Oxford Dictionary of National Biography

2005–2008

Oxford Dictionary of National Biography

2005–2008

Edited by
Lawrence Goldman

OXFORD UNIVERSITY PRESS

Great Clarendon Street, Oxford, OX2 6DP,
United Kingdom

Oxford University Press is a department of the University of Oxford. It furthers the University's objective of excellence in research, scholarship, and education by publishing worldwide. Oxford is a registered trade mark of Oxford University Press in the UK and in certain other countries

First published in 2013
Impression: 1

British Library Cataloguing in Publication Data
Data available

ISBN 978–0–19–967154–0

Typeset in OUP Swift by Interactive Sciences Limited, Gloucester
Printed in Great Britain by CPI Group (UK) Ltd, Croydon, CR0 4YY

PREFACE

This is the second printed supplement to the *Oxford Dictionary of National Biography*, which was published in 2004 in sixty volumes and online, and which then included biographies of more than 55,000 notable figures who shaped British history to the year 2000. Since 2004 we have extended our survey of the recent past by adding biographies of men and women who died in the opening years of the twenty-first century, initially online and then in supplementary print volumes. The first print supplement, published in 2009, included biographies of those who died between 2001 and 2004. This second supplement volume includes the lives of a further 865 people who died in the four years from January 2005 to December 2008. The earliest of them by birth date is Alfred Anderson, the last surviving soldier to have gone to the Western Front in 1914, who died in 2005 aged 109. The youngest is the world champion rally driver, Richard Burns, who died in the same year, aged thirty-four.

Included here are people responsible for major developments in all areas of British life: from politics, the arts, business, technology, and the law, to military service, sport, education, science, and medicine. Many were closely connected to specific periods in Britain's recent history. There are lives in this volume bound up with the Second World War—individuals such as the submariner, Ian Fraser, who won the Victoria Cross for a daring raid in midget submarines on Japanese cruisers moored off Singapore; Tony Brooks, the SOE agent who ran the 'Pimento' resistance network in France and whose campaign of sabotage in summer 1944 frustrated German efforts to reinforce the Normandy battlefields; and Alex Henshaw, the unsung test pilot who put more than 2000 Spitfires through their paces during the conflict. The 1950s are recalled in the lives (to name a few) of the actor John Mills, whose films from the era included *The End of the Affair* (1955) and *Ice Cold in Alex* (1958); the young Harold Pinter whose first plays, notably *The Birthday Party* and *The Caretaker*, changed British theatre; and the Yorkshire cricketer, Fred Trueman.

From the 1960s, the footballer George Best, photographer Patrick Lichfield, and the Pink Floyd musician, Syd Barrett epitomize different aspects of a period notable for its style, social experimentation, and the overturning of convention. In 1965 the prime minister of Rhodesia, Ian Smith, unilaterally declared his country independent of Britain under a white minority government. His biography personifies a clutch of historic themes, from the end of empire to the struggle for democracy and racial equality in modern Africa. It is difficult to look back to the 1970s without thinking of two very different figures, the prime ministers Edward Heath and James Callaghan, who led the country for seven years in that turbulent decade. That time is also closely associated with Freddie Laker, pioneer of cheap air travel, and the comedians Dave Allen and Ronnie Barker who entertained television audiences with their jokes, sketches, and situation comedies. A decade later Britons browsed in Anita Roddick's Body Shops, and (if young enough) danced to the music of Factory Records, established by the Manchester entrepreneur and club owner, Tony Wilson. The subsequent era of 'New Labour' is recalled in the biographies of two of its most prominent figures, the cabinet ministers Robin Cook and Mo Mowlem.

Many in this volume are remembered for lives dedicated to a profession or vocation. They include, from the world of journalism, for example, Bill Deedes and Conor Cruise O'Brien, former editors of the *Daily Telegraph* and *The Observer* respectively. Ned Sherrin, who is credited with the invention of television satire in *That Was the Week That Was* (1962), enjoyed more than half a century as a broadcaster. Humphrey Lyttelton spent a lifetime playing jazz and spreading an interest in it, and was latterly known as a broadcaster in his own right. Over seven decades, Arthur C. Clarke explained the opportunities, and challenges, of space exploration in numerous works of fiction and non-fiction. Others in this volume were responsible for discoveries or innovations with a lasting legacy and benefit—among them the epidemiologist Richard Doll, who made the link between smoking and lung cancer; Cicely Saunders, creator of the hospice movement; Peter Benenson, barrister and founder of Amnesty International; and Chad Varah, clergyman and founder of The Samaritans.

With the politician John Profumo (who gave his name to a scandal that fatally undermined the government of Harold Macmillan in 1963), the detective Malcolm Fewtrell (who investigated the Great Train Robbery of that year), and the Russian dissident Aleksandr Litvinenko (who was killed in London in 2006) we include individuals caught up in crime and malpractice which has always found a place in the original *Dictionary of National Biography* and its successor, the *Oxford DNB*. Other figures are synonymous with popular objects and brands evocative of recent decades. These include the BBC quiz programme *Mastermind* with the polymath Magnus Magnusson in the chair; the chimpanzees from the ever-popular advertisements for 'PG Tips' tea who were trained by the conservationist Molly Badham; John DeLorean's 'gull-wing' car, a stylish outcome of a criminal conspiracy; or the new British

Library designed by Colin St John Wilson. However, as rounded and balanced accounts, *Oxford DNB* articles also set such events and symbols of an era in the wider context of a person's life story.

Authoritative and accessible, the biographies in this volume have been written by specialist authors, many of them leading figures in their fields. Here you will find Michael Billington on Harold Pinter, the late Tony Howard on the BBC correspondent Charles Wheeler, Michael Crick on George Best, Richard Davenport-Hines on Anita Roddick, Brenda Hale on the pioneer woman barrister and judge Rose Heilbron, Simon Heffer on John Profumo, Alex Jennings on the actor Paul Scofield, Hermione Lee on the literary agent Pat Kavanagh, Geoffrey Wheatcroft on Conor Cruise O'Brien, and Peregrine Worsthorne on Bill Deedes. The lives of the two prime ministers have been written by their colleagues in government: Douglas Hurd was private and political secretary to Edward Heath while Roy Hattersley sat in cabinet with Jim Callaghan. These are just a few of the 596 contributors who have written one or more biographies for this volume. Their knowledge, judgement, and generosity—like that of the more than 450 specialist advisers who guide us on matters of selection—is central to the *Oxford DNB*. All those who contributed to this volume will have collaborated with Dr Alex May, the in-house research editor, who commissions and edits the biographies of dictionary subjects who died after 2000. Most of the articles published in this volume were prepared for publication by Ralph Evans, historical scholar and production editor of the *Oxford DNB* until his untimely death in 2011.

Many of the people included in this volume are household names. But a good number are also remembered for influential lives away from the headlines. What in the 1980s became 'Thatcherism' owed much to the behind-the-scenes advice from the economist, Ralph Harris, and the political activist (and former communist), Alfred Sherman. Children who learned to read with Ladybird Books in the 1950s and 1960s must thank their creator, Douglas Keen. Without its first producer, Verity Lambert, there would have been no *Doctor Who*. Others were 'ordinary' people capable of remarkable acts. Take, for instance, Arthur Bywater who over two days in 1944 cleared thousands of bombs from a Liverpool munitions factory following an explosion—only to do the same, months later, at another factory. Awarded the George Cross and the George Medal, Bywater remains the only non-combatant to have received Britain's two highest awards for civilian bravery.

According to the Victorian author and sage, Thomas Carlyle, 'History is the essence of innumerable biographies'. Each of the essays included in this volume may be read on its own for evidence of the life of a notable figure. Taken together, however, they help illuminate and explain the collective experience of Britain's recent past.

LAWRENCE GOLDMAN

NOTES TO READERS

- The articles in this volume were first published between 2009 and 2012 in updates to the online edition of the *Oxford Dictionary of National Biography* (www.oxforddnb.com).

  The version of each article is as it appeared in the online edition in January 2013: five subjects who died between 2005 and 2008, whose biographies appear online as part of another person's article, are here published as stand-alone entries, for example Helen Violet Caroline Delfont.

  Six articles also include the biography of a related individual who died before 2005. In these instances the name of the subsidiary subject appears in bold in the article text, for example Clara Ethel (Clare) Deniz (1911–2002) under Deniz, Francisco Antonio (1912–2005).

- The selection of biographies included in this volume is based on the recommendations of more than 450 advisers in 43 subject panels, from archaeology to zoology.

- 250 of the biographies in this volume are illustrated with a portrait. Likenesses have been selected in consultation with the National Portrait Gallery, London, from their own collection and from other sources.

- Cross-references are included within articles to direct readers to other relevant entries. Cross-references relate to subjects with entries in this volume, in the first print supplement (2009), or in the 60-volume print edition of the *Oxford DNB* (2004).

- Articles in this volume follow the same format as those published in the *Oxford DNB*. A complete guide to articles is available in volume 1 of the print edition (pages xxvii–xx) and at www.oup.com/oxforddnb/info/print/intro/guide/

GENERAL ABBREVIATIONS

1. *General abbreviations*

AD	*anno domini*
AFC	Air Force Cross
AIDS	acquired immune deficiency syndrome
A-level	advanced level [examination]
appx *pl.* appxs	appendix(es)
ARP	air-raid precautions
ATV	Associated Television
Aug	August
b.	born
BA	bachelor of arts
BAFTA	British Academy of Film and Television Arts
BBC	British Broadcasting Corporation / Company
BC	before Christ
BCG	bacillus of Calmette and Guérin [inoculation against tuberculosis]
BCh	bachelor of surgery
BChir	bachelor of surgery
BCL	bachelor of civil law
BCom	bachelor of commerce
BD	bachelor of divinity
BL	bachelor of law / letters / literature
BLitt	bachelor of letters
BMus	bachelor of music
BP	British Petroleum
BS	(1) bachelor of science; (2) bachelor of surgery; (3) British standard
BSc	bachelor of science
BSc (Econ)	bachelor of science (economics)
BSc (Eng)	bachelor of science (engineering)
bt	baronet
c.	*circa*
CB	companion of the Bath
CBE	commander of the Order of the British Empire
cc	cubic centimetres
CD	compact disc
CH	Companion of Honour
ChB	bachelor of surgery
CIA	Central Intelligence Agency
CID	Criminal Investigation Department
Cie	Compagnie
CLit	companion of literature
cm	centimetre(s)
Cmd	command [identifier for published parliamentary papers]
CMG	companion of the Order of St Michael and St George
Cmnd	command [identifier for published parliamentary papers]
Co.	company
co.	county
CSE	certificate of secondary education
CVO	commander of the Royal Victorian Order
$	(American) dollar
DBE	dame commander of the Order of the British Empire
DCVO	dame commander of the Royal Victorian Order
DD	doctor of divinity
Dec	December
dem.	demolished
DFC	Distinguished Flying Cross
diss.	dissertation
DLitt	doctor of letters
DMus	doctor of music
DNA	deoxyribonucleic acid
DPhil	doctor of philosophy
DSC	Distinguished Service Cross
DSc	doctor of science
DSO	companion of the Distinguished Service Order
DTh	doctor of theology
DUniv	doctor of the university
ed. *pl.* eds.	edited / edited by / editor(s)
edn	edition
EEC	European Economic Community
EFTA	European Free Trade Association
EMI	Electrical and Musical Industries (Ltd)
ENSA	Entertainments National Service Association
ex	sold by (*lit.* out of)
exh.	exhibited
FA	Football Association
FBA	fellow of the British Academy
Feb	February
FM	frequency modulation
fol. *pl.* fols.	folio(s)
FRS	fellow of the Royal Society
GBE	knight or dame grand cross of the Order of the British Empire
GCB	knight grand cross of the Order of the Bath
GCE	general certificate of education
GCHQ	government communications headquarters
GCMG	knight or dame grand cross of the Order of St Michael and St George
GCSE	general certificate of secondary education
GCVO	knight or dame grand cross of the Royal Victorian Order
GEC	General Electric Company
GP	general practitioner
GSO	general staff officer
HIV	human immunodeficiency virus
HM	his / her majesty('s)
HMS	his / her majesty's ship
HMV	His Master's Voice
Hon.	Honourable

ibid.	*ibidem*: in the same place
ICI	Imperial Chemical Industries (Ltd)
illus.	illustration
Inc.	Incorporated
IRA	Irish Republican Army
ITV	Independent Television
Jan	January
JP	justice of the peace
jun.	junior
KBE	knight commander of the Order of the British Empire
KCB	knight commander of the Order of the Bath
KCMG	knight commander of the Order of St Michael and St George
KCVO	knight commander of the Royal Victorian Order
KGB	[Soviet committee of state security]
km	kilometre(s)
£	pound(s) sterling
lb	pound(s) unit of weight
LittD	doctor of letters
LLB	bachelor of laws
LLD	doctor of laws
LLM	master of laws
LRCP	licentiate of the Royal College of Physicians
LSD	lysergic acid diethylamide
LVO	lieutenant of the Royal Victorian Order
MA	master of arts
MBA	master of business administration
MBE	member of the Order of the British Empire
MCC	Marylebone Cricket Club
MD	doctor of medicine
MEd	master of education
MEP	member of the European parliament
MG	Morris Garages
MGM	Metro-Goldwyn-Mayer
MI5	military intelligence department later Security Service
MI6	Secret Intelligence Service
MLitt	master of letters
Mlle	Mademoiselle
mm	millimetre(s)
MP	member of parliament
m.p.h.	miles per hour
MPhil	master of philosophy
MRCP	member of the Royal College of Physicians
MRCS	member of the Royal College of Surgeons
MS *pl.* MSS	manuscript(s)
MSc	master of science
MSc (Econ)	master of science (economics)
MusB	bachelor of music
MV	motor vessel
MVO	member of the Royal Victorian Order
NAAFI	Navy Army and Air Force Institutes
NASA	National Aeronautics and Space Administration
NATO	North Atlantic Treaty Organization
NBC	National Broadcasting Corporation
NCO	non-commissioned officer
NHS	National Health Service
NKVD	[Soviet people's commissariat for internal affairs]
no. *pl.* nos.	number(s)
Nov	November
OBE	officer of the Order of the British Empire
Oct	October
OECD	Organization for Economic Co-operation and Development
OEEC	Organization for European Economic Co-operation
O-level	ordinary level [examination]
op. *pl.* opp.	opus *pl.* opera
p. *pl.* pp.	page(s)
para.	paragraph
PhD	doctor of philosophy
priv. coll.	private collection
pt *pl.* pts	part(s)
pubd	published
PVC	polyvinyl chloride
QC	queen's counsel
RA	Royal Academy / Royal Academician
RAF	Royal Air Force
RAMC	Royal Army Medical Corps
RCA	Royal College of Art
repr. *pl.* reprs.	reprint(s) / reprinted
rev.	revised / revised by / reviser / revision
Revd	Reverend
RIBA	Royal Institute of British Architects
RN	Royal Navy
RNA	ribonucleic acid
RNVR	Royal Naval Volunteer Reserve
RO	Record Office
r.p.m.	revolutions per minute
RRS	royal research ship
Rt Hon.	Right Honourable
S4C	Sianel Pedwar Cymru
SAS	Special Air Service
ScD	doctor of science
Sept	September
ser.	series
SIS	Secret Intelligence Service
SS	(1) Santissimi; (2) Schutzstaffel; (3) steam ship
STP	doctor of theology
TA	Territorial Army
TUC	Trades Union Congress
U-boat	*Unterseeboot*: submarine
UN	United Nations
UNESCO	United Nations Educational Scientific and Cultural Organization
UNICEF	United Nations International Children's Emergency Fund
VC	Victoria Cross
VE-day	victory in Europe day
Ven.	Venerable
VJ-day	victory over Japan day
vol. *pl.* vols.	volume(s)
WAAF	Women's Auxiliary Air Force
WRAF	Women's Royal Air Force
YMCA	Young Men's Christian Association

2. *Institution abbreviations*

All Souls Oxf.	All Souls College, Oxford
BBC WAC	BBC Written Archives Centre, Reading
BFI	British Film Institute, London
BFINA	British Film Institute, London, National Archive
BL NSA	British Library, National Sound Archive
BLPES	British Library of Political and Economic Science
Bodl. Oxf.	Bodleian Library, Oxford
Bodl. RH	Bodleian Library of Commonwealth and African Studies at Rhodes House, Oxford
Borth. Inst.	Borthwick Institute of Historical Research, University of York
CAC Cam.	Churchill College, Churchill Archives Centre, Cambridge
CCC Cam.	Corpus Christi College, Cambridge
Christ Church Oxf.	Christ Church, Oxford
Christies	Christies, London
CKS	Centre for Kentish Studies, Maidstone, Kent
Courtauld Inst.	Courtauld Institute of Art, London
CUL	Cambridge University Library
CUL, department of manuscripts and university archives	Cambridge University Library, department of manuscripts and university archives
Derbys. RO	Derbyshire Record Office, Matlock
DWL	Dr Williams's Library, London
Eton	Eton College, Berkshire
FM Cam.	Fitzwilliam Museum, Cambridge
Garr. Club	Garrick Club, London
Hult. Arch.	Hulton|Archive, Getty Images, London
IWM	Imperial War Museum, London
JRL	John Rylands University Library of Manchester
King's Cam.	King's College, Cambridge
King's Lond.	King's College, London
King's Lond., Liddell Hart C.	King's College, Liddell Hart Centre for Military Archives, London
Leics. RO	Leicestershire, Leicester, and Rutland Record Office, Leicester
Linn. Soc.	Linnean Society of London
LPL	Lambeth Palace London
Lpool RO	Liverpool Record Office and Local Studies Service
Magd. Oxf.	Magdalen College, Oxford
Merton Oxf.	Merton College, Oxford
NA Scot.	National Archives of Scotland, Edinburgh
NHM	Natural History Museum, London
NL Scot.	National Library of Scotland, Edinburgh
NL Wales	National Library of Wales, Aberystwyth
Norfolk RO	Norfolk Record Office, Norwich
NPG	National Portrait Gallery, London
Nuffield Oxf.	Nuffield College, Oxford
Parl. Arch.	Parliamentary Archives of the United Kingdom
Pembroke Cam.	Pembroke College, Cambridge
priv. coll.	private collection
PRONI	Public Record Office of Northern Ireland, Belfast
RA	Royal Academy of Arts, London
Ransom HRC	Harry Ransom Humanities Research Center, University of Texas
RBG Kew	Royal Botanic Gardens, Kew
RCP Lond.	Royal College of Physicians of London
RGS	Royal Geographical Society, London
RIBA	Royal Institute of British Architects, London
RIBA BAL	Royal Institute of British Architects, British Architectural Library, London
Royal Arch.	Royal Archives, Windsor Castle, Berkshire [with gracious permission of her majesty the queen]
Royal Scot. Acad.	Royal Scottish Academy, Edinburgh
RS	Royal Society, London
St Ant. Oxf.	St Antony's College, Oxford
St John Cam.	St John's College, Cambridge
Scot. NPG	Scottish National Portrait Gallery, Edinburgh
Scott Polar RI	University of Cambridge, Scott Polar Research Institute
SOAS	School of Oriental and African Studies, London
TCD	Trinity College, Dublin
TNA: PRO	National Archives of the United Kingdom, Public Record Office, London
Trinity Cam.	Trinity College, Cambridge
U. Aberdeen	University of Aberdeen
U. Birm.	University of Birmingham
U. Birm. L.	University of Birmingham Library
U. Cal.	University of California
U. Cal., Santa Barbara, Arts Library	University of California, Arts Library, Santa Barbara
U. Cam.	University of Cambridge
UCL	University College, London
U. Durham	University of Durham
U. Edin.	University of Edinburgh
U. Glas.	University of Glasgow
U. Glas. L.	University of Glasgow Library
U. Hull	University of Hull
U. Leeds	University of Leeds
U. Leeds, Brotherton L.	University of Leeds, Brotherton Library
U. Lond.	University of London
U. Lpool	University of Liverpool
U. Lpool L.	University of Liverpool Library
U. Oxf.	University of Oxford
U. Reading	University of Reading
U. Reading L.	University of Reading Library
U. Southampton L.	University of Southampton Library
U. Sussex	University of Sussex, Brighton
U. Warwick Mod. RC	University of Warwick, Modern Records Centre, Coventry
V&A	Victoria and Albert Museum, London
Wellcome L.	Wellcome Library for the History and Understanding of Medicine, London
W. Yorks. AS	West Yorkshire Archive Service
Yale U.	Yale University, New Haven, Connecticut

3. *Bibliographic abbreviations*

ArchR	*Architectural Review*
AusDB	D. Pike and others, eds., *Australian dictionary of biography*, 16 vols. (1966–2002)
b. cert.	birth certificate
BMJ	*British Medical Journal*
Burke, *Peerage*	J. Burke, *A general* [later edns *A genealogical*] *and heraldic dictionary of the peerage and baronetage of the United Kingdom* [later edns *the British empire*] (1829–)
CCI	*Calendar of confirmations and inventories granted and given up in the several commissariots of Scotland* (1876–)
CGPLA Eng. & Wales	Calendars of the grants of probate … made in … HM court of probate [England and Wales]
CGPLA NIre.	Calendars of the grants of probate … made in … HM court of probate [Northern Ireland]
Crockford	*Crockford's Clerical Directory*
CS	Camden Society
d. cert.	death certificate
DLitB	Dictionary of Literary Biography
EdinR	*Edinburgh Review, or, Critical Journal*
FO List	*Foreign Office List*
GEC, *Peerage*	G. E. C. [G. E. Cokayne], *The complete peerage of England, Scotland, Ireland, Great Britain, and the United Kingdom*, 8 vols. (1887–98); new edn, ed. V. Gibbs and others, 14 vols. in 15 (1910–98); microprint repr. (1982) and (1987)
GJ	*Geographical Journal*
LondG	*London Gazette*
m. cert.	marriage certificate
Memoirs FRS	*Biographical Memoirs of Fellows of the Royal Society*
MT	*Musical Times*
Munk, *Roll*	W. Munk, *The roll of the Royal College of Physicians of London*, 2 vols. (1861)2nd edn, 3 vols. (1878)
New Grove	S. Sadie, ed., *The new Grove dictionary of music and musicians*, 20 vols. (1980); 2nd edn., 29 vols. (2001)
Parl. papers	*Parliamentary papers* (1801–)
PBA	*Proceedings of the British Academy*
PICE	*Proceedings of the Institution of Civil Engineers*
PRO	Public Record Office
TLS	*Times Literary Supplement*
VF	*Vanity Fair*
Wisden	*John Wisden's Cricketer's Almanack*
WW	*Who's who* (1849–)
WWW	*Who was who* (1920–)

Abse, Leopold [Leo] (**1917–2008**), politician, was born at 5 Clare Street, Cardiff, on 22 April 1917, the second of three sons and third of four children of Rudolph Abse (1887–1964), a cinema manager then serving as a private in the Lancashire Fusiliers, and his wife, Kate, *née* Shepherd (1900–1981). His older brother, Wilfred, was later a professor of psychiatry at the University of Virginia; his younger brother was the poet Dannie Abse.

Of immigrant stock—both sets of his grandparents had arrived in south Wales from, respectively, Germany and tsarist Poland in the 1870s—the young Abse was brought up in a secular Jewish household, attending Howard Gardens high school in Cardiff. Although his paternal grandfather had been a relatively rich man, owning a chain of cinemas in south Wales, his fortune had been dissipated well before his second grandson left secondary school. The young Abse was forced to go to work in a factory before enrolling in the late 1930s to read law at the London School of Economics, where he fell under the influence of Harold Laski. In 1941 he volunteered for the RAF and it was as Aircraftsman Abse that he made his début in the columns of *Hansard*, being the subject of a Commons debate in 1944 arising out of the enforced winding up of the forces parliament in Cairo. A leading figure in it, the young Abse was compulsorily posted back to Britain and, while no disciplinary action was taken, the future legislator could be said from that moment on to have made his mark as a rebel. But in fact he had already done that by becoming chairman of the Cardiff Young Socialists, joining the Labour Party at the age of seventeen, and fighting his first (unsuccessful) election for a Cardiff council seat at the then earliest permissible age of twenty-one.

When Abse re-entered civilian life in 1946, going on to found his own firm of solicitors in Cardiff, he rapidly became chairman of the Cardiff City Labour Party and of the city council's watch committee, supervising relations with the local police. He also chaired the governors of the city's art college, where he met the fabric collage artist Marjorie Iris Davies (1918–1996), daughter of Joseph Davies, clerk of works, whom he married at Cardiff New Synagogue on 17 July 1955. They had a son and a daughter.

In the year that he married, Abse contested the tory-held parliamentary seat of Cardiff North and, though he lost, three years later was chosen to fight a by-election in the safe Labour constitency of Pontypool caused by the elevation to the peerage of its previous member, Daniel Granville West. A diminutive, pixie-like figure, Abse almost immediately made a splash at Westminster. It was his habit to dress exotically—one of the traits he shared with Disraeli—and on budget days in particular he would turn up in the Commons looking as if he had just escaped from a road company production of Jerome K. Jerome's *Three Men in a Boat*. (Abse's excuse for his increasingly outrageous costumes was that he wished to draw attention to the textile products of his constituency, but the truth was that he never lost a theatrical taste for dressing up.) He soon, however, proved a painstaking and conscientious back-bench MP, who possessed the ability to hold the

Leopold [Leo] **Abse** (**1917–2008**), by Godfrey Argent, 1967

attention of the house, though the rapidity of his speech made him something of a nightmare for the press gallery shorthand writers.

More interested in issues of individual freedom than any current controversy between the parties, Abse's first private member's bill was on homosexual law reform in 1961, which was talked out. Undeterred, in the following year he introduced his Matrimonial Causes and Reconciliation Bill, from which he was compelled by opposition from the churches to remove its central proposal for divorce by consent. Six years later, however, he returned to the charge, this time getting through much the same scheme with the condition of 'the irretrievable breakdown of a marriage'. It was the same story with homosexuality: although at first rebuffed in 1961, in 1967 Abse successfully piloted through the Commons his Sexual Offences Act, which allowed homosexual conduct between consenting adults in private. In the same year he also introduced his Family Planning Act, permitting local authorites to open birth-control clinics and to distribute contraceptives. There followed David Owen's Children Act of 1975, when he materially assisted the ministerial sponsor with proposals to govern the law of fostering and adoption throughout the land and to allow adopted children to seek details of their birth parents. Abse also led the parliamentary campaign that resulted in the final abolition of capital punishment in 1969.

Altogether it was not surprising that the future Labour prime minister James Callaghan once wrote to Abse that he had done 'much more good in terms of human happiness than 90 per cent of the work done in Parliament on what are called "political issues"' (*The Times*, 21 Aug 2008). Not that he was always an easy colleague even for members of his own party. Between 1974 and 1979 he emerged as a fierce opponent of the Labour government's proposals for devolution, successfully leading—along with Neil Kinnock—the 'no' campaign in the Welsh referendum of 1979 in which the Callaghan government's constitutional plan was trounced four to one. Yet Abse also had the capacity to work with senior colleagues, as he did with the Wilson government's first housing minister, Dick Crossman, over the leasehold enfranchisement reform of 1965, and as he consistently also did with the home secretary, Roy Jenkins, over the social changes in areas supervised by the Home Office in 1965–7. Having a safe seat, and possessing no evident ambition for ministerial office himself, Abse was in many ways the ideal outrider for reforms to which the government, for good reasons or bad, did not wish its own reputation to be officially attached. He was helped, of course, by the fact that his own constituents do not appear to have resented even the more adventurous liberal positions that he took up. That may have been a tribute to their broad-mindedness but it seems more likely to have arisen from a recognition that—whatever they felt about his views on hanging, homosexuality, or even divorce—he was in every other respect an admirable constituency MP. Abse himself probably put it best. 'An MP', he once said, 'can do anything provided he has a love affair with his constituency'.

Abse's love affair with his own constituency lasted nearly thirty years—he sat first for Pontypool from 1958 to 1983 and then for the renamed seat of Torfaen until 1987. Increasingly deaf, he retired from the Commons at the age of seventy, having fought seventeen national and local elections, nine of them for his parliamentary seat. Yet anyone who thought that he would be lost without his regular outings to Westminster—rather meanly, as some thought, he was never offered a peerage—could not have been more mistaken. A man of some wealth—the solicitors' firm he founded in Cardiff became one of the largest in Wales—he simply set about launching a new career as an author. His first book, saucily entitled *Private Member* and in effect amounting to a rather unorthodox form of autobiography, had been published in 1973 while he remained an MP but once he retired from the Westminster treadmill it was swiftly followed by others, all of them applying psychoanalytical theories: *Margaret, Daughter of Beatrice: a Psychobiography of Margaret Thatcher* (1989), *Wotan, My Enemy: Can Britain Live with the Germans?* (1994), *Tony Blair and the Politics of Perversity* (1996 and 2003), *Fellatio, Masochism, Politics and Love* (2000), which included comments about the supposed repressed homosexual elements in the relationship between Tony Blair and Gordon Brown, and *The Bisexuality of Daniel Defoe* (2006). Although no book that he produced became a best-seller, each successive work provoked (as it was designed to do) considerable controversy, and his courage in putting forward unpopular viewpoints—the forthright attack, for example, on Tony Blair came when the young Labour leader was at the height of his fame as a national idol—was fearless and penetrating. At the time of his death he was at work on a volume of Freudian commentaries on biblical stories.

On 2 August 2000, four years after the death of his first wife, Abse married Ania Czepulkowska, a textile designer from Poland fifty years younger than he was. She was the daughter of Lech Czepulkowska, architect, and they married at Hounslow register office. He lived latterly in a Georgian house at Strand on the Green, Chiswick, where he and his second wife frequently entertained. He was also a valued member of London's Savile Club, where—before he nearly totally lost his hearing—he used to enjoy lunching. In his final years he developed cancer of the oesophagus. He died at Charing Cross Hospital on 19 August 2008, of a brain haemorrhage. His funeral, attended by both the first minister of Wales and the secretary of state for Wales, took place at St Gabriel's Church in Cwmbran in his former constituency on 29 August 2008. His body was cremated at Gwent crematorium, Cwmbran. He was survived by his second wife, Ania, his daughter, Bethsheba, and his son, Tobias, a historian.

ANTHONY HOWARD

Sources L. Abse, *Private member* (1973) · *The Times* (21 Aug 2008) · *Daily Telegraph* (21 Aug 2008) · *The Guardian* (21 Aug 2008); (23 Aug 2008); (2 Sept 2008) · *The Independent* (21 Aug 2008) · *Western Mail* (21 Aug 2008); (30 Aug 2008) · *Western Morning News* (21 Aug 2008) · *South Wales Echo* (21 Aug 2008); (30 Aug 2008) · A. Abse, 'Leo Abse, 22 April 1917–19 August 2008', exhibition booklet, Pontypool Museum, 2009 · *WW* · personal knowledge (2012) · private information (2012) · b. cert. · m. certs. · d. cert.

Archives NL Wales, papers | NL Wales, Dannie Abse papers | FILM BFINA, current affairs and documentary footage | SOUND BL NSA, current affairs and documentary recordings

Likenesses photographs, 1965–9, Getty Images, London · photographs, 1965–2007, Rex Features, London · J. Hedgecoe, bromide print, 1966 (*The Humanist Society*, with Alfred Ayer, Brigid Brophy, Edward Francis Williams, Ludovic Kennedy, and Basil Martin), NPG · photographs, 1966–86, Photoshot, London · photographs, 1966–2008, PA Photos, London · G. Argent, bromide print, 1967, NPG [*see illus.*] · J. Roberts, acrylic on board, 1988, NL Wales · J. Roberts, pen and watercolour, 1988, NL Wales · J. Roberts, pencil drawing, 1988, NL Wales · F. Topolski, caricature; Sotheby's, 15 July 1998 · obituary photographs · photographs, Camera Press, London

Wealth at death £1,164,271: probate, 28 May 2010, *CGPLA Eng. & Wales*

Ackner, Desmond James Conrad, Baron Ackner (1920–2006), judge, was born at 90 Highbury New Park, Islington, London, on 18 September 1920, the son of an immigrant Viennese dentist, Conrad Ackner, who had a fashionable practice in Wimpole Street, and his wife, (Rosine) Rhoda, née Tuck. Although both his parents were Jewish and he was reared in the Jewish faith his own children were baptized and confirmed as Anglicans. He was educated at Highgate School and Clare College, Cambridge, where he read law. His unremarkable 2:2 in his tripos gave no hint of his future success. During the Second World War he served first in the Royal Artillery, and then, as a result of polio which left him permanently lame, transferred into the Admiralty's naval law branch. In 1945 he was called to the bar by the Middle Temple, with a third in his bar finals. Without the advantage of physical presence he used a powerful voice, emphatic elongations, and precise, if sometimes florid, language to build up a substantial practice. He betrayed no hesitation in court: he used to say that he was paid for his certainties, not his doubts. On 24 August 1946, at St Marylebone register office, he married Joan May Spence, the 22-year-old widow of K. B.

Spence, and daughter of John Evans, mining engineer. Ackner became stepfather to her daughter Moelwyn, and they had two further children, Martin and Claudia.

Ackner took silk in 1962 and appeared in many high-profile libel cases for both plaintiffs such as Lee Kuan Yew, prime minister of Singapore, and John Bloom, the washing machine tycoon, and defendants ranging from *The Spectator* to the *International Herald Tribune*. He had a facility to be equally persuasive before a jury and an appellate court. His commercial practice included a celebrated dispute over ownership of a tanker, *Vergottis* v. *Onassis and Calogeropoulos* (the last better known as Maria Callas), in which his cross-examination of Aristotle Onassis exposed, to Onassis' understandable concern, the latter's early courtship of Jacqueline Kennedy. But the briefs for which he was best known fell outside these specialist spheres. In 1964 he represented the chief constable of Brighton, and won a judicial review in the House of Lords on the grounds that the officer's dismissal by the watch committee, without notice of the charges or an opportunity to rebut them, was a clear breach of natural justice. The case *Ridge* v. *Baldwin* (1964) is generally recognized to mark the revival of English administrative law. In 1966 he accepted instructions to represent the victims of the drug thalidomide (and was obliged in consequence to turn down a later and more lucrative offer of a brief to defend the drug's manufacturer). He came further into the public eye in consequence of his representation of the Aberfan Parents and Residents Association at the tribunal of inquiry into the collapse of a coal tip in south Wales in October 1966, which had resulted in 144 deaths. He was rightly praised not only for his forensic skills but for his humanity. Lord Robens, chairman of the National Coal Board, the victim of his advocate's assault, declined to speak to him when they were both members of the upper house more than two decades on.

Ackner became chairman of the Bar Council—then a two-year appointment—in 1968, but his judicial career had already begun when he became recorder of Swindon in 1962, and in 1967 a judge of the courts of appeal of Jersey and Guernsey, one of several who proceeded thence to the highest judicial office on the mainland. He was made a high court judge, receiving the customary knighthood, in 1971 (moving to the commercial court in 1973), presiding judge on the western circuit in 1976, and a lord justice of appeal in 1980. He was president of the senate of the inns of court and the bar between 1980 and 1982 and treasurer of the Middle Temple in 1984. He was made a law lord in 1986, taking the title Baron Ackner, of Sutton, Sussex, and the motto *Non servimus justitiae silendo* ('justice is not served by our remaining silent').

While he enjoyed a reputation for fairness, the views Ackner expressed on the bench were unashamedly conservative. As a first instance judge he cited pornography as a cause of crime, declared that the Explosive Substances Act of 1883 was insufficient to deal with 'the modern cult of terrorism', and during the 'winter of discontent', in 1978–9, enjoined transport union officials from secondary picketing disruptive of the supply of cooking oils to United Biscuits' factories, saying that to hold otherwise would mean that parliament had written a recipe for anarchy. This decision prompted a motion in the House of Commons for his removal from office, which, after attracting an opposing amendment praising his judicial qualities, was withdrawn. When in the House of Lords he supported the interim ban on media reporting of Peter Wright's *Spycatcher* memoirs in opposition to the minority who realistically recognized that the government's case was bound to founder (as it did) before the European Court of Human Rights. His Holdsworth address to the University of Birmingham in 1992, entitled 'Cet animal est méchant: one judge's view of the media', was a sustained attack on press irresponsibility.

Ackner's intellect was practical, not academic, and he left few landmarks in jurisprudence. His leading speech in *Walford* v. *Miles* (1992), where the house refused to imply a term in an agreement to negotiate in good faith, describing such a term as 'inherently repugnant to the adversarial position of parties involved in negotiating [and] unworkable in practice', encapsulated both his pragmatic approach and his trenchant style.

After retirement as a law lord in 1992, three years before the obligatory date, Ackner returned to the defence of his profession with an untrammelled zest. (He had indeed been regarded in the Lord Chancellor's Department as the law lords' shop steward.) At every juncture of the law reforms from the late 1980s to the early 2000s he took the hardest of lines. Lord Mackay's pioneering of the grant of rights of audience to solicitors in the higher courts (while Ackner was still a law lord) was said to be 'deluded by dogma' (*The Independent*, 22 Feb 1989). Lord Irvine's creation of a state criminal defence system was described as 'the dismantling of our system for the administration of justice as we know it' (Ackner, 'Access to justice', *Middle Templar*, Hilary 2000, 6), and the abolition of the traditional role and the title of lord chancellor by Lord Falconer an act of 'constitutional vandalism' (Ackner, 'Constitutional vandalism', *Middle Templar*, Trinity 2004, 5–7). The pungency of his assaults was not always considered to be conducive to the achievement of his objectives.

Ackner kept a flat in Pimlico as well as a house in Sutton, near Pulborough, Sussex. He was president of the Society of Sussex Downsmen in 1993–6. He died at St Thomas's Hospital, Lambeth, on 21 March 2006, of respiratory failure and pulmonary oedema. He was survived by his wife, Joan, his stepdaughter, Moelwyn, his son, Martin (a commercial airline pilot), and his daughter, Claudia (like her father a barrister and judge). MICHAEL BELOFF

Sources *The Times* (23 March 2006) · *Daily Telegraph* (23 March 2006) · *The Guardian* (24 March 2006) · *The Independent* (25 March 2006) · Burke, *Peerage* · *WW* (2006) · personal knowledge (2010) · private information (2010) · b. cert. · m. cert. · d. cert.

Archives FILM BFINA, current affairs footage

Likenesses Elliott & Fry, half-plate negative, 1961, NPG · photographs, 1990–98, Photoshot, London · obituary photographs

Wealth at death £1,103,046: probate, 22 Aug 2006, *CGPLA Eng. & Wales*

Ackrill, John Lloyd (1921–2007), philosopher, was born on 30 December 1921 at 49 Green Road, Reading, the youngest child of Frederick William Ackrill (1875–1956), elementary school headmaster, and his wife, Jessie Anne, *née* Davies (1881–1969). He was educated at Reading School, and in Trinity term 1940 went to St John's College, Oxford, as a Sir Thomas White scholar to read Greats. After attaining a first in classical moderations in 1941 he served until 1945 in the Royal Berkshire regiment and on the general staff, seeing active service in Europe and attaining the rank of captain. He returned to Oxford in 1945, gaining a first in *literae humaniores* in 1948.

Ackrill was appointed assistant lecturer in logic at Glasgow University in 1948, and the following year was elected to the newly created post of university lecturer in ancient philosophy at Oxford. The terms of this appointment included an initial two-year period of study leave to enable him to prepare for his new teaching duties; he studied first in Berne and then at the Institute for Advanced Study in Princeton. He took up the post in 1951, but resigned it in 1953 on his election to a tutorial fellowship at Brasenose, which he held until 1966. For most of that period his tutorial colleague in philosophy was his former pupil Michael Woods; Ackrill had strongly supported Woods's appointment, and it is generally acknowledged that in those years they constituted one of the strongest tutorial teams in Oxford, especially in ancient philosophy. In August 1953, in Perth, Western Australia, he married Margaret Walker Kerr (*b.* 1928), an economic historian, and daughter of Cyril Kerr, chartered surveyor and estate agent. They had three daughters and a son.

In 1966 Ackrill was again elected to be the first holder of a new university post in Oxford, in this case the professorship of the history of philosophy. Though the post was linked by statute to a fellowship at Keble, Ackrill invoked a university rule that allowed the first holder of a university post, if already a fellow of a college, to remain at that college. He remained a fellow of Brasenose until his retirement from the chair in 1989, and was subsequently both emeritus professor and emeritus fellow until his death. He served as vice-principal of Brasenose College from 1978 to 1980. He was elected to a fellowship of the British Academy in 1981, and to an honorary fellowship of St John's College in 1996. In 1986 a special volume of *Oxford Studies in Ancient Philosophy* was published in his honour.

The early 1950s were years of intense and diverse philosophical creativity in the English-speaking world, especially in Oxford; ancient philosophy in particular was revitalized by the application of modern analytic methods and standards of rigour to the more traditional examination of texts. Ackrill's methods of work were admirably suited to these developments. He did not attempt to advance any large theses or to construct synoptic surveys of past philosophers, preferring to proceed by scrupulously exact and detailed dissection of specific questions, which not infrequently threw light on major issues. Most of his work was in the form of articles, some of which, notably his discussions of Plato's *Sophist* (published in the *Bulletin of the Institute of Classical Studies of the University of London* in 1955 and the *Journal of Hellenic Studies* in 1957), of Aristotle's theory of the soul (published in the *Proceedings of the Aristotelian Society* in 1973), and of Aristotle on *eudaimonia* (published in the *Proceedings of the British Academy* in 1974), came to be acknowledged as fundamental to their respective topics. His single monograph, *Aristotle the Philosopher* (1981), applied the same method to Aristotle's work as a whole; throughout the book the reader is encouraged to see Aristotle less as a dogmatic teacher than as an explorer of problems, and to engage with him in the same critical spirit.

In 1960 Ackrill was appointed general editor of the Clarendon Aristotle Series, a post he held for forty years. The series had been founded by J. L. Austin, with the aim of providing students of philosophy with accurate translations accompanied by notes elucidating the philosophically significant features of the work. The second volume to appear, in 1963, was Ackrill's own translation of and notes on the *Categories* and *De interpretatione*. This remained in print throughout his lifetime, and is recognized as a paradigm of exact, yet not inelegant, translation and lucid commentary. The series, comprising over twenty volumes by 2010, constitutes a resource of permanent value to students and professionals.

During his tenure of the chair of the history of philosophy Ackrill's main duties were giving lectures and graduate classes and supervising graduate students. He brought to these activities the same meticulousness, unpretentiousness, and careful attention to the views of others that had characterized his work as an undergraduate tutor (and which were equally characteristic of his written work). The graduate students on whom he lavished this attention repaid him not only with esteem but with affection. After retirement he remained in Oxford, and despite failing health continued to interest himself in the doings of former colleagues and students. He died at his home, 22 Charlbury Road, Oxford, on 30 November 2007, of heart failure. He was survived by his wife and children. C. C. W. Taylor

Sources J. L. Ackrill, *Essays on Plato and Aristotle* (1997), introduction · *The Independent* (18 Dec 2007) · *The Times* (20 Dec 2007) · *PBA*, 161 (2009), 3–16 · *WW* (2007) · personal knowledge (2011) · private information (2011) · b. cert. · d. cert.

Archives FILM European Cultural Centre of Delphi, television interview with Vassilis Karasmanis, 2001

Likenesses photograph, repro. in http://phi.ruc.edu.cn/pol/?action-viewnews-itemid-3331 · photograph, repro. in M. Woods, ed., *A Festschrift for J. L. Ackrill* (1986), frontispiece

Wealth at death £1,199,760: probate, 10 March 2008, *CGPLA Eng. & Wales*

Ackroyd, Peter Runham (1917–2005), Old Testament scholar, was born on 15 September 1917 at 66 Stone Hill Road, Derby, the son of Jabez Robert Ackroyd, Congregational minister, and his wife, Winifred, *née* Brown. When the family moved to Harrow, Middlesex, he attended the county boys' school. He matriculated from Downing College, Cambridge, in 1935 to read modern and medieval languages as an exhibitioner, and graduated in 1938. After theological study in London (BD, 1940; MTh, 1942) he returned to Cambridge as Stanton student at Trinity College (1941–3), and received the degree of PhD in 1945 for a thesis on the criteria for the Maccabean dating of psalms. Meanwhile he was ordained a minister of the Congregational church in 1940. On 25 July the same year he married Evelyn Alice Nutt (*d.* 1990), a 25-year-old schoolteacher, and daughter of William Young Nutt, auctioneer and valuer. They had five children (two sons and three daughters).

Ackroyd served as minister of Congregational churches in Roydon, Essex (1943–7) and Balham, London (1947–8). In 1948 he was appointed lecturer in Old Testament and Hebrew studies at Leeds University and in 1952 he became lecturer in divinity at the University of Cambridge. In 1957 he was ordained deacon in the Church of England and in 1958 priest, serving as honorary curate of Holy Trinity Church, Cambridge. In 1961 he was elected to the Samuel Davidson chair of Old Testament studies at King's College, London, which he held until his retirement in 1982.

Drawing on his competence in German Ackroyd published, in 1957, an English translation of Ernst Würthwein's *The Text of the Old Testament* and, in the same year, a translation of Ludwig Köhler's *Hebrew Man*. These were followed in 1965 by *The Old Testament: an Introduction*, a translation of the comprehensive work by Otto Eissfeldt, which was extensively revised and updated from the first German edition of 1934. These books provided major study tools for English-language readers; the latter volume in particular presented detailed surveys of the complex literary analyses of the sources, structures, and forms of the Hebrew Bible. In 1968 Ackroyd published a revised version of his Hulsean lectures given in Cambridge in 1960–62, as *Exile and Restoration: a Study of Hebrew Thought of the Sixth Century* BC. This was his most original published writing and marked a fundamental rethinking of the literary consequences of the sixth century BC in the formation of the Hebrew Bible. It proved a seminal work of historical research, highlighting the theme of continuity through experiences of crisis which Ackroyd also explored in several short essays and articles. He contributed a chapter on this Persian period to the first volume of the *Cambridge History of Judaism* (1983).

The theme of continuity provided the subject of Ackroyd's inaugural lecture at King's College in 1962, in which he affirmed his regard for the Bible as the church's primary vehicle for upholding spiritual values. Both within the Bible and in its subsequent literary history, he traced the theme of continuity through periods of crisis and upheaval, returning to the theme repeatedly in numerous short perceptive studies. Both prophets and historians he regarded as agents fulfilling such a role.

Throughout his career in London he also made an extensive contribution as editor and promoter of popular commentaries, dictionaries, and surveys of current biblical research, encouraging a new generation of younger scholars to place a modern understanding of the Bible at the service of the church. He edited the Old Testament volumes of the Cambridge Commentaries on the New English Bible for Cambridge University Press and, with James Barr, the Old Testament Library and Studies in Biblical Theology for the SCM Press. He was also instrumental in promoting and editing, with C. F. Evans, the *Cambridge History of the Bible* (vol. 1, 1975), which marked a new departure in awakening interest in the contribution of the Bible to the history of ideas and to world literature. His short commentaries on several of the biblical historical books—*1 Samuel* (1971), *2 Samuel* (1973), *1 and 2 Chronicles, Ezra and Nehemiah* (1973), and *The Chronicler in his Age* (1991)—reflected his close interest in historical writing as an expression of moral and spiritual vitality.

Ackroyd was assiduous in engaging and encouraging friends and colleagues to write for a wide readership, offering advice and urging the necessity of combining scholarship with piety and social commitment. He himself lectured extensively abroad and maintained close links with colleagues and former students internationally. He was honorary secretary of the Palestine Exploration Fund (1962–70), editing its quarterly journal, and the annual *Book List* of the Society for Old Testament Study (1967–73), becoming the society's president in 1972. He served as dean of the faculty of divinity at King's College, London, in 1968–9 and was elected a fellow of the college in 1969; he served as dean of the university faculty of theology in 1976–80. He was made a DD of the University of London in 1970 and an honorary DD of the University of St Andrews the same year.

Following the death of his first wife, on 7 September 1991 Ackroyd married Ann Golden, aged fifty-seven, also a schoolteacher, and the daughter of Arthur James Golden, sales representative. He died on 23 January 2005 at Littleport Grange nursing home, Grange Lane, Littleport, Cambridgeshire, and was survived by his second wife, two sons, and two daughters, one daughter having predeceased him. RONALD E. CLEMENTS

Sources R. Coggins, A. Phillips, and M. Knibb, eds., *Israel's prophetic tradition: essays in honour of Peter Ackroyd* (1982) · *Daily Telegraph* (29 Jan 2005) · *The Times* (15 Feb 2005) · *The Independent* (19 Feb 2005) · *The Guardian* (30 March 2005) · R. Coggins, 'Peter Ackroyd (1917–2005)', *Palestine Exploration Quarterly*, 137/1 (April 2005), 5 · *WW* (2005) · personal knowledge (2009) · private information (2009) [M. D. Hooker; G. N. Stanton; M. A. Knibb; R. Coggins; J. Bowden, SCM Press; C. F. Evans; K. Carley; A. Phillips; G. Wenham] · b. cert. · m. certs. · d. cert.

Likenesses photograph, 1979, Photoshot, London · obituary photographs · photographs, repro. in *Prophetic tradition*

Wealth at death under £101,000: administration, 15 March 2005, *CGPLA Eng. & Wales*

Adams, Carol (**1948–2007**), educationist, was born on 28 July 1948 at Hackney Hospital, London, the daughter of (James) Gordon Adams, wine merchant, and his wife, Daisy Ellen, *née* Matthews. At the time of her birth registration her parents lived at 103 Glyn Road, Hackney. She grew up in working-class east London at the height of the *Windrush* era, and saw first-hand the influence and impact that a multi-ethnic London, rich with immigrants, would have during the next decades. She won a scholarship and was educated at Christ's Hospital Girls' School, Hertford, a school founded in 1552 to provide a first-class education for disadvantaged children, and it was there that the roots of her enduring commitment to an education system open to and fit for all began to grow.

Adams read history at Warwick University in the 1960s and during this decade of counterculture and revolution she began to explore issues of equality, particularly within the feminist movement. She spent time at the University of California at Berkeley during the peak of the civil rights movement and then returned to London to obtain a postgraduate certificate of education at the Institute of Education. She started teaching history in 1970 at a number of inner London state secondary schools before a stint as the Tower of London's education officer. She then managed the inner London education authority's history and social sciences centre, which ignited her lifelong passion for the promotion of professional development opportunities for all teachers. During this early period of her career she began to write and publish books, including *The Gender Trap* (with Rae Lauriekietis, three volumes, 1976) and *Ordinary Lives: a Hundred Years Ago* (1982), along with numerous teaching and in-service training materials focusing on equal opportunities within the school setting and gender issues. Meanwhile, on 26 March 1978, at Hendon Reform Synagogue, she married Richard Louis Noss (*b*. 1950), schoolteacher, and son of Michael John Noss, company director. They had two children, Joseph (Joe) and Amy. The marriage ended in divorce and he remarried, but she and Richard Noss remained lifelong friends.

The next stepping stone for Adams was to become a chief inspector for equal opportunities for the inner London education authority in 1983 and concurrently to study for an MA in human rights at the Institute of Education, awarded in 1984. From 1965 until its abolition in 1990 the education authority for the twelve inner London boroughs promoted and celebrated not just history, but feminist history, to all teachers in Greater London, in over 1000 schools. (Adams had already contributed to the burgeoning literature on women's history as co-editor of Cambridge University Press's Women in History series, and as a member of the editorial advisory board of Virago, the feminist publishing company.) When the authority was abolished in 1990 she was sought out to become the London borough of Haringey's assistant chief education officer and later the director of education in Wolverhampton. These roles next led her to Shropshire in 1994, where she became the first female chief education officer in England.

In 1997, after Labour's election victory, Adams joined a task force to explore the establishment of an independent professional body for teachers in England. When the General Teaching Council for England was established by the Teaching and Higher Education Act of 1998 she took the helm as chief executive to set up what would become a globally recognized model of self-regulation and registration for over half a million qualified teachers in England. She worked alongside Lord Puttnam (first chair of the council) as well as a broad coalition from across the education landscape in the UK to create an organization that would benefit the teaching profession. After its launch in September 2000 she and the organization faced criticism from teachers who felt they had not been properly consulted or briefed (despite an extensive consultation period with the public as well as the teaching unions and other bodies). Undaunted, she shouldered much of the criticism and worked indefatigably to reassure teachers around the country that the council was in their best professional interest, and would work both with and for them.

Never afraid to speak her mind, or to swim upstream against public opinion, Adams brought her determination to make evidence count in educational policy-making to Whitehall, and fought tirelessly to ensure that all children experienced a high quality of learning. She believed that education was the key to life chances and always worked to promote a high standard of achievement by all pupils. Her ability to bring the reality and expertise of the classroom to the corridors of Whitehall and Westminster contributed greatly to the influence and impact of the council's advice relating to professional development opportunities and entitlements for teachers.

Adams made sure that she did not get 'lost' in the bureaucracy of her role by visiting schools and education settings around the country on a regular basis, even when it meant catching the milk train to start her day. When one letter-writer to the *Times Educational Supplement* proclaimed the General Teaching Council for England a 'government poodle' (23 April 2004), she responded by marching into a meeting with education ministers wearing a pink T-shirt emblazoned with a poodle. Critical of many of the previous government's policies, she was not afraid to tell the Labour government to resist further changes to school grant-maintained status because it distracted governing bodies from more important preoccupations, such as literacy and numeracy. The fearless advocacy of equality and diversity and opposition to bigotry and prejudice of her early days as an adviser was continued in her role of commissioner for the Commission for Racial Equality, a non-departmental public body that aimed to combat racial discrimination and promote racial equality.

A keen follower of jazz, Adams played the clarinet and saxophone and retained a love of nineteenth-century industrial history along with swimming and travelling. Fearless and forthright, she fought against cancer privately for several years and finally lost her battle on 11 January 2007, a month after retiring as chief executive of the General Teaching Council. Her dedication to the teaching profession was recognized in small part through the council's sponsorship of the Carol Adams memorial award for excellence in professional development, equalities and diversity. She was survived by her children.

KEITH BARTLEY

Sources *The Guardian* (19 Jan 2007) · *Times Educational Supplement* (19 Jan 2007) · *The Times* (26 Feb 2007) · personal knowledge (2011) · private information (2011) · b. cert. · m. cert.

Wealth at death £287,645: proabte, 9 Oct 2007, *CGPLA Eng. & Wales*

Adams, Norman Edward Albert (1927–2005), artist, was born on 9 February 1927 in a flat at 74 Shernhall Street,

Walthamstow, Essex, the only child of Albert Henry Adams (1900–1975), a London Transport clerk, and his wife, Elizabeth Winifred Rose, *née* Humphries (1906–2000). The family moved shortly afterwards to Hendon and later Burnt Oak to be nearer their families, the house in which most of his childhood was then spent being one of the many 'sunshine semis' of the suburbs of north London. In 1940 he won a free place at Harrow Art School, where he stayed until 1946, meeting Anna Theresa Butt (*b.* 1926), daughter of George Baseden Butt, magazine editor, in 1944 when they were both students of painting. They married at Hendon register office on 18 January 1947, just in time for the great Europe-wide snowfall.

From Harrow Adams had won a scholarship to the Royal College of Art but his call-up papers had swiftly followed. He registered as a conscientious objector, but spent 'seven terrifying weeks' in Wormwood Scrubs prison for refusing to attend an army medical as ordered by the tribunal that turned him down (Usherwood, 12). Never a church-goer, and later calling himself a 'sort of freelance agnostic' (*Sunday Telegraph*, 14 May 1995), he credited that short but intense experience, during which he was much impressed by the prison chaplain, with convincing him that art had to have a message. Throughout his life he read considerably on religion and various mythologies, and his painting from the very first reflected a deep concern for both spiritual matters and music. He had discovered William Blake at the age of sixteen and Blake remained his great hero. He received no formal musical education but there had been a classical record society at Harrow, attended by staff as well as students; and the new BBC Third Programme became his musical university from 1947.

In 1948, after two years as a farm labourer in lieu of army service, Adams was able to take up his place at the Royal College of Art. He left three years later with the bronze medal for painting, having been taught by many talented figurative artists of the period, notably John Minton, Francis Bacon, Rodrigo Moynihan, and particularly Carel Weight, who continued to take a helpful interest in the young artist. His first solo exhibition was at Gimpel Fils in 1952, which led to a commission to design the sets for a ballet called *A Mirror for Witches*, choreographed by Andrée Howard and staged at Covent Garden. In 1955 he designed costumes as well as sets for *Saudades*, choreographed by Alfred Rodrigues and performed at Sadler's Wells. By this time he had moved to Roland, Browse, and Delbanco in Cork Street as his dealers, who gave him two-yearly shows until the late 1970s.

Another early commission, completed in 1954, was for murals of *The Odyssey* for the library of one of the earliest comprehensive schools, Broad Lane in Coventry, Adams and his wife having met the architect, Michael Smith. The school was later listed and renamed the Woodland School and Sports College. Parallel with these early successes Adams undertook stints of part-time teaching at Hammersmith and Maidstone art schools and then for nine years at St Albans. Among his colleagues at this lively school run by Mary Hoad were the experimental sculptor George Fullard and the painter Euan Uglow.

In the spring of 1955, while camping at Clapham in the Yorkshire dales, Adams and his wife found an affordable cottage with a barn that had studio potential. It stood on Butts Hill in Horton-in-Ribblesdale, so called from the ancient village archery location: it was simply a coincidence it matched Anna's maiden name. In 1956 their eldest son, Jacob, was born, soon followed in 1958 by Benjamin, and the routine of wintering in London and summering in Yorkshire continued for six years. Then in 1962 Adams was appointed head of painting at Manchester College of Art, where he stayed until 1970: for the first four years he stayed for three nights a week in a camper van in Manchester, returning for long weekends at Horton. In 1967, the year Adams was elected an associate of the Royal Academy, he was among several young and up-and-coming artists asked by Oxford University Press to illustrate parts of the Old Testament in five volumes. His colleagues in this project, including John Bratby and Alan Reynolds, all upheld in their own distinctive ways the English tradition. Adams held a particular distrust of the American influence on European painting, and maintained a missionary zeal that serious painters should be involved in higher education.

Ever enthusiastic explorers (though Adams never flew), the family had spent more than a month in the west of Scotland in 1963 and crossed to the Outer Hebrides. They paid a brief visit to the tiny island of Scarp, where six years later they bought a crofter's shieling where much of the 1970s was spent. This was a very productive decade, being almost free of teaching commitments apart from part-time lecturing at Leeds University from 1975 to 1978. In 1971 St Anselm's Church, in Kennington, commissioned Adams to paint large-scale murals on both sides of its aisle. The theme he chose was the Pilgrim's Progress, though he portrayed Bunyan's images in a semi-abstract language. In 1975 he made fourteen ceramic panels depicting the stations of the cross for the Roman Catholic church of Our Lady of Lourdes in Milton Keynes. Anna Adams's work as a ceramic sculptor and writer flourished and they began to visit Provence frequently, finding new sources of creativity together: he would say later, 'hardly a day goes by when I don't discover a new colour' (Usherwood, 80). In the spring of 1981, after returning from one of these first expeditions without their sons, Adams applied for the chair of fine art and director of King Edward VII College, Newcastle University, a post he held for five years.

The post for which Adams was best known, keeper of the Royal Academy Schools, was offered in 1986: he was glad to return to London and work in an establishment run by fellow artists. He had been elected a full member in 1972, and after nine years became in 1995 professor of painting, a post he held until he retired in 2000. The major part of his new salary consisted of a spacious and sky-lit residential studio at the top of Burlington House, just off Piccadilly. The academy respected his view that the work of professional artists involved in the training of the young should not be hampered, else they would have little to teach. Adams eschewed bureaucracy in all art schools, managing to tread the fine line between dealing with it while not letting it overtake the primacy of discussion and practical involvement with each student. His facility for watercolour resulted in his being invited by the Royal Watercolour Society to become an honorary member in 1987. In 1988 he illustrated Anna's book of mainly urban poems, *Angels of Soho*, and in 1991 contributed eight watercolours to *Island Chapters*, a book about their life on Scarp. In 1994 an anthology of articles about their life in Yorkshire, *Life on Limestone*, originally written for *The Guardian* and the *Craven Herald*, reproduced eight Ribblesdale watercolours. Earlier he had also illustrated books written by Glyn Hughes, *Alibis and Convictions* (1978), and John Milner, *A Decade of Painting, 1971–81* (1981).

In 1994 Dennis Clinch, the visionary parish priest of the oldest Roman Catholic church in Britain, St Mary's, Mulberry Street, Manchester, advised by Wendy Beckett, commissioned what Adams himself considered the greatest work of his life, the cycle in oils for the stations of the cross. Proving more easily comprehensible than the cycle at St Anselm's and more modern, even African in their influence, than his murals at Milton Keynes, they were summarized by Anna Adams as illustrating 'everything that has happened in the outside world in the way of men's ongoing crucifixion of one another' (*Stations of the Cross*, 9). Moving many visitors to tears, they were shown at the Royal Academy's Sackler galleries before being installed at the church, affectionately known as the 'hidden gem', in 1995.

Soon after the dedication of the stations, worrying symptoms Adams had gradually been experiencing were diagnosed as Parkinson's disease. While both his travelling life and his ability to draw direct from nature were curtailed his passion for painting from the imagination continued apace, still inspired by an enduring love of Blake and, to name but two others, Giotto and Grünewald. He worked on large watercolour compositions for eight years until his right hand lost its cunning. He last used the studio in Yorkshire in 2003 and thereafter, when not in hospital, he lived in the studio in Gainsborough Road, Chiswick, that he and Anna had bought in 1990. Anna was caring for him there when in August 2004 a violent rainstorm caused the main sewers in the road to overflow and their ground floor was completely flooded: Adams's bed became an island. While the water subsided the ensuing damage made life very difficult, so at the beginning of February 2005 he was moved into the Dudley House nursing home at Isleworth. He died there of bronchopneumonia on 9 March 2005 and was buried over the wall from the cottage in Yorkshire, at the Norman church of St Oswald, Horton, next to his mother, who had moved to Settle in her widowhood. He was survived by his wife, Anna, and their two sons. His gravestone is inscribed with a line from John Donne, 'I shall be made thy music'.

MAGDALEN EVANS

Sources *The stations of the cross by Norman Adams RA in Manchester's hidden gem* (1995) · *Sunday Telegraph* (14 May 1995) · A. S. Byatt, *Modern painters* (summer 1995) · P. Reyntiens, *The Tablet* (19 Oct 1996) · *The Spectator* (12 Dec 1998) · *Daily Telegraph* (14 March 2005) · *The Guardian* (15 March 2005) · *The Independent* (15 March 2005) · *The Times* (18 March 2005) · N. Usherwood, ed., *Norman Adams* (2006) [exh. cat., 108 Fine Art Gallery, Harrogate, 20 Nov – 9 Dec 2006] · *WW* (2005) · private information (2009) · b. cert. · m. cert. · d. cert.

Archives priv. coll. | RA | SOUND BL NSA, National Life Story Collection, artists' lives, interviews with M. Roberts, 2000, 2001, F8724–F8739, F9432–F9434

Likenesses N. Adams, self-portrait, etching, *c.*1947, priv. coll. · N. Adams, self-portrait, watercolour, 1981; Bonhams, 21 March 2006, lot 75 · T. Stubley, drawing, in or before 1982, priv. coll. · N. Adams, self-portrait, watercolour, exh. Fieldborne Galleries, London 1985 · J. Niblock, photograph, repro. in *East Anglian Daily Times* (11 March 2000)

Wealth at death £440,362: probate, 29 June 2006, *CGPLA Eng. & Wales*

Ahm, Povl Borge (1926–2005), civil and structural engineer, was born in Aarhus, Denmark, on 26 September 1926. He was educated at the Polyteknisk Laereanstalt in Copenhagen, graduating in 1949. He came to England in 1952 to join the consulting engineers Ove Arup & Partners, which had been established by a fellow Dane, Ove Arup, six years earlier. He remained with that firm for the whole of his working life, becoming a partner in 1965, a director in 1977, and chairman in 1989.

The year before Ahm joined Arups the firm had been appointed to work with Basil Spence on the new Coventry Cathedral. Spence's winning competition design had been developed without engineering advice, so Ahm and Ove Arup were called upon to devise a structure that would preserve the integrity of his initial concept. The solution was to provide a vaulted ceiling to the nave, consisting of a network of diagonal beams infilled with slatted timbers, carried on slender cruciform columns. The ceiling and columns, which narrow towards the east end of the cathedral, are separate from the roof above, which spans between the outer walls. Other aspects of the cathedral, such as the roof over the baptistry and the main porch, express their structure more explicitly.

Coventry Cathedral was not consecrated until 1962, by which time Ahm had worked on many other projects. Again with Spence he helped design the first buildings for the University of Sussex and also the British embassy in Rome. With his fellow Dane Arne Jacobsen he worked on St Catherine's College, Oxford (1959–64), producing a geometry of reinforced concrete walls and beams that matches the formality of the college layout. At Smithfield market in London he answered the need for a new column-free market hall by creating a domed concrete shell roof, rising 30 feet from its corners to the centre and mostly only 3 inches thick. Completed in 1963, it was one of the most daring shell structures of its time.

Ahm married Birgit Moller, whom he had known since childhood, in 1953; they had two sons, Carsten and Peter. In 1962 he and his wife built their own house at Harpenden, Hertfordshire, designed with the help of yet another Dane, Jørn Utzon. It was largely single storey beneath a sloping copper roof, linked to the garden by terraces. Listed grade II by English Heritage, it was described by one critic as 'probably the best modern house in the world' (*Sunday Times*). At the time of its construction, work on Utzon's masterpiece, the Sydney Opera House, was progressing and Ahm was one of the Arup team working on its engineering aspects.

The collective ethos of the Arup firm discouraged singling out the contribution of individual engineers on a project like the Sydney Opera House. However, Ahm had particular responsibility for the design of the podium on which the building stands, and for the spectacular beams of the concourse roof. The principal sail-like roofs for which the building is famous were first thought of as concrete shells: when eventually it was conceded that a simpler geometry, based on segments of a sphere built from concrete ribs, was the only sensible solution, this owed much to Ahm's work on the concourse beams. Utzon's resignation from the project in 1966 reflected the immense challenges it had posed, in politics and finance as much as design. Ahm was one of those who tried to persuade him to return.

As an engineer Ahm was known to be a brilliant analyst, but even more a designer eager to explore alternative solutions and to experiment. 'Engineering', he said, 'is really an art, and unless an engineer is able to use his knowledge and expertise in an imaginative and creative way, the whole discipline is not of much use' (*Concrete*, Jan 1970, 23). As he rose through the Arup hierarchy Ahm had to take on more administrative responsibility. When another famous cultural icon, the Centre Pompidou in Paris, came the firm's way in 1971 it was members of his team (Edmund Happold, Lennart Grut, and Peter Rice) who led on the design, while he kept an overview on the whole operation. During the same years he helped steer the firm towards bridge design and transport projects, particularly after winning the competition to design the Gateshead viaduct in 1965. His responsibilities extended beyond the firm: he was, for instance, a member of the council of the Institution of Civil Engineers (1972–5 and 1983–6) and chairman of the Association of Consulting Engineers (1992–6). He was made a CBE in 1993 and the same year received the first gold medal of the Institution of Civil Engineers. He received an honorary degree from Warwick University in 1994.

Ahm was tall, energetic, and self-assured. Among engineers, who are not naturally rhetorical, he stood out as someone who made his presence felt. He enjoyed team sports, and played football for Corinthian Casuals, taking part in the 1956 amateur cup final at Wembley Stadium. He remained with Arups until his retirement in 1992. He died at his home, 44 West Common Way, Harpenden, on 15 May 2005, of cancer of the oesophagus. He was survived by his wife, Birgit, and their two sons.

ROBERT THORNE

Sources P. Ahm and E. J. Perry, 'Design of the dome shell roof for Smithfield Poultry Market', *PICE*, 30 (Jan 1965), 79–108 • P. Ahm, 'Some thoughts on engineering design', *Concrete* (Jan 1970), 22–6 • P. Ahm and others, 'Design and construction of the Centre National D'Art et de Culture Georges Pompidou', *PICE*, 66/1 (Nov 1979), 557–93 • P. Ahm, 'Design and structure', *To build a cathedral*, ed. L. Campbell (1987), x–xii • P. Murray, *The saga of Sydney Opera House* (2004) • *The Independent* (23 May 2005) • *The Times* (4 June 2005) • *ARUP Bulletin*, 193 (July 2005), 22–3 • *Sunday Times* (3 Feb 2005) • personal knowledge (2009) • private information (2009) • d. cert.

Archives SOUND BL NSA, Ove Arup architecture interviews, interviews with L. Brodie, 11 Dec 1996, 17 and 24 Feb 1997, C765/15/01–06

Likenesses obituary photographs • photographs, Ove Arup & Partners

Wealth at death £851,696: probate, 11 Nov 2005, *CGPLA Eng. & Wales*

Aitken, Laurel [*real name* Oliver Anthony Stephens] (**1925–2005**), singer, songwriter, and record producer, was born on 22 April 1925, in Jamaica, one of six children of a Jamaican father and a Cuban mother. His early years were spent in Havana, Cuba, but the family moved to Kingston, Jamaica, in 1938. When fifteen years old he reputedly won a talent show at Kingston's Ambassador Theatre with his rendition of 'Pennies from Heaven'. Later he worked for the Jamaican tourist board, welcoming arrivals from the incoming cruise ships with currently popular songs. By the early 1950s he had assumed the name Laurel, or sometimes Lorenzo, Aitken, becoming a regular feature on the island's entertainment circuit, performing songs drawn from the popular hits of the American charts as well as jump blues, boogie, rhythm and blues, and indigenous material from the genres of mento and calypso.

Laurel Aitken first recorded at the Motta Recording Studios of Stanley Motta, based at 93 Hanover Street in Kingston. Just around the corner was Motta's store on Harbour Road, where the records were sold. Aitken sang his own composition in the popular mento style 'I Met a Senorita', coupled with a merengue entitled 'Merenguita'. Going on to secure a residency at the Colony Club in Half Way Tree, he was able to finance the production of more songs in the studio. His first hit record was a rhythm and blues based calypso–spiritual, 'Roll Jordan Roll', released by another local entrepreneur, Dada Tewari.

Reflecting the common practice of many of the American artists who influenced him, Aitken had two distinct sides to his recorded output. On the one hand he dealt with secular subject matters, usually based around the themes of women, alcohol, and good times; on the other he recorded material that reflected a different context. 'Ghana Independence' and 'Nebuchanezer' were released about 1957 on Caribou 78s, and he recorded a series of gospel songs for a number of different producers, including 'Zion' and 'Judgement Day' for Duke Reid, and 'What a Weeping' and 'Zion City Wall' for Leslie Kong. One unusual element that distinguished many of these recordings was the use of a trio of drums known as the 'burro'—bass drum, funde, and repeater—that would later be popularized by Prince Buster's recording of the Folks Brothers' 'Oh! Carolina', the work of Count Ossie and the Mystical Revelation of Rastafari, and eventually too in many examples of the most widespread of Jamaican musical genres, roots reggae.

In 1958 Aitken began recording for the producer Chris

Blackwell's newly created Island label. His single 'Boogie in My Bones', backed by 'Little Sheila', was the label's début release and also one of the earliest examples of the emerging genre that was to become known as 'ska'—a music indigenous to Jamaica but based on the shuffle blues originating in New Orleans. Aitken had taken a step in this direction the year earlier with the release of 'Aitken's Boogie' on Ken Khouri's Federal label. But 'Boogie in My Bones' was a huge breakthrough hit in Jamaica and topped the Jamaican Broadcasting Company chart for almost three months. Its success warranted a domestic release in Britain, thereby gaining the distinction of the first Jamaican pop record to be issued there.

In 1960 Emil Shallit's Kalypso label released 'Aitken's Boogie' in Britain, and in that year Aitken emigrated to England, settling in Brixton, where there was an established Jamaican community. He was prominent in the development of Shallit's Blue Beat label, a name that became synonymous with the music it showcased, releasing a further sixteen titles on the label over the following few years. Through this decade, as ska changed into rocksteady and rocksteady to reggae, Aitken established himself as a producer. He worked with such bands as the Bees, the Cimarons, and the Rudies, all of whom acted as backing and support bands for Aitken's own material, as well as with the singer Winston Groovy and the all-white reggae band Inner Mind. He also occasionally recorded under the pseudonym King Horror on a number of comedy talkover deejay tracks such as 'Loch Ness Monster', 'Dracula, Prince of Darkness', and 'The Hole'.

Laurel Aitken, Jamaica's first genuine recording star, became famous not only for his groundbreaking and popular records but also for his snappy dress sense, Italian-styled mohair suit, pork pie hat, and shades. His appearance earned him the sobriquets Godfather of Ska and Boss Skinhead, and created an icon that lived on through the 2 Tone era when the sound of ska was revived across Britain by bands like the Specials, Madness, and the Beat. During this period Aitken's career went through a resurgence when he had a hit with 'Rudie Got Married' as an answer to the Specials' 'A Message to You, Rudie'. In the 1980s he regularly toured the UK and recorded with the British act Potato 5. In 1986 he appeared alongside David Bowie in the film *Absolute Beginners*. He also recorded with Japan's Ska Flames, Germany's Busters, and America's Toasters.

In 2003 Aitken was treated for double pneumonia but recovered and went on to perform again; his last concert was in January 2005. Having lived in Leicester since the 1970s, he died at Glenfield Hospital, Leicester, on 17 July 2005, of chronic respiratory failure and heart failure. He was survived by his wife, Sandra Olga Stephens, and his daughter. STEVE BARKER

Sources *Daily Telegraph* (22 July 2005) · *The Times* (26 July 2005) · *Leicester Mercury* (28 July 2005); (29 July 2005) · *The Independent* (24 Aug 2005) · www.laurel-aitken.surf3.net, 17 July 2008
Archives SOUND BL NSA, documentary recording · BL NSA, performance recordings
Likenesses obituary photographs · photographs, Redferns Music Picture Library, London
Wealth at death under £2000: administration, 3 Oct 2005, *CGPLA Eng. & Wales*

Akehurst, Sir John Bryan (1930–2007), army officer, was born on 12 February 1930 at Marlow, Harsted Avenue, Chatham, Kent, the only child of Geoffrey Guy Akehurst (1901–1956), bank cashier, later bank manager, and his wife, Doris Jessie, *née* Kerwin (1903–1990). Educated at Cranbrook School, Kent, he enlisted in the army as a private soldier in 1947. The following year he was selected to attend the Royal Military Academy, Sandhurst; he was commissioned a second lieutenant in the Northamptonshire regiment on 16 December 1949. In 1952, after two years' service in Trieste, he volunteered to be seconded to the Malay regiment, serving as a lieutenant with its 5th battalion in operations against communist guerillas and gaining a mention in dispatches. With promotion to captain, he married, on 18 May 1955 in Malaya, Shirley Ann Webb (*b.* 1935/6), daughter of Major W. G. Webb, a Malayan civil servant. Their two children died young, of cystic fibrosis.

Between 1956 and 1960 Akehurst resumed duties with the Northamptonshire regiment, serving in Hong Kong and England. He attended the Staff College, Camberley, in 1961, earning a posting the following year as brigade major to 12 infantry brigade in the British army of the Rhine. In 1965 he was a company commander with the 2nd Royal Anglian regiment in Cyprus before being recalled to the staff college to join the directing staff there. Early in 1968, after two years at Camberley, he was given command of the 2nd Royal Anglian regiment. As part of 19 infantry brigade in the strategic reserve his battalion had to be ready to serve anywhere at short notice; and over the next two and a half years, besides participating in exercises in Cyprus, Kenya, and Malaysia, it was also called upon—at a time of Spanish sabre-rattling in 1968–9—to reinforce Gibraltar. Between 1970 and 1974 he was successively on the directing staff of the Royal Defence College in London and, newly promoted to colonel, commandant of the junior division of the Staff College at Warminster. By now he had long been regarded as a man of promise: his confidential report acknowledged that while the best officers should appear able to do their job one-handed: 'With John, however, I have sometimes heard a whisper of "Look, no hands!"' (*Generally Speaking*, 150).

In January 1974 Akehurst was chosen to command the Dhofar brigade in the sultan of Oman's service. The brigade, British-officered but otherwise comprising Omani and Baluchi troops, was embroiled in a nine-year-long civil war in Oman's Dhofar province against communist-inspired tribesmen backed by neighbouring South Yemen. After his arrival in south Arabia, a chance conversation with a Special Air Service non-commissioned officer, who told him that the *firqats*—groups of rebels who had surrendered and taken up arms for the sultan—were eager to return to their tribal areas, led Akehurst to initiate a strategy 'to secure Dhofar for civil development' (*We Won a War*, 65). He would capture rebel-held territory, drill water holes for the *firqats*' cattle, create the beginnings of villages, and—after warning the *firqats* that if the rebels reappeared the water supply would be cut off—left them to it. Writing to London on 4 November 1974, the British ambassador in Oman was enthusiastic: 'John Akehurst's decision to get the Firqat back into their own tribal areas and to take responsibility for them instead of sheltering in strong points … seems to be paying off' (TNA: PRO, FCO 8/2216). Later, in the final push for victory in October 1975, Akehurst showed his ability to exploit a fast-changing tactical situation. A diversionary attack launched from the mountain fastness of Sarfait having achieved unexpected results, he promptly ripped up his plans and reinforced success instead. 'Meet your flexible brigadier', he smilingly announced (Jeapes, 223). The war was now won, although on Christmas day 1975 rebel gunfire was still capable of forcing down Akehurst's helicopter.

Akehurst moved to the Ministry of Defence as deputy military secretary in 1976 and, as a major-general, commanded 4th armoured division in Germany in 1979–81. His subsequent term as commandant of the Staff College, Camberley, was considered notably successful. In 1984, on promotion to lieutenant-general as commander, United Kingdom field army, and inspector, general territorial army, he was created KCB. His last appointment, in 1987–90, as a full general, was as deputy supreme allied commander Europe, 'the perfect bridge between working and not working', as Akehurst, who believed that the position carried little influence, described it (*Generally speaking*, 208).

In retirement Akehurst wrote an amusing memoir, *Generally Speaking* (1999). He achieved wider public recognition as an expert on BBC TV's *Newsnight* during the Gulf War of 1990–91. The *Sunday Times*, in a poll on the performance of war pundits in the media, awarded him 10/10. He lived at Dresden Cottage, 46 Vicarage Street, Warminster, Wiltshire, which he had bought in 1981. In retirement he was involved in many organizations, including as a member of the Commonwealth War Graves Commission (1993–8), chairman of the governors of Harrow School (1991–7) and Princecroft primary school, Warminster (1995–2000), and president of the Warminster Civic Trust (1998–2007). He died on 20 February 2007 at the Royal United Hospital, Bath, after a stroke, and was survived by his wife, Shirley. A memorial service was held in the Royal Memorial Chapel, Sandhurst, on 3 June 2007.

ALASTAIR W. MASSIE

Sources T. Jeapes, *SAS: Operation Oman* (1980) • J. Akehurst, *We won a war: the campaign in Oman, 1965–1975* (1982) • J. Akehurst, *Generally speaking: 'then hurrah for the life of a soldier'* (1999) • *The Times* (27 Feb 2007) • *Daily Telegraph* (6 March 2007) • *Castle: Journal of the Royal Anglian Regiment*, 14/3 (June 2007), 83–4 • *Army List* • TNA: PRO, FCO 8/2216, 2456, 2707; DEFE 13/779, 24/1875 • *WW* (2007) • Burke, *Peerage* • b. cert. • d. cert.

Archives TNA: PRO, FCO 8/2216, 2456, 2707 • TNA: PRO, DEFE 13/779, 24/1875

Likenesses obituary photographs • photographs, repro. in Akehurst, *Generally speaking*

Wealth at death under £79,000: probate, 17 May 2007, *CGPLA Eng. & Wales*

Alexander, Robert Scott [Bob], **Baron Alexander of Weedon** (**1936–2005**), barrister and banker, was born on 5 September 1936 at 12B Kingsway West, Newcastle under Lyme, Staffordshire, the son of Samuel James Alexander, motor engineer and garage proprietor, and his wife, Hannah May, *née* Trevitt, an accountant's secretary. He was privately educated at Reading School, Brighton College, and King's College, Cambridge. At Cambridge he took advantage of the flexible tripos system to switch after two years from English, under the supervision of Dadie Rylands and F. R. Leavis, to law; he was taught by Kenneth Polack, a South African research student who had just completed a pupillage in the Temple, and who diverted him from his original plan of becoming a solicitor. He obtained a 2:1. Inspired by his reading of the lives of great advocates, he studied for his professional examinations by correspondence course, and was called to the bar—a route, as he once put it in a British Council lecture in Pakistan, 'traditionally said to be followed by many actors manqués'—by the Middle Temple in 1961 with the aid of a Harmsworth scholarship. During this time he earned extra money by sub-editing the *Times* law reports.

Alexander's path to the pinnacle of his profession was not negotiated in a smooth upward trajectory. At university he had indulged in amateur theatricals without notable success and he never spoke at the union. For five years he practised on the western circuit, selected by indigent defendants for the occasional dock briefs by reason of his conspicuous presence, and he only moved to Brick Court in the Temple on the recommendation of Eustace Roskill, chairman of the Hampshire quarter sessions and an enthusiastic patron of the talented young. The chambers, whose alumni included Patrick Devlin, specialized in commercial work, but in the doldrums of the mid-1960s the head, Sam Cooke, was not in favour of his tenancy. He was persuaded by the senior clerk, Ron Burley, to take a chance, a shrewd piece of advice that in the long term made Burley the doyen of the clerking fraternity. During Alexander's membership and not least because of his own growing reputation Brick Court became part of the chambers' magic circle. But he was no solitary star. His contemporaries included Nicholas Phillips, later lord chief justice, and Sydney Kentridge, the celebrated South African advocate.

Height is not a necessary or even a sufficient guarantee of success at the bar but it is an advantage; and at 6 feet 6 inches Alexander had the physical attributes to dominate a court. His advocacy was fluent but not florid, his voice plummy but not pungent, purged, save in his own view, of the midland accent of his youth. He was always immaculately dressed. He ascribed his forensic achievements to meticulous preparation. 'I would prepare my questions', he said, 'so that if I got the answer yes, I would go one way, and if not, another. It meant that you thought through the various permutations in advance' (*The Independent*, 8 Nov 2005). Lord Denning described him as 'the best advocate of his generation' (ibid.). He took silk in 1973 after a bare twelve years.

Consistent with Brick Court's traditional culture Alexander practised primarily as a commercial lawyer, but he ranged beyond the traditional fields of banking, shipping, and insurance. He held briefs for government, successfully in denying trade union rights to workers at the Government Communications Headquarters in Cheltenham, unsuccessfully in trying to prevent publication of *Spycatcher*, a book written by the rogue former MI5 officer Peter Wright. His private clients included Kerry Packer, whom he helped to defeat the cricketing establishment, and Jeffrey Archer, for whom he won a famous libel trial. Archer's subsequent imprisonment for perjury in no way detracted from the praise accorded to Alexander's conduct of the case, including his cross-examination of the prostitute who claimed—contrary to his client's denial—to have had sexual relations with Archer. When in 1985 *The Guardian* assessed his annual earnings at £1 million, Alexander publicly offered to disclose the true figure if the newspaper paid 20 per cent of the difference to charity. It declined the offer. But that his fees were at the top end of the market was indisputable, and enabled him to purchase, in addition to his London home, properties near Aylesbury, in the Dordogne, and in Spain, as well as to indulge a hobby of collecting paintings by young artists.

Alexander's courtroom battles with Tom Bingham, later holder of the judicial 'triple crown', successively master of the rolls, lord chief justice, and senior law lord, were the forensic equivalent of the pugilistic struggles of Muhammad Ali and Joe Frazier. Many thought he would choose—as he certainly could have chosen—the same judicial career as his sometime opponent, not least after his chairmanship of the Bar Council in 1985–6, a post that then gave legitimate expectation of appointment to the bench. He decided, however, on a complete career change. After a two-year stint as chairman of the Panel on Takeovers and Mergers, from 1987 to 1989 (during which time he was made a life peer, as Baron Alexander of Weedon, in 1988), he became chairman of National Westminster Bank from 1989 to 1999, acquiring *en route* non-executive directorships of the Stock Exchange, RTZ Corporation, and Total Oil. He was not the first nor last of those who spurned judicial office, but he was a notable example of a barrister, eminently *papabile*, who (like an increasing number of his generation) recognized the virtues of life beyond the law.

Alexander shone somewhat less as a banker than he had as a barrister, seeking to balance the interests of shareholders with stakeholders to (inevitably) the entire satisfaction of neither, and at the conclusion of his bank chairmanship he returned to practice, in 2001. His second coming was not an unalloyed success. Unwilling to retread the path of trial work he did not return to Brick Court, but became instead joint head of chambers (with Michael Crystal) at 3–4 South Square, a specialist insolvency set, where his son David practised. He promoted himself as an appellate advocate, arbitrator, and expert in constitutional and international law, but although he became treasurer of the Middle Temple in 2001, the complete break he had made for a decade meant that he never wholly recovered his earlier pre-eminence. He was in any event occupied by a collection of distinguished extracurricular posts. He once lectured on 'My passions, Shakespeare and cricket', which explained his chairmanship of both the Royal Shakespeare Company (2000–04) and the MCC (2001–4). He was, as well, a trustee of *The Economist* and of the National Gallery. His interest in education brought him the chancellorship of the University of Exeter, from 1998 (where a building dedicated to drama was posthumously named after him), a governorship of Wycombe Abbey School, and a quintet of honorary degrees.

A consensual man by temperament, and schooled by the disciplines of his profession to see and to articulate both sides of any argument, Alexander was an early member of the Social Democratic Party but subsequently switched his allegiance, becoming a Conservative life peer in 1988. Although both a Europhile and a one-nation tory, he none the less was an admirer of Margaret Thatcher. He had well-known ambitions to become lord chancellor, but the vagaries of politics denied him a post to which he would have been well suited. He nevertheless rendered his public service without partisanship. He was on the government panel for sustainable development during the Major and the Blair premierships (1994–2000), was a member of the Jenkins commission on electoral reform (1997–8), and advised Gordon Brown (as chancellor) on the fiscal regime for the shipping industry. He also chaired the House of Lords delegated powers and deregulation scrutiny committee (1995–2002).

If Conservative by party, Alexander was liberal by temperament. He served as chairman of Justice, the human rights organization (1990–2005), and of Crisis, a charity for single homeless people (1990–96). He wrote a book on constitutional reform, *The Voice of the People* (1997). He was a vigorous defender of judicial independence and of the interests of the bar. But usually he carried his emollient style from his profession into his public life, always balancing his criticism of particular policies with words of general praise for their authors. His broadside against the legitimacy of the invasion of Iraq ('scraping the bottom of the legal barrel'; *The Guardian*, 15 Oct 2003) and his assault on the government's hastily announced plans for constitutional reform in 2003 ('apparently written on the back of an envelope'; *The Independent*, 8 Nov 2005) were exceptions to the rule: the consummate diplomat could on occasion adopt the mien of the warrior.

Alexander was married three times: first on 26 October 1963 to Frances Rosemary Heveningham Pughe, a 22-year-old student, and daughter of Major Richard Pughe, army officer; secondly on 27 July 1978 to Elizabeth Frances Warrens Norman, a 25-year-old fashion designer, and daughter of Colonel Charles Richard Warrens Norman, army officer; and thirdly on 9 July 1985 to Mary (Marie) Anderson, a 38-year-old Irish-born barrister and former model, and daughter of Daniel Joseph Sugrue, farmer. The first two marriages ended in divorce but the third lasted until his death. With his first wife Alexander had three children, David (*b.* 1964), Mary (*b.* 1966), and William (*b.* 1969), and with his second a son, Mathew, who died in infancy. There was another daughter, Rosemary (*b.* 1962). He himself died at St Thomas's Hospital, Lambeth, London, of a stroke on 6 November 2005, having risen from a provincial background to the summit of the establishment—a classic illustration of the opportunity for upward mobility in post-war Britain. MICHAEL BELOFF

Sources *Daily Telegraph* (8 Nov 2005) • *The Guardian* (23 Oct 1989); (8 Nov 2005) • *The Independent* (18 March 1989); (8 Nov 2005) • *The Times* (8 Nov 2005) • *The Argus* [Brighton] (10 Nov 2005) • *The Economist* (12 Nov 2005) • *WW* (2005) • Burke, *Peerage* • personal knowledge (2009) • private information (2009) • b. cert. • m. certs. • d. cert.

Archives FILM BFINA, current affairs footage | SOUND BL NSA, current affairs recording

Likenesses Bassano, eight half-plate film negatives, 1978, NPG • G. Levine, photograph, *c.*1994, Getty Images, London • photographs, 1995–9, Photoshot, London • S. Whyte, bronze, exh. Society of Portrait Sculptors, London 1996 • F. Terry, portrait, 1998, repro. in *Francis Terry: recent paintings* (2000) • I. Walton, photograph, 2001, Getty Images, London • obituary photographs • photograph, MCC, Lord's, London

Wealth at death £720,723: administration with will, 13 June 2007, *CGPLA Eng. & Wales*

Allan, Elkan Philip (1922–2006), journalist and television producer, was born Elkan Philip Cohen at 16 Hoveden Road, Cricklewood, London, on 8 December 1922, the son of Allan Cohen, (*d.* 1952), furrier, later an owner of printing presses, and his wife, Rose, *née* Prager. During the 1930s or 1940s his parents changed their surname from Cohen to Allan; Allan's father also adopted a middle name, Michael. Allan himself changed his name by deed poll on 7 December 1940. Alongside his business interests Allan's father was both a gambler and a tirelessly inventive entrepreneur, driven by the same energy and creativity that would characterize his son's versatile professional life.

Educated at Quinton School, and exempted from Second World War service on medical grounds, Allan started his career in 1941 as an assistant editor of the trade magazine *The Outfitter*. His column, 'Dress circle', in which he reviewed theatrical costumes as a way of securing free tickets for West End openings, was the beginning of a lifetime of genially creative opportunism. The following year, after entering the *Daily Express* building in Fleet Street by the back entrance to avoid the commissionaires, he introduced himself to the news editor and was immediately given a job as a reward for his ingenuity. By 1945, as a junior reporter on *Picture Post*, he was assigned to cover the expected losers in the general election, thus finding himself alongside Clement Attlee when he received the dramatic news of Labour's victory. There followed spells as features editor of *John Bull* magazine and assistant editor of *Illustrated* before he moved into radio and television broadcasting. Meanwhile on 27 November 1947, at Kensington register office, he married Dorotheen Mary Ingham, a fellow journalist a year Allan's senior, daughter of William Ingham, schoolteacher. They had two sons and a daughter.

In 1945 Allan had already shown an instinct for the evolving genres by creating (and writing the questions for) BBC radio's first quiz shows, *Quiz Time* and *Quiz Team*. He moved into television (in which he would prove an imaginative pioneer) in 1953, as a presenter of the BBC's *Armchair Traveller*. With the advent of ITV two years later he became a reporter, then a producer for Associated Rediffusion's current affairs programme *This Week*. In 1960 he started writing and producing television documentaries, including *Freedom Road*, an exploration of negro protest songs that won all three prizes at the Berlin television festival in 1961. The following year he became Rediffusion's head of entertainment, responsible for such popular shows as Hughie Green's *Double Your Money* and Michael Miles's *Take Your Pick*.

It was in this capacity, in 1963, that Allan created and produced *Ready, Steady, Go!*, a seminal Friday night pop music show whose catchphrase 'The weekend starts here' became emblematic of the 'swinging sixties'. As well as showcasing all the groups of the moment—the Beatles, the Rolling Stones, the Kinks, the Who, the Moody Blues, and many more—it also featured a nineteen-year-old typist from Streatham, Cathy McGowan, as one of its presenters, thus offering new horizons to British youth in a manner entirely typical of Allan's creative imagination. The show lasted until December 1966, when it fell victim to the BBC's *Top of the Pops*, a hasty replacement for *Juke Box Jury*.

After a less successful attempt at cinema production with Rediffusion, including the bold documentary *Love in Our Time* (1968), while also writing scripts for the television series *Batman*, Allan returned to print journalism, persuading the equally dynamic editor of the *Sunday Times*, Harold Evans, to let him pioneer the art of critical television previewing. Thanks to his contacts in the business, and his inside knowledge of programme making, he wrote shrewd and balanced advance reviews that at first attracted envious hostility from rivals who were soon, of course, following his lead, finally breaking the monopoly long enjoyed by the *Radio Times*. His first marriage having ended in divorce, he married, at Hampstead register office on 5 September 1970, Angela Joy (Angie) Willment, daughter of Clifford Samuel Willment, timber manufacturer. She was also a journalist, then aged twenty-five. They collaborated on three encyclopaedic film guides, and had a son and a daughter.

Allan was lured away from the *Sunday Times* in 1979 by Sir James Goldsmith, to help launch his short-lived news magazine *Now!* In 1986 he joined another new publication, *The Independent*, as listings editor. By his seventieth birthday in 1992 he had moved to Los Angeles, where he spent four years as Hollywood correspondent of the *Mail on Sunday* and a contributor to *Variety*, while also writing television scripts. There he resumed his lifelong passion for poker, which he liked to call his 'pension' back in London, where he worked into his eighties as a poker journalist and website consultant.

Allan died of a stroke in the Whittington Hospital, Islington, London, on 25 June 2006. He left unfinished a comprehensive 'Poker Encyclopaedia', lovingly completed by his young friend Hannah Mackay, who had dealt to him at a London poker club. 'Don't be too sad,' he told his family in a moving farewell note, 'I've had a long, marvellous and happy life, and know I'm loved as well as loving.' He was survived by his second wife, Angie, and his five children. ANTHONY HOLDEN

Sources *The Guardian* (13 Feb 2006); (30 June 2006) · *The Independent* (29 June 2006) · *The Times* (1 July 2006) · personal knowledge (2010) · private information (2010) · b. cert. · m. certs. · d. cert.
Archives FILM BFINA, light entertainment footage
Likenesses E. Allan, photograph, 1965, PA Photos, London · D. Hoffmann, photograph, 1965, Rex Features, London · obituary photographs

Allbeury, Theodore Edward Le Bouthillier [Ted] (**1917–2005**), intelligence officer and novelist, was born on 24 October 1917 at 478 Manchester Road, Stockport, Lancashire, the son of Theodore Allbeury, cotton goods buyer, and his wife, Florence, *née* Bailey. He had one sister. His father died when Allbeury was young, though the circumstances are unclear; Allbeury later claimed both that his father was an officer in the Black Watch, killed a few days before the armistice in 1918 (no such casualty is recorded by the Commonwealth War Graves Commission), and that he died in Africa when Allbeury was five. Allbeury was prone to story-telling about his own life. After his father's death he and his mother and sister lived first in Birmingham, where he attended Slade primary school in Erdington, then in Ilford, where he attended Ilford county high school, then again in Birmingham, where he attended the King Edward VI Grammar School in Aston. He showed a particular flair for art, and on leaving school worked in the drawing office of an iron foundry, while also taking evening classes and teaching himself French and German.

Shortly after the outbreak of the Second World War Allbeury responded to an advertisement in *The Times* seeking linguists for special work with the army. He was interviewed in the back room of a barber's shop off Trafalgar Square, an encounter that he later wrote into several of his novels. Accepted into the intelligence corps, he served in Somalia, Ethiopia, the Sudan, Italy, and finally occupied Germany. He was demobilized in 1947 with the rank of lieutenant-colonel.

It is unclear whether, to what extent, and how long Allbeury continued in intelligence work after his official release in 1947; his own accounts varied. From the 1950s through to the late 1970s he worked in advertising and public relations, except for a few years in the early 1960s when he farmed chickens on the Isle of Oxney, Kent (which he found tedious and unrewarding). In the late 1950s he ran J. W. Southcombe, an advertising agency, and in 1964 he co-founded Allbeury Coombs & Partners. In 1965 he took over a pirate radio station, King Radio, which broadcast from the Red Sands fort in the Thames estuary. He renamed the station Radio 390 (from its wavelength) and relaunched it to provide middle-of-the-road, 'easy listening' music, mainly to housewives. It broadcast Allbeury's own show, *Red Sands Rendezvous*. The station was closed, along with other pirate radio stations, in 1967. In 1968 Allbeury stood unsuccessfully as a Liberal candidate at Petersfield. He was married several times, the last on 13 May 1972 to Grazyna Maria [Graz] Felinska (*d.* 1999), a 25-year-old secretary, and daughter of Richard Marian Felinski, businessman. He had a son and three daughters in total.

It was the experience of losing contact with one of his daughters that in part inspired Allbeury to write his first novel, *A Choice of Enemies* (1973), a spy thriller set largely in occupied Germany. Its main protagonist, Ted Bailey, clearly based in part on Allbeury himself, is sympathetically portrayed, faced with a recurrent choice between obeying orders and following his conscience (the latter with dire consequences). Allbeury went on to write some forty books under his own name, as well as others under the pseudonyms Richard Butler and Patrick Kelly; at one point he was publishing four books a year. Most were spy thrillers, set apart from most others in that genre by their preoccupation with character and psychology rather than action and gadgetry, though his early books in particular contained their fair share of spy chases. Perhaps his best books were *The Lantern Network* (1978), a story about honour and betrayal in the Special Operations Executive in France, and a sequel, *As Time Goes By* (1994), written from the perspective of its women agents in France. Other notable books included *The Special Collection* (1975), about KGB infiltration of British trade unions, and *The Alpha List* (1979), in which the narrator has to investigate his closest friend. Allbeury's books were commercially successful, and in one year he received a penny more under public lending right than Barbara Cartland, an achievement he relished.

Allbeury gradually gave up his work in advertising in order to concentrate on writing. He continued writing into his eighties, his last book published in his own lifetime being *Hostage* (2004). Several more were published after his death. The death of his wife, Grazyna, was a hard blow. Living latterly at 7 Lanthorne Mews, Tunbridge Wells, he died on 4 December 2005 at the Kent and Sussex Hospital, Tunbridge Wells, of bronchopneumonia. He was survived by his four children. ALEX MAY

Sources *The Independent* (15 Dec 2005) · *The Guardian* (3 Jan 2006) · *The Times* (5 Jan 2006); (7 Jan 2006) · b. cert. · m. cert. [1972] · d. cert.
Archives FILM BL NSA, documentary footage | SOUND BL NSA, documentary recordings
Likenesses G. Davies, resin print, 1980, NPG · obituary photographs
Wealth at death £716,373: probate, 23 Feb 2006, *CGPLA Eng. & Wales*

Allen, Dave [*real name* David Edward John Archer Cullen Tynan-O'Mahony] (**1936–2005**), comedian, was born on 6 July 1936 at Merrion House, Lower Fitzwilliam Street, Dublin, the youngest of three sons of (Gerard John) Cullen Tynan-O'Mahony (*b.* 1900), journalist and managing editor of the *Irish Times*, and his wife, Jean Ballantyne, *née* Archer, an English nurse. He was brought up in Ireland as a Roman Catholic by a mother who was a converted Anglican and a

Dave Allen (1936–2005), by Trevor Leighton, 1999

father who was an agnostic. During his first stage appearance, in a Firhouse national school play at the age of four, he played a frog and found that the faulty fly of his costume prophetically revealed too much for the scandalized nuns. His childhood became impoverished after his father took to drink and gambling. He died when David was twelve. No longer well dressed, the boy went to Terenure College, Dublin, but the loss of his father affected him profoundly. He became awkward. He liked drawing, but did not like the priests telling him what to draw. He was eventually expelled and went to the Catholic University School, Leeson Street, Dublin, but left without gaining a leaving certificate, to take dead-end jobs selling draught excluders and manning the toy counter in a department store. He then went to Independent Newspapers, where his brother Johnny (*b.* 1933) was working, later moving to the *Drogheda Argus* to work with his other brother, Peter (1930–2000), as tea and copy boy before doing reporting. Soon bored, he followed his mother and brother Johnny to England. Having joined Johnny as a Butlin's Redcoat he was, aged nineteen, guiding a party near Brighton when it began to rain heavily. The soaked holiday makers were taken into the ballroom of the Ocean Hotel in Brighton until the rain stopped. He saved the day by grabbing a stool, setting it down facing the audience, and telling stories from it for a full hour. In various formats, with the addition of a large glass of whiskey, a languidly-held cigarette, and rumbustious sketches, it was to be the core of his professional act.

Having obtained the services of an agent, and having adopted the stage name Dave Allen, because his agent did not have any names beginning with the letter A above him on his clients list, he embarked on a career as a professional entertainer. His first booking outside holiday camps was at the London Casino, and he went on to tour clubs and the variety circuits and to appear in pantomimes. In 1959 he appeared on the *New Faces* television talent show on ATV, which led to longer appearances on BBC television. In 1962 he appeared with the popular singer Helen Shapiro in a show at Brighton, and when the Beatles joined its tour the following year he took over as compere at thirty dates around the country. After this he went to try his luck in Australia, beginning as a supporting act to the operatic singer Helen Traubel at the Chevron Hotel, Sydney, where she advised him to base his jokes more on things that had happened in his own life. His first Australian television show was *In Melbourne Tonight*, for which he leapt on to a desk and did a form of one-man pantomime. Eventually he was given his own show, *Tonight with Dave Allen*, consisting of gags, rambling stories, and interviews with people who did strange things like breeding lethal spiders and 'proving' that the universe was no more than 1000 miles across. In 1964 he interviewed on Australian television the actress Judith Mary Stott (*b.* 1929), who was appearing in Sydney in *The Private Ear and the Public Eye*. They married on 9 March 1964. In the same year he received his first award—a Logie for 'most popular male'—and his *Tonight with Dave Allen* was voted the most popular programme.

Later in 1964 Allen returned with his wife to Britain, where their daughter Jane was born in 1966 (they had a son, Edward, in 1968). In 1966 he was asked to present *The Blackpool Show*, the comedian Tony Hancock being ill. It was a significant date: he was now top of the bill, and presented what was to become his irreverent and often abrasive mixture of religious jokes and social comment from his bar stool. In 1967 he hosted *Sunday Night at the London Palladium*, and then recorded thirteen episodes of *Tonight with Dave Allen* for ITV, for which he gained the Variety Club's ITV personality of the year award. He resisted attempts to place his late-night show in an earlier prime-time slot, because the late slot meant he could use more 'adult' material. His frequent channel-hopping between the BBC, ITV, and television in Australia and New Zealand was often due to such scheduling disagreements. A typical sketch—he wrote many himself—was one in which the pallbearers carrying two coffins race one another to the same graveyard; they were bound, like his irreverence from the bar stool, to affront many people.

Allen's brief return to Australia in 1971 for a 90 minute special, called simply *Dave Allen*, proved to be even more abrasively irreverent. The anarchic comedians Peter Cook and Dudley Moore were waiting to be interviewed by Allen when Cook, a heavy drinker, disappeared. When Allen asked Moore on air where Cook was, Moore replied, 'Taking a piss', to which Allen responded, 'Fuck him then'. The switchboard was jammed with protesting calls, and all three performers were banned from Australian television for two years. But the following year the second series of *Dave Allen at Large*, on BBC2, attracted the biggest audience ever for the channel. In 1974 his anthology of horror stories, *A Little Night Reading*, was published. When in 1975 the BBC showed a sketch with him as the pope stripping off as he went up church steps, there were 200,000 complaints from viewers. In 1977 RTE, Ireland's public service channel, banned all programmes by him. Once again scandal perhaps helped him, because the following year, when *An Evening with Dave Allen* had a UK tour, it beat previous box office records in many theatres, and the *Dave Allen At Large* special on BBC2 won the silver rose at the Montreux festival, and was nominated for an Emmy award.

In the 1980s a new wave of hard-hitting, machine-gun-talking comics to an extent eclipsed Allen's star. In 1981 he gave up smoking after puffing eighty Gauloises a day. He began to look more like an academic, with cardigan and 'granny' spectacles; and when he made a tour of the USA he received poor reviews. He and his wife Judith were divorced in 1983 on the grounds that they had lived apart for over two years. After more tours of New Zealand he returned to Britain, and to critics sniping that he was not the equal of the new 'alternative' comedians. One of the few encouragements in this decade was meeting Karin Stark, a theatre producer twenty-seven years younger than him, and the daughter of William David Pinkerton Stark, musician; they were to remain partners until his death.

In 1990, after four years' absence from British television, Allen returned with *Dave Allen*, originally a stage show, explaining that he was retired but in order to keep himself in the manner to which he had become accustomed he had to work. One of his jokes was that a worker clocked on and off and did everything by the clock, and when he retired, what did they give him? 'A fucking clock!' The BBC switchboards were again jammed and there were questions in the House of Commons. His 1991 season at the Strand Theatre, London, was a sell-out despite the fact that no free seats were sent to critics. About this time he was diagnosed with emphysema, claiming, improbably, that he had developed it as a result of passive smoking in clubs. In 1996 he was given an award for lifetime achievement at the British comedy awards.

Still doing work for charities until near the end of his life, Allen died at the Chelsea and Westminster Hospital, London, on 10 March 2005 of heart failure caused by chronic obstructive pulmonary disease. He was acclaimed by his fellow professionals as a great artist who assuaged his irritation with any sort of authority by enabling his audiences to laugh off the oppressions of everyday life. Five weeks after his death Karin, whom he had married on 9 December 2003, had their son Cullen.

DENNIS BARKER

Sources *The Guardian* (12 March 2005) • *The Independent* (12 March 2005) • *The Times* (12 March 2005) • *Daily Telegraph* (12 March 2005) • C. Soutar, *Dave Allen: the biography* (2005) • The best of Dave Allen, BBC dvd, 2005 • m. cert. [2003] • d. cert.

Archives FILM BFINA, *Aspel and company*, N. Phillips (director), ITV, 3 Sept 1988 • BFINA, *The Clive James show*, C. Longton (director), ITV, 8 March 1998 • BFINA, documentary footage; performance footage | SOUND BL NSA, AIRC programme sharing collection, interview with R. Holness, LBC, 1987, C1000/004/87/1 • BL NSA, performance recordings

Likenesses photographs, 1960x69–2000, Rex Features, London • photographs, 1974–99, PA Photos, London • photographs, 1975–2001, Camera Press, London • C. Poole, bromide print, *c*.1979, NPG • photograph, 1986, Photoshot, London • T. Leighton, photograph, 1999, Camera Press, London [*see illus.*] • B. E. Fantoni, pencil and gouache drawing, NPG • obituary photographs

Wealth at death £3,189,394: probate, 4 Dec 2006, *CGPLA Eng. & Wales*

Allen, Percival [Perce] (**1917–2008**), geologist and sedimentologist, was born on 15 March 1917 into a large family in Brede, near Hastings, Sussex, the son of Norman William Allen, grocer and draper, and his wife, Mildred Kathleen, *née* Hoad. He was educated at Rye grammar school and the University of Reading, from which he graduated with a BSc in geology in 1939. During the early Second World War he worked in photographic intelligence in the Royal Air Force, meanwhile researching for his PhD on the early Cretaceous sediments of the Weald of Kent and Sussex. In 1941, while still a student, he married a fellow geologist, (Frances) Margaret Hepworth (*d.* 2007), with whom he had three sons and one daughter.

Demobilized early, Allen became a university demonstrator in geology at the University of Reading in 1942, was awarded his PhD in 1943, and was promoted assistant lecturer in 1945. In 1947 he moved to Cambridge, where he was university demonstrator in geology from 1946 to 1947 and subsequently university lecturer until 1952. At the International Geological Congress of 1948 he successfully proposed the formation of the International Association of Sedimentologists, which was formally launched in 1952.

In that year Allen returned to Reading as professor of geology and head of the geology department, succeeding the distinguished palaeontologist Herbert Leader Hawkins, positions which he held for the next thirty years until his retirement in 1982. There he continued his research into Wealden rock formations, and became secretary of Philpots Quarry, West Hoathly, Sussex, enabling him to carry out research on the puzzling sandstones there. In 1975 he published a highly influential paper in the *Proceedings of the Geologists' Association*, which provided a 'new model' for the deposition of the Wealden beds that was subsequently widely accepted. Until then it had been thought that the Wealden beds accumulated in a delta, but Allen argued that instead they represented a broad coastal plain of alluviation traversed by numerous rivers and intermittently flooded by the tide; the sedimentary facies in the two cases are much the same, but their disposition and sources of supply are quite different. Another important paper by him had been published in 1959, predicting that the North Sea would contain substantial oil reserves, and advocating exploration there.

In 1962 Allen founded with funds from industry the sedimentology research laboratory at Reading; to mark its opening he organized a conference which, at his suggestion, led to the foundation of the British Sedimentological Research Group, which became the main forum for sedimentologists, especially younger ones, in the UK. The group later created the Perce Allen Award in his honour. Allen also chaired the first European earth and planetary physics colloquium in 1971 and the first meeting of the Association of European Geological Societies in 1975; the latter body instituted in his honour the Percival Allen medal for promoting international relations between geoscientists, which was awarded for the first time in 2007. His other international activities of an early date included contributing scientific advice toward German post-war reconstruction. In 1971 he received the Lyell medal of the Geological Society of London, of which he was president from 1978 to 1980. He was elected a fellow of the Royal Society in 1973 and served as a vice-president from 1977 to 1979. He received an honorary doctorate from Reading in 1992, and was an honorary member of the geological societies of America, India, and Bulgaria.

From boyhood Allen had displayed a great aptitude for science. As a youth he kept a detailed nature notebook based on his travels by bicycle—the latter practice one he vigorously pursued all his life—through the rural and coastal landscapes of his native place. He was passionate about the geology of Wealden rocks, especially in south-east England but also on the European mainland, and throughout his whole career worked on little else. His published writings were not extensive, partly because of a compulsion toward almost endless revision with the help of razor blades, so that his draft manuscripts, the bane of his secretaries, looked as though attacked by mice. But what he did publish was of the highest quality.

Two strands in particular illustrate Allen's interests and methods. His earliest efforts were directed at reconstructing the sources of Wealden sediments, that is, essentially the geology of the considerable region that supplied detritus to the Wealden basin of deposition. This he did by the meticulous analysis of detrital heavy minerals and pebble assemblages, and the application of geochemical techniques to suitable detrital sediment components. In these activities he broke decisively with the past and used statistical methods as a basis for conclusions; he was greatly encouraged in these endeavours by his friend Walter C. Krumbein of Northwestern University, USA. To this kind of research Allen added penetrating analyses of the depositional environments in which the Wealden sediments formed. His method was a detailed application of the longstanding Lyellian principle of the present being the key to the past, a safe enough bet for rocks just 125–145 million years old. His interpretations, the fruit of a controlled scientific imagination, were based on direct comparisons at a variety of spatial scales of Wealden rocks with modern sediments and environments he had seen for himself or found described. Although this work set a new standard, Allen was prepared radically to revise his interpretations of his previous facts. Few subsequent sedimentologists have accepted his precepts so fully, preferring generalized facies models or merely interpreting one sequence of rocks in terms of another.

To have conversed with Allen was to have known that here was no ordinary clay. He was a person of humility—indeed he could be exasperatingly self-effacing—and also of great humanity, as many colleagues and students found in time of need. As a teacher he was considerate and encouraging. He could be playful and amusing, but also had a ruthless streak and loathed with a special fervour those academics he saw as meretricious, publicity-seeking and failing, as he put it, 'to keep the faith'. The part of the Sussex rustic he often chose to play concealed a shrewd and guileful person who mostly got his way. Some condemned him for what they described as 'enthusiasm', and there can be little doubt that occasionally he succumbed. In 1959 he achieved a degree of national notoriety after he collaborated with rag students in announcing that diamonds had been found in the gravels of the Thames Valley, a patent geological absurdity. Most newspapers, tongue in cheek, gave the 'news' a brief notice, except *The Times*, which accorded the announcement great and portentous coverage including many photographs and, when the hoax emerged, published a leader condemning his behaviour. For some time thereafter, however, *The Guardian*, whenever *The Times* misinterpreted or misreported an important national event, would mischievously allude to the dangers of 'talking to professors at Reading'.

Allen was passionate about his family, his garden, and chess: within the family circle his entirely characteristic watchword was 'nothing is boring!' He remained active in retirement, but was much affected by the death of his wife, Margaret. He subsequently moved to the Avon Park Care Centre, Limpley Stoke, Wiltshire, where he died on 3 April 2008, of kidney failure and ischaemia. He received a woodland burial near Thornbury, Bristol, where family and friends cast into his grave rock specimens, fossils, and other items which they associated with him. His four children survived him. J. R. L. Allen

Sources *Daily Telegraph* (26 May 2008) · *Geology Today*, 24/5 (Sept–Oct 2008), 168 · *Wealden News*, 8 (Feb 2010), 2–3 · www.geolsoc.org.uk/gsl/society/history/obituaries/page5809.html, 7 June 2011 · www.bsrg.org.uk/history.html, 7 June 2011 · *WW* (2008) · personal knowledge (2012) · private information (2012) · b. cert. · d. cert.
Likenesses obituary photographs
Wealth at death £441,366: probate, 2 Dec 2008, *CGPLA Eng. & Wales*

Allen, Philip, Baron Allen of Abbeydale (1912–2007), civil servant, was born at 17 Edgedale Road, Sheffield, on 8 July 1912, the younger son of Arthur Allen (1875–1962), schoolmaster, and his wife, Louisa Mary (Louie), *née* Tipper (1883–1966). From elementary school he won a scholarship to King Edward VII School in Sheffield, and from there a scholarship to Queens' College, Cambridge, before graduating in 1934 with firsts in both parts of the history tripos. He then came first in the civil service examination for the administrative class. He started as a civil servant in the Home Office in 1934, and married early in his career, on 2 July 1938 at Christ Church, Dore, Sheffield, Marjorie Brenda Coe (1914–2002), daughter of Thomas James Colton Coe, provision merchant. There were no children of the marriage.

Allen's first Home Office posts were in the police and criminal divisions. He served in the private offices of the

Philip Allen, Baron Allen of Abbeydale (1912–2007), by Walter Bird, 1964

two home secretaries (Sir John Anderson and Herbert Morrison) during the Second World War. He also had a spell in the offices of the War Cabinet, where he was secretary to the speaker's conference on electoral reform. After the war he was awarded a Commonwealth Fund scholarship, which took him to the United States for a study of police and prison practices there. From 1950 to 1952 he was the deputy chairman of the Prison Commission.

From 1952 to 1955 Allen was responsible for all the work of the police and criminal divisions of the Home Office. One of his duties (as it had been for a short time in the late 1940s) was to help Sir Frank Newsam, the permanent secretary, with death penalty cases, where the home secretary had to decide whether there should be a reprieve or whether 'the law should take its course', as the official documents would say. Allen read the complete transcripts of the trials, often at the weekend or on holiday, and after discussion with Newsam, and with the doctors when the prisoner's mental state was an issue, he drafted the memorandum on the case for the home secretary, usually adding his own recommendation.

In 1953 Newsam and Allen recommended a reprieve for Derek William Bentley, aged nineteen, who was convicted with Christopher Craig of murdering a police officer. Craig, who fired the fatal shot, was sixteen and could not be executed. Bentley, it was alleged, had incited Craig to fire the shot. The home secretary, Sir David Maxwell Fyfe, did not accept the advice, and Bentley was hanged. This decision continued to be bitterly opposed for many years. In 1993 a royal pardon was granted for Bentley, and in 1998 the Court of Appeal quashed the murder conviction. At this time the official papers on the case were made public, bringing out that the two key officials had advised in favour of a reprieve for Bentley. But Allen, a constitutional purist, nevertheless regretted this departure from the confidentiality of officials' advice to ministers. Allen had also been involved in the decision in 1950 not to reprieve Timothy John Evans, who was convicted of strangling his young daughter. (In view of this conviction, a charge of murdering his wife remained on the court file.) In 1953 John Christie, who lived in the same house, was convicted of strangling a number of women there. An inquiry by Scott Henderson QC before Christie was executed concluded that Evans was nevertheless guilty of killing his wife and daughter. But the issue rumbled on. The Bentley and Evans cases figured prominently in the campaign against capital punishment, which was finally abolished in 1964. These two cases convinced Allen of the case for abolition, if only because of the arbitrariness of the reprieve decisions.

In 1955 Allen was promoted to be a deputy secretary in the Ministry of Housing and Local Government, dealing with planning issues and the reorganization of water authorities. Duncan Sandys was the minister and the redoubtable Dame Evelyn Sharp the permanent secretary. Allen was amused rather than irritated by Duncan Sandys's need to consider nineteen separate drafts of the planning decision about a road across Christ Church meadow in Oxford. On returning to the Home Office in 1960 his knowledge and experience were further enlarged. For the first time in his career he was responsible for work in the aliens department and the civil defence department. In 1963 he went to the Treasury, where he helped to set up the Fulton committee on the civil service, and became a member of it. He joined in the committee's recommendations for a civil service department and a civil service college. He was in no way complacent about the civil service, but it was not his view or his style to start with the sweeping assumption in some of the evidence to the committee that he and his colleagues were a bunch of amateurs. He was knighted KCB in 1964, having been made a CB in 1954.

In 1966 Allen returned to the Home Office as permanent secretary; Roy Jenkins was home secretary. He declined Dick Crossman's invitation to be permanent secretary at the Ministry of Housing and Local Government. Allen's own performance as permanent secretary at the Home Office belied the assumptions surrounding the Fulton committee. He won the approval and admiration of the four home secretaries he served (Jenkins, James Callaghan, Reginald Maudling, and Robert Carr). As principal adviser he saw his role as helping the home secretary to get things right. Ministers needed to know that he was on their side and that responsible officials could advise ministers directly. Honest dialogue with ministers was what he sought, and largely secured. From Roy Jenkins on, parliament and interest groups were no longer the only influences on policy. Public opinion and the media were now an additional currency, and these new relationships were to be managed like the others. Allen realized that a new public style was needed. The Home Office became more open, and his leadership of the Home Office was much admired.

One of Allen's first issues was a further chapter in the Evans–Christie case. Jenkins had quickly appointed another inquiry, by Sir Daniel Brabin, who concluded that Evans probably killed his wife and not his daughter, but that a jury knowing about Christie would have found it very difficult to convict Evans of either murder. This was still not sufficient on the Home Office precedents for granting a free pardon, for which innocence had to be established; and there were some legal doubts about issuing a free pardon posthumously, without further legislation. Jenkins took the view that after Brabin's inquiry Evans's conviction could not be allowed to stand, and a free pardon was the only way of recognizing this. Allen did not disagree, and a free pardon was issued.

The recurrent crises of the Home Office took up much of Allen's attention and required his steady hand: for instance the escape from Wormwood Scrubs prison of George Blake, who was serving forty-two years for espionage, scandals concerning excessive use of corporal punishment at Court Lees approved school, and the demonstrations in London against the war in Vietnam. Then Northern Ireland preoccupied his last years as permanent secretary. In 1972 he gave Brian Faulkner, the prime minister of Northern Ireland, the cabinet's decision that direct rule was to be imposed.

Allen was ready for policy changes, but preferred to make one well-considered change at a time, and he knew that lasting improvements were delivered only by constant attention. The announcement of the policy decision was but the first step towards progress. Longer-term issues in his day included the modernization of the police, the amalgamation of police forces, police appointments, technological changes, and the investigation of complaints, as well as the growth in the prison population and Commonwealth immigration. Allen remained attached to the importance of the police and criminal divisions of the office, and they provided most of the issues he had to deal with. (This was before the creation in 2007 of a separate Ministry of Justice.) For most of his career the Home Office was also responsible for the child-care work of local authorities. His sympathy for those in trouble valued the location of the children's department in the Home Office, and he resisted its move to the Department of Health and Social Security in 1971. He was promoted GCB in 1970.

After retirement from the civil service in 1972 Allen embarked on a second career of virtually full-time public service for the next thirty years. In 1975 he was chief counting officer for the referendum on continued membership of the European communities. He continued in the public eye when he investigated the leakage of Harold Wilson's resignation honours list in 1976; the culprit was not identified. In the same year he became a life peer, as Baron Allen of Abbeydale (taking his territorial designation from the area of Sheffield where he was born and brought up), and the House of Lords provided him with a new stage. He was a prime example of the new generation of life peers with huge practical experience who were ready to work on committees of the house examining issues and government proposals. His intelligent and slightly ironic questions could turn debates round, and government legislation on charities in 1992 was largely the result of his efforts. He was a leading figure in the counsels of the cross-bench peers. He was soon asked to chair a committee considering the case for a human rights bill, which produced an authoritative analysis that was much quoted in subsequent debates. He was chairman or member of a number of committees, particularly on European issues, and his views had great influence in the house.

Allen was chairman of the Occupational Pensions Board until 1978 and a member of the royal commission on compensation for personal injury (1973–8). He relished learning about the complex area of pensions, contrasting it with Home Office topics, which everyone thought they understood. He was a member of the Gaming Board and then its chairman from 1977 to 1985. He operated a powerful system of control, keeping undesirables out of high-profile casinos, but dealing more sympathetically with bingo halls. He was a member of the Security Commission from 1973 to 1991, a member of the royal commission on standards of conduct in public life (1974–6), a member of the tribunal of inquiry into the crown agents (1978–82), and chairman of Mencap (1982–8). He lived for many years in Englefield Green, Surrey, and was able to take an interest in Royal Holloway College nearby, becoming chairman of the governing body on its merger with Bedford College in 1985. His eye for detail and possible compromise steered the merger successfully. As a member of the House of Lords he was able to guide the legislation that was required. This introduction to the educational world stimulated him to make further contributions in debates on education in the House of Lords.

Allen was a wise man, with a very good brain and powers of concentration. He could appear austere and private but he was comfortable with people from all walks of life. He rarely raised his voice and was quietly self-confident. All this made him a man of great influence and much respected. He won the trust of leading politicians of all parties. He combined experience, keen judgement, and a wish to get things right on fashionable and unfashionable subjects alike. He was subtle but straightforward. He saw the need for change, without slipping into 'campaigns' for 'reform'. His style was understated and relaxed, but precise. He routinely deleted *therefore*, *however*, and *of course* from drafts put up to him. In discussion he would introduce a crippling objection with the words 'Isn't this perhaps a point to consider'. He was a very human and private man, who took quiet pride in his minor triumphs. He worked out that he was the only person who had been a member of two royal commissions at the same time. As permanent secretary of the Home Office he was the sole authority for issuing ivory passes, which entitled the holder to drive through Horse Guards, and took moderately quiet satisfaction from following the precedents by refusing a pass to junior ministers, while having one himself. He was constant in his friendships. He did not advertise himself. He never smoked, drank, or swore, but had a taste for fast cars, owning at one time an elderly Bentley, which was followed by a series of Bristols, Alfa Romeos, and Mercedes. He supported Sheffield Wednesday Football Club through thick and (mostly) thin. He was attached to nonsense verse and could quote at length from Lewis Carroll's *The Hunting of the Snark*.

Marjorie, Allen's devoted wife of over sixty years, died in 2002. In 2007 he suffered briefly from bronchial pneumonia, from which he died at the Princess Margaret Hospital, Windsor, on 27 November 2007. A memorial service was held in the chapel of Royal Holloway, University of London, on 18 November 2008. BRIAN CUBBON

Sources P. Allen, memoir, priv. coll. • *Daily Telegraph* (29 Nov 2007) • *The Independent* (29 Nov 2007) • *Yorkshire Post* (1 Dec 2007) • *The Times* (4 Dec 2007) • *The Star* [Sheffield] (6 Dec 2007) • *The Guardian* (11 Dec 2007) • *WW* (2007) • personal knowledge (2011) • private information (2011) • b. cert. • m. cert. • d. cert.

Archives SOUND BL NSA, documentary recording

Likenesses W. Bird, bromide print, 1964, NPG [*see illus.*] • photographs, 1973–8, Photoshot, London • obituary photographs

Wealth at death £2,103,207: probate, 17 April 2008, *CGPLA Eng. & Wales*

Almeida [*née* Hart]**, June Dalziel** (1930–2007), virologist, was born on 5 October 1930 at 10 Duntroon Street, Glasgow, the daughter of Harry Leonard Hart, bus driver, and his wife, Jane Dalziel, *née* Steven. On leaving school in 1947 she became a laboratory technician in histopathology at Glasgow Royal Infirmary on a salary of 25*s.* per week. She then moved to St Bartholomew's Hospital, London, working in the same discipline. On 11 December 1954, at Hampstead register office, she married Enriques Rosalio (Henry) Almeida (1913–1993), a Venezuelan artist, and son of Cirilo Almeida Crespo, also an artist. They had one daughter, Joyce.

After their marriage June Almeida and her husband emigrated to Canada, where she was appointed an electronmicroscopy technician in the Ontario Cancer Institute in Toronto. On the other side of the Atlantic there was less emphasis on formal training requirements and the necessity of having to overcome academic hurdles. Within a short time her skills and enthusiasm became apparent, her name being included on numerous scientific publications, particularly relating to viral structure. Fortuitously, in 1964 A. P. Waterson, recently appointed to the chair of microbiology at St Thomas's Hospital medical school, visited Toronto, was impressed by her work, and persuaded her to join him at St Thomas's. She moved with him to the Postgraduate Medical School of London three years later. These years were the start of a particularly fruitful period in June Almeida's career; her numerous high-quality publications were rewarded with the degree of DSc, and by the time of her death most virology review articles and chapters in textbooks contained her photoelectronmicroscopy of viruses.

The technique employed and pioneered by June Almeida, immuno-electronmicroscopy employing negative contrast, had a simplicity and originality that characterized her work. Virus preparations were mixed with specific antibodies to the virus, which resulted in the clumping of virus particles that could be visualized by electronmicroscopy; the concentration of antibody could then be reduced to reveal details of the fine structure of the virus, sometimes with bridging of the virus particles by the specific antibody. This technique made it possible to visualize directly the fine structure of viruses that failed to grow to sufficiently high concentrations to display by negative staining. Notable among her achievements with this technique was the first visualization of the fine structure of the rubella virus. One of her most important discoveries, which provided a landmark for those investigating hepatitis B, again using the technique of immune electronmicroscopy on detergent-treated virus particles, revealed a new antigen-antibody system. There were two immunologically distinct components to the virus, an outer coat and a small inner component. She also collaborated with David Tyrrell, director of the Common Cold Research Unit in Salisbury, who had developed a new technique employing organ cultures from respiratory material. They jointly characterized new viruses—the coronaviruses—which caused acute respiratory infections; SARS is now recognized as belonging to this group of viruses.

It was particularly fortunate that in 1970 Albert Z. Kapikian, from the National Institutes of Health in the USA, spent six months' sabbatical in Waterson's department, at the suggestion of his laboratory chief, R. M. Chanock, and while there attained first-hand experience of immuno-electronmicroscopy from June Almeida. He took the technique with him on returning to the USA and exploited it at the National Institutes of Health with his colleagues, leading to the discovery of viruses hitherto unseen. These included the virus responsible for an outbreak of non-bacterial gastroenteritis in a school in Norwalk, Ohio. By immuno-electronmicroscopy of clinical samples from this outbreak fed to volunteers, aggregates of small-structured round virus particles were visualized and antibody responses could be assessed, employing acute and convalescent phase serum samples. These viruses, considered to be the first viruses identified in the etiology of infectious gastroenteritis, were originally named Norwalk viruses (now noroviruses, a term June Almeida vehemently disliked) and similar viruses are now known to be the commonest cause of non-bacterial gastroenteritis among adults. A further notable achievement deriving from Almeida's technique was the visualization for the first time of the elusive hepatitis A virus, using similar immuno-electronmicroscopy methods to those of the Norwalk virus discovery, by Stephen M. Feinstone, Kapikian, and Robert H. Purcell, at the National Institutes of Health. Although the epidemiology and clinical features of hepatitis A had long been established, not least because of epidemics of infection in wartime and in institutionalized populations, the virus had not itself been seen until Almeida's techniques were used.

Almeida had a remarkable enthusiasm and the ability to interact equally well with her technical, scientific, and medical colleagues, regardless of their seniority. Meetings with her were full of fun. She taught many virologists, whether working on the more fundamental or the clinical aspects of virology. She enabled laboratory workers to identify viruses within a few minutes of clinical specimens arriving in the laboratory, which contrasted with the hitherto more laborious and time-consuming techniques then available. Almeida had the capacity to put over her methods and ideas in a delightfully direct and simple way, whether this was to one or two sitting beside her in the electronmicroscope suite, or to an audience of several hundred in a lecture theatre.

Almeida finished her career at the Wellcome Research Laboratory, where she worked on developing diagnostic assays and vaccine development. Her first marriage having ended in divorce, on 1 December 1982 at Greenwich register office she married a fellow virologist, Phillip Samuel Gardner, formerly Weidengarten (1925–1994), son of Arnold Weidengarten, diamond merchant. In 1985 they retired to Bexhill. In the late 1980s she returned to St Thomas's in an advisory role, publishing with colleagues in virology some of the first high-quality negative staining electronmicrographs of human immunodeficiency virus. Nevertheless her career took different directions. She trained and qualified as a yoga teacher, running several successful classes in the town, and (having developed an interest in collecting antiques through regular visits to East Street bric-a-brac market in Walworth) also trained in china restoration and achieved considerable expertise, which led to a productive and enjoyable career trading in antiques with her husband, Phillip. In later life she enjoyed being a grandmother, providing daycare for her two granddaughters during holidays and taking great pleasure in learning the computer skills beloved of their generation.

The career of June Almeida demonstrated how an academically able Scottish schoolgirl, despite leaving school aged sixteen, became an internationally renowned clinical scientist whose skills in electronmicroscopy enabled her not only to identify viruses the structure of which had hitherto been unknown, but also to shed light on the pathogenesis of virus infections and to pioneer and improve techniques for the diagnosis of virus infections. She died on 1 December 2007 at her home, 56 Sea Road, Bexhill, after a heart attack, and was survived by her daughter, Joyce, a consultant psychiatrist, and her granddaughters. J. E. BANATVALA

Sources A. Z. Kapikian, 'The discovery of the 27-nm Norwalk virus: an historic perspective', *Journal of Infectious Diseases*, 181/suppl. 2 (2000), S295–302 · '2005 Albert B. Sabin Gold Medal: address delivered by award recipient Albert Z. Kapikian MD, tributes by R. M. Chanock, MD and R. I. Glass, MD, PhD, and memorial tribute to J. R. La Montagne, PhD', 10 May 2005 · *The Times* (18 Feb 2008) · *BMJ*, 336 (28 June 2008), 1511 · personal knowledge (2011) · private information (2011) · b. cert. · m. certs. · d. cert.
Likenesses photograph, repro. in *The Times* (18 Feb 2008)
Wealth at death £677,094: probate, 22 May 2008, *CGPLA Eng. & Wales*

Anderson, Alfred (1896–2005), joiner and soldier, was born on 25 June 1896 at 20 Kinloch Street, Dundee, the third son of Andrew Anderson (1864–1945) and his wife, Christina, *née* Emmerson (1868–1945). His parents had emigrated to Chicago, Illinois, and were married there in 1888. However, nostalgia for Scotland or a downturn in the American economy sent them home in the 1890s. One of Alfred Anderson's earliest memories was associated with the celebrations accompanying the end of the South African War. Dundee was *en fête* and, at a victory parade, a sergeant picked him up and carried him on his shoulder through the cheering crowds. Soon afterwards the family left Dundee for the nearby planned village of Newtyle, over the Sidlaw Hills on the edge of Strathmore. Alfred went to school there and at the Harris Academy in Dundee. Meanwhile his father's business as an undertaker and joiner flourished. From an early age Alfred became used to the sight of bodies and helped with the 'coffining' before funerals. The village 'killing house' or abattoir also accustomed him to the ever-present slaughter of animals. He claimed that this long experience of death meant that the sights he encountered at the western front had a less powerful effect upon him than on many of his comrades.

In 1912 Anderson joined the Territorial Army for no other reason than that it would introduce him to friends, provide an opportunity for physical activities and sports, and, most important, offer a week's holiday during the annual camp in nearby locations in Perthshire. The 1914 camp was in late July, soon after Alfred turned eighteen, and most of the young men with whom he trained died in the trenches. With the outbreak of the First World War, these members of the Territorial Army were enrolled in the 5th battalion of the Black Watch, which recruited mainly in Perthshire and Angus. After a relatively brief training the battalion left for the front, crossed the channel in a cattle boat, and the kilted men found themselves laughed at and molested by village women as they marched through northern France.

For well over a year Anderson remained at the front, experiencing all the rigours of the trenches. He was batman to Lieutenant Bruce-Gardyne and then to Fergus Bowes-Lyon, the son of the earl of Strathmore and brother of Elizabeth, later Queen Elizabeth, the queen mother. Throughout this period the only relief for the troops was rest periods behind the lines. Anderson retained vivid memories of the sudden and unexpected peace of the Christmas truce, of the conditions in farms where they were billeted, of encounters with Indian soldiers, and many of the terrifying features of trench warfare. At the battle of Loos in September 1915 the Black Watch took severe casualties with Bowes-Lyon among the dead. Anderson, however, survived. Some weeks later he was injured by shrapnel at a forward listening post. Evacuated in great pain hours later, he was repatriated to a hospital in England. His war was over and his injuries saved him. Promoted sergeant, he became an army physical trainer at a camp in Yorkshire. There he met his future wife, Susannah Iddison (*d.* 1979), daughter of a watchmaker. They were married at St Andrew's Church, Kirkby Malzeard, near Ripon, on 2 June 1917, when both claimed to be twenty-one (though Anderson was in fact twenty). They had two sons and three daughters.

At the end of the war Anderson was keen to stay in the army with the rank of sergeant-major, but familial duties called. He was summoned home to take over the family business. His subsequent life was uneventful apart from a period running the Home Guard in Newtyle during the Second World War, but his great longevity was to bring him considerable fame in his last years. He lived long enough to become an emblem of the past and a representative of an entire generation. Although a few veterans of the First World War survived him, he was, by the end of his life, the last living member of the pre-1914 Territorial Army, the last soldier to have gone to war in the autumn of 1914, and the last survivor of the celebrated Christmas truce of that year. He became a chevalier of the Légion d'honneur, and was repeatedly featured in newspapers, in television documentaries, and in a number of books about war veterans. His sharpness of mind, his great dignity, and his acute wit marked him out as a striking figure, physically active until he was past 105. The cricketer and artist Jack Russell painted his portrait when he was 107. Shown the result, Anderson said 'You've made me look older than I am' (private information). Lionized in the Black Watch, he enjoyed having generals pay court to him. The prince of Wales met him on several occasions, at Anderson's home and at regimental events, and he later unveiled a memorial to him in Alyth, where Anderson spent his final years, except for the last six weeks, which he spent at Mundamalla Nursing Home in nearby Newtyle. He died there of bronchopneumonia on 21 November 2005. His funeral, at Alyth parish church on 25 November, was attended by a representative of Prince Charles, the French consul-general, senior politicians, and army officers, as well as many soldiers past and present. Obituaries and accounts of the funeral were printed in the national newspapers and there were items on television news. His remains were cremated at Perth crematorium. He was survived by two daughters and two sons (one daughter having predeceased him), and by ten grandchildren, eighteen great-grandchildren, and two great-great-grandchildren.

JOHN M. MACKENZIE

Sources J. M. MacKenzie, *Alfred Anderson: a life in three centuries* (2003) • R. van Emden, *Britain's last Tommies* (2005) • R. van Emden, *Boy soldiers of the Great War* (2005) • *Daily Telegraph* (22 Nov 2005) • *The Times* (22 Nov 2005) • *The Scotsman* (22 Nov 2005) • *The Herald* [Glasgow] (22 Nov 2005) • *The Guardian* (23 Nov 2005) • *The Independent* (23 Nov 2005) • personal knowledge (2009) • private information (2009) • b. cert. • m. cert. • d. cert.

Likenesses photographs, 1998–2004, PA Photos, London • photographs, 2004–5, Camera Press, London • G. Price, C-type colour print, 2005, NPG • obituary photographs • photographs, repro. in Mackenzie, *Alfred Anderson*

Anson, Thomas Patrick John, **fifth earl of Lichfield** [*known as* Patrick Lichfield] (**1939–2005**), photographer, was born on 25 April 1939 at 16 Embankment Gardens, Chelsea, London, the only son and elder child of Thomas William Arnold Anson, Viscount Anson (1913–1958), army officer, and elder son and heir of the fourth earl of Lichfield, and his wife, Anne Ferelith Fenella Bowes-Lyon (1917–1980), later (following their divorce in 1948 and her remarriage in 1950 to Prince Georg of Denmark) Princess Anne of Denmark. His mother was a niece of Queen Elizabeth, later Queen Elizabeth, the queen mother, who stood sponsor at his christening, and he was first cousin once removed of Queen Elizabeth II. He and his sister, Elizabeth (*b.* 1941), a party organizer, grew up with their father and grandfather at the family seat, Shugborough Hall in Staffordshire, with its 5000 acre estate.

Thomas Patrick John Anson, fifth earl of Lichfield [*known as* Patrick Lichfield] **(1939–2005)**, by Sir Cecil Beaton, 1968

Anson was educated at Harrow School, where he began his career as a professional photographer by charging his friends 9*d.* for the leaving pictures he took with his Kodak Retinette, and at the Royal Military Academy, Sandhurst, where in 1957 he joined the regular army as an officer cadet, and was commissioned lieutenant in the Grenadier Guards in 1959. On 14 September 1960 he succeeded his grandfather as fifth earl of Lichfield, and ran what was left of the Shugborough estate after making over most of it to the National Trust, though he retained a thirty-five-room apartment. He resigned his commission in 1962 to take up photography, and worked as a darkroom technician for Dmitri Kasterine and Michael Wallis. A technically proficient craftsman, he was never afraid of advances, and enthusiastically embraced digital photography.

Though born to be a society photographer (and he did many portraits of débutantes, signed Lichfield rather than Patrick Lichfield, which he reserved for his more serious work), Lichfield was lucky to start out in an era when photography was a chic profession—whose members, though mostly working-class, included two earls, Snowdon, who, as Lichfield said, was a photographer who became a lord, and himself, a lord who became a photographer. He created some of the defining images of the

1960s and 1970s, such as a 1968 photograph of a nude Marsha Hunt, the African-American star of the rock musical *Hair*. (He had shrewdly invested in *Hair* and *Oh! Calcutta!*) Mick Jagger and David Bailey posed for him, as did Joanna Lumley and Jane Birkin, and he made the iconic 'Swinging London' group portrait with Roman Polanski, David Hockney, and Lady Antonia Fraser. Later he took pictures of his own relatives in the royal family, of which the best known were those of a relaxed duke of Windsor (his good humour helped by Lichfield having fallen through the seat of a chair), and his pictures of Prince Charles and Lady Diana Spencer's wedding in 1981. Clicking his tongue to make the noise of a shutter, he deceived his rival photographers into using up their quota of exposures, leaving him alone to capture the famous shot of the bridal group collapsing in a heap of giggles after the formal shoot was finished. The portraits he made of most members of the royal family at work and on holiday contributed a good deal to the prevailing spirit of informality of the Windsors.

Lichfield married, to great fanfare on 8 March 1975, Lady Leonora Mary Grosvenor (*b.* 1949), daughter of Robert George Grosvenor, fifth duke of Westminster, and sister of the sixth duke of Westminster. He was a devoted father to their three children, Rose (*b.* 1976), Thomas (*b.* 1978), and Eloise (*b.* 1981), though the marriage ended in divorce in 1986, owing something, he thought, to the fact that he was a workaholic who spent an average of 200 nights a year in hotels.

Slim and elegant, despite his slightly absurd bouffant hair-do, with his beautifully tailored clothes, and seldom without a crisp, white pocket handkerchief, Lichfield was a fixture of the glamorous London social scene that began in the 1960s. He was a director of some London restaurants, including the casual chain Deals, which he ran with Eddie Lim and David Linley, and a dining club in Mayfair called Burke's that he opened with Doug Hayward, the society tailor. Thanks to Diana Vreeland, the celebrated (and helpfully snobbish) editor of American *Vogue*, he had a ten-year contract with the magazine that put him in the highest rank of British photographers, which included Cecil Beaton, Lord Snowdon, David Bailey, and Norman Parkinson. He published a dozen books, mostly of his photographs.

At his holiday home on Mustique in 1991 Lichfield suffered serious injuries in a fall. He was cared for by his partner, Lady (Mary) Annunziata Asquith (*b.* 1948), with whom he had done a stint as models for a Burberry advertising campaign in the late 1980s. She was the eldest daughter of Julian Edward George Asquith, second earl of Oxford and Asquith. Lichfield died of a stroke, arterial disease, and emphysema on 11 November 2005 in the John Radcliffe Hospital, Oxford. He was survived by Lady Annunziata Asquith and by the three children of his marriage, and was succeeded as sixth earl by his son, Thomas.

PAUL LEVY

Sources *The Times* (12 Nov 2005); (1 May 2008) · *Daily Telegraph* (12 Nov 2005) · *The Guardian* (12 Nov 2005) · *The Independent* (12 Nov 2005) · 'Lichfield shoots Bailey', *Times Magazine* (29 March 2008) · 'The lord's work', *Sunday Times Magazine* (4 May 2008) · 'Sharp shooter', *The Independent* (12 May 2008) · *WW* (2005) · Burke, *Peerage* · personal knowledge (2009) · private information (2009) · b. cert. · d. cert.

Archives FILM BFINA, 'Aspel in New York', G. Nunes (director), LWT, 4 Jan 1991 · BFINA, 'The spirit of Cuba', LWT, 24 Dec 1994 · BFINA, 'Lord Lichfield', *Open house with Gloria Hunniford*, J. Morgan (director), Channel 5, 17 Aug 2003 · BFINA, documentary footage · BFINA, performance footage | SOUND BL NSA, AIRC programme sharing collection, interview with R. Holness, broadcast LBC, 12 Oct 1986, C1000/177/86/1 · BL NSA, millennium memory bank, interview with A. Ingram, 20 Nov 1998, C900/16522 · BL NSA, documentary recording · BL NSA, performance recording

Likenesses photographs, 1960x69–2005, Rex Features, London · photographs, 1964–2005, Getty Images, London · C. Beaton, bromide print, 1968, NPG [*see illus.*] · photographs, 1968–2004, PA Photos, London · photographs, 1968–2004, Photoshot, London · photographs, 1968–2005, Camera Press, London · three photographs, 1974, NPG · R. G. Clark, two bromide prints, 1979, NPG · J. Swannell, bromide fibre print, *c.*1980, NPG · I. Sodlecka, resin bronze bust, exh. Society of Portrait Sculptors, London 1983 · T. Leighton, two bromide fibre prints, 1986, NPG · N. Waymouth, portrait, Shugborough Hall, Staffordshire · obituary photographs

Wealth at death £5,550,524: probate, 19 June 2006, *CGPLA Eng. & Wales*

Appiah [*née* Cripps], **Enid Margaret** [Peggy] (1921–2006), anthologist and charity worker, was born on 21 May 1921 at Filkins, Gloucestershire, the youngest child in the family of three daughters and one son of Sir (Richard) Stafford *Cripps (1889–1952), barrister and politician, and his wife, Isobel, *née* Swithinbank [*see* Cripps, Dame Isobel (1891–1979)], daughter of Commander Harold William Swithinbank. Her father, knighted in 1930, had a distinguished political career, culminating in the chancellorship of the exchequer in 1947–50; her mother was made a GBE in 1946 for her work in organizing aid for China.

Growing up at Goodfellows, the family's manor house in the heart of rural Gloucestershire, Peggy Cripps spent a happy childhood playing in the stream that ran through the garden and going for early morning walks, sometimes accompanied by three goats and a dog. Educated at Norland Place and Queen's College in London, then at Maltman's Green School at Gerrards Cross in Buckinghamshire, she rejected university in favour of spending a year in Florence studying art history. After returning to London in 1939 she enrolled at the Whitehall Secretarial College. Travelling out via Canada, the Pacific Ocean, and then Manchuria with her mother and her sister Theresa in order to join her father in Moscow, she provided him with valuable secretarial help during the following eight months in his work there as the British ambassador. The next move, after the German invasion of Russia, was to Iran, where she was employed in the Tehran consular department, mainly working with the British army, which was at that time running the railways there. Finally returning home in 1942, she relocated to the Russian section of the Ministry of Information. Increasingly frustrated in an occupation she no longer saw as vital, she suffered a nervous breakdown in 1947. This was put right by a period of recuperation in Switzerland, after which she accompanied her mother on an aid mission to China.

Enid Margaret [Peggy] **Appiah** (**1921–2006**), by Terry Fincher, 1955

Back in London, Peggy Cripps worked in the youth department of the World Council of Churches. She also served on the executive committee of Racial Unity, a group dedicated to achieving harmony between different ethnic groups that had been set up by Prime Minister Clement Attlee's sister Mary, a former missionary in South Africa. It was at a student dance organized by Racial Unity that she met Joseph Emmanuel (Joe) Appiah (1918–1990), a charming, high-born Ghanaian studying law at the Middle Temple and also president of the West African Students Union. Their wedding on 18 July 1953, at St John's Anglican Church opposite Lords Cricket Ground in London, was attended by Aneurin Bevan, Hugh Gaitskell, and Michael Foot, in addition to the Indian politician Krishna Menon and assorted African chiefs. The marriage and Peggy's move to Ghana in 1954 caused a predictable flutter in the British press. Four years later, on a visit home, the *Daily Sketch* described her son (Kwame) Anthony and her daughter Ama (Isobel) as the 'best-connected piccaninnies ever to hit an English village'.

Settled in Kumasi, the capital of the Ashanti region, Peggy Appiah had two more daughters, Adwoa and Abena. She also spent much time supporting her husband, an early opponent of the Nkrumah government who suffered periods in jail or under house arrest as a result. By now deeply knowledgeable about Asante culture, she decided to start writing, drawing on native folklore with the intention that Ghanaian children could thereby have access to a literature of their own. Her first book of collected folk stories, *Ananse the Spider: Tales from an Ashanti Village*, was published in 1966. It was followed by numerous other titles including *The Children of Ananse* (1968) and *The Lost Earring* (1971). *Why the Hyena does not Care for Fish and Other Tales from the Ashanti Gold Weights* (1977) drew on her extensive collection of traditional weights made of brass, known locally as abrammuor and used for weighing gold dust. Each one was always crafted to encapsulate a proverb, some of which made up the stories in this book. Her folktale collections finished with *Kyekyekulee, Grandmother's Tales* (1993). There were also two adult novels, *Smell of Onions* (1971) and *A Dirge Too Soon* (1976).

A popular and tireless philanthropic figure in Kumasi, Peggy Appiah constantly found new ways in which to put her lifelong Christian socialist beliefs into action. With the assistance of her family she founded a school for the disabled at Jacchia and also contributed to the education of many local children. Missing her always entertaining but sometimes erratic husband, who died from cancer in 1990, she produced a widely used primer on AIDS called *A Dreadful Mistake* (2001). A short book of poems, *Thought Birds* (2001), came out on her eightieth birthday. Her last major work was *Bu Me Be: Proverbs of the Akans* (2001, revised edition 2008), co-written with her son Anthony, a professor of philosophy at Princeton University, and Ivor Agyeman-Duah. It included over 7000 proverbs taken from Twi, the language of the Asante. In 1996 she was appointed MBE 'for services to UK/Ghanaian relations and community welfare'. She died in Kumasi on 11 February 2006, and was survived by her four children.

NICHOLAS TUCKER

Sources C. Bryant, *Stafford Cripps: the first modern chancellor* (1997) · P. Appiah, 'The attic of my mind', *Something about the author* [Autobiography Series], 19 (1995) · P. Clarke, *The Cripps version: the life of Sir Stafford Cripps* (2002) · *The Independent* (17 Feb 2006) · *Daily Telegraph* (24 Feb 2006) · *The Guardian* (6 March 2006) · *The Times* (17 March 2006) · Burke, *Peerage* · b. cert.

Archives SOUND BL NSA, documentary recording

Likenesses T. Fincher, photograph, 1955 (with Joe Appiah), Getty Images, London, Hult. Arch. [*see illus.*]

Appleby [*née* Walley], (**Florence**) **Lucy** (**1920–2008**), cheese-maker, was born on 1 February 1920 at Lighteach Farm, Whitchurch, Shropshire, one of eight children of Alfred Edward Walley (1886–1954), a farmer and Baptist minister, and his wife, Sarah, *née* Pierpoint (1891–1964). She was educated at the high school at Whitchurch, before being sent to Reaseheath Agricultural College at Nantwich, where she learned cheese-making from a Miss Bennion, an inspirational teacher who believed in the virtues of unpasteurized milk and unwaxed Cheshire cheese. Soon after leaving college in 1940 she met and on 16 October the same year, at Wern Baptist Chapel (she later became a Methodist), married a local farmer, Arthur Lancelot (Lance) Appleby (1908–2003), son of Arthur Appleby, farmer. In 1942, already an accomplished cheese-maker, Lucy and her husband moved to Hawkstone Abbey Farm in Shropshire, where she halted her cheese-making

(Florence) Lucy Appleby (1920–2008), by unknown photographer, 1960s

temporarily to bring up their seven children. Though the front view of the Applebys' farmhouse looked very grand, in fact the house was never part of an abbey, but was gentrified in the late Victorian era, giving it windows that might well have graced a monastery. The more prosaic back of the house gave onto the dairy.

In 1952 it was Lucy Appleby's idea to revive a cheese that was nearly extinct, and it was always known as Mrs Appleby's Cheshire. Though in the 1930s more than 400 farms made genuine, unwaxed, cloth-bound Cheshire cheese from their own unpasteurized milk, at the time of her death only the Applebys kept this tradition alive, and they sold more than 1½ tons of it each week. Although in Shropshire, Hawkstone Abbey Farm was on part of the Cheshire plain, and only 10 miles over the border with Cheshire. Its soil contained the alum and the salts that gave the cheese its particular tang, and supported the plant life that expert tastes could identify in the milk from the farm's Friesian herd.

Cheshire cheese is made much like Cheddar or Lancashire. The cheese-maker introduces a very small amount of starter into the milk, then the vegetable rennet that causes the separation of curds and whey, plus some natural dye made from annatto seeds (the latter to give the cheese its characteristic reddish colour, a substitute for the less controllable carrot juice formerly used). The finesse of Appleby Cheshire was due to the small quantity of starter, which protected it from the over-acidity that marred some other Cheshire cheeses.

Wax binding was just becoming fashionable when Lucy Appleby resumed her career as a cheese-maker, but she refused to have anything to do with it, on the grounds that the proper ripening and flavour of the cheese depended on its ability to breathe; so she stuck to her principles and her calico. She also flatly refused to use pasteurized milk, which killed the flavour-giving enzymes in the cheese. In these respects, as in others, she was out of step with her contemporaries. However, in the early days she followed most other Cheshire cheese-makers and sold her product, superior though it was, through the Milk Marketing Board. This was before the board turned bully, and began discouraging small producers from marketing their own cheeses. When this happened in the early 1980s, most cheese-makers caved in to the pressure from the big supermarkets, who insisted on buying cheese in industrial quantities. This, of course, meant that it had to be made by industrial methods. Lucy Appleby then went her own way, and insisted on marketing her cheese under the family name. This allowed her to continue to make artisanal cheese, but it was not always easy to sell.

In 1982, having broken with the Milk Marketing Board, Lucy Appleby found herself with a good deal of surplus cheese. So she loaded a 40 lb wheel of it into the family's Land Rover and drove to the Covent Garden premises of Randolph Hodgson's Neal's Yard Dairy. Her natural ally, Hodgson said he had never before tasted anything like Mrs Appleby's cheese, and that it gave him a different view of what Cheshire cheese ought to taste like. Hodgson's marketing skills made Appleby cheeses a commercial success, and in 1989 he and Lucy Appleby together founded the Specialist Cheesemakers' Association, with the aim of lobbying for the preservation of cheeses made with unpasteurized milk at a time when public hysteria over listeria prompted most supermarkets to ban such cheeses. She encouraged fellow cheese-makers in Lancashire to return to using cloth binding.

Until near the end of her life Lucy Appleby remained crucial to the cheese-making part of the business. She was her own cheese's most severe critic and a one-woman quality control. In 1994 the prince of Wales visited the farm and in 2000 both she and her husband were appointed MBE. She died on 24 April 2008 of heart failure and chronic kidney disease at Whitchurch Hospital, Shropshire. Her achievement was nothing less than to have rescued, preserved, and secured a future for a vital part of Britain's cultural heritage. She was survived by four daughters and two sons, one son as well as her husband having predeceased her. The family cheese-making business was continued at Hawkstone by her son Edward and his wife, Christine. PAUL LEVY

Sources *Daily Telegraph* (3 May 2008) · *The Times* (10 May 2008) · *The Independent* (13 May 2008) · *The Guardian* (30 May 2008) · personal knowledge (2012) · private information (2012) [R. Hodgson] · b. cert. · m. cert. · d. cert.

Likenesses photograph, 1960×69, priv. coll. [*see illus.*] · obituary photographs · photographs, priv. coll.

Wealth at death under £164,000: probate, 5 June 2009, *CGPLA Eng. & Wales*

Aprahamian, (Abraham) Felix Barter (1914–2005), music critic and concert organizer, was born on 5 June

(Abraham) **Felix Barter Aprahamian (1914–2005)**, by Pete Wicker

1914 at 16 Inderwick Road, Hornsey, London, the son of Avedis Aprahamian, formerly Hovhanessian (*b.* 1870), carpet dealer, and his wife, Araxie, *née* Garabedian. His parents were both immigrants from Armenia. In 1919 the family moved to 8 Methuen Park, Muswell Hill, London, where Aprahamian lived for the rest of his life, for many of the later years sharing his house with his widowed mother. He was educated at Tollington School, Muswell Hill, where he developed a love of music, particularly organ music, so strong that it was detrimental to his schoolwork. On leaving school he was found a job by his father as an office boy in Fenchurch Street, then Mincing Lane, but he had no real interest in business. Meanwhile he took organ lessons, and became lifelong friends with another organist, William Lloyd Webber, father of the composer Andrew Lloyd Webber and the cellist Julian Lloyd Webber. He was assistant secretary of the Organ Music Society from 1931, and secretary from 1935 to 1970. In these capacities he began an extensive correspondence with composers, conductors, and musicians, both in Britain and elsewhere (particularly France), which he preserved (along with diaries, notebooks, autographs, and scores) in an ever-burgeoning archive in Muswell Hill. In 1932 he and two friends visited Frederick Delius at Grez-sur-Loing, and on the same trip he sat in an organ loft beside Charles-Marie Widor.

During the Second World War Aprahamian served as concert director of the London Philharmonic Orchestra, and as an ARP warden. He also, with Tony Mayer, the cultural attaché at the French embassy, organized an extensive series of concerts of French music, including contemporary music, and broadcast for the BBC in French, in which he was fluent. He came to be most closely associated with the promotion of French music, and, during the war and later, organized concerts for, and got to know, all of the leading lights of contemporary French music. He played host to Messiaen and his wife, and liked to point out to visitors the plane tree outside his house where Poulenc had relieved himself.

From 1946 to 1984 Aprahamian acted as a consultant to United Music Publishers, the principal publisher of French music in the UK; he kept an office there, which he used primarily as a base from which to promote French music. He pursued a parallel career as a music critic, having penned his first contribution to the music press in 1931. From 1948 to 1989 he was deputy music critic on the *Sunday Times*, initially working under the increasingly eccentric Ernest Newman; later, in 1956 and 1958, he edited two volumes of Newman's essays. His own reviews were appreciated for their elegance, perceptiveness, and breadth of interest. He also wrote record reviews for *The Gramophone* from 1964 to 1975, and innumerable programme notes, which were invariably stylishly written and informative. His career as a music critic was not without controversy. He was dropped by *The Gramophone* for failing to meet deadlines, and by the *Sunday Times* for submitting a review of a Gennady Rozhdestvensky concert when Rozhdestvensky had in fact cancelled the concert because of illness.

Bespectacled, with a neatly trimmed goatee beard, and frequently in the evenings dressed in white tie and opera cloak, Aprahamian was an exotic and larger-than-life character, and a raconteur of notable wit. He had many friends, and was a hospitable host at his home in Muswell Hill. He kept two pianos and an organ there, the latter brought from the Basque country in 1982 specifically for the use of Aprahamian's friend and protégé David Liddle (who later took Aprahamian as a middle name). He also held open house for younger scholars and enthusiasts anxious to make use of his archive of scores and other materials. The 'conversation … at the kitchen table would always range from the extremely intellectual and musically involved, through to the most uproarious and ribald' (Liddle). He published *Conversations with Olivier Messiaen* in 1976, a translation of Claude Samuel's original, and selections of his correspondence with Messiaen, Poulenc, and Charles Tournemire were published in 1998, 2000, and 2003, edited by Nigel Simeone.

Aprahamian reputedly refused appointment as an OBE in 1987, but in 1996 became officier de l'ordre des Arts et des Lettres, in recognition of his promotion of French music. He lectured widely, including at Morley College and Surrey University. From 1989 he was a visiting professor at the University of East London, and in 1991 at the University of California. He received an honorary doctorate from City University in 1995. His last years were clouded by a series of strokes, with increasingly debilitating effect. He died on 15 January 2005 at St Mary's wing, Whittington Hospital, Islington, London, of heart failure. He never married and had no known descendants. ALEX MAY

Sources *The Independent* (18 Jan 2005) · *The Times* (20 Jan 2005); (21 Jan 2005); (26 Feb 2005) · *Daily Telegraph* (20 Jan 2005) · *The Guardian* (21 Jan 2005) · N. Simeone, 'Aprahamian, Felix', Grove Music online, www.oxfordmusiconline.com, 18 Aug 2008 · D. Liddle, 'Recollections of Felix Aprahamian (1914–2005)', www.davidliddle.org, 18 Aug 2008 · b. cert. · d. cert.
Archives priv. coll.
Likenesses J. Mendoza, portrait, oils, exh. Royal Society of Portrait Painters, London 1986, repro. in http://www.junemendoza.co.uk/music-gallery.html · C. Adams, colour print, 1990, NPG · R. Bray, drawing, 1990, priv. coll. · E. Lake, acrylic on canvas, 1995, priv. coll. · J. Mendoza, portrait, oils, repro. in http://www.junemendoza.co.uk/music-gallery.html · P. Wicker, bromide fibre print, NPG [*see illus.*] · P. Wicker, bromide fibre print, NPG · obituary photographs · photograph, repro. in http://www.davidliddle.org
Wealth at death £570,165: probate, 31 Oct 2005, *CGPLA Eng. & Wales*

Arden, Don [*real name* Harry Levy] (**1926–2007**), rock music manager and promoter, was born on 4 January 1926 at 123 Crescent Road, Crumpsall, Manchester, the son of Lazarus Levy, a machinist in a factory making waterproof garments, and his wife, Sarah (Sally), *née* Black. Both parents were of Jewish descent. His schooling was limited and he dropped out to embark on a showbusiness career, adopting the name Don Arden in 1944. On 21 April 1950, at Lambeth register office, he married Hope Tubb (1916–1999), an acrobat and dancer, daughter of James Shaw, also a variety artiste, and former wife of Richard Edward Tubb. One year later she gave birth to their son, David, followed in 1952 by a daughter, Sharon.

Arden's years on the variety circuit as a singer, comedian, and impressionist were the perfect apprenticeship for a new role as an agent and impresario. By the beginning of the 1960s he was promoting UK tours for American rock 'n' roll acts, including Gene Vincent, Bo Diddley, Chuck Berry, and Little Richard. A sea change in the British music business with the arrival of the Beatles encouraged Arden to switch his attention towards upcoming beat groups. He promoted the Animals but failed to secure their management. Later in 1964 he signed the Nashville Teens, who enjoyed several UK hits, most notably with 'Tobacco Road'. They were followed by the Small Faces, whose first hit, 'Whatcha Gonna Do about It' (1965), Arden claimed to have 'hyped' into the charts via multiple purchases in selected shops. Thereafter they were chart regulars and enjoyed their biggest hit with 'All or Nothing' (1966), on which Arden was credited as producer.

By the late 1960s Arden had enshrined his reputation as one of the most successful and feared managers in British pop music. Glorying in the nickname the Al Capone of Pop, he was fiercely proprietorial of his chart acts and enjoyed a number of feuds with rival managers. These eventually became part of pop folklore. Recalling a conflict with the impresario Robert Stigwood, whose experience was by no means unique, Arden described a visit to his office, full of drama.

> I gave him a lecture. It was arranged with the boys that when I gave him this speech I was to say, 'See that balcony … you're going to go over the top'. The arrangement was that the boys were to say, 'Don't give him a chance. Throw him over now.' But the boys had a joke planned for me. What they did was they rushed forward, ignored me, and said, 'Get him over *now*.' And they picked him up and walked towards the balcony … and he thought it was all over. (personal knowledge)

Don Arden (1926–2007), by unknown photographer, 1968

In the late 1960s Arden inherited the management of two other major chart acts, Amen Corner and the Move. Similar controversies and conflicts attended his involvement with them. Meanwhile he built up an agency, Galaxy Entertainments, whose clients included such diverse acts as the Applejacks, the Action, the Attack, Neil Christian, and the Skatalites. In 1967 he attempted to revive his own singing career with the single 'Sunrise Sunset', adapted from the musical *Fiddler on the Roof*. He acknowledged in a written legal statement that he had paid £250 in an unsuccessful attempt to 'buy' the single into the charts.

By the 1970s the music business had become more corporate and Arden adapted to the changes by forming his own record company, Jet Records. His son and daughter became key players in Jet's early success, which was boosted by the international success of ELO, one of the biggest selling stadium acts of the era. Arden also managed Black Sabbath, whose lead singer, Ozzy Osbourne, subsequently married Arden's daughter, Sharon, who took over as his manager. A family feud followed and the pair did not speak for the best part of two decades. In the interim Arden moved to Los Angeles and lived in opulent splendour in a mansion once owned by Howard Hughes. Back in England, in 1979 he was the subject of a BBC investigative programme, *Checkpoint*, which detailed his more dubious financial and thuggish activities. He responded with a libel suit that never reached the courts. In 1985 he was arrested in the USA on two separate counts of false imprisonment and blackmail. The victim was his accountant, Harshad Patel, who claimed he was held prisoner and assaulted in various gruesome ways. His bloodied clothes were presented at trial. In November 1987 Arden was found not guilty.

Thereafter Arden led a quieter life, although there were still family conflicts, reconciliations, a television documentary, and a vainglorious autobiography, before the onset of Alzheimer's disease and his death in Los Angeles on 21 July 2007. His body was flown from Los Angeles and buried four days later at Manchester's Agecroft Jewish cemetery. He was survived by his son and daughter. His self-mythologizing and gangster reputation often distracted from his impressive achievements as an agent, manager, record company mogul, and impresario. Few contemporaries spanned as many decades in the business as the self-styled Al Capone of Pop. JOHNNY ROGAN

Sources *Checkpoint*, BBC Radio, 1979 • J. Rogan, *Starmakers and svengalis: the history of British pop management* (1988) • *Don Arden: Mr Rock 'n' Roll*, Channel 4, 1997 • D. Arden, *Mr Big* (2004) • *New Musical Express* (24 July 2007) • *Daily Telegraph* (24 July 2007) • *The Times* (25 July 2007); (4 Aug 2007) • *The Guardian* (25 July 2007) • *The Independent* (25 July 2007) • *Daily Mail* (25 July 2007) • interviews with J. Rogan, 12 Feb 1997; 29 July 1997; 25 April 1999 • personal knowledge (2011) • private information (2011) • b. cert. • m. cert.

Archives FILM BFINA, *Mr Rock & Roll*, F. Hanly (director), Channel 4, 19 Sept 1999 | SOUND BL NSA, performance recordings • BL NSA, documentary recordings

Likenesses F. Bunt, photographs, 1961–8, Getty Images, London • photographs, 1967–75, Photoshot, London • photographs, 1967–2002, Rex Features, London • photograph, 1968, Rex Features, London [*see illus.*] • R. Young, photographs, 1978, Rex Features, London • photograph, 1979, PA Photos, London • C. Limpkin, photographs, 1991, Rex Features, London • S. Cook, photograph, 2002, Rex Features, London • C. McAndrew, photographs, 2003, Camera Press, London • obituary photographs

Argent, (Bernard) Godfrey (1937–2006), photographer, was born on 6 February 1937 at Taringa, Eastbourne Road, Willingdon, Sussex, the only son of Godfrey Stanley Albert Argent, a motor engineer for a local builders' merchant, and his wife, Helena, *née* Smith. The couple also had two daughters. He was educated at Bexhill grammar school and, after a brief spell in the police force in Eastbourne (where he was introduced to photography), he entered the Household Cavalry in 1954 in which he served as a corporal in the Life Guards for nine years.

Argent's interest in portrait photography developed while he was stationed at regimental headquarters, Whitehall. In 1960 he won the army's photographic competition and was appointed an associate member of the Royal Photographic Society. Two years later he was asked to photograph Sir Gerald Templer, chief of the imperial

(**Bernard**) **Godfrey Argent** (**1937–2006**), self-portrait, 1972

general staff, in full dress uniform, on his appointment as colonel of the Royal Horse Guards. Templer's pleasure at the portrait led to further commissions, including an invitation to photograph Prince Philip's uncle, Earl Mountbatten, in the following year. Templer also advised Argent on where his future might lie, informing him that he was 'a much better photographer than you will ever be a soldier', and warning him not to 'get to my age and then regret what you might have done' (*The Independent*, 15 June 2006). He duly left the army and, as Godfrey Argent, began work as a freelance photographer in June 1963. Initially his portfolio comprised portrait photography of friends and former army connections, as well as picture postcards of regimental ceremonies and English and Welsh beach scenes. By now he had a young family of three daughters to support, having married Janet Rosemary Boniface (1937–1969), daughter of Robin Boniface, nightwatchman, on 17 November 1956 at St John's Church, Polegate, Sussex. After her death he married, on 29 December 1969, Ann Yvonne Coxon (*b.* 1939/40), physician, and daughter of James Coxon, businessman, at St Edward's Roman Catholic church, Sutton Park, Woking. They had no children and were divorced in 1973.

On the recommendation of Templer, Argent was invited to provide the illustrations for a forthcoming study of the Royal Mews, published in 1965 as *The Queen Rides*. This led to an introduction to the monarch, who evidently warmed to the young photographer, and opened the way to Argent's emergence in the late 1960s as a leading royal portraitist specializing in elegant black and white images. In June 1966 he was invited to photograph Princess Anne on her sixteenth birthday and followed this with studies of the eighteen-year-old Prince Charles (also in 1966), the last portraits of Prince Philip's mother, Princess Andrew of Greece (1967), a portrait for the postage stamp marking Charles's investiture as the prince of Wales in 1968 (one of many studies of the prince to 1974), and group portraits for the royal family's Christmas cards (1966–74). Part of the success of these commissions lay in Argent's ability—a skill perhaps honed in the army—to combine deference to his sitters with a charming, relaxed, sometimes playful manner. Even so, he admitted to feeling 'physically sick with tension' before sittings throughout his career (*The Times*, 30 June 2006).

Argent's work as a royal photographer coincided with his growing reputation as an artist and businessman. An invitation to join the prestigious Camera Press picture agency (whose clients included lords Snowdon and Lichfield, Cecil Beaton, and Yousuf Karsh, whose work Argent greatly admired), was followed in 1967 by his purchase of the business of another leading portrait photographer, Walter Bird. This brought Argent both a new studio, at 49 Queen's Gate, London, and the post (replacing Bird) of official photographer of the National Photographic Record, a collection of portraits of noteworthy Britons established on behalf of the National Portrait Gallery in 1917. Argent's appointment came soon after Roy Strong's as director of the NPG. With Strong eager to see the record broadened to include studies of 'people who are actively doing things', Argent's four-year tenure included photographs of David Attenborough, Alan Bennett, John Betjeman, Sir Noël Coward, and Spike Milligan. A selection of the 650 portraits Argent created for the record was exhibited as a one-man show at the NPG in 1972. From 1967 until 1993 he was also the official portrait photographer for the Royal Society, for whom he undertook 750 portraits, including studies of Sir Ernst Chain, Dorothy Hodgkin, Francis Crick, and Stephen Hawking.

Alongside these official positions Argent continued to develop his private business. In 1967 he began a long-running association with the theatre as cast photographer for *The Mousetrap*, a commission he undertook annually on a further twenty-two occasions and combined with similar records for other productions. In 1974 he moved to new premises at 8 Holland Street, Kensington, and in the same year he purchased the Mayfair studio of the dance and society photographer Baron (Sterling Henry Nahum); the sale also gave Argent the lucrative copyright to Baron's negatives, which in turn he presented to the NPG in 1998.

Now established as one of the capital's leading society photographers, with a speciality in corporate, military, and family studies, Argent undertook a number of overseas commissions from the 1970s. In 1976 an exhibition in Johannesburg included portraits of the politicians John Vorster, P. W. Botha, and Helen Suzman, the transplant surgeon Christiaan Barnard, the author Alan Paton, and Archbishop Desmond Tutu. Argent had written to these and other prominent South Africans to request a sitting while visiting the country on honeymoon with his third wife, Sally Dorothy McAlpine (*b*. 1951/2), whom he married on 25 April 1975 at Westminster register office; the couple had one daughter and were divorced in 1990. Further shows in Cape Town and Durban (1977) were followed by several visits to Los Angeles, where he photographed the city's mayor Tom Bradley and exhibited in 1978. Argent later worked from his London home, 8 Ladbroke Walk, near Holland Park, and from the late 1990s combined this with portrait painting in oils. In 2005 he held his final exhibition at the Special Photographers' Gallery, London, by which time his photographic commissions and other work totalled more than 9000 images.

Godfrey Argent died on 1 June 2006 from cancer of the oesophagus at Pembridge palliative care centre, St Charles's Hospital, Kensington, London. He was survived by his four daughters. Between 2007 and 2009 his contribution to photography was marked with the Godfrey Argent award for the most outstanding black and white photograph or the best photographer aged twenty-five and under at the NPG's annual portrait competition.

PHILIP CARTER

Sources T. Teeman, 'The great, the good, and the downright difficult', *The Times* (1 Feb 2006) • *The Independent* (15 June 2006) • *Daily Telegraph* (20 June 2006) • *The Times* (30 June 2006) • G. Argent, CV, NPG • b. cert. • m. certs. • d. cert.

Likenesses self-portraits, photographs, 1970–79, NPG [*see illus.*] • T. Blau, photograph, 1982, Camera Press, London • obituary photographs

Wealth at death under £207,000: probate, 13 Sept 2006, *CGPLA Eng. & Wales*

Arnold, Sir Malcolm Henry (1921–2006), trumpeter and composer, was born at Fairview, Cliftonville, Northampton, on 21 October 1921, the fourth son and fifth and youngest child of William Arnold, shoe manufacturer, and his wife, Annie, *née* Hawes. Coincidentally, two other well-known British composers of the twentieth century, Edmund Rubbra and William Alwyn, were also born in Northampton. The town had long been a centre for shoe manufacture, and Arnold's father ran the family shoemaking firm. The family background was strict Methodist. His mother was musical, her ancestors including William Hawes, a master of the Chapel Royal in the early years of the nineteenth century. She both encouraged her son to take violin lessons when very young, and took pains to foster the musical talent that was soon apparent.

Arnold's youthful liking for music took a decisive turn when, during a family holiday in Bournemouth, aged twelve, he heard Louis Armstrong's band playing at the Royal Bath Hotel. Encouraged in particular by his sister Ruth, he began to collect Armstrong's records, and became a devotee. The results were to last a lifetime, and included a love of the blues that regularly surfaced in his music, a belief that rigid demarcations between different styles of music are artificial, a desire to bring something of the free-for-all and collaborative, even improvisatory, spirit of jazz into classical music, and a particular interest in the trumpet.

Arnold's first school was Eaglehurst College, near the family home; his later school career was turbulent and

Sir Malcolm Henry Arnold (1921–2006), by Erich Auerbach, 1961

often short-lived. Meanwhile he devoted himself to mastering the trumpet, and began serious study with a local musician, Philip Pfaff. At the age of sixteen he won a scholarship to study at the Royal College of Music in Kensington, London, which he entered in 1937 as a pupil of one of the leading trumpeters of the day, Ernest Hall. An interest in composition also being apparent (he had regularly written short pieces for his mother on her birthday), composition became his second study, under the composer and teacher Gordon Jacob. He also studied piano, but although he soon acquired some keyboard facility he never described himself as a pianist.

Arnold's expertise on the trumpet was such that he could easily have enjoyed a career as a professional performer on that instrument. Even before he had formally completed his studies, he was deputizing in the London orchestras, although the lure of jazz was still strong: he even once ran away from the Royal College of Music and played in a dance band in Plymouth, and was only persuaded to return by the open-mindedness of the director, Sir George Dyson. In 1941, owing to the absence of many professionals in the armed forces, he was appointed second trumpet in the London Philharmonic Orchestra, the ensemble with which he remained associated until he finally decided to cease playing altogether to concentrate on composition. It was not long before he moved up to the position of first trumpet. On 3 January 1942 he married, at Hendon register office, Sheila Nicholson (1919–2009), a violinist (and daughter of Herbert Nicholson, insurance agent). They had three children, the first a stillborn daughter whose loss affected them deeply; then a daughter, Katherine (*b.* 1948), and a son, Robert (*b.* 1950).

The Second World War affected Arnold in many other ways too, including the loss of an admired elder brother, Philip (the closest in age to Malcolm), who was killed in 1941 during a bombing mission while serving in the RAF. On first being called up himself, Arnold registered as a conscientious objector, and appeared successfully before a tribunal. Later he changed his mind; but on volunteering in 1943 and going through a full infantry training he was subjected to what he felt was the humiliation, not to say irony, of being posted to a military band. He protested by shooting himself in the foot in order to be discharged, an action that could have resulted (but did not) in his being court-martialled. This would turn out not to be Arnold's last physical assault on himself. In later years he more than once attempted suicide.

At the end of the war, after a brief spell with the BBC Symphony Orchestra, Arnold returned to his old orchestra, the London Philharmonic. Since his time at the Royal College of Music he had been composing more and more, usually chamber-sized works for colleagues and acquaintances to perform: he scored a particular success with the *Three Shanties* for wind quintet, first performed in an aircraft hangar near Bristol in 1943. In that same year an orchestral tone-poem, *Larch Trees*, was performed under the auspices of the Society for the Promotion of New Music. Eventually, and triggered in part by the award in 1948 of the Mendelssohn scholarship, which enabled him to give up performing for a year and go to Italy to study, he decided to compose full-time.

A symphony soon followed; it would become the first of nine, which after Beethoven, Dvořák, Bruckner, and Mahler had become a canonical number for symphonists. Written at various critical points in his career, Arnold's symphonies are the core of his extensive output, and although they are strongly subjective and it is often tempting to interpret them in autobiographical terms, they can also be seen as powerful musical statements capable of standing on their own without the kind of excessive hermeneutic zeal that results from unprovable speculation and a simplistic view of the creative process. It is also the case that the composer himself occasionally tended to write uncommunicative or misleading programme notes, in the firm belief that music should speak for itself.

Though completed in 1949, Arnold's first symphony had to wait a couple of years before its first performance, at the Cheltenham festival. The second followed in 1953, and was an immediate success; the third, begun about the time of his mother's death, was completed in 1957. Numbers four and five were written almost back-to-back, in 1960 and 1961, and to some extent represent opposite poles of the composer's musical personality. The sixth (1967) is in some ways the most compressed, the seventh (1973) both the most expansive and the most turbulent. The eighth (1978) is a powerful synthesis of the dark and light sides of the composer's personality; the valedictory ninth followed after a long period of illness and depression, and its brooding pessimism has led to comparisons with Tchaikovsky and Mahler. The variety of the canonical nine is both impressive and disturbing: the composer's ability not to repeat himself is striking. This seems to have disconcerted his critics: reviews were occasionally savage, and since the composer was abnormally sensitive his relations with the musical press could be abrasive.

Musical correctness during this period, particularly in the music department at the BBC led by William Glock, required obeisance towards continental Europe, avant-garde serialism, atonality, and experimental thought-processes and sound-worlds; Arnold's radicalism often took a different form, involving surprises within a conservative language. His musical gods remained constant throughout his life: Berlioz, Sibelius, Mahler.

A further significant development in Arnold's career took place in 1947. A musical colleague suggested he send some of his early scores to the Denham film studios, outside London, in case they should be able to offer any work composing music for films. From initial assignments writing scores for short factual documentaries, he soon graduated to larger projects, and eventually feature films for international producers. His fluency, natural melodic gift, and responsiveness to the medium and to stories and plot-lines made him a natural for the screen: there is an argument for saying that film replaced opera as an outlet for his dramatic gifts (he never wrote a full-length opera, yet surely would have been capable of doing so successfully). His career as a composer for the cinema threatened at times to swamp his career as a composer for the concert hall, not least because it imposed enormous demands on him, of time and energy. The music was always the last stage in the making of a film before its release, and therefore had to be tailored not only to the very precise requirements of the nearly complete picture itself (a stopwatch was an essential tool), but also to be written to almost impossible deadlines: *The Bridge on the River Kwai* (1957), one of his most famous scores, for which he won an Oscar, was completed in ten days.

Eventually Arnold gave up writing film music, but not before he had completed nearly 130 scores, ranging from his first, *Avalanche Patrol* (1947), to *David Copperfield* (1969). Many others became classics, including *I am a Camera* (1955), *The Inn of the Sixth Happiness* (1958), *The Angry Silence* (1960), *Tunes of Glory* (1960), and *Whistle Down the Wind* (1961). Directors like David Lean, Carol Reed, and John Huston became regular collaborators, although after three masterpieces, in April 1962 Arnold turned down the chance to write the score for Lean's *Lawrence of Arabia*, feeling that it was unlikely to succeed, and never worked with the director again. Partly for his work in films, in 1970 he was appointed CBE and his public profile was at its zenith.

The 1960s saw not only the eventual decision to give up writing film music but various other changes in Arnold's life. His first marriage having ended in divorce in 1962, on 2 November 1963 he married Isobel Katharine Gray (*d.* 1992), a schoolteacher twelve years his junior (and daughter of David Inglis Wood Gray, farmer). They had a son, Edward, whose autism once diagnosed became a source of tension and pressure, as well as uncertainty as to how it should be treated. Determined on a different lifestyle, the family moved to Cornwall, and the composer readily and quickly identified with the local community, socially and even musically, as in the well-known *Padstow Lifeboat March*. But the marriage became subject to increasing strain, Arnold began drinking heavily again, and eventually there was a separation.

Yet Arnold's Cornish period was initially one of his happiest and most prolific. From the outset of his career he had always been willing to write music to commission, particularly if the request came from friends in the musical profession. In the 1950s he had begun to write concertos for them, if an orchestra was available. By the end of his life he had written seventeen instrumental concertos as well as a handful of other works involving a solo instrument. Among the various dedicatees were the violinist Yehudi Menuhin, the horn-player Dennis Brain, the oboist Leon Goossens, and the guitarist Julian Bream. In the late 1980s, inspired by performers half his age, he produced a recorder concerto and two other pieces for the Danish virtuoso of the instrument Michala Petri, and a cello concerto and a solo fantasy for the cellist Julian Lloyd Webber.

Among other commissions, one from the BBC in 1954 was a particular challenge. The harmonica was not then taken seriously as a concert instrument. But the harmonica had a champion in the shape of Larry Adler, who wanted a piece to perform at the Henry Wood Promenade Concerts; so, true to his non-snobbish instincts, Arnold accepted the challenge. The resulting piece was not only expertly tailored to the unusual capacities of the solo instrument, but also genuine music rather than the parody or pastiche or comedy that some had expected. For there was a pronounced humorous side to the composer, who could be a debunking musical joker if offered the opportunity: he loved jokes in real life, practical as well as verbal. His musical humour took many forms, from the dry wit of the *Three Shanties* to the drunken parody in one of his *Four Scottish Dances* to the aping of jazz and ragtime in the second clarinet concerto, written for the American virtuoso Benny Goodman. He incorporated bizarre effects, most extremely in the *Toy Symphony* (1957), which includes parts for instruments imitating a quail and a cuckoo. However, the most celebrated examples of his musical wit derived from his friendship, and collaboration, with the subversive German-born humorist Gerard Hoffnung. Hoffnung trained as a tuba player: among his bewildering range of achievements was an arrangement of a Chopin mazurka for a quartet of tubas. Hoffnung was also an impresario, for some years arranging an annual concert at the Royal Festival Hall devoted to musical pranks of all kinds. Arnold regularly devised new pieces for these occasions: they included a *Concerto for Hosepipe*, the *Grand Grand Overture*, which ends with a firing-squad of rifles assassinating a cohort of vacuum-cleaners and a floor-polisher, *United Nations*, in which a number of military bands march through the auditorium playing a variety of different national anthems, simultaneously, and the *Grand Concerto Gastronomique*, op. 76. Described as being 'for eater, waiter, food, and large orchestra', the music includes a movement called 'Oysters' and another called 'Peach Melba'.

The year 1973 saw the start of a further effort to change

course and even to rebuild his life, when Arnold, with Isobel and Edward, went to live in Dublin. It did not work. Physical, social, financial, and psychological troubles became compounded by isolation, and culminated in a failed suicide attempt. Eventually the marriage was dissolved, in 1975, and a court order prevented Arnold from approaching his former wife and his son. Yet from this relatively brief period dates some of his finest if darkest music, including the *John Field Fantasy* (1975), as well as the seventh and eighth symphonies, the masterly second string quartet (also 1975) and the *Symphony for Brass Instruments* (1978).

By the end of 1977 Arnold was back in England, being treated in the psychiatric department of the Royal Free Hospital, Hampstead; a year later, he was admitted to St Andrew's Hospital in his home town of Northampton, to be treated for psychosis compounded by alcoholism and depression. He had become almost impossible to live with and had been deserted by many friends as a result. The resulting breakdown and creative silence lasted four years, and his health seemed permanently impaired: in 1984 he was given two years to live, and in 1988 suffered a minor heart attack. The fact that he survived into his mid-eighties was due entirely to the devotion offered by his long-term carer Anthony Day, for many more years than he can have expected at the outset when agreeing to assist the ailing composer. There was even a return to composition, in a leaner and more austere vein: the ninth symphony, dedicated to Day, is its most outstanding exemplar: a work shot through with tragedy, it nevertheless resolves on to a luminous chord of D major. In 1990, though, with inspiration at an end, Arnold gave up composition altogether, continuing to lead a quiet life in Norfolk. His last decade was increasingly clouded with mental and physical illness, but until shortly before his death he was often a visible presence at festivals, concerts, and award ceremonies: honours including a number of honorary doctorates began to accumulate, culminating in the award of a knighthood in 1993.

Arnold lived long enough to see a growing revival of interest in his music, including three biographies and many recordings; he died at the Norfolk and Norwich University Hospital, Norwich, on 23 September 2006, as a result of complications following a chest infection. His first wife and his children survived him.

It is almost traditional for British composers to experience partial eclipse for years after their death. Elgar and Britten may have been exempt but Holst, Delius, Tippett, and many others have shared this fate. Arnold suffered eclipse in his lifetime, although his many film scores contrived to keep his name in circulation outside the usual musical milieux. Oddly, his music also enjoyed considerable success in recorded form while struggling to maintain a hold on the concert platform (at the time of his death none of his symphonies had been played at the BBC Proms for many years). The sheer variety and quantity of his output means that there are many Arnolds, not one. But unquestionably, at his best, he deserves a place in the pantheon. PIERS BURTON-PAGE

Sources R. M. Schafer, *British composers in interview* (1963) • A. Poulton, *The music of Malcolm Arnold: a catalogue* (1986) • H. Cole, *Malcolm Arnold: an introduction to his music* (1989) • P. Burton-Page, *Philharmonic concerto: the life and music of Sir Malcolm Arnold* (1994) • P. R. W. Jackson, *The life and music of Sir Malcolm Arnold: the brilliant and the dark* (2003) • A. Meredith and P. Harris, *Malcolm Arnold: rogue genius* (2004) • *The Times* (25 Sept 2006) • *Daily Telegraph* (25 Sept 2006) • *The Guardian* (25 Sept 2006) • *The Independent* (25 Sept 2006) • R. D. Thöne, *Malcolm Arnold, a composer of real music: symphonic writing, style and aesthetics* (2007) • www.malcolmarnold.com, 11 June 2009 • *Beckus*, 74 (2009) [obituary of Sheila Arnold] • Burke, *Peerage* • *WW* (2006) • private information (2010) • b. cert. • m. certs. • d. cert.

Archives Royal College of Music, London | FILM BFINA, 'Malcolm Arnold at 70', *Omnibus*, K. Rusmanis (director), BBC, 11 Oct 1991 • BFINA, *South Bank show*, T. Palmer (director), ITV1, 25 Sept and 3 Oct 2004 • BFINA, documentary footage | SOUND BL NSA, documentary recordings

Likenesses M. Ambler, photographs, 1951, Getty Images, London, Hult. Arch. • L. Moser, photograph, 1953, NPG • photographs, 1953–74, Photoshot, London • H. Coster, glossy bromide prints, 1954, NPG • photographs, 1958–93, PA Photos, London • E. Auerbach, photographs, 1961, Getty Images, London, Hult. Arch. [*see illus.*] • Keystone, group portrait, photograph, 1969, Getty Images, London, Hult. Arch. • C. Ware, photograph, 1969, Getty Images, London, Hult. Arch. • N. Drabble, bromide fibre print, 1991, NPG • J. P. Arnold, oil on board, 1993, NPG • G. Newson, bromide print, 1994, NPG • R. Noakes, clay bust, 1996, NPG • G. Hoffnung, caricature, priv. coll.; repro. in www.music-webinternational.com/arnold/arnsco.htm • K. Jones, portrait, Guildhall, Northampton • K. Jones, portrait, Royal College of Music, London • obituary photographs • photographs, repro. in *Malcolm Arnold: a life in pictures* (2008) • portraits, repro. in www.malcolmarnold.co.uk

Wealth at death £1,071,229: probate, 13 Feb 2008, *CGPLA Eng. & Wales*

Ashton, Eric (1935–2008), rugby league player, was born on 24 January 1935 at 87 Mulberry Avenue, St Helens, Lancashire, the only son of Ernest Ashton, a glassworks labourer, and his wife, Sarah, *née* Dixon. He attended Rivington Road high school in St Helens and signed for Wigan rugby league club in 1955 immediately after finishing his national service in the army. As a schoolboy he had taken part in trials for his hometown St Helens team but the club had ignored him. When he joined Wigan—St Helens's fiercest sporting and civic rival—he received £150. On 18 October 1958 he married Doreen Grady (*b.* 1934), also from St Helens. The daughter of John William Grady, labourer, she was then working as a secretary. They had two daughters, Beverley and Michelle.

The bare facts of Ashton's career—497 games for Wigan, twenty-six caps for Great Britain, and over 1900 points scored—are impressive enough, but tell little about his artistry as a player or his capabilities as a leader. For much of his career with Wigan he played alongside one of rugby's greatest wingers, Billy Boston, in partnership as right centre-threequarter and right wing-threequarter respectively. It is difficult to say which player was most fortunate. Many of Boston's 479 tries for Wigan were created by Ashton's subtle tactical play, while Ashton himself could be confident that the burly yet light-footed Boston would take advantage of even the slightest try-scoring opportunity presented to him.

Ashton was a 'classical' rugby centre-threequarter in the tradition of Huddersfield's Harold Wagstaff and Bradford's Ernest Ward: a player who saw his role as creating space for his winger to score tries. He was a master of delaying the pass to his winger until the very last fraction of a second, thus drawing in his opposing centre-threequarter and causing the defending winger to turn his attention away from Ashton's winger, who would streak through the gap for a try. Ashton was also an unrivalled exponent of the 'scissors move', whereby he would run diagonally to the wing, forcing the defending centre-threequarter to follow him, and then pass the ball back inside to Boston, who would charge through the space left by the defender to score. This combination of precise timing, geometric artistry, and sheer physical power allowed Ashton and Boston to score over 700 tries for the Wigan club.

Both on and off the rugby pitch Ashton represented one of the archetypes of the newly fashionable north of England in the late 1950s and early 1960s. As he was tall, slim, and good looking—he resembled a clean-cut Albert Finney—Ashton's photograph was used at least twice on posters advertising David Storey's rugby league-based play *The Changing Room* (1971). Yet, whereas contemporary players like Alex Murphy, Vince Karalius, and Mick Sullivan revelled in the aggressive, confrontational image of the northern working-class male—best exemplified in contemporary popular culture by Arthur Seaton in Alan Sillitoe's *Saturday Night and Sunday Morning*—Ashton was polite, modest, and reserved. This self-effacement was highlighted in his autobiography, *Glory in the Centre Spot* (1966), which neglected to mention the author's date of birth and spent six of its eleven chapters describing other players.

Nevertheless Ashton's modesty concealed considerable leadership skills. He was appointed captain of Wigan at the age of twenty-two and first captained Great Britain at the age of twenty-three, against New Zealand in Auckland. (Ashton was so proud of captaining the national side that he named his house Auckland.) In 1962 he captained the Great Britain team that toured Australia and New Zealand and won the rugby league 'Ashes'. The journalist Eddie Waring later noted of the 1962 tour that Ashton 'was the only man who could keep control of players like Alex Murphy and the older men such as Vince Karalius and Dick Huddart. They looked up to Eric because they respected him' (Eric Ashton testimonial souvenir programme, 8). At the age of twenty-eight he was appointed player-coach of Wigan, leading them to victories in the challenge cup, Lancashire cup, and BBC2 floodlit trophy finals. After he retired from playing in 1969 he coached Leeds and then St Helens until 1980. In 1996 he was appointed chairman of St Helens, in which capacity he oversaw one of the club's most successful eras. Alongside his work as a rugby league coach he also built a career as a brewery sales representative, first with Webster's brewery and then with Scottish and Newcastle, with whom he eventually became an area sales manager.

In 1966 Ashton became the first rugby league player to be honoured by a reigning monarch when he was made an MBE. At the time of his death he remained the only person to have won the rugby league challenge cup as player, coach, and club chairman. In 2005 he became only the sixteenth player to be inducted into the rugby league hall of fame. He died at Willowbrook Hospice, St Helens, of prostate cancer on 20 March 2008, and was survived by his wife, Doreen, and their two daughters. TONY COLLINS

Sources E. Ashton, *Glory in the centre spot* (1966) • Eric Ashton testimonial souvenir programme, Wigan, 26 May 1969 • E. Waring, *Rugby league: the great ones* (1969) • R. Gate, *Billy Boston: rugby league footballer* (2009) • R. Gate, *Rugby league lions* (2008) • *St Helens Reporter* (20 March 2008) • *The Guardian* (21 March 2008) • *The Times* (23 March 2008) • *Daily Telegraph* (25 March 2008) • *The Independent* (25 March 2008) • *St Helens Star* (2 April 2008) • b. cert. • m. cert. • d. cert.

Likenesses photographs, 1959–66, Photoshot, London • B. Thomas, photographs, 1963–9, Getty Images, London • photographs, 1966–78, Rex Features, London • obituary photographs

Askham, Janet Mary (1941–2008), sociologist, was born on 27 October 1941 at Paxton Park, Little Paxton, St Neots, Huntingdonshire, the only daughter of the Revd Leonard Charles Askham (1898–1983), vicar of Godmanchester, and his wife, (Grace) Hilda, *née* Mallett (1908–1952). She had four brothers, Roger (*b.* 1939) and Michael (*b.* 1943), and, by her father's second marriage, Timothy (*b.* 1956) and Andrew (*b.* 1958). She was educated at the Perse School for Girls, Cambridge, and the London School of Economics, from which she graduated in sociology in 1963. In that year she joined Research Services Ltd, run by the pioneering social scientist and market researcher Mark Abrams. This was the beginning of Askham's research career and it occupied the rest of her life. On 8 October 1966, at the parish church of St Peter, Barton, Cambridgeshire, she was married (by her father) to Peter John Kennedy (*b.* 1943), son of John Kenneth Kennedy, customs and excise officer. In 1967 she and Kennedy took up posts at Aberdeen University, she in the Medical Research Council's Institute of Medical Sociology, he as a research assistant in the politics department. On expiry of his contract in 1970 she moved with him to London where she resumed working with Mark Abrams, this time at the Social Science Research Council's survey unit. In 1972, with her marriage dissolved, she returned to Aberdeen and remained there until 1983.

During this period Janet Askham's brilliance, independence of mind, and vivid sympathy with the frail and the marginalized began to shape her research. Equally skilled in quantitative and qualitative methods of analysis, her favoured method of data collection was, and remained, in-depth interviewing and observation. She combined sympathy and rigour when probing for responses on the most personal of subjects; always she learned more about people than they knew they were revealing.

As a sociologist Askham gave her main effort not to proposing new theories but to seeking to illuminate and refine existing theories by the study and interpretation of real, complex, human life, especially when lived under prolonged strain from illness, social stigma, or disadvantage. Her book *Fertility and Deprivation: a Study of Differential Fertility amongst Working-Class Families in Aberdeen* (1985) was considered ground-breaking in its use of face-to-face interviews and its exploration of sexual and family issues in a working-class context. *Identity and Stability in Marriage* (1984), based on her Aberdeen University doctoral thesis of 1980, was again much cited; it examined married couples' negotiation of sexual activity, sexual fidelity, and other sensitive topics. While in Aberdeen she met Byron John Criddle (*b.* 1942), a political scientist and son of the Revd Levi Criddle, Congregational minister; they married at Weston-super-Mare register office on 3 April 1980. They had a daughter, Rosamond, and Janet became stepmother to Matthew.

In 1983 Askham extended her research interests to later life and old age, joining the Age Concern Research Unit (again founded by Abrams), which soon became the Age Concern Institute of Gerontology at King's College, London. She was awarded a personal chair in 1997 and became director of the institute in 1998. Her publications during this period include *Dementia and Home Care* (1990, with Catherine Thompson) and *Caring: the Importance of Third-Age Carers* (1992, with Emily Grundy and Anthea Tinker). Often the only sociologist in an institute which covered many social sciences and some medical and biological disciplines, she continued to educate her colleagues and students in the types of knowledge and language in which theories could be developed. Old age was a stage of the life course particularly rich in untested assumptions and outrageous stereotypes, and these she energetically challenged.

With Anthea Tinker, a specialist on social policy concerning later life, Askham led a series of multi-disciplinary research programmes and trained a succession of young researchers. She was essential to the continuing survival of the institute, one of very few centres for social research on later life, and almost the only centre for postgraduate education in gerontology, in the UK. Askham's ability to formulate hypotheses which could be empirically tested and to relate the findings both to existing theory and to policy was exceptional, and her superb written style ensured that the results could be widely disseminated. Her interest in influencing policy on behalf of disadvantaged people led her in 2004 to become research director of the Picker Institute (Europe) at Oxford, a non-governmental organization devoted to recording the experiences of patients and advocating their use to improve the operation of the health services. In the same year she became a founder member of the media regulatory body Ofcom's advisory committee on older and disabled people; she also served as a governor of the Pensions Policy Institute, and as a member of the scientific committee of the Alzheimer's Society. For five years until her death she acted as the Department of Health's reviewer to the research programme connected with the National Service Framework for Older People. Her great kindness often led her to place heavy burdens on her own energies. She was always an advocate for research conducted with rigour and integrity, and for the application of results to improve the lot of those less able to make their voices heard among the influential. The quality of her research was recognized when she was made an academician of the Academy of Social Sciences.

Janet Askham died suddenly following a spontaneous intracerebral haemorrhage, on 7 July 2008, at Kingston Hospital, Kingston upon Thames (near her home on Richmond Hill). She was survived by her husband, Byron, her daughter, and her stepson. Although she never experienced retirement or old age herself, her life's work made an important contribution to knowledge of that and other areas of the life course. ANTHEA TINKER

Sources *The Times* (1 Aug 2008) · *The Independent* (4 Aug 2008) · *The Guardian* (13 Aug 2008) · *The Scotsman* (30 Aug 2008) · personal knowledge (2012) · private information (2012) [Byron Criddle, husband; Rosamond Criddle, daughter] · b. cert. · m. certs. · d. cert.
Likenesses obituary photographs

Aspinall, Neil Stanley (1941–2008), music executive, was born at Chatsworth House, Prestatyn, Flintshire, on 13 October 1941, the son of Stanley Arthur Aspinall, a dock labourer then serving as a petty officer in the Royal Navy, and his wife, Ivy, *née* Shaw. His mother had been evacuated to north Wales from Liverpool, and returned there not long after his birth. The family home was at 117 Belmont Road, Liverpool. He was educated at the Liverpool Institute High School for Boys, leaving in 1959 to train as an accountant. His best friend at this time was Pete Best, and while studying for his accountancy examinations he lodged with the Best family in their large Victorian house in West Derby. Best's mother, (Alice) Mona Best (1924–1988), ran an informal beat club called the Casbah in the basement of the family home which quickly established itself as a rehearsal room and venue for many of the upcoming Liverpudlian bands, and Aspinall helped to run the club.

It was through his involvement with the Beatles that Aspinall embarked on his career as a music executive. Such was the closeness of his relationship with the group that he was often described as 'the Fifth Beatle'—although several other key figures of the period, including the group's manager Brian Epstein and their long-time recording manager George Martin, could also stake a strong claim to the epithet. His involvement with the 'Fab Four'—as they were frequently dubbed by the 1960s media—dated back several years prior to their first hit single 'Love Me Do' in 1962. Paul McCartney and George Harrison were also pupils at the Liverpool Institute. Next door to the school was the Liverpool College of Art, whose students included John Lennon. The nucleus of the future Beatles was created (they were variously known as Johnny and the Moondogs, the Quarrymen, and the Silver Beetles prior to their final name change) in 1958. Pete Best joined the line-up as drummer in August 1960. On their return from Hamburg in December 1960 they invited Aspinall to become their road driver, a job that also involved loading and unloading their stage equipment, and numerous other duties.

In July 1962 Mona Best gave birth to Aspinall's son, Vincent Roag Best (the paternity was never disputed). Pete Best was sacked from the Beatles the following month. Aspinall's and Best's friendship survived these events, and indeed Best persuaded Aspinall to continue with his road manager duties. Three years later the former Cavern Club bouncer Mal Evans took over as road manager. The move enabled Aspinall to become the Beatles' personal assistant. Aspinall became the group's gatekeeper and guardian of their business secrets. He was also credited with coming up with the idea behind the pioneering concept album *Sgt Pepper's Lonely Hearts Club Band* (1967), which took the theme of a Victorian brass band giving a 'live' show on record. He also sang as part of the choir on 'Yellow Submarine' and played harmonica on 'Being for the Benefit of Mr Kite'.

Aspinall's role changed dramatically in August 1967 when Brian Epstein died suddenly from a drugs overdose. Aspinall effectively became the Beatles' new manager, although it was rumoured that their long-time record producer George Martin was none too happy with the situation because he felt that Aspinall lacked the social qualifications required to speak to executives at EMI Records and elsewhere. Aspinall nevertheless in effect then became chief executive of Apple Corps, formed after Epstein's death to represent the Beatles' interests, although he accepted 'only until they found someone else' (Granados, 12), and in the early chaotic days of the company he had no formal title. There was a brief split between Aspinall and the Beatles when John Lennon brought in the controversial US accountant Allen Klein (who also became acrimoniously involved with the Rolling Stones' business affairs) in 1969 to run the group's financial affairs, but it proved to be short-lived. Klein had taken the decision to fire Aspinall from Apple but was forced by the four Beatles to reinstate him. A year later the Beatles and Klein were in litigation with each other, and it was Aspinall who dealt with the ensuing lawsuits. Meanwhile, on 30 August 1968 he married Susan Mary (Suzy) Ornstein, daughter of George Herbert (Bud) Ornstein, a United Artists executive who oversaw the production of the Beatles' films, *A Hard Day's Night* and *Help!* (he and Suzy had met on the set of the first film). They had three daughters and a son, and Aspinall also became stepfather to her son by a previous marriage, to John Bramley.

In the years following their split in 1970 Aspinall was credited with developing the Beatles' brand and he oversaw the repackaging of Beatles music, film, and memorabilia. He was instrumental in organizing the *Anthology* series of hits and out-takes (1995–6), and Apple Corps revealed that during the last twenty years that Aspinall was at the helm the Beatles sold over 70 million albums worldwide. It was estimated that in 2008 the combined wealth of the surviving Beatles and their heirs was £2 billion. Among his final duties performed for the former Beatles, Aspinall led Apple's dispute with Apple Computers over logo rights, and also a long-running royalties dispute between EMI Records and the band. Shortly after the Apple case was settled, he resigned from his role, offering no explanation for his decision. It was rumoured within the music industry that he had become frustrated by attempts within the company to cheapen the Beatles' legacy in the pursuit of profits.

Aspinall was deeply affected by the deaths of John Lennon and George Harrison, and also that of Derek Taylor, the Beatles' former publicist, who had also been very much part of their early story. He suffered a heart attack, no doubt partly induced by the stress of running Apple, several years before his death, but recovered sufficiently to continue for some further years with his Apple Corps duties. He lived latterly in Twickenham but died at the Memorial Sloan-Kettering Cancer Center, New York, on 23 March 2008, from lung cancer following a short illness. His funeral was held at St Mary the Virgin, Twickenham, on 7 April, and he was buried in Teddington cemetery. He was survived by his wife, Suzy, and his five children. On

Neil Stanley Aspinall (1941–2008), by Bernard Gotfryd, 1964 [front centre, standing in for George Harrison at a rehearsal for The Ed Sullivan Show]

hearing the news of his death the two surviving Beatles, Sir Paul McCartney and Ringo Starr, issued a joint statement that he was 'a great man who would be missed', while Yoko Ono and Olivia Harrison, the widows of John Lennon and George Harrison, added: 'As a loyal friend, confidant and chief executive, his trusting stewardship and guidance has left a far-reaching legacy for generations to come' (Press Association news release, 24 March 2008).

CHRIS WHITE

Sources P. Best, R. Best, and R. Best, *The Beatles: the true beginnings* (2002) · S. Granados, *Those were the days: an unofficial history of the Beatles Apple organization, 1967–2001* (2002) · B. Spitz, *The Beatles: the biography* (2005) · *The Times* (25 March 2008); (1 April 2008) · *Daily Telegraph* (25 March 2008) · *The Guardian* (25 March 2008); (7 April 2008) · *The Independent* (25 March 2008) · *New York Times* (25 March 2008) · *Daily Post* [Liverpool] (25 March 2008) · *Daily Mail* (26 March 2008) · *The Economist* (5 April 2008) · personal knowledge (2012) · private information (2012) · b. cert. · m. cert.
Likenesses photographs, 1963–2006, Rex Features, London · B. Gotfryd, group portrait, photograph, 1964, Getty Images, London [*see illus.*] · photographs, 1964–2006, Getty Images, London · photographs, 1964–2006, PA Photos, London · P. Townsend, group portrait, bromide fibre print, 1967 (*The Beatles with Maharishi Mahesh Yogi*), NPG · photographs, 1969–95, Camera Press, London · photographs, 1995–2006, PA Photos, London · obituary photographs
Wealth at death £6,947,818: probate, 23 July 2008, *CGPLA Eng. & Wales*

Auld, William [Bill, Viljo] (**1924–2006**), Esperanto poet and writer, was born on 6 November 1924 at Hainault, Lesney Park Road, Erith, Kent, the son of George Auld, a draughtsman and structural engineer, who composed and recited comic verse, and his wife, Williamina Rose (Minnie), *née* Roy, shorthand typist. At the time of his birth his parents lived at 24 Bexley Road, Crayford, Kent. His father's ambition to become an actor had been thwarted at the age of fifteen, on the death of his own father (a soldier in a Scottish regiment). Auld's mother came from a more well-to-do family: her father owned a company that produced a particular type of cloth used in mines. Auld had a sister, almost eight years younger than him. Perhaps because of the age difference, they had little in common and were brought up almost as only children.

When Auld was nine the family left Kent and returned to its roots in Scotland. He won a scholarship to the prestigious Allan Glen's School in Glasgow, where he excelled at sport. He ran, and played football, rugby, and hockey. He was also an avid reader. From the age of ten he was a regular visitor to the public library in the Gorbals district of Glasgow, where he found books in such languages as Russian and Polish, reflecting the cosmopolitanism of the city. It was in another library, this time in Glasgow itself, that Auld discovered books in the international language Esperanto. In addition, as a twelve-year-old boy scout, he encountered the scout promise in Esperanto, and asked his troop-leader if he knew about the language. The scoutmaster obliged by giving Auld *Step by Step in Esperanto*, by Montagu C. Butler. From this book Auld acquired a sound theoretical knowledge of the language. However, it was not until he was sixteen that he persuaded his friend John Francis (subsequently a member of the so-called Scottish school of Esperanto writing) to learn Esperanto, and they began to use the language between themselves. At this time Auld's mother bought him a Bible in Esperanto, hoping—unsuccessfully—to convert her son from his atheism.

At the outbreak of the Second World War Auld's family moved to Helensburgh, where he completed his schooling. In 1942 he volunteered for the RAF and underwent pilot training in Rhodesia. Two years later he came top of fifty candidates for high-level reconnaissance work. In this capacity he piloted Spitfires in north Africa, the Near and Middle East, Italy, Greece, and Palestine. After the war he was briefly a test pilot.

In 1947 Auld enrolled at Glasgow University to study English language and literature, meanwhile continuing to hone his Esperanto. He would meet John Francis and the Esperanto poet and essayist Reto Rossetti, and the three would test each other's knowledge of obscure Esperanto vocabulary. Encouraged by Rossetti, Auld began to read widely in Esperanto, and to contribute to the periodical *Esperanto en Skotlando*.

Also in 1947 Auld became engaged to Margaret Barr (Meta) Stewart, two years younger and whom he had known since he was fifteen. She was the daughter of William Stewart, ship plater. At her request they decided not to marry until 1952, to allow her to complete her training as a nurse. They eventually married in Clydebank on 8 August 1952. To help support his wife and family (a daughter, Judith, was born in 1954, and a son, Roy, in 1956), Auld found work in a factory manufacturing bogies for railway vehicles. He finally graduated MA from Glasgow University in 1955 and obtained a teaching qualification in 1956. He taught in Johnstone and Paisley before moving in 1960 to be head of department at Lornshill Academy, Alloa, where two years later he was promoted to depute rector (deputy headteacher). He remained at the school until retirement. In 1963 the family moved to Dollar, Clackmannanshire, and set up home at 20 Harviestoun Road, where Auld lived for the rest of his life.

Much of Auld's most important writing dates from his time as a teacher or trainee teacher, including the epic poem *La infana raso* ('The infant race'), published in 1956 and described in a contemporary review as 'almost without parallel' in Esperanto (Waringhien, 116). The poem deals with the insignificance of the human race in the vastness of space and time. A collection of poems, *Unufingraj melodioj* ('Melodies for one finger'), followed in 1960. In 1952 appeared the first of many translations into Esperanto, Jack London's *The Whale Tooth*. Auld's translations later encompassed Byron, Burns, *The Rubaiyat of Omar Khayyam*, and, by 1997, Tolkien's *The Lord of the Rings*.

In 1999 Auld became the first Esperanto writer to be recommended for the Nobel prize in literature, by PEN. He was again nominated in 2004 and 2006. He died on 11 September 2006 at Hillview Court Care Centre, Sauchie, near Dollar, after a stroke. He was survived by his wife, Meta, and their two children. He was buried according to family wish in the parish church in Dollar on 18 September. PAUL GUBBINS

Sources G. Waringhien, 'Recenzo: *La infana raso*' [review], *La Nica Literatura Revuo*, 2/3 (1956), 116–20 · W. Auld, 75 *jaroj* [75 years] (Yekaterinburg, 1999) · *Sunday Times* (5 June 2005) · *The Guardian* (19 Sept 2006) · *Daily Telegraph* (22 Sept 2006) · H. Tonkin, 'Forpasis granda poeto kaj verkisto' [Death of a great poet and writer], *Esperanto*, 99 (Nov 2006), 219 · E. de Kock, 'William Auld kaj la originala Esperanto-poezio' [William Auld and original Esperanto poetry], *Esperanto*, 99 (Nov 2006), 224–5 · personal knowledge (2010) · private information (2010) · b. cert. · m. cert. · d. cert.
Archives NL Scot., Auld Esperanto collection | British Esperanto Association, Barlaston, Staffordshire, Biblioteko Butler | FILM priv. coll., recorded lecture
Likenesses obituary photographs
Wealth at death £213,986.35: confirmation, 17 April 2007, *CCI*

Badawi, (Mohammed Aboulkhair) Zaki (1922–2006), scholar of Islam and Muslim community leader, was born on 14 January (or possibly 11 August) 1922 at Sharkia, outside Cairo, Egypt, the son of Zaki Badawi, a university lecturer. He entered al-Azhar University in Cairo, arguably the most prestigious major place of learning for Sunni Muslims, where he first studied for his al-aliyah degree (the equivalent of a bachelor of arts) from its college of theology. In 1947 he gained his al-alimiyah (or master's) degree from al-Azhar's faculty of Arabic language and literature, winning the King Farouk first prize for the best postgraduate student in the same year. In 1951, after being awarded a doctorate and teaching for a short period at al-Azhar, he enrolled once again as an undergraduate student, this time at University College, London, where he studied psychology and graduated BA in 1954. He was later awarded another doctorate, for a thesis on 'Modern Muslim thought', by the University of London. During this period he met his fellow psychology student (Joyce) Mavis (later Maryam) Anderson (1922–2008), daughter of James Cornelius Anderson, bookseller; they married at St Marylebone register office on 20 September 1956 and had a son, Faris, and a daughter, Laila.

Badawi returned briefly to teach in Cairo, and was then sent by al-Azhar to Malaya, where he established a Muslim college and taught Arabic and Islamic studies at the University of Malaya in both Singapore and Kuala Lumpur. In 1964 he moved to Nigeria, where he became professor of Islamic education at Ahmadu Bello University in Zaria, later combining this role with that of the dean of arts at Abdullahi Bayero College in Kano. In 1976 he was appointed research professor for the Hajj Research Centre of the Abdul Aziz University in Jiddah, Saudi Arabia, and in this capacity returned to London. Two years later he took up the post of director of the Islamic Cultural Centre, together with that of chief imam of the London Central Mosque, in Regent's Park.

A passionate believer in 'home-grown' Islam and interfaith dialogue, Badawi actively used his position as a prominent religious and community leader to seek positive ways of reconciling Islamic beliefs and values with those of British society more generally. In 1982 he helped to establish the Islamic Shariʿa Council, a body of scholars

(Mohammed Aboulkhair) Zaki Badawi (1922–2006), by Gemma Levine, 1998

representing many Sunni Muslim institutions in the United Kingdom, which sought to overcome conflicts between Islamic law (*shariʿa*) and the British civil code. Other initiatives included efforts to introduce financial facilities that complied with *shariʿa* (such as *halal* mortgages) for British Muslims. In 1982 he joined the board of the Islamic Banking System, based in Luxembourg, and then negotiated with the Bank of England to permit the licensing of Islamic financial institutions in the United Kingdom. The result was the Islamic Finance House, which he managed for three years. In 1984 he was elected chairman of the Imams and Mosques Council by the National Conference of Imams and Mosque Officials of the United Kingdom.

Badawi's commitment to what he described as a 'British form of Islam' meant that he wanted imams based in Britain to be trained to operate more effectively in the Western cultural environment. This led him in 1986 to establish the Muslim College in Ealing, west London, which was the first Muslim body in the United Kingdom to offer university-accredited qualifications for Islamic theological training. Badawi had long been critical of the ability of 'traditional' imams, operating in languages other than English, to reach out to younger generations of British Muslims. The idea of creating a graduate seminary had first been proposed at a conference of Muslim leaders at the Islamic Cultural Centre in 1978. Plans had then been drawn up and presented to Muslim ambassadors to the United Kingdom in their capacity of trustees of the Islamic Cultural Centre and the London Central Mosque. It was not until 1984, however, that Badawi secured the necessary financial backing from the World Islamic Call Society and an agreement was signed for the establishment of the college. The college, whose curriculum included the study of both Islam and Western society and emphasized inter-faith dialogue, began functioning as an educational institution for graduate studies in 1987, with the first MA students graduating in 1990. Badawi remained its principal until the time of his death.

Badawi's other commitments included his involvement in a range of community and religious organizations, such as the Arabic Forum, the Islamic Religious Council, and the National Council for the Welfare of Muslim Prisoners (established in 1999). His unparalleled devotion to inter-faith dialogue meant that he was closely associated with many senior figures in British Christian and Jewish life (including Cardinal Basil Hume and Rabbi Hugo Gryn). Dedicating much time to the Maimonides Foundation (committed to building better understanding between Jews and Muslims), he was also co-founder (with the Jewish philanthropist Sir Sigmund Sternberg and the Anglican priest Marcus Braybrooke) of the Three Faiths Forum in 1997, vice-chairman of the World Congress of Faiths, a director and trustee of the Forum Against Islamophobia and Racism (FAIR) established in 2001, and a founder and trustee of the Festival of Muslim Cultures launched in January 2006. For many years Badawi advised the prince of Wales on matters concerning Islam. He edited the *Islamic Quarterly* for four years, co-edited *Encounter Magazine*, and published and lectured on a wide range of issues.

Badawi's promotion of moderation and tolerance meant that he often spoke out in the media against terrorism by Muslims, describing the attacks of 11 September 2001 in New York as 'a violation of Islamic laws and ethics', and writing that taking revenge on the innocent was abhorrent to Islam (*The Times*, 19 Sept 2001). While condemning fiercely the suicide bombings in London on 7 July 2005, he also remained critical of the Iraq war but accepted the right of British Muslim soldiers to carry out their duties to 'queen and country'. In 1998, having chosen to retain his Egyptian nationality, he was appointed an honorary OBE, and in 2004 an honorary KBE. He was also a member of the Athenaeum.

Badawi was not immune from controversy. In 1980, for instance, the Union of Muslim Organisations called for his replacement as director of the Islamic Cultural Centre, accusing him of advocating 'non-Islamic' teaching and creating 'divisions within the Muslim community'. In response Badawi emphasized his commitment to projecting Islam in the West more effectively by taking a 'middle course' (*The Times*, 7 July 1980). In 1989, against the backdrop of the *Satanic Verses* furore, he incurred further criticism when he stated that he was prepared to support its author, Salman Rushdie, despite his dislike for the book itself. Likewise, in 2005, shortly after the London bombings in July, he urged Muslims to be especially vigilant, and advised Muslim women to remove their veils as a precaution against faith-hate crimes, noting that, according to Islam, clothes are for protection and not to harm the individual. Not surprisingly, perhaps, this comment was condemned by some British Muslims. The same month, having been invited by the Chautauqua Institution in New York to deliver a speech on law and religion in society, he was refused entry upon arrival in the United States, despite having already obtained a visa. While he subsequently accepted a government apology, he did not again visit the United States.

Badawi died of a heart attack at St Mary's Hospital, Westminster, on 24 January 2006, after being taken ill while speaking at the fifth annual Islamic finance summit at the Millennium Hotel in London. His *salaat al-janaza* (funeral) took place on 27 January at the London Central Mosque, and he was buried in north Watford cemetery directly afterwards. He was survived by his wife and two children.

KHIZAR HUMAYUN ANSARI

Sources *The Times* (7 July 1980); (25 Jan 2006) · *Daily Telegraph* (25 Jan 2006) · *The Guardian* (25 Jan 2006) · 'Zaki Badawi dies', 25 Jan 2006, www.aljazeera.net, 30 June 2009 · *The Independent* (27 Jan 2006) · personal knowledge (2010) · m. cert. · d. cert.

Archives FILM BFINA, current affairs footage

Likenesses G. Levine, photograph, 1998, Getty Images, London, Hult. Arch. [*see illus.*] · photographs, 2001–5, PA Photos, London · photographs, 2003–4, Rex Features, London · obituary photographs

Wealth at death £516,791: probate, 15 Sept 2006, *CGPLA Eng. & Wales*

Baddiley, Sir James [Jim] (**1918–2008**), biochemist, was born on 15 May 1918, at Glencoin, Fog Lane, Didsbury, Manchester, the second of four children of James Baddiley (1885–1951), an industrial chemist, and his wife, Ivy (*d.* 1966), daughter of Logan Cato, a watch and clock maker in Manchester. James senior came from a farming family in south Yorkshire and was the first to embark on a scientific career. He played an important part in the dye industry during the First World War and became director of research of Imperial Chemical Industries (ICI) Dyestuffs in 1926. Jim Baddiley was educated at Manchester grammar school and Manchester University. He graduated with first-class honours in 1941 and, inspired by the lectures of A. R. (Alex) Todd, the future Nobel laureate, on vitamins and other natural products, joined Todd's research group to study the synthesis of nucleosides. With Basil Lythgoe he pioneered a new route to ribosides of adenine and was awarded his PhD in 1944. With others he was also involved in the wartime collaboration on the chemistry of penicillin. On 20 September 1944 he married Hazel Mary Townsend (1920–2007), textile designer, of Salford, daughter of Wesley Wilfrid Townsend, master tailor. They had a son, Christopher.

Baddiley moved to Cambridge with Todd in 1944 as an ICI fellow and synthesized the important coenzyme adenosine triphosphate (ATP), completed in 1948. After eighteen months at the Wenner-Gren Institute in Stockholm he returned to Cambridge where he met Fritz Lipmann, who had just discovered coenzyme A, a nucleotide derivative of pantothenic acid (one of the B vitamins) later shown to be involved in the metabolism of fatty acids and the tricarboxylic acid cycle. They agreed to collaborate in determining its chemical structure, an ideal project when Baddiley moved as an independent researcher to the Lister Institute of Preventive Medicine in London. The structure was determined, with Malcolm Thain, by 1952, and other problems in coenzyme chemistry were addressed, including a synthesis of codecarboxylase and active methionine. Tony Mathias, in the course of a study of the biosynthesis of coenzyme A, discovered two new cytidine nucleotides in extracts of *Lactobacillus arabinosus*.

In 1954 Baddiley was appointed to the chair of organic chemistry at King's College, Newcastle, then part of Durham University (but from 1963 the separate University of Newcastle). In Newcastle the cytidine nucleotides became his main research interest and when their structures were determined as cytidine diphosphate glycerol and cytidine diphosphate ribitol in 1956 their biochemical role was examined. A search for polymers of ribitol phosphate and glycerol phosphate was immediately successful and similar polymers were shown to be associated with the cell walls of Gram-positive organisms; they were given the name teichoic acids (from the Greek teichos, a fortified wall). The further exploration of the teichoic acids, their structures, biosynthesis, immunology, and most importantly the part they played in the functioning of the bacterial cell, occupied Baddiley and his research group for the next twenty-five years. Many people contributed to this programme over that period, perhaps most notably Ron Archibald and Ian Hancock. Baddiley established a separate microbiological research laboratory and in 1977 became professor of chemical microbiology. Many of his research collaborators, obtaining MSc or PhD degrees under his guidance, later made names for themselves. In 2004 the Centre for Bacterial Cell Biology was established in Newcastle under the direction of Jeffrey Errington, and the work on teichoic acids continued. A Baddiley lecture was established and Baddiley himself was able to be present at the inaugural lecture by Sir John Walker in 2008.

Meanwhile Baddiley had left Newcastle in 1981 to take up a senior research fellowship in the department of biochemistry in Cambridge. There he was able to continue his research, with post-doctoral assistance, and helped to set up the Cambridge Institute of Biotechnology with support from the university and from industry. He became a fellow of Pembroke College and used his experience to serve on a number of university and national committees.

Although Todd was a major influence in his life Baddiley was much more interested in the biological aspects of chemistry and felt at home in the company of biochemists and biologists. He used his chemical skills to unravel major problems in biology and believed that it was easier for a chemist to acquire the necessary knowledge of biology than the other way round. He was determined and single-minded, as befits a rock climber, one of his activities as a young man.

Baddiley had many interests in later life which he himself attributed in part to a happy childhood and a lack of specialization at school. He was keen on music, both classical and jazz, and on art and photography. In all of these he was supported by his wife, Hazel, who was also active in the wider sphere of Newcastle University and later in Cambridge. His many honours included the Meldola medal of the Royal Institute of Chemistry (1947), the Corday-Morgan medal and prize (1952), the Tilden medal and lecture (1959) and Pedler lecture (1978) of the Chemical Society, and the Leeuwenhoek lecture (1967) and Davy medal (1974) of the Royal Society. He was elected a fellow of the Royal Society in 1961 and of the Royal Society of Edinburgh in 1963, and was knighted in 1977. He was an honorary member of the American Society of Biological Chemists and was actively involved in a number of scientific societies and the scientific research councils. He received honorary doctorates from Heriot-Watt and Bath universities (in 1979 and 1986 respectively), to add to his own PhD, his Manchester DSc (1953), and his Cambridge ScD (1986). He spent the last year of his life at Grange Court, Grange Road, Cambridge, and died at Addenbrookes Hospital, Cambridge, on 19 November 2008, of a pancreatic malignancy. His funeral service was held at Pembroke College, Cambridge, on 1 December, and a memorial service was held there on 9 May 2009. He was survived by his son. J. GRANT BUCHANAN

Sources *The Independent* (3 Jan 2009) · *The Guardian* (29 Jan 2009) · J. Grant Buchanan, memorial service address, Pembroke College, Cambridge, 9 May 2009 · *Memoirs FRS*, 56 (2010), 3–23 · *Royal Society of Edinburgh Review*, 2010, www.royalsoced.org.uk/cms/files/fellows/obits_alpha/baddiley_j.pdf, 25 April 2011 · Professor Sir James Baddiley in conversation with Professor Sir Hans Kornberg FRS, Oct 1990, www.filmandsound.ac.uk/collections/records/0028-0000-2467-0000-0-0000-0000-0.html, 25 April 2011 · Burke, *Peerage* · *WW* (2008) · J. Baddiley, personal papers and offprints, RS · personal knowledge (2012) · private information (2012) · b. cert. · m. cert. · d. cert.

Archives RS, papers | FILM Professor Sir James Baddiley in conversation with Professor Sir Hans Kornberg FRS, Oct 1990 (http://www.jiscmediahub.ac.uk/record/display/012-00002467;jsessionid=0C769AA55D60BADB561BBE018A3A60DC) | SOUND BL NSA, documentary and performance recordings

Likenesses obituary photographs · photograph, repro. in *Memoirs FRS* · photograph, repro. in *Royal Society of Edinburgh Review*

Wealth at death £665,453: probate, 17 Feb 2009, *CGPLA Eng. & Wales*

Badham, Molly Winifred (1914–2007), zoo proprietor and conservationist, was born on 12 May 1914 at 3 Waterside, Evesham, Worcestershire, the daughter of Arthur James Badham (1889–1965), then a boot shop assistant and later a homeopath, and his wife, Edith Annie, *née* Sharp (1889–1980). She was educated at Town School, Sutton Coldfield, after which she pursued her childhood passion for animals by establishing a boarding kennel and by breeding dogs. In the early 1940s the profits from these ventures allowed her to buy a pet shop on Station Street, Sutton Coldfield, where she also lived in the flat above the premises. In 1949 she purchased a monkey from another pet shop in the town and this brought her into close contact with the shop's proprietor, Nathalie Evans, with whom she would subsequently collaborate in the founding of Twycross Zoo. The two women combined their businesses and took up residence in Badham's flat. Following the death of the first monkey they acquired two chimpanzees along with other unwanted animals who shared their cramped quarters.

In 1954 Badham and Evans moved to Hints, near Tamworth, where they opened their first zoo—the Hints Zoological Society—on a three-quarter acre site. With their collection of animals continuing to grow they moved again in 1962 to a Victorian rectory at Twycross, ten miles to the east of Tamworth, which they purchased for £12,000. The dilapidated house came with grounds of twelve acres which became home to a range of rare animals, including elephants, leopards, giraffes, and sealions, as well as chimpanzees and monkeys. Twycross opened to the public on 26 May 1963 and proved an instant attraction, drawing large crowds.

Notwithstanding this success, the zoo's running costs required Badham to seek additional sources of income. The spectacle of 'chimps' tea parties' had long been a popular zoo entertainment and in late 1956 the tea merchants Brooke Bond had begun a series of television advertisements using chimpanzees, originally loaned from Billy Smart's circus. Badham was first approached to supply animals to take part in a Brooke Bond tea party for an exhibition at Olympia; thereafter Twyford's chimpanzees made regular appearances in a series of adverts in which, dressed in adult clothing, they performed sketches as housewives, parents and children, handymen, and cyclists in the tour de France, each sketch ending with the drinking of Brooke Bond (and later PG Tips) tea. The commercials became Britain's longest-running television campaign and were aired until 2002. A year later the chimpanzees topped a poll of the nation's favourite advertising characters, having given rise to a string of catch phrases, among them: 'Coo-eee Mr Shifter', 'You hum it, I'll play it!' (Mr Shifter's reply to his son's question 'do you know the piano's on my foot?'), and 'Avez vous un cuppa … Can you ride tandem?' (from a cyclist to a race spectator who proffers tea). Badham countered occasional criticism of the use of her animals in advertisements with the claim that 'Chimps love dressing up. They have such a sense of humour' (*The Independent*, 26 Oct 2007).

In fact Badham's willingness for the Twycross chimpanzees to be used on television and in public performances ran hand in hand with her commitment to research and animal conservation at the zoo. She was a noted expert on the breeding of primates and in 1969 the first colobus monkey to be bred in captivity in Britain was born at Twycross, followed in 1994 by the successful rearing of bonobos. Badham took a central role in this work, often hand-rearing monkeys at her home (which she stopped only in 2002) and compiling a series of stud books on primates. Her other publications, which she co-wrote with Nathalie Evans, were *Chimps with Everything* (1979), a history of Twycross Zoo, and *Molly's Zoo* (2000), an account of life at Twycross that followed a documentary television series broadcast in 1999.

In 1972 Badham and Evans established Twycross as a charitable foundation, the East Midlands Zoological Society. A founding member of the National Federation of Zoological Gardens of Great Britain, Badham was appointed an inspector of licensed zoos, under legislation in 1981. In recognition of her conservation work she was awarded an honorary degree by Leicester University in 1982 and was appointed MBE in 2002. Only in 2003, on her appointment as director emeritus of the zoo, did she step back from the day-to-day running of Twycross, though she remained active in its work until her death on 19 October 2007 at her home, Tree Tops Bungalow, in Norton-juxta-Twycross. By the time of her death her zoo had become the world's largest centre for primate conservation and study, and a popular attraction with an estimated half a million visitors per year. PHILIP CARTER

Sources M. Badham, *Chimps with everything: the story of Twycross Zoo* (1979) • M. Badham, *Molly's zoo: monkey mischief at Twycross Zoo* (2000) • *Daily Telegraph* (22 Oct 2007) • *The Independent* (26 Oct 2007) • *The Times* (27 Oct 2007) • b. cert. • d. cert.

Likenesses photographs, 2001–3, Rex Features, London • obituary photographs • photographs, repro. in Badham, *Molly's zoo* • photographs, Twycross Zoo

Wealth at death under £257,000: probate, 6 Aug 2008, *CGPLA Eng. & Wales*

Bagot, Milicent Jessie Eleanor (1907–2006), intelligence officer, was born on 28 March 1907 at 68 York Mansions, Battersea, London, the younger daughter and second of three children of Cecil Villiers Bagot (1865–1940), a London solicitor, and his wife, Ethel (*d.* 1944), younger daughter of Jesse Garratt of Wateringbury, Kent. On her father's side she was descended from a line of clerics (her great-grandfather was Richard Bagot, bishop of Oxford 1829–45, then of Bath and Wells 1845–54), and was distantly related to the barons Bagot of Bagot's Bromley. She was educated at home by a French governess before going to Putney high school and Lady Margaret Hall, Oxford, where she was awarded a fourth class in classical moderations in 1927. After leaving Oxford without a full degree, she joined the Metropolitan Police as a clerk, and found her *métier* in collating sensitive information for special branch.

At Scotland Yard Bagot worked with a small group of civilian analysts led by three former army officers, Hugh Miller, Guy Liddell, and Nigel Watson, who studied domestic communist subversion. However, their work, monitoring radical socialists, became increasingly frustrating as it emerged that the branch itself had been penetrated by disaffected detectives who had participated in the 1919 police strike, which had created lasting bitterness and resentment within the force. Evidence seized during the arrest in April 1929 of several serving detectives, including Inspector Hubert Ginhoven and Sergeant Charles Jane, and their former colleagues dismissed during the strike, suggested a link between them and two suspected Soviet espionage fronts, the Vigilant Detective Agency and the Federated Press of America, a news agency with offices in the City and in Paris.

Conscious that special branch had been compromised, perhaps permanently, Liddell and Miller took the best of their clerical staff, including Bagot, to the security service (MI5). The Statute of Westminster of 1931 had given MI5 jurisdiction for the investigation of espionage, sabotage, and subversion within the empire. Under Liddell's sponsorship Bagot concentrated on the growing threat from the Comintern. She initiated a massive card index listing every personality mentioned in the MASK traffic, a wireless interception operation tapping into a covert radio channel on which the Communist Party of Great Britain, and other front organizations across the globe, received instructions from Moscow encrypted in a cipher based on *Treasure Island*. The MASK material would continue to provide an unprecedented insight into the Comintern's activities until December 1936, when Moscow changed its communications procedures.

When an expanded, wartime MI5 was reorganized in 1940 Bagot was moved to F2(b), a sub-section of the counter-subversion division headed by Roger Hollis, where her encyclopaedic knowledge of Communist Party of Great Britain personalities provided vital information to support counter-espionage investigations conducted by her colleagues. In particular she undertook a lengthy survey of contacts cultivated by Oliver Green, a wireless operator who had fought in the Spanish Civil War before running his own printing business in the Edgware Road. Technical surveillance on Green led MI5 to six members of his network and strong evidence that the GRU, the Soviet military intelligence service, had developed a group of agents in military establishments across the country known as the Robson–Gibbons ring. Although none of its members was prosecuted Bagot's painstaking survey proved a model for subsequent studies.

By 1944 Bagot was acknowledged as MI5's expert on Soviet espionage, and on one occasion in June she severely embarrassed her counterparts in the Secret Intelligence Service (SIS) by demonstrating that a supposed intelligence goldmine in Madrid, purporting to be a document about British communists prepared at the headquarters of the Spanish Falange, listing fifty people, was hopelessly inaccurate and referred to three personalities she recognized and who she knew had died years earlier. Her ambition to serve on the British control commission for Austria was thwarted by MI5's director-general, Sir David Petrie, who believed her too valuable to lose and threatened that she would have to resign if she insisted. Instead, anxious for a change, she was transferred briefly to SIS before returning to MI5 to head a new research section, designated E1, with the rank of assistant director, the first woman to be promoted to so senior a position within the intelligence services. She was made an MBE in 1949.

When Kim Philby came under suspicion in 1951, following the defection in May of his old friend Guy Burgess, Bagot confided in Arthur Martin, one of the molehunters conducting the investigation into Philby's background, that she possessed a secret source that indicated he had been a communist. She never revealed the precise nature of her information but it predated Philby's suspiciously swift pre-war conversion from his leftist views to membership of the pro-Nazi Anglo-German Fellowship. Bagot's reservations about Philby's loyalty would prove justified when he defected to Moscow in January 1963.

As she never married, and had devoted her life to the study of international communism, there was a widespread belief that David Cornwall, the writer John le Carré, himself a former MI5 and SIS officer, had based his character of Connie Sachs, the obsessive, eccentric spinster and mole expert who appeared in his novels, on Bagot, who shared many of Sachs's personality traits.

On her retirement in 1967 Bagot was advanced to CBE and commissioned by MI5's director-general, Sir Martin Furnival Jones, to answer charges made the same year in *The Zinoviev Letter* by three *Sunday Times* journalists (Lewis Chester, Stephen Fay, and Hugo Young), that British intelligence officers had deliberately peddled a forged letter to influence the October 1924 general election and damage the Labour Party's prospects of re-election. Bagot spent three years on the project and produced a memorandum in which she asserted that SIS personnel had leaked what they believed to have been an authentic directive to the Communist Party of Great Britain issued by the Soviet president of the Comintern, Grigory Zinoviev. Her report remained classified in MI5's registry, but in 1999 the Foreign Office historian Gill Bennett relied heavily on it for her own conclusions, which were published at the demand of the new foreign secretary, Robin Cook, who had long believed in a plot mounted by MI5 to replace Ramsay MacDonald with Stanley Baldwin in 1924.

One of Bagot's colleagues later recalled that 'As a boss she was a bit fierce, as a woman absolutely lovely' (*The Times*, 3 June 2006). Her part-time retention by MI5 after her formal retirement, which enabled her to continue to participate in the service's choir, came to a conclusion in 1976, and after suffering a stroke in 2001 she moved into Jubilee House nursing home in Godalming, Surrey, where she died on 26 May 2006. NIGEL WEST

Sources L. Chester, S. Fay, and H. Young, *The Zinoviev letter* (1967) • N. West, *A matter of trust: MI5, 1945–72* (1982) • N. West and O. Tsarev, *The crown jewels: the British secrets at the heart of the KGB's archives* (1998) • G. Bennett, *'A most extraordinary and mysterious business': the Zinoviev letter of 1924* (1999) • N. West, *MASK: MI5's penetration of the Communist Party of Great Britain* (2005) • *The Guy Liddell diaries: MI5's director of counter-espionage in World War II*, ed. N. West, 2 vols. (2005) • *The Times* (3 June 2006) • *The Guardian* (17 June 2006) • Burke, *Peerage* • b. cert. • d. cert.

Likenesses photograph, repro. in *The Times* (3 June 2006)

Wealth at death £472,820: probate, 28 July 2006, *CGPLA Eng. & Wales*

Bailey, David Roy Shackleton (1917–2005), classical scholar, was born on 10 December 1917 at School House, Lancaster, the youngest of the four children (three sons and one daughter) of the Revd John Henry Shackleton Bailey (1875–1956), mathematician and headmaster, and his wife, Rosamond Maud, *née* Giles (*d.* 1949). The family was a very unhappy one, which may go some way to account for 'the intense shyness and self-protection that many mistook for a lack of humanity' (Thomas, *PBA*, 5). He was educated at Lancaster Royal Grammar School, where his father was headmaster, and where he drilled himself to read privately every day a substantial quota of Greek and Latin. He then went to Gonville and Caius College, Cambridge. After obtaining a first class in part one of the classical tripos and part two of the oriental studies tripos he left Cambridge in 1941 for wartime service in British intelligence at Bletchley Park. On his release from war service and return to Cambridge in 1944 he was elected a fellow of Gonville and Caius College, and in 1948 was appointed university lecturer in Tibetan, a post he held until he left Cambridge in 1968. In 1955 he moved to Jesus College, as fellow and director of studies in classics, returning to Caius in 1964, first as deputy bursar and then a year later as senior bursar. On 12 December 1967 he married Hilary Ann (1928–2010), the former wife of Kingsley Amis, and daughter of Sidney Leonard Bardwell, a clerical officer in the Ministry of Agriculture. There were no children of the marriage.

In 1968 Shackleton Bailey left Cambridge to become professor of Latin at the University of Michigan at Ann Arbor, where his wife kept a fish restaurant called Lucky Jim's. Their marriage was dissolved in 1974, and in 1975 Shackleton Bailey moved to Harvard as professor of Greek and Latin; from 1982 he was Pope professor of the Latin language and literature. His academic distinctions included an honorary LittD from Trinity College, Dublin (1984), and, in recognition of his work on Cicero's letters, the Kenyon medal of the British Academy (1985), to which he had been elected in 1958. On retirement from Harvard in 1988 he returned to Michigan, and in 1994 married Kristine Zvirbulis, continuing to teach as an adjunct professor until 2002.

Between 1948 and 1955 Shackleton Bailey had produced a number of articles and reviews on Sanskrit and Tibetan topics, and a critical edition of two Buddhist hymns, *The Śatapañcāśatka of Mātrceta* (1951). These texts called for the application of sophisticated editorial techniques, an experience that he turned to account in 1975 in an examination of the analogous problems confronting the editor of classical texts ('Editing ancient texts', republished in *Selected Classical Papers*, 1997, 324–5). As early as 1953 he had been seriously considered for election to the Kennedy professorship of Latin; and his move to Jesus College two years later signalled a return to his original classical allegiance, which was confirmed by the publication of *Propertiana* (1956), his first book on a classical subject. This was a collection of notes on passages of critical interest in the text of Propertius which, apart from its value to future editors, was a rich source of information on Latin poetic usage. Meanwhile he had begun to publish a series of notes and articles extending over the next forty years on textual and interpretative problems in Latin writers ranging in date from Lucilius to Nigel de Longchamp, and critical editions of Latin authors including Horace, Lucan, and Martial, culminating in eighteen volumes in the Loeb Classical Library, a total unequalled by any other editor in the series.

These bilingual editions were critically important and testified also to Shackleton Bailey's gifts as a translator. Nowhere were these displayed to more effect than in his seven-volume edition of Cicero's letters to Atticus (1965–70), his *magnum opus*. Of these letters he wrote: 'Nothing comparable … has issued out of the classical world … In Cicero's letters we see a Roman Consular, on any reasonable estimate one of the most remarkable men of his eventful time, without his toga' (*Selected Classical Papers*, 364). It was Cicero as a human being, 'sometimes petty, sometimes heroic' (*Cicero: Select Letters*, 1980, 11), who fascinated him and brought out the best in him as a commentator. There was the added attraction that they posed the sort of critical and historical problems that he was pre-eminently well qualified to solve.

Propertiana had been dedicated to the memory of A. E. Housman, whose unpublished edition of Propertius had been destroyed at his death in accordance with his will. Housman himself he had seen only once, at the last lecture Housman gave, shortly before his death. It was his admiration for Housman's scholarship and his relentless emphasis on accuracy as a duty, not a virtue, that focused his own approach to establishing and interpreting the texts that he edited. In one crucial respect, however, he differed from his exemplar. Manilius's *Astronomica* had offered Housman a uniquely appropriate field for the exercise of his critical talents, and his commentary is in a class of its own as a source of information on Latin usage; but for the poet himself he felt nothing but contempt. Shackleton Bailey's work on Cicero was a labour of love. Even when he was critical of his authors he was rarely dismissive. Like Housman he despised 'literary gush' (*Selected Classical Papers*, 1997, 344) and what he termed 'noörrhea', the uncontrolled flow of whatever enters the interpreter's head (ibid., 359).

To those who did not know him well Shackleton Bailey could seem unapproachable, but close friends found in him 'a true but lovable eccentric' (Luck, 3) and a lover of good food and wine. His criticism was informed by a sensibility of which his responses to poetry and music were testimony. This trait was seen most appealingly in his love of cats. The first and most beloved of many was Donum (so called because given him by a friend), to whom he dedicated his *magnum opus*; and it was reputed that his move from Jesus back to Caius had been occasioned by the college's refusal to allow him to put a cat flap in the door to his rooms. 'Everybody who met Shack had Shack stories', according to one of his students (*Michigan Daily*, 12 July 2005). In his final years he suffered from Alzheimer's disease, and he died in Ann Arbor on 28 November 2005. He was survived by his wife Kristine. E. J. Kenney

Sources R. F. Thomas, *Harvard University Gazette* (8 Dec 2005) · G. Negri, *Boston Globe* (19 Dec 2005) · *The Times* (22 Dec 2005) · *The Independent* (4 Jan 2006) · G. Luck, 'Remembering Shackleton Bailey', *Exemplaria classica*, 10 (2006), 3–17 · J. T. Ramsey, *Proceedings of the American Philosophical Society*, 152/2 (2008) · *WW* (2005) · R. F. Thomas, *PBA*, 153 (2008), 3–21 · personal knowledge (2009) · private information (2009) · b. cert. · m. cert. [1967]

Archives Jesus College, Cambridge, archives · Needham Research Institute, Cambridge, Joseph Needham MSS

Likenesses photographs, 1944–89, Gonville and Caius College, Cambridge · obituary photographs · photograph, British Academy

Bailey, Derek (1930–2005), guitarist and musical theorist, was born on 29 January 1930 in Nether Edge Hospital, Sheffield, the only child of George Edward Bailey (*d.* 1965), barber, and his wife, Lily, *née* Wing (*d.* 1996). His maternal grandfather, Percy Wing, played banjo and pub piano, his mother played piano, and his mother's younger brother, George, became an early musical influence, providing access to gramophone and radio and being one of the first musicians in Sheffield to play electric guitar.

Bailey attended Nether Edge grammar school from 1941 to 1946. An early thirst for the popular music of the day—jazz, swing, and big band—coupled with the lure of American cinema, was tempered by the strictures of school music lessons and regular trips to the Hallé Orchestra, which in his later view acted as major disincentives to a potential life in music. From July 1950, after eighteen months in the navy on national service, he combined day jobs with paid musical work in pubs in Sheffield, Bradford, and Glasgow. From 1955 to 1968 he worked continuously across the UK and occasionally on the continent as a commercial musician, playing in pubs, jazz clubs, and restaurants, doing broadcasts, performing for American forces dances, in dance halls, and in variety shows such as the *Morecambe and Wise Show* in Blackpool, and doing some recording studio work. Many of these working situations offered opportunities for exploring and practising on the job, and Bailey used these to develop his interest in improvisation, serialism, and non-time playing. On 24 September 1956, at Sheffield register office, he married Doris Priest, a 31-year-old shorthand typist, and daughter of Arthur Guest, steelworks furnaceman.

Bailey first met the bass player Gavin Bryars and the percussionist Tony Oxley in 1963 in Chesterfield, and for the next three years, playing regularly at The Grapes pub on Trippett Lane in Sheffield, they moved away from conventional jazz and by 1965 were playing totally improvised pieces. An example of this period is 'Rehearsal Extract'. They used the name of Joseph Holbrooke, once described as the cockney Wagner, as 'a good cover for our activities' (D. Bailey, *Improvisation: its Nature and Practice in Music*, 1992, 86). In a period of great activity and hectic travel Bailey's first marriage broke up and on 23 March 1964, at Manchester register office, he married Joan Burns, a 30-year-old secretary, and daughter of Thomas Burns, painter and decorator. His son, Simon, was born in 1966 and he separated from Burns the same year.

Moving to London in 1966, Bailey was well prepared to participate, over a period of time, with like-minded exploratory musicians based around John Stevens and the Spontaneous Music Ensemble: Evan Parker, Dave Holland, Trevor Watts, Paul Rutherford, Barry Guy, and Kenny Wheeler. The Music Improvisation Company (Parker, Bailey, Hugh Davies, Jamie Muir, and latterly Christine Jeffrey) appeared in 1969, by which time freely improvising musicians across Europe—including Peter Brötzmann, Alexander von Schlippenbach, and Peter Kowald from Germany, Han Bennink and Misha Mengelberg from the Netherlands, Fred Van Hove from Belgium, and Irène Schweizer from Switzerland—had begun to play together in all manner of combinations.

Incus, one of the first musician-owned independent record labels in the UK, was formed in 1970 by Tony Oxley, Derek Bailey, and Evan Parker, with the initial finance coming from Michael Walters. Following the departure of Oxley and then Parker, Bailey took on the mantle of label owner, though from the mid-1980s it was run by his partner Karen Anne (daughter of William Brookman, company manager) from their home at 14 Downs Road, Hackney, London. The label's first release was *The Topography of the Lungs* (1970). Bailey's solo performances invariably proved popular with audiences (less so with Bailey himself, who preferred interaction with other musicians), and his first solo recording was released on Incus as *Solo Guitar* (1971). Another solo recording on the label, *Lot 74* (1974),

Derek Bailey (1930–2005), by Mephisto, 2001

included the first of his 'chats', 'In Joke', poking fun at the po-faced free improvisation scene.

The idea of free improviser as organizer might seem to be a combination of opposites and yet only by managing their own affairs could such musicians hope to survive. Bailey took this several steps further by combining his philosophical approach to music-making—that things are most interesting before musicians get settled and a style develops—with organizing annual 'company weeks' for nearly twenty years. He chose the players and increasingly invited musicians from outside the improvising sphere. The first 'company' concert took place at the Purcell Room in 1976 and resulted in four LPs over the following months. The first 'company week' occurred in 1977 at the Institute of Contemporary Arts and the last 'company' event was in 2001 in New York city.

Bailey the theorist made his appearance known through the publication in 1980 of *Improvisation: its Nature and Practice in Music*. At the time, a well-researched monograph on this largely ignored musical development was unusual. Rather than seeing improvising as solely a form of jazz—the common (mis)understanding of the time—Bailey explored major idioms in which improvisation could form an integral part: Indian music, flamenco, baroque, organ music, rock, and jazz. It was particularly influential in introducing the term 'non-idiomatic improvisation', which has since been criticized, largely because in the intervening years there came to be a slightly broader understanding of what is entailed in playing freely improvised music and what it sounds like. The impact of the monograph was substantial, with a second edition following from the British Library in 1992, an American edition, and translations into Dutch, French, German, Italian, Japanese, Spanish, and Turkish. The second edition coincided with the appearance in February 1992 on Channel 4 television of *On the Edge*, a series of four 55 minute films written and narrated by Derek Bailey and produced and directed by Jeremy Marre.

By the early 1990s Bailey had become internationally recognized as a major contributor to the music, recording, theory, and promotion of free improvisation. Refusing to rest on his laurels, he undertook a series of encounters that were criticized for their lack of improvisational purity, but steadfastly followed his desire to explore unexpected playing situations. Many of these were encouraged and recorded by John Zorn and included *Saisoro* (1994) with the Ruins, *Guitar, Drums 'n' Bass* (1995) with DJ Ninj, and *Mirakle* (1999) with Jamaaladeen Tacuma and Calvin Weston. Further eyebrows were raised when, in 2002, he released *Ballads*. He used early standards of popular songs to test out his recently purchased archtop Epiphone Emperor guitar over Christmas 2001; his practising was heard by Zorn and quickly recorded. A recording that no one was expecting from him, this represented an important point in his recorded legacy of over 200 LPs and CDs.

Bailey and Karen Brookman were married on 22 November 2000 and moved to Barcelona for two years in 2003. In the summer of 2004 he experienced problems in holding his plectrum; he adapted his playing technique and was eventually diagnosed with carpal tunnel syndrome. He returned to London, and, after several tests, he was correctly diagnosed with motor neurone disease. He died at his home shortly before midnight on 24 December 2005. The funeral took place at the City of London crematorium and his ashes were scattered on Elizabeth Street, New York, by his wife. His son, Simon, also survived him.

PETER STUBLEY

Sources *The Guardian* (7 May 1976); (29 Dec 2005) · B. Watson, *Derek Bailey and the story of free improvisation* (2004) · *The Independent* (29 Dec 2005) · *The Times* (4 Jan 2006) · www.efi.group.shef.ac.uk, 20 June 2008 · private information (2009) [Karen Bailey, wife; Simon Bailey, son] · personal knowledge (2009) · b. cert. · m. certs. · d. cert.
Archives SOUND BL NSA, oral history of jazz in Britain, interview with B. Priestley, 15 July 1987, T9639–T9641 · BL NSA, 'Impressions', interview with B. Morton, 1994, H3617/3 · BL NSA, documentary recordings · BL NSA, performance recordings
Likenesses Mephisto, photograph, 2001, Rex Features [*see illus.*] · photographs, 2001, Rex Features, London · obituary photographs · photographs, repro. in http://www.efi.group.shef.ac.uk/
Wealth at death under £233,000: probate, 10 April 2006, *CGPLA Eng. & Wales*

Baker, Harold Brooks Brooks- (1933–2005), publisher, was born Harold Brooks Baker in Washington, DC, USA, on 16 November 1933, the son of Charles Silas Baker (1888–1943), head of the law firm of Baker, Beedy, and Magee, and his wife, Elizabeth, *née* Lambert. As a child he contracted polio and nearly died; he never recovered from the physical effects of his illness, and in his final years was confined to a wheelchair. For two years he languished in a sanatorium in Georgia, reading novels and day-dreaming; and his susceptibility to titled society perhaps dated from this time. At the age of fifteen he resumed his interrupted education, and entered Trinity College, a private school at Hartford, Connecticut; afterwards he studied at the University of Virginia law school. He is said to have been a press officer in the White House during the Eisenhower presidency. He worked as a foreign correspondent of the *Washington Observer* in 1960–63, and then as a bond dealer in Paris and Geneva for six years. In 1964 he married Irene Marie, daughter of Count Robert Elliott Le Gras du Luart de Montsaulnin and his wife, Elisabeth de la Rochefoucauld—a marriage that gave him the gratification of a connection with such exclusive French families as Polignac, de Luynes, and Murat. There were two daughters of this marriage. He adopted the surname of Brooks-Baker to circumvent the French laws of birth registration, which prevented him from bestowing the family name of Brooks as his daughters' middle forename.

Brooks-Baker came to London in 1976 as managing director of Debrett's Peerage Ltd, which had recently been acquired by new owners. Under his direction the firm published a lucrative series of books on etiquette, manners, and protocol, notably Douglas Sutherland's *The English Gentleman* (1978) and *The English Gentleman's Wife* (1979). Brooks-Baker oversaw the launch in 1981 of *Debrett's Handbook*, a new biographical dictionary to rival *Who's Who*, retitled *Debrett's Distinguished People of Today* from 1988. His office's affairs fell into disarray, and insolvency was only

Harold Brooks Brooks-Baker (1933–2005), by unknown photographer, 1986

averted by the timely publication of a book marking the marriage of the prince of Wales in 1981. The London Trust Company bought a 75 per cent holding in *Debrett's* at this time, and installed Ian McCorquodale as chairman of its subsidiary. Shortly afterwards Brooks-Baker was locked out of the office, and his dismissal was confirmed at a stormy board meeting on 9 November 1981, at which his cause was championed by the quixotic figure of Sir Iain Moncreiffe of that ilk.

In 1984 Ravensdale Securities bought the company that published *Burke's Peerage*, a rival of *Debrett's*, which could not however meet its debts to the Inland Revenue and was wound up in 1985–6. It would have been sensible to merge the two competing reference books, but instead, during this period of financial vulnerability, Brooks-Baker acquired the right to publish spin-off books under the *Burke's* imprint. But he had nothing to do with compiling or publishing *Burke's Peerage*, of which no new edition was published between 1970 and 1999. Instead his flair for publicity and self-advertisement was put to the service of an enterprise that published books on history and manners, and which undertook remunerative work as genealogical researchers for clients in Britain, North America, and Australasia. Subsequently he acted as a middleman who enabled his clients to buy Scottish feudal baronies at prices reportedly exceeding £50,000. These were not titles of honour, but dignities tied to specific lands, carrying powers and responsibilities over the property to which they were attached, and rather less empty than manorial lordships in England. Holders of Scottish feudal baronies were entitled to an armorial grant by the lord Lyon king of arms in Edinburgh. These dealings were exempt from the Honours (Prevention of Abuses) Act of 1925, although the Scottish parliament's Abolition of Feudal Tenure Act of 2004 stripped feudal baronies of their powers and reduced them to mere titles of dignity, which could be bought and sold without any land. Brooks-Baker and his associates also designed and sold bogus coats-of-arms: bona fide heralds of the College of Arms held his activities in contempt. He was companionable, but had a reputation for being unreliable in money matters, and some of those who had business dealings with him were left smarting. People nicknamed him Brookie to his face, and Crooks-Faker behind his back.

It was chiefly as a 'rentaquote' that Brooks-Baker reached prominence. In the 1980s he became a self-appointed arbiter of the habits and conduct of the British royal family and nobility. He was always ready with a pithy and provocative comment for journalists, and indeed issued bombastic public statements before being approached by newspapers. His opinions carried a spurious air of authority because of his association with *Burke's*, but were generally glib, ill-informed, smug, and malicious, and part of the culture of irresponsible, inaccurate, and defamatory comment on the house of Windsor that became so prevalent in the 1980s. There seemed no limit to his effrontery. Some senior journalists tried to inhibit the publication of his pronouncements, but they were usually foiled by lazy or ill-informed younger reporters, who found his quotes readily available and reliably catchy.

His first marriage having ended in divorce, Brooks-Baker married secondly, in 1997, Catherine Mary Neville-Rolfe (*b.* 1947), writer, and daughter of Edmund Neville-Rolfe, agricultural economist and later an artist. His health failed after a fall in the autumn of 2004, and in his final years he suffered from post-polio syndrome. He died on 5 March 2005 at the Chelsea and Westminster Hospital, of heart and respiratory failure. He was survived by his second wife, Catherine, and the two daughters of his first marriage. RICHARD DAVENPORT-HINES

Sources *The Scotsman* (24 Nov 2003) · *New York Times* (8 March 2005) · *The Times* (8 March 2005) · *Daily Telegraph* (8 March 2005) · *Mail on Sunday* (13 March 2005) · *The Herald* [Glasgow] (14 March 2005) · *The Guardian* (12 April 2005) · personal knowledge (2009) · private information (2009) · m. cert. [1997] · d. cert.
Archives FILM BFINA, performance footage
Likenesses double portrait, photograph, 1982 (with Douglas Sutherland), PA Photos, London · photograph, 1986, Photoshot, London [*see illus.*] · J. Ford, photograph, 1992, Rex Features, London · obituary photographs
Wealth at death under £152,000: probate, 30 June 2005, *CGPLA Eng. & Wales*

Baker, Laurence Wilfred [Laurie] (**1917–2007**), architect in India, was born on 2 March 1917 at 6 Kings Road, Erdington, Birmingham, the third son and youngest of four children of Charles Frederick Baker, a clerk at the local gasworks, and later chief accountant of Birmingham's gas distribution authority, and his wife, Milly, *née* Fleming. He came from a Methodist family, but later converted to Quakerism. He grew up in Birmingham, attending King Edward VI Grammar School, Aston. His early interest in drawing took him to the Birmingham School of Architecture, where he graduated in 1937 with an engineering degree. But his training as an architect was cut short by the Second World War. He opposed the war on moral grounds and became a conscientious objector, enlisting in the Friends Ambulance Unit. As a part of a surgical unit tending to the war wounded he was sent to China. The hardships he endured there took a toll on his own health, and in 1944 he was forced to return to England to recuperate.

Stranded in Bombay, waiting for a steamer to England, Baker, living with Quaker friends, had a chance encounter with Mahatma Gandhi. Gandhi stressed that India's biggest architectural challenge lay in finding a solution to housing the poor. Whether this encounter with Gandhi had an immediate impact on him is hard to say, but in 1945 he returned to India to work for an organization dealing with leprosy. His job involved the conversion of refugee centres into hospitals and building low-cost homes and health centres in the United Provinces, northern India. During the course of his stay there he met Elizabeth Chandy, a young Indian doctor who specialized in leprosy treatment. Working with the same organization, once the two married in 1948, they were posted to the Himalayan district of Pithoragarh. They had two daughters, Vidya and Heidi, and a son, Tilak.

Baker's instinctive response to Gandhi's ideology and his acceptance of the frugal lifestyle of Pithoragarh as his own, along with his Quaker background, appeared in the rugged, direct nature of his architecture. Despite his training as a conventional architect his use of such materials as rock, mud, laterite, and cowdung was anything but conventional. As he built in the Himalayan setting he began to understand that simplicity was at the base of all effective living architecture. 'To me this Himalayan domestic architecture was a perfect example of vernacular architecture: simple, efficient and inexpensive', he said in 1980 (Bhatia, 11). The sort of burdened functionalism that modernism enforced with elaborate theory came naturally to one whose religious beliefs expressed in his handiwork the desire to build simply, willingly, and honestly.

In 1963 the Bakers left Pithoragarh and settled in the similarly mountainous region of Vakamon, in the southern Indian state of Kerala. Though the stay lasted barely three or four years the lessons he derived from this as well as his Himalayan experience remained with him when he resumed his practice in Trivandrum (later Thiruvanthapuram). He remained there for over forty years, working on remarkably varied projects, ranging from institutional buildings, churches, hospitals, and cathedrals to housing for the poor. In Thiruvanthapuram alone he built over a thousand private houses, each project demonstrating design ideas specific to his client's requirements while making use of local materials. 'Low cost', he maintained, 'was not just for the poor, but for all' (*Hindustan Times*, 17 Jan 1974). But while many of these were middle-class homes his heart was always with those who could not afford the services of an architect. His most important institutional project, the Centre for Development Studies, was established in 1965 to promote economic development in Kerala, and with the explicit message of projecting its socially conscious goals in a progressive architecture. He worked on the rolling, deeply forested site like a true craftsman, plotting the plans on the natural terraces, thereby fragmenting the buildings—libraries, dormitories, classrooms, and student centre—into smaller components set within the existing landscape. No contour was disturbed, no tree uprooted.

In all Baker's work there remained a continuous restraint of personal expression, an idea that was the direct outcome of his working like a traditional craftsman. Supporting the production and assembly of standardized building elements in his work—whether a home, a school, or a cathedral—he established a clear visible link in all his architecture. The peculiarly Bakeresque forms of the screen, the walled courtyard, the terracotta roof made of discarded tile, and the steep overhanging eaves, in varying combinations, produced open-plan structures with obvious references to the climate and ecology of Kerala. Their inclusion in all his projects suggested their values as definitions of useful space as well as visible symbols of a regionally identifiable architecture. From his body of work stemmed an entire ideology of architectural practice—a pattern that, compared with the clumsy form of modernism spawned in India by imitations of Le Corbusier's Chandigarh, was revolutionary in its simplicity and transformative in its interpretation of traditional and local technology. 'In most countries of the world architects are being accused of failing to produce a modern form of their own previous distinctive styles', he argued in 1986 (Bhatia, 30).

Despite many years of a rigorous practice rooted in a single place Baker's architecture never succeeded in winning government backing. His adage—'a better building at half the cost'—was unacceptable to an unimaginative and elephantine bureaucracy, controlling large public housing projects and working within wasteful budgets and antiquated norms. Years later, when recognition came, it came grudgingly; in the late 1980s the government began to seek his advice on large-scale construction projects. He was nominated to a number of national committees on housing. Besides being a member of the governing committee of the Housing and Urban Development Corporation and the National Institute of Design he received the Indian Institute of Architects' gold medal. In 1981 the Royal University of the Netherlands awarded him an honorary doctorate for 'outstanding work in the Third World'. In 1992 he received the United Nations habitat award, and in 1993 he won the International Union of Architects award. Though the only honour that Baker actively sought from the Indian government for forty years was Indian citizenship, eventually granted in 1989, the government also conferred on him the Padma Shree (1990), a civilian honour. His last few years were spent nursing a recurring heart condition, but he remained actively involved in practice, doing his drawings on scraps of envelopes and visiting building sites, committed, as always, to bringing change through his trademark brick buildings that dotted his home state of Kerala. He died in Thiruvanthapuram on 1 April 2007 and was survived by his wife, Elizabeth, and their three children.

GAUTAM BHATIA

Sources G. Bhatia, *Laurie Baker: life, works, writings* (1991) · A. Deulgaonkar, *Laurie Baker* (1994) · E. Baker, *The other side of Laurie Baker* (2007) · *Indian Express* (1 April 2007) · *Hindu* (2 April 2007); (15 April 2007) · *Daily Telegraph* (2 April 2007) · *New York Times* (8 April 2007) · *Building Design* (13 April 2007) · *Hindustan Times* (13 April 2007) · *Times of India* (21 April 2007) · *The Times* (3 May 2007) · *Birmingham Post* (3 May 2007) · *The Guardian* (11 May 2007) · lauriebaker.net, 5 July 2010 · el.doccentre.info/website/RDC/docsweb/Booklet-Laurie%20Baker/1stpg-laurie-baker-main.php, 5 July 2010 · www.archiplanet.org/wiki/Laurie_Baker, 12 July 2010 · personal knowledge (2011) · private information (2011) · b. cert.
Archives priv. coll.
Likenesses S. Gopakumar, photograph, repro. in www.hindu.com/2007/04/02/stories/2007040203471300.htm · R. S. Iyer, photograph, PA Photos, London · obituary photographs · photographs, repro. in Bhatia, *Laurie Baker* · photographs, repro. in Deulgaonkar, *Laurie Baker* · photographs, repro. in Baker, *Laurie Baker* · photographs, repro. in lauriebaker.net · photographs, repro. in el.doccentre.info/website/RDC/docsweb/Booklet-Laurie%20Baker/1stpg-laurie-baker-main.php · photographs, repro. in www.archiplanet.org/wiki/Laurie_Baker

Balchin, William George Victor [Bill] (1916–2007), geographer, was born on 20 June 1916 at 1 Ivy Cottages, Bellevue Road, Aldershot, the only child of Victor Balchin (1884–1944), steam lorry driver, and later publican, and his wife, Ellen Winifred Gertrude, *née* Chapple (1891–1988). His family life in Hampshire was extended by the summers he spent with his grandparents in Cornwall. His academic ability began to show through at a very early age and he was 'fast-tracked' through Aldershot county high school. He sat for higher school examinations at the age of fifteen and needed to qualify for a scholarship to go on to university. He was successful but because of his age had to defer entry to university; he left Aldershot county high school a year later to study geography at St Catharine's College, Cambridge, with a state scholarship. As an undergraduate he became centrally interested in geomorphology and in the record in landscape of former sea levels. A modified version of his dissertation on this theme, based on Cornwall, won the first Royal Geographical Society essay prize and was published in the *Geographical Journal* when he was still only eighteen.

After graduating from Cambridge, Balchin was appointed to the staff of the university as a demonstrator and in 1938 he joined an expedition to the Arctic. He had considerable skills in geodetic and topographic survey and applied these to the research area near Spitsbergen. He was able to provide significant evidence for isostatic uplift and his mapping endeavours were rewarded when the Norwegian government accepted his naming of a 5000 foot high glaciated peak at latitude 81° N as Mount Balchin (Balchinfjellet).

After Balchin came back from the Arctic, other events took over. On the outbreak of the Second World War, he was enlisted in the Admiralty's hydrographic department at Bath. Shortly afterwards he was married. He had met Lily Kettlewood (1912–1999) when he was seventeen. The daughter of Henry Gordon Kettlewood, lithographic artist, she was from Otley in Yorkshire; they were married at Bramhope parish church, Yorkshire, on 10 December 1939. They had three children, Peter, Joan, and Anne. Balchin's family life was of great importance to him.

During the Second World War Balchin worked mainly on the compilation of marine charts and special air maps. Towards the end of this period he collaborated with Norman Pye in the development of a new research field of microclimatology or local climates. They constructed their own Stevenson screens to record weather data and with help from local botanists examined the relationship between flowering dates of plants and height along the valley sides in the Bath region.

In 1945, with the end of the war, Balchin's work with the hydrographic department came to an end and he joined King's College, London, as a lecturer in geography. There he completed a PhD degree under the supervision of S. W. Wooldridge on the theme of erosion surfaces; he later completed a book on Cornwall, which revealed his interest in landscapes and his admiration for the writings of W. G. Hoskins on the making of landscapes. He collaborated with Norman Pye on climatology and also on the arid landscapes of Arizona. At this time he was an established and respected researcher with a range of interests in geomorphology, climatology, and cartography. Although he had a lifelong interest across the breadth of the discipline of geography, it was the physical environment that held his major focus.

An important change in Balchin's career path came in 1954 when he became the first professor of geography and head of department at the University College of Swansea. Among his responsibilities was the planning and design of a new purpose-built geography department in the natural sciences building, a building shared with geology and biological sciences. Academically his instinct was to create a new department (though there had been a geographical presence at Swansea since 1931) with a strong concentration on physical science and cartography. Perhaps he recognized that, within the University of Wales, Aberystwyth provided a similar focus on human geography and anthropology. As the Swansea department developed it gradually acquired a better balance and had strengths across the broad range of the discipline. Balchin quickly revealed his considerable ability as an administrator and manager. His attention to detail and careful planning was well known, and these activities commanded more of his time and energy. He was head of department for twenty-four years and held other important university roles, including a spell as vice-principal. During these years he continued his academic activities, though perhaps inevitably the scientific research components of his contributions became much less prominent with the passage of time. He wrote, with Alice Coleman, a number of valuable and interesting studies of the concept of graphicacy (that is the ability to understand and interpret information in the form of graphics, and the argument that graphicacy should rank as a skill alongside literacy and numeracy) and he had a strong interest in water resources and conservation. His affiliation with bodies such as the Geographical Association (of which he was president in 1971 and whose history he wrote on its centenary in 1993) and the Royal Geographical Society (of which he was vice-president from 1978 to 1982) was always maintained and he became a senior figure within the discipline, able to comment authoritatively on a range of issues of national and international importance.

Balchin retired from Swansea in 1978 and made a new home in Ilkley, Yorkshire, where he and Lily had family connections. He was remembered in Swansea as a kindly and helpful man who set up a thriving department at the university. He kept in touch by regular correspondence and visits and made a point of attending, at the age of eighty-seven, the retirement dinner of a former student. In his own retirement he remained active. He was much involved with the Balchin Family Society, a family history group of which he became president in 1993. He died at Troutbeck Nursing Home, Crossbeck Road, Ilkley, on 30 July 2007, of heart failure, and was survived by his son, Peter, and daughter Anne; his daughter Joan and his wife, Lily, predeceased him. He was an active participant and leader in the emergence and consolidation of geography as a major discipline in the British university system. His legacy embraced many aspects of the discipline and took specific form in the department he founded at Swansea.

DAVID T. HERBERT

Sources *The Times* (6 Sept 2007); (1 Oct 2007) · www.balchin-family.org.uk, 4 Jan 2011 · *WW* (2007) · personal knowledge (2011) · private information (2011) · b. cert. · m. cert. · d. cert.
Likenesses photographs, repro. in www.balchin-family.org.uk
Wealth at death £821,598: probate, 16 Nov 2007, *CGPLA Eng. & Wales*

Baldry, John William [*known as* Long John Baldry] (**1941–2005**), singer and guitarist, was born at East Haddon Hall, East Haddon, Northamptonshire, on 12 January 1941, the first of three children of William James Baldry (1915–1990), a Metropolitan Police constable, and his wife, Margaret Louisa, *née* Parker (1915–1989). At the time of the registration of his birth his parents lived at 18 Frinton Road, East Ham, London. He obtained the sobriquet Long John as a baby, being remarkably long, and by his mid-teens he was six feet seven inches tall. He was raised in Queensbury, Middlesex, attended Downer County Grammar School, Edgware, and sang in the choir at St Lawrence's Church, also in Edgware. By 1953 he was listening to American blues performers and learning twelve-string guitar. He made his first public appearance as a guitarist and blues singer in 1956 and also played with the renowned guitarist Davey Graham.

After leaving school Baldry worked for an advertising agency, but soon joined Alexis Korner and Cyril Davies in their group, Blues Incorporated. The fluid line-up included Jack Bruce, Ginger Baker, and Charlie Watts alongside such vocalists as Baldry, Mick Jagger, and Paul Jones. His commanding presence was heard on the album *R&B from the Marquee* (1962). In 1962 Baldry toured Germany working with the vibraphonist Günther Hampel and his quartet. He returned to find Korner and Davies at loggerheads. As Baldry later recounted, 'Both Alex and Cyril were anxious for me to join their bands, and I joined Cyril on the toss of a half-crown' (BBC Radio Merseyside, 13 July 2002). Exactly one year later Davies died of leukaemia. Baldry assumed leadership of his band but renamed it Long John Baldry and the Hoochie Coochie Men. The musicians ranged from nineteen to forty-eight, the youngest being Rod Stewart, whom Baldry had heard playing harmonica on Twickenham railway station. Rod Stewart later remarked, 'In those days the only music we fell in love with was the blues and John with his wonderful voice was the first white guy singing it' (*The Independent*, 25 July 2005).

In 1966 Baldry, Stewart, Brian Auger, and Julie Driscoll formed Steampacket. They toured with the Rolling Stones, but there were management problems. Baldry wanted another new band but did not want the rigmarole of forming another line-up. He recalled, 'I was at a gambling casino opposite the V&A, the Cromwellian Club. There was live music in the basement and this night it was Bluesology with Reg Dwight [later known as Elton John] playing keyboards, and I gave them the job *en bloc*' (BBC Radio Merseyside, 13 July 2002). Baldry's rich voice was appreciated by a songwriting and production team at Pye Records, Tony Macaulay and John MacLeod. They offered him a polished pop–soul ballad, 'Let the Heartaches Begin'. Macaulay remembered, 'Long John Baldry [sang] it extraordinarily well, thanks to three-quarters of a bottle of Courvoisier' (*The Independent*, 25 July 2005). The record climbed to the top of the charts and Baldry performed it at the royal variety performance in 1968. It is often assumed that he hated the song, but he said in 2002 that 'I liked doing anything in the studio and I was very happy that Pye was employing me. I was hugely flattered to be backed by a large orchestra, and it's not a bad song' (BBC Radio Merseyside, 13 July 2002).

Baldry had further hits with 'When the Sun Comes Shinin' Thru' (written by Manfred Mann's new vocalist, Mike D'Abo), 'It's Too Late Now', and 'Mexico'. Of the latter Baldry said, 'That was done for the Olympic Games in 1968 and it was constantly on the radio. I wanted to scream every time I heard the damn thing, talk about overkill' (BBC Radio Merseyside, 13 July 2002). His albums *Let the Heartaches Begin* (1968) and *Wait for Me* (1969) included some excellent cover versions, including 'Stay with Me' and 'Man Without a Dream'. When Dwight told Baldry that he was leaving Bluesology to pursue a career as a singer and songwriter the band gave him a new name. They took Elton from their saxophone player, Elton Dean, and Dwight added John as a tribute to Baldry. Baldry had prevented the emotional Dwight from committing suicide, the subject of Elton John's song, 'Someone Saved my Life Tonight'.

In 1971 Baldry released the album *It Ain't Easy* produced by Elton John and Rod Stewart. He promoted it in North America and liked Canada so much that he moved to Vancouver and became a Canadian citizen in 1981. A witty and friendly man, he quickly became acclimatized to the Vancouver musical scene. He had a Canadian hit with 'Don't Try to Lay No Boogie Woogie on the King of Rock and Roll' and recorded several albums including *It Still Ain't Easy* (1991), *Right to Sing the Blues* (1996), and *Remembering Leadbelly* (2001). His main income came from lending his deep voice to commercials and cartoons including *Sonic the*

Hedgehog. He died from a chest infection in Vancouver, British Columbia, on 21 July 2005. He was survived by a sister. Spencer Leigh

Sources *The Guardian* (23 July 2005) • *The Times* (25 July 2005) • *Daily Telegraph* (25 July 2005) • *The Independent* (25 July 2005) • interview, BBC Radio Merseyside, 13 July 2002 • personal knowledge (2009) • private information (2009) • b. cert.
Archives film BFINA, performance footage | sound BL NSA, documentary recording; performance recordings • interview, BBC Radio Merseyside, 13 July 2002
Likenesses photographs, *c*.1960–1965, Getty Images, London • photographs, 1960x69–2000x05, Rex Features, London • photograph, 2001, PA Photos, London • H. Goodwin, photographs, priv. coll. • obituary photographs • photographs, Redferns Music Picture Library, London

Ball, Alan James (1945–2007), footballer and football manager, was born on 12 May 1945 at 2 Brookhouse Avenue, Farnworth, Lancashire, the son of (James) Alan Ball, builder's joiner, later publican, and his wife, Violet, *née* Duckworth. His father was an occasional professional footballer with Southport, Oldham Athletic, and Rochdale, whose later career as a football manager was ended prematurely by his death in a road accident in Cyprus in 1982. It was a household in which football was an important part of family life. One of Ball's earliest memories was the smell of liniment, dubbin, and sweat that permeated the dressing rooms of his father's teams. Young Alan's relationship with his father was a crucial part of his own footballing life. He went to Farnworth grammar school but left with no qualification save that of being an outstanding footballer. He was the best player in the school team at the age of fifteen but was already missing school matches to turn out for Ashton United in the semi-professional Lancashire Combination, a team managed by his father. When it had become clear that the young Ball had talent, his father instituted a strict regime of physical training that included running 5 miles from home to school and back and sprinting between houses on his newspaper rounds. He also insisted on an hour's ball practice every night. Ball would later remember that his father not only taught him how lucky he was to be such a good player but would never let him forget it. As his professional career developed, his father would accompany him when new contracts were being discussed and insist that rewards should be performance-related.

It was inevitable that so talented a young player who had a parent who was already part of the football subculture would arouse the interest of professional clubs. Both Bolton Wanderers and Wolverhampton Wanderers decided that at 5 feet 6 inches Ball was too small for the tough, physical games of the English league. But Blackpool, then in the first division of the Football League, took him on as a sixteen-year-old in 1961, and he signed his first professional contract with them the following year. He was paid £7 10s. per week. He was soon exhibiting the qualities, good and not so good, that would characterize him throughout his career. He was a very hard worker with a strong belief in his own ability based on endless practice and formidable physical stamina. He also held strong views about the shortcomings of others, which he was not afraid to express. At Blackpool he criticized Stanley Matthews for not running hard enough in a practice match to collect one of his passes. When Matthews returned to Stoke City Ball became the star of a fading Blackpool team often only kept afloat, in 1965–6, by the goalkeeping of Tony Waiters at one end and the perpetual motion, tackling, passing, and scoring of Alan Ball everywhere else. In November 1964 he had been selected for the England under-23 team, which was a sure sign that a move to a bigger club was not far away.

Alan James Ball (**1945–2007**), by Bob Thomas, 1975

Don Revie was particularly keen to sign Ball for Leeds United and not only encouraged him to escalate a contract dispute with Blackpool but made him what were essentially a number of illegal payments. Ball was later charged by the Football Association with bringing the game into disrepute and fined £3000. In August 1966 he signed for Everton, the fee of £110,000 being then a record for a player moving between two British clubs. By then Ball had been the man of the match in England's world cup final victory over Germany.

Ball received his first England cap against Yugoslavia in May 1965 just a few days before his twentieth birthday, but had not been able to hold down a regular place. He had played in the opening match of the world cup of 1966, a disappointing goalless draw against Uruguay, but was left out for the next two games as the manager, Alf Ramsey, persisted with the use of an orthodox wing forward on the right. Ball was recalled for the quarter-final against Argentina and played well in the semi-final against Portugal but in the final he surpassed himself, tormenting the experienced German left back, Karl Heinz Schnellinger, by his irrepressible energy, running, and invention. With the score at 2–2, during extra time he helped create the third English goal (the one that only the Soviet linesman, Tofik Bakhramov, thought was over the line), and his performance throughout the game was remarkable. Ramsey, famously stinting in his praise, told him afterwards, 'Young man, you will never play a better game of football in your life than you did today' (*The Independent*, 26 April 2007).

All this meant high expectations for Ball's first season at Everton, and with Howard Kendall and Colin Harvey to help him in midfield a good team was transformed into a better one. Although the cup final was lost in 1968, the championship was won by nine points in 1969–70. It is not entirely clear why this success was not developed. The Everton management seemed to lose its way, and it was a surprise when Everton accepted an offer for Ball from Arsenal (of £220,000, again an English record) in December 1971. Arsenal had won both cup and league in 1970–71, but five frustratingly unsuccessful seasons followed. Ball broke a leg in 1974 and won the last of his seventy-two England caps the following year. Meanwhile, on 21 May 1967, at the parish church of St Stephen, Kearsley, Lancashire, he married (Janet) Lesley Newton (1947–2004), a ladies' hairdresser, and daughter of Jack Newton, gentlemen's hair dresser. They had two daughters, Keely and Mandy, and a son, Jimmy.

Ball was transferred to Southampton, then in the second division, in 1976 for £60,000. Under a manager with whom he got on well he thrived and so did the Saints, winning promotion to the first division in 1977–8 and reaching a league cup final in 1979. Ball briefly boosted his summer wages by two terms in North America but then made the first of what would be a series of calamitous career moves when he returned to Blackpool as player–manager in 1980. The team was weak and was eventually relegated to division four. He was sacked after seven months. But there was to be one last hurrah on the field. Ball was still very fit, and his enthusiasm for playing was undiminished. He rejoined Southampton, now back in the first division, and in his thirty-seventh year played sixty-three more games for them, including forty-one out of forty-two in the 1981–2 season, when the club finished in seventh place.

One of the minor curiosities about the after-life of the players who brought England its world cup win in 1966 is that only Jack Charlton was a success as a manager. It is probable that one of the reasons is the impatience good players often exhibit when asked to supervise those of lesser ability. This certainly seems to have been true of Ball, although he could be good on the training pitch if not very diplomatic off it. As a manager he seems to have too often chosen the wrong club at the wrong time. Four of his appointments ended in relegation. After taking the job at Portsmouth in May 1984 he oversaw their promotion to the first division in 1987, but financial difficulties accompanied relegation in 1988 and Ball was dismissed four months into the new season. Fifteen traumatic months at Stoke City also ended in relegation in 1989–90. At this point he seems to have decided that football management was too stressful and took a pub near Ascot. But his passion for football tempted him back again to third-division Exeter City, where his two seasons, 1991–2 and 1992–3, both involved narrowly avoiding relegation to the fourth division.

Ball had enjoyed his time as a player at Southampton and perhaps his most successful period as manager was also at the south-coast club. He returned in January 1994, saved them from relegation, and took them to tenth place in 1994–5. But he could not resist the call from a bigger club, Manchester City, though it was heavily in debt and with a well-earned reputation for underachievement. City was relegated from the premier league in 1995–6 and Ball, predictably, lost his job. He returned to Portsmouth in 1998 but was sacked for the last time in December 1999.

Looking back on his footballing life and the fame and rewards it brought, Ball insisted that it was playing that he had really loved. It was 'everything you wanted to do in your life. Get up in the morning, go and train, play football, get paid for it' (Hattenstone, 114). He worked hard, but his commitment and aggression meant he often upset other players and referees. He was only the second England player to be sent off in a full international (against Poland in 1973) and when he was appointed captain for a match against Germany in 1975 one MP, Walter Johnson, complained that it set a bad example to youth. He was appointed MBE in 2000. He did make a good living from the game. At Southampton, for example, he was thought to have been the highest paid player in Britain, earning £500 a week. Yet he retained the 'wonderful feeling that we were still part of the people', unlike the multi-millionaire stars of the later game (*The Guardian*, 26 April 2007).

In 2001 both Lesley and Mandy Ball were diagnosed with cancer, within six weeks. Mandy survived. Lesley died in 2004, but not before she had persuaded Alan Ball to sell his world cup winner's medal in order to help secure the financial future of the family. It was sold in May 2005 for £164,800. Ball died from a heart attack while putting out a fire in the garden of his home in Hook Lane, Warsash, Hampshire, on 25 April 2007. He was survived by his three children. TONY MASON

Sources A. Ball, *Playing for extra time* (2004) · S. Hattenstone, *The best of times: what became of the heroes of '66?* (2006) · *The Times* (26 April 2007) · *Daily Telegraph* (26 April 2007) · *The Guardian* (26 April 2007) · *The Independent* (26 April 2007); (27 April 2007) · D. Porter, 'Egg and chips with the Connellys: remembering 1966', *Sport in History*, 29 (2009), 519–39 · b. cert. · m. cert.

Archives FILM BFINA, 'Alan Ball, Mick Channon', *Yesterday's heroes*, ITV, 21 April 1996 · BFINA, documentary footage | SOUND BL NSA, performance recording

Likenesses photographs, 1964–2006, Rex Features, London · photographs, 1964–2006, PA Photos, London · photographs, 1966–2006, Getty Images, London · photographs, 1966–2007, Photoshot, London · B. Thomas, photograph, 1975, Getty Images, London [*see*

illus.] · obituary photographs · photographs, repro. in Ball, *Extra time*

Wealth at death £358,164: probate, 5 Sept 2007, *CGPLA Eng. & Wales*

Banbury, (Frederick Harold) Frith (1912–2008), actor, theatre director, and producer, was born on 4 May 1912 at 8 The Terrace, The Hoe, Plymouth, the elder child of Captain Frederick Arthur Frith Banbury (1874–1951), naval officer, and his wife, Winifred, *née* Fink (1876/7–1960). His sister Joan was born six years later. Their father was a paymaster in the Royal Navy who eventually rose to the rank of rear-admiral. Winifred Banbury was a cosmopolitan Jew who taught her son to play the piano and took him to his first play, *Joy Bells*, at the age of six, thus beginning his infatuation with all things theatrical. Returning home from a long period of overseas service, Banbury senior found his eight-year-old son's immersion in all things artistic and theatrical baffling and disappointing, a position he held all his life.

Banbury was educated at Stowe School, a progressive public school where his headmaster described him as ploughing 'a lonely furrow'. 'You know what this means, don't you?', Banbury's father allegedly boomed, 'the other boys don't like you' (*Saga Magazine*, 2003). Banbury preferred to assert that 'I didn't like the other boys', but despite the insouciance of this remark his schooldays were unhappy; he detested games and refused to join the Officers' Training Corps, a commitment to pacifism he maintained throughout his life. He sustained himself by imagining his future theatrical career and going to the theatre with religious assiduity; as he once remarked, 'some get Christianity, I've got theatre' (interview, 2005). In 1930 he went to Oxford to read modern languages at Hertford College and immediately joined the Oxford University Dramatic Society, where he acted alongside Terence Rattigan, and 'went to parties' (Duff, 9). By the end of the year it was clear that he and Oxford were not suited and in the autumn of 1931 he enrolled at the Royal Academy of Dramatic Art (RADA), where he studied alongside Joan Littlewood (whose future theatre practice would be diametrically opposite to his) and Rachel Kempson. RADA was the making of him as he discovered an aptitude for learning that Oxford and Stowe had never stimulated. He enjoyed lessons at RADA (unlike Littlewood) and was sufficiently inspired to undergo further training with Michel St Denis, whom he had approached offering his language skills in exchange for a chance to work with the director.

Ten days after graduating, in June 1933, Banbury had his first job playing piano and understudying in Sholom Aleichem's revue, *Hard to be a Jew*, at the Shaftesbury Theatre. The show, renamed *If I Were You* in view of Hitler's rise to power, closed after ten days. Next came a small part in the touring production of *Richard of Bordeaux*, directed by John Gielgud. Banbury had a small part and also understudied Glen Byam Shaw as Richard, eventually playing the role for a week in Hammersmith when Shaw fell ill. Although he apparently struggled with the period costume, he was considered good enough to be offered the part of Marcellus in Gielgud's *Hamlet* by producer Donald Albery. At the first rehearsal, however, Gielgud demoted him to Courier and reallocated most of his lines; an unpropitious beginning to what became an enduring personal and professional friendship. Banbury worked as an actor and revue performer until 1947 (including throughout the Second World War; he was deemed unsuitable for farm work), when he was invited back to RADA to take over direction of Pinero's *The Times* and then to direct two more plays of his own choosing. RADA's principal, Kenneth Barnes, was sufficiently impressed to offer him a post but Banbury was about to embark on his first commercial production, *Dark Summer*, written by his fellow pacifist Wynard Browne.

In 1947 Banbury used his savings to buy a six-month option on *Dark Summer* and took the play to the leading West End producers of the day, H. M. Tennent Ltd, who eventually agreed to produce it at the Lyric Hammersmith via their non-commercial arm, Tennent's Productions. Banbury proved an able director with a talent for dealing with difficult personalities. The play was well reviewed, which gave him the courage to ask his mother for £10,000 to establish a commercial company. She agreed and Banbury began a long career producing the work of new writers such as Browne (whose *The Holly and the Ivy*, 1950, was a long-running West End hit and repertory staple), Errol John (whose *Moon on a Rainbow Shawl*, 1958, was probably the first play with an all-black cast to be given a mainstream London production), Robert Bolt, N. C. Hunter, John Whiting, and Rodney Ackland, alongside established authors such as J. B. Priestley and Terence Rattigan. Banbury was later celebrated for tirelessly championing Ackland's work—often difficult, abstruse, and uncommercial—and in particular for persuading Rattigan to invest his profits from *The Deep Blue Sea* (1951), which Banbury had directed, in Ackland's *The Pink Room* (1952). Directed by Banbury, the play exposed the seamy underbelly of post-war London in forensic detail and was a flop of such magnitude that Rattigan apparently never spoke to Banbury again. But Banbury's vision was vindicated when *The Pink Room* was rediscovered and revised as *Absolute Hell* in the late 1980s, subsequently staged at the National Theatre, and filmed for the BBC. *The Pink Room* was also something of a personal watershed for Banbury as Christopher Taylor, the young Canadian actor engaged to play the part of the Canadian airman, became his closest personal and professional companion, working as play-reader, play-doctor, and adapter alongside him. For all his rebellion against his father, and his assertion that he was 'a homosexual, half-Jewish conchie' (*The Independent*, 17 May 2008), Banbury, like many men of his generation, was a discreet homosexual, who habitually referred to Taylor as his 'chum' in public (*Saga Magazine*, 2003).

Among Banbury's later successes were a revival of Henry James's *The Aspern Papers* at the Haymarket in 1984, starring Wendy Hiller, Vanessa Redgrave, and Christopher Reeve, Emlyn Williams's *The Corn is Green* (Old Vic, 1985), with Deborah Kerr as the schoolmistress, and D. L. Coburn's *The Gin Game* (Savoy, 1999), with Joss Ackland and

Dorothy Tutin. In 2003 he directed a revival of Rodney Ackland's *The Old Ladies*, in Richmond and on tour.

Banbury was synonymous with Tennent's and the style of well-made theatre they espoused. But his love of theatre was by no means confined to this style and he was a regular and conspicuous figure in London's fringe theatres, as well as in the West End, well into his nineties. He was appointed MBE for services to drama in 2000, an honour both well-deserved and long overdue. He died of cancer at his home in St James's Terrace, overlooking Regent's Park, on 14 May 2008. He was survived by his partner of fifty-four years, Christopher Taylor, who died on 18 August 2008. Early collectors of David Hockney and other modern artists, Banbury and Taylor left two works by Hockney, *Study for Doll Boy* and *The Berliner and the Bavarian*, valued at £234,000, to the Tate collection in lieu of tax.

KATE DORNEY

Sources C. Duff, *The lost summer: the heyday of the West End theatre* (1995) · 'Life lessons', *Saga Magazine* (Sept 2003) · *The Times* (16 May 2008) · *Daily Telegraph* (16 May 2008) · *The Guardian* (16 May 2008) · *The Independent* (17 May 2008) · R. Wilton, interview with Frith Banbury, 2005, V&A, theatre and performance department · *WW* (2008) · private information (2012) · b. cert. · d. cert.

Archives Ransom HRC · V&A | FILM BFINA, documentary and performance footage · V&A, theatre and performance department | SOUND BL NSA, National Life Story Collection, interview · BL NSA, documentary and performance recordings

Likenesses photographs, 1942–2004, Getty Images, London · photograph, 1999, Photoshot, London · obituary photographs

Wealth at death £1,919,002: probate, 24 July 2008, *CGPLA Eng. & Wales*

Anthony Louis [Tony] **Banks, Baron Stratford (1942–2006)**, by David Mansell, 2002

Banks, Anthony Louis [Tony], **Baron Stratford (1942–2006)**, politician, was born on 8 April 1942 at Jubilee Maternity Hospital, Belfast, the only son and elder child of Albert Herbert Banks, a sergeant in the Royal Army Service Corps, who before the Second World War had been a toolmaker, and his wife, Olive Irene (Rene), *née* Rusca. After the war his father worked at the Board of Trade then, from 1963, at the Foreign Office, serving in Nigeria, Saudi Arabia, Trinidad and Tobago, South Vietnam, and the European capitals of Helsinki and Warsaw.

Banks was brought up in Brixton, London, where he attended St John's primary school and Archbishop Tenison's Grammar School in Kennington. Some indication of his childhood experiences may be gleaned from the fact that he later expressed resentment at the pigeonholing of children into the clever ones who read books and the stupid ones who did sports. He enjoyed both, though with typical humour he said that 'I could have been a serious athlete, only to have my promise cut short when I discovered Woodbines and women' (*Hansard*, 5L, 673.1547, 20 July 2005). The 'brash cheek' of the schoolboy resulted in a stormy relationship with his teachers (*The Times*, 26 Jan 2006) and he failed his exams, left school, and worked as a clerk while attending night school to gain the necessary qualifications for university. He studied politics at the University of York, where he was president of the student representative council and graduated with an upper second class degree in 1967, then undertook further study at the London School of Economics.

Banks's first career was as a trade union official, first for the Amalgamated Union of Engineering Workers from 1969 to 1975, then as assistant general secretary of the Association of Broadcasting Staff from 1976 to 1983. Concurrently he was pursuing a career in local government, having joined the Labour Party in 1964. He was a member of Lambeth council from 1971 to 1974. His shrewd political brain was apparent when, newly elected, he looked at the committee budgets, picked the one with the second biggest spending power, and said to a colleague, 'You and I will take that one over', which he did (private information). He was also a member of the Greater London council (GLC) for Hammersmith and Fulham from 1970 to 1973, then for Fulham to 1977, and for Tooting from 1981 to 1986.

It was as a Greater London councillor, notably when he was chairman of the GLC's arts and recreation committee in 1981–3, that Banks first attracted national attention. He abolished the champagne bar at the Royal Festival Hall, something that contributed to the jibe that the GLC under Ken Livingstone was addicted to 'loony left' gesture politics; though as the bar was unprofitable this was a measure of prudent economics. He also promoted 'community-based' arts projects with the emphasis on inclusivity, particularly of London's large ethnic minority community, which had previously been neglected by arts funders. He was chairman of the GLC from 1985 until its abolition by Margaret Thatcher's government in 1986, leaving London without an elected governing body until the establishment of the Greater London Authority in 2000. He claimed to have been the first to suggest a directly elected mayor for London, a post for which he unsuccessfully attempted to become the Labour Party's candidate in the 2004 election; this would have meant challenging Livingstone, the incumbent, who until shortly before the election was expected to run again as an independent. Banks did not secure the Labour Party's nomination and the contest embittered relations between him and Livingstone, an erstwhile friend and colleague.

Banks stood unsuccessfully for the parliamentary seats of East Grinstead in 1970, Newcastle upon Tyne North in October 1974, and Watford in 1979, before winning Newham North West in 1983. He represented this east London seat until 2005, through its expansion under boundary changes and its renaming as West Ham in 1997. His causes were many and he was forever putting forward motions in the House of Commons to do such things as denounce foreign dictators, or decriminalize cannabis, and on one notable occasion invited his fellow MPs to condemn the entire human race for its cruel treatment of animals. In the 1983–7 parliament he asked more questions of ministers than any other MP. He was a vegetarian and particularly noted as a supporter of animal rights. Among many campaigns related to animals he took a leading role in the long campaign to ban fox hunting; the ban was passed in England and Wales in 2004. When it appeared that the government might block the anti-hunting legislation he threatened to resign his seat and fight a by-election on the issue, a threat he would certainly have carried out.

In his career as an MP, both inside and outside the house, Banks's fruity turns of phrase were more reminiscent of eighteenth-century than late twentieth-century political dialogue. He called Prime Minister Thatcher 'a half-mad old bag lady' (Dale, 16); of one of her successors, William Hague, he said, 'they have elected a foetus as leader. I bet a lot of them wish they had not voted against abortion now' (ibid., 129). He described one political opponent (Terry Dicks) as 'living proof that a pig's bladder on a stick can be elected as a member of parliament' (ibid., 28). Despite the acid tongue he maintained many friendships across the political divide; he spoke with acerbity, but without malice. He used to attend Chelsea football matches with the former Conservative minister David Mellor, who later said, 'the match was so often very boring, but Tony was never boring' (memorial, House of Lords, 13 July 2006).

Banks was appointed minister for sport in the Department for Culture, Media and Sport after Labour's 1997 election victory, perhaps a surprise appointment but a popular one among the sport-loving public; he was never at a loss for words on the media or the public platform. But ministerial office did not sit well with his cheerfully rebellious nature and he resigned from the government in 1999 to lead the unsuccessful bid to host the football world cup in London in 2006. His happiest House of Commons role was as chairman of the works of art committee, where he worked to expand and to make publicly accessible what was in effect a private collection. He was himself a collector of political memorabilia, in particular of items connected with Charles James Fox. His only publication, *Out of Order* (1993; 'a survivor's guide to the Palace of Westminster'), written with Jo-Ann Goodwin, gives a flavour of his irreverent humour. He stood down at the 2005 election and accepted a peerage that year, taking what he called the 'nom de politics' of Baron Stratford, after his East End home in Stratford High Street.

Banks was short and trim of appearance, dapper in dress, and played on his reputation as an outspoken cockney 'cheeky chappie'. Paradoxically he was an extremely private person and many biographical facts are obscure. He was a humanist and a republican, but, unlike many people of decided views, he combined his stands of principle with a wit that spared him from the besetting sin of earnestness. His wide range of interests, his restless passions, and his need for excitement meant that he was never considered a safe pair of hands, hence his single, brief, junior ministerial appointment. He was always better at heckling from the sidelines than at playing the high political game for which his intellect and experience qualified him. He suffered a stroke on 5 January 2006 while having lunch on Sanibel Island in Florida, where he and his long-term partner, Sally Anne Jones, were visiting their friend Brian Davies, founder of the International Fund for Animal Welfare. He was flown by helicopter to a hospital in Fort Myers but died there on 8 January without regaining consciousness. JAD ADAMS

Sources T. Banks and J. Goodwin, *Out of order* (1993) · I. Dale, ed., *The wit and wisdom of Tony Banks: a tribute to a parliamentary character* (1998) · *The Times* (9 Jan 2006); (26 Jan 2006) · *Daily Telegraph* (9 Jan 2006) · *The Guardian* (9 Jan 2006) · *The Independent* (9 Jan 2006) · *Stage, Screen and Radio* (Feb 2006) · transcript of speeches at memorial service, 13 July 2006, queen's robing room, House of Lords · *WW* (2005) · private information (2009) [York University Archive] · b. cert.

Archives FILM BFINA, *Kirsty Young interviews*, F. Clark (producer), transmitted Channel 5, 19 July 1998 · BFINA, current affairs footage [also BL NSA] · BFINA, documentary footage [also BL NSA] · BFINA, light entertainment footage | SOUND BL NSA, current affairs recording · BL NSA, documentary recording · BL NSA, performance recording

Likenesses P. O'Connell, bromide fibre print, 1995, NPG · J. Anderson, bromide fibre print, 1996, NPG · D. Mansell, photograph, 2002, Camera Press, London [*see illus.*] · J. Murphy, oils, GLC Heritage Collection, London · obituary photographs · photographs, Rex Features, London · photographs, Camera Press, London · photographs, Getty Images, London · photographs, Photoshot, London · photographs, PA Photos, London · portrait, repro. in A. Mitchell, Lord Crathorne, and Baroness Wharton, *Parliament in pictures: inside the House of Commons and the House of Lords* (1999), 90

Wealth at death £177,919: probate, 16 May 2006, *CGPLA Eng. & Wales*

Banks, Joseph Ambrose [Joe] (1920–2005), sociologist and historian, was born at 66 Montague Road, Edmonton, Middlesex, on 5 January 1920, the only child of Joseph William Banks, a boot and shoe dealer who later became a master tailor, and his wife, Louisa Mary Ann, *née* Wellman. He was educated at Enfield grammar school, where his mathematics teacher persuaded his father not to take him out of school for a cutter's apprenticeship in tailoring. During the Second World War he was a conscientious objector (as his father, an atheist socialist, had been in the First World War). On 22 June 1944 he married Olive Lucy Davies (1923–2006) [*see* Banks, Olive Lucy], also from a 'respectable' working-class background. (She was the daughter of Herbert Davies, builder and contractor.) Although there were no children, their lifelong partnership was fruitful in every other way. Both became leading sociologists of their generation, and shared enthusiasms for dancing, hill-walking, gardening, cinema, and the opera. They each went to read sociology at the London School of Economics in 1947, both excelling sufficiently to qualify for a master's degree under David Glass's supervision. Banks then embarked on the study of the Victorian family, which was to lead to *Prosperity and Parenthood* (1954).

Banks's early intellectual and personal formation was profoundly influenced by his participation in the co-operative movement, through which he and Olive had met. From July 1942 for three years he was on the first editorial board of the British Federation of Young Co-operators' monthly magazine, *Comrade*, and a member of the education committee of the Enfield Highway Co-operative Society, subsequently serving as secretary of the Southern Co-operative Education Committees Association. The first issue of *Comrade* contained a short article, prophetically entitled 'Invitation to the Dance' by a certain Olive Davies (they met the following year at the Enfield Co-operative youth group and she taught him ballroom dancing during their courtship). Banks's lifelong local friend Harold Campbell, later national secretary of the Co-operative Party from 1964, was their best man at Enfield register office.

In 1952 Banks was appointed lecturer in the sociology department at Leicester, headed by Ilya Neustadt. Joe—as he was known—was insistent that Olive should also have the career she merited and in 1954 this became possible when both took up posts in the sociology and social work department at the University of Liverpool. They stayed until 1969 when Banks returned to the chair of sociology at Leicester and Olive became reader in sociology (in 1973 she became the first female professor at Leicester). They both took voluntary early retirement in 1982, thereby saving five posts for younger scholars in their department.

Banks became the leading authority of his generation on the fertility decline that took place in Britain between about 1870 and 1914. He was the first to read beyond official statistics into the diverse literary, pamphlet, and newspaper primary sources of the Victorian era and produced a trilogy of contextualized studies that transformed understanding of late nineteenth-century demographics. *Prosperity and Parenthood* became a much-republished classic and the starting point for all serious students of the subject. Through a brilliantly innovative analysis of such sources as the changing guidance on etiquette set out in the seven successive editions between 1861 and 1906 of *Mrs Beeton's Book of Household Management* Banks documented the phenomenon of rising aspirations for 'the paraphernalia of gentility' among the middle classes. He showed how escalating costs of secondary education became a crucial element, leading to greatly delayed marriage and ultimately the resort to birth control within marriage. *Feminism and Family Planning* (1964, published jointly with Olive Banks) argued that Victorian feminism was wary of association with the subject of contraception and so did not promote family planning. *Victorian Values: Secularism and the Size of Families* (1981) explored how respectable upper- and middle-class Victorians squared their religious sensibilities with family limitation.

Banks's inaugural lecture, 'Sociology as a vocation', eloquently echoed Weber and exemplified the 'Leicester school' of Norbert Elias and Ilya Neustadt: sociology's specific disciplinary role was the ambition to provide a causal explanation of the current and future course of social change. This was to be through an interpretative understanding of social action, striving to integrate and evaluate all relevant historical and comparative knowledge to arrive at these carefully weighed insights and predictions. Specialization of knowledge of all kinds in commerce, science, professional life, and the academy had, he argued, rendered sociological skills of communication ever more valuable and valued throughout society and the economy. A stream of publications ensued, many based on his collaborative research with the industrial sociology research team led by W. H. Scott in Liverpool, applying a Weberian methodology to industrial relations and technological change. With his schooling in voluntarist co-operation, Banks was critical of Marxist class reductivism and also published widely on the importance of associations and social movements.

In accord with these views, Banks played a leading role in sociology's own professional body, the British Sociological Association. His exceptionally open, warm, and entirely unaffected personality helped enormously—all who came into contact with him found him instantly likeable. Joining as a student at its foundation in 1951, he became an executive member from 1956, secretary from 1964, and chairman in 1971. These were certainly not easy times for a discipline experiencing break-neck institutional expansion and acquiring a reputation for radicalism and subversion. Nevertheless Banks was remembered as a particularly effective leader of his profession. Indeed, his inaugural lecture had characteristically offered a penetrating sociological analysis of precisely these troubling issues in relation to a careful, interpretative evaluation of the significance of the sit-in of March 1967 at the London School of Economics.

In retirement Banks and his wife lived at 30 Lismore Grove, Buxton, Derbyshire. He died on 13 November 2005 at Stepping Hill Hospital, Stockport, following a heart attack. S. R. S. SZRETER

Sources *Comrade*, 1 (July 1942–June 1943) · 'Editor's foreword', J. A. Banks and G. N. Ostergaard, *Co-operative democracy* (1955) · J. A. Banks, *Sociology as a vocation: an inaugural lecture delivered in the University of Leicester, 18 February 1971* (1971) · *The Guardian* (14 Dec 2005);

(22 Dec 2005) · personal knowledge (2009) · private information (2009) [Olive Banks, wife] · b. cert. · m. cert. · d. cert.

Archives FILM 'The middle classes', R. Bell (editor), BBC2, Feb 2001

Likenesses photograph, repro. in *The Guardian* (14 Dec 2005) · photograph, repro. in *The Guardian* (22 Dec 2005)

Wealth at death £302,937: probate, 17 Jan 2006, *CGPLA Eng. & Wales*

Banks [*née* Davies], **Olive Lucy** (**1923–2006**), sociologist, historian, and feminist, was born at 10 Riley Road, Enfield Highway, Middlesex, on 2 July 1923, the only child of Herbert Alfred Davies, a house decorator, and later builder and contractor, and his wife, Jessie Louise, *née* Tebby, the widow of his brother. Her parents came from a working-class background and her awareness of feminism arose at an early age when she observed the dissatisfaction of her hard-pressed mother. Although there were no books at home and neither of her parents encouraged her to succeed at elementary school, in 1933 she won a scholarship to the local grammar school for girls, determined that a full-time domestic life was not for her. It was at Enfield county school that she developed a love of reading, music, and the theatre, despite the fact that she felt she did not fit in well among her predominantly middle-class peers. Her feminist awareness was sharpened when, at fifteen years old, a debate with the boys' grammar school on the motion that 'a woman's place is in the home' angered her; she was horrified both by the arguments advanced by the opposite sex and by the feeble replies given by the girls. The lesson was brought home more forcibly a few months later when she applied for a job at the local public library and was promptly informed that only boys could apply. As she later commented, 'From that day my feminist commitment has never wavered' ('Reflections', 403). As expected, she left school at sixteen and then worked as a clerk and later as a laboratory assistant until, on 22 June 1944, she married Joseph Ambrose (Joe) *Banks (1920–2005), also from a 'respectable' working-class family. During these years her appetite for further study had been awakened when she attended classes run by the local co-operative society and by the Workers' Educational Association.

Marriage did not end Olive Banks's desire for an academic career of her own, and Joe was supportive of her ambitions. In 1947 both entered the London School of Economics to read sociology, and both stayed on for postgraduate work. Her PhD thesis, completed in 1953, was turned into a book, *Parity and Prestige in English Secondary Education: a Study in Educational Sociology* (1955). This, with its emphasis upon the interplay between the educational system, the class structure of modern Britain, and the labour market, became very influential in the emerging discipline of sociology—as well as in policy-based discussions about how to make Britain a more equal society. Yet despite the recognition that she received for her book, she found it difficult to find a post in higher education. Eventually, in 1954, she was offered a temporary research post in the sociology and social work department of the University of Liverpool, where Joe had been appointed a senior researcher. Typically for women academics, she was kept on short-term contracts until 1959, when her post was made permanent. This enabled her to investigate a topic she had long wanted to study, the history of British feminism. In 1964 she published, with Joe, *Feminism and Family Planning in Victorian England*. However, this book attracted little notice until a decade later when a generation of feminist academics emerged in the USA.

During the 1960s Olive Banks went through a period of depression about the discipline of sociology, largely due to the rejection of any kind of historical scholarship and the growing influence of Marxist theory, which emphasized the importance of social class rather than gender. By now she was teaching and publishing in the newly expanding field of the sociology of education. Her reputation as a leading scholar in the area was sealed with the publication of her highly successful and influential textbook, *The Sociology of Education* (1965). In 1970 she was appointed a reader in sociology at the University of Leicester (where Joe had been offered a professorship) and in 1973 became the first woman to hold a chair at that university.

During the 1970s, despite her regular attendance at the annual conferences of the British Sociological Association, Olive Banks's discontent with sociology increased. She found herself trapped in a field of expertise in which she had no abiding interest and in a male-dominated department that had no interest in gender issues. The advent of 'second-wave' feminism and the renewed interest in feminism generally among women academics at this time spurred her on to return to the subject that interested her, the history of feminism. *Faces of Feminism*, a historical and comparative study of feminism in Britain and the USA from the early nineteenth century to the 1970s, appeared in 1981. It sold extremely well, hitting the academic market at a time when women's studies courses were being established. The following year Olive and Joe Banks both took early retirement, thus helping to save the jobs of five younger colleagues.

Retirement brought Olive Banks more time for such leisure interests as opera, the arts, and gardening, but especially for research and writing. Her two-volume *Biographical Dictionary of British Feminists* (1985–1990) soon became an important reference source, while *Becoming a Feminist: the Social Origins of 'First Wave' Feminism* (1986) pioneered collective biography as an approach to the subject. *The Politics of British Feminism, 1918–1970* (1993) was her last book. With increasing age she began to suffer from deafness and arthritis. When Joe died in 2005 she was heartbroken. They never had any children and Olive lamented the lack of a close extended family. She died at her home, 30 Lismore Grove, Buxton, Derbyshire, on 14 September 2006, following a heart attack. JUNE PURVIS

Sources O. Banks, 'Some reflections on gender, sociology and women's history', *Women's History Review*, 8/3 (1999), 401–10 · *The Guardian* (12 Dec 2006) · J. Purvis, 'Olive Banks (1923–2006): an appreciation', *Women's History Review*, 16/2 (April 2007), 137–43 · personal knowledge (2010) · private information (2010) · b. cert. · m. cert. · d. cert.

Likenesses photograph, repro. in *Guardian* (12 Dec 2006)

Wealth at death £1,023,232: probate, 23 Nov 2006, *CGPLA Eng. & Wales*

Barber, Anthony Perrinott Lysberg, Baron Barber (1920–2005), politician, was born at Bornholm, Northfield, Kingston upon Hull, on 4 July 1920, the youngest of three sons of John Barber (*d.* 1958), businessman, and his wife, Ellen Katty (Mussee) Lysberg (*d.* 1945). His father was managing director of a confectionery firm in Doncaster and at one time a personal assistant to Lord Leverhulme. His mother was Danish. His brother Noel (1909–1988) became a respected journalist and author and his brother Kenneth became a banker.

Barber was educated at Retford grammar school in Nottinghamshire. Plans for him to be articled as a solicitor were aborted by the outbreak of the Second World War in 1939. He joined the Doncaster branch of the territorials, was commissioned into the Royal Artillery, and went to France in 1940. He was in the withdrawal from Dunkirk in the same year and on his return to Britain was transferred to the RAF as a pilot in the photographic reconnaissance unit. On a mission in 1942 he ran out of fuel and bailed out over France. He was captured and remained a prisoner for the rest of the war. He made a number of escape attempts (one in which he was involved inspired the film *The Wooden Horse*) and once managed to reach Denmark—thanks to his Danish mother he could speak the language—but was recaptured. He then decided to concentrate on studying by correspondence for a law degree from London University. He relied on materials supplied by the International Red Cross and gained a first-class degree. He was already showing the qualities of application, intellect, and ambition that marked his later career. Following the war he spent two years in the war-shortened philosophy, politics, and economics course at Oriel College, Oxford, emerging with a second-class degree. He was called to the bar by the Inner Temple in 1948, and practised as a barrister specializing in taxation. He was also set on a political career and, as the only applicant for the Conservative nomination, was selected to fight the safe Labour seat of Doncaster in the general election of 1950. Helped by redistribution, he substantially reduced the majority. In the general election of 1951 he was narrowly elected. On 5 September the previous year he had married Jean Patricia Asquith (*d.* 1983), the thirty-year-old daughter of Milton Asquith, businessman, of the Manor House, Wentbridge, Yorkshire. She had also fought the election of 1950 as a Conservative candidate. They had two daughters, Louise (*b.* 1951) and Josephine (*b.* 1953).

In parliament Barber had a three-year stint as a parliamentary private secretary and between 1955 and 1958 a three-year spell as a junior whip. Significantly for his later career the chief whip at the time was Edward Heath, later Conservative leader and prime minister. In 1958 Barber became parliamentary private secretary to the prime minister, Harold Macmillan. In October 1959 he was promoted to the Treasury, serving first as economic secretary and from July 1962 as financial secretary. In October 1963 Sir Alec Douglas-Home became prime minister and he appointed Barber to the cabinet as minister of health, in succession to Enoch Powell, who had refused to serve. Barber was also sworn of the privy council and held the health post for twelve months. In the general election of October 1964 he lost Doncaster but in February 1965 was returned in a by-election for Altrincham and Sale. He held that seat until his retirement from the House of Commons in the general election of 1974. During the period of opposition he built up a successful business career. He was a non-executive director of Chartered Bank (later merged with Standard, and to figure in his later career), a director of British Roads, and chairman of his father-in-law's company, Redfearn National Glass. In 1965, following Douglas-Home's resignation as leader of the Conservative Party, he managed Edward Heath's successful campaign for the post. His reward came in 1967 when Heath appointed him party chairman. He diligently toured the local associations, explaining party policy and listening to complaints, which he passed on to Heath and the shadow cabinet. Among the grass roots he loyally backed Heath against the supporters of Enoch Powell, whom Heath had sacked from the shadow cabinet following his notorious 'rivers of blood' speech.

Barber held his nerve during the general election of June 1970, which produced a surprise victory for the Conservatives. The press and many of Heath's colleagues, prompted by the opinion polls, expected a comfortable majority for the Labour government. British entry to the European Economic Community was central to Heath's plans for reviving the British economy and strengthening Britain's place in the world. He appointed Barber chancellor of the duchy of Lancaster with special responsibility for negotiating Britain's entry to Europe. But a month later the chancellor of the exchequer, Iain Macleod, died suddenly. Heath needed a replacement. Recalled from Brussels to meet Heath in number 10, Barber said to a friend in a lift going up to see the prime minister: 'I hope he's not going to ask me to be Chancellor' (*The Independent*, 19 Dec 2005). Barber had already decided that he would return to a business or City career in the next two to three years. Nevertheless Heath persuaded him to take the post, and on 25 July he was appointed chancellor of the exchequer. During his tenure of 11 Downing Street he was caught between a prime minister set on a course of economic expansion and a more cautious Treasury, and his reputation has suffered because of the onset of a savage inflation, some of it caused by his policies.

It might have been expected that with his specialist legal background in taxation and his previous Treasury experience Barber would be a successful chancellor. In fact the verdict of most commentators places him near the bottom of the list of effective chancellors. Most of the tax reforms he inherited from Macleod. In his October 1970 statement Barber abolished purchase tax and selective employment tax, and introduced value added tax (VAT). He also announced a reduction in the basic rate of income tax of 6*d.* in the pound as well as cutting spending, notably in housing subsidies and welfare, imposing charges for entry to museums and art galleries, and ending free milk for primary school children. In his 1971 budget statement Barber had referred to the 'baffling combination of evils', rising unemployment and rising inflation. Old Keynesian methods of trading off unemployment and price increases no longer worked. His initial priority was to combat inflation. But in 1972 these policies were put into reverse, and the new imperative was to stem the rise in unemployment. In January the unemployment figure had passed the 1 million mark. The government, however, continued to face numerous inflationary pressures. There was a steep rise in commodity prices and in 1973 Arab oil prices were quadrupled, following the Arab–Israeli War, and militant trade unions were pressing for large wage increases.

Edward Heath increasingly relied for economic advice on Sir William Armstrong, head of the civil service. The two men shaped the expansionist budget of 1972, which combined tax cuts, incentives for investment, and increased public spending. The government set a target of 5 per cent growth in the hope that a dynamic British economy would be able to take advantage of its access to a larger European market. Heath was determined to end the stop-go British economy and, faced with a declining currency, floated the pound in June 1972. But Barber added to inflationary pressures by presiding over a large increase in the money supply in 1972 and 1973, after his removal in November 1971, on the recommendation of the Bank of England, of quantitative controls on bank advances. Heath resisted the obvious alternative—raising interest rates—because he wanted business to invest. The economy grew rapidly but at an unsustainable pace and the balance of payments went into heavy deficit. Barber later conceded that the budget of 1972 had proved inflationary and expressed regret. The Treasury proved unable to withstand the political influence of the prime minister and spending ministers. The government then reversed its previous disavowal of prices and incomes policies in autumn 1972, introducing the statutory prices and incomes policy to head off rising inflation. By December 1973 the government was forced to reverse economic policy again, imposing cuts in public spending, increases on surtax, and controls on the money supply. The incomes policy meanwhile led to conflict with the trade unions, notably the miners at the end of 1973, a general election, in February 1974, and the downfall of the government.

Barber was made a life peer in Edward Heath's dissolution honours list and entered the House of Lords as Baron Barber, of Wentbridge, Yorkshire. He had left politics aged only fifty-four. Politics may have had little to offer him, however. He lacked a base in the parliamentary party and his reputation had plummeted; 'the Barber boom' was an enduring and unfortunate appellation. His legacy when the government fell in February 1974 was rapidly rising inflation and a record balance of payments deficit. He became chairman of Standard Chartered Bank (the merger had been completed in 1969), and remained in post until 1987. It was an overseas bank and Barber spent a lot of time travelling, particularly in Africa and Asia. (At one time the young John Major was one of his advisers.) He was also a director of BP. In 1982 he was a member of the Franks inquiry into the conduct of the war with Argentina over the Falklands. Interested in conservation, he was chairman of the council of the Royal Society for the Protection of Birds. He was one of the Commonwealth eminent persons group who visited South Africa in 1986 to explore ways in which the tensions in the country might be eased. He was in a minority of one in opposing tougher sanctions to force the South African regime to abandon apartheid. Critics noted that Standard Chartered did much business in South Africa. In fact Barber detested apartheid, but he feared that sanctions would have an impact largely on the black population. In 1991 he was chairman of the RAF Benevolent Association's appeal launched for the fiftieth anniversary of the battle of Britain, which raised over £25 million. He had a low profile in the House of Lords and avoided public comment on Conservative Party politics. In private, however, he was critical of what he regarded as the divisive conduct first of Edward Heath, after he had lost the party leadership to Margaret Thatcher in 1975, and then of Thatcher after she lost the leadership in 1990. In 1996 he published privately a discreet and little noted memoir, *Taking the Tide*.

Anthony Barber was a professional politician, largely self-made, and one of the so-called 'Heathmen' who had been to grammar schools or minor public schools. Sir Alec Douglas-Home's last cabinet contained eleven old Etonians, Heath's only three. In private he was modest, witty, and charming, as well as being businesslike. In public some interpreted his directness as abruptness, and he was a pugnacious debater. Proud of his Yorkshire background, he retained a home there until late in life. He was relatively short, wiry, prematurely bald, and a desperate smoker. Smoking was forbidden in Heath's cabinet meetings and Barber regularly withdrew from cabinet to enjoy a cigarette. Until he was enlightened the prime minister thought that his chancellor's sudden withdrawals were designed to check for a change in the bank rate or some other dramatic economic news.

Following the death of his first wife, on 8 September 1989 Barber married Rosemary Ann (*d.* 2003), the 61-year-old daughter of Canon Fearnley Algernon Cyril Youens, and the former wife of John Surgenor. Following her death he decided to move to Suffolk to be near his daughter Josephine. He suffered from Parkinson's disease and died at Ipswich Hospital of bronchopneumonia, on 16 December 2005. He was survived by his two daughters. A memorial service was held on 27 April 2006 at St Margaret's, Westminster. DENNIS KAVANAGH

Sources A. Barber, *Taking the tide* (1996) • *The Times* (19 Dec 2005) • *Daily Telegraph* (19 Dec 2005) • *The Independent* (19 Dec 2005) • *The Guardian* (20 Dec 2005) • Burke, *Peerage* • *WW* (2005) • private information (2009) • b. cert. • m. certs. • d. cert.

Archives FILM BFINA, party political footage | SOUND BL NSA, current affairs recordings; documentary recording; party political recordings; recorded speeches

Likenesses Bassano, six half-plate film negatives, 1947, NPG • Bassano, five half-plate film negatives, 1948, NPG • photographs, 1951–73, Getty Images, London • Elliott & Fry, half-plate negative, 1955, NPG • Bassano, two half-plate film negatives, 1959, NPG • W. Bird, bromide print, 1963, NPG • Vicky, political cartoon, 1965;

Sothebys, 7 Nov 1973, lot 100/8 • photographs, 1968–73, PA Photos, London • group portraits, photographs, 1970–86, Photoshot, London • M. Boxer, ink drawing, 1971, NPG • caricatures, repro. in G. Scarfe, *Line of attack* (1988) • obituary photographs • photograph, NPG

Wealth at death £83,583: probate, 26 July 2006, *CGPLA Eng. & Wales*

Barker, Ronald William George [Ronnie] (**1929–2005**), actor and comedian, was born on 25 September 1929 at 70 Garfield Street, Bedford, the only son and second of the three children of Leonard William Barker, a clerk for Shell, and his wife, Edith Eleanor, *née* Carter. His father's work took the family to Ilford and eventually to Oxford, where Barker attended Donnington junior school and the City of Oxford High School. On leaving school he began to train as an architect but after a few months abandoned his studies and took a job at the local Westminster Bank. A childhood bout of nephritis and surgery for a tubercular gland ensured his rejection for national service.

While working at the bank Barker joined a local amateur dramatics group, where he caught the attention of the director, Margarethe Bayliss, who suggested that he might become a professional actor. His audition for the Young Vic school in London in 1947 was unsuccessful; but in 1948 he auditioned for the Manchester Repertory Company, at that time located in Aylesbury, and was taken on as assistant stage manager. After serving a week's notice at the bank, on 8 November 1948 he entered the hectic world of weekly repertory, and a week later made his professional stage début as Lieutenant Spicer in J. M. Barrie's *Quality Street*. He recalled playing mostly 'upper-class idiots' but, intoxicated by the sound of an audience's laughter, he realized that his natural instinct was for comic roles: 'This is what I want to do, I thought. I want to make people laugh. Never mind Hamlet. Forget Richard the Second. Give me Charley's Aunt' (*Dancing in the Moonlight*, 38). He would later commemorate his early stage career, together with his offstage sexual conquests, in a lively memoir.

In time the company left Aylesbury for Rhyl, and Barker went with it; but the company's days were numbered, and Barker soon found himself back home in Oxford. He worked as a hospital porter until, in January 1950, he joined Clifford Williams's touring mime company. After a few weeks of 'misery and despair' (*Dancing in the Moonlight*, 72) the tour collapsed in Cornwall without even enough money for everyone's train fare, and Barker was left to walk home to Oxford. He then joined Frank H. Fortescue's Famous Players in Bramhall, Cheshire, where he was influenced by Glenn Melvyn, 'who was to teach me everything I ever learned about comedy' (ibid., 80)—including how to stutter. While still in Bramhall, Barker applied to the Oxford Playhouse and was taken on, albeit initially in the publicity department. His young contemporaries included Maggie Smith, whom Barker advised to give up acting. Fortunately she took no notice.

The first major turning point in Barker's career came with the arrival of Peter Hall as the new director of the Oxford Playhouse. He recognized Barker's talent, and when he left Oxford for London to become director of the Arts Theatre he invited Barker to join him for a production of Eugene O'Neill's *Mourning Becomes Electra* (1955). This marked the beginning of Barker's career on the West End stage, which would include a role in Peter Brook's production of *Irma La Douce* (1958)—an unhappy experience that left Barker with an aversion to long runs—and perhaps reached its high point when he played two characters in two plays in different theatres on the same evening. On 8 July 1957, at All Saints, Harrow Weald, Barker married Beryl Joyce (Joy) Tubb, a 24-year-old actress, and daughter of George Tubb, painter and decorator. They had two sons, Laurence (Larry; *b.* 1960) and Adam (*b.* 1967), and a daughter, Charlotte (*b.* 1963).

Ronald William George Barker (**1929–2005**), by unknown photographer, 1975

Barker also began to find work in radio and television. The long-running series *The Navy Lark*, in which he played the malcontent Able Seaman Johnson, made him a distinctive radio personality; he stayed with the show for seven years (1959–67). His television career took a decisive turn in 1966 when the BBC producer Jimmy Gilbert proposed that he should join Ronnie Corbett and John Cleese in *The Frost Report*, David Frost's new series of themed satirical shows on various aspects of contemporary British society. The series, which would make television stars of all three men, was memorable mainly for its comic visual representation of the British class structure, with Barker standing between the tall Cleese and the diminutive Corbett to speak for the middle class. The show later moved to ITV as *Frost on Sunday* (1968–70). *The Frost Report* also saw the emergence of Barker as a prolific comedy writer. He began to submit material under assumed names, ostensibly so that his colleagues would judge the material on its own merits. His favourite *nom de plume* was Gerald Wiley.

In 1968 Barker was given his own show, *The Ronnie Barker Playhouse*, a series of six individual comedies. He had gained his first experience of the 'playhouse' format, presenting different characters and situations in each episode, when he had appeared with the comedian Jimmy Edwards in *The Seven Faces of Jim* (1961) and its two sequels, and such series would prove particularly fruitful in Barker's career: *Hark at Barker* (1969, 1970), *Six Dates with Barker* (1971), and *Seven of One* (1973) would yield characters and ideas that Barker was later able to develop.

Barker enjoyed only a modest film career, making little impact, and came to realize that his future lay in television; but with *Futtock's End* (1970), which he wrote himself, he discovered the genre of the 'almost silent' film. He made two others, also starring Ronnie Corbett: *The Picnic* (1976) and *By the Sea* (1982), which reflected Barker's love of seaside postcards. He had become an avid collector of printed ephemera, and in 1974 he published his *Book of Bathing Beauties*, the first of several such volumes derived entirely from his own collection.

The next major development in the career of Ronnie Barker—and of Ronnie Corbett—came about by accident. When a live broadcast of an awards ceremony from the London Palladium was interrupted by a technical problem, the two Ronnies gave an impromptu performance to entertain the audience. The BBC's head of light entertainment, Bill Cotton, was so impressed that he suggested that the two men be brought together for their own series. *The Two Ronnies* ran from 1971 to 1986. The format never changed. Opening and closing with spoof announcements and news items, each show contained sketches, monologues, a comedy drama serial, and a musical finale, with the sign-off line, 'It's goodnight from me—and it's goodnight from him'. The stand-up comedian Corbett delivered his monologues directly to the audience, but Barker the actor was invariably in character, usually a spokesman for some fictitious organization or government department. The serials, all written by Barker, included 'The Worm that Turned', portraying a future Britain ruled by women and with the men wearing women's clothes; 'The Phantom Raspberry Blower of Old London Town', elaborating an episode contributed by Spike Milligan to *Six Dates with Barker*; and 'Death can be Fatal', featuring the two clueless detectives Piggy Malone (Barker) and Charley Farley (Corbett). The sketches frequently displayed Barker's love of wordplay, most notably in 'Four Candles/Fork Handles', which became an established favourite and which the two Ronnies later performed live (with a new ending) during their season at the Palladium in 1978. In the same year Barker and Corbett were appointed OBE.

Two situation comedies in the 1970s, *Porridge* and *Open All Hours*, confirmed Barker as the country's foremost comedy actor. *Porridge* (1974–7), written by Dick Clement and Ian La Frenais, retrieved Norman Stanley Fletcher, a convicted criminal, from *Seven of One*, and captured the tedium of daily prison life and the sweetness of little victories over authority. A feature film with the same title followed in 1979; but *Going Straight* (1978), a series tracing Fletcher's life after his release, was less successful. *Open All Hours* (1976 and 1981–5) saw the revival of another character from *Seven of One*: the stuttering, miserly grocer Arkwright, who exploited the good nature of his downtrodden nephew Granville and lusted after the buxom nurse Gladys Emmanuel. *Open All Hours* was written by Roy Clarke, whose next series, *The Magnificent Evans* (1984), about a flamboyant Welsh photographer, gave Barker his first real taste of failure. A similar fate would befall *Clarence* (1988), his last series, written by Barker himself. Revived from *Six Dates with Barker*, Clarence the short-sighted removal man also failed to impress.

In late 1985 Barker decided to retire. He had begun to find writing difficult but had also developed heart disease (he underwent surgery in 1996). He planned his retirement carefully and finally stopped working at the end of 1987, walking away from show business to open an antique shop in Chipping Norton. 'I lose money every week, but it's a hobby', he said (*Daily Express*, 23 Dec 2003). Fortunately his retirement was not absolute. In 1988 his daughter, Charlotte, opened at London's King's Head Theatre in *Mum*, a play he had written for her. It received a cool reception from the critics. He returned to film acting in *The Gathering Storm* (2002), playing Churchill's butler, David Inches, and in *My House in Umbria* (2003), in which he was reunited with Maggie Smith. In 2004 he suggested that some *Two Ronnies* material might be shown again; and the popularity of *The Two Ronnies Sketchbook* (2005), in which Corbett and Barker presented a personal selection, demonstrated that the shows had retained their appeal. Barker was visibly frail, and the Christmas special, recorded in July 2005, marked his final television appearance.

Secure in his own talent—he knew what he could do and knew that he was good at it—Barker was spared the anxieties that haunted the careers of many of his comedy contemporaries. Peter Hall, whose early admiration for Barker had only grown over the years, identified Barker's 'gift of total relaxation', and praised his 'immaculate comic timing' and the way in which he 'completely inhabited what it was he was being, even if it was a north country charlady' (McCabe, 36). In the late 1980s Hall invited Barker to play Falstaff at the National Theatre. (In the mid-1960s Barker had appeared on Caedmon recordings of *The Merchant of Venice* as Launcelot Gobbo and *Measure for Measure* as Barnardine. These performances suggest that he could have justified Hall's belief in him.) Barker cited Hall's remarkable offer, or more particularly the summary fashion in which he rejected it, as the immediate cause of his decision to retire; but the truth is that Hall's invitation had simply come too late—failing health and loss of motivation had already made Barker's decision for him. He died of heart disease at Katharine House Hospice, Adderbury, Oxfordshire, on 3 October 2005. He was cremated after a humanist funeral service at Banbury crematorium on 13 October. A service of thanksgiving for his life and work was held at Westminster Abbey on 3 March 2006. He was survived by his wife, Joy, and their children Laurence, Charlotte, and Adam. In a late interview with Terry Wogan, Ronnie Barker had composed his own epitaph: 'I suppose I would like to be remembered as one of the funniest men people have seen on TV. "He did make us laugh. God bless him"' (*The Independent*, 4 March 2006). It was an assessment with which few would have disagreed. EDWARD LEESON

Sources R. Barker, *Dancing in the moonlight: early years on the stage* (1993) • R. Barker, *'All I ever wrote': the complete works*, ed. B. McCabe, rev. edn (2001) • B. McCabe, *Ronnie Barker: the authorized biography* (2004) • *The Times* (5 Oct 2005); (4 March 2006) • *Daily Telegraph* (5 Oct 2005) • *The Guardian* (5 Oct 2005); (8 Sept 2006) • *The Independent* (5 Oct 2005); (14 Oct 2005); (4 March 2006) • *Sunday Express* (9 Oct 2005) • *Daily Express* (17 Dec 2005); (4 March 2006); (11 March 2006) • *Daily Mail* (17 Dec 2005) • R. Corbett and D. Nobbs, *And it's goodnight from him …: the autobiography of the two Ronnies* (2006) • J. Evans, *The Penguin TV companion*, 3rd edn (2006) • *WW* (2005) • b. cert. • m. cert. • d. cert.

Archives FILM BFINA, 'Ronnie Barker, a life in comedy: a man of character', E. Cornish (producer), BBC1, 24 Aug 1997 • BFINA, 'Ronnie Barker, a life in comedy: Wiley by name', E. Cornish (producer), BBC1, 28 Aug 1997 • BFINA, *Heroes of comedy*, J. Fisher (producer), Channel 4, 28 Dec 2000 • BFINA, 'Ronnie Barker, a BAFTA tribute', S. Donnelly (producer), BBC1, 7 Feb 2004 • BFINA, current affairs footage • BFINA, documentary footage • BFINA, performance footage | SOUND BL NSA, AIRC programme sharing collection, interview with R. Holness, LBC, 14 Dec 1986, C1000/220/86/1 • BL NSA, documentary recording • BL NSA, performance recording

Likenesses photographs, 1964–2004, Getty Images, London • photographs, 1964–2004, Rex Features, London • photographs, 1966–2004, PA Photos, London • photographs, 1968–2004, Photoshot, London • photographs, 1971–2003, Camera Press, London • photograph, 1975, Getty Images, London [*see illus.*] • B. Fantoni, double portrait, pencil and gouache drawing, 1976 (with Ronnie Corbett), NPG • obituary photographs • photographs, repro. in Barker, *Dancing in the moonlight* • photographs, repro. in McCabe, *Ronnie Barker*

Wealth at death £300,337: probate, 4 Sept 2006, *CGPLA Eng. & Wales*

Barkworth, Peter Wynn (1929–2006), actor, was born at 26 Madeira Road, Margate, Kent, on 14 January 1929, the son of Walter Wynn Barkworth, a sales manager in the motor trade, of 56a High Street, Margate, and his wife, Irene May, *née* Brown. When his father took up a post in Manchester the family moved to Bramhall, near Stockport, Cheshire, and Barkworth was educated at Stockport School. Gaining a love of performing, he perfected an impersonation of Winston Churchill reciting 'Mary had a little lamb' as a party piece for friends, accompanied by his mother on the piano and father on the Swanee whistle. He also acted at school, once starring as Macbeth, and appeared at the Hippodrome Theatre, Stockport, in *For What We Are* (1942), aged thirteen.

On leaving school Barkworth won a scholarship to train as an actor at the Royal Academy of Dramatic Art (RADA) (1946–8) and made his professional début as Jack Read in *The Guinea Pig* (1948) with Folkestone Repertory Theatre, where he performed with the Arthur Brough Players (1948–9). After national service (1949–50) he joined the Sheffield Repertory Company (1950–51), then made his first appearance in London's West End, as Gaston Probert in *Letter from Paris* (Aldwych Theatre, 1952). He followed it with the roles of Gerald Arbuthnot in *A Woman of No Importance* (Savoy Theatre, 1953), Stefan in *The Dark is Light Enough* (Aldwych Theatre, 1954), Bernard Taggart-Stuart in *Roar Like a Dove* (Phoenix Theatre, 1957), Sir Benjamin Backbite in a revival of *The School for Scandal* (Haymarket Theatre, 1962), which he also played on Broadway (Majestic Theatre, 1963), and Edward VIII in Royce Ryton's play about the abdication crisis, *Crown Matrimonial* (Haymarket Theatre, 1972), a role he repeated in 1974 in a television adaptation, winning him a BAFTA best television actor award. Then came the roles of a government minister attending an old boys' reunion in *Donkeys' Years* (Globe Theatre, 1976) and a corporate architect in *Can You Hear Me at the Back?* (Piccadilly Theatre, 1979).

Barkworth made his television début in 1948, when he appeared in a live, twenty-minute BBC play while still studying at RADA. His first feature film was *You Know What Sailors Are!* (1953), starring Donald Sinden, in which he acted a naval lieutenant. He took a similar role in *A Touch of Larceny* (1959), alongside James Mason, and was in the political drama *No Love for Johnnie* (1961). Although he later appeared in the films *Where Eagles Dare* (1968), *Mr Smith* (1976), and *Escape from the Dark* (1976), and in *Champions* (1984), as the racehorse owner Nick Embiricos in a film about Bob Champion, the jockey who conquered cancer to win the Grand National, television became the medium in which Barkworth had most success, usually playing professional types.

After character parts in plays and episodes of popular series like *No Hiding Place* (1963) and *The Avengers* (1963), Barkworth became a household name in *The Power Game* (1965–6, 1969), playing Kenneth Bligh, the son of the founder of a civil engineering company that was taken over by John Wilder (Patrick Wymark), whose success as an aerospace tycoon had been featured in a previous series, *The Plane Makers*. The executive that Barkworth acted was typical of the middle-class, besuited roles for which he would become best known on television. After playing the British agent Vincent in the thriller series *Manhunt* (1970), set in occupied France during the Second World War, and Tsar Nicholas II in Ronald Eyre's play *Rasputin* (1971), he took a rare comedy role as the grumpy television executive Eustace Morrow in the sitcom *The Good Girl* (1974), played Guy Foster in the three-part Francis Durbridge thriller *Melissa* (1974), and won both BAFTA and Royal Television Society awards for best actor for his performance as the philosophy professor Anderson in Tom Stoppard's play *Professional Foul* (1977).

Barkworth again won BAFTA's award for best television actor for his role as the stockbroker turned country restaurateur Richard Elkinson in *The Country Party* (1977). But his biggest screen success was as the international banker Mark Telford seeking a less stressful life by becoming a provincial bank manager in *Telford's Change* (1979). The BBC series was Barkworth's own idea, and had originally been rejected by ITV eleven years earlier. On television he also acted Stanley Baldwin in *Winston Churchill: the Wilderness Years* (1981) and Geoffrey Carr, a computer magnate raising the ransom for his kidnapped wife and stepchild, in the thriller series *The Price* (1985), which again was his own idea. His final screen role was as the prosecutor

Charles Gill in *Wilde* (1997), a film about Oscar Wilde starring Stephen Fry. His last West End stage roles were in *Hidden Laughter* (Vaudeville Theatre, 1990) and *The Winslow Boy* (Globe Theatre, 1994).

Barkworth taught at RADA from 1955 to 1963, when his students included Anthony Hopkins, Diana Rigg, and Simon Ward, and served as a RADA council member from 1985 to 2001. He wrote the books *About Acting* (1980), *More About Acting* (1984), and *The Complete About Acting* (1991), based on insights gathered while he was teaching at RADA. He was also the author of *First Houses* (1983), a memoir of his early years as an actor, and *For All Occasions* (1997), collected poetry and prose for public speakers. For more than forty years he lived in an eighteenth-century house in Flask Walk, Hampstead, and he also had a seaside flat in Folkestone, Kent. He died of bronchopneumonia at the Royal Free Hospital, London, on 21 October 2006, ten days after suffering a stroke. He never married.

ANTHONY HAYWARD

Sources T. Vahimagi, ed., *British television: an illustrated guide* (1994) · *The Times* (25 Oct 2006) · *The Independent* (25 Oct 2006) · *Daily Telegraph* (26 Oct 2006) · *The Guardian* (26 Oct 2006) · *The Stage* (30 Oct 2006) · BFI SIFT database, www.bfi.org.uk/filmtvinfo/ftvdb, 24 July 2009 · internet movie database, www.imdb.com, 24 July 2009 · BAFTA website, www.bafta.org, 24 July 2009 · *WW* (2006) · b. cert. · d. cert.

Archives FILM BFINA, *This is your life*, R. Mayoh (director), Thames Television, 14 March 1979 · BFINA, current affairs footage · BFINA, performance footage · BFINA, documentary footage · BFINA, light entertainment footage | SOUND BL NSA, performance recordings · BL NSA, documentary recordings

Likenesses A. Buckley, photographs, 1952–72, NPG · photographs, 1964–93, Rex Features, London · photograph, 1979, Hult. Arch., London · J. Downing, photograph, 1990, Hult. Arch., London · photographs, 1992–2001, Photoshot, London · photographs, 1997–2001, PA Photos, London · C. Jones, photograph, 2004, Getty Images, London · obituary photographs

Wealth at death £2,256,862: probate, 4 July 5007, *CGPLA Eng. & Wales*

Barnes, Clive Alexander (1927–2008), dance and drama critic, was born on 13 May 1927 at St Thomas's Hospital, Lambeth, London, the only child of Arthur Lionel Barnes (1898–1940), ambulance driver, and his wife, Freda Marguerite, *née* Garratt. After their divorce when Clive was seven his mother brought him up (reconciliation later on was cut short by Arthur's sudden accidental death). Her work as secretary to a theatrical agent brought free tickets, and she took him to plays regularly from the age of ten. He attended Emanuel School, Battersea. During the Second World War the Old Vic Theatre Company shared the New Theatre with the Sadler's Wells ballet and opera companies and he began going also to them, seeing his first ballet in 1943 and being quickly hooked. His initial intention was to become a psychiatrist and he studied medicine for a year at King's College, London, but abandoned that after finding that the sight of blood made him faint. Conscripted into the Royal Air Force, he managed to stay in London by exaggerating his grandmother's illness, and spent his time preparing psychological tests, helping with adult education, and playing rugby football. While still serving in the RAF, on 4 January 1947 he married Joyce Elizabeth Tolman (*b.* 1928), a music student, and daughter of Reginald Edgar Tolman, motor driver. There were no children of the marriage.

After national service Barnes changed his studies to English language and literature and secured a place at St Catherine's Society, Oxford. By now he wished to become a critic of drama and dance, and started writing about ballet in 1949 for the Oxford University magazine *Isis*. In 1950 he and John Percival jointly revived the Oxford University Ballet Club's wartime magazine *Arabesque*; it lasted only one issue but helped get them both into a new national magazine, *Dance & Dancers*. There Barnes became associate editor, then (from 1961 to 1965) executive editor (also of *Music and Musicians* and *Plays and Players* for the same publisher) and eventually New York editor until it closed in 1998.

Meanwhile, after graduating with a third-class degree in English in 1951 (the result, perhaps, of his extra-curricular activities), Barnes first supported himself by working (from 1952 to 1961) as an administrative officer for the Greater London Council's town planning department, while he gradually built up his freelance work. Among the many publications he served, the one that kept him busiest was the *Daily Express*, where he covered dance, drama, film, music, and television. He was also, inter alia, dance critic at different times of the *New Statesman* and of the literary weekly *The Spectator*. What he was most proud of, however, even though it was subject to the paper's customary anonymity, was becoming, in 1961, the first specialist dance critic of *The Times*; hitherto dance had fallen to the chief music critic. One of his beliefs was that every major newspaper should have its own dance critic and he was very happy when, largely through his urging and example, that eventually came about. From 1956 he was also London correspondent for New York's *Dance Magazine*, beginning an association that continued until his death. His first—and in many ways most original—book appeared in 1953, *Ballet in Britain since the War*; although only a slim paperback it discussed every British company and their visiting counterparts. Other early books were *Frederick Ashton and his Ballets* and *Ballet Here and Now* (both 1961). His first marriage having ended in divorce, on 26 July 1958 he married Patricia Amy Evelyn Winckley (*b.* 1930/31), a production assistant for ATV, and daughter of George Clifford Winckley, a colonel in the Royal Corps of Signals. They had a son, Christopher, and a daughter, Maya.

Needing extra income, Barnes asked the *New York Times* if he could become their London correspondent; hesitant at first, in 1963 they were persuaded by some who knew him to agree, and when the top dance post fell vacant two years later they invited him with his family to move at their expense to New York. Another two years on saw him become both dance and drama critic of the *New York Times*. In 1977, however, because of changes in other papers, the paper's management decided that one man should not hold so much power and took drama from him. Thereupon Rupert Murdoch, owner of the *New York Post*, personally persuaded Barnes to transfer there with the two functions, which he held for more than thirty years. His second marriage having also ended in divorce, he was married twice more, to Amy Pagnozzi, a journalist, in 1985 and after a third divorce to Valerie Taylor, a former Royal Ballet dancer and more recently a dance teacher, in 2004.

After his move to New York, Barnes wrote also for the European magazine *Ballet 2000*, published in Italian and French, and for the London weekly *The Stage*. There were three further books by him: *Dance Scene USA* (1967), with photographs by Jack Mitchell, *Inside American Ballet Theatre* (1977), and a biography, *Nureyev* (1982). Moreover, he conducted lectures and seminars, and appeared often on television. But what he did best of all was his writing as a critic, watching many performances of drama and dance (sometimes as many as nine in a week) and writing an account and assessment of them straight afterwards for publication in the paper the next morning. Nobody could equal him in this. What made it possible was his vast experience, his quick, sure judgement, his immense enthusiasm, and the speed with which he produced writing marked by clarity, incisiveness, and a great deal of humour.

Barnes was diagnosed with cancer in October 2008 and admitted to Mount Sinai Hospital, New York, where he died on 19 November 2008, surrounded by his wife, his two surviving former wives, and his children. His work did not lack recognition. For his love of Danish dance he was appointed a knight of the order of Dannebrog in 1972, and in 1975 he was appointed CBE, receiving his award from Queen Elizabeth, visiting New York, for his services to British theatre arts in America. Honorary degrees came to him from Adelphi University in 1976 and Albright College in 1982. In a unique tribute, the theatres of Broadway all dimmed their external lights for a minute the day after his death. JOHN PERCIVAL

Sources *New York Post* (20 Nov 2008); (21 Nov 2008) · *New York Times* (20 Nov 2008) · *Washington Post* (20 Nov 2008) · *The Times* (20 Nov 2008); (24 Nov 2008) · *Daily Telegraph* (21 Nov 2008) · *The Guardian* (21 Nov 2008) · *The Independent* (21 Nov 2008) · *Sunday Times* (23 Nov 2008) · *WW* (2008) · personal knowledge (2012) · private information (2012) · b. cert. · m. certs. [1947, 1958]
Archives FILM BFINA, current affairs and documentary footage | SOUND BL NSA, performance recordings
Likenesses C. Rene Perez, photograph, 1977, PA Photos, London · A. Bergman, selenium-toned bromide print, 2003, NPG · obituary photographs

Barr, James (1924–2006), Old Testament scholar, was born on 20 March 1924 at 5 Melville Street, Glasgow, the son of Allan Barr, schoolteacher, later minister of religion and professor of New Testament language and literature at the United Free Church college in Edinburgh, and his wife, Agnes Christina, *née* Dryburgh. His paternal grandfather was James *Barr (1862–1949), United Free Church minister and Labour MP; Elizabeth Brown *Barr (1905–1995), the first woman to be ordained as a Presbyterian minister in Scotland, was an aunt. He was educated at Daniel Stewart's College, Edinburgh, and from 1941 the University of Edinburgh, where he read classics, his studies being interrupted by war service from 1942 to 1945 in the Fleet Air Arm of the Royal Naval Volunteer Reserve. He returned to Edinburgh in 1945 and took his degree in 1948. Following study at New College, Edinburgh, he was ordained in 1951 to the ministry of the Church of Scotland and served for two years as minister in Tiberias, Israel. On 10 February 1950, at Trinity Church, Perth, he married Jane Jackson Stewart Hepburn, a schoolteacher (and daughter of James Hepburn, postal inspector), whom he had met as a student of classics in Edinburgh. They had two sons and a daughter.

From 1953 to 1955 Barr was professor of New Testament literature and exegesis at the Presbyterian College, Montreal, and having embarked on an academic career was successively professor of Old Testament literature and theology at Edinburgh University (1955–61), professor of Old Testament literature and theology at Princeton Theological Seminary (1961–5), professor of Semitic languages and literatures at Manchester University (1965–76), Oriel professor of the interpretation of holy scripture at Oxford University (1976–8), and regius professor of Hebrew at Oxford University (1978–89). Following his retirement from Oxford he accepted the position of professor of Hebrew Bible at Vanderbilt University in Nashville, Tennessee, a post he held until 1998. His university career was such that he was able to escape the worst of the financial constraints and need to meet government targets that increasingly diverted attention away from academic matters in universities in Britain, although he played an important part in helping the Oxford theological faculty to gain adequate administrative accommodation.

Barr made a contribution to Old Testament and biblical scholarship that was unrivalled in the latter part of the twentieth century. He was driven by a desire for clarity and accuracy and he brought to this task a competence in disciplines previously outside the normal range of Old Testament scholars, including linguistics. He had a penetrating and searching intellect and expressed his criticisms formidably, if always fairly. The severity of some of his writing contrasted strikingly with his personal manner. He was a soft-spoken, diffident, almost shy man, who looked much younger than he was, and who seemed to be blessed with eternal youth and vitality. He spoke with a uvular 'r', which became especially noticeable in pronouncing words like 'retroversion'. His lecturing style was characterized by clarity and originality.

Barr's first major work, *The Semantics of Biblical Language* (1961), was an attack on a way of using the Bible that assumed that it was a privileged medium of divine revelation accessible through studies of the Hebrew language, especially etymologies that underlay key theological concepts. This approach was known generally as 'biblical theology' and it had deep roots in some continental European scholarship as well as in Britain and North America. Barr showed that it was based on an inadequate knowledge of semantics, as understood in linguistics, and argued that theology had to take account of larger linguistic units than verbal 'roots'. He showed that biblical studies could not operate in ignorance of other disciplines pertinent to its study, and he opened the door to the later interdisciplinary study of the Bible, in the process rescuing the field from becoming moribund and introspective. His second major work, *Comparative Philology and the Text of the Old Testament* (1968), was a critique of a method of understanding biblical Hebrew that used other Semitic languages to recover 'lost' Hebrew words. While Barr did not reject the validity of the approach he showed that in practice it assumed that there had been far too many homonyms in ancient Hebrew, which raised the question how the language could have been an effective means of communication. When the Old Testament section of *The New English Bible* was published in 1970 it was found to be so vulnerable to the criticisms that had been made in Barr's book that a revision was seen to be necessary. It appeared in 1989 in *The Revised English Bible*. In between these two works appeared *Old and New in Interpretation* (1966) based upon the Currie lectures. This book was addressed not only to academics, but indicated Barr's concern that students preparing for ministry should be enabled to use the Bible effectively in their work and preaching. It reviewed ways in which Christian theology had sought to relate the Old and New testaments and was critical of what Barr called 'purist' approaches that argued that only principles derived from the Bible itself could yield satisfactory criteria for interpretation. (He was later unsympathetic to B. S. Childs's influential 'canonical criticism' for this reason.) Barr argued for a readiness to interpret the biblical text in a way that involved exposure to other disciplines, including philosophy. Such ideas were unusual at the time and helped to shape future thinking on the subject. These books laid down the principles that were expanded in Barr's later works, notably the major studies *Fundamentalism* (1977) and *The Concept of Biblical Theology: an Old Testament Perspective* (1999, based on the 1968 Cadbury lectures), as well as *Holy Scripture: Canon, Authority, Criticism* (1983), *Escaping from Fundamentalism* (1984), and *The Garden of Eden and the Hope of Immortality* (1992). In 2000 he published *History and Ideology in the Old Testament: Biblical Studies at the End of a Millennium*, based on the Hensley Henson lectures. This masterly survey evaluated the state of a discipline that Barr had helped to shape, while expressing trenchant criticisms of some of its developments.

Barr was able to accept many invitations to lecture in Britain and abroad, and to deliver special series of lectures. He held visiting professorships at the Hebrew University, Jerusalem (1973), Chicago University (1975, 1981), Strasbourg University (1975–6), Brown University, Providence, Rhode Island (1985, 1994), Otago University, New Zealand (1986), the University of South Africa, Pretoria (1986), Vanderbilt University (1987–8), and, following his retirement from Oxford, at Heidelberg University (1993) and the Chinese University of Hong Kong (2003). Special lecture series included the Currie lectures (Austin Seminary, Texas, 1964), the Cadbury lectures (Birmingham University, 1968), the Croall lectures (Edinburgh University, 1970), the Grinfield lectures on the Septuagint (Oxford University, 1974–8), the Sprunt lectures (Richmond Theological Seminary, Virginia, 1982), the Schweich lectures of the British Academy (1986), the Hensley Henson lectures, Oxford University (1997), and the Gifford lectures (Edinburgh, 1999). Many of these series became the basis for his books. Honours flowed to him from many parts of the world. He was elected a fellow of the British Academy in 1969, and corresponding member of the Göttingen Academy of Sciences (1976), the Norwegian Academy of Science and Letters (1977), and the Royal Society of Sciences, Uppsala (1991). Honorary degrees were conferred upon him by nine universities or colleges around the world.

During the second part of the twentieth century there was no scholar who could match Barr's combination of mastery of the minutiae of biblical scholarship with his insights into the wider and theological implications of the use of the Bible. Inevitably there were disappointments. In 1974 Barr took over the *Oxford Hebrew Dictionary* project, which up to then had proceeded on principles not exactly those of Barr. There was no one better qualified to reorganize and direct the work, but in 1980 Oxford University Press decided that it could no longer fund the project and it was abandoned. Again, Barr's acceptance of so many visiting professorships and requests for special lectures necessitated absences from his institutions that perturbed some of his colleagues, and resulted in his having few research students. This was a price that had to be paid for the books and lectures that were such an important contribution to biblical scholarship.

After his retirement from Vanderbilt Barr moved to Claremont in California, although he continued to travel and to accept invitations to lecture. In 2005 he sustained serious head injuries from a fall at a meeting of the American Philosophical Society in Philadelphia. Another fall the following year was the prelude to his death in Claremont on 14 October 2006, although the cause of death was given as bone cancer. After the funeral in California his ashes were interred near Christ Church Cathedral, Oxford. He was survived by his wife and children.

J. W. Rogerson

Sources *The Times* (18 Oct 2006) · *The Guardian* (8 Nov 2006) · *The Independent* (11 Nov 2006) · E. Nicholson and J. Barton, *PBA*, 153 (2008), 25–51 · *WW* (2006) · personal knowledge (2010) · private information (2010) · b. cert. · m. cert.

Likenesses W. Stoneman, bromide print, 1930, NPG · A. Newman, group portrait, bromide print, 1978 (*Regius professors*), NPG · obituary photographs · photograph, repro. in *PBA*

Barraclough, Sir John (1918–2008), air force officer, was born on 2 May 1918 at 394 Hanworth Road, Hounslow, Middlesex, the son of Horatio Leonard Barraclough (1874/5–1956), construction engineer, and his wife, Marguerite Maude (1882–1965), daughter of Conrad Bührer. He was educated at Cranbrook School, and for three years from 1935 was a volunteer in the Artists' Rifles while working in the City. In May 1938 he was accepted for training in the RAF, initially on a four-year commission. He was posted to Coastal Command, and in 1939, flying an Anson, was involved in the search for the submarine *Thetis* in Liverpool Bay.

On the outbreak of the Second World War Barraclough was sent on a flying boat conversion course, then posted to 240 squadron. He flew in support of the unsuccessful British expeditionary force to Norway, and was then engaged in anti-submarine patrols and convoy escorts, from Invergordon and Sullom Voe. In 1941 he was made chief instructor of the flying boat conversion unit at Invergordon, and was awarded an AFC for his innovations in training. In February 1942 he joined 209 squadron, equipped with Catalina flying boats, and in June of that year he was posted with the squadron to the Indian Ocean. Based initially in Mombasa, in September it was involved in the attack on Madagascar, then held by the Vichy French, and in particular the successful amphibious operations to capture Tamatave and Majunga, the island's two main ports. In 1943 he was awarded a DFC for his role in the campaign, the citation referring to his 'initiative, leadership and resourcefulness'. He was subsequently involved in the planning of the chain of coastal and island RAF bases in the western Indian Ocean and, promoted wing commander, from early 1943 he commanded the airfield at Mogadishu, recently captured from the Italians. He returned to Britain in May 1944 as chief instructor at Killadeas, the main flying boat conversion unit, on Lough Erne.

After the war Barraclough expected to be compulsorily demobilized and contemplated a career in the law, but in 1946 he was offered a permanent commission in the RAF, which he accepted with enthusiasm. That year he married Maureen Mary Jane McCormack (1913–2001), daughter of William John McCormack, medical practitioner, of Wicklow, Ireland, and niece of George Noble, Count Plunkett. They had one daughter, Rosalind Mary (Moyra) (*b.* 1950).

After staff training at Haifa, and staff duties (which he never liked) at RAF Headquarters Middle East and Air Headquarters Malta, in 1948 Barraclough joined the Central Flying School where he was responsible for standards of instruction throughout the RAF. While there he wrote a paper on the advantages of using a basic jet aircraft, rather than a propeller aircraft, for initial pilot training. His suggestion was well received, and in 1951 he flew the first Vampire training aircraft (a short-range, single-engine jet aircraft) to South Africa and back, for which he was awarded a queen's commendation for valuable services in the air.

Barraclough was station commander of RAF Biggin Hill from 1954 to 1956, and of Middleton St George from 1956 to 1958. For the next three years, by now a group captain, he was based in Singapore as senior operations and training officer at Headquarters Far East Asia Force, during the last stages of the Malayan 'emergency'. In 1961 he was appointed CBE and became director of public relations at the Air Ministry; his tasks included defence of the nuclear deterrent and of the planned TSR 2, which was subsequently cancelled by the Labour government. From 1964 to 1967 he was air officer commanding no. 19 group, with NATO responsibility for the eastern Atlantic, and the rank of air vice-marshal.

Unusually, in 1967 Barraclough took annual leave to attend, at his own expense, the advanced management program at Harvard Business School. On his return he was made the last air officer (administration) for Bomber Command, which in 1968 was subsumed within Strike Command, of which he was air officer (administration) until 1970. In the latter year he became vice-chief of the defence staff and was also promoted air marshal and knighted KCB (having been made a CB in 1969). He was air secretary from 1972 to 1974 and commandant of the Royal College of Defence Studies (his final posting) from 1974 to 1976. He was promoted air chief marshal in 1973.

In his retirement Barraclough was an underwriting member of Lloyd's (1979–85) and vice-chairman of the British Export Finance Advisory Council (1982–9), but threw most of his considerable energies into supporting various air- and defence-related organizations. He was chairman of the council of the Royal United Services Institute (1977–80), then a vice-president (1980–90) and a vice-patron (1990–2008); president of the Air Public Relations Association (1976–99, and thereafter a vice-patron); vice-chairman of the Air League Council (1977–81); honorary inspector-general of the Royal Auxiliary Air Force (1984–9); chairman (1999–2003) and then president (2003–8) of the Maritime Air Trust; president of the Coastal Command and Maritime Air Association (1999–2008); and vice-president of the Bomber Command Association (2000–8) and of the Aircrew Association (2001–8). He was editorial director (1978–81) then vice-chairman of the editorial board (1981–6) of *Nato's Sixteen Nations*, and collaborated with General Sir John Hackett on the bestselling book *The Third World War* (1978) and its sequel *The Third World War: the Untold Story* (1982).

A tall man with a commanding presence, yet modest and kindly, Barraclough was a keen horseman and sailor, and a member of the Royal Western Yacht Club. He lived latterly at 28 Royal Crescent, Bath, and was president of the Royal Crescent Society from 1990 to 2003. He was much saddened by the death of his wife, Maureen, but bore his own final illness stoically. He died on 10 May 2008 at his home in Bath, of cancer of the colon, and was survived by his daughter, Moyra. ALEX MAY

Sources *Daily Telegraph* (12 May 2008) · *The Times* (15 May 2008) · *The Independent* (21 May 2008) · www.unithistories.com/officers/RAF_officers_B01.html, 16 Aug 2011 · www.rafweb.org/Biographies/Barraclough_J.htm, 16 Aug 2011 · *WW* (2008) · Burke, *Peerage* · b. cert. · d. cert.

Archives King's Lond., Liddell Hart C.

Likenesses W. Bird, bromide print, 1964, NPG · photographs, 1998, Photoshot, London · group portrait, photograph, 2004, PA Photos, London · H. Wrightson, bromide print, NPG

Wealth at death under £220,000: probate, 27 Nov 2008, *CGPLA Eng. & Wales*

Barrett, Roger Keith [Syd] (**1946–2006**), musician and songwriter, was born on 6 January 1946 at 60 Glisson Road, Cambridge, the fourth of five children of Arthur Max Barrett, medical practitioner, and his wife, Winifred Flack, *née* Heeps. Educated at the Cambridge and County High School for Boys, the young Roger Barrett was good-

Roger Keith [Syd] **Barrett (1946–2006)**, by Gems, 1969

looking, blessed with an ebullient, positive personality, a quirky outlook, and a talent for music and art. By his mid-teens he had acquired the nickname Syd, some proficiency with ukulele, banjo, and electric guitar, and was playing in various Cambridge groups. The only apparent shadow that fell across his youth was the death of his father when he was fourteen.

In 1964 Barrett enrolled at Camberwell Art College, in London. A year later the earliest incarnation of Pink Floyd (named after the American bluesmen Pink Anderson and Floyd Council) took shape, playing the rock 'n' roll and R 'n' B covers typical of aspiring groups. Eventually a line-up of Barrett (guitar and vocals), Roger Waters (bass), Nick Mason (drums), and Richard *Wright (keyboards) was established. Waters, Mason, and Wright were students of architecture at Regent Street Polytechnic, and Barrett's friendship with Waters dated back to his Cambridge school days.

Pink Floyd made their presence felt on the London music scene from February 1966 when they began gigging regularly at the Marquee Club in Soho. They soon gained a following as the unofficial band of the developing London counter-culture 'underground' scene, and their first manager, Peter Jenner, encouraged the more experimental music that soon found a visual complement in an innovative light and projection show. The band played before 2500 people in October for the *International Times* at the Roundhouse in London, with a return gig in December and an appearance at the Royal Albert Hall. At the end of 1966 they became the house band at the UFO Club on the Tottenham Court Road.

Having signed to EMI for £5000, Pink Floyd's début single 'Arnold Layne' (written by Barrett about a transvestite) was released in January 1967, reaching number twenty-five in the British charts. In April 1967 they played at the 'Fourteen-Hour Technicolour Dream Festival' at the Alexandra Palace. Barrett's ability to perform was by now adversely affected by his frequent use of the drug LSD. It is said that Barrett's first 'trip' was in 1965 when he was at art school, and an eleven-minute film purportedly captures this experience. Friends like June Child (later married to Marc Bolan) recalled that Barrett was taking three or four LSD doses a day. It did not help that for a time Barrett lived at 101 Cromwell Road with some militant 'acid-heads' gripped by an anarchic zeal for forcing hallucinogenics on the unwary.

In May 1967 Pink Floyd played the 'Games For May' concert at the Queen Elizabeth Hall. A second single, the darkly enchanting 'See Emily Play', written for this concert, reached number five in July, leading to an appearance on BBC television's *Top of the Pops*. ('Emily' was later covered by David Bowie on his 1973 *Pin-Ups*.) A début LP, *The Piper at the Gates of Dawn* (released by EMI Columbia in August 1967), was recorded in studio 3 at Abbey Road during March and April, while the Beatles were completing *Sgt Pepper* in the next studio. A key album of English psychedelia, *Piper* was named after a chapter in Kenneth Grahame's *The Wind in the Willows*. Barrett wrote most of the eleven songs, and the album included two staples of the Floyd's live performances, 'Astronomy Domine' and 'Interstellar Overdrive'.

As a guitarist Barrett's technique was largely rudimentary chording, but crucially he saw the electric guitar as more than merely an amplified acoustic. He created washes of sound through effects such as echo and reverb, in conjunction with substitutes for a bottleneck that gave glissandi that pitched higher than the fretboard, effects that were continued by his successor David Gilmour. Barrett's musical legacy consists of about sixty songs, many hardly more than Bedlam watercolours. His songwriting was highly idiosyncratic and marked by little use of minor chords (by pop standards); plentiful non-diatonic major chords, so that a Barrett song nominally in the key of A major might feature, in addition to A, D, and E, major chords on any other pitch; angular chord changes based on a tritone, for instance A to E♭ and sequences of chords moving in semitone steps. All of these traits helped to shape his melodies. The songs often had irregular beats or phrases. His lyrics were pictorial, whimsical–portentous, and surreal, often sounding like sinister nursery rhymes, and were sung in a British accent, rather than the American accent affected by many British groups at the time.

In 1967 Pink Floyd's music had two conflicting aesthetics: Barrett's idiosyncratic pop songs, exemplified by 'Arnold Layne' and 'See Emily Play', and the band's partly improvised longer live pieces, as captured in Peter Whitehead's film *Tonite, Let's All Make Love in London* (1967). Audiences were often baffled by their longer pieces, but the band, and Barrett in particular, was uneasy with being seen as a chart-aiming pop group. Pink Floyd's performances explored the possibility, then current in the 'underground', of travelling to the margins of normal consciousness. Drug-use (especially hallucinogenics), high volume, repetition, powerful beats, sound-effects, and light-shows reached for a romantic ideal of sensory overload that promised a triple reward of insight, transcendence, and pleasure. The psychedelic concert was a metaphor for, but also a means to, the desideratum of altered consciousness. If Barrett had undiagnosed mental problems, or a fragile psyche, he had embraced a lifestyle and an aesthetic that carried a high probability of unbalancing him.

Barrett's mental health began to break down not long after the release of the group's first album. Members of the band recalled that a sudden, alarming change took place in Barrett during the summer of 1967. It was said that he was no longer 'there'. By the time Pink Floyd toured the USA in October and the UK in November, he was behaving erratically, refusing to mime on TV when required or to play during live concerts. A third single, 'Apples and Oranges', released in November, flopped. Alarmed by the psychological decline of their friend and principal songwriter, the group tried to formulate a *modus operandi* by which Barrett could be retained as a studio-based member. In February 1968 another friend from Cambridge, the guitarist David Gilmour, stepped in to cover for Barrett during live shows, and this evolved into a permanent replacement from April 1968. One day in the spring of 1968, when it was time to pick Barrett up for a gig, they simply decided not to. Only one Barrett song, 'Jugband Blues', featured on the band's second album, *A Saucerful of Secrets* (1968).

After a lengthy hiatus, which included treatment at a Cambridge psychiatric hospital, Barrett tried to revive his career, contacting EMI in March 1969 (the year of Jenny Fabian's novel *Groupie*, in which Barrett appears as Ben). Various musical sketches and fragments were captured during difficult sessions for two solo albums, *The Madcap Laughs* and *Barrett* (both 1970; later re-issued with increasing numbers of alternative recordings as *Opel*, 1988, *Crazy Diamond*, 1993, and *Wouldn't You Miss Me?*, 2001). Barrett also made brief returns to the stage at Olympia in June 1970 (exiting after only four songs) and in a one-off gig in 1972 at the Cambridge Corn Exchange with a group called Stars. He then retreated from the music business to live quietly in Cambridge with his mother, and to paint, supported by an invalidity pension and royalty cheques. He reverted to being known as Roger. In the 1990s large offers of money for new songs made by record companies, aware of his cult status, were ignored.

Pink Floyd remembered Barrett in later albums and songs. Perhaps the greatest musical tribute to him was the live version of 'Astronomy Domine' on *Ummagumma* (1970). The internationally successful *Dark Side of the Moon* (1973) had several songs about madness and depression. Its follow-up, *Wish You Were Here* (1975), featured a song about Barrett, 'Shine On You Crazy Diamond'. When Roger Waters was patching vocals for this song in the mixing studio, Barrett, now bald, overweight, and obviously mentally unwell, turned up unannounced, initially unrecognized by any of the group. In later years it is said that mention of Pink Floyd caused him distress, though he is reported to have watched the BBC *Omnibus* documentary about himself. For most of his life he was as significant as a symbol for counter-cultural assumptions as he was for his songs, a focus for rock music's questionably romanticized connections between innocence, rebellion, creativity, and mental illness. He died of cancer on 7 July 2006 at his home, 6 St Margaret's Square, Cambridge. He was unmarried, and had no children. RIKKY ROOKSBY

Sources J. Green, *Days in the life: voices from the English underground, 1961–1971* (1988) · P. Anderson and M. Watkinson, *Crazy diamond: Syd Barrett and the dawn of Pink Floyd* (1991); new edn (2006) · B. MacDonald, *Pink Floyd* (1996) · P. Humphries, *Pink Floyd: an illustrated history* (1997) · J. Palacios, *Lost in the woods: Syd Barrett and the Pink Floyd* (1998) · *The Pink Floyd and Syd Barrett story*, DVD (2001) · D. Parker, *Random precision: recording the music of Syd Barrett, 1965–1974* (2001) · T. Willis, *Madcap: the half-life of Syd Barrett, Pink Floyd's lost genius* (2003) · *The Times* (12 July 2006) · *Daily Telegraph* (12 July 2006) · *The Guardian* (12 July 2006) · *The Independent* (12 July 2006) · b. cert. · d. cert.

Archives FILM priv. coll., film footage of Pink Floyd, *c.*1965–7 · *Tonight let's all make love in London*, Peter Whitehead (producer), 1967 · EMI promotional video for Pink Floyd singles, 1967 · BBC Omnibus documentary, 2001 | SOUND BL NSA, documentary recordings · priv. coll., performance recordings

Likenesses photograph, 1960–69, Photoshot, London · photographs, 1960–2006, Rex Features, London · photographs, 1966–79, Getty Images, London, Redferns music picture library · C. Walter, photographs, 1967, Getty Images, London, WireImage · photographs, 1967, Hult. Arch., London · photographs, 1967, PA Photos, London · photographs, 1967–70, Getty Images, London, Michael Ochs archives · Gems, photograph, 1969, Getty Images, London, Redferns Music Picture Library [*see illus.*] · M. Rock, photographs, repro. in M. Rock, *Psychedelic renegades: photographs of Syd Barrett by Mick Rock* (2007) · obituary photographs

Wealth at death £1,250,455: probate, 8 Nov 2006, *CGPLA Eng. & Wales*

Barron, John Penrose (1934–2008), classical scholar and college head, was born on 27 April 1934 at 13 Thornfield Terrace, Morley, Yorkshire, the son of George Barron, a secondary school teacher, and his wife, Minnie Leslie, *née* Marks (1908–1994). His father was the head of mathematics at the local grammar school and his mother, from a Cornish family, was the daughter of a builder. Barron spent many childhood holidays in Cornwall at St Just in Penwith and was deeply attached to the area. He was educated at Wakefield grammar school and then at Clifton College: his father undertook two jobs to send his son there. He went up to Balliol College, Oxford, as an exhibitioner in 1953 to read Greats, graduating in 1957. Among others, he was tutored at Balliol by Kenneth Dover and the ancient historian Russell Meiggs. He remained close to them both thereafter.

Barron's doctoral research was on the island of Samos in the sixth century BC, then a centre of intellectual life in the Greek world. He took his DPhil in 1961 and from it he published *The Silver Coins of Samos* in 1966. It was more than a work in numismatics; Barron pieced together various types of literary and archaeological evidence as well to present a broad history of Samos and its flourishing culture in the period. The book displayed his aptitude for hunting down pieces of information, linking them together, and making wider intellectual connections. Indeed his talent for making connections, whether in his study of ancient Greek history and art, or among his colleagues, friends, and students, was an aspect of his approach to scholarship and to life.

Towards the end of his doctoral research Barron met an undergraduate historian from Somerville College, Oxford, Caroline Mary Hogarth (*b.* 1940), the daughter of William David Hogarth, publisher, and granddaughter of the archaeologist David George Hogarth. After her graduation they married at the church of St John-at-Hampstead on 1 September 1962. As Caroline Barron she became a leading historian of medieval London and held a chair in the history department at Royal Holloway, University of London. They had two daughters, Catherine (Katie) and Helen. Together the Barrons made a remarkable academic team, noted for their hospitality in London at their home in St John's Wood and later in Oxford, and for the enthusiasm they imparted to their students and colleagues. Barron's first appointment at Bedford College, London, then a women's college, and his support for his wife's career, made him a noted promoter of academic opportunities for women.

Much of Barron's academic career was spent in different colleges of the University of London, to which he was as devoted as to Oxford. He was an assistant lecturer and then lecturer at Bedford College between 1959 and 1964. He moved to University College as a lecturer in archaeology (1964–7), became reader in archaeology and numismatics, and was then elected to the chair of Greek language and literature at King's College, London, in 1971 at the age of only thirty-seven. He held the chair for twenty years, combining it with several senior positions at King's and in the University of London more widely. He was director of the Institute of Classical Studies in London between 1984 and 1991 and dean of all the London institutes for advanced study for the last two years of that period. He was instrumental in setting up the University of London Institute for Advanced Study. He also had two spells as the university's public orator.

Barron had wide academic interests and published in the leading classical journals. His study *Greek Sculpture* (1965, rev. edn 1981) was a very well-received introduction to the subject. His work on numismatics, focusing on Kos as well as Samos, showed the relevance of coins to an understanding of the wider history of the ancient world. Most at home in Greek literature in the era between Hesiod and the early classical period of the first half of the fifth century BC, he collaborated with Patricia Easterling in writing on the authors of this period for the *Cambridge History of Classical Literature* (1985). His interests were more than merely classical and extended to the contemporary culture of Greece which he came to appreciate through frequent visits to the country, including as a lecturer for Swan Hellenic cruises. He was also widely known among leading figures in the Greek community in London.

In 1987 Barron chaired a national review of the teaching of classics in British universities under the auspices of the University Grants Committee, which came to the conclusion that the subject should be concentrated in fewer but stronger departments. Unpopular at the time, the Barron report (*Review of Classics*, 1987) was quickly vindicated and was seen to have saved the subject from decline. This led on to membership between 1989 and 1993 of the University Funding Council (UFC) which was established by the Conservative government to replace the University Grants Committee and oversee changes to the British university system. The UFC was also unpopular in British universities, not least because its members included a majority of non-academics. Barron's position on it was indicative of his long-standing view that it was better to influence an institution from the inside, making it easier to defend what was of value, than to raise impotent opposition from outside. He also supported the overall expansion of the British university system which was planned and set in motion while he was a member of the UFC and which saw participation rates rise from approximately 12 per cent to more than 30 per cent in less than a decade.

Returning to Oxford in 1991 as master of St Peter's College, Barron encouraged initiatives to improve access to the university, especially as chairman of the Oxford Colleges' Admissions Committee (1997–2000). During his mastership there was a notable increase in the proportion of female students and fellows at the college. Founded as recently as 1928 and with limited resources, St Peter's came of age under Barron. The college increased the number of undergraduates and postgraduates; it began a successful visiting students programme for undergraduates from the United States; and its academic position in Oxford improved, not least because Barron showed a personal interest in every student, meeting with them individually at the end of each term to review progress. Barron was at ease with all comers: he often said that the most important quality for a successful head of house in Oxford was gregariousness.

St Peter's expanded physically as well. Barron had a sharp eye for architecture and design and was involved from the outset with plans to redevelop the site of Oxford Castle, until recently a prison, to the west of the city centre and close to the college. He accepted reluctantly that it was too big a project for the college to manage alone, but his interest in it led St Peter's to build three elegant student residences in the vicinity, contributing to the regeneration of this previously run-down quarter of the city.

In recognition of Barron's success as master the fellows extended his term for two years beyond the usual retiring age. He stood down in 2003 and devoted himself to historical and educational interests. He was president of Clifton College, a member of the council of the Society of Antiquaries, and chairman of the committee for Lambeth Palace Library. He died of pancreatic cancer on 16 August 2008 at University College Hospital, Camden, London. His funeral service was held at St Peter's on 27 August 2008 and he was buried in St Just in Penwith. He was survived by his wife, Caroline, and their two daughters.

LAWRENCE GOLDMAN

Sources *The Times* (29 Aug 2008) • *Daily Telegraph* (29 Aug 2008) • *The Independent* (10 Sept 2008) • *The Guardian* (19 Sept 2008) • *WW* (2008) • personal knowledge (2012) • private information (2012) • b. cert. • m. cert. • d. cert.
Likenesses obituary photographs
Wealth at death £1,328,162: probate, 22 Oct 2008, *CGPLA Eng. & Wales*

Baskett, Peter John Firth (1934–2008), anaesthetist, was born in Belfast on 26 July 1934, the eldest of three sons of Sir Ronald Gilbert Baskett (1901–1972), agriculturist, and his wife, Joan Shirley Staples, *née* Firth (1903–1982). His parents were originally from Essex. At the time of his birth his father was head of the chemical and animal nutrition division of the Ministry of Agriculture for Northern Ireland; later he was the professor of agriculture at Queen's University, Belfast, and a Ministry of Agriculture adviser. In 1959 he became director of the National Institute for Research in Dairying at Shinfield, Berkshire; he was knighted in 1966.

Peter Baskett's schooldays were in Belfast. After preparatory schools he went to Belfast Royal Academy from 1945 to 1949 and as a boarder to Campbell College from 1949 to 1952. A schoolfellow later remembered him as a 'happy-go-lucky individual who was never serious for a moment' (*The Times*, 19 June 2008). His medical studies were at Queens' College, Cambridge, from 1952 to 1955, with his clinical training back in Belfast at Queen's University medical school from 1955 to 1958. On graduating he undertook postgraduate training in the recently launched department of anaesthetics at Belfast, led by the outstanding young anaesthetist John Dundee. His training in Dundee's department from 1958 to 1961, mainly at Belfast's Royal Victoria Hospital, included early involvement in intensive care, which was just being introduced. His invaluable apprenticeship encompassed assisting with a recently introduced treatment for tetanus in which patients were paralysed by curare for several weeks and their breathing taken over mechanically until the antitoxin had worked through the disease. Northern Ireland then had Britain's highest incidence of tetanus.

Baskett moved to Bristol in 1962, where he completed his training in anaesthetics. He became a consultant to the United Bristol Hospitals and Frenchay Hospital in 1966, posts he retained until his retirement in 1999. An early contribution to Frenchay Hospital was the intensive care unit that he and his colleague John Zorab established in 1967.

Baskett's most notable contribution to patient care started in 1970 when he began campaigning for ambulance crews to be equipped and trained to provide pre-hospital pain relief. This arose from his insistence that they ought to be capable of using the simple Entonox analgesia dispensers that midwives used to relieve childbirth pain. Until he began transforming the situation ambulance crews had never been trained in more than first aid, which left many patients transported to hospital in severe pain. Baskett's plan to trial the use of Entonox (premixed nitrous oxide and oxygen analgesia) by Bristol ambulance crews was not initially accepted. The idea of lowly ambulance staff being entrusted with pain relief was a step too far for most medical authorities. However, support came from the medical officer of neighbouring Gloucestershire, Allan Withnell, who authorized the training of a dozen of his ambulance personnel in Entonox use.

The uptake of Baskett's idea by ambulance services across the country began with the success of this pilot scheme, on which early training courses and promotional lectures were based. Two years later Baskett piloted short-term hospital attachments, at Frenchay, for ambulance personnel to acquire emergency care skills. By then he had formed collaborative links with two other leading campaigners for better pre-hospital care: the Belfast cardiologist Frank Pantridge, who in 1966 had invented the portable defibrillator and put the first into an ambulance ready to enhance the chances of heart attack victims, and the Brighton cardiologist Douglas Chamberlain, who was training local ambulance crews to use defibrillators. This trio's ideas and campaigning were at the leading edge of a growing movement in the 1970s for ambulance service reform, which led in the 1980s to the evolution of modern paramedic services in Britain.

By the late 1970s Baskett was intent on improving the resuscitation capabilities of emergency care professionals and in 1977 he became a founder member of the British Association for Immediate Care Schemes, of which he was chairman from 1981 to 1985. In 1981 he had a leading role in establishing a national resuscitation advisory council, which in 1984 became the Resuscitation Council (UK). In 1989 he helped found the European Resuscitation Council and served as chairman until 1994. In 1997 he became the chief editor of its journal, *Resuscitation*, and admirably guided it for a decade.

Baskett was a man of many roles, infectious in enthusiasms, and gifted in charm and rhetoric that sometimes shone in outspokenness. He made prominent contributions to the College of Anaesthetists (from 1992 the Royal College of Anaesthetists) as a council member from 1983 to 1995, and to the Association of Anaesthetists of Great Britain and Ireland, of which he was a council member from 1976 to 1980 and 1986 to 1992, and president from 1990 to 1992. By the later 1980s he was internationally acknowledged as a leading expert in cardiopulmonary resuscitation and airway management, and also in emergency and disaster medicine, his status assisted by more than a hundred publications, including several major texts that he wrote or edited. He became the president of the World Association for Emergency and Disaster Medicine from 1989 to 1993 and of the International Trauma Anaesthesia and Critical Care Society from 1995 to 1998. His influence on the development of trauma services in the UK was profound, and overseas he introduced into more than twenty countries the advanced life support course that he helped the European Resuscitation Council develop. In 2005 he was named a 'Resuscitation Giant' by the American Heart Association.

Baskett was an elegant man of fine lifestyle. His leisure interests were principally focused on family, motor racing, rugby football, and regular visits to Northern Ireland. He was married four times: first on 29 August 1959 to Hazel McCurdy (*b.* 1934/5), a schoolteacher from Belfast, and daughter of William McCurdy, farmer; second on 15 March 1973 to Margaret Jean Snelgar (*b.* 1949), a nurse in Bristol, and daughter of Victor John Snelgar, a civilian instructor in the Royal Navy; third on 6 April 1989 to Christine Mary Reynolds, *née* Day (*b.* 1948), a hospital theatre superintendent, also from Bristol, and daughter of Reginald John Day, personnel manager; and fourth on 4 January 1995 to Fiona Mary Gilroy (*b.* 1959), a medical practitioner in Cheltenham, and daughter of George Gilroy. He had a son and daughter with his first wife, a daughter with his second wife, and another daughter with his fourth wife. His first three marriages ended in divorce. He suffered at the end of his life from cancer of the colon, chronic obstructive airways disease, and chronic heart failure; he died of left lower lobe pneumonia at the Frenchay Hospital on 18 April 2008. He was survived by his wife, Fiona, and his four children. MAX BLYTHE

Sources *Wiltshire Times* (2 May 2008) • *The Times* (20 May 2008); (19 June 2008) • *BMJ*, 336 (31 May 2008), 1254 • *The Guardian* (13 June 2008) • www.erc.edu/index.php/news/en/nid=200/, 14 July 2011 • P. Baskett, audio interviews with Max Blythe, 15 Feb 2001 and 15 March 2001, priv. coll. • P. Baskett, video interviews with Max Blythe, 26 June 2001 and 7 Aug 2001, Oxford Brookes University, Medical Sciences Video Archive, MSVA 198, 200 • personal knowledge (2012) • private information (2012) • m. certs. • d. cert.

Archives FILM Medical Sciences Video Archive, Oxford Brookes University, interviews with M. Blythe, 26 June 2001 and 7 Aug 2001, MSVA 198, 200 | SOUND priv. coll., interviews with M. Blythe, 15 Feb 2001 and 15 March 2001

Likenesses obituary photographs

Wealth at death £495, 738: probate, 19 June 2008, *CGPLA Eng. & Wales*

Battiscombe [*née* Harwood], **(Esther) Georgina (1905–2006)**, biographer, was born on 21 November 1905 at 68 South Audley Street, Mayfair, London, the elder daughter of George Harwood (1845–1912), a master cotton spinner and Liberal MP for Bolton from 1895 to his death, and his second wife, Ellen, *née* Hopkinson. Her maternal grandfather, Sir Alfred *Hopkinson, was the first vice-chancellor of Manchester University, and her stepfather, John *Murray, was principal of the University College of the South-West, Exeter. Like her father both these men and other members of her family were members of parliament. Her father died when she was a child and her family moved first to Chipping Campden and then to Oxford. She was educated at St Michael's School, Oxford, run by the sisters of the Society of the Holy and Undivided Trinity. She went to Lady Margaret Hall, Oxford, in 1924 and gained a second-class degree in modern history in 1927. Her contemporaries at the university included Mary Rosalie Glyn Grylls, Richard Acland, and Dingle Foot. For a time she considered following a political career in line with the family tradition. She married Lieutenant-Colonel Christopher Francis Battiscombe (1890–1964), a civil servant and former officer in the Grenadier Guards (and son of Christopher William Battiscombe, brewer), on 1 October 1932 in the Grosvenor Chapel, Hanover Square. After spending two years in Zanzibar, where her husband worked as secretary to the sultan, they moved in 1935 to Durham, where he was appointed chapter clerk and librarian to the cathedral. In 1955 they went to live in the King Henry III tower at Windsor Castle, because of his work as the honorary secretary of the Friends of St George's. They had one daughter, Aurea.

Georgina Battiscombe's literary career began in 1943 with the publication of *Charlotte Mary Yonge: the Story of an Uneventful Life*. Given wartime conditions and the 'extraordinary paucity of material' (*Yonge*, 7) that she found, it is hard to differ from E. M. Delafield's opinion in her introduction to the book that she showed 'enterprise and a real appreciation of Charlotte Yonge's importance as a writer' (ibid., 15). At a period when Trollope was enjoying a vogue, the biography was favourably received. Even Q. D. Leavis, despite serious reservations, admitted that it was 'an attractive book' (Leavis, 234). *Two on Safari* was published in 1946, followed by *English Picnics* (1949), which she described as a 'gallimaufry' intended 'to amuse rather than to instruct' (*Picnics*, v). She returned to biography with her focus on a great man's wife: *Mrs Gladstone: the Portrait of a Marriage* (1956). Acknowledgement of her achievements came with the award of the James Tait Black memorial prize for *John Keble: a Study in Limitations* (1963). She had already explored Keble's influence on Charlotte Yonge, and now she had been 'fortunate enough to gain access to a great mass of manuscript material, much of it unpublished' (*Keble*, ix). Further recognition came with her election in 1963 as a fellow of the Royal Society of Literature.

With Marghanita Laski, Georgina Battiscombe edited *A Chaplet for Charlotte Yonge* (1965), an elegant volume of essays and other material by members of the Charlotte Yonge Society, including Lettice Cooper, Elizabeth Jenkins, Violet Powell, and Kathleen Tillotson. After a brief study of Christina Rossetti (1965), she wrote *Queen Alexandra* (1969), which was probably her most popular book—it was about the royal family, and it was enthusiastic and colourfully descriptive. Although she was unable to find as much source material as she wanted, she said in the foreword that she was given 'unrestricted access' to Queen Alexandra's correspondence with King George V and Queen Mary and to 'all other relevant material now in the Royal Archives at Windsor'. She interviewed several members of the royal family, including the duke of Windsor. Like Queen Alexandra she suffered from deafness (alleviated in her case from the age of fifty by a hearing aid) and so wrote with sympathetic understanding of the queen's predicament: 'Only those who have been deaf themselves can realise the full meaning of deafness' (*Alexandra*, 86).

For the next ten years or so Georgina Battiscombe continued to write well-received full-length biographies. *Shaftesbury: a Biography of the Seventh Earl, 1801–1885*, was published in 1974. She had a grateful regard for the subject of her next book, *Reluctant Pioneer: a Life of Elizabeth Wordsworth* (1978). Yet again she indicated Charlotte Yonge's influence on a person's life, this time on the thought and conduct of the woman who became the long-serving first principal of Lady Margaret Hall. She included in the book a long account of Elizabeth Wordsworth's childhood and youth written by Evelyn Jamison in the late 1930s. She returned to another of her favourites in *Christina Rossetti: a Divided Life* (1981). Her last biography was the topical *The Spencers of Althorp* (1984), appearing three years after the marriage of Prince Charles and Lady Diana Spencer. In 1992 came *Winter Song: an Anthology of Poems on Old Age*.

Besides her biographical work Georgina Battiscombe was concerned for many years with the conservation of ecclesiastical buildings, serving, for example, from 1958 to 1981 as a member of the Oxford diocesan advisory committee for the care of churches. In *Who's Who* she gave 'looking at churches' as her recreation. She always retained a close interest in politics and a fondness for travel. Her daughter, who married George Morshead, son of Sir Owen Morshead, librarian at Windsor, died in 1997, but she had three grandchildren and several great-grandchildren. She died of respiratory failure at Thamesfield nursing home, Henley-on-Thames, Oxfordshire, on 26 February 2006. DONALD HAWES

Sources G. Battiscombe, *Charlotte Mary Yonge* (1943), author's note; E. M. Delafield, introduction • G. Battiscombe, *English picnics* (1949) • G. Battiscombe, *John Keble: a study in limitations* (1963), foreword • G. Battiscombe, *Queen Alexandra* (1969), foreword • Q. D. Leavis, *Collected essays*, ed. G. Singh, vol. 3: *The novel of religious controversy* (1989) • *The Times* (2 March 2006) • *Daily Telegraph* (2 March 2006) • *The Guardian* (2 March 2006) • records, Royal Society of Literature, London • *WW* (2006) • private information (2010) [archivist, Lady Margaret Hall, Oxford] • b. cert. • m. cert. • d. cert.
Likenesses photograph, repro. in *The Times* (2 March 2006)

Baxandall, Michael David Kighley (1933–2008), art historian, was born on 18 August 1933 at 22 Gordon Road, Cardiff, the only son and eldest child of David Kighley Baxandall (1905–1992), museum director, and his wife, (Sarah) Isobel Mary, *née* Thomas (1905–1990). His twin sisters, Edith and Jennifer, were born in 1938. At the time of Baxandall's birth his father was an assistant keeper at the National Museum of Wales; he was later keeper of the department of art there and (after war service in the RAF) director of Manchester City Art Galleries (1945–52) and of the National Galleries of Scotland (1952–70). His grandfather, too, had worked in museums, having been the curator of instruments at the Science Museum in South Kensington.

Baxandall received a classical education at Manchester grammar school and went on to read English at Downing College, Cambridge (1951–4). In an interview Baxandall later singled out F. R. Leavis as an abiding presence for his intellectual and scholarly attitudes. Leavis and William Empson both imparted to Baxandall the centrality of the linguistic, while Leavis also engendered a respect for nonconformity and an appreciation of the vernacular in culture.

In 1955 Baxandall went to Italy for a year, staying at the Collegio Borromeo and studying in Pavia, and then proceeded to St Gallen, Switzerland, in 1956–7 for a year teaching English and studying German. In the following year (1957–8) he went to the University of Munich and sat in on classes with Hans Sedlmayr, a well-known and somewhat controversial figure (he had sympathized with the Nazis) who had published a popular book on art called *Verlust der Mitte* in 1948 (published in English as *Art in Crisis: the Lost Centre*, 1957). Sedlmayr introduced Baxandall to the challenging problems of relating artistic content and style to culture and history. In Munich, Baxandall also studied at the Central Institute for Art History with Ludwig Heydenreich in a seminar dedicated entirely to Federico da Montefeltro and his Renaissance court at Urbino.

In the summer of 1958 Baxandall returned to London from his continental wanderings. He was given a job in the photograph collection at the Warburg Institute by the director Gertrude Bing, who was to nurture Baxandall's professional development over the next few years. There he met Katharina Dorothea (Kay) Simon (*b.* 1926), who worked in the same department. She was the daughter of Francis Eugen *Simon, professor of physics at Oxford. They married at Oxford register office on 6 April 1963 and had a daughter, Lucy (*b.* 1963), and a son, Thomas (*b.* 1968).

During these early years at the Warburg, Baxandall also developed a friendship with the British art historian Michael Podro, who remained a colleague and intellectual sounding board for decades. In 1959 Baxandall was awarded a two-year Warburg research fellowship. He studied with the scholar with whose work he would have the most complex dialogues: Ernst Gombrich, who became Baxandall's dissertation adviser on the topic of decorum and restraint in the Renaissance, a thesis that Baxandall, with characteristic mischievousness, never completed. In 1961 he took a job at the Victoria and Albert Museum where he was eventually given responsibility for cataloguing the collection of German sculpture. His work there, augmented by summer trips to Germany sponsored by the museum and discussions with his colleague Terence Hodgkinson, led to the research that resulted in his book *The Limewood Sculptors of Renaissance Germany* (1980). Meanwhile, in 1965 Gombrich offered Baxandall a lectureship in Renaissance studies at the Warburg, an institution to which he would remain professionally connected for the next twenty-two years, but intellectually and emotionally tethered for the rest of his life. He was promoted reader in 1973 and professor in 1981. It is reported that some of his last thoughts were concerns about the future of the Warburg Institute, the same worries, he noted in his posthumous memoir, *Episodes* (2010), expressed by Gertude Bing in her last moments. In 1986 he was offered a chair in the history of art at the University of California at Berkeley, where he became a permanent member of the department the following year and stayed until his retirement in 1996.

Baxandall's two-year Warburg fellowship in 1959–61

and his collaboration with Gombrich led to his first publication, a short entry co-authored with Gombrich, in the *Journal of the Warburg and Courtauld Institutes* (Jan 1962). There followed, in quick succession, a series of three articles in the same journal over the next three years (1963–5). Each of these articles examined humanist texts that dealt with art. Baxandall's contribution was to focus on humanist writings that were not as professionally directed as Alberti's more famous works like *On Painting*, such as Bartholomaeus Facius's *De viris illustribus*. In such texts he fleshed out a more encompassing picture of the relationship between humanism and the visual art of the Renaissance. These articles laid the foundations for his ground-breaking book *Giotto and the Orators* (1971), in which not only the vocabulary of the humanists but the conventions and even the styles of humanist writing were correlated with aspects of pictorial culture. The book opened up an entirely new and expansive way of considering the relationship between writing and painting. A striking feature was that the book's method was strongly reminiscent of structuralism, which in these years had emerged from the anthropology of Claude Lévi-Strauss. The measure of the book's influence can be seen in the myriad books and articles subsequently written on Renaissance art that at least partly utilized Baxandall's approach: an attention to language and a sophisticated analysis of the social and literary relationships between patrons, painters, and humanists.

This book was immediately followed by another, the even more influential *Painting and Experience in Fifteenth Century Italy* (1972). This remarkable volume could be argued to have dramatically changed the direction of art history. It represented the cutting edge of art historical methodology and reconnected art history with the other humanities and social sciences in a profound way, which is why, for example, the French sociologist Pierre Bourdieu took such admiring notice of it. Without question, its legacy for the discipline was profound, especially with the advent of 'visual culture', a concept proposed in that book through its conception of the 'period eye'. If *Giotto and the Orators* marked a linguistic turn in art history, *Painting and Experience* indicated an anthropological or cultural turn; in fact, the latter book merged these concerns. In these books and in subsequent scholarship Baxandall dealt with issues of historicized visuality and how perceiving art might be stimulated by other social or intellectual cultural activities tangentially related to art, and, further, how artists' ideas about looking, seeing, and perception may have put certain pressures on their representations' organization or style.

Baxandall's book *The Limewood Sculptors of Renaissance Germany* (1980) examined the social, political, and practical world of German patrons and sculptors in a sophisticated fleshing out of their historical context. Extending and reworking concerns brought up in *Painting and Experience*, in this book Baxandall again took as his subject the visual world in which artists, consumers, and institutions were embedded. One section dealt with the nature of the material, limewood, while other sections examined the conditions of trade, guilds, and competition; and a chapter on the 'period eye'—echoing *Painting and Experience*—described how barrel gauging and calligraphy played major roles in colouring the visual attention and aesthetic attitudes of fifteenth- and early sixteenth-century German artists and patrons.

Through the 1970s Baxandall found himself at odds with certain disciplinary trends. In his article 'The language of art history' (published in *New Literary History*, 1979), he offered a response to contemporary inclinations in art history to define its objectives:

> On the other hand, what I do like is there being a manifold plurality of differing art histories, and when some art historians start telling other art historians what to do, and particularly what they are to be interested in, my instinct is to scuttle away and existentially measure a plinth or reattribute a statuette. (p. 454)

In some respects, the remainder of Baxandall's career was testing the parameters of this 'manifold plurality of differing art histories'. With the rise of what came to be called 'the new art history', which was partially synonymous with 'the social history of art', it was common to take jabs at those art historians who practised formalism, a method that took the work of art as an independent aesthetic object created by a person with clear expressive intentions. The work of Ernst Gombrich, too, came under criticism in these years. But Baxandall respected much in the legacy of formalism and connoisseurship, in Gombrich's work, and even in the English art critical tradition represented by John Ruskin or Roger Fry. In some ways he moved to show how these traditions and their sensibilities could be merged with newer concerns and still be invaluable tools for an art historian. Indeed, he sought to demonstrate—perhaps recuperate—their centrality and even necessity in studying art by pushing them to new extremes to test their range and viability in myriad case studies.

The book *Patterns of Intention* (1985) might be seen as testing out some such cases. Based on a series of lectures, it also resembled a series of experiments or demonstrations with objects and how to verify them from various perspectives such as artists' intentions or motivations, the limitations of style and materials, the visual and professional worlds of the artist and patrons or spectators, and so on. At the same time, Baxandall tried to refine his own concepts, such as the concept of the 'period eye'. The book *Tiepolo and the Pictorial Intelligence* (1994), a collaboration with his long-time companion and Berkeley colleague Svetlana Alpers, was a *tour de force* assessment of Tiepolo's painting at Würzburg and how the works functioned visually on varied levels of engagement: with the architecture, with the movement of the spectators, within discrete and broad compositional frameworks, with light and shadows—both real and fictive—and how the painter approached these visual problems. The treatment at times bordered on the joyful, and at times on the playful, but at all times focused on the process of the painter's mind and the solutions to various complex pictorial challenges, tracing both intended and unintended expressions and their potential pictorial results. The range of concerns vacillated elegantly between an individual's contribution—the painter's—to the broader stratagems of rococo art.

One of the more difficult aspects of Baxandall's scholarship was its relation to the work of Gombrich, and perhaps especially *Art and Illusion*. When it came out in 1960 Baxandall and others met weekly to discuss its chapters. The book became a rich resource from which to quarry several concepts and problems that called for elaboration and investigation; and perhaps even for refutation, such as the notion of 'projection' and the 'beholder's share', which Baxandall would play with in the most sophisticated manner in later works, finding expression, for example, in *Shadows and Enlightenment* (1995), in which Baxandall made forays into the realm of scientific studies on perception of shape and form to enrich our understanding of the role and comprehension of shadows. While admitting the limitation of his expertise, he didn't shy away from the complex psychological, physiological, and technical literature most art historians would find intimidating.

In *Words for Pictures: Seven Papers on Renaissance Art and Criticism* (2003) Baxandall revisited some of his early subjects and topics: humanist writers such as Leon Battista Alberti and Angelo Decembrio, and the painter Piero della Francesca, on whom Baxandall had written a monograph in 1966. His engagement with his work continued to be an ongoing project, ever susceptible to revision and new insights. Such was Baxandall's devotion to his interests. He never tired of the problems offered by art and our involvement with it. His love of the challenge of writing was also an enduring characteristic, and many admired him for his style as an author as much as his ideas as an intellectual. In two posthumously published works, *Episodes: a Memory Book* (2010) and *A Grasp of Kaspar* (2010)—the former an autobiography and the latter a novel—he demonstrated his considerable abilities with other modes of writing.

Baxandall's contributions were among the most significant in the history of the discipline. His work heralded art history through one of its most transformative eras, and his scholarship was without doubt a major component of those transformations. Ironically, he declined to call himself an art historian. Indeed, he liked to dodge any such attempt to label his professional activities. Still, he had a soft spot for the Warburg Institute in London, where he had had the title 'professor of the history of the classical tradition', which he probably preferred to any other label, though in a characteristic gesture of both playfulness and dead-seriousness, he listed his occupation in his passport as 'antiquary'. An intellectual but not an academic, someone who liked to resist the trends and who found normativity in scholarship troubling, he believed that scholars should be sharp enough to think themselves out of whatever the latest fashion was. As a teacher he tried to unlock this latent capacity for original critical thought in his students.

In addition to the award of the Mitchell prize, the highest accolade for an art history book (for *Limewood Sculptors*), Baxandall was awarded the Edmund Gardner prize for his contribution to Italian studies in 1972, appointed Slade professor of fine art at Oxford in 1974 (his Slade lectures leading to *Limewood Sculptors*), and made a fellow of the British Academy in 1982. In the United States he was A. D. White professor-at-large at Cornell University from 1982 to 1988 and was the recipient of a MacArthur Foundation award in 1988. Also in 1988 he was awarded the city of Hamburg's Aby M. Warburg prize. He was a Getty scholar in 1994–5. He died at the Royal Free Hospital, Camden, London, on 12 August 2008 of aspiration pneumonia, and was survived by his wife, Kay, and his two children.

ALLAN LANGDALE

Sources A. Langdale, 'Art history and intellectual history: Michael Baxandall's work between 1963 and 1985', PhD diss., U. Cal., Santa Barbara, 1995 • A. Langdale, 'Aspects of the critical reception and intellectual history of Baxandall's concept of the period eye', *Art History*, 21/4 (Dec 1998), 479–97 • 'Substance, sensation, and perception', interviews by R. C. Smith, 1998, Getty Research Institute, Art History Oral Documentation Project • A. Rifkin, ed., *About Michael Baxandall* (1999) • *Daily Telegraph* (18 Aug 2008) • *The Independent* (19 Aug 2008) • *The Guardian* (26 Aug 2008) • *New York Times* (26 Aug 2008) • *The Times* (27 Aug 2008); (15 Sept 2008) • *Times Higher Education Supplement* (11 Sept 2008) • *San Francisco Chronicle* (11 Sept 2008) • A. Langdale, 'Interviews with Michael Baxandall, February 3rd and 4th, 1994, Berkeley, CA' and 'Linguistic theories and intellectual history in Michael Baxandall's *Giotto and the orators*', *Journal of Art Historiography*, 1 (2009); arthistoriography.wordpress.com/number-1-december-2009/, 30 July 2011 • M. Baxandall, *Episodes: a memory book* (2010) • J. Tanner, 'Michael Baxandall and the sociological interpretation of art', *Cultural Sociology*, 4/2 (2010), 231–56 • P. Hills, 'Art history reviewed, XIII: Michael Baxandall's *Painting and experience in fifteenth century Italy*, 1972', *Burlington Magazine*, 153 (June 2011), 404–8 • *WW* (2008) • personal knowledge (2012) • private information (2012) • b. cert. • m. cert. • d. cert.

Archives CUL, corresp. and papers

Likenesses M. Whitaker, cibachrome print, 1989, NPG • obituary photographs

Wealth at death under £184,000: probate, 6 Feb 2009, *CGPLA Eng. & Wales*

Baxter, Raymond Frederic (1922–2006), broadcaster and writer, was born on 25 January 1922 at 132 Cranbrook Road, Ilford, Essex, the son of Frederic Garfield Baxter (1881–1968), science teacher, and his wife, Rosina Ellen, *née* Retzbach (1884–1934), also a teacher. At the time of his birth registration his parents lived at 168 Wellesley Road, Ilford. He was taught at home until he was seven and attended Ilford county high school from 1933, leaving in 1940 to take a clerical job with the Metropolitan Water Board, through which he joined the Home Guard.

Following his first flight in 1936 Baxter's ambition had been to join the RAF. Called up in March 1941, he went for training to a British flying training school in Oklahoma. After returning to England, in August 1942 he piloted his first Spitfire and joined 65 squadron and, in March 1943, 93 squadron in north Africa, where he flew numerous

Raymond Frederic Baxter (1922–2006), by unknown photographer, 1951

Spitfire sorties. After a spell as a pilot instructor he joined 602 squadron, with which he dive-bombed V2 sites in 1944 and was mentioned in dispatches. On 17 September 1945 he married an American army nurse, Sylvia Kathryn Johnson (*d.* 1996). They had a son and a daughter.

Baxter began broadcasting in 1946 while posted in Cairo. 'I was an unemployed fighter pilot, and … had become interested in broadcasting … so I went to the forces broadcasting station … and said "please can I have a job?"' (*Desert Island Discs*). He became an announcer and then in 1947 joined the British Forces Network radio station in Hamburg as civilian deputy director. 'It was a complete course in broadcasting. One was expected to be able to do everything oneself … and to teach other people to do it, too' (ibid.).

In 1949 Baxter joined the BBC, where he became respected for the clarity, knowledge, and gravitas he brought to commentaries, particularly on major state occasions. These included the funeral of George VI (1952) and the coronation of Elizabeth II (1953). He was both commentator and crew member for the 1953 London to New Zealand air race. He took a dual role also in twelve Monte Carlo rallies, including the 1954 event, in which he was injured. He covered the Farnborough air show for thirty unbroken years, and many other events involving powered transport. From 1967 to 1968 he was director of motoring publicity for the British Motor Corporation.

Eye on Research (broadcast on BBC television in 1959–62) capitalized on Baxter's enthusiasm for technology and revealed his skill in conveying it to television audiences. He described his approach thus: 'I … read up everything on the subject I can … and get the [scientists] to explain their stuff to me. Then I … write it down on the back of a dirty envelope. If it won't go on the back of a dirty envelope … I keep on trying till it does' (*News Chronicle*, 6 March 1959). Television's interest in science continued to grow, and with it Baxter's involvement. He was the reporter–interviewer at Goonhilly covering the first exchange of live television pictures across the Atlantic, via the satellite Telstar, in July 1962.

When *Tomorrow's World*, a weekly live science programme, started in 1965, Baxter became its presenter. The brief was to explain how technology was changing the world. Studio demonstrations, for instance of how glass fibre optics worked, and short films about new products drew healthy audiences of more than eight million. Advances covered included the use of computers in the classroom (1965), breathalyser tests (1967), and digital watches (1972). Spectacularly, in 1967 Baxter interviewed Christiaan Barnard on the phone from South Africa shortly after he had carried out the world's first heart transplant. He also covered the first flights of the British and French Concordes in 1969. 'As a presenter [he] was first class. He had no fear in a live studio and always finished on time. His knowledge could not be faulted' (private information, Sir Paul Fox). However, by 1977 Baxter's style had become out of tune with the programme's then editor, who decided that he should appear less. Unhappy with this plan, Baxter left the programme at the end of what his department head described as 'a long and distinguished innings' (P. Daly to R. Baxter, 15 Sept 1976, BBC WAC). He continued commentating almost until his death on his familiar subjects, including the seventy-fifth anniversary of the RAF (1993) and the Royal British Legion festival of remembrance, which he covered for thirty-three consecutive years until 1995.

A keen interest in boats led Baxter in the 1960s to buy *L'orage*, which had taken part in the Dunkirk evacuation of 1940. On the twenty-fifth anniversary he skippered her for a repeat journey with other Dunkirk veterans; the Association of Dunkirk Little Ships was born, with Baxter its honorary admiral. In 1971 he was elected as a fellow of the Royal Society of Arts for services to broadcasting. He was a vice-president of the Royal National Lifeboat Institution (1987–97) and a member of the Air League Council (1980–85). He was the first recipient in 2000 of the Raymond Baxter award for science communication and in 2003 he was appointed OBE for 'services to heritage'. His publications included *Tomorrow's World*, volumes 1 and 2 (1970–71, with James Burke and Michael Latham), film commentaries, articles, and reports on motoring and flying.

Baxter was described as 'tall, good-looking, with a raffish air, and a loud laugh … a caricature of an RAF pilot' (private information, Sir Paul Fox) and as 'a typical Englishman: well-mannered and very considerate … He had no side and never let his fame go to his head' (private information, Peter Dimmock). He died of bronchopneumonia on 15 September 2006 at the Royal Berkshire Hospital, Reading. Two RAF Spitfires flew past at his funeral on 29 September at Ewelme parish church, Oxfordshire, where his ashes were buried. There was a thanksgiving service at the RAF church, St Clement Danes, London, on 19 April 2007. He was survived by his two children.

NICHOLAS MOSS

Sources *News Chronicle* (6 March 1959) · *Desert island discs*, BBC Home Service, 9 Sept 1963, BBC WAC, S133/18/187 · staff files, BBC WAC · R. Baxter and T. Dron, *Tales of my time* (2005) · *The Times* (16 Sept 2006) · *Daily Telegraph* (16 Sept 2006) · *The Guardian* (18 Sept 2006) · *The Independent* (18 Sept 2006) · *WW* (2006) · private information (2010) [Graham Baxter, son; M. Cormack; P. Dimmock; P. Fox; P. Lewis; P. Massey; B. Reader; RAF Museum; Royal Society of Arts] · b. cert. · d. cert.

Archives BBC WAC | FILM BFINA, performance footage · BFINA, documentary footage | SOUND BFI NSA, current affairs recordings · BFI NSA, documentary recordings · BFI NSA, documentary recordings

Likenesses photograph, 1951, BBC [*see illus.*] · photograph, 1952, Getty Images, London, Popperfoto · photographs, 1957–2003, PA Photos, London · H. Todd, photograph, 1959, Hult. Arch., London · photographs, 1960–97, Photoshot, London · photograph, 1971, Getty Images, London, Popperfoto · photographs, 1972–2003, Rex Features, London · R. Taggart, photograph, 1979, Hult. Arch., London · photographs, 2000–03, Camera Press, London · obituary photographs · photographs, BBC

Wealth at death £579,332: probate, 23 Feb 2007, *CGPLA Eng. & Wales*

Bayliss, Sir Richard Ian Samuel [Dick] (**1917–2006**), physician, was born on 2 January 1917 at Glenmore, Tettenhall, Staffordshire, the son of Frederick William Bayliss, mechanical engineer and Wolverhampton ironmaster, and his wife, Muriel Anne, *née* Sanderson. He early developed an interest in science and medicine, reading up on whooping cough when he was suffering from the disease. Later he had a laboratory in an attic for which his grandfather gave him a microscope and where he dissected a frog. When he exploded a flask on a Bunsen burner his eyesight may have been saved by the spectacles needed for his myopia. He was educated at Rugby School and then Clare College, Cambridge, obtaining an upper second in his preclinical studies. He graduated MB BChir at Cambridge and was admitted MRCS LRCP in 1941 at St Thomas's Hospital medical school, London. On 19 April 1941, while still a medical student, he married Margaret Joan Hardman Lawson (*d.* 1994), five years his senior, and daughter of William Henry Lawson, merchant. They had one son and one daughter.

At Cambridge Bayliss was active in the amateur dramatics club, but not the Footlights, and was in charge of the lighting; indeed he obtained the unusual distinction of being elected president of the club, even though he was not an actor. He composed and played songs, becoming for a while a gramophone record critic. He played the piano beautifully from an early age, and this was put to good use at the students' Christmas shows at St Thomas's. With his natural ear he played jazz spontaneously throughout his life; for three months in 1935 he was a professional musician in a Munich nightclub.

After qualifying, Bayliss was successively student, casualty officer, house physician, registrar, and resident assistant physician at St Thomas's Hospital during the Second World War, and his reminiscences of hospital life during repeated bombing were fascinating and often amusing. The staff worked all the time, every day of the week, dealing with harrowing injuries in restricted conditions, particularly after bombings nearby, including one that landed on a double-decker bus. He was renowned for his cool diagnostic skills under these circumstances. Once he is reputed to have diagnosed atropine poisoning in a medical student, and traced the source to the muslin handkerchief that the landlady had used both to mop up the atropine eye drops of her daughter and to strain the student's breakfast coffee. He passed the MRCP examination only a year after qualifying; indeed, he seemed to excel at everything that he did.

Bayliss's initial interest was in cardiology, and he wrote his MD thesis, awarded in 1946, on cardiac metastases from bronchogenic carcinoma. After the war he spent three years in India as a medical specialist with the rank of major, in charge of the British military hospital in Delhi. At that time diarrhoea was afflicting officers who drank either whisky and soda, or gin and tonic. He showed that this was due to *E. coli* contaminated water, and that the soda and tonic were made locally from water that came from tanks in the roof, which he personally inspected, finding that they contained drowned birds and mammals, or 'sewerage', as the bacteriologist pithily described it. In 1948 he returned as tutor in medicine at the Postgraduate Medical School of London under John McMichael, and in 1950 became a lecturer in medicine and consultant physician at the Hammersmith Hospital. In 1950–51 he was a Rockefeller fellow at Columbia University in New York, where he sought the elusive salt-retaining hormone aldosterone in urine: this quest was unfortunately impaired by an ether explosion in the laboratory refrigerator, a crime of which he was uncharacteristically innocent; this destroyed all his samples. In 1954 he moved to the Westminster Hospital, initially as assistant physician and endocrinologist, remaining there until 1981. He was also consulting physician to King Edward VII Hospital, London, 1952–81, and Midhurst, 1973–82.

Everyone who knew Bayliss described him as an outstanding physician; immaculately dressed, with a penchant for striped shirts, and with dark hair, large horn-rimmed glasses, and a piercing twinkle in his eye. He was renowned for his diagnostic skills, so much so that some patients called him the 'magician'. He was adept at eliciting important details of their histories. A charismatic teacher, he was revered by students. He was dean of Westminster Hospital medical school in 1960–64, which he succeeded in modernizing, but his term was cut short, at the age of forty-eight, by a heart attack, which he treated in his own way by getting out of bed as early as possible, against the current medical advice, and skiing three weeks later. In 1964 he joined the medical household as physician to the royal household, and he was physician to the queen from 1970 to 1982, and head of the medical household from 1974 to 1982. He handled this varied and sometimes difficult post with skill, discretion, and aplomb. He was created KCVO in 1978.

In addition to about one hundred papers and thirty-three chapters in books Bayliss's book *Practical Procedures in Clinical Medicine*, first published in 1950, went to three editions. *Thyroid Disease: the Facts*, first published in 1982, went to four editions. He also made a film on examination of the central nervous system. He gave the Royal College of Physicians Croonian lecture in 1974, 'Idiopathic oedema in women'. He was an examiner for the college, 1961–6, councillor, 1953–4 and 1967–70, second vice-president, 1983–4, assistant director of the research unit, 1982–8, and chairman of the joint committee for independent health care, 1979–83. Among numerous other posts he was secretary of the Association of Physicians, 1958–63, and its president, 1980–81, a member of the council of the British Heart Foundation, 1976–87, civilian consultant to the Royal Navy, 1975–82, adviser to the Merck Institute of Therapeutic Research, 1973–89, medical adviser to the Nuffield Hospital Trust, 1980–88, chairman of the board of Private Patients Plan Medical Centres, 1981–7, chairman of the editorial board for medical sciences of Pergamon Press, 1980–86, and chairman of the medical advisory panel of the Independent Television Commission from 1983. He had become a fellow of the Royal College of Physicians of London in 1956 and gave its Harveian oration, on 'Thyroid disease as the expression of auto-immune disease', in 1983 (the year in which he was made an honorary fellow of his Cambridge college). He was made an honorary fellow of the Royal College of Pathologists in 1994 and a founding fellow of the Academy of Medical Sciences in 1998.

Bayliss's first marriage was dissolved in 1956, and on 12 January the following year he married Constance Ellen Frey, a sub-editor ten years his junior, and daughter of Wilbur James Frey, manager of a telephone company. They had two daughters. Following the dissolution of this marriage Bayliss married, on 24 February 1979, Marina Audrey Felicité Rankin (*b.* 1932), widow of Charles Rankin, and daughter of Count Baudouin de Borchgrave d'Altena, head of military intelligence for the Belgian government in exile during the Second World War. They had an extremely happy marriage, and together entertained their many friends in their penthouse flat in Onslow Square.

After retirement in 1982 from the National Health Service Bayliss continued in private practice and as medical adviser to many organizations, and was consulted both in Britain and abroad. He read voraciously and maintained an active interest in medical writing, taking to the computer like a duck to water. In 2004 he caught out a bogus meter reader at his flat who filched some silver boxes, but unwisely talked about his recent operation. Later realizing his loss, Bayliss contacted the police with the details, and they quickly traced and apprehended the burglar, who was later gaoled.

Throughout his life Bayliss had a succession of illnesses and afflictions to which he applied his interest and diagnostic skills, including a coronary infarction, leaking abdominal aortic aneurysm, and a perforated Meckel's diverticulum. These were followed by a recrudescence of the unusual fungal disease histoplasmosis a few years before his death, probably contracted years before in the United States. He gave, with characteristic gusto, a noteworthy lecture recounting the difficult diagnosis of this esoteric disease. Finally, he quickly succumbed to cancer after returning from a skiing holiday abroad and planning celebrations for his ninetieth birthday. He was a lifelong smoker, which may have been the ultimate cause of his death, and in his eighties he accidentally set fire to his flat. He finished his memoirs, *In Sickness and in Health: a Physician Remembers*, in 2006, and they were published after his death. These include a memorable account from 1935 of the appalling racist behaviour of the Hitler Youth in the Allgau, and fascinating details of medical life at St Thomas's Hospital during bombing, in India in the 1940s, and in London during the second half of the twentieth century. He died on 21 April 2006 in the London Clinic, Devonshire Place, Westminster, and was survived by his third wife, Marina, and three children, his eldest daughter having predeceased him. His memorial service was held on 27 September 2006 at St Luke's Church, Chelsea.

RICHARD THOMPSON

Sources R. I. S. Bayliss, 'Almost like any other day', *As you were: VE day, a medical retrospect* (1984) • *Metro* [newspaper] (10 May 2006) • *Daily Telegraph* (25 April 2006) • *The Independent* (26 April 2006) • *The Times* (2 May 2006); (8 May 2006) • *BMJ* (13 May 2006) • Munk, *Roll* • R. Bayliss, *In sickness and in health: a physician remembers* (2007) • Burke, *Peerage* • *WW* (2006) • personal knowledge (2010) • private information (2010) • b. cert. • m. certs. • d. cert.

Archives RCP, Lond. | FILM Oxford Brookes University, interview with Lord Walton of Detchant, 1992

Likenesses photograph, 1973, Photoshot, London • photograph, 1978, Photoshot, London • G. R. Sinclair-Hogg, bronze bust, 1985, priv. coll. • Lady Bayliss, photograph, repro. in Bayliss, *Sickness*, jacket • obituary photographs

Wealth at death £588,116: probate, 30 Aug 2006, *CGPLA Eng. & Wales*

Baynes, Pauline Diana (1922–2008), illustrator, was born on 9 September 1922 at 67 Brunswick Place, Hove, Sussex, the younger daughter of Frederick (otherwise Frederic) William Wilberforce Baynes (1889–1967), a first-class magistrate in the Indian Civil Service, and his wife, Jessie Harriet Maud, *née* Cunningham (1888/9–1958). While still a baby she was taken to Agra where her father was stationed, and her formative experiences were of growing up in India and, in particular, of summers spent at the hill station of Mussoorie. When she was five, her mother left her father and brought her and her sister back to Britain. Baynes found the move very upsetting; she missed her Indian way of life and later recalled with great affection in particular her ayah and her pet monkey. Her first educational experience at a local convent school, where she was mocked for her imagination, her home-made and eccentric clothes, and her ability to speak Hindi, was the source of many unhappy memories. She was happier when she moved to Beaufront School, Camberley, Surrey, aged nine. In particular she enjoyed art 'because it was easy' (*The Independent*, 6 Aug 2008). She later returned briefly to teach art at the school. In 1937 she enrolled at Farnham School of Art and spent two terms studying design before following her much admired elder sister, Angela, to the Slade School of Art, which was relocated to Oxford in 1939. At the Slade she studied illustration and was particularly influenced by Rex Whistler, Arthur Rackham, and the French illustrator Jacques-Marie-Gaston-Onfray de Breville (JOB), whose finely painted animals in the style of medieval illuminations provided inspiration for her own work. She cited the latter and her sister as the biggest influences on her while at the Slade; she also benefited from the mentoring of E. H. Shepard, the highly successful illustrator of A. A. Milne's *Winnie the Pooh* and Kenneth Grahame's *The Wind in the Willows*, who encouraged her illustration and became a lifelong friend.

In 1940 Baynes (who admitted that she had wasted too much of her student career on socializing and parties) left the Slade without completing her course, and with her sister, Angela, volunteered with the Royal Engineers' camouflage development and training centre, based in Farnham Castle, where they made models for use on training courses. She worked there until 1942 when she moved to the hydrographic department at the Admiralty in Bath, where she drew naval charts and maps until 1945. While at Farnham Castle she received her first commission to illustrate a children's book, *Question Mark*, through a fellow worker whose family ran Perry Colour Books. Other commissions followed, both while she was still working at the Admiralty and later when she was acting as housekeeper for her father. These included collections of fairy tales and illustrated children's books for *Country Life* as well as the first book she both wrote and illustrated, *Victoria and the Golden Bird* (1948), the story of a young girl who flew around the world which gave Baynes the chance to illustrate scenes from other cultures.

In 1948 Baynes's work was first seen by the publishers George Allen and Unwin, who showed it to their author J. R. R. Tolkien. Tolkien had discussed his books with other illustrators but had failed to find one whom he felt suited the work. He liked Baynes's work and persuaded his publisher to commission her to illustrate *Farmer Giles of Ham* (1949), an entertaining novel for younger readers about an unsuccessful dragon. Baynes created detailed and witty illustrations in the style of a medieval manuscript which delighted Tolkien, who later complimented Baynes on the illustrations by saying that she had 'reduced my text to a commentary on her drawings' (*Daily Telegraph*, 9 Aug 2008). Baynes illustrated several of Tolkien's later books, including *The Adventures of Tom Bombadil and Other Verses from the Red Book* (1962) and *Smith of Wootton Major* (1967). She also illustrated *Bilbo's Last Song* (1974) after his death. Tolkien's ambition that Baynes would illustrate *The Lord of the Rings* was never fulfilled as to illustrate such a big book would have been unviable financially, but she did create some sketches and maps. As the popularity of *The Lord of the Rings* grew after the reissue of the series in 1966 Baynes redrew and coloured her own versions of Tolkien's original maps, as well as creating images for other ephemera including posters and a slip case for a paperback set of the three volumes. She also designed the cover for the Puffin edition of *The Hobbit* (1961).

Tolkien recommended Baynes as an illustrator to his friend and fellow academic C. S. Lewis, who was enthusiastic about her work; she was commissioned to illustrate the text and create the dust jackets for the original hardback editions of the whole *Chronicles of Narnia* sequence. *The Lion, the Witch and the Wardrobe* (1950) was followed by a book a year for the next six years: *Prince Caspian* (1951), *The Voyage of the 'Dawn Treader'* (1952), *The Silver Chair* (1953), *The Horse and His Boy* (1954), *The Magician's Nephew* (1955), and *The Last Battle* (1956). Black and white and drawn in pen and ink, Baynes's illustrations remained the iconic images of the best-selling stories, especially for the Puffin editions, despite the publishers' attempts to try other 'looks'. For new editions to celebrate the centenary of Lewis's birth in 1998 she hand-coloured her illustrations, adding a new depth to the line. Despite their close association, Baynes only met Lewis twice: first on new year's eve 1949 at a lunch arranged by Tolkien in Magdalen College, Oxford, and second, briefly, at Waterloo Station. Despite the success of the books and her illustrations for them, Baynes never replicated with Lewis the close working relationship she had had with Tolkien and she was hurt by knowing that Lewis, although polite about the illustrations to her face, was critical of them publicly, opining in particular that she could not draw lions.

While her immediate association with magic on account of her Narnia illustrations led to obvious commissions such as for Amabel Williams-Ellis's *The Arabian Nights* (1957), Baynes also illustrated many other kinds of books including *The Puffin Book of Nursery Rhymes* (1963), edited by her friends Iona and Peter Opie. She developed a close working relationship with her editor at Puffin from 1961, Kaye Webb. In 1968 she was awarded the Library Association's Kate Greenaway medal for her illustrations to Grant Uden's *A Dictionary of Chivalry*, published by Longmans in the same year. A substantial volume with almost 600 illustrations and margin decorations, it gave Baynes the opportunity to show many versions of the exquisite and detailed work that characterized her illustrations. She was a great admirer of medieval art and passionate about illuminated manuscripts in particular, and much of her work referenced it. Working in tempera and wash using a dry brush and pen and ink, she was an expert letterer and created many illuminations, frequently depicting the natural world. Overall she illustrated more than a hundred books and in doing so created the definitive look of many modern classics such as Mary Norton's *The Borrowers Avenged* (1982) and Ursula Moray Williams's *The Adventures of the Little Wooden Horse*, for which she created a new Puffin cover in 1985. She was particularly well known for her illustrations of animal stories including the paperback editions of Richard Adams's *Watership Down* (1972) and Rosemary Harris's *The Enchanted Horse* (1981). She worked mostly, in her later years, on religious stories including *All Things Bright and Beautiful* (1986) and *Noah and the Ark* (1988); although a Christian, she was interested in the stories of all religions and was working on an illustrated edition of stories from the Koran in the years before she died. As commissions for her work dwindled, she wrote two further books of her own, *How Dog Began* (1985), a story set in prehistoric times, which she dedicated to eleven of her own dogs, and *King Wenceslas* (1987). She also edited *In the Beginning* (1990), a collection of prayers from around the world, and wrote and illustrated *Questionable Creatures* (2006), a highly entertaining and visually stunning version of a traditional medieval bestiary, complete with a delightful range of unlikely creatures with credible but unproven powers.

Baynes's work was not confined to books. Having sold her illustrations for the *Chronicles of Narnia* for a flat fee rather than a royalty, initially she needed to continue to earn her living. She took on commissions for magazines including the *Illustrated London News* as well as designing and illustrating greetings cards and working on advertising campaigns for Huntley and Palmers biscuits. In 1970 she designed the world's largest crewel embroidery for Plymouth Congregational Church, Minneapolis, and later designed a stained-glass window for her local church in Dockenfield, Hampshire.

On 18 March 1961 Baynes married Fritz Otto Gasch (1919–1988), a German former prisoner of war who was working as a van driver delivering dog's meat, whom she had met only a month earlier. They had one baby who was stillborn and no subsequent children. He later worked as a contract gardener. After his death she was bereft, despite having many friends. Two years later, however, his daughter from his first marriage in Germany rang her up; it was only after the fall of the Berlin Wall that she had been able to find out what had happened to her father and to discover Baynes's relationship to him. The two remained in close touch, and Baynes also developed a relationship with Gasch's grandchildren. She died on 2 August 2008 in Hampshire at her home, Rock Barn Cottage, Heath Hill, Dockenfield, of ischaemic heart disease.

JULIA ECCLESHARE

Sources H. Carpenter and M. Prichard, *The Oxford companion to children's literature* (1984) • 'Illustrating Narnia', *Books For Keeps*, 113 (Nov 1998); booksforkeeps.co.uk/issue/113/childrens-books/articles/other-articles/illustrating-narnia, 20 Sept 2011 • V. Watson, ed., *The Cambridge guide to children's books in English* (2001) • *The Guardian* (6 Aug 2008) • *The Independent* (6 Aug 2008) • *The Times* (9 Aug 2008) • *Daily Telegraph* (9 Aug 2008) • V. Grove, *So much to tell* (2010) • P. Baines, *Puffin by design* (2010) • *WW* (2008) • b. cert. • m. cert. • d. cert.

Archives SOUND BL NSA, interview recording

Likenesses obituary photographs

Wealth at death £990,695: probate, 6 Nov 2008, *CGPLA Eng. & Wales*

Beadle, Jeremy James Anthony Gibson (1948–2008), broadcaster and author, was born at 262 Victoria Park Road, Hackney, London, on 12 April 1948, the son of Marjorie (Marji) Beadle (1921–2004), of 25 St George's Road, Leyton, a clerk for a boxing promoter. His father was a married Fleet Street sports reporter who left Beadle's mother when he discovered she was pregnant. From birth Beadle suffered from Poland's syndrome in the form of a withered right hand, with the fingers joined together, which were to be the subject of many operations. He was brought up on a Kent housing estate by his mother, who influenced his future career by buying him the *Guinness Book of Records* and inspiring his interest in odd facts.

Finding in practical jokes a release from depression, Beadle employed them at Midfield Road junior school, St Paul's Cray, where he discovered little except the fact that he didn't like being told what to do in any context whatsoever. His sympathetic mother frequently had to do her best to smooth things over. When he was ten he was given three years' probation for the theft of a pound note from a teacher's handbag. He failed his eleven-plus examination, and was later expelled from Orpington secondary modern school. He went on CND marches, worked for Oxfam, and played a pantomime dame in a youth club production.

After school came a number of dead-end jobs. Never losing his taste for practical jokes, even if it was not shared by his colleagues, Beadle worked for short periods in a bakery; in a hospital as a porter; for a magazine publisher as a messenger (when he drummed up trade for the magazine's leisure trips by walking fully clothed into the sea); as a fruit picker in Spain; and in Germany, where he had pursued a girlfriend, as a lavatory attendant. There he deliberately allowed the cubicles to run out of toilet paper and filled the urinals with tea in order to suggest that they were overflowing. His tricks on unenthusiastic workmates once led to their stealing all his clothes, leaving him naked in front of 400 women arriving for their shift.

When he returned to Britain Beadle's jobs had more connection with the father he had never met. After a spell as a street photographer in Brighton he founded the town's listings magazine, *What's on in Brighton*, writing its television column before he progressed to the London listings magazine *Time Out*. For the North West Arts Association in 1972 he organized the Bickershaw Festival, a rock festival near Wigan, at which the Grateful Dead appeared. Other festivals followed. 'I was dealing with bullshitters, conmen, hustlers, shady characters and drug addicts', he wrote in his autobiography (*Watch Out!*, 86). He began sending in ideas to television stars including Russell Harty and Kenny Everett. For the *Daily Express* he wrote a 'Jeremy Beadle's today's the day' strip, about odd anniversaries, reflecting his lifelong interest in and collection of esoteric facts. He also began supplying these to radio and television game shows, and later published compendia, beginning with *Today's the Day* (1979) and ending with *Beadle's Miscellany* (2007).

From 1979 Beadle began presenting *Nightline* on LBC Radio. His earliest participation in television was as a writer. In 1980 he wrote *April Fool* for the BBC, a history of practical jokes hosted by Dave Lee Travis. He first achieved fame as a performer in the television show *Game for a Laugh* (1981–5), a revamp of his 'Gotcha!' formula, which was turned down by the BBC, in which he staged and recorded the reactions of victims of various practical jokes, such as shocking an office worker on the fifth floor who thought her husband was miles away but suddenly saw him outside her window (on a window cleaner's cradle). Originally he was meant to be solely a writer for the show, but so many celebrated presenters turned down appearing on the programme that he was drafted in.

Only a year after *Game for a Laugh* ended, Beadle had his own show, *Beadle's About*, which ran from 1986 to 1996 through eleven series. Instead of studio-bound adventures Beadle went on location with increasingly daring and dangerous tricks. These included telling a man that his house had been taken over for a car park—this being the only occasion on which the victim actually hit his torturer. The programmes sold well around the world. Starting at the same time, but lasting only a year, came his solo show, *People Do the Funniest Things* (1986–7), in which he presented archive material of, in effect, assorted pratfalls. The quiz show *Chain Letters* lasted from 1987 to 1988. Beadle also achieved high audience ratings with *You've Been Framed!* (1990–97), in which viewers were allowed to film their own mishaps for themselves (usually in the form of pratfalls), and *Beadle's Hot Shots* (1996–7), based on viewers' camcorder spoofs of star turns.

The public on the whole vastly enjoyed thinking Beadle a terrible man, as indicated by a 2001 public survey to establish who was the most hated man in Britain. Beadle was second only to Saddam Hussein. He had a mental attitude that resisted such put-downs. 'The fact that people don't like me has nothing to do with me', he said. 'It's because they feel guilty about laughing at the practical jokes I play. So they transfer their guilt on to me' (*Daily Mail*, 1 Jan 1993). He was appointed MBE in 2001. He was a fund-raiser for the Foundation for Children with Leukaemia long before he himself was diagnosed with it, and he helped many other charities; it was estimated that he had raised some £100 million for various charities by the time of his death. He lost a kidney to cancer in 2004. He died of pneumonia at the London Clinic, 20 Devonshire Place, Westminster, on 30 January 2008, three years after the diagnosis of leukaemia. He was survived by his wife, Susan Maria (Sue; *b.* 1944), daughter of James Marshall, secondary school teacher, whom he had married on 6 February 2004 after they had been partners for twenty-one years, his daughters Cassie and Bonnie, and his stepchildren Leo and Clare. DENNIS BARKER

Sources J. Beadle, *Watch out!* (1998) • *The Times* (31 Jan 2008) • *Daily Telegraph* (31 Jan 2008) • *The Guardian* (31 Jan 2008) • *The Independent* (1 Feb 2008) • b. cert. • m. cert. • d. cert.

Archives FILM BFINA, 'Jeremy Beadle: a tribute', ITV Productions, ITV1, 4 Feb 2008 • BFINA, 'An audience without … Jeremy Beadle', M. Thomas (director), ITV1, 16 May 2008 • BFINA, current affairs, documentary, light entertainment, and performance footage | SOUND BL NSA, documentary and current affairs recordings

Likenesses photographs, 1972–2007, Getty Images, London • photographs, 1980–2007, Rex Features, London • photographs, 1983–2006, Photoshot, London • photographs, 1983–2007, PA Photos, London • obituary photographs • photographs, Camera Press, London

Wealth at death £1,983,197: probate, 22 May 2008, *CGPLA Eng. & Wales*

Beckett, Allan Harry (1914–2005), engineer, was born on 4 March 1914 at 294 Central Park Road, East Ham, London, the son of George William Harry Beckett, accounting clerk, and his wife, Emma Louise, *née* Stokes. He was originally given the first name Basil, soon changed to Allan. He was educated locally in east London and at London University, where he graduated in engineering. After serving an apprenticeship with Sanders and Foster, steel work and structural engineers, in 1936 he became an engineering assistant with A. J. Brindle, consulting engineers.

At the outbreak of the Second World War in September 1939 Beckett volunteered for service. In January 1940 he was posted to no. 13 war party for training as a sapper. He was selected as a potential officer and commissioned at no. 2 Railway Training Establishment where he was greatly influenced by Lieutenant-Colonel W. T. Everall, who had gained inventive experience repairing railway bridges, destined to be invaluable in Normandy. Under Everall, Beckett produced drawings and design models for bridging companies in the field and won a reputation for getting things done.

Planning for a return to the continent began after Dunkirk. Winston Churchill must have recalled the landings on open beaches at Gallipoli in 1915. In his historic minute of 30 May 1942 to Admiral Lord Louis Mountbatten, chief of combined operations, outlining the basic design of a landing dependent on a floating roadway connecting pierheads for unloading cargo vessels that would rise and fall with the tide, he urged that this problem be solved immediately, concluding his note, 'Don't argue the matter. The difficulties will argue themselves.' In September 1943 at Quebec the allied high command agreed that the assault across the Channel should take place on a Normandy beachhead not later than May or June 1944. Artificial harbours, codenamed Mulberry, would supply the armies until the great port of Cherbourg should receive troops and their weapons from across the Atlantic.

Much experimentation on the various components was by then in progress, the floating roadway and pierhead taking shape at Wigtown, where the rise and fall of the tide was similar to that in Normandy. As a member of the War Office transportation group, Beckett kept a close eye on developments, which were a well-kept secret. (The supremacy of the Royal Air Force ensured that the Germans gained little knowledge of what was afoot.) In particular he provided technical advice for the two floating roadways known by the codename Whale. Everall was able to design a pontoon bridge able to ride a rough sea without over-stressing any of its components. Beckett was advised by him to strengthen the moorings of the British and American bridges. This led to Beckett's invention of mooring shuttles for severe weather. Known as Camel, they had trumpet-shaped restrainers (later called kite anchors).

In the weeks before D-day the Mulberry components had to be assembled all over the country, ending up at Marchwood, near Southampton, and Richborough (once used by the Romans). On 2 June 1944 Beckett set sail with a tow from the Isle of Dogs and attached himself to 21st army group, the British invading force, as technical adviser in the field. He arrived at Arromanches, the only disturbance being attacks from German E-boats. During the early days of the landings he became concerned about the skill of the American 'seabees' who were trying to complete their floating roadways before the British. His advice to anchor them 'As tight as a lady's bodice' was ignored. When a storm began to blow on the evening of 19 June a number of caissons and an ill-conceived floating breakwater broke up the American Mulberry, rendering it useless. The British Mulberry now became the only artificial harbour for unloading stores and equipment for the allied forces in the battle area. It continued to be used until Antwerp, the nearest port to the German frontier, had been cleared of mines by 19 November 1944.

Beckett was made a military MBE for his work on the indispensable floating roadways and received a £3000 award for his invention of the kite anchor. With this money he was able to build a house in Farnborough, Kent, where he lived until his death. After being demobilized in 1946 he became a partner with Sir Bruce White, Wolfe Barry & Partners. He now began to play an important role in port construction. He was responsible as senior partner for the development of techniques for the mini hydraulic model studies as a tool for designing new ports and their application for Brunei, Dammam in Saudi Arabia, and Tripoli in Libya. He was responsible for London's flood mitigation proposals including a feasibility study and subsequent design of lifting sector gates for the Thames Barrier.

Beckett married Ida Gwladys James in 1949, and they had two sons, Michael and Tim, and a daughter, Siân. Tim Beckett followed in his father's footsteps as a civil engineer. When Allan Beckett retired in 1987 he became consultant to Beckett Rankine, a firm of marine consulting engineers set up by Tim Beckett with Sir Bruce White's grandson, Gordon Rankine. Allan Beckett was himself a keen yachtsman and had kept his boat afloat throughout the war. He liked to sail in the English Channel, exploring the tidal waters. At the same time he kept abreast of engineering developments. In 1977 he had built a cupronickel yacht. Even in his early eighties he was experimenting with new types of breakwater and lifesaving equipment. He died at his home, Thistledown, Wood Way, Farnborough Park, of peripheral vascular disease, on 19 June 2005, a year after he had been present at Arromanches for the unveiling of a memorial to the engineers and contractors who were involved in the building of Mulberry. He was buried in Oare churchyard, almost in sight of the Thames estuary where the Whale convoys sailed to the Channel. He was survived by his wife and their three children.

GUY HARTCUP

Sources W. J. Hodge, 'The Mulberry invasion harbours', *Structural Engineer*, 24/3 (March 1946), 125–98 • *The civil engineer in war*, 2: *Docks and harbours* (1948) • G. Hartcup, *Code name Mulberry* (1977) • A. Harris, 'The Mulberry harbours', *Royal Engineers Journal*, 108 (April 1994) • A. E. M. Walter, 'The Mulberry harbours', *Royal Engineers Journal*, 112 (April 1998) • A. H. Beckett papers, priv. coll. • H. H. Hickling and I. MacKillop, 'The story of the Mulberries', TNA: PRO, CAB 106 • *The Times* (11 July 2005) • *Daily Telegraph* (30 June 2005) • private information (2010) [Tim Beckett, son] • b. cert. • d. cert.

Archives priv. coll.

Likenesses T. Beckett, photograph, 2004, priv. coll.

Wealth at death £2,312,490: probate, 10 Nov 2005, *CGPLA Eng. & Wales*

Bedford [*née* von Schoenebeck], **Sybille** (1911–2006), writer, was born on 16 March 1911 at Charlottenburg, on the outskirts of Berlin, Germany, the second daughter of Maximilian Josef von Schoenebeck (1863–1925) and only child of his second wife, Elizabeth, *née* Bernhardt. Her father was descended from a long line of bureaucrats and minor landed gentry; his father, August von Schoenebeck, was a judge, both of whose sons entered the army. Maximilian von Schoenebeck's first wife, Melanie Herz, died in 1905, leaving a daughter, Maximiliana Henrietta, born in 1899. His second marriage, in 1910, enabled him to buy a small estate at Feldkirch in Baden, south Germany, and it was there that Sybille spent her childhood. Her half-Jewish mother was a Catholic convert, and Sybille was brought up in the Roman faith, educated somewhat haphazardly at home and for a brief period at a nearby Ursuline convent.

As her mother was frequently absent, absorbed in a series of glamorous love affairs, Sybille von Schoenebeck was left mainly in the care of her father. It was from him that she imbibed a knowledge and love of food and wine that lasted a lifetime. Her parents divorced in 1921, and four years later her father died, consigning her to the care of her mother and of an Italian stepfather, an architect, Norberto Marchesani. For the next few years this threesome travelled through Italy, with Sybille at intervals dispatched to England to continue her education. It was while attending hearings at the law courts in the Strand that she first became fascinated by the judicial process, the subject of much of her non-fiction writing.

The family finally settled in Sanary sur mer in the south of France, and there Sybille met the novelist and philosopher Aldous Huxley and his wife, Maria Nys, 'the two people I owe most to,' she wrote, 'who educated me morally [and] intellectually' (*Quicksands*, 18). She later completed an acclaimed two-volume biography of Huxley, published in 1973–4. At Sanary, too, she came to know a number of English writers, among them Cyril Connolly and Brian Howard, and was drawn into a circle of German refugee intellectuals, forming a particular friendship with the children of Thomas Mann, Klaus and Erika. In 1933 she contributed an article to Klaus Mann's magazine, *Die Sammlung*, criticizing the Nazi regime, and this, together with the discovery by the German authorities of her Jewish ancestry, led to her bank account being frozen. Aware of the danger of her situation, she left for London, where the Huxleys helped to arrange a marriage of convenience to a club attendant sixteen years her senior, Walter Croan, otherwise Walter Bedford. They married at Westminster register office on 15 November 1935, with Aldous Huxley as a witness. Although the union was quickly dissolved, it had crucially conferred not only a British passport but the name by which Sybille Bedford became known to generations of readers.

Although her mother had by this time died, Sybille Bedford returned to France, remaining until 1940 when she left for California, scraping a living as a secretary, journalist, and translator. After the war she spent a year travelling in Mexico before moving to Rome. Determined to pursue

Sybille Bedford (1911–2006), by Lucinda Douglas-Menzies, 1990

a literary career, she was much encouraged by two writer friends, Martha Gellhorn and Allanah Harper, the latter supporting the almost penniless Bedford with a small income. Fluent in four languages, she chose to write in English, the rope that saved her, as she put it, 'from drifting awash in the fluidities of multi-lingualism that surrounded me' (*Jigsaw*, 70). In 1953 she published her first book, *The Sudden View: a Mexican Journey*, later reissued as *A Visit to Don Otavio*, widely regarded as a classic of travel literature. This was followed in 1956 by a novel, *A Legacy*, the first stage in a journey of imaginative autobiography culminating in 1989 in her penultimate work, *Jigsaw*. *A Legacy* was widely acclaimed, Evelyn Waugh referring to its author as 'a new writer of remarkable accomplishment' (*The Spectator*, 13 April 1956). There were further novels, *A Favourite of the Gods* (1963) and *A Compass Error* (1968), as well as four works of non-fiction: *The Best We Can Do* (1958), an account of the murder trial of Bodkin Adams, *The Faces of Justice* (1961), describing proceedings in European courts of law, and two volumes of collected articles, *As It Was* (1990) and *Pleasures and Landscapes* (2003). Her last book, *Quicksands* (2005), was a remarkable if elusive work of autobiography, dedicated to her long-term companion and executor, Aliette Martin.

For over thirty years Bedford led a peripatetic existence until in 1979 she made a permanent home in Chelsea, London. She was a fellow of the Royal Society of Literature, a vice-president of PEN, appointed OBE in 1981, and elected a companion of literature in 1994. Small and slender, with an almost heroic disregard for personal adornment, she had a mesmerizing personality and was intensely curious, fiercely intelligent, prone to frightful anxieties, and endowed with enormous kindness, sensitivity, and charm. She conducted several intense love affairs, one with a married woman in Rome, Evelyn Gendel, and for twenty years with the American novelist, Eda Lord. Despite tormenting difficulties with her eyesight, she was a dedicated writer, who brought to all her work a great sensitivity, a supremely elegant style, and an incorruptible morality. She died at the Lister Hospital, London, on 17 February 2006 and was cremated at Mortlake crematorium ten days later. A memorial meeting was held at the Reform Club, Pall Mall, on 5 June 2006.

SELINA HASTINGS

Sources *Genealogisches Handbuch des Adels: adelige Haüser*, vol. 17 (1989) · S. Bedford, *Jigsaw* (1989) · S. Guppy, *Paris Review*, 126 (1993) [interview] · S. Bedford, *Quicksands* (2005) · *The Independent* (20 Feb 2006) · *The Times* (21 Feb 2006) · *Daily Telegraph* (21 Feb 2006) · *The Guardian* (21 Feb 2006) · *WW* (2006) · Ransom HRC, Bedford archive · personal knowledge (2010) · private information (2010) · m. cert.

Archives Ransom HRC

Likenesses Snowdon, photographs, 1957–89, Camera Press, London · T. Smith, photograph, 1989, Camera Press, London · L. Douglas-Menzies, bromide fibre print, 1990, NPG [*see illus.*]

Wealth at death £1,264,417: probate, 20 June 2006, *CGPLA Eng. & Wales*

Beeson, Paul Bruce (1908–2006), physician, was born at 112 South Sixth Street, Livingston, Montana, USA, on 18 October 1908, the second son of John Bradley Beeson (1872–1969), surgeon and general practitioner, and his wife, Martha Gerard, *née* Ash (1878–1969), schoolteacher, and daughter of Thomas Ash of Missouri. The family left Livingston in 1916 for Anchorage, Alaska, where Beeson's father became surgeon to the Alaska Railroad. After Anchorage high school, which he left aged sixteen, Beeson studied business administration at the University of Washington, but within three months was persuaded by his mother to change to medicine. He later followed his brother to McGill University, and graduated MD in 1933. After an internship at Philadelphia, he joined his father and brother in Wooster, Ohio, where the work combined family practice with general surgery, obstetrics, gynaecology, and urology. Beeson had no talent for surgery and after two years decided on further training in medicine. After an unpromising beginning in the private service of New York Hospital, he found a post in Oswald Avery's team at the Rockefeller Institute, where he was immediately stimulated by his first experience of research, in the use of serum antibodies in the treatment of pneumonia. There began a lifelong interest in infectious disease. In 1939, after two years at Rockefeller, he became chief resident to Soma Weiss at the Peter Bent Brigham Hospital at Harvard. Weiss was an inspirational bedside clinician and teacher, a man whom Beeson greatly admired and on whom he modelled his own career.

In 1940 the American Red Cross–Harvard Field Hospital Unit was established in Salisbury, Wiltshire, to study the

Paul Bruce Beeson (1908–2006), by unknown photographer

epidemiology of diseases resulting from crowded conditions in the armed forces and in bomb shelters. Beeson was appointed its chief physician. Nurses came from the USA, among them Barbara Neal (*b.* 1917), who had graduated from the school of nursing at St Luke's, Chicago, in 1936. The daughter of Ray Cursons Neal of Buffalo, New York, she first met Beeson in London and they soon became engaged. But in July 1942 the unit was disbanded and its staff returned to America. Beeson had a congenital abnormality of the urinary tract and so was unfit for military service. Eugene Stead, a colleague at Harvard who had become professor of medicine at Emory University, offered him an associate professorship there. He and Barbara sailed home from Bristol, married at Snyder, New York, on 10 July 1942, and a month later were in Atlanta. They had two sons, John and Peter, and a daughter, Judith.

Beeson delighted in his clinical work and teaching and soon linked the development of the hepatitis occurring after blood transfusion in patients at Emory with that arising after administration of anti-mumps serum to soldiers in England, and so was one of the first to associate blood products with hepatitis. It was at Emory too that he began his work on bacterial endocarditis and the mechanisms of fever. In 1946 he succeeded Stead as professor of medicine at Emory. He continued his work on the nature of bacterial pyrogens and the role of white cells in producing fever. In 1948 began his co-editorship of *Harrison's Principles of Internal Medicine*, which became the rival of the *Cecil–Loeb Textbook of Medicine*, then the leading authority in the field. His reputation as a clinician and teacher was growing and in 1952 he took on the Ensign professorship and chair of the department of medicine at Yale, where he was soon recognized to be an inspirational chief. At Yale he struggled to preserve general medicine against the increasing trend to ever narrower specialization. Meanwhile his demonstration that polymorphonuclear white cells could produce a substance capable of raising body temperature (what he called endogenous pyrogen, now known as interleukin-1) foreshadowed the later discovery of the cytokines. In the 1950s infectious diseases were thought to have been largely defeated by antibiotics and Beeson's interest in them was unusual and prescient.

Increasing administrative work at Yale began seriously to impede Beeson's teaching and research and in 1958 he took a sabbatical year at St Mary's Hospital in London, investigating the susceptibility of the kidney to infection. In the same year he returned to editorial work, joining Walsh McDermott as the new co-editor of the *Cecil–Loeb Textbook of Medicine*; he remained one of the editors until 1982. Back at Yale, in 1961 he and Robert Petersdorf published, in the journal *Medicine*, one of the most quoted papers in the medical literature, 'Fever of unexplained origin'. Over the next four years he continued to lead a remarkably talented group of juniors, many of whom were to go on to prestigious posts. Increasingly, though, he became irked by ever more administrative work, so that when Sir George Pickering, regius professor of medicine at Oxford, invited him to consider the Nuffield professorship of clinical medicine, he was immediately attracted and took up that chair, together with a fellowship of Magdalen College, in 1965. Among the reasons he gave for moving was the possibility of continuing as a generalist, to nurture bedside clinical skills and escape from the narrow specialization he so deplored in America. He was concerned, too, about the 'industrialization of medicine' with the mechanical overuse of investigations driven by the rigid protocols of 'cook-book' medicine. In 1966, as president of the Association of American Physicians, he spoke controversially of his concern about the increasing tendency of academic physicians to devote most of their time to laboratory research and ever growing clinical specialization, commenting that 'I don't see how these tendencies can fail to have detrimental effects on our competence as physicians and as teachers of clinical medicine' (Rapport, *Physician*, 218).

Of his arrival in Oxford Beeson wrote 'There I had a firm with 40 beds, a house staff of six and five full members of the department. I could work again with the young, with patients and could even return to some research activity. It was wonderful' (private information). Soon he was to lead distinguished research into bacterial endocarditis and the pathophysiology of eosinophil cells. Although Beeson found that getting things changed in Oxford could be deeply frustrating, he managed to achieve by personality and leadership what was not possible solely by virtue of his professorial position. Together he and Pickering presided over an extraordinary rise in the national and international standing of the Oxford clinical school.

Beeson returned home in 1974 to take up a veterans administration distinguished professorship at the University of Washington, continuing clinical work, teaching, editing, and supporting new causes by travelling the country to argue against nuclear proliferation and for the need for better care of the elderly. He served on the National Research Council on Aging and became editor of the *Journal of the American Geriatric Society*, greatly raising the profile of a neglected area in education and clinical practice.

He retired at last in 1981, but remained active, in 1986 producing the *Oxford Companion to Medicine*, with Sir Ronald Bodley Scott and (after Scott's death) Sir John Walton. He also remained concerned about the way his profession was moving. In 2000 in an interview in the *Annals of Internal Medicine* he said, 'I fear losing sight of the relationship between the doctor and the patient ... and it seems that many trends in the last half of this century have conspired against it' (Lee, 78).

Beeson was a reserved, even shy man of immense integrity, revered by patients, students, and colleagues alike. Richard Rapport wrote of him 'sitting beside a patient on an open ward, surrounded by students, listening to the clues, fears, and questions embedded in the story of a single sick person' (Rapport, *Physician*, 258). Others wrote of his graciousness, diligence, and intense concern for people. He was frequently likened to Sir William Osler in that both grew up on frontiers; both went to McGill; both edited the foremost textbooks of medicine in their time, and both held chairs at Oxford. Both also founded their reputations on their skills as great bedside clinicians and inspirational teachers.

Beeson became an honorary KBE in 1973 and received honorary degrees from Emory, McGill, and Yale universities, and from Albany and Ohio medical colleges. He was an honorary fellow of Magdalen College, Oxford, a fellow of the American Academy of Arts and Sciences, and served both as president of the Association of American Physicians and master of the American College of Physicians. The Paul B. Beeson professorship of internal medicine at Yale was endowed in 1981 and the medical service at Yale also carried Beeson's name. Paul B. Beeson career development awards in aging research began in 1995. He died of aspiration pneumonia following a stroke, on 14 August 2006, in Exeter, New Hampshire, where he and his wife had moved in 2002. She survived him, along with their three children. JOHN G. G. LEDINGHAM

Sources R. V. Lee, 'Changing times: reflections on a professional lifetime, an interview with Paul Beeson', *Annals of Internal Medicine*, 132/1 (2000), 71–9 • R. Rapport, *Physician: the life of Paul Beeson* (Fort Lee, NJ, 2001) • *New York Times* (18 Aug 2006) • *Yale Bulletin and Calendar*, 35/1 (1 Sept 2006) • *The Independent* (11 Sept 2006) • *The Lancet*, 368/9543 (2006), 1232 • *BMJ*, 333 (16 Oct 2006), 604 • G. H. Stollerman, 'Remembering Paul Beeson', *Journal of the American Geriatrics Society*, 54/11 (2006), 1637–8 • T. T. Yoshikawa, 'Paul Beeson, MD: today's Sir William Osler', *Journal of the American Geriatrics Society*, 54/11 (2006), 1639–40 • J. Ledingham, 'Paul Bruce Beeson', *Oxford Medicine* (Feb 2007), 14–15 • R. Rapport, 'Infectious disease, internal medicine and Paul Beeson', *Yale Medicine* (winter 2007) • *WW* (2006) • private information (2010) [Barbara Beeson, widow; John Beeson, son; W. C. Gibson; American Federation for Aging Research] • personal knowledge (2010)

Likenesses obituary photographs • photograph, Yale University, school of medicine [*see illus.*] • photographs, repro. in Rapport, *Physician* • photographs, repro. in Lee, 'Changing times'

Bell, (Ernest) Arthur (1926–2006), plant chemist, was born on 20 June 1926 at 7 Balmoral Terrace, Gosforth, Northumberland, the son of a Northumbrian chartered accountant, Albert Bell, and his Welsh wife, Rachel Enid, *née* Williams. He liked to be known by his second name,

(Ernest) Arthur Bell (1926–2006), by A. McRobb

Arthur. He was educated at Dame Allan's School, Newcastle, and graduated BSc in 1946 from King's College, Newcastle upon Tyne, then part of the University of Durham, before gaining a doctorate from Trinity College, Dublin, in 1950. He married Jean Swinton Ogilvie in 1952 and they had two sons and one daughter.

Bell was trained as a chemist and began his career working for a brief period at ICI in 1946 but soon moved back to an academic position at Trinity College, Dublin, in 1947; he became a lecturer in biochemistry at King's College, London, in 1953 and a reader from 1964 to 1968. He then held a professorship of botany at the University of Texas, Austin, from 1968 to 1972 before returning to King's College, London, in 1972 as professor of biology and head of the department of plant sciences. While there he also served as chairman of the school of biological sciences (1974–80) then dean of natural science (1980–81). In 1981 he somewhat surprised his chemical colleagues by accepting the directorship of the Royal Botanic Gardens, Kew, a post he held until 1988.

Bell had a distinguished career both as a scientist and as a botanic garden director. His work in plant biochemistry concentrated on non-protein amino acids of plants. He applied this knowledge to problems of plant ecology, systematics, and the use of forage plants for the developing world. His study of plant toxins was of considerable significance to medicine and nutrition. On a visit to Australia he collected seeds of the Moreton Bay chestnut and later his research team isolated the polyhydroxyalkaloid castanospermine that shows activity against HIV. A toxic substance that Bell and his collaborators isolated from a species of *Cycas* has been shown to be the cause of some types of motor neurone disease. He published over 140 scientific papers, beginning in 1948 with a paper in *The Lancet* on the mode of action of the sulphonamide derivatives and later including ten in *Nature*. His varied scientific researches gave him a great interest in sustainable living and the conservation of topsoil as vital to human survival, and he was an early proponent of both these areas. As director of the Royal Botanic Gardens he saw them through the difficult transition from being a government department to semi-autonomy as a non-departmental government body, as was called for in the National Heritage Act of 1983. During his time as director the historic palm house at Kew was restored to its original glory, the new state-of-the-art Princess of Wales Conservatory was built, and opened in January 1987, and the Sir Joseph Banks Centre for Economic Botany was completed. This last was a pioneer building for its environmentally friendly design incorporating a turf roof and a heat pump system in the water table. Bell had to cope with the effects of the storm that destroyed many trees at Kew and its sister garden, Wakehurst Place, in October 1987. Bell's sense of humour and personnel skills helped to maintain the morale of Kew's staff during this traumatic period. On retirement from Kew he continued his chemical research through honorary appointments in Texas and at King's College. He continued his interest in botanic gardens by helping with the development of gardens in Austin and Galveston, Texas, and at Marks Hall, near Coggeshall in Essex.

Bell had the straightforward frankness and friendliness frequently associated with Northumbrians, and this was complemented by his great sense of humour. He always saw the funny side of any situation. He was what might be termed a 'people person' and his former staff and students were struck by his understanding and accessibility. He was equally at home with royalty, government ministers, and the most junior member of his staff, whose name he would always know. He was an excellent teacher and in his lectures his humour was always evident. He served on the council of the Royal Horticultural Society (1985–9), as vice-president of the Linnean Society of London (1982–6), as president of the plant biology section of the British Association for the Advancement of Science (1985–6), and as honorary botanical adviser to the Commonwealth War Graves Commission (1982–8). During his career he held visiting professorships at the University of Reading and King's College, London, and at the universities of Kansas, Texas, British Columbia, and Sierra Leone. He was made a fellow of the Royal Institute of Chemistry (later the Royal Society of Chemistry) in 1961 and of the Institute of Biology in 1987, became an honorary life member of the Phytochemical Society of Europe in 1985, and was appointed CB in 1988. Latterly he lived in Wimbledon, London, and he died on 11 June 2006 at St George's Hospital, Tooting, of bronchopneumonia and heart failure. He was survived by his wife, Jean, and their three children.

GHILLEAN T. PRANCE

Sources *The Independent* (22 June 2006) • *Daily Telegraph* (27 June 2006) • *Evening Chronicle* [Newcastle] (27 June 2006) • *The Times* (17 July 2006) • P. Nunn, memorial service address, 17 Oct 2006, www.kcl.ac.uk/schools/biohealth/news/nunn.html, 5 Feb 2008 • *WW* (2006) • A. Bell, curriculum vitae, priv. coll. • personal knowledge (2010) • private information (2010) [Jean Bell, widow; P. Churcher; G. Lucas] • b. cert. • d. cert.

Likenesses A. McRobb, photograph, RBG Kew [*see illus.*] • obituary photographs

Wealth at death £747,255: probate, 10 Nov 2006, *CGPLA Eng. & Wales*

Bell, (Alexander) Scott (1941–2007), insurance and financial services executive, was born on 4 December 1941 at Dunrowan, Falkirk, the son of William Scott Bell, physician, and his wife, (Catherine) Irene Alexandra, *née* Traill. He was educated at Daniel Stewart's College in Edinburgh. After leaving school at the age of seventeen he went to work as a trainee actuary for the Edinburgh-based Standard Life Assurance Company, where he remained for the next forty-four years. At the time Standard Life had withdrawn from many of its overseas markets, but was still a powerful force in the United Kingdom, Ireland, and Canada. On 12 October 1965, at Wardie parish church, Primrose Bank Road, Leith, he married Veronica Jane (Nicky) Simpson, a 21-year-old hairdresser, and daughter of James Flucker Simpson, company director. They had two sons and a daughter.

Bell qualified as an actuary in 1966 and was assigned as assistant, later deputy, actuary for the Canadian business, but based in Edinburgh. In 1971 the sales organization in the United Kingdom was split up on a regional basis and in 1974 Bell was appointed to run the south-east of England. He was joined by Tom King and Jim Stretton. The experience they gained in London and the south-east was to be invaluable when they later came to manage the whole enterprise.

Bell returned to Scotland in 1979 as assistant general manager (finance) with responsibility for investments. The removal of controls on overseas investments by the incoming Conservative government allowed him to follow a much more adventurous investment strategy than his predecessor, with the proportion of the 'free funds' held in overseas securities raised to 15 per cent. When the management was restructured in 1985 he was promoted to be general manager (finance), with Stretton in charge of operations and King marketing. The new team focused on developing Standard Life as a brand, raising its profile in an increasingly competitive market place.

Bell was appointed group managing director and actuary in March 1988, with Stretton as his deputy. From the outset they realized that if Standard Life was to hold its own against Prudential, Legal and General, Norwich Union, and Scottish Widows, it was essential to develop a ten-year strategic plan. The core objective was to provide

> with profits contracts on which the ultimate returns will be considerably greater than those available on comparable policies of other life offices, and to do so in the maximum volume consequently possible without detriment to the maintenance of an appropriate level of financial strength (Moss, 321)

This was a bold agenda. A business model was developed

to ensure that the company could withstand the worst possible investment conditions, like the 1974 bear market. An essential component of the strategy was to extend the company's product range, to invest in the existing businesses in Canada and Ireland, and to explore new business opportunities in overseas markets.

The strategy had also to take into account the likely impact of the Financial Services Act of 1988 on independent financial advisers, the company's principal distribution channel. In February 1989 it was announced that the Halifax was to become a tied agent of Standard Life, only marketing its products under the terms of the act. This link with one of the country's biggest building societies reflected the excellent working relationship between Bell and Jim Birrell, the chief executive of the Halifax. This was to lead to proposals for greater co-operation that were rejected by the Standard Life board in 1994.

By the end of 1992 the first attempt at coherent planning was complete. Bell wrote to all employees in the United Kingdom and Ireland outlining the organizational and procedural changes, particularly the need to shorten chains of communication. Central to success was the engagement of all staff in delivering 'total customer satisfaction' at a time when the industry was facing serious criticism for mis-selling (Moss, 339–40). Fundamental to the strategy and dear to Bell's heart was the concept of mutuality, which in the financial services sector as a whole was under threat, with a raft of public flotations of mutual societies. For Bell the advantage of mutuality was that all the profits were available for distribution to with-profits policy holders. The disadvantage was the lack of capital provided by shareholders.

In 1998 a new state of the art head office was opened at the foot of Lothian Road, symbolizing the growing confidence of Bell and his team. At the same time, after a review of investment management, Bell decided to create a separate company to manage all Standard Life's assets and market a range of investment products and services. It was anticipated that this initiative would allow Standard Life to compete effectively for managed funds. The new company was launched with £60 billion of managed funds in November 1998. A component of the review was the decision in 1996 to sell Standard Life's 32 per cent stake in the Bank of Scotland. Free of this connection, the following year Standard Life Bank was launched to provide deposit taking services for customers and to sell mortgages. Overseas Bell drove through the merger of the Canadian business with the Calgary-based Sovereign Life in 1992–3 and the launch of a new range of savings and retirement products. From the time he assumed office he was determined to take Standard Life back into the European market, which it had left in the inter-war years. Acquisitions were made in Spain and Germany in 1993 and 1994. More adventurous was the return to the Far East with joint ventures in India and China in 1995.

The end of the century was marked by an aggressive campaign led by the Australian Fred Woollard to force Standard Life to demutualize. This was against all Bell's cherished principles and, backed by the board, he resolutely defended the concept of mutuality. Stretton recalled that the campaign 'showed the loyalty of his staff and the extent to which he inspired them' (*The Independent*, 28 Aug 2008). The policy holders voted 54 to 46 per cent to remain mutual. Bell retired in 2002 and remained silent about the company's problems that led finally to flotation in 2004.

Scott Bell was a commanding presence in the insurance and financial services sector in Edinburgh. He was a big man in every sense of the word. Under his leadership Standard Life had remained independent when others, such as Scottish Widows, had been taken over, and had increased its business both in the United Kingdom and abroad at a very difficult time for the sector. His directorships included the Bank of Scotland (1988–96), Hammerson plc (1988–98), the Universities Superannuation Scheme (1996–2005), and the Dumfermline Building Society (2002–7). He was honorary Canadian consul in Scotland (1994–2004), and was awarded an honorary doctorate by Heriot-Watt University in 1997. He was a keen golfer. He died of cancer of the colon at St Columba's Hospice, Edinburgh, on 23 August 2007, and was survived by his wife and children. MICHAEL S. MOSS

Sources M. Moss, *The building of Europe's largest mutual life company: Standard Life, 1825–2000* (2000) • *The Independent* (28 Aug 2008) • *The Times* (3 Sept 2007) • *Daily Telegraph* (3 Sept 2007) • *WW* (2007) • personal knowledge (2011) • private information (2011) • b. cert. • m. cert. • d. cert.

Likenesses B. Curtis, photographs, 2000, PA Photos, London • photograph, 2000, Photoshot, London • obituary photographs • photographs, Standard Life plc, Edinburgh

Bell, Thomas George [Tom] (**1933–2006**), actor, was born at 33 Ramsey Road, Allerton, Liverpool, on 2 August 1933, one of seven children of James Guthrie Bell, a ship's carpenter in the merchant navy, and his wife, Gladys May, *née* Smith. During the Second World War he was evacuated to Morecambe, Lancashire, where he lived with three different families and attended Euston Road secondary modern school. After acting in school plays he sought a career on the stage and joined a local repertory company before training at the Bradford Civic Theatre. He subsequently acted in rep in Liverpool, Swansea, and, with the Shannon Players, in Dublin. On 22 October 1960 he married Lois Dainty, a twenty-year-old actress (as Lois Dane), and daughter of John Dainty, civil servant. They had one son, Aran.

Bell had made his television début in 1959, as a boxer in an episode of the crime drama *Dial 999*, before being cast in two productions in ITV's groundbreaking *Armchair Theatre* series of contemporary plays: as one of three sailors on shore leave in Liverpool in the writer Alun Owen's *No Trams to Lime Street* (1959) and as the young clerk Albert Stokes, whose controlling mother worries about his leading an 'unclean' life with girls, in Harold Pinter's *A Night Out* (1960). He also starred on stage in Owen's first full-length play, *Progress to the Park*, about four friends who pass from youth to manhood during a warm summer weekend in Liverpool, which was performed at the Saville

Theatre in London's West End in 1961. These dramas were part of the revolution taking place in the arts, which were beginning to depict working-class culture as it really was, and Bell followed his first feature film, *The Criminal* (1960), written by Owen, with *The Kitchen* (1961), an adaptation of the Royal Court Theatre's production of Arnold Wesker's play set in the basement kitchen of a large restaurant and illustrating the dehumanizing nature of the workplace.

Bell made his greatest impact in *The L-Shaped Room* (1962), one of the landmark film dramas of the period, adapted by its director, Bryan Forbes, from Lynn Reid Banks's best-selling novel. Bell acted Toby, the brooding, bitter young writer in a seedy London boarding-house who falls for a pregnant, unmarried Frenchwoman, played by Leslie Caron. Great predictions were made for Bell, but he found that good starring roles in film were in short supply after his anti-establishment attitude led him to heckle the duke of Edinburgh at the 1963 British Film Academy awards dinner with the words, 'Make us laugh, tell us a joke!' (*The Guardian*, 6 Oct 2006). He shone on the big screen as a cat-burglar in *He Who Rides a Tiger* (1965), and appeared in another dozen films over the next twenty years, but won his best roles on television.

Bell followed the single drama *The Sailor's Return* (1978), in which he played a nineteenth-century seaman returning from his travels, with the role of the Nazi war criminal Adolf Eichmann in the epic American series *Holocaust* (1978). Then came his most memorable small-screen performance, as Frank Ross in *Out* (1978), the writer Trevor Preston's gangland drama about a bank robber being released from jail and obsessed with tracking down the informer responsible for his conviction. After playing Feliks Dzerzhinsky, the cold, amoral head of the Soviet secret police, in *Reilly: Ace of Spies* (1983), he starred in *The Detective* (1983) as Commander Kenneth Crocker, whose principles extended to reporting his own brother-in-law for a breach of the peace. He then acted an equally disliked, but far from principled, policeman in the original *Prime Suspect* mini-series (1991). As the sexist Sergeant Bill Otley, he opposed the appointment of Detective Chief Inspector Jane Tennison (played by Helen Mirren) to take over a murder inquiry. After initially refusing to reprise the role, he did so for *Prime Suspect 3* (1993) and *Prime Suspect: the Final Act* (2006). He was twice nominated for a BAFTA television award as best actor, for *Out* and *Prime Suspect*.

On television Bell also played the coalminer Walter Morel in *Sons and Lovers* (1983) and Old Tom, Ursula's grandfather, in *The Rainbow* (1988), as well as making a rare switch to comedy to star as Harry Nash, the cantankerous wax museum owner, in *Hope It Rains* (1991–2). However, Bell was best known for acting menacing, sinister characters, particularly in his later film roles, such as that of Uncle Philip, the controlling toymaker, in *The Magic Toyshop* (1987), and the petty thief Jack 'the Hat' McVitie, whose murder brought down the East End gangster brothers, in *The Krays* (1990). Although his stage appearances were rare he won acclaim for his performance as Horst, companion of the promiscuous Max (played by Ian McKellen), in the world première of Martin Sherman's *Bent* (at the Royal Court Theatre, 1979), an examination of Hitler's persecution of homosexuals, set in Dachau.

Bell's marriage to Lois Dainty was dissolved in 1976, and his partner for the last thirty years of his life was the television and film costume designer Frances Tempest. He became stepfather to her daughter Nellie, and they had another daughter, Polly. Having lived latterly in College Terrace, Brighton, he died of bronchopneumonia, cirrhosis of the liver, and ischaemic heart disease at the Royal Sussex County Hospital, Brighton, on 4 October 2006 and was survived by his partner Frances, his two children, and his stepdaughter. ANTHONY HAYWARD

Sources J. Wintle, ed., *Makers of modern culture* (1981) • *The Times* (6 Oct 2006) • *The Guardian* (6 Oct 2006) • *Daily Telegraph* (7 Oct 2006) • *The Independent* (7 Oct 2006) • BFI screenonline, www.screenonline.org.uk/people/id/482498, 28 Nov 2008 • BFI SIFT database, www.bfi.org.uk/filmtvinfo/ftvdb/, 28 Nov 2008 • internet movie database, www.imdb.com, 28 Nov 2008 • b. cert. • m. cert. • d. cert.

Archives FILM BFINA, performance footage

Likenesses obituary photographs

Wealth at death under £26,000: probate, 31 Aug 2007, *CGPLA Eng. & Wales*

Benenson, Peter James Henry (1921–2005), barrister and human rights campaigner, was born on 31 July 1921 at 6 Albert Court, Knightsbridge, London, the only child of Lieutenant-Colonel Harold Josiah Solomon (1885–1930), army officer, and his wife, Flora (1895–1984), daughter of the Jewish Russian banker Grigori Benenson. He became known as Peter Solomon-Benenson in 1939, following the death of his grandfather, before formally adopting the surname Benenson in 1949. After education at home (where his tutors included W. H. Auden) he studied at Summer Fields preparatory school in Oxford, Eton College, and—briefly, due to the onset of the Second World War—at Balliol College, Oxford. While at Eton he actively supported the cause of the Spanish republic and assisted child refugees from Nazi Germany. During the war he served in military intelligence at Bletchley Park. On 25 August 1941 he married Margaret Susan Anderson (1917–2004), daughter of Hector James Anderson, a civil servant in South Africa. They had two daughters.

After the war Benenson, who was called to the bar in 1948, became involved in Labour Party politics, standing unsuccessfully in all four general elections of the 1950s. More significantly for his later career, however, he had become active in monitoring political trials in Franco's Spain from 1948 onwards, and by the mid-1950s this had broadened into a more general interest in violations of human rights. His interest was sharpened by his experiences in Cyprus, which he first visited in October 1956, where he called for the proper investigation of Cypriot allegations of abuses by the British authorities. In 1957 he played a central role in the establishment of Justice, a cross-party organization of British lawyers dedicated to upholding the rule of law.

In the late 1950s Benenson went through a period of profound personal reassessment. He retired from the bar due to ill health in 1960 and went to recuperate in his beloved

Peter James Henry Benenson (1921–2005), by Carolyn Djanogly, 1999

Italy. He had converted to Catholicism in 1958 and distanced himself from party politics. On his return to Britain in the autumn of 1960 he conceived the idea of a year-long campaign for the release of those imprisoned for their beliefs—the 'prisoners of conscience'. He galvanized the support of a group of like-minded lawyers, journalists, and other opinion formers, and the Appeal for Amnesty, 1961 (which formally became known as Amnesty International in 1962) was launched with Benenson's clarion-call article on 'The forgotten prisoners' in *The Observer* on 28 May 1961. The article, which received much international attention, evoked a remarkable response and Benenson soon found himself at the head of a voluntary movement with branches across Britain and western Europe. He also contributed a Penguin Special entitled *Persecution 1961*, which presented case studies of nine political prisoners.

Between 1961 and 1966 Benenson was at the height of his powers. His tireless and charismatic leadership, as well as his willingness to draw on his great range of political and personal connections, all greatly facilitated Amnesty's rapid early growth. During its first three years alone Amnesty adopted 1367 prisoners (of whom 329 were released) and organized 360 groups in 14 countries. Although others played a valuable role, Benenson was Amnesty's unquestioned inspiration and leader: in the words of one colleague 'Amnesty was Peter'. He oversaw the development of an archive of information on political prisoners, and addressed countless meetings of the local groups that campaigned for their release. His idea that these groups should campaign for three prisoners (from the West, the communist states, and the third world) was highly innovative and reinforced the movement's impartiality. He undertook some early investigative missions, notably to Haiti where he posed as an artist while researching the crimes of the Duvalier regime. He also had a keen eye for the power of symbols and provided the concept for the famous Amnesty motif—a candle in barbed wire.

Even during these early years, however, there were signs of problems to come. Benenson had little time for administration, and organization was often chaotic. Tellingly, he would later confide that 'It has always seemed to me that a humanitarian movement should decide its actions from the heart not from the book of law' (Benenson to Marie-José Protais, 11 July 1991, Amnesty International papers). He was also overly trusting of Harold Wilson's new Labour government. In 1966–7 Amnesty was engulfed in a complex crisis that had two distinct components. First, there was the damaging revelation that Benenson had agreed for Amnesty to channel secret British government funds to the families of political prisoners in Rhodesia. Second, Amnesty crossed swords with Wilson's government over its allegations of torture in the crown colony of Aden. The crisis culminated in the allegation by Benenson, now under severe mental strain, that British intelligence had infiltrated Amnesty. In March 1967 he was forced to stand down as president. Benenson's break with Amnesty was a cause of great sadness on both sides, but was not permanent. He formally rejoined the organization in 1978, and Amnesty's leaders continued to seek out his advice. He remained very proud of his creation—especially when it was awarded the Nobel peace prize in 1977—although he also continued to argue that its headquarters should move to a neutral country.

In 1967 Benenson withdrew to farm near Aylesbury, but he remained an active campaigner for human rights, and created a number of new organizations. These included Pour l'Imaginaire (1978), a trust fund to aid persecuted artists and writers, and Nevermore (1980), a campaign to address the roots of conflict. He later became chairman of Action by Christians against Torture. However, his most significant contribution in these years was arguably his role as co-founder of the Coeliac Society in 1968 (Benenson himself had been recently diagnosed with the condition). His first marriage ended in divorce in 1973, and on 3 August the same year he married Susan Elizabeth Booth (*b.* 1944), daughter of James Booth, heating engineer. They had a son and a daughter. Benenson suffered a car accident in 1993 and his final years, which he spent at Nuneham Courtenay near Oxford, were marked by serious ill health.

Peter Benenson was offered—and refused to accept—an honour from the British state. However, he accepted the Gandhi peace award in 1978 (for pioneering a method of checking the 'vicious devices in various lands for the suppression of political dissent'), and an honorary fellowship of Balliol College (2002). His reputation will always be associated with Amnesty International, his finest achievement. Those who worked with Benenson at that time saw him as an inspirational, dynamic force. In the words of one close associate, Peggy Crane, he was an 'evangelist with a divine spark' (Buchanan, 'Truth will Set You Free', 597). His thinking was coloured by a deep spirituality, and he presented his thoughts on the role of religion in world history in *The Other Face*, a short book privately published in 1977. However, he never lost sight of the need to employ practical—and sometimes shocking—means to arouse what he termed 'the world conscience'. He was a man of powerful and impulsive enthusiasms, and these qualities were essential to the founding and early advance of Amnesty International. He died on 25 February 2005 at the John Radcliffe Hospital, Oxford. TOM BUCHANAN

Sources F. Solomon and B. Litvinoff, *Baku to Baker Street: the memoirs of Flora Solomon* (1984) • E. Larsen, *A flame in barbed wire: the story of Amnesty International* (1978) • J. Power, *Like water on stone: the story of Amnesty International* (2001) • Peter Benenson interview, *New Review*, 4/47 (Feb 1978) • T. Buchanan, '"The truth will set you free": the making of Amnesty International', *Journal of Contemporary History*, 37/4 (2002), 575–97 • T. Buchanan, 'Amnesty International in crisis, 1966–1967', *Twentieth Century British History*, 15/3 (2004), 267–89 • *Daily Telegraph* (28 Feb 2005) • *The Times* (28 Feb 2005) • *The Independent* (28 Feb 2005) • *The Guardian* (28 Feb 2005); (3 March 2005) • *The Lancet*, 365/9466 (April 2005), 1224 • Amnesty International papers, Internationaal Instituut voor Sociale Geschiedenis, Amsterdam • private information (2009) • b. cert. • m. cert. • d. cert.
Archives priv. coll. | Internationaal Instituut voor Sociale Geschiedenis, Amsterdam, Amnesty International papers
Likenesses S. Dack, photograph, 1981, Getty Images, London • E. Goldsmith, bronze bust, in or before 1992, priv. coll. • C. Djanogly, bromide print, 1999, NPG [*see illus.*] • obituary photographs • photograph, PA Photos, London
Wealth at death £414,340: probate, 12 July 2005, *CGPLA Eng. & Wales*

Bennett [*née* Fisher], **Mary Letitia Somerville** (**1913–2005**), civil servant and college head, was born on 9 January 1913 at 37 Norham Road, Oxford, the daughter of Herbert Albert Laurens *Fisher (1865–1940), historian, politician, and college head, and his wife Lettice [*see* Fisher, Lettice (1875–1956)], daughter of Sir Courtenay *Ilbert. She was educated at Oxford high school and Somerville College, Oxford, where she obtained a second in classical moderations in 1933 and a first in *literae humaniores* in 1935. One of her close friends was Isaiah Berlin, then a young prize fellow at All Souls. After graduating she gave tutorials in Roman history and started research on the Roman grain supply. In 1941 she joined the staff of the Joint Broadcasting Committee, a wartime propaganda organization, and later transferred to the transcription service of the BBC. In 1945 she joined the Colonial Office, where she initially joined the Mediterranean department, and later the east African department. She left the civil service after marrying, on 17 September 1955, a Colonial Office colleague (and musicologist), John Sloman Bennett (1914–1990), son of Ralph Bennett, veterinary surgeon. There were no children of the marriage.

After her marriage Mary Bennett served as secretary of the Society for the Promotion of Roman Studies and a part-time teacher at Westminster Tutors, and served on the selection board of the Elizabeth Nuffield Trust. She was an unexpected choice as principal of St Hilda's College, Oxford, in 1965, but an inspired one. Her unflappability, attention to detail, great interest in young people, and liberal tolerance were qualities highly appropriate to a college head in an age of financial strain and increasing student assertiveness. (It was thought by some of her colleagues that she indeed encouraged her students to take part in demonstrations and sit-ins.) A reassuring figure, she frequently conducted interviews with a cat on her lap, a distraction that helped calm even the most anxious of students. She oversaw a period of expansion, including a doubling of the number of fellows and the erection of several new buildings, before her retirement in 1980. When the move to open the men's colleges to women students was first mooted—by New College, as it happened—she shared the hostility to the idea of the principal of Lady Margaret Hall, Dame Lucy Sutherland, seeing it not as a move to expand women's access to higher education but as a self-interested device to get 'stupid men out and clever girls in' (*Daily Telegraph*, 21 Nov 2005). She subsequently changed her mind, and thought St Hilda's was being much too slow in following suit. It was only after her death that her old college started to admit men. In retirement in Alma Place, Oxford, and Thursley, Surrey (where she had inherited a cottage after her mother's death), she pursued historical research relating to her forebears, including her maternal grandfather, Sir Courtenay Ilbert, and her paternal great-grandfather, John Jackson, a professor at Calcutta Medical College, published in *The Ilberts in India* (1995) and *Who Was Dr Jackson?* (2000). She remained active until near the end of her life. She died on 1 November 2005 at Rock Cottage, Highfield Lane, Thursley, Surrey, of breast cancer.

Sources *Mary Bennett: an autobiography* (privately printed, St Hilda's College, Oxford, 2006) • *The Times* (4 Nov 2005) • *The Independent* (19 Nov 2005) • *Daily Telegraph* (21 Nov 2005) • b. cert. • m. cert. • d. cert.
Likenesses obituary photographs • photograph, repro. in www.st-hildas.ox.ac.uk
Wealth at death £600,107: probate, 5 July 2006, *CGPLA Eng. & Wales*

Benney, (Adrian) Gerald Sallis (**1930–2008**), goldsmith and silversmith, was born at 56 Westbourne Avenue, Sculcoates, Hull, on 21 April 1930, the younger son of Ernest Alfred Sallis Benney (1894–1966), an artist and designer who was then principal of the City of Hull College of Arts and Crafts and later (from 1934 to 1958) principal of Brighton College of Art, and his wife, Aileen Mary, *née* Ward (1898–1975), a silversmith. The young Benney benefited from a creative upbringing. This fed both his lifelong appreciation of colour and texture and his commitment to the handmade, allied to a keen commercial sense. His integrated approach to the design of his homes and workshops was typical of the arts and crafts tradition, although *The Studio* described 'a definitely modern feeling' in his first workshop.

Educated at Brighton, Hove, and Sussex grammar school, Benney moved in 1945 to Brighton College of Art, learning from and later working with Dunstan Pruden, the silversmith at Eric Gill's Guild of St Joseph who reinforced his commitment to handwork. After national service in the Royal Army Service Corps (1948–50), which stimulated his enthusiasm for motorcycles, he attended the Royal College of Art (RCA) in London under Robert

Goodden. He won the Prince of Wales scholarship for a tea service in the design spirit of the Festival of Britain of 1951. With typical enterprise, he bought a gold- and silver-plating business off Tottenham Court Road, while still at the RCA. It extended into cadmium plating for the needs of atomic energy and chromium plating for irons. This subsidized his nascent silversmithing business. In 1956 he established his first workshop, at Whitfield Place, London. His flatware designs in stainless steel for Viners from 1957 to 1969 sold well. Undergraduates at the new University of Sussex recalled removing his Chelsea cutlery from the refectory although they were indifferent to his silver beer and water jugs, funded by the Goldsmiths in the belief that 'such gifts would help to form the taste of students'. Meanwhile, on 4 May 1957 at St Andrew's Church, Sherborne St John, Hampshire, he married Janet Edwards, journalist, later events organizer, daughter of Harold Neville Edwards, building contractor. They had three sons and one daughter.

In a talented generation, including David Mellor and Robert Welch, Benney caught the eye of Graham Hughes, art director at Goldsmiths' Hall and later Benney's biographer. As Hughes commented, 'Patronage in the arts grows with exhibition enthusiasm'. Benney's work toured the USA and Canada in the Goldsmiths' Company's exhibition 'Art in Craftsmanship'. In 1962 the company commissioned his eye-catching Beetle Bowl, a large piece set with peridots devised 'as a forceful representation of new British design'. His Thistle Vase, made for Goldsmiths' Hall thirty years later, enamelled in deep crimson, combined chasing with colour. Benney was especially associated with his successful commercial revival of enamelling in strong colours. His other successful innovation, of bark-like textures contrasting with polished surfaces, was accidentally discovered in 1964, from picking up a scarred hammer head, and subsequently exploited in almost all his work. It had the great advantage of resisting finger prints and so delaying tarnishing.

For fifty years, through fluctuations in the trade and craft, Benney ran a series of workshops, employing twenty-nine workmen in the early 1970s. Confident in his artistic and business judgement, he was notable for attracting and retaining patrons, both personal, such as Michael Behrens and Alistair McAlpine, and institutional. From 1963 commissions for Reading town council built up over twenty-six years to an exceptional civic collection of 176 objects, for entertaining and ceremonies. Benney's successful standard designs for retail and export attracted high prices. But rent increases, plus the imposition in 1975 of value added tax (VAT) at 25 per cent on luxury items, forced him to move out of London in 1974 to Beenham in Berkshire. Meanwhile from 1974 until 1983 he was part-time professor of silversmithing and jewellery at the RCA.

Appointed a royal designer for industry in 1971 and elected a fellow of the Society of Industrial Artists and Designers in 1975, Benney held four royal warrants, and was consultant to the Silver Trust. He was appointed CBE in 1995. Admitted to the Goldsmiths' Company as a freeman in 1958, and to the livery in 1966, in 1981 he became a member of the court of assistants but resigned on a matter of principle in 1983, a decision he later regretted. His long and close relationship with the Goldsmiths' Company, celebrated in one-man shows in 1973 and 2005, led to a sixty-person service of flatware for lunches, handsome balanced items with his characteristic bark textured handles. A tall, imposing figure, with broad shoulders and a beard, giving him an almost Russian air, Benney was excellent company. He died at his home, the Old Rectory, Cholderton, Salisbury, Wiltshire, on 26 June 2008, of lung cancer. He was survived by his wife, Janet, and their four children, one of them a silversmith and another an artist. A memorial service was held at Southwark Cathedral on 30 October 2008. PHILIPPA GLANVILLE

Sources G. Hughes, *Gerald Benney, goldsmith* (1998) • *The Independent* (2 July 2008) • *The Times* (11 July 2008); (31 Oct 2008) • *The Guardian* (25 July 2008) • *WW* (2008) • personal knowledge (2012) • private information (2012) • b. cert. • m. cert. • d. cert.
Archives FILM BFINA, documentary footage
Likenesses obituary photographs
Wealth at death £1,733,533: probate, 15 Dec 2008, *CGPLA Eng. & Wales*

Beresford, Maurice Warwick (1920–2005), economic historian, was born on 6 February 1920 at 403 Boldmere Road, Sutton Coldfield, Warwickshire, the only son of Harry Bertram Beresford, a manager in a warehouse supplying chemists' shops, and his wife, Nora Elizabeth, *née* Jefferies. He had a particularly close relationship with his mother, and later dedicated a book to her. He attended local elementary schools and Bishop Vesey's Grammar School in Sutton Coldfield. He went to Jesus College, Cambridge, in 1938 to take a history degree, and was drawn to aspects of the subject that did not belong in the conventional syllabus. He was interested in maps and visual evidence, and was encouraged by excursions from Cambridge led by John Saltmarsh to observe the historic landscape. After graduating with first-class honours in 1941, having been exempted from military service as a conscientious objector, he did social work, to which throughout his life he was passionately committed. He was warden of an adult education centre in Rugby in Warwickshire from 1942 to 1948.

In 1948 Beresford published an article that demonstrated, using maps and aerial photographs, that 'ridge and furrow' preserved the outlines of the medieval open fields. This was based on part-time research without formal training: in later years he gave a lecture, 'On never being a research student'. When planning the remains of fields in Leicestershire he came upon an area of mounds and hollows, which he realized marked the site of the medieval village of Bittesby. He then discovered 100 deserted villages in Warwickshire, expanded the work to the rest of the country, and published *The Lost Villages of England* in 1954. He argued that there had been a phase of deliberate depopulation by profit-conscious landlords in the late fifteenth and early sixteenth centuries to create enclosed sheep pastures.

Maurice Warwick Beresford (1920–2005), by Zigmund Baumann

By the time *Lost Villages* appeared Beresford was well established as a lecturer in economic history at the University of Leeds, a post to which he had been appointed in 1948. Investigating deserted villages in Yorkshire, he discovered the site of Wharram Percy hidden in a valley in the wolds. He began to dig there with the help of friends, to find and date the foundations of houses. J. G. Hurst, newly graduated from Cambridge, who was keen to develop medieval archaeology, took over the excavations, which were henceforth conducted on a larger scale, using the latest techniques. Beresford and Hurst made an effective team, though they were very different in personality. Beresford talked and enthused, while Hurst, an inspector of ancient monuments, quietly exercised his influence. Together they recruited a group of collaborators who listed and mapped all known deserted medieval villages in England. The fruits of their labours appeared in 1971 as *Deserted Medieval Villages: Studies*. Deserted villages had a great impact on the general public; they set archaeologists and geographers on a quest to answer questions about the origins of villages, village planning, and peasant houses. The new discipline of 'landscape history' developed out of these enquiries, inspired by Beresford's writings as well as those of W. G. Hoskins. In 1957 came *History on the Ground*, in which Beresford showed the potential of studying parks and planned towns as well as villages. He published, with Kenneth St Joseph, a collection of aerial photographs with a commentary in *Medieval England: an Aerial Survey* in 1958. His main contribution to village studies in the next three decades was organizing the camp for the Wharram Percy excavators. When the digging ended he wrote with Hurst *Wharram Percy: Deserted Medieval Village*, which appeared in 1990.

In the mid-1950s Beresford's research on medieval towns began, focusing on the new generation of planned towns of the twelfth and thirteenth centuries, which led him to visit south-west France as well as all parts of England and Wales. His *New Towns of the Middle Ages* was published in 1967 at the very beginning of a new wave of academic interest in urban history. Beresford investigated the past of his adopted town of Leeds, and wrote a history of its chamber of commerce soon after his arrival. This interest culminated in his study of the modern growth of the town, *East End, West End* (1988), in which he traced the advance of streets and houses.

Beresford's well-written and much read books influenced both landscape history and urban history. His striking phrases drew the readers' attention: *Lost Villages* and *New Towns* were typical choices of apt and attractive titles. He lectured with enthusiasm and wit, using illustration, and he frequently gave talks to adult education classes and local societies as well as audiences in universities and academic conferences. He contributed generously his time and energy to the Yorkshire Archaeological Society and the Thoresby Society. He was active in university administration, holding a chair from 1959 until retirement in 1985, and serving as dean and chairman of the school of economic studies. In the university senate those critical of the management relished his contributions to debate. His conversation could be waspish, but he was always engaging and wide-ranging. Music, opera, ballet, theatre, and cinema were all enthusiasms of his, and he was addicted in later years to continental travel. He had remarkable powers of persuasion, so he relied on others to take him to sites, as he did not drive. From student days he had taken an interest in prisoners and young offenders, and devoted a great deal of time to befriending, advising, and educating them. His well-attended evening class in Wakefield prison ran for many years. He was actively engaged in public life, serving on many committees and advisory bodies: these ranged from the parole review committee of Leeds prison to the Royal Commission on Historical Monuments (England). His achievement was marked with honours, including four honorary degrees, two volumes of essays written in his honour (presented in 1989 and 2000), and election as a fellow of the British Academy in 1985.

From the late 1990s Beresford's health deteriorated, but he was able to attend conferences well into his eighties. He died on 15 December 2005 of a chest infection and septicaemia in St James's University Hospital, Leeds. He never married and had no surviving relative, but his numerous friends visited him in hospital, attended his cremation ceremony on 30 December, and took part in a subsequent memorial meeting on 4 July 2006 at Leeds University.

CHRISTOPHER DYER

Sources M. W. Beresford, *Time and place: collected essays* (1984) · M. W. Beresford, 'Forty years in the field: an exaugural lecture', *University of Leeds Review*, 29 (1986–7), 27–46 · Y. M. Fennell, ed., *Northern History*, 37 (2000), 307–20 [M. W. Beresford issue] · *The Guardian* (22 Dec 2005) · *The Times* (2 Jan 2006) · *The Independent* (14 Jan 2006) · C. Dyer, 'Maurice Beresford and local history', *Local Historian* (May 2006), 128–30 · H. S. A. Fox, *Newsletter, Society for Landscape Studies* (spring–summer 2006) · L. Butler, *Yorkshire Archaeological Journal*, 78 (2006), 243–5 · M. Aston and others, 'Founders: Maurice Beresford', *Landscapes*, 7/2 (2006), 90–104 · *WW* (2005) ·

personal knowledge (2009) • private information (2009) • b. cert. • d. cert.
Archives U. Hull, papers, including papers relating to Wharram Percy • U. Leeds, Brotherton L., papers and corresp. • Yorkshire Archaeological Society, notebooks | Bodl. Oxf., O. G. S. Crawford papers
Likenesses T. Stubley, gouache, exh. Royal Society of Portrait Painters, London 1988 • Z. Baumann, photograph, priv. coll. [*see illus.*] • obituary photographs
Wealth at death £665,889: probate, 13 June 2006, *CGPLA Eng. & Wales*

Berman, Nestor Montague [Monty] (1913–2006), film and television producer, was born on 16 August 1913 at 25 Whitechapel Road, London, the son of Israel (otherwise Isadore) Reuben Berman, musician, and his wife, Fanny, *née* Josephvitz. He was of Jewish descent. He was educated at University College School, Hampstead, and entered the film industry in 1930 as a camera assistant at Twickenham Studios. He then worked as a camera operator at Teddington Studios (1934–8), where he filmed Michael Powell's *The Edge of the World* (1937), and at Ealing Studios (1938–40). On 11 November 1940, at Hendon register office, he married Ella Barbara Joan Humphrey, an eighteen-year-old hairdresser, and daughter of Stanley Frederick Humphrey, commercial traveller.

During the Second World War Berman served in the army, attaining the rank of sergeant, and was transferred to the Eighth Army kinematograph unit in north Africa, where he met Robert S. Baker; they worked on the documentary *The Way from Germany* (1946). After demobilization Berman continued as a camera operator on several films before forming a production company, Tempean Films, with Baker. They made two low-budget comedies, *A Date with a Dream* (1948), financed by friends and relatives, and *Melody Club* (1949), both starring Terry-Thomas, before becoming firmly established as second feature producers. They were a complementary team: Berman looked after the finances and cinematography, while Baker focused on script development and direction. Their reputation as efficient and capable producers came through a very tight control of budgets, scripting, casting, and direction, using a limited number of actors and directors (principally John Gilling). To reduce costs they often filmed on location, which allowed Berman more scope as the cinematographer and gave Tempean films a distinctive look in what was a largely undifferentiated market.

Tempean's output of over thirty, mainly crime, films changed from the staunchly British early ones—including *The Frightened Man* (1952)—to faster paced American thrillers using second-drawer American stars and designed for the American market. Many, including *Impulse* (1954), starring Arthur Kennedy and directed by the blacklisted Cy Endfield, were indebted to *film noir*. Under a separate banner, CIPA, Baker and Berman produced three films in Ireland, before graduating into first features, beginning with *Sea of Sand* (1958), a gripping war film set in the north African desert. Berman directed as well as produced *The Siege of Sidney Street* (1960), based on the events of 1911, and the luridly melodramatic *The Hellfire Club* (1961), shot in colour. His first marriage having ended in divorce, on 2 November 1956 Berman married Ursula Anne Sharp (*b.* 1934), actress, and daughter of Percy William Sharp, colliery agent; they had one daughter.

The strict discipline of low-budget film-making was the foundation of Berman's and Baker's success after they moved into television production, working for Lew Grade's Independent Television Corporation, having secured the rights to Leslie Charteris's gentleman outlaw, the Saint. Roger Moore proved to be perfect casting as Simon Templar, and *The Saint* (1962–9) was a major international success, changing to colour halfway through. By contrast *Gideon's Way* (1964), based on the novels by J. J. Marric (John Creasey), was a sober, realistic police procedural starring John Gregson as Commander George Gideon of Scotland Yard, making expert use of London locations. *The Baron* (1966) blended the two, with the American Steve Forrest playing a London antiques dealer who is also a secret agent.

Having broken with Baker, Berman set up Scoton Productions with the scriptwriter Dennis Spooner, who had written over half the episodes of *The Baron*. With Berman as producer and occasional writer, Spooner as script supervisor, and a stable team of writers and directors, Scoton produced five further series, beginning with *The Champions* (1968–9), a conflation of the spy thriller and superhero adventure story. *Department S* (1969–70), in which the three protagonists solve cases that have baffled conventional law agencies, was more popular, especially the foppish character of Jason King (Peter Wyngarde), the professional crime writer turned amateur detective. In *Jason King* (1971–2) Wyngarde's hair, clothing, and mannerisms became more extravagantly camp. In between Berman and Spooner produced *Randall and Hopkirk (Deceased)* (1969–70), a combination of supernatural fantasy and hard-boiled thriller about two slightly seedy London-based private detectives, Jeff Randall (Mike Pratt) and Marty Hopkirk (Kenneth Cope), the latter dead but returning to give his partner a helping hand. Scoton's final series, *The Adventurer* (1972–3), starring Gene Barry as a wealthy government agent posing as a film star to travel the world, was stale and lacklustre.

A talented cinematographer, Berman prided himself on his efficiency, 'orderliness', and quality control, and he had a reputation of being ruthless. These qualities enabled him to prosper in an intensely competitive market. However, his best-remembered films and television series also showed a degree of imagination and inventiveness that testified to his creativity as well as his business acumen. He retired after *The Adventurer*, but lived to see several of his television series becoming cult hits and remade. He died on 14 June 2006 at the Chelsea and Westminster Hospital of bronchopneumonia and severe aortic stenosis. He was survived by his wife, Ursula, and daughter, Charlotte. ANDREW H. SPICER

Sources P. Noble, ed., *The British Film Yearbook, 1949–50* (1950) • 'Tempean Films to make bigger pictures', *Kinematograph Weekly* (21 April 1957), 37 • T. Gruner, 'Baker and Berman: a saint goes marching on — and on', *Kinematograph Weekly* (13 Aug 1964), 15–16 • interview with Robert S. Baker, B. McFarlane, *An autobiography of British* *cinema* (1997), 4–48 • J. Chapman, *Saints and avengers: British adventure series of the 1960s* (2002) • B. McFarlane, 'Value for money: Baker and Berman, and Tempean Films', *British cinema of the 1950s: a celebration*, ed. I. MacKillop and N. Sinyard (2003), 176–89 • B. McFarlane, ed., *The encyclopedia of British film* (2003) • R. Sellers, *Cult TV: the golden age of ITC* (2006) • *The Independent* (4 Aug 2006) • *The Guardian* (14 Aug 2006) • *The Stage* (31 Aug 2006) • *Stage, Screen and Radio* (Sept 2006) • D. Mann, *Britain's first TV/film crime series and the industrialisation of its film industry, 1946–1964* (2009) • interview with Berman, BFI, BECTU, no. 360 • interview with Johnny Goodman, BFI, BECTU, no. 388 • L. Marcus and S. Hulse, *Baker and Berman: a saintly combination*, www.televisionheaven.co.uk/saint4.htm, 14 July 2009 • b. cert. • m. certs. • d. cert.

Archives FILM BFINA, current affairs footage | SOUND BFI, BECTU oral history project, interview, 360

Likenesses photograph, 1949, Rex Features • Barratts, photograph, 1962, PA Photos, London • obituary photographs

Wealth at death £574,439: probate, 31 Aug 2007, *CGPLA Eng. & Wales*

Best, George (1946–2005), footballer, was born on 22 May 1946 at the Royal Maternity Hospital, Belfast, the elder son and eldest of six children of Richard (Dickie) Best (1919–2008), an iron-turner in the Harland and Wolff shipyard, and his wife, Ann Mary (Annie), *née* Withers (1922–1978), who worked in Gallaher's tobacco factory. He was originally named Ronald Samuel Best, but two weeks after his birth was renamed George.

Belfast and Manchester The Best family lived on the newly built Cregagh council estate in east Belfast, a predominantly protestant area. They were Free Presbyterians who attended church twice on Sundays; as a teenager George Best joined the protestant Orange order. His father was a keen amateur footballer and his mother played hockey to almost international standard, but Best credited his maternal grandfather, George Withers, with encouraging his passion for football. Family photographs show the young Best kicking a ball at the age of about fifteen months. Later he played football in the street, or in a field behind the family home, and honed his skills by dribbling a tennis ball to and from school. It was said that he even took a football to bed with him.

Best attended Nettlefield primary school and won a scholarship to Grosvenor High School, a grammar school where he often played truant because it was a rugby school and because his daily journey took him through a Catholic area where he suffered taunts and stone-throwing. After a year he was transferred to Lisnasharragh intermediate school, a secondary modern school where he played for the football team. He also began playing for Cregagh Boys' Club, and earned a reputation for dedicated practice. Advised that his left foot was weak, he spent several days wearing a plimsoll on his right foot and a football boot on his left, hitting a tennis ball until both feet were equally strong.

Although the teenage Best drew admiration for his dribbling he was considered too frail to become a professional player, and was rejected by the Belfast club Glentoran. 'I looked like a stick of rhubarb', he later said. 'I weighed about seven stones' (Parkinson, 14–15). When he was fourteen, however, a friend of his father, Bud McFarlane, recommended him to Bob Bishop, the scout in Northern

George Best (1946–2005), by Sefton Samuels, 1968

Ireland for one of England's top clubs, Manchester United. Bishop, too, was worried about Best's physique, but then successfully tested him in games against older and bigger players. 'I think I've found you a genius', Bishop is said to have told Matt Busby, the United manager, by telegram (B. Best, 62).

In July 1961, a week after qualifying to become a printer's apprentice, Best crossed the Irish Sea for a two-week trial in Manchester. It began badly: United officials neglected him on his arrival, and Best felt homesick. Within forty-eight hours he returned to Belfast, but his father gently encouraged him to go back to Manchester. For the next two years Best remained an amateur with United, since Football Association rules barred Irish players from becoming professional until they were seventeen. Initially he worked as an errand-boy for the Manchester Ship Canal Company, and later he was given a bogus job with a local electrical firm. Yet within five months of becoming professional (in May 1963), and having played barely a few games for the reserves, Best had made his début in the United first team—a 1–0 win over West Bromwich Albion at United's Old Trafford ground on 14 September 1963. Although he played well it would be more than three months before he appeared for the first team again. On Boxing day 1963 United had been thrashed 6–1 at Burnley, and Busby made radical changes for the return fixture two days later. Best scored the first goal as Manchester United beat Burnley 5–1, and he stayed in the side thereafter.

Footballing legend Best possessed a wide range of skills, including pace, acceleration, stamina, and physical strength. He beat defenders easily with an extraordinary control that made it look as if the ball was tied to his feet, and his repertoire of feints, swerves, and spurts once prompted his team-mate Pat Crerand to say he left opponents with 'twisted blood' (*The Times*, 26 Nov 2005). Above all he had remarkable balance, and an elasticity that enabled him to bounce back quickly from the ground, ride challenges, and avoid serious injury. He was never afraid to tackle, could head the ball, was a master at passing, and deadly in front of goal. Although he was a shy and very private character he showed huge confidence even in his youth, unaffected by noisy crowds. He frequently played on the wing, especially in his early career, and could easily play as a forward, but was often given licence to roam the midfield. What made him special was his showmanship: to him football was entertainment. Crowds loved his cheeky, mischievous smile, and the way he played with his socks around his ankles. They responded with loud, expectant roars whenever he got the ball. His weaknesses were a tendency to perform unnecessary tricks, and an occasional selfishness that stopped him passing to colleagues who were better placed. He also had a volatile temperament.

In a Manchester United career that lasted just over ten years Best scored 179 goals in 470 competitive appearances. He joined the side amid Matt Busby's rebuilding following the 1958 Munich air crash, in which eight players were killed. Along with Bobby Charlton and Denis Law he was one of the 1960s 'holy trinity' of world-class forwards who helped restore United to greatness. He won two English championship medals, in 1965 and 1967, but it was in Europe that he really made his mark. Perhaps his greatest game was United's European cup quarter-final in March 1966 against Benfica, the Portuguese champions, in Lisbon. Matt Busby warned his players against taking risks, but they produced an astonishing 5–1 win. Best scored twice in the opening minutes, and took most of the headlines. 'George just went out and destroyed them', said Busby. 'I ought to have shouted at him for not following instructions, but what could you say?' (Lovejoy, 95–6). He was still only nineteen.

George Best—Georgie to fans, or sometimes Geordie in Ireland—soon became English football's first modern superstar, part of the 'swinging sixties', and it was said that his appearance added from 5000 to 10,000 to the attendance at any Manchester United fixture. It was an era when managers weren't used to handling wealthy stars whose fame extended beyond football, and here lay the seeds of Best's downfall. 'It might have been better if Matt had been harder on me', he later remarked. 'The normal laws of the club didn't seem to apply to me' (*Blessed*, 114). Endowed with the perfect surname and blue eyes, he grew his hair long like the Beatles; indeed he was sometimes called the fifth Beatle. Although he still lived in the modest council home of his United club landlady, Mary Fullaway, in Chorlton-cum-Hardy, he was the 1960s 'man about town', wearing fashionable clothes and driving expensive sports cars. Like the Beatles he attracted screaming schoolgirls, though when many of them wrote requesting a lock of hair, he responded with tufts shorn from the Fullaway family's black dog. Over the years his many lovers included famous actresses, two holders of the Miss World title, and several married women who were a lot older than him, including the wife of the prominent Manchester QC George Carman (who would later unsuccessfully defend Best in an assault case).

Best soon needed three secretaries to handle his fan mail. He was one of the first footballers to employ a commercial agent, and before long his income from outside activities outstripped his player's wages. He wrote ghosted columns for several newspapers and magazines, and in 1966 opened the first of several fashion boutiques in Manchester. He modelled clothes, too, and over the next few years he advertised sausages, oranges, aftershave, his own brand of football boots, and even women's bras. The Egg Marketing Board used him to promote eggs for breakfast, under the slogan 'E for B and Georgie Best' (*The Guardian*, 10 May 2008).

During the 1967–8 season Best was joint leading scorer in the English league, with twenty-eight goals (and four more in other competitions), a remarkable tally for a winger. At the end of the season, in May 1968, he scored his team's second goal as Manchester United became the first English club to win the European cup, with a 4–1 win over Benfica at Wembley Stadium. It was a typical Best strike, as he knocked the ball through a defender's legs and then dribbled round the goalkeeper. That year Best was chosen as footballer of the year in both England and Europe, the youngest player to win either award.

Best's contribution to Manchester United's victory in the European cup, ten years after the club had lost almost a whole team at Munich, would prove to be the pinnacle of his achievements, even though he was barely twenty-two. 'Although I was not to know it at the time', he would subsequently admit, 'it was the beginning of the end' (*Where Do I Go from Here?*, 13). He had a sense that there was nothing else to do at United. Busby stepped down as manager, but released from the burden of Munich the club seemed to lack ambition: the supply line of youth players dried up and United failed to exploit the transfer market. For five successive seasons Best was the team's top goalscorer, but felt the side relied too much upon him. 'I was finding it increasingly difficult to get motivated as the team was so poor', he later confessed (*Blessed*, 141).

Frustrated with football, Best adopted a more carefree lifestyle. First signs came with a succession of driving offences, one of which led to a six-month ban. This was followed by increasingly regular disciplinary measures, by Manchester United for missing training sessions, and by the football authorities for offences on the pitch. His bookings and dismissals were rarely for malicious conduct, but often stemmed from anger that referees weren't giving him protection from the violent attempts of defenders to stop him. In 1970 he was suspended for a month for knocking the ball out of the referee's hands after a defeat by Manchester City. On his return he scored six times as United won 8–2 in an FA cup tie at Northampton Town. Nevertheless by this time he had started to drink heavily, often all night long. Among his favourite haunts were the Brown Bull, a pub in the centre of Manchester, whose landlord gave him a key so that he could drink as he pleased, and Phyllis's, an unlicensed club that was open all hours. The pressure grew with the troubles in Northern Ireland, and a serious death threat delivered before a game at Newcastle in 1971.

Best left his club landlady to live in a futuristic house he had had built in Bramhall, equipped with numerous electronic gadgets. But the property was too exposed, and he felt trapped in a 'goldfish bowl' by gawping fans outside (*Where Do I Go from Here?*, 117). Before long he was annoying team-mates such as Bobby Charlton, who felt that Busby and his successors as manager, Wilf McGuinness and Frank O'Farrell, treated him too leniently. Relations got so bad that Charlton and Best rarely passed the ball to each other. If he had lived in later decades Best would almost certainly have moved to a leading Spanish or Italian club, but this was an era when there was little international movement in players. An alternative might have been a transfer to one of the big London clubs, since he loved playing in the capital, but Best felt huge loyalty to Manchester United.

Best found little solace in playing for Northern Ireland, for whom he had made his début against Wales on 15 April 1964. Aged just seventeen, he was then the youngest player ever to appear for his country. He envied his Manchester United team-mates Bobby Charlton and Nobby Stiles, who had helped England win the world cup in 1966, and he feared, rightly, that he would never achieve much with his national team. Northern Ireland never qualified for the world cup finals or the final stages of the European championship during the years he was at his peak. His best game for Northern Ireland was probably a 1–0 win over Scotland in October 1967, but he rarely performed well for his country. 'Recreational football', he later called his Northern Ireland games (Lovejoy, 162). He played in just thirty-seven international matches between 1964 and 1977, and scored nine goals, but had he played for a more successful country, it might have extended his ambitions, career, and reputation.

In May 1972 Best announced from holiday in Majorca that he was giving up the game. 'I am no longer a footballer—and that is final', he declared (Lovejoy, 227). It took only two weeks for Manchester United to persuade him to change his mind, but he was far less effective the following season. When Best again skipped training United first fined him and then put him up for sale for £300,000. It was a sign of his unreliability that the club received no offers, and shortly afterwards Best again announced his retirement from English football. He toyed with the idea of playing in North America, but in the summer of 1973 Busby and the latest Manchester United manager, Tommy Docherty, again persuaded him to return to the club. He trained hard, but this latest comeback did not last long. In January 1974 he missed training once more and was dropped for a cup tie, though it is disputed whether he was then sacked or quit. He had played his last game for Manchester United in a 3–0 defeat at Queen's Park Rangers on new year's day 1974. He was twenty-seven, an age when most players approach their peak, but he would never play top-flight English football again.

Decline Best continued to live in Manchester, where he had opened his first nightclub, Slack Alice's, in 1973, and a second, Oscar's, the following year. Gambling became his latest addiction, and he would often fritter away his clubs' nightly takings in a nearby casino. The sums were huge: one night he was losing £17,000, only to finish £9,000 in profit. Yet it was only a temporary retirement from football. Over the next decade his career stuttered on, as he played for more than a dozen different clubs on five different continents. In many cases these were purely money-making ventures, involving just a handful of games, and Best would be excused from training. Such deals were struck with a club called the Jewish Guild in Johannesburg, South Africa (1974), followed by Dunstable Town (1974–5) and fourth division Stockport County (1975) in England, and then Cork Celtic (1975–6) in Ireland. He was next lured by the emerging North American Soccer League, which had already attracted such ageing world-class stars as Pele and Franz Beckenbauer. For the next six years Best spent the summer months playing in the United States, with the Los Angeles Aztecs (1976–8), the Fort Lauderdale Strikers (1978–9), and the San Jose Earthquakes (1980–81), for whom he also played indoor six-a-side football. In all he played 150 competitive games in the USA, and scored fifty-seven goals. He combined this American summer football with winter performances in Britain. Between 1976 and 1978 he played for the London second division club Fulham, and scored ten goals in forty-seven games. In 1979 and 1980 he also scored three times in twenty-two matches for the Edinburgh club Hibernian.

These were years of sad decline, as Best became slower and overweight, and more troubled by his addictions. He enjoyed the anonymity of living in America, where he settled in Hermosa Beach, and in 1977 opened a beach bar called Bestie's. During long drinking sessions in California he would disappear for days, walking or hitch-hiking from one clandestine bar to another, going without food, and sometimes sleeping in doorways and on the beach. Often he went penniless, and later admitted that he was once so desperate for a drink that he stole money from a woman's purse. There were violent mood swings, though he would often go for several months without drink, and he also felt guilty for neglecting his mother. She had died in 1978 of a heart attack that was probably brought on by alcoholism, and Best wondered whether his own troubled life had driven her to drink. The same year Best married Angela MacDonald (Angie) Janes, from Essex. They had one son, Calum, born in 1981 (the year in which Best entered a rehabilitation clinic in Los Angeles, the first of many), but separated a year later and divorced in 1986. After Best's death his sister revealed that he had also fathered a daughter back in 1969, though he never met her, and her identity has never been made public.

Occasionally crowds saw flashes of the old Best brilliance. While playing for San Jose in 1981, when his drinking problems were acute, he scored what many regard as the greatest goal of his career. Playing against his former club, Fort Lauderdale, he dummied left and right, shaking off every defender in his path, before shooting past a helpless goalkeeper. That same year he entered negotiations about returning to the English first division, to play for Middlesbrough, with an eye to returning to the Northern Ireland squad that had just qualified for the 1982 world cup finals. In 1983 he was also approached by Manchester United about yet another comeback. After giving the idea 'serious thought', he declined, fearing 'I might go back and make a fool of myself' (*Blessed*, 269). Instead he played five games for third division Bournemouth, and had brief spells with two teams in Hong Kong, non-league Nuneaton Borough in England, and two clubs in Australia. His last competitive match was for Tobermore United in Northern Ireland in 1984. 'It was a freak show', Best later said of these nomadic years. 'People were coming to see me fall over, or whatever. The problem was that I had to do it. I needed the money' (Lovejoy, 305).

For most of his post-football years George Best lived in Cheyne Walk, Chelsea, London, where his personal troubles worsened. In 1984 he was imprisoned for eight weeks for assaulting a policeman in an argument over a drink-driving offence. Another humiliating moment occurred in 1990 when he appeared on the BBC chat-show *Wogan* and, obviously drunk, told viewers 'I like screwing' (Lovejoy, 341). In 1982 he was declared bankrupt in an action taken by the Inland Revenue over an unpaid tax bill for £22,000. By 1991 he was estimated to have debts of £100,000, though his bankruptcy was discharged the following year. His fortunes were restored with the help of his partner from 1987 to 1995, Mary Shatila, who acted as his agent in securing personal appearances. Best employed his wit and high intelligence to become a pundit on football, notably for Sky Television, and also delivered after-dinner speeches and stage shows, often in a double-act with Denis Law and his Fulham team-mate Rodney Marsh. He produced half a dozen editions of autobiography and reminiscences. On 24 July 1995 he married Alexandra Jane (Alex) Pursey, an air stewardess who was less than half his age, but they divorced in 2004 after she accused him of violence.

Final years Best's final years were a battle against his addictions, which involved regular trips to health farms (where he still managed to drink), and programmes of anti-abuse tablets sewn into his stomach. But the restoration of his finances only encouraged more gambling. When friends raised £20,000 at a testimonial dinner he lost it all the same night at a casino. At times he seriously contemplated suicide. In 1999 he was found to have severe cirrhosis of the liver. The following year he was admitted to hospital in London and came close to death, and in 2002 he was given a liver transplant, on the understanding that he would give up alcohol. He failed to do so. In October 2005 he entered the Cromwell Hospital in London for the last time, suffering from a kidney infection that was a side-effect of the drugs taken for his liver transplant. He spent seven weeks in intensive care, and he allowed one newspaper to photograph his haggard condition to warn people off drink. He died on 25 November 2005. The cause of death was a combination of pneumonia, septicaemia, multi-organ failure, and gastrointestinal bleeding. His funeral, in Belfast on 3 December 2005, was almost a state occasion, with a service held at the Northern Ireland assembly at Stormont, broadcast live on British television. An estimated 100,000 people watched the cortège pass through the streets to Roselawn cemetery.

The Brazilian player Pele, who perhaps deserved the title himself, once described Best as 'the greatest footballer in the world' (*The Times*, 26 Nov 2005). Certainly he is a prime contender as the greatest player in British history. Comparisons are difficult, as his early departure from the English first division and his absence from top international tournaments probably ensured that he never reached his true potential. 'I spent a lot of my money on booze, birds and fast cars', he once joked. 'The rest I just squandered' (Smith and Hunt, 59). He was the archetypal flawed genius. He was one of the most talented and entertaining players of the twentieth century, yet he was brought down by his other obsessions—sex, gambling, and especially drink.

Best's life was portrayed in the film *Best* (2000), starring John Lynch, and celebrated in the 1970 song 'Belfast Boy', by Don Fardon. In 2006 the harbour airport in Belfast was renamed George Best Belfast City Airport. He was featured on a limited edition five pound banknote issued by Ulster Bank on the first anniversary of his death. He was also depicted on several of Northern Ireland's murals, a distinctive form of political street art of this period, and featured in a three-man statue at Old Trafford, alongside Bobby Charlton and Denis Law. There is a plaque on the family home in Burren Way, Belfast. The George Best Foundation was established in 2006 to help research into liver disease and alcoholism, and to promote football as an alternative to drink and drugs. MICHAEL CRICK

Sources G. Best, *Best of both worlds* (1968) · D. Meek, *Anatomy of a football star: George Best* (1970) · J. Roberts, *George Best: fall of a superstar* (1973) · M. Parkinson, *Best: an intimate biography* (1975) · G. Best, *Where do I go from here? George Best: an autobiography* (1981) · G. Best, *The good, the bad and the bubbly* (1990) · G. Best, *The best of times* (1994) · J. Lovejoy, *Bestie: a portrait of a legend* (1998) · G. Best, *Blessed: the autobiography* (2001) · A. Best, *George and me* (2001) · D. Carman, *No ordinary man* (2002) · G. Best, *Scoring at half time* (2003) · G. Best, *Hard tackles and dirty baths* (2005) · A. Best, *Always Alex: my story* (2005) · D. Meek, *Tribute to a legend* (2005) · C. Hilton and I. Cole, *Memories of George Best* (2005) · G. Burn, *Best and Edwards: football, fame and oblivion* (2006) · R. Williams, ed., *George Best: a life in the news* (2006) · B. Best, *Our George: a family memoir of George Best* (2007) · B. Smith and M. Hunt, *George Best: a celebration* (2007) · *The Times* (26 Nov 2005) · *Daily Telegraph* (26 Nov 2005) · *The Guardian* (26 Nov 2005) · *The Independent* (26 Nov 2005) · *Belfast Telegraph* (8 Oct 2007) · b. cert. · m. cert. [1995] · d. cert.

Archives FILM BFINA, *This is your life*, M. Baker (director), Thames Television, 17 Nov 1971 · BFINA, 'Best intentions', B. Milliard (director), ITV, 9 Sept 1989 · BFINA, 'Best night', B. Boseley (executive producer), BBC2, 19 May 1996 · BFINA, *Stars and their lives*, C. Vorderman (presenter), ITV, 22 July 2000 · BFINA, 'George Best's stories', *Football stories*, D. Lavery (director), Channel 4, 25 June 2001 · BFINA, *Rich and famous*, A. Linares (director), ITV1, 20 Oct 2001 · BFINA, 'There's only one George Best', S. Walker (director), BBC1, 25 Sept 2002 · BFINA, *This is your life*, M. Baker (director), BBC1, 25 Sept 2002 · BFINA, 'Alex Best: my life with George',

J. Smith (director), Channel 4, 12 Feb 2004 · BFINA, 'The truth about George Best', J. Alexander (director), Five, 28 June 2004 · BFINA, current affairs footage · BFINA, documentary footage · BFINA, light entertainment footage · BL NSA, 'The Best thing', M. Parkinson (presenter), 1996 | SOUND BL NSA, 'George Best has … a word with Williams', interview with G. Williams, NP8831BW · BL NSA, documentary recordings

Likenesses photographs, 1964–2005, Getty Images, London · photographs, 1964–2005, Photoshot, London · photographs, 1964–2005, Camera Press, London · N. Libbert, bromide print, 1965, NPG · photographs, 1966–2005, PA Photos, London · photographs, 1967–2005, Rex Features, London · S. Samuels, bromide print, 1968, NPG [*see illus.*] · S. Samuels, two bromide prints, 1968, NPG · A. Catlin, bromide fibre print, 1987, NPG · T. R. Hart, C-type colour print, 1995, NPG · D. Goode, resin bronze, exh. Society of Portrait Sculptors, London 1997 · obituary photographs

Wealth at death £135,853: probate, 25 Jan 2007, *CGPLA Eng. & Wales*

Bethell, Nicholas William, fourth Baron Bethell (1938–2007), politician and writer, was born on 19 July 1938 at 7 Herbert Crescent, Chelsea, London, the son of William Gladstone Bethell (1904–1964), stockbroker, and his wife, Ann Margaret Frances, *née* Barlow (1919–1996). His grandfather John Henry Bethell, a politician and stockbroker, had been created a baronet in 1911 and was raised to the peerage as the first Baron Bethell in 1922. Bethell's parents were divorced in 1946, and his mother subsequently remarried three times.

Bethell was educated at Harrow School, and during national service from 1956 to 1958 was trained as a Russian interpreter, sparking a lifelong interest in the politics, language, and culture of the east. At Pembroke College, Cambridge, he read oriental languages, specifically Arabic and Persian. On 7 April 1964 he married Cecilia Mary Lothian Honeyman (*d.* 1977), daughter of the distinguished Arabist Alexander Mackie Honeyman. They had two sons, James (*b.* 1967) and William (*b.* 1969).

On leaving Cambridge Bethell spent two years (1962–4) writing for the *Times Literary Supplement* before joining the BBC's radio drama department as a script editor (1964–7), specializing in east European drama. Having befriended a number of Polish undergraduates at Cambridge he was inspired to write his first biographical work, *Gomulka: his Poland and his Communism* (1969). His lifelong love of Poland would eventually earn him the Polish order of Merit at the commander's level in 1991. Bethell's life, however, had taken an unexpected turn in 1967, when his 39-year-old cousin, Guy Anthony John, third Baron Bethell, was found dead in a guest house in Tenby. Nicholas Bethell became fourth Baron Bethell and joined the Conservative benches, and on the election of a Conservative government in 1970 was appointed a whip in the Lords.

By this stage Bethell's literary career had begun to blossom, as he completed translations of leading east European dissidents, including Slawomir Mrozek, Joseph Brodsky, and Alexander Solzhenitsyn. But the last of these, Solzhenitsyn's *Cancer Ward* (1968), led to a long-lasting dispute with the author and a libel case against *Private Eye*, which, although Bethell won, cut short his political career in the Lords: he was obliged to stand down as a whip after only ten months in the post. In his memoirs, *Spies and Other Secrets* (1994), Bethell revealed that his ministerial career had been cut short and that the prime minister, Edward Heath, had vetoed his inclusion on a list of Conservative candidates for seats in the European assembly on suspicion that he was a security risk. Despite years spent campaigning for the release of leading Russian dissidents, including Andrey Sakharov (and helping to found the Sakharov prize in 1985) he became an unfortunate victim of the cold war, accused of being a Soviet spy and a member of MI6 in almost equal measure. Whatever the exact truth he remained staunchly anti-communist throughout his adult life.

In 1975 the election of a new Conservative leader, Margaret Thatcher, breathed fresh life into Bethell's political career: he was nominated to the European assembly in 1975, and when the first direct elections took place four years later to the renamed European parliament he was elected as MEP for London North-West, a seat he held until defeated in 1994. He returned as one of London's MEPs in 1999, before the effects of Parkinson's disease eventually forced him to retire in 2003. Throughout his career in Strasbourg Bethell proved himself a committed pro-European, believing that Britain's commerce was inextricably tied up with that of the EEC. In the 1980s he led a Freedom of the Skies campaign against the fixing of European air fares. Although a legal action against some of the airlines failed through lack of funds, his actions helped pave the way for an era of low-cost air travel. On leaving the European parliament in 2003 he was awarded the Robert Schuman medal by the European People's Party, a Christian Democrat grouping that he had been determined to join in 1992 against the wishes of the more Eurosceptic members of his own party.

Bethell, however, will be best remembered as both a gifted linguist and a distinguished author. Perhaps his most important work was *The Last Secret: Forcible Repatriation to Russia, 1944–7* (1974), which exposed Britain's role in repatriating over 50,000 Cossacks and other refugees to the Soviet Union after the end of the Second World War. Two other books, *The War Hitler Won, September 1939* (1972) and *Russia Besieged* (1977), also focused on war themes from an eastern perspective. *The Palestine Triangle: the Struggle between the British, the Jews and the Arabs, 1935–1948* (1979) was an acclaimed introduction to the origins of the Palestinian conflict, while *The Great Betrayal* (1984) shed new light on Kim Philby's efforts to stop the Anglo-American attempts to free Albania from the Soviet sphere of influence. Bethell also completed another translation, of Chingiz Aitmatov's *Ascent of Mount Fuji* (1975).

Bethell's first marriage, to Cecilia, was dissolved in 1971. However, he found new happiness in 1992, when on 13 July he married Bryony Lea Morgan Griffiths (*b.* 1966), daughter of Brian David Griffiths, farmer, of Llanrhystud, Cardiganshire, and Arguignac, France. They had one son, John (*b.* 1995). Bethell died of heart failure at his home, 11 Anley Road, Fulham, London, on 8 September 2007, and was succeeded as fifth Baron Bethell by his elder son,

James. Annabel Markov, the widow of a murdered Bulgarian dissident, rightly recalled Bethell as 'a seemingly completely English person, whose real interests and passions lay in the east' (*The Guardian*, 13 Sept 2007).

MARK STUART

Sources N. Bethell, *Spies and other secrets* (1994) • *The Times* (11 Sept 2007) • *Daily Telegraph* (11 Sept 2007) • *The Guardian* (11 Sept 2007); (13 Sept 2007) • *The Independent* (13 Sept 2007) • Burke, *Peerage* • *WW* (2007) • b. cert. • m. cert. [1992] • d. cert.
Archives U. Birm. L., Avon MSS | FILM BFINA, current affairs footage | SOUND BL NSA, documentary recordings
Likenesses A. Lentati, photograph, 1994, Rex Features, London • photographs, 1994, Photoshot, London • obituary photographs
Wealth at death £4,538,005: probate, 27 Feb 2008, *CGPLA Eng. & Wales*

Bevan [*née* Ackenhausen], **Natalie Alice** (**1909–2007**), artist, muse, and collector, was born on 22 May 1909 at 2 Pembroke Cottages, Edwardes Square, London, the elder daughter and eldest of three children of Kurt Bernhard Heinrich Carl Ackenhausen (1878/9–1954) and his wife, Alice Katherine Inchbold, *née* Denny (*d.* 1964/5). Her father was a German textile merchant and her mother a children's book illustrator. The family adopted Denny as their surname in response to the First World War, and her father also changed his first name to Court.

Natalie Denny attended Norland Place School, London. She received an unorthodox artistic training from her mother and from the various artists she befriended as a popular figure among the creative milieu of London in the late 1920s. She met Christopher Nevinson in 1927 and went on a painting holiday in France the following year with him, his wife Kathleen Knowlman, and the painter Henry Jonas. Indeed she spent extended periods in France in 1927 and 1928, including a spell studying at Ossip Zadkine's studio in Paris. At a party held by Augustus John in 1927 she met Mark Gertler and thereafter sat for two portraits by him. *Supper* (*Natalie Denny*) (now known as *Natalie Bevan* [*née Ackenhausen, later Denny*], NPG) exudes the sensuality of the nineteen-year-old model and the artist's passion for her. Recalling her life at this time, based around fashionable nightclubs, and her introduction to the painter John Armstrong, she wrote, 'The Cave of Harmony, the Gargoyle, endless lovely parties and beautiful, beautiful people; but most of all the long serious talks about Painting and Love made a golden glorious beginning to our life-long friendship' (Strang, 14).

Gertler summed up Natalie Denny's position as one of the most beautiful and charismatic women of her generation, declaring in 1928: 'She is a nice girl, but too popular—there is a waiting list of six men, all of whom have proposed to her—but she cannot as yet make up her mind—meanwhile they all buzz around her like so many amorous bees—what a life!' (M. Gertler to M. G. Hodgkinson, 29 Feb 1928, priv. coll.). Among her suitors was the advertising copywriter Robert Alexander Polhill (Bobby) Bevan (1901–1974). However the victor was the writer and pioneering radio and television producer Lancelot de Giberne *Sieveking (1896–1972), whom she married on 24 August 1929; they had two daughters, the artist Victoria

Natalie Alice Bevan (**1909–2007**), by Mark Gertler, 1928

Burroughs (1930–1988) and the photographer Anthea Sieveking (*b.* 1933), and lived in Chelsea and Snape, Suffolk. Through Sieveking she developed her friendships with such artists as Paul Nash, who designed covers for Sieveking's books, and his brother John Nash. During her first marriage her own art flourished. She concentrated on painting in oils and watercolours, creating lively images of the landscape around Snape, as well as of France and Mexico. In 1936 she met the book collector and writer A. J. A. (Alphonse) Symons; his passion for her lasted until the end of the decade.

Natalie's marriage to Sieveking was dissolved in 1939. During the Second World War she worked for the Ministry of Works, organizing the collection of scrap metal throughout East Anglia. The post came with a petrol ration, allowing her to indulge her enthusiasm for fast and accomplished driving. When Bobby Bevan returned from war service in Washington he was delighted to discover that Natalie was single once more. They married on 11 July 1946 and lived in Knightsbridge and at Boxted House, Boxted, on the Essex–Suffolk border. Bevan had a distinguished career in advertising, becoming chairman of the agency S. H. Benson Ltd. He was involved in campaigns like that under the slogan 'Guinness is good for you' and was the inspiration for Mr Ingleby in Dorothy L. Sayers's crime novel *Murder Must Advertise*.

Bobby Bevan was the son of the painters Robert Polhill *Bevan and Stanislawa de Karlowska, leading figures of the London art world of the early twentieth century. He inherited and purchased works by his parents, as well as their Camden Town Group friends and other associates, including Walter Sickert, Paul Gauguin, and Henri Gaudier-Brzeska. Their works hung on the walls of Boxted House, where they were joined by paintings and drawings by the Bevans' own artist friends, including John Armstrong and Frederick Gore, and others more closely associated with East Anglia, including Cedric Morris, Lett Haines, and John Nash. Thanks to Natalie's skills as a hostess and Bobby's wine cellar, Boxted soon became a gathering place for artists, writers, and gardeners. Weekend guests included Maggi Hambling, Francis Bacon, A. P. (Alan) Herbert, Ronald Blythe, Beth Chatto, Robert Gathorne-Hardy, and Randolph Churchill, with whom Natalie had a close relationship from 1958 until his death ten years later. The Bevans did much to support the visual arts, not least through Bobby's lengthy chairmanship of the Minories gallery in Colchester and his promotion of his father's work, including a substantial gift to the Ashmolean Museum, Oxford, in 1957.

In the 1960s Natalie resumed her own artistic activities, attending classes at Colchester School of Art and Chelsea Pottery and exhibiting as a member of Colchester Art Society. She made and fired ceramics in a kiln in the conservatory-studio at Boxted and had a solo exhibition at Anthony d'Offay's gallery in London in 1968. However, perhaps her greatest creation was Boxted House itself. A Georgian square-built house of 1820, it contained a colourful profusion of pictures, objects, furniture, and plants. Bobby's collection of eighteenth-century furniture and Natalie's collections of Staffordshire and Chelsea ceramics mingled with patterned carpets and textiles, books, and arrangements of marble eggs, shells, and stones collected during extensive travels. The walls were covered with pictures, every one of which had a personal link to the couple. The ensemble was brought to life by Natalie's charisma; she was very glamorous, with golden hair swept up in elegant arrangements, often wearing knickerbockers with matching silk stockings, high-necked silk shirts, and hats galore. She greeted visitors on the door step with an offer of champagne, provided gourmet food and wine, and brought out the best in people, exclaiming 'Oh *do* try a bit' if she felt they were failing to provide interesting company. She had a great talent for friendship and sense of fun.

On 26 March 1986 (twelve years after Bobby's death) Natalie Bevan married the sailor and writer Samuel (Sam) Barclay (1920–2000), with whom she and Bobby had been friends for years. After Sam's death Boxted House was sold and Natalie moved to a nearby nursing home, Great Horkesley Manor, Great Horkesley, where she died on 15 August 2007. She was buried at St Peter's church, Boxted, on 29 August. An exhibition celebrating Natalie and Bobby Bevan and their life at Boxted House was held at the Scottish National Gallery of Modern Art, Edinburgh, in 2008, toured in part to Gainsborough's House, Sudbury, that year, and was recreated at Brighton Museum and Art Gallery in 2010. Following Natalie's death nine major works of twentieth-century British art were accepted in lieu of inheritance tax and allocated to the National Galleries of Scotland, the National Portrait Gallery, and the Tate collection. ALICE STRANG

Sources *The Independent* (29 Aug 2007) · *The Times* (10 Sept 2007) · A. Strang, *From Sickert to Gertler: modern British art from Boxted House* (2008) · personal knowledge (2011) · private information (2011) · b. cert. · m. certs. · d. cert.

Archives Tate archive, London, Natalie Bevan papers | Tate archive, London, personal papers of Cedric Morris and Arthur Lett-Haines

Likenesses G. Spencer Watson, oils, 1920–29, priv. coll. · H. Jonas, oils, *c.*1927, priv. coll. · M. Gertler, oils, 1928, NPG [*see illus.*] · photographs, *c.*1928–*c.*1968, repro. in Strang, *Sickert to Gertler* · obituary photographs

Wealth at death £3,731,776: probate, 17 June 2008, *CGPLA Eng. & Wales*

Beyer, Ralph Alexander (1921–2008), letter carver and sculptor, was born on 6 April 1921 in Rathenower Strasse in the Tiergarten area of Berlin, the elder son and eldest of three children of Oskar Wilhelm Laurenz Georg Beyer (1890–1964), art historian, and his wife, Margarete (1893–1945), daughter of Wilhelm Löwenfeld, lawyer. His brother, Frank Michael Beyer (1928–2008), was a composer. During his early years the family lived in Berlin, first in an apartment adjacent to his maternal grandparents and subsequently in a small house near Potsdam. The family moved in 1928 to Dresden, where Oskar Beyer set up Kunst-Dienst, an exhibition and information centre specializing in contemporary religious art. Beyer's parents were part of a circle that included the artist and typographer Rudolf Koch, the architect Erich Mendelsohn, and the theologians Paul Tillich and Martin Buber, both of whom lectured at Kunst-Dienst. At a young age Beyer was introduced to the New Typography movement, the New Photography, the products of the Bauhaus, and Rudolf Koch's innovative lettering and calligraphy produced at the Offenbacher Werkstatt.

Beyer's education was thoroughly radical. He attended the experimental Versuchsschule in Dresden and from 1932 was taught at home at Ahrenshoop on the Baltic coast, where his parents were living a communal existence with the architect Bernhard Hopp and the theologian Gottfried Schmidt and their families, working on a collaborative translation of the New Testament into contemporary German. This idealistic, cultivated life ended when Hitler became chancellor. The Beyers departed for Crete in the summer of 1933, then briefly joined the Bruderhof in Liechtenstein in 1936, and finally moved to Switzerland where Beyer attended the trilingual progressive École d'Humanité.

In 1937 Beyer was sent to England to work as an apprentice with Eric Gill at Piggotts in Buckinghamshire at the suggestion of Erich Mendelsohn, by then living in London. Although Beyer was only sixteen Gill immediately gave him challenging work. Gill's neo-medieval way of life was a shock but Beyer saw the sense in Gill's robust teaching methods. After six months he decided to attend the Central School of Arts and Crafts in London, lodging with his mother's cousin Margaret Lowenfeld, the child psychologist. He also attended life-modelling classes given by Henry Moore at Chelsea School of Art. After the war he collaborated with Moore, cutting lettering for the Northampton *Madonna*, the Dartington Hall *Reclining Figure*, and a memorial to Edith Sitwell at St Mary's, Weedon Lois, Northamptonshire.

On 7 March 1940 Beyer married Anne Yvonne Poole, also aged eighteen, daughter of Sydney Ernest Poole, electrical engineer; they had three daughters and a son. In the same year as his marriage he was interned as an enemy alien and sent to Huyton Camp near Liverpool, where he met the choreographer Kurt Joos and shared a house with Nikolaus Pevsner, who read and discussed with Beyer the early drafts of his *An Outline of European Architecture* (1942). Beyer was subsequently drafted into the pioneer corps, finally working as an interpreter in the intelligence corps in Germany where he found his father, brother, and sister 'in a pitiful state' outside Berlin (BL NSA interview, 2001) and was given the shocking news that his mother (who was Jewish) had been arrested in 1943 and had died in Auschwitz in April 1945. After serving in the army for six years he returned to art school for a couple of terms, taught briefly at St Christopher's School, Letchworth, worked in Cambridge for the ecclesiastical builders and carvers Rattee and Kett, and then, more fruitfully, spent a year at David Kindersley's workshop before setting up on his own.

In 1953 Beyer saw examples of David Jones's painted inscriptions in Nicolete Gray's *Architectural Review* article 'Theory of classical', and a year later his father Oskar Beyer's *Frühchristliche Sinnbilder und Inschriften: Lebenszeugnisse der Katacombenzeit* appeared, a small picture book of early Christian symbols and inscriptions. Inspired by these two sources, Beyer began to develop his own informal approach to carved lettering. This was seen to great effect in his collaborations with the architects Maguire and Murray, at the Royal Foundation of St Katherine, Butcher Row (1954), and at St Paul's, Bow Common (1958–60). The bold cast concrete lettering for the St Paul's Church porch that declaims 'This is the Gate of Heaven' had a particular poignancy sited in a then deprived area of east London.

In 1956 Beyer embarked on a commission for Coventry Cathedral, where his contributions included monumental letters cast in bronze set into the cathedral floor, a typeface for signs and notices, and the eight nave inscriptions carved in situ with his assistant Michael Watson on Hollington stone panels measuring fifteen by six feet. Beyer persuaded Spence that standard Trajanic lettering would not do, showing him his father's book of 1954. The eight 'Tablets of the Word' reflected post-war ecclesiastical interest in the early church; strikingly innovative examples of lapidary art, they constituted one of the most ambitious epigraphic projects of the twentieth century. While he was working at Coventry, Beyer married second (his first marriage having ended in divorce) Hilary Stephenson Reynolds (*b*. 1935), a secretary at the BBC (later a librarian), and daughter of Edward Robert Bernard Reynolds, schoolteacher. They had two daughters.

In the early 1970s Beyer completed another prestigious commission, for Paul Tillich Park in the historic utopian community of New Harmony, Indiana, sandblasting quotations from Tillich's writings on boulders and carving the ten commandments for the Waddams Chapel. For his inscriptions in Turkish and German at the Maguire and Murray KITA day-care centre for children in Berlin-Kreuzberg (1985–7) he developed a special child-friendly relief lettering in plaster. The commission was of particular personal importance, being a homecoming to the city of his birth.

Throughout his life Beyer also practised as a sculptor, sometimes combining his sculptures with lettering as at Hull College of Technology (1970). He also carried out the innumerable smaller commissions—memorial stones, plaques, and signs—that are the usual work of the letter cutter. This more modest work was informed by a passionate interest in typography. He believed in clear communication and avoided prettiness. All his inscriptions were, therefore, powerful and unadorned and his memorial stones—to figures as various as Noël Coward, Edith Sitwell, and Rolf Gardiner—were unflinching, meeting death head-on. Some of his most moving work was made for his own pleasure, in the form of carved inscriptions from the writings of Saint-John Perse, Rainer Maria Rilke (whom he translated elegantly from the German), and Rabindranath Tagore. He carved lettering for the artist and garden designer Ian Hamilton Finlay briefly in the late 1980s. He was one of the few British letter cutters to continue to work in an entirely modernist spirit in a field that from the 1980s became increasingly dominated by the eclectic and the decorative. He was an inspirational teacher of typography and letter forms at the University of Reading from 1968 to 1986 and at the City and Guilds of London Art School from 1983 to 1994.

Encountering Beyer and his wife, Hilary, at their house in St Winifreds Road, Teddington, was an uplifting experience. His manner combined fierce intensity and delightful humour. Casually but stylishly dressed, fond of wearing an anarchist beret or a cloth cap, his persona was perennially youthful, even boyish. In his company it seemed conceivable that the battle for heroic modernism in art and design might yet be won, with a fairer society just around the corner. Active to the end, he died at home of a heart attack on 13 February 2008. He was cremated at Mortlake cemetery, London, and was survived by his wife and six children. TANYA HARROD

Sources N. Gray, 'Lettering in Coventry Cathedral', *Typographica*, 6 (1962) • A. Bartram, *Lettering in architecture* (1975) • S. Raw, 'Interview with Beyer on Gill', *A Letter Exchange Occasional Paper*, 1 (1975) • J. Stevenson, 'Ralph Beyer: a study of informality and expression', in 'Lettercutting', BA diss., Department of Typography and Graphic Communication, U. Reading, 1988 • R. Beyer, 'The first forty years', *Dot the I: Journal of Letter Exchange* (spring 1991), 48–53 • L. Campbell, *Coventry Cathedral: art and architecture in post-war Britain* (1996) • T. Harrod, *The crafts in Britain in the 20th century* (1999) • interview with Ralph Beyer, 2001, BL NSA, National Life Story Collection: Crafts Lives • *The Guardian* (7 March 2008) • *Coventry Tele-*

graph (11 March 2008) · *The Times* (17 March 2008) · *Architects' Journal* (17 March 2008) · *The Independent* (27 March 2008) · S. Hill, *Howard's End is on the landing: a year of reading from home* (2010) · G. Learner, 'How to build a cathedral', *The agister's experiment* (2011) · J. Neilson, *Ralph Beyer* [forthcoming] · personal knowledge (2012) · private information (2012) · m. certs. · d. cert.
Archives University for the Creative Arts, Crafts Study Centre, papers, drawings, carved inscriptions | Royal Commission on the Ancient and Historical Monuments of Scotland, Edinburgh, Sir Basil Spence archive | SOUND BL NSA, National Life Story Collection: Crafts Lives, interview, 2001
Likenesses J. Donat, portrait, repro. in Gray, 'Lettering' · obituary photographs
Wealth at death under £270,000: probate, 3 July 2008, *CGPLA Eng. & Wales*

Bide, Sir Austin Ernest (1915–2008), chemist and industrialist, was born at 3 Blithfield Street, Kensington, London, on 11 September 1915, the son of Ernest Arthur Bide (1886/7–1918) and his wife, Eliza, *née* Young (1884–1976). He was brought up by his mother after his father, a gardener who had become a lance bombardier in the Royal Garrison Artillery, was killed in France in October 1918.

Bide showed an early interest in science, encouraged by visits to the nearby Science Museum, and left Acton county school at sixteen to join the department of the government chemist, while studying in the evenings for a chemistry degree through Birkbeck College and Chelsea Polytechnic. Unusually for a part-time student, he was awarded a first. In 1940 he was rejected for the Royal Air Force, but seconded instead to work for Glaxo Laboratories, whose work was seen as vital for the war effort. He worked on the synthesis of vitamin B1 and on the development of penicillin. On 28 June 1941 he married Irene Ward (*b*. 1920/21), a milliner, and daughter of Ernest Auckland Ward, upholsterer; they had three daughters. In 1944 his appointment as department head, with responsibility for patents and chemical development, began a career in management which led to his acting as personal assistant to the deputy managing director and further studies in economics and law at the London School of Economics.

Glaxo's Chairman, Sir Harry Jephcott, posted Bide to Montrose in 1951 to establish a factory for the manufacture of cortisone. Three years later he was back in London as deputy company secretary, then company secretary in 1959, and a director in 1963. The detailed understanding he gained in these posts of the often dysfunctional management of a business that was effectively a loose federation of companies was a key to his subsequent success. He became deputy chairman in 1971 and was already starting to merge some wholesale operations when the company was the subject of what was then the largest ever contested takeover bid in Britain, from Beecham. With the chairman suffering a breakdown, Bide was one of the small group who successfully fought off the approach, which was ruled out by the Monopolies Commission in 1972 on the grounds that it would damage the UK's research into new drugs. Ironically a defensive merger planned by Bide, with Boots, was ruled out on the same grounds, that innovation declined when companies exceeded a certain size. Subsequently Glaxo merged on its own terms with Beecham and later with the American group Smith Kline.

Bide succeeded as chairman and chief executive of Glaxo in 1973 and set about reordering the company's management. He instituted a management committee, organized the businesses on functional reporting lines, and began a step-by-step programme to establish a single company identity. He also reviewed the company's geographical profile, with strong export links and manufacturing concentrated on the Commonwealth. In 1978 Glaxo took the first step to what became a key to its subsequent success—the acquisition of an American company, Meyer Laboratories. At the time it was seen as a rather cautious step and Bide had to explain that 'we thought it sensible to start with a business which was viable ab initio. We did not have the right to be over-venturesome' (*The Independent*, 24 May 2008). But his approach paid off and was the basis of a major American expansion under his successor, Sir Paul Girolami. Bide also benefited from the discovery of Zantac, the blockbuster anti-ulcer drug launched in 1981, which had become the world's best-selling drug by 1986. It reinforced his determination to step up the company's research activities with an increasing share of turnover devoted to them. When Bide retired as chairman in 1985, Glaxo was Britain's most successful pharmaceutical company and one of its most admired. In recognition he was appointed life president. He had been knighted in 1980.

Bide was a quiet, kindly, unassuming man who was proud of being a scientist and enjoyed mending his own car and fishing. His qualities of determination and cool analytical detachment gave him an effectiveness in business that was much sought after. One contemporary said, 'He looks things in the face and does not flinch' (*The Guardian*, 4 Feb 1986). But while his advice was greatly valued by other top businessmen, none more so than the combative chairman of the British Leyland Motor Corporation, Sir Michael Edwardes, his dislike of the public stage became a fatal weakness when he succeeded Edwardes in 1982 in what was the most high-profile job in British industry.

In 1977 Edwardes had been appointed as chairman of what became British Leyland (BL), a huge sprawling company which had once accounted for 40 per cent of the UK's motor car output but now was in public ownership and still in difficulties even with hundreds of millions of pounds of government subventions. He turned to Bide to become one of two new non-executive directors on a six-person board. As Edwardes cut numbers, sought new models, and confronted unions and shop stewards, he found Bide a dependable ally. Bide became deputy chairman in 1980 and Edwardes said, 'he proved a tower of strength as we hit problem after problem' (Edwardes, 46). Bide was a key part of the BL team as they argued with the prime minister, Margaret Thatcher, for more financial support and she in turn stressed her desire for privatization of the company. By 1982 it was clear that Edwardes was losing favour with the government and a new chairman would be required. Edwardes made the case for a part-time non-executive chairman, arguing that the group's managing directors were now competent enough to need less close supervision. In the absence of an obvious candidate Bide was appointed. There was criticism of his continuing to hold his Glaxo post and he did not help matters by remarking in an interview that 'my expertise in management is total' (*The Times*, 29 Oct 1982). His lack of public visibility was also increasingly commented on.

As chairman of BL, Bide did a reasonable job of managing his directors and did not shirk the difficult decisions. Confronted by the Labour MP Tam Dalyell over the closure of the Bathgate factory, he refused to bend and told him years later, 'in the long run, facing reality as soon as possible causes the least hurt' (*The Independent*, 24 May 2008). He saw his role as 'getting BL to the point where someone might want to buy it' (*The Guardian*, 4 Feb 1986), a rather understated reflection of Margaret Thatcher's insistent demands. But he failed. He came close in 1985 with a potential deal first with Ford, and then, for part of the business, with General Motors, but the Ford deal was leaked and the government vetoed the sale. Bide was furious. The bid from General Motors for Land Rover and Leyland Trucks then collapsed over the government's insistence that General Motors' British board—and not the Americans—should have majority control. But Bide did not help himself when he opined that 'I am not sure that BL will attract better workers or managers if it were out of the Government's hands' (ibid.). Jaguar was finally sold in 1986 but the volume cars struggled against fierce competition. Bide's fate was sealed when the company had to apply for £1.5 billion more aid in 1985. The following year Thatcher brought in a favourite, Sir Graham Day, from British Shipbuilders.

Bide was committed to the encouragement of better technology. He chaired the Confederation of British Industry's Research and Technology Committee for ten years and wrote a government report on technology skills in 1986. On his retirement, in conjunction with his friend the former prime minister Edward Heath he chaired the Salisbury Cathedral Spire Appeal Committee. He was active in a wide range of bodies including the Medical Research Council, the British Institute of Management, the Freight Transport Association, and the British Shippers' Council. In 1993 he founded the World Humanity Action Trust to study issues of governance for a sustainable future. He was an honorary fellow of the Institute of Chemical Engineers and the Institute of Biotechnological Studies, and received several honorary degrees. He died on 11 May 2008 in St Anthony's Hospital, North Cheam, of bronchopneumonia following a stroke; he was survived by his wife and their three daughters.

MARTIN ADENEY

Sources *The Guardian* (4 Feb 1986); (5 June 2008) · *Daily Telegraph* (20 May 2008) · *The Independent* (24 May 2008) · *The Times* (29 Oct 1982); (28 May 2008) · M. Edwardes, *Back from the brink* (1983) · M. Thatcher, *The Downing Street years* (1993) · M. Adeney, *The motor makers* (1988) · Burke, *Peerage* · *WW* (2008) · b. cert. · m. cert. · d. cert.

Likenesses L. Woon, semi-matte bromide print, 1985, NPG · obituary photographs

Wealth at death £554,649: probate, 22 Dec 2008, *CGPLA Eng. & Wales*

Biffen, (William) John, Baron Biffen (1930–2007), politician, was born on 3 November 1930 at the Drummuir Nursing Home, Northfield, Bridgwater, Somerset, the son of Victor William Biffen (1896–1987), tenant farmer, of Hill Farm, Otterhampton, Bridgwater, and his wife, Edith Annie (Tish) (1908–1996), *née* Bennett. His mother had come to the farm as a housemaid and married her employer. From Dr Morgan's School, Bridgwater, where despite his lack of prowess at games he became head boy, Biffen won a scholarship to Jesus College, Cambridge, to read history. He took up his place after two years' national service as a clerk in the Royal Engineers, in which he reached the rank of lance-corporal. He graduated in 1953 with first-class honours in both parts of the tripos. He was offered places at Yale and Cornell universities to do graduate research but lacked the funds to take them up. Instead from 1953 to 1960 he worked for Tube Investments Ltd, a holding company for specialized engineering businesses, and from 1960 to 1961 he worked in the Economist Intelligence Unit.

Biffen had developed a strong interest in politics at Cambridge, and was chairman of the university Conservative association. His first attempt to enter parliament was at Coventry East in the general election of 1959, against Richard Crossman. Even in an election that brought the tories a third term in power with a large majority Crossman won comfortably, though he expressed his admiration for his opponent. Biffen was selected to fight Oswestry at a by-election in November 1961 caused by David Ormsby-Gore's appointment as ambassador to Washington, the former lance-corporal defeating a major and two colonels to secure the candidacy. He would become one of the parliamentary party's most dedicated opponents of membership of the Common Market. It was ironic, therefore, that he was the only contender for the seat to endorse wholeheartedly at the selection meeting the attempt by Harold Macmillan to take Britain into it. On winning the seat (renamed Shropshire North in 1983) he held it until his retirement from the House of Commons at the general election of 1997.

Backbencher Biffen was a close friend and supporter of Enoch Powell and one of just fifteen tory MPs who voted for Powell in the 1965 Conservative Party leadership contest. Partly innately, but also partly because of Powell's influence over him, Biffen was very much an independent member once on the back benches. Perhaps as a result his considerable intellect was not, except briefly, rewarded by a place on the front bench until after Edward Heath had been removed from the leadership in 1975. The exception was when Sir Alec Douglas-Home appointed him technology spokesman in opposition in 1965 under Ernest Marples. He resigned soon after Heath became leader later that year, citing ill-health: in fact, he had had a poor relationship with Marples. Biffen's Powellite sympathies, notably on economic matters and Europe, made him suspect so far as Heath was concerned. However, sounded out

(William) **John Biffen, Baron Biffen** (1930–2007), by unknown photographer, 1986

about a job after the tories returned to power in 1970, Biffen replied that he could not in all honour consider such a thing.

Biffen was wise to say so. In October 1971 he voted against his own party on the principle of British entry to the EEC; he maintained that stance in the divisions on the European Communities Bill during 1972, a bill enacted only with Labour Party support. This further alienated him from the leadership. After Heath's defeat in the October 1974 general election the leader, pressed to make a gesture towards the right of the party in the interests of unity, offered Biffen a place on the front bench. Biffen wrote to Heath—and asked that the correspondence be published—declaring that the party would benefit from a new leader. Heath did not promote him.

Nor, initially, did Biffen accept shadow office from Margaret Thatcher after she replaced Heath in 1975. However, in January 1976 he agreed to become energy spokesman, and in the autumn of that year he moved to industry; yet he resigned after three months, again pleading illness. This time it was true: he had been diagnosed with clinical depression, caused, it turned out, by a blood disorder. It was not until November 1978 that he was well enough to return to the front bench, this time as small businesses spokesman. He performed with sufficient conviction and commitment in the few months that remained of that parliament to secure his place in the Thatcher government; he and she were the only grammar-school products in the cabinet.

Cabinet minister Biffen was sworn of the privy council and appointed chief secretary to the Treasury after the Conservative victory at the 1979 general election. He soon showed he was entirely in tune with Thatcher's economic doctrine of reduced public spending and lower taxes. He wholeheartedly endorsed the deflationary policies of Sir Geoffrey Howe, the chancellor of the exchequer, and spoke of 'three years of unparalleled austerity' that lay ahead for Britain (*The Times*, 22 Jan 1980). On 2 November 1979 he married Sarah Wood (*née* Drew) at Wandsworth register office, becoming stepfather to her two children. The daughter of John Albert Cyril Drew, she had been Biffen's secretary. Until then Biffen had appeared to be a confirmed bachelor, and friends and colleagues were surprised when he married. Michael Foot, soon to become leader of the opposition, congratulated him on his 'own personal U-turn'.

Biffen's conduct of public spending rounds as chief secretary—he was one of the toughest and most resolute in that office's short history—was sufficient for him to be promoted to secretary of state for trade in 1981, though some felt his ability to see all sides of every argument had held him back from wielding the axe as much as he might. His most controversial decision at trade was to approve Rupert Murdoch's purchase of Times Newspapers without any reference to the Monopolies and Mergers Commission, which many were confident would have blocked it. He was never happy running a department: he lacked the stamina, and also confessed to 'mind-numbing terror and absolute funk' over his responsibilities (*Daily Telegraph*, 15 Aug 2007). And the job of trade secretary was one unsuited to a man who disliked going abroad.

Biffen had felt almost uncritical admiration for Margaret Thatcher from the moment of her victory: but, ironically, it was her handling of the event that confirmed her international reputation and secured her a landslide at the 1983 general election—the Falklands War—that caused him for the first time to question her judgement. In a reshuffle caused by the resignation of Lord Carrington, the foreign secretary, and Humphrey Atkins, who spoke for the Foreign Office in the Commons, Biffen was moved to be leader of the House of Commons, a post he held until the election of June 1987. He sat in the cabinet as lord president of the council from 1982 to 1983, and as lord privy seal from 1983 to 1987.

By common consent Biffen was one of the great Commons leaders of modern times. The combination of his intelligence, courtesy, modesty, and reasonableness won him friends in all parties and ensured that business was transacted smoothly at a time when the most contentious Thatcherite measures were being put through parliament, including trade-union reform and privatization. He was popular not least because he could be very funny: as when he told the left-wing tribune Dennis Skinner that 'we grammar school boys must stick together' (*The Guardian*, 8 June 1985). However, the steep decline of his relationship with Thatcher dated from his assumption of this office. He took issue with her most devout supporters and their attempt to turn toryism into a 'raucous political faction' (*The Times*, 10 Feb 1986). There was an irony, because he agreed with her entirely on her most controversial policy—monetarism—and was ahead of her on scepticism about the European project.

Always his own man—a difficult thing when bound by collective responsibility—Biffen began to signal his opposition to certain policies, provoked largely by what he saw as Thatcher's refusal to engage in debate. He was opposed to her determination to ban staff at GCHQ, the government's secret communications centre, from belonging to trade unions, which caused him to be 'shouted down' in a cabinet meeting (*The Times*, 15 Aug 2007). He opposed the attacks on the BBC by Norman Tebbit, the party chairman, which made him unpopular in the party apparatus. However, his greatest error was to go on television in 1986 and call for a 'balanced ticket' of senior Conservatives by the time of the next general election (*Weekend World*, LWT, 11 May 1986), which was interpreted as an attack on Thatcher's and Tebbit's control of the party.

This heresy was compounded by Biffen's statement that the party should 'consolidate' for a while rather than pursue more radical reforms. Thatcher was tempted to sack him at once, but was talked out of that by Lord Whitelaw and John Wakeham, two of her closest confidants. Instead she used her press secretary, Bernard Ingham, to brief against him—Ingham called him 'semi-detached' and a 'licensed court jester' (*The Times*, 13 May 1986)—and he was frozen out of important decision making. He was determined not to be forced into resignation: 'I would sooner leave on my feet than crawl on my knees', he said (*The Times*, 1 June 1987). He also fought back at Ingham, describing him as 'a rough-spoken Yorkshire Rasputin who is manipulating government' and as 'not the sewage, only the sewer' (*The Guardian*, 1 Feb 1989).

By the time of the 1987 election campaign Biffen was effectively a non-person in the cabinet. He was given no national role in the campaign and, to the anger of many in the parliamentary party, was sacked in the post-election reshuffle. Given how well, by any standards, he had done his job of keeping 'the usual channels' open and ensuring parliamentary business got through, his sacking was widely interpreted as a vindictive act. At least on the back benches he could give full vent to his contrary opinions, and did. He attacked the government's policy on Europe—his Powellite approach to that question remained undiluted and, in fact, Thatcher moved towards it. However, he took her on directly over the question of the community charge, or poll tax, which he believed unduly regressive.

Last years Once Thatcher had been deposed and the poll tax—described as her 'flagship' policy—went with her, Biffen commented that 'when a flagship becomes a navigational hazard, the best thing to do is to scupper it' (*The Independent*, 22 March 1991). Her successor, John Major, soon ran into trouble over the question of Europe. Although Biffen voted against the third reading of the bill to ratify the Maastricht treaty in 1993, he never joined in the organized militancy against the bill, and against Europe, that made Major's time in office so difficult. He did, though, make an outspoken attack on Major for his role in taking Britain into the European exchange rate mechanism in 1990.

After leaving government Biffen had a number of business interests. He was a director of Glynwed International from 1987 to 2000, of J. Bibby & Sons from 1988 to 1997, of the Rockware Group from 1988 to 1991, and of Barlow International from 1998 to 2000. He was also a trustee of the London Clinic from 1994 to 2002, and was appointed a deputy lieutenant for Shropshire in 1993. He wrote two short and well-received books about political and parliamentary life: *Inside the House of Commons* (1989) and *Inside Westminster* (1996). He became a regular contributor to newspaper comment pages, notably in *The Guardian*.

Biffen took a peerage in 1997 as Baron Biffen, of Tanat, in the county of Shropshire, though his elevation coincided with a serious deterioration in his health: he underwent a major operation immediately upon leaving the Commons. He suffered total renal failure in 2000 and had to go on dialysis three times a week: nonetheless he attended the Lords as regularly as he could until his health became too poor in 2005. He spent his last years in a Georgian rectory on Shropshire's border with Wales at Llanyblodwel, nursed by his devoted wife. He died of heart failure on 14 August 2007 at the Royal Shrewsbury Hospital. His funeral was at Llanyblodwel on 21 August, and his memorial service at St Margaret's, Westminster, on 19 February 2008.

Biffen had the best traits of the highly intelligent man: he was self-deprecating, low-key, modest, and diffident, without a trace of intellectual arrogance. Like many naturally witty people he was also intense and complex, and could be brooding. Though idiosyncratic, and not the best team player, he was loyal and of impeccable integrity. He was no great political innovator, but he represented a strain of intelligent and principled conservatism that was an important element in his party. SIMON HEFFER

Sources *The Times* (15 Aug 2007) · *Daily Telegraph* (15 Aug 2007) · *The Guardian* (15 Aug 2007) · *The Independent* (15 Aug 2007) · Burke, *Peerage* · *WW* (2007) · personal knowledge (2011) · private information (2011) · b. cert. · m. cert. · d. cert.

Archives FILM BFINA, documentary footage | SOUND BL NSA, current affairs, documentary and performance recordings

Likenesses W. Bird, bromide print, 1966, NPG · photographs, 1979–86, Getty Images, London, Hult. Arch. · photographs, 1979–98, PA Photos, London · photographs, 1980–98, Photoshot, London · photographs, 1982–93, Rex Features, London · photograph, 1986, Getty Images, London, Hult. Arch. [*see illus.*] · N. Sinclair, photographs, 1991–*c*.1993, NPG · Marc [M. Boxer], ink caricature, repro. in *The Observer* (23 Oct 1983) · obituary photographs

Wealth at death £2,395,014: probate, 26 June 2008, *CGPLA Eng. & Wales*

Bingley [*née* Vick], **Juliet Martin**, **Lady Bingley** (**1925–2005**), social worker, was born on 18 July 1925 at St Clere's Hall, Danbury, Essex, the third of four daughters of Reginald Martin Vick (1884–1971), consulting surgeon at St Bartholomew's Hospital, London, and his wife, Mary Kate (*b.* 1891), elder daughter of Sir Reginald James Neville Neville, first baronet, barrister and judge, of Sloley, Norfolk. She grew up with her three sisters in London in one of only two family houses in Harley Street. She attended King Alfred's School, Hampstead, which was co-educational and run without punishments or homework. Among her activities she attended spirited and energetic country dancing sessions at Cecil Sharp House. At the London School of Economics, then evacuated to Cambridge, she studied social administration. A life-changing experience was her placement with the Personal Services Society in Liverpool. For the first time she met racism, religious persecution, and poverty. She qualified as an almoner (medical social worker) in 1945 and started work at St Bartholomew's Hospital in London.

On 7 August 1948 Juliet Vick married Alexander Noel Campbell (Alec) Bingley (1905–1972), a captain in the Royal Navy, and son of Robert Noel Glanville Bingley, tea planter. After their marriage they bought Hoddesdonbury, in Hoddesdon, Hertfordshire, a farm mentioned in Domesday Book. There she created a family home to which she was devoted for the rest of her life. She and her husband had three children: twins—William and Charlotte Elizabeth (Liza; *b.* 1950)—and Penelope (Polly; *b.* 1954). In 1959 her husband, by now an admiral, was knighted KCB and appointed commander-in-chief, Mediterranean. The family went to live at Admiralty House in Valletta, Malta, where Juliet Bingley found full expression for her many talents. She became closely involved in reform of aspects of the Maltese health and social care system. The first president of Malta later said that her memorial was the change in attitude there to the importance of proper social welfare systems, especially for the old. She had met and become friends with Dom Mintoff, the prime minister, before she went to Malta. He was at odds with the British government, and she became an unofficial envoy, or 'messenger' as she put it, between him and the government. She continued to fulfil this role in the 1970s and 1980s, long after leaving the country, and for this and her work in promoting social welfare in Malta the Maltese government granted her its highest award, the companionship of Honour, in 1976.

In 1961 Sir Alec Bingley was appointed commander-in-chief, Portsmouth, and Juliet Bingley became involved in improvements of the naval family welfare services. Two years later he retired from active service and returned to Hoddesdonbury. Juliet Bingley then began a long involvement with the National Association of Mental Health (later MIND), which culminated in four tumultuous years from 1979 as its national chairman. During this period the association changed from being an organization dominated by professional interests to one focused on the rights of those with mental health problems. MIND made a major contribution to the drafting of the Mental Health Act of 1983. Another important development was an increased emphasis on the contribution of volunteers.

In 1972 Alec Bingley died suddenly, at the age of sixty-seven, a devastating blow to his wife. Four days after his death Juliet Bingley decided that she should return to work as a medical social worker after an interval of twenty-four years. She obtained a part-time post at a small hospital in London, St Mark's, which specialized in disorders of the intestinal tract, and which was associated with St Bartholomew's. Many patients suffered from chronic or recurrent inflammatory bowel disease, and others suffered disorders of bowel function with an important emotional component. Juliet Bingley's warm and empathetic personality captivated patients and staff alike. She built up a close working relationship with both medical and nursing staff, and also with a psychotherapist. Her concern extended to the welfare of every member of the hospital staff, and she chaired a heads of staff committee. For this work she was awarded the Ellison Nash prize by St Bartholomew's Hospital in 1988, and was appointed MBE in 1990.

In 1979 Juliet Bingley was a founding member of the National Association for Colitis and Crohn's Disease (NACC) and served on its governing council for twenty-three years, including a period as vice-chairman. During this time membership increased to 30,000. One of her particular contributions was the development of NACC In-Contact, a telephone enquiry and support service run by trained sufferers for sufferers. She also instigated and helped to run a welfare fund for those in financial need, and established a system of competitive awards for research into the psychological and social consequences of inflammatory bowel disease.

Juliet Bingley was well built, with a fresh, open face and blue eyes. She was outgoing and fun to be with. She had a kind of inner radiance that brought out the best in those she came into contact with, and gave them the self-confidence to do themselves justice. People felt that she cared and that they could trust her implicitly. However, she had a steely resolve as well as charm and good humour in pursuing her goals. In later years she discovered a love of writing poetry and enjoying it with the Ware Poets Group. She published a volume of her poems, *What It Was and What It Was Not* (2002), and circulated privately some charming books of illustrated stories written for her grandchildren. She collected Staffordshire figures and took great delight in the practical details of running Hoddesdonbury, and creating there a place of welcome for her family and wide circle of friends.

After retirement from St Mark's in 1990 Juliet Bingley worked for twelve years as counsellor for a large general practice in Welwyn, and later for Danesbury, a unit providing care, rehabilitation, and respite for adults, especially young adults with serious physical illness. She supported innumerable local activities and good causes. The local newspaper in its obituary called her 'the People's Champion' (*Hertfordshire Mercury*, 21 Jan 2005). She died on 16 January 2005, at Queen Elizabeth II Hospital, Welwyn Garden City, following a stroke. Hoddesdon parish church was packed for her funeral, as was Christ Church, Spitalfields, London, for her memorial service on 17 October that year. She was survived by her three children.

JOHN LENNARD-JONES

Sources *Washington Post* (28 July 1983) · 'Lady Juliet Bingley', *St Mark's Hospital Annual Report* (1990), 31 · *The Guardian* (10 Feb 2005) · 'Juliet Bingley: a tribute', *NACC News* (spring 2005) · 'Lady Juliet Bingley', *St Mark's Hospital Annual Report* (2005), 64 · 'Remembering Juliet Bingley', booklet prepared for memorial service at Christ Church, Spitalfields, London, 17 Oct 2005 · Burke, *Peerage* · *WW* (2005) · personal knowledge (2009) · private information (2009) · b. cert. · m. cert. · d. cert.

Likenesses M. Zanolin, photograph, repro. in J. Bingley, *What it was and what it was not* (2002), cover · photograph, repro. in *The Guardian* · photograph, repro. in *St Mark's Hospital Annual Report* ·

photograph, repro. in *NACC News* · photograph, repro. in *Remembering Juliet Bingley*
Wealth at death £1,178,583: probate, 29 June 2005, *CGPLA Eng. & Wales*

Birley, Marcus Oswald Hornby Lecky [Mark] (**1930–2007**), club owner, was born at midnight on 29–30 May 1930 (his birth was recorded as 30 May), at the Corner House, 62 Wellington Road, St John's Wood, London, the only son of Sir Oswald Hornby Joseph *Birley (1880–1952), portrait painter, and his wife, Rhoda Vava Mary (1900–1981), daughter of Robert Lecky Pike, high sheriff of co. Carlow. His only sister was Maxime de la Falaise (1922–2009), designer, fashion writer, food columnist, and *gallante*. He was educated at Eton College, and had a year of philosophy, politics and economics at University College, Oxford, before failing his prelims. On 10 March 1954 he married Lady Annabel Vane-Tempest-Stewart (*b*. 1934), younger daughter of Edward Charles Stewart Robert Vane-Tempest-Stewart, eighth marquess of Londonderry. They had two sons, Rupert (1955–1986, presumed drowned off the coast of west Africa) and Robin (*b*. 1958), and a daughter, India Jane (*b*. 1961). In 1964 his wife became *maîtresse-en-titre* of his boon companion Jimmy Goldsmith: the Birleys subsequently separated, and were divorced in 1975 after she had had two of Goldsmith's children. Although Birley was a considerable philanderer, who ranked sex before cigars, wine, and dogs as life's four chief pleasures, he was profoundly depressed when his wife left him.

During the 1950s Birley worked for J. Walter Thompson's advertising agency. Beginning as David Hicks's successor as the art department's paste-up boy, he was later art director of the Horlicks advertising campaign and redesigned *Tatler*. In 1959 he opened the first London shop of the luxury-goods firm Hermès in Jermyn Street. There he honed his skill in convincing customers that spending large sums on trifles showed discernment.

In 1962 Birley's friend John Aspinall opened the Clermont gambling club at 44 Berkeley Square, and leased its basement to him. He started with a piano bar of two rooms, dug out the garden, extended his premises to Hay's Mews, and opened a nightclub with dining tables and dance floor in 1963. It was named Annabel's after his wife. As the son of artists he had a good eye for pictures, and indeed for visual impact: his eclectic collection of paintings and sketches (many of them canine), together with rich textiles, created an air of Edwardian luxury. He was often said to have devised a country-house effect, but his arrangements were too flawless and contrived for country-house living. The balance between Birley's stylish, old-money clients and the parvenus, who were indispensable to the profitability of his club, was always precarious. There was an influx of property developers and ill-starred secondary bankers in the 1970s. During the 1980s Arab businessmen with their escorts were conspicuous at its dining tables. The crisis in the Lloyds insurance market had a greater impact on Annabel's than any other event: the old-money membership greatly receded in the early 1990s. After 2000 Annabel's membership lists were revived and enhanced by his daughter, India Jane, who refitted the club and made Annabel's a sexy brand for the rich young crowd working in the hedge funds and private equity companies with headquarters near Berkeley Square.

Birley opened a second club, Mark's, at 46 Charles Street in 1969. This was a luncheon and dining club, serving English fare, intended to vie with Wilton's restaurant in Jermyn Street. Men could talk business there, which was prohibited in St James's Street clubs, in a luscious atmosphere of country-house living in the Sassoon or Rothschild manner. It was a thundering success with its members. In 1975 Birley leased a former wine merchant's premises at 26 South Audley Street, where he created a restaurant, Harry's Bar. Named after Giuseppe Cipriani's famous bar in Venice, the restaurant had a Milanese menu (Alberico Penati was renowned among London chefs) and Venetian décor, in which Fortuny fabrics were juxtaposed with works by the New York cartoonist Peter Arno. Unlike Mark's Club it was intended to attract women habituées. For thin ladies who lunched, as well as American visitors and devotees of Italian cuisine, the food and ambience were sublime. Prices were exorbitant: at one time Harry's Bar was the highest grossing restaurant per square foot in the world. Birley considered it to be his apogee.

In 2001 Birley opened another dining club, George, at 87–8 Mount Street. The Bath and Racquets Club, a private men's gymnasium at 49 Brook's Mews, was another Birley operation, with his hallmarks of elegance, luxury, and exclusion. Its steam-rooms, showers, and urinals were made of green onyx. He also opened an interiors emporium in Pimlico Road in 1973 and a cigar-shop and vintners in Fulham Road in 1978.

Birley's mother had been cruelly unloving: he detested her memory. As a result he found his satisfactions in objects rather than people, in material perfectionism rather than demonstrative affection. He lacked empathy with women, preferred dogs to humans, was mistrustful and emotionally constipated, sometimes melancholic. Standing 6 feet 5 inches tall, he had daunting manners, chill formal elegance, and despotic habits. His temperament was imperious, peremptory, irritable, and impatient. Selfish about his personal convenience, and self-indulgent about his comforts, he was nevertheless Berkeley Square's Beau Brummell, who set the fashions of his set. People savoured his dry, dismissive wit: when asked at a dinner what the French excelled at, he paused for effect before replying, 'they are very good at raking gravel'. Although he was loyal to select friends there was a lifelong rupture with Aspinall. He could be charming when in a good mood, but was intolerant of failure or imperfection. His businesses were ruled with a close scrutiny and relentless insistence on quality. He travelled widely to copy good ideas or filch staff. Employees were carefully selected, and treated with paternalistic generosity: Annabel's head doorman earned enough to put his son through Harrow and Cambridge.

Birley smoked ten cigars a day even after a threatening heart by-pass operation. In his final years he suffered long spells of hospitalization, had a publicized estrangement from his surviving son, Robin, and in June 2007 sold all his club interests for a reported £90 million to Richard Caring, who had made his first fortune in the garments trade and already owned The Ivy and Le Caprice restaurants. Birley died at Charing Cross Hospital, Fulham, London, on 24 August 2007, of a spontaneous intracranial haemorrhage. His funeral at St Paul's, Knightsbridge, on 19 September 2007 was attended by, among others, Prince and Princess Michael of Kent.

RICHARD DAVENPORT-HINES

Sources *The Times* (27 Aug 2007) · *Daily Telegraph* (27 Aug 2007) · *The Guardian* (29 Aug 2007) · *The Independent* (3 Sept 2007) · M. Orth, 'Hurley Birley', *VF* (Feb 2008) · Burke, *Peerage* · personal knowledge (2011) · private information (2011) · b. cert. · d. cert.

Likenesses photographs, 1954–2001, Photoshot, London · photographs, 1954–2006, Getty Images, London · photographs, 1961–2004, Rex Features, London · T. Jenkins, photographs, 2003, Camera Press, London · J. Becker, photograph, repro. in www.vanityfair.com/culture/features/2008/02/birley200802 · obituary photographs · photographs, repro. in A. Goldsmith, *No invitation required: the Pelham Cottage years* (2009)

Wealth at death £104,805,718: probate, 30 June 2009, *CGPLA Eng. & Wales*

Bishop, Sir Frederick Arthur (1915–2005), civil servant and director-general of the National Trust, was born on 4 December 1915 at 118 Hampstead Road, Brislington, Bristol, the son of Alfred John Bishop, foreman for a wholesale stationers, later factory manager, and his wife, Mary Maria, *née* Shaw. He was educated at Colston's Hospital School in Bristol. He joined the Inland Revenue in 1934. For financial reasons he had not been able to go to university, but he took an external law degree at London University in 1938. He served during the Second World War as a ferry pilot in the Air Transport Auxiliary. On new year's day 1940 he married Elizabeth Finlay Stevenson (1915–1999), a fellow civil servant, and daughter of Samuel Brown Stevenson, of Belfast; they had two sons and a daughter.

Bishop returned to the civil service in 1947, initially in the Ministry of Food. There his abilities were soon recognized; within two years he was principal private secretary to the minister, John Strachey, and to his successors Maurice Webb and Gwilym Lloyd George. He was moved to be assistant secretary to the cabinet in 1953. He was an effective manager of the cabinet's economic business, and secretary of its building committee during the government's drive to build 300,000 houses a year, led by Harold Macmillan as minister of housing. He worked closely with the powerful cabinet secretary, Sir Norman Brook, who in 1956 secured his move to 10 Downing Street to become Anthony Eden's principal private secretary. His calm efficiency won the respect, and the ear, of an increasingly embattled prime minister. Some historians believe that even under Eden his advice, and his 'hawkish' views on international affairs, began to acquire the influence that was to be more marked under Eden's successor Macmillan.

Macmillan kept Bishop on when he took over as prime minister in 1957. Over the next four years Bishop played a key role in the policy process, exercising influence out of all proportion to his formal responsibilities. With a weak foreign secretary in Selwyn Lloyd, Macmillan relied heavily for advice on international affairs on his civil service private secretaries, whose primary loyalty was increasingly to him personally, treating them as a virtual 'kitchen cabinet' (Aldous, 'Family affair', 14), 'more akin to American national security advisers than mere private secretaries' (McNamara, 67). Working closely with his colleague Philip de Zulueta, Bishop did not hesitate to disagree with, and brief the prime minister against, the official Foreign Office line. He and de Zulueta have been described as the '"change agents" essential to any process of [policy] redefinition, [giving] access to ideas that had not been dulled by slow passage through the bureaucratic machine' (Aldous, 'Family affair', 15). When in 1957 Macmillan wanted to ensure American collaboration in resisting communist infiltration into Syria, it was Bishop whom he sent to Washington for talks with the secretary of state, John Foster Dulles. Dulles was charmed and impressed by Bishop, declaring that there was 'genuine, intimate and effective co-operation, stemming directly from Macmillan' (McNamara, 100). Bishop often travelled with Macmillan, for instance to the Bermuda conference in March 1957 and to Moscow in 1959, the scene of a celebrated row between Macmillan and Nikita Khrushchov. His role and his influence were openly resented by the Foreign Office and the foreign secretary.

Bishop became deputy secretary to the cabinet in 1959. Although in principle he should now have been impartially serving the cabinet as a whole, he remained very close to the prime minister; he has been described as acting at this time in some respects as though he were still Macmillan's principal private secretary, advising him on European matters. During the protracted debates about Britain's relations with the European Economic Community (EEC), pro-Europeans used Bishop as their direct link to the prime minister. He was appointed CB in 1960, having been made CVO in 1957.

Bishop returned to the Ministry of Agriculture, Fisheries, and Food in 1961. Even there he continued to be influential in international affairs, especially in relation to the EEC. One historian, Jacqueline Tratt, has described him as a leading member of the small group—including Harold Macmillan, Edward Heath, and Sir Frank Lee, permanent secretary to the Treasury—that connived to bring about a major change of policy orientation, almost surreptitiously planning and putting into action the ultimately unsuccessful first approach to the EEC in 1961. He also played a significant part in creating the National Economic Development Council. He intended this in part to rival a department he disliked, the Treasury, arguing that there was a need for 'a more planned approach to the national economic problem … a partnership with employers and unions' (Ringe and Rollings, 342–3). His draft terms of reference were reproduced largely verbatim when the creation of the council was announced by the chancellor of the exchequer, Selwyn Lloyd.

After three years in the Ministry of Agriculture, Fisheries, and Food Bishop's government career seemed to be moving towards a climax when, in 1964, he was appointed permanent secretary of the Ministry of Land and Natural Resources, newly created by Harold Wilson. Wilson's aim was to speed up the planning process by removing it from what some saw as the dead hand of the Ministry of Housing and Local Government. Others felt that the new department, with a remit to bring forward more land for development by taxing landowners and developers, never had a chance. It was doubly unfortunate for Bishop both that his new minister, Fred Willey, was out of his depth and that the Ministry of Housing and Local Government was led by one of the most formidable civil servants of the post-war period, Dame Evelyn Sharp. She was determined that her department should lose no important responsibilities. Exploiting the access of her own minister, Richard Crossman, to Wilson, she fought ruthlessly to ensure, first, that the new ministry was given no real powers and, second, that it was wound up as soon as possible. Willey's complaints and Wilson's resentment were unavailing. Bishop, who had no illusions about either his ministry or his minister, found himself in a non-job. By June 1965 he had let it be known that he wished to resign from the civil service and Crossman was exulting in his diary, 'He should be sent off as soon as possible. Let's get rid of him this summer' (Crossman, 261).

Bishop was an able and well-liked public servant who, in his most senior Whitehall post, was unlucky to be frustrated by such fierce bureaucratic and political infighting. He left the civil service in 1965 and took a number of part-time posts, most notably on the board of S. Pearson & Son. In 1968–9 he was a member of a group of former senior officials set up to advise Edward Heath, then leader of the opposition, on reforms to the machinery of government. The Pearson board brought him into regular contact with Patrick Gibson, a committee member (and later chairman) of the National Trust. One result was that in January 1971 Bishop took up his final full-time position, as director-general of the National Trust. He succeeded another former senior official, Sir John Winnifrith, whose name he had suggested himself.

The National Trust, whose ethos Bishop was to describe as 'amateurism, in the real and best sense of the word' (Jenkins and James, 258), was trying to bring its style more into line with modern needs; it had opened its first shop in 1970, and during Bishop's tenure enlarged its professional staff and saw its membership double (to 500,000). Described by a former colleague as 'by nature a manipulator and negotiator' (Gaze, 235), Bishop used his Whitehall experience and contacts assiduously on behalf of the trust, in particular helping to secure valuable changes in the rules governing the tax treatment of bequests and gifts. Not all was smooth sailing, however: the 1975 annual report noted that 'a high level of inflation will make it impossible to maintain the high standard of conservation which both members and the general public have come to expect'. When Bishop that year outlined to staff the executive committee's proposals for a 20 per cent cut in real expenditure, the need for this was hotly questioned and tempers ran high. But in general Bishop was popular, both with members of the trust's committee and with staff, for whom he obtained better salary levels and pension arrangements. His management style was described as 'unobtrusive', without undue intervention in matters of detail (Gaze, 244).

Bishop (Fred to his family, but Freddie more widely) took early retirement for health reasons from the National Trust in May 1975, having been knighted in January that year, and he and his wife moved to Cornwall. He had already been a member of the BBC's general advisory council (1971–75), a director of Pearson Longman (1970–77), and chairman of the Home Grown Timber Advisory Committee (1966–73); in Cornwall he took up directorships with English China Clays Ltd (1975–86) and Lloyd's Bank (1976–86). He continued to practise his skills as an amateur painter and his gift for friendship, not only with the Gibsons and others but also with Harold Macmillan, who visited the Bishops several times and remained in close touch until his own death. In 1987 Bishop and his wife moved to Hampshire to be closer to their grandchildren. He died at his home, Manor Barn, 65 Church Road, Bramshott, Hampshire, on 2 March 2005, of an acute transformation of chronic lymphatic leukaemia. He was survived by his three children, his wife having predeceased him. WILLIAM PLOWDEN

Sources H. Wilson, *The Labour government, 1964–1970: a personal record* (1971) • H. Macmillan, *Riding the storm, 1956–1959* (1971) • R. Crossman, *The diaries of a cabinet minister*, 1: *Minister of housing, 1964–1966* (1975) • R. Rhodes-James, *Anthony Eden* (1986) • J. Gaze, *Figures in a landscape: a history of the National Trust* (1988) • A. Horne, *Macmillan, 1957–1986*, 2 (1989) • I. Clark, *Nuclear diplomacy and the special relationship: Britain's deterrent and America, 1957–1962* (1994) • J. Jenkins and P. James, *From acorn to oak tree: the growth of the National Trust, 1895–1994* (1994) • P. Weideger, *Gilding the acorn: behind the façade of the National Trust* (1994) • R. Aldous, 'A family affair: the art of personal diplomacy', *Harold Macmillan and Britain's world role*, ed. R. Aldous and S. Lee (1996), 9–35 • J. Tratt, *The Macmillan government and Europe: a study in the process of policy development* (1996) • T. G. Otte and C. Pagedas, eds., *Personalities, war and diplomacy: essays in international history* (1997) • P. Giddings, review of *The Macmillan government and Europe*, *Political Studies*, 46/1 (May 1998), 179 • A. Ringe and N. Rollings, 'Responding to relative decline: the creation of the National Economic Development Council', *Economic History Review*, 53/2 (2000), 331–57 • R. McNamara, *Britain, Nasser and the balance of power in the Middle East, 1952–1967: from the Egyptian revolution to the Six-Day War* (2003) • R. Aldous, *Macmillan, Eisenhower and the Cold War* (2005) • R. Hyam, *Britain's declining empire: the road to decolonisation, 1918–1968* (2006) • *Daily Telegraph* (14 March 2005) • *The Times* (5 April 2005) • *WW* (2005) • Burke, *Peerage* • archives, National Trust • personal knowledge (2009) • private information (2009) • b. cert. • m. cert. • d. cert.

Likenesses obituary photographs

Wealth at death £566,348: probate, 3 Aug 2005, *CGPLA Eng. & Wales*

Black, Dorothy [Kitty] (1914–2006), theatrical agent and translator, was born on 30 April 1914 in Johannesburg, South Africa, the younger daughter and youngest of six children of Francis Black (*d.* 1918), quantity surveyor, and his wife, Elizabeth Johanna, *née* Albertyn. A brother, Brian Black, a rugby international, was killed in a flying accident in 1940.

Black was educated first at Roedean School, Johannesburg, then in England, at St Albans, and finally, having passed her university entrance examination, at a finishing school in Paris. There she was persuaded by her music teacher to train as a concert pianist. She gave her first public recital in the Maison Pleyel when she was seventeen, then spent four years travelling in Europe, North and South America, and the West Indies with her mother. 'Sober reflection' during her travels (Black, 15) persuaded her that a career as a concert pianist was unlikely and so she learned to use a stenography machine and registered with a secretarial agency in London.

Black's first job was as a junior shorthand typist at H. M. Tennent Ltd, a theatrical management company. She arrived in 1937, impressing both Hugh (Binkie) Beaumont, one of the firm's directors, and Harry Tennent, the managing director, with the ease and speed with which her stenography machine could manage dictation. By the end of her first month she was able to reflect: 'Not only was the theatre my abiding passion, but I was actually going to be allowed to earn my living working in it. The square peg had found the square hole and I was supremely happy' (Black, 7). Tennents was already a major player when Black arrived, and as the firm's status rose, so she assumed a greater part in the organization, liaising with clients and acting as the company's unofficial casting director for minor roles, as well as off-stage pianist and audition accompanist. In 1939 she became Beaumont's secretary, then, having assisted John Gielgud with the transcription of *Early Stages*, became his secretary as well in 1940. Following Beaumont's creation of a non-profit making arm of the company Black became increasingly involved in organizing and overseeing tours of airforce bases and regional theatres. A confident and sometimes overbearing woman, she was supremely loyal to Tennents, and was much annoyed when they appointed a casting director: 'half my job and much of the fun disappeared' (Black, 96). After the war Beaumont invited John Perry, formerly Gielgud's lover and now his, to join the firm—in what Black described as a 'fairly unspecified capacity'—which only increased her sense of grievance (ibid., 110). As a result she moved, at Beaumont's suggestion, to become assistant to Murray Macdonald, administrator of the Company of Four (Tennents' non-profit making subsidiary), at the Lyric Theatre, Hammersmith.

The Company of Four's brief was to produce new plays with new directors and designers and to provide jobs for actors returning from the forces. Black and Macdonald worked happily together for many years, and presided over some major theatrical and box office triumphs, including *The Relapse*, *The Holly and the Ivy*, *Let's Make an Opera!*, and John Gielgud's season of classical revivals (*Richard II*, *Venice Preserv'd*, and *The Way of the World*). Despite their success Perry made it clear that she would never be the administrator of the company. Black therefore left in 1953 to become head of drama at the leading literary agency Curtis Brown. Already enormously well connected, she transformed the fortunes of the department through her tireless networking (much of it on the golf course) and powers of persuasion. Among her clients were Angus Wilson, Somerset Maugham, and Samuel Beckett.

Black's years in Paris had resulted in a profound Francophilia that earned her the nickname Noir. The war had kick-started her career as a translator and adaptor: years of reading plays and watching productions take shape had instilled in her a respect for dramaturgical principles, which, married with her facility for languages, earned her a considerable reputation. In 1940 she provided Noël Coward with a literal translation of a Parisian hit, *Histoire de rire* by Armand Salacrou. Although Coward declared himself delighted with the result, her efforts came to nothing when the fall of France ended any chances of negotiating rights for an English production. Immediately after the war her fluent French and can-do attitude got her the job of technical adviser and interpreter to the Old Vic's victory in Europe tour, organized by the British Council. She subsequently found success with her translations of Sartre's *Crime passionel* and Kean and Anouilh's *Point of Departure*. She also provided the literal translation for Anouilh's *L'invitation au château*, adapted by Christopher Fry into *Ring Around the Moon*, directed by Peter Brook, and she produced and edited translations for Peter Daubney's World Theatre seasons.

In 1957 Black left Curtis Brown and England when she became engaged. This period of her life is tantalizingly blank, but she returned to England unmarried within a year and went on to work in television. She was also, thanks to her friendship with Allan Crawford, an unlikely supporter and financial backer of one of the first 'pirate' radio stations, Radio Atlanta. For many years she lived in a large terrace house in Brunswick Gardens, Kensington, where she entertained prodigiously until her last years, which were clouded by the onset of Parkinson's disease. She died on 26 December 2006 at the Chelsea and Westminster Hospital, London, of ischaemic heart disease. She never married, and had no children. KATE DORNEY

Sources K. Black, *Upper circle: a theatrical chronicle* (1984) • *The Times* (12 Jan 2007) • *The Guardian* (13 Feb 2007) • C. Nicol, The pirate radio hall of fame: Kitty Black, www.offshoreradio.co.uk/kitty.htm, 8 May 2009 • d. cert.

Archives Mander and Mitchenson Theatre Collection | FILM BFINA, documentary footage

Likenesses obituary photographs • photographs, repro. in Black, *Upper circle*

Wealth at death £2,274,569: probate, 2 April 2007, *CGPLA Eng. & Wales*

Blackmore, Frank Cuendet (1916–2008), road traffic engineer, was born on 16 February 1916 at La Maison Lugon, rue Michelet, Fort National (later Larbaa Nath Irathen), Algeria, the third of four children of a British father, Josiah Thomas Cullum Blackmore (1880–1961), a Plymouth Brethren missionary who established an eye hospital there, and his Swiss wife, Clarisse, *née* Cuendet (1889–1962). He grew up bilingual and spoke French-accented English throughout his life. He held dual British and French nationality until France was occupied during the Second World War, when he relinquished his French passport. Meanwhile he attended a French lycée in Algiers and received his baccalauréat in 1933. He then studied at the University of Lausanne, where he gained a diploma in civil engineering in 1937. He joined his brother in England in 1936 when appointed civil engineer's assistant in the borough of Colchester's engineering department. He enlisted in the RAF volunteer reserve and at the outbreak of the Second World War held the rank of sergeant.

On 7 September 1939, four days after war was declared, Blackmore married his childhood friend, Geneviève Claire Dufour (1916–1942), daughter of Pierre Thomas Dufour, a Swiss civil engineer. They had no children; Geneviève died of tuberculosis. On 26 October 1945, Blackmore married Eva Margaret Johnson (1918–1986), daughter of Harrison Johnson. They had two daughters and a son. The marriage ended in divorce in 1969. From 1970 until she died in April 2008, his partner was Eliane Lavallée, whom he had known since adolescence in Algeria.

During the Second World War Blackmore piloted Wellington bombers and was involved in testing the Leigh light, a device fitted to airplanes to assist the detection and destruction of surfaced U-boats at night. He was commissioned as a pilot officer in April 1941 and ended the war as a flight lieutenant, war substantive rank. He survived an emergency landing on a beach at Ardnamurchan Point in the western highlands of Scotland and in 1944 was awarded the Air Force Cross. He remained in the RAF until 1959, attaining the rank of wing commander. After the war he worked for the Air Ministry in London, for NATO in France, and as air attaché at the British embassy in Beirut, where one of his duties was to help train Lebanese pilots.

In 1960 Blackmore joined the Road Research Laboratory at Langley, Buckinghamshire, where he worked on traffic efficiency and safety at junctions. His interest in junction design became a passion and later obsession. During family holidays he spent much time inspecting and photographing road layouts. Roundabouts were his main interest. These were not new in the 1960s but Blackmore's concept of small or mini-roundabouts governed by the 'offside rule' of traffic priority was ground-breaking. Such was the resistance to his ideas, however, that he undertook much of his early work in his own time. He also battled with bureaucrats and others who misunderstand or rejected his vision. His first small roundabout, the Peterborough 'pimple', opened in 1969. His first 'overrunable' mini-roundabout followed at South Benfleet in 1970. He gradually refined his designs until the mini-roundabout became no more than a small white circle functioning as a guide to driver priority and lane discipline.

Blackmore's most famous design was for the Swindon ring junction, or 'magic roundabout' as it became known, a complex of five mini-roundabouts arranged in a circle around a small central roundabout. It was notable for its combination of clockwise and anti-clockwise flows and multiple paths between feeder roads. Opened in 1972, it attracted public comment ranging from derision and hostility to admiration. It regularly featured in polls for the 'worst' or 'scariest' junctions in the UK, but both its traffic throughput and safety records were good. Similar roundabouts and variations on the ring junction were soon constructed elsewhere in Britain, across much of western Europe, and further afield. Blackmore received the Wolfe award for his 'outstanding contribution to research on junction design' in 1976 and was appointed OBE in 1977. He retired in 1981 but for some years worked as a consultant on projects in Europe and beyond. He wrote little aside from reports for the Road Research Laboratory and a few articles for traffic journals.

Blackmore was an original thinker on junction design and 'one of the great pioneers' of mini-roundabouts (www.miniroundabout.com). His innovations helped alleviate traffic congestion and reduce accidents. Although shy and self-effacing, he could be great fun. He was kind, hospitable, and generous, but 'also had very much his own way of doing things [and] could be argumentative, stubborn and difficult' (ibid.). For years he lived in Finchampstead, Berkshire. He suffered a stroke while in France in 2002. In his last years, when afflicted with dementia, he resided at Kensington Nursing Home, Ladbroke Grove, London. After fracturing a hip in a fall he died from heart failure at the Chelsea and Westminster Hospital on 5 June 2008. He was cremated at the West London crematorium on 14 June 2008 and was survived by his three children. P. W. J. BARTRIP

Sources G. Charlesworth, *A history of the Transport and Road Research Laboratory, 1933–1983* (1987) • M. Brown, *The design of roundabouts* (1995) • *The Times* (14 June 2008) • *The Guardian* (21 June 2008) • *The Independent* (28 June 2008) • *Peterborough Evening Telegraph* (3 Oct 2008) • 'Tributes to Frank Blackmore', www.miniroundabout.com/tribute.htm, 15 Aug 2011 • *Air Force List* • personal knowledge (2012) • private information (2012) • m. certs. • d. cert.

Likenesses obituary photographs

Wealth at death £90,869: probate, 25 Nov 2008, *CGPLA Eng. & Wales*

Blatch [*née* Triggs], **Emily May**, **Baroness Blatch** (**1937–2005**), politician, was born on 24 July 1937 at the Maternity Hospital, Birkenhead, Cheshire, the only daughter of Stephen Joseph Triggs, a butcher's shop assistant and later electrician, and his wife, Sarah Ann, *née* Carpenter. She was educated at Prenton secondary school for girls in Birkenhead and at Huntingdonshire College. At the age of eighteen she joined the Women's Royal Air Force and became an air traffic assistant. In 1959 she left the WRAF and went to work in the civilian branch of air traffic control, at the Aeroplane and Armament Experimental Establishment at Boscombe Down. There she met and, on 7 September 1963, married John Richard Blatch, RAF officer and test pilot; they lived first in Wiltshire and then at Spaldwick (which until 1974 was in Huntingdonshire and thereafter in Cambridgeshire). They had four children.

Blatch's political career did not start until 1977, when she was asked by the Conservatives to stand for Cambridgeshire county council and won, assisted by the unpopularity of the Labour government, in what was seen as a natural Labour seat, with many London 'overspill' electors. Crucially her forcefulness and ability had won her the support of the leader of the Cambridgeshire Conservatives, Robert James. In 1981 he promoted her move to

Emily May Blatch, Baroness Blatch (1937–2005), by David Wimsett, 1992

the leadership of the county council. She ran a tight and effective ship in Cambridgeshire during the next four years. The county council was singled out as an example of good government by the Audit Commission when it reduced costs by 25 per cent and was chosen to take a lead in introducing local financial management for schools because of its reputation for getting things done. She was appointed CBE in 1983 and remained a councillor until 1989, but stood down as council leader in 1985 when the Conservatives lost political control.

In 1987 Blatch was elevated to the House of Lords as Baroness Blatch, of Hinchingbrooke, Cambridgeshire, by Margaret Thatcher, who had been impressed by Blatch's leadership in Cambridgeshire. She was reportedly astounded by her elevation, and at first wondered if she was the victim of a practical joke. She made her maiden speech in a debate on primary and secondary education. There she set out what were later to be her watchwords as education minister—that the fundamental objectives of Conservative policy were:

> The raising of standards; the retention of diversity and choice and the strengthening of the accountability of schools to parents; the recognition of good professional performance by teachers and more importantly, promotion of their standing within the community, and a more stable environment free from industrial strife, within which our children can enjoy a rich and full education. (*Hansard 5L*, 488.1048, 15 July 1987)

Blatch served as a government whip from January 1990, but it was with the arrival of her friend John Major as prime minister in November 1990 that her career took off. In 1976 she got to know John Major soon after he was selected as parliamentary candidate for Huntingdonshire, and the two families became very close. Politically they, Gillian Shepherd, and other political neighbours became known as the East Anglia (or fenland) mafia. Major appointed her, in November 1990, parliamentary under-secretary at the Department of the Environment, where she took responsibility for heritage issues and piloted the Local Government Bill through the Lords. In 1991 she was promoted to minister of state at the Department of the Environment, in which post in February 1992 she had the unusual duty of announcing to their lordships' cheers that the department's unloved modern building at 2 Marsham Street (known from its appearance as 'the toast rack') was to be demolished.

In April 1992 the newly re-elected John Major appointed Blatch minister of state for education, and it was in this post that she had her most tumultuous political experience. The Conservative election manifesto had promised a bright future for grant-maintained schools. The secretary of state chosen to deliver the policy was John Patten, a former Oxford don, in his first cabinet appointment. The task was made more difficult because an entirely new administrative and financial structure was needed to manage the transfer of schools from local authority control to grant-maintained status. The education establishment, which ministers failed to cultivate, opposed such schools. This opposition, and the impression that there was no policy to look after the interests of an opted-out school where things might go wrong, meant that the ballots of parents to approve the transfer of a school often failed or did not take place, and the policy stalled. The issue of testing was another minefield: the National Association of Schoolmasters / Union of Women Teachers successfully defended a legal challenge to its right to take industrial action on the testing arrangements and the government then announced a review of the curriculum and testing to be carried out by Sir Ron Dearing. Patten's health broke down under the strain of these events and he was absent from the department until the autumn of 1993. Blatch carried on the struggle for grant-maintained status in the Lords debates, and on Patten's disappearance to recuperate she took over as acting secretary of state; in this capacity she accepted the compromises in the Dearing review. In July 1994 she was moved to become minister of state at the Home Office, her last ministerial appointment, where she largely avoided the controversies surrounding the secretary of state, Michael Howard.

In opposition from the election of the Blair government in May 1997, Blatch was successively Conservative spokesperson on home affairs (1997–8) and education (1998) in the House of Lords, and finally deputy opposition leader in the Lords until her death. In her last years in politics she supported Baroness Young (Janet Young) in her campaigns on sex education. She also had the ironic pleasure of watching the Labour government travelling the same agonizing road to freeing schools from local authority control through the construction of separately funded academies. Her commitment and willingness to fight for her convictions shone through her political speeches in this as in earlier periods, and she proved to be an authentic voice for middle Britain at the highest level. She died of complications induced by pancreatic cancer at the London Clinic, 20 Devonshire Place, Westminster, on 31 May 2005, and was survived by her husband, John, two sons, and a daughter, one son having predeceased her.

CAROLINE JACKSON

Sources *The Times* (1 June 2005) • *Daily Telegraph* (1 June 2005) • *The Guardian* (1 June 2005) • *The Independent* (1 June 2005) • D. Callaghan, *Conservative party education policies, 1976–1997* (2006) • *WW* (2005) • Burke, *Peerage* • personal knowledge (2009) • private information (2009) [John Blatch, husband; J. Major] • b. cert. • d. cert.
Archives FILM BFINA, current affairs footage
Likenesses photographs, 1990–99, Photoshot, London • D. Wimsett, photograph, 1992, Photoshot, London [*see illus.*] • obituary photographs
Wealth at death £498,680: probate, 14 Oct 2005, *CGPLA Eng. & Wales*

Bleaney, Brebis (1915–2006), physicist, was born on 6 June 1915 at 423 King's Road, Chelsea, London, the second son of Frederick Bleaney, a house painter then serving as a sapper in the 3rd London field company of the Territorial Army, and Eva Petersen. His father did not register the birth until 4 May 1916 (when he mistakenly gave the birth date as 5 June). Bleaney's mother was Danish and his father was English. His unusual name of Brebis came from the village of La Brebis, near Ypres, where his father was serving when Brebis was born. His brother, Paul, was born three years earlier. His parents were not well off financially and because of this, in 1919, Paul was sent to Denmark to live with his grandparents. The family lived in a succession of barely legal flats and Bleaney attended Cook's Ground elementary school from 1921 until 1926 when he won an entrance scholarship that enabled him to go to Westminster City School. He won a number of prizes at the school and obtained distinctions in his school certificate examinations in mathematics and in physics.

In 1933 Bleaney was awarded an open scholarship at St John's College, Oxford, which he took up the following year, despite his family's continuing financial difficulties. He undoubtedly enjoyed his experience as an undergraduate at Oxford. He played football and other sports for his college and chess for the university, which he represented against Cambridge from 1936 until 1938. He obtained a first-class degree in physics in 1937. Francis Simon was his supervisor for the DPhil degree from 1937. Bleaney shared a room with Nicholas Kurti and successfully modified a cryostat so that he could cool samples below 1K and then perform various experiments on the properties of materials at what were then very low temperatures. In 1939 he was awarded his DPhil and obtained a senior studentship from the Goldsmiths' Company to continue his research for another two years.

However, towards the end of 1939 many university physicists were drafted into the military and some from Oxford were sent to radar stations around the coast. Bleaney went to stations at Pevensey in Sussex and at Crail in Fife. In 1940 he returned to Oxford to work in the team assigned the task of designing and building the electromagnetic generators for radar waves. He contributed to the design of klystrons that produced 10 cm wavelength electromagnetic radiation; the wavelength was subsequently decreased to 3.2 cm, then 1.25 cm. The designs were easier to manufacture than those developed in the USA, and in 1943 Bleaney and his colleague J. Griffiths went to the USA by plane and arranged for the Raytheon Company to build klystrons to the Oxford design. The klystrons were later described as the most important single package to cross the Atlantic at that time.

In 1945 Bleaney was appointed a university lecturer in Oxford, and he became a fellow of St John's College in 1947. Initially he started to extend his work with microwaves by studying their propagation and attenuation in gases and in particular in ammonia. This was important work but the spectra were very broad, so he decided to concentrate on the properties of magnetic solids and how microwaves can provide a vast amount of information about magnetic solids. The technique parallels nuclear magnetic resonance, which had just been developed in the USA but requires the use of much higher frequencies because the electronic magnetic moments are much larger than the nuclear moments. Initially he and his co-workers found that the resonance lines were broad, due to interactions with neighbouring atoms. Bleaney's experience of cooling samples below 1K enabled him at least partially to overcome this problem, especially when they were combined with materials in which the magnetic ions were diluted, so that it was much harder for them to interact with one another. These experiments enabled Bleaney and Roger Penrose in 1948 to establish electron paramagnetic resonance (EPR) as an invaluable tool for determining the magnetic state of ions and the local environment in which they occurred. Unknown to Bleaney a successful electron paramagnetic experiment had been performed in Kazan in Russia, in 1944, but this work was not subsequently followed up. At this time one of his collaborators was Betty Isabelle Plumpton, daughter of Herbert Francis Plumpton, stockbroker. They married at St Nicholas's Church in Compton, Surrey, on 15 March 1949; she was then aged twenty-two. They had a son and a daughter.

For the next ten years Oxford was the leading establishment for EPR measurements and theory. Experimentally Bleaney and his team explored the electronic ground state of the transition metals and of the actinides, how this depended on the electronic environment produced by the neighbouring atoms, and how it was influenced by the interactions with the nuclear ground state through the hyperfine coupling. The experiments were performed in close collaboration with theory. Maurice Price, Roger Elliott, Ken Stevens, and Anatole Abragam emphasized the importance of symmetry and introduced the 'spin Hamiltonian' and other concepts to explain the experimental results. EPR soon became studied worldwide and used particularly by chemists and biologists for the determination of the location and environment of magnetic impurities in materials.

In 1956 F. A. Lindemann (Lord Cherwell) resigned from both Dr Lee's chair of experimental philosophy and the headship of the Clarendon Laboratory and Sir Francis Simon was appointed to succeed him. Unfortunately a month later Simon died and in due course Bleaney was appointed to the chair and took over the headship of the laboratory in 1957. A period of institutional and personal difficulty followed. Willis Lamb had been appointed to a chair in theory in 1956 and Denys Wilkinson was appointed to a chair in experimental (nuclear) physics in 1959. Although Bleaney was nominally responsible for both new professors they each wanted their own department, and, encouraged by the university, the departments of theoretical physics and nuclear physics were set up in 1962 as independent departments in buildings on the opposite side of Parks Road from the Clarendon Laboratory. It is likely that Bleaney did not approve of this break-up of physics in Oxford, but Simon had already promised Wilkinson a new department. The three departments were eventually reunited, together with astronomy and atmospheric physics, in 1990.

At the beginning of the 1960s there was a marked increase in the number of undergraduates in physics. This pressure on space was alleviated by obtaining funds from the Mullard Company to build the Mullard Cryomagnetic Laboratory in 1962 and by the move of the theoreticians and the nuclear physicists out of the Clarendon Laboratory. Most of the undergraduate practical teaching remained in the Clarendon under the supervision of Bleaney. There was comparatively little change in the research activities in the Clarendon Laboratory for the next twenty years. There was a large group concerned with electron spin resonance and another group concerned with low temperature physics. Tony Stradling initiated a group working on semiconductors and Colin Webb introduced laser physics into the department, to develop a high resolution optical spectroscopy group.

In 1977 Bleaney resigned from his chair and from the headship of the laboratory because he wished to devote more energy to his research. He became a Warren research fellow of the Royal Society and then a Leverhulme fellow from 1980 to 1982. He continued to produce excellent contributions to electron spin resonance and nuclear ordering in solids, and to be active in the laboratory until he was over eighty-five. He wrote over 300 scientific papers, many of which were ground-breaking publications on electron spin resonance. He and his wife wrote the textbook *Electricity and Magnetism* (1957), which was an excellent description of much of solid state physics as well as of electromagnetism, concentrating on the physics instead of the mathematics, unlike so many books on electromagnetism. It went through a number of editions, culminating in a revised edition in two volumes in 1989. Together with Anatole Abragam he also wrote *Electron Paramagnetic Resonance* (1970; rev. edn, 1986), a clear and comprehensive account of EPR experiments and theory, and a primary source for those interested in the low energy states of magnetic ions.

Bleaney was awarded many honours. He was elected a fellow of the Royal Society as early as 1950. He was awarded the Charles Vernon Boys prize of the Physical Society in 1952, the Hughes medal of the Royal Society in 1962, the Holweck medal and prize of the Institute of Physics and the Société Française de Physique in 1984, and the Zavoisky prize in 1992. He was appointed CBE in 1965 and held many visiting professorships at universities including MIT, Columbia, Berkeley, and Pittsburgh. He enjoyed travelling and meeting people.

Bleaney was an excellent tutor and supervisor who took a personal interest in his students and their progress. He had an impish sense of humour, as shown by the photograph he displayed of himself on a beach with his trousers rolled up to the knees. With Betty he enjoyed playing and listening to chamber music, and they were an active tennis pair until he was over seventy-five. He was an excellent product of the pre-war educational system, and made the best possible use of the opportunities it provided. He died on 4 November 2006 at his home, Garford House, Garford Road, Oxford, and was cremated at Oxford crematorium; he was survived by his wife and by their two children.

R. A. Cowley

Sources B. Bleaney, autobiography, priv. coll. • A. J. Croft, 'Oxford's Clarendon laboratory', priv. coll. • M. Baker, '90th birthday of Brebis Bleaney', *EPR Newsletter* (15 Feb 2005), 7–8 • *Daily Telegraph* (30 Nov 2006) • *The Independent* (30 Nov 2006) • *The Times* (6 Dec 2006) • *The Guardian* (8 Jan 2007) • *WW* (2006) • personal knowledge (2010) • private information (2010) [W. Hayes; M. Baker; R. J. Elliott] • b. cert. • m. cert. • d. cert.
Archives RS, scientific notebooks
Likenesses W. Stoneman, photograph, 1950, RS • obituary photographs
Wealth at death £649,779: probate, 23 March 2007, *CGPLA Eng. & Wales*

Bloom, Alan Herbert Vauser (1906–2005), horticulturist, was born on 19 November 1906 in Over, near Swavesey, Cambridgeshire, the son of Charles Herbert Bloom, grocer and draper, and later market gardener, and his wife, Katherine Annie Jane, *née* Whitworth. His father's family is thought to have been descended from Huguenots who had come to East Anglia with Cornelius Vermuyden in the reign of Charles I. Interested in plants from the first, Bloom worked in a number of East Anglian nurseries when he left school, then joined his father's business. By the age of twenty-four he had his own thriving wholesale nursery in Oakington, Cambridgeshire, where he bred new aubrietas, dianthus, and campanulas, the last remaining a special favourite. He named his first new variety *Dianthus* 'Oakington' in 1927. On 16 April 1931 he married Doris Hilda Heavens, the twenty-year-old daughter of Henry John Heavens. By 1938 Blooms Nurseries in Oakington was one of the largest in England but following the outbreak of the Second World War food crops became the priority and Bloom turned his hand to agricultural production, about which he wrote in *The Farm in the Fen* (1944).

Bloom bought Bressingham Hall, with 228 acres of land at Bressingham, Norfolk, in 1946, and spent nearly all of his life there except for a brief, unsuccessful sojourn with his young family to try farming in Canada from 1948 to

Alan Herbert Vauser Bloom (1906–2005), by Tessa Traeger, 2000

1950. He returned to revive the fortunes of his nursery and from then on he focused on his chief love, hardy perennial plants, breeding new kinds and skilfully propagating and promoting good old varieties. The handsome semi-evergreen hybrid *Heuchera* x *brizoides* named by his father 'Blooms' variety' won a Royal Horticultural Society award of merit in 1930–31 at a time when such perennials were usually disparaged except in cottage gardens. To give his plants the best advantage Bloom introduced island beds (his first notable example was at Bressingham itself in 1953) which sailed like stately floral galleons through ample lawns. Less labour-intensive than borders, they allowed plants to be viewed from all sides, permitted easy access for the gardener, and allowed more light so plants were more sturdy and needed less staking. They could also be introduced into the smaller gardens whose owners were buying more plants than the old estates. In 1957 Bloom became founding chairman of the Hardy Plant Society, an important body for stimulating enjoyment in herbaceous hardy plants, which by the time of his death had 10,000 members. His first marriage having ended in divorce, on 30 October 1956 he married Flora Elizabeth Mackintosh, the 27-year-old daughter of Alfred Mackintosh.

Bloom introduced into cultivation more than 200 plants that he had bred and named and was responsible for thousands of others that were distributed from the Blooms nurseries. Many of them became staples of European and North American gardens, but despite his remarkable skill he remained humble before the workings of the natural world; he did not consider his plants so much a matter of pride as 'of pleasure' and always gave credit to those that had come his way not through a breeding programme but 'as chance or self-sown seedlings', as was the case with *Dianthus* 'Oakington'. His great skill was in perceiving the potential of new varieties, discerning their qualities, coaxing them into growth, and working up stocks for commercial sale. He believed that for 'the gardening public' a 'plant stands or falls on its own merits, for beauty and reliability' (A. Bloom, 'Introductions from Bressingham', in R. Bird, ed., *Plantsmen on Plants*, 1990, 204).

Bloom was always a hands-on gardener but he had a shrewd business sense and realized that speedier propagation methods and new methods of retail trading and of attracting customers were the coming trend. His two sons, Robert and Adrian, joined him in the business in 1962. A steam enthusiast from a young age, Bloom had the previous year bought his first traction engine, and by the end of 1962 had collected fourteen engines, which formed the nucleus of Bressingham Steam Museum. In 1965 he laid the first of several narrow- and standard-gauge tracks. In 1972 he handed over the running of Blooms Nurseries to his sons, formed the steam collection into a trust (of which he was founding chairman and later president), and retired to his six acre private garden at Bressingham Hall with its nursery in which he and a small band of helpers raised by hand special plants 'which objected to mechanisation' (personal knowledge). His elder son Robert died in a car crash in 1995 but his younger son Adrian and grandson Jason continued the family business at Bressingham Gardens, though the Plant Centre was taken over in 2007.

Bloom had a wild streak though brought up strictly and remaining a Quaker throughout his life. At seventy he had his ears pierced. He wore hoop earrings and let his hair grow long, and looked like a kind of horticultural pirate. Though he had been a sickly child, outdoor life had improved his health and even in his nineties he was an attractive and charismatic figure. He wrote about thirty books, including an autobiography, *Come You Here, Boy!* (1995), and made regular broadcasts, the last occasion only a few months before he died. Proud that his was the only family in which the Royal Horticultural Society's prestigious Victoria medal of honour had been awarded to both father and son (Adrian), he also received the Veitch memorial medal and was appointed MBE in 1997. He died of bronchopneumonia at Bressingham Hall on 30 March 2005 and was survived by his wife, Flora, his son Adrian, and his four daughters. FRANCESCA GREENOAK

Sources A. Bloom, *The farm in the fen* (1944) · *The Times* (3 Aug 1991); (9 April 2005) · A. Bloom, *Come you here, boy!* (1995) · *The Independent* (5 April 2005) · *The Guardian* (6 April 2005) · *Daily Telegraph* (9 April 2005) · 'Bressingham Steam Museum's Alan Bloom dies at 98', *Old Glory* (May 2005), 6–7 · www.bloomsofbressingham.com, 23 April 2008 · www.bressingham.co.uk, 23 April 2008 · personal knowledge (2009) · private information (2009) · b. cert. · m. certs. · d. cert.

Archives FILM BFINA, 'Squire of a Norfolk cabbage patch', K. Ackrill (director), Channel 4, 1 Jan 1990 | SOUND BL NSA, 'Down to earth: an oral history of British horticulture', interviews with L. Brodie, 7–9 Nov 2001, F11479–F11489

Likenesses photograph, 1969, PA Photos, London • M. Warren, photograph, 1984, Photoshot, London • L. Douglas-Menzies, bromide fibre print, 1990, NPG • M. Young, oils, exh. Contemporary Portrait Society, Medici Gallery, London 1992 • T. Traeger, silver gelatine print, 2000, NPG [*see illus.*] • obituary photographs
Wealth at death under £72,000: probate, 10 June 2005, *CGPLA Eng. & Wales*

Blow, Isabella [*née* Isabella Delves Broughton] (**1958–2007**), fashion journalist and stylist, was born on 19 November 1958 at the London Clinic, 20 Devonshire Place, Westminster, the eldest child in the family of three daughters and a son of Major Sir Evelyn Delves Broughton, twelfth baronet (1915–1993), soldier and landowner, and his second wife, Helen Mary, *née* Shore, barrister. The Broughton baronetcy was created in 1661 but the family traced its descent from the Vernon family, who arrived in England at the time of the Norman conquest. Isabella's romantic engagement with her family history stimulated an interest in history and architecture. Her grandmother Vera Edyth, Lady Broughton, the first wife of Sir Henry John Delves (Jock) *Broughton, eleventh baronet [*see under* Hay, Josslyn Victor], was an important influence in her life. She was an explorer, anthropologist, photographer, big game hunter, and fisherwoman, who until 2000 held the record for the largest ever tuna (weighing some 700 lbs) caught in European waters. She was also considered one of the best-dressed women of her generation. However, the Broughton family was also tainted with scandal and instability. Isabella's grandfather (Vera's husband), Sir Jock Broughton, having sold off most of the family's assets to fund his extravagant lifestyle, was acquitted of the murder of the twenty-second earl of Erroll in Kenya in 1941 and committed suicide on his return to England in 1942.

Isabella's parents owned a house at 17 Cadogan Square, Chelsea, London, but she was brought up in a house on the Broughton estate at Doddington Park, Cheshire. Her brother John (*b.* 1962) died in an accident that she witnessed in 1964. Her parents were very distressed by their only son's death and Isabella felt that it led them to distance themselves from their daughters. One of Isabella's fondest memories of her childhood was trying on a 'giant pink hat' of her mother's. 'There's a photograph of me … and I look as happy as anything to be wearing it' (*Philip Treacy*, 11). When her parents separated in 1972 Isabella's mother left the children in the care of their father. After their divorce in 1974 her father married his third, much younger, wife, Rona Crammond, *née* Clifford Johns. Her father's remarriage strained his relationship with Isabella. On his death in 1993 his wife inherited the bulk of his estate, with each daughter receiving a token £5000.

Isabella Delves Broughton (known variously as Issy, Issie, Izzie, or Izzy) was a boarding pupil at Heathfield School, Ascot, from 1969 to 1975. She belonged to the Church of England and was head of chapel at school. When she left school she went to secretarial college and did various jobs before going to the United States. In the autumn of 1980 she attended the school of general studies at Columbia University in New York, where one of her classes focused on the arts in China. She lived briefly in west Texas before returning to New York. While still in the USA, in 1981 she married an Englishman, Nicholas Taylor, but they divorced in 1983. In 1982 the musician Brian Ferry and his wife, Lucy, introduced her to Anna Wintour, the editor of American *Vogue*, who hired her as her assistant. She went on to work at *Vogue* for André Leon Talley, organizing fashion shoots. In New York she became a friend of the artists Andy Warhol and Jean-Michel Basquiat. After her return to London she worked as a fashion assistant and then assistant editor at *Tatler* magazine from August 1985 to December 1989. On 18 November 1989, at Gloucester Cathedral, she married Detmar Hamilton Lorenz Arthur Blow (*b.* 1963), barrister, later art dealer and gallery owner. Detmar's family home, Hilles House, at Harescombe in Gloucestershire (designed by his grandfather, the architect Detmar Blow), became very important to Isabella and she enjoyed throwing it open to her friends and protégés.

Isabella Blow (1958–2007), by Mario Testino, 1998

After eighteen months working as a freelance for the magazine, in 1991 Isabella Blow joined the staff of British *Vogue* as a features associate, working there for the next three years. During this period she met the milliner Philip Treacy (in 1989) and the fashion designer Alexander McQueen (in 1991). Both were students but she immediately recognized their talent and craftsmanship and made it her mission to nurture and develop their careers. She was a confrontational and demanding mentor but affectionate, hugely enthusiastic, and generous with her contacts and her knowledge of history and art. She provided Treacy with space to live and work in the basement of her London home and purchased McQueen's entire degree show collection, paying in instalments. She also discovered the model Sophie Dahl and promoted the careers of the fashion designer Hussein Chalayan and the model Stella Tennant. They in turn loved her crazy imagination, daring flights of fancy, and earthy humour, which informed her fashion shoots. She was a natural member of the avant-garde. Her ability to spot new talent at an early stage and to facilitate it was her greatest gift and pleasure.

Blow was also passionate about finely crafted clothes

and dressed with eccentric, theatrical flair. She had a vulnerable and fragile personality and considered herself ugly, but defied her looks and low self-esteem by drawing attention to her creativity and appreciation of beauty through her clothes. Treacy's hats, which she wore constantly, performed the function of exquisite, hand-made armour, and McQueen's skilful tailoring, which flattered her excellent figure, excited her and gave her confidence.

In 1997 Blow joined the *Sunday Times* as editor of *Style* magazine, working there until 2001. In 1998 she became a consultant for Swarovski and in 2002 for DuPont Lycra. In 2002 London's Design Museum celebrated her creative collaboration with Treacy with the exhibition 'When Philip Met Isabella' (also the title of a book). In the same year she rejoined *Tatler*, working as its fashion director until 2006 and then as a freelance fashion editor-at-large until May 2007. In 2004 she and her husband separated over money problems and their inability to conceive a child. They were reunited eighteen months later, but in 2006 she was diagnosed with cancer. Her illness, and fears that that her career had stalled, led to bouts of depression and several attempts at suicide. She died on 7 May 2007 at Gloucestershire Royal Hospital, Gloucester, from the effects of paraquat poisoning. Her funeral took place on 15 May 2007 at Gloucester Cathedral and her body was cremated. A memorial service was held at the Guards' Chapel, Wellington Barracks, London, on 18 September 2007. After her death the British Fashion Council renamed its fashion creator award as the Isabella Blow award for fashion creator in acknowledgement of her unerring support of British designers and her contribution to the international fashion industry. In June 2010 Daphne Guinness, a close friend, saved her wardrobe from dispersal at auction by purchasing it in its entirety in a private treaty sale. EDWINA EHRMAN

Sources I. Blow, H. Bowles, and P. Treacy, *Philip Treacy: when Philip met Isabella* (2002) · *The Observer* (23 June 2002) · *The Independent* (10 Sept 2005); (9 May 2007) · *The Times* (8 May 2007); (12 Aug 2007); (19 Sept 2007) · *Daily Telegraph* (8 May 2007); (19 Sept 2007) · *The Guardian* (8 May 2007); (12 May 2007); (19 Sept 2007) · K. Bernard, 'Crowning McQueen', *Tatler* (April 2010) · *Financial Times* (3 July 2010) · D. Blow and T. Sykes, *Blow by blow: the story of Isabella Blow* (2010) · M. Rink, *Isabella Blow* (2010) · *WW* (2007) · Burke, *Peerage* · b. cert. · m. cert. · d. cert.
Archives FILM BFINA, documentary footage
Likenesses M. Testino, photograph, 1998, priv. coll. [*see illus.*] · R. Young, photographs, 1998–2005, Rex Features, London · photographs, 1999–2006, PA Photos, London · T. Noble, S. Webster, taxidermy, wood, fake moss, light projector, and installation template, 2002, NPG · J. Almasi, photographs, 2005, Photoshot, London · photographs, 2005–7, Getty Images, London · photographs, 2006, Rex Features, London · obituary photographs · photographs, repro. in Blow, Treacy, and Bowles, *When Philip met Isabella* · photographs, repro. in Blow and Sykes, *Blow by blow* · photographs, repro. in Rink, *Isabella Blow*

Blow, Sandra Betty (1925–2006), painter and collagist, was born on 14 September 1925, at 64 Manor Road, Stoke Newington, London, the only daughter of Jacob (Jack) Blow, a fruit wholesaler at Spitalfields market in Shoreditch, and his wife, Leah (Lily), *née* Rubinstein. She was of Jewish descent. Her brothers, Stanley and Morris, were,

Sandra Betty Blow (1925–2006), by Roger Mayne, 1966

respectively, sixteen months older and nine years younger. She was an infant when the family moved to north London, as was the case with many Jewish families who had prospered in the East End. If her father was businesslike and solitary, single-minded, and emotionally undemonstrative, her mother was lively, affectionate, and domestically haphazard: both, it may be thought, contributed aspects of their character to their daughter, who grew up to be independent of mind and spirit, capable of an intensely focused creative solitude, personally passionate, sociably gregarious, and inclined to informality in her style of life.

Throughout her childhood Blow spent idyllic Sundays and holidays on her grandparents' fruit farm at Paddock Wood in Kent. In early 1934 she contracted scarlet fever and, soon after, rheumatic fever, which left her with a permanently damaged heart, and the awareness of mortality that frequently accompanies it: in later life she spoke of 'my Russian Roulette existence' (BL NSA, interview). It seems to have had no effect on an adventurous and ardent temperament and a remarkable zest for the creative life. She attended Northfield Road primary school in Stamford Hill, north London, and after the age of eleven she was sent to a small private girls' school near Hampstead Heath. At fourteen, for safety as the Second World War broke out, she moved with her mother and brothers to Paddock Wood. In the orchards and hopfields of wartime Kent, her schooldays over, she read deeply, and began to draw and paint.

After returning to London in 1941 Blow was encouraged by her mother's spirited sister, Rose, to enrol at St Martin's School of Art, one of the few colleges to remain open in wartime London, and from 1941 until 1946 she studied there. Ruskin Spear was her most helpful teacher. The curriculum was traditional—life drawing and strictly tonal painting—but for Blow 'art school was like paradise, a totally new world' (BL NSA, interview); she had found her vocation. By the mid-1940s she was also familiar with Soho's night-life bohemia, and acquainted with Francis Bacon, Lucian Freud, John Minton, and others. Early in 1947 she attended the Royal Academy Schools, but was disappointed by the dreary ambience and the dullness of the teaching. In the summer of 1947 she travelled alone to Italy, intending to study classic Italian art at first hand.

In Rome, excited by conversations about abstract painting with the gifted American-Italian painter Nicolas Carone, Blow took leave of absence from the Royal Academy Schools (she never returned) and enrolled at the Accademia di Belle Arti, where Carone was a mature student. Carone espoused the high-principled existential approach to colour and space in painting expounded by his influential pre-war teacher Hans Hofmann, and through him Blow became aware of currents in American artistic thought and practice that had yet to be felt in London. Also through Carone she met the Italian artist Alberto Burri who, already over thirty, was just beginning his own artistic career. He was to progress towards a distinctive abstract *art informel*, utilizing non-art 'poor' materials like sacking and burnt plastics. Blow became his lover—'the fundamental bond was work' (Bird, *Sandra Blow*, 37)—and travelled with him throughout Italy in the spring and summer of 1948, learning from him to look at fresco painting and at the weathered architecture of Italy with a modernist eye to abstract and textural values. As they travelled she was able to observe, intently, close-up, a great artist developing his vision through a rigorous daily practice of drawing and painting. Although much was later made of his influence on her use of 'poor' materials, it was the burning intensity of Burri's commitment to art and his preternatural sensitivity to the surfaces of the world that had the most profound and enduring effect on Blow's own artistic sense and sensibility.

In the winter of 1948–9 Blow worked alongside Burri in Paris, but with little professional success. Their affair over, they remained friendly, and a critical awareness of his great work of the 1950s continued to provoke creative responses in her own painting throughout the 1950s and 1960s. After solitary sojourns abroad, and unsure of the direction and quality of her work, she returned to London in late 1950, and set out on what Hofmann, her mentor at one remove, had (in the title of a book published in 1948) called 'the search for the real'. She started as a pure painter, but it was through the use of mixed media—sacking, hessian, PVC, paper, plaster, ash, tea, sawdust, sand, and so on—and, above all, the chances and changes of collage, that Blow in the mid-1950s found herself as an artist of natural space, material surfaces and forms, and elemental energies. Independently committed to her own experimental mode of abstract practice, she did not ever align herself with any group or tendency in British art.

The basis of Blow's abstraction, as she always acknowledged, was Carone's 'exposition of space and pictorial space, which really goes back [by way of Hofmann] to Cézanne … of there being a connection between one area and the other to make … a spatial movement or balance' (Bird, *Sandra Blow*, 46). The search for a dynamically poised formal relation between pictorial elements, however many intuitive adjustments and re-adjustments this might require, was constant. For Blow the creative process was analogous to an existential quest for 'rightness': it was driven, she had no doubt, by an inner demand for psychic composure. A painting was a visual and tactile metaphor for an instant of harmonic, naturally asymmetric poise in the circumstantial welter of the material world. Blow's consistent and compulsive resort to rough-and-ready, robustly 'poor' materials served to emphasize this phenomenological reality.

After notable appearances in prestigious group exhibitions Blow began to exhibit successfully as a solo artist in 1960. There followed a brilliant career culminating in magisterial retrospectives, at the Royal Academy in 1994 and Tate St Ives in 2001. Teaching painting at the Royal College of Art from 1960 to 1975, with a large studio in Sydney Close, Chelsea, she was an animated and attractive presence at a vibrant centre of artistic life at a time of great vitality and diversity in British art, much loved and admired by her contemporaries. Of these colleagues it was with the abstract painter Roger Hilton, a friend from the early 1950s, that she felt the closest affinity of artistic attitude and style. In 1978 she was elected to the Royal Academy. From 1994 until her death she lived and worked in St Ives, at Bullans Court, Bullans Lane.

Fiercely intelligent, individualistic, and highly principled in her practice, Blow was never inclined to intellectual theory, for she had a light-footed ability to live with unanswered questions and creative uncertainties; she could wait, sometimes for years, for a painterly intuition, whether technical or thematic, to find material form in her work. In the studio she could disguise her creative confidence by admitting to doubts, playfully seeking advice and reassurance. At once innocent and canny, she could be fey and inconsequential, only to disconcert a visitor or a friend with an alarming directness of address. She died at the Royal Cornwall Hospital, Truro, on 22 August 2006, of a cerebral haemorrhage caused by treatment for a heart valve replacement. She never married, and in later life was said to have regretted not having children.

MEL GOODING

Sources Royal Academy of Arts exhibition catalogue, 1994 • M. Gooding, *Sandra Blow: space and matter, 1958–2001* (2001) • M. Bird, *Sandra Blow* (2005) • *Daily Telegraph* (23 Aug 2006) • *The Guardian* (23 Aug 2006) • *The Independent* (23 Aug 2006) • *The Times* (24 Aug 2006) • *Jewish Chronicle* (26 Oct 2006) • *The Cornishman* (31 Aug 2006) • M. Bird, exhibition catalogue, Beaux Arts, London, 2009 • interview by A. Lambirth, 1996, BL NSA • *WW* (2006) • personal knowledge (2010) • private information (2010) • b. cert. • d. cert.

Archives BL NSA, National Life Story Collection, artists' lives, interview with A. Lambirth, 1996, F5201–F5207 | SOUND BL NSA, documentary recordings

Likenesses I. Kar, photographs, 1955, NPG • R. Mayne, modern bromide print from original negative, 1966, NPG [*see illus.*] • E. Lucie-Smith, bromide print, *c.*1970, NPG • A. Purkiss, bromide fibre print, 1994, NPG • G. Scott, photographs, 2003, Camera Press, London • E. McCabe, C-type colour print, 2005, NPG • E. McCabe, photographs, 2005, Camera Press, London • S. Walia, photograph, repro. in C. Parry-Crooke, ed., *Contemporary British artists* (1979) • obituary photographs • photograph, repro. in *Royal Academy magazine*, 67 (2000) • photographs, repro. in Bird, *Blow*

Wealth at death £1,241,545: administration, 14 Feb 2007, *CGPLA Eng. & Wales*

Bolton, Sir Frederic Bernard [Tim] (**1921–2005**), shipowner, was born on 9 March 1921 at 1 Lower Terrace, Hampstead, London, the only son among the four children of Louis Hamilton Bolton (1884–1953), shipowner, and his wife, Beryl (*d.* 1977), daughter of Bernard Dyer. Usually known as Tim, he was educated at Rugby School, where his main achievements were sporting rather than academic. After leaving school he worked for six months on the broking side of his family firm, before enlisting for war service in July 1940. He was commissioned into the Welsh Guards, and from 1942 saw active service in the north African and Italian campaigns. He proved 'fearless and indefatigable' according to the citation for the Military Cross awarded to him in 1945. After demobilization in 1946 he rejoined the family business, and on 19 April 1950 he married Valerie Margaret Barwick (*d.* 1970), daughter of George Short Barwick, company director. They had two sons.

In 1953 Bolton succeeded his father as chairman of the family business. Originally known as the Bolton Steam Shipping Company, the business had been established by his grandfather, Sir Frederic Bolton, who had started as a Lloyd's underwriter in 1874. The company specialized in small cargo vessels, all named after artists whose names began with R, such as *Raphael* and *Rubens*. Initially successful in trade with the Mediterranean, after 1945 it became an operator of tramp steamers and ore carriers and diversified into such other areas as broking, underwriting, and agency work, becoming the Bolton Group. Not all Bolton's attempts to broaden the business were successful, however; he acquired a stake in Transglobe Airways in 1966, for instance, which went into liquidation two years later. Bolton himself became a director of the Atlantic Steam Navigation Company in 1960, of BP's tanker division in 1968, and of British Rail's shipping operations (later Sealink) in 1970. The Bolton Group's core business of shipping dwindled steadily, however, as Britain's share of world trade declined and the industry was transformed by containerization, and the last two Bolton ships were sold to an American company in 1982. Bolton carried on as chairman of the group's remaining interests until his retirement in 1991.

Bolton achieved greater prominence through his role as a leading representative of the British shipping industry. He joined the general committee of Lloyds Register of Shipping in 1961, and by 1964 was a member of the Port of London Authority and also a very active chairman of the Chamber of Shipping's research committee. By 1965 he was vice-president of the chamber, and in 1966 became its second-youngest ever president. His impact was felt when he delivered 'a whirlwind speech which helped to knock half an hour off the usually sluggish ritual of the chamber's annual meeting', in which he posed searching questions about the performance of the industry, including 'are our management as efficient as they could be?', and 'have we too many small and family-dominated companies?' (*The Times*, 25 Feb 1966). When the Geddes report on the future of British shipbuilding was published in the following month, Bolton was quoted as saying that 'surely the problems of British shipping are the problems of Britain', and posed the question, 'why is this country not working any longer?' (*Daily Telegraph*, 25 Aug 2005). This gave a hint of his hostility to the strength of trade unionism in his industry, further demonstrated during the strike of the National Union of Seamen in May 1966, which he declared would be 'disastrous for the nation' (*The Times*, 3 May 1966).

From 1972 to 1975 Bolton was president of the British Shipping Federation, and he became president of the General Council of British Shipping (created through the amalgamation of the Chamber of Shipping and the British Shipping Federation) in 1975–6. In this post he was vociferous in the campaign to prevent the extension of the national dock labour scheme to non-scheme ports and to all freight-handling services within 5 miles of the coast. The scheme dated from 1947 and had been a significant step in decasualizing dock labour, providing a minimum guarantee of earnings for dockers and safeguards against dismissal. Its proposed extension sought to prevent undercutting of the scheme by ports outside it that could recruit labour on a casual basis, and equally to stop inland container bases taking work away from scheme ports. Bolton instead argued that 'the crying need is for efficient, reliable and trouble-free ports' (*Port of London News*, Sept–Oct 2005, 4). After intensive lobbying the extension bill was wrecked by amendments in the Lords. Bolton (who was knighted in 1976) was also president of the International Shipping Federation between 1973 and 1982. His last major posts were as chairman of the Dover Harbour Board (1982–8) and chairman of the British Ports Association (1985–8), in which posts he campaigned for the abolition of the national dock labour scheme, finally enacted by the Conservative government in 1989.

Tim Bolton was an enthusiastic and forceful figure with a 'deep sense of fun and cheerfulness' (*Lloyd's List*, 14 Sept 2005), much respected in the shipping industry. He was perhaps an example of a 'third generation' entrepreneur who accepted the 'aristocratic embrace', for despite his thoroughly industrial and urban origins he moved to a large farm at Pudlicote, near Charlbury in Oxfordshire, listed his recreations in *Who's Who* as 'country sports', and for many years was joint master and chairman of the Grafton hunt. Between 1991 and 1995 he was treasurer of the West Oxfordshire Conservative Association. After his first wife's death he married, on 4 February 1971, Vanessa Mary Ann Robarts, a 31-year-old sales assistant and daughter of Lieutenant-Colonel Anthony Vere Cyprian Robarts. With her he had a further two sons and two daughters. He died in his sleep while holidaying in the French Alps on 27 July 2005. His funeral took place in Chadlington, Oxfordshire. The service was preceded by a medley of Gilbert and Sullivan songs, and at the end the coffin was borne out to the theme tune of *The Archers*. SAM DAVIES

Sources *Daily Telegraph* (25 Aug 2005) · *The Times* (6 Sept 2005) · *Lloyd's List* (14 Sept 2005) · *Port of London News* (Sept–Oct 2005), 4 · *Ear Foundation News*, 28 (winter 2005), 2 · *WW* (2005) · Burke, *Peerage* · b. cert. · m. certs.

Likenesses obituary photographs

Wealth at death £1,531,984: probate, 15 Feb 2006, *CGPLA Eng. & Wales*

Bond, Derek William Douglas (1920–2006), actor, was born on 26 January 1920 at 17 Sandyford Place, Glasgow, the youngest of three sons of Frank Herbert Bond, commercial traveller, and his wife, Dorothy Blanche, *née* Pennington, beautician. His parents had married in London in 1912. The family moved back to London two years after his birth and he was educated at Holmwood preparatory school and Haberdashers' Aske's School, Hampstead. He left at the age of sixteen to become briefly a cub reporter on the *Golders Green Gazette* and then a junior postal clerk with Brown Shipley & Co., merchant bankers. However, he was to find his true vocation as an actor, gaining some initial experience at the Finchley Amateur Dramatic Society alongside his mother. His father's grudging consent was eventually forthcoming and Bond picked up some work on an early BBC television play by Karel Capek, *R.U.R* (1938), and as understudy and assistant stage manager on the pre-London tour of *As Husbands Go*. He was promoted to stage manager and played a small role during the successful three-month London run at the Garrick Theatre. Afterwards he gained a permanent position as stage manager and juvenile lead at the Colchester Repertory Company, one of the leading repertory companies in the country.

Following the outbreak of the Second World War in September 1939 Bond responded to a BBC announcement and applied to join the brigade of guards. He was quickly put forward for officer training and passed out of the Royal Military College, Sandhurst, as a second lieutenant in the Grenadier Guards, eventually attaining the rank of captain. He first saw action in north Africa during the allied landings in 1942 and was wounded in the leg on 19 December leading a night attack on some German self-propelled guns near Medjez al-Bab. Invalided back to England, he was awarded the Military Cross and on recovery spent time training new recruits. In July 1944 he returned to active service in Italy and was captured by a forward German patrol while visiting what he believed to be the liberated city of Florence. He saw out the last eight months of the war as a prisoner of war at Stalag 7a, in Moosberg, Bavaria, where among other things he took responsibility for the camp shows. He later wrote a play, *Sentence Deferred*, which was broadcast on BBC Radio 4, addressing one of the troubling experiences he had during incarceration. In 1990 he published an entertaining account of his war experiences as *Steady Old Man! Don't You Know There's a War On?* On 28 January 1942 he had married Grace Ann D'Eath, a 25-year-old widow whom he had first met at the Colchester Repertory Theatre. The daughter of Gilbert Edward Trubody, grocer, she had a son by her first marriage, Larry. A second son, Anthony, was born in 1944.

During the period in England recovering from his wound Bond had met Diana Morgan, a scriptwriter at Ealing Studios. During the war the film industry was chronically short of young leading men and Bond gave an audition for a role in the historical film *Champagne Charlie* (1944). Though he was successful, the War Office refused his release and he gained instead a contract with the studio that was to commence fully upon his demobilization. He was somewhat dismayed following his return to England after liberation to discover that his first role for Ealing was in *The Captive Heart* (1946), a film about British prisoners of war. He was required to return to Germany immediately to film the location scenes in the former prisoner-of-war camp at Westertimke. In fact the experience laid to rest some ghosts and Bond was fortunate to play in an acclaimed and commercially successful film a sensitive musician who confronts the torture of discovering an unfaithful wife back home.

Bond's big break came with Ealing's ambitious plan to film *Nicholas Nickleby* (1947) with Bond cast in the lead. The film was only a modest success and suffered in comparison to David Lean's striking adaptations of Dickens's *Great Expectations* (1946) and *Oliver Twist* (1948). Bond continued to play in such Ealing films as *The Loves of Joanna Godden* (1947), and as Captain Oates in *Scott of the Antarctic* (1948), but no longer in the lead role. As his name began to appear further down the cast list in British films like the first Norman Wisdom comedy, *Trouble in Store* (1954), Bond accepted more parts in the burgeoning television service, while continuing to act on the stage. Among his numerous television appearances were roles in episodes of *The Vise* (1955), *Errol Flynn Theatre* (1957), and *William Tell* and *The Invisible Man* (both 1959). Briefly, in 1956, he accepted the assignment, untypical for an actor, of television announcer for the BBC, and in the early 1960s he co-presented *Picture Parade* and *Tonight* for the service.

Bond continued to act regularly on stage and television in the 1960s and 1970s, most memorably as one in a line of section chiefs in the popular spy series *Callan* (1969), and his play *Unscheduled Stop* was produced for ATV's celebrated *Armchair Theatre* (1968). However, the later part of Bond's career was most notable for his controversial term of office as president of the actors' union, Equity, from 1984 to 1986. Deeply conservative and a believer in individual conscience, he clashed with more radical elements in the union following his stage appearances in South Africa. He narrowly escaped a vote of no confidence within the council, but later resigned after the membership voted for a total ban on working in South Africa. In 1989 he also resigned his posts within the council and executive.

His first marriage having ended in divorce, on 11 November 1977 Bond married Margaret Ann (Annie), the 35-year-old daughter of Captain Philip Foster Glover, naval officer. They had one daughter, Belinda. Having lived latterly at 15 Chester Close, Queen's Ride, Barnes, London, he died on 15 October 2006 at St George's Hospital, Tooting, London, of bronchopneumonia following a fall. He was survived by his wife Annie, son, stepson, and daughter. A memorial service was held on 18 January 2007 at St Paul's Church, Covent Garden. ALAN BURTON

Sources D. Bond, *Steady, old man! Don't you know there's a war on?* (1990) · *The Times* (19 Oct 2006); (19 Jan 2007) · *The Independent* (20 Oct 2006) · *Daily Telegraph* (25 Oct 2006) · *The Guardian* (8 Nov 2006) · b. cert. · m. certs. [1942, 1977] · d. cert.
Archives SOUND BL NSA, performance recording

Likenesses Vivienne, vintage bromide print, 1954–6, NPG · photographs, 1959–75, Rex Features, London, GTV archive · photographs, 1967, Rex Features, London, Thames–Nicholas Young archive · photographs, 1971, Rex Features, London, ITV archive · obituary photographs

Bond, Sir Kenneth Raymond Boyden (1920–2006), accountant and industrialist, was born on 1 February 1920 at 38 Harborough Road, Streatham, London, the son of James Edwin Bond, a Post Office sorter who had served as a sergeant-major in the Royal Engineers during the First World War, and his wife, Gertrude Deplidge, *née* Boyden. Educated at Selhurst grammar school, he joined a City accounting firm, Cooper and Cooper, in 1936. After service in the Territorial Army in Europe and the Middle East during the Second World War, he returned to Cooper and Cooper, qualified as a chartered accountant, and became a partner in 1954. On 11 September 1958 he married Jennifer Margaret Crabbe (*b*. 1937), a dental receptionist, and daughter of Sir Cecil Crabbe, the chief registrar of Friendly Societies. They had three sons and three daughters.

One of Cooper and Cooper's clients was Electrical and Musical Industries (EMI), and it was a transaction involving that company that brought Bond into contact with Arnold Weinstock, who was to become one of Britain's leading industrialists. Weinstock's father-in-law, Michael Sobell, had started a company assembling radio and television sets but had sold that business to EMI in 1953. In the following year he bought it back, renamed the company Radio and Allied Industries and asked Weinstock to help manage it. Bond had acted for EMI in its dealings with Sobell, and Weinstock was sufficiently impressed by his financial skills to offer him a job. After considering several other offers from industrial companies, Bond joined Radio and Allied in 1957. He said later that he chose Radio and Allied because it seemed more likely than the others to 'get things done' (Jones and Marriott, 216).

This was the start of a partnership that was to change the face of the British engineering industry. Weinstock's intense focus on cost reduction and manufacturing efficiency, coupled with the financial controls introduced by Bond, made Radio and Allied a highly profitable company. After floating the company on the stock exchange in 1958 Sobell and Weinstock began to look for acquisitions. At the end of 1960 a merchant banker, Harry Moore of Philip Hill, Higginson, suggested the idea of a merger between Radio and Allied and the General Electric Company (GEC). GEC was one of the three big British electrical groups, the others being English Electric and Associated Electrical Industries (AEI), and it had a loss-making radio and television business that needed new management. The merger, in 1961, took the form of a takeover by GEC of Radio and Allied, which was a much smaller company, but Weinstock soon emerged as the dominant figure in the enlarged group; he was made managing director in 1963.

What then ensued was a sweeping reform of GEC's management, in which Bond—who became finance director in 1962 and deputy managing director in 1966—played a crucial role. Under Bond's direction

> the managers of each company or division were given specific reports to make monthly and required to budget, something which they had never had to do before … Each unit was given its own bank account; before, everyone had helped themselves relatively unchecked from a central account at headquarters. (Jones and Marriott, 218)

The financial disciplines devised by Bond and rigorously enforced by Weinstock underpinned a remarkable improvement in GEC's profitability.

In 1966, while Weinstock was consolidating his position in GEC, Harold Wilson's Labour government set up the Industrial Reorganization Corporation (IRC), whose remit was to promote rationalization in industries that were deemed to be too fragmented. One of the industries targeted by the corporation was electrical engineering, and Weinstock was seen, in the light of his achievements at GEC, as the man best qualified to take the lead. In 1967, after failing to promote a friendly merger between GEC and AEI, the Industrial Reorganization Corporation encouraged Weinstock to make a hostile takeover bid, which despite fierce resistance from the AEI board was successful. In the following year the third member of the 'big three' electrical companies, English Electric, received an unwelcome takeover approach from Plessey. Lord Nelson, English Electric's chairman, turned to GEC as a more congenial partner, and a merger was quickly agreed.

GEC was now the titan of the British electrical industry. Weinstock was the driving force, but Bond, who remained with the company until his retirement in 1990, was his indispensable partner and adviser. Weinstock looked to Bond not as a source of ideas but as a frank and objective critic of all major investment proposals. If it was rare for Bond to initiate things, it was even rarer for Weinstock to go against Bond's advice. The two men were not personal friends and they had very different lifestyles—unlike Weinstock, Bond had no interest in opera or the arts—but they were completely at one in how they wanted GEC to be run. The few disagreements were generally over personnel matters, with Bond restraining Weinstock from what he regarded as unfair treatment of managers who had failed to meet their profit targets.

Bond was a man of simple tastes, a quintessentially British accountant, commuting into London each day from his home in Gerrards Cross, rarely travelling overseas either on business or holiday. He also had great charm and a sense of humour that helped to lighten the austere atmosphere at GEC's Stanhope Gate headquarters. He was unpretentious and never sought publicity for himself, nor did he try to accumulate great wealth. He took no outside directorship, but served on several government bodies, including the Wilson committee on the functioning of financial institutions (1977–80), the Audit Commission (1983–6), and the Civil Justice Review Advisory Committee (1985–8). He was knighted in 1977. After his retirement from GEC he continued to live at Woodstock, Wayside Gardens, Gerrards Cross, until his death, of cardiac failure and peritonitis, at Wexham Park Hospital, Slough, on 13 May 2006. He was survived by his wife, Margaret, two sons and three daughters, one son having predeceased him. GEOFFREY OWEN

Sources R. Jones and O. Marriott, *Anatomy of a merger: a history of GEC, AEI, and English Electric* (1970) • A. Brummer and R. Cowe, *Weinstock: the life and times of Britain's premier industrialist* (1998) • S. Aris, *Arnold Weinstock and the making of GEC* (1998) • *Daily Telegraph* (30 May 2006) • *The Times* (7 June 2006) • *Financial Times* (15 June 2006) • Burke, *Peerage* • *WW* (2006) • private information (2010) • b. cert. • m. cert. • d. cert.

Wealth at death £1,537,331: probate, 3 Aug 2006, *CGPLA Eng. & Wales*

Bondi, Sir Hermann (1919–2005), applied mathematician and scientific administrator, was born on 1 November 1919 in Vienna, Austria, the son of Samuel Bondi (*d*. 1959), a doctor and heart specialist with a deep interest in science, and his wife, Helene, *née* Hirsch (*d*. 1960). His parents were distant relatives, his paternal grandmother also being a member of the wider Hirsch family. The family was Jewish but non-observant.

Education, internment, and wartime research Bondi showed an early aptitude for mathematics; by the time he was nine he was helping his sister, Gabriele, who was five years his senior, with her school homework, and taught himself calculus from a book he found on a visit to his uncle Joseph. His interest in mathematics was further encouraged by a distant relative, Abraham Frankel, who was a professor at the University of Kiel. In 1936 he met Sir Arthur Eddington, who advised him to apply to Trinity College, Cambridge. He was accepted and arrived in England in September 1937, going straight into the second year of the maths tripos. By the following Easter he was convinced that he wanted to pursue a career as a mathematician and his success in the June examinations led the college to award him a senior scholarship. These were troubled times: Bondi was deeply worried at the rising power of Nazi Germany, and when the Austrian referendum on union with Germany was announced, he telegrammed his parents saying they must immediately leave Austria. They heeded his advice, taking the train to Budapest on the morning of 11 March 1938; Hitler marched into Austria the next day.

On 10 May 1940 Hitler invaded France, Belgium, and the Netherlands, and two days later, as an Austrian citizen, Bondi was interned in an army barracks in Bury St Edmunds. There he met a fellow 'alien', Thomas [Tommy] *Gold; the two became lifelong friends and colleagues. He was transported to Camp L in Canada where, under the leadership of Max Perutz, the internees set up a camp 'university', in which several subsequently distinguished scientists participated. Bondi gave lectures on mathematics without the aid of notes or books. This moulded his lecturing style, and with few exceptions he subsequently gave lectures, radio, and television broadcasts without notes.

In June 1941 Bondi was released and returned to Cambridge as a research student under the supervision of Harold Jeffreys, but in April 1942 he joined the radar research team in the Admiralty Signals Establishment. There he formed a theory group with Fred *Hoyle and Tommy Gold. During this period he worked out the theory of the magnetron used to produce high-powered radar beams, and developed the first comprehensive study of wave clutter. Such spare time as he had in the evenings was spent working on astronomy with Hoyle and Gold in the cottage they had rented; in 1943 he was awarded a fellowship at Trinity College on the basis of his research on accretion on stars.

Research in Cambridge Bondi returned to Cambridge to take up his fellowship in the summer of 1945 and was also appointed to an assistant lectureship, and from 1948 to a lectureship, in mathematics. His rooms in Trinity became the meeting place for renewed research collaboration with Gold and Hoyle. In 1947 he met Christine Mary Stockman, a fellow mathematician four years his junior who was one of Hoyle's research students, and daughter of Henry Watson Stockman, civil servant. They married on 1 November 1947 at Cambridge register office, with Gold among the witnesses. They had three daughters, Alison, Elizabeth, and Deborah, and two sons, Jonathan and David.

Bondi's research interests included waves on compressible liquids, the structure of the solar corona and chromosphere, the rotation of the earth, gravitation, and cosmology. A major paper at this time was 'Spherically symmetric models in general relativity', published in the *Monthly Notes of the Royal Astronomical Society* in 1947. This clarified and extended earlier work by Georges Lemaître and Richard C. Tolman, giving a physical interpretation to the co-ordinates, evaluating the properties of the model, and showing that rapidly collapsing matter might force a light ray passing through it to travel inwards, thus anticipating future results on black hole formation. This paper became a classic and was still frequently referred to more than fifty years later.

One of the major problems of cosmology, much discussed by Bondi, Gold, and Hoyle, was the time-scale problem: the time constant of the 'Hubble expansion' of the universe was estimated by Edwin Hubble to be 1.8 billion years, very short compared with contemporary estimates of 4 billion years for the ages of the oldest rocks of the earth, of meteorites, and of the sun. The Bondi–Gold–Hoyle trio struggled to reconcile these apparently contradictory data until, in late 1947, Gold came up with the thought that if matter were being continually created perhaps it was possible to solve the age problem. The three of them worked out the idea, leading to the 'steady state' theory of cosmology, which envisaged new matter being created as the universe expanded, so that on the large scale the universe was unchanging, since it had always existed and always would. Some astronomers were attracted by the theory, others hated it. It made the names of Bondi, Gold, and Hoyle widely known to the general public and to numerous students of science, and was admirably described in Bondi's book *Cosmology* (1952). One of the strengths of the steady state theory was that it gave specific predictions that could be tested but, over the following decades, mounting observational evidence on radio source counts and cosmic background radiation were not in agreement with the theoretical predictions, and almost all astronomers abandoned the theory.

When Bondi met his wife, Christine, she was working on stellar structure and they combined their talents to develop techniques for solving the structure equations, introducing the 'Bondi homology variables' to minimize the numerical calculations required to obtain a stellar model. This was before the age of computers at a time when developing efficient algorithms was a prime consideration, and their work was a fine example of the British applied mathematical approach to problems of theoretical physics.

Bondi's work on accretion began while he was collaborating with Hoyle during the war; it was his detailed analysis of accretion on stars as they moved through the interstellar medium that gained him his research fellowship at Trinity. In 1951 Bondi asked himself what would happen if the star were stationary and embedded in a cloud. This was a relatively straightforward problem, which he completed in a few days, deriving the rate of accretion in terms of the mass of the star and the density and speed of sound in the cloud. He regarded this as a simple piece of work and did not plan to publish it, but Ray Lyttleton persuaded him to do so and the paper, 'On spherically symmetric accretion', published in the *Monthly Notes of the Royal Astronomical Society* in 1952, became another widely cited classic.

King's College, and gravitational waves In 1954 Bondi moved to King's College, London, as professor of applied mathematics. There he established a major international research centre in general relativity. The work of Bondi and his team led to an influential series of papers, 'Gravitational waves in general relativity', published in the *Proceedings of the Royal Society* from 1958 to 2004. Two of these papers deserve special mention. In the mid-1950s there was debate as to whether general relativity predicted the existence of gravitational waves, and in a paper of 1959, 'Exact plane waves', by Bondi, F. A. E. Pirani, and Ivor Robinson, the first exact solution was given, thus finally demonstrating that general relativity did indeed predict gravitational waves. In a paper of 1962, 'Waves from axisymmetric isolated systems', by Bondi, M. G. J. van der Burg, and A. W. K. Metzner, the authors conveyed a clear understanding of the transport and reception of energy in such waves, introducing the 'Bondi radiation coordinates', the 'Bondi mass', the 'news function', and the 'Bondi–Metzner–Sachs group', thereby laying the foundation for much future work on the subject. Bondi considered this his most important scientific paper. He continued working in this field throughout his subsequent career in scientific administration, and his last paper in the series, 'Standing waves', was published in 2004.

During his period at King's Bondi became increasingly involved in public education about science, giving series of talks on radio and television, always lucid and inspirational. He wrote several popular books, including *The Universe at Large* (1961), *Relativity and Common Sense* (1964), and *Assumption and Myth in Physical Theory* (1968), which were translated into many languages. It was also during this period that he became friends with the playwright and poet Ronald Duncan, visiting the Duncans' farm in Welcombe on the north Devon–Cornwall border, and having long discussions about science that culminated in Duncan's epic poem *Man* (1970–4), which he dedicated to Bondi.

Scientific administration At King's College Bondi was increasingly drawn into administration, advising new universities in the West Indies, Nigeria, and Ghana, planning the rebuilding of King's College, serving as secretary of the Royal Astronomical Society, advising on the Anglo-Australian telescope, and serving as a member, then chairman of the Meteorological Research Committee. He was invited to join the Defence Scientific Committee, and to chair a committee to look at British defence interests in space. Then came a request to produce a one-man report on a proposed Thames barrier to protect London in times of floods. His report of 1967 recommending the building of a barrier near Woolwich was subsequently acted on and the Thames barrier was officially opened on 8 May 1984. Bondi regarded this as one of his major achievements.

In 1967, while remaining professor of mathematics at King's, Bondi accepted the post of director-general of the European Space Research Organization (ESRO). At this time the organization was in deep financial crisis and there had been no successful satellite launches since its foundation in 1964. Due in major part to Bondi's leadership almost all problems had been resolved by the end of 1968; ESRO I and II and HEOS A had been launched, political difficulties overcome, and a sound budget agreed. New projects were also approved: ESRO Ib was launched in 1969, and HEOS A2 and ESRO IV in 1972.

Bondi's three-year contract was extended but other events intervened; in 1971 he accepted an invitation from Lord Carrington, the secretary of state, to become the full-time chief scientific adviser to the Ministry of Defence, working with successive ministers, Lord Carrington, Ian Gilmour, Roy Mason, and Fred Mulley. After six years in this post he moved in 1977 to be chief scientific adviser at the Ministry of Energy; during his tenure he led the UK delegation to the International Fuel Cycle Evaluation, and chaired the Severn Barrage Committee. It is a tribute to his chairmanship skills that this very heterogeneous committee, with representatives of water authorities, ecologists, and parliamentarians, reached a unanimous report which recommended that a 16 km barrage be built between Brean Down and Lavernock Point that would generate 7200 MW. The committee's recommendations were not acted upon but remained as the basis of subsequent studies and proposals. Following civil service rules, Bondi retired from the Ministry of Energy at the end of September 1980 but was then appointed chairman and chief executive of the Natural Environment Research Council; during his term of office remote-sensing blossomed, the modern British Geological Survey was born, the council joined the new International Ocean Drilling Program, the RSS *Charles Darwin* was built, and the council's budget for Antarctic research increased.

In 1983 Bondi accepted the position of master of Churchill College, Cambridge, moving into residence in 1984. His chairmanship skills, honed over the years with ESRO and in numerous government scientific bodies, were much appreciated by the fellows. A charismatic, warm, and inspiring person, he got on easily and informally with both students and fellows, engaging them in discussions on a wide range of subjects and telling jokes, of which he had a large repertoire, sustaining a vigorous intellectual environment and communal life. Under his leadership the college received a munificent donation from the Danish Maersk Foundation.

Honours, and final years Bondi was elected a fellow of the Royal Society in 1959 and knighted KCB in 1973. He was awarded the gold medal of the Einstein Society in 1983, the gold medal of the Institute of Mathematics and its Applications in 1988, the Austrian decoration of honour for science and art in 1999, and the gold medal of the Royal Astronomical Society in 2001. He served as secretary of the Royal Astronomical Society (1956–64), president of the Institute of Mathematics and its Applications (1974–6), president of the Hydrographic Society (1985–7), and chairman of the International Federation of Institutes of Advanced Study (1982–90). He was awarded honorary doctorates by the universities of Bath, Birmingham, Plymouth, St Andrews, Salford, Southampton, Surrey, Sussex, York, and Vienna.

Both Hermann and Christine Bondi were very active in the British Humanist Association from the 1950s onwards, and he served as president from 1982 to 1999 and as president of the Rationalist Press Association over the same years. In 1990 he was awarded the G. Birla international award for humanism. He was similarly active in education and the public understanding of science, serving as president of the Association of British Science Writers (1981–3), president of the Association for Science Education (1982–4), and president of the Society for Research into Higher Education (1981–97).

Following his retirement from Churchill College in 1990 Bondi and his wife moved to a house in Impington, outside Cambridge, from where he continued to pursue his research on gravitational waves. He also remained a tireless worker for Save the Children, delivering envelopes and collecting funds in his home village for as long as he was mobile. In his final years he developed Parkinson's disease, and he died at Addenbrooke's Hospital, Cambridge, on 10 September 2005, of bronchopneumonia. He was survived by his wife, Christine, and their five children. He will be remembered for his foundational work in science, particularly for his fundamental contribution to our understanding of gravitational radiation, and for his work on accretion and cosmology. He will also be remembered for his many major contributions to government science and administration, especially on the Thames barrier, and his leadership of ESRO, and for his outstanding communication skills and contributions to the public understanding of science. IAN ROXBURGH

Sources H. Bondi, *Science, Churchill and me* (1990) • J. Krige and A. Russo, *A history of the European Space Agency, 1958–1987* (2000) • *The Independent* (12 Sept 2005) • *The Times* (13 Sept 2005) • *Daily Telegraph* (13 Sept 2005) • *The Guardian* (13 Sept 2005) • I. Roxburgh, *Memoirs FRS*, 53 (2007), 45–61 • Burke, *Peerage* • *WW* (2005) • personal knowledge (2009) • private information (2009) • m. cert. • d. cert.

Archives CAC Cam., papers, *c*.1940–2000 | Bodl. Oxf., Society for Protection of Science and Learning MSS • CUL, G. B. B. M. Sutherland MSS | FILM BFINA, documentary footage | SOUND BL NSA, current affairs recordings • BL NSA, documentary recordings • BL NSA, recorded talks

Likenesses photograph, 1959, RS • R. M. Duncan, black wash, 1967, priv. coll. • photograph, 1980, PA Photos, London • N. Sinclair, bromide print, 1993, NPG • obituary photographs

Wealth at death under £244,000: probate, 23 Dec 2005, *CGPLA Eng. & Wales*

Bonham, Derek Charles (1943–2007), industrialist, was born at Swanbourne, Buckinghamshire, on 12 July 1943, the son of Thomas Bonham (1909–1995), farmer, and his wife, Marjorie Ellen, *née* Jenkins (1914–2003). His father, who rented 500 acres from Lord Cottesloe, was determined that his son should not follow him into farming. However, Bonham worked on the farm as a boy, and having been given a lamb as a seven-year-old, grazed sheep on neighbours' land, and had a profitable flock by the age of eighteen. He was educated at Bedford School, where he was strong at science, and took articles with a London firm of chartered accountants at £7 a week. On 24 September 1966, by now qualified, he married Dinah Chapman (*b.* 1942), secretary, and daughter of Godfrey Percival Chapman, army officer. They had two daughters.

In 1971 Bonham became deputy financial controller at Hanson Trust—one of only a handful of trusted staff working in the company's headquarters. While Gordon White and James Hanson made big deals in Britain and the USA, Bonham (who was promoted to be finance director in 1981) studied the figures, hatched schemes that limited tax liabilities, devised and enforced controls over expenditure of subsidiaries, monitored investments, and suggested the prices at which to sell off unwanted subsidiaries. Bonham became Hanson Group's first chief executive in 1992 and deputy chairman in 1993. The last big successful bid, £2.5 billion for Eastern Electricity, came in 1995. Thereafter Hanson Group chose to dismantle itself, and when Imperial Tobacco was demerged in 1996 Bonham became its chairman. He left Hanson's board in 1997. Meanwhile, his first marriage having ended in divorce, on 21 August 1992 he married Karen Beryl Levy, a 46-year-old financial public relations consultant who had worked for Hanson, and daughter of Lawrence Morton Levy, merchant.

In 1997–8 Bonham was chairman of Energy Group, which included the former Eastern Electricity, until Texas Utilities took control after a takeover battle with Pacific Corporation. He was also chairman of Cadbury Schweppes from 2000 to 2003, but it was as chairman of Imperial Tobacco and of Marconi that he had greatest impact.

Imperial Tobacco had been bought by Hanson in a bitterly contested takeover battle in 1986 at a cost of almost £2 billion. Bonham became chairman in 1996 just as smokers finally began to win litigation in the American courts against tobacco companies, and the imposition of advertising bans was recognized as inevitable. Faced with falling sales in Britain, Imperial Tobacco's target after its demerger was to double the proportion of its profits earned overseas by 2000. The company bought Rizla in 1997 and Van Nelle Tabak the next year, spending about £900 million on these two acquisitions, and consequently met its diversification target ahead of schedule. Steady rises in British tobacco excise duty pushed the price of a packet of twenty premium cigarettes towards £4 by 1999. Smokers consequently defected from Gallaher's long-term market-leading brand, Benson and Hedges, to Imperial Tobacco's cheaper Lambert and Butler brand. By 1999 Lambert and Butler held 17 per cent of the British cigarette market, 5 per cent ahead of Benson and Hedges. Bonham's drive for economies led to the closure of several factories. During the decade after its demerger from Hanson, Imperial Tobacco's sales and profits trebled, although plaudits for this corporate success were muted because they were achieved with tobacco. Bonham was not squeamish about his product.

Early in 2001 Bonham was recruited to the board of Marconi, the renamed incarnation of Arnold Weinstock's GEC. In Weinstock's final year at GEC (to March 1997) it had made profits of over £1 billion on sales of £11 billion, and had cash reserves of £1.1 billion. GEC, which had been vitiated by Weinstock's obstinate insistence on building a cash-pile, was soon destroyed by the profligate ineptitude of the strategy overseen by his successor, Lord Simpson of Dunkeld. Simpson sold GEC's defence electronics business and spent about $7 billion buying American telecom equipment firms. Marconi plunged into broadband communications equipment and top-of-the-market optical switches despite analysts' misgivings. Some suspected that GEC's transformation into Marconi, with its accompanying strategy, was meretricious manoeuvring to create a business that would be bought for a huge sum by a world-dominant company such as Lucent or Nortel. Simpson and his cohorts dissipated Weinstock's cash-pile. A misleading profits forecast in July 2001, and the withholding of accurate figures for two months, caused an explosive crisis. In September 2001 Bonham led the ousting of Simpson as Marconi's chief executive, and of its chairman Sir Roger Hurn. He was shocked by what had happened, spoke with brutal enmity of Simpson and his finance director, and opposed their severance pay-outs. He restructured Marconi's board, persuaded lenders to write off immense debts, and left the meagre remnants of the business with less dismal prospects in 2002 (it was taken over by Ericsson, the Swedish telecommunications firm, in 2005).

Bonham was a non-executive director of the pharmaceutical giant Glaxo Wellcome from 1995 until he was forced to resign in 2001 by activist shareholders indignant at his Imperial Tobacco connection. He was master of the Feltmakers Company in 2006–7.

Bonham's reputation was that of a hard, incisive, ruthless man with formal manners who did not shy from unpopular courses. Hard work was a pleasure to him. He was considered to have tenacious integrity, with an entrenched sense of right and wrong, in an environment where these qualities might have slackened. He was personally reticent. An aggressive skier and a tennis player who liked to win, he owned a home in Knightsbridge, a hobby-farm near Newbury, and a chalet at Verbier. His second marriage having also ended in divorce, on 16 January 2005 he married Derkje Septima (Dicky) Ulmer, a 61-year-old widow, and daughter of Cornelis Adrianus Meijer, patent lawyer. He died of prostate cancer at University College Hospital, Camden, London, on 3 September 2007, and was survived by his third wife and the two daughters of his first marriage. RICHARD DAVENPORT-HINES

Sources *Economist* (8 Sept 2001) · *The Times* (3 Nov 2004); (12 Sept 2007) · *Daily Telegraph* (17 Sept 2007) · *The Independent* (19 Sept 2007) · *WWW* · b. cert. · m. certs. · d. cert.

Likenesses photographs, 1994–5, Photoshot, London · Butler, photographs, 1996, PA Photos, London · S. Adler, photographs, Camera Press, London · obituary photographs

Wealth at death £5,743,438: probate, 9 May 2008, *CGPLA Eng. & Wales*

Boston, Richard (1938–2006), journalist and author, was born on 29 December 1938 at Stonefield nursing home, Blackheath, London, the elder son of Frank Boston (*b.* 1903), a dairy farmer of Shernden, Edenbridge, Kent, then serving as an engineer officer in the RAF, and his wife, Janet, *née* Vessey (*b.* 1904). He was educated at Stowe School and spent a year studying art at the Regent Street Polytechnic in London before going to King's College, Cambridge, where he read English. He went to Sweden in 1963–4, once running in a marathon there. He spent 1964–5 in Paris, living in a garret high above the Gare du Nord. He taught English, wrote occasional feature articles, and appeared in Jacques Tati's film *Playtime*. After returning to Britain he moved into a flat in Covent Garden and worked for *Peace News*, later claiming that MI5 had compiled a file on him. He then worked at the *Times Literary Supplement*, where he was a sub-editor and took great pleasure in headlines such as one he wrote for a review of a book on Pearl Harbor, which read 'Nasty nip in the air'. He became books editor of *New Society* magazine, and edited a critical volume on the British newspapers, *The Press We Deserve* (1970). On 27 January 1968, he married (Elizabeth) Anne Caulkin (*b.* 1945), then a secretary but later (as Anne Boston) a journalist and author, daughter of Lieutenant David Howard Caulkin, army officer. There were no children of the marriage, which was dissolved in 1976, though they remained close friends.

After returning from a convivial spell living in a former hunting lodge in the Sologne region of France Boston signed a contract in 1972 as a features writer for *The Guardian*, a relationship that would last for nearly all the rest of his life and took a number of forms. He became celebrated for championing 'real ale' and attacking the big brewers in a weekly column, 'Boston on beer', which he began in 1973, shortly after the founding of the Campaign for Real Ale (CAMRA). Though he always said he preferred a pink gin to a pint of beer, the column became a great success with readers, and won a Glenfiddich award for food and drink writing as well as providing material for a book, *Beer and Skittles* (1976). When *The Guardian* launched its Saturday supplement Boston appeared on the cover of the first issue, naked in a deck chair and with a portable typewriter strategically placed in his lap, to illustrate an article about a nudist colony in the south of France. The article was entitled 'Starkness at noon', which later became the title of a collection of his pieces (1997). A similar pun had given him the title for another book bringing together his best articles, *Baldness be my Friend* (1977).

Though he listed procrastination as a recreation in *Who's Who* (in another reference book he chose 'soothsaying, shelling peas and embroidery'), Boston was always pursuing new avenues. In 1974 he published the first book he had written rather than edited, *An Anatomy of Laughter*, a fluent, characteristically wry, but also extremely erudite account of the subject ranging from the Marx brothers to Henri Bergson. He wrote or edited a dozen more books on subjects ranging from the first English translator of Rabelais, Sir Thomas Urquhart (*The Admirable Urquhart*, 1975) to a British Film Institute monograph on the classic French film *Boudu sauvé des eaux* (1994). His fondness for practical jokes led to a book recounting the tomfoolery of an invented character whom he named C. O. Jones (*cojones*), *The C. O. Jones Compendium of Practical Jokes* (1982, with illustrations by Posy Simmonds). When the book was published a BBC interviewer asked him on air if practical jokes were possible on radio. Boston replied by saying nothing and, after an interval, everybody in the studio began to giggle. Apart from his regular writing for *The Guardian* Boston contributed to a wide range of publications, mainly on literary or country matters, though he also did a spell as restaurant critic for the newspaper. Towards the end of his life he was working on a book about Cézanne and Zola.

In 1977 Boston founded the environmental magazine *Vole*, working out of a cramped basement room in his accountant's office beside Regent's Park. Though it was in constant financial straits and closed in 1980 the magazine was ahead of its time and was home to a fine collection of writers and illustrators. He also edited the literary journal *Quarto* from 1979 to 1982. He used his wit to full effect as a presenter of the television press review programme *What the Papers Say*, and as a panellist on such radio programmes as *The News Quiz*. He also maintained his artistic interests with sketches and watercolours, and on one occasion presented the newly appointed editor of *The Observer* with a tie he had decorated with vivid variants of the newspaper's masthead and a quiz question on the back.

After living in Islington during his first marriage Boston rented a cottage in the Berkshire village of Aldworth from the cartoonist and designer Osbert Lancaster, the subject of a biography he published in 1989 (*Osbert: a Portrait of Osbert Lancaster*). He then bought the converted village schoolhouse that was his home for the rest of his life, becoming an integral part of Aldworth life, often seen sitting outside the nearby pub on summer evenings, munching on pork scratchings and drinking something other than beer. In the European parliament election of 1994 he formed the Boston Tea Party and ran for the local constituency on the slogan 'It's a big trough and I want to get my nose in it'. He received only 1018 votes, but wrote a high-spirited account of his campaign for *The Guardian*. His politics remained rooted in anarchism, usually coloured by his contrary spirit, which rebelled against any form of authority. His companion for the last twenty-three years of his life was Marie-Claude Thérèse Chapuis, a tour guide thirteen years his junior, and daughter of Marcel Chapuis, commercial traveller. Together they spent winters at her family home outside Aix-en-Provence where Boston pursued his research into Cézanne. They married on 7 December 2004. Boston died in the Royal Berkshire Hospital in Reading on 22 December 2006, of bronchopneumonia following a haemorrhagic stroke. He was survived by Marie-Claude, and by Anne Boston. JONATHAN FENBY

Sources *The Guardian* (23 Dec 2006); (28 Dec 2006) · *The Times* (29 Dec 2006) · *The Independent* (30 Dec 2006) · *L'écossais de Mourjou* (privately printed, 1999) · *WW* (2006) · personal knowledge (2010) · private information (2010) · b. cert. · m. certs. · d. cert.
Archives SOUND BL NSA, performance recordings · BL NSA, light entertainment recordings
Likenesses obituary photographs
Wealth at death £437,335: probate, 23 Feb 2007, *CGPLA Eng. & Wales*

Bowen, Denis Arthur (1921–2006), painter, was born on 5 April 1921 at Zantespans Drift Farm, near Kimberley, South Africa, one of two sons and two daughters of Alan Bowen, a farmer originally from Cardigan, and his wife, Bertha, *née* Jones. Orphaned young, he went to England with his brother and sisters in 1926. From then until 1933 he lived first with his maternal grandmother then with an aunt in Manchester. Thereafter he lived under the protection of a paternal aunt in Huddersfield, Yorkshire, and completed his schooling at King James I Grammar School in Almondbury. His artistic talent was already apparent and in 1938 he entered Huddersfield School of Art, where he was encouraged by the local painter Reginald Napier, a former Royal College of Art student who pointed his charge towards further studies at the college.

As with many of his generation, Bowen's education was put on hold by the Second World War. He served in the navy, travelling on Atlantic convoys to Canada as well as sailing to Africa and the Far East. Experience at sea was seminal for Bowen's developing iconography and early informalism. In particular, the mercurial energy of the sea inspired his loose, gestural, and liquid paint handling, which exploited chance, accident, and the 'organic' processes of painterly image formation. From the deck of his frigate in Portsmouth harbour at night Bowen was intrigued by searchlight beams that unified the sky with the mysterious dark waters below. In his work vertical abstract marks deriving from these experiences countered the lateral orientation of most landscape-derived compositions.

Bowen resumed his studies in 1946, entering the Royal College of Art with a borough scholarship from Huddersfield. His benign tutor, Kenneth Rowntree, together with charismatic teachers like Carel Weight and John Minton, saw him develop notable tonal skills that instilled even into gestural abstraction a naturalism related either to landscape or, in later work, to an extra-terrestrial cosmological vision. He took his diploma in 1949. What became a lifelong teaching career ensued; after graduating he taught part-time in the interior design department at Kingston School of Art. This was followed by teaching stints on the intermediate course at Hammersmith during the early 1950s and in the school of industrial design first at the Central School of Art (1953–6) and then at the Royal College of Art (1956–61). Not only did Bowen create in these colleges a network of professional contacts among staff and students that would last a lifetime, but the experimental tenor of his work was consolidated within a climate of radical innovation informed by the Bauhaus-inspired teaching methods introduced by Victor Pasmore and others.

While Bowen's emerging abstract style was influenced by New York abstract expressionism and by contemporary French 'tachism', gleaned from the magazines *Cimaise* and *Art d'Aujourd'hui*, a more direct spur to his evolving language came through meeting in London artists he admired, such as Alberto Giacometti, Pierre Soulages, Georges Mathieu, and later Mark Rothko. He also stayed in Paris with Yves Klein. An intrepid gallery-goer, he became a well-informed artist whose talents extended beyond his own artistic practice to embrace exhibition organizing and critical writing. Accordingly he opened his own gallery, the avant-garde New Vision Centre Gallery in London, with help from Halima Nalecz and Frank Avray Wilson, in April 1956.

Both inspired by, and a reaction to, the Institute of Contemporary Art, founded in 1948, the New Vision Centre Gallery formed itself out of the Free Painters Group. As its title implies, this group represented a more open, democratic forum than the institute and during its decade-long existence (1956–66) the gallery devoted itself to promoting a broad spectrum of both hard-edged, geometric and informal abstract art by British, continental, and international artists. Among the many distinguished exhibitors were Peter Blake, Paul Feiler, Roy Turner Durrant, Piero Manzoni, Robert Goodnough, and the comedian Charlie Drake. Meanwhile Bowen's own exhibition career blossomed beyond the walls of the subterranean New Vision Centre Gallery to take in such prestigious West End galleries as the Redfern, O'Hana, Tooth, and Grabowski. Always an internationalist, he also exhibited in Paris, New York, Rome, and other major cities. He participated in the Redfern Gallery's landmark 'Metavisual, Tachist, Abstract' exhibition (1957) alongside leading young abstract artists like Gillan Ayres, Robyn Denny, and Roger Hilton. The Atomic Landscape series, produced during a furious two-day burst of spontaneous production, frequently made up his gallery displays.

During the early 1960s Bowen was inspired by space exploration, and his painterliness was formalized into geometrical symbols and stellar or planetary discs. *Re-entry Colonel Glenn* (1962) and *Triptych for a Venusian* (1963) epitomized these developments. By 1965 his output had peaked and he latterly refined the explosive gestures, as in the Projectile series based on rocket launches, and the astronomical symbols. There were, however, innovations like his passing flirtation with 'op' and kinetic art, where he experimented with relief and with new, optically vibrant, fluorescent or luminous paints.

Bowen married twice: first, on 7 April 1949, Eve Elizabeth Reinhardt, an 18-year-old art student, and daughter of Ernest Joseph Reinhardt, button manufacturer, and second, on 11 August 1962, Judith Ann Stapleton, a 22-year-old art teacher, and daughter of John William Stapleton, secondary school teacher. Both marriages were brief and ended in divorce. He became a British citizen in 1962. Although his teaching career took him to the University of Victoria, British Columbia, in 1969–72, he kept his rented flat at 4 Seymour Place, Marble Arch, above what had been the New Vision Centre Gallery. Latterly he taught at High Wycombe and devoted more time to writing art criticism for *Arts Review* and *Art International*. He was an active member of the Association of International Art Critics and travelled to their conferences across Europe. His penchant for travel took him regularly to the Venice Biennale and to workshops in Macedonia during the 1980s and 1990s. Finally, alongside younger artists he participated in the Celtic Vision, Cosmopolis, and Sharing a View painting groups during the 1990s and 2000s. A burst aorta suffered in his flat in March 2005 led to months in St Mary's Hospital, Paddington. Although he recovered he died from pneumonia at the same hospital on 23 March 2006. He was survived by a daughter, Amanda Groome. He was cremated at Golders Green crematorium.

PETER DAVIES

Sources M. Garlake, *New Vision, 56–66* (1984) • M. Garlake, *New art, new world: British art in postwar society* (1998) • P. Davies, *Denis Bowen* (2000) • *The Independent* (28 March 2006) • *The Guardian* (31 March 2006) • *The Times* (29 April 2006) • C. Lotz, 'A tribute to Denis Bowen', www.aica-uk.org.uk/members/denisbowen_clotzarticle_0306/htm, 27 April 2009 • C. Lotz, 'The other story of British abstract art', www.aworldtowin.net/reviews/Bowen.html, 27 April 2009 • www.denisbowen.com, 27 April 2009 • Tate collection, Denis Bowen archive • personal knowledge (2010) • private information (2010) • m. certs. • d. cert.

Archives Tate collection | SOUND BL NSA, documentary recordings

Likenesses M. Wood, photograph, 1988, priv. coll. • J. A. Maguire, photographs, 2004, Rex Features, London • N. P. James, photograph, repro. in www.thecentreofattention.org/dgnewvision.html • T. Reed, photograph, repro. in www.imperial.ac.uk/college.asp?P=3516 • obituary photographs

Wealth at death under £64,000: probate, 26 May 2006, *CGPLA Eng. & Wales*

Bowie, Malcolm McNaughtan (1943–2007), scholar of French and comparative literature, was born on 5 May 1943 at 1 Hollesley Villa, Saxmundham Road, Aldeburgh, Suffolk, the elder of two children (both sons) of George Alexander Bowie (*b.* 1913), a private in the Royal Army Medical Corps, and his wife, Beatrice Georgina (Betty), *née* Strowger (*b.* 1920). On discharge from the army his father trained as a psychiatric nurse and eventually, in partnership with his wife, became superintendent of a home for psychiatrically infirm elderly people in Aldeburgh. Bowie grew up in the Aldeburgh area; his secondary education was at Woodbridge School. Intrigued by the children's books his father had brought back from war service in France, he warmed to French at school and chose to study French and English at Edinburgh University. On 30 August 1964, while still a student, he married, at the West Central Liberal Synagogue, London, Eva Zwalf, a 21-year-old graduate student of English, and daughter of Meyer Zwalf, research economist. Having graduated with a first in 1965, he studied for a DPhil at Sussex University, focusing on the complex verbal and visual universe of the poet Henri Michaux, and thus launching a lifelong engagement with what he saw as the transformative power of poetic language.

While writing his thesis Bowie served for two years as assistant lecturer at the University of East Anglia (1967–9), and was then appointed lecturer at the University of Cambridge and fellow of Clare College (1969–76). At Cambridge he formed close associations with Lloyd Austin, the Drapers professor of French, and Alison Fairlie, fellow of Girton, leading scholars of nineteenth-century French poetry. These friendships continued to flourish after his appointment, in 1976, to a professorship at Queen Mary College, London. His first marriage having ended in divorce, on 17 March 1979 he married Alison Mary Finch (*b.* 1948), daughter of Joseph Finch, schoolteacher. A fellow literary scholar, then carrying out pioneering work on Proust's manuscripts, Alison Finch had studied with Alison Fairlie at Girton and was a university lecturer and French fellow at Churchill College. The union was exceptionally happy and well balanced (Bowie was a natural feminist). They lived in Cambridge, Bowie commuting to London; they had a son, Sam, and a daughter, Jessica.

Bowie's second book, *Mallarmé and the Art of Being Difficult* (1978), confirmed his exceptional gifts as a reader of literary texts, while also revealing another of his enduring strengths, the conviction that the new critical theories emanating from Paris could contribute significantly to the understanding of complex literary works. While showing what Julia Kristeva, Roland Barthes, or Michel Serres could bring to the reading of Mallarmé, Bowie took up the challenge of interpreting the difficult and often abstruse psychoanalytic thought of Jacques Lacan for a non-specialist audience, providing an incisive essay in John Sturrock's *Structuralism and Since* (1979), and later a pellucid monograph, *Lacan*, in the Fontana Modern Masters series (1991). While from this point on non-doctrinaire psychoanalysis provided some of the impetus for Bowie's writing, his wide and eclectic reading in philosophy, art history, and musicology (music was an abiding passion) helped him forge a unique and multifaceted critical idiom. His remarkable virtuosity as a prose stylist emerged fully at this juncture, for example in the scintillating inaugural lecture he delivered at Queen Mary College in 1978, 'Proust, jealousy, knowledge', incorporated as a chapter of his third book, *Freud, Proust and Lacan: Theory as Fiction* (1987), where the three writers are seen as 'portraitists of the mental life' (p. 7) and as theorists of desire.

As head of the French department at Queen Mary, Bowie progressively involved himself in the affairs of London University while establishing his position as a figurehead for French studies in the UK, a role he retained for the rest of his life. From 1980 to 1987 he succeeded Austin as general editor of *French Studies*, the leading journal in the discipline, and also in 1980 became founding general editor of Cambridge Studies in French, a monograph series that, for the next fifteen years, published a stream of outstanding books (forty-two in all), each benefiting from his painstaking advice, and at their best characterized by the editor's own ability to combine meticulous scholarship with new critical vistas. In 1983 he was instrumental in the creation of the Modern Critical Theory Group and its journal, *Paragraph*, which became a leader in its field. He showed a similar dynamism when in 1989 he persuaded the University of London to establish the Institute for Romance Languages. Almost overnight the institute, subsequently subsumed into London's School of Advanced Study, was buzzing with the cross-disciplinary energies Bowie increasingly came to incarnate. Stepping down from the headship and other administrative burdens at Queen Mary, Bowie, as founding director (1989–92), made the institute's premises on the third floor of Senate House his headquarters, presiding over a dazzling range of lectures and colloquia that brought world-class quality to the sometimes parochial world of modern languages in Britain.

In 1992 Bowie was appointed to the Marshal Foch professorship of French literature at Oxford and became a fellow of All Souls. From 1995 to 2002 he was actively involved in the recently established European Humanities Research Centre at Oxford, serving as director from 1998 to 2002, and setting up its imprint, Legenda. Under his guidance Legenda developed monograph series in various European literatures, including Yiddish, as well as in comparative literature, and became a leading academic publisher of outstanding work across modern languages and beyond. At All Souls, and in the sub-faculty of French, he organized numerous high-level research seminars, inviting distinguished critics to Oxford, including speakers at the annual Zaharoff lecture connected with the Foch chair, and the holders of the Weidenfeld visiting professorship in European comparative literature, which he helped to inaugurate. Once he had settled in, the family moved to Oxford, Alison becoming a fellow of Jesus, and then of Merton College. During his Oxford years Bowie was made a fellow of the British Academy (1993) and the Royal Society of Literature (1999) and served as president of the Society for French Studies (1994–6) and the British Comparative Literature Association (1998–2002).

Bowie's decade in Oxford saw the fruition of his many years of close study of Proust. Building on the insights of *Freud, Proust and Lacan*, and the essays collected in *Psychoanalysis and the Future of Theory* (1993), which include a marvellous chapter on the 'European unconscious' that placed Freud in his cultural and historical context by way of interconnections with Mahler and Schoenberg, he progressively composed his masterly *Proust among the Stars*, published to great acclaim in 1998 and awarded the Truman Capote award for literary criticism in 2001. Bowie's *Proust* is the work of a supreme stylist. On page after page, elegant and enriching formulations of the essentials of Proust's achievement, gathered under plain headings ('Self', 'Time', 'Art', 'Politics', 'Morality', 'Sex', 'Death'), incite readers to refine their appreciation of the multitudinous ways in which Proust's alter ego charts 'the inscrutable inwardness of human desire' (p. 327). Bowie's contribution (on the nineteenth and twentieth centuries) to *A Short History of French Literature* (2003), co-written with Sarah Kay and Terence Cave, placed Proust in a wider context and demonstrated afresh the breadth as well as the depth of Bowie's knowledge of French literature (a breadth apparent from the beginning of his career in the range of his reviewing). At Oxford he was able to give full rein to his outstanding qualities as a doctoral supervisor. As Clive Scott noted, he 'encouraged in his students not only the adventurousness and fearlessness of his own thinking, but attention to the revelations of textual detail, and scrupulous scholarship' (*The Independent*, 5 Feb 2007). Scott added that 'there are many academic careers that have prospered thanks to his careful and caring guidance' (ibid.), an observation that applied more widely to the many younger colleagues for whom Bowie served as an ideal older brother, unfailingly generous with his time, sagacious in his advice, and delightfully amusing in conversation (as with everyone: a colleague remarked of him that he was able to make the most boring meeting seem fun).

In 2002 Bowie returned to Cambridge to be master of Christ's College, where he took pleasure in welcoming visitors to the college of Milton and Darwin and relished his role in spearheading the college's celebrations of its 500th anniversary in 2005. He proved a popular master, held in esteem and affection by fellows and students alike. But his tenure was short-lived. In 2004 he was diagnosed with multiple myeloma, an incurable form of cancer. A bone-marrow operation offered the possibility of lengthy remission but the disease returned and he stood down from the mastership two months before he died, at Arthur Rank House, a hospice in Cambridge, on 28 January 2007. His funeral took place at Cambridge crematorium on 7 February. He was survived by his wife, Alison, and their two children. In 2008 the Society for French Studies inaugurated an annual Malcolm Bowie prize for the best article published by a young researcher in the field of French studies.

The uncomplaining fortitude and good humour with which Bowie had carried on his work after the diagnosis were entirely characteristic. Visitors to the master's lodge observed the enduring delight he evidently took in the powers of literature, thought, and art, as well as the joy he derived from his family life. In the wake of his work on Mallarmé and Proust he had come to give increasing prominence to music and painting. In the outstanding programme notes he wrote for Covent Garden, essays on Mallarmé and Debussy, or Proust and Italian painters, or in his last publication, a magnificent review of books on the German Lied for the *Times Literary Supplement*, he articulated a broad and generous vision of the humanities, whose cause he sought to advance with great urgency in his last years. 'Why Art Matters', the title of a symposium in his honour, held in Cambridge in December 2005, summed up the essence of Bowie's legacy. Through the power and originality of his intellect, the warmth and generosity of his personality, the flair and commitment with which he created contexts where research could flourish, and through the brilliance and humanity of his writing, Bowie was not only the leading figure in French studies of his generation but a scholar of lasting importance in the wider fields of literary and cultural study. MICHAEL SHERINGHAM

Sources *Daily Telegraph* (5 Feb 2007) · *The Independent* (5 Feb 2007) · *The Times* (6 Feb 2007); (20 Feb 2007) · *The Guardian* (14 Feb 2007) · C. Scott, funeral tribute, 7 Feb 2007, www.bcla.org/bowie.htm, 28 July 2010 · *French Studies*, 61/4 (2007), 570–73 · *Paragraph*, 30/2 (2007), 117–19 · *PBA*, 161 (2009), 41–59 · *Pieces* [Christ's College, Cambridge], 10 (spring 2007), 2 · *WW* (2007) · personal knowledge (2011) · private information (2011) · b. cert. · m. certs. · d. cert.
Archives SOUND BL NSA, documentary recordings
Likenesses obituary photographs · photograph, repro. in www.sfs.ac.uk/bowieprize.htm · photograph, repro. in www.ehrc.ox.ac.uk/announcements.htm · photograph, repro. in *PBA*
Wealth at death £17,620: probate, 5 March 2007, *CGPLA Eng. & Wales*

Box, John Allan Hyatt (1920–2005), film production designer, was born on 27 January 1920 at 80 Fordwych Road, Hampstead, London, the first child and elder son of Allan Cyril Box (1887–1974), a civil engineer then serving as a lieutenant in the Royal Engineers, and his wife, Albertha Jane (Bertha), *née* Storey (1885–1933). When he was less than a year old the family moved to Ceylon. Film was to be a lifelong love; he saw his first films in Ceylon as a schoolboy, later remembering an outdoor screening of a film accompanied by mosquitoes and fireflies. His imagination was also seized by a classics teacher who read *Treasure Island* aloud. He was also encouraged to draw and sketch. When he was thirteen he and his younger brother David Charles, who was born in Ceylon, went home with their mother to Maryport, Cumberland, a cold, grey mining district far from the heat and sun of Ceylon. His mother died very shortly afterwards, and he and his brother went to live with an uncle near London, where he attended Highgate School.

As befitted his surname Box was good at boxing, and it was suggested he join the Metropolitan Police; but with the support of his father he chose instead to study architecture, applying to the Polytechnic of North London, on Holloway Road. This choice laid the groundwork for his future film career. The very first day, the instructor told the students that making the first line was all-important, a dictum that Box never forgot. He also learned the intricacies of working drawings and scale models. The Second World War broke out three years into his five-year course, and he enlisted. He spent the next six years in the Royal Armoured Corps, and was mentioned in dispatches for his bravery in Normandy in 1944. He ended the war commanding a tank regiment, in the vanguard of troops entering Paris after the liberation. On 15 January 1944, at St Peter's Church, St Albans, he married Barbara Courtenay, the 21-year-old daughter of Charles Henry Linton, civil engineer. There were no children of the marriage, which ended in separation soon after the war and divorce in 1951.

Demobilized in 1946, Box finished his architecture degree at Holloway, and was made an associate of the Royal Institute of British Architecture in 1948. However, in the years of post-war austerity and continued rationing, there was not much to design, at least in the real world. Inspired by John Bryan's stunning black-and-white design of David Lean's *Great Expectations* (1947) Box decided to try cinema. He entered the film industry in 1948 as a draughtsman at Denham Studios, assisting the veteran designer Alec Vetchinsky on *Escape* (1948), a thriller starring Rex Harrison. The studio system taught Box the basics of building sets, budgets, and time-saving short cuts and tricks of the trade. Another valued early influence was the designer Carmen Dillon, for whom he worked on Anthony Asquith's *The Browning Version* (1951) and *The Importance of Being Earnest* (1952). His first big break came on *The Black Knight* (1954), an Alan Ladd film largely made on location in Spain; Vetchinsky came down with typhoid, and Box took over. Working on this film he also met his second wife, the 27-year-old costume designer Doris Lee (1926–1992), whom he married on 15 April 1954 at the register office in Kensington; their happy marriage lasted until her death. Lee retired from designing in the late 1950s to be a full-time mother to their two daughters, Susan and Deborah.

Box's first film as full art director, *The Million Pound Note* (1953), directed by Ronald Neame and starring Gregory Peck, was produced by his idol John Bryan. In the mid-1950s, when Box's contract with Rank expired, he signed with Warwick Films. Working on films like *Malta Story* (1953) and *Cockleshell Heroes* (1955) he practised his craft and went from strength to strength. The peak in this period was Twentieth Century Fox's *The Inn of the Sixth Happiness* (1958), directed by Mark Robson, Box's first epic production, set in China and starring Ingrid Bergman and Robert Donat. Box thought Wales had the quality of Chinese watercolours, and employed it very convincingly as a stand-in for China. Fox offered him *Cleopatra*, which was then to be made in Britain, but he turned it down for the chance to work with Carol Reed, a director he much admired, on *Our Man in Havana* (1959), which was filmed on location in Cuba just as Castro was coming to power.

These films brought Box to the attention of David Lean. *Lawrence of Arabia* (1962) marked the start of nearly thirty years with the noted director, stretching to his last, uncompleted, film project, Joseph Conrad's *Nostromo* (1986–91). Lean was a perfectionist, with a great sense of visual style. Box always maintained that he studied film-making at the 'David Lean School', acknowledging how much he learned from Lean about imaging, and the value of sudden inspiration. He often cited the instance of how he impulsively painted a white line in the desert to create the memorable effect of Omar Sharif emerging from a mirage, one of the classic images of modern cinema. *Lawrence*'s company was also the first to film in Almería, Spain, later a famous location. There, in sand dunes standing in for the Arabian desert, they constructed their own railway, which they blew up for a battle scene. Seville became Cairo; Aqabah was a set, completely built in Spain.

Box earned the nickname the Magician when he recreated snowy Russia in scorching midsummer Spain for David Lean's *Doctor Zhivago* (1965). Owing to the political situation, filming on location in Russia was impossible. Eventually Box realized that they would have to create Russia themselves, in Spain: 'We ran out of winter; we had to completely create it. But that is making movies. It's the art of the impossible' (*The Independent*, 17 March 2005). He created a hauntingly memorable 'snow palace' interior, invaded by snow and ice, by ingeniously melting hot candle wax and then freezing it with cold water, forming eerie shapes. Equally memorable was the visual impact of a train with red flags crossing the wintry steppes, an example of Box's understanding of the use and effect of colour.

When asked, Box said he was most proud of *A Man for All Seasons* (1966), Fred Zinnemann's film about Thomas More's conflict with Henry VIII. For this film Box accomplished a more low-key miracle, perceptible only upon close scrutiny: Hampton Court was entirely recreated at Shepperton Studios, and is one storey lower than the actual palace. The film was also testimony to Box's unerring ability to visualize the character of a scene, notably the confrontation of Cardinal Wolsey (Orson Welles) and More (Paul Scofield), shot against a simple background, to focus on Wolsey's overwhelming presence. Another highlight of the 1960s was his work on Carol Reed's *Oliver!* (1968), one of the first large-scale musicals made in England. Box and his crew spent eighteen months building two huge sets at Shepperton Studios. For his visual references Box used the same sources John Bryan used for Lean's 1948 *Oliver Twist*: Gustave Doré's book of 1872, *London*, and a collection of late nineteenth-century photographs recording parts of London that were doomed to demolition.

Box continued producing distinguished film designs throughout the 1970s and 1980s. The historical epic *Nicholas and Alexandra* (1971) took him back to 'Spanish Russia'. *The Great Gatsby* (1974), evoking F. Scott Fitzgerald's jazz age story, was shot mostly at Pinewood, with some American locations. But Box was still up to a challenge. *Rollerball* (1975) marked a real departure, to a futuristic world of violent sport. Sport was another lifelong interest for Box, a great lover of cricket. The film's director, Norman Jewison, first had him invent the fast-moving game for the film, before any sets or costumes were designed. At a slower pace *A Passage to India* (1984) reunited him with Lean. Made on a smaller budget than the earlier epics, it still offered opportunities for art department invention, blending locations hundreds of miles apart into one seamlessly edited vista for Peggy Ashcroft's arrival in Bombay, a scene otherwise impossible in practical terms.

Box thrived on cinema projects, and continued working after Lean's death. His last two films were *Black Beauty* (1994), made at Pinewood, and *First Knight* (1995), for which he transformed a Welsh reservoir into Camelot. He always valued the team work that went into making films, and was genuinely pleased to see many of his former colleagues and assistants make good. He was delighted to work with old friends and employ younger hopefuls, and was especially conscious of 'handing on the baton' to a younger generation.

By the 1990s Box was one of the grand old men of British cinema, with four Oscars, or Academy awards (*Lawrence of Arabia*, 1962; *Doctor Zhivago*, 1965; *Oliver!*, 1968; and *Nicholas and Alexandra*, 1971), two Oscar nominations (*Travels with My Aunt*, 1972, and *A Passage to India*, 1984), three BAFTA awards (*A Man for All Seasons*, 1966; *The Great Gatsby*, 1974; and *Rollerball*, 1975), and a special BAFTA lifetime achievement award (1991). He became a fellow of the Royal Society of Arts in 1992, and a royal designer for industry in 1993. He was appointed OBE in the queen's birthday honours in 1998.

A soft-spoken man, Box nevertheless waxed eloquent, telling fascinating stories of the productions he worked on, tales peppered with the names of noted directors, producers, cameramen, and stars. But he was also generous in sharing credit with assistants and crew, invariably mentioning many minor technicians, stressing that every one of them was important.

Before Box began to lose his eyesight in his last years, he enjoyed painting, and visiting art galleries and museums. He particularly loved Constable's quick watercolour sketches of Hampstead Heath, and the French impressionists at the National Gallery. Another great joy was poetry; the *Oxford Book of English Verse* was a favourite travelling companion. He divided his time between homes in Barnes, overlooking the Thames, and Devon. He died on 7 March 2005, at the Princess Alice Hospice, in Leatherhead, Surrey, of end-stage peripheral vascular disease. He was survived by his two daughters, Susan and Deborah. The main collection of his film designs was deposited with the British Film Institute, London.

CATHERINE A. SUROWIEC

Sources *The Times* (11 March 2005) · *Daily Post* [Liverpool] (14 March 2005) · *Herald Express* [Torquay] (15 March 2005) · *The Independent* (17 March 2005) · *The Guardian* (26 March 2005) · *WW* (2005) · personal knowledge (2009) · private information (2009) · b. cert. · m. certs. · d. cert.

Archives BFI, film designs | FILM BFINA, documentary footage

Likenesses obituary photographs

Wealth at death £356,147: probate, 19 Sept 2005, *CGPLA Eng. & Wales*

Boyce, (Nora Elisabeth) Mary (1920–2006), scholar of Zoroastrianism, was born on 2 August 1920 in Darjeeling, India, where her parents were staying. Her father, William H. Boyce, was a judge in the Calcutta high court. Her mother, Nora, *née* Gardiner, was a granddaughter of the historian Samuel Rawson Gardiner. Mary had one older brother. The family returned to England when she was young and she went to Wimbledon high school and then to Cheltenham Ladies' College before going (after brief service in the Land Army) to Newnham College, Cambridge, where she studied English for part one of the tripos and archaeology and anthropology for part two, obtaining a double first in 1943. She studied under Hector Munro Chadwick, an international scholar in the field of orally transmitted literatures, which deeply influenced her later Zoroastrian studies. She became friends with Chadwick's wife and they studied Persian under Professor Vladimir Minorsky, who, with other staff from the School of Oriental and African Studies, had moved from London to Cambridge at the outset of the Second World War. In 1944 she was appointed assistant lecturer in Anglo-Saxon literature and archaeology at Royal Holloway College, London, continuing her study of Persian at SOAS, which had now returned to London. There she was influenced by the brilliant Iranist Walter Bruno Henning, who inspired her to learn ancient Iranian languages. Henning organized a seminar, with another leading Iranist, Mujtaba Minovi, on the Sasanian document the 'Letter of Tansar'. She attended the seminar and prepared an annotated English translation, eventually published in 1968.

In 1946 Boyce returned to Cambridge to study for a PhD on 'The Manichaean hymn cycles in Parthian' under the joint supervision of Professor Sir Harold Bailey and Henning. The following year she was appointed to the newly established lectureship in Iranian studies at SOAS. After completing her thesis, at Henning's suggestion she worked on a *Catalogue of the Iranian Manuscripts in Manichaean Script in the German Turfan Collection* (1960), involving regular visits to Germany to check with the originals. She also developed an interest in the transmission of epic traditions and published articles on that subject. In 1955 she became secretary to a new project to publish the historical inscriptions of Iran, the *Corpus inscriptionum Iranicarum*, working under Henning. In 1958 she was appointed reader in Iranian studies at SOAS. She was active in various societies, being on the council of the Royal Asiatic Society in 1956–60 and 1965–8, and on the editorial board of the journal *Asia Major* from 1962 to 1975. After Henning's move to Berkeley she was made professor of Iranian studies at SOAS in 1963.

In 1964 Boyce undertook a year's fieldwork in remote orthodox Zoroastrian villages in Iran, notably Sharifabad near the desert town of Yazd. This transformed her approach to Zoroastrianism. Previously she had studied ancient texts from a purely linguistic perspective, but after living with devout families she became interested in the religious dimension of the Zoroastrian community. Furthermore, it provoked her to argue for the great continuity of Zoroastrianism. Previously it was common to search for the 'true' Zoroastrianism simply from the prophet's hymns, the *gathas*, and to characterize subsequent eras as the resurgence of pre-Zoroastrian paganism as Zoroaster's followers deviated from his teaching. She developed her theory of the continuity of Zoroastrian belief and practice from the time of the prophet (which she dated as about the late twelfth century BC) down to modern times, and therefore interpreted some ancient texts in the light of modern practices. She summed this up in an article published in 1978:

> It has been a weakness in the western study of Zoroastrianism that it has concentrated largely on texts … In a purely academic study of Zoroastrianism it is possible to make a subjective choice of what seems significant whereas encounters with a living faith force one to accept its adherents' own understanding of its essentials, which are likely, moreover, to be embodied in its main observances. (Boyce, 'Early days', 613)

She took seriously Zoroaster's description of himself as a priest. She postulated that as he was a trained Indo-Iranian priest the *gathas* were, in part at least, meditations on the ritual (see for example 'Zoroaster the priest').

After returning from Iran, Boyce (who thereafter was forced to write lying on her back due to a painful injury sustained before her Iranian visit but undoubtedly aggravated by life in the villages) continued temporarily to write on Manichaeism and Parthian issues, but gradually evolved her theories of the continuity of Zoroastrianism. She increasingly wrote about the religion and especially its rituals. The first substantial indicator of her theory of the continuity of Zoroastrianism emerged in the first volume of her magisterial three-volume *History of Zoroastrianism* (1975, 1982, and 1991). This opened with a substantial study of pre-Zoroastrian religion, against which backcloth she located Zoroaster, and she also saw in his teaching many of the beliefs and practices expounded in the later Middle Persian texts, for example on animal sacrifice.

Boyce soon became prolific in the field of Zoroastrian belief and practice. Her next major work was *A Persian Stronghold of Zoroastrianism* (1977), the published version of public lectures in Oxford in which she gave a vivid and substantial account of the Zoroastrians with whom she had lived in Sharifabad. She concluded that the best people to interpret the prophet's religion were not academics in their Western studies but rather the devout priests living in an isolated place, cut off from outside influences and transmitting the tradition orally. She therefore saw them as crucial primary sources. The summation of her theories on the prophet's dates and the continuity were set forth in *Zoroastrianism: its Antiquity and Constant Vigour* (1992).

Throughout her life Boyce encouraged others to study Zoroastrianism, being generous with her time to all students. She also wrote for students. *Zoroastrians: their Religious Beliefs and Practices* (1978; revised editions, 1984 and 2000) was important because it was the first book to trace the story of the religion from pre-Zoroastrian times down to the twentieth century, both in Iran and among Indian Parsis. The book encapsulated her convictions on the continuity of Zoroastrianism. A second student textbook, *Textual Sources for the Study of Zoroastrianism* (1984), was a compendium of translations of texts both ancient and modern, so that students could study the texts for themselves.

Mary Boyce was among the most prolific and radical scholars in the study of Zoroastrianism. Her work on Zoroastrians in Iran earned her the Burton memorial medal of the Royal Asiatic Society in 1972 and the Sir Percy Sykes memorial medal of the Royal Society of Asian Affairs in 1985. She never married, being wedded, as she put it, to her work. She died in hospital after a short illness, on 4 April 2006. She was survived by her brother Peter, with whom she spent part of each year in Somerset.

JOHN R. HINNELLS

Sources M. Boyce, *A Persian stronghold of Zoroastrianism* (1977) · A. D. H. Bivar and J. Hinnells, 'Professor Mary Boyce', *Acta Iranica*, 24 (1985), xi–xx · A. Mama, 'SOAS's commitment to Zoroastrianism', *Parsiana*, 20 (July–Aug 1997), 36–8 · *The Guardian* (11 April 2006) · *The Times* (13 April 2006) · *Daily Telegraph* (28 April 2006) · *The Independent* (28 April 2006) · *Asian Affairs*, 37 (2006), 421 · *Iran: Journal of the British Institute of Persian Studies*, 44 (2006), vii–ix · *Ushta Newsletter*, 27 (Jan–March 2006) · *Center for Iranian Studies Newsletter*, 18 (spring 2006), 1, 11 · *Jam-e Jamshed* (16 April 2006) · *Vision: Ontario Zoroastrian Community Foundation*, 4 (April 2006), 6 · *British Institute of Persian Studies Newsletter*, 29 (May 2006), 4 · *Manashni: Australian Zoroastrian Association of New South Wales*, 24 (June 2006), 6 · *Newsletter of the Zoroastrian Society of British Columbia*, 14 (June 2009–July 2006), 7 · *East and West*, 56 (2006), 447–59 · *Studia Iranica*, 35 (2006), 279–84 · *Zoroastrian Trust Funds of Europe News* (Sept 2006), 8–9 · *Hamazor*, 41 (2006), 10–11 · A. Hintze, *Bulletin of SOAS*, 70/1 (2007), 143–9 · *SOAS People*, 29 (winter 2006), 8 · *FEZANA*, 19 (March 2006), 125 · *AIIT News: the Newsletter of the Ancient India and Iran Trust* (summer–autumn 2006), 2 · *Parsiana*, 29 (7 Aug 2006), 30–32 · *Nāme-ye Irān-e Bāstān: the International Journal of Ancient Iranian Studies*, 5 (2005–7), 3–7 · F. de Blois, 'Professor Mary Boyce and the quest for Zoroaster', Mary Boyce memorial lecture, Royal Asiatic Society, 13 March 2008 · F. Vajifdar, 'Mary Boyce memorial lecture: Professor Mary Boyce and the quest for Zoroaster', *Hamazor*, 49 (2008), 16–18 · *Zoroastrian Trust Funds of Europe News* (Sept 2006), 6–7 · 'Mary Boyce library', *AIIT News: the Newsletter of the Ancient India and Iran Trust*, 2 (spring–summer 2007), 1 · *British Association for the Study of Religions Bulletin*, 111 (2007), 4 · 'ZTFE's friends', *Parsiana*, 30 (7 Oct 2007), 22 · *Zoroastrian Trust Funds of Europe News* (May 2009), 4–5 · personal knowledge (2010) · private information (2010)
Archives SOAS · Ancient India and Iran Trust, Cambridge
Likenesses photograph, repro. in *World Zoroastrian* [Souvenir Issue: The 1st World Conference on Zoroastrian Religion, Culture and History] (1984) · photograph, repro. in *Parsiana* (1977) · P. Fox, photograph, Zoroastrian Centre, Harrow · obituary photographs
Wealth at death £1,426,455: probate, 3 Jan 2007, *CGPLA Eng. & Wales*

Boyne, (Donald Arthur) Colin Aydon (1921–2006), architectural journalist and editor, was born on 15 February 1921 at Holnest, Farway, Honiton, Devon, the only child of Captain Lytton Leonard Boyne (*b.* 1887), formerly of the 3rd Royal Sussex regiment, and his wife, Millicent, *née* Nisbet (*b.* 1885). He was brought up by his mother and an unmarried aunt after his father's early death, and attended Tonbridge School as a day boy. They determined that Boynes had to be farmers or military men, not architects, so when the war came Boyne joined the forces, choosing the Indian army as being far from his mother. An officer in the 8th battalion of the 13th frontier force rifles, he was badly wounded in Burma when a careless Pathan shot him in the ankle and his horse fell on top of him, wounds made worse in hospital. Invalided out, in 1943 he was awarded a scholarship to the School of Architecture of the Architectural Association, although standing over a drawing board aggravated the constant pain that he endured for the rest of his life. He qualified in 1947, and on 4 July the same year he married Rosemary Barnaschone, *née* Pater, a 27-year-old secretary, daughter of Richard Albert Macaulay Pater, sales manager, and former wife of Richard Barnaschone. They had a daughter and twin sons.

Boyne turned to journalism at the suggestion of his wife, who spotted an advertisement for an editorial assistant at the Architectural Press. Originally rejected by the editor, Jim Richards, he was contacted two months later, the first appointment having been a disaster. Boyne proved an outstanding success, rising in two years to become *de facto* editor in 1949 of the *Architects' Journal*, leaving Richards to concentrate on his first love, the *Architectural Review*; he became executive editor of the *Architects' Journal* in 1953.

In the 1930s and 1940s there were only two serious architectural magazines. The monthly *Architectural Review* was glamorous and glossy, with articles from John Betjeman, John Piper, Gordon Cullen, and Nikolaus Pevsner that mixed modernism with an appreciation of Britain's past. Boyne took the weekly *Architects' Journal* from being its poor relation and made it essential reading for the profession: campaigning, perceptive, and presenting the latest technical information. It pioneered the promotion of cost analysis in case studies written by outside experts, and reinspected buildings after a few years to see if they had met their brief. Design guides, begun in 1961, boosted sales by a third in that year alone. By 1970, when Boyne became chairman of the editorial board of both magazines, the *Architects' Journal* was supporting the *Architectural Review*. He served as chairman until 1974, and continued as editorial director of the Architectural Press for another decade.

Boyne was committed to modern architecture, but above all to architecture as a service for the public good. He never wavered from this social commitment, which dominated architecture in the late 1940s and early 1950s, and he regretted the subsequent return of what he termed 'conspicuous display' (*Architects' Journal*, 5 Oct 2006, 16). He encouraged public sector architects, whose work was until then published anonymously and generally disregarded by the profession. One of Boyne's first campaigns was to return responsibility for London council housing to the architect's department after it had been passed to London county council's valuer. He succeeded in 1949, but more than fifty years later still remembered with embarrassment that the valuer, Cyril Walker, had tears in his eyes when they met to hear the council's decision.

Boyne was astute, but his sense of justice was tempered with humility and warmth. His friends in the profession were the public-sector architects he championed. He did much to promote the revival of interest in the Hertfordshire prefabricated schools of the late 1940s when he brought together many of the architects who designed them as part of a team that briefed the historian Andrew Saint in the writing of *Towards a Social Architecture* (1987). This was a history of the prefabricated school movement and in particular its driving force, Stirrat Johnson-Marshall, designer of the Commonwealth Institute, a leading member of the 'chain gang' of public architects who met regularly in the Architectural Press's own bar, the Bride of Denmark, and perhaps the architect Boyne most admired.

When Boyne finally retired in 1984 the architect Hugh Morris wrote that 'behind the dry, quizzical, abrupt, sometimes paramilitary manner and the conservative dark suit hides the 100 per cent, unreconstructed, inveterate, unrepentant hair-shirted radical … that's about the highest praise I can think of' ('Gentlemen of the press'). Physically tough despite his disability, in 1959 Boyne had taken on management of a 40 acre wood in Kent, where he and Rosemary built themselves a house, designed with Robert Maguire. They sought an easier life in Wells in the early 1990s, but Boyne soon became chairman of the planning committee of the local civic society and of the local branch of the Council for the Preservation of Rural England, campaigning for Wells and its environs. He died on 28 September 2006 at West Mendip Hospital, Glastonbury, Somerset, of uraemia, lymphoma, and spinal stenosis, after a short illness, and years of pain that did not prevent him from being one of the kindest if sharpest of critics. His wife, Rosemary, died a week later. They were survived by their three children. ELAIN HARWOOD

Sources 'Gentlemen of the press', *Architects' Journal* (18 July 1984), 26 · *Architects' Journal* (5 Oct 2006), 16 · *The Independent* (11 Oct 2006) · *The Times* (18 Oct 2006); (13 Nov 2006) · *The Guardian* (26 Oct 2006) · *ArchR* (Dec 2006), 11 · *WW* (2006) · personal knowledge (2010) · private information (2010) · b. cert. · m. cert. · d. cert.

Archives SOUND BL NSA, documentary recordings

Wealth at death £375,090: probate, 25 April 2007, *CGPLA Eng. & Wales*

Boyse, Edward Arthur [Ted] (**1923–2007**), immunologist, was born on 11 August 1923 at St Botolph's Lodge nursing home, Richmond Road, Worthing, Sussex, the son of Arthur Boyse (1859–1940), organist and choirmaster, and his wife, Dorothy Vera, *née* Mellersh (1888–1964). At the time of his birth registration his family lived at 32 Grafton Road, Worthing. After his education at Worthing grammar school, in 1941 Boyse joined the Royal Air Force, in which he served throughout the Second World War. During his initial training as a pilot he was awarded the navigation cup, and he spent the latter part of the war as a pilot trainer, achieving the rank of flight lieutenant.

After the war Boyse attended St Bartholomew's Hospital medical school, University of London, where he graduated MB BS in 1952. On 24 May 1951, while still a student, he married Jeanette Grimwood, a state registered nurse and daughter of Ralph Vere Grimwood, tea planter, and Violet, *née* de Wet. They had two sons, Conrad and Dominic, and a daughter, Adrienne. Meanwhile, under the mentorship of George Payling-Wright, he completed his MD thesis in 1957 at Guy's Hospital, London, on the spread of herpes virus in the cerebrospinal fluid of rabbits. From 1957 to 1960 he continued his research at Guy's Hospital in the laboratory of Peter Gorer, who had recently discovered the H-2 major histocompatibility complex in mice—the white blood cell counterpart to the well-known red blood cell system. These early research experiences and relationships with his mentors at Guy's Hospital, including Peter Medawar (a cordial rival), formed the foundation of Boyse's subsequent lines of investigation.

In 1960 Boyse accepted a postdoctoral fellowship in the department of pathology at New York University under the scientific leadership of Baruj Benacerraf, another influential mentor. At New York University he initiated the breeding of inbred (congenic) mouse strains, which provided unique animal modelling systems to study how the body recognizes and fights off disease and other foreign substances. In 1964, as an associate member, he joined the staff at the Sloan-Kettering Institute for Cancer Research, where he became a member in 1967 and American Cancer Society research professor in 1977; he remained there for the next twenty-two years, conducting studies in diverse immunogenetic systems and establishing a congenic mouse production facility. His work was among the first to define antisera and later monoclonal antibodies and formed the backbone of the field of immunogenetics. At this time and throughout his career he was renowned for his generosity, freely sharing and distributing mice and reagents, and participating in many productive collaborations, most notably with Lloyd Old at Sloan-Kettering in the 1960s and Harvey Cantor at Harvard medical school in the 1970s. From 1969 to 1989 he was concurrently professor of biology at Cornell University medical school and in 1989 he moved to the University of Arizona, where he served as distinguished professor of microbiology and immunology until his retirement in 1994.

Boyse initiated a series of innovative and paradigm-shifting studies. Most notably he discovered many of the fundamental elements of cellular immunology, pioneered research in odour-type genetics, and envisaged cord-blood transplantation. His early research at Sloan-Kettering pioneered the field of mouse immunogenetics to dissect the cellular basis of the immune response to foreign proteins or antigens. Later a standard practice in biomedical research, the use of congenic mice, in which only one gene differs, allowed definition of the precise effects of each gene on the immune response. He used antibodies to develop a strategy to differentiate between defined populations of cells according to their surface protein antigens. This work formed the cornerstone of later understanding of the cellular immune response and was translated in large part by others to the human immune system.

In a parallel yet distinct line of inquiry during his research on mouse histocompatibility factors Boyse and his fellow scientist Lewis Thomas discovered that H-2 genes in mice generate specific scents that allow recognition of family members and olfactory signals that determine mate selection and prevent interbreeding. In subsequent studies, in collaboration with Gary K. Beauchamp from the Monell Chemical Senses Center, similar effects were defined in humans. This early work catalysed the development of a new field of odour-type genetics research.

Boyse's third major research innovation came from his realization that haematopoietic stem cells harvested from umbilical cord blood might be useful for human clinical transplants. In collaboration with Judith Bard, his research associate and partner, he discovered that cord blood from mice could be frozen, preserved, and successfully restored for use as a source of blood-forming bone marrow stem cells. Boyse and his colleagues successfully translated this paradigm to humans and in the first cord blood transplant in 1988 in France cured an American child of Fanconi's anaemia. Later, cord blood harvest at birth and its reconstitution for life-saving transplants became a widely accepted practice, and it was estimated that more than 10,000 children and adults had been saved by this procedure by the time of Boyse's death.

In recognition of his scientific achievements Boyse received numerous awards during his career, including the Cancer Research Institute William B. Coley award for distinguished research in immunology (1975), the Isaac Adler award from Rockefeller and Harvard universities (1976), the outstanding investigator award of the National Cancer Institute of the National Institutes of Health, and the C. Chester Stock award from the Memorial Sloan-Kettering Cancer Center. Indeed Boyse was the first individual to hold full membership of the American Academy of Arts and Sciences (1977), the Royal Society (1977), and the American National Academy of Sciences (1979). During his career he published more than 250 articles in peer-reviewed journals; his last paper, in 2002, described odour-specific changes in mice with mammary tumours.

In addition to his scientific accomplishments Ted Boyse was known for his dry wit and sense of mischief. He was passionate about his work and a perfectionist in all he undertook. He loved all animals but particularly his experimental mice, which were extremely well cared for. Always physically active, he enjoyed running, skydiving, playing squash, and cycling, as well as making and restoring furniture. He also enjoyed planting trees and working in his desert garden in Arizona. His lifelong passion for flying was fulfilled by parachuting, spending time with aviators, and building ultra-light aircraft. He also maintained a keen appreciation of classical music, a legacy from his father, and particularly enjoyed the works of J. S. Bach. What perhaps most distinguished Boyse was his remarkable intellectual curiosity and innate ability to integrate and synthesize data from diverse fields, which yielded scientific innovations that became essential elements of biomedical research. His first marriage having ended in divorce, on 24 June 1987 he married his colleague Judith Bard. He succumbed to pneumonia on 14 July 2007 in Tucson, Arizona. He was survived by his wife Judith and by two children, his son Dominic having predeceased him. A private family memorial service was held on 27 July.

Harvey Cantor

Sources opa.ahsc.arizona.edu/newsroom/news/2007/pioneer-immunologist-edward-ted-boyse-dies, 6 Aug 2010 • *New York Times* (27 July 2007) • *The Independent* (29 Aug 2007) • *The Times* (25 Sept

2007) • *Nature Immunology*, 8 (Oct 2007), 1011 • *WW* (2007) • personal knowledge (2011) • private information (2011) • b. cert. • m. cert. [1951]
Likenesses obituary photographs

Brabourne. For this title name *see* Knatchbull, John Ulick, seventh Baron Brabourne of Brabourne (1924–2005). For other subjects who held this title name *see Oxford DNB*, 7.137.

Bracewell, Dame Joyanne Winifred (1934–2007), judge, was born on 5 July 1934 at 5 Orville Drive, Burnage, Manchester, daughter of John William Bracewell, cotton manufacturer, and his wife, Lilian, *née* Gibson. By the time of her birth the family was comfortably off, her father having worked his way up from humble origins to become director of a cotton manufacturing company. She was educated privately and became a talented child actor, appearing in a number of *Children's Hour* productions of E. Nesbitt's plays and also in two films produced by Film Studios Manchester in 1948, *Cup-tie Honeymoon*, starring Sandy Powell, and *Holidays with Pay*, starring Frank Randle and Tessa O'Shea. No doubt this experience contributed to the beautiful voice and outstandingly clear diction that she later deployed in court.

Bracewell studied law at the University of Manchester, from which she graduated LLB in 1954 and LLM in 1956. She was one of the law faculty's star students of the early 1950s (her achievements were later recognized with an LLD degree in 1991). Perhaps it was her early acting career that drew her to a career at the bar. This was still an inhospitable place for a woman, despite the pioneering example of Rose Heilbron, with whom she had brains, beauty, courage, and determination in common. She was called to the bar by Gray's Inn in 1955, did pupillage with Godfrey Heilpern (later leader of the northern circuit) from 1955 to 1956, and became a tenant in his chambers, then at 60 King Street in Manchester. Women were not then allowed to attend the bar mess dinners, where men were elected to the circuit, and were elected at the 'business court' instead. By dint of ability and sheer hard work, she built up a strong common law practice. It is reputed that such was her dedication to work that one day, unusually, she asked her colleagues whether her undefended divorce cases could be taken ahead of theirs because she was getting married that day. True or not, it was certainly in character. She married Roy Copeland, a 34-year-old textile merchant (son of Jack Copeland, also a textile merchant), on 12 September 1963, at Manchester register office. They adopted a son in 1965 and a daughter in 1967.

After her marriage and the arrival of her children Bracewell continued her career without interruption. She was an inspiration to the women who followed her to the Manchester bar, including Brenda Hale in 1969 and Janet Smith in 1972. She took silk in 1978 and became head of her chambers, masterminding the move to their own premises at 28 St John Street. She was appointed a recorder in 1975 and a circuit judge on the northern circuit in 1983, transferring to the western circuit in 1986. She and Roy bought a large and beautiful house and garden in Somerset, which they ran as a guest house. Roy was also a talented jazz musician, playing both saxophone and clarinet, and their hospitality both in Manchester and in Somerset was legendary.

Bracewell's 'big break' came with the passing of the Children Act 1989. The lord chancellor, Lord Mackay of Clashfern, recruited her to help with the implementation of the act and to act as its ambassador in winning over the 'hearts and minds' of those who would have to make it work on the ground. She was a great success. In 1990 she was rightly rewarded with promotion to the High Court (and the accompanying appointment of DBE), only the fifth woman (after Elizabeth Lane, Rose Heilbron, Margaret Booth, and Elizabeth Butler-Sloss) to hold that office. She was also family division liaison judge for London from 1990 to 1997 and chaired the Children Act Advisory Committee from 1993 to 1997. She was responsible for the invaluable *Annual Report* and *Handbook of Best Practice in Children Act Cases* (1997). She was consulting editor of *Family Court Practice* and of *Butterworth's Family Law Service*.

In court Bracewell was known for her 'air of quiet authority, a measured approach, great courtesy of manner, and an almost superhuman power to maintain those qualities when faced with difficult or emotional litigants, or insensitivity on the part of any advocate who appeared before her' (Potter, memorial address). She was a tough judge, expecting the same high standards of others—be they local authorities in their child protection work or parents in the care of their children—as she expected of herself. She hit the headlines in 2004 with an open-court judgment transferring children from the care of their mother to their father because the mother had obstructed their contact with him. She took an even stronger line when she transferred the care of two children born to a lesbian couple from their birth mother to their other mother, because of the birth mother's attempts to deny the importance of the children's relationship with their other mother and her son. (Unusually, in that case the law lords thought she had been too tough.) She supported proposals for early intervention, to nip such problems in the bud before they escalated into a court dispute, and also for more flexible and constructive approaches to enforcing contact orders once made, which were implemented in the Children and Adoption Act 2006.

Tough she may have been, but Joyanne Bracewell was also friendly and approachable, enjoying the company of other family lawyers at Family Law Bar Association conferences (where she would label herself Joyanne rather than Mrs Justice Bracewell). She was unfailingly cheerful and optimistic, continuing to work for as long as she possibly could during her final illness. This she faced with typical courage—the same courage with which she faced a frustrated litigant who threatened the Court of Appeal with a (convincing replica) gun. She and her fellow judges then had the unusual experience of giving evidence at the Old Bailey, where she had also sat as a judge. She died of breast cancer on 9 January 2007 at St Margaret's Hospice, Yeovil,

Somerset, and was survived by her husband, Roy, and their two children. A celebration of her life was held at Gray's Inn Hall, London, on 19 March 2007.

Brenda Hale

Sources *Daily Mail* (5 July 2004) • D. Lynch, *Northern circuit directory, 1876–2004* (2005) • J. Bracewell, 'Family law: rights and consequences', *Graya*, 119/Hilary (2006), 28–37 • M. Potter, memorial address, Royal Courts of Justice, 12 Jan 2007 • Mr Justice Ryder, eulogy, Manchester Crown Court, 12 Jan 2007 • *Daily Telegraph* (15 Jan 2007) • *The Times* (16 Jan 2007) • *The Guardian* (25 Jan 2007) • *Graya*, 121/Hilary (2008), 103–7 • www.imdb.com, 7 July 2010 • Mancunian Film Studios website, www.itsahotun.com, 7 July 2010 • J. Munby, 'Re D (a child) (intractable contact dispute: publicity)', 2004, EWHC 727, [2004] 1; *Family Law Reports*, 1226, para 38 • J. Bracewell, 'V *v* V (children) (contact: implacable hostility)', 2004, EWHC 1215 (fam), [2004] 2; *Family Law Reports*, 851 • 'Re G (children) (residence: same sex partner)', 2006, UKHL 43, [2006] 1; *Weekly Law Reports* [House of Lords], 2305 • Burke, *Peerage* • *WW* (2007) • personal knowledge (2011) • private information (2011) [D. Hart, B. Hytner, J. Smith] • b. cert. • m. cert. • d. cert.

Likenesses photographs, 1983–2000, Photoshot, London

Wealth at death £2,074,134: probate, 21 Aug 2007, *CGPLA Eng. & Wales*

Braden, Bernard Chastey (1916–1993). *See under* Kelly, Barbara (1924–2007).

Bradshaw, Anthony David [Tony] (1926–2008), evolutionary biologist and restoration ecologist, was born at 214 Kew Road, Richmond, Surrey, on 17 January 1926, the youngest of three sons of Harold Chalton Bradshaw (1893–1943), architect, and his wife, Mary Norah Lupton, *née* Taylor (1890–1967), archaeologist. At the time of his birth registration his family lived at 35 The Avenue, Richmond, but they later moved to Hampstead. His parents provided an environment in which achievement was expected but with the freedom to explore and develop his interests, particularly when they holidayed in the Norfolk broads, an area for which he developed a lifelong passion. He attended The Hall preparatory school, Hampstead, and then St Paul's School, Hammersmith. His biology teachers at St Paul's unusually encouraged an interest in independent research and when he went up to Jesus College, Cambridge, in 1943 to read natural sciences, his interest in plants was stimulated by interaction with two great botanists, Harry Godwin and Alex Watt. After Cambridge he undertook a PhD in Aberystwyth in the department of agricultural botany and the Welsh plant breeding station on population differentiation in the grass *Agrostis tenuis* (later renamed *Agrostis capillaris*), a project that was almost entirely his own conception. The discoveries that he made then set the path for the rest of his career.

In 1952 Bradshaw moved to Bangor as a lecturer in agricultural botany, and consequently did not submit his PhD until 1959. On 3 September 1955, at All Hallows, Whitchurch, Hampshire, he married Betty Margaret Alliston (1925–2000), physiotherapist, and daughter of Archibald William Alliston, banker. They had three daughters, Jane (*b.* 1956), Penelope (Penny) (*b.* 1958), and Sarah (*b.* 1961). In 1968 he was appointed professor of botany at Liverpool University, where he remained until his retirement. He was an exceptionally gifted teacher and postgraduate supervisor, transmitting his enthusiasm for his subject with a natural ease and, for his sixty PhD students, understanding intuitively when to intervene and when to allow free rein.

Tony Bradshaw was one of the leading evolutionary biologists of the twentieth century and one of the few to bridge the gap between fundamental and applied science, excelling in both. His early work on population differentiation in grasses was influential in overturning the then orthodox view that gene flow between populations would swamp any selection pressures leading to evolutionary divergence. He showed that distinct populations of grasses could occur within a few metres of each other, especially on mine wastes, where toxic metals in the soil created very strong selection pressures. What this showed was that evolutionary differentiation could happen much faster than had previously been assumed, and his studies were one of the finest demonstrations of evolution in action. Although initially he developed this finding in a conventional academic context, with important advances in the study of genotype–environment interactions and of phenotypic plasticity, he soon realized that the adaptation of plants to toxic soils had practical implications and began to develop a research programme on the use of plants to reclaim such derelict sites.

Bradshaw's move to Liverpool in 1968 was a very deliberate project to apply these novel ideas in an urban context. His team in Liverpool worked on a wide range of derelict sites, from coal spoil in Lancashire and metal mines in Wales to china clay waste in Cornwall. The key goal was to create functioning ecosystems on these damaged and degraded sites, using suitably adapted plants and attention to soil fertility and nutrient cycles. This work was fundamental to the development of the new science of restoration ecology, and his book *The Restoration of Land* (1980), written jointly with M. J. Chadwick, was influential. This combination of high quality fundamental science with applied work was unusual at the time, and he was eager to use it to deliver effective solutions for environmental improvement. In 1974 he established the environmental advisory unit at the University of Liverpool, which became a model for many subsequent environmental consultancies because it was based in firm science.

Bradshaw received many accolades for his work. He was elected a fellow of the Royal Society in 1982 and was president of the British Ecological Society (BES) from 1982 to 1984 and an honorary member from 1988. One of his ambitions was to create professional accreditation for the emerging profession of ecologist, and when it became clear that the BES was unlikely to offer that route, he persuaded the society to give financial support to a new institute, the Institute of Ecology and Environmental Management. In recognition of his efforts, he was appointed its first president in 1991 and was awarded its gold medal in 2007. He was also awarded the Ted Sperry award of the Society for Ecological Restoration in 1996 and honorary degrees from Lancaster and Hong Kong Baptist universities (in 1998 and 2000 respectively).

Bradshaw was also active in environmental matters beyond the academy, for example as a member of council of the Nature Conservancy Council (1969–78), of the Groundwork Trust (1981–2006), and of the National Wildflower Centre, which he was instrumental in creating in 2000. After retirement he remained active in environmental affairs both locally in Liverpool, and nationally and internationally. His commitment to the Liverpool and Merseyside environment was immense, and was recognized in his final year when the city, then the European Capital of Culture, made him its first citizen of honour. He lived for forty years at 58 Knowsley Road, Liverpool, and died in Fernlea Nursing Home, North Mossley Hill Road, Liverpool, of ischaemic heart disease, on 21 August 2008. He was survived by his three daughters.

Alastair Fitter

Sources *Daily Post* [Liverpool] (28 Aug 2008) · *The Guardian* (11 Sept 2008); (23 Sept 2008) · *Western Morning News* [Plymouth] (13 Sept 2008) · *Restoration Ecology*, 16/4 (2008), 525 · *Memoirs FRS*, 56 (2010), 25–39 · *WW* (2008) · personal knowledge (2012) · private information (2012) · b. cert. · m. cert. · d. cert.
Archives SOUND BL NSA, documentary recording
Likenesses photograph, repro. in *The Guardian* (11 Sept 2008) · photograph, repro. in *Memoirs FRS*, 56 (2010)
Wealth at death £1,051,054: probate, 5 May 2009, *CGPLA Eng. & Wales*

Brainin, Norbert (1923–2005), violinist, was born on 12 March 1923 in Vienna, Austria, the son of Adolf Brainin (*d.* 1930), furrier, and his wife, Sophie (*d.* 1938). He was raised in the Jewish faith. Even though his parents must have felt the impact of the economic downturn that brought the country to its financial knees in the early 1920s, he seems to have enjoyed all the trappings of a relatively wealthy central European childhood. Like others from similar backgrounds, he was introduced to music at an early age. As a boy of six he heard the thirteen-year-old Yehudi Menuhin play in Vienna in 1929. Overwhelmed by the experience, the young Brainin immediately decided to become a violinist, a course from which he never wavered. He began violin lessons at the age of seven with his cousin, Max, an architect and a passionate amateur musician. Under his tutelage Brainin progressed quickly on his quarter-size instrument and it was soon clear that he needed to be taught professionally. After being tutored by a series of teachers that included Theodore Paschkus, Solomon Auber, and Heinrich Schwarz, Brainin became a pupil of the nineteen-year-old leader of the Vienna Philharmonic, Ricardo Odnoposoff, at the Vienna Conservatory from 1933 to 1935. But it was Rosa Hochmann-Rosenfeld who probably influenced him most, because it was she who introduced him both to chamber music and to the great violin pedagogue Carl Flesch.

In 1938 Brainin was struck by two severe blows: the death of his mother and the annexation of Austria by Nazi Germany. Having been orphaned at the age of fifteen, he was raised by one of his paternal uncles, with whom he later fled to London. Although the Brainins were émigrés and were unfamiliar with Britain, they quickly recognized the commercial possibilities that Europe's biggest metropolis had to offer and soon began to trade as furriers in fashionable New Bond Street. Nevertheless, Brainin must have felt the trauma of displacement, because shortly

Norbert Brainin (1923–2005), by Milein Cosman, 1960s [Amadeus Quartet: Brainin (left) with (left to right) Siegmund Nissel, Peter Schidlof, and Martin Lovett]

after arriving in England he became involved with some of the refugee groups that had sprung up around the capital. As an affable and talented young man he rapidly became a familiar face at those gatherings by playing at some of their concerts. His education also progressed apace in England, where he attended a boarding school at Leigh-on-Sea and where he began to take lessons with Carl Flesch. But Brainin's relationship with Flesch was short-lived, since Flesch fled London for The Hague in anticipation of the blitz. (He subsequently spent two years in Nazi-occupied Holland before being allowed to move first to Budapest and then to Lucerne, where he died in 1944.) Continuity was achieved at least in part, however, when Brainin was accepted as a pupil by Flesch's assistant, Max Rostal.

Brainin's musical education was again interrupted when in 1940 he was interned as an enemy alien at a camp in Prees Heath, Shropshire. Although he worked as a machine tool fitter at the camp, music remained his passion and he soon sought out others who shared his enthusiasm. As a teenager he was naturally drawn to other internees of the same age, and among the friends that he made at the camp was the young Austrian violinist Peter Schidlof (1922–1987). Schidlof was also of Jewish descent but had been educated at a Roman Catholic boarding school. His early musical education was equally unconventional, because his first violin lessons were with the local blacksmith's son. After arriving in Britain as a refugee in 1938 he attended Blundell's School at Tiverton in Devon, before being interned. After Brainin was released later in 1940, Schidlof was moved from Shropshire to a camp on the Isle of Man, where he befriended yet another young Austrian-Jewish violinist, Siegmund Nissel (1922–2008), who had fled Vienna on the last *Kindertransport* in 1938.

By 1941 Brainin, Schidlof, and Nissel had all been released from internment and were able to continue their studies with Max Rostal. After the war they joined the Rostal Chamber Orchestra and it was as members of that group that they met the young English cellist Martin Lovett (*b.* 1927), the fourth member of what was to become the Amadeus Quartet. Brainin was now part of an exciting nexus of young musicians and his playing went from strength to strength; he won the gold medal at the international Carl Flesch violin competition in London in 1946 with a performance of Brahms's violin concerto, and went on to play Beethoven's violin concerto with the London Philharmonic Orchestra at the Royal Albert Hall in January 1948.

For a young virtuoso the lure of a solo career must have been very tempting, but chamber music was never far from Brainin's thoughts and when Schidlof converted successfully from the violin to the viola, they joined with Nissel and Lovett to form the Brainin Quartet. With a unified playing style that benefited from their close contact with Rostal the group quickly came to the attention of some of Britain's leading musicians. One of the first to be impressed by the quartet's playing was Imogen Holst, who invited them to perform at Dartington Hall on 13 July 1947. For Brainin that performance was an artistic epiphany, and in later life he recalled that:

> something decisive happened, in my head, my soul, and my heart; and this was entirely caused by the music we played. Above all, by Beethoven's quartets, but also by those of Schubert, Mozart, and Haydn ... I couldn't *think* about anything else ... Already in 1947 I sensed, that playing string quartets would become the purpose of my life. (www.schillerinstitute.org)

With the success of the Dartington Hall concert behind them Brainin, Schidlof, Nissel, and Lovett made their Wigmore Hall début as the Amadeus Quartet on 10 January 1948, having decided that a more neutral name would serve their purposes better. News of this sensational band of young players spread like wildfire through the close-knit chamber music community. Demand for tickets for their Wigmore Hall concert soon far outstripped supply and those lucky enough to secure a seat began to sing the quartet's musical praises, both nationally and internationally. Central Europe was conquered next and it was at Hamburg that the quartet made its German début in 1950. There the young players caused a sensation, prompting 'the audience in its enthusiasm almost [to] smash ... the entire hall' (www.schillerinstitute.org). News of that success soon attracted wider interest and the group then toured America and the world in 1953 and 1954 respectively. On 17 April 1948 Brainin had married Kathe, the 29-year-old former wife of Hans Helmut Block, and daughter of Hugo Kottow, a German grain merchant; they had one daughter, Anne.

Although clearly gifted the quartet benefited greatly from the advent of long-playing records and it was through these that its fame and performance style reached a wider audience. As three of the ensemble's members had been born in central Europe, it was almost inevitable that the group would become associated with the works of Haydn, Mozart, Beethoven, and Schubert. Their interpretations of Schubert's music were particularly highly regarded and their recordings of that composer's 'Trout' quintet with the pianist Clifford Curzon and of the C major quintet, first with William Pleeth and later with Robert Cohen, became benchmarks against which all other recordings of those works were judged. For Brainin, however, it was the music of Beethoven that was the greatest challenge for a chamber musician, and he later argued that if 'a violinist ... cannot play the Beethoven quartets, that is who hasn't the equipment to play them, [he] is not a violinist in the fullest possible sense'. Moreover, he felt that a 'certain technique is involved' in playing those works and that in order 'to do justice to the music, the expression, and all that is necessary, you must have this technique'. According to Brainin the style of violin playing that was taught in Vienna equipped a player best for this music, and:

> it is exactly [that] kind of violin playing which you need in order to play Beethoven's music ... It means producing a certain singing *tone*. It's like the *bel canto* technique in singing. And, like a singer, you have to rehearse this every day. Every day. (www.schillerinstitute.org)

As time progressed, the Beethoven quartets became increasingly important to the group and it was while re-recording those works in 1987 that Peter Schidlof died of a heart attack. Because of the personal and musical relationships that had developed over the previous forty years, the remaining members of the quartet felt that it would no longer be possible to continue as a unit without him. It was agreed, therefore, that they should pursue independent careers and that they should disseminate their performance style by teaching and giving masterclasses. Brainin was particularly sought after as a teacher and was affiliated to the Hochschule für Musik in Cologne and the Royal Academy of Music in London from 1976 and 1986 respectively.

Brainin's performance style was that of a musical literalist, who looked to *Urtext* scores as the basis for his interpretations. He argued vigorously against the use of poor editions and was a particularly strong advocate of consistency in performance. He was a musician whose roots were planted firmly in the fertile artistic soil of central Europe, and his performance aesthetic had much in common with that of other musical giants from that tradition. Nevertheless, he was a cosmopolitan musician who maintained that his playing was not the product of a single method but the synthesis of the Russian and Viennese schools: the Russian through Flesch and the Viennese through his experiences as a boy in Vienna. During his career he played on at least two instruments made by distinguished Cremonese makers: the first was a violin made by Pietro Guarneri, which was bought for him by the founders of Dartington Hall, Leonard and Dorothy Elmhirst, in 1947, and the second was the Stradivarius of 1713 known as the Gibson, which he bought in 1988.

From the 1980s Brainin became particularly interested in pitch. He argued that A=440 Hz, the pitch used commonly in Britain and elsewhere, was harmful to singers and inappropriate for performing music from the late eighteenth and early nineteenth centuries. He advocated the widespread adoption of A=432 Hz, a pitch that he felt made early music both fuller and more transparent and vocal music less hazardous to perform. Brainin was not the first musician to address this thorny question: Sir Henry Wood had also challenged existing trends when he adopted French pitch for the Promenade Concerts in London in 1895, a drop of approximately a semitone from that used normally in Britain at that time. But unlike Wood, Brainin was keen to pursue his argument scientifically, and in tests supervised by Bruno Barosi of the International Institute of Violinmaking at Cremona in Italy, he tuned a number of Stradivarius's instruments to the lower pitch and played the same work under the same conditions. As the instruments responded by resonating more fully at A=432 Hz, Brainin felt that his thesis had merit and that further investigations into this fundamental aspect of performance practice were essential.

A large man with a large appetite for life, Brainin was known both for his wit and for his absent-minded behaviour. He was admired greatly for his musical honesty and his devotion to his art. At the time of his death he was involved with the establishment of the Norbert Brainin Foundation at Asolo in Italy, which he hoped would have both a pedagogic and an archival role. He was appointed OBE in 1960 and received honorary degrees from institutions in Britain and abroad. He died of cancer of the colon at Northwick Park Hospital, Brent, London, on 10 April 2005. He was survived by his wife, Kathe, and their daughter, Anne. RAYMOND HOLDEN

Sources D. Snowman, *The Amadeus Quartet: the men and the music* (1981) • *The Times* (17 Aug 1987); (18 Aug 1987); (12 April 2005); (23 May 2008) • *New York Times* (20 Aug 1987); (16 April 2005); (24 May 2008) • S. Rozsa-Lovett, ed., *The Amadeus: forty years in pictures and words* (1988) • A. Jacobs, *Henry J. Wood: maker of the proms* (1994) • M. Nissel, *Married to the Amadeus* (1998) • *Daily Telegraph* (11 April 2005); (23 May 2008) • *The Guardian* (11 April 2005); (23 May 2008) • *The Independent* (11 April 2005); (26 May 2008) • Schiller Institute website, www.schillerinstitute.org, 20 May 2008 • *WW* (2004) • personal knowledge (2009) • private information (2009) • m. cert. • d. cert.

Archives FILM BFINA, performance footage | SOUND BL NSA, *Focus on the fifties*, interview with H. Burton, 1996, H6817/3 [joint Amadeus Quartet] • BL NSA, documentary recordings • BL NSA, performance recordings

Likenesses M. Cosman, group portrait, pen and ink sketch, 1960–69 (Amadeus Quartet), NPG [*see illus.*] • G. Maiteny, group portrait, glossy bromide print (Amadeus Quartet), NPG • obituary photographs

Wealth at death £322,894: probate, 13 March 2006, *CGPLA Eng. & Wales*

Bramall [*née* Taylor], **Margaret Elaine** (1916–2007), social worker and charity director, was born on 1 October 1916 at 17 Thornsett Road, Penge, Kent, the daughter of Raymond Taylor, metallurgist, and his wife, Nettie Kate, *née* Turquand (1890–1969). She was educated at St Paul's Girls' School, Hammersmith, and Somerville College, Oxford. She was active in the university Labour Club (through which she met her future husband), took part in anti-fascist demonstrations in London, and helped feed the Jarrow marchers. She graduated with a second-class degree in modern history in 1939, and on 2 September that year married (Ernest) Ashley *Bramall (1916–1999), politician and educationist. They had met through the Labour Club at Oxford. They had two sons. After the war she served briefly on Twickenham borough council as a Labour councillor. When her sons had entered school and her marriage was breaking up (it was dissolved in 1950) she studied for a certificate in social science at the London School of Economics, under Richard Titmuss; in 1951 she followed this with a certificate from the Institute of Almoners. Bringing up her two sons on her own, she worked as an almoner at Ashford Hospital and Mortlake Chest Clinic before joining Middlesex county council, working primarily with lone parents. In 1962 she became director of the National Council for the Unmarried Mother and her Child, which had been founded by Lettice Fisher in 1918 primarily as a welfare agency. Under Margaret Bramall's direction it gained a much higher profile as an organization campaigning to end discrimination against single parents and their children, and in 1973 it became the National Council for One Parent Families. It was highly successful in influencing the report of the departmental committee on one-parent families set up under the chairmanship of Sir Morris Finer in 1969; Margaret Bramall was disappointed that so few of the report's recommendations were implemented immediately, though the report continued to have an impact on policy many years later. Bramall was kind and warm, and she was greatly respected by many of those who worked with her, but she found it hard to delegate and could be authoritarian. She also had difficulty in adapting to the increasingly bureaucratized context in which she worked. She was eased out of the directorship of the National Council for One Parent Families in 1979. She then lectured in applied social studies at the University of Surrey for ten years. She remained committed to the Labour Party into her retirement. She had been an active campaigner for the anti-apartheid movement, and was closely involved in securing the release of her friend Hannah Stanton, a Christian missionary imprisoned by the apartheid regime in South Africa. Initially an agnostic, she was latterly a regular attender at St James's Church, Hampton Hill. She was appointed OBE in 1969. She died on 11 August 2007 and was survived by her two sons.

Sources *The Guardian* (17 Aug 2007); (30 Aug 2007) • *Richmond and Twickenham Times* (18 Aug 2007) • *Daily Telegraph* (15 May 2007) • *WW* • b. cert. • m. cert.

Likenesses photograph, repro. in *Richmond and Twickenham Times* (18 Aug 2007)

Wealth at death £679,326: probate, 18 Aug 2007, *CGPLA Eng. & Wales*

Brandt, George William (1920–2007), film-maker and scholar of film, television, and drama, was born Georg Wilhelm Brandt in Berlin on 8 October 1920, the eldest child of a Jewish businessman. The family left Germany in 1933 and eventually settled in England, where he completed his secondary education at King Alfred's School, Hampstead. He studied modern languages at University College, London. In 1940, at the end of his second year, the college's arts faculty was evacuated to Aberystwyth. In the panic following Dunkirk he was seized as an alien and put before an internment tribunal, but successfully pleaded to be allowed to take his final exams (under armed guard) before being interned at a camp near Liverpool and then deported to a camp in Canada where he was detained for sixteen months. He subsequently graduated MA from the University of Winnipeg. In 1945 he joined the National Film Board of Canada at the invitation of its director, John Grierson; he worked as a writer and editor on propaganda films, and then progressed to writing and editing documentaries. In 1949 he married Christiane Adrienne (Toni) Lafrenière, primary school teacher, and shortly afterwards returned to London.

Back in England, Brandt worked first as a freelance documentary scriptwriter, and in 1951 was appointed a junior fellow in the newly formed department of drama at the University of Bristol. Working closely with Glynne Wickham, he developed an approach to the study of film and theatre that combined the rigour of academic scholarship with practical engagement through the production of plays and films, introducing practical film and television studies to British universities. He was a gifted linguist and a brilliant lecturer, and truly international in his artistic and scholarly interests. His early achievements included a European tour of *The Duchess of Malfi* in 1953, with a cast of staff and students; in Vienna it was the first post-war performance of an English-language production. Subsequent cultural activities included supervision of the production of Harold Pinter's first play, *The Room*, in the department of drama (1957) and the presentation in Bristol of the first Japanese Noh company with female performers to visit the UK (1981). These diverse commitments reflected a lifelong love of language and European culture, and a later interest in Japanese theatre. He was a brilliant extemporary speaker, bilingual in English and German, fluent in French and Spanish, with good Italian and Dutch. In the early 1980s he learned Japanese and was a visiting professor at Shizuoka University.

In 1968 Brandt founded the graduate programme in radio, film, and television at Bristol, which achieved an international reputation through the accomplishments of its many distinguished alumni. He was appointed director of film and television in the department of drama in 1971, and was awarded a personal chair in 1983. He provided generations of students with challenging but generous attention, pushing them to discover creative potential with sometimes tough but always perceptive comment. His particular strengths lay in a sensitivity to structure and rhythm in staging and film, qualities that informed his scrupulous attention to each element of film-making from first scenario to final edit. However, his encounters with technology, from camera to projector, were rarely short of disastrous, and his technical colleagues spent many hours repairing or attempting to prevent the consequences of his enthusiastic commitment. This foible was the source of many anecdotes, some of which attained almost mythical proportions. He retired from the department in 1986.

Brandt engaged in a broad range of scholarly activity. He edited *British Television Drama* (1981), one of the first books to approach the subject as a serious academic study. Other work included *British Television Drama in the 1980s* (1993), *German and Dutch Theatre, 1600–1848* (1993), and *Modern Theories of Drama: a Selection of Writings on Drama and Theatre, 1850–1990* (1998). He contributed to the *Continuum Companion to Twentieth Century Theatre* (2002) and wrote articles for *New Theatre Quarterly* on subjects as diverse as Bristol's Shakespeare at the Tobacco Factory company (2002) and the first staging in 1782 of *The Robbers* by Friedrich Schiller (2006). He maintained his wide range of research and writing interests to the end, completing his final work, 'German baroque theatre and the strolling players, 1550–1750' (published in *A History of German Theatre*, 2008), shortly before his death.

Brandt believed in the transformative power of film and television culture; he believed that these media should be 'able to relate individual experiences to an implicit moral structure and scale of values, able to broaden the viewer's sympathies beyond their normal confines, to lead them to a greater insight into interpersonal and social relationships' (Brandt, *British Television Drama in the 1980s*, 1993, 5). He was himself a passionate campaigner on social and political issues. He lacked pomposity, acted impulsively, and possessed an infectious sense of fun. Physically as well as mentally vigorous, he practised gendai budo and achieved a brown belt in judo. He died of cancer of the prostate at Bristol Royal Infirmary on 24 September 2007. The music he chose for his funeral (at Canford crematorium, Bristol, on 3 October 2007) included the theme for *Citizen Kane* and 'Give a Little Whistle' from Disney's *Pinocchio*—from which the refrain 'always let your conscience be your guide' stands as a fitting epitaph for a remarkable man. He was survived by his wife, Toni, and their two children, Peter and Maya. JOHN ADAMS

Sources *Western Daily Press* (6 Nov 2007) · *Daily Telegraph* (23 Nov 2007) · *The Guardian* (27 Nov 2007); (3 Dec 2007) · records, University of Bristol · personal knowledge (2011) · private information (2011) · d. cert.

Archives FILM University of Bristol, department of drama, documentary footage | SOUND BL NSA, documentary recording

Likenesses photograph, repro. in www.bristol.ac.uk/news/2007/5674.html

Wealth at death £366,500: probate, 14 Dec 2007, *CGPLA Eng. & Wales*

Brech, Edward Francis Leopold (1909–2006), management consultant, theorist, and historian, was born Edward Franz Leopold Brech at 84 Brook Street, Kennington, London, on 26 February 1909, one of four children of Franz Josef, later Francis Joseph, Brech (1876–1933), an Austro-Hungarian restaurant manager, and his wife, Anna Maria Magdalene, *née* Bachmaier (1880–1961), originally from Bavaria. His family suffered considerably when his father was interned during the First World War. Educated at Clapham College, a Catholic grammar school, he seemed destined for the priesthood and was selected for a pilot scheme whereby priests took a degree before entering the church. But having obtained a London University BA (general) degree in 1929, he abandoned the church and worked briefly for a fur trader and at the Swiss Commercial College before joining the German Commercial School in Ealing in 1931. In the following year he graduated with a London University BSc degree in economics, and in January 1933 became the German Commercial School's director at the precocious age of twenty-three.

On 1 September 1936, at the Roman Catholic church of Saints Peter and Paul, Northfields, London, he married Irene Ella Levien-Thompson (1912–2000), the daughter of Henry Levien-Thompson, commercial clerk. They had a son, Robert, and two daughters, Lorna and Wendy.

Brech's interest in management and commercial education was nurtured during the difficulties of the great depression, and in 1938 he obtained the diploma of industrial administration from the Institute of Industrial Administration. However, it was his relationship with Lyndall Urwick that was to prove a key factor in his working life. In the same year Urwick, impressed by Brech's diploma results, asked him to undertake some unpaid research on the development of industrial management in Britain, then sponsored his appointment as research officer to the education research project of the British Management Council. The outbreak of the Second World War interrupted this work, and in December 1939 Brech joined the management consulting firm of Urwick, Orr & Partners as Urwick's personal assistant. He was subsequently co-author with Urwick of the pioneering three-volume *The Making of Scientific Management* (1945–8). This was followed by his own major contributions, first *The Nature and Significance of Management* (1946), then *The Principles and Practice of Management* (1953), both of which ran to several editions (the former as *Management: its Nature and Significance*). *The Principles and Practice of Management* remained in print for thirty years, sold 90,000 copies, and was the standard text for management studies in the national curriculum. In 1957 Brech published *Organization: the Framework of Management*, which explored managerial delegation, and the second edition of which was the first in an eighteen-volume series in management studies edited by Brech for Longmans.

A believer with Peter Drucker in the social and educative importance of management, Brech championed a professional, institutional response to management theory and practice. He also did much to create a central institute for management. His wartime work laid the basis for post-war management training, and the foundation of the British Institute of Management in 1947. At Urwick Orr he was an active consultant, providing services to companies like Lotus Shoes, John Laing, Macleans, BOAC, George Wimpey, and Unilever. He was also a founding director of MSL, a management recruitment agency, in 1955. From 1961 to 1963 he was a vice-president of the American firm Booz-Allen and Hamilton, and managing director of its London subsidiary, though he was less comfortable with the American approach to consultancy. After a period of part-time work, notably with Shell-Mex, he became chief executive of the newly established Construction Industry Training Board in September 1965. There he flourished for a time, making a major contribution to the training of the skilled and semi-skilled and editing a hefty volume, *Construction Management in Principle and Practice* (1971), before a somewhat messy departure the same year: essentially he was sacked for having been too successful. In 1974 he was co-founder of Intex Executives, which provided an innovative executive leasing service.

In 1964 Brech was offered, but turned down, the post of principal of Manchester Business School, one of the pioneering business schools in Britain. While these institutions gained momentum in the 1970s, he felt that the study of management and the institutional history of management remained neglected areas, and he proved to be a lively and enduring advocate. A man of indefatigable energy, he set new standards in his attitude to ageing. Embarking on an Open University doctorate in 1990 he completed his thesis, entitled 'The concept and gestation of Britain's Central Management Institute, 1902–1976', in 1994 and became, at the age of eighty-five, Britain's oldest doctoral graduate. He went on to publish a monumental series of five volumes for Thoemmes Press entitled *The Evolution of Modern Management* (2002), which provided an institutional history of British management practice and knowledge. Making a significant contribution to the Open University's business school, he founded and led a management history research group in the 1990s. He was also a regular attender of the LSE business history unit's seminars. A modest and self-effacing man possessed of enormous integrity and humour, he was always provocative and constructive in debate, putting scholars half his age to shame. Many a speaker was disconcerted by his remark: 'I know the answer to this. You see, I was there'.

Brech's contribution to the development of management science in Britain was significant but limited. The British Institute of Management did not achieve all that he had hoped, and his attempt to encourage business schools to embrace the history of management did not prove very successful. While he did much to encourage accounting, business, and economic historians to see management as a science, there were others who saw management as more intuitive and who did not share his interest in the detailed history of management institutions. He was appointed MBE in 2003, became an honorary freeman of the City of London in 2004, and a DLitt of the Open University in 2005. He died on 22 September 2006 at his home, 1 Littlemead, Esher, Surrey, of heart failure. He was survived by his three children. His papers and books were donated to the Open University after his death.

TERRY GOURVISH

Sources *The Independent* (6 May 1999) • M. Witzel, ed., *Biographical dictionary of management* (2001) • J. F. Wilson and A. Thomson, *The making of modern management: British management in historical perspective* (2006) • *The Guardian* (10 Oct 2006) • *The Times* (13 Oct 2006) • E. F. L. Brech and R. Brech, 'A man in management: autobiographical notes', 2006/7, Open University business school • personal knowledge (2010) • private information (2010) [Robert Brech, son] • b. cert. • m. cert. • d. cert.

Archives Open University business school

Likenesses obituary photographs • photograph, repro. in *Independent* (6 May 1999) • photographs, priv. coll.

Wealth at death £1,107,679: probate, 14 Dec 2006, *CGPLA Eng. & Wales*

Brett, Sir Charles Edward Bainbridge (1928–2005), solicitor and architectural historian, was born on 30 October 1928 at Glenard, Holywood, co. Down, the eldest son of Charles Anthony Brett (1897–1988), solicitor, and his wife, (Elizabeth) Joyce, *née* Carter. His father was senior partner

Sir Charles Edward Bainbridge Brett (1928–2005), by Jill Jennings

of L'Estrange and Brett, an old-established firm of solicitors in Belfast. After schooling at Aysgarth in Yorkshire and at Rugby School Brett went up to New College, Oxford, with a scholarship in history. At Oxford he pursued what became a lifelong interest in literary and artistic matters and people, becoming chairman of the University Poetry Society and enjoying a convivial friendship with Dylan Thomas. He graduated in 1949. Following a gap year working as a journalist in Paris he returned to Belfast to commence his legal career. He qualified as a solicitor in 1953, and in the same year married Joyce Patricia Worley (*b.* 1927), with whom he had three sons.

Brett became a partner of L'Estrange and Brett in 1954. But he did not confine himself to what he called 'the conventional life of a provincial lawyer' (*Long Shadows*, 47), though he became in time a distinguished practitioner in company and commercial law, whose advice was highly valued. He immersed himself with enthusiasm in the cultural life of Belfast and plunged into local politics as an active member of the Northern Ireland Labour Party. If this caused some raised eyebrows among his firm's more conservative clients, it was only because they failed to appreciate the radical streak in generations of the Brett family. For some twenty years Brett was involved in constituency canvassing and pamphleteering controversy, serving a term as chairman of the party.

In 1956 Brett was invited to join the Northern Ireland committee of the National Trust, and he later (from 1975 to 1989) served as a member of the national council. In the former capacity he was one of the pioneers of the Ulster coastline appeal, which became the model for the trust's wider Enterprise Neptune campaign. On discovering the lack of books on local architecture he proceeded to fill the gap himself. His book *The Buildings of Belfast* (1967) was followed by a stream of authoritative and attractively written books and monographs, mostly on the buildings of Ulster but also extending to architectural studies in such diverse places as the Channel Islands and the Crimea.

Brett's concern for the preservation of the built heritage led him to play a pivotal role in the foundation in 1968 of the Ulster Architectural Heritage Society, of which he was the first chairman and then president from 1979 until his death. Architectural preservation in Northern Ireland was then in a critical state, the result of many depredations from developers and later from bomb damage. Over the succeeding years he spearheaded the society's activities, campaigning tirelessly to raise the profile of conservation, institute the listing of buildings and a historic buildings record, and create conservation areas. A signal early achievement of the society was the restoration of Belfast's Grand Opera House after it sustained serious bomb damage, a project that sparked the revival of Belfast's cultural and night life, which had almost disappeared as a result of the civil disturbances. To assist in the preservation of endangered buildings Brett was instrumental in setting up the conservation charity Hearth, a novel concept consisting of a revolving fund and housing association, the latter offering advantages that Brett was quick to seize when the governing legislation came into force. Under his aegis Hearth successfully acquired and restored many historic buildings at risk and made them available as social housing at affordable rents or offered them for resale.

In 1971 Brett was appointed a member of the Northern Ireland housing executive, newly formed to administer the stock of public dwellings. The responsible Unionist minister, Roy Bradford, later said that he was taking a chance politically in making this appointment, but few public appointments can have been more fruitful. Brett served for thirteen years on the executive, the last five as chairman, and made an immense and unique contribution to ensuring quality in design, construction, and layout of public housing and the fairness of its allocation. There followed another public appointment in 1986, as founding chairman of the International Fund for Ireland, financed largely by the United States and the EEC 'to promote economic and social advance and reconciliation'. Brett created the framework and guided it with Robespierrian integrity into its pattern of activity in the application of its funds, refusing to allow its resources to be diverted into the partisan projects of political parties.

All this Brett undertook at the same time as carrying a full working load in his solicitor's practice. He was able to do so by channelling his energy into concentrated and effective work in his practice and other activities. His record of public service was recognized by his appointment as CBE in 1981 and a knighthood in 1990. Queen's University, Belfast, conferred the honorary degree of LLD on him in 1989 and he was made an honorary member of the Royal Society of Ulster Architects and the Royal Institute of Architects of Ireland, and also of the Royal Institute of British Architects, a unique distinction that he valued highly.

Brett was tall, slim, and upright, with a good head of sandy hair. With his questioning mind and a never failing willingness to engage in controversy he was regarded by many as formidable, but that exterior concealed a warmer persona. With wide cultural interests and reading he rejoiced in entertaining conversation, and discussion ranging over a wide field. His literary output in his many publications was idiosyncratic, entertaining, and a trifle iconoclastic, but his writing flowed with deceptive ease. He had a complete lack of interest in all organized sports, amounting to marked disapproval. He reserved his particular spleen for golf, which he called the most wasteful land-use in the world. His marriage to Joyce, a fellow Labour sympathizer and party worker, was a great solidifying factor in his life. Possessed, like her husband, of an independent spirit and an inquiring mind, she gave Brett unfailing support in all his activities during a long and happy marriage. They complemented each other in their multifarious activities and interests, made many enduring friendships, and dispensed much warm hospitality. Brett retired from his solicitor's practice in 1994, but he remained a consultant for four more years, and he continued to serve on various public and civic bodies with distinction. He died on 19 December 2005 at Belfast City Hospital, of chronic obstructive pulmonary disease, and was buried in the old graveyard in Holywood, co. Down. He was survived by his wife, Joyce, and their three sons.

ROBERT CARSWELL

Sources C. E. B. Brett, *Long shadows cast before* (1978) • R. Bradford, 'Expert on city skyline', *Ulster News Letter* (11 Jan 1993) • *Belfast Telegraph* (21 Dec 2005) • *The Times* (23 Dec 2005) • *The Independent* (24 Dec 2005) • *The Times* (5 Jan 2006) • *The Guardian* (14 Feb 2006) • Burke, *Peerage* • *WW* (2005) • personal knowledge (2009) • private information (2009) [Aden T. G. Brett, son] • b. cert. • d. cert.
Archives PRONI, papers relating to National Trust
Likenesses J. Jennings, photograph, Country Life Picture Library, London; repro. in *The Times* (23 Dec 2005) [*see illus.*] • J. Morgan, oils, Ulster Architectural Heritage Society, Belfast • photograph, repro. in *Ulster Newsletter* (11 Jan 1993)
Wealth at death £1,398,656: probate, 6 March 2006, *CGPLA NIre.*

Brewer, Derek Stanley (1923–2008), literary scholar and college head, was born on 13 July 1923 at 49 Canada Road, Gabalfa, Cardiff, the younger son of Stanley Leonard Brewer (1892–1963), a clerk at an electrical fittings factory, and his wife, Winifred Helen, *née* Forbes (1896–1985). His older brother, Douglas (*b.* 1925), was later a distinguished physicist.

Brewer was educated at Marlborough Road elementary school, Cardiff (1928–34), and the Crypt Grammar School, Gloucester (1934–41), before entering Magdalen College, Oxford, as a demy in 1941. His tutors there included C. S. Lewis and J. A. W. Bennett. (He and his brother were the first of their family to go to university, a heavy financial burden for their family, but one gladly borne.) His undergraduate career was interrupted by war service: he was commissioned as a second lieutenant in the Worcestershire regiment in 1942, and later served in Italy in 1944–5 as adjutant of the 1st battalion of the Royal Fusiliers, with the rank of captain. On demobilization he returned to Oxford, where a disappointing second in English in 1947 was rectified by his winning the Matthew Arnold prize in 1948. In 1949 he was appointed to an assistant lectureship, soon followed by a full lectureship, at the University of Birmingham, where he remained, with the exception of the years 1956–8, when he was professor of English at the International Christian University in Tokyo, until 1964. On 17 August 1951, at St Mary's Church, Patshull, Staffordshire, he married Lucie Elisabeth Hoole (1923–2008), daughter of Elijah Basil Hoole, vicar of Burnhill Green, Wolverhampton. She was at the time of her marriage a schoolteacher, and later a lecturer at Homerton College, Cambridge, and author of books on the poetry of the *Gawain* manuscript, and on T. H. White. They had three sons and two daughters.

In Birmingham Brewer laid the foundation of his career in Middle English studies and published his first book, *Chaucer* (1953), periodically rewritten and brought up to date, and continuously in print throughout his lifetime. He taught and wrote articles on a wide range of subjects from Old English onwards. He loved his time in Japan, a bold move for him and his family, which by then included three very young children, with a fourth born there. His second book, *Proteus: Studies in English Literature* (published in Tokyo in 1958), gives in about 260 pages a better idea of his literary range, and of his humanity, than any other single work among his very many publications. Wherever he was, he got on well with his colleagues, and with his students.

In 1965 Brewer moved to Cambridge, as a lecturer in English and fellow of Emmanuel College. He became a reader in medieval English in 1976, and professor of English in 1983. He chaired the English faculty board at Cambridge (1984–6 and 1989), and also Fitzwilliam Museum Enterprises Ltd (1978–90) and the syndics of Cambridge University Library (1980–93). He served as master of Emmanuel College from 1977 to 1990. His election as master proved an excellent choice. He was liked as head of house by the fellows who had appointed him, by undergraduates and graduates, and by old members of Emmanuel College throughout the world, who showed their loyal generosity when appealed to by him for financial support, enabling the college to make significant investments. He was a very good fund-raiser, for the same reason that he was a very good and generous tutor, supervisor, and, more generally, colleague and friend: he was wholly trusted. Brewer wrote twenty-eight books, some of them jointly, and about 175 articles, chiefly on Chaucer, Malory, and the *Pearl* poet, and he was widely regarded as the foremost Chaucer scholar of his generation. He was interested in textual problems, and therefore participated in the production of facsimiles of several manuscripts. In 1960 he edited Chaucer's *Parlement of Foulys*; the importance of this edition lies partly in the use of Cambridge University Library manuscript Gg.IV.27, and partly in its valuable introduction. He was twice president of the English Association (in 1982–3 and 1987–90).

Brewer enjoyed a parallel, and also important, career as a publisher of academic books, chiefly on medieval subjects. He was hurt and annoyed by the difficulty many young medievalists faced in getting their work published by the university presses. Excellent doctoral theses, when expanded into readable and significant books, were rejected; young lecturers fared no better. He thought it must be possible to publish such books successfully in small print runs, perhaps not making a huge profit, but not making a loss either. The legacy of £5000 given to Elisabeth by her aunt, Catherine Cowell, enabled them to start in 1972 a small publishing firm, D. S. Brewer, later an imprint of Boydell and Brewer Ltd. At the time of his death this had become a major publishing enterprise of scholarly books centred on the middle ages: in 2008 30 titles bore the imprint D. S. Brewer, and 192 titles bore the imprint of the Boydell and Brewer group worldwide.

Brewer gave many distinguished lectures, including the Sir Israel Gollancz memorial lecture at the British Academy in 1974, and was elected to many honorary fellowships and visiting professorships in the UK, Japan, the USA, and Belgium. He was an honorary member of the Japan Academy (1981) and a corresponding fellow of the Medieval Society of America (1987). He won the Seatonian prize at Cambridge ten times between 1969 and 1990 (once jointly), and in 1991 was Sandars reader at the university. He received honorary degrees from Keio (1982), Harvard (1984), Birmingham (1985), York (1985), Paris-Sorbonne (1988), and Liège (1990) universities, and from Williams College, Massachusetts (1990). He was president of the International Chaucer Society (1982–4) and chairman of the trustees of the Chaucer Heritage Trust (1992–8), as well as of the British Taiwan Cultural Institute (1990–98). A committed Anglican, he was a founder of the Church of England Record Society (and honorary vice-president from 1996), and a member of the committee of the Society for the Study of Medieval Christianity and Culture (2000–8).

Brewer became an emeritus professor at Cambridge and life fellow of Emmanuel College on his formal retirement in 1990, but he remained active for many years longer. His last major book, *Chaucer's World*, was published in 2000. In his later years he suffered from motor neurone disease. He died of heart failure at his home, 240 Hills Road, Cambridge, on 23 October 2008. He was survived by his five children, his wife, Elisabeth, having predeceased him by five weeks. He was cremated, and a memorial service was held at Great St Mary's Church, Cambridge, on 7 February 2009. E. G. STANLEY

Sources *Daily Telegraph* (3 Nov 2008) · *The Independent* (4 Nov 2008) · *The Guardian* (17 Nov 2008) · *The Times* (18 Nov 2008); (9 Feb 2009) · *WW* (2008) · personal knowledge (2012) · private information (2012) [Michael Brewer, son; B. Windeatt] · b. cert. · m. cert. · d. cert.

Archives SOUND BL NSA, documentary and performance recordings

Likenesses obituary photographs · portrait, Emmanuel College, Cambridge

Wealth at death £861,642: probate, 28 May 2009, *CGPLA Eng. & Wales*

Bridge, Nigel Cyprian, Baron Bridge of Harwich (1917–2007), judge, was born on 26 February 1917 at Mill House, Codicote, Hertfordshire, the second son of Cyprian Dunscomb Charles Bridge (1885–1939), commander in the Royal Navy, and his wife, Gladys, *née* Steel, daughter of a wealthy Lancashire cotton manufacturer. His elder brother, Antony Cyprian Bridge (1914–2007), became dean of Guildford. He never met his father, who abandoned his mother shortly after his birth. But he saw him: one day in his boyhood he was on the upper deck of a London bus with his mother, who pointed to a man in the street and said that that was his father.

Bridge was educated at Marlborough College but disliked what he regarded as its dreary athleticism and went to Europe, where he learned French and German. Back in England he worked as a journalist for a spell. He volunteered for the Fleet Air Arm before the Second World War was declared in 1939 but was rejected as colour blind. He was called up in 1940 and after a year in the ranks was commissioned into the King's Royal Rifle Corps. He served in Italy, north-west Europe, and Germany, and was demobilized with the rank of captain in 1946. Before that he had met and on 8 January 1944, at Christ Church, Mayfair, married Margaret Swinbank (1922–2006), a blond beauty then working as a secretary in the War Office, daughter of Leonard Heseltine Swinbank, commercial manager for ICI. The marriage was long and happy; they had a son and two daughters.

Wartime brought Bridge not only marriage but also an experience that was to point the way to his future career. Shortly after he was commissioned he was detailed to represent a soldier at his court martial for desertion. A plea of guilty was expected but Bridge, after obtaining and studying the *Manual of Military Law*, realized that the soldier had a complete defence. He was duly acquitted. Thereafter Bridge was in much demand as a defending officer for the rest of the war. And so he came to be called to the bar by the Inner Temple in 1947. Having been pupil to Martin Jukes he was first a member of a new set of chambers specializing in personal injury cases. That was not greatly to his liking and in 1950 he joined John Widgery's set at 3 Temple Gardens, where he made a name in local government and planning law.

In 1964 Bridge was appointed first junior counsel to the Treasury (common law)—the 'Treasury devil', that is the member of the bar appointed by the attorney general to undertake the leading cases for the government of the day (of whatever colour) in civil matters. By this time the amount of government work was so pressing that it was practically impossible for the Treasury devil to retain any private cases. Bridge was the last devil to do so: he held over one House of Lords appeal from his previous practice. Though the great expansion of the judicial review jurisdiction in England still lay ahead (it accelerated after enlightened procedural reforms in 1977), Bridge's practice, before and during his time as Treasury devil, in the overlapping fields of town and country planning and local government law, foreshadowed the future growth of public law as a major dimension of the common law.

The practice at that time (as it had been for very many years) was that, except in exceptional circumstances, after five years or so the Treasury devil would be translated to the High Court bench. Bridge was appointed a judge after just under four years, in 1968, when he was also knighted: the lord chief justice, Lord Parker (himself a former Treasury devil) was anxious to have his talents serve and strengthen the judiciary.

Bridge's reputation as a judge is mixed. The intellectual rigour he brought to the task is beyond question. He upheld in many cases an objective firmness in the law, which is a quality of the first importance. This was exemplified in some of his muscular disagreements with Lord Denning in the Court of Appeal (to which Bridge was appointed in 1975); Lord Denning was sometimes inclined to take an over-romantic view of the law. Bridge came under criticism, however, for what in some quarters was seen as an excessive sympathy for establishment causes. His judgment in the Birmingham Six case was often cited as a primary example. The trial took place in 1975. The defendants' convictions depended heavily on confessions they had made to the police. Their case was that the confessions had been beaten out of them. After hearing evidence in the absence of the jury Bridge disbelieved their account and ruled that the confessions had been voluntarily given and should be admitted before the jury. In 1991 (after they had spent sixteen years in prison) their convictions were quashed in the face of new evidence tending to show that their version of events was, in its essentials at least, right after all. There was however no criticism of the trial judge. Lord Justice Lloyd in the Court of Appeal (the case was finally disposed of in the House of Lords) stated it was 'not surprising' that Bridge had ruled as he did given the absence of any bruising on the men when they appeared before the magistrates.

Bridge's conduct of his office as a member from 1977 (chairman, 1982–5) of the security commission, his report on the Geoffrey Prime case (after which the issue of trade union membership at GCHQ was reconsidered), his conduct of the inquiry into the case of Michael Bettaney, and his report into the authorization by ministers of telephone-tapping by the Security Service have all been variously prayed in aid to show that he was (as at one stage an exasperated Roy Jenkins described him) 'the poodle of the executive' (*The Times*, 12 March 1985). But the soubriquet was unjust. His minority judgment in the *Spycatcher* case in 1987 in the House of Lords (to which he had been promoted in 1980, taking the title Baron Bridge of Harwich) showed him excoriating the government's attempts to stifle dissemination of a book that was already, effectively, in the public domain as 'a significant step down the very dangerous road to censorship—the indispensable tool of the totalitarian regime' (*The Guardian*, 14 Aug 1987). He showed a genuine concern for civil liberties in some of his judgments and opinions on asylum and immigration cases, and his independence of mind was again in evidence in his opinion on a case involving the Greenham Common protesters, when he decided that local by-laws had been too widely interpreted. Bridge's guiding lights were reason and fairness. These were the engines of all his conclusions. If some of his decisions seemed unduly pro-establishment, that was never the upshot of any bias towards those in power, but only the product of his judgement as to what reason and fairness (and the rigorous interpretation of any relevant statutory provision) in context required.

Bridge could be a hard man to appear before. Counsel who was not meticulously prepared, or had only a stupid point to make, could expect short shrift. On one occasion in the House of Lords he was addressed by a QC representing a local authority who took a spectacularly bad point on the facts of the case. By a few questions Bridge ruthlessly exposed its vacuity. He was, however, by no means a natural bully, as unhappily one or two judges among his contemporaries were. He simply had an almost visceral intolerance of very bad points.

Bridge made a lasting contribution to the common law, particularly in the areas of public law, as witness his opinions in *Gillick* v. *West Norfolk and Wisbech Area Health Authority* (1985, dealing with the legality of government guidance about contraceptive advice for girls under sixteen), *R.* v. *Secretary of State for the Home Department ex parte Khawaja* (1984, interpretation of key provisions in the immigration legislation), and *R.* v. *Secretary of State for the Home Department ex parte Brind* (1991, the government ban on reporting the live speech of supporters of terrorism); and also the law of tort (the seminal case of *Caparo* v. *Dickman*, 1990). Outside court he was a delightful companion, wholly without pomp.

Bridge served in the House of Lords until he was time-expired at the age of seventy-five in 1992. On leaving office he referred (in a judgment delivered on his last day) to the 'statutory judicial incapacity' that had overtaken him. In retirement he enrolled with the Open University and took a degree in mathematics in 2003, at the age of eighty-six. His erstwhile colleague in the House of Lords, Lord Slynn of Hadleigh (another former Treasury devil) was not above teasing him: 'How are the sums going, Nigel?' was met with a somewhat gruff response. He greatly enjoyed sudoku puzzles. He had a number of minor strokes in the last year or so of his life. But virtually until the very end he retained the sharp intellect that had so well served him and his profession. He died on 20 November 2007, of cancer at Homerton University Hospital, Hackney, London, and was survived by his three children. JOHN LAWS

Sources *The Times* (26 Nov 2007); (29 Nov 2007) · *Daily Telegraph* (26 Nov 2007) · *The Guardian* (28 Nov 2007); (4 Dec 2007) · *The Independent* (28 Nov 2007) · Burke, *Peerage* · *WW* (2007) · personal knowledge (2011) · private information (2011) · b. cert. · m. cert. · d. cert.

Archives SOUND BL NSA, documentary recordings

Likenesses photographs, 1975–99, Photoshot, London · N. Sinclair, bromide print, 1992, NPG · obituary photographs

Wealth at death £1,121,669: probate, 6 Feb 2008, *CGPLA Eng. & Wales*

Brien, Alan (**1925–2008**), journalist and novelist, was born at 4 Mowbray Terrace, Sunderland, on 12 March 1925, the youngest of five children of Ernest Brien, a journeyman engineer and fitter for the city tram service, and his wife, Isabella, *née* Patterson. At the time of his birth registration the family lived at 16 Guildford Street, Sunderland. He went to Bede Collegiate Boys' School, Sunderland, where a friend remembered him as tall, thin, shabby, mischievous, and good at English. Brien had already determined to be a newspaper columnist—he thought something along the lines of the New York drama critic Alexander Woollcott—and had started writing. While at school he submitted the first episode of a series featuring a hero named Hercules Standpoint to D. C. Thomson, the Dundee-based publishers of *Rover*, *The Wizard*, *Hotspur*, and other weekly 'bloods'. Thomson accepted the proposal but, for once short of ideas, Brien was stuck for a sequel. Nothing came of it.

The family was far from rich, and Brien never forgot the way things were in the working-class Sunderland of his youth. As a teenager he joined the Young Communist League, and when in 1943 he was accepted for an Oxford University short course—combining English literature with RAF training—he picked Jesus College for its Welsh connection and supposed political links with the miners. He was trained as a pilot but had no knack for it: after he made a spectacularly bad landing his commanding officer told him he would have to pay for a new aeroplane out of his service pay, luckily an empty threat. Instead he was made an air-gunner, a vulnerable role he disliked. He used to take *Paradise Lost* to read on long flights. In another bad landing the tail-end 'pod' of his bomber broke off and rolled about the airfield. Brien was shaken, but not otherwise hurt. While serving in the RAF he met Pamela Mary Jones (1922–1998), a sergeant in the Women's Auxiliary Air Force and daughter of Edmund Merrello Jones, commercial traveller; they married on 14 December 1946 at Abingdon register office (he was then based at RAF Abingdon and she at RAF High Wycombe) and had three daughters.

Demobilized in 1948, Brien returned to Jesus. Colleges had the option of allowing short-course cadets to re-enter the university as undergraduates. A senior don at Jesus had not taken to Brien, and told colleagues, 'That man will come back here over my dead body.' Brien (the don having died before the war was over) used to say: 'And that is exactly what I did.' Brien became a pupil of F. W. Bateson, a fellow of Corpus Christi, a radical and dissenting voice in the Oxford English faculty, and founder-editor of the influential quarterly *Essays in Criticism*. Brien was thereafter Bateson's loyal champion. Brien and his wife had a flat in Walton Well Road, and he became a prominent Oxford figure, as a writer and, in 1948, as editor of *Isis*, the weekly undergraduate magazine. By now he had grown a beard. His *Isis* was irreverent, amusing, and festooned with puns, parodies, and paradoxes. One leading article began, 'Like adversity, and I dare say perversity, university makes strange bedfellows'. The editor of *Cherwell*, the rival undergraduate magazine, who made no secret of his own appointment as a papal count, foolishly picked a fight with Brien's *Isis*: Brien demolished *Cherwell* when he described it as 'count-struck'.

After graduating with a second-class degree in English in 1950 Brien found a job in London on a magazine for home-movie fans, *Mini-Cinema* (he called it 'Mini-Enema'), but was fired in 1952 for unpunctuality and over-long lunch hours. About this time Randolph Churchill took him on as a researcher, and he also worked on the monthly magazine *Courier*. In 1953 he joined the political weekly *Truth* as columnist and film critic, and from there in 1954 he became television critic of *The Observer* and simultaneously columnist and film critic on the *Evening Standard*. He held both jobs until Lord Beaverbrook, the *Standard*'s proprietor, objected to his writing also for the left-leaning *Observer* and hired him exclusively for the *Standard* at a higher salary than he had earned for both newspapers combined. He also became one of three presenters of an early evening television chat show for Associated Rediffusion, *Three After Six*, and the host of a BBC literary quiz game, *Take It or Leave It*. But he hankered after something more serious and when the Hungarian uprising took place in 1956 he asked his editor to send him to Budapest as a reporter. The editor refused, but sent him to America as the paper's New York correspondent. There he met Nancy Newbold Ryan (1930/31–1987), a writer, and daughter of Allan Ryan, company director. Brien's first marriage having ended in divorce, she became his second wife on 29 April 1961. They had a son and a daughter. Meanwhile Brien had left the *Evening Standard* in 1958, joining *The Spectator* as its drama critic and features editor at a time when the weekly was attracting many talented younger journalists.

In 1961 Brien was hired as theatre critic for the newly launched *Sunday Telegraph*. His witty and acerbic reviewing for that paper twice won him the 'critic of the year' accolade in the Hannen Swaffer awards. In 1967 he was poached by the editor of *The Times*, Harold Evans, to write a back-page column, 'Alan Brien's week' (which was regularly parodied by Auberon Waugh in *Private Eye*). He also spent time in Moscow and Saigon for the paper. In 1976 he became the *Sunday Times*'s film critic, filling that post to general acclaim until 1984. While working at the *Sunday Telegraph* and the *Sunday Times* he also wrote at various times for the *Daily Mail* (as the columnist John Jelley), *The Spectator* (1963–5), the *New Statesman* (1966–72), and *Punch* (1972–84). After leaving the *Sunday Times* he continued to write as a freelance journalist and a frequent book reviewer for the *London Review of Books* and the *Literary Review*. He published two books: *Domes of Fortune* (1979), celebrating women's breasts, and in 1987 *Lenin: the Novel*, a fictionalized biography. Neither book was a success with critics. He was working on a novel about Cicero when he died, and had started an autobiography, to be called 'All Right for Some'.

Brien's second marriage also ended in divorce, and on 24 December 1973 he married Jill Sheila *Tweedie (1932–1993), a fellow journalist. After her death he married, on 8

June 1996, Jane Hill (*b.* 1958/9), a librarian, curator, and writer, daughter of Peter John Hill, builder. They set up home in Northamptonshire before returning to London, to live in reputedly the most ancient cottage in Highgate village.

Brien never quite lost the dry, crackly tone of voice of his native Sunderland, nor his left-wing political views. He was a lifelong Labour supporter and he took part in several Aldermaston marches. He was a generous friend and boon companion, and his writing was colourful and funny. Harold Evans said that Brien could get interesting copy out of the fluff in his navel. His writing, like his conversation, was salted with sharp opinions and outlandish comparisons. He was always wittily disputatious, and never pedestrian. He remained cheerful and gregarious even when afflicted by Lewy body disease. In January 2008 he moved to Denville Hall nursing home, Northwood, London, where he died of bronchopneumonia on 23 May 2008. He was survived by his fourth wife, Jane, and his five children from his first two marriages.

PAUL VAUGHAN

Sources *The Times* (26 May 2008); (20 Nov 2008) · *The Guardian* (26 May 2008) · *The Independent* (31 May 2008) · *Daily Telegraph* (4 July 2008) · *WW* (2008) · personal knowledge (2012) · private information (2012) · b. cert. · m. certs. · d. cert.

Archives FILM BFINA, current affairs footage | SOUND BL NSA, documentary and interview recordings

Likenesses obituary photographs

Wealth at death £368,831: probate, 28 Oct 2008, *CGPLA Eng. & Wales*

Brightman, John Anson, **Baron Brightman** (1911–2006), judge, was born on 20 June 1911 at Cintra, Sandpit Lane, Sandridge, St Albans, Hertfordshire, the second son of William Henry Brightman, solicitor, and his wife, Minnie Boston, *née* Way. He attended Doon House preparatory school in Kent and Marlborough College before reading law at St John's College, Cambridge. He was called to the bar by Lincoln's Inn in 1932 and two years later joined the chambers of Fergus Morton, practising at the chancery bar. In 1939 he volunteered as an able seaman; he was commissioned lieutenant in the Royal Naval Volunteer Reserve in the following year. Based in Tobermory on the Isle of Mull he served on an anti-submarine frigate in convoy duties in the Atlantic and later in the Mediterranean. Selected for the Royal Navy staff course at Greenwich in 1944, he was promoted lieutenant-commander on passing out, and sent to Ankara as assistant naval attaché. There he met and in 1945 married Roxane, the stepdaughter of Gerasimo Abatielo, the Greek consul-general in Istanbul. They had one son, Christopher.

Returning from the war in 1946, Brightman developed his practice and became an expert in trusts and taxation, especially in matters relating to inheritance and estate duties. He was elected a member of the Bar Council in 1956, took silk in 1961, and was a bencher of Lincoln's Inn. In 1969 he became attorney-general of the duchy of Lancaster and attorney and serjeant within the county palatine of Lancaster. But he relinquished these offices on his appointment as a judge of the High Court's Chancery Division in 1970. He was given the customary knighthood the same year.

The qualities of clarity in exposition, courtesy, and persuasiveness that had served Brightman well at the bar were even more in evidence from the bench. As a judge he was fair-minded, balanced, and exact. He brought out the facts of a case and then applied the law effectively. His judgments were rarely overturned. Conservative by disposition and pragmatic by inclination, he also displayed independence of mind. One of his first cases concerned relations within his own profession. A former Labour MP, William Wells, had excluded his co-head of chambers from their set in the Middle Temple on being, as he claimed, defamed by his colleague. Brightman found in favour of Wells because he was the acknowledged titular head of the chambers whereas his colleague, as co-head, had only a licence. Brightman therefore refused to order the latter's reinstatement. In 1971 he banned publication of a pirated edition of the novel *August 1914* by Alexander Solzhenitsyn, rejecting the argument that because the book was a *samizdat* publication that had not been approved by the Soviet censors it was therefore not subject to English copyright law.

In a judgment that found much more popular favour in the following year Brightman decided that neither Bobby Moore nor Geoff Hurst, respectively England's captain and highest goalscorer in the 1966 world cup-winning football team, should have to pay tax on the bonuses and cash gifts they were given after that competition. These, he argued, had more 'the quality of a testimonial or accolade than remuneration for services rendered'. In view of this liberality the press dealt kindly with his admission that he did not know how often the world cup was staged. In 1975 he demonstrated his credentials in defence of civil liberties and his prescient concerns about the rights of individuals in a case in which a German-owned engineering company sued for alleged breach of copyright. Opposing the so-called Anton Piller order, a civil instrument providing the right to search premises and seize evidence without prior warning, which would have severely curtailed the opportunity of the defendant, Manufacturing Processes Ltd, of Hayes, to prepare its defence, Brightman complained that such an order 'might become an instrument of oppression'. He was subsequently overruled by Lord Denning, master of the rolls.

It was in the 1970s that Brightman was involved in the most controversial phase of his career, his membership between 1971 and 1974 of the National Industrial Relations Court set up by the administration of Edward Heath under the 1971 Industrial Relations Act. The act and the court were subject to intense criticism from trades unions and the Labour Party, who opposed the use of the law rather than the exercise of free collective bargaining to resolve industrial disputes. Widely seen as tools of the Conservative government, both act and court were swept away by the incoming administration of Harold Wilson in 1974, and Brightman, along with the court's president, Sir John Donaldson, was sent back to the High Court.

Brightman's association with this ill-fated institution and the belief held by many on the Labour benches and in the press that its judges were unfavourably disposed towards trade-unionists might have hampered his career in the long as well as the short term. But Margaret Thatcher had been one of Brightman's former pupils, and after the Conservative election victory in 1979 he was elevated to the Court of Appeal. As a lord justice of appeal he soon ruled that exempting women from doing dirty work in government armaments factories was unlawful sex discrimination. He also questioned the charitable status of the Moonies cult when he presided over their unsuccessful libel action against the *Daily Mail*. After three years, in 1982, he was appointed a lord of appeal and elevated to the House of Lords, as Baron Brightman.

As a law lord Brightman's experience, knowledge of the law, and sure grasp of human nature combined successfully, though his appointment at seventy-one allowed him only four years before reaching the retirement age. In 1983 in a case attracting much public interest and jocularity, he found that the barrister Ann Mallalieu could not claim tax relief on the clothes she wore beneath her gown when pleading in court. In the following year a judgment in the Dawson family tax case, concerning a scheme for the avoidance of capital gains tax, was received much more critically by the financial sector. In a case involving two men, Dean Hancock and Russell Shankland, accused of murdering a minicab driver during the coalminers' strike in 1984, Brightman upheld the substitution of a verdict of manslaughter for that of murder, with implications for the definition of intent in murder cases.

After 1986 Brightman served as a judge on a part-time basis and remained active in the House of Lords, where he was a member of several select committees including those investigating property law (1994) and domestic violence (1995). He chaired the Lords select committee on abortion, which in 1988 urged that there should be no time limit on abortion when the baby was diagnosed as 'grossly abnormal and unable to lead any meaningful life', providing a definition of 'serious handicap' that was used widely in subsequent debates on this matter. A member of the Lords' select committee on charities in 1983–4, he was chairman of Tancred's Charities from 1982 to 1996. In 1988, in one of the most public episodes in his career, he was one of the law lords who declined to grant the government a permanent ban on newspaper coverage of allegations contained in the memoirs of the former MI5 officer Peter Wright entitled *Spycatcher*. In his judgment Brightman made evident his disapproval of Wright (for breaking his professional duty of confidence) and of the *Sunday Times* (for publishing his stories). But like his fellow peers he could see no grounds for an injunction when material from *Spycatcher* had been spread so widely already. In this and other cases Brightman brought to bear not only his legal expertise but a strong dose of realism.

Brightman had a notable interest in the Arctic, which he visited several times. He was a keen sailor. He was elected to the Geographical Club within the Royal Geographical Society in 1987, and he became an honorary fellow of the society in 2001. He died on 6 February 2006 and was survived by his wife and son. LAWRENCE GOLDMAN

Sources *Daily Telegraph* (8 Feb 2006) • *The Times* (17 Feb 2006); (14 March 2006) • Burke, *Peerage* • *WW* (2006) • b. cert.
Likenesses photograph, 1998, Photoshot, London • obituary photographs
Wealth at death £432,255: probate, 19 Oct 2006, *CGPLA Eng. & Wales*

Bronhill, June [*real name* June Mary Gough] (**1929–2005**), singer, was born on 26 June 1929 in Broken Hill, New South Wales, Australia, a mining town some 700 miles west of Sydney. Broken Hill had always had a strong connection with the arts, and as a daughter of this fiercely proud town June Gough was encouraged by friends and family to pursue her early aspirations as a singer. At the age of nineteen she travelled to Sydney, where, encouraged by her singing teacher, Marianne Mathy, whom she described as a 'second mother' (Carmody, 329), she entered and won the coveted Sun aria competition in 1950, a prize awarded the year before to Joan Sutherland.

Like many young Australians before and since, June Gough felt the need to visit Britain, where she hoped to realize her dream of becoming a professional singer. The cost was daunting, if not prohibitive, but outback communities had a habit of rallying around in times of need and it was decided by family and neighbours to raise the necessary funds to send her. She arrived in London in 1952. As a young singer competing in a market awash with graduates from leading conservatories in Britain and abroad she attempted to stand out from the crowd by changing her name. Her teacher suggested that she should adopt the name Chrystal Belle, but she dismissed this as too undignified and decided instead (and in tribute to those who had financed her journey) that her stage name should be Bronhill, a contraction of Broken Hill.

In London Bronhill studied with Dino Borgioli before making her European début as Adèle in the Sadler's Wells production of Strauss's *Die Fledermaus* in 1954. That performance marked the beginning of a long relationship with the company, during which she explored much of the soprano literature. Her ability to hold the stage, her secure coloratura voice, and her capacity for hard work made her the natural choice for such roles as Norina in Donizetti's *Don Pasquale*, Gilda in Verdi's *Rigoletto*, the Queen of the Night in Mozart's *Die Zauberflöte*, and Zerbinetta in Richard Strauss's *Ariadne auf Naxos*. As a member of a busy ensemble company she was also expected to perform works that were new to Sadler's Wells and was cast as Lucy in Menotti's *The Telephone*, and as Vixen Sharpears for the British première of Janáček's *The Cunning Little Vixen* in 1961. But it was her work as an operetta singer that was most popular with audiences, and it was her performances in works like Strauss's *The Gypsy Baron*, Offenbach's *Orpheus and the Underworld* and *La vie parisienne*, and Lehar's *The Merry Widow* that defined her career. Of these *The Merry Widow* was the operetta with which she was most frequently associated. During her career she gave some 200 performances of the operetta, both in Britain and in Australia, and the Vilia aria soon became known in musical circles as 'June's tune'. With William Reid, a British conductor who ended his career with the Australian Opera, she recorded the work for EMI, one of a series that the company made with Bronhill and the Sadler's Wells troupe performing works from the operetta canon.

Bronhill's success was not restricted to the Sadler's Wells Theatre; she also made an impact with other companies and in other genres and media. In 1959 the distinguished Australian soprano Joan Sutherland was indisposed during a regional tour of England with the Covent Garden company. She was scheduled to sing the title role in Donizetti's *Lucia di Lammermoor* at Oxford but was replaced at short notice by Bronhill. Although Sutherland was near the beginning of her long career, she had already made this role her own and subsequently recorded it with her husband, Richard Bonynge, and the renowned British conductor John Pritchard. For some the prospect of replacing such an illustrious colleague might have been daunting, but Bronhill rose to the challenge, performed with distinction, and won the admiration of the critics.

Having carved a niche for herself in British operatic life by the mid-1960s, Bronhill decided to explore the possibilities that the West End and television had to offer. In 1964 she was cast in Ron Grainer's *Robert and Elizabeth*, a musical version of the play *The Barretts of Wimpole Street*. Directed by Wendy Toye, the show was an outstanding success. It ran for 948 performances and was later taken to Australia. The fame that she achieved in live theatre and her easy manner with audiences meant that she was also an ideal choice for radio and television. In the 1960s and early 1970s she was a regular guest on BBC radio's light music programmes *Friday Night is Music Night*, *Variety Playhouse*, and *Palm Court*, and on Yorkshire Television's religious musical programme, *Stars on Sunday*.

For Australians living abroad the need to return to their homeland in maturity is often overwhelming. Bronhill eventually left Europe for Australia and made her home in Sydney from 1976, the year she was appointed OBE. At that time, however, she had no intention of retiring, and appeared successfully in a variety of opera, theatre, and television roles ranging from Rosalinde in the State Opera of South Australia's production of Strauss's *Die Fledermaus* in 1979, through Mrs Slocombe in Australian television's version of *Are You Being Served?* (from 1980), to the mother in Peter Williams's production of *Straight and Narrow* (1994). She published her autobiography, *The Merry Bronhill*, in 1987. She continued to work until 1995, when deafness caused by tinnitus forced her to retire. She was twice married: first, before leaving Australia for England, to Brian Martin, and second, in 1963, to the television producer Richard Finny, with whom she had one daughter. Both marriages ended in divorce. She died of breast cancer in Sydney, New South Wales, on 25 January 2005. She was survived by her daughter, Caroline.

RAYMOND HOLDEN

Sources J. Bronhill, *The merry Bronhill*, 1987 · W. Bebbington, ed., *A dictionary of Australian music* (1998) · J. Carmody, 'Mathy, Marianne Helene Sara', *AusDB*, 15.329–30 · D. M. Cummings, *International who's who in classical music* (2003) · *Daily Telegraph* (26 Jan 2005) · *The Guardian* (27 Jan 2005) · *The Independent* (28 Jan 2005) · *The Times* (16 Feb 2005) · personal knowledge (2009) · private information (2009)

Archives FILM BFINA, performance footage | SOUND BL NSA, *Leading ladies*, interview with V. Lee, BBC Radio 2, 31 Mar 1981, T3886BW · BL NSA, performance recordings · National Library of Australia, interviews with Bill Stephens, 1985–7

Likenesses photographs, 1956–61, Getty Images, London · obituary photographs · photograph, Lebrecht Music and Arts, London, priv. coll.

Brooks, Anthony Morris [Tony] (**1922–2007**), special operations and intelligence officer, was born on 4 April 1922 at The Cottage, Orsett, Essex, the son of Douglas Charles Morris Brooks, construction engineer and businessman, and his wife, Beryl, *née* Anderson. His father had undertaken secret missions during the First World War, though Brooks only discovered this in 1945 towards the end of his own clandestine wartime service. His parents separated when he was a child and Brooks and his brother were taken by their mother to live with relatives in France and Switzerland. He was educated at Chillon College, near Montreux, and then, after his mother's death, at Felsted School in Essex. He spoke perfect French.

Brooks encountered the French resistance in the early stages of the Second World War. At its outbreak he was living with relatives and working in his uncle's timber yard in the Jura. When he attempted to join up he was rejected as too young. After the German invasion in May 1940 he and his relatives headed for Montauban in the south-west to stay with other relatives. When the family returned home after the Franco-German armistice he remained in Montauban, however, making contact with members of the resistance and assisting a British soldier to escape over the Pyrenees to Spain. When he followed his family back to the Jura he discovered that his aunt was also engaged in helping British soldiers to make their escape and he became a courier for fugitives on the journey south to Marseilles. When in May 1941 he was warned that he was about to be interned by the Vichy authorities he followed the same line of escape himself, leading a small party into Spain. They were arrested by the Spanish authorities and interned at the concentration camp at Miranda de Ebro, where he spent six weeks before his release was arranged by the British embassy.

On his return to Britain Brooks was rejected by the established security agencies, the Secret Intelligence Service and MI9, as too young for service in France. But the new Special Operations Executive, established to assist resistance behind enemy lines in Europe, sent him for training, at which he excelled. At the beginning of July 1942 he was dropped into France near Limoges, but was badly injured in his back and knee when his ill-designed parachute failed to open correctly. He was nursed back to health by a local farmer.

By a remarkable coincidence Brooks's contact in Toulouse, 'Robert', was someone known to him: René Bertholet, from Switzerland, whom he had already met at Montauban. Brooks took the codename Alphonse and

Anthony Morris [Tony] **Brooks (1922–2007)**, by unknown photographer

worked as a garage mechanic, ostensibly going about the French countryside collecting parts from abandoned vehicles. Through Bertholet he recruited a range of people in the Toulouse and Lyons areas, many of them industrial workers and railwaymen, and then took control of the network thus created, which was known as Pimento. Brooks declined a radio link with the Special Operations Executive. Instead messages were passed to London on microfilm; this was taken by an engine driver to the Swiss border and transferred in a handshake to the Swiss turntable operator at Annemasse who sent it on to Geneva. The operator's mate passed on any message London might have for Pimento.

Brooks created a remarkably successful network that was never penetrated by the Germans to any significant extent. He was able to summon up and organize many successful drops of equipment and arms by the RAF, keeping the agents well supplied with the tools of the trade of railway sabotage—not only explosives but even abrasive grease to be smeared over axles—in which they specialized. After the war Brooks used to say 'that the most effective work he did was not blowing up trains but rather switching destination labels on trucks in freight yards' which 'caused at least as much disruption' (*The Times*, 25 May 2007).

After some setbacks, including the capture of several of his comrades, Brooks was recalled to London in August 1943. Promoted to the rank of captain, while in Britain he married, at Leverington parish church, Cambridgeshire, on 9 November, Hope Munday (*b*. 1922), daughter of George Campbell Munday, farmer and landowner, of Leverington Hall. She was then serving in the WAAF. Brooks was parachuted back into France at the end of December 1943 and resumed command of Pimento. The network increased the frequency and daring of its operations to disrupt German communications in the months before operation Overlord (D-day, on 6 June 1944). There followed Pimento's finest hour: the obstruction of 2nd SS Panzer division in its efforts to move up from its base in the south-west and join the defence against the allied invasion in Normandy in June 1944. It is said that no train moved between Marseilles and Lyons between 6 June and 25 August without experiencing at least one derailment.

It was at this time, in July 1944, that Brooks came closest to capture. Based in Lyons, ostensibly working as a clerk in the post office, he was picked up and interrogated after being kept for two days without food. He had been found with 72,000 francs on him, funds he was going to use to pay his agents later that day. He managed to convince his German captors that he had won the money in a bet (summoning the testimony of one his comrades, a bookie, in his support), and that he was going to spend it on a new suit (a story supported by another of his agents, a tailor). On another occasion Brooks and his deputy in Pimento, who was a customs policeman, had arrived at Toulouse railway station when a full-scale security sweep was underway: they escaped using the pretence that Brooks was a prisoner, handcuffed and under the arrest of the French agent. When the German forces retreated from Lyons, Brooks tried personally to neutralize explosive charges set to blow up the bridges over the Rhône. He was on hand to lead the first American armoured column into the city. He spent the remainder of the war travelling through France and evaluating the successes and failures of the Special Operations Executive sabotage operations there.

Brooks was awarded the MC and DSO in 1943 and 1944 respectively, and the Croix de Guerre and Légion d'honneur in 1944. He ended the war with the rank of major at the age of twenty-three. He was invited to join the Secret Intelligence Service (known popularly as MI6) and in 1947 was sent for three years to Sofia. Back in England, his first marriage having been dissolved, in 1952 he married (Elizabeth) Helene Moncrieff (Lena) Erskine, whom he had met in Lebanon. He resigned from the security services in 1952 on being told that he was to be sent to Hanoi on his own: he wrote his letter of resignation in green ink on a memo pad taken from the chief's own desk. Four years later, after a spell working in the family business—a plaster works—in France, he rejoined the Secret Intelligence Service. He was on standby (but never called upon) to engage in sabotage during the Suez crisis, served in Cyprus, and was posted to Paris and Geneva. In later years, working for the Security Service (MI5), he specialized in the investigation of those who had defected from the Soviet Union.

Brooks retired from MI5 in 1977 and resumed his business career. In his last years he suffered from chronic heart disease. He died on 19 April 2007 in St Mary's Hospital, Praed Street, Westminster, of pneumonia. He was survived by his second wife. There were no children of either marriage. LAWRENCE GOLDMAN

Sources M. R. D. Foot, *SOE in France: an account of the work of the British Special Operations Executive in France, 1940–1944* (1966); rev. edn (2004) · M. Hastings, *Das Reich: resistance and the march of the 2nd SS Panzer Division through France, June 1944* (1981) · M. R. D. Foot, *SOE: an outline history of the Special Operations Executive, 1940–46* (1984) · M. Ruby, *F section, SOE: the Buckmaster networks* (1988) · *The Independent* (30 April 2007) · *Daily Telegraph* (15 May 2007) · *New York Times* (21 May 2007) · *The Times* (22 May 2007); (25 May 2007); (30 May 2007) · *The Guardian* (26 June 2007) · special forces roll of honour, www.specialforcesroh.com/browse.php?mode=viewiaward&awardid=4030, 5 Jan 2010 · b. cert. · m. cert. [1943] · d. cert.

Likenesses photograph, 1995, Photoshot, London · obituary photographs · photograph, repro. in *Daily Telegraph* (15 May 2007) [*see illus.*]

Wealth at death £1,599,823: probate, 3 Aug 2007, *CGPLA Eng. & Wales*

Brown, William Christopher (1928–2005), civil engineer, was born on 16 September 1928 at Beech House, Croesyceiliog, Monmouthshire, the second of two sons of William Edward Brown (1892–1965), joiner, cabinet-maker, and sometime county councillor, and his wife, Margaret Eliza, *née* Hughes (1891–1953), descended from a family of farmers. Brown's grandfather had established a joinery and cabinet-making business, which was continued by his two sons on his death. Brown, later a self-styled 'hands-on' engineer, derived pleasure as a boy from visiting the workshop, making articles in wood (including toys during war time), and using tools fashioned by his grandfather and father, the latter having served apprenticeship to a blacksmith. From Monmouth School, he was awarded a state scholarship for a two-year degree course in civil engineering at University College, Southampton. A first-class degree led to a two-year graduate studentship (extended to three years) at Imperial College, London, under A. J. S. Pippard and S. R. Sparkes. His research topic concerned the buckling behaviour of metal plates in structural engineering, which contributed to his first professional paper in 1956.

Brown joined Freeman, Fox & Partners (FFP) in 1951. He worked on the design of the Volta Bridge, a trussed arch, when he was seconded to Halcrow to work on site during 1956. He then returned to FFP where he developed a close working relationship with Gilbert Roberts, taking over leadership of Roberts's engineering team on his retirement in 1969. Roberts was undoubtedly the leader in the resurgence of British expertise in the design of long-span road bridges after the Second World War, a role that Brown inherited and further developed. He became a partner of FFP in 1970. Meanwhile, in 1964 he married Celia Hermione Emmett; there were no children of the marriage.

The most spectacular consequence of changes in bridge-building techniques was seen in the (first) Severn Bridge (span 988 metres, completed 1966) with its 'aerofoil' deck form, which saved approximately 25 per cent in weight by comparison with the trussed deck of the Forth Road Bridge (span 1006 metres, completed 1964) and with rectangular box (as opposed to cellular) bridge towers. A cross-braced truss design had been considered for the Severn Bridge but the destruction of its model during wind tunnel testing provided a fortuitous opportunity for a successful trial of an aerofoil form. The optimization of bridge decks remained a special interest of Brown throughout his further career, in relation particularly to their dynamic and aerodynamic characteristics. In 1974 he designed his own simple wind tunnel, which was rebuilt in 1988 with greater capability, to test and improve aerofoil forms to minimize air resistance and avoid risk of 'flutter'—potentially catastrophic wind-induced oscillation. Some of his later designs introduced slots in the deck between two or more box structures beneath carriageways or rail-tracks.

In 1969 FFP shared the first annual MacRobert award, for the Severn Bridge superstructure, designed by the team led by Roberts and Brown. The citation described it as 'awesome in its striking simplicity'. The following year saw a setback for FFP's reputation as a leading bridge designer, with the collapse during construction of the Milford Haven Bridge in June, followed by the more serious collapse of the West Gate Bridge across the River Yarra in Melbourne in October. The royal commission report on this latter event identified numerous factors contributing to the accident, criticizing Brown and other partners of FFP. Such experiences led to the Merrison report on design and construction of box-girder bridges (1974), which identified the need for clear codes of practice supported by research, which lagged behind practice, coupled with independent design checks.

Brown's last major bridge project with FFP that proceeded to construction was the (first) Bosphorus Bridge (span 1074 metres, completed 1973), for which, after supervising design, he was resident partner for construction in 1972–3. He resigned from FFP in 1985. In 1987 he set up his own consultancy, Brown Beech and Associates (Beech being a toponym recalling his birthplace). His principal commission was as engineer and project director for the second Bosphorus Bridge (span 1090 metres, opened 1988). He prepared preliminary designs for a number of other major bridges. He was appointed lead designer for the Messina road and rail bridge (span 3300 metres), but a change of government led to suspension of the project. This would have been by far the longest span bridge, made possible by Brown's multi-box form of bridge deck.

Brown was an innovative, ingenious, and highly numerate engineer. He contributed also to techniques of bridge construction including, for example, to notable savings in cost in forming the suspension cable. He was appointed OBE in 1966 and elected a royal designer for industry in 1977, serving as master of the Faculty of Royal Designers for Industry from 1983 to 1985. He was elected an honorary fellow of the Royal Institute of British Architects in 1978 and a fellow of Imperial College in 1987. He received several honours from overseas. From 1967 Brown lived at 1 Allen Mansions, Allen Street, Kensington, London. His death at the Chelsea and Westminster Hospital from a heart attack on 16 March 2005 was followed by cremation at Mortlake crematorium. He was survived by his wife, Celia.

ALAN MUIR WOOD

Sources *The Times* (10 April 2005) · *Evening Times* [Glasgow] (14 April 2005) · *South Wales Echo* (5 May 2005) · T. A. Wyatt, 'Dr W. C. Brown: an appreciation', *International Association of Bridge and Structural Engineers Newsletter*, 21 (spring 2005) · *WW* (2005) · curriculum vitae, 2005, priv. coll. · private information (2009) [Celia Brown, widow; Imperial College archives] · personal knowledge (2009) · b. cert. · d. cert.

Archives priv. coll.

Likenesses obituary photographs

Wealth at death £1,569,482: probate, 19 Sept 2005, *CGPLA Eng. & Wales*

Browne, George Edric (1920–2007), singer, songwriter, and actor, was born Edric Browne on 4 May 1920 in Corbeau Town, Port of Spain, Trinidad, the only son and youngest of three children of Ernest Browne, a government printer, and his wife, Frances, *née* Noriega, a domestic servant. His paternal grandmother was Barbadian and his parents Trinidadian. He grew up listening to 'shango and shouting', religious practices based in African ritual traditions, and played in tamboo-bamboo bands, which used sets of tuned bamboo tubes beaten rhythmically against the ground. He absorbed a wide repertoire of songs through listening to records played by shopkeepers competing for custom. He added George to his given name while working in the library of the writer and intellectual Richard E. Braithwaite. It was Braithwaite who introduced him to the work of early black activists and writers, and the possibilities beyond island life.

Browne spent a year at sea as a mess boy on a Norwegian oil tanker, and travelled to Australia and New Zealand before signing off in Scotland in December 1941 in the company of a fellow crewman, John Clarke. Dancing at a Glasgow ballroom they met Trinidadian musicians who persuaded them to move to London; there Clarke won a singing competition at a West End club for merchant seamen. Recruited for a minstrel show compèred by the veteran African-American singer Ike Hatch, the pair sang spirituals on the same bill as an all-white banjo band, then appeared in a revival of *Show Boat* before Browne left to work as an actor and to sing with the band of the Jamaican saxophonist Bertie King.

Browne's show-business career was unplanned. He had envisaged becoming a writer, but the upheaval of the Second World War created opportunities for individuals with talent, and a rich baritone voice gave him a natural advantage. While working as a waiter at the Caribbean Club he watched the proprietor, Rudy Evans, singing and learned how to deliver a song. He formed a vocal quintet with Clarke and others, and as the Peanut Vendors they gave swinging renditions of American hits and secured broadcasts and concerts before going their separate ways. Browne then learned to play the double bass to work with the guitarist Lauderic Caton; he then, with the increasing popularity of the Trinidadian calypso, began featuring songs of contemporary relevance. At the Orchid Room he followed the Caribbean practice of composing impromptu calypsos in honour of visiting dignitaries; when he did this for the duke of Edinburgh, the management considered it audacious but was forced to recant when a larger royal party returned the following night to hear the song.

Encouraged by this reception, Browne took singing and tap dancing lessons, then formed a singing trio, later a quartet. In France the Four Just Men met American jazz musicians who assisted them with presentation. They worked with the swing trumpeter Bill Coleman, but Kenny Clarke, James Moody, and Art Simmons had a greater influence for they were modernists, and while Browne still sang traditional material, he was 'head over heels in love with' bebop, the new music epitomized by the saxophonist Charlie Parker, with whom the quartet

George Edric Browne (1920–2007), by V. Wilmer, 2005

toured France in 1949 (interview, 2005). When they disbanded Browne formed a relationship with a bookmaker's cashier from Manchester named Diana and found work in Paris at a restaurant on the left bank. He was encouraged by the New Orleans veteran Sidney Bechet but chastised by Roy Eldridge for singing folk songs and spirituals, a repertoire that the trumpeter considered anachronistic and racially demeaning. Chastened, Browne revised his act. On returning to London he took the calypsonian's name of Young Tiger and began a long recording career with songs of social commentary.

Two compositions ensured Browne's lasting fame: 'I Was There', his observations on the coronation of Queen Elizabeth II in 1953 (broadcast on radio and television on the day of the coronation), and 'Calypso Be', its name a witty twist on the title of a George Russell composition for Dizzy Gillespie, and its lyrics a reflection on the collision between calypso and modern jazz. Connections with African activists led to his composing a Nigerian national anthem—though it was never used—and his most significant recording, 'Freedom for Ghana': 20,000 copies of the latter were imported by the Gold Coast to help that nation's independence campaign.

For two years (1952–3) Browne lived with the guitarist Lauderic Caton, whom he credited as his 'mentor and guru' (interview, 2005). Caton introduced him to vegetarianism and fasting and helped burnish his instrumental ability. He toured with Humphrey Lyttelton's band, then developed a sophisticated nightclub act. His band became a fixture for society and university functions, and in 1955 he sang the credits for the BBC Television series *Port Calypso*. He acted at the National Theatre and Theatre Royal, Stratford, London, and in 1966 travelled to Dakar, Senegal, for the First World Festival of Negro Arts, playing Christ in the Negro Theatre Workshop's passion play *The Dark Disciples*. He continued to work as an entertainer until 1970 when he retired from music and joined Post Office Telephones as an operator, then instructor.

Browne was a small, modest man who dressed neatly, wore a red bebopper's beret, and sported a beard. He designed his musical offerings to suit the needs of the day and, while retaining some traditional material, explored several popular styles. He helped win a new audience for the calypso through an appearance in the rock-and-roll film *Rock You Sinners* (1957)—and composed a 'Marilyn Monroe Calypso' and a 'Davy Crockett Calypso'—but in the purist view, a repertory embracing mambos and ephemeral pop songs disqualified him from the ranks of long-serving calypsonians.

After separating from Diana in 1964 Browne formed a relationship with Liesel Scotland, a schoolteacher and the daughter of Wilhelm Steffens, schoolmaster; she was German and the divorced wife of Legent Hugh Alphonso Scotland, concert promoter and artists' agent. They married at Lewisham register office on 9 May 1970 and Browne brought up his stepson, Hugh K. Scotland (*b.* 1964), with their daughter, Annette Liesel (*b.* 1970). In 1979 he and Liesel opened a restaurant and health club in London, before moving to the USA, where they ran a restaurant in Florida. Seasonal trade made this unviable and after playing a season in the Cayman Islands Browne moved with his family to California and opened another restaurant. He separated from Liesel in 1986 but remained in the USA and studied computers and accountancy. In 1990, after divorce, he returned to England. He settled in Croydon, where he performed at a local hostelry before retiring to his high-rise flat to play the stock market for modest returns. The re-release of his early recordings on compact disc sparked a revival of interest in his work and illuminated his final years. In 2002 Mark Ainley and Richard Noblett included 'I Was There' on the compilation CD and album *London is the Place for Me*. Engulfed in his impressive white beard and still resonant of voice, he was interviewed, broadcast, appeared in concert (including the BBC's *Electric Proms* series at the Roundhouse in 2006), and was delighted: 'It's miraculous, really. To come to London is more than a Cinderella story. And to live to tell the tale—it's all a miracle' (interview, 2005). He died at the Mayday Hospital, Croydon, of a chest infection secondary to prostate cancer, on 23 March 2007 and was cremated on 2 April at Croydon cemetery and crematorium. He was survived by his daughter and stepson. VAL WILMER

Sources *New Musical Express* (5 Aug 1955) • S. Hall, 'Calypso kings', *The Guardian Friday Review* (28 June 2002) • R. Noblett and M. Ainley, *London is the place for me*, 2 (2005), notes [CD] • *Daily Telegraph* (14 July 2005) • V. Wilmer, 'Put a tiger in your tank', *Mojo* (Dec 2005) • *The Guardian* (7 April 2007) • *The Independent* (10 April 2007) • *Mojo* (May 2007) • J. Collins, 'The importance of African popular music studies for Ghanaian/African students', www.codesria.org/IMG/pdf/Collins.pdf, 14 July 2010 • interview with V. Wilmer, 2005, priv. coll. • personal knowledge (2011) • private information (2011) [L. Caton; R. Henderson] • m. cert. • d. cert.

Likenesses Studio Zwirn, photograph, *c.*1950–1959, repro. in *Calypso time no. 2* [Parlophone EP record; repro. in *London is the place for me*, 2, Honest Jon's CD, 2005] • photograph, 1955, repro. in *New Musical Express* (5 Aug 1955), 12 • S. Lee, photograph, 2002, repro. in *The Guardian* (28 June 2002) • V. Wilmer, photograph, 2005, repro. in *The Guardian* (7 April 2007) • V. Wilmer, photograph, 2005, priv. coll. [*see illus.*] • V. Wilmer, photographs, 2005, priv. coll.

Wealth at death under £7000: administration (will), 19 May 2010, *CGPLA Eng. & Wales*

Browse, Lillian Gertrude (1906–2005), art dealer and art historian, was born at 2 Carlton Mansions, West End Lane, Hampstead, London, on 21 April 1906, the younger child of Michael Browse, entrepreneur, champion cyclist, and son of a Jewish White Russian émigré who had settled in southern Africa, and his wife, Gladys Amy, *née* Meredith, a member of a large, close-knit, well-established Anglo-Jewish family. She was originally named Lily Gertie, but later adopted first Gertrude then Lillian. Aged three, she, her elder brother, Jack (*b.* 1904), and their mother emigrated to Johannesburg to rejoin their father, who had established himself as a racehorse trainer in the Transvaal. She was educated at Barnato Park High School, Johannesburg. She returned to London in 1928 to train under Margaret Craske at the Cecchetti Ballet School.

In 1930, on tour with Anton Dolin's company to Amsterdam, Browse realized she would never be pre-eminent as a dancer. The following year, despite knowing nothing of

Lillian Gertrude Browse (1906–2005), by Ida Kar, late 1950s

the fine arts, she persuaded Harold Leger to take her on, unpaid, to file old master photographs in his Bond Street gallery. Over the next eight years she trained her eye, became familiar with the auction rooms, learned the essential skills of a cataloguer, absorbed the financial and negotiating skills of the commercial art world, and engaged deeply with the work of nineteenth- and twentieth-century French and British artists. In due course Leger made her manager of the gallery and allowed her to mount a series of adventurous one-man shows, as well as mixed thematic shows of contemporary work. On 3 September 1934 she married, in the Liberal Jewish synagogue at St John's Wood, her first cousin Ivan Harold Joseph. Four years her junior, he was a businessman then working as a depot inspector for a catering company, and the son of Walter Gordon Joseph, company secretary for a builders' merchants. They had little in common, and the marriage did not survive. They separated, but did not formally divorce until 1944.

On the outbreak of the Second World War, Browse joined the London ambulance service. However, her unique wartime contribution was to persuade Kenneth Clark, director of the National Gallery, to let her organize exhibitions of contemporary British art to cover the bare walls of his gallery in place of the old masters removed to Wales for safe keeping. In 1940 she mounted 'British painting since Whistler' and 'Drawings of Augustus John'; in 1941 the first major, non-commercial Walter Sickert retrospective; in 1942 a two-man show of William Nicholson and Jack Yeats. She scoured the country gaining the trust and friendship of private owners and museum curators, and assembling an unrivalled personal archive of work by early twentieth-century British artists. She thus established the bedrock of her future attainments as dealer and scholar. In 1941 she initiated her career as an author by bringing together, in *The Drawings of Augustus John*, illustrations of the works she had collected for the 1940 exhibition. 1943 saw the publication of her first volume on Sickert, which included a fine selection of his works with informative catalogue notes.

At the end of the war, together with Henry Roland and Gustav Delbanco, Browse became a founding partner of Roland, Browse, and Delbanco at 19 Cork Street, London. The firm held a succession of well-chosen and well-researched exhibitions, many featuring Browse's favourite artists. In 1946 she became general editor of Ariel Books on the Arts, overseeing publication of slim volumes on Constantin Guys, James Dickson Innes, Barbara Hepworth, Lesley Hurry, and Eric Ravilious.

Degas Dancers, published in 1949, brought together Browse's twin passions, dance and art. Widely reviewed and praised, this book led to her appointment from 1950 to 1954 as ballet critic of *The Spectator*. A catalogue raisonné of paintings by William Nicholson followed in 1956. 1960 saw the summit of her achievement as a Sickert scholar. She selected the Arts Council centenary retrospective and her second, substantial, monograph on Sickert was published. The essence of her achievement as a scholar rested in the combination of individual discrimination and scrupulous research. She trusted her eye.

Browse's second marriage, at the Westminster register office on 17 June 1964, to Sidney Henry Lines (1912–2000), was full and happy. The son of Sidney Augustus Lines, a buyer of oriental goods, he was a widower six years her junior, and a director of Wiggins Teape. They entertained their wide circle of friends in London and indulged their enthusiasm for gardening both in London and at their cottage in Petworth. Although childless, Browse had a clutch of godchildren, several the progeny of theatrical families.

In 1977 Roland and Delbanco retired from their gallery, to be replaced by William Darby. After four years Browse withdrew all but her name and goodwill from the business. In 1978 she published her last monograph, *Forain, the Painter*, and in 1999 her autobiography, *Duchess of Cork Street*. This sobriquet, bestowed by Rex Nan Kivell, director of the Redfern Gallery next door in Cork Street, alluded to her dignity and astounding elegance. She made many of her own clothes, favouring an Edwardian look with high ruffled necks. She always wore fabulous hats. Her gracious entry into the auction rooms, to take her reserved seat in the front row, held all in thrall.

In 1982, honouring a promise she had made to Anthony Blunt some twenty years earlier, Browse gave much of her private collection of paintings, drawings, and sculpture to the Courtauld Institute of Art. She later bequeathed an important Degas sculpture, *Préparation à la danse*, to the Courtauld, and a few of her favourite pictures to the Fitzwilliam Museum, Cambridge. Her many contributions to the visual arts were recognized in 1998 when she was appointed CBE. She died at her home, 29 Bloomfield Terrace, Westminster, of pneumonia on 2 December 2005, less than five months short of her hundredth birthday.

She was cremated at Putney Vale cemetery on 15 December. A memorial exhibition was held at Browse and Darby in November 2006. WENDY BARON

Sources L. Browse, 'The National Gallery in wartime: and other memories', *Apollo* (Feb 1997) • L. Browse, *Duchess of Cork Street: the autobiography of an art dealer* (1999) • *Daily Telegraph* (9 Dec 2005) • *The Times* (10 Dec 2005) • *The Independent* (17 Dec 2005) • *The Guardian* (21 Dec 2005) • *Burlington Magazine*, 148/1237 (April 2006) • *WW* (2005) • personal knowledge (2009) • private information (2009) • b. cert. • m. certs. • d. cert.

Archives Tate archive, personal and research papers, papers relating to gallery | Tate archive, stock books of Roland, Browse, and Delbanco

Likenesses E. Mané-Katz, oils, 1936, Courtauld Inst. • I. Kar, photograph, 1956–9, NPG [*see illus.*] • I. Kar, two group portraits, vintage bromide prints, 1959 (with Henry Roland and Gustav Delbanco), NPG • J. Herman, oils, 1973, priv. coll. • Snowdon, double portrait, photograph, 1984 (with Howard Hodgkin), Camera Press, London • obituary photographs • photographs, repro. in Browse, *Duchess of Cork Street* (1999)

Wealth at death £4,783,135: probate, 7 July 2006, *CGPLA Eng. & Wales*

Bruce, Donald William Trevor, **Baron Bruce of Donington** (**1912–2005**), politician, was born at 76 Norbury Court Road, Norbury, Surrey, on 3 October 1912, the son of William Trevor Bruce (*d.* 1934), a wealthy insurance broker, and his wife, Mary Frances, *née* Law. The family left Norbury for Lincolnshire when Donald was quite young but had already started at Norbury preparatory school. He received his secondary education at Donington grammar school in Lincolnshire. He did not go on to university but, under his father's influence, trained locally to become a chartered accountant. In 1930 he moved to London, where he was articled to a City firm of accountants. He qualified as a chartered accountant and industrial economist.

By the early 1930s Bruce had established himself with sufficient confidence to become involved in Conservative Party politics. He joined the North Paddington branch of the Junior Imperial League and was an active campaigner for the local Conservative MP in the lead-up to the crisis of 1931 that brought the collapse of Ramsay MacDonald's Labour government and the formation of a national government led by MacDonald and Stanley Baldwin. By then Bruce, a firm young patriot, had also enlisted in the Territorial Army (the Middlesex yeomanry), in which he served for four years. He had the build of a guardsman, broad-shouldered, a craggy face even as a young man, with beetle brows covering sharp eyes. Altogether it was a combination that appeared to prepare him for a military career or possibly that of a traditional Conservative MP. That would certainly have reflected the Bruce family background. Despite all this Donald Bruce underwent an extraordinary transformation to end up a left-wing member of the Labour Party, which he joined in 1935 after a short spell with the still more radical Independent Labour Party. This remarkable change took root following the collapse of the MacDonald government of 1931 at a time of economic crisis, widespread depression, and social deprivation, all of which made a profound impression on the young Bruce. Nevertheless, it was clearly a highly unusual conversion. On 15 July 1939 he married Joan Letitia, the 22-year-old daughter of Henry Claud Butcher, cycle manufacturer. They had one son and three daughters.

Immediately following the outbreak of the Second World War in 1939 Bruce rejoined the army, eventually rising to the rank of major in the Royal Signals. After taking part in the Normandy landings, which brought a mention in dispatches, he was recruited to General Eisenhower's intelligence staff. None of this affected his by then well-developed political convictions, and while still in uniform he was selected as Labour candidate to contest the hitherto safe Conservative seat of North Portsmouth in the general election of 1945—which he went on to win by a majority of 1042. Bruce followed up his political transformation by joining the Fabian Society and the campaigning Keep Left group within the Labour Party, which included new MPs from the 1945 intake like Michael Foot. He quickly made a reputation as a powerful advocate of socialism and came to the attention of Aneurin Bevan, who had just been appointed minister of health by Prime Minister Attlee. Soon afterwards Bevan accosted Bruce in the doorway of the Commons' smoking room and offered to make him his parliamentary private secretary. Bruce was stunned and flattered but grasped the opportunity. He became Bevan's chief lieutenant during the preparation of legislation to establish the National Health Service and Bevan sent him to Sweden and Denmark to study the socialized health systems in both those countries. He became devoted to Bevan and was soon regarded in the inner sanctum of government as 'Nye's hairshirt'—chiefly because he was always prepared to argue with Bevan himself against compromises the minister was under pressure to make, most notably to the medical profession in the critical months when the NHS was struggling to be born. By the time the NHS was launched in July 1948 the two men had become firm and close friends. Indeed, Bruce was—and remained—among the few men around him whom Bevan trusted. Bruce in turn always insisted that his election as a Labour MP in the Labour landslide of 1945 was a crowning moment and his association with Aneurin Bevan his greatest achievement.

In the general election of 1950 Bruce lost his redrawn Portsmouth West constituency by 945 votes. When he tried again for a parliamentary seat in the Wrekin in the general elections of 1959 and 1964, he failed each time. By then he had already set up his own accountancy firm, which he personally ran until 1974 when it merged with Halpern and Woolf, with Bruce remaining a senior partner. Halpern and Woolf were later taken over by Casson Beckman, which eventually merged with Baker Tilly, for whom Bruce was still working as a consultant well into his later years. Yet he never ceased his active role as a left-wing campaigner in the Labour Party and a committed Bevanite.

In 1974 Harold Wilson, on returning to office, created Bruce a life peer as Baron Bruce of Donington. He was one of the first British appointees to become a member of the European parliament after Britain's entry into the EEC. He was rapporteur for the Labour Group but resigned in 1979 when direct elections for the European parliament were introduced. In fact he had never really believed in the European project. On one occasion in 1979, before he resigned as rapporteur, he sensationally refused to sign the EC accounts because, he claimed, there was evidence of 'scandalous duplicity' in the handling of financial controls. When in 1979 he was appointed in the House of Lords as opposition spokesman on Treasury economic and industrial questions, he was a constant critic of European institutional practices. He continued in that role until 1990, when he decided to stand aside. Throughout those active years he established a reputation as one of the predictably sternest, often infuriating, critics of virtually everything proposed in the name of the European Union.

Bruce remained an active and assiduous attender in the Lords to the end of his life, never hesitating to become involved in controversy—especially where Europe was concerned. By the end of his life he was the last remaining member of the Parliamentary Labour Party of 1945 still to be sitting in parliament, a badge he wore with great pride. His first marriage ended in divorce in 1980 and on 12 February 1981 he married Cyrena Shaw Heard, a 64-year-old widow and daughter of Cyril Charles Shaw, mining engineer. He died of prostate cancer at Avon House nursing home, Kensington, London, on 18 April 2005. He was survived by his wife, son, and one daughter, two daughters having predeceased him. GEOFFREY GOODMAN

Sources *The Times* (20 April 2005) • *Daily Telegraph* (20 April 2005) • *The Guardian* (20 April 2005) • *The Independent* (20 April 2005) • *Labour History* (winter 2006–2007) • *WW* (2005) • Burke, *Peerage* • private information (2009) • personal knowledge (2009) • b. cert. • m. certs. • d. cert.

Likenesses Bassano, five half-plate film negatives, 1947, NPG • W. Stoneman, three photographs, 1949, NPG • photograph, 1993, Photoshot, London • obituary photographs

Wealth at death £364,232: probate, 27 June 2005, *CGPLA Eng. & Wales*

Brunt, Peter Astbury (1917–2005), ancient historian, was born on 23 June 1917, at 16 Highfield Road, Coulsdon, Surrey, the only child of Samuel Brunt, Wesleyan Methodist minister, and his wife, Gladys Eileen, *née* Blewett. He was educated at Ipswich School, and won an open scholarship in history to Oriel College, Oxford, in 1935. In the event he switched to classics, gaining a first in classical moderations and in *literae humaniores*, after a formal viva. By then, if not earlier, any trace of religious belief had disappeared. It was never as far as is known a subject of conversation between him and his mother, although almost everything else from his childhood onwards was: his mother was a frequent visitor to the house he bought in Oxford in 1970, first from the south coast, then from her own sheltered flat in Oxford.

Frail in health as a child, Brunt was not fit for military service in 1939, and served instead in the Ministry of Shipping. He believed to the end of his life that his generation of Oxford students had been traduced by the public misunderstanding of the 'king and country' debate: the public ignored the subsequent vote of the Oxford Union to fight over the German occupation of the Sudetenland, and never understood that the first vote had not been a vote either against country or for tyranny. Reflecting later on his wartime service, he recalled with emotion the patriotism of shipowners who insisted that their best ships were taken, despite knowing that the compensation if they were sunk would not be in full. His time at the Ministry of Shipping also created a lifelong friendship with Derek Allen, allowed him to observe the beginnings of the cold war, with the conspiratorial obstructiveness of Russian delegates to meetings either side of the end of the war, and made it clear to him that he had substantial administrative gifts, to be deployed later in his career.

In 1946 Brunt took up a demyship at Magdalen College, Oxford, and the Craven fellowship that had been awarded to him in 1939, choosing as a topic for research the relations between governed and governors in the Roman empire, and set off for the British School at Rome. Some of his later interest in Roman stoicism derived from that period, but his stay in Rome did not inspire him with a concern for the iconographic or archaeological sources for Roman history: archaeological evidence either told you something you knew already or was not to be believed. He was appointed to a lectureship at St Andrews in 1947, but succeeded in returning to Oxford in 1951, to Oriel, his former college, as fellow and tutor in ancient history in succession to M. N. Tod. He had by that time read, in the original Greek or Latin and in chronological order, all the major sources for Greek and Roman history, in preparation for a career as a teacher of ancient history: he stopped with Julian, on his appointment to Oxford, on the grounds that he would never need to teach any later period. It was also while he was at St Andrews that he formed a close friendship with one of his students that did not in the end lead to their marriage; the student in due course moved to America, and did marry, but she and Brunt remained close, with intermittent meetings. He never contemplated marriage thereafter, her photograph remaining on his bookcase to the end.

Brunt claimed later that his published work arose out of teaching; but it certainly did not arise out of the ritualistic puzzle-solving that constituted much teaching of ancient history at Oxford during his period as tutor. He clearly rejected from the start, given his initial topic for research, the widely held view that the history of the ancient world is essentially the history of its governing class; and he set out to try to understand the ancient world as a whole, beginning with its economic and demographic structure. Hence his admiration both for A. H. M. (Hugo) Jones, whom he got to know when Jones simply knocked on his door one day, and Moses Finley. His style, however, was not that of either man, lacking both the effortless, often descriptive, lucidity of the former and the off-the-cuff epigrammatism of the latter.

Brunt read and made notes on an astonishing range of material, both ancient and modern; and although some of his published work consisted of a snappy demonstration that current views of parts of Alexander's army or of the chronology of Cicero's letters were most unlikely to be right, his more substantial pieces are shot through with a sense of the obscurity and difficulty of his subject. Part of the reason for this is that he not only insisted on analysing every level of ancient society, but also saw the importance of philosophy, law, politics, and rhetoric. One of the themes that occupied him during the period from 1951 to 1968 was that of ancient slavery: some of his work issued in a devastating review of William L. Westermann's *Slave Systems* (1955); but more of it flowed into the project that increasingly occupied his time and his attention, the demography of Roman Italy and of the Roman world in general.

Despite the publication in 1962 of one of the most important articles on Roman republican history of the second half of the twentieth century, on the army and the land in the revolution that replaced the Roman republic with an empire, Brunt assumed that the Camden chair of ancient history would go to A. N. Sherwin-White, not him. Partly because of this, partly to get more time for writing, he became in 1968 bursar of Gonville and Caius College, Cambridge, which promised a professorial salary and time for research. In fact, he was elected a fellow of the British Academy in 1969, and when the time came Hugo Jones insisted that the electors receive an application for the Camden chair from Brunt, the electors were given the page proofs of *Italian Manpower*, and the election was made. The book appeared in 1971, the year after he took up the chair, forming the most sustained attempt ever made to argue for the view that the Emperor Augustus changed the basis of the Roman census, and that up to that point the figures represented adult males, thereafter men, women, and (some) children. A rather different work was *Social Conflicts in the Roman Republic*, written at the instance of Moses Finley and also published in 1971: it was at the time and for many years remained the best introductory account of the Roman republic. It was also at Finley's behest that Brunt took over from him as chair of the ancient history committee of the Joint Association of Classical Teachers, overseeing the latter's A-level in the subject. His service to the national classics community also included a period as president of the Roman Society and as a member of the council of the British School at Rome.

In the end Brunt was not at ease as Camden professor, disliking particularly the expectation that he should be able to think of topics for research students to work on, and not finding the atmosphere of the graduate seminar congenial. He was not sorry when the cuts in university funding imposed by the government of Margaret Thatcher in 1982 created an opportunity for him to retire, two years early. The years that followed were occupied by collecting for publication, with revisions and additional pieces, his articles on the Roman republic (1988), the Roman empire (1990), and Greece (1992), and by increasingly intensive work on Roman stoicism. The volume of articles on the Roman republic, in particular, contained new material that showed undiminished power, notably a long essay on the fall of the Roman republic that provided the title for the whole volume, and a piece setting out to demolish the importance of client relations for an understanding of Roman republican politics. It is a curious irony, and perhaps a measure of the extent to which the two men had lost contact, that at about the same time Finley was busy arguing that client relations provided the key to understanding Athenian politics.

It was Roman stoicism, however, that claimed more and more of Brunt's attention; this took him into detailed analysis of the fragmentary and difficult evidence for the views of the founders of the school and of Panaetius, perhaps the single most important intermediary between Greek and Roman stoicism. From about 2000 onwards progressively failing physical powers led him to change his plan to write a book about Roman stoicism and collect his earlier articles on the subject with a number of new studies instead. Even this project was in the end defeated; but the undiminished intellectual ambition to try to get something difficult right led him to form plans with his executors for posthumous publication. By this time complaints of physical weakness were all too evidently justified, complaints of loss of memory much less so: to the end, Brunt combined an astonishing knowledge of English literature and British history with a sharply critical view of the politics and the follies of the world around him. In the autumn of 2005 he refused treatment for a cancerous growth in the oesophagus, and died in Sobell House, Oxford, on 5 November 2005.

MICHAEL H. CRAWFORD

Sources P. A. Brunt, unpublished memoir, priv. coll. • *Daily Telegraph* (16 Nov 2005) • *The Times* (23 Nov 2005); (25 Nov 2005); (2 Dec 2005) • *The Independent* (25 Nov 2005) • *The Guardian* (28 Nov 2005) • M. Crawford, 'Peter Astbury Brunt 1917–2005', *PBA*, 161 (2009), 63–86 • *WW* (2005) • personal knowledge (2009) • private information (2009) • b. cert. • d. cert.

Likenesses obituary photographs • photograph, British Academy, London; repro. in *The Independent*

Wealth at death £484,535: probate, 15 May 2006, *CGPLA Eng. & Wales*

Budden, Julian Medforth (1924–2007), musicologist and radio producer, was born on 9 April 1924 at Brynmor, The Promenade, Hoylake, Cheshire, the only son of Lionel Bailey Budden (1887–1956), lecturer in, and later professor of, architecture at Liverpool University, and his wife, Dora Magdalene, *née* Fraser, an Edinburgh-born writer, poet, and (as Maud Budden) author of the *Liverpool Echo*'s 'Curly Wee' cartoons. He was educated at Stowe School, and then, in 1942, went to Queen's College, Oxford, to read classics. Declaring himself a conscientious objector, he worked in the Friends' Ambulance Unit from 1943 to 1946, serving both in Italy and in Austria. Returning to Queen's, he graduated BA in 1948 and then studied piano (with Thornton Lofthouse), composition (with Patrick Hadley), and bassoon (with Archie Camden) at the Royal College of Music.

In 1951 Budden started at the BBC, where he remained for his entire working life. His first post was as a clerk and script editor (although he found time to take a BMus degree at Trinity College of Music in 1955); he then rose through the BBC ranks to become a producer (1956–70), chief producer of opera (1970–76), and external services music organizer (1976–83). His time at the BBC was a golden age for broadcast opera: little-known works were produced regularly, there were numerous broadcasts from elsewhere in Europe, and Budden was personally responsible for many important revivals, including the resurrection of a number of Verdi's more obscure titles (including the original versions of *Macbeth*, *La forza del destino*, and *Simon Boccanegra*).

Remarkably, though, Budden's work at the BBC continued in tandem with a second occupation as a writer on music. At first this *deuxième carrière* took the form of articles and reviews for *The Listener* and other publications, but in the 1970s and early 1980s it flowered into his monumental three-volume study *The Operas of Verdi*. It is difficult to overestimate the effect these books had. Their scholarship was impeccable and in many instances entirely original: no source, however obscure, was overlooked, and the assessments of Verdi's literary source material were always fresh, with a formidable cultural background worn lightly. Most impressive of all, though, were the musical judgements. Budden's first volume, covering the operas from *Oberto* to *Rigoletto*, came out in 1973, at a time when Verdi's early operas were by no means universally respected among musicians. Budden somehow managed to communicate the force of these still rather alien works by looking at them within their own cultural and musical context. His authorial personality was uncommonly welcoming and generous: to his hero Verdi, of course, and to past scholars who had tried to understand him, but also to his readers. His prose was full of wit and relaxed communication, never striving merely to impress.

Budden took early retirement from the BBC in 1983 and then divided his time between a modest flat in London and homes in or near Florence. He became a feature of the Italian operatic scene in his role (by no means self-consciously assumed) as *un vero gentleman inglese*. His Italian was extraordinary: its elegance of expression and command of the lexicon were praised by the most discriminating judges, and the fact that he continued to deploy these skills within a resolutely English cadence was part of the charm. His books were translated into Italian and inspired a younger generation of Italian Verdians; and he condensed and revised his three-volume *Verdi* into a Master Musicians volume (1985). His last years as a writer were mostly devoted to Puccini: a monograph (more modest in size than the Verdi project, but on the same high level critically) about the life and works appeared in 2002. He was also a member of the editorial board of the Verdi complete edition, served loyally and conscientiously as president of Lucca's Centro di Studi Giacomo Puccini until his death, and was much involved in the Istituto Nazionale di Studi Verdiani in Parma. He was elected a fellow of the British Academy in 1987 and appointed OBE in 1991.

This was Julian Budden the scholar and writer. The man was harder to know. Particularly in later years he could sometimes cut a lonely figure at the social jamboree of conferences. But the generosity that so characterized his writing also characterized the man: it was harder to locate, but never entirely submerged. During his Italian years he became close to the Innocenti family in Florence: to Luigi, who was the son of the landlady who housed him during his first Florence sojourn in the 1960s; and to Luigi's son Jimmy, who lived with him for a time in his last house, in Pontassieve. He died in Florence on 28 February 2007 and was buried in a little cemetery outside Doccia, in the undulating Tuscan hills, in the shade of a large cypress tree. ROGER PARKER

Sources *The Guardian* (7 March 2007) · *The Times* (13 March 2007); (27 March 2007) · *The Independent* (26 March 2007) · *PBA*, 153 (2008), 115–22 · *WW* (2007) · personal knowledge (2011) · private information (2011) [P. Petrobelli] · b. cert.
Archives SOUND BL NSA, documentary recordings
Likenesses obituary photographs · photograph, repro. in www.puccini.it/bollettino/Julian_Budden_1924-2007.htm · photographs, repro. in *PBA*
Wealth at death £338,948: probate, 8 Jan 2008, *CGPLA Eng. & Wales*

Bullard, Sir Julian Leonard (1928–2006), diplomatist, was born in Athens on 8 March 1928, the third of four sons and fourth of five children of Sir Reader William *Bullard (1885–1976), diplomatist, and his wife, Miriam Catherine (Biddy), *née* Smith (1888–1973), daughter of Arthur Lionel *Smith, master of Balliol College, Oxford. At the time of his birth his father was consul in Athens, about half way through a consular and diplomatic career that was to end with the ambassadorship in Tehran during the Second World War.

Bullard was educated at the Dragon School in Oxford, then as a scholar at Rugby School. He was noted as academically outstanding, excelling at team sports, and for a talent for the stage that embraced both Shakespeare and a tuneful Gilbert and Sullivan. From Rugby, where he was head of school, he won a demyship at Magdalen College, Oxford, at the age of sixteen. He went to Magdalen in 1946, and quickly established himself as one of the stars in a highly talented group of classical scholars. He won the Gaisford prize for Greek verse in 1947 and a Craven scholarship a year later, gained firsts in classical moderations (1948) and *literae humaniores* (1950), and went on to scale still greater Oxford academic heights by winning a prize fellowship at All Souls in the autumn of 1950. Meanwhile 'Magdalen teams benefited from his appearance on the field of sport' (Neill, memorial address) and he was elected president of the junior common room for the final year of his undergraduate life. He was then called up to do his national service, commissioned into the rifle brigade, and posted to the 1st battalion, stationed at Celle, just north of Hanover. There he commanded a platoon in a motor company, learned German, developed his taste for opera, and summed up his military experience by saying that he had not expected to enjoy it as much as he did. Bullard had passed top into the foreign service in 1951, and took up his appointment in 1953. On 27 March the following year he married Margaret Ruth Alleyn Stephens, the 24-year-old daughter of Archibald Collingwood Stephens, Church of England clergyman. They had first met when she was an undergraduate at St Hilda's, and she was to prove the best of partners throughout the years, and the moves, that followed. They had two sons and two daughters.

Bullard's early Foreign Office postings were certainly testing. In his first five years he was involved in three major rounds of negotiation: the Geneva conference ending the Korean War, the negotiations that preceded the signing of the Austrian state treaty, and those ending the treaty relationship with Jordan. In 1958, during his service in Jordan, he contracted polio, which he fought with determination. He was left, however, with damage to muscles on his left side, serious enough to interfere with both cricket and tennis, and to leave him with a slight limp.

In 1968, after spells in the Foreign Office, Bonn, and Moscow, Bullard was sent to Dubai as political agent. The Trucial States were about to enter a critical period, and the announcement that British forces would be withdrawn from the Gulf foreshadowed the end of the special relationship between them and Britain. There was concern that political instability would follow. Someone of Bullard's calibre was well placed to maintain the confidence of the rulers, to resolve the numerous issues arising from the imminent transfer to them of Britain's special responsibilities in this area, and to encourage them to move towards a federation. A major flashpoint was narrowly averted in 1970, when the shah of Iran, re-asserting the Iranian claim to the disputed Gulf islands of Abu Musa and the Tunbs, challenged an oil concession granted by one of the Trucial States to Occidental Petroleum. Bullard's coolness and energy were substantial factors in preventing the crisis developing into military conflict.

From Dubai, Bullard returned to London, as head of the eastern European and Soviet department. He ran this conspicuously well from 1971 to 1975, but his tenure was chiefly remembered for the expulsion in September 1971 of 105 members of the Soviet official establishment in London. The Soviet intelligence presence had been allowed over the years to build up to a wholly unacceptable level, and occasional attempts to deal with it piecemeal, by expelling egregious offenders, achieved little beyond Soviet retaliation. The choice was thus a stark one: to do nothing very much, and go on being rolled over; or to do something radical. To Bullard the answer was clear. The upper reaches of the Foreign and Commonwealth Office were persuaded, and so was the foreign secretary, Sir Alec Douglas-Home. Voices spoke darkly of future damage to the political influence of Britain and to the opportunities for trade. These predictions proved wide of the mark, and the chapter was given a pleasing symbolic end in November 1973, when Bullard accompanied Douglas-Home on an official visit to Moscow.

After a further posting to Bonn, this time as minister, Bullard returned to the Foreign and Commonwealth Office in 1979 as deputy under-secretary of state, in which capacity he acted as political director. The permanent under-secretary, Sir Michael Palliser, was due to retire in early 1982. Widely regarded within the Foreign and Commonwealth Office as the outstanding British diplomat of his generation, Bullard was an obvious choice to succeed him. The views of Margaret Thatcher must undoubtedly have weighed in the decision in favour of Antony Acland, also then serving in London as a deputy under-secretary. In parallel with the announcement of Acland's succession Bullard was promoted *ad hominem* to the post of deputy permanent under-secretary, and both he and Acland were appointed KCMG in 1982. Bullard's outstanding abilities made him hugely effective as the British political director in what was then a European Community of twelve countries, and as the principal foreign policy adviser to successive secretaries of state, who held him in the highest regard. His contribution might not have been as striking had his strengths been dispersed across the spectrum of accounting, ceremonial, economic, and managerial tasks that fall additionally to the permanent under-secretary, and the outcome may be seen in hindsight as a not unreasonable deployment of different talents.

Bullard's final years in the diplomatic service were spent as ambassador to Bonn, where he built on an already formidable reputation as an authority on the politics of the federal republic and on the history, culture, and language of Germany. The Chamberlain lecture that he delivered at the University of Birmingham in October 1990 provided a short glimpse of the sympathy, depth of knowledge, and wise judgement on which his influence, and many friendships, in Germany were based.

Bullard's immediate task on retiring from the foreign service in 1988 (having been advanced GCMG the previous year) was to act as an unexpectedly busy associate author to Valéry Giscard d'Estaing in the production of a report to the Trilateral Commission on East-West Relations, for which Henry Kissinger and Yasuhiro Nakasone were the other principals. The report, based on extensive consultation that included discussion with Mikhail Gorbachov and other Soviet leaders in Moscow, was published in April 1989. It was an intelligent and forward-looking view of the policy options envisaged at the time, but was soon overtaken by the collapse of the Berlin wall in November 1989.

Bullard returned to Oxford, where he was welcomed back to All Souls with a distinguished fellowship. He was also, in 1987, elected to an honorary fellowship of St Antony's College, and subsequently took an active part in the work of its European studies centre. Meanwhile, from his home base at All Souls, he worked in partnership with the Chichele professor of the history of war, Robert O'Neill, in planning and establishing the All Souls foreign policy studies programme. This was to result over many years in a highly regarded series of seminars and occasional weekend conferences to which academics, diplomats, and politicians were invited. O'Neill later described Bullard as 'a superb partner in this enterprise', noting that he brought to it wisdom, expert knowledge, a high reputation in Britain and abroad, a fine sense of humour, and exceptional ability as a chairman (Neill, memorial address). Bullard brought all these qualities to bear at the University of Birmingham during his years as a member of council (1988–97) and chairman of council and pro-chancellor (1989–94). He took particular pleasure in persuading the German authorities that the University of Birmingham should be the place for their Institute of German Studies, and in seeing the institute establish itself as a leader in its field in Britain. With his wife as co-author he made another significant contribution to European studies in 2000, with the publication of *Inside Stalin's Russia*, the edited text of the diaries which his father had kept during the years 1930–34 while serving as consul-general in Leningrad.

Bullard was a man of great intellect and ability; wide-ranging and cultivated in his interests and talents; modest without false modesty; committed to family and friends; and generous to younger colleagues, for whom he was a source of inspiration. He was an outstanding British public servant, and a convinced European. The final years of his life were increasingly subject to the progress of Parkinson's disease; his wife, Margaret, was an unfailing support. He died at his home in Northmoor Road, Oxford, on 25 May 2006, and was survived by his wife and their four children. A memorial service was held at the university church of St Mary the Virgin (where he and Margaret had married more than fifty years previously) on 14 October.

BRIAN FALL

Sources 'Around the world in diplomatic ways', *Birmingham Magazine*, 9 (Oct 1997) • *The Times* (30 May 2006) • *The Independent* (31 May 2006) • *The Guardian* (2 June 2006) • *Oxford Times* (2 June 2006) • *Daily Telegraph* (6 June 2006) • Lord Neill, memorial service address, university church of St Mary the Virgin, Oxford, 14 Oct 2006 • Burke, *Peerage* • *WW* (2006) • personal knowledge (2010) • private information (2010) • m. cert. • d. cert.

Archives SOUND BL NSA, documentary recordings

Wealth at death £69,638: probate, 3 Aug 2006, *CGPLA Eng. & Wales*

Burnett, Sir John Harrison (1922–2007), botanist and university administrator, was born on 21 January 1922 in Ripon, Yorkshire, the son of Thomas Harrison Burnett (1887–1970), Methodist minister, and his wife, Florence, *née* Waite. The family moved soon thereafter to Paisley, where his father was appointed a minister. Burnett was educated at the Methodist Kingswood School, near Bath, and at Merton College, Oxford. His Oxford studies were interrupted by the Second World War and (having gained a distinction in the war-shortened botany course) in 1942 he joined the Royal Naval Volunteer Reserve. He served with distinction in several theatres including the Russian convoys, reaching the rank of lieutenant and being mentioned in dispatches. While a marine commando in the Mediterranean he once found himself sharing a cave with Marshal Tito. On 22 September 1945, while still serving in the RNVR, he married, in the cathedral at Chichester, (Enid) Margaret Bishop (*b*. 1921), schoolmistress, and daughter of Edgar William Bishop, schoolmaster. They had two sons, Nicholas and Andrew.

After the end of hostilities Burnett completed his studies at Merton and in 1947 graduated with a first-class degree in botany. He was awarded a Christopher Welch scholarship and in 1948 was appointed to a lectureship at Lincoln College, Oxford, while working towards a DPhil (awarded in 1953), but in 1949 moved to Magdalen College with a fellowship gained by examination. During this period (1949–53) he held the posts of university lecturer and demonstrator. He then left Oxford and began a journey around some of the élite universities of Britain, with a one-year lectureship at Liverpool followed by three distinguished chairs of botany: at St Andrews (1955–60), at King's College, Newcastle, from 1963 Newcastle University (1960–68), and as regius professor at Glasgow (1968–70).

Glasgow, eminent position as it was, was only ever likely to be a stopping place because three relevant professorships were about to become vacant in Oxford. In 1969 forestry, renamed forest science, was filled after a short interregnum by Jack Harley, returning to Oxford from the botany chair in Sheffield; Geoffrey Blackman retired from the Sibthorpian chair of rural economy (agriculture) in 1970; then Cyril Darlington vacated the Sherardian chair of botany in 1971. It was to the agriculture building in Parks Road and the Sibthorpian chair that Burnett went in 1970 with a fellowship at St John's, where he joined Harley, another eminent scientist who bridged the boundary between botany and mycology. It promised a golden age for Oxford plant scientists and mycologists but one that in the minds of many, especially the more traditionally minded, never quite materialized; at least not for many years. But that was no fault of Burnett. The undergraduate course in forestry had come to an end and forestry was by then a graduate department, while Oxford agriculture was hardly at the forefront of the subject. Burnett, with Harley's support, oversaw the amalgamation of their old schools into a new department of agricultural and forest science. It was probably the first department of applied science at Oxford but was simply following a trend already taking place elsewhere. Darlington's botany department stayed out and it was not until after his retirement that the three became plant sciences. The sadness for mycologists was that their subject largely fell through the cracks, and although Burnett and Harley between them could and should have left Oxford with a rich mycological legacy, it was not to be, at least as far as whole-organism studies were concerned.

In 1979 Burnett moved again, this time back to Scotland as principal and vice-chancellor of Edinburgh University, a position he held for eight years. It was a difficult time to be in university administration because under Margaret Thatcher's government the funding process both for higher education and for scientific research was changed. Much more research was commissioned, but for the short term only. Projects taking many years became increasingly difficult to justify or sustain, and there was much less scope for adventurous 'blue skies' study. Burnett fought long and hard through this period for the raising of university standards and was absolutely committed to academic excellence. He was widely credited with having been the saviour of Edinburgh University at a time when less able and determined administrators would have caved in to the cuts. It was said that his response to a suggestion that poorly performing areas of endeavour should be axed was to demand increased support so that they could improve. Even with such a huge administrative burden, however, Burnett never let go of his research and maintained mycological studies through his students.

Outstanding academic as he was, it was outside the university world that Burnett made his most enduring contribution. From 1961 to 1987 he served on various committees of Nature Conservancy and then for two years was a member of the Nature Conservancy council. Seeing conservation as a national not a regional matter, he was vehemently opposed to the break-up of the body and its restructuring into separate agencies in each of the United Kingdom's countries. He was, however, largely instrumental in the establishment of a United Kingdom-wide body in the Joint Nature Conservation Committee, which was to advise the national bodies.

Like other thinking conservationists Burnett recognized that obtaining and recording data was essential if the understanding and management of Britain's biodiversity was to be meaningful. To this end he became chairman in 1989 of the new Co-ordinating Commission for Biological Recording and then, following the United Kingdom response to the 1992 United Nations convention on biological diversity (the Rio treaty) assisted in the establishment of the National Biodiversity Network Trust, serving as its chairman from 2000 to 2005. He was committed to this collaborative body, set up to collect and use data from government and other agencies, environmental bodies, local records centres, and many voluntary groups, and make it widely available to the public. It became recognized internationally as a world leader in the field and it was appropriate that one so passionate about it should have served as executive secretary of the World Council for the Biosphere from 1987 to 1993 and chairman of the International Organisation for Plant Information from 1991 to 1996. Among numerous other responsibilities Burnett served as a long-time trustee of the *New Phytologist*, one of the pre-eminent British botanical journals. He was a committed member of the British Mycological Society and served as its president in 1982–3.

Burnett, alone and with his students and collaborators, published extensively in scientific journals. For mycologists his seminal work was *Fundamentals of Mycology* (1968), which went through several editions and served generations of mycologists. Among his other publications were *Mycogenetics* (1975), *Speciation and Evolution in Fungi* (1989), and *Fungal Populations and Species* (2003), and (as editor) *The Maintenance of the Biosphere* (1989) and *Surviving with the Biosphere* (1994).

Burnett was a short, dapper man with a penetrating smile; a kindly, personable individual with a sharp sense of humour and wit. But the genial appearance belied a quick, incisive, and meticulous mind, and he certainly kept a close eye on the management and finances of the British Mycological Society long after he had left its council: his presence at the society's annual general meeting always gave rise to anxiety, if not abject terror, in the heart of the treasurer of the day. The observation 'Sir John is in the audience' kept everyone on their toes in many organizations.

Honours and awards, including several honorary degrees and fellowship of the Royal Society of Edinburgh, came inevitably and abundantly. Despite his difficulties in the Thatcher era—she was said to have called him her 'favourite dissident scientist' (*The Times*, 17 Aug 2007)—he was knighted in 1987, at the end of his time in Edinburgh. To the mystification of his many friends and colleagues one major honour eluded him, however: he was never elected to fellowship of the Royal Society. He died at his home, 13 Field House Drive, Oxford, on 22 July 2007, of cancer of the brain. He was survived by his wife, Margaret, and their two sons. STEFAN BUCZACKI

Sources *The Independent* (27 July 2007) · *The Herald* [Glasgow] (15 Aug 2007) · *The Times* (17 Aug 2007) · *The Guardian* (2 Oct 2007) · Burke, *Peerage* · *WW* (2007) · personal knowledge (2011) · private information (2011) · b. cert. · m. cert. · d. cert.

Likenesses obituary photographs · photograph, repro. in www.nbn.org.uk/News-and-Events/NBN-news/John-Burnett-memorial-lecture.aspx · portrait, repro. in *Transactions of the British Mycological Society*, 81 (1983), 1

Wealth at death £591,239: probate, 30 Nov 2007, *CGPLA Eng. & Wales*

Burns, Richard Alexander (1971–2005), rally driver, was born on 17 January 1971 at the Royal Berkshire Hospital, Reading, the first of two children born to Alexander Kenmir (Alex) Burns, computer manager, and his wife, Denise Ann, *née* Pettafor. He was brought up in Henley-on-Thames, then Hook End, Checkendon. His interest in motor cars became apparent at a very early age and by the time he was eight he was to be found practising his driving skills on a circuit of some 165 yards around the yard of his parents' farmhouse. He also gained driving experience by volunteering to reverse horse trailers at his sister's pony club, and eventually became a member of the Under 17 Car Club. However, it was a visit to Jan Churchill's rally driving school in Wales, a fifteenth birthday present, that prompted him to commit his future to motor sport. He worked part time in order to raise the funds to support his ambitions but it was the backing of family and friends that was instrumental in allowing him to pursue them. His father was particularly supportive, providing him with his first rally car, a Sunbeam, which, with a friend, he converted to rally specification. This was the first and only rally car he actually owned, the remainder coming from supporters who admired his driving ability, including members of the Craven Motor Club in Reading. After honing his technique in a number of secondary meetings in 1988 and 1989 Burns participated in the 1990 RAC rally, his first involvement in a world championship event.

David Williams, a rally enthusiast who had appreciated the young Burns's potential, was another important influence in his emergence as a key figure in British motor sport, providing finance and introducing him to Prodrive, Subaru's rally team in Britain. Prodrive became important in improving Burns's understanding of rallying and, with their support, in 1993 he became the youngest ever driver to win the British rally championship. It was during this period that Burns got to know Robert Reid, who became his principal co-driver for thirteen years.

Burns's opportunities with Prodrive became limited by the success of his team-mate, Colin McRae, in the world championships of 1995, so he moved to Mitsubishi to further his career. He gained valuable experience during his three seasons with Mitsubishi, benefiting from partnering Tommi Mäkinen, the Flying Finn. His successes even enabled him to challenge Mäkinen as the team's principal driver. In 1998 he won the gruelling Safari rally in Kenya, his first victory in the world rally championship, and in the same year enjoyed success in the British rally.

With his status in motor sport greatly enhanced, Burns left Mitsubishi in 1999 to rejoin Prodrive and Subaru as the team's lead driver. He won a number of events with Prodrive and came second two years running in the world championship, in 1999 and 2000, before securing the title in 2001. He was the first Englishman and only the second Briton after Colin McRae to win the world rally championship, the sport's highest achievement. The reasons for his subsequent move in 2001 from Prodrive to the Peugeot team based in France are not entirely clear. It turned out to be a two-year low in his career, and he was overshadowed by the success of his team-mate, Marcus Grönholm, who had narrowly beaten him to the world title in 2000. Burns had already decided to return to Subaru when he suffered a blackout *en route* to the Wales rally GB in November 2003. He was later diagnosed with astrocytoma, a form of brain tumour.

Burns claimed that he was not particularly blessed with natural talent as a driver, though he was recognized as being courageous, thoughtful, and tactically astute. Although determined to succeed, he did not drive beyond the limit of where he felt in control of the car. He believed strongly in the importance of personal fitness, including an appropriate diet, as well as the value of sports psychology in tackling the physical and mental problems that accompanied rallying at the highest levels. He was held in high regard, both personally and professionally, by his many followers and colleagues in the sport. His success contributed to the popularity of rallying as a television spectacle. His autobiography, *Driving Ambition*, was published in 2002. About 2001 he formed a relationship with Zoë Keen, a television producer, who supported him through his final illness. He died on 25 November 2005 at the Wellington Hospital (North), 27 Circus Road, Westminster, and was survived by her and his father Alex, his mother having predeceased him. A memorial service was held at St Luke's Church, Chelsea, on 22 December 2005, and the following year the Richard Burns Foundation was launched, to 'inspire and support people with serious injury and illness'. DAVID THOMS

Sources C. McRae and D. Allsop, *The real McRae* (2001) • R. Burns and J. Desborough, *Driving ambition* (2002) • A. Henry, *Driven man: David Richards, Prodrive and the race to win* (Osceola, 2005) • *The Guardian* (28 Nov 2005) • *The Independent* (28 Nov 2005) • *Daily Telegraph* (29 Nov 2005) • *The Times* (29 Nov 2005) • www.richardburnsfoundation.com, 25 May 2010 • b. cert. • d. cert.

Archives FILM BFINA, documentary footage • BFINA, performance footage

Likenesses photographs, 1993–2003, PA Photos, London • photographs, 1997–2003, Getty Images, London • photographs, 2001, Rex Features, London • photographs, 2001–3, Photoshot, London • obituary photographs

Wealth at death £1,419,228: probate, 14 Aug 2006, *CGPLA Eng. & Wales*

Burns, Thomas [Tommy] (**1956–2008**), footballer and football manager, was born on 16 December 1956 at 43 Soho Street, Calton, in a tenement building in Glasgow's east end, the second of three children of Thomas Burns, steel erector, and his wife, Margaret, *née* McInnes. He had two sisters, Elizabeth and Anne. He was born in the parish of St Mary's Roman Catholic Church, in whose parochial hall Celtic Football Club was founded by a group of Irishmen led by Marist Brother Walfrid in November 1887 (with the new team playing its first game in May the following year). Burns received the sacraments of his Catholic faith there and also attended mass regularly throughout his life. Ironically, his faith was nurtured by his protestant mother as his Catholic father was often away working in the oil industry. He was educated at St Mary's Roman Catholic School in Calton, and St Mungo's Academy, run by the Marist brothers. When he was fifteen his parents separated, though his father remained supportive of his family. In the mid-1990s his aged mother converted to Catholicism.

The red-headed, left-footed Burns's leisure time as a youngster was mainly spent playing and watching football, and like the rest of his family he supported Celtic. After playing with the local Catholic parish in Boys' Guild football he played for Eastercraigs Boys' Club, a successful youth team in Glasgow. As he began to excel on local football fields, he received offers to go to England to play professionally, but he turned these down and, despite some initial hesitation in case he did not get an opportunity to play first team football, signed in 1973 for Celtic. This meant moving to Celtic Boys' Club and subsequently being farmed out to the local Maryhill Juniors side for experience.

Burns made his first appearance for Celtic under manager Jock Stein as a substitute in the 1974–5 season, but it was another two years before he made his mark as a gifted midfield player, thereafter becoming a regular until the 1989–90 season. During that time he made 503 competitive appearances and scored eighty-two goals for Celtic. In the process he won six league championships, five Scottish cups, and one league cup. He was an integral part of the team that won the league and cup double in the club's centenary year of 1987–8. Despite his winner medals, he regarded his greatest success as a Celtic player to have been his longevity at the club. After making his début in May 1981 he played another seven times for Scotland, the last at Wembley in the Rous cup against England in a 1–0 defeat in May 1988.

In late 1989 Burns departed Celtic for Kilmarnock. He played 167 times (scoring nineteen goals) as player and player–manager before retiring from playing in the 1993–4 season. In 1994 he returned to Celtic as manager in acrimonious circumstances since Kilmarnock did not want him to leave: the Scottish Football Association subsequently fined Celtic £100,000 for 'tapping' him and Billy Stark his assistant. As manager of Celtic from July 1994 until May 1997, he led the club in 140 matches and experienced 78 victories, 38 draws, and 24 defeats. Under his management Celtic won the Scottish cup in May 1995.

This was Celtic's first trophy since Burns was a player with the team that won the same cup against Glasgow Rangers in the final of 1989. It was also the last trophy won until November 1997: these years reflecting the arduous period on and off the field experienced at the club. In the 1995–6 season Celtic lost only one league game but failed to wrest the title from a vibrant and wealthy Rangers team that won more games. Burns's time as manager of Celtic was significantly tempered by the presence of Fergus McCann, the Scottish-born, Canadian-based owner of the club from 1994 to 1999. McCann and Burns did not have a good relationship, with Burns solely focused on a successful Celtic team and McCann emphasizing stadium redevelopment, a sound financial footing for the club, and making a large profit from his venture. Eventually Burns was sacked, three weeks before the end of the 1996–7 season. McCann's tenure deeply divided fans but Burns retained the Celtic supporters' affections, recognizing as they did that he was one of them and that he knew what Celtic meant in Catholic/Christian, Irish, moral, and marginalized class terms. Burns modestly wrote that he was 'the supporter who was lucky enough to get the hooped jersey to wear and become the people's representative on the park' (Burns, 144). Likewise he once said of his beloved club: 'When you pull on that jersey you're not just playing for a football club, you're playing for a people and a cause' (Cuddihy, 1).

Burns subsequently encountered another turbulent time in a football club's history when after a short spell assisting Kenny Dalglish at Newcastle, he temporarily and unsuccessfully managed Reading between March 1998 and October 1999, during which time the team was demoted from the first to the second division of English football. He returned to Celtic to assist temporary manager Dalglish in early 2000 and was subsequently put in charge of youth development by new manager Martin O'Neill in June of that year. Aware that a club of Celtic's stature required a modern training facility—as opposed to the one traditionally used by the club at Barrowfield near to Celtic Park—he was instrumental in achieving this at Lennoxtown near the Campsie Hills. While still head of youth development at Celtic, he also assisted Bertie Vogts in his position as Scotland manager from March 2002 to November 2004. He subsequently managed Scotland for one match, against Sweden, before the appointment of his former Glasgow Rangers managerial rival, Walter Smith (assisted by former Rangers player Ally McCoist), as manager. He continued in his supportive role with Scotland until Smith left the post in 2007.

Burns married Rosemary Smith, a computer operator, and daughter of Matthew Hendry Smith, builder's labourer, on 24 June 1980 (Rosemary's twenty-fifth birthday) at St Francis's Roman Catholic Church in Glasgow's Gorbals district. Hundreds of children and adults surrounded the wedding party as it left the church, greeting them with Irish and Celtic flags and singing the Celtic club anthem, 'Hail Hail, the Celts are here'. The Burns family subsequently comprised Tommy, Rosemary, and four children, Emma, Jenna, Michael, and Jonathan.

Reflecting his personal faith and the founding ethos of the club he represented for most of his life, Burns organized and attended many hundreds of charitable events and as a talented singer, as well as a genuinely humorous individual, he was often requested to sing the Bobby Darin classic, 'Mack the Knife'. He would almost always enthusiastically comply and such a rendition was usually forthcoming at the annual 'Burns Night Supper' (dedicated to Tommy not Robert) held by the Heriot-Watt and Edinburgh universities Celtic Supporters' Club.

Burns was diagnosed with skin cancer in July 2005, and despite treatment he died at his family home, in Newton Mearns, on 15 May 2008, shortly after a visit to the Catholic Marian shrine at Lourdes. His requiem mass was concelebrated by forty-one priests, including two bishops, at St Mary's Roman Catholic Church in Calton on 20 May 2008. A reported 20,000 people attended his funeral at the church and in the vicinity of the parish and Celtic Park. He was buried in Linn cemetery, Castlemilk, Glasgow, and was survived by his wife, Rosemary, and their four children.

Joseph M. Bradley

Sources Scottish Press Association, press release, 15 March 2008 • *The Scotsman* (16 May 2008) • *The Herald* [Glasgow] (16 May 2008); (21 May 2008) • *The Times* (16 May 2008) • *Daily Telegraph* (16 May 2008) • *The Guardian* (16 May 2008) • *The Independent* (16 May 2008) • *Evening Times* [Glasgow] (16 May 2008); (17 May 2008); (20 May 2008) • J. M. Bradley, ed., *Celtic minded 3: essays on religion, politics, society, identity — and football* (2009) • P. Cuddihy, *Tommy Burns: a supporter who got lucky* (2009) • T. Burns, *Twists and turns: the Tommy Burns story* (1989) • b. cert. • m. cert. • d. cert.

Likenesses obituary photographs • photographs, repro. in Cuddihy, *Burns*

Burtt, Brian Laurence [Bill] (**1913–2008**), botanist and plant taxonomist, was born on 27 August 1913 at Homeleigh, Claygate, Surrey, the youngest of three children, and only son, of Laurence Buckley Burtt (1878–1963), a bank clerk with Coutts & Co., and his wife, Mabel Johnston, *née* Hall (1882–1972). His childhood was spent largely in Lewes and Godalming, where he acquired an early love of natural history. A move to south London followed, where he attended Dulwich College, which he left at seventeen with distinctions in Latin and Greek. It was the time of the depression, and university was out of the question, so an interview was arranged with his father's First World War commanding officer, T. F. Chipp, by now assistant director of the Royal Botanic Gardens, Kew. In September 1930 Burtt was offered the post of technical temporary assistant (at a weekly salary of 23*s*.), on condition that he took evening classes in natural science at Chelsea Polytechnic. At Chelsea he was secretary of the 'evening' section of the Natural History Society; he took a second-class degree from the University of London in 1936.

At Kew Burtt was assigned to the African department under John Hutchinson, and acquired a sound training in herbarium skills, concentrating on the family Compositae, which resulted in his first scientific paper in 1932. The following year he became an assistant botanist (at an annual salary of £150), working in the office of the director, Sir Arthur W. Hill, who emphasized the importance of observing living plants and introduced Burtt to what would become two abiding interests: the African violet family, Gesneriaceae, and the study of living processes, including atypical developmental and morphological processes, that might be useful in producing good natural classifications. There could have been no better botanical training ground for a bright young man with a classical education than Kew in the 1930s, with its great herbarium, living collections and library, and the reception for study and naming (and delineation by his older contemporary and lifelong friend Stella Ross-Craig) of plants from all over the empire and from private British gardens (like that of E. A. Bowles). T. A. Sprague, an expert on botanical nomenclature, was also a significant influence.

On 13 October 1942, at St Mary's Church, Reading, Burtt married Joyce Daughtry (1913–2003), dispenser, the daughter of Edmund Osmond Daughtry, music scholar; they had two sons. In April of that year he had been commissioned into the Royal Ordnance corps; he was transferred to the Royal Electrical and Mechanical Engineers, and later reached the rank of captain. A spell in Nigeria, testing radar, provided his first brief exposure to tropical plants. On returning to Kew in 1946 he was put under W. B. Turrill in the Europe and Middle East department. While undertaking this work assiduously—a misidentified herbarium specimen was recognized as *Koenigia islandica*, new to Britain, and he published on the flora of Kuwait—his heart was never in European or floristic work. In 1951 he seized the opportunity to run the herbarium of the Royal Botanic Garden in Edinburgh, under the ageing Sir William Wright Smith, who insisted that any research should be undertaken in Burtt's own time.

The Edinburgh garden was the focus for the rest of Burtt's long and productive life, nominal retirement taking place in 1975. He played a vital role in rebuilding both the fabric and the intellectual life of a moribund establishment, being the intellectual power behind the productive flamboyance of the regius keepership of Harold R. Fletcher. Highlights included Burtt's role in the International Botanical Congress of 1964, which coincided with the opening of the magnificent new herbarium and library building, to the planning of which he had contributed greatly; his reinvigoration of the *Notes of the Royal Botanic Garden, Edinburgh*; and teaching (especially of plant geography) on the influential graduate diploma course on taxonomy set up by Peter H. Davis.

Despite heavy administrative duties Burtt's own research flourished; the first of five field trips to Sarawak in 1962, part of his ever increasing work on the family Gesneriaceae, saw the start of an interest in the ginger family, Zingiberaceae. In 1964 he met the South African botanist Olive Mary Hilliard (*b.* 1925), daughter of David Henry Spencer Hillary, company manager. They formed an outstanding intellectual partnership: there followed nineteen visits to South Africa, resulting in major collections of herbarium specimens, plant introductions, and monographs of the genera *Streptocarpus* (1971) and *Dierama* (1991). Hilliard and Burtt undertook pioneering explorations of the botanically almost unknown mountain range of the southern Natal Drakensberg, leading to a *Flora* of the area in 1987. The collaboration continued after Hilliard retired from a research chair at Pietermaritzburg in 1985 and settled in Edinburgh. An amicable separation of Burtt from his first wife had taken place after the second of their two sons left school. Following her death Hilliard and Burtt married, at Edinburgh register office on 30 March 2004. The second of Burtt's most important collaborations was with Anton Weber of Vienna, who stimulated, and jointly wrote, a series of publications on Gesneriaceae, including the collected volume *Taxonomic Studies in South East Asian Gesneriaceae* (1998).

Burtt's publication record (256 singly and 128 jointly written papers, containing some 570 new species and 27 new genera across 47 plant families) spanned an almost unparalleled period of 76 years. The publications covered the full gamut of classical taxonomy: revisionary work (from tribal down to species level), nomenclature, bibliography, and functional morphology (for example, on the flowering head of the daisy family; and unusual development, including unequal growth and persistence of one seed leaf, 'anisocotyly', in certain Gesneriaceae). His love of and extensive knowledge of literature was reflected in more than 75 book reviews. Though he was scrupulously modest in person, his wisdom was widely recognized and used by colleagues (distant ones by means of an extensive correspondence). Only a moderate amount of academic recognition came his way: he was elected a fellow of the Royal Society of Edinburgh (1954), was awarded the Linnean medal for botany by the Linnean Society of London (1981), and had twenty-seven species named for him. His love of living plants and horticulture was demonstrated in daily visits to the garden—in part to follow the progress of his own introductions. Of these the South African wand flowers (*Dierama*) and twinspurs (*Diascia*), introduced with Hilliard, proved to be of major horticultural significance. This aspect of Burtt's work was recognized in the award of a gold Veitch memorial medal by the Royal Horticultural Society (1977). He died at Pine Villa, 4 Hawthorn Gardens, Loanhead, Midlothian, on 30 May 2008 of vascular dementia, and was survived by his two sons and his second wife. H. J. Noltie

Sources M. J. van Steenis-Kruseman, *Cyclopaedia of Collectors*, suppl. 2: *Flora Malesiana*, Cyclopaedia of Collectors, ser. 1, vol. 8 (1974) [19] · 'Report of the council of the Royal Horticultural Society for 1977', *The Garden*, 103/2 (1978), viii · 'Report of the proceedings of the 174th A. G. M. of the R. H. S.', *The Garden*, 103/4 (1978), x · 'Linnean medal for botany: Brian Laurence Burtt', *Biological Journal of the Linnean Society*, 16 (1981), 365 · B. L. Burtt, 'My time at Kew', *Journal of the Kew Guild*, 15 (2008), 343–8 · *The Independent* (13 June 2008) · *The Times* (21 June 2008) · *Taxon*, 57 (2008), 1366–9 · D. J. Middleton and I. Hedge, 'Brian Laurence Burtt: a celebration of longevity and productivity', *Edinburgh Journal of Botany*, 66 (2009), 1–5 · A. Weber and D. J. Middleton, 'Plants named in honour of B. L. Burtt', *Edinburgh Journal of Botany*, 66 (2009), 6–7 · A. Weber and others, 'Botanical publications of B. L. Burtt', *Edinburgh Journal of Botany*, 66 (2009), 8–26 · K. Jong, 'Reflections on working with a botanical giant: B. L. Burtt', *Botanical Society of Scotland News*, 92 (2009), 9–12 · personal knowledge (2012) · private information (2012) [Olive Hilliard, widow; Julian Burtt, son] · b. cert. · m. certs. · d. cert.

Archives Royal Botanic Garden, Edinburgh, papers (incl. corresp. and field notebooks) and herbarium specimens

Likenesses photograph, *c.*1970, repro. in van Steenis-Kruseman, *Cyclopedia* · L. Boulos, photograph, *c.*1990, repro. in *Taxon* · D. White, photograph, 2002, repro. in Middleton and Hedge, 'Brian Laurence Burtt'

Wealth at death £565,104: confirmation, 2008, *CCI*

Buzás, Stefan (1915–2008), architect, was born István Buzás into a liberal Jewish family in Tapolca, Hungary, on 16 January 1915, the second son of Desiderius Buzás (1879–1944), lawyer and linguist, and his wife, Eugenie, *née* Lessner (1888–1944), who came from a family of wine producers in the Lake Balaton region. His father was a committed socialist and took part in the short-lived Hungarian Soviet Republic of 1919, but with its collapse the family moved to Vienna, Austria. Influenced by his uncle, Mano Lessner, an architect who was designing in the modernist style, Buzás enrolled in architecture at the Vienna Technische Hochschule in 1935. However, with increased persecution of Jews, and the German Nazi annexation of Austria, he left Hungary in April 1938 for England, sponsored by a Jewish family with whom he lived for a short period in Hampstead, London. He never saw his parents again; they both died in concentration camps in 1944, his father in Dachau, his mother in Auschwitz. His brother József (1914–1975) survived and became a civil servant in post-war communist Hungary. Buzás spoke little about his parents' deaths, and returned to Hungary only once, for his brother's funeral.

When Buzás enrolled at the Architectural Association, his term in Vienna was given credit, enabling him to graduate in 1940. During the Second World War he worked with a firm of architects in St James's Square while performing night watch duties. Between 1944 and 1949 he taught at Kingston School of Art, where he was known as an inspirational teacher. On 2 May 1942, he married the opera singer Joan Marjory Mills (1916–1996), with whom he had two daughters, Eugenie Elizabeth (*b.* 1943) and Katherine Mary (Kate) (*b.* 1945).

In 1948, with fellow students from the Architectural Association—James Cubitt, Fello Atkinson, and Dick Maitland—Buzás formed the architectural practice of James Cubitt and Partners. The Australian-born Cubitt put the money up to take offices at 25 Gloucester Place, London, and decided to concentrate on work abroad, having spent much of the war in west Africa. The partners first opened an office abroad in Accra, Gold Coast, where Buzás designed the Agricultural Development Corporation building. The overseas practice grew and became very successful, especially the office established in Lagos, Nigeria, in 1957, where Buzás went regularly for many months at a time to supervise.

Buzás, however, worked mainly in the London office, where he was much in demand for his beautiful draughtsmanship and his eye for creating fine detail. It was the smaller projects in which he excelled. He was commissioned to assist the architect Ralph Tubbs with interior displays in the Dome of Discovery for the 1951 Festival of Britain, making a beautiful set of more than a dozen designs in pastel (now in the drawings collection of the Royal Institute of British Architects). Shop interiors and their window displays became a speciality. On Piccadilly he fashioned the tourist offices for South Africa on one side of the street and for Iceland on the other. In the window of the Qantas Airlines building he placed a great aeroplane propeller and, nearby, in the window of the Time-Life building in New Bond Street, he made a weather window with sleek electronic forecasting dials set in glass boxes like contemporary jewellery caskets.

Buzás's best-known interior was for Manchester's Ringway airport terminal building, opened in 1962, for which he commissioned four enormous glass chandeliers from the Venetian glassmaker Paolo Venini, each weighing 2 tons and made of 1300 pieces of blown crystal droplets. A great admirer of Italian design, Buzás befriended the Italian architect Carlo Scarpa and contributed essays to several books about his work. They also shared a common love of Sir John Soane's Museum, about which Buzás wrote a very personal text for a book published in 1994, with photographs by Richard Bryant.

Although Buzás created only a few houses, he said that he found domestic design very satisfying, enabling him to express his client's most private desires. His most notable architectural work was the pair of small brick houses on adjacent plots that he created in 1951 at Ham Common, in south-west London: one for his own family and the other for a friend and his family. Although these houses were built during the time of post-war building restrictions, with their flat roofs, expanses of floor to ceiling glass walls, and open room planning, they epitomized the optimism of the possibilities of stylish modern living for the middle classes in an era of mass social housing.

Buzás left James Cubitt and Partners in 1965 to open a joint office with the younger architect Alan Irvine, who became his son-in-law the following year, after marrying Kate. Buzás now became known as an architect of high modern interiors furnished in rich and expensive materials. His Standard Bank offices in Northumberland Avenue, London, led to further jobs with City banks such as Schroder Wagg and Lazards. With sponsorship from the Worshipful Company of Goldsmiths, he designed the treasuries at Chichester and Norwich cathedrals, the latter set dramatically high and in open view within a fifteenth-century arch. He finally retired in 1992.

Coming from a cultured middle European family, Buzás was fluent in Hungarian and German, and learned French in his late teens from a private tutor, and later Italian. His spoken English had only a hint of an accent. He had a gentle manner but could be outspoken, especially on the state of architecture as it moved away during the Thatcher years from his own socialist roots, as his many published letters to the architectural journals so strongly expressed. His marriage ended in divorce in 1974. He died on 2 October 2008 and his ashes were buried in Richmond Park beneath an ancient oak. He was survived by his two daughters. NEIL BINGHAM

Sources recording, 1999, BL NSA, National Life Story Collection: Architects' Lives · *The Guardian* (23 Oct 2008) · *The Times* (17 Nov

2008); (24 Nov 2008) • *Almanac of Architecture and Design*, 2010 (266) • personal knowledge (2012) • private information (2012) [Katherine Irvine, daughter] • m. cert.
Archives SOUND BL NSA, National Life Story Collection: Architects' Lives, interview
Likenesses obituary photographs

Bywater, (Richard) Arthur Samuel (1913–2005), munitions factory official, was born on 3 November 1913 at 1 Teignmouth Road, Selly Oak, Birmingham, the third son of Walter Bywater, clerk at a tinplate works, later chief clerk of stores at the Austin Motor Company, Longbridge, Birmingham, and his wife, Florence Amy, *née* Mould. He won a scholarship to Kings Norton grammar school, graduated from the University of Birmingham with a first in chemistry, and received the degree of MSc in 1936. After three years as chief chemist at Boxfoldia Ltd, packaging manufacturers, in Redditch, Worcestershire, at the beginning of 1939 he became a technical assistant at the Royal Filling Factory at the Royal Arsenal, Woolwich. After the outbreak of the Second World War Bywater applied to join the RAF, but was turned down because he was in a reserved occupation, and was put in charge of the experimental department at the Woolwich Arsenal. In the summer of 1940 he took charge of the fuse section.

Because the munitions factories were in London, and at risk from enemy bombing, new factories were built in the west and north-west of the country, areas regarded as safe. One of the new factories was the Royal Ordnance Factory no. 7, a large filling factory built at Kirkby, Lancashire, north-east of Liverpool, which opened in March 1941. The filling factory at the Woolwich Arsenal had been destroyed in an enemy raid in September 1940, and Bywater moved to Kirkby as factory development officer. Most of the employees, mainly women, had the hazardous job of filling anti-tank mine fuses with explosives, and by the beginning of 1944, in preparation for D-day, 150,000 fuses a week were filled by women working a three-shift system, twenty-four hours a day. On 22 February 1944 a fuse exploded, detonating a tray of twenty-five fuses, killing one woman and badly damaging the factory. When Bywater reached the scene with Lawrence Gale, the superintendent of the factory, he realized the danger of further explosions and arranged the evacuation of the building, volunteering to lead a team of volunteers in removing the remaining 12,000 fuses. It was discovered that the original explosion had been caused by a defective striker in the fuse, and 4000 of the remaining fuses were also found to have faulty strikers. They were removed to a site a mile away and detonated: twenty-three were in such a critically sensitive state that he carried each out individually to be destroyed. The operation took two days. He was awarded the George Cross, the highest civilian award for bravery, for his leadership and disregard for personal safety.

A few months later, on 15 September 1944, there was another incident at the Kirkby factory, while workers were filling a set of 8 pound bombs into a container attached to a parachute. Fourteen people were killed in a series of explosions, and again Bywater organized the evacuation of the building: when the fires were extinguished he led the team in the dangerous operation to clear the debris of unexploded ammunition. Each of the 4000 bombs had to be handled separately and taken away for destruction, a job that took three months. In his report the director-general of filling factories wrote: 'the work in progress was possibly the most dangerous ever attempted in an industrial factory' (Hay, 79). For this he was awarded the George Medal, and became the first and only civilian to hold both the GC and the GM.

After the war Bywater became works manager of R. N. Coate and Co., cider makers, at Nailsea in Somerset, near Bristol. In 1947 he married Patricia Ferneyhough; they had one son and one daughter. In 1954 they emigrated to New South Wales, Australia, where he worked for the Mulwala explosives factory and later became assistant manager of St Mary's explosives factory. After moving to Melbourne he became general manager of the banknote printing works of the Reserve Bank of Australia. He retired in 1976 and bought a 240 acre farm at Cobram, on the Murray River in Victoria, before moving to Albury in New South Wales in 1980 to help his daughter and son-in-law in the running of their equestrian business. He died on 6 April 2005 in Australia, and was survived by his wife and their two children. ANNE PIMLOTT BAKER

Sources I. Hay, *R.O.F.: the story of the Royal Ordnance Factories, 1939–1948* (1949), 79–81 • W. Hornby, 'Factories and plant', *History of the Second World War: U.K. Civil Series, War Production Series* (1958), 91–107 • *R.O.F. Kirkby, 1940–1946: a photographic history* (1995) • *Daily Telegraph* (8 April 2005) • *The Times* (8 April 2005) • *The Guardian* (18 April 2005) • b. cert.
Likenesses photograph, repro. in *The Times* (8 April 2005) • photographs, repro. in *R.O.F. Kirkby*

Cabrera Infante, Guillermo (1929–2005), novelist and writer, was born on 22 April 1929 in Gibara, Cuba, the eldest son of Guillermo Cabrera López (*c*.1900–1990) and his wife, Zoila Infante Castro (1909–1965). His parents founded the Cuban Communist Party and were imprisoned in 1936 for their political activities. In 1941 the family moved to Havana, which came to occupy the centre of his literary imagination.

Cabrera Infante began studying medicine at the University of Havana in 1949 but soon devoted himself to journalism and literature, entering the school of journalism, where he studied from 1950 to 1954. His journalism focused on the cinema, a lifelong passion, and in 1951 he co-founded the Cinemateca de Cuba (Cuban Film Archive). He contributed to the magazine *Bohemia*, and in 1952 was briefly jailed for publishing a story containing 'obscenities', and forbidden to write under his own name. He subsequently adopted the pseudonym G. Caín (a characteristic pun based on the first syllables of his surnames). Between 1954 and 1960 he wrote film reviews for the weekly *Carteles*, of which he became editor from 1957 to 1960. His knowledge of film was wide-ranging, and his collection of film criticism from this period, *Un oficio del siglo XX* (1960; published in translation as *A Twentieth-Century Job*, 1991) is urbane and perceptive. In 1953 he married Marta Calvo, with whom he had two daughters, Carola

Guillermo Cabrera Infante (1929–2005), by Bryn Colton, 1985

and Ana. They divorced in 1961 and that same year he married the actress Miriam Gómez, a relationship which endured until his death.

When Fidel Castro came to power in 1959 Cabrera Infante initially supported the new regime. He was appointed a director of the new film institute (ICAIC) and also edited *Lunes de Revolución*, the weekly literary supplement of the communist newspaper, *Revolución*. He published his first book of short fiction, *Así en la paz como en la guerra* in 1960 (this was subsequently published in translation as *Writes of Passage*, 1993). In 1961 he clashed with the government over the censorship of the film *PM*, directed by his brother, and a polemical discussion appeared in *Lunes de Revolución*. The latter was closed down and Cabrera Infante banned from publishing. Distancing himself from increasing political control, he accepted appointment in 1962 as cultural attaché in Brussels, becoming chargé d'affaires in 1964–5.

In Brussels Cabrera Infante worked on what became his most acclaimed novel, *Tres tristes tigres* (1967; *Three Trapped Tigers*, 1971). The novel's tongue-twisting title perfectly captures its wit. It is a celebration of Havana's pre-revolutionary night life, full of word play, often humorous and sexual in nature. An initial note insists that it is an attempt to capture the human voice on the wing and that it is written in 'Cuban'. The linguistic improvisation and passages of rumination are reminiscent of jazz, by turns joyous and reflective. Displaying immense technical sophistication, the novel has little conventional narrative (the structure is akin to collage), but storytelling is not the point. It is an exploration of Havana voices, as well as having elements of scintillating parody, questioning the very nature of literary representation. Faulkner and Sterne are antecedents, but it is above all James Joyce (Cabrera Infante referred to him as 'J'aime Joys') who inspired the intoxicating invention. It won the prestigious Biblioteca Breve award in Spain.

Cabrera Infante returned to Havana in 1965 for his mother's funeral and then opted for exile and never returned. He initially went to Spain but the Franco regime refused him resident's status, and in 1966 he moved to London where he remained until his death, becoming a British citizen in 1979. In a BBC interview he later expressed the view that exile had made him a professional writer. But exile was demanding and he experienced severe depression, which curtailed his writing. He recovered and his later output was diverse. He wrote screenplays for the cinema (*Wonderwall*, 1968, and *Vanishing Point*, 1971) and adapted *Tres tristes tigres* for the screen (2005, as *The Lost City*). Other notable works of his exile years were *Vista del amanecer en el trópico* (1974; *A View of Dawn in the Tropics*, 1978), exploring the story of Cuba from discovery to the present; the experimental *Ejercicios de esti(l)o* (1976; 'Exercises in style'); a second volume of film writing, *Arcadia todas las noches* (1978; 'Arcadia every night'); and, above all, his second novel, *La Habana para un infante difunto* (1979; *Infante's Inferno*, 1984). This semi-autobiographical novel is a nostalgic examination of growing up in middle-class Havana during the 1940s and 1950s. He also published *Holy Smoke* (1985), a celebration of smoking (he was a devoted smoker of cigars), written in English. He won a Guggenheim fellowship in 1970, and the foreign book prize (France) in 1971.

Cabrera Infante's writings on Cuba under Castro were collected in *Mea Cuba* (1992), which reveals his contempt for the regime. In an interview in 1968 he attacked Castro, and he was then declared a traitor. He insisted that he was never a communist, but his anti-Castroism did not derive from a commitment to the right. In political terms he is probably best described as liberal. In his last years he remained prone to depression and illness. He died in Charing Cross Hospital on 21 February 2005 of MRSA and a chest infection caught after fracturing his hip. He was survived by his wife and the two daughters of his first marriage.

Cabrera Infante was the leading Cuban novelist of his generation and one of the most distinguished Latin American writers of his time. For his lifetime achievement he was awarded the Premio Cervantes in 1997, the leading literary award in the Spanish-speaking world. His masterpiece was *Tres tristes tigres*, but he had considerable achievements beyond that. He wrote with wit and elegance, and had a fascination with words and their plasticity that was allied to daring humour or sarcasm. He said that Havana was the greatest discovery of his life, and his themes and ideal readers undoubtedly remained Cuban. Never a political writer like other leading Latin American writers, none the less he articulated trenchant anti-Castro views. In Cuba *Tres tristes tigres* was classified as counter-revolutionary, and from 1968 until his death his books were banned. He remained devoted to the island of his birth and it was his wish that his ashes be kept for burial in Cuba after the death of Castro. MARK MILLINGTON

Sources R. D. Souza, *Guillermo Cabrera Infante: two islands, many worlds* (1996) · V. Smith, ed., *Encyclopedia of Latin American literature* (1997) · D. Balderston and M. Gonzalez, *Encyclopedia of Latin American and Caribbean Literature, 1900–2003* (2004) · *The Times* (23 Feb 2005) · *The Guardian* (23 Feb 2005) · *Daily Telegraph* (24 Feb 2005) · *The Independent* (24 Feb 2005) · personal knowledge (2009) · d. cert.

Archives Princeton University Library | SOUND BL NSA, documentary recordings

Likenesses B. Colton, photograph, 1985, Camera Press, London [*see illus.*] · photographs, 1987–98, Getty Images, London · photographs, 1998–2000, Camera Press, London · obituary photographs

Wealth at death £0—net: administration, 13 Feb 2006, *CGPLA Eng. & Wales*

Cadbury, Peter Egbert (1918–2006), aviator and businessman, was born on 6 February 1918 at 6 Kimberley Terrace, Great Yarmouth, the elder son of Sir Egbert Cadbury (1893–1967), then a flight commander in the Royal Naval Air Service, and his wife, Mary Forbes, *née* Phillips. He attended Leighton Park School, the Quaker establishment founded by his grandfather George Cadbury, a member of the Cadbury chocolate family, and then went to Trinity College, Cambridge. But his interests were fired more by the exploits of his father, a First World War air ace who shot down two zeppelins and was promoted air commodore before becoming managing director of the chocolate business (and being knighted in 1957).

Cadbury was taught to fly by his father at the age of seventeen and in 1940 he joined the Fleet Air Arm. He was seconded to the Ministry of Aircraft Production, where he became one of the test pilots assigned to test the new Meteor jet aircraft. It was a high-risk profession and many of his colleagues died. But Cadbury survived to become a caricature of the dashing pilot, rarely without a fast car, a pretty girl, and a gung-ho quip, and always looking for an argument. He rejoiced in his nickname, the Cad. When he married Eugénie Benedicta Down-Byrne at Westminster register office on 13 December 1947 the legendary fighter pilot Douglas Bader was best man. Cadbury's first wife was three years younger than him, daughter of Major Ewen Cameron Bruce, army officer, and the former wife of St John Down-Byrne. They had a son and a daughter.

In 1945 Cadbury had accepted an invitation from the Liberals to contest Stroud in the election of that year, because of his family's traditional links with the party. He reputedly told the electors, 'If you don't like any of [my views], I can change them because I only learned them yesterday' (*Daily Telegraph*, 18 April 2006). Nevertheless he still managed to win 30 per cent of the vote. Soon afterwards he joined his natural home, the Conservative Party, and spent eight years at the bar (1946–54). This included a spell as an assistant prosecutor at the Nuremberg trials, where he accompanied his godfather, the formidable Norman Birkett. He showed no interest in working for the family business and his own high-profile commercial exploits were later a contrast, and often an embarrassment, to the rigorous standards of corporate governance associated with his more strait-laced Cadbury cousins.

Cadbury's business career began in 1954 when he borrowed £75,000 from his father to buy the Keith Prowse ticket agency. Block bookings by Prowse could determine success or failure in the West End theatre and when Cadbury, who backed his own middlebrow tastes, declared that he only supported shows that his mother would like, John Osborne bemoaned the fact that plays should depend on 'catching the fancy of a tasteless man's tasteless mother' (*Daily Telegraph*, 18 April 2006). He floated the business in 1960 for £1.5 million, a rapid profit. He remained chairman until 1971, in spite of a rebellion by his fellow directors about his autocratic style in 1964.

Cadbury was attracted by the profits in commercial television, launched in 1955 and memorably described by Lord Thomson as 'a licence to print money'. He became a director of Tyne Tees in 1957. Then he sought what the *Daily Express* called 'the last big plum' (*Daily Express*, 17 Dec 1959), the west country franchise. He had few local connections and later described himself as driving down with only a copy of *Who's Who*. He still assembled a formidable consortium including the TUC, lord lieutenants, and Daphne du Maurier. It beat eleven other bids. Westward Television was launched on 29 April 1961. But extravagant spending on local promotion and an overrun on purpose-built studios combined with a new government-imposed advertising duty to bring an early crisis and lay-offs. Cadbury fulminated publicly against the duty and the encroachment of neighbouring franchises, and demanded the expansion of the region to take in Bristol. In 1970 the board voted him out; one member said he was 'sick and tired of his wild statements' (*Daily Telegraph*, 18 April 2006). However, he was back eight days later thanks to his control of the majority of voting shares.

Cadbury's control of Westward brought him to public notice. The station made a genuine connection with its region and was consistently regarded as the friendliest, if sometimes the most amateur, of the ITV stations. He ran it mainly from London. When he drove down to Plymouth in one of his fast cars—a Ferrari or a Bentley—he would head for the bar, the pretty girls, and the fruit machine. Many of the staff idolized him and he treated them with a mixture of challenging demand 'if at first you don't succeed, you are fired' (private information)—and encouraging delegation. As one producer put it, 'he was good to work for particularly when he wasn't there' (private information).

As television became more regulated, however, Cadbury's autocratic style and choleric behaviour, usually in full public view and often in the newspaper letter columns, led to problems. Speeding led to confrontations with the police, and he began a vendetta against the local chief constable, attempting to keep him off Westward transmissions. He was charged with wasting police time over an anonymous letter alleging local authority corruption and also for shooting protected geese. It didn't help that his letters were routinely written on Westward notepaper. When, in frustration with local airline services, Cadbury founded his own airline on the Westward budget, the licence renewal due in 1980 looked increasingly unlikely. His solution was to bring in Lord Harris of Greenwich, a former minister in the Home Office (which allocated the licences). The tactic backfired as Harris sniffed the political wind and told Cadbury that with his behaviour, they did not stand 'a snowball's chance in hell' of renewal. Harris persuaded the board to vote him out but the staff petitioned for reinstatement. Cadbury reluctantly decided not to force the issue and left the company in early 1980. When the franchise was refused, he sent Harris a telegram asking what it was like 'to be a snowball in hell' (*The Guardian*, 27 April 2006). Later he attempted and failed to buy MG and the Playboy Club but bizarrely acquired a loss-making magazine, *Working Woman*, where he sacked the feminist editor and soon closed it.

Cadbury's first marriage was dissolved in 1968 and on 15 April 1970, at Kensington register office, he married Jennifer Mary Victoria Morgan-Jones (later well known as the businesswoman Jennifer *D'Abo (1945–2003)), whom he had employed at Keith Prowse. The daughter of Michael William Vernon Hammond-Maude, land agent, she had already supported him through Westward crises and he later explained their divorce in 1976 by saying that 'she was a better entrepreneur than I am' (*Daily Telegraph*, 18 April 2006). They had a son. On 29 July 1976 he married, as his third wife, at Chelsea register office, (Angela) Jane Mead, a 36-year-old divorcee, and daughter of Harry St George, army officer. They had two sons. Cadbury meanwhile ran through a succession of grand country houses, where he regularly quarrelled with neighbours, at Preston Candover, near Basingstoke, Hampshire, where he had his own airstrip, at Lyneham House in Devon, where he complained of 'police harassment', and finally at Upton Grey Lodge, Upton Grey, also near Basingstoke. When it was burgled in 1994, he resigned from the Conservative Party criticizing its failure on law and order, and announced that he slept with a shotgun under his pillow. In 1999 thieves broke in again and their haul included his shotgun. He replaced it with a crossbow. Over 400 of his former staff turned out at a dinner in his honour in 2001, and others regularly visited after he suffered a major stroke in 2004. He died of a further stroke at Upton Grey Lodge on 17 April 2006, and was survived by his third wife, Jane, and five children. MARTIN ADENEY

Sources *Daily Telegraph* (18 April 2006) · *The Independent* (21 April 2006) · *The Guardian* (27 April 2006) · *The Stage* (3 May 2006) · www.users.zetnet.co.uk/itw/Westward/history.html, 11 May 2009 · *WW* (2006) · private information (2010) · b. cert. · m. certs. · d. cert.

Archives FILM BFINA, documentary footage

Likenesses photograph, 1988, Photoshot, London · photographs, 1991–9, Rex Features, London · A. Davidson, photograph, 1999, Photoshot, London · N. Rogers, photograph, repro. in *The Guardian* (27 April 2006)

Wealth at death £4,994,303: probate, 9 Oct 2006, *CGPLA Eng. & Wales*

Cahn, Robert Wolfgang (1924–2007), materials scientist, was born on 9 September 1924 in Fürth, Bavaria, the first of two children of Martin Cahn (1896–1963), accountant and merchant, and his wife, Else, *née* Heinemann (1896–1962). His family was Jewish, assimilated into the business community. His maternal grandfather, Hugo Heinemann, co-founder of a successful glass-finishing business in Fürth, recognized early the danger posed by Nazism, deposited a large portion of his fortune outside Germany, and in September 1933 arranged for the family to escape to Zürich, ostensibly for a skiing holiday. Cahn's father moved to establish a business in London, while Cahn, his mother, and sister, Irene, settled in Palma, Mallorca, where he attended the École Internationale. In 1936 the family was further dispersed by the Spanish Civil War, Cahn ultimately joining his father while the rest of the family stayed in Italy and Switzerland, returned to Spain in 1940 and then to Germany in 1948.

In England Cahn attended the Maiden Erlegh boarding school. Aged fifteen, and with his father interned as an enemy alien, he sought a better education in the sciences and enrolled at Haberdashers' Aske's Boys' School in Cricklewood, north-west London. After a few weeks his father's concern about the blitz and a near miss in the bombing led to a move to Workington technical school in Cumberland. He entered Trinity College, Cambridge, in 1942 to read metallurgy. In September 1945 he started his PhD work under Egon Orowan at the Cavendish Laboratory, and thus began his research career on the structure and deformation of metals and alloys. While an undergraduate his interest in mountaineering led to his meeting Patricia Lois (*b.* 1926), daughter of Daniel Hanson, head of the department of physical metallurgy at Birmingham; they married at Cambridge register office on 26 July 1947, and had two sons and two daughters. He became a British citizen the same year.

In October 1947 Cahn left Cambridge to complete work for his PhD degree at the Atomic Energy Research Establishment, Harwell, working under Bruce Chalmers. In 1951 he moved to a lectureship at the physical metallurgy department at Birmingham and in 1962 to a professorship focused on semiconductor materials at the University College of North Wales, Bangor. Soon recognizing this as not a good fit with his interests, in 1965 he was appointed, at Sussex, to the UK's first professorship of materials science. He was involved in setting up the Science Policy Research Unit, and later became dean of the school of engineering and applied science (1973–8). In 1981 he took up the chair in metallurgy at the University of Paris XI, but found that French academic bureaucracy left little opportunity for research. In 1983 he retired to Cambridge, where in 1986 his former department (now the department of materials science and metallurgy) elected him to an honorary distinguished research fellowship. He remained an active scholar until his death.

Cahn was one of the creators of the modern academic discipline of materials science, its development chronicled in his book *The Coming of Materials Science* (2001). He was a founding editor of the *Journal of Nuclear Materials*, the

Robert Wolfgang Cahn (1924–2007), by Godfrey Argent, 1992

Journal of Materials Science, and *Intermetallics*, and an inaugural principal editor of the *Journal of Materials Research*. His multi-author text, *Physical Metallurgy* (1965), went into four editions, the last two edited jointly with Peter Haasen. Twenty years (1972–92) as an editor of the Cambridge Solid State Science Series were followed by co-editing *Materials Science and Technology: a Comprehensive Treatment* (1991–2000) and the Pergamon Materials Series. Cahn also served as section editor, editor, or co-editor of the *Encyclopedia of Materials Science and Engineering* and the *Encyclopedia of Advanced Materials*. His interests in materials ranged very widely; his 'News and views' articles in *Nature* (many collected in *Artifice and Artefacts: 100 Essays in Materials Science*, 1992) were particularly notable, making him a source of reference in fields well outside his own specialism.

In his PhD work Cahn found that metallic single crystals, after plastic deformation and annealing, reformed into a series of strain-free crystallites. Together with Alan Cottrell he showed that his observations could only reasonably be explained by dislocation rearrangement into walls, termed 'polygonization'. This was a metallurgical breakthrough, being the first unambiguous experimental evidence for dislocations (hypothesized in 1934) that are the basis for understanding the plasticity of metals. At Harwell he performed important early work on the plastic flow of uranium, elucidating the mechanism of deformation twinning. His later research ranged widely, with authoritative studies of recrystallization, ordering in alloys and intermetallics and its effects on creep and ductility, rapid solidification of alloys, and metallic glasses.

Cahn was elected a fellow of the Royal Society in 1991. He was elected to academies in Germany, China, Spain, and India, and held further honours from the USA, France, and Italy. He travelled extensively, and had a very international outlook on science. He was eager to promote the careers of others, and to recognize new ideas from young scientists. He had many deep interests outside science: mountains, music, art, literature, and photography. He died at the Nuffield Hospital, Cambridge, on 9 April 2007, of myeloid leukaemia, and was survived by his wife and their four children. A. LINDSAY GREER

Sources H. M. Chan, introduction, *Journal of Materials Science* [special issue dedicated to Robert W. Cahn], 39 (2004), 3861 · R. W. Cahn, *The art of belonging* (2005) · *Daily Telegraph* (4 May 2007) · *The Times* (7 May 2007) · *The Guardian* (22 May 2007) · *Materials Today*, 10/6 (June 2007), 57 · *Nature Materials*, 6 (July 2007); www.nature.com/naturematerials, 13 July 2010 · *WW* (2007) · personal knowledge (2011) · private information (2011) · m. cert. · d. cert.

Likenesses G. Argent, photograph, 1992, RS [*see illus.*] · obituary photographs · photograph, repro. in www.nature.com/nmat/journal/v6/n7/full/nmat1941.html

Wealth at death £349,420: probate, 21 Jan 2008, *CGPLA Eng. & Wales*

Calder, Angus Lindsay Ritchie (1942–2008), historian and literary critic, was born at Cedar Court Nursing Home, Sutton, Surrey, on 5 February 1942, the second son and third of the five children of Peter Ritchie *Calder, later Baron Ritchie-Calder (1906–1982), journalist and author, and his wife, Mabel Jane Forbes, *née* McKail (1906–2001). Educated at Wallington county grammar school and King's College, Cambridge, where he read English literature, he was active in student politics and, like his father, a socialist and supporter of the Campaign for Nuclear Disarmament. On 1 October 1963 he married Jennifer Rachel (Jenni) Daiches (*b.* 1941), historian and literary scholar, and daughter of the literary historian David *Daiches. They lived at first in London, where Calder completed a PhD thesis on the wartime Common Wealth Party under the supervision of Asa Briggs at the University of Sussex. He was also at work on *The People's War: Britain, 1939–1945* (1969), a prodigiously researched narrative that challenged conventional accounts of unity and solidarity on the home front.

Published to widespread acclaim, *The People's War* would have guaranteed Calder a full-time academic career if he had wanted one. He opted instead for the life of a freelance, living off the proceeds of literary work and occasional teaching jobs. After three years (1968–71) during which he and Jenni taught at the University of Nairobi, they set up home in Edinburgh with their children, a boy and two girls. In 1979 Calder was appointed staff tutor in arts at the Open University in Scotland, a role well suited to his romantic socialist convictions. An inspirational tutor and lecturer, he journeyed far and wide meeting tutors and students, but took early retirement in 1993 with the title of reader in cultural studies. 'It seems clear to me', he wrote in 2003, 'that every child should be encouraged to deviate as far as possible from careerist norms' (*Gods, Mongrels and Demons*, 4).

In 1971 Calder embarked on another *magnum opus*, a one-volume history of the British empire. It soon expanded into a proposal for three volumes, of which the first, *Revolutionary Empire: the Rise of the English-speaking Empires from the 15th Century to the 1780s*, was published in 1981. A dazzling blend of stupendous research, narrative art, and provocative argument, enriched by his own travels to parts of the former empire, it was probably his most important book, but the response was appreciative rather than enthusiastic: imperial topics lacked the emotional resonance of the home front. Having twice climbed an academic Everest, Calder may perhaps have lacked the stamina for another ascent. At any rate the second and third volumes never appeared and his writing increasingly took the form of essays and shorter works.

History was only ever one component of Calder's literary life. A prominent literary critic, editor, and commentator, he wrote a history of Russian fiction from Pushkin to Chekhov, a study of Byron and Scotland, and luminous introductions to classics by Sir Walter Scott, Charles Dickens, and Evelyn Waugh. An enthusiast for the post-colonial literature of Africa and the Caribbean, he co-edited the *Journal of Commonwealth Literature* from 1981 to 1987. The Scottish strands in his work, always present, multiplied in response to the cultural debates stimulated by the rise of nationalism. He co-edited three volumes of the uncollected writings of Hugh MacDiarmid and published two collections of essays on the myths and realities of Scottishness: *Revolving Culture: Notes from the Scottish Republic* (1994) and *Scotlands of the Mind* (2002). Politically he described himself as a 'socialist home ruler' (*Revolving Culture*, vii).

Calder was contemptuous of Thatcherite values but generous in the range of his sympathy for individuals, which transcended ideology. Rebels, romantics, and oddballs all commanded his interest and admiration. Intellectually he towered above most of his contemporaries but his modesty was genuine. In his own estimation he probably never matched up to the exacting standards he set himself. Nor was he entirely confident of his identity as a Scot or his credentials as a man of the people. In *The Myth of the Blitz* (1990) he revised *The People's War* by deconstructing what he saw as an English national myth of 1940. In a sense the book was an apology for his English upbringing and accent and relatively privileged background. 'All your life', wrote his friend Joy Hendry, 'you longed to wrench the shining spoon of privilege from your mouth … to know the sweat and strain of workers in the fields and factories and to sing the songs in their hearts' (Berengarten and Calder, 51).

Calder suffered bouts of depression which he relieved with alcohol, cigarettes, and the camaraderie of the pub. His growing dependence on drink contributed to the break-up of his first marriage in 1982. On 19 December 1986 he married Catherine Janet (Kate) Kyle, *née* Young (*b.* 1949), a schoolteacher, and daughter of William Young, a scientific and technical officer in the Ministry of Defence. They had one son. Eventually, however, his second marriage also broke up and Calder opted for a bohemian existence in a city centre flat whence he could sally forth to the theatres, bookshops, and howffs of Tollcross. Sadly his descent into alcoholism continued and plunged him into predicaments from which he had to be rescued by long-suffering friends, but something of his old creativity remained.

Ever since Cambridge Calder had written and published occasional verse, and he was one of the prime movers in the establishment of the Scottish Poetry Library in 1984. Poetry was his spiritual home: in the company of his fellow 'makars', with a bottle of malt whisky to hand, he was halfway to paradise. The publication in 1997 of a collection of his poems, *Waking in Waikato*, marked a late flowering in the course of which he published another four volumes of verse. *Horace in Tollcross* (2000), an updating of the Odes of Horace, gave enduring expression to his caustic wit, his most tender feelings, and his reaffirmation of life in the shadow of his approaching death. In 2007 he suffered a loss of short-term memory and in 2008 he was diagnosed with lung cancer and transferred to the Elsie Inglis Nursing Home in Spring Gardens, Edinburgh. 'It's been a helter-skelter existence', he told one of his visitors, 'and mainly my own fault' (private information). He died in the nursing home on 5 June 2008 and was survived by his four children. PAUL ADDISON

Sources J. Calder, *Not Nebuchadnezzar: in search of identities* (2005) • *The Scotsman* (6 June 2008) • *The Herald* [Glasgow] (6 June 2008) • *The Guardian* (10 June 2008); (14 June 2008) • *The Independent* (10 June 2008) • *Daily Telegraph* (13 June 2008) • *The Times* (16 June 2008); (21 June 2008) • *Times Higher Education Supplement* (26 June 2008) • R. Berengarten and G. Calder, eds., *For Angus: poems, prose, sketches and music, May–July 2008* (2009) • *History Workshop Journal*, 70 (autumn 2010), 299–304 • *Chapman*, 110 (2010) • personal knowledge (2012) • private information (2012) • b. cert. • m. certs. • d. cert.

Archives NL Scot., papers | FILM BFINA, current affairs footage | SOUND BL NSA, current affairs, documentary and performance recordings

Likenesses obituary photographs

Callaghan, Leonard James [Jim], **Baron Callaghan of Cardiff** (**1912–2005**), prime minister, was born at 38 Funtington Road, Copnor, Portsmouth, on 27 March 1912, the only son and younger child of James Callaghan, formerly Garoghan (1877–1921), a sailor who rose to the rank of chief petty officer in the Royal Navy, and his wife, Charlotte Gertrude, widow of Daniel Speare, seaman, and daughter of William Henry Cundy, naval shipwright, of Tavistock, Devon. His sister, Dorothy, was born in 1904.

Family, marriage, and early career Petty Officer James Callaghan was of Irish descent (his grandfather had left Ireland at the time of the potato famine). He had changed his name from Garoghan, without recourse to deed polls, when he joined the fleet. He was by birth and upbringing a Roman Catholic. But when he met and fell in love with Charlotte Speare, a Baptist, he left the church after being refused permission to marry her and became a member of a Baptist chapel. His decision was to prove crucial to the life of his son. Although there is much doubt about how much belief Callaghan retained into adult life, the nonconformist ethic was a profound influence on all of his public and private life. By telling his son stories of ships and the sea Callaghan's father also encouraged in the young boy a romantic attachment to all things naval that, although uncharacteristic of his essentially down-to-earth character, remained with him for all his life.

After the First World War Callaghan's father left the Royal Navy and became a coastguard at Brixham (where Callaghan attended Furzeham School). Three years later, at the early age of forty-four, he died suddenly of a heart attack. Callaghan was nine. From then on his mother was the dominant influence in his life. But his attachment to his father's memory never faded. In 1975 he had decided that his duties as foreign secretary—particularly the renegotiation of the United Kingdom's membership of the European Community—would make it impossible for him to accompany the queen on a visit which took the royal yacht down the Kiel Canal. It was not a decision that he took lightly or with any great pleasure, for he was an ardent admirer of the queen. However, on the day before *HMS Britannia* was due to set sail he sent for his minister of state—the reluctant substitute—and said that he had changed his mind. Affairs of state would have to wait. He had discovered that on the only previous occasion when the royal yacht had sailed that way his father had been on board. Callaghan was determined to make a devotional repetition of the journey.

After her husband's unexpected death, and the consequent loss of the coastguard's house in Brixham, Charlotte Callaghan returned with her children to Portsmouth, where they lived in a variety of rented properties and varying degrees of poverty. Leonard, as he was then called, attended Portsmouth northern secondary school—and found it generally unsatisfactory. One of the landladies, of whom the Callaghans were subtenants, encouraged them to rejoice at the election of Ramsay MacDonald's Labour Government in 1924. The family's allegiance was cemented by the award, after a long battle, of a naval widow's pension—16*s*. a week with an additional 10*s*. for her son.

Callaghan borrowed books from the Carnegie Library in Portsmouth, but the real influence on his adolescence was the Baptist church. At the age of fourteen, a year before his formal baptism, he became a Sunday school teacher. A year later he took the Oxford senior certificate. He passed

Leonard James [Jim] **Callaghan, Baron Callaghan of Cardiff (1912–2005)**, by Bryan Organ, 1983

with second-class honours. This qualified him for employment by the Inland Revenue. At the age of seventeen he became a clerk in the Maidstone office on a salary of one pound a week plus cost of living allowances. The Portsmouth Baptists made sure that their Kent co-religionists found him comfortable, and respectable, lodgings.

In 1934, four years after he joined the Inland Revenue, Callaghan became a trade unionist. His membership of the Association of the Officers of Taxes was, initially, prompted more by the attraction of the correspondence courses they offered than by a feeling of class solidarity or the hope of becoming part of an irresistible movement for improved wages and conditions. Nevertheless he became impatient with what he regarded as the incompetence of the local branch and the inefficiency of the national organization and successfully contested the election for branch secretary, defeating the long-serving incumbent. He was regarded, for the first and perhaps only time in his life, as a young revolutionary—particularly by Douglas Houghton, the effective head of the union (who was later to serve as chancellor of the duchy of Lancaster in the 1964 Labour government). Promoted to the London office, he became an official of the union's City East branch and was reconciled with Houghton, who recognized that the man who became his protégé was ambitious not anarchic.

Perhaps Callaghan had been tamed by a seismic change in his personal life. At the Maidstone Baptist church he met Audrey Elizabeth Moulton (1913–2005), then only sixteen but, like Callaghan, a Sunday school teacher. It was something approaching love at first sight, and it lasted for a lifetime. Callaghan's feelings were illustrated by an uncharacteristic willingness to embrace energetic physical activity. He joined the local tennis club, though he did not excel. The relationship was cemented by his almost instant acceptance by the Moulton family. Frank Moulton, Audrey's father, was the managing director of a Maidstone machine-tool company and deacon of the Baptist church. On Callaghan's promotion to the London office he was neither surprised by, nor opposed to, his daughter following. Audrey Moulton registered at the Battersea College of Domestic Science. She qualified as a teacher and began work in a school in Eltham. Many of her evenings were spent—in a combination of conviction and companionship—at Fabian Society meetings. She and Callaghan married on 28 July 1938 at the Baptist chapel in Maidstone, with Audrey's parents as witnesses. They had two daughters, Margaret (*b.* 1939), later Baroness Jay of Paddington, and Julia (*b.* 1942), and a son, Michael (*b.* 1945).

In August 1936 Callaghan had stood for election as full-time assistant general secretary of the union. He won against a selection of more experienced candidates, and also Cyril Plant, who became both president of the union and chairman of the Trades Union Congress (and was an invaluable ally of his old opponent during the Labour government's fractious negotiations with the unions in the turbulent 1970s). Callaghan's salary was spectacularly improved. The basic pound a week of his apprenticeship had increased to £2 16*s.* a week with an allowance of £30 a year. Both Callaghan and the union prospered. The assistant general secretary, happy in suburban Norwood, began to meet the great names of the trade union and labour movement and always treated them—as throughout his life he treated everyone—with a mixture of courtesy, genuine interest, and cautious suspicion. Later in 1936 the association joined with the National Association of Assessors and Collectors of Taxes and the Valuation Office Clerical Association to form the Inland Revenue Staff Federation—a union of which Callaghan initially aspired one day to become general secretary. But by 1940 his ambition had grown and, much to Douglas Houghton's distress, he applied first to be general secretary of the Ministry of Labour Staff Association then general secretary of the Federation of Post Office Supervising Officers. Neither application was successful.

War service and early political career Technically a civil servant, Callaghan was in a 'reserved occupation' following the outbreak of the Second World War. But in June 1940—perhaps the low point of the allies' fortunes, for the war in France had just ended with the evacuation of Dunkirk—he applied to join the Royal Navy and was told he could enlist as an ordinary seaman. His release from the Inland Revenue Staff Association required Douglas Houghton's approval. It was not given until the autumn of 1942, so Callaghan did not get to sea until the summer of 1943. In April 1944 he was promoted sub-lieutenant and was about to see active service when he was diagnosed as suffering from a mild form of tuberculosis. After his discharge from hospital he was employed writing a manual on Japan, its people and customs, in preparation for victory in the Far East. But, eventually, he saw action of a sort. On VE-day he was on board *HMS Queen Elizabeth* on its way to cover the allies' landing at Rangoon.

The months ashore, although regretted and resented, had in reality been a stroke of good fortune. At some point—possibly before his naval service, for his latter-day detractors claimed that it was the reason why he volunteered—Callaghan had decided to aim for a seat in parliament. Once again there were objections from the union and once again Callaghan dismissed them out of hand. Hopes in co. Durham, Birmingham, and Reading were not realized. But he was selected for Cardiff South—beating, in the final ballot, George Thomas, who was later to become speaker of the House of Commons. According to Thomas's biography—which Callaghan greeted with the comment 'Until I read it, I thought that we were friends'—he introduced himself by saying 'My family call me Leonard, but for politics I'm going to use my second name James' (Thomas, 49). Whatever the truth of the story, James (or, more often, Jim) is what he became.

Callaghan was a personable candidate, appearing at meetings in his naval uniform and then, as always, careful that his shoes were polished and his trousers creased. But his success in the selection process for Cardiff South, by a single vote, might well have been the result of his reputation as a 'genuine socialist' preceding him to Wales. At the Labour Party conference, in December 1944, Ian

Mikardo (the successful aspirant to the Reading candidature) had moved a resolution that committed a future Labour government to the public ownership of the basic industries. Jim Callaghan had supported it with a call for a 'restatement of our fundamental principles' (*Report of the Labour Party Conference*, 1944, 169). When the resolution was carried—against the wishes of the leadership—Herbert Morrison, deputy leader and once the philosopher of public ownership, told its supporters 'You've lost us the general election' (I. Mikardo, *Back-bencher*, 1988, 77). In fact Labour won 393 seats to the Conservatives' 213 in the election of July 1945. Callaghan defeated his tory opponent with a majority of 5944.

Callaghan's maiden speech on 20 August 1945 dealt—with an absence of party polemic appropriate to such occasions—with the difficulty of establishing a stable government in defeated Japan. He received the usual formal congratulations and spent the next few weeks working, assiduously, on questions related to taxes, the subject he knew best, and Wales, the topic which he was expected to air. He was invited to join the XYZ Club—a Labour group that was usually confined to professional economists. To less surprise at the time than the memory of the event caused thirty years later, he exhibited both his independence of mind and radical inclinations by voting (alongside more durable left-wingers) against the $3.75 billion American loan that John Maynard Keynes had negotiated with the American treasury. He was not called during the debate that endorsed the decision. But later that day, during a discussion on the civil war in China, he referred (gratuitously, his critics thought) to 'economic aggression by the United States' and declared that 'as a socialist' he demanded international control of industrial investment (*Hansard 5C*, 417.750 13 Dec 1945). As a result of his rebellion he was forced to step down from the first rung of the promotion ladder. He had, briefly, been parliamentary private secretary to the under-secretary for the colonies.

The trivial set-back did not dampen Callaghan's radical ardour. In October 1946 he was one of twenty-two backbenchers—most of whom were involved in the Keep Left group—who signed a letter calling for a more sympathetic attitude towards the Soviet Union and was open in his criticism of, perhaps even hostile towards, Ernest Bevin as foreign secretary. But he was increasingly regarded as a 'coming man'. Hugh Dalton, who usually only cultivated young Oxbridge 'intellectuals', added Callaghan to his protégés. And in October 1946 he was invited to join a parliamentary delegation to Russia. It was led by A. V. Alexander, the first lord of the Admiralty, who insisted that Sub-Lieutenant Callaghan, still not formally demobilized, should travel in his naval uniform. Although Callaghan continued to express reservations about some government policies he managed, with remarkable facility, to avoid being labelled as a pathological rebel. Nevertheless, when in October 1947 he joined the government as parliamentary secretary to the Ministry of Transport it was not clear whether his promotion owed most to a recognition of his undoubted ability or the wish to stifle his criticism.

Largely thanks to Dalton's patronage, in the summer of 1950 Callaghan was asked to act as deputy leader of the British delegation to the Council of Europe—an unusual appointment for a serving minister. It was his first experience of the conflicting claims of national interest and European unity, and he gladly articulated the government's belief that no international institution should diminish the sovereign powers of national governments. It was a view that he was to hold until, in 1976, he attended a meeting of foreign ministers in Schloss Gymnich and became convinced that, in some particulars, co-operation was better than competition.

The general election of 1950 (which, after boundary redistribution, Callaghan fought and won as candidate for Cardiff South-East) marked the effective end of what had been one of the great radical administrations of the twentieth century. In the reshuffle that followed Labour's victory Callaghan became parliamentary and financial secretary to the Admiralty—not technically a promotion, but a clear sign of growing importance as the first lord, Viscount Hall, was in the upper house and his junior minister had, therefore, to answer for all naval matters in the Commons.

After the Conservative victory in November 1951 Callaghan was ideally placed to represent a new generation of MPs in the Labour leadership. Only two MPs from the 1945 intake were elected to the post-election shadow cabinet. The parliamentary party shrewdly chose two future prime ministers: Jim Callaghan and Harold Wilson. Callaghan became spokesman on transport, often the graveyard of ambition, and then on fuel and power, but found more excitement (as well as important additions to his income) in journalism and broadcasting. His weekly column for the *Women's Sunday Mirror* had the dated title of 'The intelligent women's guide to world affairs', and the 'Free speech' debates on BBC television often ended in a verbal brawl. But the young shadow minister was becoming known to the general public. Together with his appointment as parliamentary adviser to the Police Federation (on an annual retainer of £500 a year, with £300 expenses) his freelance employment removed all financial worries. His family was secure in their modern flat overlooking Blackheath. It was at this time that Audrey Callaghan began to play her own part in public life. It culminated—after some years on the London county council—in her becoming chairman of Great Ormond Street Children's Hospital. Her work there was so distinguished that Margaret Thatcher, when prime minister, wanted her to become a dame of the British empire. Audrey Callaghan declined with thanks.

There is little doubt that Jim Callaghan agreed to advise the Police Federation (effectively the trade union of junior officers) for no better reason than that he wanted the money. But once on the pay roll he became emotionally committed to their cause. That was always his way. The trade unions, the Royal Navy, the police: once an association was established, his loyalty was unwavering, and his pride in the various partnerships was never hidden. As chancellor of the exchequer he described his economic policy 'in the old naval term, steady as she goes' (*The Times*,

12 April 1967), and he told Rear-Admiral Morgan Giles MP, 'I have never slept in the captain's cabin, but I have slung my hammock on the quarterdeck'. His abiding, and obvious, affection for the police and the trade unions was to prove a source of both strength and pain. In his years in Downing Street he was more loyal to them than they were to him.

After a brief period as spokesman on education (a subject that, over the years, he continually claimed to be his primary interest) Callaghan succeeded Aneurin Bevan as shadow colonial secretary in 1956. It was a period of colonial transition. Iain Macleod became colonial secretary in 1959 with a clear mandate to dissolve the empire—a view that Alan Lennox-Boyd, his predecessor, had not shared. But the dissolution of empire proved barely less painful than its acquisition. The idea of federation, in the Caribbean and in Central Africa, although fashionable in Britain was unpopular in the colonies themselves. Callaghan was deputy leader of a parliamentary delegation to the Central African Federation that, in a unanimous report, predicted that the union of Nyasaland and the two Rhodesias would only succeed if the African population within them was given a stronger voice in the eventual government. The predictions proved depressingly correct and unrest turned into open revolt. After a state of emergency was declared and nationalist leaders arrested in 1959, Macleod asked Lord Monckton of Brenchley—sometime adviser to Edward VIII, tory cabinet minister, and friend of Sir Stafford Cripps—to chair a royal commission to inquire into the federation's future. Callaghan was asked to become a member, an appointment that required him to be a member of the privy council. Membership was offered him but, according to his autobiography and an account he gave to the cabinet during a discussion on the 'Lib-Lab pact', he replied that to accept the distinction from a Conservative prime minister would be like 'a Welsh rugby forward accepting an English cap' (*Time and Chance*, 142). In fact he disagreed with the commission's terms of referral. It should, in his opinion, have been empowered to consider the desirability of any one of the constituent states seceding from the federation.

In 1960—Harold Macmillan's 'never had it so good' election having secured the third consecutive Conservative victory a year before—Aneurin Bevan died, leaving vacant the post of shadow foreign secretary. Harold Wilson was chosen to succeed him and Callaghan became the shadow chancellor. After fifteen years in the House of Commons he had become an indisputable member of the Labour leadership. Three years later that status was confirmed when in February 1963, after Hugh Gaitskell's death, he stood for election as leader of the Labour Party. It is impossible to believe that he ever thought that he could win—an assumption supported by the brevity with which the subject was dealt in his autobiography. It is far more likely that he was establishing his credentials as one of Labour's 'big three'. He came bottom of the poll with just forty-one votes and, like many candidates in subsequent Labour leadership contests, boasted about the quality rather than the size of his support. He was particularly flattered by the endorsement of Tony Crosland, a man of vastly different background and temperament. It was Crosland, not Roy Jenkins, he chose to make foreign secretary in 1976.

Chancellor of the exchequer, 1964–7 Reginald Maudling—shadowed as chancellor of the exchequer by Callaghan for two years before the 1964 election—believed that the solution to Britain's economic malaise was expansion at all costs. The result was increased pressure on the already precarious pound. When Labour won the election with an overall majority of four seats Callaghan was required to wrestle with a sterling crisis that was likely to be exacerbated by the arrival of a government in which international creditors did not repose immediate confidence. Maudling, packing to leave the chancellor's residence in Downing Street, passed on the torch to his successor with an apology: 'Sorry old cock to leave it in this shape. I suggested to Alec [Douglas-Home] this morning that perhaps we should put the bank rate up but he thought it best to leave it to you' (*Time and Chance*, 162). Callaghan was about to make the first of the two great mistakes which removed at least a little of the shine from an otherwise glittering career.

On the day that Callaghan became chancellor Harold Wilson, the new prime minister, called a meeting in Downing Street to discuss the outline of government economic policy. Only two other ministers were present, Callaghan and George Brown, the first secretary of state for economic affairs, and head of the new department that was supposed, when pitted against the Treasury, to provide the energy that comes from 'creative tension'. In the months that lay ahead the tension was more apparent than the creativity. But at that first meeting of the Labour government the two ministers—and the four senior officials who accompanied them—were unanimous in support of the wrong decision. It was agreed that the pound should not be devalued, virtually without discussion and completely without thought of consulting cabinet colleagues.

It was later often argued that Callaghan—despite taking a course in economics while a visiting fellow of Nuffield College, Oxford—lacked the intellectual self-confidence to argue against the decision not to devalue. In fact the decision was based more on patriotism and politics than economics. Wilson, Callaghan, and Brown took an old-fashioned pride in the integrity of sterling. Devaluation was, to them, capitulation. It was also a betrayal. Two years later, during his visit to see President Lyndon Johnson in Washington, Callaghan asked a young backbencher—who had impatiently argued for devaluation back in 1964—if he realized that the pound was a reserved currency and that to have reduced its value would have been to rob the developing nations of the Commonwealth that held sterling balances in the Bank of England. There was also the government's reputation to consider. To economists devaluation was no more than an economic adjustment. To the general public it was both a humiliation and proof that Britain was a step nearer to bankruptcy. Ramsay MacDonald (admittedly after he formed the National Government) and Clem Attlee had both presided over a devaluation. Wilson and his ministers did not want it to seem a Labour habit.

Callaghan's first budget had therefore to respond to the nation's traditional weakness with traditional methods. The reduction in international confidence and the inevitable run on sterling that followed was to be combated with spending cuts of approaching £240 million—though the increases in pensions, national assistance, and national insurance benefits (promised in the budget) were honoured. The standard rates of income tax and petrol duty were increased by 6*d.* and a new capital gains tax and corporation tax were introduced. The hope that the bank rate would not have to be raised was confounded within days. On 23 November 1964 it was increased by two points to 7 per cent.

The balance of payments deficit was tackled by an 'import surcharge', a temporary financial imposition which was intended to make foreign purchases more expensive and therefore less attractive. The European Free Trade Area, of which Britain had retained its membership after President de Gaulle vetoed the application to join the Common Market, claimed that the scheme was an infringement of Britain's treaty obligations. The foreign secretary, at an EFTA summit meeting, had to agree to limiting the life of a policy that was clearly an inhibition on free trade. But the crisis, which could not be avoided, had been postponed. An electioneering budget on St David's day 1966, which included the promise of a decimalized currency, was followed by a general election on the last day of March, which Labour won with an overall majority of ninety-six seats. The chancellor of the exchequer's stock was high. In the autumn of 1967 he was elected treasurer of the Labour Party with an automatic seat on the national executive. It was an eminence which could not last—though for a time public attention was diverted from the economy by the rebellion in Rhodesia and the attempts by George Brown (transferred from the Department of Economic Affairs to the Foreign Office) to prepare the way for another British application to join the Common Market.

A forced devaluation was only a matter of time. It came on 18 November 1967, the day that the trade figures for October were released showing a monthly deficit of £107 million, the largest on record. What doubts there might have been about taking that drastic decision were removed on 16 November when Robert Sheldon (a Labour back-bencher and accountant) asked, during questions to the chancellor of the exchequer, if Callaghan would confirm that a £1000 million loan had been negotiated with foreign banks. The question was followed by supplementary questions about the prospects of devaluation. Despite Callaghan's impassive procrastination £1500 million was lost in twenty-four hours in an attempt to prop up sterling. The chancellor's performance got very near to deceiving the House of Commons. Everyone agreed that deception had been justified. Callaghan made a statement to the House of Commons that spoke of both his 'great personal regret' and the prospects of 'a lasting and substantial improvement in the balance of payments'. Iain Macleod, the shadow chancellor, accused the chancellor of having 'broken faith' 'devalued his word'. He ended his philippic with the dubious compliment that, since Callaghan was 'an honourable man, he should resign' (*Hansard 5C*, 754.939, 20 Nov 1967).

Home secretary, 1967–70 After defending his decision in the House of Commons debate, Callaghan told the prime minister that he must return to the back benches. Wilson urged him to stay. Callaghan agreed and asked to become secretary of state for education and science. That, the prime minister said, was too junior a portfolio. A move there would look like punitive demotion. The best—and easiest—solution would be a straight swap with Roy Jenkins at the Home Office. Callaghan took up the new post on 30 November. The new department was to prove his passport to the triumphs that were to follow.

Callaghan's period as home secretary began badly. On 20 February 1968, following a number of suspicious deaths in Fulham and Acton, he informed the House of Commons that 'the murderers' had been arrested—and refused, absolutely, to apologize for stigmatizing the men while they were still only suspects. But he dealt with the anti-Vietnam war protests outside the American embassy in Grosvenor Square with a mixture of strength and sensibility that the public applauded. He received—generally unfairly—much criticism for the introduction of the 1968 Commonwealth Immigrants Bill. He began the press conference at which the bill was unveiled with the announcement—brazen in the opinion of many of his critics—that the proposed legislation was the work of Jenkins, his predecessor at the Home Office. The disclaimer was an indication of his acceptance that succeeding the conspicuously 'liberal' Jenkins would be a difficult task. But it was also a tacit admission that the bill was a moral embarrassment to a government that prided itself on taking a stand against racism. When Kenya and Uganda had been granted independence the British government of the day had made an explicit promise to the Asian minorities within those countries that if the process of 'Africanization' drove them out of east Africa, they could always find a home in Britain. The Commonwealth Immigrants Bill legalized the breaking of that promise. But there were other initiatives that illustrated Callaghan's own libertarian instincts. Rudi Dutschke, a German radical, was, despite a tabloid outcry, allowed into Britain to study for a research degree at Cambridge. And Callaghan expressed strong and public opposition to all-white South African sports teams touring Britain. A more truly characteristic initiative was *Children in Trouble*, a white paper of May 1968, which prepared the way for the Children and Young Persons Act 1969, which provided a more humane system of detention for young offenders. There was a moment of deep embarrassment before the general election of 1970 when, as home secretary, Callaghan performed his statutory duty of presenting the boundary commission's report to the House of Commons but then—knowing that the redistribution of seats disadvantaged the Labour

Party—recommended that his honourable friends vote against it.

If Callaghan performed the domestic duties of the office of home secretary with mixed success and acclaim the task of supervising the governance of Northern Ireland, then one of the home secretary's responsibilities, was discharged with undisputed brilliance. The late 1960s marked the beginning of new Irish 'troubles'. Callaghan proved the ideal man to deal with them. His period as effective viceroy, lord lieutenant, and chief secretary lasted for less than a year. It began with mass riots in Belfast on 2 August 1969 and ended with Labour's general election defeat on 18 June 1970. Throughout August 1969 the situation—bad at the beginning of the month—deteriorated. Peace had barely been restored in Belfast when the Apprentice Boys' march in Londonderry provoked an outbreak of even greater violence than that which had scarred the provincial capital. Then it was Belfast again. Nationalists, reinforced by members of the Irish Republican Army, fought with police and B special paramilitaries, who made no secret of their support for continued protestant domination of the Northern Ireland government. On 14 and 15 August two hundred houses were burned down in Belfast's predominantly Catholic Falls Road area. Seven people, including a nine-year-old boy, were killed. In the Short Strand area of the city a massacre of Catholics was only averted by the intervention of republican gunmen.

On 7 August the Londonderry police had made an official request for 'the military to come to the aid of the civil power'. The Ministry of Defence, conscious of the implications of taking such a step, recommended the home secretary to tell the chief constable that the time had not yet come to put soldiers on the streets of a city in the United Kingdom. Wilson supported that view with the comment, 'Once the troops go in, they could be there for weeks' (personal knowledge). But on 14 August the line could be held no longer. Reinforced by a plea from Bernadette Devlin—later a republican MP—the home secretary accepted that British soldiers were needed to prevent Irish deaths. The Prince of Wales's Own Yorkshire regiment entered Londonderry and imposed something approaching martial law. Callaghan realized that nothing in Northern Ireland could ever be the same again and that if the situation was to improve rather than deteriorate a political, rather than a military, solution would have to be found.

The solution—only partial, but clearly a great leap forward—had to be imposed on the protestant majority on behalf of Catholic communities that had suffered a whole range of gross injustices. The RUC was disarmed and the B specials disbanded and replaced by the Ulster Defence Regiment, operating under strict military discipline. The Whitehall government provided money for slum clearance and house building, on the strict understanding that the allocation of the new tenancies should be even-handed between Catholics and protestants. But Callaghan's greatest contribution to the fragile peace was the atmosphere of calm that his persona exuded and the promise of a fairer society that he bravely made. His year in charge of the troubled province is best remembered by the photograph taken on his second visit, in October 1969, in which an obviously adoring crowd listened to him speak from the bedroom window of a terraced house. Asked, years later, what he remembered about the moment of triumph Callaghan said that all he could recall was that his special branch escorting officer lost a shoe in the crush—and charged for a new pair on his expenses.

Callaghan's year of Ireland was not all triumph, however. Barbara Castle, first secretary of state and secretary of state for employment and productivity, had never been one of his favourite politicians and in the dying days of 1968 she had compounded all the other causes of his criticism by circulating the draft of a white paper that proposed that the conduct of trade unions should be regulated by an industrial relations act. (A royal commission, under the chairmanship of Lord Donovan, had come to quite the opposite conclusion, but the ever active Mrs Castle wanted direct government intervention.) Her proposals—paradoxically set out in a command paper entitled *In Place of Strife* (1969)—were anathema to the TUC. Negotiations between employers and employees had always been carried on by the process of 'free collective bargaining' and in 1969 there were many influential figures in the Labour movement who could not imagine why that should change. Callaghan, still loyal to his trade union roots, was among them.

In his biography Callaghan insisted that he had always believed that industrial reform was necessary but had no doubt that the best way to bring it about was for the trade unions to make the changes themselves. Indeed, before the royal commission reported he told the Fire Brigades Union that the TUC should anticipate its recommendation with reform proposals of its own. He should have known, and perhaps did know, that there was no chance of the unions accepting his advice. He nevertheless argued against Castle's proposals in cabinet and organized against them in the Parliamentary Labour Party and in the party in the country. Ministers—before and since—have been known to do the same. But Callaghan took his rebellion a step further. On 26 March 1969, at the meeting of Labour's national executive, he voted in favour of a resolution that condemned government policy. Not surprisingly his cabinet colleagues (at least those who supported *In Place of Strife*) regarded his conduct as unforgivable. Dick Crossman, secretary of state for health and social security and a Castle ally, shouted that he should resign. Wilson removed Callaghan from the management committee—known colloquially as the inner cabinet—and made his demotion public.

Callaghan was not deflected from his purpose. In any event it was too late for him to recover his colleagues' esteem by recanting his strongly held views. And he had little doubt that feeling was running too strongly in his favour to leave him, at the end of the argument, on the losing side. The climax of the drama came at a meeting of the Parliamentary Labour Party with Douglas Houghton, Callaghan's old trade union boss, in the chair. That afternoon, speaking at a trade union conference, Callaghan had reiterated his opposition to the statutory control of collective bargaining. Houghton began the meeting with a resounding declaration that the party 'simply would not accept' the proposed legislation. His proclamation was greeted with thunderous applause. Barbara Castle's parliamentary secretary hurried to her department with the news, 'It's dead', she said. 'It's dead. That bastard Callaghan has killed it' (personal knowledge).

It is at least arguable that the defeat of *In Place of Strife*—both because of the popularity of trade union reform and the inevitable consequences of so obvious a cabinet split—was the cause of Labour's unexpected general election defeat in June 1970. Other possible explanations were canvassed, including the publication, in the week before polling day, of balance of payments figures that were made to look far worse than they were by the inclusion of the cost of several commercial aircraft bought from America. But the general view was that the dispute over *In Place of Strife* had made the government seem divided and its eventual abandonment had caused the prime minister to appear ineffectual. The defeat was as substantial as it was surprising. Edward Heath's Conservatives enjoyed a majority of thirty over all other parties. However, in the post mortem Labour did not turn on Callaghan and accuse him of ensuring a tory victory. In the shadow cabinet elections that followed the convening of the new parliament it was Barbara Castle who failed to gain a place. Callaghan—always able to judge the mood of the party—came a respectable fifth.

Opposition, 1970–74 Anthony Barber, chancellor of the exchequer in the Heath government after the death of Iain Macleod, suggested to Callaghan that he might be interested in becoming managing director of the International Monetary Fund (IMF). For a time he was tempted, even though Audrey Callaghan had expressed her doubts about moving to America. But before he had made up his mind the French vetoed his nomination. His career was saved for British politics.

Callaghan played a remarkably passive role in the four years of opposition that followed Labour's 1970 defeat. As shadow home secretary he dominated the debates on Ireland which preceded the suspension of Stormont and the imposition of direct rule. But the real issue of the 1970 parliament was Europe. Heath secured Britain's entry into the Common Market—an achievement that eluded Labour in government and one the party opposed in opposition. Sixty-nine Labour MPs, under the leadership of Roy Jenkins, the deputy leader of the party, voted with the government in favour of British entry. Callaghan was a passionate—at times it seemed pathological—opponent of British membership.

In the spring of 1972 Jenkins, unable to reconcile his conscience to the need to vote with his party during the long committee stage of the Common Market Entry Bill, resigned as Labour's deputy leader. Several prominent trade unionists urged Callaghan to contest the consequent vacancy. In all probability he would have won an election, which in those days was carried out exclusively in the Parliamentary Labour Party. However, he declined. But he was again the beneficiary of events outside his control. Denis Healey became shadow chancellor in place of Jenkins, and Callaghan moved from shadowing the Home Office to become shadow foreign secretary.

The Heath administration ended with the election in which the prime minister invited the voters to decide 'Who governs Britain?' In 1972 the National Union of Mineworkers had—after much agitation, a strike, and an arbitration award—won a wage increase that flouted the government's pay guidelines. Faced with a second confrontation the Conservatives decided to appeal to the electorate for a mandate to put the mineworkers' union in its place. The election was anticipated weeks before it was declared. In Birmingham, at Labour's local government conference, Callaghan, that year's chairman of the Labour Party, spoke solemnly about the 'constitutional outrage' of holding a general election on a voters' register that was out of date. 'Surely', he said, 'the Prime Minister will wait for the new register' (*The Times*, 14 Jan 1975). In private he conceded, 'Of course he won't'. Nor did he. The election was held on 28 February 1974 and, to general surprise, Labour won 301 seats to the Conservatives' 297 (though on a lower share of the vote). After a futile attempt to attract the Liberals into a coalition Heath resigned. Wilson became prime minister again and Callaghan his foreign secretary.

Foreign secretary, 1974–76 During the campaign—as the Labour Party struggled to distract the public's attention from the striking miners—Callaghan had constantly warned the country about what, according to Labour's manifesto, were the dangers of Common Market membership. Chief among them was the rising price of food. The shadow foreign secretary had gone so far as to appear on platforms carrying a basket of groceries that illustrated, or were said to illustrate, Europe's influence on the cost of living. There is no doubt that many of the Foreign Office staff who watched his performances comforted themselves with the belief that the grocery stunt proved that his antagonism was no more than cheap populism. They discovered they were wrong during his first week in the Foreign Office, when he convened a meeting of British ambassadors to the Common Market capitals. Immediately, before he addressed them, he gave each one a copy of Labour's election manifesto. One of the more senior ambassadors, anxious to demonstrate independence of mind, thought it would be amusing to ask if he and his colleagues were expected to buy their copies. 'No', the foreign secretary replied, 'just implement them' (private information). There was a gasp of amazed realization that Callaghan really meant 'to renegotiate the terms of British membership'—or leave the Common Market.

The 'renegotiation' began in Luxembourg on 1 April 1974. Callaghan had rejected all official advice to seek the new terms in a spirit of friendship and compromise. Emollience was not to be part of his negotiating technique. He could not address the council of foreign ministers until a debate had been concluded on the export of cattle between France and Germany. The delay neither improved his temper nor softened his approach. As a result both the content and the manner of his speech (which became a government white paper) shocked his fellow foreign ministers into believing that not only was Britain prepared to leave but that withdrawal was the option Callaghan wanted. The Foreign Office officials, who still hoped that they might rescue British membership, were certain that Callaghan's aggressive attitude had made an acceptable outcome more difficult to achieve. Even other ministers, present with him at those early meetings, were unsure if he wanted the renegotiation to fail or to succeed. And they feared that if he had made a calculated decision to begin hard and gradually soften he might well not win the support of Europe but lose the support of the Labour Party. Fortunately for those who believed Britain's destiny to lie in Europe, his attitude changed, almost overnight.

Two months after he became foreign secretary Callaghan attended a 'political co-operation meeting' at Schloss Gymnich in Germany. His suspicion that much of the talk about European unity was rhetorical was confirmed. He was reinforced in the view that heady promises about closer integration would not be matched with either hard thought about how it could be achieved or a willingness to make the sacrifices necessary to achieve it. But although he was irritated by his colleagues' style, the absence of substance made him realize that Britain need not fear being sucked into a federation. Equally important, he enjoyed the discussions with his fellow foreign ministers and welcomed the opportunity of the European powers to combine their strength in voluntarily agreed policy positions. From then on he wanted the renegotiations to succeed. But a renegotiation there had to be.

The two key issues that had to be resolved were Britain's budget contribution and access for Commonwealth agricultural products, particularly sugar from the Caribbean and New Zealand cheese, butter, and lamb (known in the Common Market as 'sheep meat'). The argument over the budget illustrated a difference in logic between Britain and her European colleagues. The United Kingdom paid a contribution of between 10 and 12 per cent of the total Common Market budget, and received 8 per cent of Brussels' expenditure in return. Worse still, the contribution was estimated to rise to 20 per cent of the total after the transition period consequent on Britain's entry. The French and Germans did not think the arithmetical discrepancy was important. Britain did not behave in a way that attracted expenditure. They did.

Callaghan found the Common Market's methods hard to accept. British empiricism often clashed with the continental reverence for rigorous rules. Occasionally the tension turned into violent dispute. Discussions on the proposed meeting of oil producers were proceeding peacefully until Callaghan discovered that Britain, an oil producer, was not to participate directly but would be represented by Gaston Thorn, prime minister and foreign minister of Luxembourg, and temporary president of the council of ministers. That was the requirement of the rules, but Callaghan would not accept it. After a morning of angry confrontation it was agreed that Britain should be added to the list of participants.

Even as Callaghan edged closer to a deal both he and Wilson were careful to protect their position within the party by preserving the appearance of scepticism. Callaghan's autobiography later suggested that they welcomed the French proposals that heads of government should meet regularly in a formal European council. But at the time the idea was proposed both he and Wilson were so cautious about appearing to support the idea that they refused to attend the inaugural meeting. A trembling junior minister went in their place. The early vicissitudes of the Foreign Office were also made more tolerable by retreat to his farm (on the Weald of Sussex) and his family. One day, leaving unexpectedly by the ambassadors' entrance in Horse Guards Parade, he told a startled junior minister, 'You take the meetings this afternoon. I'm going to see my granddaughter' (personal knowledge).

There were other moments of drama during Callaghan's eighteen months at the Foreign Office. The Turks, having given assurances to the contrary, invaded Cyprus. Callaghan, impatient to get to Whitehall at the first opportunity, refused to wait for his official car to arrive and commandeered a milk float. Idi Amin, the president of Uganda, arrested a British citizen, Denis Hills, and, accusing him of imperfectly defined crimes, threatened execution unless Callaghan visited east Africa and pleaded for his release. Callaghan duly complied. Britain fought (and lost) a 'cod war' with Iceland. The Armed Forces Movement restored democracy to Portugal and Callaghan insisted to Henry Kissinger that the new government should not be ostracized. But the real issue was the Common Market. By the end of the negotiations—the principle of a budget rebate being conceded, and sugar and dairy product imports having won a temporary stay of execution—Callaghan felt able to announce that the renegotiation had succeeded. But the Labour Party still had to be convinced. The solution (a tribute to Wilson's traditional tactical ingenuity) was a referendum on continued membership—a constitutional innovation the prime minister had dismissed out of hand two years earlier. A special Labour Party conference, basing its debate on a general 'anti' party document and the government's unequivocally 'pro' white paper, agreed that 'the government proposes and the people decide'. On 5 June 1975 the people duly decided that Britain should remain a member of the Common Market.

Callaghan enjoyed the Foreign Office. And, after the Foreign Office got used to his occasionally irascible ways, the Foreign Office enjoyed him. Often his short temper was the result of a (usually mistaken) view that he was being patronized by the over-educated. The suggestion that Bryan Gould (a former diplomat and Oxford don, now Labour MP for Southampton Test) should be made a parliamentary secretary was greeted with the announcement that he did not promote anyone who 'talks to me as if I have just come down from the trees' (private information). The intellectual parity of his relationship with officials was confirmed when, frustrated by an abstruse explanation of what he regarded as a simple point, he quoted Roy Campbell, the South African poet:

I'm with you there of course:
They use the snaffle and the curb all right
But where's the bloody horse?

Prime Minister, 1976–79 On 16 March 1976—much to general surprise—Harold Wilson first told the queen, then the cabinet, and eventually the general public, that he proposed to resign his seals of office as soon as a successor was appointed. Long after the event, *soi-disant* close friends claimed that they had known of his decision long in advance. Few of the claims were justified. But it does seem that Callaghan knew at least the night before the announcement. He asked a couple of carefully selected ministers of state which cabinet job they would most like in what he described as an imminent reshuffle. It seems that none of them realized that it would not be Wilson who carried it out. Wilson predicted to his staff that the following day's headlines would proclaim 'It looks like Jim'. The prediction proved to be correct.

Before the outcome of the leadership election was determined, Callaghan, already a declared candidate, announced to parliament the details of an initiative, unsuccessful as it turned out, by which he had hoped to break the deadlock in negotiations with still unlawfully independent Rhodesia. Cynics said that it was part of his election campaign. In fact it was the result of another facet of his character which became more apparent as the years passed. A few days earlier he had sat next to the queen at dinner in the Italian embassy and had told her of his hopes of moving towards a peaceful settlement. She had expressed her approval of the plan. Callaghan, a monarchist who held the royal family in personal esteem, accepted his sovereign's implicit command. His reverence for the institution and the individuals who embodied it increased with the years. During his retirement he developed the habit of writing to the queen, who invariably replied.

At this time the leader of the Labour Party was elected by Labour MPs. Six candidates contested the election held on 5 April 1976: Callaghan, Roy Jenkins, Michael Foot, Denis Healey, Tony Benn, and Tony Crosland. Callaghan—with a strong following in parliament—was sure that he would top the first ballot. He came second, with 84 votes to Michael Foot's 90. Jenkins, Crosland, and Benn pulled out or were eliminated. On the second ballot Callaghan won 141 votes to Foot's 133 and Healey's 38. He won on the third ballot by the decisive, but not overwhelming, majority of 39 votes. The next day he was prime minister.

A new prime minister has to put his decisive stamp on the cabinet. Callaghan accomplished that necessity by sacking Barbara Castle, his old adversary from the days of *In Place of Strife*. It was a controversial beginning to what was to remain a controversial premiership. At the first party conference he addressed as leader Callaghan, encouraged by Peter Jay, his son-in-law and sometime economic correspondent of *The Times*, renounced John Maynard Keynes's belief in a 'cosy world … where employment could be guaranteed by the stroke of a pen'. He went on to argue that Keynes was not just outdated but plain wrong. 'We used to think that we could spend our way out of recession … That option no longer exists … In so far as it ever did exist, it only worked on each occasion … by injecting a bigger dose of inflation into the economy.' Reality—as the prime minister saw it—burst in on the conference next day when Denis Healey, the chancellor of the exchequer, returned from Heathrow airport, where he had been about to board a plane for New York and a meeting of the IMF, to deal with a sudden deterioration in the value of sterling. There followed the IMF crisis, during which the government boosted international confidence in the pound by reducing what was thought to be a public sector borrowing requirement of £12 billion. In fact the deficit was barely £8 billion. But, working on the overestimate, the cabinet struggled through October 1976 to cut public expenditure and services to a level at which the imagined deficit was reduced by half.

For the next three years the government was derided for accepting a more rigorous fiscal regime imposed on it by the IMF. In fact Callaghan used the pressure of international opinion to implement policies he had meant to employ from the day on which he became prime minister. Public expenditure had been cut by £1 billion during the previous July, but that clear indication that the government intended to operate a more stringent economic policy had little effect on either the balance of payments (in deficit by £3 billion) or the value of the pound (almost two dollars in January 1976 but only $1.64 in September and forecast to fall by a cent a day until it reached $1.50). The crisis made the need for dramatic action more urgent and the justification easier to explain. But accepting the IMF's stern advice was what Healey called a 'Pyrrhic defeat'. He allowed himself to be forced to do what he had always wanted to do.

Concern for the state of the economy did not prevent Callaghan from pursuing what, back in 1967 when he resigned from the Treasury, he had described as his 'real interest'—education. Within days of becoming prime minister he had sent a memorandum to the secretary of state for education asking about the quality of basic teaching, the relevance of the curriculum for older children in comprehensive schools, and the examination system's competence to test ability and attainment. While the department was still composing its answer the prime minister laid the foundation stone for a new hall of residence at Ruskin College, Oxford. The speech that accompanied the ceremony horrified the education establishment. Its insistence that the purpose of education was 'to equip children to the best of their ability for a lively and constructive place in society and also fit them to do a job of work' (*The Times*, 19 Oct 1976) was interpreted—almost certainly correctly—as an expression of doubt about the non-selective (comprehensive) system of secondary education and a declaration that the traditional freedom of teachers to teach how and what they chose could not continue. It began a debate about teachers and teaching that was still raging decades later.

The economic policy the Callaghan government had

inherited from its predecessor was crucially dependent on income restraint, which its economic advisers believed was vital to the defeat of inflation. Experts later disagreed about how much the reduction of the retail price index, from over 20 per cent to single figures, was the result of the wages policy and the price code that accompanied it (largely to convince the unions that profits, like earnings, were being held down). What is certain is that, at the time, it was believed to be crucial. Callaghan, unlike Wilson, felt emotionally involved in the campaigns to encourage the trade unions to co-operate in holding wages down. He supported the trades unions and they should support him.

In the summer of 1977 Callaghan was at least privately sympathetic towards the moderate ministers who joined the picket lines outside the Grunwick film processing laboratory in Willesden, where the largely female and Asian workforce had been refused the right of trade union membership. And although he supported—indeed initiated—the cabinet's hard line towards the Fire Brigades Union (which was on strike in support of demands for a 30 per cent wage increase and a reduction in the working week) he admitted to feeling deep regret that a generally devoted group of men and women were being used, by less worthy comrades in other unions, to blow a hole in wages policy.

The feeling of mutual affection survived, despite some strain, until the summer of 1978, when it became clear that trade unions were unlikely to accept any level of wage restraint and certain to reject the 5 per cent ceiling (with exceptions for the lowest paid) on which Callaghan personally insisted. Co-operation broke down in part because of two misconceptions. One was that real wages would be higher if freely negotiated. The other was that the IMF settlement had marked the end of the Labour government's commitment to high levels of public expenditure providing a constantly improving level of public services—regarded by the TUC as the *quid pro quo* of old justifications for pay policy. And, since the economy was obviously improving, was pay policy still necessary?

The path towards full rejection of income restraint was marked by a series of mile posts that should have left the prime minister in no doubt that the 5 per cent limit on earnings increases would be impossible to enforce. But he remained determined to impose it on the unions. Indeed, he was far more resolute (or inflexible) in pursuit of the impossible than was Healey and actually sent messages to some cabinet ministers that, if they argued for an even lower figure, he would have no objection. Throughout 1977 it was nevertheless clear that support for a voluntary incomes policy had ebbed away. The TUC general council was evenly tied on a vote proposing support of the government's proposal and Tom Jackson—chairman, leader of the Post Office union, and himself a supporter of 'restraint'—thought it his constitutional duty to declare the resolution 'not carried'. The biennial conference of the Transport and General Workers Union not only rejected 5 per cent but shouted down Jack Jones, the general secretary, when he asked the delegates not to risk the re-election of a tory government.

By the time the prime minister addressed the TUC in Brighton, in September 1978, it was clear that pay policy was dead. But as the economy improved so did the government's opinion poll rating. Pundits agreed that if there were to be an autumn election Labour would—at worst—be the largest single party. At dinner with the general council on the night before he addressed the delegates Callaghan gave the impression that an announcement was imminent. Even his speech, which included an embarrassing version of 'There was I, waiting at the church', did not convince them that the election would not be announced before the end of the week.

At the end of the last cabinet meeting before the summer recess Callaghan—in typical style—had told ministers that he did not want letters advising him what the election date should be. When the cabinet reassembled, on the day after his TUC speech, he informed them of the decision he had taken by reading a letter he had sent to the queen earlier that morning. He clearly enjoyed the atmosphere of increasing tension as he went through the opening paragraphs which set out the state of the nation—inflation down, sterling stable, productivity improving. However, there was much work still to be done. There was a dramatic pause before the last paragraph. 'I therefore do not propose to ask Your Majesty for an early dissolution of Parliament.' There was a second pause and then—the style maintained—he added, 'You can discuss it if you want to. But I doubt if you'll persuade me to write to the Queen again, telling her that I've changed my mind.' There was a ripple of half laughter round the Cabinet table. 'You're laughing with relief', the prime minister said. 'But if we have trouble with the unions during the winter, we lose our majority and are forced out, you'll all feel differently' (personal knowledge). Few prime ministers have made a more prophetic announcement.

The alternative to an incomes policy accepted by the unions was a statutory pay code enforced by penalizing companies that agreed to wage increases above the government's stipulated maximum. Sustaining such a controversial policy—indeed making progress in any field of government—required a robust House of Commons majority. And the Callaghan administration, with never more than a handful of votes more than the combined opposition, lost by-elections. The only way to retain office was to forge a pact with the Liberal Party. It was a stratagem that Michael Foot, effectively the deputy prime minister, pursued with enthusiasm. Callaghan himself regarded it as no more than a tedious necessity, even though the Liberal Party never imposed one of its policies on the government as the price of co-operation. The pact offended his partisanship and his pride. And it was those emotions that prevented him, in the end, from extending the government's life by the arrangement of another humiliating deal.

Although the Liberals asked for very little Callaghan asked his cabinet to throw a crumb in their direction by supporting, in a free vote, proportional representation as the method by which members of the European parliament should be elected. Some ministers responded to his wishes. But indiscipline was becoming endemic. The government lost the vote on the annual estimates and was beaten in the major attempt to impose sanctions on companies that breached pay policy. On both occasions Labour back-benchers had made the difference between victory and defeat. There was only one moment, during those fractious days, when members of the cabinet thought the prime minister looked less than composed. That was when a note was passed to him from an official and he immediately—and peremptorily—left the meeting. Audrey, his wife, had received slight injuries in a motor accident.

In the middle of what came to be called the winter of discontent Callaghan joined the presidents of the United States and France and the chancellor of Germany on the island of Guadeloupe. There was no doubt about the importance of their discussions. They tried to lay the foundations of a world stability pact that would underwrite the value of currencies and they examined the emergence of militant Islam in Iran and the pressure that might be brought on the apartheid regime in South Africa. A new round of arms limitation talks was initiated. But they met in the sun while Britain was in the grip of a politically bitter winter. On his return the prime minister's staff urged him not to hold a press conference at the airport. But Callaghan—happiest when he was talking to other world leaders—insisted on giving the newspapers an immediate account of his discussions. A reporter from *The Sun* asked if it had been right to abandon Britain at such a time. The prime minister replied with a homily on discussions about great international events putting domestic issues in perspective. It ended, 'I don't think other people in the world would share the view that there is a crisis'. *The Sun* paraphrased his comments on its front page as 'Crisis. What Crisis?' (11 January 1979). Support, in and out of parliament, continued to ebb away.

There was, however, one policy that—as long as its implementation remained possible—was guaranteed to ensure that the Liberal Party would keep the Labour government in power. It was the devolution of power from Westminster to Edinburgh and, to a lesser degree, to Cardiff. It was not a policy for which Callaghan felt any great enthusiasm. But, although it was an initiative with too intangible benefits to stir his passions, he realized the advantages of pursuing the idea with resolute determination.

The devolution bill made slow progress through parliament. However, trade union dissatisfaction with government policy accelerated more quickly. It was the public service unions which took the most dramatic action. Hospital porters picketed hospital gates, allowing the entry only of patients whom they regarded as emergencies. Refuse collectors refused to empty dustbins, forcing householders to leave rubbish in black bags at street corners and thus creating ideal photographs for use by anti-government newspapers. In a cold winter school caretakers neglected to switch on classroom heating and local government workmen left icy roads ungritted. In Liverpool members of the General and Municipal Workers Union parks and cemeteries branch refused to bury the dead.

Parochially minded MPs in the House of Commons—uncertain about the constitutional propriety of a bill to devolve power from the Westminster parliament—inserted a clause that required the proposal to be subject to a referendum that must endorse the notion not only with a majority of the votes, but with 40 per cent of the electorate voting in favour. When the referenda were held on 1 March 1979 Wales voted against it, Scotland just in favour, but with only 33 per cent of the registered electorate in favour. Devolution was dead and the nationalists withdrew their support from the government. Margaret Thatcher, the leader of the opposition, knowing that the government no longer commanded a majority, tabled a vote of no confidence that was debated on 28 March 1979. Much work was done to persuade individual MPs from the minority parties to support the government—but not by Callaghan. Indeed, when Enoch Powell offered at least the abstention of the Ulster Unionists, in return for a gas pipeline joining the province to the mainland, he explicitly vetoed the idea on the grounds that it had not been properly discussed by the cabinet. He had grown weary of cobbling together fragile and temporary majorities and lost patience with the indignity of modifying policies to meet the whims of fractious back-benchers. The vote of no confidence was carried by one vote.

The cabinet and the national executive of the Labour Party met in the Waterloo room of 10 Downing Street to consider the election manifesto. There was argument about almost every paragraph. But the fiercest argument was over a proposal to promise the reform of the House of Lords. Although it was fierce it did not last for long. It had barely begun when Callaghan announced that, if the party fought the election on a promise to make radical changes to the upper house, it would do so under another leader. During the campaign that followed Callaghan put on a convincing show of optimism. But, at least according to Bernard Donoughue, the head of his political office, he always believed that the tide had turned irrevocably. The likelihood was, however, that he would have won in the previous autumn and might well have been equally successful a year later when the memory of the winter of discontent had begun to fade. Choosing the wrong election date was Callaghan's second great mistake—greater even than his reluctance to devalue the pound in 1964. In the event, the Conservatives won 339 seats to Labour's 269.

Defeat, and later years Some of Callaghan's closest friends advised him to resign as leader of the Labour Party immediately after the new parliament assembled. He rejected the idea on the grounds that he should 'take some shine off the ball' in the hope of making the batting easier for Denis Healey, his preferred successor. The months that followed were, he freely admitted, among the unhappiest in his life. The Labour Party was in open revolt—not simply hell-bent on moving policy to the left, but equally determined to change its constitution in a way that made the leftward shift permanent. The leader should be elected by the party at large. Candidates should be subject to re-selection (or not) by their constituency parties. The Parliamentary Labour Party should be denied all influence over the contents of the manifesto. In an effort to hold back the tide Callaghan met those he believed to be the most tractable trade union leaders at the Association of Scientific, Technical and Managerial Staffs training college at Bishop's Stortford. The re-selection of MPs was conceded but the battle over the method of electing the leader went on. It was still raging when Callaghan resigned his leadership of the Labour Party, on 15 October 1980. He was succeeded not by Denis Healey but by Michael Foot.

Callaghan stayed to fight the 1983 election in the re-drawn Cardiff South and Penarth constituency, dissociating himself from the party's defence policy in a speech made there. But his interest increasingly turned to international affairs. He was never so happy as when he was with the other great men of his era—Helmut Schmidt, Gerald Ford, Valéry Giscard d'Estaing—discussing how to put right the world they could no longer influence. He became father of the House of Commons and, much to his monarchist delight, in 1987 a knight of the Garter. True to both his affection for Wales and his well-ordered life, he arranged—long before he died—to have his Garter banner hung in the cathedral at Llandaff. On retirement from the Commons he was made a life peer, as Baron Callaghan of Cardiff, later in 1987.

The abiding feature of Callaghan's final years was his devotion to Audrey, his wife. For the last decade of her life she suffered from accelerating Alzheimer's disease. Towards the end she was cared for by nuns at St George's Retreat, Burgess Hill, a home for the elderly near the Callaghans' farm near Ringmer in Sussex. Callaghan visited her every day and sat by her bedside for hours. At the party in Downing Street given by Tony Blair to celebrate Callaghan's ninetieth birthday he confided to an old associate, 'She does not recognise me. But I recognise her. And that's what matters' (personal knowledge). Audrey Callaghan died on 15 March 2005. In the words of Peter Jay (his son-in-law), in the week after her death, 'He decided that there was nothing else he had to do. The work was finished'. He settled down in the room at St George's Retreat which she had occupied during her final days and went peacefully to his rest on 26 March; the causes of death were given as lobar pneumonia, cardiac failure, and kidney failure.

Jim Callaghan risks the judgements of history that haunt almost all prime ministers whose tenure was brief and ended in defeat. But he deserved much better. He inherited an administration that would not, or could not, face up to Britain's burgeoning economic crisis and he left office with sterling stable, the balance of payments in surplus, and inflation moving down. He was a good prime minister. Given another four or five years he might have become a great one. ROY HATTERSLEY

Sources H. Wilson, *The Labour government, 1964–1970: a personal record* (1971) • R. H. S. Crossman, *The diaries of a cabinet minister*, 3 vols. (1975–7) • H. Wilson, *Final term: the Labour government, 1974–1976* (1979) • B. Castle, *The Castle diaries*, 2 vols. (1980–84) • G. Thomas, *George Thomas, Mr Speaker: the memoirs of the Viscount Tonypandy* (1985) • J. Callaghan, *Time and chance* (1987) • B. Donoughue, *Prime minister: the conduct of policy under Harold Wilson and James Callaghan* (1987) • T. Benn, *Out of the wilderness: diaries, 1963–67* (1987) • T. Benn, *Office without power: diaries, 1968–72* (1988) • D. Healey, *The time of my life* (1989) • T. Benn, *Against the tide: diaries, 1973–76* (1989) • T. Benn, *Conflicts of interest: diaries, 1977–1980* (1990) • R. Jenkins, *A life at the centre* (1991) • K. O. Morgan, *Callaghan: a life* (1997) • A. Seldon and K. Hickson, eds., *New Labour, Old Labour: the Wilson and Callaghan governments, 1974–1979* (2004) • *The Times* (28 March 2005) • *Daily Telegraph* (28 March 2005) • *Financial Times* (28 March 2005) • *The Guardian* (28 March 2005) • *The Independent* (28 March 2005) • Burke, *Peerage* • *WW* (2005) • personal knowledge (2009) • private information (2009) • b. cert. • m. cert. • d. cert.

Archives Bodl. Oxf. | Bod. RH, Fabian Bureau MSS • Bod. RH, Welensky MSS • CAC Cam., John Silkin MSS • King's Lond., Liddell Hart MSS • NL Wales, Lord Cledwyn MSS • NL Wales, Viscount Tonypandy MSS | FILM BFINA, 'Government', *Callaghan*, J. Bush (director), Channel 4, 10 April 1987 • BFINA, 'Society', *Callaghan*, J. Bush (director), Channel 4, 17 April 1987 • BFINA, 'Britain and the world', *Callaghan*, J. Bush (director), Channel 4, 24 April 1987 • BFINA, current affairs footage • BFINA, documentary footage • BFINA, party political footage | SOUND BL NSA, current affairs recordings • BL NSA, documentary recordings • BL NSA, parliamentary recordings • BL NSA, party political recordings • BL NSA, recorded speeches

Likenesses Bassano, six half-plate film negatives, 1947, NPG • Elliott & Fry, vintage print, 1947, NPG • W. Stoneman, bromide print, 1947, NPG • photographs, 1954–2002, Getty Images, London • photographs, 1955–2002, PA Photos, London • *Daily Herald*, bromide print, 1960–69, NPG • P. Keen, 35mm colour slide, *c*.1965, NPG • P. Keen, double portrait, 35mm colour slide, *c*.1965 (with Lady Callaghan), NPG • photographs, 1965–2002, Rex Features, London • photographs, 1965–2003, Photoshot, London • photographs, 1975–2002, Camera Press, London • B. L. Schwartz, dye transfer print, 1977, NPG • A. Newman, bromide print, 1978?, NPG • J. Pannett, drawing, 1980, priv. coll. • R. Spear, oils, exh. RA 1980 (*I told you so*) • B. Organ, oils on canvas, 1983, NPG [*see illus.*] • J. Mendoza, group portrait, oils, 1986–7, House of Commons, Westminster, London • G. Jones, pastel on paper, 1991, House of Commons, Westminster, London • H. Ocean, portrait, exh. RA 1991 • F. Topolski, black chalk drawing; Sothebys, 15 July 1998, lot 288

Caminer, David Tresman (1915–2008), computing systems engineer, was born David Solomon Treisman on 26 June 1915 in Hackney, London, the only son of Henry Jacob (Jack) Treisman (1892–1918), tailor, and his wife, Rachel (Raie), *née* Simmons (1891–1982), milliner. Following his mother's remarriage, to Felix Caminer in 1921, his name was altered to David Tresman Caminer. His mother subsequently gave birth to a daughter, Adèle. The Treisman family had arrived in London in the late nineteenth century as refugees from anti-Semitic pogroms in Lithuania. Having married Raie in 1914, Jack Treisman was called up to serve as a soldier and was killed in the trenches in the final year of the First World War.

Caminer spent his childhood in Fulham, south-west London. He attended Sloane School, but was so engaged with socialism and anti-fascism that he gave little thought to his future career. He failed the scholarship examination for Cambridge University through lack of preparation, which caused him some regret at the time. His parents arranged for an interview with the catering company J. Lyons & Co, best known for its 250-branch national teashop chain and Corner House restaurants in London. In 1936 he began as a trainee in management accounts at the Cadby Hall headquarters in Hammersmith, work that suited his fine, analytical mind. He was called up on the outbreak of the Second World War and served in an infantry regiment, the Green Howards. In 1943 he lost his right leg at the battle of Mareth in Tunisia. Invalided out of the army, he returned to Lyons in 1944 and assumed responsibility for the systems research office, which had been set up in the 1930s to increase the efficiency of accounting and other clerical operations. On 22 July the following year, at Wembley town hall, he married Joyce Jacqueline (Jackie) Lewis (*b.* 1922), daughter of Leonard Lewis, company director. They settled in Richmond and had two daughters and a son; Jackie later became a schoolteacher.

In 1947, led by its chief accountant, John Simmons, Lyons began to think about using a computer to carry out clerical work. From 1949 its own engineers built the Lyons electronic office (LEO), based on the Cambridge EDSAC (electronic delay storage automatic calculator). Caminer's office assessed the systems supporting the Lyons businesses and drew up specifications to convert them from manual to computer operation. He insisted that a system should be meticulously analysed through flow charts before a job was programmed; every program was checked and rechecked long before it reached the computer. 'David … saw immediately that the computer could do more than copy what was being done in offices by clerks', wrote one of his colleagues; 'With proper design, the computer could be used to support management activities and improve the way the company was run' (*The Guardian*, 11 July 2008). From November 1951 LEO ran a weekly costing of the materials that went into the bread and cakes at Lyons' twelve bakeries. It was the first computerized, regularly scheduled office job in the world. Gradually Lyons brought its payroll onto the computer, together with an ordering and distribution system for the teashops. Caminer and his team took note of everything from the multiple written orders submitted by teashop manageresses to the pre-dawn loading of the vans in the yard at Cadby Hall, and came up with a system that incorporated daily 'online' updates by telephone.

In 1954 Lyons established a computer manufacturing subsidiary, Leo Computers Ltd, to sell machines and expertise to other companies. Caminer led the systems side of the business, joining the board as head of marketing in 1959. The Leo team designed each system to meet the needs of its user. While this led to many satisfied customers, the level of available investment never kept pace with the costs. In 1963 Leo Computers was merged with the computer interests of English Electric and in 1968 absorbed into International Computers Ltd (ICL). In the following decade Caminer supervised the successful development and installation of the computer and communications network for the European Community.

Caminer was one of the first to recognize that computers were not just tools for scientists, but part of a technological revolution that would change all our lives. On retiring in 1980 he was appointed OBE 'for services to British commercial interests in Luxembourg'. In his retirement he co-edited *LEO: the Incredible Story of the World's First Business Computer* (1998) and organized a conference at London's Guildhall in 2001 to mark fifty years of business computing. In his address to the conference he observed that had the Leo pioneers' concern for error-free programming and the user's perspective survived into the modern era, many expensive failures might have been avoided. He received an honorary doctorate from Middlesex University in 2006.

To his colleagues Caminer was a man driven by the demands of his work, but he led a very full life outside Cadby Hall. He was proud of his Jewish heritage; he retained a passionate belief in social justice, and chaired his local branch of the Labour Party. Having visited South Africa on business in the early 1960s, he became a staunch campaigner against apartheid and invited Desmond Tutu to visit Richmond. There he arranged for local schoolchildren to greet their visitor with what was then the African liberation anthem, 'Nkosi Sikelel' iAfrika'. Although his injury put an end to his active involvement in sport, he was a supporter of Chelsea Football Club and a member of the MCC, and also followed rugby and athletics. He and his wife loved travel, theatre, and music, especially opera. Poor health clouded his final years as his kidneys failed but, indomitable as ever, he submitted to twice-weekly dialysis and lobbied successfully for a new unit for kidney patients in his area. He died of end-stage kidney failure at his home, 9 Parkgate Gardens, East Sheen, Richmond upon Thames, on 19 June 2008, and was cremated at Golders Green on 24 June 2008. He was survived by his wife, Jackie, and their three children. GEORGINA FERRY

Sources D. Caminer and others, *LEO: the incredible story of the world's first business computer* (1998) • G. Ferry, *A computer called LEO: Lyons teashops and the world's first office computer* (2003) • *Daily Telegraph* (25 June 2008) • *The Independent* (26 June 2008) • *The Times* (30 June 2008) • *The Guardian* (11 July 2008) • H. Caminer, 'David's life – apart from the computers!', paper for Computer Conservation Society/ LEO Foundation conference 'The legacy of LEO in business applications: a tribute to David Caminer', 11 Sept 2008 • private information (2012) • m. cert. • d. cert.

Likenesses obituary photographs

Wealth at death £356,457: probate, 2 Oct 2008, *CGPLA Eng. & Wales*

Cammaerts, Francis Charles Albert (1916–2006), special operations officer and teacher, was born on 19 June 1916 at 17 Launceston Place, South Kensington, London, the elder son and third of the six children of Emile Leon Cammaerts (1878–1953) and his wife, Helen Geralda Louise, *née* Braun (1879–1964), an actress with the stage name Tita Brand. His Belgian father was a journalist, a respected poet, and professor of Belgian studies at the University of London from 1933 to 1947. His wife, Cammaerts's mother, was the daughter of the Wagnerian diva Marie Brema. Cammaerts was brought up at Radlett, Hertfordshire, going to preparatory school in Harpenden followed by Mill Hill School and then St Catharine's College, Cambridge, where he got a poor degree in English and history. He became a schoolteacher, first in Belfast and then in Penge in Kent. A pacifist from childhood, he resigned in 1940 and went to work as a farm labourer in Lincolnshire.

On 15 March 1941, at the register office in Caistor, Lincolnshire, he married Nancy (Nan) Findlay (1916–2001), daughter of James Smith Findlay, architect. They had a son and three daughters (one of whom died young).

Cammaerts's brother Pieter's death in the RAF cured him of pacifism. A chance meeting with Harry Rée, a friend and colleague from Penge, led him into the Special Operations Executive (SOE), where his perfect fluency in French commended him to the independent French section. He had one great disadvantage as a secret agent—he stood six feet four inches tall, and thus caught policemen's eyes. Moreover, the training staff did not notice his qualities of leadership, and pronounced him no more than a competent instructor in sabotage. As such, ranked as a lieutenant in the intelligence corps but wearing plain clothes, he went to France by Lysander aircraft on the night of 23–4 March 1943 to join the circuit of Peter Churchill, who returned by the same aircraft to England for rebriefing. Churchill's circuit had just moved from the riviera to Annecy, near the Swiss frontier. Cammaerts found it dangerously insecure, separated himself from it at once, and settled down in Nice to discover what life in Nazi-occupied France was like, pretending that he was recovering from tuberculosis.

With the help of some retired policemen Cammaerts gradually assembled a powerful circuit of his own, codenamed Jockey, in some of the départements to the east of the Rhône, mainly in the Drôme. His own codename was Roger. With the help of Auguste Floiras, his radio operator, he was able to secure parachuted drops of supplies, and so to arm the saboteurs he trained. In parallel with his sabotage circuits he had a private circuit of safe houses round which he rotated, never staying more than two nights in any one place; nobody else, not even Floiras, knew where he would be—an invaluable safety precaution. He carried the papers of an electricity inspector, which enabled him to travel widely. In the spring of 1944—by now a lieutenant-colonel—he effected some useful sabotage, both of railways and of electric power supplies. He redoubled his efforts after the allied landings in Normandy in June 1944. He visited the Vercors during its rising, but escaped from it when the Germans attacked, with his courier, the Polish countess Krystyna Gizycka. The *état-major des forces françaises de l'intérieur* gave him command of all resistance forces east of the Rhône, but no orders. The Germans offered two million francs for his capture; no one turned him in.

By bad luck Cammaerts fell into enemy hands at a road block on 13 August, was identified, and condemned to death. The night before he was to have been shot his courier appeared with a vast sum in francs and bought his release. His teams offered invaluable help to the American troops who landed on the riviera on 15 August and inflicted heavy casualties on the retreating Germans. He was awarded a DSO by the British, the Croix de Guerre and the Légion d'honneur by the French, and the medal of freedom by the Americans. He and Floiras rescued the latter's wife and daughter from Ravensbrück concentration camp.

After the war Cammaerts served briefly in the allied military government in Berlin, before being posted to Brussels—where his family could join him—as deputy director of the Inter-Allied Reparations Agency (1946–8). He then spent four years running an international bureau for educational visits and exchanges, before he went back to teaching. He became headmaster of Alleyne's Grammar School at the new town of Stevenage, which in nine years (1952–61) he built up into a flourishing eight-hundred-strong comprehensive school. He then spent five years (1961–6) as principal of Scraptoft teacher training college, Leicester, treating trainees as his equal, and instilling his theories of how children should be taught. He always stressed the importance of bringing out each child's individuality, rather than cramming them with data. Staff and pupils alike warmed to his outgoing personality. In 1966 he became professor of education in Nairobi, Kenya, as that former colony recovered from the ravages of Mau Mau, and assured Kenyan predominance over former missionary schools of several faiths. From 1972 to 1981 he was principal of Rolle College, Exmouth, again sustaining teacher training. His last official post was in Botswana, where from 1982 to 1988 he set up a teacher training system at Molepolole from scratch.

Cammaerts and his wife, Nan, retired to Combemaure in the Drôme, and then moved on to Le Pouget in the Hérault, where she died in 2001. He lived another five years, dying in his house at Le Pouget on 3 July 2006. He was survived by his son and two daughters. He often said he would rather be remembered as a teacher than as a secret agent. M. R. D. FOOT

Sources A. L. Funk, *Hidden ally: the French resistance, special operations, and the landings in southern France, 1944* (1992) • M. R. D. Foot, *SOE in France: an account of the work of the British Special Operations Executive in France, 1940–1944*, 3rd edn (2004) • *Daily Telegraph* (7 July 2006) • *Leicester Mercury* (12 July 2006) • *The Times* (6 July 2006); (17 July 2006) • *The Guardian* (7 July 2006); (22 July 2006); (24 July 2006); (26 July 2006) • *Francis Cammaerts: 1916–2006* [commemorative booklet, privately printed] • personal knowledge (2010) • private information (2010) • b. cert. • m. cert.

Archives TNA: PRO, IWM SOE files, HS 6/586, 568, 9/258/5

Likenesses obituary photographs • photograph, Rex Features, London • photographs, repro. in *Francis Cammaerts, 1916–2006*

Campbell, Sir Alan Hugh (1919–2007), diplomatist, was born at the Lodge Nursing Home, Stoke Abbott Road, Worthing, Sussex, on 1 July 1919, the son of Hugh Elphinstone Campbell (1873/4–1943), silk merchant, and his wife, Ethel Marion, *née* Warren (1879/80–1951), whose father Sir Pelham Warren ended his career as consul general in Shanghai. At the time of his birth his parents lived at Beresford, Winchester Road, Worthing. His father was managing director of the firm Ilbert & Co. in Shanghai, with a long background of business in China, where Campbell's mother was born. His father had rebuilt a large house near Kingsbridge in Devon and Campbell was proud of his west-country connections. He used to return to the area in his retirement to paint.

Campbell was educated at Sherborne School and at Gonville and Caius College, Cambridge, where he read modern languages. He was fluent in French and German. He took a first in part one before serving in the Devonshire regiment during the Second World War, much of it spent as a staff officer in the Special Operations Executive. In 1946 he was demobilized with the rank of major, joined the Foreign Office, and was posted to Singapore as third secretary. All the jobs he subsequently held in the Foreign Office were important and interesting—a tribute to his abilities. He was not a large man physically, but had great energy, particularly intellectual. He was a supremely competent diplomat, shrewd, well-informed, thorough, and of good judgement. In 1947 he married Margaret Jean Taylor (1918–1999), daughter of Gilbert Taylor, of Sydney, New South Wales, and they had three daughters. Margaret was a skilled and meticulous hostess and supported Campbell admirably in all his posts. In 1950 he became private secretary to the permanent under-secretary, Sir William Strang. He learned much from someone whom he greatly admired, including the need for sensitive management of the diplomatic service and careful handling of the intelligence agencies. The Maclean and Burgess defections took place while he was with Strang.

In 1959 Campbell was appointed assistant head of the news department. Journalists appreciated the clarity of his mind, the shrewdness of his assessments, his manifest integrity, and his amused sense of the absurd. A relationship of trust was established. He was then transferred to the mission to the United Nations, a posting he particularly enjoyed. He was head of chancery—in effect chief of staff—to Sir Patrick Dean and then Lord Caradon, appointed minister of state by the Labour government. Campbell quickly mastered the intricacies of UN procedures and both ambassadors relied heavily on his skill. In the security council he was deeply involved in the drama of the Cuban missile crisis. After a short time in the western department a move to Paris as head of chancery to Sir Patrick Reilly, and then Christopher Soames, produced several challenges; first the student riots in 1968, when plans had to be made for evacuating the embassy (happily not implemented), and then the 'Soames affair', the publication by the British government of proposals concerning European integration made privately by President de Gaulle to the ambassador. Relations between British and French officials were soured for a considerable time. Campbell, after his retirement, wrote a brief memoir describing in more detail what had happened.

Campbell's first ambassadorial appointment was to Ethiopia (1967–72). He found his life in Addis Ababa not unlike that described in Evelyn Waugh's *Black Mischief*. He formed a close relationship with Haile Selassie, admiring the emperor's dignity and close control of all aspects of government, but recognized that change had to come. After the revolution of 1974 members of the emperor's family sought refuge in London, and Campbell tried to ensure that they were adequately provided for. From 1972 to 1976 he was assistant and then deputy under-secretary dealing with African affairs. He travelled to southern Africa with Sir Alec Douglas-Home and Jim Callaghan, both of whom admired his clear mind and negotiating skills. After a brief return to European affairs as political director in the Foreign Office his last post was as ambassador to Italy (1976–9), where he had previously served. His time there was enjoyable but not easy. The Red Brigade terrorists were active, and the former prime minister Aldo Moro was murdered. NATO needed bases in Italy and European Community affairs were strained. Numerous British organizations needed support. He was made GCMG on completing his term in 1979, having been made CMG in 1964 and knighted KCMG in 1976.

After his retirement from the diplomatic service Campbell worked as a foreign affairs adviser to Rolls-Royce and as a director of the National Westminster Bank. He was a governor of his old school, Sherborne, and was active in Anglo-Italian organizations. A man of many parts, he enjoyed watercolour painting and music and until his eyes failed him he was a competent and wily tennis player. He relished lively company and was often to be found lunching at the Beefsteak or searching for new books in the library at Brooks's. He took up bridge and, always welcoming and gregarious, he enjoyed visits and telephone calls from friends. In 1988 he published an autobiography, *Colleagues and Friends*, an appropriate title as he always kept in touch with both. In retirement he deplored the financial pressures on the Foreign Office and the scaling down of personnel. Indeed the office, and particularly European affairs, remained his main interest. In later life his wife suffered from severe back problems and spent her last years in a nursing home near their flat; she died in 1999. Campbell suffered from osteoporosis and increasing frailty himself and died at his flat, 45 Carlisle Mansions, on 7 October 2007 after a stroke. He was buried near his family home at Kingsbridge and was survived by his three daughters. A memorial service was held on 31 January 2008 at Chelsea Old Church, where he had regularly worshipped. ANTONY ACLAND

Sources A. Campbell, *Colleagues and friends* (1988) • A. Campbell, *L'affaire Soames* • *Daily Telegraph* (9 Oct 2007) • *The Independent* (13 Oct 2007) • *The Times* (18 Oct 2007) • *The Guardian* (26 Oct 2007) • Burke, *Peerage* • *WW* (2009) • personal knowledge (2011) • private information (2011) • b. cert. • d. cert.

Likenesses obituary photographs • photographs, repro. in Campbell, *Colleagues*

Wealth at death under £110,000: probate, 10 July 2008, *CGPLA Eng. & Wales*

Campbell, Ambrose (1919–2006), musician and bandleader, was born Oladipupo Adekoya Campbell in Lagos, Nigeria, on 19 August 1919, the third of four sons in the family of six children of James, G. M., or Adekoya Campbell, a minister in the West African Episcopal church, and his wife, Phoebe Ibidun Adekoya. His father was an Ijebu of Sierra Leonean descent and his mother was Ijebu-Yoruba. Oladipupo (Oladipo) Campbell sang in his father's church choir as a child, and at night, accompanied by his fellow choristers, escaped from the family compound to join seamen and 'rascal boys' at the palm-wine shops where they gathered to drink and make music, playing guitars and simple percussion instruments. Singing and playing on a tin can with these well-travelled older men, he absorbed a wide variety of cultural influences, and adopted the name Ambrose to avoid bringing his family into disrepute: his father believed that playing music made his son a beggar. He left home aged fourteen in reaction to his father's restrictions, and found shelter in the home of the Nigerian nationalist Herbert Heelas Macaulay. At the age of sixteen he was apprenticed as a newspaper printer. He bought a guitar but when he joined an itinerant band he was playing a tambourine, known as 'eight corners' in Lagos, where it was an instrument of symbolic significance believed to have the power to stimulate mental and spiritual consciousness. With the Jolly Boys Orchestra, a group distinguished by the penny-whistle flute of Sunday Harbour Giant, he played for tips, and made his first recording in 1939.

In wartime Campbell found work as a seaman. He saw England for the first time in 1940; he jumped ship in Liverpool two years later and moved to London. A slight physique ill equipped him for seafaring, but on a third voyage he reached South America, where he encountered Latin American music, and New York, where he and his shipmates played their guitars and drums in Harlem bars. He was greatly affected by the deaths of comrades at sea and did not want to return. He managed to prosper in wartime London in the face of widespread racial antipathy and deprivation, and made a mark in Camden Town, where he joined Cockney pub 'sing-alongs' and played music with friends. In 1942 he formed a relationship with Ida Margaret Gould (*b.* 1924/5), a restaurant waitress, and daughter of Noah Gould, a general dealer. They had a daughter, Dawn Adeyinka (*b.* 1944), and a son, Ambrose Oladipo (*b.* 1945).

After the war Campbell formed a band with percussionist friends in response to taunts about the integrity of African music; he was joined by the guitarist Brewster Hughes, another member of the Jolly Boys from Lagos. They played 'highlife', the popular west African dance music, for student dances, and in 1946 accompanied the Ballets Nègres, the first black British dance company, and visited Paris. With Campbell playing guitar as well as percussion, and after several changes of personnel, the band became the West African Rhythm Brothers, the name under which most of their 10 inch 78 rpm shellac records were made. Campbell's attractive singing voice, with its 'sad, strong, life-loving tones' (MacInnes, *Highlife today*), marked him out as leader, although Hughes was the group's main guitarist and its spokesman. The association with dancers continued when they formed a working relationship with the African-American choreographer and dance-teacher Buddy Bradley. In 1949 Campbell concentrated on the guitar. He studied with Ade Bashorun, a Lagosian who had joined the band playing bongos, and with the Trinidadian jazz musician Lauderic Caton, and was seen playing this instrument when the band made their television début in 1948 supporting the work of the Nigerian sculptor Ben Enwonwu.

In London Campbell's joyful music was an antidote to post-war austerity. More than two decades before the popularity of Afro-beat as a genre, he reinvigorated popular music with the gentle 'sunshine' sound of highlife, singing in Yoruba and accompanied by plangent guitars and by drummers who played melodies as well as keeping time. In 1952 the band found a base in London's West End when the Nigerian entrepreneur Ola Dosunmu opened the Abalabi, immortalized as the Beni Bronze by MacInnes (1957). Musicians, journalists, jazz fans, and intellectuals went there and to its successor, Club Afrique, to dance and drink, to savour the Nigerian atmosphere and food, and mix with Soho's African contingent. Nor did Campbell neglect the wider African community; his was the first visiting African band to play in Manchester's Moss Side.

The West African Rhythm Brothers became a ubiquitous presence in jazz circles, where their intricate 'Afro-rhythms' coincided with a growing awareness of the African origins of black American music. Yoruba music was rooted in religious symbolism and cultural function, but in Britain Campbell moved beyond tradition. The influence of jazz and calypso was strong in west Africa during this period, and Campbell's own association with jazz musicians fired his imagination, leading him to augment the band with Caribbean instrumentalists—their clarinet, saxophone, and muted trumpet attracted a wider audience—and Adam Fiberesima, a Nigerian Ijo whose percussive piano playing emphasized the Latin American element present in highlife and built a fuller sound. When the band visited Nigeria in 1957 Campbell recruited exponents of the talking drum (*gan-gan*), in order, he said, to further 'enrich' the texture.

In 1962 Campbell spent six months on Italy's Adriatic coast, where his audience included Jacqueline Kennedy, but back in London the growing popularity of music based on rock 'n' roll forced him to diversify from his earlier repertory and he flirted with a group of younger musicians, and played the twist. On 12 December 1964 he married Elizabeth Jane Graham-Smith (*b.* 1940), a riding instructor, and daughter of Richard Alan Graham-Smith, schoolmaster. They had two sons, Danny Adekoya (*b.* 1962) and Christopher Oladipo (*b.* 1964). When they separated Campbell formed a nightclub act with Cleo Howard, an Englishwoman whom he taught to play drums.

Gentle, balding, and softly spoken, Campbell was a dreamer who lived for the day. He survived through his ability to attract support and friendship across class and cultural divides. The record producer Denny Cordell was an admirer, and in 1972 he persuaded Campbell to move to the USA and join him and the Oklahoman singer and pianist Leon Russell in a production company. He toured and recorded with Russell's band as a percussionist, returning briefly to Nigeria in 1979 to refute rumours of his death, then moved to Nashville and continued working with Russell and other popular musicians. In 1980, in order to support the man he claimed as his spiritual adviser, Russell opened the Ambrose Campbell World Video Studio in Burbank, California. In the USA Campbell married Antoinette (surname unknown) about 1973; their daughter, Funmilayo, was born in 1976. In 2004 he returned to England, precipitating a revival of interest in his work; he was interviewed and some of his recordings were reissued on

CD. He died in Plymouth on 22 June 2006 from an acute upper gastrointestinal haemorrhage and cancer of the stomach.

Campbell occupied a unique position as a traditional African artist. Respected by the jazz community and admired for his 'authenticity' by musicians like the saxophonist Ronnie Scott, who described Campbell as 'a bit special … a musicologist' (interview with V. Wilmer, 1991), he was exposed to jazz modernism, itself in part an outcome of African-American movements for self-determination and racial equality. Appreciation of his music developed in a context in which Afro-Cuban rhythms, associated with black cultural nationalism, crossed the Atlantic and remained a component in popular music. Predicting figures of future significance, in 1952 the critic Ernest Borneman chose Campbell's drummers for their potential to 'provide tomorrow's British hornmen with backing as interesting as any that [the Cuban percussionists] Machito and Chano Pozo … provided for [Charlie] Parker and [Dizzy] Gillespie' (*Melody Maker*, 22 March 1952). VAL WILMER

Sources *West African Review* (Sept 1946); (Nov 1952); (July 1953); (Sept 1956) • *Illustrated* (12 April 1947) • *Melody Maker* (25 Feb 1950); (22 March 1952) • *Daily Times* [Nigeria] (25 April 1951); (7 Sept 1951); (7 March 1952); (20 Nov 1957); (8 April 1970) • *Beat*, 1/3 (Feb 1957), 30–31 • C. MacInnes, *City of spades* (1957) • C. MacInnes, 'City after dark', *The twentieth century* (1957) • *West Africa* (28 Nov 1959) • C. MacInnes, 'Welcome, beauty walk', *England, half English* (1961) • C. MacInnes, *Highlife today*, LP notes, 1966 • *Billboard* (22 Oct 1980) • A. Alaja-Browne, 'A diachronic study of change in juju music', *Popular Music*, 8/3 (Oct 1989), 232–42 • *The Blacklisted Journalist* (1 Feb 2001) • *Mojo*, 145 (Dec 2005), 70–72, 74 • V. Wilmer, *London is the place for me 3*, CD notes, 2006 • *The Guardian* (8 July 2006) • *The Times* (21 July 2006); (31 July 2006) • A. Abeke, 'No foreign land like homeland', *Universal Journal*, [Lagos], 2008, http://ayjw.org • personal knowledge (2010) • private information (2010) [Dawn Hammond, daughter; C. Bashorun; A. Bashorun; H. Beckett; A. Fiberesima; I. Pedro; R. Scott; J. Sikuade] • m. cert. • b. certs. [children] • d. cert.

Archives FILM BFINA, current affairs footage

Likenesses A. McBean, photograph, 1946, repro. in *West African Review* (Sept 1946) • M. Severn, photograph, 1946, Hult. Arch. • photographs, *c.*1952–1964, priv. coll. • photograph, *c.*1954, repro. in *The Guardian* • photographs, *c.*1954, repro. in *Mojo* • photographs, *c.*1956, repro. in *West African Review* (Sept 1956) • photograph, *c.*1957, repro. in *Beat* • photograph, *c.*1959, repro. in *West Africa* (28 Nov 1959) • D. Hoffmann, photograph, *c.*1964, repro. in *Mojo* • M. Joseph, photograph, 1966, repro. in *Highlife today* (1966) [record album sleeve] • H. Borden, photographs, 2005, repro. in *Observer Music Monthly* (Jan 2006) • H. Borden, C-type colour print, 2006, NPG • C. Saville, photograph, 2006, repro. in *fRoots* (May 2006)

Campbell, Gordon Thomas Calthrop, **Baron Campbell of Croy** (**1921–2005**), diplomatist and politician, was born on 8 June 1921 in Quetta, India, one of two sons of Major-General James Alexander Campbell (1886–1964), army officer, and his wife, Violet Constance Madeline, *née* Calthrop (*d.* 1978), artist and writer. Educated at Wellington College and, at the outbreak of the Second World War, the Royal Military Academy, Woolwich, Campbell served briefly as an instructor, then with the 15th Scottish division. He was promoted captain at nineteen, and major at twenty-one. As the Germans retreated after D-day, he commanded the 320 field battery in the 15th Scottish division and became embroiled in some of the fiercest fighting of the war. Having earned the nickname Lucky following close shaves on the Siegfried line and in Normandy, he found himself on 29 April 1945 with one more river to cross, the mighty Elbe. Just minutes after his division set off in assault boats, a bullet smashed through Campbell, severing his sciatic nerve and disabling him for life. 'Here's another bloody Jerry!', shouted one of his rescuers as they carried him to a padre, failing to recognize Campbell beneath the blood and mud. 'That's not a bloody Jerry,' replied the padre, having spotted his MC and bar, 'it's Major Gordon Campbell!' (*The News*, Nov 2002). He survived, unlike his brother Ian, a Spitfire pilot who was shot as an escaping prisoner in 1943 after baling out over Italy.

Campbell was flown back to Britain where he spent more than a year in hospital. He took the entrance examination for the Foreign Office while still on crutches, and began his diplomatic career with a desk job covering eastern Europe. He got to know the foreign secretary, Ernest Bevin, and would often wake him during the Berlin blockade to pass on telegrams. During this period the so-called 'Campbell solution' was adopted over Trieste, marking the border between Italy and Yugoslavia. At the Foreign Office Campbell formed a close friendship with Anthony Montague Browne, later Churchill's last private secretary, who remembered Campbell being 'in pain a good deal of the time and partially disabled' (his left leg was in a calliper), although it 'did not stop him being both remarkably efficient and the most jolly and humorous of companions' (Browne, 68–9). Browne was Campbell's best man when on 21 July 1949, at St Mary's, Bryanston Square, London, he married Nicola Elizabeth Gina Madan, a 28-year-old Foreign Office colleague. She was the daughter of Captain Geoffrey Spencer Madan, and a descendant of Isambard Kingdom Brunel. They had two sons and one daughter. Shortly after his marriage Campbell was transferred to New York as part of the UK delegation to the United Nations. His regime of daily hospital care continued in the United States, and three years later he returned to London, first as Foreign Office liaison officer with MI5, MI6, and Government Communications Headquarters (GCHQ), and then as private secretary to the cabinet secretary, Sir Norman Brook.

It was apparently Brook who suggested Campbell to the former Conservative Scottish secretary James Stuart as the latter's successor in the Moray and Nairn constituency. He was duly adopted, resigned from a diplomatic posting in Vienna, and worked in the Conservative research department until the general election of 1959, when he was elected to parliament. After two years on the back benches he became a Scottish whip, and in 1963 joined the Scottish Office as parliamentary under-secretary for local government and housing. In opposition from 1964, he joined Edward Heath's front bench (despite voting for Reginald Maudling in the 1965 leadership contest) as a shadow defence spokesman before replacing Michael Noble (to whom Campbell's wife was also related) as shadow Scottish secretary in February 1969. He earned a reputation as a stickler, often contesting Hansard's grammatical corrections of his speeches.

In 1970 Campbell became secretary of state for Scotland in Heath's government, arriving at St Andrew's House to applause from civil servants, something that reportedly infuriated his predecessor (and successor) as Scottish secretary, Labour's Willie Ross. From Ross, Campbell inherited the report of a royal commission on local government in Scotland. He broadly supported its recommendation for two-tier local authorities, and stood firm despite opposition from Conservative activists fearful that a Strathclyde regional council would consolidate Labour dominance in the west of Scotland. Always uncomfortable with the political aspects of his cabinet post, Campbell also faced hostility because of his refusal to overrule Scottish councils that wanted to abolish selective schools. But there were some successes. The NHS in Scotland was overhauled through the creation of individual health boards, while Campbell was especially proud of fast-tracking construction of the A9 road. Industrial relations, however, were not so smooth. Campbell infuriated the Scottish Trades Union Congress when he described the upward trend of unemployment in Scotland as 'worrying, though not unexpected' (*The Times*, 18 Feb 1972), while the Upper Clyde Shipbuilders forced Heath into a disastrous economic U-turn. Campbell also faced growing discontent over Heath's lack of commitment to a devolved Scottish assembly, a proposal that was not implemented despite a report from the Kilbrandon commission in October 1973. The Scottish National Party was then on the march with its compelling cry of 'It's Scotland's oil'. Unfortunately for Campbell, voters in Moray and Nairn largely agreed and he was beaten by the Scottish Nationalist Winnie Ewing at the general election of February 1974 and jeered when, uncharacteristically, he claimed his defeat was a vote against the disabled. Campbell was unfailingly courteous, but what John Biffen remembered as 'an engaging lack of flamboyance' (*The Guardian*, 30 April 2005) did not serve him well as a politician and he was one of the weakest post-war Scottish secretaries.

Appointed to the House of Lords as Baron Campbell of Croy, he served as opposition spokesman in the upper house on Scottish affairs, and spoke on rather esoteric subjects reflecting his interests in ornithology and nature, including a campaign to exterminate the highland midge. More fruitful was his long campaign on behalf of disabled people. In the 1960s he had campaigned against discrimination and succeeded in strengthening the statutory duty of employers to provide access for disabled workers. He resumed his championship of the disabled after leaving the Commons. His work was recognized with the Nuffield Trust's first Queen Elizabeth, the queen mother, fellowship in 1980, after which he published *Disablement: Problems and Prospects in the UK* (1981). He also campaigned for greater understanding of schizophrenia.

Campbell was active in the upper house until the early years of the new millennium, but the constant travelling between his home in Nairnshire and parliament eventually took its toll. He moved, with his wife, to the St George's Nursing Home at 61 St George's Square, London, and died at St Thomas's Hospital, Lambeth, on 26 April 2005, of a pulmonary thrombo-embolism. He was survived by his wife and their three children.

DAVID TORRANCE

Sources A. Montague Browne, *Long sunset* (1995) · G. Pottinger, *The secretaries of state for Scotland, 1926–1976* (1979), 176–84 · *The News* [Magazine of the Thomson Foundation] (Nov 2002) · *The Times* (18 Feb 1972); (28 April 2005) · *Daily Telegraph* (28 April 2005) · *The Independent* (29 April 2005) · *The Guardian* (30 April 2005) · D. Torrance, *The Scottish secretaries* (2006), 270–81 · Burke, *Peerage* · *WW* (2005) · private information (2009) · m. cert. · d. cert.

Archives priv. coll. | NA Scot., Scottish Office papers | SOUND NL Scot., *The office of secretary of state for Scotland*, acc. 7330

Likenesses W. Bird, bromide print, 1959, NPG · photographs, 1959–74, *The Scotsman*, Edinburgh · photographs, 1959–74, *The Herald*, Glasgow · J. Mendoza, group portrait, oils, 1986–7, House of Commons, Westminster · photographs, 1998, Photoshot, London · H. More Gordon, group portrait, watercolour, 1999 (*Eight secretaries of state for Scotland*), Scot. NPG · obituary photographs · photograph, NPG

Wealth at death £345,896.31: confirmation, 17 Aug 2006, *CCI*

Campbell, Steven Macmillan (1953–2007), painter, was born on 19 March 1953 at 204 Brownside Road, Cambuslang, Glasgow, the son of George Campbell (1922–1995), bricklayer, later clerk of works, and his wife, Martha Dallas, *née* Macmillan (*b.* 1924). He was educated at Rutherglen Academy, but left at the age of sixteen to serve an apprenticeship with British Steel. He then worked as a time-served maintenance engineer in the steel mill at Cambuslang. On 4 July 1975, at St Cuthbert's and Queens Cross Church, Glasgow, he married Carol Ann Thompson (*b.* 1953), schoolteacher, and daughter of Andrew Crossen Thompson, wire worker. They had two daughters, Lauren and Greer, and a son, Rory.

After gaining the necessary qualifications at night school, in 1978 Campbell went to Glasgow School of Art. His first interest was in performance art, reflecting his enduring love of cinema, especially Hitchcock, Chabrol, and *film noir*. Cinema's freedom from the constraints of linear narrative combined with the surrealist approach to dreams inspired his own approach. He also extended the idea of performance into his pictures, often appearing in them in the *alter ego* of Dracula's nemesis, Van Helsing. His farouche but nevertheless always studied appearance also extended performance into his daily life. When he graduated in 1982 Glasgow School of Art recognized his originality with the Bram Stoker gold medal, devised specially for him. He was seen as the leader of his generation at the art school, but it was not a position that he either sought or enjoyed.

Campbell first made his mark in an exhibition at the New 57 Gallery in Edinburgh in 1982. The paintings he showed were big, improvised with great energy, and crowded with huge figures. He had decided that the greatest art of the past was figurative and could only be emulated by an artist who was prepared to take on that challenge. In 1982 he was awarded a Fulbright scholarship, which allowed him to fulfil his ambition to go to New

York. It was intended that he should follow a course at the Pratt Institute, but his attendance was nominal. He held several exhibitions in America and enjoyed considerable success from his first showing of just two paintings, at the Barbara Toll Gallery in June 1983. Unhappily a dispute with his dealer later developed into a lawsuit that left a legacy of some bitterness. His painting in these years tended to be of young men, often identified as hikers or travellers, for example *Man Amazed at the Height He is Up*, and dressed in tweeds. Like characters in P. G. Wodehouse's novels, which he admired, they face the baffling unreliability of the world they travel with imperturbable naïvety.

Campbell anticipated his return to Scotland with a major exhibition at the Fruitmarket Gallery, Edinburgh, in 1985 (first shown at the Riverside Studios in London in late 1984). Two years later he was a central figure in the exhibition 'The Vigorous Imagination' at the Scottish National Gallery of Modern Art. In 1987 he also held his first one-man show with Marlborough Fine Art in London, who remained his dealers thereafter. In 1989 he moved with his young family from Glasgow to a house on the edge of the village of Kippen, Stirlingshire. In Kippen he organized 9V (Nine Villages), an ambitious series of evening classes for local teenagers.

Campbell went to Australia in 1990 as artist-in-residence at the Art Gallery of New South Wales, but later that year he also held a major one-man exhibition at the Third Eye Centre in Glasgow. Called 'Steven Campbell: on Form and Fiction', the exhibition, which subsequently toured in England and Wales, was characteristically ambitious and original, both in form and content. His exhibitions were always planned as artworks, not merely as the sum of their parts. At the Third Eye Centre, the *mise-en-scène* was cinematic. A series of large, square paintings, lit like cinema screens, were framed by smaller, monochrome works on paper, unframed and mounted edge to edge so that the whole wall was covered with images. His work had grown lighter, both in tone and in mood. It was also more studied and less dramatic in execution. As both the titles of this show and of individual works, such as *Portrait of a Nude Encouraging Significant Form*, indicated, he had begun to explore the fictions on which painting depends, the paradoxes that they entail and often too the puns and other jokes that they suggest.

The title of Campbell's next major show, 'Pinocchio's Present', held at the Talbot Rice Gallery, Edinburgh, in 1993, suggested the paradox of seeking truth in any kind of fiction, whether in words or pictures. He returned to a more improvised approach to the construction of his pictures, but nevertheless gave a great deal of thought to composition. However complex and dream-like it may be, the space in his pictures is always coherent. Before this exhibition, however, deeply discouraged, he had almost given up painting and only returned to it through a series of extraordinary tapestry-like collages. These were included in the exhibition along with some of his finest paintings, notably *Painting in Defence of Migrants* (1993). The image of flight and insecurity in this picture, in which birds, nature's migrants, take pity on human migrants displaced by war, reflected current events in the former Yugoslavia. Nevertheless the beautifully painted birds, like the flowers that also often appear in his work, were typical of a kind of naturalism that linked even his most bizarre visions back to his love of the natural world. St Francis of Assisi was one of his great heroes.

In 1995 Campbell travelled in Italy on a Leverhulme scholarship. In 1996 'Chesterfield Dreams', shown first at the Pier Arts Centre in Orkney and the following year at Marlborough Fine Art in London, saw him reinvent himself yet again with a remarkable series of surrealist, low-relief collages. In 2000 he produced an installation at the Scottish National Portrait Gallery in honour of Edwin Morgan. In the same year he received a Creative Scotland award. The work he produced with the award was shown at the Talbot Rice Gallery in 2003 in an exhibition entitled 'The Caravan Club'. It was typical of Campbell's fertile imagination to see an analogy between painting and caravans, which carry within them a simulacrum of domestic life. It was the illusion of suburban security within the caravan's flimsy shell that intrigued Campbell, however. His dark vision in these paintings was of the forces that lurk beneath that cosy illusion, or in a different metaphor, of what is hidden under the carpet. The painting *No Bathroom Evidence Painting can Explain the Fact that there is no Rug in Psycho* is simply a painting of a carpet, but its surface surges with life, birds and flowers above, the corpse of the murdered girl in the film looming beneath.

Steven Campbell died of a ruptured appendix on 15 August 2007, and was survived by his wife and children. At the time of his death he was working on another major exhibition, and in 2008 the work he left was shown posthumously at the Glasgow School of Art. The title he had chosen was 'Wretched Stars, Insatiable Heavens' a quotation from the libretto for Monteverdi's *Orfeo* that proved sadly apt. The carpet metaphor reappeared as a sinister Axminster metamorphosing into a crocodile in *The Childhood Bedroom of Captain Hook* (2006–7). In a series inspired by the apprentice's column at Rosslyn Chapel he reflected obliquely on his own time as an apprentice. Many of these works were rich in naturalistic detail of birds and flowers, and several include the Green Man, a pagan personification of nature. At the time of his death he was as vigorous and inventive a painter as he had always been.

DUNCAN MACMILLAN

Sources *Steven Campbell: new paintings* (1984) · *The vigorous imagination: new Scottish art* (1987) · J. Collins, 'Interview with Steven Campbell', *Flash Art* (Feb–March 1987) · *Steven Campbell: recent work* (1988) · K. Hartley, *Scottish art since 1900* (1989) · S. Campbell, *On form and fiction* (1990) · D. Macmillan, *The paintings of Steven Campbell: the story so far* (1993) · D. Macmillan, *Scottish art in the 20th century* (1994) · S. Campbell, *Outside right at the sunset gate* (1994) · *Contemporary British art in print: the publications of Charles Booth-Clibborn and his imprint, the Paragon Press, 1986–95* (1995) · S. Campbell, *Chesterfield dreams* (1997) · *The Caravan Club: new paintings by Steven Campbell* (2002) · S. Campbell, *Steven Campbell, Jean-Pierre Léaud* (2004) · *The Scotsman* (17 Aug 2007); (22 Aug 2007) · *The Herald* [Glasgow] (17 Aug 2007) · *The Times* (21 Aug 2007) · *The Guardian* (3 Sept 2007) · *The Independent* (4 Sept 2007) · *Sunday Herald* [Glasgow] (10 Aug 2008) · personal knowledge (2011) · private information (2011) · b. cert. · m. cert.

Archives SOUND BL NSA, documentary recordings
Likenesses self-portrait, oils, *c*.2006 (*Scratched out, it's all in the wrists*), National Galleries of Scotland · W. Cheung, photographs, Camera Press, London · obituary photographs

Carpenter, Humphrey William Bouverie (1946–2005), author, broadcaster, and musician, was born on 29 April 1946 at the Radcliffe Maternity Home, Oxford, the only child of Harry James Carpenter (1901–1993), warden of Keble College and later bishop of Oxford, and his wife, Urith Monica, *née* Trevelyan (1909–1995), a Froebel-trained teacher who went on to read English at Oxford. He grew up in an atmosphere of purposeful activity, mental and physical, and was encouraged by his mother in particular to take his own line and think for himself. Contemporaries remembered a small, determined figure tricycling round the Keble quadrangle and lighting up pantomimes with spirited and mischievous performances. He was educated at the Dragon School in Oxford (at the time offbeat and bohemian in character), at Marlborough College, where he was less comfortable, and at Keble College, Oxford, where he read English. He followed this with a year's teacher training in Oxford, but in 1968 accepted a BBC general traineeship, with placements in television, regional news, the World Service, and (the then experimental) local radio.

Carpenter's crackling intelligence and fluency could have taken him a long way inside the BBC, but in 1970 he chose to return to his beloved Oxford to work on the fledgeling BBC local radio station, where he moved with ease between serious and intellectual programming, surreal comedy, and a manically giggly disc-jockey show entitled *Humf*. On 31 March 1973 he married a colleague at that radio station, Mari Christina Prichard (*b*. 1947), daughter of the Welsh poet and novelist Caradog *Prichard. They had two daughters, Clare (*b*. 1978) and Kate (*b*. 1981), and lived at 5 Polstead Road, Oxford, until 1977, 61 Observatory Street until 1980, and then 6 Farndon Road until the end of his life. All these homes lay within a small patch of north-west Oxford, where he was a familiar part of the community, singing in the St Barnabas church choir intermittently for much of his life, although his formal religious belief ran out, according to close friends, around 1980 (when he was working on the Oxford University Press Past Masters biography of Jesus).

From the mid-1980s Carpenter ran, with considerable brio, a children's theatre group called Mushy Pea. 'It is not', he said, 'a kind deed to be looking after other people's children on Saturday mornings. It is a way of getting my own works performed by enormous casts' (*The Times*, 19 May 1993). His taste for the music and shows of the first half of the twentieth century found a spectacular outlet when in 1993—largely at his own expense and with the observation that 'oh, some people spend that kind of money on a car' (ibid.)—he took a company of some sixty children to perform two of his shows at the Shaw Theatre in London. The youngest of the cast was only four years old. One show was *Mr Majeika: the Musical*, based on his own children's books, the other *Babes*, about the lives of Hollywood child stars. Both his daughters performed, the younger doing a startlingly Mermanesque impression of Ethel Meglin, dance school proprietress.

Humphrey William Bouverie Carpenter (1946–2005), by Mark Gerson, 2003

Meanwhile, however, Carpenter's work as a biographer was flourishing. After his authorized biography of J. R. R. Tolkien (1977) he turned to group biography, evoking with great skill C. S. Lewis's Oxford friends (in *The Inklings*, 1978, which won the Somerset Maugham award). Later he was to do the same with American writers in 1920s Paris (*Geniuses Together*, 1987), the Evelyn Waugh circle (*The Brideshead Generation*, 1989), the 1960s satirists (*That Was Satire That Was*, 2000), and the 1950s rebels (*Angry Young Men*, 2002). It is significant that he excelled in this area, for sociability was one of his most marked characteristics. John Walsh, the journalist, observed that 'He loved company, harmony, communion, the humming convivium of a party, the shared endeavour of musicians, the sight and sound of human beings working together' (*The Independent*, 6 Jan 2005). With his wife, Mari, he edited the *Oxford Companion to Children's Literature* (1984) and a year later published *Secret Gardens*, a study based on a lifelong interest in the personalities and beliefs of children's authors in the 'golden age'. He began to write his own books for children with *The Joshers* (1977) and from 1984 the Mr Majeika series, about an irrepressible, eccentric, and accident-prone wizard working as a primary school teacher.

Carpenter's individual biographies included those of W. H. Auden (1981, which won the E. M. Forster award of the American Academy of Arts and Letters), Ezra Pound (1988, which won the Duff Cooper memorial prize), Benjamin Britten (1992), Robert Runcie (1996), Dennis Potter

(1998), and Spike Milligan (2003), but in the course of writing them he confessed that he often discovered such marvellous stories that it was a torment to keep them to himself until publication, and he was tempted to tell all at parties. Sometimes he did. Some attacked him for his breezy openness about the sexual oddities of his subjects, notably Britten and Potter, and his inclusion of remarks by Runcie that were indiscreet, though not 'off the record', caused the latter some embarrassment; but his research was rigorous, his sources solid, and if there was a difference between him and those who criticized him it was that he was slower to condemn the strange byways down which life leads nervous and creative people. It was notable that even if his work was treated intemperately by rival writers, he managed to forget the slight and return to cordial relations with them in no time. As one contemporary said, 'He didn't do feuds, he didn't do grudges' (private information). His family life was conspicuously happy and stable.

Carpenter's performing career continued through much of his life; he was a regular radio presenter on Radio 3 and Radio 4, and in 1983 he founded Vile Bodies, a mixed group of professionals and amateurs who played dance music and jazz from the 1920s to the 1940s. This combo had a residency at the Ritz Hotel in London from 1987 to 1994, thus providing possibly the only opportunity to see a leading literary biographer and arts broadcaster wrapped up in a giant sousaphone under pink lighting. In 1994 he became programme director of the Cheltenham literary festival for three years, and livened up the hitherto rather staid world of English literary festivals by introducing jazz, cartoonists, and numerous children's and science events, in between the interesting unknowns and the literary and intellectual big-hitters. He often personally chaired sessions, rushing from room to room in a happy blur. His own book reviews were acute, occasionally mischievous, but generous in spirit.

Suffering from Parkinson's disease in the last years of his life, characteristically Carpenter continued working, kept quiet about it as long as he could, and gathered information and helpful gadgets. He also began writing a musical about the illness entitled *Shake it all About*, with a lament on the difficulty of 'putting on my socks' set to the tune of 'Puttin' on the Ritz'. After his sudden death from a heart attack on 4 January 2005 (he was pronounced dead at the John Radcliffe Hospital, Oxford) it was performed by his friends as a fundraiser for a project on public awareness of the illness. He was buried on 14 January in Wolvercote cemetery. His untimely death brought an avalanche of tributes from friends, all trying to evoke the vivid, beaky, dishevelled tornado that was Humphrey Carpenter. One fellow church choir singer wrote, 'He is the only person I know competent to sing any of the four parts of choral music—treble, alto, tenor or bass', adding that 'during the more boring parts Humphrey, naughty choirboy of 34, his uncombed mop poking from his surplice, could be seen bent over a novel' (*Evening Standard*, 10 Jan 2005). Another observed, 'he seemed to want to clasp the world to his manly bosom, gleefully, greedily, to have as much going on simultaneously as one life could bear' (*The Independent*, 6 Jan 2005). His wife, Mari (who survived him, along with their two daughters), oversaw the publication of his final works. Two were published posthumously: the fourteenth Majeika story, which owed something to his experience of Parkinson's disease, and a history of the publisher John Murray, which was once again an account of what he loved best: the world of creative, turbulent literary and artistic co-operation. LIBBY PURVES

Sources *Daily Telegraph* (5 Jan 2005) · *The Guardian* (5 Jan 2005); (27 Jan 2005) · *The Times* (6 Jan 2005); (12 Jan 2005); (14 Jan 2005); (20 Jan 2005); (3 Feb 2005) · *The Independent* (6 Jan 2005) · *Sunday Times* (9 Jan 2005) · *Evening Standard* (10 Jan 2005) · *WW* (2005) · personal knowledge (2009) · private information (2009) [Mari Prichard, widow] · b. cert. · m. cert. · d. cert.
Archives FILM BFINA, current affairs footage | SOUND BL NSA, current affairs recordings · BL NSA, documentary recordings · BL NSA, performance recordings
Likenesses photographs, 1996–2003, Rex Features, London · M. Gerson, bromide fibre print, 2003, NPG [*see illus.*] · photographs, 2003, Camera Press, London · obituary photographs
Wealth at death £643,760: probate, 14 June 2005, *CGPLA Eng. & Wales*

Carrier, Robert (1923–2006), writer on cookery and restaurateur, was born Robert Carrier McMahon on 10 November 1923, at Tarrytown, New York state, USA, the third son of a wealthy property lawyer of Irish descent. His mother was of German descent, and also from a wealthy background. (His middle name, later his assumed surname, was that of one of his grandmothers, chosen because it looked good in print and was easy to pronounce in French.) When his parents lost their money following the Wall Street crash he became a child actor, taking the juvenile lead in musicals; he eventually appeared on Broadway, in Leonard Sillman's revue *New Faces*, probably in 1943. After leaving school, when not acting he took art courses. He first came to Britain with the American armed forces in 1943, as a member of the Office of Strategic Services (OSS), the forerunner of the CIA. He later stated bluntly, 'I was a spy' (personal knowledge). His wartime duties were in intelligence. After D-day he moved to Paris as a cryptographer, and worked in the headquarters of General de Gaulle. He became editor of a magazine, *Spectacle*, that supported de Gaulle's party, the Rassemblement du Peuple Français, until the publication folded in 1947. He then stayed on in Europe, working as a radio journalist for an American English-language station, and acting (he took the part of a cowboy in a musical revue in Italy), and eventually arrived in not yet fashionable St Tropez. There he received the only professional kitchen training he ever had (he never called himself a chef), at Chez Fifine, where the proprietor took the tall, good-looking young man under her wing.

Invited by a friend to return to London for the coronation, Carrier fell in love with the place, though rationing had not yet ended, and the food was poor. However, he cooked for a dinner party where the food was so impressive that one of the guests, Eileen Dickson, offered him a job writing about food for *Harper's Bazaar*. He went on to write for *Vogue*, and then a weekly column in the *Sunday*

Robert Carrier (1923–2006), by Barry Marsden, 1998

Times Magazine. He was probably the first cookery writer to make use of cookery cards, stiff wipe-clean cards with a glossy photograph of a dish on one side and the recipe on the other. He also worked in public relations, which gave great scope for his flamboyant charm. His accounts included stock cubes, New Zealand apples, and cornflour; conflict of interest was not then a consideration in the world of food journalism. In 1957 he and his long-term partner, Oliver Lawson Dick, published *The Vanished City: a Study of London*, featuring architectural prints of seventeenth- and eighteenth-century London's temples, gardens, parks, and squares.

Carrier's heyday was the late 1960s and the 1970s. Though he had two notable restaurants, his real sphere of influence was the domestic dinner party. *Home* magazine called him 'London's gayest gourmet'. In his *Great Dishes of the World* (1963) he introduced a large readership to foods that had previously been the province of self-styled 'gourmets', including not only the classics of French bourgeois and regional cookery, but also moussaka and a properly made *ragù bolognese*. This was a time when post-war, post-Spam cooks cherished their recent access to cream, butter, and the brandy bottle, and Carrier, now a portly man, encouraged all three. *Great Dishes* in its various guises and permutations was said to have sold over 10 million copies worldwide. Many cookery titles followed, including some ingenious part-works for Marshall Cavendish from 1981 to 1983, for which he styled the photographs himself. His recipes were more specific and easier to follow than Elizabeth David's, and made it possible for tens of thousands of middle-class women to prepare food that would impress their guests.

In 1966 Carrier bought a restaurant in Camden Passage, Islington. The Greek couple he had intended to run it for him disappeared, and he ended up cooking himself. An outlet for his showmanship and flair, Carrier's was done up in imaginative French provincial style, with Provençal fabrics and wood that looked and felt expensive. Avocado starters, fresh herbs used with profligacy, generous servings of country terrines, rich desserts, and lots of main courses beyond the usual steak, appealed both to those who knew the food of France and to those who could only aspire to such knowledge. Something new on the London restaurant scene, Carrier's attracted people whose names featured in newspaper gossip columns. There was a show-business touch of camp in all Carrier's enterprises—the service in his restaurants was elaborate and the food itself as over-decorated as in the photographs in his books and cookery cards. In 1967 Carrier opened a specialized cookware department in Harrods.

His talents needing a new theatre, in 1971 Carrier paid £32,000 for Hintlesham Hall near Ipswich, a huge, grade one listed Tudor brick house with a Georgian front and 175 acres. He had failed to commission a survey, and its tumbledown state meant that, though he had a workforce of sixty, he never achieved the vision he had for it as a country house in which he could live and entertain, so in August 1972 he opened it as a hotel and restaurant. Later he invested another £300,000 to turn it into a state-of-the-art cookery school, but in 1981, when the instructor he had in mind failed him, he began teaching the courses himself. His career as a genial television cook had begun in 1975 with *Carrier's Kitchen*, and clients flocked to his cookery school. But the repetitiveness of teaching bored him, and he closed the school in 1982 and sold Hintlesham the next year. In 1984 he also gave up the Camden Passage restaurant, which had become a nursery for talented chefs, including Shaun Hill.

Carrier travelled a good deal, bought a house in Marrakesh, took up painting, and published an excellent book, *A Taste of Morocco* (1987). He made further television series in the 1980s, and had a success in his native America with a weekly magazine. In 1984 he became the public face of the British restaurant industry, arguing effectively for changes to the licensing laws, and he was made an honorary OBE in 1987. He returned to London in 1994 from Morocco (having passed a few years in New York), then lived his last few years in Provence. Oliver Lawson Dick predeceased him, and the octogenarian Carrier was looked after by his close friend and former editor, Liz Glaze. He died in France on 27 June 2006. PAUL LEVY

Sources *The Guardian* (28 June 2006) · *The Times* (28 June 2006) · *The Independent* (1 July 2006) · personal knowledge (2010) · private information (2010)

Archives FILM BFINA, light entertainment footage

Likenesses photographs, 1963–86, PA Photos, London · photographs, 1968, Getty Images, London, Popperfoto · photographs, 1981–2000, Rex Features, London · M. Birt, bromide print, 1982, NPG · J. Downing, photographs, 1982, Getty Images, London, Hult. Arch. · H. Schwarz, watercolour, gouache and conte, 1994; Bonhams, 21 Nov 2006, lot 13641 · H. Schwarz, oil on board, 1994–5;

Bonhams, 17 Feb 2004, lot 11037 • B. Marsden, colour transparency, 1998, NPG [*see illus.*] • photographs, Photoshot, London

Carter, Denis Victor, **Baron Carter** (**1932–2006**), farmer and politician, was born on 17 January 1932 at 39 Hayles Street, Southwark, London, the son of Albert William Carter (*d.* 1973), tea warehouseman, and his wife, Annie Julia, *née* Tynan (*d.* 1972). The family later moved to Hove, Sussex, where they ran a sweetshop and later a café. After attending six different schools in seven years, Carter was sent to Xaverian College in Brighton, where he met his future wife, Teresa Mary May Greengoe, daughter of Cecil William Walter Greengoe. They eventually married on 3 August 1957; Carter was an agricultural student by that time, and she a primary school teacher. They had one son, Andrew (*b.* 1963), who died at the age of nineteen, and one daughter, Catherine (*b.* 1959), who died at the age of forty-four. Both suffered from the hereditary degenerative condition retinitis pigmentosa, and in addition Andrew had a defective heart.

Carter, a city boy with no agricultural connections who was to become one of the most knowledgeable men in Britain on agriculture, had developed the idea of becoming a farmer between 1950 and 1952 when he was doing his national service in the Suez Canal zone working as an audit clerk. After returning to England he went back into accounting and worked for a company in London but the 'call of the land' was persistent, and two years later he enrolled at the East Sussex Institute of Agriculture, followed by Writtle Agricultural College, Essex, where he obtained the national diploma in agriculture and the queen's award for the country's highest marks. Much later, in 1970, he was awarded a two-year senior research fellowship in agricultural marketing at the Institute of Agricultural Economics at Worcester College, Oxford, where he gained a BLitt in 1972.

In 1957 Carter founded and became director of an agricultural accounting and management company, AKC Ltd, which grew to manage and handle the accounts of a large number of farms, mainly in southern England. He held this position for forty years until 1997, when he entered government. At the same time he also began farming himself, first in Oxfordshire and then on a larger scale in Wiltshire and Hampshire. In 1968 he founded and then worked for thirty years with United Oilseeds, which expanded, largely under his guidance, into a substantial farm trading operation. United Oilseeds was responsible for introducing large-scale oilseed rape marketing into Britain and later encouraged the production of opium poppies as a profitable medical crop.

Carter stood once for parliament. Encouraged by Wilfred Cave, a Wiltshire farmer and staunch Labour supporter, he contested Basingstoke as the Labour candidate in the election of 1970 but was unsuccessful. In the mid-1970s, during the boom in agricultural land prices, Carter served on the Northfield committee, investigating especially the effect of City funds on land prices. Other farming appointments followed including, in 1982, being elected chairman of the Farmers' Club, of which he was later a trustee. Many other organizations gained from Carter's enthusiasm, expertise, sharp mind, down-to-earth approach, and dry humour. He chaired the BBC rural affairs and agriculture committee from 1987 to 1990; in 1993 Michael Heseltine appointed him to chair the UK Co-operative Council, a post he held until 1997; he was president of the Guild of Agricultural Journalists from 1994 to 1996 and of the British Institute of Agricultural Consultants from 1992 to 1997. He was also a member of two agricultural discussion clubs, Turners (in Stockbridge) and Grasshoppers (in Amesbury).

Denis Victor Carter, Baron Carter (**1932–2006**), by unknown photographer, 1997

In 1987, on Neil Kinnock's recommendation, Carter was created a life peer as Baron Carter, acting for his first ten years as an authoritative opposition spokesman on rural affairs. He was also opposition spokesman on social security from 1988 to 1990 and health from 1989 to 1992, the latter with special reference to the disabled. His experience of bringing up children with a degenerative disease causing increasing disability made him a sensitive spokesman in the Lords on these complex and important issues. In 2003, when he chaired the joint committee on the draft Mental Capacity Bill, he won cross-party support for the legislation and was particularly successful in ensuring that people with learning disabilities could present evidence to his committee. In memory of their children the

Carters set up the Andrew and Catherine Carter Foundation Trust to help disabled people. He was made an honorary fellow of the Royal College of Psychiatrists in recognition for his work for the disabled.

From 1990 to 1992 Carter was deputy opposition chief whip in the House of Lords, and when Labour gained power in 1997 he was appointed captain of the Honourable Corps of Gentlemen at Arms (government chief whip), deputy chairman of various committees and deputy speaker, and was sworn of the privy council. For five years until 2002 he steered a heavy legislative programme including the Human Rights Act through the House of Lords, and he was involved in the negotiations that led to the compromise in the House of Lords Act 1999, which retained ninety-two hereditary peers in the first stage of reform. Carter himself was a strong supporter of Lords reform. A year after the start of Tony Blair's second term as prime minister he stood down as chief whip in the Lords, having reached the age of seventy. Still farming, he remained an active member of the House of Lords and became vice-chairman of the English Farming and Food Partnership and the British Association for Biofuels and Oils, and president of the Forestry and Timber Association and the Royal Association of British Dairy Farmers. He was voted peer of the year in 2003.

Carter was a man of courage and vision who was respected by all members of the House of Lords, loyal to his political party and its values, committed to those who lived and worked in rural enterprise, dedicated to his wider belief in caring for the disabled, and, above all, a committed Roman Catholic. He died of cancer of the pancreas at the Royal Marsden Hospital, Chelsea, London, on 18 December 2006. Baroness Amos, leader of the House of Lords, in paying tribute to him, recalled that she had visited him only a few hours before his death, to find him filling in his tax return. He was survived by his wife, Teresa.

PLUMB OF COLESHILL

Sources *Daily Telegraph* (20 Dec 2006) · *The Independent* (20 Dec 2006) · *The Times* (21 Dec 2006) · *The Guardian* (22 Dec 2006) · *WW* (2004) · Burke, *Peerage* · personal knowledge (2010) · private information (2010) · b. cert. · m. cert. · d. cert.
Likenesses photographs, 1995–2001, Photoshot, London · photograph, 1997, Photoshot, London [*see illus.*]
Wealth at death £2,380,515: probate, 14 Dec 2007, *CGPLA Eng. & Wales*

Carter, Sir John Gregorio (1919–2005), lawyer and diplomatist, was born on 27 January 1919 in Cane Grove, East Coast Demerara, British Guiana, the only son and youngest of five children of Kemp R. Carter, pharmacist, and his wife, Gertrude, *née* Humphrys. His parents were both from British Guiana. He attended Queen's College, Georgetown, leaving for England in 1939 with a scholarship to study law at London University. He studied hard during the week and played cricket at weekends, benefiting from a captain who understood how precarious student finances were. He graduated in 1942, and was called to the bar by the Middle Temple in the same year.

In 1942 Carter was appointed general and travelling secretary of the League of Coloured Peoples founded in 1931 by the Jamaican-born Harold Moody. It had functioned as a welfare organization chiefly for the small native-born, non-white population in Britain and campaigned actively against the colour bar in British society. When Carter joined, the presence of black servicemen from Africa and the Caribbean, but especially the relatively large number of African-American servicemen, brought new problems, often within the American armed forces rather than with the local population. In 1944 he was involved in a celebrated case in which an African-American serviceman was sentenced to death for rape by an American military court. Following a public campaign in which the League of Coloured Peoples and Carter played a prominent role the sentence was commuted. During this period Carter spoke regularly for the Caribbean services of the BBC.

Returning to British Guiana in 1945, Carter took over the practice of the man who had encouraged his study of the law and had died in 1944. His links with the League of Coloured Peoples and his BBC work made him well known. When in 1948 the pioneering trade unionist Hubert Nathaniel Critchlow was unseated from the legislative council after a legal challenge, Carter, who had recently represented a trade union, won the subsequent by-election, becoming at twenty-nine the youngest member of the colony's legislature. In many ways he was the last member of the old politics of a restricted franchise in British Guiana, where mass parties were unknown. In 1952 he founded the United Democratic Party with Rudy Kendall. In the election of 1953 the strongly anti-communist line of the party worked only for Kendall, and Carter lost to the new, mass-based People's Progressive Party of Cheddi Jagan and Forbes Burnham. After another failure to be elected in 1957, Carter and Kendall merged the United Democratic Party with Forbes Burnham's wing of the People's Progressive Party to form the People's National Congress in 1958. In the election of 1961 Carter was finally elected to a seat in the capital, Georgetown. He became pro-chancellor of the newly founded University of Guyana in 1962, serving until 1966. Meanwhile, in 1959 he had married Sara Lou Harris, with whom he had two sons, John and Brian. He was also stepfather to Robin, Sara Lou's daughter from her first marriage, and had two daughters, Gillian and Jennifer, from his own first marriage, to Dorothy Fraser (1923–2001) in 1947, which had ended in divorce.

Carter did not stand in the election of 1964 in which a coalition of the People's National Congress and Peter D'Aguiar's United Force unseated Cheddi Jagan's People's Progressive Party. Knighted in 1966 when British Guiana became independent (as Guyana), he became Guyana's ambassador to the United States of America and high commissioner to Canada, serving briefly as the country's representative at the United Nations. In 1970 he became high commissioner to the United Kingdom, being also accredited to France, West Germany, the Soviet Union, and Yugoslavia. About his duties in London he once remarked that the greatest difficulty he faced was that of the relations between the police and black youngsters, since the police would never admit to wrongdoing and the mothers of the youngsters could not imagine that their children could do any wrong. At the level of foreign relations Carter's duties increasingly involved the defence of his country's radical shift in policies. Guyana had become a prominent member of the Non-Aligned Movement and an increasingly radical trend internally led in 1976 to the nationalization of Bookers, the British sugar company chiefly founded on sugar in Guyana but which by 1971 had diversified out of the country. During this period Carter's anti-communism was eclipsed by his nationalism and his great admiration for the intelligence and political skills of Forbes Burnham.

As part of this trend Carter's next posting was to China in 1976, being accredited simultaneously to North Korea, but significantly not until 1979 to Japan. He remained in this post until 1981 when, expecting to retire, he was asked to take over the post of high commissioner to Jamaica, where relations with the newly elected conservative (Jamaica Labour Party) government of Edward Seaga needed to be repaired. His charm and urbanity appeared to have worked and he retired in 1983, settling in Bethesda, Maryland, USA. He continued to work as a consultant and for charitable causes in the USA and Guyana. In his later years he was much interviewed by researchers and consulted on political matters, especially after the Soviet Union collapsed and his original brand of politics appeared to have triumphed. He died on 23 February 2005 at Suburban Hospital, Bethesda, of pulmonary hypertension, and was buried on 2 March at the Gates of Heaven cemetery, Silver Spring, Maryland, following a funeral service at the Chevy Chase United Methodist Church. He was survived by his wife, Sara Lou, his four children, and his stepdaughter. PETER D. FRASER

Sources *L. C. P. Newsletter* (1942–5) · C. Jagan, *The West on trial: my fight for Guyana's freedom* (1966) · M. St Pierre, *Anatomy of resistance: anti-colonialism in Guyana, 1823–1966* (1999) · C. Seecharan, *Sweetening 'bitter sugar': Jock Campbell's British Guiana, 1934–1966* (Kingston, 2003) · *The Guardian* (4 June 2005) · Sir John Carter papers, priv. coll. · curriculum vitae, priv. coll. · *WW* (2005) · Burke, *Peerage* · personal knowledge (2009) · private information (2009) · b. cert. · d. cert.

Archives priv. coll.

Cartwright, Thomas William [Tom] (**1935–2007**), cricketer, was born on 22 July 1935 at 248 Alderman's Green, Coventry, the youngest of four children of William Thomas Cartwright, a transport driver for a motor company, later a fitter in an aircraft factory, and his wife, Lily Irene, *née* Whitmore. He appeared on his birth certificate as William Thomas (like his father), but in all subsequent documents was Thomas William. The Cartwrights were Labour folk with a strong sense of right and wrong, and even in the conservative world of English cricket Tom Cartwright retained their values. He attended Foxford School, an elementary school in Coventry, until the age of fifteen. Despite rudimentary facilities he achieved outstanding success on the sports field, captaining Coventry schools in both football and cricket. He began work at the Rootes car factory, admiring the skills and the dedication of the craftsmen who hand-built cars like the Humber Pullman. In time, with a cricket ball in his hand, he too would become a master craftsman, hard-working and proud.

In April 1952 Cartwright joined the staff of Warwickshire County Cricket Club, making his début in the first team in the last match of that summer, against Nottinghamshire at Trent Bridge. A shy lad, he played as a specialist batsman, scoring 82 and 22 not out. However, after national service in the Royal Artillery he took some years to establish himself as a regular in the Warwickshire side. He never quite fulfilled the county's hopes for his classical batting, but three times he passed 1000 runs in a season, his best 1668 in 1961. At Nuneaton in 1962 he hit a double century. His bowling did not come to the fore until the late 1950s, but he quickly developed a reputation for unflagging accuracy, for an ability to move the ball both ways even in unhelpful conditions, and for a capacity for hard work. In 1962 he took 100 wickets in a season for the first time, thereby becoming the only Warwickshire professional ever to complete the double of 1000 runs and 100 wickets. In 1967, when an experimental regulation prevented any polishing of the ball, he was the leading wicket-taker in the country with 147.

Cartwright played five tests for England. In his first in 1964, when the Australian Bobby Simpson hit 311 on the flattest of Old Trafford pitches, he bowled 77 overs on the first two days, never losing control and taking two wickets for 118 runs. In his last in 1965, at Trent Bridge, when the South African Graeme Pollock hit a magnificent 125, he was at his most testing, taking six for 94. Unfortunately his thumb was fractured as he attempted a return catch, and he never regained his England place.

On 24 September 1960, at the Methodist church in Skewen, Glamorgan, Cartwright married Joan Morwen Rees (*b.* 1929/30), a schoolteacher, and daughter of Meredith Rees, platelayer. They had a son and a daughter. They spent the winter following their marriage in Johannesburg, where Cartwright coached at the Wanderers Club and where, radicals both, they became unsettled by the inhumanity of the apartheid system. He toured South Africa four years later with the MCC, and in August 1968, despite being out of the game with a shoulder injury, he was surprisingly selected to tour there again. The party did not include the 'Cape coloured' cricketer Basil D'Oliveira, who had just scored 158 at the Oval in the final test against Australia. Many believed that the MCC had made a political decision, fearing that D'Oliveira's selection would lead to the tour's cancellation, and a great controversy ensued. Cartwright, meanwhile, became uneasy. His shoulder needed rest, he had two young children whom he never liked leaving for long, and he grew disturbed when he saw a news item in the paper reporting that the MPs in the South African parliament, told of D'Oliveira's omission, had all stood up and cheered. 'When I read that', he said, 'I went cold. I started to wonder if I wanted to be part of it' (personal knowledge). After visiting a specialist about his shoulder he withdrew, D'Oliveira replaced him, and the tour was cancelled. When the South Africans were due to visit England in 1970

Cartwright had just moved from Warwickshire to Somerset and he made it clear that he did not wish to play against the tourists.

For Somerset, Cartwright continued his supremacy with the ball: the country's leading wicket-taker in 1972, and top of the first-class averages in 1973. Somerset appointed him as coach, and he successfully negotiated for £1000 each for six young cricketers to join the staff for the summer of 1974. They were 'Tom's boys', and they included Ian Botham, Viv Richards, Vic Marks, and Peter Roebuck. Botham had been on the ground staff at Lord's, where his bowling was considered a joke, but under Cartwright's guidance that soon changed.

In 1977 Cartwright moved to Glamorgan, where he played one last summer of county cricket and served as team manager. Then for twenty-three years he was the full-time director of coaching in Wales, passing on his technical expertise and inculcating into young cricketers the best values of the game. In 1999 he was the first cricketer to be inducted into the National Coaching Federation's hall of fame; in the new year honours of 2000 he was appointed MBE. 'Tom's tremendously respected by his fellow cricketers', Dennis Silk, the former MCC president, once said of him. 'He's kept up such high personal standards without making a meal of it. And he's put so much back into the game, patiently and generously. He's one of the great unsung heroes of English cricket' (Chalke, 215). 'A cricketer's cricketer' was how Mike Smith described him (*Daily Telegraph*, 1 May 2007). He was still running the Wales under sixteens when he was struck down by a heart attack. He died six weeks later at Neath Port Talbot Hospital, Baglan, on 30 April 2007. He was survived by his wife, Joan, and their two children.

STEPHEN CHALKE

Sources S. Chalke, *Tom Cartwright: the flame still burns* (2007) • *The Times* (1 May 2007); (7 May 2007) • *Daily Telegraph* (1 May 2007) • *The Guardian* (1 May 2007) • *The Independent* (1 May 2007) • *Birmingham Post* (1 May 2007); (14 May 2007) • *South Wales Evening Post* (1 May 2007) • *South Wales Echo* (22 May 2007) • personal knowledge (2011) • private information (2011) • b. cert. • m. cert. • d. cert.

Likenesses S & G, photographs, 1955–68, PA Photos, London • photographs, 1961–8, Rex Features, London • photographs, 1964–81, Getty Images, London • photographs, 1969–2000, PA Photos, London • obituary photographs • photographs, repro. in Chalke, *Cartwright*

Wealth at death under £24,000: probate, 1 Aug 2007, *CGPLA Eng. & Wales*

Cary, Tristram Ogilvie (1925–2008), composer, was born at 12 Parks Road, Oxford, on 14 May 1925, the third of the four sons of (Arthur) Joyce Lunel *Cary (1888–1957), author, and his wife, Gertrude Margaret, *née* Ogilvie (1891–1949). His eldest brother was Sir (Arthur Lucius) Michael *Cary (1917–1976), civil servant. The family home was at 12 Parks Road, Oxford. His early interest in music was encouraged by his mother and he was already composing and playing the piano as a pupil at the Dragon School in Oxford. He attended Westminster School, London, where he was a king's scholar. His developing interest in technology and engineering saw him go up to Christ Church, Oxford, as an exhibitioner to study science. His studies were interrupted in 1943 when aged seventeen he volunteered, joining the Royal Navy where after further technical training he became involved in the development and testing of specialized ship-borne radar. It was at this point that his two passions, music and technology, started to come together. He saw the potential of the tape recorder, being developed in Germany, as a tool for manipulating natural sounds, and also the possibility of using pure electronic tone as a musical source.

On demobilization in 1946, Cary returned to Oxford and then enrolled at Trinity College of Music in London, where he studied composition. Always practical and imaginative, he constructed his first rudimentary electronic music studio using redundant military equipment, a 78 rpm disc cutter, and a very basic tape recorder. All this came with him when, on 7 July 1951, he married Doris Enid (Dorse) Jukes (*b.* 1922), artist, and daughter of Joseph William Jukes, and moved to a house in Nevern Road, Earls Court. They had three children, John (*b.* 1952), Robert (*b.* 1955), and Charlotte (*b.* 1960).

Cary's early compositions were not solely in the rarefied world of electronics. He wrote a series of chamber works; *Partita* for piano was given its premiere at the Wigmore Hall in 1949. As with many new graduates he supplemented his income by taking teaching jobs. It was at this time that he was approached by the film director Alexander Mackendrick who asked him to write the incidental music for *The Ladykillers* (1955). This was a turning point in his career as it led to more film commissions and to work in the theatre, television, and radio. The financial rewards that came with his success enabled him to buy a cottage in Fressingfield, Suffolk, where he moved in 1963 and where he constructed a new studio. As a professional composer with a family to support he now had to find a balance between working on commissions for the media and writing music for concert performance. He was not alone among composers in finding this balance sometimes difficult to achieve.

Cary continued to create electronic music, gradually improving the equipment in his studio. *Solfeggio* for tape (1959) was the first of many concert pieces to be performed in this medium. He began to have opportunities to introduce electronic music into many of his scores for the media, notably in *Dr Who* (1963) for BBC Television, and the film *Quatermass and the Pit* (1967). This helped to bring electronic music to the notice of a wider public but the natural conservatism of the average listener often led to controversy. Over the next few years he created several concert pieces scored for conventional instruments playing alongside tapes such as *Narcissus* (1968), for flute and two tape recorders.

In 1967 Cary founded the electronic music studio at the Royal College of Music. His search for new ways to create electronic music led, in 1969, to a collaboration with the composer Peter Zinovieff and the inventor David Cockerell. Together they created the EMS line of synthesizers, the VCS3 being the best known (used, for instance, by Pink Floyd on their album of 1973, *The Dark Side of the Moon*). It was his affinity with the EMS Synthi 100 that led to his first visit to Australia when, in 1973, Melbourne University invited him to spend a term working as visiting composer in their newly opened electronic music studio. He then joined the music department of Adelaide University, where he was to stay for twelve years. This move to academic life in Australia was a significant milestone in his life. He was able to free himself from the financial and professional pressures that until then had dogged him despite his successes. In 1986 he became a full-time composer once again; he took Australian citizenship and in 1991 received the medal of the Order of Australia for his services to Australian music. His first marriage had been dissolved in 1978 and in the early 1980s he began a relationship with Jane Delin; they married in 2003. He died in Adelaide on 24 April 2008 of cancer. A memorial plaque at the Royal College of Music describes him as 'The Father of British Electronic Music'. ROGER LIMB

Sources *Daily Telegraph* (26 April 2008) • *The Times* (29 April 2008) • *The Independent* (29 April 2008) • *The Guardian* (2 May 2008) • biographical notes, Tristram Cary Creative Music Services, priv. coll. • J. Cary, 'Tristram Cary, O. A. M., 14 May 1925–24 April 2008', priv. coll. • 'What the future sounded like', film, Porthmeor Productions, 2007 • personal knowledge (2012) • private information (2012) [John Cary, son] • b. cert. • m. cert. [1951]

Archives SOUND BL NSA, documentary and performance recordings

Likenesses M. Barnes, photograph, 1968, Getty Images, London • obituary photographs

Cass, Frank (1930–2007), publisher, was born on 11 July 1930 at 31 Leweston Place, Stamford Hill, London, the son of Simon (Sid) Cass (1891/2–1959), cabinet manufacturer, and his wife, Fanny, *née* Greenwich (1900–1985). His parents were Jewish immigrants, from Russian Poland. His career as a publisher arose from a love of books that he discovered as a child while attending St Thomas's School near his home in Clapton, east London. He spent much of his leisure time at the local library where, according to his biographer, Gerry Black, he was interested in the style and appearance of books as much as their content. One day his mother, worried that he had failed to come home from school at his usual time, found him in the local library, sitting on the floor, comparing two versions of *Robinson Crusoe*. His education was interrupted by the London blitz, when he, his parents, two sisters, and a brother were evacuated to Merthyr Tudful. He began school there, but for two years was confined to home with rheumatic fever. He did, however, recover in time to win a scholarship to Merthyr Tudful grammar school. When the war ended the family returned to London, where he spent a year at Hackney Downs grammar school. (Previously the Grocers' Company's School and even in the late 1940s usually referred to as 'The Grocers', the school was the nursery of dozens of scientists, politicians, and writers, among them Harold Pinter.)

In October 1949 Cass took his first job, working at the Economist Bookshop, close to the London School of Economics. At the age of twenty-two he struck it lucky when a 'to rent' sign fell on his foot as he was doing up a shoelace outside the Bedford Hotel in Southampton Row, London. He took up the offer—for £3 a week—and was in business on his own. Before long he was known as an antiquarian dealer as well as a specialist in old academic volumes.

On 3 February 1957, at Hendon Synagogue, he married Audrey Esme Steele (*b.* 1937), dressmaker and daughter of Davis Steele. They had a son, Stewart, and a daughter, Hayley. Audrey liked to say of her husband, who always more resembled a jolly-looking businessman than a publisher (usually ready with a joke to begin important discussions), that he had a photographic memory 'except when I asked him to do things'. It helped him run a business without much resort to writing letters or rereading important documents.

The year of Cass's marriage was a defining one, professionally as well as privately, since it was when he became a publisher. He had the idea of not just selling old volumes, but reprinting them. He realized that he was frequently receiving requests for books that still existed only in single copies that he had managed to buy at auctions and that if he could reprint them he would meet a demand that he knew existed. This was the beginning of Frank Cass & Co. He was soon successful enough to move to larger premises at Woburn Walk, close by but more part of Bloomsbury. *The Guardian* wrote at the time:

> The House of Cass is one room, and a miniscule office in the back … Wedged in between a boutique and an antique shop (and across the street from Yeats's London home), the sign above the door reads merely 'The Book Shop'.

Cass's operation was described as 'a publisher version of the two-men-and-a-handcart success story' (Black, *Frank's Way*, 52).

Cass began publishing new books and in the early 1960s established the Cass Library of African Studies. In time he would publish a number of (expensive leather-bound) biographies of and polemics by African leaders, some of whom were overthrown after deals had been made—and, fortunately for him, paid for. Black studies was also the perfect introduction for him to the American market, after the inauguration of President John F. Kennedy. In 1966 he was able to expand his business and take on new premises at Great Russell Street, thanks to selling 45 per cent of his enterprise to Trinity Holdings, who, among other things, could offer printing facilities that were superior to anything he had had at his disposal hitherto. The agreement did not last, however, and Cass bought back the shares in the company that Trinity held. With them had gone the rights to a project that was typical of his enterprise, the publication of British parliamentary papers of the early nineteenth century. Eventually he regained control of the papers and presented sets of them to the libraries of the houses of parliament.

Another vital trademark of the Cass business was the publication of academic journals, which began in 1964 with *Middle East Studies* and over the years was followed by *The Journal of Development Studies*, *Terrorism and Political Violence*, *International Peace Keeping*, *Immigrants and Minorities*, *The Journal of Legislative Studies*, *Business Studies*, *Military History*, and *The Journal of Intelligence and National Security*. He also launched *Cold War History* and, in a totally different context, journals on sport. There was eventually a total of sixty-five of these journals, which Cass would say were responsible for 70 per cent of the firm's turnover and 100 per cent of its profits. They certainly allowed him the luxury of publishing a highly eclectic list, or rather lists, since his publishing business sense made sure that he had square pegs for square holes, with a series of different imprints. They were a reasonable outcome of his own personality, which was very different from that of most publishers. He lived neither in an ivory tower nor among the cocktail party circuits. His closest friends were 'ordinary' businessmen, professional people, Jewish communal workers, and possibly only a sprinkling of writers. He was a big supporter of the Jewish community centre Sinclair House, in Ilford, Essex, and established the *Essex Jewish News*. He was, people said, never happier than when discussing the politics of his local synagogue as well as British and Israeli politics. His conversation was as eclectic as his publishing list. He had the reputation of telling the best Jewish jokes around, which he sprinkled with the latest anecdotes of his favourite football team, the failing Leyton Orient, to which he was devoted. He published a number of volumes on football.

Cass had set up a company called Woburn Books as an education publisher, but before long it became the home of books on entertainment—including collections of *Goon Show* scripts (1972 and 1973), which were so popular with the heir to the throne that Prince Charles came to its official launch and wrote Cass a long letter extolling both the programmes and the book. Similar script books from *Round the Horne* followed in 1974, along with biographies of such people as the American entertainer Sophie Tucker and the British comedian Arthur Askey. He also published the definitive history of the Jewish entertainer, *So Let's Hear the Applause* (1984), and a book on Frank Simon, an American brass-band leader who worked with John Philip Sousa.

Perhaps Cass's own favourite imprint—although not for the profits it accrued because there were never any—was Vallentine Mitchell, which he bought from the *Jewish Chronicle* in the 1970s and which became the most important publisher of Jewish thought in Britain. Before the takeover the firm had been the first to publish the diaries of Anne Frank in English. Israel, the holocaust (including the publication of *The Journal of Holocaust Studies*) and, during the Soviet era, the problems of 'refuseniks', formed an important part of its output. Some were light-hearted, others more serious, and included the *Jewish Year Book* and the *Jewish Travel Guide*. Ireland was another culture close to Cass's heart. In 1974 he bought the Irish Academic Press, which, although responsible for the publication of the British parliamentary papers and a fourteen-volume collection of documents pertaining to the American War of Independence, was chiefly concerned with publishing books by Irish authors, particularly academics. More than 300 titles covered the traumas of the potato famine and the Easter rising of 1916 as well as military, social, and women's studies, and books on local history and the arts and media in the country. He also published Irish law journals. To prove, further, how varied his output was, in 1999 he wrested the government's official history programme from Her Majesty's Stationery Office, producing, among others, official histories of the armed services.

In 2003 Cass sold Frank Cass & Co. to the British publishers Taylor and Francis for more than £11 million, with an additional £3.7 million once certain sales targets had been achieved. The sale included all the firm's imprints, titles, and journals, except Vallentine Mitchell and the Irish Academic Press. He died on 9 August 2007 at Hammersmith Hospital, London, of leukaemia, an illness that had dogged him for ten years without most people knowing it for most of that time. He was survived by his wife, Audrey, and their two children. MICHAEL FREEDLAND

Sources *Jewish Chronicle* (16 Aug 2007) · *Jewish Quarterly*, 207 (autumn 2007) · *Irish Times* (22 Sept 2007) · *The Guardian* (29 Oct 2007) · *The Times* (13 Nov 2007) · *Immigrants and Minorities*, 27/1 (March 2009), 118–22 · G. Black, *Frank's way: Frank Cass and fifty years of publishing* (2008) · personal knowledge (2011) · private information (2011) · b. cert. · m. cert. · d. cert.
Likenesses obituary photographs
Wealth at death £5,562,428: probate, 24 Sept 2008, *CGPLA Eng. & Wales*

Castleman, Christopher Norman Anthony (1941–2006), merchant banker, was born Christopher Norman Phillips on 23 June 1941 at St Joseph's Nursing Home, Beaconsfield, the son of Stanley Howard Phillips, a P&O purser then serving in the Royal Naval Reserve, and his wife, Joan Doris, *née* Bennett-Levy. He was given the third name Anthony as an infant and adopted his stepfather's surname of Castleman as a schoolboy. He was educated at Harrow School and Clare College, Cambridge, where he took a first in law. After graduation in 1963 he joined the middle-ranking merchant bank M. Samuel & Co. Two years later it was acquired by Philip Hill Higginson, the combined firm, Hill Samuel, becoming one of the City's largest merchant banks. Hill Samuel was the creation of Kenneth Keith, one of the most forceful merchant bankers of the post-war decades. His ambition was to build a top City firm, and his philosophy was 'big is beautiful'. Keith insisted on hard work and professionalism, and disdained the gentlemanly amateurism that was widespread in the City at that time. Castleman became his foremost protégé. The year of the creation of Hill Samuel also saw another merger—Castleman's marriage on 30 October 1965 to Sarah Victoria Stockdale (1942/3–1979), a secretary, and daughter of Frank Alleyne Stockdale, a county court judge. They had a son and a daughter.

Working on the corporate finance side of the business, Castleman advanced rapidly in the firm. Keith entrusted him with the launch of Hill Samuel Australia, of which he was general manager from 1970 to 1972. (In 1985 it combined with other interests to become Macquarie Bank, one of Australia's leading financial institutions, and Castleman joined the board.) After returning to London in 1972 he was promoted to director in the corporate finance department. In 1976 he became chief executive of the New York office and in 1978 he was dispatched to run the South African subsidiary. Profits grew 60 per cent over the two years he was at the helm in Johannesburg, establishing him as heir-apparent among the younger generation of executives.

Castleman's elevation came sooner than expected. In 1980 Keith abruptly resigned from Hill Samuel, having fallen out with the board over unsanctioned takeover talks with Merrill Lynch, precipitating a reshuffle. Castleman became group chief executive. In the first half of the 1980s under his leadership Hill Samuel's profits quadrupled to £32 million, making it the most profitable of the merchant banks. This performance was achieved by strong cost control and the firm's transformation into a pocket financial conglomerate with five divisions: merchant banking, fund management, employee benefit consultancy, insurance broking, and shipping services.

The mid-1980s saw the deregulation of the UK securities industry in a series of stages, culminating in the 'big bang' in October 1986. Relaxation of the rules regarding the ownership of stock exchange firms led to a scramble by merchant and commercial banks to acquire brokers and market makers. Though Castleman recoiled at the prices being paid for securities firms Hill Samuel took a stake in the broker Wood Mackenzie. 'We felt that to ignore big bang developments and basically go on as we were would have relegated our investment banking side to the role of a niche player', he told *The Banker* (Travers, 'Castleman interview'). Castleman's strategy was the development of Hill Samuel as a British investment bank with a growing emphasis on the provision of personal financial services, unlike some other City houses that sought to meet the challenge of the Wall Street 'bulge bracket' firms in the global capital market, an idea that he described as 'lunacy'. In 1987 Hill Samuel was approached about a merger by Union Bank of Switzerland (UBS), which was keen to establish a substantial presence in investment banking in London. Castleman opposed a merger, believing that UBS would jettison the non-banking businesses, and advised against opening discussions with UBS, fearing that it would put the firm 'in play'. When the board disagreed he resigned. Within weeks of his departure UBS withdrew from the talks and the foundering firm was bought by the Trustee Savings Bank and later broken up when that bank merged with Lloyds Bank.

Castleman was immediately hired as chief executive of Blue Arrow, a fast-growing employment agency, though he clashed with the chairman and left after only a few months. After a spell as an independent consultant, in 1989 he became chief executive of the transatlantic financial services group Johnson Fry, then from 1991 to 1995 its chairman. Also in 1991 he became an executive director at Standard Chartered, which was undergoing a major restructuring. He handled more than 100 acquisitions and disposals in the 1990s and contributed significantly to the bank's refocusing and substantial increase in profits. He retired from Standard Chartered in 2001, but remained an advisory director. He was also, at various times, chairman of National Investment Holdings, a director of Consolidated Goldfields, and an adviser at UBS Investment Bank, being valued for his extensive international contacts and experience.

Highly competitive and passionate about sport, Castleman was a keen cricketer and ran marathons for charity. Following the death of his first wife, in 1980 he married Caroline Clare Westcott, a South African with whom he had two daughters. The marriage was dissolved in 1990 and on 5 July the same year he married another South African, the 34-year-old Susan Mary (Suzy) Diamond, a dress designer, and daughter of Geoffrey Michael Twycross, farmer; they had a daughter and a son. Castleman lived latterly at Tofte Manor, a seventeenth-century manor house in Sharnbrook, Bedfordshire, with a holiday home in South Africa. He was diagnosed with leukaemia in 2003, but remained active until shortly before his death, on 26 April 2006, at St Anthony's Hospital, North Cheam, Surrey. He was survived by his wife, Suzy, and his six children. RICHARD ROBERTS

Sources 'Hill Samuel: on with the new', *The Economist* (14 June 1980) · N. Travers, 'Castleman interview: Hill Samuel seeks a bigger role', *The Banker* (March 1986), 34–9 · 'Big bang brief: Christopher Castleman', *The Economist* (20 Oct 1986) · 'Protecting the City: Christopher Castleman speaks out', *Banking World* (Nov 1987), 12–13 · R. Whipp, R. Rosenfeld, and A. Pettigrew, 'Culture and competitiveness: evidence from two mature UK industries', *Journal of Management Studies*, 26/6 (Nov 1989), 561–83 · *Daily Telegraph* (9 May 2006) · *The Times* (19 May 2006) · *WW* (2006) · b. cert. · m. certs. [1965, 1990] · d. cert.
Likenesses obituary photographs
Wealth at death £5,461,761: probate, 14 Nov 2006, *CGPLA Eng. & Wales*

Cattermole, James [Jim] (1910–2007), political organizer, was born on 11 December 1910 at 138 Newcombe Road, Coventry, the son of Harry Cattermole, leather worker and saddler, and his wife, Elizabeth, *née* Norris. He was a bright boy, and despite his working-class background and Birmingham accent, entered the prestigious King Edward's Grammar School, Birmingham. However, his father—an active trade unionist and a target for discrimination by anti-union employers—was often out of work, and his family could not afford to support him while at school. He left at sixteen and found a job as a messenger boy in Birmingham. He went on to join a smelting firm, but by 3 October 1936, when he married Phyllis Taylor (*b.* 1908/9), an overseer in a chocolate factory (and daughter of Jacob Taylor, licensed victualler), he was a bullion dealer's clerk. He and Phyllis had two children, Philip and Roy.

In 1931 Cattermole had joined the Labour Party, which was to be the chief focus for his working life for more than thirty years, and also the white-collar, and quintessentially moderate, National Union of Clerks. It was not until 1945, however, that his career as a political organizer really began. In that year he was appointed agent and organizer of the Birmingham Labour Party. The job brought him into contact with a number of young Labour high-fliers, fresh from war service and thirsting for peacetime preferment. Among them were the then modishly left-wing Major Woodrow Wyatt, later a vociferous Thatcherite *frondeur*; Wing Commander Eddie Shackleton, a future leader of the House of Lords and knight of the Garter; and Captain Roy Jenkins, a future home secretary and chancellor, and then leader of the Social Democratic Party. Not only did Cattermole make useful personal contacts, but his pivotal role in Birmingham Labour politics at a key moment in the party's history made his reputation as a canny and resourceful organizer. Traditionally Birmingham—the city of the Chamberlains—had been a bastion of working-class Conservatism. In 1945, however, Labour won ten of the thirteen Birmingham seats—all of them gains from the Conservatives. In that *annus mirabilis* for the left this might have happened in any case. But among his fellow Labour organizers, at any rate, Cattermole had become a man to watch.

In 1947 Cattermole was appointed assistant regional organizer for London. Housing was desperately short, and for a while he shared accommodation with Roy Jenkins—laying the foundations for an enduring friendship. His London stint ended in 1952, when he was promoted to be regional organizer for the east midlands, a post he held for twenty years. He was based in Nottingham, and it was at the register office in Basford, Nottingham, that, his first marriage having been dissolved, he married on 26 March 1956 Joan Eileen Mitchell (*b.* 1920), economist and university lecturer, daughter of Albert Henry Mitchell, paper merchant. They were a happy, hospitable, and fulfilled couple, and had two children, Nick and Jackie. Joan Mitchell became professor of economics at Nottingham University (1978–85), and served on the short-lived National Board for Prices and Incomes set up by the Wilson government in 1965.

Despite an engagingly laid-back manner and impish sense of humour that irked some of the more angular constituency Labour parties he dealt with, Cattermole was perhaps the most redoubtable Labour regional organizer in the country. Organizing the east midlands was not an easy task. The region had no common identity and no obvious centre. Margaret Thatcher's birthplace of Grantham and the cathedral city of Lincoln had little in common with the mining strongholds of the Nottinghamshire–Derbyshire coalfield or the fiercely independent township of Glossop on the edge of greater Manchester. Cattermole could cajole, but he could not command. His troops marched, insofar as they marched at all, to their own rhythms. Where he excelled was as a mixture of talent scout and marriage broker, drawing promising would-be parliamentary candidates to the attention of suitable constituency parties. Dick Taverne's selection as prospective candidate for Lincoln was one example; David Marquand's selection for the mining constituency of Ashfield was another. It was not an accident that both were committed Gaitskellites and, in the jargon of the day, 'multilateralists', opposed to unilateral nuclear disarmament.

In 1972 Cattermole retired from his Labour Party post and left the east midlands to become director of the Labour Committee for Europe, a pro-European party pressure group that swam stubbornly, though at first unsuccessfully, against a swelling anti-European tide, both in the most powerful trade unions and in the constituency parties. The committee could not stem the tide, but it could and did give much-needed practical and psychological support to beleaguered Labour pro-Europeans. When the referendum on continued British membership of the European Community came in 1975, the Labour Committee for Europe played an important part in the 'yes' campaign within the Labour movement. That was the high point of Cattermole's directorship, but he remained in that post until 1998 and went on working for the wider European movement for another five years. Unlike Roy Jenkins and a number of other personal and political friends he stayed in the Labour Party when they seceded from it to form the Social Democratic Party in 1981, but with characteristic tolerance and good humour he took care to stay on good terms with them. It was Roy Jenkins who organized a celebratory dinner for him following his retirement as director of the Labour Committee for Europe.

Cattermole was a warm and kindly man, a tower of strength to political friends in need, and a lover of good food and wine—important qualifications for a member of the National Liberal Club wine committee, which was one of his happiest roles in old age. He died at St George's Hospital, Tooting, on 11 January 2007, of sepsis and pneumonia following a urinary tract infection, and was survived by his second wife, Joan, and his four children.

DAVID MARQUAND

Sources *The Independent* (17 Jan 2007) · *The Guardian* (9 Feb 2007) · personal knowledge (2011) · private information (2011) · b. cert. · m. certs. · d. cert.

Archives U. Warwick Mod. RC, Labour Party east midland region papers

Likenesses obituary photographs

Wealth at death under £44,000: probate, 28 Feb 2007, *CGPLA Eng. & Wales*

Caulfield, Patrick Joseph (1936–2005), painter, was born on 29 January 1936 at 17 All Saints Road, Acton, London, the son of Patrick Caulfield, plate layer, and his wife, Annie, *née* Gill. During the Second World War the family lived in Bolton, Lancashire, where Caulfield's father worked for the De Havilland aircraft factory; in later years Caulfield took elocution lessons to lose the accent he had picked up there. The family moved back to Acton with the return of peace.

At the age of fifteen Caulfield left Acton secondary modern school and worked drilling gas rings in a factory before moving to the advertising department of Crosse and Blackwell, where his duties included varnishing chocolates for display purposes. At seventeen he enlisted in the RAF, pre-empting call-up for national service, and, while stationed at RAF Northwood, in his free time began going to evening classes at Harrow School of Art. Having admitted in his interview with William Coldstream at the Slade School of Fine Art that he did not know the name of any important British artist, Caulfield won a place at Chelsea

School of Art in 1956. It was at Chelsea that he met (Anna) Pauline Jacobs, a fellow student eight years his junior (later a fabric designer), and daughter of Christopher Gage Jacobs, architect. They eventually married at the Sacred Heart Church, Lambourn, Berkshire, on 22 June 1968, and had three sons.

Caulfield had a particular aversion to Walter Sickert, and the dark and damp, seedy atmospheres of the paintings of the Camden Town Group. At Chelsea one of his tutors was Jack Smith, well known then as a 'kitchen sink' realist, a style that Caulfield may be thought to have simultaneously flooded with colour and stripped of emotion. He started out in the 1960s painting black-outlined objects against plain colour fields. The paint surface was 'dumb' and uninflected, like a poster or a page in a magazine. Almost from the beginning the pictures were pleasant, clean, and bright, although Caulfield's detractors saw them as bland, even blank, and devoid of conventional 'humanist' content. 'I didn't like misty brush-strokes and atmospheric painting', Caulfield later said. 'This was my reaction against the Englishness of English painting which so greatly valued a slightly understated, tentative figuration' (personal knowledge).

A turning point was Caulfield's first trip abroad in 1960, shortly before taking his place at the Royal College of Art (1960–63). He was in Athens, *en route* to Crete, and, having grown accustomed to the drabness of austerity Britain, was unprepared for the pre-war American Cadillacs and Fleetwoods cruising the ancient streets looking for fares. The combination of the chromed and finned petal-pink Cadillacs against the backdrop of the Acropolis—the conjunction of the Old World with the New—became one of the characteristic ideas of his work. While many of his contemporaries and near-contemporaries—David Hockney, Derek Boshier, and Richard Smith among them—emigrated to America both actually and in the temper and content of what they produced, Caulfield, always resistant to any kind of mid-Atlanticism and no convert to the notion of 'hip', triumphantly combined European manners and conceptually complex, intellectually challenging, cutting-edge art.

Because they were students together at the Royal College of Art, Caulfield was often aligned with the 'third wave' of British pop artists, which included Hockney, R. B. Kitaj, Peter Phillips, and Allen Jones. Caulfield always resisted the association. As late as the Royal Academy's big survey exhibition of pop art in 1991, in which his work featured prominently, he defined pop art dismissively as 'social realism without the realism' (*The Times*, 1 Oct 2005). But among the things Caulfield had in common with his contemporaries was a rejection of the gestural painting favoured by the 'abstract expressionists' and other abstract painters, and the personal agonizing associated with Frank Auerbach, Francis Bacon, and what would come to be known as the School of London. He wished to exclude himself as far as possible from his art, making it as apparently objective, dispassionate, and anonymous as the work of the twentieth-century artists whom he most admired, such as Fernand Léger and Juan Gris. His *Portrait of Juan Gris*, painted while he was still at the Royal College of Art, was one of the last of his paintings to include a human figure, in line with his belief that 'Picasso had pulled the plug on interpreting the human form' (*Daily Telegraph*, 30 Sept 2005).

Caulfield's main subject as a painter was the blissful, occasionally transcending melancholy of human absence and solitude. The bars and restaurants and other social spaces he painted were devoid of people. The 'exit' sign that is the focus of one of his later paintings, *Happy Hour* (1996), is the direction in which his fellow drinkers have all already headed. The figure reflected in the single filled glass at the centre of the canvas is the painter pursuing his solitary practice. Indeed, it was characteristic of Caulfield that even a visit to the theatre could become a way of experiencing his separateness and enveloping aloneness, even (indeed especially) in the teeth of what, for others, was a convivial social occasion. 'The trouble with the theatre', he liked to say, 'is that it so interferes with one's evening' (private information, J. Hoyland). Nobody who went to the theatre with him, whether it was to see something in the West End or at Covent Garden (where he created a long talked-about set for Michael Corder's ballet *Party Game*, for the Royal Ballet in 1984, based on big, billboard-sized versions of the burgundy-shaded boudoir lights that cast their dim glow over the stalls) ever expected to see him back in his seat after the interval. The reverie going on in his head was the one he invariably wanted to stay with.

Caulfield was an urbanite, with no taste for the pastoral in art or in life, or for the trappings of country living. He delighted in referring to the country as 'the mud museum' (personal knowledge). When he was invited to choose from works in the National Gallery for the 'Artist's Eye' series in 1986, he ruled out religious pictures ('I didn't want paintings of angels') and concentrated on paintings that reflected his interest in urban imagery. Half of his selection was drawn from the gallery's basement, the repository of paintings that were, on the whole, considered less remarkable than the ones in the grand rooms. The still lifes of drink and food, and scenes set in music halls and taverns, tended to be equally modest. *Lunch-time* (1985), the painting of his own that Caulfield chose to include, was typical of his sense of humour in that there is no food to be found in it. It shows the nicotined corner of a City pub decorated with a pot of geraniums and generic bric-à-brac, and crowded with deep, all-too-solid shadows. If, as Grey Gowrie once maintained, Francis Bacon was unique in the twentieth century 'in his ability to render the indoor, overfed, alcohol and tobacco-lined flesh of the average urban male' (*Mail on Sunday*, 11 April 1993), then this surely is a portrait of his comfily recessed, button-backed set and lair.

Caulfield was constantly alert to the everyday excitements of living in a major city. It is unlikely that he ever read Virginia Woolf ('seemed to deal with a middle-to-upper-class society that I didn't know anything about and it meant nothing to me', he once said of the mid-century English novel) (B. Robertson, 'Patrick Caulfield: prints',

Waddington Gallery, 1981), but he shared with Woolf a love of urban experience, seen quite vividly in a novel like *Mrs Dalloway*, for example, in all its hallucinatory particulars. And yet for the forty years of his career Caulfield painted places that offered respite from the noise and sheer teeming variety of city life. These included restaurants, cafés, hotel foyers, and other public places, as well as bars. For several years his first call of the day after leaving his home in Belsize Park in north London was at his local pub, a few minutes after the bolts had been drawn in the morning. He liked to breathe in the opening-time cellar smells and observe the shapes the slanting light cut through the fixtures and fittings; he liked to stare into the distance and listen to London. Early paintings such as *View of the Rooftops* (1965) and *Lit Window* (1969), and later ones such as *Trou Normand* (1997), *Rust Never Sleeps* (1996), and *Terrace* (2002), are proof that this was time well spent. The arrival of fellow customers he took as a sign that it was time for him to be on his way.

Caulfield's place on the fault-line of European and American experience was occasionally alluded to directly in his work. From the 1980s on, he started squeezing acrylic paint straight out of the bottle to recreate the textures of anaglypta and lincrusta and other serviceable, lodging-house surfaces that were begining to disappear. Above and alongside them Caulfield would introduce passages of photorealist painting that conveyed the luridly patterned, wype-cleen Vymura wallpapers that had been imported from America and, for a time, enjoyed a fleeting popularity. A sly gap at floor level betrayed the fact that a regency or art deco column had been encased in formica or a cheap plastic veneer. He mixed in Victorian ceiling sconces and Tiffany-style lamps with affectless contemporary prints. A single Caulfield painting, the critic Marco Livingstone noted, could be an inventory of 'the full range of everything imaginable that painting can encompass—*trompe l'oeil* realism set against geometric abstraction, careful delineation abutting freely brushed areas, forceful sensations of three-dimensionality adjacent to surfaces of the most extreme flatness' (Livingstone, 158).

Caulfield started off using decorator's gloss paint on hardboard because he liked the impersonal surface it produced. By the time of his major work, he had moved on to acrylic (and occasionally oil) on canvas. Where he never wavered was in his commitment to impure, industrial, non-art colour; colours that were more the colours of things than atmospheres; that referred, directly or indirectly, to the experience of modernity. The post-war period was the period of the digitalization of colour in art. This, the British artist David Batchelor argued, 'was an entirely new conception of colour … More urban colours than the colours of nature. Artificial colours, city colours, industrial colours. Colours that are consistent with the images, materials and forms of an urban, industrial art' (D. Batchelor, *Chromophobia*, 2000, 98, 106). It was Caulfield's unabashed fondness for impure colours and sharp finishes, his determination to deal head-on with modern kitsch and artificiality, that made him an artist's artist. It seems likely, however, that it was these same qualities that throughout his life denied him the interest of collectors, and so the material rewards, that so many of his contemporaries enjoyed.

Caulfield was a Royal Academician (1993); a senior fellow of the Royal College of Art (1993); an honorary fellow of the London Institute (1996); winner of the Jerwood prize (in 1995, with Maggi Hambling); and nominee for the 1987 Turner prize. He was appointed CBE in 1996, and enjoyed major retrospectives at the Tate Gallery (1981), the Serpentine Gallery (1992), and the Hayward Gallery (1999). Unusually for a modern-minded visual artist, he was a voracious reader of books. He was introduced to the poems of Jules Laforgue as a student and in 1972 produced a series of twenty-two prints based on Laforgue's work. In the 1980s he started reading Raymond Carver's short stories, which also appealed to him for their refusal of floridity and long-windedness, and for the unflinching way they addressed the problem of drink. When Carver visited England before his own premature death, Caulfield, who was unwell at the time, made a heroic effort to cross London to see him read.

Caulfield was found to be suffering from cancer of the mouth and tongue in November 1992, a condition that, with characteristic candour and courage, he didn't hesitate to attribute to his love of whisky. He never recovered his health after the operation that followed. His first marriage having ended in divorce, on 17 November 1999, at Burgh House, Hampstead, he married his fellow artist Janet Nathan, the 61-year-old daughter of Harold Poster, industrialist. He died of squamous cell cancer on 29 September 2005 at his home, 19 Belsize Square, Belsize Park, London, and was survived by his wife and the three sons of his first marriage. 'The most inexplicable thing about Patrick was his work', Caulfield's lifelong friend the painter John Hoyland said at his funeral. 'It was and remains an enigma. Patrick was charming, graceful and seemingly impassive; he rarely showed his inner passions. He concealed everything that mattered to him from all but a few' (private information, J. Hoyland). He was nevertheless recognized as one of the great British painters of the late twentieth century.

GORDON BURN

Sources C. Finch, *Image as language: aspects of British art, 1950–1968* (1969) · M. Livingstone, *Patrick Caulfield: paintings* (2005) · *Daily Telegraph* (30 Sept 2005) · *The Times* (1 Oct 2005) · *The Independent* (1 Oct 2005) · *The Guardian* (3 Oct 2005); (21 Jan 2006) · *WW* (2005) · personal knowledge (2009) · private information (2009) [J. Hoyland and others] · b. cert. · m. certs. · d. cert.

Archives SOUND BL NSA, National Life Story Collection, artists' lives, interviews with A. Lambirth, 27 March and 17 July 1996, 21 April and 25 Aug 1998, F6302–F6307, F6851 · BL NSA, Andrew Graham-Dixon Recordings, interview with A. Graham-Dixon, 13 April 2000, F16501 [closed] · BL NSA, 'Artists talking', interview with B. Robertson, 13193 · BL NSA, 'Conversations with artists', interview with E. Lucie-Smith, NP5466R

Likenesses photographs, 1964–2000, Camera Press, London · M. Cooper, bromide fibre print, 1966, NPG · J. Edelstein, bromide fibre print, 1989, NPG · K. Govier, bromide print, 1992, NPG · photographs, 1993–5, Rex Features, London · photographs, 1995, Getty Images, London · J. Bellany, double portrait, oils (with John Hoyland), priv. coll. · P. Caulfield, self-portrait, black kohl pencil drawing; Bonhams, 30 May 2008, lot 172 · G. Deblonde, photograph, Tate collection · obituary photographs

Chadwick, Henry (1920–2008), theologian and church historian, was born on 23 June 1920 at St Andrews, Oaklands Road, Bromley, Kent, the third of four sons and the fourth of six children of John Chadwick, barrister, and his wife, Edith Mary, *née* Horrocks, a gifted musician. The four sons all became men of distinction: Sir John Chadwick (1911–1987) as a diplomat, (William) Owen Chadwick (*b.* 1916) as a church historian (he was appointed KBE in 1982 but, like Henry himself, was an ordained clergyman and so did not use the title), and Martin Chadwick (1927–1998) as a churchman.

Henry Chadwick was a king's scholar at Eton College (1933–8), from where he won a music scholarship to Magdalene College, Cambridge. He was said to have been sent into the organ loft at Eton to study with the school's famous teacher, Henry Ley, because his Greek was considered weak. However, throughout his long career his patristic Greek and Latin left nothing to be desired. In Cambridge his reputation as a virtuoso keyboard player was quickly established. In his very first term Boris Ord of King's College, whom Chadwick described as then the greatest influence on him, summoned him one evening to entertain his dinner guests with Chabrier's arrangement of his *España* for two pianos. Chadwick had to read his extremely difficult part at sight. Patrick Hadley, professor of music, turned the pages for him, at every turn thumping him in the back, shouting 'Bravo!' (Darlington, 2). He retained his musical brilliance into old age, and saw music as giving to his whole life a vital sense of elevation, 'a ladder of ascent' as he called it in a sermon preached in the chapel of King's College, Cambridge, in 1991 (ibid., 3). In 1995 he gave a lecture at Oxford of astonishing range and insight on the power of music.

After obtaining the MusB in 1941 Chadwick turned to the study of theology, mainly because as a committed evangelical Christian he felt a vocation to the church's ministry. One of the relatively hidden aspects of his personality was his pastoral gift, as would be revealed by his many letters of encouragement and compassion to diverse individuals. Studying at Ridley Hall, Cambridge, he was ordained deacon in 1943 and priest in 1944. He held a harrowing curacy in south Croydon (1943–5), which suffered much German bombing. On 24 August 1945, at Holy Trinity Church, Brompton, he married Margaret Elizabeth (Peggy) Brownrigg, a talented singer who sometimes maintained that she had married her accompanist. The daughter of William Pemell Brownrigg, she was later a secondary school teacher. The marriage was a long and happy one; to each of their three daughters (Priscilla, Hilary, and Juliet) Chadwick dedicated one of his books. His wife was always a vital support to Chadwick, watcher over his well-being, co-host in his generous hospitality, proofreader of his books, and insister on clarity in his sermons and scholarly writings. Chadwick was a prodigious accumulator of books, but he could not always find them. Peggy usually could.

After a few months as assistant master at Wellington College, Chadwick was from 1946 to 1958 fellow and chaplain of Queens' College, Cambridge. His lectures there

Henry Chadwick (1920–2008), by David Poole

showed him to be a born communicator; each would end with a cliff-hanger—some exciting question or problem for the following week. Published in 1953, his monumental work on Origen's *Contra Celsum* placed him at once in the front rank of patristic scholars. This work was remarkable for its fine translation and 'succinct introduction and notes, which reveal a great deal about the engagement between the Christian apologist and the Greek philosophical heritage' (*SBL Forum*). Chadwick always loved footnotes and excelled in the art of composing them. Other early works included *Alexandrian Christianity* (with J. E. L. Oulton, 1954), *Lessing's Theological Writings* (1956), and *The Sentences of Sextus* (1959). Chadwick was also editor of the important *Journal of Theological Studies* from 1954 to 1985, and contributed many of its most distinguished book reviews.

Early in 1959 Chadwick became regius professor of divinity at Oxford and a canon of Christ Church. In 1966 appeared a book of massive erudition and clear judgement, *Early Christian Thought and the Classical Tradition*, on how, in the second and third centuries, Christianity defined itself and gained credibility in its own eyes by its relation to Greek philosophy. Thus the book followed up his interest in *Contra Celsum*. With a mastery of Platonism and neo-Platonism, it related the kind of paradox in which Chadwick delighted: the harsher the words about Greek philosophy of Justin, Clement, and Origen became, the more deeply impregnated with Platonism was their actual theology. Earlier, in 1961, he had given a paper at a major classical conference in Oxford on the same subject.

Its preparation was to him 'a nightmare': 'I sat up working at the wretched thing each night and somehow it wouldn't go' (letter to Peggy Chadwick, 11 Aug 1961, priv. coll.). However effortless the end product looked, Chadwick's scholarship always involved struggle. The paper was in fact a success, and Arnaldo Momigliano, as chairman, said that it marked a change of emphasis in classical studies that for the first time their conference was addressed by a professor of divinity. In 1967 Chadwick's brilliant and much reprinted survey, *The Early Church*, was published in the Pelican History of the Church.

In 1969 Chadwick became dean of Christ Church, Oxford. As such he was both the head of a college and the dean of a cathedral, a demanding position. Emollient, ready to see all sides of an argument, reluctant to say no, he could hardly feel entirely comfortable in the role. His days were filled with often none-too-calm meetings, and with committees and administration, which by no means always played to his gifts, let alone to his inclinations. He felt for Augustine, who 'wanted to be a monk rather than a busy town pastor constantly beset by unreasonable people' (Chadwick, *Augustine*, 1986, 58). To his (eminently reasonable) colleague Peter Oppenheimer, who once offered him a cup of coffee after lunch, he replied soulfully, 'Ah! My dear Peter, it might keep me awake during Hebdomadal Council!' (private information). But if it came to a great occasion in the college or the university, whether at the lectern or in the pulpit of the cathedral, he displayed a clarity of utterance and dignity of bearing which, together with his pre-eminent scholarship, were the pride of his colleagues. He thought that he would never be able to write a book while dean, but by rising exceptionally early, and working on it for three hours before the morning office in the cathedral, he wrote a highly original one on the Spaniard *Priscillian of Avila* (1976), defending with verve Priscillian's orthodoxy against his enemies. He relished conflict of this kind in a past age, as much as he hated it around him.

During his deanship fell the greatest part of Chadwick's work in the Anglican–Roman Catholic International Commission (ARCIC), of which he was a member from 1969 to 1981 and again from 1983 to 1990, and on which he was the leading figure. Here his emollience became a positive virtue, and his scholarship was massively deployed. In the ARCIC statement *Salvation and the Church* (1976), for instance, a range of the writings of Augustine of Hippo, as of the early Anglican divines on whom Chadwick was if anything even more learned at the time, served to point up possible theological resolutions of much that seemed to divide Anglicans and Roman Catholics. The hand of Chadwick can be seen, not exclusively, but in large measure here. He was at pains to show, as in his later book on Boethius, how linguistic usage rather than substance could be theologically divisive. His brilliant footnote on transubstantiation in the ARCIC *Agreement on the Eucharist* (1971, ed. Julian Charley) was a case in point.

Chadwick well knew that the resolution of theological difficulties would not in itself lead to Christian unity. There were also intractable problems of authority and ecclesiology. In his view progress here depended on the continuation within the Roman Communion of the Second Vatican Council's emphasis on the collegiality of all bishops as well as on the Roman primacy. In 1969 he brought Cardinal Leo Suenens to Oxford to lecture on collegiality. This attitude of Chadwick's went back a long way. In his Oxford inaugural lecture of 1959, 'The circle and the ellipse', he argued that from very early on the church was conceived to have not one centre but two, Jerusalem and Rome, and thus the local churches were not united with each other by a circular line centred on one church, but by an elliptical line centred on two. This idea was pregnant with consequences for his later thinking about primacy and episcopal collegiality. The retreat from collegiality in Rome, which he traced back to Pope Paul VI, was the first cause of disappointment in his ecumenical hopes which Chadwick would come to feel deeply. Notwithstanding his disappointment, however, the degree of unity in 2000 was vastly greater than in 1950, and he had played a significant role in that change.

Early in 1982 Chadwick went to Rome as Archbishop Runcie's emissary, to discuss directly with Pope John Paul II in particular the form of service at Canterbury during the pope's forthcoming visit to England. Afterwards he wrote of his impression that Anglicans had come 'to seem a bore to the top administrators of the Roman Catholic Church' (Carpenter, *Robert Runcie*, 241). But he personally was held in great respect by the pope, who presented him with a splendid embroidered stole, a mark of specifically priestly honour, which at his funeral lay on his coffin.

From 1979 to 1983 Chadwick was regius professor of divinity at Cambridge. In 1981 his book on Boethius was published. This was a subject peculiarly congenial to him. Boethius was a deeply Platonist thinker, ever searching after the One that bound the whole cosmos together, and Chadwick's book integrated into a coherence all the intellectual aspects, including music, of this early sixth-century Italian nobleman. During the 1980s Chadwick's interest in Augustine was always deepening, stimulated by his work in ARCIC, as well as by his friendship with Peter Brown and others. His *Augustine* (1986) was intended as a short introduction, but it represented the distillation of great learning and insight. It also represented a large investment of his own personality; for, always compatibly with critical scholarship, he seemed often to identify himself with Augustine's faith and humanity. Even more arresting was a book on Augustine which had been abandoned for the one published in 1986; it was discovered after his death by Peggy and published posthumously as *Augustine of Hippo: a Life* (2009). In his foreword Peter Brown wrote that no one else could seize with greater clarity and firmness the nerve centres of entire systems of thought, without ever freezing them into static structures. Besides its profundity this book contained some fine examples of Chadwick's characteristic wit, such as his description of Augustine's biographer Possidius as 'an honest uninventive man, gasping with astonishment in the presence of personal greatness' (*Augustine of Hippo*, 4). As regius professor in Cambridge he was a fellow of Magdalene College, where the many fond memories of him included his own delight when he returned some books to the college library late and with profuse apologies, to be answered by the kindly assistant, 'don't worry dear, I'm a slow reader myself' (private information).

Chadwick came out of retirement in 1987 to become, for six years, an eirenic master of Peterhouse, Cambridge. There he worked on his two last books, *The Church in Ancient Society: from Galilee to Gregory the Great* (2001), a summation of his life's scholarship; and the much shorter but even more remarkable *East and West: the Making of a Rift in the Church* (2003), about what he called 'the greatest Christian split of all' (*East and West*, 1). The epilogue of the latter book harked back to his long ecumenical experience, when he observed that the characteristic of those against ecumenism always was, in effect, their refusal to bring themselves out of the past into the present. This book had a hero in Photius, the ninth-century patriarch of Constantinople. Photius was an urbane churchman, and a great collector and reviewer of books. For one glorious moment it looked as if he and Pope John VIII had resolved all the then disputes between Rome and Constantinople. The pope sent him a pallium and other vestments, but after his death all was to end in disappointment.

In 1960 Chadwick was elected a fellow of the British Academy and thereafter he was showered with many honorary doctorates and fellowships. He was an honorary or corresponding member of learned societies in America, France, Germany, and Belgium. He was made a KBE in 1989 (but as an ordained priest did not use the title 'Sir'), and in 1993 was elected to the German Order Pour le Mérite, an order of truly world-class scholars and scientists. This election reflected not only his personal distinction, but also his study of German theology and his sympathetic friendships with German theologians immediately following the Second World War and subsequently. In the memorial address about Chadwick, delivered for the order by his fellow theologian Eberhard Jüngel, Jüngel called him a great builder of bridges (*pontes*), bridges between different kinds of people, and between the early Church and our own present; truly a *pontifex*, who even sought to build bridges to the Roman *pontifex maximus*. For all his Olympian presence, his tall form and slight stoop, his fine forehead and piercing eyes, his sing-song diction, he was so courteous, so compassionate, so good a listener, and so engaged with people, as to be also a most loveable person. He lived latterly in St John Street, Oxford, and died on 17 June 2008 at the John Radcliffe Hospital, Oxford, of pneumonia. He was survived by his wife, Peggy, and their three daughters. Memorial services were held at Christ Church Cathedral, Oxford, on 27 September 2008, and at Great St Mary's, Cambridge, on 22 November 2008.

HENRY MAYR-HARTING

Sources *The Times* (19 June 2008) • *Daily Telegraph* (19 June 2008) • *The Guardian* (19 June 2008) • *The Independent* (21 June 2008) • *New York Times* (22 June 2008) • *Le Monde* (1 July 2008) • *SBL Forum*, 6/6 (2008); www.sbl-site.org/publications/article.aspx?ArticleId=782, 16 May 2011 • H. Mayr-Harting, memorial address, Christ Church, Oxford, 27 Sept 2008, www.chch.ox.ac.uk/news/2008/henry-chadwick-memorial, 16 May 2011 • S. Darlington, memorial address, Christ Church, Oxford, 27 Sept 2008, www.chch.ox.ac.uk/sites/default/files/stephen-darlingto-chadwick-address.pdf, 16 May 2011 • H. Carpenter, *Robert Runcie: the reluctant archbishop* (1996) • Burke, *Peerage* • *WW* (2008) • personal knowledge (2012) • private information (2012) • b. cert. • m. cert. • d. cert.

Likenesses W. Bird, bromide print, 1966, NPG • S. Malin, oils, Christ Church Oxf. • D. Poole, oils, Peterhouse, Cambridge [*see illus.*] • obituary photographs

Wealth at death £421,526: probate, 30 March 2009, *CGPLA Eng. & Wales*

Challenor, Harold Gordon [Harry; Tanky] (**1922–2008**), soldier and police officer, was born on 16 March 1922 at 3 Caledonia Street, Bradley, near Wolverhampton, Staffordshire, the second of five children of Thomas Henry Challenor, then working in an iron foundry, and his wife, Ellen, *née* Barnes. He grew up in a family controlled by an unskilled, brutal father, 'a mean, cruel, sadistic tyrant who terrorised his family, made few friends and left not one endearing memory' (Challenor, 21). His father eventually found work in what was then known euphemistically as an asylum, one of those custodial institutions whose architecture and regime bore great similarity to those of prisons and in which disturbed patients were often harshly manhandled by the attendants. After leaving school, and a series of other jobs, Harry Challenor eventually joined his father working in the same institution.

It was the outbreak of the Second World War that gave Challenor's talents their full rein. In 1941 he joined the army and, because of his nursing experience, was at first posted to the Royal Army Medical Corps, later describing himself as 'the most aggressive medical orderly' they ever had (Challenor, 30). While serving in north Africa he volunteered for 62 commando, which became part of the 2nd Special Air Service (SAS) regiment. He lost his commando beret and made do with a tank corps one, hence the nickname Tanky, which stuck. In September 1943, by now a lance-corporal, he and five other SAS soldiers were dropped by parachute near Borgo Val di Taro, north of La Spezia, Italy, several hundred miles behind enemy lines. Four of his colleagues were never seen again. Challenor and Lieutenant Thomas (Tojo) Wedderburn succeeded in derailing three trains before running out of explosives. Wedderburn was captured and spent the rest of the war as a prisoner. Challenor was captured twice but escaped twice, and finally reached allied lines after seven months in German-occupied territory. He was awarded the Military Medal. He was again parachuted behind enemy lines in northern France soon after D-day, and his unit was among the first to cross the Rhine in March 1945. Promoted sergeant, he saw the end of the war in Norway. He had developed a visceral hatred of Germans, and later confessed to acts of unprovoked violence against German prisoners of war. He told a friend that 'when a man is obliged to spend months behind enemy lines and is taught to take a pleasure in killing, it is bound to leave some mark on his personality' (*The Times*, 19 Sept 2008). He remained with the SAS until 1947, latterly as a company quartermaster sergeant in Palestine. Meanwhile, while on leave, on 1 August 1944 he had married Doris May Broome (1921–1992), then a coil winder in an ammunition factory.

She was the daughter of William James Broome, iron foundry worker. They had one son.

On demobilization Challenor worked briefly in an iron foundry before joining the Metropolitan Police in 1951. Based initially in Mitcham, he was promoted detective constable in 1956 and in 1958 joined the flying squad. In 1962 he transferred to West End Central in Savile Row (covering Soho) as a detective sergeant. He impressed his seniors in the police force as he waged a personal campaign against crime in Soho, which he described in graphic terms as swimming 'against a tide of sewage' (Challenor, 54). Over the course of a police career lasting twelve years he amassed 600 arrests and eighteen commendations; he also earned a fearsome reputation among London's criminal fraternity, with allegations of brutality, forced confessions, planted evidence, and increasingly erratic behaviour. Colleagues later testified, for instance, that he had repeatedly punched a Barbadian named Padmore (arrested on suspicion of living off immoral earnings) while singing a popular song of the day, 'Bongo, bongo, bongo, I don't want to leave the Congo'. At this time the abuse of those detained in police stations was perhaps commonplace, and in some instances routine, part of a culture that was endemic and almost impossible to eradicate.

Challenor would no doubt have died unknown to other than a narrow circle of former police and army acquaintances save for the fact that in 1963 he was exposed not merely as a brutal policeman but also as a serial perverter of justice. The case not only brought down Challenor but was also a severe embarrassment to both the home secretary, Henry Brooke, and the commissioner of the Metropolitan Police, Sir Joseph Simpson.

On 11 July that year a protest demonstration took place outside Claridge's Hotel against Queen Frederika of Greece, who was on a controversial state visit to Britain. Large numbers of the communists who had been defeated in the Greek civil war were still imprisoned, while Frederika had Nazi associations in her past. The police attempted to break up the demonstration and among those arrested was a young cartoonist for *Peace News*, who also happened to be a member of the National Council for Civil Liberties, Donald Rooum. Although Rooum offered no resistance, back at Savile Row he was struck about the ear by Challenor and violently knocked to the floor before being locked in a room where Challenor again assaulted him. Then, from his pocket and wrapped in newspaper, Challenor produced the half brick that was to be his nemesis. This was the 'offensive weapon' that Challenor claimed he had found in Rooum's pocket. The same was done to three other protesters who had been arrested with Rooum. Challenor, however, had not reckoned with the high intelligence of Rooum's solicitor, who at the earliest opportunity brought Rooum a complete change of clothing and took away all that he had been wearing at the time of arrest. Examined in an independent forensic laboratory, it was found to contain no trace whatever of the telltale dust that is found in any receptacle in which bricks are carried.

The establishment of Rooum's innocence led to the reopening of no fewer than twenty-six cases of other innocent men convicted on Challenor's mendacious testimony after being subjected to violence in custody. In June 1964 Challenor was indicted to stand trial at the Old Bailey, accused of conspiracy to pervert the course of justice. Three other detectives stood in the dock with him. While they were each subsequently sentenced to three years in prison, Challenor himself was found unfit to plead owing to mental illness, a very rare event in criminal trials and one almost exclusively confined to defendants in homicide cases. Instead of standing trial, he was committed to a psychiatric hospital near his home. The trial judge was Sir Frederick Lawton, an unimpeachable champion of truth and justice. His remarks at the trial led to a subsequent inquiry, headed by Arthur James QC, into how Challenor had been allowed to remain in the police force and how evidence of his erratic behaviour had gone unheeded, but the report of the inquiry (published in 1965) was widely regarded as a whitewash.

On release from psychiatric hospital many years later, Challenor found work as a clerk in the office of the solicitors who had represented him. In 1990 he published a memoir, co-written with Alfred Draper, *Tanky Challenor: SAS and the Met*, whose front cover featured his medals and a half-brick. He was visited regularly by his former SAS colleagues. His wife, Doris, who supported him throughout his illness and incarceration, predeceased him. He died on 28 August 2008 at Amberley Lodge care home, in Downlands Road, Purley, Surrey, of a chest infection and bronchopneumonia. He was survived by his son.

Whether Challenor was a paranoid schizophrenic, as was claimed at the time, or suffering from post-traumatic stress disorder after his time behind enemy lines (as he suggested in his autobiography), or from a long-established personality disorder, is not a question that can perhaps ever be conclusively answered. What can be said is that, a tragic anti-hero, Challenor was a man in whom were combined opposing characteristics: the noble quality of courage in battle and the ignoble quality of injustice. Though subsequently mellowed by age and infirmity, he was a brutal man, in his prime a committed racist, and wholly without pity for his victims. Nevertheless, at the time of his death some internet posts lauded his methods and portrayed him as a hero brought down by liberal opinion. Though undoubtedly suffering from mental disorder, his fate has been to be remembered less for his bravery in war than for his brutality and corruption in public office. Bernard Toms's novel, *The Strange Affair* (1966, made into a film in 1968) was based on his case. He was reputedly also the model for the brutal Inspector Truscott in Joe Orton's farce, *Loot* (1965), and for the deranged Inspector Potter in Clive Exton's television drama, *The Bone Yard* (1966).

TERENCE MORRIS

Sources *Report of the Challenor Inquiry*, 1965, Cmnd. 2735 • M. Grigg, *The Challenor case* (1965) • B. Smoker, 'The Challenor case', *British Journal of Criminology*, 6 (1966), 68–71 • H. Challenor, *Tanky Challenor: SAS and the Met* (1990) • *Daily Telegraph* (16 Sept 2008) • *The*

Guardian (18 Sept 2008); (11 Oct 2008) · *The Times* (19 Sept 2008) · *The Independent* (23 Sept 2008) · b. cert. · m. cert. · d. cert.
Likenesses obituary photographs
Wealth at death under £135,000: probate, 6 Jan 2009, *CGPLA Eng. & Wales*

Chan, Michael Chew Koon, Baron Chan (1940–2006), paediatrician, was born on 6 March 1940 in Singapore, the only son of James Chieu Kim (Michael) Chan (1916–1979), a headmaster, and his wife, Rosie (1916–2000). He had a younger sister, Janette. His parents had both been born in Singapore, part of Singapore's small Chinese Christian community. He was educated at the Raffles Institution, Singapore, and went on to study medicine at Guy's Hospital in London. While there he met his future wife, Irene Wei-Len, daughter of Shin On Chee, from East Malaysia. They married on 13 November 1965 and had two children.

Paediatrics was Chan's chosen speciality and he returned to Singapore to train in this, becoming a lecturer in the department of paediatrics at the University of Singapore in 1970 and a senior lecturer and consultant paediatrician in 1973. In 1974 he returned to the UK on a British Paediatric Association Heinz fellowship to undertake research into Von Willebrand's disease, a disorder of blood coagulation, at Great Ormond Street Hospital, where he worked with Roger Hardisty. From there he was recruited in 1976 to the Liverpool School of Tropical Medicine, where he spent the next eighteen years as a senior lecturer and consultant paediatrician. During his time in Liverpool his academic work included research into and teaching about the special issues of children in the developing world. He worked with the British Council to set up courses for doctors from India, and was always keen to look for practical solutions to problems of caring for children, especially in the newborn period. In 1991 he was the joint editor of the fourth edition of a textbook, *Diseases of Children in the Subtropics and Tropics*.

Chan's background and professional work made him acutely aware not only of the health problems of children in developing countries, but also of the challenges faced by those from ethnic minority communities working in the UK. In 1994 he moved his work to Leeds, where he became director of a new NHS ethnic health unit. He was also appointed a visiting professor in ethnic health at the University of Liverpool in 1996, a non-executive director of the Wirral and West Cheshire community NHS trust (1999–2001) and the Birkenhead and Wallasey NHS primary care trust (2001–5), and adviser on ethnic health to the NHS north-west region (2000–06). He was very supportive of his wife, who set up and for many years ran the Wirral Multicultural Organisation, which he chaired from 1997 to 2003, and which became a model for others to emulate. In a letter to *The Times* in 2004 he warned that 'Equality of opportunity and equity of access to employment and promotion are essential safeguards against the dangerous voices of extremism' (*The Times*, 8 April 2004). He was born into a strongly Christian family and religion played a very important part in all he did. He was chairman of the Chinese Overseas Christian Mission and it was

Michael Chew Koon Chan, Baron Chan (1940–2006), by G. Lee, 2001

for his work with the Chinese community in the UK that he was appointed MBE in 1991. He increasingly became involved in national affairs and was a patron of the Family Matters Institute and chaired the Chinese in Britain Forum (1996–2006). In the latter capacity he voiced the concerns of Chinese restaurant owners that new immigration laws would decrease the availability of suitable kitchen staff. He joined the Sentencing Panel in 1999 and the Commission on the Future of Multicultural Britain under the chairmanship of Lord Parekh in 2000, contributing a chapter on health to the commission's final report.

In 2001 Chan was made a life peer, as Baron Chan, one of the first 'people's peers'. He was the first person of Chinese origin to be elevated to the House of Lords, and sat on the cross benches. It was no surprise that he was active in both health and ethnic minority issues as well as being a member of the Press Complaints Commission from 2002. He was never afraid to voice his opposition when he thought it necessary. He spoke out about the Labour government's health reforms, warning very presciently of the dangers of major infection problems like MRSA. With Baroness Cox he condemned the Burmese military dictatorship, defending Aung San Suu Kyi, the opposition leader under permanent house arrest, and also voicing concern for the Burmese Christians who were a special target of the military forces. He raised questions about preparedness for avian flu and joined Baroness Rendell of Babergh's appeal for more racial diversity in the theatre. Singapore was always close to his heart, and following his ennoblement he visited that country to see relatives, but was invariably invited to meet politicians and attend official dinners. When London was bidding to become host city for the 2012 Olympic Games he was part of the team that flew out to Singapore to try to win the bid. Chan believed that the greatest impact on the voting members of the International Olympic Committee was made by a group of children representing London's ethnic minority communities.

Michael Chan was a quiet, unassuming man who was passionately devoted to children and their health. He was highly valued by his colleagues and students. He was not shy and was always prepared to talk to those who he thought needed assistance or who might help him solve the problems of others. He had a gentle but highly effective manner which made people feel that he valued their opinions and points of view. If he had a fault it was that he could never say 'no' and probably took on too many issues. He always remembered his roots and was never arrogant. He had a great sense of humour and said that he would have liked to be a comedian. He was much in demand to be a patron of charities and was heavily involved with many both in Merseyside and nationally. As a church elder at Liverpool's Chinese Gospel Mission he claimed to enjoy preaching and listed it as one of his hobbies, along with Chinese cooking, travel, and gardening. He died unexpectedly at Arrowe Park Hospital, Birkenhead, on 21 January 2006, following complications of acute pancreatitis. His memorial service in Liverpool's Anglican cathedral was attended by over 600 mourners, including several of his fellow peers. In 2007 one of the Pearl awards, which recognize contributions of the Chinese community to Britain, was named after him. He was survived by his wife and their two children, Stephen, a general practitioner, and Ruth, a midwife and psychologist, who had worked as his personal assistant when he was in the House of Lords.

ALAN W. CRAFT

Sources *Daily Telegraph* (26 Jan 2006) • *The Times* (8 Feb 2006) • *The Guardian* (13 Feb 2006) • *The Lancet*, 367/9510 (18 Feb 2006), 562 • Burke, *Peerage* • *WW* (2006) • personal knowledge (2010) • private information (2010) • d. cert.

Likenesses G. Lee, C-type colour print, 2001, NPG [*see illus.*] • photographs, 2001, Photoshot, London • obituary photographs

Wealth at death £187,234: probate, 5 June 2006, *CGPLA Eng. & Wales*

Chandler, Tony John (1928–2008), geographer and climatologist, was born on 7 November 1928 at the City Maternity Home, Westcotes Drive, Leicester, the second son of Harold William Chandler (1893–1975), hosiery factory manager, and his wife, Florence Ellen, *née* Moore (1894–1973). At the time of his birth registration his parents lived at 17 Equity Road, Leicester. He was educated at Hinckley grammar school (1939–42) and Alderman Newton Boys' School in Leicester (1942–6). In 1946 he entered King's College, London, to read geography and mathematics, before graduating in 1949 with a first. A diploma in education followed in 1950. He spent his national service teaching meteorology to servicemen at RAF Cranwell. In 1952 he was appointed assistant lecturer in geography at Birkbeck College, London. On 4 September 1954 he married, at St Anne's Church, Leicester, Margaret Joyce Weston (1927–2001), daughter of Willie Bertram Weston. They had two children, Kathryn (*b.* 1957) and Adrian (*b.* 1960).

In 1955 Chandler completed his MSc thesis on the historical geography of Leicestershire and began research on London's climate. At the time, Henry Clifford Darby, professor of geography at University College, London, was looking for a climatologist and encouraged Chandler to apply. In 1956 he joined University College as a lecturer, becoming reader in 1965 and professor in 1969. He left for a chair at the University of Manchester in 1973, becoming head of department and chairman of the pollution research unit.

At University College Chandler taught meteorology, climatology, and cartography, and contributed to masters courses in architecture, conservation, hydrology, and planning. His delivery was clear and unambiguous, reflecting his training and belief in the power of rigorous scientific principles. His doctoral thesis, 'Studies of the climate of London' (University of London, 1964), gave rise to *The Climate of London* (1965). This pioneering work used results from his London Climatological Survey that involved schools and private individuals maintaining weather stations and Chandler employing a legendary mobile recording station, housed in a Land Rover that he drove along carefully chosen traverses through London and its suburbs. The survey revealed how the atmospheric environment of a great city functioned; Chandler's accounts of airflow, fog, air pollution, and the 'heat island' of the built-up area were outstanding. The survey attracted much attention and was extended by government grants enabling automatic temperature recorders to be installed on the Post Office communications tower in the West End. Its results helped to shape subsequent urban climatological research across the globe. Chandler shared his expertise with his doctoral students working on urban thunderstorms, air pollution, evapotranspiration, transport of atmospheric smoke and sulphur dioxide, and the influence of surface roughness and temperature on urban airflow.

Following the appearance of *The Climate of London*, Chandler was invited to be the World Meteorological Organization rapporteur on urban climates (1965–9), and president of the joint World Meteorological Organization/World Health Organization symposium on urban climates and building climatology (1968). He was a consultant to the United Kingdom Atomic Research Establishment, Aldermaston, and in 1970 chaired a working group preparing evidence for the royal commission on environmental pollution. He was on the council of the Royal Meteorological Society (1961–4), and became secretary in the early 1970s. He served on the editorial boards of *Weather* and of *Boundary Layer Meteorology*. He received the prestigious Back award from the Royal Geographical Society in 1963.

During the 1970s his professional commitments included being vice-president of the Royal Meteorological Society (1973–5); a member of the World Meteorological Organization committee on climate and environmental problems (1972–4), of the royal commission on climate and environmental pollution (1973–7), of the Clean Air Council, and of the council of the Natural Environment Research Council (1974–9); and scientific secretary of the Royal Society study group on pollution and the atmosphere (1975–7).

Chandler published *Selected Bibliography of Urban Climate* (1970) and *Urban Climatology and its Relevance to Urban Design* (1976), as well as a textbook, *Modern Meteorology and Climatology* (1972; rev. edn, 1981). He contributed 'The climate of towns' to *The Climate of the British Isles* (co-edited with Stanley Gregory, 1976), and wrote many scholarly articles and scientific reports. He was a pioneer in climatological science and led the way in using geographical knowledge to inform environmental planning.

In 1977 Chandler was invited to become master of Birkbeck College, and took up his post in October. Despite the honour attached to the mastership, dealing with difficult personnel issues at the college proved too great a challenge for Chandler, who resigned on medical grounds in January 1979. His decision to leave Birkbeck was devastating for his colleagues, and his later decision to abandon academic work was tragic, since he was arguably the world's leading urban climatologist. He spent his retirement collecting clocks, reading, listening to music, and travelling. In 1989 he was made an honorary research fellow at University College, London, and a visiting professor at King's College. He spent his final years near Eastbourne, his wife having predeceased him in May 2001. He died at his home, 15 Durrell Close, Langney, on 17 July 2008, and his funeral was in Leicester on 5 August. He was survived by his daughter and son. HUGH CLOUT

Sources *The Times* (29 Sept 2008) · *Leicester Mercury* (14 Nov 2008) · *GJ*, 175 (2009), 82–3 · *Weather*, 64/2 (2009), 53–4 · *International Association for Urban Climate Change Newsletter*, 31 (March 2009), 2–3 · T. R. Oke, 'Classics in physical geography revisted: Chandler, T. J., 1965: *The climate of London*', *Progress in Physical Geography*, 33/3 (2009), 437–42 · *WW* (2008) · personal knowledge (2012) · private information (2012) · b. cert. · m. cert. · d. cert.
Likenesses obituary photographs

Channon, (Henry) Paul Guinness, Baron Kelvedon (1935–2007), politician, was born on 9 October 1935 at 21 St James's Place, Westminster, the only child of Sir Henry (Chips) *Channon (1897–1958), politician, and his wife, Lady Honor Dorothy Mary, *née* Guinness (1909–1976). Few twentieth-century politicians have inherited so many advantages of wealth and family connections. His mother was the daughter of the second earl of Iveagh and heiress to a brewing fortune. His American-born father wrote one of the most celebrated political diaries of the twentieth century and was a Conservative MP for the last twenty-three years of his life. He had taken over the seat, Southend-on-Sea, from his mother-in-law, Lady Iveagh, who in turn had replaced her husband, the Hon. Rupert Guinness, as MP when he became second earl of Iveagh.

(Henry) Paul Guinness Channon, Baron Kelvedon (1935–2007), by unknown photographer, 1986

Guinness had first won Southend in 1912. Thus in January 1959, when following his father's death Paul Channon won a by-election for what had become the constituency of Southend West, he was maintaining an unbroken family connection with the seat that had already persisted for the best part of five decades. When he was selected as the Conservative candidate against stiff opposition, led by Lord Beaverbrook's *Daily Express*, his grandmother, Lady Iveagh, told the constituency party that 'you have done the right thing by backing a colt when you know the stable he was trained in' (*The Times*, 14 Jan 1959).

Certainly Channon would not have entered parliament at the age of twenty-three if he had relied on his own proven merits. Educated at Lockers Park, Hertfordshire, and Eton College, he had undertaken a year's national service in the Royal Horse Guards before entering Christ Church, Oxford. His father's death, and the ensuing by-election, occurred at the start of Channon's final year, and he never took a degree. But in this truncated academic career he won the presidency of Oxford's Conservative Association and his maiden speech, which drew on his experiences of national service in Cyprus, showed that he had more to offer than an exalted pedigree.

The first steps of Channon's path towards ministerial office were assisted by Conservatives who had been associated with his father. In 1959 he was appointed parliamentary private secretary (PPS) to the minister of power, Richard Wood, son of Lord Halifax, before serving 'Rab' Butler (successively home secretary, first secretary of state, and foreign secretary) in the same capacity from 1960 to 1964.

Channon's father had been Butler's PPS in 1938–41, when the latter was under-secretary at the Foreign Office. On 7 August 1963 Channon married Ingrid Olivia Georgia Guinness, *née* Wyndham (*b.* 1931), daughter of Major Guy Richard Charles Wyndham, army officer and artist, and former wife of Channon's cousin Jonathan Guinness, later third Baron Moyne. It was a happy union that produced three children, Olivia (*b.* 1964), Georgia (*b.* 1966), and Henry (*b.* 1970).

The tories lost office in 1964, not least because of their close connections to the aristocratic establishment. Yet Channon's origins were not held against him by colleagues who had come to appreciate his personal qualities. His voting record placed him clearly on the 'progressive' wing of his party, alongside most other senior Conservatives of the time. In 1965 he was elected to the executive of the Conservative backbench 1922 committee, and when Edward Heath became leader of the party in the same year he gave Channon a front-bench speaking role, on public building and works. In 1967 he was given an even more congenial job, covering the arts. A love of art was almost the only trait that he shared with his father. However, when the Conservatives returned to office in 1970 a more senior figure, Viscount Eccles, was given the arts portfolio. For most of the period until the government fell in February 1974 Channon was a junior minister within the Department of the Environment, working on housing. His housing duties were interrupted briefly in 1972 by a spell as a junior minister for Northern Ireland. During this time his historic London home, 96 Cheyne Walk, Chelsea, was the venue of a controversial and abortive meeting between the secretary of state, William Whitelaw, and representatives of the Provisional IRA.

In opposition again after 1974, Channon continued to speak for the Conservative Party on environment issues, though still in a junior capacity. Despite his relative youth, by 1974 he had been in parliament for fifteen years and could have expected promotion. Instead when Heath was replaced as Conservative leader by Margaret Thatcher in 1975 his prospects sharply declined; the new leader spoke of him slightingly as 'that millionaire' (*Daily Telegraph*, 30 Jan 2007). With no constructive outlet for his energies in London he turned towards Europe for political engagement, serving as deputy leader of the Conservative delegation to the Council of Europe and the Western European Union from 1976 to 1979, but in the latter year he failed to secure a nomination for the first elections to the European parliament. After the Conservative victory in the general election of 1979 Thatcher indicated that her view of Channon was unchanged by floating the idea that he should take a peerage. After his refusal she relented to the extent of appointing him to another junior post, this time in the Civil Service Department, under Christopher Soames. Since Soames was soon dispatched to oversee the transition to majority rule in Rhodesia, Channon was effective head of the department for much of the time. In 1981 he finally became arts minister, but unlike Heath, Thatcher did not believe that the state should have an active role in this field. Having recognized that Channon was an able administrator and an energetic lobbyist on behalf of his department she moved him in 1983 to the newly established Department of Trade and Industry, again as a junior minister.

In January 1986 the secretary of state for trade and industry, Leon Brittan, was forced to resign as a result of the Westland affair. Channon (seen as a safe pair of hands) took Brittan's place, sixteen years after his first appointment as a junior minister. For the first time since his selection for Southend West, he had found himself in the right place at the right time. Unfortunately he had used up his ration of good fortune. Within a few months of joining the cabinet he lost his daughter Olivia to a drugs overdose after a party to celebrate the end of her final examinations, at Channon's old college. Even if Channon had never entered politics the death of his daughter in such circumstances would have attracted prurient media interest.

Channon's political life provided no respite from this personal tragedy. When he took over trade and industry the department was engaged in negotiations to sell off parts of the state-owned British Leyland motor company to the American firms General Motors and Ford. Although Channon managed to block both deals the incident aroused patriotic anger within parliament and among the general public, and Channon was not the kind of man to deal effectively with emotional diatribes. At trade and industry he was also faced with a series of controversial takeover battles, including the attempt of the Guinness brewing firm to take control of Distillers. Channon delegated oversight of this transaction to his junior minister, Michael Howard, but allegations of 'insider dealing' in shares led to lengthy legal proceedings against three prominent businessmen, inevitably harming both Channon and the family firm.

After the 1987 general election Thatcher moved Channon to transport. Although this was clearly a demotion within the cabinet, it signalled that the prime minister retained her faith in Channon's administrative abilities. Unfortunately for Channon transport had just been afflicted by the sinking of the ferry *Herald of Free Enterprise*, costing almost 200 lives; and in his relatively brief spell as secretary of state the department would be hit by an additional trio of tragedies. In November 1987 thirty-one people were killed in the King's Cross fire; in December 1988 there were thirty-five fatalities after a collision between two trains outside Clapham Junction; and just nine days later a bomb exploded inside a Pan Am jet flying over Lockerbie, killing 270 people on the plane and in the town. Channon was much criticized when, two days after the Lockerbie disaster, and while questions were being asked of the Department of Transport's failure to pass on warnings, he left Britain for a holiday on the island of Mustique, which was particularly identified in the public mind with aristocratic debauchery thanks to publicity surrounding Princess Margaret and her friends. By this time looking hopelessly accident-prone, in the cabinet reshuffle of July 1989 he left the government. In the Conservative leadership election of the following year he voted for Michael Heseltine rather than Thatcher, but this decision was entirely consistent with his ideological inclinations on domestic and European issues.

Channon's first years in his new role as a backbench MP were marked by skilful chairmanship of the Commons' transport select committee. In 1992 he hoped to follow three family members by serving as speaker of the house. Instead, amid procedural wrangling, he was forced to withdraw from the fray. Later in the 1992–7 parliament his old ally Willie Whitelaw asked him if he intended to stand for election again. Channon replied: 'You must be mad! I don't want anything to do with this lot, and hope I'll never see them again' (private information). He announced his decision to stand down in 1995. Finally accepting a peerage after the election of 1997, he took the title of Baron Kelvedon from the main family home in Essex, Kelvedon Hall. However, he made little mark in the House of Lords, and his health was poor for many years owing to the onset of lewy body disease. He died at the Lister Hospital, Westminster, on 27 January 2007, and was survived by his wife and two of his children. A memorial service was held at St Margaret's, Westminster, on 12 June 2007. Essentially a pragmatist rather than a Thatcherite ideologue, he had continued to uphold an ethic of public duty long after he had been overtaken by more self-serving colleagues. In stark contrast to his garrulous, extrovert father, he was discreet even in retirement, when he could have helped his reputation by publishing an exculpatory account of his long years of ministerial service. As it was, at the time of his death he was remembered, perhaps unfairly, as a maladroit minister whose daughter had died after a decadent party. MARK GARNETT

Sources A. Clark, *Diaries* (1993) · M. Thatcher, *The Downing Street years* (1993) · *The Times* (30 Jan 2007) · *Daily Telegraph* (30 Jan 2007) · *The Guardian* (31 Jan 2007) · *The Independent* (31 Jan 2007) · Burke, *Peerage* · *WW* (2007) · private information (2011) · b. cert. · m. cert. · d. cert.

Archives FILM BFINA, current affairs footage | SOUND BL NSA, documentary recordings · BL NSA, current affairs recordings

Likenesses photographs, 1970–2002, Getty Images, London · photographs, 1983–2002, Rex Features, London · photograph, 1986, Getty Images, London [*see illus.*] · photographs, 1986–93, PA Photos, London · photographs, 1988–97, Photoshot, London · Marc [M. Boxer], caricature, repro. in *The Observer* (23 Feb 1986) · obituary photographs

Wealth at death £78,437,281: probate, 22 Feb 2008, *CGPLA Eng. & Wales*

Chapple, Derek Barton- [*performing name* Derek Waring] **(1927–2007)**, actor, was born on 26 April 1927 at St Clair, 30 Goodwyn Avenue, Mill Hill, London, the son of Wing Commander Harry John Barton Chapple (1898–1978), RAF officer and electrical engineer, who assisted John Logie Baird with his early television experiments, and his wife, Ada Marian, *née* Chuter (1897–1998). He was educated at Dulwich College. After national service with the army in India he declined a place at St Edmund Hall, Oxford, to read modern languages, and went instead to the Royal Academy of Dramatic Art, where he adopted the stage name Derek Waring, before spending five years in repertory theatre. He made his West End début in *The World of Suzie Wong* (Prince of Wales Theatre, 1958). From 1962 to 1964 he acted with the Royal Shakespeare Company, where he met the actress Dorothy *Tutin (1930–2001). They married on 23 December 1963 and had a son, Nicholas, and a daughter, Amanda, who both followed their parents into the acting profession.

As Derek Waring, Barton-Chapple played Albert to his wife's Victoria in *Portrait of a Queen*, both in the West End (Vaudeville Theatre, 1965) and on Broadway (Henry Miller's Theatre, 1968). Other stage appearances included Michael Pertwee's *Sextet* (Criterion Theatre, 1977), the Agatha Christie thriller *Cards on the Table* (Vaudeville Theatre, 1981), George Bernard Shaw's *You Never Can Tell* (Haymarket Theatre, 1987), and the musicals *Cowardy Custard* (Mermaid Theatre, 1972) and Leslie Bricusse's *Sherlock Holmes* (Cambridge Theatre, 1989), in which he played Dr Watson. He was perhaps better known for his roles on film and especially television. He made his cinema début as a surgeon in the Ealing comedy *Barnacle Bill* (1957), starring Alec Guinness. There followed a large number of character parts in a wide variety of largely forgotten British films of the 1960s and 1970s. His television appearances included *The Adventures of Sir Lancelot* (1957) and *The Adventures of Robin Hood* (1957–8), *Z Cars* (1969–73, as Detective Inspector Neil Goss), *Moody and Pegg* (1974–5, as the antique dealer Roland Moody awkwardly sharing a house with the civil servant Daphne Pegg, played by Judy Cornwell), *Partners* (1981, written by his brother Richard, who had adopted the pen name Richard Waring), the sketch show *The Funny Side* (1985), and *Keeping up Appearances* (1995). He was described by one television executive who worked with him as an excellent 'company chap' but 'lightweight' (*The Guardian*, 22 Feb 2007). He was an enthusiastic and talented cook as well as gardener. He died on 19 February 2007 at Petworth Cottage Nursing and Convalescent Home, Petworth, Sussex, of cancer. He was survived by his two children.

Sources *The Guardian* (22 Feb 2007) · *The Independent* (23 Feb 2007) · *The Times* (27 Feb 2007) · *Daily Telegraph* (27 Feb 2007) · b. cert. · m. cert. · d. cert.

Likenesses S. & G. Barratts, photograph, 1962, PA Photos, London · photographs, 1975–89, Rex Features, London · obituary photographs

Wealth at death £484,758: probate, 25 Jan 2008, *CGPLA Eng. & Wales*

Charles, Dame **(Mary) Eugenia (1919–2005)**, prime minister of Dominica, was born on 15 May 1919 at Pointe Michel, near Roseau, on the south-west coast of Dominica, the daughter of John Baptiste Charles (who died in 1983, at the age of 107), businessman, and his wife, Josephine, *née* Delauney. Her father was a successful fruit exporter and the founder of the Dominica Co-operative Bank, a 'penny bank' for small savers. She was educated at the Convent High School, Roseau, and St Joseph's Convent, Grenada, and remained a devout Roman Catholic throughout her life. She read law at the University of Toronto and was called to the bar at the Inner Temple, London, in 1947. She began private practice in Dominica in 1949. She wrote

Dame (Mary) Eugenia Charles (1919–2005), by B. Dale, 1983

anonymous articles for *The Herald* and later *The Star* newspapers that were highly critical of the ruling Dominica Labour Party. She was in the vanguard of those who founded the Dominica Freedom Party in 1968 following demonstrations against the passing of a Seditious and Undesirable Publications Act in July by the Dominica Labour Party, then under the premiership of Edward Oliver Le Blanc. She failed to win the Roseau North seat in the general election of 1970, contesting it against the future prime minister, Patrick John, but entered the House of Assembly as a nominated member that year.

In the general elections of 1975 Charles contested and won the Roseau Central seat and became leader of the opposition in the new parliament. She was a delegate at the constitutional conference held at Marlborough House, London, in 1977, and was an active spokesperson in the public meetings related to the constitution in the run up to independence in November 1978. During political upheavals and a constitutional crisis leading to the resignation of Patrick John in 1979 she served as a member of the Committee for National Salvation that brokered the creation of an interim government under the premiership of the Dominica Labour Party's Oliver Seraphine to administer Dominica until a general election could be organized. She became the first Caribbean woman prime minister when she led the Dominica Freedom Party to victory in the 1980 general election. During this time she was given the nickname Mamo, by which she was popularly known for the rest of her life. Regionally she immediately became part of a formidable team of Caribbean leaders including Edward Seaga of Jamaica and Tom Adams of Barbados, who dominated Caribbean public life in the 1980s.

Charles's first term was dedicated to the reconstruction of housing, roads, and other infrastructure destroyed by Hurricane David, which had hit Dominica on 29 August 1979, and in getting the business of government and foreign relations back into order. This was made more difficult by destabilization and the attempted coups to overthrow her government in 1981 and the court cases that followed. (Patrick John was jailed for twelve years for his part in one such attempted coup, in conjunction with North American white supremacist groups.) Her government was re-elected in 1985 with a reduced majority and again in 1990 when the United Workers' Party, formed in 1988, became the main opposition in parliament.

In 1991 Charles was made a DBE by Elizabeth II at Harare, Zimbabwe, during the Commonwealth heads of government meeting. She retired from the House of Assembly in 1995 and her Dominica Freedom Party lost the general election of that year after fifteen years in power. During that time the country rose to an economic peak in 1988 but the momentum was not maintained and by 1993 there was evidence of the beginning of an economic decline, due mainly to changes in international trade affecting the banana industry, the reduction of foreign aided projects, and the economics of scale in relation to small independent island states. Conflict over her domination of the cabinet and her views on a successor marred the last two years of her leadership. Her firm and forthright character and clear-cut opinions were seen by some to be abrasive and she made many enemies, but her admirers cited these as the only means by which to accomplish results in difficult circumstances. She was best known outside Dominica for her staunch anti-communism during the last years of the cold war in the Caribbean and, as chairman of the Organization of Eastern Caribbean States, for leading the invitation to the United States government under President Ronald Reagan to invade Grenada in October 1983. For this she was often referred to as the Iron Lady of the Caribbean.

Following her retirement in 1995 Charles watched from the sidelines as the fortunes of the Dominica Freedom Party rapidly declined under new leadership, eventually losing all of its seats in the House of Assembly at the general election of 2005. By then Charles's memory and mental capacity to absorb what was going on around her were fading and in the opinion of those close to her she had lost the will to live by the time she fell and fractured her left hip on 27 August 2005. She was flown to Martinique for treatment, but died of a pulmonary embolism in Fort de France, Martinique, on 6 September. She was buried in Pointe Michel on 14 September, after a funeral service at La Sallette Roman Catholic church. She never married and had no children. Her death removed another of the core group of regional leaders, including Tom Adams of Barbados, Sir John Compton of St Lucia, Sir Vere Cornwall Bird of Antigua, and Sir James Mitchell of St Vincent and the Grenadines, who dominated the politics of the eastern Caribbean during the latter part of the twentieth century, when the islands attained independence from Britain. LENNOX HONYCHURCH

Sources O. Opfell, *Women prime ministers and presidents* (1993), 88–94 · L. Honychurch, *The Dominica story*, 3rd edn (1995) · *The Times* (8 Sept 2005) · *Daily Telegraph* (8 Sept 2005) · *The Guardian* (8 Sept 2005) · *The Independent* (8 Sept 2005) · *New York Times* (9 Sept 2005) · *Washington Post* (14 Sept 2005) · *Weekly Gleaner* (15 Sept 2005) · *The Economist* (17 Sept 2005) · L. Honychurch, 'Dame Mary Eugenia Charles', www.lennoxhonychurch.com/article.cfm?id=434, 12 July 2008 · Burke, *Peerage* · *WW* (2005) · personal knowledge (2009) · private information (2009)
Archives University of the West Indies, Cave Hill, Barbados | SOUND BL NSA, current affairs recordings
Likenesses B. Dale, photograph, 1983, National Geographic, Getty Images, London [*see illus.*] · photographs, 1983–5, Getty Images, London · photographs, 1983–2001, PA Photos, London · photographs, 1996, Rex Features, London · obituary photographs · photographs, CUL, Royal Commonwealth Society collection
Wealth at death Eastern Caribbean $51,000,000

Charlot [*née* Huber], **Monica** (1933–2005), historian and political scientist, was born at 6 Maitland Park Villas, St Pancras, London, on 31 May 1933, the second of three children of Joseph Jacob (Jack) Huber, consular official, and his wife, Doris May, *née* Fickling. Her Swiss father had met her English mother while he was working in London for a Swiss tourist association. He was subsequently Swiss consul in London, New York, and finally in Australia, where he died. Monica was brought up in London and Manchester before moving back to London as an undergraduate student at Bedford College. Her father had encouraged her to study German but she had other plans. She took a BA degree in French before transferring to Paris at the age of twenty-one, where she was employed as 'English assistante' in a French lycée. She then met Jean Charlot (1932–1997), a French political scientist whom she married in 1956. They had three daughters. When Jean was called up to serve in Algeria at the height of the uprising there, the whole family followed him across the Mediterranean.

Monica Charlot was already thinking of making her way through the French academic qualification system. This meant sitting the *agrégation* exam, a highly selective and competitive process that turned out qualified lycée teachers. On becoming *agrégée* in English, she spent a couple of years teaching English in two Paris lycées before being recruited as lecturer by the University of Nanterre, where she watched the hatching of the 1968 student protest that started there with the setting up of the Mouvement du 22 Mars. During these years she had been working on a doctoral thesis, which she eventually defended at the Sorbonne in 1971. Devoted to the study of the general election campaigns in Britain between 1933 and 1970, it was published the following year by the Presses de la Fondation Nationale des Sciences Politiques under the title *La démocratie à l'anglaise*. Retrospectively this seminal book was seen as a turning point in the tradition of British studies in France, which until then had been almost exclusively identified with literary studies.

Appointed professor of British civilization—the French umbrella term encompassing political and social culture as well as cultural studies—at the Sorbonne Nouvelle University, also known as Paris III, Monica Charlot set out to win British and American political and social studies official recognition as a legitimate branch of British and American studies in general. This she achieved by convincing the higher education department to create a 'civilization' paper, alongside linguistics and literature papers, in the *agrégation* exam with a view to giving future lycée teachers a proper grasp of British (and American) politics and society. A born organizer, she brought together the university civilization specialists within a national research centre called CRECIB (Centre de Recherches et d'Études en Civilisation Britannique), which by the time of her death had some 250 members spread across France. She also provided inspiration and support to the numerous students—over a hundred of them—who wrote their doctoral dissertations under her supervision.

Charlot was also a prolific writer. She published some fifteen books in her own name and contributed to seventeen collective works on various aspects of British politics and society. Her textbooks on British government and politics became standard fixtures on students' reading lists in France but her own preferred productions were *La démocratie à l'anglaise* (1972), *Le temps des incertitudes*, a hefty account of Britain's political history between 1945 and 1980, published in 1981 by the prestigious Imprimerie Nationale, and *L'Angleterre, cette inconnue: une société qui change* (1980). It is regrettable that none of her books was translated into English except the first volume of her biography of Queen Victoria, *Victoria: le pouvoir partagé* (1989), which was published two years later by Blackwell's under the title *Victoria: the Young Queen*. The second volume was never completed.

A longtime member of the Franco-British Council, a bilateral think-tank created by Edward Heath and Georges Pompidou, in 1984 Charlot was appointed director of the Maison Française at Oxford. The perfect candidate to fill this post, she remained there until 1991, and with the support of two Oxford political scientists in particular, David Butler and David Goldey, fulfilled her passion to be a mediator between the two countries. Her outstanding contribution in this field was rewarded with the highest distinctions both in France (Palmes Académiques, ordre national du Mérite, Légion d'honneur) and in Britain, where she was appointed OBE.

Monica Charlot retired from academic life in 2002, five years after the death of her beloved husband Jean. She died of a stroke in Rennes on 20 May 2005 and was cremated. Her ashes were subsequently scattered over the Channel, as those of Jean Charlot had been. She was survived by her three daughters, two of whom followed in their parents' academic footsteps.

JEAN-CLAUDE SERGEANT

Sources *The Guardian* (27 March 1997); (13 June 2005) · *Le Monde* (27 May 2005) · S. Halimi, ed., *Les institutions politiques au Royaume-Uni: hommage à Monica Charlot* (Paris, 2006) · personal knowledge (2009) · private information (2009) · b. cert.
Likenesses photograph, repro. in Halimi, *Institutions politiques*

Chipp, David Allan (1927–2008), journalist and news agency executive, was born on 6 June 1927 at 199 Kew Road, Kew, the son of Thomas Ford Chipp (1886–1931), botanist and assistant director of the Royal Botanic Gardens, and his wife, Isabel Mary, *née* Ballinger (1888–1979). He had an older sister, Rosemary (*b.* 1924). On the death of his father, Chipp, his sister, and his mother (who never remarried) moved to Cheltenham, where he attended the nursery class of Cheltenham Ladies' College before switching to Hillstone School in Malvern. He was visiting a relative in Malaya in 1939 when the Second World War began, and his mother decided that he should not risk the long sea journey home but instead move to Australia, where he was educated at Geelong grammar school in Melbourne. He thrived there: the headmaster, James Darling, and the senior history master, the radical Manning Clark, became his friends, and he made several return visits to Australia after the war.

Chipp returned to Britain in 1944 to serve in the Middlesex regiment. Before being demobilized in 1947 he passed the entrance examination for King's College, Cambridge, where he indulged his enthusiasms for acting (he was a gifted mimic) and rowing. A skilled and enthusiastic oarsman, he rowed for his college team and for many years served as a steward at Henley regatta. After graduating in English in 1950 he was accepted as a trainee by Reuters, the international news agency based in London, initially working on the sports desk. 'I really just slid into journalism', he later wrote, 'and it was not long before I knew that this was what I wanted. It's something I have never regretted' (Chipp, 7). As a trainee he was paid very little, so he spent much of his free time working as a dishwasher at a Lyons Corner House in London's West End. Yet Reuters' management soon recognized that he had the qualities to make an excellent news agency reporter—principally an eye for accuracy and the persistence to pursue all aspects of a story until the full facts were uncovered.

In 1952 Chipp was transferred to the general news desk and the following year received his first foreign posting, to Pakistan. Soon he moved his base to Rangoon, Burma, and travelled frequently in south-east Asia—notably Vietnam, where he covered the aftermath of the Indo-China War. In Rangoon he underwent a personal crisis when he learned that he had fathered a son by a Burmese woman he met in a cinema. He arranged for the boy to be looked after by a Roman Catholic orphanage and gave them £500 to support him. 'It meant I was going to be in debt for years', he wrote in his posthumously published memoir (Chipp, 86). He had not spoken of the incident during his lifetime and his acquaintances were surprised to hear of it, given the widely held belief that he was homosexual—an assumption that he did not challenge.

In 1956 the government of the People's Republic of China, which had refused to admit resident correspondents from the West since the revolution of 1949, agreed to lift the ban in the case of Reuters, such was the agency's international reputation for impartiality. Chipp was chosen as its representative. 'It was a dream assignment for a 28-year-old', he wrote later (Chipp, 79). Although there were severe restrictions on what he was allowed to see and report, he forged a friendship with Chou En Lai, the prime minister, and was able to meet other leaders of the regime. When he trod on the toe of Chairman Mao Zedong at a social event, the incident provided material for many an anecdote in later life, as well as the title of his memoir.

After two years in Peking, Chipp returned to London, where he occupied a series of editorial and executive positions at Reuters' Fleet Street headquarters until he was appointed the agency's editor in 1968. After a successful year in that post he was asked to become editor-in-chief of the Press Association (PA), the domestic news agency owned by national and regional newspapers, with which Reuters shared offices and facilities.

Chipp's task at the PA was to revive an organization perceived to be underperforming, its output stodgy and lacking flair. Because its journalists were regarded as beneath those on national newspapers in the professional pecking order, there was a constant turnover of staff and morale was low. His priority was to reverse this. At his first editorial conference he declared: 'Journalism is fun. If we don't find it so we might as well be bank clerks' (Chipp, 34). He urged reporters to seek out offbeat stories and write them with a lighter touch, without sacrificing the agency's reputation for accuracy and impartiality. To motivate them he introduced bylines on their formerly anonymous reports. With Britain soon to join the European Economic Community he appointed a correspondent in Brussels, the PA's first overseas bureau. It was not long before the agency's clients began to notice a marked improvement in the quality and range of its journalism. His dedication to the PA was demonstrated in 1979 when, during an industrial dispute, the National Graphical Association—the union whose members put material onto the wire—refused to handle anything that had not been subedited and initialled by Chipp. For the seven weeks that the dispute lasted he complied with this condition, working long hours to keep the service going, returning late at night to his flat at Crane Court, just two minutes from the office.

Chipp was a fervent campaigner for freedom of information and press access to official sources. He disliked the 'lobby rules' of unattributable briefings to political correspondents and opposed the 'D notice' system by which governments sought to control reporting of security matters. In 1980 he authorized the publication by the PA of leaked documents about proposed defence cuts: 'I think people have a right to know and that open government should be more than just platitudes' (*UK Press Gazette*, 3 Nov 1980). He elaborated on the theme in his memoir: 'At times when liberty is in danger, it must always be the task of journalists to challenge, to investigate and provoke … If they do not do it, no one else will' (Chipp, 264). It was as a result of his pressure that the government increased the number of reporters travelling with the British task force to the Falkland Islands in 1982.

After retiring from the PA in 1986 Chipp became an adviser on human rights and press freedom to the Commonwealth Press Union and was soon recruited to the boards of a number of media organizations, including *The Observer* and the Reuters Foundation. From 1991 to 1993 he was a member of the Press Complaints Commission, the self-regulating body of the newspaper industry. A keen churchman of the high Anglican variety, he also served as a beadle of St Bride's Church in Fleet Street. He was an enthusiastic clubman and sparkling conversationalist, and in his later years he spent many hours at the Garrick, where he was a popular and gregarious member of the Old Codgers, an informal lunch club composed of former editors. He maintained an ebullient social life until his death, from a ruptured abdominal aortic aneurysm, in his flat, 2 Wilton Court, 59–60 Eccleston Square, Pimlico, London, on 9 September 2008. A memorial service was held at St Bride's on 20 November. MICHAEL LEAPMAN

Sources *The Times* (11 Sept 2008); (17 Sept 2008) · *Daily Telegraph* (12 Sept 2008) · *The Guardian* (21 Nov 2008); (12 Sept 2009) · *The Independent* (12 Sept 2008); (15 Sept 2008) · D. Chipp, *Mao's toe: memoirs of the life of David Chipp, a serious correspondent*, ed. D. Freeman (2009) · *WWW* · personal knowledge (2012) · private information (2012) · b. cert. · d. cert.
Archives King's Cam., Archive Centre, corresp.
Likenesses photograph, 1985, PA Photos, London · obituary photographs
Wealth at death £467,056: probate, 1 June 2009, *CGPLA Eng. & Wales*

Chisnall, (James) Arthur White (1925–2006), social worker and club and concert promoter, was born on 3 June 1925 at 33 Birkenhead Avenue, Kingston upon Thames, Surrey, the son of Elizabeth Goater Chisnall, of no fixed occupation, then residing at 7 Cambridge Road, Kingston upon Thames. The identity of his father was never confirmed, although as an adult he speculated that his father was a local shopkeeper to whom he was sent as a young boy with an empty basket and a note from his mother. The man would look him over and then fill the basket and send him on his way. The young Chisnall spent his earliest years living with his mother in his maternal grandparents' home. George and Rosella Chisnall ran a shop in Kingston. By the end of 1930 both had died. Chisnall took the death of his grandfather particularly badly, describing it as a 'major trauma' (personal knowledge). His mother continued to run the family shop for several years and sent him to a local church school. He struggled through his education; although left-handed, he was forced to write with right-handed pens and was scolded 'for spoiling charitably given church property' (ibid.). He left at fourteen. His first job was working for the carpet department of a Kingston-based store, Hide & Co. In 1942 he volunteered for military service and joined the Royal Engineers. He served in a specialist communications unit in north Africa and took part in Field Marshal Montgomery's operation Bertram, which saw him involved in the deployment of dummy tanks in the largest deception plan of the desert war.

After demobilization Chisnall was employed on the groundnut scheme in Tanganyika; there he formed a jazz club in Nachingwea. He returned to England in 1951 and took a course in social science at Coleg Harlech in Merioneth. His interest in social trends and what was happening to the post-war generation took on more impetus after he returned in 1952 to Kingston, where he initially worked in a junk shop. At the same time he joined a group of academics, among them Leslie T. Wilkins of the Home Office research unit, and Brian Lewis, later deputy director of the Institute of Educational Technology at the Open University, who were interested in the views and problems of young people; several believed that the impact of two world wars had created a gap in the nation's cultural heritage and structure, which left a generation of young people lost and alienated from society.

Through his work in the junk shop in Kingston Chisnall had witnessed the popularity of jazz and blues records among students from the various arts schools, and decided to utilize this in his social research. In 1956 he convinced Michael Snapper, the owner of the dilapidated hotel on Eel Pie Island, just down the River Thames from Kingston, to give him free rein to organize music sessions on Wednesday and Sunday nights. (Snapper had started letting out the hotel's ballroom to jazz musicians a few months earlier.) He started by booking traditional jazz musicians like Ken Colyer, Cy Laurie, George Melly, Acker Bilk, and the Temperance Seven. The hotel's secluded location (initially it could be reached only by a small ferry, though this was soon replaced by a footbridge) and Chisnall's supportive attitude towards the emerging rhythm 'n' blues scene helped nurture many artists who went on to revolutionize pop culture. At the hotel musicians could experiment with their song styles and band line-ups, and play for an audience who, like them, wanted to change the world. Chisnall booked the Rolling Stones in 1963 (all members of the band having previously played on the island as part of other outfits). He also gave stage time to such up-and-coming British rhythm 'n' blues bands as the Cyril Davies All Stars, the Yardbirds, John Mayall's Bluesbreakers, the Artwoods, the Downliners Sect, Jeff Beck and the Tridents, and Long John Baldry and his Hoochie Coochie Men (featuring the young Rod Stewart).

Chisnall never saw the club as a commercial operation: he booked bands primarily to attract young people into the club so that he and other members of his social research group could help them to write CVs and apply for grants and entry to colleges and universities. He would later be described as an outreach social worker, although he attracted young people to him by using what he referred to as the 'carrier wave', popular music, rather than going out to find them himself (personal knowledge). There was a network of people whom he invited to Eel Pie Island to talk to the clubbers and to encourage them to develop their potential; politicians, scientists, and policy makers thus mixed with art students and young music fans at the island's gigs. Chisnall himself steered many young people towards higher education, several going to Coleg Harlech, which became well known as a 'second chance' college, often for people who for economic or social reasons had never had a first chance of a university education. An altruistic man, he used his own time and the little money he had to run a social club that almost incidentally became fertile ground for talented bands to showcase their music.

By 1967 the shabby hotel was in urgent need of repair, and since neither Chisnall nor Snapper could afford the estimated £200,000 cost, the police forced its closure. (It briefly reopened as Colonel Barefoot's Rock Garden in 1969 before being occupied as an anarchist commune and then being destroyed by fire in 1971.) In the late 1960s and throughout the 1970s Chisnall continued to work in social research and for the BIT Information Service in London (formed by supporters of the *International Times*), which provided a range of information to young people, published a number of alternative travel guides, and nurtured the British Communes Network. In addition, it helped and supported the *Arts Lab Newsletter*, the Community Levy for Alternative Projects (CLAP), and Cope, an anti-psychiatry information and help service. In 1974, with Brian Lewis and Auriol Hall, he published *Unattached Youth*, based on a study commissioned by the Joseph Rowntree Memorial Trust. His last years were spent in Strawberry Hill, Twickenham. He died on 28 December 2006 at the Princess Alice Hospice, Esher, Surrey, of cancer. He was survived by his wife, Susanne Fischer, a decorator. JO MEEK

Sources L. T. Wilkins, *Unofficial aspects of a life in policy research* (1999) · *The Independent* (4 Jan 2007); (5 Jan 2007) · *The Times* (29 Jan 2007); (23 Feb 2007) · 'The Eel Pie Island hotel', BBC Radio 4, 30 Jan 2007 · *Richmond and Twickenham Times* (1 June 2007) · D. Van der Vat and M. Whitby, *Eel Pie Island* (2009) · personal knowledge (2010) · private information (2010) · b. cert. · d. cert.
Likenesses obituary photographs
Wealth at death £345,478: probate, 20 April 2007, *CGPLA Eng. & Wales*

Chissell, Joan Olive (1919–2007), music critic, was born on 22 May 1919 at 115 Mill Road, Cromer, Norfolk, the only child of George Ernest Chissell (1880–1936), railway clerk, and his wife, Eva Ellen, *née* Lennard (1884–1954). She was educated at the Manor School in Sheringham, from which she won a scholarship in 1937 to the Royal College of Music. There she studied the piano with Kendall Taylor and theory with Herbert Howells, intending a career as a pianist and becoming sufficiently accomplished to give the first British performance of Ravel's concerto for the left hand under the baton of Constant Lambert. Though an injury to her right hand meant that by 1942 she had been obliged to abandon this ambition, she had also studied history with Frank Howes, and in 1943 began teaching at the Royal College of Music and lecturing for the extramural departments of the universities of Oxford and London. In 1948 she was invited by Howes, now chief music critic of *The Times* and an influential mentor, to become his assistant together with William Mann. In the same year she published her first book, a volume on Schumann in the Master Musicians series that remained a valuable and much consulted work.

On *The Times* Chissell's inside knowledge of the repertory meant that she concentrated largely on covering piano and song recitals. Though the paper's reviews were then unsigned, anonymity was no bar to her work being recognized for its critical discrimination and fairness, and she was soon invited to broadcast and write more widely, making valuable contributions to musical journals and symposia (including one on Benjamin Britten). It also brought her a circle of friends in the musical profession that, exceptionally for a critic, included many well-known artists who liked her and admired her writing. She had the respect of the débutant performers whose first appearances were then generously covered by the paper, and whose recitals she treated sympathetically but honestly; and she was often asked to sit as an adjudicator on panels, including that of the Leeds piano competition, where her quiet but knowledgeable voice was paid as much attention as those of celebrated performers.

Chissell's interests continued to centre on nineteenth-century song and piano music, and in particular Schumann. Her 1972 BBC guide to Schumann's piano music covered the ground with the capacity for succinct, scrupulous judgement she had developed in her years as a *Times* journalist, while her two contributions to the Faber Great Composers series, aimed primarily at young musicians, on Chopin (1965) and Brahms (1977), earned respectful opinions for their perceptions. She retired from *The Times* in 1979 to general regret, not shared only by the paper's typesetters, who had been required to decipher her handwriting. By now having won international recognition as a Schumann scholar she went on to publish in 1983 her study *Clara Schumann*. Subtitled 'a dedicated spirit', the book discussed Clara's dedication to her life as a piano virtuoso and a composer as much as to her family and her often difficult husband and his tragic decline into insanity. It was written in the judicious, graceful style that marked all her work. The two books on the Schumanns, coupled with her other scholarly work, won her the Robert Schumann prize in Germany in 1991.

In a sense the anonymity of her early *Times* writing suited Joan Chissell admirably. Shy and unassertive by nature, she was always guided by a wish not to draw attention to herself at the expense of performer or music. She found broadcasting a trial, and approached the microphone warily, but once launched she gave talks, especially in the BBC's 'Music Magazine', that were as illuminating and as much appreciated as her writing. To her wide circle of friends she was a warm and generous hostess in her Abbey Road flat in London and especially on the boat she kept moored on the Thames at Newbridge, where she would entertain visitors with convivial excursions up river. Her other great love was Greece, to which she made frequent visits and where she had close friends. Her private life was not happy, and having suffered one particularly painful disappointment she never married, but her charm and her gift for companionship saw to it that she was well surrounded by friends and was regularly visited in the care home in St John's Wood where she spent her final years. Beautiful as a young woman, she retained her fine looks to her last days. She died at the St John's Wood Care Centre, Boundary Road, St John's Wood, London, on 31 January 2007, following a stroke. A memorial concert was held for her on 27 September 2007 at the Royal College of Music, where in 2009 the Joan Chissell Schumann prize was launched in her memory. JOHN WARRACK

Sources *The Times* (5 Feb 2007); (7 Feb 2007); (23 Feb 2007) • Royal College of Music memorial concert programme, 27 Sept 2007 • personal knowledge (2011) • private information (2011) • b. cert.

Archives SOUND BL NSA, performance recordings • BL NSA, documentary recordings

Likenesses photograph, repro. in www.johnctibbetts.com/World%20of%20Robert%20Schumann/assets/gallery.htm • photographs, repro. in memorial concert programme

Wealth at death £851,834: probate, 4 April 2007, *CGPLA Eng. & Wales*

Chrysostomides, Iouliane [Julian] (**1928–2008**), Byzantine scholar and teacher, was born in Constantinople on 21 April 1928 (two years before the city was renamed Istanbul), the daughter of Chrysostomos Chrysostomides, a Cappadocian entrepreneur, and his wife, Victoria, *née* Rizas, a Phanariot from whom she inherited her sensitivity, perseverance, and love of beauty, and who remained a major influence in her life. She was educated at the Zappeion, the Greek lyceum for girls in Istanbul. In 1950, with the Greek community under increasing pressure, she came to England to read *literae humaniores* at Oxford, having found the Sorbonne less congenial. She was accepted at St Anne's College a year later. The tutor who interviewed her, Iris Murdoch, was impressed by her 'proud humility' (P. J. Conradi, *Iris Murdoch: a Life*, 2001). For the next five decades they would remain close and loyal friends. Chrysostomides inspired the character of Rain Carter in Murdoch's *The Sandcastle* (1957).

After graduating at Oxford with a third-class degree in 1955 Chrysostomides pursued her BLitt at Royal Holloway College, University of London, under the distinguished Byzantinist Joan Mervyn Hussey, whom in 1988 she honoured with a Festschrift entitled *Kathēgētria* (translated both as 'teacher' and 'guide'). Chrysostomides chose to study the scholar-emperor Manuel II Palaeologus (*r.* 1391–1425) and his policy *vis-à-vis* the Ottomans, which in turn led her to research in Venetian documents, an incomparable source for Byzantine history, society, and economy in the Palaeologan period. On completion of the first stage of her research, with the help of Iris Murdoch she secured a library post in the Society of Antiquaries. In 1963, thanks to a Virginia Gildersleeve fellowship awarded by the International Federation of University Women, she pursued further research in the Venetian archives. There she met the eminent Byzantinist Raymond-Joseph Loenertz, who would leave an indelible mark on her approach towards scholarship.

In 1965 Chrysostomides was appointed lecturer in history at Royal Holloway College, where she taught Byzantine history and political theory for almost three decades. In 1983 she was appointed senior lecturer and in 1992 reader in Byzantine history. She was a dedicated teacher;

Iouliane Chrysostomides (1928–2008), by unknown photographer, 1963

indeed many MA and research students who had no official association with Royal Holloway were the beneficiaries of her generous help, encouragement, and guidance. In 1985 she established, with Joseph Munitiz and Athanasios Angelou, the University of London graduate working seminar on editing Byzantine texts, with the aim of bringing together graduate students, university teachers, and visiting scholars interested in editing texts from manuscripts. This seminar was at the time the only one of its kind in Britain. Chrysostomides's co-operation with King's College, London, remained a special one. Originally she shared the undergraduate teaching of Byzantine history with Donald Nicol. In 1988, together with Jonathan Riley-Smith and Athanasios Angelou, she established the MA in Byzantine studies, designed especially for those who were interested in progressing to doctoral research in this field. This led to further co-operation with Nicol's successor, Averil Cameron, and with Charlotte Roueché, which eventually led to the establishment of the MA in late antique and Byzantine studies. Chrysostomides was a fervent supporter of the University of London's federal system. Over the last decade of her life she observed with increasing concern the decentralization of the university and the independent stance of many colleges, which in her view put the future of the University of London at risk.

During her long academic career Chrysostomides published articles and books on various aspects of Byzantine history and historiography, political theory, economy, and society, including Byzantine women, Venetian commercial activities in the Byzantine empire, Byzantine perceptions of war and peace, and, finally, Byzantium and the rise of the Ottomans, which in a sense closed the circle from where she had started her research, only now with greater detachment and maturity. Among her major contributions were the annotated critical edition and translation of Manuel II Palaeologus's *Funeral Oration on his Brother Theodore* (1985), and her volume *Monumenta Peloponnesiaca* (1995), which was widely acclaimed. She also produced a number of volumes in co-operation with other scholars, including *The Letter of the Three Patriarchs to Emperor Theophilos* (with Joseph Munitiz and others, 1997), *The Greek Islands and the Sea* (with Charalambos Dendrinos and Jonathan Harris, 2004), *'Sweet Land …': Lectures on the History and Culture of Cyprus* (with Charalambos Dendrinos, 2006), and a *Catalogue of the Greek Manuscripts in Lambeth Palace Library* (with John Barron and others, 2006).

On her retirement in 1993 Chrysostomides was awarded an emeritus readership in Byzantine history by the University of London. Despite her retirement she remained active in both teaching and research, supervising graduate students, continuing her research on the Byzantine Peloponnese and her collaborative projects on the Greek population in Rhodes under hospitaller rule, and Greek palaeography, co-directing the graduate seminar on editing Byzantine texts, and giving papers and lectures in Britain and abroad. In 1998 she was appointed director of the Hellenic Institute at Royal Holloway. For the next decade she worked indefatigably (and without remuneration) to reorganize the institute, establishing it as a research centre for the diachronic and interdisciplinary study of Hellenism, at the same time securing funds for the establishment of full-time lectureships, fellowships, graduate studentships, and bursaries. In recognition of her long services to Hellenism and her major contribution to Byzantine studies she was given the title of ambassador of Hellenism by the Greek state (1999), and was honoured by former students and colleagues, headed by Judith Herrin, with a Festschrift appropriately entitled *Porphyrogenita* ('Born in the purple', 2003). She lived in Camberley, Surrey, and died at Frimley Park Hospital, Frimley, Surrey, on 18 October 2008, after a seven-month fight against cancer. She never married, but adopted the younger son of her twin brother Nikos, John, who survived her.

CHARALAMBOS DENDRINOS

Sources C. Dendrinos and others, eds., *Porphyrogenita* (2003) · *Daily Telegraph* (26 Nov 2008) · *The Times* (9 Jan 2009) · www.rhul.ac.uk/hellenic-institute/Julian-Chrysostomides/Julian-Chrysostomides.html, 2 Nov 2010 · J. A. Munitiz, funeral oration, web.rhul.ac.uk/hellenic-institute/Julian-Chrysostomides/Funeral-Oration.html, 2 Nov 2010 · *The Ship* [St Anne's College, Oxford] (2008–9), 50 · personal knowledge (2012) · private information (2012) · d. cert.

Likenesses photograph, 1963, Royal Holloway College, Egham, Hellenic Institute [*see illus.*] · obituary photographs

Wealth at death under £226,000: probate, 22 Dec 2008, *CGPLA Eng. & Wales*

Clark, (Anna) Mary Hawthorn Kitson [*married name* Mary Chitty] (**1905–2005**), archaeologist, was born in Leeds on 14 May 1905, the only daughter and youngest of three children of Edwin Kitson Clark (1866–1943), mechanical engineer, and his wife, Georgina, *née* Bidder. The younger of her two brothers was George Sidney Roberts Kitson *Clark (1900–1975), historian. She was educated at Leeds Girls' High School and Girton College, Cambridge, where she read history and stayed on for a year of archaeology. Returning to Yorkshire, in 1929 she became secretary of the Roman Antiquities Committee for Yorkshire, of which her father was treasurer, holding that post until 1943. In 1935 she published the acclaimed *Gazetteer of Roman Remains in East Yorkshire*, and from 1941 to 1943 she served as curator of Roman antiquities at the Yorkshire Museum, in York. On 5 July 1943 she married Derwas James Chitty (1901–1971), Church of England clergyman and archaeologist, and the son of James Charles Martin Chitty, also a clergyman. They had met in 1929 in Palestine, where she had joined Dorothy Garrod excavating palaeolithic sites and he was excavating the monastery of St Euthymius. After their marriage they settled in Upton, Berkshire, where he was vicar, though she remained involved in the Yorkshire Philosophical Society (which ran the Yorkshire Museum) and the Roman Antiquities Committee for Yorkshire for a number of years. They had one daughter. After her husband's retirement in 1968 they moved to Llangwnnadl, on the Llŷn Peninsula, Caernarvonshire, near Bardsey Island (Ynys Enlli). As Mary Chitty she published *The Monks of Ynys Enlli* in two volumes, covering the years 500–1252 (1992) and 1252–1537 (2000). In 1988 her earlier contributions to Roman archaeology in Yorkshire had been recognized in *Recent Research in Roman Yorkshire: Studies in Honour of Mary Kitson Clark*. She died at Môr Awel, Llangwnnadl, on 1 February 2005 and was survived by her daughter.

Sources *The Independent* (18 March 2005) · C. S. Briggs, 'A century of Yorkshire archaeology and history, 1900–2000: the Kitson Clarks of Meanwoodside and beyond', *Yorkshire Archaeological Journal*, 77 (2005), 263–81 · m. cert. · d. cert.

Likenesses photographs, 1929, Bibliothèque du Musée des Antiquités Nationales de Saint Germain-en-Laye, fonds Suzanne Cassou de Saint-Mathurin

Wealth at death £129,800: probate, 26 May 2006, *CGPLA Eng. & Wales*

Clarke, Sir Arthur Charles (**1917–2008**), science and science fiction writer, was born on 16 December 1917 at 4 Blenheim Terrace, Minehead, Somerset, the eldest of the four children of Charles Wright Clarke (1888–1931) and his wife, (Mary) Nora Jessie, *née* Willis (1892–1980). His father was a Post Office telegraphist then serving as a second lieutenant in the Royal Engineers; his mother also worked as a telegraphist. Following the war, after a first unsuccessful attempt at farming, a career decided upon because of lung injuries Clarke's father had received, the family took up a smallholding at Ballifants, near Bishop's Lydeard, Somerset, in 1924. There Clarke and his younger siblings, Fred (*b.* 1921), Mary (*b.* 1923), and Michael (*b.* 1928), grew up.

Education, early writings, and move to Ceylon As a schoolboy, Clarke developed a passionate interest in science, which his family and school (Huish Grammar School, Taunton) encouraged. His brother Fred recalled, in an article published in the journal *Foundation* to celebrate Clarke's seventieth birthday, experiments with rockets, wireless, and photography. In a collection of contributions from the *Huish Magazine* published in 1996 Clarke's own contributions included spoofs and skits written under the spell of the science fiction magazines he was already reading at the time, while he was teased as 'Professor Larke' and 'Clericus' (one of his pseudonyms) in essays by others. His later contributions were clearly influenced by the effect upon him of Olaf Stapledon's epic future-history *Last and First Men* (1930), which he was several times to remark had changed his life, and his discovery of the British Interplanetary Society, which Clarke joined in 1934 shortly after its formation. He was later to serve the society, established to argue the case for space exploration by a young Wallasey engineer, P. E. Cleator, as chairman in 1946–7 and again in 1950–53.

On leaving school to join the civil service Clarke's early life was dominated by these interests. He attended the first science fiction convention in Leeds in January 1937, and his first work of fiction, 'Travel by Wire', was published in *Amateur Science Stories*, a fanzine published in that year by the newly founded Science Fiction Association. Much of his early writing appeared in similar organs produced by the small but active group of science fiction devotees of the time, such as *Novae Terrae*, or as part of the overlapping activity of the British Interplanetary Society. His enthusiasm for both was satirized by his friend and fellow writer William Temple, with whom he shared a London flat at 88 Gray's Inn Road (the title of Temple's later book of reminiscences) until 1939. His affectionate nickname 'Ego' reflected the focus and ambition that he brought to his scientific and literary projects (his regular newsletters to friends and fans in later life were 'Egograms'). Clarke was already working on a novel, which appeared as 'Against the Fall of Night' in *Startling Stories* in 1948, was published in book form in 1953, and extensively revised as *The City and the Stars* in 1956. His first professional fiction sales, 'Loophole' and 'Rescue Party', appeared in *Astounding* in April and May 1946.

Volunteering for RAF service in 1941, Clarke became a technical officer working on radar systems until his demobilization in 1946, when he began a degree course at King's College, London, graduating with first-class honours in mathematics and physics. Before then, however, he had published what was perhaps his most prophetic work: the essay 'Extra-terrestrial relays' in the technical journal *Wireless World* (1945). Here he suggested using rocket technology to place a system of satellites in geosynchronous orbit around the earth, from which signals could be bounced to blanket the earth with a communications network. Apart from the fact that Clarke envisaged manned satellites, this is essentially the system used today. While this was by no means the first suggestion of the idea—and Clarke was himself at pains later to point out that others were thinking similar thoughts at the time—Clarke's essay was the first in print at a crucial time. Rocket missiles had been used in war against Britain, designed by the space enthusiast Wernher von Braun, and many of Clarke's engineer friends in the British Interplanetary Society were developing new technologies. Suddenly the 'oddball' ideas of the pre-war rocket societies were ripe with promise. Clarke's first book, *Interplanetary Flight* (1950), its successor, *The Exploration of Space* (1951), and a novel he had written in 1947, *Prelude to Space* (1951), were visionary propaganda for the forthcoming space age.

The 'bright renaissance' following the achievement of

Sir Arthur Charles Clarke (1917–2008), by unknown photographer, 1968

lunar travel in *Prelude to Space* and the ambiguous ending of the influential short story 'Sentinel of Eternity' (better known as 'The Sentinel'), published in the same year, expressed a feeling that somewhere in the universe was the end to a sense of loneliness, and that space travel was a means to that end. 'Sentinel' ended with the triggering of a kind of signal device left on the moon by an alien race. The narrator contemplates the result: will it be a welcome or a threat? Clarke's most influential novel, *Childhood's End* (1953), along with stories like 'The Nine Billion Names of God' (1953) or 'The Star' (1955), explored some of the more transcendental versions of these anxieties. Although Clarke's reputation was built upon his exercises in futurology, enthusiasm for technology, and an interpretation of his fiction as 'hard science fiction', these stories undermined the comfort that the gadgets of hard science fiction tended to offer readers, and accepted the possibility of unease. The utopia of *Childhood's End* which humanity has to accept under the rule of alien Overlords is a false paradise. It is merely a step towards the end of humanity as we know it and sublimation into a new trans-species identity, a step that the Overlords themselves are poignantly eternally barred from making.

These books and others brought Clarke success, with his reputation among the British science fiction readership assured. (At this point he was a regular attendee at meetings of the London science fiction circle at the White Horse pub, later The Globe.) His gifts for clear and visionary explanation of factual science gave him a wider audience among the general public, dramatically increasing sales in the USA thanks to the choice of *The Exploration of Space* as a Book of the Month Club selection. On 15 June 1953, in New York, he married Marilyn Torgenson (*née* Mayfield), a 22-year-old American divorcee with a young son, and they returned to Britain just before the publication of his breakthrough novel, *Childhood's End*. The marriage was not a success, and the couple separated after a matter of months, although the formal divorce was not until 1964. Following another of his interests, diving, in 1954 Clarke joined a friend, Mike Wilson, on an expedition to the Australian Great Barrier Reef. On the way they stopped at Ceylon, where they returned in 1956, eventually to establish a diving business with a Ceylonese partner, Hector Ekanayake. Clarke was to make Ceylon (renamed Sri Lanka in 1972) his home for the rest of his life. His companion, Leslie Ekanayake, Hector's brother, died in a motorcycle accident in 1977.

Doyen of science fiction His growing reputation, and the space race that had erupted with the successful launch of the Russian sputnik satellite in 1957, made Clarke increasingly in demand for lectures, fiction, and non-fiction. He was awarded the UNESCO Kalinga prize for science writing in 1961. His collection of speculative essays, *Profiles of the Future*, was published in 1962, to be reissued and revised (with wry comments about what he had got 'wrong') several times thereafter. In the same year he contracted polio, which was to result in the post-polio syndrome with which he was diagnosed in 1988. He was to spend his last years wheelchair-bound.

In 1964 Clarke was contacted by Stanley Kubrick, who had expressed an interest in making a science fiction film. The result was *2001: a Space Odyssey* (1968), partly based upon 'The Sentinel' but also echoing the transcendental elements of *Childhood's End*. The film showed Kubrick's obsessive detail and Clarke's visionary realism at work in sometimes uneasy partnership. Clarke's own novelization differed in significant respects from the film. In the end he wrote several sequels, *2010: Odyssey Two* (1982), *2061: Odyssey Three* (1987), and *3001: the Final Odyssey* (1997). Various sequences in Kubrick's film—a bone used as a weapon hurled into the air in triumph and seguing into a spaceship, the spacecraft docking to the tune of Strauss's 'Blue Danube' waltz, and especially the chilly rebellion of the sentient computer HAL 9000 which jeopardizes the mission—were especially striking. It was almost inevitable that Clarke was among the science fiction writers asked to commentate on the Apollo 11 moon landing in July 1969, and asked to speak at the UNESCO space communications conference later that year. *The Lost Worlds of 2001* (1970) added more background to the film.

By this time Clarke was perhaps the best-known science fiction writer in the world and one of the few with genuine best-seller status. Subsequent novels received the science fiction field's highest awards. *Rendezvous with Rama* (1972) brought its author British Science Fiction Association, Nebula, Hugo, Campbell and *Locus* magazine awards. Also winning the Hugo and Nebula awards, *The Fountains of Paradise* (1979) was set in a version of his adopted home, Sri Lanka, and featured yet another mammoth technological idea, the 'space elevator', based upon ideas suggested by the Russian scientist Yuri Artsutanov. The 'elevator' consisted of a cable lowered from a satellite in geostationary orbit which when secured at a fixed point on the earth's surface could transport material from the earth's surface to orbit.

With these awards for Clarke's fiction came a growing reputation as a commentator upon science and technology which resulted in numerous accolades and appointments, among them the Bradford Washburn award from the Boston Museum of Science (1977). In 1979 he was appointed chancellor of Moratuwa University in Sri Lanka, where he served until 2002. In 1982 he received the Marconi fellowship award, which was used to fund an Arthur C. Clarke Centre for Modern Technologies in Sri Lanka. In the same year he addressed the UN committee on disarmament. In 1987 he received the Charles A. Lindbergh award for many years of significant contributions towards balancing technology and nature, and in 1989 he became the first chancellor of the International Space University in France, which offered advanced courses in space studies. In 1995 his pioneering visions of space exploration resulted in his being awarded the NASA distinguished public service medal. He was kept in public view with the television series *Arthur C. Clarke's Mysterious World* (1980), in which he looked at unexplained phenomena. The combination of scepticism and fascination with which current enthusiasm for the 'unexplained' was treated attracted a large audience and it was followed by two other similar series in 1985 and 1994.

In addition Clarke was a patron of the Science Fiction Foundation and president of the British Science Fiction Association, to whose publications he would respond with encouraging comments and anecdotes. In 1986 he funded the Arthur C. Clarke award for the best science fiction novel of the year published in the UK. He received honorary DLitt degrees from Bath (1988), Liverpool (1995), conferred, appropriately, by satellite link, and Baptist University, Hong Kong (1996). He was awarded Sri Lanka's highest civil honour, Sri Lankabhimanya ('pride of Sri Lanka'), in 2005.

Many of Clarke's later novels were collaborations with other writers in, for example, inferior sequels to *Rendezvous with Rama*, although the solo *The Ghost from the Grand Banks* (1990) was well received. With *The Light of Other Days* (2000) and the *Time Odyssey* trilogy (2003–7) he teamed up with Stephen Baxter. In Baxter, a writer strongly influenced by Clarke but whose own cosmological speculations and sense of time and history made him very much his own man, Clarke seemed to have a collaborator who understood his fiction and shared his sense of vision.

Clarke 'retired' several times, and several novels were proclaimed as his 'last' book, but he kept on writing to the end, although *3001: the Final Odyssey* was probably his last unaided work. Perhaps his last true novel, and certainly one of his finest, was *The Songs of Distant Earth* (1986), in which Thalassa, an idyllic, utopian colony, is visited by a ship from a destroyed earth *en route* to its destination to terraform a new world. The starship's crew have to decide whether to stay, and possibly disrupt the Thalassan idyll, or continue, shattering the bonds of contact that have developed. In this book Clarke revisited the tension between transcendence and the physical, and the ambiguous utopianism, found in earlier fiction. The melancholy in *Songs* may be in part an echo of the numinous in previous works, in which Clarke, a lifelong atheist, nevertheless imagined godlike parental aliens. He was widely reported to have quipped, 'I don't believe in God, but I'm very interested in her'.

Final years and reputation Having been appointed CBE in 1989, Clarke was awarded a knighthood for services to literature in 1998, although he was not formally knighted until 26 May 2000, as previous plans had been postponed following unfounded allegations of sexual impropriety in a tabloid newspaper. While Clarke was as reticent about his private sexuality as he was about including sex in his novels—it was perhaps after the introduction of a gay character in *Imperial Earth* (1975) that reporters would ask Clarke if he was gay, invariably to be told, 'merely mildly cheerful'—his orientation was no secret to his friends and admirers.

Clarke's ninetieth birthday was marked by an address in which he noted the rapid change in space and communications technologies and presented as his 'three wishes' evidence of extraterrestrial life, the replacement of coal and oil with clean energy sources, and a lasting peace in his adopted country, Sri Lanka. His final novel, *The Last Theorem* (2008), was written in collaboration with the American author Frederik Pohl, one of his few surviving peers. Clarke died in Colombo, following breathing difficulties, on 19 March 2008. He was buried in the General Cemetery, Colombo, on 22 March, in accordance with his wishes that 'no religious rites of any kind … should be associated with my funeral'.

Arthur C. Clarke was the poet of a particular vision which saw space travel as a challenge willingly to be met. It is a dream itself, of course, with its own contradictions. The 1950s fantasy that Britain would play a major role in the forthcoming age of space was a simple fantasy, but this was not quite so clear-cut at the time as it became with hindsight: for many it offered a possible shape for a new post-empire Britain. British science fiction writers of local disaster and catastrophe such as John Wyndham and John Christopher showed more clearly the social anxiety of the 1950s, and later writers such as J. G. Ballard dismissed altogether stories of 'outer space' as irrelevant to the exploration of a psychological 'inner space' in which science fiction was a literary tool rather than a means of propaganda or reuse of stale clichés. Clarke's early novels and stories, though, showed the dream of mid-century science fiction: that history does not have to be the way it is, and that humanity can take control of its destiny. His non-fiction and science writing, harnessed to a visionary internationalism, emphasized this mould. What became noted as his 'three laws' (expounded in the revised version of his *Profiles of the Future*, 1973) expressed the often playful working of his imagination as applied to all aspects of his writing: (1) When a distinguished but elderly scientist states that something is possible, he is almost certainly right. When he states that something is impossible, he is very probably wrong. (2) The only way of discovering the limits of the possible is to venture a little way past them into the impossible. (3) Any sufficiently advanced technology is indistinguishable from magic.

Clarke's reputation will remain attached to a vision of the future that assumed, years before it happened, that space travel was both possible and desirable. Much of his fiction can be seen as speculations of the space age by someone who was trying both to make it happen, and to explain to a wide audience why it was so important that it should indeed happen. While firmly committed to the project of knowing and understanding the universe, Clarke's writing did not unquestioningly assume the project's success. He was occasionally seduced by the visionary rather than the practical implications of science, as with his enthusiasm for cold fusion, and a rather too easy assumption that global communications and space exploration would link nations and promote peace and understanding. He was, however, much more than a propagandist. His science writing was both informative and genuinely inspirational: he was, simply, a great communicator curious about the world and passionate in sharing that curiosity. His best fiction (which includes much of his early work) echoed a sense of personal and cosmic loneliness which evoked a sense of awe at the thought of the immensity and potential of the universe. As the critic John Clute wrote in an obituary of Clarke, 'He spoke for the highest hopes of the 20th century' (*The Independent*, 20 March 2008). ANDY SAWYER

Sources F. Clarke, 'Arthur C. Clarke, the early days', *Foundation: The International Review of Science Fiction*, 41 (1987), 9–15 · E. James, 'The future viewed from mid-century Britain: Clarke, Hampson and the Festival of Britain', *Foundation: The International Review of Science Fiction*, 41 (1987), 42–51 · A. C. Clarke, *Astounding days* (1989) · N. McAleer, *Odyssey: the authorised biography of Arthur C. Clarke* (1992) · F. Clarke, *Four heads in the air* (1995) · D. Aronowitz, ed., *Childhood ends* (1996) · A. C. Clarke, *Greetings, carbon-based bipeds! Collected essays, 1934–1998* (1999) · W. Temple, *88 Grays Inn Road* (2000) · A. C. Clarke, *The collected stories* (2001) · E. James, 'Arthur C. Clarke', *A companion to science fiction*, ed. D. Seed (2005), 431–40 · P. Weston, ed., *Relapse*, 16 (Feb 2010) · *The Times* (20 March 2008) · *Daily Telegraph* (20 March 2008) · *The Guardian* (20 March 2008) · *The Independent* (20 March 2008) · clarkefoundation.org, 18 July 2011 · *WW* (2008) · personal knowledge (2012) · private information (2012) · b. cert.

Archives 25 Barnes Place, Colombo, Sri Lanka, H. Ekanayake, 'Leslie's House' · Boston University Library, corresp. and papers | Bodl. Oxf., C. S. Lewis MSS, corresp., 1943–53 | FILM BFINA, *This is your life*, B. Klein (director), BBC1, 11 Jan 1995 · BL NSA, current affairs, documentary, and performance recordings | SOUND BL NSA, current affairs, documentary, and performance recordings

Likenesses photographs, *c.*1918–2003, Getty Images, London · photographs, 1952–2008, PA Photos, London · photograph, 1968, Rex Features, London [*see illus.*] · photographs, 1968–2003, Rex Features, London · C. Adams, colour print, 1976, NPG · photographs, 1980–89, Lebrecht Music and Arts Photo Library, London · A. George, crayon, 1995, NPG · N. Sjoman, portrait, priv. coll. · caricature, Lebrecht Music and Arts Photo Library, London · obituary photographs · photographs, Camera Press, London · photographs, repro. in McAleer, *Odyssey*

Clarke, Nicholas Campbell [Nick] (**1948–2006**), broadcaster and writer, was born on 9 June 1948 at Mount Alvernia Nursing Home, Godalming, Surrey, the son of John Campbell Clarke, journalist, and his wife, (Wilda) Ruth, formerly Massy, *née* McNeile. He was educated at Bradfield College, Berkshire, and Fitzwilliam College, Cambridge, where he read modern languages. After graduating he spent two years as a reporter on the *Yorkshire Post*, before joining the BBC in Manchester in 1973, 'on condition', he recalled, that 'I shaved off my very large beard' (*Radio Times*, 11 Dec 1993). Within three years he had been appointed industrial correspondent, and by 1980 was reporting for BBC2's *The Money Programme*. In the mid-1980s he appeared on BBC2's *Newsnight* as political correspondent and presenter. However, it was radio rather than television that increasingly appealed to his sense of seriousness. From 1989 he took the presenter's job on BBC Radio 4's Sunday lunchtime current affairs programme, *The World This Weekend*, and over the next five years he frequently stood in on *Any Questions?*, *Any Answers?*, and *The World at One*. During the Gulf War of 1991, when Radio 4 turned one of its frequencies into a 'rolling-news' service, he was a key anchorman, at ease occasionally conducting an interview in fluent French while simultaneously providing his own running translation. It was, one reviewer suggested, largely through the 'sober tact' of Clarke and his fellow presenters that the

Nicholas Campbell Clarke (1948–2006), by Jeff Overs, 2002

BBC's first rolling-news service established itself as 'urgent without being hysterical', confounding the worst expectations of its critics (*Daily Telegraph*, 22 Jan 1991; Hendy, 348).

Clarke's skill as a political interviewer was put to best use after 1994 when he became the full-time presenter of *The World at One*. Politicians, journalists, and listeners noted that he always asked clear questions and insisted on proper answers, though he would never 'growl, bark or nip' (*Daily Telegraph*, 7 Aug 1993). 'I don't like interruptions', he once explained; 'I believe it's nearly always possible to find a pause, however microscopic, into which a question can be inserted' (*The Times*, 4 Oct 1995). Commentators regarded such unyielding civility, and the 'surgeon's instinct for the political raw nerve' it belied, as something to be cherished in what seemed like an increasingly frantic media culture (*Sunday Times*, 27 Feb 1994). This was confirmed in 1999 when the Voice of the Listener and Viewer organization made him radio broadcaster of the year and again in 2000 when the Broadcasting Press Guild voted him broadcaster of the year. Both awards acknowledged not just the quality of his journalism but his wider contribution to the medium of radio. When Radio 4's *Round Britain Quiz* was revived in 1997 Clarke's inquiring but unobtrusive style made him the obvious choice as question-master. He was equally well suited to chairing *Straw Poll*, a live public debating series broadcast in 2004 and 2005.

Clarke, once described by a columnist as 'Radio 4 personified' (*The Guardian*, 24 Nov 2006), briefly contemplated writing a history of his favourite network. He had already published in 1999 a well-received biography of another Radio 4 figure, Alistair Cooke, and it had sold well. In the event his follow-up was *Shadow of a Nation* (2003), an elegiac and highly personal reflection on the changing character of Britain, in which he despaired of a growing celebrity culture and lamented the 'draining away' of social cohesion. The national psyche, he believed, was gradually being debased through television's 'staple diet of spurious fame' (*Shadow of a Nation*, 3–7).

Away from this diminishing public realm, Clarke found regular consolation in the private pleasures of fine wine, cooking, cricket, and, above all, family life. His first marriage, on 13 October 1973, was to the journalist Susan Katharine (Sue) Armstrong. Aged twenty-one at the time of their marriage, she was the daughter of Philip Bryan Armstrong, solicitor. They had two sons and one daughter (twins Alison and Tom, followed by Pete) before the marriage was dissolved in 1990. In the following year he married the television producer Barbara Want, with whom he had twin boys. Benedict and Joel were still young children when, in November 2005, Clarke (whose father had died of cancer when Clarke was eighteen) discovered a lump on his left buttock, a metastatic sarcoma that forced him to have his left leg amputated. He and his wife recorded an audio diary throughout his illness, and much of it was heard on Radio 4 in June 2006 as the documentary *Fighting to be Normal*. Clarke worried that broadcasting a personal story was 'inappropriate' for BBC presenters, but listeners wrote in their thousands to say how moved they had been and how much he was being missed. Soon after its broadcast he returned to presenting *The World at One*. But the respite was brief. The cancer had spread, and Clarke died on 23 November 2006 at his home in Highlever Road, Kensington. He was survived by his wife and his five children.

DAVID HENDY

Sources *Daily Telegraph* (9 Oct 1990); (27 April 1993); (7 Aug 1993); (4 Oct 1993); (24 Nov 2006) • *The Times* (22 July 1993); (4 Oct 1995); (4 Dec 1995); (24 Nov 2006) • *The Observer* (8 Aug 1993); (26 Nov 2006) • *Radio Times* (11 Dec 1993); (6 April 1996) • *Sunday Times* (27 Feb 1994) • *Fighting to be normal*, BBC Radio 4, 23 June 2006; 12 Jan 2007 • *The Guardian* (24 Nov 2006) • *The Independent* (24 Nov 2006) • D. Hendy, *Life on air: a history of Radio Four* (2007) • *WW* (2006) • personal knowledge (2010) • private information (2010) • b. cert. • m. cert. [1973] • d. cert.

Archives FILM BFINA, current affairs footage

Likenesses J. Overs, photograph, 2002, BBC [*see illus.*] • M. Pope, photographs, 2003, Camera Press, London • W. Conran, photograph, 2004, Getty Images, London • obituary photographs • photographs, BBC

Wealth at death £442,920: probate, 26 June 2007, *CGPLA Eng. & Wales*

Clarke, Peter William Hanwell (1948–2007), social worker and children's commissioner, was born on 7 October 1948 at the Maternity Home, Oxford Road, Llandudno, Caernarvonshire, the son of William Arthur Clarke, a captain in the army, and his wife, Jean Barbara, *née* Hanwell. At the time of his birth his parents lived at 2 Abbey Road, Llandudno. He attended fourteen schools, owing to his father's peripatetic life. He withdrew from the Royal Military College, Sandhurst, after six months when he realized he was only doing what was expected of him and started work as an untrained social worker at Stamford remand centre, London, before reading philosophy and politics at Sussex University, while working in an old people's home at night. He then graduated MA in philosophy, again at Sussex. After qualifying as a social worker at Warwick University he became a field social worker in London and Brighton. In 1985 he joined the Spastics Society as a community care adviser. In 1987 he married Jennifer Mary (Jenny) Thompson; they had two sons, Liam and Bryn.

Clarke moved back to Wales in 1991 to become the first director of the National Schizophrenia Fellowship Wales. In 1995 he became head of ChildLine Cymru, a twenty-four hour helpline for children. His own childhood gave him empathy with many of the children with whom he worked. There had been, he admitted, 'difficulties' about which he preferred not to speak. This personal attachment to those with whom he worked was perhaps allowed its fullest expression when, in March 2001, he was appointed children's commissioner for Wales, the first children's commissioner in the UK.

Between 1997 and 2000 an inquiry headed by Sir Ronald Waterhouse had investigated abuse in children's homes in north Wales and its report recommended that such a post be created. Countries in Europe and elsewhere had established children's ombudsmen (the first post was created in Norway in 1981) but the idea had been rejected by successive UK governments. Following the Waterhouse report the government relented (but stipulated that the commissioner and his staff be funded by the Welsh Assembly). After the Welsh post came into being others followed in Scotland in 2004 and Northern Ireland in 2007. In 2005 a children's commissioner's role was created in England but in a far more circumscribed form. Clarke's passion, and his involvement of children and young people in his job, underpinned by his independence and considerable powers, set the tone for the others.

As well as the more obvious children's issues—health, education, and social services—Clarke was charged with considering planning, transport, the environment, economic development, and rural affairs. He also had the power to consider and make representations to the Welsh Assembly on any matter he deemed to affect children's rights and welfare in Wales. When 'listening to children' was too often honoured in the breach than the practice, Clarke showed consistently how children and young people could influence services for the better (he pioneered using children for the commission's appointments panels). He used the means by which children and young people communicated, including emails, message boards, and texting by mobile phone, to draw them in. He set up an advice line that children could call at any time.

Clarke was tireless in his advocacy of children's rights. In 2004 he said that an additional £700,000 for what were then the new child and adolescent mental health services in Wales was welcome but 'totally inadequate' in the face of the growing crisis in provision (*Times Educational Supplement*, 19 Nov 2004). Just before he died he was threatening legal action against the assembly on how it took decisions about children. In *Telling Concerns* (2003) he reviewed social services departments, and he produced practice guides on whistleblowing, children's advocacy, and children's complaints, as well as training materials. Like his other publications, these were written in formats accessible to children and young people. His major inquiry was the 'Clywch' inquiry (*clywch*, significantly, being the Welsh command to listen) into child sexual abuse at Rhydfelen secondary school. This was published in 2004 and resulted in new safeguards for children in Wales and influenced thinking elsewhere in the UK. In addition to his work in Wales Clarke was involved at a UK level with the Family Justice Council and other bodies, and was president of the European Network of Ombudspersons for Children (ENOC) in 2005–6. He was also a board member of Voices from Care.

Young people were frequently characterized, Clarke opined, as 'angels or demons and rarely as human beings' (*South Wales Evening Post*, 21 May 2005). He believed that the failure of systems, procedures, and professionals stemmed from a failure to allow the needs and rights of children and young people the same importance as those of adults. By making respect the foundation of his own work he provided a model of a children's advocate and of a good service for children. Even after being diagnosed with lung cancer he remained fully committed to his role and continued to speak up for children's rights. He died at Ty Bryngwyn Hospice, Prince Philip Hospital, Llanelli, on 21 January 2007, and was survived by his wife, Jenny, and their two sons. TERRY PHILPOT

Sources *Western Mail* (22 Jan 2007); (25 Jan 2007) · *South Wales Echo* (22 Jan 2007) · *Daily Post* [Liverpool] (22 Jan 2007) · *Community Care* (25 Jan 2007) · *Children Now* (31 Jan 2007) · *The Times* (12 Feb 2007) · *The Guardian* (15 Feb 2007) · personal knowledge (2011) · private information (2011) · b. cert. · d. cert.

Likenesses obituary photographs · photographs, repro. in news.bbc.co.uk/1/hi/wales/6285193.stm

Wealth at death £366,176: probate, 14 May 2007, *CGPLA Eng. & Wales*

Cleland, William Paton [Bill] **(1912–2005)**, cardiothoracic surgeon, was born on 30 May 1912 in Sydney, New South Wales, Australia, the only son and third of five children of Sir John Burton Cleland (1878–1971), pathologist and naturalist, and his wife, Dora Isabel, *née* Paton. His father became professor of pathology at the University of Adelaide in 1920 and his dedication to the environment was recognized by the naming of Cleland Conservation Park in the Mount Lofty Ranges in South Australia. The Cleland family had been involved in law, viticulture, and medicine in Australia since 1852.

Cleland was educated at Scotch College and graduated in medicine from the University of Adelaide in 1934. After junior appointments at the Royal Adelaide Hospital he worked his way as a ship's doctor to England at the age of twenty-seven in order to specialize as a physician in chest medicine. He gained a post at the Brompton Hospital for

William Paton Cleland (1912–2005), by unknown photographer, 1959 [Cleland (centre) with (left to right) Denis Melrose, a Russian surgeon, John Beard, and A. N. Bakulev]

Diseases of the Chest, from where he obtained membership of the Royal College of Physicians of London in 1939 (becoming a fellow in 1967). But encouraged by the senior surgeon, Tudor Edwards, who thought that he would make a good surgeon, he then became the resident surgical officer at the Brompton. His mother did not approve, commenting, 'Bill was never any good at carpentry'. Cleland was later to say, 'Little did mother know that cardio-thoracic surgery owes more to plumbing than to carpentry' (*Courier Mail*, 4 May 2005). During the Second World War he served in the Emergency Medical Service at the Horton Hospital, Epsom, where he operated on both military and civilian patients, removing bomb fragments from the heart and lungs and also operating for pulmonary tuberculosis. Meanwhile on 18 May 1940, at the Church of St Mary the Virgin, Hampstead, he married Norah Goodhart (1914–1994), daughter of George Elijah Goodhart, a stockbroker. They had a daughter, Janet, and two sons, Peter and John.

In 1946 Cleland became a fellow of the Royal College of Surgeons of England and started out on his lifetime's work as a consultant cardiothoracic surgeon, gaining appointments concurrently at King's College Hospital and the Brompton Hospital (from 1948) and Hammersmith Hospital, at the Postgraduate Medical School of London (from 1949). The appointment at Hammersmith was to prove the highlight of his surgical career. He also served as civilian consultant to the Royal Navy and adviser in thoracic surgery to the Department of Health and Social Security.

Cardiac surgery developed rapidly after 1945 when the first 'blue baby' operation was carried out in America, but such operations were all done with an intact beating heart and there was an urgent need to be able to open the heart and fully correct the defects. For this a heart-lung machine was needed and at Hammersmith Hospital Denis Melrose invented a pump oxygenator in 1952, with which Cleland performed the first such open heart operation in Britain in 1957. Having seen the apparatus, Alexander Bakulev from Moscow was keen to buy one and start open heart surgery in the Soviet Union. He invited Melrose to bring the Hammersmith team, with Cleland and Hugh Bentall as the surgeons, and four others, to visit Moscow in May 1959. Four children with congenital heart disease were selected for surgery. Two of them were very blue children with the tetralogy of Fallot, a condition on which the team had never before operated. But all four operations were successful and the deputy prime minister, Anastas Mikoyan, embraced the theatre sister, Phyllis Bowtle, saying, 'Doctors are clean, but politicians are dirty' (*Daily Mail*, 16 May 1959). This was probably the first time that a foreign medical team had actually worked in the Soviet Union, as distinct from just being shown around.

In 1968 an article by Cleland and his colleagues in *The Lancet* entitled 'A decade of open heart surgery' gave details of 1200 operations, which showed the safety of using extra-corporeal circulation, and he published a landmark paper in *Thorax* in 1983, 'The evolution of cardiac surgery in the United Kingdom'. He wrote chapters on heart surgery for several textbooks and over seventy papers. He continued to do pulmonary operations and his paper in *The Lancet* in 1963 comparing surgery with radiotherapy gave details of what remained throughout his lifetime one of the very few randomized trials in lung cancer surgery. He edited the *Journal of Cardiovascular Surgery* from 1978 to 1983.

Cleland was an unflappable and meticulous surgeon, and the theatre was always calm when he was operating. Although he was seemingly unhurried, quite suddenly an operation would be finished. Many surgeons and physicians from Britain and abroad came to Hammersmith to learn new techniques and Cleland lectured and performed heart operations in Europe and the Middle East. For his work in their countries he was made a commander of the order of the Falcon of Iceland and a commander of the order of the Lion of Finland. He was the first director of surgery at the Institute for Diseases of the Chest at the Brompton Hospital, London, where one of his colleagues was the pioneer chest and cardiac surgeon Russell Claude Brock. Cleland was an extremely hard worker and outside the operating theatre he was very active in promoting his specialism by teaching, writing, and lecturing, and he trained many young surgeons from abroad who later themselves became leaders in their own countries.

Cleland, known to all as Bill, was a strongly built man with a soft Australian accent. He was warm hearted, always a pleasure to be with, and someone who others felt instinctively could be completely trusted and reliable. Latterly he and his wife lived in Green Meadows, an eighteenth-century mill house in Goodworth Clatford, near Andover in Hampshire, with a trout stream running through the property. He was an outstanding angler, fishing being his main hobby, and the salmon of the River Spey, Lapland, and Iceland were magnets for him. At home he was a keen gardener and beekeeper, and he usually won top prizes in the annual village show at Goodworth Clatford, where he was much loved for his modesty, wisdom, and wit. Second only to fishing was his great love of opera, with Angela Gheorghiu latterly his favourite diva. He was proud of his ancestry and he became the twenty-sixth head of an ancient Scottish family that traced its history back to a cousin of William Wallace. In his nineties he was physically frail but as alert as ever. He died comfortably and peacefully at home in his own bed on 29 March 2005 after only a short illness. A lifelong friend remarked, 'How typical of Bill to have arranged his death so well' (private information). The main cause of death was malignant neoplasm of the prostate. He was cremated at Salisbury and survived by his three children.

ARTHUR HOLLMAN

Sources *Courier Mail* [Queensland] (4 May 2005) • *The Independent* (9 May 2005) • *The Guardian* (21 May 2005) • *BMJ*, 330/1212 (2005) • A. Hollman, 'Cleland, William Paton', Munk, *Roll*, 12, 2007, www.rcplondon.ac.uk, 29 May 2008 • 'Cleland, William Paton', *Plarr's Lives* (2007); www.livesonline.rcseng.ac.uk, 29 May 2008 • W. P. Cleland archive, RCP Lond. • *WW* (2005) • personal knowledge (2009) • private information (2009) • m. cert. • d. cert.
Archives RCP Lond.
Likenesses group portrait, photograph, 1959 [*see illus.*] • obituary photographs
Wealth at death £2,278,891: probate, 2 Nov 2005, *CGPLA Eng. & Wales*

Clements, Richard Harry [Dick] (**1928–2006**), journalist, was born on 11 October 1928 at 60 Warwick Gardens, Kensington, London, the third child and second son of Harry Clements, osteopath, and his American-born wife, Sophia Victoria (Sonia), *née* Edelman. His father, born in rural Gloucestershire in the 1890s, had been a conscientious objector during the First World War, and after a spell in jail he spent the rest of the war as a farm labourer in a Tolstoyan community at Whiteway, near Stroud, Gloucestershire. After the war he crossed the Atlantic to join a similar community in New England, where he studied osteopathy. There he met Sonia Edelman, an anarcho-syndicalist of Russian Jewish parentage, whom he married in the early 1920s. After the birth of a son (John) and a daughter (Barbara), the family moved to England, and Harry set up in practice, first at Whiteway and later in London. The practice prospered, and the family moved to Hampstead Garden Suburb so that Dick (as he was universally known throughout his life) and his siblings could go to King Alfred School, a progressive co-educational school nearby.

When the Second World War came and France fell, Clements was sent to the United States to stay with an uncle, John Edelman, who was a well-known Washington lobbyist for the Congress of Industrial Organizations (roughly the equivalent of the British TUC). His formal education continued at Western High School in Washington DC, and he gained a valuable knowledge of American liberal politics by meeting his uncle's friends and colleagues. But after his brother was killed as a pilot in Bomber Command, Clements insisted on returning to England, where the V1 flying bomb campaign was in full swing. He went first to Regent Street Polytechnic to matriculate, then joined the Merchant Navy as an apprentice in 1946.

After eighteen months in the navy Clements won a

place at the London School of Economics but he dropped out in 1949 to become a reporter, first on the *Middlesex Independent* and then, in 1951, on the *Leicester Mercury*. While there, he tried to establish his own left-wing weekly in the midlands. It failed, but it led to an offer in 1953 of the editorship of the Labour Party's youth paper, *Socialist Advance*. In 1954 this led in turn to a job as industrial reporter at the TUC-owned *Daily Herald*. For much of this post-war period he was living with his parents in Baker Street, where his mother kept court over a remarkable assembly of young people, most of them either stray Americans or students at the London School of Economics. On 28 November 1952 he married Bridget Mary MacDonald, the 27-year-old daughter of Alister MacDonald, architect, and granddaughter of the former prime minister Ramsay MacDonald. They had met in a pub near his parents' country cottage, where she was acting as a temporary barmaid. The pub's owner was her aunt, Ishbel MacDonald, daughter of the former prime minister. They had two sons.

After two years at the *Herald* Clements was invited in 1956 to join the staff of the left-wing weekly, *Tribune*. The paper was then edited by Michael Foot, who was at the time in conflict with his old friend and ally Aneurin Bevan over Bevan's rejection of unilateral nuclear disarmament. With his pacifist background, Clements backed Foot in this dispute, and when he was eventually appointed editor in 1961 he proudly attached the slogan 'The Paper that Backs the Anti-H Bomb Campaign' to its masthead. It was to remain there throughout his subsequent twenty-one years in the editor's chair—a stint that covered some of the nastiest and most bad-tempered years in Labour Party history. The easiest part was probably putting the paper together each week. Indeed his greatest achievement may well have been keeping it solvent for twenty-one years, because *Tribune* was chronically hard up, and much of the editor's time was taken in raising funds. Among Clements's most successful fund-raisers was Neil Kinnock.

Though firmly committed to democratic socialism, Clements's *Tribune* remained a beacon of comradely debate at a time when an array of Trotskyist factions were competing to take over the party. This even-handed fairness, combined with his good humour and optimism, made him liked and respected across the ideological divide—so much so that Jim Callaghan offered to 'parachute' him into a safe east London seat just before the 1979 election. Had he accepted, he would almost certainly have sat on Labour's front bench. But he was too much of a democrat to agree to this, and he insisted that there must be several candidates for the local party to choose from. Callaghan gave way, a selection conference took place, and Clements lost.

Clements eventually resigned the editorship in 1982 to become an adviser to Michael Foot when he became leader of the party in succession to Callaghan. He remained in the leader's office after Kinnock succeeded Foot a year later, and stayed there as office manager until 1987, becoming a popular figure at Westminster. After his retirement in 1993 he took a job as director of the Citizens' Income Trust, using his contacts to advance the radical concept of a guaranteed minimum income for all citizens. He retired finally in 1996 after being diagnosed with Parkinson's disease.

Clements's amiability may well have been responsible for the final twist to his career in 1999, when a Soviet defector, Vasily Mitrokhin, named him long after his retirement as a KGB 'agent of influence' with the code name Agent Dan. It was claimed that he had been a channel of propaganda for the Soviet Union, printing KGB-inspired articles in *Tribune*. Clements laughed this off, pointing out (accurately) that his paper had published masses of anti-communist material. He argued that the KGB agents had probably been exaggerating their successes to impress their bosses, although it is equally possible that they had been deceived by his affability into a belief that he really was on their side.

One surprising aspect of Clements's character was that, in spite of his geniality, he exhibited a ferocious competitive drive in sport. A first-class tennis player (he once took a set off Jaroslav Drobný), he was also a fanatical captain of *Tribune*'s cricket team, especially in its annual contest with its great rival, the *New Statesman*. These confrontations had, in the pre-Clements days, been largely an excuse for a picnic, whose main purpose was the consumption of vast quantities of beer and white wine. Under Clements *Tribune* was out to win. People who knew only the affable Clements were startled to encounter this other one. They put it down to his spell in America.

Clements's Parkinson's disease got progressively worse over the last ten years of his life, and his final months were spent in the Arkley Nursing Home in Barnet (near his home in Strafford Road). He died there of end-stage complications of the disease on 23 November 2006. He was survived by his wife, Bridget, and their two sons.

IAN AITKEN

Sources *Daily Telegraph* (24 Nov 2006) · *The Guardian* (24 Nov 2006) · *The Independent* (24 Nov 2006) · *The Times* (28 Nov 2006) · *WW* (2006) · personal knowledge (2010) · private information (2010) · b. cert. · m. cert. · d. cert.

Likenesses obituary photographs

Wealth at death £318,742: probate, 27 April 2007, *CGPLA Eng. & Wales*

Cockfield, (Francis) Arthur, Baron Cockfield (1916–2007), businessman, politician, and international civil servant, was born on 28 September 1916 at 26 Devonshire Road, Horsham, Sussex, the second son of Charles Francis Cockfield (1890–1916) and his wife, Louisa, *née* James (1890–1974). He never knew his father, a second lieutenant in the Royal Garrison Artillery, who had been killed in action at the battle of the Somme on 27 August 1916. He was educated at Dover grammar school and subsequently at the London School of Economics, where he read law and economics and graduated both LLB and BSc (Econ).

Civil servant, businessman, and politician In 1938 Cockfield embarked on a career in the Inland Revenue while also studying law (he was called to the bar at the Inner Temple in 1942). At the outbreak of the Second World War most of

(Francis) **Arthur Cockfield, Baron Cockfield** (1916–2007), by unknown photographer, 1988

the administration of the Inland Revenue was evacuated to Wales, but Cockfield had the good fortune to find himself part of a relatively small, central staff that remained in London, where his formidable intelligence and energies found rapid and widespread recognition. By 1945 he was already an assistant secretary and director of statistics, and in 1951 he was appointed a commissioner of Inland Revenue at the astonishingly early age of thirty-five. Meanwhile, on 23 July 1943, at the King's Chapel of St John the Baptist, Savoy, London, he had married Ruth Helen Simonis (1914–1998), daughter of Henry Solomon Simonis, academic lawyer. They had a daughter, Hilary Ann (*b.* 1944), and a son, Roger Edmund (*b.* 1947). The marriage ended in divorce in the early 1960s, a profound rift with his family which remained total until his death.

Despite his rapid rise to the upper ranks of the Inland Revenue, Cockfield soon began to feel frustration at the slow pace of public administration and the political constraints on the Whitehall machine. Along with an increasing number of senior mandarins, he decided to follow the lure of a more challenging and risky life in the commercial world. In 1953 he left the Inland Revenue and moved to the Boots Pure Drug Company, initially as its finance director (1953–61) and then, as managing director and chairman of the executive management committee (1961–7), presiding over a steady expansion of its retail, manufacturing, and international export businesses.

Even while micro-managing Boots, Cockfield still nurtured his interest in the functioning of the economy at large, for instance chairing a study, for the Royal Institute of Public Administration, of potential new sources of local revenue—which, interestingly, came down firmly against the idea of a poll tax as regressive and likely to be massively unpopular. He also served on Selwyn Lloyd's National Economic Development Council from 1962 to 1964. Within a short time of the Conservative government's defeat in 1964 he became intimately involved in the party's rethinking of its economic policies, working closely as economic adviser to the shadow chancellor, Iain Macleod, on the development of a taxation strategy in preparation for a return to government. From 1968 to 1969 he was president of the Royal Statistical Society and in 1970 he married his second wife, (Aileen) Monica Mudie, *née* Blurton (1919–1992), a choreographer. There were no children of this second marriage.

When Macleod died in 1970 within days of becoming chancellor of the exchequer in the new Conservative government under Edward Heath, Cockfield was both personally and professionally bereft, but he continued to serve as adviser to Macleod's successor, Anthony Barber, for whom he devised a radical tax credit system. In 1973 he received a knighthood. In March of that year, as inflation reached well into double figures and industrial relations became increasingly polarized, the Heath government set up a pay board and a price commission in an attempt to bring wage and price inflation under control. Cockfield was appointed chairman of the price commission. Although a profound believer in the free market, he devoted himself wholeheartedly to making sense of the job with the intellectual rigour and meticulous attention to detail that were already his hallmark. Such was his zeal in holding back price rises that he felt able to claim before the end of the first year that he had already saved the shopper £320 million.

When the new Labour government came to power in 1974 it promptly abolished the pay board but retained the price commission. It was a tribute to his manifestly fair-minded and balanced approach to competition that Cockfield, though openly a staunch Conservative, was retained in post by the incoming secretary of state, Shirley Williams. For three more years he continued to use his remorselessly penetrating analytical powers to corner companies into cutting back or even abandoning their proposed price increases as inflation peaked at 25 per cent in 1975 and then began to fall back. In July 1977 he left the price commission to return full-time to his role as an adviser to the Conservative Party, playing a leading part in the work of its economic reconstruction group under Geoffrey Howe, planning the party's economic strategy and policies on public expenditure and reform of the tax system. He was made a life peer in 1978, as Baron Cockfield.

When the Conservatives returned to power in 1979, Cockfield became minister of state at the Treasury, in charge of the Inland Revenue and a strong influence behind the tax-reforming budgets that followed. In 1982 he was promoted to the cabinet, being sworn of the privy council and becoming secretary of state for trade. When, only a year later, the Department of Trade was once again merged with Industry after the general election of June 1983, he became chancellor of the duchy of Lancaster. Freed from departmental responsibilities and with a seat in the cabinet and most key cabinet committees, he earned himself few friends over the next fifteen months as he frequently and fearlessly ambushed his colleagues' proposals over a wide policy front.

European commissioner: the single market and the Single European Act The most important turning point in Cockfield's professional life came in the summer of 1984, with the decision of the prime minister, Margaret Thatcher, to send him to Brussels as the senior British member (at that point Britain chose two European commissioners, by convention one Conservative and one Labour) and vice-president of the new European Commission which was to take office in January 1985. He resigned as chancellor of the duchy and absented himself from the House of Lords in order to devote himself entirely to preparing for Brussels. He was in many ways an unexpected choice for the job, having taken very little interest in European Community matters until then, but by the time he arrived in Brussels (asking warily whether it was safe to drink the water) he had read the treaty of Rome from cover to cover three times—he would later often tartly remark that some of his colleagues had clearly never even read it once—and had briefed himself exhaustively on every conceivable area of community activity. His predecessors also advised him to learn French, as the all-important language of the Brussels corridors; he tried, but soon gave up, so that when a visiting minister once asked if he might speak French, Cockfield replied 'By all means. [*pause*] But I shan't understand a word you say' (personal knowledge).

To appreciate the scale of what was to turn out to be Cockfield's crowning achievement, it is important to recall the extent to which the process of European integration had slowed to a snail's pace in the preceding years, reflecting economic stagnation, sluggish progress on enlargement, and above all the stalling power of the United Kingdom government in pursuit of its claims for a rebate on its contributions to the community budget. That and other thorny issues had at last been resolved at the Fontainebleau European council in June 1984. The new president of the commission, Jacques Delors, who had been one of the main players, as French finance minister, in reaching agreement on the British budget refund, was determined to make a fresh start and to use his presidency to restore momentum to the community's development. Even before the new commission took up office, Delors and Cockfield had agreed that completing the internal market was the biggest single area of community business left unfinished. It was also the objective most likely to be supported by most member governments—not least by the United Kingdom—and by the overwhelming majority of the commercial and industrial community.

Delors and Cockfield shared the analysis that, for the economies of Europe to compete successfully with those of the United States and Japan, all the obstacles that prevented them from functioning as a single market needed systematically to be removed. With characteristic ambition and thoroughness, and with total confidence in his own ability to hold all the parts together, Cockfield not only successfully claimed the internal market portfolio for himself but persuaded Delors that it should be significantly enlarged to include company and indirect taxation, financial institutions and the customs union, many of the manufacturing industries with the strongest interest in a single market (such as food, chemicals, and pharmaceuticals, wholesale and retail distribution, textiles, and the construction industry), and the implications for the internal market of all other policies. That such a raid on the traditional definition of portfolios should have been achieved without the bloodletting usually associated with incoming commissions was a measure of Delors's ability to persuade his colleagues to accept from the outset the primacy and the scale of ambition of the single market project as the flagship of his term of office. It also suited Cockfield's personality, giving him the autonomy to master and resolve for himself the dossier's many inherent complex and intractable policy conflicts, which would have tested his limited skills in handling people had they involved trying to reconcile his own and his colleagues' interests. Not that he was afraid of confrontation: he positively relished it in the council of ministers and, if necessary, even within the commission itself, where only the very brave dared to cross him—and often regretted it. Members of his team soon learned that, faced with an impasse at their own level, the suggestion that 'maybe your commissioner had better discuss it with mine' could yield capitulation within minutes (personal knowledge).

Within days of taking office Delors and Cockfield set the commission a deadline of June and the next European council summit in Milan to produce a white paper outlining a comprehensive plan for completing the internal market. Cockfield called on the whole commission to draw up an inventory of all the measures that would be needed to remove all the barriers that prevented member states from functioning as a single market. Within weeks hundreds of pieces of legislation had been identified, some of them already on the negotiating table, some lurking in desk drawers waiting for the commission to have the courage to put them forward, many others still to be conceived and drafted. As word spread that the internal market was the bandwagon to climb aboard, long-neglected drafts were dusted off and put forward as vital to the cause. In response Cockfield was ruthless in repelling all boarders who were not absolutely needed on the voyage, and the programme finally settled at a formidable 300 measures.

With a programme of such immense scope, Cockfield's study of community history had taught him that the council's tendency would be to back the easy winners and leave the rest to lag behind or fall by the wayside altogether. He, however, stuck uncompromisingly to the insight that, for the physical, technical, and fiscal barriers to the free market to be abolished, every single pretext for their continued existence had to go. With the rigorous logic of the super-bureaucrat that he was, and certain that it had to be all or nothing, he therefore built in a detailed timetable, with deadlines measure by measure, monitored by annual progress reports, reinforced by periodic high-profile strategic reviews in 1988, 1990, and 1992, and, most importantly, committed to an overall political deadline of the end of 1992 for completion of the entire project. (1992 would mark the end of two commission terms of office and, at that time, Cockfield, who was in Thatcher's good books, could expect to be reappointed to see the programme through.)

By early June 1985 Cockfield and his team had the whole programme sewn up. His fellow commissioners were bowled over by the sheer magnitude and audacity of the plan, whose unanswerably detailed logic they were all able to follow without interpretation as Cockfield laid it out before them in his slow, lugubrious drone. By the end of June the commission had bounced the Milan European council into committing itself to 'a precise programme of action based on the White Paper … with a view to achieving completely and effectively the conditions for a single market in the Community by 1992 at the latest in accordance with … a binding timetable', and to convening the intergovernmental conference that would give birth the following year to the Single European Act, the change in the rules (introducing qualified majority voting in the council for a wide variety of measures) needed to make the target credible and legally binding.

Alongside the widespread applause from all quarters for the ambition of the project, there was no shortage of voices asserting that it simply could not be done. This was a red rag to a bull, and for the next three and a half years Cockfield ploughed doggedly on with his programme, determined to prove the Jeremiahs wrong, harrying his own troops to keep to the timetable, facing down the member states in the council of ministers, and roundly denouncing faint-heartedness, foot-dragging, or outright obstruction wherever he sniffed it out. Inevitably he particularly relished tearing strips off British ministers and, though this undoubtedly boosted his credibility with his colleagues in Brussels and the other capitals of Europe, it was eventually to cost him his job.

As far as Cockfield's lifeline to London was concerned, the rot had, in fact, set in almost from the start. Thatcher had first taken issue with Cockfield as early as the publication of the white paper itself, over what she saw as his unwelcome 'invention' of the need for tax harmonization. His own account of the clash recorded:

> Myself: It was in the Treaty of Rome.
> The PM: It was not.
> Myself: It was.
> The PM: It was not.
> Myself: It was.
>
> This unproductive conversation was brought to an end by the Private Secretary being sent to find a copy of the Treaty of Rome. I asked him to read out Article 99, which reads as follows: 'The Commission shall present proposals for the harmonisation of indirect taxes …' This was greeted in complete silence. I was to learn over the years that silence was always the Prime Minister's response when in difficulties. But thinking, as I then did, that it was possible to penetrate this iron defence, I said:
> Myself: You ought to have read it before you signed it.
> The PM: I didn't sign it.
> Myself: I know you didn't. But you were a member of the Cabinet which did sign it.
> Silence. (Cockfield, 56–7)

The writing had been on the wall ever since then, made more indelible by what Thatcher saw as his complicity in trapping her into agreeing to the Single European Act. His appetite for pillorying British ministers in council meetings eventually lost him the support of the Foreign Office, which considered such public shows of national discord unseemly. By June 1988 he knew that he would not be reappointed, confirmation of which first reached him, as was the new vogue for the out-of-favour, through a Downing Street leak. But in that same month the Hanover European council declared that progress towards the single market was now 'irreversible', so that, sad though he was not to have a chance to steer the flagship home himself, he felt confident that he had set it on its course and that the momentum he had generated would see it in on time to a safe harbour. It certainly did not detract from his sense of ownership of the project: his own account of how it was all achieved, *The European Union: Creating the Single Market* (1994), was written almost entirely in the first person singular.

Four years after Cockfield's departure from Brussels, in December 1992, the vision became reality and, despite delays in implementation by some member states, the Edinburgh European council declared the single market complete in all essential respects. Not everything was as Cockfield had originally designed it—his radical proposals on VAT and excise duties, too extreme in their logic to be swallowed by finance ministers, were denatured as soon as his back was turned—and in some important respects, such as the energy market, there was still more to be done. But the whole unprecedentedly ambitious project as set out in the white paper had been substantially realized.

Final years, and assessment Cockfield's role in the creation of the European single market was recognized in a series of honorary doctorates and fellowships from universities on both sides of the Atlantic as well as by the award by Belgium of the grand cross of the order of Leopold II. From 1988 he worked for some time as an adviser on European affairs to the London accountants Peat, Marwick, McLintock, and he was much in demand as a speaker at conferences on the single market. 1992 was, however, also the year in which his wife Monica, his constant companion, suddenly died, leaving him a lonely and isolated figure in his final years, though he continued to attend regularly and to speak in debates in the House of Lords until shortly before his death at the John Radcliffe Hospital, Oxford, on

8 January 2007, of gastro-intestinal bleeding. He was survived by his two children.

Over an exceptionally long working life Cockfield had several distinguished careers, each of which would have earned him a solid footnote in the history books. But in the twilight of those years, arguably in just six months of superhuman intellectual effort, he made a whole chapter his own. The completion of the single market has been called the greatest leap forward in the process of European integration, profoundly altering the balance of economic power between the world's major trading blocs. Cockfield was perhaps an unlikely candidate for the status of European hero, but with his formidable, all-encompassing ability to hold both the detail and the wider picture together, combined with an unwavering loyalty to the rightness of his cause, he proved that the apparently impossible can, just occasionally, be achieved.

SEBASTIAN BIRCH

Sources A. Cockfield, *The European Union: creating the single market* (1994) · *The Times* (10 Jan 2007) · *Daily Telegraph* (11 Jan 2007) · *The Guardian* (11 Jan 2007) · *The Independent* (20 Jan 2007) · Burke, *Peerage* · *WW* (2007) · personal knowledge (2011) · private information (2011) · b. cert. · m. cert. [1943] · d. cert.
Archives SOUND BL NSA, current affairs recordings
Likenesses Elliott & Fry, quarter-plate glass negative, 1952, NPG · photographs, 1978–82, Photoshot, London · photograph, 1982, PA Photos, London · photograph, 1988, Getty Images, London, Popperfoto [*see illus.*] · obituary photographs
Wealth at death £4,233,794: probate, 4 May 2007, *CGPLA Eng. & Wales*

Cohn, Norman Rufus Colin (1915–2007), historian, was born on 12 January 1915 at 41 Alleyn Park, Dulwich, London, the youngest of six sons of August Sylvester Cohn (1867/8–1947), barrister, and his wife, Daisy Annie, *née* Reimer (1872/3–1951). His father was a German Jew who became a naturalized British citizen in the 1880s after hearing Gladstone expound liberalism. His mother was partly German, a Catholic, who spent most of her childhood in South Africa, where his father on holiday met and married her. His brothers and cousins fought on opposite sides in the First World War.

Cohn was educated at Gresham's School, and in 1933 won a scholarship to Christ Church, Oxford, to read French. He graduated with a first-class degree in 1936, and uniquely at that time in the modern language school was awarded a further three years to read German. The outbreak of the Second World War prevented his pursuing immediate plans for graduate research, although his linguistic skills would be used to advantage in his war service and in the books he wrote after the war ended. He married on 3 September 1941 a Russian, Vera Broido (1907–2004), who had lived for seven years in a *ménage à trois* with a much older man, the founder of Dada, Raoul Hausmann, and his complaisant wife. She and Cohn had one son, Nik (*b.* 1946). In the same month as their marriage Vera's mother was shot as a Menshevik traitor after solitary confinement in Russia since 1927, but only after the archives were opened following the collapse of the Soviet Union did she know of her mother's fate. Vera was a close friend of Frederic Voigt, the Berlin correspondent of the *Manchester Guardian*, and the thesis of his book *Unto Caesar* (1938), that communism and Nazism were both forms of secularized millenarianism, had made a great impression on her. It would be developed to great effect by her new husband.

Cohn volunteered for the army in 1940 and was commissioned in the Queen's Royal regiment; he was transferred to the intelligence corps in 1942, and from Bletchley at the end of the war was sent to Austria, where he listened to Nazi prisoners talking among themselves when they thought that their captors could not understand them. In peacetime he resumed his academic interests in languages between 1946 and 1962, first as a lecturer in French at Glasgow University and then as professor of French, at Magee University College, Londonderry (1951–60), and later at King's College, University of Durham (1960–3).

It was as a professor of French that Cohn published his first major book, *The Pursuit of the Millennium* (1957), but in the ten years that it took him to write it he had turned himself into a historian. The book met with instant acclaim. His brilliant evocation of John of Leyden's reign of terror in Münster—and of the flagellants who seemed to have walked straight out of Ingmar Bergman's movie *The Seventh Seal*, released in that same year—stayed in the reader's mind. Cohn intended it to do so, but not at the price of failing to recognize that millenarian speculations could have stabilizing effects as well as destabilizing ones. He was particularly sensitive to the power of belief in the idea of a 'last world emperor' as a secular companion figure to that of the 'angelic pope'. There are thirty-one entries on the emperor cult in the *Pursuit of the Millennium* index, which will only surprise those who accept a simplified reading of the Cohn thesis. The book remained in print throughout Cohn's lifetime and was translated into French, German, Italian, Spanish, Portuguese, Norwegian, Greek, Hebrew, and Japanese. The *Times Literary Supplement* in 1975 listed it among the 100 non-fiction works that had had the greatest influence on the way in which post-war Europeans perceived themselves. At the time it was published there was no systematic history of millenarianism into which a book could be slotted. Cohn's book went a long way to filling that gap. However, in its concluding chapter, he restated his still uncompleted mission to recover the historical roots of twentieth-century persecution and genocide.

Between 1957 and 1963 the career of the professor of French was in a sort of limbo. Rescue came in 1963 with Cohn's appointment as director of the newly established Columbus Centre at the University of Sussex. Its origins were to be found in April 1962 at a meeting held to commemorate the uprising of the Warsaw ghetto. The editor and proprietor of *The Observer*, David Astor, gave an address that was printed in *Encounter* the following August. He argued that contemporaries were still far from grasping the full implications of the holocaust and called for an academic study of the processes that led up to it. Astor's address provoked much interest between 1962 and

1963, which led to discussions in which the author of *The Pursuit of the Millennium* was invited to participate, and culminated in Astor's offering Cohn the directorship of the Columbus Centre in 1963. Although the centre was based at Sussex University, it was the trust set up by Astor, not the university, that paid Cohn's salary, and with it a small annual fee to the university. Its remit was research, not teaching, and a number of books were published under the centre's auspices bearing the imprint of the Sussex University Press, not least of them Cohn's own two publications for the centre. The first, *Warrant for Genocide* (1967), established that the key document of a supposed Jewish world conspiracy, *The Protocol of the Elders of Zion*, was a nineteenth-century tsarist forgery. Cohn's book was translated into French, German, Italian, Spanish, Portuguese, Serbian, Russian, Hebrew, and Japanese. In the Soviet Union the Russian translation circulated as samizdat before its open publication in 1990. In the United States the book gained the Anisfeld-Wolf award for its contribution to race relations. More than forty years after its original publication the English version was still in print. His second publication for the centre, *Europe's Inner Demons* (1975), was translated into French, Spanish, Hungarian, Norwegian, and Japanese, and also remained in print at the time of Cohn's death. In it he showed how the idea of the satanic pact was at the heart of the European witch craze, and on the way put to rest the once influential thesis of Margaret Murray's *The Witch-Cult in Western Europe* (1921) that witches really existed as a survival of an ancient pagan religion.

Cohn held the title of Astor-Wolfson professor of history at Sussex from 1973, and after his retirement in 1980 was made an emeritus professor. He was elected a fellow of the British Academy in 1978. Within a year of retiring as director of the Columbus Centre he was invited to Concordia University, Montreal, to help to launch the Institute for Genocide Studies, which came into existence in 1985. He published two further books, *Cosmos, Chaos and the World to Come* (1993) and *Noah's Flood: the Genesis in Western Thought* (1996). His wife Vera predeceased him in 2004, having compiled her memoirs in her ninety-first year under the title *Daughter of Revolution* (1998). On 10 December 2004 he married another remarkable Russian, Marina Voikhanskaya (*b.* 1933/4), a psychotherapist (and daughter of Israel Fridlender, scientist), who had been expelled from the Soviet Union in the 1970s for protesting against the compulsory detention of political dissidents in psychiatric hospitals. Cohn died of heart failure at his home, 20 Garden Walk, Cambridge, on 31 July 2007, and was survived by his second wife and his son, Nik, a celebrated writer, one of whose books gave rise to the musical *Saturday Night Fever*. WILLIAM LAMONT

Sources V. Broido, *Daughter of revolution* (1998) • *Daily Telegraph* (3 Aug 2007) • *The Guardian* (9 Aug 2007) • *The Times* (23 Aug 2007) • *The Independent* (29 Sept 2007) • *PBA*, 161 (2009), 87–108 • *WW* (2007) • British Academy, London, Norman Cohn papers • Lord Dacre's private papers [loaned by his trustee, B. Worden] • personal knowledge (2011) • private information (2011) • b. cert. • m. certs. • d. cert.

Archives FILM BFINA, documentary footage
Likenesses photograph, repro. in *PBA* • photograph, repro. in www.richardwebster.net/norman_cohn_obituary.htm
Wealth at death under £68,000: probate, 13 Dec 2007, *CGPLA Eng. & Wales*

Coldstream, (John) Nicolas (1927–2008), archaeologist and historian, was born on 30 March 1927 in Lahore, India, the only son of Sir John Coldstream (1877–1954), a member of the Indian Civil Service then serving as a judge at the high court in Lahore, later chief minister of Kapurthala state, and his wife, Phyllis Mary, *née* Hambly (1896–1972). The family returned to England in 1939, settling in St John's Wood, and in 1952 took up residence at 180 Ebury Street, the eponymous house of what was later to be christened 'Mozart Terrace'.

Coldstream attended St Cyprian's School, Eastbourne, then became a king's scholar at Eton College. Before progressing to King's College, Cambridge, he did his national service in the canal zone and Palestine with the Highland light infantry. He graduated from Cambridge with a double first in the classics tripos in 1951. He then taught classics at Shrewsbury School for four years before commencing a more archaeological career with a post in the Greek and Roman department of the British Museum in 1956. He had already visited Cyprus during his military service, and Greece then became another focus of his interest when he took up the MacMillan scholarship at the British School of Archaeology in Athens in 1957. There he commenced work on the material that was to become his own, the pottery of the Geometric period of Greek culture, *c.*1000–700 BC.

In 1960 Coldstream gained a post in the University of London, where he spent the rest of his career, initially at Bedford College, as a lecturer in Greek, rising to a personal chair in Aegean archaeology in 1975; he then transferred to the Yates chair of classical archaeology at University College in 1983, during a period of considerable turbulence in the area of classical studies both in the country and in the university. He remained in post there until retirement, becoming emeritus professor in 1992 and honorary fellow in 1993. On 4 July 1970, at Oxford register office, he married a historian of medieval art and architecture, and fellow university lecturer, (Imogen) Nicola Carr (*b.* 1942), daughter of Charles Francis Carr, factory inspector. There were no children of the marriage.

As an excavator Coldstream worked at Motya on Sicily, at the port site of Kastri on Kythera (with George Huxley), and on various occasions at Knossos, in particular in the sanctuary of Demeter, on the hillside south of the palace. All such work was promptly published and gave clear evidence of his mastery of areas well beyond the narrower range of his acknowledged speciality. His publications amounted in all to some 140, many of them highly influential. Among his more general works, *Greek Geometric Pottery* (1968, second edition 2008) was an indispensable tool for those working in the field, and *Geometric Greece* (1977, second edition 2003) placed the pottery and other artefacts in the fuller setting of the period, so poorly provided with other sources.

Coldstream's wish was to write history, and is exemplified in the many articles he wrote devoted to the relationships between the Greek world, Cyprus, and the 'biblical' Near East during the earlier first millennium BC. In this area in particular he was at pains to stress the importance of considering all the evidence, not the individual piece which might point in a different direction. Plus or minus a decade or two, his chronological scheme for this period came to be widely accepted. With respect to Greeks further west, his study of a well-known Greek amphora of the eighth century from Kourion on Cyprus was one catalyst in a reassessment of their role; his 'new address' for the piece, as a work from the island of Euboea, connected with further historical, and ever increasing archaeological sources, to confirm the role of the Euboeans in travelling beyond Greek frontiers in the tenth to eighth centuries BC, first to the east, Cyprus and Phoenicia, and then west, to Italy.

Coldstream's work at Knossos was dedicated to the millennium or so after the fall of the Palace of Minos. His studies of the pottery of the early Iron Age, summarized well in his contribution to the *Knossos Pottery Handbook: the Iron Age* (2001), included treatment of much material excavated since 1950, notably a number of pots with precocious figured scenes, a group often neglected in broader studies of Greek art of the period—though not his own—which concentrated on the dour scenes of battle and funerals on the burial vases made in Athens.

Coldstream's teaching was always careful and clear. The theoretical aspects of 'modern' archaeology were of no interest, although he was happy to embrace scientific evidence where relevant; his second-best subject at school was mathematics. The efficacy of such teaching and the general acknowledgement of the quality of his work were reflected in the large number of postgraduate students he attracted; successful students at that, for there were few who did not succeed in gaining employment in or around the profession, from Atlanta to the Dead Sea. Two publications illustrate this well: a Festschrift, *Klados* (1995), composed largely of articles by former students, some twenty-five in all, and the writing up of a tomb group from Cyprus housed in the Institute of Archaeology, written, under guidance, by the group of students taking his MA course in Cypriot archaeology and published in the *Bulletin of the Institute of Classical Studies* for 1991–3. The course was the only such one in Britain at the time, encouraged and materially nurtured by another, contemporary, fellow of University College, Vassos Karageorghis, director of Cypriot antiquities.

Coldstream was Geddes Harrower visiting professor at Aberdeen in 1983 and visiting fellow at the Australian Institute of Archaeology in Melbourne in 1989. He was elected a fellow of the Society of Antiquaries in 1964 and a fellow of the British Academy in 1977. He was an honorary or corresponding member of archaeological institutes in Germany, Greece, and the USA. In 2003 the British Academy awarded him the Kenyon medal for classical studies. When the tenth International Conference of Classical Archaeology was held in London in 1978, he stepped into the breach when the original chairman of the organizing committee withdrew, not only pulling irons from the fire but even making a profit. He kept up lasting connections with the British School at Athens; he edited its *Annual* between 1968 and 1973, and was chairman of its managing committee from 1987 to 1991.

Nicola Coldstream's professional status as a historian of medieval architecture happily fitted in with Nicolas Coldstream's own interest in travel. His other main interest was music, fittingly for the occupier of the house where Mozart composed a few early pieces. He played the piano with the University College chamber orchestra from his joining the college until the end. The Kreutzer sonata was in rehearsal when he fell ill, and he died of heart failure at his home, 180 Mozart Terrace, Ebury Street, on 21 March 2008. He was cremated at Putney Vale crematorium. Memorial meetings were held at the British School at Athens on 29 March 2008 (originally planned as a symposium to mark his eightieth birthday) and at St Mary's, Bourne Street, on 17 April. He was survived by his wife, Nicola. ALAN JOHNSTON

Sources *Daily Telegraph* (4 April 2008) • *The Times* (9 April 2008) • *The Independent* (15 April 2008) • *The Guardian* (4 July 2008) • *PBA*, 166 (2010), 103–16 • *WW* (2008) • personal knowledge (2012) • private information (2012) [Nicola Coldstream, widow] • m. cert. • d. cert.
Archives British School at Athens
Likenesses photograph, *c*.1950, repro. in *The Guardian* (4 July 2008) • photograph, *c*.1985, repro. in *PBA*, 103 • photograph, *c*.1991, repro. in *Klados: essays in honour of J. N. Coldstream* (1995), ix
Wealth at death £219,699: probate, 25 June 2008, *CGPLA Eng. & Wales*

Cole, Grace Elizabeth Agnes Annie [Gracie] (**1924–2006**), trumpeter, was born at Ivy Cottage, Rowlands Gill, co. Durham, on 8 September 1924, the only child of Albert Ernest Cole (1904–1986), miner and musician, and his wife, Elsie, *née* Lee (1905–1972). Her four first names were those of two grandmothers and two great-grandmothers. Her father played cornet in colliery bands in Yorkshire and was also a popular children's entertainer, going by the name of Albertino the Clown, and whenever he changed bands the family moved, so that Gracie's schooling was somewhat unsettled. When she was twelve her father taught her to play the cornet, and within a few months she was playing in her first brass band, the Rossington Welfare, and in two years was playing alongside her father with Firbeck Colliery Band. In 1939 she made her first broadcast on *Children's Hour* when *Brass Band News* advised all bandsmen to listen, saying, 'they will be surprised to hear such fine playing from a girl'.

Gracie Cole was making brass band history in the 1930s when brass bands were very much a male preserve, with none of the top bands using female musicians. It therefore created quite a stir when, in 1940, an invitation to be guest soloist with the Besses o' th' Barn Band led to her being featured with them for the next three years. She was soon in demand by the noted brass band conductors of the day, including Harry Mortimer, broadcasting and performing with the likes of Fairey Aviation, Foden's, and Grimethorpe Colliery, whose band she joined in 1942, becoming

Grace Elizabeth Agnes Annie [Gracie] **Cole (1924–2006)**, by Val Wilmer, 1986

the first female to compete in the Belle Vue championships. Another landmark was reached in 1942 when she competed for the Alexander Owen memorial scholarship, something no other woman had attempted, and which she won by an astonishing twenty-one points, the biggest winning margin in the history of the competition, not to be repeated for another thirty-eight years.

Later in 1942 Cole became eligible for call-up into the armed forces or 'war work'. On her father's advice she switched to the trumpet and joined Gloria Gay's All Girls Band, working with ENSA, followed by a brief spell with Rudy Starita's Starlites. In November 1945 she joined the Ivy Benson Band as lead trumpet and soloist at the start of the band's second European ENSA tour, and was featured on a live broadcast from Hamburg immediately following George VI's speech on Christmas day. She spent the next five years with Ivy Benson, the most famous 'girls' band in Europe, playing the Russian sector of Berlin and Egypt and the Suez Canal zone, as well as headlining variety theatres in the UK with summer residencies at Butlins holiday camps.

In 1950 the Ivy Benson Band was in Grimsby where a photo call was arranged with the George Evans Band, which was also appearing in town. So impressed was Evans with Gracie Cole's playing that he invited her to join his previously all-male band. She needed no persuading even though she would be taking a cut in salary, having fallen for Evans's trombonist William (Bill) Geldard (*b.* 1929), whom she married in 1951. It seemed like a dream ticket when both were invited to join the legendary Squadronaires, but male prejudice soon made life uncomfortable and Gracie left having decided to form her own 'girls' band. She continued fronting this until the birth of her first daughter in 1957. She led a male band for Mecca ballrooms in 1958 and then played with the Denny Boyce Band at Wimbledon Palais before joining Sydney Lipton at Grosvenor House in 1960. The birth of her second daughter later that year led to her playing on a freelance basis from then onwards. Together with her husband she did much to encourage local brass bands, and in 1990 she was made a freeman of the City of London. Having lived in Thames Ditton, Surrey, since the mid-1960s, she developed Alzheimer's disease towards the end of the 1990s and spent the last six months of her life in Westcott House, Guildford Road, Westcott, where she died on 28 December 2006. Her funeral at All Saints' Church, Weston Green, Surrey, on 19 January 2007 was followed by cremation at Randalls Park crematorium, Leatherhead. She was survived by her husband and their two daughters.

Gracie Cole, along with her contemporary, the Hallé Orchestra's trombonist Maisie Ringham, was a prime innovator of the musical emancipation of women, changing the face of brass bands in the 1930s and 1940s, although it would be many more years before female musicians were finally accepted as the equals of their male counterparts. SHEILA TRACY

Sources *The Guardian* (20 Jan 2007) · *The Times* (23 Jan 2007) · personal knowledge (2010) · private information (2010) · b. cert. · d. cert.

Archives SOUND BL NSA, documentary recordings

Likenesses V. Wilmer, photograph, 1986, priv. coll. [*see illus.*] · H. Smead, photographs, repro. in www.ivybenson-online.com/Press_cuttings/Blowing%20her%20own%20trumpet.htm · obituary photographs · photograph, repro. in www.ivybenson-online.com/Biographies/gracie_cole.htm

Wealth at death £326,588: probate, 23 March 2007, *CGPLA Eng. & Wales*

Cole, Henry Alfred [Harry] **(1930–2008)**, police constable and author, was born on 12 July 1930 at 48A Lower Road, Rotherhithe, Bermondsey, London, the son of Henry Alfred Cole, furrier, and his wife, Emma Elizabeth, *née* Shipgood. Born and raised in south London, he left school during the Second World War when he was fourteen and became in turn a cricket-bat maker, soldier, and stonemason. On 20 September 1952 he married Joan Barbara Shipgood (*b.* 1931), a telephonist, and daughter of John William Shipgood, packer. They had one daughter, Christine.

In the same year as his marriage Cole joined the Metropolitan Police. He later recalled: 'my family looked on the police with a good deal of suspicion. They were not nice, the police I mean, and my family were not great upholders of the law' (Parker, 300). He was sent to Carter Street police station, off the Walworth Road in south London, as a cadet, straight out of police training college. For twenty-nine years, until he retired in 1983, he served as a police constable at Carter Street and became a well-known and popular figure in the local community, often cycling through the streets with his helmet at an angle and a smile for his many friends and acquaintances.

Cole was just a few years away from his retirement when he discovered he could write: 'That was a great novelty. People were amazed that a policeman could string two words together. I didn't start until I was 49. I wish I had started earlier. But if I had, I wouldn't have been in the police and wouldn't have had anything to write about' (*The Mercury*, 19 July 1984). When his first book, *Policeman's Progress*, was published in 1980 he became something of a national celebrity. Andrew Hogg commented in the *Evening News* (23 July 1980) that Cole's book 'could do for the police force what James Herriot stories did for vets'. Cole told his stories in anecdotal style with a wry, worldly humour. The book captured what life was like for an ordinary 'bobby' on the beat and became a bestseller. In the *Daily Express* (29 July 1980) Janice Morley described Cole's Walworth beat as 'not a pretty area. But certainly a lively one—bodies dead, alive and drunk, fighting and violent, frightened and victims, old and lonely, young and helpless.' In the same article Morley described Cole as 'the first to tell the tale of a London constable'. This was probably true, for serving police officers were until then not allowed to publish their life stories. Cole's original manuscript for *Policeman's Progress* had to be vetted by Scotland Yard and given official clearance. *This Small Cloud*, the autobiography of another London police constable, Harry Daley, who died in 1971, was published posthumously in 1986.

When *Policeman's Progress* was published Cole was invited by the television presenter Russell Harty to make a guest appearance on the BBC programme *All About Books*. This was probably the first time a serving police officer had been given permission to be interviewed on television. With the publication of Cole's second book, *Policeman's Lot*, came an appearance on BBC Radio 2's *John Dunn Show*. Reflecting on the changes he had seen during his police service, Cole told Dunn that when he joined the police the uniform 'would literally do the job for you. Now it is counterproductive' (*John Dunn Show*, 30 July 1981). He also explained that he wrote *Policeman's Progress* to dispel the cosy image of the 'bobby on the beat' popularized by BBC Television's *Dixon of Dock Green* drama series, which ran from 1955 to 1976. In 1983 Tony Parker interviewed Cole for *The People of Providence: a Housing Estate and Some of its Inhabitants*, a study of the Brandon estate in Walworth. Disguising him as 'PC Arthur "Fuzzer" Davidson', Parker described Cole as 'a slightly wirily built man, whose appearance hardly matched in any way the conventional figure of a policeman. When he wore his helmet it always looked far too big … most of his time appeared to be spent in chatting amiably in shops or with people on the street … He talked easily and naturally, as one ordinary person to another: he never pretended the police were above criticism and he never tried to put himself in a position where he himself was above it' (Parker, 301).

In total Cole wrote nine books in the *Policeman* series, as well as three novels, *Queenie* (1994), *Billie's Bunch* (1995), and *Julia's War* (1997), and three non-fiction books. He also wrote *Policeman's Prelude* (1984), an autobiographical account of his childhood and teenage years in Bermondsey before and during the war. For many years he contributed a weekly column to the *South London Press*.

In his spare time Cole was a football coach and worked tirelessly for Southwark's Charterhouse boys' club. He was also an enthusiastic Millwall fan and supported them from the age of four. In 1978 he was awarded the British empire medal for his voluntary work. In 2006 he was honoured with a Southwark blue plaque, placed on the Charles Dickens Primary School in Lant Street, Southwark, where he had been a pupil from 1934 to 1940. He died of kidney failure in King's College Hospital, Denmark Hill, London, on 17 April 2008, and was survived by his wife and daughter. Chief Superintendent Malcolm Tillyer, borough commander for Southwark Police, described him as 'a talented man with a tremendous sense of humour. His books did much to enhance the reputation of the police service—his amusing anecdotes showed the other side of policing, the "human" side. He had a real sense of loyalty and passion for policing and for Southwark borough' (*South London Press*, 22 April 2008).

STEPHEN BOURNE

Sources H. Cole, interview with Russell Harty, *All about books*, BBC1, 24 July 1980 • H. Cole, interview with John Dunn, *John Dunn show*, BBC Radio 2, 30 July 1981 • T. Parker, *The people of Providence: a housing estate and some of its inhabitants* (1983) • H. Cole, *Policeman's prelude* (1984) • *The Mercury* [Streatham] (19 July 1984); (17 July 1986) • *South London Press* (25 April 2008) • personal knowledge (2012) • private information (2012) • b. cert. • m. cert.

Cole, Michael (1928–2008), scientist and inventor, was born on 18 October 1928 at 27 Welbeck Street, Marylebone, London, the oldest child in the family of two sons and one daughter of Captain Awdry Valentine Connor (Henry) Cole (formerly Witkowsky), and his second wife, Marguerite Eleanor Mary Agnes, *née* Gooch, daughter of Charles Edwin Gooch, of Wivenhoe Park, Colchester, Essex. His father, born and educated in India, was descended from a Polish Jewish family which had emigrated to Chicago in 1848. Having amassed a fortune at a very young age by selling insurance in India, he came to England in 1906, was commissioned in the British army, and (by then a captain in the 7th North Staffordshire regiment) was wounded in 1916 at Gallipoli.

Cole grew up in Cannes, where his parents had started a fashionable tennis club, and in the late 1930s the family moved to Salcombe, Devon, where Cole's father was occupied in ship salvage, and later in farming. Cole was educated at Eton College, and after national service in the Royal West African Frontier Force in the Gold Coast, where he arrested Kwame Nkrumah, wrongly suspected of being responsible for the riots of 1948, he went up to Trinity College, Cambridge, in 1948 to read natural sciences. He graduated with an upper second in 1951, and after completing a PhD in metallurgy, awarded in 1955, he won a King George VI fellowship and spent 1954–5 at the University of Chicago. He returned to Cambridge as a research fellow at the Cavendish Laboratory. On 26 November 1960 he married Susan Mary Fellowes (*b.* 1936), daughter of William Albemarle Fellowes, land agent, of Sandringham, Norfolk; they had two daughters and two sons.

Cole did not want to become an academic, and in 1957 he founded Metals Research, in a loft over a garage in King Street, Cambridge, and began work on the processes required for growing and preparing samples of single metal crystals, then beginning to be in great demand in solid state physics laboratories, especially in the aircraft, space, weapons, and semi-conductor industries. Single metal crystals allowed the structure of the metals to be studied in its purest form, but were difficult and expensive to produce. Over the next few years Cole developed both the processes for crystal growing, and a range of innovative equipment, including specialized furnaces and a spark erosion machine, the Servomet, which could cut and shape crystals without damaging their structure. In 1960 he was joined by his brother David to manage the business side of the company, leaving him free to concentrate on technical matters and product development. With the invention of the Quantimet Image Analysing Computer, which used a television camera, a microscope, and a computer to analyse the appearance of surfaces and images, and was developed by Colin Fisher, later technical director of Metals Research, into a highly versatile and powerful instrument with applications in a wide range of industries, the company grew rapidly. In 1965 Metals Research was able to buy Moat House, Melbourn, a country house outside Cambridge, and build a new laboratory and workshops in its grounds. In 1969 Cole introduced the Quantimet 720, which used a digital image analysis system, and the workforce grew to some 500 by the early 1970s. Subsidiary companies were established in France, Germany, the United States, and Russia, and about three-quarters of production was exported. Metals Research won three queen's awards for Industry. In 1975, looking to expand further and exploring the possibility of acquiring another company, and with support from the Labour government and the National Enterprise Board, Metals Research made a reverse takeover of Scientific and Medical Instruments Ltd, part of the former Cambridge Instrument Company, founded by Horace Darwin, son of Charles Darwin, a century earlier. The new company, Cambridge Analysing Instruments Ltd, despite receiving a queen's award in 1976, ran into difficulties from falling sales levels in the difficult financial climate of the late 1970s, especially after the change of government in 1979, and in 1979 Cole resigned.

In 1982 Cole bought Genevac, a company that made laboratory vacuum pumps, with the intention of improving its products. This led to the invention of a vapour vacuum pump, based on the principle of 'lift', which worked according to the 'Cole vacuum principle'. This could pump corrosive acids and solvent vapours quickly, without the need for regular maintenance, whereas a normal pump would disintegrate. Sales of the new pump were slow in taking off, and as the cost of the development of the pump escalated, and despite successive refinancing, Genevac was forced into liquidation, following the breakdown of a proposed collaboration with an American company. Cole was left deeply in debt, and lost both his house and his pension. At this point his brother bought the defunct company from the receiver, and with the help of his wife and his son Harry, Cole resumed work on the development and sale of his pump. Later, in 1994, he invented an evaporator for use in the pharmaceutical research industry which could process hundreds of samples simultaneously and evaporate many times faster than previous evaporators without overheating the thermolabile samples, leaving a purer substance. This was a huge success, and Cole opened an office in New York, increased the workforce to 150, and achieved a turnover of £15 million. After winning his fifth queen's award in 2000, Cole sold the company to an American instrument company, after a bidding war between two instrument groups.

After the sale of Genevac, Cole started a new research company to explore ways of cultivating cep (or porcini) mushrooms (*Boletus edulis*) commercially, something that people all over the world had been working on, unsuccessfully, for years. Although he failed to find a solution, he came to the conclusion that the explanation lay with electricity, and that there was a correlation between the charged air caused by thunderstorms, and the growth of ceps. To test this hypothesis he experimented with a metal tree with platinum roots, planted in his garden. At the end of his life Cole became interested in climate change, reaching the conclusion that there was little scientific basis for the view that man-made carbon dioxide caused global warming, and that the predictive computer models used were based on false assumptions. Cole was mentioned in the debate on climate change in the House of Lords on 21 May 2009.

As an inventor, Michael Cole was a genius, and his confidence and determination kept him going. Even when facing enormous financial difficulties, over and over again he refused to accept that something was impossible, and thought of a way to do it. Metals Research was one of the first high technology companies in the country, and Cole was a key figure in the industrial renaissance in Cambridge in the 1960s. A big man and a bon viveur, he enjoyed flying, sailing, and skiing, was passionate about music, and was also a keen gardener and a fine bridge player. He and his brother bought Osea Island, off the Essex coast, and used to fly their families there for their holidays. He also often flew to France and back for lunch in his favourite restaurant in Le Touquet. He died on 6 April 2008 at his home, Moor Farm, Friston, Saxmundham, Suffolk, of cancer, and was survived by his wife and children. ANNE PIMLOTT BAKER

Sources R. Falk, *The business of management*, 5th edn (1978), 213–18 · *Daily Telegraph* (23 May 2008) · private information (2012) · b. cert. · m. cert. · d. cert.

Likenesses photograph, repro. in *Daily Telegraph* (23 May 2008)

Wealth at death £3,255,957: probate, 24 Sept 2008, *CGPLA Eng. & Wales*

Colledge, (Magdalena) Cecilia (1920–2008), figure skater, was born at 36 Belsize Grove, Hampstead, London, on 28 November 1920, the younger child of Lionel Colledge (1883–1948), an ear, nose, and throat specialist, and his wife, Margaret Mary (1884–1966), daughter of Admiral John Brackenbury. Her elder brother, Maule, a flight lieutenant in the Royal Air Force, was shot down over Germany in 1943.

Cecilia and her mother attended the 1928 world figure skating championships, held in London, where Sonja Henie won the second of ten consecutive world titles. Cecilia was entranced by Henie's balletic skating and remarked, 'I should like to skate like that' (Hines, *Figure Skating*, 110). Encouraged by Gertrude Vinson, the mother of the American skater Maribel Vinson, Cecilia's mother arranged lessons for her. She was taught initially by the British ice dancers Eva Keats and Eric van der Weyden, a husband and wife couple who wrote an important book on skating and who invented four compulsory dances later employed in international competition. Mother and daughter went to Norway, the home of Henie, for coaching, but during a visit to see her brother, who attended school in Zuoz, Switzerland, they met Jacques Gerschwiler, one of three members of an important Swiss coaching family. Gerschwiler became Cecilia's coach, living initially in the Colledges' home, and remained her coach throughout her competitive career.

In 1932 both the Olympic winter games and the world figure skating championships were held in North America for the first time, the Olympics at Lake Placid, New York, on 4–15 February and the world championships at Montreal, Quebec, on 19–20 February. Fifteen ladies competed at Lake Placid, fourteen at Montreal, the largest number at that time for a world championship. Among them were four from Great Britain: Megan Taylor, Colledge, Mollie Phillips, and Joan Dix. They were placed seventh to tenth in that order at both competitions. For all of them these were their first international competitions. All except Phillips were aged eleven. Colledge was the youngest at eleven years and eighty-three days, a record for ladies at the world championships that still stood at the time of her death. Taylor was thirty-four days older.

Colledge and Taylor provided one of figure skating's great rivalries. At many competitions only one of them competed, but from 1931 to 1939 they competed against each other sixteen times, each beating the other eight times. On only four occasions were those placements not first and second. Six national competitions resulted in three titles each. At the Olympic trials in 1931 and the Olympic winter games in 1932 Taylor beat Colledge. At four European championships, Colledge beat Taylor every time, winning three titles (in 1937, 1938, and 1939). At the world championships Taylor was placed ahead of Colledge in 1932 and 1933, Colledge won the world title in 1937, the year after Henie's retirement from amateur competitions, and Taylor won in 1938. Their rivalry reached its peak in 1939. Colledge won her third consecutive European title with Taylor a close second, but Taylor was the reigning world champion. The anticipated showdown at

(**Magdalena**) **Cecilia Colledge** (**1920–2008**), by unknown photographer, 1932

the world championships did not occur. An injury kept Colledge out of the competition; Taylor easily won her second world title. It was the last competition before the Second World War, and neither skater competed internationally after the war, although Colledge won a sixth British title in 1946.

Colledge and Taylor were the most prominent skaters during a golden age for ladies' skating in Great Britain. Not since Madge Syers in 1906 and 1907 had there been a British world champion and there had been only a handful of medallists. After this remarkable period only Jeannette Altwegg claimed European, world, and Olympic titles for Britain (all in 1951–2) during Colledge's lifetime. Colledge's cumulative record included six national titles, three European titles, and one world title.

After turning professional in 1946 Colledge skated in several shows, first an ice review at the Stoll Theatre in London, and later in shows at Brighton and at the Roxy Theater in New York. She moved to the United States in 1951 and taught skating for one season in Lake Placid, the site of her first Olympic effort nineteen years earlier. She then moved to Boston, where she taught at the Skating Club of Boston for forty-three years, retiring in 1995. Many of her students competed nationally and internationally, among them Lorraine Hanlon, and the ice dancers Sidney Foster and Franklin Nelson, and Judy Lamar and Ronald Ludington.

Colledge's place in figure skating history was sealed by a remarkable competitive record followed by her career as a respected coach, but also by several skating firsts. Most important was the parallel spin, later known as the camel spin, an invention of Colledge and her coach, Jacques Gerschwiler. Colledge was also the first skater to do a layback spin, later included in most ladies' programmes. In jumping Colledge was the first female competitor to do a two-revolution jump in competition, a double Salchow (included in her programme at the 1936 European championships). She also invented the one-foot Axel Paulsen jump, in which the landing is on an inside edge and on the same foot as the takeoff. Colledge was thus the inventor of more standard jumps and spins in figure skating than any other skater. She was a balanced skater with strong compulsory figures, which at that time accounted for 60 per cent of the score. Commenting on the elimination of compulsory figures from competition in 1990 she echoed the opinion of many coaches: 'I really liked figures and I think it's a terrible shame that they removed [them]. I think it has reduced the quality of skating' (Stevenson, 55).

Colledge was elected to the world figure skating hall of fame in 1980 and on her retirement from coaching in 1995 was named an honorary member of the Skating Club of Boston. Having lived latterly in Lexington, Massachusetts, USA, she died in Cambridge, Massachusetts, on 12 April 2008. She never married. JAMES R. HINES

Sources N. Brown, *Ice skating: a history* (1959) • D. L. Bird, *Our skating heritage: a centenary history of the National Skating Association of Great Britain, 1879–1979* (1979) • B. T. Wright, 'The hall of fame: Cecilia Colledge, Great Britain', *Skating* (April 1981), 14–15, 28–9 • B. T. Wright, *Skating around the world, 1892–1992: the one hundredth anniversary history of the International Skating Union* (1992) • A. Stevenson, 'A visit with Cecilia Colledge, 1937 world champion', *Blades on Ice* (July/Aug 2001), 54–6 • J. R. Hines, *Figure skating: a history* (2006) • *The Times* (16 April 2008) • *Globe and Mail* [Toronto] (16 April 2008) • *Daily Telegraph* (17 April 2008) • *The Guardian* (18 April 2008) • *The Independent* (21 April 2008) • *New York Times* (24 April 2008) • J. R. Hines, *Historical dictionary of figure skating* (2011) • personal knowledge (2012) • private information (2012) • b. cert.

Archives FILM BFINA, light entertainment and news footage

Likenesses photographs, 1927–38, Getty Images, London • Madame Yevonde, bromide print, 1930–39, NPG • photograph, 1932, Lake Placid Olympic Museum, Lake Placid, New York [*see illus.*] • World Wide Photos, bromide print, 1933 (with Megan Taylor), NPG • Bassano, photographs, 1936–8, NPG • photographs, 1938–98, PA Photos, London • photograph, 1950 (with Jeannette Altwegg and Daphne Walker), Rex Features, London • obituary photographs • photographs, repro. in *The Guardian* (14 Jan 1989)

Collins, Philip Arthur William (1923–2007), literary scholar, was born at 38 Fletching Road, Clapton, Hackney, London, on 28 May 1923, the second child and elder son of Arthur Henry Collins, master printer, and his wife, Winifred Nellie, *née* Bowmaker, teacher. In his early childhood his family moved to Little Burstead, near Billericay, Essex, and he attended Brentwood School with a scholarship. In 1941 he entered Emmanuel College, Cambridge, and took a first in part one of the English tripos in 1942. He was then conscripted into the army and served as a sergeant in the Royal Army Ordnance Corps before being commissioned into the Royal Norfolk regiment in 1945.

After demobilization Collins returned to Cambridge, where he took a first in part two of the tripos in 1947. During his time at Cambridge he was a very active member of the Marlowe Society and his lifelong passion for the theatre later led him to become founding secretary of both the Phoenix and the Haymarket theatres in Leicester. He also served on the Arts Council's drama panel (1970–75) and the board of the National Theatre (1976–82). In 1947 he was appointed staff tutor in adult education at the University College of Leicester and in 1954 became warden of Vaughan College. When the University of Leicester obtained its royal charter in 1957 he joined the English department as senior lecturer while remaining strongly committed to adult education. He was closely involved with the University of Leicester Press and its highly successful Victorian Library reprint series. In 1964 he was appointed to a chair and twice served as head of department (1971–6 and 1981–2). In 1982 he took early retirement with the title of professor emeritus. He was married twice: first on 1 November 1952 to Mildred Lowe (*b.* 1911), a lecturer in education at the University College of Leicester, and daughter of Ernest Lowe, railway inspector, and second (his first marriage having ended in divorce in 1963), on 18 August 1965, to Joyce Dickins (*b.* 1942), then a graduate student, later a publisher, daughter of James Wilfred Dickins, security officer. With his second wife he had two sons and a daughter.

Reading Edgar Johnson's biography of Charles Dickens, published in 1952, stirred Collins's interest in the great Victorian novelist, who was at that time not much regarded in the English departments of most British universities, largely as a result of the influence of F. R. Leavis. Collins became especially interested in Dickens as a social commentator and campaigner for reform and, in 1955, published the first of upwards of a hundred articles that he was, over the years, to write about the novelist. In 1962 came his classic study *Dickens and Crime*, which after half a century remained one of the indispensable books in the field. It was followed in 1963 by *Dickens and Education*. His deep and practical interest in Dickens's career as a public reader (he was himself a splendid platform performer of passages from Dickens's work) led to his magnificent edition for Oxford University Press of the novelist's specially prepared reading texts in 1975. Among his other major contributions to Dickens scholarship were his volumes devoted to the novelist in Routledge's Critical Heritage series (1972) and in Macmillan's Interviews and Recollections series (1981).

Collins's great distinction as a Dickens expert and his ease and brilliance as a lecturer resulted in his being regularly invited to undertake lecture tours in many different countries and from 1986 to 2000 he was a much valued 'faculty member' at the annual Dickens Universe conferences at the University of California at Santa Cruz. In 1976 he was elected president of the Dickens Society of America, and he served also as president of the International Dickens Fellowship in 1983–5. From 1984 to 1992 he chaired the board of trustees of the Dickens House Museum, London.

Collins's interest in Victorian literature and culture was by no means confined to Dickens. He also published important studies of Tennyson, Trollope, and other major (and some minor) writers, and he served a term as chairman of the Tennyson Society. With the historians H. J. (Jim) Dyos and Jack Simmons he co-founded in 1966 the Victorian Studies Centre at Leicester. This flourished, hosting international conferences and welcoming as visiting professors distinguished scholars from all over the world. It was also responsible for some landmark publications, including *The Victorian City* (1973), to which Collins contributed a notable essay on Victorian London.

Philip Collins was a man of great warmth and geniality who was unfailingly generous with his time and encouraging towards younger scholars seeking his help and advice. He was a devotee of classical music, jazz, and, above all, opera. He lived in Leicester for most of his life. After enduring considerable ill health with cheerful stoicism during his last years, he died on 6 May 2007 at the Royal Infirmary, Leicester, of heart failure, and was buried at Scraptoft natural burial ground, outside Leicester, on 16 May. He was survived by his wife, Joyce, and their three children. MICHAEL SLATER

Sources *The Independent* (12 May 2007) · *Daily Telegraph* (14 May 2007) · *The Guardian* (15 May 2007) · *The Times* (23 May 2007) · *The Dickensian*, 472 (March 2007), 187–90 · *WW* (2007) · personal knowledge (2011) · private information (2011) · b. cert. · m. certs. · d. cert.
Likenesses obituary photographs
Wealth at death £566,400: probate, 5 Nov 2007, *CGPLA Eng. & Wales*

Colvin, Sir Howard Montagu (1919–2007), architectural historian, was born on 15 October 1919 at Inglenook, 4 Longlands Park Road, Foots Cray, Kent, the elder son of Montagu Colvin (1888–1938), an engineer's buyer, and his wife, Annie Winifred, *née* Randle (1888–1944), daughter of George Beavis Randle, photographer. He grew up in Sidcup, attending Merton Court School until 1933, when he became a boarder at Trent College in Nottinghamshire. This provided an excellent education and also an escape from home, where the death of his only brother had precipitated the breakdown of his parents' marriage.

As a young boy Colvin was chiefly interested in the natural world. But as he grew older he became more and more intrigued by the built environment. He cycled round west Kent in search of architecture when at home, and at school was permitted to do the same in place of cricket during the summer term, exploring the buildings of the east midlands. A trip to Cleeve Abbey in Somerset awoke a fascination with medieval architecture and he led a schoolboy dig at Dale Abbey in Derbyshire, publishing his findings in five articles. By the time he was ready to leave school he was determined to become an archaeologist. Advised by Sir Mortimer Wheeler to read history as preparation, he entered University College, London, in 1937. There he specialized in medieval history. He was also involved in successive digs at Clarendon Palace near Salisbury. The disruption of the Second World War and the college's evacuation to Aberystwyth provided no obstacle to his achieving the highest academic honours—though it did prompt a publication on the buildings of the town. He graduated in 1940 with a first-class degree and the Rosa Morrison medal.

Colvin left college with more than just a degree. It was there that he met Christina Edgeworth Butler (1919–2003), a fellow student, daughter of the professor of Latin, Harold Edgeworth Butler, and granddaughter of Arthur Gray Butler, first headmaster of Haileybury College, and of the historian Albert Frederick Pollard. They were engaged in 1941 and married on 16 August 1943. Christina shared many of his interests and herself later published on

Sir Howard Montagu Colvin (1919–2007), by Lucy Anne Dickens, 2001

eighteenth-century literature as well as contributing to the Victoria County History series. They had three children: a daughter who died in infancy and two sons. It was at university, too, that Colvin first came up with the idea that was to make his name, a biographical dictionary of architects. He and a fellow student, David Young, knew little of modern art-historical methods but, as he later recalled, they 'did realise that the factual basis of English architectural history was hopelessly amateurish'. They concluded that the solution 'was to apply to architecture the ordinary processes of historical scholarship' (Colvin, *Essays*, 292). From 1938 onwards Colvin worked steadily on a book intended to do just that.

The war did not derail this work. In 1940 Colvin joined the RAF and became an aerial photography interpreter. In 1941 he was posted to Malta, where 'To watch—as we did almost daily throughout the first half of 1942—60 or 70 Stukas diving through the massed fire of more than 100 guns was to experience both the Awful and the Sublime' (Colvin, 'Early life', 8). It was an exciting time, and in later years the usually reserved scholar would become animated when describing it. Malta had its scholarly side, too. Inevitably the island inspired an article on its architecture. The well-stocked Garrison Officers' Library proved to possess numerous books on British building, not least the nineteenth-century *Biographical Dictionary of British Architects*, which was to be central to Colvin's future work.

Demobilized in 1946, Colvin abandoned his ambitions of becoming an archaeologist and accepted John (J. E.) Neale's offer of an assistant lectureship in medieval history back at University College, London. A condition of his appointment was that he should register for a doctorate. 'As it seemed unlikely that anything architectural would find favour with Neale (who was a ruthless sacker of those who lost his favour)' he decided to work on the Premonstratensian order, which had founded Dale Abbey (Colvin to Nigel Ramsay, 24 April 2004, Colvin MSS). A year later his circumstances changed completely. The election of the historian Austin Lane Poole as president of St John's College, Oxford, created a vacancy there for a tutor. Almost certainly pushed by his supervisor, Vivian (V. H.) Galbraith, who was a close friend of Lane Poole and who believed that Colvin was 'probably the best young mediaevalist since [Richard] Southern' (Galbraith to OUP, 2 Dec 1949, OUP archives, PB/ED 006473), he beat the formidable early modernist John (J. P.) Cooper to the job. In December 1947 Colvin was elected a fellow of St John's. Initially his term of appointment was only three years. In fact he was to stay for six decades.

Colvin had been hesitant about moving to Oxford. He would be the first fellow of St John's not to have been educated in the university and he subsequently observed that the closest any member of his family had ever come to such a role was the Victorian comic actor J. L. Toole, who had once starred in a play called *The Don*. But he was encouraged by his wife, whose family had taught in Oxford and Cambridge for generations, and whose brother, David Butler, had just arrived at Nuffield College. Colvin was always grateful that he had listened to her advice. He found 'that Oxford was a place where, once established, one could do whatever one liked provided only that one did not neglect one's pupils' (Colvin, 'Early life', 11). He thus began what he called 'a double life as a medievalist and an architectural historian' (Musson, 120). The thesis was completed (but never submitted) and published as *The White Canons in England* (1951). It was well received. None the less, the real focus of his research quickly became the *Biographical Dictionary of English Architects, 1660–1840*, the contract for which was signed in 1949.

The *Dictionary* was published in 1954 and marked a revolution in architectural history. Colvin had done just what he planned when he was still a student at University College, London. He had applied the ordinary standards of historical scholarship to a subject still mired in amateur antiquarianism and what he called 'irresponsible attributionism' (Colvin, *Essays*, 294), that is the tendency to attribute buildings to the most famous architect of the period. Travelling the country, often accompanied by Rupert Gunnis, 'who used his old Etonian network ruthlessly', or Lawrence Stone, 'who got us into one reclusive ducal house by charming the Duke's former nanny over the phone' (Musson, 120), he pored over manuscripts and rewrote the architectural history of the period. Frequently he was only just in time: arriving at Malmesbury Abbey in 1949 he found the verger tearing out pages from the churchwardens' accounts to light his pipe.

Colvin's *Dictionary* transformed the field. His careful use of documents and systematic survey of sources made it a model for subsequent studies. He was to rewrite it three more times. In 1978 the second edition extended the chronological range, starting in 1600. It also widened the geographical scope by including numerous Scottish architects. The third edition in 1995 was swelled by the inclusion of more minor names and Welsh architects. Finally, in 2008, the fourth edition was still bigger and more detailed. The work was not just exacting, it was also a good read. On publication of the second edition John Betjeman wrote to say that 'Each entry is as good as a thrilling short story … You have lifted architecture out of German art history into literature' (Betjeman to Colvin, 19 June 1978, Colvin MSS).

Colvin's achievements did not end there, however. Between 1951 and 1982 he was the general editor of the *History of the King's Works* (1963–82), a six-volume, multi-author account of the department of state responsible for building between the middle ages and the modern day. He wrote much of it and edited the remainder ruthlessly. He also published scores of articles, edited collections of building accounts and architectural drawings, and supervised a number of important doctoral theses. He wrote *Unbuilt Oxford* (1983), a history of failed architectural projects, and *Architecture and the After-Life* (1999), an ambitious survey of funerary buildings. His achievement in securing a significant building for the National Trust was celebrated in *Calke Abbey: a Hidden House Revealed* (1985).

This academic industry was rather grudgingly recognized by the University of Oxford, which made Colvin a reader in architectural history in 1965 (and abolished the post on his retirement in 1987); he was never made a professor. Outside the university, however, he was in great demand. He sat on the Royal Fine Arts Commission (1962–1972), the Royal Commission on Historical Monuments (1963–76), the Historic Buildings Council (1970–84), and the Royal Commission on Historical Manuscripts (1981–8). He was also a founding commissioner of English Heritage in 1984. He became a fellow of the British Academy in 1963, was appointed CBE in 1964 and CVO in 1983, and was knighted in 1995.

Howard Colvin was a small, shy, reserved man, often formal and sometimes a little remote. But he came alive when discussing architecture. He had an extraordinary visual memory and was hugely proud of having designed his own house, as well as an addition to the senior common room at St John's. He was also pleased to have been instrumental in commissioning the Architects' Co-Partnership to build the first modernist addition to the college. None the less, his real memorial was undoubtedly the *Dictionary*. He finished proofreading the fourth edition on 24 December 2007 and died in his sleep on 27 December at his home, 50 Plantation Road, Oxford. He was survived by his two sons. WILLIAM WHYTE

Sources *Home and Garden* (May 1960), 72–3; (May 1978), 110–11 · D. Watkin, *The rise of architectural history* (1980) · *Design and practice in British architecture: studies in architectural history presented to Howard Colvin* (1984) [*Architectural History*, 27, special issue] · K. Powell, 'Historian with modern views', *Architects' Journal* (2 Nov 1995) · H. Colvin, *Essays in English architectural history* (1999) · H. M. Colvin, 'The Historic Buildings Council and the country house', *The twentieth century great house*, ed. M. Airs (2002), 101–8 · G. Tyack, *Modern architecture in an Oxford college: St John's College, 1945–2005* (2005) · J. Musson, 'Leading architectural historian', *Country Life* (3 May

2007) • *The Times* (1 Jan 2008); (11 Jan 2008); (23 Jan 2008) • *The Independent* (1 Jan 2008); (3 Jan 2008) • *Daily Telegraph* (7 Jan 2008) • *The Guardian* (15 Jan 2008) • *History Today* (April 2008), 7 • *Newsletter of the Society of Architectural Historians of Great Britain*, 94 (summer 2008), 1–4 • *Burlington Magazine*, 150 (2008), 613–14 • *Oxoniensia*, 73 (2008), ix–x • R. Hewlings, 'A scholar's lair', *Country Life*, 202 (2008), 60–63 • *Sir Howard Montague Colvin, 1919–2007* (privately printed, 2008) • *WW* (2007) • Burke, *Peerage* • priv. coll., Colvin MSS [inc. 'Early life of Howard Colvin'] • J. Summerson, autobiography, RIBA BAL • OUP archives, PB/ED 006473 • personal knowledge (2011) • private information (2011) • b. cert. • m. cert.

Archives priv. coll. | Derbys. RO, papers relating to Calke Abbey and Harpur Crewe family

Likenesses T. S. LaFontaine, pen and ink sketch, 1981, St John's College, Oxford • H. C. G. Matthew, bromide print, 1998, NPG • L. A. Dickens, C-type colour print, 2001, NPG [*see illus.*] • obituary photographs • photograph, Bloomsbury Auctions, 25–6 Sept 2008

Wealth at death £2,204,212: probate, 22 May 2008, *CGPLA Eng. & Wales*

Cook [*née* Lansley], **Beryl Frances** (1926–2008), painter, was born at Helmsley, Pooley Green Road, Egham, Surrey, on 10 September 1926, the third of four daughters of Adrian Stephen Barton Lansley, mechanical engineer, and his wife, Ella, *née* Farmer-Francis, an office worker. Her parents separated four years later, and Beryl's mother moved to Reading with her four daughters. When Beryl was ten a boy called John Victor Cook moved in next door (his father, Victor Harry Cook, was a tax officer with the Inland Revenue), and was soon her childhood sweetheart. She went to Kendrick Girls' School, but excelled at nothing, including art, and left when she was fourteen to train as a typist. In 1944 the family moved to London where she took a variety of jobs including performing as a chorus girl in a production of *The Gypsy Princess* and working as a model for Goldberg's fashion showroom in Bond Street. She was attracted to the limelight but didn't make a career on the boards or catwalk. In 1947 she moved with her mother and sisters to Hampton to help run a tea room. She met up again with John Cook, who was now an officer in the merchant navy, and they married on 2 October 1948. Their son, John, was born in 1950. They lived briefly in Leigh-on-Sea in Essex and then, in 1955, took a tenancy together of the White Horse pub in Stoke by Nayland in Suffolk, in the heart of Constable country. They kept pigs and chickens but, as Beryl quipped later, 'it may have been healthy, but we hated the life' (*The Independent*, 30 May 2008). A year later they moved to Salisbury, Southern Rhodesia, where Beryl worked as a bookkeeper in an insurance office, while John worked in car sales. It was there that her life suddenly switched gear.

Most art grows out of art—the natural flowering of a childhood talent, encouraged by parents or at school, or born in an atmosphere of art. Beryl Cook's art, apparently, came out of nowhere. When they were still in Salisbury in 1960 she and John gave their ten-year-old son a child's oil painting set. He painted a typical child's picture with a strip of sky at the top and a band of grass at the bottom with a little house standing on it. Beryl commented that there was nothing in the middle. Young John replied, reasonably enough, that there *was* nothing in the middle. 'I'll paint you a picture with something in the middle', Beryl replied, and she painted two large, naked breasts with a woman's face above them with big eyes glancing furiously right, as if to say 'what are you looking at?'. She had no idea how to paint a waist, so she painted in a broad black band, as if the woman were leaning over a shellacked fence. Her husband immediately dubbed it 'The Hangover', and this bright gem of a painting hung in her house ever after. She later said that she felt as if she had been kicked in the stomach when she saw what she had done. She had no idea where it came from, and had at first no idea what to do with the creative power she had found within herself (personal knowledge).

Beryl Frances Cook (1926–2008), self-portrait, 1977

It not until about five years later, when she and her family had moved back to live in East Looe in Cornwall, that Beryl Cook began to see scenes around her, particularly in their local pub, which she thought she would like to paint. There are hints of Stanley Spencer and Edward Burra as well as Picasso, Manet, and Matisse in her very early attempts, but what is remarkable is how rapidly she developed her instantly recognizable style; she soon became famous for her 'fat ladies'. But it is not only the ladies in her paintings that are fat: everything is fat, the cigarettes and wine glasses, the shoes (she loved painting shoes), the fur coats, the ice creams and Cornish pasties, the hairdos, and the dustbins. She never painted nails on her fingers, not because she couldn't but because such finicky details would have distracted from their fullness. The only details on her ballooned features were the lines of mouths and the angles of glances. These were crucial and take one to the heart of the start of each picture. They spring from direct observations of unguarded moments when someone reveals their true feelings, relaxes with a fag, dances with joy, or surreptitiously eyes up a sailor, moments that make us, the viewers, smile, and sometimes laugh out loud, as we recognize these feelings in ourselves.

In 1968 the Cooks bought a bed and breakfast in Plymouth, and soon the walls were covered with her paintings. If guests commented on them she pretended that they were by her son, or husband. But in 1975 Bernard Samuels, the director of the Plymouth Art Centre, heard about this boarding house full of paintings, and went to see it. He immediately offered Beryl Cook an exhibition. The show drew crowds, many sales, priced between £40 and £60, and attention from local and then national media. In 1976 her painting of the knowingly smiling barmaid of their local pub, the Lockyer Tavern, starred on the cover of the *Sunday Times* colour magazine. The London art dealer Lionel Levy saw it and invited her to show in his Portal Gallery. She subsequently held eighteen hugely successful exhibitions there. Her paintings began to be reproduced as greetings cards which were sold around the world. The first of eleven books of her art, *Beryl Cook: the Works*, was published by John Murray in 1978, and in the following year Melvyn Bragg featured her on his *South Bank Show* on ITV.

As she became more and more successful Beryl Cook's horizons widened. She travelled to New York, flying out on Concorde and sailing back on the *QE2*, searched out tango dancers in Buenos Aires, and followed in the footsteps of the painter Edward Burra in Marseilles, all the while making tiny sketches in her handbag, occasionally pretending to snap John so that she could photograph a background detail. She became Britain's most genuinely popular living painter in the 1980s.

Cook's popularity to a large extent excluded her from the established contemporary art world that lauded avant-garde work that offended public taste. A few critics liked her work, such as Edward Lucie-Smith, but curators were much derided when they bought her work for public collections. Modern art was supposed to be angst-ridden, the critics claimed, so Beryl Cook's paintings couldn't be modern or, as one eminent gallery director once announced, even art. They are, and gloriously so, each image a memorable insight into contemporary life. The warmth in them is palpable. Cook said, 'I can see things that horrify me and upset me, but I don't want to paint them. If I thought that by painting something very meaningful it would change things then perhaps I would want to, I don't know. But I don't believe that. Instead I think people are getting dulled by the amount of horror. I only paint when I'm excited by something, and what excites me is the joy, the animation, the pleasure in life' (press cutting, 1985, Beryl Cook archive). She was appointed OBE in 1996. Typically she couldn't face going to Buckingham Palace to receive it. She died of cancer, painting almost until the last, in Plymouth, on 28 May 2008. She was survived by her husband and their son. JULIAN SPALDING

Sources B. Cook, *The works* (1978) • B. Cook and C. O'Hare, *Seven years and a day* (1980) • B. Cook, *One man show* (1981) • E. Lucie-Smith and B. Cook, *Bertie and the big red ball* (1982) • N. Newman and B. Cook, *My Granny was a frightful bore (but she isn't any more)* (1983) • *Beryl Cook's New York* (1985) • *Beryl Cook's London* (1988) • B. Cook, *Bouncers* (1991) • B. Cook, *Happy days* (1995) • B. Cook, *The bumper edition* (2000) • J. Wilder and J. Sans, *The world of Beryl Cook* (2007) • *The Times* (29 May 2008) • *Daily Telegraph* (29 May 2008) • *The Guardian* (29 May 2008) • *The Independent* (29 May 2008); (30 May 2008) • Portal Gallery, London, Beryl Cook archive • www.berylcook.org, 1 April 2011 • www.berylcookusa.com, 15 Aug 2011 • *WW* (2008) • personal knowledge (2012) • private information (2012) • b. cert. • m. cert.

Archives Portal Gallery, London | FILM BFINA, 'Beryl Cook and Joint Stock Theatre Group', *South Bank Show*, A. Snell (director), ITV, 25 March 1979 • BFINA, documentary and light entertainment footage • Portal Gallery, London | SOUND BL NSA, performance recording • Portal Gallery, London

Likenesses C. Ware, photograph, 1976, Getty Images, London • B. Cook, self-portrait, 1977, priv. coll. [*see illus.*] • photographs, 1978–2001, Rex Features, London • D. Farson, semi-matte bromide print, 1985, NPG • T. Mercer, C-type colour print, 1987, NPG • B. Cook, self-portrait, oils (*Art and artists RIP*); Bonhams, 19 Nov 2008 • G. Duley, photograph, repro. in *Independent on Sunday* (9 July 1995) • C. Hopkinson, photographs, Camera Press, London • T. Mercer, photograph, repro. in *The Observer* (23 Feb 1986) • S. Norfolk, photograph, repro. in *Sunday Times* (2 Dec 2001) • C. Saville, photograph, repro. in *The Times* (29 Aug 2006) • obituary photographs • portraits, London, Beryl Cook archive

Wealth at death £889,721: probate, 13 Oct 2008, *CGPLA Eng. & Wales*

Cook, Robert Finlayson [Robin] (**1946–2005**), politician, was born in the County Hospital, Bellshill, Lanarkshire, on 28 February 1946, the only child of Peter Cook (*d.* 1994), schoolteacher, and his wife, Christina, *née* Lynch (*d.* 2003). His paternal grandfather was a collier, blacklisted after the 1926 general strike. Peter Cook, who grew up in Fraserburgh, was a scientist of great ability, who passed the Second World War years as a researcher for Imperial Chemical Industries but regretted involvement in its military work; Cook's mother also worked in the same factory in this period. After the war his father became a teacher in Aberdeen, head of science at the Royal High School, Edinburgh, and latterly rector of Kirkcudbright Academy.

School, university, and Edinburgh corporation Cook was educated at Aberdeen grammar school and the Royal High School, Edinburgh, where he was a pupil for three years. At Edinburgh he was one of the talented leftish generation that included the political scientist Iain McLean, the economist John Kay, Brian Lang, later principal of the University of St Andrews, the actor Ian Charleson, and the poet John Whitworth. Cook was an academic high achiever and passionately bookish, but also developed an early interest in left-wing politics. As a prefect he daringly sported Campaign for Nuclear Disarmament and anti-apartheid badges, getting away with it because no master fancied a rhetorical fencing match. Both at school and at the University of Edinburgh (1964–8) he excelled in debating.

At university Cook read English literature, with an original intention to enter the ministry of the Church of Scotland; later he was one of the very few MPs who described himself as an atheist. He was very politically active, campaigning for the Labour Party in the 1964 general election, and went on to become chair of the university Labour club and co-chairman (with George Robertson, a future Labour cabinet minister) of the Scottish Association of Labour Student Organizations. Earnestness was relieved by a complex social life, run from his own flat

Robert Finlayson [Robin] **Cook** (**1946–2005**), by Flying Colours, 2005

(quite unusual at the time for a Scottish student) in Goldenacre, shared with, among others, John Whitworth. For a time Cook simultaneously had two girlfriends, Maureen Clarke, and Margaret Katherine Whitmore (*b.* 1944), daughter of Lewis Arthur Whitmore, a former RAF officer and aeronautical engineer from Somerset. Margaret studied medicine at Edinburgh and was active in the university's nationalist club. He ultimately became engaged to her in 1967, and the couple married at St Alban's Church, Westbury Park, Bristol, on 15 September 1969. Later they lived rather separate lives as Margaret pursued her medical career in Scotland (rising to become a hospital consultant) and Robin his political career. Their bonds included their two sons, Christopher (*b.* 1973) and Peter (*b.* 1974), and a love of horse-riding.

Cook graduated in 1968 with a disappointing upper second in English literature. He started, but did not complete, a doctorate on Charles Dickens and Victorian serial novels, supervised by John Sutherland, who admitted to being overawed by his charge. Having abandoned his thesis, Cook taught for a time in West Lothian secondary schools. In 1970 he took over from his friend Ian Jordan (focal point of an agreeable leftish Edinburgh bohemia) as tutor-organizer of the Workers' Educational Association for Lothian, under Jack Kane, leader of the Labour group on Edinburgh corporation. This was usually seen as a post more political than educational, and involved such duties as running conferences on poverty and housing and weekend schools for trade unionists.

In 1971 Cook, now secretary of the Edinburgh city Labour Party, was elected to Edinburgh corporation (the local authority) as a councillor. The corporation, run by the nominally independent Progressive Party (in reality a Conservative–Liberal coalition), was at the time unduly influenced by the building interest. This influence extended to Labour members of the corporation whose relations with the city party were remote. Cook was one of a group of young left-wingers who reimposed party control and was instrumental in defeating a cross-party lobby that favoured a highly destructive inner-city ring road. Out of this came a well-organized, reforming Labour Party that captured key committee chairs from the Progressives and held full power from 1980 until 2007. Cook, as convener of the housing committee (1973–4), played a major part in this. By changing the emphasis of the slum clearance programme from demolition to renovation he succeeded in saving 3000 properties in central Edinburgh, an achievement of which he remained very proud. Cook's time at Edinburgh corporation was brief but important in revealing his approach to politics, notably a concern for the effective operation of democratic institutions, and in laying the foundations for Labour's long dominance in what had been Scotland's most conservative city.

By this time Cook had parliamentary ambitions. He had already stood unsuccessfully in the Conservative-held seat of Edinburgh North in the 1970 general election. When the MP for Edinburgh Central subsequently announced his retirement, Cook sought selection for the seat. He was seen as the candidate from the party's left and his main opponent, George Foulkes (himself later to become a Labour minister), as the candidate from the party's right. Cook won the selection, and went on to win the seat in the general election of February 1974—on his twenty-eighth birthday—extending his small majority in the second election of October that year. He held it until redistribution in 1983, whereupon he switched to the safer seat of Livingston (beating Tony Benn to the selection), which he represented until his death.

Early parliamentary career As a new backbencher Cook quickly joined Labour's centre-left Tribune group, to which he emotionally belonged throughout his life. He built a strong political relationship in particular with Neil Kinnock, another ginger-haired Tribunite with a background in the Workers' Educational Association, who had entered parliament in 1970. Cook rapidly gained a reputation as a formidable and meticulous debater, who (unlike many other MPs) spent far more time in the House of Commons library than in the bars. His interests continued to include housing and nuclear disarmament, and he also pursued issues such as the transparency and accountability of arms sales and the security services. During his early years in parliament Cook championed several liberalizing social measures, to mixed effect. He repeatedly (and unsuccessfully) introduced a private member's bill on divorce reform in Scotland, but succeeded in July 1980—and after three years' trying—with an amendment to bring the Scottish law on homosexuality into line with that in England.

Cook's entry to the Commons had coincided with Harold Wilson's second, crisis-ridden Labour administration, and with the growing prominence and effectiveness of the Scottish National Party (SNP) in the two elections of 1974. The SNP's challenge caused the Labour leadership to impose a policy commitment to devolution on its Scottish party in time for the October contest. Cook had previously been hostile to devolution, but expressed support in his October 1974 election address. In the following year, in an essay on housing for the *Red Paper on Scotland* edited by Gordon Brown (then rector of Edinburgh University), Cook declared himself reconciled to a Scottish parliament, though he argued that the existence of this alone would not improve the poor living conditions of many Scots. However, in 1978 Cook reverted to his original position when Labour sought to proceed with Scottish devolution and took a militantly hostile line against the policy, much to the chagrin of his friend and constituency party chairman, the American political scientist Henry Drucker. Along with some in the Scottish Labour Party he was involved with the 'No to devo!' campaigns, while others such as Gordon Brown supported the proposals for a new Scottish assembly. Cook, unlike some Labour opponents of devolution, notably Tam Dalyell, was accused of working with the opposition to undermine the proposals. This episode earned him lasting distrust among some of his fellow Scots.

After Labour lost power in May 1979 Cook encouraged Michael Foot's bid to become party leader and joined his campaign committee. Foot's success over Denis Healey was seen as a victory for the left. But when Tony Benn challenged Healey for the party's deputy leadership in September 1981 (a move which split the left) Cook accepted *realpolitik*, declaring of Healey 'I will down four double-whiskies and give him my vote' (private information). Foot's leadership brought Cook his first position on the Labour front bench in 1980, as a junior member of the shadow Treasury team under Peter Shore. In this role he further developed his growing reputation as a highly effective parliamentarian and a sharp and well-informed debater.

Following Labour's defeat at the polls in June 1983 Cook worked again with Gordon Brown (the newly elected member for Dunfermline) to edit *Scotland: the Real Divide* (1983). This was a collection of essays on Scottish social conditions, intended to reassert the primacy of social policy against the obsession with Scottish identity. But Cook and Brown fell out over the book, which Brown believed Cook had hijacked. The dispute proved lasting, and their subsequently acrimonious relationship had important implications for Cook's career.

Shadow minister In the wake of Labour's 1983 electoral defeat Cook managed the successful campaign of his ally Neil Kinnock to replace Foot as party leader. He was also elected for the first time to the shadow cabinet in June 1983, and given the position of spokesperson on European affairs by the new party leader. On Europe, as on devolution, Cook showed a facility for U-turns, deftly executed. In 1973–5 he had shared the hostility of the Labour left to the EEC, but he was now brought in by Kinnock to manage the party's transition to more united pro-European views. Later both men warmed to the European Commission presidency of Jacques Delors (1985–94), whose combination of market integration with the idea of a 'social Europe' appealed to the moderate left and the trade unions. However, Cook remained in the post for only a year, and was then appointed by Kinnock as party campaign co-ordinator. His subsequent low parliamentary profile contributed to his being voted off the shadow cabinet in 1986, only to return a year later when he was appointed to the far more satisfying post of shadow secretary of state for health and social security. This allowed him to lead with flair in parliament on Labour's most salient policy issue and to score a number of victories over Conservative ministers. One of the most notable encounters took place in April 1988 when Cook contrasted the government's generosity to high earners in the recent budget with the impact of imminent reforms to social security payments on the least well-off. The principal victim of Cook's attack was John Moore, secretary of state at the Department of Health and Social Security, who, as one of Margaret Thatcher's good-looking dauphins, was then regarded as a potential successor. Moore's political career suffered greatly from encounters like these and he left the cabinet a year later.

Cook's successes won him a seat on the party's national executive committee in 1988, which he held continuously for ten years, often topping the poll. He also regularly came first in the poll of MPs for the shadow cabinet. But he remained a man more respected—for his retentive memory, forensic analysis, and fluent oratory—than widely liked. His reputation was as 'a cat who walks by himself': not always trustworthy, never clubbable, and with little patience for the kind of work required to build up a 'Cook faction' or to woo political journalists. 'Those of his rivals who had got where they were through schmoozing as much as by intellectual rigour distrusted a man who regarded raw argument as the only legitimate route to success' (Kampfner, 66). The Conservatives saw him as a threat, but so did some on his own front bench. His erudition could be combined with a wit and charm many political opponents—and many women—found winning, though to others he could appear pompous and smug. In his spare time, having been introduced to horses by his wife, he was, unusually for a Labour MP, often to be found at the races. Between 1991 and 1998 he wrote a weekly tipster's column for the Glasgow *Herald* newspaper and from 1989 was, to the surprise of many, a close friend of the television racing pundit—and arch-Conservative—John McCririck.

Defeat for Labour in the 1992 general election brought about another change of leader, with Cook again acting as kingmaker—this time as campaign manager for John Smith. Smith appointed Cook as shadow secretary of state for trade and industry, a position which he had long coveted but been denied, partly because Gordon Brown had insisted he be kept out of economic affairs. The collegial John Smith appointed Brown as his shadow chancellor, and induced the two to co-operate. When Smith died unexpectedly in May 1994 Cook gave serious consideration to running for the leadership himself, but prevaricated. It was not clear whether he had a sufficient following to win a contest, and he also famously commented that he did not have the looks for leadership in the television age (his gnomish appearance was often highlighted by political cartoonists). Ultimately he was overtaken by the negotiations that brought Tony Blair to the Labour leadership through the 'Granita compact' with Gordon Brown. Thereafter the two men contrived to keep Cook out of domestic politics, and he was made shadow foreign secretary: a prestigious but not wholly welcome appointment. One exception to this sidelining was the position he was given brokering a deal with the Liberal Democrats over Labour's plans for constitutional reform. The 1997 'Cook–Maclennan report' (with the Liberal Democrat Robert Maclennan) set out a blueprint for devolution, a human rights act, freedom of information legislation, House of Lords reform, and modernization of the House of Commons. Much of this was implemented when Labour came to power.

Cook's reputation as a formidable parliamentary performer received one further boost in opposition when, on 15 February 1996, he led the Commons debate on the report from Sir Richard Scott's inquiry into the 'arms to Iraq' affair. This followed the collapse of a trial of the three directors of Matrix Churchill, a British manufacturing company, charged with misleading ministers on the end use of machine tools exported to Saddam Hussein's Iraq. Scott's inquiry established that ministers were aware of the company's actions and of the tools' potential military application, and the report criticized both the Thatcher and Major governments for not announcing to parliament that rules on exports to Iraq had been relaxed. John Major, his administration in free fall since 'black Wednesday' in September 1992, tried to scupper the opposition's challenge by making Scott's 1800-page report available to Cook alone only three hours before the debate began; government ministers, by contrast, had received multiple copies eight days earlier. But Major reckoned without Cook's intelligence and assiduity in good forward planning and preparation, based in part on his attendance at several of the original inquiry hearings. This resulted in the composition and delivery of a devastating analysis of government dissimulation. In a subsequent adjournment debate, on 26 February, Major carried a vote of confidence by a majority of one. Just over a year later Labour was returned to office with the largest parliamentary majority since 1935.

Foreign secretary, 1997–2001 The balance of power in the 1997 Labour cabinet remained much as it was in opposition. The effective division was between the prime minister (Blair) and the chancellor of the exchequer (Brown). The economy (generously defined) was 'Gordon's thing', while Cook was made foreign secretary. In this role he shared control of foreign policy with Blair and Clare Short, in charge of the Department for International Development. Making any sort of concert against the Blair–Brown dyarchy would have required solidarity between Cook and Short: but, despite both coming from the party's 'soft left', this was ruled out by a mutual hostility that deepened in office following disputes over departmental responsibilities. Meanwhile Blair's advisers were distrustful of both ministers, and Downing Street retained a tight control of all government departments.

Cook sought to make his mark early, launching a new mission statement for the Foreign Office within two weeks of the election. This called for 'an ethical dimension' to British foreign policy, which 'must support the demands of other peoples for the democratic rights on which we insist for ourselves' (*The Times*, 13 May 1997). Cook wanted to see closer scrutiny of arms sales and more focus on environmental protection and human rights, alongside greater British co-operation in Europe. He built good relations with Madeleine Albright, American secretary of state in the administration of President Bill Clinton, and with key players in Europe including Joschka Fischer, German foreign minister in Gerhard Schröder's coalition. Cook also sought to change the internal culture of the Foreign Office, for example by encouraging young non-white and female candidates to consider careers in the foreign and diplomatic service. The distinctly informal style that he adopted pleased some, but by no means all, of his civil servants, and was to cause some difficulties with foreign leaders.

Cook's tenure at the Foreign Office saw a number of important policy initiatives. In May 1997 he announced a ban on the use and stockpiling of landmines and later that year oversaw the handover of Hong Kong to China; he negotiated the trial, under Scots law, of the Libyan suspects accused of bombing Pan Am flight 103 over Lockerbie; and helped press Iraq's Saddam Hussein into readmitting UN weapons inspectors. He also supported NATO intervention on behalf of the Kosovo Albanians in May 1999, and punitive strikes against the Serbs, hitherto regarded by Foreign Office orthodoxy as a dependable *force majeure* in the region.

But Cook's ministerial career also faced an early threat when on 3 August 1997 the *News of the World* broke the story of his long-standing relationship with his Commons secretary, Gaynor Regan (*b.* 1957). Pressed by the prime minister's official spokesman Alastair Campbell, Cook announced immediately that he would be separating from his wife. Despite this quick decision, and Blair's full public support, Cook faced a barrage of media comment. Margaret, from whom he was divorced in March 1998, began writing news columns that were often critical. In 1999 she went further, publishing a book (*A Slight and Delicate Creature*) recording the marriage, which criticized him as a man and a politician, alleging insensitivity, drunkenness, adultery, and depression. This significantly weakened Cook's position, and enhanced the prime minister's power of manoeuvre with respect to policy. None the less Cook's personal life quickly became more settled, and he married Gaynor Regan, daughter of Alan and Joan Wellings, at Tunbridge Wells register office on 9 April 1998.

The realities of office imposed themselves elsewhere. The economic importance of the UK's defence industry and the prominence of politically well-connected companies like British Aerospace meant that Downing Street was distinctly less keen than Cook on new controls on arms exports. Cook's 'ethical' approach was severely challenged when the government failed to reverse a 1996 agreement to deliver Hawk jets to Suharto's Indonesia, which was actively supporting repression in East Timor. Similarly Cook was seriously embarrassed in summer 1998 by the disclosures that followed an intervention by a British security firm, Sandline International, to restore the democratically elected ruler of Sierra Leone who had been ousted in a coup in the previous year. Claims that Sandline—under investigation for contravening a UN embargo to supply arms to Sierra Leone—had been advised by Foreign Office officials, coupled with disputes over the extent to which ministers were aware of the investigation, pointed to a department in turmoil. Cook also got into difficulties over the delicate issue of Kashmir when accompanying the queen on a state visit to Pakistan and India in October 1997, which led to the British delegation being snubbed by the Indian prime minister.

From 2000 onwards transatlantic relations became far more difficult for Cook. He had worked well with the Clinton administration, but found himself less comfortable than Blair in switching allegiance to the new right-wing Republican president, George W. Bush. He was also, thanks to the Matrix Churchill affair, all too well-versed in Anglo-American collaboration with Saddam Hussein. But despite Cook's concern over the new Republican administration many on the left of the Labour Party remained critical of what they saw as his neglect of former principles. According to the journalist Jackie Ashley, the Foreign Office years saw the eclipse of 'Radical Robin': 'New Cook lived in big houses, was photographed in foreign parts wearing funny hats and was peppery rather than dry. He was not a popular success' (*The Guardian*, 7 Jan 2002).

In late 1998 one alternative had presented itself to Cook that might have had significant constitutional consequences. In the wake of the referendum in August 1997 paving the way for the establishment of a Scottish parliament, Donald Dewar, secretary of state for Scotland, had taken a bruising getting the Government of Scotland Act through Westminster. Dewar was undecided about whether he wanted to stand as first minister of Scotland, and Cook considered putting himself forward. Despite his early reservations he had become a convert to devolution as long ago as 1983, and was now a firm proponent. Had he taken the job he would have been a formidable (and to Whitehall not always a friendly) performer. But, as with the Labour leadership in 1994, he prevaricated—bogged down by a Foreign Office workload and the fallout from his personal difficulties. Ultimately he held back, probably much to the relief of Blair and Brown.

Leader of the house, 2001–2003 In June 2001 Blair demoted Cook to leader of the House of Commons in his second government. The Bush–Cook incompatibility may have played a part, along with Europe, as Brown was widely believed to have demanded the Europhile Cook's removal from foreign affairs. He was replaced by the more Eurosceptic Jack Straw. Cook felt the humiliation, but managed to retain the foreign secretary's flat in Carlton Gardens, briskly rallied, and set about work on another of his passions: constitutional reform. Unlike his predecessors since 1997 he was seen as a reforming leader of the house, more in the mould of Richard Crossman or Norman St John Stevas. As (*ex officio*) chair of the modernization committee he oversaw changes to strengthen the select committees, responsible for scrutinizing government departments, and to reform the legislative process, including publication of more bills in draft form. Here he paid close attention to the new Scottish parliament, which was getting into its stride in Edinburgh, with family-friendly hours and a powerful committee structure. His ambitions were, however, constantly reined in by number 10 and the Labour whips, who orchestrated a humiliating defeat of one of his key proposals, to reform select committee appointments, in May 2002.

During this period Cook also took a lively interest in questions of political disengagement (much discussed following the slump in voter turnout in 2001), exploring ways to reconnect parliament with the public and possibilities such as online voting. His own preference would have been a move to proportional representation, but this was off the political agenda. Instead he intervened in the debate on House of Lords reform. Working with sympathetic Labour MPs (and some from the opposition parties), he essentially derailed proposals from the lord chancellor, Derry Irvine, for a largely appointed house with a minority elected element, though Cook's own preference for a mainly elected upper chamber was also defeated in a free vote in February 2003. Cook's enthusiasm for a largely elected second chamber was certainly not calculated to make him more popular with the prime minister, who publicly expressed concern that a democratically legitimate upper house would challenge the primacy of the Commons.

The tensions with Blair finally came to a head over a different matter. In the aftermath of the attacks on New York and Washington on 11 September 2001, Cook became steadily more distrustful of the prime minister's pursuit of an American alliance in the Middle East at the expense of the United Nations. The cabinet's circumspect discussions of policy towards Iraq seemed increasingly to be paralleled by pro-American initiatives hatched by Blair in his private office. To Cook the consequence of this would be the emasculation of the international rule of law in favour of submission to the will of the United States as a 'hyper-power', alongside greater instability in the Middle East. Having advocated Britain's need to be at the heart of the European Union while foreign secretary, Cook also warned that Blair's approach was detrimental both to relations with France and Germany and to the chances of winning a proposed referendum on Britain's entry into the euro. He repeatedly spoke out in cabinet and expressed his concerns behind the scenes. The Matrix Churchill affair had given him a deep knowledge of the ambiguous coils of previous British policy towards Iraq. This, combined with his continued links with foreign affairs specialists at home and overseas (not least as the elected president of the Party of European Socialists, 2001–4), made Cook severely doubtful over claims about 'weapons of mass destruction', which Blair cited as the *casus belli*. Cook's efforts to encourage the prime minister to seek a second UN resolution prior to military action in March 2003 against Iraq, and for Britain to refuse to participate without one, proved unsuccessful. However, as leader of the house Cook did work closely with Jack Straw to persuade Blair that a prior vote in parliament was necessary in order to legitimate military action. He finally resigned from the government on 17 March 2003, denouncing the prime minister's actions in a measured speech that asserted Britain's interests as 'best protected not by unilateral action but by multilateral agreement and a world order governed by rules'. The speech resulted in that rare (and officially 'unparliamentary') thing, a standing ovation in the House of Commons. As a back-bencher for the first time in twenty years, he was one of 139 Labour MPs to vote against the invasion of Iraq on the following day. None the less the vote was won with Conservative support. Two days later the invasion of Iraq by American, British, and coalition forces had begun.

Since 2001 Cook had kept a diary and in October 2003 he published an edited version as *The Point of Departure*, his account of the Iraq crisis and other events of the period. The book stood out from other ministerial memoirs, usually evasive and self-serving, of the Thatcher–Blair era. Its style was fluent and sophisticated, and the account of cabinet government under New Labour was analytical and frank, but never vitriolic. Cook also took up a weekly newspaper column, initially in *The Guardian* and later in *The Independent*, where he reflected upon national and international issues, including Iraq, the Middle East, and the state of British democracy. Again he was often critical of the Blair–Bush line, but his words—frequently laced with wit—were chosen carefully to be constructive rather than hostile.

Despite his criticisms of the government Cook remained an unrepentant Labour loyalist. With Blair's popularity waning, he campaigned vigorously in the run-up to the 2005 general election to persuade Labour doubters to remain with the party. This almost certainly helped save some seats, though many others were lost and the government was returned with a reduced Commons majority of sixty-six. Cook himself won Livingston with—against the trend—an increased majority. The future remained unclear, but there was much speculation that he would return to the cabinet once Gordon Brown (as expected) took over as prime minister—particularly given that, since Cook's resignation, the two had finally been reconciled. But no such opportunity was to present itself. On 6 August 2005 he and Gaynor were walking near the top of Ben Stack in the far north-west of Scotland when he suffered a heart attack and a fall from the path. A nearby climber summoned a helicopter from RAF Kinloss, but Cook was pronounced dead on arrival at Raigmore Hospital, Inverness. On 12 August he was accorded something akin to a state funeral at St Giles's Cathedral in Edinburgh, where his old rival Gordon Brown delivered a secular eulogy from the pulpit of John Knox. Cook's popularity had grown, particularly since his resignation, and the genuine warmth with which he was now regarded was demonstrated by the crowds that lined the streets. Large numbers of MPs broke off from their holidays to attend the service and the only notable absence among cabinet members, pointedly criticized from the pulpit by John McCririck, was Tony Blair. A later memorial service at St Margaret's Church, Westminster, included a reading by Blair and warm tributes by Brown and Madeleine Albright. Cook's friend and election agent since 1983, Jim Devine, won the resulting by-election with a reduced majority.

Assessment Robin Cook was often accused of immodesty. He once recorded his proudest achievements at the Foreign Office as 'Breaking the deadlock in the Lockerbie case; defending Kosovo; saving lives and relieving suffering in Sierra Leone; contributing to the fall of Milosevic; transforming Britain's relations with Europe; rebuilding respect for Britain in the world' (*The Guardian*, 10 April 2001). In 2007, when his gravestone was erected in Edinburgh's Grange cemetery, the inscription, chosen from *The Point of Departure* by his wife, Gaynor, and his two sons, was simpler: 'I may not have succeeded in halting the war, but I did secure the right of Parliament to decide on war.'

Cook will certainly be remembered first and foremost as a parliamentarian, and probably the most accomplished orator of his generation. He was also one of only two cabinet members under Blair to resign on a point of principle (his resignation was followed by that of Clare Short). In many ways his strengths were also his weaknesses. More than many of his contemporaries he struggled with reconciling his strongly held left-wing values with the compromises his party made in order to gain and hold on to power. Skill in debate meant the ability to construct a powerful case, but his language also put down vivid markers of conviction that were often difficult to depart from. He suffered many obstacles, both in opposition and in government. Like a rider over the sticks, he excelled by staying on. But many of the hurdles were self-made; someone less cocky might have employed more diplomacy to dismantle or evade them. Had his government posts been reversed—had he been leader of the house first and subsequently foreign secretary—the movement he built up behind him might have sustained him against the 'government by cabinet faction' that marked the Blair years. Had he built this movement earlier, his achievements could have been even greater.

Another personal aside perhaps comes closest to the man: 'The two most exciting sights and noises I know are these: first, a large field coming into a steeplechase fence; the other is the clang of the tin-ballot boxes as they hit the floor on election night' (*The Independent*, 26 Sept 1998).

CHRISTOPHER HARVIE

Sources C. Harvie, *Fool's gold: the story of North Sea oil* (1993) · P. Anderson and N. Mann, *Safety first: the making of New Labour* (1997) · J. Kampfner, *Robin Cook* (1998) · M. Cook, *A slight and delicate creature* (1999) · A. Rawnsley, *Servants of the people* (2000) · P. Toynbee and D. Walker, *Did things get better?* (2001) · C. Hill, 'Foreign policy', *The Blair effect*, ed. A. Seldon (2001) · R. Cook, *The point of departure* (2003) · P. Toynbee and D. Walker, *Better or worse?* (2005) · *The Times* (8 Aug 2005) · *Daily Telegraph* (8 Aug 2005) · *The Independent* (8 Aug 2005) · *Financial Times* (8 Aug 2005) · *The Guardian* (12 Aug 2005) · *WW* (2005) · personal knowledge (2009) · private information (2009) · b. cert. · m. certs.

Archives FILM BFINA, current affairs footage · BFINA, documentary footage · BFINA, party political footage | SOUND BL NSA, current affairs recordings

Likenesses photographs, 1958–2005, Rex Features, London · photographs, 1971–2004, Camera Press, London · photographs, 1974–2004, Photoshot, London · photographs, 1982–2005, PA Photos, London · photographs, 1983–2005, Getty Images, London · M. Glover, charcoal drawing, 1984, priv. coll. · J. Mendoza, group portrait, oils, 1986–7, House of Commons, Westminster, London · S. Humphrey, drawing, 1995, priv. coll. · H. Jones, oils, in or before 2000, priv. coll. · S. Amery, bust, clay model, in or before 2001, priv. coll.; cast, U. Edin. · K. Mar, oils, 2003, priv. coll. · Flying Colours, photograph, 2005, Getty Images, London [*see illus.*] · F. Carlisle, portrait, House of Commons, Westminster, London · obituary photographs

Coombs, Robert Royston Amos [Robin] (1921–2006), immunologist, was born Robert Royston Amos on 9 January 1921 at 4 Laurel Bank, Hoop Lane, Golders Green, London, the younger son of Charles Royston Amos (1892–1929), company director and former RAF officer, and his wife, Edris Owen, *née* Coombs (1891–1960x69). His maternal grandfather, Robert Coombs, was a founder in 1872 of the firm of Clarke, Nickolls, and Coombs, abbreviated as Clarnico, the well-known confectioners. Charles Amos left the family shortly after Robin was born, taking no further part in the care of his sons. Grandfather Coombs took on their financial support. Edris resumed her maiden name and the two boys later adopted Coombs as their surname. In 1929 she emigrated with her sons to South Africa. Robin Coombs was sent to the Diocesan College in Rondebosch near Cape Town. Reading *Microbe Hunters* (1926) by Paul de Kruif turned his ambitions towards becoming a bacteriologist. He became friendly with a local veterinarian who fired his interest in a career in veterinary medicine.

After finishing his schooling in South Africa in 1938 by taking the London matriculation examination when he was only seventeen, Coombs returned on his own to the UK to study veterinary medicine at the University of Edinburgh. He was a highly successful veterinary student and won all the available prizes. He qualified as a veterinarian in 1943. He was then directed to war work at the Ministry of Agriculture's veterinary research laboratory at Weybridge to work with Norman Hole on glanders, a fatal disease of horses, which was then considered as a possible biological warfare agent. This was a seminal event in Coombs's life and largely influenced the course of his subsequent scientific career. The sero-diagnostic test then used for glanders was complement fixation and this aroused his interest in techniques for measuring antibodies; in the complement system; and, indeed, in immunology in general. These interests he maintained throughout his life. Norman Hole formed a high opinion of Coombs's abilities and suggested that he study for a PhD in immunology. He duly went to Cambridge in 1944 and never lived anywhere else again.

During the Second World War the Galton Laboratory serum unit, including Robert Race and Arthur Mourant, was evacuated to the Cambridge pathology department. The unit was interested in the recently described Rhesus blood groups. Antibodies against Rhesus antigens do not agglutinate cells bearing these antigens, which made their measurement extremely difficult. This problem excited Coombs's interest. The story goes that he was returning from London on a dark wartime train when the image of a Christmas tree on the station platform suggested to him that red cell membrane could be viewed as having protrusions and valleys with the rhesus antigen so low in the valleys that an antibody reacting with it would not rise above the protrusions and so be out of reach of Rhesus antigens on another red cell. He recognized that when the antibodies reacted with red cells they would coat them with immunoglobulin and postulated that a further anti-immunoglobulin antibody should then produce agglutination. He rapidly showed that an antiglobulin would indeed agglutinate Rhesus positive cells carrying anti-Rhesus antibodies. This work made his name internationally well-known even before he finished his PhD. He always called the technique the 'antiglobulin reaction' but in the wider immunological and haematological world it became known as the Coombs test. Subsequently Coombs produced an extensive stable of variants of the antiglobulin reaction which could be used for detecting antigens as well as antibodies. These included tests for blood group antigens in blood smears, which proved of some forensic value; and very simple tests for 'near patient' detection of infectious organisms.

In 1946 Coombs was elected John Lucas Walker student in the department of pathology. He obtained his PhD in 1947 for a thesis entitled 'The conglutination and sensitization reactions', the first half being devoted to work on the conglutinating complement fixation reaction and only the second to the antiglobulin reaction. In 1947 he was elected Stringer fellow of King's College, Cambridge. In 1950 he became assistant director of research in animal pathology. In 1953 this appointment was transferred to the department of pathology, and he remained assistant director of research there until 1963 when he was promoted to reader. Meanwhile in 1962 he had been elected a fellow of Corpus Christi College and remained a fellow there happily for the rest of his life. In 1968 he was elected to the Quick chair of biology, which he held until his retirement in 1988. He married, on 13 September 1952, at the parish church in Beccles, Suffolk, Anne Marion Blomfield, a 29-year-old pathologist who had been his first graduate student, daughter of Charles Geoffrey Blomfield, architect. They had a son and a daughter.

In pursuing his chosen research projects Coombs sought out collaborators with their own expertise, and he liked to build a team of such workers. He attracted graduate students and post-doctoral workers from all over the world, and his laboratory was always an extremely interesting mix of immunologists from different countries and with different scientific backgrounds. He was keen to connect immunology to the clinic, and in the mid-1970s moved a section of the immunology division to laboratory space at the new Addenbrooke's Hospital site. He saw enormous diagnostic potential for simple red blood cell-based immunoassays. He demonstrated that such assays had great potential in many types of real-world situations with unmet needs. One such situation was the detection of pathogens, particularly viruses, directly in clinical samples.

A major contribution that Coombs, together with his close friend Philip Gell, professor of immunology at the University of Birmingham, made in their textbook *The Clinical Aspects of Immunology* (1963) was to classify the allergic mechanisms of tissue damage, that is the mechanisms by which the results of the immune response could give rise to tissue damage rather than to immunity. The four types then described proved extremely durable. Coombs explored for many years the theory that cot death, at least in part, could be explained by an allergic reaction to cows' milk regurgitated and inhaled when children are asleep. While it is almost certain that cot death has no single cause, the idea that anaphylaxis to inhaled cows' milk is one causative factor remains highly plausible.

During the Second World War immunology in the United Kingdom had gone into some decline and in the immediate aftermath of the war, the discovery of penicillin and the promise of antibiotics led to the (mistaken) view that the problems of infectious disease were likely to be fully conquered very quickly. The renaissance of immunology after the war was led by a remarkable group of people who formed the core of what became the British Society of Immunology. They included, besides Coombs and Gell, John Humphrey, head of immunology at Mill Hill; John Marrack, who had been professor of chemical pathology at the London Hospital but joined Coombs in Cambridge after his retirement; and Robert White, professor of microbiology and immunology at Glasgow. Slightly separate was another group that was greatly involved in the birth of transplant immunology, in which Peter Gorer and Peter Medawar were the main figures. The British Society for Immunology was founded in 1955 and Coombs became its first general secretary. He devoted a great deal of energy and effort to establishing it and it became, and remained, a remarkably successful society. Its meetings were never short of exciting scientific controversy and maintained a very high standard. Coombs was devoted to the idea that immunology should stand as an independent discipline for university teaching and among the pathological disciplines. The fact that this largely became the case was in no small part due to his efforts. After he retired from office at the society in 1965 he never again involved himself in the public aspects of the subject and decided that what he really liked was to be in his laboratory with his students and that the world of London committees was perhaps not one in which he would care to be too closely involved. He nevertheless received many honours, including the Gairdner Foundation award (1965), the Henry Steele gold medal of the Royal College of Veterinary Surgeons (1966), the James Calvert Spence medal of the British Paediatric Association (1967), the Philip Levine award of the American Society of Clinical Pathology (1969), and the British Society for Haematology medal (1993). He was elected a fellow of the Royal Society in 1965 and of the Royal College of Pathologists in 1969, and an honorary fellow of the Royal College of Physicians in 1973. He received honorary doctorates from four universities.

When he retired in 1988 Coombs gave up all scientific work but this didn't entirely suit him and he returned to writing up his theories on cot death. His last few years were blighted by progressive dementia and he died at Midfield Lodge nursing home, Oakington, Cambridge, of bronchopneumonia, on 25 January 2006. He was survived by his wife, Anne, his son, Robert, a neonatologist, and his daughter, Rosalind, who worked in the book trade.

PETER J. LACHMANN

Sources *The Times* (6 March 2006) · *The Independent* (6 March 2006) · *The Guardian* (8 March 2006) · *Daily Telegraph* (30 March 2006) · *The Lancet*, 367 (15 April 2006), 1234 · *BMJ*, 332 (24 June 2006), 1514 · A. A. Konugres, *Transfusion*, 46/10 (Oct 2006), 1845–6 · A. B. Kay, *Vox Sanguinis*, 91 (2006), 93–4 · A. B. Kay, *Clinical and Experimental Allergy*, 36/6 (2006), 687–8 · D. H. Pamhilon and M. L. Scott, 'Robin Coombs: his life and contribution to haematology and transfusion medicine', *British Journal of Haematology*, 137/5 (June 2007), 401–8 · *Memoirs FRS*, 55 (2009), 45–58 · Munk, *Roll* · M. Scott, Professor Robin Coombs, www.bbts.org.uk/news/details.cfm?newsId=54, 5 Feb 2009 · *WW* (2006) · personal knowledge (2010) · private information (2010) · b. cert. · m. cert. · d. cert.
Archives Wellcome L., papers
Likenesses W. Bird, photograph, RS · obituary photographs
Wealth at death £238,508: probate, 30 Nov 2006, *CGPLA Eng. & Wales*

Corbet, Philip Steven (1929–2008), entomologist, was born on 21 May 1929 in Kuala Lumpur, Malaya, the eldest child in the family of three boys and one girl of (Alexander) Steven Corbet (1896–1948), a soil microbiologist at the Rubber Research Institute in Kuala Lumpur, and his wife, Irene, *née* Trewavas. His two brothers died in infancy. His father's love of natural history, and of entomology in particular (he was an authority on the butterflies of Malaya), was a strong influence on his two surviving children, who both became distinguished professional entomologists. The family returned to England in 1932, but during the Second World War Philip moved with his mother and sister to New Zealand, where he attended Nelson Boys' College, set in a rural province in the north of the South Island. Meanwhile his father was appointed to the staff of the British Museum (Natural History), to work on the butterfly collections, where he rose to become deputy keeper of entomology. His sister-in-law, Ethelwyn Trewavas, an authority on African lake fish, was also on the staff of the museum. When the war ended the family were reunited and lived in Reading, but Corbet's father died of a heart attack soon after, following a butterfly-collecting trip in Hampshire.

Corbet completed his schooling after spending a year as a boarder at Dauntsey's School, Wiltshire (1945–6), where he had his first formal lessons in biology. He took a place at Reading University to read zoology (1946–50), where he took a first-class honours degree and received the Colin Morley prize for zoology. From 1950 to 1953 he studied the seasonal regulation in dragonflies at Gonville and Caius College, Cambridge, under the supervision of V. B. Wigglesworth, for his PhD thesis. This work confirmed his love for dragonflies and led to the publication in 1960 of the seminal book *Dragonflies* in the New Naturalists series, which he co-wrote with Cynthia Longfield and Norman Moore. This and a second book, *A Biology of Dragonflies* (1962), established Corbet's reputation as the world's leading authority on dragonflies and a master of scientific synthesis.

Corbet's first professional appointment, from 1954 to 1957, was as invertebrate zoologist at the east Africa high commission laboratories in Jinja, Uganda, where he studied the ecology and feeding strategies of fish in Lake Victoria. From 1957 to 1962 he was transferred to the East African Virus Research Institute at Entebbe, Uganda, to work on the behaviour and ecology of mosquitoes and the discovery of the mosquito vector of o'nyong-nyong fever, which at the time affected over two million people in Uganda and Kenya.

When Uganda achieved independence in 1962 Corbet took a post at the Entomology Research Institute in Ottawa, where he investigated the breeding strategies of mosquitoes in the Canadian high Arctic. He was also instrumental in identifying and eliminating the nuisance caused by biting flies on the St Lawrence River before Expo 1967 in Montreal. In 1967 he was appointed director of the Canada Agriculture Research Institute at Belleville, Ontario, where the focus of his work was on developing methods of pest management that reduced the use of synthetic organic pesticides. During this period he crystallized his ideas on the role of human populations in destabilizing ecosystems and precipitating pest outbreaks. Thereafter he took every opportunity to call for national policies on sustainable development.

These convictions led Corbet to accept posts first as professor and chairman of the biology department at the University of Waterloo, Ontario, in 1971, and then, in 1974, as professor and director of the Joint Centre for Environmental Sciences at the University of Canterbury, New Zealand, where he was able to pursue his ideas on integrated holistic environmental studies. In New Zealand he had the opportunity to present an ecological perspective on various influential forums by serving on the Environmental Council, the government fact-finding group on nuclear energy, the Demographic Society, and the Club of Rome. By 1978 he considered that the job as director of the Joint Centre had become too political and insufficiently scientific so he resigned to take a chair in the department of zoology at the University of Canterbury. Soon afterwards he was awarded a Commonwealth visiting professorship in the department of applied biology at the University of Cambridge.

Corbet was married three times. He married his first wife, Hildegard Gertrud Keller, a teacher who later became a psychiatrist, in Germany on 9 February 1957. They were divorced in 1979. On 15 October 1980, in New Zealand, he married his Swedish second wife, Laila Kristin Kjellström, who held various jobs and was latterly a member of a counselling service. The birth of their daughter, Katarina Alexandra, prompted them in 1980 to return to Britain, where Corbet took the foundation chair in zoology in the department of biological sciences at the University of Dundee. There he was head of department from 1983 to 1986. His second marriage having also ended in divorce, on 31 December 1987 he married Mary Elizabeth Canvin (*b.* 1933), a medical practitioner, in Edinburgh. While at Dundee he served on the Nature Conservancy Council committee for Scotland and chaired the science committee of the Scottish Wildlife Trust. He also brought his considerable scientific and organizational powers to help shape the British Dragonfly Society, which was formed in 1983 and of which he was elected first president, a post he held until 1992. He retired from the University of Dundee as professor emeritus of zoology in 1990 and then spent six years as honorary professor in the department of zoology at Edinburgh University. It was during this period that he was able to complete the highly regarded and comprehensive *Dragonflies: Behaviour and Ecology of Odonata* (1999), which included 830 pages and 4000 references. For this definitive synthesis on dragonflies he was awarded the Neill medal for natural history by the Royal Society of Edinburgh in 2002.

In 1997 Corbet left Scotland and moved to Crean Mill, near St Buryan in the far west of Cornwall, close to the home of his sister and where, his third marriage having also ended in divorce, he met Sarah Jewell, who became his close partner. There he was able to enjoy dragonflies in the mill's garden, which had a stream and large ponds. While living in Cornwall he served on the council and executive of the Cornwall Wildlife Trust and completed his last major project, a new book on *Dragonflies* (co-written with S. J. Brooks) in the New Naturalist series, published a few months after his death.

Corbet was awarded doctorates or honorary doctorates by the universities of Reading (1962), Cambridge (1976), Edinburgh (2003), and Dundee (2005). He was elected a fellow of the Institute of Biology (1967), the Entomological Society of Canada (1977), of which he was president (1971–2) and from which he received the gold medal for outstanding achievement (1974), the Royal Society of Tropical Medicine and Hygiene (1985), the Royal Society of Edinburgh (1987), and the Royal Society of Arts (1991). From 2001 to 2003 he was president of the Worldwide Dragonfly Association.

Corbet was courteous, thoughtful, and quietly spoken. He was incisive, and had a powerful personality and strongly held convictions, valuable assets on the various bodies on which he served. He also had a thorough grasp of the English language and a prodigious memory, which served him well when synthesizing facts on the world's dragonflies. He died at the Royal Cornwall Hospital, Treliske, on 13 February 2008, after suffering a heart attack in the post office at Crean. He was survived by Sarah Jewell and by his daughter, Katarina. STEPHEN J. BROOKS

Sources *The Independent* (28 Feb 2008) · *Daily Telegraph* (6 March 2008) · *The Guardian* (17 March 2008) · *The Times* (31 March 2008) · *Agrion* [special issue] (May 2008) · personal knowledge (2012) · private information (2012) [Sarah Corbet, sister] · m. cert. [1987] · d. cert.

Likenesses obituary photographs · photographs, repro. in *Agrion*

Wealth at death £281,314: probate, 30 June 2008, *CGPLA Eng. & Wales*

Coren, Alan (1938–2007), humorous writer, was born on 27 June 1938 at 2 Queensdown Road, Hackney, London, the son of Samuel Coren, builder and plumber, and his wife, Martha, *née* Coren, hairdresser. At the time of his birth registration his parents lived at 214 Upper Clapton Road, Hackney. Evacuated to Blackpool during the Second World War, he was educated at East Barnet grammar school. An inspirational English teacher there, Annie Brooks, encouraged him to apply to Oxford, where he took a first in English from Wadham College. He remarked later to a friend that you 'can always get a first just by phrase-making' (personal knowledge). The making of wonderful phrases, indeed, was a linchpin of his career. He rejected academe after a graduate Commonwealth fellowship at Yale and Berkeley. Having sent hilarious dispatches on the American university scene to *Punch*, he was made assistant editor of that magazine at the age of twenty-four, and rapidly became an immensely valued writer in other periodicals ranging from *The Spectator* to the *Mail* group of newspapers. He also began writing for television, though the only series he wrote entirely by himself, *The Losers* (1978), starring Leonard Rossiter as a wrestling promoter, was not a success. Meanwhile, on 14 October 1963, at Marble Arch Synagogue, he had married Anne Doris Kasriel (*b*. 1940), then a medical student, later a consultant anaesthetist, daughter of Michael Kasriel, civil engineer. Theirs was a long and famously happy marriage, and produced two children, Giles (*b*. 1969) and Victoria (*b*. 1973).

Coren served as *The Times* television critic from 1971 to 1978, showing both critical acumen—he championed several programmes others ignored—and a fearless willingness to make jokes at the expense of the medium's darlings. Having become deputy editor of *Punch* in 1969 under William Davis, he became editor in 1978. He was noted for his willingness to turn down or demand improvements in copy even from long established or famous contributors. 'Sometimes', he remarked, 'I feel like a wartime RAF officer telling someone their son's bought it' (personal knowledge). But he brought on young writers—Steve Punt, Miles Kington, Michael Bywater, among others—and encouraged women, among them Tina Brown and Libby Purves, at a time when the female 'humorist' and essayist was still regarded with suspicion.

Although his own friendships were broad, eclectic, and often very distinguished indeed, and his cultural frame of reference breathtakingly wide, Coren had a lifelong scorn for establishment self-protection and old-boy networks. Working-class Jewish by birth, he relished the position of an observant, mocking outsider, although serious political satire never much interested him. He found the British class system immensely amusing and a little reprehensible, and for a period there was an uncomfortable hostility between his *Punch* and the public-school establishment satirists over at *Private Eye*.

Alan Coren (1938–2007), by Terry O'Neill, 1990

Coren ran a cheerful office, often playing cricket with a tennis ball along the corridor: Kington recalled the occasion when the ball toppled a pile of magazines and Coren spontaneously exclaimed, 'Spot of trouble among the Spectators, I see' (*The Independent*, 20 Oct 2007). One of his endearing characteristics was an abundant freedom with impromptu jokes, whether in public or among friends and casual acquaintances: he never saved them up for best, or for profit. His daughter, Victoria, remembered such asides as the reply—during the Arab–Israeli War of 1973—to someone asking what kind of artichoke was in the soup: 'Today Jerusalem; tomorrow the globe' (*Daily Mail*, 16 Oct 2008). His years as host of the legendary *Punch* table lunches were convivial—guests, veiled in a heavy fug of cigar smoke, ranged from senior royalty to government ministers, among them his own staff and cartoonists and any unknown writer to whom he had taken a fancy. Although the taking of offence was vanishingly rare, no guest could expect to be immune from mockery: the joke, as ever, came first.

At the time of the oil crisis and City panic in the 1970s

Coren famously amused himself by dressing as an Arab and turning up at the stock exchange, causing considerable uproar. Indeed, he felt no compunction in mocking any target that either deserved it or was just too tempting to resist. His spoof 'Idi Amin' letters in *Punch* were considered uncomfortable by some, with their deliberate parody of black verbal style as well as Amin's savagery and vanity, but he shrugged off criticism. His fearlessness, speed, and thoroughness of research in the odder corners of newspapers made him a treasured member of the *News Quiz* team on Radio 4 from 1975 until his death, although some of his comments were inevitably edited by a nervous BBC. When he died, a memorial edition concluded with a recording of Coren suddenly bursting into song, rendering 'Lili Marlene' in German. Fellow panellists shed genuine tears.

After leaving *Punch* in 1987 Coren edited *The Listener*, again encouraging new writers who later blossomed, such as Lynne Truss. It was his last staff job, but his freelance career remained highly active, notably in *The Times*, on Radio 4, and on television as a long-time panellist on *Call My Bluff*. A devoted father himself within a long marriage, he wrote successful children's books about a character called Arthur who moved from the Wild West to Victorian London. His journalism was widely anthologized in books with surreal titles like *Golfing for Cats* (1975) and *The Lady from Stalingrad Mansions* (1978), yet he claimed to regret that he had not written a novel. Miles Kington remembered him saying seriously:

> When I was writing my piece last night, my wife Anne came and looked over my shoulder as I typed away, and she suddenly said, halfway through reading it: 'When you are 60 years old, are you still going to be writing little pieces about men called Norman Foskett?', and my blood ran cold. (*The Independent*, 20 Oct 2007)

Perhaps his meticulousness, gift of parody, and finicky perfectionism impeded any effort to write the great novel he intended: but as Coren said, humour was to him the most precious of art forms. 'I respond to a bit of sentimentality or nostalgia, but comedy moves me more than anything' (*The Times*, 20 Oct 2007). Alan Hamilton of *The Times* defined his skill as 'a distorted prism. Shine a fact, the more trivial the better, at one side and out of the other would come a refracted rainbow of lateral thinking that would take wing on an updraught of preposterous imagination' (ibid.). His confidence in his own wit and inventiveness made him generous to friends and rivals, often ringing them up to congratulate them on a good line. He was voted by Radio 4 listeners 'the wittiest man in Britain' in 1994, and awarded an honorary doctorate by Nottingham University in 1993 for 'outstanding services to modern literature'. He was known to his readers as the Sage of Cricklewood, and Cricklewood featured in much of his writing. Latterly, though, he lived on the east side of Regent's Park. A smoker, he died on 18 October 2007 at his home, 2 St Katharine's Precinct, Camden, of lung cancer. He was survived by his wife, Anne, and their two children, both of whom had become journalists and broadcasters, and jointly edited a final collection of his work, *Chocolate and Cuckoo Clocks* (2008). A memorial service was held at St Bride's, Fleet Street, on 8 September 2008.

LIBBY PURVES

Sources *Evening Standard* (19 Oct 2007) · *The Times* (20 Oct 2007); (22 Oct 2007); (23 Oct 2007) · *Daily Telegraph* (20 Oct 2007) · *The Guardian* (20 Oct 2007); (25 Oct 2007) · *The Independent* (20 Oct 2007); (29 Oct 2007) · *Sunday Times* (21 Oct 2007) · *The Observer* (21 Oct 2007); (4 Nov 2007) · *Daily Mail* (16 Oct 2008) · *WW* (2007) · personal knowledge (2011) · private information (2011) · b. cert. · m. cert. · d. cert.

Archives FILM BFINA, light entertainment footage | SOUND BL NSA, light entertainment recordings · BL NSA, performance recordings · BL NSA, documentary recordings

Likenesses photographs, 1971–98, PA Photos, London · photographs, 1972–2004, Rex Features, London · G. Howard, bromide fibre print, 1973, NPG · photographs, 1977, Getty Images, London, Hult. Arch. · photographs, 1977–96, Photoshot, London · J. Blau, bromide print, 1978, Camera Press, London · G. Levine, photographs, 1978–85, Getty Images, London, Hult. Arch. · T. Leighton, bromide prints, 1987, NPG · T. O'Neill, photograph, 1990, Getty Images, London [*see illus.*] · M. Dunkerton, photograph, repro. in *Sunday Times* (28 May 1989) · obituary photographs

Wealth at death £3,173,948: probate, 19 March 2008, *CGPLA Eng. & Wales*

Corley, Sir Kenneth Sholl Ferrand (1908–2005), industrialist, was born at Rosthwaite, Westley Road, Acocks Green, Birmingham, on 3 November 1908, the son of Sydney Walter Corley, insurance inspector, and his wife, Annie Louise, *née* Sholl. He was educated at St Bees School in Cumberland. At the age of nineteen he joined the Birmingham firm of Joseph Lucas & Son Ltd, which specialized in electrical components for the automotive and aviation industries. He remained with the firm until his retirement forty-five years later.

On joining Lucas, Corley was sent to the firm's depot in Leyton, where he learned the technical side of the business before returning to Birmingham to learn the commercial side by being 'office boy' to F. H. Walker, the firm's general manager and a future director. Corley first came to prominence in the firm when he was dispatched to Lowestoft in 1929 to act on behalf of the company when it acquired a major shareholding, valued at £8696, in the motor accessory firm D. V. A. Rist. Lucas's holding in Rists was kept secret for thirty-four years, for most of which Corley acted as the sole link between the two establishments. His business acumen attracted the attention of Oliver Lucas, the grandson of Joseph Lucas, who by 1921 had become a director. Lucas often took the young Corley with him when conducting business negotiations, including on a trip to the United States in 1933. On 19 June 1937 Corley married, at the Methodist Church, Oaklands Gate, Northwood, Middlesex, the 24-year-old Olwen Mary Yeoman (*d.* 1999), daughter of Maurice Hart Yeoman, a principal assistant for London county council. They had a son, Peter, and a daughter, Ann.

On the outbreak of the Second World War several Lucas directors and managers found themselves being seconded to other electrical firms at the request of the ministries of Aircraft Production and Supply. Corley was kept on at Lucas as Walker's assistant in spite of strenuous efforts made by another director, Peter Bennett, to appoint him to his staff at the Ministry of Supply. Corley's wartime effort was therefore spent entirely in Birmingham as part of the skeleton senior management team led by Bertram Waring, who became joint managing director with Peter Bennett following the death of Oliver Lucas in 1948. In the same year Corley was elevated to the position of company director.

The early 1950s saw considerable organizational change at Lucas. In 1951 this entailed dividing the board of directors into two, creating a main board and an executive board, with the latter taking responsibility for running Lucas's various subsidiary companies. Corley was transferred from the main to the executive board, but quickly found himself part of a small, tight-knit coterie of managers surrounding Waring who in effect ran the organization. In 1955 Corley also took over the committee responsible for executive organization and development, and a year later was made chief administrative officer.

Lucas harboured plans to expand into the European market and in 1959 Corley was given responsibility for initiating a partnership with Ducellier-Bendix-Air Equipment in France. A new enterprise was formed to manufacture a full range of electrical automotive components, known as Ducellier & Cie. In the same year, 1959, Lucas perceived that it would have to diversify its products following the Sandys report on the future of Britain's air defences, which had come out in favour of guided missiles at the expense of manned aircraft. It considered manufacturing electrical systems for British Rail. Corley was closely involved in this plan, but little had been achieved before British Rail announced that it preferred to remain with its tried and tested suppliers. Greater success was obtained in supplying electrical equipment for the machine tool industry, though the financial benefits for the company were not as great as the potential gains that might have been garnered from more profitable railway supply contracts. Also in 1959, as part of the diversification exercise, Corley spearheaded Lucas's attempt to move into all-glass, sealed beamed light units for cars. A separate manufacturing company was proposed. British Sealed Beams Limited was registered in 1959 with Corley as chairman. Initial production was small, with Vauxhall being the first main customer, but over time orders were received from Ford and the British Motor Corporation, and heralded the success of the new subsidiary.

In 1965 Corley was appointed commercial director of the executive board, while at the same time being vice-chairman (commercial) for the whole group as well as chief executive of Lucas Electrical. In 1969 he was appointed chairman and combined that role with that of chief executive. During his tenure as chairman he was responsible for streamlining the groups from nineteen more or less independent firms to seven. Under pressure from the Industrial Reorganisation Corporation in the late 1960s Lucas made a number of acquisitions in the aircraft industry. Corley promoted that side of the business, including a partnership with Rolls-Royce in developing the RB211 engine. However, the increasing costs of the RB211 eventually forced Rolls-Royce into crisis, leaving Lucas with debts of £20 million. On hearing of this all Corley is reputed to have said is 'Mmm, well, well'.

Outside Lucas, Corley was a life governor of Birmingham University, a governor of the Royal Shakespeare Theatre, chairman of the Birmingham chamber of commerce in 1964, president of the Society of Motor Manufacturers and Traders in 1971, and a governor of his alma mater, St Bees (and chairman, 1978–84). He was knighted in 1972 and made a chevalier of the Légion d'honneur in 1975 for his services to the automotive industry. After his retirement he instigated and presided over the Lucas Festival of Arts. A quiet unassuming man who got on with things, he retired to Cumbria where he enjoyed bee-keeping and fell walking, even climbing Scafell Pike on his eightieth birthday, yet still finding time to be an inveterate letter writer to the *Daily Telegraph* newspaper. He died of prostate cancer at his home, Bradbury House, Gosforth, Cumbria, on 6 March 2005, and was survived by his two children.

TOM DONNELLY

Sources H. Nockolds, *Lucas: the first hundred years*, 2 vols. (1976–8) · *Daily Telegraph* (30 March 2005) · *Birmingham Post* (31 March 2005) · *Birmingham Evening Mail* (1 April 2005) · 'Lucas Industries', company history, www.answers.com, 30 April 2008 · *WW* (2005) · Burke, *Peerage* · b. cert. · m. cert. · d. cert.

Likenesses obituary photographs

Wealth at death £991,484: probate, 14 July 2005, *CGPLA Eng. & Wales*

Corner, Beryl Dorothy (1910–2007), paediatrician, was born at 7 Waterford Road, Westbury-on-Trym, Bristol, on 9 December 1910, the eldest of three children of Edward Graham Corner (1881–1952), a clerk in the port of Bristol authority, and his wife, Cicely Rose, *née* Menzies (1885–1976). She won a scholarship to Redland High School for Girls, then became a prize-winning medical student at the London School of Medicine for Women at the Royal Free Hospital, where she qualified in 1934 and sailed through her higher medical exams in 1936. It was during her student years that her interest in paediatrics took hold, when she attended ward rounds at Great Ormond Street Hospital and was taught by Robert Hutchison. After house officer posts at the Royal Free and the Elizabeth Garrett Anderson Hospital the realistic option for her, as a woman doctor, was to try to obtain a post in general practice or in public health. She was all set to join a general practice in Bristol when a surgeon friend of the family suggested that she apply for a vacant post as resident medical officer at the Bristol Children's Hospital.

Paediatrics was only just beginning to be developed as a speciality separate from adult medicine and, contrary to the view of the professor of medicine at Bristol, Corner became convinced of the need for doctors who specialized in the care of children and were based at the Children's Hospital rather than adult physicians who dropped in to do rounds. Seeking further training in paediatrics she found she could not apply to Great Ormond Street Hospital, which had an official policy of not employing women house physicians. She applied for a post as registrar at the Westminster Children's Hospital only to be told in a letter from Donald Paterson, consultant paediatrician and secretary of the British Paediatric Association, that although she was the outstanding candidate they could not appoint her because she was a woman. Eventually she obtained a post at the Brompton Hospital before returning to Bristol, where she was appointed honorary physician to the outpatients in 1937 and became one of the first full-time paediatricians in the UK, surviving with money from lecturing to nurses and some private practice.

Seeing the need to improve the care of newborn babies Corner ventured onto the maternity wards at Bristol, but was told by the obstetricians that her presence was not welcome. She simply ignored this instruction and set about improving the medical and nursing care of babies, which almost certainly was a major factor in reducing perinatal mortality in Bristol. With the support of the medical officer of health, appointed consultant paediatrician in 1942, and influenced by the work of Julius Hess in the USA and Mary Crosse in Birmingham, she went on to set up the special care baby unit at Southmead Hospital, which opened in 1946, gained an international reputation, and provided the example and stimulus for many other units in the UK. She was a founder member of the Neonatal Society and became an adviser to the World Health Organization in neonatology. Among a wider public she reached worldwide attention for the successful care of the Good sisters (the first quadruplets in the world all to survive a birth by caesarean section) in 1948, and in 2006 gained fame through the BBC2 programme *Beryl's Babies*, about her pioneering work as a paediatrician.

Between 1942 and 1947 Corner was the only paediatrician in the south-west of England. She was an enthusiastic teacher, and as well as lecturing to nurses she started one of the first courses in the UK in paediatric medicine for medical students. She published many research papers and was one of the first to use exchange transfusion to prevent brain injury due to jaundice in premature babies, was innovative in introducing a breast-milk bank, employed outreach neonatal nurses to help with the care of premature babies after discharge from hospital, and wrote a widely read book, *Prematurity* (1960).

Corner made a tactical decision to try not to be seen as a campaigning feminist but was very supportive of women doctors who came to her for help with problems of discrimination. She waited until 1954 before she joined the Medical Women's Federation, at which time both she, and perhaps the federation itself, had become a part of the medical establishment. She later became its president. Her achievements and those of other women who were pioneering paediatricians brought into focus the inequity of barring women from the male bastions of medicine, and in 1945 she and four other distinguished women paediatricians were finally allowed to become members of their own professional body, the British Paediatric Association.

Short of stature and given to travelling at speed around Bristol in a large white Mercedes which could at first sight seem driverless until it passed by and her distinctive profile was revealed behind the wheel, Beryl Corner had an unforgettable personality. Sociable and charming with friends and colleagues, loyal and supportive to her extended family, helpful to young paediatricians who showed commitment, she had no hesitation in showing disapproval at work, with her ire typically directed at everyone on a ward-round including the innocent, and there were occasions when her handbag was swung and made contact. None of this was personal and the anger disappeared as quickly as the morning dew. Most of those who worked for her came to regard her with great affection and respect. Among parents there were many who were devoted to her and welcomed her certainty and authority, but there were some, including the mother of the Good sisters, who were upset by what they perceived as a failure to respect their views.

Corner enjoyed conversation, taking centre stage whether in a small group, in a medical meeting, or with parents. She was less comfortable in a purely listening role. She was an accomplished amateur musician, made contributions to the study of medical history, and became 'paediatrician' to the Bristol Zoo, where she was an innovator in the care of sick newborn primates. On at least one occasion she admitted a sick primate into an incubator alongside the babies in the neonatal unit. She was a committed Christian and an active member of Christ Church, Clifton. Appointed OBE in 2006, she kept her sharp intellect until her death from a stroke in Southmead Hospital, Bristol, on 4 March 2007. She was unmarried.

DAVID STEVENS

Sources M. Good, *The Good story* (1998) • D. Stevens, 'Pride, prejudice and paediatrics (women paediatricians in England before 1950)', *Archive of Disease in Childhood*, 91 (2006), 866–70 • *The Independent* (15 March 2007) • *Daily Telegraph* (20 March 2007) • *The Guardian* (22 March 2007) • *The Times* (23 March 2007) • *BMJ*, 334/906 (28 April 2007) • http://munksroll.rcplondon.ac.uk/biography/details/5610, 9 Aug 2010 • personal knowledge (2011) • private information (2011) • b. cert. • d. cert.

Archives SOUND BL NSA, documentary recording

Likenesses obituary photographs • photograph, repro. in news.bbc.co.uk/1/hi/health/113844.stm • photograph, repro. in goodquads.co.uk/Intropage1.htm • photograph, RCP Lond. • photograph, Institute of Child Health, Bristol

Wealth at death £1,470,439: probate, 18 July 2007, *CGPLA Eng. & Wales*

Cosgrove, Denis Edmund (1948–2008), geographer, was born on 3 May 1948 at 16 Kenilworth Road, Liverpool, the second of the six children of Peter Cyril Cosgrove (1910–1980), bank clerk, later bank manager, and his wife, Gwendoline Brenda, *née* Mackrill (*b.* 1922). He was raised in a lower middle-class, devoutly Catholic, household, his father being of Irish descent. He was educated at St Francis Xavier's College, a prominent Jesuit secondary school which his father had also attended. As an academic high flyer he was initially obliged to give up the study of geography in favour of Latin and Greek, but later selected the subject for study at a higher level. The first member of his family to attend any university, he won an open scholarship to read geography at St Catherine's College, Oxford

(1966–9), and completed a masters degree at the University of Toronto (1969–70).

Cosgrove's return to Oxford in 1970 was inspired by personal commitment as much as academic ambition: Isobel Thubron (*b.* 1943), whom he married in New York on 25 September 1970, had recently been appointed to the post of demonstrator in the university's school of geography. She was the daughter of Samuel Thubron, financial director of Clarke Chapman Engineering. They had two daughters, Emily and Isla. After their marriage Cosgrove registered for a postgraduate degree and was eventually awarded a DPhil in 1976, though by then he was well established as an academic. His first professional employment, in 1971–2, was as a researcher in the built environment research group of the Polytechnic of Central London, where his job was to assist in the development of computer planning models. In 1972 he was appointed as lecturer in human geography at Oxford Polytechnic, where he flourished as a teacher and administrator, rising to principal lecturer and chair of the geography section.

In 1980 he moved to the recently established department of geography at Loughborough University as lecturer, becoming reader in 1983. There he helped to create an influential new school of cultural geography, oriented towards historical studies of landscape iconography. Having previously held visiting professorships at the University of Toronto, the University of Texas at Austin, and the University of Oregon, he was now set on widening his horizons further. In 1994 he was appointed to a chair in human geography at Royal Holloway, University of London. There he established a new masters programme in cultural geography and became dean of the graduate school, as well as being founder editor (also in 1994) of *Ecumene* (subsequently renamed *Cultural Geographies*). In 2000 he was appointed to the newly endowed Alexander Von Humboldt chair of geography in the University of California, Los Angeles. Meanwhile, his first marriage having ended in divorce, on 2 December 1989 he married Carmen Patricia Mills (*b.* 1964), daughter of Richard Aldous Mills, geologist. They had one son, Leon.

One of Cosgrove's principal achievements as a scholar was to develop a compelling rationale for geography as a humanities discipline at a time when the subject was dominated by models drawn from the physical and social sciences. In his view geographical enquiry was equally concerned with the technical, material, and imaginative engagement between people and places. Early in his career he was drawn to the works of Ruskin, and Renaissance ideas of landscape as reflected in sixteenth-century Vicenza and the Veneto. These concerns were reflected in a series of influential books, including *Social Formation and Symbolic Landscape* (1984), *The Palladian Landscape* (1993), and *The Iconography of Landscape* (1988, co-edited with Stephen Daniels). His later writings on mapping drew him to fruitful collaborations with scholars and artists in England and North America. Throughout his career he maintained an enduring interest in the relationships between geography and cosmography, resulting in his *magnum opus* on imaginative geographies of the globe, *Apollo's Eye: a Cartographic Genealogy of the Earth in the Western Imagination* (2001). His publications had a significant impact well beyond his chosen discipline, notably within architecture and the visual arts, and were widely translated. In 1988 he won the Back award of the Royal Geographical Society for contributions to human geography, and in 2008 he was awarded an honorary doctorate by the University of Talinn, Estonia.

Cosgrove's academic outlook was inspired by a strong sense of the connections between scholarship, pedagogy, and ethics. He was a humane scholar who made possible a more expansive vision of geography as a creative discipline, an inspiring teacher who changed the way his students thought about the world and their place within it, and a trusted colleague and mentor, whose convivial and generous approach to life inspired many of those who knew him. He died on 21 March 2008 at his home in West Hollywood, Los Angeles, California, having been diagnosed with stomach cancer in 2006. Memorial meetings were held in May 2008 at the UCLA Fowler Museum, Los Angeles, and at the Royal Geographical Society, London. His ashes were scattered, according to his wishes, at two of his favourite places: Malibu, Los Angeles, and Parliament Hill, London. He was survived by his wife, Carmen, and his three children. FELIX DRIVER

Sources D. Cosgrove, *Geographical imagination and the authority of images: Hettner-Lecture* (2006) · D. Cosgrove, *Geography and vision* (2008) · M. Heffernan, 'Denis Edmund Cosgrove', *Geographers Biobibliographical Studies*, 29 (2010), 127–50 · T. Freitag and H. Jöns, 'A biographical interview with Denis Cosgrove', *Die Erde*, 136 (2006), 205–16 · *The Independent* (8 April 2008) · *The Times* (10 April 2008) · *Daily Telegraph* (24 April 2008) · *Environment and Planning A*, 40 (2008), 1179–82 · *Imago Mundi*, 61 (2009), 97–100 · www.geog.ucla.edu/cosgrove.php, 18 June 2011 · personal knowledge (2012) · private information (2012) · b. cert. · m. cert. [1989]

Archives SOUND BL NSA, current affairs and documentary recordings

Likenesses obituary photographs

Cotton, Sir William Frederick [Bill] **(1928–2008)**, television executive, was born on 23 April 1928 at 175 Saltram Crescent, Paddington, London, the younger son of William Edward (Billy) *Cotton (1899–1969), bandleader, and his wife, Mabel Hope, *née* Gregory (1895–1989). He grew up as his father's career as a popular bandleader was in full swing. With his radio catch phrase 'Wakey! Wakey!', Billy Cotton was a household name and 'young' Bill observed his father's career at first hand. This understanding of the vagaries and temperaments, pressures and worries that accompany stars enabled him in later life to become one of the most trusted, respected, and sympathetic of talent patrons in British broadcasting.

Cotton had a very promising academic career, finishing at Ardingly College, where he excelled both on the sports field and in the classroom; he turned down an offer of admission to Downing College, Cambridge. He completed his national service in the Royal Army Service Corps, and through family contacts began life as a music publisher, a grand title for his real job, which was essentially song 'plugging'—visiting the stars and trying to sell them the

Sir William Frederick [Bill] **Cotton** (**1928–2008**), by unknown photographer, 1957

publisher's latest copyright. He started with the Noel Gay company, and then moved to Chappells publishing. He was very good at his job because he knew most of the stars and had a keen ear for a good song. This led him to join Johnny Johnson as joint managing director of Michael Reine Music. He was particularly proud of promoting the song 'I Saw Mommy Kissing Santa Claus' and selling it to the Beverley Sisters in 1951; it subsequently became a number one hit and perennial favourite Christmas song. Meanwhile, on 21 October 1950, in Felpham, Sussex, he married Bernadine Maud (Boo) Sinclair (1926–1964), daughter of Bernard Charles Henry Sinclair. They had three daughters, Jane, Kathryn, and Lisa.

When commercial television expanded the universe of viewers in 1955, and became the most important distribution outlet for entertainment, Cotton saw his future and successfully applied for a producers' training course at BBC television. Variety was in vogue and BBC and ITV became magnets for many people of talent with experience in the variety theatre. Not only had Cotton followed his father around the 'halls', learning the trade, he had also appeared on stage. If his father was unable to appear through illness, promoters like his agent Leslie Grade would ask young Bill to hold the baton—that way, 'a' (if not the) Billy Cotton was actually appearing and no money needed to be refunded.

Cotton's career as a young television producer flourished. He was given shows such as *Six Five Special*, Jack Payne's *Off the Record*, and the performance-based *Starlight* series. His father was watching with unspoken admiration the skills and mastery that his son brought to these and other shows and decided he was just the man to produce the television version of his *Billy Cotton Band Show*. Tense family negotiations followed. It wasn't until Billy agreed to defer to his son on editorial and production matters in the event of a difference and that they would never row publicly that young Bill was persuaded to produce his father's Saturday night variety show, which lasted from 1956 to 1968.

The mid- and late 1960s were marked for Cotton by a series of grievous losses. His first wife, Boo, died of breast cancer in 1964 after fourteen years of marriage. It took Cotton decades of grief to overcome this loss. They were a devoted couple. In 1966 his older brother, Ted, to whom he was very close, died prematurely at the age of forty after an aneurysm. Then, in 1969, his father died. Cotton idolized his father, from whom he inherited a gift for plain speaking and a straightforward approach to problems that combined looking someone in the eye and telling him or her the truth—but always with sympathy and understanding. In an entertainment industry seemingly kept afloat on an ocean of flattery and sycophancy, Cotton's blend of common sense and directness were rare qualities indeed. To counter the pain of this succession of losses, he threw himself into his BBC career. He also, on 28 May 1965, at Westminster register office, married Ann Corfield Henderson, *née* Bucknall (*b.* 1929), a make-up supervisor, former wife of Andrew V. Henderson, and daughter of Lieutenant-General Gerard Corfield Bucknall, army officer. There were no children of the marriage, which ended in divorce in 1989.

Meanwhile, Cotton's ascent of the BBC greasy pole was as swift as it was inevitable given the talents he was displaying: he was in turn assistant head of light entertainment (1962–7), head of variety (1967–70), head of light entertainment (1970–77), then controller of BBC1 (1977–81). During this time his talents came together: his taste, his ability to attract and spot talent, that unerring ear he had for a song which had now become an unerring eye for a television show. He invented the *Top of the Pops* format and launched it in 1964. He signed the Two Ronnies (Ronnie Barker and Ronnie Corbett), and Morecambe and Wise; he encouraged writers such as Johnny Speight (*Till Death Us Do Part*), Alan Simpson and Ray Galton (*Steptoe and Son*), Jonathan Lynn and Antony Jay (*Yes Minister*); he launched Michael Parkinson as a talk show host; and picked great barons to run the drama series with a string of hits including *All Creatures Great and Small*. This was truly a golden age for BBC television. 'If BBC1 is working', he was fond of saying, 'the BBC is OK' (personal knowledge).

Many offers came Cotton's way to enrich himself by switching to ITV. He always remained loyal to the BBC, despite a period in the wilderness. In 1982 he was passed over for the post of managing director of the television service in one of those customary BBC political upheavals and was moved to run the embryonic satellite broadcasting ambitions of the BBC. The chairman changed from

George Howard to Stuart Young, who was quick to recognize that BBC television needed Cotton's talents, and in 1984 appointed him managing director. The fortunes of the BBC television service were revived in double quick time under Cotton—and with his signature wit and wisdom. At a particularly fractious meeting, he found himself presiding over an argument about the size of the new breakfast show's audiences versus its commercial rival. He brought the debate to a halt with an apparent non sequitur: 'Remember the Battleship Potemkin'. The debate was halted; quizzical stares ensued. With his customary exquisite timing Cotton explained: 'They placed too much faith in the ratings' (private information).

Cotton was always alert to the internal and external politics of the corporation, but never a political 'machinator'—which probably explains why he never became director-general, a post for which he was eminently better suited than most of those he served under. Irrespective of his own assessment of individuals, he respected their positions, not least Alasdair Milne, director-general from 1982 to 1987. He was courageous under fire, and never afraid to defend his beloved corporation. When Margaret Thatcher made public her extreme displeasure at the BBC coverage of the Falklands conflict, relations between the prime minister and the corporation were best described as non-existent. After some months the prime minister was prevailed upon to re-enter BBC premises for a 'clear the air' dinner with the senior management. Mrs Thatcher spent most of the first hour berating the BBC's lack of patriotism, left-wing anti-war bias, and so on. The senior managers responsible for the war coverage were stunned into silence. Cotton was the first to intervene: 'Prime Minister, are you accusing the BBC of treachery? If so you are wrong!'. A stunned silence. A long pause. Then the prime minister responded: 'I have said all I intended to say.' That was the turning point; someone at last had the gumption to stand up to the prime minister. Relations were subsequently restored (private information).

Cotton's tenure at the BBC came to an end with his retirement in 1988, hastened by another changing of the guard at the top. Marmaduke Hussey became chairman, fired Milne, and appointed Michael Checkland, an accountant, as director-general. He in turn, aware of the weakness in his journalistic qualifications, recruited John Birt to watch his editorial back. Cotton judged this the moment to retire and Sir Paul Fox was hastily recruited from Yorkshire Television to succeed him. 'I am making way for an older man', quipped Cotton of his longstanding friend Fox, two years his senior (personal knowledge). From 1988 to 1997 he was chairman of Noel Gay TV and a director of the Noel Gay Organization, and from 1998 he was a director of Billy Marsh Associates. He was also from 1990 a vice-president of the Marie Curie Foundation.

Any misgivings Cotton might have felt about the manner of his departure from the BBC were more than compensated for in his personal life. After he and Ann divorced, he found happiness with Kathryn Mary (Kate) Burgess, *née* Ralphs (*b.* 1946), a homes officer for the Marie Curie Foundation, daughter of Frederick Ralphs, chief education officer, and former wife of David P. H. Burgess. They married on 21 April 1990. It was an idyllic period of personal fulfilment for Cotton and ended his years of pain, searching, and struggling to rediscover the happiness he had found with his wife Boo. He was knighted for his services to broadcasting in 2001, having been appointed OBE in 1976 and a CBE in 1989. He died at the Royal Bournemouth Hospital on 11 August 2008 of idiopathic pulmonary fibrosis, and was survived by his wife, Kate, and the three daughters of his first marriage.

Media academics may argue for many years about whether or not the second half of the twentieth century represented the golden age of British broadcasting. Whatever their conclusions, among the names that emerge as the outstanding television impresarios of the period, that of Bill Cotton will always find its rightful place. From the day he arrived at the BBC television service as a trainee producer in 1956 to the day of his retirement as managing director of BBC television in 1988, he remained committed to the highest standards of popular, quality entertainment. At the time of his death two decades later, BBC screens were still alive with repeats of his legacy.

MICHAEL GRADE

Sources B. Cotton, *Double Bill: 80 years of entertainment* (2000) · *The Times* (12 Aug 2008); (4 Sept 2008); (13 Sept 2008); (27 Feb 2009) · *Daily Telegraph* (13 Aug 2008) · *The Guardian* (13 Aug 2008) · *The Independent* (13 Aug 2008) · *WW* (2008) · personal knowledge (2012) · private information (2012) · b. cert. · m. certs. · d. cert.

Archives FILM BFINA, *Bill Cotton*, BBC1, 3 April 1991 · BFINA, *This is your life*, M. Aspel (presenter), BBC1, 22 March 1995 · BFINA, *The man who made Eric and Ernie*, A. Briscoe (producer), 26 Dec 2008 · BFINA, documentary and light entertainment footage | SOUND BL NSA, documentary, light entertainment, and performance recordings

Likenesses photograph, 1957, BBC [*see illus.*] · photographs, 1957–84, BBC · photographs, 1986–97, Photoshot, London · photographs, 1995–2002, PA Photos, London · photograph, 2002, Camera Press, London · obituary photographs

Wealth at death under £174,000: probate, 12 Nov 2008, *CGPLA Eng. & Wales*

Court [*née* Brown], **Audrey Kathleen** (**1913–2005**), athlete and family planning reformer, was born on 24 May 1913 in Bankura, Bengal, India, the third of five children and the only daughter of Arthur E. Brown, Methodist minister and principal of Bankura College, and his wife, Gertrude, *née* Parsons. Her four brothers 'were all keen sportsmen and above average athletes' (Daniels and Tedder, 30): Ralph (1909–2003) was the Amateur Athletic Association 440 yards hurdles champion in 1934 (and later, as Sir Ralph Kilner Brown, a high court judge), and Godfrey *Brown (1915–1995) was Britain's leading 400 metres runner, a Cambridge blue, and Olympic gold medallist.

At the age of nine Audrey Brown was sent to England to be educated in Birmingham under the guardianship of her maternal uncle, Sir Leonard Parsons, a noted paediatrician. She went to Birmingham University to study social and political science in 1932. While there she developed a passion for running and was coached by W. W. Alexander of Birchfield Harriers—a famous club and 'my athletic salvation' (*Birmingham Magazine*, 110). She blossomed as a sprinter and was picked for the inter-university team at the world student games in Turin in 1933. A chest infection ruled her out of competition for 1934–5, but she came back to fitness in her final university year and, after a strong performance in the national championship at the White City stadium, was picked for the small British women's Olympic team of 1936, for the 100 metres and the 4 x 100 metres relay. With typical modesty she later confessed to being 'amazed at my inclusion' (Birmingham University House Association, 2).

There were only twelve competitors in the British women's Olympic team. They were provided with a 'parading uniform' by the British Olympic Association but they had to sew their own running vests and buy their own running shorts and shoes. On the outward journey the couchettes were not attached to the train and the women arrived sleepless without having even trained together until they got to Berlin. 'Knowing we had little chance in the individual races', she recalled, 'we trained very hard together to run the best we could' and were 'delighted' to reach the 4 x 100 metres final (personal communication). It was a dramatic race. The German team had broken the world record in the semi-final heat but then dropped the baton in the final handover when they were leading, giving the gold medal to the Americans and the silver to the British team, with Audrey Brown running the third leg. On the same day her brother Godfrey, who had already won silver in the individual 400 metres, brought home gold in the anchor leg of the 4 x 400 metres. They remain the only British brother and sister Olympic medallists on the track in the same games.

Brown's parents had planned a trip to Berlin to see her brother compete and 'it was an added bonus when I unexpectedly joined him' (personal communication). Their unprecedented joint success was 'a great joy' to their Methodist missionary parents, who 'never saw any difference between my taking up athletics and my brothers doing so' (Daniels and Tedder, 30). She confessed to being 'irked by … the German aim to prove themselves as a superior nation', preferring to dwell on the comic aspects of the Nazi regime with its 'rather ridiculous' oakleaf laurels; she thought Leni Riefenstahl, who directed the official film of the games, was 'a bit of a nuisance' (ibid., 101, 117).

Audrey Brown gave up running competitively in 1938 when she moved to York to take up a post as personnel officer at Rowntrees. On 30 March 1940 she married her former tutor at Birmingham, the economic historian William Henry Bassano (Harry) Court (1904–1971), son of William Henry Hallewell Court. Her husband was subsequently professor of economic history at Birmingham from 1947 to 1970. They had three daughters, Sarah, Bridget, and Alison, between 1943 and 1949. Audrey Court kept a link with athletics while bringing up her children, but from 1949 she devoted most of her energy to her work for the Family Planning Association (FPA). She started as a volunteer but soon joined the Birmingham FPA committee, becoming its honorary secretary and finally its chairman in 1961. There followed a huge increase in the activity of the Birmingham FPA, the largest and most dynamic in the country, spreading its services throughout the city as the demand for the birth control pill and the right to abortion became stronger throughout the 1960s. She fought hard to extend the services of the FPA to the new ethnic minority communities and to the unmarried, especially the young, 'who could find very little help and none from the FPA' (Court and Walton, 53). In 1968 the FPA handed over responsibility for unmarried women to the newly formed Brook Advisory Centre in Birmingham and Audrey Court moved across to head it, doing 'fantastic work', according to her successor, Penny Barber; 'when she saw a need she'd move mountains to meet it … Audrey was very far-seeing' (*Birmingham Post*, 17 June 2005). She retained the chair of the Birmingham Brook Advisory Centre from 1968 until her retirement in 1990, and was appointed MBE in 1991 for service to family planning in Birmingham. Her life combined sporting achievement and public service in the best traditions of her family and of British voluntarism. She moved from Birmingham to Gatley, Cheshire, to be closer to her family in 2003 and died on 11 June 2005 at Wythenshawe Hospital, Manchester, of heart failure. Her funeral took place on 20 June at Lodge Hill crematorium, Selly Oak. She was survived by her three daughters.

RICHARD HOLT

Sources Birmingham University House Association, *50th anniversary of the 1936 Berlin Olympics* (1986) · 'The making of an Olympian', *Birmingham Magazine*, 12 (Oct 2000), 101–12 · S. Daniels and A. Tedder, *A proper spectacle: women Olympians, 1900–1936* (2000) · A. Court and C. Walton, *Birmingham made a difference: the Birmingham Women's Welfare Centre and the Family Planning Association in Birmingham* (2001) · A. Court, 'The 1936 Berlin Olympics', 7 Feb 2001 [personal communication] · *Birmingham Evening Mail* (16 June 2005) · *Birmingham Post* (17 June 2005); (18 June 2005) · *The Guardian* (29 Sept 2005) · www.olympicwomen.co.uk, 10 June 2008 · m. cert. · d. cert.

Archives SOUND BL NSA, oral history of British athletics, interviews with R. Cutler, Oct–Dec 1996, F5269–F5271, F5352

Likenesses photograph, repro. in Daniels and Tedder, *Proper spectacle*, 30 · photograph, repro. in *Birmingham Magazine*

Wealth at death under £152,000: probate, 19 Aug 2005, *CGPLA Eng. & Wales*

Court, Hazel Marjorie (1926–2008), actress, was born Margery Hazel Court at 134 Heathfield Road, Handsworth, Birmingham, on 10 February 1926, the younger daughter of George William Court, a stores clerk, and former professional cricketer with Durham County Cricket Club, and his wife, Mary Magdalene (Madge), *née* Blockley. When she was ten months old the family went to live at Eastern Road, Wylde Green, where her father worked for the United Yeast Company. His brief was to create a sports ground and club for the company's workers. By her own account Hazel enjoyed an idyllic childhood, entering fully into the seasonal delights of her environment. From a very early age she was drawn to acting, loved dressing up and performing in church shows, and was powerfully attracted to the great movie stars of the period, acting out their roles after leaving the cinema. The Second World War intervened when she was a teenager, and when her elder sister Audrey's husband was killed she went to live with her in Ealing. By happy chance Audrey showed the producer Norman Loudon and the director Anthony

Asquith a photograph of the eighteen-year-old Hazel, which led to her first film role—a one-line assignment in Ealing's valentine to the music-hall heyday, *Champagne Charlie* (1944). It also led to an affair of several years with Loudon, who was more than twice her age. In the early 1940s she had some stage experience with the Birmingham Alexander Theatre, appearing in *School for Scandal*, and studied acting at the London Academy of Music and Dramatic Art.

In the immediate post-war period Court appeared mainly in modest movies made with largely domestic consumption in mind, but she made the most of the limited opportunities they offered her. She had the female lead opposite the popular comedians Flanagan and Allen in *Dreaming* (1945), a farce that gave her the chance to appear in several guises and a bizarre range of costumes. Her pert prettiness and shapeliness ensured a steady stream of films, with *Holiday Camp* (1947) perhaps the highlight from this period. In this hymn to post-war egalitarianism she played sympathetically a young war widow with a baby who finds romance at the eponymous venue. She had supporting roles to such 1940s stars as Sally Gray in the romance *Carnival* (1946), Phyllis Calvert in the feebly feminist *The Root of All Evil* (1947), Greta Gynt in the thriller *Dear Murderer* (1947), and Jean Kent in *Bond Street* (1948). In the latter she was the bride whose wedding dress gives rise to a multi-storied plot, but a demure Court could hardly compete with Kent in full cry as a tough prostitute. Court had leads in the minor period comedy *Meet Me at Dawn* (1947), in the dim thriller *My Sister and I* (1948), and in the surprisingly robust *film noir Forbidden* (1949), in which her purposeful heroine takes the sexual initiative in ways uncommon among her more genteel compeers. However, busy and often effective as she was in the 1940s, she never quite took her place with the major female stars of the decade, perhaps as a result of starting a little later than they had.

Court's co-star in *My Sister and I* was another Rank hopeful, (James Patrick) Dermot Walsh (1924–2002), whom she married on 2 July 1949 and with whom she had a daughter, Sally. They appeared together in three above-average B movies: the semi-supernatural thriller *Ghost Ship* (1952), the oddly suburban *Counterspy* (1953), and *A Woman of Mystery* (1958), a Danziger Productions mystery in which she played a tediously subservient girlfriend. There were several other B movies in the often-anodyne 1950s, including two trim thrillers, *Behind the Headlines* and *The Narrowing Circle* (both 1956), in which she enjoyably sparred with the Canadian actor Paul Carpenter. The 1954 release *Devil Girl from Mars* became a camp classic among the cheeseparing science-fiction films of the decade, but Court's role was inevitably overshadowed by the showier types involved, especially Patricia Laffan, the titular visitor in search of virile male earthlings.

Hammer Studio's first venture into Technicolor horror revealed Court in all her red-haired, green-eyed, ample-bosomed glory as she was exposed to the danger of *The Curse of Frankenstein* (1957), which launched the studio's hugely profitable horror cycle and her career as Hammer's 'scream queen'. At roughly the same time she came to wider notice in the television series *Dick and the Duchess* (1957–8), opposite the American actor Patrick O'Neal. The rest of her career reflected her success in both horror and television. She made three well-regarded period shockers for the American director Roger Corman, *The Premature Burial* (1962), *The Raven* (1963; co-starring Vincent Price, Boris Karloff, and Peter Lorre), and *The Masque of the Red Death* (1964), all derived from Edgar Allan Poe. She was also a frequent guest star on American television from the late 1950s, including appearances in *Alfred Hitchcock Presents*, one episode of which was directed by the former actor Don Taylor (1920–1998), whom she married on 25 March 1964, having divorced Dermot Walsh the previous year.

Apart from an uncredited cameo in *The Final Conflict* (1981), directed by Taylor, Hazel Court retired from acting in the early 1970s, and took up painting and sculpture, for which she trained in Italy. She settled permanently in the USA on her second marriage, which produced two further children, Courtney and Jonathan. After Taylor's death in December 1998 she went to live in their cabin at Lake Tahoe, California, in the High Sierras, where she died on 15 April 2008. Her autobiography, *Hazel Court: Horror Queen*, was published a week after her death. It is a somewhat fulsome account but, in refusing to dish dirt on colleagues, she emerges as a likeable enthusiast. She was survived by her three children. BRIAN MCFARLANE

Sources H. Court, *Hazel Court: horror queen* (2008) · 'Dermot Walsh', *An autobiography of British cinema*, ed. B. McFarlane (1997) · G. Brown, 'Holiday Camp', *The cinema of Britain and Ireland*, ed. B. McFarlane (2005) · B. McFarlane, *The encyclopedia of British film*, 3rd edn (2008) · *Daily Telegraph* (18 April 2008) · *The Independent* (18 April 2008) · *The Times* (19 April 2008) · *The Guardian* (22 April 2008) · www.uk.imdb.com · b. cert. · m. cert. [1949]

Archives FILM BFINA, documentary and performance footage

Likenesses photographs, 1945–66, Getty Images, London · photographs, 1947–58, PA Photos, London · photographs, 1947–2004, Rex Features, London · bromide print, NPG · obituary photographs · photographs, Camera Press, London

Cowgill, (George) Bryan (1927–2008), television producer and executive, was born on 27 May 1927 at 19 Cowper Avenue, Clitheroe, Lancashire, the son of John Clifford Cowgill (1899–1969), printer and stationer, and later proprietor of the Clitheroe *Advertiser and Times*, and his wife, Ada Gertrude, *née* Hartley (1902–1999). He had one brother. He attended Clitheroe grammar school from 1938 to 1942 and left at the age of fifteen with few formal qualifications. His grandfather's connections in the regional newspaper industry helped him secure his first job as a copy boy with the *Lancashire Evening Post* in Preston.

In 1943 Cowgill enlisted in the Royal Navy's Y scheme, introduced to allow boys aged sixteen and seventeen to pursue a career in the navy. He was selected for officer training in the Royal Marines king's squad, and at eighteen became the youngest officer in the 3rd Royal Marine commandos. He reached the rank of lieutenant, and in 1945 was billeted to a small fishing village, Tai O, on the island of Lantau, near Hong Kong. On demobilization in 1947 he returned to work at the family-run newspaper, where he became editor. On 16 October 1951 he married Doreen Thompson, a 23-year-old shop assistant, and daughter of Harold Thompson, transport manager. They had two daughters.

Cowgill could have built a career in the family business, but in 1954 he responded to an advertisement for the job of 'stage manager' in the BBC's television outside broadcast department, based at Lime Grove, London. The following year he started work as a 'floor manager', the very same day (22 September) that the BBC's competitor, Associated-Rediffusion, began broadcasting in London. He quickly learned the grammar of live television production and within months was a production assistant on the outside broadcast series *Saturday Night Out*, which introduced the BBC's 'roving eye' camera. In the same year, he directed his first television programme, *Dancing Club*, featuring Victor Sylvester and his orchestra. From then on he regularly directed outside broadcasts, including sport.

In 1957 the BBC's director of outside broadcasting (television), Peter Dimmock, asked Cowgill to produce *Sportsview*, the BBC's popular midweek sports magazine programme. The slick, fast-paced programme, edited by Paul Fox, mixed live studio interviews with filmed highlights from sport, and demanded disciplined direction. Cowgill excelled in the role, later admitting that his naval background helped him to call the shots with a commanding voice. It was in this role that he earned the nickname Ginger, partly because of his red hair, but more because of his reputation as a loud, fiery taskmaster, a tag he claimed did not reflect his 'true character' (*Mr Action Replay*, 25).

After directing the coverage of athletics during the 1958 Commonwealth games in Cardiff, Cowgill and Fox approached Dimmock with an idea for *Grandstand*, which became the BBC's flagship sports programme until its demise in 2007. As head of BBC television sport from 1963, Cowgill was involved in a number of ground-breaking initiatives. In 1964 alone these included a deal with the Football League that led to the launch of *Match of the Day* on BBC2, satellite coverage from the Olympic games in Tokyo, and forty-over Sunday league cricket. Cowgill won three BAFTA awards, including one for the coverage of the 1966 world cup finals, in which 'action replay' technology (a phrase introduced by Cowgill) was used for the first time in Britain. Throughout the 1960s *Grandstand* became synonymous with the BBC's coverage of sport, and so did Cowgill's working relationship with its presenter David Coleman. On 10 November 1966, Coleman was Cowgill's best man when, his first marriage having ended in divorce, he married Jennifer Elizabeth (Jenny) Baker (*b.* 1939), a BBC television secretary, and daughter of Sidney James Abbott Baker, an insurance official. They had two sons.

With the arrival of colour television in 1967, Cowgill drove the BBC's negotiations with the All England Tennis Club to abolish the amateur–professional distinction, and in 1968 Wimbledon became an open championship. From 1972 he was head of the Television Outside Broadcast Group, and two years later he succeeded Paul Fox as controller of BBC1. It was a role he relished and from 1974 to 1977 his scheduling strategy transformed the performance of the channel, with series including *Porridge*, *The Good Life*, *All Creatures Great and Small*, *Mastermind*, and *Jim'll Fix It*.

In 1977 Cowgill was invited to become director of news and current affairs, with a place on the BBC's board of management. However, the job entailed a reduction in salary, so when an offer came to become managing director of Thames Television he left the BBC and doubled his salary. In 1979, and again in 1984, he was embroiled in a battle with the engineering unions, and infamously locked out members of the Association of Cinematograph, Television and Allied Technicians from the Thames building. In spite of the disputes he led Thames to eight years of commercial success and critical acclaim, in the process enticing his friends Eric Morecambe and Ernie Wise to flit from the BBC to ITV. However, his tenure ended abruptly in 1985 when he broke a concordat with the BBC and poached the rights to the American soap *Dallas*. Cowgill's former colleague Sir Paul Fox later assessed the *Dallas* affair as a 'monumental misjudgement'. The International Broadcasting Authority forced Thames to relinquish the rights and Cowgill smartly offered his resignation. This effectively ended his professional career, save for a brief period with the sports agent Mark McCormack's IMG, and consultancy with British Satellite Broadcasting, which was establishing a sports channel. He retired to Stratford upon Avon, and published his autobiography, *Mr Action Replay*, in 2006. He died of a heart attack on 14 July 2008, and was survived by his wife, Jenny, and his children. RICHARD HAYNES

Sources B. Cowgill, *Mr Action Replay* (2006) · P. Fox, 'Who shot Bryan Cowgill?', *Television Magazine*, 43/6 (2006) · *Daily Telegraph* (16 July 2008) · *The Times* (17 July 2008); (22 July 2008) · *The Independent* (17 July 2008) · *The Guardian* (18 July 2008) · *Sunday Times* (20 July 2008) · *WW* (2008) · b. cert. · m. certs.

Archives BBC WAC | FILM BFINA, *Face the press*, P. Martin (producer), Channel 4, 12 Jan 1986 · BFINA, current affairs footage · *More than a game*, Channel 4, 1996 · *Sport in the sixties*, BBC4, 2006 | SOUND BL NSA, current affairs recording

Likenesses photographs, *c.*1962–*c.*1980, repro. in Cowgill, *Replay* · photographs, 1971–85, PA Photos, London · photograph, 1978, Photoshot, London · photograph, *c.*1980, repro. in *The Guardian* (18 July 2008)

Wealth at death under £5000: probate, 26 Sept 2008, *CGPLA Eng. & Wales*

Cowling, Maurice John (1926–2005), historian, was born in a nursing home at 210 Knights Hill, Norwood, London, on 6 September 1926, the elder child of Reginald Frederick Cowling (1901–1962) and his wife, May, *née* Roberts. Then living at 176 Camberwell New Road, the family soon moved to Streatham. His father, who had left school at fifteen, was technical assistant to a patent agent, and qualified as an agent himself in 1929.

Education and military service In 1937 Cowling won a place at Battersea grammar school, being evacuated with it following the outbreak of the Second World War to Worthing and then Hertford. In August 1943 he gained a major scholarship to read history at Jesus College, Cambridge. After his first-year examinations in 1944 he was called up for war service. Attached to the Queen's Royal regiment, he was sent to Bangalore as an officer cadet in 1945. In 1946 he was assigned to the Kumaon regiment and travelled to various garrisons across India; the following year he was redeployed to Egypt as a camp adjutant and then to Libya as a captain. He saw no military action. He returned to Cambridge in January 1948 and completed his history degree in eighteen months, taking firsts in part 1 in 1948 and in part 2 in 1949. He also rowed enthusiastically for the college, aided by a strong physique that he maintained well into later life.

Cowling's early experiences shaped him permanently. The ferociously hard-working grammar-school boy never lost his admiration for the respectable, aspirational values of the lower middle-class suburbs. Then, arriving in Cambridge in mid-war, he fell under the spell of 'three Anglican reactionaries', the history dons Kenneth Pickthorn, Edward Welbourne, and Charles Smyth, who reinforced his disdain for liberal-left values. Smyth introduced him to the views of E. C. Hoskyns, that reason could not grasp, or effectively attack, the mystical core of the Christian religion, and also impressed on Cowling—who was already fascinated by power—the historical importance of religion in upholding intellectual and political regimes. Cowling developed a 'strong polemical Christianity' and briefly considered ordination (Attallah, 129). Finally, his years in the army broadened his social experience, deepened his admiration for and curiosity about the processes of imperial rule, and loosened his vocabulary (to permanent effect—four-letter Anglo-Saxonisms were to be important and sometimes disconcerting elements in his academic self-presentation).

Journalism and history After graduation Cowling registered to write a PhD thesis on the policy and politics of British India from 1860 to 1890, and spent time in 1950–51 studying in Delhi, Calcutta, and Bombay. With the support of his college mentor, Charles Wilson, and on the basis of a paper about the economic policy of Bartle Frere as governor of Bombay in the 1860s, he was elected to a research fellowship at Jesus, which he held until 1953. He abandoned the doctorate, though some of the research appeared in a *Manchester Guardian* feature of July 1954 and an academic article of 1961, on the origins of the Anglo-Afghan War of 1878. Instead he started to read widely in nineteenth-century thought. He fell in with a faction in the university that sought to challenge the developing post-war consensus, becoming influenced particularly by Herbert Butterfield of Peterhouse and Michael Oakeshott of Caius.

Cowling adored the idea and reality of Cambridge and was bitterly disappointed at having to leave in 1953. Having attended Jesus College chapel regularly, he now ceased to be a practising Anglican, though he claimed to experience 'no recession in certainty about Christianity' (*Religion and Public Doctrine in Modern England*, 1, 1980, xvii). A research fellowship at Reading (1953–4) convinced him that he did not want to lecture in a 'provincial' university. He won late entry to the Foreign Office, working for six months on the Jordan desk, but then resigned. In 1955 he became a leader writer on *The Times* for a year before being sacked. Later he worked more briefly on the *Daily Express* and *Daily Telegraph*, and no more successfully, since he would not compromise on either the rebarbativeness of his views or the complexity of his prose style. However, he made close friendships with such hard-hitting conservative-minded journalists as Peregrine Worsthorne, Colin Welch, Henry Fairlie, and T. E. Utley, as well as his undergraduate contemporary George Gale, and these helped to shape his conception of politics. At the 1959 election he sought a political career, as Conservative candidate for the Labour-held seat of Bassetlaw in Nottinghamshire, but was again a failure, finding the blandness and small talk required especially challenging.

Throughout these years Cowling returned frequently to Cambridge and began to supervise undergraduates at the weekends, with great success. Eventually, convinced that he should write books, he moved back to the city permanently, teaching at one stage for forty hours a week. In 1960 Wilson arranged for him to be director of studies in economics and politics at Jesus, and in 1961 he became university assistant lecturer in history. In 1963 he moved from Jesus to Peterhouse at the invitation of Butterfield, the master there. He remained in the history faculty until he took early retirement in 1988 (having been promoted to reader in 1975) and a fellow of Peterhouse until 1993.

In two short books of 1963 Cowling worked out his major intellectual concerns since the late 1940s. *The Nature and Limits of Political Science* was an Oakeshottian critique of the disciplines of political science and political philosophy. It argued that social science's claim to offer accurate analysis of human behaviour was bogus, and that the political process was far too complex and fluid to be rationalized by theorists, being fully intelligible only to those within the system. *Mill and Liberalism* was less a scholarly study of John Stuart Mill than a polemic against 'liberalism' and 'the liberal mind'. Cowling's most fundamental hostility was to liberal writers who argued that reason and abstract, secular good intentions could create a more beneficent society. He thought them ignorant of human behaviour, unwilling to admit the self-interestedness of their own prejudices, and self-deceiving about their ability to smooth away the conflicts that would always remain inherent in society and politics. They could not, he believed, see that their views were no more authoritative, no more tolerant of alternatives, and no more likely to ensure social stability than the traditional (usually Christian) attitudes that they dismissed as blinkered but that had underpinned national solidarity for centuries. His resentment of the naïvety and power of the liberal intelligentsia was fuelled by its fervent opposition to the use of force, and its faith in the United Nations, particularly during the Suez crisis of 1956. Declaring personal lifelong guerrilla warfare against solemnity and earnestness, his standard conversational technique was to use 'irony, geniality and malice as solvents of enthusiasm, virtue and political elevation' (Cowling, *Mill and Liberalism*, 1963, xxx).

For the next twelve years Cowling worked hard to produce three books on British history that set out to challenge some widely held assumptions about how politicians behaved—that is, that they responded straightforwardly to either electoral opinion or rational principles. *1867: Disraeli, Gladstone and Revolution* (1967) was followed by *The Impact of Labour, 1920–1924* (1971) and *The Impact of Hitler, 1933–1940* (1975). These books argued that politicians acted 'situationally', in a rapidly changing context. They emphasized contingency and complexity, and challenged popular liberal-left readings of key moments in modern British history, such as the assumption that democratic pressures prompted the major extension of the franchise in 1867, or the social inevitability of the emergence of a Labour government in 1924. *The Impact of Hitler* suggested that the guarantee to Poland in March 1939 was the result of a high political calculation swayed by ill-informed indignation among the intelligentsia, and that it led Britain to fight a war on unsuitable terms that permanently weakened her power. The three volumes marked a significant increase in the professionalization of political history, being based on numerous archival collections of letters and diaries, on the grounds that these were the best guides to politicians' motives.

Cowling's seriousness as a historian was often underestimated, since one element of his assault on the solemnity of *bien pensant* academics was to insist that professional history was an illusion, since all history reflected authorial bias. But this did not mean—as his detractors suggested—that for him writing was just a game. Rather, proper history should involve significant personal reflection on some major problem of human society. Serious academics embarked on a never-ending journey to tackle such questions; certainly he saw himself in that light. By the 1970s he saw his task as understanding the interrelationship of practical politics and ideas, his two lifelong fascinations. He became progressively more interested in politicians' public language and the role played by a 'clerisy' of writers and newspaper editors in shaping the dominant mood. Conscious that social stability could never be taken for granted, he became more aware of the difficulties and challenges of political leadership. He vehemently denied the charge that his work, and that of a small number of pupils and colleagues who followed his techniques and who were dubbed the Peterhouse or 'high political' school, ignored the role of ideas in politics.

In 1977 Cowling announced that modern English political development would best be understood by charting the relationship between politics, religion, scholarship, art, literature, and morality: 'the basis for all public doctrine in England in the past century and a quarter' (Bentley, 343–4). He devoted the rest of his life to that project. To this end, he toyed with a number of ideas for books, but the only output was a three-volume inquiry into the continuing significance of views about religion in modern England. *Religion and Public Doctrine in Modern England* (1980, 1985, and 2001) occupied twenty-five years, and the last volume had to be reduced from 700,000 words. It became all-engrossing because Cowling found the process of studying for it much more congenial than the tiring archival visits of the previous fifteen years. He spent his days in his college rooms, muscularly grappling with books, indeed often physically ripping them apart. Made up of hundreds of essays on the thought of individuals, the work neither engaged with other scholarship nor developed an interpretative model for understanding modern Britain. However, it asserted the centrality of religion to English culture after 1840, sought to rescue unfashionable approaches, demonstrated that opponents of traditional Christianity usually retained crucial religious assumptions and prejudices, and suggested that secularization had been neither straightforward, rapid, nor complete. It reflected his conception of intellectual life as a relentless conflict between minds, most of which were less coherent, original, and effective than they supposed themselves to be. He had long lost his adolescent Christian mysticism, and defenders of orthodoxy as well as their assailants were subjected to pithy, provocative irony. He made clear that his admiration of the former was based mainly on the quality of their enmity towards the latter.

Peterhouse and politics Cowling's day-to-day life reflected his belief that the academy was an arena for the development, assertion, and clash of opinions. That was the point of his undergraduate teaching style over forty years, which was charismatic but never dogmatic. The supervisions usually took place after dinner, well lubricated with whisky. He swore at priggishness and naïve solemnity, but by example led undergraduates to think and talk deeply about ideas. He ridiculed established authorities, but also prescribed an extraordinary variety of books, including much Marxist and post-modernist criticism. He groaned at pupils' inanities, but with an impish playfulness that hinted at an unusual tolerance for and interest in them. His approach offended some of the more arrogant and panicked some of the less imaginative, but forced most to examine their illusions and look at the world through keener eyes. Peterhouse was already a strong college for history but he made it the most intellectually serious in Cambridge, while the electricity that he generated made him a guru to receptive young men throughout the university, who were encouraged to think that their ideas mattered—and that those of the great and the good were mostly superficial.

Cowling had little time for the solemnities of professional academic life. He never went to conferences and hardly to seminars. He delivered his lectures in a monotone. Believing that colleges were the core institutions of Oxford and Cambridge, he intervened in faculty politics only if he could find a foolish reform to oppose. Promotion, therefore, was not rapid. He was neither very willing nor very competent as a supervisor of PhD students. Advising students to ignore secondary work except if it could be ridiculed, to head straight for the archives in search of inspiration, and to complicate the narrative as much as possible, was an unsuccessful strategy: few of them completed a thesis. His taste for conflict greatly increased divisiveness within the Peterhouse governing body, to the alarm of Butterfield, who had governed more effectively as an autocrat. Cowling was addicted to schemes, and his artless openness about them, his tendency to overplay them, and his sheepish amusement when they misfired, were endearingly Hancockian. For twelve years after Butterfield's retirement in 1968 a conservative faction dominated the college, mainly by preventing almost all new permanent appointments. Key to this strategy was the election of two aged and conservative masters, and in an attempt to pull off the same trick again Cowling secured the post for Hugh Trevor-Roper, Lord Dacre, in 1980. Ideologically, this was not the error that was often alleged. Dacre was not a natural reformer, and when he left Peterhouse in 1987 it was more out of touch with the Cambridge mainstream than it had been in 1980. The admission of women in 1984 was not his initiative but the result of a volte-face by Cowling's party undertaken for academic reasons, and on their own terms, once the intellectual quality of arts undergraduates began to decline (now that most other colleges had gone mixed). The difficulties between Cowling and Dacre stemmed instead from Cowling's assumption that Dacre was as addicted to conspiracy and oppositional politics as he was—a self-fulfilling prophecy, especially once Dacre became bored with the social and cultural insularity of the college. The result was a long-running and increasingly public slanging match which both men found immensely life-enhancing.

Throughout these years Cowling retained his interest in politics and journalism. He sat as a Conservative on Cambridgeshire county council from 1966 to 1970. When Gale became editor of *The Spectator* in 1970 Cowling became literary editor, writing several pieces critical of the Conservative leader Edward Heath and his pro-EEC policy. However, he resigned in 1971 when the acting editor, in Gale's absence, refused to publish Cowling's protest against his publication of an article by Tony Palmer that claimed that the significant question about Princess Anne was whether she had had sex. At this time Cowling was broadly a Powellite, opposed to extra government expenditure, taxation, and European entry. He wanted a blunt defence of the social order, social inequality, and the traditional 'stabilities and decencies of English political life' against government interference (as he put it in a letter to *The Times*, 14 June 1968).

It was often stated that Cowling had a considerable influence on the direction of Conservative thought in the 1970s and 1980s, either personally or in association with academic and political co-conspirators in and beyond Peterhouse. The college was widely regarded as a conservative seminary, partly because several of Cowling's pupils went to work for the Conservative research department or Conservative newspapers. Cowling himself became a more active propagandist in the late 1970s, helping to found the Salisbury Group, which aimed to provide a forum for serious discussion of Conservative political philosophy, and editing the collection *Conservative Essays* (1978). He approved of the general direction and tone of the Thatcher governments, but *Conservative Essays* was in part a warning to the party not to place too much emphasis on rigorous *laissez-faire* doctrines, which he called 'Jacobin' and which he felt were likely to be expressed in too unrestrained and socially divisive a manner. He saw Hayek, and many of the philosophical converts to Thatcherism, as painfully earnest and doctrinaire social scientists with narrowly economic preoccupations who lacked perspective, worldly wisdom, and tactical skill. On Margaret Thatcher's only visit to Peterhouse, to address a Conservative gathering in 1977, she waved his intervention aside with the remark that 'we don't want pessimists in our party' (Bentley, 288). Later, still anxious to prick illusions, pomposity, and earnestness, he denied that the 'new right' had been very original or that Thatcher had transformed Britain, since governments could, in his view, achieve little. He also denied intellectual influence for himself, claiming instead that his various political interventions over thirty years had merely reflected the 'suburban, backwoods and provincial opinion' that was 'the core and heart of English Conservatism' (*Independent on Sunday*, 10 Oct 1993).

Cowling's academic and other writings helped to make newspaper commentary on politics much more sophisticated during his lifetime, an achievement that he shared with his like-minded journalist friends—including Frank Johnson, Patrick Cosgrave, and Charles Moore, as well as Gale, Worsthorne, Welch, and Utley. Though in term-time he maintained a bachelor lifestyle in Peterhouse rooms, in the vacations he lived with Gale and his wife in their houses in Wivenhoe, Essex, and then Tattingstone, Suffolk. He also rented a flat in The Albany, London, from Peterhouse, the landlord. The main attractions of Wivenhoe and Tattingstone were political gossip, poker, and the salon run by Gale's wife, Patricia Marina (Pat), *née* Holley, daughter of Charles Francis Holley, cable manufacturer. She and Gale were divorced in 1983. Cowling married her on 5 September 1996, though they had been lovers for decades previously; he was always particularly close to her youngest son.

Retirement On leaving Peterhouse Cowling retired to Caswell Bay on the Gower peninsula, and he hardly set foot in the college again, reflecting his iron will and lack of nostalgia. On becoming Olin visiting professor of religion at Columbia University in 1989 he discovered the ideological and financial attractiveness of parts of the American university system. In 1993 his admirer Hilton Kramer arranged for him to be distinguished service professor at Adelphi University, but a heart attack in 1996 led to retirement from Adelphi and a triple bypass operation in 1997. From this point he lived almost entirely in Wales, especially after a second bout of illness in 2002, which left him weak. Quiet domestic life was no hardship to him, for though always willing to be sociable he was at his most content in a room with lots of books, a telephone, and whisky for the evenings. He died at the Singleton Hospital, Swansea, on 24 August 2005, of angiodysplasia of the colon and cerebrovascular disease. He was survived by his wife, Pat.

JONATHAN PARRY

Sources N. Attallah, ed., *Singular encounters* (1990), 128–48 · M. Bentley, ed. *Public and private doctrine: essays in British history presented to Maurice Cowling* (1993) · P. Ghosh, 'A bibliography, 1948–1991', *Public and private doctrine: essays in British history presented to Maurice Cowling* (1993), 345–53 · *The Times* (26 Aug 2005); (29 Aug 2005) · *Daily Telegraph* (26 Aug 2005); (29 Aug 2005) · *Sunday Telegraph* (28 Aug 2005) · *The Spectator* (3 Sept 2005) · *The Guardian* (6 Sept 2005) · *The Independent* (6 Sept 2005) · *WW* (2005) · personal knowledge (2009) · private information (2009) · b. cert. · m. cert. · d. cert.

Archives CUL, department of manuscripts and university archives, Butterfield papers | SOUND BL NSA, documentary recording

Likenesses obituary photographs

Wealth at death under £117,000: administration with will, 13 Nov 2006, *CGPLA Eng. & Wales*

Cox, (Charles) Brian (1928–2008), poet, literary critic, and educationist, was born on 5 September 1928 at 142 Humberston Road, Grimsby, Lincolnshire, the second son of Hedley Ernest Cox, coal exporter's clerk, and his wife, Rose, *née* Thompson, lady's maid. Attendance at Nunsthorpe elementary school laid principles of academic rigour and coherent ethics that stayed with him throughout his life. He took from his family's Methodism an almost secular sense of kindness. The importance of family and community was reinforced by his mother's death when he was aged ten; he remained thereafter close to his father and older brother. Much of his poetry expressed a sense of human vulnerability and love. His subsequent education built on that foundation, but was in itself less fulfilling. He transferred at the age of eleven to Wintringham secondary school, and thence to Pembroke College, Cambridge, on an open scholarship gained in 1946 but deferred to 1949 for army service. He graduated with a first in English literature in 1952, and then took an MLitt for a thesis on Henry James in 1954. His experience of academic study throughout these fifteen years was worthy but, as he later wrote, somewhat unconnected to his real pleasure in reading and writing.

Nevertheless several experiences at Cambridge had a permanent impact on Cox. He properly met his future wife, Jean Willmer (though they been acquainted at secondary school), who was a schoolteacher; they married at the Memorial Mission Hall in Grimsby on 7 August 1954, and their partnership he later described as 'completely happy' (*Great Betrayal*, 85). He formed a lasting, close friendship with A. E. (Tony) Dyson, a fellow student of literature. While a postgraduate student he taught on two days each week for the Workers' Educational Association, resuming an involvement in adult education that had started when he had been recruited into the Royal Army Education Corps and confirming his belief that great literature ought to be made available to everyone.

Cox was appointed in 1954 to a post as assistant lecturer in English at Hull University, staying until 1966. His colleagues included Richard Hoggart, Malcolm Bradbury, and Barbara Everett, and he became friends also with the university librarian, Philip Larkin; it was a politically diverse group, but all were committed to the wide dissemination of high literary standards. Cox's most lasting contribution to that end came in 1959 when, with Dyson, he founded *Critical Quarterly*, aiming to provide informed debate about literature to an educated public. It was highly successful, achieving over 5000 subscribers, among whom were English teachers in more than half the grammar schools of Britain. The journal ran summer schools for teachers and senior school students. It held poetry competitions which encouraged the work of several of the new voices of the 1960s including Sylvia Plath, Ted Hughes, R. S. Thomas, Thom Gunn, and Larkin, who remained a strong supporter of the journal and a source of advice. It also led to two volumes by Cox and Dyson, *Modern Poetry* (1963) and *Practical Criticism of Poetry* (1965).

The journal always had educational aims, but this became more overt and controversial when it published a series of five *Black Papers* on education from 1969 to 1977. These collections, edited by Cox and Dyson, provided platforms for polemical protest against student militancy in universities, comprehensive secondary schooling, and 'child-centred' methods of teaching. Cox remained ambivalent about the achievement of the *Black Papers* for the rest of his life. On the one hand he believed that they had shifted the terms of debate, ensuring the acceptance that 'standards of excellence must be maintained' (*Black Papers on Education*, 1971, 33). On the other he deeply regretted being labelled as right-wing, especially by critics on the left who seemed not to have read what he wrote.

Cox insisted that he was a liberal, both in the sense of respecting diversity and equal rights, and also in his belief in human reason and the importance of liberal education for all. His textbook with Dyson on the practical criticism of poetry had established—well before these controversies—that the engaged academic ought to support schoolteachers constructively. His greatest contribution to education policy was to chair (in 1988–9) the official working group that created the English national curriculum for schools in England and Wales, publishing a report that sought high standards and knowledge of a literary canon alongside free expression—drama, creative writing, discussion, and reading for pleasure. The report was also well informed by research on how children become literate, and showed a respect for dialect and for bilingualism alongside an insistence on the importance of standard linguistic forms. The price of this balance was that the resulting curriculum was gradually eroded by the mechanistic preferences of both Conservative and Labour governments from the mid-1990s onwards.

Cox, who was appointed CBE in 1990, was widely acknowledged to be an extraordinarily courteous man with a firm commitment to public service, a belief in teaching as a powerful force for good, and loyalty to what he called early in his career the 'ideals of progress, liberty, tolerance and reason' (C. B. Cox, *The Free Spirit*, 1963, 161). The tragedy for his optimism was that he lived at a time when faith in such ideals was widely contemned.

Cox's poems were published in *Two-Headed Monster* (1985), *Collected Poems* (1993), *Emeritus* (2001), and *My Eightieth Year to Heaven* (2007). Among his other works were a study of Joseph Conrad (1974) and an edited collection of profiles of African writers (2 vols, 1996). He lived latterly at

20 Park Gates Drive, Cheadle Hume, near Stockport, and died there on 24 April 2008, of cancer of the prostate. He was survived by his wife, Jean, and their three children.

LINDSAY PATERSON

Sources C. B. Cox and A. E. Dyson, 'Word in the desert', *Critical Quarterly*, 10 (1968), 1–7 · C. B. Cox, '*Critical Quarterly*: twenty-five years', *Critical Quarterly*, 26 (1984), 3–16 · B. Cox, *The great betrayal* (1992) · M. Schmidt, 'C. B. Cox: pragmatic patron', *Critical Quarterly*, 35 (1993), 17–20 · *The Guardian* (28 April 2008) · *The Independent* (29 April 2008) · *The Times* (30 April 2008) · C. MacCabe, editorial, *Critical Quarterly*, 50 (2008), iii–vi · B. Cox, '*Critical Quarterly* and Hull', *Critical Quarterly*, 50 (2008), 1–4 · C. Atherton, 'Public intellectuals and the schoolteacher audience: the first ten years of the *Critical Quarterly*', *English*, 58 (2009), 75–94 · *WW* (2008) · personal knowledge (2012) · private information (2012) · b. cert. · m. cert. · d. cert.

Archives JRL

Likenesses photographs, 1966–77, Photoshot, London · photograph, *c.*1992, repro. in Cox, *Great Betrayal*, jacket · obituary photographs

Cox, Sir Geoffrey Sandford (1910–2008), journalist and broadcasting executive, was born on 7 April 1910 at Palmerston North, New Zealand, the youngest of three sons of Charles William Sandford Cox (1873–1965), bank manager, and his wife, Mary, *née* MacGregor (1875–1960). From Southlands High School in Invercargill he went to Otago University to read history and thence, as a Rhodes scholar, to Oriel College, Oxford, where he opted for philosophy, politics, and economics. More relevant to his immediate future was his travel in Europe during the vacations and, challenged by a German fellow scholar to see the Nazi way of life for himself, he spent three weeks under canvas with the *Arbeitsdienst*, the military-style youth labour service. An account he wrote of this adventure was picked up by the *New York Times* and in Britain by *The Spectator*, and brought him to the attention of Fleet Street.

After graduating from Oxford with a second-class degree in 1934—and on 25 May 1935 marrying a young woman he had met there, Cecily Barbara Talbot Turner (1912–1993), daughter of Alexander Forrest Turner, artist—he was taken on by the *News Chronicle*, a liberal newspaper with a tradition of forthright reporting. In Spain, where civil war broke out in 1936, its celebrated foreign correspondent Arthur Koestler had been imprisoned for criticizing General Franco. The veteran Vernon Bartlett was about to be sent in his stead when it was decided not to risk losing another of the paper's eminences. Despite his recent marriage Cox was considered more expendable, with the added advantage that his New Zealand passport might confuse suspicious fascists. In the event his coverage was confined to the beleaguered capital, and gave him the material for a book, *The Defence of Madrid* (1937), that brought him a rival Fleet Street offer, this time from the all-powerful *Daily Express*, as a foreign correspondent. Based in Vienna, then Paris, but sooner or later pursuing every lurch towards world war, he covered the *Anschluss* of Austria into the German Reich, the Munich crisis, the Russo-Finnish winter war, the blitzkrieg through the low countries, and so to the fall of France, from where he escaped on the last P&O steamer to leave Bordeaux.

Deciding it was time to fight in the war rather than report it, in 1940 Cox joined a New Zealand infantry brigade that had been switched to Britain when an immediate invasion was feared, but now that Mussolini's declaration of war had extended the conflict to the Mediterranean, was returning to its original destination, the Middle East. Cox served in Greece, Crete, and the western desert as an intelligence officer and was mentioned in dispatches. At this point his native country decided it should have a voice in the deliberations of the wartime alliances. Cox was plucked from the army and sent to the newly established New Zealand legation in Washington as first secretary and chargé d'affaires. His superior there was still a minister in the New Zealand government and had to spend much time back home. It fell to Cox, aged thirty-two, to debate and eventually sign historic treaties, on one occasion immediately ahead of the Soviet Union's formidable ambassador to the United States, Andrei Gromyko. Then in 1944 he was able to rejoin what was now the 2nd New Zealand division for the final slog of the Italian campaign, from Monte Cassino to Trieste, which enclave staged the first of the many vengeful small wars that flared up once the big war ended, and gave Cox another subject for a book.

Spurning a diplomatic or military career, in 1945 Cox went back to the *News Chronicle* as a lobby correspondent but was soon making his name as a commentator on international as well as domestic affairs. When the *Chronicle* made him an assistant editor in 1954 he determined on an executive career in newspapers. Two years later he was offered the deputy editorship. His letter of acceptance was in his pocket, ready to be delivered, when he heard the snatch of gossip which—once more—tempted him to change course. Aidan Crawley, who had successfully set up Independent Television's news service, ITN, when commercial television went on the air in 1955, was sick of the cost-cutting and general interference now emanating from hard-hit programme contractors, and was resigning in protest. Cox stalled on the *Chronicle* offer and applied for the ITN job. He was summoned to lunch by Captain Tom Brownrigg, the brusque former naval officer who was general manager of Associated-Rediffusion, the main London contractor, and also chairman of ITN. They had been reluctant allies, they now discovered, when in 1941 German airborne forces were landing on Crete and the navy was dispatched to take off British and New Zealand troops. 'Would have left you there if I'd had my way', Brownrigg grunted. 'We had already lost half the Mediterranean Fleet. It was madness to risk losing more ships' (*See it Happen*, 21–2).

Nevertheless Brownrigg gave Cox the post of editor, ITN. It was a daunting challenge. Crawley's great innovation had been to replace the impersonal newsreaders of BBC television with 'newscasters,' as he termed them, who would be involved in the writing and delivery of each item, and who might even turn to interview a witness to the story or a specialist in its subject. The public's favourite was the athlete Christopher Chataway. Only now did Cox learn that he too was quitting. There happened to be an approach from the then little-known Ludovic Kennedy, whose Sunday afternoon arts programme had just been axed, while young Robin Day was showing promise. Cox, whose knack of picking the right people for the right job would distinguish his whole career, pushed them both to the forefront.

On a visit to the United States Cox had been impressed by the authority of such news moguls as Charles Collingwood and Ed Murrow, and even more by their live transmission of events and debates and hearings as they took place, notably Murrow's showing-up of Senator McCarthy. 'See it happen' became his watchword (and in due course the title of his memoir). When President Kennedy arrived in London in 1961 his namesake Ludovic collared him in the street for an on-air interview. Another time viewers were abruptly switched to cameras deep under the Alps for the moment when engineers driving a new road tunnel from both ends met in the middle. All this enterprise was still confined within fifteen-minute bulletins out of peak viewing hours. Cox's goal was a full half-hour timed to harvest all the main news of the day. In 1967 he was finally able to launch *News at Ten*, the first half-hour, peak-time news programme on British television.

Cox (who was made a CBE in 1959 and knighted in 1966) was a member of a consortium bidding for one of the last programme contracts, Yorkshire TV. When in 1968 they succeeded he became its deputy chairman and had to leave ITN. In 1971 Yorkshire Television took over Tyne Tees Television, and Cox become chairman of the latter. In 1977, however, he returned to his old haunts as chairman of UPITN, an international agency formed by ITN and United Press. He was also chairman of LBC Radio from 1978 to 1981.

Cox finally retired in 1981 to enjoy country walks and fishing in local waters, though he also served as an independent director of *The Observer* for another eight years. He and Cecily had had two sons, Peter and Patrick, and twin daughters, Rosamond and Evelyn. Their home from 1976 was in Coln St Dennis, Gloucestershire. Cox, who survived his wife by fifteen years, died on 2 April 2008, at Moreton Hill Farm Care Centre, Standish, Gloucestershire, of cancer. He was cremated at Cheltenham crematorium on 11 April and his ashes, along with his wife's, rest in the burial annexe of St James the Great Church in Coln St Dennis. They were survived by their four children.

PHILIP PURSER

Sources G. Cox, *See it happen* (1983) · *The Times* (4 April 2008) · *Daily Telegraph* (4 April 2008) · *The Guardian* (4 April 2008) · *The Independent* (4 April 2008) · *WW* (2008) · Burke, *Peerage* · personal knowledge (2012) · private information (2012) · m. cert. · d. cert.

Archives FILM BFINA, current affairs footage | SOUND BL NSA, documentary recording

Likenesses S & G Barratts, photographs, 1965, PA Photos, London · obituary photographs

Wealth at death £772,767: probate, 10 Nov 2008, *CGPLA Eng. & Wales*

Cox, Lawrence Jack [John] **(1920–2007)**, civil engineer and advocate of organ donation, was born on 18 August 1920 at 19 Phoenix Street, Wolverhampton, the only son of John Cox, a grinder at a motor car works, and his wife, Gladys, *née* Booth. He left Wolverhampton intermediate school at the age of fourteen and then did small jobs to supplement the family income, but every weekday attended night school to learn about building construction. At the age of eighteen he secured employment with the Bernard Sunley Group and worked at Samlesbury on enlarging an aircraft factory and constructing an airfield for production of the Hampden twin-engined bomber. In 1940 his occupation was classified 'reserved', and he found himself in technical charge of constructing on a greenfield site near Selby (with plant improvised from open-cast coal mining) runways first for fighters, then for twin-engined bombers, building on his own initiative to dimensions sufficient for taxiing four-engined bombers. As Britain's battle of the Atlantic required long-distance air cover, he was transferred to Farrars Ltd, Belfast, and engaged in constructing airfields at Ballykelly, Ballyhalbert, and Aldergrove (later Northern's Ireland's international airport).

In 1946 Cox was promoted his company's agent on projects. One such was the Belfast harbour power station. As post-war reconstruction supervened he was engaged in building houses and factories, mainly in concrete as the most readily available material in Britain. In 1948 he returned to England to work on utilities in Cornwall and in 1949 joined Tarmac Ltd. By then the conditions of cold war prevailed and required large new airfields for the United States Air Force and for the RAF's V-bombers that could carry the atomic bomb as a deterrent. At Machrihanish he built the NATO airfield by moving and spreading over higher ground 1 million cubic yards of peat by using water jets. Continuing to work with Tarmac at Alconbury and then Elvington, he happened to be on hand when in February 1953 the east coast floods breached coastal defences. On site that night he contracted by handshake with Lincolnshire River Authority to repair the breach in three weeks with rock, earthworks, and concrete. In 1956 he met Anne Rosemary (Ro) Marshall (*b.* 1939), daughter of James Saddler Marshall, gas engineer, and the next day asked her to marry him. They were married on 25 June 1960 at the parish church of St Nicholas, Lincoln, and had two children, Peter and Christine.

Also in 1956 came the most far-reaching redirection of Cox's industrial life when the minister of transport, Harold Watkinson, launched a sixteen-year programme to construct the first 1000 miles of motorway network in Britain. Cox was Tarmac's agent on site to build, in spite of interruption by months of heavy rainfall, the first 8¼ miles of motorway, forming the Preston bypass within the plans of motorways for Lancashire vigorously advocated by James Drake, the county surveyor and bridgemaster. The £2.84 million bypass was opened on 5 December 1958 by the prime minister, Harold Macmillan.

Thereafter until 1983 Cox carried responsibility in top management roles for major industrial construction projects including Drax power station, nuclear accelerators at Culham and CERN (Geneva), and the Thames barrier. He masterminded sequences of contracts to build sections of motorway such as the M50, and major parts of the M5, M6, M74, M25, and others, including numerous bridges and split-level junctions. In 1966 he became a director of Tarmac Construction and later chairman of Tarmac National and vice-chairman of Tarmac International. As the bipartisan motorway building programme spluttered through the last quarter of the twentieth century he proposed in 1981 the engagement of private finance to design, build, and operate motorways in return for incomes related to the volumes of traffic using them over a long subsequent period (an idea taken up very much later).

In 1977 Cox became a member of the council of the Institution of Highway Engineers and in 1981 its president, redirecting it as the Institution of Highways and Transportation (later the Chartered Institution of Highways and Transportation). He became a member of the Institution of Civil Engineers' road board, the Department of Transport's liaison committee, the council of the Federation of Civil Engineering Contractors and the council of the Export Group of Construction Industries, and the Conseil National des Ingénieurs et des Scientifiques de France. He served as a member of the Transport and Roads Research Laboratory advisory committee from 1978 to 1983, and visitor to the same laboratory between 1988 and 1991.

Cox's success as an engineer was overshadowed by the death in 1989 of his son, Peter, caused by an inoperable brain tumour. Peter asked that his kidneys be taken to prolong another life. The family secured this. His sister, Christine, launched in his memory the concept of voluntary organ donation cards, even while she worked as the private secretary to the chairman of Rolls-Royce. Cox, over two decades, took on the roles of travelling advocate, fund-raiser, and political lobbyist. Thence emerged the National Register of Organ Donors, launched in 1994. (A kidney donor card had been launched in 1971.) He was awarded a commemorative medal for raising the largest total of funds in 'statemented' causes nationally by Age Concern in 2006.

In 1995 Cox responded with Tom Williams and Ron Bridle to Sir Peter Baldwin's plan that there be assembled by voluntary effort a comprehensive national archive of first-hand experience of the construction of Britain's motorway system. Cox (always using an old typewriter) and his collaborators made contact with hundreds of former colleagues who contributed writings of their own. The Motorway Archive Trust (incorporated with charitable status on 28 August 1999 with Cox as one of its trustees) went on to publish a series of encyclopaedic books under the title *The Motorway Achievement* and created a website detailing the archival sources. Cox put a sustained effort into fund-raising for it and wrote two keynote chapters for the first volume, on the Preston bypass and contracting relationships; he later made contributions to other volumes in the series. He also had several articles published in *Tarmac Papers* but made no other notes detailing his own pioneering achievements. In his final years cancer of the prostate and bone cancer confined him to a wheelchair. He died at his home, 10 The Parklands, Finchfield Hill, Wolverhampton, on 4 March 2009, and was survived by his wife, Rosemary, and daughter, Christine.

PETER BALDWIN

Sources G. Charlesworth, *A history of British motorways* (1984) · R. Bridle and J. Porter, eds., *The motorway achievement: frontiers of knowledge and practice* (2002) · P. Baldwin and R. Baldwin, eds., *The motorway achievement: the British motorway system, visualisation, policy and administration* (2004) · P. Baldwin, R. Baldwin, and D. I. Evans, eds., *The motorway achievement: building the network in southern and eastern England* (2007) · W. J. McCoubrey, ed., *The motorway achievement: building the network* (2009) · J. M. Carrington, ed., *The motorway achievement: building the network in the midlands* (2009) · B. Hawker and H. Stevens, eds., *The motorway achievement: building the network in Wales* (2010) · *The Independent* (19 April 2007) · *The Times* (7 June 2007) · personal knowledge (2011) · private information (2011) · b. cert. · m. cert. · d. cert.

Archives Motorway Archive Trust, corresp. with Sir Peter Baldwin

Likenesses photograph, Chartered Institution of Highways and Transportation, London · photograph, repro. in Baldwin and Baldwin, eds., *British motorway system*, 498

Wealth at death £780,527: probate, 21 June 2007, *CGPLA Eng. & Wales*

Craig, Stella Ross- (1906–2006), botanical artist, was born on 19 March 1906 at 61 Gordon Road, Aldershot, Hampshire, one of the three children of John Ross Craig, pharmacist, and his wife, Christina Sinclair, *née* Lauder. Both her parents were Scottish. On her birth certificate her father signed himself J. Ross Craig, and by the time of her marriage she had added a hyphen. During her childhood in Hampshire and Kent her father, who was an amateur botanist, stimulated her interest in flowers, and her brother encouraged her to draw. After her mother's early death she left school at the age of fourteen to look after the family home. At eighteen she undertook a course lasting four years at Thanet Art School, where she studied life drawing, print-making, photography, and embroidery. At the same time she attended evening classes on botany. She subsequently extended her botanical knowledge at the Chelsea Polytechnic but took no qualification. There she met Joseph Robert Sealy, known as J. Robert Sealy (1907–2000), a fellow student, and son of Joseph Sealy, a sergeant in Kew Gardens constabulary; they eventually married on 24 October 1936. Sealy had entered the Royal Botanic Gardens at Kew about 1925. Two years later he was transferred to the Kew herbarium to assist Otto Stapf, botanist and editor of *Curtis's Botanical Magazine*.

Curtis's Botanical Magazine published floral paintings, especially those of horticultural appeal. In 1929 it engaged Stella Ross-Craig as a botanical artist; it is not clear whether her future husband played any part in this appointment. The Royal Horticultural Society, which owned the periodical, paid her salary but she reported to Stapf at Kew Gardens. (She was never a member of Kew's staff.) Her first drawing was published in 1932, lithographed by Lilian Snelling, at that time the periodical's principal artist. From 1935 the floral dissections that accompanied every illustration were transferred to the text pages as line drawings, and most of them were executed by Ross-Craig. She succeeded Snelling when the latter retired in 1952 and was joined by Ann Webster (whom she claimed to have trained) and later by Margaret Stones as fellow artists. When her last painting was published in

1980, she had contributed 333 plant portraits to the magazine.

In 1932 the Bentham-Moxon Trust at Kew Gardens employed Ross-Craig to produce line drawings for *Hooker's Icones Plantarum*, a periodical that Sir William Hooker had founded in 1837. Originally it had selected new or rare specimens from Hooker's personal herbarium, but it was now portraying species in the Kew herbarium. By 1956 Ross-Craig had drawn 397 plates, which included 25 for a small monograph that she compiled, *A Revision of the Genus Sphaeranthus* (1955). She also produced 50 line drawings for W. B. Turrill's *Studies in the Genus Fritillaria*, which was completed by her husband after Turrill's death. It appeared as a separate issue of *Hooker's Icones Plantarum* in 1980.

Through her contributions to *Hooker's Icones Plantarum* Ross-Craig perfected her skill as a black and white illustrator and was ready to contemplate her *magnum opus*, *Drawings of British Plants*. It was to be a compendium of British native species, excluding Gramineae (grasses) and Cyperaceae (sedges), which other publications had adequately covered. She was not the first to conceive of such a project. W. H. Fitch had produced *Illustrations of the British Flora* (1880) as a companion to George Bentham's *Handbook of the British Flora*. Its small line drawings, four to a page, in a portable form, deserved their popularity with the general public, but they lacked detail. Much more in accord with Ross-Craig's concept was Roger W. Butcher's *Further Illustrations of British Plants* (1930), with competent line drawings by Florence E. Strudwick.

Ross-Craig planned a line drawing of every species incorporating magnified dissections of its flower and fruit. She emulated the woodcuts in medieval herbals by occasionally including roots whenever they were a pertinent diagnostic detail. Charles Hubbard, a Kew botanist, encouraged her, and the director, Sir Edward Salisbury, introduced her to the publisher George Bell & Son. The publisher chose good quality paper to facilitate hand colouring by the purchaser. The first part appeared in 1948 and during the next twenty-five years she produced, on average, about two drawings a week, amounting to 1316 full-page plates in thirty-one parts. Her husband and their friend Bill Burtt joined her in collecting specimens, members of the Botanical Society of the British Isles volunteered to find rare species, and dried specimens in the Kew herbarium were consulted. Her husband, Burtt, and Noel Sandwith, a Kew botanist with a comprehensive knowledge of the British flora, advised her on any taxonomic problems. Issued in paperback parts, initially 6*s*. each—which had soared to £2 when the last part, the index, appeared in 1974—it was welcomed by teachers and students, for whom it was largely intended. Sir Edward Salisbury pronounced it to be 'a magnificent work of scientific investigation and recording'. It rapidly became a classic in its particular genre of botanical art.

Ross-Craig's line drawings appeared in other publications: 69 in J. Hutchinson and J. M. Dalziel's *Flora of West Tropical Africa* (vol. 2, pts 1–2, 1931–6); 16 in F. C. Stern's *Study of the Genus Paeonia* (1946); and a few in H. J. Elwes's *Monograph of Genus Lilium* (supplement, 1938–40). She contributed three colour plates to G. H. Johnstone's *Asiatic Magnolias in Cultivation* (1955), but only the frontispiece to her husband's *Revision of the Genus Camellia* (1958). It proved too expensive to include the other Camellia paintings she had executed (seven of them are now in the Kew library) but she compensated for their absence by drawing 102 line figures for the volume. When Sir Jeremiah Colman's fine collection of living orchids was bequeathed to Kew Gardens early in 1942, she painted 49 of them over the next four years and generously presented the paintings to Kew in 1968.

Ross-Craig described her technique of painting and drawing in W. Blunt and W. T. Stearn's *The Art of Botanical Illustration* (1994), and in an article in *Medical and Biological Illustration* (1953). Before attempting any plant portrait she would absorb what she called its 'character or personality'. Only then would she lightly pencil in her composition, adroitly inserting floral dissections in appropriate spaces on the sheet. The smoothness and whiteness of hot-pressed Whatman paper gave her the purity of colour she sought. She objected to being grouped with 'flower painters', seeing herself as a botanical artist subject to the discipline of scientific accuracy. In an undated note, now in the Kew library, she affirmed that, for her, 'painting was never routine, always an endeavour to do justice to the plants' (Ross-Craig to Gren L. Lucas, Ross-Craig papers). As a botanical artist she will be remembered best for her accomplished line drawings, which project three-dimensional images through confident line and stipple shading. She drew in waterproof Indian ink with a flexible lithographic pen on Bristol board. Whenever living plants were not available she would consult Kew herbarium's collections. She had confidently mastered the difficult technique of recreating a plant from a lifeless specimen through a combination of precise draughtsmanship and botanical knowledge.

Volume 182 (1978–80) of *Curtis's Botanical Magazine* was dedicated to Ross-Craig and her husband, who had been its editor in all but name. Both had 'diligently upheld its high standards' for more than half a century. In November 1999 she was presented with the Kew award 'in recognition of her outstanding contribution to botanical art'. She received the Royal Horticultural Society's prestigious Veitch memorial medal in 2002. In the same year a selection of her work was exhibited in the Edinburgh Botanic Garden, and it was shown again at Kew in 2003.

Ross-Craig was a modest, unassuming person—some called her self-effacing—but this natural reticence concealed firm resolve and stamina, qualities she needed to complete her ambitious *Drawings of British Plants*. She cared for her husband during his last years while he suffered from dementia. She spent her declining years at Abbeyfield Nursing Home in Ennerdale Road, Kew, and died in the West Middlesex Hospital in neighbouring Isleworth of bronchopneumonia on 7 February 2006, just six weeks short of her hundredth birthday. The residue of her estate was divided equally between Kew's Bentham-Moxon Trust, which had once employed her, and the Kew

Guild, of which her husband had been secretary for many years. She had prepared the preliminary drawings in the application of the guild for a coat of arms and a badge. She expressed a wish that her bequest should be used primarily for travel and plant expeditions and general research. Much of her published art work, miscellaneous watercolours and pencil drawings, a few sketchbooks, and a small archive of correspondence are housed in the Kew library.

RAY DESMOND

Sources *Journal of Kew Guild*, 13 (2000), 470–71 [obituary of J. Robert Sealy] · *Daily Telegraph* (10 Nov 2001); (9 Feb 2006) · *Sunday Telegraph* (13 Jan 2002) · U. Buchan, 'Stella Ross-Craig, botanical artist', *Plantsman*, 2/3 (2003), 152–9 · *The Times* (18 Feb 2006) · *The Independent* (20 Feb 2006) · *Curtis's Botanical Magazine*, 23 (2006), 255–7 · *Journal of Kew Guild*, 15 (2007), 116–17 · RBG Kew, Ross-Craig papers · personal knowledge (2010) · private information (2010) · b. cert. · m. cert. · d. cert.

Archives RBG Kew, corresp.

Likenesses obituary photographs · photograph, repro. in Buchan, 'Stella Ross-Craig, botanical artist'

Wealth at death £722,662: probate, 14 March 2006, *CGPLA Eng. & Wales*

Crampsey, Robert Anthony [Bob] (**1930–2008**), head teacher, writer, and broadcaster, was born on 8 July 1930 at 75 Clincart Road, Mount Florida, Glasgow (appropriately in the shadow of Hampden Park, the home of Scottish football), the eldest of the five children of an Irishman, Daniel Frederick Crampsey, a spirit merchant's manager and later publican and newsagent, and his Scottish wife, Catherine Arnot (Kitty), *née* McNaughton. He was educated first at Holy Cross Primary School and then at Holyrood School, Crosshill, the first co-educational Catholic secondary school to be opened in Glasgow, where he played in goal for the school team. At Holyrood he developed his love of history and English and his facility for languages, though he never comprehended mathematics, apart from goal averages. At home he 'devoured' the contents of an eight-volume set of encyclopaedias (Crampsey, 125).

Crampsey took a history degree at Glasgow University and, after national service in the RAF, began a teaching career in the city's Catholic schools, culminating in the rectorship of St Ambrose High in Coatbridge. Meanwhile on 7 April 1958, at Holy Cross Roman Catholic Church, Glasgow, he married Veronica Rose (Ronnie) Carson (*b.* 1929/30), medical practitioner, and daughter of Andrew Edward Carson, schoolteacher. They had four daughters. Crampsey was a devout Roman Catholic but he never forced his faith on others, although one pupil recalled having to write out the word 'Catholicism' fifty times because he had misspelled it. As a teacher he was apt to deviate from the core curriculum; a religious instruction lesson on St Joseph also covered the price of sten guns in the Second World War. As a head he was old-fashioned, more interested in the pastoral care of his pupils than being accountable to governors and others. Allegedly the Scottish comedian Chic Murray's portrayal of a quirky, piano-playing headmaster in the film *Gregory's Girl* (1981) was based on Crampsey.

Crampsey retired from teaching in 1987 to concentrate on broadcasting, a career that he had run in tandem with his school work since first commentating for STV in 1955. In those early days of television and its associated technical hitches Crampsey could draw on his remarkable recall to talk authoritatively, wittily, and virtually indefinitely in his instantly recognizable mellifluous tones. From 1987 he was part of BBC Radio Scotland's *Sportsound* team, though he also contributed extensively to sports programmes on STV and Radio Clyde. Although his uncles all supported Celtic, 'out of sheer cussedness', Crampsey chose Rangers, though he later transferred his allegiance to Queen's Park, a staunchly amateur side whose history he was later to write (Crampsey, 29). Yet football was not his sport of preference. His greatest sporting pleasure was watching Somerset County Cricket Club, of which he was a member. Indeed he was a missionary for schoolboy cricket in Lanarkshire, though he acknowledged that it was difficult to interest his pupils 'until they realised what kind of pain could be inflicted with a cricket ball' (*The Herald*, 28 July 2008).

Crampsey's knowledge of sport, and Scottish football in particular, was encyclopaedic, but his interests were much broader and he was a keen musician, historian, and linguist. Bert, as he was known to family and close friends (though as a broadcaster he was known as Bob Crampsey), was, his son-in-law proclaimed, 'Google before Google, Wikipedia before Wikipedia' (*Sunday Herald*, 3 Aug 2008). He learned the piano from his mother and won talent competitions playing classical music. He was an associate of the Royal College of Music and his tastes ranged from opera to American musicals. In 1965 he won BBC Radio's *Brain of Britain* quiz, and seven years later he reached the semi-finals of the corporation's televised *Mastermind* competition, in which his special subject was the American Civil War, a topic for which he had won a Churchill scholarship in 1970 and on which he later lectured as part of Glasgow University's lifelong learning programme.

Crampsey was a writer with a varied and prolific output. It included a novel and two plays; several chronicles of Scottish golf and football, the latter including histories of Queen's Park Football Club and the Scottish Football League; biographies of Sir Thomas Lipton and Jock Stein; travel books, which began when an offer by Crampsey to write about the Isle of Bute turned into a contract to cover Puerto Rico; and a forty-year stint producing 'Now you know' for the *Glasgow Evening News*, a column that settled many a sporting debate. His last book, written in his seventies, was on the 1938 Glasgow empire exhibition. In 1999 he received an honorary doctorate from the University of Stirling, in recognition of his contribution to Scottish sports studies.

The onset of Parkinson's disease forced Crampsey's retirement from regular broadcasting in 2001. He died on 27 July 2008 at Mearnskirk House care home, Newton Mearns, of general debility. A memorial mass, attended by around 500 mourners, was held on 1 August 2008 at Holy Cross Church, where fifty years before he had married his wife, Ronnie, who survived him with their four daughters. On hearing of his death the first minister of Scotland, Alex

Salmond, described him as 'an extraordinary man', and 'a legend in broadcasting and in Scottish football' (Salmond, press release). Crampsey was a modest man who played down his cerebral achievements, but he was pleased to be the first non-footballer elected to the Scottish Football Museum hall of fame, in 2007. WRAY VAMPLEW

Sources B. Crampsey, *The young civilian: a Glasgow wartime boyhood* (1987) · *The Scotsman* (28 July 2008) · *The Herald* [Glasgow] (28 July 2008); (2 Aug 2008) · *Daily Record* (28 July 2008) · *The Sun* (28 July 2008) · *Evening Times* [Glasgow] (28 July 2008); (1 Aug 2008) · *The Times* (29 July 2008) · *Sunday Herald* (3 Aug 2008) · *Sunday Times* (3 Aug 2008) · *Times Educational Supplement* (8 Aug 2008) · *The Guardian* (12 Aug 2008); (16 Aug 2008) · A. Salmond, press release, 28 July 2008, www.scotland.gov.uk/news/releases/2008/07/28120928, 9 May 2011 · b. cert. · m. cert. · d. cert.

Archives NL Scot., literary papers, broadcasts, press cuttings (1970–98)

Likenesses obituary photographs

Cresswell, (Elizabeth) Helen (1934–2005), children's author, was born on 11 July 1934 at Orchard House nursing home, Kirkby in Ashfield, Nottinghamshire, the second of three children of Joseph Edward Cresswell and his wife, Annie Edna, *née* Clarke. She was originally named Edna Helen Cresswell, but throughout her life was known, and published, as Helen Cresswell. At the time of her birth her father, the son of a miner, had his own business as a wholesale fruit merchant. The family lived in West Bridgford, a comfortable suburb of Nottingham, but were unhappy. Her father, who bore the physical and mental scars of the First World War, was frequently drunk and violent, and bullied his wife who would, but for her children, she told them, 'leave him tomorrow' (*Something about the Author*, 106). His eventual bankruptcy was a shameful secret long kept from his children. Annie Cresswell came from a better-off Nottinghamshire family: she had been to grammar school, was well-read and a good pianist. She encouraged her children to read widely, and taught other children so as to afford fee-paying schools for her own. In Cresswell's account of her childhood in *Something about the Author* (1995) she wrote that when she first read D. H. Lawrence's *Sons and Lovers* 'it was as though the writer had lifted the roof of our own house to find his characters' (ibid., 115).

Cresswell enjoyed school ('a world of calm and order, a predictable world with its own framework'; *Something about the Author*, 110) and at the age of ten won a scholarship to Nottingham Girls' High School. Her parents were Christian Scientists, not consistently, but enough to pass on to their children the belief that illness was one's 'own fault for not thinking the right thoughts' (ibid., 103). At the age of twelve she suffered a back problem which, neglected, led to her being hospitalized, and missing school for most of a year. Back at school she felt she was two people: 'the popular class clown, one of the top clique. But my real, secret self is the one who sits up into the early hours to finish poems … constantly aware of a mystery beyond the banalities of everyday life' (ibid., 114). She had been writing poems from the age of six and regarded her early writing in the style of Keats, Wordsworth, and de la Mare as her apprenticeship, 'my five finger exercise, my scales' (*Author Zone*, 42). Encouraged by her mother to enter competitions, she won a Poetry Society prize when she was sixteen and assumed that she would be a poet when she grew up.

(Elizabeth) Helen Cresswell (1934–2005), by David Worthy, 1990

Cresswell went to King's College, London, and took a degree in English in 1955. She then did a variety of jobs, including fashion buying, secretarial work, and teaching at a Nottingham school, and on 14 April 1962 she married (Leslie) Brian Rowe (1934–2000), the son of Leslie Baker Rowe, a Nottingham lace manufacturer. At the time of their marriage he was marketing director for the family factory but lost his job after a takeover, and then ran a corner shop. They had two daughters, Caroline (*b.* 1963) and Candida (*b.* 1971). Her husband was even-tempered, and a successful foil for Cresswell while the children grew up, but they then separated without acrimony. The marriage was dissolved in 1995.

Cresswell's first published book was *Sonya-by-the-Shore* (1960), about a girl who lives by a lake with her grandparents, thinking that is the whole world until she hears about a big city full of people across the lake. In 1963 she started on a completely different tack—a series of stories about Jumbo Spencer, an eleven-year-old boy with no intention of being like anyone else his age. The second book, *Jumbo Back to Nature* (1965), introduced one of her enduring themes—a tramp or wanderer who represents freedom and living for what's round the corner.

Cresswell tried various settings and styles until she made her name with *The Piemakers* (1967), about Gravella Roller, daughter of one of the hereditary piemaking families of Danby Dale. For this book she received the first of her four nominations for the Library Association's Carnegie medal. The others were for *The Night Watchmen* (1969), *Up the Pier* (1971), and *The Bongleweed* (1973). *The Night Watchmen* (which won the Children's Literature Association's phoenix award in 1989) was perhaps her most personal fantasy, seamless and poetic, full of hard-to-catch meaning. In it a boy meets two tramps, 'Do-as-you-pleasers', who tell him, 'You've got Here … and you've got

There. We're from There' (*The Night Watchmen*, 50). Her other favourite among her books was *The Winter of the Birds* (1975).

Cresswell also became an expert and enthusiastic writer for children's television, starting with the BBC's *Jackanory* programme. She sometimes wrote for book publication and television simultaneously, with specified locations, as in *Moondial* (1987), set at Belton House, Grantham. Her *Lizzie Dripping* series (1973 onwards) was filmed around her home, and the television series and books made Lizzie Dripping perhaps her most enduring character. (Her *Bagthorpe Saga*, also televised, was her most sustained series of books.) She was also a good adapter of other authors, with a particular affinity for Edith Nesbit. She liked the collaboration and teamwork inherent in television. The medium rewarded her: in 2000 she was joint winner of the British Academy of Film and Television Arts (BAFTA) children's writer's award.

Cresswell was equally at home with high humour and deep mystery, fantasy, pastoral and fairy story, slapstick and menace, the numinous and the anarchic. Her books celebrated the singular and eccentric, timeless craft, ceremony and community, and the natural world. She wrote over 100 children's books for a variety of publishers and said of them, 'Whatever the outward settings of my stories, the adventures they chart are essentially inner ones' (*Author Zone*, 42). She wrote early in the morning, sitting on the floor, and drafted stories at speed, without prior plotting, in bound blank books, changing very little thereafter. While writing she was happy, but she suffered from depression (for which she had a variety of treatments) and sometimes couldn't write for months. When elated she spent money on antiques and on statues for her garden.

Five feet ten inches tall, with long blonde hair, Cresswell cared how she looked. In middle age, with still-long hair, and stylish but unusual clothes, her appearance was particularly striking. She was independent-minded but easy to work with, ambitious, practical, and businesslike, but averse to the metropolitan literary scene. Despite her shyness she was good at talking to audiences of all ages. She listed her recreations as watercolour painting, collecting pictures, books, antiques and coincidences, and sundial watching. She was married in an Anglican church, and considered herself Christian, but not conventionally. She believed in ghosts. Her politics were Labour, veering later to Liberal Democrat. She remained attached to her family and her Nottinghamshire roots and bought a Georgian farmhouse, Old Church Farm, in the small village of Eakring, near Rufford Abbey, where she set another of her books (*The Secret World of Polly Flint*, 1982). She died at her home in Eakring on 26 September 2005, of cancer, and was cremated at Mansfield crematorium. Her memorial service was at Southwell Minster on 25 November 2005. She was survived by her two daughters.

MARI PRICHARD

Sources *Something about the Author*, 20 (1995), 101–21 • *Author Zone*, 4 (Sept 2002) • V. Watson, ed., *The Cambridge guide to children's books in English* (2001) • *The Independent* (28 Sept 2005) • *Daily Telegraph* (29 Sept 2005) • *The Guardian* (29 Sept 2005) • *The Times* (30 Sept 2005) • *WW* (2005) • papers, H. Cresswell papers, priv. coll. • private information (2009) [Caroline Rowe, daughter; A. Home; M. Thomas; G. Cross] • personal knowledge (2009) • b. cert. • m. cert. • d. cert.

Archives priv. coll., letters, typescripts • University of Minnesota Libraries | FILM BFINA, current affairs footage

Likenesses D. Worthy, photograph, 1990, PA Photos, London [*see illus.*] • D. Worthy, photographs, 1990, PA Photos, London • obituary photographs

Wealth at death £572,978: probate, 23 Nov 2007, *CGPLA Eng. & Wales*

Crick, Sir Bernard Rowland (1929–2008), political scientist and biographer, was born on 16 December 1929 at 77 Circle Gardens, Merton, London, the son of Harry Edgar Crick (*d.* 1968), insurance official, and his wife, Florence Clara, *née* Cook (1890–1986). He attended Whitgift School, Croydon, then read economics at University College, London, switching to government in his third year and gaining first-class honours in 1950. He had started attending lectures at the London School of Economics, including the final lectures of the ailing Harold Laski, an early influence. On completion of his first degree he registered for a PhD, but initially it made little headway, and he spent the years from 1952 to 1956 teaching and researching at North American universities, Harvard (1952–4), McGill (1954–5), and Berkeley (1955–6), which allowed him to avoid national service. His encounter with American political science was formative. He reacted strongly against the scientific pretensions of American behaviouralism, and wrote a critique of it for his doctoral thesis, which was subsequently published as *The American Science of Politics* (1959). Meanwhile, on 15 September 1953, in Cambridge, Massachusetts, he married Joyce Pumfrey Morgan, a lecturer in German, and they had two sons, Oliver and Thomas.

In 1957 Crick was appointed to an assistant lectureship in the department of government at the London School of Economics, where he stayed until 1965, being promoted to lecturer and then senior lecturer. The London School of Economics government department at this time was dominated by the conservative scepticism of Michael Oakeshott, which discouraged engagement in practical politics. Crick responded by writing his classic work, *In Defence of Politics* (1962). Translated into many languages, it went through five editions, and sold over 400,000 copies. It celebrated political engagement and active citizenship, arguing that politics is the condition of a free society, the activity of finding out what people want and how their divergent interests can be reconciled. The essence of politics, he emphasized, is negotiation, compromise, argument, and debate, which often appears messy and unprincipled, but is far preferable to the utopian anti-politics of the left and the reactionary anti-politics of the right. In 1964 Crick published *The Reform of Parliament* and became active in campaigning for greater accountability through more parliamentary scrutiny of the executive. In the same year he co-founded the Study of Parliament Group, which brought together the leading academic specialists on parliament, and he acted as its first secretary until 1968.

Following the recommendation for the expansion of the universities in the Robbins report of 1963 a new

Sir Bernard Rowland Crick (1929–2008), by Colin McPherson, 2003

department of politics was created at the University of Sheffield, and Crick was appointed to the first chair, in 1965. At his insistence the department was named the department of political theory and institutions, which captured the breadth of his interests. It soon developed into one of the leading departments of politics in the UK. As its first professor, from 1965 to 1971, Crick had the opportunity to make many new appointments. He created a lively and unorthodox department with representatives from all parts of the ideological spectrum. He appreciated vigorous debate and the clash of opinions and perspectives, arguing that this was the best environment for university teaching. Stories abounded of his time at Sheffield, particularly his habit of sleeping overnight in his office in the university's Arts Tower, to the consternation of the cleaners and the university authorities. Although he greatly enjoyed Sheffield he also missed London, but after his return to the capital in 1971 he continued to visit friends in Sheffield often, and kept in close touch with some of his academic colleagues, particularly Stuart Walkland and Patrick Seyd. He attended departmental anniversaries and was delighted to be awarded an honorary degree by the university in 1990.

In 1971 Crick become professor of politics at Birkbeck College, London, where he helped create another new department. The Birkbeck style of evening teaching and degrees for part-time and mature students suited him, and he appointed several scholars who became leaders in their field, including Paul Hirst and Ben Pimlott. His heart was never in university administration, however. While at Birkbeck he was approached by George Orwell's widow, Sonia, to write the first authorized biography of Orwell. It was published as *George Orwell: a Life* in 1980 and was a major critical success, the starting point for all subsequent Orwell biographies, noted for its shrewd analysis of Orwell's politics and its appreciation of his style of writing, although some critics thought it less good at capturing the personal side of Orwell. He took early retirement in 1984 (at a time of deep cuts in university budgets) partly to give himself more time for writing and other activities.

One of Crick's lifelong engagements was with the *Political Quarterly*, a journal established by Leonard Woolf, Kingsley Martin, and William Robson in 1930. He was joint editor (1966–80), chairman of the board (1980–93), and literary editor (1993–2000). The aim of the journal was to provide a bridge between the academic and the public world, accepting articles written in plain English on issues of public importance. With the royalties from his book on Orwell and further financial assistance from Richard Blair and David Astor, he helped set up the Orwell Memorial Trust, which funded lectures at Birkbeck and at Sheffield, and then with the help of additional sponsorship from the *Political Quarterly* established the Orwell prizes in 1993, two annual awards for the best political writing in journalism and literature. He chaired the panel of judges and saw the prizes develop into one of Britain's leading literary awards, and the pre-eminent prize for political writing.

Another of Crick's abiding passions was political education. In 1969 he founded the Politics Association, a body dedicated to the teaching of politics and government in schools. He helped revive the Hansard Society for Parliamentary Government, and became chief examiner for the government and politics A level at the University of London. In this latter capacity he revolutionized the curriculum, moving it away from rather dull questions on the constitution to political ideas and political issues, which produced a dramatic increase in the number of candidates. The education secretary, David Blunkett, one of his former students at Sheffield, asked him to chair the advisory group on the teaching of citizenship and democracy in schools in 1997. He brought together a team of enthusiasts including Betty Boothroyd and Kenneth Baker and produced a report in 1998 which led to citizenship education being incorporated into the national curriculum. In 2002 he was knighted for services to citizenship in schools and to political studies. He continued to advise David Blunkett on citizenship issues after the latter had moved to the Home Office, and in 2003–4 he chaired the Living in the UK advisory group, which helped devise tests and naturalization ceremonies for new British citizens.

Crick was a public intellectual and a democratic socialist in the Fabian tradition. One of the great political essayists and reviewers of his generation, he addressed himself to the general reader and the active citizen. A lifelong gadfly, he was forever starting new associations and launching new projects, many of which endured. He never lost his enthusiasm for political engagement and political argument, but he feared populism, particularly the trivialization and dumbing down of citizens by the modern media. The structures that can preserve an open and pluralist democracy, Crick warned, had continually to be fought for, otherwise they can all too easily be lost. In his passion for citizenship education he sought to counter the 'empty mob' of contemporary political culture. Only through arguing and engaging with one another, he suggested, could citizens find ways to express their interests and their hopes. This for Crick was the process of political education itself, which is never-ending, and the purpose of citizenship education was not just to teach how government works, but to develop the capacity for active citizenship. He himself had fierce views about most political subjects, from the Falklands and Iraq wars to Northern Ireland and presidential prime ministers. His view of politics did not mean a watered down consensus. He maintained that no progress of any kind was possible without political argument, political education, and political participation, and that to achieve these the political class had to stop talking to itself and engage with citizens, however uncomfortable and messy, and less than ideal, real politics might turn out to be.

Crick had an unforgettable presence. Jean Seaton, who worked with him on the Orwell prize committee, described him as 'a magnificently impossible person—clever, at times overbearing, absurd, self-centred, and yet at times humane, and certainly very human. He was no collaborator, but communities formed in his slipstream' (*The Guardian*, 27 Dec 2008). After the end of his first marriage he was married twice more, first on 17 February 1978 to Margaret Emily Cahill, *née* Smith (*b.* 1935/6), schoolteacher, former wife of Michael T. P. Cahill and daughter of Herbert Smith, carpenter, and then on 21 December 1989 to Freda Ivy Edis, a university tutor, daughter of Frederick James Cook, tailor. Both marriages ended in divorce. His partner in latter life was Una MacLean. After retiring from Birkbeck in 1984 he had moved to Edinburgh. In 2000 he received a lifetime achievement award from the Political Studies Association. He died on 19 December 2008 from prostate cancer at St Columba's Hospice, Edinburgh, and was cremated on 6 January 2009 at Warriston crematorium after a humanist service. The funeral procession was led by a New Orleans-style jazz band, because his family felt that this was the kind of noise he would have wanted to be played upon his departure. He was survived by his partner, Una, and his two sons.

ANDREW GAMBLE

Sources E. Levenson and others, eds., *Fabian thinkers: 120 years of progressive thought* (2004) • *The Guardian* (20 Dec 2008); (27 Dec 2008) • *The Times* (22 Dec 2008); (23 Dec 2008) • *Daily Telegraph* (22 Dec 2008) • *The Independent* (22 Dec 2008) • *New York Times* (22 Dec 2008) • *The Scotsman* (23 Dec 2008) • S. Katwala, 'On reading Bernard Crick', *Our kingdom*, 23 Dec 2008, www.opendemocracy.net/article/ourkingdom-theme/on-reading-bernard-crick, 14 July 2011 • *Evening News* [Edinburgh] (7 Jan 2009) • Burke, *Peerage* • *WW* • b. cert. • m. certs. [1978 and 1989] • d. cert.

Archives Birkbeck College, London | NL Scot., *Political Quarterly* papers | FILM BFINA, current affairs and documentary footage | SOUND BL NSA, current affairs and documentary recordings

Likenesses photographs, 2002–3, Camera Press, London • C. McPherson, photograph, 2003, Corbis [*see illus.*] • C. McPherson, photographs, 2003, Corbis • K. Wigglesworth, photograph, 2003 (with David Blunkett), PA Photos, London • photographs, 2003, Rex Features, London • obituary photographs

Croll [*née* Sprackett], **Elisabeth Joan** [Lisa] (**1944–2007**), Sinologist and anthropologist, was born on 21 September 1944 in Reefton, South Island, New Zealand, the daughter of Colston Robert (Bob) Sprackett (1916–1993) and his wife, Kathleen Joan (*b.* 1917). Her father was a Presbyterian minister from a poor background, and had defied the church's directives not to register as a conscientious objector during the Second World War. Her mother came from a long line of academics who in the mid-nineteenth century had been involved in setting up New Zealand's first university at Dunedin. Bob Sprackett visited Hong Kong in the 1950s to serve with an American social service organization, and this led to his eventual relocation to Sydney in 1963 to work with Chinese refugees and orphans. These early influences all had their part to play in shaping the young Lisa's future, not only her interest in China, but also her strong sense of social justice, responsibility, and thrift, as well as her love of learning.

Lisa Sprackett went to school in Christchurch and took bachelor's and master's degrees in history at the University of Canterbury, where she met her future husband, James George Arthur (Jim) Croll (*b.* 1943), civil engineer. After their marriage in 1966 they moved to London, where Jim Croll began a long academic career at University College, London, and Lisa obtained a second MA, in Far Eastern studies, in 1971 and a doctorate in anthropology in 1977, both from the School of Oriental and African Studies (SOAS). During the following years she had two children, Nicholas and Katherine, and a series of short-term research fellowships at the Contemporary China Institute at SOAS, the Institute of Development Studies at the University of Sussex, Queen Elizabeth House and Wolfson College, Oxford, the department of east Asian studies at Princeton, and the Institute of Social Studies at The Hague. It was only in 1990, however, that she obtained her first stable academic post when she was appointed lecturer in anthropology at SOAS. Her promotion was then rapid, and she was appointed senior lecturer in 1991, reader in 1992, and professor of Chinese anthropology in 1995. After several years as first holder of the chair of SOAS's Centre of Chinese Studies and head of the department of development studies, in 2002 she was appointed vice-principal of SOAS with special responsibility for external relations.

Lisa Croll was one of a pioneering group of Anglophone scholars who, in large part inspired by Western 'second-wave' feminism, began to write about women in the People's Republic of China. Her first books, *Feminism and*

Socialism in China (1978) and *The Politics of Marriage in Contemporary China* (1981), granted insights into social, political, and gendered worlds to which students at the time had little access. Numerous books, papers, and reports on women and gender followed, some of which became required reading for undergraduates in Chinese and women's studies, including *Changing Identities of Chinese Women: Rhetoric, Experience and Self-Perception* (1995) and *Endangered Daughters: Discrimination and Development in Asia* (2000). Inspired by her commitment to identifying the sources of social injustice and poverty, Croll's interests broadened to result in a host of other publications including *The Family Rice Bowl: Food and the Domestic Economy in China* (1982), *From Heaven to Earth: Images and Experiences of Development in China* (1994), and *China's New Consumers: Social Development and Domestic Demand* (2006).

Croll had an abiding interest in the applied and policy implications of her research in China. Many of the short-term research methods she elaborated became the basis for the field manuals used by multilateral development agencies. She regularly worked in an advisory capacity for all the UN's main multilateral agencies, the International Labour Organization, the World Bank, the Overseas Development Administration, the Ford Foundation, Oxfam, and the Nederlandse Organisatie voor Internationale Bijstand. She advised the Chinese government and the All-China Women's Federation on issues concerning gender discrimination, the alleviation of poverty, the supply of agricultural labour, investment, and migration. With international recognition for her work on daughter discrimination in Asia she was appointed in 1998 to the United Nations University Council in Tokyo, where she was elected vice-chair and then chair (2002–4). She was equally committed to putting China's social development on the agenda of public and policy-making bodies in the UK, and in 2005 joined the British government's China task force, set up to foster co-operation between the British and Chinese governments. She was appointed CMG in 2007, but died before she could be invested.

Behind her successful public profile Croll's trajectory was far from smooth. She began her village-based fieldwork in China years before it was possible to spend the length of time there that ethnographic fieldwork conventionally expected of anthropologists. Her interest in women's lives long predated the entry of gender and women's studies into mainstream social science. Her unconventional scholarly profile brought her many successes, but this did not diminish her sense that she had to fight for recognition of her work, as a woman, an anthropologist, and an outsider. She also struggled to combine the roles and responsibilities of mother and partner with those of researcher and teacher, and her marriage ended in divorce in 1997.

Lisa Croll was known to many as a friend more than as a scholar and public figure, and a number of her long-term friendships dated back to the early days of her arrival in the UK, sustained by her generosity of spirit, her wisdom, and her warmth. Her interests ranged from music and embroidery (at which she was expert) to travel. Having lived latterly in Despard Road, Islington, London, she died at St John's Hospice, Westminster, on 3 October 2007, of cancer of the colon. She was survived by her two children. Harriet Evans

Sources T. Lu, 'Nutong wenti xin gainian' ['New ideas about the question of girls'], *Zhongguo Funu* ['Women of China'], 11 (2000), 8 · *The Guardian* (10 Oct 2007) · *The Times* (16 Oct 2007) · *The Independent* (17 Oct 2007) · *Daily Telegraph* (18 Oct 2007) · *New Zealand Herald* (27 Oct 2007) · www.presbyterian.org.nz/archives/Page200.htm, 20 June 2010 · *WW* (2007) · personal knowledge (2011) · private information (2011) · d. cert.
Likenesses S. Baker, photograph, repro. in users.ox.ac.uk/~cccrw/events.html · obituary photographs
Wealth at death £374,667: probate, 25 Sept 2008, *CGPLA Eng. & Wales*

Cuckney, John Graham, Baron Cuckney (1925–2008), intelligence officer and industrialist, was born on 12 July 1925 in India, the only surviving son of Ernest John Cuckney (1896–1965), Royal Air Force officer, and his wife, Lilian, *née* Williams (1898–1976). His father was air officer commanding No. 43 Group Royal Air Force in 1944–5, and ended his career as an air vice-marshal and director of planning at the Ministry of Supply. After schooling at Shrewsbury, Cuckney went to St Andrews University intending to become a surgeon but joined the army, serving with the Royal Northumberland Fusiliers and the King's African rifles. He was posted to Africa and shortly after the end of the Second World War was involved in an accident in Cairo which left him with back pain for the rest of his life. Returning to St Andrews, he completed a degree in history, remarking later that he had seen enough of hospitals during the war. His career then disappeared into the shadows which Cuckney, who cultivated an elegantly enigmatic profile, did little to dispel, describing it in his *Who's Who* entry as 'attachment to the War Office (civil assistant, General Staff) until 1957'. On 15 September 1950 he married Elizabeth Mitchell, *née* Bateman (*b.* 1919), daughter of Osborne Robert Sacheverell Bateman, accountant, and former wife of Peter Duncan Felton Mitchell. The marriage was short-lived. The couple were divorced in 1956.

Cuckney had become an MI5 officer, a fact revealed in 1987 when another former operative, Peter Wright, published an unauthorized memoir, *Spycatcher*, which government lawyers tried, and failed, to suppress. Wright named Cuckney as the 'tough, no nonsense officer' who supervised his training programme in 1955:

> Cuckney could be downright rude but I soon realised he was just tired of knocking into shape young MI5 recruits of generally poor calibre. He was altogether different from the average MI5 officer. He refused to submit to the monotony of the dark pinstripe, preferring bolder styles. Cuckney was his own man and had broader horizons beyond the office.

Among the advice Cuckney gave was that if operatives were caught illegally entering buildings or invading privacy, there was little the office could do, and he was blunt that MI5 work 'very often involves trangressing propriety or the law' (Wright, 31–3).

John Graham Cuckney, Baron Cuckney (1925–2008), by unknown photographer, 1977

In 1957 Cuckney left the intelligence service to work for a stockbroker, Standard Industrial Group. On 8 December 1960 he married another divorcée, Muriel Band, *née* Boyd (1911–2004), landscape painter, daughter of Walter Scott Boyd, businessman, and former wife of Geoffray Band. From 1964 he was a director of the merchant bank Lazards, where one recruit noted his trademark world-weary detachment: 'he didn't seem that enthusiastic about the place' (*The Independent*, 19 March 1994). In 1970 he became the first Lazards director in living memory to resign when he set up the Anglo-Eastern Bank to finance trade with the Middle East. His partner was the Iranian-born textile magnate David Alliance, later to become chairman of Coats-Viyella. At the same time he embarked on a string of public appointments which marked him out as one of the most astute industrial 'fixers' of his time, the man to whom successive governments turned to resolve intractable and embarrassing problems. In parallel, he maintained a strong and persistent association with the defence industries and arms sales, where his Middle East connections and acute political antennae made him a formidable player.

Cuckney had been appointed by Labour to the Railway Policy Review Committee in 1966, but his first big public sector job was as chairman of the Mersey Docks and Harbour Board from 1970 to 1972, under a Conservative government. The old board had been bankrupted by the building of the deepwater Seaforth dock, in an attempt to reverse a decline due to changing patterns of trade, the beginnings of containerization, and old-fashioned practices ingrained in management and powerful trade unions. In two years Cuckney demonstrated his ability to bring together conflicting interests and achieved a painstaking capital reconstruction which necessitated a private bill in parliament. This was the beginning of a career as a government troubleshooter that led Margaret Thatcher to refer to his 'extraordinary talents' (Thatcher, 426), not least of which was his ability to deal with both businessmen and politicians with confidence and understanding. Sir Kenneth Durham, chairman of Unilever, described him later as 'one of the best non-executive Chairmen in the country' (*Daily Telegraph*, 1 Nov 2008).

In 1972 Cuckney was appointed to help sort out the government's Property Services Agency as chief executive, followed in 1974 by another difficult assignment to rescue the Crown Agents, traditionally the procurement agency in the UK for overseas British territories, who had rashly used their funds to become property investors and effectively bankers to property concerns. The secondary banking crisis and the collapse of the property market had left the agents with a £236 million black hole. Cuckney did what he could to stabilize matters, writing off debts with the help of a further £85 million from the government and carrying out a reorganization that included separating the agents' military equipment interests into a separate company, International Military Services. He chaired the latter until 1985, during a period in which it successfully sold tanks and missiles, notably to the Iranian government under the shah. In 1977 he became chairman of the Port of London Authority, which faced similar problems to Liverpool, but this time his recipe for recovery, which included the closure of the huge Royal docks and large redundancies, was opposed by the unions and was not accepted by the Labour government, which was under extreme pressure from the trade unions in the 'winter of discontent' of 1979.

A tall man with bushy eyebrows, with a courtly manner and a liking for large-spaced pinstripes, Cuckney was adept at dealing pleasantly with journalists, a half-smile on his lips, but giving nothing away. Brushing aside personal queries, he joked that his hobbies included 'yak-stalking' and 'dipping worry beads into cold water' (*Daily Telegraph*, 1 Nov 2008). In board meetings he was commanding, insisting on keeping briskly to time and giving short shrift to those who could not command their brief. Knighted in 1978, he then undertook a succession of chairmanships of usually troubled public companies including the travel agency Thomas Cook (1978–87), Brooke Bond Tea (1981–4), and the engineering group John Brown (1983–6), where he continued to build his reputation as a 'company doctor' (a term he disliked) who never lost a patient.

In 1985, however, Cuckney's appointment as chairman of the nearly bankrupt Westland helicopter company sparked a political controversy that resulted in the resignation of two cabinet ministers, and represented a severe threat to the continuance of Margaret Thatcher as prime minister. Emollient Cuckney could be, but it was his steely determination and a ruthlessness that led him to play very close to the wire that brought him through as the one obvious winner in what became known as the Westland affair. He described it as being fought out on two levels, high political and corporate, adding disingenuously that 'I've concentrated on the corporate problem and try hard to keep out of the political battle' (*Daily Telegraph*, 1 Nov 2008). Cuckney operated throughout on the basis that Westland was a quoted company and that the shareholders would decide. But it was his ability to handle the politicians and the trust in which he was held by Margaret Thatcher that ensured his success.

Westland, the UK's only helicopter manufacturer, was a small company with a turnover of only about £300 million a year, and it needed refinancing. A bid from the maverick helicopter operator Alan Bristow was withdrawn when the government refused his demand to guarantee work and write off £40 million of launch aid. Cuckney's solution was to approach the American helicopter manufacturer Sikorsky to take a stake, with the prospect of Westland receiving some subcontract work and potentially building Sikorsky's Black Hawk helicopter for the Ministry of Defence. Although this was strictly a commercial decision, because Westland depended on government orders he sought clearance from the minister of defence, Michael Heseltine, who agreed that the Sikorsky option should be explored but also undertook to investigate a European alternative, which Cuckney said he had no time to investigate. Heseltine then summoned a meeting of the national armaments directors of Germany, Italy, and France, which agreed that their helicopter requirements should be met solely by helicopters designed and built in Europe. Cuckney realized that this would preclude a Sikorsky deal. Heseltine insisted that Westland should delay and consider a European offer but Thatcher and the responsible minister, the secretary of state for industry, Leon Brittan, argued that Westland should press ahead with the Sikorsky option.

Cuckney's closeness to Thatcher was obvious when he was asked, most unusually, to attend a sub-committee of the cabinet's economic committee to set out his case and answer questions. Four days later the Westland board approved the Sikorsky deal, dismissing outline proposals from the European consortium. When a formal offer was also rejected, Heseltine offered to drive to Cuckney's home on Christmas eve. A furious Cuckney, whose wife had just come out of hospital, said he had no power to do as Heseltine asked. The Ministry of Defence then sent a letter to the Europeans' bankers stating that only by joining with the consortium would Westland be able to share in European projects. Cuckney sought clarification from the prime minister and received a suitably ambiguous reply. But the argument escalated when a further letter from Heseltine was judged by the government's solicitor-general, Sir Patrick Mayhew, to 'contain material inaccuracies'. The leaking of Mayhew's letter to the press brought a furious reaction from Heseltine, contributing to his resignation a few days later. The leaking of the sensitive material subsequently led to the resignation of Brittan.

Cuckney still had to get the deal through. It needed agreement from 75 per cent of shareholders but Alan Bristow, opposed to the deal, had increased his shareholding. Meetings were held at Claridge's Hotel the day before the special shareholders' meeting, involving Bristow, Cuckney, Sir Gordon White of the Hanson Group, which had just bought shares, and a representative of Sikorsky's parent company, United Technologies Corporation. Bristow claimed he was offered a high price to sell his shares but declined. Cuckney claimed to have left the room before the offer was made. The meeting failed to vote the required 75 per cent but subsequently the deal was passed on a lower vote, after extraordinary activity in Westland shares that saw 20.33 per cent in the hands of six mystery shareholders, with four holding companies whose ultimate owners were not known. Cuckney had won but not without questions to his reputation. A stock exchange inquiry investigated the possibility of an illegal 'concert party' but without conclusion while the all-party House of Commons trade and industry committee said it 'entertained substantial suspicions' falling 'short of proof'. Asked for his view, Cuckney commented drily that it was a 'fan club' (*Financial Times*, 3 Nov 2008).

The Westland affair enhanced Cuckney's reputation, at least in the short term, though Sikorsky ultimately did little for Westland. He became chairman of the investment group 3i (1987–92), vice-chairman of the pharmaceutical group Glaxo (1993–5), and chairman of the Orion Publishing Group (1994–7). From 1985 to 1990 he was deputy chairman of the engineering group TI. Conspiracy theorists noted that TI Group had sold Matrix Churchill and that 3i was a shareholder in Astra, a munitions group, both of which had connections to the Iraqi 'supergun' affair of 1991–2, the subject of an official government investigation in 1996. But there was no suggestion that Cuckney was involved. One out-of-character, high-profile failure came in 1989 with a short-lived excursion as the chairman of a consortium, Metsun, put together by his old bank Lazards, which briefly talked of mounting a £7 billion bid for the electronics and defence group GEC. His final hurrah came with his resolution of the Maxwell pensions scandal. On the death of the tycoon Robert Maxwell in 1991, a £450 million shortfall was found in his companies' pension schemes. Cuckney was appointed as head of a trust to seek donations to assist the pensioners. He carried it through to a triumphant conclusion, raising an immediate £6 million and cajoling and encouraging City institutions including those involved in the transferring of pension moneys to produce a £276 million settlement.

Cuckney was made a life peer as Baron Cuckney, of Millbank in the city of Westminster, in 1995. Following the death of his second wife, on 12 April 2007 he married Priscilla Jane Newell, *née* Watts (*b.* 1944), a pensions expert who had been a trustee of the Maxwell Pensioners' Trust. She was the daughter of Arthur Ronald Watts, Royal Air

Force officer, and a widow. Cuckney died at his home, Flat 18, 68 Vincent Square, Westminster, on 30 October 2008, of heart failure and vascular dementia. He was survived by his third wife, Priscilla. A memorial service was held at St John's, Smith Square, London, on 9 March 2009.

MARTIN ADENEY

Sources P. Wright, *Spycatcher* (1987) • M. Thatcher, *The Downing Street years* (1993) • *The Independent* (19 March 1994); (13 Nov 2008) • M. Heseltine, *Life in the jungle* (2000) • *The Guardian* (12 Jan 2006); (3 Nov 2008) • *Daily Telegraph* (1 Nov 2008) • *The Times* (3 Nov 2008); (10 Nov 2008) • *Financial Times* (3 Nov 2008) • *Western Morning News* [Plymouth] (4 Nov 2008) • Burke, *Peerage* • *WW* (2008) • personal knowledge (2012) • private information (2012) • m. certs. • d. cert.
Likenesses photographs, 1966–96, Photoshot, London • photograph, 1977, Museum of London [*see illus.*] • J. James, photograph, 1992, PA Photos, London • obituary photographs
Wealth at death £628,280: probate, 6 March 2009, *CGPLA Eng. & Wales*

Cudlipp, Reginald William [Reg] (1910–2005), journalist and promoter of Anglo-Japanese relations, was born on 11 December 1910 at 118 Lisvane Street, Cardiff, the second of three sons and second of four children of William Christopher Cudlipp, commercial traveller for a provision merchant, and his wife, Bessie Amelia, *née* Kinsman. The sons—Percy *Cudlipp (1905–1962), Reginald, and Hubert (Hugh) *Cudlipp (1913–1998)—were unique in that, for a brief period in 1953, they all had editorial control of London-based national newspapers.

The three boys were educated in Cardiff, at Gladstone elementary school and Howard Gardens secondary school, which they all left in their early teens to become apprentice journalists. Reginald occupied a lowly position on the *Penarth News*, a small weekly paper serving the seaside resort just south of Cardiff, which later gave Hugh his first job. Reginald had been assiduous in acquiring the basic skills of shorthand and typing and, while still a teenager, was hired as a reporter and sub-editor by the *Western Mail*, the national newspaper of Wales. He stayed in Cardiff until 1938, when he moved to London to work as a sub-editor on the *News of the World*. When the Second World War broke out in 1939 he joined the Royal Artillery and was posted to Gibraltar, where he edited a monthly magazine for servicemen, *The Rock*. Towards the end of the war he was made a captain and sent to Calcutta as associate editor of a similar publication, in which capacity he witnessed the surrender of the Japanese in Singapore in September 1945. The same year he married Rachel Joyce Braham. There were no children of the marriage.

On demobilization Cudlipp returned to London and in 1946 rejoined the *News of the World*, which sent him to New York as its United States correspondent. In 1948 he returned to London as features editor, rising to deputy editor two years later, and inheriting the editorial chair in 1953 when his predecessor, Arthur Waters, died in office. He was the last of the brothers to achieve this status: Percy was by then editor of the *Daily Herald* and Hugh editor-in-chief of the *Daily Mirror* and *Sunday Pictorial*. When Reginald won his promotion the three met for a celebratory dinner—but Percy was dismissed by the *Herald* ten days later.

The *News of the World*'s circulation was then above 8 million—more than any other British newspaper has achieved before or since. It was notable for its thorough reporting of divorces and court cases involving sexual offences. 'We'd have one page for the dirtiest cases of the week,' Cudlipp recalled in 2002, 'although they wouldn't raise an eyebrow these days' (Hagerty, 27). Yet he was probably not the most suitable editor for that kind of newspaper. A tall, lean man of studious demeanour, he was known by his colleagues as the Bishop. By 1959 the *News of the World*'s circulation had fallen to just over 6 million and he was replaced by his deputy, Stafford Somerfield, a portly *bon vivant*.

Unemployed at forty-nine, Cudlipp took some time to find a new career path; and when he did it was a surprising one for a former editor of a mass-market newspaper. In 1961 he became director of the Anglo-Japanese Economic Institute and editor of its quarterly journal, *Japan*. The institute's primary mission was to foster trading links between Britain and the nation that had emerged from wartime defeat to develop the most powerful economy in the Far East. Cudlipp also became enthused by the possibilities of co-operation between Japan and developing countries, especially those in Africa. He took on his role with energy and became deeply attached to Japan. In a booklet in 1973 he wrote: 'I always tell diehard sceptics who prefer to think of Japan in terms of sweated labour and shoddy products that they really ought to go there some time' (R. W. Cudlipp, *Japan: Some of the Problems of the Seventies*, 1973, 6). In the numerous articles and pamphlets that he wrote for the institute he adoped a schoolmasterly tone, urging British exporters to redouble their efforts to break into this expanding market, however great a challenge it represented. His commitment made a powerful impression on the Japanese and in 1982 he was awarded their equivalent of a knighthood when admitted to the order of the Sacred Treasure.

Cudlipp regarded himself as a journalist first and foremost, and when he stepped down from the institute in 1986, at the age of seventy-five, he was proud to declare that he had served sixty years in the profession. He spent an active retirement with his wife in Arundel, Sussex, writing and lecturing well into his eighties on Japan and its relations with the rest of the world. He died from prostate cancer at St Richard's Hospital, Chichester, on 21 January 2005, and was survived by his wife.

MICHAEL LEAPMAN

Sources H. Cudlipp, *Walking on the water* (1976) • B. Hagerty, 'The forgotten Cudlipp', *British Journalism Review*, 13/3 (2002), 22–7 • *The Independent* (26 Jan 2005) • *Daily Telegraph* (27 Jan 2005) • *The Guardian* (28 Jan 2005) • *The Times* (27 Jan 2005); (21 Feb 2005) • *WW* (2005) • personal knowledge (2009) • private information (2009) • b. cert. • d. cert.
Likenesses photograph, repro. in *Daily Telegraph* (27 Jan 2005) • photograph, repro. in *The Times* (27 Jan 2005)

Cummings [*née* Halverstadt], **Constance** (1910–2005), actress, was born on 15 May 1910 in Seattle, Washington,

USA, the younger child and only daughter of Dallas Vernon Halverstadt, lawyer, and his wife, Kate Logan, *née* Cummings, who had trained as a concert soprano. She was educated at St Nicholas's Girls' School in Seattle. Her parents separated when she was ten, and her mother, who had never fulfilled her own ambitions, transferred her aspirations to her daughter. She never saw her father again.

Constance had wanted to be a classical dancer, but at the age of sixteen made her début (as Constance Cummings) in a walk-on part as a prostitute in *Seventh Heaven* (1926), with the San Diego Stock Company. She moved to New York, and in 1928 made her Broadway début in the chorus line of the George and Ira Gershwin musical *Treasure Girl*, which starred Gertrude Lawrence. She was also in the chorus of *The Little Show* (1929) at the Music Box, and took over the role of the showgirl Miss Rixey in George S. Kaufman and Ring Lardner's Tin Pan Alley musical comedy *June Moon*, on its post-Broadway tour (1930). Her dazzling looks caught the eye of the film mogul Sam Goldwyn, who brought her to Hollywood to star opposite Ronald Colman in *The Devil to Pay!* (1930), only for her to be replaced at the last minute by Loretta Young. Colman, however, helped her find an agent, and the following year she made her début at Columbia Pictures, in *The Criminal Code*, a well-received prison drama directed by Howard Hawks and starring Walter Huston. For the next four years she worked exclusively in films. The most notable were *American Madness* (1932), directed by Frank Capra, *Movie Crazy* (1932) with Harold Lloyd, and *Night after Night* (also 1932) with George Raft and, making her screen début, Mae West. Her last film in Hollywood before moving to England was a comedy-whodunit with Robert Young, *Remember Last Night?* (1935).

In Hollywood Cummings had met the British playwright Benn Wolfe *Levy (1900–1973), who was there as a screenwriter. He was the son of Octave Levy, a wealthy wool broker, and his wife, Nannie Joseph. They were married on 3 July 1933, and while on their honeymoon in Venice she received an offer to film in England. She won a legal battle with Columbia Pictures that enabled her to make the move, and thereafter her career and family life were largely centred on the United Kingdom. Her husband was active in political circles, and from 1945 to 1950 served as Labour MP for Eton and Slough. They had a son and a daughter.

Cummings made her London stage début in 1934 in *Sour Grapes*, at the Apollo Theatre, and shortly after returned to New York and had a big personal success in Samuel Raphaelson's comedy *Accent on Youth* at the Plymouth. She also started to appear in plays, mostly boulevard comedies, written for her, and directed by, her husband—*Young Madame Conti* (1936), *The Jealous God* (1939), and *Clutterbuck* (1946) among them—and she developed a sophisticated comedic skill, elegant and with a light touch, that dominated her acting choices until the more demanding roles of her later years. Levy also directed his wife in his own adaptation of Flaubert's *Madame Bovary* (1937), in New York, and the following year in London she had a big success as Mrs Chipping in *Goodbye, Mr Chips* (1938), at the Shaftesbury. In 1939 she joined the Old Vic Company, then in wartime exile in Buxton and Streatham Hill, to play Juliet, opposite the Romeo of Robert Donat, and Shaw's Saint Joan, but neither production was considered a great success. She had better luck in a revival of Oliver Goldsmith's *Good Natur'd Man*, in another Raphaelson play, *Skylark* (1942), and in Robert Sherwood's *The Petrified Forest* (1943).

On film Cummings and her fellow American Robert Montgomery were oddly cast as Dorothy L. Sayers's quintessentially English sleuths, Harriet Vane and Lord Peter Wimsey, in an adaptation of *Busman's Honeymoon* (1940). She played an American ally in *The Foreman Went to France* (1942) and was stylishly good as Ruth, the upper-middle-class second wife of Rex Harrison's Charles Condomine in David Lean's film of Noël Coward's *Blithe Spirit* (1945). She had made her television début in 1938, as Roxane in a live broadcast of *Cyrano de Bergerac*, with Leslie Banks and James Mason, and although television and film were to offer her fewer, and less satisfying, opportunities than the theatre, she did make some notable appearances on television, including in *The Scream* (1953) with Douglas Fairbanks junior, an adaptation of Scott Fitzgerald's *The Last Tycoon* (1959), and in televised versions of two of her later stage successes, *Long Day's Journey into Night* (1973) and *Wings* (1983). On film she had good roles as a movie star in Joseph Losey's *The Intimate Stranger* (1956), and was wonderfully unsympathetic as Mrs Barrow, the American efficiency expert murderously pursued by Peter Sellers's mild-mannered accountant, in Charles Crichton's *The Battle of the Sexes* (1959).

On stage in London Cummings showed evidence of her emotional capabilities in Clifford Odets's *Winter Journey* (1952) with Michael Redgrave, in Joseph Kramm's *The Shrike* (1953) with Sam Wanamaker, and in her husband's *The Rape of the Belt* (1957, and in New York in 1960). At the Oxford Playhouse the director Frank Hauser encouraged her to increase her range still further, first as Aristophanes' Lysistrata (1957), and then as the sadistic lesbian Inès in Sartre's *Huis clos* (1962), which she played in a double bill with Max Beerbohm's *A Social Success*. She was especially fine, taking over from Uta Hagen, as Martha in the London production of Edward Albee's *Who's Afraid of Virginia Woolf?* (1964), opposite Ray McAnally. Cummings was never averse to venturing outside the West End, where she was able to tackle some great roles in plays by great writers—Tennessee Williams's *The Milk Train Doesn't Stop Here Any More* in Glasgow; G. B. Shaw's *Mrs Warren's Profession* in Bristol and Vienna; Edward Albee's *All Over* in Brighton; Somerset Maugham's *The Circle* in Guildford; and Friedrich Dürrenmatt's *The Visit* in Coventry.

In 1969 Cummings played Gertrude in Tony Richardson's production of *Hamlet* with Nicol Williamson, in London and New York, and in 1971 joined the National Theatre Company, where she gave some good performances in poorly received productions—as Volumnia to the Coriolanus of Anthony Hopkins, in Bertolt Brecht's version of Shakespeare; as Leda in Laurence Olivier's production of *Amphitryon 38*, by Jean Giraudoux and S. N. Behrman; and as Agave in Euripides' *The Bacchae* (1973). The National also gave her what was perhaps her greatest opportunity, as the morphine-addicted Mary, wife of Olivier's blistering James Tyrone, in Michael Blakemore's production of Eugene O'Neill's *Long Day's Journey into Night* (1971). Cummings's delicate and fragile performance won huge plaudits and the Evening Standard drama award as best actress.

Further success followed, as Madame Ranevsky in *The Cherry Orchard* (1973) at the National, and as the widowed matriarch in A. R. Gurney's *Children* (1974), which Cummings performed shortly after the death of her own husband. On returning to New York she triumphed in a captivating solo performance as Emily Stilson, a former aviator and wing-walker struggling to recover from a cerebral haemorrhage, in Arthur Kopit's memory-play *Wings* (1979). She considered this to be her greatest performance. The public and critics agreed, and she won the Antoinette Perry (Tony) and Drama Desk awards. She also played the role at the National Theatre in London, and in 1982 made her final appearance in New York as the formidable Mrs St Maugham in an off-Broadway revival of Enid Bagnold's *The Chalk Garden*, with Irene Worth as the governess. In 1994 she played the part again at the King's Head, a tiny pub theatre in London, then toured in a one-woman show as Fanny Kemble, and made her final stage appearance as Maman in *Uncle Vanya* (1996) at the Chichester Festival Theatre, finishing a career that had started seventy years before as a chorus girl on Broadway.

After her husband's death Cummings maintained their country home at Cote House in the Oxfordshire village of Cote, a 600 acre dairy farm where they bred Friesians, and a house in Chelsea designed by Walter Gropius. She later moved to The Old Cow House, Cote. She supported a number of political and charitable causes, including Amnesty, Liberty, and the Actors' Charitable Trust. She was appointed CBE in 1974. She died at Wardington House nursing home, Wardington, Oxfordshire, on 23 November 2005, and was survived by her two children, Jonathan and Jemima. ALEX JENNINGS

Sources M. R. Gartside, *For all seasons: the story of stage and screen star Constance Cummings* (1999) • *Daily Telegraph* (25 Nov 2005) • *The Guardian* (25 Nov 2005) • *The Independent* (26 Nov 2005) • *The Times* (28 Nov 2005) • *New York Times* (29 Nov 2005) • *WW* (2005) • I. Herbert, ed., *Who's who in the theatre*, 1 (1981) • www.imdb.com, 15 Aug 2008 • www.ibdb.com, 15 Aug 2008 • personal knowledge (2009) • private information (2009) • d. cert.

Archives FILM BFINA, performance footage | SOUND BL NSA, performance recordings

Likenesses photographs, 1931–85, Rex Features, London • photographs, 1932–69, Getty Images, London • J. Oppenheim, oils, 1934, Garr Club, London • photographs, 1935–7, Photoshot, London • glossy unglazed bromide print, 1936, NPG • G. Anthony, bromide fibre print, *c.*1939, NPG • photographs, 1944–83, PA Photos, London • A. McBean, vintage bromide print, 1946, NPG • D. Wilding, half-plate film negative, NPG • obituary photographs • photographs, repro. in Gartside, *For all seasons*

Wealth at death under £48,000: probate, 30 Jan 2007, *CGPLA Eng. & Wales*

Curran [*née* Brennan], **Agnes** (**1920–2005**), prison governor, was born on 12 February 1920 at 25 Lyle Street, Greenock, Renfrewshire, the eldest of nine children of Mark Brennan, shoemaker, and his wife, Agnes, *née* Hendry. Her first career was as a registered mental nurse and she rose to be deputy matron of Ravenscraig Hospital. She later studied at the Royal College, Edinburgh, for a nursing administrative certificate. She was married first to John Reynolds, a mechanical engineer, but the marriage ended in divorce. On 3 October 1952 she married, second, Edward Curran (*d.* 2005), a fellow registered mental nurse. She had three children, Mark, John, and Angela. She also cared for some of her siblings while bringing up her own family, after her father died at the early age of forty-six.

After twenty-two years in nursing Curran changed the direction of her career. She began to work for the prison service, having previously undertaken voluntary work in prisons for a number of years. In 1969 she was appointed assistant governor at Gateside prison for women and remained there until its closure in 1975, when she was transferred as deputy governor to Cornton Vale, a new prison for women. She nevertheless retained an interest in nursing and was chairwoman of the Greenock branch of the Royal College of Nursing.

In 1979 Curran became the first female governor of a male prison when she was appointed governor of Dungavel prison, near Strathaven. Her achievement was marked that year at a women of the year luncheon. In a television interview in 1982 she said that she was 'taken aback' by her appointment (*Women of Today*). She had thought that she might be appointed deputy governor but was surprised that the government had been courageous enough to appoint a woman governor to a male prison. She believed that there were differences between managing men's and women's prisons. The relationships between women prisoners and between prisoners and staff were well developed and nuanced. For example, women were not afraid to tell her that she had been missed if she had been away from the prison or to tell her if they liked the dress she was wearing. When she arrived at Dungavel she found the all-male environment hostile and men (both staff and prisoners) adopting either 'hunter' (aggressive or seductive) or 'filial' (protective) attitudes towards her. In her time at Dungavel she managed to change this culture into one more closely resembling 'normality'(ibid.).

Curran's time as governor was a success and she was appointed MBE in 1984. She explained her success by saying 'I don't see them as murderers, rapists and robbers. I see them as men and I expect them to behave like men.' She claimed that she was annoyed when she had to punish a man—'annoyed that he could be so stupid'—and acknowledged that she ran the institution by courtesy of the prisoners, recognizing that if they chose to be 'nasty and aggressive', the tables could turn very quickly. She challenged the public to think about what prisons were expected to do with men serving long sentences, arguing that it was not enough 'to give him a bed and three square meals and see that the workshops conform to the Factory Acts' (*The Herald*, 11 Oct 2005). She introduced an innovative regime at the medium security prison, where long-term prisoners were preparing for release. Up to 20 of the 100 prisoners worked outside the prison every day, undertaking unpaid work in the community. At a time when the attention of Scottish penal reformers was on the high-profile Barlinnie special unit, Agnes Curran was quietly developing a similar regime for equally serious offenders as they progressed through the prison system from high to medium security. She also encouraged contact between prisoners and members of the public by inviting the latter into the prison twice a year for sales of prisoners' work in aid of charities.

Curran set up In-work Ltd, a programme that offered work to those with mental health problems. She retained an interest in mental health after she retired and was always actively involved with various local charities. She was a member of the Scottish Association for Mental Health, chairwoman of the Inverclyde association, and a member of the community care forum. She was also a district organizer for the Women's Royal Voluntary Service in Inverclyde. A gifted communicator, she was in great demand as a speaker, invariably on the themes of caring for less fortunate people and not dismissing them because they were in prison or had a disability.

Curran's achievement as the first female governor of a male prison became embedded in the history of women's achievements. When asked by a television interviewer in 1982 what other career she might have chosen if she had her life to live again, she replied 'I always wanted to be a surgeon. I knew I had a sensitivity to people but I came to realise that my sensitivity was perhaps not so geared to the flesh as to the mind' (*Women of Today*). Her husband, Edward, died in September 2005. She herself died a fortnight later, on 29 September, at the Inverclyde Royal Hospital, Greenock. The causes of death were given as bronchopneumonia, immobility, general frailty, and depression secondary to her husband's death. She was survived by all three children. ANNE WORRALL

Sources *Women of today: prison governor*, ITV, 18 Aug 1982 • *The Times* (12 Oct 2005) • *The Herald* [Glasgow] (11 Oct 2005); (15 Oct 2005) • b. cert. • m. cert. [1952] • d. cert.
Archives FILM BFINA, *Women of today: prison governor*, ITV, 18 Aug 1982
Likenesses obituary photographs
Wealth at death £51,322: confirmation, 1 Dec 2005, *CCI*

Cushing, David Henry (1920–2008), marine ecologist, was born on 14 March 1920 at 10 Prudhoe Street, Alnwick, Northumberland, the son of William Ewart Wittrick Cushing (1891–1980), schoolmaster, and his wife, Isobel, *née* Batchelder (1892–1988). He attended Duke's School, Alnwick, and the Royal Grammar School, Newcastle upon Tyne. In 1938 he went as a Horsley scholar to Balliol College, Oxford, to complete a war-shortened degree in zoology. (In 1950 he completed his DPhil thesis on the vertical migration of zooplankton under Sir Alister Hardy.) In April 1941 he was commissioned, from the officer cadet training unit, into the Royal Artillery. He served in various anti-aircraft regiments, ending in 1945 with service with the 1st Royal Fusiliers and the 8th Indian division. On 29 April 1943, at St Barnabas's Church, Dulwich, he married Diana Romola Camilla Antona-Traversi (*b.* 1919), daughter of Hugo Antona-Traversi, a translator for the BBC; they had one daughter, Camilla.

In 1946 Michael Graham persuaded Cushing to join an expanding team of oceanographers and fisheries scientists at the government's Fisheries Laboratory in Lowestoft (later the Centre for Environment, Fisheries, and Aquaculture Science). He remained at Lowestoft for the rest of his career, eventually becoming deputy director and head of the fish population dynamics division from 1974 to his retirement in 1980.

Cushing's early work was immediately innovative. The new technologies developed in the war years allowed him to investigate acoustic means of mapping the movements of fish and zooplankton, and 'calibrate' the returned signal strength to estimate the abundance of fish stocks. He was also interested in how production was regulated in the sea—whether it was determined primarily by a bottom-up nutrient input or a top-down predation. In 1954 he followed a North Sea plankton patch with thirteen research cruises over three months, and mathematically modelled the processes and results to show the different roles of nutrients and predators. The use of observation and modelling was to continue throughout his career; but events took an abrupt change.

The East Anglian herring fishery, off Lowestoft and Yarmouth, was without equal, and for hundreds of years fed Europe. In 1955 it failed. Cushing was called in as part of the team at Lowestoft to solve the herring crisis. This had a profound effect on the direction of his, and future, science, and on his view of science serving society. Only in 1977 was the fishery closed, by which time a 5 million tonne breeding stock had fallen to 50,000 tonnes. A fishery, a market, and a culture were lost. Cushing considered that the failure was as much one of science as of management. Managers needed better science based on fuller understanding and not just empiricism.

Out of this crisis came some outstanding science. Cushing demonstrated that the failure was due to reduced 'recruitment' (young fish) caused by a diminished parent stock. The science of the relationships between stock and recruitment was born. It is this relationship that determines the sustainability of fish stocks, and failures of recruitment due to fishing Cushing termed 'recruitment overfishing'. Fish stocks are also very variable, due to extreme fluctuations in the numbers of recruits from year to year or over longer periods. Both the form of the stock–recruit relationships and the causes of this variability lie in the very early life history of the fish, as larvae. Cushing explained the variability in his 'match-mismatch' hypothesis, wherein good recruitments follow the coincidence of larval production with the production of larval food determined by weather or climate.

Cushing produced ten books, including *The Arctic Cod* (1966), *Fisheries Biology* (1968), *Marine Ecology and Fisheries* (1975), *Climate and Fisheries* (1982), and *The Provident Sea* (1988). His last book was *Towards the Science of Recruitment* (1996). His global recognition can be appreciated from his various awards: the Rosenstiel gold medal (1980), the

Albert medal for oceanography (1984), and the Ecology Institute prize (1993). He was elected a fellow of the Royal Society in 1977. Approaching retirement, he instigated the *Journal of Plankton Research* and remained as editor until 2001. His last scientific paper, published in this journal in 2000, was written with his close colleagues Joe Horwood and Tim Wyatt. It was on stock and recruitment. The journal instituted an annual David Cushing prize for the best publication by a young scientist.

Cushing enjoyed art and wine, spending many summers touring southern Europe. He died at the James Paget Hospital, Gorleston, Norfolk, on 14 March 2008, after suffering a stroke; he was survived by his wife and daughter. He had been driven by the need for the understanding and application of marine ecology in the management of fisheries. He was an iconoclast whose influence was truly global. In Cushing's Festschrift Robert Dickson's use of Samuel Johnson's quotation was not out of place: 'The true genius is a mind of large general powers, accidentally determined to some particular direction.'

JOSEPH HORWOOD

Sources D. H. Cushing, 'A link between science and management in fisheries', *Fishery Bulletin*, 72 (1974), 859–64 · K. M. Brander and R. R. Dickson, 'Papers in appreciation of David Henry Cushing, FRS', *Fisheries Oceanography*, 2 (1993), 109–13 · *The Times* (27 March 2008) · *The Independent* (11 April 2008) · R. Harris, editorial, *Journal of Plankton Research*, 30 (2008), 491–4 · *Balliol College Register* · *WW* (2008) · personal knowledge (2012) · private information (2012) · b. cert. · m. cert. · d. cert.

Wealth at death £141,934: probate, 22 May 2008, *CGPLA Eng. & Wales*

Cutler, Ivor (1923–2006), humorist and singer, was born Isadore Cutler on 15 January 1923 at 3 Ralston Drive, Govan, Glasgow, the second son and third of five children of Jack Morris Cutler, draper and jeweller, and his wife, Paulina (Polly), *née* Goldberg. Both his parents were Jewish, and had arrived in Scotland in the wake of pogroms in eastern Europe; their original surname of Kushner was changed to Cutler by immigration officials. Though named Isadore on his birth certificate, Cutler was always known as Ivor, as he appeared in all subsequent documentation.

Cutler later put his creative urge down to a neurosis created by the arrival of his younger brother: 'He took my place as the centre of the universe. Without that I would not have been so screwed up as I am and therefore as creative. Without a kid brother I would have been quite dull, I think' (*The Times*, 7 March 2006). He once said that he had, at the age of three, tried to kill the perceived usurper with a poker, only to be stopped by an intervening aunt. School at Shawlands Academy, Glasgow, was not a happy time. He said he was victimized by antisemitic schoolteachers for not being a 'real Scot' and claimed that he was on the receiving end of the strap over 200 times (*The Independent*, 9 March 2006). That brutality informed his own more benign teaching methods when he went into education, after a short spell in the Royal Air Force during the Second World War as a trainee navigator. He was dismissed, he said, for being 'too dreamy and absent minded' (*The Times*, 7 March 2006).

Ivor Cutler (1923–2006), by Angela Deane-Drummond, 1974

Cutler was a teacher for over thirty years. His unorthodox approach caused alarm to some parents yet delighted his pupils. One former student later recalled him rewriting the lyrics to 'Moon River' thus: 'Fried liver, where are you tonight? I'd like to take a bite of you. And fried onions, as big as mum's bunions, and stronger than things from the zoo' (*Daily Telegraph*, 10 March 2006). Such an eccentric style, though, made him a suitable member of staff for A. S. Neill's Summerhill, the progressive 'school with no rules', and of course helped form his idiosyncratic voice as an artist and performer, which he discovered concurrently with his teaching career. He, in fact, claimed that teaching unlocked his creativity. 'I used them,' he once said of his pupils, 'but they used me. It was a mutual thing.' He likened the classroom to his audience:

> In a way I am still carrying on with the kids. And those who come to my gigs probably see life as a child would. It's those who have been busy making themselves into grown-ups, avoiding being a child—they're the ones who don't enjoy it. (*The Guardian*, 12 August 1999)

On 4 September 1954 he married Virginia Pearson, ten years his junior, and daughter of George Howard Pearson, factory manager. They had two sons, but the marriage ended in the 1960s.

While married and teaching Cutler tried hawking his songs for sale around Tin Pan Alley, before deciding to perform them himself. His first gig was at the Blue Angel in London in 1957, which he described as an 'unmitigated failure' (*The Independent*, 9 March 2006). His singing and songwriting nevertheless got him noticed by the BBC, who booked him for broadcast appearances. He performed on both television and radio, on the *Acker Bilk Show* and *Late Night Line-Up*, and on the BBC's Home Service. This flurry of success coincided with the release of *Ivor Cutler of Y'hup* in 1959 and *Who Tore Your Trousers?* in 1961. His television appearances and quirky humour brought him to the attention of the Beatles, who asked him to appear in their film *Magical Mystery Tour* (1967). He played the part of a bus conductor called Buster Bloodvessel who announced to his passengers 'I am concerned for you to enjoy yourselves within the limits of British decency', and then developed a passion for Ringo's aunt Jessie. So taken with Cutler were the Beatles that they asked him to educate their children, an offer he declined. In a further creative connection their producer, George Martin, helped him to record *Ludo* (1967), which featured Cutler singing his offbeat lyrics in his rich baritone voice to the accompaniment of a wheezy harmonium—the elements that formed his distinctive performance style.

Poetry followed, although Cutler said that he didn't begin writing it until he was forty-two and didn't become any good at it before he was forty-eight. Yet he produced numerous books—which often carried his illustrations—and he was included in Faber's collection of Scottish verse edited by Douglas Dunn. He set the exact time of writing next to most of his poem manuscripts, including this one, written at 23:58 in July 1999:

> Why don't you sit down and go away?
> You can't sit down and go away.
> Yes you can, I said, and sat down and went away.
> She was too shocked to follow me.
> Wow, I thought, now I can get rid of all my stupid boring friends.
> So I did.
> I've done it ever since, it gives me a real buzz.
> (*The Guardian*, 12 Aug 1999)

Besides the Beatles and poetry editors Cutler's fans included the philosopher Bertrand Russell, the comedian Billy Connolly, and the influential BBC Radio 1 disc jockey John Peel, who introduced his work on his late-night programme to what became a loyal following. One such fan, Alan Magee, a fellow Scot and the record label manager who discovered the rock band Oasis, reissued some of Cutler's recordings in the 1990s, including *Ludo* and *Life in a Scotch Sitting Room Vol. 2*, spreading his appeal to a new generation.

Cutler lived for the large part of the years following his divorce in a one-bedroom flat on Laurier Road in London's Parliament Hill Fields, surrounded by a selection of eccentric artefacts including a set of ivory cutlery (a pun of course), stuffed birds, and an indoor washing line on which his recent paintings were hung to dry. He became a local figure, often seen cycling around on his sit-up-and-beg bicycle with cow-horned handlebars, or transforming the pavement detritus of dog faeces into smiley faces with a piece of chalk, or handing out small sticky labels with gnomic statements like 'Made of dust', 'True happiness is knowing you're a hypocrite', 'Changing your pants is like taking a clean plate', 'Imperfection is an end. Perfection is only an aim', and the tersely political 'Thatcher is an eight-letter word'. He seemed, in part, to live by some of these statements. He listed his recreations in *Who's Who* as 'catalyst' and 'hypocrite' and maintained that art was, for him, therapy. It was said of him that he was 'a man for whom the tag "eccentric" seems pitifully inadequate' (*The Times*, 7 March 1995). He developed a close friendship with the writer Phyllis King, with whom he sometimes collaborated, and who, on occasion, watched him perform on stage, while knitting in the wings.

Cutler was still performing into his eighties, receiving excellent reviews for his inspired performances, but as he grew older he feared losing his memory and succumbing to Alzheimer's disease, as his brother and father had both done. It was, sadly, to be his fate. His last months were spent at Osmond House, a Jewish care home in Bishops Avenue, Finchley, London. He died at the Royal Free Hospital, Camden, on 3 March 2006 after an intracerebral haemorrhage, and was survived by his two sons.

MARK ESPINER

Sources *The Guardian* (12 Aug 1999); (3 Feb 2004); (7 March 2006); (8 March 2006); (10 March 2006) · *The Times* (7 March 2006) · *Daily Telegraph* (7 March 2006); (10 March 2006) · *The Independent* (9 March 2006) · *Sunday Times* (12 March 2006) · *Financial Times* (18 March 2006) · www.ivorcutler.org, 11 July 2009 · www.benbecula.com/archive/ivor_cutler.shtml, 11 July 2009 · *WW* (2006) · personal knowledge (2010) · private information (2010) · b. cert. · m. cert. · d. cert.

Archives FILM BFINA, *South of Watford*, N. Miller (director), ITV, 9 May 1986 · BFINA, *Ivor Cutler: looking for truth with a pin*, P. Spencer (director), BBC4, 15 April 2004 · BFINA, documentary footage · BFINA, light entertainment footage | SOUND BL NSA, documentary recordings · BL NSA, performance recordings

Likenesses L. Morley, group portrait, resin print, 1963, NPG · R. Stevenson, photographs, 1970–79, Rex Features, London · A. Deane-Drummond, photographs, 1974, Hult. Arch., London [*see illus.*] · C. Mills, photograph, 1983, Getty Images, London, Redferns music picture library · M. Marnie, photographs, 1997, Getty Images, London, Redferns music picture library · S. Townsley, photographs, 1997, Rex Features, London · photographs, 1999, Photoshot, London · R. Greig, photographs, 2004, Camera Press, London · P. Millson, photographs, 2004, Camera Press, London · P. Edwards, oils, priv. coll. · obituary photographs

Wealth at death £385,188: probate, 14 Sept 2006, *CGPLA Eng. & Wales*

Dacie, Sir John Vivian (1912–2005), haematologist, was born at 30 Montserrat Road, Putney, London, on 20 July 1912, the son of John Charles Dacie (1860–1928), accountant, and an ardent collector of snails and especially shells, and his wife, Lilian Maud, *née* Vivian (1877–1960), a gifted amateur musician. He had three half-sisters through his father's previous marriage, and one sister, Barbara Gertrude (*b.* 1910), later a schoolteacher. He was educated at King's College School, Wimbledon. His main extracurricular activities during his schooldays, undoubtedly influenced by his parents, were lepidoptery and music, both of which remained absorbing interests throughout his life. After his father died his mother decided to sell his collection of shells, and two of his conchological colleagues offered to catalogue his collection prior to auction. One of them, Colonel Peele, took an interest in

Sir John Vivian Dacie (1912–2005), by Godfrey Argent, 1970

Dacie's future and suggested that he should think of a career in medicine. In 1930 he obtained a leaving exhibition from King's College School, a London county council senior county scholarship, and a scholarship to King's College Hospital. He had a brilliant career as a medical student, winning prizes for anatomy, clinical pathology, surgical pathology, and medicine. He had acquired a microscope and particularly enjoyed staining and examining blood films, building up his personal collection of interesting films. This, together with his continuing enthusiasm for collecting butterflies and moths, gave him the training and skill of a meticulous collector and classifier that would serve him well in his future professional career. After qualifying he held posts in rotation as a house physician, resident biochemist, and resident pathologist. On 8 January 1938 he married Margaret Kathleen Victoria Thynne, a 25-year-old staff nurse at King's College Hospital whom he had met while he was working as a house officer on a medical ward. She was the daughter of Arthur Victor Thynne, minister of religion. They had three sons and two daughters.

After completing his early clinical training Dacie obtained a Medical Research Council studentship that enabled him to work for six months with Janet Vaughan at the University of London British Postgraduate Medical School at Hammersmith Hospital, and then for the next six months with John Wilkinson and Martin Israels at the Manchester Royal Infirmary. Then, with a Will Edmonds fellowship, he returned briefly to King's. On the outbreak of the Second World War in 1939, when King's was largely evacuated, he remained in London as blood transfusion officer until January 1940, when he was moved to the Central Pathology Laboratory at Epsom. In 1943 he joined the Royal Army Medical Corps, serving at a casualty clearing station in Normandy six days after D-day, and then in Italy with the rank of lieutenant-colonel. In Italy he saw an advertisement in *The Lancet* for the position of senior lecturer in clinical pathology at the British Postgraduate Medical School at Hammersmith Hospital, the post that Janet Vaughan had vacated on becoming principal of Somerville College, Oxford. He was appointed to this post in September 1946 and he remained at Hammersmith Hospital for the rest of his career. In 1950 he was appointed reader in haematology by London University, and in 1957 he became the first professor of haematology in the UK. He held this post until his retirement in 1977, when he became an emeritus professor.

Dacie had been attracted to Janet Vaughan's department at Hammersmith by her book *The Anaemias*, the second edition of which, published in 1936, included a chapter on haemolytic anaemias. Her tuition was to inspire his life's work on the haemolytic anaemias, complementing his earlier appreciation of blood cell morphology. In 1952 he was awarded the degree of MD by London University for a thesis entitled 'Auto-antibodies in acquired haemolytic anaemia in man'. He developed simple diagnostic tests using test tubes and a Pasteur pipette, from which, together with examination of stained blood films, he was able to make astute observations on the behaviour of blood in various haemolytic anaemias. He never felt quite at home with the advent of automatic analysers—not because they were too complex, but because he would not trust a procedure in which blood was put in at one end and a result was printed out at the other. He needed to know exactly how the sample behaved during the process. His simple tests enabled him to detect minor differences in reaction of different blood samples, from which he could recognize variants of haemolysis. By analysing the features that might be present in the blood of a patient, especially blood cell morphology by microscopy, together with critical assessment of the clinical and laboratory data, he could solve the most complex diagnostic problems.

While he was a well-qualified physician, having obtained his membership (1936) and subsequently fellowship (1956) of the Royal College of Physicians, Dacie was not attracted to clinical practice, preferring to study the pathophysiology of blood in the laboratory, though always in close consultation with his more clinically oriented colleagues. He investigated a large number of patients with various haemolytic anaemias who were referred to him from all parts of the UK as well as from overseas, and also reviewed blood films with unusual features sent to him for elucidation. In his office he maintained carefully classified files on all these patients, and contacted them regularly to assess their progress. This enabled him to make careful notes of the clinical course of their illnesses as well as to examine changes in their blood films, which he filed for future reference.

At the same time Dacie was building his department into the leading haematology centre in Britain for all aspects of the speciality. London University had established a one-year postgraduate diploma course in clinical pathology, in which he ran the haematology section; he was also attracting to his department other graduate trainees, initially from the dominions and former British colonies, but also from countries of western Europe and the United States, and from as far afield as China. Thus he greatly influenced the practice of haematology in many other countries besides the UK. He was in great demand to lecture in these countries and to participate in international congresses. Although he enjoyed meeting his old post-doctoral students and trainees, many of whom became distinguished academic and consultant haematologists, he would accept invitations with some reluctance as he preferred to spend his free time at home with his close-knit family—but when he did accept invitations he would at least compensate by including in his luggage his equipment for augmenting his lepidoptera collection.

Dacie had been a member (and later chairman) of a Medical Research Council working party on the treatment of leukaemia. In 1966, at the request of the Department of Health and the Medical Research Council, he established the council's leukaemia unit at Hammersmith, with David Galton as director. This unit became a national (and international) reference centre for research in and diagnosis and management of leukaemias and lymphomas. He helped create the Leukaemia Research Fund and was, from 1975 to 1985, the first chairman of its medical and scientific advisory panel.

During his academic career Dacie published over 170 scientific papers, while a further 670 papers were published independently by other members of his department. He respected their academic freedom and he would not have his name attached to any paper if he had not made a significant contribution and had not been personally involved in its writing. His published papers were later listed in an annotation in the *British Journal of Haematology* (2005). He was also the author of two major books, both published by Churchill-Livingstone. The first of these was *Practical Haematology*, which was originally published in 1950 and subsequently (with S. M. Lewis as co-author) went into nine editions, becoming a standard textbook worldwide, with translated editions in several languages. The tenth (multi-author) edition, entitled *Dacie and Lewis Practical Haematology*, maintained the principles of good laboratory practice that had been established by Dacie; he had an affinity with his technical staff, and in 1953 he was invited to be an honorary fellow of the Institute of Medical Laboratory Technology. His other major undertaking was *Haemolytic Anaemias*. The first edition of this unique treatise appeared in 1954; the third edition was published in five volumes, the first in 1985 and the last in 1999, a *magnum opus* that was a fitting memorial to his intellect, to the breadth of his scientific and technical knowledge of the subject, and also to his scholarly style of writing. When his retirement had deprived him of his secretary he continued his writing at home in his study, with Margaret in the breakfast-room typing the drafts on their faithful Remington typewriter and pasting in any corrections by hand: as with his attitude to the automated blood counters, he could not bring himself to start using the newfangled computer.

Dacie's influence on haematology was further extended by his distinguished editorship of the *British Journal of Haematology*, which was launched by Blackwells in 1955. His dedication and insistence on an impeccable standard of both scientific content and literary style ensured that the journal quickly acquired an international reputation. When he relinquished the editorship in 1962 he remained as chairman of the editorial board, providing valued advice to the next six editors who successively took up the mantle. He was a co-founder of the British Society for Haematology, and became its president in 1964. He was also president of the European–African division of the International Society of Hematology for its congress in London in 1975. Many awards testified to his contributions to British haematology. He was elected FRS in 1967, served as president of the Royal College of Pathologists (1973–5), and of the Royal Society of Medicine (1977), and received honorary degrees from the universities of Uppsala (1961) and Marseilles (1977). He was knighted in 1976.

Dacie's lifelong interest in lepidoptera and his skill and devotion to collection and classification led him to become distinguished in that field too. To this hobby he applied the same scholarly and scientific aptitude as he did with his professional work. He enjoyed inviting selected visitors to inspect his mounted display of various species. He was very proud to have become a member of the British Entomological Society, with three papers published in the *Entomologists' Record*. He lived latterly at 10 Alan Road, Wimbledon, and died at St George's Hospital, Tooting, on 12 February 2005, of peritonitis. He was survived by his wife, Margaret, and by four of their children: Janet, a diagnostic radiologist at St Bartholomew's Hospital, Julian, a general practitioner, (Mary) Jocelyn, a teacher of children with learning difficulties, and (Adrian) James, a teacher of English. His eldest son, John, who worked in advertising, died of a brain tumour in 1985.

S. Mitchell Lewis

Sources 'Studies in haematology', *British Journal of Haematology*, 23 (1972) [A supplement in honour of J. V. Dacie on his 60th birthday] • H. Swan, *The founding of the British Society for Haematology*, 1989, www.bloodmed.com/home/bshhistorypdf, 1 Nov 1007 • *Daily Telegraph* (19 Feb 2005) • *The Independent* (26 Feb 2005) • *The Guardian* (11 March 2005) • *The Times* (17 March 2005) • M. Lewis, 'Annotation: Sir John Dacie', *British Journal of Haematology*, 130 (2005), 834–44 • M. Lewis, 'Dacie, Sir John Vivian', 2005, www.rcplondon.ac.uk/heritage/munksroll/munk_details.esp?ID=5374, 16 July 2007 • M. Lewis, P. Mollison, and D. Weatherall, *Memoirs FRS*, 52 (2006), 67–82 • annual reports of (Royal) Postgraduate Medical School, 1950–80, Imperial College library, London, Hammersmith campus library • Burke, *Peerage* • *WW* (2005) • personal knowledge (2009) • private information (2009) • b. cert. • m. cert. • d. cert.

Likenesses G. Argent, bromide print on card mount, 1970, NPG, RS [*see illus.*] • W. Narraway, portrait, 1975, Royal College of Pathologists, London • W. Bird, bromide print, RS • L. Boden, pencil or chalk on paper, Royal Society of Medicine, London · obituary photographs · photograph, repro. in *British Journal of Haematology* (1972) · photograph, repro. in *British Journal of Haematology* (2005) · photograph, repro. in *Memoirs FRS*

Wealth at death under £235,000: probate, 9 June 2005, *CGPLA Eng. & Wales*

Dacres, Desmond Adolphus [*known as* Desmond Dekker] (**1941–2006**), singer and songwriter, was born on 16 July 1941 in St Andrew, on the outskirts of Kingston, Jamaica. Little is known about his childhood except that after his mother's early death his father, desiring a proper education for his son, sent him to live with relatives in the quiet country town of Seaforth in the parish of St Thomas, where he began singing gospel in the local church. He completed his musical education under the supervision of Sister Mary Ignatius Davies at the Alpha Boys' School on South Camp Road, Kingston. After being apprenticed as a tailor he switched direction and took a job as a welder at Standard Engineering where his singing around the workplace received encouragement from his co-workers, including the young Bob Marley. He took to visiting local sound system dances in the Maxfield Road area. In 1961 he auditioned without success for the producers Clement Dodd at Studio One and Duke Reid at Treasure Isle before later moving on to Leslie Kong's record label, Beverley's, where he auditioned in front of the label's biggest star, Derrick Morgan. After repeated attempts he finally entered the Federal studios on Marcus Garvey Drive in 1963 to cut his début single in the fashionable ska style of the era; 'Honour Your Mother and Father' was credited to Desmond Decker and Beverley's Allstars. The song became a number one hit locally and led to further recording success with follow-up singles such as 'Parents', 'Dracula' (as Desmond Dekkar) and 'Labour for Learning' (as Desmond Dekker).

From the mid-1960s 'groups' began to dominate the music scene both in Jamaica and internationally; Dekker's success allowed him to co-opt one of Kong's groups, the Cherry Pies, as back-up on another big hit, the rumbustiously boastful 'King of Ska', a tune establishing him as a major star of the ska genre. In turn this led to Dekker joining the Four Aces, with whom he later became internationally famous as Desmond Dekker and the Aces after the release in 1964 of '007 (Shanty Town)' in the newly fashionable rock steady style. Influenced by the 'rude boy' fashion and attitude popular at the time, the song was a reflection of the reality of everyday life, with a message that carried across the ocean and into the working-class movement of skinheads in Britain, who adopted both Desmond Dekker's music and his nattily attired appearance as part of their own cultural, if not political, stance.

Mirroring the emergence of America's 'black power' movement, for many Jamaican artists the late 1960s was also an era of protest given voice by 'songs of freedom' whose lyrics echoed the tribulations of everyday life. In 1968, after a series of grittily direct singles including 'Rudy got Soul', 'Keep a Cool Head', 'Hanging Tree', and 'Unity', Dekker changed musical direction by utilizing the new beat called reggae and producing a single that would define his career. Originally called 'Poor Me Israelites', its retitling as 'Israelites' for the British and American markets was the only concession made to commerciality, for the song was sung in pure patois. 'Israelites' was the first native Jamaican recording to reach number one on the British 'hit parade' (in April 1969) and the first to break into the American top ten, and its success paved the way for the coming of Jimmy Cliff and Bob Marley, and the growth in worldwide interest in reggae that was a marked feature of the mid-1970s. On its release, and in subsequent reissues, 'Israelites' found its way into the hearts of young and old, especially when featured in the 1990s parody for Vitalite margarine, after which children could be heard on streets singing 'Oh, oh, me ears are alight!'—a version appreciated by the artist himself. Even the Beatles' Paul McCartney was a fan and referred to Dekker by name in the opening line of 'Ob-La-Di, Ob-La-Da' ('Desmond has a barrow in the market-place') on the band's *White Album* (1968).

Desmond Adolphus Dacres [Desmond Dekker] (**1941–2006**), by David Corio, 1985

In the early 1970s Dekker moved to the UK, useful as a base for constant touring, and although he continued to record new songs the big hits dried up, even though the quality of his output remained high. His last major hit was a cover of Jimmy Cliff's 'You Can Get It If You Really Want', which reached number two in the UK singles chart in 1970. Following the early death of his mentor Leslie Kong his recording career became less focused, but he was always in demand for live shows. He was perhaps best remembered by the audiences of BBC television's *Top of the Pops* for flashing sideways leers at the camera in the middle of his always charismatic performances. At the end of the 1970s he signed with the British record label Stiff, in the wake of the successful locally bred ska sound of 2 Tone, leading to the release of the album *Black and Dekker* (1980), followed by an album produced by Robert Palmer, *Compass Point* (1981). Neither album sold well and Dekker was forced to file for bankruptcy in 1984. Nevertheless the succession of 'Israelites' reissues and re-recordings, including its use in a television advertisement for Maxell tapes in the early 1990s and a new reggae version with Apache Indian in 2005, ensured he remained in the public eye, as did an album with the 2 Tone ska revival band the Specials, *King of Kings* (1992). He also continued performing, his last concert being at Leeds University on 11 May 2006.

Dekker's vast catalogue of excellent early material literally defined the ska, rocksteady, and early reggae periods, but was often unjustifiably overlooked, falling as it did under the shadow of the international success of his major hits. He died suddenly from a heart attack on 25 May 2006 at his home, 66 Harcourt Road, Thornton Heath, Surrey. He was married but divorced, and was survived by a daughter, Desrene Theresa, and a son, Desmond.

STEVE BARKER

Sources C. Larkin, ed., *The Guinness who's who of reggae* (1994) • S. Barrow and P. Dalton, *Reggae: the rough guide* (1997); 2nd edn (2001) • *Jamaica Observer* (26 May 2006) • *The Times* (27 May 2006) • *Daily Telegraph* (27 May 2006) • *The Guardian* (27 May 2006) • *The Independent* (27 May 2006) • K. Roberts, 'Desmond Dekker and the music of the shantytowns', www.counterpunch.org/roberts06102006.html, 21 July 2009 • P. Scholtes, 'Desmond Dekker came first', http://blogs.citypages.com/pscholtes/2006/06/desmond_dekker_.php, 21 July 2009 • d. cert.

Archives FILM BFINA, current affairs footage • BFINA, documentary footage • BFINA, light entertainment footage

Likenesses H. Goodwin, photographs, 1960–69, Rex Features, London • D. Hoffmann, photographs, 1960–79, Rex Features, London • photographs, 1960–2005, Getty Images, London, Redferns music picture library • photographs, 1970–80, Getty Images, London, Michael Ochs archives • photographs, 1974, Hult. Arch., London • D. Corio, photograph, 1985, Getty Images, London, Redferns music picture library [*see illus.*] • D. Tafari, photograph, 1995, NPG • G. Williams, photographs, 1996, Rex Features, London • H. Valentine, photographs, 2001, PA Photos, London • I. Dickson, photographs, 2002, Rex Features, London • C. Walter, photographs, 2002, Getty Images, London, WireImage • obituary photographs • photographs, Photoshot, London • photographs, repro. in http://blogs.citypages.com/pscholtes/2006/06/desmond_dekker_.php

Wealth at death £290,456: probate, 20 July 2007, *CGPLA Eng. & Wales*

Daiches, David (1912–2005), literary scholar, was born at 2 Salem Hill South, Sunderland, co. Durham, on 2 September 1912, the younger son of Salis *Daiches (1880–1945), rabbi and author, and his wife, Flora, *née* Levin (1890–1983). He and his elder brother, Lionel (1911–1999), later an advocate, were the first generation to break with the rabbinical family tradition: they and their two sisters, Sylvia (1914–1996), subsequently a noted French scholar and university lecturer, and Beryl (1923–1964), were descended

David Daiches (1912–2005), by Joyce Gunn-Cairns

from a long line of rabbis going back at least 500 years. In March 1919 the family moved from Sunderland, where his father had been minister to its Jewish community, to Edinburgh, where Salis Daiches became minister at the Graham Street Synagogue and subsequently the unofficial Scottish-Jewish spiritual leader. In his first autobiography, *Two Worlds: an Edinburgh Jewish Childhood* (1956), David Daiches wrote that the move to Edinburgh 'was the true beginning of my life as I remember it for I remember my childhood as a developing relation between family tradition and my sense of Edinburgh' (p. 17). This sense of duality, of existing in two worlds, of accommodation, pervaded Daiches's life and work.

Educated at George Watson's College, the 'bastion of gentile Edinburgh education' (*The Times*, 25 July 2005), Daiches was unable to participate in school games, sports, or the literary society which met on Friday evenings. It was at that time that he

> became acutely aware of living in two worlds, or rather of moving freely between one and the other. Bagpipe music and synagogue melody represented the two poles between which my sensibility moved. I accepted this dualism as part of the nature of things. (*Two Worlds*, 60)

He was already writing poems: his first publication, a poem 'The Fountain in Moonlight', appeared in the school magazine, *The Watsonian*, in December 1923. In his final year at school, 1930, he walked away with various prizes, including a scholarship to Edinburgh University, where he graduated in 1934 with first-class honours in rhetoric and English literature. He chose English because of his passion for poetry. At Edinburgh special influences were H. J. C. Grierson, the great John Donne and Walter Scott scholar, and the Shakespearean scholar John Dover Wilson. Daiches wrote articles, reviews, poems, and letters for *The Student* during the years 1932–4, under the pseudonym Quidam, and ran the university English Literature Society. The first book he edited belongs to this period: *Private Business* (1933), a collection of poems by him and his contemporary student poets in the society including Sorley MacLean and Robert Garioch.

In 1934 Daiches won an Elton exhibition to Balliol College, Oxford. In a memorial address to the English department at Aberdeen University sixty years later, with characteristic frankness he recalled that 'because I wasn't used to handling money I spent my three years' money in my first year and I had nothing left to complete my Oxford doctorate'. He 'wrote to Grierson … and I asked him if he could give me an assistant lectureship at the University for a year so that I could recoup my finances and go back to Oxford to finish my doctorate. By return of post … I got a letter of appointment' ('Memories of Grierson', 31). After a year as assistant in English at Edinburgh (1935–6) he returned to Balliol as Andrew Bradley fellow for 1936–7. In 1937 he married Isobel (Billie) Mackay (*d.* 1977), a fellow student at Edinburgh who became a librarian. They had one son, Alan (1940–2006), later a photographer, and two daughters, Elizabeth (Liz; 1946–2008) and Jennifer (Jenni; *b.* 1941), who married the historian and literary critic Angus *Calder; as Jenni Calder she became a distinguished poet and literary critic, and wrote movingly about both her parents in *Not Nebuchadnezzar: in Search of Identities* (2005).

Daiches received his DPhil degree in 1939 for a thesis on the development and sources of the King James version of the Bible with special reference to the Hebrew tradition (published as *The King James Version of the English Bible*, 1941). In the same year he accepted an academic position in America at the University of Chicago, partly for his father's sake: Daiches's marriage to a gentile had placed his father, an orthodox rabbi, in an embarrassing situation. Following four years at Chicago, and war service in the British embassy in Washington and British information services in New York (1944–6), Daiches became a very popular and influential professor at Cornell University. He wrote of this American period in his second volume of autobiography, *A Third World* (1971). His students included the prolific author Harold Bloom. His friendship with a colleague, the distinguished critic of Romanticism, Meyer H. Abrams, led to the influential textbook *The Norton Anthology of English Literature*. First published in 1962, by the year 2000 it was in its seventh edition. Daiches was responsible for the twentieth-century section in the first four editions, from 1962 to 1979. During these years, in addition to producing thirty-six books, innumerable academic articles, and reviews, Daiches wrote poetry published in the *New Yorker*.

In 1951, making what Daiches subsequently described as an unfortunate career move, he and his family returned to Britain. His real motive was to obtain a chair at a Scottish university. He spent the years 1951–61 as a university lecturer in English at Cambridge (he was a fellow of Jesus College from 1957), and writing prolifically. His *Critical Approaches to Literature* (1956; 2nd edn, 1981) and his scholarly and analytical multi-volume *A Critical History of English Literature* (1960; 2nd rev. edn, 1994), as so much of his work, anticipated future literary fashions and concerns, recognizing the crucial role played by literary criticism and theory in literary study. Alastair Fowler, the eminent Renaissance literary scholar, viewed Daiches's extensive treatment of Milton in the critical history as anticipating subsequent work by Stanley Fish and others. Milton had already been the subject of a book-length study by Daiches (1957; new rev. edn, 1969) and various individual essays. His earlier books, *Virginia Woolf* (1942; rev. edn, 1963) and *Willa Cather: a Critical Introduction* (1951; new edn, 1962), anticipated later feminist interests. *The Novel and the Modern World* (1939; rev. edn, 1960) and *Poetry and the Modern World: a Study of Poetry in England between 1900 and 1939* (1940) prefigured many of the concerns of later historians of modernism, while his earlier *Literature and Society* (1938) had explored the complex relationship between the production of literature and the social conditions in which the writer lives, a central concern of academics in the field of cultural studies at the end of the twentieth century.

At Cambridge Daiches continued his reviewing activities in the *Manchester Guardian*, *Times Literary Supplement*, *New Republic*, *New Statesman*, *New York Times Book Review*, *Commentary*, and similar newspapers and journals on both sides of the Atlantic. He also began broadcasting frequently on the radio: his appearances on the *Brains Trust* made him a national celebrity and radio voice.

Recruited by Asa Briggs in 1961, Daiches was one of the founding fathers of the University of Sussex. *The Idea of a New University: an Experiment in Sussex* (1964; 2nd edn, 1970), edited by Daiches, explained the ideas behind the university and its foundation. In his essay 'The place of English studies in the Sussex scheme' he described his differing experiences of the academic study of English and his conception of a new school of English and American studies. Janet Burroway described him at this time as

> large-hearted, witty, erudite, and vain. He expected to be the centre of attention, but he had no tinge of the little-man's Napoleonic meanness. His natural state of being was delight: delight in language, family, history, babies, rhyme schemes, verbal trickery, anybody's happiness, unblended whisky, high discourse, repartee and praise. (Baker and Lister, 31–2)

Daiches's lectures were replete with brilliant insights. His explication of Shakespeare's sonnets emphasized the relationships in them between personal affection and money contained in a word such as 'dear'. Comments on Yeats's 'Byzantium' poems contained an overwhelming sense of mutability, the line 'Of what is past, or passing, or to come' having all the tenses subsumed. He also drew attention to the illusion of all time conquered in Keats's 'Ode to Autumn', and the brilliant observation in Wallace Stevens's 'Sunday Morning' that in a secular world the pigeon replaces the dove.

The first of Daiches's 100 or so books, *The Place of Meaning in Poetry*, was published in 1935. The last, *A Weekly Scotsman and Other Poems*, containing seventy-five of his poems spanning six decades, appeared in 1994. Aside from a mass of journalism and academic articles, he was also the editor of general series including Studies in English Literature, published by Arnold from 1961 to 1985, to which he contributed what was regarded by many as the best short critical analysis of George Eliot's *Middlemarch* (1963). He published extensively on Walter Scott's achievement as a novelist, and advocated Scott's cause as a consummate artist in the years in which Scott was out of critical fashion. In 1984 he became the vice-chairman of the advisory board of the Edinburgh edition of the Waverley novels; indeed he was described as the godfather of this edition. Hugh MacDiarmid, whose *At the Sign of the Thistle* Daiches favourably reviewed in *Life and Letters* in 1934, referred to Daiches as the 'foremost living authority on [Scottish] literature' (MacDiarmid, 97). Daiches also served as the chair of the advisory board for the edition of *The Collected Works of James Hogg*. A pioneer of American studies in Britain, Daiches made significant contributions to many areas of literary studies, including the modern novel, as well as English, biblical, and eighteenth- and nineteenth-century studies. But poetry was his first love. As well as writing poetry, he produced powerful new critical explications of passages from writers as diverse as Marlowe, Shakespeare, Milton, Yeats, and Dylan Thomas. In addition to his frequent broadcasts on the radio and appearances on television, his sound recordings included a memorable discussion with the critic Barbara Hardy on George Eliot and Jane Austen, and readings with L. C. Knights from *Hamlet* and *The Tempest*.

Daiches's contributions to Scottish literature and culture may perhaps be regarded as his most significant. All his writing was pervaded with the sense of duality that he experienced growing up in Edinburgh. He saw dualities in the work of many Scottish writers, including Stevenson, Allan Ramsay, MacDiarmid, and James Thomson. The range and depth of his knowledge of Scottish literature was extensive: from Henryson and Dunbar to Fergusson and Burns, through to the late twentieth century. As his daughter Jenni observed, 'There is no one who has done more than he has to regenerate engagement with Scottish literature and the wider Scottish cultural context' (Calder, 'Reading, writing and reverberations', 11).

Daiches's non-literary works extended from his evocation of the history and topography of Scotland's two first cities, *Glasgow* (1977) and *Edinburgh* (1978), to *Literary Landscapes of the British Isles: a Narrative Atlas* (written with John Flower, 1979), *Charles Edward Stuart: the Life and Times of Bonnie Prince Charlie* (1973), and *Scotland and the Union* (1977). His father had been a connoisseur of Havana cigars; Daiches became known for his expertise in the national drink. His *Scotch Whisky: its Past and Present* (1969, 3rd rev. edn, 1978) was something of a best-seller, especially in Japan, and remained long in print. His enthusiasm could be infectious. Joel Sayre recalled that at Cornell Daiches had mentioned that Mortlach single malt was sold in New York, at Macy's: 'On his next trip to Manhattan he dropped in at Macy's to stock up his Mortlach supply. "Sorry, but some damn fool prof up at Ithaca recommended it to his students, and we're all out"' (Sayre, 6).

Following his retirement in 1977 Daiches moved back to Edinburgh, where he became actively involved in the cultural and intellectual life of Scotland. From 1980 until 1986 he was director of the Institute for Advanced Studies in the Humanities at Edinburgh University, and he played an active role in the university's summer programme and its creation. His last years were spent in his Belgrave Crescent flat, whose study was lined with books towering upwards to the high ceiling, threatening to collapse upon the frail bald dome beneath. One of the last polymaths, he was a self-confessed eclectic. The publication at eighty-one of his poems gave him great pleasure, as did the increasing recognition of his role in the rediscovery of Scottish literature. In 1981 he became a fellow of the Royal Society of Edinburgh, and in 1991 he was appointed CBE.

Daiches did not lack his share of personal and professional disappointments. These included his rejection by Scottish universities when he applied for positions in the post-war years, his failure to get the chair at Edinburgh he was so evidently qualified for, or a knighthood, and the death of his first wife, Billie, within days of their return to Edinburgh. In 1978 he married his second wife, Hazel Neville, *née* Newman. She died in 1986. Daiches himself died in Edinburgh on 15 July 2005. He was buried in the Jewish section of the Piershill cemetery in Edinburgh on 18 July. A well-attended celebration of his life was held on 2 October 2005 at the Playfair Library of the University of Edinburgh. He was survived by his three children, though two of them died soon after. WILLIAM BAKER

Sources D. Daiches, *Two worlds: an Edinburgh Jewish childhood* (1956) • H. MacDiarmid, *A drunk man looks at the thistle*, 4th edn (1962) • J. Sayre, *Book World* (8 March 1970) • D. Daiches, *A third world* (1971) • D. Daiches, 'Memories of Grierson', *Aberdeen University Review*, 193 (spring 1995), 23–32 • J. Calder, 'Reading, writing and reverberations', *Scottish Book Collector*, 7/6 (2003), 7–11 • J. Calder, *Not Nebuchadnezzar: in search of identities* (2005) • *The Independent* (18 July 2005) • *Daily Telegraph* (19 July 2005) • *The Scotsman* (20 July 2005) • *The Herald* [Glasgow] (19 July 2005); (21 July 2005) • *The Guardian* (19 July 2005); (20 July 2005); (12 Aug 2005) • *The Times* (25 July 2005); (4 Oct 2005) • W. Baker and M. Lister, eds., *David Daiches: a celebration of his life and work* (2008) • M. Drabble, 'A happy dualism', *TLS* (22 May 2008) • *WW* (2005) • personal knowledge (2009) • private information (2009) [Jenni Calder, daughter; M. Lister; J. Stallworthy; K. James] • b. cert.

Archives NL Scot., corresp. and papers • Queen's University, Canada, corresp. and literary MSS • U. Sussex, papers | *Manchester Guardian* archives, letters to *Manchester Guardian* • Yale U., Sterling Memorial Library, Osborne collection, corresp., annotated lectures, papers | FILM BFINA, current affairs footage | SOUND BL NSA, millennium memory bank, interview with J. Firth, 14 Nov 1997, C900/21039 • BL NSA, current affairs recordings • BL NSA, documentary recordings

Likenesses J. Gunn-Cairns, pencil and red chalk drawing, 1999, Scot. NPG • A. Daiches, photograph, repro. in Baker and Lister, *Daiches*, jacket • D. Dingsdale, photograph, repro. in *The Herald* (4 June 1994) • J. Gunn-Cairns, drawing, repro. in *Drawing David Daiches: extracts from writings by David Daiches* (2004) [*see illus.*] • J. Gunn-Cairns, drawings, repro. in *Drawing David Daiches: extracts from writings by David Daiches* (2004) • obituary photographs • photographs, repro. in Calder, 'Reading, writing and reverberations'

Dalitz, Richard Henry [Dick] (**1925–2006**), particle physicist, was born in Dimboola, Victoria, Australia, on 28 February 1925, the son of Frederick William Dalitz and Hazel

Blanche, *née* Drummond. His father, originally a blacksmith, fought in the First World War, then entered the civil service; his mother was a schoolteacher. When he was two the family moved to Melbourne. After his secondary education at Scotch College, Melbourne, he took degrees in mathematics (1944) and physics (1945) at the University of Melbourne, coming top in both of these subjects. In 1946 he won an Aitchison travelling scholarship and went to Trinity College, Cambridge, to study for a PhD in nuclear physics, taking with him his wife, Valda, *née* Suiter, whom he had married in Melbourne earlier that year; they were to have three daughters and a son.

Dalitz's thesis was on 'Zero-zero transitions in nuclei', processes where the emission of a single photon is forbidden by the principle of conservation of angular momentum. Dalitz showed that the nuclear transition can occur if an electron and a positron are produced. It was this early insight that would later bear fruit with the concept of 'Dalitz pairs' in particle physics. During the preparation of his thesis he took a one-year post at the University of Bristol as student-assistant to Neville Mott. There he became enthralled by the fundamental discoveries being made by Cecil Powell's group in the field of cosmic radiation, such as the pion, carrier of the force that binds atomic nuclei, and 'strange particles'. Among the latter he took interest in the 'tau' meson, later known as the K meson, which on decay transformed into three pions.

In 1949 Dalitz joined Rudolf Peierls's group in the mathematical physics department at the University of Birmingham. After completing his thesis in 1950 it was in Birmingham in 1951 that he made his first seminal contribution, by demonstrating that the electrically neutral pion could decay into a photon and an electron–positron pair—the Dalitz pair. The technique of measuring Dalitz pairs was used to measure the parity of the pion and the tau meson. Parity concerns the relation of something to its mirror image and, according to the received wisdom at the time, remains unchanged when particles decay. Dalitz's work was about to overthrow this, though at first he did not realize it. The tau meson decayed into three pions, but sometimes exhibited a 'theta' mode where it decayed into two. When a heavy particle decays into lighter ones they share the parent's energy in different proportions. Thousands of examples are studied whereby the distribution of energy can reveal the properties of the parent particle. Dalitz invented a way of mapping the data on a diagram, the 'Dalitz plot', and showed that the tau and theta modes were from the same particle. This could only be true if nature distinguished left from right, which ran counter to the received wisdom. It was T. D. Lee and C. N. Yang in the USA who later realized that this 'law' had never been tested in weak interactions, which were responsible for these decays. Dalitz's plot thus set in train the sequence of events that led to Lee and Yang's Nobel prize in 1957.

In 1953 Dalitz moved to Cornell University, and in 1956 to the chair of physics at the Enrico Fermi Institute at the University of Chicago. During his time there he became the world's leading expert on the theory of hypernuclei—atomic nuclei where one of the normal protons or neutrons has been replaced by a heavy unstable particle known as a hyperon. At the end of the 1950s Dalitz plots were made of the data emerging from bubble chambers in the new high-energy particle accelerators. As a result, within three years the first examples of what would turn out to be scores of short-lived particles known as 'resonances' were found.

Dalitz was elected a fellow of the Royal Society in 1960 and retained a connection with Chicago until 1966, but in 1963 Rudolf Peierls, who had just moved from Birmingham to Oxford, persuaded him to join him in Oxford as Royal Society research professor, a post he held for twenty-seven years. On taking up this position Dalitz was the first physical scientist to become a fellow of All Souls College since the seventeenth century. At about this time Murray Gell-Mann proposed his 'eightfold way' scheme as a mathematical description of the host of newly discovered particles, many of which were being discovered by means of Dalitz plots. In 1964 Gell-Mann proposed that this scheme would emerge naturally if the particles were composites of more fundamental entities: quarks. While experimentalists quickly realized the power of the quark model, Gell-Mann was ambiguous. The quarks' electrical charges were fractions of a proton's charge, the smallest charge that had ever been seen. They are so strongly bound together that a single one has never been separated, even though they act like independent particles in many ways. Dalitz took them seriously, and proposed that they are basic blocks within a proton analogous to electrons inside atoms. The laws that determine the rotary and spinning motions of electrons were applied in Dalitz's model to quarks and resonances.

In 1965 Dalitz showed how the quark model explained the magnetic properties of the proton and neutron, and then took a more radical step: he proposed that quarks could be raised into different energy states following the established laws of non-relativistic quantum mechanics. This implied the existence of many short-lived resonances similar to, but heavier than, the proton. Some were already known and fitted the scheme perfectly, while in the subsequent decades many other examples were found, invariably by application of Dalitz plots. The quark model thus became established as the explanation of what had become a menagerie of particles. By about 1970 the experimental evidence as interpreted by Dalitz and others convinced physicists that quarks were real, and the standard model of particle physics includes them as essential ingredients. Dalitz's key pioneering role was arguably never adequately recognized. He was suspicious of theorizing and saw his job as understanding the data, of which he had an encyclopaedic knowledge, supported by meticulously kept notebooks.

Dalitz was a member of council of the Royal Society (1979–81), and a corresponding or foreign member of the national academies of science in Australia (1978), Poland (1980), India (1990), and the USA (1991). He won many awards, including the Maxwell medal of the Institute of Physics (1966), the Hughes medal of the Royal Society

(1975), the J. Robert Oppenheimer prize of the University of Miami (1980), and the Harrie Massey prize of the Institute of Physics and Australian Institute of Physics (1990).

Dalitz was a shy, modest man of few words, but with a dry sense of humour. His interests outside physics included travelling, biographical research, and the history of the Wends, or Sorbs, pre-German inhabitants of Brandenburg who speak a Slavonic language, inhabit a few villages between Cottbus and Berlin, and from whom he was descended. Having discovered that his great-grandparents had emigrated to Australia in 1858, he identified their village as Werben, and when he went there he discovered that the local historian and he were related. He published work that casts new light on aspects of the history of the Wends. Following his retirement he continued also to be active in physics, attending seminars and pursuing research in the Oxford theoretical physics department, later the Rudolf Peierls Centre for Theoretical Physics. Having lived latterly in Jack Straw's Lane, Headington, Oxford, he died at the John Radcliffe Hospital, Oxford, on 13 January 2006, of bronchopneumonia following a stroke. He was survived by his wife and their four children. FRANK CLOSE

Sources *The Guardian* (24 Jan 2006); (31 Jan 2006) · *The Times* (17 Feb 2006); (21 Feb 2006); (28 Feb 2006) · *The Independent* (24 Feb 2006) · G. Ross, *Nature*, 440 (9 March 2006), 162 · I. J. R. Aitchison, F. E. Close, A. Gal, and D. J. Millener, 'The scientific heritage of Richard Henry Dalitz, FRS (1925–2006)', *Nuclear Physics*, 771 (2006), 8–25 · R. Dalitz, autobiographical notes, www-thphys.physics.ox.ac.uk/people/SubirSarkar/dalitzmeeting/Dalitzhistory.pdf, 14 Aug 2008 · *WW* (2006) · personal knowledge (2010) · private information (2010) [Rod Dalitz, son] · d. cert.
Archives RS, Howard Florey papers · RS, Thomas Gold papers
Likenesses W. Bird, photograph, RS · obituary photographs
Wealth at death under £95,000: probate, 6 March 2006, *CGPLA Eng. & Wales*

Dally [*née* Mullins], **Ann Gwendolen** (1926–2007), doctor and medical historian, was born on 29 March 1926 in a nursing home at 27 Welbeck Street, Marylebone, London, the first of the three children of Claud William *Mullins (1887–1968), reforming magistrate and author, and his wife, Elizabeth Gwendolen (Gwen) Brandt (1904–1997), craftswoman. Her mother belonged to a wealthy German-Russian banking family; her father was the son of the prominent Victorian sculptor, Edwin Roscoe Mullins. Aged two, Ann moved with her parents from 24 Eldon Road, Kensington, to Summerdale, Burgh Heath Road, Epsom.

A voracious reader from the age of four, Ann Mullins attended small progressive schools, first the 'enlightened but not freakish' Sherwood House near her home, then Wychwood School in Oxford as a boarder because, according to her father's diary, the eleven-year-old Ann was completely unmanageable, not to mention 'rude', 'detached', and 'stubborn'. She had defeated the child psychiatrist Emanuel Miller by refusing to say a word at their twice-weekly sessions. She flourished at Wychwood, benefiting from its wartime collaboration with the academically rigorous Oxford high school, although her 'disdain for authority or any form of control' remained noteworthy. Expelled on her sixteenth birthday, she continued at the high school and won an open exhibition to Somerville College, Oxford, the following year.

In her first term at school Ann Mullins was befriended by a classmate's mother, Dorothea Nasmyth, a doctor who had served in the Mediterranean during the First World War and who was an important influence on Ann's life. After taking a second-class degree in modern history in 1946 Ann worked for the War Office, giving history lectures to British troops in Germany and Austria, before starting medical training at St Thomas's Hospital in 1947 (the first year women were admitted). On 1 April 1950 she married Peter John Dally (1923–2005), a fellow medical student, with whom she rapidly produced six children, two before she graduated MB BS in 1953. From 1955 the family lived in Dulwich, Peter training in psychiatry, the children and their nanny (and her child) staying frequently with Ann's parents and sister in Graffham, Sussex. (In 1963 Ann's mother bought them a farmhouse in the village, which eased the congestion.)

With the move to Dulwich, Ann Dally had intended to work part-time until her children were in school, but later that year Peter contracted polio and became almost completely paralysed for several months, forcing her to focus on her career. She worked as a research registrar in general medicine and acquired a diploma in obstetrics before finally leaving hospital jobs in 1959. Over the next decade she had a small general practice, worked in other people's practices, conducted baby clinics, worked for the Family Planning Association, and was an active medical journalist and broadcaster. From 1960, as Ann Mullins, she produced regular columns and articles for the *Sunday Telegraph*, *Evening News*, and *Family Doctor* that related to her interests in mothers, children, and psychological medicine, with titles like 'What is normal?' and 'The child who won't conform'. A steady stream of books followed, starting with *An Intelligent Person's Guide to Modern Medicine* (1966), *A Child is Born* (1966), and a biography of Cicely Williams (1968), which entailed a research trip in 1962 to Beirut, where Williams was teaching. She also recorded and transcribed in the early 1960s a series of interviews with Sylvia Payne about the early history of the psychoanalytical movement. Later Ann Dally became one of the first radio psychiatrists, on a pioneering Radio London programme presented by Robbie Vincent.

In 1968 Ann and Peter Dally bought 13 Devonshire Place, a large house in the heart of medical London, where Peter, by now a consultant psychiatrist at Westminster Hospital, had a thriving private practice. Their intention was that Ann would assist with Peter's patients while building a practice of her own, and that a great deal of commuting time would be saved. Ann occupied one consulting room, Peter another, two more were rented out, the receptionists worked at desks in the enormous hallways, and the family lived on the top three floors, Peter occupying the mews flat above the garage. Their marriage was over, but Ann and Peter did not divorce until 1969, seeing no need to upset Ann's father (founder of the Marriage Guidance

Council) while he lived. The two Dallys shared a medical practice until they retired, and remained intellectual soulmates all their lives. On 29 June 1979 Ann Dally married Philip Wellsted Egerton (*b.* 1920), a management consultant.

By the 1980s Ann Dally was seeing a large number of opiate addicts (often referred to her by other doctors), whom she viewed with a sympathy that was at odds with the increasingly punitive emphasis on criminalization and rapid withdrawal favoured by the medical and political establishments. She argued instead that such people could, by means of maintenance programmes (and not being forced to seek drugs on the black market, often at great risk to themselves), be enabled to hold down jobs, look after their families, and generally lead normal lives; indeed, she went further, to argue that prohibition was the real problem, not the opiates themselves. She was twice found guilty of professional misconduct by the General Medical Council, in 1983 and 1987, for allegedly issuing prescriptions for controlled drugs in an irresponsible manner, though she was not struck off, and restrictions on her right to prescribe drugs were removed in 1988. She and her supporters felt that she was being victimized by the medical establishment, not so much because of her work with addicts but because she spoke out about the problems she encountered. 'Had I kept silent and simply treated patients, as other doctors did, I might never have got into trouble', she wrote later in her autobiography, *A Doctor's Story* (1990).

Ann Dally spent much of her later life working on medical history, based at the Wellcome Institute in London. Her history of gynaecology, *Women under the Knife*, was published in 1991. When the house on Devonshire Place was sold in 1994 she and her husband, Philip, moved to a flat on Wimpole Street, but thereafter lived mainly at Wiblings Farm in Graffham, where Ann wrote books and welcomed grandchildren until she suffered a stroke, dying shortly after, on 23 March 2007. She was survived by her husband, Philip, and by two sons and two daughters from her first marriage, two sons having predeceased her. Her friend Margaret Drabble admitted to using Ann's house on Devonshire Place in her novel *The Radiant Way* (1987), but further parallels can be discerned between its protagonist (a Harley Street child psychiatrist raising a large family above the shop) and Ann Dally.

CATHERINE CRAWFORD

Sources A. Dally, *A doctor's story* (1990) • E. Dally, *Dying twice: a sister's tale* (2000) • *The Independent* (30 March 2007); (5 April 2007) • *The Times* (4 April 2007); (18 April 2007) • *The Guardian* (23 May 2007); (1 June 2007); (5 June 2007) • *The Lancet*, 370/9582 (14 July 2007), 128 • A. Mold, *Heroin: the treatment of addiction in twentieth-century Britain* (2008) • Dally papers, Wellcome L., PP/DAL • personal knowledge (2011) • private information (2011) • b. cert. • m. certs.

Archives Wellcome L., PP/DAL | FILM BFINA, documentary footage | SOUND BL NSA, documentary recordings

Likenesses obituary photographs • photograph, repro. in www.thelancet.com/journals/lancet/article/PIIS0140-6736(07)61074-5/fulltext • photographs, Wellcome L., PP/DAL/A/4, 5; B/1/2/5

Wealth at death £787,812: probate, 21 Aug 2007, *CGPLA Eng. & Wales*

Dalton, Sir Howard (1944–2008), microbiologist, was born at Woodside Nursing Home, Epsom Road, Sutton, Surrey, on 8 February 1944, the son of Leslie Alfred Dalton, lorry driver, and his wife, Florence Gertrude, *née* Evans. At the time of his birth registration his parents lived at 121B Manor Drive North, New Malden, Surrey. From a young age it was clear that he was a very bright boy with an inquiring mind and a scientific bent, and there were many escapades with cocktails of chemicals which marked his early interest in science. His family were extremely proud of his attending Raynes Park grammar school after passing his eleven plus examinations and he subsequently seized the opportunity to study at Queen Elizabeth College, University of London. After graduating in 1965 with a BSc in microbiology he began research with John Postgate at the world-renowned unit of nitrogen fixation at the University of Sussex, which led to his DPhil in 1968. During this time he published a number of important scientific papers in the field of microbial physiology which explained how the soil bacterium *Azotobacter* protects its nitrogenase enzyme from damage by oxygen.

In 1968 Dalton moved to the USA and worked for two years as a postdoctoral fellow on the biochemistry of nitrogenase in the anaerobic bacterium *Clostridium* in the laboratory of Len Mortensen at Purdue University, Indiana. It was while he was in the USA that he met his future wife, Kira Rostislavavna De Armitt, *née* Rozdestvensky, five years his junior, the Russian-American daughter of Rostislav Sergevich Rozdestvensky, a college professor; she was later an employment counsellor and management consultant. They married at Lewes register office on 5 October 1971 after her divorce. While in the USA, Dalton successfully avoided the possibility of being drafted to Vietnam by his ordination, achieved through a correspondence course, into the Universal Life Church. This subsequently became a running joke, with friends frequently referring to him as the Reverend Howard Dalton, despite his being a lifelong atheist.

In 1970 Dalton returned to the University of Sussex to work with Bob Bray in the department of chemistry, where he developed his interest in spectroscopy techniques to study two molybdenum-containing enzymes, nitrate reductase from *Aspergillus nidulans* and xanthine dehydrogenase from *Veillonella alcalescens*. The following year he accepted the offer of a lectureship in microbiology at the department of biological sciences, newly established by Roger Whittenbury, at the University of Warwick. Dalton and his wife, Kira, settled in the village of Radford Semele, near Leamington Spa, Warwickshire, at the start of what would become a long and highly successful tenure at the University of Warwick. He and Kira had a son and a daughter, in addition to the two sons of her earlier marriage.

During his time at Warwick, Dalton established a large research group, pioneering work on two fascinating enzymes catalysing the oxidation of methane by bacteria. These remarkable enzymes, called methane monooxygenases, convert methane into methanol. Dalton and his colleagues were able to purify and characterize these enzymes at the biochemical and molecular level. This work firmly established much of the subsequent knowledge of their structure and catalytic mechanisms. Dalton was also perceptive enough to realize that these enzymes had remarkable co-oxidation properties, which stimulated a long-standing interest in biocatalysis, biotransformations, and 'green chemistry', using microbial oxygenases. He became a consultant for the New Jersey company Celanese and joined the scientific advisory board for the spin-out biotechnology company Celgene (formed in 1986 immediately prior to the merger of Celanese with the American Hoechst Corporation), which gave him considerable insight into the chemical and industrial aspects of microbiology, which he used to good effect in his biotransformation research.

Dalton's research at Warwick gave him a high international reputation, yielded many seminal publications in a career generating well over 250 scientific papers, and opened up whole new research fields in the microbiology of one-carbon compounds. He was awarded a personal professorship at Warwick in 1983 and became chair of the department of biological sciences from 1999 to 2002. As his scientific career flourished he was elected fellow of the Royal Society in 1993, appointed president of the Society for General Microbiology from 1997 to 2000 and of the Marine Biological Association from 2007, awarded the Leeuwenhoek medal lecture at the Royal Society in 2000, and knighted in the new year's honours list in 2007.

Dalton was seconded to become chief scientific adviser to the Department for Environment, Food and Rural Affairs (Defra) in 2002, a role in which he sought to instil scientific rigour into policy-making decisions. He led the scientific advisory team generating the UK contingency plan for dealing with avian influenza virus, and was instrumental in raising the profile of climate change as a significant threat, delivering lectures on this and other topics such as biofuels and genetically modified crops at many national and international meetings. He was able to observe at first hand the effects of global warming in Antarctica during a two-week visit to the British Antarctic Survey in 2006 and his great skills as a communicator were evident from his highly entertaining blog in which he described his visit.

Dalton was a down-to-earth, self-effacing man, outgoing, witty, and very popular with all of his colleagues. He was extremely generous with his time and an inspirational mentor for well over a hundred PhD students and postdoctoral researchers, many of whom went on to very successful careers in academia and industry. His penetrating questions and insightful comments at national and international scientific meetings always made for lively and stimulating debate, and colleagues found that discussing science with him was always rewarding.

Dalton had an immense zest for science and life in general. His extensive knowledge of Japanese garden design resulted in the creation of two fine gardens on the University of Warwick campus. He was a keen sportsman and played with distinction in the Rowington village cricket side (once, though exceptionally, taking eight for fifteen). A lifelong Spurs supporter, he was in his early days at Warwick a regular member of the biological sciences football team, aptly named 'Biohazard', which in the 1970s played a memorable friendly match against the Saudi Arabia national team. He also had a great passion for real tennis and was a member of Leamington Real Tennis Club where his competitive spirit, guile, and ability won him many tournaments. It was there, while playing in a friendly doubles tournament, that he suffered a heart attack on 12 January 2008; he was declared dead at Warwick Hospital later the same day. He had just returned from a month in the Gambia assisting his wife, Kira, in her extensive humanitarian work, setting up new medical centres and schools there. He was survived by her, their two children, and his two stepsons. COLIN MURRELL

Sources *Daily Telegraph* (15 Jan 2008) • *The Times* (16 Jan 2008) • *The Independent* (19 Jan 2008) • *The Guardian* (25 Jan 2008) • *Microbiology Today* (May 2008) • *WW* (2008) • personal knowledge (2012) • private information (2012) • b. cert. • m. cert. • d. cert.
Likenesses obituary photographs
Wealth at death £601,028: probate, 10 April 2008, *CGPLA Eng. & Wales*

Daly, John (1937–2008), film and music producer and promoter, was born on 16 July 1937 at Lambeth Hospital, London, one of five children of Thomas Daly, a dock labourer and manager of a boxing gym in Bermondsey, and his wife, Emily Louise, *née* Bennett. At the time of his birth registration his parents lived at 30 Barrett Road, Lambeth. He attended St Joseph's Roman Catholic School in Camberwell, and left at fifteen to pursue a series of temporary occupations including that of boxer (like his father and uncle), waiter in the merchant navy, and insurance salesman. On 27 July 1963, at St Patrick's Roman Catholic Church, Soho, he married Brigitte Gisela Becker, a twenty-year-old interpreter, and daughter of Ernst Heinrich Becker.

Daly's fortunes were transformed through a chance encounter with David Hemmings, with whom he founded Hemdale Corporation in June 1967, a group of fourteen interlocking companies acting as a talent agency that enabled participants to exchange higher-taxed income for lower-taxed capital investment, together with a package of financial, legal, and publicity services. Hemdale enjoyed considerable success, but Hemmings departed in August 1970 after an acrimonious boardroom battle.

Through a merger with Equity Enterprises, run by David Frost and Jim Slater, Hemdale diversified its activities, managing rock bands including Yes and Black Sabbath, staging West End musicals—notably *Grease* and Lionel Bart's *Oliver!*—and co-promoting, with Don King, the world title fight in Zaire on 30 October 1974 between Muhammad Ali and George Foreman. There was even a chain of betting shops. However, Hemdale's principal activity was film production, and Daly co-ordinated a 'package' as executive producer: 'I assemble the project team—actors, director, technicians, specialists—for the picture and oversee every element, from funding through production to marketing' (*The Guardian*, 10 Nov 2008). Hemdale's output included *Melody* (1971), which launched the film careers of David Puttnam and Alan Parker, and Ken Russell's *Tommy* (1975). The merger with Equity ended with Frost's departure in 1974, and by 1976 Daly was Hemdale's sole owner. Even though he concentrated on distribution, more profitable and less risky than production in a contracting market, he, like many others, could not survive the continual upheavals of the crisis-ridden British economy and relocated to Los Angeles in 1978.

In America Daly continued with a packaging approach to film-making—finding investment partners, setting up tax shelters, negotiating foreign pre-sales, overseeing distribution—but also producing films for the burgeoning cable and video rental markets. However, he struggled to establish himself in America until the huge success of *Terminator* (1984). Shrewdly he made medium-budget films and championed projects judged too difficult by the major studios, including James Foley's *At Close Range* (1985) and two by Oliver Stone, *Salvador* (1986) and *Platoon* (1986). Stone thought Daly embodied 'the tradition of European, liberal, ironic thinking' (*Sunday Times Magazine*, 23 Oct 1988), while Daly confessed that he enjoyed being associated with 'the renegades, the outlaws, the controversial film-makers' (Stabinier, 33). *Platoon* became a major hit for Daly, receiving four Oscars. Film-makers appreciated the creative freedom they were given and Daly's willingness to support films critical of American values. Hemdale also financed films in Britain, Europe, and Australia, and Daly became wealthy, with homes in Bel-Air and Bayswater.

To keep costs down Daly trimmed budgets and drove hard bargains, exhibiting a ruthlessness that could descend into sharp practice. He was the subject of numerous lawsuits, including that of the producer Tom Fox, who took Daly to court over alleged improprieties on *Return of the Living Dead* (1985), and was quoted as saying that 'if Daly's body was found murdered, there would be 7,000 suspects' (Matousek, 93). Daly's fortunes were severely dented when he had to pay $15.7 million to Vestron Video in compensation for lost revenue. (Vestron Video had originally negotiated the video distribution rights to *Platoon* and *Hoosiers*, also 1986, but Daly had then allowed distribution by another company, HBO Video, which had offered Hemdale a larger share of the profits.) Although Hemdale re-entered UK film distribution in 1990 and continued to back unconventional films, including Ken Loach's *Hidden Agenda* (1990), the company went bankrupt in 1992 after its major financier, Credit Lyonnais, called in its loans. Daly continued in the business, managing Global Assets Entertainment Corporation, setting up Greenhills Films, a European-based production company, and, from 2003, becoming chairman and chief executive of Film and Music Entertainment Inc. He tried his hand at writing and directing, enjoying critical success with *The Aryan Couple* (2004), a film set during the holocaust.

In 2005 Daly received a lifetime achievement award at the Milan international film festival. He was working on several films at the time of his death from cancer on 31 October 2008 at Cedars-Sinai Medical Center, Los Angeles. He was survived by four children, Jennifer, Michael, Julian, and Timothy. Even his numerous detractors recognized his flair, shrewd judgements, and hard work, qualities that enabled him to mould Hemdale into an important force in the British and American film industries for nearly thirty years, supporting a number of respected films and aiding the careers of several talented film-makers. ANDREW H. SPICER

Sources J. Deighton, 'Hemdale takes Tiger for growth', *Today's Cinema*, 9780 (17 Feb 1970) • 'Big blow up in Hemdale Group', *Kine Weekly*, 3279 (15 Aug 1970), 3, 17 • 'What will happen to Hemdale', *Today's Cinema*, 9838 (11 Sept 1970), 10 • 'The Hemdale row is dissolved', *Today's Cinema*, 9856 (13 Nov 1970), 2 • H. Hollinger, 'Hemdale of Hollywood seen as alternate source of pic financing', *Variety* (6 Feb 1980) • N. Willmott, 'Hitting bulls-eye in Hollywood', *The Observer* (29 March 1987) • 'Hemdale bids for Goldcrest', *Screen International*, 594 (4 April 1987), 4 • C. Peachment, 'Platoon 'n true Brit', *The Times* (6 April 1987) • A. Timker, 'How Platoon boss made £80m in movies', *The Sun* (24 April 1987) • *Films and Filming*, 393 (June 1987), 15–17 • K. Stabinier, 'Fast times at Hemdale Films', *American Film*, 12/9 (July–Aug 1957), 33–5 • M. Matousek, *Interview*, 18/8 (Aug 1988), 92–5 • R. Wheatley, 'Daly bread', *Sunday Times Magazine* (23 Oct 1988), 21–3 • *Screen International*, 755 (5 May 1990), 1, 4 • D. Hemmings, *Blow up … and other exaggerations: the autobiography of David Hemmings* (2004) • R. Johnson, 'The battle of the little big films', *Screen International* (4 Feb 2005), 19–20 • *Variety* (2 Nov 2008) • *The Guardian* (10 Nov 2008) • *The Times* (15 Nov 2008) • *Daily Telegraph* (16 Dec 2008) • www.imdb.com/name/nm0198460/bio, 10 Feb 2011 • d. cert. • m. cert.

Likenesses C. Court, photographs, 2006, Camera Press, London • obituary photographs • photograph, repro. in *Interview*, 93

Darling, Julia Rose (1956–2005), poet, playwright, and novelist, was born on 21 August 1956 at 8 College Street, Winchester, Hampshire, the eldest daughter and second of five children of John Ramsay Darling, a science teacher at Winchester College, and his wife, Patricia Rosemary (Vicky), *née* Vickers, a nurse and a Quaker. She was educated at Winchester County High School for Girls and St Christopher's School, Hertfordshire, from where she was expelled at the age of fifteen. She then did a cordon bleu cookery course before studying fine art at Falmouth School of Art. She grew up in the house where Jane Austen died and remembered its being constantly visited during her childhood. When she plastered anti-apartheid and 'women's right to choose' posters on the windows of the house, the Jane Austen Society complained. She later drew on her early experiences for her first novel, *Crocodile Soup* (1998).

In 1980 Darling moved to the north-east. She never returned south, falling in love with Newcastle—the bridges, the architecture, and the way people talked. (She was also particularly attached to the Isle of Wight, where she went every summer with her family.) She worked with community arts in Pennywell, and set up the Women's Intellectual Group (WIG). In the same period she created the political cabaret *Sugar and Spikes* with Ellen Phethean. She was always drawn to working collaboratively across a range of art forms: she worked with musicians, glass artists, and film-makers. On 13 October 1984 she married Ivan Paul Sears, a 28-year-old trade union organizer later known as Ieuan Einion, and son of John Sears, furniture maker. After the birth of her two daughters, Scarlet (*b.*

1984) and Florence (Florrie; *b.* 1986), she started to write in earnest. Her first collection of poems, *Small Beauties* (1988), was published by Newcastle Libraries. Her group Poetry Virgins was formed to perform the poems in *Small Beauties*. She wrote a number of plays for the theatre (notably for Live Theatre, Quondam, and Northern Stage) and the radio. Her plays included *Doughnuts Like Fanny's* (2002), a comic play about the life of Fanny Cradock, *Attachments* (2002), and *Manifesto for a New City* (2004), a musical. She also wrote short fiction—*Bloodlines* (1995) was a collection about different women coping with difficult lives. It was her publishers who encouraged her to embark on a novel. Like almost all of her writing, *Crocodile Soup* (1998) is the work of a comic spirit, a wholly unexpected tale of love, knowledge, and eccentricity, driven by endless invention. It brought Darling's work to a national readership and established her reputation.

In 1990 (her marriage having ended in divorce) Darling met her long-term partner, Beverley Anne (Bev) Robinson, and brought her daughters up with her; they made a welcoming home together in Heaton. The house was always teeming with friends, teenagers, neighbours, dogs, and cats. In 1995 Darling was first told that she had breast cancer. She dealt with cancer in an extraordinary way and passionately believed in living in the moment. She was the most uplifting and exhilarating of company.

Darling held a Royal Literary Fund fellowship at the University of Newcastle from 2000. Later, she became a fellow in creative writing and health there, enjoying the company of other writers enticed there by the innovative head of department, Linda Anderson: Jo Shapcott, Cynthia Fuller, Margaret Wilkinson, Linda France, Bill Herbert, Tom Shakespeare, Sean O'Brien, and Jackie Kay among others. She loved the sense of a writers' community. She belonged to many groups, yet still retained a strong sense of her own individuality. She was instrumental in establishing successfully Proud Words, the first gay and lesbian literary festival in England.

When her cancer returned Darling started writing poetry as a way of coping with the illness. She did an MA in creative writing at Newcastle University, specializing in poetry. Afterwards she produced two collections, edited by Jo Shapcott, *Sudden Collapses in Public Places* (2003) and *Apology for Absence* (2004), both inspired by her experiences. Having cancer made her work harder, as if she was attempting to cram it all in. In 2003, the year in which she won the prestigious Northern Rock Foundation writer's award, she published *The Taxi Driver's Daughter*, a witty novel about a family on the verge of collapse. Even when dealing with difficult subjects, her work exhibited both lightness of touch and humour. She believed that poetry should be a part of the life of every hospital; her last book was an anthology about illness, *Poetry Cure* (2005), compiled with Cynthia Fuller, which she hoped would be read by doctors and patients everywhere.

'Dying is very surreal', Darling said. 'Death is such a palaver. Ho hum the nurses come' (personal knowledge). In her weblog, which appeared sporadically but was eagerly awaited, she wrote that there were positive things about dying—one was that she was in no pain unless she tried to dance the hokey cokey, and another that you only had to 'do' death once. The weblog was later dramatized on BBC Radio 4, produced by Sue Roberts, who produced many of Darling's radio plays, and acted by her close friend Charlie Hardwick. Darling took control of her own death. She chose her own funeral, burial plot, and gravestone. She said, 'You don't see many lesbian gravestones' (personal knowledge) and wanted to acknowledge her much loved partner and her daughters on hers. She managed to predict her own peaceful death in her poem *End*: she died at home on 13 April 2005 in the late afternoon, with the sun shining. She was survived by her partner, Bev, and her two daughters. JACKIE KAY

Sources *The Guardian* (16 April 2005) · *The Independent* (16 April 2005) · *The Times* (20 April 2005) · www.juliadarling.co.uk, 1 May 2008 · personal knowledge (2009) · private information (2009) [Bev Robinson, partner] · b. cert. · m. cert. · d. cert.
Archives SOUND BL NSA, current affairs recording
Likenesses obituary photographs · photographs, repro. in http://www.juliadarling.co.uk
Wealth at death under £132,000: probate, 20 Jan 2006, *CGPLA Eng. & Wales*

Datta [*née* Goddard], **Naomi** (**1922–2008**), microbiologist, was born on 17 September 1922 at 2 Cleveland Square, Bayswater, London, the second daughter of Alexander Goddard (1867–1956), secretary to the Chartered Surveyors' Institution, and his wife, Ellen Henrietta, *née* Illingworth (1878/9–1946). When their father retired in 1932 the family moved to Kings Head House, Northleach, Gloucestershire. He had a wide knowledge of the countryside which he passed on to Naomi. She went to St Mary's School, Wantage, Oxfordshire, where her sister, Helen, who was twelve years older than her, had also been a pupil. In 1937 Helen married George Paling Wright, a well-known pathologist. It was probably his influence that helped Naomi decide to study medicine. Initially she went to the Sorbonne in Paris, but returned to England when war was declared in September 1939. She enrolled on the pre-medical course at University College, London (UCL). The students were evacuated to Bangor, north Wales, and later to Leatherhead, Surrey. Naomi studied medicine at the West London Hospital medical school, London. On 9 April 1943 she married (Satya) Prakash Datta (1920–2010), whom she had met on the pre-medical course. The son of Surendra Kumar Datta, principal of Forman Christian College, Lahore (and a delegate to the Indian round table conference in 1931), by the time of their marriage he was a medical student at UCL; he later became professor of medical biochemistry there. They had two daughters and a son.

Naomi Datta qualified in medicine in 1946, and worked for a year in junior hospital medical posts. From 1947 to 1957 she was a senior bacteriologist at the Public Health Laboratory Service in Colindale, north London. She studied part-time for a diploma in bacteriology from the University of London, gaining it in 1950 and qualifying MD in 1952. In 1957 she was appointed assistant lecturer in the department of bacteriology, Royal Postgraduate Medical

School, Hammersmith Hospital, University of London. Later she was promoted to professor of microbial genetics.

At Hammersmith, Datta was expected to do some original research as well as teaching and diagnostic work. In 1959 there was an outbreak of infection in staff and patients with *Salmonella typhimurium*. For her research it was suggested that she could collect *Salmonella typhimurium* cultures during the outbreak and examine them later to see if they had changed while travelling through the human host. Although the antigenic, metabolic, and lysogenic results and phage type were the same, of the 309 cultures she found 25 were drug-resistant. Fifteen of these were resistant to three antibiotic drugs—sulphonamides, streptomycin, and tetracycline. None of the patients had been treated with all three drugs. In 1961 Tsotomu Watanabe and Toshio Fukasawa published Japanese research on the transfer of drug resistance, mainly in *Shigellae*. Datta set up cultures of *Shigella sonnei*, incubated them with resistant *Salmonella typhimurium*, and then plated them with streptomycin and/or tetracycline. She discovered that *Shigella sonnei* had acquired resistance to these antibiotics. Her results were published in the *Journal of Hygiene* in 1962, a relatively obscure journal. It was some time before bacteriologists realized that she was the first in Europe to describe the transfer of antibiotic resistance in bacteria, and the importance of her results. The resistance genes were shown to be carried on self-replicating loops of DNA called plasmids. Datta and her co-researchers investigated the properties of plasmids. They classified them into about forty 'incompatibility groups'. The members of each group had similarities such as size, host range, and transfer genes. Using molecular analysis her group showed that when a particular resistance gene was transferred into a plasmid, its molecular weight increased. In fact a specific fragment of DNA was inserted into the plasmid. This process is called 'transposition' and the genetic unit is a 'transposon'. Antibiotic resistance thus spreads at three levels: it is carried on transposons between plasmids, plasmids between bacteria, and bacteria between people and animals. In 1983, with Victoria M. Hughes, Datta showed that bacteria isolated in the pre-antibiotic era carried the same types of plasmids as present-day resistance plasmids, but without the genes for drug resistance.

Datta became a fellow of the Royal College of Pathologists in 1973, and a fellow of UCL in 1981. In 1984 she retired and was made an emeritus professor. She was elected a fellow of the Royal Society in 1985. In 1989 she was made an honorary member of the Society for General Microbiology, which she had joined in 1952. In the course of her career she co-authored over eighty research papers, and contributed chapters to several important textbooks and edited others. She enjoyed participating in conferences worldwide. She was an immensely creative and caring person and a valued leader. She was interested in the activities of her colleagues and students and was remembered for her enthusiasm and encouragement.

Datta's family were very important to her and she ensured that her children had interesting and challenging holidays abroad and in Britain. Often she rose at 5 a.m. on holiday to write up reports so that she could dedicate the day to her children. After retirement she and her husband travelled extensively. She continued to enjoy cooking and gardening. She contributed two chapters to *But the Crackling is Superb* … (1988), edited by Nicholas and Giana Kurti. One was entitled 'Domestic science', describing some of the problems of bringing up children while working as a full-time scientist. 'Orange marmalade' gave two recipes handed down from her mother and her mother-in-law. In 1996 for her own interest she studied part-time at UCL for an MSc degree in human evolution at the Centre for Genetic Anthropology. She died on 30 November 2008 at Charing Cross Hospital, Fulham, London, from a spontaneous intracerebral haemorrhage. A private funeral took place on 11 December. A celebration of her life was held on 20 February 2009 at UCL. She was survived by her husband and two daughters, her son having predeceased her.

CATHARINE M. C. HAINES

Sources N. Datta, 'Domestic science' and 'Orange marmalade', *But the crackling is superb: an anthology on food and drink by fellows and foreign members of the Royal Society*, ed. N. Kurti and G. Kurti (1988) · N. Datta, 'Early encounter with resistance plasmids', *Current Contents*, 20 (1989), 14 · *The Guardian* (19 Dec 2008) · S. Falkow, 'The fortunate professor', *Annual Review of Microbiology*, 62 (2008), 1–18 · *BMJ*, 338 (14 Feb 2009), 413 · *Microbiology Today* (Feb 2009), 59 · *The Independent* (10 March 2009) · citation for Naomi Datta, 1980, RS, EC/1985/11 · *WW* (2008) · personal knowledge (2012) · private information (2012) [S. Prakash Datta, husband; Jessica Datta, daughter; Alexis Datta, daughter; H. Richards; P. Barth] · b. cert. · m. cert. · d. cert.

Archives SOUND BL NSA, documentary recording

Likenesses Godfrey Argent Studios, photograph, RS · obituary photographs

Wealth at death £900,311: probate, 10 March 2009, *CGPLA Eng. & Wales*

Davie, George Elder (1912–2007), philosopher and historian, was born on 18 March 1912 at 4 Baxter Park Terrace, Dundee, the only child of George Myles Davie, master pharmacist, and his wife, Isabella Calder, *née* Elder, schoolteacher. He was a pupil at Dundee high school and then, offered a place at both Edinburgh University and Oxford, chose the former, where he read classics and philosophy, graduating with first-class honours in 1935. For the following six years he was assistant to Norman Kemp Smith, professor of logic and metaphysics at Edinburgh, before serving, from 1941 to 1945, in the signals corps in north Africa and Italy. On 5 October 1944, at Bonnyrigg church, he married Elspeth Mary Dryer [*see* Davie, Elspeth Mary (1919–1995)], who was later to achieve high distinction as a novelist and short-story writer. Anne, their only child, was born in 1946.

In 1945 Davie joined the moral philosophy department at Queen's University, Belfast, and he stayed there until 1960, when he took up a lectureship in the department of logic and metaphysics at Edinburgh University, where he remained (latterly as a reader) until his retirement in 1982. By 1960 he had already spent many years of intensive work on Scottish philosophy from the eighteenth century to the twentieth, one result of which had been a thesis, 'A

Scotch metaphysics: the theory of knowledge in the Scottish universities 1730–1860', for which in 1953 he was made DLitt by Edinburgh. While preparing the thesis for publication Edinburgh University Press asked him to write an introductory chapter on the intellectual and social background of the Scottish philosophers. It was the series of insights he had while doing this that led to his writing instead a separate, rather long, book, *The Democratic Intellect: Scotland and her Universities in the Nineteenth Century*. This was published in 1961, quickly gained many admirers in the fields of educational philosophy and Scottish intellectual history, and was never out of print in Davie's lifetime.

Davie argued in *The Democratic Intellect* that the great strength of Scottish education through the eighteenth century and well into the nineteenth was its generalist approach, the promotion of the idea that a broadly based education encompassing arts and sciences, as against one requiring early specialization, had distinct advantages in respect of the intellectual flexibility and depth that it instilled. He also noted as part of the Scottish educational scene a democracy not only in respect of the disciplines, in that all had a place in the sun, but also in respect of the recipients, in that education, and especially higher education, was available to the generality of the population and not just the privileged few. Within the Scottish way of education, philosophy held pride of place because it taught universal principles that gave strength to a person's thinking in any and all the academic disciplines. Davie's DLitt dissertation was eventually published in 2000, under the title *The Scotch Metaphysics*, nearly half a century after it was written.

Davie's retirement in 1982 was marked by a Festschrift in his honour, entitled *Philosophers of the Scottish Enlightenment*. In 1983 he was elected a fellow of the Royal Society of Edinburgh, and three years later he published his second major book, *The Crisis of the Democratic Intellect: the Problem of Generalism and Specialisation in Twentieth-Century Scotland*. In this he criticized modern Scotland's failure to prevent the encroachment of the bad English habit of requiring early specialization in the educational field. Thereafter two volumes of his essays appeared, *The Scottish Enlightenment and Other Essays* (1991) and *A Passion for Ideas: Essays on the Scottish Enlightenment* (1994). In 2003 he published *Ferrier and the Blackout of the Scottish Enlightenment*, in which he claimed that James Ferrier's a priori thinking about human consciousness brought down the curtain on the Scottish Enlightenment, a claim later disputed but in such a way as to acknowledge the importance of Davie's argument. His writings were in the main far removed from the concerns of most professional philosophers in Scotland and beyond, but he was quite unconcerned by this fact.

Davie was a prominent member of the Edinburgh literati, on close terms with distinguished figures like Hugh MacDiarmid and Sorley MacLean. In 1987, five years after his retirement, he was made reader emeritus by Edinburgh University. Among other awards conferred on him were honorary doctorates of the universities of Dundee and Edinburgh. His wife, Elspeth, died in 1995 and ten years later he moved from Edinburgh to Sutton Veny, Wiltshire, to be near his daughter, Anne, and her family. He died at Sutton Veny House nursing home on 20 March 2007 of cerebrovascular disease.

Alexander Broadie

Sources *The Herald* [Glasgow] (23 March 2007) · *The Independent* (29 March 2007) · *The Times* (18 April 2007) · personal knowledge (2011) · private information (2011) · b. cert. · m. cert. · d. cert.
Likenesses obituary photographs · photograph, repro. in www.sorleymaclean.org/english/literary_associates.htm

Davie, Michael (1924–2005), journalist and author, was born at Belhaven, Cranleigh, Surrey, on 15 January 1924, the second son and youngest of three children of Russell Davie, head of a stock-jobbing firm in the City of London, and his wife, Harriet Selina Hatton, *née* Browne. He went to Haileybury College, where he appeared in the cricket eleven with Alan Ross, the poet, whom he was later to appoint as cricket correspondent of *The Observer*. He spent a year at Merton College, Oxford, as an exhibitioner reading English under Edmund Blunden, before following his elder brother, Peter, into the Royal Navy, serving the last two years of the Second World War in the Pacific. He returned to Merton in 1946, changing to study history.

Davie's tutor at Haileybury, Martin Wight (later famous as an international relations scholar), passed on to David Astor, *The Observer*'s new editor, a letter Davie had sent him about a holiday at Sandwich, in Kent. Astor was so impressed by the undergraduate's writing that he dined him at Boodle's and surprisingly offered him the post of diplomatic correspondent. Davie had to turn the offer down because he had not completed his course, but, having graduated with a second-class degree in modern history, he joined the paper in 1949—this time in the equally surprising role of religious correspondent—after a short training spell on the *Manchester Evening News*. Religious correspondent was apparently the only position the news editor had available. Davie, though describing himself as a 'middle-stump Anglican' (*The Guardian*), was not drawn to the subject, especially after being lectured at Cliveden on the virtues of Christian Science by the editor's mother, the redoubtable Nancy Astor. On 8 November 1954 he married Mollie Robin Atherton, the 24-year-old daughter of Guy Atherton. They had a son and two daughters.

As sports editor in the late 1950s, in partnership with Christopher Brasher, the former Olympic athlete, Davie created a new form of sports journalism for which he recruited unlikely contributors, such as the Oxford dons A. J. Ayer and John Sparrow. He demanded a quality of writing on sport that matched that on the literary and arts pages. He also persuaded current players, such as the footballer George Eastham, to file a report after a match from the dressing-room, which had not been done before. He was fanatical about cricket and used to slip away from the office to watch Len Hutton or Gary Sobers batting. On one memorable occasion he persuaded Groucho Marx to accompany him to Lord's; 'It's great', Marx is reputed to have replied when Davie asked if he was enjoying himself, 'When does it start?' (*Daily Telegraph*). He covered the Melbourne Olympics of 1956 and went with the England cricket team on their Australian tour in 1959–60. He later wrote a book, *Anglo-Australian Attitudes* (2000).

After a brief spell in Washington, Davie next became news editor and earned the respect of reporters by showing a talent for handling both them and their copy. Two of his injunctions became famous: he sent back one over-excited story with the comment 'Not dull enough' and always insisted 'If necessary, cut the facts, never the jokes' (personal knowledge). Following his American heroes, H. L. Mencken and A. J. Liebling, he regarded the title of 'reporter' as the highest a paper could bestow. His authority rested partly on his easygoing personality, but also on his own graceful style of writing—a grace that disguised a sharp cutting edge. Astor's *Observer* was characterized by the brilliant writing of journalists like Patrick O'Donovan, John Gale, Kenneth Tynan, and Gavin Young, and Davie played an important role in finding talent to maintain that tradition.

Astor chose Davie as launch editor of the colour magazine in 1964, where he worked closely with his friend Anthony Sampson; Astor then brought him back to the main paper as his deputy. Davie, however, torn between writing and editing, took every opportunity to go on reporting assignments. He was fascinated by American politics, especially by the Kennedy family, and wrote some highly regarded pieces on their so-called 'Camelot court'. A book about President Lyndon Johnson (1966) was much admired by American journalists. Richard Nixon was another favourite subject and later he followed the twists and turns of the Watergate saga.

In the mid-1960s Davie looked like Astor's inevitable successor. In 1969, however, when his first marriage broke up, he disappeared for several weeks, infuriating Astor, at whose behest he gave up his executive role and turned fully to writing. He began a new column on the newspaper's back page called 'Notebook', in which he displayed his wide range of interests and his fluency—authoritative and gossipy at the same time. A former colleague said: 'His prime gift was for concentration … he was a spectator of acute talent' (*The Guardian*). He obtained exclusive stories about cabinet committees as well as a rare interview with P. G. Wodehouse, who talked proudly of a try he had scored for Dulwich College against Haileybury in 1899. He was named journalist of the year in 1976. His second book, *California: the Vanishing Dream*, was published in 1972, and he had a big publishing success by editing Evelyn Waugh's waspish diaries (1973–6), which were serialized in *The Observer* and then the *Sunday Times*. Meanwhile on 6 September 1975 he married Anne Katharine Chisholm, a 35-year-old journalist and author whom he had met through *The Observer*. She was the daughter of Archibald Hugh Tennent Chisholm, oil company executive and former editor of the *Financial Times*, and the granddaughter of Hugh Chisholm, editor of the *Encyclopaedia Britannica*. They adopted one son.

As well as America, Davie always had a special affection for Australia, where his first wife came from, and in 1977 he accepted an offer to join *The Age* in Melbourne as an associate editor, becoming editor from 1979 to 1981. He was remembered there for his pursuit of investigative stories and campaigns, for persuading prominent Australian authors to write for the newspaper, and for promoting young journalists, especially women. In 1981 he returned to England and to *The Observer*, where he resumed his 'Notebook' column, mixing this with his book writing; his account of the *Titanic* appeared in 1986. He retired from the paper in 1987, the year in which he published, with his son Simon, the *Faber Book of Cricket*. He then produced, with his second wife, his most successful book, *Beaverbrook: a Life* (1992), which won high critical praise. He had been fascinated by the legendary press lord ever since Beaverbrook had summoned him to his villa in the south of France in 1956 to offer him a job, impressed by an article he had written for *The Observer* about Marilyn Monroe.

Michael Davie was one of the most brilliant journalists of his generation. Some of his admirers believed that his equal facility at writing and editing may have prevented him reaching the professional heights that his talents deserved; others put this down to a natural diffidence. In any event, he was not a man to harbour regrets. He had great charm and modesty and was always, with his lifelong alertness for news and gossip, the best of company. He was described by a colleague as 'a quintessential Englishman … with his matinee idol good looks and faultless public school accent and manners … he would have looked completely at home at a 1930s country house party' (*Daily Telegraph*). He died at his home, Chaucer Cottage, in Ewelme, Oxfordshire, on 6 December 2005, following a heart attack. He was survived by his wife, Anne, and the three children of his first marriage, his adopted son having predeceased him. DONALD TRELFORD

Sources *The Independent* (8 Dec 2005) · *The Times* (12 Dec 2005) · *Daily Telegraph* (13 Dec 2005) · *The Guardian* (14 Dec 2005) · private information (2009) · personal knowledge (2009) · b. cert. · m. certs. · d. cert.

Archives Guardian and Observer Archive and Visitor Centre, Observer archives

Likenesses group portrait, photograph, 1960–69, Topham Picturepoint, London · obituary photographs

Wealth at death £415,534: probate, 1 Nov 2006, *CGPLA Eng. & Wales*

Davies, (Albert) Meredith (1922–2005), organist and conductor, was born on 30 July 1922 at 27 Beresford Road, Upton, Birkenhead, Cheshire, the second son of Elias Aaron Davies, Presbyterian minister, and his wife, Norah Annie Margaretta, *née* Parry. At the age of eight he became a junior exhibitioner at the Royal College of Music as a cellist. Showing aptitude for the organ, he was taken as a pupil by the organist George Thalben-Ball. In 1936 he was admitted as a fellow of the Royal College of Organists, and in 1941 he went as an organ scholar to Keble College, Oxford. Called up in 1942, during the Second World War, he served for three years in the Royal Artillery, before returning to Oxford after the war to complete his degree, graduating with a second-class degree in philosophy, politics, and economics in 1947.

Davies, appointed organist and choirmaster at St Albans Cathedral in 1947, was married there on 29 January 1949 to Betty Hazel, the 21-year-old daughter of Kenneth Leslie Bates. There were four children of the marriage, three sons and a daughter. Later in 1949 he moved to Hereford Cathedral where, as well as his duties as organist, he conducted at the Three Choirs festivals of 1952 and 1955. Encouraged by Sir Adrian Boult to become a full-time conductor, Davies took courses at the Accademia di Santa Cecilia in Rome during 1954 and 1956, before leaving Hereford to become organist at New College, Oxford, a post from which he resigned in 1959. Meanwhile he was conductor of the City of Birmingham Orchestra (1957–60) and the City of Birmingham Choir (1957–64).

Davies had a particular affinity with the work of Benjamin Britten. A performance of Britten's *Spring Symphony* in 1960 led to the composer's inviting Davies to conduct with the English Opera Group (EOG) at the Aldeburgh festival. During the next five years Davies conducted many of Britten's operas with the EOG, on tour, at Aldeburgh, and at Sadler's Wells Theatre in London. These included *The Rape of Lucretia*, *A Midsummer Night's Dream*, *Albert Herring*, and *The Turn of the Screw*. Davies made a very successful Covent Garden début in November 1960, conducting Britten's *Peter Grimes*; his handling of the big choral scenes won particular praise. He gave the North American première of *A Midsummer Night's Dream* in Vancouver in July 1961, then conducted the Covent Garden production of the opera at the Edinburgh festival and in London. Davies had perhaps his greatest triumph in May 1962 when he conducted the main orchestra, choir, and soprano soloist (Heather Harper, who had had only ten days in which to learn her part) at the première of Britten's *War Requiem* in the newly built Coventry Cathedral; Britten, who had been expected to conduct the whole work, instead conducted the chamber orchestra accompanying the tenor and baritone soloists. Davies also conducted the triumphant first performance of the work in Westminster Abbey in December 1962. Britten had complete confidence in Davies's skill as a conductor and his interpretation of his works.

Also in 1962 Davies conducted Delius's *A Village Romeo and Juliet* for Sadler's Wells Opera; the South American première, in Buenos Aires, of *A Midsummer Night's Dream*; and *The Turn of the Screw* for the EOG at the Edinburgh festival. During 1963 he conducted a new production of *Peter Grimes* for Sadler's Wells, which the company took to Germany, and Poulenc's *Dialogues des carmélites* at Covent Garden. At the 1964 Aldeburgh festival he conducted the première of Malcolm Williamson's *English Eccentrics*, based on the book by Edith Sitwell. Other composers with whose work Davies became associated included Ralph Vaughan Williams (Davies's recordings of his *Riders to the Sea* and *Sir John in Love* were highly acclaimed), Anthony Milner, Alan Bush, and Jonathan Harvey.

In September 1964 EOG made a historic tour of the Soviet Union, visiting Riga, Leningrad, and Moscow. During the tour Davies began a five-year relationship with Cara Lancaster, a stage manager for EOG, with whom he had two children, a son and a daughter. Davies, who had been appointed conductor of the Vancouver Symphony Orchestra, travelled to Canada directly from Russia. He returned to Britain several times during his seven years in Vancouver: in 1965 to conduct Britten's *Billy Budd* at Covent Garden; in 1967 to conduct the première of Lennox Berkeley's *Castaway* at Aldeburgh; and in 1969 to take the EOG's *Midsummer Night's Dream* to the Flanders festival and to conduct *English Eccentrics* for the London Opera Centre.

Davies was appointed conductor of the Royal Choral Society in 1972, and the same year joined the teaching staff of the Royal College of Music. He continued to conduct opera from time to time, including the London première of Alexander Goehr's *Arden Must Die*, given by the New Opera Company at Sadler's Wells, and Puccini's *La rondine*, presented by the EOG at the same theatre, both in 1974. He conducted *The Turn of the Screw* for English Music Theatre (successor to the EOG) at the 1976 Brighton festival and in 1980 took over *Mary, Queen of Scots* from the composer, Thea Musgrave, when she became ill and was unable to conduct it for Scottish Opera. In 1979 Davies was appointed principal of Trinity College of Music, London, where he remained until 1988, inaugurating an opera group at the college, which gave yearly performances at the Bloomsbury Theatre; he also worked with the London Schools Symphony Orchestra. He was appointed CBE in 1982.

On retirement Davies went to live in Alresford, Hampshire. He was chairman of the Delius Society from 1991 to 1997; a great admirer of Delius, he made fine recordings of his operas *A Village Romeo and Juliet* and *Fennimore and Gerda*. He died at his home, 10 Mallard Close, New Alresford, on 9 March 2005, of congestive cardiac failure. A memorial service was held in St Albans Cathedral on 2 October 2005, and the students of Trinity College performed the *War Requiem* in his memory at Rochester, Southwark, and Brighton in March 2006. He was survived by his wife, Betty, two sons, and two daughters, one son from his marriage and the son from his relationship with Cara Lancaster having predeceased him. ELIZABETH FORBES

Sources *Opera Magazine*, 11–31 (1960–80) · E. W. White, *Benjamin Britten: his life and operas* (1970) · *New Grove* (1980) · S. Sadie, ed., *The new Grove dictionary of opera* (1992) · *The Independent* (29 March 2005) · *The Guardian* (30 March 2005) · *The Times* (2 April 2005) · *Daily Telegraph* (2 April 2005) · *WW* (2005) · personal knowledge (2009) · private information (2009) · b. cert. · m. cert. · d. cert.

Archives FILM BFINA, performance footage | SOUND BL NSA, documentary recordings · BL NSA, performance recordings

Likenesses Fayer, photograph, Camera Press, London · obituary photographs

Wealth at death £611,017: probate, 28 Sept 2005, *CGPLA Eng. & Wales*

Davies, Sir (Robert) Rees (1938–2005), historian, was born on 6 August 1938 at Glanddwynant, Llanfor, near Llandderfel, a village in the upper Dee valley, Merioneth, the youngest of four sons of (William) Edward Davies (1904–1967), tenant farmer, and his wife, Sarah Margaret (Maggie), *née* Williams (1906–1984). His parents shortly afterwards moved a few miles eastwards and upwards, to the hill farm of Blaengwnodl Uchaf, where Rees (as he always wished to be known) was brought up. The family home, with its superb vista of the Berwyn range on the opposite side of the valley, and its region, the historic commote of

Edeyrnion, left a profound and lifelong impression on him. It was the country of Owain Glyn Dŵr, still at that time almost wholly Welsh in speech, ever in creative tension with the English influences from just across the mountains or downstream. Questions of identity and borderlands became central to his interests as a historian.

Davies attended school at the village of Cynwyd, then as a weekly boarder at the boys' grammar school in Bala. There he proved a brilliant pupil, and also learned the English that he subsequently employed with such elegance and precision. In 1956 he went to University College, London, where he studied history with Geoffrey Barrow, Alfred Cobban, and May MacKisack. Anxious for a pupil described as 'the ablest undergraduate we've had in the department since the war', they were advised that it would be a 'great mistake for a medieval historian, even if Welsh, to *start* his postgraduate work by tackling Welsh history' (Morgan and Davidson, 6). Wisely Davies opted for a halfway house: study of the lords of the Anglo-Welsh marches. This would in many ways determine his life's work. For the present—the year was 1959—it took him to Merton College, Oxford, as a student of the redoubtable K. B. McFarlane at Magdalen.

After one or two monosyllabic initial encounters McFarlane clearly hit it off with Davies, who later recalled McFarlane's friendship as 'utterly direct and totally equal', his 'intellectual honesty and integrity' as sometimes 'terrifying'. McFarlane appreciated 'some Welsh sharpness' in his pupil, 'not wholly blunted by good nature'. The fruit of their collaboration was Davies's DPhil dissertation of 1965 on the Lancaster marcher lordships in the fourteenth century, carefully matured, for, as McFarlane observed, 'he can't bear a slovenly sentence, a misplaced comma, or a reckless generalisation' (McFarlane, 210–13, 215–17, 226–7, 251–2). Another reason for delay was Davies's burgeoning academic career in both his countries. Appointed as an assistant Welsh-medium lecturer at Swansea in 1961, he was then recalled to University College as a lecturer two years later.

In London Davies had joined Welsh circles, just as he later took an active role in the Cymdeithas Dafydd ap Gwilym at Oxford. Through the Welsh Presbyterian Church he met Carys Lloyd Wynne, and they married at Zion Chapel, Wrexham, on 29 July 1966. A schoolteacher, aged twenty-eight at the time of her marriage, Carys was the daughter of Ifor Lloyd Wynne, bank manager. They had one son and one daughter. Meanwhile the subject-matter of Davies's thesis broadened into a stream of highly suggestive articles over a further decade, before being reconfigured as his first book, *Lordship and Society in the March of Wales, 1278–1400* (1978). Critical acclaim was immediate for this momentous *thèse*, which interwove political, administrative, legal, and social approaches. Opening up a vast, rich, and intricate world, the work nevertheless rested on a single basic juxtaposition, within and between the myriad petty jurisdictions it examines: that of native Welsh and immigrant English.

Two years before the book's publication Davies had taken a chair at the University College of Wales, Aberystwyth, partly from his and Carys's desire for their children to grow up in a Welsh-language environment. At Aberystwyth he was the prime mover in a complete redesigning of the history syllabus, and served between 1988 and 1991 as vice-principal. He assumed a far wider pedagogical brief too when in 1989–91 he chaired the National Curriculum History Committee for Wales. This body achieved truly pioneering work, and laid out for the first time a vision (and a fully bilingual one) for the study of history in Wales. In the meantime Davies had delivered, for a new and authoritative History of Wales series published by Oxford University Press, one of the finest treatments of any period in the country's past. His *Conquest, Co-Existence and Change: Wales, 1063–1415* (1987), brilliantly conceived and pellucidly executed, won him the Wolfson prize and constituted a high point in the renaissance of Welsh historiography that coincided so exactly with his career. Davies, however, having become a historian of his homeland largely in England, was now in the process of retooling himself as a British historian while in Wales. His Wiles lectures of 1988 at the Queen's University of Belfast, which were published as *Domination and Conquest: the Experience of Ireland, Scotland and Wales* (1990), disclosed a whole new research territory. It was a logical consequence of this trajectory for him to be appointed to the Chichele chair of medieval history at Oxford in 1995.

Davies's move back to Oxford followed a hard decision. He was always quizzical about Oxford, and felt something of an outsider. Yet he brought an immensely fertile blend of shrewdness, dedication, and imaginative creativity to his university duties. As a devoted supervisor or mentor to nearly a hundred graduate students at any one time he turned doctoral research on medieval topics into a more coherent academic enterprise, with an enhanced *esprit de corps*. At the same time, though setting no store by such things in themselves, he initiated major and overdue reforms in the structure and conduct of faculty business. Above all he supplied intellectual leadership, beginning with a memorable inaugural, which told a disturbingly Oxford-centred story of the replacement of the British heritage by the 'Matter of England', as the main strand in the grand historiographical narrative of the British Isles, first in the twelfth century, then confirmed with full professional gravitas in the later nineteenth, by the likes of Stubbs and Freeman. The theme was soon elaborated in his Ford lectures at Oxford, published as *The First English Empire* (2000). These analysed an Anglicization of the British Isles, from 1093 to 1343, and of course beyond, which confirmed the exclusion, and the passive or active resistance, of the 'Celtic' lands. He described a deep divide within Britain, with 'two political culture zones', and a border between (as they came to be perceived from the centre) 'sweet civility' and 'barbaric rudeness' (*First English Empire*, 110 ff).

The Anglo-Welsh border was the frontier that Davies had known since his youth in Edeyrnion, though he and Carys could also build on long-standing Welsh traditions at Oxford, within the university and beyond. The chronicler of the identity of others had by now constructed his own, which straddled that notional border he wrote of. This was reflected in the multiplying accolades and commitments of his latter years. He became a fellow of the British Academy in 1987—and typically knuckled down to some very hard work for it. Alongside a CBE in 1995 and a fistful of honorary fellowships and degrees in both countries, he was awarded the Medlicott medal for his services to the Historical Association in 1994, even as he presided over its sister organization in London, the Royal Historical Society (1992–6). On the Welsh side of the fence his longest involvement was with the Ancient Monuments Board for Wales, of which he had been the youngest member ever in 1977, and became chairman in 1995. In the Honourable Society of Cymmrodorion too, the oldest and broadest-based of Welsh learned societies, Davies played a leading role, being elected president in 2002.

During this time political debates about Welsh nationhood, within or beyond Britishness, were intensifying. Davies had long experienced a *crise de conscience* before he articulated it in historical terms through his most deeply felt and popular work, *The Revolt of Owain Glyn Dŵr*, in 1995. This was, above all, a gripping and definitive narrative of the independence struggle of late medieval Wales. The phenomenon of Glyn Dŵr helped inspire Davies to his maturest reflections on the identity of nations in general and of the Welsh in particular. In an eisteddfod talk in 1998 he spoke from the heart about the British dimension of his Welshness and vice versa: how England's unique achievement of a '1000-year Reich' had undermined the pristine equilibria of the 'Matter of Britain'. Now in its decline there was a need to rebuild the crumbling edifice of Britishness, as the best carapace for the survival of Welsh culture too. For all his emphasis on identity, mythology, and other cultural markers Davies always saw material authority as very real, enduring, and irreducible. Thence his feeling for those looser-limbed traditions of marcher lordship, with which he began his career, and to which he returned, in the widest European context of *seigneurie* and *Herrschaft*, in some of his last, uncompleted work.

Rees Davies was a deeply unassuming man, dutiful, utterly professional, who bore huge burdens with never a complaint, and whose daunting organizational skills were always deployed to achieve results through a gentle, even diffident, but infinitely patient manner, through painstaking and selfless application, and through a radiant generosity of spirit. He was a brilliant teacher; a colleague whose sometimes slightly reserved exterior soon dissolved into quick wit and good humour; a correspondent whose letters and memoranda, in what has been called a 'hand as meticulous as that of a medieval Chancery scribe' (*The Independent*, 23 May 2005), apparently never needed correction; a walker and lover of the natural world, with the eye of a countryman (though more of an urban turn of speed) and a sharp sense of place and landscape; an active devotee of music and literature; above all a man of firm, humble, quiet spirituality, and of unswerving devotion to his family and friends. He was knighted in the new year's honours of 2005, by which time he was suffering from cancer. He died at his home, 9 Dale Close, Oxford, on 16 May 2005, and was survived by his wife, Carys, and their two children. R. J. W. EVANS

Sources K. B. McFarlane, *Letters to friends, 1940–1966*, ed. G. Harriss (1997) · R. R. Davies, *Beth yw'r ots gennyf i am Brydain?* (1999) · R. R. Davies, 'On being Welsh: a historian's viewpoint', *Transactions of the Honourable Society of Cymmrodorion*, new ser., 9 (2003), 29–40 · *The Independent* (23 May 2005) · *Daily Telegraph* (25 May 2005) · *The Guardian* (26 May 2005) · *The Herald* [Glasgow] (28 May 2005) · *The Times* (9 June 2005) · R. Griffiths, *Royal Historical Society Newsletter* (spring–summer 2005) · *Heritage in Wales*, 31 (summer 2005), 22–3 · *Y Bedol: Papur Bro Rhuthun a'r Cylch*, 28/7–8 (July 2005) · B. F. Roberts, *Transactions of the Honourable Society of Cymmrodorion*, new ser., 11 (2005), 232–6 [in Welsh] · N. Campbell, *Postmaster and the Merton Record* (2005), 142–4 · R. Griffiths, *Y Traethodydd*, 161 (2006), 9–14 · R. A. Griffiths, *Welsh History Review*, 23 (2006–7), 158–63 · D. A. L. Morgan and J. Davidson, *Power and identity in the middle ages: essays in memory of Rees Davies*, ed. H. Pryce and J. Watts (2007) [with Davies's 'Farewell speech'] · *WW* (2005) · personal knowledge (2009) · private information (2009) · b. cert. · m. cert. · d. cert.

Archives NL Wales, papers

Likenesses obituary photographs · photograph, U. Oxf., faculty of modern history · photograph, Swansea University; repro. in *The Times*

Wealth at death under £86,000: probate, 30 Aug 2005, *CGPLA Eng. & Wales*

Davis, John Michael Newsom- (1932–2007), neurologist, was born John Michael Newsom Davis on 18 October 1932 at Bamville Wood, Harpenden, Hertfordshire, a twin and the youngest of three children of John Kenneth Newsom Davis (1905–2001), company director of an iron foundry, later managing director of the Davis Gas Cooker Company, and his wife, Dorothy Eileen, *née* Tate (1907–1998), a doctor's daughter. At the time of his birth registration his parents lived at Appletree House, Park Avenue, Harpenden. Newsom-Davis, as he later liked to be known, was educated at Sherborne School, Dorset. During national service (1951–3) he flew Meteors and at one point considered a career in the Royal Air Force. Instead, after reading natural sciences at Pembroke College, Cambridge (graduating in 1957), he went on to the Middlesex Hospital medical school, University of London, where he graduated MB BChir in 1960; his Cambridge MD was awarded in 1966. On 8 October 1963, at Kensington register office, he married Rosemary Elisabeth Schmid (*b.* 1939), an English-Swiss national (daughter of Werner Oskar Schmid, businessman) who later became an educational psychologist. They had two daughters and one son.

Moran Campbell fostered Newsom-Davis's interest in investigative medicine, and Michael Kremer attracted him into neurology. He first studied the neural control of breathing in patients with lesions of the spinal cord with Tom Sears at the Institute of Neurology and National Hospital for Nervous Diseases, Queen Square, where Newsom-Davis was lecturer in the university department of clinical neurology from 1967 to 1969. He then spent a year as a research fellow at Cornell Medical Center, New York, working with Fred Plum. Although loyal to Queen Square, as a young man he was not comfortable with the uncritical hagiography that characterized this famous hospital, being branded a 'communist' when, as resident medical officer in 1968, it fell to him to inform the medical committee that payments to junior staff looking after private patients would now be required. Nevertheless, he joined the consultant staff at Queen Square and the Royal Free Hospital in 1970. His expertise in the neurology of breathing led to his directing the intensive care unit (the Batten unit) at the National Hospital, where patients sometimes spent months dependent on assisted ventilation. At that time he interacted with the leading neurophysiologist Ricardo Miledi, who wanted access to human intercostal muscle. Among others, Newsom-Davis provided a sample from himself which led to an acute pneumothorax (punctured lung), described to his wife during the night on which it developed as 'like a wet fish [the collapsed lung] flapping around in my chest' (private information).

Newsom-Davis's work changed direction in 1976 when, because antibody had already been implicated in the pathogenesis, it was suggested to him that plasma exchange might be used to treat myasthenia gravis (a disorder caused by the body's immune system attacking the junction between nerve and muscle, resulting in severe but reversible weakness). The remarkable effect of this novel treatment inspired Newsom-Davis to focus the rest of his career on neuro-immunology. The availability of antibody removed from patients with myasthenia gravis undergoing plasma exchange provided experimental opportunities that benefited from Newsom-Davis's background in experimental neurophysiology. With Angela Vincent, who joined him at the Royal Free Hospital school of medicine in 1977, the group systematically unravelled disease mechanisms in many different categories of myasthenia gravis. The work was recognized by Newsom-Davis's appointment, in 1980, to the first Medical Research Council clinical research professorship, held at the Royal Free Hospital and the Institute of Neurology. In 1981 came the second major discovery when another, hitherto unknown, auto-antibody responsible for a closely related disorder, the Lambert Eaton myasthenic syndrome, was identified, also helping to explain many mysterious disorders that constitute remote effects of cancer.

In 1987 Newsom-Davis was elected action research professor of clinical neurology in the University of Oxford. There followed a highly productive decade for the loyal group that moved with him from London. A third immunological scalp was added in the form of a novel auto-antibody implicated in a rare disorder, acquired neuromyotonia (Isaac's syndrome). More was to follow with the realization that the auto-immune ion-channel disorders have effects in the brain as well as on nerve and muscle.

Newsom-Davis brought authority and the international perspective of someone who had served academic medicine for many years to his clinical, research, and administrative work. He was a member of the Medical Research Council from 1983 to 1987 and, having served on the neurosciences grants committee from 1978, he chaired the council's neurosciences board from 1983 to 1985. Active also in the British Association for the Advancement of Science, he was president of its biomedical section in 1982–3. The impressive catalogue of his scientific achievements was further recognized by election as a fellow of the Royal Society (1991), foundation fellow of the Academy of Medical Sciences (1998), whose council chamber in Portland Place was named after him in recognition of a donation from the Welton Foundation which he served as a trustee for many years, and foreign associate member of the Institute of Medicine of the National Academy of Sciences of the USA (2001). He was appointed CBE in 1996.

Few could rival Newsom-Davis as a communicator. Lectures were carefully crafted. The preparation was meticulous, the delivery lively, the arguments presented with impeccable logic, the language precise but never indulgent, and the recognition of good performance sincerely given and gladly received. However, writing a book in his thirties (the second edition of *The Respiratory Muscles: Mechanics and Neural Control*, 1970, with Moran Campbell and Emilio Agostini) made him wary of repeating that experience, and he did not consider himself to be an especially natural writer. But he approached original data with appetite and enthusiasm, showing a fluency that led to many original research papers of lasting value. He understood and could guide younger colleagues through the many and complex vicissitudes of academic life—the ups and downs of giving presentations, crafting papers, and securing funding, and the uncertainties of career advancement. He always had the right word of encouragement, made the thoughtful telephone call, sent the sensitive handwritten letter or email, and showed personal interest in those with whom he worked. His mentorship and loyalty were exemplary. His recreation was music but family life was his main source of pleasure, based in London (or Oxford) and Dorset, where he would toil in the garden and, after several hours poring over recipe books, cook sumptuously for family and friends.

In retirement from 1998, Newsom-Davis returned to London but needed new challenges. As a former secretary (1981–4) and medallist (1999) it was natural that he should be elected president of the Association of British Neurologists (1999–2000). He felt that the association had drifted away from its origins in 1932 as a forum for discussing the best of British scientific neurology, and took several steps to merge the interests of an expanding membership focused on providing a high quality clinical service with presentation of the best clinical neuroscience being carried out in the United Kingdom. From 1997 to 2004 he edited *Brain: a Journal of Neurology*, founded in 1878, which he had already served as secretary and treasurer (1977–81) and as chairman of the guarantors (1994–9). The journal grew in stature under his editorship. He had a knack for identifying work that was forward-looking and would command attention. He introduced electronic processing and online publication well ahead of other journals in the field.

For over forty years removal of the thymus gland (located behind the sternum) had been performed as a treatment for myasthenia gravis but without formal evidence either for efficacy or safety. In association with experts in the United States, Newsom-Davis obtained funding from the National Institutes of Health to conduct a multicentre trial involving over eighty centres. His death occurred in a road accident at Adjud, Romania, on 24 August 2007, after a morning visit to a participating hospital in Bucharest. He was survived by his wife, Rosemary, and their three children.

John Newsom-Davis (generally known as JND) changed the lives of people with myasthenia gravis. He earned respect for the clinical neurosciences in a changing climate of academic medicine. He led by example and motivated others to adopt careers in clinical neuroscience. He valued ability, intellectual honesty, and curiosity. He inspired loyalty and affection and reciprocated both, especially to young people, with whom he interacted easily at home and abroad. He flourished at a time when developments in other branches of medicine threatened to leave neurology in their wake. His legacy was successfully to have steered clinical neuroscience, traditionally descriptive and rooted in neurophysiology, into the age of molecular medicine. He effected this transition through excellence as a clinical neurologist, his own grounding in neurophysiology, his preparedness to master new disciplines, and the opportunism that favours the prepared mind. ALASTAIR COMPSTON

Sources *The Independent* (18 Sept 2007) • *The Guardian* (21 Sept 2007) • *The Times* (24 Sept 2007) • *World Neurology*, 22/3 (Sept 2007), 16 • *The Lancet*, 370/9594 (6 Oct 2007), 1205 • *BMJ*, 335/7624 (20 Oct 2007), 830 • *Advances in Clinical Neurology and Rehabilitation*, 10/1 (March–April 2010), 30–31 • *WW* (2007) • personal knowledge (2011) • private information (2011) • b. cert. • m. cert.

Likenesses obituary photographs • photograph, repro. in www.mgauk.org/mganews/9901-02.htm • photograph, repro. in archneur.ama-assn.org/cgi/content/extract/64/12/1796 • photographs, RCP Lond. • photographs, Association of British Neurologists, London • photographs, RS

Wealth at death £784,038: probate, 24 March 2009, *CGPLA Eng. & Wales*

Deakin, Sir (Frederick) William Dampier [Bill] (**1913–2005**), special operations officer, historian, and college head, was born on 3 July 1913 at 30 Temple Gardens, Golders Green, London, the elder son of Albert Whitney Deakin, motor engineer and farmer, and his wife, Bertha Mildred, *née* Measures. At Westminster School an inspiring teacher reported in 1930 that 'He has a fine critical intelligence, plenty of drive and a command of words which is sometimes brilliant' (Deakin papers, priv. coll.). After brief spells at a college in America and at the Sorbonne in Paris, Deakin entered Christ Church, Oxford, in 1931. He flourished there, took a first in modern history in the summer of 1934, and went to teach for a while in Germany, where he met and disliked Anthony Blunt. On 22 October 1935 he married Margaret Ogilvy Beatson Bell, the 21-year-old daughter of Sir Nicholas Dodd Beatson Bell, vicar of Cornish Hall End, Essex, and former governor of Assam. They had two sons, Nicholas (*b.* 1936) and Michael (*b.* 1939). The marriage ended in divorce in 1940.

Sir (Frederick) William Dampier Deakin (1913–2005), by Bassano, 1961

Research for Churchill In 1936 Deakin was appointed a fellow of Wadham College, Oxford. Before then an even more momentous event had occurred. Winston Churchill, seeking help with the later stages of his work on Marlborough, sought advice from Keith Feiling at Christ Church. Feiling recommended Deakin, a man of 'great spirit and courage, as I have seen in several trials' (Feiling to Churchill, 2 Dec 1935, Churchill papers, CHAR 8, 506/23). The elder statesman and the new recruit, separated in age by almost forty years, took to each other swiftly. Deakin's knowledge, orderliness, and zeal impressed Churchill. For his part Deakin admired Churchill's fierce concentration and loved his company. Soon he was regarded almost as a member of Churchill's family. He also won within a couple of years his master's complete confidence in political matters. 'Mr. Deakin is a young man of the highest character and intelligence', Churchill wrote to the president of Czechoslovakia in the spring of 1938, 'and shares my outlook on European affairs' (Churchill to E. Beneš, 1 April 1938, Churchill papers, CHAR 8/595). Marlborough completed, Churchill embarked on *A History of the English-Speaking Peoples* with Deakin as his chief coadjutor. The two often laboured until the early hours in the library at Chartwell; Deakin would then drive to Oxford and teach at Wadham from 9.00.

With Churchill's blessing Deakin had before the outbreak of the Second World War joined the Queen's Own Oxfordshire hussars. During the first winter of the conflict he combined his military duties with research and drafting. In April 1940, while the battles for Norway raged, he found himself late at night in Admiralty House discussing the Norman conquest, and he lunched alone with Churchill at the height of the battle of Britain that summer. Briefly posted to Northern Ireland, he then went for a time to work for British security co-ordination under Sir William Stephenson in New York, before returning on his own insistence to Europe. He was recruited into the Special Operations Executive, sent to Cairo, and there met Livia Stela (Pussy) Nasta (*d.* 2001), daughter of Liviu Nasta of Bucharest. They married in 1943.

SOE in Yugoslavia In May 1943 Deakin was dispatched to Yugoslavia, to find out what he could about the mysterious Tito, of whose identity and whereabouts the British were ignorant. He pretended to no expertise in the tangled affairs of Yugoslavia and did not speak any of the local languages. His senior officer in Cairo, a strong supporter of General Mihailović, apparently hoped that he would not return. When the tiny British party landed by parachute in Montenegro, near Mount Durmitor, the enemy forces were all around. Within a few days Deakin's fellow officer was killed in an attack during which Tito, Deakin, and others were wounded. As Churchill later remarked in the House of Commons, to be wounded by the same bomb constituted 'a bond between people, but a bond which, I trust, we shall not have to institute in our own personal relationships' (*Hansard 5C*, 22 Feb 1944, 397.694).

Neither then nor later did Deakin doubt that Tito, revealed to be Josip Broz, was a man of distinction and quality; Tito appears to have reached with equal speed the same conclusion about Deakin. They spent many hours in each other's company. Deakin admired the fortitude, calmness, and determination that Tito displayed in often desperate circumstances. He knew that the partisans—starving, living sometimes on nettle soup or handfuls of grass, infested by lice, daily witness to acts of heroism and terror—were doing the allies a service of the first order by engaging so many German and Italian divisions, a diversion of forces that became the more significant as the campaigns in Sicily and Italy developed. Because Tito spoke no English and Deakin no Serbo-Croat, they plotted the downfall of the Führer entirely in German. In his own account Deakin made no attempt to glide around the horrors of this guerrilla warfare. When the cries of the wounded, soldiers of a Croat division that had fought under German leadership, sounded from the pathways and ditches, 'Pity had long drained out of us. Edging my horse among the bodies, a flick of the rein would have avoided the trampling of the imploring shadows. But in our triumphant wrath and the explosion of our release, we crushed them' (*Embattled Mountain*, 22). In Cairo towards the end of 1943, when Churchill passed through on his way from the conference with Stalin and Roosevelt at Tehran, Deakin found himself seated next to a trim figure in the uniform of a field marshal. This was Jan Smuts. 'And what do you do?' he asked. 'I think I am some sort of bandit', Deakin replied. Smuts winked. 'So was I once' (ibid., 261).

In due course a larger mission under Fitzroy Maclean was sent to Yugoslavia. The two of them, and others, advised that the most effective opposition to the axis in Yugoslavia came from the partisans rather than from Mihailović, and the British government decided eventually to withdraw support from the latter and concentrate it on the former. That Maclean and Deakin had contributed to this decision is not in doubt; what counted for far more, it is now plain, was the interception of many enemy communications revealing links between Mihailović and the Italians and Germans and the fact that it was the partisans, not Mihailović, who caused them most trouble.

In 1944 Deakin became head of SOE's Yugoslav section in Cairo and, later that year, was transferred to the staff of Harold Macmillan and became adviser to a new command, Balkan Air Force, responsible for all military operations into central and south-eastern Europe. Macmillan valued him as highly as Churchill did. After the war he served for a while as first secretary in the British embassy at Belgrade, confronted hourly by obstruction and outright hostility on the part of the Yugoslav authorities, of which he did not fail to provide many examples when taking official farewell of Tito at the end of January 1946. For his services in Yugoslavia Deakin was awarded the DSO and the Russian order of Valour, and later the Yugoslav Partisan Star, first class.

Churchill had already resolved to follow the habit of a lifetime; having lived in the eye of the storm for six years, he would write about the war. On his return to England Deakin found himself intercepted and asked to deal with all the political and diplomatic side of the memoirs. To this task he devoted himself for years, combining it with his duties at Wadham. By his mastery of languages, wide intellectual interests, coiled energy, cordial relations with colleagues in Whitehall, readiness in drafting, and harmony with Churchill, Deakin made the enterprise possible. Describing himself as 'one who surrendered without terms long ago to the magic of the man' ('Churchill the historian', 1), he felt the tension immanent in the position of a research assistant who was also a professional historian. 'It was always Winston's book', he nevertheless said long afterwards; 'the rest of us were there to help as best we could, not to interpose our own views' (private information).

St Antony's College At the instance of Churchill, Wadham College converted Deakin's post in 1949 to a research fellowship. But it chanced that Antonin Besse, a French citizen whose main enterprises were based in Aden and east Africa, had offered Oxford over £1 million for the foundation of a college. Negotiations dragged; Besse became impatient; there was a risk that the benefaction would be lost. It was probably the warden of Wadham, C. M. Bowra, who proposed that Deakin should become head of the new enterprise. At all events it was he who explained the position to Churchill. 'I was delighted to hear of this plan which will give Bill Deakin the opportunity his talents have so long deserved', Churchill replied. 'I do not think you could have made a better choice' (Churchill to Bowra, 20 March 1950, Churchill papers, CHUR 2/168B).

St Antony's might have taken any one of several forms; indeed, it might have proved little more than a hostel. Deakin, however, saw and seized the opportunity. Oxford could now build up a purely graduate international college. He travelled to meet Besse in the south of France and expounded his plans. Between the two an immediate alliance of respect was forged, soon reinforced by strong affection. Besse judged Deakin to be 'altogether a superior man', who had in him 'a spark of adventurous spirit which endears him to me' (Footman, 185–6). Within weeks Deakin surmounted innumerable difficulties. He gathered the nucleus of a staff, looking for people of high talent who would not only bring distinction on the nascent college by their research but also devote themselves to their pastoral and teaching duties.

St Antony's opened in October 1950 with seven students. It concentrated largely, but in no rigid fashion, on the study of modern international history, politics, and economics, acquiring buildings by lease or purchase. Student numbers grew rapidly. The college's areas of expertise expanded almost by the year. It became and remained a renowned centre of 'regional studies' of a distinctive kind, firmly rooted in established academic disciplines. Like the warden himself it provided a bridge between the worlds of public affairs and of academic study.

Somehow Deakin combined these duties with research and drafting for the last three volumes of *The Second World War* (1951–4), paying a heavy price in respect of his own scholarly interests, but with a dividend beyond calculation; for in the study at Chartwell he had learned 'vastly more of the sense of history than my formal education as a student, and later as a teacher, ever taught me' ('Churchill the historian', 12). After Churchill retired exhausted from the prime ministership in 1955 Deakin helped at every stage with the revision of *A History of the English-Speaking Peoples*, issued in four volumes between 1956 and 1958. Then the way was at last open for pursuit of his own academic interests. His masterly account of the relations between Hitler and Mussolini, and of the implosion of the fascist regime in 1943, appeared as *The Brutal Friendship* in 1962, and *The Case of Richard Sorge*, written with his close friend and colleague at St Antony's, Dick Storry, in 1966.

The original endowment had proved inadequate to support St Antony's as its work and reputation grew. Though he always said he disliked the activity Deakin sought funds assiduously and successfully; Besse's family made further generous donations, as did a wide variety of foundations. With support from Macmillan, now chancellor of the university and prime minister, and Churchill, he obtained a handsome grant from the Ford Foundation. From a conference he organized at St Antony's in 1962 sprang the British National Committee for the History of the Second World War, over which he presided for thirty-five years. He also served as vice-president of the international committee to which the British organization was affiliated, and did much to sustain contacts with former enemies and especially with the countries behind the iron curtain. His genius for friendship, accessibility, and reputation as a scholar and as a man of action gave him unique standing and he remained quietly determined that justice should be done to the role which Britain and the Commonwealth countries had played. Deakin's other concerns while warden were numerous, not least when he yielded to the urgent entreaty of Macmillan to serve as one of the five who under the chairmanship of Lord Radcliffe scrutinized security procedures in the public service. The committee examined the techniques of communist penetration, and in November 1961 made numerous recommendations that were accepted by the government in full.

Later years With the college on a sounder financial footing at last, and after nearly two decades as warden, Deakin retired to Le Castellet, in the south of France, in 1968. There he wrote *The Embattled Mountain* (1971), a candid account of the horrors and heroics he had witnessed in Yugoslavia, followed by an examination of the same events in the light of facts and evidence largely unknown at the time. He could make but guarded reference to the mass of intercepted evidence on which the British government had chiefly relied in deciding to support Tito. That policy had been strongly criticized from the start, and over a period of some sixty years Deakin found himself censured in wounding terms. This fate he endured with stoicism.

Clubbable and hospitable to a degree, Deakin (who was knighted in 1975) loved in retirement to visit London and old haunts in Yugoslavia. He travelled widely to conferences, and delivered numerous lectures. Self-effacing and unpretentious, he resisted suggestions that he should write an autobiography or an account of his time with Churchill. 'You are so modest', exclaimed Macmillan, 'that you do not realise the high reputation that you have' (Macmillan to Deakin, 22 April 1981, Deakin papers, priv. coll.). He did however leave behind a large body of unpublished material about Yugoslavia, and his papers were later housed alongside those of his mentor at Churchill College, Cambridge.

Deakin was intuitively aware of subtleties of personality and situation that eluded others. His natural dignity enabled him to disdain the frailties of old age; his spirit and courage remained undimmed to the last. Shortly before his death the nurses asked him, 'Is there anything we can do for you, Monsieur Deakin?' 'Certainly', he replied with decision, 'champagne for everyone' (private information). He died on 22 January 2005 at Le Castellet, and his ashes were buried there a week later. A memorial meeting was held on 23 April 2005 at St Antony's College. He was survived by his two sons.

Bill Deakin had achieved high academic distinction; he had played the dominant role in the creation of a pioneering college; he had fought with the utmost valour; he had been a trusted friend and servant of the greatest Englishman of his time. That no one else in his generation had achieved this combination of feats is not a thought likely to have crossed his mind; had it done so, he would have dismissed the notion instantly. DAVID DILKS

Sources F. W. D. Deakin, 'Churchill the historian', *Schweizer Monatshefte* [Zurich] (1969–70) · F. W. D. Deakin, *The embattled mountain* (1971) · H. Macmillan, *War diaries: the Mediterranean, 1943–1945* (1984) · D. Footman, *Antonin Besse of Aden* (1986) · C. S. Nicholls, *The history of St Antony's College, Oxford, 1950–2000* (2000) · J. Cripps, 'Mihailović or Tito? How the codebreakers helped Churchill choose', *Action this day*, ed. R. Erskine and M. Smith (2001) · D. Reynolds, *In command of history* (2004) · *The Times* (25 Jan 2005) · *Daily Telegraph* (25 Jan 2005) · *The Independent* (27 Jan 2005) · *The Guardian* (31 Jan 2005) · 'Tributes to Sir William Deakin', *St Antony's College Record* (2005), 126–48 · *WW* (2005) · Burke, *Peerage* · F. W. D. Deakin, 'What really happened in Yugoslavia during the war?', unpub. typescript, Deakin papers, CAC Cam. · Deakin papers, CAC Cam. · Deakin papers, priv. coll. · Churchill papers, CAC Cam. · Wheeler-Bennett papers, St Ant. Oxf. · personal knowledge (2009) · private information (2009) · b. cert. · m. cert. [1935]

Archives CAC Cam. · priv. coll. | CAC Cam., Churchill papers, corresp. · St Ant. Oxf., Wheeler-Bennett papers · U. Birm. L., Eden/Avon papers

Likenesses Bassano, half-plate film negative, 1961, NPG [*see illus.*] · Bassano, two half-plate film negatives, 1961, NPG · O. Nemon, bust, 1976, St Ant. Oxf. · E. Sargeant, portrait, 1983, St Ant. Oxf. · obituary photographs

Wealth at death €241,321.97—estate in France · £13,858—estate in UK: probate, 1 July 2005, *CGPLA Eng. & Wales*

Deedes, William Francis [Bill], **Baron Deedes** (**1913–2007**), journalist and politician, was born on 1 June 1913 at The Nook, Holford Road, Hampstead, London, the only son and eldest of four children of (Herbert) William Deedes (1881–1966), who had served as a lieutenant in the 60th rifles during the South African War, and his wife, (Melesina) Gladys, *née* Chevenix Trench (1884–1966), second daughter of Philip Francis Chevenix Trench. At the time of his birth his parents were living at Symnel, Aldington, Kent.

Born the heir to great landed estates—including Sandling Park and the Norman Saltwood Castle—on the North Downs, where his family had lived since the fifteenth century, Deedes was sent first to Wellington House preparatory school, Westgate-on-Sea, and then to Harrow School in 1927. Two years later, however, he had to be withdrawn suddenly because there was no money to pay the fees. This was not the fault of the great depression, which was just beginning, but rather that of his mentally unbalanced father who in the course of the previous decade had squandered a fortune that had taken 450 years to accumulate. So instead of going on to Oxford along with his well-heeled Harrovian contemporaries Deedes had to join his parents in their relatively modest rented house in Marine Parade, Hove, where in the course of the next five years a private tutor helped him to pass his school certificate, the only educational qualification he ever acquired. More usefully Miss Clough's Secretarial School in Folkestone taught him to type—a skill that helped his distinguished soldier uncle, Brigadier-General Sir Wyndham Deedes, to get him apprenticed, in 1931, as a cub reporter on the financially ailing *Morning Post*. This involved a further

William Francis [Bill] Deedes, Baron Deedes (1913–2007), by Andrew Festing

uprooting, since in order to have free lodging near his place of work off Fleet Street he was sent to live with the same uncle, who, after retiring from the army to take up social work, had bought a house in working-class Bethnal Green: not at all the right kind of address for a young man about town, which in other circumstances young Deedes might well have been.

Such 'riches to rags' reversals of fortune, common enough in America during the slump, were much more exceptional in Britain, and although Deedes came to see his own as having been a blessing in disguise—releasing him from the traditional upper-class trajectory—missing out on the university experience could well have done him lasting damage. Certainly his contemporaries thought so, blaming it for the sense of inadequacy Deedes suffered from in the company of intellectuals in later life, whether politicians, journalists, or, most challenging of all, civil service mandarins.

Not that intellectual inadequacy would have been much of a disadvantage in the *Morning Post* newsroom, since in those days very few reporters would have been near a university, and the days when Coleridge and Disraeli were leader writers on the paper were long since past. The qualities Deedes soon proved that he most certainly did have were of much greater potential value: an easy charm, a way with words, a natural gift for getting to the heart of human interest stories, and a natural gift for socializing gregariously and bibulously with colleagues late into the night in one or other of Fleet Street's ill-favoured watering holes. So promotion came quickly and in 1935, after only four years in the newsroom, Deedes, who had never before been out of Britain, was appointed special correspondent to cover Mussolini's invasion of Abyssinia—the foreign news story of the year—in competition with a formidable array of veteran foreign and war correspondents, national and international, including the already famous young novelist Evelyn Waugh, representing the *Daily Mail*. Although Deedes, characteristically, always said that he only got the job because, as he was a bachelor, the financially strapped *Morning Post* could insure him on the cheap, it seems much more likely that his work had already shown him to be a journalist of promise.

In the event, cooped up in Addis Ababa, Abyssinia's dusty and dilapidated capital, far from the war front, the journalists had very little news to report. Indeed the journalists, and their idiosyncrasies, rivalries, duplicities, and eccentricities, were the news, as Waugh's famous satirical novel about them, *Scoop* (1938), made all too clear. Waugh partly based the book's ingenuous young reporter, Boot, on Deedes, but however ingenuous young Deedes may indeed have been when he went out to Addis, he undoubtedly came home for Christmas in 1937 with a far subtler and more realistic understanding of the ways and wiles of the world than ever he would have acquired as an undergraduate at Oxford. More important, unlike Waugh, he returned home an ardent anti-appeaser long before other old Harrovians, including the former prime minister Stanley Baldwin, had seen the light.

Having proved his worth in Abyssinia, Deedes was soon promoted to be the *Morning Post*'s political correspondent and assigned to the main news stories of the period, including Edward VIII's abdication and the antisemitic British Union of Fascists' marches in London's East End. Even more significantly, so far as his career was concerned, he was put in charge of the paper's Christmas Toy Fund, a charity that proved so astonishingly successful that when in 1937 the failing *Morning Post* eventually merged with the prospering *Daily Telegraph* the latter's proprietor, Lord Camrose, insisted that Deedes should be kept on especially to run it, over and above his reporting duties. One of these in 1938 was to report on the return to Heston airport of Neville Chamberlain from the ill-fated Munich conference. Deedes made clear his scepticism about Chamberlain's promise of 'peace in our time' by writing a series of articles on the necessity of air-raid precautions, articles later put together as a best-selling pamphlet that made so much money for the *Daily Telegraph* that Camrose felt it only proper to send Deedes a substantial royalty cheque. Possibly it was this cheque, and a salary rise about the same time, that enabled him to give much needed financial help to the other, more hard-up members of his family. Then, early in 1939, believing that war was inevitable, he joined the Queen's Westminsters, a territorial battalion of the King's Royal rifle corps, transferring soon to a new battalion specially formed to accommodate the many other journalists and actors volunteering to serve in its ranks.

As his authorized biographer, Stephen Robinson, shrewdly observed, Deedes was 'by temperament … ideally suited to life as a junior officer, placing his faith in his superiors and winning over the men under his command by his charm and diligent example' (Robinson, 113); and such problems as he experienced during his wartime years of arduous training were primarily caused by the half-hearted—on both sides—courtship he began while stationed in Yorkshire with Evelyn Hilary Branfoot (1915–2004), daughter of Clive Branfoot, scion of a well-established shipping family. They eventually married (at the parish church in Stonegrave, Yorkshire) on 21 November 1942. When the first child, Jeremy, was born in November 1943 Deedes failed to be present, and although on this occasion military duties might seem a good excuse, his in-laws suspected him of not having tried hard enough to get leave—a worrying foretaste of his future neglect of family duties, in such marked contrast to his model dutifulness as comrade in arms, colleague, and friend. When the invasion of Normandy eventually came in 1944 Deedes's battalion, scheduled to go over on D-day itself, was delayed for six days by striking dockers who refused to load the tanks—a disgraceful strike that meant that the suicidally obstructive behaviour of the Fleet Street print unions in the 1980s came to him as no surprise.

Even by the highest standards Deedes had a 'good war': a record of almost unbroken active service, culminating in an act of gallantry—for which he won the MC—when, as company commander, he saved the life of one of his junior officers. Never afterwards, however, did he take pride in his 'good war', always painfully aware of the men under his command who lost their lives. Indeed in his letters to the widows can be discerned his gift for communicating human sympathy, which towards the end of his life turned him into a national treasure.

Emotionally drained—and not much enjoying family life in the Victorian farmhouse he had bought near Aldington—Major Deedes was glad to be able to return to the *Daily Telegraph*, albeit in the somewhat humble role of deputy editor on 'Peterborough', the paper's diary column. Aldington in east Kent, of course, was where his roots lay, and when the sitting conservative MP for Ashford let it be known that he would not be standing at the next election, Deedes—whose great-grandfather and great-great-grandfather had been Kent MPs—successfully applied for the nomination, going on to win the seat in the general election of 1950. Not until 1954, however, did his name catch the public eye when, because of his media connections, he was chosen by the whips to introduce Harold Macmillan, minister for housing, on one of the first political broadcasts to be televised in Britain. Deedes's profile having been much raised, the prime minister, Winston Churchill, offered him the junior ministerial job of parliamentary secretary to the minister of housing, and subsequently other junior ministerial jobs; but the mental strain of holding his own with a succession of brilliant mandarin minds—as he freely confessed—eventually undermined his health and in January 1957 he voluntarily returned to the back benches. Rather to the amazement of his old *Telegraph* colleagues he gratefully resumed his old, very modest job on that paper, supplemented this time by occasional leader-page articles in support of 'one nation' conservatism.

Then in July 1962 Deedes received an urgent invitation from the prime minister, Harold Macmillan—who had just perpetrated a panic government reshuffle, known as the 'night of the long knives'—to return to the front bench as minister without portfolio with a seat in the cabinet, charged with using his media skills to restore the public image of a government already moving irreversibly towards the rocks. Unfortunately for Deedes, however, the Profumo scandal broke on his ministerial watch. Jack Profumo—a fellow Harrovian—was the minister of war who became involved, at the same time as the Russian military attaché, with the beautiful call girl Christine Keeler, and Deedes was one of the five ministers involved in the scandal's naïve mishandling. At an emergency meeting in the small hours of the morning this group of ministers encouraged Profumo to make later that day a statement to parliament claiming that 'no impropriety whatever' had taken place; a manifestly mendacious statement that, in the absence of any secretary at that early hour, Deedes himself had to type out. (In fact he was the only one of the ministers who knew how to type.) Two months later Profumo admitted lying, and resigned. For Deedes it was a particularly damaging incident, because it highlighted his conspicuous lack of the very worldly wisdom and Machiavellian realism that Harold Macmillan was looking to him to provide. As a high flying politician his reputation never recovered, and when in 1964 the Conservatives, led by then by Sir Alec Douglas-Home, lost the next general election, Deedes—who held his own Ashford seat—happily returned to the back benches and, once again to the surprise of his *Telegraph* colleagues, to his old job on 'Peterborough', from where he contributed more mildly right-wing, agreeably expressed political articles. Only on South Africa—where he was an unapologetic supporter of the apartheid regime—did he put his head above the parapet.

In 1974, hearing that Maurice Green, the *Daily Telegraph*'s editor, had decided to retire, Deedes, with a degree of dexterity that Harold Macmillan had looked for in vain, manoeuvred successfully in persuading Lord Hartwell to let him take Green's place. It was, for the most part, a popular appointment not only because Deedes had become a much loved colleague, but also because the staff hoped that a former war hero editor might, at long last, have the courage to tell the proprietor a most unwelcome home truth: that under the divide and rule editorial policy he had inherited from his all-powerful father, the first Lord Camrose, the paper was stagnating. Hating confrontation, Deedes demurred, telling colleagues that 'it was not the job of the adjutant to tell the commanding officer how to run the show' (private information)—an argument rather devalued by the fact that in this case the adjutant carried the authority of a former cabinet minister. Nor did it help that Deedes, the most unideological of men, was in charge of the *Telegraph* during the ideologically charged Thatcher years. For the proprietor was a dyed-in-the-wool Keynesian, in marked contrast to the leader writers, who were Thatcherite fundamentalists, and Deedes's efforts not to displease either did not result in a *Telegraph* line that gave much pleasure to number 10. Deedes's characteristically civilized way of making up for this was by playing a lot of golf and drinking a lot of gin and tonic with Denis Thatcher—a friendship immortalized in *Private Eye* by the satirical letters entitled 'Dear Bill'. Deedes's very considerable speech-writing skills were also made available, most memorably in the draft he produced for Margaret Thatcher's historic address to a joint session of the American congress in 1985, during Ronald Reagan's presidency. He was made a life peer, as Baron Deedes, in 1986.

Deedes's editorship ended, after eleven years, when Hartwell's obdurate mismanagement allowed the Canadian financier Conrad Black to take the *Daily Telegraph* over and appoint a new, more masterful young editor, Max Hastings, under whom Deedes, always loyal to a fault, agreed to serve as a columnist and foreign correspondent. Under Charles Moore, who succeeded Hastings in 1995, these roles allowed Deedes to come at last into his own as a brave and formidable champion, all over the world, of humanitarian causes: most notably over landmines in Angola and the Balkans, alongside Princess Diana. In 1997 he published his autobiography, *Dear Bill*, which mentioned his wife only once; this was followed by *At War with Waugh: the Real Story of 'Scoop'* (2003), *Brief Lives* (2004), a collection of memoirs of contemporaries, and *Words and Deedes: Selected Journalism, 1931–2006* (2006). He was appointed KBE in 1999. He died, still in harness, on 17 August 2007, at his home, New Hayters, Forge Hill, Aldington, of bronchopneumonia, and was mourned on a scale that befitted the passing of a national institution, which is what by then he had become. His burial took place privately on 20 August at the Church of St Martin, Aldington, and his memorial service was held at the Guards' Chapel, Wellington Barracks, on 26 November. He was survived by his son Jeremy, a director of the Telegraph group of companies, and three daughters, one son having predeceased him. PEREGRINE WORSTHORNE

Sources W. F. Deedes, *Dear Bill* (1997) · W. F. Deedes, *At war with Waugh: the real story of 'Scoop'* (2003) · W. F. Deedes, *Brief lives* (2004) · *The Times* (18 Aug 2007) · *Daily Telegraph* (18 Aug 2007); (23 Nov 2007); (27 Nov 2007) · *The Guardian* (18 Aug 2007); (27 Nov 2007) · *The Independent* (20 Aug 2007) · S. Robinson, *The remarkable lives of Bill Deedes* (2008) · Burke, *Peerage* · *WW* (2007) · personal knowledge (2011) · private information (2011) · b. cert. · m. cert. · d. cert.

Archives FILM BFINA, documentary footage · BFINA, current affairs footage | SOUND BL NSA, current affairs recordings · BL NSA, documentary recordings

Likenesses photographs, 1953–2005, Getty Images, London · photograph, 1954, PA Photos, London · W. Bird, photograph, 1963, NPG · photographs, 1970–2005, Camera Press, London · photographs, 1977–2005, Rex Features, London · photographs, 1986–2002, Photoshot, London · N. Sinclair, bromide print, 1992, NPG · T. Leighton, photographs, 1996–2000, NPG · photograph, 1997–2003, Corbis · A. Festing, oils, priv. coll [*see illus.*] · J. Wilde, photograph, repro. in *Sunday Telegraph* (13 Jan 2007) · obituary photographs · photograph, repro. in Robinson, *Remarkable lives*, cover · photographs, repro. in Deedes, *Dear Bill*

Wealth at death £200,670: probate, 10 Jan 2008, *CGPLA Eng. & Wales*

Deer, William Alexander [Alex] (**1910–2008**), petrologist and college head, was born on 26 October 1910 at 82 St Ives Road, Rusholme, Manchester, the eldest son of William Deer, warehouseman, and his wife, Davina, *née* Cunningham. He completed his education at the Central High School in Manchester and in 1929 went on to read natural sciences at the university there. With a Beyer fellowship

(1933) he started geological research, a Strathcona scholarship taking him to St John's College, Cambridge, and a place in C. E. Tilley's newly formed department of mineralogy and petrology. There he came to the notice of L. R. Wager, veteran of Everest and seasoned Arctic explorer, who was then planning an expedition to study a remarkable layered intrusion that he had discovered in East Greenland. So Deer went as second geologist with the party, which spent a year in 1935–6 with Inuit support on the Skaergaard. During their stay the superbly exposed Skaergaard intrusion was mapped and studied in detail; also some 35,000 square kilometres of difficult and dangerous country was mapped in reconnaissance, an extraordinary feat carried out by two two-man sledging teams. Deer returned from the Arctic a firm friend with his famously perfectionist and exacting leader.

In 1937, on completion of his PhD, Deer was appointed assistant lecturer at Manchester University. On 11 April 1939, at St Paul's Methodist Church, Didsbury, he married Margaret Marjorie Kidd (1912–1971), daughter of William Kidd, electrical engineer. They had two sons and a daughter. The award of a senior 1851 exhibition in the same year as his marriage brought him back to Cambridge where he was elected a research fellow of St John's. Also in 1939 his and Wager's Skaergaard memoir was published in the Danish series Meddelelser on Grønland. This, one of the more important petrological memoirs of the twentieth century, was the first quantitative study of the successive layers of crystal accumulation in a large magma chamber and in its detailed correlation of field observation with chemical and microscopic laboratory study set the standard for all subsequent investigations.

The outbreak of the Second World War only months later stifled the impact of the Skaergaard memoir and put the careers of its authors on hold. Although in a reserved occupation, Deer joined up, trained as a gas officer in the Royal Engineers, and served on the general staff in Iraq and Iran. Posted to organize a new Indian corps, he fought with it in the desperate battle of Kohima, which finally denied the Japanese access to India. Seconded to Mountbatten's staff in Ceylon planning an invasion of Japan, he ended the war with the rank of lieutenant-colonel.

Deer could have remained in the War Office but preferred a return to Cambridge, where he was appointed demonstrator in mineralogy and petrology and in 1946 junior bursar of St John's; he proved an energetic improver of the rather primitive facilities of that venerable institution. Three years later he accepted a tutorship at St John's, and made a summer return to the Arctic, prospecting for layered intrusions in the then unmapped mountains of Baffin Island. He was accompanied on this mini-expedition by his pupil Chris Brasher, later an Olympic gold medallist athlete and founder of the London marathon. Deer would later tell, with a chuckle, how he had nearly rejected the eager but spare young man, as having insufficient stamina for this enterprise.

In 1950 Deer was elected professor of geology at Manchester, where through eleven years of hard work he expanded a tiny department into a leading school of geology, boasting among its innovations the first hydrothermal high-pressure experimental laboratory in Britain. On Tilley's retirement in 1961, Deer returned to Cambridge and to St John's College, to succeed him as professor of mineralogy and petrology. His unaffected friendliness and easy accessibility stood in marked contrast to the rather Olympian professorial style of the day, and his way with bureaucracy soon had welcome funds flowing. His talents did not long escape the notice of the wider university, which appointed him to its general board. He also chaired the strategic committee which produced the Deer report in 1965, which argued the case for expansion into the cornfields of west Cambridge. As master of Trinity Hall from 1966 to 1975 he presided over an extensive building programme, and concurrently served as university vice-chancellor from 1971 to 1973 during a frustrating period of student unrest. He was instrumental in modifying university structures by placing fuller responsibility for academic management and long-term planning in the general board's hands, and developing the role of the secretary-general of the faculties.

Outside Cambridge, Deer served as president of the Mineralogical Society (1967–70), and of the Geological Society (1970–72). He was a trustee of the British Museum (natural history) from 1967 to 1975, a member of the Natural Environment Research Council (1968–71), and served on the Marshall Aid Commemoration Commission (1973–9). He was awarded the Murchison fund of the Geological Society in 1946 and its Murchison medal in 1974. He was elected FRS in 1962 and received an honorary DSc degree from Aberdeen University in 1984.

Deer was able to return to the Skaergaard on two further expeditions. In 1953 that of Oxford and Manchester universities was led jointly by Wager and Deer. While in preparation for the 1966 Oxford–Cambridge expedition Deer suffered the blow of Wager's death. Leading probably the last expedition to travel to Greenland from the UK by chartered vessel, Deer took deep drilling equipment and Canadian drillers to explore the 'hidden zone' beneath the exposed layers of the intrusion. The 380 metres of core recovered under difficult conditions continued for many years to provide an invaluable resource for research.

Although Deer's scientific reputation rested firmly on Skaergaard, his name became more familiarly known through the monumental work *Rock-forming Minerals* by Deer, R. A. Howie, and Jack Zussman. The first edition of five volumes (1962–3) was replaced from 1978 by a greatly expanded second edition, which had become at the time of his death an encyclopaedia of eleven volumes.

As a leader and administrator Deer was clear-minded, far-sighted, and decisive. His puffing on a small pipe complemented a gruff, laconic persona. Generally tolerant, he remained essentially a private man of simple tastes, devoted to his family. After Margaret's death in 1971, he married, on 22 December 1973, Rita Tagg, *née* Vincent (1916–2006), secretary, daughter of William Henry Vincent, chief engineer, and former wife of Robert Tagg. As a boy, he had shown talent with the violin; at a ripe age he became a competent bassoon player. Later restricted by physical infirmity, he remained in his Cambridge flat until a few days before his death, a cheerful and convivial companion with formidable recall and acuity. He died on 8 February 2009 at The Hollies nursing home, 11 Queen Ediths Way, Cambridge, of sepsis, and was survived by a son and a daughter, one son having predeceased him. He was buried beside his second wife in the Arbory woodland burial ground, Barton, near Cambridge. A memorial service was held on 31 October 2009 at Trinity Hall, Cambridge. GRAHAM CHINNER

Sources *The Times* (12 March 2009) · *Mineralogical Magazine*, 73/3 (June 2009), 511–14 · www.geolsoc.org.uk/page5814.html, 18 June 2012 · *WW* (2009) · personal knowledge (2013) · private information (2013) · b. cert. · m. certs. · d. cert.

Dehn, Olive Marie (1914–2007), poet and children's writer, was born on 29 September 1914, at 13 Belfield Road, Didsbury, the only daughter and second of three children of Frederick Edward Dehn (1881/2–1947), cotton merchant, and his wife, Helen, *née* Susman (1880–1976). Her elder brother was Paul Edward *Dehn (1912–1976), writer and film critic. Her contrariness developed early: at the age of four she proclaimed that she actually liked corners when told to stand in one. She was educated at a girls' school in Seaford, Sussex, an unhappy experience. By the age of eighteen she was already contributing to *Punch* and *Country Life*. In 1933, while staying in Germany with relatives, she wrote a satirical poem, 'Goebelchen (a Half-Aryan Ballad)', for *Punch*. She was promptly arrested and deported from the country under armed guard. Back in England she became an established writer, with stories for the BBC radio programme *Children's Hour*, poetry illustrated by E. H. Shepard, children's plays, and a notably successful book for children, *The Basement Bogle* (1935).

On 5 June 1937 she married the actor (Peter) David Markham (1913–1983); they had four daughters. During the Second World War her husband, a libertarian anarchist and pacifist, was sentenced to twelve months' hard labour as a conscientious objector. Olive Dehn shared his political beliefs, and like him joined the Committee of 100 soon after it was founded in 1960. She was also arrested with him in Moscow in 1974 and deported when, as founding members of the Campaign Against the Abuse of Psychiatry, they campaigned for the release of Soviet dissidents. She thus had the unusual distinction of having been deported by both the Nazis and the KGB.

After the Second World War she and her husband had bought Lear Cottage, near Coleman's Hatch in Ashdown Forest, Sussex. There, in a clearing in the forest, they farmed organically, becoming largely self-sufficient, raising sheep, pigs, geese, and hens, growing a wide variety of fruit and vegetables, and taking pride in the prizes awarded for their animals and produce. Dehn continued to write, though she published less frequently. Her children's book *The Pike Dream* (1958), illustrated by her eldest daughter, Sonia, was a particular success, as was *Spectacles for the Mole* (1968). Her last children's story was *Goodbye Day* (1980). She continued to write poetry, and in 2006 published *Out of My Mind: Poems, 1929–1995*. She died in Wych Cross, Sussex, on 21 March 2007, and was survived by her four daughters.

Sources *The Guardian* (31 March 2007) · *The Independent* (27 April 2007) · b. cert. · m. cert.

Wealth at death £842,025: probate, 6 Sept 2007, *CGPLA Eng. & Wales*

Delfont [*née* Haymen; *other married name* Farr], **Helen Violet Carolyn, Lady Delfont** [*performing name* Carole Lynne] (1918–2008), actress and singer, was born on 16 September 1918 at 217 Maidstone Road, Rochester, Kent, the daughter of Victor Cecil Haymen (1895–1968), recently demobilized as a lieutenant in the Royal Munster Fusiliers, and his wife, Helen Elizabeth, otherwise Helen Debroy, *née* Somers. She was educated at St Hilary's School, Cliftonville, and, adopting the stage name Carole Lynne, made her professional début in 1937 playing Miss Thing in J. M. Barrie's *A Kiss for Cinderella* with the Canterbury Repertory Players. The following year she made her London début in the Hungarian musical romance *Paprika*, at His Majesty's Theatre. Her first appearance in revue was in *The Gate Revue* at the Gate Theatre (1939), starring Hermione Gingold and Michael Wilding. A glamorous, shapely blonde with a fine soprano voice, she was much in demand for revue, and scored a particular success with Pat Kirkwood in *Black Velvet* at the Hippodrome (1939), which opened shortly after the outbreak of the Second World War; the revue ran for 620 performances.

She had on 18 June 1939 married the actor Derek Capel Farr (1912–1986), but the marriage did not survive his enlistment. She met Bernard *Delfont [formerly Boris Winogradsky] (1909–1994), theatrical impresario, in 1943 when he was producing *Old Chelsea* at the Prince's Theatre, in which she starred opposite the popular tenor Richard Tauber; the latter was best man at their wedding on 22 January 1946. Meanwhile she scored further West End successes in *Cinderella* (Her Majesty's, 1943) and *Jill Darling* (Winter Garden, 1944), and appeared in two films, both comedies, *The Ghost Train* (1941) and *Asking for Trouble* (1942). After the war she appeared in *Big Ben* (Adelphi, 1946), *Cinderella* again (London Casino, 1947), and *Touch and Go* (Prince of Wales, 1950), before retiring to concentrate on raising her children and performing to a fault the role of impresario's wife. She became Lady Delfont when her husband was knighted in 1974; he was raised to the peerage in 1976. After his death she was fiercely and publicly critical of the restructuring of his entertainment company, First Leisure, by his nephew Michael Grade, and also of the latter's refusal to rename the Prince of Wales Theatre (where Delfont had kept his office) the Delfont Theatre. She was involved in a range of charities, especially theatrical ones, but also as an early supporter of the Museum of Immigration and Diversity in London's East End. She died at her home in Sussex on 17 January 2008 and was survived by her three children.

Sources *The Stage* (21 Jan 2008) · *The Times* (22 Jan 2008); (16 Feb 2008) · *Daily Telegraph* (25 Jan 2008) · *The Independent* (9 April 2008) · b. cert. · m. certs.

Likenesses obituary photographs

DeLorean, John Zachary (1925–2005), motor car manufacturer, was born on 6 January 1925 in Detroit, Michigan, USA, the eldest of four sons of Zachary DeLorean, a Romanian-born foundry worker in the Ford motor car works, and his wife, Kathryn, *née* Pribak, a factory worker of Austro-Hungarian antecedents. His father was a violent alcoholic whose family suffered many deprivations and terrors. John DeLorean, who was educated at Cass Technical High School, Detroit, was drafted into the US army for three years midway through his course at the Lawrence Institute of Technology in Detroit, but graduated in 1948. He joined the Chrysler Corporation before transferring in 1952 to the Packard company, where he worked in the research and development of hydraulics and transmissions systems.

In 1956 DeLorean was recruited to the Pontiac division of General Motors (GM), serving first as director of advanced engineering, then as chief engineer from 1961 and general manager from 1965. He incorporated vertically stacked headlights, racing stripes, cockpit-style interiors, angled instrument panels, and other accessories into the designs of Pontiac models such as the GTO and Firebird, which greatly raised sales to young male buyers, and he was a vice-president of GM by the age of thirty-nine. After being promoted in 1969 to be general manager of GM's Chevrolet division, he turned around its profitability. Subsequently he assumed responsibility for GM's five American car divisions (Chevrolet, Buick, Oldsmobile, Pontiac, and Cadillac), its American truck and coach division, and its Canadian operations. Nevertheless his flamboyance, egotism, and unconventionality jarred with his colleagues at GM, and he left the corporation in 1973. Next he registered the DeLorean Corporation, specializing in cars, camper vans, and trailers, and was involved in several business initiatives, including an avocado farm and a ski school, that ended in failure and litigation. He tried to attract government funding to set up a bus factory in the high unemployment area of South Bronx, but above all wanted to build an exotic sports car. Adapting a discarded Porsche design, he determined to build a rear-engined, two-seater sports car with an all-plastic chassis, stainless steel exterior, and gull-wing doors which, if both were open, gave the look of a bird in flight.

In June 1978 DeLorean approached the Labour government in London with a plan to build this sports car at a government-subsidized factory in Northern Ireland. Despite expert misgivings, Roy Mason, the secretary of state for Northern Ireland, assured his cabinet colleagues that DeLorean's initiative would bring great political, social, and economic benefits to the province and prove a hammer-blow against the Irish Republican Army. Mason, who had an entrenched socialist faith in government intervention in industry, concluded a deal with DeLorean, after hectic negotiations, on 28 July. A site was selected at Dunmurry, south-west of Belfast, a beleaguered area of high unemployment straddled by both Catholic and Protestant districts, and a factory was erected that created

John Zachary DeLorean (1925–2005), by unknown photographer, 1981

2500 jobs. The accession to power in 1979 of a Conservative government altered the way in which Whitehall responded to DeLorean's urgent, honeyed words. The Thatcher cabinet mistrusted government subsidies of feeble industrial enterprises, and when DeLorean approached Mason's successor, James Prior, for another £40 million of government money to develop a sedan car, Prior proved more interested in reducing the company's £25 million overdraft, which carried a government guarantee. Prior initially found DeLorean suave, handsome, self-confident, and commanding, but decidedly tricky; later he decided that DeLorean was a confidence trickster. Engineering work on the DeLorean car DCM12 was assigned to the Lotus company in Norfolk. Production began in December 1980 with high hopes, but the car was underpowered, boring to drive, and expensive at $25,000 each—especially at a time when the USA, its only market, was in recession. 6000 DMC12s were supplied to the USA in the period to January 1982, but only 3000 were sold. The slipshod Belfast workers produced vehicles of such poor quality that they had to pass through rectification plants in the USA before they could be sold. The DeLorean Corporation was undercapitalized and hoped to raise $12 million by a float on the New York stock exchange, but the float was indefinitely postponed on the advice of its investment bankers.

The Belfast company was insolvent by January 1982, and Sir Kenneth Cork, who was appointed as its receiver, began to unravel the squalid mess. He found DeLorean pompous, sly, and blustering. When DMC12 production ceased in October 1982, British taxpayers had contributed £78 million to produce 8500 vehicles. Cork soon discovered that $17.5 million paid for the development costs of the car had been diverted through Panama to Switzerland, and had then been pocketed by DeLorean, Colin Chapman, the head of Lotus, and a Lotus executive, Frederick Bushell. Chapman died in 1982, and Bushell was jailed in 1992, but DeLorean evaded attempts to extradite him from the USA to face British criminal prosecution. In 1986 he was unwarrantably acquitted of related charges by an American court.

DeLorean had been genuinely dedicated to producing his own motor car, and longed to be the commander-in-chief of a motor corporation, but failed to control his venality or manage his headstrong talents. A desperate man who could not face failure, he hoped to save his toppling empire by a last desperate ploy, and after returning from Colombia he was arrested on 19 October 1982 in Los Angeles for importing 220 lb of cocaine worth £14.7 million into the USA. Despite strong evidence of his guilt, he was acquitted in August 1984 after arguing that he had been a victim of entrapment by the FBI. He was finally bankrupted in 1999, and his 434 acre estate in New Jersey (bought in 1981) was seized by a federal court in 2000. About the time of his arrest he became a born-again Christian.

DeLorean married first, in 1954 or 1957, Elizabeth Elaine Higgins. They had an adopted son and two daughters. After this marriage was dissolved, he married, on 31 May 1969, Kelly Harmon (*b.* *c.*1949), from whom he was divorced in 1972. On 8 May 1973 he married a model named Cristina Ferrare, from whom he was divorced in 1985. His fourth wife was Sally Baldwin. He died after a stroke on 19 March 2005 at Overlook Hospital, Summit, New Jersey. He was survived by his fourth wife and the children of his first marriage.

RICHARD DAVENPORT-HINES

Sources H. Levin, *Grand delusions* (1983) • M. Edwards, *Back from the brink* (1983) • J. DeLorean and T. Schwarz, *DeLorean* (1985) • I. Fallon and J. Srodes, *Dreammakers* (1985) • W. Haddad, *Hard driving* (1985) • J. Prior, *A balance of power* (1986) • K. Cork, *Cork on Cork* (1988) • R. Mason, *Paying the price* (1999) • *The Guardian* (21 March 2005) • *The Times* (22 March 2005) • *Daily Telegraph* (22 March 2005) • *The Independent* (21 March 2005)

Archives FILM BFINA, 'A little bit of money', *World in action*, B. Blake (producer), Thames Television, 24 June 1985

Likenesses photographs, 1961–98, Getty Images, London • photograph, 1979–86, Rex Features, London • photograph, 1981, Getty Images, London [*see illus.*] • photographs, 1981–7, PA Photos, London • obituary photographs • photographs, Camera Press, London

Dempster, Nigel Richard Patton (1941–2007), journalist, was born near Calcutta, India, on 1 November 1941, the youngest of three children of Eric Richard Patton Dempster (1890–1980), an Australian who worked as the managing director of the Indian Copper Corporation, and his wife, Angela Grace, *née* Stephens (1909–2000), who was British. His mother acquired a British passport for him

Nigel Richard Patton Dempster (1941–2007), by Trevor Leighton, 1981

and packed him off at the age of six to be educated at St Peter's preparatory school, Lympstone, Devon, and subsequently at Sherborne School in Dorset, from where he was expelled for being a disruptive influence. His first job, at sixteen, was as a porter at Westminster Hospital. In 1958 he became a broker at Lloyd's, and a year later a bluebutton at a firm of City stockbrokers. In 1960 he moved into public relations, working as an account executive for the earl of Kimberley until 1963.

A keen party-goer, Dempster had been making a modest freelance income contributing items to the 'William Hickey' column in the *Daily Express*, and in 1963 a chance meeting at Cowes with the newspaper's proprietor, Lord Beaverbrook, led to a staff job. He worked on the newspaper until 1971, when he was recruited by David English, the new editor of the *Daily Mail*, to assist Paul Callan in establishing a diary to rival Hickey. English was in the business of creating his own stable of star writers and saw in Dempster a keen and malleable young man who was willing to play the part required of him. In 1973 English allowed Dempster to usurp Callan as the *Mail*'s diary editor.

Dempster proved an excellent conduit for society gossip, but he was not a natural writer. English rewrote a lot of Dempster's early columns himself—as he did for Lynda Lee-Potter—to establish a distinctive voice for the columnist, and later entrusted the job to Peter Donnelly, one of English's favourite sub-editors. Sporting long hair and shirts unbuttoned almost to his midriff—in keeping with the trends of the day—Dempster soon became one of

Fleet Street's most recognizable characters and made frequent appearances on television. His column was all the while notching up some remarkable scoops: it disclosed, three months before it happened, that Harold Wilson intended to resign as prime minister, and it apprised the actress Vivien Merchant of the fact that her husband, Harold Pinter, was having an affair with Lady Antonia Fraser. For many years in the 1970s and 1980s Dempster was the most notorious and best informed of all the newspaper gossip columnists.

Dempster married, on 17 May 1971, Countess Emma Magdalen de Bendern (*b.* 1950), daughter of Count John Gerard de Bendern and his wife, Lady Patricia Sybil, *née* Douglas (daughter of the eleventh marquess of Queensberry). The couple divorced in 1974. On 30 July 1977 he married Lady Camilla Dorothy Godolphin Harris (*b.* 1950), former wife of Robert Julian Brownlow Harris and only daughter of John Osborne, eleventh and penultimate duke of Leeds, and his second wife, Audrey Young, a painter. Dempster had a stepdaughter, Emily Kate Godolphin Harris (*b.* 1972), and a daughter, Louisa Beatrix (*b.* 1979). His marriage to Camilla was dissolved in 2002.

After Paul Dacre became editor of the *Mail* in 1992 Dempster was marginalized. In 1996 Dacre revived a rival diary called 'Ephraim Hardcastle', which was written by Peter McKay, and, for a while, also ran a column called 'Wicked Whispers' under the editorship of John McEntee, who had previously been Dempster's rival on the *Daily Express*. Obsessively fit throughout his early life—playing squash most mornings and often competing in marathons—Dempster fell victim to progressive supranuclear palsy. By the eve of the millennium he had noticeably slowed down and instead of seeing in the new year he retired to bed early at his home in South Kensington. By 2002 it was fashionable in the industry to talk disparagingly about his column, but he was still able that year to beat all of his 'so-called rivals' to the story of Bryan Ferry's separation from his wife, Lucy.

In his final decade Dempster embraced the Roman Catholic church and wore around his neck a chain bearing the image of the Virgin Mary. He resigned as the diarist of the *Daily Mail* and *Mail on Sunday* (for which he had begun writing in 1986) in 2003, and, very frail, he was taken in by his former wife Camilla, who cared for him with the assistance of a nurse at her home on Ham Common in Richmond, south London. He was succeeded as the *Daily Mail*'s diarist by Richard Kay, who, much to Dempster's amusement, led his inaugural column with a 'world exclusive' on the duke of York's readiness 'to take the huge step of marrying again', to a businesswoman named Amanda Staveley. Dempster succumbed to his illness at home in Ham on 12 July 2007. A requiem mass was held for him at Brompton Oratory on 18 July and a memorial service on 17 October at St Bride's, Fleet Street. TIM WALKER

Sources *The Times* (13 July 2007); (17 July 2007); (18 July 2007); (23 July 2007) • *Daily Telegraph* (13 July 2007) • *The Guardian* (13 July 2007); (14 July 2007) • *The Independent* (13 July 2007); (14 July 2007) • *New York Times* (13 July 2007) • *WW* (2007)

Archives FILM BFINA, documentary footage • BFINA, light entertainment footage | SOUND performance recordings • light entertainment recordings

Likenesses photographs, 1961–2003, Rex Features, London • G. Scarfe, pen and indian ink, 1972, NPG • photographs, 1977–2000, Getty Images, London • photographs, 1977–2001, PA Photos, London • T. Leighton, bromide fibre print, 1981, NPG [*see illus.*] • T. Leighton, bromide fibre print, 1981, NPG • photographs, 1997–8, Photoshot, London • obituary photographs • photographs, Camera Press, London

Wealth at death under £107,000: probate, 18 April 2008, *CGPLA Eng. & Wales*

Deniz, Clara Ethel (Clare) (1911–2002). *See under* Deniz, Francisco Antonio [Frank] (1912–2005).

Deniz, Francisco Antonio [Frank] **(1912–2005)**, guitarist and bandleader, was born at 9 Christina Street, Cardiff, on 31 July 1912, the eldest of three sons of Antoni (or Antonio) Francisco Deniz, formerly Diniz (1878–*c.*1931), a donkeyman (engine-room sailor), and his wife, Gertrude Blanch (or Blanche), *née* Boston (1886–1974). His younger brothers were José William (Joe) *Deniz (1913–1994) and Laurence Richard (Laurie) *Deniz (1924–1996); a sister died in infancy. Their father was an African from Cape Antonio in the Cape Verde Islands, and their mother, born in Cardiff, was of English and African American descent.

Deniz was born while his father was away at sea and baptized twice as a result. As Frank he was christened at St Mary's Church, Cardiff, under the rites of the Church of England, but when his father came home, he was baptized again as a Roman Catholic with the name Francisco Antonio. He grew up in Cardiff with his half-siblings, Maria Margaret Correa (1907–1978) and Manoel Edward Correa (*b.* 1909), the children of their mother's first marriage, to Manoel or Manuel Correa, a ship's cook. Correa was a Cape Verdean, too, and thus, like Antoni Deniz, a member of what is believed to have been the first and oldest immigrant community in Cardiff's docks. As a boy Deniz heard African and Caribbean airs, sea shanties, and popular songs. He knew traditional Portuguese music through his father, who played violin, mandolin, and guitar, and learned to play by listening to Portuguese-speaking Cape Verdean Africans at Sunday sessions where his mother played piano.

Deniz attended South Church Street school and on leaving, aged fourteen, sold newspapers in the streets. When the newspaper's photographer hired Deniz to carry his equipment, he experienced a new life, attending race meetings where he observed Cardiff 'society'. But his father disapproved and with an eye to the future took his eldest son to sea at fifteen, against his mother's wishes. For three years he worked on tramp ships, sometimes with his father, travelling to India, Malaya, Australia, China, and as far as Vladivostok. When his father was taken ill in Odessa, he was forced to leave him in hospital, where he died. He continued going to sea for nearly ten years, eventually qualifying as a donkeyman, while playing guitar and taking the opportunity to hear music wherever he travelled. In Jacksonville, Florida, he heard African American longshoremen singing work songs and blues, and encountered segregation. In Galveston and

Francisco Antonio Deniz (1912–2005), by Val Wilmer

Charleston he came across 'holy-roller' preachers and in Boston joined a gospel congregation.

Between voyages Deniz stayed in Cardiff. In 1934 he heard and met Louis Armstrong at the Empire Theatre, and the same year started playing music with his brother Joe, and with his future wife, Clara Wason; their Blue Hawaiians included another guitarist, Victor Parker. He played also with the dance band of the saxophonist Syd Clements and for a while he, too, played saxophone, mainly because of the limited role then available for stringed rhythm instruments in a band. His experiences in the Americas had shown him that he did not want to strum a banjo or play Hawaiian-style guitar; what inspired him was the single-string work of Teddy Bunn and Eddie Lang, pioneering American jazz guitarists who played clear melodic lines on the instrument.

On 8 August 1936 Deniz married Clara Wason at the church of St Mary the Virgin, Cardiff. Born in Cardiff on 30 September 1911, **Clara Ethel (Clare) Deniz** [*née* Wason] (1911–2002), pianist, was the daughter of Frederick Wason (*c*.1883–1913), a merchant seaman from Barbados, and Bessie Louise Bryant from Somerset, who had some French ancestry. She grew up with her mother in Grangetown, Cardiff, in the home of a Mrs Knight, who came from a mixed-race theatrical family in Bristol, and who was married to a ship's steward from the Caribbean; there Clara learned to play the piano, inspired by Louisa (Louie) Erskine, aunt of the heavyweight boxer Joe Erskine.

After their marriage Frank and Clara Deniz moved to London and immediately found their way into the raffish world of bottle-parties that dominated the capital's nightlife. They joined forces with other British-born musicians of colour, and moved around Soho, taking whatever work they could find. With the guitar yet to come into its own as a dance-band instrument, they often relied on Clara's income, and eventually it was she rather than Frank who (as Clare Deniz) joined an up-and-coming band when she replaced Yorke de Souza in the 'all-black' orchestra of the Guyanese dancer Ken 'Snake Hips' Johnson. In 1937 Frank Deniz spent a brief period as Johnson's second guitarist, playing alongside his brother Joe. The intention was to feature Joe on the amplified Hawaiian guitar, then a popular instrument, and another guitarist was needed to carry the rhythm. The birth of the Denizes' first daughter, Lorraine, in 1937, brought about his departure from the band, although he did so with the blessing of its leader. He then returned to the bottle-parties and jam-sessions. He met prominent American musicians including Art Tatum and Fats Waller, but it was not until he joined the Nigerian pianist Fela Sowande at the Florida Club in 1938 and accompanied the American singer Adelaide Hall that he received the exposure warranted by his developing abilities.

In May 1940 Deniz joined the merchant navy, and survived the dive-bombing of his ship. In San Francisco he heard Louis Armstrong again and met his hero, Teddy Bunn, then in Brazil encountered the Afro-Portuguese rhythmic music that would determine his artistic direction. The chance to practise came by playing 'Latin' music with Edmundo Ros between voyages. In November 1941 he was among the leading musicians participating in the first recorded public jam session, organized by *Melody Maker*, the music trade's weekly newspaper. He played jazz and Latin American music with other bands, but because of his earlier seagoing career, was unable to escape his maritime commitments, despite being torpedoed twice. He continued to broadcast between voyages and joined ENSA to entertain troops with the accordionist Eric Winstone. Leading his own Spirits of Rhythm, named in homage to Teddy Bunn's group of the same name, his guitar playing drew accolades, while Clare also played with the band. Their second daughter, Claire Frances, was born in 1945.

At Rudy Evans's Caribbean Club, where he preceded Lauderic Caton in the house trio, Deniz drew the attention of the music profession's burgeoning modernists. He continued as a featured artist with Winstone, with whose band Clare also played, but although he worked with many jazz notables including the violinist Stéphane Grappelli and at the Caribbean Club, where he returned in 1946, his goal lay elsewhere. To shake off the negative image that was attached—unjustly—to local black artists, he dropped the Americanisms he had adopted as a 'jazzman', and changed his presentation, demeanour, and dress. His fellow guitarist Ivor Mairants helped him initially but his breakthrough came about through the pianist Stanley Black, an admirer of the Deniz brothers who loved Latin American music. When Black became leader of the BBC Dance Orchestra in 1944 he gave Deniz his entrée to radio by employing him regularly and introducing him to other leaders and arrangers—and, importantly, contractors and producers, thereby helping to establish him as a session musician.

In 1953, Frank and Clare Deniz were reunited with Fela Sowande when they appeared in the BBC radio series *Club Ebony*, where Clare sang in Sowande's choir. The same year, inspired by an encounter with Carmen Miranda's musicians, Frank formed a Latin American band, Hermanos Deniz, which included his brother Joe, and later also their younger brother Laurence. For several years the band held prestigious residencies in London's West End. As the guitar grew in popularity, Deniz began writing and playing with his group for films. He created music for Orson Welles's *Three Cases of Murder* (1953) and, with Laurence, co-wrote thirty original pieces for Carol Reed's *Our Man in Havana* (1959).

Regarded as one of the leading guitarists of his generation, Deniz was a thoughtful and serious individual for whom respectability was crucial. The example of Ken 'Snake Hips' Johnson's success with an 'all-black' orchestra inspired him and determined him to organize an equally businesslike band. He did this through excellent musicianship and a capacity to adapt. His uncredited session work ranged from light music to rock 'n' roll but his favourite job came accompanying the American songwriter Hoagy Carmichael. His forte was reproducing the warmth, interplay, and percussive colour of African–Portuguese and African–Spanish rhythms. He continued to organize bands for private functions until 1980 when he and Clare moved to Spain. They worked occasionally in local bars and Frank studied Spanish guitar, but when Clare contracted Parkinson's disease in the 1990s they returned to England where he became her full-time carer. She died in Whitford, Hertfordshire, on 7 December 2002. Frank Deniz died at home, at 12 Amwell Lane, Stanstead Abbots, Hertfordshire, on 17 July 2005; like Clare he was cremated at Harlow crematorium. He was survived by his two daughters, Lorraine and Claire, the latter a successful cellist, known as Clare Deniz. VAL WILMER

Sources programme, Jazz Jamboree 1939 · *Melody Maker* (8 March 1941); (13 Nov 1943) · *Accordion Times and Musical Express* (18 Oct 1946) · *Record Mirror* (23 Feb 1957); [Nov 1958] · *South Wales Echo* (11 July 1964) · I. Mairants, *My fifty fretting years* (1980), p. 67 · 'Clare Deniz', *The Guardian* (3 Jan 2003) · 'Clare Deniz', *Wales on Sunday* (5 Jan 2003) · *The Independent* (29 July 2005) · *The Guardian* (30 July 2005) · *The Stage* (11 Aug 2005) · Val Wilmer and Frank Deniz, interview, 1989, BL NSA · Val Wilmer and Clare Deniz, interview, 1989, BL NSA · personal knowledge (2009) · private information (2009) [Lorraine Rowley, daughter] · b. cert. · m. cert. · d. cert.

Archives FILM BBC, documentary film [about Ken 'Snake Hips' Johnson; includes interviews with Frank and Clare Deniz] | SOUND BL NSA, oral history of jazz in Britain, interview with V. Wilmer, 18 Aug 1989, T9910–T9912Y · BL NSA, oral history of jazz in Britain, interview with V. Wilmer, 21 July 1989, T9809–T9810Y [Clare Deniz] · BL NSA, performance recordings

Likenesses photographs, *c.*1928–2005, priv. coll. · photograph, *c.*1935, Getty Images, London · Nissen, photograph, 1944, repro. in *Banjo, mandolin and guitar* · photograph, 1945, repro. in *Sound Wave Illustrated* (July 1945), 16 · Yvonne, photographs, *c.*1950, priv. coll. · H. P. Newby, group portrait, photograph, *c.*1953 (Hermanos Deniz), Photowork Studios · V. Wilmer, photograph, 1989, priv. coll. [*see illus.*] · V. Wilmer, photograph, 1989, repro. in *The Guardian* · photograph, repro. in Mairants, *Fifty fretting years*, 165

Wealth at death under £180,000—Clare Deniz: probate, 14 April 2003, *CGPLA Eng. & Wales*

Denman, Sir (George) Roy (1924–2006), civil servant and diplomatist, was born at 10 Lisburn Road, Wavertree, Liverpool, on 12 June 1924, the elder son of Albert Edward Denman of Ardwyn, Morfa Nefyn, Caernarvonshire, and his wife, Gertrude Ann, *née* Harrison. His father was a Post Office telephone engineer; his grandfather was a docker. At Harrow grammar school an inspirational teacher instilled in him an undying fascination for all things German. He won a scholarship to read modern languages at St John's College, Cambridge, but after a year his studies there were interrupted by active service in the Far East campaign. Called up in 1942, he joined the Royal Signals. A major at twenty-one, he commanded a detachment of the 3/1st Gurkha rifles which after VJ-day was sent to Indo-China to disarm Japanese troops and contain the growing Vietminh independence movement. To his amusement a squad of dutiful fully armed Japanese guards was placed under his command. Back at St John's after demobilization he took a first in modern languages, and there was talk of a fellowship in Germanic language and literature. An older and wiser don advised him that he would be bored to tears within ten years.

Denman took the tests for entry into the foreign service, but missed narrowly. Despite a distaste for the bureaucracy he had met during a spell in army administration in Delhi he took up an appointment with the home civil service, where in 1948 he was, improbably to him, assigned to the Board of Trade. He soon took the high-flying route to the president's private office, where his first master was Harold Wilson. Denman was not easy to please, but he admired Wilson's intelligence and energy and had no harsh word to say of him. He subsequently went round various departments of the board, until in 1957 an opportunity to serve abroad opened for him. The Foreign Office wanted to strengthen its role in trade promotion by attaching trade specialists to selected posts. No matter that the remuneration was to be below that of a regular diplomat, Denman leapt at the chance of serving in the Bonn embassy. There, fluent in the language, he steeped himself ever deeper in German culture and history. He was something less than impressed by the general run of his embassy colleagues, with their scant linguistic ability and distaste for Germans.

Although other peregrinations in his home department followed, Denman's bent was by now what it remained—the twin track of Europe and trade liberalization. There followed postings, in the board's gift, to the British delegation to the General Agreement on Tariffs and Trade (GATT) in Geneva (1960–61, 1965–7), working with congenial colleagues on the Kennedy round, and negotiating with big hitters notably in the European Commission and the American delegation. The discussions continued in favourite haunts where Denman's palate for fine wines was an important part of his success. By 1970 he had been promoted to deputy secretary in the renamed Department of Trade and Industry, which made him, *inter alia*, chief UK negotiator in the GATT Tokyo round. On 2 April 1966, at the parish church in Ightham, Kent, he had married Moya Frances Gabrielle Lade, a 24-year-old publisher, and daughter of John Mourier Lade, businessman. They had a son and a daughter.

When in 1970 the team was formed to discover on what terms the UK might enter the European Economic Community Denman was the automatic choice for the trade chapter, which along with managed agriculture was virtually all the EEC covered at the time. It was hard going—long hours round the table (and bibulously in the haunts), with weekly trips to London for briefings and discussion. He greatly welcomed the result, which saw Britain join the EEC on 1 January 1973. Then in 1975 he was head-hunted by the cabinet office to be its second permanent secretary, with special responsibility for European affairs. With Whitehall profoundly uninformed about the European institutions it was necessary for someone with knowledge to have the guiding hand. Almost simultaneously came an offer that Denman could not refuse. Christopher Soames, first British vice-president of the European Commission and in charge of commercial policy, asked Denman to fill the vacancy of director-general, trade. Denman agreed, subject to seeing out his work in the cabinet office. He was later asked, along with others, why he wanted to work for Europe. The others elaborated, feelingly. Denman replied simply that he had been in the last war and he did not want another. On leaving the cabinet office in 1977 he was knighted KCB, having been made CMG in 1968 and CB in 1972.

As the European Commission's director-general for external affairs, Denman found his task double-edged. On the one hand he was engaged with the rest of the world—Russia trying to put its 'community', the Council for Mutual Economic Affairs, on a par with the EEC; the USA tenaciously defending its own trade unilateralism and continuously attacking EEC trade barriers; Japan expansionist and hungry; the less developed world demanding special favours. On the other, no less insistent or noisy, were the member states, holding back concessions and demanding gains, while suspicious of their commission negotiator. He attracted particular controversy when one of his thinkpieces was leaked to the press, with its account of the Japanese as workaholics living in rabbit hutches. This was not an outpouring of scorn, but a wake-up call to realization of the task the commission faced in creating conditions for European industry to compete.

In 1982, as the Brussels stint reached its five-year term, another challenge was offered. One of the commission's nerve centres was its office in Washington. When the post of ambassador and head of the European Communities delegation fell vacant Denman was once again ideally suited for the job. In the GATT fraternity he already had American friends-cum-adversaries. He was well steeped in American history and politics and was a master of trade policy. (His subordinates recalled that he never had to ask them for briefs on any issue.) For seven years he travelled widely in the USA, entertained royally, and lobbied mightily, all the time keeping the member states' ambassadors, jealous of their ancient privileges, on side.

After retirement in 1989 Denman taught for a year at the John F. Kennedy School of Government at Harvard; briefly practised business consultancy, and most notably wrote for the *International Herald Tribune*. In his 'op-eds' for this paper and in other writings, including a book, *Missed Chances: Britain and Europe in the Twentieth Century* (1996), he bemoaned in choice prose the continuing capacity of British governments, like their predecessors, to miss chances to make the most of EEC membership. He wrote freely to those editors who would publish him. In his final appearance in print before he fell ill he foresaw Britain isolating itself from Europe and 'sleepwalking into international oblivion' (*Financial Times*, 8 April 2005). He published a memoir, *The Mandarin's Tale*, in 2002. At the end of his life he was deep into a major and probably revisionist history of Anglo-German relations. He died on 4 April 2006 at his home, 26 St Luke's Street, Kensington, London, of a chest infection, and was survived by his wife, Moya, and their children. WILLIAM NICOLL

Sources M. D. Kandiah, ed., *Britain and Europe* (1988) • C. O'Neill, *Britain's entry into the European Community* (2000) • R. Denman, *The mandarin's tale* (2002) • *Daily Telegraph* (8 April 2006) • *The Independent* (11 April 2006) • *The Times* (19 April 2006) • *The Guardian* (21 April 2006) • Burke, *Peerage* • *WW* (2006) • personal knowledge (2010) • private information (2010) • b. cert. • m. cert. • d. cert.

Likenesses photograph, 1970, Photoshot, London • photograph, repro. in Denman, *Mandarin's tale*, endpaper • portrait, priv. coll.

Wealth at death £2,028,171: probate, 20 July 2006, *CGPLA Eng. & Wales*

Denton, Sir Eric James (1923–2007), marine biologist and physiologist, was born on 30 September 1923 at 53 Denby Street, Bentley, Yorkshire, the only child of George Denton, a fitter at a colliery, later a grocer, and his wife, Mary Ann, *née* Ogden, who ran a dress shop. He won a scholarship to Doncaster grammar school and a state scholarship to St John's College, Cambridge, where he read physics for two years before joining the Telecommunications Research Establishment at Malvern in 1942. There he worked on radar technology and met Nancy Emily Wright, whom he married at Christ Church, Doncaster, on 19 December 1946. She was the daughter of Charles Henry Wright of Doncaster. They had a daughter, Susan Mary (*b.* 1948), and two sons, Andrew (*b.* 1950) and Christopher (*b.* 1954).

In the same year as his marriage Denton joined the biophysics group of the Nobel laureate A. V. Hill at University College, London. During this period he graduated BSc in physiology with first-class honours. Denton often remarked that this was the most important period in his career, as it allowed him to begin to apply physical principles to physiology—an approach that underpinned much of his subsequent career. In 1948 he gained a full lectureship at the University of Aberdeen, focusing his research on the physiology of vision. He spent eight years in teaching and research in Aberdeen before moving in 1956 to the Plymouth laboratory of the Marine Biological Association (MBA) as a physiologist. He became concurrently a Royal Society research professor at the University of Bristol in 1964.

The MBA provided the perfect environment for Denton's research endeavours, being one of the foremost physiological and marine biological laboratories and attracting world-class scientists, including the Nobel prize-winning squid physiologists Alan Hodgkin and Andrew Huxley, along with many others. Denton's research interests began to broaden further at Plymouth. His research on vision extended from the study of the visual pigments of vertebrates to obtaining a deeper understanding of the structure of the eyes, luminescent organs, and external reflective surfaces of fish. He greatly improved the understanding of camouflage in fish and how they use reflective scales that, in the light environment under the sea, enable them to render themselves largely invisible to predators. His research was punctuated with groundbreaking discoveries, such as the finding that a species of deep sea dragonfish could use a 'searchlight' to illuminate its prey. He went on to make major discoveries relating to buoyancy in fish and cephalopods. In his later researches he developed a fruitful collaboration with Sir John Gray (former secretary of the Medical Research Council) through which they applied a combination of physiological and theoretical approaches to deepen the understanding of how fish perceive sound, movement, and distance, and in particular how their anatomy allows particularly efficient coupling between the swim bladder and the ear. Denton's skills in the laboratory were matched by his enthusiasm for working at sea on research vessels like *Sarsia* and *Discovery*, which helped him to place his biophysical work into a broad biological and ecological context. It was his view that all scientific staff at the MBA should have experience of working at sea.

Denton was elected a fellow of the Royal Society and made ScD of Cambridge, both in 1964. He served as a council member and vice-president of the Royal Society, sat on many committees, and was a member of the royal commission on environmental pollution (1973–6). He was appointed CBE in 1974. Also in 1974 he became director of the MBA, taking on a substantial administrative load. He continued to develop the reputation of the MBA as a premier marine biological research laboratory, in particular making its facilities open to its many visitors, whom he regarded as being as important as the resident staff. His directorial style allowed scientists and visitors the freedom to explore the most interesting and exciting problems of the time and he engaged fully and enthusiastically with all researchers in Plymouth. He continued to carry out his own experiments, dividing his time between the laboratory and the director's office. Those who worked with him were struck by his desire for rigorous analysis and scientific discussion, driven by his natural curiosity. Coffee breaks would invariably turn into discussion sessions and he would simply, and often unexpectedly, drop into a laboratory or office to find out what was going on—and what had been discovered recently—from whoever was there. He was an extremely sociable individual and he and Nancy received many guests at their family home in St Germans, Cornwall.

Denton received a number of the highest academic accolades, the most notable of which were (both in 1987, the year of his retirement) the Zoological Society's Frink medal and the Royal Society's royal medal. He was also knighted in 1987 for services to marine biology. He was awarded the Japan international prize for biology in 1989. He carried on with his research as an honorary fellow of the MBA after his retirement for a number of years. The progression of Parkinson's disease made it increasingly difficult for him to continue and eventually to communicate. True to his character, however, he developed a keen scientific interest in the condition and invented numerous devices to allay the symptoms based on his increasing understanding of its neurological basis. His family cared for him in his final years and he died on 2 January 2007 at Poldhu Nursing Home, Poldhu Cove, near Helston, Cornwall. He was cremated at Bodmin crematorium in January 2007, and was survived by his wife, Nancy, and their three children. COLIN BROWNLEE

Sources annual reports, 1954–2007, Marine Biological Association of the UK · *Western Morning News* (5 Jan 2007) · *The Times* (15 Jan 2007); (20 Jan 2007) · *The Independent* (27 Jan 2007) · *The Guardian* (19 March 2007) · *Yorkshire Post* (7 April 2007) · *Memoirs FRS* (2009), 59–76 · personal notebooks, National Marine Biological Library, Plymouth · Burke, *Peerage* · *WW* (2007) · personal knowledge (2011) · private information (2011) · b. cert. · m. cert. · d. cert.

Archives National Marine Biological Library, Plymouth | CAC Cam., A. V. Hill MSS

Likenesses K. Howard, oils, National Marine Biological Library, Plymouth · obituary photographs · photographs, National Marine Biological Library, Plymouth

Wealth at death £388,987: probate, 17 July 2007, *CGPLA Eng. & Wales*

Dobrée, Georgina (1930–2008), clarinettist, was born on 8 January 1930 at 74 Sutherland Avenue, Maida Vale, London, the only child of Bonamy *Dobrée (1891–1974), literary scholar, and his wife, Gladys May Mabel (Valentine), *née* Brooke-Pechell (1894–1974), artist, author, and poet. She was brought up first at Mendham Priory, Harleston, Norfolk, and then from 1936 at Earls Colne, Essex. From an early age she studied violin and piano and when the Second World War broke out was evacuated to the United States to stay with friends of her parents. She attended the Peabody Conservatory in Baltimore, where she discarded her violin studies and began playing the clarinet, having found one by chance in the home of the people she was staying with, and discovering an immediate affinity for the instrument.

After returning to London at the end of the war Dobrée spent three years at the Royal Academy of Music (1946–8), studying piano under Harold Craxton and clarinet under George Anderson. In 1949 she won a scholarship offered by the French government to study in Paris with Gaston

Hamelin, principal clarinettist in the Orchestre Nationale. In the 1951 Hoveringham Festival she played in association with the Griller quartet, led by the violinist Sidney Griller. The following year she made her first broadcast from this festival for the BBC Third Programme. During the summer she travelled to Darmstadt and won the Kranichsteiner music prize for new music, returning to London in the autumn to take part in a series of lectures and recitals on twelve-tone music at Morley College, London's contemporary music hub in this era. Her concerts in London during the 1950s featured regular recitals for the Society for the Promotion of New Music and appearances with the McNaughton New Music Group. At Thea King's invitation she joined the Portia Wind Ensemble and later on created the Chantry Ensemble with the flautist William Bennett, who was succeeded by Patricia Lynden, and with the pianist Alexander Kelly. Elisabeth Lutyens dedicated her Fantasie Trio op. 55 (1963) to the ensemble. Among the many other works written for her was Gordon Jacob's Miniature Suite for clarinet and viola. Alexander Kelly was to remain her most regular pianist and in 1973 they gave a series of concerts in Leighton House, Holland Park, to celebrate twenty-one years of this partnership.

Dobrée was always aware of the Huguenot origins of her father, which perhaps explains her affinity with French music. She felt very much at home with the French style of clarinet playing and with French instruments but was also able to adapt to the more contemporary German sound. From 1953 to 1964 she appeared regularly in the Darmstadt Festival, where she performed the music of and worked with composers such as Peter Maxwell Davies, Olivier Messiaen, Luciano Berio, Karlheinz Stockhausen, and Pierre Boulez.

Dobrée started playing the basset horn in 1952 and it began to make an appearance in her programmes in 1957, when she performed the sonata for piano and basset horn by Franz Danzi and, with Thea King, the Mendelssohn Konzertstücke op. 114. She recorded the Mendelssohn piece for Hyperion with Thea King and also edited this music in the 1990s. Meanwhile her performing career continued with such momentum and vitality through the 1950s and 1960s that it would be easy to overlook her other activities and achievements. Her contributions in researching, editing, and performing early repertoire for clarinets and basset horn can reasonably be said to have begun with Johann Melchior Molter's concertos for D clarinet, recorded for EMI in 1968. From making this recording the idea came to form her own record company, Chantry Records, which continued until 1985. Eight vinyl recordings were reissued on compact disc by Clarinet Classics in 1995.

From the late 1960s Dobrée also became increasingly in demand as a teacher and began this aspect of her career as clarinet tutor at the Watford School of Music. She was subsequently professor of clarinet at the Royal Academy of Music, London, from 1967 until 1986. Editorial commissions came from publishers such as Schott, Musica Rara, Oxford University Press, and Chester Music. Alongside the Chantry record label, she had her own publishing company, Chantry Publications, which was transferred to Emerson Edition in 1999. In that year she also completed one of her last editions, a collection of four French clarinet works published by Kevin Mayhew and consisting of clarinet and piano sonata no. 12 by Jean Xavier Lefèvre, *Première Rhapsodie* and *Petite Pièce* by Claude Debussy, and the sonata op. 167 by Camille Saint-Saëns. She also continued to extend the contemporary repertoire for the basset horn in the 1990s, commissioning new works from a number of British and eastern European composers including Paul Drayton, David Gow, Sarah Rodgers, Petr Pokorný, Jaroslav Rybář, Karel Janovický, Marta Jiráčková, Alois Piňos, and Iris Szeghová.

Georgina Dobrée was notable not only for the mastery of the instruments that she played but also for her initiation of new and discovery of old works that enriched the repertoire for clarinet and basset horn players and listeners. She was a meticulous musicologist, dedicated to the furthering of scholarly information about the instruments she loved, as well as a fine musician and in great demand as a teacher. She was an indefatigable ambassador for the clarinet and basset horn in both Europe and the USA, and her home in north London was a magnetic hub, often becoming the base for visiting instrumentalists and composers. There were regular parties for colleagues and friends to meet the foreign visitors, and to enjoy her legendary hospitality. Latterly she suffered from Alzheimer's disease and moved to a nursing home in Hitchin, Hertfordshire. In early April 2008 she suffered a fractured left femur and underwent surgery; she died of a chest infection at the Lister Hospital, Stevenage, on 27 April 2008. She was unmarried. GERALDINE ALLEN

Sources *Music and Musicians* (Dec 1953) · G. Allen, 'Georgina Dobrée: a musician of her time', *Clarinet and Saxophone*, 17/3 (autumn 1992) · *Clarinet and Saxophone*, 33/3 (autumn 2008) · *The Guardian* (9 May 2008); (17 May 2008) · personal knowledge (2012) · private information (2012) · b. cert. · d. cert.

Wealth at death £295,000: probate, 26 Aug 2008, *CGPLA Eng. & Wales*

Doll, Sir (William) Richard Shaboe (1912–2005), physician and epidemiologist, was born at 15 Park Road, Hampton Hill, Middlesex, on 28 October 1912, the elder son of Henry William Doll, physician and surgeon, and his wife, Amy Kathleen, *née* Shaboe, concert pianist. He was educated at Westminster School, where he showed a flair for mathematics and considered studying it at university. Instead he studied medicine and by chance became an epidemiologist—an ideal vocation for a numerate doctor with a social conscience, since it permitted him to apply his talents to major public health problems around the world.

Early influences Much of Doll's upbringing at home was by his Victorian grandmother. When he left school in 1931 he was turning away from religion and towards pacifism and socialism, influenced by the First World War and by the growing numbers of demoralized unemployed. As a medical student at St Thomas's Hospital, London (1931–7), he delivered babies in the slums of Lambeth and was appalled by the living conditions, malnutrition, and poverty. He became increasingly aware that much disease and premature death could be prevented by social change. He helped organize the St Thomas's Socialist Society, joined the Communist Party, and visited Soviet Russia (and, for different reasons, Nazi Germany). He participated in the Jarrow march in 1936, a mass protest against unemployment, providing first aid to the marchers, and energetically helped raise funds for medical aid to the republicans in the Spanish Civil War.

Soon after Doll qualified, the Second World War began. By then he had already predicted and accepted the necessity of war with Nazi Germany and had volunteered for the Royal Army Medical Corps, with which he served throughout the war. Three days after the outbreak of hostilities he went to France as medical officer to a regular battalion, the First Loyals. He treated and helped evacuate many wounded through the chaotic retreat to Dunkirk, despite sustained shelling and air attack, taking charge when other officers were lost, and leading men to safety. In 1941 he was sent to Egypt, travelling via the Cape (with Archie Cochrane), and served as medical officer in a Cairo infectious disease ward and then on a hospital ship in the Mediterranean that was closely involved with the Salerno landings. He developed renal tuberculosis and was repatriated in 1944; the kidney was removed, and he recovered.

He met his future wife, Joan Mary Faulkner (1913–2001), who was at the time married to Hugh Charles Faulkner, at a meeting of communist doctors. She was the formidably intelligent daughter of Charles Duncan Blatchford (a son in Blatchford and Sons, artificial limb manufacturers) and Susan Margherita, *née* Rota (a forceful Italian who had grown up in the Lambeth area, and eventually lived with Richard and Joan for many years). Like Doll Joan was committed to political change, only partly to improve health, and both campaigned for the establishment of a national health service in Britain, in 1948 jointly writing a pamphlet entitled *Humanise our Hospitals*. They remained communists (although increasingly uneasily so, after the 1948 Lysenko affair) for some twenty years, but a year after the Soviet invasion of Hungary in 1956 and Khrushchov's secret speech describing the realities of the Stalin era they resigned, and came to accept the impracticality and undesirability of centrally planned command economies.

Doll proposed marriage to Joan on 8 May 1945 (VE-day, when war ended in Europe). She divorced, and they eventually married on 4 October 1949, at Kensington register office, Doll thereby becoming stepfather to her son, Tim. As Joan could not have further children they wanted to adopt, but the Dolls were atheists and at that time adoption agencies required evidence of the Christian commitment of prospective adoptive parents. With advice from the British Humanist Association they set up the Agnostics' Adoption Society. It was initially based in their home, and the Dolls used their own funds to help hire its first social worker. The society grew considerably, changing its name in 1964 to the Independent Adoption Society and expanding its remit. The Dolls themselves adopted two children, Nicholas in 1954 and Catherine in 1956. Initially to help with child and grandmother care, Isabelle (Steve) Sutherland kept house for the Dolls for four decades.

At the suggestion of Joan, by then a rising administrative star at the Medical Research Council (MRC), Doll began his research at the Central Middlesex Hospital with the eminent gastroenterologist Francis Avery Jones, studying peptic ulcer, and conducting perhaps the first factorial randomized clinical trial. Although Doll soon moved elsewhere he was considerably influenced by Avery Jones's scientific temperament, and continued to do some research and clinical work in gastroenterology at the Central Middlesex until moving to Oxford in 1969.

Concurrently Doll (along with several other post-war

Sir (William) Richard Shaboe Doll (1912–2005), by Michael Crabtree, 2004

doctors who wanted to help make a better world) began to study medical statistics at the London School of Hygiene and Tropical Medicine under an extraordinarily influential epidemiologist and teacher, Austin (Tony) Bradford Hill, just as Hill was introducing the medical profession to randomization. In 1947 Hill was asked by the MRC to investigate the reasons for the rising mortality from lung cancer in the UK. Hill had observed the quality of Doll's research with Avery Jones and offered him a research post, seeking new causes of lung cancer. Doll and Hill's long collaboration discovered the main hazards of smoking, helped change the ways in which causes of disease would be investigated and understood, and greatly strengthened the discipline of epidemiology.

Smoking, lung cancer, and other diseases The mortality attributed to lung cancer in the UK (among people of a given age) had been increasing rapidly for decades. It was known by 1947 that part of this increase was an artefact, caused by the increasing ability of doctors to recognize the disease. Such artefacts should, however, have affected men and women similarly, yet the increase was far steeper in men. These lung cancer trends did not attract much attention until after the Second World War. Many then blamed increasing atmospheric pollution, perhaps from coal smoke, and Doll himself originally thought the increase might well be due chiefly to occupational factors, or to the tarring of roads, as there were known animal carcinogens in tar.

The results of Doll and Hill's first study were, however, clear: the one consistent difference between lung cancer patients (cases) and other patients (controls) was that almost all of the lung cancer patients had smoked. Doll and Hill published their conclusion in 1950 that smoking was 'a factor, and an important factor, in the production of carcinoma of the lung' (R. Doll and A. B. Hill, 'Smoking and carcinoma of the lung: preliminary report', *BMJ*, 1950, 2.746). Four American studies also published in 1950 (including one of comparable size, by Ernst L. Wynder and Evarts A. Graham) independently found the same association, as had two smaller German studies published in 1939 and 1943 that had been largely or wholly overlooked in England and America. Doll and Hill's second report, published in 1952, cited all these American, German, and British studies as being mutually supportive (and Doll consistently cited all of them in his historical perspectives written in the 1980s and 1990s). Extraordinarily, even with such strong evidence so clearly presented from case-control studies, most of the medical and scientific community in the early 1950s, many of whom themselves smoked, still did not accept that smoking could cause lung cancer, and argued that there must be other explanations for the association.

Although Doll and Hill understood that there was already proof beyond reasonable doubt that smoking was an important cause of lung cancer, they also understood that further research was needed, partly to help convince sceptics and partly to see whether smoking also caused other diseases. In 1951 they enrolled 40,000 British doctors into a new type of study, asking them about their smoking habits and then following them prospectively over many years to see what the doctors died of. On 26 June 1954 the *BMJ* published the first prospective results, confirming that lung cancer rates were much higher in smokers, and increased with the amount smoked. In 1956 Doll and Hill reported that smokers also had higher death rates from heart disease, chronic lung disease, and many other conditions. In 1957 the British (because of Doll and Hill) and Dutch were the first governments to accept officially that smoking caused lung cancer; now, all governments do so. Doll succeeded Hill as director of the MRC statistics unit in 1962, and their ten-year findings appeared in 1964. By then competent scientific doubt about smoking as a cause of lung cancer was past, and a consensus was emerging that smoking also killed even more people by other diseases.

Doll continued for fifty years to follow meticulously every British doctor he had originally recruited in 1951 who still lived in Britain. Richard Peto, statistician and (eventually) epidemiologist, joined Doll in 1967 and collaborated closely on the prospective study of doctors, and much else, until Doll's death in 2005. Over these decades the epidemic of smoking-related deaths in Britain (and elsewhere) was evolving in complex ways. On 26 June 2004 the *BMJ* published the fifty-year follow-up, showing that persistent cigarette smokers born in the first few decades of the twentieth century died, on average, ten years earlier than otherwise similar non-smokers. Importantly, they also showed that stopping smoking was remarkably effective at reducing the risk of dying prematurely. By then the situation in Britain had been transformed. Doll lived long enough to see widespread cessation of smoking in Britain, and to see the proportion of the male population killed by tobacco before the age of seventy fall from 20 per cent at 1970 death rates (half of all male deaths in middle age) to just 5 per cent at 2005 rates. In 1970 British men had the worst rates in the world of premature death from tobacco, but over the next few decades they had the world's greatest decrease in such deaths.

Strengthening epidemiology and improving public health Although best known for his work on smoking, Doll made an extraordinary range of other contributions to epidemiology and public health. Before the 1950s most epidemiological studies had been of infectious diseases, often with a relatively fast-acting organism as a necessary cause. Different concepts were needed to study non-infectious causes of disease, some of which, such as smoking, took decades to have their full effect on risk. Moreover, the fact that many people could smoke yet not develop lung cancer and that a few with lung cancer were non-smokers troubled many with traditional views on how to attribute and understand causation. Hill and Doll helped introduce new guidelines for assessing causality—based, among other things, on the presence of a dose-response relationship and the time sequence of events. By 1950 the leading causes of death in developed countries (heart disease, stroke, and cancer) were no longer the infectious diseases, and subsequent investigations into their causes relied heavily on the criteria clearly articulated by Hill and Doll. Furthermore, much of the proper understanding of the relative merits of different types of epidemiological study design can be traced to Hill and Doll's careful discussion of the implications of their various studies. Doll's influential Rock Carling lecture, published as a monograph in 1967 entitled *Prevention of Cancer: Pointers from Epidemiology*, summarized the understanding that had by then developed of the avoidability of each major type of cancer.

In the late 1950s Doll embarked on a series of studies with Michael Court Brown of the long-term effects of medical exposures to moderate doses of X-rays (by following up people who had been treated with X-rays to alleviate spinal disease). Although heavy exposure was known to cause cancer they demonstrated that moderate doses could also cause cancer, particularly leukaemia, establishing for the first time within one study a dose-response relationship between radiation and cancer. For the rest of his life Doll collaborated extensively in several quantitative epidemiological studies of low-dose radiation of various types.

Doll also instigated successful studies of cancer in the coal gasification, nickel refining, and asbestos industries. In 1955 he completed a study (in collaboration with the company) of the mortality of men who had worked at Turner Brothers Asbestos in Yorkshire. The striking results, with a tenfold increase of lung cancer in heavily exposed workers, led the company's lawyers to attempt to suppress the research, claiming the military importance of asbestos, the irrelevance of long-past occupational exposures, and private ownership of the employment records. Despite legal threats Doll and Hill promptly published their findings, after which the company agreed to continue indefinitely to provide Doll with current and past employment records for independent analysis, which were eventually used to demonstrate a significant continuing hazard.

Soon after the contraceptive pill became available in 1960 reports of adverse effects, particularly venous thrombosis, began to appear. Doll immediately realized that systematic epidemiological investigations were needed to obtain reliable evidence about the effects of the pill on health and helped others initiate and interpret them. He continued until 2005 to be closely involved in studies of the effects of the pill on cancer, participating actively in worldwide meta-analyses of all relevant epidemiological studies. These eventually showed that there was only a small and transient increase in the incidence of breast cancer, which was outweighed by a lifelong decrease in that of ovarian cancer.

Doll also showed, more clearly than anyone, that cancer arose, sometimes over a period of many decades, from a combination of nature, nurture, and luck. During the 1960s he was a key figure in bringing together evidence from cancer registries in five continents that showed that each type of cancer that was common in one population was rare in another. He argued that these differences were not chiefly genetic, so wherever one type of cancer was common, it did not have to be. In 1981 Doll and Peto set about quantifying the avoidable causes of cancer in countries such as the UK and USA, presenting their findings in a report to the American Congressional Office of Technology Assessment that was published in the *Journal of the National Cancer Institute* (vol. 66, 1981, 1191–308). They found that the hazards of smoking were more than twice the sum of every other reliably known cancer hazard, and that man-made environmental pollutants played a relatively minor role.

Doll made major contributions to epidemiological methodology and disease prevention for more than fifty years, and played a central role in strengthening public health institutions and supporting the careers and inspiring the work of later generations of epidemiologists and medical statisticians. He tried to help whoever sought his advice, and made a point of finding time to provide concise and constructive comments on their research plans and scientific reports.

Expanding medical education and research in Oxford Doll moved to Oxford in 1969 as regius professor of medicine, the most senior medical post in the university. He quickly set about expanding the medical school and enhancing the quality of research. He made a series of new professorial appointments, broadened the scope of the medical curriculum, and helped his successors transform the faculty into one of the top medical institutions in the world.

While regius professor Doll also managed to found Green College (since 2008 Green Templeton College). This was a difficult task, requiring considerable diplomatic skills not only to raise money but also to get Oxford medical students and the university to agree to a new graduate college that would initially specialize in one main subject, medicine. Doll took early retirement to become the first warden of Green College. He and Joan (who had by then retired, but had been the first woman with a senior MRC position) treated the students, staff, and fellows as their extended family, from which they got much interest and pleasure.

The twenty-five years after Doll's retirement in 1979 as regius professor were extraordinarily productive. He wrote, travelled, and lectured, and collaborated with many others in new research on tobacco, alcohol, radiation, breast cancer, and vascular disease. Half a century earlier he had helped Bradford Hill to establish randomized trials, and was delighted to see the clarity with which large-scale randomized evidence could answer important questions.

Until weeks before his death Doll continued working every day in the Cancer Epidemiology Unit (directed since 1989 by Valerie Beral) or the Clinical Trial Service Unit (co-directed since 1985 by Rory Collins and Richard Peto). In June 2005 both units moved into the newly built Richard Doll Building, devoted to large-scale population studies of the causes, prevention, and treatment of cancers, heart attacks, strokes, and other major diseases. Doll worked in the building only briefly before his death, admiring its spaciousness, but still more the large research projects that it was already facilitating.

International recognition and influence The importance of Doll's work was soon recognized throughout the world.

He won many awards, including the United Nations award for cancer research in 1962, and was the first recipient of the General Motors cancer research prize in 1979. He was elected a fellow of the Royal Society in 1966, was its vice-president in 1970, and received the society's royal medal in 1986. He was knighted in 1971 and made a Companion of Honour in 1996. He received numerous honorary doctorates and fellowships, both in the UK and elsewhere.

Doll's integrity, courtesy, sharp mind, and precise use of language made him an effective chairman of many committees and an impartial adviser to various government departments and industries. His strategic aims in such work were to ensure that the epidemiological evidence would be described accurately, distinguishing between established and unproven claims, and to ensure that employment records would be kept and analysed in ways that would ensure that any real hazards were discovered sooner rather than later, and that mistaken claims of hazard or safety would be minimized. He was open about his dealings with industry, received no retainers, and always gave away whatever consultancy fees or honoraria he received, usually to Green College. He also gave away some of the prizes he was awarded. He was regularly invited to deliver major lectures, and in the last year of his life he lectured in seven different countries on five different continents.

Personal qualities Elegant and well-mannered, Doll thought, wrote, and spoke clearly, choosing his words carefully; his publications, although concerned with factual matters, were often a pleasure to read. Having lived through the 1930s he understood how greatly medical science in general, and epidemiology in particular, could improve people's lives. Thus motivated, he worked efficiently, and for long hours. He found good epidemiology beautiful and intellectually satisfying, considering himself to have been extraordinarily lucky professionally.

Many found Doll's apparent severity daunting, but behind the sometimes austere exterior was a mischievous interior that enjoyed nonconformity, and his wit was delightful. He dressed immaculately, and wore vivid ties in later life that he enjoyed people noticing. He and Joan loved and depended on each other, and had similar professional values. For two years after she died in 2001 grief predominated in private, but in his last two years he had more internal peace, and retained his intellect and humour. He liked to say that old people should take risks, and in his ninety-third year he rode on a camel in the Arabian desert, flew in a glider, and climbed a jungle tree in Australia.

Doll had a remarkable ability to interpret, assimilate, and remember population-based evidence and to put into perspective the major and minor avoidable causes of disease. This was not a theoretical exercise; he was conscious that his conclusions must not be wrong, as people's lives and livelihoods were at stake. The more closely people worked with Doll, the more they respected him. His wide experience, careful judgement, integrity, and rigour—all obvious to those who worked with him—meant that he was rarely wrong, and never stubbornly wrong. He was one of the most important medical scientists of the twentieth century. He died with dignity at the John Radcliffe Hospital, Oxford, on 24 July 2005, of heart failure, and was survived by his adopted children.

As a result of the twentieth-century epidemiological studies of smoking, of which Doll's were among the most influential, many millions of premature deaths had already been prevented by the time he died; according to the World Health Organization, hundreds of millions of deaths from tobacco would be prevented during the twenty-first century. Doll's own words (of 1994) are engraved on his memorial stone in the Richard Doll Building:

> Death in old age is inevitable but death before old age is not. In previous centuries 70 years used to be regarded as humanity's allotted span of life and only about one in five lived to such an age. Nowadays, however, for non-smokers in Western countries, the situation is reversed; only about one in five will die before 70 and the non-smoker death rates are still decreasing, offering the promise, at least in developed countries, of a world where death before 70 is uncommon. But, for this promise to be properly realised, ways must be found to limit the vast damage now being done by tobacco and to bring home, to not only the many millions of people in developed countries but also the far larger populations elsewhere, the extent to which those who continue to smoke are shortening their expectation of life by so doing.

RICHARD PETO and VALERIE BERAL

Sources R. Doll, 'Experiences of a battalion medical officer in the retreat to Dunkirk, parts I–V', *BMJ*, 300 (1990), 1183–6; 1256–9; 1324–8; 1385–7; 1449–52 · G. Phillips, *Best foot forward: Chas A. Blatchford & Sons Ltd, artificial limb specialists* (1990) · R. Doll, 'Uncovering the effects of smoking: historical perspective', *Statistical Methods in Medical Research*, 7 (1998), 87–117 · R. Doll, 'Tobacco–a medical history', educational videotape produced by J. Watt, distributed by Victoria Cancer Council, 1999 · *The Observer* (7 July 2002); (24 April 2005) · S. Darby, 'A conversation with Richard Doll', *Epidemiology*, 14 (2003), 375–9 · R. Doll, 'Fisher and Bradford Hill: their personal impact', *International Journal of Epidemiology*, 32 (2003), 929–31 · C. Cook, 'Oral history—Sir Richard Doll', *Journal of Public Health*, 26 (2004), 327–36 [full transcript held by the Faculty of Public Health] · A. Wagstaff, 'Richard Doll: science will always win in the end', *Cancer World* (Dec 2004), 28–34 · *The Times* (25 July 2005); (13 Aug 2005) · *Daily Telegraph* (25 July 2005) · *The Guardian* (25 July 2005); (13 Aug 2005); (25 Aug 2005) · *The Independent* (26 July 2005) · *New York Times* (26 July 2005) · *BMJ*, 331/7511 (2005), 295 [and additional website material] · *Tobacco Control*, 14 (2005), 289–90 · *The Lancet*, 366 (2005), 448 · *Nature*, 438 (2005), 41 · R. Peto, 'Sir Richard Doll, 1912–2005', *Cancer Research UK Scientific Yearbook, 2004–2005* (2005), 6–9 · R. Peto, 'Nature, nurture, and luck: Richard Doll, who made sense of the causes of cancer', *Oxford Today*, Michaelmas term (2005), 13 · L. Kinlen, 'Sir Richard Doll, epidemiologist: a personal reminiscence, with a selected bibliography', *British Journal of Cancer*, 93 (2005), 963–6 · J. M. Samet and F. E. Speizer, 'Sir Richard Doll', *American Journal of Epidemiology*, 164 (2006), 95–100 · R. Wakeford, 'Letter to the editor re. secret ties to industry and conflicting interests in cancer research', *American Journal of Industrial Medicine*, 50 (2007), 239–40 · C. Keating, *Smoking kills: the revolutionary life of Richard Doll* (c.2009) · *Munk's Roll* online, vol. 12, www.rcplondon.ac.uk/heritage/munksroll/munk_details.asp?ID=5595, 9 Aug 2008 · *Plarr's Lives of the Fellows* online, http://livesonline.rcseng.ac.uk/biogs/E000163b.htm, 9 Aug 2008 · www.deathsfromsmoking.net, 9 Aug 2008 · *WW* (2005) · Burke, *Peerage* · personal knowledge (2009) · private information (2009) · b. cert. · m. cert. · d. cert.

Archives Wellcome L., papers | UCL, L. S. Penrose papers · Wellcome L., Sir Ernst Chain papers
Likenesses G. Argent Studio, two photographs, 1977–86, RS · A. Newman, bromide print, 1978 (*Regius professors*), NPG · T. Stubley, sanguine, exh. Royal Society of Portrait Painters 1984, Green Templeton College, Oxford · photograph, 1987, PA Photos, London · N. Sinclair, bromide print, 1993, NPG · N. Sinclair, bromide print, 1994, NPG · A. di Stefano, oils, 1996, NPG · photograph, 1997, Photoshot, London · photographs, 1998–2005, Camera Press, London · M. Crabtree, photograph, *c.*2004, Troika Photos; repro. in www.deathsfromsmoking.net [*see illus.*] · R. Judges, four photographs, 2004, Rex Features, London · T. Stubley, portrait, St Catherine's College, Oxford · F. L. T. Tolkien, bronze bust, Green Templeton College, Oxford · obituary photographs
Wealth at death £2,385,461: probate, 24 Jan 2006, *CGPLA Eng. & Wales*

Donaldson, John Francis, **Baron Donaldson of Lymington** (**1920–2005**), judge, was born on 6 October 1920 at 6 King Street, St Marylebone, London, the son of Malcolm *Donaldson (1884–1973), consultant gynaecologist, and his first wife, Evelyn Helen Marguerite, *née* Gilroy. He was educated at Charterhouse School and at Trinity College, Cambridge, where he obtained a lower second-class degree in law. He became secretary of debates in the Cambridge Union and acted as chairman of the Federation of University Conservative and Unionist Associations. Called up in 1941, he served with the Royal Signals and the guards armoured divisional signals for the remainder of the Second World War, rising to the rank of captain. It was during the war that he met (Dorothy) Mary Warwick [*see* Donaldson, Dame (Dorothy) Mary, Lady Donaldson of Lymington (1921–2003)], who was then working as a nurse. She later became the first woman to be lord mayor of London, in 1983. They had two daughters, Margaret-Ann (*b.* 1946) and Jennifer Mary (*b.* 1948), and a son, Michael (*b.* 1950). In 1945–6 Donaldson worked in the allied military government of Schleswig-Holstein before being demobilized with the rank of lieutenant-colonel.

Donaldson was called to the bar in 1946 as a Harmsworth scholar at Middle Temple. He joined the chambers of Henry Willink at 3 Essex Court, which specialized in shipping, marine insurance, and banking. There he built up a thriving commercial practice and initiated his lifelong enthusiasm for maritime law, perhaps arising from his love of sailing. He was a joint editor of *Lowndes and Rudolf on General Average* for the eighth, ninth, and tenth editions (1955–75). He found time to take an active part in local politics and was an Independent Ratepayer councillor in Croydon between 1949 and 1953. He was also a member of the Bar Council from 1956 to 1961. He took silk in 1961 and was appointed a judge of the queen's bench division in 1966, on the recommendation of Lord Gardiner. One of his early decisions was *Baker* v. *Willoughby* (1969), on the allocation of damages between successive tortfeasors.

Donaldson had taken an early interest in the reform of industrial relations, contributing to the influential *A Giant's Strength*, published in 1958 by the Inns of Court Conservative Association. Edward Heath's Conservative government, elected in 1970, was pledged to take action against trade-union power. This included restraints on the

John Francis Donaldson, Baron Donaldson of Lymington (1920–2005), by unknown photographer, 1992

right to strike and a legal framework for settling disputes over unfair dismissal. Donaldson assisted in drafting the Industrial Relations Act 1971. This complex legislation established a National Industrial Relations Court, and Donaldson became its first (and only) president. His vision was strongly managerial. The court would be informal, with no wigs or gowns, and would welcome an early opportunity of involvement in the hope it could nip disputes in the bud. As he used to boast, it was 'the fastest court in the west'. In characteristic fashion he issued a *Presidential Statement* (1972) to mark the opening of the court:

> Once the court and each party knows what the essence of the dispute is about, arrangements will be made for a speedy investigation of the dispute. At this stage procedures will differ according to circumstances, but a common procedure will be to invite the parties to an informal meeting with the court at which the best method of hearing and determining the issues can be selected. At such a meeting it will be possible to find out what are the real issues—what the case is really about—and to do so much more quickly, cheaply and effectively than by a lengthy exchange of formal documents.

Donaldson cherished the independence of his presidency. Years later he told the House of Lords about an encounter with Robert Carr, Edward Heath's employment secretary:

> [Carr] asked me, 'To whom are you responsible as President?' I understood him to be referring to the National Industrial Relations Court. He said, 'I take it that you are responsible to the Lord Chief Justice'. I said, 'Certainly not'. He said, 'Then,

to the Lord Chancellor'. I said, 'Certainly not. I am responsible solely to my conscience and to the law'. (*Hansard 5L*, 596.1149, 28 Jan 1999)

As the court's president, Donaldson was exposed to attack as the government's personal instrument in curbing trade unionism. Matters quickly came to a head with a series of disputes over containerization in the docks. In *Heatons Transport (St Helens) Ltd* v. *T&GWU* (1972) Donaldson's court fined the union for the 'unofficial' action of its shop stewards in blacking container depots. That decision was overturned on appeal, Lord Denning holding that the stewards' actions were not the union's responsibility since they had not been authorized by the national executive. Donaldson immediately told the lord chief justice, Lord Widgery, that he could not continue as president if the Denning decision was allowed to stand since it would create individual martyrs. Before the matter could be resolved, five London dockers refused to obey an injunction to cease unlawful picketing at a depot. Donaldson felt he had no option but to gaol them for contempt. Predictably, London dockers and print workers went on strike in support of the 'Pentonville five'. Within days the House of Lords had overturned the Court of Appeal decision in *Heatons*, clearing the way for the intervention of the official solicitor and the dockers' release. Donaldson was embroiled in fresh controversy in 1973, when he ordered sequestration of the funds of the Amalgamated Union of Engineering Workers for refusing to call off a strike at a small Surrey engineering factory. An early day motion was signed by 182 Labour MPs calling Donaldson's action 'an act of political prejudice and partiality' and urging that he be sacked (*The Times*, 4 Dec 1973).

The Labour government elected in 1974 made repeal of the 1971 act a priority. His presidency abolished, Donaldson returned to the High Court. He officiated in some prominent criminal trials, notably those of the 'Guildford four' in 1975 and the 'Maguire seven' in 1976. These were high-profile miscarriages of justice, in which police witnesses had lied and forensic evidence favourable to the defence had been suppressed, though it was more than a decade before the miscarriages were acknowledged; Sir John May, appointed by the government to inquire into the Maguire trial, found in 1990 that Donaldson had misunderstood and mishandled critical evidence.

When Margaret Thatcher came to office in 1979 she promoted Donaldson to lord justice almost immediately, and in 1982 he succeeded Lord Denning as master of the rolls. He soon showed himself to be a champion of reform of civil procedure in the interests of closer case management and greater efficiency. He introduced skeleton arguments in civil appeals, and the practice of handing down judgements, which had until then routinely been read out in open court. He initiated the publication of an annual report on the work of the Court of Appeal. In 1988 he was made a life peer, as Baron Donaldson of Lymington.

It was characteristic that, given the opportunity, Donaldson favoured the extension of judicial review jurisdiction to cover a wide range of regulatory bodies. In *R* v. *Panel on Take-overs and Mergers, ex parte Datafin Plc* (1987) the Court of Appeal extended the supervisory jurisdiction of the High Court to any body exercising what were in effect public powers judicially when the source of its power was not purely contractual. His ruling in *Sutcliffe* v. *Pressdram Ltd* (1991) set the trend towards limiting jury awards in libel cases, regarded as a considerable fetter on press freedom. In *M* v. *Home Office* (1992), where the Conservative home secretary, Kenneth Baker, ignored an order to return a man deported to Zaire in defiance of an undertaking given to the Divisional Court, Donaldson held him personally in contempt. Donaldson held that ministers and civil servants were accountable to the law and to the courts for their personal actions and could be proceeded against for contempt of court. 'It would be a black day for the rule of law and the liberty of the subject if ministers were not accountable to the courts for their personal actions', he said (*Daily Telegraph*, 2 Sept 2005). It demonstrated his boldness as a constitutional innovator and his reluctance to see the court's powers in its own sphere fettered or diminished. He displayed a similar boldness in *X* v. *Morgan-Grampian* (1991), where the appellant journalist was defying a court order to name the source of his story. Donaldson refused to hear the appellant while he was in contempt of court. The decision was subsequently reversed by the House of Lords, which found that the contemner was entitled to challenge the court's jurisdiction to make the order.

Donaldson retired as master of the rolls in 1992. He was called in to undertake a number of important marine inquiries, writing *Safer Ships: Cleaner Seas* (1994), a report on the prevention of maritime pollution, examining the sinking of the oil tanker MV *Braer* in 1993 and the loss of the *Aegean Sea* the previous year. In 1995 he was asked to investigate the disappearance of the bulk carrier MV *Derbyshire* off the Japanese coast in 1980. It was his firm advocacy of an expedition to find the wreckage of the carrier and discover why it had sunk that eventually, in 2000, resolved what had been a great mystery for some twenty years. Donaldson's review of salvage and intervention following the *Sea Empress* disaster in 1996 uncovered serious deficiencies in the provision for dealing with oil spillages at sea and led to important changes in the supervision of oil rigs and tankers.

After 1997, with a Labour majority in the Commons apparently bent on abolishing hunting with dogs, Donaldson became exercised about the role of the House of Lords. In 2000 he introduced the Parliament Acts (Amendment) Bill in the Lords on the premise that the Parliament Act of 1949 was of doubtful validity. He worried that the House of Commons might use the Parliament Acts to extend the life of a parliament beyond five years. One of his last speeches, in February 2004, was a trenchant critique of proposals to abolish the office of lord chancellor and replace the judicial committee of the House of Lords with a supreme court.

Standing more than six feet tall, and bespectacled, Donaldson was known for sucking boiled sweets in court and wearing his judicial wig at an angle. His hobbies were sailing and do-it-yourself: 'He's a dreadful embarrassment in people's houses', his wife said. 'He fishes out his penknife and tightens loose screws' (*Daily Telegraph*, 2 Sept 2005). He died suddenly on 31 August 2005 at his home, 5 Kingsfield, Lymington, Hampshire, after a heart attack. He was survived by his three children.

MAUREEN SPENCER and JOHN SPENCER

Sources J. Donaldson, 'Lessons from the industrial court', *Law Quarterly Review*, 181 (1975) • *The Times* (1 Sept 2005); (2 Sept 2005) • *Daily Telegraph* (2 Sept 2005) • *The Guardian* (3 Sept 2005) • *The Independent* (3 Sept 2005) • J. Spencer and M. Spencer, 'The judge as "political advisor": behind the scenes at the National Industrial Relations Court', *Journal of Law and Society*, 33/2 (June 2006), 199–220 • bench book entry, Middle Temple, London • *WW* (2005) • Burke, *Peerage* • b. cert. • m. cert. • d. cert.

Archives SOUND BL NSA, current affairs recording

Likenesses photographs, 1961–96, Photoshot, London • W. Bird, bromide print, 1967, NPG • photograph, 1992, Photoshot, London [*see illus.*] • obituary photographs

Wealth at death £686,624: probate, 29 Nov 2006, *CGPLA Eng. & Wales*

Donaldson, (Charles) William [Willie; *pseud.* Henry Root] (**1935–2005**), writer and impresario, was born in Sunningdale, Berkshire, on 4 January 1935, the son of Charles Glen Donaldson (1904–1956), shipowner, and his wife, Elizabeth (Betty), *née* Stockley (*d.* 1955). His father was co-chairman of the Donaldson Line, a family shipping firm established as Donaldson Brothers in 1854, which owned a fleet of nineteen passenger and cargo ships. Although the company was based in Glasgow he had moved south five years after marrying Elizabeth Stockley in 1927. For complicated psychological, and less complicated comical reasons, Donaldson was later to portray his mother as an overbearing snob. The truth was rather different: she was a loving, occasionally indulgent mother to her two children, Eleanor Jane and Charles (as Donaldson was known at the time).

From 1942 Donaldson attended Woodcote House preparatory school, where he became a boarder in 1944 at the age of nine. By the time he went to Winchester College in 1948 he had become known as William, or Willie. He was remembered by old Wykehamists with varying degrees of fondness as a restless and subversive figure who had great charm but also a well-developed talent for disruption. When Lord Wavell inspected the college corps, it was Donaldson who right-turned and quick-marched, while the rest of his house platoon turned left. He did his national service in the submarines, developing an intense friendship with a fellow old Wykehamist, Julian Mitchell, with whom he shared a passion for ballet, the arts, and intellectual discussion. Mitchell already knew that he wanted to be a writer; Donaldson's ambition was to be a ballet critic. In April 1955 the two sailors travelled to Paris vowing to lose their virginity. After a week the mission was accomplished after a fashion but, on his return to London, Donaldson was summoned to Sunningdale. There he was told that his mother had been killed in a car crash near Winchester. The tragedy was particularly devastating to Donaldson's father who effectively gave up on life,

(**Charles) William Donaldson** [*pseud.* Henry Root] (**1935–2005**), by Sam Barker, 2005

staying at home and drinking heavily. He died less than two years later.

Now rich, Donaldson went to Magdalene College, Cambridge, where his most notable achievement was to set up and edit, with Julian Mitchell, who was at Oxford, a literary magazine called *Gemini* whose contributors included Sylvia Plath, Ted Hughes, and Geoffrey Hill. Meanwhile his personal life was becoming complicated. While attending Ascot and smart parties in the expected way, even becoming engaged to a beautiful, tennis-playing débutante, Sonia Iris Avory (daughter of Edward Raymond Avory, stockbroker), in his last year at Cambridge, he spent increasing amounts of time in the company of the girls he was truly attracted to—those who plied their trade around Curzon Street. 'I knew that I was a pervert when I was twenty', he said years later (Blacker, 48). He nevertheless married Sonia Avory, at Holy Trinity Church, Brompton, on 17 July 1958. She was then aged twenty.

On leaving Cambridge, Donaldson became a theatrical producer. His first enterprise, an atom bomb satire by John Bird called *Here Is the News*, was a brave and expensive failure but Donald Langdon, agent to Peter Cook, was sufficiently impressed by Donaldson's nerve to offer him another satire, *Beyond the Fringe* (1961), which became a huge hit in the West End and on Broadway. Characteristically, Donaldson finessed failure out of triumph, investing what money he had made in a series of original, eccentric, money-losing revues. Although he was among the first to recognize the talent of Spike Milligan, Marty Feldman, Terry Jones, and Michael Palin, he was more or less broke by 1964 and definitively bankrupt by 1966.

Donaldson's personal life was equally eventful. For the

first part of the 1960s he lived the life of a typical wealthy, fun-loving bachelor of the time. Unfortunately he was married. In 1960 Sonia gave birth to his son, Charlie. The marriage ended in divorce in 1965. For a while Donaldson lived with the actress Sarah Miles (*b.* 1941), a period interrupted when he moved out, soon becoming engaged to the young American singer Carly Simon (*b.* 1945). When Simon returned to America to prepare for marriage, he revived his relationship with Miles. The relationship was again short-lived. In 1967, broke and on the run from creditors, Donaldson travelled around the country with Claire Gordon (*b.* 1941), an actress. They were married on 1 September 1967. The following year, after the death of a grandmother, Donaldson received his last family bequest, which he spent on buying model agencies and throwing famously exotic, drug-fuelled, and debauched parties at the flat in Ranelagh Gardens, Chelsea, where they lived.

After one final theatrical disaster, a production of Oscar Panizza's *The Council of Love* (1970) that was unsuccessfully sued for blasphemy, Donaldson debunked to Ibiza, where he spent what money he had left on a glass-bottomed boat called (coincidentally) *Capitan-Wylly*. His relationship with Gordon broke down during this period, although they were not finally divorced until 1975. In Ibiza Donaldson contacted a colonel's daughter who had become a successful call-girl. In October 1972 he returned to England to move in with the woman he called Emma Jane Crampton. Surrounded by a wealth of comic material, Donaldson began to write, reworking the events of his life in the form of semi-fiction, with himself as the fall guy and villain. *Both the Ladies and the Gentlemen*, whose first line was 'Living in a brothel isn't everything it is cracked up to be', was published in 1975 to some favourable reviews. By this time, Crampton had been replaced in Donaldson's affections by his former secretary Cherry Jane Hatrick (daughter of David Lindsay Hatrick, production engineer), with whom he lived at 139 Elm Park Mansions, off the Fulham Road in Chelsea, for several years.

In 1980 Donaldson's most successful book, *The Henry Root Letters*, was published. Inspired by an American book, Don Novello's *The Lazlo Letters* (1977), it took the form of a series of letters (often accompanied by a £1 note) written to politicians, policemen, and media stars by a vulgar and ferociously right-wing wet-fish merchant, many of which received gratifyingly vain and stupid replies. The book became one of the great best-sellers of the decade. Briefly fashionable, Donaldson was the first gossip columnist of the *Mail on Sunday* and replaced Julian Barnes as restaurant critic of *The Tatler*. There was a second book of Root letters and *Henry Root's World of Knowledge* (1982), an application of the idea behind Flaubert's dictionary of received ideas to Thatcher's Britain.

For the rest of his life Donaldson regularly wrote comic volumes—'toilet books', as he called them (Blacker, 203)—sometimes in collaboration with other authors. A gleeful literary impersonator, he created a series of alternative personae, including the oleaginous court correspondent Talbot Church, the French intellectual Jean-Luc Legris, and the demented TV producer Liz Reed. His more directly autobiographical work, from the semi-factual novel *Is This Allowed?* (1985) to the semi-fictional memoir *From Winchester to This* (1997), and his memorably frank column 'William Donaldson's week' in *The Independent*, reflected with lacerating, self-immolating humour and wildly varying degrees of accuracy the downward spiral of his private life. In 1985 he became passionately involved with Melanie Soszynski, an escort agency girl with a fondness for cocaine. At the end of an exciting and destructive relationship Soszynski was in a rehabilitation clinic and Donaldson had developed a liking for crack cocaine, which he continued to take for the next fifteen years. Having confessed his infatuation to Cherry Hatrick, he married her on 5 August 1986 (after she had insisted they either marry or separate), but the relationship was already over. Hatrick moved out of Elm Park Mansions nine months later, though they never divorced.

Although Donaldson continued to write with a brilliant, savage wit, his life in the 1990s took a melancholy turn. After another doomed affair with a call-girl, he was declared bankrupt for the third and final time in August 1994. His final years were brightened by two things: a relationship with the model Rachel Garley, and his last great triumph as a writer, *Brewers' Rogues, Villains and Eccentrics* (2002), a 300,000 word compendium of bad behaviour. 'Willie Donaldson has never had the recognition he deserves as a comic genius', Francis Wheen wrote in the *Mail on Sunday*. 'Perhaps this magnificent volume will do the trick' (*Mail on Sunday*, 15 Dec 2002).

Throughout his life, Donaldson acquired a reputation as a corrupting influence, but in person he was a respectable, quietly spoken, slightly frayed figure of naval bearing, beguiling company, and as funny at first hand as he was on the page. His years of recreational crack abuse finally caught up with him on 22 June 2005 when, during a heatwave, his lungs finally gave out and he died of respiratory failure, alone in his Elm Park Mansions flat. He was cremated at a sparsely attended funeral at Mortlake cemetery. A memorial reading of his work at the Lyttelton Theatre six months later was, however, a sell-out.

TERENCE BLACKER

Sources *The Times* (22 June 2005) • *The Guardian* (25 June 2005) • *The Independent* (25 June 2005) • *Daily Telegraph* (27 June 2005) • T. Blacker, *You cannot live as I have lived and not end up like this: the thoroughly disgraceful life and times of Willie Donaldson* (2007) • personal knowledge (2009) • private information (2009) • m. certs. [1958, 1986] • d. cert.

Archives FILM BFINA, documentary footage | SOUND BL NSA, documentary recordings

Likenesses T. O'Sullivan, group portrait, photograph, 2003, Camera Press, London • S. Barker, photograph, 2005, Getty Images, London [*see illus.*] • obituary photographs • photographs, repro. in Blacker, *You cannot live*

Donkin, Robert Arthur [Robin] **(1928–2006)**, geographer, was born on 28 October 1928 at Southgate, Morpeth, Northumberland, the son of Arthur Donkin, draper and shopkeeper, later civil servant, and his wife, Elizabeth Jane, *née* Kirkup, solicitor's secretary. At the time of his birth registration his parents lived at 78 Commercial

Road, Jarrow. His father had enlisted in the army on leaving school and fought in the trenches during the First World War; he enlisted again in 1939 and was posted to India and Burma, where his unit was reported for nine months as missing. Despite this latter interruption Donkin had a stable, modest, home life that was musical, bookish, and Anglican. From a local elementary school at Monkton he went to Jarrow grammar school, where in 1947 he took his higher school certificate in English, geography, and history. He next read geography at King's College, Newcastle upon Tyne, under the aegis of the University of Durham. He graduated with a first-class degree in 1950 and became a research student, supervised at Newcastle by M. R. G. Conzen, a historical geographer and expert on medieval towns who had fled Germany in the mid-1930s to escape the National Socialist regime. Donkin's dissertation was on the contribution of the Cistercians to the geography of England in the twelfth and thirteenth centuries, for which he was awarded the degree of PhD in 1953.

Donkin's national service from 1953 to 1955 was in Egypt as a lieutenant in the Royal Artillery. He then spent 1955–6 as a King George VI memorial fellow in the department of geography at the University of California, Berkeley, attracted there by his having read as a student some of the writings of the cultural landscape geographer Carl Sauer. Donkin's sojourn at Berkeley laid the foundations for the interests he was later to pursue in the historical geography of Latin America and in the domestication of plants and animals globally.

On returning to the United Kingdom Donkin was an assistant lecturer in geography at the University of Edinburgh from 1956 to 1958 and then assistant lecturer, subsequently lecturer, in geography at the University of Birmingham from 1958 to the end of 1970. In January 1971 he moved to a lectureship in geography at the University of Cambridge, where he was promoted in 1990 to be a reader in historical geography, a post he held until his retirement in 1996. He was elected a fellow of Jesus College in 1972 and a fellow of the British Academy in 1985, and was made LittD by Cambridge in 1992. On 12 September 1970, a few months before moving to Cambridge, he married (at St Oswald's Church, Grasmere, Westmorland) one of his former Birmingham students, now working as a librarian, Jennifer Gay Kennedy (*b.* 1941), daughter of Joseph Edward Kennedy, sales director. They had one daughter, Lucy (*b.* 1977).

Donkin was an exceptional scholar in both substance and style. He set for himself very high standards of research and teaching and he expected others to do likewise for themselves. Between 1957 and 1969 he published twenty papers in peer-reviewed journals on the geographical impact of the Cistercian order in Europe (and especially in England and Wales) during the middle ages. In 1969 he published *The Cistercian Order in Europe: a Bibliography of Printed Sources*, a pioneering listing of about 1500 printed works relating to the Cistercian order as a whole. In 1978 he published *The Cistercians: Studies in the Geography of Medieval England and Wales*, a thorough updating of his doctoral dissertation written twenty-five years previously.

When Donkin moved to Cambridge in 1971 it was to a lectureship in the geography of Latin America, enabling him to develop the interests that had enthused him at Berkeley fifteen years earlier. But his focus on Latin America was gradually subsumed in a broader theme, the early domestication of plants and animals and related cultural interactions between the Old and New worlds. These issues inspired Donkin to produce a remarkable series of meticulously researched monographs: on cochineal, a red dyestuff that Mexican and Peruvian Indians had for centuries collected from an insect and that came to be the most widely traded and, next to gold and silver, the most valuable product of the Spanish Indies (*Spanish Red*, 1977); on terracing for agriculture (*Agricultural Terracing in the Aboriginal New World*, 1979); on the cultural use of manna from the sixteenth century onwards (1980); on the historical geography of the New World peccary (1985); on the origins and dispersal of the Muscovy duck (1986); on the anthropogenic dispersal of the guinea fowl (1991); on pearls and pearl-fishing from its origins to the age of discoveries (1998); on the Indonesian origins and diffusion of camphor, the source of a powerful perfume (1999); and on the Indonesian archipelago of the Moluccas and the traffic in spices until the arrival of the Europeans in the fifteenth century (2003). Donkin's research was principally library-based, and involved painstakingly collecting, dating, sorting, tabulating, and mapping masses of data drawn from printed sources. In addition to research in libraries in England, he travelled abroad extensively to work both in libraries and in the field. While based in Birmingham he visited Mexico, Guatemala, Haiti, the Dominican Republic, and the northern and central Andes. At Cambridge his travels embraced Bolivia, Argentina, Ecuador, Brazil, Mexico, Guatemala, India, Pakistan, China, Hainan Island, Macau, and Hong Kong. Adventurously, he travelled alone, using local transport and basic accommodation.

Teaching was important to Donkin. His lecture courses at Birmingham and Cambridge reflected closely his own research interests. His empirical lectures on origins and dispersals of early domesticated plants and animals and on relations between the New and Old worlds contrasted not only with the kind of geography undergraduates had learned at school but also with the quantitative and theoretical geography being promoted by many geographers during the 1960s, 1970s, and 1980s. He delivered fluent, polished lectures, articulating memorable phrases precisely in an apparently spontaneous manner, although they had usually been carefully prepared. To rapt audiences, issued with famously extensive reading lists, he conveyed a depth of enthusiasm and breadth of scholarship that impressed his listeners.

So, too, did his dress and demeanour. He was smart in appearance, often in what many undergraduates and some colleagues considered to be an old-fashioned brown tweed suit, proudly wearing his Gunner tie and sporting a silk handkerchief from his breast pocket. For many years he smoked small cigars and then wonderfully aromatic tobacco in his cherished pipe. From his days as a graduate student until his death his increasingly antediluvian but still used Olivetti typewriter graced his office desk. At Birmingham he drove a large, Burgundy-coloured convertible Alvis car, replaced when he moved to Cambridge by a sand-coloured, short wheelbase Land Rover (which, although an expeditionary vehicle, he never took abroad).

Donkin was an erudite, modest, somewhat shy man, possessing high standards of scholarship and of integrity. He was admired by many of his colleagues while being distinctively different from almost all of them. He was a highly productive scholar in the pursuit of what he called 'esoteric knowledge'. He was also a very independent scholar—he never became involved administratively with any professional society, he attended very few academic conferences, he supervised only two graduate students, and he interacted minimally with other scholars. But by thus guarding time for his own work, he was able to produce a corpus of published work high in quality and considerable in quantity.

Donkin died at Addenbrooke's Hospital, Cambridge, on 1 February 2006 of heart failure. His funeral service was held on 13 February in Jesus College's chapel. In October of that year his ashes were interred in the burial ground of St Oswald's Church, Grasmere, the Lake District parish where his family had a house inherited from his wife's parents and where he had indulged his enjoyment of gardening. His wife and daughter survived him.

Alan R. H. Baker

Sources *The Independent* (10 May 2006) • *Jesus College Annual Report* (2006), 91–2 • T. Jenkins, eulogy, www.geog.cam.ac.uk/people/donkin/, 12 Oct 2010 • personal file, Jesus College, Cambridge • personal file and minutes of the degree committee of the faculty of earth sciences and geography (1992–2006), U. Cam., department of geography • minutes of the degree committee of the faculty of earth sciences and geography, 1970–92, CUL • *WW* (2006) • personal knowledge (2011) • private information (2011) [Jennifer Donkin, widow; W. M. Adams; T. P. Bayliss-Smith; M. D. Billinge; M. D. I. Chisholm; M. C. Cleary; I. Edwards; J. H. Galloway; N. Gates; R. E. Glasscock; B. Giles; D. J. Gregory; J. D. Hamshere; G. Harcourt; D. Harris; P. N. Jones; G. Kearns; J. Langton; R. Munton; L. Newson; K. S. Richards; D. J. Robinson; M. Sharp; R. M. Smith; T. Spencer; J. Stargardt; C. W. J. Withers; P. A. Wood] • b. cert. • m. cert. • d. cert.

Likenesses photograph, repro. in *The Independent* (10 May 2006)

Wealth at death £429,886: probate, 21 June 2006, *CGPLA Eng. & Wales*

Dougan, (Alexander) Derek (1938–2007), footballer and author, was born on 20 January 1938 at 41 Susan Street, Belfast, Northern Ireland, the son of John Dougan, a boilermaker in the riveting department of Harland and Wolff, and his wife, Josephine, *née* Kitchen. Most of his childhood was spent in east Belfast, in the shadow of the shipyard. He was educated at Mersey Street primary school and Belfast Technical High School.

Having shown early promise Dougan represented Northern Ireland schools at football and, while playing for Cregagh Boys' Club, was signed by the Irish league club Distillery in 1953. He worked in a toy factory and then became an apprentice electrician in the shipyard until further evidence of his potential as a goal-scoring forward, and international representation at amateur level, led to a £4000 transfer in 1957 to Portsmouth Football Club. The following year he won his first full international cap for Northern Ireland at the world cup finals in Sweden. In 1959 he was transferred to Blackburn Rovers for the sum of £11,000, but his stay at Ewood Park ended controversially. He helped his new team to reach the FA cup final in 1960 but then submitted a transfer request on the eve of the game. His request was not granted until 1961, when he was sold to Aston Villa for £15,000. The next two years saw a dip in his form, resulting in a shock transfer in 1963 to third division Peterborough United, the transfer fee being £21,000. In the meantime, on 10 July 1963 at Birmingham register office, he had married Jutta Maria Fichtl, a twenty-year-old bank clerk, daughter of Franz Fichtl, a German-born electrician. They had two sons.

In 1965 Dougan was transferred again, this time to Leicester City for the sum of £25,000. Following a now familiar pattern, he stayed at Filbert Street for only two years, and moved to Wolverhampton Wanderers in 1967 for £50,000. This transfer ushered in the most successful period of his career, lasting from 1967 until 1975, and Wolves was to become the club with which he was subsequently most closely identified. Wolves were promoted to the first division during his first season at Molineux. They lost 2–3 to Tottenham Hotspur in the two-leg 1972 UEFA cup final but then beat Manchester City 2–1 in the 1973 league cup final. Dougan played 323 games for Wolves, scoring 123 goals in a career during which he played 546 games and scored 222 goals. He represented Northern Ireland at senior level on forty-three occasions, scoring eight times, and captained his country from 1969 until 1973.

During the latter stages of Dougan's playing career politics and writing began to occupy some of his spare time. From 1970 to 1978 he served as chairman of the Professional Footballers' Association and fought strenuously for his members in an industry that still bore some of the hallmarks of feudalism. He also took an interest in the political situation in Northern Ireland and, in 1973, controversially played for what was in reality an all-Ireland national team (thinly disguised as a Shamrock Rovers eleven) against Brazil. Like his near contemporary George Best, Dougan consistently advocated the cause of a united Ireland football team. The idea had little support, however, within the Irish Football Association, Northern Ireland's governing body, which had not sanctioned the appearance of its players in the Brazil game. Dougan was not selected for his country again.

Dougan's frustrations with traditional Ulster unionism had already been made explicit in 1972 with the publication of *The Sash He Never Wore*, part autobiography and part political treatise. Among his other books were an autobiography, *Attack!* (1969), a novel, *The Footballer* (1974), and a revised edition of *The Sash He Never Wore* (1997), which Dougan himself clearly regarded as a contribution to cross-community understanding in Northern Ireland in the context of the peace process. Ironically, given his concerns about unionism, but in keeping with his lifelong reputation as a maverick, he subsequently joined the

United Kingdom Independence Party and appeared on behalf of his party on BBC TV's *Question Time*. Long before this, though, he had already established himself as a television personality on Independent Television, in the early days of football punditry.

On leaving Wolverhampton Wanderers, Dougan worked as player-manager of Kettering Town. However, in 1982 he was lured back to Molineux as chairman and chief executive of Wolverhampton Wanderers, a club that was soon to find itself in financial difficulty. Dougan resigned in 1985, thereby ending his formal association with football. Latterly he worked in marketing and continued the charity work he had begun while still playing football. In 2005 he was a coffin bearer at the funeral of his former Northern Ireland team mate George Best. He died at his home in Love Lane, Stockwell End, Wolverhampton, on 24 June 2007, as a result of a heart attack associated with ischaemic heart disease and a history of hypertension. 'Flamboyant, outspoken, periodically combustible' (*The Independent*, 26 June 2007), the Doog (as he was known by his fans) was a man of many talents and diverse enthusiasms. He will best be remembered not for his political views, challenging as they were, but for his goal-scoring record and for his charisma in a sport that was becoming increasingly devoid of genuine personalities. He was survived by his wife and two sons. ALAN BAIRNER

Sources D. Dougan, *Attack!* (1969) • D. Dougan, *The sash he never wore* (1972) • M. Brodie, *100 years of Irish football* (1980) • *The Times* (25 June 2007) • *Daily Telegraph* (25 June 2007) • *The Guardian* (25–6 June 2007) • *The Independent* (26 June 2007) • *Irish Post* (26 June 2008) • *Soccer History*, 17 (autumn 2007) • *Winger: the Review of British Football*, 80 (Oct 2007), 10–11 • www.londonwolves.com/html/the_doog.html, 22 April 2010 • *WW* (2007) • b. cert. • m. cert. • d. cert.

Archives FILM BFINA, current affairs footage • video, www.londonwolves.com/html/the_doog.html

Likenesses photographs, 1959–80, Getty Images, London • photographs, *c*.1960–*c*.1980, Rex Features, London • photographs, 1960–2005, PA Photos, London • photographs, 1963–83, Photoshot, London • obituary photographs • photographs, repro. in www.londonwolves.com/html/the_doog.html

Wealth at death £168,177: administration, 15 Nov 2007, *CGPLA Eng. & Wales*

Douglas, Margaret Elizabeth (1934–2008), television producer and executive, was born at 107 Abbott Road, Poplar, London, on 22 August 1934, the only child of Thomas Mincher Douglas, Metropolitan police constable, and his wife, Dorothy May, *née* Jones, teacher. She was brought up in Islington and would later call herself a 'blitz kid', having remained in London throughout the Second World War, apart from a brief spell with her grandmother in Glasgow. She was educated at Parliament Hill grammar school, but left at the age of seventeen. It was her choice to train as an office worker rather than enter higher education. After joining the BBC in 1951 on the lowest secretarial grade she spent almost her entire working life at the corporation.

Douglas's career reflected well on the BBC. Without any academic qualifications (other than the school certificate), she was chosen for the production secretaries' course and was bright enough to join the television service at a time when it was expanding rapidly. Her first job was as production secretary to Michael Peacock, the first editor of *Panorama*, the BBC's innovative and most prestigious current affairs programme. She worked at the Lime Grove Studios, in Shepherd's Bush, London, during what became known as television's golden age. *Panorama*'s Monday night audiences were at that time averaging 8 million people and it was to Douglas that many contributors came for guidance and sustenance. She progressed within current affairs, becoming a researcher, director and then producer for programmes such as *Gallery* and *24 Hours*. She was happiest in political broadcasting and when Ian Trethowan and Robert McKenzie set out on long interviews with two former prime ministers, Lord Avon (Anthony Eden) and Lord Stockton (Harold Macmillan), it was Douglas both sides wanted as the producer. Anne Glyn-Jones, assistant to Lord Stockton, described her as 'magnificently decisive' (private information).

In 1972 Douglas became responsible for the BBC's television coverage of the party political conferences. This was an onerous job that involved many hours of television from Blackpool, Brighton, and Bournemouth. It also led to numerous rows between the BBC and politicians. But Douglas had the resolve and the charm to calm matters. By now, she was as comfortable in 10 Downing Street as she was in the television studio, supervising countless party political and election broadcasts.

When Alasdair Milne became director-general of the BBC in 1982 he remembered Douglas from his Lime Grove days and appointed her as his chief assistant, responsible for the BBC's relations with the political parties. This was a senior role, previously held by such luminaries as Harman Grisewood, Oliver Whitley, and John Crawley. At a time of increasing political turbulence between the broadcasters and the politicians, Douglas did her best to ensure that the interests of the viewers and the listeners were not forgotten. Her patience was often tested; her quiet persistence usually, but not always, won the day. Her judgement was sound. When Michael Checkland succeeded Milne as director-general in 1987 he promoted Douglas to chief political adviser, the first woman to hold such a senior post in the BBC. Even John Birt, who thought he understood politics well, found it necessary to retain her services when he became director-general in 1992.

In 1993, however, Douglas decided she had had enough, and left Broadcasting House for the Palace of Westminster to become supervisor of parliamentary broadcasting, succeeding her former boss, John Grist. Televising parliament, which had been delayed for far too long, was now running smoothly and Douglas ensured that there were no problems. For six years Westminster was her second home until she retired in 1999.

Douglas was slight in build with sparkling eyes and a courteous and confident manner, and, in the hothouse that was political television, trusted by all sides. She was appointed OBE in 1994. For some years she was close to Terence Lancaster [*see below*] and they were married (after his first wife died) on 25 April 2000. Their home was a riverside flat in the Anchor Brewhouse on Shad Thames, near Tower Bridge. Politics—alongside football—

remained her principal interest. She survived her husband by ten months, and died on 20 August 2008 at the Cromwell Hospital, Kensington, of cancer. She had no children but was survived by her two stepsons.

Douglas's husband, **Terence Roger** [Terry] **Lancaster** (1920–2007), journalist, was born in Salisbury on 29 November 1920, the son of Reginald Froude Lancaster, master printer, and his wife, Dorothy, *née* McMahon. On leaving school he joined the *Salisbury Gazette* as a junior reporter. In 1939 he joined the RAF, serving as an intelligence officer in north Africa and Italy. On 19 August 1941 he married Brenda Christine Abbott (1918–1998), schoolteacher, and daughter of Frederick William Abbott, manager of an employment exchange; they had two sons. On demobilization he returned to journalism, initially at the *Southern Daily Echo*, based in Southampton. In the early 1950s he moved to London to join the staff of *The Star*, an evening paper. He unsuccessfully contested Finchley for Labour in the 1955 general election. After moving to the *Daily Express* under Lord Beaverbrook, he pulled off a scoop by interviewing Nikita Khrushchov immediately after his speech denouncing Stalin at the twentieth communist party congress in 1956, and was made foreign editor, organizing acclaimed coverage of the aftermath of John F. Kennedy's assassination in 1963. He next joined *The People* as political columnist, before becoming political editor of the *Daily Mirror* in 1970. He was particularly influential during the Labour governments of Harold Wilson and Jim Callaghan from 1974 to 1979. He resigned from the *Mirror* soon after Robert Maxwell took over the paper in 1984. He worked briefly for Eddy Shah's new paper, *Today*, and was later the first public affairs officer of the Speaker of the House of Commons, working for Betty Boothroyd. He was highly regarded by his colleagues and by politicians, and noted for his charm, wit, and integrity. He died at the London Clinic, 20 Devonshire Place, Westminster, of aspiration pneumonia on 6 October 2007.

PAUL FOX

Sources *The Times* (9 Oct 2007); (12 Oct 2007) · *The Guardian* (9 Oct 2007) · *The Independent* (10 Oct 2007); (18 Oct 2007) · *The Independent* (25 Aug 2008) · *The Times* (26 Aug 2008) · *The Guardian* (4 Sept 2008) · *WW* (2008) · personal knowledge (2012) · private information (2012) · b. cert. · d. cert. · m. certs. [1941, 2000] · d. cert. [Terence Lancaster]

Wealth at death £1,607,925: probate, 3 Feb 2009, *CGPLA Eng. & Wales* · £200,881—Terence Roger Lancaster: probate, 6 Oct 2007, *CGPLA Eng. & Wales*

Douglas [*née* Tew], **Dame (Margaret) Mary (1921–2007)**, social anthropologist, was born on 25 March 1921 in San Remo, Italy, where her parents, Phyllis Margaret Twomey (1900–1933) and Gilbert Charles Tew (1884–1951), had disembarked to take a late honeymoon on their passage home from Burma, where they had married the previous year. Their second daughter, Patricia (Pat), was born two years later.

Gilbert Tew, the son of a gasworks manager, had been educated at Warwick School; he won a scholarship to read classics at Emmanuel College, Cambridge, before entering the Indian Civil Service. He was posted to Burma in

Dame (Margaret) Mary Douglas (1921–2007), by Mayotte Magnus, 1976

1908 as an assistant commissioner; he became private secretary to the lieutenant-governor for a year before his marriage, and was confirmed as a deputy commissioner in 1924, discharging a range of responsibilities as 'custodian of enemy property', and as an excise commissioner with responsibilities for the government monopolies of opium and salt. Phyllis Twomey's father, Sir Daniel Harold Ryan Twomey (1864–1935), son of a Queenstown butcher and ship's chandler, had joined the Indian Civil Service in 1884 after education at St Stanislaus College, Leinster, and University College, London. He was called to the bar in 1895, becoming a judge in 1909, and serving as chief judge of the court of lower Burma from 1917 until he retired in 1920, when he and his wife, May (*née* Ponsford) set up house in Totnes, Devon, to be joined in 1926 by Mary (as she was always known) and her sister. Mary, and later also Pat, attended Stoodley Knowle, a French convent primary school in Ilsham, Torquay, as weekday boarders. In 1932 their parents returned home when Phyllis Tew developed incurable cancer. She entrusted her daughters to the nuns of the Sacred Heart convent in Roehampton, her old school, where they became boarders in 1933, some months before their mother died. Gilbert Tew retired from the Indian Civil Service in 1934 to take his children into his care.

On finishing school, and after six months spent in Paris at the Sorbonne, Mary Tew passed the Oxford entrance examination, electing to read philosophy, politics, and economics at St Anne's College. She graduated with a second-class degree in 1943. There followed four years of war service (1943–7) as a temporary assistant principal in the Colonial Office, where she began to meet social anthropologists, including Audrey Richards and Raymond Firth. In 1947 she returned to Oxford to study for a diploma and then a BSc in anthropology, submitting her thesis, 'Bride wealth in Africa', in May 1948. She then became a research assistant to Daryll Forde at the International African Institute, writing the volume of the *Ethnographic Survey of Africa* for Nyasaland (1950). The fieldwork in the Belgian Congo on which she based her DPhil dissertation was carried out between May 1949 and April 1950 under the supervision of E. E. Evans-Pritchard. She immediately secured a lectureship in Oxford, which she held for a year before moving to London, after her marriage to James Alexandre Thomas Douglas (1919–2004), economist, and son of Colonel Herbert Archibald Douglas of the Indian army, at the Roman Catholic church of Our Most Holy Redeemer, Cheyne Row, on 31 March 1951. As Mary Douglas she took up a lectureship in anthropology at University College, London, later that year. The couple's first child, Janet, was born late in 1951 (followed by two sons, James and Philip) and they moved from James's flat in Kensington to a house on the Holly Lodge estate in Highgate, which remained the family home until 2006 when, two years after James's death, Mary moved to an apartment in Bloomsbury, near the University of London. Meanwhile her husband pursued a career in the Conservative research department, which he joined in 1951 and of which he was director from 1970 to 1974 until the electoral defeat of Edward Heath saw his 'one nation' brand of conservatism eclipsed. James and Mary shared lifelong commitments to the Roman Catholic church (both having Catholic mothers), to inclusive social forms, not least in the hospitality of their own home, and to social theory as a practical tool in the remedy of society's problems.

In 1953 Mary Douglas undertook a second spell of fieldwork among the Lele in the Belgian Congo, which proved her last trip to Africa, apart from a brief visit in 1987, since the civil war in the Congo rendered it unsafe from soon after independence. The Lele researches gave rise to a monograph, *The Lele of Kasai* (1963), influential essays on comparative economy, kinship, and classificatory systems, and case studies in many of her later books of social theory. But Mary Douglas's wider reputation does not rest on her African research.

During her Oxford years Mary Douglas had come to know the Czech refugee Franz Steiner and attended his series of lectures on taboo (published posthumously under that title in 1956). The ideas of this Jewish thinker struck a chord with her Roman Catholic precepts. In 1966 and 1970 Douglas published her two most influential books, *Purity and Danger* and *Natural Symbols*. Reduced to its most basic, *Purity and Danger* offered a comparative analysis of systems of classification cross-culturally. Readers were particularly seduced by her demonstration of the strict logic underlying the dietary codes of Leviticus, and this unlikely case study emerged as the exemplary demonstration in her work of the general idea that boundaries important to purity were produced by and patrolled by rules that were sanctioned by dangers. Societies invested their shared classifications with a taken-for-granted character most evident when the breach, or threatened breach, of rules risked dangers being unleashed automatically. The insight was derived from combining Emile Durkheim on social order with Franz Steiner on taboo, as filtered through the post-war concerns of the Oxford Institute of Social Anthropology, but the ability to make the argument so vividly was essentially Mary Douglas's. The argument of *Natural Symbols* gained impetus from the introduction of the reforms of the Second Vatican Council, notably changes to the Latin liturgy, which Douglas believed not only to be insensitive to the contribution of ritual to social solidarities but also to represent the social interests of reformers, which were at variance with those of many of their parishioners. Here she leant upon the work of the educationist Basil Bernstein to suggest a relationship between subjects' experience of belonging to social groups and networks, and their cultural bias in respect of ritual and symbols. In her experience of Roman Catholicism, a commitment to hierarchical organization went along with receptivity towards condensed symbolism and governance by explicit rules. The converse of this would be a more individualized society which relied on individuals' capacity to form their own networks of relations, and welcomed competition rules more than it did a regulated environment. These ideas were the germ of what she initially called 'grid and group theory', an initiative to correlate cultural value with social environment. Later she sought to develop these ideas with an international circle of like-minded researchers, calling it 'cultural theory'.

During the 1970s Douglas began working more explicitly on Western society, initially on British food habits with Michael Nicod, then in collaboration with Baron C. Isherwood on an ambitious attempt to rewrite economists' consumption theories on the assumption that consumption was about social relations rather than individual desires. The resulting work, *The World of Goods*, appeared in 1979, by which time she had moved in 1977 to the Russell Sage Foundation in New York to become director of research on culture. There she extended her interests in an edited volume on food festivals, but also embarked on research on environmental movements with Aaron Wildavsky, published as *Risk and Culture* (1982), that in its ambition to root perceptions of environmental dangers in the social experience of those who espoused them proved as provocative as *Natural Symbols* had been a dozen years earlier.

Douglas's next position, from 1981 until retirement in 1985, was as Avalon professor at Northwestern University, in Evanston, Illinois, a chair supported to foster the interdisciplinary study of the humanities: in Douglas's case a joint appointment in the departments of anthropology and of the history and literature of religions. A lecture series delivered at the end of this period offered the most extensive and explicit statement of her theoretical ambitions. *How Institutions Think* (1986), based on the 1985 Frank W. Abrams lectures at Syracuse University, New York, explored the grounds for shared ideas about subjects like fairness and entitlement, and argued that the common capacity to produce shared ideas was similar to the economists' preoccupation with a nation's ability to produce those public goods from which no user can be excluded. Both were essential to society. A later volume, *Missing Persons* (1998, with Steven Ney), can be read as complementary to this in its emphasis on the different kinds of people produced by different social institutions.

A visiting professorship at Princeton University from 1986 to 1988 was Mary Douglas's last position in the USA, after which she and James (who had also held visiting professorships at various American universities) returned to live in the north London house they had bought in 1951. It was during this period, in 1987, that she read the book of Numbers for the first time in its entirety in preparation for delivering the Gifford lectures in the Edinburgh divinity school. This led her to reproach herself for having earlier mined Old Testament sources for apt illustrations, rather than treating them holistically, as her anthropological method recommended. The late harvest of a twenty-year period would be a trilogy, and its coda. *In the Wilderness* (1993) argued that the book of Numbers had been edited by its priestly redactors into a ring, and that only by appreciating this literary structure in the whole book was it possible to recover the inclusive social vision that was their message. *Leviticus as Literature* (1999) revisited the example that had been central to *Purity and Danger* to suggest that the book of Leviticus seen as a whole was a textual composition in three parts intended by its priestly editors to be analogous to other tripartite distinctions, including that of the courtyard, sanctuary, and shrine of the covenant in the tabernacle. *Jacob's Tears: the Priestly Work of Reconciliation* (2004) makes the most explicit argument associating the vision of the priestly editors of the Pentateuch of a religion that was strictly monotheistic and entirely rejected icons with their promotion of an inclusive social settlement meant to encompass all the descendants of Jacob. The priestly editors emerge as the heroes of the trilogy: wise, benign, and possessed of the artistry to express their ideas in literary forms that became invisible to readers for centuries. This last observation paved the way to a coda on the priestly books.

Thinking in Circles: an Essay on Ring Composition (2007), the final book to appear in Mary Douglas's lifetime, was completed after she had been diagnosed with terminal cancer in 2006. At first sight it is a light-hearted book, sharing her enjoyment in the discovery of archaic literary genres in sources as diverse as the Old Testament, the *Iliad* and Laurence Sterne's *Tristram Shandy*. But there was a more sombre point: our lost abilities to create or appreciate these complex literary constructions spoke also of our social impoverishment. The last book completed in Mary Douglas's lifetime, published posthumously, was an edition of her father's fishing essays, *Being Fair to Trout* (2008), for which she threw herself into understanding fishing with the same relish that she had tackled Lele hunting six decades earlier.

In addition to numerous honorary degrees, Mary Douglas was elected to the American Academy of Arts and Sciences in 1974, and a fellow of the British Academy in 1989 on her return from the USA; she was appointed CBE in 1992, and a week before her death was invested DBE. She died on 16 May 2007 shortly after being admitted to University College Hospital, Camden. Following a funeral mass at the Roman Catholic church of St Patrick in Soho Square, London, on 25 May, she was buried in Highgate cemetery, rejoining James, her husband. They were survived by their three children. RICHARD FARDON

Sources R. Fardon, *Mary Douglas: an intellectual biography* (1999) · M. Douglas, 'A feeling for hierarchy', Marianist Award Lecture, University of Dayton, 2002 · *The Times* (18 May 2007) · *The Guardian* (18 May 2007) · *Daily Telegraph* (22 May 2007) · *The Independent* (22 May 2007) · *New York Times* (22 May 2007) · *Prospect*, 135 (30 June 2007) · *Anthropology Today*, 23/5 (Oct 2007), 24–7 · *American Anthropologist*, 110/3 (Sept 2008), 404–7 · *PBA* (2011) · *India List and India Office List* (1906–35) · *WW* (2007) · personal knowledge (2011) · private information (2011) · m. cert. · d. cert.

Archives Northwestern University, Illinois, papers · UCL, papers | FILM interview, 26 Feb 2006, www.alanmacfarlane.com

Likenesses M. Magnus, bromide print, 1976, NPG [*see illus.*] · N. Sinclair, bromide print, 1993, NPG · obituary photographs · photograph, Photoshot, London

Wealth at death £493,276: probate, 12 Nov 2007, *CGPLA Eng. & Wales*

Drake, Charles Edward [Charlie] (**1925–2006**), actor and comedian, was born Charles Edward Springall on 19 June 1925 at 185 Westmoreland Road, Walworth, London, the second child in the family of three sons and three daughters of William Springall, newspaper vendor, and his wife, Winifred, otherwise Violet, *née* Drake. He attended Victory Place junior school and Paragon Row senior school, leaving the latter aged fourteen. Congenitally restless and fired by memories of accompanying Harry Champion singing 'Any old iron' at the South London Palace aged eight, he was determined to succeed as an entertainer. His short stature (five feet one and a half inches), quick wits, and acrobatic ability made him a natural comic. His boyish face, wispy strawberry-blond curls, and blue eyes gave his persona an innocence belied by a truculent determination to get his own way. He enlisted in the RAF in 1943 as a wireless operator and rear gunner, finding occasional opportunities to perform. After demobilization he worked part-time at working men's clubs as a stand-up comedian, adopting his mother's maiden name.

After the war Drake turned professional, initially working as Dick Emery's feed touring provincial variety theatres, but his career took off after pairing with Jack Edwardes, whose height and lugubrious persona complemented Drake's whirlwind, maniacal energy. Their double act, featured on the children's magazine television programme *Jigsaw* (BBC, 1954–5), blossomed in their own show on ITV, *Mick and Montmorency* (1955–8). Drake's 'Hello, my darlins' became a national catchphrase. Unwilling to be typecast as a children's entertainer he dissolved the partnership to star in several series built round his own impish persona: *Drake's Progress* (1957–8), *Charlie Drake In …* (1958–60), and *The Charlie Drake Show* (1960–61) for the BBC. A perfectionist dedicated to the comedian's craft, Drake, who wrote or co-wrote his material, often with his long-time writing partner Lew Schwarz, gained a reputation as 'difficult' because of his uncompromising demands in décor, lighting, and set design. The latter was a necessity as his shows were built round inventive and perilous slapstick set pieces—'The reluctant tightrope walker' or 'The little picture hanger'—that required absolute exactitude. During an episode of the live television show *Bingo Madness* (1961) he was seriously injured and lay in a coma for several days. However, Drake always felt that a live show provided 'the edge and fear that … are essential to all of the performing arts' (*Drake's Progress*, 98).

After a two-year break Drake returned with what became his best-remembered series, *The Worker* (1965–70), for ITV, playing a willing but accident-prone handyman who fails at every job he is given. The central scenes of mayhem were bookended by his sparring with Henry McGee's dead-pan labour exchange clerk Mr Pugh, always mispronounced as 'Poo'. The culmination of his television career came in 1968 when a compilation of set pieces from the BBC series *The Charlie Drake Show* won the coveted golden rose at Montreux. It included the celebrated nine-minute sequence in which he conducted an orchestra performing Tchaikovsky's *1812 Overture* and played every instrument, a masterpiece of comic invention, timing, and the megalomania that characterized many of his creations.

Drake's cinema career—he starred in four films for the Associated British Picture Corporation—was less successful. *Sands of the Desert* (1960) was undistinguished, but *Petticoat Pirates* (1961) made more inventive use of the anarchic and lubricious side of his persona. *The Times* reviewer referred to him as a 'battered Botticelli cherub' (*The Times*, 1 Dec 1961), an epithet he treasured. In *The Cracksman* (1963) and *Mister Ten Per Cent* (1967) he explored the dilemma of the artist whose integrity and yearning for acceptance is spurned by an uncomprehending and venal world.

Drake also enjoyed recording success with sentimental or comic songs, produced by George Martin, notably 'Old Mr Shadow' (1960) and 'My Boomerang Won't Come Back' (1961) and continued to perform on stage, including prestigious appearances at the London Palladium, starring in nine royal variety shows (he had missed his first invited appearance as a result of the accident while filming *Bingo Madness*). He concentrated on his stage act after 1970 but was suspended by Equity after refusing to pay a fine for employing a non-member—a local housewife—in a Christmas pantomime at the Bradford Alhambra (1974–5). During eighteen months of inactivity he lost both income and familiarity and his return with *Slapstick and Old Lace* was undermined by the extraordinarily hot summer of 1976 when audiences plummeted. After several further lean years he faced bankruptcy in 1979, unable to support a sybaritic lifestyle that included a Surrey mansion, yacht, racehorses, sports cars, and inveterate gambling (poker and horse racing).

Accepting whatever work was offered in order to clear his tax debts, Drake branched out into serious acting, starring in a production of Alfred Jarry's *Ubu Roi* (1980). He played Touchstone in *As You Like It* at the Ludlow festival in 1981 and gave acclaimed performances as Davies in *The Caretaker* (1983) and as the grotesque moneylender Smallweed in the BBC adaptation of *Bleak House* (1985). After playing Nagg in Beckett's *Endgame* (1992) he returned to the stage for Jim Davidson's adult pantomime *SINderella* (1994) as Baron Hardon.

Drake's first marriage, on 11 March 1954 to Heather Evelyn Barnes, an eighteen-year-old professional dancer (and daughter of Edward Barnes, department store manager), whom he had met on tour, produced three sons but ended in divorce in 1971. His second marriage, on 12 May 1979, to

Charles Edward [Charlie] **Drake (1925–2006)**, by Popperfoto, 1967

Elaine Ann Bird, another professional dancer thirty-two years his junior (and daughter of Frank George Bird, telegraphist), also ended in divorce, in 1985. Following a stroke in 1995 he stopped performing and lived at Brinsworth House, Twickenham, a retirement home for actors and performers run by the Entertainment Artistes Benevolent Fund, where he died on 23 December 2006 from bronchopneumonia and heart failure. He was survived by his three sons.

Drake's cultural roots were in music hall but he was one of the first generation of variety comedians for whom television provided their main audience. He was part of the long tradition of diminutive British working-class comedians who played the 'little man', the underdog muddling his way through all adversity. But there was a darker, harsher side to his comedy, exploring the pressures and torment that performers experience. This ambivalence made him the most distinctive, if not the best-loved, comedian of his generation.

ANDREW H. SPICER

Sources *News of the World* (20 Oct 1968) • *The Sun* (27 Feb 1971); (25 May 1985) • J. Fisher, *Funny way to be a hero* (1973) • *Daily Mirror* (2 March 1974) • *Daily Telegraph* (23 June 1975); (26 Dec 2006) • *Daily Mail* (24 June 1975); (31 March 1984); (17 April 1985); (6 Oct 1995) • *Sunday Express* (8 Jan 1978); (5 July 1981) • *Daily Star* (11 Aug 1984) • *Western Mail* (20 April 1985) • C. Drake, *Drake's progress* (1986) • *Mail on Sunday* (9 June 1991) • A. Spicer, *Typical men* (2001) • *The Times* (26 Dec 2006) • *The Independent* (26 Dec 2006) • *The Scotsman* (27 Dec 2006) • *The Guardian* (28 Dec 2006) • *The Stage* (11 Jan 2007) • b. cert. • m. certs. • d. cert.

Archives FILM BFINA, *The entertainers*, A. Rippon (presenter), LWT, 9 Aug 1992 • BFINA, *Arena*, M. Dickinson (director), BBC2, 25 Dec 2001 • BFINA, light entertainment footage • BFINA, documentary footage | SOUND BL NSA, performance recordings

Likenesses photographs, 1955–78, Hult. Arch., London • photographs, 1957–71, Getty Images, London, Popperfoto • photographs, 1958–93, PA Photos, London • photographs, 1958–95, Rex Features, London • photographs, 1959–63, Photoshot, London • photograph, 1967, Getty Images, London, Popperfoto [*see illus.*] • T. Leighton, photograph, 2003, Camera Press, London • obituary photographs

Wealth at death under £5000: probate, 24 April 2008, *CGPLA Eng. & Wales*

Drummond, Sir John Richard Gray (1934–2006), television producer, broadcaster, and music administrator, was born on 25 November 1934 at 64 Holland Park, London, the only child of Archibald Richard George Drummond, a tone-deaf Scottish master mariner, and his wife, Esther Wynne, *née* Pickering. At the time of the registration of his birth his parents lived at 3 Cavendish Road, Willesden, London, but his father was away at sea for years on end before being obliged to retire through ill health. Drummond's mother was the dominant influence on his childhood. Born and bred in Australia, she had studied singing at the Royal Academy of Music in London, though a weak heart had prevented any chance of an operatic career. Drummond spent his infancy in Kensington, only a few hundred yards from Campden Hill, on whose slopes he was to live most of his adult life. Evacuated to Dorset at the outbreak of the Second World War, he was able to attend

Sir John Richard Gray Drummond (1934–2006), by unknown photographer, 1984

concerts given by the Wessex Players (conducted by Reginald Goodall), and aged eleven he heard a recital by Kathleen Ferrier, whose biography he filmed twenty years later. His mother imbued him with her passions for poetry and painting, while a friendly local librarian allowed him to borrow as much music as he wanted. His mother's accompanist gave him piano lessons; he was later to describe his style of playing as 'splashy and erratic' (*Tainted by Experience*, 39).

In 1948 Drummond won a scholarship to Canford School, in Dorset. A studious, intellectually inclined teenager, he was a devoted fan of the BBC's recently inaugurated Third Programme. He gained eight distinctions in his nine school certificate subjects: ironically it was poor aural tests that let him down in music. He left school as head boy with a major history scholarship to Trinity College, Cambridge, but first spent two years of national service in the Royal Navy, a period largely devoted to the study of Russian—an invaluable asset in his later career. He described himself at university as 'an unattractive, bespectacled six-footer' (*Tainted by Experience*, 73), but his peers (among them John Tusa and John Tydeman) recalled a brilliant conversationalist whose cabaret turns for the Footlights were matched by enough histrionic talent to see him play Baldock opposite Derek Jacobi in Marlowe's *Edward II*, a student production that briefly transferred to

London. He also tried his hand at writing a musical, *The First Resort*, set in regency Brighton, but it was damned by the critic Ken Tynan, who castigated Cambridge for 'wasting time on trash like this, when they could be producing Brecht' (ibid., 81).

In 1958 Drummond was picked out as a general trainee on the BBC's fast-track recruitment scheme. After shuttling between religion, fledgling drama documentaries, and low-budget schools programmes, he was offered the number two position in the Paris office. He was soon in Moscow, translating for a high-powered BBC delegation, and over the next two years his energy and commitment, not to mention his linguistic prowess, impressed most of the top brass—save only the arts chief Huw Wheldon who, to Drummond's chagrin, passed over his application to join *Monitor*, the flagship arts magazine programme. But in 1965, when Wheldon's department expanded after the launch of BBC2, Drummond became an original member of BBC television's new music and arts department. Among his production and directorial credits over the next few years were *The Golden Ring*, an award-winning documentary about Georg Solti's recording of Wagner's Ring cycle; *A Question of Stature*, a BBC1 feature about Chopin; the master classes given by French cellist Paul Tortelier; and an affectionate behind-the-scenes film about the 1966 Leeds piano competition, for which he won the best director award at the Prague TV festival the following year. When his friend and boss Humphrey Burton left for ITV in 1967, Drummond should have been a contender for the succession, but Wheldon, by now controller of programmes, distrusted his restless and highly strung personality and instead hived off music programmes from the other arts to create two departments. Arts features went to Stephen Hearst. Music, including ballet (Drummond's special love since his years in Paris), was handed to the former recording producer John Culshaw. It proved a somewhat frustrating period for Drummond, though he turned in a fascinating pair of documentaries for *Omnibus* about Serge Diaghilev, whose example as an impresario was to fuel the second half of his own life. Meanwhile he made his first mark in the field of contemporary music with a monthly magazine series entitled *Music Now*, featuring such composers as Harrison Birtwistle, Hans Werner Henze, Nicholas Maw, Peter Maxwell Davies, and John Tavener, many of whom became personal friends.

In 1969 Drummond accepted Hearst's invitation to become executive producer of arts features. Entrusted with the simultaneous development of half a dozen projects concerned with art and architecture, he was in his element, yet dissatisfied because in the laissez-faire conditions then prevailing at the BBC he did not have the power to order individual producers as to which programmes should be undertaken. No sufferer of fools, he also found it difficult to put up with what he felt to be the arrogance and in some cases, so he felt, the laziness of his colleagues. In the BBC Club and office corridors his critiques were legendary. 'Saw your programme last night', he would exclaim. 'So good to see you back on form at last.' Or, 'I saw your programme last night; I've been defending it all morning' (personal knowledge). In 1975 he achieved a critical hit with *The Spirit of the Age*, a series of eight programmes about British architecture down the centuries, for which he recruited a luminous group of cultural commentators that included Hugh Casson, Alec Clifton-Taylor, and John Summerson. Nevertheless Drummond's hopes of running a BBC department were to be dashed several times. In 1974, after Hearst had been promoted to controller of Radio 3 and his successor Norman Swallow had returned to Granada TV, Drummond's name was again mooted as a potential chief, but a group of senior producers privately lobbied against his appointment. Instead Burton resumed control of the joint department, insisting from the outset that Drummond should be his second-in-command. *In Performance*, the strand Drummond edited on BBC2, was a model of eclectic programming, incorporating the best of ballet, opera, and concert music. But by 1977 he was convinced that his way forward at the BBC would be blocked so long as Wheldon was in command. Relief came in the shape of an advertisement for the general manager's post at the Edinburgh International Festival. Wheldon supplied a glowing testimonial: 'I have never met an artist who did not respect and admire him' (*Tainted by Experience*, 214).

At Edinburgh Drummond was at last his own master. He set about building a team and creating a witty, sharp, name-dropping, erudite personal style: it was as if he had spent half a lifetime at the BBC preparing for the role of arts impresario in the Diaghilev tradition. (Indeed, he opened his first Edinburgh festival, devoted to Diaghilev, on the fiftieth anniversary of Diaghilev's death.) Over the next five years (1978–83) he entertained prodigiously (he delighted in recalling one of his parties that featured 'wall to wall duchesses') and scoured the world for theatrical and operatic talent that would create a stir. 1980 was his best year for opera: the Cologne company (whose music director, John Pritchard, became a staunch supporter) brought Mozart's *Così fan tutte* and Cimarosa's *Il matrimonio segreto*, Glasgow provided Berg's *Wozzeck* and Janacek's *The Cunning Little Vixen*, and the festival itself produced a distinguished world première of Maxwell Davies's *The Lighthouse*. In the field of theatre Drummond never bettered his first season, 1979, when he presented Georgia's astonishing Rustaveli Company in Brecht and Shakespeare. The following year he fell out spectacularly with the gifted but demanding Polish director Tadeusz Kantor but put the Assembly Hall to effective use with Bill Bryden's masterly adaptation of the York and Wakefield mystery plays. Under Drummond's aegis the main thrust of the festival remained its classical music programmes at the Usher Hall. Innovations at the festival included master classes (first with the formidable Elisabeth Schwarzkopf), the inauguration of the book festival, and the commissioning of the Queen's Hall as a venue for chamber music. But financial constraints were arduous and negotiations with the burghers interminable; after five years he had had his fill and he declined the invitation to renew his contract. His final festival (in 1983) was dedicated to the fruitful theme of Vienna 1900.

The riskiness of Drummond's decision to cut loose without having secured a new position was a sign of the strain under which he had been operating. But he was soon hired by the Arts Council to write a report on the provision of a permanent home for dance in London. His recommendation—to take over the Theatre Royal, Drury Lane—was a pipe dream and the report was shelved, but Drummond's enhanced prestige in the field of dance enabled him to create (and administer from 1986 to 1994) the national dance co-ordination committee.

After a year in the doldrums Drummond returned to the BBC when he was picked out by the new director-general, Alasdair Milne, to succeed Robert Ponsonby as radio's controller of music. During William Glock's time in office the controller's power had been undisputed but a long-standing anomaly meant that while the in-house symphony orchestras and the music broadcasts, including the Proms, were administered by Drummond's department, the scheduling was in the hands of the controller of Radio 3, a post then held by Ian McIntyre, a journalist and biographer with no great sympathy for music. But in 1987 the two controllerships were merged, and Drummond, whatever his abrasiveness, perhaps indeed because of his powerful personality, proved to be the right man for the new job. His intention, he later wrote, was to change the perceived style of the network from that of a senior common room to an artists' cafe. The announcers (characterized by Drummond as 'the sulkiest group of grown men that I can ever recall') were ordered to drop 'elucidatory notes' and instead talk in spoken rather than written English (*Tainted by Experience*, 351, 355). He made a good choice of Andrew Davis as chief conductor of the BBC Symphony Orchestra in 1989. Working with his old friend John Tusa he inaugurated multi-faceted weekends of broadcast reportage from as far afield as Berlin and Minneapolis–St Paul.

Drummond's chief joy and satisfaction during his second stint at the BBC derived from the planning of the annual two-month Prom season. His enthusiasm for new music was balanced by an acute historical perspective, a very wide acquaintance with the leading conductors, ensembles, and performers, a flair for the discovery of new talent, and a love of young people: he greatly increased the number of appearances by youth orchestras. His European outlook also prompted an increase in the number of foreign orchestras. In 1992 he gave up his controllership (Nicholas Kenyon succeeded him) but held on to Proms planning. He was granted a six-month sabbatical that year in order to mastermind a European arts festival all over the UK, the brainchild of the prime minister, John Major, who wanted something spectacular to celebrate Britain's chairmanship of the European Community. As Thelma Holt remarked, Drummond turned Major's poisoned chalice into a crock of gold, devising a programme whose highlights included visits by Giorgio Strehler's Piccola Scala company from Milan, Ariane Mnouchkine's Théâtre du Soleil from Paris, and the Netherlands Dance Theatre. He was knighted in 1995, having been appointed CBE in 1990.

Openly hostile to the philosophy and management style of the new director-general, John Birt, Drummond was only sixty when he finally left the BBC after presiding over the Proms centenary celebrations which, cunningly, he spread over two seasons. His last 'last night' (in 1995) ended with calculated controversy when he commissioned Birtwistle to compose a twenty-minute work for saxophone and orchestra entitled *Panic*. He had earlier raised a different type of storm by dropping Mark Elder from the 1990 last night on the eve of the first Gulf War, after Elder had talked to the press about his hostility to government policy.

That Drummond possessed the vision and guts to run another major arts organization was not in doubt, but he failed to prepare the ground and was passed over in the botched succession to Jeremy Isaacs at Covent Garden in 1997. Without an official platform, he withdrew to his study. He had already published a gentle miscellany about churchyard gravestones, *A Fine and Private Place* (with Joan Bakewell, 1977), and an entertaining account of his quest for Diaghilev, *Speaking of Diaghilev* (1997), based on the interviews contained in his television documentary. His assistant on that earlier film, Robert David Lockyer-Nibbs, known as Bob Lockyer, became a close friend—'central to my life for over thirty years' was Drummond's laconic description (*Tainted by Experience*, 176)—though they did not share the same roof until in 1997 Lockyer bought a cottage in Lewes, Sussex, where they lived throughout a long and worrying period of illness. When he eventually recovered, Drummond bought himself a separate home in the town but their friendship was unaffected. In 2000 Drummond published his exceptionally frank autobiography under the self-mocking title *Tainted by Experience*—which was how he had been described by a 'henchperson' (his word) of John Birt (*Tainted by Experience*, xi).

Birt's apparatchik had added disparagingly that despite his alleged experience, Drummond had not achieved very much. In fact, he made a substantial impact on two of the nation's greatest cultural institutions and spoke out all his life for what he believed in, even when his comments made uncomfortable listening and cost him friends. His withering assessments of such cultural icons as his erstwhile colleague Melvyn Bragg and the violinist Nigel Kennedy were eagerly anticipated at his annual Proms press conferences, at least by those who were not the object of his barbs. Characteristically Drummond used the launch of his memoirs (at the Edinburgh International Book Festival) to dish out more headline-gathering insults. Alan Yentob, by then a leading figure in the BBC hierarchy, was dismissed as 'a prat'; the government, Drummond claimed, knew nothing about culture and Tony Blair was 'a professional philistine'; even Lord Evans, Drummond's publisher at Faber, was attacked as 'one of those middle-aged men who wear baseball caps turned the wrong way round because they don't want to grow up'. It was what David Attenborough described as Drummond's 'unlimited capacity for indignation' (*Tainted by Experience*, xvii) that seems to have ruled him out of further employment in a conformist world dependent on public support and sponsorship. He continued to write and lecture (notably the Royal Philharmonic Society's annual lecture in 1998, entitled 'Taking music seriously'), but his energies were sapped by a debilitating illness that affected his spine; walking became difficult and he was prevented from attending the performances that had brought him joy all his life. There was a year or two of recovery when he was able to indulge his lifelong love of travel and visit his mother's Australian homeland. He celebrated his seventieth birthday in some style with a gathering of friends in Lewes. His final illness, a year later, was brief, and he died of multi-organ failure at the Royal Sussex County Hospital, Brighton, on 6 September 2006, with Bob Lockyer at his bedside. In 2007 a late night Prom consisted entirely of works he had commissioned. HUMPHREY BURTON

Sources H. Carpenter, *The envy of the world: fifty years of the BBC Third Programme and Radio 3, 1946–1996* (1996) · J. Drummond, *Tainted by experience: a life in the arts* (2000) · *The Times* (8 Sept 2006) · *Daily Telegraph* (8 Sept 2006) · *The Guardian* (8 Sept 2006) · *The Independent* (8 Sept 2006) · Burke, *Peerage* · *WW* (2006) · private information (2010) · personal knowledge (2010) · b. cert. · d. cert.

Archives FILM BFINA, documentary footage | SOUND BL NSA, documentary recordings · BL NSA, current affairs recordings · BL NSA, performance recordings

Likenesses photographs, 1978–85, Photoshot, London · photograph, 1984, BBC [*see illus.*] · obituary photographs · photographs, repro. in Drummond, *Tainted* · photographs, BBC

Wealth at death £530,895: probate, 27 March 2007, *CGPLA Eng. & Wales*

Duckworth, (David) Keith (1933–2005), automotive engineer, was born at 112 Accrington Road, Blackburn, Lancashire, on 10 August 1933, the son of Frank Duckworth, a textile engineer who also sold cotton cloth on the Manchester cotton exchange, and his wife, Emma, *née* Hardman, a cooker demonstrator in electricity board showrooms. Following his education at Giggleswick, a boarding school in Yorkshire, Duckworth joined the Royal Air Force as a national serviceman. He undertook pilot training, moving from Tiger Moths to Chipmunks and then to twin-engine Oxfords. Eventually he was rejected as a pilot as he fell asleep in the cockpit during a night training flight owing to an allergy to medication he was taking for an ankle injury. Nevertheless his conduct was considered incompetent and dangerous. Subsequently he was offered training as an RAF navigator, but owing to differences of opinion with his navigational instructor the RAF released him. (Later in life he succeeded in gaining a helicopter pilot's licence.) Immediately he took up a place at Imperial College, London, to study engineering. He obtained, as he fully anticipated, only a pass degree, as his dissertation comprised primarily a critique of his BSc course, its content, and methodology.

Duckworth's interest in practical engineering dated back to his childhood and he was encouraged by his father, who provided him with a lathe, a vertical drill, and a grinder. He made model steam and aero engines and won local popularity for dealing with the neighbours' mechanical and electrical malfunctions. It was at university that his fellow undergraduates introduced him to motor racing, and he bought a sports kit car from Colin Chapman, which after three outings he crashed at Goodwood. During his student holidays he found employment in Chapman's gear and transmission department at Lotus's factory in Hornsey, which at that time was headed by the racing driver Graham Hill. It was there that he met Mike Costin, who was to become his business partner. On Hill's departure from the company in 1957 Duckworth succeeded him in charge of gearbox engineering. Almost immediately he pointed out the deficiencies in Chapman's product and left the firm.

In 1958 Duckworth joined forces with Mike Costin and established Cosworth Engineering, with an authorized original capital of £100. Duckworth focused on design and Costin on engineering development. The new firm was depicted as a no-frills operation, and its first premises were in Shaftesbury Mews before it moved to rat-infested premises at Friern Barnet and then on to Edmonton in 1961, before finally moving to a purpose-built complex in Northamptonshire in 1964. On 10 January 1959, at All Saints' Church, Carshalton, Surrey, Duckworth married (Dorothy) Ursula Cassal, the 22-year-old daughter of Charles Victor Cassal, electrical engineer. They had a son, Roger, and a daughter, Tricia.

Duckworth had been aware of the potential of the Ford 10E 1100 engine that powered the Ford Anglia saloon, and began experimenting. The firm's big break came in 1965 when Colin Chapman and Walter Hayes, public relations director of Ford, persuaded Sir Patrick Hennessy, chairman of Ford of Britain, to fund the design and manufacture of a new 3 litre formula one car, a category that was due to be launched on the racing circuit the following year. In essence, for the cost of £100,000, this brought Duckworth, Ford, and Lotus together. Rather than work in the factory, Duckworth designed the new engine in the quietness of his own home, losing forty pounds in weight in the process. The initial outcome was a four cylinder, 1600 cc formula two engine from which was developed the V8 Cosworth–Ford DFV (double four valve). Production of this new engine was timely for British motor racing, as it had been announced that Coventry Climax would no longer produce racing engines. The DFV changed the face of formula one racing in that, following Jim Clark's victory in a DFV-powered Lotus in the Dutch grand prix in 1967, it and its subsequent derivatives went on to dominate formula one racing down to 1983, winning 155 events. It was also used in formula two, three, and junior races with considerable success, and DFV-engined cars won the Le Mans twenty-four-hour race and several American speedway races. The key to the engine's success lay in Duckworth's precision in the use of a narrow angle, four-valve-per-cylinder, twin overhead camshaft cylinder head layout, which other firms had to acquire or develop themselves to remain competitive. More important, this was an off-the-shelf engine that was sold to independent firms like Brabham, Tyrrell, McLaren, Hesketh, and Wolf. It contributed significantly to the repeated success of such British racing drivers as Jackie Stewart, Damon Hill, and James Hunt.

Duckworth suffered a heart attack in 1973, which ultimately resulted in bypass surgery in 1987. As he owned 85 per cent of the company, his failing health and the prospect of crippling death duties persuaded him in 1980 to sell his interest in the business to United Engineering, and soon after he gave up his chairmanship of the company in favour of Mike Costin and retired to live in his hilltop house, Buckby Folly, in the village of East Haddon, Northamptonshire. His first marriage having ended in divorce in January 1986, on 18 April that year he married Gillian Mary (Gill) Reeve, the 43-year-old daughter of Thomas Francis Cockerill, farmer.

A bluff Lancastrian, Duckworth 'could always be relied upon to upset an otherwise tranquil discussion with one incisive comment' (*The Times*, 23 Dec 2005). He also enjoyed a talent for conjuring up pithy phrases and aphorisms, which became popular throughout the world of formula one racing and were known as Duckworthisms. He died of a ruptured abdominal aortic aneurysm at Northampton General Hospital on 18 December 2005, leaving an estate valued at over £10 million. He was survived by his wife, Gill, and the two children of his first marriage.

TOM DONNELLY

Sources G. Robson, *Cosworth: the search for power* (2003) · *The Guardian* (21 Dec 2005) · *Daily Telegraph* (22 Dec 2005) · *The Times* (23 Dec 2005) · *The Independent* (28 Dec 2005) · www.keithduckworth.co.uk, 30 April 2008 · 'Keith Duckworth', 19 Dec 2005, www.grandprix.com/ns/ns16050.html, 30 April 2008 · C. Corliss, 'The Cosworth story', www.motormarques.com, 30 April 2008 · 'Cosworth racing and the history of the Cosworth engine', www.madabout-kitcars.com, 30 April 2008 · b. cert. · m. certs. · d. cert.

Archives SOUND http://www.sidepodcast.com/tag/keith-duckworth

Likenesses group portraits, two photographs, 1970, Photoshot, London · obituary photographs · photograph, repro. in *The Times* · photographs, Heritage Image Partnership, London

Wealth at death £10,095,075: probate, 14 Feb 2007, *CGPLA Eng. & Wales*

Duke, Neville Frederick (1922–2007), air force officer and aviator, was born on 11 January 1922 at 82 Hadlow Road, Tonbridge, Kent, the son of Frederick Herbert Duke (1881–1957), managing clerk for a corn merchant, and his wife, Jane, *née* Tarbit (1888–1971). Educated at Judd School, Tonbridge, he was early obsessed by aeroplanes, making his first flight in an Avro 504K biplane trainer with Alan Cobham's flying circus at Biggin Hill, Kent, before unsuccessfully applying to join the Fleet Air Arm at the outbreak of the Second World War in 1939 at the age of only seventeen and then enlisting as a Royal Air Force cadet in June 1940.

After a year's training, Duke joined 92 fighter squadron at Biggin Hill in March 1941, flying Vickers-Supermarine Spitfires on sweeps over northern France, scoring his first victory over Dunkirk in June. In November he was posted to north Africa, where he spent most of the Second World War. Initially serving with 112 squadron, equipped with the inferior American Curtiss Tomahawk, he was shot down twice within six days before the squadron was re-equipped with the superior Kittyhawk. With eight more victories he was awarded the DFC in 1942. After six months as an instructor at a fighter school in Egypt, he returned to operations in 1943 as a flight commander, again with 92 squadron, now in Tunisia, and within three months shot down a further twelve enemy aircraft, to be awarded a bar to his DFC and a DSO, before reverting to the fighter school as chief instructor. He returned to operations in February 1944 and was ultimately posted to command 145 fighter squadron in Italy, flying the powerful Spitfire VIII and over the next few weeks claiming another five victories and being awarded a second bar to his DFC. Hit by anti-aircraft fire on 7 June, he encountered great difficulty in bailing out before landing in Lake Bracciano, north-west of Rome, his parachute dragging him through the water. He was sheltered by Italian partisans until the arrival of American troops. He returned to his squadron on 7 September and achieved two more victories to bring his ultimate score to twenty-eight enemy aircraft destroyed, having logged 486 sorties and becoming the RAF's highest-scoring fighter pilot in the Middle East theatre.

Neville Frederick Duke (1922–2007), by Charles E. Brown

Duke returned to England in October 1944 to be seconded to Hawker Aircraft as a production test pilot in January 1945. A year later he was selected to attend the Empire Test Pilots' School at Cranfield, Bedfordshire, where he flew a jet fighter, a twin-jet Gloster Meteor, for the first time and in June 1946 was one of three pilots who formed the RAF high speed flight at Tangmere, Sussex. In 1947–8 he was assigned to the Aeroplane and Armament Experimental Establishment at Boscombe Down, Wiltshire, for research with Meteors at high Mach numbers and altitudes up to 50,000 feet, exploring the then little understood aerodynamic phenomenon of compressibility at speeds approaching that of the so-called sound barrier. He was awarded an AFC for this work in 1948. Displaying a Meteor in Prague, he was also presented with the Czech military cross for his wartime military service. On 15 March 1947 he had married Gwendoline Dorothy Fellows (Gwen) (*b.* 1920), the daughter of Stanley Litchfield Fellows, company director, and former wife of Herbert Herman Louis Lohnberg. She had reverted to her maiden name by the time of their marriage, at the parish church in Dorney, Buckinghamshire.

Duke resigned from the RAF in 1948 with the rank of squadron leader and rejoined Hawker Aircraft as assistant chief test pilot. He also joined the Royal Auxiliary Air Force, flying Spitfires and Meteors from Biggin Hill at weekends until 1950, commanding 615 county of Surrey squadron, whose honorary air commodore was Winston Churchill. Delivering Hawker Furies to the Pakistani and Egyptian air forces, he established point-to-point speed records between London and Rome, London and Karachi, and London and Cairo.

By the end of 1949 Hawker had developed a series of experimental jet fighters that led to the highly successful transonic Hunter, with which Duke's name became closely associated after he made the first flight on 20 July 1951. By now Hawker's chief test pilot, on 7 September 1953 he established a world speed record of 727.63 m.p.h. flying a Hunter, and twelve days later another world record of 709.2 m.p.h. on a 100 km closed circuit. His brilliant flying of a Hunter in August 1955 after engine failure earned him the queen's commendation for valuable services in the air. Two days later he encountered further engine trouble and had to make a forced landing at 200 m.p.h. at RAF Thorney Island, suffering serious back injuries from which he never fully recovered. In October 1956 he resigned from Hawker. For his outstanding contribution to the exploration of high speed flight and his achievements with the company he had been appointed OBE in 1953.

Taking up freelance flying and consultancy, in 1960 Duke formed Duke Aviation, also becoming personal pilot to Sir George Dowty, the aeronautical engineer and industrialist. After selling his company in 1982 he concentrated on test flying light aircraft. He and his wife owned and displayed numerous light aircraft over the years. He also gave great support to the Tangmere Military Aviation Museum, of which he was honorary president, and where his world-record-breaking red Hunter WB188 is on permanent display. He wrote five books, of which *Sound Barrier* (1953) came to be regarded as a classic for its day. He was a keen sailor, but his passion remained flying. He died on 11 April 2007. Flying with his wife, he suddenly felt unwell and, although he landed safely at Popham airfield in Hampshire he collapsed as he left the aircraft and died that evening at St Peter's Hospital, Chertsey, of a ruptured abdominal aortic aneurysm. NORMAN BARFIELD

Sources G. Dorman, *British test pilots* (1950) • N. Duke, *Sound barrier* (1953) • N. Duke, *Test pilot* (1953) • N. Duke, *Neville Duke's book of flying* (1954) • N. Duke, *Neville Duke's book of flight* (1958) • N. Duke and E. Lanchbery, eds., *The crowded sky* (1959) • D. Middleton, *Test pilots: the story of British test flying, 1903–1984* (1985) • N. Duke, *The war diaries of Neville Duke*, ed. N. Franks (1995) • *Daily Telegraph* (13 April 2007) • *The Guardian* (14 April 2007) • *The Times* (16 April 2007) • *The Independent* (18 May 2007) • *Royal Aeronautical Society Aerospace Professional* (Aug 2007) • *WW* (2007) • personal knowledge (2011) • private information (2011) • b. cert. • m. cert. • d. cert.
Archives Brooklands Museum, Weybridge, Surrey • RAF Museum, Hendon • Tangmere Military Aviation Museum, West Sussex
Likenesses photographs, 1941–93, Rex Features, London • photographs, 1946–53, Photoshot, London • photographs, 1946–54, Getty Images, London, Hult. Arch. • photographs, 1951–3, PA Photos, London • C. E. Brown, photograph, Royal Air Force Museum [*see illus.*] • obituary photographs
Wealth at death under £32,000: probate, 12 Dec 2007, *CGPLA Eng. & Wales*

Dundy, Elaine [*real name* Elaine Rita Brimberg] (**1921–2008**), novelist and biographer, was born on 2 August 1921 in Manhattan, one of three daughters of Samuel M. Brimberg, a Jewish garment manufacturer who later turned to the manufacture of office equipment. Her father was violent and it was an unhappy childhood. She was educated at Mills College in Oakland, California, Sweet Briar College in Virginia, and then, after wartime service in the Army Signals Corps based in Arlington, Virginia, at the Jarvis Theatre School, Washington, DC, where she adopted the stage (and eventually pen) name, Elaine Dundy. Moving to Europe, she spent a year in Paris before arriving in London, scraping a living in both cities by taking small parts in plays. On 25 January 1951 she married the theatre critic Kenneth Peacock *Tynan (1927–1980). They had one daughter. She married him three months after meeting him, attracted by his romantic and larger-than-life character, and did her best to cope with his mercurial temperament. She originally wrote *The Dud Avocado* (1958), a comic novel about a young American woman in Paris, subtitled 'The Vie Amoureuse of Sally Jay in Paris', because she thought it would please him, but the overnight success of the book instead filled him with envy. Eventually his violent temper and infidelities became unbearable; she started drinking heavily, and finally left him after suffering a broken nose and two black eyes. They divorced in 1964. From then until the 1980s she divided her time between New York and London (where she kept a house in Mayfair). She wrote two more novels, *The Old Man and Me* (1964) and *The Injured Party* (1974), but neither enjoyed the success of *The Dud Avocado*. She also, after a period of rehabilitation for drink and drug addictions, wrote a biography of the actor Peter Finch, also well known for his hell-raising (1980); *Elvis and Gladys* (1985), about Elvis Presley's relationship with his mother; *Ferriday, Louisiana* (1991), a study of a small town in America which claimed to have produced more famous people per square mile than anywhere else in America; and an autobiography, *Life Itself!* (2001), which several critics slated for its relentless name-dropping. She had meanwhile moved to Los Angeles in the 1980s, and died there on 1 May 2008 following a heart attack. She was survived by her daughter, Tracy, a costume designer and film director.

Sources K. H. Tynan, *The life of Kenneth Tynan* (1987) • *Kenneth Tynan: letters*, ed. K. H. Tynan (1995) • *The diaries of Kenneth Tynan*, ed. J. Lahr (2001) • E. Dundy, *Life itself!* (2001) • *Daily Telegraph* (7 May 2008) • *The Guardian* (8 May 2008); (17 May 2008) • *The Times* (9 May 2008); (13 May 2008) • *The Independent* (10 May 2008) • *New York Times* (10 May 2008); (13 May 2008)
Likenesses obituary photographs

Dunlop, (Stephen) Robert (**1960–2008**), racing motorcyclist, was born on 25 November 1960 at the Robinson Hospital, Ballymoney, co. Antrim, the son of William Dunlop, motor mechanic, and his wife, May, *née* Barkley. His oldest brother was William Joseph (Joey) *Dunlop (1952–2000), also a racing motorcyclist. He made his road race début in 1979, in the Temple 100, and his professional début at Aghadowey in 1981. In 1985 he won the first of eight victories in the Cookstown 100 race; he would also win a record fifteen North West 200 races. In 1983 he won the newcomers' 350 cc Manx grand prix, and went on to win the 125 cc Isle of Man TT race three years in succession, from 1989 to 1991 (and in the latter year also won the junior TT). He finished second in that race in 1992 and 1993, but the following year a serious accident in the formula 1 TT, when the back wheel of his 750 cc Honda collapsed, almost killed him; he remained out of competition for the next two years, and was left with a shortened leg which required extensive operations. He nevertheless resumed racing in 1996. In 1998 he won the 125 cc TT race (his fifth TT victory), and in 2000 and 2002 achieved third place in the same event; in 2004 he came second. He again retired from racing in 2004–6, while undergoing further operations on his leg, but in 2006 he returned to win the 125 cc North West 200. During practice for the 250 cc race at the North West 200 on 15 May 2008 he was flung from his bike when it seized at over 150 m.p.h. He died later that day from injuries sustained in the accident. He was survived by his wife, Louise, whom he had married around 1984, and by their three sons, two of whom had themselves become racing motorcyclists. (Michael went on to win the North West 200 250 cc race in which his father had been killed in practice, dedicating his victory to his father's memory. Michael subsequently became a TT winner himself.)

Sources *Irish Times* (16 May 2008); (19 May 2008) · *Belfast Telegraph* (19 May 2008); (26 Feb 2009) · *The Independent* (19 May 2008) · b. cert. · d. cert.
Likenesses obituary photographs
Wealth at death £180,000: administration, 7 Sept 2000, *CGPLA NIre*

Dunlop, Samuel Clarke (1922–2008), master mariner, was born on 27 November 1922 at Carnlough, co. Antrim, Northern Ireland, the son of William Dunlop, master mariner, and his wife, Mary Ann, *née* Clarke. He was educated at Belfast Royal Academy. He first went to sea on 3 April 1939 as an indentured cadet in the Bank Line tramp steamer *Cedarbank*, circumnavigated the world via Turkey and Japan, and was in Buenos Aires when the Second World War broke out. After helping to paint *Cedarbank* grey and black and load with a cargo of grain he sailed for Freetown to join one of the first wartime convoys, and then served eleven months in *Teesbank*. Both these ships were torpedoed shortly after he left them. His next ship was *Myrtlebank*, but he was hospitalized with malaria for several weeks at Long Island College Hospital, New York. By July 1942 he was well enough to join the 17,000-ton tanker *Empire Marvell*, after which he passed his mate's certificate and served in her as third and then second officer.

Dunlop volunteered for the Royal Navy but was not released from a reserved occupation until August 1943, when he joined the Royal Fleet Auxiliary oiler *Cederdale* in Alexandria. For several months he was continually at sea, apart from two days in Australia, ferrying oil from the Gulf to the British Pacific Fleet. In August 1945 *Cederdale* was one of the first ships to enter newly liberated Hong Kong, and was employed to repatriate British and Commonwealth prisoners of war. Dunlop was appointed MBE in 1946 for his wartime services.

In September 1946 Dunlop became second officer of the tanker *Brown Ranger*, which fuelled the battleship HMS *Vanguard* during King George VI's state visit to South Africa. In March 1948, at a relatively early age, he passed his master's certificate and joined the tanker *Broomdale*, on which he was navigator and ship's doctor. When one of the crew fell into an empty tank and was badly injured Dunlop followed instructions given by radio on how to fit a catheter; his patient survived. He was promoted to master in 1958, and was particularly delighted, while in command of the aviation training ship *Engadine*, to be made a member of the Fleet Air Arm Officers' Association. On 20 August 1960, at Duncairn Presbyterian Church, Shankill, Belfast, he married Joyce Gertrude Scott Allen, a 27-year-old dental receptionist, and daughter of Norman Scott Allen, insurance official. They had a daughter and then a twin son and daughter.

In May 1977 Dunlop was appointed commodore of the Royal Fleet Auxiliary, and one of his last duties before his imminent retirement was to host a visit on 26 June 1981 to the ammunition and stores ship *Fort Austin* by the queen, a first by royalty since the Royal Fleet Auxiliary was established by order in council in 1911. However, on the outbreak of the Falklands War he retained command of *Fort Austin* and during the British landings in May 1982 kept her in San Carlos Water as a helicopter base while he unloaded hundreds of tons of ammunition. During one low-flying air attack he claimed he could read the pilot's name, Rodriguez, written on the side of the aircraft. Reassuring a junior officer, he said: 'You don't have to worry about going down in this ship [with her cargo of explosives], you'll only ever go up' (private information, M. Nurse). *Fort Austin* was continuously at sea for ninety-one days and steamed some 18,000 miles, and Dunlop became the first Merchant Navy officer since the Second World War to be awarded the DSO, for 'considerable qualities of leadership, steadiness and aggression', and for 'his immense inspiration to those under him' (*London Gazette*, 14 Dec 1982). He was also appointed CBE, and received his DSO and his CBE at the same investiture, when he made it known that he regarded these awards as not his personal awards, but for all who served in *Fort Austin* and the Royal Fleet Auxiliary.

On retirement, after more than forty years at sea that had begun and ended in war, Dunlop called for the Royal Fleet Auxiliary in any future war to be placed under the white ensign. This so upset civil servants in the Ministry of Defence that he was not invited to the unveiling of a memorial to the dead of the Royal Fleet Auxiliary at Marchwood, on Southampton Water.

Dunlop was honest, hardworking, and hospitable, with

a mischievous sense of fun, but he expected high standards in all aspects of life. He was known as 'Black Sam' because of the colour he turned while serving in the tropics. His passion was sailing. In the 1970s he helped to establish the annual Weymouth trawler race. He was also chairman of the South Dorset Sail Training Association, which later gave him the opportunity in retirement to navigate several tall ships, and in 1975 he organized the Royal Dorset Yacht Club's centenary. His three generations of boxers were called Bruce, Bess, and Buster. He lived latterly in Weymouth, Dorset. His final years were affected by cancer. He died on 17 July 2008 at Dorset County Hospital of bronchopneumonia, after a long illness. He was survived by his wife, Joyce, and their three children.

PETER HORE

Sources *RNSTS Journal* [passim] • *Daily Telegraph* (19 Aug 2008) • *The Times* (28 Aug 2008) • private information (2012) [Mike Nurse] • b. cert. • m. cert. • d. cert.
Likenesses obituary photographs
Wealth at death under £47,000: probate, 7 Oct 2008, *CGPLA Eng. & Wales*

Dunwoody [*née* Phillips], **Gwyneth Patricia** (1930–2008), politician, was born at 25 Rosaville Road, Fulham, London, on 12 December 1930, the elder child and only daughter of Morgan Walter *Phillips (1902–1963), political organizer, and his wife, Norah Mary [*see* Phillips, Norah Mary, Baroness Phillips (1910–1992)], schoolteacher and politician, and daughter of William Lusher. Her father had been a coal miner in south Wales and subsequently an official in the West Fulham Labour Party. He rose through the party's organization to become national secretary in 1944. Her convent-educated mother worked as a teacher and became an extremely active life peer in 1964.

Educated at Fulham County Secondary School and the Convent of Notre Dame, Gwyneth Phillips left school at sixteen and worked as a local journalist, an actress in repertory, and at Radio Hilversum in the Netherlands. Her most significant education was within the culture of the Labour Party, not least the convivial political evenings at the Phillipses' home. There she met a medical student, John Elliott Orr Dunwoody (1929–2006), son of William Orr Dunwoody, medical practitioner. They married at the Roman Catholic Church of the Most Holy Trinity, Brook Green, Hammersmith, on 29 May 1954 and had a daughter and two sons. From 1956 the family lived in Totnes, Devon, where she became a rare Labour presence on the local council in 1960.

Both Gwyneth Dunwoody and her husband had parliamentary ambitions. In the 1964 election she was narrowly defeated in Exeter but became the city's first Labour member in the March 1966 landslide. Her husband joined her, successful in the marginal Cornish seat of Falmouth and Camborne. She became a junior minister at the Board of Trade in 1967; late in 1969 her husband went to the Department of Health and Social Security. They were the first husband and wife team to hold ministerial office. However, in June 1970 each lost both office and seat. They responded to defeat in contrasting ways. John Dunwoody

Gwyneth Patricia Dunwoody (1930–2008), by Jane Bown, 2003

became a family doctor in south London. Gwyneth Dunwoody returned to the Commons in February 1974 as MP for Crewe. Their marriage was dissolved in 1975.

Dunwoody's return to the Commons did not mean a return to ministerial office. A critic of the European Economic Community, she served as a nominated member of the European parliament from 1975 until the introduction of direct elections in 1979. Greater influence came with the ideological disputes and personal antipathies that engulfed the Labour Party after its 1979 election defeat. Dunwoody became thoroughly involved in the tough loyalist response to the left's growing influence. She was a member of the loyalist slate for elections to the party's national executive committee in 1981 and became a member of the executive's women's section. This bloc of politically reliable women was thoroughly hostile to the agenda of the left and Dunwoody's opposition was expressed in notably robust terms. The major unions, and therefore a largely male electorate, had the preponderant role in determining the membership of the women's section. Successful candidates were rarely sympathetic to the increasing demands of Labour women for institutional and procedural reforms to end the marginalization of women within the party. Dunwoody aroused anger among women delegates at the 1982 conference when she spoke for the national executive committee in opposition to their proposals.

Dunwoody became more significant within the parliamentary party as defections weakened the resources of the right. Michael Foot as leader from November 1980 was desperate to reconcile the contending factions. He gave Dunwoody responsibility for leading the opposition attack on the Thatcher government's health policies. In 1981 she was elected to the shadow cabinet. Elevation did not assuage her reservations about Foot's leadership. By August 1982 she was complaining to him that she and her fellow loyalists felt taken for granted. Foot's resignation as leader after the heavy electoral defeat in June 1983 meant contests for leader and deputy leader. She was a late and hopeless entrant to the latter contest. Her vote was derisory (amounting to around 1.3 per cent of the weighted ballots). Under Kinnock she retained her front bench position with responsibility for transport but her standing declined. She lost her shadow cabinet position in 1985 and by 1989 diminishing union support meant her removal from the national executive committee. The initiative within the party was shifting to a younger generation. Her personal circumstances deteriorated; financial problems led to her acceptance of a retainer from the Fur Trading Association. Her response to critics was a blunt insistence that she needed the money. At one point her house was repossessed. Even her electoral position had become perilous. Secure Crewe had become highly marginal Crewe and Nantwich; she survived in 1983 and 1987, but with small majorities.

Dunwoody's renaissance came as an effective critic of misgovernment, most notably from 1997 as chair of the select committee on the environment, transport, and regional affairs. She presided with authoritative rigour over hearings, not least on the problematic legacies of rail privatization. New Labour ministers became apprehensive about her ability to probe their vulnerabilities. In mid-2001 the Blair government clumsily attempted to remove her and another committee chair. The strategy failed spectacularly as Labour backbenchers revolted. She became a powerful symbol of resistance to New Labour's intolerance of dissent. Her opinions like her dress sense were emphatically 'off message' (she was described as looking 'as if she had not so much dressed but rolled herself up in the bedroom carpet' *Daily Telegraph*, 19 April 2008). She was Eurosceptic, opposed to electoral reform, dismissive of changes in the Commons' working hours, and voted against the equalization of the age of consent for homosexuals. She was president of Labour Friends of Israel from 1988 to 1993. Her effectiveness was enhanced because this one-time paragon of party discipline personified the ethos of the party's old right that was insensitively dismissed by New Labour zealots. She was named 'Battle-axe of the Year' in 2002 by *The Oldie* magazine. A further redrawing of constituency boundaries in 1997 proved beneficial and she remained MP for Crewe and Nantwich until her death. She died in the John Radcliffe Hospital, Oxford, on 17 April 2008 of sepsis and bronchopneumonia a week after heart surgery. She was survived by her three children.

DAVID HOWELL

Sources T. Benn, *The end of an era: diaries, 1980–90* (1992) · T. Benn, *Free at last! Diaries, 1990–2001* (2002) · J. Golding, *Hammer of the left* (2003) · R. Cook, *The point of departure* (2003) · D. Hayter, *Fightback! Labour's traditional right in the 1970s and 1980s* (2005) · *The Times* (19 April 2008) · *Daily Telegraph* (19 April 2008) · *The Guardian* (18 April 2008) · *The Independent* (19 April 2008) · C. Mullin, *A view from the foothills: the diaries of Chris Mullin*, ed. R. Winstone (2009) · C. Mullin, *Decline and fall: diaries, 2005–2010*, ed. R. Winstone (2010) · *WW* (2008) · b. cert. · m. cert. · d. cert.

Archives People's History Museum, Manchester, Michael Foot Papers, MF/M10/5/1; Labour Party National Executive Committee minutes; Parliamentary Labour Party minutes · University of Hull, Brynmor Jones Library, Labour Solidarity Campaign archives | FILM BFINA, current affairs and party political footage | SOUND BL NSA, current affairs, documentary, and interview recordings

Likenesses photographs, 1954–87, Getty Images, London · photographs, 1966–2001, PA Photos, London · photographs, 1966–2005, Photoshot, London · Madame Yevonde, bromide print, 1967, NPG · V. Carew Hunt, photograph, 1998, repro. in V. Carew Hunt, *One two one: women in parliament* (1998), 31 · J. Bown, photograph, 2003, Camera Press, London [*see illus.*] · J. Bown, photographs, 2003, Camera Press, London · obituary photographs

Wealth at death £578,576: administration, 24 Sept 2008, *CGPLA Eng. & Wales*

Durham, Sir Kenneth (1924–2005), businessman, was born on 28 July 1924 at 104 Stanley Street, Blackburn, Lancashire, the son of George Durham, house painter, and his wife, Bertha, *née* Aspin. He was educated at Queen Elizabeth Grammar School, Blackburn, and briefly read physics at Manchester University before serving in the Royal Air Force between 1942 and 1946, during which he qualified as a pilot and attained the rank of flight lieutenant. On 29 June 1946, while still an RAF officer, he married Irene Markham, a 22-year-old shop assistant from Blackburn, daughter of James Markham, overlooker. They went on to have a son and a daughter.

After leaving the RAF, Durham returned to Manchester, where he won a Hatfield scholarship and graduated with first-class honours in physics. He then briefly joined the Atomic Energy Research Establishment at Harwell as a theoretical physicist before joining Unilever's Port Sunlight research laboratory in 1950. Port Sunlight was then the largest research laboratory owned by Unilever. This company had been formed in 1929 through a merger between the British-owned Lever Brothers and the Dutch-owned Margarine Union. It remained a highly unusual case of a business owned ultimately by two parent companies located in different countries, Britain and the Netherlands. Its chief executive was the three-person special committee consisting of the British and Dutch chairmen and a third executive. It was probably the largest European company at the time of its creation, and during the post-war decades it remained the leading European manufacturer of margarine and of soap and detergents. The giant global business also sold processed foods, ice cream and frozen products, tea, toothpaste and other toiletries, animal feeds, and chemicals; it owned vast plantations in Africa and elsewhere, and operated extensive shipping and other transport facilities. Unilever's research laboratories supported this vast enterprise, and were widely regarded as a major source of scientific innovation.

Durham's career flourished at Port Sunlight. He was recognized as not only a first-class scientist but also someone who understood that his company needed to commercialize its basic research by utilizing it to create products consumers wanted to buy. This was a major weakness of Unilever, a sprawling colossus noted for its inability to take decisions quickly and without innumerable internal discussions. In the late 1940s Unilever had faced the decimation of its large American laundry business after its American rival Procter and Gamble launched synthetic detergents. In 1961 Durham was appointed head of the Port Sunlight laboratory, and in the following year he was sent to attend the advanced management programme at the Harvard business school, the best executive educative programme in the world at the time, to which Unilever sent its potential future leaders. In 1965 he was appointed to head Unilever's fast-growing laboratory at Colworth in Bedfordshire. In 1970 Unilever transferred him to line management. He joined the large animal feeds business, which was performing poorly. In the following year he became chairman of BOCM Silcock, Unilever's British affiliate that made oilseed cake and other compound feeds for animals. Durham rapidly reduced the workforce from 10,000 to 3500, rationalized the product line, and moved production from the large oil mills located at ports which were dominated by confrontational trade unions to smaller mills scattered around the country. Durham's decisive, even aggressive, personality brought success within Unilever. He was appointed to the boards of the British and Dutch parent companies in 1973.

In 1978 Durham became the 'third man' on the special committee. His years on Unilever's special committee coincided with a time of crisis for the firm. Its financial performance in Europe had deteriorated sharply earlier in the decade following the oil price rises of 1973, while poor local management had led to a catastrophic decline in market share and profitability in its American business. The company was so diversified that managerial attention was spread too thinly. The special committee functioned primarily as a reactive rather than proactive force. Durham became one of the major forces behind change. Crucially he helped force through shifts in Unilever's American business. In 1978 Unilever acquired the well-run National Starch Company in the United States, which became a catalyst for change. Durham was instrumental in the sacking of the chief executive of its largest American affiliate, long protected by ties of loyalty and friendship.

As the American business slowly turned round, Durham became chairman of the British company in 1982. Over the following four years he formulated, with his other colleagues on the special committee, Floris Maljers and Michael Angus, a radical programme of divestment of so-called non-core businesses, enabling the company to focus managerial time and financial resources on a narrower range of categories led by detergents, foods, personal care, and chemicals. The new strategy resulted in improved financial performance by a company that had looked like a potential target for takeover at the end of the 1970s.

Durham was knighted in 1985, and appointed commander of the order of Orange Nassau the same year. Following his retirement as chairman of Unilever in 1986 he went on to hold several other senior positions in British business. He served as chairman of Woolworth Holdings between 1986 and 1990, and as deputy chairman of British Aerospace between the same years (having been a director since 1980), and was also a director of the electrical components maker Delta (1984–2004) and the merchant bank Morgan Grenfell (1986–90). He served on various industry and government bodies, for example as chairman of the economic development committee for the food, drink, and packaging machinery industries (1981–6), the economic policy committee of the Confederation of British Industry (1983–6), and the Ministry of Agriculture's priorities board (1984–7). He was also a trustee and later chairman of the Leverhulme Trust from 1974 to 1998. He devoted considerable time to charitable causes, and led a £6 million fund-raising campaign for the charity Help the Aged. As president of the British Association for the Advancement of Science (1986–7) he was a strong supporter of scientific research, and criticized governments for insufficient funding. He was made an honorary fellow of the British Academy in 1997, and received honorary doctorates from the universities of Manchester and Loughborough, and Queen's University, Belfast. He lived latterly at Dove Cottage, Middle Entrance Drive, Storrs Park, Bowness-on-Windermere, Cumbria. He died on 17 February 2005 at Westmorland General Hospital in Kendal of myocardial infarction and acute renal failure.

GEOFFREY JONES

Sources C. Wilson, *Unilever, 1945-1965* (1968) · G. Jones, 'Control, performance and knowledge transfers in large multinationals: Unilever in the United States, 1945–1980', *Business History Review*, 76 (autumn 2002), 435–78 · G. Jones, *Renewing Unilever: transformation and tradition* (2005) · *Unilever Magazine*, 45 (June–July 1986) · *Daily Telegraph* (18 April 2005) · Burke, *Peerage* · *WW* (2005) · private information (2009) · b. cert. · m. cert. · d. cert.

Archives Unilever, Port Sunlight, Cheshire, historical archives · Unilever, Rotterdam, historical archives | SOUND BL NSA, current affairs recording

Likenesses B. Organ?, portrait, Unilever, London; repro. in *Unilever Magazine*, 45 (June–July 1986)

Wealth at death £474,238: probate, 14 Sept 2005, *CGPLA Eng. & Wales*

Eames [*née* Graham], **Elizabeth Sara** (**1918–2008**), archaeologist and expert on medieval tiles, was born on 24 June 1918 at 62 Stimpson Avenue, Northampton, the daughter of Arthur Frederick (Fred) Graham, an industrial chemist then serving as a second lieutenant in the Royal Field Artillery, and his wife, Eveline Lucy (Eva), *née* Garrett (1887–1945). In 1937 she went from Rugby high school to Newnham College, Cambridge. There she read English in part 1 of the tripos, changing to archaeology and anthropology for part 2, choosing to read section B, Anglo-Saxon and kindred studies (which included an archaeological component). After graduating in 1940 she started work towards a PhD, but soon joined the Auxiliary Territorial

Service. In 1943 she was commissioned. Ending the war as an education officer in charge of a camp in Guildford, she was demobilized in 1946. Her academic interests had shifted during the war and, having spent a year at the University of Oslo, she submitted a thesis on women in Viking society and was made a Cambridge MLitt. On 15 October 1949, at St Andrew's Church, Rugby, near where her parents then lived, she married Herbert Wells Eames (1919–1983), a solicitor and for some time Conservative leader of Lewisham borough council, with whom she had a son and two daughters.

Elizabeth Eames joined the staff of the British Museum in 1949, as a part-time special assistant, working three days a week (initially on £1 a day), a position she held for thirty years. She was given the job of sorting and cataloguing the museum's vast collection of (mainly British) medieval tiles, which had recently been substantially augmented by the accession of the tenth duke of Rutland's collection of 9000 decorated English tiles. Apart from a few exceptionally interesting early fourteenth-century tiles from Tring and thirteenth-century tiles from Chertsey, acquired many years previously, which were displayed in the galleries, the museum's tile collections were stored in chaotic conditions in unheated and dusty basements. Eames had to sort these out and, in many cases, assist in their conservation. Many tiles were suffering from efflorescence and had to be washed and dried out, without damaging the glazes, before they could be handled and placed in proper storage. At the same time she was involved in the rescue of the remains of the pavements and tile-kiln uncovered in the 1930s at Clarendon Palace, Wiltshire, by Tancred Borenius; these were lifted and removed to the museum. She also excavated kilns and pavements at, among other places, Meaux Abbey in Yorkshire, Ramsey Abbey in Huntingdonshire, and Haverholme Priory in Lincolnshire, and advised on many other sites investigated in the 1960s and 1970s, from which many tiles were acquired by the museum.

In 1975 Eames arranged a major display of medieval tiles in a dedicated gallery in the museum, including the remains of the mid-thirteenth-century kiln from Clarendon Palace, together with the important pavements from the king's chapel and the queen's chamber at the same site. In 1980 she published her major work, the groundbreaking, two-volume *Catalogue of Medieval Lead-Glazed tiles in the Department of Medieval and Later Antiquities in the British Museum*, which described 13,882 tiles, dating from the late Anglo-Saxon period to the sixteenth century, many of which were illustrated by drawings. This work was supplemented in 1988 by a monograph written jointly with Thomas Fanning on Irish medieval tiles, and published by the Royal Irish Academy.

When Eames began her work on tiles, the subject had been severely neglected. A handful of papers on tiles from specific sites and small regions had been published in archaeological journals, while the Victoria and Albert Museum's medieval tiles had been briefly surveyed in Arthur Lane's *Guide to the Collection of Tiles* (1939). Consequently she had to start from first principles. In a series of articles, particularly in the *Journal of the British Archaeological Association* from the 1950s onwards, and in two small popular booklets published by the British Museum, she constructed a chronology for the surviving material that was of crucial importance in the burgeoning field of medieval archaeology, also examining the tiles in their art-historical, economic, and social contexts. She also contributed greatly to an understanding of the medieval tile industry and of its manufacturing methods, taking part, for example, in various experiments that replicated the use of kilns.

Eames was a considerable figure in the study of medieval building construction, not only through her work on tiles, but also through the work of the brick section of the British Archaeological Association (of which body she was a long-serving council member and vice-president). She was elected a fellow of the Society of Antiquaries in 1958 (and served on its council), and was appointed MBE in 1978. A bubbly enthusiast, she inspired many students in further education, teaching courses on archaeology until well into her eighties. She had an infectious laugh and a sense of humour that occasionally bordered on the bawdy. Welcoming to specialists and amateurs alike, she gave generously of her deep knowledge. She died at the Royal Free Hospital, Camden, London, on 20 September 2008, of acute heart failure, and was survived by her three children. DAVID M. WILSON

Sources *The Guardian* (30 Sept 2008) · *The Times* (11 Oct 2008) · *The Independent* (11 Oct 2008) · *Daily Telegraph* (14 Oct 2008) · personal knowledge (2012) · private information (2012) · b. cert. · m. cert. · d. cert.

Likenesses obituary photographs

Wealth at death £494,117: probate, 28 Jan 2009, *CGPLA Eng. & Wales*

Eames, (Gwladys) Marion (1921–2007), novelist and radio producer, was born on 5 February 1921 at 86 Raffles Road, Tranmere, Birkenhead, Cheshire, the second of the three daughters of William Griffith Eames (1885–1959), greengrocer and later proprietor of a general store, and his wife, Gwladys Mary, *née* Jones (1891–1979). Both her parents were of Anglesey stock but she was sent to school in Dolgellau in Merioneth, where from 1932 to 1936 she attended (as a day pupil) Dr Williams's School for Girls, which was notorious in her day on account of the wholly English education it dispensed. She was to complain in later life that she had not received a single Welsh lesson while at the school and this lack she felt keenly. She made strenuous efforts to regain the language of her early childhood and, after leaving school at the age of fifteen, became fluent while working with the county's library service and in the library of the University College of Wales at Aberystwyth. She also worked as an organizer for Plaid Cymru in north Wales and as editor of *Y Dydd*, a weekly newspaper published in Dolgellau. Among the foreign writers she grew to admire was Simone Weil, author of *L'enracinement* (1949), which had a profound effect on her thinking about the obligations of the individual and the state.

It was in London, where she had gone to study the piano and harp at the Guildhall School of Music, that Eames met the journalist Griffith Williams (1917–1977), the son of a coalminer, John Henry Williams. They married at the Welsh Tabernacle in Finsbury on 25 August 1955. Though they married in a Congregational church he was already attracted to the faith of the Quakers and introduced her to the Society of Friends, in which she retained a general interest. There were no children of the marriage. They returned to Wales in 1955 on her appointment as a producer of radio programmes for the BBC in Cardiff, making their home at Bonvilston in the Vale of Glamorgan. Among the programmes she made was *Merched yn bennaf*, the Welsh equivalent of *Woman's Hour*; she also wrote scripts for the nightly soap *Pobol y cwm*.

Marion Eames made her name as a historical novelist and one of the most consummate prose writers to have taken the matter of Wales as her theme. Her books were admired for their literary quality as much as for the meticulous research on which they were based. Making no concession to readers expecting mere entertainments or romantic yarns, she produced six novels of high seriousness which were among the finest written in Welsh during the latter half of the twentieth century.

Eames's first two novels, *Y stafell ddirgel* (1969) and its sequel *Y rhandir mwyn* (1972), announced the emergence of a new talent that was to reinvigorate the writing of novels on Welsh historical subjects. These books, translated as *The Secret Room* (1975) and *Fair Wilderness* (1976), tell the story of Rowland Ellis (1650–1731), a member of the minor gentry who joined the Society of Friends in 1672, and of his emigration to Pennsylvania and the settling of the Welsh tract there. The name of his old home near Dolgellau, which still stands, is preserved in that of Bryn Mawr College. The novels, which tell an exciting tale with restraint and perception, proved a huge success when televised in serial form by BBC Cymru. So authentic were they that it was hard to believe that the author had never set foot in Philadelphia. Although patriotism was at the heart of all her books, she never allowed propaganda to interfere with her writing, for which reason they are all the more convincing in their account of the Welsh people at critical points in their history.

Eames's third novel was *I hela cnau* ('To gather nuts', 1978), in which she dealt with the migration of young people from rural north Wales to the docks and cotton mills of Merseyside; an English translation appeared as *The Golden Road* in 1990. It was followed by three more novels: *Y gaeaf sydd unig* ('The winter is lonely', 1982), set in the thirteenth century during the reign of Llywelyn ap Gruffudd, the last prince of independent Wales; *Seren gaeth* ('Captive star', 1985), about a troubled marriage between an academic and a talented music student, which bears some resemblance to the relationship between Ernest Jones, Freud's biographer, and his first wife, the young composer Morfydd Llwyn Owen; and *Y ferch dawel* ('The quiet girl', 1992), in which the subject of incest is broached. She also published *A Private Language?* (1997), based on a series of lectures on Welsh literature that she had given (under the auspices of the Workers' Educational Association) to English incomers into the Welsh-speaking heartlands of Gwynedd.

Marion Eames was a shy, softly spoken woman whose mild manner belied a steely commitment to her craft and a clear-eyed view of people and events. These, together with her gifts as a storyteller, equipped her well as a novelist. When asked whether she had thought of how much money she could have made had her novels been written in English, she would reply that financial reward meant nothing to her while the Welsh language, in all its richness, was there for her to write in. She died of cancer at Dolgellau and Barmouth District Hospital, Dolgellau, on 3 April 2007, and was cremated in Aberystwyth on 24 April 2007 after a memorial service held at Salem Chapel, Cader Road, Dolgellau, on the same day; her remains were interred with those of her husband at Pendine church, Carmarthenshire. MEIC STEPHENS

Sources *The Independent* (6 April 2007) • *Daily Post* [Liverpool; north Wales edition] (12 May 2007) • personal knowledge (2011) • private information (2011) • b. cert. • m. cert. • d. cert.
Archives NL Wales, papers, diaries, corresp.
Likenesses J. Sheppard, photographs, NL Wales • photograph, repro. in *Daily Post* (12 May 2007) • photographs, repro. in news.bbc.co.uk/welsh/hi/newsid_6520000/newsid_6525500/6525579.stm • sculpture, priv. coll.
Wealth at death £402,870: probate, 23 Aug 2007, *CGPLA Eng. & Wales*

Edwards, John Hilton (1928–2007), human geneticist, was born on 26 March 1928 at Ingleborough Lodge, Dulwich, London, the elder son of Harold Clifford Edwards (1899–1989), consulting surgeon at King's College Hospital medical school, London, and his wife, Ida Margaret Atkinson, *née* Phillips (1900–1981). His younger brother, Anthony (*b.* 1935), was professor of biometry at Cambridge University until his retirement in 2003.

Edwards went to Uppingham School in 1942 and left in 1946 with a distinction in physics at higher school certificate level and a passion for gliding obtained during his time in the officers' training corps air section. The university gliding club, of which he became secretary, featured prominently during his three years' preclinical course at Trinity Hall, Cambridge, and this, with some uninspiring lecture courses, he regarded as the probable reasons for his graduating in 1949 with a third in part one of the natural sciences tripos. However, he greatly enjoyed the zoology lectures and this influenced his later career. He went on to clinical studies at the Middlesex and Central Middlesex hospitals, during which he joined the Territorials (Artists' Rifles), and graduated MB BChir in 1952. Instead of moving on to pre-registration house jobs he joined, as medical officer with an interest in zoology, the research ship *John Biscoe* of the Falklands Islands Dependencies Survey and spent nine months in Port Stanley and the South Atlantic. Outbreaks of diphtheria and German measles occupied time not spent in reading. On his return in July 1953 he sought a post as a junior house officer and, on 18

July, at the parish church of East Harling, Norfolk, married Felicity Clare Toussaint (*b.* 1928), a fellow medical student at the Middlesex, and daughter of Charles Hugh Christie Toussaint, consulting chest physician at the Central Middlesex Hospital. They had four children, Vanessa, Conrad, Penelope, and Matthew.

Edwards's first hospital post was in neurology (with Douglas McAlpine) at the Middlesex. This was interrupted by the discovery of a tuberculous lesion in one lung during a routine medical examination for army national service. After six months' treatment at the Central Middlesex, employed partly in reading up on statistical methods, he took a second house job in gastroenterology (with Francis Avery Jones) and then six months as senior house officer in psychiatry at Knowle Hospital, near Fareham in Hampshire. There he became interested in brain pathology, and this led to a job as senior house officer in pathology at the Central Middlesex. In 1956, using his statistical knowledge, he successfully applied for a lectureship in epidemiology at Birmingham University to work with Thomas McKeown and Lancelot Hogben in the department of social medicine. In the same year he became a member of the Royal College of Physicians. He was greatly influenced by Hogben and learned to apply statistics to information in the malformation register, namely to studies of the epidemiology of dislocation of the hip and of neural tube defects that he published in 1958. He pursued his clinical interests by going on ward rounds at the Birmingham Children's Hospital once a week and this led him to an interest in genetics. His first publication (on Peutz-Jegher's syndrome, in 1956) stems from this time. McKeown suggested that he join the new Medical Research Council unit in population genetics at Oxford directed by Alan Stevenson, an expert on congenital malformations. Edwards was at the unit from 1958 to 1960, but kept regular contact with the Children's Hospital in Birmingham and this resulted in an acclaimed paper on trisomy 18, published in *The Lancet* in 1960. He resigned from the unit in 1960 to take a year's sabbatical at the Children's Hospital in Philadelphia, where he consolidated his cytogenetics interests, learning how to make chromosome preparations from small blood samples and interacting with Peter Nowell and David Hungerford.

In 1961 Edwards returned to the vacant lectureship at the department of social medicine at Birmingham, this time with a half-time connection with Douglas Hubble's department at the Nuffield Institute of Child Health. Edwards set up there a small cytogenetics laboratory to study Down's syndrome and to provide a chromosome diagnostic service. Promotion to senior lecturer followed in 1965, and to reader in human genetics in 1966. At this point he took a year's sabbatical at Cornell Medical Center and the New York Blood Center with James German. On his return he was awarded a personal professorship in human genetics and moved the cytogenetics service and genetics clinic to the Women's Hospital. He was elected a fellow of the Royal Society in 1979 for 'contributions to human cytogenetics and genetic epidemiology including elucidation of the threshold model for multifactorial traits and pedigree linkage analysis'. In the same year he accepted the professorship of genetics at Oxford University after Walter Bodmer's resignation to become director of research at the Imperial Cancer Research Fund in London. He retired from his Oxford appointments in 1995.

At the time Edwards entered academic medicine in 1956 genetics played virtually no part in the practice of medicine. The molecular structure of DNA had been solved only three years earlier, and the discovery that humans had forty-six chromosomes and not forty-eight was made in the year in which he was appointed lecturer. By the time of his death genetics was at the heart of medicine and DNA was the basis of diagnostic pathology. Edwards was one of the pioneers who helped to make this remarkable transformation possible. Jerome Lejeune was another, and his contribution with Marthe Gautier was to discover in 1959 the extra chromosome 21 responsible for Down's syndrome. One year later Edwards, working with David Harnden, discovered the next chromosome disorder, due to an extra chromosome 18. This condition, trisomy 18, became known as Edwards's syndrome. The discovery was no chance observation. It was due to sound clinical intuition. Edwards appreciated that the pattern of multiple minor malformations and mental handicap in Down's syndrome could be the clues that could lead to other chromosomal syndromes.

In the years that followed Edwards continued his interest in chromosome abnormalities and described patients with mosaic trisomy, triploidy, and various translocations. He established a small laboratory for this work in the Nuffield Institute of Child Health in Birmingham. In one important study he analysed personally the chromosomes of 128 patients with Down's syndrome born to young mothers in order to determine to what extent inherited translocations and maternal mosaicism contributed to the frequency of the condition. Only one inherited translocation was found and he rightly concluded that routine analysis of affected children caused unnecessary distress and was unwarranted. When prenatal diagnosis was introduced in 1970 the recurrence of Down's syndrome in women with an affected child was found to be less than 0.5 per cent. The option of prenatal diagnosis, however, gave couples the reassurance necessary to contemplate further pregnancies. Edwards's laboratory was one of those that were early in the field in providing prenatal diagnosis. Indeed as early as 1956 he had written to *The Lancet* drawing attention to its possible use in the diagnosis of fetal genetic disorders.

Edwards's contribution to the development of diagnostic cytogenetics was very important, but he also made outstanding contributions to other aspects of human genetics, including the epidemiology of malformations, twin studies, linkage mapping, genetic susceptibility to common disease, clinical genetics, and comparative genomics. He was expert in designing simple diagrams to convey important concepts. He attended all eleven Human Gene Mapping Workshops from 1973 to 1991. These workshops provided the chromosome maps that led eventually to the human genome project and the complete DNA sequence of the human genome in 2001. Edwards's contribution was to provide novel computing methods for assigning and ordering genes onto their specific chromosomes. He made original contributions to statistical genetics and was one of the pioneers of the application of computers to human genetics, writing his own computer programmes. He insisted that his colleagues make their primary data freely available and was an early advocate of openness in human genetics.

From the beginning of his career Edwards was interested in how to determine genetic susceptibility to such common diseases as diabetes and heart disease. His aim was to distinguish the effects of single genes of low penetrance from the combined effects of a multiplicity of genes. His ideas were encapsulated in a paper entitled 'The simulation of mendelism', published in *Acta Genetica et Statistica Medica* in 1960, widely considered one of his best papers. Another was 'A marker algebra', published in *Clinical Genetics* in 1972. He returned to these themes on many occasions up to the last year of his life, with many critical papers on the proper use of sib-pair analysis, on haplotype mapping, and on various aspects of allelic association.

Edwards's interest in the conservation of linkage groups between species led in the 1980s to a series of papers written with Mary Lyon, Tony Searle, and other mouse geneticists at Harwell, comparing the chromosomal homologies of mouse and human. He designed a graphical representation of homologies based on comparative mapping that became known as the Oxford grid. With the help of Frank Nicholas from the University of Sydney a database was created in which the genomes of many species, including farm animals, were compared in this way. These grids proved themselves valuable for evolutionary studies, as well as being a demonstration of the extraordinary conservation of chromosome structure within the animal kingdom.

Among clinical geneticists Edwards was an outstanding diagnostician and his clinical experience led to notable papers on the characterization of X-linked hydrocephalus due to stenosis of the aqueduct of Sylvius, and on the delineation of the Cornelia De Lange and Peutz-Jeghers syndromes. He ran genetic counselling clinics throughout his professional life and he had an excellent rapport with his patients. He was always extremely helpful to his clinical and scientific staff and was a kind and generous supervisor of graduate students. He had a particular talent for inspiring his students and staff. Besides his posts in Birmingham and Oxford his appointments included consultant to the University of Iceland from 1967, where he helped to establish record linkage of all Icelandic births from 1840. He was also visiting professor of human genetics at the Memorial University of Newfoundland from 1977, consultant in human genetics to the World Health Organization from 1972, and visiting professor at the University of Sydney from 1998 to 2006.

Edwards had a quick wit and was good company. His conversation was full of amusing anecdotes and he always had an apt analogy to emphasize a particular point. He would often discuss several different subjects simultaneously and this sometimes confused the listener, especially on the telephone. When his mind was concentrating on other interests he appeared to lose account of time and this may have been responsible for the numerous stories of his absent-mindedness. Deciphering his handwriting was always a problem but this, and other eccentricities, did not detract from the respect in which he was held. Sir David Weatherall described him as 'One of the nicest and cleverest [scientists] of our field' (*The Independent*, 17 Nov 2007). Oliver Mayo wrote that 'no one else in my scientific world combined insight, keen humour and capacity to confuse and illuminate simultaneously' to the same degree (Ferguson-Smith, memorial address). Sir Walter Bodmer noted that 'He had a fine feel for human genetics, including a historical perspective, and always an original way of looking at problems and presenting them' (*The Independent*, 17 Nov 2007). Similarly, Sir Ed Southern commented, 'He had a brilliant mind; lesser intellects had difficulty following his reasoning and, in my case, it would often take months for the penny to drop—but what pennies!' (Ferguson-Smith, memorial address).

In retirement Edwards continued actively in his research with his bioinformatics and veterinary colleagues at the University of Sydney to develop the Oxford grid website, producing grids for an increasing number of species and using DNA sequence data rather than gene mapping information. The identification of sequences that have been conserved, gained, or lost between species contributes to knowledge on speciation and evolution, and the molecular mechanisms involved. Edwards's other scientific interests were not neglected and he was a critical commentator on publications on allelic association and genome-wide screening. He died of prostate cancer at St Luke's Nursing Home, Latimer Road, Oxford, on 11 October 2007, and was survived by his wife, Felicity, and their four children. MALCOLM A. FERGUSON-SMITH

Sources *The Independent* (17 Nov 2007) · *BMJ*, 335/1269 (15 Dec 2007) · *Nature Genetics*, 39/12 (Dec 2007), 1417 · *The Times* (17 Jan 2008) · *The Record* [Keble College] (2008), 10–12 · M. Ferguson-Smith and F. Nicholas, memorial addresses, 19 April 2008, oxgrid.angis.org.au/johnedwards/addresses.pdf, 2 March 2010 · *WW* (2007) · personal knowledge (2011) · private information (2011) · b. cert. · m. cert. · d. cert.

Archives University of Cardiff, special collections and archives

Likenesses photograph, repro. in *Nature Genetics* · photograph, repro. in *The Record*

Wealth at death £721,404: probate, 11 Dec 2007, *CGPLA Eng. & Wales*

Elgar [*née* Craymer], **Sybil Lillian** (**1914–2007**), educationist, was born on 10 June 1914 at 88 Tubbs Road, Harlesden, Middlesex, the daughter of Frederick Green Craymer (1892–1939), railway locomotive fireman and later engine driver, and his wife, Ellen, *née* Thomas, who worked in the local Pathé News factory. At some point her family adopted the surname Green-Craymer. She was brought up in Willesden. During the Second World War she was a local government clerk responsible for accommodating evacuees in north London, and trained as a mortician. On

8 June 1940 she married John William Elgar (1914–1994), then a sapper in the Royal Engineers, formerly a railway clerk, and later a surveyor and civil servant. They had one daughter, Jacqueline (Jackie).

After the war Sybil Elgar worked as a school secretary. On deciding to become a teacher she became a student of the Montessori method and owing to lack of financial resources she embarked on a correspondence course to gain her diploma. In 1958, while studying, she went to see the Marlborough Day Hospital for 'severely and emotionally disturbed children'. She was horrified by the scene she was confronted with and 'could not get out of her mind how soul-destroying the place was and how miserable the children were' (*The Guardian*, 24 Jan 2007). At the time of the visit children with autism were viewed as being 'psychotic' and Leo Kanner's 'refrigerator mother' theory was prevalent. Parents, particularly mothers, were thought to be largely responsible for their offspring's difficulties due to a 'genuine lack of maternal warmth' and 'parental coldness', and it was widely accepted that children with disabilities should be placed in institutions (L. Kanner, 'Problems of nosology and psychodynamics of early infantile autism', *Journal of American Orthopsychiatry*, 19/3, 1949, 416–26). On visiting the hospital for a second time, in 1960, it was clear to Elgar that nothing had changed. Frustrated, she resolved to provide an alternative.

In 1962 Elgar succeeded in setting up her own school for autistic children in the basement of her home in St John's Wood, London. There she developed a new and innovative way of teaching, allowing her pupils time to internalize what they needed to do, through clear instructions that she would write down or present in pictorial form. In doing so she became one of the first teachers able to see beyond the difficult, often severely challenging or withdrawn behaviour of autistic children to the underlying child, and to act on her belief that every child had the capacity to learn. As word spread, demand from parents grew. In September 1965, with support from the Autistic Children's Aid Society of North London (renamed the National Society for Autistic Children in 1966 and the National Autistic Society in 1975), she was able to open a residential school for children with autism, in Ealing. The school, initially named the Society School for Autistic Children, was the first of its kind in the UK, and, it is thought, the world.

Although Elgar faced some critics who described the project as over-ambitious, the school quickly gained an international reputation as an example of how autistic children should be taught. At first nine children with an age range of five to fourteen years were accommodated within one building, which included a live-in flat for Sybil Elgar and her husband. However, within five years the school grew rapidly and the society was able to purchase three more adjoining houses, with the pupil intake growing to forty. Elgar's work was widely admired and she influenced, for example, Eric Schopler from North Carolina, USA, who came to view her work in 1965 and went on to develop the structured teaching model known as TEACCH (the treatment and education of autistic and related communication-handicapped children), which became part of the essential toolkit for teaching children with autism.

In October 1969 Elgar celebrated a historic moment when an inspection by the Department of Education and Science granted the school formal recognition. The following year a visit from Edward Short, the secretary of state for education, gave further credibility to the pioneering work of Elgar and her team. In 1972 the National Society for Autistic Children marked its tenth anniversary. In the commemorative issue of the society's magazine, *Communication*, Elgar stated that 'Children need praise and congratulation but most of all they need the opportunity to continue their education and training so that they can maintain and extend educational capabilities, develop social and personal ability and acquire occupational skills' (*Communication*, June 1972). This vision was shared by a growing number of educationists and carers, and reflected Elgar's determination to promote the rights of all children and adults with autism to learn and to have that learning facilitated throughout their lives.

Despite celebrating tremendous success within the field of education Elgar was increasingly drawn to a similarly pioneering role for adults with autism. Soon after establishing the school she recognized that while the children improved considerably in their behaviour and awareness they still remained autistic, and if they did not continue to receive appropriate support into adulthood they could easily regress or struggle to cope with daily life. So, after an enormous fundraising effort, in 1974 she founded the first residential service for adults with autism. Still working with the National Society for Autistic Children, she oversaw the purchase of Somerset Court, a large house at Brent Knoll in Somerset. Moving twenty of the older children from the Ealing school, she set about showing how the skills the children had acquired at school could be developed and built on, greatly enhancing their lives as adults as well as their ability to function within society. According to Wendy Brown, the founding head of two later National Autistic Society schools (Helen Allison School and Broomhayes School), it was at Somerset Court that Elgar 'showed the effectiveness of a person with autism's functioning within society was based on other factors, including an appropriate education, the fostering of motivation, and a stimulating environment'. She also observed that Elgar 'was perhaps also the first person to realise that the language disorder was close to the heart of the condition' (private information, W. Brown).

Sybil Elgar was appointed MBE in 1975 and retired in 1984, having made a major contribution to the body of expert knowledge, understanding, and experience of autism. She was an inspirational leader who had true determination and tenacity. Her last years were spent in Dawlish, Devon, where her daughter, Jackie, and her family lived. She died at Palm Court Nursing Home, Dawlish, on 8 January 2007, of pneumonia, and was cremated at Exeter crematorium. She was survived by her daughter. The principles of her work continued to inform the education and care of children and adults with autism throughout the UK and the world and she was commemorated by the renaming of her pioneering school as Sybil Elgar School. Each year at the school's graduation ceremony the Sybil Elgar cup is presented for 'most progress made'.

CHLOE PHILLIPS

Sources *Communication* [National Society for Autistic Children] (June 1972) • *The Guardian* (24 Jan 2007) • *National Autistic Society*, Jan 2007, www.autism.org.uk • *Awares News*, [Autism Cymru], Jan 2007, www.awares.org • H. G. Allison, 'Perspectives on a puzzle piece', www.autism.org.uk/en-gb/about-autism/autism-library/magazines-articles-and-reports/article-collection/perspectives-on-a-puzzle-piece.aspx, 28 June 2010 • personal knowledge (2011) • private information (2011) [Jackie Cragg, daughter; L. Wing; W. Brown] • b. cert. • m. cert. • d. cert.
Archives priv. coll.
Likenesses photograph (with Robert Morley), repro. in www.newman-family-tree.net/Hill%20Brow%20School/
Wealth at death under £101,000: probate, 20 April 2007, *CGPLA Eng. & Wales*

Ellenshaw, Peter (1913–2007), special effects artist and landscape painter, was born William Samuel Cook Ellenshaw at 76 Chatham Road, Battersea, London, on 24 May 1913, the son of Adeline Eyles. His mother was named on his birth certificate as Alice Ellenshaw, formerly Eyles, and his father as William Ellenshaw, engine driver at a laundry. The origin of the name Ellenshaw was unknown to him and he always understood that his father was James S. Alcock (*d.* 1921), an Irishman whose family came from Enniscorthy, co. Wexford, who had once owned a silver mine in Rico, Colorado, but now operated a laundry in the Wandsworth area. Although the names William Samuel appeared on official documents well into his adult life, he was known as Peter from childhood. He had two older sisters (registered as Eyles), Dorothy and Lulu, with whom he was evacuated during the First World War to Vange, Essex. At one point he briefly attended a preparatory school in Deal, Kent. He acquired a younger half-sister, Irene, after his mother married Edward James Hook, a gardener, in 1920. Sent to school in Chipstead, Surrey, he left at the age of fourteen and worked as a garage mechanic.

A talented, self-taught amateur artist, Ellenshaw spent his evenings making copies of paintings by the old masters that earned the encouragement of the Royal Academician Walter Percy ('Pop') Day (1878–1965), a pioneering special effects artist at Alexander Korda's London Films. Day specialized in creating hand-painted mattes: paintings on large sheets of glass which, suspended in front of the camera, or double exposed, created the illusion of scenery, thus obviating the need for elaborate sets or location filming. Day became Ellenshaw's mentor and, in the early 1930s, engaged him as his apprentice; Ellenshaw gave uncredited assistance with the creation of mattes for films including *The Scarlet Pimpernel* (1934), *Things to Come* (1936), *Fire over England* (1937), *The Four Feathers* (1939), and *The Thief of Baghdad* (1940). The closeness of Ellenshaw's relationship with his employer led to his introducing his mother, Adeline, to the widowed Day. She left James Hook and moved in with him, initially as his 'cook', although she subsequently adopted his surname, and in 1953 they married.

Ellenshaw joined the Civil Air Guard in 1938, and served as a fighter pilot in the RAF during the Second World War. In 1941 he was posted to Albany, Georgia, USA, for training. There he met Bobbie Palmer (*d.* 2000), a nurse at the Lawson General Hospital. They married in 1942 and had a son, Peter (known as Harrison), and a daughter, Lynda. On demobilization he returned to work with Day, most notably on three films produced and directed by Michael Powell and Emeric Pressburger, *A Matter of Life and Death* (1946, chosen for Britain's first charity royal film performance), *Black Narcissus* (1947), and *The Red Shoes* (1948).

Ellenshaw's long association with Walt Disney began in 1947, when he undertook the matte paintings for the producer's first live-action film, *Treasure Island* (1950), filmed in England. The tutelage of Day paid off and Ellenshaw created highly convincing shots of Bristol harbour crowded with three-masted schooners as well as giving the English locations the appearance of an exotic Caribbean island. In an era before computer-created effects the work of the matte artist was indispensable and Ellenshaw's ability to render paintings with a photographic realism resulted in his becoming rapidly established as a master of the craft.

The success of Ellenshaw's work on *Treasure Island* led to his painting a vista of ancient Rome for Mervyn LeRoy's MGM epic *Quo vadis?* (1951) and two more projects for Disney that involved a year's work painting fifty-two and sixty-two matte paintings respectively for *The Story of Robin Hood and his Merrie Men* (1952) and *The Sword and the Rose* (1953). The skill with which he discharged this huge undertaking resulted in his moving to California in 1953 to enter into an exclusive contract with Walt Disney Productions, although this did not prevent his taking on occasional uncredited jobs for other studios, including more scenes of ancient Rome, this time for Stanley Kubrick's *Spartacus* (1960).

Between 1953 and 1979 Ellenshaw painted the mattes for every live-action film Disney produced (some thirty-four in total) as well as contributing to the concept art and special effects for many films and, on some titles, acting as production designer. Significant work included the underwater sequences in *20,000 Leagues under the Sea* (1954), which were shot in the demanding format of Cinemascope; the astonishing sequences set in the underground leprechaun kingdom in *Darby O'Gill and the Little People* (1959); and the vertigo-inducing alpine landscapes of *Third Man on the Mountain* (1959). Among other notable films to which he contributed were *Swiss Family Robinson* (1960), *Kidnapped* (1960), *In Search of the Castaways* (1962), and *Summer Magic* (1963). Between films he worked on Disney's television shows, including *Davy Crockett* (1955), *Zorro* (1957–60), and *Walt Disney's Wonderful World of Color* (1955–65). He also painted one of the first aerial maps of Disneyland, featured on early guidebooks and postcards, as well as contributing to the design of several attractions at the theme park.

Ellenshaw won an Academy award (or Oscar) for best visual effects for his work on *Mary Poppins* (1964), which memorably featured the title character's flight across the skyline of Edwardian London, the 'feed the birds' sequence set around St Paul's Cathedral, and the rooftop antics of the chimneysweeps, whose dance number, 'Step in Time', was inspired by his recounted memories of the London pub dance 'Knees Up, Mother Brown'. He was Oscar-nominated three more times, for *Bedknobs and Broomsticks* (1971), on which he served as art director, and for *The Island at the Top of the World* (1974) and *The Black Hole* (1979), on both of which he acted as production designer.

Throughout his career Ellenshaw painted powerful landscapes and seascapes, notably of the south-west coast of Ireland (where he kept a holiday home), the Mojave Desert, the American Pacific coastline, and the Himalayas. After his official retirement in 1979 he devoted more time to his paintings, which fetched high prices at leading New York galleries, although, with a defensiveness born out of his lack of formal art training, he disarmingly confessed that 'sophisticates think they're corny' (*New York Sun*, 15 Feb 2007). He came out of retirement to work with his son, providing mattes for *Superman IV: the Quest for Peace* (1987) and Disney's *Dick Tracy* (1990). He also contributed somewhat over-prettified paintings of scenes from Disney animated films, which became a line of best-selling lithographs for the Disney studio's merchandising arm. Designated a 'Disney legend' in 1993, Ellenshaw was a man of huge charm who concealed a considerable ego beneath a cloak of self-effacing modesty. He died at his home in Santa Barbara, California, on 12 February 2007 and was survived by his two children, both of whom had followed him into the film industry, Harrison as an Oscar-nominated visual effects artist and Lynda as a visual effects producer. BRIAN SIBLEY

Sources P. Ellenshaw, *The garden within: the art of Peter Ellenshaw* (1996) · P. Ellenshaw, B. Gordon, and D. Mumford, *Ellenshaw under glass, or, 'Going to the matte for Disney'* (2003) · *Hollywood Reporter* (15 Feb 2007) · *Daily Variety* (15 Feb 2007) · *New York Sun* (15 Feb 2007) · *Boston Globe* (16 Feb 2007) · *The Times* (20 Feb 2007) · *Daily Telegraph* (31 March 2007) · *The Independent* (4 April 2007) · b. cert.

Likenesses M. Germana, photograph, 2004, Photoshot, London · obituary photographs · photograph, repro. in www.filmreference.com/Writers-and-Production-Artists-Ei-Gi/Ellenshaw-Peter.html · photographs, repro. in Ellenshaw, *Garden within*

Elliott, Walter Archibald [Archie], **Lord Elliott** (**1922–2008**), advocate and judge, was born at 8 Cheyne Walk, Chelsea, London, on 6 September 1922, the second son, and the second of the five children, of Thomas Renton *Elliott (1877–1961), physician and physiologist, and his wife, Martha Sara Mary, *née* McCosh. The young Walter (as he remained to some of the family, while the world came to know him as Archie) spent his early childhood at Cheyne Walk. In 1936 his parents commissioned a home in the Scottish borders. Their architect was the young Basil Spence, and at Broughton Place, surrounded by grouse moors, he produced a superbly stylish tower house. On the adjacent slopes Martha Elliott created gardens worthy of the house. Thanks to her, Elliott already knew plants in Latin; but at Broughton his lifelong love of gardening took root.

From Eton College, Elliott went to Trinity College, Cambridge, to read modern history. But after two years, in 1943, he was commissioned as an ensign in the 2nd battalion, Scots Guards. The north African campaign was ending, with a brief respite near Tripoli: 'On the table in my tent I always had a vase of those most beautiful of African lilies, the pearl white amaryllis, which grew wild nearby. Their perfume hung sweet and heavy on the desert night' (Elliott, 20). Ahead, within days, lay his twenty-first birthday, on the very eve of the horrors of Salerno; almost immediately the award of an MC; capture and escape; battling on to the Garigliano, and in due course the Rhine and Germany itself; wounds, and the unrelenting deaths of brothers-in-arms of all ranks. Yet amid all the scars of war and its aftermath, Elliott found an abiding focus for heart and mind: esprit de corps, and 'how human identities (with their consequent loyalties) can be created and retained' (ibid., 9).

Demobilized in 1947 as a captain, Elliott turned to the law. He joined the Inner Temple, but it was at the Scottish bar that he chose to practise. He took a law degree at Edinburgh and 'devilled' for Ian Fraser (the future Lord Fraser of Tullybelton), a kindred spirit and lifelong friend. He was admitted to the Faculty of Advocates in 1950, the same year that he was called to the English bar. On 30 July 1954 he married Susan Isobel Mackenzie Ross (*b.* 1929), scientist, and daughter of Philip Mackenzie Ross, golf course architect. In 1964, soon after Elliott had taken silk and now with two sons, they moved to Morton House, Winton Loan, on the southern edge of Edinburgh. This outstanding house—with its ever more imaginative garden and grounds—was to be his home for the rest of his life.

In the 1950s and 1960s there was an increasing demand for counsel in matters such as planning, where there was not merely a legal dispute, but a need for tribunals or inquiries to resolve conflicts between private and public interests. Elliott was particularly suited to such work. He was deeply fair-minded. He recognized the need for both development and conservation. He could feel the tensions, but also the bonds, between society and individuals. His reflective mind was more naturally attuned to the complexities of public and administrative law than to cut-and-thrust litigation or the judicial impatience which was then customary in the court of session. Along with work in trust, land, and taxation cases he specialized in planning law. This reached its culmination in the Edinburgh inner ring road inquiry in 1967. Planning inquiries in Scotland were conducted by an independent QC. Elliott's discharge of this quasi-judicial role, and above all his handling of the controversial ring road proceedings, was exemplary.

Commitment to public service led to Elliott's involvement in the Bow Group and standing for parliament as a Conservative three times, coming dangerously close to winning Leith from Labour in 1970. A more durable public service was imminent. A lands tribunal for Scotland had been envisaged since 1949. The Conveyancing and Feudal

Reform (Scotland) Act 1970 made it urgent. In 1971 Elliott accepted appointment as the first president of the tribunal. This jurisdiction included a controversial power to vary or discharge binding conditions in feudal title deeds. The new president evolved principles of fairness which would justify such intervention; and he did so with a clarity that ensured lasting acceptance. The tribunal's ground-breaking decisions provided a calmly decisive step towards an overall transformation of Scottish land tenure.

Until 1978 the Scottish land court was chaired by Lord Birsay. Elliott succeeded him, acquiring the judicial title of Lord Elliott. Like the lands tribunal, the land court's jurisdiction was broad, covering all the notorious problems of agricultural and crofting law. Elliott was none the less asked to head both bodies. He did so until his retirement in 1992. The two separate jurisdictions were so successfully managed that the custom of combining the presidency and the chair survived him. Elliott's character and abilities made him an admirable and popular chairman of the court. His somewhat patrician bearing was combined with a wholly genuine affection for people of all kinds. In an itinerant court sitting locally, perhaps in a village hall, the chairman was able, in wig and judicial robes, to blend legal acumen with an obviously friendly understanding. The tangles of statutes and highland boundaries alike were brought to comprehensible order.

If gardening was his passion, Elliott's delight in the country and country pursuits ran much wider. His work let him travel all over Scotland, especially in the isles and crofting counties. Meanwhile his profound interest in human nature bore fruit with the publication in 1986 of *Us and Them: a Study of Group Consciousness*. This thoughtful, perceptive work ended with a credo: 'The Brotherhood of Man needs to be *cultivated* and based on a deeper sense of humanity.' Always and everywhere both Archie and Susan Elliott cultivated a sense of total humanity. Their travels took them to Latin America and to India, to the sites of the American Civil War, to the Middle East, and the Silk Road—wherever there were other histories and peoples. Elliott's other book, *Esprit de Corps: a Scots Guards Officer on Active Service, 1943–1945*, was published in 1996, but written some fifty years before. When at last he was prevailed upon to edit and publish it, it was recognized as a small masterpiece; it revealed not only his modesty and his courage, but already that all-embracing decency which continued to the end of his days. He died at Colinton Nursing Home, Edinburgh, on 9 August 2008, following a stroke, and was survived by his wife, Susan, and their sons. WILLIAM D. PROSSER

Sources W. A. Elliott, *Esprit de corps* (1996) • *Daily Telegraph* (4 Sept 1996) • W. D. Prosser, memorial tribute, 19 Aug 2008, priv. coll. • *The Scotsman* (21 Aug 2008); (25 Aug 2008) • *Daily Telegraph* (27 Aug 2008) • *The Herald* [Glasgow] (28 Aug 2008) • *Sunday Times* (5 July 2009) • personal knowledge (2012) • private information (2012) [Lady Elliott, widow] • *WW* (2008) • b. cert. • m. cert. • d. cert.

Likenesses H. Lamb, group portrait, 1935, City of Edinburgh Art Collection, Edinburgh • H. Lamb, pencil sketch, 1935, City of Edinburgh Art Collection, Edinburgh • H. Lamb, sketch, oils, 1935, City of Edinburgh Art Collection, Edinburgh • obituary photographs

Ellis, Susan Caroline Williams- (1918–2007), ceramics designer and manufacturer, was born on 6 June 1918 at Durbins, Guildford, Surrey, the eldest in the family of one son and two daughters of Sir (Bertram) Clough Williams-*Ellis (1883–1978), architect and creator of the holiday resort of Portmeirion in Caernarvonshire, and his wife (Mary) Annabel Nassau (Amabel) Strachey (1894–1984), writer, and daughter of John St Loe Strachey, proprietor and editor of *The Spectator*. Susan was born in a house belonging to Roger Fry, in a room decorated by Duncan Grant, and grew up in London at the centre of the Bloomsbury set: her parents' friends included Bertrand Russell, Augustus John, Rudyard Kipling, and Virginia Woolf. Summer holidays were spent at Plas Brondanw, the family home in Merioneth.

In 1934 Susan Williams-Ellis's parents, influenced by Bertrand and Dora Russell and their progressive views on education, sent her to Dartington Hall School in Devon, where she was taught pottery by Bernard and David Leach. Interested in painting from an early age, she was taken by her Strachey grandmother to European art galleries every year, and decided to enter the art school at Chelsea Polytechnic in 1936. There she was taught book illustration by Graham Sutherland and sculpture by Henry Moore. While there she also did the illustrations for *In and Out of Doors* (1937), a family activity book produced by all the members of her family, which remained in print for over twenty years. Leaving without a certificate, at the beginning of the Second World War, she taught art at Dartington for a short time before getting a job at the Air Ministry, drawing maps for bombing raids. At St Brothen's Church, Llanfrothen, Merioneth, on 28 April 1945 she married Euan Stewart Cooper-Willis (*b*. 1920), who had shared rooms at King's College, Cambridge, with her brother (killed at Monte Cassino in 1944). The son of Guy Cooper-Willis, civil servant, at the time of their marriage he was a captain in the army; he later became a stockbroker, economist, and investment adviser. They had one son and three daughters.

After a year in Cambridge the family moved to Glasgow, where Euan Cooper-Willis spent a year working for Blackie and Son, the publishing firm owned by his family, but in 1947, with their two small daughters, they moved to Wales, taking over Cefn Cyffin, a remote cottage on Susan's father's estate near Plas Brondanw and Portmeirion. Working the farm they became almost self-sufficient, while Susan (who continued to be known by her maiden name) worked as a freelance book illustrator and textile designer and her husband became an investment adviser for the City firm Grieveson, Grant. In 1946 a set of twelve tiles made by Poole Pottery to her designs was shown in the exhibition Britain Can Make It, organized by the Council of Design at the Victoria and Albert Museum in London, and she painted four panels for the dome of discovery at the 1951 Festival of Britain.

At the same time Susan and her husband were becoming more involved in the management of Portmeirion village, and in 1953 Clough Williams-Ellis asked them to take over the running of the gift shop. In order to increase the range of goods for sale, Susan Williams-Ellis sent designs to the pottery decorating firm of A. E. Gray & Co. Ltd in Stoke-on-Trent, where they were used to decorate blank pottery shapes, and soon she was commissioning exclusive designs, to be used only in the Portmeirion shops. One of the first of these was the Portmeirion Dolphin (1958). They opened more shops in the village, and in 1957 a Portmeirion shop opened in Pont Street, London, selling ceramics, rugs, tweeds, quilts, and other textiles designed by her. She developed the Malachite range of pottery and textiles in 1959 for the Pont Street shop. On the death of A. E. Gray in 1960 she and her husband bought the workshop, and in 1961 this was followed by the acquisition of Kirkhams Ltd, a pottery manufacturing business, also in Stoke-on-Trent. The two firms were amalgamated, and Portmeirion Potteries Ltd was established at the beginning of 1962.

With the pottery manufacturing and decorating sides of the business in her hands, Susan Williams-Ellis was able to turn her attention to designing and making pottery shapes on which to transfer her designs, and in 1962 she introduced the 'cylinder' shape, including the tall, straight coffee pot, which became one of Portmeirion Potteries' most famous shapes. One of her most successful designs was the Totem embossed range of tea and coffee sets, launched in 1963. During the next decade her new shapes included Meridian (1971), and she created many popular designs, including Magic City (1966), but it was the popularity of the Botanic Garden range of tableware, launched in 1972, that made Portmeirion Potteries famous. Botanic Garden, based on illustrations in Thomas Green's *The Universal Herbal* (1817), offered a choice of over thirty different plant designs, with the same leaf border, so that each plate, cup, and bowl in a set would be different. Botanic Garden was soon accounting for half of total sales, as she continued to add new motifs, including plants illustrated in Rebecca Hey's *The Moral of Flowers* (1835): in the end over sixty plant designs were used. With the success of Botanic Garden the factory was greatly expanded in 1976. Susan Williams-Ellis continued to be responsible for most of the new designs, including Birds of Britain (1978), using illustrations from Edward Donovan's *Natural History of British Birds* (1793), and Pomona, a new botanical range based on the *English Pomological Magazine* from the early 1800s. There were also such new shapes as Romantic (1982), inspired by an early Carthaginian cup in a museum in Ibiza.

The popularity of Portmeirion pottery in the United States led to the formation of Portmeirion USA in 1986, and in 1988 Portmeirion Potteries, by now exporting to thirty-four countries, was floated on the stock market and became a public company. The family continued to run the company, and when Portmeirion China was launched in 1994 Susan Williams-Ellis contributed one of the new designs, Ladies Flower Garden (her daughters Angharad and Anwyl were responsible for the other three). In 1995 she produced a new cup shape, Traditional.

Susan Williams-Ellis had always loved the sea, and early in her career she illustrated two books, 'Shore Life in Britain' and 'The Complete Mermaid', both unpublished. She became fascinated by the underwater world of coral reefs, taking up underwater diving, first with an aqualung and later with a snorkel. On holidays in the Indian Ocean, Hawaii, and the Caribbean she went sketching underwater, using a waterproof board, transferring her sketches later. Magic Gardens, an exhibition of her paintings, was shown at Plas Glyn-y-weddw gallery in 2002.

One of the best ceramic designers of her day, Susan Williams-Ellis was unusual in combining the creation of pottery shapes and the design of patterns to go on them. It was also unusual for a woman to design shapes—most famous potters were men—but her early training with Bernard Leach as well as lessons in wood-turning at Dartington equipped her with the right skills. Her early very contemporary shapes and abstract patterns gave way to more traditional designs as the business developed, but she was always very clear that her ceramics should be both functional and affordable. Portmeirion Potteries became known worldwide, to such an extent that for many people Portmeirion meant the pottery and not the place. In 2002 she was awarded an honorary degree by the University of Keele for her outstanding contribution to the ceramics industry. She retired in 2005, and died of bronchopneumonia at her home, Ty'n yr Ardd, Minffordd, Penrhyndeudraeth, Merioneth, on 27 November 2007. She was survived by her husband and their four children.

ANNE PIMLOTT BAKER

Sources V. Stanton and E. Cooper-Willis, *The story of Portmeirion Potteries, 1960–1995: a collectors' guide* (1995) · J. Jones, *Clough Williams-Ellis* (1996), 150–53 · S. Jenkins and S. P. McKay, *Portmeirion Potteries* (2000) · A. Turner, ed., *Portmeirion* (2006) · *The Independent* (29 Nov 2007) · *Daily Telegraph* (30 Nov 2007) · *The Times* (10 Dec 2007) · *The Guardian* (28 Jan 2008) · A. Turner and T. Marsh, *Magic gardens: the underwater art of Susan Williams-Ellis* (2008) · A. Turner, *Susan Williams-Ellis: a life in design*, booklet accompanying exhibition at Chelsea Futurespace, 2009 · private information (2011) · b. cert. · m. cert. · d. cert.

Archives FILM *Magic gardens*, television documentary, BBC Wales, 2002

Likenesses obituary photographs · photograph, repro. in Jenkins and McKay, *Portmeirion*, 104 · photographs, repro. in www.portmeirion.co.uk

Wealth at death £1,735,952: probate, 6 May 2009, *CGPLA Eng. & Wales*

Eltringham, (Stewart) Keith (1929–2006), zoologist, was born on 21 June 1929 in Edgerton, Alberta, Canada, the second son of George Alexander Eltringham, farmer, originally from the west country. The family struggled to make ends meet during the great depression, and returned to Britain. Eltringham was brought up in Bristol, where he attended St Brendan's College and was an enthusiastic visitor to the city's zoo. After national service in the RAF (some of it spent as ground staff during the Berlin airlift) he went to Southampton University, where he studied zoology and joined the university air squadron. After graduating he stayed on at Southampton to complete a PhD on the environmental impact of a new electrical power station on the River Test, specifically on the populations of gribble (*limnoria lignorum*), a marine isopod crustacean. (The study had practical implications, in that the gribble is a wood-borer and any increase in its population would pose a threat to wooden boats.) In the course of his research Eltringham discovered that two other species of gribble, *limnoria tripunctata* and *limnoria quadripunctata* (both particularly destructive), were present in British waters, as he reported in *Nature* in 1958. On 23 August that year he married Susan Penelope (Sue) Tonge, daughter of Stanley Vincett Tonge, local government officer. They had two daughters.

From 1958 to 1961 Eltringham combined his zoological and aviation skills as a pilot–biologist for the Severn Wildfowl Trust in Slimbridge, Gloucestershire, the organization founded by the ornithologist Peter Scott in 1946. Eltringham's role was to undertake aerial surveys of waterfowl populations, in the process devising new methods for bird-count surveys that were widely adopted elsewhere. In 1962 he became an assistant lecturer at King's College, London, where he lectured primarily on marine biology and conservation. He also developed links with staff and students at Makerere College in Kampala, Uganda.

In 1967 Eltringham moved to Mweya, Uganda, as director of the Nuffield Unit of Tropical Animal Ecology, the first wildlife research station in Africa. There he directed research on a wide variety of animals and plants in the Queen Elizabeth National Park. His own interest was in the large mammals, and he conducted numerous aerial surveys of animal populations, refining a constant height, constant width transect method, using visible ground markers at set distances. Initially his surveys confirmed the over-population of elephants (leading to the erosion of the national park habitat and problems for neighbouring farmers), but from the early 1970s the surveys revealed an alarming decline in elephant populations as a result of poaching and the disintegration of law and order under the dictatorship of Idi Amin. Eltringham was forced to leave Uganda in 1973, but he remained in touch with researchers there, and followed with concern the further deterioration in African elephant numbers, which led eventually to the international ban on the trade in ivory in 1989.

In 1973 Eltringham returned to Britain to take up a post as lecturer in applied biology at the University of Cambridge. He remained there (as university lecturer in zoology from 1989) until his retirement in 1997. He was a fellow of Wolfson College from 1988, and admissions tutor there from 1995 to 1997. It was during his time at Cambridge that he was most productive in terms of publications. His book *The Ecology and Conservation of Large African Mammals* (1979), delineating the interactions between large mammal species and between them and humans, represented an important step beyond single-species studies, and was welcomed by Brian Bertram as providing 'a much needed dose of general knowledge, experience and common sense' in this field (*Nature*, 285, 19 June 1980, 597). His other publications included *Elephants* (1982), *Wildlife Resources and Economic Development* (1984), and *The Hippos* (1999). His lobbying on behalf of the latter species was credited with helping to add it to appendix 2 of the CITES convention in 1995, which ensures regulation of the trade in endangered species. From 1981 to 2002 Eltringham was associate editor of the *East African Wildlife Journal* (from 1979 the *African Journal of Ecology*). He was also for many years a trustee of the Kora Wildlife Preservation Trust (renamed in 1988 the George Adamson Wildlife Preservation Trust) and of the Elsa Conservation Trust (of which he was chairman from 2001 until his death).

As a teacher, mentor, and supervisor Eltringham was much valued by his students. One of them remembered him as 'reassuringly steady, calm and apparently unruffled … Very kind and exceedingly patient', another his 'exceedingly dry sense of humour and his unflappable disposition' (G. Norton and R. Malpas, in Kayanja and others, 296, 298). Many of his students went on to occupy important positions in the World Bank and the United Nations Development Programme as well as organizations like the World Wildlife Fund and Conservation International, and universities worldwide.

Eltringham lived latterly in Gilbert Road, Cambridge. His final years were clouded by the onset of Parkinson's disease. He died on 19 January 2006 at Addenbrooke's Hospital, Cambridge, of heart failure. He was survived by his wife, Sue, and their two daughters. ALEX MAY

Sources *The Independent* (22 Feb 2006) • F. I. B. Kayanja and others, *African Journal of Ecology*, 44 (2006), 296–9 • Eltringham African Collection, www.zoo.cam.ac.uk/library/eltringham.html, 20 Aug 2009 • private information (2010) • m. cert. • d. cert.

Likenesses photograph, repro. in www.zoo.cam.ac.uk/library/eltringham.html

Wealth at death £191,000: probate, 22 March 2006, *CGPLA Eng. & Wales*

Elvin, (Herbert) Lionel (**1905–2005**), educationist, was born on 7 August 1905 at 2 Laurel Villas, Hills Road, Buckhurst Hill, Essex, the eldest of the three sons of Herbert Henry Elvin (1874–1949), engineer's clerk, trade unionist, and lay preacher, and his wife, Mary Jane (Dolly), *née* Hill (1874–1962). There was an older sister, who died in infancy. He was educated at elementary schools and from 1917 at Southend high school where, still known as Herbert or Bert, he achieved academic and sporting success and was the author of a new school song. A scholar at Trinity Hall, Cambridge, from 1924 to 1928, he gained first-class honours in history and English and an athletics blue, and was president of the Union and chairman of the Labour Club. After two years as a Commonwealth fellow at Yale he returned to Trinity Hall as the college's first fellow with responsibility for the teaching of English. On 3 April 1934 (by which time he was using the forename Lionel) he married a 24-year-old schoolteacher, Mona Bedortha (Margaret) Dutton (*d.* 1997), at the Hampstead register office. She was the daughter of Dr Caleb Samuel Simeon Dutton, minister of religion, of San Francisco. They had one son, (John) Mark Dutton Elvin (*b.* 1938).

Although unsuccessful as Labour candidate for Cambridge University in the parliamentary election of 1935,

Elvin served on the town council and its education committee. He also became an active member of the Workers' Educational Association and treasurer of its eastern district. War service in the Air Ministry (1940–42) and the Ministry of Information (1943–5) was followed by appointment as principal of Ruskin College, Oxford, which reopened in September 1945. His chief rival for the post was Richard Crossman. Elvin was firmly committed to Ruskin and fully in accord with its educational, political, and social principles. Moreover there were family connections, and the Elvin room at Ruskin was named not for Lionel but for his father, Herbert, general secretary of the National Union of Clerks, who had served on the college's governing council. The Ruskin post involved a considerable drop in salary, but in his autobiography Elvin recorded that 'I do not think any five years in my career were more enjoyable than those I spent at Ruskin' (*Encounters with Education*, 96). Elvin taught courses in English literature and politics and oversaw the acquisition of new premises and the introduction of students from the USA. His educational experience was further broadened by appointments to national bodies, including the Secondary School Examinations Council and the University Grants Committee (1946–50).

In 1950 Elvin took up a less congenial but more lucrative post as director of the UNESCO department of education, based in Paris. There he encountered new challenges of education in the developing world and of international diplomacy. In 1956 he returned to England as professor of education in tropical areas at London University's Institute of Education. Two years later, following the death in post in 1957 of G. B. Jeffery, he was appointed director of the institute. At this time the Institute of Education comprised not only the 'central' institute but also a 'wider' institute or area training organization of some thirty colleges of education. Elvin thus found himself head of an organization at a peak of power and influence that was training one-quarter of the teachers in England. Though he had neither trained as a teacher nor taught in a school, Elvin's broad experience and numerous contacts within the worlds of education and politics made him uniquely fitted for the role. Expansion was in the air and he played a crucial role in securing a new building in Bedford Way and in overseeing the introduction of the BEd degree. Nevertheless, by 1973 when he retired with the title of emeritus professor, a sharp decline in the projected numbers of teachers had led to crisis in the colleges. William Taylor, Elvin's successor, would oversee the ending of the area training organization.

Elvin was active in numerous causes, for example as president of the English New Education Fellowship and of the Council for Education in World Citizenship, as chairman of the Commonwealth Education Liaison Committee, and as a member of the Central Advisory Council for Education (England) and the government of India education commission. He also played a major role on the committee on higher education chaired by Lord Robbins, which reported in 1963. His publications included *Men of America* (1941), *An Introduction to the Study of Literature (Poetry)* (1949), *Education and Contemporary Society* (1965), *The Place of Commonsense in Educational Thought* (1977), and his autobiography, *Encounters with Education* (1987).

Throughout his career Elvin remained a man of the left, a humanist, and a champion of 'peace and the making of a more just society' (*Encounters with Education*, 191). Adherence to his principles led him to refuse many honours, but he did accept the honorary fellowships awarded by Trinity Hall and the Institute of Education, in 1980 and 1993 respectively. His final years were spent at 4 Bulstrode Gardens, Cambridge. Suffering from bronchial cancer and heart disease, he died at Midfield Lodge nursing home, Oakington, Cambridgeshire, on 14 June 2005, less than two months before his 100th birthday. He was survived by his son, Mark, a distinguished scholar of Chinese history.

RICHARD ALDRICH

Sources C. Crawley, *Trinity Hall: the history of a Cambridge college, 1350–1975* (1976) • H. Pollins, *The history of Ruskin College* (1984) • C. W. Dixon, *The institute: a personal account of the history of the University of London Institute of Education, 1932–1972* (1986) • L. Elvin, *Encounters with education* (1987) • H. Carmichael, *With future and with past: a history of Southend High School for Boys on the occasion of its centenary* (1995) • G. Andrews, H. Kean, and J. Thompson, eds., *Ruskin College: contesting knowledge, dissenting politics* (1999) • W. R. Niblett, *Life, education, discovery* (2001) • R. Aldrich, *The Institute of Education, 1902–2002: a centenary history* (2002) • *The Independent* (17 June 2005) • *Times Educational Supplement* (24 June 2005) • *Southend High School Parent Bulletin* (16 Dec 2005) • L. Elvin, 'Last words', *New Humanist*, 121/1 (2006) • D. E. Samara, 'A grandfather's note', website, East of London FHS, www.eolfhs.org.uk/membdata/elvin.htm, 24 Sept 2007 [rept. from *Cockney Ancestor*] • *WW* (2005) • Institute of Education archives, U. Lond. • personal knowledge (2009) • private information (2009) • b. cert. • m. cert. • d. cert.

Archives Trinity Hall, Cambridge, diaries, corresp. | Rice University, Woodson Research Center, corresp. with Sir Julian Huxley

Likenesses Elliott & Fry, two quarter-plate glass negatives, 1960, NPG • M. Noakes, pencil drawing, 1974, Institution of Education, Newsam Library; repro. in Dixon, *The institute* • obituary photographs • photographs, repro. in Elvin, *Encounters* • photographs, Ruskin College, Oxford

Wealth at death £589,900: probate, 7 Oct 2005, *CGPLA Eng. & Wales*

Emmanuel, Ivor Lewis (1927–2007), singer and actor, was born on 7 November 1927 at 3 Prince Street, Port Talbot, Glamorgan, the elder son and eldest of three children of Stephen John Emmanuel (1905–1941), steelworker, and his wife, Ivy Margaretta, *née* Lewis (1908–1941). When he was six months old the family moved up the Afan valley to the picturesque industrial village of Pont-rhyd-y-fen to live with his mother's family. On the night of 11 May 1941 a German bomber, returning after bombing nearby docks, jettisoned a high-explosive bomb which directly hit the family home in Morgans Terrace. Ivor's parents, his three-year-old sister Mair, and his grandfather were all killed while Ivor, his younger brother, John, and an uncle were rescued by neighbours and the ARP and were found to have only minor injuries. The brothers were subsequently brought up separately, Ivor by his mother's sister Flossie.

Leaving school at the age of fourteen Emmanuel worked first in a mine and later in the steelworks. He had trained as a boy soprano and sang with local choirs and in eisteddfodau before joining the Port Talbot Amateur Operatic Society. From the age of twenty he was auditioning in London theatres and on visits there he stayed with his friend, the actor Richard Burton, who had been born in Pont-rhyd-y-fen. It was Burton's intervention that gained him a small part in *Oklahoma!* at the Theatre Royal, Drury Lane. He spent a year with the D'Oyly Carte Company before landing parts in *South Pacific* (1951) and *The King and I* (1953), again at the Theatre Royal. Later there were lead parts in a number of short-run shows: *Damn Yankees* (Coliseum, 1957), *Finian's Rainbow* (New Shakespeare Theatre, Liverpool, 1958), *A Time for Singing* (Broadway, 1966) and *110 in the Shade* (Palace Theatre, 1967). On 19 May 1951 he married Jean Dorothy Beazleigh (*b.* 1927), a member of the D'Oyly Carte chorus and daughter of Francis Beazleigh, carriage attendant. They had a daughter, Siân, and a son, Simon. The marriage ended in divorce, and on 31 May 1963 Emmanuel married Patricia Anne Bredin (*b.* 1935), actress and singer, and daughter of James Henry Bredin, merchant seaman. There were no children of this marriage.

Emmanuel was a performer whose strong, versatile, and very even baritone voice, strapping appearance, and convincing American accent were exactly right for the big American musicals. There were doubts, however, as to whether he had the ambition to pursue the transatlantic career that his qualities warranted. Meanwhile Wales presented alternative opportunities. While performing in Liverpool he went to Manchester to appear in a Granada Television Welsh-language show. His potential was spotted by the Cardiff company Television Wales and the West (TWW), who signed him for *Land of Song* (*Gwlad y gan*), a weekly bilingual show that was to run in the ITV national network's Sunday evening religious slot for seven years (1958–64), attracting an audience of 10 million. The show helped establish the popular notion of Wales as a musical culture, and Emmanuel's distinctive voice and engaging smile made him something of a national personality.

In 1963 Emmanuel met his friend Stanley Baker in London's White Elephant restaurant and this led to his involvement in the movie *Zulu* that Baker was about to produce in South Africa. The film, starring Stanley Baker and Michael Caine and released in 1964, depicted the battle of Rorke's Drift in 1879. Emmanuel's character, Private Owen, was given some memorably comic lines and then led the men in a rendering of the Welsh tune *Men of Harlech*, for which he had written the English lyrics. The film somewhat exaggerated the Welsh involvement in the Zulu wars but subsequently it was this morale-boosting musical dimension that accounted for the film's popularity and its place in Welsh cultural mythology.

With the demise of *Land of Song* Emmanuel concentrated on provincial summer shows, pantomimes, and television guest spots. There had been a royal command performance in 1960, the first to be televised, and, for TWW, he recorded a series in which he sang with local choirs. A cruise ship on which he was performing took him to Spain and led to his buying a home in the hilltop village of Benelmadena, near Malaga. Meanwhile his marriage to Patricia Bredin had failed. In 1981 he opted for retirement in Spain and for anonymity. He was accompanied by his third wife, Malinee Samakarn Oppenborn (*b.* 1954/5), an American of half-Thai descent, daughter of Frederick Oppenborn, radio station erector; they had married on 25 April 1978 (when she was aged twenty-three), and had one daughter, Emily. With the collapse of the Bank of Credit and Commerce International in 1991 Emmanuel lost his life savings. After a period of some difficulty during which a friend organized a collection for him, he was able to recover over half of what he had lost.

In the new culturally devolved Wales a degree of curiosity developed with regard to the fate of an entertainer who had been much loved. In 1997 in an HTV programme, *It's My Life*, Emmanuel reminisced about his career and friendships, and there was a documentary with Bryn Terfel. His recordings, especially those featuring the music of Ivor Novello, were still in demand. Perhaps no other British singer had seemed so well equipped to perform the great American musicals of the mid-twentieth century, but there was a reserve and lack of confidence that had held him back. He died in Malaga, Spain, on 20 July 2007, and was survived by his wife Malinee and his three children. PETER STEAD

Sources D. Berry, *Wales and cinema: the first hundred years* (1994) • D. Parsons, *In war and peace: Port Talbot, 1939–99* (2000) • T. Herbert and P. Stead, *Hymns and arias: great Welsh voices* (2001) • K. Tucker, ed., *Keeping the past alive: Neath Antiquarian Society, 1923–2003* (2003) • R. Shail, *Stanley Baker: a life in film* (2008) • *The Independent* (24 July 2007) • *Daily Telegraph* (26 July 2007) • *The Times* (29 Aug 2007) • *The Guardian* (17 Aug 2007) • *The Stage* (18 Sept 2007) • BBC South West Wales, hall of fame, www.bbc.co.uk, 13 May 2010 • www.musical-theatre.net, 13 May 2010 • b. cert. • m. certs.

Archives FILM BFINA, light entertainment footage • ITV Wales, Television Centre, Cardiff • National Film and Sound Archive of Wales, Aberystwyth | SOUND BL NSA, performance recordings

Likenesses photograph, 1960, Rex Features, London • obituary photographs

Erskine, Ralph (1914–2005), architect and town planner, was born on 24 February 1914 at 30 Victoria Road, Mill Hill, London, the second child and only son of George Erskine, shipping clerk, and his wife, Mildred Goepel, *née* Gough. His paternal grandparents were Scottish. His father was unambitious, but his mother held a degree from London University and was described by Erskine as intellectually frustrated. Fabian socialists, they sent their son to the Friends' School at Saffron Walden as they admired its values. There Erskine met his future wife, Ruth Monica Francis (1914–88), and, while he was never a Quaker himself, the pacifist and humanist ideals of the Quakers strongly informed his life and work. Wanting a career involving fresh air and drawing, he entered Regent Street Polytechnic in 1931 to study surveying, but changed to architecture as more interesting; he qualified in 1937. Gordon Cullen, with whom Erskine's ideas of townscape have often been compared, was in the year above. Modernism appealed to Erskine's social conscience, but he quickly became wary of white walls and flat roofs that aped the monumental; he was also suspicious of the classical details he was expected to apply to housing when he went in 1936 to work for C. W. Glover and Partners in Welwyn Garden

City, and to factories when a year later he joined Ewart Culpin and Partners.

A study tour of central Europe made little impression on Erskine's work. But in Sweden a social democratic government had come to power in 1932 with a programme of slum clearance and new building that adopted a gentle modernism that Erskine admired as functional and contextual. As he said, 'housing is a small "a" architecture. It should be friendly, intimate and have little there to make it monumental' (BL NSA, interview, 23 Jan 1997). Perhaps it was fortunate that the Swedish climate made it impossible to follow the modernist dogma of flat roofs and thin concrete walling. He headed in May 1939 for Stockholm by ferry and bicycle, and found work there. He then sent for Ruth, and on 29 August 1939 they married. The Second World War broke out a few days later; Erskine lost his job and they were stuck with no work and no money. Yet, as a pacifist, he decided to stay in neutral Sweden. In 1941 he and Ruth built themselves a small house in timber at Lissma, and a few commissions with friends followed. In 1945 they decided not to return to Britain.

Erskine's buildings from the early 1950s were modest in scale, yet many of the structures were experimental. Most were new rural settlements for the timber industry, including Gyttorp, begun in 1945, and Hammarby, begun in 1947. Terraces of housing had arched or steeply pitched roofs in a variety of picturesque forms, set around open spaces, and at Gyttorp accompanied by a school, added in 1955. In his industrial work of this period Erskine sought to break down factories' bulk into smaller components with sculptural forms expressive of their function, as for a cardboard factory at Fors, in 1950–53. In 1948 he designed the Borgafjäll Hotel in Lapland, with a ski slope on its roof. The Engström weekend house on Lisön took the form of an igloo. In 1954 he designed Sweden's first indoor shopping centre at Luleå, a response to the bleak northern climate; though inspired by North American models, it was more friendly in its variety of shapes, materials, and signage.

A concept for an Arctic town brought Erskine international recognition, initially through a project of 1958 that he presented at the Congrès International d'Architecture Moderne at Otterlo in the Netherlands the next year. He selected a south-facing slope, then provided additional shelter by means of a wall of flats that sheltered lower housing in its lee from north winds. The wall was largely blind on the north side, but had extensive areas of south-facing glazing, with balconies devised to avoid cold bridging, and roofs and porches to shield them from snow. In 1963 a revised version won a competition for Svappavaara, a new mining village in northern Sweden, but only the wall building and a few cottages were realized. In 1973 he produced a similar scheme for a new town at Resolute Bay, Canada, but again only part of the perimeter wall was built, with heavy timber sidings, before economic changes obviated the need for the town. Erskine was an associate of Team 10, attending several of its meetings as a way of keeping in touch with architects from southern Europe, but he felt the discussion was often academic and philosophical, with little relevance to the people really using the buildings—very different from the humane approach he admired in Scandinavian architecture. He claimed that his sense of urban planning was indebted to medieval models such as Stockholm's Gamla Stan more than modern ideals, admiring their slow change and limited materials.

The most extensive of Erskine's Arctic works was in Kiruna (1961), consisting of five blocks of offices and flats with curved walls of storey-height slabs and sharply angled roofs, up to thirteen storeys high. Similar forms were realized in brick from 1962 at Barberaren, in Sandviken, where a strong social democratic council offered many commissions. The slabs and curved corners were repeated in the house and office he built for himself at Drottningholm, outside Stockholm, in 1963, two parallel buildings of similar proportions that reflected his informal lifestyle and the strong sense of his office as an extended family. Between 1955 and 1963 his employees and their families moved the office each summer to an island at Rågö, via *Verona*, a Thames barge he sailed over from England. The Erskines had a son and three daughters, the youngest born with Down's syndrome, who died in childhood.

In the mid-1960s architectural work in Sweden was limited by the government's encouragement of large-scale system building for its project of a million new homes. Only a few low-rise schemes were built, including Landskrona (1969–70). Instead Erskine secured commissions for town planning and housing work in England. He produced a town planning study for Cambridge University in 1962, which led to his appointment at Clare Hall in July 1964, where he produced an informal design appropriate for a new graduate college, built of red brick with brightly stained timber details that included distinctively overscaled downpipes, balconies, and seating. He also designed private housing for Bovis in Newmarket and Milton Keynes, and for the builders Stanley Miller at Killingworth. The latter led him to be recommended for rebuilding Byker, an area of Newcastle already partly demolished for a motorway scheme, where a new Conservative administration was looking for an alternative to large slab blocks. Byker shines out among British public housing of this period for the intimacy of its detailing and landscaping in a massive scheme of 2000 units, and it was the most completely realized and intricate of all Erskine's housing designs. Built piecemeal over a decade, 1969–80, Byker was a model of early public consultation with the eventual tenants following the 1969 Skeffington report, Erskine opening an office and 'drop-in' centre in a former undertaker's shop within the redevelopment. The Byker wall was a snake of multi-coloured brickwork and blue roofs across the north of the site, with tiny windows facing the projected motorway to the north, while the south wall was a riot of fenestration and balconies. The low-rise housing in its lee featured children's playgrounds, and more timber decoration—or what the critic Reyner Banham termed 'a tidal wave of sheddery and pergolation' (Banham, 330). Fragments of demolished

Newcastle buildings were also incorporated in the landscape.

From the late 1970s Erskine designed a prodigious number of buildings, increasingly using practices set up by former assistants to realize the working drawings. Housing included Myrstuguberget outside Stockholm (1977–80), on the Byker model to give shelter from a motorway. At Ekerö, near Drottningholm (1985–90), he realized a new town centre, with modestly scaled housing, shops, and community facilities; this was his personal favourite among his designs. He worked extensively at Stockholm University's Frescati campus, including its library, student centre, and sports hall (1974–81), and the Aula Magna (great hall) (1997). In 1984 he received the Wolf Foundation prize for art, using the prize money to found a scholarship for young architects, and in 1987 he won the royal gold medal of the Royal Institute of British Architects.

Erskine's most adventurous late projects were a pair of offices for the building firm Skanska; Lilla Bommen in Göteborg (1987–90), a twenty-two-storey landmark whose bright colours were derived from the ships in the surrounding harbour; and The Ark (1988–91), an atrium building tucked between a gyratory and the underground in Hammersmith, London. The atrium was filled with distinct spaces—pods or shelves for up to four firms on each floor, with different stairs and lifts or access across flying bridges. Erskine explained that 'in a liberal democratic society you have concern for those not at the top … as those at the top can look after themselves' (BL NSA, interview, 23 Jan 1997). Among his last designs was the initial part of the Millennium Village in Greenwich, won in competition in 1998: another wall of flats to give protection from north winds, it was completed in 2007 by Tovatt architects. Erskine died on 16 March 2005 in Drottningholm, and was survived by his son and two daughters.

ELAIN HARWOOD

Sources nomination papers, 1938, RIBA • C. Amery, 'Byker by Erskine', *ArchR*, 156/934 (Dec 1974), 346–54 • R. Banham, 'The great wall of Tyne', *New Society*, 31/644 (6 Feb 1975), 330–31 • R. Erskine, *The Byker redevelopment* (Newcastle, 1981) • M. Egelius, *Ralph Erskine, architect* (Stockholm, 1990) • P. Collymore, *The architecture of Ralph Erskine*, rev. edn. (1994) • J. Lever and R. Erskine, interview, 23 Jan 1997, BL NSA, National Life Story Collection, architects' lives • E. Harwood, 'Home from home', *Crafts Magazine*, 191 (Nov–Dec 2004), 56–61 • *Architecture and Urbanism*, 414/3 (March 2005) [special issue] • M. Risselada and D. van den Heuvel, eds., *Team 10, 1953–81: in search of a utopia of the present* (Rotterdam, 2005) • *Daily Telegraph* (18 March 2005) • *The Times* (19 March 2005) • *The Independent* (21 March 2005) • *The Guardian* (22 March 2005) • *WW* (2005) • personal knowledge (2009) • private information (2009) • b. cert.

Archives RIBA, drawings and archives • Tovatt Architects, Drottningholm, Sweden | SOUND BL NSA, National Life Story Collection, architects' lives, interview with J. Lever, 23 Jan 1997 • BL NSA, National Life Story Collection, architects' lives, interviews with J. Lever 23–24 Jan 1997, F5338–F5345

Likenesses L. Hellman, portraits, 1991, repro. in L. Hellman, *Archi-têtes* (1992) • J. Forsman, photograph, 1994, Rex Features, London • J. Henriksson, photograph, 1998, Camera Press, London • J. Mikrut, photograph, 2004, PA Photos, London • obituary photographs

Ervine, David Walter (1953–2007), paramilitary and politician, was born on 21 July 1953 at 11 Chamberlain Street, Belfast, the third son and youngest of the five children of Walter Ervine, engineering worker, and his wife, Elizabeth (Dolly), *née* Tate. As a boy he attended Sunday school at the local Presbyterian church but gradually drifted away from formal religious observance. He was educated at Orangefield Boys' Secondary School but left formal education in June 1968, shortly before his fifteenth birthday. He subsequently worked in a number of manual and administrative jobs. On 1 March 1972, at the Megain Memorial Presbyterian Church, Knockbreda, Belfast, he married Jeanette Cunningham, a tobacco factory worker three years his senior, daughter of Robert Alexander (Bobby) Cunningham, fitter. They had two sons.

Following the outbreak of civil conflict in Northern Ireland in August 1969 Ervine became involved in low-level vigilante activity, including the manning of barricades against the threat of republican bomb attacks. At the age of nineteen he joined the loyalist paramilitary group the Ulster Volunteer Force (UVF). His decision, he said, was inspired by the events of 21 July 1972, known as bloody Friday, when the Provisional IRA exploded some twenty-two bombs across Belfast, killing nine people. Ervine saw the decision to join the UVF as a means of defending his community.

In November 1974 Ervine was arrested while driving a vehicle containing a 5 pound explosive device. He was tied to the vehicle by members of the security forces and forced to disarm the bomb himself. He was subsequently convicted of possessing explosives and served six years of an eleven-year sentence before he was released in 1980. While in the Maze prison he discovered a renewed interest in education, which led to his taking GCE O-level examinations and beginning an Open University course. He was one of a number of UVF prisoners influenced by their fellow prisoner Augustus (Gusty) Spence, a founding member of the UVF, who encouraged the organization to pursue a more directly political strategy. After his release from prison Ervine had a number of jobs including running a newsagent's shop, but he was increasingly drawn towards the world of politics. In 1984 he became associated with the Progressive Unionist Party, which was popularly viewed as the political wing of the UVF. He was a candidate in the district council elections of 1985 but was not elected.

As the Northern Ireland peace process developed in the early 1990s Ervine played a significant role in discussions with other political actors, not least those from the Republic of Ireland. After the loyalist paramilitary groups declared a ceasefire in October 1994 he made an increasing number of media appearances, in which he was presented as someone who was close to the thinking of the UVF. His eloquence and ability to explain the loyalist position to a wide, and often critical, audience won him many admirers outside his own political constituency as well as the somewhat back-handed compliment of the nickname Dictionary Dave. He was elected to the Northern Ireland forum from the East Belfast constituency in May 1996. This was an area that for generations had been dominated by employment in heavy engineering companies and had returned Northern Ireland Labour Party members to Stormont in the 1950s and 1960s, before the outbreak of the 'troubles'. Indeed, Ervine's father had been a member of the Northern Ireland Labour Party. In May 1997 Ervine became a member of Belfast city council when he was elected in the Pottinger ward, also in east Belfast. He retained his seat in the May 2005 council elections.

After the signing of the Good Friday agreement in April 1998 Ervine was a strong proponent of the agreement and for a 'yes' vote in the subsequent referendum on it. In 1998 he was elected to the Northern Ireland assembly to represent East Belfast and was again returned to the assembly in 2003. In April 2002 he succeeded Hugh Smyth as leader of the Progressive Unionist Party. In May 2006 he announced that he was supporting the Ulster Unionist Party group in the assembly, a move which, under the D'Hondt mechanism used to allocate ministerial posts in the Northern Ireland executive, potentially gave the Ulster Unionists a third seat in the executive. In September, however, the speaker of the assembly ruled against this arrangement, leading an angry Ervine to complain that, although the Northern Ireland executive required a compulsory coalition between parties, a voluntary coalition was not permitted.

Ervine died at the Royal Victoria Hospital, Belfast, on 8 January 2007 following a heart attack and stroke. He was buried at Roselawn cemetery near Belfast on 12 January 2007. A funeral service held earlier that day at Newtownards Road Methodist Church was attended by many leading political figures including Sinn Fein's president, Gerry Adams. Adams's presence, in a staunchly Unionist area, was in itself perceived as a measure of success for the peace process in which Ervine had played a significant part. He was survived by his wife, Jeanette, and their two sons. GORDON GILLESPIE

Sources H. Sinnerton, *David Ervine: uncharted waters* (2003) · *The Times* (9 Jan 2007) · *Daily Telegraph* (9 Jan 2007) · *The Guardian* (9 Jan 2007) · *The Independent* (9 Jan 2007) · *Belfast Telegraph* (9 Jan 2007) · *Irish Times* (13 Jan 2007) · E. Moloney, *Voices from the grave* (2010) · www.davidervine.com, 16 April 2010 · personal knowledge (2011) · private information (2011) · b. cert. · m. cert. · d. cert.

Archives FILM BFINA, current affairs footage

Likenesses photographs, 1994–8, Getty Images, London · photographs, 1994–2006, PA Photos, London · photographs, 1995–8, Photoshot, London · R. Wilson, mural, 2008, Belfast [*see illus.*] · obituary photographs · photographs, repro. in Sinnerton, *Ervine*

Evans, Gwynfor Richard (1912–2005), politician, was born on 1 September 1912 at Y Goedwig, 24 Somerset Road, Barry, Glamorgan, the eldest of the three children of Daniel James (Dan) Evans, ironmonger, and his wife, Catherine Mary, *née* Richard, shopkeeper. His industrious and godly parents established the Dan Evans department store in the booming coal-exporting port of Barry, and it was in this vibrant town of constantly shifting cultural borders on the periphery of 'Welsh' Wales that Evans was brought up.

Education and early career The supreme irony of Evans's upbringing is that perhaps the greatest Welsh patriot of the twentieth century saw more of England than of Wales during his youth, with the family home directly in the shadow of the west country. Initially the politics of identity were of little consequence to the Liberal-supporting Evans family as the language of the home shifted from Welsh to English. Such a situation was not uncommon for the handful of Welsh-speaking families in Barry. This linguistic shift was reinforced by the thoroughly English education Evans received at the Barry county school, where he excelled at cricket. During these adolescent years this sickly child developed into a handsome young man but the key change was psychological. In 1929 he experienced a quasi-religious conversion and came to see Wales as a Christian nation in need of salvation from Englishness, modernism, and war.

Evans fervently believed that he had been called to save a nation (a familiar Welsh nonconformist trope) but his messianic fervour while at the University College of

David Walter Ervine (1953–2007), by Ross Wilson, 2008

Gwynfor Richard Evans (1912–2005), by unknown photographer, 1970

Wales, Aberystwyth, where he studied law between 1931 and 1934, was initially directed towards the town's pacifist and Christian societies, believing the recently formed Plaid Cymru to be too irrelevant to make any impact. However, after graduating with a second-class degree Evans did join Plaid Cymru, having reconsidered his earlier view that the party was in thrall to the prelapsarian ideas of its brilliant but utterly maverick president, Saunders Lewis. Though Evans and Lewis shared more in common than either would perhaps care to admit, Evans from the outset intended to change Plaid Cymru and make it a wholly pacifist and constitutional party, much to Lewis's extended and very public chagrin. These moves (and a somewhat exaggerated rediscovery of his command of the Welsh language) were adumbrated during a two-year period at St John's College, Oxford, between 1934 and 1936, where he obtained a further second-class degree in law. But it was upon his return to Wales and a period as an articled clerk with W. B. Francis, solicitors, in Cardiff that Evans's precocious vision of transforming Plaid Cymru began to mature.

Evans's pacifism crystallized into a clearly defined absolutist stance under the influence of the Peace Pledge Union. With war looming ever larger he resolved to save his dream of a peaceful Wales through selfless proselytizing. By 1939 he had abandoned the legal profession, deciding instead (much to his family's horror) that he would work on the family's farm in Llangadog, Carmarthenshire. This financial security and an unconditional discharge from military service allowed him to become an assiduous secretary of the Welsh Pacifists and a young tyro within the ranks of Plaid Cymru in extremely trying days. He also became a central figure in the more ecumenical New Wales Union, a body that proved vital in maintaining a sense of Welshness in the age of total war. Nevertheless, his stance proved extremely difficult for his family in Barry, since Evans combined two ideologies that were inimical to many. On 1 March 1941, at the Welsh Calvinistic Methodist chapel, Crwys Road, Cardiff, Evans married Rhiannon Prys Thomas (*d.* 2006), daughter of Adolphus Daniel (Dan) Thomas, bank manager. They made their first home at Wernellyn, Llangadog, where they had seven children. Thus was set a pattern of political widowhood for Rhiannon, who bore her husband's frequent campaigning absences and self-absorption with remarkable forbearance.

The summer of 1943 saw Evans assume the *de facto* presidency of a rudderless Plaid Cymru with the nominal president, Abi Williams, indisposed because of a 'nervous condition'. Despite the enormous difficulties and the suspicion that Plaid Cymru was a crypto-fascist party, Evans set about transforming the party's sect-like image. First he saved the party from disappearing completely and then started to make a deliberate pitch for the votes of Welsh-speaking, Liberal Wales by conjuring a gentle vision of Wales as a historic nation. Shedding the declamatory excesses of Saunders Lewis was vital, as was Evans's readiness to develop an eclectic political philosophy that combined elements of socialism, conservatism, pacifism, nationalism, and enviromentalism. Despite this 'big tent' approach, his first foray into parliamentary politics was utterly inauspicious as a candidate in Merioneth during the general election of 1945.

President of Plaid Cymru Undaunted, and despite his natural reserve, Evans became party president in August 1945. He quickly became ever more convinced that nationalist failure should be ascribed to too little engagement with constitutional politics. At a local level this plunged Evans into vicious and landmark battles with the Labour Party on Carmarthenshire council, a body to which he was elected in 1949 and on which he sat until 1974, over the Welsh language. At a national level his repeated denunciation of Labour policy towards devolving power in Wales saw extended bouts of fisticuffs that, despite Plaid Cymru's ostensible insignificance, set the rhetorical tone for much of Welsh politics over the next five decades. He also exerted influence through such bodies as the BBC's Welsh advisory council and the court of the University of Wales. These moves were of a piece with his view that Plaid Cymru could not be exclusivist about how best to defend the interests of Wales. Crucially Evans also saw the need for a wider body of people to campaign for a Welsh parliament along the lines of the Scottish Covenant Association. In 1949 the Parliament for Wales campaign was launched—the first mass campaign for devolution since the ill-starred venture of Young Wales half a century earlier.

Despite these ventures and ceaseless campaigning, electoral success proved elusive for Evans personally and his party in the general elections of 1950 and 1951. Two years later he moved to Talar Wen, Llangadog, Carmarthenshire, a beautiful house designed by his brother-in-law, Dewi Prys Thomas, which served as both family home and an assertion of the potentialities of Welsh architecture. Another significant consolation came in his being nominated president of the Welsh Congregationalists in 1954—the radical denomination to which he was by now utterly devoted. But this accolade and a record number of parliamentary candidates for Plaid Cymru at the general election of 1955 failed to prevent further electoral ignominy. Evans became an increasingly divisive figure within his party and by the latter part of the decade two clear camps had developed. His acolytes saw him as an eirenical figure who deserved beatification for having devoted his life to the defence of Wales. Others, though, particularly supporters of Saunders Lewis, saw Evans as having turned a once radical party into a cult of insufferably nice pacifists wedded to a pointless constitutional cause.

These tensions over nationalist strategy exploded in the late 1950s over the question of how best to resist the construction by Liverpool corporation of the Tryweryn dam in Merioneth, the parliamentary constituency that Evans was still coveting. The unsuccessful fight to prevent the drowning of the village of Capel Celyn proved a pivotal moment in Welsh political history and nobody did more than Evans to expose what for many was a shocking injustice. However, the Tryweryn battle came close to destroying his political career as he vacillated between the polar opposites of parliamentary pressure and non-violent direct action. Having procrastinated for two years, he ultimately plumped for the former course in 1959, fearing that a long term of imprisonment would destroy the party. The financial future of his market gardening business was also a consideration, as was his fervent belief that he and Plaid Cymru could make a long-promised electoral breakthrough in Merioneth at the general election of that year; but a familiar fate awaited him and he came last.

This and other similarly disappointing results provoked five years of internecine strife within Plaid Cymru, as an epic battle between 'constitutionalists' and 'actors' raged. In 1961 Evans, in despair, had to be dissuaded from resigning, though nothing could prevent him from relinquishing the Merioneth parliamentary nomination in 1962. In middle age Evans had little of the iconic about him, as Welsh nationalist politics fractured shortly before the nadir of Plaid Cymru's electoral fortunes, the general election of 1964. By then some activists espoused violent and non-violent action; others argued for the party to adopt a more republican, left-wing stance and abandon the *via media* that Evans carefully trod. The latter tendency had by now brought him into lethal battle with Emrys Roberts, the party's mercurial but hubristic general secretary, who engineered what Evans (not without reason) perceived to be a coup. Roberts's sacking plunged the party into another bout of melancholy introspection between 1964 and the general election of March 1966. The upshot of this was that Evans's hopes of a parliamentary breakthrough in his newly adopted Carmarthen constituency looked as fanciful as ever.

Evans, predictably, lost to Labour's Lady Megan Lloyd George but the event, as one unwittingly prescient journalist put it, was a 'strange, listless affair', partly because of her absence through illness (*Western Mail*, 24 March 1966). Within a few weeks of her victory Megan Lloyd George died, leaving Evans to fight a by-election in July 1966 in which the most optimistic nationalists hoped he would come second. To the surprise of everyone (not least himself) he won the seat. As election upsets go, it was one of the greatest shocks ever. True, Evans was the legatee of a truly gruesome period for the Wilson government, but he was also the beneficiary of a patriotic and to a lesser extent nationalist shift in Welsh political consciousness that he himself had helped to create in Carmarthen and elsewhere.

The effect of the Carmarthen victory transformed Evans's image. From now on he was seen as a national redeemer by many in his hyperventilating party, the man who had led Wales to freedom after centuries of servitude. Despite his loathing of Westminster, the new member for Carmarthen (and member for Wales, as he was colloquially known) skilfully used his parliamentary position to ask hundreds of questions about Wales—a tactic that in turn prompted the Labour Party and in particular the Welsh secretary, George Thomas, to attack Evans with a fanatical zeal. Almost inevitably Evans lost the Carmarthen seat at the general election of 1970 but the effect of his by-election win on his party and Welsh politics would be profound. From now on Welsh and, from 1967, Scottish parliamentary nationalism became permanent fixtures in a new and plural British politics.

Evans spent the next four years trying to regain his Carmarthen seat and to propagate a love for Welsh history among a new generation of patriots. This he achieved through his extremely popular (and tendentious) history of Wales, *Land of My Fathers*, published in 1974. He regained the Carmarthen seat in the general election of October 1974. He returned to Westminster accompanied by Dafydd Elis-Thomas and Dafydd Wigley, two younger and tougher MPs who made the next five years less of a parliamentary penance for him, though by the end he was suffering from mental exhaustion. Together this triumvirate exacted a number of concessions, first from the Wilson and then from the Callaghan governments—the most notable being the promise to hold a referendum on an assembly for Wales in 1979. The overwhelming rejection of an assembly by the people of Wales was a crushing blow for Evans, who interpreted the vote as a denial by the Welsh of their own existence. In the subsequent general election of 1979 he lost his seat. Utterly dispirited, he began to plan an act of patriotic martyrdom during 1980 in order to reinvigorate Welsh nationalism. This plan never came to fruition because the Conservative government handed him a cause on a plate when they broke their own manifesto commitment to create a separate

Welsh-language television channel. In May 1980 Evans threatened to fast to the death unless the government capitulated. Amid scenes of mounting apprehension verging on blind panic when it became apparent that Evans was deadly serious, the government capitulated for fear Wales would become ungovernable. In 1982 the Welsh fourth channel, S4C, was launched—a living monument to the suicidal threat of a somewhat inconsistent pacifist.

Later years Evans relinquished the presidency of Plaid Cymru in 1981 after thirty-six years—a record of unbroken leadership only bettered at the time by Marshal Tito in Yugoslavia. A last and misguided attempt to regain Carmarthen at the 1983 general election did not dim his passion for politics nor his prolific writing. In 1986 he and Rhiannon moved to Pencarreg, Carmarthenshire, though their latter years were difficult ones, with Rhiannon succumbing to Parkinson's disease almost immediately after the move. Eventually old age and osteoporosis ravaged his body too, though as he faded from public view his revered status grew in equal measure. He had already received an honorary doctorate from the University of Wales in 1973 and the Cymmrodorion medal in 1984, but the ultimate proof of his popularity among a section of the Welsh people came in 2004 when the Welsh public voted him the greatest living politician and fourth in a list of all-time Welsh heroes, after Aneurin Bevan, Owain Glyn Dŵr, and the singer Tom Jones.

Evans died at his home, Talar Wen, Pencarreg, on 21 April 2005. His funeral service at Bethel Congregationalist Chapel, Aberystwyth, on 27 April was described as the nearest Wales has ever seen to a state funeral. His ashes were scattered a few weeks later on the hill fort of Garn Goch, Carmarthenshire, a part of Wales which provided emotional solace to this complex and sometimes contradictory man. Despite his unconventional personality and the fact that he did not bequeath a coherent political philosophy Evans's legacy was by the time of his death secure. Though all parties contributed to the process of political devolution for Wales, it is arguable that the national assembly for Wales would not exist were it not for Gwynfor Evans and his simple love for his nation at a time when the concept of Wales as a political nation did not exist. RHYS EVANS

Sources G. Evans, *Bywyd Cymro* (1982) • G. Evans, *For the sake of Wales* (1986) • R. Evans, *Gwynfor: rhag pob brad* (2005) • R. Evans, *Gwynfor Evans: a portrait of a patriot* (2008) • *The Times* (22 April 2005) • *Daily Telegraph* (22 April 2005) • *The Guardian* (22 April 2005) • *The Independent* (22 April 2005) • *South Wales Echo* (22 April 2005) • *South Wales Evening Post* (22 April 2005) • *Wales on Sunday* (24 April 2005) • *Carmarthen Journal* (27 April 2005) • *Western Mail* (28 April 2005) • *WW* (2005) • www.gwynfor.net, 5 Aug 2008 • personal knowledge (2009) • private information (2009) • b. cert. • m. cert. • d. cert.

Archives NL Wales | NL Wales, Huw T. Edwards papers • NL Wales, Dafydd Elis-Thomas papers • NL Wales, Thomas Iorweth Ellis papers • NL Wales, Emyr Humphreys papers • NL Wales, Harri Webb papers | FILM BFINA, current affairs footage | SOUND BL NSA, performance recordings

Likenesses photograph, 1970, PA Photos, London [*see illus.*] • A. Davies, photograph on canvas, 1980–89, NL Wales • J. Roberts, acrylic, watercolour, 1989, NL Wales • D. Griffiths, oils, 2001, NL Wales • obituary photographs

Wealth at death under £36,000: administration, 18 July 2005, *CGPLA Eng. & Wales*

Evans, Sir (William) Vincent John (1915–2007), international lawyer, diplomatist, and judge, was born on 20 October 1915 at 163 Albert Road, Wood Green, Middlesex, of Welsh ancestry, the son of Charles Herbert Evans (*d.* 1978), bank clerk, later bank manager, and his wife, Elizabeth (Lizzie), *née* Jenkins (*d.* 1965). After Merchant Taylors' School, Northwood, Middlesex, he went to Wadham College, Oxford, where he gained first-class honours in jurisprudence in 1937 and the BCL a year later. Elected a Cassel scholar at Lincoln's Inn in 1937, he was called to the bar in 1939.

Despite poor eyesight Evans served in the army through the Second World War, including with the Eighth Army in north Africa, and was made a military MBE in 1945. From 1945 to 1946 he was legal adviser to the British military administration in Cyrenaica, with the rank of lieutenant-colonel. On demobilization he joined the Foreign Office as an assistant legal adviser. On 4 January 1947, at Fox Lane Congregational Church, Palmers Green, Middlesex, he married Joan Mary Symons (1919/20–2010), daughter of Angus Bryant Symons, mechanical engineer. They had two daughters, Marion (*b.* 1948) and Jane (*b.* 1952), and a son, David (*b.* 1950). Evans served as chairman of his wife's family's firm, Bryant Symons and Co. Ltd, from 1964 to 1985.

After rapid promotion to legal counsellor Evans was posted as legal adviser to the UK permanent mission to the United Nations, in New York, in 1954, where he remained for five years, a period in which many of the UN's legal forms and practices found themselves hammered on the anvil of harsh experience, and Evans's patient influence was felt in their development. In 1956, though, the Suez crisis burst (the Foreign Office lawyers having been deliberately excluded from the Anglo-French planning by Eden), and unleashed harsh criticism of the two states at the UN in particular; the refusal of American support in the security council led to the humiliation of having to rescue the diplomatic position in the general assembly, convened in emergency session, without the protection of the veto. And in that setting Suez led also to the invention of UN peacekeeping by creative interpretation of the unspoken potential of the UN charter, though the UN system proved incapable of handling the Soviet invasion to crush the uprising in Hungary the same year.

Evans returned to the Foreign Office in 1959 (being gazetted CMG that year), where he was once again marked out for his prodigious capacity for work, attention to detail, and mastery of his briefs. Following promotion to deputy legal adviser in 1960 he served for a year as acting legal adviser in 1965, and was appointed to the post substantively in 1968. This was, however, at the time of the successive amalgamation of the three external affairs ministries under the Wilson administration, so he served for a brief period conjointly with the former legal adviser to the old Colonial Office (later Commonwealth Office) before becoming, in 1969, the sole legal adviser to the combined Foreign and Commonwealth Office, which had inherited not simply relations with independent members of the Commonwealth but the still extensive responsibility for colonial administration as well. His skill and tact, and his kindness at the personal level, contributed in a major way to the successful integration of three widely differing legal staffs into one close unit, and stood the Foreign and Commonwealth Office in good stead in coping with the manifold problems of administration as Britain's overseas commitments were harshly scaled down and the trickle of decolonization turned into a torrent, all against the background of hostile barracking from within the UN. He was knighted KCMG in 1970 and appointed QC in 1973. He retired at the statutory age of sixty in 1975, and was promoted GCMG the following year. He was a member of the Permanent Court of Arbitration from 1987 to 1997, and Lincoln's Inn elected him an honorary bencher in 1983. His Welsh descent was not forgotten, and in 1987 he was made a vice-president of the Honourable Society of Cymmrodorion.

At the Foreign and Commonwealth Office Evans had become closely involved in the work of the Council of Europe, chairing its committee on legal co-operation from 1969 to 1971, and its steering committee on human rights from 1979 to 1980. He was elected a member of the UN human rights committee set up under the international covenant on civil and political rights from 1977 to 1984. All this made him a natural choice to be nominated and elected a judge of the European Court of Human Rights in Strasbourg in 1980, in which capacity he served until 1991. Evans's style in the court was, however, noticeably different from his predecessor's: less pugnacious, less prone to dissent, persuasive not by the brilliance of his reasoning but out of respect for his character and principles and his straightforward good sense, as well as his sheer hard work in mastering every detail of the cases with which he dealt. He was said to have been the first judge to put questions to counsel from the bench. In the court's judgements he was mostly with the majority, nudging the court from within towards a realistically liberal view of the development of European convention rights. The great respect in which he was held throughout government in Britain contributed materially to the acceptance of adverse decisions out of Strasbourg when they came, and he was wholeheartedly in favour of the incorporation of the convention into UK law when in due course that occurred.

A caring and sympathetic man, and generous with his time, Evans took seriously his responsibilities to the law and to the developing field of human rights, even after his retirement from the court. He helped to set up and was chairman of the advisory board of the Centre for International Human Rights Law at the University of Essex from 1982 to 1994 (he received an honorary doctorate from the university in 1986). He was a vice-president of the British Institute of Human Rights from 1992 to 2004. Retaining fond memories of his schooldays he was president of the Old Merchant Taylors' Society in 1984–5 and a member of the scholarships committee of the Merchant Taylors' Company from 1985 to 1993. He remained deeply attached to Wadham, his Oxford college, which made him an honorary fellow in 1981, and was the founding president of the college law society. He was a keen and knowledgeable gardener. He lived for years in Moor Park, Northwood, at the centre of a notably happy and devoted family circle. He died of a heart attack on 18 May 2007, at Luton and Dunstable Hospital, Luton, and was survived by his wife and their three children. F. D. BERMAN

Sources *The Times* (5 June 2007) • University of Essex press release, www.essex.ac.uk/wyvern/extra/evans.htm, 18 Aug 2010 • *British Yearbook of International Law*, 78 (2008), 1–6 • *Wadham College Gazette* (2008), 165–8 • diplomatic service and FO lists, 1948–75 • Burke, *Peerage* • *WW* (2007) • private information (2011) • b. cert. • m. cert. • d. cert.

Archives Albert Sloman Library, University of Essex, papers relating to European Court of Human Rights

Wealth at death £218,773: probate, 13 Nov 2007, *CGPLA Eng. & Wales*

Ewing [*née* McAdam; *married name* Bain], **Margaret Anne** (**1945–2006**), politician, was born on 1 September 1945 at Fairhaven, Hyndford Road, Lanark, the daughter of John McAdam, ploughman, later builder's labourer, and his wife, Margaret Jamieson Cuthbert (Peggie), *née* Lamb. She was born to the rural working class rather like Chris Guthrie, heroine of Lewis Grassic Gibbon's *A Scots Quair* (1932–34), whom in passion and radicalism she resembled. She retained an interest in rural affairs and the environment throughout her life. She attended the primary and high school at Biggar from 1950 to 1962, with the exception of the years 1957–8, when she was recovering from tuberculosis. After graduating with a second-class degree in French from Glasgow University in 1967 and taking a teacher training course at Jordanhill College she became an assistant teacher at Our Lady's High School in the then new town of Cumbernauld. In 1970 she moved to St Modan's High School, Stirling, as a special assistant teacher, and from 1973 principal teacher for remedial education. Her childhood illness and work as a remedial teacher gave her an empathy and a quality of kindness that made even her political opponents regard her with affection. On 20 July 1968 she had married a political scientist, Donald Straiton Bain, son of Donald Bain, veterinary surgeon. Both were already active in the Scottish National Party (SNP), and in the early 1970s her husband became an economic adviser to the party. Along with Gordon Wilson he investigated and impressively deployed the cause of North Sea oil, which won Margo MacDonald the Govan by-election in November 1973 on the eve of the report of the Kilbrandon commission. Also in 1973, Margaret Bain (by now a member of the SNP national executive) gained the nomination for East Dunbartonshire (really Cumbernauld New Town).

1974 brought two general elections. Margaret Bain was heavily defeated in February but was returned to the House of Commons in the October contest with the truly hairsbreadth majority of 22 votes in a close three-way contest. In a sense, however, the election had already shot the SNP's fox. Labour, after conceding the principle of devolution, started to recover. By the autumn of 1977 it was steadily winning by-elections against the SNP. Margaret Bain, tall, arresting, blonde, and described by one parliamentarian not normally regarded as a chauvinist as having 'the best legs in the house since the eighteenth century' (private information), settled in well at Westminster, but her party's chances were soon ebbing away. A left-wing Scottish Labour Party was founded in 1975 by Jim Sillars as compromises were written into Labour's bill, most notoriously when a Scottish-born London MP, George Cunningham, inserted an amendment requiring a minimum 'yes' vote of 40 per cent of the *entire* electorate. The referendum took place on 1 March 1979 during the bleakest winter in years, complicated by endemic labour problems. In Scotland the 'yes' vote was carried by a small margin, but failed to reach the 40 per cent threshold; in Wales devolution was rejected outright. The prime minister, James Callaghan, tabled the repeal of the bill: the eleven SNP MPs countered with a vote of no confidence. In this Plaid Cymru ultimately took Labour's side, but on a motion of no confidence carried by only one vote on 1 April the Labour government was forced to the polls. In the election of May 1979 Bain lost her seat by a wide margin, coming third behind both the Labour and the Conservative candidates.

The aftermath of the 1979 election was scarcely less traumatic for the SNP. A left-wing pressure group, the '79 Group, headed up by Jim Sillars, now in the SNP, attracted many talented younger members, including Alex Salmond. In this confrontation Margaret Bain (who supported herself as a freelance journalist and later co-ordinator of the west of Scotland certificate in social service scheme) took the side of the party establishment against what was perceived as a 'party within a party', and supported the group's expulsion in 1982 (they were readmitted in 1983). She contested Strathkelvin and Bearsden, unsuccessfully, in 1983 and was senior vice-chair of the party from 1984 to 1987. Meanwhile her marriage to Donald Bain had ended in 1980, and on 30 November 1983 she married Fergus Stewart Ewing (*b.* 1957), solicitor and politician, son of Stewart Martin Ewing, lecturer in tax legislation, and his wife Winifred Ewing, then MEP for the Highlands and Islands in the European parliament (having previously served as SNP MP for Hamilton in 1967–70 and Moray and Nairn from 1974 to 1979).

In 1987 Margaret Ewing returned to the House of Commons as MP for Moray and Nairn, retaining the seat in the elections of 1992 and 1997. She followed her mother-in-law in involving herself in European matters through the Commons select committee on European legislation from 1987 to 1999. In 1990, when the Soviet Union was about to invade Lithuania, democratic forces had barricaded themselves in the parliament buildings. Margaret Ewing took up their cause and set out with volunteers to support President Landsbergis, much to the apprehension of her colleagues. She was also deeply committed to improving the condition of elderly people and children. She was widely respected for her compassion and reasonableness, her assiduousness on behalf of constituents, and the sincerity of her nationalist beliefs. From 1987 to 1999 she was leader of the SNP parliamentary group, and in 1990 was widely tipped to succeed Gordon Wilson as party leader, but in the event was defeated at the party conference by Alex Salmond, by 486 votes to 186.

Following the success of the 1997 referendum on devolution, Margaret Ewing was returned for Moray to the new Scottish parliament in July 1999, and held a dual mandate until 2001, when she gave up her Westminster seat. Her husband meanwhile served as SNP member of the Scottish parliament for Inverness East, Nairn and Lochaber, and her mother-in-law for the Highlands and Islands.

Margaret Anne Ewing [Bain] **(1945–2006)**, by Victoria Carew Hunt, 1998

In April 2002 Margaret Ewing was diagnosed with breast cancer and had a mastectomy. She took six months off but was returned to the Scottish parliament for Moray in 2003. In this session she took a particular interest in Africa and led a delegation to Malawi, which decided on a partnership with Scotland. According to her husband 'She insisted it was too important a cause to ignore' (*Daily Record*, 24 March 2006). She recovered from the breast cancer therapy, but the long-term impact gravely impaired her health and increased her liability first to pneumonia, then to anaemia. She died suddenly of a heart attack at her home, Burns Cottage, Tulloch's Brae, Lossiemouth, Moray, on 21 March 2006, while dealing with constituents' correspondence. The widespread affection she enjoyed was reflected in the turnout at her funeral, at St Geraldine's High Church, Lossiemouth, on 25 March. She was survived by her husband Fergus. There were no children of either marriage. CHRISTOPHER HARVIE

Sources *The Herald* [Glasgow] (22 March 2006) • *Aberdeen Press and Journal* (22 March 2006) • *The Times* (22 March 2006) • *Daily Telegraph* (22 March 2006) • *The Independent* (22 March 2006) • *The Guardian* (23 March 2006) • *Daily Record* (24 March 2006) • *Cumbernauld News* (30 March 2006) • *Sunday Times* (14 May 2006) • *WW* (2006) • www.alba.uk/moray/index • personal knowledge (2010) • private information (2010) • b. cert. • m. certs. • d. cert.

Archives FILM BFINA, party political footage | SOUND BL NSA, current affairs recording

Likenesses photograph, 1995, Photoshot, London • photographs, 1995–2003, PA Photos, London • V. Carew Hunt, bromide fibre print, 1998, NPG [*see illus.*] • obituary photographs

Exton, Clive [*real name* Clive Jack Montague Brooks] (**1930–2007**), screenwriter, was born at 123B Pentonville Road, Islington, London, on 11 April 1930, the son of Jack Ernest Brooks (1901–1970), a certified bailiff who later became an administrative officer with the Inland Revenue, and his wife, Marie, *née* Rolfe (1901–1986). He attended Christ's Hospital, Horsham, Sussex, and left at the age of sixteen to become a clerk with an advertising company. His two years' national service were spent with the British army of the Rhine in West Germany, where he took part in stage shows.

After completing his national service Brooks trained at the Central School of Speech and Drama and, with the actors' union Equity already having an actor called Clive Brook on its books, chose Exton as his professional name, randomly taking it from the character of Sir Piers of Exton in *Richard II*. He subsequently wrote as well as acted as Clive Exton. From 1951 he performed in repertory theatre and, in 1954 with Brian Rix's company, in the farce *Reluctant Heroes* at the Whitehall Theatre in London's West End. However, he gave up acting after watching the film version of *Richard III* (1955), declaring that he could never be as good as Laurence Olivier. He decided to work behind the scenes and became a stage manager, first at the Albery Theatre, then the Criterion Theatre. He married first, on 16 August 1952, Patricia Fletcher Ferguson (*b.* 1928), office instructor, and daughter of Peter McNab Ferguson, engineer, with whom he had two daughters, and second, on 30 August 1957 (his first marriage having been dissolved earlier that year) Margaret Josephine (Mara) Reid (*b.* 1933), actress, with whom he had another two daughters and a son.

Exton turned to writing after being told a story by Harry Korris, formerly a member of the music-hall act Ramsbottom, Enoch and Me, and the result was his first play, *No Fixed Abode*, about four men in a doss-house. Although intended for the theatre, it was broadcast by ITV in 1959, in the TV Playhouse series, as was his second play, *The Silk Purse*. This led to eight commissions for the commercial channel's prestigious Armchair Theatre series over the next five years, when his style changed from one of social realism to surrealism. The former was represented by his first play for the series, *Where I Live* (1960), about a brother and sister fighting about the care of their unwanted, widowed father. When surrealism was used for *The Trial of Dr Fancy* (1964), about a Harley Street doctor who cut shorter the legs of tall people embarrassed by their height, ITV tried to ban the play but finally broadcast it after the director, Ted Kotcheff, mounted a press campaign to get it screened. By then Exton had already written another play that was in fact banned—*The Big Eat* (1962), about a promotional campaign culminating in an eating contest in which a competitor dies from overeating. ITV saw it as an attack on advertising, which funded the commercial channel, but the play was eventually shown by the BBC three years later. Switching to the BBC's Wednesday Play series, Exton wrote *The Bone Yard* (1964), about a police inspector who had psychic visions, but this was also delayed, because it was considered too close to a contemporary case involving a corrupt Metropolitan Police detective, and was eventually shown in 1966. Exton's other single plays for television included *The Boundary* (co-scripted with Tom Stoppard, 1971) and *The Rainbirds* (for the BBC's Play for Today series, 1971).

Most of Exton's scripts for the cinema were adaptations. They included *A Place to Go* (1963), based on Michael Fisher's novel *Bethnal Green*, Emlyn Williams's suspense drama *Night Must Fall* (1964), Joe Orton's comedy *Entertaining Mr Sloane* (1970), and *10 Rillington Place* (1971), from the book by Ludovic Kennedy about the serial killer John Christie. Uncredited, he also rewrote the script of the comedy *Georgy Girl* (1966). Later, during a fairly unfruitful, ten-year stay in Hollywood, he co-wrote *Red Sonja* (1985), an action-adventure film starring Arnold Schwarzenegger, and—again uncredited—contributed to the script of *The Bounty* (1984).

A new era of television success followed Exton's return to Britain, where he wrote the first Ruth Rendell Mysteries adaptation, *Wolf to the Slaughter* (1987), and from 1989 to 2001 was the lead writer for the Poirot adventures, starring David Suchet as Agatha Christie's Belgian detective. He injected an element of comedy into the scripts, which was lacking in Christie's books. He also scripted Jeeves and Wooster (1990–93), featuring Stephen Fry and Hugh Laurie in P. G. Wodehouse's comic stories, and many episodes of Rosemary and Thyme (2003–6), starring Felicity Kendal and Pam Ferris as green-fingered sleuths. His few stage plays included *Murder Is Easy* (Duke of York's Theatre, 1993), based on the Agatha Christie novel. At the time of his death at the Marie Curie Hospice, Camden, London, from brain cancer on 16 August 2007 he was planning productions of two of his own plays, *Neddy and Bumps* and *Barking in Essex*. His funeral was held at Golders Green crematorium. He was survived by his wife, Mara, and by his five children. ANTHONY HAYWARD

Sources *The Independent* (18 Aug 2007) · *Daily Telegraph* (20 Aug 2007) · *The Times* (22 Aug 2007) · *The Guardian* (21 Aug 2007); (25 Aug 2007) · BFI, SIFT database · internet movie database, www.imdb.com, 1 Feb 2010 · BFI screenonline, www.screenonline.org.uk, 1 Feb 2010 · www.doollee.com/PlaywrightsE/exton-clive.html, 1 Feb 2010 · *WW* (2007) · b. cert. · m. certs. · d. cert.

Likenesses obituary photographs · photograph, repro. in www.hometheaterforum.com/forum/thread/267249/the-htf-film-and-necrology-report-for-2007-part-ii

Wealth at death £567,237: probate, 17 Nov 2008, *CGPLA Eng. & Wales*

Farnon, Robert Joseph (1917–2005), composer and musical arranger, was born on 24 July 1917 in Toronto, Ontario, Canada, the second son and third of four children in a musical family: his father, a clothier, played the violin, and his mother played the piano. He himself learned to play the violin, piano, percussion, and trumpet, while still young. He gained experience on radio as a teenager and became, at nineteen, lead trumpet in the Canadian Broadcasting Corporation Orchestra (conducted by Percy Faith). He was also, from 1937 to 1943, a member of the Happy Gang, broadcasting skits, comedy routines, and a variety of musical items each weekday lunchtime on CBC Radio. On trips to New York he played in jam sessions with Dizzy Gillespie and Oscar Peterson, both of whom became lifelong friends. He studied composition with Louis Waizman, and initially had high-art ambitions, composing two symphonies (the first given a performance by Eugene Ormandy and the Philadelphia Orchestra in 1942). In September 1944, as a Canadian army captain, he came to Britain as conductor of, and arranger for, the Canadian band of the allied expeditionary forces. His forces' post gave him an opportunity to experiment creatively within lighter idioms.

Farnon decided to settle in England after the war. British bandleaders like Bert Ambrose and Lew Stone had already taken to his music, and he soon found work as an arranger for Geraldo, whose band he took over when Geraldo embarked on an American tour in 1947. The next year the Robert Farnon Orchestra was heard frequently on radio, and he was also working for Decca as a house conductor and arranger. His reputation was clinched with Decca's release of the vinyl 78 rpm disc number F9038 towards the end of 1948. This became one of the most celebrated of all light music recordings containing, as it did, 'Portrait of a Flirt' on one side, and 'Jumping Bean' on the other. The latter has been used more widely as a signature tune than any other piece of light music. 'Jumping Bean' begins with a snarling brass tritone (the 'devil's interval' or *diabolus in musica*), but then menace turns unexpectedly to comedy as the tension suddenly evaporates. The tritone was also used to comic effect in 'Peanut Polka' (Decca LF1020, 1950). It is a mark of Farnon's talent that the tritone loses its usual associations with the demonic in the context of his musical idiom and becomes, instead, a source of amusement.

Farnon became interested in composing for screen, and made his first individual and distinctive contribution to film music with his score to *Just William's Luck* in 1947, in which he created an influential vocabulary of comic musical devices. Humour in music was always something at which Farnon excelled. The next year he was composing for another William film, as well as providing music for *Spring in Park Lane*, one of Britain's commercially most successful films, starring Anna Neagle and Michael Wilding. The closing titles music, for orchestra and wordless chorus, revealed his orchestral palette at its richest. The opening titles music anticipated his arrangements of traditional material on Frank Sinatra's album *Great Songs from Great Britain* (1962). Sinatra (who nicknamed Farnon the Guv'nor) was just one of many singers for whom he composed and arranged; the list included Tony Bennett, Gracie Fields, and Vera Lynn, as well as such lesser-known figures as Beryl Davis, Denny Dennis, and Donald Peers. Farnon's film score to *Captain Horatio Hornblower RN* (1951) showed his ability to compete with the swashbuckling Hollywood style of Erich Korngold. Among the many other films for which he composed were *Expresso Bongo* (1959), starring Cliff Richard, and the final Bob Hope and Bing Crosby collaboration, *Road to Hong Kong* (1962). In the mid-1950s, in Toronto, he married Patricia (Pat) Smith, a casting director, with whom he had five sons and two daughters. About 1959 they moved to Guernsey, where Farnon continued to compose prolifically. During the 1970s, when interest in light music had faded, he was writing scores for TV series, including *Colditz* (1972–4) and *Secret Army* (1977–9).

Farnon was a versatile composer who could turn his hand to any musical mood, but he was without equal in his ability to communicate joy through music. André Previn reputedly called him 'the greatest living writer for strings in the world' (*The Times*, 27 April 2005). His polished technique can be heard to effect in 'Westminster Waltz' (Decca F10818, 1956), which won for Farnon one of his four Ivor Novello awards; another was given for outstanding services to British music (1991). In 1996 he received a Grammy award for best instrumental arrangement (for 'Lament', performed by J. J. Johnson and the Robert Farnon Orchestra). He was honoured with the order of Canada in 1988.

Farnon was influenced early in his career by the British light music composer Eric Coates, especially regarding the care taken over orchestral effects, but became himself a major influence on the sound of light music after the Second World War. Many of his characteristic devices, such as the use of divided strings sweeping up and down in parallel motion, as well as decorative wind phrases, harp glissandi, and other musical devices that he termed 'gingerbread', were widely imitated. His music had an influence on the film composers Quincy Jones and John Williams. He never lost his interest in more classically oriented composition, as is evident in his rhapsody for violin and orchestra (a BBC commission of 1958), or one of his last works, the third symphony (first performed in Edinburgh in the month after his death). He regretted that he did not have more opportunity to work with jazz players he admired, especially with personal friends like Gillespie and Peterson.

Early in the twenty-first century there was a revival of interest in Farnon's compositions, thanks to their being championed by the conductors Ronald Corp and John Wilson. He was therefore enjoying renewed attention in the years before he died peacefully, during the early hours of 23 April 2005, in St Martin's, Guernsey. He was survived by his wife, Pat, and their seven children. A memorial service was held at St Paul's, Covent Garden, on 24 July.

DEREK B. SCOTT

Sources *The Guardian* (26 April 2005) • *Evening News* [Edinburgh] (26 April 2005) • *The Times* (27 April 2005) • *Daily Telegraph* (28 April 2005) • *The Herald* [Glasgow] (13 May 2005) • *The Independent* (14 May 2005) • *Daily Post* [Liverpool] (17 May 2005) • *The Stage* (26 May 2005) • D. Jacobs, *The Guv'nor: the Robert Farnon story*, 5 June 2005 [BBC Radio2 tribute] • D. Ades, *Melody fair*, CD notes, two-disc set, JASCD 661 (2007) • website, Robert Farnon Society, www.rfsoc.org.uk, 3 Dec 2007 [incl. biography, discography, online issues of *Journal Into Melody* and index, 1992–2006]

Archives FILM BFINA, performance footage | SOUND BL NSA, documentary recordings; performance recordings

Likenesses two photographs, 1949, Getty Images, London • D. Boulton, photographs, Redfern Music Picture Library, London • obituary photographs

Farr, Dennis Larry Ashwell (1929–2006), art historian and museum director, was born on 3 April 1929 at 30 Leagrave Road, Luton, Bedfordshire, the youngest of three children of Arthur William Farr, who sold, and later manufactured, hats, and his wife, Helen Eva, *née* Ashwell. Educated at Luton grammar school, where he was encouraged in his ambition to study the history of art by Ronald Smoothey, the enthusiastic senior art master, he went to the Courtauld Institute of Art, University of London, in 1947 (graduating BA in 1950). At the time Anthony Blunt had just become director and the student body consisted predominantly of former servicemen and -women. At Blunt's suggestion he wrote his MA dissertation on William Etty, the early nineteenth-century painter of nudes, which was subsequently published with a full catalogue, as *William Etty* (1958).

In 1954 Farr was appointed assistant keeper at the Tate Gallery, just when the National Gallery and Tate Gallery Act gave full independent status to the Tate for the first time. Farr described his early years there in an illuminating reminiscence in the *Burlington Magazine* (Jan 2006) containing numerous amusing anecdotes, including a description of the occasion when the then director, John Rothenstein, punched the well-known, irascible collector, Douglas Cooper, on the nose. He worked on several exhibitions, notably a Duncan Grant retrospective, and he was on the committee of the legendary Romantic Movement exhibition, celebrating the tenth anniversary of the Council of Europe in 1959. But the long-term fruit of his period at the Tate was the catalogue *Modern British Paintings, Drawings and Sculpture* (1964), which he wrote with Mary Chamot and Martin Butlin, and a general book, *British Sculpture since 1945* (1965). On 6 June 1959 he married Diana Pullein-Thompson (*b*. 1925), a successful author of childrens' books, and daughter of Captain Harold James Pullein-Thompson. They had two children, Benedict and Joanna.

Relatively brief interludes as curator of the Paul Mellon Collection in Washington (1965–6) and then as senior lecturer in fine art at Glasgow University (1967–9) led to the appointment that turned out to be central to Farr's career, the directorship of Birmingham City Museums and Art Gallery (1969–80). The Art Gallery is outstanding among the regional collections in England and under Farr's direction it enjoyed a golden period, marked by major acquisitions, notably a Giovanni Bellini altarpiece and two views of Warwick Castle by Canaletto. His calm and modest demeanour and human kindness and the encouragement he gave to his staff were widely recognized and appreciated. His high standing in Birmingham was attested in a variety of ways, not least in his appointment as JP (1977–80) and the award of the honorary degree of DLitt by the university (1981).

In 1980 Farr was appointed director of the Courtauld Institute Gallery, where his first task was the integration and display of the recent munificent bequest of Count Antoine Seilern, the Princes Gate collection. This was mainly of Flemish and Italian paintings and drawings, and it added a new dimension to Samuel Courtauld's original collection of French impressionists and post-impressionists. A few years later Farr planned and supervised the collection's move from its modest home in Woburn Square to grand surroundings in the fine rooms at Somerset House. The new galleries were opened to the public in 1990 and Farr was appointed CBE in the following year. His popularity with his colleagues at all levels was attested by the security staff, who insisted on giving him their own leaving party when he retired in 1993.

Farr's rather easygoing manner belied a great deal of energy and commitment. As well as the administrative tasks of his directorships he engaged in research, particularly, though by no means exclusively, on twentieth-century British art, and produced numerous publications. Most notable was his volume in the Oxford History of English Art series, *English Art, 1870–1940* (1978), and his monumental book on the sculptor Lynn Chadwick, written with Eva Chadwick (1990). Nor did he shirk the demands of the public arena of his profession. A valued member of numerous committees, he was, uniquely, both president of the Museums Association (1979–80) and chairman of the Association of Art Historians (1983–6). On the academic side he was editor of Clarendon Studies in the History of Art (1985–2001).

Retirement from the Courtauld gave Farr more time for his favourite hobby, riding, in pursuit of which he and his wife moved to Haslemere in Surrey. Yet he continued to be in demand as a guest curator of exhibitions and he took on a Francis Bacon retrospective at the Yale Center for British

Art in New Haven in 1999. He also contributed fourteen entries to the *Oxford Dictionary of National Biography*, including a substantial article on William Etty. His career provides an eloquent example of an able manager who was also a gifted curator and a productive scholar. He died of a cerebral haemorrhage at the Royal Surrey County Hospital, Guildford, on 6 December 2006, and was cremated at Guildford crematorium following a funeral service at St Bartholomew's Church, Haslemere, on 14 December. A memorial service was held at St Mary-le-Strand on 19 April 2007. Farr was survived by his wife, Diana, and their two children. C. M. KAUFFMANN

Sources D. Farr, 'A student at the Courtauld Institute', *Burlington Magazine*, 147 (2005), 539–47 · D. Farr, 'A curator at the Tate Gallery', *Burlington Magazine*, 148 (2006), 25–30 · *The Independent* (14 Dec 2006) · *The Times* (21 Dec 2006); (11 Jan 2007) · P. Cormack, 'Dennis Farr remembered', *Courtauld Institute Newsletter*, 23 (spring 2007) · R. Green, *Burlington Magazine*, 149 (2007), 414 · *WW* (2006) · personal knowledge (2010) · private information (2010) · b. cert. · m. cert. · d. cert.
Archives Tate collection, corresp., MSS, and notes | SOUND BL NSA, documentary recording
Likenesses J. Cope, bromide print, 1979, NPG · UPPA, photograph, 1990, NPG · photographs, 1990, Photoshot, London · obituary photographs
Wealth at death £295,009: probate, 5 April 2007, *CGPLA Eng. & Wales*

Farrah, Abd'Elkader [Abdel] (**1926–2005**), theatre designer, was born in Ksar al-Boukhari, Algeria, on 28 March 1926, the son of Brahim Farrah and his wife, Fatima-Zohra Missoumi. His first ambition was to be a painter, but with fundamentalist strictures against figurative painting he found the theatre a three-dimensional alternative and ran a touring company with his brother until it was censored and closed by the authorities in 1950.

With the political situation in Algeria deteriorating, Farrah headed for Paris. He initially intended to work as a painter, but again found himself in the theatre. He designed his first production, *Samson and Delilah* (1953), at the Stadsschouwburg in Amsterdam and then joined Michel St Denis in Strasbourg, where he became head of the city's theatrical design course at the national theatre school from 1955 to 1962. During these years he worked mainly in Strasbourg with St Denis on a wide repertory that included Brecht, Shakespeare, and Mozart, and also with John Blatchley and Jean Dasté at St Etienne. During this time he married Simone Pieret, with whom he had two children, Safi and Leïla.

In 1960 Farrah designed *Oedipus rex* for St Denis at Sadlers Wells. It was a triumph and attracted the attention of Peter Hall, then setting up his new Royal Shakespeare Company (RSC). Hall invited both St Denis and Farrah to join him in Stratford upon Avon. The war in Algeria was at its height—Farrah was effectively an exile from both France and north Africa—and Stratford offered a safe haven for Farrah and his family. It also offered him perfect working conditions—a wonderful ensemble, superb workshops, and a theatre community dedicated to excellence. It was the start of a long association with the RSC, as resident associate designer from 1961 to 1991, and honorary associate artist thereafter.

For Michel St Denis, Farrah designed *The Cherry Orchard* in 1961 and *Puntila* in 1965; for Peter Brook, *The Tempest* in 1963; and for Clifford Williams, a long-time friend, several productions, including *Dr Faustus* (1968), *Oh! Calcutta!* (1970), *The Duchess of Malfi* (1971), and Pirandello's *Henry IV* (1974). But it was for his collaborations with Terry Hands that he came to be best known. Over a twenty-year period they mounted twenty-five productions together, which encompassed among others Genet's *The Balcony* (1971), premières of two Peter Barnes plays, *The Bewitched* (1974) and *Red Noses* (1985), *Coriolanus* (1977), starring Alan Howard, *Poppy* (1982) by Peter Nichols and Monty Norman, *Richard III* (1972) and *Le Cid* (1977) at the Comédie Française, and two productions, *Troilus and Cressida* (1978) and *As You Like It* (1979), for the Burgtheater, Vienna. Nevertheless it was the cycle of all eight of Shakespeare's history plays at Stratford between 1975 and 1980 that most defined their working relationship and indeed careers. Farrah introduced the bare black stage with a steep incline, thrusting into the audience, which one critic described as like 'the great deck of an aircraft carrier' (James N. Loehlin, *Henry V*, 2000, 54), upon which all the plays would take place, and then concentrated on the detail of costuming, richness of decoration, and careful selection of hand and scenic props. He also demanded that the lighting should carry an equivalent impact. It put huge demands on the actors—'it wasn't a stage where you could hide weakness', he said (S. Beaumann, ed., *The Royal Shakespeare Company's Production of Henry V*, 1976, 31)—but Alan Howard, Helen Mirren, Julian Glover, David Suchet, and Emrys James (among many others) revelled in the challenges.

The period from 1975 to 1985 has been called the golden age of the RSC. Apart from the histories it included *Macbeth* (1976), starring Ian McKellen and Judi Dench, Trevor Nunn's *Nicholas Nickleby* (1980), Buzz Goodbody's *Hamlet* (1975), starring Ben Kingsley, *Cyrano de Bergerac* (1983), starring Derek Jacobi, and many other award-winning productions. The Other Place, Stratford, became a regular new-play theatre, the Donmar and the Barbican were opened, and work was completed on the Swan. In this extraordinary ten-year period Farrah designed twenty-one productions.

Farrah's personality was as rich and mysterious as his work. A central figure in the growth of the RSC, an advocate for the Arab world (he maintained a lover's quarrel with Algeria till his death), he came without traditional baggage to the RSC and drew upon images from a civilization that others knew only from books but he knew from life. He was exotic and un-English. Among his peers—the other world-class designers then associated with the RSC, including John Bury, John Napier, Ralph Koltai, and Timothy O'Brien—he was respected and liked. John Napier dubbed him 'the wisest of us all' (personal knowledge). He died on 18 December 2005, and was survived by his two children, Safi and Leïla, his wife, Simone, having predeceased him. TERRY HANDS

Sources *The Guardian* (5 Jan 2008) · *The Times* (11 Jan 2006) · personal knowledge (2009) · private information (2009)
Likenesses obituary photographs

Faulkner, (Herbert Gustavus) Max (1916–2005), golfer, was born at 36 Havelock Road, Bexhill, Sussex, on 29 July 1916, the eldest son of Gustavus Kirkham (Gus) Faulkner, a professional golfer then based at Selsey, and his wife, Eliza Ellen, *née* Hussey. His early education was in Wales, while his father was the professional at Pennard on the Gower peninsula, then in Surrey when he moved to Bramley. Max Faulkner worked first as his father's assistant, then became the professional at Leamington Spa. As a player he first came to prominence in 1937 when he won both the Berkshire championship and the Addington foursomes. On 20 August 1938 he married Joan, the 21-year-old daughter of William Frederick Weller, farmer, of Amberley Farm, Milford, Surrey. They had three children, Guy, Hilary, and John.

Like so many sportsmen of his generation Faulkner was deprived of some of his best competitive years by the Second World War. During the conflict he served as a physical training instructor with the RAF, concentrating on boxing far more than on golf (he claimed later to have played only one round during the entire war). None the less after demobilization he returned to his first love, and victory in the west of England professional championship of 1947 helped secure his selection in the British Ryder cup team of that year. In all he played in five Ryder cup matches (1947, 1949, 1951, 1953, and 1957), although his personal record was disappointing and he won one solitary point from eight games played. In 1949 he won both the Penfold and Lotus tournaments, and tied for sixth place in the open championship, four strokes behind the winner, Bobby Locke. In the following year Locke won again, with Faulkner coming fifth.

These experiences of contending at the highest level paved the way for Faulkner's greatest triumph, and the feat for which he is best remembered, his victory in the open championship of 1951, held that year for the first (and at the time of his death only) time at Royal Portrush in Northern Ireland. Three opening rounds of 71, 70, and 70 gave Faulkner a substantial lead of six strokes with eighteen holes to play, and, although the Argentinian golfer Antonio Cerdá chased him hard on the final afternoon, Faulkner held on to win by two shots with a score of 285. This proved to be the only home win in the open championship between Henry Cotton's third and final victory in 1948 and Tony Jacklin's triumph of 1969, which ushered in an altogether different era in the history of British, and indeed European, golf. In all Faulkner won sixteen European professional tournaments, including the Dunlop masters of 1951, the Spanish open championship three times (in 1952, 1953, and 1957), and the Portuguese open title of 1968. In 1953 he won the *News of the World* tournament (then effectively the Professional Golfers' Association match-play championship) at Ganton, defeating Dai Rees in the final.

Faulkner's style was distinctive, elegant, and powerful, with immense ball-striking ability. He regularly won long-

(Herbert Gustavus) Max Faulkner (1916–2005), by Bob Thomas, 1960

driving competitions, and always maintained a high level of physical fitness. He was an inveterate fixer and manipulator of golf clubs, and was rumoured to possess more than 300 putters, many of his own design. That said, Faulkner never forgot that golf was a game, and that paying spectators deserved to be entertained. He was a 'personality' before the term was invented, and something of a flamboyant dresser, in contrast to many of his fellow competitors, whose often austere demeanour reflected the prevailing drabness of the years after the war, when many golf clubs were struggling for survival. 'Faulkner stories' abounded among golf journalists, for whom he was always good copy, and Henry Longhurst always claimed that he witnessed Faulkner signing autographs at Portrush in 1951 with the appendage 'open champion 1951' when two rounds still remained to be played.

In later life Faulkner received several honours, including being appointed OBE (2001) and being made a freeman of the City of London. He played numerous exhibition matches for charitable causes, and was involved in both personal and professional ways in nurturing young golfing talent. In particular he headed the 'Butten boys' initiative of the businessman Ernest Butten, who wanted to develop a cohort of British golfers capable of challenging the very best American and international players. Among these was Brian Barnes, who not only married Faulkner's daughter, Hilary, but later followed his father-in-law as champion of Spain and Portugal, played in the Ryder cup on several occasions, and in 1995 secured a memorable triumph in the British seniors open, watched in person by Faulkner over the same Portrush links where the latter had won the open forty-four years previously. Barnes also shared with Faulkner a love of fishing. Having lived latterly at Pulborough, Sussex, Faulkner died on 26 February 2005 at St Richard's Hospital, Chichester, of pneumonia.

RICHARD FISHER

Sources M. Faulkner and L. T. Stanley, *The Faulkner method* (1952) · H. Longhurst, *Only on Sundays* (1964) · *Golfer's handbook* [various edns] · *The Times* (1 March 2005) · *Daily Telegraph* (15 July 2001); (2 March 2005) · *The Independent* (18 July 2001); (2 March 2005) · *The Guardian* (5 April 2005) · D. Barnes, www.maxfaulkner.com, 5 May 2008 · b. cert. · m. cert. · d. cert.

Archives SOUND BL NSA, recorded talks

Likenesses photographs, 1947–73, Getty Images, London · photographs, 1947–95, PA Photos, London · group portraits, photographs, 1958–60, Photoshot, London · B. Thomas, photograph, 1960, Getty Images, London [*see illus.*] · obituary photographs

Wealth at death £484,374: probate, 11 Nov 2005, *CGPLA Eng. & Wales*

Feilden, Sir Bernard Melchior (1919–2008), conservation architect, was born on 11 September 1919 at 31 Meadway Court, Hampstead Garden Suburb, London, a twin son and one of five brothers born to Robert Humphrey Feilden (1884–1925), a mechanical engineer and major in the Royal Field Artillery special reserve, and his wife, Olive, *née* Binyon (1888–1971), who was descended from a family of engineers and architects, including the chief engineer of the Stockton to Darlington railway. Having been gassed in France in the First World War, his father took the family to a ranch in British Columbia to recover his health. It was there that Feilden received the distinctive scar on his face from a brother wielding a pickaxe. In 1925, in a traumatic incident witnessed by the young Feilden, his father drowned in a lake. At the age of nine he returned to Britain, where he was raised in Bedford by his mother and aunts.

At Bedford School Feilden developed his passion for architecture, which he perhaps inherited from his maternal grandfather, Brightwen Binyon (1846–1905), an architect, furniture designer, and former pupil of Alfred Waterhouse. After winning a scholarship to the Bartlett School of Architecture at University College, London, his education was interrupted by the Second World War, during which he served with the Bengal Sappers and Miners in India, Mesopotamia, Iran, and Italy, before completing his studies at the Architectural Association, from which he qualified in 1949. On 23 April the same year, at St Mary's Church, Great Plumstead, Norfolk, he married Ruth Mildred Bainbridge (1927–1994), daughter of Robert John Bainbridge, fruit farmer; they had two sons, Henry (*b.* 1956) and Francis (*b.* 1964), and two daughters, Harriet (*b.* 1958) and Mary (*b.* 1960).

Feilden secured his first job at the Norwich-based practice of Edward Boardman & Son, where he designed the Trinity Presbyterian Church (later the Trinity United Reformed Church), Norwich, one of only a handful of post-war church buildings to be listed. In 1954, undeterred by a shooting accident in which he lost his left eye, he used the compensation to set up his own architectural practice with David Mawson. Over the next fifty years Feilden and Mawson grew into a highly successful and respected firm involved in a wide range of projects, with offices in London, Cambridge, and Prague as well as Norwich. Feilden replaced Denys Lasdun as the consultant architect to the University of East Anglia and soon made his name as a thoughtful and innovative moderate modernist responsible for overseeing the design of the university and, in particular, The Square, which became the lively social focus of the entire campus.

In 1962 Feilden was invited by Launcelot Fleming, the bishop of Norwich, to advise on the repair of the tottering bomb-damaged spire of Norwich Cathedral, one of the most challenging conservation dilemmas of its time. Scaling the outside of the spire, he felt physically sick as it swayed in the wind, but together with Bertrand Monnet, who had worked on Chartres and Strasbourg cathedrals, he devised an ingenious system for strengthening the existing structure using spring-loaded tensioning and steel wires. Other commissions soon followed. Between 1965 and 1971 he was surveyor to the fabric of York Minster, where he boldly inserted new foundations beneath the sinking central tower. From 1969 to 1977 he was surveyor to the fabric of St Paul's Cathedral where, after an exhaustive survey, he identified serious subsidence, bomb damage, and a huge backlog of repairs. His response was to put in place a visionary forty-year conservation strategy, while carrying out radical improvements to the visitor facilities, and creating a new setting in the crypt for the heroes of empire. In Edinburgh he created an entirely new floor for the High Kirk of St Giles, and in 1982 he intervened to save the historic heart of Chesterfield from destruction, for which he won the Europa Nostra silver medal.

From 1972 to 1994 Feilden lectured on the architectural conservation course at UNESCO's International Centre for the Study of the Preservation and Restoration of Cultural Property (ICCROM) in Rome, where he moved in 1977 after resigning as surveyor of St Paul's. He served as director of ICCROM from 1977 to 1981, during which time he advised on the conservation of the dome of the Al-Aqsa mosque in Jerusalem, for which he received the Aga Khan award in 1986. Other UNESCO commissions followed, including advising the government of India on the Taj Mahal and the thirteenth-century Sun Temple at Konarak, and the government of China on the conservation of the Forbidden City, the Great Wall, the Buddhist Mogao caves, the Terracotta warriors in Xian, and the buildings on Mount Tai. In New Zealand he guided the conservation of the Parliament Buildings (the largest timber structure in the world), and in Canada he helped the state of Alberta with the management of its world heritage sites.

Alongside a formidable lecture programme at home and overseas, Feilden still found time to advise on Marlborough House and Hampton Court Palace. Meticulous, energetic, and with a quiet spiritual commitment to his ecclesiastical work, he maintained a lifelong passion for English cathedrals, serving on the Church of England's cathedrals advisory commission for England from 1981 to 2000, and on the fabric committees of Bury St Edmunds, Ely, and Norwich cathedrals from 1990 to 2000. He also served on the Ancient Monuments Board from 1962 to 1977, and as a member of the Royal Institute of British Architects' council from 1975 to 1977. In 1973–4 he was Hoffman Wood professor of architecture at Leeds University. He was president of the Ecclesiastical Architects' and Surveyors' Association in 1975, and of the Guild of Surveyors in the following year. Between 1981 and 1987 he was president of the International Council on Monuments and Sites.

Feilden's book *Conservation of Historic Buildings* (1982), on the fundamental principles of conservation, immediately established itself as the most important single authority on the subject. His other publications included *The Wonder of York Minster* (1976), *An Introduction to Conservation of Cultural Property* (1979), *Between Two Earthquakes: Cultural Property in Seismic Zones* (1987), *Guidelines for Conservation in India* (1989), and *Management Guidelines for World Cultural Heritage Sites* (1993), as well as numerous articles in professional journals. His books did much to raise the status and understanding of conservation worldwide. He was regarded as the leading conservation architect of his generation, and the father of the profession.

Feilden was a kindly and modest man with immense energy. His nephew Hugh Feilden, a partner at Feilden and Mawson, recalled that 'He had a very moral sense of the world and was always looking to do right in the way he treated people', whether they were clients, fellow professionals, students, or contractors (*Building Design*, 20 November 2008).

In his later years Feilden continued to work from his family home at Stiffkey Old Hall, near Wells next the Sea, Norfolk, and later the Old Barn, Hall Farm Place, Bawburgh, near Norwich. He enjoyed sailing, painting, fishing, and devouring histories and biographies. After the death of his first wife, on 21 October 1995 he married Christina Matilda Beatrice (Tina) Murdoch (*b*. 1940), secretary; she was the daughter of Henry Frederick Erskine Tufnell, bank director, and the former wife of Ian Lindsay Murdoch.

Feilden was appointed OBE in 1969, advanced to CBE in 1976, and knighted for his cathedral work and international activities in 1985. He became a fellow of the Royal Institute of British Architects in 1968, the Society of Antiquaries in 1969, and the Royal Society of Arts in 1973. In 1976 he was appointed to the order of St William of York for his work on York Minster. He was made an honorary fellow of University College, London, in 1985, and of the American Institute of Architects in 1987. He was bestowed with honorary degrees from Gothenburg in 1988 and the University of East Anglia the following year. In 2007 a fellowship was endowed in his name at York University to promote the teaching of craft skills in architectural conservation. He died at his home in Bawburgh on 14 November 2008 from renal failure and chronic obstructive pulmonary disease. He was survived by his second wife, Tina, and the four children of his first marriage. A memorial service was held in Norwich Cathedral on 7 February 2009. PHILIP DAVIES

Sources *Daily Telegraph* (17 Nov 2008) · *The Independent* (20 Nov 2008) · *Building Design* (20 Nov 2008) · *The Guardian* (21 Nov 2008); (26 Nov 2008) · *The Times* (2 Dec 2008); (9 Feb 2009) · S. Restorick, 'Feilden and Mawson: Sir Bernard Feilden: a tribute, a personal memoir', priv. coll. · Burke, *Peerage* · *WW* (2008) · b. cert. · m. certs. · d. cert.

Likenesses obituary photographs

Wealth at death £1,277,944: probate, 22 May 2009, *CGPLA Eng. & Wales*

Fewtrell, (Ernest) Malcolm (1909–2005), police officer, was born on 28 September 1909 at the police station in Newport Street, Ryde, Isle of Wight, one of six sons of Ernest George Fewtrell, police officer, and his wife, Minnie Albanette, *née* Simms. At the time of his birth his father was a police constable; later he was a detective in the Criminal Investigations Department (CID), and later still a newsagent. Three of Fewtrell's brothers also became detectives. He attended school in Reading, then worked for a year on a sheep station in Australia before returning to join the Buckinghamshire police force in 1927 as a cadet. On 4 June 1934 he married Ann Thomas, a 24-year-old nurse at the King Edward VII Hospital, Windsor (they had met when Fewtrell had had an appendix operation), and daughter of George Thomas, railway fireman. Fewtrell later described her as (like all successful policemen's wives) 'patient, tolerant and understanding' (Fewtrell, 8). They had one son and one daughter.

Fewtrell gradually rose through the ranks of the Buckinghamshire police force, and was noted as a calm and capable officer. During the Second World War he was, as a policeman, prohibited from joining the armed forces, to his disappointment. In 1950 he was promoted to detective inspector, and in 1954 to detective superintendent, and head of Buckinghamshire CID.

Fewtrell was looking forward to his retirement, then less than a year away, when he found himself charged with solving one of the most celebrated crimes of the twentieth century. At about 4.30 a.m. on the morning of 8 August 1963 he was woken by a phone call from the police headquarters in Aylesbury, with the message 'There's been a train robbery at Cheddington, sir' (Fewtrell, 9). Within half an hour he was at Bridego Bridge, near Linslade, to find the Glasgow to London mail train in two parts (the engine and high-value carriage having been decoupled from the other carriages, which had been left a mile behind at Sears Crossing), sixty-five bewildered postal sorters, and a badly coshed driver; 120 mail bags containing Scottish banks' takings after a bank holiday weekend were missing. At first it was thought (in amazement) that £1 million had been stolen, but over the next few days it became clear that nearer £2.6 million had been taken, in what the press immediately dubbed the 'great train robbery'. At lunchtime on the day of the robbery Fewtrell advised his chief constable to call in Scotland Yard, and from that point he shared responsibility for the investigation with Detective Superintendent Gerald McArthur of the Yard.

Initially there were few clues to go on. Eyewitness reports from the train crew and postmen told of around fifteen men, wearing balaclavas and gloves, operating

(Ernest) **Malcolm Fewtrell (1909–2005)**, by Ralph Crane, 1963 [left]

swiftly in a highly professional, military-style operation. Fewtrell's first thought was that the robbers would have made their getaway using the nearby M1 back to London. However, the train's fireman had been told to lie still for half an hour while the gang made their getaway. Fewtrell correctly surmised that the gang was holed up in a hideaway relatively near the abandoned train. He and McArthur therefore decided to search the surrounding countryside from the train outwards up to a 30 mile perimeter. 'I have kicked myself thousands of times for not having ordered the search the other way round', he later wrote; (Fewtrell, 44). They also took the calculated risk of calling a press conference to publicize their hunch. The result was spectacular: 'the whole country seemed to be in the grip of detective fever', Fewtrell wrote (ibid., 57). One particular tip-off proved decisive: a local cowman, John Maris, reported suspicions about Leatherslade Farm, near Oakley in Buckinghamshire. The two officers sent to investigate found a house well stocked with food, beer, and entertainments, and, in the basement, several mailbags stuffed with bank wrappers and Post Office chits. 'The whole place is a clue', Fewtrell was reported as saying (ibid.). Evidence from Scotland Yard's fingerprinting unit proved crucial in the subsequent course of the investigation, as did further tip-offs from the general public, and chance discoveries of some of the money. Fewtrell's own role was particularly important in trapping in interview Brian Field, the smooth-talking solicitor's clerk who had helped the robbers buy the farm.

Fewtrell also had responsibility for the security of the courtroom in which the subsequent trials were held, and for the detention and transport of the defendants. No local court was big enough to accommodate the trial, so Aylesbury district council offices were temporarily converted into a courthouse, with additional security challenges. Fewtrell was later proud that none of the defendants escaped while in the custody of his officers. He was in court on 16 April 1964 to hear the sentences on the twelve convicted men, most for thirty years. He disagreed with the view that the robbers had been handed unduly harsh sentences, and especially disliked the romanticization of their crime, emphasizing the ruthlessness of the men, and the deterrent value of the sentences. 'It is easy in this country for people to forget that we all live on a biscuit-thin crust above violence and social upheaval below', he later wrote (Fewtrell, 143).

Having retired, Fewtrell was free to write about the investigation, unlike serving officers; he wrote two long articles that appeared in the *Sunday Telegraph* on 19 and 26 April 1964, and subsequently a book, *The Train Robbers* (1964). In this he was at pains to emphasize that he had 'no desire to take more than a very modest share of the credit' (Fewtrell, 10). On leaving the police he worked for ten years as accommodation officer for Portsmouth Polytechnic before retiring to a bungalow in Swanage, Dorset; there he organized the local neighbourhood watch and played golf into his nineties. He died at Poole Hospital on 28 November 2005, following a stroke. He was survived by his son and daughter, his wife having predeceased him.

Alex May

Sources M. Fewtrell, *The train robbers* (1964) • *The Times* (1 Dec 2005) • *Daily Telegraph* (21 Dec 2005) • b. cert. • m. cert. • d. cert.

Likenesses R. Crane, double portrait, photograph, 1963 (with Gerald McArthur), Getty Images, London, Time and Life Pictures [*see illus.*] • two photographs, 1963, PA Photos, London • obituary photographs • photograph, repro. in Fewtrell, *Robbers*

Wealth at death £411,335: probate, 6 Feb 2006, *CGPLA Eng. & Wales*

Figures, Sir Colin Frederick (1925–2006), intelligence officer, was born at 34 Primrose Lane, Hall Green, Birmingham, on 1 July 1925, the son of Frederick Joseph Figures, insurance clerk, and his wife, Muriel Nellie, *née* Hadwell. He was educated at King Edward's School, Birmingham. He then served in the Worcestershire regiment from 1943 to 1948; his postings included the inter-service Russian language course at Cambridge and the British military missions in Romania and Hungary. On demobilization he went to Pembroke College, Cambridge, where he took a degree in French and Russian. A keen sportsman, he had played rugby for King Edward's and for Pembroke College and had a chance of a Cambridge blue. Perhaps to console himself for not achieving this, towards the end of his time at university he co-founded the Woodpeckers, a combined Oxford and Cambridge touring rugby side. He was also an enthusiastic cricketer.

Figures joined the Secret Intelligence Service (SIS, also known as MI6) directly from university in 1951. After two years at the head office in London he was attached to the Allied Control Commission in Germany from 1953 to 1956, then to the embassy in Amman from 1956 to 1958. After a year back in London, in 1959 he was appointed head of the important station in Warsaw, which gave him the chance to demonstrate his ability to recruit and run foreign spies under hostile conditions. His reputation within the service for competence and reliability was by this time growing into the realization that he was potentially a high-flying senior officer. In 1956 he had married a secretary at the Foreign Office, Pamela Ann (Pam) Timmis, with whom he had a son and two daughters.

Figures returned to London in 1962 and spent most of the next ten years dealing with operations behind the iron curtain, including a period from 1966 to 1969 as head of a station in a Vienna that would still have seemed atmospherically familiar to Harry Lime. This was a busy time politically as well as professionally, coinciding with the 'Prague spring' of 1968, and led to his being appointed OBE in his last year there. Over the next ten years he broadened his relationship with the Foreign and Commonwealth Office and, especially during four years directing SIS operations in Northern Ireland, with the Security Service (MI5) and the military. His east European experience proved extremely useful in the Irish context and during this period SIS shook off the adverse effects of the Philby and Blake disasters and scored a number of significant recruitment successes against the hardest east European targets. He was involved in the operational planning of several of these. By the time he handed over the Northern Ireland responsibility he had established himself as a leading member of the Whitehall intelligence community and was appointed CMG in 1978.

Figures was a natural choice to take over as deputy chief of SIS under Sir Arthur (Dickie) Franks in 1979, then to replace him as chief in 1981. Figures's four years as chief were conspicuously successful. He combined a background founded on solid midland middle-class values with practical common sense and an ability to lead by example. Self-effacing but quietly self-confident in manner, he exemplified SIS's stated policy of employing not risk seekers but risk takers. His door remained metaphorically, and often actually, open; and through it could sometimes be heard ball-by-ball test match commentary, turned down very low. He was approachable by the whole staff, a good delegator who was liked, respected, and trusted by his subordinates. A man of total integrity, he combined an infectious sense of humour with an absence of pomposity; never a puritan, he was always staunchly loyal to his family and he was unusually fortunate in having a wife who also established herself firmly in the affections of the service and took great interest in questions of welfare in what could sometimes be quite stressful professional circumstances.

Figures had not been long in the chair when Argentina invaded the Falkland Islands in 1982. SIS initially came in for some criticism for not having forecast the invasion, as did the Foreign and Commonwealth Office, but it was soon rightly accepted that foreign intelligence and diplomatic services faced an impossible task in monitoring the unpredictable policies of an erratic dictator. More importantly, and with some invaluable help from their excellent relationships with allied liaison services in North and South America, western Europe, and the Commonwealth, SIS was able to contribute significantly to the achievements of the armed forces in their successful military campaign. Among SIS's achievements was the monitoring of the commercial availability of Exocet missiles that might have replenished Argentinian stocks, the missiles having been deployed with considerable effect against the Royal Navy at a time when the outcome of the campaign was still far from clear. SIS was also able to complement Government Communications Headquarters (GCHQ) in reporting on the Argentinian air force and navy. A less glamorous preoccupation for Figures as chief of SIS was the growing Treasury pressure to trim the budgets of the intelligence community and to improve the working relationships between SIS, the Security Service, and GCHQ. He was ideally suited for this role, lacking as he did any hint of pretentiousness or bombast but having a good eye for detail, and under his leadership SIS's relations with the other two services and with the Foreign and Commonwealth Office were all harmonious. He was knighted KCMG in 1983.

During Figures's time as chief SIS was still unavowed, in other words the existence of the service was not officially acknowledged and still less was the identity of the CSS (chief of the secret service) himself known to the public. With increasingly open government, a press that rejected traditional attitudes towards secrecy, and not least because of the building of a relatively high-profile new headquarters beside the Thames to replace the nondescript building near Lambeth North tube station, it became impossible to maintain the pretence. The former low-profile existence had suited the inherently modest Figures very well, but it became much harder for him to avoid the limelight when in 1989 he was appointed intelligence co-ordinator in the cabinet office in succession to Sir Tony Duff. This job formalized the responsibility he had been given in SIS for budgetary control and joint intelligence co-operation, but now he had to oversee all three services and their relationships with Whitehall in general and with the joint intelligence committee, under Sir Percy Cradock, in particular. Rigorous financial controls were imposed by the Treasury, but making good use of his high reputation and popularity in the intelligence community Figures presided over four harmonious and successful years for British intelligence. One of his outstanding achievements in this period was the reorganization of the intelligence machinery in Northern Ireland, especially after the Ballygawley incident of August 1988, when eight British soldiers were killed and twenty-eight injured by an IRA bomb. His previous responsibility for SIS operations in the territory gave him an invaluable background for this task and meant that his views carried appropriate weight.

After his retirement in 1989 Figures and his wife divided their time between Thames Ditton, Surrey, and the Isle of Wight. He even listed beachcombing as one of his pursuits, but he also keenly followed sport. During the last few years of his life he became increasingly incapacitated by Parkinson's disease and was fortunate to have a supportive wife and family. On 8 December 2006 he died peacefully after quite a long period in Emberbrook Care Centre, Thames Ditton. He was survived by his wife and children. ALASTAIR RELLIE

Sources *The Times* (15 Dec 2006) · *The Guardian* (18 Dec 2006) · *Birmingham Evening Mail* (19 Dec 2006) · *Daily Telegraph* (21 Dec 2006) · *The Independent* (29 Dec 2006) · *WW* (2006) · Burke, *Peerage* · personal knowledge (2010) · private information (2010) · b. cert. · d. cert.
Likenesses obituary photographs
Wealth at death £371,723: probate, 8 May 2007, *CGPLA Eng. & Wales*

Finlay, Ian Hamilton (1925–2006), poet, artist, and gardener, was born in Nassau, Bahamas, on 28 October 1925, the son of James Hamilton Finlay and his wife, Annie Whitelaw, *née* Pettigrew. According to his son James Finlay was a bootlegger who smuggled rum into the United States during prohibition. When he was six Finlay was sent back to boarding school in Scotland. His education there lasted only until he was thirteen, when he was evacuated to Orkney on the outbreak of the Second World War. He briefly attended Glasgow School of Art before being called up for military service in 1943. He served in the Royal Army Service Corps until 1947, spending part of the time in Germany. He was married, in 1945, to Marion Fletcher.

After demobilization Finlay returned to Orkney to earn his living as a shepherd and agricultural labourer. While there he began to write short stories and plays, some of which, in the 1950s, appeared in the *Glasgow Herald* and were produced on BBC radio. His first book, *The Sea-Bed and Other Stories*, was published in 1958 by Castle Wynd, a small press in Edinburgh, and consisted of forty-eight stapled pages. His first collection of poems, *The Dancers Inherit the Party*, was published in 1960 but, significantly, was the product of an American small press run by a Scottish exile, Gael Turnbull, from Ventura, California. Turnbull's *Migrant* magazine was founded in 1958 and had published poems by Finlay in its last two issues in 1960 before transforming itself into a publisher of new collections of poetry. Finlay's book was one of the earliest on its list and he thus became a recognized figure in the avant garde of American poetry—his influence acknowledged by poets like Robert Creeley and Lorine Niedecker—before he gained recognition in Scotland. What appealed to these American writers was the deliberate simplicity of Finlay's work, with its roots in folk tradition. The combination of popular culture and avant-garde experimentalism produced, in 1961, Finlay's groundbreaking collection of poems in contemporary Glasgow vernacular, *Glasgow Beasts, an a Burd, Haw, an Inseks, an, aw, a Fush*, which paved the way for some of the most experimental Scottish writing of the next two decades.

Glasgow Beasts, an a Burd was the first production of the Wild Hawthorn Press, which Finlay founded with Jessie McGuffie in 1964 on the model of Turnbull's Migrant Press. Becoming his own publisher was indicative of the ways in which Finlay sought to control the environment of his art. The Wild Hawthorn Press launched, in the following year, the magazine *Poor. Old. Tired. Horse.* (a title taken from the poem 'Please' by Robert Creeley), of which twenty-five numbers were produced by 1968. Edwin Morgan summarized it as a magazine in which 'well-crafted thing-y poetry was preferred to expressionist or confessional "depth"', and observed that while it did 'publish concrete poetry, semiotic poetry, and sound-poetry' it also included poets who 'dealt with the larger socio-political issues: Mayakovsky, József, Neruda, Günter Grass'. The result, Morgan suggested, was 'an eclecticism that two decades later seems to belong so much to the spirit of the sixties as to have gained more unity and harmony than it appeared to possess at the time' (E. Morgan, 'Early Finlay', in Finlay, ed., *Wood Notes Wild*, 20–21). It was Morgan who had directed Finlay to a letter about 'concrete poetry' by E. M. de Melo e Castro in the *Times Literary Supplement*, where Finlay discovered that 'it was just what in my little naïve, home-made, Scottish way, I had been thinking about' (Finlay, afterword, 98). Finlay published his first concrete poetry in *Rapel* in 1963 and contributed to the first international concrete poetry festival in Brighton in 1967. His role as a pioneer was acknowledged when he and Morgan were nominated as the Scottish representatives on the committee of the international concrete poetry movement. By the late 1960s, however, he was already moving towards a broader conceptual art in which language was situated in a specific environment, as in the series of boat names and numbers printed on wood and wrapped in fishing nets he produced in the late 1960s. One of these, *Starlit Waters*, inspired a campaign against the Tate Gallery when the latter acquired it in 1976.

In 1964 Finlay married Sue MacDonald-Lockhart and in 1966 they moved into an abandoned croft at Stonypath in Lanarkshire, with their two children, Alec and Ailie. They began to develop the land round the croft as a garden that would provide the setting for Finlay's works. The joint work of Finlay and his wife in creating the garden was to become typical of how Finlay's work was produced, being made in collaboration with typographers, sculptors, architects, potters, glassmakers, and others, who produced the objects required by this 'environmental' art. As the garden developed the Wild Hawthorn Press continued to publish postcards, pamphlets, and booklets in which Finlay experimented with language and design in ways that would often prefigure the motifs inscribed on the plaques, the plinths, the sundials, and the sculptures around which the garden was built. 'What you compose with is neither here nor there', Finlay commented, 'you compose with words, or you compose with stone, plants and trees, or you compose with events' ('The death of piety').

Growing recognition of Finlay's achievement came with exhibitions in Sunderland in 1970, at the Scottish National Gallery of Modern Art in 1972, at the National Maritime Museum in 1974, and at the Serpentine Gallery in London in 1977. One room of the exhibition at the Serpentine Gallery was described as 'a small temple opening upon a garden' (Abrioux, 7, quoting the exhibition catalogue), an image that was being created in reality at Stonypath by the transformation of an old cowshed into a gallery that, in the light of Finlay's increasing concern with classical Greece, would later be declared to be a temple. Stonypath itself would be renamed Little Sparta to signify its resistance to Edinburgh as the Athens of the North. Commissions from the Max Planck Institute Garden in Stuttgart in 1975 and from the Kröller-Müller Museum in Holland in 1980, followed by others from the Schweizergarten in Vienna, the Maritime Village in Swansea, and the Villa Celle in Italy, confirmed Finlay's growing international reputation both as a poet-artist and as a garden designer.

Increasing prominence, however, also meant increasing conflict with the cultural establishment. As early as 1962 Finlay had been involved in an acrimonious exchange of letters in *The Scotsman* with Scotland's leading poet, Hugh MacDiarmid (who had been best man at Finlay's first wedding). Challenged by Edwin Morgan with ignoring the new developments in Scottish literature represented by Wild Hawthorn Press publications, MacDiarmid queried whether 'progress to any desirable end will be achieved under the impetus of a group of teddyboy poetasters who have in any case written little enough in justification of their own attitude' (*The Scotsman*, 18 May 1962; Bold, 811–14). In return Finlay and Jessie McGuffie accused MacDiarmid of being a Stalinist trying to ignore the thaw represented by younger writers. Rumours of an attack by a Wild Hawthorn zeppelin on the International Writers' Conference held as part of the Edinburgh Festival in 1962, and of a protest march, proved to be the prologue to a long-running confrontation between Finlay and arts institutions, often involving the use of art as a 'mythological' mode of attack, a confrontation that culminated in 1984 in what Finlay described as 'the Little Spartan War'. In 1978 Finlay had withdrawn his Serpentine exhibition from a Scottish Arts Council space, declaring the absence of the artworks to be more meaningful than their presence. As a consequence the Arts Council broke off all communication with Finlay, which in turn resulted in Strathclyde region revoking relief on the local tax that had been granted to Finlay's gallery, since it was no longer in receipt of Arts Council funding. When the cowshed was declared to be a temple in 1980 Finlay argued that it was therefore entitled to the exemption from taxation allowed to religious buildings, a status that Strathclyde region refused to accept. A raid by a sheriff officer appointed by the courts to seize assets as a form of payment was repulsed (in a well-prepared publicity event, with television and newspaper reporters in attendance) in February 1983 by a group of Finlay's supporters whom he had dubbed the Saint-Just vigilantes, after a leading figure in the French Revolution. A month later a second raid resulted in the removal of a number of works, some of which did not actually belong to the Finlays, but only succeeded in raising public awareness of Finlay's art when the events were transformed into a touring exhibition of 'Heroic Ephemera from the Little Spartan War'.

The naming of this confrontation as the Little Spartan War was emblematic of Finlay's concern with the iconography of war (a bird table in the garden is in the shape of an aircraft carrier). The iconography of the French Revolution—particularly the guillotine and the decapitated head—also came to play a central role as Finlay explored the revolution's relation to classical models. The attention that Finlay's 'classicism' received in France, with several exhibitions taking place in 1987, led to his being commissioned by the French ministry of culture to design a garden commemorating the French Revolution for the bicentenary celebrations in 1989. In 1984, however, an exhibition entitled 'The Third Reich Revisited' had merged imagery from Nazi Germany with contemporary Edinburgh and, in particular, with the Arts Council office in Charlotte Square, the object of several assaults by the Saint-Just vigilantes. In Paris a campaign began against Finlay because of his use of what were perceived to be Nazi emblems (such as the double 'S' associated with the Nazi SS in one of his inscriptions), a campaign fuelled by the publication of extracts from Finlay's letters to one of his collaborators, Jonathan Hirschfeld, which were represented as being antisemitic. Finlay brought and won a case for libel against a Paris magazine and radio station, but he was awarded derisory damages of one franc, and by the time the case was concluded the commission for the bicentenary garden had already been cancelled by the French government. The stress of this episode fell substantially on Sue Finlay who, because Finlay suffered from a form of agoraphobia and rarely left his garden, undertook most of the organization of exhibitions. After it the couple separated.

By the 1990s Finlay's work was appearing in major exhibitions in North and South America and across Europe, but it was only in 1991 that he received his first commission for a garden in the UK, at Stockwood Park Nurseries, Luton. The garden at Stonypath was, however, increasingly acknowledged as one of the major artistic achievements of the second half of the twentieth century, and Finlay was awarded honorary degrees by the University of Aberdeen (1987), Heriot-Watt University (1993), and the University of Glasgow (2001), and was made an honorary professor at Dundee from 1999. He was appointed CBE in 2002 and was presented with the Scottish horticultural medal by the Royal Caledonian Horticultural Society the same year. In 2003 he was awarded a £30,000 creative Scotland award by the Scottish Arts Council. On his seventieth birthday a trust was established to safeguard the future of the garden, which was declared in December 2004, by a poll of Scottish artists and gallery directors, to be the most important single work of Scottish art. Finlay had suffered a stroke in 1999, a side-effect of which was his release from agoraphobia, so that in the following years he was able to attend some of the events at which he was honoured. He died at Strachan House Care Home, Craigcrook Road, Edinburgh, of renal cancer, on 27 March 2006, and was survived by his two children. CAIRNS CRAIG

Sources E. Morgan, 'The beatnik in the kailyard', *New Saltire Review*, 3 (1962) • *The letters of Hugh MacDiarmid*, ed. A. Bold (1984) • I. H. Finlay, 'Liberty, terror and virtue: the Little Spartan War and the Third Reich revisited', *New Arcadians Journal*, 15 (1984) • Y. Abrioux, *Ian Hamilton Finlay: a visual primer* (1985) • A. Finlay, ed.,

Wood notes wild: essays on the poetry and art of Ian Hamilton Finlay (1995) • A. Finlay, afterword, in I. H. Finlay, *The dancers inherit the party* (1996) • 'The death of piety: Ian Hamilton Finlay in conversation with Nagy Rashwan', *Jacket*, 15 (Dec 2001) [http://jacketmagazine.com/15/rash-iv-finlay.html, accessed April 2009] • J. Campbell, 'Avant gardener', *The Guardian* (31 May 2003) • *The Times* (28 March 2006); (3 April 2006) • *Daily Telegraph* (28 March 2006) • *The Guardian* (29 March 2006) • *The Independent* (29 March 2006) • *Scotland on Sunday* (2 April 2006) • *Art Monthly* (1 May 2006) • J. D. Hunt, *Nature over again: the garden art of Ian Hamilton Finlay* (2009) • *WW* (2006) • personal knowledge (2010) • private information (2010) • d. cert.

Archives Ian Hamilton Finlay Trust • Scottish National Gallery of Modern Art | Getty Research Institute for the History of Art and the Humanities, papers and corresp. • Indiana Universtiy, Lilly Library, papers, corresp., incl. letters to Derek Stanford • Kettle's Yard Museum and Art Gallery, Cambridge, letters to H. S. Ede • NL Scot., corresp. with Alastair Fowler, Duncan Glen, Robert Nye, Derek Stanford • Orkney Archive, letters to E. W. Marwick • Tate collection, papers, corresp., incl. letters to Stuart Mills | SOUND BL NSA, documentary recording

Likenesses A. Moffat, pastel, 1975, National Galleries of Scotland • K. Collie, cibachrome print, 1982, NPG • photographs, 1983, Scotsman Publications Ltd • J. Röhrscheid, photograph, 1994, repro. in www.littlesparta.co.uk/ihf.htm • R. Gillanders, composite photograph, 1995, National Galleries of Scotland • T. Traeger, silver gelatin print, 2001, NPG • photographs, 2001, Photoshot, London • N. McBeath, bromide fibre print, 2003, NPG • M. Macleod, photograph, repro. in *The Guardian* (26 March 2009) • obituary photographs

Finnis, Valerie Margaret Steriker [*married name* Valerie Margaret Steriker Montagu Douglas Scott, Lady Montagu Douglas Scott] (**1924–2006**), gardener and photographer, was born on 31 October 1924 at Wyke Cottage, Crowborough, Sussex, the younger daughter of Steriker Finnis, a paymaster commander in the Royal Navy, and his wife, Constance Mary Katharine, *née* Barford. At the age of five she moved with her family to Earlswood, near Reigate, where she created her first garden, with encouragement from her mother. She attended the Kerry School in Reigate. From the age of thirteen she boarded at Hayes Court, Kent; when it was closed at the beginning of the Second World War she moved to Downe House School, near Newbury. In 1942 she enrolled as a student at Waterperry Horticultural School for Women, a rigorous but happy establishment founded by the redoubtable Beatrix Havergal, which trained young women, including Land Army girls. When the course ended she stayed on as a gardener and teacher, eventually becoming head of the alpine department. She became extremely knowledgeable on alpines and, in time, an internationally noted expert on Kabschia and Engleria saxifrages. She was a particularly good cultivator of plants, with a prodigious memory for names.

In 1955 Valerie Finnis took up plant photography, partly as a means of making a little money to augment her modest salary. Her first images appeared in a learned article on crocus, but she soon started to sell them to Gordon Fraser for greetings cards and calendars, and to EMI for record covers. Later her pictures illustrated gardening magazines and books, such as the *Collins Guide to Alpines and Rock Garden Plants* (1972). She maintained that she only ever took one exposure of a subject, as film was so expensive. Her plant portraits, especially her carefully assembled bouquets of seasonal garden flowers, were immensely appealing and became very popular. In 1961 she won a gold medal from the Royal Horticultural Society and exhibited her photographs at Kodak's headquarters. Her powers of observation, honed by the culture of small alpine plants, naturally disposed her to expertise in this field. She strongly influenced many of the garden photographers who appeared on the scene in the 1970s and 1980s to satisfy demand when gardening magazines began to be printed in full colour. She also gave illustrated lectures all over Britain and, after she was invited as a guest lecturer on a Swan Hellenic cruise in 1961, abroad as well. She appeared as a guest presenter on Percy Thrower's *Gardening Club* programme on television. She constructed miniature rock gardens at Chelsea flower show and was a longstanding judge for the Royal Horticultural Society from 1962. She received the Victoria medal of honour of the Royal Horticultural Society in 1975.

One day in 1968, while in the potting-shed in the alpine department at Waterperry, Finnis heard a visitor point out the unusual American woodland herbaceous plant *Gillenia trifoliata* to his companion. She called out, 'You're the first person who's ever known that plant' (*The Guardian*, 30 Oct 2006). The person was Sir David John Montagu Douglas Scott (1887–1986), a widower and retired head of the consular service, as well as an avid gardener. They married on 31 July 1970 at the parish church in Weekley, Northamptonshire; she was forty-five, he eighty-three. He lived at the Dower House, a wing of Boughton House near Kettering, Northamptonshire, renting it from his cousin, the eighth duke of Buccleuch and tenth duke of Queensberry. He had told Finnis that he lived in a semi-detached house outside Kettering, which was true—in a way. He had already made a fine two-acre tree and shrub garden on a north-facing slope with his first wife, Dorothy (*née* Drummond), who died in 1965. The year after Valerie Finnis (who continued to use her maiden name) moved to Boughton, Waterperry closed as a horticultural college for women, so she imported many thousands of alpine plants; 150 yards of raised beds were built for these against the north- and south-facing walls of the kitchen garden. For a number of years the Montagu Douglas Scotts opened the garden to visitors very successfully under the charitable National Gardens Scheme twice a year. As popular as the garden was the sale of unusual plants, mainly propagated by David, who worked all day in the garden until well into his nineties, usually accompanied by a pug dog.

David Montagu Douglas Scott had, over many years, assembled an important collection of Victorian and twentieth-century paintings and drawings. His most famous acquisition was *No Walk Today*, by Sophie Anderson. Valerie Finnis fully shared his love of art, having herself a very good eye; she later curated the pictures. She and her husband were excellent company and entertained a wide variety of friends at the Dower House, until David became ill about three years before he died. Everyone who came to visit—from the Aga repair man to Princess Alice, duchess of Gloucester—was photographed and asked to write something about him- or herself in a succession of Smythson leather-bound scrapbooks, which chronicled the Montagu Douglas Scotts' life together, and which she later willed to the British Library. Valerie Finnis was full of fun, gossip, and practical jokes, and could be mischievous. She had a wide circle of friends and got on especially well with children. Although she had an attractive and lively personality, which drew people to her, she could also sometimes be a trouble-maker, which made them wary; she was said to enjoy a good row.

In 1990 Valerie Finnis founded a charity, the Merlin Trust, to fund travel scholarships for young gardeners. It was named in memory of her husband David's only child, Merlin, who had been killed while serving as a second-lieutenant in the rifle brigade in the Middle East during the Second World War. In her seventies arthritis forced her to give up gardening, although she lived on at the Dower House. She remained a judge for the Royal Horticultural Society until 2002. On retirement from judging she selected pictures of plants and gardeners that she had known, from her collection of 50,000 transparencies; these were included with her reminiscences in a book published in 2007, *Garden People: Valerie Finnis and the Golden Age of Gardening*. She died in Kettering General Hospital on 17 October 2006, of an upper gastro-intestinal bleed. Her brain was willed to scientific research, and her remains cremated at Kettering crematorium on 1 November. She directed that all her assets, including the picture collection, be sold for charitable purposes. The Finnis Scott Foundation was set up in 2007, with the purpose of giving grants to horticultural and art-related projects, reflecting the abiding interests of Valerie Finnis and her husband.

URSULA BUCHAN

Sources U. Buchan, A. Pavord, and B. Elliott, *Garden people: Valerie Finnis and the golden age of gardening* (2007) • *The Times* (23 Aug 2006); (4 Nov 2006) • *The Independent* (21 Oct 2006) • *Daily Telegraph* (28 Oct 2006) • *The Guardian* (30 Oct 2006) • Burke, *Peerage* • personal knowledge (2010) • private information (2010) • b. cert. • m. cert. • d. cert.

Archives SOUND BL NSA, documentary recording

Likenesses N. Parkinson, C-type colour print, 1976 (with Sir David Montagu Douglas Scott), NPG • J. Baldwin, cibachrome print, 1993, NPG • T. Traeger, silver gelatin print, 2000, NPG • H. Sooley, 2006, repro. in Buchan, *Garden people* • M. Warren, photograph, Photoshot, London • obituary photographs

Wealth at death £7,865,489: probate, 27 March 2007, *CGPLA Eng. & Wales*

Fisher, Sir Henry Arthur Pears [Harry] (**1918–2005**), barrister, judge, and college head, was born at The Hall, Repton, Derbyshire, on 20 January 1918, the eldest of six sons of the Revd Geoffrey Francis *Fisher (1887–1972), then headmaster of Repton School, and his wife, Rosamond Chevallier, *née* Forman, daughter of the Revd Arthur Forman, a former master at Repton. Geoffrey Fisher later became bishop of Chester, bishop of London, and finally, in 1945, archbishop of Canterbury; he was made a life peer, as Baron Fisher of Lambeth, on retirement in 1961. On both sides of the family Fisher was descended from long lines of clerics and schoolmasters. His paternal great-great-grandfather, great-grandfather, and grandfather were all rectors of Higham on the Hill, Leicestershire, in continuous succession from 1792 to 1910. His great-grandfather on his mother's side was Steuart Adolphus Pears, the dynamic headmaster of Repton from 1854 to 1874, who created the modern school, and his great-great-grandfather was the Revd James Pears, headmaster of Bath grammar school. It might have been expected that with such an ancestry Harry Fisher would himself have gone into the church or become a schoolmaster. In the event, in his public life at least, he manifested a total lack of religious belief. Nor did he feel any call to be a schoolmaster. The fact that three of his brothers did become headmasters of public schools sufficiently perpetuated the family tradition.

War service and the bar Fisher was educated at Marlborough College (where his father had also been a pupil and, for a short period, a master) then Christ Church, Oxford, where he won the Gaisford Greek prose prize in 1937 and obtained a first in classical moderations in 1938. The advent of the Second World War compelled him after one and a half years to take a war-shortened (unclassified) degree. In 1940 he joined the Leicestershire regiment. While an officer cadet he displayed his characteristic independence of mind by refusing to attend church parade on the ground that he was an agnostic. He was posted to India and served also in Burma and Malaya. He went to the Staff College in Quetta in 1943, became a GSO2 in that year and GSO1 at the headquarters of the Fourteenth Army in 1945. He was mentioned in dispatches 'in recognition of gallant and distinguished services in Burma' (*London Gazette*, 9 May 1946).

Demobilized in 1946 with the rank of lieutenant-colonel, Fisher decided to read for the bar and was called by the Inner Temple in 1947. The previous year he had entered the prize fellowship examination at All Souls College. He applied as a candidate in law, notwithstanding the fact that he had not read for a law degree. (A college tradition holds that he received from an Oxford law don a reading list and expert advice as to the type of questions that might be put by the law examiners.) His successful election in November 1946 began a long connection with the college, in various different categories of fellowship. Between 1961 and 1966 he held the office of estates bursar, an appointment that coincided with most of the period when he was heavily engaged as a silk, appearing regularly in court, and giving advice in weighty matters. On 18 December 1948, at the Church of Our Most Holy Redeemer, Chelsea, he had married Felicity Sutton, a 26-year-old artist, and daughter of Eric Sutton, author. They had one son and three daughters. The marriage was extremely happy and Felicity gave Harry continuous support in all his activities.

Fisher was a junior counsel from 1946 to 1960. Much of the work was of a standard commercial type, though some specialist cases came his way. Thus when the coal industry was nationalized he became involved in claims for compensation for expropriation. Another unusual area in which he was briefed concerned the liability of the

Air Ministry as the owner of rectorial property to pay a share of the costs of repairing the chancel of the local parish church (*Chivers & Sons Ltd* v. *Air Ministry*, 1955). Fisher, who was briefed by the Treasury solicitor, always claimed that he was instructed in this abstruse matter because he was the son of the archbishop of Canterbury and could be assumed to be a master of ecclesiastical law. Sadly this was not true and Fisher had to carry out much antiquarian research in his attempt (ultimately unsuccessful) to protect the Air Ministry from the claim.

In 1960 Fisher took silk. His first major brief arrived out of the blue in January 1961. He had about ten days in which to prepare for a case in the restrictive practices court on behalf of the cement manufacturers. He was ready to open the case on time and after a three-week hearing won the case. It brought Fisher's name to the attention of solicitors, and he became much in demand. However, he did not confine himself to his own work but deployed his energy and skills on behalf of the profession. After service on the Bar Council he was chairman of the bar from 1966 to 1968. He was also recorder of Canterbury from 1962. He was asked to act as counsel in one case where two senior silks had in succession returned the brief on accepting appointment to the bench (first Fred Lawton, next Stanley Rees). When Fisher met the client he observed: 'You have been unfortunate in your choice of counsel', to which came the reply, 'We don't have to worry with you. Your clerk says you will never be a judge' (private information). Though true for the particular case this prophecy was not fulfilled.

High Court, and resignation At the beginning of 1968 Fisher accepted appointment as a High Court judge, in the Queen's Bench Division. He did not take the oath on appointment. Instead he affirmed. His tenure of office was short and there was hardly time for him to make his mark on the law. He was in any event unsympathetic to innovative decision-making by judges. Law reform he thought was a matter for the Law Commission and parliament. However, in July 1968 he was the junior member in a Court of Appeal decision that quashed the conviction for obscenity entered against the publishers of *Last Exit to Brooklyn*. This case sounded the death knell for prosecutions on the ground of obscenity of books with literary merit (real or plausibly claimed).

As a judge Fisher spent much of his time out of London on circuit. During the day he would try criminal cases and in the evening he was expected to entertain official guests in the company of his fellow judges. This lifestyle proved to be totally unsatisfying for him. In particular he sorely missed the intellectual challenge of arguing complex cases as counsel. He concluded that he had made a mistake and resigned from his judicial appointment at the end of July 1970. There is reason to believe that his first preference would have been to return to practice at the bar but there was a convention at the time that prevented this, so instead he took up a directorship of J. Henry Schroder Wagg, the merchant bankers, at the invitation of his friend Gordon Richardson (later governor of the Bank of England). Ignoring the traditional advice, 'Never explain, never apologize', he wrote a letter to many of his friends to explain his decision:

> I am not resigning on the ground of ill health. I am not resigning in protest about anything. I have not been asked to resign. Nothing disreputable has occurred. I am resigning because I find judicial work uncongenial, and I do not enjoy the life which Judges are expected to lead … I find a Judge's life a dull life, and I have found myself becoming dull as a result. The art of advocacy is a fascinating one to practise, but to sit and listen day after day to other people's advocacy I find a wearisome ordeal.

He had given much consideration to the question: 'Ought I in the public interest to disregard my own personal feelings and stay on the bench?', and had concluded that 'there is no sufficient reason' (letter of 1 August 1970).

Within the legal profession Fisher's resignation caused emotions ranging from shock and surprise to indignation and hostility. A critical article in the *Solicitors Law Journal* deplored the precedent Fisher's move created and concluded that 'It should not be too much for the country to ask that, in return for the invaluable constitutional guarantee of security in their appointments, High Court judges should themselves refrain from resigning to take other jobs unless circumstances are exceptional' ('Current topics', *Solicitors Law Journal*, 114/32, 7 Aug 1970, 593). By contrast the *New Law Journal* reacted with calm and restraint, observing that 'A judge is entitled like anyone else, to make his life where he honestly believes he can best be himself' ('On retiring from the High Court bench', *New Law Journal*, 120, 13 Aug 1970, 746–7). The controversy took some time to die down, however. As late as 19 November 1970 Viscount Dilhorne, a former lord chancellor, took the opportunity of a debate on the Courts Bill to criticize as 'inexcusable' the action of any judge who resigned in order to take up a career in business: 'having embarked on a judicial career, one is under a moral obligation to do the job and not to give it up in favour of one that appears more attractive' (*Hansard 5L*, 312.1288, 19 Nov 1970).

Fisher remained with Schroders for five years, also serving on the board of Schroder International and other companies, including Thomas Tilling and Equity and Law Life Assurance. Later in his career he returned to the City as chairman of the appeal committee of the Takeover Panel (1981–7). He was also involved in self-regulation in the City in his capacity as founder chairman of the Investment Management Regulatory Organisation.

Public inquiries Notwithstanding the disfavour with which Fisher continued to be regarded by much of the legal establishment after he left the bench, the government was quick to appreciate that there was now available an individual of exceptional skills who could be called upon to undertake the role of chairman in difficult inquiries. The first such appointment came the year after Fisher ceased to be a judge. In March 1971 he was asked by the ministers for social services and for employment and productivity to head a committee to investigate and report on abuse of social security benefits. By October 1972 the committee had produced a painstaking report that included eighty-eight recommendations aimed at minimizing the number of benefit frauds. Although, as with any committee report, it is difficult to spot the fingerprints of any particular member, a couple of the recommendations may be noted as exemplifying Fisher's approach in public affairs. The committee recommended that the departments should not be inhibited in their efforts to detect those working while drawing benefits 'by fear of criticism for excessive zeal', but that the departments 'should not take any positive steps to encourage the general public to inform' (*The Independent*, 14 April 2005). The first recommendation advocated right conduct by public officials notwithstanding the risk of criticism; the second abhorred the creation of a Stasi-like informer society.

In the Confait inquiry (1975–7) Fisher was asked by the crown to examine a gravely flawed prosecution that had resulted in the conviction of three young men, all for arson, one for murder, and another for manslaughter. On a reference by the home secretary the Court of Appeal, presided over by Lord Scarman, had quashed all the convictions. In the ensuing investigation Fisher heard evidence from numerous witnesses and scrutinized a mass of documents. He concluded that there had been blatant disregard by the police of the 'judges' rules' (designed to secure fair procedures for the interrogation of suspects). His cogent report recommended radical changes in the system. This led directly to the appointment of a royal commission under Sir Cyril Philips and thence to the enactment of the Police and Criminal Evidence Act 1984 and the Prosecution of Offences Act 1985. The following year the Crown Prosecution Service was established. Fisher's report laid the groundwork for all these reforms. However, it did not satisfy all who read it. Sir Louis Blom-Cooper QC, who had represented the three young men at the Fisher inquiry, commented after his death that Fisher should have held on the facts that there had been no sustainable case against any of the accused.

In 1979 Fisher was asked by Lloyd's of London to conduct an inquiry into self-regulation at the institution. The following year he produced a seminal report recommending the adoption of a new constitution he had drafted. One aspect of this was the creation of a new governing council. Effective disciplinary machinery was also put in place. A novel feature was a clause protecting council members from claims of negligence; liability was made to depend on bad faith. However, the recommendation to which the greatest financial consequences attached was one to the effect that all Lloyd's brokers should over a five-year period divest themselves of their underwriting interests, on the ground that there was an inherent conflict of interest between the two roles. When Lloyd's presented a private bill to parliament to implement what Fisher had proposed this particular recommendation was omitted. But the House of Commons insisted on its inclusion and the necessary amendments were made before the bill was enacted.

Wolfson, Imperial, and retirement In 1975 a new opportunity for service had presented itself. On the retirement of Sir Isaiah Berlin, the first president of Wolfson College, Oxford (a college for graduate students, many of them from overseas and many married), Fisher was elected as his successor. This proved to be a brilliant appointment. The Fishers got to know all the students by name and what each was studying. It was a point of pride with Fisher to acquire sufficient knowledge of such subjects as mathematics and physics that he was able to discuss the research projects being undertaken by all members of the college. An exceptional degree of pastoral care was displayed by the Fishers to these students and their families. No visitor to the college could fail to be struck by the warmth of these relationships.

Fisher also had a lifelong interest in scientific developments. It was very appropriate that Lord Sherfield should in 1973 have introduced him to Imperial College as a member of the governing body. From 1975 to 1988 he was its much-respected chairman. Another role he undertook was the presidency of the Howard League for Penal Reform (in succession to Lord Gardiner) from 1983 to 1991. He was a successful fund-raiser on behalf of the league and a gracious host at its annual September conference in Oxford.

Fisher was one of the most brilliant lawyers to appear in the generation after the Second World War. His time on the bench was short, but his career also straddled the City, public service, and the world of academe in a manner for which it would be hard to find a parallel. Such leisure as his restless spirit allowed him was spent with his wife, Felicity, and children and friends, or at the keyboard. His passion was J. S. Bach, whose works he performed with great ability and affection. The music of the romantic composers generally received a cool reception.

For the last few years of his life Fisher lived quietly in retirement at Marlborough, Wiltshire, where he had been a member of the governing council of the school for many years. He walked on the downs, read, listened to and played music, and with his wife travelled abroad. She supported him with the help of the children during his last painful illness. He died at his home in Marlborough on 10 April 2005, following a stroke, and was survived by his wife and children. PATRICK NEILL

Sources *The Times* (4 Aug 1970); (6 Aug 1970); (27 June 1980); (18 April 2005); (27 April 2005); (5 May 2005) · *The Independent* (14 April 2005); (7 May 2005); (24 June 2005) · *Daily Telegraph* (15 April 2005) · *The Guardian* (19 April 2005); (21 April 2005) · *Derby Evening Telegraph* (5 May 2005) · Burke, *Peerage* · *WW* (2005) · personal knowledge (2009) · private information (2009) · b. cert. · m. cert. · d. cert.

Likenesses F. Sutton, portrait, 1949, repro. in *The Times* (18 April 2005); priv. coll. · G. Argent, bromide print, 1969, NPG · R. Moynihan, oils, exh. RA 1985 · obituary photographs

Wealth at death £284,751: probate, 3 Aug 2005, *CGPLA Eng. & Wales*

Fitt, Gerard Martin [Gerry], **Baron Fitt (1926–2005)**, politician, was born in the Union Workhouse, 51 Lisburn Road, Belfast, on 9 April 1926, the son of Rose Martin, a thirty-year-old unmarried servant, and an unidentified father. Only the birth of an unnamed male infant was civilly registered by the master of the workhouse but the day after his birth he was baptized a Catholic there and given the name Gerald (later he preferred Gerard) by his natural mother before being handed over for adoption by George

Gerard Martin Fitt, Baron Fitt (1926–2005), by Powell, 1968

Patrick Fitt (1899–1935) and his wife, Mary Ann, *née* Murphy (1901–1989), who brought him up as a member of their own family. At that time they already had a daughter and a son. Later another son and two daughters were born. He had no more contact with his natural mother.

Childhood, merchant navy, and marriage The Fitt family lived in grinding poverty in a spartan end-of-terrace house at 1 Welbeck Street, in the New Lodge area of Belfast. After his adoptive father, a council labourer, lost a leg in a work accident and died in 1935, Gerry Fitt toiled before and after school earning money by delivering groceries and selling newspapers to help the family make ends meet. Although his teachers at St Patrick's Christian Brothers School identified his ability, especially the fact that he was highly articulate for his age, an uninterested Fitt persuaded his adoptive mother to let him leave school at the earliest opportunity, which he did, in 1940. He intended to follow his elder brother, George, to sea when he was old enough and in the meantime drifted through a number of menial jobs, ending up as a soap-boy in a barber-shop in Donegall Street, Belfast.

One morning, in March 1942, while Gerry Fitt was lathering a customer for shaving, George arrived to say he had found him a job as a fireman on a coaster carrying coal from Salford to Belfast. Fitt promptly abandoned the customer in the chair and headed for the docks, but after a couple of return voyages the captain discovered that his crewman was under age and sacked him. Fitt then overstated his age by a year and volunteered for the merchant navy and, over the remaining wartime years, as a fireman shovelling coal deep in the ships' boiler rooms, he made a number of hazardous transatlantic crossings and trips to Russia in convoys under constant threat of attack. One return from Murmansk was especially perilous, when his ship suffered engine trouble and was forced to limp home without escort. Fitt saw many friends perish in vessels torpedoed by U-boats or sunk from the air, and he lost his adopted brother, George, who had gone on to join the Irish Guards and was killed in northern France in July 1944, shortly after the D-day landings.

Fitt's first-hand experience of war and the austere years immediately afterwards, when he travelled by sea to every continent and saw at first hand the ravages of conflict and the destruction and poverty left in its wake, were defining influences. During the long voyages he read avidly, once fighting for access to the officers' library on board ship because he wanted to read Hemingway rather than the cowboy novels favoured by his crewmates. He also developed a deep interest in Irish history and adopted as his lifelong inspiration James Connolly, the Scottish-born trade unionist who was executed by the British administration for his part in the 1916 Easter rising in Dublin.

On 5 November 1947, at the Roman Catholic Church of the Immaculate Conception in Crossgar, Fitt married Susan Gertrude (Ann) Doherty (1922–1996), daughter of William Doherty, a tailor from Castlederg, co. Tyrone. They had six daughters, affectionately known as the Miss Fitts. With his growing family to support, Fitt gave up the sea in 1953 and settled permanently in Belfast, where between voyages he had already been tentatively drawn into local politics.

Belfast corporation, Stormont, and Westminster In 1958 Fitt was elected to Belfast corporation as a councillor for Dock ward and four years later won the Dock seat in the Northern Ireland parliament at Stormont, which he retained until Stormont was prorogued in 1972. His energetic representational activities on behalf of Unionist as well as nationalist electors undoubtedly helped in creating for him a unique cross-community political power-base transcending the traditional sectarian and political divides. Although he was publicly committed to the eventual and peaceful reunification of Ireland, the cornerstone of Fitt's political philosophy, which he described as 'Republican Labour', was to champion working-class rights, and he enhanced his reputation by successfully fighting cases against bureaucrats and in tribunals for his constituents regardless of their political or religious allegiance. Such was his reputation as an advocate that once, after he had collapsed at Stormont, an ambulance-man conveying him to hospital lobbied him about a problem and thrust a note with his address into Fitt's breast-pocket for attention when he recovered.

Fitt's political success was also very much attributable to his mastery of the black arts of Irish electioneering. Outplaying his Unionist rivals at their own game, he built up a small but formidable team of 'markers', who monitored newspaper death notices, house moves in every street, and apathetic sympathizers, to identify voters on the electoral roll who could be impersonated by 'pluggers' on election days. These were men and women, kitted out from jumble sales, who changed their clothing and travelled from polling station to polling station stealing often crucial votes in close-run contests. Fitt was privately embarrassed by such activities but felt compelled to participate to deny any advantage to his opponents.

Fitt's real political breakthrough came in 1966 when he was returned to Westminster as MP for West Belfast.

Becoming an MP provided him with personal financial security for the first time. Beforehand he mainly existed on state benefits or the proceeds of casual work and had to rely on donations from sympathizers and even borrow from family members and moneylenders to raise the cash deposits necessary to stand for election.

Fitt's victory sundered the long-standing Unionist grip on the turbulent West Belfast constituency, where sectarian differences counted far more than conventional political issues despite appallingly poor housing and serious social deprivation. Fitt's political priority therefore was not to campaign for a united Ireland, but instead to persuade the British government of the need to overrule the unchanging Unionist administration at Stormont and introduce a wide-ranging reform programme to improve social and economic conditions for all in Northern Ireland, and to bring to an end general discrimination against Catholics, notably in housing and public service employment. An equally fundamental demand was for an end to the rigging of electoral boundaries to maintain Unionist political control and for a universal franchise, later encapsulated in the slogan 'one man, one vote'. In a widely acclaimed maiden speech at Westminster on 25 April 1966 Fitt said: 'I am not asking for preferential treatment, or making an outlandish request on behalf of my constituency; I am asking for exactly what British constituents have' (*Hansard* 5C, 727.442, 25 April 1966).

Fitt quickly proved to be a skilled propagandist adept at using the newspapers, radio, and television to promote his causes and, as an epic drinker, he found it easy to forge influential alliances with other politicians in the bars at Westminster. This contributed to his most lasting achievement at this time, which was to lead sympathetic Labour MPs, with the firm but private encouragement of the prime minister, Harold Wilson, in breaking the long-standing convention that internal Northern Ireland affairs were never scrutinized by the London parliament. As a result, for the first time since the partitioning of Ireland in the early 1920s, Fitt succeeded in focusing national attention on the activities and shortcomings of the Unionist administration in Belfast. Back home, as his reputation as a formidable constituency worker grew, people seeking assistance queued in the rooms and even along the stairs of his Belfast house at 85 Antrim Road, often round the clock. In his frequent absences his wife and daughters patiently served endless cups of tea until he returned.

At this time Fitt was significantly inspired by the ongoing campaign for civil rights by the black community in the United States, and he soon emerged at the vanguard of similar groups dedicated to highlighting injustice and discrimination in Northern Ireland. He became an even more widely recognized political figurehead after he was batoned by officers of the Royal Ulster Constabulary while leading a banned civil rights march in Londonderry on 5 October 1968. His picture, with blood streaming from a head wound, symbolized the outbreak of what became known as 'the troubles'. As the growing violence propelled the problems of Northern Ireland to the forefront of the international news agenda Fitt was a much sought after proponent of the case for long overdue reform.

As civil disorder escalated and widespread terrorism engulfed Northern Ireland in the early 1970s Fitt was a central figure in the valiant but vain efforts to head off bloodshed and create a durable political solution. In 1970 he joined with other nationalists elected to Stormont on a civil rights ticket to form the Social Democratic and Labour Party (SDLP), becoming its founding leader, but it was always an uneasy coalition, not least because he was an instinctive political loner. At an earlier stage of his career, when he formed what proved to be a short-lived alliance with a like-minded contemporary, a supporter remarked that two one-man parties had become one two-man party.

In 1973 the SDLP entered into the Sunningdale agreement, with Fitt, as deputy chief minister, joining the moderate Unionist, Brian Faulkner, in forming an unprecedented power-sharing executive. He was the first Catholic politician to occupy such a senior office at Stormont. But in May 1974, after scarcely five months in power, hardline Ulster loyalists mounted a general strike in protest at plans for a council of all Ireland. Some of Fitt's colleagues, most notably the forceful John Hume, would not compromise on the timescale for achieving this and, with the newly elected British Labour government unwilling to confront the strikers, to Fitt's lasting dismay, the bold experiment in political co-operation promptly collapsed. At the height of the crisis Fitt refused to join Faulkner in resigning and later liked to boast that for the succeeding seventeen hours until he was sacked by the British government he was effectively prime minister of Northern Ireland.

The episode nourished the estrangement between Fitt and the SDLP and he eventually left the party in 1979, because of his distaste for its uncompromising Irish nationalism and the ambivalence on the part of many party members towards the violence of the Irish Republican Army (IRA), which he found repugnant. At a time when considerable courage was required to do so, Fitt unreservedly condemned all violence. He had much first-hand experience of it. The first rioter to be shot dead by the British army was killed close to the front door of his home, and the first soldier to be murdered by the IRA was also shot close by. In 1973 Paddy Wilson, then his closest political ally, was abducted and murdered by loyalist killers. One troubled night in 1976 Fitt was forced to spring from bed to defend his family at gunpoint when a mob of IRA sympathizers broke into his home. As a result bullet-proof windows, reinforced doors, and other security measures were built into his home, which thereafter was always known as Fortress Fitt.

Fitt never forgave the British Labour Party, which he had staunchly supported since 1966, for failing to confront the 1974 loyalist workers' strike and on 28 March 1979 this lingering resentment heavily contributed to his refusal to support James Callaghan's Labour government in a confidence motion, which it lost by a single vote, and which paved the way for the Conservatives, led by Margaret Thatcher, to come to power.

Towards the end of 1980 a group of Provisional IRA prisoners at the Maze prison, near Belfast, began a hunger strike to the death, escalating their campaign to be classified as prisoners of war. What they wanted was a recognition by the British government that their offences—murder, bombing, and shooting, the most serious in the criminal law—were politically, not criminally, motivated. With his acute understanding of Irish history Fitt recognized from the very outset the strong emotional impact a hunger strike would have on the Catholic community throughout Ireland. 'If I was a shrewd politician', he told his family, 'I would keep my head down and say nothing. If I was a dishonest politician, I would support the prisoners and lead the inevitable protest marches through my West Belfast constituency to ensure my permanent popularity' (Ryder, 353). But Fitt decided he could not live with his principles or his conscience by following either of these courses.

Fully conscious of the consequences, that it might provoke the IRA into trying to shoot him or could lead to his political defeat at the ballot box, Fitt decided to make a speech in the House of Commons in London on 10 November 1980 condemning the Provisional IRA and the hunger strike, and advising the British government to make no concessions whatever to the prisoners. 'I had walked behind the coffins of far too many victims of the Provisional IRA and other terrorists to do anything else', he later explained (Ryder, 353). The speech provoked immediate hostility, and one evening soon afterwards there was an eerie demonstration outside Fitt's Belfast home. With stones glancing off the brickwork and paint tins squelching against the fortifications around the front door, he listened to the steady thump of tramping feet, shouts, and the intermittent beating of a drum.

> I put the room lights out and slipped open the curtain. Outside in the darkness there was a large crowd, some holding flaming torches. In the flickering torchlight I could pick out some familiar faces, people who had been among my staunchest political supporters, until then. That demonstration was a decisive turning point in my life as a politician and marked the beginning of the end of my career in the House of Commons. (Ryder, 354)

Fitt continued to oppose the ongoing IRA hunger strikes at the Maze prison, and within a year he lost his seat on Belfast city council as Sinn Féin, the political front for the Provisional IRA, capitalized on the emotions raised by the deaths of ten hunger strikers and steadily emerged as a significant political force on the Catholic side. In June 1983, when a British general election was called, Fitt's uncompromising stand against the IRA, as he expected, cost him the West Belfast seat at Westminster. He was, though, especially embittered that the SDLP, now led by John Hume, helped to undermine his remaining support by running against him, and that so many of his erstwhile supporters voted to eject him from parliament in favour of Gerry Adams, the leader of Sinn Féin, whose methods and activities so revolted him that he had come to hate the word 'republican'.

Altogether over three stormy decades Fitt had fought nineteen elections and lost only three: his first Belfast council poll in 1956; and his final contests, for the Belfast council in 1981 and Westminster in 1983. At one time he held an unparalleled triple mandate, simultaneously serving as a Belfast councillor and member of both the Stormont and Westminster parliaments. He was a uniquely colourful, unorthodox political character once described as having the back-slapping style of a minor American senator. Public or parliamentary speeches were always delivered off-the-cuff, reflecting his shrewd political instincts and highly retentive memory. He rarely wrote letters, usually conducting his business on the telephone or, more often, holding court in public houses where he was an unrivalled raconteur. He once said that his filing cabinets were the inside pockets of his jackets and his desk the nearest window ledge in Belfast city hall, Stormont, or Westminster.

House of Lords, and final years Fitt's growing unpopularity had led to more sustained attacks on his house, and immediately after the election, while he and his wife were absent in London, Republican sympathizers succeeded in breaking in and setting it alight, this time causing destruction on such a scale that he had to move out permanently. Soon afterwards he bought a flat at 25 Vincent Square in London. Fitt then defied nationalist convention by accepting, in the same year, a life peerage. He really wanted to be known as Lord Fitt of Dock but because of the rules he was created Baron Fitt, of Bell's Hill, from the co. Down townland where his adopted mother had lived after being evacuated from Belfast during the Second World War.

In the House of Lords, as he had done throughout his political career, Fitt maintained a non-sectarian political stance and, from the crossbenches, earned widespread admiration for his courage in promoting reconciliation and speaking out trenchantly against the ongoing violence in Northern Ireland. As the 1990s 'peace process' developed Fitt was appalled that so many former terrorists were being elected to public office, and he especially resented the very public emergence of John White, who had murdered Paddy Wilson, as a prominent advocate of the Ulster loyalist cause. Fitt doubted that the ascendant hardliners on both sides had any appetite for the great compromises that would be necessary to create lasting peace and stability, and feared that the long-standing political intransigence would prevail 'until God sees Fitt' and beyond. Thus he remained cynical about the prospects for agreement in Northern Ireland until the end of his life.

In 2005 Fitt suffered declining health and when he developed serious heart trouble in July that year his daughters moved him to Ashford in Kent, where three of them lived. He died at 58 Lower Queens Road, Ashford, on 26 August 2005, of heart failure, and, after requiem masses at Westminster Cathedral and St Joseph's Church, Crossgar, on 31 August, was buried beside his wife in the churchyard of St Lawrence's at Godmersham, Kent. He was survived by five daughters, one daughter having predeceased him. CHRIS RYDER

Sources Sunday Times Insight Team, *Ulster* (1972) • G. Fitt, When God sees Fitt, MS autobiography, 1982 • *The Times* (27 Aug 2005) • *Daily Telegraph* (27 Aug 2005) • *The Guardian* (27 Aug 2005) • *The Independent* (27 Aug 2005) • C. Ryder, *Fighting Fitt* (2006) • M. Murphy, *Gerry Fitt: a political chameleon* (2007) • *WW* (2005) • Burke, *Peerage* • Belfast workhouse records, PRONI • parish records (baptism), St Brigid's, Belfast • *Belfast street directory* (1925–7) • merchant navy records, TNA: PRO • Northern Ireland Office papers, TNA: PRO • personal knowledge (2009) • private information (2009) • b. cert. • m. cert. • d. cert.

Archives FILM BFINA, 'My own native land', *The light of experience*, F. Dickey (director), BBC2, 16 Jan 1982 • BFINA, *Out on a limb*, J. Wilcox (producer), BBC1, 17 Oct 1982 • BFINA, *Questions*, D. Coulter (director), Channel 4, 19 Aug 1984 • BFINA, *Regrets?*, D. Heather (producer), ITV 13 Aug 1985 • BFINA, current affairs footage • BFINA, documentary footage | SOUND BL NSA, documentary recordings • BL NSA, parliamentary recordings • BL NSA, reorded talk

Likenesses Powell, photograph, 1968, Getty Images, London [*see illus.*] • photographs, 1968–73, Getty Images, London • R. Friers, drawing, *c.*1972, priv. coll. • photographs, 1973–83, PA Photos, London • R. Young, photograph, 1983, Rex Features, London • R. Friers, pen and ink drawing, NPG • obituary photographs • photograph, repro. in C. Ryder, *Fighting Fitt* (2006)

Wealth at death £658,321: probate, 30 Dec 2005, *CGPLA Eng. & Wales*

Fitter, Richard Sidney Richmond (1913–2005), naturalist, was born on 1 March 1913 at 14 Mount Nod Road, Streatham, London, the only son of Sidney Harry Fitter, produce broker, and his wife, Dorothy Isacke, *née* Pound. He was educated at Eastbourne College (1926–9), where his enthusiasm for natural history was encouraged by his headmaster, E. C. Arnold, and at the London School of Economics (1929–32), where he graduated in economics and became research assistant to Ivor Jennings. He was recruited in 1936 to the think-tank Political and Economic Planning (PEP) by its general secretary, Max Nicholson, whom he had met the year before through their common interest in ornithology. On 19 April 1938 he married Alice Mary (Maisie) Stewart Park, the 25-year-old daughter of Robert Stewart Park, medical doctor. They had two sons and a daughter. In 1940 Fitter moved from PEP to Mass-Observation (led by another ornithologist, Tom Harrisson), to investigate civilian morale for the Ministry of Information. He was then recruited to the operational research section of Coastal Command in 1942, as assistant editor of *Coastal Command Review*, in which post he spent the remainder of the Second World War. These posts developed his ability to write technical reports in the brief but lucid style that became the bedrock of his later career.

Fitter had become active in the London Natural History Society about 1934, assisting with surveys, sitting on committees, serving as 'recorder' for various sorts of animals, editing journals, and writing reports, with papers in *Nature* on the colonization of England by the black redstart and on the effects of the war on birds. Like many of his contemporaries he took the war as an opportunity to plan for a better world. He was a member of the Post War Aims Group, which within a month of the outbreak of war published a statement on war aims, and later he was invited to become secretary of the Wildlife Conservation Special Committee, chaired by Julian Huxley (another ornithological contact). Fitter's main role was to draw up lists of potential nature reserves, making many site visits in his spare time. The committee's report, *Conservation of Nature in England and Wales* (Cmd 7122, 1947), led to the establishment of national parks and the Nature Conservancy.

Fitter's first book, *London's Natural History* (1945), was a masterly synthesis in urban ecology, showing how the interaction of man and wildlife had developed over the centuries. It established him as a writer and was followed by *London's Birds* (1949) and several other contributions to urban natural history. In 1946 he left London for Burford, Oxfordshire, having been appointed assistant editor of *The Countryman*, a position he held for thirteen years while his own writing career blossomed. In 1952 he published the first modern 'field guide', the *Collins Pocket Guide to British Birds*, illustrated by R. A. Richardson. Designed to allow even the inexperienced to identify birds, it unusually (but helpfully) arranged the species by habitat and size. It was hugely successful and he produced about a dozen other field guides, including the *Pocket Guide to Nests and Eggs* (1955, also superbly illustrated by Richardson) and the *Collins Guide to Bird Watching* (1963). The *Pocket Guide to Wild Flowers* (1956, co-written with David McClintock) and *Birds of Britain and Europe with North Africa and the Middle East* (1972, with illustrations by Herman Heinzel and maps by John Parslow) were again innovative: the former abandoned the traditional dry keys and focused on the colour, form, and size of flowers to guide the inexperienced to an identification, while the new bird book had the pictures of each species opposite the relevant text rather than in separate blocks. With his wife, Maisie, he also wrote the *Penguin Dictionary of British Natural History* (1967).

Fitter became the most influential natural history author of the second half of the twentieth century in Britain, through his field guides, his approximately twenty other books, and his articles, especially his notes, 'Fitter's rural rides', in *The Observer* newspaper. The *Ark in Our Midst* (1959) was a masterly compilation of the attempts to introduce alien vertebrate species into Britain, and *Penitent Butchers* (1978) a useful history of the Fauna Preservation Society, later the Fauna and Flora Preservation Society.

Fitter was also a pioneer of the post-war nature conservation movement, largely in a voluntary capacity. He served as director of the intelligence unit of the Council for Nature (1959–63); on the species survival commission of the International Union for the Conservation of Nature (1963–88, chairman from 1975); and as honorary secretary (1964–71), and later chairman (1983–7) and vice-president (1988–2005) of the Fauna and Flora Preservation Society, at one point its British business being effectively run by him and his wife. He was much involved in the Berkshire, Buckinghamshire, and Oxfordshire Naturalists' Trust and served the World Wildlife Fund, the Royal Society for the Protection of Birds, the British Trust for Ornithology, and many other bodies in honorary positions. His contributions were based on his deep knowledge of the facts and issues, his capacity for organization, and the easy warmth of his modest personality. He was appointed an officer of the order of the Golden Ark, in the Netherlands (1978), and awarded the Christopher Cadbury medal of the Royal Society for Nature Conservation (1998) and the Peter Scott medal of the British Naturalists' Association (also 1998).

Fitter remained active until the end of his life. In 2000 his presidential address to the London Natural History Society was about the likely impacts of global warming on wildlife, and two years later he wrote, with his son Alastair (professor of biology at the University of York), a paper in the journal *Science* on changes in flowering time of British plants, based on forty-seven years' observation of 385 species around his home in Chinnor in the Chilterns. At the time of his death he was revising his book *Finding Wild Flowers*, first published in 1971, preparing a flora of France, and working on an unusual autobiography, based on the influences that the places he had visited had had on him. Having lived latterly in Great Shelford, Cambridge, he died at Addenbrooke's Hospital, Cambridge, on 3 September 2005, of complications of prostatic cancer. He was survived by his three children, his wife, Maisie, having predeceased him in 1996. JEREMY J. D. GREENWOOD

Sources *The Independent* (5 Sept 2005) · *Daily Telegraph* (6 Sept 2005) · *The Times* (10 Sept 2005) · *The Guardian* (28 Sept 2005) · R. Fitter, MS autobiography, priv. coll. · *WW* (2005) · personal knowledge (2009) · private information (2009) · b. cert. · m. cert. · d. cert.

Archives Bodl. Oxf. | CUL, Sir Peter Scott papers, corresp. · Linn. Soc., Council for Nature papers · London School of Economics and Political Science, PEP papers | SOUND BL NSA, recorded talk

Likenesses Elliott & Fry, vintage print, 1958, NPG · photograph, 1970, Hunt Institute for Botanical Documentation, Pittsburgh, Pennsylvania · obituary photographs

Wealth at death £381,234: probate, 20 March 2006, *CGPLA Eng. & Wales*

FitzHerbert, Luke Jos (1937–2007), charity campaigner and social activist, was born Luke Joseph FitzHerbert on 28 October 1937 at 15 Lower Hatch Street, Dublin, the younger son of Captain Henry Charles Hugh (Harry) FitzHerbert (*d.* 1945), army officer, and later stockbroker, and his wife, Sheelah, *née* Murphy. His father was protestant and his mother Catholic; he was brought up in the latter's faith. His brother, Giles (*b.* 1935), became a diplomat, his final posting being as British ambassador to Venezuela, and his younger sister, Caroline, a librarian. He was educated at Ampleforth College and won an exhibition to Christ Church, Oxford, to read modern history. Before going to university he joined the army as a commissioned officer in the Irish Guards (his father's regiment), guarding the vaults at the Bank of England and vigorously opposing the Suez invasion while in Egypt. At university he espoused left-wing and anti-religious causes while at the same time flourishing as part of the establishment. He became master of the Christ Church and New College beagles and a member of the exclusive Gridiron and Bullingdon clubs, replacing the buttons on his Bullingdon jacket with CND buttons.

After graduating in 1960 FitzHerbert joined Caps, a Soho printing firm spearheading the use of microfilm technology. In 1966 he set up the Caps New York office, spending a happy year travelling the length and breadth of America. When the office was taken over by an American company he taught history for a year in a Massachusetts high school. After returning to England in 1968 he became secretary to the National Economic Development Council's engineering committee, but he didn't find life as a civil servant congenial. After a further stint with Caps, in 1974 he resumed teaching. The pupils at Brentside high school in Hanwell, London, warmed to his stock of improbable facts, energy, wide experience, and teaching brilliance. It was at this time that he found his voice as a community activist, initiating the Brent River and Canal Society, which campaigned to open up 4½ miles of riverside to public access. He was non-confrontational, charming, yet essentially uncompromising. The popular Brent River Park, including a FitzHerbert Walk, was his first success.

In 1983 FitzHerbert changed career yet again. His friend Peter Jay recruited him to the National Council of Voluntary Organizations to develop payroll giving. Under this scheme, which had worked well in the USA, employers encouraged their employees to make monthly deductions from their pay as donations to charity. The hope was that this might be replicated in the UK, which it eventually was but without the same success. In 1984, when the Charities Aid Foundation took over the project, FitzHerbert approached Michael Norton, founder of Directory of Social Change, a new and fast-growing centre of information, training, and advice for charities, offering himself as a volunteer. Directory of Social Change had just published the first guide to giving by companies in the UK, and FitzHerbert proposed a companion guide to giving by foundations. At that time foundations tended to be secretive, and their accounts at the Charity Commission were often seriously out of date. Foundations are private institutions for public benefit, whose finances are enhanced substantially by tax reliefs at public expense. FitzHerbert believed that increased public accountability would lead to better grant making, putting the money where it was more needed and could be better used. He also wanted to campaign for better practice in how foundations were run: to report delays in submitting accounts to the Charity Commission; to widen trusteeship, so that foundation boards included people with a more diverse experience of needs and solutions; to encourage the diversification of assets where a major shareholding in a company had been vested in the foundation, so if the company hit hard times the foundation would not become seriously diminished (as had happened with the Nuffield Foundation); to highlight unnecessarily high expenditure on such things as entertainment and professional fees; and to put pressure on foundations to spend their income rather than accumulating it for the future.

When drafts for the first edition of the *Guide to the Major Trusts* were sent to foundations for comment, some replied with positive suggestions, many didn't and a few sent letters threatening legal action. These were ignored and this readable, anecdotal, and affordable book was published to critical acclaim in 1985. FitzHerbert followed this with the publication of other titles (on educational foundations and foundations for individuals in need, on smaller and regional foundations, and on specific themes such as youth, peace, and the arts). In 1994 the UK's national lottery was launched, which at its peak generated over £1.5 billion annually for good causes. FitzHerbert developed a similar approach to promoting greater accountability and more effective grant making by the lottery distribution boards. With the support of the Joseph Rowntree Foundation, he collected, analysed, and published information about all grants made, exposing policy anomalies and areas not receiving their fair share of funding, while also organizing training courses for applicants.

By 1986 FitzHerbert had become co-director of Directory of Social Change, but when Michael Norton left in 1995 to start a new venture he decided to concentrate on research and campaigning as senior researcher. In his latter years he became something of an elder statesman in the charity world, with special insight into such important issues as private schools, charitable support for the health service, and government contracting. His opinions were highly valued. He inspired a whole generation of charity staff and volunteers through his training, which reached more than 30,000 people, and through his book *Effective Fundraising* (2003). In the early 1990s he also ran fund-raising workshops in Russia, Hungary, the Czech Republic, Slovakia, and Romania. He was given a lifetime achievement award by *Third Sector* (2005) and an outstanding individual achievement award by *Charity Times* (2007).

FitzHerbert had two other passions. The first was his wife, Katrin (Kay) Norris, formerly Vickers, *née* Thiele (daughter of Eberhardt Thiele, mechanical engineer), an anthropologist, journalist, and author (whose work included the seminal *Jamaica: the Search for an Identity*, 1962), whom he married on 15 May 1964 when she was twenty-seven, and with whom he had one daughter, Kitty (*b.* 1966), and adopted a second daughter, Monica (*b.* 1968), in 1974. He supported Kay energetically in two projects. The first was to create the National Pyramid Trust, providing a framework for primary teachers to identify children at risk and develop effective preventive strategies. The second was Kay's family's history (her grandfather was a German émigré barber in Hampstead who after the First World War was deported to Germany, where her grandmother and mother had to cope with being English through the Second World War, while her father had become a Nazi functionary). Kay's memoir was published as *True to Both my Selves* (1997) and won the J. R. Ackerley prize in 1998. FitzHerbert's second passion was water. He was a keen and expert sailor, and sailed across the Atlantic and raced around Britain (three times). He and Kay owned a small canal boat, and spent weeks and weekends exploring Britain's waterways, and when he half-retired to Totnes they also kept a shrimper on the River Dart. On 7 January 2007 Luke and Kay FitzHerbert were both hit by a car when crossing the A5 near Weedon, Northamptonshire, after a day on their canal boat. Luke died instantly. Kay was seriously injured but survived. Luke was buried in Totnes cemetery on 22 February 2007.

MICHAEL NORTON

Sources *Regeneration and Renewal* (12 Jan 2007) • *Western Morning News* [Plymouth] (15 Jan 2007) • *The Guardian* (15 Jan 2007) • *Third Sector* (17 Jan 2007); (24 Jan 2007) • *The Independent* (21 Feb 2007) • *Herald Express* [Torquay] (22 Feb 2007); (23 Feb 2007) • personal knowledge (2011) • private information (2011) • b. cert. • m. cert. • d. cert.

Likenesses obituary photographs • photograph, repro. in www.allenlane.org.uk/lectures.html

Wealth at death £653,522: probate, 26 June 2007, *CGPLA Eng. & Wales*

Fletcher, Alan Gerard (1931–2006), graphic designer, was born on 27 September 1931 in Nairobi, Kenya, the only child of Bernard Wolfe Fletcher, an executive in the Kenyan government, and his wife, Dorothy, *née* Murphy. His father died in 1936, and he and his mother then returned to his maternal grandparents' house in Shepherd's Bush, west London. At the outset of the Second World War in 1939 he was evacuated to Christ's Hospital, Horsham, Sussex. Leaving school in 1949 he took a place at Hammersmith College of Art, assuring his anxious mother that it would equip him for a teaching career. He transferred to the Central School of Arts and Crafts a year later, where his classmates included his future colleagues Colin Forbes and Theo Crosby, and his ambitions expanded. He spent an interim year in Barcelona teaching English, before returning to London in 1953 to embark on postgraduate study at the Royal College of Art. During this time he worked on the student publication *Ark* and met artists and designers including Peter Blake, Joe Tilson, and the future spy novelist Len Deighton.

Finding early 1950s London gloomy, Fletcher longed for the bright lights of the United States of America, a nation he understood largely through Hollywood films. In 1956 he arranged an exchange for himself between the Royal College of Art and Yale University. After marrying his long-term Italian girlfriend Paola (*b.* 1927), daughter of Raffaele Biagi, bank manager, at Kensington register office on 5 July 1956, he applied for visas for them both to enter the USA on the white Kenyan quota. Once at Yale he was exposed to the teaching of seminal modern art and design talents including Josef Albers and Paul Rand. He visited New York where he also met prominent designers including Robert Brownjohn, Ivan Chermayeff, and Tom Geismar. These young practitioners were an important inspiration for Fletcher, particularly in encouraging him to establish an independent studio on his return to London.

Fletcher often made the modest claim that his career sprang from being at the right place at the right time. In 1957 he presented his portfolio to Lio Lionni, then the art director of the Time and Life publication *Fortune*. He was immediately offered the opportunity to design the magazine's cover, on the strength of which he won a job in the marketing department of Time and Life. Setting up home in the West Village, Fletcher would have settled in New

York, but for his wife's homesickness. After a tour across the USA, during which he worked briefly for the film titles designer Saul Bass, he and Paola returned to Europe via Venezuela. Their brief South American adventure was the product of a fantasy, Fletcher envisaging himself designing rugs to be woven by local artisans. The idea was cut short by the outbreak of a revolution on their arrival, which prompted the couple to take the last boat out of Caracas, heading to Genoa. Fletcher worked for a few months in Milan for the tyre manufacturer Pirelli before returning to London.

In 1959 Fletcher set up home in Notting Hill and rented a desk in Colin Forbes's studio. His daughter, Rafaella, was born in 1961. Continuing to work for Pirelli, Fletcher was also a regular designer of Penguin paperback covers, commissioned by the innovative art director Germano Facetti. His bold, ideas-driven graphic style and his ability to communicate directly with top management indicated a formidable new direction in design. In 1962 Fletcher and Forbes teamed up with the American émigré Bob Gill to form the firm Fletcher/Forbes/Gill. Later the same year they teamed up with others, including David Bailey and Terence Donovan, to found the Designers and Art Directors Association, of which Fletcher acted as president in 1973.

Between 1962 and 1972 Fletcher/Forbes/Gill evolved into the multidisciplinary design studio Pentagram. During that period Gill resigned and Fletcher and Forbes were joined by the architect Theo Crosby, the product designer Kenneth Grange, and the art director Mervyn Kurlansky. Occupying a large former warehouse in Paddington basin, Pentagram acquired many large-scale corporate clients, including the news agency Reuters and the cruise line Cunard. Fletcher remained at Pentagram for two decades, successfully reconciling his taste for graphic play with his facility for consummate professionalism. In 1993 he left to establish a studio in his mews home in Pembridge Crescent.

Working independently, Fletcher combined an emphasis on long-standing personal projects with the position of art director, both at Phaidon Press and at the Novartis Campus, a pharmaceutical research facility in Basel. He retained these appointments until the end of his life. He received many honours during his career, including appointment as a royal designer for industry in 1972, presidency of the Alliance Graphique Internationale in 1982, and fellowship of the Royal College of Art in 1989. He was inducted into the New York-based Art Directors Club hall of fame in 1994. His numerous books included the monograph *Beware Wet Paint* (1996) and the 1066 page masterwork *The Art of Looking Sideways* (2001). After a short illness he died of lung cancer on 21 September 2006 at his daughter's house, Merrilies, Woodcote Road, Forest Row, Sussex. Both she and Paola survived him. He was described in his obituaries as 'a man uniquely responsible for defining British graphic design … from the late 1950s onwards' (*The Guardian*, 25 Sept 2006), 'the father figure of British graphic design' (*The Independent*, 26 Sept 2006), and 'the most highly regarded graphic designer of his generation' (*Daily Telegraph*, 29 Sept 2006). A later tribute described him as 'Britain's best ever graphic designer' (*The Observer*, 12 Nov 2006). EMILY KING

Sources A. Fletcher, *Beware wet paint* (1996) · *The Guardian* (25 Sept 2006); (11 Nov 2006) · *The Times* (26 Sept 2006); (8 Nov 2006) · *The Independent* (26 Sept 2006); (7 Nov 2006) · *Daily Telegraph* (29 Sept 2006) · *The Observer* (12 Nov 2006) · *WW* (2006) · interview with Linda Sandino, BL NSA, C464/34 · personal knowledge (2010) · private information (2010) · m. cert. · d. cert.

Archives SOUND BL NSA, interview, C464/34

Likenesses Snowdon, photographs, 1995, Camera Press, London · photograph, 1998, Photoshot, London · T. R. Hart, C-type colour print, 2005, NPG · obituary photographs

Wealth at death £2,027,833: probate, 13 Jan 2009, *CGPLA Eng. & Wales*

Fletcher, Cyril Trevellian (1913–2005), comedian and impresario, was born on 25 June 1913 at Dunoon, Hagden Lane, Watford, Hertfordshire, the only son and younger child of George Trevellian Fletcher, deputy town clerk of Watford, and his wife, Maude Mary, *née* Ginger. Both parents were keen on amateur dramatics. He attended a preparatory school in Trowbridge, Wiltshire, where his father had become town clerk, then Woodhouse School in Finchley, where he persuaded the headmaster to allow him to produce a concert in aid of library funds and cast himself as leading performer: 'How did I know, I wonder, that I could do this, never having even been in an amateur concert of any kind?' Nevertheless, after its success, 'the school magazine proclaimed the advent of a new comedian' (*Nice One Cyril*, 41–2).

Having disappointed his father by failing his French matriculation three times, Fletcher could not bring himself to announce the fact that his real ambition was to make the stage his profession. He decided to work in London, first for a timber firm, then for the Scottish Union and National Insurance Company, where he produced an unofficial office magazine in which he published the first 'Odd Odes' that were later to bring him lasting fame. Just as significantly he enrolled at the Guildhall School of Music as an evening drama student. One of his tutors was Kate Rourke, who had been Henry Irving's leading lady. To help pay for his lessons he performed as a comedian at club socials and dinners. Through this he first made contact with the Concert Artistes Association, which enabled him to obtain more contacts for after-dinner engagements. He became a member and was proud of being elected president several times in the 1950s and 1960s; he later became one of their patrons.

After appearing at a Sunday night concert at the Prince of Wales Theatre in 1936, when his droll act had received an enthusiastic response, Fletcher was approached by Greatrex Newman, whose seaside show the Fol-de-Rols was one of the most popular of the day. Newman offered him a season at the White Rock Pavilion, Hastings, for £7 a week. The same week his manager at Scottish Union and National asked if he would like to be their junior representative in Rangoon:

> 'Thank you for your confidence in me', I said, 'but I was coming to see you at the end of the week to resign'. 'Oh,' he

> said, rather deprecatingly, 'and what sort of job had you in mind?' … 'I am going to be a comedian', I said. To say he was considerably disconcerted by my answer is a grave understatement. (*Nice One Cyril*, 54–5)

Fletcher enjoyed two successful seasons at Hastings with the Fol-de-Rols and was one of the first comedians to appear on the newly opened BBC television service from Alexandra Palace. He also started to become a popular voice on radio via broadcasts for Radio Luxembourg and the BBC.

In 1938 Fletcher was booked at Llandudno and, short of material for a broadcast from the show, decided to recite Edgar Wallace's *Dreaming of Thee: a Lovesick Tommy's Dream of Home*, a sub-Kipling piece delivered in a nasal cockney accent. Within days Fletcher realized what an impact he'd made when he heard a bus conductor distributing tickets and impersonating his comic voice: 'I became a household name like Guinness or Harpic' (*Nice One Cyril*, 64). Fletcher started recording his 'Odd Odes' in 1938 for Columbia and Decca which, together with such radio series as *Thanking Yew* (named after his catchphrase), consolidated his popularity.

In 1940, when booked for a programme to be broadcast from Bristol, where the BBC's variety department had been relocated during the London blitz, Fletcher met the actress, singer, and scriptwriter **Betty Astell** (1912–2005). Born Betty Julia Hymans at 54 Cranhurst Road, Willesden, London, on 23 May 1912, she was the daughter of Herbert Hymans, drug merchant, and his wife, Estella, *née* Oppenheimer. Trained as a dancer, she first sang on BBC radio at the age of twelve, and four years later made her West End stage début in John Galsworthy's *Escape* at the Ambassadors Theatre. She took part in John Logie Baird's early '30-line' television experiments from his studio in Long Acre from 1931, and in the BBC's first 30-line transmission in 1932. After the BBC launched its regular television service from Alexandra Palace in 1936 she appeared frequently until the closure of the service during the Second World War. She also appeared in some two dozen films before the war, including *A Tight Corner* (1932) with Frank Pettingell, *This Is the Life* (1933) with Gordon Harker and Binnie Hale, *Jack of All Trades* (1936) with Jack Hulbert, and *The Mind of Mr Reeder* (1939) with Will Fyffe. At the time she met Cyril Fletcher she was undoubtedly better known than he was. They first appeared together in a Home Guard concert and married within a year at St Martin-in-the-Fields, London, on 18 May 1941. They would often work together on radio in such comedy series as *Fletcher's Fare* (1952) and *Mixed Doubles* (1957), both written by Bob Monkhouse and Denis Goodwin. They had one daughter, Jill Fletcher, also an actress and comedian.

In parallel with his broadcasting work Fletcher was in demand for variety, and appeared on the bill with several music hall veterans, including Harry Tate, George Robey, Nellie Wallace, Billy Bennett, and Harry Champion. He was flattered when Max Miller took an interest in his act and advised him how to improve it: 'For the placing of a gag and for the timing of a joke he had and has no equal' (*Nice One Cyril*, 80). After taking part in some Pathé Pictorials, Fletcher's first major film appearance was in the wartime thriller *The Yellow Canary* (1943), with Anna Neagle. He most notably played a flamboyant Alfred Mantalini in Alberto Cavalcanti's Ealing production of *Nicholas Nickleby* (1947). He appeared in the wartime show *Keep Going*, the first of many with words and music by Betty Astell in which they were to appear together. For twenty-five years he played fruity-voiced and, at over six feet, strikingly tall pantomime dames in stylish productions written and directed by his wife (who frequently co-starred in them). These often incorporated a harlequinade reflecting the early pantomime tradition. For a memorable production of *Mother Goose* at the Cambridge Arts Theatre (1950) their friend the artist Edward Seago painted sixteen watercolours as scenery for his first professional stage commission. They also collaborated on summer shows throughout the 1950s and 1960s which were shrewdly presented under their own management, giving early encouragement to such fresh talents as Harry Secombe, Sheila Hancock, and Anna Quayle. As the 1950s progressed Fletcher's broadcasting career continued with appearances on BBC television's popular *What's My Line?* and the long-running radio comedy panel game *Does the Team Think?*

Fletcher was discovered by a new generation when he was invited to contribute 'Odd Odes' to reflect situations brought to the attention of Esther Rantzen's BBC1 consumer programme *That's Life!* (1974–81). His resurgence in the public eye led to a series of witty books including *Odd Odes* (1974), an autobiography, *Nice One Cyril* (1978), and several devoted to gardening, including *Cyril Fletcher's Gardening Book* (1974).

After he left *That's Life!* Fletcher continued his television career by presenting gardening programmes for a few years. In the mid-1980s he and Betty Astell moved to Guernsey. He presented several series about his showbusiness life and friends for BBC Radio 2. On at least one occasion during his final years BBC radio referred to him as 'the late Cyril Fletcher', which amused him greatly. He died at his home in St Peter Port, Guernsey, on 2 January 2005. Betty Astell died in Guernsey on 27 July 2005. Their daughter, Jill, survived them.

MICHAEL POINTON

Sources C. Fletcher, *Nice one Cyril* (1978) · *The Times* (3 Jan 2005) · *Daily Telegraph* (3 Jan 2005) · *The Guardian* (3 Jan 2005) · *The Independent* (3 Jan 2005) · *The Herald* [Glasgow] (3 Jan 2005) · *The Independent* (29 July 2005) [B. Astell] · *The Times* (30 July 2005) [B. Astell] · *Daily Telegraph* (30 July 2005) [B. Astell] · personal knowledge (2009) · private information (2009) · b. cert. [Cyril Fletcher] · b. cert. [Betty Hymans] · m. cert.

Archives FILM BFINA, *This is your life*, R. Mayoh (director), Thames Television, 16 March 1977 · BFINA, current affairs footage · BFINA, documentary footage · BFINA, performance footage | SOUND BL NSA, interviews with S. Williams, C704/01–02 · BL NSA, documentary recordings · BL NSA, performance recordings

Likenesses H. Coster, fourteen half-plate film negatives, 1936, NPG · E. Seago, oil on board, 1940–49; Christies, 8 May 2008, lot 134 · photographs, 1942–65, Getty Images, London · photographs, 1952–80, PA Photos, London · photographs, 1968–87, Rex Features, London · obituary photographs

Fogg, Gordon Elliot [Tony] (1919–2005), botanist and ecologist, was born on 26 April 1919 at Langar, near Bingham, Nottinghamshire, the eldest of four children of Leslie Charles Fogg, Wesleyan minister, and his wife, Doris Mary, *née* Elliott. His early schooling was complicated by his father's frequent moves between circuits as a Methodist minister, from Northumberland to Lancashire and subsequently in a series of circuits in the London area. His boyhood hobbies ranged from chemical experiments to watercolour painting; an increasing interest in the living world (and particularly plants) was stimulated by frequent visits to his maternal grandparents' home in Nottinghamshire. He was also an active boy scout, and went camping on many occasions. When the family moved to London he won a London county council scholarship to Dulwich College, where his interest in biology was fostered, and on leaving school he went to Queen Mary College, University of London, as an exhibitioner and, later, scholar. He graduated with first-class honours in botany in the summer of 1939, planning to embark on research at Queen Mary College with the algologist F. E. Fritsch, professor of botany there.

With the Second World War impending Queen Mary College was evacuated to Cambridge. Fogg had registered as a conscientious objector, and was given that status on condition that he undertook research work. This he did at Cambridge under Fritsch's supervision, embarking on research into the so-called blue-green algae—soon to be reassigned as bacteria rather than plants, under the designation of cyanobacteria. This group was to remain the focus of Fogg's research for much of his career—organisms playing a major role as plankton in the world's oceans and in many freshwater bodies. In addition to contributing to the beginning of the food web for many marine and other aquatic organisms they share with a few other bacteria the capacity to take nitrogen gas from the air and convert it to ammonia and thence to protein. This 'nitrogen fixing' capacity of cyanobacteria became a central feature of the subsequent research of Fogg and his students. In the later part of the war, from 1942 onwards, Fogg was directed by the Ministry of Supply to join a research team under V. J. Chapman (later to become a world renowned algologist, and professor of botany at the University of Auckland), together with two young colleagues, to conduct a survey of seaweeds of the western coast of Britain. Their research contributed later to the exploitation of the red seaweeds to make culture media for medical microbiology, but the brown seaweeds were used to make (among other things) a water-soluble parachute silk for the air-dropping of sea mines. Fogg was later to ponder his role in this, as a conscientious objector.

After completing his PhD on cyanobacteria Fogg went on in 1943 to work for Pest Control Ltd in Cambridge, where he met (Elizabeth) Beryl Llechid-Jones (*d.* 1997), who was working there on anti-malarial drugs. Two years younger than him, she was the daughter of Thomas Llechid-Jones, clergyman. They were married on 7 July 1945 in Colwyn Bay, Denbigh, her family home. They had a daughter, Helen, and a son, Timothy. Earlier in 1945 Fogg had been appointed an assistant lecturer in the botany department of University College, London, where he resumed his research on cyanobacteria, but also on other aspects of algal plankton ecology and physiology. He and his growing research group fitted well into the ecologically slanted department headed by W. H. Pearsall, and he was soon promoted to reader. This led, very appropriately, to his nickname of Gentle Reader, with a teasing reference both to his status and his personality. Fogg's work laid the foundation for the discovery that the specialized colourless cells in the cyanobacterial filament known as heterocysts were the site of nitrogen fixation—a process that has enormous significance in the sustained cropping of rice as a global food source, for the rice obtains much of that vital element 'second hand' from cyanobacteria. Using carbon-14 to 'label' organic compounds, a technique he acquired while on a Rockefeller fellowship in Chicago, Fogg was able to demonstrate that marine microalgae could leak up to 50 per cent of their products of photosynthesis back into the sea. This came to be recognized as a previously unsuspected feature of the global carbon cycle.

In 1960 Fogg was appointed to the chair of botany at Westfield College, London University. Now head of his own department, he appointed staff so as to cover the major fields of botany while also building up a group of specialists in cyanobacteria. The latter included Bill Stewart, who was later to become chief scientific adviser to the government. Much of the work of that group was summarized in *The Blue-Green Algae* (1973), by Fogg and others. In 1968 Fogg gave the Royal Society's Leeuwenhoek lecture, based on his cyanobacterial work.

Fogg's final move was in 1971 to take the chair of marine biology at the University College of North Wales, Bangor, where he remained until his retirement in 1985. While this brought his wife Beryl back home to Wales, and brought Fogg the chance of defending the importance of algal ecology within the field of marine biology, it also brought him a range of administrative problems that he had been largely spared in Westfield. These ranged from rivalries with colleagues in the Marine Science Laboratories in Menai Bridge on Anglesey, to conflict with the university administration over resources. He later gave a diplomatic version of some of these events in his memoir for the Royal Society of his colleague Dennis Crisp (1992). Despite these distractions Fogg continued the research on the extracellular products of marine algal plankton that he had started at Westfield, with a number of research students.

An important and separate phase of Fogg's life, which extended from his time in Westfield well into his retirement, was his enthusiastic commitment to Antarctic ecology and algology. His first visit was in 1966 while still at Westfield College, when he spent two months in the South Orkneys studying primary production and nitrogen fixation by marine algae in the Antarctic marine environment. Over the following years he made a number of other visits to Antarctica. When the British Antarctic Survey was placed under the control of the Natural Environment Research Council, Fogg was appointed to its Antarctic committee. He continued to visit Antarctica after his retirement, in the capacity of lecturer on cruise ships. He published three books on Antarctic science, the last of which, *The Biology of Polar Habitats* (1998), he dedicated to his late wife, who had accompanied him on his last voyage south. He was very proud that his son, Timothy, became involved in work in Antarctica in the late 1970s, with the British Antarctic Survey; the family name is commemorated in the name of the Fogg Highland at 72°45′ S, 60°50′ W.

Fogg played an active role in many societies and other bodies involved in his research fields. He was secretary, vice-president, and then president (1976–7) of the Institute of Biology, president of the British Phycological Society (1961–2) and of the International Phycological Society (1964), and a trustee of the Royal Botanic Gardens, Kew (1983–9), and of the British Museum (Natural History) (1976–85). He was elected FRS in 1965 and appointed CBE in 1983.

Tony Fogg (as he was always known to friends and family) was an outstanding lecturer and a very approachable, calm, and diplomatic colleague. He was the scientist who more than any other elucidated the mechanism of nitrogen fixation by the cyanobacteria, and illuminated their role in the global ecosystem. He also made a unique contribution to the record of Antarctic exploration and ecology. He died shortly after suffering a stroke, at the Gwynedd Hospital, Bangor, on 30 January 2005. He was survived by his two children. WILLIAM G. CHALONER

Sources G. E. Fogg, R. H. Richens, and R. A. Lewin, *Strictly marginal* (1995) · G. E. Fogg, The blooming of phytoplankton ecology, Fogg lecture, 2002, www.sbcs.qmul.ac.uk/news/lecture_series.shtml #fogg, 24 April 2008 · *The Independent* (18 Feb 2005) · A. E. Walsby, *Memoirs FRS*, 52 (2006), 99–116 · *WW* (2005) · personal knowledge (2009) · private information (2009) · b. cert. · m. cert. · d. cert.

Likenesses photograph, 1972, Hunt Institute for Botanical Documentation, Pittsburgh, Pennsylvania · R. A. Lewin, group photograph, photograph, 1976, repro. in *Memoirs FRS* · G. Argent, photograph, repro. in *The Independent* · W. Bird, photograph, RS · photograph, repro. in *Memoirs FRS*, frontispiece

Wealth at death £566,181: probate, 26 July 2005, *CGPLA Eng. & Wales*

Foggon, George (1913–2006), civil servant and industrial relations adviser, was born at 88 Station Lane, Hebburn, co. Durham, on 13 September 1913, the elder son and eldest of five children of Thomas Foggon (1891–1965), copperworks labourer, and later laboratory technician, and his wife, Margaret Burn, *née* Martin (1892/3–1957). He attended Hebburn colliery board school, from where, in 1924, he gained a scholarship to Jarrow grammar school. Entering the civil service at 16, he began his working life as a clerk in the Ministry of Labour at Felling labour exchange, Gateshead, in 1930. The 1930s were his formative years. He saw the Jarrow marchers, and he dealt daily with large numbers of the unemployed. This experience imbued him with great compassion, kindness, and a sense of fairness. He had already inherited a marked desire for knowledge and improvement. He read widely and developed an interest in modern history. His regional controller where he began his working life was Jameson Adams, who had been with Sir Ernest Shackleton in 1908 on his historic journey to within 97 miles of the south pole. This sparked such an interest in Foggon that he studied in great detail all of Shackleton's expeditions and he later regaled his friends with his knowledge of this topic, with infectious enthusiasm. On 25 June 1938, at the church of St John the Evangelist, Hebburn, he married Agnes McIntosh (1912–1968), daughter of James Robert McIntosh, carpenter. They had one son, Miles (*b*. 1951).

Following the outbreak of the Second World War, in 1940 Foggon volunteered for the Royal Air Force and trained as an armourer. Commissioned in 1943, he led the RAF armaments team at the Normandy landings, finding himself among the first members of the RAF to go ashore after D-day. In the course of following the armies from Normandy to Berlin he rose in rank to wing commander. He was appointed MBE in 1945. Shortly after hostilities ceased he was seconded to the Foreign Office to work on the staff of the British military government in Berlin, as an adviser for labour affairs. In this capacity he assisted in the restoration of German social structures in West Berlin and contributed to the efforts of the Allied Control Commission in the re-establishment of the West German trade unions and employers' organizations. He was promoted OBE in 1949.

Later in 1949 Foggon entered the Colonial Office as a principal. After two years' service in London he was promoted to assistant secretary and appointed to the West African Inter-Territorial Secretariat, based in the Gold Coast. In 1952 he became commissioner for labour in Nigeria. During his service in Africa he argued for the establishment of properly democratic trade unions and employer organizations as well as governmental and legal institutions to support social and labour affairs. His pleasant personality and fairness towards all sides gained the trust of many leading African politicians, trade unionists, and employers. He did much then and later in pursuit of these essentials and, in doing so, contributed greatly to limiting Soviet and later Chinese influences, which were intruding into this facet of developing countries.

In 1958 Foggon was brought back to London as labour adviser to the secretary of state for the colonies. In 1961 he was appointed CMG. In 1962, when most of the colonies began to move towards independence, he became a member of the Secretariat for Technical Co-operation. In 1965 his appointment was transferred to the Ministry of Overseas Development. By then he was emerging as a considerable expert in all matters of international labour affairs and industrial relations legislation. He was clearly one of the most appropriately qualified civil servants when appointed, in 1966, to the post of overseas labour adviser to the Foreign Office, in which post he remained until his retirement from the civil service in 1976. He established close working relationships with the Trades Union Congress and the Confederation of British Industry, particularly with their international departments. He pressed for the secondment to his office of representatives of both bodies, and, until the election of the Conservative government of Margaret Thatcher, TUC officers were attached to the overseas labour adviser's office of what was now the Foreign and Commonwealth Office. Meanwhile Foggon strove, with the help of a diminishing number of Labour attachés, to ensure that his knowledge of international labour problems was accurate and up to date. In one year he covered 100,000 miles, with visits to Egypt, Turkey, Iran, and Sri Lanka. In the same year he went to advise on the resolution of a general strike in the Gilbert Islands. Such journeys gave him much enjoyment as well as hard work, and provided him with a fund of stories always told with masterly detail and with kindly humour. His great strength was his ability to make the acquaintance of a wide mix of people and to see which of them were, or would become, key figures.

Such was now his standing, internationally as well as in the UK, that Foggon had already been invited by the International Labour Office in Geneva to head their London office. He took up this new task on retirement from the British civil service and served until his ultimate retirement in 1982. All those with whom he worked, then as before, liked him, sought his advice, and enjoyed his company. His great knowledge and efficiency, his charm, kindness, generosity, humour, and dedication all contributed to his popularity.

Following the death of his first wife, on 30 August 1969 Foggon married Audrey Clarissa (1932–2002), the daughter of Joseph William Blanch, diplomat. There were no children of the marriage. They lived for most of Foggon's retirement in Pimlico, which provided easy access to his office and his clubs. He had long been a member of the Athenaeum and the Oriental Club, and his joy was to entertain his many friends to long and informative lunches in these venues. In 2000 he and Audrey moved to 3 Castle Hill House (the former Wylam Manor), in Wylam, Northumberland, where they bought an additional guest apartment to accommodate their visitors. Foggon died, at Castle Hill House, on 18 February 2006, of prostate cancer. He was cremated at Newcastle crematorium on 25 February and his ashes were later buried in Hebburn cemetery. He was survived by his son, Miles. EDWARD TOMS

Sources *The Times* (20 Feb 1951); (10 Feb 1976); (1 March 1976); (24 March 2006); (30 March 2006) • *The Guardian* (24 March 2006) • *WW* (2004) • private information (2010) [Audrey Morgan, sister; Miles Foggon, son] • personal knowledge (2010) • b. cert. • m. certs. • d. cert.

Archives priv. coll.

Likenesses pencil sketch, 1946–9, priv. coll. • photograph, repro. in *The Times* (24 March 2006)

Wealth at death £1,811,739: probate, 9 June 2006, *CGPLA Eng. & Wales*

Ford, Sir Edward William Spencer (1910–2006), courtier, was born on 24 July 1910 at The Hall, Repton, Derbyshire, the son of Lionel George Bridges Justice Ford (1865–1932), headmaster of Repton School, later headmaster of Harrow School and dean of York, and his wife, Mary Catherine, daughter of Edward Stuart *Talbot, bishop of Winchester. The cricket writer William Justice Ford was his uncle. Ford was the fourth (twin) son. There were also two daughters. His twin, Christopher, was killed at Anzio in January 1944, while serving as a major in the Grenadier Guards.

Ford was educated at Eton College as a king's scholar and excelled at sport. (For many years he was the oldest surviving member of an Eton or Harrow Lord's cricket team, and cricket remained an abiding pleasure to him all his life.) From Eton he moved on to New College, Oxford (where he was an open scholar). He took a first in classical moderations in 1931 and a second in *literae humaniores* in 1933. He was called to the bar by the Middle Temple in 1937. His already burgeoning reputation as a counsellor was at that time being tested during a brief appointment as private tutor to the young King Farouk of Egypt, where it seems that his wise words may have fallen on deafer ears than at other stages of his life. He practised at the bar until 1939 then served throughout the Second World War in the Grenadier Guards. He was mentioned in dispatches twice, seeing action at Dunkirk and in north Africa, Italy, and Belgium.

In 1945, while instructing at the Staff College in Haifa, Ford was invited to join the three-strong team of private secretaries in King George VI's household at Buckingham Palace. He accepted with alacrity and worked happily for two sovereigns, King George VI and Queen Elizabeth II, throughout the ensuing twenty-two years as assistant private secretary, with first Sir Alan Lascelles and then Sir Michael Adeane as principals. Ford's mixture of wisdom, humour, knowledge, and self-effacement fitted him ideally for the task, and he was a popular and jovial member of the royal household, known by many as the Pasha. On 1 December 1949 he married Virginia Polk (1918–1995), elder daughter of the leading banker Robert Henry *Brand, Baron Brand, and widow of John Metcalfe (Jack) Polk, of the family of the American president of that name. Virginia was a niece of Nancy Astor. Ford's marriage, an exceptionally happy one, was based from 1963 to 1982 at Virginia's Palladian house, Eydon Hall, in Northamptonshire, which she inherited from her father. Virginia had already had two sons with Jack Polk, and was mother to two more with Ford.

In 1967 came the other, besides his marriage, defining moment of Ford's life. Adeane was due to retire in 1972, and the private secretarial succession was complicated by the two contenders, Ford and Charteris, being close in age. Ford, typically, made way for Charteris. This caused him much sadness, but it was done with the good grace, good humour, and dignity that were variously his hallmarks. The move though, was not the end of his connection with the queen. He remained until the end of his life her valued correspondent (in one of his letters he coined the phrase 'annus horribilis', later used by her to describe the events of 1992, a poor year for the royal family's fortunes), adviser, and friend. And he retained, together with some vivid memories, a lifelong admiration for the queen and the duke of Edinburgh. In this respect his guardianship of the Order of Merit from 1975, as secretary and registrar, was impeccable. His notes on candidates, successful and otherwise, made good reading and reflected the extraordinary breadth of his knowledge on matters cultural and scientific, to name but two, which was the envy of his many friends. He was also, at various times, high sheriff and a deputy lieutenant of Northamptonshire, secretary of the Pilgrims Trust (1967–75), and, to his delight, prime warden of the Goldsmiths' Company in 1979. He had been made an MVO in 1949 and CB in 1952, knighted KCVO in 1957 and advanced to KCB in 1967, and in 1998 he was made GCVO.

Virginia predeceased him, after a long illness, in 1995 but Ford, who had devotedly cared for her, recovered from this blow and continued to make energetic forays from his base in Little Venice into London society, country houses, family occasions, and, even in his nineties, homes abroad where he was entertained by the great and good. When asked how he entered one hostess's swimming pool in his exceedingly old age, he replied 'I always dive'. Such was the man that his interlocutor was not surprised. He died, still entirely in control of his faculties, of a heart attack at his home, 23 Blomfield Road, Westminster, on 19 November 2006, and was survived by his two sons and a stepson, one stepson having predeceased him. The queen and the duke of Edinburgh were among those who filled the Guards' Chapel, Wellington Barracks, London for a memorial service on 28 February 2007.

ROBERT FELLOWES

Sources *The Times* (21 Nov 2006) · *Daily Telegraph* (21 Nov 2006) · *The Independent* (23 Nov 2006) · *The Guardian* (28 Nov 2006) · Burke, *Peerage* · *WW* (2006) · personal knowledge (2010) · private information (2010) · b. cert. · m. cert. · d. cert.

Archives Bodl. Oxf., family papers

Likenesses photographs, 1949–76, Photoshot, London · G. Argent, bromide print, 1969, NPG · Bassano, photograph, Camera Press, London · obituary photographs

Wealth at death £6,617,020: probate, 12 March 2007, *CGPLA Eng. & Wales*

Fort, Dame Maeve Geraldine (1940–2008), diplomatist, was born on 19 November 1940 at Elmswood, North Mossley Hill Road, Wavertree, Liverpool, of Anglo-Irish descent, the only child of Frank Leslie Fort (1908–1969), a clerk at an aircraft factory, and later a hospital administrator, and his wife, Ruby Elizabeth, *née* Galbraith (*d.* 1982), a district nurse and midwife. Her parents had run a maternity nursing home but later worked for the newly established National Health Service. The family moved to Nantwich, Cheshire, where she grew up. She was educated at Nantwich grammar school, and Trinity College, Dublin, where she took a degree in English and French, before going to the Sorbonne, Paris, on a French government scholarship.

Told that her qualifications were insufficient to get her into the fast stream of the Foreign Office, Maeve Fort determined to enter the executive or junior branch, which she achieved in 1963 as one of two women out of twelve successful candidates. In 1964 she spent some

Dame Maeve Geraldine Fort (1940–2008), by John Stillwell, 1996

months in New York as a second secretary at the general assembly of the United Nations. In 1965 she was seconded to the South-East Asia Treaty Organization in Bangkok and from there went to Lagos in 1971. She returned to the Foreign and Commonwealth Office (as it had become) in 1973 and was subsequently promoted a 'fast stream' first secretary. In 1978 she went on a substantive posting to the British mission to the United Nations in New York, where she dealt with African affairs. In 1982 she returned to London on promotion to counsellor. In 1983 she spent a year at the Royal College of Defence Studies. In 1984 she was posted to Santiago, Chile, as counsellor, head of chancery, and consul-general. From 1986 to 1989 she was head of the west African department at the Foreign and Commonwealth Office and non-resident ambassador to Chad. She was appointed ambassador to Mozambique from 1989 to 1992 and ambassador to the Lebanese republic from 1992 to 1996, and her final posting was as high commissioner to South Africa from 1996 to 2000.

At the United Nations in New York Fort was a key member of the contact group working with the secretary-general's special representative, Maarti Ahtisaari, to bring Namibia to independence. It was at the United Nations that she began to develop her reputation as a tough and skilful negotiator. Her stint as head of the west African department strengthened further her African credentials. These were put to good use in Mozambique, where she was closely involved in the international negotiations to bring the rival Frelimo and Renamo movements together in an effort to end the bloody civil war. These were ultimately successful in 1992. At this stage Fort's career took a change of direction. She volunteered, typically her friends would say, for the arduous and at times dangerous role of ambassador to Lebanon. The civil war there may have ended in 1991 but life had by no means returned to normal. She saw her mission there as public British support for the government and people of Lebanon but also as a way of developing a real understanding of the situation on the ground. In so doing she was not inclined to sit behind the fortifications of the embassy, and travelled widely (with six military policemen as her bodyguards). This was a posting made for her and she described life in Beirut as the best kept secret in the Middle East.

Fort's appointment as high commissioner to South Africa came two years after Nelson Mandela had been elected president and South Africa had moved out of the apartheid era. Britain was consolidating its ties with the new democracy and Fort developed a strong relationship with Mandela. In 1999 Thabo Mbeki became president. There were major problems with his stance on HIV and AIDS and his ambivalent attitude towards Robert Mugabe, president of Zimbabwe. In an interview in 2000, just as she retired, Fort was strongly critical of African leaders who failed to stand up to Mugabe. A source of personal and professional satisfaction was the visit of the queen and the successful Commonwealth heads of government meeting in Durban in 1999. She had been appointed CMG in 1990, DCMG in 1998, and, on the occasion of the queen's visit to South Africa, DCVO in 1999.

Fort never married but was accompanied in later years by her beloved dog Chloe, a Maltese toy Pomeranian cross, which was not too shy to be photographed sitting on Nelson Mandela's lap. Throughout her life Fort was stylish and sociable, developing a huge network of friends, colleagues, and contacts, with whom she never lost touch. Her staff loved her. She thrived on political gossip and information gathering, had good political instincts, an iron will, an intrepid spirit, and immense charm. These strengths underpinned her career. One of her former colleagues said that she had 'a knack for getting on with awkward people' (*The Times*, 9 Oct 2008). She had no truck with gender politics but was gratified to have been one of the few women who, up to her time, had reached the highest echelons of the diplomatic service.

In retirement Fort was a trustee of the Red Cross, the Beit Trust, and the Chalker Foundation, and was a governor of Benenden School. She loved her mews house in Notting Hill and her London life of theatre, cinema, and above all shopping, which she turned into an art form. She divided her year between London and her home in France, where she spent her time gardening and entertaining her many friends. She died after a brief illness at St Mary's Hospital, Paddington, on 18 September 2008. A memorial service was held at Holy Trinity Church, Sloane Street, on 28 November 2008. GRAHAM BURTON

Sources *Daily Telegraph* (25 Sept 2008) · *The Independent* (30 Sept 2008) · *The Guardian* (2 Oct 2008) · *The Times* (9 Oct 2008); (1 Nov 2008); (28 Nov 2008) · *Irish Times* (11 Oct 2008) · *Cape Times* [South Africa] (5 Feb 2009) · diplomatic service lists, 1963–2000 · Burke, *Peerage* · *WW* (2009) · personal knowledge (2012) · private information (2012) · b. cert. · d. cert.

Likenesses J. Stillwell, photograph, 1996, PA Photos, London [*see illus.*] · J. Stillwell, photographs, 1996, PA Photos, London · obituary photographs

Forte, Charles, Baron Forte (1908–2007), caterer and hotelier, was born on 26 November 1908 in the hamlet of Mortale, outside the village of Casalaticco, in an area of Italy known as the Ciociaria, the eldest son of Rocco Giovanni Forte and his wife, Maria Luigia, daughter of Michelangelo Antonio Forte. His parents were distantly related. The name of his birthplace was altered in his honour from Mortale to Monforte some eighty years later. People from the Ciociaria had been settling in Scotland since the 1880s; in 1911 Rocco Forte joined his brother and cousin, who had several small shops there. He opened a business, the Savoy Café in Alloa, that boasted the earliest American soda fountain and Italian espresso coffee-machine in Clackmannanshire. In 1913 Rocco's wife with her adored eldest child joined him there. The five-year-old had hitherto been called Carmine Forte, but his forename was soon Anglicized. He was educated in Alloa, briefly at a boarding-school run by Marist fathers in Dumfries, then at Collegio Scheppers and the Liceo Mamiami in Rome. In 1926 he took a six-month course in accountancy and bookkeeping in Scotland.

Forte first worked in an ice-cream parlour and sandwich bar in Weston-super-Mare, which his father owned with two cousins, and then in his father's cafés in Bournemouth and Weymouth. In 1929 he became manager of the Venetian Lounge in Brighton, which his father had started in partnership with another cousin. In 1935 he opened his own milk-bar adjacent to Regent Street Polytechnic in London, and began serving a novelty called milkshakes. Failing to draw enough passers-by, he decided that he needed more conspicuous premises but lower costs. Accordingly he sacked three staff, and extended into an abutting shop. Thereafter he always understood that the sites of his enterprises were decisive to their success, and never relented in his strict costing. The Mayfair property dealers Howard and Basil Samuel helped him to find good sites for further milk-bars in Charing Cross Road, Oxford Street, and Leicester Square. By the outbreak of the Second World War in 1939 Forte had nine milk-bars in central London, and was saving 20 per cent on buying costs by supplying them from centralized premises where cakes, sandwiches, and fruit syrups were prepared.

When Italy entered the conflict as an axis ally in 1940, Forte was briefly interned as an enemy national on the Isle of Man. In January 1943 he married Irene Mary (1920/21–2010), only daughter of Olga Chierico, a redoubtable Venetian widow who ran a delicatessen in Soho; her long-dead husband had been Giovanni Chierico. They had one son and five daughters. Forte became a British subject after the war.

Charles Forte, Baron Forte (1908–2007), by Baron, 1953

During the depths of post-war austerity Forte began collaborating with a jovial cockney property developer, Joe Levy. Levy had an estate agent's credo: 'If you can't make a damned good living within three square miles of Piccadilly Circus, don't try in this profession. And never go into a back street' (Marriott, 182). Forte learned much from Levy, including the buying and leaseback of property. At Levy's prompting he bought the Lyons tea-room at Rainbow Corner on Shaftesbury Avenue, near Piccadilly Circus, with a £35,000 loan from Prudential Assurance. By leasing part of the site to himself at a rent of £4000 a year, and leasing the rest at £8000, he achieved an annual income of £12,000. Thereafter he enlarged his fortune by property deals as well as catering, and became known to the City pages as a property financier as much as a restaurateur. In 1950 he leased the resplendent Criterion building on the south side of Piccadilly Circus at an annual rent of £12,000, used its Marble Hall restaurant as a cafeteria serving chicken Maryland, ice gâteaux and the like, and leased back other parts of the building. As an expert in mass feeding and the costing of cheap food he secured half of the catering concession for the Festival of Britain in 1951. In 1953—again advised by Levy—he bought the Café Monico site at Piccadilly Circus from the Express Dairy. Finally, in 1953, he and Sir Leslie Joseph obtained a twenty-one-year lease from London county council to run a funfair in Battersea Park, and to turn the Cremorne beer garden into a restaurant (he severed his connection when the funfair gained an insalubrious reputation as a haunt of hooligans). These deals made Forte a millionaire. Journalists nicknamed him Mr Piccadilly (Hennessy, 5).

In April 1954 Forte was co-opted onto the board of the Café Royal, and soon stretched his resources by buying its Regent Street building. At critical moments of expansion he dared to take on high leverage, and there were phases of his career in which he was personally short of money. The glamorous Café Royal was Forte's favourite property: for years he kept a private penthouse office there. In July 1954—ten months after an earlier offer of 6*s*. 6*d*. per share had been rejected—Forte paid 10*s*. per share to buy the entire Criterion site, including the Criterion Theatre. The deal cost about £800,000. At the same time, after convoluted manoeuvres, he bought the caterers Slaters and Bodega, with a valuable property portfolio. In 1955 he formed a new subsidiary, Forte's Popular Restaurants, and received the first catering concession at Heathrow airport. In 1957 he went into partnership with Bernard Delfont to convert the London Hippodrome music-hall into a theatre restaurant called Talk of the Town. His ambition to have a luxury restaurant was satisfied by buying the Hungaria restaurant in Lower Regent Street.

Forte befriended the Labour politician Alf Robens, who introduced him as a potential sympathizer to the party leader, Hugh Gaitskell. Gaitskell, who described him in 1956 as '*the* great caterer in the country', was delighted when Forte undertook to give an annual subsidy of £5000 to the Glasgow socialist weekly *Forward* (*Diary of Hugh Gaitskell*, 470). In 1959 Gaitskell offered to recommend him for a peerage. Forte, who was by then expending his extra-business energies as chairman of the charity fund-raising National Sporting Club, declined, for he was far from a socialist and fixed in his resistance to union recognition in his operations. In 1980 only about 10 per cent of his staff was unionized: he frequently voiced his dislike of being bullied by union officials or anyone else.

Until 1948 Forte lived in flats off Portland Place, a short walk from that stretch of London, Regent Street between Oxford Circus and Piccadilly Circus, which was the focus of his interests. He then moved to 7 Greenaway Gardens in Hampstead, and installed his parents and other relations nearby. In 1970 he took over Chester House in Upper Belgrave Street from Lord Bruntisfield, and subsequently moved to nearby Lowndes House. A keen shot, in 1965 he bought the 1500 acre Ryde farm estate at Ripley in Surrey. His interests were controlled by his privately owned company, Forte Holdings, with headquarters at 251–9 Regent Street, overlooking Oxford Circus.

During the 1950s Forte was chairman of the London Publicity Committee, a forerunner of the London Tourist Board (on which he also served). He envisaged a vast expansion of tourism, and recognized that this could not be accomplished while holiday visitors to London, 'the greatest city in the world', remained seasonal. His strategy to attract off-season visitors was to promote London's conference business by a publicity drive. In an article for *The Times* (25 March 1958), he wrote:

> Paris, Geneva, Brussels and many continental cities, most of which are not only smaller than London but have a fraction

> of London's amenities, do far better at encouraging conferences. We in this city are too complacent in a world which is becoming more publicity-conscious than ever … many Continental cities are vying to become the capital of a more united Europe. Why should this not be London?

In the 1960s Swan Tours and Milbanke Travel became wholly owned Forte subsidiaries, and he held a stake in Thomas Cook until 1970. By 1978 almost half of Forte's guests in British hotels came from abroad.

In 1958 Forte bought his first hotel, the Waldorf Hotel at Aldwych, for £600,000, which he raised by selling his lease of the Monico site in Piccadilly to Jack Cotton for £500,000. He then arranged a sale and leaseback deal with Prudential Assurance on the Waldorf. The following year he bought the Quality Inn chain of restaurants and extended his ownership of lower-grade provincial hotels: there were about 100 in 1980. By 1960 Forte was a top table guest at Cotton's famous annual luncheon at the Dorchester Hotel. He did several property deals with Sir Isaac Wolfson, from whom he bought Jay's fashion store at Oxford Circus in 1961, and by 1962 Anthony Sampson was writing, 'the era of Nuffield and de Havilland is being succeeded by the era of Charles Forte and Jack Cotton' (Sampson, 499). In 1969 Forte bought the Frederick Hotels group, with eight hotels including the Russell in Bloomsbury. In 1970 he bought three Paris hotels, the George V, Plaza Athénée, and Trémoille. Subsequently he acquired the Ritz Hotel in Madrid and the Hôtel des Bergues in Geneva. His company built airport hotels at Heathrow, Birmingham, Manchester, and Glasgow as well as the Golden Sands Hotel near Famagusta in Cyprus. He bought three hotels in Bermuda from Sir Harold Wernher and another hotel in Jamaica, and erected a village of holiday cottages in Sardinia.

Forte's other acquisitions included the Kardomah coffee houses and Henekey wine-bar chains, Fuller's tea-shop and chocolate business (1959), Bellevue Stadium in Manchester (1962), the Mr Whippy ice-cream business (1962), and Joseph Terry, chocolate manufacturers, for £4.3 million (1963). He invested £50,000 in the publishers Sidgwick and Jackson in 1956, and joined the board: later the firm published his anodyne and forgetful memoirs, *Forte* (1986).

Forte successfully tendered to run the Newport Pagnell service-station cafeteria on the M1 motorway from London to Leeds, which opened in 1959. Another eight Forte motorway cafeterias were opened over the next twenty years, and damaged the Forte brand by the poor quality of the food. In 1961 he opened (outside Oxford) the first of his Travelodge chain of motels, with restaurants and petrol stations attached, sited on trunk roads. It was rumoured that Enrico Mattei, Forte's friend who was the controversial chairman of the Italian state oil company ENI, would join him in the motel business. In 1961 Forte became chairman of the wholly owned English subsidiary of AGIP, the marketing arm of ENI. AGIP began opening petrol stations on prime English sites. After Mattei's aircraft crashed in dubious circumstances in 1962 Forte was stunned into speechlessness for the only time in his life. He assisted the sale of AGIP's English petrol stations to Esso for about £12 million, but did not take up share options worth £1.5 million.

Forte looked distinctively Italian, standing five feet four inches tall, dapper, with a neat moustache, bristling energy, and formal punctilio. He was a smiling, courteous martinet. At home, he liked order and refinement: he was stern and exacting with his children. In business, he was a forceful, even imperious presence who vitalized, chivvied, and rewarded his employees. Always he was self-consciously dignified. Punctuality was a passion with him. He prided himself on working openly with a team of trusted deputies, strove to be considerate, and enjoyed the admiring dependence of his senior managers. Wages in his group were higher than average in the sector, but the annual turnover of his low-paid staff of about 70 per cent was also above average. He did not take defeat well, but never repined over reverses: his driving will spurred him forward to jump at the next challenge. The future for him was not problematic but promised satisfactions.

Forte Holdings was one of the largest privately owned businesses in Britain. In 1961 he agreed a £30 million merger with Mecca, a publicly quoted company operating bingo halls, ballrooms, ice-rinks, and diners. This news delighted the stock exchange, which was eager for investors to get a stake in Forte's flourishing, fast-expanding business. The deal however collapsed because of the difficulties met by accountants in valuing the diverse components of Forte Holdings at a price acceptable to its owner. Speculators who bought heavily in Mecca shares as a way of getting a slice of Forte's earnings lost heavily when the amalgamation was discontinued. Mecca was subsequently acquired by Sir Max Joseph's Grand Metropolitan Estates. Despite this stumble Forte was impatient to stride into the motel business, and to develop his chain of steak houses, but with each motel costing about £250,000 his organization's financial needs were too big for his resources. Forte Holdings was therefore floated on the stock exchange in 1962 to raise the necessary millions. The issue proved a resounding success, being heavily oversubscribed. Control of this holding company was retained by its founder's specially created private company, Forte Investments. Effectively he had 71 per cent voting control.

About this time Forte bought the City catering group Ring and Brymer (which catered for the lord mayor's banquet, Chelsea flower show, and Farnborough air show), the restaurant Gennaro's of Soho, and an amusements business, Fairwater Glides. In 1969 he bought Lillywhite's clothes store on the corner of Lower Regent Street and Piccadilly Circus. He took over the promenade piers at Blackpool, New Brighton, and Llandudno, and opened the Serpentine restaurant in Hyde Park. When Forte acquired provincial hotels their interiors were gutted, their furnishings were given a monotonous modernity that soon dated, their purchasing was centralized, their meals were ruled by 'portion control', and their prices were standardized. The beautiful gilt mosaic ceiling of the Marble Hall at the Criterion was hidden by a shoddy, lowered ceiling and forgotten for several decades under Forte's stewardship. His view was that his Little Chef and Happy Eater diners, and Travelodges, were reliable, hygienic, and affordable. Detractors complained of their soul-immolating uniformity, indifferent cooking, and stifling mediocrity.

By 1970 Forte's company employed 16,000 and had assets of £70 million. It vied with Trust Houses, long known for its medium-sized provincial hotels with old-fashioned charm but embarrassing plumbing. Under an ambitious chairman, Lord Crowther, Trust Houses had lately developed a bland but lucrative chain of Post House motor-hotels. In 1970 it was agreed to merge the two businesses in a new company, Trust House Forte, which with assets of £120 million surpassed Maxwell Joseph's Grand Metropolitan as Britain's largest hotelier. These assets included 215 hotels in Britain, thirteen foreign hotels, 250 restaurants and cafés, and 1500 canteens, catering for fifty airlines, ten piers, seven motorway service areas, and four amusement parks. Trust House was strong in industrial catering and English hotels (including the Grosvenor House, Hyde Park, Brown's, and Cavendish hotels) while Forte's strengths lay in public catering and foreign hotels. Forte expected his own way: if someone submitted a carefully argued policy paper that went against what he wished to do, he ignored it. This attitude riled both Crowther and the Trust House management, whose methods Forte found cumbersome and bureaucratic. There were other tensions: Trust House headquarters staff left work at 5.30 sharp, but Forte's management was instilled with his habit of long, punishing hours. Crowther had intimated that he would retire after a year as chairman to be succeeded by his deputy chairman, Forte, but reneged on this deal. The two men came to loathe one another, and traded public insults: Crowther accused Forte of costing the company a million pounds a year in trappings and expenses. Whereas Crowther relied on the support of old Trust House directors Forte nominated Sir Charles Hardie and the Conservative Party chairman, Lord Thorneycroft (who had an Italian wife), to the merged board: their backing proved decisive.

In October 1971 Allied Breweries launched a £128 million takeover bid which intensified the animosity. Forte outmanoeuvred Crowther by jockeying onto the board his friend Alf Robens (by then a peer), and thus obtained a majority among the directors. Recognizing that his grip on the chair was precarious, Crowther supported Allied's offer. Forte, who owned the largest stake in the company, borrowed £2 million to outbid Allied for shares in the market: he mustered friends such as Delfont and Max Joseph to buy with him, and paid for an adroit public relations campaign to sway shareholders. Allied's bid was defeated, Crowther and his cohorts resigned, and Forte's merger with Trust House evolved into a delayed takeover. Crowther dropped dead a few days later.

Forte installed Thorneycroft as chairman of Trust House Forte and served as chief executive until he replaced Thorneycroft in 1978. (The two men were co-trustees of the Italian Hospital in Bloomsbury, which they abruptly shut in 1989.) During the 1970s Forte participated in several huge overseas hotel projects, notably the al-Jazira in Bahrain, the Plaza of the Americas in Dallas, and the Riyadh Palace in Saudi Arabia. In 1973 he acquired 460 American hotels and motels by purchasing TraveLodge International of California. The Pierre Hotel in New York was bought soon afterwards. In 1976 Trust House Forte paid £25 million for the Lyons group of thirty-four hotels, including the Cumberland, Strand Palace, and Regent Palace hotels in London; in 1981 it bought the entertainment interests of Sir Jules Thorn's Thorn-EMI, including three London theatres; and in 1986 paid £186 million for the hotel and catering interests of the Imperial group, which Lord Hanson had recently taken over. Forte injured his reputation by a prolonged attempt—beginning in 1981 with the backing of Kuwaiti investors, and fizzling out in 1989—to wrest control of the Savoy Hotel from interests led by Sir Hugh Wontner. Forte's siege of the Savoy and antagonism to Wontner were comparable to Tiny Rowland's siege of Harrods and loathing of Mohamed Fayed in 1981–92. Both episodes were in all senses vain. Forte spent £38 million to buy 69 per cent of Savoy's equity, but held only 42 per cent of voting capital.

Forte was knighted in 1970, and received a life peerage in 1982 on the recommendation of Margaret Thatcher. He was one of the entrepreneurs—along with Kenneth Keith, Arnold Weinstock, Marcus Sieff, John King, and James Hanson—who were promoted to the House of Lords in Thatcher's first term, and signalled the capitalism she admired: despite her commitment to reviving small businesses, her favourite businessmen were despotic rulers of colossal fiefs. Forte venerated Mrs Thatcher, who spoke at his eightieth birthday dinner, attended by 1200 guests, at the Grosvenor House Hotel. This gala was described in acidulous detail in Woodrow Wyatt's diary for 22 November 1988:

> Charles Forte made a speech, far too long. He kept on saying how much he loved his wife and how marvellous she was. Then came the cutting of the cake ceremony which was preceded by a fanfare of Household Cavalry trumpeters, or Life Guard trumpeters, with their great banners, all looking very royal … and somewhat overdoing it for vulgarity. Then we had Vera Lynn who sang the most appalling song, 'from all the women especially, and Irene Forte, to Charles Forte'. (*Journals of Woodrow Wyatt*, 1.670)

In 1983 Forte appointed his son Rocco as chief executive, while retaining the chairmanship. The corporate name was changed in 1991 to Forte plc. Sales in that year were worth £2641 million, and shareholders' funds stood at £2961 million—of which nearly two-thirds represented freehold land and buildings. Institutional shareholders grew restive at his baronial style of management, and complained that Forte's board was a gerontocracy. Finally, in 1992, he relinquished the chairmanship to his son, and was named life president, but his renunciation was too late. After a fierce takeover battle, control of his vulnerable empire was seized by Granada for £3.9 billion in 1996. Latterly, although physically hale, Forte was afflicted by senile dementia. He died at his London house, Lowndes House, Belgravia, on 28 February 2007, and was survived by his wife and their six children. His son Rocco and eldest daughter Olga had by then built up a chain of luxury hotels throughout Europe, Rocco Forte Hotels Ltd.

RICHARD DAVENPORT-HINES

Sources A. Sampson, *Anatomy of Britain* (1962) • O. Marriott, *The property boom* (1967) • E. Hennessy, *The entrepreneurs* (1980), 1–34 • *The diary of Hugh Gaitskell, 1945–1956*, ed. P. M. Williams (1983) • C. Forte, *Forte: the autobiography of Charles Forte* (1986) • D. Stewart, 'The growth and development of Trusthouse Forte', *Tourism Management*, 12 (1991), 341–51 • R. Teare and others, 'The Granada takeover of Forte', *Management Decisions*, 35 (1997), 5–9 • *The journals of Woodrow Wyatt*, ed. S. Curtis, 3 vols. (1998–2000) • *The Times* (1 March 2007) • *Daily Telegraph* (1 March 2007) • *The Guardian* (1 March 2007) • *The Independent* (1 March 2007) • Burke, *Peerage* • *WW* (2007)

Archives SOUND BL NSA, documentary recording

Likenesses Baron, photograph, 1953, Getty Images, London [*see illus.*] • photographs, 1953–85, Getty Images, London • photographs, 1954–91, PA Photos, London • R. Coleman, photograph, 1959, NPG • R. Franks, photograph, 1964, NPG • F. Goodman, photograph, 1966, NPG • photographs, 1970–94, Photoshot, London • B. L. Schwartz, photograph, 1977, NPG • F. Greer, photograph, 1990, NPG • H. Mee, oils, exh. London Hop Exchange, London 1990, repro. in H. Mee, *British eminencies* (1990), 49 [exhibition catalogue, London Hop Exchange, 23 May - 13 June 1990] • S. Whyte, bronze bust, repro. in *Portrait in the round: 33rd exhibition of the society of portrait sculptors* (1996) • obituary photographs • photograph, repro. in *Sunday Telegraph* (11 Oct 1987)

Wealth at death £80,150,694: probate, 24 Aug 2007, *CGPLA Eng. & Wales*

Forth, Eric (1944–2006), politician, was born on 9 September 1944 at 30 Balshagray Avenue, Glasgow, the son of William Forth, deputy harbourmaster, of 3 Churchill Drive, Glasgow, and his wife, (Helen) Aileen, *née* Fraser. He was educated at Jordanhill College School, where he stood in a mock election as a communist, but later became secretary of the Conservative Club at the University of Glasgow, where he studied politics and economics. After university he worked in industry for Ford Motors and Rank Xerox, and served on Brentwood urban district council for four years from 1968. On 11 March 1967 at the register office in Redbridge he had married Linda St Clair, a schoolteacher also aged twenty-two, and the daughter of Peter Linn St Clair, steel fixer. They had two daughters.

At both 1974 general elections Forth stood unsuccessfully against Jo Richardson in the safe Labour seat of Barking. In 1979 he was elected to the European parliament for Birmingham North, but by the time he had entered parliament as Conservative MP for Mid-Worcestershire in 1983 his early Euro-enthusiasm had given way to strong Euroscepticism.

Forth gained an early reputation for being 'politically incorrect', using his maiden speech to launch a scathing attack on the Sex Equality Bill. His House of Commons office was adorned with a poster of the glamour model Samantha Fox; in 1988 he opposed Clare Short's bill to ban 'page three' nudity in newspapers on the grounds that topless models who had chosen 'to display whatever assets they possessed for profit were successfully exploiting the male population' (*The Times*, 14 April 1988). He opposed spending public money on combating AIDS, which he regarded as 'largely self-inflicted' (*The Times*, 28 March 1987); he once advised a constituent who wrote to complain that his son could not afford to buy a house in his constituency to 'move to a grottier part of town' (*Evening Standard*, 6 April 1998); and at a private dinner he said, 'All this sucking up to minorities is ridiculous. There are millions of people in this country who are white, Anglo-Saxon and bigoted and they need to be represented' (*The Times*, 8 Oct 2001). Few politicians have been as outspoken as Eric Forth. Yet such outspokenness did not preclude ministerial advancement.

In the 1980s Forth formed part of Margaret Thatcher's right-wing praetorian guard, as a member (later convenor) of the No Turning Back group, formed to keep the Thatcherite revolution on track. (From 1997 to 2001 he also served as chairman of the Thatcherite Conservative Way Forward group.) In 1986 he was appointed parliamentary private secretary to Angela Rumbold, minister of state at the Department of Education and Science. In 1988 Thatcher promoted him to the Department of Trade and Industry as parliamentary under-secretary of state in charge of consumer protection. He described staff at the Citizens' Advice Bureau as a 'bunch of Trots' (*Daily Telegraph*, 19 May 2006). But there were moments of unshowy decency: he won praise for curbing the sharp practices of estate agents, and bringing pressure to bear on British Telecom to improve their services for the deaf. In 1990, by now parliamentary under-secretary of state at the Department of Employment under Michael Howard, Forth played a key role in persuading other Thatcherites to support John Major as her most suitable successor. As parliamentary under-secretary of state for education (1992–5) he spearheaded the government's drive against truancy, and as minister of state for higher education (1995–7) he did much to further the cause of special education. He was sworn of the privy council in 1996.

In 1997 boundary changes put Forth's parliamentary career in jeopardy, but he was selected to fight the redrawn and newly named Bromley and Chislehurst, which he duly won. Nevertheless the tory 'landslide' defeat of 1997 claimed his favourite to succeed John Major as leader of the Conservative Party, Michael Portillo. Forth became campaign manager for Peter Lilley, switching his support to John Redwood, and finally to William Hague. By the time Portillo returned to parliament in 2001 Forth had become a fan of David Davis, sensing that Portillo had abandoned his Thatcherite credentials. Ironically Forth's greatest hour came after he left ministerial office. During the 1997 parliament he led the 'awkward squad', a small ginger group of tory backbenchers who embarked upon what he described as 'trench warfare' (*The Times*, 19 Oct 2001): disrupting normal parliamentary proceedings to block non-contentious legislation, especially private members' bills, and continually harassing government ministers. Resentment on the Labour side towards Forth's activities was partly responsible for the government's decision to timetable all government bills. In 1997 he was closely involved with David Maclean in setting up the Parliamentary Resources Unit, a subscription briefing service for Conservative backbenchers which, unlike its Labour equivalent, was publicly funded from MPs' expenses.

In 2001 Iain Duncan Smith appointed Forth shadow leader of the House of Commons, a post in which he revelled, especially in his weekly jousts with Robin Cook, leader of the house. The two became firm friends. Forth's instinctive dislike of authority always shone through: he would make animated gestures behind Duncan Smith's back at prime minister's questions, to the delight of Labour MPs. Unsurprisingly he was one of four frontbenchers dismissed by Michael Howard in 2003. It later became clear that Forth, who had been a supporter of David Davis in the Conservative leadership contest of 2005, disapproved of the consensual approach of the new tory leader, David Cameron. At a meeting of the backbench 1922 committee, Forth asked Cameron, 'I believe in lower taxes, grammar schools and big business. Mr Cameron, am I still a Conservative?' (*The Independent*, 20 May 2006).

Over the years Forth became renowned for his sartorial extravagance: with his garish ties and waistcoats, sideburns, and chunky jewellery, he resembled a latter-day Elvis Presley—fitting, given his love of the singer. His first marriage was dissolved in 1994, and later the same year he married a lawyer, Carroll Goff, in a $25 ceremony in New Mexico, thereby acquiring one stepson. He died of cancer at Charing Cross Hospital, London on 18 May 2006 and was survived by Carroll, his stepson, and the two daughters of his first marriage. MARK STUART

Sources P. Cowley, *Revolts and rebellions: parliamentary voting under Blair* (2002) • *The Times* (19 May 2006) • *Daily Telegraph* (19 May 2006) • *The Guardian* (19 May 2006) • *The Independent* (20 May 2006) • *WW* (2006) • b. cert. • m. cert. [1967] • d. cert.
Archives FILM BFINA, current affairs footage • BFINA, documentary footage | SOUND BL NSA, parliamentary recording
Likenesses A. Butler, photograph, 1988, PA Photos, London • photograph, 1990, PA Photos, London • photographs, 1995–9, Photoshot, London • D. Mansell, photographs, 2001–2, Camera Press, London • photographs, 2002, PA Photos, London • Flying Colours, photograph, 2005, Getty Images, London • D. Wimsett, photographs, 2005, Photoshot, London • obituary photographs
Wealth at death £119,372: probate, 25 June 2008, *CGPLA Eng. & Wales*

Foster, Trevor John French (1914–2005), rugby league player, was born at the Church House Inn, 14 Portland Street, Newport, Monmouthshire (the childhood home of the poet W. H. Davies), on 3 December 1914, the third son and sixth and youngest child of Richard Foster, innkeeper and former soldier, and his wife, Mabel Elizabeth Janet, *née* Bower. He was educated at St Joseph's convent school then Holy Cross School, Newport, leaving at fourteen to assist his father, whose sight was failing. He played rugby union at Holy Cross, and joined the former pupils' club Newport Hibernians in 1935, progressing via Pill Harriers to join Newport for the 1937–8 season. He was an instant success as a blindside wing-forward, leading Newport's scorers with twelve tries in thirty-four matches. Within a few months he played for the Possibles in the final Welsh trial and was travelling reserve for Wales against Ireland at Swansea.

Noticed by rugby league scouts even while still in junior rugby, Foster was visited at the start of the 1938–9 season by Harry Hornby, chairman of Bradford Northern. When Hornby put £400 on the table he initially declined, keen to secure his Welsh rugby union cap and concerned about his parents and the family business. His elder sister Freda told him, 'What if you break your leg next Saturday? You may never again get such a chance in your life. I'll look after Mum and Dad' (Foster, Gate, and Lush, 13). He later described signing as 'the greatest thing I ever did' (Collins, 55). Among the last of nearly 400 Welsh players to 'go north' between the wars, he formed a bond with Bradford that lasted long beyond his playing days.

Foster took rapidly to rugby league as a second row forward, finding that 'There was a lot more space and room to move. This suited my style of play' (Foster, Gate, and Lush, 18). Conscripted in 1940 into the King's Own Yorkshire light infantry, he joined the Army Physical Training Corps as a sergeant-instructor. Successive postings in Yorkshire allowed him, until posted to Egypt early in 1945, to continue playing rugby league with great success. Trophyless since 1906, Bradford won championships in 1940 and 1941 and the challenge cup in 1944. He also played for Wales in five rugby league internationals and, under the wartime dispensation allowing league players in the services to play union, seven union internationals. He also played in two league versus union matches played under union rules but won by the professional code.

Demobilized in 1946, Foster went that year with the first post-war Great Britain touring team, known as the Indomitables after the aircraft carrier on which they travelled, to Australia and New Zealand. Injury ruled him out of the Ashes tests but the captain, Gus Risman, reckoned him 'the most popular member of the party' (Foster, Gate, and Lush, 174) and he received, and declined, an offer to emigrate and play for South Sydney. Instead, aged thirty-one, though claiming (as he would until very old) to be two years younger, he returned to a leading role in Bradford's unprecedented feat of playing in three consecutive challenge cup finals at Wembley (1947–9). Foster scored tries in the two victories, in 1947 and 1949. On 13 June 1949 he married, at St Patrick's Church, Westgate, Bradford, Jean Florence Unsworth, a 23-year-old nurse from Bradford, and daughter of Leonard Unsworth, assistant racing manager. They had four children, Simon, Jane, Sara, and Bridget, and for five years from the late 1950s fostered Joseph Elston. They separated in the mid-1970s.

Always a prolific try-scorer by forward standards—his career total of 144 remained at his death a record for a Welsh forward—Foster peaked with twenty-two in 1947–8, including six in one match against Wakefield Trinity. Contemporaries admired his mix of power and pace with subtlety and fine judgement. The New Zealander Cecil Mountford called him 'one of the greatest forwards it has been my pleasure to watch', noting his 'ability to hold the ball until he could part with it to advantage and to take the tackle if such was inevitable, rather than let a colleague do so' (Foster, Gate, and Lush, 87 and 169).

Foster retired in 1955 after 432 matches for Bradford, 16 for Wales (including 7 as captain), and 3 Great Britain tests. By then he was the club's assistant coach and had been, in

1949, rugby league's first national coaching organizer before resigning to concentrate on his playing duties. In 1958 he became a director at Bradford and in 1960 chief coach, resigning both posts at the end of 1960 when significant decisions were made without consulting him. In 1963 Bradford went out of business. Foster, now coaching at Leeds after a short spell with Keighley, and his former team-mate Joe Phillips drove the public campaign that led to the club's re-formation and readmission to the rugby league in 1964. The local paper said that 'but for his enthusiasm … it is doubtful that the club would exist today' (*The Independent*, 6 April 2005). This was the most public expression of a remarkable record of service to his adopted community—as an education welfare officer from 1957 to 1981, youth sports coach, and active supporter of the Bradford Police Club for Young People—that earned copious recognition late in life. He was the first recipient (in 1998) of the lord mayor of Bradford's lifetime achievement award, appointed MBE in 2001, and awarded an honorary doctorate by Bradford University in 2002, the same year that a road near Bradford's Odsal Stadium was named Trevor Foster Way.

Foster remained a vigorous and genial presence at Bradford matches, acting as timekeeper from 1986 until 2004. Aged eighty-nine he had to be dissuaded, on a wet day when he had no raincoat, from accompanying charity walkers on the Bradford leg of a trek around rugby league grounds. Only three days before his death he attended the launch of a book celebrating his life. A lifelong Catholic, he appeared as Christ in a 1956 pageant at Odsal and in 2001 received the Benemeriti medal from Pope John Paul II for his work in the church. He died on 2 April 2005, the same day as the pope, in Bradford Royal Infirmary following a heart attack. He was survived by his wife, Jean, two daughters, and a son, his daughter Jane having died in 1992. HUW RICHARDS

Sources R. Gate, *Gone north: Welshmen in rugby league*, 2 (1988) • N. Williams, *Bradford Northern: the history, 1863–1989* (1989) • G. Moorhouse, *A people's game: the centenary history of rugby league football, 1895–1995* (1995) • D. Hadfield, *Up and over: a trek through rugby league land* (2004) • S. Foster, R. Gate, and P. Lush, *Trevor Foster: the life of a rugby league legend* (2005) • *The Times* (5 May 2005) • *The Independent* (6 April 2005) • *Daily Telegraph* (20 May 2005) • T. Collins, *Rugby league in twentieth century Britain* (2006) • b. cert. • m. cert. • d. cert.

Likenesses obituary photographs

Wealth at death £85,042: probate, 5 July 2005, *CGPLA Eng. & Wales*

Fournier, Robert Charles Privett (1915–2008), potter, was born on 16 March 1915 at 5 Mount Road, Wimbledon, Surrey, the son of Alphonse Robert William Fournier (1884–1954), a woodworking engineer who helped to build aircraft in the First World War and later motor cars, and his wife, Helen Maude, *née* Privett (1890–1965), who became a Labour alderman. It was a happy childhood. At grammar school Fournier did well in art and also composed poetry, which astonished his teacher who refused to believe he had written it. In Fulham he became a member of an amateur dramatics company where, in addition to acting, he painted the scenery. Keen to live in the country, he moved to Hertfordshire with his then partner, Sylvia, but their plans to settle were thwarted when they bought a piece of land from a con man and lost all their money. For a time he and Sylvia worked as farm labourers, horrifying their neighbours by living together in a shed.

Having refused to enlist following the introduction of conscription in the Second World War, Fournier was arrested and imprisoned in Wormwood Scrubs prison, where, as the bombs fell on London, he helped to write and produce the prisoners' magazine. The death of his only brother, Victor, a navigator in the Royal Air Force, in a plane crash over Wales, served to confirm his pacifist beliefs. Intent on pursuing a career in art he modelled animals seen in London Zoo. Enthralled by clay, on his release from prison he attended evening classes at the Central School of Arts and Crafts in London, coming under the watchful eye of Dora Billington, an outstanding teacher and potter. Far from following the established approach that was based on an aesthetic of quietude advocated by Bernard Leach, she encouraged a more eclectic, challenging view that included Mediterranean and industrial wares. Finding it difficult to afford the fees, Fournier took a job as a technician at the school, becoming Billington's assistant.

In 1946 Fournier set up Ducketts Wood Pottery in Hertfordshire where he produced slipware, tin-glaze, and later mosaics. In 1948 he established the pottery department at Goldsmiths' College, London. There he met Sheila Lord (1930–2000), one of his students, a divorced schoolteacher, and daughter of Robert Cook, railway clerk. They married on 22 July 1961. For a time they had a studio in Greenwich before moving to Castle Hill in Kent in 1965, where they produced tableware as well as making individual pieces. Aware of the growing educational interest in ceramics, Fournier issued 500 colour slides of historical ceramics, then a revolutionary educational aid much used by schools and individual potters. In 1971 they settled in the beautiful village of Lacock in Wiltshire, leasing, on a peppercorn rent, an old workhouse owned by the National Trust, carrying out much needed extensive renovation.

At Lacock Fournier consolidated his ceramics, producing what became his signature pieces, a range of 'pebble' pots that were based on natural form. With a sure understanding of the organic structures of stones, rocks, and plants, he translated these into clay through the use of simple, hand-built or moulded dish shapes or tall flattened bottles. These were decorated with areas of unglazed clay and poured textured white glaze, and dotted with small patches of rich, saturated colour. He was particularly renowned for producing a vibrant turquoise blue. The pots were successfully shown at galleries in Britain, Germany, and France.

In addition to potting, Fournier pursued his interest in writing. A book on building electric kilns with clear instructions and much practical advice dispelled the mystique around constructing simple but efficient structures.

As an inveterate compiler of information relevant to studio pottery he was assiduous in scouring available technical texts, bringing it together and presenting it in dictionary form. Titles included *The Illustrated Dictionary of Practical Pottery* (1952), *The Illustrated Dictionary of Pottery Form* (1981), and *The Illustrated Dictionary of Pottery Decoration* (1986). Later he collaborated with Eric Yates-Owen on *British Studio Potters' Marks* (1999), a thoroughly researched and comprehensive survey of the stamps and marks used by studio potters in Britain. Ever curious about the history and diversity of studio ceramics, he collaborated with John Anderson to make films of Rosemary and Denise Wren, Ladi Kwali, and David Leach. He also filmed Isaac Button, one of the last surviving makers of traditional terracotta garden pots. In line with his interest in film, as a founder member and council member of the Craftsmen Potters Association he arranged three successful film festivals showing potters' films from round the world. These were exhilarating events in introducing diversity and thought into what was often seen as the narrow world of studio pottery. He also organized the Craftsmen Potters Association archive at Aberystwyth University.

In 1987 the Fourniers retired from potting and settled in a more convenient if less exciting semi-detached property in Market Lavington, near Devizes. Visits to ancient sites in Crete and other Mediterranean islands enabled them to pursue their interest in early ceramics, while, as ardent wine buffs, they enjoyed wine tastings. Following Sheila's death in 2000 Robert Fournier continued to write, completing several novels and starting a memoir, which remained unfinished. He did, however, record his life story for the British Library National Sound Archive.

Slightly built and with a mischievous look, Robert Fournier was an amusing and wry companion, his success as a writer often overshadowing his fine and inventive work as a potter. By their very nature some potters are lifelong rebels, often selecting their profession because of its quirky, 'alternative' lifestyle. Such is the case with Fournier. He was a lifelong pacifist and atheist, whose decision to become a potter was, in part, a refusal to compete in what he saw as an increasingly consumer-led society. He died in Market Lavington on 19 January 2008.

EMMANUEL COOPER

Sources *The Independent* (12 March 2008) · *The Times* (20 March 2008) · personal knowledge (2012) · private information (2012) · b. cert. · m. cert.
Archives SOUND BL NSA, National Life Story Collection: Crafts Lives, interview
Wealth at death under £260,000: probate, 20 May 2008, *CGPLA Eng. & Wales*

Fowden, Sir Leslie (1925–2008), plant biochemist, was born on 13 October 1925 at Birch Hill House, Wardle, Rochdale, Lancashire, the only child of Herbert Fowden (1878–1960), an iron turner at Turner Brothers, ironfounders, and his wife, Amy Dorothy (1891–1960), a cotton minder and daughter of Frank Goodridge Rabbich, a school caretaker and former baker. At the time of his birth registration his parents lived at 133 Royds Street, Rochdale. He was brought up a Baptist, but was never baptized. After education at Rochdale grammar school, Fowden (pronounced *Foeden*) won a state scholarship to read chemistry at University College, London, in 1943. Part of his intensive two-year wartime degree course was undertaken at the Aberystwyth campus of the University of Wales, where the chemistry department was evacuated. He graduated with first-class honours in 1945 after the department had returned to London. He continued at University College, working under Christopher Kelk Ingold on a kinetic study of aliphatic nucleophilic substitution, for which he was awarded his doctorate in 1948. On 9 July the following year, at the Methodist chapel in East Ham, he married a fellow chemistry student, Margaret (Peggy) Oakes (1923–2006), daughter of Arthur George Murell Oakes, fireman, who worked as a chemistry teacher except when their two children, Abigail and Jeremy, were young.

Fowden could easily have made a research career as a physical organic chemist as part of the influential 'Ingold school'. Instead he began work in the Medical Research Council's human nutrition research unit in 1947, and this stimulated what became a lifelong interest in plant chemistry. The fiasco of the post-war Labour government's Tanganyika groundnuts (peanuts) scheme from 1946 to 1951 serendipitously provided the opportunity for Fowden's ground-breaking discoveries in the early 1950s. His initial research on the protein content of peanuts (*Arachnis hypogaea*) led to the discovery of a new amino acid, 4-methyleneglutamine, in 1951, and this was followed by the isolation of more than fifty other non-protein soluble nitrogenous compounds from different fruits, nuts, and algae. Many of these substances were found to be toxic when absorbed by animals, fungi, and bacteria, and therefore potentially useful in a wide range of biocides. He spent many years investigating the structure, metabolism, and biosynthesis of these amino and imino acids in plants using the analytical techniques of paper and ion-exchange chromatography, nuclear magnetic resonance, and spectroscopy, and identifying the enzymes that prevented plants from self-harm.

In 1950, on Ingold's recommendation, Fowden was appointed a lecturer in plant biochemistry in the botany department at University College, with promotions to a readership (1956–64), and a personal chair (1964–73). He acted as dean of the faculty of science from 1970 to 1973 and, unusually, he was made an honorary fellow of University College in 1966. During this London period he also held visiting appointments at Cornell University (1955), the Biochemical Institute in Helsinki (1957), the University of California at Davis (1963), and the University of Hong Kong (1967). He was elected a fellow of the Royal Society in 1964 and served on its council from 1970 to 1972.

At the end of 1971 Fowden was asked by Lord Rothschild to become the first chief scientist in the Ministry of Agriculture, Fisheries, and Food, but he turned the offer down because he was not wholeheartedly in favour of Rothschild's policy of pushing scientific research into the marketplace. However, on being appointed director of the

Rothamsted Experimental Station in Harpenden in 1973 in succession to Sir Frederick Bawden, he found himself heading a private institution largely financed by the government-customer-client principle. Although the administration of such a large research institution took him away from the laboratory bench, Fowden provided inspirational leadership by reading and criticizing all of his colleagues' manuscripts before publication. Under his leadership Rothamsted was twice awarded the queen's award for technological achievement, in 1976 and 1980, for its development of synthetic pyrethroid insecticides. In 1986 Rothamsted and the Long Ashton Research Station at Bristol were merged to form the Institute of Arable Crops Research. By the time of his retirement in 1988 Fowden had extended the range of Rothamsted's agricultural research and its commercial activities and ensured its financial soundness. As well as publishing nearly 200 papers, he edited eight monographs on agricultural and environmental issues.

Fowden deeply believed science to be a global activity. In retirement he travelled and lectured widely as chairman of the plant chemistry working group division (1987–90) of the International Organization for Chemical Science in Development, which helped to train phytochemists in developing countries to exploit their crops and biotechnology, and as chairman of the British Council's agricultural and veterinary advisory committee (1987–95). His many advisory positions included one at the Royal Botanic Gardens, Kew, where he was also a trustee (1983–93). He was knighted in 1982 for his services to agriculture and awarded an honorary doctorate by the University of Westminster in 1993. In addition he was elected a foreign member of the Deutsche Akademie der Naturforscher Leopoldina, a corresponding member of the American Society of Plant Physiologists, and chairman of the Phytochemical Society of Europe.

Fowden never lost his Rochdale accent. While his work was of profound international importance, his colleagues chiefly remembered him as being 'cheerful, friendly, direct, and unpretentious' (*ChemUCL Newsletter*). He died from renal and heart failure at Etheldred House care home, Clay Street, Histon, Cambridgeshire, on 16 December 2008 after coping with Parkinson's disease for some years, and was cremated at Cambridge crematorium on 29 December. He was survived by his two children. The main lecture theatre at Rothamsted had been named after him in 1987.

W. H. Brock

Sources *The Times* (22 Jan 2009) · *ChemUCL Newsletter* (2009) · Fowden papers, Rothamsted Research, Harpenden, Hertfordshire · UCL, student and staff files · University of Westminster archives · Burke, *Peerage* · *WW* (2009) · private information (2012) [Abigail Fowden, daughter; P. Lea] · b. cert. · m. cert. · d. cert.
Archives Rothamsted Research, corresp., papers, speeches
Likenesses R. Shephard, oils, 1987, Fowden Hall, Rothamsted Research, Harpenden, Hertfordshire · obituary photographs · photograph, repro. in *Memoirs FRS* · photographs, Rothamsted Research, Harpenden, Hertfordshire, Fowden collection
Wealth at death £1,790,110: probate, 23 June 2009, *CGPLA Eng. & Wales*

Fowles, John Robert (1926–2005), author and museum curator, was born on 31 March 1926 at Waygate, 37 Fillebrook Avenue, Westcliff-on-Sea, Essex, the only son and elder child of Robert John Fowles and his wife, Gladys May, *née* Richards. While his father commuted into London, where he managed the family tobacco firm, Allen and Wright, his mother cheerfully assumed the traditional role of housewife, looking after their small but comfortable semi-detached home and the son who would remain their only child until the late arrival of a daughter, Hazel, in 1942.

Fowles enjoyed a conventional middle-class childhood, attending Alleyn Court preparatory school in Westcliff-on-Sea, where he demonstrated an aptitude for both learning and sports. Among the teachers at the school was his mother's brother Stanley, who took his nephew on nature expeditions into the countryside, hunting for caterpillars and lappet-moths on the Thames estuary marshes. The experience helped to develop a lifelong interest that equalled if not surpassed his passion for literature. Indeed, the two pursuits would often coincide: his first published essay, 'Entomology for a schoolboy', which appeared in the Alleyn Court school magazine in 1938, offered an obvious foreshadowing of his first novel, *The Collector*, and through his life he regularly found opportunities to write about the nature that he loved.

In 1939 Fowles won an exhibition to Bedford School. Having enjoyed an unusually sheltered and serene childhood, he found the experience of being a boarder at public school a shock. After enduring a year of homesickness and bullying, he was withdrawn from the school for a term, which coincided with his family evacuating to Ipplepen, a village halfway between Newton Abbot and Totnes in Devon. It was a sudden, dramatic change in his circumstances that reinforced his sense of nature as a restorative refuge and also marked the beginning of a strong identification with the west country, from where his mother's family had come. He returned to Bedford for the spring term of 1941 with a new-found resilience that enabled him to resume his school career with considerable success. He eventually became captain of cricket and head of school. Responsible for imposing discipline on 500 boys, he carried out his duties with an outward seriousness and respect for the rules of the school, but this display of conformity and convention hid a more sensitive and dissenting side. He would later compare his character in these years to a caddis-fly larva, which builds around itself a tough protective casing out of whatever surrounding material happens to be available.

In 1944 Fowles left Bedford to join the Royal Marines. After completing his officer training, he was posted to Okehampton camp on Dartmoor as an instructor in charge of training commando units. Prizing the opportunity that the post offered to explore the natural world he loved, he considered continuing his military career into peacetime, but was persuaded by a visit from the mayor of Plymouth, Isaac Foot, to take up a place at Oxford. In 1947 he began at New College, where he read French and German, although he soon dropped German

John Robert Fowles (1926–2005), by Tomas Watson, 2001

to focus on French language and literature; in later years he would cite his dislike of the *Lieder* evenings of the German department as the reason. His time at Oxford was a period of significant self-discovery, in which a thirst for adventure caused him, once and for all, to cast off the skin of the rather conservative-seeming public school boy and Marine officer. A friendship with a fellow student and committed Marxist, Fred (Podge) Porter, caused him to challenge many of his previous preconceptions, laying the ground for views that would mature into a radical socialist outlook.

As transforming an experience was a visit to the south of France during the long vacation of 1948. Befriending an elderly French millionaire, Monsieur Jullié, and his young companion, Micheline Gilbert, Fowles was invited to join the crew of their yacht, as it travelled along France's Mediterranean coast. Confiding details of a past in the resistance and a present divided between her rich lover and a husband in Paris, Micheline provided the young Oxford student with an insight into the complexities of grown-up life. Fowles would later confess a 'calf love' for Micheline; there was no prospect of his feelings being returned, but another lesson in his sentimental education quickly followed when he began an affair with the yacht's young Danish cook, Kaja Juhl, thus completing a memorable summer. During the long vacation of the following year Fowles joined an ornithological trip to the Finnmark region of Norway, which had been organized by the naturalist Peter Scott's Severn Wildfowl Trust. Journeying to the Arctic tundra and fir forests, Fowles encountered a northern landscape of spectacular solitude that, as much as his Mediterranean sojourn, helped to stir the imagination of the future novelist.

At Oxford Fowles found himself free to think about, and to engage with, the world around him. The desire to express this new independence of thought tilted him decisively into becoming a writer. The journal that he began to keep consistently from this time marked the beginning of a long and determined literary apprenticeship, which also expressed itself in a continuous output of short stories, poems, plays, ideas for film scripts, and various other fragments of writing.

After graduating with a second-class degree in 1950, Fowles, with the help of his tutor at New College, Merlin Thomas, secured a year-long post as a *lecteur* at Poitiers University. While becoming a published writer had emerged as his chief ambition, entries in his journal for this period reveal the exacting standards that would put off his début for many years: 'At twenty-five I have created nothing that I can venture to publish. All of it is derivative, or faulty in technique or conception' (*Journals*, 1.108). Arriving in Greece the following year to teach English at the Anargyrios and Korgialeneios school on the island of Spetses, Fowles set to work on a novel, 'Journey to Athens'. In his own words 'a jewel, a Treasure Island, a paradise' (*Journals*, 1.150), Spetses would play a critical role in determining both his career and his life. It introduced him to his future wife Elizabeth, *née* Bradley (*d.* 1990), who arrived on the island with her husband Roy Christy and their young daughter Anna. (She was the daughter of Edgar Bradley, electrical engineer.) It also helped him to break away from the impasse of 'derivative' writing: the unpublished 'Journey to Athens' itself may have marked only one more stage in his apprenticeship, but what he saw, found, and did in Greece provided him with the inspiration for the novel that would, after many mutations, eventually be published as *The Magus* (1965). If falling in love with Elizabeth in such an idyllic setting made the period in Spetses a highly romantic, fulfilling time for Fowles, it was also an extremely painful one, with the blossoming of their relationship involving the break-up of another. Fowles eventually married Elizabeth at Hampstead register office on 2 April 1957, but there was a heavy cost as Elizabeth struggled through a difficult divorce and separation from her daughter.

Having returned with Elizabeth to England in July 1953, Fowles taught for a year at Ashridge College in Hertfordshire, and then, in 1954, became a teacher of English at St Godric's secretarial and language college in Hampstead, London. There he would remain until the successful publication of his first novel, *The Collector*, in 1963. Turned into a Hollywood film, starring Terence Stamp and directed by William Wyler, the recipient of three academy awards, the novel instantly established Fowles as a leading novelist on both sides of the Atlantic. Although over the course of his career Fowles would enjoy a huge worldwide audience, such fame was not something that he had consciously courted. His second book, *The Aristos* (1964), a collection of numbered philosophical observations after the manner of Pascal's *Pensées*, was an example of how he would always follow his own instinct as a serious writer rather than the market. It was this uncompromising attitude that would help him over the next twenty years to push forward the boundaries of modern fiction in a series of works that were never content to repeat past success but always sought to experiment with the narrative form.

Embracing his new career as a best-selling author, Fowles in 1965 left London with Elizabeth to live near the town of Lyme Regis on the Dorset coast. The move provided him with easy access to the nature and wildlife he loved, but also encouraged a new passion for local history. He referred to the collection of his different selves as the John Fowles Club, but whether writer, naturalist, or historian, those selves all found a common source in an extreme sensitivity to environment and a flair for describing it. Another way Fowles would explain this was to speak of 'the domain'—the garden, literal or figurative, where one was free to wander. This sense of domain accounted for the often strong autobiographical vein in his novels. Just as *The Magus* drew on his experience as a teacher on Spetses, *The French Lieutenant's Woman* (1969) explored the past of the town in which he lived, and the eponymous hero of *Daniel Martin* (1977), who is a screenwriter, provided another obvious alter ego.

For the first few years of life in Dorset the domain was to be found at Underhill Farm. The house stood to the west of Lyme, on a geologically unstable stretch of coast known as the Undercliff. Overlooking the coast, the fields of the farm ran down to the cliff's edge. The sea's expanse complemented a rugged landscape that, inaccessible to human habitation, gave the impression of having been made over entirely to nature. Fowles derived a profound contentment from this setting, in his journals describing it as 'a huge, complex poem' (*Journals*, 1.646). But the taste of paradise would be short-lived. When in February 1968 a large area of the farm slid into the sea, Fowles and his wife, Elizabeth, were forced to leave. Moving to Lyme Regis, they made their new home in Belmont House. A large Georgian property situated high above the town, it overlooked the Cobb, the harbour that Fowles's novel *The French Lieutenant's Woman* would make famous.

Published in 1969, *The French Lieutenant's Woman*, which won the W. H. Smith award, was a huge critical and commercial success, remaining on *The New York Times* best-seller list for over a year. But although it firmly established its author as one of Britain's most important novelists, Fowles himself felt increasingly remote from what he regarded to be the narrow concerns of the literary world, with the often restrictive criteria that it applied to writers. After the appearance of a volume of poems in 1973 offered some defiance of this tendency to pigeonhole, Fowles published a collection of long stories, *The Ebony Tower*, in 1974, and then the novel *Daniel Martin* in 1977, but through the decade his fiction writing formed an increasingly intermittent part of a literary output that, in such works as *Shipwrecks* (1974), *Islands* (1978), and *The Tree* (1979), was as notable for its engagement with the natural world.

In 1978 Fowles was appointed curator of Lyme Regis's local museum, the Philpot. Although the position was intended to be honorary, he made of it a full-time occupation, as he set about organizing repairs to the dilapidated building and cataloguing a rich and varied collection of fossils, local artefacts, and old photographs. His work as local historian and naturalist was interspersed with long trips to Greece or France, which had remained continuing sources of inspiration since his first discovery of them as a young man. Although Fowles published only two more novels, *Mantissa* (1982) and *A Maggot* (1985), he remained as industrious a writer as ever, producing a steady stream of essays, translations, reviews, forewords, and introductions. Gathered together in the collection *Wormholes* (1998), they formed a mosaic of varied but passionately pursued interests that reflected a wilfully eclectic cast of mind.

In 1988 Fowles suffered a serious stroke and two years later his wife, Elizabeth, died. But over time he rediscovered an equilibrium, which was greatly aided by his marriage on 3 September 1998 to his second wife, Sarah Smith (*b.* 1943/4), advertising director, and daughter of Peter Smith, farmer. In the last years of his life Fowles prepared for publication two remarkable volumes of journals (2003 and 2006). Forthright and uncompromising, they were highly controversial, but, in the words of one reviewer, amounted to 'what may come to be seen as one of the very best of his works' (*Literary Review*, Oct 2003). After many years of poor health he died of heart failure at Axminster Hospital, Devon, on 5 November 2005. He was survived by his second wife, Sarah. He did not believe in an afterlife. Thirty years earlier, he had named his new home, Underhill Farm, *Nil manet*, 'Nothing remains', aware of what lay in store for this house on a cliff-face even as he took possession of it. Careless of his fame and reputation, he would undoubtedly have taken the same attitude to his place in posterity, although the quality of his work will ensure that his name lasts longer than most. CHARLES DRAZIN

Sources D. L. Vipond, ed., *Conversations with John Fowles* (1999) • J. Fowles, *The journals*, ed. C. Drazin, 2 vols. (2003–6) • E. Warburton, *John Fowles: a life in two worlds* (2004) • *The Times* (8 Nov 2005) • *Daily Telegraph* (8 Nov 2005) • *The Guardian* (8 Nov 2005) • *The Independent* (8 Nov 2005) • *WW* (2005) • personal knowledge (2009) • private information (2009) [D. Sharrocks, F. Porter, R. Payne] • b. cert. • m. certs. • d. cert.

Archives Dorset History Centre, papers relating to Lyme Regis • Exeter University Library, photocopies, corresp., and diaries • Ransom HRC | FILM BFINA, 'The magus', *Robinson country*, T. Smith (director), Channel 4, 9 Aug 1984 • BFINA, 'Dorset', *The literary island*, G. Greenwood (director), Channel 4, 2 July 1991 • BFINA, current affairs footage • BFINA, documentary footage • BL NSA, 'The return of the magus', *c*.2000 | SOUND BL NSA, interview with M. Barber, *c*.1977, C1141/9–10 • BL NSA, *Third ear*, interview with C. W. E. Bigsby, BBC Radio 3, 25 Feb 1992, B9106/2 • BL NSA, documentary recordings

Likenesses photographs, 1970–85, Getty Images, London • photographs, 1970x79–1999, Rex Features, London • R. Mayne, bromide print, 1974, NPG • photographs, 1987–2001, Camera Press, London • G. Bird, portrait, 2000, priv. coll. • T. Watson, oil on linen, 2001, NPG [*see illus.*] • obituary photographs

Wealth at death £1,481,463: probate, 5 June 2006, *CGPLA Eng. & Wales*

Fox [*née* Henderson], **Aileen Mary**, **Lady Fox** (**1907–2005**), archaeologist, was born on 29 July 1907 at 12 Kensington Square, London, the eldest of three daughters of Walter Scott Henderson (1871–1945), a solicitor, and his wife, Alice Livingstone, *née* McClean (*d.* 1966). She was educated at Downe House School, Berkshire (1921–5), and, after a court presentation, read English at Newnham College, Cambridge (1926–9). Early continental travels with her father had sparked her interest in archaeology. After graduation she obtained an introduction to the inspector of ancient monuments, J. P. Bushe-Fox, and started unpaid work at the Roman site at Richborough: in the 1930s there was no formal archaeological training in Britain. She gradually became well known among the rising generation of archaeologists and on 6 July 1933 married Cyril Fred *Fox (1882–1967), director of the National Museum of Wales at Cardiff, who was knighted in 1935. They had three sons. She collaborated in her husband's fieldwork in south Wales and initiated her own projects, notably excavations at Caerleon Roman fortress, published in *Archaeologia Cambrensis* (1940). These experiences established her interest and expertise in later British prehistory and the Roman occupation of Britain. During the Second World War she lectured in archaeology at University College, Cardiff.

In 1945 Aileen Fox was invited to undertake rescue excavation on bombed sites in the Roman city of Exeter, in which she used a range of pioneering open area methods. This led to *Roman Exeter: Excavations in War-Damaged Areas, 1945–7* (1952). She became lecturer in archaeology at the University College of the South West at Exeter in 1947. On her husband's retirement in 1948 the family moved to Exeter, where she remained as senior lecturer until her retirement in 1972, five years after her husband's death. Throughout her time at Exeter (which obtained university status in 1955) she promoted the teaching of archaeology with a strong practical bias.

South-west England in the late 1940s was an open research field to a dynamic archaeologist, and Aileen Fox was known for her energy. On Dartmoor there had been no systematic research for decades and her excavations of settlements at Kestor and Dean Moor, published in the *Transactions of the Devonshire Association*, remain classics. A series of papers established significant regional variations among Iron Age hillforts. With William Ravenhill, she investigated a range of Roman military sites, and produced the first evidence of the Roman army's presence in Cornwall, at the fort of Nanstallon near Bodmin. She drew all this research together in her significant synthesis *South West England* (1964), written in her distinctive, clear and definite style. She continued rescue work in Exeter but by the late 1960s the scale of archaeological work was changing. She was instrumental in setting up the Exeter Archaeological Field Unit, later Exeter Archaeology, which in 1971 produced dramatic proof of the presence of Legio II Augusta in the cathedral close. The publication *The Legionary Bath-House and Basilica and Forum* was both dedicated to, and prefaced by, her. Successive directors of the unit owed much to her practical help and encouragement. She helped revitalize the Devon Archaeological Society and was elected its president for 1963–4. She also served as a vice-president of the Council for British Archaeology.

By Fox's retirement in 1972 local archaeological provision was much expanded, largely due to her efforts. She felt the need for a new arena for research and moved to Auckland, New Zealand, and left her local successors, mainly in positions she had helped establish, to 'get on with things' (in her own words). In New Zealand she found a small but thriving archaeological community to which she could make a major contribution. She remained for ten years, first as visiting lecturer at the university, then as acting archaeologist at Auckland Museum, and finally in a voluntary capacity. Her research in New Zealand ranged from excavations on Maori pas—in some ways similar to British hillforts—to studies of artefacts. Significant publications were *Prehistoric Maori Fortifications* (1976) and *Carved Maori Burial Chests* (1983). Her colleagues contributed to an affectionate Festschrift, *A Lot of Spadework to be Done*, on her return to England in 1983.

Aileen Fox was elected a fellow of the Society of Antiquaries of London in 1944. A highlight of her later years in England was the award by Exeter University of an honorary doctorate of letters in 1985. Another valued award was honorary membership of the Prehistoric Society in 1998. She remained active in archaeological life in Devon, publishing papers well into her late eighties. She suffered from ill health in her last years and died at the Royal Devon and Exeter Hospital in Exeter on 21 November 2005, following a stroke. Her body was cremated on 29 November at the Devon and Exeter crematorium, Topsham, Exeter. Her final work was her delightfully readable autobiography, *Aileen: a Pioneering Archaeologist* (2000). This is a graphic inside portrait of a career that brought about major developments in the understanding and organization of archaeology in two very different areas, south-west England and New Zealand, and made her a valued influence on scholars and amateurs in both areas. She was survived by her three sons. HENRIETTA QUINNELL

Sources W. L. D. Ravenhill, 'Aileen Fox: an appreciation', *Proceedings of the Devon Archaeological Society*, 37 (1979), 3–6 • A. Fox, *Aileen, a pioneering archaeologist: the autobiography of Aileen Fox* (2000) • *The Independent* (16 Dec 2005) • *The Times* (21 Dec 2005) • *The Guardian* (20 Jan 2006) • H. Quinnell, 'Aileen Fox, 1907–2005', *Cornish Archaeology*, 43–4 (2004–5), 203–9 • H. Quinnell, 'Aileen Fox: an obituary', *Proceedings of the Devon Archaeological Society*, 64 (2006), 348–51 • J. Davidson, V. Maxfield, and H. Quinnell, 'Aileen Fox: a bibliography of published works', *Proceedings of the Devon Archaeological Society*, 64 (2006), 352–59 • personal knowledge (2009) • b. cert. • m. cert. • d. cert.

Archives Newnham College, Cambridge | SOUND BL NSA, millennium memory bank, interview with E. Hawkey, 14 Dec 1998, 1CDR0009265

Likenesses A. Sorrell, group portrait, oils, *c.*1946 (with family), priv. coll. • obituary photographs • photograph, repro. in Ravenhill, 'Aileen Fox', facing p. 3

Wealth at death £589,621: probate, 9 Jan 2006, *CGPLA Eng. & Wales*

Fox, Levi (**1914–2006**), historian and conservationist, was born on 28 August 1914 at Woolrooms, Worthington,

Leicestershire, the sixth of seven children of John William Fox, coalminer, and his wife, Julia Sophia, *née* Stinson. He was educated at Ashby-de-la-Zouch grammar school before proceeding in 1933, with scholarships, to Oriel College, Oxford, where he read history; he graduated with first-class honours in 1936. Research awards from Oxford and Manchester universities led to articles and other publications on medieval Leicestershire. He was appointed Coventry's first archivist in 1938, and on 27 August the same year he married Jane Richards (1914–2002), whom he had known since he was a boy (she was the daughter of another miner, John William Richards). The Methodist ceremony reflected his background. For some time he had been a lay preacher, later retaining his faith but without formal expression. They had a son and twin daughters.

Establishing Coventry's record office enabled Fox to further his historical interests, but after the outbreak of the Second World War he had to pack up many archives for safety. Luckily most of the medieval documents were moved to Stratford. Following the devastating air raids on Coventry in 1940 he was tasked with supervising food distribution in the city, where some 60,000 people had been made homeless; this was a valuable and never forgotten experience. In 1941 he served as an instructor in the Royal Army Ordnance Corps but, on health grounds, soon returned to civilian life. Scouring the bombed cellars of offices in the city centre for archives, he was credited by a later city archivist with saving a lot of extremely important Coventry records for posterity (*Coventry Evening Telegraph*, 23 Sept 2006).

In 1945 Fox became director of the Shakespeare Birthplace Trust in Stratford upon Avon, Warwickshire, responsible then for four houses linked with the dramatist's family on whose admission fees from visitors the organization depended for its income. The trust also maintained a library and archive relating mainly to Shakespeare and his town. Fox's directorship lasted forty-four years, during which the trust transformed its historic houses into major heritage attractions, extended its educational mission, and gained an international profile. The eighteen full-time staff, and some part-timers, he inherited grew to over two hundred by the time he retired in 1989; and he witnessed annual numbers of visitors rise from about 150,000 to 1 million.

In his first decade Fox refurbished the Shakespeare houses, raising the integrity and appeal of their displays. In 1949 he persuaded his trustees to take a bank loan and purchase Hall's Croft, believed to be the home of John Hall and his wife Susanna, Shakespeare's eldest daughter; after restoration the building opened to the public in 1951. Fox also pursued a policy of acquiring property near the Shakespeare houses, primarily for conservation purposes but also as a long-term investment. The purchase in 1968 of Glebe Farm, adjacent to the supposed girlhood home of Mary Arden, Shakespeare's mother, turned out to be particularly fortunate since evidence discovered in 2000 proved it to be the Arden homestead.

A high point of Fox's career was creating the Shakespeare Centre, to replace the trust's inadequate headquarters. He worked closely with its architect on the design, supporting a modernistic approach rather than a traditional building, as favoured by some trustees. Overlooking the Shakespeare Birthplace garden, the centre accommodated offices, study facilities, and the libraries of the trust and the Royal Shakespeare Theatre. Its opening on 22 April 1964 was a key event in Stratford's quatercentenary celebrations of Shakespeare's birth, organized by a committee led, inevitably, by Fox. Among his achievements was persuading the Post Office to break with custom and allow Shakespeare to appear with the monarch on commemorative stamps. In recognition of his work for the quatercentenary he was appointed OBE, though he noted in his memoirs that many people thought he deserved a higher award. In 1980–81 he oversaw the completion of a coach terminal serving the Shakespeare Birthplace and an extension to the Shakespeare Centre, which improved amenities for visitors and educational facilities.

Throughout his career Fox found time for research, writing, and lecturing. Aside from hosts of guidebooks, pocket anthologies, and pamphlets relating to Shakespeare and Stratford, he published histories of the town (1953) and his Ashby school (1967), and edited, for the Dugdale Society, three collections of Warwickshire records, including *The Correspondence of the Rev. Joseph Greene* (1965) and *Minutes and Accounts of the Corporation of Stratford-upon-Avon, 1593–1598* (1990). He was secretary and general editor of the Dugdale Society from 1947 to 1977, then chairman until his death. His strong sense of duty, allied to his aptitude for managing committees, resulted in his holding leading offices, often for years, on other historical societies, Shakespeare associations, conservation groups, and school boards. These involvements were another channel for the administrative skills and entrepreneurial energy, combined with academic interests, with which he led the trust, and helped to sustain the public recognition he enjoyed.

In his roles Fox pursued what he believed was right and opposed what he judged unacceptable, whether harmful development, shoddy work, or threats to grammar schools. Outward affability masked an essentially private person, whose centre of being was his own family, and the extended family of trust staff, most of whom he personally appointed. He died at his home of almost fifty years, Silver Birches, 27 Welcombe Road, Stratford-upon-Avon, on 3 September 2006, of cerebrovascular disease and renal failure, and was buried in Stratford cemetery after a funeral in the Guild Chapel, next to Shakespeare's old school in Stratford. Many of his papers and books were bequeathed to the trust. He was survived by his three children. ROGER PRINGLE

Sources L. Fox, *The Shakespeare Birthplace Trust: a personal memoir* (1997) • *Coventry Evening Telegraph* (5 Sept 2006); (23 Sept 2006); (9 Oct 2006) • *The Times* (12 Sept 2006); (25 Sept 2006) • *The Guardian* (12 Oct 2006) • *Stratford-upon-Avon Herald* (9 Nov 2006) • *Leicestershire Archaeological and Historical Society Transactions*, 81 (2007) • personal knowledge (2010) • private information (2010) • b. cert. • m. cert. • d. cert.

Archives Shakespeare Birthplace Trust, Stratford upon Avon | Herbert Art Gallery and Museum, Coventry, Coventry history centre, academic and personal papers • Leics. RO, research and personal papers | FILM Shakespeare Birthplace Trust, Birmingham University degree congregation, 12 Dec 1986, video tape 94.5 | SOUND BL NSA, documentary recording • Shakespeare Birthplace Trust, interview, 8 July 1991, DR 730/23

Likenesses P. Vincze, bronze plaque, 1989, Shakespeare Centre, Stratford upon Avon • obituary photograph • photographs, Shakespeare Birthplace Trust, Stratford upon Avon

Wealth at death £546,313: probate, 11 April 2007, *CGPLA Eng. & Wales*

Fox, Sir Michael John (1921–2007), judge, was born at Lyndon Lodge, Golden Manor, Hanwell, Middlesex, on 8 October 1921, the youngest of the four children of Michael Fox, civil servant, and his wife, Norah (or Nora), *née* Houlihan. His father came from Dublin, his mother from Killarney. He was brought up in Hanwell. In 1930 an older brother died in a shooting accident and a month later his father died. His mother remarried in 1932. In his stepfather, John Gallagher, a civil servant in the Inland Revenue, Fox found a true substitute father who introduced him to the world of books and encouraged him to read widely. He was an avid reader throughout his life.

Fox was educated at Drayton Manor School, then a recently founded county grammar school. From there he went to the London School of Economics to read law, but his studies were interrupted by the Second World War. His poor eyesight did not permit him to serve in the armed services, but from 1943 to 1945 he was an assistant principal in the Admiralty's intelligence section headed by Rodger Winn, who later became a lord justice of appeal. Fox's work consisted of processing material obtained from the Enigma machine at Bletchley Park. In 1945, instead of continuing his studies at the London School of Economics, he applied for a place at Magdalen College, Oxford. An interview with Magdalen's president, Sir Henry Tizard, gained him entry; he graduated BA in jurisprudence in 1947 and BCL in 1948. He had as his tutor the distinguished legal scholar John Morris; it was probably because of Morris that Fox was encouraged to try for the Chancery bar.

Fox was called to the bar by Lincoln's Inn in 1949. He became the pupil of John Sparrow, the future warden of All Souls, in the élite Chancery chambers at 3 New Square, Lincoln's Inn, which had a lord chancellor, Viscount Maugham, and a master of the rolls, Lord Greene, among its previous heads, and whose then head was Sir Cyril Radcliffe. Radcliffe, shortly after Fox's arrival, achieved the rare distinction of being appointed a law lord directly from the bar. Fox provided Sparrow's biographer with a description of those chambers in 1949 that exemplifies his characteristically dry humour. The chambers

> had a flavour of their own. They were extremely shabby, not to say dirty, but they had a great reputation because of the Maugham, Greene, Radcliffe succession; the three most eminent lawyers of their time. The Clerk was Mr Thresher. The great years had left on him a certain glaze of prosperity. On arrival at Chambers, he went to his room and telephoned his stockbroker. It used to be said that anybody could be a successful clerk to the likes of Maugham, Greene and Radcliffe. But I think there is no doubt that he was a highly competent (and tough) clerk. He was extremely civil to me in a crushing sort of way. (Lowe, 124)

As a junior in those chambers Fox gradually built up a good practice of typical Chancery work involving property, trusts, tax, and estate duty, leavened with cases involving wards of court. The 1950s were not an easy time for the Chancery bar, primarily because of the unfortunate reputation of some of the senior Chancery judiciary. However, the appointment of a fresh generation of Chancery judges and the passing of the Variation of Trusts Act 1958 were to bring a sea change in prosperity for Chancery barristers like Fox.

On 5 June 1954, at the parish church of Cuckfield, Sussex, Fox married Hazel Mary Stuart (*b.* 1928), then a junior barrister in the common law chambers of Harry Phillimore, the future lord justice of appeal. Her father, John Matthew Blackwood Stuart, a civil engineer, had died in 1941 and in 1945 her mother, Joan, had married Tom Denning, then Mr Justice Denning. Fox met her when after a moot in Magdalen presided over by its most famous alumnus he chanced to encounter Denning walking round the Magdalen gardens with his stepdaughter. The autobiography of Robin Dunn, a member of the same chambers and another to reach the Court of Appeal, records that Fox and she were married to the chagrin of all the members of those chambers. His wife enjoyed a distinguished legal career of her own. They had three sons and a daughter.

In 1968 Fox took silk. A man of transparent integrity, he coupled a deep knowledge of the law with an analytical mind that enabled him to see through the intricacies of a case to the nub of the problem. In the 1960s and early 1970s, when taxes were punitively high and many of the ablest Chancery minds were engaged on how to keep their clients' wealth out of the Inland Revenue's clutches, he was in great demand for his wide knowledge of fiscal law and his skills as an advocate. But it was not only in tax cases that Fox was briefed. He appeared in some of the leading cases in other fields, such as *Gissing* v. *Gissing* (1970), a seminal case concerning a wife's entitlement to a beneficial share of the matrimonial home placed in the husband's sole name; Fox appeared in the House of Lords as *amicus curiae*.

In 1975 Fox was appointed a High Court judge in the Chancery Division, receiving the traditional knighthood. He remained modest and self-effacing. In court he was a model of patience, courteous, quick to grasp the point and slow to interfere, preferring to let counsel get on with their submissions. His judgments were characterized by the clarity of their exposition of the facts, the rival contentions, and his reasoning. His style was elegantly simple and lucid. Appeals from his court rarely succeeded and after six years as a High Court judge he was elevated to the Court of Appeal and sworn of the privy council. He sat in the Court of Appeal for eleven years. Many cases attracting public attention came before him. They included the *Gillick* v. *West Norfolk and Wisbech Area Health Authority* case (1984), in which the court held that a doctor could not give contraceptive advice to a girl under sixteen without her parents' consent; that decision was narrowly reversed by the House of Lords the following year. His more permanent contribution to the law lay in the leading judgments he gave in several cases deciding important issues of property and trust law, such as *Re Duke of Norfolk's Settlement Trusts* (1981), *Ashburn Anstalt* v. *Arnold* (1988), and *Agip (Africa) Ltd* v. *Jackson* (1990). In 1992, after breaking his leg in a fall, he took early retirement.

Fox and his wife resided in Notting Hill and Nuthanger Farm, near Ecchinswell, Hampshire, the latter made famous by Richard Adams's book *Watership Down*. His final years were marred by his failing eyesight and vascular dementia. He died at St Mary's Hospital, Praed Street, Westminster, on 9 April 2007, of bronchopneumonia, and was survived by his wife and their four children.

PETER GIBSON

Sources R. Dunn, *Sword and wig* (1993) • J. Lowe, *The warden: a portrait of John Sparrow* (1998) • *Daily Telegraph* (14 April 2007) • *The Times* (23 April 2007) • *The Guardian* (26 April 2007) • Burke, *Peerage* • *WW* (2007) • personal knowledge (2011) • private information (2011) • b. cert. • m. cert. • d. cert.

Likenesses S & G Barratts, photograph, 1982, PA Photos, London • obituary photographs

Wealth at death £2,719,457: probate, 21 Sept 2007, *CGPLA Eng. & Wales*

Franca, Celia [*real name* Nita Celia Franks] (**1921–2007**), ballet dancer, choreographer, and ballet director, was born on 25 June 1921 at 57 Nicholas Street, Mile End, London, the daughter of Solomon Franks, boot salesman, later ladies' outfitter, and his wife, Gertie, *née* Feigenbaum. Her parents were of Jewish descent. She started dance lessons at the age of four, and won scholarships to the Guildhall School of Music and Drama and the Royal Academy of Dance. She made her professional début as a tap dancer in the musical comedy *Spread It Abroad*, aged fourteen. Its choreographer, Walter Gore, recommended her to Marie Rambert, and she joined the Ballet Rambert in 1936, also attending Rambert's school, where she was taught by Stanislas Idzikowsky, Vera Volkova, and Antony Tudor. Having adopted the stage name Celia Franca, over the next few years she danced in over two dozen ballets with the company, including Tudor's acclaimed *Jardin aux lilas* (1936) and *Dark Elegies* (1937), and his *Suite of Airs* (1937, broadcast on television), a revival of Frederick Ashton's *Les masques* (playing both the wife and the lady friend), Frank Staff's *Peter and the Wolf* (1940), and work by Ninette de Valois, Andrée Howard, and others. She also produced her own choreography, notably *Constanza's Lament* (1938), to Beethoven's music, and *Midas* (1939) to a score by Elizabeth Lutyens.

Following the closure of Ballet Rambert in 1941 as a result of the disruption of the Second World War, and after a brief engagement with the International Ballet,

Celia Franca (1921–2007), by Janine, 1960

Franca joined Sadler's Wells, initially replacing the injured June Brae. Among her most notable roles were as the Queen in Robert Helpmann's *Hamlet* (1942), the Prostitute in his *Miracle in the Gorbals* (1944), Wrath in Ashton's *The Quest* (1943), and the Spider in Howard's *Le festin de l'araignée* (1944). She was reputed by many to be the company's best dramatic dancer. For Sadler's Wells Theatre Ballet (when the main company moved to Covent Garden she decided she would be bored by three months of *Sleeping Beauty*, so did not follow) she choreographed *Khadra* (1946), to Sibelius's music, and *Bailemos* (1947) to Massenet's. In 1947 she joined the small Metropolitan Ballet as soloist and ballet mistress, choreographing *Dance of Salome* (1949) and *Eve of St Agnes* (1950), both televised. After performances with the Ballet Workshop she then returned briefly to Ballet Rambert. Meanwhile, on 27 February 1941, at Watford register office, she had married a fellow Ballet Rambert dancer, Leo Kersley (*b.* 1920), son of Edwin Charles Kersley, art dealer. They subsequently divorced, but remained close friends.

In 1950 Ninette de Valois was asked to recommend someone to run a new national Canadian ballet. There were then already two Canadian ballet companies, the Russian-influenced Volkoff Ballet and the largely amateur Winnipeg Ballet, but a group of Canadians had decided that they would like a new ballet company, in the style of Ballet Rambert or Sadler's Wells (who had toured triumphantly in North America in 1949). De Valois recommended Franca, who for the next twenty-three years (1951–74) was artistic director and effective shaper of the new National Ballet of Canada, based in Toronto. At first she found the going tough—the ballet's first base was a dilapidated building with pigeons in the rafters, rats in the basement, and barely functioning heating, and Canadians, used to the more flamboyant and athletic style of Russian ballet, did not initially take to Franca's more nuanced repertoire—but she persevered, and succeeded in building a company of international standing. She nurtured local talent, especially through the National Ballet School, which she set up in partnership with Betty Oliphant, but also formed long associations with such stars as Erik Bruhn (with whom she had worked at the Metropolitan Ballet) and the temperamental Rudolf Nureyev (whom she disliked on a personal level).

Franca danced many leading roles with the National Ballet until 1959, when she handed over to a succession of dancers she had trained herself, though she continued to dance the occasional role. She also choreographed, her notable creations including versions of *Nutcracker* (1964) and *Cinderella* (1968, which was televised, and won Canada's first Emmy award in 1970). In 1964 she oversaw the company's move to the O'Keefe Centre in Toronto. She also organized and accompanied many international tours by the company. Always demanding as a choreographer and taskmaster and direct in speech, she was increasingly dictatorial in the way she ran the company; one of her leading stars, Karen Kain, described her as 'ferocious' (*The Independent*, 21 Feb 2007). Already exhausted by constant battles with her board of directors over finance and other matters and disappointed by the reception of some of her more daring productions, she was eventually manoeuvred into resignation in 1974 (blaming a falling out with Betty Oliphant, whom she suspected of trying to usurp her). She nevertheless, after a few years, and particularly after Frederick Ashton's lover Alexander Grant was appointed the company's artistic director, continued to choreograph for the National Ballet, and in 1978 she published a history of the company in collaboration with the photographer Ken Bell. She also served as joint artistic director of the Ottawa School of Dance.

Franca was appointed an officer of the order of Canada in 1967, and a companion of the order in 1985. She was married twice while in Canada: in 1952 to a theatre technician, Hubert Anderson (*d.* 2004), whom she divorced in 1954; and in 1960 to the clarinettist James Morton (*d.* 1997). She died in Ottawa on 19 February 2007. She had no children. The Celia Franca Centre, the Canadian National Ballet School's new studio facilities, had been opened in 2006. She was described by the choreographer James Kudelka as 'the icon of ballet in Canada' (*The Guardian*, 22 Feb 2007).

ALEX MAY

Sources C. Franca and K. Bell, *The National Ballet of Canada* (1979) • J. Neufeld, *Power to rise: the story of the National Ballet of Canada* (1996) • *Daily Telegraph* (21 Feb 2007) • *The Independent* (21 Feb 2007) • *The Guardian* (22 Feb 2007) • *The Times* (28 Feb 2007) • b. cert. • m. cert. [1941]

Likenesses photographs, 1942–53, Getty Images, London, Hult. Arch. • Janine, photograph, 1960, The National Ballet of Canada Archives [*see illus.*] • photographs, 1978–2001, PA Photos, London • obituary photographs

Francis, Frederick William [Freddie] (**1917–2007**), cinematographer and film director, was born on 22 December 1917 at 32 Offord Road, Islington, London, the son of Frederick William Francis, railway worker, and later commission agent, and his wife, Mary Ann, *née* Wilkins. About the age of thirteen he developed an interest in photography, and when he left school at sixteen he was apprenticed to a stills photographer. However, a visit to a film studio ignited a passion for film-making and he took a job as clapper boy at British International Pictures at a time when British cinema was experiencing one of its periodic booms. He slowly worked his way up through the camera department, and on the eve of the Second World War was already an experienced camera assistant, recently having served on Carol Reed's acclaimed *The Stars Look Down* (1940).

Francis spent seven years in the army, gaining considerable experience with the army kinematograph unit, making training and propaganda films. On 12 May 1940, at St Luke's Church, Islington, he married Gladys Florence Dorrell (*b.* 1919), daughter of William James Dorrell, caterer. They had a son, but the marriage ended in 1961. After the war Francis re-entered the British film industry when it was once more in an optimistic mood, his first assignment being second-unit photography on *The Macomber Affair* (1947). He was fortunate, from the late 1940s onwards, to serve as camera operator for two of the industry's leading cinematographers. He assisted Christopher Challis in the shooting of Michael Powell's *The Small Back Room* (1949), *The Elusive Pimpernel* (1950), *Gone to Earth* (1950), and *The Tales of Hoffman* (1951), and then worked with Oswald Morris on the John Huston pictures *Moulin Rouge* (1952) and *Beat the Devil* (1953). Francis later acknowledged the significance of this experience and the opportunity to work with two such adventurous directors. The demanding Huston worked Francis to near death on the difficult production of *Moby Dick* (1956).

With ambitions beyond simply operating a camera, Francis accepted the opportunity to serve as director of photography on *A Hill in Korea* (1956), directed by Julian Aymes. He built a reputation on some modest productions, including Joseph Losey's *Time without Pity* (1957), and quickly established himself as a leading cinematographer, especially with his trend-setting work in black and white on the 'new wave' dramas *Room at the Top* (1959) and *Saturday Night and Sunday Morning* (1960). He then extended his range to two period dramas shot in black and white Cinemascope, winning an Oscar for his stunning visual treatment of D. H. Lawrence's *Sons and Lovers* (1960), while brilliantly evoking the chilling atmosphere of *The Innocents* (1961), based on the celebrated novella by Henry James. In the latter film Francis captured a remarkable intimacy within the widescreen frame and his work on this production ranked among the cinematographer's own proudest achievements. On 20 April 1963 Francis married Pamela Anne Mann (*b.* 1927), a script supervisor, and daughter of Raymond Claude Mortlake Mann, proprietor of a finance company. They had a son and a daughter.

Francis's ambition led him to directing, and in this capacity he worked on three minor films in 1962: the uninspired comedy *Two and Two Make Six*, the low-budget horror *The Brain*, and some additional scenes for *Day of the Triffids*, a production that had fallen into trouble. It was with his success on his fourth film, *Paranoiac* (1963), that he was unrewardingly typecast in the modestly budgeted horror film. He worked extensively for the leading production companies in the genre, contributing Dracula and Frankenstein tales to the lucrative cycle of Gothic horrors produced at Hammer, and varied shockers for its rival Amicus. However, his best work at Hammer was a series of contemporary psychological thrillers made in the wake of Hitchcock's *Psycho* (1960), which began with *Paranoiac* in 1963 and included *Nightmare* (1964) and *Hysteria* (1965); while his most influential productions at Amicus were a cycle of anthology horror stories, including *Dr Terror's House of Horrors* (1965), *Torture Garden* (1967), and *Tales from the Crypt* (1972), films that later acquired cult status. He worked regularly with the horror star Peter Cushing, for whom he developed a great admiration, and also with his son from his first marriage, Kevin, who had formed Tyburn Pictures and produced *The Ghoul* (1975) and *Legend of the Werewolf* (1975). But Francis was essentially unhappy within the limitations of genre film-making. Too often he was shackled to intractable material and unsympathetic producers, and had to face the professional humiliation of seeing his name attached to such 'stinkers' as *The Deadly Bees* (1967), *Trog* (1970), and *Vampire Happening* (1971). He was greatly disappointed when his own cherished production, the perverse black satire on class and the family, *Mumsy, Nanny, Sonny and Girly* (1970), confused audiences and critics, and flopped. During this period he returned only once to the camera, shooting the moody *Night Must Fall* (1964) as a favour to its director, Karel Reisz.

In the mid-1970s the low-to-medium budget horror film lost its market and Francis himself became disenchanted with the genre:

> I used to get invited to all these horror film festivals, and I'd start talking about the directors I most admire, the Billy Wilders and the William Wylers, and they didn't know who I was talking about … And I suddenly realised that most of these people were only interested in horror—not just horror films, but horror pure and simple. Well, you know, that wasn't for me. I'm not a weirdo at all. (*Sight and Sound*, Nov 1992)

Francis gave up directing for a number of years, but was eventually lured back into a highly successful second career as a leading lighting cameraman in Britain and Hollywood. The opportunity arose when the American director David Lynch wanted to shoot *The Elephant Man* (1980) in black and white, and Francis was approached for his experience and expertise in what was rapidly becoming a lost art. It proved the last major monochrome film made in Britain. He shot two further productions for the idiosyncratic Lynch, *Dune* (1984) and *The Straight Story* (1999), the final picture on which Francis worked. Other significant productions included *The French Lieutenant's Woman* (1981), which reunited Francis with Karel Reisz, and Martin Scorsese's remake of *Cape Fear* (1991), where the director relied on the cameraman's developed sense of the Gothic. Francis won a second Oscar for his work on the American Civil War epic *Glory* (1989), making him the only British cinematographer to pick up Academy awards for both black-and-white and colour cinematography. In 1997 he received the lifetime achievement award of the British Society of Cinematographers, and the following year was granted the prestigious international award of the American Society of Cinematographers. He never lost the ambition to direct and gratefully accepted the opportunity to lead the production of *The Doctor and the Devils* (1985), a strong moral tale of grave robbing that he had harboured for a number of years; however, it was not a success, possibly the victim of a producer's tinkering to raise the requisite horror levels.

Francis also worked regularly as a director in television, contributing to such hit series as *The Saint*, *Man in a Suitcase*, and *The Champions* in the 1960s, and supplementing dwindling feature assignments in the 1970s with work on *The Adventures of Black Beauty* and *Star Maidens*. Late in his career, and as a personal tribute, he photographed a television documentary on his friend Peter Cushing. In time the best of his own horror films acquired the status of classics of the genre. The films offered a pronounced compositional sense, incorporated long graceful camera movements, and managed a visual richness that belied their limited budgets, raising them alongside the very best of horror film production in Britain at the time. He died of complications arising from bronchopneumonia at the Atfield House nursing home, St John's Road, Isleworth, London, on 17 March 2007; he was survived by his wife Pamela and his three children. ALAN BURTON

Sources W. W. Dixon, *The films of Freddie Francis* (1991) · 'Gothic shadows: Freddie Francis talks with Kevin Jackson', *Sight and Sound* (Nov 1992) · P. M. Jensen, 'Freddie Francis', *The men who made the monsters* (1996) · D. Petrie, *The British cinematographer* (1996) · J. Rigby, *English gothic: a century of horror cinema*, 2nd edn (2002) · *Daily Telegraph* (21 March 2007) · *The Independent* (21 March 2007) · *The Times* (22 March 2007) · b. cert. · m. certs. · d. cert.

Likenesses photographs, 1946–93, Getty Images, London · photographs, 1963–2000, PA Photos, London · R. Blanshard, photographs, 1999, Camera Press, London · obituary photographs · photograph, Photoshot, London

Wealth at death £110,028: probate, 23 Nov 2007, *CGPLA Eng. & Wales*

Frankel, William (1917–2008), barrister and newspaper editor, was born Woolf Frankel at 1A Eastman Court, Whitechapel, London, on 3 February 1917, the second of three sons of Isaac Frankel, a street trader and synagogue beadle, and his wife, Hannah (Anna), *née* Lacker. His parents had arrived from the Galician area of Poland a few years before his birth. Isaac Frankel changed his surname on arrival in London to that of his mother's maiden name, having been advised that his own, Kiesel, sounded 'very foreign' (Frankel, 1). The Frankel family lived in impoverished conditions at a variety of addresses in London dictated primarily by Isaac's chequered work career. Living in an Orthodox Jewish milieu (an upbringing that flavoured and influenced his life), Frankel attended a succession of East End schools. But, at the age of eleven, the unconventionality that was to be his hallmark showed itself when, after matriculation, he enrolled in the Polytechnic Secondary School in Regent Street. However, that institution failed to inspire any career ambition and he turned, in his sixth-form year, to the Davenant Foundation School, hoping it might provide him with the background in classics needed for admission to Jews' College, the training establishment for the Jewish ministry. But that school, too, bored young Frankel, and he left.

Frankel's first paid job after school, with an East End scrap merchant, did not last long. Nor did the next, as a warehouseman with a company importing Japanese goods. He was happier, but still without ambition, when, aged twenty, having moved through a couple of office posts with Orthodox Jewish organizations, he was appointed secretary of the Mizrachi Federation of Great Britain and Ireland, a leading religious Zionist organization. On 16 April 1939, less than five months before the outbreak of the Second World War, he married, in a ceremony at the prestigious Great Synagogue in the City, Gertrude Freda Reed (*b.* 1916), daughter of Louis Reed, a travelling salesman—and exhausted their savings with a wedding party at the Ritz Hotel. They had two children, Anne and John. Having moved to Cambridge in 1940 to escape the Blitz, Frankel and the Mizrachi Federation agreed to part company. Taking advantage of the wartime installation of the London School of Economics in Cambridge, and with the help of his wife's occasional earnings, fees from teaching Hebrew to local Jewish children, and sporadic family handouts, Frankel (who had been rejected as unfit for military service) enrolled in its law school. He graduated LLB with upper second-class honours. He later repaid what he felt was his debt to Cambridge by becoming a major fund-raiser for the university's Centre for Modern Hebrew Studies.

Back in London Frankel was called to the bar by the Middle Temple in 1944 while working for a year as assistant secretary to the foreign affairs committee of the Board of Deputies, the representative body of Anglo-Jewry. It was through this appointment that he established what was to be a life-long connection with the American Jewish Committee (a major Jewish advocacy group operating worldwide), whose London representative he became on a part-time basis, an engagement that, despite his membership of the Middle Temple and well-regarded chambers, gave him more satisfaction than his time at the bar. It was at an American Jewish Committee dinner that he first met the managing director (later chairman) of the *Jewish Chronicle*, David Kessler, who a few years later offered him the job of general manager at the paper, the world's oldest Jewish weekly newspaper (established 1841), which he took up in 1955. It was a surprise to Frankel and the staff of the *Jewish Chronicle* when, three years later, Kessler asked him to become editor.

At the time Frankel became editor of the *Jewish Chronicle* it was a worthy and respected communal journal, but he swore to make of it 'a stimulant for and accurate mirror of Jewish life' (Frankel, 122). He largely succeeded in his purpose, opening its columns to the best young Jewish writers of the day, vastly expanding the newspaper's foreign coverage, and bringing from Glasgow a young columnist, Chaim Bermant, whose weekly commentary on world Jewish affairs was to become for many years the most read column in the paper. Frankel, whose association with American Jewry had exposed him to new thinking about the nature and practice of the Jewish religion, was not averse to controversy in his columns, frequently challenging the authority of the established Orthodox rabbinate. One episode, which earned him both condemnation from the Jewish religious establishment and national recognition as a campaigning editor, was his support for Rabbi Louis Jacobs during the so-called Jacobs affair, beginning in 1961. Jacobs, a major young scholar, seen by some as a future chief rabbi, was barred by the chief rabbi, Israel Brodie, from taking up the post of moral tutor at Jews' College because of writings in which he rejected the divine origin of the Torah, the main part of the Hebrew Bible. Frankel put his personal and his newspaper's prestige totally behind Jacobs and was to the fore in the founding in 1964 of a new synagogue movement in Britain, Masorti, headed by Jacobs. Reflecting half a century later, Frankel wrote: 'I readily concede I may have been too passionate in my pro-Jacobs advocacy in the JC' (ibid., 171).

Frankel's first marriage ended in divorce in 1971, and on 16 December 1973 he married Claire Neuman of Baltimore, Maryland, who had three daughters from her former marriage. Four years later, in 1977, on his sixtieth birthday, Frankel (who had been made CBE in 1970) retired from the editorship of the *Jewish Chronicle*, though he maintained his connection, serving as chairman from 1991 to 1994. His years after giving up the editorial chair were among the most active of his life; they included service as a special adviser to *The Times* (1977–81), president of the Mental Health Review appeal tribunal (1978–89), and chairman of the Social Security appeal tribunal (1979–89), as well as an officer of a number of national and international Jewish organizations and a member of the governing bodies of various educational institutions. He took great delight in writing a weekly column for *The Statesman* of India, an association which lasted for over twenty years, and from 1982 to 1992 he edited an annual *Survey of Jewish Affairs* for the Institute of Jewish Affairs (later the Institute for Jewish Policy Research, of which he was a vice-president). He and his wife established a pattern of living at their home in Washington, DC, during the winter months and spending the summer at their apartment in Montagu Square, Marylebone, London (he was a regular at Lords during the cricket season). He published his memoirs, *Tea with Einstein and Other Memories*, in 2006, the title being taken from the occasion he visited the great scientist at home in Princeton in 1947; he had earlier published *Friday Nights* (1973), an anthology of *Jewish Chronicle* pieces, and *Israel Observed: an Anatomy of the State* (1980). In his final years, he developed Parkinson's disease. It was while walking in Washington on 18 April 2008 that he fell and suffered a cerebral haemorrhage from which he died. He was buried in London on 24 April 2008. A memorial service was held at the (Masorti) New London Synagogue, St John's Wood, on 12 June 2008. He was survived by his second wife, Claire, and his son, John, his daughter, Anne, having died in 1989 (a source of much grief in his later years). GEOFFREY D. PAUL

Sources W. Frankel, *Tea with Einstein and other memories* (2006) · *The Times* (24 April 2008); (26 April 2008) · *Jewish Chronicle* (24 April 2008); (19 June 2008); (1 May 2008) · *The Guardian* (25 April 2008) · *New York Times* (3 May 2008) · *The Independent* (27 June 2008) · *WW* (2008) · personal knowledge (2012) · private information (2012) · b. cert. · m. cert. [1939]
Archives U. Southampton L.
Likenesses obituary photographs
Wealth at death £2,842,138: probate, 15 Sept 2008, *CGPLA Eng. & Wales*

Franks, Sir Arthur Temple [Dick] (1920–2008), special operations and intelligence officer, was born on 13 July 1920 at 12 Heath Drive, Hampstead, London, the son of Arthur Franks, managing director of W. B. Dick Ltd, which evolved into Castrol, and his wife, Kate Isabel (Kitty), *née* Robins. His mother had wanted to name him Richard Arthur Franks but his father insisted on his being named Arthur Temple Franks instead. Despite this, Kitty still called her son Richard and he became known to his many family and friends as Dick. In 1934 his parents sent him to Rugby School and in 1938 he went to Queen's College, Oxford, obtaining a war-shortened law degree in 1940, before joining the Royal Corps of Signals in August that year.

Short-sighted but absolutely fit, Franks was commissioned into the Hertfordshire regiment in September 1941 and posted to the Middle East during 1942 as a battalion intelligence officer to the Libyan Arab force in the western desert. In July 1943, two months after the final defeat of axis forces in north Africa, he was promoted to staff captain and in September joined the Special Operations Executive (SOE), Britain's wartime clandestine sabotage agency. Based in Cairo, he undertook his special operations training for force 133, the cover name for SOE in the Middle East, and carried out his parachute training at military establishment 102 in Haifa, one of the first SOE training schools to have been opened overseas, moving to Italy when conditions allowed.

Franks's first operation for SOE was to have been to parachute into Hungary with a small party to locate an alleged reception group, but after several sorties no lights were seen and the operation was cancelled. Franks was then reassigned to carry out sabotage against enemy transport on the Danube and gather intelligence on the potential use of the river for the allies once the Germans were forced to abandon the Balkans. He was put in charge of a small party of saboteurs dropped just outside Sikole in Serbia on the night of 14–15 September 1944. Code-named 'Dolphin', the party moved to the headquarters of the 25th partisan division and with their permission began to interrogate river men who had been captured as prisoners of the partisans. Only ten days into his mission, however, Franks was alerted that elements of the Red Army were in the area and he realized that his original intention of sabotage could not now be carried out. As the Dolphin party was ordered back through the lines of advancing Soviet forces Franks and his team, along with a Russian escort, came under German counter-attack. Two drivers and a Red Army officer were killed, while one of Franks's team was captured although he subsequently escaped. The whole Dolphin party eventually returned to Bari on the night of 13–14 October, having managed to collect intelligence about the Danube, the effects of mining, and the steps taken by the Soviets towards river organization.

In early 1945 Franks returned to the United Kingdom and joined the team of instructional staff at Beaulieu, Hampshire, SOE's 'finishing school'. On 24 March that year he married Rachel Marianne Ward (1922–2004), a member of the Women's Royal Naval Service attached to SOE, and daughter of the Revd Arthur Easton Stanley Ward, clergyman. She would go on to play an important role at her husband's side throughout his career, and they had a son and two daughters. Their marriage had barely begun when the war in Europe ended in May 1945 and Franks was appointed diplomatic secretary to the political division of the British element of the Allied Control Commission for Germany. He found himself at the forefront of allied post-surrender planning to oversee de-Nazification and democratization but also increasing Western attempts to gather intelligence on Soviet activity in eastern Europe.

Franks was demobilized in June 1946, at first undertaking provincial press work for Staffordshire Sentinel Newspapers Ltd, and then joining the *Daily Mirror* in May 1948 as a sub-editor. As a married man with (then) two children Franks did not find his work in Fleet Street congenial, often having to work into the early hours of the morning. Only a year after joining the *Daily Mirror* he was recruited into the Secret Intelligence Service (SIS), or MI6 as it was popularly known. The qualities he had shown while working for SOE must have been attractive to SIS, an organization now fully engaged in the emerging cold war.

Franks's first overseas posting was to Cyprus in October 1952, where he covered Middle Eastern affairs. Despite his youth and relative inexperience he served in Tehran from 1953 to 1956, carrying out well the very difficult job of maintaining contact with the new young shah of Iran, who had just been restored to the throne. His wife, Rachel, was active socially while in Tehran and the couple proved popular then as subsequently within the diplomatic corps. His next major posting abroad was to Bonn in July 1962, where he stayed for four years and struck up a lifelong friendship with David Cornwell, the spy novelist known as John Le Carré. His posting to Bonn, a key station in SIS's targeting of Soviet bloc countries, indicated that senior management within SIS had come to regard him as one of the service's most outstanding officers among his peer group. During the 1970s his reputation continued to rise within SIS and he eventually became assistant chief of SIS in 1977. Throughout this period he showed himself to be an all-round performer, who could produce far-seeing plans coupled to realistic recommendations for practical action. One of his best attributes was his ability to identify the important while firmly rejecting the trivial.

It came as no surprise when Franks succeeded Sir Maurice Oldfield as chief of SIS in February 1978, a post he held until 1981. Reportedly he told his board of directors at his first staff meeting as chief that 'I want the Directors' Board to be a collegiate body. I will be listening to you, you will not be listening to me' (Davies, 287). As chief he sought to get the best out of his staff and to continue to develop good relations with Whitehall and, in particular, the Foreign and Commonwealth Office. Indeed he was regarded not only as a first-rate political operator but also as an able organizer with a sure touch for staff management and the gift of generating loyalty; it was these attributes that helped to continue to professionalize the service and kept morale high under his leadership. He was knighted KCMG in 1979, having been appointed CMG in 1967.

After his career in SIS had finished Franks accepted a job with the Wilkinson Group, advising on their overseas marketing of civil protection products. In retirement he purposely kept a low profile, refusing to talk about his career in SIS by making himself inaccessible to researchers and journalists. His principal interests lay in Aldeburgh, Suffolk, where he lived at Roefield, Alde Lane, and where he became captain of Aldeburgh Golf Club and was also chairman of the local British Legion. Throughout his life he always found time for his family, to whom he was devoted, and for the Travellers' Club, which he greatly enjoyed. He died of cancer of the liver at Aldeburgh Hospital, Park Road, Aldeburgh, on 12 October 2008; he was survived by his three children.

CHRISTOPHER BAXTER

Sources A. Glen, *Footholds against a whirlwind* (1975) • A. Glen and L. Bowen, *Target Danube: a river not quite too far* (2002) • P. H. J. Davies, *MI6 and the machinery of spying* (2004) • *The Times* (20 Oct 2008) • *Daily Telegraph* (20 Oct 2008) • *The Guardian* (28 Oct 2008) • *The Independent* (30 Oct 2008) • TNA: PRO, HS5/195–212 • *WW* (2008) • Burke, *Peerage* • b. cert. • m. cert. • d. cert.

Likenesses obituary photographs • photograph, repro. in www.specialforcesroh.com/awards-7061.html

Wealth at death £805,909: probate, 15 Jan 2009, *CGPLA Eng. & Wales*

Fraser, Sir (James) Campbell (1923–2007), industrialist, was born on 2 May 1923 at Dunard, Cawdor Crescent, Dunblane, Perthshire, the son of Alexander Ross Fraser, a post office clerk and later postmaster, and his wife, Annie McGregor, *née* McLaren. He was educated at McLaren High School in Callander and briefly at the University of Glasgow before being called up during the Second World War. He served as an RAF navigator from 1941 to 1945, and studied at McMaster University in Canada during training. Following demobilization he took a BCom degree at the Dundee School of Economics in 1950. On 12 July the same year, at Logie Kirk, Bridge of Allan, he married Maria Harvey (Myar) McLaren (1923/4–1995), a nurse, and a friend from his teens. She was the daughter of James Shands McLaren, motor driver. They had two daughters.

After his marriage Fraser moved to Liverpool as an economist for the Raw Cotton Commission, and two years later to the Economist Intelligence Unit in London. He helped bring together the handful of economists then working for businesses into the Business Economist Group. He also indulged what was a lifelong interest in journalism, carving out a parallel career as a freelance radio broadcaster that included presenting *Woman's Hour* on BBC radio. He earned the nickname Ten o'Clock Fraser for his insistence on early nights.

In 1957 Fraser crossed the road from the *Economist* offices to the headquarters of Dunlop, an international icon of British manufacturing that had held the first patents for pneumatic tyres, and was one of the world's largest manufacturers. After a short time as a public relations officer, then a little regarded skill, he moved quickly into marketing, and then the overseas division and caught the eye of the influential director (soon to be chairman), Reay Geddes. In 1967 he was given his management test—sent to New Zealand to close down operations. His achievement in rescuing the business instead led to rapid promotion to executive director in 1969, joint managing director in 1971, managing director from 1972, and executive chairman in 1978, the year he was knighted (and made a fellow of the Royal Society of Edinburgh).

Fraser took over as managing director of Dunlop at the moment when British industry, temporarily sustained by tariffs and imperial markets, was falling apart, and foreign competition reviving. Dunlop had expanded UK tyre production in the 1960s on the basis of forecast expansion but from 1972 British motor production declined and imports multiplied. Dunlop's setbacks were compounded by the 1973 oil shock and recession. The introduction of radial tyres, which lasted twice as long, increased the company's difficulties. The fact that Dunlop's continental competitors had also built up production and suffered similarly, with Michelin's losses dwarfing Dunlop's, made things worse. Fraser had been a member of the board that in 1971 backed a tie-up between Dunlop and Pirelli, but it proved disastrous, with Pirelli's losses bleeding Dunlop. Although it was hailed as a forerunner for European co-operation, by 1981 Fraser was being praised for the way he achieved its dissolution. Other problems were self-inflicted, and long-running. The company was slow in developing radials, and UK quality and productivity were poor: salesmen preferred supplies from Dunlop's continental factories. Fraser could reasonably claim that he started to rationalize ahead of many competitors, but it was too late and Dunlop's resources were too limited to succeed. In 1977 he hired Alan Lord, a civil servant previously in charge of national industrial policy, to accelerate the programme of closing factories and halving the UK workforce. But in 1983, with losses of a fifth of its capital and reserves in a year, the company sold its European tyre business to the Japanese company Sumitomo. It was against Fraser's wishes, but he was blamed by its largest, Malaysian, shareholder, which had its own ambitions, and he was dismissed.

The gravity of the crisis at Dunlop had not been appreciated when the gregarious and plausible Fraser agreed to become president of the Confederation of British Industry (CBI) in 1982, after vigorously promoting that organization as a counterweight to the trade union-dominated agenda of the 1970s. His term was fraught with embarrassment. He exhorted business 'to get off our butts, get on our bikes and improve our share of the world's market' (*The Times*, 9 Nov 1983) and pressed Japan to open its markets just as Sumitomo plotted its takeover of Dunlop. When he received a 21 per cent pay increase, swollen by a bonus for disentangling the Pirelli link, Fraser's criticism that Britain was 'bonkers on pay' (ibid., 8 Nov 1978) was rapidly quoted back. And his commitment to good industrial relations was questioned when the sale to Sumitomo cost 1000 jobs. His speeches expressing concern about unemployment rang hollow. He helped mend the CBI's bridges with the government of Margaret Thatcher but drew criticism for breaking convention in publicly backing her in the election of 1983.

Fraser's chairmanship of Scottish Television from 1975 to 1991 was more successful. He improved profits, and secured franchise renewal at a bargain price, while, as a former broadcaster, he took a lively interest in programming and was a keen supporter of Channel 4. He was a director of British Petroleum (1978–92), BAT Industries (1980–93), and many other companies, and an active trustee of *The Economist* (1978–2006). He maintained his Scottish links and served on the courts of three Scottish universities. Temperamentally he was a Conservative moderate who favoured employee participation, but his consensual style was overwhelmed by the scale of the economic storm that fell upon an over-extended company, far from alone in British industry for its poor productivity and quality. He lived latterly at 4 Silver Lane, Purley, Surrey, and died on 27 April 2007 at the Mayday Hospital, Croydon, of gastro-intestinal bleeding. He was survived by his two daughters. MARTIN ADENEY

Sources *Financial Times* (20 Sept 1983) · M. Adeney, *The motormakers* (1989) · *The Times* (11 May 2007) · *Daily Telegraph* (23 May 2007) · *The Guardian* (24 May 2007) · *The Independent* (18 June 2007) · www.royalsoced.org.uk/fellowship/obits/obits_alpha/fraser_c.pdf, 4 May 2010 · Burke, *Peerage* · *WW* (2007) · b. cert. · m. cert. · d. cert.

Archives U. Warwick Mod. RC, papers as president of CBI | FILM BFINA, current affairs footage | SOUND BL NSA, current affairs recording

Likenesses photograph, 1982, Photoshot, London · obituary photographs · photograph, repro. in www.royalsoced.org.uk/fellowship/obits/obits_alpha/fraser_c.pdf · photograph, repro. in www.ecademy.com/node.php?id=90805

Wealth at death £2,041,898: probate, 21 Aug 2007, *CGPLA Eng. & Wales*

Fraser, George Macdonald (1925–2008), journalist, novelist, and screen-writer, was born on 2 April 1925 at 48 London Road, Carlisle, Cumberland, the son of William Fraser, medical doctor, and his wife, Annie Struth, *née* Donaldson, nurse. His original aim, during his schooldays at Carlisle Grammar School and later at Glasgow Academy, was to read medicine at university. But he was an indifferent student and in 1943, feeling that he would

George Macdonald Fraser (1925–2008), by Neil Drabble, 1999

never amass the qualifications necessary to enter the University of Glasgow's medical school, he enlisted in the Border regiment and was sent to India. *Quartered Safe Out Here* (1992), his memoir of the Burma campaign, recounted his wartime experiences in some detail. Among other exploits he was hung upside down by his heels while strafed by Japanese sniper fire as he foraged for water, and promoted to lance-corporal on four occasions but three times returned to the ranks for minor infringements of army discipline. One of these involved losing a tea urn. Subsequently he was given a commission in the Gordon Highlanders and served with the regiment in the Middle East and north Africa. This period of his life offered material for the semi-autobiographical 'McAuslan' stories, collected in *The General Danced at Dawn* (1970), *McAuslan in the Rough* (1974), and *The Sheikh and the Dustbin* (1988).

After returning to Carlisle on demobilization in 1947 Fraser embarked on a career in journalism. This began with a post on the *Carlisle Journal*, then took him to Canada, where he worked on the *Regina Leader-Post*, and finally to Glasgow, where he moved with his family in 1953. On 16 April 1949 he had married Kathleen Margarette Hetherington, a reporter on a rival Carlisle paper, and daughter of George Hetherington, baker. They had three children. By the mid-1960s, however, Fraser had become disillusioned. Passed over for ultimate preferment on the leading Scottish newspaper, the *Glasgow Herald*, when it came under new ownership (he served as deputy editor between 1964 and 1969 and at one point rose to the position of acting editor) he determined, as he put it to his wife, 'to write us out of this' (private information).

Fraser's literary imagination had been stirred by preteenage exposure to sanguinary historical fiction, notably Raphael Sabatini's *Captain Blood*, which he read at the age of ten. This undoubtedly informed his first novel, *Flashman* (1969), supposedly one among a trunk-full of manuscripts discovered at a sale in Leicestershire, but in fact deriving from Fraser's own historical research. The distinguishing mark of the twelve-volume Flashman series, which found the villain of Thomas Hughes's morality tale *Tom Brown's Schooldays* purposefully yet pusillanimously at large at the upper levels of Victorian society, was its relish of historical detail. While its animating force was merely an inspired invention the world in which Flashman moved was sharply and convincingly laid out. To the comparatively rare spectacle of an unreal person intervening in a real world Fraser added a further refinement. Unlike the conventional heroes of historical fiction Harry Paget Flashman was a coward, a bully, and a satyromaniacal philanderer. The honours and decorations with which he was routinely showered (these included the Victoria Cross, a knighthood, and the thanks of parliament) were invariably the result of grotesque accidents. This worm's eye view of history gave the novels a significant internal dynamic. Knowing that Flashman was a self-advertised moral absence, the reader believed everything he said, on the grounds that he had no reason to dissemble. All this produced an acute, but often bitterly humorous, critique of the Victorian imperial project, in which the folly and mismanagement of some of its military endeavours was never allowed to disguise Fraser's transparent admiration for some of the personalities on display.

Although turned down by nearly every publisher in London, until its eventual acceptance by the firm of Herbert Jenkins, *Flashman*, which followed its anti-hero ingloriously through the First Afghan War of 1841–2, was an instant success, inspiring in P. G. Wodehouse what he called 'that-watcher-of-the-skies-when-a-new-planet-stuff' (book cover). Charlie Chaplin was also a fan. In later instalments Flashman starred in a reworking of Anthony Hope's Ruritanian romance of 1894, *The Prisoner of Zenda* (*Royal Flash*, 1970), mistakenly stormed the Russian guns at Balaklava (*Flashman at the Charge*, 1973), sailed a war canoe with Rajah Brooke in Borneo (*Flashman's Lady*, 1977), was the solitary survivor of Custer's last stand at the battle of Little Big Horn (*Flashman and the Redskins*, 1982), and assisted the US abolitionist John Brown at Harper's Ferry (*Flashman and the Angel of the Lord*, 1994). Among a riot of encounters with celebrated nineteenth-century personalities he became the intimate of Queen Victoria, Ulysses S. Grant, Bismarck, Palmerston, and Queen Ranavalona, the deranged and lustful monarch of 1840s Madagascar. The vigour of Fraser's prose led to comparisons with Robert Louis Stevenson and the tough-minded eighteenth-century Scottish novelist Tobias Smollett. A small part of his vast international fan-base—mostly Americans—believed that the books were genuine historical documents.

Meanwhile, from the early 1970s, and on the back of the Flashman series' success, Fraser pursued a yet more lucrative career as a Hollywood screen-writer. His credits included *The Three Musketeers* (1973) and its sequel, *The Four Musketeers* (1974), *Royal Flash* (adapted from his novel, and starring Malcolm McDowell and Britt Ekland, 1975), *The Prince and the Pauper* (1977), the James Bond vehicle *Octopussy* (1983), and *Red Sonja* (1985), featuring the young Arnold Schwarzenegger. As his Hollywood memoir, *The Light's On at Signpost* (2002), made clear, he came from a generation for whom the novelty of cinema never waned: the shaky transit of an ageing Gregory Peck across a restaurant foyer always had him delightedly turning his head. Fraser's other novels included *Mr American* (1980), *The Pyrates* (1983), *The Candlemass Road* (1993), and *Black Ajax* (1997), a spirited re-imagining of the career of the black Regency-era prize-fighter Tom Molineaux. He also wrote a history of the Anglo-Scottish border reivers, *The Steel Bonnets* (1971).

In personal dealings Fraser combined an occasionally rugged reserve with an extreme courtesy. He was devoted to his wife, Kathleen, to whom all the Flashman books were dedicated, to his sons, Simon and Nicholas, and to his daughter, Caro, herself a successful novelist, and doted on his grandchildren (who by the time of his death numbered eight). As he grew older, living in the tax exile's seclusion of the Isle of Man, his political and social views became steadily more hard-line. *The Light's On at Signpost* was interspersed by periodic teeth-gnashings on the subject of law and order, and on 'New Labour' and other abominations. Exposure to a typical Fraser audience, which tended to magnify and in some cases to distort these opinions, could occasionally unnerve the more literary of his admirers. A younger friend who conducted an interview with him at the National Army Museum, where the crowd consisted largely of serving soldiers, confessed that the experience made him feel 'vaguely homosexual and left-wing' (private information).

Apart from an OBE (1999) for services to literature and a belated fellowship of the Royal Society of Literature (1998) Fraser received little formal recognition for his work, the 1973 *Playboy* editorial award notwithstanding. He did not seem cast down by this neglect. A final novel, *The Reavers* (2007), appeared shortly before his death, of cancer, at Nobles Hospital in Strang on the Isle of Man on 2 January 2008. He was survived by his wife and children.

D. J. TAYLOR

Sources *The Times* (4 Jan 2008) · *Daily Telegraph* (4 Jan 2008) · *The Guardian* (4 Jan 2008) · *The Independent* (4 Jan 2008) · *WW* (2008) · personal knowledge (2012) · private information (2012) · b. cert. · m. cert.

Archives FILM BFINA, *Borderers*, W. Cartner (director), ITV, 9 Sept 1975 · BFINA, *South Bank Show*, B. Bee (director), ITV, 12 Nov 2000 · BFINA, current affairs footage

Likenesses photographs, 1982–2005, Rex Features, London · photographs, 1988–2006, Getty Images, London · N. Drabble, C-type colour print, 1999, NPG [*see illus.*] · obituary photographs · photographs, Camera Press, London

Fraser, Ian Edward (1920–2008), submariner, was born on 18 December 1920 at 79 Uxbridge Road, Ealing, London, the elder son of Sydney Fraser, marine engineer, and his wife, Florence Irene, *née* McKenzie. At the time of his birth his parents lived at 65 The Vineyard, Richmond, Surrey. He was educated at the Royal Grammar School, High Wycombe, and on the training ship HMS *Conway*. He

Ian Edward Fraser (1920–2008), by unknown photographer, 1946–7

entered the Merchant Navy in 1937, joining the Blue Funnel Line and going to sea as a cadet in the *Tuscan Star* and *Sydney Star*. He enlisted in the Royal Naval Reserve and underwent statutory training as a midshipman in the battleship *Royal Oak* in July 1939. After the outbreak of the Second World War he served in the destroyers *Keith*, *Montrose*, and *Malcolm*, taking part in the Dunkirk evacuations in May 1940 and the sinking of the German submarine U-651 in June 1941.

'For no valid reason which I can now recall' (*Frogman VC*, 84), Fraser volunteered for submarines and after serving in the elderly P35 and H43 went to the Mediterranean to join the *Sahib* (under Lieutenant J. H. Bromage) in the Fighting Tenth submarine flotilla. He was awarded a DSC for his contribution to several successful patrols which sank supply shipping and, in January 1943, a U-boat, U-301. At a lively party aboard a depot ship, Fraser suffered a broken bone in his foot when someone dropped a heavy brass ashtray. He thus missed *Sahib*'s final patrol when she was damaged and scuttled, all save one of her crew surviving to become prisoners of war. He was next appointed to the training submarine H44 as second in command at Londonderry where he responded to a signal from flag officer submarines calling for volunteers for 'special and hazardous service'. This was to lead to command of the midget submarine XE3 which, after crew training, was loaded with five others onto the former Clan Line heavy lift ship HMS *Bonaventure*, departing for the Far East in November 1944. Meanwhile on 26 June 1943 he had married Melba Estelle Hughes (*b*. 1922), who was serving in the Women's Royal Naval Service. She was the daughter of Stanley Kellett Hughes, commercial traveller. They were to have four sons and two daughters.

As part of the campaign to recover the Malayan peninsula from the Japanese, *Bonaventure*'s brood of midget submarines, now based at Brunei Bay, North Borneo, was set various tasks—to cut the telegraph cables to Saigon and Hong Kong and to sink the formidable cruisers *Takao* and *Myoko*, both of 10,000 tons with 8 inch guns, lying in the Johore Straits near Singapore dockyard. Fraser's three-man crew were Sub-Lieutenant William Smith (a New Zealander), Artificer Charles Reed, and a frogman diver, Leading Seaman James Magennis. XE3 was towed to the straits by the submarine *Stygian* while XE1 was towed by the *Spark*, XE3 to attack the *Takao* and XE1 the *Myoko*.

Slipping from the *Stygian* at 11 p.m. on 30 July, Fraser was confronted with an intricate and dangerous passage of some 40 miles, avoiding a known minefield and acoustic hydrophones. At 4.30 a.m. he hit the bottom and damaged the log when forced to dive hurriedly by a tanker and its escort that loomed out of the dark. He was able to negotiate the British anti-submarine boom which had been opened for an enemy vessel. As navigation buoys were unlit, he sat astride the semi-submerged casing for much of the passage, looking ahead with a pair of binoculars. At 12.50 p.m. he saw the target but was forced deep by a Japanese liberty-boat full of sailors. He actually hit the *Takao*'s hull with a clang, and had great difficulty forcing XE3 underneath amidships as the target was nearly aground fore and aft and the tide was falling. Magennis made his way out of the wet-and-dry airlock compartment but found that the *Takao*'s hull prevented the top hatch from fully opening, so had to take a deep breath, take off his diving set, get out, and then put it on again. He found that much marine growth had to be scraped off before the magnets on his limpet mines would adhere. With a slight oxygen leak in his diving gear, he returned via the wet-and-dry compartment, utterly exhausted. Fraser now tried to release the two large amatol explosive charges that were secured each side of the submarine, each weighing, in air, two tons. The starboard side stuck. Fraser wanted to go out to release it, but Magennis insisted he was the diver, took a large spanner, and after a long five minutes released the charge. Great difficulty was experienced in extricating the submarine. At one point Fraser thought they might have to abandon ship and face capture, but eventually he got XE3 out from under the *Takao*. Meanwhile XE1 had been delayed by patrol craft and was not able to precede XE3 as planned; it was likely that if XE1 had gone on past the *Takao* to reach the *Myoko*, she would have been returning as Fraser's charges detonated. She dropped her side charges near the *Takao* and both X-craft made it back to their parent submarines, reaching Labuan on 4 August. *Takao* sank onto the river bed with a huge hole in her hull. Ironically, the Japanese surrendered ten days later. Both Fraser and Magennis were awarded the VC, Fraser's citation saying that 'his courage and relentless determination to get right under the *Takao* were beyond praise'. Fraser was also appointed an officer of the United States Legion of Merit in 1945.

Fraser used his VC and underwater experiences to good effect. Immediately after the war he formed a troupe of frogmen who displayed their skills and re-enacted their wartime underwater exploits in a 20,000 gallon glass-sided tank at the Belle Vue Zoo in Manchester and then at other locations. In 1947 with other naval frogmen he formed Universal Divers Ltd, an underwater engineering company which he turned over to his brother in 1965. With others, he then formed North Sea Diving Services which met the needs of the offshore oil industry until the company was acquired by Blue Star Line in 1975; he then served on the board of Star Offshore Services until retirement in 1982. He remained in the Royal Naval Reserve until 1965, retiring with the rank of lieutenant-commander, having been awarded the Reserve decoration with long-service bar. He was appointed a justice of the peace for Wallasey in 1957 and elected a younger brother of Trinity House in 1980. In 1957 he published a memoir, *Frogman VC*, which dealt with his wartime exploits and his commercial struggles. He lived latterly at 1 Lyndhurst Road, Wallasey, and died of heart failure on 1 September 2008 at Arrowe Park Hospital, Birkenhead. He was survived by his wife, Melba, and five children, one daughter having predeceased him. GUY LIARDET

Sources I. E. Fraser, *Frogman VC* (1957) • E. N. Poland, *The torpedomen: HMS Vernon's story, 1872–1986* (1993) • A. Hezlet, *British and allied submarine operations in World War II* (2001) • *The Times* (3 Sept 2008) • *Daily Telegraph* (3 Sept 2008) • *The Independent* (4 Sept 2008) • *The Guardian* (11 Sept 2008) • *WW* (2008) • b. cert. • m. cert. • d. cert.

Likenesses obituary photographs • photograph, repro. in *Daily Telegraph* (2 Sept 2008); priv. coll. [*see illus.*] • photographs, repro. in Fraser, *Frogman VC*

Wealth at death under £49,000: probate, 10 Nov 2008, *CGPLA Eng. & Wales*

Fraser, Jill (1946–2006), theatre director, was born on 15 April 1946 at Ravenswood Nursing Home, Kentish Town, London, the daughter of Alec Fraser, actor–manager, and his second wife, Guinevere Blanche, *née* Fellowes, actress and singer. At the time of her birth her parents lived at 4 Chalcot Gardens, Hampstead. She attended South Hampstead high school, where she was head girl, and then won a scholarship to study stage management and theatre production at the Central School of Speech and Drama. After graduating she worked for the City of London festival, Liverpool Playhouse, and the Edinburgh festival, where she stage managed Frank Dunlop's production of *A Midsummer Night's Dream*. In 1971 she joined the stage management team of the Royal Shakespeare Company and went on to be Buzz Goodbody's first production manager at the opening of the Other Place in Stratford in 1974. She then worked for Welsh National Opera and the Actors' Company, and was administrator for the Cambridge Theatre Company, working with its artistic director, Jonathan Lynn. On 21 March 1980 she married James Edmund Sargant, who was then administering the Royal Shakespeare Company's move from the Aldwych into the Barbican Centre. Eleven years her senior, he was the only son of Sir (Henry) Edmund Sargant, solicitor and sometime president of the Law Society. They had a son, Sam (*b.* 1983), and a daughter, Charley (*b.* 1985).

In 1981 Fraser and Sargant bought the Watermill Theatre, a converted 1830s redbrick mill in Bagnor, just outside Newbury, Berkshire, from Judy Gollins, whose eldest son, David, had masterminded the conversion of the mill into a theatre in 1965. Fraser soon extended the performing schedule from twenty-three weeks a year to all year round. Between 1981 and 2006 she broadened the Watermill's repertory on an unprecedented scale, not only increasing the range of the theatre's work, but also touring both in the UK and to over twenty-one countries. In the year 2004–5 the Watermill reached over 100,000 people with its work in the theatre, in schools and colleges, and on tour. This took in rural touring, workshops for schools and further education colleges, and an active and highly successful youth theatre. Fraser fostered work involving primary school children, people with special needs, the homeless, and a number of community projects in which adults, children, and artists could work side by side.

Fraser helped John Doyle to pioneer a new style of musical theatre, dispensing with some of the excesses of the large-scale musical. In these productions the actors played their own musical instruments, fusing the band–actor relationship into one. The style and success of these shows, including *Cabaret* (1998), *Irma La Douce* (1999), *The Gondoliers* (2001), *Piaf* (2001), *Fiddler on the Roof* (2002), and *Sweeney Todd* (2004), had a major impact. *The Gondoliers* and *Sweeney Todd* both transferred to the West End, and the latter opened on Broadway in November 2005. The *New York Times* described the production as being 'ferociously inventive' (*New York Times*, 4 Nov 2005). The Watermill also became the home of Propeller, which Fraser and Edward Hall founded in 1997. The idea grew from an all-male production of *Henry V* in which part of the performance was played outside the auditorium, with the actors taking to the roof of the theatre to represent the walls of Harfleur. This style of promenade production was repeated on tour, and at the National Theatre of the Philippines a company of twelve actors took an audience of nearly 2000 into the streets to enact the battle of Agincourt. Five further highly successful Shakespeare productions followed, supported by Fraser.

Fraser believed that theatre could break down social barriers and loved seeing 'the student in tatty jeans sitting next to the leader of a corporate conglomerate' (personal knowledge). She made it her mission to 'provide people with opportunities of exploring different aspects of their life' (*The Independent*, 1 June 2006). She was famous for giving young artists opportunities and there were countless theatre professionals in every field from directing, acting, designing, and lighting to writing, marketing, and production who owed their first break to her. In 2001 the theatre won the highly coveted Peter Brook empty space award and in 2005 Fraser was appointed MBE for her services to drama.

Fraser perhaps harboured a secret wish to be a vet or a florist—she surrounded herself with animals that lived in the grounds of the theatre, nurturing young ducklings, dogs, and cats, while also employing her eye for design on the beautiful garden that was often the venue for a battle, a love scene, songs, or music. She was as much at home feeding the ducks, doing the school run, coping with blocked drains, doing the weekly shop, being a car park attendant, cooking for seventy in the restaurant in a crisis moment, as she was attending a dress rehearsal, a critical funding meeting, or a Broadway opening. Having battled with breast and bone cancer since 2002, she died on 10 February 2006 at the Royal Berkshire Hospital, Reading, from rampant pneumonia. She was survived by her husband, James, and their two children. In October 2008 it was announced that a £3 million fund-raising appeal, launched by Fraser in June 2005 to secure the future of the theatre, had reached its target. EDWARD HALL

Sources *The Guardian* (15 Feb 2006); (23 Feb 2006) · *The Times* (16 Feb 2006) · *Daily Telegraph* (16 Feb 2006) · *The Stage* (23 Feb 2006) · *The Independent* (1 June 2006) · personal knowledge (2010) · private information (2010) · b. cert. · m. cert. · d. cert.
Likenesses obituary photographs
Wealth at death £150,190: probate, 6 Feb 2007, *CGPLA Eng. & Wales*

Fraser, Peter Marshall (1918–2007), classical scholar and historian, was born on 6 April 1918 at 45 Blakehall Road, Carshalton, Surrey, the son of Archibald Fraser, bank clerk, and his wife, Lily Louisa Fraser, *née* Sydenham. He was educated at the City of London School and Brasenose College, Oxford, where his degree course in *literae humaniores* was cut short by the Second World War; he took a second in classical moderations in 1939, qualifying later for his degree on just two sections of a special examination (under emergency wartime provisions) taken one year early (1940). He took his BA in absentia in 1943.

When on 8 October 1940 he married (May Alwine) Catherine Heaton-Renshaw (*b.* 1913), daughter of William Heaton Heaton-Renshaw, vicar of St Mary Magdalen, Taunton, Fraser was described as 'gunner R.A.'. His wartime service was with the Seaforth Highlanders and, despite never living in that country, Fraser always considered himself a Scot. He served first in north Africa, where he was wounded at El Alamein, and later volunteered for service with the Special Operations Executive. After training in Palestine and learning modern Greek in Alexandria, in July 1943 he was parachuted into western Messenia, and was based in Greece until 1945, active in various areas. He ended the war a captain, in effective charge of Volos, aged just twenty-seven. The MC, awarded him in 1944, recognized his act of sabotage at an airport near Argos, and his role in negotiations. This wartime experience had a lasting effect on the course of his later scholarly life in two respects: it left him with a fascination with Alexandria, then as earlier a key cosmopolitan city, and with a deep affection for Greece and its people, on whose friendship and help he had so often relied. People in their landscapes were important to him.

After returning to Oxford in 1946 Fraser was appointed to a senior scholarship at Christ Church (1946–7), followed by a short-term teaching job at Balliol. Influenced, he later claimed, by meeting William W. Tarn at an impressionable age, he worked primarily on the Hellenistic period when, following Alexander's conquests, Greeks settled throughout the previous Persian empire, where the challenges of survival and adaptation resulted in a new Greek world. It was the Greeks, both of old Greece and the new diaspora, who held Fraser's interest rather than the native populations of the new kingdoms. In Oxford he worked under the supervision of Hugh Last, and in 1950 successfully submitted his DPhil thesis entitled 'Studies in the History and Epigraphy of Hellenistic Rhodes'. He never took his doctorate but was awarded the prestigious Conington prize for this work (1954). Two books followed: *The Rhodian Peraea and Islands* (1954), jointly with George E. Bean, and *Rhodian Funerary Monuments* (1977). The same concern found in these for the written and material record (both inscriptions and monuments) was displayed in his *Boeotian and West Greek Tombstones* (1957), written jointly with T. Rönne. His study *Samothrace: the Inscriptions on Stone* (1960) treated inscriptions only. Fraser's written output (both of books and of numerous articles) was impressive, starting in the same year (1948) that he won the Arnold historical essay prize and was appointed in Oxford to a specially created university lectureship in Hellenistic history (1948–64), later a readership (1964–85).

In 1954 Fraser was elected to an extraordinary research fellowship at All Souls College, and on 14 June 1955 he married his second wife, Ruth Elsbeth Renfer (*b.* 1930/31), daughter of Franz Renfer, bank manager, of Bern, Switzerland. All Souls served as his main institutional base for the rest of his life. He was junior proctor of the University of Oxford (1960–61) and served All Souls as junior bursar (1962–5), sub-warden (1980–82), and, newly emeritus, acting warden for two years (1985–7). All Souls was important to him, representing a continuum in an otherwise varied life; he viewed the ways of his college with a somewhat ironic detachment tempered by fondness.

Throughout his career and perhaps as a result of his wartime experiences, Fraser seems to have enjoyed the responsibility of administrative or other involvement alongside his scholarly work. From 1968 to 1971, still at All Souls, he held the directorship of the British School at Athens during politically difficult years in Greece. He then became chairman of the management committee of the Society for Afghan Studies (1972–82) and vice-president of the Society for South Asian Studies (1985–90). On 9 May 1973 (his second marriage, like his first, having ended in divorce) he married his third wife, (Barbara) Ann Stewart (*b.* 1921), daughter of Lionel Edward Close Norbury, surgeon, and former wife of John G. Stewart. In the same year he took up a visiting professorship at Indiana University (1973–4), where he relished the opportunity to teach modern Greek literature (Cavafy was a favourite poet). If Alexandria was the centre of Greek developments, Afghanistan too had its part to play in Hellenistic studies. Fraser was hands-on in his interest in that country, which he visited more than once and where he encouraged the excavation of Old Kandahar (Alexandria in Arachosia). There is a link here with his later study, *Cities of Alexander the Great* (1996), in which he critically investigated the many city foundations ascribed to Alexander, just a few of which survived his scrutiny. The sense of place and irrepressible curiosity displayed in this book were characteristic of much of his work.

In Oxford (and London) Fraser gave some lectures on Hellenistic history and epigraphy, but his main teaching took the form of seminars held in an All Souls room on a wide range of Hellenistic subjects. The few who attended were richly rewarded. He was generous with his knowledge and his scholarship, which ranged as widely as did his library. He was an avid and discriminating collector of books. In his library rare archaeological reports joined a fine collection of texts, English and Greek literature (both ancient and modern), papyrological and epigraphical volumes. A similar depth and breadth of stimulus benefited the graduates whom he supervised.

The output of the powerhouse that was Fraser's college room was multifarious in both subject and form. Detailed epigraphical articles were joined by larger undertakings. When older works of importance needed updating Fraser was selfless in undertaking the task, which he completed in a timely fashion. In 1957 M. I. Rostovtzev's *Social and Economic History of the Roman Empire* in two volumes was given a second and revised edition. In 1978 Alfred J. Butler's *The Arab Conquest of Egypt and the Last Thirty Years of the Roman Dominion* (1902) was reprinted in a second edition by Fraser with the addition of two further works and a 39 page critical bibliography, bearing witness to its editor's knowledge of Arabic and his mastery of the subject. He translated two works from Swedish—Einar Lofstedt's *Roman Literary Portraits* (1958) and Ernst Kjellberg and Gösta Säflund's *Greek and Roman Art* (1968)—and in 1965 Faber published a collection of (mainly literary) essays of the writer Alice Meynell, *The Wares of Autolycus*, selected and introduced by Fraser.

Ever since his first acquaintance during the Second World War, Fraser had regularly visited Alexandria, where he had close friends among the international, cultured élite of that ever-changing city. His three-volume study *Ptolemaic Alexandria* (1972) was dedicated (in Greek) to his 'Alexandrian friends'. Volume one aimed to place before the reader not just the topography and history of a city now lying beneath the sea, but an overview too of Hellenistic science, scholarship, philosophy, and literature, the products of Ptolemaic patronage. The range was truly Alexandrian and, though expertise in so many fields is probably unattainable, this remains the standard work on that city. Volume two, *Notes*, with its storehouse of references regularly quoted in full, seems likely to have an even longer life than the study itself.

Ptolemaic Alexandria was an exemplar of individual research, a bold and immense scholarly work taking years in the making. But Fraser also excelled in research on the alternative model—the large joint enterprise resulting in a widely consulted online database as well as published volumes. As early as 1950 (in an article published in the *Classical Quarterly*), Fraser had shown an interest in Greek names, in where these occurred and what they might show. His interest developed over the years and he started collecting names classified by locality. His project was adopted as a major research project by the British Academy in 1972 and *A Lexicon of Greek Personal Names* started to appear some fifteen years later: volumes 1, *The Aegean Islands, Cyprus, Cyrenaica* (1987), 2, *Attica* (1994), 3a, *The Peloponnese, Western Greece, Sicily and Magna Graecia* (1997), 3b, *Central Greece, from the Megarid to Thessaly* (2000), and 4, *Macedonia, Thrace, Northern Regions of the Black Sea* (2005). Volume 5a, *Coastal Asia Minor: Pontos to Ionia* (2010), was published after his death, with further volumes underway. Fraser was general editor and chairman of the British Academy committee supervising the project. The appointment of Elaine Matthews as assistant editor and later director was crucial to the successful form that it ultimately took. Overall, however, Fraser's conception and questions remained at its heart: many aspects of cultural, religious, and social history (especially the process of migration) are illuminated through the study of names; recorded for individuals in their different dialect forms, these also allow philologists to trace linguistic developments. The *Lexicon* speedily became a standard reference work. Fraser's final book, *Greek Ethnic Terminology* (2009), a masterly study displaying familiarity with the full range of documentary and literary texts of antiquity, formed a supplementary volume to the *Lexicon*.

Fraser was elected a fellow of the British Academy in 1960 and a foreign member of the Athens Academy in 2003. He received honorary doctorates from Trier, Athens, and La Trobe universities. He died on 15 September 2007 at Sobell House, Oxford, from cancer of the bile ducts and, as he wished, his ashes were buried in the Commonwealth War Graves Commission cemetery on Cephalonia. He was survived by his wife, Ann, the three daughters and one son of his first marriage, and the two sons of his second.

DOROTHY J. THOMPSON

Sources *The Independent* (25 Sept 2007) · *The Times* (12 Oct 2007) · *The British School at Athens, Annual Report of Council for the Session 2006–2007*, 62 · *Annual of the British School at Athens*, 103 (2008), 1–7 · S. Kalyvas, F. Millar, and T. Honoré, commemoration event booklet, 31 May 2008 · E. Matthews, preface, *A lexicon of Greek personal names*, ed. T. Corsten, 5a (2010) · TNA: PRO, War Office records, HS 5/698 S6557 · sound recording of interview on wartime experiences, *c*.2007, priv. coll. · *WW* (2007) · personal knowledge (2011) · private information (2011) [E. Matthews; S. Hornblower] · b. cert. · m. certs. · d. cert.

Likenesses photograph, repro. in *The Times* (11 Oct 2007) · photograph, repro. in *Annual of the British School at Athens*, 103 (2008), 2 · photograph, repro. in www.lgpn.ox.ac.uk/names/PeterMarshallFraser.html

Wealth at death £761,934: probate, 3 April 2008, *CGPLA Eng. & Wales*

Freeman, Alan Leslie (1927–2006), disc jockey, was born on 6 July 1927 in Melbourne, Victoria, Australia, the son of a foreman in a timber yard and his wife, a waitress. After leaving school he worked in the accounts office of a timber company. As a teenager he studied classical music and had early ambitions to be a professional singer but realized that his baritone voice lacked the qualities required for a successful career in opera, and so decided to develop his distinctive communication skills and work in radio. His first job in radio was in 1952 as an announcer on the 7LA station in Launceston, Tasmania. The following year he joined the Melbourne station 3KZ as a presenter and disc jockey, reading out the commercials and, utilizing his musical training, even singing the occasional ballad. In 1957 he visited England, ostensibly for a holiday. His visit coincided with the arrival of American rock 'n' roll music on the British music scene. Unimpressed by the BBC's musical output of the time, which largely ignored this

Alan Leslie Freeman (1927–2006), by S. & G. Barratts, 1969

teenage-oriented music genre (he recalled a BBC Light Programme announcer saying stiffly with a BBC accent 'and that was a new gramophone record sung by Frank Sinatra'), Freeman decided to stay on in Europe and became a summer relief disc jockey for the rather more pop-conscious listeners of Radio Luxembourg.

Freeman's broadcasting skills came to the attention of BBC radio and he was invited to join the Light Programme two years later, initially presenting *Housewives' Choice*, followed by his own show *Records Around Five* in 1961, when he first introduced his familiar signature tune, 'At the Sign of the Swinging Cymbal', written by Brian Fahey. In September 1961 he was asked to present *Pick of the Pops*, which was then a segment of the Saturday evening radio show *Trad Tavern*. It was the programme that saw the birth of his familiar catchphrase, 'Greetings, pop pickers'. His later catchphrases included 'Not 'arf', 'Erm …', and 'Alright?'. His fellow BBC Light Programme disc jockey David Jacobs had already been presenting *Pick of the Pops* for some time when Freeman took over. Freeman later recalled:

> Trad was happening and I loved the music. David Jacobs was presenting *Pick of the Pops* and they wanted to incorporate that into *Trad Tavern*, a live show with an audience. David didn't care for standing up in front of a jazz audience, so I was asked to do it. It was a suit, collar and tie job for me, and all the jazz freaks wondered who I was. (*The Independent*, 29 Nov 2006)

Such was the success of Freeman's stewardship of *Pick of the Pops* that the BBC decided to move the programme to Sunday afternoons. However, his early years with the show were not without in-house controversy, and he was frequently censured by BBC bosses for his ebullient presenting style. Indeed, the urbane David Jacobs was reinstated as *Pick of the Pops* presenter late in 1962 but two years later Freeman returned to the helm and remained with the show for the next eight years. In 1972 he took over from Terry Wogan as an afternoon presenter on Radio 1, and in 1973 he introduced the first Radio 1 roadshow and also launched the long-running documentary series *The Story of Pop*.

In 1973, with the emergence of the progressive rock genre, Freeman became the host of Radio 1's *Saturday Rock Show*, championing the likes of Genesis, Led Zeppelin, Jethro Tull, Bachmann Turner Overdrive, Yes, Vangelis, and Rush. He eventually left the BBC in 1979 and spent the next ten years at the London station Capital Radio, presenting *Pick of the Pops Take Two* on Saturday mornings, although he continued his association with the BBC through television's *Top of the Pops*, which he had regularly introduced since its arrival in 1964.

In 1987 Freeman was awarded the Radio Academy's outstanding contribution to UK music radio award and the following year he was named Sony Radio Awards' personality of the year. On the strength of these prestigious accolades he was in 1989 invited back to Radio 1 to present a new version of *Pick of the Pops* as well as returning to the *Saturday Rock Show*. In 1994 he returned to Capital Radio for a second stint, presenting *Pick of the Pops Take Three*, while also hosting a regular rock programme for Virgin Radio.

Freeman found time for other professional activities, including television commercials (most notably for Brentford Nylons and OMO soap powder) and even dabbled in some lightweight film acting. He appeared in *Dr Terror's House of Horrors* (1965) and as a disc jockey in the Dirk Bogarde film *Sebastian* (1968). In Julien Temple's musical *Absolute Beginners* (1986) Freeman played the sleazy TV host, 'Call Me Cobber'. In 1984 he poked fun at himself in the television special *Smashey and Nicey: the End of an Era*, the final appearance of the two spoof disc jockeys created by the comedians Harry Enfield and Paul Whitehouse. Freeman's ebullient style was wickedly parodied by Enfield as the disc jockey Dave Nice. He also appeared as God in drag in the television comedy *The Young Ones*.

By the late 1990s Freeman was suffering from encroaching arthritis and from the age of seventy-two he was forced to use a walking frame. However, his broadcasting days were not yet over: he joined Radio 2 in 1997 to present, once again, *Pick of the Pops*, and also the Tuesday night show *Their Greatest Bits*, which harnessed his great knowledge and love for classical and opera music. In 1998 he was appointed MBE. In early 2000, after two falls at his Maida Vale penthouse, he became a resident at Brinsworth House in Twickenham, a retirement and respite home for people who had worked in the entertainment industry. For some time, however, he continued to prerecord his shows for Radio 2, being chauffeur-driven to the BBC studios. Eventually he passed on the mantle of *Pick of the Pops* presenter to the television and radio personality Dale Winton. 'I didn't have the bite I used to, and if you're frightened of doing something then it's probably a good idea to pack it in', he said (*The Independent*, 29 Nov 2006). His last show was broadcast on 21 April 2000. In May 2000 he was presented with a lifetime achievement award at the Sony Radio Awards in London and received a standing ovation as Dale Winton described him as 'a man who has served and is held in the highest affection by every sector of our industry' (BBC News, 28 Nov 2006).

During his long career Freeman, known affectionately as Fluff (either on account of the woolly jumpers he wore, or because he occasionally fluffed his lines), became one of the best-known voices on radio in the UK. His long-time personal manager Tim Blackmore summed up Freeman's style succinctly:

> He cared passionately for music of all kinds, for his family and his friends, yet through all this professional success he retained a total bewilderment that so much success and affection should have come his way. His was the creation of the chart countdown, his was the stunning combination of rock music and classical music, and his was the creation of minimalism in the art of the DJ. (BBC News, 28 Nov 2006)

Freeman died at Brinsworth House retirement home, 72 Staines Road, Twickenham, on 27 November 2006, of broncho-pneumonia. His funeral was held on 7 December at South-West Middlesex crematorium, followed by a wake in the great hall of Hampton Court Palace, which was attended by friends, former colleagues, and contemporaries. His niece Louise travelled from Melbourne to deliver one of the eulogies. He was unmarried.

CHRIS WHITE

Sources BBC News obituary, 28 Nov 2006, http://news.bbc.co.uk/1/hi/entertainment/2940413.stm, 14 July 2009 • *The Times* (29 Nov 2006) • *Daily Telegraph* (29 Nov 2006) • *The Guardian* (29 Nov 2006) • *The Independent* (29 Nov 2006) • personal knowledge (2010) • private information (2010) • d. cert.

Archives FILM BFINA, *This is your life*, T. Yarwood (director), Thames Television, 14 Oct 1987 • BFINA, documentary footage • BFINA, light entertainment footage | SOUND BL NSA, documentary recordings • BL NSA, performance recordings • BL NSA, light entertainment recordings

Likenesses L. Morley, 2 resin prints, 1960–69, NPG • photographs, 1960–94, Getty Images, London, Redferns music picture library • photographs, 1962–72, Hult. Arch., London • Bentley, photograph, 1964, Getty Images, London, Popperfoto • photographs, 1964–2000, Rex Features, London • photographs, 1964–2003, PA Photos, London • photograph, 1965, Getty Images, London, Michael Ochs archives • photographs, 1965–2000, Photoshot, London • S & G Barratts, photograph, 1969, PA Photos, London [*see illus.*] • I. Cook, photograph, 1994, Getty Images, London, Time and Life pictures • P. Borland, bromide print, 1999, NPG • P. Borland, photographs, 2000, Getty Images, London, Premium archive • T. Sheehan, photograph, Getty Images, London, Sony music archive • obituary photographs • photographs, Camera Press, London

Wealth at death £522,775: probate, 29 June 2007, *CGPLA Eng. & Wales*

Frend, William Hugh Clifford (1916–2005), church historian, was born on 11 January 1916 at the Vicarage, Shottermill, Haslemere, Surrey, the youngest of four children, a late child and second son, of Edwin George Clifford Frend (1871–1937), a high-church Anglican vicar, and his wife, Edith, *née* Bacon (1877–1966). He was baptized by his father in St Stephen's parish church, Shottermill, on 2 March 1916. An uncle, John Palliser Frend, was also a clergyman. The cleric William Frend (1757–1841), controversialist in politics and theology, was a great-great-uncle.

After Fernden School and Haileybury College, Frend went to Keble College, Oxford, to read modern history, a curriculum that enabled his participation in the Augustine seminar of the professor of divinity, F. L. Cross. He graduated with a first-class degree in 1937, and won a Craven fellowship for graduate research in classical antiquity. This enabled him to study at the Humboldt University, Berlin, which exposed him to challenging standards. After the iconic figures of Adolf von Harnack and Karl Holl, Hans Lietzmann carried the torch of thesis history rather than conviction history. Frend attended his *Oberseminar*. Lietzmann's influence was formative. He endorsed the interweaving of literary and material sources and pointed to models. He helped Frend shape as his project the socio-economic context of Donatist religious dissent in north Africa, and supported his trip to Tunisia to study early Christian archaeological sites. Frend's thesis (for which he was awarded an Oxford DPhil in 1940) was co-supervised externally by the London Byzantinist and official translator of Hitler's speeches, Norman H. Baynes. The thesis evolved into a groundbreaking book, *The Donatist Church* (1952), which concentrated on non-theological dimensions.

During the Second World War Frend worked successively in the War Office, the Cabinet Office, and the Foreign Office, in political intelligence, and in the latter part of the war was posted to north Africa, Italy, and Austria. He was decorated by the Polish government-in-exile. He remained with the Foreign Office until 1947, when he became an army officer, and for the next four years he helped analyse seized German foreign ministry documents. He was proud of his war effort, not sharing early Christian dissent on matters of military service. On 2 June 1951 he married Mary Grace Crook (1928–2002), daughter of Eric Ashley Crook, surgeon. They had a son, Simon, and a daughter, Sally. Frend's wife's family had historical Quaker associations (as indeed the Frend family had too) so that even his marriage was perhaps a symptom of his fondness for dissent.

After a brief spell as research fellow at Nottingham University (1951–2), from 1952 to 1969 Frend's seminal work on the frontiers between archaeology, church history, and theology was done at Cambridge, based at Gonville and Caius College, of which he was a bye-fellow from 1952 and fellow from 1956. He also lectured in the divinity faculty. He published *Martyrdom and Persecution in the Early Church* (1965), valuable for source orientation, and *The Early Church* (1965), a textbook for students that was popular. In 1966 he was made an Oxford DD. In 1967–8 he gave the Birbeck lectures at Trinity College, Cambridge, later published as *The Rise of the Monophysite Movement* (1972). This further exemplified his interest in alternative or submerged Christian traditions.

From 1969 until 1984 Frend was professor of ecclesiastical history at Glasgow in the faculty of divinity, which also incorporated Trinity College (which trained candidates for Church of Scotland ministry, and where his office was located until 1976). The cultural challenge was mutual. His background of English 'home counties', Oxbridge, the Church of England, and civil religion did not fit comfortably into a Scottish university divinity faculty, orientated partly to the Presbyterian ministry, and located in declining industrial Glasgow. Frend remained unreconstructed. Some staff perceived quasi-proconsular attitudes. However, his scholarship excelled—acknowledged by an Edinburgh DD in 1974—and he delighted undergraduates. His service as dean of the divinity faculty from 1972 to 1975 and as (an apparently unlikely) chairman of the Association of University Teachers (Scotland) from 1976 to 1978 was idiosyncratic. Involvement in university politics did not help his discipline, as his chair was suppressed on his retirement. He was and remained incandescent, although he magnanimously made a bequest to Glasgow University in his will. His earlier foray into Liberal Party politics at Cambridge took a different turn in Glasgow, where he canvassed for a Conservative and Unionist candidate against Roy Jenkins in 1982. He found Glasgow tenement politics chastening. Moreover, he had security anxieties due to the IRA shadow, since he had a Territorial Decoration and a son on military service in Northern Ireland. He was reassured when told he might only qualify for a 'knee job'. Glasgow, however, was the workshop of Frend's magnum opus, *The Rise of Christianity* (1984), a huge tome unmatched by any modern English-speaking scholar in the field. It followed his tardy election as a fellow of the British Academy (1983).

On his retirement and return to England in 1984 Frend remained active in research and in church ministry. Ambivalent towards the church and having a reductionist concept of Christianity, his colours were 'low church' and 'liberal'. He served variously. He had edited the *Modern Churchman* (1963–82). A Church of England lay reader since 1956, he later became a deacon (1983) and minister (1984) of the Scottish Episcopal Church, serving in Aberfoyle parish. He then became priest-in-charge of the linked parishes of Barnwell with Thurning and Luddington in Peterborough diocese until 1990. Thereafter he officiated intermittently as assistant priest in the Fulbourn group of parishes in the diocese of Ely. Mildly Trollopian, he focused more on pastoral work than on order, liturgy, or preaching, but a humane spirit made him effective in that role.

Other marks of esteem were Frend's fellowships of the Society of Antiquaries (a society for which he later endowed the Frend medal for archaeology), the Royal Historical Society, and the Royal Society of Edinburgh. He served on committees of national and international learned societies. As president of the International Commission for Comparative Ecclesiastical History (1980) he refused the affiliation of a South African society on the grounds of its failure to reflect ethnic and denominational diversity. He was nevertheless a guest lecturer in South Africa as well as in the USA. One such lecture-set became his attractive *Saints and Sinners in the Early Church* (1985). He was on the editorial board of *The Coptic Encyclopedia*.

Frend's self-appraisal appeared in *From Dogma to History* (2003) and in an essay published in *The American Scholar* in 1985 on his *The Rise of Christianity*. He was a new broom in early church studies. That he was an amusing lecturer and a fluent writer helped. His descent into uncensored history contrasted with the flight from history of many British theological historians. His attention to history's losers or rejects was significant. However, the bifurcation of the subject remained. The interdisciplinary and empirical approaches that he inherited, albeit imperfectly, from Berlin (and ultimately Ranke) were viewed with scepticism. Respected at home, lauded abroad, he did not establish a research school. Paradoxically his last years saw much that he stood for become a new orthodoxy—interdisciplinarity, national and international collaborative projects, research council commitment, and diversified public dissemination.

Burly, mentally agile, charming, prone to seeing red mist, gregarious, and complex, William Frend died at Addenbrooke's Hospital, Cambridge, on 1 August 2005, of heart failure, having lived latterly at Clerk's Cottage, 31 Rectory Farm Road, in Little Wilbraham, Cambridgeshire. His funeral service took place at St John's Church, Little Wilbraham, on 12 August. After the committal at Cambridge crematorium his ashes were interred alongside those of his wife in the churchyard at Barnwell, Northamptonshire. He was survived by his two children.

W. Ian P. Hazlett

Sources W. H. C. Frend, 'The rise of Christianity', *American Scholar*, 54 (1985), 397–402 · W. H. C. Frend, conclusion, *Saints and sinners in the early church: differing and conflicting traditions in the first six centuries* (1985) · W. H. C. Frend, preface and introduction, *The early church: from the beginnings to 461* (1991) · select bibliography of W. H. C. Frend, to 1991, *Early Christianity, origins and evolution to AD 600: in honour of W. H. C. Frend*, ed. I. Hazlett (1991) · M. Wiles, 'Orthodoxy and heresy', *Early Christianity, origins and evolution to AD 600: in honour of W. H. C. Frend*, ed. I. Hazlett (1991) · J. Kelly, 'Why study early church history?', *Early Christianity, origins and evolution to AD 600: in honour of W. H. C. Frend*, ed. I. Hazlett (1991) · H. Chadwick, preface, *Early Christianity, origins and evolution to AD 600: in honour of W. H. C. Frend*, ed. I. Hazlett (1991) · P. Denis, 'From church history to religious history', *Journal of Theology for Southern Africa*, 99 (1997), 85 · W. H. C. Frend, *From dogma to history: how our understanding of the early church developed* (2003) · *Daily Telegraph* (11 Aug 2005) · *Church Times* (12 Aug 2005) · *The Independent* (19 Aug 2005) · *The Times* (24 Aug 2005); (7 Sept 2005) · *The Herald* [Glasgow] (25 Aug 2005) · 'University of Glasgow story: biography of William Frend', www.universitystory.gla.ac.uk/biography/?id=WH0905&type=P, 5 July 2008 · W. Liebeschuetz, 'William Hugh Clifford Frend, 1916–2005', *PBA*, 150 (2007), 37–54 · *WW* (2005) · Crockford (1985–2005) · 'William Hugh Clifford Frend', *Wikipedia*, http://en.wikipedia.org/wiki/William_Hugh_Clifford_Frend, 5 July 2008 · personal knowledge (2008) · private information (2008) [Sally McIntyre, daughter; R. Jones] · parish register, 1916, St Stephen, Shottermill, Surrey [baptism] · b. cert. · m. cert. · d. cert.

Archives U. Glasgow archives, corresp. and working papers, personal and institutional | CAC Cam., papers from work during the Second World War · Society of Antiquaries, London, report on Christianity in the Nile Valley | SOUND priv. coll., interview with D. Talbot

Likenesses obituary photographs · photograph, repro. in Hazlett, *Early Christianity*, back cover · photograph, repro. in 'University of Glasgow story' · photograph, repro. in Liebeschuetz, 'Frend' · photograph, British Academy, London

Wealth at death £1,001,142: probate, 5 May 2006, *CGPLA Eng. & Wales*

Fretwell, Elizabeth Drina [Betty] **(1920–2006)**, singer, was born on 13 August 1920 in the suburb of Murrumbeena, south-east of Melbourne, Victoria, Australia. As the daughter of a city that boasted internationally renowned sopranos like Nellie Melba and Marjorie Lawrence as former residents she would have been aware of her musical antecedents. As a child she dreamt of becoming a ballerina, but having grown particularly tall as a teenager she abandoned her ambitions as a dancer and studied singing instead. Hopes of a professional career were encouraged by her reaching the final of the prestigious Sun aria competition in 1947. That competition was an important showcase for many young Australian singers and previous first-prize winners included Joan Sutherland and June Bronhill, both of whom went on to successful careers in Britain. Fretwell then enrolled in the opera school of the National Theatre Movement in Melbourne the same year. There she sang a variety of roles, including Donna Anna, Fiordiligi, and Cherubino in Mozart's *Don Giovanni*, *Così fan tutte*, and *Le nozze di Figaro*; Elsa and Senta in Wagner's *Lohengrin* and *Der fliegende Holländer*; and the eponymous heroine in Puccini's *Tosca* between 1950 and 1954. In later life many of these parts were associated with her and these early experiences laid the foundations for her future career. For the company she also sang Antonia in Offenbach's *The Tales of Hoffmann*, which she performed at a royal performance during Princess Elizabeth's visit to Australia in 1952. At that time Australia was fiercely loyal to the British crown and it was a feather in both her professional and private caps to have sung at such an important event.

With an eye fixed firmly on her future Fretwell travelled to London in the early 1950s to become a student of Joseph Hislop. But that visit was relatively short and after she returned to Australia for a tour of *Tosca* she met her future husband, the baritone Robert Simmons. Although Simmons was married they soon engaged in an extra-marital affair that became the talk of Australia's close-knit opera community. For a country that would be scandalized shortly afterwards by the sexual exploits of the British composer–conductor Sir Eugene Goossens, when he was chief conductor of the Sydney Symphony Orchestra, such 'scandalous' behaviour was unacceptable. Fretwell and Simmons decided therefore to move to England in 1955. They married in 1958, lived happily for the rest of their lives, and had two children, John and Geraldine.

After her return to Europe Fretwell's first professional engagement was with the Dublin Grand Opera, for which she sang the title role in Verdi's *Aïda* and Musetta in Puccini's *La Bohème*. But it was her work with the Sadler's Wells Opera between 1955 and 1965 that defined her career in Britain and that brought her to the attention of Europe's opera-going public. Billed as Betty Fretwell (the name by which she was known to friends and colleagues throughout her life) for her début with the company as the First Lady in Mozart's *Die Zauberflöte* in October 1955, she quickly secured a reputation as a singer of professionalism, reliability, and technical brilliance. With a voice that was both adaptable and musical she explored much of the soprano repertoire with Sadler's Wells Opera, including leading roles in Puccini's *La fanciulla del West*, *La Bohème*, *Madama Butterfly*, and *Suor Angelica*, Verdi's *La traviata*—performed first by her in February 1956, after which she was billed as Elizabeth Fretwell—Wagner's *Der fliegende Holländer*, Tchaikovsky's *Eugene Onegin*, Strauss's *Ariadne auf Naxos*, John Gardner's *The Moon and Sixpence*, Lehár's *Das Land des Lächelns*, and Britten's *Gloriana* and *Peter Grimes*. As Ellen Orford in the latter opera she sang the role for the company on a tour that visited regional centres throughout the United Kingdom as well as Münster, Frankfurt, Munich, West Berlin, and Kassel in Germany. That tour took place in the autumn of 1963, shortly after she returned from a series of performances for the Elizabethan Opera Trust in Australia, where she sang Leonore in Beethoven's *Fidelio* and Countess Almaviva in *Le nozze di Figaro*.

While much of Fretwell's career in Britain was spent with Sadler's Wells Opera she also accepted a number of other important engagements elsewhere. In 1958 she was involved in the celebrations commemorating the centenary of Puccini's birth and was invited to sing the role of Anna in a broadcast of the composer's rarely heard first opera, *Le villi*, for BBC Radio. With the English Opera Group she sang the role of Miss Jessell in Britten's *The Turn of the Screw* in Edinburgh and London and, for Scottish Opera, she performed Donna Anna in *Don Giovanni*. In November 1964 she sang the eponymous role in *Aïda* for an indisposed colleague at Covent Garden, before returning to that house in April 1965 to sing Giorgetta in Puccini's *Il tabarro*. Curiously she never again performed at the Royal Opera, a house with a long tradition of encouraging talented Australian singers. In 1966 and 1967 she returned to Scottish Opera to sing Sieglinde in Wagner's *Die Walküre* and then Freia in that composer's *Das Rheingold*.

In 1970 Fretwell returned permanently to Australia, where she joined the Australian Opera. For that house she sang principal soprano roles in Verdi's *Falstaff*, *La forza del destino*, and *Aïda*, Mussorgsky's *Boris Godunov*, Janáček's *Jenufa*, Puccini's *Tosca* and *Il tabarro*, and Sitsky's *Lenz*. In 1973 she performed with the company during the opening season of the Sydney Opera House; in 1977 she was appointed OBE. She retired from the stage in the late 1980s. Keen to retire quietly she left the Australian Opera without any formal announcement. She was a passionate gardener. She died of a ruptured cerebral artery aneurysm at her home in the north-east suburbs of Sydney on 5 June 2006. She was survived by her son and daughter, her husband having predeceased her. RAYMOND HOLDEN

Sources *The Times* (22 June 2006) · *The Independent* (10 July 2006) · *WW* (2006) · *Playbill arts*, www.playbillarts.com, 28 June 2008 · *It's an honour: Australia celebrating Australians*, http://itsanhonour.gov.au/, 28 June 2008 · ABC Classics FM website, www.abc.net.au/, 28 June 2008 · ABC Television website, www.abc.net.au/, 28 June 2008 · National Library of Australia website, http://protocat.nla.gov.au/, 20 June 2008
Likenesses R. Wilson, photograph, 1967, Rex Features, London · obituary photographs

Frost, Robert William [Rob] **(1950–2007)**, Methodist minister and evangelist, was born on 27 April 1950 at the Halifax General Hospital, the only child of Ronald William Frost (*b.* 1920), Methodist minister, and his wife, Freda

Mary, *née* Williams (1917–1980). At the time of his birth registration his parents lived at 7 Beech Villas, Sowerby Bridge, Yorkshire. As his father served in a succession of Methodist circuits, Rob Frost's education took place in Stoke-on-Trent, at Plymouth College (1961–5), and at King Edward's School, Birmingham (1965–6). He began preparing for a career in television and secured a place at the Regent Street School of Film and Television. However, a committed evangelical Christian from the age of seventeen, he enrolled instead for a year's course at Cliff College, Derbyshire, the Methodist institution for training lay evangelists. After being accepted as a candidate for the Methodist ministry in 1971 he trained at Hartley Victoria College, Manchester (1971–5), and graduated BA from Manchester University. These years established significant patterns for the future. At a time when conservative evangelicalism and evangelism were discounted in many quarters Frost gathered a group of like-minded students and spent college vacations running missions in Britain and the USA. He became involved in local radio, laying the foundations for a lifetime of broadcasting. He volunteered for work with the homeless and also developed contacts with Christians in Yugoslavia, a precursor of his later presidency of Release International, supporting persecuted Christians overseas. The combination of a traditional message with modern methods of communication, the blend of evangelism and social action, an openness to the wider world, boundless energy, an entrepreneurial ability to seize opportunities and launch new ventures, a gift for building teams and inspiring loyalty, and a sometimes uneasy relationship with the denominational establishment, remained hallmarks of Frost's ministry for the next thirty-five years. It was also in Manchester that Frost met Jacqueline (Jacqui) Thornton (*b.* 1955), civil servant, and they were married at the parish church of St Edmund, Whalley Range, on 28 June 1975. They had two sons, Andrew and Christopher.

Frost was sent to South Elmsall, Yorkshire, in the summer of 1975. Ordained in 1977, he moved in 1978 to Mitcham in south London. Echoes of these appointments appeared in his novels *Gospel End* (1991) and *Broken Cross* (1992). In 1983 he moved to the Sutton circuit, where reduced local church responsibilities facilitated a wider role with Methodist home missions and the Methodist Association of Youth Clubs. His first publications were bible-study materials for youth groups. Meanwhile the *Gospel Roadshow*, a 'zany comedy presentation' of the Christian message (*Breaking Bread*, 146), toured the country from 1981, followed by the musical *Daybreak* (1983), telling the story of the resurrection. The *Daybreak* model—a touring production with a core professional cast supported by a chorus of local volunteers—was replicated with *Visions* and *Breaking Bread* (1988). In these productions Frost sought to engage young people, to revitalize worship, and to present a gospel message, and he developed the creative arts as an effective means to achieve these goals. With the *Pilgrims* programme (1990) he reached beyond evangelism and worship to explore models of spirituality. Concern for social and spiritual issues was also reflected in the millennium musical *Hopes and Dreams* (1999), which featured Cliff Richard's hit single 'The Millennium Prayer'.

In 1986, supported by Donald English, general secretary of the home mission division, Frost became Methodism's first national evangelist. Working with Frost was likened to 'riding a roller-coaster, sometimes exhilarating, sometimes terrifying, as yet another big vision unfolded' (*Methodist Recorder*, 13 Dec 2007). In 1988 he booked the Camber Sands holiday camp for Easter People, a week-long annual convention, which ran in various venues until Easter 2007, with attendances growing to exceed 10,000. Methodist districts were invited to host a 'Share Jesus' summer mission, co-ordinated by the Frost team and delivered by hundreds of volunteers. A 'seed team' programme was developed to mentor young people in evangelistic placements in local churches and communities. Meanwhile Frost's broadcasting work expanded, and he hosted a current affairs programme on Premier Radio and a weekly television show on the God Channel.

Frost's commitment to the renewal of the church and to effective evangelism remained constant. Working late into the night, he undertook research into the church's mission in 'new towns' after the Second World War for a London PhD (awarded in 1995). *Which Way for the Church?* (1997) drew on his findings, presenting a searing critique of contemporary denominational leadership and strategy. Admired by many, but regarded by some in the Methodist church as a maverick, Frost never attained high office in his own denomination, although nominated several times for the presidency of the Methodist conference, and for the post of general secretary of the Methodist church in 2003. His links were increasingly with a wider evangelical constituency, reflected in the board of Share Jesus International, established in 2001, with Frost as director.

Frost was outstanding in his ability to motivate people and in his willingness to take risks. Rooted in Methodist evangelicalism, but also open to new currents of spirituality and environmental concern, he did much to reinvigorate his denomination's evangelical tradition, while experiencing the strains of working in an increasingly pluralist church. Diagnosed with skin cancer in June 2007, he died on 11 November 2007 at St George's Hospital, Tooting. His funeral was at Raynes Park Methodist Church, London, on 25 November, and a memorial service was held at Methodist Central Hall, Westminster, on 12 January 2008. He was survived by his wife and two sons.

MARTIN WELLINGS

Sources K. B. Garlick, *Garlick's Methodist registry* (1983) · R. Frost, *Break me, shape me: working out commitment in the real world* (1986) · R. Frost, *Breaking bread* (1988) · A. Frost and others, *Destiny* (2004) · *Methodist Recorder* (22 Nov 2007); (13 Dec 2007) · *Church Times* (23 Nov 2007) · *The Times* (18 Dec 2007) · *Minutes of the Methodist Conference* (2008) · personal knowledge (2011) · private information (2011) · b. cert. · m. cert. · d. cert.

Likenesses photograph, repro. in *Church Times* (23 Nov 2007)

Fry, Christopher (1907–2005), playwright, was born at 65 Sussex Place, Bristol, on 18 December 1907, the second son of a former builder and Anglican lay preacher, Charles John Harris (*b.* 1869), and his wife, Emma Marguerite, *née* Hammond (*b.* 1871/2). He was originally named Arthur Hammond Harris. His father died when he was still young, and at some point in his childhood he adopted the surname Fry from his maternal grandmother, Emma Louisa Fry, on the unproven assumption that she may have been part of the prominent Quaker family. Although he was known legally as Arthur Hammond Fry into his late twenties he always wrote, and became known, as Christopher Fry.

Educated at Bedford Modern School, Fry wrote his first play at eleven and his first verse drama at eighteen and also taught himself to play the piano and to compose songs. After a brief spell as an actor in Bath and a schoolteacher in Surrey, in 1934 he became director of a repertory theatre in Tunbridge Wells, where he staged the first English production of G. B. Shaw's *Village Wooing*. He developed his interest in theatre by becoming a composer–lyricist, and writing several songs, including 'I'll Snatch the Man from the Moon', for a 1935 London revue, *She Shall Have Music*. A year later he directed a tour of Ivor Novello's *How Do, Princess!* that ended ignominiously after the producer spent the investment-money playing strip poker with the chorus-girls and an assistant stage manager was imprisoned for bigamy. On 3 December 1936 Fry married Phyllis Marjorie Hart (1906–1987), from Southborough, the 29-year-old daughter of Ernest Stephen Hart. They adopted one son, Tam.

Fry's serious writing career began with an invitation from a vicar in the Sussex village of Coleman's Hatch to write a play celebrating St Cuthman who, according to local legend, pushed his mother from Cornwall to Steyning in a wheelbarrow. The resulting play, *The Boy with a Cart* (1938), was heavily influenced by the choric style of T. S. Eliot's *Murder in the Cathedral*, as was a subsequent pageant-play, *The Tower* (1939), on the history of Tewkesbury Abbey. Eliot's influence on Fry took a more practical turn when they first met in 1939. Fry later recalled asking Eliot what he could do in wartime that didn't mean shooting people. 'He suggested the fire service and, when I told him that I had no head for heights, he said "You must specialise in basements"' (personal knowledge).

After a brief spell as director of the Oxford Repertory Players in 1940 and four years as a non-combatant in the Pioneer Corps, Fry resumed his writing career in 1946 with *A Phoenix Too Frequent*, staged at London's Mercury Theatre. Taken from a story by Petronius, later adapted by Jeremy Taylor, it dealt with an Ephesian widow who is dissuaded from incarcerating herself in her husband's tomb by the arrival of a handsome young centurion. It starred a young Paul Scofield, and, with its serio-comic treatment of life's triumph over death, struck a chord with a society debilitated by war. In 1946 Fry also wrote an early version of *The Firstborn* (later revised), describing the struggle between Moses and the pharaoh at the time of the plagues, for Oxford Playhouse. He followed this with *Thor With Angels*, written for the Canterbury festival and again combining Christian principles with verbal dexterity.

Fry's breakthrough came with *The Lady's not for Burning*, commissioned by Alec Clunes for the Arts Theatre Club. Written in the arctic winter of 1946–7 and first performed in the spring of 1948, it became a flagship for the revival of poetic drama. Concerning an encounter between a life-hating former soldier who wants to be hanged and a suspected witch who does not want to be burned, the story had a tragic outline: Fry's language, however, was a cascade of puns, paradoxes, metaphors, and similes that was Elizabethan in origin and affirmatively exuberant in impact. After its initial showing at the Arts, the play enjoyed a long West End run in 1949 with John Gielgud and Pamela Brown in the central roles and a young Richard Burton and Claire Bloom in support. The play's success—coterminous with that of T. S. Eliot's *The Cocktail Party*—seemed to signal a return to poetic drama. For some it was a path to the future. For others, spearheaded by Kenneth Tynan, the return to verse was a retrograde move after a half-century in which prose had been established as a valid instrument of theatrical expression. As Tynan later wrote, 'writing verse-plays, like speaking Latin, is an enjoyable intellectual exercise for a minority' (Beaton and Tynan, 45).

In the immediate post-war decade Fry was a dominant figure in British drama. In 1950 he found himself working simultaneously on a translation of Jean Anouilh's *L'Invitation au château* as *Ring Round the Moon* for Peter Brook and a new play, *Venus Observed*, for Laurence Olivier's management at the St James. The latter play proved to be an exquisitely wrought, if sometimes overwrought, autumnal comedy about an amorous astronomer who bids three former mistresses to a solar eclipse and invites his son (typically introduced as 'my extension in time') to choose a stepmother from among them. Although Olivier's presence guaranteed the play's success, Fry seemed on surer ground in *A Sleep of Prisoners*, written for Festival of Britain year (1951) and performed in churches in Oxford and London's Regent Street. It deals with four prisoners of war who, in their dreams, re-enact Old Testament stories including those of Cain and Abel and Abraham and Isaac. But without abandoning his old pun-loving self ('Amor vincit insomnia' ran one line), Fry eloquently and movingly advocated, at a time of increasing cold war tension, peace, charity, and goodness, which he saw as 'stronger than anger, wiser than strategy' (C. Fry, *Selected Plays*, 1985, 252). His Christian values, however, were always combined with a highly professional versatility. In 1953 he wrote the screenplay for a notoriously troubled film of *The Beggar's Opera* starring Olivier and directed by Peter Brook. In 1954 he produced the third of his seasonal plays, *The Dark is Light Enough*, which, although set in an Austrian country house in 1848–9, was clearly a contemporary metaphor for the need to overcome the cyclical nature of war. In 1955 Fry's translations of Anouilh's *L'alouette* (as *The Lark*) and Giraudoux's *La guerre de Troie n'aura pas lieu* (as *Tiger at the Gates*) played concurrently in the West End.

This, however, was Fry's perihelion. He became a victim of the radical changes instituted by the upsurge of realistic prose drama at the Royal Court Theatre in 1956. As his mixture of Christian charity, rhetorical richness, and high-flying verse went out of theatrical fashion, Fry turned increasingly to film-writing. In the late 1950s he was invited to Rome for six weeks to rewrite parts of William Wyler's film of *Ben Hur*. In the event he stayed more than a year and virtually rewrote the whole movie. He returned to script-writing with *Barabbas* (1962) and the early sections of a projected film of *The Bible* (1966). Even during his long years in the theatrical wilderness Fry continued to write plays. *Curtmantle* (1961) dealt with the conflict between Henry II and Thomas à Becket but was overshadowed, ironically, by a play on the same theme by Anouilh, whom Fry had done so much to promote. He also completed his quartet of seasonal plays with *A Yard of Sun*, dealing with family reunions in the aftermath of war, premièred at Nottingham Playhouse in 1970. At the age of ninety-three he was commissioned to write a play, *A Ringing of Bells*, by his old school and lived to see it revived at the National's Olivier Theatre.

Although marginalized by the post-Osborne British theatre, Fry remained a magnanimous, cheerful figure who praised the work of such younger writers as Harold Pinter and Tom Stoppard. He also brought colour, spiritual fervour, and an irrepressible verbal élan to post-war British theatre. In 1962 he was elected a fellow of the Royal Society of Literature and in 1999 saw *The Lady's not for Burning* voted one of the hundred best plays of the twentieth century in a poll organized by the National Theatre. He lived latterly at The Toft, East Dean, Chichester, Sussex. He died of septicaemia and a urinary tract infection at St Richard's Hospital, Chichester, on 30 June 2005. He was survived by his son, Tam. MICHAEL BILLINGTON

Sources D. Stanford, *Christopher Fry: an appreciation* (1951) • J. C. Trewin, *Dramatists of today* (1953) • C. Beaton and K. Tynan, *Persona grata* (1953) • E. Roy, *Christopher Fry* (1968) • B. Nightingale, *An introduction to fifty modern British plays* (1982) • G. Leeming, *Christopher Fry* (1990) • *The Times* (4 July 2005) • *The Guardian* (4 July 2005) • *The Independent* (4 July 2005) • *New York Times* (5 July 2005) • *WW* (2005) • personal knowledge (2009) • private information (2009) • b. cert. • m. cert. • d. cert.

Archives U. Birm. L., Nicoll papers, letters • V&A, theatre collections, papers and corresp. | FILM BFINA, documentary footage | SOUND BL NSA, British Council tapes, 'The poet speaks', interview with P. Orr, 4 Oct 1970, 1CDR0003955 BD13 • BL NSA, *Desert island discs*, interview with R. Plomley, 10 Oct 1978, NP3314W • BL NSA, interviews, 1979, 1985–6, 1988, 1989, 1990, 1995, 2000, 2003, 2005, F16035, F16332–F16341, F16342–F16344, F16345, F16353, F16390 • BL NSA, current affairs recordings • BL NSA, documentary recordings • BL NSA, performance recordings • BL NSA, recorded lectures • BL NSA, recorded talks

Likenesses photographs, 1944–77, Getty Images, London • A. McBean, bromide print, 1950, NPG • P. Lambda, bronze bust, 1951, NPG; plaster version, 1951, priv. coll. • Elliott & Fry, three quarter-plate negatives, 1952, NPG • photographs, 1952–93, Camera Press, London • C. Beaton, photograph, 1953, repro. in C. Beaton, *The face of the world* (1957), 204 • Elliott & Fry, five photographs, 1953, NPG • photograph, 1953, repro. in Beaton and Tynan, *Persona grata* • Y. Karsh, bromide print, 1954, NPG • N. Parkinson, bromide print, 1954 (*The dark is light enough*), NPG • F. Topolski, charcoal, crayon and wash drawing, *c.*1955, priv. coll. • photographs, 1964–82, Rex Features, London • G. Argent, bromide print, 1970, NPG • P. Keen, C-type colour print, 1970, NPG • D. Fraser, resin print, 1982, NPG • G. Davies, bromide fibre print, 1986, NPG • J. Pannett, charcoal drawing, 1998; Bonhams, 3 Oct 2005, lot 53 • W. Legge, resin bronze bust, exh. Society of Portrait Sculptors, London 2003 • B. Brandt, photograph, priv. coll. • I. Penn, photograph, repro. in I. Penn, *Moments preserved* (1960) • obituary photographs

Wealth at death £175,217: probate, 4 Aug 2006, *CGPLA Eng. & Wales*

Fry, Jeremy Joseph (1924–2005), inventor and businessman, was born on 19 May 1924 at Grove House, Frenchay, Winterbourne, Gloucestershire, the youngest child in the family of two sons and one daughter of Cecil Roderick Fry (1890–1952), chairman of J. S. Fry & Sons Ltd, chocolate manufacturers, and his wife, Olave Kate (*d.* 1949), daughter of W. C. Anderson of Keston, Kent. He was educated at Gordonstoun School in north-east Scotland, which was evacuated to Llandinam in Montgomeryshire in 1940: before the evacuation he overlapped briefly with Prince Philip of Greece, later duke of Edinburgh. Already interested in cars, he managed to avoid playing games at school in return for keeping the headmaster's car running, and was captain of the engineering guild.

After leaving school in 1942 Fry joined the RAF, serving as air crew, and later trained as a pilot in North America. When the Second World War ended he studied at the Architectural Association School of Architecture, but left without qualifying to join his brother at the Frenchay Products Company, which they set up to manufacture components for the aviation industry. He also founded the Parsenn Car Company, and designed, built, and raced the Parsenn car (named after his favourite ski-run). On 20 March 1954 he married Camilla (*d.* 2000), the twenty-year-old daughter of Geoffrey Norman Grinling, landscape painter; their family consisted of two sons and two daughters. After his marriage he bought Widcombe Manor, a Georgian manor house near Bath. In 1960 Antony Armstrong-Jones (later earl of Snowdon), one of his closest friends, asked him to be best man at his wedding to Princess Margaret, but a month before the wedding Fry stood down, ostensibly on the grounds of ill health. Rumours abounded at the time and later as to the real reason for his withdrawal (later it emerged not only that he had in 1952 been found guilty of importuning men for sex, but also that Armstrong-Jones was the biological father of Camilla's daughter, Polly Fry), but he remained a close friend of the Snowdons.

Frenchay Products had acquired Rotork, a small electrical and mechanical engineering company in Frenchay, after the war, and Fry re-formed it as a separate company. He began work on the design of motorized valve actuators for pipelines, and in 1957 the Rotork Engineering Co. Ltd workshop moved to Widcombe Manor. A major innovation was the flameproof actuator, and by 1958 Rotork was supplying actuators for the BP, Esso, and Shell oil refineries in Britain, Europe, and the Middle East. In 1960 Fry introduced O ring sealing, which made the electrical actuator waterproof as well as explosion-proof. While the manufacture of the actuators had originally been contracted out, in 1960 Fry converted an old mill into a factory, and in 1962 built a new factory in Brassmill Lane, Bath, which became the company's headquarters. One of

Rotork's main customers in these early years was the French atomic energy authority, which placed an order in 1962 for more than 1000 actuators for a new uranium enrichment plant. In 1968 Rotork became a public company, Rotork Controls Ltd, with Fry as majority shareholder. He opened a manufacturing plant in Maryland in the United States in 1970, to supply American oil companies and the American nuclear power industry, and continued to expand and innovate throughout the 1970s. By the time Fry retired in 1984 Rotork was the leading valve actuation company in the world, with subsidiaries in nine countries and revenues of £21 million a year.

Fry was an inventor, not a trained engineer, teaching himself what he needed to know as he went along, and trying different methods until he found one that worked, rather than sitting at a desk making calculations. According to his protégé James Dyson 'he had no regard for experts from other fields … and he was an engineer interested in building things that derived not only excellence from their design, but elegance as well' (Dyson, 49). He also liked to nurture talented young people with ideas, and this had led Dyson, a student at the Royal College of Art, to approach Fry in 1968 with an idea for an aluminium, mushroom-shaped theatre. Although Fry did not offer to finance this project, he offered him a different one, to help him to design the auditorium for the Roundhouse theatre in London, which was being converted from a former locomotive turning house. Then Fry asked Dyson to help with the design of the Sea Truck, a high-speed, flat-bottomed landing craft: in 1970 Fry set up Rotork Marine to make and sell it, with Dyson in charge. When Bangladesh was devastated by floods in 1972 Fry sold 100 Sea Trucks to the Bangladeshi government to help in landing supplies for the victims, and spent several months there managing the service depot. Fry and Dyson set up Prototypes Ltd to develop new products and produce working prototypes which would then be manufactured elsewhere: joint projects included the Squirrel, an outdoor wheelchair with four-wheel drive and power steering, manufactured in collaboration with Lord Snowdon, which was never a commercial success, and a bagless vacuum cleaner. Dyson later bought Fry out of Prototypes Ltd and set up his own company, the Air Power Vacuum Cleaner Company (later Dyson Ltd), which very successfully developed the upright dual cyclone vacuum cleaner.

In 1958 Fry bought Le Grand Banc, an uninhabited hamlet on the northern slopes of the Luberon valley in Provence, and restored the derelict houses, intending it as a holiday home and a base for engineers and artists to work together. He also bought a seventeenth-century castle in Malta. He loved travel, and went on expeditions to India, Sri Lanka, Japan, and Guatemala, often in the company of his friend the film director Tony Richardson. He travelled across the 'empty quarter' of Saudi Arabia with his disabled friend the writer Quentin Crewe (whom he housed in Le Grand Banc for a decade). After his divorce in 1967, and the sale of Widcombe Manor, he moved to the Royal Crescent, Bath, and later to The Brewery, Freshford. After restoring the brewery, he financed a number of other restoration projects: in 1979 he bought the dilapidated Theatre Royal in Bath, restored it, and formed a charitable trust, endowing it in perpetuity for the people of Bath. It reopened in 1982. In 1985 he became chairman of the Arnolfini gallery, an arts centre in Bristol, and engaged the architect David Chipperfield to restore it. A ballet lover, Fry became chairman of the Northern Ballet Company in 1989, and with Christopher Gable as artistic director it became one of the most successful ballet companies in the country. He was also the first chairman of the Michael Clark Dance Company, formed in 1984. Always willing to give young and inexperienced people a chance, he was an important figure in the Eaton Hall Design Workshops, started by Sally, duchess of Westminster, to help young engineering designers. He met the young Canadian Robert Carsen (*b.* 1955), later a well-known opera director, in 1975, and they were devoted companions for the rest of Fry's life.

In 1994 Fry moved to Kerala in southern India. He bought the wooden former palace of the raja of Travancore, dismantled it, moved it up the mountain to a tea and cardamom plantation, restored it, and then, after years of difficulties with officials and neighbours, dismantled it again and moved it over the mountains to Tamil Nadu, where he spent the rest of his life. Described by his close friends as charismatic, magnetic, original, unconventional, charming, clever, and good-looking, Jeremy Fry died on 18 July 2005 in Madurai, Tamil Nadu, and his body was cremated there on a funeral pyre. The Jeremy Fry memorial scholarship at the University of Bath was set up after his death by the James Dyson Foundation, to be awarded annually to the engineering student who demonstrated the most inventive flair. As Dyson said when announcing the award:

> Jeremy was the most charismatic and inventive of engineering designers … He was such a great inventor, and was very keen to encourage invention and creativity. His real brilliance was to nurture and help young engineers, to whom he showed huge generosity. (*Bath Chronicle*, 17 Nov 2005)

Anne Pimlott Baker

Sources T. Richardson, *Long distance runner* (1993), 187–90 · J. Dyson, *Against the odds* (1997) · *Rotork: 40 years in control* (1997) · *Daily Mail* (20 Dec 2004) · *Daily Telegraph* (20 July 2005); (12 Nov 2005) · *Daily Express* (22 July 2005) · *The Times* (26 July 2005) · *The Independent* (27 July 2005) · *Bath Chronicle* (17 Nov 2005) · A. de Courcy, *Snowdon* (2008) · 'Rotork: 50 years, 1957–2007', www.rotork.com, 20 June 2008 · 'History of Rotork plc', www.referenceforbusiness.com, 20 June 2008 · private information (2009) · b. cert. · m. cert.

Likenesses photographs, 1954–79, Getty Images, London · A. Buckley, modern bromide print from original negative, 1960, NPG · photographs, 1960–65, Photoshot, London · obituary photographs

Fryer, Peter James (1927–2006), journalist and historian, was born on 18 February 1927 at Hull Maternity Home, Cottingham, Sculcoates, Yorkshire, the only child of Cyril Fryer, master mariner, of 285 Beverley Road, Hull, and his wife, Elsie Frances, *née* Gill, legal secretary. His father had been born in Hull, his mother in Revelstoke, British Columbia, Canada. He won a scholarship to Hymers College, Hull, in 1938, and left at the age of sixteen to join the *Yorkshire Post*. He had joined the Young Communist League in 1942 (having initially been attracted to anarchism). His political views proved too much for the *Yorkshire Post* so he resigned, moving to the *Daily Worker* in 1947. Two events soon occurred that shaped his life and work. First he went to Tilbury docks to report the arrival of the *Empire Windrush* in 1948; then in 1949 he was sent to Hungary, where he followed the official party line in his reporting on the Rajk show trial.

In early 1956 Fryer returned to Hungary for Rajk's rehabilitation. Sent there again in October 1956 when the Hungarian uprising started—the worst decision his editor claimed to have made—Fryer from first-hand knowledge dissented from the party line that the uprising was a counter-revolution. His reports to the *Daily Worker* were not published. However, his support for the actions of those taking part in the uprising and the fact that he was a member of the Communist Party left a lasting impression on the Hungarians he met. (He died before he could be honoured by the Hungarian government in person but not before his contributions in 1956 were acknowledged.) After the brutal intervention by the Soviet Union he wrote his first book, *Hungarian Tragedy* (1956), in two weeks, demonstrating the effects of Stalinism on Hungary and the courageous resistance of the Hungarian people, and rebutting the claims of counter-revolution. Not surprisingly he was expelled from the Communist Party of Great Britain. He edited *The Newsletter* and co-edited the *Labour Review* as a member of Gerry Healy's Trotskyist group, the Socialist Labour League. Expelled quickly, years after Healey's own expulsion he wrote a weekly column for its *Workers' Press*. He remained non-sectarian, willingly helping other writers with editing, proof-reading, or indexing. He wrote a short book on writing for journalists, *Lucid, Vigorous, and Brief* (1993).

Fryer and his long-term partner, Norma Meacock, had one son and two daughters, and it was partly the need to provide for his family that led him to write prolifically, mainly on topics that drew together themes of freedom and resistance to oppression. After *The Battle for Socialism* (1959), he co-wrote, with Elizabeth McGowan Pinheiro, *Oldest Ally: a Portrait of Salazar's Portugal* (1961), combining travel writing with a political critique of Salazar's regime. The most interesting of his early books was *Mrs Grundy: Studies in English Prudery* (1963). This survey of forbidden words and actions through the ages showed Fryer at his anarchistic best. Always on the side of liberated humanity, he trawled the British Library, seeking out the etymology of indecent words, explored the temperance movement, and discussed the origins and reactions to striptease. Two years later his book *The Birth Controllers* appeared. The research for these two books led to a third, *Private Case–Public Scandal* (1966), in which he poked fun at the British Library's policy of shielding readers from indecent texts. Several other books followed. Some laid the groundwork for his later work on black history: he came across evidence that black people were part of the eighteenth-century *demi-monde* and early nineteenth-century radical politics.

In 1981, at a conference on blacks in Britain, Fryer presented a paper on black musicians in Britain. That paper marked a shift from his previous focus on purely British and European subjects. His intention at that time was to write a history of black music and musicians in Britain; he was himself an accomplished jazz pianist. In 1984 *Staying Power: the History of Black People in Britain* was published. It adopted the British political definition of 'black' by including people of Asian ancestry, though the book focused mainly on people of African ancestry. Widely acclaimed, it immediately became a standard text, emphasizing the effects of and the resistance to racism. Its radicalism attracted many readers and its scholarship won academic approval. Music and literature after the First World War were, given Fryer's literary and musical interests, surprisingly neglected; less surprising was Fryer's neglect of religion, the importance of which Fryer later admitted that he had, as a Marxist, completely underestimated. From then on his books focused on aspects of the African diaspora, with the exception of *Crocodiles in the Streets: a Report on Latin America* (1987), written after a tour of several Latin American countries.

Short, amiable, yet forceful, and by the 1980s looking like a kindly uncle, Fryer mostly overcame opposition from those who believed that a white author should not write about black people, delivering more than two hundred lectures on black British history. A number of shorter works appeared, including *The Politics of Windrush* (1999). More substantial (based on research in Brazil) was *Rhythms of Resistance: African Musical Heritage in Brazil* (2000), which marked a return to his original interest in music, as did his book on African-American music, provisionally entitled 'Behind the Blues', nearly finished at the time of his death. He remained active to the end, and in his last few weeks he won excellent reviews for his piano playing at the Caipirinha jazz club, in Archway, north London. He died of a ruptured aortic aneurysm at the Whittington Hospital, Islington, London, on 31 October 2006, and was survived by his partner, Norma, and their three children.

PETER D. FRASER

Sources *The Guardian* (3 Nov 2006); (11 Nov 2006) · K. Flett, *Socialist Worker*, 2026 (11 Nov 2006) · J. O'Mahony, *Solidarity*, 16 Nov 2006, www.workersliberty.org/node/7307, 25 May 2009 · P. Fraser, 'Peter Fryer (1927–2006): an appreciation', *Immigrants and Minorities*, 27/1 (March 2007), 123–7 · T. Brotherstone, *Critique*, 35/2 (Aug 2007), 297–302 · personal knowledge (2010) · private information (2010) [Norma Meacock, partner; R. Visram] · b. cert. · d. cert.
Archives SOUND BL NSA, documentary recordings
Likenesses obituary photographs
Wealth at death under £7000: probate, 16 May 2007, *CGPLA Eng. & Wales*

Ganz, Peter Felix (1920–2006), German scholar, was born on 3 November 1920 in Mainz, Germany, the son of Hermann Friedrich Ignaz Ganz, who was company secretary in the family carpet business, and his wife, Charlotte (Lotte), *née* Fromberg. Both parents had doctorates in law. His father's was a long-established Mainz family, which had converted in the previous generation from Judaism to Lutheranism. Peter attended the Realgymnasium in Mainz. On being forced to leave school on the grounds that under the Nuremberg laws he counted as Jewish, and after the family firm had been 'Aryanized', he became an apprentice leatherworker. In November 1938, after the *Kristallnacht*, he was taken to the concentration camp at Buchenwald, to be released six weeks later, after which he went to join his father in England, followed by his mother early in 1939. He enrolled as a student of languages at King's College, London (at that time evacuated to Bristol), was interned for a period in 1940 on the Isle of Man, and then recruited by the Pioneer Corps. Subsequently he joined the Combined Services Detailed Interrogation Centre, where he worked transcribing the conversations of captured German prisoners. At the end of the war he was sent to Farm Hall, where he belonged to the team who eavesdropped on captured German nuclear scientists (including Otto Hahn and Werner Heisenberg) as they received news of the bomb at Hiroshima.

After the war Ganz resumed his studies, opting to read German. He graduated BA in 1947, MA in 1951, and PhD in 1955. In 1948 he was appointed assistant lecturer in German philology at Royal Holloway College in London, and then in 1949 at Westfield College. On 27 June 1949 he married Rosemary Norah Allen, a 22-year-old zoologist working for the Ministry of Agriculture, and daughter of Norman Arthur Allen, electrical engineer. They had two sons and two daughters. In 1960 Ganz was appointed reader in German at the University of Oxford and subsequently a fellow of Hertford College, where he was one of a group of dons who devoted themselves to encouraging applicants from schools with no tradition of sending pupils to study at Oxford. In 1972 he was elected professor of German and became a fellow of St Edmund Hall. On retiring from Oxford in 1985 he took up the position of resident fellow at the Herzog August Bibliothek in Wolfenbüttel, which he held in conjunction with an honorary professorship at the University of Göttingen (1985–8). His first wife died in 1986, and on 23 March the following year he married the Dutch historian (Marianne Elisabeth Henriette) Nicolette Mout (*b.* 1945; daughter of Arie Mout, lawyer), with the result that his last years were divided between England and the Netherlands. His academic honours included an honorary fellowship at Hertford College, Oxford (1977), election to a fellowship of the Medieval Academy of America (1987), and an honorary doctorate from the University of Erlangen–Nürnberg (1993). In 1973 he was awarded the Grosses Bundesverdienstkreuz of the Federal Republic of Germany.

Ganz's specific contribution to German studies resulted from his commitment to Jacob Grimm's broad conception of a discipline devoted to the literary, legal, and social culture of the past founded on the commonality of language. His first book, *Der Einfluss des Englischen auf den deutschen Wortschatz, 1640–1815* (1957), was on the influence of English on the German vocabulary. His work as an editor of medieval texts culminated in his edition of Gottfried von Strassburg's *Tristan* (1978), a work to which he brought the full range of German literary and historical scholarship, and which he was proud to present as a poem worthy to be enjoyed alongside the writings of classical antiquity and the European literature and music of later times by which he set his aesthetic standards. His contribution to German studies stood out among the writings of his generation for his exceptional range of interests, which took him from Old High German Bible translation to the *Dukus Horant*, a medieval German poem written in a form of Yiddish, in Hebrew characters, to the poetry of his own contemporary Paul Celan. Towards the end of his career he reversed his priorities and devoted himself to editing and providing commentary on the writings of the Swiss historian Jacob Burckhardt, whose symbiosis of scholarly rigour and honest commitment to personal judgement, which the professionals disdained as amateurism, he so greatly admired. This work culminated in his edition, in 1982, of Burckhardt's lectures, *Über das Studium der Geschichte* ('On the study of history'), previously better known as the *Weltgeschichtliche Betrachtungen*, which was followed up by a second edition as volume ten of the *Kritische Gesamtausgabe* in 2000. He also served as joint editor of the *Beiträge zur Geschichte der deutschen Sprache und Literatur* (1976–90), and of *Oxford German Studies* (1978–90).

Ganz's contribution to the academic world went far beyond his writing, and he was perhaps the leading figure of his generation within the medieval German disciplines of the British universities, when it came to bringing Anglo-American and German scholarship together, providing a context, through lectures, colloquia, and collaborative publications, for the robust and critical exchange of ideas. Firmly agnostic, he espoused social democratic views, though by temperament and upbringing he was more conservative. He died on 17 August 2006 at the John Radcliffe Hospital, Oxford, of peritonitis, and was survived by his wife, Nicolette, and the four children of his first marriage. NIGEL F. PALMER

Sources *The Times* (7 Sept 2006) · *The Independent* (15 Sept 2006) · *Wolfenbütteler Bibliotheks Informationen*, 31/1–4 (2006), 46 · *German Life and Letters*, 60 (2007), 1–3 · *Speculum*, 82 (2007), 823–6 · A. Ganz, 'Listening to the generals', BBC Radio 4, 15 April 2009 · *WW* (2006) · personal knowledge (2010) · private information (2010) · m. certs. · d. cert.

Likenesses obituary photographs

Wealth at death £499,929: probate, 1 Sept 2006, *CGPLA Eng. & Wales*

Gardiner, Margaret Emilia (1904–2005), patron of the arts, was born on 22 April 1904 in Berlin, the only daughter and second of the three children of Sir Alan Henderson *Gardiner (1879–1963), Egyptologist, and his wife, Hedwig (Heddie), *née* von Rosen (*d.* 1964), who was of part Hungarian Jewish and part Scandinavian descent. Her elder brother was (Henry) Rolf *Gardiner (1902–1971), ecological campaigner. The family was wealthy, in large part through inheritance from her paternal grandfather.

In 1911 the family moved from Berlin to London, where Gardiner attended the Froebel School in Hammersmith before going on to Bedales School, Hampshire. In 1923 she went to Newnham College, Cambridge, to read modern

Margaret Emilia Gardiner (1904–2005), by unknown photographer, *c.*1980

languages, switching in her second term to moral science. Later she dropped her university studies in favour of Russian. She wrote, 'I wasn't taking work very seriously. For me there was too much else in Cambridge, all the intoxicating excitements of meeting people, of talk and ideas. And besides, I didn't really need to work', noting that 'I took it for granted that every young man I got to know would fall in love with me' (*Footprints*, 4–5). Many did. She was attractive, with an intelligent, eager face and a bob of thick hair. Later in life she wore jewellery from the south seas or Asia and loose colourful clothes. Her scarlet nail polish horrified Barbara Hepworth during the Second World War.

Gardiner's first great love was (Arthur) Bernard *Deacon (1903–1927), an anthropologist she met in 1925 just before he left Cambridge to study marriage systems in Malekula in the New Hebrides. Unresolved before they parted, love developed through a series of letters in which he called her 'Margou … the pet name my family sometimes used' (*Footprints*, 2). He died of blackwater fever aged twenty-four in 1927, just as Gardiner was poised to live with him in Australia. She travelled to Vanuatu to visit Deacon's grave on the fifty-sixth anniversary of his death and in 1984 published a memoir, *Footprints on Malekula*.

After Deacon's death, rudderless, Gardiner studied at the Froebel Institute of Education and briefly became an elementary school teacher in Cambridgeshire, but her liberal ideas, influenced by A. S. Neill, clashed with those of the headmaster and parents. She moved to Hampstead, initially lodging in Elm Row with H. S. (Jim) Ede, then an assistant at the Tate Gallery and later the creator of Kettle's Yard, Cambridge, to be near Barbara Hepworth, to whom she had been introduced by the zoologist Solly Zuckerman, Gardiner's then boyfriend. When her affair with Zuckerman ended Gardiner became involved with Adrian Stokes, the painter and art critic. He described her 'genius for friendship' (*The Times*, 10 Jan 2005); Gardiner herself recognized that 'everything in my life has resulted from friendships' (*Scatter of Memories*, 22), which included those with Louis MacNeice, W. H. Auden, Stephen Spender, and Stevie Smith. Some of her pieces of writing, fictional, autobiographical, or memoir, were later published together in 1988 as *A Scatter of Memories*, while her friendships inspired a Channel 4 documentary, *Time is a Country*, broadcast on Christmas day the same year.

Gardiner became Hepworth's confidante when the sculptor first met Ben Nicholson. Later unofficial godmother to Hepworth and Nicholson's triplets, Gardiner often visited the circle of artist friends who moved to St Ives during the Second World War. Enjoying a private income, she supported Hepworth and Nicholson through purchases of their work as well as practical help like cooking. Gardiner and Hepworth later travelled to Greece together and she provided the guarea wood for some of Hepworth's finest sculptures. She also acquired works from many other artists, including Naum Gabo and Alfred Wallis, the fisherman painter. She saw these works, and others bought from a younger generation of St Ives artists, not as a formal collection but as evidence of personal connections. She said she was not fundamentally interested in visual art but loved the company of artists. Nevertheless she was later one of the founders of the Institute of Contemporary Arts.

The art Gardiner acquired was of a domestic scale appropriate to the small regency house with its modernist interior in Hampstead where she lived from 1937 until her death. She lived there with her son, Martin (*b.* 1937), but not with his father, (John) Desmond *Bernal (1901–1971), a distinguished Cambridge scientist with active interests in art and politics and a complex relationship with women. Once, introduced as Mrs Bernal and being challenged, Gardiner is supposed to have replied brightly, 'Oh. There are hundreds of us' (private information).

Politically Gardiner was on the left, like Bernal, but she was never a member of the Communist Party. Swept up in the anti-fascist movements of the 1930s and a brilliant organizer, she was the driving force behind For Intellectual Liberty, and its secretary. A close political colleague at this time was Leonard Woolf, whom she liked, but whose wife Virginia she found 'very snubbing, very unpleasant' (*Daily Telegraph*, 7 Jan 2005). She later supported American draft resistance during the Vietnam War and the Campaign for Nuclear Disarmament, and was treasurer of the International Confederation for Disarmament and Peace.

Gardiner's most remarkable achievement was the permanent home she created for her works of art. She and Martin Bernal visited Orkney in 1956 while he was on leave from national service in the RAF and discovered

Orcadian archaeology and hospitality. On a whim, she purchased a house on Rousay and later, at her son's suggestion, gave the people of Orkney the bulk of her art collection. As the collection was enlarged by numerous gifts from artist friends who had become highly successful, this was an outstandingly generous gesture. Her organizing skills and persuasive talents created a museum, the Pier Arts Centre, which linked Stromness to the sites most associated with British modernism and with her life: Hampstead, Cambridge, and St Ives. Ben Nicholson commented that the Pier was so far away. 'It all depends where you start from', retorted Gardiner (private information). Having reached a century, she died on 2 January 2005 at Heathgrove Lodge nursing home, 837 Finchley Road, Golders Green, London, of cardiopulmonary degeneration. She was survived by her son, Martin, a distinguished sinologist. GILL HEDLEY

Sources M. Gardiner, *Barbara Hepworth: a memoir* (1982) [inc. autobiographical elements] • M. Gardiner, *Footprints on Malekula: a memoir of Bernard Deacon* (1984) • M. Gardiner, *A scatter of memories* (1988) • A. Brown, *J. D. Bernal: the sage of science* (2005) • *The Guardian* (5 Jan 2005); (13 Jan 2005) • *Daily Telegraph* (7 Jan 2005) • *The Scotsman* (7 Jan 2005) • *The Times* (10 Jan 2005) • *The Independent* (21 Jan 2005) • personal knowledge (2009) • private information (2009) • d. cert.

Archives FILM BFINA, *Time is a country*, T. Neat (director), Channel 4, 25 Dec 1988 • BFINA, current affairs footage | SOUND BL NSA, National Life Story Collection, architects' lives, interviews with C. Courtney, 10 Nov–16 Dec 1999, F7865–F7868 • BL NSA, documentary recording

Likenesses photograph, *c*.1980, Pier Arts Centre, Stromness, Orkney [*see illus.*] • obituary photographs

Wealth at death £377,361: probate, 16 Sept 2005, *CGPLA Eng. & Wales*

Garrity, Frederick [Freddie] (**1936–2006**), singer, was born at 123 Crescent Road, Crumpsall, Manchester, on 14 November 1936, the son of Frederick Garrity, general labourer, later dye mixer, and his wife, Elsie, *née* Clynes. At the time of his birth his parents lived at 11 Chandley Street, Ancoats, Manchester. He went to school in Sale, but left at the age of sixteen to become an apprentice engineer. His heart was in entertaining, however, first in a skiffle group, the Red Sox, with his brother, Derek, from 1957, and then from 1959 with the Dreamers Rhythm Group, which he established. The diminutive, bespectacled Garrity led the 'five boys in red' with Derek Quinn (lead guitar and harmonica), Roy Crewdson (rhythm guitar and keyboards), Pete Birrell (bass), and Bernie Dwyer (drums). Garrity was sacked several times from day jobs for lacking concentration as he was pursuing club work and writing songs. His girlfriend, Josephine Ida (Josie) Tideswell, machinist, and daughter of Ernest Tideswell, railway inspector, encouraged his talent and they married at the parish church in West Didsbury on 28 October 1961. She was then nineteen. They had one daughter.

The month following Garrity's marriage the Dreamers broadcast on the BBC's Light Programme, and, as Freddie and the Dreamers, they made their début at the Cavern in Liverpool on July 1962. Appearing with the Beatles two months later, they purloined one of the Beatles' stage numbers, 'If You Gotta Make a Fool of Somebody'. Garrity sang an impassioned version of Roy Orbison's 'Crying', but they established themselves as clowns with 'Short Shorts' during which Garrity would pull down the Dreamers' trousers. Five feet three inches tall, thin, and with horn-rimmed glasses, he was an unlikely looking pop star.

In 1963 Freddie and the Dreamers secured an audition for EMI and 'If You Gotta Make a Fool of Somebody' was their first single. 'We got a lot of plays for it on Radio Luxembourg, although James Ray's original version was much better', Garrity reflected in 1995. 'We were seen on TV for the first time on *Thank Your Lucky Stars* and I came running down steps, swinging my arms from right to left. The single leapt up the charts, and those dance routines helped as our sound was thin and weedy' (private information). 'If You Gotta Make a Fool of Somebody' went to number three and Garrity wrote the follow-up, 'I'm Telling You Now', with the Denmark Street songwriter Mitch Murray. He developed a new routine and the single reached number two. Freddie and the Dreamers subsequently topped the bill over the Rolling Stones on a British tour, but the group was more suited to pantomime, appearing first in *Cinderella* at Chester's Royalty Theatre in 1963. Their Christmas hit was Mitch Murray's 'You Were Made for Me', nursery-rhyme pop which had been written for, and rejected by, the Searchers. It climbed to number three and sold 750,000 copies in the UK alone. Their first album, *Freddie and the Dreamers*, also sold well, although their versions of beat standards were ruined by Garrity's manic laugh. For publicity purposes Garrity claimed to be unmarried and four years younger than he was, but this came to light when he appeared in court for a motoring offence.

Freddie and the Dreamers appeared in the film *What a Crazy World* with Joe Brown and Marty Wilde in 1963 and made a guest appearance in *Everyday's a Holiday* (1965). They also starred as dim-witted boy scouts in the inane *Cuckoo Patrol* (1965). They had further chart hits with 'Over You', a revival of Paul Anka's 'I Love You Baby', 'Just for You', and an update of 'Auld Lang Syne', 'I Understand'. In 1965 they topped the American charts with 'I'm Telling You Now' (their only number one hit in either country), which they promoted on *The Ed Sullivan Show*. They had further American hits, including a song about their ridiculous dances, 'Do the Freddie'. They toured the USA for three weeks for $90,000, but had not appreciated that they had to pay the supporting acts and meet all expenses. They returned home $7000 in debt. This led to their demise.

Following the break-up of the original Freddie and the Dreamers Garrity became a children's TV star with *Little Big Time* (1971–3), appeared in summer seasons and pantomimes, and continued to perform the group's songs, recruiting existing bands to be the Dreamers as and when needed. He also featured in a succession of unlikely tabloid stories. In 1988 he demonstrated how he was keeping his thick, curly locks with hair fusion. A few years later it was reported that he had lost his singing voice and mimed while somebody else sang. Eventually one musician had had enough, stopped singing, and left the stage with Garrity in pursuit. A tabloid set up a hot line to reveal how the real Garrity sounded. After his voice recovered he took part in oldies tours and played pantomime.

Garrity's first marriage ended in divorce, and on 24 November 1975, at Bournemouth register office, he married Deirdre Violet (Dee), daughter of Kenneth William Andexser, hotelier. A 26-year-old divorcee, she had changed her name to Garrity before their marriage. They had a son and two daughters. When they divorced Dee and her new partner invited Garrity for Christmas. 'There is no reason why we can't go on being one big happy family', said Garrity. In 1989, while performing at a holiday camp, he met his third wife, Susan Christine Lea, a sales assistant who had been Mrs Perfect on a reality show. Eighteen years his junior, she was the daughter of Ronald James Floy, painter and decorator. They were married at Congleton United Reformed church on 29 October 1990. There were no children of this marriage.

In 2001 Garrity collapsed on a plane and became an invalid. Although confined to a wheelchair, he was joking until the end. He died of severe pulmonary arterial hypertension and systemic sclerosis on 19 May 2006 at Gwynedd Hospital, Bangor, Caernarvonshire. Histories of popular music have been unkind to Garrity, but there is always room for entertainers who refuse to take themselves seriously and are out to have fun. His stage shows were as much about comedy as music, and although he did not change popular music in any way he made his audiences happy. SPENCER LEIGH

Sources *The Times* (22 May 2006) • *Daily Telegraph* (22 May 2006) • *The Guardian* (22 May 2006) • *The Independent* (22 May 2006) • personal knowledge (2010) • private information (2010) • b. cert. • m. certs. • d. cert.

Archives FILM BFINA, performance footage

Likenesses photographs, 1963–6, Getty Images, London, Hult. Arch. • photographs, 1963–2000, Getty Images, London, Redferns Music Picture Library • photographs, 1964–99, Rex Features, London • photographs, 1967–89, PA Photos, London • obituary photographs

Wealth at death £244,000: probate, 27 Sept 2006, *CGPLA Eng. & Wales*

Garson, Mary Sunniva (1921–2007), nun and founder of the Benedictine sisters of Grace and Compassion, was born on 3 October 1921 at Denend, Udny, Aberdeenshire, the only daughter and eldest of four children of David Garson, merchant seaman and later harbour master, and his wife, Jessie, *née* Anderson. She was educated at Invergordon Academy and at the University of Aberdeen, where she graduated MA in psychology. During the Second World War she served as an officer in the Women's Auxiliary Air Force, working on the interviewing procedures for RAF recruits, and was seconded to the army to assist the diagnostic testing of soldiers returning from Burma. On demobilization she worked as an industrial and educational psychologist.

Mary Garson had been brought up as a presbyterian but in 1947 was received into the Roman Catholic church. She was at first, by her own admission, a reluctant Catholic. Her contacts with a Jesuit priest, Bernard Bassett, who had been involved in RAF leadership courses, persuaded her

Mary Sunniva Garson (1921–2007), by unknown photographer, 1993

that she had a religious vocation, but its character was discerned slowly. While practising as a psychologist in Brighton she began to work, encouraged by the local clergy, among the many elderly in the town and witnessed their desperation and loneliness. Perhaps her inspiration was similar to that of her fellow Catholic converts Leonard Cheshire and Sue Ryder and so many other former service personnel of her generation. She had great determination and an ability to overcome a shortage of funds for her initiatives: 'If we do our best, God will do the rest' she would say (personal knowledge).

Mary Garson was small in stature, about 5 feet 2 inches in height, and of average build. She had a personal serenity and meekness and was quietly spoken with a faint Scottish lilt. She was a woman of few words but they were always well chosen. She had a shrewd business sense and a determined character. She always believed that what good she did was simply God's will.

Garson's residential home for the elderly in Brighton, St Mary's House, Preston Road, which opened in 1954, was always a place of prayer as well as of work. Her co-workers gradually turned themselves into a religious community not resident in one place but united in purpose and lifestyle. In 1959, only five years after the first home opened, Cyril Cowderoy, the Roman Catholic bishop of Southwark (whose diocese then included Brighton) recognized the community as a 'pious association'. Holy Cross Priory, near Heathfield in Sussex, became the headquarters of Mary Garson's charitable and religious activities in 1965. Gradually habits were adopted, blue in colour and with black veils, and in 1978 the rule of St Benedict, with its moderation and wisdom, was adopted. She was greatly influenced by the monks of Worth Abbey in Sussex and in particular by their first abbot, Victor Farwell. Her spirituality, in her early Catholic days, was Jesuit-inclined and her houses hosted 'cell' meetings inspired by Bernard Bassett. She gradually saw that the Benedictine rule, in its origins intended for a closed community, was easily adapted for an active congregation, as for similar groups like the Sisters of the Good Samaritan in Australia. She lived in a convent within the grounds of Worth Abbey, which served as her generalate from 1977 until 1994. The sisters remained there until 2003. In 1992 Cormac Murphy O'Connor, bishop of Arundel and Brighton, had recognized them as a diocesan congregation. Their dedication to ecumenism would particularly have appealed to him.

On 18 September 1992 the sisters were admitted into full association with the international Benedictine confederation. Garson was by then styled Mother Mary Garson, prioress general of the Benedictine sisters of Grace and Compassion. Their life was not that of the cloistered nuns but their observance was centred on shared liturgical prayer; their active work was compassion, especially for the elderly. It was a mixed life, fully informed by the Second Vatican Council and with a strong emphasis on collaboration with lay professionals and helpers. It attracted many vocations and by the time of her death there were more than 200 sisters in Europe, Africa, and Asia, representing a truly multinational community, running twenty-seven care homes for the elderly and needy. This was a key part of the congregation's charisma and explains, alongside Garson's own inspiration and initiatives, why, at a time when many European Catholic congregations of women were in decline, the sisters of Grace and Compassion flourished.

Mary Garson celebrated the jubilee of her first foundation in Arundel Cathedral in 2004, a year before her retirement as prioress general in 2005. She was appointed MBE in 2004 'for devoting her life to the care of others', having both promoted 'the vision of individual dignity' and 'engendered an overwhelming family feeling about the charity, attracting people of all religious faiths', who, by her example, 'foster participation and unity'. She died on 8 March 2007 at St Joseph's Home, Albert Road, Bognor Regis, Sussex, and, after a requiem at Worth Abbey, she was buried at Holy Cross Priory, Heathfield, Sussex, on 27 March 2007. DOMINIC AIDAN BELLENGER

Sources *The Independent* (17 March 2007) • *The Times* (23 March 2007) • *Daily Telegraph* (24 March 2007) • *The Guardian* (19 April 2007) • *Calendar for the Year of our Lord 2008* [Benedictine Sisters of Grace and Compassion] (2008) • personal knowledge (2011) • private information (2011) • b. cert. • d. cert.
Likenesses photograph, 1993, Grace and Compassion Convent, Brighton [*see illus.*] • obituary photographs • photographs, repro. in www.tamilnadunursingcouncil.com/institution/st.benedicts College/focus.htm • photographs, Grace and Compassion Convent, Brighton

Gaster, Jacob [Jack] **(1907–2007)**, solicitor and communist activist, was born on 6 October 1907 at 193 Maida Vale, London, the twelfth of thirteen children of Moses *Gaster (1856–1939), scholar and rabbi, and his wife Leah Lucy, *née* Friedlander (1871–1940), the only child of Michael Friedlander, principal of Jews' College, London. He spent a year at the London School of Economics before becoming an articled clerk in 1925; he qualified as a solicitor in 1931. A talented speaker and organizer, he joined the Independent Labour Party in 1926 and was active in its revolutionary policy committee. In 1935, following the Comintern's endorsement of the idea of a 'popular front' against fascism, he, along with the other members of the committee, joined the Communist Party of Great Britain (CPGB). It was through the party that he met his wife, Maire Lynd (1912–1990), daughter of Robert Wilson Lynd, journalist; they married on 7 October 1938 and had two daughters and a son. On the outbreak of the Second World War (and following the Nazi–Soviet pact) Gaster voted against the CPGB's policy of 'revolutionary defeatism' but reluctantly acquiesced in it. After the German invasion of the Soviet Union he volunteered for active service, and joined the Royal Sussex regiment. Injured in training, he spent the remainder of the war in the army education corps. From 1946 to 1949 he was one of two Communist members of London county council. In 1946 he was a member of the CPGB's national Jewish committee, which submitted a memorandum for the Anglo-American commission on the future of Palestine, arguing vehemently against the creation of a Jewish state, proposing instead a Palestinian state with safeguards for the Jewish minority. In 1952 he was a member of the delegation of the International Association of Democratic Lawyers that visited Korea to investigate claims that the USA had engaged in germ warfare. On his return he published a pamphlet, *I Saw the Truth*, that claimed to provide evidence of the use by the Americans of biological weapons. As a solicitor he represented a wide variety of left-wing individuals and causes, from anti-fascists in the 1930s to striking miners in the 1980s; among his clients were Joe Slovo and Tariq Ali. He finally retired in 1990. After the dissolution of the CPGB in 1991 (which he opposed, and regretted) he joined the Socialist Labour Party. He had a reputation of being abrasive and even aggressive, but was a devoted family man. He died at his home, 1 Antrim Road, Belsize Park, London, on 12 March 2007, and was survived by his three children.

Sources *The Guardian* (13 March 2007) • *The Independent* (16 March 2007) • *Morning Star* (21 March 2007) • *The Times* (11 April 2007) • personal knowledge (2011) • b. cert. • m. cert. • d. cert.
Likenesses obituary photographs
Wealth at death £2,085,496: 13 June 2007, *CGPLA Eng. & Wales*

Gearing, Harold William George (1912–2005), statistician and computer manager, was born on 6 February 1912 at 3 Felix Road, Ealing, London, the fourth child of Charles William Edward Gearing, watchmaker, and his wife, Florence Eleanor, *née* Foster. He won a scholarship to Ealing grammar school, but left at the age of sixteen to start work as an audit clerk in an accountancy firm. He continued his studies in evening classes at Regent Street Polytechnic, and completed his chartered secretary examinations in 1931. He won an evening student exhibition to the London School of Economics in 1931 and graduated BSc (Econ) in 1935, having won the Farr prize for statistics. After graduation he continued his part-time studies at the London School of Economics towards a master's degree, which was awarded in 1939. His first employment after graduation was as a statistician with the Co-operative Building Society, but in 1939 he joined the Metal Box Company in Acton, London, as a financial and cost accountant. He remained with Metal Box all his working life.

The manufacture of tin cans, one of Metal Box's primary products, was a protected industry during the Second World War, so Gearing was not called up, but instead joined the ARP as a night watchman. In 1941 he moved to Metal Box's Perry Wood offices in Worcester to manage their machine-accounting division, which was using automated accounting systems, in particular punched-card systems from Powers-Samas. During a short period at the Metal Box factory in Aintree, Liverpool, he met his future wife, Florence Grace (1908–1990), daughter of Herbert John Parsons, branch manager. They married in Ealing on 17 January 1942, and had a son and a daughter.

After the war Gearing moved back to London as Metal Box's head of budgets and financial accounts. His academic interests remained, and in 1951 he was a founder member of the Institute of Statistics. In July 1954 he attended a course at Northampton Polytechnic, in Northampton Square, London, on 'Computers with cost accounting and management control'. These courses, which were organized by a group of individuals who would shortly go on to found the London Computer Group, were the first to look at commercial applications for the new electronic computers that would replace the electro-mechanical systems already in use. In 1956 he was asked to head a new division at Metal Box to investigate applications of the new technology and the potential benefits to the company. After much research, including the preparation of test programs on Northampton Polytechnic's Pegasus computer and a visit to IBM in the USA in 1956, an intention to order a Pegasus II was placed with Ferranti in 1961. In fact Metal Box subsequently took delivery in 1964 of a Ferranti Orion computer, which was installed in the Worcester office. This was one of the first computers to be used by a commercial company in the UK. Although Gearing used the new Ferranti language, NEBULA, provided by the manufacturer, he went on to extend the system using his own machine-code programs. He reported on this increasingly sophisticated system at a conference organized by the International Federation for Information Processing in 1968, and presented a flexible report generator that provided Metal Box's management with accurate and timely financial reports, and which had the ability to respond quickly to changes in their requirements.

Gearing was a founder member of the British Computer Society (BCS). On 20 May 1957 representatives of the London Computer Group (in which he was now active) and the National Research and Development Corporation met at Metal Box's London offices and agreed to form the BCS. The BCS was incorporated in October 1957 and granted charitable status in 1966. Throughout the early years Gearing served on the BCS council and was joint founder editor with Eric Mutch of the *Computer Journal* and the *Computer Bulletin*. He was made an honorary fellow of the society in 1969. By the time of his death the society had more than 60,000 members.

Gearing retired from Metal Box in 1973, but continued to provide advice and expertise to a number of small companies, including one run by his son. He remained an active member of the BCS, and in 1991 became the first archivist of the Computer Conservation Society ('a specialist group' within the BCS) and put in much dedicated work collecting important documentation and artefacts from early British computing that were at risk of being lost. He remained a member of the committee of the Computer Conservation Society until his death.

Gearing was highly regarded by those who worked with him, and he provided support and encouragement both to new statisticians in the form of a series of lectures at Wolsey Hall starting in 1951, and also to the programmers and technicians who supported the systems at Metal Box. During one period he made the machine over to the manufacturer each night to test new programs and was particularly concerned to see the programmers were properly looked after and well fed. In his spare time his interests included photography and music. Having lived latterly at 14 Croft Way, Steeple Morden, near Royston, Hertfordshire, he died on 4 September 2005 at Addenbrooke's Hospital, Cambridge, from pneumonia and bowel cancer. A service of remembrance was held at St Peter and St Paul's Church, Steeple Morden, on 16 September 2005. He was survived by his son and daughter, his wife, Florence, having predeceased him. KEVIN MURRELL

Sources N. E. Enticknap, 'British computer industry: summary of a debate held at Science Museum [24 Feb 1994]', priv. coll. · *The Times* (11 Oct 2005) · P. Barnes, 'How the BCS was born', *Resurrection*, autumn 2005, www.cs.man.ac.uk/ccs/res/res36.htm#6, 18 June 2008 · E. Swires-Hennessy, 'Harold William George Gearing', *Journal of the Royal Statistical Society: ser. A*, 169/2 (March 2006), 381–2 · personal knowledge (2009) · private information (2009) · b. cert. · m. cert. · d. cert.

Likenesses photograph, 1956, repro. in 'Pictures of the past', *Resurrection*, 37 (spring 2006) · photograph, repro. in *The Times*

Wealth at death £243,000: probate, 1 Nov 2005, *CGPLA Eng. & Wales*

Ghoussoub, Mai (1952–2007), writer, publisher, and artist, was born in Beit Shabab, a town in the mountains above Beirut, Lebanon, on 2 November 1952, the second daughter of Raymond Ghoussoub, lawyer and amateur footballer, and his wife, Maggie Bridi, mathematics teacher. Her parents were Maronite Christian Arabs. She was educated at the Lycée Franco-Libanais, Beirut. As an eighteen-year-old she gave early evidence of intelligent determination when she wrote, and tried unsuccessfully to publish, an article defending a maid condemned by the Lebanese media for killing her newborn baby, born after rape by the

Mai Ghoussoub (1952–2007), by unknown photographer

girl's employer. Ghoussoub took a degree in French literature at the Lebanese University simultaneously with a degree in mathematics at the American University in Beirut.

When in 1975 the Lebanese civil war broke out, Mai Ghoussoub was a member of a Trotskyite splinter group who refused to join the fighting; she and her childhood friend André Gaspard helped distribute medical supplies in a poor, mixed area of Beirut that the doctors had left. Her car was hit by a shell when she was driving a casualty to hospital, and aged twenty-three, she lost an eye and left Beirut for treatment in England. Despite her facial injuries she remained strikingly attractive, with a dancer's slender body, long dark hair, and a penchant for dramatic clothes and jewellery.

In 1976, while working as a journalist in Paris, she wrote, together with André Gaspard, a book about the society they had both left, *Comprendre le Liban* (1977), under the pseudonyms Magida Salma and Selim Accaoui. Back in London in 1978 Ghoussoub realized that London had no Arabic bookshop, rang Gaspard, and suggested that they start one. Although they lacked funds, work permits, and premises, they founded the Al-Saqi Bookshop at 26 Westbourne Grove, near Paddington, London, in the same year. It became the centre of Middle Eastern cultural life in London, and survived her, as did the publishing house that sprang from it, Saqi Books. In 1990 Ghoussoub and Gaspard co-founded a sister publishing house in Beirut, Dar-al-Saqi. Meanwhile she married, in 1978 at Islington register office, Jonathan Isaiah Rothschild, a translator five years her senior, and son of Jack Rothschild, management consultant. The marriage ended in divorce, and on 4 February 1991 she married the Lebanese writer and journalist Hazim Saghie, otherwise Hazem Saghieh (*b.* 1951), son of Rashid Saghie, merchant. Theirs was a notably happy relationship full of laughter and argument.

In the 1980s Mai Ghoussoub (as she continued to be known) had begun a parallel career as a visual, literary, and performance artist, studying sculpture at the Henry Moore Sculpture Studio, Morley College, London, but always seeing her creative practice as a unity. The issues she explored as a publisher were equally central to her art: freedom and censorship; sexual, cultural, and gender stereotyping; the power of women. She also saw fun and beauty as ends in themselves, so her sculptures were often playful, with witty, cartoonish lines. *Divas*, her 2000 monologue with sculptures, featured vividly energetic caricatures of such female icons as Josephine Baker, the Egyptian singer Umm Kulthum, and Edith Piaf, and Ghoussoub attached scraps of cloth, wire wool, beads, earrings, and 'frivolous' accoutrements like a little gold bag to the strong, dark single lines of metal that defined the women's bodies. She exhibited nationally and internationally, in Beirut, Berlin, Copenhagen, and Chicago. In 2004, sharing a show with the Israeli artist Anna Sherbany, she dressed up in a white *chador* and dark glasses and walked around Shoreditch with a tennis racquet: no one batted an eyelid, proving her point that London was basically tolerant.

During the 1990s Mai Ghoussoub was effectively creative director of the Saqi publishing house. She entertained visiting artists and intellectuals generously and was a source of inspiration on the alternative London arts scene. In 1998 she published her semi-autobiographical *Leaving Beirut*, a remarkable sequence of fluidly linked chapters that told the story of life during the civil war and in its bitter aftermath through a series of character studies; she managed to understand both the freedom fighter and the torturer. The book was framed by the lightly fictionalized story of an assignment Ghoussoub wrote as a girl at the French *lycée* that glorified revenge, incurring the displeasure of her revered Jewish teacher. This subtle, brilliant book explained the difficulty but absolute necessity of forgiveness.

Under Ghoussoub's and Gaspard's leadership Saqi Books published international literary fiction in English by writers including Ismail Kadare, first winner of the international Man Booker prize, brought key Western texts to the Arab world in translation, and published many books banned in Arab countries. In 2005 Ghoussoub spoke to the Freemuse Conference on Freedom of Expression and Music in Beirut, citing her central principle *mamnouʾ al-mane* ('it is banned to ban') and the Arabic saying *kul mamnouʾ marghoub* ('what is banned is desired'). 'Words do not kill: people do', she said. Her art and journalism continued to challenge censorship, prejudice, and abuses of human rights.

In 2006 the Israeli invasion of the Lebanon sent Mai Ghoussoub into creative overdrive. She organized readings, co-curated an exhibition for the Liverpool Biennial, and published *Lebanon, Lebanon*, an elegiac anthology for the country she loved, in aid of child victims of the war. In 2007 she contracted severe gastroenteritis, was hospitalized (at St Mary's Hospital, Praed Street, Westminster) on 16 February, and died suddenly the following morning of heart failure. She was cremated at the west London crematorium, Kensal Green, and was survived by her husband, Hazim Saghie, her parents, and her sister Houda. Her obituary in the *Daily Star* of Lebanon praised her work but also evoked her restless cosmopolitan glamour: 'Ghoussoub was cool. Seeing her around Beirut or London … was like catching sight of Debbie Harry in New York … [She] made things happen' (*Daily Star*, 19 Feb 2007).

MAGGIE GEE

Sources *Daily Star* [Lebanon] (19 Feb 2007) · *Open Democracy* (22 Feb 2007) · *The Guardian* (23 Feb 2007) · *The Independent* (23 Feb 2007) · *Independent on Sunday* (25 Feb 2007) · *New York Times* (2 March 2007) · *The Times* (14 March 2007) · M. Ghoussoub, *Leaving Beirut: women and the wars within* (1998); new edn. (2007) [introduction by M. Gee] · M. Ghoussoub, *Selected writings* (2008) · personal knowledge (2011) · private information (2011) · m. certs. · d. cert.
Likenesses obituary photographs · photograph, repro. in Ghoussoub, *Selected writings* · photograph, Saqi Books, London [*see illus.*] · photographs, Saqi Books, London
Wealth at death £385,966: probate, 10 Dec 2007, *CGPLA Eng. & Wales*

Gill, (George) Michael (**1923–2005**), television producer, was born on 10 December 1923 at a maternity home, The Firs, Weeke Hill, Winchester, Hampshire, the only child of (George) Arnold Gill, a bank cashier, and later manager with the Midland Bank, and his wife, Mary, *née* Taylor. His mother's family were Yorkshire mill owners, and his father's mill workers. He was educated at Wootton Court preparatory school, Kent, and St Edmund's School, Canterbury. His childhood was blighted by tuberculosis, which forced him to spend most of five years on his back, and by bullying: he described his school years as 'the most unhappy of my life' (*Growing into War*, 46). Early ambitions to become a doctor were set aside when the outbreak of the Second World War prompted him to join the intelligence branch of the RAF. Having seen service in Holland and, at the end of the war, Germany, he returned to England, decided against a career in medicine, and went to Edinburgh University to read philosophy and psychology. There he met Yvonne Janette Gilan, an actress, and daughter of Louis Gabriel Gilan, dentist. They married at the (Episcopalian) church of St John the Evangelist, Edinburgh, on 21 January 1952, when she was twenty. They had two sons, Adrian and Nicholas.

In 1954, after a couple of years as a journalist on *The Scotsman*, Gill joined BBC radio, switching in 1958 to television to work in schools programmes, then on *Monitor*, the arts series edited by Huw Wheldon that trained a remarkable band of programme makers including Ken Russell, John Schlesinger, Melvyn Bragg, and Jonathan Miller. Gill brought in the writer, critic, and sociologist John Berger (who later made the seminal art series *Ways of Seeing*) as a presenter, and for five years the two of them rode around on Berger's motorcycle, arguing the toss and using the dialogue between writer and presenter to construct their programmes.

In 1967, with BBC2 about to launch colour television, the network controller David Attenborough decided that snooker and art were prime candidates to exploit the new technology, thinking that led to *Pot Black* (1969–86) and *Civilisation* (1969). Attenborough asked Sir Kenneth Clark, the former director of the National Gallery and the author of several art books, to present the arts series, and Gill was chosen to produce and direct it. Although Gill began by distrusting Clark, the patrician aesthete, finding him 'glittering, self possessed, armed with precise certainties' (*The Independent*), the very antithesis of the attitudes adopted by Gill and Berger, in the end Gill and Clark achieved a remarkably successful working relationship, and Gill came to have a high regard for Clark's erudition and quiet passion. They ended up firm friends. It was not unusual for Gill to discover in this way qualities in an individual that clashed with his political or philosophical attitudes. Though he described himself as 'a doctrinaire socialist' (*The Times*) and distrusted the very idea of an aristocracy, he developed a great admiration for the queen when he produced *Royal Heritage* in 1976 to mark the silver jubilee.

The making of *Civilisation* proved to be an important milestone in television history. Clark had assumed that he would give studio lectures for which Gill would find suitable colour slides or clips of library film as illustrations, but Gill's ambitions went far beyond that. In the end Gill persuaded Clark to travel for two years all over Europe and beyond, to stand in front of paintings, sculptures, and buildings using a portable autocue to deliver terse but articulate descriptions and opinions which, with Gill's beautifully shot and edited sequences of pictures, conveyed a vivid impression of the history of western civilisation. Between them Gill and Clark had invented the authored documentary series, which became a staple first of BBC television in the 1970s and then of television everywhere in the 1980s and 1990s. *Civilisation* became a *succès d'estime* in Britain, eventually winning enormous prestige and worldwide sales for the corporation. Selling to America initially proved tricky, but when lunchtime screenings of the series with seats for 300 were arranged at Washington's National Gallery of Art 24,000 people turned up on the first day, including Jackie Onassis and half of President Nixon's cabinet.

Gill went on to work with the veteran radio broadcaster Alistair Cooke to make the thirteen-part series *America* (1972–3), which some critics regarded as even better than *Civilisation*, while Adrian Malone produced *The Ascent of Man* (1973) for the BBC as a scientific counterpart to *Civilisation*, with Jacob Bronowski as presenter. Later Gill and Malone formed their own company to make programmes in the UK and the USA. After he left the BBC, Gill's series included *The Commanding Sea* (1981), on the history of seafaring, *Vintage: a History of Wine* (1991), *The Buried Mirror: Reflections on Spain and the New World* (1992), and *Highlanders* (1995), on the Scottish clans. His last series, in 1997, was *The Face of Russia*.

Gill's first marriage was dissolved and on 12 July 1978 he married Georgina Jane Denison, a publisher twenty-four years his junior, and daughter of Colonel William Maxwell Evelyn Denison, army officer. They had one daughter, Chloe. In his final years Gill wrote an account of his early life up to the end of the Second World War, *Growing into War* (2005). It reveals him as a quintessential example of one particular type of middle-class Englishman: the product of brutal private schools yet gentle, diffident, a lover of poetry and the English countryside. 'Only the look of the countryside, though', according to his son

Adrian, 'not the reality. Picnics were okay but not nature red in tooth and claw or even vaguely pink. He was terrified of heifers' (private information). The last years of his life were clouded by the disappearance in 1998 of his son Nicholas, a Michelin-starred chef, and by Alzheimer's disease, diagnosed in 2000. He died at the Chelsea and Westminster Hospital, London, on 20 October 2005, of septicaemia and bronchopneumonia. He was survived by his wife, Georgina, their daughter Chloe, and his son Adrian, the journalist and author known as A. A. Gill.

CHRISTOPHER DUNKLEY

Sources M. Gill, *Growing into war* (2005) • *The Independent* (24 Oct 2005) • *Daily Telegraph* (26 Oct 2005) • *The Guardian* (28 Oct 2005) • *The Times* (29 Oct 2005) • personal knowledge (2009) • private information (2009) [A. A. Gill, son] • b. cert. • m. certs. • d. cert.

Likenesses obituary photographs • photographs, repro. in Gill, *Growing into war*

Wealth at death under £30,000: probate, 10 May 2006, *CGPLA Eng. & Wales*

Gilmour, Ian Hedworth John Little, **Baron Gilmour of Craigmillar (1926–2007)**, politician and author, was born Ian Hedworth Gilmour on 8 July 1926 at 16 Devonshire Terrace, London, the only son (there was an older daughter) of Lieutenant-Colonel Sir John Little Gilmour, second baronet (1899–1977), stockbroker and company director, and his first wife, the Hon. Victoria Laura Cadogan (1901–1991), supposed youngest daughter of Henry Arthur Cadogan, Viscount Chelsea. The Gilmours had been landed gentry in Fife and Midlothian since at least the sixteenth century; several of Gilmour's ancestors had sat in both the Scottish and United Kingdom parliaments as MPs for Midlothian or Edinburgh. At the age of just two Ian Gilmour inherited from his step-grandfather (who, he subsequently discovered, was in fact his biological grandfather), Admiral the Hon. Sir Hedworth Meux, the income from the Meux brewery fortune, the capital of which amounted to the then very substantial sum of £500,000. (The trust was broken up in the 1950s, and Gilmour was then awarded 40 per cent of the capital.)

Gilmour was educated at Eton College from 1939 to 1944, where one of his main occupations was cricket, though he also started to show an interest in politics. He was commissioned into the Grenadier Guards on leaving school. After demobilization in 1947 in the rank of lieutenant he went to Balliol College, Oxford, where he read modern history; he graduated with a second-class degree in 1950 and was called to the bar by the Inner Temple in 1952. At Windsor Castle, where he had been invited with his mother (who had been a lady-in-waiting to the queen when she had been duchess of York), he met Lady Caroline Margaret Montagu Douglas Scott (1927–2004), younger daughter of Walter John Montagu Douglas Scott, eighth duke of Buccleuch and tenth duke of Queensberry. They were married on 10 July 1951 in Westminster Abbey, and had four sons and a daughter.

Press proprietor to politician Gilmour spent two years as a tenant in the chambers of Lord Hailsham, but practised law only briefly: he chose instead to pursue a career in

Ian Hedworth John Little Gilmour, Baron Gilmour of Craigmillar (1926–2007), by unknown photographer, 1974

journalism, and in 1954 used part of his inheritance (which also included ownership of Temple Bar) to buy *The Spectator* from Sir Evelyn Wrench. He edited it until 1959, when he handed over the editorship to Brian Inglis; he continued to own it until 1966. He attracted a stable of talented young writers, notably Bernard Levin, Henry Fairlie, and Katharine Whitehorn, and established a lively rivalry with the *New Statesman*. The liberal nature of his toryism was apparent from the tone of the magazine; he was appalled by Anthony Eden's conduct of the Suez crisis, and had a lifelong sympathy for the Arab cause. *The Spectator*, under his ownership, also attracted a celebrated libel action from three prominent Labour figures—Aneurin Bevan, Richard Crossman, and Morgan Phillips—whom the magazine accused of having been drunk at a conference in Venice. The accusation was true, but they sued nonetheless, and won. 'Bevan wanted the money', said Gilmour (*The Times*, 24 Sept 2007).

Inglis became more critical of the Macmillan government, a stance that pushed up the circulation, but which also caused him and Gilmour to fall out; Inglis resigned for a job in television. Gilmour's unhappiness with the direction of the magazine was connected with his political ambitions: he had decided to try to become a tory MP. He was encouraged in this by the chairman of the party, Iain Macleod, who told him: 'stop criticising us—do something!' (*The Times*, 24 Sept 2007). He unsuccessfully sought candidacies at Pontefract, Lincoln, and Hexham, but finally secured one in Central Norfolk, for which he was returned at a by-election in November 1962 (caused by the death of the Conservative MP, Group Captain Richard Collard) by just 220 votes. He held the seat until it was abolished as a result of boundary changes at the election of February 1974; he then became MP for Chesham and Amersham, which he held until 1992. He soon specialized in defence and foreign affairs, but early on showed a progressive streak in his support for female and racial equality. He was one of only two Conservatives who during the 1960s voted on the liberal side of all the great causes of the day—reform of abortion, divorce, homosexual law, and capital punishment.

In the 1963 leadership crisis in his party that followed the resignation of Harold Macmillan, Gilmour backed Hailsham, who soon renounced his peerage and became Quintin Hogg. However, when Lord Home became leader of the party (also renouncing his peerage, and becoming Sir Alec Douglas-Home), Gilmour surprised everyone by offering Macleod the editorship of *The Spectator*; Macleod, having embarrassed Gilmour by leaking the news of his appointment before the incumbent editor, Ian Hamilton, had been told, then wrote an attack on the 'magic circle' that had chosen Home as leader, an article (published on 17 January 1964) that became perhaps the most famous in *The Spectator*'s history.

Gilmour was parliamentary private secretary to Hogg, lord president and minister for science and education, from 1963 to 1964. When his party went into opposition in the latter year he served as vice-chairman of its committees on broadcasting and on agriculture, fisheries, and food. Always one of the more cerebral figures in a party short of them, he had confirmed his credentials with his first book, *The Body Politic* (1969), which had suggested various reforms to the way Britain was governed, including the introduction of elected mayors.

Minister When the tories won power again in June 1970 under Edward Heath, Gilmour was appointed parliamentary under-secretary for the army in the Ministry of Defence, then run by Lord Carrington, with whom he had a close working and personal relationship. He was promoted to minister of state for defence procurement in April 1971, and was formally made Carrington's deputy—answering for the department in the House of Commons—in November 1972. He was sworn of the privy council in 1973 and joined the cabinet as secretary of state for defence in January 1974, weeks before the end of the Heath government. Although he discharged his duties meticulously, his closest colleagues felt he lacked the 'killer instinct' needed to defend a big department of state (*Daily Telegraph*, 24 Sept 2007).

With the party in opposition and Heath under siege Gilmour spent a short time as defence spokesman before being made Northern Ireland spokesman; and he was simultaneously made chairman of the Conservative research department. He served as Heath's link man between the back benches and the leadership at a time of massive discontent. He wrote, with Chris Patten, the manifesto for the October 1974 election, which the tories also lost, and which was Heath's final undoing. He urged Heath to resign after the defeat so that William Whitelaw might succeed him. Heath's refusal to do so, and the hardening of opinion against the direction Heath had followed, helped enable Margaret Thatcher to force, and win, a leadership contest in the following February.

On becoming Conservative leader Thatcher moved Gilmour to the mainstream of the shadow cabinet, making him shadow home secretary. He was never comfortable in a role that was a perennial target for the party's regiment of hangers and floggers, and happily moved back to shadow the defence brief from 1976 to 1979. He consolidated his reputation as an intellectual with his book *Inside Right* (1977), which attacked an ideological approach to politics and made a plea for consensus. It caused Enoch Powell to describe Gilmour as 'a fine survivor of the species low Tory, alternatively classifiable as high Whig' (*The Times*, 3 March 1983).

After Thatcher's victory in May 1979 Gilmour (now Sir Ian Gilmour, having inherited his father's baronetcy in 1977) joined the cabinet as lord privy seal, speaking for the Foreign Office in the Commons because the secretary of state, Lord Carrington, was in the upper house. Gilmour was never happy with Thatcher's brand of Conservatism and became one of the faction in the cabinet known as 'the wets'. This group was characterized by its hostility to monetarist economics—which Gilmour described as 'the uncontrollable in pursuit of the indefinable' (*The Times*, 15 Oct 1981), and to the acceptance of high unemployment by the Thatcherites, who saw it as an inevitable concomitant of the exercise.

At the Foreign Office Gilmour was removed from any direct influence over economic policy. He found himself, somewhat to his chagrin, having to engage alongside the prime minister in her assault on the European Community, as she sought to obtain a British rebate. The settlement she in fact achieved in 1980 was brokered by Gilmour and Carrington, and initially rejected by her: he later described, in his book *Dancing with Dogma* (1992), how they had threatened to resign unless she accepted it, and then briefed the press about the triumph she had won. He was also closely involved in handling the final independence of Rhodesia, as Zimbabwe, and with trying to bring the Palestine Liberation Organization back into talks about the future of the Middle East.

Despite his air of diffidence Gilmour never lacked the courage of his convictions. On her first weekend as prime minister Thatcher had received a letter from him and Chris Patten protesting at her plan—subsequently executed—to incorporate the research department, which had always been a separate entity, into Conservative central office. He also found ways of delivering oblique attacks on monetarism and economic dogma, notably in a lecture at Cambridge in 1980 in which he attacked Friedrich Hayek, one of Thatcher's leading influences: he described Hayek's philosophy as 'not a safeguard of political freedom but a threat to it' (*The Times*, 11 Feb 1980). Thatcher slapped him down the next day. Gilmour believed that the economic experiment would collapse, and the Conservative Party would resume its usual course: at the time he underestimated not merely the determination with which Thatcher would pursue her goals and the popularity she would enjoy that helped her win two further elections, but also the anger against him that his 'sniping' provoked in some of those around her. He and other 'wets' chose not to resign when confronted with the deflationary budget of 1981, which took the then considerable sum of £3.5 billion out of borrowing.

Gilmour had been saved only by Carrington's intervention from being sacked in January 1981. However, the level of dissent rose, and by the following September the prime minister had had enough, and dismissed him. Gilmour took it as might have been expected, with sang-froid: 'It does no harm to throw the occasional man overboard', he said as he left Downing Street, 'but it does not do much good if you are steering full speed ahead for the rocks' (*The Times*, 15 Sept 1981). The Social Democratic Party was launched shortly before Gilmour left the government, and it tried to recruit him: he refused, determined to fight for his idea of toryism from within the party.

Critic of Thatcherism Thereafter Gilmour became one of the main advocates of what came to be classified as 'one nation' toryism (though it did not always bear much relation to what the One Nation group had put in its original pamphlet in 1950). He espoused such causes as the incorporation of the European convention on human rights into statute law, electoral reform, and increased child benefit, and was a committed supporter of Palestine. He was a vocal opponent of the community charge—or 'poll tax'—that played such a prominent part in Thatcher's downfall in 1990. His fundamental objection to Thatcherism was that it had stranded the poor, who were unable to participate in the Thatcher revolution. He was often to be found voting against his party during the 1980s, but always with grace, honesty, and good manners: he was never a plotter or conspirator. He did, however, support Sir Anthony Meyer's 'stalking horse' challenge to Thatcher in 1989. He decided to leave the Commons at the 1992 election, and accepted a life peerage, becoming Baron Gilmour of Craigmillar.

Gilmour wrote a succession of serious and thoughtful analyses of politics from a Conservative-left viewpoint. Informed by his disenchantment with Thatcherism and its legacy, they were also elegant critiques: *Britain Can Work* (1983), which attacked his party for causing so much unemployment, *Dancing with Dogma* (1992), and *Whatever Happened to the Tories?* (1997), of which he was co-author with Mark Garnett. He began to turn his intellectual interests towards history and literature. Also in 1992 he published *Riot, Risings and Revolution: Governance and Violence in 18th Century England*, which was well received; and he derived the greatest pleasure from, and won much acclaim for, his literary study *The Making of the Poets: Byron and Shelley in their Time* (2002), a second volume of which he was working on at the time of his death. In the last twenty-five years of his life he was also a prolific journalist—most notably in the pages of *The Guardian*—and book reviewer. He read widely and deeply. He added a modern library to his neo-Georgian house by the River Thames in Isleworth, and filled it with thousands of volumes, none of them ornamental. He and his wife entertained frequently and generously there. He also served as president of Medical Aid for Palestinians from 1993 to 1996, and was chairman of the Byron Society from 2003 until his death. Balliol College elected him an honorary fellow in 1999.

Gilmour retained much vigour into his late seventies until troubled by back pain, which necessitated a series of operations. He was stricken by the death of his wife in 2004, after a long illness, but immersed himself even more in his family, his friends, and his books. He died of pneumonia after a stroke on 21 September 2007 at the West Middlesex Hospital, Isleworth.

'Getting to the top? I don't believe I have the combination of skills and traits of character necessary', Gilmour had said during the factionalism of 1980 (*Daily Telegraph*, 24 Sept 2007). He was tall, languid—his friend Sir Julian Critchley described him as being like 'the reincarnation of Arthur Balfour' (*The Guardian*, 24 Sept 2007)—shy, and urbane, with an elegance of appearance and manner that sat ill with the politics of his time. Gilmour always had an enviable perspective on politics, not just because of his wealth, but also because of his intellect and his wide range of cultural and other extra-political interests. His languor concealed deeply held beliefs and a vigorously open mind that responded to intelligent opinion of whatever cast. That is what made him a success as an intellectual, but less so as a politician. SIMON HEFFER

Sources *The Times* (24 Sept 2007) · *Daily Telegraph* (24 Sept 2007) · *The Guardian* (24 Sept 2007) · *The Independent* (24 Sept 2007) · M. Garnett and K. Hickson, *Conservative thinkers: the key contributors to the political thought of the modern Conservative Party* (2009) · Burke, *Peerage* · *WW* (2007) · personal knowledge (2011) · private information (2011) · b. cert. · d. cert.

Archives FILM BFINA, documentary footage | SOUND BL NSA, documentary recordings · BL NSA, current affairs recordings

Likenesses photographs, 1962–89, Photoshot, London · Bassano and Vandyk Studios, half-plate film negatives, 1969, NPG · photograph, 1974, Photoshot, London [*see illus.*] · photographs, 1979–81, PA Photos, London · C. Arrowsmith, photograph, repro. in *The Times* (5 Feb 1980) · obituary photographs

Gish [*née* Gash], **Sheila** (1942–2005), actress, was born Sheila Anne Syme Gash, at Bromhead Maternity Home, Lincoln, on 23 April 1942, the only daughter and elder child of Major Ivan Henry Gash, an officer in the East Lancashire regiment, and his wife, Margaret Elsie, *née* Millar. At the time of the registration of her birth her parents lived in Welton, Lincolnshire. Her early years were spent in Germany, the Sudan, and Egypt. At the age of twelve she was sent to the Royal School for Daughters of the Officers of the Army, a boarding-school in Bath. She went straight from school to study as an actress at the Royal Academy of Dramatic Arts, and (with the stage name Sheila Gish) began her professional life in repertory theatres, including Birmingham and Pitlochry, where she met her first husband, the actor Roland Kingsford Curram (*b.* 1932), son of Bernard Kingsford Curram, who worked in insurance. They were married at Holy Trinity Church, Stratford upon Avon, on 12 December 1964. They had two daughters, Lou Gish [*see below*] and Kay Curram (*b.* 1974), both of whom followed their parents into acting.

Gish's first role in the West End was as Bella in *Robert and Elizabeth* at the Lyric Theatre in 1964, a musical adaptation by Ronald Millar and Ron Grainer of *The Barretts of Wimpole*

Street. The following year she made her film début, alongside her husband, in *Darling* (1965), directed by John Schlesinger and starring Julie Christie, both of whom became lifelong friends. Her early career was spent largely in comedic roles, and in 1975 she made a notable West End appearance alongside Pauline Collins and John Alderton in Alan Ayckbourn's five short plays that made up *Confusions*, for which she won the Clarence Derwent award as best supporting actress. In 1977 she was cast as the fading southern belle in the West End production of Tennessee Williams's New Orleans-set *Vieux Carré* at the Piccadilly Theatre, but late cuts to the text made her feel that her role had been compromised, and she left the production shortly after the opening night, amid much press attention.

While playing the title role in Christopher Fettes's production of Racine's *Berenice* (1982) at the Lyric Theatre in Hammersmith, Sheila Gish was finally recognized as a major actress. Dressed simply in a Fortuny gown, on a smoked-mirrored set, she was riveting as Racine's love-consumed queen, disintegrating in despair. Her performance was a revelation, with a complete vocal mastery of Racine's alexandrines, and a depth of passion that surprised some people, but as she said 'I've worked for this step by step. I'm ready for more' (*The Times*, 12 March 2005). That same year her delicate beauty was perfect for Chekhov's Yelena in *Uncle Vanya* at the Haymarket, but despite a glossy cast (which included Donald Sinden, Frances de la Tour, Ronald Pickup, and Harry Andrews) the production was not a success. In 1983 she returned to Tennessee Williams, when she played Blanche DuBois in Alan Strachan's production of *A Streetcar Named Desire* at the Greenwich Theatre, despite attempts by Williams's wilfully protective and eccentric editor, Maria St Just (thinking she was wrong for the part and perhaps remembering their previous encounter on *Vieux Carré*), to prevent her. She gave a moving and original performance, portraying all of Blanche's fragility, vulnerability, and tenderness, but combined with a formidable intelligence and self-awareness. She was 'almost a figure of Greek tragedy, relentlessly pursued by the Furies' (ibid.). Her affinity with Williams's work was unusual in a British actress.

Gish then played in a revival of Osborne's *A Patriot for Me* (1983) with Alan Bates at Chichester, directed by Ronald Eyre, and made her National Theatre début in Tom Stoppard's adaptation of Molnar's *Rough Crossing* (1984). She and Curram were divorced in 1985, but that same year she met and fell in love with the actor Denis Lawson (*b*. 1947), the son of Laurence Lawson, watchmaker and jeweller. Meanwhile her stage successes continued: she played Celia in a West End revival of T. S. Eliot's *The Cocktail Party* (1986) with Alec McCowen, directed by John Dexter; convinced completely as Isadora Duncan in Martin Sherman's *When She Danced* (1989) at the King's Head; was perfectly cast as Mrs Prentice in *What the Butler Saw* (1990); and played Clytemnestra to the Electra of Fiona Shaw in Deborah Warner's production of *Electra* at the Riverside Studios (1991).

On returning to the National in 1993 Gish scored a huge success as Yvonne, the monstrous mother to Jude Law in Sean Mathias's production of Jean Cocteau's *Les parents terribles*, and was rightly disappointed to lose the role to the more 'starry' Kathleen Turner when the production was staged on Broadway. At the Donmar Warehouse she gave an acclaimed performance as Joanna, the raddled alcoholic, in Sam Mendes's hugely successful production of Stephen Sondheim's *Company* (1995), deservedly winning an Olivier award as best supporting actress in a musical, and challenging the memory of that role's creator, Elaine Stritch, with her desperate and funny rendition of 'The Ladies who Lunch'. She then returned to the Riverside Studios to play Racine's Phaedra (2002), again directed by Christopher Fettes, and scored once more in Tennessee Williams, as Violet Venable, the terrifying matriarch in *Suddenly Last Summer* (1999).

Film and television were never to offer Gish the same kind of opportunities as the theatre, but she had a good role in the film of Peter Nichols's *A Day in the Death of Joe Egg* (1972), and shone alongside Maggie Smith, Alan Bates, and Isabelle Adjani in the Merchant–Ivory film of Jean Rhys's *Quartet* (1981). She made her television début in *Z Cars* in 1968, and later appearances included roles in *The First Churchills* (1969), in two adaptations of Kingsley Amis novels, *That Uncertain Feeling* (1985) and *Stanley and the Women* (1991), as an outrageous opera diva in an episode of *Inspector Morse* (1993), and as Nancy Mitford's Lady Montdore in *Love in a Cold Climate* (2001).

Gish loved the theatre and knew it was her element. She was a serious and dedicated actress whose theatrical career was neatly divided in two. After the early years largely spent in comedy and farce, she then had a triumphant second half as a tragedienne, playing 'women on the verge of breakdown—and women long past the verge, women ravaged, women in a frenzy, tortured and torturing' (*Daily Telegraph*, 12 March 2005). These included Racine's Berenice and Phaedra, Williams's Blanche and Violet Venable, Cocteau's Yvonne, and Sondheim's Joanna. In 2003 the director Steven Pimlott asked her to play Arkadina in his production of Chekhov's *The Seagull* at the Chichester Festival Theatre. By this time Gish had been stricken with a rare facial cancer, and when her illness led to corrective surgery and the removal of her right eye, she offered to withdraw. However, Pimlott suggested she play the role with an eye patch, and Gish rose magnificently to the challenge, giving an immensely brave and heartbreaking performance. Her daughter Kay appeared alongside her as Masha, the only time they were to act together. It was Gish's last stage role.

Gish faced her illness with great courage, surrounded by family and friends. She worked once more, in a BBC radio production, partly recorded in her home, of two short pieces, *Roman Fever* by Edith Wharton, and one final Tennessee Williams, *Something Unspoken*. In March 2004 she and Denis Lawson married, in Antigua. She died on 9 March 2005 at Edenhall Nursing Home, Camden, London, of cancer, and was buried in Highgate cemetery. She was survived by her husband, Denis, and her daughters.

Gish's elder daughter, **Louise Mikel Henrietta Marie**

Curram [*performing name* Lou Gish] (1967–2006), actress, was born in London on 27 May 1967. She was educated at Macaulay Church of England primary school in Clapham, Furzedown School in Wandsworth, Alleyn's School in Dulwich, and Camberwell School of Art. She then worked in a variety of jobs (including as assistant to the theatrical agent Jeremy Conway) before embarking on a career as an actress. Her first professional role was in Grigory Gorin's *Forget Herostratus!* at the White Bear Theatre, Kennington. Subsequent stage roles included Helen Carver in Sean Mathias's revival of Noël Coward's *Design for Living* at the Donmar Warehouse (1994), Marge in Phyllis Nagy's adaptation of Patricia Highsmith's *The Talented Mr Ripley* at the Watford Palace (1998), Ann in Denis Lawson's production of David Halliwell's *Little Malcolm and his Struggle against the Eunuchs* at the Hampstead Theatre and subsequently in the West End (1998–9), Helena in John Osborne's *Look Back in Anger* at the Bristol Old Vic (2001), and the title role in John Webster's *The Duchess of Malfi* at the Salisbury Playhouse (2002). In each of these roles she was applauded by critics for her intelligence and her ability convincingly to portray complex characters. On television she appeared in such popular series as *Game On*, *Holding the Baby*, *Coupling*, *Casualty*, *The Vice*, and *EastEnders*. She was also a talented artist, and in 2004 held an exhibition of line drawings and watercolours at a gallery in West Hampstead. She was first diagnosed with cancer in 1999, and fought it with the same heroic and ferocious determination as her mother. Her last stage role was as Goneril in Steven Pimlott's version of *King Lear* at the Minerva Theatre, Chichester (2005), in which her sister played Cordelia; they had agreed to return to Chichester in part as a tribute to their mother, whose last stage performance had been there. Lou Gish died at St Mary's Hospital, Westminster, on 20 February 2006. She was survived by her partner of six years, the actor Nicholas James Sebastian (Nick) Rowe (*b.* 1966).

ALEX JENNINGS

Sources *The Guardian* (11 March 2005) · *The Independent* (11 March 2005) · *The Times* (12 March 2005) · *Daily Telegraph* (12 March 2005) · *The Herald* [Glasgow] (14 March 2005) · www.imdb.com, 30 July 2008 · *The Guardian* (24 Feb 2006) · *The Independent* (25 Feb 2006) · personal knowledge (2009) · private information (2009) · b. cert. · m. cert. [1964] · d. cert. · d. cert. [Lou Gish]

Archives FILM BFINA, performance footage | SOUND BL NSA, performance recordings

Likenesses photographs, 1972–2004, Rex Features, London · photographs, 1992–9, PA Photos, London · photographs, 1994–2001, Photoshot, London · photographs, 1997–8 (Lou Gish), Photoshot, London · photographs, 1997–2005 (Lou Gish), Rex Features, London · photographs, 1999–2004, Camera Press, London · photographs, 2004, Getty Images, London · M. Pope, photographs, 2005 (Lou Gish), Camera Press, London · obituary photographs · obituary photographs (Lou Gish)

Wealth at death £369,637: probate, 19 July 2005, *CGPLA Eng. & Wales* · under £52,000—Louise Curram: administration, 16 June 2006, *CGPLA Eng. & Wales*

Glossop, (Cyril) Peter (1928–2008), singer, was born on 6 July 1928 at 20 Milden Road, Hillsborough, Sheffield, the son of Cyril Glossop, a manager for a cutlery manufacturer, and his wife, Violet Elizabeth, *née* Wright. He was educated at High Storrs grammar school and worked as a bank clerk while studying singing with two local teachers, Leonard Mosley and Eva Rich. In 1949 he made his amateur stage début as a baritone with the Sheffield Operatic Society as Coppelius and Dr Miracle in Offenbach's *The Tales of Hoffmann*.

Glossop joined the chorus of Sadler's Wells Opera in 1953, becoming a principal the following year. On 8 January 1955 he married Joyce Elizabeth Blackham (*b.* 1934), daughter of Albert Blackham, a maintenance engineer. Joyce Blackham, a mezzo-soprano, was also a member of the Sadler's Wells company. In 1956 Glossop sang his first major Verdi role, the Count of Luna in *Il trovatore*. His voice, smoothly produced and warm-toned, was a perfect vehicle for the great Verdi baritone roles, and he sang some sixteen of them during his career. At Sadler's Wells, after Gerard in Giordano's *Andrea Chénier*, Figaro in Rossini's *The Marriage of Figaro*, Zurga in Bizet's *The Pearl Fishers*, and the title role of Tchaikovsky's *Eugene Onegin*, in 1961 he sang the title role of *Rigoletto* for the first time; it soon became his favourite Verdi interpretation, and one for which he was widely acclaimed.

After winning first prize in the first International Competition for Young Opera Singers, held in Bulgaria in 1961 (an event which gained him much publicity), Glossop made his début with the Royal Opera the same year, singing Lysander in Britten's *A Midsummer Night's Dream*, first at the Edinburgh festival and later at Covent Garden. At Covent Garden he became immersed in Verdi, singing Renato in *Un ballo in maschera*, Amonasro in *Aida*, Giorgio Germont in *La traviata*, Posa in *Don Carlos*, Iago in *Otello*, the title roles of *Simon Boccanegra* and *Nabucco*, and of course Rigoletto. After winning over the notoriously demanding opera-going citizens of Parma, Palermo, and Naples, in 1965 he made his début at La Scala, Milan, as Rigoletto (an achievement compared by Frank Johnson in the *Daily Telegraph* to allowing an Italian to open the batting for England at Headingley), and first sang in the USA with the American International Opera at Indianapolis as Verdi's Falstaff. In 1966 he made his Paris Opéra début as Posa and then appeared as Posa and Rigoletto in San Francisco, returning there in 1968 as Don Carlo in Verdi's *Ernani*.

Glossop made a notable appearance at the 1970 Salzburg festival under the direction of Herbert von Karajan (whom he described as 'a dictator [but] not a bully in the way Solti was' *Story of a Yorkshire Baritone*, 147) as Iago, probably his best Verdi role after Rigoletto. The recording of the production was critically acclaimed, but the accompanying film was not a great success. Glossop made his début at the Metropolitan Opera, New York, in 1971 as Baron Scarpia in Puccini's *Tosca*, returning as Don Carlos in Verdi's *La forza del destino*, Falstaff, and Berg's Wozzeck. At Covent Garden during the 1970s he sang Mozart's Don Giovanni, the title role of Britten's *Billy Budd*, Escamillo in Bizet's *Carmen*, Choroebus in Berlioz's *Les Troyens*, John the Baptist in Strauss's *Salome*, and two Wagner roles, Donner in *Das Rheingold* and the Herald in *Lohengrin*. Described by one obituarist as 'an uncompromisingly direct ladies' man who made the most of his international tours' (*Daily Telegraph*, 10 Sept 2008), in 1977 he divorced Joyce Blackham and on 25 June the same year he married Michèle

Yvonne Amos, formerly Siebert (*b.* 1954), ballet dancer, and daughter of David Charles John Siebert, builder and decorator. They had two daughters.

Glossop returned to the Metropolitan in 1978 as Mr Redburn in *Billy Budd*, repeating the role at Covent Garden the following year. He added to his Verdi collection with two versions of the title role of *Macbeth*, the first, 1847, version at a Promenade Concert in 1978 and the second, 1865, version for Northern Ireland Opera, Belfast, in 1981. He returned to English National Opera in 1980 for Mandryka in Strauss's *Arabella*, sang Captain Balstrode in Britten's *Peter Grimes* at San Diego in 1984, and made his final Metropolitan appearance the same year as Paolo in *Simon Boccanegra*. He appeared in numerous recordings throughout his career.

Glossop and his second wife, Michèle, were divorced in 1986. This event appears to have triggered a loss of faith in his own abilities, and he gave up performing, though after his retirement to Axminster, Dorset, he gave lessons in singing. After he was diagnosed with cancer of the oesophagus his first wife, Joyce, and her new partner moved to be near him. In 2004 he published a revealing autobiography, *The Story of a Yorkshire Baritone*. A lover of jazz, he amassed a huge collection of jazz recordings. He died at Pinhay House, Rousdon, Lyme Regis, Dorset, on 7 September 2008, of cancer. He was survived by his two daughters. ELIZABETH FORBES

Sources *Opera Magazine*, 5–35 (1954–84) · P. Glossop, *The story of a Yorkshire baritone* (2004) · *The Times* (9 Sept 2008); (26 Sept 2008) · *Daily Telegraph* (10 Sept 2008) · *The Guardian* (10 Sept 2008); (16 Sept 2008) · *The Independent* (13 Sept 2008) · *WW* (2008) · personal knowledge (2012) · b. cert. · m. certs. · d. cert.
Archives SOUND BL NSA, current affairs, interview, and performance recordings
Likenesses D. De Marney, photograph, 1956, Getty Images, London · photograph, 1960, Photoshot, London · bromide prints, 1970–73, NPG · S. Toepffer, photograph, Lebrecht Music and Arts Photo Library, London · obituary photographs · photographs, repro. in *Opera Magazine*
Wealth at death £506,995: probate, 27 Jan 2009, *CGPLA Eng. & Wales*

Glyn, Andrew John (1943–2007), economist and socialist, was born on 30 June 1943 at Attington House, Tetsworth, Oxfordshire, the younger son and third of four children of John Patrick Riversdale Glyn (1913–1988), later briefly sixth Baron Wolverton, banker, and his wife, Audrey Margaret, *née* Stubbs (1914–2007). At the time of his birth his father was serving as a captain in the Grenadier Guards; he was demobilized with the rank of major, became managing director of the family bank, Glyn, Mills & Co., in 1950, and succeeded his cousin as Baron Wolverton in 1986.

Glyn, like his father, was educated at Eton College and New College, Oxford. After graduating with a first-class degree in philosophy, politics, and economics in 1964 he spent two years as an economic assistant at the Treasury and Department of Economic Affairs. On 17 July 1965 he married (Elizabeth) Celia Antonia Molteno Laws (*b.* 1945), secretary, and daughter of Frederick Laws, journalist. They had two children, Miles and Lucy. From 1966 to 1969 Glyn did graduate research at Nuffield College, Oxford, as well as some teaching, and in 1969 he was appointed to a teaching fellowship at Corpus Christi College, a post he held until his death, taking only two extended periods of leave—to be visiting associate professor at Tokyo University (1979) and visiting fellow at the Wissenschaftszentrum in Berlin (1994–5).

Andrew John Glyn (1943–2007), by Wendy Glyn

From his tranquil Oxford study Glyn participated directly and indirectly in some of the central political and economic conflicts of the time. He was one of the most prolific and influential of a generation of left-wing scholars in the social sciences that emerged in the late 1960s. In 1972 he co-wrote with Bob Sutcliffe a book, *British Capitalism, Workers and the Profits Squeeze*, which attributed the mounting world economic crisis to the twin pressures on profits coming from rising wages (and trade-union strength) on the one side and greater inter-capitalist rivalry on the other. Following Marx, the book saw the capitalist system as precariously balanced between interclass and intra-class pressures. Such ideas were developed during several years of research in his more comprehensive *Capitalism since World War II* (1984, co-written with Philip Armstrong and John Harrison, and updated in 1991 as *Capitalism since 1945*). Notwithstanding his social background his works of economic analysis were pervaded by a strong antagonism to the capitalist system. While most of his contemporary economists embraced 'neo-classical' economics, Glyn's central concerns were closer to those of the classical economists and in particular those of Marx—inequality, class struggle (including the labour market), and the instability of capitalism. He was in some ways, however, unusual among economists of the left, first because of his ability to interweave Marxist with more orthodox economic approaches, and second because he paid exceptional attention to empirical questions and data (in daunting quantities).

Capital's weakness during the 1960s and 1970s inevitably produced a counter-attack. When it came, in the forms of the Thatcher and Reagan governments, Glyn seized the opportunity to play a significant role in the politics of the struggle. A central issue during the miners' strike of 1984–5 was the validity of the Coal Board's contention that a large number of mines should be closed because they had become economically unviable. Glyn rejected this, presenting a trenchant and detailed case against pit closures, in newspaper articles, pamphlets (notably *The Economic Case against Pit Closures*, published by the National Union of Mineworkers in 1984), and in broadcasts and public speeches. His convincing economic justification of keeping mines open provided a powerful weapon to the strikers. Even after the strike was defeated he continued for several years to call attention to the severe social and economic costs of the pit-closure programme in a series of reports to the Mineworkers' Union, the TUC, and the House of Commons' employment and trade and industry committees.

In 1981 Glyn's first marriage ended and on 27 June 1986 he married a fellow economist, Wendy Joan Carlin (*b.* 1957), daughter of Brian Frederick Carlin, agricultural scientist; they had two children, Tessa and Jonathan. Over the next two and a half decades Glyn was to collaborate with many economists, Carlin included. He became a central participant in a broad informal international research network studying his favourite issues of economic inequality, wages, and profits, and touching on such other subjects as globalization and the environment. A major theme in this work was strong opposition to inequality, on grounds of both equity and efficiency. He became increasingly convinced that the more liberal world economic policies that followed the crisis of the 1970s not only increased economic injustice but also were steering the world economy towards a new economic disaster. In his final book, *Capitalism Unleashed* (2006), he foresaw many aspects of the crisis that broke out in 2008.

The subject matter and approach of Glyn's economics were strongly motivated by his socialist beliefs. He was politically both committed and active. He was involved in Labour Party politics up to the 1980s and for many years supported the Trotskyist Militant Tendency. After the miners' strike his political activities did not diminish but became more eclectic. He was the least sectarian of socialists, however, and as a result maintained the respect of a broad spectrum of the left. Glyn was greatly appreciated as a teacher—for his ability 'to challenge students' minds without challenging their dignity' as one student put it (private information), for his compelling enthusiasm for the subject and his gift for explaining it intelligibly, and for the generous amounts of time he allocated to students. He was also a prolific writer of books, articles, and pamphlets (amounting to over sixty items), not to mention a connoisseur of jazz. His final article ('Functional distribution and inequality', published in *The Oxford Handbook of Inequality*, 2009) was a new analysis of the division of income between the social classes (between wages and profits), the dichotomy that had been the theme of his earliest published work and remained for him a key pointer to the erratic and destructive movements of the world capitalist economy. He died at Sobell House hospice, Oxford, on 22 December 2007, of a brain tumour, and was survived by his wife, Wendy, and his four children.

BOB SUTCLIFFE

Sources *The Guardian* (1 Jan 2008); (4 Jan 2008) · *Financial Times* (2 Jan 2008) · *In Defence of Marxism* (3 Jan 2008) · *The Independent* (7 Jan 2008); (10 Jan 2008) · *The Times* (8 Jan 2008) · *Red Pepper* (Feb–March 2008) · S. White, 'Must equality and efficiency conflict? The economics of Andrew Glyn', *Oxford Review of Economic Policy*, 25/1 (spring 2009), 155–63 · 'The writings of Andrew Glyn (1943–2007)', *Oxford Review of Economic Policy*, 25/1 (spring 2009), 164–72 · Burke, *Peerage* · personal knowledge (2011) · private information (2011) [Celia Glyn, former wife; Wendy Carlin, widow; Lucy Glyn, daughter; P. Armstrong] · b. cert. · m. certs. · d. cert.

Likenesses W. Glyn, photograph, priv. coll. [*see illus.*] · obituary photographs

Wealth at death £118,000: probate, 29 Feb 2008, *CGPLA Eng. & Wales*

Godwin [*née* Simmonds], **Fay Suzette** (1931–2005), photographer, was born on 17 February 1931 in Berlin, the elder child of Sidney Simmonds (1899–1978), British consular official, and his first wife, Stella, *née* MacLean (1896–1948), an American artist. The family moved regularly to different countries. Godwin was educated first by her mother, then in a series of nine schools across the globe, the last of which was Luckley School in Berkshire, where she gained her school certificate. She was an intelligent and competitive child who excelled in most activities, sporting and academic, and had a career mapped out in the international arena using her considerable language skills. However, the loss of her mother (on Fay's seventeenth birthday) put an end to her academic aspirations as she was obliged to assist her father with his official duties. In 1952 she was able to set up base in London, but spent much of the decade working as a travel representative in mainland Europe. It was during this period that she seriously damaged her knee in a skiing accident, which affected, but did not curtail, her lifelong passion for walking.

While working at John Murray publishers, Fay Simmonds met Anthony James Wylie (Tony) Godwin (1920–1976), publisher, who was to become an important and innovative figure in publishing, as chief editor at Penguin Books. They married in 1961 and had two sons, Nicholas and Jeremy. Throughout the 1960s she focused on her role as a mother and played hostess to her husband's career needs. Her interest in photography began as a hobby. She discovered its creative and documentary facilities while producing the family albums and entertaining her children by exploring the developing process to make negative imprints of leaves and flowers. When the marriage terminated, very abruptly, in 1969, it proved to be the catalyst for turning her hobby into a profession, as she resolved to control her own destiny.

In the early 1970s Fay Godwin set up her own business, taking portraits of authors for publicity purposes, and exhibiting them at Swiss Cottage Library (1974). Though largely self-taught, she took some classes with Euan Duff, and it was through this connection that her work appeared in various social documentary articles, especially in the Camden area. Godwin attended, then eventually taught at, photographic workshops, and was a strong champion of the support and community they engendered. At the start of her career she was strongly drawn to photojournalism, but, needing to be home-based, she eventually combined her documentary skills in the landscape images that began to emerge in a serious form during 1974.

Godwin's abiding interest in nature stemmed from her childhood. She joined the Ramblers' Association during the 1950s, later becoming its president (1987–90), and vice-president thereafter. A visit to the Lake District using a Wainwright guide inspired her to produce the first of a series of walkers' guidebooks: *The Oldest Road: an Exploration of the Ridgeway* (1975), co-written with J. R. L. Anderson. Her collaboration with established authors was a formula that opened her work to widely different audiences; probably her best-known was *Remains of Elmet* (1979), with Ted Hughes.

Godwin received an Arts Council bursary to fund her landscape work in the British Isles in 1978, which formed a significant percentage of the images in *Land* (1985), a reflection on the relationship between man and nature. This was the most celebrated body of her work, demonstrating her outstanding artistic and technical abilities. *Land* was shown nationally and internationally, and accompanied by her monograph of the same name. However, it was her defence of the environment that brought forth the absolute passion and politics in Godwin. In her fourteenth book, *Our Forbidden Land* (1990), she launched a multi-pronged offensive against the various bodies that prevented public access to a large percentage of land across the British Isles. It was dedicated to the Ramblers' Association, and won the first Green Book of the Year award.

Godwin earned many accolades during her professional life. She was the first photographer to have an entire programme of *The South Bank Show* feature her work, in 1986, an event that reflected not only her personal standing within the profession, but also changing attitudes of the establishment towards fine art photography. In 1987 she was the second photographer to take part in the fellowship scheme at the National Museum of Photography, Film and Television in Bradford, choosing the opportunity to experiment more formally with colour. Other awards followed, including honorary fellowships of the Royal Photographic Society and the Royal Incorporation of Architects in Scotland, in 1990 and 1992 respectively, and an honorary doctorate from De Montfort University in 2002.

Despite a determined move across the genres of her craft in the 1980s Godwin remained wedded to the welfare of the land. Thus in 1995 she used her award from the Erna and Victor Hasselblad Foundation to revisit Cumbria to investigate the relationship between the landscape and those who farm it. In 2001 the Barbican Centre hosted a major retrospective of her work, once again revealing the wide spectrum of subjects and equipment with which she continued to experiment throughout her professional life. Her state of health was a significant preoccupation throughout much of her life, and she was a devotee of alternative medicine and therapies. She managed to recover from two life-threatening illnesses but died at the Conquest Hospital, St Leonards, Sussex, near to her home at 6 Coastguard Cottages, Toot Rock, Pett Level, Hastings, on 27 May 2005, of heart failure, and was buried at Hastings borough cemetery, The Ridge, Hastings. She was survived by her two sons. GERALDINE ALEXANDER

Sources R. Taylor, 'Topographer with attitude', in F. Godwin, *Landmarks: a survey* (2001) · *The Guardian* (28 May 2005); (31 May 2005); (2 June 2005) · *Daily Telegraph* (30 May 2005) · *The Times* (31 May 2005); (7 June 2005) · *Western Morning News* (31 May 2005) · *The Independent* (2 June 2005) · *Yorkshire Post* (4 June 2005) · G. T. L. Alexander, 'Crossing the landscape: a journey from uncontested to contested space', MA diss., U. Sussex, 2006 · Fay Godwin website, www.djclark.com/godwin, 2 May 2008 · British Council collection, http://collection.britishcouncil.org/html/artist/artist.aspx?id=18161, 2 May 2008 · Fay Godwin papers, BL · *WW* (2005) · personal knowledge (2009) · private information (2009) · d. cert.

Archives BL | FILM BFINA, *The South Bank show*, H. Chadwick (director), LWT, 9 Nov 1986 · BFINA, current affairs footage | SOUND BL NSA, oral history of British photography, interviews with V. Williams, F3675–F3680 C1 · BL NSA, current affairs recordings · BL NSA, documentary recordings

Likenesses obituary photographs

Wealth at death £1,358,137: probate, 19 March 2007, *CGPLA Eng. & Wales*

Goldberg, Sir Abraham [Abe] **(1923–2007)**, physician, was born at 1 Buccleuch Terrace, Edinburgh, on 7 December 1923, the youngest of five children of Julius Judah Goldberg, Hebrew teacher and travelling salesman, and his wife, Rachel, *née* Varinofsky. His parents, of Jewish descent, were immigrants from Lithuania and Ukraine respectively and later set up a draper's business. He was educated at George Heriot's School, Edinburgh, and studied medicine at the University of Edinburgh; he graduated MB ChB in 1946. He said in later life that he had decided on his future career at the age of ten when he contracted rheumatic fever. This illness kept him bedridden for six months and eventually contributed to the stroke that disabled him greatly in the last year of his life.

After junior hospital medical posts and two years' national service with the Royal Army Medical Corps in Egypt, in 1952 Goldberg obtained a Nuffield fellowship in the department of chemical pathology at University College Hospital, London, where he learned the techniques that were to underpin his future research studies on the blood pigment haem and its relation to the disease porphyria. Having spent two years on an Eli Lilly travelling fellowship in Salt Lake City, Utah, with the haematologist Max Wintrobe, in 1956 he returned to the UK as a lecturer in medicine in the University of Glasgow, where he was to spend the rest of his professional career. With a doctorate of medicine with honours and a doctorate of science for his work on porphyria, he was successively appointed to a senior lectureship, a personal chair (1967), the regius chair of materia medica and therapeutics (1976), and finally the regius chair of the practice of medicine (1978). On 3 September 1957, at Queen's Park Synagogue, Glasgow, he married Clarice Cussin, a 25-year-old shorthand typist, and daughter of Jacob Cussin, fruiterer; they had two sons, David and Richard, and a daughter, Jennifer.

Goldberg was best known for his research on the basis of and treatment for porphyria, a disease that has several forms and many precipitant causes, including prescription medicines and herbal remedies, and which, according to some authorities, was responsible for the periodic madness of George III. Goldberg's work in this field stimulated his interest in clinical pharmacology and toxicology and led to his appointment to the directorship of the Medical Research Council's group on iron and porphyrin metabolism and his first regius chair. He became one of the few world authorities on porphyria and his group contributed extensively to the understanding of this difficult condition. His research also highlighted the risk of lead poisoning from water pipes and its links to brain damage. As a direct consequence of this work he became involved in public health controversies and was influential in improving the safety of the water supply to Glasgow.

Few academics with as busy a career as Goldberg placed such emphasis on the importance of improving medical education. He was responsible for modernizing the curriculum in his medical school and introducing then quite novel audio-visual aids to learning throughout the Glasgow hospitals. Generations of medical students and junior doctors in Glasgow recalled the enthusiasm and originality of his lectures and teaching ward rounds. (For instance, he devised a 'dermatome dance' to help students remember the nerve supply of the skin in different regions of the body.) He also took a personal interest in his patients, sending many of them Christmas cards until his death.

Not surprisingly, Goldberg was early drawn into administration at both local and national level. He served on the Glasgow health board, was made chairman of the grants committee of the clinical research board of the Medical Research Council (1973–7) and chairman of the biomedical research committee of the Scottish Home and Health Department's chief scientist's office (1977–83), and became founder president of the faculty of pharmaceutical medicine of the Royal College of Physicians (1989–91). Perhaps his most important outside appointment was as chairman of the Committee on the Safety of Medicines, a position he held from 1980 to 1986. The documentation traditionally presented to the committee was voluminous, but at each meeting it was known that Goldberg would have read every page of every submission. His tenure of the position was not altogether happy as he became involved in an episode of aggressive and unfair television journalism in connection with a BBC *Panorama* programme on Opren (a drug for arthritis linked to liver disease), which did not present him or the committee in the best light. This hurt him greatly at the time and for many years after.

Goldberg was knighted in 1983, and among many other honours was given the lord provost's award for services to the city of Glasgow in 1988. He retired in 1989, and was made a professor emeritus. He was prone to chronic back pain, and in retirement his ability to travel was limited. But, always interested in history, he developed as a writer on many historical topics, not all medical, and was appointed an honorary senior, then professorial, fellow in the department of modern history in his university (1990–96 and 1996–9). He also became especially interested in ways of promoting better understanding between those of his faith and others.

Throughout his professional life Goldberg demonstrated a tenacious and single-minded pursuit of what he thought was correct, sometimes irrespective of prevailing opinion. He was one of a breed of professors of medicine with a breadth of interest and achievement unusual in later generations. He died of heart failure at Burnfield Care Home, Giffnock, near Glasgow, on 1 September 2007, and was survived by his wife, Clarice, and their three children. ALASDAIR BRECKENRIDGE

Sources *Daily Record* (6 Sept 2007) • *Evening Times* [Glasgow] (7 Sept 2007) • *The Herald* [Glasgow] (9 Oct 2007) • *The Times* (17 Oct 2007) • *BMJ*, 335/7625 (27 Oct 2007), 891 • www.rcpe.ac.uk/publications/obituaries/2007/goldberg.php, 17 March 2010 • www.rse.org.uk/fellowship/obits/obits_alpha/goldberg_a.pdf, 17 March 2010 • *WW* • Burke, *Peerage* • personal knowledge (2011) • private information (2011) • b. cert. • m. cert. • d. cert.

Likenesses obituary photographs • photograph, repro. in www.universitystory.gla.ac.uk/images/UGSP00902.jpg

Goldman, Sir Samuel (1912–2007), civil servant, was born in a three-roomed tenement at 225 Brady Street Buildings, Whitechapel, London, on 10 March 1912, the seventh and youngest son of Jewish immigrants who had settled in London in 1898, Philip Goldman, who worked in the clothing trade, and his wife, Sarah, *née* Shineman. He was educated at Davenant Foundation and Raines Foundation schools, and at the age of seventeen gained a scholarship to the London School of Economics. He graduated BSc (Econ) after two years, instead of the normal three, and in 1931 was awarded first-class honours and the Gladstone memorial prize for the highest aggregate marks of any candidate for the degree from all faculties. He was influenced by Friedrich Hayek, who gave four lectures at the school in 1930–31, and whom he visited in Vienna in 1932. Goldman's MSc (Econ) dissertation was on the English theory of capital from a Hayekian viewpoint, and Hayek was one of the examiners. Goldman was later one of the school's first honorary fellows.

On 24 December 1933, while still a research student, Goldman married, at Willesden register office, Pearl

Moshinsky, otherwise Marre (1909–1941), daughter of Joseph Moshinsky, tobacconist. They had a daughter, Janet (*b.* 1937), who died in infancy, and a son, Antony (*b.* 1940). From 1934 Goldman worked for the London subsidiary of Moody's Economist Services and then in 1938–9 for the stockbrokers Joseph Sebag & Co. With the outbreak of the Second World War the Bank of England had to strengthen its collection and assessment of financial data so as to administer the new exchange controls and to mobilize and sell privately owned foreign exchange assets, and Goldman was one of a number of recruits from the City in 1940. On 27 November 1943, at Marylebone register office, following the death of his first wife, he married Patricia Rosemary Bond (1915–1990), widow of Geoffrey Bond and daughter of Thomas Hodges, mining engineer. There were no children of this second marriage.

In 1947 Goldman joined the civil service as a statistician in the Central Statistical Office. There was a sterling crisis that summer that exposed the danger of reliance on sometimes tardy information from the Bank of England and in September he was appointed head of a new statistical division in the Treasury's overseas finance group. In 1948 he became the department's chief statistician. He took part in discussions in Paris in 1947–8 that led to the setting up of the Organization for European Economic Co-operation to help administer Marshall aid. In 1949 he was one of a small group of officials who flew to Washington for talks with the Americans and Canadians in preparation for the devaluation of sterling.

Goldman decided to develop his professional career by transferring to the administrative class, which he did in 1952 as assistant secretary in charge of the exchequer division in the Treasury's home finance group. Subsequently he had experience of overseas finance and supply services divisions. He was promoted under-secretary in 1960, and in 1961–2 he was deputy head of the Treasury and supply delegation in Washington and UK alternate director at the World Bank. From 1962 he was a third secretary with oversight of the home finance divisions and domestic and external aspects of the monetary and credit system. From March to May 1968 he was a member of a hastily convened committee drawn from the Treasury and the Bank of England to consider what should be done about a run on the reserves following the sterling devaluation of 1967. The Treasury advisers favoured wholesale blocking of sterling balances; the bank preferred to float the pound, but was overruled, and the Bretton Woods system of fixed but adjustable exchange rates survived a few more years.

In the summer of 1968 Goldman became second permanent secretary, initially with responsibility for home and overseas finance, but from December he was head of the public sector group with responsibility for the planning and control of public expenditure. In order to make a success of devaluation it was necessary to reverse the rise in the public sector's share of the national income, and by 1970 that share had fallen two percentage points from its 1968 peak. He oversaw rapid development of the public expenditure survey system that Sir Richard Clarke had pioneered in the early 1960s. From 1970 he had to adapt the system to the ideas of Edward Heath's government, notably the policy analysis and review scheme for scrutinizing whether the instruments used to achieve policy aims were cost-effective. He was knighted KCB in 1969, having been made a CB in 1964.

Six months before Goldman was due to retire in 1972 the prime minister ruled that he should cease to be engaged in normal Treasury duties since he planned to take employment in the City. In order to tap his experience it was agreed he should write a pamphlet, *The Developing System of Public Expenditure Management and Control* (1973), which he drafted with a view to its use as a Civil Service College training manual. In it he said he doubted whether the use of constant prices encouraged inflation by removing any incentive to minimize costs or wage increases. In the event, however, the system proved to be ill adapted to the high inflation of the mid-1970s and cash control was introduced in 1976.

In 1972 Goldman joined Orion Bank as an executive director and was managing director from 1974 until 1976, when he became chairman of Henry Ansbacher Holdings Ltd and Henry Ansbacher Ltd. He was chairman of the Covent Garden Market Authority from 1976 to 1981. In 1982 he retired from the City to care for his wife, who died in 1990. He then moved into a flat in a house in Wonersh, near Guildford, and set about restoring its grounds, which had been designed by Gertrude Jekyll.

Goldman had a sharp, analytical mind and good judgement. He was held in high esteem and acquired many friends. His conversation was punctuated with a sometimes wicked sense of humour. He died at Bridge House nursing home, Farnham Road, Elstead, Surrey, on 28 July 2007 and was survived by his son, Antony.

G. C. PEDEN

Sources S. Goldman, 'My early life, or, An East End childhood, 1912–1931', BLPES • 'First report for select committee on procedure, 12 Feb 1969', *Parl. papers* (1960–69), 15.153 • 'Third report for the expenditure committee', 36.729, *Parl. papers* (1970–71), HC 549 • TNA: PRO, T 199/702–703, 919, 1239; 295/489–90; 331/529, 665–6, 679–80, 685–6, 947 • H. Heclo and A. Wildavsky, *The private government of public money: community and policy inside British politics* (1974) • R. Clarke, *Public expenditure, management and control*, ed. A. Cairncross (1978) • L. Pliatzky, *Getting and spending: public expenditure, employment and inflation* (1982) • *The Robert Hall diaries*, ed. A. Cairncross, 2 vols. (1989–91) • A. Cairncross, *The Wilson years: a Treasury diary, 1964–1969* (1997) • A. Hamilton, 'Beyond the sterling devaluation: the gold crisis of March 1968', *Contemporary European History*, 17 (2008), 73–95 • *The Times* (10 Aug 2007) • Burke, *Peerage* • *WW* (2007) • private information (2011) [Antony Goldman, son] • b. cert. • m. certs. • d. cert.

Archives BLPES

Likenesses G. Argent, bromide print on card mount, 1970, NPG • obituary photographs

Wealth at death £382,874: probate, 4 March 2008, *CGPLA Eng. & Wales*

Gomm, Richard Culling Carr- (1922–2008), army officer and charity founder, was born at Mancetter Lodge, Mancetter, near Atherstone, Warwickshire, on 2 January 1922, the third of four sons of Mark Culling Carr-Gomm (1883–1963), civil engineer, and his wife, Amicia Dorothy, *née*

Heming (1880–1962). He went to Stowe School and won a place at Oriel College, Oxford. However, the Second World War was declared in his last year at school and he declined the place and volunteered to join the army. First enlisting in a young soldiers' battalion in the Royal Berkshires, he was commissioned into the Coldstream Guards in 1941. He was twice injured by shrapnel, fought in Normandy in the 6th guards tank brigade, and visited Belsen. He was awarded the Croix de Guerre (silver star) and mentioned in dispatches. From Europe he went to Palestine, where he spent two and a half years during the mandate. He applied for a regular commission and reached the rank of major. Carr-Gomm was an ambitious soldier, so much so that he longed to achieve what his great-great-uncle, Sir William Carr-Gomm, had achieved—a field marshal's baton.

However, in 1955 and to the astonishment of his friends and family, Carr-Gomm threw over his military career, resigned his commission, and became an unpaid home help, working with old and disabled people. He left his comfortable billet in London's Chelsea barracks and took a bedsit in Bermondsey, a deprived area of south London, where his family owned property. He was known as the Scrubbing Major.

Carr-Gomm's career charge was determined by the fact that in various of his postings he had encountered scenes of deprivation and poverty unknown to one of his background, but also the fact that beginning in 1953 he had undergone a religious conversion that deepened his already existing Christian faith. Travelling back from a posting in the Suez canal zone by way of Malta and Sicily to Naples, he took the slow train the length of Italy. He travelled as a tramp, sleeping rough, foraging for food, drinking from public water taps, washing in the sea—and, unbeknownst to her, at one time in Gracie Fields's swimming pool in Capri. He did this 'to see what it was like' (*Push on the Door*). He found that the worst deprivation of all was loneliness. Looking like a tramp, he was treated like one, and people gave him a wide berth. He said that on that long journey only once did he meet kindness. However, in Turin, on his way to the cathedral to see the Turin shroud, he chanced upon the Cottolengo ('the little house of divine providence'), run by nuns for 8000 people suffering various kinds of distress. There he saw, he said, 'deaf and dumb children trying to speak and the deformed playing football. I saw the aged lying in their beds at the foot of a crucifix and madmen walking about, declaiming' (ibid.). He was initially shocked by how the children of friends and family were allowed to wander about. But 'it's not infectious', he was told (ibid.). He returned to Britain wondering how his own country looked after the poor, disabled, and marginalized. His own beliefs were undergoing revaluation. He returned to the Guards but spent a weekend retreat with Franciscans in Dorset, where he slept in a cell and found silence companionable. He felt, he said, 'a clarity of vision and a peace, feeling very rare for me' (ibid.). His critical point of departure came when he attended a rally in Harringay stadium addressed by the American evangelist Billy Graham. As a result he decided to leave the Guards, with a small gratuity of £250 but no pension.

At the end of 1955 Carr-Gomm used the gratuity for a deposit on a run-down house in Bermondsey. Decorating it with the help of volunteers, he then invited four lonely people—two men and two women—to share it with him while he acted as housekeeper and offered two hot meals a day. He wished to combine support, companionship, and independence. Within two years, he had opened five more sheltered houses and in 1956 he formed the Abbeyfield Society. He did this with the help of Susan Gibbs (1927–2007), daughter of Ralph Gibbs, stockbroker, whom he married on 21 October 1957, and with whom he had two sons and three daughters.

The Abbeyfield Society grew into a national organization and by the time of its founder's death it ran 700 sheltered houses and eighty homes for those too frail to care for themselves, providing homes for more than 8000 people. But in 1963, to his shock and distress, after months of debate about the way that the society should go, he was at first banned from the central office and then sacked by a central committee. It accused him, he complained, of 'power complexes and egotism' (*Push on the Door*). He feared that a central administration and all that went with it would destroy the idealistic voluntary spirit. He had also always and controversially encouraged a strong spiritual element with hymn singing, albeit within a non-denominational ethos. He was later reconciled with the organization.

After working as a librarian for two years, Carr-Gomm founded the Carr-Gomm Society, again starting with one house in Bermondsey. This society aimed to help those of all ages who were lonely or had mental health problems or other difficulties. This, too, grew into a national charity and one that by the time Carr-Gomm died provided accommodation for 1500 people, with thousands more receiving support in their own homes. More than 60 per cent of those helped were under forty-five years of age. In 1975 he founded the Morpeth Society (later Morpeth Society Housing Association), buying two flats in Victoria for rent to people able to afford their own properties but who did not wish to live alone.

Carr-Gomm was appointed OBE in 1985 and was awarded the Templeton UK project award in 1984. On 27 October 2008, almost a year after the death of his wife, he suffered a pulmonary embolism while out walking near his home in Batheaston, Somerset. He was declared dead on arrival at the Royal United Hospital, Bath. A service of thanksgiving was held at Southwark Cathedral on 29 April 2009. He was survived by his five children.

TERRY PHILPOT

Sources R. Carr-Gomm, *Push on the door* (1979) · *The Times* (30 Oct 2008) · *Daily Telegraph* (30 Oct 2008) · *The Independent* (3 Nov 2008) · *The Guardian* (6 Nov 2008) · *WW* (2008) · b. cert. · m. cert. · d. cert.

Likenesses G. Konig, photograph, *c.*1960 (with Mutesa II), Getty Images, London · F. Monaco, photograph, 1983, Rex Features, London

Wealth at death £654,396: probate, 9 March 2009, *CGPLA Eng. & Wales*

Goobey, Alastair Ross (1945–2008), pension fund manager, was born at 29 The Avenue, Wanstead, Essex, on 6 December 1945, the son of George Henry Ross *Goobey (1911–1999), pension fund manager, and his wife, Gladys Edith, *née* Menzies (*b.* 1911). He was brought up in Clevedon, near Bristol, and educated at Marlborough College and Trinity College, Cambridge, where he studied economics. A keen student actor, he met Sarah Georgina Mary Stille (*b.* 1949) in a production of *Hamlet*; she was a secretary, the daughter of Cedric Ernest Stille, a flower bulb importer. They married on 26 July 1969 and had a son and a daughter.

Ross Goobey's father, the in-house investment manager of Imperial Tobacco Company's pension fund from 1947 to 1975, was a legendary figure in fund management as the pioneer of the 'cult of the equity', the shift from government bonds to equities in the 1950s. Ross Goobey junior joined the merchant bank Kleinwort Benson, a leading City merchant bank, as a graduate trainee in 1968. Subsequently he worked for Hume Holdings (1972–7), Courtaulds pension fund (1977–81) as investment manager, and the investment boutique Geoffrey Morley and Partners (1981–7) as a director. From 1987 to 1993 he held the relatively prominent post of chief investment strategist at the leading City stockbroker James Capel & Co.

Ross Goobey became a high-profile financial figure as chief executive of Hermes Pensions Management, manager of the Post Office and British Telecom staff pension fund, from 1993 to 2001. Hermes was one of Britain's biggest institutional investors with sizeable holdings in many quoted companies. They provided Ross Goobey with an opportunity to pursue better corporate governance through institutional shareholder activism. Soon after his appointment he wrote to all the chairmen of FTSE 100 companies informing them that Hermes opposed three-year rolling contracts for chief executives, which ensured huge pay-offs regardless of performance. He was an early proponent of the separation of the roles of chairman and chief executive and of greater corporate transparency, and took a dim view of directors remaining beyond normal retirement age. Hermes even opposed the re-election of Ross Goobey's septuagenarian father as chairman of a quoted property company. His ideas were taken up by official inquiries into corporate governance and incorporated into the Combined Code of 2003. 'It's quite difficult to argue with some of the things we suggest', he observed to the *Financial Times* in 2002, 'such as the principle that we're not against people being paid well but please can they earn it first' (*Financial Times*, 9 Jan 2002). He was a founder and from 2002 chairman of the International Corporate Governance Network, which brought together shareholder activist investors from across the world. 'The big change is that companies are now listening to shareholders', he said. 'When we started this, they didn't even talk to shareholders' (*Financial Times*, 19 July 2001).

Like his father, Ross Goobey developed pension fund investment in new directions, especially commercial property, being 'one of the most forceful advocates of

Alastair Ross Goobey (1945–2008), by unknown photographer, 2003

property as a financial asset' (*Financial Times*, 10 Nov 1994). From 1995 to 2004 he was president of the Investment Property Forum, a body that promoted commercial property to institutional investors. He wrote a monthly column in the *Estates Gazette* and was author of *Bricks & Mortals* (1992), an account of the 1980s property boom and bust. His other book, *The Money Moguls* (1986), was a study of the investment management industry. He created the Hermes Focus Funds that invested actively in underperforming companies and helped to turn them round, and after retiring as chief executive of Hermes Pensions Management Ltd he continued as chairman of Hermes Focus Asset Management Ltd. He was much in demand as an adviser. He played a key role in the development of the investment strategy of the Wellcome Trust, the world's largest medical charity, of which he was a governor from 2002. He was a member of the council of Lloyd's (1997–2003) and on the European advisory board of Morgan Stanley, where he was a senior adviser from 2002. Directorships included Scottish Life (1978–86), Cheltenham and Gloucester Building Society (1989–91 and 1992–7), TR Property Investment Trust (1994–2004), and John Wainwright & Co. (1997–2008). From 2002 until his death he was a senior adviser at Morgan Stanley.

A free-market Conservative, Ross Goobey unsuccessfully contested the safe Labour seat of Leicester West in the general election of 1979. This brought him to the notice of Nigel Lawson, leading to stints as special adviser to chancellors Nigel Lawson in 1986–7 and Norman Lamont in 1991–2. He later observed that he was 'jolly glad' he had not become a politician (*The Times*, 5 Feb 2008). His Whitehall experience led to several senior official appointments, including the Goode committee on pensions law (1992–3), the Middleton committee on film industry finance (1995–6), and the chairmanship of the private finance initiative panel (1996–7). He was appointed CBE in 2000 for services to pensions; many City colleagues felt that he deserved a higher honour, particularly for his role in improving corporate governance.

Ross Goobey became known beyond the City through newspaper articles and as a panellist on seven series of BBC Radio 4's light-hearted business quiz, *The Board Game*. Interviewed on the *Today* programme in March 2003, during a stock market downturn, he correctly called the bottom and famously exhorted listeners to 'fill your boots' with equities (*The Independent*, 6 Feb 2008). He was, in his own phrase, 'a card-carrying capitalist' who admired successful entrepreneurship, though, observed an obituarist, 'he certainly had a puritanical streak, emphasized by an appearance that had something of the 19th-century Nonconformist preacher' (*Daily Telegraph*, 8 Feb 2008). He disclosed his own pay package, never claimed his lunch expenses, and turned down opportunities of more lucrative employment. 'I just think I missed out on the greed gene', he remarked (*The Times*, 5 Feb 2008). Nigel Lawson recalled in his memoirs that Ross Goobey 'never could resist a joke' (Lawson, 658).

Ross Goobey's recreations included club cricket, supporting Arsenal, and music. He played the piano and the clarinet, notably at the wedding of Clive James. Charitable and voluntary contributions included membership of the boards or investment committees of the Royal Academy of Music, the National Gallery, the National Opera Studio Foundation, and the Royal Opera House. CancerBACUP, the cancer information charity, was an active interest in acknowledgement of the help provided after his diagnosis of blood cancer in 1997. He was successfully treated, but died at his home, 22 Alwyne Road, Islington, from a recurrence, on 2 February 2008. He was survived by his wife, Sarah, and their two children.

RICHARD ROBERTS

Sources N. Lawson, *The view from no. 11: memoirs of a tory radical* (1992) · *Financial Times* (10 Nov 1994); (19 July 2001); (9 Jan 2002) · *The Times* (5 Feb 2008) · *The Independent* (6 Feb 2008) · *Daily Telegraph* (8 Feb 2008) · *The Guardian* (11 March 2008) · *WW* (2008) · b. cert. · m. cert. · d. cert.

Archives SOUND BL NSA, documentary recording

Likenesses photograph, 2003, Rex Features, London [*see illus.*] · photographs, 2003, Rex Features, London · obituary photographs

Wealth at death £3,151,270: probate, 19 Nov 2008, *CGPLA Eng. & Wales*

Goodwin, Leonard George [Len] **(1915–2008)**, pharmacologist and medical protozoologist, was born on 11 July 1915 at 5 Cheapside High Road, Wood Green, London, the son of Harry George Goodwin (1886–1964), manager of a shoe shop, and his wife, Lois, *née* Steel (1889–1979), daughter of a gamekeeper in Rutland whose early influence established Len's interests in natural history and keenness for practical skills. He grew up in Hampstead and, after attending the William Ellis School, Camden, from 1926 to 1932, he went as a county scholar to study pharmacy at the College of the Pharmaceutical Society in Bloomsbury Square, as advised by his admired uncle, Percy Goodwin, who managed a pharmacy in London's Wigmore Street. He completed the recently introduced BPharm degree in 1935. He then became a demonstrator at the Pharmaceutical Society College for four years under the powerful influence of its dean, the eminent pharmacologist J. H. Burn, who advised him to combine this appointment with part-time studies of physiology at nearby University College. This he did, graduating BSc in 1937 and going on to complete second MB studies just before the outbreak of the Second World War.

When the Pharmaceutical Society College was evacuated to Cardiff, Goodwin remained in London and in October 1939 joined the staff of the tropical medicine laboratories of the Wellcome Bureau for Scientific Research in Euston Road, the outstanding international centre of tropical disease research. On 24 August 1940 he married a fellow pharmacist, Marie Evelyn Coates (1916–2004), daughter of Frank Arnold Coates, sales manager. Meanwhile, under the direction of the eminent protozoologist Cecil Hoare he began investigating protozoan parasites of the tropics. There was intense pressure to assist Allied forces overseas by developing more effective drugs and treatments for tropical infections. His early contributions were in refining the assaying of potentially therapeutic compounds being synthesized for screening by the Wellcome Bureau's chemistry laboratories. By 1942 his value as a pharmaceutical protozoologist secured his release from the tank corps just days after call-up. Soon afterwards he had a major part in research leading to the anti-leishmaniasis drug sodium stibogluconate, or Pentostam. With the German drug Stolustibosan no longer available and leishmaniasis a problem among troops invading Sicily, Wellcome chemists took up the challenge of synthesizing a similar organometallic pentavalent antimony compound. Goodwin undertook the screening of the numerous versions they created, eventually finding a British equivalent of Stolustibosan, which was trialled on American servicemen after initial testing on hamsters. Pentostam proved a timely addition to the wartime drugs arsenal and went on to widespread peacetime use.

Goodwin introduced the Syrian or golden hamster into drugs testing after finding that European hamsters, which German pharmacologists had used in assaying anti-leishmoniasis compounds, were slow in developing the disease. It was later sometimes claimed that pet golden hamsters originated from the laboratory colony that Goodwin established. As Goodwin pointed out, however, his breeding stock came from the zoologist Edward Hindle, who in turn had received his from the original laboratory colony bred by Saul Adler, professor of parasitology at the Hebrew University of Jerusalem, from a wild litter found at Aleppo. The domestication of golden hamsters began with Adler.

After the war Goodwin's attention turned to antimalarial and trypanosomiasis research. ICI had brought out Paludrine, but the Wellcome laboratories were intent on finding a better antimalarial drug. By 1947 the biochemist George Hitchings at the Wellcome Research Laboratories in New York had begun investigating nucleic acids and synthesizing purine and pyrimidine analogues, some of which he hoped to be therapeutic. Ones worth testing for antimalarial properties he sent to Goodwin's laboratory. The sixty-third of these, pyrimethamine, received in 1950, assayed well both as a therapeutic and protective agent. Goodwin's first of several trips to Africa to trial drugs in the field came in the same year. By then he had qualified MB BS, having since 1947 combined clinical training at University College Hospital with night and weekend research in the Wellcome laboratories. His trip to Nigerian cattle stations in 1950 was mainly to trial the effectiveness of three phenanthradine compounds that in laboratory tests had looked promising against cattle trypanosomiasis. But these compounds proved too toxic and the latter part of his trip he used to arrange trials of pyrimethamine in Lagos. He also undertook preliminary tests on himself and was exposed to falciparum infection without harm. The trials he arranged fully validated pyrimethamine, which remained in use at the time of his death.

In the 1950s Goodwin made several long visits to Africa to trial chemotherapeutic products that had assayed well against tropical scourges, including potential anthelmintics. With increased responsibility these had become part of his research remit at a time when the pharmaceutical industry was under pressure to produce drugs against the main worm diseases of the tropics. Recollections of the adventures and trials and tribulations of a visit to Tanganyika in 1954 to trial a *p*-aminophenoxyalkane, that laboratory tests had shown strongly anti-schistosomal, were later recorded in the autobiography of his trials companion Owen Standen. Although the main trial was abandoned when a number of subjects reported visual disturbances, a pilot trial of piperazine, a standby product they had with them, had a better outcome, revealing its strong worming action. It was to become a major product. Goodwin accounted for his late-life blindness as stemming from personal testing of the *p*-aminophenoxyalkane trialled on this trip.

Goodwin became the head of the Wellcome Laboratories of Tropical Medicine in 1958, but six years later, with the Wellcome Trust going through major change not entirely to his liking, took the post of director of the newly created Nuffield Institute of Comparative Medicine at the Zoological Society of London which he led innovatively until 1980, combining this role with that of the society's director of science from 1966. Under his direction the institute became a leading international research centre with unique databases covering the comparative physiology of the Zoo's spectrum of exotic species. He also led research into such areas as arteriosclerosis, sleeping sickness, and the anticoagulant properties of pig saliva.

It was as a tropical medicine pharmacologist of the 1940s and 1950s that Goodwin's career had most impact, through the five major drugs he helped establish: sodium stibogluconate to combat leishmaniasis, pyrimethamine to combat malaria, piperazine to combat ascariasis, bephenium to combat ankylostomiasis, and phenanthridine derivates to combat trypanosomiasis.

Goodwin's list of scientific publications was impressive, including part authorship of several textbooks, including *Biological Standardization* (1950) and *A New Tropical Hygiene* (1960). In 1976 he was elected a fellow of the Royal Society and a year later appointed CMG. His down-to-earth affability and considerable modesty masked his distinction. His main leisure interests were painting, opera, travels in Italy, gardening, and small-scale animal husbandry at his Finchampstead smallholding; at one point he kept four wallabies, as well as sheep, ducks, geese (and cats). A talented artist, on overseas journeys he had recorded places visited with easy watercolour brush strokes instead of photography, capturing their spirit as well as form. The loss of the ability to paint and to attend to his garden and smallholding were afflictions he bore with stoicism. He died of bronchopneumonia at the Royal Berkshire Hospital on 25 November 2008. He had no children.

MAX BLYTHE

Sources O. Standen, *The fellow travellers: an autobiography* (1994) • *Daily Telegraph* (15 Jan 2009) • *The Guardian* (24 Feb 2009) • *The Times* (10 March 2009) • munksroll.rcplondon.ac.uk/biography/details/6072, 8 Aug 2011 • G. Wolstenholme, video interview, 28 June 1989, Oxford Brookes University, Medical Sciences Video archive, MSVA 043 • M. Blythe, video interview, 16 July 1996, Oxford Brookes University, Medical Sciences Video archive, MSVA 134 • *WW* (2008) • personal knowledge (2012) • private information (2012) • b. cert. • m. cert. • d. cert.

Archives FILM Oxford Brookes University, Medical Sciences Video archive, interviews with G. Wolstenholme, 28 June 1989, MSVA 043, and M. Blythe, 16 July 1996, MSVA 134

Likenesses Elliott & Fry, photograph, 1962, NPG • obituary photographs

Wealth at death £1,272,648: probate, 5 March 2009, *CGPLA Eng. & Wales*

Graham, Colin (1931–2007), opera director and librettist, was born on 22 September 1931 at 17 Fourth Avenue, Hove, Sussex, the son of Frederick Eaton Graham-Bonnalie (1897–1979), physician and medical author, and his first wife, Alexandra Diana Vivian (Anore), *née* Finlay (1909–1988). His parents divorced while he was still young and both subsequently remarried. Educated at Northaw preparatory school, Hertfordshire, and Stowe School, Buckinghamshire, he had an early interest in singing but soon realized that his voice lacked the necessary lustre for a professional career. Instead he turned to acting and while still a student at the Royal Academy of Dramatic Art, in 1950, he worked as an assistant stage manager at the Royal Opera House, Covent Garden, during his holidays. This inspired him to investigate the possibilities that stage management had to offer, and after leaving the academy he worked briefly as an actor, and later as a stage manager at the Nottingham Repertory Theatre.

When Graham was appointed assistant stage manager for the English Opera Group in 1953 he quickly came to the attention of Benjamin Britten. The company was soon central to Graham's career path and Britten's music dominated his activities to the end of his life. In 1956 Graham co-directed the composer's *Let's Make an Opera* and he staged a revival of *Albert Herring* the following year. Clearly gifted, he was then invited to direct the world première of *Noye's Fludde* at Orford church for the Aldeburgh festival in 1958. With masks and costumes designed by the Welsh artist Ceri Richards and a cast that included Owen Brannigan and Gladys Parr conducted by Charles Mackerras, the production was Graham's first major success. In 1959 he revived *The Rape of Lucretia*; in 1963 (the year in which he became director of productions for the English

Opera Group) he directed Britten's performing version of Gay's *The Beggar's Opera*; and in 1964 he took charge of the première of *Curlew River*, the first of Britten's three church parables. Staged and designed by Graham and performed by Peter Pears and Bryan Drake, the work brought him into increasingly closer contact with Britten. Throughout the preparatory period Graham visited Britten regularly in Venice, where he consulted him fully. Britten was concerned that the staging should avoid ostentation and should complement fully both the libretto and the score, later defining features of Graham's production style. In 1966 he designed and directed Britten's second church parable, *The Burning Fiery Furnace*, at Orford, and in 1968 he was responsible for staging the third church parable, *The Prodigal Son*, again at Orford. By the late 1960s Graham's name was closely associated with Britten and Aldeburgh, and he became artistic director of the festival between 1969 and 1989 and of the English Music Theatre Company (formerly English Opera Group) between 1975 and 1979. With those companies he worked tirelessly on behalf of the composer's music and, in 1973, took charge of the first performance of *Death in Venice* at The Maltings, Snape. He also wrote the libretto for Britten's *The Golden Vanity* (1966), a 'vaudeville' for boys and piano.

During his time with the English Opera Group and the Aldeburgh festival Graham maintained his links with spoken theatre and directed productions at the Old Vic, the Oxford Playhouse, and the Bristol Old Vic and for the Royal Shakespeare Company. But opera remained his passion, and as early as 1961 he had begun to spread his artistic wings by directing his first opera at Sadler's Wells: Janáček's *The Cunning Little Vixen*. Acclaimed critically, the staging was the first of a series of challenging productions that he directed at Rosebery Avenue. In 1965 he produced Richard Rodney Bennett's *The Mines of Sulphur*; in 1966 Janáček's *From the House of the Dead* and Britten's *Gloriana*; and in 1967 Richard Rodney Bennett's *A Penny for a Song*, for which Graham wrote the libretto based on John Whiting's play of the same name. That year Graham was made associate director of productions at Sadler's Wells Opera, an appointment he held until 1975.

After the company moved to the Coliseum and changed its name to the English National Opera in 1970, Graham rose to new artistic heights. For the renamed company he created a new performing version of Offenbach's *The Tales of Hoffmann* with Edmund Tracey and, for Glyndebourne Festival Opera, he directed Nicholas Maw's *The Rising of the Moon* conducted by Raymond Leppard. In 1971 he staged Wagner's *Lohengrin* and Monteverdi's *The Coronation of Poppea* (with Janet Baker) at the Coliseum and directed, jointly with Brian Large, Britten's television opera *Owen Wingrave* for the BBC. The following year he staged Prokofiev's *War and Peace* for the English National Opera, a production considered by many commentators as his greatest theatrical achievement. In 1973 he adapted his version of *Owen Wingrave* for the Royal Opera House's stage, and in 1974 made his American début with a production of the work for Santa Fe Opera. This was followed by a staging of *Death in Venice* at the Metropolitan Opera, New York, which was received coolly, a major disappointment for Graham. His spirits were restored, however, when he directed a critically acclaimed production of *The Cunning Little Vixen* at Santa Fe in 1976 and produced the world première of Stephen Oliver's *Tom Jones* for English Music Theatre the same year. For that company he then staged Britten's *Paul Bunyan* and *The Turn of the Screw*, Mozart's *La finta giardiniera*, and Weill's *The Threepenny Opera*. In 1976 he directed a revival of Walton's *Troilus and Cressida* at the Royal Opera House and in 1977 he staged the world première of Iain Hamilton's *The Royal Hunt of the Sun*, based on Peter Schaffer's play, at the Coliseum. That year he successfully directed the first performance of Thea Musgrave's *Mary, Queen of Scots* and accepted the post of director of productions at the English National Opera. He remained in that post, and an important figure with the company, until 1984, when the team of Peter Jonas, Mark Elder, and David Pountney changed the artistic direction of the company. Although he often considered his own work to be both distinctive and incisive, others began to consider it old-fashioned and representative of an earlier aesthetic.

Even though his approach had fallen from favour in London, Graham was still in great demand in the United States. Between 1985 and 2007 he was artistic director of the Opera Theatre of St Louis. There he staged the world première of Minoru Miki's *Tale of Genji* and produced operas and operettas by Mozart, Berlioz, Weber, Rossini, Tchaikovsky, and Sullivan. He taught opera production at Yale school of music, staged the world première of John Corigliano's *The Ghosts of Versailles* at the Metropolitan Opera, and was the librettist for, and director of, André Previn's *A Streetcar Named Desire* at San Francisco in 1998. While he took American citizenship and worked mainly for American institutions during his last years, he never turned his back fully on Europe, where he led the Walton Foundation's opera course at the composer's former home on the island of Ischia in Italy. During his American period he was drawn increasingly to religion, and in 1984 he announced that he was reducing his directing activities so that he could study theology. Three years later he was ordained a minister of the New Covenant church. He also took up bodybuilding at the age of sixty, and entered competitions and won championships in his age group. In 2002 he was appointed OBE. He never married. On 6 April 2007 he died of cardiac and respiratory failure at St Louis, Missouri. At the time of his death he was collaborating with the American composer David Carlson on the opera *Anna Karenina*, for which he wrote the libretto. Within weeks of his death the work was staged in Miami and his libretto was praised by the *New York Times* on 30 April 2007 for its faithfulness to Tolstoy's book, a fitting tribute to a man who devoted his life to the search for artistic truth. A memorial service was held at St Paul's, Covent Garden, on 5 October 2007. RAYMOND HOLDEN

Sources A. Porter, 'The Cunning Little Vixen', *MT*, 102/1417 (March 1961), 146–7 • J. Warrack, 'Britten's *Curlew River*', *Tempo*, new ser., 70 (autumn 1964), 19–22 • H. Keller, 'A re-affirmation', *Tempo*, new ser., 79 (winter 1966–7), 2–5 • A. Payne, 'Nicholas Maw's *The*

Rising of the Moon', *Tempo*, new ser., 94 (autumn 1970), 26–9 • R. McAllister, 'Prokofiev's Tolstoy epic', *MT*, 113/1555 (Sept 1972), 851–5 • E. Crozier, '*The Fairy Queen* revived', *Early Music*, 5/4 (Oct 1977), 605 • *St Louis Post-Dispatch* (6 April 2007) • *The Times* (9 April 2007) • *Daily Telegraph* (9 April 2007) • *Playbill Arts* (9 April 2007) • *The Guardian* (10 April 2007) • *The Independent* (11 April 2007) • *New York Times* (30 April 2007) • *WW* (2007) • private information (2011) [C. Mackerras] • b. cert.

Likenesses photograph, 1963, PA Photos, London • N. Luckhurst, bromide print, 1975 (with Isador Caplan), NPG • photograph, repro. in en.wikipedia.org/wiki/Colin_Graham

Graham, David Michael Gordon [Davey], [Davy] (**1940–2008**), guitarist and singer, was born on 26 November 1940 at Bosworth Park Infirmary, Market Bosworth, Leicestershire, the son of James McLeod (Hamish or Seamus) Graham, accountant and Gaelic scholar, and Winifred Mary Gordon Woolford (1916–1989). His father was born on Skye, his mother in Georgetown, British Guiana; she was the daughter of Sir Eustace Gordon Woolford, the first speaker of the national assembly of Guyana (1953–7). His mother did not register his birth until 1974; by then she had adopted the name Amanda and had married (in 1941) Dennis G. A. Howell and then (in 1947) James M. Doyle, and on 15 July 1972 Graham himself had married Holly Patrice Gwinn, an American teacher five years his junior. He then gave his profession as music teacher rather than musician (interestingly, since his music lessons could be notoriously eccentric and might merely entail playing LPs).

Graham grew up acutely aware of his mixed-race bloodlines, and also felt himself to be something of an outsider nestling in beside his younger half-siblings on his mother's side, Jill, Nicolas, and Jennifer. His biological father rarely figured in his life. An absentee in his life until he was eleven, he then did not reappear for twenty-three years. 'I had to think like a mongrel. Like a hybrid. You're not talking to an Englishman. You're talking to an Anglo-Scot who has got Caribbean blood', he later said (personal knowledge). In a playground fight at the Lycée Français in South Kensington in 1949 he lost most of the sight in his right eye—creating further psychological complexities.

Graham first laid hands on a guitar—a neighbour's—in 1952 and recalled how in an afternoon he worked out how to play a pavane on it from sheet music. Fired by Lonnie Donegan and the skiffle boom, he finally acquired his first guitar at the age of sixteen. 'I couldn't concentrate at school thinking of Lonnie Donegan. … I was seized with the desire to sound like that, to play that sort of music' (Hunt, 'Folk routines'). He secured his first booking the same year at the Troubadour coffee-house in Earl's Court, a hub for poetry, folk music, flamenco, and other artistic activity. He left school in 1958 in order to concentrate on his guitar playing. In 1959 Ken Russell's BBC documentary film *Hound Dogs and Bach Addicts: the Guitar Craze* was broadcast. Historically and musically its most arresting scene was one of the eighteen-year-old Graham playing his arrangement of Julie London's 1954 hit, 'Cry Me a River', for solo guitar. It later became staple footage in documentaries about the post-war British folk scene.

Handsome and debonair, bohemian and donnish, Graham cut quite a dash. He would earn money working

David Michael Gordon [Davey], **Graham** (**1940–2008**), by Brian Shuel, 1966

dead-end jobs in London in winter and in summer head south. In France he played for Elizabeth Taylor and Sean Connery. In Morocco he sampled the sticky hashish confectionery known as *majuun* (or *majoon*) and commandeered the word to title a composition. Everywhere he went he absorbed music. The image of the bohemian traveller was enhanced by his requiring consular assistance to be repatriated five times, the first in 1959. He reckoned he had had eighteen addresses in one three-month period straddling 1960–61. In London he formed a working partnership with Alexis Korner that also saw them accompanying the Australian zither player Shirley Abicair on radio, television, and stage. He obtained an engagement playing music at Nick's Diner in London's Earl's Court; this landed him a cameo as the uncredited guitarist singing 'Rock Me Mama' in Joseph Losey's *The Servant* (1963). He also worked with Long John Baldry in Blues Incorporated and, briefly, with John Mayall—though his blues guitar reportedly did not sound 'dirty' enough. In the heady mêlée of this period he recorded *3/4 AD* with Alexis Korner, a five-track demonstration session financed by the entertainer Bob Monkhouse (eventually released as *From Monkhouse to Medway, 1963–1973* in 2010), and his LP debut, *The Guitar Player* (1963). This was followed by *Folk, Blues and Beyond* (1964) and a collaboration with Shirley Collins, *Folk Routes, New Routes* (1965), both of which were critically acclaimed and (though not selling in huge quantities) extremely influential on both contemporary and later musicians.

What turned Graham (initially known as Davy, later as Davey) into one of Britain's most intrepid, innovative, and admired acoustic guitarists was not so much his formidable technique, or his compositions, or his innovative guitar tunings, highly important though they were. Above all else his influence was conceptual, notably the potency of his vision and his cool-headed inability merely to regurgitate what others had done. He tore the pre-existing acoustic guitar 'blueprint' into tatters. His arrangements were impressionistic. He transferred the jazz sounds of Charlie Parker, Sonny Rollins, Thelonious Monk, Ray Charles, Lennie Tristano, and the Dave Brubeck Quartet to the guitar. Later on, grist for the mill might be Henry Purcell, Bulgarian dance music, Mike Heron of the Incredible String Band, or Lalo Schifrin. Two pieces typified his otherness. The first was 'Angi', later standardized as 'Anji'. This was a guitar instrumental with *soleares* roots named after Angela, his Czech-English girlfriend, travelling companion, and busking assistant, which he had devised in Menton on the French–Italian border in 1959. For their recording session in April 1961 Alexis Korner convinced him to play it for their joint EP *3/4 AD*. Paul Simon and Bert Jansch went on to record it. Aside from becoming a rite of passage for umpteen thousands of guitarists it figured in the soundtracks to numerous films and documentaries. The second was 'She Moved Through the Fair', which first appeared on *From a London Hootenanny* (1963). In his hands Padraic Colum's rewriting of the traditional song became a springboard for flowing modal improvisation for guitar, earning it the nickname 'She Moved Thru' the Bizarre'. John Pilgrim's 1967 recording segueing into 'Blue Raga', released on *After Hours* (1997), captured the piece in full flight.

Much to the consternation of close friends such as Alexis Korner and Martin Carthy, from very early on Graham took to emulating his jazz heroes far too assiduously. Heroin and cocaine were not the folk scene's drugs of choice and those in the know were shocked and at a loss to help when Graham began to use them heavily. His collaboration with Shirley Collins was one of the first relationships to founder. She ascribed this to 'the personal difficulties … of working with Davy, who was quite heavily into drugs and his own peculiar way of life. And me as a young mum with two kids just couldn't cope with somebody who lived this way-out life' (Hunt, 'Shirley and Dolly Collins', 10). He was a competent rather than commanding singer, who was an early champion of songs by Cyril Tawney, the Beatles, and Joni Mitchell; it was his instrumental prowess for which he was remembered. Yet, with few exceptions, it would be individual tracks rather than whole albums that tended to impress. The major exception was his come-back album, *The Complete Guitarist* (1978). By then he had developed into a multi-instrumentalist with the adoption, in particular, of oud and sarod.

Musicians of the calibre of Martin Carthy, Graham Coxon, Ray Davies, Roy Harper, Bert Jansch, John Martyn, Ralph McTell, Jimmy Page, and John Renbourn acknowledged Graham's influence, many describing him in inspirational terms as a musical latch-lifter. The fiddler Dave Swarbrick recalled seeing him play at the Troubadour: 'He was just incredible. There wasn't anybody doing the kind of stuff that he was doing or even dreaming that it could be done' (Hunt, 'Folk routines', 39). He died at his home, 11 Lyme Street, Camden Town, London, on 15 December 2008 of lung cancer. *The Guardian* described him as a guitarist 'whose inventiveness transformed the music scene in the 1960s' (17 Dec 2008); *The Independent* (17 Dec 2008) said that his playing 'influenced a generation', and the *Daily Telegraph* that he 'influenced the leading guitarists of his age' (19 Dec 2008). At his 'leaving do' the poet Michael Horovitz read specially composed haikus in his memory. His last girlfriend, Carol Ballard, reportedly scattered his ashes at his father's grave on the Isle of Skye. He was survived by his daughters, Kim and Mercy.

KEN HUNT

Sources R. Denyer, 'Davey Graham', *Guitar* (July 1975), 15–17 · J. A. Gomez, *Ken Russell* (1976) · K. Hunt, 'Shirley and Dolly Collins: part 1', *Swing*, 51 (1979), 4–19 · J. Martyn, 'Kerrang guru court: guitar stars pick their heroes', *New Musical Express* (12 May 1990) · K. Hunt, 'Folk routines', *Folk Roots* (May 1997), 37, 39, 41 · J. Pilgrim and D. Graham, *After hours at Hull University, 4 February 1967*, CD notes, 1997 · *Living Tradition* (Jan–Feb 2008), 13 · *The Guardian* (17 Dec 2008) · *The Independent* (17 Dec 2008) · *The Scotsman* (18 Dec 2008) · *Daily Telegraph* (19 Dec 2008) · *The Times* (22 Dec 2008) · D. Graham, interviews, corresp., and unpublished autobiographical sketches, priv. coll. · J. Pilgrim, 'The man who invented world music', priv. coll. · personal knowledge (2012) · private information (2012) [Jill Woolnough, sister; M. Gavin] · b. cert. · m. cert. · d. cert.

Archives priv. coll. | FILM BFINA, 'Blame it on my youth', *The other side*, Channel 4, 18 Nov 1999 · BFINA, documentary and performance footage · *Hound dogs and Bach addicts: the guitar craze*, BBC, 1959 · uncredited cameo in *The servant*, directed by J. Losey, 1963 · *Cain's film*, directed by J. Wadhawan, 1969 · *Acoustic routes*, directed by J. Leman, 1992 · *Folk Britannia*, BBC, 2006 | SOUND BL NSA, documentary recordings

Likenesses B. Shuel, modern bromide print, 1966, NPG [*see illus.*] · B. Shuel, modern bromide prints, 1966, NPG · photographs, 1966–2006, Getty Images, London · S. Hadley, photographs, 2007, Rex Features, London · D. Peabody, photograph, priv. coll. · B. Shuel, photograph, repro. in Collections Picture Library, www.collectionspicturelibrary.com · obituary photographs

Grant, Ted [*real name* Isaac Blank] **(1913–2006)**, political activist, was born on 9 July 1913 in Germiston, South Africa, the son of Max Blank, a Russian Jewish immigrant, and his French wife. His parents divorced while he was still young, and his mother took in lodgers, including Ralph Lee, his senior by six years and a former member of the South African Communist Party, to whom he owed his teenage conversion to Trotskyism. In 1934 he left South Africa for Britain, adopting his new name en route. This was the year of the 'French turn', when Trotsky realized that the tiny groups of his supporters had more chance of exerting influence by entering larger socialist parties, as they did in France, than by trying to build independent organizations. After his arrival in London Grant joined other future notables of British Trotskyism, such as Gerry

Healy, in the Marxist group, which was engaged in such 'entryism' within the Independent Labour Party.

The fissiparous forces of British Trotskyism were not to be contained in any one organization. In 1937 Grant became a leading publicist in the Workers' International League, which came to the attention of the authorities during the Second World War. Three of its members were charged with sedition, when Tyneside shipyard apprentices took strike action in 1944. That year the Workers' International League joined with its rivals to form the Revolutionary Communist Party. By the end of the decade the latter had disintegrated and the remnants formed rival organizations within the Labour Party. Grant was now the dominant figure in one of these, initially with forty or so members, the Revolutionary Socialist League. For the next thirty years, largely unnoticed until the 1970s, the group followed Grant's prospectus of 'slow, methodical and persistent agitation' ('The present situation and our tasks', 1957, Deane archive, Manchester Metropolitan University), with bases in Liverpool and London, and the ultimate objective of transforming the Labour Party into a revolutionary organization.

Grant's short-term focus was recruitment from within the Labour Party. Progress was indeed slow. In 1964 the Revolutionary Socialist League, approaching 100 strong, launched *Militant*, a four-page monthly newspaper with Peter Taaffe as editor. Grant's authority derived from his knowledge of Marxist and Leninist-Trotskyist ideology; Taaffe was the more accomplished organizer and agitator. Grant's authority remained secure as long as his vision of crisis and transformation accorded with the British experience of economic volatility, rising industrial conflict, and turmoil within the Labour Party, as was the case in the period 1968–87. It was in this context that Grant's organization, now known as the Militant Tendency, grew to the point where it controlled the Labour Party Young Socialists and the Labour majority on Liverpool council, and could count on the support of three Labour MPs and representatives on such governing bodies as the Labour Party national executive committee (NEC) and the TUC general council—all on the basis of no more than 8000 members. Though its activities were the subject of successive inquiries in 1975 and 1976, no action was taken. The Labour Party itself had moved to the left in the 1970s and it would take shocking defeats in the general elections of 1979 and 1983 to begin to change its mood and outlook.

It was in the early stages of Labour's retreat from the socialist militancy associated with Tony Benn that Grant was expelled from the Labour Party in 1983, along with four of his colleagues on the *Militant* editorial board, following an inquiry by the national executive committee. Heading a growing organization, however, he had no intention of abandoning entryism. Strife in the Labour Party, mass unemployment, a strong sense of crisis—this was what he had always prophesied. Confrontation in Liverpool was guaranteed by the council's refusal to set a rate, in defiance of the Conservative government's rate-capping policy. Of the sixteen Labour councils that embarked on this policy only Liverpool and Lambeth persisted. In September 1985 Liverpool council issued redundancy notices to its 30,000 workforce in a final act of brinksmanship. These events backfired on the Trotskyists, adding momentum to the purge of the Militant Tendency that now swept the Labour Party.

Grant addressed a rally of 8000 supporters of *Militant* at Alexandra Palace in 1988, but he had been less important to the organization than Peter Taaffe for some time, as events were about to show. In that year the Conservative government introduced a new tax—the community charge, or 'poll tax'. *Militant* led a national campaign of non-payment whose perceived success supplied the rationale for the creation of Scottish Militant Labour in 1991 as an independent party, led by Tommy Sheridan. In May 1991 *Militant* also supported a challenge to the official candidates of the Labour Party in the Liverpool local government elections. Grant opposed this formal abandonment of entryism, insisting on the continuing validity of his belief that a crisis of British capitalism would transform Labour into a revolutionary party. He could not appreciate that all variants of socialism had been in retreat since the mid-1980s and was conspicuously slow to understand its collapse in the former communist bloc at the end of the decade. In 1992 he was expelled by the organization he created, remaining a supporter of entryism to the end of his life, together with a band of followers organized around the newspaper *Socialist Appeal*. Militant Labour was born as an open and independent party without him in 1991, taking the bulk of the Militant Tendency membership, who now believed that Labour had ceased to matter to the future of socialism. A change of name to the Socialist Party in 1997, however, could not disguise its own shrinking profile. Grant spent his last years at The Lodge nursing home in Romford, Essex, and died there of acute cardiac failure on 20 July 2006. He never married and had no known descendant. JOHN CALLAGHAN

Sources J. Callaghan, *British Trotskyism: theory and practice* (1984) • M. Crick, *The march of Militant*, 2nd rev. edn (1986) • J. Callaghan, *The far left in British politics* (1987) • P. Taaffe, *Rise of Militant: thirty years of Militant* (1995) • A. McSmith, *Faces of Labour: the inside story*, 2nd rev. edn (1997) • T. Grant, *History of British Trotskyism* (2002) • *The Times* (26 July 2006) • *Daily Telegraph* (27 July 2006) • *The Guardian* (27 July 2006) • *The Independent* (9 Aug 2006) • d. cert.

Likenesses photograph, 1982, Photoshot, London • photograph, 1992, PA Photos, London • obituary photographs

Wealth at death under £3000: probate, 9 July 2007, *CGPLA Eng. & Wales*

Gravell, Raymond William Robert [Ray] (1951–2007), rugby player, broadcaster, and actor, was born at 36 Station Road, Kidwelly, Carmarthenshire, on 12 September 1951, the first child of Thomas John (Jac) Gravell (1924–1966), coalminer and amateur rugby player, and his wife, Nina Eileen, *née* Johns (1922–1990). The family moved from Kidwelly to Mynydd-y-Garreg while he was still young. He was educated at Mynydd-y-Garreg primary school, Burry Port secondary modern school, and then, after passing the thirteen-plus examination, Queen Elizabeth Grammar School, Carmarthen, which he attended until he was seventeen. When he was fourteen his father, depressed by

Raymond William Robert [Ray] **Gravell** (**1951–2007**), by Tony Edenden, 1980

back pain following a mining accident, committed suicide. Ray found the body. He was to say that 'rugby saved me' (Parry-Jones). He captained his school and was capped in 1968 for Wales at youth level. He joined the South Wales Electricity Board as a school leaver and later held jobs in sales and as a training officer with the Manpower Services Commission. After joining Llanelli rugby club as a youth player in 1967 he graduated to the first team in 1970 and became a leading figure in a golden period for the club under its inspirational coach Carwyn James, playing in victories over the touring New Zealand All Blacks in October 1972 and in four Welsh cup finals, in effect the national championship, between 1973 and 1976. Meanwhile, on 17 March 1973, at Bethel Presbyterian church, Meidrim, he married (Sarah Elizabeth) Aurona Rees (*b.* 1949), a clerical officer in the local health authority, and daughter of Benjamin David Simon Rees, caretaker.

Thickset at 5 foot 11 inches and 13 stone 7 pounds, and bearded, Gravell was a highly effective performer in an era of unremittingly physical midfield play, 'always there to set up the second phase play or take out an opposition attacker without fuss' (Rowlands and Farmer, 120), and wont to remark that 'you've got to get your first tackle in early, even if it is late' (*The Guardian*, 6 Nov 2007). The forthright exuberance of his play belied all-consuming nerves and a need for reassurance, particularly before matches. The night before his début for Wales, against France in Paris in 1975, he told his room-mate J. J. Williams, 'I can't take the pressure, I'm not cut out for international rugby' (*The Times*, 2 Nov 2007), and had to be dissuaded from packing his bags.

Though dismissing himself as 'just a minor cog, and actually quite an ordinary player' (*The Guardian*, 6 Nov 2007), Gravell enjoyed a highly successful international career during which, according to the Welsh Rugby Union's historians, he gave 'uncompromising and emotional commitment to Welsh midfield play' (Smith and Williams, 442). Wales won sixteen of the twenty-three matches he played in between 1975 and 1982. He played in teams that won four five nations championships, three triple crowns, and two grand slams, and toured South Africa with the British and Irish Lions in 1980, playing in all four tests.

Carwyn James, coach of the British Lions as well as Llanelli, believed that 'nobody has played for Wales with a deeper sense of being a Welshman' (Davies, 21). That sense came from a bilingual upbringing that developed into a passionate commitment to Welsh language, history, and culture. Gravell sang the compositions of the folk musician Dafydd Iwan to calm himself before matches, broadcast for Plaid Cymru, was admitted to the Gorsedd of Bards as Ray o'r Mynydd in 1981, and campaigned successfully for bilingual signage at Llanelli rugby club. He captained Llanelli from 1980 to 1982 and retired in 1985 with club career totals of 485 games and 120 tries. The club historian Gareth Hughes reckoned that 'No more popular player ever wore the Scarlet shirt, and none wore it more proudly' (Hughes, 238).

Emotional, volubly articulate in two languages, and self-consciously Welsh, Gravell epitomized Llanelli's collective personality. Those qualities were by 1985 translating into a second career as an actor and broadcaster. This had costs. Gravell blamed being 'captivated by crowds and audiences' (*Grav*, 174) for the collapse of his first marriage. His second career found him equally at home with sport, talk, or music, capable of presenting, interviewing, or commentating equally fluently. He broadcast bilingually on rugby from 1983 and presented programmes including a breakfast radio show and talent contest, *Tip Top*, also the title of the cassette tape of Welsh songs he recorded in 1988. As an actor, he told the film director Louis Malle, 'I can only play myself' (*The Guardian*, 6 Nov 2007), but that persona extended to parts including the title role in the series *Bonner* for the Welsh-language television station S4C (1985) and in films including Malle's *Damage* (1992). His natural warmth and humour made him hugely successful. As his Wales team-mate Gerald Davies said, 'His greatness was not the many talents he enjoyed, it was above all his humanity' (*Daily Telegraph*, 16 Nov 2007), while the academic Hywel Teifi Edwards called him 'A social lubricant, a tidal wave of good fellowship who enhanced the lives of everybody he met' (ibid.).

On 2 August 1991, at Horeb Calvinistic Methodist Church, Mynydd-y-Garreg, Gravell married his second wife, Mari Roberts (*b.* 1962), administrative clerk, and daughter of Ivor Myrddin Roberts, opencast mineworker. They had two daughters, Manon (*b.* 1995) and Gwenan (*b.* 1998). Later life also brought numerous honours. He said that appointment in 1997 as sword-bearer to the Gorsedd of Bards at the national eisteddfod 'gave me as much pleasure as the first cap I'd won for Wales' (*Grav*, 219). He became president of Llanelli rugby club in 1998 and in 2003 Brynhyfryd in Mynydd-y-Garreg, the street where he had lived since 1954, was renamed Heol Ray Gravell. However, his final years were beset with health problems. He was diagnosed with diabetes in 2000. In April 2007 his right leg was amputated below the knee. He insisted that the artificial replacement be decorated with the Llanelli badge and colours, and he never lost his positive and optimistic outlook. He died of a heart attack while on holiday in Majorca, Spain, on 31 October 2007, thirty-five years to the day after Llanelli's victory over the All Blacks. His death unleashed a wave of emotion in Wales. Carmarthenshire council opened books of condolence, an honour usually reserved for royalty. His public funeral, held on 15 November 2007 at Stradey Park, Llanelli, attracted more than 8000 participants and was described as 'akin to a state funeral' (*Western Mail*, 16 Nov 2007). A private ceremony was held afterwards at Llanelli crematorium. He was survived by his wife, Mari, and their two daughters. He was subsequently commemorated through the Ray Gravell Charitable Trust, supporting causes in west Wales, the renaming of the press conference room at the Millennium Stadium, Cardiff, and a bronze lifesize statue at Llanelli's new ground, Parc y Scarlets, unveiled in 2009.

Huw Richards

Sources G. Davies, *Gerald Davies: an autobiography* (1979) • D. Smith and G. Williams, *Fields of praise: the official history of the Welsh Rugby Union, 1881–1981* (1980) • J. Taylor, *Decade of the dragon* (1980) • P. Bennett and M. Williams, *Everywhere for Wales* (1981) • G. Hughes, ed., *One hundred years of scarlet* (1983) • G. Hughes, *The Scarlets: a history of Llanelli Rugby Football Club* (1986) • C. Rowlands and D. Farmer, eds., *Giants of post-war Welsh rugby* (1990) • D. Parry-Jones, *The Dawes decades* (2005) • *South Wales Echo* (1 Nov 2007); (2 Nov 2007) • *The Times* (2 Nov 2007); (3 Nov 2007) • *Daily Telegraph* (2 Nov 2007); (16 Nov 2007) • *The Guardian* (2 Nov 2007); (6 Nov 2007) • *The Independent* (2 Nov 2007); (6 Nov 2007) • *South Wales Evening Post* (2 Nov 2007); (6 Nov 2007); (16 Nov 2007); (20 Nov 2007); (21 Nov 2007); (20 Nov 2008); (19 Aug 2009) • *Western Mail* (3 Nov 2007); (16 Nov 2007); (5 Aug 2008) • R. Gravell, *Grav in his own words*, ed. A. W. Bevan (2008) • D. Parry-Jones, interview, 2000, www.walesvideogallery.org, 2 Nov 2010 • personal knowledge (2011) • private information (2011) • b. cert. • m. certs.

Archives FILM BFINA, performance footage • D. Parry-Jones, interview, 2000, http://www.walesvideogallery.org

Likenesses S & G, photographs, 1976–9, PA Photos, London • T. Edenden, photograph, 1980, repro. in www.sporting-heroes.net/rugby-heroes/displayhero.asp?HeroID=6296 [*see illus.*] • photographs, 1980–2006, Getty Images, London • photographs, 2007, Rex Features, London • D. Williams-Ellis, bronze statue, Parc y Scarlets, Llanelli • obituary photographs • photographs, repro. in Gravell, *Grav*

Wealth at death £389,433: probate, 10 March 2008, *CGPLA Eng. & Wales*

Gray, (Thomas) Cecil (1913–2008), anaesthetist, was born on 11 March 1913 at the Clock public house, 31 London Road, Liverpool, of which his father Thomas Gray was the landlord. His mother, Ethel Gray, *née* Unwin, had been married before, to the Macclesfield silk manufacturer Ernest Abraham, and widowed with three children. Cecil Gray was the only child of her second marriage. A devout Roman Catholic, she arranged his school education accordingly. This began in 1920 at a residential convent primary school at Bath, and continued from 1923 until 1931 at Ampleforth College, the Benedictine public school in north Yorkshire, where he developed interests in science, acting, and music, and a calling to be a monk. Owing to 'petty transgressions', however, he lasted only two months as a novice at Ampleforth Abbey and then turned to medical studies at Liverpool University where he trained from 1931 to 1937. On 18 September 1937 he married Marjorie Kathleen Hely (1909–1978), daughter of Herbert William Byrne Hely, dental surgeon. They had a son and a daughter.

After graduating Gray went into general practice. As an assistant GP in central Liverpool he began giving dental anaesthetics, as GPs did, which is where his interest in anaesthesia began. His medical training in giving anaesthetics had been 'abysmal', consistent with the low status of a speciality still largely the province of part-time GP-anaesthetists giving ether for major surgery. After buying his own general practice at Wallasey in 1939 he volunteered to assist the most distinguished Liverpool GP-anaesthetist, Robert J. Minnitt, the inventor of the 'gas and air' analgesia apparatus that was transforming British midwifery. By employing a practice assistant Gray was eventually assisting Minnitt two days a week at Liverpool's Northern Hospital and in 1942 gained the recently introduced diploma in anaesthetics. By then he had sold his bomb-blasted practice to take a half-time post as anaesthetist at Liverpool's Sefton Hospital and assist several local surgeons in private practice, among them Charles Wells, whom he later described as the finest surgeon he ever encountered, and who was to become a major ally.

Soon Gray was working sixty-hour weeks and feeling fit for military service, for which he had been turned down in 1940 owing to the asthma he suffered. On re-applying, he was called up to the Royal Army Medical Corps (RAMC) in September 1942 and trained at Oxford for service with one of the mobile neurosurgery units designed by Oxford's leading neurosurgeon, Hugh Cairns. As a captain in the RAMC Gray was shipped with his unit to north Africa in December 1942 and served in the Tunisia campaign from February to May 1943, but not long afterwards severe bronchopneumonia ended his military service.

Soon after returning to hospital practice in Liverpool early in 1944 Gray began the research collaboration with his local colleague John Halton that laid the foundations of subsequent anaesthetic practice. Through Halton's connections with the nearby Burtonwood US Air Force base they had early knowledge of the pioneering use of curare in North America, before wartime medical journals had spread the story of how this muscle relaxant was being used as a supplement to general anaesthesia. Formerly, deep general anaesthesia had been the sole means of producing adequate relaxation of musculature during major surgery. Intrigued, Gray and Halton acquired through Halton's Burtonwood connections trial supplies of intocostrin, the purified curare being produced in the USA. Used as recommended, it produced the supplementary muscle relaxation of which they had heard, but by the time supplies ran out they were committed to further exploration of its potential. Fortune favoured them when Gray remembered d-tubocurarine chloride being used in physiology experiments at Liverpool University, from where hundreds of ampoules of this curare-related compound were acquired. Using the contents of the first of these, Gray had the breakthrough moment that led to revolutionary improvements in the use of general anaesthetics. Unsure of how much d-tubocurarine chloride to use, he dissolved the contents of an ampoule (possibly 100mg) in a pint bottle of sterile saline solution ready for dripping into a patient undergoing a cholecystectomy at Liverpool's Northern Hospital. With the patient anaesthetized with pentathol and the surgeon James Rawlinson opening the abdomen, this dripping-in began and was followed by a sudden dramatic loss of muscle tension which left surgeon and anaesthetist shocked. Once Gray had begun assisting the patient's breathing, which had dropped, the operation progressed with remarkable ease and far lighter anaesthetic, which had considerable advantages.

Gray had stumbled on the benefits of using muscle relaxant less sparingly than ever risked before and soon he and Halton, in their different hospitals, were using concentrations that produced major skeletal muscle paralysis. This meant taking over the patient's breathing by manual, air-bag ventilation, but the rewards were unprecedented muscle relaxation and the need for only light anaesthesia throughout major surgery. Gray concentrated on abdominal surgery cases in Liverpool and Halton on thoracic cases at Clatterbridge Hospital on the Wirral. They met almost weekly to discuss outcomes and refinements of their technique over a pint or two at Liverpool's historic Ye Cracke public house. Within months they had progressed to using the reversal agent prostigmine to terminate the paralysis they induced, Gray meanwhile testing for risks to the heart of their new procedure, which his laboratory animal experiments at Liverpool University showed as negligible. In just over a thousand surgical operations in 1945–6 Gray and Halton refined their procedure and validated its revolutionary effectiveness, the details of which they presented in a paper to the anaesthetics section of the Royal Society of Medicine in London in May 1946, which was justly titled 'D-tubocurarine chloride—a milestone in anaesthesia?' Its publication in the society's *Proceedings* sent reverberations through the world of anaesthetics and was the beginning of modern general anaesthesia. Although cautiously slow, its uptake by a conservative clinical speciality led to rapid advances in surgery.

Gray (known as T. Cecil Gray) received an MD degree from Liverpool University in 1947 for a thesis on his investigations of 1944–6 and in the same year was appointed head of the university's new department of anaesthetics, as reader in anaesthesia. In his first year in this appointment he created the country's first day-release course for young clinicians who were preparing for the diploma in anaesthetics. By the mid-1950s his fine teaching, leadership, and skill in the appointment of staff had secured a reputation for his department that drew postgraduate students from around the world to learn the 'Liverpool technique'. The first lecturer he appointed was Gordon Jackson Rees, who under Gray's direction pioneered paediatric anaesthetics in Britain and became his closest ally. Gray became professor of anaesthesia in Liverpool in 1959 and remained as head of the department until his retirement in 1976. From 1970 to 1976 he served also as Liverpool's dean of medicine. His research influence continued into the 1970s as a co-author of papers on the clinical monitoring of neuromuscular block by muscle relaxants. The train-of-four twitch technique of monitoring that his team devised was soon adopted by anaesthetists worldwide.

On a national level Gray made profound contributions to the development of anaesthetics as a speciality, both as a foundation member from 1948 to 1969 of the board of the faculty of anaesthetists of the Royal College of Surgeons of England, of which he was the dean from 1964 to 1967, and from 1948 to 1976 as a member of the council of the Association of Anaesthetists of Great Britain and Ireland, of which he was the president from 1956 to 1959. Between 1948 and 1964 his editorial skills lifted the status of the *British Journal of Anaesthesia*. He also edited major textbooks, including *Modern Trends in Anaesthesia* (1958) and *General Anaesthesia* (1959), both of which went through several editions. Internationally he lectured widely on the Liverpool technique and refinements to it and in 1961 was the first anaesthetist recipient of the Sir Arthur Simms travelling fellowship of the Royal College of Surgeons of England.

For his contributions to anaesthetics Gray was appointed a CBE in 1976, which many in the field thought an inadequate recognition of his achievements. His devoted contributions to the Roman Catholic Church were honoured in 1982 when he became a knight commander of the Order of St Gregory the Great. Following the death of his first wife, on 24 August 1979 he married Pamela Mary Corning (*b*. 1942/3), hospital secretary, and daughter of Charles Frederick Corning, engineer; they had one son. Gray died at his home in Ravenmeols Lane, Formby, Liverpool, on 5 January 2008, of gastrointestinal bleeding. He was survived by his wife, Pamela, and his three children.

MAX BLYTHE

Sources *The Independent* (26 Jan 2008) · *Daily Telegraph* (30 Jan 2008) · *Daily Post* [Liverpool] (30 Jan 2008) · *The Times* (8 Feb 2008); (18 Feb 2008); (26 Feb 2008) · archives, U. Lpool · T. C. Gray, audio interview with Max Blythe, 16 Aug 1996, priv. coll. · T. C. Gray, video interview with Max Blythe, 28 Aug 1996 and 25 Nov 1996, Oxford Brookes University, Medical Sciences Video Archive, MSVA 138, 145 · G. J. Rees, video interview with Max Blythe, 28 Aug 1996, Oxford Brookes University, Medical Sciences Video Archive, MSVA 139 · *WW* (2008) · personal knowledge (2012) · private information (2012) · b. cert. · m. certs. · d. cert.

Archives U. Lpool, archives | FILM Oxford Brookes University, Medical Sciences Video archive, interview with M. Blythe, 28 Aug 1996 and 25 Nov 1996, MSVA 138, 145 | SOUND priv. coll., interview with M. Blythe, 16 Aug 1996

Likenesses obituary photographs

Wealth at death under £280,000: probate, 8 July 2008, *CGPLA Eng. & Wales*

Gray [*née* Stanham], **Patience Jean** (1917–2005), writer on food, was born on 31 October 1917 at Michen Hall, Shackleford, near Godalming, Surrey, the second of three daughters of Hermann Stanham Stanham, then a major in the Royal Field Artillery, and his wife, Olive Florence, *née* Colgate, daughter of a Lincolnshire farmer. Late in life she delightedly discovered that her misogynist father, later a surgeon at the London Hospital, then a failed pig-farmer near Basingstoke, and subsequently a photographer with his own studio on the Sussex coast, was actually the son of a rabbi named Warschavski, who had fled persecution in Poland in 1861 and become a Unitarian minister. She and her sisters were brought up in an Edwardian-style household run by servants, where their overbearing father was the only male.

A very bright child, Patience Stanham passed her university entrance examinations at sixteen, but her father felt she was too young to take up her place, so sent her to Bonn to learn German and study economics, which she abandoned in favour of art history. She returned to attend Queen's College in Harley Street, living with her maternal aunt and uncle, as her own family had fallen on hard times. She then took the degree of BSc (Econ) at London University, where her tutor was Hugh Gaitskell. In the summer of 1938 she set off with her sister Tania (who became a photographer) on a mission for the Quakers to establish cultural ties with Romania. When Queen Marie died in July she wrote her first piece of journalism, which appeared in a Bucharest paper; its infatuated editor laid siege to her, filling her hotel room with tuberoses, the scent of which, she said, always filled her with remembered horror. She and her sister escaped his attentions by fleeing to the Black Sea in a monoplane piloted by a Romanian prince.

When the Second World War broke out Stanham was dismissed from the Foreign Office job she had just acquired for, she claimed, 'having too many foreign contacts' (*The Observer*, 18 Oct 1987). She had an affair with a married man, Thomas Gray, a Spanish Civil War veteran who ran a clandestine counter-insurgency course for the Home Guard at Hurlingham, London. She was secretary of this school for teaching civilians new skills 'such as how to make Molotov cocktails' (ibid.). When Thomas Gray was conscripted he left her to cope with a son and a daughter in a cottage on the South Downs; she took the name Gray by public announcement in the *London Gazette* of 17 January 1941.

In 1950–51 Patience Gray worked as research assistant to F. H. K. Henrion on the Festival of Britain. In 1957 Penguin published her *Plat du Jour, or, Foreign Food*, a highly successful mass-circulation paperback cookery book, to which her friends Primrose Boyd contributed recipes and David Gentleman the striking illustrations and pink cover. It sold 50,000 copies in its first ten months, with recipes for the sort of sophisticated dishes that chic post-war London hostesses liked to prepare for dinner parties; but it stood the test of time. The next year, following a competition for *The Observer* that was said to have attracted a thousand entrants, David Astor told her 'unenthusiastically that I had won, and they were prepared to take me on to start a woman's page' (*The Observer*, 18 Oct 1987). At first she reported happily to Nigel Gosling, but in 1961 her next boss, George Seddon, had a different idea of the paper's readership, and she left in 1962, to work as a textile designer.

In 1963 Gray met and fell in love with the sculptor Norman Mommens (1922–2000), whose own marriage was breaking up, and they began their odyssey in search of marble. This was described in her second classic book, *Honey from a Weed: Fasting and Feasting in Tuscany, Catalonia, the Cyclades and Apulia* (bravely published in 1987 by Alan Davidson's Prospect Books, for whom it turned out to be a best-seller), and finally ended when, in 1970, Mommens

Patience Jean Gray (1917–2005), by Jane Bown, 1987

bought the *masseria* of a tumbledown ruined sheep farm at Spigolizzi in Apulia. Gray settled into the house, which had neither water nor electricity until the 1990s, cultivating her female neighbours to the extent that the local peasants regarded her as the repository of lore about their native edible and medicinal plants. Despite her principled objections to the institution Gray married Mommens in 1994; after his death she continued to live in the *masseria*, where the courtyard and surrounding fields were scattered with his phallic sculptures.

Gray was a considerable prose stylist. In her writing, as in life, she achieved and celebrated simplicity and elegance. She kept up with her old friends, such as the bibliophile Irving Davis, whose book of recipes she edited in 1967 as *A Catalan Cookery Book: a Collection of Impossible Recipes*. In 2000 she published *Work Adventures Childhood Dreams*, a collection—arranged in no particular order—of anecdotes about, for instance, T. S. Eliot's envy of Henry James, shopping in Lecce before the advent of supermarkets, Stendahl's travel writing, her enthusiasm for Buster Keaton, and Irving Davis's reincarnation as a bluebottle. She died at Spigolizzi on 10 March 2005, and was survived by her son and daughter. PAUL LEVY

Sources *The Observer* (18 Oct 1987) • *Wall Street Journal* (17 Dec 1987) • *The Independent* (14 March 2005) • *Daily Telegraph* (16 March 2005) • *The Guardian* (18 March 2005) • *The Times* (21 March 2005) • personal knowledge (2009) • private information (2009) • b. cert.
Archives SOUND BL NSA, documentary recording
Likenesses J. Bown, photograph, 1987, Guardian News and Media Ltd [*see illus.*] • J. Bown, photograph, priv. coll. • obituary photographs

Gray, Sally [*née* Constance Vera Stevens; *married name* Constance Vera Browne, Lady Oranmore and Browne] (**1915–2006**), actress, was born at 16 Loraine Road, Islington, London, on 14 February 1915, one of five children of Charles Stevens, motor cab driver, and his wife, Gertrude Grace, *née* Green. Her mother, widowed early, encouraged Constance's stage aspirations by sending her to the children's section of the Fay Compton School of Dramatic Art. She made her acting début aged ten in a production of Eugene O'Neill's *All God's Chillun Got Wings*, subsequently obtaining a scholarship to continue training at the school until she was sixteen.

A blonde beauty with elegant figure and delectably husky voice, she became a considerable dramatic actress in 1940s British cinema, after a dozen largely stereotyped roles in forgotten 1930s films. Her first appearance was an uncredited 'bit' in Maurice Elvey's adaptation of *The School for Scandal* (1930), along with other hopefuls Rex Harrison and Anna Neagle. After this unpropitious start she spent several years on the London stage in the chorus of the musicals *Bow Bells* (Hippodrome, 1932) and *Jill Darling* (Saville, 1934) and had a small acting part in Cole Porter's *Shall We Dance?* (1933), starring Fred Astaire, who befriended her and influenced her in dance techniques.

The prominent agent John Gliddon signed her after seeing her on stage. She first appeared in films as Sally Gray in small roles in five 1935 releases, moving slightly up the cast for the B-movie thriller *Checkmate*. Most of her 1930s

Sally Gray (1915–2006), by unknown photographer

films required of her little more than acceptable feminine decoration, which she provided effortlessly, but matters improved later in the decade. Whereas in the earlier films she simply went through paces learned from stage musicals, in 1939 she had a strong role as an alluring wife to the illusionist Paul Lukas in *A Window in London*, and held her own opposite George Sanders in *The Saint in London*. The latter, made for the American company RKO-Radio, led to the offer of a Hollywood contract, which she declined. She also appeared in several musicals, including *The Lambeth Walk* (1940), in which she sang the title song, and *Over She Goes* (1937) and *Hold My Hand* (1938), both co-starring Stanley Lupino (*b.* 1893), with whom she lived until his untimely death in 1942.

The turning point in Sally Gray's film career was Brian Desmond Hurst's popular wartime romantic melodrama *Dangerous Moonlight* (1941), in which she played a journalist who falls in love with a Polish pianist (Anton Walbrook). He is wounded and loses his memory in the battle of Britain but all ends well, with the lovers reconciled. Richard Adinsell's *Warsaw Concerto* was specially composed for the film. *Dangerous Moonlight* was rather lugubrious but Gray had warmth, sharpness, and sex appeal in her first undeniable star performance.

Gray was off-screen for five years after this, suffering a nervous breakdown, allegedly following Lupino's death. However, she scored a major stage success in the title role of the smart American comedy *My Sister Eileen* in 1943, offering a clever foil to the wisecracking Coral Browne as her sister. When she returned to the screen in the later 1940s there was a new maturity in her persona, sometimes touched with melancholy, sometimes with a sense of hard-won knowledge. She was affecting as the tragic ballerina Jenny Pearl in *Carnival* (1946), adapted from Compton Mackenzie's novel, though one writer thought it 'like winter weather: dull and wet' (Quinlan, 198). In Sidney Gilliat's invigorating comedy thriller *Green for Danger* (1946) she was top-billed as the nurse who provides Trevor Howard's romantic interest; and she gave a real centre to Desmond Hurst's *The Mark of Cain* (1947) as the site of contestation between two brothers (Patrick Holt and Eric Portman). Her other co-star in this, Dermot Walsh, recalled that she 'was one of the most beautiful women in the business and had a lovely voice. She was also a very nice person' (McFarlane, 590). She was, indeed, warmly remembered by her colleagues.

Gray's three most notable films followed in rapid succession, all having strong *film noir* affiliations. In Cavalcanti's *They Made Me a Fugitive* (1947), described by one critic as 'the key film' in post-war British *noir* (Spicer, 187), she was the spirited former girlfriend of a very nasty gangster, again finding romance with Trevor Howard as a disillusioned former serviceman; in Lance Comfort's inventive adaptation of Michael Pertwee's play, *Silent Dust* (1948), she brought a grave authority to the role of the woman seeking to disperse the oppressive ties of a supposedly dead war-hero husband; and in *Obsession* (1949) she played the faithless wife of Robert Newton, who exacts a bizarre revenge. In these she established herself as a major star in British films. In the event, however, she made only one more film, the insignificant *Escape Route* (1952), in which she and the fading American tough-guy George Raft smash a kidnapping racket.

On 1 December 1951 Gray married Dominick Geoffrey Edward Browne, fourth Baron Oranmore and Browne and second Baron Mereworth (1901–2002), and retired from the screen to live at his remote Castle MacGarratt in co. Mayo. They lived there, where she developed a taste for gardening, until financial problems caused them to resettle in a flat in Eaton Place, London, where they lived until their deaths. There were no children of the marriage, but he had eight children by his first two marriages (one of whom had died in infancy and a further three of whom predeceased him). She never wanted to talk about her career, writing in 1994, 'I do not give interviews by meetings or telephone' (personal knowledge). By all accounts a woman of charm and character, she put fame resolutely to one side and found other fulfilments in her long life. She died in London on 24 September 2006.

BRIAN MCFARLANE

Sources P. Noble, 'Sally Gray', *Sound Wave Illustrated* (Nov 1943) · D. Quinlan, *British sound films: the studio years, 1928–1959* (1984) · 'Dermot Walsh', *An autobiography of British cinema*, ed. B. McFarlane (1997) · A. Spicer, *Film noir* (2002) · *Daily Telegraph* (29 Sept 2006) · *The Independent* (3 Oct 2006) · *The Times* (5 Oct 2006) · *The Guardian* (5 Oct 2006) · Burke, *Peerage* · BFI film and TV database, www.bfi.org.uk, 14 March 2008 · www.imdb.com, 14 March 2008 · personal knowledge (2010) · private information (2010) · b. cert.
Archives FILM BFINA, performance footage
Likenesses photographs, 1935–49, Getty Images, London, Hult. Arch. · photographs, 1946–56, Rex Features, London · obituary photographs · photograph, repro. in *Leader Magazine* (2 July 1949), cover · photograph, repro. in *True Story* (Jan 1947), cover · photograph, Mander and Mitchenson [*see illus.*] · portrait, repro. in *Picturegoer*, cover
Wealth at death £148,345: probate, 4 May 2007, *CGPLA Eng. & Wales*

Gray, Simon James Holliday (1936–2008), playwright and diarist, was born at Winton House, Beach Road, South Hayling, Hayling Island, Hampshire, on 21 October 1936, the second son of James Davidson Gray, a Scottish GP who later became a pathologist, and his wife, Barbara Cecelia Mary, *née* Holliday, a former Olympic athlete and hockey player. At the age of three he was evacuated to Canada with his elder brother, Nigel (*b.* 1934), to escape the Second World War. They stayed with their paternal grandparents and aunt for five years, coming home just before the war ended. His younger brother, Piers, was born in 1946.

Gray was educated at Portsmouth grammar school and Westminster School. He moved back to Canada in 1953 when he was seventeen, to attend Dalhousie University in Halifax, Nova Scotia, to read English. A fellow student there described him as 'a hybrid creature consisting of an animated but profound literary sage combined with a vaudevillian comic of the absurd' (Louis Greenspan, in *Critical Quarterly*, 10). He graduated in 1957 and then, attracted by the prospect of being taught by F. R. Leavis, attended Trinity College, Cambridge, as a postgraduate. He did not complete a PhD, but from 1960 to 1963 was a supervisor in English at Trinity, and in 1963–4 he returned to Canada once again as a senior instructor in English at the University of British Columbia. In 1965 he was appointed a lecturer in English at Queen Mary College, London, where he remained until 1985, when he became an honorary fellow. He was highly regarded by his students—'For all of us there are a few people in our lives who open up something inside us' (Angela Hall, in *Critical Quarterly*, 2), said one of them—although his attitude to the university itself may be inferred from his novel, *Breaking Hearts* (1997), in which he referred to a university which closely resembled Queen Mary College as 'The Dump'.

Gray wrote his first novel, *Colmain* (1963), while he was at Cambridge. He subsequently wrote four more novels, *Simple People* (1965), *Little Portia* (1967), *A Comeback for Stark* (under the pseudonym Hamish Reade, 1968), and *Breaking Hearts* (1997), all published by Faber. But the novel wasn't his natural form. An adaptation of a short story of his, *The Caramel Crisis*, was commissioned for television in 1966 by Kenith Trodd, who went on to produce most of Gray's screenplays. He wrote over twenty-five, including adaptations of his stage plays. He stopped writing for television when the commissioning process became sclerotic with 'new' management. In the best of his screen work, such as *Plaintiffs and Defendants* (1975), *Two Sundays* (1975), and *A Month in the Country* (1987), he wrote against the prevailing idiom of the time, which was largely social-realist, leftish neo-documentary. As Trodd said, 'For most of the so-called television golden age, [Gray's] territory of iffy lawyers, faded denizens of empire, self-heroising academics and

Simon James Holliday Gray (1936–2008), by Martin Pope, 2001

women trying to define their space and dignity was much less fashionable but eventually more resilient' (Kenith Trodd, in *Critical Quarterly*, 27).

Gray's first two stage plays, *Wise Child* (1967) and *Dutch Uncle* (1969), were grotesques in the style of Joe Orton, but by the time he wrote *Butley* (1971) he had appropriated the classicism of Racine. We see a character in a room: doors open, people enter and leave, and, by a remorseless accumulation of incident, that character's doom is sealed. In *Quartermaine's Terms* (1981) he took classicism to extremes by placing the violence—adultery, murder, blackmail—entirely off stage and seeing the action, or *in*action, through the eyes of a mild, good-humoured, unsuccessful tutor of English to whom nothing apparently happens at all. Gray's subject was emotional dishevelment, but his plays were all the stronger for having been written within the confines of a puritanical form.

Gray's writing for the theatre was invariably warm and approachable—a paradox given that his tone was sharp, his politics unregenerate, his central characters often rumpled wrecks whose alcohol intake is auto-destructive and whose nicotine consumption is probably poisoning half the street. His canon was enormous and perhaps he was too prolific for the good of his reputation. He wrote nearly thirty plays in as many years, many of which had a successful run in the West End. It is no coincidence that many of his plays were directed by a writer with a correspondingly puritanical aesthetic, Harold Pinter. Pinter directed nine of Gray's plays and their friendship survived a falling out over the character—or caricature—of Hector Duff, 'the world's greatest living playwright', in Gray's television play *Unnatural Pursuits* (1993). Pinter directed two of Gray's most interesting later plays, *The Late Middle Classes* (1999) and *The Old Masters* (2004).

Behind many of Gray's plays lay a kind of ghost-play, the cast of which appears in one play after another, swapping roles, suits, and moustaches like an overworked repertory company. There are, or appear to be, two leading men, one a flamboyant, clever, sexually exploitative show-off who exasperates his wife, disappoints his mistresses, and skives at work. Then there is an opposite figure, at times a diligent family man, more often an obvious loser. He is sometimes a brother, sometimes a childhood friend. Homosexuality is a constant theme, but it never erupts between the louche authorial figure and the prissy one. More to the point is the awkward closeness between two heterosexual Englishmen whose friendship is based on the fact that they were almost-lovers as boys.

Gray always wanted to write an epic play about Dickens. What he responded to in Dickens was the cascading imagination and a view of the world that was essentially comic, or at least too absurd to be able to take quite seriously, underscored by an indelible humanity. Like Dickens too, Gray had a way of exploring the world that was simultaneously so closely observed as to be hyper-real while at the same time—and for the same reasons—wild and phantasmagoric. Gray's penultimate play, *Little Nell* (2007), was partly about the relationship between Dickens and Ellen Ternan, but also about the consequences of deceit and guilt.

Gray was never a member of any of the unofficial clubs which are the central organizing principle of British society. As his friend Simon Callow (a fellow Dickens enthusiast) said,

> He had no skill at self-promotion. He raged against this, but he was resigned to it. Though outwardly a typical, cricket-loving, somewhat fogeyish, doggedly non-p.c. middle class Englishman of his generation, he never quite felt himself to be entirely part of the normal, the ordinary world. (*The Guardian*, 14 Aug 2008)

If the characteristic Gray protagonist in his plays seemed to be close to autobiographical, there was no confusion in his diaries. He published eight volumes (one posthumously) in which he wrote frankly (and very funnily) of sexual desire, failure, fantasy, and jealousy; of loneliness, guilt, and shame. The diaries, both in form and content, were unrestrained, but for all that they were no less plays than his plays, albeit monologues for a not-quite-solipsistic, sometimes bitter, often loving, amiable, humane, vulnerable, intelligent, droll, melancholy, curmudgeonly protagonist who was often fuelled by immense quantities of alcohol—mostly champagne—and always, until he renounced both, by nicotine. The pleasures of drinking and smoking and the need, with the onset of illness, to renounce them—as well as the prospect of renouncing life itself—provided the narrative momentum of much of the diaries. As the fine dramatist that he was, Gray gave the writing of them a sense of spontaneity with an artlessness that was supremely artful, using the present tense as if memories and the act of recording them occurred simultaneously. Words flew out of him as if he had discovered the secret of circular breathing: on tyranny, racism, sharks, rats, dogs, cats, flies, DTs, childhood, sex, murder, friendship, death, the power of fiction, lesbian fantasies, and more. It was the literary equivalent of the way in which thoughts come unbidden into one's mind when one is lying half awake in the early morning or drifting unmoored during the day.

Gray didn't moralize in his plays or his diaries: 'The moral is: you can learn nothing from experience, at least in my experience'. That may be true, but there were few who wrote about their experience with such honesty, self-knowledge, and, above all, such wit. The moral impulse at the heart of all his work was derived from this: the fault lies not in systems or societies or institutions but in ourselves alone. The success of the diaries brought about a reassessment of his plays. His extraordinarily fertile output came to be regarded not as a talent spreading itself thinly but as a writer whose prolific nature—like Dickens's—was part of his genius. Recognition came with the BAFTA writer's award in 1990 and a CBE in 2005 for services to drama and literature.

Gray married twice. On 25 June 1965 he married Beryl Mary De Haan (*b.* 1936), a photo researcher at the BBC, daughter of William Charles Kevern, a welfare officer. They had two children, Ben and Lucy. The marriage was dissolved in 1997, and on 22 February the same year he married a fellow lecturer at Queen Mary College, Victoria Katherine Rothschild (*b.* 1953), daughter of (Nathaniel Mayer) Victor *Rothschild, third Baron Rothschild, zoologist and public servant. His love for Victoria ran as a moving but discreet obbligato throughout the later diaries. Gray was diagnosed with cancer in 2007, perhaps not surprising for a man who wrote of himself that 'he'd smoked sixty cigarettes a day for the last fifty years and boasted of it'. But he died on 7 August 2008, ironically not of cancer, but of an aortic aneurysm, at St Mary's Hospital, Westminster. He was survived by his wife, Victoria, and the two children of his first marriage. RICHARD EYRE

Sources S. Gray, *An unnatural pursuit and other pieces* (1985) • S. Gray, *How's that for telling 'em, fat lady?* (1988) • S. Gray, *Fat chance* (1995) • S. Gray, *Enter a fox* (2001) • S. Gray, *The smoking diaries* (2004) • S. Gray, *The year of the jouncer* (2006) • S. Gray, *The last cigarette* (2008) • S. Gray, *Coda* (2008) • *The Times* (8 Aug 2008) • *Daily Telegraph* (8 Aug 2008) • *The Guardian* (8 Aug 2008); (14 Aug 2008) • *The Independent* (8 Aug 2008) • *New York Times* (8 Aug 2008) • 'Remembering Simon Gray', *Critical Quarterly* [special issue], 52/1 (April 2010), iii–iv, 1–129 • *WW* (2008) • personal knowledge (2012) • private information (2012) • b. cert. • m. certs. • d. cert.

Archives Boston University Library, papers | FILM BFINA, current affairs footage | SOUND BL NSA, documentary and interview recordings

Likenesses group portrait, photograph, 1976, PA Photos, London • D. Cooper, group portrait, photograph, 1984, Getty Images, London • M. Pope, photograph, 2001, Camera Press, London [*see illus.*] • T. R. Hart, C-type colour print, 2004, NPG • T. Buckingham, photograph, repro. in *Evening Standard* (1 April 2004) • D. Rose, photograph, repro. in *The Independent* (23 June 1987) • obituary photographs • photographs, Camera Press, London

Wealth at death under £5000: probate, 9 Feb 2009, *CGPLA Eng. & Wales*

Grayson, Edward (1925–2008), barrister, was born Isadore Edward Goldman on 1 March 1925 at 34 Moresby Road, Upper Clapton, Hackney, London, the only son of Moss David Goldman (1893/4–1948), timber merchant, and his wife, Mary, *née* Lifson. He was educated at Taunton's School, Southampton, joined the RAF for national service but was invalided out, and read law at Exeter College, Oxford, from which he graduated in 1947 with third-class honours in jurisprudence. A month after his father's death he changed his name by deed poll, to Edward Grayson.

Called to the bar by the Middle Temple in 1948, Grayson had a peripatetic career starting in chambers in Lincoln's Inn, moving to common law sets at 1 Garden Court and 4 Paper Buildings, with a brief intermission between 2002 and 2005 to become in-house general counsel to an East End firm of solicitors, Bowling & Co., and then returning to Chancery Chambers, of which he remained a member until his death. On 27 May 1958, at the New West End Synagogue, London, he married a fellow barrister, (Myra) Wendy Schockett (*b.* 1930), daughter of Henry Charles Schockett. They had a son, Harry.

Grayson had, in his prime, a criminal and common law practice. However, his claim to fame lay not in this conventional legal activity but in his development of a sports law specialism—the first person at the bar to do so. His interest in sport had germinated at school where, taking up the challenge of a master, he undertook a 20 mile bicycle ride to obtain the autograph of the England centre forward G. O. Smith, a member of the celebrated amateur team the Corinthians, who later sent him a photograph of himself with C. B. Fry. As a result Grayson was inspired to write his first book, *Corinthians and Cricketers* (1955, in which successive editions had forewords by C. B. Fry, Hubert Doggart, and Gary Lineker), an elegy to the values of the golden age of amateur sport. He was himself a supporter of Leatherhead United (of which his senior clerk was chairman), giant killers of the Isthmian League, and latterly of Corinthian Casuals. With the professional game he was increasingly disenchanted.

Grayson regretted that during his lifetime the Corinthian spirit of sport was heavily overlaid by commercialism. He responded to this by seeking to ensure that the rule of law infused not only the regulatory processes of governing bodies but the way in which games were played. His own sporting life, other than as a referee, was terminated by a broken leg sustained during the university trials and it was appropriate that, of the many significant sports-related cases in which he appeared, the most notable were those where sportsmen had suffered—as he had—physical injury on the field of play. These cases expanded the boundaries of tort law and made it clear that the sporting arena was, in Lord Atkin's memorable phrase, 'no Alsatia ... where the King's writ [did] not run'. His unpopularity with sports administrators, who disliked any erosion of their control by the courts, was matched by his popularity with the media, for whom he was for many years the first port of call for a pungent quote when a legal issue arose in a sporting context.

Grayson was a prolific, if undisciplined writer, best known for his book *Sport and the Law* (1988), the first of its kind in a later highly populated field. He did not believe that there was such a self-contained subject as 'sports law', hence the carefully chosen dichotomy in its title; no one could accuse its author of austere academic analysis but it testified to an encyclopaedic knowledge of and abundant enthusiasm for its subject. The same qualities were displayed in his long relationship with the *Daily Telegraph*, to whose offices he would sally forth, from his chambers or flat at 1 Brick Court in the Temple, providing raw material for professional sports journalists in a waterfall of words, delivered in his unmistakable high-pitched voice, dictating the odd legal opinion by telephone to his clerk, and finally and frequently sleeping at his desk. He had an unorthodox lifestyle and was sometimes unpunctual in his travel arrangements but none the less became a vocal fixture on the growing sports conference circuit. In 1977 he published, with Sir Michael Havers, *The Royal Baccarat Scandal*, later a successful West End play.

Widely acknowledged as the founding father of sports law in England, Grayson was a fellow of the Royal Society of Medicine, a visiting professor at Anglia Polytechnic University, and the first president of the British Association of Sport and Law, which later commemorated him by an annual lecture. He aspired briefly but unsuccessfully to silk and his judicial career was limited to sitting for three days as a deputy stipendiary magistrate at Bow Street. He was indeed not suited to either status. But he left a more lasting mark on the law than many who enjoyed the profession's glittering prizes. After several years of dwindling health he died on 23 September 2008 at University College Hospital, Camden, of renal and heart failure. He was survived by his wife, Wendy, and their son, a solicitor. MICHAEL BELOFF

Sources *The Times* (1 Oct 2008); (2 Oct 2008); (9 Oct 2008); (14 Oct 2008); (15 Oct 2008); (25 Oct 2008) · *Daily Telegraph* (1 Oct 2008) · *LondG* (25 June 1948) · personal knowledge (2012) · private information (2012) · b. cert. · m. cert. · d. cert.
Archives SOUND BL NSA, interview recording

Green, Guy Mervin Charles (1913–2005), cinematographer and film director, was born on 5 November 1913 at 4 Portway, Frome, Somerset, the son of Charles Frederick Green, chauffeur, and his wife, Violet Annie, *née* Smith. An enthusiastic filmgoer as a child, he gained his first technical experience operating his school's new film projector, and later used a contact at the film distributor to gain a job as assistant projectionist on cruise ships. Back in London he briefly ran a portrait studio with a friend before entering film production as a clapper boy at Sound City studios, Shepperton, on the film *Song of the Plough* (1934), directed by John Baxter.

Green methodically worked his way up through the camera departments of various production companies, working with experienced cinematographers like Claude Friese-Green and Otto Kanturek, and being particularly influenced by the German cameraman Günther Krampf. At British International Pictures, Elstree, from the mid-1930s, he graduated to camera operator. He moved over to Denham studios during the Second World War and became operator for the accomplished British cameraman Ronald Neame, shooting exteriors on *A Yank in the RAF* (1941) and operating on Michael Powell's *One of our Aircraft is Missing* (1942). Of particular importance was his participation on David Lean's *In Which We Serve* (1942) and *This Happy Breed* (1944), for the director recommended Green to Carol Reed as director of photography on *The Way Ahead* (1944), a commission he successfully completed. On 17 July 1943 he had married Ellen Mary Coleman, the 39-year-old daughter of Frank Edgar Coleman, salesman. She later died in childbirth.

When the difficult and perfectionist Lean clashed with Robert Krasker, his cinematographer on *Great Expectations* (1946), he chose Green to replace him and the result was a triumph for all concerned. Widely regarded as the most distinguished of all film adaptations of Dickens and reckoned by some to be the greatest ever achievement in black and white cinematography, it won Green an Oscar, the first British film to win the award in this category. Green was the natural choice to photograph Lean's *Oliver Twist* (1948), also for the Cineguild company, and once again he turned in a masterful treatment of light and shade and a wonderful evocation of mid-nineteenth-century London. Both of these films are celebrated for the visual force of their striking opening sequences: the terror of Pip in the eerie graveyard as he confronts Magwitch, and the pain and desperation of the heavily pregnant woman struggling through the stormy night to reach the workhouse. The two films were largely shot in the studio, which suited Green as it gave him maximum control: 'Outside you're at the mercy of the weather and the time of day, and other terrible problems. I love to be in the studio, there's a set with people on it, and it's pitch black. Then I turn it into a picture by turning light on where I think it should be. That's marvellous fun' (*Exposure*, 32). While working on *Oliver Twist* Green met (Celia) Josephine Smith, an actress with the stage name Josephine Stuart, and daughter of Nathaniel Smith, businessman. They married on 24 April 1948, when she was aged twenty-one, and had two children, Michael and Marilyn. After his marriage Green worked with Lean on two further films: *The Passionate Friends* (1949) and *Madeleine* (1950), pleasing his director with his sensitive lighting of the star Ann Todd.

In 1947 Green had photographed the costume melodrama *Blanche Fury* for Cineguild, his first film in Technicolor. Against the prevailing orthodoxy he approached the subject dramatically, explaining:

> Photography for dramatic subjects ... must reflect the emotional content of the scene ... It must not be a glorious

> spectacle all on its own. Therefore in some way it must be suppressed and made to lend itself to the subject dramatically … Monochrome or colour, it is light that sets the scene. (Petrie, 99–100)

Nevertheless, despite this understanding of the cinematographer's art, the films with Lean and Cineguild marked the high point of Green's career as a cinematographer. His other work in the early 1950s was more routine: a couple of Disney adventure stories in *The Story of Robin Hood and his Merrie Men* (1952) and *Rob Roy the Highland Rogue* (1953), and such undistinguished British films as *For Better, for Worse* (1954) and *The Dark Avenger* (1955). The challenge was not up to that posed by Lean, and Green moved over to directing, the last film he photographed being *I Am a Camera* (1955), an uncertain treatment of the Christopher Isherwood stories.

Green commenced directing on the feature *River Beat* (1954) and followed it with other routine thrillers and genre pictures, the most successful being *Sea of Sand* (1958), a war film shot largely on location in Libya. This collaboration with the actors Richard Attenborough and Michael Craig led to *The Angry Silence* (1960), a controversial story of industrial relations and Green's best-regarded film, which won the international film critics' prize at the Berlin film festival. The film was produced by Allied Film Makers, a consortium of film personnel that included Green and gave an unusual measure of control. Another controversial subject—child molestation—was tackled in *The Mark* (1961). Green then went to Hollywood to direct some big-budget social problem films, including *Light in the Piazza* (1962), *Diamond Head* (1963), and *A Patch of Blue* (1965), for which he also wrote the script. He lost his way in the later 1960s with an ill-considered adaptation of John Fowles's *The Magus* (1968) and a series of forgettable films including the ludicrous *Jacqueline Susann's Once Is not Enough* (1975). He then worked out his career in the production mill of American made-for-TV movies, an unsatisfying experience for him as director. His final production was an adaptation of Arthur Hailey's novel *Strong Medicine* (1986). In later years he stayed in touch with the industry in his role as a committee member of the Academy of Motion Picture Arts and Sciences, helping to nominate the candidates for best foreign language film. He was appointed OBE in 2004. He died at his Beverly Hills home on 15 September 2005, of kidney and heart failure, and was survived by his wife, Josephine, and their two children. ALAN BURTON

Sources D. Petrie, *The British cinematographer* (1996) • B. McFarlane, *An autobiography of British cinema* (1997) • *Eyepiece* (Oct–Nov 1997) • *Exposure* (spring 1999) • *The Times* (17 Sept 2005) • *The Guardian* (17 Sept 2005) • *The Independent* (17 Sept 2005) • BFI, oral history project, BECTU, tape no. 233 • b. cert. • m. certs.

Archives FILM BFINA, documentary footage | SOUND BFINA, 'Guy Green interview', BECTU oral history project

Likenesses photographs, 1940x49–1965, Rex Features, London • double portrait, photograph, 1960 (with Richard Attenborough), Getty Images, London • R. Blanshard, photograph, 1999, Camera Press, London • group portrait, photograph, PA Photos, London • obituary photographs

Green, Vivian Hubert Howard (1915–2005), Church of England clergyman, historian, and college head, was born on 18 November 1915 at 101 Thurlby Road, Wembley, Middlesex, the only child of Hubert James Green, law stationer's clerk, and son of a Hampstead master tailor, and his wife, Edith Eleanor Playle, *née* Howard, daughter of a civil servant. His father had at one point had a confectioner's shop in Wembley but at some time in the late 1920s the family moved to Shanklin on the Isle of Wight, where Green's mother's family lived. They again moved a few years later to Minehead in Somerset. The family was not wholly untroubled. Green had little affection for his father. He was, however, deeply devoted to his mother and to his aunt, Gertrude, who accompanied the family to Minehead. As the owner of successive confectionery shops in seaside towns, Green's father prospered modestly, and Green's mother took on additional work to help send him to Bradfield College. From Bradfield he obtained a scholarship to Trinity Hall, Cambridge, where he obtained a first in both parts of the tripos. In 1937–8 he was a Gladstone research student at St Deiniol's Library, Hawarden. He set himself the life of Bishop Reginald Pecock as an appropriate research subject. His essay on Pecock won the Thirlwall medal and prize in 1941.

Green had been ordained in 1940 and became chaplain at Exeter School and St Luke's Training College. He later vividly remembered his service as an air raid warden and the havoc that Baedeker raids inflicted on Exeter. (They incidentally destroyed his papers, delaying publication of his book on Pecock until 1945.) In 1942 he became chaplain and history master at Sherborne School, a post that suited him well. His pupils accorded him respect and liking, though they could not resist naming him Gumboil Green on account of the cyst that he bore on his cheek at that time. He travelled widely in Europe with his closest colleague, H. H. Brown, whose friendship he enjoyed for many years. Their regular trips to Switzerland resulted in a notable account, *The Swiss Alps* (1961). Green's historical works as a schoolmaster were necessarily based on secondary materials. His *The Hanoverians: 1714–1915* (1948) sold well, but ignored the Namierite revolution that was transforming eighteenth-century history. On the other hand *Renaissance and Reformation* (1952) was widely appreciated as a balanced account of European history in the sixteenth and seventeenth centuries, and remained a school textbook for many years.

In 1951 Green applied for the chaplaincy of Lincoln College, Oxford. He was placed *proxime accessit*. Fortunately for Green the successful candidate felt unable to give communion to the rector of the day, Keith Murray, a keen supporter of chapel but a Scottish Presbyterian. Green had no reservations on the subject and was duly appointed. In addition to the chaplaincy he taught medieval history, held various offices including the senior tutorship, and was sub-rector from 1970 to 1983. In that role he was esteemed by an expanding fellowship. He enjoyed reminding his colleagues that sub-rectors had once had a whip with which to keep order among them. He was entirely lacking in malice though he was not incapable of

Vivian Hubert Howard Green (1915–2005), by unknown photographer

sending up humbug. His good nature and congeniality extended to all he knew and met. He was an unfailing source of good sense and judgement, though he never patronized his juniors. He was a conscientious but not a rigorous and demanding tutor. He was, however, exceptionally empathetic and supportive. He was never taken in, but neither did he betray a confidence.

Though he gave up his chaplaincy in 1969 Green did not lose his love of the liturgy, the poetry, and the music of traditional Anglicanism. In his later years he increasingly doubted its supernatural doctrines. If his latitudinarianism turned to agnosticism he avoided controversial debate. None the less, his wide-ranging book *A New History of Christianity* (1996) reflected his belief that the church was increasingly remote from modern life.

Green was perhaps at his best as the historian of an ancient, small, and beautiful Oxford college, preserved mainly because it was for long one of the poorest Oxford colleges. Immersed in its archives, he wrote a succession of books that reflected great scholarship, as well as deep affection for the collegiate tradition that Lincoln maintained. His instinctive tolerance always carried over into his historical world. *Oxford Common Room* (1957) was a delightful evocation of an intimate, sometimes factious little world of nineteenth-century fellows. *The Young Wesley* (1961) portrayed Wesley before his heart was 'strangely warmed', struggling with his own impulses and thoughts, relishing the wine, cards, and evening parties of early eighteenth-century Oxford, and not a little attracted by young women whom he encountered among the Cotswold families with which he became acquainted. Among other things Green identified the room that Wesley had occupied in his younger days, where the Holy Club met and Methodism had its origins, distinct from the so-called Wesley Room, restored by American Methodists in 1929. It seems likely that Wesley lived in the latter during his last years as a fellow. Green's magnum opus was *The Commonwealth of Lincoln College* (1979), a work of scholarship applied to five centuries of the college's history. His mastery of the college's records never obscured his appreciation of the human colour of its changing community. He always took a particular interest in Mark Pattison, for many years a formidable figure in Lincoln, a leading intellectual light in the university as a whole, and not least a likely model for George Eliot's Edward Casaubon. He never published the biography that he had worked on. He did, however, write up the story of Pattison's deep affection for a young woman of tender years in *Love in a Cool Climate* (1985), as well as editing his *Memoirs of an Oxford Don* (1988).

In 1983 Green became rector of Lincoln College in succession to Lord Trend, albeit for only four years since it was known that he would retire at seventy. In the event his tenure proved more than a sentimental gesture. He was a force for moderation and toleration, and showed astuteness in managing colleagues and students alike. He treasured the opportunity to lead the little *collegiolum* that Richard Fleming, bishop of Lincoln, had founded, somewhat precariously, in 1427. Green's portrait by Richard Foster was hung in college with that of Lord Trend, but more characteristic was the cover photograph on the student magazine of the day, *The Lincoln Imp*, which displayed him astride a motorbike, kitted out in black leather.

In later life Green was identified publicly as the partial original of John le Carré's inscrutable Smiley, a character rendered all the more plausible by Alec Guinness's television performance. le Carré (David Cornwell) owed Green a considerable debt for his friendship and support both at Sherborne and Lincoln, a debt that he amply returned in later life. Green seemed an unlikely spy to other friends and colleagues, but in his construction of Smiley, le Carré was aiming to convey that spies or 'spooks' were not at all what most people supposed.

Green's retirement was a happy one. His friendship with William Scoular was a source of great strength to him. It began with Scoular's casting of Green as Canon Chasuble in his production of *The Importance of Being Earnest* at the Apollo Theatre in Oxford (1979). In 1988 they published jointly *A Question of Guilt: the Murder of Nancy Eaton*, an investigation of a Canadian crime that had uncomfortable implications. The case was subsequently made the subject of a film by Scoular in 2003. Green continued to write to the end. In his last days he edited the proofs of the second edition of his *The Madness of Kings*, a study of the psychiatric disorders of monarchs throughout history which he had first published in 1993. He died on 18 January 2005 at Old Prebendal House, a nursing home in Shipton-under-Wychwood, Oxfordshire, a few miles from his delightful if somewhat decaying residence, Calendars, in Burford, where he had over many years entertained students, colleagues, friends, and acquaintances with characteristic generosity, kindness, humour, and charm. He never married, and had no children.

PAUL LANGFORD

Sources *The Independent* (25 Jan 2005) · *The Times* (26 Jan 2005); (7 Feb 2005) · *Daily Telegraph* (26 Jan 2005) · *The Guardian* (5 March

2005) · *WW* (2005) · personal knowledge (2009) · private information (2009) · b. cert. · d. cert.

Likenesses D. Elliott, bromide fibre print, 1984, NPG · R. Foster, portrait, Lincoln College, Oxford · obituary photographs · photograph, Lincoln College, Oxford [*see illus.*]

Wealth at death £467,340: probate, 19 Sept 2005, *CGPLA Eng. & Wales*

Greenwood, Ronald [Ron] (**1921–2006**), footballer and football manager, was born on 11 November 1921 at 15 Lennox Street, Worsthorne, near Burnley, Lancashire, the son of Sam Greenwood, cotton weaver, and later painter and decorator, and his wife, Margaret, *née* Holden, who also worked in a local cotton mill. He would later recall his own introduction to the world of work, helping on local farms and on a milk round wearing leather-topped clogs with wooden soles. Well-paid jobs were not easy to come by in east Lancashire during the years between the wars. One uncle had already moved to London and Sam Greenwood did the same in the 1920s, followed by the rest of the family in 1931. They lived in Alperton, where Greenwood went to the local school. While he was there his Lancashire accent was transformed as he experienced the pressure felt by many young migrants to conform to their new surroundings. He left school at fourteen and his father used his influence to arrange an apprenticeship with a firm of signwriters that had Lancashire connections. Some of its jobs took it to leading London sporting venues including Wembley, where his father would eventually become maintenance manager. It must have seemed a dream job to both son and father: Wembley was home to the most celebrated matches in the English football calendar, including the FA cup final and the biannual visit of Scotland, and football had already become an important part of the young Greenwood's life.

Greenwood later recalled watching Burnley Football Club with his father in the 1920s, and he played the game from an early age both at school and in local church leagues. By his early teens he had appeared for several clubs, played for a youth side at Wembley, and, with a friend, had a trial at Queen's Park Rangers. Chelsea offered him a contract in the late 1930s and he soon began to play for the reserves as a centre-half. In 1940 he joined the Royal Air Force. He served with a mobile radio unit in Northern Ireland, where he played regularly for Belfast Celtic before a posting back to London enabled him to play a few games for Chelsea. In 1944 he went to France after D-day as a member of a radar unit. However, appendicitis led to a posting to Yorkshire, where his wife was staying with relatives. Fit again, he signed for Bradford Park Avenue. The club liked him so much that they paid their then record transfer fee to Chelsea to keep him in 1946. After three seasons in Bradford he followed his manager to Brentford. But he was thirty before he played in the first division, after he had been re-signed by Chelsea in October 1952. He won a championship medal when Chelsea won the title for the first time in 1955. Two unhappy years at Fulham completed his playing career.

Greenwood was unlike most of his footballing contemporaries. As a centre-half for Chelsea he preferred marking space as much as the opposing number nine, and generally tried to use the ball constructively. He became interested in coaching while a player at Brentford, attending courses run by the Football Association and coming under the influence of Walter Winterbottom. While at Chelsea he coached at Oxford University and also worked with Ealing grammar school and Walthamstow Avenue. He was convinced that even good players could be improved by teaching. No footballer could have too much intelligence. The Hungarians had impressed him in 1953 by their movement on and off the ball; they not only knew where to go, but when to go.

In 1956 Eastbourne asked Greenwood to coach them and he gave up playing after they agreed to match the £1000 a year he was earning at Fulham. Sussex County Football Association made him their chief coach and he was soon putting on courses at the National Physical Recreation Centre at Lilleshall in Shropshire, and also helping to develop the England youth team. His reputation grew, especially in the south, and eventually Arsenal appointed him their first ever full-time coach. He spent three years at Highbury, during which he gained some experience of European football as manager of the England under-twenty-three team. In 1961 West Ham appointed him as only their fourth ever manager, in succession to Ted Fenton. He was paid £2000 a year, was living in Twickenham, and had just bought his first car, a Morris Minor. It would be his job for the next sixteen years.

During the 1960s West Ham became one of the most popular clubs, especially among the new male, middle-class, metropolitan football audience that appreciated their intelligent, free-flowing style. Greenwood inherited a goldmine of young players, but most of them would later acknowledge the help they received from him, including the three England giants of 1966, Bobby Moore, Martin Peters, and Geoff Hurst. Greenwood converted Hurst from an ordinary wing-half into a successful striker; he moved Moore to play on the left side of central defence, and eventually found a free role for Peters behind the two main strikers. West Ham won the FA cup in 1964 and the European cup winners' cup in 1965. Many critics and fans thought that these were merely the overtures to future triumphs, but they did not materialize. West Ham never finished higher than sixth in the first division. Greenwood thought it was his fault. There were in fact several factors involved, a lack of defensive solidity, a football style that though pleasing to the eye was unsuited to the boggy pitches of winter, and an inability to fill such key positions as goalkeeper and centre-half being perhaps the most crucial. Players became dissatisfied, and first Peters and then Hurst and Moore moved to other clubs. By 1974 the directors and many supporters felt that a different approach and a younger manager were needed. Greenwood became general manager and John Lyall took his place on training ground and match days.

If Walter Winterbottom had succeeded Stanley Rous as secretary of the FA in 1962, Greenwood might have become manager of England instead of Alf Ramsey. He would certainly not have done so if Don Revie had not resigned from the England job in 1977, towards the end of the qualifying competition for the following year's world cup. The FA, desperate for a caretaker, appointed Greenwood, initially for three games, not only because he was available but because he was known and respected at Lancaster Gate. He would later be preferred to Brian Clough, Lawrie McMenemy, and Bobby Robson, who were also interviewed for the permanent position. As with West Ham Greenwood's management of England was successful up to a point. The home international championship was won three times in five years and qualification was achieved for the finals of the European championship of 1980 and the world cup of 1982. Both ended in disappointment, particularly in Spain in 1982, when England were unbeaten in five matches and conceded only one goal but suffered injuries to key players and were not helped by the tournament's eccentric structure. Greenwood resigned after the tournament finished.

Greenwood certainly had some of the qualities required for international football management. He did not believe that British was best and was convinced that British insularity was an obstacle to progress. He was critical of those players who refused to practise either to improve skills or to eliminate weaknesses. He liked to think of football as a battle of wits, and disliked the British tendency to reduce it to a conflict of speed and aggression. To him it was a game of risk and teams should gamble, but with intelligence and skill. He could talk fluently about the game, but as he grew older he developed a pompous side that led to nicknames like the Vicar. He was a thoughtful man, yet one who believed that northern players were harder than those from the south; his approach could probably be summed up as old-fashioned with touches of modernity.

Greenwood lived in Sussex after retirement and was briefly a director of Brighton and Hove Albion in 1984. He was appointed CBE in 1981. Towards the end of his life he was cared for at The Beeches residential home, in Ixworth, Suffolk, where he died of heart failure on 8 February 2006. He was survived by a son and daughter, along with his wife of over sixty years, Lucy Joan. Perhaps she summed up the difficulties of the football manager's life when she advised the young women of Britain to think carefully before marrying one. TONY MASON

Sources T. Brooking, *An autobiography* (1981) · T. Francis and D. Miller, *The world to play for* (1982) · R. Greenwood and B. Butler, *Yours sincerely* (1984) · C. Korr, *West Ham United: the making of a football club* (1986) · J. Powell, *Bobby Moore: the life and times of a sporting hero* (1993) · T. Moore, *Bobby Moore, by the person who knew him best* (2005) · M. Peters and M. Hart, *The ghost of '66* (2006) · *The Times* (10 Feb 2006) · *Daily Telegraph* (10 Feb 2006) · *The Guardian* (10 Feb 2006) · *The Independent* (10 Feb 2006) · *WW* (2006) · b. cert. · d. cert.

Archives FILM BFINA, documentary footage | SOUND BL NSA, documentary recording

Likenesses photographs, 1952–78, Rex Features, London · photographs, 1953–88, PA Photos, London · photographs, 1961–81, Hult. Arch., London · photographs, 1977–80, Getty Images, London, Popperfoto · B. Thomas, photographs, 1979–86, Getty Images, London, Bob Thomas Sports · photographs, 1980–82, Photoshot, London · obituary photographs

Grierson, Philip (1910–2006), historian and numismatist, was born on 15 November 1910 at Portobello House, Dublin, one of four children of Philip Henry Grierson, landowner and surveyor, of Kilcarberry House, Clondalkin, and his wife, Roberta Ellen Jane, *née* Pope. He was educated at Marlborough College and Gonville and Caius College, Cambridge (1929–32), where he was admitted to study medicine but immediately switched to history. He graduated with high distinction, and won the Lightfoot scholarship for ecclesiastical history. In 1935 he was elected to a college research fellowship. He remained a fellow of Caius, and a resident bachelor don, throughout his long life. He was most sociable, entertaining numerous guests in college. He also served the college as librarian (1944–69), director of studies in history, and president (deputy head of house; 1966–76). At the same time he held university teaching appointments in the faculty of history, successively as assistant lecturer (from 1938), lecturer (1945–59), reader in medieval numismatics (1959–71), and professor of numismatics (1971–8). Bibliography was an active interest throughout his career, and he served for thirty-five years as a syndic of the university library, eventually as chairman.

When he was a young man Grierson's political sympathies lay with the Soviet Union, which he visited in 1930. In 1943 he published *Books on Soviet Russia, 1917–42*, and he continued with regular bibliographical work on Russia for twenty years. To the end of his life he was hostile to religious belief, and he left strict instructions that his funeral should be entirely secular in character. It is curious, therefore, that the historical research he undertook as Lightfoot scholar and in the first stage of his long career concerned the abbeys of medieval Flanders. As well as writing articles for learned journals, he edited an important text, in *Les annales de Saint-Pierre de Gand* (1937). His personal inclination in scholarship, however, deriving perhaps from his early education in the natural sciences, was for wide-ranging and systematic review. This found expression in the *Shorter Cambridge Medieval History* (1952), a two-volume distillation of the original eight volumes, for which Grierson succeeded to the editorial responsibility in 1947. His breadth of experience as a medieval historian was further developed by his serving as literary director of the Royal Historical Society (1945–55).

It was in a sense a chance event that redirected Grierson's intellectual interests, and set him on a new course in his career, which he followed unswervingly and with growing distinction for sixty years. In 1945 he happened to find among his father's belongings a Byzantine copper coin, which he puzzled over and eventually identified only with difficulty. He then visited a London firm of coin dealers, intending just to buy a few medieval coins with which to enliven his tutorials and university lectures. But collecting quickly became a passion. In the post-war years some distinguished old coin collections came onto the market, and it was possible to acquire significant material without much competition. Grierson soon laid the foundations of what was to be the world's finest and most wide-ranging private collection of medieval European coins. For country after country throughout Europe it eventually became second only in scope and range to the national collection of that country. Collecting on that scale and at that level of discernment would, for most scholars, have consumed all their energies. Grierson found time and energy also for critical study of the chronology and exact attribution of his coins. His academic familiarity with medieval European history enabled him to place a vast miscellany of individual coin-types into their political context—an intellectual approach that had its roots in nineteenth-century taxonomy, and that might be described as *l'art de vérifier les médailles*. With such an Olympian agenda, and with disciplined hard work, he became Europe's most distinguished numismatic scholar. From 1948 until 1981 he held, in addition to his Cambridge appointments, a professorship of numismatics and the history of coinage in the University of Brussels. In 1953 and 1954 he ran summer schools in New York, under the auspices of the American Numismatic Society; and in 1955 he was appointed by Harvard University as adviser on numismatics at its Byzantine Institute in Dumbarton Oaks, Washington, DC, with the plan, and the funding, to build up the finest collection of Byzantine coins in the world, and to publish a catalogue of it. Grierson sold his own collection of Byzantine coins to Dumbarton Oaks, leaving him better able to concentrate his resources on building up his collection of European coins—again with a view to publishing a catalogue of the widest scope, and of a thoroughness that would guarantee its pre-eminence for the foreseeable future. Thus he laid claim to an overview of the medieval numismatics of two-thirds of the Mediterranean and Western world; Islamic coinage lay, essentially, outside his expertise.

Grierson pursued his two monumental projects single-mindedly for the rest of his career. He lived to see the completion of the five lavish volumes of the Dumbarton Oaks collection, amounting to over 3000 pages of text, in addition to copious illustration. This was a collaborative venture, with Alfred R. Bellinger and others, but volume 5 (published in 1999), covering the coinage of the years 1258–1453 with magisterial skill and discretion, was written by Grierson himself. The medieval European project was even more ambitious: fifteen large volumes were envisaged. The first of these (*Medieval European Coinage*, vol. 1, 1986), written jointly with Mark Blackburn and published by Cambridge University Press, covered all the coinages of the West from the fifth century to the tenth—the post-Roman successor states, the Visigoths, Merovingians, Carolingians, Frisians, and early Anglo-Saxons. It is for this early period that numismatics is of greatest value to the medieval historian. Another volume, written jointly with Professor Lucia Travaini, was published, describing the subsequent coinages of southern Italy, as volume 14 in the series, in 1998. Some eight or ten other volumes were already in preparation at the time of Grierson's death.

Grierson was elected a fellow of the British Academy in 1958, and was president of the Royal Numismatic Society from 1961 to 1966. He received honorary doctorates from the University of Ghent in 1958 and from Leeds in 1978. In addition to his LittD degree (1971), Cambridge made him an honorary LLD in 1993. He listed his hobby in *Who's Who* as science fiction, and as well as an extensive library of the genre he owned some 2000 videos and DVDs. His extremely hard-working and productive career as a historian and as a collector earned him a unique international reputation as a polymath in medieval numismatics. When at his death he bequeathed his collection of some 20,000 medieval coins (and an outstanding numismatic library) to the University of Cambridge, its value was estimated at between five and ten million pounds. He died on 15 January 2006 at Cottenham Court nursing home, Cottenham, near Cambridge, of bilateral pulmonary emboli. He never married. D. M. METCALF

Sources *The Times* (20 Jan 2006) · *Daily Telegraph* (20 Jan 2006) · *The Independent* (20 Jan 2006) · *WW* (2006) · personal knowledge (2010) · private information (2010) · b. cert. · d. cert.
Archives Gonville and Caius College, Cambridge
Likenesses obituary photographs
Wealth at death £5,189,096: probate, 22 Sept 2006, *CGPLA Eng. & Wales*

Griffith, Kenneth Reginald (1921–2006), actor and documentary film-maker, was born Kenneth Reginald Griffiths on 12 October 1921 at his paternal grandparents' home, Rhos Cottage, Church Park, Tenby, Pembrokeshire, the son of Harold Sydney Griffiths, railway booking clerk, and his wife, Margaret (Peggy), *née* Davies. Six months after his birth his parents went their separate ways, leaving him behind with his Wesleyan Methodist grandparents, Ernest and Emily Griffiths. As a boy he showed some indications of the individualistic film-maker and presenter he was to become, wheedling, hectoring, and incredulous at the world's folly and duplicity. He felt himself to be always the odd man out, 'not so much at the bottom of the hierarchy as slightly to the side of it' (Griffith, 11). He attended Tenby council school and gorged on films, especially *Ben Hur*, at the Royal Gate House cinema, imitating the actions of the players for fellow junior school pupils. At Greenhill grammar school, Tenby, his talent for acting was encouraged by his English teacher, Evelyn Ward. When he was fifteen the headmaster, J. T. Griffith, told him that if he wanted to become an actor he should change his name to Griffith, since Griffiths was an Anglicization.

Though his mother, who had reappeared, found a job for him in an ironmonger's shop in Cambridge, Griffith did not like the job. He soon found the Festival Theatre on the Newmarket Road, presented himself at the stage door, auditioned twice, and at the age of sixteen was given the part of Cinna in a modern-dress *Julius Caesar*. The director of the local repertory company saw the play and offered him the part of the cheeky office boy in *London Wall*. During the summer season he played the sinisterly plausible and murderous psychopath Danny in *Night Must Fall*; intangibly threatening and odd characters were to become his forte.

Turned down for the weekend pilots scheme for the RAF City of London air squadron (he had displayed his ruthless regard for the truth by telling the recruiters that he was 'prepared' rather than 'keen' to fly), Griffith was accepted as a student at St Martin's School of Art in London and carried on acting, Emlyn Williams giving him a small role as a coachman in *The Corn is Green*. His first part for the cinema was in the film of Eden Phillpotts's play *The Farmer's Wife* (1941). While rehearsing *Macbeth* at Burnley for a production by Tyrone Guthrie, who was to become a mentor, he volunteered a second time for the RAF. At last called up, he carried a copy of Adolf Hitler's *Mein Kampf* with him for the remainder of the Second World War, because he wanted 'to understand fully what the war was about' (Griffith, 68), an early illustration of his indifference to other people's possible view of him. Suffering from scarlet fever, he was invalided out in 1942. Having recovered, he then toured Britain as Heathcliff in *Wuthering Heights*. At a cadets' ball in Stratford upon Avon he had, meanwhile, met Joan Mary Stock, a schoolteacher a year his senior, daughter of Archibald George Stock, journalist. They were married in Heysham parish church on 11 March 1944, and had two sons.

During the latter stages of the Second World War, Griffith appeared with Guthrie's Old Vic company at Liverpool in a number of plays, including *The Tragedy of Doctor Faustus*, *Scandal at Barchester*, and *John Gabriel Borkman*. Following the Old Vic's return to London he remained with the company. He was due to play the poet Villon, the major role in *The Other Heart*, in 1951, but Hugh Hunt (Guthrie's successor) decided instead to assign Alan Badel to the role, offering Griffith a smaller part. Griffith regretted accepting it, and his meagre facility for compromise shrank even further. When he went to South Africa with the Old Vic one member of the company was Doria Noar, whom he married following his divorce from his first wife, Joan; they had one daughter, the actress Eva Griffith.

As an actor Griffith preferred the cinema to the theatre, and in a career lasting more than fifty years he appeared, often in warped, threatening, or eccentric roles, in some eighty or more films, including *Private's Progress* (1956), *Lucky Jim* (1957), *I'm All Right Jack* (1959), *The Lion in Winter* (1968), *The Wild Geese* (1978), *Four Weddings and a Funeral* (1994), and *The Englishman Who Went up a Hill but Came down a Mountain* (1995). He also enjoyed a long career in television, from *The Shop at Sly Corner* (1946), to *The Prisoner* (1967–8), to *Holby City* (2003). He claimed that he saw these film and television parts as a plumber might see his job.

It was after Griffith was interviewed on the British–Boer conflict on BBC television's *Tonight* programme in 1964 that Huw Wheldon and David Attenborough asked him to make a film about any one of his enthusiasms. Griffith suggested the siege and relief of Ladysmith, resulting in *Soldiers of the Widow* (1967), which he wrote and presented, and in which he acted most of the roles (as he did with most of his documentaries). From that point he was able to turn his desire to tilt at received opinion into his life's work. Inevitably, however, his career as a film-maker was marked by controversies and conflicts. In 1973 he made *Hang Up Your Brightest Colours*, about the Irish nationalist Michael Collins, for Lew Grade's ATV company, but the Independent Broadcasting Authority asked Grade not to submit it to them (because they did not want to have to refuse him permission to screen it). Griffith included a reference to the 'suppression' of this documentary in his *Who's Who* entry, and in 1974 made *The Public's Right to Know*, dealing also with the problems encountered in making a documentary on Lord Baden-Powell, as a result of the trade union boycott of South Africa. (Griffith himself had joined the actors' union, Equity, only under protest.) His film about Napoleon, *The Man on the Rock* (1975), would have been less controversial had he not seen himself as Napoleon's advocate. As part of the bicentenary in 1976 he was asked by the American Broadcasting Corporation to make a film about the American War of Independence, but he found his script emasculated and the title changed. His projected film in the late 1970s called *Curious Journey*, based on talking to IRA survivors of the Easter rising and Anglo-Irish War, was taken up by Harlech Television, but predictably ran into trouble; Harlech later offered him all rights for 1*p*. provided the company's name was taken off the film.

In the 1980s Griffith's clashes with authority continued. His film about Tom Paine for BBC Wales, *The Most Valuable Englishman Ever* (1982), had been opposed behind the scenes, and he believed that attempts had been made to dissuade BBC commissioning editors from using him in future. When Channel 4 approached him, he suggested a film on William Gladstone and Paul Kruger, having already come to the view that the Afrikaners had been unfairly maligned by the British. Two weeks later his business partner David Swift was told by a Channel 4 executive, 'Kenneth can't work here'. Asked by Indira Gandhi to make a film about her father, Jawaharlal Nehru, he filmed all over the country. The resultant film, *But I Have Promises to Keep* (1989), was suppressed and not screened until 1993. He was in even worse diplomatic difficulties when he planned a film on the life of Dr Ambedkar, the political leader of India's untouchables. He was obstructed in his efforts to film in India itself, with the result that the film was not made, though Thames Television paid his salary in full. *Zola Budd: the Girl Who Didn't Run* (1989) was about the Afrikaner barefoot runner who had twice broken the women's 5000 metre world record, then after taking British citizenship had competed for England, only to be suspended by the International Amateur Athletics Association for supposedly running in an event in South Africa. Griffith, who quixotically saw her as a victim, wrote that 'there are no bigger racists than the Blacks' (Griffith, 362), and similarly disparaged western left-wingers who supported what he regarded as persecution of her.

Altogether Griffith made over twenty documentaries. In 1993 he had one made about himself, called *The Tenby Poisoner*, an epithet given to him by the Welsh writer Alun Richards. Roy Davies, head of BBC Wales's documentaries department, also made sure his long-banned film *Hang Up Your Brightest Colours* was screened as part of a season of Griffith documentaries, resulting in death threats against him by protestant unionists. But he found that his one real problem was what he called 'this support and expression of approbation' (Griffith, 384). He had grown so used to vetoes, opposition, and denunciation, that friendly approval temporarily threatened his *raison d'être*, which was to use the truth as he perceived it to shake up establishments of any kind. Late in life he said, 'I've been accused of being a Marxist, a fascist, a traitor and probably worst in most people's eyes, inconsistent. I was a radical Socialist. I'm now a radical Tory. It has been a very painful journey' (*The Times*, 21 Oct 1992). His autobiography, *The Fool's Pardon*, was published in 1994.

Griffith's third marriage, to Carole Hagar (with whom he had a son and a daughter), ended, like the first two, in divorce, after which he had relationships lasting two years with Madeline Bell, a singer, and seven years with Margret Kopala (*b.* 1945), a Canadian-born BBC production assistant (and later a conservative activist in Canada). He died at his home, 110 Englefield Road, Islington, London, on 25 June 2006, from the effects of Alzheimer's disease and diabetes. He was survived by his five children.

DENNIS BARKER

Sources K. Griffith, *The fool's pardon* (1994) · *The Independent* (26 June 2006) · *The Times* (27 June 2006) · *Daily Telegraph* (27 June 2006) · *The Guardian* (27 June 2006) · *WW* (2006) · personal knowledge (2010) · private information (2010) · b. cert. · m. cert. [1944] · d. cert.

Archives NL Wales, Emyr Humphreys papers | FILM BFINA, current affairs footage · BFINA, documentary footage · BFINA, performance footage | SOUND BL NSA, performance recordings

Likenesses J. Chillingworth, photograph, 1953, Getty Images, London, Hult. Arch. · obituary photographs · photographs, repro. in Griffith, *The fool's pardon* · photographs, Rex Features, London

Wealth at death £608,147: probate, 7 Dec 2006, *CGPLA Eng. & Wales*

Griffiths, Philip Jones (1936–2008), photojournalist, was born on 18 February 1936 at Monfa, Hylas Lane, Rhuddlan, Flintshire, the oldest of three sons of Joseph Griffiths (1903–1962), a railway master fitter who worked at Llandudno Junction, and his wife, Lizzie (Catherine) Jones (*d.* 1973), a district nurse. His younger brothers were Penri Jones Griffiths (*b.* 1938) and Gareth Jones Griffiths (*b.* 1944). He spoke Welsh as his first language. He attended Rhuddlan county primary school until passing the eleven-plus examination and moving up the valley to St Asaph's Grammar School. For a short time his grandfather Henry Griffiths moved the village general store into the front room of the family home from where he traded until he was suddenly struck blind.

As a teenager Griffiths became a conscientious objector and a member of the Peace Pledge Union. His commitment to pacifism, together with his Welsh-bred partisan empathy for the underdog, became fixed ideals generating an emotive force visible in much of his work. While still at school he worked as a trainee pharmacist at Boots the chemists in Rhyl. The Rhyl Camera Club was situated upstairs, and it was there that he became exposed to the work of Henri Cartier-Bresson and nurtured his passion for photography. He began to explore north Wales on his motorbike, documenting the plight of Welsh villagers displaced by flooding. At home the back yard was turned into a chemistry laboratory and the bathroom was converted into a darkroom, complete with an enlarger that swung up on a sprung shelf. Prints, such as his portraits of the theatre director Sam Wanamaker, were dried on a line in the kitchen. He never lost his boyish fascination with the technical aspects of his craft: processing, printing, cameras, and optics. As a teenager he saved up for camera equipment by photographing group portraits of convalescing Derbyshire miners at Pengwern Hall, a short ride from Rhuddlan.

After moving to Liverpool to study pharmacy Griffiths photographed the nascent arts scene in the city, accompanying the poet Adrian Henri, an old school friend from St Asaph's, and photographing the Beatles' first concert at the Liverpool Empire. He completed his studies in Sunderland then moved to London, where he worked in the pharmacy at St Mary Abbot's Hospital, Kensington, and as the night manager of Boots in Piccadilly, often managing the needs of drug addicts. By day he photographed Soho life and bunked in a brothel near Leicester Square with his brother Penri. His support for pacifism led him to photograph the first and subsequent Aldermaston marches. His first break came when the influential editor of *Photography* magazine named the aspiring Welshman as one of the five best photographers of 1960. This led to a job with *The Observer* in 1961. A year later his reputation as an international photojournalist blossomed with his scoop on the *regroupement* programme during the Algerian War. When the *Sunday Times* and *Sunday Telegraph* colour magazines were launched in 1962 and 1964 he went on to freelance for them on assignments in Mongolia and Ethiopia.

In 1966 Griffiths joined Magnum Photos as an associate, and in the same year set out to report on the Vietnam War, a five-year odyssey that was to become the defining juncture of his career. He lambasted the stupidity of war, yet at the same time photographed with intimate tenderness its victims on both sides of the conflict, resulting in some of the finest war photographs of the twentieth century. *Vietnam Inc.*, a classic in the history of photojournalism, was finally published in 1971, with most of the printing, text, and design having been prepared with his partner, Heather Holden, in London and New York. *Vietnam Inc.*—its moving photographs and accompanying polemic—helped turn public opinion against the war in south-east Asia, although by 1971 there was already widespread disaffection. Following the critical success of the book Griffiths sought to build on the impact that it had made. During the 1970s he went on to photograph Cambodia, the Yom Kippur War, the conflict in Northern Ireland, and Rhodesia where, in the most frightening incident of his life, he had a hood placed over his head and was taken out to be shot.

In 1980 Griffiths was elected president of Magnum Photos for a five-year term during which, he claimed, he 'dragged Magnum kicking and screaming into the twentieth century' (private information). He moved to 36th Street in New York and in 1981 began a ten-year relationship with the photographer Donna Ferrato. His later books included *Dark Odyssey* (1996), *Agent Orange: Collateral Damage in Vietnam* (2004), *Vietnam at Peace* (2005), *Recollections* (2008), and a new edition of *Vietnam Inc.* (2006).

Griffiths was courageous, charismatic, disarmingly

funny, and caring—especially about the plight of the disempowered. He was also stubborn and unforgiving. He had entrenched opinions on a wide range of things he abhorred such as smoking, military power, and perceived disloyalty. He was 'the spirit of contradiction' but at the same time gave to photojournalism its moral soul. He died at his home in 195A Goldhawk Road, Shepherd's Bush, London, on 19 March 2008 of colon cancer. He was survived by his two daughters, Katherine Holden and Fenella Ferrato (both born in 1982). STUART FRANKLIN

Sources *The Times* (20 March 2008) · *The Guardian* (21 March 2008); (24 March 2008); (1 April 2008) · *The Independent* (22 March 2008) · personal knowledge (2012) · private information (2012) [Heather Holden, partner; Donna Ferrato, partner; Katherine Holden, daughter; Fenella Ferrato, daughter; Gareth Jones Griffiths, brother; Penri Jones Griffiths, brother; E. Erwitt; J. Bulmer; I. Berry; D. Hurn] · b. cert. · d. cert.
Archives SOUND BL NSA, documentary recordings
Likenesses obituary photographs

Grima, Andrew Peter (1921–2007), jeweller, was born in Rome on 31 May 1921, the son of John Grima, a Maltese-born embroidery designer, and his Italian wife, Leopolda, *née* Farnese. The family moved to Britain when Andrew was aged five. After attending St Joseph's College in south-east London he studied mechanical engineering at University College, Nottingham. During the Second World War he served with the Royal Electrical and Mechanical Engineers in India and Burma, was mentioned in dispatches, and developed his talent for improvisation as an engineer and his interest in craftsmanship. After demobilization he hoped to study at art college but this proved impossible. Instead he took a secretarial course, where he met Hélène Marianne Haller (*b.* 1923/4), daughter of the Viennese-born Josef Schwaighofer, who ran a small jewellery-making business. They married on 5 July 1947 at St George's Roman Catholic Church, Wembley, and had two daughters and one son.

Grima was initially employed by his father-in-law as the firm's accountant but in 1948 he changed course when the company acquired a suitcase of Brazilian semi-precious stones with which he was able to begin a career as a designer. Untrained in jewellery design, Grima pursued an unorthodox and radical approach; many of his ideas developed from paintings (his first creative passion) or facsimiles of natural patterns and shapes. From his initial assortment of tourmalines, rough amethysts, and aquamarines he put together a collection distinctive in its use of large, rough stones and natural textures fashioned into sculpted, abstract shapes. In 1951 he took over the business following Josef Schwaighofer's death, and sold it to a Knightsbridge stone dealer on the condition that he remain as designer.

In 1960 Grima's work was recognized by Graham Hughes, then art director at the Worshipful Company of Goldsmiths, who invited him a year later to participate in the world's first exhibition of modern art jewellery at the Goldsmiths' Hall, London. For the exhibition Grima designed pieces based on wax models submitted by the sculptors Elisabeth Frink, Kenneth Armitage, and Bernard Meadows. Hughes also began to promote Grima's work to influential clients, while Grima made his own telling introduction to royal circles when he invited Lord Snowdon, the husband of Princess Margaret, to tour his workshop. The invitation followed a public lament by Snowdon on the dullness of contemporary jewellery design. So began Grima's emergence as one of the decade's most sought-after jewellery designers for the British royal family and fashionable society. Snowdon's visit prompted him to acquire pieces for Princess Margaret; Prince Philip purchased a brooch of rubies for the queen in 1966. Thereafter Grima was commissioned by the queen to design state gifts for royal visits. In the same year he began trading at 80 Jermyn Street, London, in premises—designed by his brothers Godfrey and George, and opened by Snowdon—that, with their mix of steel, slate, and a perspex spiral staircase, mirrored the boldness and modernity of his jewellery. Commercial success was matched by professional recognition, which included twelve De Beers diamond international design awards (1964–76) and a queen's award for industry (1966) and culminated in 1970 in Grima's appointment as jeweller to the queen.

The royal warrant came a year after one of Grima's most celebrated creations: a collection for Omega of eighty-five individual watches encased in gemstones rather than glass. Known as About Time, the work took sixty-four craftsmen a year to complete and was influential in highlighting the potential for watches as jewellery and art works as well as timepieces. Grima's Omega exhibition toured the world and his international appeal was further established with the opening in 1970 of a New York gallery, followed by premises in Sydney and Tokyo. As the decade came to a close his creations—defined by flamboyance, organicism, and wit—were regularly worn by members of the British royal family, as well as by Jacqueline Onassis, Ursula Andress, and others. In the early 1970s Grima used notably large, rough, and unusual minerals for his Rock Revival collection (1972) which he followed with further themed exhibitions including 'Supershells' (1975) and 'Sticks and Stones' (1977). In 1975 he met Joanne Jill (Jojo) Maughan-Brown (*b.* 1950/51), daughter of Nigel Maughan-Brown, farmer, and granddaughter of the diamond magnate Sir Thomas Cullinan, and two years later he divorced his wife. He and Jojo married at Westminster register office on 20 December 1977; their daughter, Francesca, was born in 1980 and joined the family business in 1998.

In 1975 Grima had opened another gallery in Zürich, again based on a striking design by his brother George. However, further expansion of the firm in 1980 ended in failure when his business partner was declared bankrupt soon after. In 1986, with great regret, Grima resigned the royal warrant and moved to Switzerland, where he set up a business specializing in private commissions, initially at Lugano and from 1993 at Gstaad. Biannual exhibitions of his work were mounted in London between 1998 and 2006, in which year Bonhams held an auction of his work. He died on 26 December 2007 at Gstaad, Switzerland, and was survived by his wife and four children. For her annual

Christmas broadcast, shown the day before Grima's death, the queen again wore his brooch with rubies purchased in 1966. PHILIP CARTER

Sources G. Hughes, *Grima: a jeweller's world* (2003) · *Daily Telegraph* (21 Dec 2007) · *The Times* (5 Jan 2008) · *The Guardian* (18 Jan 2008) · *The Independent* (18 Jan 2008) · www.grimajewellery.com, 12 Aug 2010 · *WW* (2007) · b. cert. · m. certs.
Likenesses obituary photographs · photograph, repro. in www.peteredwardsjewels.com/jewellery-Designers/Andrew-Grima.aspx · photographs, Getty Images, London, Hult. Arch. · photographs, repro. in www.grimajewellery.com

Guest, Val (1911–2006), film director and screenwriter, was born Valmond Maurice Grossmann at 116 Sutherland Avenue, Maida Vale, London, on 11 December 1911, the son of John Simon Grossmann, jute broker, and his wife, Julia Anne Gladys, *née* Emanuel. His parents were of Jewish descent. He spent his infancy in India, returning to London after his parents' divorce, which was kept secret from him (he was told that his mother had died). He was educated at Seaford College, Sussex, and left in 1927 to work briefly as a bookkeeper. After beginning his career as an actor he went on to form a successful song-writing partnership with Ivan Keith, and to sample journalism with *Film Weekly* and the *Los Angeles Examiner*, and as the London editor of the *Hollywood Reporter*. His work was noticed by the film director Marcel Varnel, who invited him in 1935 to join Gainsborough Studios as a writer. There he associated with such outstanding creative talents as Alfred Hitchcock and showed a genuine flair for comedy writing, contributing scripts (co-written with George Marriott Edgar) for Will Hay classics like *Oh, Mr Porter* (1937) and *Convict 99* (1938) and for madcap comedies featuring Arthur Askey and the Crazy Gang. Varnel signed him to an exclusive partnership, and enabled him to gain directorial experience on Varnel's second unit. On 25 March 1936, at St Marylebone register office, he married a 'Gaiety girl', Violet Johnston, known as Pat Watson (*b.* 1913), daughter of David Johnston, music hall artist. They had a son, David (*b.* 1939), but the marriage did not survive the Second World War. By the time of his marriage he had adopted the name Val Guest, and he confirmed it by deed poll in March 1939.

Moving to Lime Grove Studios at the outbreak of war Guest continued to write hit comedies, while also serving as an auxiliary fireman. He was finally given his first directorial commission by the Ministry of Information: to write and direct *The Nose Has It!* (1942), a short film starring Askey that warned of the dangers of coughs and sneezes. On the strength of its success Gainsborough consented to Guest directing two feature-length scripts for Askey: the racy musical comedies *Miss London Ltd* (1943) and *Bees in Paradise* (1944). However, the director's most original film of the war years was *Give Us the Moon* (1943), a screwball comedy that gave the teenage Jean Simmons her first major part. The serious political undertones that Guest gave to the comedy pointed the way to the issue-based cinema he would develop a decade later.

In the post-war years Guest enhanced his reputation for sharp and pacey comedies, working with a variety of producers, notably Daniel M. Angel. Increasingly his films featured the vivacious American actress Yolande Donlan, otherwise Yolande Donlan Truex (*b.* 1920; daughter of James Donlan, actor), whom Guest married, at St Marylebone register office on 11 September 1954, also becoming stepfather to her son, Christopher Truex (*b.* 1946). Guest created eight starring roles for her, beginning with *Miss Pilgrim's Progress* (1949), in which an American girl saves a British village from the ravages of town planning, and including *Mr Drake's Duck* (1950), which satirized cold war paranoia and military inefficiency, and the alpine fantasy *Penny Princess* (1952), which Guest also produced.

When Hammer Studios hired Guest to direct his friends Ben Lyon and Bebe Daniels in two 'spin-offs' from their successful television series *Life with the Lyons* it seemed he was firmly type-cast in comedy, but Hammer surprisingly also offered him the chance to explore new genres. In adapting a Nigel Kneale television play, Guest pointed to a new direction for Hammer with *The Quatermass Xperiment* (1955), one of the high points of British science fiction cinema. The same team followed it with *Quatermass II* (1956) and *The Abominable Snowman* (1957), two thoughtful films that tapped into widespread fears about government secrecy and nuclear proliferation.

Although Guest did not abandon comedy—*Expresso Bongo* (1959), for instance, was a memorable satire on Tin Pan Alley—his new trajectory led him to write, produce, and direct British cinema's definitive expression of post-war anxiety and ambivalence about scientific progress, *The Day the Earth Caught Fire* (1961). The film won the BAFTA award for best screenplay. Guest's genre films were distinguished by their honesty and conviction, and the use of techniques more conventionally associated with social realist cinema—such as overlapping dialogue, location filming, and hand-held camera—to keep his narratives credible. *The Camp on Blood Island* (1957) and *Yesterday's Enemy* (1959) did not flinch from showing the horrors of the war in east Asia, or the amorality encouraged by survival conditions. In *Hell is a City* (1960) and *Jigsaw* (1962) Guest enlisted the aid of local police forces to facilitate location shooting and brought a new level of authenticity to the crime melodrama and police procedural. His fondness for a documentary approach to drama and his increasingly accomplished use of Arthur Grant's shimmering widescreen cinematography were exemplified in *80,000 Suspects*, Guest's homage to one of the main influences on his film-making, Elia Kazan's *Panic in the Streets* (1951).

In 1960 Guest and his family moved to Peartree Cottage, a former royal hunting lodge and venue for the clandestine affair between George IV and Mrs Fitzherbert, in London's St John's Wood, and, as the 1960s began to swing Guest's cinema also became more decadent and flippant, eventually returning to its comedic roots via the shenanigans of the James Bond spoof *Casino Royale* (1967) and the salaciousness of *Confessions of a Window Cleaner* (1974). Thereafter he worked more in television than cinema, and made his last film, *The Boys in Blue*, a slipshod retread of his script for *Ask a Policeman* (1939), in 1983. After a few years in a mews house in Belgravia and a holiday home in Malta he moved in 1989 to Palm Springs, California, where he died of prostate cancer on 10 May 2006. In a career that stretched over six decades he had proved himself a uniquely versatile film craftsman. He was survived by his wife and son. STEVE CHIBNALL

Sources Y. Donlan, *Shake the stars down* (1976) · S. Swires, 'Interview with Val Guest', *Starlog*, 162 (Jan 1991); 163 (Feb 1991) · T. Weaver, M. Brunas, and S. Scrivani, 'Interview with Val Guest', *Scarlet Street*, 15 (1994) · A. Jezard, 'Reel life', *Hammer Horror*, 7 (1995) · W. Kinsey, 'Val Guest', *The House that Hammer Built*, 11 (1999) · V. Guest, *So you want to be in pictures?* (2001) · *The Times* (16 May 2006) · *Daily Telegraph* (16 May 2006) · *The Guardian* (16 May 2006) · *The Independent* (16 May 2006) · J. Fox, 'Versatile Val and the guest stars', *The Veteran*, 114 (2007) · www.imdb.com, 1 June 2009 · b. cert. · m. certs.
Archives FILM BFINA, documentary footage · BFINA, performance footage · BFINA, light entertainment footage · interviews, 2004, on DVDs of *Up the creek*, *Further up the creek*, *The Quatermass experiment*, *Quatermass II*, and *Expresso bongo* · *The making of Casino Royale* (2008) · interview, *Flesh and blood: the Hammer heritage of horror*, E. Newsom, director (1994) [video recording] | SOUND BL NSA, performance footage · BL NSA, documentary footage · commentaries on DVDs of *The Quatermass experiment*, *Quatermass II*, and *Expresso bongo* (2004), *The abominable snowman* (c.1997), *Hell is a city* (c.2000), *The day the earth caught fire* (c.2002)
Likenesses obituary photographs

Gutteridge, William Frank [Bill] (1919–2008), international relations scholar, was born on 21 September 1919 at 33 Sandy Lane, Beddington, Surrey, the son of Frank Leonard Gutteridge (1891/2–1956), assistant rate collector, and his wife, Norah Conwy, *née* Tighe (1891–1947). He had a younger sister, Elizabeth (*b*. 1923). Brought up in Mellows Road, in suburban south London, he was sent to Stamford School, Lincolnshire. He was called up for military service in 1939 and after attending the Royal Military College, Sandhurst, was commissioned in February 1940 into the Manchester regiment. As a general staff officer he worked under Sir Montagu Stopford and participated in the battle of Imphal-Kohima, the British counter-offensive to the Chindwin, the seizure of the bridgehead at Kalewa, and the drive on Mandalay. Throughout these taxing operations his calm industry earned high praise. Eschewing a military career he left the army in 1946 with the rank of major and a military MBE. In 1944 he had married Margaret McCallum Parker (*b*. *c*.1922), a state registered nurse; shrewd, sympathetic, and sensible, she remained a loyal source of strength and stability throughout his life. They had three daughters.

In 1946 Gutteridge matriculated at Hertford College, Oxford, graduating in 1948 with a second-class degree in modern history. The following year he accepted the offer of a senior lectureship in Commonwealth history and government at Sandhurst. In 1947 Sandhurst had transformed itself into the Royal Military Academy, offering a two-year course, strong on academic content. Gutteridge played a substantial part in creating an environment in which cadets (including African and other foreign cadets) could imbibe the Sandhurst ethos and grasp the complexities of the conditions under which they would serve in the post-war world.

From 1963 to 1971 Gutteridge served as head of the department of languages and modern studies at Lanchester Polytechnic, Coventry, and henceforth the midlands became his home. At Lanchester he joined several other Africanists, including Brian May and Catherine Hoskins. In 1960–61 he had received a Nuffield Foundation travelling fellowship that enabled him to study the role of armed forces in Africa. The resulting four books—*Armed Force in New States* (1962), *Military Institutions and Power in New States* (1965), *The Military in African Politics* (1969), and *Military Regimes in Africa* (1975)—established him as one of the world's foremost authorities on post-colonial Africa. Together they constituted a pioneering achievement, exhibiting arguments and approaches easily transferred to other parts of the world.

In 1971 Gutteridge joined the University of Aston, first as director of complementary studies, and then from 1976 as professor of international studies. African affairs always remained central to his world view. After 1990 his focus switched to southern Africa and the emerging social and political structures that would replace apartheid. His interest in the region was not new, for he had been a founding member of the Southern Africa Study Group established at the Royal Institute for International Affairs and he took a leading role in shaping its work for over twenty-five years. He published three studies on this theme, *South Africa from Apartheid to National Unity, 1981–1994* (1995), *South Africa's Defence and Security Force in the 21st Century* (1996), and (edited with J. E. Spence) *Violence in Southern Africa* (1997).

Gutteridge knew many African leaders personally and he would talk discreetly but charmingly of being entertained by the likes of Julius Nyerere. In such circles he exerted much informal influence. It was never stronger than in 1989–90 when he skilfully acted as an interlocutor between the African National Congress and the South African Defence Forces, successfully persuading the ANC that their former enemies should not be purged because they had much to teach the newcomers about the organization and training of formal armed forces.

Bill Gutteridge (though always William to his family) was a large and imposing man, well over six feet in height with a strong frame; he never lost his officer's bearing. This did not deter acquaintance because he dispensed affability and good cheer in an avuncular manner; his ruddy face was kindly, with omnipresent spectacles and a full head of hair. He had a dry, level-toned but pleasing voice, and was a brilliant teacher, always approachable, encouraging, and innovative—by no means stuck in traditional moulds. He was extraordinarily generous with his time in helping young people, and dealt with his colleagues, senior as well as junior, with sensitivity and perceptiveness. A devoted family man, he had few interests outside his work, except for cricket, but he was far from dull. He was a man of strong and liberal opinions, and occasionally his zeal would outrun his discretion. This happened less in the presence of Margaret, who, while seeming to attend to her embroidery, would good humouredly call him to order. He was a skilful and well-organized administrator and a shrewd academic politician. When he served in 1978–84 as chairman of the Council for National Academic Awards committee for arts and social sciences he brought a deep knowledge of the workings and aspirations of polytechnic institutions.

In the early 1980s Gutteridge became acutely aware of the deteriorating financial position of the social sciences at Aston University and in 1982 he accepted early retirement. It was typical of him that this indicated greater not lesser activity. He had worked as the secretary of the British Pugwash Group since 1965. By the 1980s he had become increasingly preoccupied with the renewed nuclear arms race; in 1983 he edited *The Dangers of New Weapons Systems*. He also became involved with an Anglo-Italian offshoot of Pugwash, the International School on Disarmament and Research on Conflicts. He brought an air of realism to the deliberations of such bodies without puncturing the overall enthusiastic and idealistic atmosphere. He never ceased to remind people that the root of the arms race must be located in 'political factors, national pride, suspicion and fears', not technology (D. Carlton and C. Schaerf, *Reassessing Arms Control*, 1984, 10). The other direction he pursued embraced terrorism. He was prescient in warning of the dangers represented within societies arising from the fanatical pursuit of special interests within states. From 1984 to 1994 he served as editorial director of the Research Institute for the Study of Conflict, and produced a monthly digest of the world's areas of turmoil. He continued writing until his eightieth year, and produced a monograph, *South Africa: Potential for Mbeki's Presidency*, in 1999. However, in the following decade his health deteriorated and he entered a nursing home in Kenilworth, dying on 22 May 2008 at University Hospital, Coventry, of an abdominal aortic aneurysm.

Gutteridge personified all that was best about his generation of British academics in his dedication and his thoughtful, disinterested pursuit of learning. He proved himself a creative and pioneering scholar, publicist, and man of affairs. His wide-ranging and widely read works were based on historical understanding and informed both by social science methodology and by his profound understanding of the policy-making process. He made a lasting contribution in particular to the study of the relationship of armed force and the problems of the international environment, notably in Africa.

BRIAN HOLDEN REID

Sources *The Times* (11 June 2008) · *The Independent* (29 Aug 2008) · *WW* (2008) · personal knowledge (2012) · private information (2012) [D. Carlton, J. E. Spence, J. M. O. Sharp] · b. cert. · d. cert.
Archives SOUND BL NSA, documentary recording
Likenesses obituary photographs
Wealth at death under £284,000: probate, 9 Oct 2008, *CGPLA Eng. & Wales*

Guyatt, Richard Gerald Talbot [Dick] (**1914–2007**), graphic designer, was born on 8 May 1914 in La Coruña, Galicia, Spain, the third son and last of the six children of Thomas Guyatt (1872–1924), British vice-consul at La Coruña and later consul at Vigo, and his wife, Cecil Katherine, *née* Chetwynd-Talbot (1878–1957). He spent his early childhood in Spain. His father died when Guyatt was nine, and he was dispatched to Charterhouse School in 1924, where his talent for drawing—inherited, he claimed, from his Spanish grandmother—was first recognized. He went on to serve as apprentice to Oliver Messel's theatre design studio, and in the evenings attended life-drawing classes at Westminster School of Art, taught by Bernard Meninsky. He was later to recall that 'Meninsky's love of drawing was truly infectious and through it he was able to impart something of the wonder he knew to be lying behind the drab façade of ordinary vision' (Guyatt, speech on receiving Sir Misha Black medal for distinguished services to design education, 2000, RCA archives). It was at one of these classes that he met Elizabeth Mary (Lizzie, or Min) Nicholls (1907–2005), former wife of John Francis Nicholls and daughter of Colonel Arthur Henry Nicholas Corsellis of the dragoon guards. She had a two-year-old daughter, Julie, whom Guyatt brought up as his own. There were no children of the marriage. Elizabeth had appeared, briefly, in the Apache dance sequence of the silent film *Piccadilly* (1929), and was a budding illustrator. They married on 24 February 1941 at Westminster register office. Both Richard and Elizabeth Guyatt had been deeply influenced by the teachings of the Russian philosopher and mystic P. D. Ouspensky on the part played by the emotions in human understanding and self-knowledge: the emotional drive generated by an idea needed practical skill as well as intellectual analysis to test its feasibility. Guyatt was introduced to Ouspensky's work in 1933 and they attended his meetings together until 1947.

Richard Guyatt (known to everyone as Dick) was described on the marriage certificate as a 'commercial artist'. He had begun his career as a freelance graphic designer in 1935, notably with lithographic lorry-bills for Shell Mex commissioned by Vernon Nye in the series Visit Britain's Landmarks and These People Use Shell. Two of these, *Ralph Allen's Sham Castle in Bath* (1936) and *Racing Motorists* (1939), which featured a cut-out tinted photograph of the designer himself, characteristically smoking a cigarette, became classics among historians of advertising and collectors. From the mid-1930s he also designed for BP, and taught part-time at Hackney School of Art.

During the Second World War, in 1940, Guyatt was recruited by the Ministry of Home Security to join the camouflage directorate, based in Leamington, where he became involved in the concealment of factories; he later specialized in naval camouflage for the Admiralty and became regional camouflage officer for Scotland. His strongest memories of this were of aerial reconnaissance, crouched in the hull of a Sunderland flying boat. The work was a sort of advertising in reverse. In the camouflage directorate he first met, as fellow 'camoufleurs', several of the post-war design professors of the Royal College of Art (RCA), including Hugh Casson, Robert Goodden, Edwin La Dell, David Pye, and the future principal and rector, Robin

Darwin, who became secretary to the camouflage committee in 1942.

In 1947 Darwin wrote an influential report for the Council of Industrial Design on the RCA and postgraduate design education—one of several official reports since the mid-1930s—complaining about the college's drift towards producing art teachers and career academics rather than preparing students for working lives in the specialized design professions just beginning to emerge. When Darwin became principal of the RCA as a result, he invited Guyatt in 1948 to become the youngest in the group of professors he was assembling in South Kensington to reform and restructure the institution. Guyatt had since 1946 been director and chief designer of Cockade Ltd, set for a full-time career in commercial art and exhibition design, but he abandoned this two years later to join the college. The new RCA mission involved subject specialization, the use of teachers who were also active practitioners, a new status for designers—no longer occupying 'a small back room', as Darwin put it (Frayling, 130–31)—a nourishment of design from fine art, and encouraging the students, within these boundaries, to find their own voices.

Guyatt's new specialist department was to be called 'design for publicity'. It was only after an irate article in *The Times* welcoming the reorganization but complaining about the vulgarity of the phrase 'publicity design'—mirroring discussions within the RCA—that a new title was sought. As Guyatt wrote in 1963, with typical deadpan humour, 'with a certain sense of relief, but not much conviction, the name "graphic design" was chosen. No-one was quite sure what it meant but it had a purposeful ring' (*Graphics RCA*). The phrase avoided the pejorative associations of 'commercial art' as well as the educational limitations of 'publicity design'. Guyatt has been widely credited with coining the phrase 'graphic design'. It was in fact coined in the United States at least as early as 1922 (by the designer William Addison Dwiggins), but Guyatt does seem to have been the first to use the phrase publicly in Britain, and the first to apply it to education. This helped to propel it into general usage.

Over the next few years the school of graphic arts expanded to consist of a complex set of interrelated specialisms: graphic design, typography, illustration, and printmaking (art-meets-design), joined in the mid-1950s by photography and in the late 1950s by film and television design, with research units devoted to the readability of print (especially dictionaries and telephone books), experimental cartography, natural history illustration, and graphic information. The student magazine *ARK*, based in the school, was launched in 1950 and the Lion and Unicorn Press published limited editions of finely printed books. The purpose of all these elements, said Guyatt, was to create the richest possible educational environment for graduate graphic designers, and to launch them into their professional worlds.

As part of the Festival of Britain on London's South Bank in 1951, at Robin Darwin and Hugh Casson's invitation, Guyatt designed—with his RCA colleagues Robert Goodden (a trained architect, and professor of silversmithing and jewellery) and Dick Russell (a furniture designer, who headed the wood, metal, and plastics department, which was to become 'industrial design')—the Lion and Unicorn Pavilion, celebrating in a 'contemporary' way as twin aspects of Britishness the solidity and strength of the lion and the imagination and eccentricity of the unicorn. After the festival closed there was a short-lived plan to move the pavilion to a site in South Kensington, as a permanent annex to the RCA, but it came to nothing. Guyatt's inaugural lecture, 'Head, heart, and hand', published in the same year as the festival—a characteristic mixture of Ouspensky's philosophy, John Ruskin's ideas on art education, and Robin Darwin's pragmatism—argued that while reflection and craftsmanship were central to the experience of art and education, teachers should never forget the promptings of the human heart.

An exhibition, and catalogue, of 1963 called 'Graphics RCA', which toured Europe, took stock of fifteen years' work by the graduates of the school in the Guyatt years. It reads like a *Who's Who* of the best in early 1960s British graphic design: posters by David Gentleman, Michael Foreman, and Brian Tattersfield; book covers and advertisements by Alan Fletcher; a cookery strip by Len Deighton; the set of BBC television's *Quatermass and the Pit* by Cliff Hatts; and a still from Ridley Scott's recently completed student film, *Boy on a Bicycle*, starring his younger brother, Tony. As Robin Darwin wrote in his foreword to the catalogue, the school of graphic arts had by then become a focus and a communication hub for the entire college—with its magazine, posters, prints, photographs, printing press, its philosophy of art-meets-design like the RCA in microcosm—and its creative atmosphere was directly attributable to 'Professor Guyatt's own ruminative imagination', and his fastidious attention to detail (*Graphics RCA*). Just down the corridor in the Exhibition Road painting studios next to the graphics studios, the British pop art generation had just graduated. Guyatt had been a visiting professor at Yale University in 1955 and 1962—on exchange with Alvin Eisenman—and often liked to visit New Haven in vacations, much impressed by the latter-day Bauhaus principles of graphic communication. A treasured possession was a series of abstract geometric prints given to him by Josef Albers.

In parallel with his professorship and teaching—in a double life that was very important to him—Guyatt was consultant designer for Josiah Wedgwood & Sons (1952–5 and 1967–70); the Central Electricity Generating Board (1964–8); the British Sugar Bureau (1965–8); and W. H. Smith (1970–87), producing letterheads, logos, packaging, print advertising, or assorted graphics for all of them. He designed for the Royal Mint a silver medal (1972) and a commemorative crown piece for the eightieth birthday of the queen mother (1980, featuring bows and lions, a witty reference to her maiden name of Bowes-Lyon). For the Post Office and Royal Mail he designed the postal order forms (1964), the 700th anniversary of parliament stamp (1965, the largest stamp ever issued by the Post Office up to that time), and the silver jubilee stamps (1977), and he served on the stamp design advisory committee (1963–74). He also served on the Bank of England design advisory committee (1968–75). From 1968 to 1981 he was chairman of Guyatt-Jenkins Design Group, a small design consultancy in partnership with Nicholas Jenkins, his former colleague as senior tutor (from 1965 to 1975). His best-known designs were the elegant, dignified, and charming commemorative mugs and plates he created for Wedgwood—for the coronation (1953), the prince of Wales's investiture (1969), the royal silver wedding anniversary (1972), the marriage of Prince Charles and Lady Diana Spencer (1981), the millennium (2000), the golden jubilee (2002), and the fiftieth anniversary of the coronation (2003). Usually these featured delicate, flowing ribbons, and a beauty and clarity of line—an unfussy tribute by a designer to the establishment and its rituals. His last mug was produced in 2005, for the bicentenary of the battle of Trafalgar. At the RCA he designed a Phoenix dinner service—with the college's post-war symbol of regeneration prominently displayed—for Robin Darwin's beloved senior common room.

Guyatt was described as 'one of the last remaining examples of a genuine Edwardian gentleman, to whom the qualities of duty, fidelity, truthfulness and manners were paramount' (*The Independent*, 29 Oct 2007). He enjoyed driving large cars—always calling them 'she'—very fast along the M4 motorway, from his flat in Onslow Square, South Kensington, to his large cottage with studio and romantic garden in Ham, Wiltshire. He always wore to work the same lovingly patched blue denim jacket—doubling up as an artist's smock—which he had designed himself.

In 1969 Guyatt was appointed CBE. He was pro-rector of the RCA, to Lionel Esher's rector, from 1974 to 1978, then rector from 1978 to 1981. He launched his rectorship by saying that he might appear an old broom, but his bristles were in excellent condition. It was an unsettled time, though, involving angry arguments with the painting staff (he wanted to bring back drawing classes), confrontation with the incoming Conservative government over the college's role in industrial regeneration, and a divided college council. Some of his disappointment was captured in Peter Blake's perceptive portrait of him, made in 1981. By the time he retired, he had worked at the RCA for thirty-three years. He had been at the centre of a revolution in British art education—and in attitudes towards design—and, as Hugh Casson put it in July 1981 in a speech on his retirement, in his professional life, his teaching, and his professorship, he had shown 'the qualities of the true professional—the ruthless determination to achieve by rational methods aims that have been conceived in passion' (retirement brochure, RCA archives).

By the time of Elizabeth Guyatt's death in 2005, at the age of ninety-seven, she had been suffering from dementia for several years. Dick Guyatt looked after her at home with patience and love, and died on 17 October 2007 at home, at Forge Cottage, Ham, of congestive cardiac failure and chronic pulmonary obstructive disease. On his bed was his family's frayed donkey blanket from Spain and on the wall of his bedroom was Josef Albers's series of abstract geometric designs. CHRISTOPHER FRAYLING

Sources R. Darwin, ed., *The anatomy of design* (1951) • R. Guyatt, ed., *Graphics RCA* (1963) • *Queen* [Royal College of Art special issue, ed. R. Guyatt] (21 June 1967) • R. Guyatt, *Two lectures* (1977) • T. Sheppard and J. Hoole, eds., *That's Shell that is!* (1983) • C. Frayling, *The Royal College of Art: one hundred and fifty years of art and design* (1987) • H. Goodden, *Camouflage and art* (2007) • *The Guardian* (27 Oct 2007) • *The Independent* (29 Oct 2007) • *The Times* (5 Dec 2007) • *WW* (2007) • personal knowledge (2011) • private information (2011) • m. cert. • d. cert.

Archives Royal College of Art, London

Likenesses P. Blake, mixed media on board, 1981, Royal College of Art, London

Wealth at death £826,573: probate, 12 June 2008, *CGPLA Eng. & Wales*

Hall, Clifford Samuel [Cliff] (**1925–2008**), singer and guitarist, was born of Jamaican parents in Oriente Province, Cuba, on 11 September 1925. His father, Arthur Bertram Hall, was a plantation worker. As a child he studied at both Spanish and English schools, but following the death of his mother, and his father's subsequent remarriage (together with the outbreak of the Second World War), he relocated with his father to Jamaica. Arthur Hall could not afford further education for his son, so Cliff, at the age of fourteen, became an agricultural worker.

During the Second World War the RAF recruited many West Indian servicemen and, after lying about his age, Hall joined the RAF and came to Britain for basic training as a mechanic in November 1942. He was based in Hartlebury in Worcestershire for most of the war, but his job involved travelling across Britain delivering and installing aircraft parts. Prior to demobilization he studied for an electrical engineering qualification in Leeds. There he met a Scottish factory worker, Janet Greer Massie (1922–1985), and they were married on 10 November 1947 at Leeds register office. They had a daughter, Lynn (1949–2007), and two sons, Clifford junior (*b.* 1951) and Robert (*b.* 1962).

Hall later recalled that he

> always enjoyed listening to the sound of guitar music; I liked to listen to country and western music on the American Forces Network radio station, so I bought a cheap guitar in Leeds and learned to strum along to the radio and the odd record Janet and I had, just to amuse myself. (personal knowledge)

In 1953 he was working as an electrician in Leeds when he was subcontracted to the atomic site at Capenhurst, outside Chester. There he met Tony Davis, who invited him to hear his jazz group in Liverpool; Hall was soon playing along on bongos. These jazz jam sessions led to the formation in September 1958 of the Spinners folk group: Cliff Hall, Tony Davis, Mick Groves, Hughie Jones, and Jacqui McDonald were the original members. Jones was the only Liverpudlian in the group, but the group was often referred to as 'the Liverpool Spinners', in part to distinguish them from the American Motown group of the same name. From their beginnings in the basement of Samson and Barlow's restaurant in London Road, Liverpool, the Spinners came to specialize in folk, maritime, and 'folk revival' material, although Hall, like Tony Davis, always had a penchant for a wider variety of music genres, and he added many Caribbean songs to the Spinners' repertoire. They were, therefore, an eclectic combination, which did not always go down well in certain 'purist' folk circles. However, by the late 1950s and early 1960s their cheerful and entertaining performances had built the group a steady following in Liverpool, and they opened one of Liverpool's first folk clubs, which soon found a home at Gregson's Well public house in Low Hill. Hall was by this time an accomplished guitarist, and also added occasional harmonica to the Spinners' sound.

When Jacqui McDonald left the Spinners in 1962 she was not replaced, and the musical balance within the group changed. In contrast to the more raucous sea songs sung by the whole group McDonald had sung the quieter songs, so Hall, with his gentle baritone, took on the key role of providing contrast and grain. His quiet, textured voice gave the Spinners a different, more commercial, sound with 'a unique and captivating flavour' (Stuckey, foreword). However, while his voice changed the Spinners' sound, his very membership raised their profile, for the group was undoubtedly the first multiracial singing group to enjoy major success in the UK. While by the 1960s the folk revival was regarded by its protagonists as creating a kind of musical space for everyman, it largely consisted of white music played in white environments. Indeed, it was very unusual in the early 1960s for a folk group to include a black member. This fact brought some racist comments during the Spinners' early days, for jibes concerning their so-called 'lack of authenticity' were usually directed at the Caribbean material. (Similarly, black Liverpudlian attitudes to the group could also be mixed, some regarding Hall as a rather less than authentic representation of Liverpool's black community.) Racism also reared its head by the time the group had commenced recording in 1962: when the Spinners came to release their first album, *Quayside Songs Old and New*, that year, EMI (who owned the HMV label) was uncomfortable about promoting a multiracial group. Instead of a photograph of the group, a cartoon adorned the LP cover, and all the members appeared to be white. However, the group's second album, *The Spinners* (1963), issued by Fontana, sported a photograph of the four musicians round a spinning wheel.

Regular weekends in London spent consulting the archives in the English Folk Dance and Song Society's Vaughan Williams Library together with singing at The Troubadour and other folk clubs in the capital expanded the Spinners' repertoire and live reputation. But invitations to sing at folk events around the country placed strain on their day jobs. The Spinners turned fully professional in 1963. Encouraged by Michael Flanders and Donald Swann, they hired St George's Hall in Liverpool and quickly sold out a concert. The following year they booked the city's Philharmonic Hall: recordings of the concert were released on two subsequent LPs, *Folk at the Phil!* (1964) and *More Folk at the Phil!* (1965). Turning professional meant that they looked to concert halls rather than folk clubs for their gigs. This further alienated the purists, but also meant that they achieved a reputation far beyond the rather closeted folk circles, especially after they embraced the ever expanding medium of television. They had already appeared in episodes of the Associated-Rediffusion series *Looking About* in 1961 and ABC's *Hullabaloo!* in 1963. Several further guest appearances were followed by seven series of *The Spinners* for the BBC, broadcast between 1970 and 1981, and by regular Christmas broadcasts until 1985. They also sang the theme to the film *Funeral in Berlin* (1967), starring Michael Caine. Meanwhile, they continued to produce new LPs on a regular basis, one of them entitled *Not Quite Folk* (1969).

In 1965 fellow Fontana artists Wayne Fontana and the Mindbenders 'borrowed' Cliff Hall to add his deep voice to the word 'love' in the recording of 'Game of Love', which reached number one in the American singles chart and number two in the UK. This was the nearest any Spinner came to singles success of their own. Like many of their folk-based contemporaries, the Spinners did not to any great extent flirt with singles releases; however, the group became synonymous with contemporary songs such as 'Dirty Old Town' (by Ewan MacColl), 'In My Liverpool Home' (by Pete McGovern), 'Black and White' (by Earl Robinson), and 'The Family of Man' (by Karl Dallas). 'Black and White' was thought to be a nod towards Hall's race. The Liverpool historian Ray Costello later commented:

> Some felt that this song was overly sentimental, as it played upon black and white children sharing a blissfully idyllic school-life, but such was the appeal of this well-loved group and their genial style, that they managed to carry it off with some success. (Costello, 76)

Indeed, Hall's very presence in a 'white folk group' helped to shape the discourse surrounding not only the Liverpool black community (of which he was not ostensibly a member), but also music, race, representation through genre, and black realization.

Like his fellow Spinners, Hall was awarded the gold badge of the English Folk Dance and Song Society. The group supported many charities and humanitarian causes, and raised money for Mother Teresa through War on Want, as well as for Queen's Park School, Lincoln, a school for young people with learning difficulties where Hall was on the board of governors. The group disbanded in 1988, although there were several reunions, including when the group led the community singing at the all-Merseyside FA cup final in 1989. Following a knee operation Hall convalesced in Australia, where he met a Spinners' fan, Dorothy, who was a nurse from Birkenhead. By this time he had been widowed twice; he stayed in Australia and they were soon married. He died in Adelaide on 26 June 2008 and was survived by Dorothy, as well as by the two sons of his first marriage. MICHAEL BROCKEN

Sources D. Stuckey, *The Spinners: fried bread and brandy-o!* (1985) · R. Costello, *Liverpool black pioneers* (2007) · *Daily Echo* [Liverpool] (26 June 2008); (8 July 2008) · *Daily Post* [Liverpool] (27 June 2008) · *The Independent* (27 June 2008) · *The Guardian* (30 June 2008); (2 Aug 2008) · *The Times* (1 July 2008); (4 July 2008) · personal knowledge (2012) · private information (2012) · m. cert. [1947]

Likenesses D. Redfern, group portraits, photographs, 1960–70, Getty Images, London · B. Shuel, group portraits, photographs,

1962–8, Getty Images, London · J. Morris, photographs, 1970, Rex Features, London · group portraits, photographs, 1970, Getty Images, London · obituary photographs · photographs, repro. in Stuckey, *Spinners*

Hall, Mary [*name in religion* Mother Rosario] (**1928–2008**), nun and educationist, was born on 30 November 1928 at 106 North Circular Road, Dublin, the elder child of Michael Hall, a clerk and administrator, and his wife, Nora, *née* Deegan, who had been a buyer for Arnotts department store in Dublin before her marriage. At the time of her birth registration her parents lived at 19 Sword Street, Dublin. Her younger brother, John, was an officer in the Irish army and member of the United Nations peacekeeping forces. Her mother, Nora, had a profound influence on her, as she had had a successful career and passed on her love of fashion.

After primary education at St Mary's parish school in Dublin, Mary Hall won a scholarship to the Jesus and Mary Secondary School, Gortnor Abbey, Crossmolina, co. Mayo, where a love of music and drama led to her qualifying as an associate of the Irish Academy of Music. The school, run by the religious Congregation of Jesus and Mary, was her inspiration at the age of eighteen to enter the order with a vocation to teach, taking the name Mother Rosario. Before taking up teaching in Lahore in Pakistan, she studied at University College, Galway, and then took a master's degree in education at the Institute of Education and Research in Lahore. She went on to become headmistress of the senior Cambridge high school in Lahore, lecturer in educational psychology at the Lahore Teacher Training College, and education adviser to the Lahore Board of Education. Her many pupils included Benazir Bhutto, the future prime minister of Pakistan. Through a contact at the British Council she formed a lifelong friendship with Tom McCready, a civil engineer and vice-president international of the engineering company Gilbert Commonwealth Associates, who played a central role in building schools and convents, though a grand master of the masonic order. It was under his protection that at one point in the India–Pakistan conflict she escaped across the mountains to the north.

Mary Hall's second career began when she was encouraged by her order to study for a doctorate in mission at Selly Oak Colleges in Birmingham. She supported herself by bilingual teaching in inner-city primary schools in Birmingham and by lecturing in ecclesiology and religious education at St Mary's Seminary, Oscott, and in the department of mission and social studies at Selly Oak Colleges. When she was invited in 1978 by Bishop Gerald Mahon, at the instigation of Cardinal Pignedoli of the secretariat for non-Christians in the Vatican (subsequently renamed the Pontifical Council for Inter-Religious Dialogue), to undertake research to build relationships between Roman Catholic and ethnic communities in Britain, she was executive officer of the Birmingham International Council for Overseas Student Affairs and had many contacts within the ethnic minority communities in Birmingham. She initiated a project that brought together over three years a group of 156 people from fourteen communities within Birmingham and developed a unique methodology of dialogue, culminating in the establishment of the first multi-faith centre in the UK, of which she was the director.

Hall's key principle in dialogue was to place the interlocutors firmly in their own faith identity and make them clear about their own relationship with their faith community before entering dialogue with others. The next stage was to learn about the beliefs and practices of other faiths from articulate practitioners rather than theologians. She worked on this with the Grubb Institute of Behavioural Studies, based in north London. The model that evolved took its ground of dialogue as the shared local community, in this case the city of Birmingham. The project grew into an established centre, first the Multi Faith Resource: a Foundation for Education and Citizenship, and then the Multi Faith Centre: a Partnership for Education and Citizenship, with certificated courses in the various religions. The centre sponsored dialogical encounters in other countries, including Australia, Belgium, Canada, Denmark, Germany, the Netherlands, Sweden, and the USA. It was the people, Christians, Hindus, Muslims, Sikhs, Buddhists, and Jews, who constituted the 'resource'. When by 1991 the Multi Faith Centre had its headquarters in Harborne Hall in Birmingham, its conferences had drawn in such distinguished visitors as Cardinal Arinze, then president of the Pontifical Council for Inter-Religious Dialogue, Cardinal Hume of Westminster, and Douglas Hurd, the home secretary. Visiting lecturers included John Hick, Donald Nicholl, Rewata Dhamma, Norman Solomon, Khalid Alawi, and Gopal Singh Puri. Within ten years 500 students had taken the certificate courses. The Multi Faith Centre produced two publications: a journal containing thoughtful papers and poems, *Encounter with the Birmingham Multi-faith Resource Unit*, and a newsletter, *Mosaic*.

Hall was in the forefront of the Catholic church's teaching initiated by the declaration *Nostra aetate* of the Second Vatican Council. This set in train an approach to mission that was very open to other faiths, and was slow to be understood and put into practice within the church. Hall was encouraged and inspired by the life and spirituality of Helder Camara in Brazil and conducted a series of interviews with him (in French) in Recife, published under the title *The Impossible Dream: the Spirituality of Dom Helder Camara* (1979). Her other publications included *Strangers in Birmingham: a Study of Overseas Students* (1978), and *A Quest for the Liberated Christian* (1980).

Hall held the first Roman Catholic lectureship at Selly Oak Colleges, and was a recognized lecturer in the department of theology of the University of Birmingham. She retained her international contacts by serving as a member of the executive board of Pro Mundi Vita, an international documentation and research centre in Brussels. She was named UK Catholic woman of the year in 1983, made a fellow of the World Academy of Art and Science in 1987, and received the Templeton award for progress in religion in 1988.

Hall had a powerful personality, a true *mulier fortis*, with vision and intelligence, and a balanced perspective on life founded on a good sense of humour. She continued to have a great love of music and theatre and when she ceased to wear the religious habit so as to facilitate her civic contacts, the dress sense she inherited from her mother always made her appearance both elegant and striking. She developed Alzheimer's disease and her final years of helplessness proved the affection and devotion she had inspired in others. She died on 5 September 2008, and her funeral was held at St Paul's Convent, Selly Park, on 10 September 2008. The Multi Faith Centre did not survive her. WILLIAM I. OZANNE

Sources M. Hall, 'The Multi Faith Centre at Harborne Hall', *Harborne Society News*, 21 (summer 1991), 6–7 · *Mosaic* ['Tenth anniversary issue: a decade of dialogue'] (spring 1992) · *Birmingham Post* (11 Sept 2008) · *The Times* (26 Sept 2008) · *The Tablet* (27 Sept 2008) · *Newsletter of the Birmingham Council of Faiths* (Sept 2008) · Birmingham archdiocesan archives · personal knowledge (2012) · private information (2012) [Karen Hall, niece] · b. cert.
Likenesses photographs, repro. in *Mosaic* [various issues]

Hall, Terence [Terry] (**1926–2007**), ventriloquist and children's author, was born on 20 November 1926 at 635 Middleton Road, Chadderton, Oldham, Lancashire, the son of James Emanuel Hall, a dyer's labourer, and later publican, and his wife, Catherine, *née* Ward. He was educated at St Patrick's School, Oldham, and De la Salle College, Salford.

As a boy of eight Terry Hall became fascinated with Hollywood prison dramas in which inmates communicated plans for a breakout without moving their lips. Imitating these scenes, he discovered a natural gift for ventriloquism. On his fourteenth birthday his parents bought him a second-hand dummy for 50s., and within twelve months he and 'Bert Williams' were touring in the *Carroll Levis' Discoveries* show with other amateur talents—including a young singer named Kathleen Mary (Kath) Whitehouse (1927–1978), daughter of Charles Whitehouse, steelworker, of Oldham, whom he married five years later, on 2 January 1947.

For years Hall was on the road, living out of a caravan with his young wife and their daughter Beverley. (A second daughter, Melanie, followed.) He was using a conventional doll named Mickey Flynn when the act was booked for the London Palladium to support Gracie Fields in 1953. While appearing at the north pier, Blackpool, the following year Hall visited the town's zoo and was inspired by the almost human reactions of a lion there to devise a new—animal—character. A local properties man, Fred Drummond, made Lenny the Lion out of papier mâché and fur, with a golf ball nose and white-painted muzzle, for £150. Hall later insured Lenny for £10,000. On the same bill that summer was the vocalist Anne Shelton, who advised Hall to lose the puppet's realistic teeth, which only frightened the children, and soften the growling voice. The de-fanged, effeminately lisping Lenny was an unqualified success.

Hall's national television début was in March 1956 in *Dress Rehearsal*, Eric Sykes's 'deconstruction' of preparations for a BBC spectacular. 'Lenny the Lion with Terry Hall' (there was no doubt who was the main attraction)

Terence Hall (1926–2007), by unknown photographer, 1960s

was an instant hit and rapidly became popular in the BBC's children's television schedules, featuring on *Hopscotch* and *Crackerjack*. From June 1956 Lenny was the front-page star of the children's magazine *TV Comic* in a full-colour strip. Originally depicted *au naturel*, with a proper complement of arms and legs (and his 'minder' nowhere to be seen), Lenny joined in the fun and games with human playmates. Next the BBC gave Hall and his companion a ten-minute television slot all to themselves, and before Christmas they also enjoyed a number of cabaret dates at the Eve nightclub on Regent Street. For the 1956–7 pantomime season, the midland-based producer Derek Salberg put them into *Babes in the Wood* at the Alexandra Theatre, Birmingham, along with eccentric dancer Jack Stanford and the 'harmonica rascals' the Three Monarchs. Salberg's casting observed a long tradition of infiltrating variety turns into pantomime storylines, and was the first of many such bookings for Hall.

The duo returned to BBC television in 1957 for a series of 45-minute programmes entitled *The Lenny the Lion Show* that continued until 1959. By that time everyone was repeating Lenny's coy, self-mocking, catchphrase 'Oh, don't embawwas me', delivered with a limp-wristed gesture from one large paw (concealing Hall's right arm: Lenny was more glove puppet than fully articulated ventriloquist's doll) accompanied by a fluttering of the eyelashes. Over the next decade spin-off merchandizing included brightly illustrated annuals, story books, jigsaw puzzles, card games, and the toy manufacturer Chad Valley's authorized hand-puppet.

In 1957 *Val Parnell's Saturday Spectacular* introduced commercial television viewers to a new character. Jeremy the

Giraffe (sporting an Eton collar and striped tie around his long neck) was a bashful, dopey creature, sounding like Walt Disney's Goofy. Hall, with trademark fixed grin and clenched teeth, delivered a fluent rendition of 'Old MacDonald Had a Farm' as Jeremy interpolated the animal noises. Hall consolidated his celebrity with an appearance on the *Ed Sullivan Show* in America, and then returned for another BBC television series, *Lenny's Den*, a regular ten-minute Sunday teatime slot that started in 1959. That same year Lenny and Terry released a 45 rpm 7 inch disc for the Christmas market on which they sang 'I Wish I Could Be Father Christmas': the B side was their cover version of an American novelty hit from 1953, 'I Want a Hippopotamus for Christmas'.

When the Royal Navy's cruiser *HMS Lion* was commissioned in 1960 Hall offered the Admiralty his puppet's services as ship's mascot, and it was agreed that a flag would be made bearing Lenny's image, to be raised on suitable occasions. The first of these was a children's party for *HMS Lion*'s favoured charity, the Dorton House School for the Blind, Sevenoaks, Kent, and Lenny's antics had everyone on board enthralled.

The next BBC television series, *Pops and Lenny*, ran for two years from 1962. In May 1963 the Beatles topped the bill with a medley of their recent hits. One of the production team, Hayward Stenton Jones (whose teenage son, later known as David Bowie, adored Lenny), started up an official Lenny the Lion fan club. There was another single release, 'Lenny's Bath Time' / 'Lenny Has a Cold', and the pair ended the year travelling to Scotland for the Glasgow Alhambra's traditional Christmas show, *A Love for Jamie*.

In 1965 Lenny fronted a number of television commercials for Trebor Mints, with the punch-line 'a minty bit stronger', while Hall capitalized on 'James Bond mania', devising a board game for Waddington, Spy Ring, in which players diced to obtain top-secret information from enemy agents. The duo continued to appear in variety theatres from Dover to Harrogate, and in ABC Television series like *Big Night Out* and *The Blackpool Show*. During the 1970s they visited ATV's regional studios in Birmingham more than once to dodge the custard flans on Chris Tarrant's *Tiswas*, the anarchic Saturday morning riot of cartoons, competitions, and slapstick.

In 1977 Terry Hall reinvented himself. *Reading with Lenny* was made by Granada Television for ITV Schools to teach children between four and six years of age the basics of the English language. Stories were written around a kitten named Kevin (a cool young cat in T-shirt and jeans) and through his everyday mishaps infant viewers were introduced to the small learning experiences of life. For twenty-eight episodes, broadcast between 1977 and 1980, a leonine paw would run along the bold-printed words in a large picture book, while Hall carefully enunciated the text and Lenny repeated key words for emphasis. Hall also wrote the scripts, and *Kevin the Kitten* books to accompany the series were published from 1978.

On 15 November 1980, now a widower and living in Solihull, Hall married Denise Eileen Parsons (*b.* 1944), a dance teacher, daughter of Joseph Charles Francis, schoolteacher, and former wife of Geoffrey Parsons. Hall became stepfather to her children Tracey and Nigel, and moved to Earlsdon, a suburb of Coventry. During his last years he experienced the onset of Alzheimer's disease and became a resident at the Wolston Grange private care home in Wolston, near Rugby, where he died of heart failure on 4 April 2007. In 2009 his widow unveiled a blue plaque at the corner of Middleton Road, Chadderton, near to the site of his childhood home. The plaque is perhaps unique: below the main text is a cameo portrait of Lenny the Lion's smiling face. CY YOUNG

Sources *Radio Times* (1956–9); (1962–3) · *TV Mirror and Disc News* (1956–8) · *What's On* (1956) · *TV Times* (1957); (1964); (1966); (1975–80) · *Television Mail* (1965) · D. Salberg, *Once upon a pantomime* (1981) · *Coventry Telegraph* (11 April 2007) · *Daily Telegraph* (12 April 2007) · *The Independent* (12 April 2007) · *The Times* (14 April 2007) · *The Guardian* (30 May 2007); (4 June 2007) · *Oldham Evening Chronicle* (14 Sept 2009) · 'HMS Lion, first commission, 1960–1962', *c.*1962, www.axfordsabode.org.uk/pdf-docs/lion04.pdf, 7 June 2010 · private information (2011) · b. cert. · m. certs. · d. cert.
Archives FILM BFINA, performance footage
Likenesses photographs, 1958–65, Getty Images, London, Hult. Arch. · photograph, 1960–65, priv. coll. [*see illus.*] · photographs, 1960–91, Rex Features, London · obituary photographs · photograph, repro. in news.bbc.co.uk/1/hi/england/coventry_warwickshire/6544083.stm · photographs, repro. in *Radio Times*
Wealth at death under £32,000: probate, 17 Oct 2007, *CGPLA Eng. & Wales*

Hall, Willis Edward (1929–2005), playwright, was born on 6 April 1929 at 20 Addington Street, Hunslet, Leeds, the only son and elder child of Walter Hall, an engineer's fitter, and his wife, Gladys, *née* Gibbon. Raised in the back-to-back terraces of Hunslet—when his first West End director, the aesthetic Lindsay Anderson, paid a visit to his old home in the interests of research he found himself 'stranded in a world I had no relationship with' (Anderson, 68)—he was educated at local council schools then Cockburn High School. He thereafter drifted through a variety of dead-end jobs—as factory worker, trawler hand, and amusement park attendant, most of which were to serve him well when he turned to writing for television—until, anticipating national service, he volunteered for the regular army. In due course he found himself serving as a signals corporal in Malaya. Having dabbled with writing for radio at home, he now passed the time by composing plays for Chinese children on Radio Malaya—a useful writer's discipline in that he was confined to an English vocabulary of about fifty words.

On leaving the army, Hall settled in Nottingham, where he established himself as a scriptwriter for the BBC, and on 16 September 1954 married Kathleen May (Kay) Cortens, who ran the secretarial agency that typed up his early scripts. A 32-year-old divorcee, she was the daughter of William Edis, civil servant. Establishing himself at once in the pattern he was to continue all through his working life, Hall rented an office in a commercial block and from there worked a nine-to-five day. He began by writing radio plays, but soon moved on to television. The mid-1950s was the beginning of the golden age of the single television play, and Hall, with his command of what he called 'doorstep English' and his intuitive knowledge not only of how ordinary people talked but what they thought, was a natural.

In 1958 the television director Peter Dews invited Hall to write a stage play for eight Oxford undergraduates in a production he was taking to the Edinburgh Festival. The only proviso was that there could be but one entrance and exit, owing to the limitations of the hall. It was just the kind of theatrical problem that appealed to Hall. He gave Dews a play called *The Disciplines of War*, which accommodated the restrictions imposed upon it by being claustrophobically set in the Malayan jungle, where half a dozen squaddies, plus a Japanese prisoner, await the inevitable onslaught by the enemy. The play was enthusiastically received in Edinburgh and transferred first to the Royal Court Theatre and then the New Theatre under a title, *The Long and the Short and the Tall*, provided by its London director, Lindsay Anderson. Described by the *Guardian* critic Philip Hope-Wallace as 'a *Journey's End* of the Malayan war' (*The Guardian*, 9 Jan 1959), it was an instant success, propelling its leading light Peter O'Toole into stardom and its industrious young writer (who by now had some forty radio and television plays to his credit) to the ranks of the so-called 'new wave' of writers or 'angry young men,' as they were dubbed.

At about this time Keith Waterhouse, an old youth club friend of Hall's from their Leeds days, was achieving some success with a new novel, *Billy Liar* (1959). Hall called him out of the blue and observed, 'There's a play in this just screaming to get out.' Thus began a fruitful collaboration that lasted over thirty years. Starring Albert Finney and later Tom Courtenay, *Billy Liar* (1960) played for 582 performances before being taken out on a series of national tours. It was filmed by John Schlesinger (1963), with Courtenay in the leading role and Waterhall Productions Ltd, as the pair now styled themselves, providing the screenplay. It became a long-running Drury Lane musical, *Billy* (1974), starring Michael Crawford, and a television situation comedy both in Britain (1973–4) and, as *Billy*, in the United States (1979).

With offers pouring in for Waterhall, the team, working from an office in New Bond Street, turned out a series of north-country plays of varying success, as well as situation comedies, sketches, and screenplays (starting with *Whistle Down the Wind*, 1961, and *A Kind of Loving*, 1962). They were regular contributors to Ned Sherrin's groundbreaking television satire show *That Was the Week That Was* and its successors. Wishing by now to get rid of their cloth-cap image, they wrote a middle-class comedy, *Say Who You Are* (1965). Starring Ian Carmichael and Patrick Cargill, it filled Her Majesty's Theatre for fifteen months, before transferring to the Vaudeville and then proceeding on an extended post-West End tour. Meanwhile Waterhall, among other enterprises, had two long-running television series in the pipeline—*Budgie* (1971–2), starring Adam Faith, and *Worzel Gummidge* (1979–81), with Jon Pertwee.

Hall's first marriage ended in divorce, and he was married three more times: on 24 January 1962 to the actress (Nora Noel) Jill *Bennett (1929?–1990), daughter of (James) Randle Bennett, company director; in 1966 to Dorothy Kingsmill-Lunn; and on 2 November 1973 to Valerie Shute, a 28-year-old dancer and actress, and daughter of Alfred Shute, advertising director. His second and third marriages ended in divorce, but his fourth lasted until his death. In all he had four sons.

After three non-stop decades the Waterhall machine was beginning to slow down, and Hall and Waterhouse agreed to pursue separate projects, though they remained close friends. Hall, with his wife Valerie, settled in the West Riding of Yorkshire and devoted himself to writing children's books—he wrote about twenty, between *The Royal Astrologer* (1960) and *Vampire Island* (1999)—the occasional stage musical adaptation, and his hobby of magic. He was a member of the Magic Circle and the International Brotherhood of Magicians, as well as the magicians' societies of the United States and Malta. He died at his home in Ghyll Mews, Ilkley, on 7 March 2005, of cancer of the oesophagus, leaving his wife Valerie and four sons. A celebration of his life and work was held at St Paul's, Covent Garden, on 6 November 2005.

KEITH WATERHOUSE

Sources J. Dexter, *The honourable beast* (1993) • O. Lewenstein, *Kicking against the pricks: a theatre producer looks back* (1994) • K. Waterhouse, *Streets ahead* (1995) • L. Anderson, *The diaries*, ed. P. Sutton (2004) • *The Guardian* (12 March 2005) • *The Independent* (12 March 2005) • *The Times* (14 March 2005) • *Daily Telegraph* (14 March 2005) • *WW* (2005) • personal knowledge (2009) • private information (2009) • b. cert. • m. certs. [1954, 1962, 1973] • d. cert.

Archives FILM BFINA, light entertainment footage | SOUND BL NSA, documentary recordings • BL NSA, performance recording

Likenesses L. Morley, double portrait, bromide print, 1960 (with Keith Waterhouse), NPG • obituary photographs

Wealth at death £350,668: probate, 11 Aug 2005, *CGPLA Eng. & Wales*

Halliwell, David Wiliam (1936–2006), playwright and theatre director, was born on 31 July 1936 at Lynn Lea Maternity Home, Clifton, Yorkshire, the elder son of Herbert Halliwell, company secretary, and his wife, Ethel, *née* Spencer. At the time of his birth his parents lived at 24 Upper Green Lane, Brighouse, Yorkshire. As a child he had ambitions to become a comic actor, and his hero was Charlie Chaplin. Educated at Victoria secondary modern school, Rastrick, and Hipperholme grammar school, he attended Huddersfield College of Art (1953–9), from which he was expelled and then allowed to return. The incident inspired him to write his most famous play, *Little Malcolm and His Struggle against the Eunuchs*, in which the protagonist, Malcolm Scrawdyke, is expelled from a technical college before starting the Dynamic Erection Party, whose main purposes are power and revenge against the college's principal. The anti-hero Malcolm is an instantly recognizable human figure, a mixture of frustrated ambition and absurd self-delusion.

Halliwell studied acting at the Royal Academy of Dramatic Art (RADA), and, after graduating, worked as an assistant stage manager at Nottingham Playhouse. He moved back to London (living at 28 Chepstow Court) and in 1964 wrote *Little Malcolm*. 'It occurred to me that if I could write a successful play I might rocket to the top of the profession', he said (*The Times*, 21 March 2006). Initially running for six hours, the play was first directed by Mike Leigh at London's left-wing Unity Theatre in 1965. When first produced, it was seen as a ground-breaking political satire and was noted for its extraordinary display of verbal fireworks. Substantially rewritten, it was revived at the Garrick Theatre the same year, with John Hurt giving a critically acclaimed performance in the title role. The play won for its author the *Evening Standard*'s most promising playwright award for 1967. It was seen in Dublin and then in New York (where it was pointlessly retitled *Hail Scrawdyke!*), filmed in 1974 (again starring John Hurt, and with George Harrison as producer) and revived at the Hampstead Theatre in 1998 in a sell-out production starring Ewan McGregor. Reassessing the play after three decades Michael Billington commented: 'If the play makes for a good evening it is because it pins down the bedsit revolutions of much of 1960s student life and accurately shows how dreams of power spring from emotional deprivation' (*The Guardian*, 19 Nov 1998).

In 1968 Halliwell set up, with David Calderisi, his own pioneering fringe theatre company, Quipu, which operated until 1973 variously at the Arts Theatre, the Mercury Theatre in Notting Hill, and the Little Theatre, off St Martin's Lane. Halliwell's purpose was to create 'a new kind of organisation in which the means of production are owned, controlled and developed by the artists whose work is being produced' (*The Guardian*, 22 March 2006). As well as directing premières of new works, including his own, he oversaw successful productions of Shaw, Strindberg, Poliakoff, and Pinter. A staple of 1960s fringe theatre was his own play *The Experiment* (1967), in which a group of actors struggle to explore the significance of the assassination of the American president James Garfield in 1881. Throughout the 1970s Halliwell continued to write prolifically, notably *K. D. Dufford* (1970), a shocking and controversial drama in which a man seeks notoriety by murdering a child. Other plays included *A Last Belch for the Great Auk* (1971) and *The Freckland Bum* (1975). In 1976 he spent a year as the literary manager of the Royal Court Theatre in London.

In his later writing career Halliwell's nuanced psychological stage plays began to fall out of fashion, but he did write a host of well-received television dramas including *Triple Exposure* (1972) and *Steps Back* (1973). He also contributed scripts to several television crime series, including *Crown Court* and *The Bill*. Radio plays included *Was It Her / Spongehenge*, *There's a Car Park in Witherton*, *Crossed Lines*, and, most famously, *Who's Who of Flapland*, which brought two of his paranoiacs together, characteristically using language drawn from his native Yorkshire as the site of their confrontations.

Few British dramatists have enjoyed such international acclaim with their first play as Halliwell did with *Little Malcolm and His Struggle against the Eunuchs*, and although he never repeated the triumph he remained a highly influential figure in British theatre during the 1960s and early 1970s. His work, both as an experimental and political dramatist, and as a visionary fringe theatre director, was championed by such figures as Alan Strachan, Mike Leigh, and Dan Crawford. A bluff northerner, who never married, he was renowned in theatrical circles as being a maverick, a loner with few social graces. His close friendships were few but to those who knew him well he remained a fiercely loyal and witty companion. He died alone on 17 March 2006 at his home, 8 Crowborough Villas, Charlbury, Oxfordshire, following a heart attack. His brother Roger survived him. PATRICK NEWLEY

Sources *The Guardian* (22 Jan 1998); (19 Nov 1998); (22 March 2006) · *The Times* (21 March 2006) · *The Independent* (5 April 2006) · *The Stage* (12 April 2006) · personal knowledge (2010) · private information (2010) · b. cert. · d. cert.
Archives SOUND BL NSA, documentary recordings
Likenesses obituary photographs
Wealth at death under £27,000: probate, 8 May 2006, *CGPLA Eng. & Wales*

Hamburger, Michael Peter Leopold (1924–2007), poet, translator, and literary critic, was born in Berlin on 22 March 1924, the elder son and third of the four children of Richard Hamburger (1884–1940), an eminent paediatrician of Polish origin, and his wife, Lilli, *née* Hamburg (1887–1980), who came from a very wealthy banking family. Both parents were Jewish, very musical, and secular. Hamburger's younger brother Paul (1926–2001), who subsequently changed his name to Paul *Hamlyn, became a prominent publisher, businessman, and philanthropist.

Hamburger went to a private preparatory school in Berlin and briefly to a *Gymnasium*. With considerable foresight, his father decided to emigrate and in November 1933 the family moved to Edinburgh, where Richard Hamburger gained British medical qualifications before settling in St John's Wood, London, in a private practice. Michael Hamburger briefly attended George Watson's College, Edinburgh, and subsequently the Hall School, Hampstead. He became proficient very early on in English. Late in 1934 the family went to live in Hove with grandparents and an uncle who had also emigrated from Germany, and Hamburger briefly attended Brighton, Hove and Sussex grammar school. In 1937 he went to Westminster School, where he became friendly with Tony Benn and, as recounted in Hamburger's autobiographical *A Mug's Game: Intermittent Memoirs, 1924–1954* (1973), his first published poem appeared in his house magazine, *The College Street Clarion*, in April 1939. A Petrarchian sonnet, 'The Death of a Nation', its subject was the German annexation of Czechoslovakia. Early in 1941 Hamburger won a Westminster exhibition to Christ Church, Oxford, to read modern languages. There he formed firm friendships and was heavily influenced by T. S. Eliot, Dylan Thomas, and W. B. Yeats. An Oxford contemporary, Philip Larkin, was later the subject of a moving memoir, *Philip Larkin: a Retrospect* (2002).

Hamburger spent four terms at Oxford in 1941–2. Through the good offices of Herbert Read, with whom

Hamburger had become friendly, Nicholson and Watson published his translations as *Poems of Hölderlin* in their Editions Poetry London series in 1943. Hamburger initially encountered Hölderlin's verse while at school. He continued to produce translations of Hölderlin, a major influence, throughout his life. His identification with Hölderlin's final years, his 'homelessness', his change of identity, and attempt to find a home in English for the German poet may have had something to do with his own sense of displacement: 'I should never have started translating in my adolescence if that hadn't been a bridge to a culture lost to me in every regard' (*The Independent*, 11 June 2007). His 'Hölderlin in 1842' appeared in *Oxford and Cambridge Writing in 1942*, and 'Charles Baudelaire', 'The Rebels', and 'La vita vecchia' in *Oxford Poetry, 1932–1942* (1943), alongside work by his Oxford friends John Heath-Stubbs, Sidney Keyes, Philip Larkin, Michael Meyer, David Wright, and others. A long poem, 'Profuse Dying', was published by M. J. Tambimuttu in his *Poetry London X* in 1944.

While waiting for call-up in wartime London, Hamburger mixed in bohemian poetic circles in Soho and Chelsea. In June 1943 he joined the Queen's Own Royal West Kent regiment. During his infantry training, following a review of *Poems of Hölderlin* in *Punch*, he was invited by the Poetry Society to read for them. The society contacted his company commander who ordered him to accept and represent the regiment. Subsequently he trained as a signalman and spent a period on garrison duty in the Shetlands, meanwhile working on his Baudelaire translations, an introduction to which he had begun when nineteen. His edition of Baudelaire's *Twenty Prose Poems* was published by Editions Poetry London in 1946, and reflected his scholarship, critical acumen, and lucid and informative prose style.

The war in Europe ended in May 1945 and Hamburger was posted to Italy, where he taught himself Italian so that he could read Dante in the original. He was then sent to Austria as an army interpreter and in the winter of 1945–6 he became the headmaster 'of a co-educational boarding school for the children of British soldiers and military government officials in Austria' (Hamburger, *A Mug's Game*, 139). About this time he managed to visit Berlin and track down elderly relatives, the experience leaving an indelible impression upon him. He was demobilized with the rank of lieutenant in July 1947. He then returned to Oxford in October 1947 and after four terms took his finals in the summer of 1948, obtaining second-class honours in German and French. He subsequently travelled to France, seeing the sights and writing poetry.

In the late 1940s and early 1950s Hamburger's poems appeared in such journals as the *Poetry Review* and *Penguin New Writing*, and in the United States in *Tomorrow*. He lived in his mother's Maida Vale house. He worked as a freelance writer, producing book reviews and longer critical pieces on a regular basis, and also did some broadcasting. The journals to which he contributed included the *Times Literary Supplement*, for which between 1949 and 1986 he wrote over 175 reviews, largely on German and French books, and on the post-war German cultural scene; the *PEN Bulletin*, for instance 'Contemporary German poetry' (July 1954); the *New Statesman*, *Encounter*, and *The Spectator*; and little magazines in Britain, America, and Germany. There were frequent visits to Italy and elsewhere, powerfully recounted in *A Mug's Game*. On one of these trips in Palermo he met Edwin Muir and his wife, Willa, whose work he subsequently championed. He also translated for Thames and Hudson, for instance the letters, journal, and conversations of Beethoven, published in 1952. On 28 July 1951 he married Anne Ellen File (*b.* 1928), a poet under the pseudonym Anne Beresford, and daughter of Legh Richmond File, film company's representative. They had two daughters, Mary Anne (*b.* 1953) and Claire (*b.* 1957), and a son, Richard (*b.* 1955). Hamburger and his wife divorced in 1970, but remarried on 22 March 1974.

In London during the 1950s Hamburger first met Paul Celan, who had a profound influence upon him, and whose work he advocated. In 'On translating Celan' (1984) he wrote of 'the urgency of [Celan's] vision' (Hamburger, *Testimonies: Selected Shorter Prose, 1950–1987*, 1989, 277). Hamburger's 'translations are attempts, however incomplete or provisional, to keep faith with [Celan's] texts' (ibid., 285). His highly acclaimed translations of Celan were published in 1988 and 1995. The Hand and Flower Press, of Aldington, Kent, published in 1950 a pamphlet from Hamburger's early poetic collections, *Flowering Cactus: Poems, 1942–1949*, and in 1952 his *Poems, 1950–1951*. In 1952 he took up a post as assistant lecturer in German at University College, London, and in 1955 he became a lecturer in the German department at Reading University and moved with his family to Westwood House, Tilehurst, near Reading. He began cultivating the land, and stayed at Reading until 1964, rising to the rank of reader, meanwhile continuing with his translating, writing, criticism, and poetry. After resigning his position at Reading he lived a peripatetic existence in the USA, holding temporary appointments in German at Mount Holyoake College (1966–7), Buffalo (1969), Stony Brook (1970), Wesleyan University (1971), the University of Connecticut (1972), the University of California at San Diego (1973), the University of South Carolina (1973), and Boston University (1975 and 1977). He resettled permanently in England in 1978, the year he became a part-time professor at Essex University.

Hamburger's poetic style transformed over the course of five decades, changing 'from a formal, symbolic and Yeatsian style to more colloquial work in free verse' that explored 'evolving rather than fixed patterns of meaning' (P. Schmidt, 132) and was evident in *Real Estate* (1997) and *Variations* (1998). His poetry 'explored the dilemma of the modern European Jew, survivor of the Holocaust and wanderer through the ruins of war' (*Contemporary Authors*, 2008). Many of the late poems published in *In Suffolk* (1981), *Trees* (1988), *Intersections* (2000), *Wild and Wounded* (2004), and *Circling the Square* (2007) celebrated the Suffolk landscape, transplantation, and renewal.

Hamburger was prolific, the author of innumerable reviews, over twenty volumes of translations, and various poetry volumes; his most influential critical work was *The Truth of Poetry* (1969, new edn 1996). Michael Schmidt commented in a special issue of *Agenda* devoted to Hamburger's work that 'no book gives a clearer or more comprehensive sense of European poetry from Baudelaire through the 1950s' (M. Schmidt, 'Michael Hamburger's *The Truth of Poetry*', *Agenda*, 35/3, 1997, 116). Admirers of his poetry included Donald Davie, Jon Silkin, and M. L. Rosenthal. Davie, writing in *Under Briggflatts*, regarded Hamburger's poem 'To Bridge a Lull', published in memory of George Oppen, as 'an admirably suave and monumental poem' (Davie, 223). Many honours were bestowed, including Bollingen Foundation fellowships in 1959–61 and 1965–6, a fellowship of the Royal Society of Literature in 1972, honorary doctorates of the University of East Anglia (1968) and the Technische Universität Berlin (1995), the coveted Cholmondeley award for poetry in 2000, the Hölderlin prize in 1991, the Goethe medal in 1986, and the Austrian state prize for literary translation in 1988. In 1992 he was appointed OBE.

Hamburger's last years were spent with Anne in a rural retreat at Middleton, near Saxmundham, Suffolk, writing some of his finest poetry; translating, for instance, W. G. Sebald, a fellow East Anglian; gardening, and preserving rare varieties of apple trees, cultivating them from seeds. He died of a ruptured abdominal aortic aneurysm at his home, Marsh Acres, The Causeway, Middleton, surrounded by his beloved East Anglian orchards, on 7 June 2007, the 164th anniversary of Hölderlin's death. Nominally an Anglican, he was buried at Middleton parish church on 18 June 2007. To honour Hamburger's Jewish roots his wife Anne asked the poet and translator Anthony Rudolf to recite the kaddish at his funeral.

WILLIAM BAKER

Sources M. Hamburger, *A mug's game: intermittent memoirs, 1924–1954* (1973) · M. Davis, ed., *Conversations: Jon Silkin, George Macbeth, Adrian Henri, Michael Hamburger, Roger McGough* (1975), 35–41 · P. Schmidt, 'Michael Hamburger', *Poets of Great Britain and Ireland, 1945–1960*, ed. V. B. Sherry, DLitB, 27 (1984), 130–37 · R. Jeutter, 'The publications of Michael Hamburger: a bibliography', *Comparative Criticism*, 10 (1988), 346–76 · D. Davie, *Under Briggflatts: a history of poetry in Britain, 1960–1988* (1989) · *Agenda*, 35/3 (1997) [tribute to Michael Hamburger] · M. Hamburger, *Michael Hamburger in conversation with Peter Dale* (1998) · M. Hamburger, 'Autobiographical essay', *Contemporary Authors*, 196 (2002), 133–50 · T. Lowth, 'The traveller: a tribute to Michael Hamburger', *Modern Poetry in Translation*, 3/1 (spring 2004) · *Daily Telegraph* (9 June 2007) · *The Times* (11 June 2007) · *The Guardian* (11 June 2007) · *The Independent* (11 June 2007) · *Contemporary Authors*, 261 (2008), 141–2 · J. Crick, M. Liebscher, and M. Swales, eds., *From Charlottenburg to Middleton: Michael Hamburger (1924–2007), poet, translator, critic* (2010) · *WW* (2007) · private information (2011) [Richard Hamburger, son; P. Jay; A. Rudolf; S. Stuart-Smith] · m. certs. · d. cert.

Archives JRL · priv. coll. · Ransom HRC · State University of New York, Buffalo State College, poetry collection | FILM BFINA, *First reaction*, K. Jackson (series editor), Channel 4, 5 Oct 1990 | SOUND BL NSA, documentary recordings · BL NSA, performance recordings

Likenesses R. B. Kitaj, screenprint on paper, 1974, Tate Collection · R. Dupré, bromide print, 1999, NPG · R. B. Kitaj, portrait-study, repro. in Dale, *Hamburger* · J. P. Tripp, portrait, repro. in *Book Collector*, 58/4 (2009), 541 · obituary photographs · photograph, repro. in *Agenda* · photographs, repro. in Hamburger, 'Autobiographical essay' · photographs, repro. in 'Michael Hamburger', *Poets of Great Britain and Ireland, 1945–1960*

Wealth at death £804,689: probate, 23 Nov 2007, *CGPLA Eng. & Wales*

Hand, (Geoffrey) David (**1918–2006**), archbishop of Papua New Guinea, was born on 11 May 1918, the son of William Thomas Hand, Church of England clergyman, and his wife, Constance, *née* Jowett, at Clermont, Queensland, where his father was rector. His maternal great-great-uncle was Benjamin Jowett. Following his parents' return to Britain in 1920 he was educated at Gresham's School in Norfolk, where he was an organ scholar, and at Oriel College, Oxford. His tutor there was Maurice Powicke. He graduated with a second-class degree in modern history in 1941, then trained for the ministry in 1941–2 at nearby Cuddesdon Theological College. He was ordained deacon in 1941 and priest in 1942, the third of three brothers to become priests. He served his curacy at Heckmondwike in the West Riding of Yorkshire between 1943 and 1946. While there he read in the press, and was moved by, the final letter to his father of Vivian Redlich, a missionary priest killed after the Japanese landing at Gona on the northern coast of Papua: 'If I don't come out of it just be content that I have tried to do my duty faithfully' (letter of 27 July 1942, now on display at St Paul's Cathedral, London). He volunteered to take Redlich's place, and arrived in Papua in November 1946.

After initial training at the Anglican head station, Dogura, Hand was appointed in 1947 to the Sefoa mission station. There he discovered he possessed a 'gift of languages for which I had not dared to hope' (Hand, 27), and eventually became fluent in twenty of Papua New Guinea's 800 languages. After serving at Redlich's mission district of Sangara (1948–50) he was chosen by Philip Strong, bishop of New Guinea, as assistant bishop, and consecrated on 29 October 1950; at the age of thirty-two he was the youngest bishop in the Anglican communion.

In addition to the trauma of war, on 21 January 1951 came the Mount Lamington volcanic eruption, which caused the deaths of 4000 Papuan people living in the area, including government officers and eighteen Papuan and expatriate Anglican mission staff. Hand's remarkable energies were prominent in the months of reconstruction following the disaster. He opposed the popular notion of the eruption as God's vengeance for the betrayal by some Papuans of allied servicemen and missionaries to the Japanese.

At this time the Anglican New Guinea mission was experiencing a period of critical opportunity. There was a demand for extension of the church's work, especially in education, to the thickly populated New Guinea highlands, which were being brought under government control. Happiest when on 'walkabout', Hand was well fitted for strenuous physical activity. Known among his fellow missionaries by the sobriquet Butch, he was heavily and strongly built, and had incisive eyes and a commanding presence. Not only was he a lifelong supporter of Norwich City Football Club, but he was no stranger to fisticuffs and, at least before his consecration, had a reputation as a man with a fiery temper. He restored Anglican activity in post-war New Britain and then moved to the highlands. Beginning at Aiom in 1953, he and his Papuan assistant Blake Kerina (later assistant bishop) were the pioneer missionaries in the Siane valley. Like most Anglican missionaries before him, Hand was sensitive to much village culture and continued to introduce elements of it into the church's liturgy through traditional costume as well as in carving and painting, singing, and dance.

In 1969, 97 per cent of the land in Papua New Guinea still belonged to the indigenous people but the alienated 3 per cent included some of the best and most accessible land, and Hand felt this to be an injustice. One of the first occasions when he crossed swords with the Australian administration was over land in the Sangara area, near Mount Lamington, which was leased to timber companies, but which he wanted restored to the original owners. He promoted the Papuan co-operatives begun earlier by James Benson instead of the Australian soldier-settlement schemes that were being mooted in the early 1950s, leading some European critics to label the Anglican co-operative schemes as 'Communist-inspired' (Hand, 131–2). The co-operative movement was ended by the intervention of the Australian minister for territories, C. E. (Ceb) Barnes.

Within the New Guinea church there were high points: the consecration in Brisbane of George Ambo as first indigenous bishop in the south Pacific in 1960 and the creation seventeen years later of the self-governing Anglican province of Papua New Guinea. Hand succeeded Strong as bishop of New Guinea on Strong's translation to the archbishopric of Brisbane in 1963. With Sir Donald Cleland, former administrator of Papua New Guinea and chancellor of the Anglican diocese, Hand began the planning that led in 1977 to the subdivision of the Anglican church in Papua New Guinea into five dioceses. He became the first bishop of Port Moresby and archbishop of Papua New Guinea in 1977.

Hand's cordial relations with other churches in Papua New Guinea, especially the Roman Catholic church, were reflected in the Melanesian Council of Churches, of which he was a co-founder. In 1972 both Roman Catholic and Anglican bishops took part in a 150 mile walk across the Kokoda Track to raise funds for the indigent Anglican church. He was deeply saddened by the divisive effects of American Pentecostal movements on family life. He was also a resolute opponent of Jehovah's Witnesses and Seventh Day Adventist missions, for whose converts, in a land where the only large animal was the wild pig, the eating of pork was forbidden.

In the move towards political independence Hand was keen for political evolution to come earlier rather than later, a position that was opposed by Bishop George Ambo, who felt that the movement towards nationhood was being rushed. Later Hand revised his earlier views and supported the conservative United Party. It is a measure of his stature that upon applying for citizenship as a foreigner in independent Papua New Guinea in 1975 he was enrolled as the country's 'citizen number 1'. He was appointed CBE in 1975 and KBE in 1984.

Retiring on his sixty-fifth birthday in 1983, Hand moved to Norfolk and became vicar of Tatterford, where his father had been incumbent. He returned to Port Moresby in 1986, and was appointed to the chair of Papua New Guinea's censorship board. Among the books banned on his recommendation was Salman Rushdie's *Satanic Verses* (1988). In 2005 he was awarded Papua New Guinea's highest honour, the grand companionship of the order of Logohu, conferred on him by the princess royal. He died in Port Moresby on 6 April 2006. His fifty-nine years in Papua New Guinea had made him the country's longest-serving Anglican missionary, and his nearly fifty-six years as a bishop one of the longest-serving in the Anglican communion. He was given a state funeral in Port Moresby on 18 April and was buried at Popondetta, Oro province; a memorial service was held at St Philip's Church, London, on 26 May. DAVID WETHERELL

Sources *Occasional Papers of the Papua New Guinea English Committee*, 124 (Dec 1947), 27; 127 (June 1950), 1–3; 128 (Feb 1951), 1; 139 (Jan 1963), 1; 140 (Easter 1963), 3–4, 23; 166 (Nov 1963), 3–4 · D. Hand, *Modawa Papua New Guinea and me* (privately printed, Port Moresby, 2002) · *Daily Telegraph* (19 April 2006) · *The Times* (3 May 2006); (13 May 2006) · *The Guardian* (15 May 2006) · *The Independent* (16 May 2006) · private information (2010)

Archives University of Papua New Guinea, New Guinea collection, Anglican papers

Likenesses photograph, repro. in *Occasional Papers*, 140 (1963) · photographs, repro. in Hand, *Modawa*

Handford, Peter Thomas (1919–2007), film sound recordist, was born on 21 March 1919 at 34 Albert Road, St Marylebone, London, the son of Hedley William Mounteney Handford (1883–1929), Church of England clergyman, and his wife, Helen Beatrice, *née* Crosse (*b*. 1891). At the time of his birth his parents lived at 14 Ellerdale Road, Hampstead. He was educated at Christ's Hospital, Horsham, Sussex, but his main training lay elsewhere. From an early age he was fascinated by the cinema, and in March 1936 he was taken on as an unofficial apprentice at Denham film studios. There was no formal training available for those interested in sound recording: decades later, Handford said,

> I don't think you can train sound recordists. Technical knowledge, yes, because we have to understand the working of our equipment and its limitations ... So far as the technique of recording is concerned, however, I don't believe you can teach it. I think you have to learn by experience. (McFarlane, *British Cinema*, 280)

The films he worked on at this time included *A Yank at Oxford* (1938), *On the Night of the Fire* (1939), and *The Thief of Bagdad* (1940), but he did not receive credit on the pre-war films he was involved with at Denham, where his official designation was as 'sound loader' or 'sound camera operator'.

Handford joined the British expeditionary force on the outbreak of the Second World War, and subsequently spent some time with the army film unit, both in England and north-western Europe. Having been evacuated from France early in the war, he returned there as a cameraman filming the D-day landings. He was shot two days later, but his life was saved by a diary and a silver cigarette case in his coat pocket. Meanwhile, on 20 April 1942, at St Cuthbert's Church, Kensington, he had married Freda Austen (*b.* 1921), a hairdresser's receptionist, and daughter of Charles Austen. They had two daughters, Marilyn and Pamela.

After the war Handford had varied experience with the Crown Film Unit and the Fox and MGM units in Britain on documentary films (including *Theirs is the Glory*, 1946, about the battle of Arnhem) and on fiction films (including *While I Live*, 1947). He had a contract with MGM but that proved 'a catastrophe because they didn't make any films' (McFarlane, *British Cinema*, 280–81) and he had an acrimonious departure, having first made sure he had a job with the producer and director Herbert Wilcox to go to. He stayed with Wilcox until Wilcox suffered a financial collapse in 1954. Thereafter Handford was a freelance, and was never out of work again.

Handford's first full credit as sound recordist was on Alfred Hitchcock's *Under Capricorn* (1949), and, though the director's pre-planning left his collaborators little scope for experiment, Handford was delighted when Hitchcock tracked him down twenty-odd years later for *Frenzy* (1972), his first British film in that time. By then, however, Handford had acquired a formidable reputation in his particular branch of film art and craft. He had worked for the Boulting brothers (*Private's Progress*, 1956), Carol Reed (*The Key*, 1958), and others in the 1950s, but his real distinction belongs to the period evoked by the term the British new wave.

Handford was sound recordist on Jack Clayton's *Room at the Top* (1959), a watershed film in its social and cultural realism and sexual candour, and he relished the sense of a new 'authenticity' in British films. 'At last we got away from the studios, using real locations and real people. There had been nothing like it before … It involved a marriage of drama and documentary' (McFarlane, *British Cinema*, 282). He went on to work with the director Tony Richardson on such other new wave films as *The Entertainer* (1960), *A Taste of Honey* (1961, uncredited), and *Tom Jones* (1963), with John Schlesinger on *Billy Liar* (1963), with Karel Reisz on *Saturday Night and Sunday Morning* (1960), and with Clayton again on *The Pumpkin Eater* (1964). He became a pioneer of sound recording on location, aiming to use 'entirely natural sounds' as opposed to studio recordings, which he felt tended to deaden the reality of sound.

After making his reputation on the new wave films Handford was in constant demand for high-profile films, and not just in the field of gritty northern realism. The expatriate American director Joseph Losey sought him several times, notably on the period romantic drama *The Go-Between* (1970), for which Handford intricately captured the diversity of sounds and voices at a cricket match. He also worked for such other distinguished American directors as Sidney Lumet (*Murder on the Orient Express*, 1974), Sidney Pollack (*Out of Africa*, 1985, for which he won an Oscar for best sound), and Clint Eastwood (*White Hunter Black Heart*, 1990). The first of these may well have drawn on Handford's encyclopaedic knowledge of steam-train sounds. The master tapes of his recordings of these are now held at the National Railway Museum in York, and in 1980 he published *Sounds of Railways and their Recording*. In the early 1980s, frustrated with film-making, perhaps prompted by his time with Michael Cimino on the crisis-ridden production of *Heaven's Gate* (1980), he turned to television and spent several years with Anglia Television in Norwich.

Handford's first marriage ended in divorce, and on 4 June 1974, at the register office in Eye, Suffolk, he married Helen Margaret Stronach (Helen Fraser; *b.* 1942), actress, and daughter of Ian Rennie Stronach, dental surgeon. They had met on the set of *Billy Liar*, her first film. There were no children of the marriage. An unpretentious man but at the same time articulate and determined, Handford came to be regarded as one of the doyens of his profession. He died at his home, the Mill House in Wickham Skeith, Suffolk, on 6 November 2007, following a heart attack. He was survived by his wife, Helen, and his two daughters.

BRIAN MCFARLANE

Sources J. Sullivan, ed., *The British Film Industry Yearbook* (1948) · P. Noble, ed., *The British Film and Television Year Book, 1956–57* (1957) · B. McFarlane, *An autobiography of British cinema* (1997) · *The Independent* (30 Nov 2007) · *Daily Telegraph* (12 Dec 2007) · *The Times* (22 Dec 2007) · *The Guardian* (9 Jan 2008) · B. McFarlane, *The encyclopedia of British film*, 3rd edn (2008) · personal knowledge (2011) · private information (2011) · b. cert. · m. certs. · d. cert.

Archives National Railway Museum, York, tapes of sound recordings, notebooks, documents | SOUND BL NSA, documentary recording · University of the West of England, Bristol, interview with Brian McFarlane

Likenesses obituary photographs · photograph, repro. in www.hitchcockwiki.com/wiki/File:PeterHandford.jpg

Wealth at death £181,286: probate, 24 April 2008, *CGPLA Eng. & Wales*

Handley, Vernon George [Tod] (**1930–2008**), conductor, was born on 11 November 1930 at 26 Vista Avenue, Enfield, Middlesex, the second son of Vernon Douglas Handley (1900–1982), a machinist in a paper mill, and his wife, Claudia Lilian, *née* George (1891–1989). He once described his family as 'very, very working-class' (*Irish Times*, 9 Nov 2000), but it was also musical. His father, who was Welsh, had once sung as a tenor in the choir at Llandaff Cathedral. His mother, who was Irish, had been a piano teacher (and also a breeder of Newfoundland dogs). By the age of eighteen months Handley could sing in tune, and early in his life acquired the nickname of Tod: this, he later explained, was because he was born with his feet turned in, and therefore 'toddled' everywhere.

Handley wanted piano lessons but his mother regarded him as 'unteachable' (*The Times*, 11 September 2008) and the family was too poor to send him elsewhere. He injured his hand at the age of eight, and thereafter his musical life consisted of studying scores and listening to recordings, most of which he borrowed from the Enfield public library. He would later place himself in the line of musicians that included Sir Thomas Beecham, Sir Edward Elgar, and Sir Adrian Boult, who, like him, were self-taught. He attended Enfield grammar school; and a music master,

Vernon George [Tod] **Handley (1930–2008)**, by Godfrey MacDomnic

sympathizing with his interests, secured him a pass to watch the BBC Symphony Orchestra rehearsing at the Maida Vale studios under Boult, who would become Handley's role model and hero. Handley was also invited to conduct the school choir, which was a revelatory experience for him.

Having completed his national service between 1949 and 1951, Handley went up to Balliol College, Oxford, to read English. He threw himself into conducting any orchestra, choir, or music society that needed direction, and did so at the cost of a good degree: he left Balliol in 1954 with a third, having conducted eight concerts in his last term. (The college appointed him an honorary fellow in 1999.) On 18 September 1954 he married, at the parish church of St Cross, Holywell, Oxford, Barbara Black, a twenty-year-old student, and daughter of Kilner Newman Black, businessman. They had a daughter and two sons, one of who died in a cot death aged thirteen months.

Handley had decided on music as a career, and after graduating took a succession of odd jobs in order to subsist while he sought to establish himself. These included working on the roads, in hospitals, as a publisher's representative, and as a supply teacher, his priority being to keep his evenings and weekends free to conduct amateur choirs and orchestras. He also sought to acquire some instrumental experience, and set about studying, at the Guildhall School of Music, the unusual combination of double bass, trombone, and violin. Eventually he plucked up the courage to write to Boult, who invited him to attend a rehearsal at the Royal Festival Hall. Several days later Boult asked him to his office and examined him more closely; and in the end promised to help him. Handley became, effectively, Boult's pupil, attending rehearsals with him and discussing the music afterwards. Meanwhile he worked from 1958 to 1961 with the Tonbridge Philharmonic Society and from 1959 to 1961 with the Hatfield School of Music and Drama. He also conducted at Morley College, where Gustav Holst had taught half a century earlier.

Thanks to Boult, Handley had his first professional engagement, with the Bournemouth Symphony Orchestra, in 1961: it attracted very good reviews. He became close to Boult and studied his rather minimal conducting style closely, and emulated it, though he also professed that the band leader Joe Loss had been a strong influence on his style. Boult was at the time a master of the English repertoire, which had grown considerably during the twentieth century, and had been a close friend of all the great English composers since Sir Hubert Parry and Elgar. Handley delved into the same repertoire, though he enjoyed composers of whom Boult disapproved, notably Sir Arnold Bax and Frederick Delius.

In 1962 Handley won the Arnold Bax memorial medal for conducting, and was appointed musical director of the Guildford Philharmonic Orchestra, from which he steadily began to build up a reputation; he was associated with the orchestra until 1986. At least a quarter of the music he programmed there was English, and audiences improved; under him, the orchestra became increasingly professional. He was appointed professor for orchestra and conducting at the Royal College of Music in 1966, a post he held until 1972. He also conducted the choral class there from 1969 to 1972. He left after a disagreement with students about his determination to teach them using the English repertoire.

Handley built up a powerful catalogue of recordings from the mid-1970s onwards, notably on the Lyrita label, which championed English music at a time when it was out of fashion. He persuaded other record companies to allow him to record music by a number of neglected composers: there was a cycle of Robert Simpson's symphonies for Hyperion, some Malcolm Arnold symphonies for Conifer, and Bax's symphonies for Chandos. He also recorded almost all of E. J. Moeran's orchestral music for Chandos, and made a definitive recording for them of Sir Arthur Bliss's *Colour Symphony*. He was a close friend of Bliss and the two men admired each other; the recording of *A Colour Symphony* showed to perfection Handley's instinctive relationship with an orchestra and deep understanding of the work and the composer who wrote it. It was this profound sympathy with the music he conducted that made him a talented interpreter of the English canon.

Among Handley's vast output of recordings of British music, particularly notable were his recording in 1979 for Lyrita of Patrick Hadley's *The Trees So High* and Gerald Finzi's *Intimations of Immortality*, and his ground-breaking account in 1984 of Ralph Vaughan Williams's piano concerto, with Howard Shelley as soloist, which was accompanied on the same disc by the first ever recording, more than half a century after it was written, of John Foulds's

Dynamic Triptych. Handley was acclaimed in the early 1980s for a series of recordings of Elgar's music on the Classics for Pleasure label, causing some critics to opine that he conducted Elgar better than anyone since the composer himself. His recording with Nigel Kennedy of Elgar's violin concerto won a *Gramophone* award, and his accounts of the symphonies were among the finest ever made. He moved on to Vaughan Williams, of whom he had an implicit understanding, and recorded a fine cycle of his symphonies in the late 1980s. At his death it was estimated that of the 160 discs he had made, 90 were of British music, and included 100 pieces never before recorded.

Handley was popular with concert audiences, conducting frequently at the Proms and all around London and the provinces. He was popular with orchestral players too, often demonstrating his particularly unstuffy sense of humour. He enjoyed huge success as principal conductor of the Ulster Orchestra from 1985 to 1989, and from 1989 to 1995 as principal guest conductor of the Royal Liverpool Philharmonic Orchestra. His Vaughan Williams cycle was made with that orchestra, and he and the orchestra also recorded a superb account of Herbert Howells's *Hymnus Paradisi*.

For all his association with the English canon, Handley was in demand as a guest conductor with numerous other orchestras. Among those with whom he performed regularly were the Strasbourg Philharmonic, the Helsinki Philharmonic, and the Amsterdam Philharmonic. He became chief guest conductor of Melbourne Symphony Orchestra and chief conductor of the Western Australian Symphony Orchestra in the 1990s, and between 1991 and 1996 spent much of his time in Australia. He was injured in a serious car accident in Brisbane in 1991 and in another in Munich in 2005, in which his taxi driver was killed. He was offered an OBE in 1988, but declined it. He accepted a CBE in 2004, but many of his admirers wondered why, unlike some conductors of equal accomplishment, he had not been knighted. He had acquired a reputation for unreliability, though to be fair to him this was largely down to poor health as he became older. Although genuinely modest—he would often point to the score during the applause at the end of a concert, as if to show where the credit was really due—he could be temperamental, and despite his success was always something of an outsider. His refusal to concentrate on the wider European repertoire might also have counted against him, as did his failure ever to hold a top post with a London orchestra, though he had a close association with the Royal Philharmonic (as guest conductor from 1961 to 1994 and associate conductor thereafter).

Handley's first marriage ended in divorce, and on 19 March 1977 he married Victoria Charlotte Parry-Jones, the twenty-year-old daughter of Vaughan Evans Parry-Jones, life assurance agent; they had one son and one daughter. That marriage also ended in divorce, and on 5 October 1987 Handley married Catherine Margaret Newby (*b.* 1961), flautist, and daughter of Kenneth Newby, sales representative. They had one son.

Handley was a stocky man with pugilistic features. He wore his hair *en brosse*: unlike some of his brethren, he set little store by appearances. He was happiest at his cottage in Monmouthshire, where he enjoyed growing roses. He was also a keen ornithologist, and a fine photographer of birds. From the 1970s to the first decade of the twenty-first century no conductor did more than him to champion British music and widen its appeal, though he was closely followed in that pursuit by Richard Hickox, who died suddenly a few weeks after him. His health was poor in the last years of his life, and he suffered from a variety of ailments. He died at his home, The Cottage, Birch Hill Farm, Skenfrith, Monmouthshire, on 10 September 2008. He was survived by his wife, Catherine, and five of his six children. SIMON HEFFER

Sources *The Times* (11 Sept 2008); (18 Sept 2008); (22 Sept 2008); (30 Sept 2008) · *Daily Telegraph* (11 Sept 2008) · *The Guardian* (11 Sept 2008); (12 Sept 2008); (3 Oct 2008) · *The Independent* (11 Sept 2008) · *WW* (2008) · personal knowledge (2012) · private information (2012) · b. cert. · m. certs. · d. cert.

Archives FILM BFINA, current affairs and documentary footage | SOUND BL NSA, current affairs, documentary, and interview recordings

Likenesses photographs, 1973–2007, Getty Images, London · photographs, 2007, Rex Features, London · photographs, 2007, Camera Press, London · photographs, 2007, PA Photos, London · G. MacDomnic, photograph, Lebrecht Music and Arts Photo Library, London [*see illus.*] · obituary photographs · photographs, Lebrecht Music and Arts Photo Library, London

Wealth at death £134,961: administration, 25 Feb 2009, *CGPLA Eng. & Wales*

Hardee, Malcolm Gerrard (1950–2005), comedian and comedy promoter, was born on 5 January 1950 in Lewisham Hospital, London, the eldest child of (Harry) Frank George Hardee, Thames lighterman, and his wife, Joan Annie Alicia, *née* Hurley. He attended St Stephen's Church of England primary school, Colfe's Grammar School, Lewisham, and Sedgehill comprehensive school, Catford, and was expelled from all three. After stealing a bicycle at the age of eleven he fell into a life of petty crime, which encompassed car theft, burglary, and cheque fraud. 'Later, when it suited me, I would claim I'd fallen in with a bad lot, but the truth was that *I* was the bad lot' (Hardee, 18–19). As a result he spent much of his youth and early adulthood in borstals and in Wandsworth, Exeter, and Grendon Underwood prisons. By the late 1970s he had got bored with crime and incarceration, and he later reflected that 'Prison is like mime or juggling: a tragic waste of time' (ibid., 49).

In 1978 Hardee joined Martin Soan and others in The Greatest Show on Legs, which performed an adult Punch and Judy show and various comedy sketches in pubs and at hippy festivals in Devon and East Anglia. The group was introduced to the emerging alternative cabaret scene by Rik Mayall and Ade Edmondson, and started appearing at the Comedy Store in London. In 1981 they developed the infamous balloon dance, which involved the three members of the group appearing naked and precariously covering their genitals with balloons. Performing it on the late-night television show *OTT* brought them national fame and cult status in Sweden.

By the time The Greatest Show on Legs split up in 1983

Hardee had already started to establish himself as a solo stand-up (with the catchphrase 'Oy Oy!'). He was described by John Connor as 'not exactly the world's greatest comic [but] probably the world's best con-man of comedy' (Connor, 27); Hardee's material was unremarkable, often consisting of old gags introduced with a bark of 'Joke number one', 'Joke number two', etc. What brought him notoriety on the comedy circuit was his tendency towards nakedness and urination. One routine involved him doing an impression of General de Gaulle with his penis, and he was once sacked for urinating on stage while compèring at the Albany Empire.

Hardee was probably more significant on the alternative comedy circuit as a promoter than as a performer, running venues and managing other acts. He set up the Tunnel Club in a pub called The Mitre in Greenwich in January 1984, and it became legendary for the boisterousness of its audience, which many comedians found terrifying. Indeed, in a notable incident that Hardee saw as the beginning of the end for the venue Babs Sutton of the double act Clarence and Joy Pickles was hit in the face by a glass which had been hurled at the stage. After the Tunnel closed, Hardee set up another Greenwich venue, Up the Creek, with a slightly less fearsome reputation. He also managed various comedians, including Jerry Sadowitz, and was credited with helping the careers of Harry Enfield, Vic Reeves, and Jo Brand (with whom he had an affair).

Perhaps Hardee's greatest attribute, though, was his genius for publicity stunts. In the 1983 Edinburgh festival fringe he disrupted the show of the American performance artist Eric Bogosian by driving a sit-down lawnmower through the tent in which he was performing. In 1986 he stole an enormous birthday cake that had been baked for Freddie Mercury's fortieth birthday party, the incident providing the title for Hardee's autobiography. He ran for parliament in Greenwich in 1987, winning 174 votes for the Rainbow Alliance Beer, Fags and Skittles Party, and again in 1991, this time as a way of exploiting the free mail shot to get leaflets promoting Off the Kerb to 10,000 constituents. This was not the only example of publicity stunts being used to promote his comedy ventures. In 1989 he got his friend and fellow comedian Arthur Smith to review his Edinburgh show and submit it to *The Scotsman* under the name of the noted comedy critic William Cook, only revealing the scam after it had been published.

From the late 1970s until 1990 Hardee's partner was Philippa (Pip) Hazelton, with whom he had two children, Frank (*b.* 1985) and Poppy (*b.* 1988). Fittingly, he married Jane Kintrea Matthews (a 35-year-old publicity officer, and daughter of Robert Ian Matthews, farmer) on April fool's day 1993. They split up in 2000, causing him to abandon his final Edinburgh show (his first was in 1982) after only two nights. About 31 January 2005 he drowned in Greenland Dock, Bermondsey, when he fell out of the dinghy that was carrying him from the boat-based pub he ran, the Wibbley Wobbley, to his houseboat; his body was found on 2 February. His funeral, at St Alfege's Church in Greenwich on 17 February, included contributions from a number of comedians, and his coffin bore a floral tribute that spelt out the words 'Knob Out'. He was survived by his two children. OLIVER DOUBLE

Sources J. Connor, *Comics: a decade of comedy at the Assembly Rooms* (1990) · W. Cook, *Ha bloody ha: comedians talking* (1994) · M. Hardee, *I stole Freddie Mercury's birthday cake* (1996) · *Evening News* [Edinburgh] (11 Aug 2000) · *Daily Telegraph* (4 Feb 2005) · *The Guardian* (4 Feb 2005) · *The Independent* (5 Feb 2005); (19 Feb 2005) · *The Times* (7 Feb 2005) · b. cert. · m. cert. · d. cert.

Archives FILM BFINA, *Funny business*, J. Reid (producer), ITV, 15 Sept 1996 · BFINA, documentary footage · BFINA, performance footage

Likenesses J. Fleming, photograph, 1996, repro. in http://www.malcolmhardee.co.uk · obituary photographs · photographs, repro. in http://www.malcolmhardee.co.uk

Hardman, Leslie Henry (1913–2008), Jewish minister and army chaplain, was born at 12 Maes-y-Dyffryn, Glynneath, Glamorgan, on 18 February 1913, the son of Abraham Hardman, draper, and his wife, Dora, *née* Priceman. His father had emigrated from Poland, his mother from Russia. He was originally named Henry Leslie, but was always known as Leslie. He was one of five children, three girls and two boys, in a family of orthodox Jews. When he was eight they moved to Liverpool, where he attended the Hope Street Jewish School. An intelligent and religiously observant young man, he spent a period at Jewish religious seminaries (*yeshivot*) in Liverpool and Manchester, studying at one stage under Rabbi Isser Yehuda Unterman, later chief rabbi of Israel, before going on to the University of Leeds where he took BA and MA degrees in Hebrew, Syriac, and biblical literature. After a period studying at Jews' College in London, in 1934 he was briefly minister of the Jewish community at St Anne's, Lancashire, before taking an appointment at the Francis Street Synagogue in Leeds in the following year. On 14 October 1936 he married Josephine (Josi) Cohen (1911–2007) in her home city of Glasgow. A bookkeeper and secretary, she was the daughter of Harry Cohen, mantle manufacturer. They had four girls, Hilarie, Hazel, Devorah, and Aviva. Josi was to be a constant support to him in his pastoral work.

Hardman joined the army as a Jewish chaplain in 1942 and was initially stationed in Hertfordshire under eastern command. Remarkably, he chose to carry a gun. In the autumn of 1944 he was sent to the Netherlands where he learned at first hand of the persecution, deportation, and murder of Dutch Jewry during the occupation. From there he was sent to Germany. On 15 April 1945 the British 11th armoured division, to which Padre Captain Hardman was attached, came upon the Bergen-Belsen concentration camp in Lower Saxony. The camp held nearly 60,000 people in the most appalling conditions, most of them driven to it as the allies advanced from east and west in 1945. Anne Frank had died there a matter of weeks earlier. Many of the captives had typhus and other diseases that would kill them; all were malnourished and in despair.

Although he was not present at the actual liberation, Hardman was called to see his commanding officer on the following day and told that he must go to Belsen and do what he could for the many thousands of Jews there. He later described the sight on entering the camp on 17 April:

> Towards us came what seemed to be the remnants of a holocaust—a tottering mass of blackened skin and bones, held together somehow with filthy rags. 'My God, the dead are walking', I cried aloud, but I did not recognise my voice. (Hardman and Goodman, 2)

Another witness to these infamous scenes was the broadcaster Richard Dimbleby, whose reports for the BBC made the liberation of Belsen a defining moment of the British experience of the Second World War.

Doing what he could to minister to these victims of Nazism, Hardman comforted and listened to them as they talked of the brutality they had experienced and the killings they had witnessed. Joseph Kierz, an inmate, recalled that 'the first day after the liberation, Rev. Leslie Hardman, a chaplain in the British army, spoke to us for about an hour in Yiddish and gave us tremendous hope … he seemed like our messiah' (BBC, People's War website). The inmates were indeed amazed that salvation had come in the shape of a rabbi with a star of David on his British uniform:

> I felt that I could help most if I could slacken a little the almost intolerable tension of their sorely afflicted minds; if I could kindle some warmth in their frozen hearts; if I could inject some emotion into their withered bodies. So I sat there for hours, smoking, talking, listening. (Hardman and Goodman, 13)

Hardman also wept, and the inmates of the camp comforted him.

When the British entered the camp there were some 13,000 unburied corpses in Belsen. In the course of the next two weeks, despite the attempts of the army to organize and sanitize the camp and give medical assistance to those who might be saved, 9000 more perished, and through May and June 1945 a further 4000 died. Hardman and another Jewish army chaplain officiated over the mass burials, remorseful that it was impossible to show the dead the respect they deserved. After two weeks he was ordered to return to normal military duties. He refused and went temporarily into hiding in the camp. He was then allowed to stay and remained until August. He attended the first interrogation of the Belsen commandant, Hans Kremer, who was unrepentant and who was hanged in December 1945.

Hardman was appointed minister of the Hendon Synagogue in north-west London in 1947. It was a large, confident, and affluent community within the United Synagogue movement, the orthodox mainstream of the Anglo-Jewish community. He was revered and loved by the congregation and remained with them until his retirement in 1982. His learning and wisdom, but above all his first-hand experience of the holocaust, made him one of the most respected figures in Anglo-Jewish life. Unsurprisingly, given this experience he was a committed Zionist. It also made him impatient with religious observance for its own sake. He demanded the highest ethical standards from his community which, he argued, were more important than the letter of Jewish law. He advocated accepting converts to Judaism who did not adhere to every religious obligation; he respected the continuing Jewish identity of those who married non-Jews. In the controversy concerning the views of Rabbi Louis Jacobs over the historical origins of the Bible which divided British Jews in the early 1960s, Hardman supported Jacobs's more liberal and scholarly approach and thus put himself outside the orthodox consensus.

He was also singular in his adoption and defence of the title of 'reverend'. He was never, in fact, accorded the status of rabbi by the rabbinical authorities in Britain, perhaps because of his liberal views and support for Jacobs. But he was content to be styled by the more Anglicized title. It suited his personality and reverend bearing, it was a statement of his strong British identity, and was a mark also of his difference from other orthodox Jewish religious leaders of his own and the next generation.

Through lecturing, writing, and his support of the Holocaust Educational Trust, Hardman did much to try to ensure that the crimes committed at Belsen and the other concentration camps were not forgotten and would never be repeated. For this work he was appointed MBE in 1998. Three years earlier he had conducted the service to commemorate the fiftieth anniversary of the liberation of Belsen, which was held at the Ravensbrück camp. The Channel 4 docudrama, *The Relief of Belsen*, broadcast in 2007, in which Hardman was played by the actor Paul Hilton, brought his role in the camp to much wider public attention. Hardman's wife died in 2007 and he himself a year later on 7 October 2008 at the Royal Free Hospital, Camden, of pneumonia and heart disease. A memorial service was held for him at the Hendon Synagogue on 18 January 2009. He was survived by two of his daughters, the eldest and youngest having predeceased him.

LAWRENCE GOLDMAN

Sources L. H. Hardman and C. Goodman, *The survivors: the story of the Belsen remnant* (1958) • J. Reilly, *Belsen: the liberation of a concentration camp* (1997) • B. Shephard, *After daybreak: the liberation of Belsen, 1945* (2006) • L. Smith, *Forgotten voices of the holocaust: a new history in the words of the men and women who survived* (2006) • *The relief of Belsen*, Channel 4, 15 Oct 2007 • *The Times* (8 Oct 2008) • *Daily Telegraph* (8 Oct 2008) • *The Guardian* (13 Oct 2008) • *The Independent* (21 Oct 2008) • *Jewish Chronicle* (23 Oct 2008) • *Jerusalem Post* (16 Oct 2008) • D. Verbov, ed., *'My dear friends': timeless words of warmth, wit, and wisdom from Rev. Leslie Hardman, MBE, MA, HCF*, 2009, Hendon United Synagogue, London • W. Hitchcock, *Liberation: the bitter road to freedom, Europe 1944–1945* (2009) • www.bbc.co.uk/ww2peopleswar/stories/15/a3901015.shtml, 7 Aug 2011 • b. cert. • m. cert. • d. cert.

Archives SOUND BL NSA, documentary recording

Likenesses K. Wigglesworth, photograph, 2003, PA Photos, London • obituary photographs

Wealth at death £534,063: probate, 22 June 2009, *CGPLA Eng. & Wales*

Harling, (Henry) Robert (1910–2008), typographic designer, novelist, and magazine editor, was born on 27 March 1910 at 27 Thorpedale Road, Islington, London, the elder son of Henry Robert Harling (1876–1954), taxi driver and former regular soldier, and his wife, Adelaide Lavinia, *née* Thomas (1876–1949). He and his younger brother, Arthur Stanley (*b.* 1912), were brought up by their parents in north London. Harling later gave a characteristically unreliable account of his upbringing in his semi-autobiographical novel *Amateur Sailor*, published in 1944 under the pseudonym Nicholas Drew, in which he claimed that his parents died young and he was brought up in Brighton by a so-called 'aunt', a family friend, and her dairyman husband. It would have delighted him that this romanticized account appeared as fact in his obituaries.

Harling, known in the family as Robbie, attended Dame Alice Owen's School in Highbury. He showed a precocious interest in the design of print and lettering and this became the ruling passion of his life. He enrolled as a student of typography at the Central School of Arts and Crafts at some point during an unsettled and somewhat frenzied early period in which he also worked for the *Daily Mail*, gained experience at the Lund Humphries printing works in Bradford and the Kynoch Press in Birmingham, and made use of a family legacy to open a bookshop selling first editions and poetry in Lamb's Conduit Street, London. His outlook was already that of the sophisticated metropolitan.

In 1932 Harling entered the then burgeoning world of modern advertising, taking a job as designer at Stuart's, an agency well known for its illustrated booklets for Fortnum and Mason. Four years later he moved to Everett Jones and Delamere, the agency financed by the young Lord Delamere, as a freelance designer. His promotion to creative director allowed him to commission work from his favourite artists, Edward Bawden, Rex Whistler, and Eric Ravilious. His redesign of the cover for *Wisden's Cricketers' Almanack* in 1938, with its Ravilious engraving of Victorian cricketers, is regarded as a typographic classic of its time. The cover used Harling's own Victorian-style typeface Playbill, developed in 1938 with the Sheffield typefounders Stephenson Blake for whom he also designed Chisel (1935), Tea Chest (1939), and Keyboard (1951).

Harling was quick on the uptake and able to predict, and indeed to stimulate, the coming resurgence of interest in Victoriana. Two books on the Victorian period—*The London Miscellany* (1937) and *Home, a Victorian Vignette* (1938)—reinforced his reputation as an authority on period design and decoration. But he was notably eclectic in tastes, his authority also encompassing the continental modern. In 1935 he organized an exhibition of Rudolph Koch's Klingspor types at Lund Humphries's office in London. This was followed by an exhibition on Jan Tschichold; Harling wrote the first article about the Swiss typographer to appear in Britain. It was published in *Printing* magazine in 1936 with the typically Harlingesque heading, 'What is this "functional" typography? The work of Jan Tschichold. The man is different!'. At this period he also made friends with the great English type designer Eric Gill, visiting him at Pigotts. Harling's later book, *The Letter Forms and Type Designs of Eric Gill* (1976), was recognized as the most authoritative study of this aspect of Gill's work.

Harling's breadth of knowledge and enormous range of contacts, as well as his sheer energy and zest for life, made him a natural magazine editor. In November 1936 the first issue of *Typography* appeared. This was an innovative periodical conceived by Harling with his slightly older friend James Shand and published by Shand's family firm, the Shenval Press. The magazine was original in its coverage of lettering of all kinds, not just fine book printing. The first issue contained an article on Kardomah tea labels; the second an analysis of train ticket typography. Harling's early championing of typographic ephemera anticipated 1960s pop culture. Eight issues were published before *Typography* ended with the outbreak of the Second World War.

Harling's war was eventful. Always a keen sailor, he volunteered for the Royal Navy and, before he had finished training, assisted in the evacuation of British forces from Dunkirk in May 1940. He described the episode in *Amateur Sailor*, a book praised by John Masefield as the best of all eyewitness accounts of Dunkirk. As a sub-lieutenant in the Royal Naval Volunteer Reserve he served as navigator of a corvette on convoy duty in the western approaches, an experience he recounted in a further vivid personal narrative, *The Steep Atlantick Stream* (1946). His close friendship with the writer Ian Fleming began in 1939 when Fleming, already working in intelligence, commissioned him to redesign the Admiralty's weekly intelligence report. In 1941 Fleming, now assistant to the director of naval intelligence, recruited Harling first to the inter-services topographical division, to work on gathering and publishing information on potential enemy targets, and later as a member of Fleming's own 30 assault unit, referred to by Harling as 'Fleming's secret army', operating in the front line at the end of the war to capture enemy code books, wireless equipment, and so on, before these could be destroyed. Harling became the unit's expert on mines and minefields.

Harling had been present when, in 1944, Fleming stated his intention to write 'the spy novel to end all spy novels'. The result was James Bond, a fictional character who bore a distinct resemblance to Harling in his sardonic elegance of manner and cool sexual expertise. In 1945, when Fleming was foreign manager at the *Sunday Times*, Harling was appointed consultant designer to the paper, remaining blissfully happy in the part-time post for the next forty years. He was also for a while the architecture critic for the *Sunday Times*. The journalistic world of power politics fascinated him and when he too began writing fiction Fleet Street provided him with a potent theme. His first novel, *The Paper Palace* (1951), was a thriller about a reporter sent out by a corrupt editor on the trail of a dead man. It gave an acute and chilling picture of English journalism at that period as did his later book, *The Hollow Sunday* (1967). Of his other five novels the most successful was *The Endless Colonnade* (1958), a suspense novel about a physician in Italy being pursued by killers. Harling loved Italy and would revisit Venice year after year.

After the war Harling resumed his typographical enthusiasms. He and James Shand inaugurated a new graphic design periodical, *Alphabet & Image*, eight issues of which appeared between 1946 and 1948. This was followed by *Image*, ostensibly a quarterly concentrating on the visual arts. Eight volumes were published between 1948 and summer 1952. Under Harling's brilliantly entrepreneurial editorship the journal published work by such important post-war artists as John Minton, Leonard Rosomon, Blair Hughes-Stanton, and Edward Ardizzone. In 1948, again with Shand, he set up the Art and Tecnics publishing firm, commissioning a series of exceptionally elegant and expert books on architecture, including John Summerson on Sir John Soane and Hugh Casson on Victorian buildings. In 1957 he started the last of his many varied but interconnected lives as editor of *House & Garden* magazine, published by Condé Nast and based at Vogue House in Hanover Square. He liked the ambience of what he called 'the glossies', relishing their absurdities and making the most of his many opportunities to encourage young illustrators and designers. He was an autocratic, effective, imaginative editor, adored by his largely female staff, who extended the potential of a magazine previously limited to decoration into architecture and social commentary, inventing the journalistic 'lifestyle' feature. He edited *House & Garden* until 1993.

Harling married first, on 25 October 1930, Mary Adelaide Homer (1910–2002), drapery saleswoman, and daughter of William Thomas Homer, cartage contractor (and a friend of Harling's father). After their divorce (in 1942 she married the advertising agent Sydney Righyni) she was quickly edited out of his life; later friends remained unaware of her existence. He then married, on 3 April 1945, a psychiatrist's beautiful assistant, Phoebe Pauline Helen Konstam, formerly Kohnstamm (1911–2006). His own version of their meeting was that he had picked her up in Leicester Square. It was apparently a very happy marriage, surviving Harling's many liaisons—some long-lasting, some less so—elsewhere. They had three children (two sons and a daughter), two of whom became journalists, the third a painter. The family lived in an exquisite house, Glebe House at Godstone in Surrey, an eighteenth-century pink-washed gothick vicarage, which Harling reconfigured by removing the top storey. When the planning authorities objected he was able to present the evidence to prove that he had simply returned the building to the architect's original intention.

Harling was a lean, handsome, raffish man who cut a figure of considerable glamour in drab London in the 1950s, wearing well-cut Edwardian-style suits and a fedora. His friend the artist Lucian Freud, noting Harling's drainpipe trousers, enquired how he managed to make quick getaways. He was loyal and affectionate to selected friends but not generally gregarious. He showed a characteristic ruthlessness in divesting himself of his family at an early stage. Ruari McLean described him as 'exceptionally non-boring. One probably never knew much about him; but one never forgot him'. He died of cancer on 1 July 2008 at Glebe House, and was survived by his three children. He was cremated at Surrey and Sussex crematorium on 10 July 2008. FIONA MACCARTHY

Sources R. Harling, 'Trio', [n.d.], priv. coll. • R. Harling, 'Ian Fleming, a discursive memoir', *c.*2002, priv. coll. • R. Harling, 'Two improbable partners', *An E. J. keepsake* (1982) • R. McLean, 'Robert Harling at ninety', *Matrix*, 21 (2002) • *The Guardian* (2 July 2008); (8 July 2008) • *The Times* (3 July 2008); (4 July 2008); (8 July 2008) • *Sunday Times* (6 July 2008) • *The Independent* (8 July 2008) • A. Powers, 'Robert Harling in the 1930s', *Matrix*, 29 (summer 2010) • personal knowledge (2012) • private information (2012) • b. cert. • m. certs. • d. cert.

Likenesses H. Coster, photographs, 1945–56, NPG • obituary photographs

Wealth at death £101,394: probate, 1 May 2009, *CGPLA Eng. & Wales*

Harris, (David) Kenneth (1919–2005), journalist and broadcaster, was born at Aberaman, Glamorgan, on 11 November 1919, the only son and elder child of David Harris, a market gardener, and his wife, Kathleen. He was educated at Trowbridge boys' high school, Wiltshire, and Wadham College, Oxford. His studies were interrupted by the Second World War, and from 1940 to 1945 he served in the Royal Artillery. He returned to Oxford on demobilization in 1945 and two years later, after graduating with a second-class degree in modern history, took part in the first post-war Oxford Union debating tour of the United States, along with Tony Benn and Sir Edward Boyle. Debating became an important theme in his life. He founded the Observer Mace debating tournaments in 1953 and was chairman of the English Speaking Union's overseas debating committee from 1960 to 1995. When he died, a spokesman for the union said, 'Kenneth's importance in developing competitive debate in this country cannot be overstated' (www.britishdebate.com).

In 1948 Harris joined the *Sheffield Telegraph* and on 16 April 1949 he married Doris Winsmore Young-Smith (*d.* 1970), a 37-year-old war widow, and daughter of Aubrey Lawrence Fullerton. There were no children of the marriage. In 1950 Harris moved on to *The Observer*, where David Astor had recently become editor of the family-owned newspaper. It was typical of Astor's inspired risk-taking that he should appoint the thirty-year-old Harris to the important post of Washington correspondent, largely on the strength of the book, *Travelling Tongues* (1949), he had written about the Oxford undergraduate debating tour. He remained on *The Observer* for thirty-two years, working on the Pendennis diary column and then as the newspaper's labour correspondent. Always assiduous at cultivating social and political contacts, he gained the trust of senior figures in the Labour Party and the trade-union movement, especially Sam Watson, the Durham miners' leader, for whom he wrote some speeches. He also succeeded where many had failed in gaining the confidence of Clement Attlee, the post-war Labour prime minister, who agreed to confide his political memories to Harris's tape-recorder. These meetings culminated, many years later, in the only official Attlee biography (1982), Harris's most successful book. He also produced books about David Owen (1987), Margaret Thatcher (1988), and Elizabeth II (1994), and several collections of his journalism.

Harris was mainly known for his in-depth interviews, both in the newspaper and on television. Some of his journalist colleagues regarded him as over-deferential in his approach to his subjects, who were allowed to read and correct his written interviews. Astor, however, believed that Harris's courteous but well-researched method paid dividends in winning over public figures who were otherwise distrustful of the media. He persuaded a number of celebrities, from President Nixon to Sir Gordon Richards, the jockey, to confide personal secrets they had never made public before. On television he conducted a famous interview with Indira Gandhi, later the Indian prime minister, in which he provoked her to defend the principle of nepotism. He secured the first interview with Alexei Kosygin when he became Soviet premier, a scoop deemed so important that it was broadcast on both the BBC and ITV. Harris also secured the final interview with the duke of Windsor in 1972, weeks before his death. Astor believed the BBC should have made him the heir to Richard Dimbleby.

Harris was an elegant, well-groomed man with an actor's voice and a suave, faintly old-fashioned style that some of his colleagues regarded as pompous; hence his office nickname, the Bishop. By the end of 1976 he was enjoying a comfortable, but not notably demanding, schedule—doing two big interviews a year for *The Observer*, organizing the newspaper's debating competitions, covering the party political conferences for the BBC, working in a leisurely fashion on his books, lunching at his club, the Athenaeum, enjoying the gaming tables at night (one of his casino companions, an elderly widow, left him a painting by Édouard Vuillard in her will)—when his life was changed by a chance meeting over dinner at Rules restaurant in Covent Garden with a visiting American friend, Douglass Cater, a former White House correspondent and presidential aide turned academic. At that meeting Cater asked Harris about *The Observer*, which was on the point of being taken over by Rupert Murdoch. He suggested calling his boss at the Aspen Institute, a think-tank funded largely by Atlantic Richfield, the giant Californian oil company. A series of telephone calls followed over the weekend between Robert O. Anderson, the chairman of Atlantic Richfield (and the biggest private landowner in the United States), and Lord Goodman, chairman of the Observer Trust. As a result the American oil company bought Britain's oldest Sunday newspaper for one pound and took over its mounting debts.

Harris (who was made a director of The Observer Ltd in 1978) was regarded as a saviour by the paper's staff and quickly established a close personal relationship with Anderson, introducing him to the elevated contacts he had developed throughout his career. They launched an annual dinner, first at Lincoln's Inn and later at Claridge's, to celebrate the 'rescue' of *The Observer*, where the speakers included Harold Macmillan and Henry Kissinger and the guest-list read like an extract from *Who's Who*. Harris and Cater, who was given an office at *The Observer*, started issuing memoranda on editorial policy, which were resented by the senior staff. Conor Cruise O'Brien, the Irish writer, diplomat, and politician, was drafted in as editor-in-chief to act as a buffer between 'Cater-Harris' (as the two were known) and the journalists. In his memoirs O'Brien described Harris as 'a poisonous presence in my professional life' (O'Brien, 366), and at the time wrote a withering column about sycophants ('lickspittles') in history, which was seen as a thinly veiled attack on him.

A crisis arose in 1981 when Anderson let it be known that he wanted Harris to represent him as deputy chairman of the newspaper. The *Observer* board, including Goodman, Astor, and O'Brien, rejected this proposal. Anderson's response was to sell the newspaper, immediately after the board meeting, to Lonrho, which owned it for the next twelve years. So Harris had the rare distinction for a working journalist of not only saving *The Observer* from Rupert Murdoch's clutches but also being the reason why it was sold on to Tiny Rowland. In 1981 Lonrho appointed him chairman of one of its subsidiaries, George Outram & Co., later Caledonian Newspaper Publishing, publishers of the Glasgow *Herald* and *Evening Times*; he held this post until 1992, when he was appointed CBE. He retired as a director of The Observer Ltd in 1993.

Harris was a keen and knowledgeable follower of horse-racing, an interest he pursued in his retirement. He listed his other recreations as walking, fishing, and reading. His first wife having died in 1970, on 13 February 1988 he married Jocelyn (Jo) Rymer, a 45-year-old secretary, divorcee, and daughter of Frederick Smithson Wilkinson, farmer; she had two daughters from a previous marriage. Having lived latterly in Mill Lane, Donington, Lincolnshire, he died of cerebrovascular disease and prostate cancer at Gosberton House Care Home, Westhorpe Road, Gosberton, Lincolnshire, on 24 June 2005. He was survived by his wife, Jo, and his two stepdaughters.

DONALD TRELFORD

Sources C. Cruise O'Brien, *Memoir: my life and themes* (1998) • *The Guardian* (2 July 2005) • *The Observer* (3 July 2005); (17 July 2005) • *The Times* (5 July 2005); (14 July 2005) • *The Herald* [Glasgow] (7 July 2005) • *WW* (2005) • www.britishdebate.com, 26 June 2008 • personal knowledge (2009) • private information (2009) • m. certs. • d. cert.

Archives Bodl. Oxf., William Clark MSS • Guardian and Observer Archive and Visitor Centre, Observer archives | SOUND BL NSA, current affairs recordings • BL NSA, documentary recordings • BL NSA, news recording

Likenesses double portrait, photograph, 1967 (with Cliff Michelmore), PA Photos, London • obituary photographs

Wealth at death £471,300: probate, 5 Aug 2005, *CGPLA Eng. & Wales*

Harris, Ralph, Baron Harris of High Cross (1924–2006), economist and free-market polemicist, was born on 10 December 1924 at 88 Langham Road, Tottenham, London, one of four children of William Henry Harris (*d.* 1941), bus inspector, and his wife, Lilian Maud, *née* Vallé. He was educated at Tottenham grammar school, and won an exhibition to Queens' College, Cambridge, where he read economics, attaining a first in 1948. At Cambridge he was influenced by Stanley Dennison, a classical economist fighting against the Keynesian message of fettered markets and government macro-economic controls.

After graduating Harris worked for Conservative central office, first as an education officer for the newly formed Conservative Political Centre and then for the Conservative research department. In 1949 he moved to St Andrews University, where he lectured in political economy with

Ralph Harris, Baron Harris of High Cross (1924–2006), by unknown photographer, 2002

great success until 1956. On 5 November 1949 he married José Pauline Jeffery, the 22-year-old daughter of Roger Frederick Jeffery, manufacturer. They had a long, happy marriage, which produced two sons and a daughter.

During his time in Scotland Harris unsuccessfully contested two parliamentary seats; the first in Kirkcaldy for the Liberal Unionist Party in 1951 and the second in Edinburgh for the Conservatives in 1955. It was also the beginning of a long association with the *Glasgow Herald*; he started as a leader writer in 1956 and continued to contribute to the paper for the rest of his life. During his time in Scotland he wrote his first book, *Politics without Prejudice*, a political appreciation and biography of R. A. Butler, then thought of as a possible future leader of the Conservative Party.

It was after a speech in 1949 given by Harris for the Conservative Political Centre in East Grinstead that Antony Fisher first mentioned to Harris his discussion with Friedrich Hayek on the setting up of an 'anti-Fabian' think-tank. It was then clear to Fisher that Harris had the necessary persuasive powers to convince a wider audience of the free-market message. Nearly eight years later, in January 1957, Harris started work at the newly formed Institute of Economic Affairs (IEA), having resigned from St Andrews in the preceding spring. It was a risky move, with the IEA's influence and financial security yet to be established. In his typically self-deprecating manner, he later reflected on his decision to give up a secure academic career with a potential move across the River Tay to an academic chair at Queen's College, Dundee, in the offing:

> [a] moment of thought was enough for me to conclude that, even if the Dundee job were offered me on a plate, I would have turned it down … I could not imagine I would ever be qualified for such a rarefied academic distinction. (*Harris in his Own Words*, 19)

Harris's role as general director of the IEA from 1957 to 1987 was to publicize the work of the institute and to act as an intellectual salesman for the Hayekian message it was to propound so effectively for the next thirty years. The IEA needed an editorial director to promote the publication of articles. In February 1957 Harris met Arthur Seldon. It was the perfect match. They both came from working-class roots yet possessed different skills. Seldon was the 'embodiment of intellectual rigour: Harris was an enthusiastic spreader of their message' (Robinson, *Seldon*, 61). In a reflective piece, 'Living with Arthur', Harris later commented on his close relationship with Seldon:

> From our first days together in 1957 I recognised and deferred to Arthur's intellectual pre-eminence … Arthur was a quite exceptional teacher and I positively revelled in my good fortune for 30 years to be his favoured perpetual pupil … I increasingly found myself looking on Arthur as a second brother with whom it would be inconceivable to fall out very seriously or for very long. (*Harris in his Own Words*, 14–16)

In the first few years of the IEA Harris and Seldon found it difficult to recruit like-minded writers due to the prevailing Keynesian paradigm with its emphasis on state intervention, so the two of them wrote many of the early publications themselves. Harris publicized the work by sending it to journalists for review and by inviting academics, journalists, and businessmen for lunch. It was through this network that he also later raised money for the continuing work of the institute. (The initial funding had been provided by Fisher, founder of the Buxted Chicken Company.) Seldon described Harris as 'a past master at selling, persuading and explaining … my salesman as it were' (*Conversation*, 36). The IEA distanced itself from any political party, with Harris abandoning his association with the Conservatives. The IEA papers avoided the constraint of what was politically possible and instead focused on winning the intellectual case for free markets and capitalism. In conversation with Fisher Hayek had suggested: 'Society's course will be changed only by a change in ideas. First you must reach the intellectuals, the teachers and writers, with reasoned argument. It will be their influence on society which will prevail, and the politicians will follow' (Blundell, 17).

The IEA's influence on the Conservative Party started after that party's defeat in the general election of 1964. Keith Joseph, later an architect of the 'Thatcher revolution', found in Harris and Seldon's IEA a theoretical underpinning for his own developing intellectual case for economic liberalism. Geoffrey Howe, later Margaret Thatcher's first chancellor, was also an avid reader of IEA publications, particularly on welfare reform. In a letter to Harris in 1977 Thatcher reflected on the contribution of the IEA to her 'assault on the post-war consensus': 'At times it must have seemed like bashing your head against a brick wall but political historians will, I believe, judge [the IEA] in proper perspective' (Cockett, 173). It was Harris who invited Milton Friedman to dine privately with Thatcher in 1978. Friedman's clear monetarist views on tackling inflation clearly helped to shape the Thatcher government's deflationary policies. Days after winning the general election of 1979 Thatcher asked Harris to take a seat in the House of Lords. The invitation came at a time of personal tragedy for Harris and his family as their son Simon had died suddenly at the age of twenty-six after a long battle 'with drugs and drink which he had at last shown signs of winning' (*Harris in his Own Words*, 22). On a professional front Harris was worried about the implications for the perceived political neutrality of the IEA if he took up a political position in the Lords. Seldon's suggestion that he take a seat on the crossbenches and thus avoid any accusation of politicking allowed him to be Thatcher's first nominee to enter the upper chamber, taking the title Baron Harris of High Cross (the territorial designation derived from the brick monument in the centre of Tottenham).

Harris had already become involved in a number of political campaigns and societies long before entering the Lords. He helped set up the Constitutional Book Club in 1970 with Rhodes Boyson, a state school headmaster and future Conservative minister, and Ross McWhirter, another aspiring Conservative MP. The club produced a series of pamphlets published by the Churchill Press, the most influential probably being the first, *Right Turn* (1970), in which Harris wrote an essay entitled 'The morality of capitalism'. He also campaigned against comprehensivization, fighting a legal battle with other parents to prevent his daughter's school changing status. As chairman of the Wincott Foundation, founded in honour of the financial journalist Harold Wincott, from 1969 to 1995, he celebrated good financial journalism through the foundation's annual awards and lectures. As secretary of the Mont Pelerin Society from 1967, and president from 1982 to 1984, he had regular contact with the leading thinkers behind the classical liberal revival, including Milton Friedman, James Buchanan, George Stigler, Ronald Coase, and Gary Becker. Inspired by Friedrich Hayek, the society brought together the economists who were to inspire the IEA's thinking. In particular Buchanan's 'public choice theory' provided a theoretical framework for an attack on 'big' government in all its guises. The theory attacked the romantic notion that civil servants always act in the public interest and instead suggested that, like those making economic choices in the private sector, their decisions were guided by self-interest. Harris's access to these thinkers, many of them Nobel prizewinners, gave the IEA a willing selection of academic giants to write papers and give lectures.

Harris was forever active in a wide variety of free-market causes. Opened in 1976, following a campaign by Harris, Seldon, and others in 1967–9, and given its royal charter in 1983, the University of Buckingham was Britain's first independent university. Harris served on its council between 1980 and 1995. In 1976 he was appointed honorary secretary of the Political Economy Club, founded in 1821 to support the principles of free trade. During the late 1970s and 1980s several liberal, right-leaning think-tanks emerged, the most notable being the Centre for Policy Studies, started by Keith Joseph in 1974, the Social Affairs Unit, founded in 1980 as an offshoot of the IEA, and the Centre for Research into Communist Economies, founded in 1983 by Harris, Fisher, and Ljubo Sirc. Harris was involved in the influential, right-wing No Turning Back group founded after the Conservative election victory of 1983 and committed to continuing Thatcher's free-market reforms. As the first chairman of the Eurosceptic Bruges Group, established in 1989 by Patrick Robertson, Harris warned of the submersion of Thatcher's reforms by a growing EU committed to socialist rather than free-market solutions. He resigned in 1991 after Robertson attacked the Major government for its policy towards Kurdish refugees. Harris held several boardroom roles after his full-time involvement with the IEA finished, most notably as a director of Times Newspapers (1988–2001).

Perhaps Harris's most controversial position was as chairman of Forest, the pro-smoking lobbying group, from 1989 until his death. An avid pipe-smoker, he abhorred the government's restrictions on smokers, and in one of his most infamous publications, *Smoking out the Truth* (2005), challenged the chief medical officer to provide the supposed evidence that passive smoking seriously damages health. He wrote: 'The imposition of a ban on smoking in so-called public places would … represent a triumph of prejudice and propaganda masquerading as science' (*Smoking*, 17). Harris also courted controversy in the late 1990s by assisting his long-standing friend Neil Hamilton in raising money to support his libel case against Mohammed Al Fayed. Harris refused to name the backers he had persuaded to contribute to the fund when Hamilton lost and Al Fayed demanded payment of his own legal fees by those backers, on the grounds that they had encouraged Hamilton in his action. Having promised confidentiality to the 400 or so contributors, Harris asserted: 'If it was a question of a week in jail for contempt of court then I suppose I'd have to do it' (*Evening Standard*, 22 Dec 1999). In the event the High Court ruled that Hamilton's backers would not have to pay Al Fayed's costs.

With over thirty years at the centre of liberal economic thinking, Harris's contribution to the political landscape of Britain was considerable. From its humble beginnings, the IEA grew to be the leading free-market think-tank in Britain and among the most influential worldwide. At its epicentre stood the unshakeable ideological partnership of Harris and Seldon. Although Seldon was the more prolific writer of the two, Harris undoubtedly provided the crucial marketing prowess to get the message across to a decreasingly sceptical audience. In measuring the IEA's contribution to the intellectual battle of ideas Milton Friedman concluded that:

> As veterans of a major … intellectual battle dating back to the end of World War II, and in the phalanx of people who have promoted ideas of freedom and human liberty, Ralph Harris and Arthur Seldon deserve a place of honour. (*Conversation*, 72)

Harris was of distinctive, and in later years somewhat old-fashioned, appearance, with a centre parting in thinning hair and toothbrush moustache, a blazer, fancy waistcoat, and deerstalker hat, and a meerschaum pipe hanging from his mouth (with several more bulging from a pocket). He was fond of bathing in the sea and was an accomplished conjuror. He was noted for his quick wit, and his speeches in the House of Lords always projected a consistent message with a persuasive eloquence and disarming humour. He died at Barnet General Hospital on 19

October 2006 of hypovolaemic shock following a ruptured aortic aneurysm, and was survived by his wife, José, and daughter, Angela, both sons having predeceased him. NICHOLAS MALONEY

Sources R. Cockett, *Thinking the unthinkable* (1994) • R. Harris and A. Seldon, *A conversation with Harris and Seldon* (2001) • J. Blundell, *Waging the war of ideas* (2001) • S. Usherwood, 'Bruges as a lodestone of British opposition to the European Union', *Collegium*, 29 (winter 2004), 5–16 • R. Harris, *Smoking out the truth* (2005) • *Ralph Harris in his own words*, ed. C. Robinson (2008) • C. Robinson, *Arthur Seldon: a life for liberty* (2009) • *The Times* (20 Oct 2006) • *Daily Telegraph* (20 Oct 2006) • *The Guardian* (20 Oct 2006) • *The Independent* (21 Oct 2006) • *The Herald* [Glasgow] (27 Oct 2006) • Burke, *Peerage* • *WW* (2006) • b. cert. • m. cert. • d. cert.

Archives SOUND BL NSA, current affairs recordings • BL NSA, documentary recordings

Likenesses photographs, 1979–99, Photoshot, London • photographs, 2000–05, PA Photos, London • photograph, 2002, Institute for Economic Affairs, London [*see illus.*] • J. Mingay, photographs, 2005, Photoshot, London • obituary photographs

Wealth at death £303,300: probate, 12 March 2007, *CGPLA Eng. & Wales*

Harrod [*née* Cresswell]**, Wilhelmine Margaret Eve** [Billa], **Lady Harrod** (**1911–2005**), architectural conservationist, was born on 1 December 1911 at New Hunstanton, Snettisham, Norfolk, the daughter of Lieutenant (later Captain) Francis Joseph Cresswell (*d.* 1914) of the Norfolk regiment and his wife, Barbara, *née* ffolkes (1884–1977). Her father was killed in action at Mons in the early stages of the First World War, aged thirty-one, and in 1918 her mother married, as her second husband, General Sir (Edward) Peter Strickland (1869–1951); she was created DBE in 1923 following a gruelling tour of duty with her husband in Ireland. Billa Cresswell's early years were peripatetic because of her stepfather's postings, and she was educated privately and then, briefly, at the Sorbonne. She then became a wardrobe mistress at various London film studios. In the early 1930s she was briefly engaged to John Betjeman, the poet and Victorian conservationist; they remained lifelong friends. She met the economist (Henry) Roy Forbes *Harrod (1900–1978) at Sezincote in Gloucestershire, then owned by the Dugdale family. They married on 8 January 1938, and had two sons. After her marriage Billa Harrod provided hospitality for generations of her husband's colleagues and students at their Oxford house, initially at 6 Beaumont Street, and after 1940 at 91 St Aldates, opposite the entrance to Christ Church meadow. (The latter home was subsequently incorporated, in the early 1980s, into a new quadrangle of Christ Church.) Nancy Mitford reputedly based the character of Fanny in *Love in a Cold Climate* on her. She was first drawn into the conservation movement by the campaign to save Beaumont Street from redevelopment. Her love of her home county had already borne fruit in her writing, with Charles Linnell, the Shell Guide to Norfolk (1957). Her two passions were brought together after her husband's retirement, and their permanent move to Holt, Norfolk, where they had acquired the Old Rectory in 1962. In 1970 she took a leading role in founding the Friends of Norwich Churches, and in 1976 she was the founding chairman of the Norfolk Churches Trust, which raised large sums for the preservation of Norfolk churches, and was in some cases able to restore parish church status to churches that had been made redundant. In 1972 she published *Norfolk County Churches and the Future*, with illustrations by Osbert Lancaster and John Piper, and an introduction by Sir John Betjeman. She was appointed OBE in 1992. She died on 9 May 2005 at her home, the Old Rectory, Holt. She was survived by her two sons.

Sources *The Times* (12 May 2005) • *Daily Telegraph* (12 May 2005) • *The Guardian* (10 June 2005) • b. cert. • m. cert. • d. cert.

Likenesses obituary photographs

Wealth at death £952,796: probate, 24 March 2006, *CGPLA Eng. & Wales*

Hart, Frederick Leslie [Fred] (**1914–2008**), automotive engineer, was born on 12 September 1914 at 25 Pendlestone Road, Walthamstow, Essex, the son of John Octavius Hart (1870–1942), a stock keeper for a provisions dealer, and his wife, Rosina Florence, *née* Callow (1873–1955). He was educated at Walthamstow grammar school. After leaving he worked in the City of London before becoming a landscape architect, meanwhile studying for his engineering qualifications at evening classes. It was not until 1940 that he entered the car industry, joining the Ford motor company as a draughtsman. Initially he was employed in designing armoured military vehicles as part of Ford's contribution to Britain's war effort. On 18 September 1943, at the parish church of St Saviour, Walthamstow, he married Margaret Lydia Bennett (*b.* 1922), daughter of George Henry Bennett, seaman. They had a son, John.

After the war Hart was engaged in designing light motor cars for Ford and by 1957 had achieved the rank of executive engineer. His rise within the company was a reflection of his remarkable talents as an engineer. The first vehicle in whose development he played a central part was the Ford Anglia 105E, a small family car, in 1959. The Anglia was a 'notchback', meaning that its rear window leant back from its base. Following the success of the Anglia, Hart was enlisted in 1960 to play a major role in the development of the Ford Cortina, which became one of the company's best selling cars for two decades. The impetus for this vehicle was to a degree born out of the rivalry between Ford Britain and Ford Germany. Essentially the Cortina project was a riposte to the news that Ford Germany was working on a new, mid-range, front-wheel drive family saloon. British products were normally rear-wheel drives, but Ford Britain then embarked on designing and constructing a rival front-wheel drive car that would be produced at the same time as the German car. The German project was already one year into its development cycle, meaning that the British operation had to be completed in two years if a simultaneous launch was to be achieved.

The Cortina project was led by Ford's project manager, Terry Beckett, with Hart as executive engineer. The British team worked fast, and hard, and its efforts bore fruit in September 1962 when the launch target was met. The Cortina subsequently went through five generations with over 4.2 million cars being sold between 1962 and 1982, when production finally ceased. A notable feature of the

Cortina which was incorporated into the 1964 variant was the innovatory aeroflow heating and ventilation system, offering flow-through ventilation to eliminate stuffiness and increase the accuracy of temperature control, thus standing in sharp contrast to previous heating systems. Hart was heavily involved in this revolutionary system and in advocating its introduction.

Hart was promoted to chief engineer of Ford Britain's car division in 1963. His team was responsible for developing the Corsair, a larger variant of the Cortina, but the Corsair never obtained the Cortina's near-iconic status in the motoring world. Hart was also closely involved in the development and launch in 1966 of the top-of-the-range mark 1V Zephyr and Zodiac models. Both were equipped with independent suspension for both their front and rear wheels, unlike their predecessors.

In 1969 GKN Sankey recruited Hart to become technical director at its Telford base in the west midlands. His expertise was required in the development of a 'proper' (four-wheeled) car for the disabled to replace the existing unstable three-wheeled invalid carriage that was commonly used throughout Britain. Hart's design was much more practical, but also costly, and despite its winning a 1978 Design Council commendation the Labour government refused to back its commercial development and the project withered. Hart retired from GKN Sankey the following year.

Hart was a highly practical man, whose son later recalled his father making for him toys that were a distinct improvement on those they had seen in department stores. In retirement Hart pursued his hobbies of bowls and gardening. He died of bronchopneumonia at his home, Lugano, 3 Powell Road, Buckhurst Hill, Essex, on 15 April 2008 and was survived by his wife and son.

TOM DONNELLY

Sources *Daily Telegraph* (17 July 2008) · 17 July 2008, www.thisisannouncements.co.uk/5858834, 28 June 2010 · b. cert. · m. cert. · d. cert.

Hart [*née* Williams], **Jenifer Margaret** (1914–2005), civil servant and historian, was born on 29 January 1914 in Chelsea, London, the third of five daughters of Sir John Fischer *Williams (1870–1947), barrister, and later a member of the British panel on the permanent court of arbitration at The Hague, and his wife, (Eleanor) Marjorie Hay, *née* Murray (1880–1961), a descendant of John Murray, third duke of Atholl. She was educated at the Lycée Molière and then the Cours Fénelon in Paris, at Downe House, Newbury, and at Somerville College, Oxford, where she graduated with a first-class degree in 1935. She joined the Communist Party later that year. In 1936 she entered the civil service, having been placed third out of 493 candidates. She chose to work in the Home Office, initially in the children's division, before becoming private secretary to Sir Alexander Maxwell in 1939. She subsequently worked as secretary to the committee hearing appeals against detention orders. She was given special dispensation to remain in the civil service after her marriage on 19 October 1941 to the legal philosopher Herbert Lionel Adolphus *Hart (1907–1992).

Two years after the return of peace Jenifer Hart resigned from the civil service, despite her promising career, to join her husband in Oxford. She initially took charge of the programme of university extension lectures in adult education organized by Oxford's extramural department. The department was then a noted centre of socialist intellectuals and teachers opposed to British policy in the early stages of the cold war, and during the two years Hart was there it was the subject of a controversial university investigation into the conduct of certain tutors. A Gwilym Gibbon fellowship at Nuffield College, Oxford, in 1950 enabled her to publish *The British Police* (1951), on the strength of which, in 1952, she was elected to a fellowship in modern history at St Anne's College, Oxford. She published little while at St Anne's, but her article 'Nineteenth-century social reform: a tory interpretation of history' in *Past and Present* (1965) was an important contribution to the academic debate on the development of the British state. Her demonstration of the intellectual and ideological factors influencing the growth of government in the nineteenth century—as opposed to the so-called tory interpretation, which emphasized the role played by well-meaning bureaucrats guided by their experience—was widely accepted by historians. She was a college tutor until her retirement in 1981. In 1992 she published her second book, *Proportional Representation: Critics of the British Electoral System, 1820–1945*, an important scholarly study of the development of ideas of electoral reform.

In 1983 Jenifer Hart's unguarded remarks to a *Sunday Times* journalist led to an article alleging that she had been a spy, and suggesting that her husband might have passed her information during his wartime work with MI5. Following legal proceedings the *Sunday Times* issued a half-hearted apology, but the episode contributed to Herbert Hart's nervous breakdown. In *Spycatcher* (1987) Peter Wright alleged that Phoebe Pool (a Soviet spy who committed suicide in 1971) had named Jenifer Hart as a member of an 'Oxford ring', a supposed covert communist cell. In 1998 Hart published her autobiography, *Ask Me No More*, in which she revealed that friends in the Communist Party had urged her to join the civil service as a 'mole' (p. 70), though she claimed that she had not been 'involved in any deception' (ibid.), that she had never been asked to pass on any secrets, and that she had left the Communist Party by 1939. She died on 19 March 2005 at the Radcliffe Infirmary, Oxford, of heart failure, and was survived by her four children.

Sources J. Hart, *Ask me no more: an autobiography* (1998) · R. Fieldhouse, *Adult education and the cold war* (1985) · L. Goldman, *Dons and workers: Oxford and adult education since 1850* (1995) · *The Independent* (31 March 2005) · *Daily Telegraph* (9 April 2005) · *The Guardian* (11 April 2005) · *The Times* (31 May 2005); (7 June 2005) · m. cert. · d. cert.

Likenesses obituary photographs

Wealth at death £1,452,546: probate, 27 Sept 2005, *CGPLA Eng. & Wales*

Hart, Philip Montagu D'Arcy (1900–2006), physician and medical researcher, was born on 25 June 1900 at 18 Pembridge Gardens, Kensington, London, into a cultivated

Jewish family, the son of Henry D'Arcy Hart (*d.* 1938), a barrister who subsequently gave up the law to become a flower painter, and his wife, Ethel, *née* Montagu (*d.* 1947), daughter of Samuel Montagu, first Baron Swaythling, founder of the bankers Samuel Montagu and Liberal MP. He was educated at Clifton College and at Gonville and Caius College, Cambridge, and completed his medical education at University College Hospital, London, qualifying in 1925. He decided soon after qualifying that clinical medicine was not for him. After spending a very profitable year in New York at the Rockefeller Institute for Medical Research with René Dubos he joined the University College Hospital medical unit. There he began to study tuberculosis, the subject which was to occupy him for most of his professional life.

At that time pulmonary tuberculosis was a major cause of illness and carried a high mortality. At the University College Hospital medical unit Hart first started investigating the usefulness of tuberculin testing (the Mantoux test) in detecting tuberculous infection in a large-scale study of schoolchildren and later in adults. He showed that it was accurately indicative, with a 98 per cent correlation with disease, and provided a valuable indicator for treatment. While silicosis had been long recognized among workers in the hard-rock coalmining industry in Wales, in the mid-1930s there was accumulating evidence that there might be comparable ill health among soft coal workers. In a study instituted by the government through the Medical Research Council in 1936, Hart found that many coalface workers were incapacitated by lung fibrosis (pneumoconiosis), which also predisposed to tuberculous infection. As a result compensation for sufferers was instituted. Hart remained with the Medical Research Council throughout the Second World War, and on 25 October 1941 he married, at St Pancras register office, Ruth Meyer, a 28-year-old hospital radiographer, and daughter of Herbert Meyer, chartered accountant. They had one son.

In 1946 the Medical Research Council created the tuberculosis research unit with Hart as director. When reports from the USA of the value of streptomycin in tuberculosis appeared, he was the secretary of one of the first randomized controlled trials organized by the Medical Research Council, which confirmed its effectiveness. However, resistance developed so frequently that there was a requirement for multiple therapy and in due course other agents came along, notably PAS and isoniazid. With triple therapy, resistance was largely eliminated and was virtually universally effective. Hart showed that treatment could be just as effective in ambulant patients, a matter of great public health importance that sounded the death-knell for sanatoria and had a tremendous importance for the treatment of tuberculosis in developing countries. The value of this was notably established as a result of a clinical trial carried out by his colleague Wallace Fox in an impoverished population in Madras. In the 1950s Hart carried out a controlled trial of bacillus Calmette-Guérin (BCG) vaccine against tuberculosis infection among schoolchildren, which showed it to be about 80 per cent effective, although with local variation.

In 1965 Hart (who was made a CBE in 1956) retired as director of the tuberculosis research unit but he moved into laboratory work at the National Institute for Medical Research, first at Hampstead and then in the new location at Mill Hill. His interest was in the biology of the mycobacterium in the host cell and he was working latterly with an electron-microscopist, John Armstrong. Their investigation concentrated on the reasons for the failure of the lysosome reaction in macrophages, which destroys most classes of ingested micro-organisms, to deal with tubercles, which thus resulted in persistence of the living bacteria in the cell. This problem was still being investigated at the time of his death.

Hart (always known as Philip or P. M. D'Arcy Hart) was deeply involved in the relation of medicine to society, particularly to its less fortunate members; he was a long-standing member of the Socialist Medical Association and was active in the pro-republican Medical Aid Committee during the Spanish Civil War. He was a member of the Tots and Quots, a dining club of scientists concerned with economic, social, and political issues. He was rather a shy person but had a wry sense of humour and could be a witty speaker. In his younger days he had been a keen flyfisher but due to increasing physical disability had to give it up. He never lost his enthusiasm for science.

Aged ninety-eight, Hart gave the keynote address at a British Medical Association conference recognizing the fiftieth anniversary of the streptomycin trial. He continued to work in the laboratory past his hundredth birthday; his mind remained very active although his deafness and failing vision finally forced him to retire for a second time in 2002. Having lived latterly at 37 Belsize Court, Camden, London, Hart died there on 30 July 2006. He was survived by his wife, Ruth, and their son, Oliver, professor of economics at Harvard University.

Arnold Burgen

Sources G. Watts, 'Why a 1940s medical committee should not be forgotten', *BMJ*, 323 (2001), 360 · *The Times* (16 Aug 2006) · *The Independent* (24 Aug 2006) · *BMJ*, 333 (26 Aug 2006), 449 · *The Guardian* (30 Aug 2006); (12 Sept 2006) · *The Lancet*, 368 (2 Sept 2006), 836 · E. M. Tansey, *Journal of the Royal Society of Medicine*, 99 (Oct 2006), 535–7 · Munk, *Roll* · E. M. Tansey, Philip Montagu D'Arcy Hart (1900-2006), www.jameslindlibrary.org/trial_records/20th_Century/1940s/MRC_lancet_1944/hart_biog.html, 24 Aug 2007 · www.mrc.ac.uk/Achievementsimpact/Storiesofimpact/Tuberculosis/index.htm, 24 Aug 2007 · *WW* (2006) · personal knowledge (2010) · private information (2010) · b. cert. · m. cert. · d. cert.

Archives FILM Oxford Brookes University, interview by Kenneth Citron, 18 Oct 2001

Likenesses N. Sinclair, bromide print, 1994, NPG · obituary photographs

Wealth at death £2,664,610: probate, 17 Jan 2007, *CGPLA Eng. & Wales*

Hartley, Marie (1905–2006), artist, historian, and collector, was born on 25 September 1905 at Middleton Road, Morley, Yorkshire, the only daughter and elder child of Harry Hartley, a prosperous shoddy, or felt, manufacturer, and his wife, Gertrude, *née* Hinchliffe, whose family made woollen cloth in the town and presented a window symbolizing Aspiration to Morley town hall. Hartley's parents were active Methodists and she and her brother John were sent to Ackworth School, near Wakefield, run by the Society of Friends, which retains a delicately drawn plan of the buildings, one of her earliest surviving illustrations. She also learned much from Morley's famously independent spirit and her family's place in it. The Hartleys owned two mills and were in the tradition of the Morley dashers, business people who could not wait to dash home from the neighbouring and rival town of Leeds. The Morley Dashers pub in the town's high street commemorates them.

The Hartleys' local business associates included the Asquith family, whose scion Herbert Henry Asquith was a leading Liberal politician throughout Marie Hartley's youth and prime minister when she was a teenager. Like him she set her horizons further afield than the clannish West Riding town of their birth, and after private painting lessons with the Yorkshire artist Owen Bowen she enrolled at Leeds College of Art, where she concentrated on engraving, taught by Owen Jennings. Her generation of students included Henry Moore and Barbara Hepworth, and like them she went to London, winning a place at the Slade School of Art in 1921. There she specialized in wood engraving and developed her 'quiet eye', an unintrusive but exact style of observation that was central to her life's work as artist and historian of the Yorkshire dales.

Family holidays in the beautiful valleys had quickened Hartley's interest in the dales' distinctive ways of life. She also knew that these were fast disappearing. Eager to record them, she returned from London after graduation to live in Wetherby, where her parents had retired. From there she conducted forays in search of views and interviews, along with her friend **Ella Pontefract** (1896/7–1945), a would-be writer from a similar textile background in Lindley Moor, near Huddersfield. She was the younger daughter of John Henry Pontefract and his wife, Emma, and had been educated at the Wheelwright Grammar School, Dewsbury, and Highfield School, Harrogate. The Pontefracts moved to Wetherby after a business setback, building a new house that spoilt the Hartleys' view, but the two families had so much in common that they became fast friends. Ella Pontefract later became vice-president of the Association of Yorkshire Bookmen.

The two women soon became impatient with day trips up the A1, and bought a caravan to tow behind their car, christening it the Green Plover, and settling like the distinctive dales bird in local communities for weeks at a time. Their collaboration gained immediate success with the publication of their first book, *Swaledale*, by J. M. Dent and Sons in 1934. This was followed by *Wensleydale* (1936) and *Wharfedale* (1938). Pontefract supplied the text in each case and Hartley the illustrations. Their curiosity was not confined to the dales, and the eleven books they produced before Pontefract's death included a collection of illustrated essays on the county's best churches that had originally appeared in the *Yorkshire Weekly Post* (1936) and a tour of the whole of Yorkshire (1939). But in 1939 they found a derelict seventeenth-century cottage, Colehouse, in the Wensleydale village of Askrigg, and the Green Plover came to rest.

War work with the ambulance service in Wetherby delayed their planned restoration of Colehouse but in 1942 Hartley and Pontefract collaborated with a team of local craftsmen, including Robert Thompson, 'the Mouseman of Kilburn', who left three of his trademark carved mice in the house. This project increased Hartley's interest in local skills and the tools involved. Forays up the valleys seldom ended without ancient examples of cooking or farming equipment being stashed in the car boot. Colehouse soon began to resemble a museum, although never a fusty one; rather it was the busy base for an early example of rescue archaeology. Typical of many expeditions, Hartley and Pontefract drove to Leyburn in 1941 when they heard that a jumble of local curiosities known as Horne's Private Museum was to be sold. They bought thirteen lots, including a rare packhorse collar with seven bells and a jug used at Wesleyan Methodist love feasts for 200 years. Ella Pontefract died in Harrogate on 23 February 1945; Marie Hartley published a memoir of her, *Yorkshire Heritage*, in 1950.

The treasures accumulated by Hartley and Pontefract formed the basis of a nationally significant collection that Hartley continued to acquire with her second companion and collaborator, **Joan Alicia Ingilby** (1911–2000). A cousin of the Ingilby family of Ripley Castle, near Ripon, she was born in North Stainley, near Ripon, on 11 December 1911, the younger daughter of Lieutenant-Colonel John Uchtred Macdowall Ingilby (1874–1948), army officer, and his wife, Marjorie Cecily, *née* Phelips (*d.* 1957). She was educated at a girls' school in Norfolk and wrote poems from an early age; some of these were published in *Country Life*, *Time and Tide*, and other publications in the 1930s. She took over Pontefract's role as Hartley's collaborator in a further twenty-two books.

Hartley developed an interest in photography, taking her own photographs and becoming skilled in tracking down a marvellous archive of both ancient and contemporary prints. She also increasingly contributed to the text of her books. Her hand is evident in such studies as *Life and Tradition in West Yorkshire* (1976), which described the snarling, bruzzing, and wuzzing of recalcitrant wool strands in her native textile town, and included two full pages of acknowledgements to local manufacturers. Its companion volume, *Life and Tradition in the Yorkshire Dales* (1968), and *The Old Hand Knitters of the Dales*, published by *The Dalesman* magazine in 1951, are considered Hartley and Ingilby's classics. Their other great lasting achievement was the Dales Countryside Museum in Hawes, Wensleydale, which developed from the Colehouse artefact collection, which they donated when it overflowed to North Riding county council in 1974. The museum opened to the public in 1979.

Hartley's warmth and enthusiasm endeared her to dales people, whose fundamental sense of content she in turn admired. She and Ingilby were awarded the silver medal of the Yorkshire Archaeological Society in 1993, were appointed MBE in 1997, and received honorary degrees from the Open University in 1999. Joan Ingilby died on 27 October 2000. Marie Hartley continued publishing after

Ingilby's death, including studies of the making of butter, boots, and cartwheels. She died of a stroke at Colehouse on 10 May 2006, only a few weeks after corresponding with the Yorkshire Archaeological Society to correct details of the history of local Wensleydale mills. She was cremated at Harrogate nine days later, and her ashes were scattered with those of Ingilby on the summit of the hill behind their home, overlooking both Wensleydale and Swaledale. A memorial service was held at Askrigg on 17 June. MARTIN WAINWRIGHT

Sources *The Times* (28 Feb 1945); (13 Nov 2000) · M. Hartley, *Yorkshire heritage: a memoir to Ella Pontefract* (1950) · *Daily Telegraph* (17 Nov 2000); (26 May 2006) · *Yorkshire Post* (13 May 2006); (20 May 2006); (24 May 2006); (26 May 2006); (30 May 2006); (4 Oct 2006); (15 Nov 2006); (3 Feb 2007) · *The Guardian* (17 May 2006) · Morley Community Archives, www.morleyarchives.org.uk, 19 Aug 2009 · www.thedales.org.uk/MarieHartleyMBE, 19 Aug 2009 · W. Yorks. AS, Hartley papers · Dales Countryside Museum, Hawes, Hartley and Ingilby collection · personal knowledge (2010) · private information (2010) [Thelma Bannister, niece] · b. cert. · d. cert.

Archives Dales Countryside Museum, Hawes · Yorkshire Archaeological Society, Leeds | SOUND BL NSA, documentary recording

Likenesses T. Spencer, photograph, 1965 (with Joan Ingilby), Getty Images, London, Time and Life pictures · obituary photographs · photographs, repro. in www.thedales.org.uk/MarieHartleyMBE · photographs (Joan Ingilby), repro. in www.thedales.org.uk/MarieHartleyMBE · photographs (Ella Pontefract), repro. in www.thedales.org.uk/MarieHartleyMBE

Wealth at death £1,540,021: probate, 15 Nov 2006, *CGPLA Eng. & Wales* · £7404 0s. 8*d*.—Ella Pontefract: administration with will, 28 June 1945, *CGPLA Eng. & Wales* · £501,815—Joan Ingilby: probate, 30 Jan 2001, *CGPLA Eng. & Wales*

Hastings, Sir Stephen Lewis Edmonstone (1921–2005), politician, was born on 4 May 1921, at 13 Washington House, Basil Street, Knightsbridge, London, the only son of Major Lewis Aloysius Macdonald Hastings (1880–1966) and his wife, Meriel Eda St John (1888–1971), daughter of Neil Edmonstone, lieutenant-colonel in the 4th hussars. His father had absconded from Stonyhurst College after being accused of homosexuality, and went to southern Africa, where he prospected for diamonds, joined the Cape Mounted Police, became a political organizer, and commanded the emergency reserves during the Johannesburg strikes of 1913. After war service he bought a tobacco farm in Southern Rhodesia in 1922, founded the Southern Rhodesian Tobacco Growers' Association, and was MP for the Lomagundi constituency in the Southern Rhodesian parliament from 1931 until his return to England in 1939 to rejoin the army. He became one of the most popular and pungent of the BBC's war correspondents, and made his first parachute jump at the age of sixty-three. Brandishing his stick, he liberated Bremen town hall in 1945, and was among the first to enter Buchenwald concentration camp. He was a remote but heroic figure in his son's boyhood; his sturdy individualism, contempt for doubters, imperial pride, intrepid war service, and mistrust of progressive beliefs were exemplary for his son.

A bout of malaria resulted in Stephen Hastings's return from Rhodesia to live in Berkshire with his maternal grandmother, who doted on him as a surrogate son and

Sir Stephen Lewis Edmonstone Hastings (1921–2005), by Bassano, 1948

encouraged his lifelong passion for horses. He was educated at Durnford School, Langton Matravers, Dorset (1929–34), Eton College (1934–9), and the Royal Military College, Sandhurst (1939). After being commissioned into the Scots Guards on the outbreak of the Second World War, he fought against the Italians and Germans in the desert until 1943, when he joined the Special Air Service and participated in daring raids in Benghazi and elsewhere. He was briefly aide-de-camp to Richard Casey, minister resident in Cairo, before training as a Special Operations Executive (SOE) agent. In 1944 he was parachuted behind enemy lines in the Apennines, and organized three divisions of about 4000 Italian partisans, who seized Piacenza and held a bridgehead over the Po for three days. He was awarded the MC. After the war he was based in Vienna as personal assistant to the head of the economic division of the control commission in Austria (1946–8).

In 1948 Hastings was recruited by a friend of his father's into the Secret Intelligence Service (MI6). Under the guise of an assistant military attaché at the British legation in Helsinki (1950–53) he watched the Russian bear during a freezing phase of the cold war. He was posted to the British embassy in Paris in 1954–8, and then to Cyprus as first secretary in the political office of the Middle East forces' headquarters during the guerrilla war with EOKA. He was in post in Paris at the time of the Hungarian uprising and the Suez débâcle, and, in disgust at the mood of national retreat in Britain, applied to Conservative central office to join the parliamentary candidates' list. This resulted in his election as Conservative MP for Mid-Bedfordshire at a by-election in 1960.

Just as Lewis Hastings scorned the influence in Britain of 'the Nancy Left' and 'bottle-party intellectuals' (L. Hastings, 224, 256), so his son regarded socialism as an egregious mixture of the ideas of Karl Marx, John Knox, and Father Christmas. He was an effective Commons performer, thorny in his questioning of ministers and adept at calling for emergency debates. A forceful speaker, with an officer's authoritative tones, he was upright and gallant, but out of tune with his parliamentary leaders, though his views chimed with many party members.

In 1961 Hastings paid the first of many political visits to Rhodesia, and he soon became a vocal opponent of official British policy in southern Africa. He opposed immediate majority black rule, and felt that the Macmillan government was surrendering to African nationalist extremism. When the Rhodesian prime minister, Ian Smith, unilaterally declared independence in 1965 Hastings rebelled against his party's line, and opposed economic sanctions. His support for the Rhodesian rebels rendered him ineligible for office under Edward Heath's leadership (1964–75). He opposed the Lancaster House agreement of 1979, which created Zimbabwe and brought Robert Mugabe to power. He was a stalwart member of the Monday Club, and deplored Whitehall defeatism, Commonwealth idealism, and American prejudice against British colonialism. Julian Amery and Ronald Bell were his diehard allies in resisting decolonization and multiculturalism.

Hastings's connection to the security services was well known, and he monitored communist infiltration of British trade unions and institutions in the 1960s and 1970s. In 1976–8 he formed a secret advisory committee, code-named Shield, which also included Nicholas Elliott of MI6 and Brian Crozier, to brief Margaret Thatcher and her shadow cabinet colleagues on communist subversion in Britain. Shield adduced evidence that there was a plot to turn Britain into a communist state on the east European model, and in the Commons in 1977 Hastings named five trade union leaders whom Czech intelligence officers had tried to suborn on behalf of the KGB. The Shield committee's recommendation of a counter-subversion executive to act as a cold war equivalent of SOE, under MI6, was defeated by Lord Carrington, the shadow foreign secretary, at a meeting in 1978 chaired by Thatcher, and attended by, among others, Sir Keith Joseph and William Whitelaw. Hastings obtained libel damages from *The Observer* in 1986 after that newspaper named him as part of an MI5 plot to oust Harold Wilson.

As a backbench MP, Hastings became a non-executive director of several companies, including Anglo-European Marketing Ltd and the Handley Page aircraft factory at Cricklewood. This led him to a keen interest in the aviation sector. He deplored the cancellation in 1965 of the TSR2 tactical strike aircraft as a betrayal both of British strategic power and of aeronautical manufacturing, and published his polemic *The Murder of TSR2* in 1966. The book was dismissed in some quarters as the result of heavy, embittered briefing by special interests. His pillorying of Lord Mountbatten and Lord Zuckerman, who had put their weight into the scales against TSR2, and of the Treasury for mishandling the project's steeply rising costs and squandering technical expertise, showed his powers of invective, but the book was thoughtful in its analysis of the difficulties when the rate of scientific development outstrips managerial organization, and in drawing lessons for the nuclear energy and electronics sectors. Hastings was also active in campaigns to stop a large airport being built in the vale of Aylesbury.

Hastings was knighted in July 1983, a month after his retirement from parliament. A painter, sculptor, and raconteur, who drank with gusto and had a great sense of fun, he loved horses and Labradors, hunted regularly with the Quorn, and was president of the British Field Sports Society in 1982. His autobiography, *The Drums of Memory*, was published in 1994.

Hastings married, on 29 September 1948, Harriet Mary Elizabeth Jephson (*b.* 1921), a widow, daughter of Colonel Julian Latham Tomlin, director of posts and telegraphs in the Sudan. They had a son and a daughter. This marriage was dissolved in 1971, and in September 1975 he married Elizabeth Anne Marie Gabrielle (1934–1997), formerly wife of Sir Vivyan Naylor-Leyland, third baronet, and ostensible daughter of the second and last Viscount Fitzalan of Derwent. Her mother, before her birth, had become the lover of the tenth and last Earl Fitzwilliam, and ultimately married him: Elizabeth Hastings inherited the Fitzwilliam estates at Milton, Castor, Cambridgeshire, and Malton, Yorkshire, on his death in 1979. Hastings became a director of the Fitzwilliam Estates Company (1980–97), partner and manager of the Milton Park stud, and joint master of the Fitzwilliam hunt. In 1995 he led an appeal for funds for the preservation and development of Peterborough Cathedral, and raised £7.3 million by the end of 2000. He died of cancer of the oesophagus on 10 January 2005, at his home, Stibbington House, Wansford, Cambridgeshire. He was buried in the churchyard of St Mary the Virgin, Marholm, on 18 January, following a funeral service at St Kyneburgha's Church, Castor, near Peterborough. A memorial service was held at Peterborough Cathedral on 17 April 2005. He was survived by the two children of his first marriage.

RICHARD DAVENPORT-HINES

Sources S. Hastings, *The drums of memory* (1994) · L. Hastings, *Dragons are extra* (1947) · B. Crozier, *Free agent* (1993) · *Daily Telegraph* (11 Jan 2005) · *The Times* (13 Jan 2005); (15 Jan 2005); (24 Jan 2005) · *Peterborough Evening Telegraph* (13 Jan 2005); (19 Jan 2005) · Burke, *Peerage* · *WW* (2005) · b. cert. · m. cert. [1948] · d. cert.

Likenesses Bassano, half-plate film negative, 1948, NPG [*see illus.*] · Bassano, two half-plate film negatives, 1948, NPG · G. Argent, bromide print, 1960, NPG · Elliott & Fry, vintage print, 1960, NPG · double portrait, photograph, 1960 (with J. More), PA Photos, London · photographs, 1960–67, Photoshot, London · obituary photographs · photographs, repro. in Hastings, *Drums of memory*

Wealth at death £589,071: probate, 10 June 2005, *CGPLA Eng. & Wales*

Hatch, Sir David Edwin (1939–2007), broadcasting executive, was born on 7 May 1939 at Hulme Walfield vicarage,

Congleton, Cheshire, the fourth and youngest son of Raymond Harold Hatch (1893–1971), Church of England clergyman, and his wife, Winifred Edith May, *née* Brooks (1900–1987). He was educated at St John's School, Leatherhead, and went to Queens' College, Cambridge, to read theology but switched to history and then gained a diploma in education. In a career-defining moment he joined the Cambridge Footlights and in 1963 performed in the summer revue, *A Clump of Plinths*, alongside Tim Brooke-Taylor, John Cleese, Graeme Garden, and Bill Oddie. The show, renamed *Cambridge Circus*, ran in London and went on to play in New Zealand and New York.

When he returned to London Hatch and several of the cast joined the BBC's radio light entertainment department and created the comedy show *I'm Sorry I'll Read That Again* (1964), billed as a 'radio custard pie'. Hatch's role in the sketches was as the straight man trying to calm the nonsense and hold things together, prefacing, some were to claim, his later life as a BBC boss. Between the first and second series of the programme, on 18 July 1964, Hatch, describing himself as a journalist, married, at the parish church of Wedmore, Somerset, Ann Elizabeth Martin (1938–1997), nurse and daughter of Christopher George Martin, carpet merchant. They had two sons and a daughter.

Hatch became producer of *I'm Sorry I'll Read That Again* while still performing in it, and began producing other radio entertainment shows, notably the first series of *Just a Minute* (1967), and in 1970 originating with Simon Brett the long-running topical sketch show *Week Ending*. He took his first step into management in 1974 as the radio network editor in Manchester, where he made an 'audacious' attempt to have the *Today* programme run from the north (Hendy, 178). In 1978 he returned to London as head of radio light entertainment, seeking to create a 'buzz' in what was a steady, traditional department (ibid., 194). He brought in writers from television and introduced a competition for new writers so that by the end of the following year there were more than forty new people writing for radio comedy. He took his showmanship with him when he became controller of Radio 2 in 1980. He brought Kenny Everett back to the BBC, brightened up the *Jimmy Young Show*, and made Gloria Hunniford the first woman to have a daily show on the network.

Hatch's next job, as controller of Radio 4 (from 1983 to 1986), posed his greatest challenge. He inherited a network that had shed 6 million listeners over the previous ten years yet had a passionate audience which, as he put it, asked, 'Please give us some new programmes—but don't change anything'. He recited to his team the network schedule from ten years earlier to show how little had changed and warned, 'Numbers are not unimportant, even on a cultural channel' (Hendy, 301). His big experiment was *Rollercoaster*, a non-stop magazine programme running throughout the morning. The press, the BBC governors, the director-general, and editorial colleagues were all sceptical or against the experiment and Hatch suffered a torrent of listener abuse. He boldly asked the audience to write, and they did: 'Go back to Radio 2' (ibid., 303). He ended the programme after a year. It had increased the audience but it was expensive and savings were required. He cherished the custodianship of Radio 4 and sought to introduce to the relentlessly serious network more joy and delight. When Brian Wenham was brought from television to be managing director of radio in 1986 Hatch was promoted to director of programmes, with a seat on the board of management, to provide the necessary knowledge and understanding of radio. He took over from Wenham the following year.

Hatch was the bold advocate of radio, recognized by colleagues on the board as canny, fair, and straight dealing. He left the converted windmill in Buckinghamshire where he lived at the crack of dawn in order to arrive at Broadcasting House early to look in on studios at radio's peak audience time and then to unleash the handwritten notes that all who worked with him recalled with fondness. He wrote to stars, producers, agents, and colleagues, to praise them, warn, commiserate, criticize, and encourage, always with warmth and a passion for the BBC. One friend received a piece of advice signed, 'Cluck, cluck. Mother Hen' (private information). Radio flourished under his leadership, though his biggest innovation, the launch of Radio 5, was an awkward mixture of education, sport, and children's programmes culled from the other radio networks as they became more focused. The network never took off and in 1994 was replaced by an all news and sports network, Radio 5 Live.

When John Birt became director-general of the BBC in 1993 he replaced Hatch as managing director of radio but kept him on the board of management as his adviser. Hatch was disappointed but with customary energy and loyalty threw himself into this new and difficult role, springing to Birt's defence when he was attacked over his employment status. He was an invaluable voice for the staff, for radio, and for old BBC values in a time of rapid change and some turmoil.

Hatch was appointed CBE in 1994 and retired from the BBC in 1995. He was appointed chairman of the National Consumer Council (1996–2000); his chairing skills, attention to detail, and motivating notes helped the organization through a testing time when relations with government were scratchy. It was a mighty blow when his wife, Ann, died of cancer in 1997. The following year his friends Terry and Helen Wogan introduced him to Mary Philomena Clancy (*b.* 1948/9), daughter of Michael Clancy and company secretary of the Clancy Docwra building company. They married on 13 February 1999 at Farm Street Catholic Church, Westminster.

Hatch had long been a JP and in 2000 became chairman of the parole board for England and Wales, the first not to come from a government-service background. He was a vigorous advocate of the board's independence and gave a shot in the arm to the morale of staff, throwing an annual party at his own expense. He defended the policy of releasing as many prisoners as possible, as he believed that it weaned them off crime and helped relieve prison overcrowding. Having been a member of the board of Services

Sound and Vision Corporation (which provided broadcasting for British servicemen and women around the world) from 1981, in 2000 he was made chairman. He was knighted in 2004 on retirement from the parole board. The last few years were a very happy time in Hatch's life—he enjoyed with his wife a house in Cape Town, racing, the theatre, walking, and parties. In the spring of 2007 he was diagnosed with pancreatic cancer. He died at home in Chalfont St Giles, Buckinghamshire, on 13 June. He was buried in Chalfont St Giles on 25 June, and a memorial service was held at All Souls, Langham Place, London, on 3 October 2007. He was survived by his wife, Mary, and the three children of his first marriage.

Hatch was one of the few in the BBC to progress from performer to senior management, and he retained the performer's ability to listen both to the public and to those who created programmes. He was the doughty champion of radio in what appeared to be the era of television and he brought a generous heart, warmth, and wit to everything he did. Shortly before his death he was visited by his old friend John Cleese, who was greeted by Hatch pulling down the sheets to reveal a T-shirt that read, 'I'm going underground'. WILL WYATT

Sources *Broadcast* (29 May 1978) · *Daily Telegraph* (12 Dec 1983) · *The Listener* (17 May 1984) · *Sunday Express* (14 March 1993) · J. Abramsky, lectures at Exeter College, Oxford, 2002 · J. Birt, *The harder path* (2002) · W. Wyatt, *The fun factory: a life in the BBC* (2003) · D. Hendy, *Life on air: a history of Radio Four* (2007) · *The Times* (14 June 2007); (15 June 2007) · *The Independent* (14 June 2007) · *Daily Telegraph* (16 June 2007) · *The Guardian* (16 June 2007) · *WW* (2007) · personal knowledge (2011) · private information (2011) · b. cert. · m. certs. · d. cert.
Archives FILM BFINA, current affairs footage | SOUND BL NSA, documentary recordings · BL NSA, performance recordings
Likenesses obituary photographs
Wealth at death £351,077: probate, 20 Dec 2007, *CGPLA Eng. & Wales*

Hatto [*married name* Barrington-Coupe], **Joyce Hilda (1928–2006)**, pianist, was born on 5 September 1928 at 65 Canterbury Terrace, Kilburn, London, the only child of Horace Hatto, a baker and confectioner who later became an antiques dealer, and his wife, Dorothy Hilda, *née* Vincent (*d.* 1994). Accounts of her schooling, musical training, and early career—many reliant on Hatto's own anecdotes—have varied considerably. She attended what is now Copthall School, Mill Hill, and took early piano lessons from her music-loving father, going on to study for the Trinity College, London, initial examination, which she passed with honours in 1938. Her first formal teacher was Marian Holbrooke (sister of the composer Joseph), from whom, according to a later interview, Hatto learned 'what it takes to be a really good teacher' (James, 'Interview').

During and after the Second World War, Hatto was mentored by the Russian-Jewish *émigré* conductor Serge Krish. Through him she met Alfred Cortot, Benno Moiseivitch, and other famous musicians about whom she was later apt to reminisce in interviews and correspondence. She attended Morley College, London, studying composition with Mátyás Seiber from 1948, and trained privately

Joyce Hilda Hatto (1928–2006), by Vivienne, 1972

between 1950 and 1954 with Frederic Jackson, professor of piano at the Royal Academy of Music, taking work through him as part-time répétiteur for the nascent London Philharmonic Orchestra Choir, which she helped prepare for concerts and recordings under Victor de Sabata, Sir Thomas Beecham, and other conductors. In 1951 she met William Halford Barrington-Coupe (*b.* 1931), a concert promoter who became her agent and whom she married on 8 September 1956. He was to be the crucial figure in her life.

Hatto's career developed promisingly through the 1950s with recitals throughout England, concerto appearances with the Haydn and Boyd Neel orchestras, and foreign tours, notably to Poland in 1958. Her impressive piano technique was honed by Ilona Kabos, and by Zbigniew Drzewiecki in Warsaw and London. From the late 1950s through to the mid-1970s she often appeared in concert programmes at London's Festival and Wigmore halls, playing popular concertos with the London Symphony and other orchestras, as well as solo recitals. Many featured the music of Liszt and Chopin, two composers suited to her theatrical, bravura style. In 1971 she became a board member of the society formed to promote the latter's work, and she gave the modern première of two recently discovered Chopin *bourrées* at the Queen Elizabeth Hall in 1973. She was also active as a teacher, both privately and at schools such as Crofton Grange, Hertfordshire, where her pupils included the novelist Rose Tremain.

When her husband served eight months in Ford prison (1966–7) for purchase tax evasion Hatto's teaching work expanded. After his release the couple mounted a series of concerts featuring the best of her pupils at the Purcell Room (1968–70). Meanwhile, for her husband's various record labels, Hatto had made some fifteen LPs or EPs of concertos and solo works during the late 1950s and 1960s, recorded in England, Germany, and France. Most positively received were two pioneering issues of music by Arnold Bax, notably the première recording of his technically demanding *Symphonic Variations*, with the Guildford Symphony Orchestra under Vernon Handley in 1970. It has been claimed that serious illness affected her work during and after those sessions; and certainly a mixture of poor houses and lukewarm reviews during the early 1970s affected her confidence. *Daily Telegraph* reviews referred to 'lapses of concentration' and 'her very overwrought condition' (Williams, 'Joyce Hatto'). Recalling her final London appearance on 7 July 1976 Andrew Ball, later professor of piano at the Guildhall School of Music and Drama, said: 'It was extraordinarily accident-prone and just very bizarre playing … it had some of the affectations of a great pianist without any of the goods' (ibid.).

After that Wigmore Hall débâcle Hatto and her husband retired from the public eye, although she continued teaching. In 1992 she was diagnosed with an inoperable ovarian cancer, but alternative herbal treatments helped prolong her life. In her last decade well over one hundred recordings attributed to her appeared on Barrington-Coupe's Concert Artist label, many receiving enthusiastic praise from internet groups and magazines such as *Gramophone*. The *Boston Globe* described her (on 21 August 2005) as 'the greatest living pianist that almost no one has ever heard of', but even then doubts were being expressed as to the feasibility of her feats, given her advanced illness and age.

Hatto died at her home, 12 Tall Trees, Royston, Hertfordshire, on 29 June 2006, of ovarian cancer and deep vein thrombosis and was cremated in Cambridge on 11 July. The obituaries were laudatory. *The Guardian* described her as 'one of the greatest pianists Britain has ever produced … Her legacy is a discography that in quantity, musical range and consistent quality has been equalled by few pianists in history' (10 July 2006). However, in February 2007 it emerged that many of the CDs attributed to her were copies, in some cases digitally altered, of published commercial recordings by other pianists. The sound engineer Roger Chatterton of Kite Studios, Cambridge, claimed his involvement amounted to manipulating the tonal balance of varied source recordings he received direct from Barrington-Coupe, to render the sound uniform. The scandal made headlines worldwide, not least for the damage done to the reputation of critics taken in by the deception.

Barrington-Coupe initially expressed bafflement, but subsequently partially admitted the fraud. He claimed that he had merged portions of other pianists' work with his wife's recordings, to cover up her 'gasps of pain' (*The Sunday Times*, 4 March 2007), and that Hatto was unaware of the deception. Many commentators doubt this version of events. In a telephone interview given to Radio New Zealand on 6 April 2006 (broadcast on 28 May) Hatto gave no indication that she was anything other than sole pianist on the CDs; several reports attest to the couple's bitterness against the musical establishment, and the likelihood is that the fraud was conceived largely to consolidate a once promising professional reputation, to which her husband too had contributed much.

Christopher Webber

Sources *The Boston Globe* (21 Aug 2005) · *The Guardian* (10 July 2006); (27 Feb 2007) · *The Times* (26 July 2006); (27 Feb 2007); (6 March 2007) · *Daily Telegraph* (28 July 2006); (27 Feb 2007) · *The Independent* (14 Aug 2006); J. Duchen, 'Joyce Hatto: notes on a scandal' (26 Feb 2007); (27 Feb 2007) · C. Joseph and A. Luck, 'Revenge of the fraudster pianist', *Daily Mail* (24 Feb 2007) · *Sunday Times* (4 March 2007) · R. Williams, 'Joyce Hatto: the great piano swindle', *Intelligent Life* (Sept 2007) · M. Singer, 'Fantasia for piano', *New Yorker* (17 Sept 2007) · B. James, 'Joyce Hatto: a pianist of extraordinary personality and promise', *Music Web International*, 2003, www.musicweb-international.com/classrev/2003/Mar03/Hatto.htm, 28 June 2008 · C. Webber, 'Bax's *Symphonic variations*: a comparative review', 10 Feb 2004, www.musicweb.uk.net/bax, 28 June 2008 · A. Orga, 'Joyce Hatto: the artist and the recordings', *Music Web International*, Jan 2006, www.musicweb-international.com/classrev/2006/Jan06/Hatto_Orga_1.htm, 28 June 2008 · 'Joyce Hatto: some thoughts, some questions and a lot of letters', *Music Web International*, Feb 2007, www.musicweb-international.com/classrev/2007/Feb07/Hatto_Howell.htm, 28 June 2008 · A. Rose, 'Joyce Hatto: the ultimate recording hoax', *Pristine Classical*, 5 March 2007, www.pristineclassical.com/HattoHoax.html, 28 June 2008 · *Gramophone* online archive, www.gramophone.net, 28 June 2008 · newsgroup archive, http://groups.google.com/group/rec.music.classical.recordings, 28 June 2009 · J. Hatto, diary, priv. coll. · private information (2010) [W. Barrington-Coupe, husband] · b. cert. · m. cert. · d. cert.

Likenesses F. Ramage, photograph, 1954, Getty Images, London, Hult. Arch. · Vivienne, photograph, 1972, priv. coll. [*see illus.*]

Wealth at death £343,661: probate, 14 June 2007, *CGPLA Eng. & Wales*

Hauser, Frank Ivor (1922–2007), theatre director, was born on 1 August 1922 at 37 Park Place, Cardiff, the fourth of five children of Abraham Hauser (1888/9–1966) and his wife, Sarah, *née* Cohn (1889–1970). His father was a Polish Jewish émigré who became a naturalized British subject, and served with the Royal Flying Corps during the First World War. He worked first as a ship's chandler in Barry dock, Glamorgan, and subsequently as a property dealer in Cardiff. There were two daughters (Rachel and Lena), followed by three sons. Frank's brothers were Lewis, who became a queen's counsel and judge, adopting the surname Hawser, and Eric, a solicitor.

Frank Hauser was educated at Cardiff high school (1932–40), where he showed promise as a pianist and actor. He began directing at Christ Church, Oxford, where he took a wartime degree in English literature (1941–7), interrupted by service as a Royal Artillery lieutenant (1942–5), first with the Eighth Army in north Africa and later with the Jewish brigade in Italy. The assistant librarian of Christ Church claimed that his college production of Jean-Jacques Bernard's *The Unquiet Spirit* 'attained the highest honours in modern Oxford stage history' (Hiscock, 195). His tutor, Lord David Cecil, recommended him to the

BBC. After taking a second-class degree in 1947 he became a radio producer with the corporation (1948–51), gaining a reputation among actors and listeners as a director of European drama. He broadcast versions of Shakespeare's *Henry V* with Richard Burton and of Anouilh's *Antigone* with Alec Guinness. He resigned regretfully (in January 1951) when Guinness invited him to co-produce a West End revival of *Hamlet*, starring Guinness himself. The production never recovered from a gremlin-plagued first night and for nearly a year Hauser was out of work, until in 1952 the Arts Council invited him to run Salisbury Arts Theatre. From there he moved in 1953 to the Coventry-based Midland Theatre Company.

In 1956 Hauser formed Meadow Players to reopen the Oxford Playhouse. He remained there for seventeen illustrious years. Inspired by his Midland Theatre Company production of Betti's *The Queen and the Rebels* with Irene Worth and Leo McKern, which transferred to the Haymarket Theatre (1955), his aim was unashamedly upmarket. He focused on the 'heavyweight' European dramas 'written about but not performed' (Hauser, 'The uncommitted theatre', *Plays and Players*, Oct 1962), casting them with the stars he had cultivated at the BBC and the promising actors he had a talent for spotting, and relying on transfers and touring to underwrite his programme.

Despite £2000 from Burton, Hauser ended his first year deep in debt. Then the English première of Anouilh's *Dinner with the Family* (1957) began a stream of London transfers. They included Achard's *Rollo* with McKern (1959), Santha Rama Rau's version of Forster's *A Passage to India* with Zia Mohyeddin (1960), *Hamlet* with Jeremy Brett (1961), Shaw's *Misalliance* with Barbara Jefford and John Turner (1963), Julian Mitchell's version of Ivy Compton-Burnett's *A Heritage and Its History* (1965), Jonson's *Volpone* with McKern and Leonard Rossiter (1966), Arbuzov's *The Promise* with Judi Dench, Ian McKellen, and Ian McShane (1967), and Sartre's *Kean* with Alan Badel and Felicity Kendal (1971). In between he gave the Greek director Minos Volanakis free rein to revive Greek classics including *The Oresteia* (1961), to introduce audiences to a number of Genet plays, and to direct classics like Giraudoux's *The Madwoman of Chaillot* with Elisabeth Bergner (1967) and Brecht's *The Good Woman of Setzuan* with Sheila Hancock (1968).

Hauser led company tours to Europe (1958, 1959) and to India, Pakistan, and Sri Lanka (1959–60). Opera productions for Sadler's Wells and Glyndebourne further enhanced his reputation; and the takeover of the Playhouse by Oxford University in 1961 and its reconstruction as a university theatre in 1963 with his former manager Elizabeth Sweeting as administrator relieved him of maintaining the fabric. But professionals and students proved uneasy bedfellows. Hauser felt the dons undervalued his work (as was made clear in his article 'A great white wail', *Oxford Magazine*, 21 Jan 1965) and the theatrical climate was against him. While Eric Shorter said critics could still look to Hauser for 'something really challenging' like Racine's *Phèdre* (*Daily Telegraph*, 11 Jan 1966), Robert Muller had compared his work unfavourably with that of Peter Hall and George Devine (*Daily Mail*, 2 Nov 1961). While continuing to champion his efforts, the Arts Council struggled to fund the growing number of regional companies and civic theatres. Hauser's decision to join the Royal Opera House and Sadler's Wells in 1969, servicing Britain's major provincial theatres for the Dramatic and Lyric Theatre Association, proved his undoing. The three lacklustre productions that followed *Kean*, a revival of *Othello* with Badel that he directed himself, and *The Merry Wives of Windsor* and *A Man for All Seasons*, for which his deputy was responsible, gave the Arts Council the excuse to cease funding Meadow Players as a major company, prompting Hauser to resign and the directors to wind up his company.

Hauser bowed out with a glittering summer festival, of which the centrepiece was Molnar's *The Wolf* with McKern, Dench, and Edward Woodward (1973), which promptly transferred to the Apollo Theatre. Even his final pantomime, *Cinderella* (1973–4), resurfaced in London with Twiggy. The farewell party the profession staged for him, *Pussies Galore* (he called all actors, regardless of gender, Pussy), showed the high regard he commanded. Judi Dench said: 'He's been too loyal to the Playhouse. It's time he shared himself round' (*Oxford Mail*, 21 Jan 1974).

Hauser's career never again scaled the heights that had earned him his appointment as CBE in 1968. Nor as a freelance director was he able to exercise the talent for breathing theatrical life into fragile literary texts that had won him acclaim at Oxford and on tour for such rarities as Auden's *The Sea and the Mirror* (1968) and Browning's *Pippa Passes* (1968). He directed the odd production in Greece, Australia, and New York as well as several in the West End, including Dryden's *All for Love* at the Old Vic (1977) and Shaw's *Captain Brassbound's Conversion* with Penelope Keith at the Haymarket (1982). He teamed up for the final time with McKern at the 1995 Chichester festival with a revival of Brighouse's *Hobson's Choice*. Meanwhile he built on the reputation he had gained as a teacher from his Playhouse schools days with valuable work for the British and American Drama Academy and the University of California, Davis. His versions of foreign classics continued to hold the stage and helped fund a Frank Hauser bursary for student directors at Birkbeck College, London. Nevertheless he failed to gain the place many thought he deserved in the theatrical establishment. He died at a residential care home, Nightingale House, 105 Nightingale Lane, Balham, of Lewy body dementia on 14 October 2007 and was cremated on the 28th at Putney Vale crematorium, Stag Lane, Putney. He never married.

DON CHAPMAN

Sources W. G. Hiscock, *A Christ Church miscellany* (1946) · *Oxford Mail* (21 Jan 1974) · *The Guardian* (18 Oct 2007) · *The Times* (19 Oct 2007) · *The Independent* (23 Oct 2007) · D. Chapman, *Oxford Playhouse: high and low drama in a university city* (2008) · taped interview with Don Chapman, 24–6 Aug 1999, Oxfordshire RO, Oxford · V&A, theatre collections, Meadow Players archive · Oxfordshire RO, Oxford, Oxford Playhouse records, Frank Hauser file · Glamorgan RO, Cardiff, Cardiff High School archive · Frank Hauser file, BBC WAC · Frank Hauser clippings and picture files, Oxford Mail and

Times Archive · *WW* (2007) · private information (2011) [Eric Hauser, brother] · b. cert. · d. cert.

Archives BBC WAC, Frank Hauser file | Oxfordshire RO, Oxford, Oxford Playhouse records · V&A, theatre collections, Meadow Players archive | SOUND BL NSA, documentary recordings · Oxfordshire RO, Oxford, interview with D. Chapman, 24–6 August 1999

Likenesses obituary photographs · photograph, Oxford Mail and Times Archive; repro. in Chapman, *Oxford Playhouse*, 162 · photograph, repro. in www.oxfordplayhouse.com/anniversary/playhouseplayers.html · photograph, repro. in www.notesondirecting.com/content/authors.html · portraits, Oxford Mail and Times Archive

Wealth at death under £76,000: probate, 17 April 2008, *CGPLA Eng. & Wales*

Hawkes, John Gregory [Jack] (**1915–2007**), botanist, was born on 27 June 1915 at 9 Clarence Place, Kingsdown, Bristol, the only child of Charles William Hawkes, a journeyman house decorator who later became a teacher in a technical school, and his wife, Gertrude Maude, *née* Chappell. He first attended a dame school in Bristol, then Stroud elementary school, followed by Cheltenham grammar school (1929–34). He won a place at Christ's College, Cambridge, and graduated with first-class honours in natural sciences in 1937; he completed his PhD in 1941 under the supervision of the noted potato breeder and historian Redcliffe N. Salaman. The university awarded Hawkes the degree of ScD in 1957. On 20 December 1941 he married, at Cambridge register office, Barbara Ellen Leather, who was working as an organizing secretary in Norwich for the Workers' Educational Association. Three years younger than Hawkes, she was the daughter of Charles Henry Leather, secondary school teacher. They had two daughters, born in 1944 and 1946, and twin sons born in Colombia in 1950.

On graduation in 1937 Hawkes had successfully applied for the position of assistant to P. S. Hudson, director of the Imperial Bureau of Plant Breeding and Genetics in Cambridge, for an expedition to Lake Titicaca in the Andes. In the event this expedition did not materialize due to Hudson's poor health, but Hawkes joined another in 1938–9 to Peru, Argentina, Bolivia, Ecuador, and Colombia, led by E. K. Balls, a professional plant collector. Thus began his lifelong interest in 'the humble spud'. In order to prepare himself for the expedition, and because he recognized that he 'knew virtually nothing about the scientific aspects of potato species' (*Economic Botany*, 2), he received permission to travel to Leningrad to meet the Russian scientists S. M. Bukasov and S. W. Juzepczuk, who had already collected potatoes in South America, and to seek their advice about the planned British expedition. It was during this visit that he met the world-famous geneticist Nikolay Vavilov, whom he described as 'a colossus among his colleagues both within and outside the USSR' (Hawkes, 11). He acknowledged that it had been 'a privilege to have known him', and was certain that Vavilov's influence helped to shape his career (ibid., 11). During the visit he also met the controversial Trofim Lysenko, whose influence with Stalin led to the banning of Mendelian genetics in the Soviet Union for a generation. Hawkes did not like Lysenko one little bit and thought him 'a dangerous and wholly repellent person … a politician rather than a scientist' (ibid., 14). Lysenko's ascendancy led to Vavilov's disgrace and early death in 1943.

John Gregory Hawkes (1915–2007), by unknown photographer

The 1938–9 expedition was the first of more than a dozen major plant-collecting trips that Hawkes made to South and Central America in search of wild potato species, which became the basis for his taxonomic treatment of potatoes, first published in 1956, with several later revisions. He had a long collaboration with the Danish botanist J. Peter Hjerting, with whom he published two major monographs on the wild potatoes of Argentina, Brazil, Paraguay, and Uruguay (1969) and Bolivia (1989), emphasizing not only the taxonomy but also breeding relationships to facilitate their use in potato improvement.

From 1948 to 1951 Hawkes was seconded to the Colombian government to establish a potato research station. Nelson Estrada, a renowned Colombian potato breeder, was one of his protégés, and their hybridization research became a model for potato breeding programmes. Not long after returning to the UK, Hawkes was appointed lecturer in taxonomic botany at the University of Birmingham in 1952, and he remained there until his retirement in 1982. In 1961 he received a personal chair in taxonomic botany, and in 1967 was appointed Mason professor of botany and head of department. In addition to his lifelong research on potatoes he spearheaded scientific interest in the *Solanaceae* plant family, which also includes the tomato, tobacco, chilli peppers, and aubergine, and many species with pharmaceutical properties. With his colleagues at Birmingham in the late 1950s he developed serological methods to study relationships between potato species. He was also one of the leading lights in the production of a computer-mapped flora of Warwickshire, a first of its kind, published in 1971.

One of Hawkes's most important legacies, stemming from his work on potatoes, was his participation in and contributions to the nascent genetic resources conservation movement of the 1960s. He joined the United Nations Food and Agriculture Organization's (FAO) panel of experts led by the eminent wheat breeder Sir Otto Frankel, which also included the plant collector Erna Bennett and the cereals expert Jack Harlan, among others. They envisaged a worldwide effort to conserve plant genetic resources in a network of gene banks, and gave impetus to international efforts to collect and conserve plant varieties that were threatened with extinction. These efforts led eventually to the establishment of the International Board for Plant Genetic Resources in Rome, under the auspices of the FAO. Hawkes was chairman of the European Association for Plant Breeding Research's gene bank committee for thirty years from 1961. He actively supported the genetic resources programme at the International Potato Center in Lima, Peru, from 1973, and several of his PhD students did their research there. He also acted as scientific adviser to the Commonwealth Potato Collection in Scotland (founded from germplasm he had collected in 1939) and the United States department of agriculture potato collection at Sturgeon Bay, Wisconsin.

Shortly after being appointed Mason professor of botany Hawkes received support from the university to develop a one-year course in plant genetic resources. In September 1969 just five students enrolled on an MSc course that was subsequently offered for almost four decades. This was significantly longer than Frankel had predicted when Hawkes first mooted the idea, and by 2008 over 1400 MSc and three-month short course students from more than 100 countries had studied at Birmingham, many becoming genetic conservation leaders in their own countries. The course (and its successor) was the only formal training of its kind in the world.

Hawkes received many honours and awards, including the Frank N. Meyer memorial award from the American Genetic Association for services to plant introduction in 1973, and the distinguished economic botanist award from the Society for Economic Botany in 1996. In 1984 he received the Linnean medal from the Linnean Society of London, of which he was later elected president (1991–4), a role that gave him immense satisfaction. He was appointed OBE for services to botany in 1994. He received many other honours, but what probably gave him most pleasure were the Vavilov medal and honorary professorship of the N. I. Vavilov Institute of Plant Industry in 1999, of which he was the second recipient and the first non-Russian. In a sense his life's work had come full circle from the moment in 1938 when he had met the great geneticist at the institute that later bore his name.

After his retirement from the university Hawkes continued to publish actively. In 2004 his memories of the 1938–9 expedition—and his initiation into the world of the potato—were published under the title *Hunting the Wild Potato in the South American Andes*. In all he published 240 scientific works. After Barbara died in 2005, and increasingly frail, he left his home of more than fifty years in Harborne, Birmingham, and moved to Reading to be near his family. He died at Austen House Care Home, Lower Earley, Reading, on 6 September 2007, and was survived by his four children. MICHAEL T. JACKSON

Sources *LondG* (11 June 1994) [suppl.] · 'J. G. Hawkes, distinguished economic botanist: reply to AWARD, 4 July 1996', *Economic Botany*, 51/1 (Jan 1997), 2–5 · M. T. Jackson, 'Jack Hawkes: plant collector, researcher, educator and visionary', *Managing plant genetic diversity*, ed. J. M. M. Engels and others (2002), xv–xvi · J. G. Hawkes, *Hunting the wild potato in the South American Andes: memories of the British empire potato collecting expedition to South America, 1938–1939* (2004) · *Daily Telegraph* (21 Sept 2007) · *The Independent* (18 Oct 2007) · *The Times* (7 Nov 2007) · R. Croston, 'Biography of Jack G. Hawkes', www.eucarpia.org, 1 Feb 2010 · *WW* (2009) · personal knowledge (2011) · private information (2011) · b. cert. · m. cert. · d. cert.

Likenesses obituary photographs · photograph, priv. coll. [*see illus.*]

Wealth at death £517,841: probate, 7 Jan 2008, *CGPLA Eng. & Wales*

Haycraft [*née* Lindholm], **Anna Margaret** [*pseud.* Alice Thomas Ellis] (**1932–2005**), publisher and novelist, was born on 9 September 1932 at 2 St John's Road, Wallasey, Birkenhead, the only child of John Richard Alfred Lindholm, a supervisor of a general stores' packing department, and later works manager, and his Welsh-born wife, (Gladys) Alexandra Irene, *née* Griffiths. She was originally named Anne, but later changed her name to Anna. She went to Bangor county grammar school after her parents moved to north Wales, and on to Liverpool School of Art. Her father was half Finnish and her parents belonged to a group called the Church of Humanity, which preached a high-minded atheism. In reaction against her parents' belief, she became a Roman Catholic at the age of nineteen because she 'no longer found it possible to disbelieve in God' (*Daily Telegraph*). After dropping out of Liverpool Art School she spent a year as a postulant nun with the order of Notre Dame in Liverpool, but left after slipping a disc: the nuns refused to take anybody with a health disorder. In later years she would occasionally announce to her husband and children that she had always intended to be a nun and would one day join a contemplative order.

Anna Lindholm moved to London, arriving in 1950s bohemian Chelsea, and found temporary work in a delicatessen. One of the customers was Colin Berry *Haycraft (1929–1994), who was living near the King's Road. With a first in Greats from Oxford, Haycraft, son of an army officer, had worked as personal assistant to his cousin Cecil Harmsworth King on the *Daily Mirror* but found his true vocation in publishing, and moved to Weidenfeld and Nicolson, where he started its academic imprint, the World University Library. He immediately fell in love with the dark-eyed beauty behind the counter, and on 15 December 1956 they married, at the Roman Catholic chapel of Our Lady of the Rosary, Dwygyfylchi, Caernarvonshire. From this time Anna Haycraft established a style that hardly changed over the years—kohl-rimmed eyes and black clothes, with the occasional Jean Muir during more prosperous years.

Anna Haycraft's stated view of human relationships was: 'There is no reciprocity. Men love women. Women love children and children love hamsters' (*The Independent*). The greater part of her life was absorbed by motherhood. She had seven children: five sons, William, Joshua, Thomas, Oliver, and Arthur, and two daughters, Sarah and Rosalind. Born prematurely, Rosalind died after two days. In 1978 her second son Joshua died, aged nineteen, after some months in a coma. He had fallen through a roof at Euston station while train-spotting. His death profoundly affected his mother, who likened the continuing pain to a form of amputation.

In the early 1960s the Haycrafts bought 22 Gloucester Crescent, Camden Town, for £4000. Within a few years the crescent of large Victorian houses had become one of the most fashionable streets in London. Their close neighbours included Jonathan Miller, Alan Bennett, A. J. Ayer and Dee Wells, and Nick and Claire Tomalin. The street even gave rise to a cartoon in *The Times* about media types, *NW1*. The Haycrafts' house became a meeting place for bohemian culture, and the champagne cocktails mixed by Colin were renowned for inducing riotous behaviour.

In 1968 Colin Haycraft decided with a partner, Tim Simon, to buy the publishing house of Duckworth, which had been founded by Virginia Woolf's half-brother in 1898. After the death of his partner from cancer, Haycraft became sole proprietor and moved the offices to the Old Piano Factory, Oval Road, close to their home. From 1970 Anna was in charge of fiction, while Colin concerned himself with the scholarly list. Beryl Bainbridge, who became a close friend of the Haycrafts, was the best known of the novelists whom Anna encouraged and published. As an editor, she was inspirational. She was unfailingly encouraging to young writers, and for a few years from 1993 ran a writing course, with the novelist Shelley Weiner, from her second home in Wales. It was notable for the après-writing, when wine and conversation flowed till the early hours.

In 1977, aged forty-five, Anna Haycraft published her own first novel, *The Sin Eater*, under the pseudonym Alice Thomas Ellis. It was published while her son Joshua was in a coma after his accident, and it was his death, she said, that made her go on writing. Her novels are spare, elegantly written black comedies, poignant with a touch of the supernatural. After *The Sin Eater*, which exposed the violent rancours of Welsh, Irish, and English, and won a Welsh Arts Council award, she published *The Birds of the Air* (1980); *The 27th Kingdom* (1982), short-listed for the Booker prize; *The Other Side of the Fire* (1983); and *Unexplained Laughter* (1985), which won the Yorkshire Post book award. Her trilogy *The Clothes in the Wardrobe* (1987), *The Skeleton in the Cupboard* (1988), and *The Fly in the Ointment* (1989), about infidelity and betrayal, was filmed for television as *The Summerhouse*, starring Jeanne Moreau. *The Inn at the Edge of the World* (1990), winner of the 1991 Writers' Guild award for fiction, alluded to Celtic myth, and *Pillars of Gold* (1992) was an urban satire. This was followed by a collection of stories, *The Evening of Adam* (1994), and a novel about the mysterious appearance of a newborn baby in a remote corner of Wales, *Fairy Tale* (1996). In 1999 she was made a fellow of the Royal Society of Literature.

Anna Haycraft also wrote non-fiction, again mainly as Alice Thomas Ellis, and her popular column 'Home life' in *The Spectator* was published in four collections by Duckworth between 1986 and 1989. This account of domestic life was like a pithy soap opera, where readers got to know and love the various characters, such as the frequently mentioned Janet, who began as nanny to the Haycraft children, and moved on to be secretary, chauffeur, and general organizer to Anna. Anna Haycraft published a volume of memoirs, *A Welsh Childhood* (1990), and books on food, beginning with her first ever book, *Natural Baby Food: a Cookery Book* (1977, as Brenda O'Casey). *Darling, You Shouldn't Have Gone to So Much Trouble*, co-written with Caroline Blackwood (1980, as Anna Haycraft) featured recipes involving such ingredients as tinned sardines, Spam, baked beans, and lashings of alcohol. Her last book also centred on food: *Fish, Flesh and Good Red Herring: a Gallimaufry* (2004), a quirky history of cookery through the ages.

In her more controversial non-fiction, Haycraft (still writing as Alice Thomas Ellis) attacked the liberal wing of the Roman Catholic Church, objecting to nuns in slacks and 'happy-clappy stuff'. She published the polemical *Serpent on the Rock: a Personal View of Christianity* in 1994. A fervent traditionalist (she attended the sung Latin mass at St Dominic's Priory in Kentish Town), she criticized progressive bishops in her column in the *Catholic Herald*. In 1996 she attacked Derek Worlock, the liberal archbishop of Liverpool, who had died three months previously of cancer. Sacked by the *Catholic Herald*, in response to demands from the Catholic hierarchy, she moved on to *The Oldie*, where she continued her column as 'The God slot'—published in 2004 in a collection as *God Has Not Changed*.

As someone who was tolerant of family chaos and friends' muddled lives, Haycraft's firm stance on religious orthodoxy seemed contradictory. And although she didn't much like eating, she enjoyed writing about food and cooking meals for her friends—though she rarely sat down to eat, preferring to throw in occasional remarks, cigarette in hand, while leaning against the Aga. Her novels featured independent-minded women, but she was staunchly anti-feminist. She despised 'new age' theologies, yet possessed a Celtic awareness of the mystic.

The Haycrafts' later years in publishing were beset by financial troubles. In 1988 Colin sold a 50 per cent share in Duckworths to an investor but in 1991 he was forced to buy back his shares in order to regain control. The stress affected his health and he died of a stroke on 24 September 1994. With Robin Baird-Smith as publisher, Anna Haycraft remained as fiction editor for several years. In 2001 she sold the house in Gloucester Crescent and moved to Trefechan, a farmhouse at Pennant Melangell in Montgomeryshire. Surrounded by mountains, reached by a single-track lane, with the nearest shop five miles away, it was not an ideal place for someone who didn't drive.

There she worked on *A Gallimaufry*, and her columns for *The Oldie* and other journals. In 2003 she was diagnosed with lung cancer and underwent an apparently successful operation. Cancer was diagnosed again early in 2005. She claimed to feel no fear at the prospect of death, only 'huge excitement' (*Daily Telegraph*). She died at Meadow House Hospice, Ealing Hospital, Southall, London, on 8 March 2005. The funeral Latin requiem mass, with plainsong, at St Ethelreda's, Ely Place, London, was officiated by Kit Cunningham, an old family friend who had also conducted Colin's funeral eleven years earlier. She was buried in the churchyard of St Melangell at Pennant Melangell, close to her husband, and her son Joshua.

CLARE COLVIN

Sources A. T. Ellis, *Home life* (1986) · A. T. Ellis, *More home life* (1987) · A. T. Ellis, *Home life three* (1988) · A. T. Ellis, *Home life four* (1989) · A. T. Ellis, *A Welsh childhood* (1990) · *The Times* (10 March 2005) · *Daily Telegraph* (10 March 2005) · *The Guardian* (10 March 2005) · *The Independent* (10 March 2005) · *The Observer* (20 March 2005) · *WW* (2005) · personal knowledge (2009) · private information (2009) · b. cert. · m. cert. · d. cert.

Archives NL Wales, Kyffin Williams MSS | FILM BFINA, current affairs footage | SOUND BL NSA, interview with B. Mooney, B7957 · BL NSA, current affairs recording

Likenesses S. Clarke, photograph, 1997, Rex Features, London · D. Santini, C-type colour print, *c*.1997, NPG · J. Bauer, photograph, repro. in *The Independent* · obituary photographs

Wealth at death £651,151: probate, 27 June 2006, *CGPLA Eng. & Wales*

Hayes, John Trevor (1929–2005), art historian and museum director, was born on 21 January 1929 at 18 Fursby Avenue, Finchley, London, the elder son of Leslie Thomas Hayes, actuary, and his wife, Gwendoline, *née* Griffiths. He was educated at Ardingly College and at Keble College, Oxford, where he graduated with a second-class degree in modern history in 1951. He went on to the University of London's Courtauld Institute of Art in 1952, where he gained a distinction in the postgraduate diploma in the history of art in 1954. In 1962 he received the degree of PhD from the Courtauld Institute for his thesis on the landscape paintings of Thomas Gainsborough.

Hayes's first post was at the London Museum, where in 1954 he was appointed assistant keeper by the director, Sir Mortimer Wheeler. Four years later he was awarded a Commonwealth Fund fellowship that took him to the Institute of Fine Arts in New York and gave him the opportunity to travel across the United States to see public and private art collections. He forged many friendships during his year there and returned regularly over the following four decades. During his early years at the London Museum he organized a number of exhibitions, including in 1956 one on Anna Pavlova, which reflected his lifelong passion for ballet. In 1970 he was appointed director of the London Museum but the following years were difficult for him, since the proposed amalgamation with the Guildhall Museum and the plans to move from Kensington Palace to new premises, designed by Powell and Moya at London Wall, were not entirely to his liking. As director he appointed younger staff, established a modern department under the direction of Colin Sorensen, and, with very modest resources, continued to organize successful exhibitions such as that devoted to Mary Quant's London in 1973.

When in 1974 he failed to be appointed director of the new Museum of London, Hayes applied successfully to succeed Roy Strong as director of the National Portrait Gallery. His twenty years as director witnessed a highly successful period in the gallery's history. Outstanding monographic exhibitions like those devoted to Van Dyck in England, Sir Peter Lely (both curated by Sir Oliver Millar), Johan Zoffany, and Sir Thomas Lawrence continued to enhance the gallery's burgeoning reputation as a centre for scholarship in historic British portraiture. Shortage of space at the gallery's cramped St Martin's Place premises was an issue that Hayes urgently wished to address and, although plans to move to the South Bank or to Canary Wharf in the later 1980s were not supported by the trustees, in 1987 Hayes persuaded Margaret Thatcher's government to purchase the freeholds on Orange Street, immediately to the north of the gallery, which allowed for expansion to house the gallery's extensive archives, administrative and curatorial offices, and conservation departments. In 1989 the newly remodelled ground floor of the gallery, with new twentieth-century galleries and the Wolfson exhibition gallery providing more space, was opened. Substantial funding for both these projects came from private donations, notably £2 million from the Heinz Foundation, and the new Orange Street extension opened in November 1993, just months before Hayes's retirement.

Hayes was a notable exponent of outstations in the regions for the National Portrait Gallery, believing in the principle of putting on public display as many of the nation's pictures as possible. In 1979 collaboration with the National Trust resulted in the opening of Beningbrough Hall, near York, where many eighteenth-century works not on display at the gallery could be shown. A few years later Bodelwyddan Castle in Denbighshire became available for the display of nineteenth-century portraits. Hayes also pioneered the 'acceptance-in-lieu' scheme, which allowed works allocated to public museums in lieu of tax to be retained in their historic setting, such as the fine group of paintings by Mytens and Gainsborough at Arundel Castle.

During Hayes's directorship the National Portrait Gallery made many important acquisitions, especially of eighteenth-century figures, including portraits by Reynolds of Laurence Sterne, by Gainsborough of J. C. Bach, and by Hogarth of the mathematician William Jones, as well as superb marble busts of Lord Chesterfield by Roubiliac and of Alexander Pope by Rysbrack. A subtle shift in policy could be detected in the gallery's attempts to ensure that acquisitions were not only of important historical figures but were high-quality works by leading artists. Hayes also had a profound interest in contemporary portraiture and in 1979 persuaded the trustees to extend the collecting policy to allow commissions. In 1980 he established the annual portrait award, initially sponsored by John Player and then later by BP, which led to the gallery's significant role in the revival of portraiture in the 1980s. In addition to acquiring important modern works like Graham Sutherland's *Self Portrait* Hayes commissioned such popular works as Bryan Organ's portrait of Lady Diana Spencer, just before her marriage to the prince of Wales in 1981, and he also encouraged talented young portrait painters like Sarah Raphael.

Throughout his tenure at both the London Museum and the National Portrait Gallery Hayes remained a prolific author. Soon after his arrival at the London Museum he began to publish learned articles in the *Burlington Magazine* and *Apollo* and he continued his profound interest in the work of the eighteenth-century painter Thomas Gainsborough. In 1960 he organized a small exhibition of the artist's work for the Arts Council and in 1970 he published the first full catalogue, *The Drawings of Thomas Gainsborough*. This was followed a year later by *Gainsborough as a Printmaker* and in 1982 by a catalogue, *The Landscape Paintings of Thomas Gainsborough*. His catalogue entries were of unprecedented thoroughness, despite the lack of hard evidence about the dating of many of Gainsborough's works, and, after the death of Sir Ellis Waterhouse in 1985, Hayes was for some time unchallenged as the leading Gainsborough scholar. He organized two further exhibitions of the artist's work for the Tate and the Grand Palais in Paris in 1980–81 and for Ferrara Arte in Italy in 1998. His last major publication on Gainsborough was an edition of *The Letters of Thomas Gainsborough* (2001). His interests were, however, much more wide-ranging and he published books on Rowlandson in 1972 and on Graham Sutherland in 1980. As an accomplished cataloguer he was also in demand internationally and his catalogue of the British paintings in the National Gallery of Art, Washington (1992), was followed by a catalogue of the British paintings in the Cincinnatti Art Museum, which remained unpublished at the time of his death.

Hayes's shy and diffident public manner could be misleading, and he enjoyed the companionship of his friends and the conviviality of the Beefsteak and Garrick clubs. He was a keen tennis player in his youth at Keble and an avid devotee of the opera and ballet. Among his greatest pleasures was foreign travel, especially by train and road. He always claimed his fearlessness as a driver resulted from learning to drive in Manhattan in the late 1950s. Excursions abroad were meticulously planned to ensure stopovers where Michelin-starred restaurants were to be found so that he could indulge his passion for excellent food. He was, however, essentially an intensely private man, and friends were often bemused that despite knowing him for decades he remained as enigmatic as on first meeting. His management style as a museum director was to delegate as much as possible, not only to give his colleagues experience but so that he could continue to pursue his own research and writing. At the time of his death he was preparing a catalogue of the subject pictures of Gainsborough and was honorary editor of the project to produce a full catalogue of Gainsborough's portraits.

Hayes was chairman of the Walpole Society from 1981 to 1996 and vice-president from 1996 until his death. He was elected a fellow of the Society of Antiquaries of London in 1971 and was appointed CBE in 1986. He never married and his only brother, Peter, predeceased him. In August 2005 he suffered a severe stroke which left him partially paralysed and with speech difficulties. He died at the Chelsea and Westminster Hospital, London, from complications related to his condition on Christmas day 2005.

BRIAN ALLEN

Sources *Daily Telegraph* (4 Jan 2006) • *The Guardian* (13 Jan 2006) • *The Times* (14 Jan 2006) • *The Independent* (24 Jan 2006) • *WW* (2005) • private information (2009) • personal knowledge (2009) • b. cert. • d. cert.

Likenesses A. Newman, bromide print on card mount, *c*.1973, NPG • N. Parkinson, group portrait, bromide print, 1981 (*The staff of the National Portrait Gallery*), NPG • C. Hafenrichter, group portrait, bromide print, 1984 (*Trustees and senior staff of the National Portrait Gallery*), NPG • T. Leighton, group portrait, C-type colour print, 1987 (*The staff of the National Portrait Gallery*), NPG • J. Ward, chalk drawing, 1990, NPG • P. Sayer, bromide fibre print, 1990–94, NPG • T. Leighton, group portrait, C-type colour print, 1993 (*The staff of the National Portrait Gallery*), NPG • J. T. Oman, group portrait, colour snapshot print, 1994, NPG • D. Weightman, group portrait, digital C-type colour print from original negative, 2004, NPG • obituary photographs

Wealth at death £657,999: probate, 16 Feb 2006, *CGPLA Eng. & Wales*

Haynes, John Norman [Johnny] (**1934–2005**), footballer and businessman, was born on 17 October 1934 at the Middlesex Hospital Annexe, St Pancras, London, the son of Edward Robert Haynes, printer's packer, later Post Office clerical assistant, of 3 Grafton Terrace, St Pancras, and his wife, Rose Clara, *née* Newton, Post Office telephonist. Brought up in Edmonton, north London, he was an outstanding schoolboy football player who quickly brought himself to the attention of a wider audience when he starred for England schoolboys against Scotland at Wembley on 15 April 1950. The match was shown on live television, a rare event in those days, and England won 8–2. His progress was noted by Tottenham Hotspur and Arsenal, the latter of which he supported. He visited Arsenal with his father but decided that to go to a club with so many good players might hinder his progress. He later wrote that Highbury seemed more like the stock exchange than a football club. A fellow north London schoolboy had already signed for Fulham and that may have influenced Haynes to do the same. Fulham were a mid-table second division club, but Haynes would be a key factor in elevating them into one of the most fashionable in the capital; their followers included many of the west London entertainment set. His first two seasons were largely spent on loan to the non-league clubs Feltham, Wimbledon, and Woodford Town, before he made his début in the football league against Southampton on Boxing day 1952. Between then and January 1970 he made a further 593 league appearances, scoring 146 league goals, 9 more in 44 FA cup games, and 2 in 20 football league cup matches.

Though right-footed, Haynes had a fine left foot and was a regular goalscorer, but it was his passing that marked him out as exceptional. He probably gave the right pass at

John Norman Haynes (1934–2005), by Ken Coton, 1966

the right moment more often than any of his contemporaries, mostly from a central midfield position. He was a master of all the distances but it was the cross-field pass from left to right, setting the wing-forward free, or the long through ball to a forward roaming clear of the centre of the opposition's defence, that were his specialities. He was a very hard worker, both on and off the field, and a supporter of coaching and a more thoughtful approach to the playing of the game, attitudes not always welcomed by his contemporaries. He was also very self-critical and could easily become frustrated not only by his own failings but by those of his colleagues.

Two defeats by Hungary and a disappointing performance in the 1954 world cup persuaded progressives at the FA to set up an under-twenty-three team to aid the process of developing a more successful national side. The England manager, Walter Winterbottom, was given more time to prepare the England team for international fixtures, and results improved. Haynes became a key player, appearing in thirteen of the sixteen unbeaten matches between November 1955 and November 1957. The death of eight Manchester United players in the Munich air crash in February 1958 disrupted the progress of the England team and thereafter they were exciting and frustrating in turn, and somewhat unlucky in the world cups of 1958 and 1962. By then Haynes had been the captain in twenty-two successive internationals and no one could have been more upset by this failure of potential.

If success at international level proved elusive Haynes was a major beneficiary of the agreement between the Football League and the Professional Footballers' Association to remove the maximum wage in 1961. The chairman of Fulham, the comedian Tommy Trinder, had occasionally joked that Haynes was worth one hundred pounds a week, and after the abolition of the maximum wage Haynes became the first English player to earn that sum, although it was only half of what he would have received if Fulham had allowed him to move to Milan. He was probably one of the first professional footballers to employ an agent and he had begun to take advantage of other commercial opportunities, replacing Denis Compton as the centrepiece of the Brylcreem advertising campaign.

Haynes's football career was severely undermined by a car accident on Blackpool promenade in 1962. He broke bones in both feet and badly injured a knee, causing him to miss most of the 1962–3 season. He was probably never quite the same player again although he regained sufficient fitness to turn out for Fulham a further 236 times. Tottenham Hotspur were apparently keen to sign him in 1963 as a replacement for John White, but Fulham refused to allow him to leave. He was not chosen for England after 1962 and it is tempting to conclude that had he not suffered serious injury he would have been the captain of the England team in the 1966 world cup, when he would still have been only thirty-one.

Haynes's later years at Fulham coincided with a decline in performance before failing crowds. He retired in 1970 and moved to South Africa, playing for Durban City and other clubs, and twice being a member of a championship-winning side for the only times in his career. He later ran a bookmaking business. He was married three times: first, on 28 December 1972, to Elizabeth Ellen (Libby) Tucker, an American actress, and later businesswoman, daughter of Allen Marshall Tucker, real estate broker; second, in South Africa in 1976, to Marjorie (Marge) Green; and third (on 8 October 2004, after a partnership lasting almost two decades) to Avril Cassidy, otherwise MacKinley, *née* Carnie (*b.* 1939), daughter of Alexander Carnie, accountant. In 1985 he returned to Britain and lived with Avril in Edinburgh, where they had a dry-cleaning and office cleaning business. On 17 October 2005 he was driving along Dalry Road in Edinburgh when he suffered a brain haemorrhage. The car veered into incoming traffic and hit a light goods vehicle. He was kept on a ventilator at the Edinburgh Royal Infirmary for some thirty hours, until it was switched off, on 18 October. His wife, Avril, injured in the accident, survived him. A month after his death it was announced that Fulham's Stevenage Road stand would be renamed the Johnny Haynes stand. In October 2008 a statue of Haynes was unveiled in front of the Craven Cottage gates. TONY MASON

Sources J. Haynes, *It's all in the game* (1963) · J. Moynihan, *The soccer syndrome* (1966) · J. Moynihan, *The soccer syndrome*, new edn (1987) · *The Independent* (19 Oct 2005); (20 Oct 2005) · *The Times* (19 Oct 2005); (20 Oct 2005); (22 Oct 2005); (26 Oct 2005); (1 Nov 2005) · *Daily Telegraph* (20 Oct 2005) · *The Guardian* (20 Oct 2005) · M. Taylor, *The association game: a history of British football* (2008) · M. Plumb and K. Coton, *Johnny Haynes: the maestro* (2008) · private information

(2009) [M. Plumb; K. Coton] • b. cert. • m. certs. [1972, 2004] • d. cert.
Archives FILM BFINA, light entertainment footage
Likenesses photographs, 1950–98, Photoshot, London • photographs, 1950–2002, PA Photos, London • photographs, 1952–68, Getty Images, London • K. Coton, bromide fibre print, 1966, NPG [*see illus.*] • obituary photographs • photographs, repro. in http://www.johnnyhaynesstatue.com/statue/ • photographs, repro. in Plumb and Coton, *Johnny Haynes* (2008) • statue, Fulham Football Club, London
Wealth at death £54,422.22: confirmation, 13 Jan 2006, *CCI*

Hayter, Alethea Catharine (1911–2006), writer and British Council official, was born in Cairo, Egypt, on 7 November 1911, the youngest of the three children of Sir William Goodenough Hayter (1869–1924), a judge in the Anglo-Egyptian service and legal adviser to the Egyptian government, and his wife, Alethea, daughter of John Henry Slessor, rector of Headbourne Worthy, Hampshire. Her brother, also Sir William Goodenough *Hayter (1906–1995), became ambassador to the Soviet Union, and warden of New College, Oxford, and her sister, Priscilla Napier (1908–1998), was a gifted writer. In Cairo the sisters were educated by governesses, a happy childhood described by Priscilla in *A Late Beginner* (1966), but after their father died they returned to England. Alethea was a pupil at Downe House School, Berkshire, from 1924 to 1929, when she won a senior scholarship to read modern history at Lady Margaret Hall, Oxford. In 1932 she graduated with a second-class degree and joined the editorial staff of *Country Life* for five years, becoming fashion editor. 'I loved it,' she said, 'although, had they needed a fly-fishing editor, I'd have done that just as readily' (*The Independent*, 5 July 1992). She also acted as a model: tall, thin, and elegant, she remained beautiful all her life.

At the outbreak of the Second World War in 1939 Hayter joined the postal censorship department and worked in highly sensitive areas, first in Gibraltar and then Bermuda, the main point for censorship of mail between the Americas and Europe. This was followed by spells in Trinidad and London. Friends later surmised that she worked for British intelligence, which she always dismissed with an amused smile. After the war, in November 1945, she joined the British Council. In 1952 she was posted to Athens, as assistant to the controversial art historian Roger Hinks (who had resigned from the British Museum after being reprimanded for his role in a disastrous 'cleaning' of the Elgin marbles). In January 1960 she became deputy representative in Paris; and from 1967 until her retirement in 1971 she was British Council representative and cultural attaché in Belgium.

Unknown to her colleagues, during the war Hayter began writing novels under the pseudonym (from a family ancestor) of J. C. Fennessy, beginning with *The Siege of Elsinore*, in which she imagined Hamlet and Ophelia married. Her five Fennessy books, between 1941 and 1952, honed her sense of narrative, and ten years later, in her flat on the Île St Louis, Paris, she wrote *Mrs Browning: a Poet's Work and its Setting* (1962), winner of the Royal Society of Literature Heinemann award. Next came the brilliantly original

Alethea Catharine Hayter (1911–2006), by Anne Hamilton

A Sultry Month: Scenes of London Literary Life (1965), interwoven scenes looping around the suicide of the artist Benjamin Robert Haydon in July 1846, involving the Carlyles, Browning, Dickens, and even the duke of Wellington, combining meticulous research with fluent storytelling.

Hayter's wit and analytic skill also appeared in *Horatio's Version* (1972), a report of an inquiry into events at Elsinore, while her pioneering use of a single moment to illuminate a broad sweep of history was evident from *A Voyage in Vain: Coleridge's Journey to Malta in 1804* (1973) to her remarkable last book, *The Wreck of the Abergavenny* (2002), about the loss at sea of Wordsworth's brother John in 1805. Her most influential work, however, was *Opium and the Romantic Imagination* (1968), a wide-ranging medical, critical, and biographical study of eight writers, including Coleridge, Keats, and Poe, which was also a study of dreams and a powerful investigation into the nature of creativity. Other works ranged from *FitzGerald to his Friends: Selected Letters of Edward FitzGerald* (1979) to *The Backbone* (1993), edited diaries of her Slessor ancestors during the Napoleonic wars, and a short life of Charlotte Yonge, a writer she considered unjustly neglected (1996).

In 1970 Hayter was appointed OBE. She never married, and lived alone at 22 Aldebert Terrace, her book-filled flat in south London, remaining extremely active as a governor of the Old Vic and Sadler's Wells theatres, and a member of the management committee of the Society of Authors. She also continued reviewing, particularly for the *Times Literary Supplement*, kept up with a wide circle of friends, and took great pleasure in the reissue of her books in the 1990s. She was profoundly affected by the death of her sister, Priscilla, in 1998 but although frail, she seemed indomitable, attending lectures at the Royal Society of Literature in her early nineties, sitting in the front row, straight-backed and alarmingly attentive. Beneath her slightly daunting exterior, she was immensely kind, indulgent to friends' lapses despite her own upright probity, a lover of gossip and parties, with a keen wit and a delight in the ridiculous. To the next generation of writers her 'sturdy independence of mind' came to represent the virtues of 'the independent scholar, unaffected by the fashions and orthodoxies of academe … essential for the healthy functioning of intellectual discussion' (Julian Barnes, *The Guardian*, 3 May 2008). She died of atrial fibrillation and coronary artery disease at King Edward VIII's Hospital, Westminster, on 10 January 2006, and was buried at Headbourne Worthy, Hampshire. Her elegant headstone is carved with two books. JENNY UGLOW

Sources P. Napier, *A late beginner* (1966) · *The Independent* (5 July 1992); (11 Jan 2006) · *Daily Telegraph* (11 Jan 2006) · *The Times* (12 Jan 2006) · *The Guardian* (13 Jan 2006) · British Council Association directories · personal knowledge (2010) · private information (2010) [Lavinia Mynors, niece; Lady Hamilton, niece] · d. cert.
Archives priv. coll. | SOUND BL NSA, documentary recording
Likenesses Lady Hamilton, pencil drawing, priv. coll.; repro. in *The Times* [*see illus.*] · obituary photographs
Wealth at death £418,602: probate, 19 July 2006, *CGPLA Eng. & Wales*

Hayward, Douglas Frederick Cornelius [Doug] (**1934–2008**), tailor, was born on 5 October 1934 at 12 Church Walk, Kensington, London, the younger son of Noel Westmacott Hayward (1897–1968), electrical engineer, and his wife, Winifred Elliott, *née* Thurston (1905–1984). He came from a working-class background (his father worked in the boiler room at the BBC before cycling to a London transport depot to wash buses; his mother worked in a munitions factory during the Second World War) and grew up in Hayes, Middlesex. He won a scholarship to Southall grammar school. He was a talented footballer and took a trial for Middlesex county football team but was unsuccessful. After leaving school at fifteen he was apprenticed to a tailor in Shepherd's Bush Green, west London. Following his apprenticeship he did two years' national service in the Royal Navy.

On his return to civilian life Hayward rejoined his former employer, whose premises were located close to Shepherd's Bush Theatre and the BBC studio at Lime Grove, giving Hayward his first contact with actors, who later formed his core clientele. On 4 October 1958, at the parish church in Ickenham, Middlesex, he married Diana Mary Smith, a twenty-year-old secretary, and daughter of Robert Scott Smith, accountant. Through his sister-in-law Melissa Smith (the actress Melissa Stribling), who was married to the film director Basil Dearden, Hayward attracted new clients, retaining their business when he went into partnership with Dimitrio Major, a tailor in Fulham Road, west London, with a similar clientele. The firm of Major Hayward offered skilfully cut, well-made suits whose flattering, fluid shapes suited the lifestyles of its young customers. Determined to work in the West End, Hayward left to set up his own business in Pall Mall in 1963. Clients such as the actor Terence Stamp followed him and in 1967 he upgraded his premises to a four-floor property at 95 Mount Street, Mayfair, where he lived on the first floor. As well as bespoke tailoring, the shop offered a range of shirts, sweaters, ties, and dressing gowns, known as 'Hayward Classics', luggage, hand-made shoes, and wrist watches. His customers, who were mostly young and successful, came from the worlds of art, media, sport, and business. He offered them, and their wives and girlfriends, a relaxed and convivial alternative to the class-conscious formality of Savile Row. In spite of his alternative approach to the business of bespoke tailor, his skills were highly rated by his fellow tailors. In 1965 he was the only non-establishment tailor to be recommended by the society magazine *Queen* in its 'Society Index'.

During the 1960s Hayward helped to redefine the classic man's suit. As a tailor and not, he emphasized, a fashion designer, his aim was to create a suit that made its wearer appear, and feel, slim, relaxed, and comfortable. He described his customers as looking 'a mixture of smart but scruffy in suits that are beautifully made' (Ross, 125). The suits he created for films brought his aesthetic to a wider audience. He dressed Terence Stamp in *Modesty Blaise* (1966), Michael Caine in *The Italian Job* (1969), and Roger Moore in *For Your Eyes Only* (1981) and *A View to a Kill* (1985). Many of his clients became lifelong friends, including Caine and the photographers Patrick Lichfield, with whom he set up Burke's dining club in Clifford Street, Mayfair, in 1969, and Terry O'Neill, who was a regular member of Hayward's amateur football team, the Mount Street Marchers' Social Club. His first marriage having been dissolved, on 31 December 1970, at Westminster register office, Hayward married Glenys Marjorie Evans, *née* Roberts, a 31-year-old journalist (as Glenys Roberts) and daughter of Stanley Roberts, bank manager. Their daughter Polly was born in 1970. The marriage was dissolved in 1978 and Hayward subsequently had a relationship with the journalist Janet Street-Porter (*b.* 1946).

According to Audie Charles, Hayward's office manager from 1967, his

> knack was to give a man a suit he could put on and forget about, knowing he looked good. He didn't want anyone to say, there goes a Hayward suit; he wanted you to know the man looked good but you weren't sure why. (Ross, 126)

He was also admired for his personal qualities and John Le Carré drew on his character and appearance when creating Henry Pendel for his novel *The Tailor of Panama* (1996). Hayward valued his privacy and independence but was a discreet and attentive listener whom many called upon for advice. He was also an amusing raconteur, bon viveur, and womanizer. In later life he moved seamlessly between his working-class roots and high society, singing Cole Porter duets with Princess Margaret in Mustique and organizing down-to-earth parties of the kind he had enjoyed as a child.

Hayward's success and personal popularity attracted customers from a wide social spectrum, with businessmen predominating towards the end of his career. He advised Ralph Lauren on his Purple Label menswear line, which was launched in 1994, and lectured on tailoring at the Royal College of Art. In 2006 his daughter Polly took over her father's business because of his failing health. He nevertheless continued to live at 95 Mount Street (and also had a country property near Henley). He died on 26 April 2008 at Meadbank Hospice, 12 Parkgate Road, Battersea, London, from bronchopneumonia and vascular dementia. Although an agnostic he received the last rites from a Roman Catholic priest. The company Douglas Hayward went into administration in 2009, and was purchased by a newly formed company, Mount Street Tailors.

EDWINA EHRMAN

Sources *The Independent* (26 June 1994) · P. Gorman, *The look: adventures in pop and rock fashion* (2001) · *Daily Mail* (29 April 2008) · *Daily Telegraph* (30 April 2008) · *The Times* (1 May 2008) · *The Guardian* (3 May 2008) · J. Brown, 'Douglas Hayward rescued', *Drapers* (29 July 2009) · G. A. Ross, *The day of the peacock: style for men, 1963–1973* (2011) · b. cert. · m. certs. · d. cert.

Archives FILM BFINA, *Now and then*, B. Braden (producer), 22 Sept 1967

Likenesses photographs, 1971–85, Getty Images, London · J. Swannell, photographs, 2003, Camera Press, London · obituary photographs · photographs, Lichfield archive, Lichfield Studios, London

Wealth at death £577,689: probate, 6 Nov 2008, *CGPLA Eng. & Wales*

Hazlehurst, Ronald [Ronnie] (**1928–2007**), musician, was born at 169 Lodge Lane, Dukinfield, Cheshire, on 13 March 1928, the son of Herbert Hazlehurst, a general labourer, later railwayman, and his wife, Lillian May, *née* Wraith. His father played wind instruments and his mother gave piano lessons, and the young Ronnie learned the cornet. He attended St John's Church of England primary school in Dukinfield and then Hyde county grammar school, Cheshire. He left school when fourteen to boost the family finances. While working as a clerk in a cotton mill he also played with George Chambers's band at a dance hall in Ashton-under-Lyne. In 1947 he was conscripted, playing cornet in the 4th/7th dragoon guards and attending the Royal Military School of Music in Twickenham.

During the 1950s Hazlehurst worked as a milkman while freelancing as a musician around Manchester and studying arranging. The bandleader Woolf Phillips employed him at the prestigious Pigalle night club in London: Hazlehurst played cornet, wrote arrangements, and deputized whenever Phillips was unavailable. He joined Peter Knight, the head of music at Granada TV, but when Knight left a year later his own position came to an end. To bide his time he worked on a record stall in Watford market. On 22 March 1952, at the parish church of Adenshaw, Manchester, he married Georgina Rowbotham (*b.* 1929), daughter of Tom Rowbotham, engineer. They had two sons.

Hazlehurst became a BBC staff arranger in 1961 and his first significant contribution was to score and arrange the programme for a concert at the Royal Albert Hall to celebrate the fortieth anniversary of the BBC in 1962. From 1964 he worked mainly for television, gaining immediate acclaim with his music for *The Likely Lads* in the same year. He also wrote music for the ground-breaking television

Ronald Hazlehurst (**1928–2007**), by Chris George

play *Vote, Vote, Vote for Nigel Barton* (1965) and the series *It's a Knockout* (1966). In 1968 he became the head of music for light entertainment, replacing Harry Rabinowitz. He was adept at writing theme music and he crafted music to fit the title. The music rises and falls at appropriate moments in *The Fall and Rise of Reginald Perrin* (1976). In *Are You Being Served?* (1972) he used a cash register in the melody. Sometimes a production was over budget and the music, the final component, had to be made at minimal cost. An ingenious example of Hazlehurst's skill in working within such constraints was his use of two piccolos to relate the title of *Some Mothers Do 'Ave 'Em* (1973) in Morse code. Reportedly he had to fight to get the second piccolo.

Hazlehurst's music for television usually reflected the comedy that was to follow, but a glorious exception was his theme for *Last of the Summer Wine* (1973), which captured the tranquillity of the Yorkshire Pennines and the gently paced stories. It became the world's longest-running sitcom, with Hazlehurst writing and conducting incidental music for over fifty episodes. He also wrote the majestic melody for *To the Manor Born* (1979), with Penelope Keith and Peter Bowles. In 1980 he used Big Ben's chimes as the inspiration for *Yes Minister*, for which his theme music was accompanied by Gerald Scarfe's acidic caricatures. He wrote the theme music for *The Two Ronnies* (1971), starring Ronnie Barker and Ronnie Corbett, *My Wife*

Next Door (1972), the first series of *Only Fools and Horses* (1981), and the generation-gap comedy *Three Up, Two Down* (1989). He also wrote the music for the frivolous quiz series *Blankety Blank* (1979), which was hosted first by Terry Wogan and then by Les Dawson, and the introductory music for Wogan's talk show. He arranged and conducted Clare Torry's 'Love is like a butterfly' for *Butterflies* (1978), starring Wendy Craig and Geoffrey Palmer, and performed a similar service for Paul Nicholas, who sang the theme song for his comedy *Just Good Friends* (1983).

Hazlehurst wrote the introductory music for the BBC's coverage of the Montreal Olympics in 1976. He was musical director for the Eurovision song contest when it was held in the UK in 1974, 1977, and 1982, and conducted the British entry on several occasions, notably for Michael Ball's 'One Step out of Time' in 1992. When it was held at Wembley in 1977, he conducted Lynsey de Paul and Mike Moran's song 'Rock Bottom' in a pinstripe suit, bowler hat, and rolled umbrella. He conducted the orchestra for the royal variety performance in 1982.

Hazlehurst recorded several middle of the road albums and made two albums of music from Laurel and Hardy films. He moved from Hendon to Guernsey in 1998. In 1999 he received a gold badge from the British Academy of Composers and Songwriters. His music was frequently derided as 'plinky plunky' or 'fiddly twiddly', but it was often memorable. He loved *Spitting Image* mocking him as having a four-second attention span. His first marriage ended in divorce. His second wife was Sita Davenport, *née* Singh, sales representative and daughter of Sugria Singh, barrister; they married at Hendon register office on 3 December 1991. At the time of his death his partner was Jean Fitzgerald. He died, following a stroke, in St Peter Port, Guernsey, on 1 October 2007. SPENCER LEIGH

Sources *The Times* (3 Oct 2007) · *The Independent* (3 Oct 2007) · *Daily Telegraph* (4 Oct 2007) · *The Guardian* (12 Oct 2007) · personal knowledge (2011) · private information (2011) · b. cert. · m. certs.
Archives FILM BFINA, performance footage
Likenesses P. Jordan, group portrait, photograph, 1999, PA Photos, London · C. George, photograph, South West News Services [*see illus.*] · obituary photographs
Wealth at death £331,308: administration with will, 29 Oct 2009, *CGPLA Eng. & Wales*

Heap, John Arnfield (1932–2006), polar researcher and civil servant, was born at St Mary's Hospital, Manchester, on 5 February 1932, the only child of David Heap, electrical engineer, and his wife, Ann Arnfield, *née* James. At the time of his birth registration his parents lived at 13 Lea Road, Heaton Moor, Lancashire. He was educated at Leighton Park School, Reading, and at Edinburgh University, where he read geography. He graduated in 1953 and that summer organized and led an undergraduate expedition to the Lyngen peninsula in Arctic Norway. He proceeded MA in 1955, and the same year joined the Falkland Islands Dependencies Survey as a research student at Clare College, Cambridge, in order to work at the Scott Polar Research Institute under Terence Armstrong, an authority on sea ice in Russian Arctic waters. For the next seven years he studied sea ice distribution in British Antarctic Territory waters from the support ship RRS *John Biscoe* and, in 1956–7, from the MV *Theron*, the ship used by Vivian Fuchs on his trans-Antarctic expedition. He then returned to Cambridge to write up his report as a thesis for the degree of PhD, which was duly awarded in 1962. The following year the thesis was published as *Sea Ice in the Antarctic*, but sold only eleven copies. Heap wryly referred to the work as a 'world worstseller' (personal knowledge). This was unsurprising, as sea ice distribution was already being monitored from aircraft and through satellite imagery. On 10 September 1960, at the church of St Peter and St Mary, New Fishbourne, Sussex, he had married Margaret Grace Gillespie (Peggy) Spicer (*b.* 1933), a state registered nurse, daughter of Captain Sir Stewart Dykes Spicer, third baronet, naval officer. They had two daughters and one son.

Heap spent the years 1962–4 at the University of Michigan, Ann Arbor, as one of a team measuring by tellurometer the movement of the Ross ice shelf in Antarctica, and studying the ice on Lake Michigan. In 1964 he returned to England to join the polar regions section of the Foreign and Commonwealth Office in London, serving initially under Brian Roberts. The rapport between the two men and Heap's ability to meet Roberts's exacting standards ensured a harmonious relationship and a smooth transition of responsibility when Roberts retired and Heap succeeded him in 1975. Heap also served as administrator for the British Antarctic Territory from 1989 until his retirement from the Foreign and Commonwealth Office in 1992.

Heap exercised a powerful influence on government policy in Antarctica. As head of the polar regions section he held one of the very few specialist appointments in the diplomatic service that did not involve overseas posting. Nevertheless he travelled widely as a member or leader of United Kingdom delegations to all meetings of the Antarctic treaty countries. This enabled him to play a leading role in the adoption of the conventions on the conservation of seals and of marine living resources (1982), and in the regulation of marine living resources, as also in the protocol for environmental protection. He edited successive editions of the *Handbook of the Antarctic Treaty System*. In 1991 he was appointed CMG. In 1986 he had been commemorated in Heap Island, one of the Biscoe Islands, off Graham Coast, Antarctica. He was also commemorated in Heap glacier, feeding the Ross ice shelf. Later he was for many years a member of the polar medal assessment committee.

As director of the Scott Polar Research Institute in Cambridge from 1992 to 1998 Heap was very successful in raising funds for building an extension to the institute in memory of Sir Ernest Shackleton and his son Eddy, Lord Shackleton. On a visit to Canada he canvassed the renowned Anglo-Canadian Arctic explorer and zoologist, and former Cambridge student, Tom Manning, who donated $1 million. Manning's generosity made the project viable, building went ahead, and the Shackleton extension was officially opened in November 1998.

In the tradition of the diplomatic service Heap was an

excellent writer, but sadly published only articles, reviews, and notes, mainly in the *Polar Record*. He was an urbane and accomplished speaker, a skill that served him well when, in retirement, he was a Liberal Democrat member of South Cambridgeshire district council. He died of lung cancer at his home, 27 High Street, Harston, Cambridgeshire, on 8 March 2006, and was survived by his wife, Peggy, and their three children.

G. HATTERSLEY-SMITH

Sources *Polar Record* (1955–2005) • *Daily Telegraph* (18 March 2006) • *The Independent* (18 March 2006) • *The Times* (24 March 2006) • *WW* (2006) • personal knowledge (2010) • private information (2010) [Margaret Heap, widow] • b. cert. • m. cert. • d. cert.

Archives FILM BFINA, current affairs footage

Likenesses J. Tichotsky, photograph, 1996, Scott Polar RI • M. Brierley, photographs, 1998, Scott Polar RI • S. Sawtell, photographs, 1998, Scott Polar RI • N. Socha, photograph, 1998, Scott Polar RI • obituary photographs

Wealth at death £295,273: probate, 27 Oct 2006, *CGPLA Eng. & Wales*

Heath, Sir Edward Richard George [Ted] (1916–2005), prime minister, was born at 1 Holmwood Villas, Albion Road, Broadstairs, Kent, on 9 July 1916, the elder son of William George Heath (1888–1976), carpenter and builder, and his wife, Edith Annie, *née* Pantony (*d.* 1951), formerly a parlour maid. Within weeks of his birth the family moved to Crayford, on the outskirts of London, where his father, under wartime arrangements, was allocated a job in the Vickers engineering factory. But factory work did not suit William Heath's independent character, and the family returned to Broadstairs when Heath was seven. During his career Heath tended to speak little of the things that meant most to him, and it was only in his last years that he began to talk and write easily about his boyhood at Broadstairs, but he described it in his memoirs as 'idyllic' (Heath, 11).

Broadstairs, Oxford, and political apprenticeship Heath's childhood contained few excitements and no extremes of happiness or tragedy. His was a thoroughly English upbringing spent on the subtle English borderline between the working and middle classes. Its two main centres were the family and the grammar school, each sustained by loyalty, mutual affection, and hard work. Talent was recognized and helped when accompanied by effort, and for Heath, his family, neighbours, and friends, this process was the core of life. The competition was softened and made human by friendships, the gentle pleasures of a seaside town, the gradual unveiling of literature and the arts, and above all the close ties of a family.

Heath's father was primarily a builder by trade, first working for others, then promoted to foreman of a small business, then taking over that business as his own. He was an energetic, outgoing man, totally without pretence, whose jokes might contain a touch of kindly mischief. The turning point of his life came when he could just

Sir Edward Richard George Heath (1916–2005), by Jane Bown, 1978

afford to buy a semi-detached house after years living in rented property. This meant a heavy mortgage that the family slowly paid off by providing rooms in their three-bedroomed house for seaside visitors during the summer. The boarders occupied the two main bedrooms. Heath and his brother slept in the small back room and their parents on a couch in one of the rooms downstairs, which also served as William's office. Heath's mother, Edith, was the dominant force in his life. He remembered her as calm, beautiful, fair-minded, and determined that her two sons should be brought up to make the best of their opportunities. She and William Heath never took holidays, but always ensured holidays for their children.

After three years at a Church of England primary school Heath won a scholarship at the age of ten to Chatham House Grammar School, Ramsgate. He had a natural aptitude for school work; at this stage he did best at mathematics and science. Chatham House, like most grammar schools of the period, worked hard to broaden the lives of its pupils well beyond the range that parents could manage on their own. A school trip to Paris at the age of fourteen created a zest for travel which never left him. He was useless with his hands, but enjoyed theatricals and above all the debating contests at which the school excelled. But alongside school a fresh influence had already entered his life. A cousin of his mother's introduced him to music and he began to take piano lessons. Characteristically his parents scraped together enough money to buy him a piano, paid for in twenty-four monthly instalments of £2 each. Soon after, he joined the choir of the local church as a treble. A love of music was thereafter the strongest single pleasure in his life.

By the time he left school, the principles and philosophy of Broadstairs were already firmly established in Heath's mind and character, and he never departed from them. Central to this philosophy was the belief that success was fragile and had to be earned by hard work. The town and Heath's family depended precariously on the business cycle; its ups and downs were part of everyone's life. One of Heath's favourite phrases in later speeches was that after a setback you must 'pick yourself up, dust yourself down, and try again'.

Heath failed to win the organ scholarship to St Catharine's College, Cambridge, in 1934, and failed again next year to win scholarships to Keble and Balliol colleges, Oxford. But Balliol offered him entry as a commoner without a scholarship. The price was steep, £220 per year. The Kent education committee lent him just under half what was needed, a friend and client of his father's another £40 a year, and his parents managed to find the rest. On a sunny afternoon in October 1935 Heath and his parents loaded his belongings into the family Hillman Minx and set off for the unknown world of Oxford. He was the first member of his family to go to a university. Theirs was a risky decision, vulnerable to any downturn in his father's business. Within weeks the anxiety was eased. The organ scholarship at Balliol unexpectedly became available; Heath entered and won. This meant not just financial help but four years instead of three at university. Those added terms and the extra £80 a year gave him the space he needed to make the most of Oxford. He could begin to buy books and records, and spend time on activities outside the lecture rooms and tutorials.

For Heath Oxford was not a place of dreaming spires and lost causes. New doors opened, and revealed opportunities that had previously only been shadowy hopes. In his memoirs he made light of the problems faced by the boy from Broadstairs who found himself sharing a world with the sons of dukes. He must have been exceptionally quick to adapt, finding solutions before difficulties became acute. One such compromise remained forever in the awkward vowel sounds with which he equipped himself, forming an accent different from those of his father and brother. Nevertheless he was skilful or lucky in his choice of college. Balliol had for years placed a greater emphasis on merit than background and received a higher than average proportion of young men with a state education. Heath's natural self-confidence saw him through. He became an agreeable if serious undergraduate with a wide range of acquaintances. His closest friend was an old Harrovian, Madron Seligman, with whom he shared a zest for music and painting as well as politics. There do not seem to have been any special girlfriends at Oxford, but he was developing a close friendship during vacations in Broadstairs with a childhood neighbour, Kay Raven, the local doctor's daughter. He was 'walking out' with her in the limited literal sense of that ancient phrase; it was with her that at home he mainly played tennis or went to concerts.

At Oxford Heath's musical life blossomed rapidly. The post of organ scholar at Balliol was no sinecure. It meant playing in the college chapel at 8 a.m. every weekday morning and on Sunday evenings, and helping to design a new college organ. He composed music for the production of two Aristophanes plays performed by the Balliol Players, and went with them on a tour of southern England. He joined the Oxford Bach Choir, and revived the Balliol Choral Society. He expanded his musical repertory and developed into a competent performer on the organ as well as on the piano. The Heather professor of music, Sir Hugh Allen, told him that he could look forward to a good career as a professional musician, if he was prepared to give up his politics.

But politics now became Heath's first passion, which he followed at different levels, combining personal ambition with a genuine interest in the underlying flow of ideas. At the outset he joined the political clubs of all three political parties so that he could hear a wide range of visiting speakers. He was powerfully influenced by the master of his college, A. D. Lindsay. Lindsay was a socialist, but he won strong enthusiasm from Heath for his undogmatic approach. Heath's Christian faith, though quietly held, stayed constant and gave him strong sympathy for the social message of Archbishop William Temple. By the time he arrived in Oxford Heath already knew that he was a Conservative, but he belonged to a particular part of that broad church. On the economic side he was convinced by Keynes and by the success of Roosevelt's new deal that the capitalist system could be run humanely with high levels of employment. On the political side he was attracted by Harold Macmillan's book *The Middle Way* (1938), which offered the prospect of a moderate, youthful Conservative Party dedicated in a fresh way to the concept of one nation. One unfair advantage that Oxford and Cambridge enjoyed over other universities was the ease with which they attracted well-known outside visitors. Heath relished the company of Macmillan, Churchill, Eden, and many others, learning at first hand something of the inner gossip and processes of politics.

Heath became president of the Oxford University Conservative Association in 1937–8, but the main vehicle for his political enthusiasm was the Oxford Union. He had for years studied the techniques of debate. He worked hard on the detail of each subject; he tackled and learned large chunks of each speech by heart. At the union he developed the style he retained through his life. His speech making fell short of greatness. He possessed neither a majestic voice (like Gladstone) nor the ability to coin a witty or dramatic phrase (like Disraeli). Like Peel he relied on intellectual honesty, a mastery of detail, and an aptitude for organizing that detail in a lucid, persuasive way. The union had achieved worldwide notoriety three years before Heath arrived when in 1933 it approved a motion refusing to fight for king and country. By 1936 the union was dominated by the left and accustomed to passing resolutions in that spirit. It was in expectation of easy success that Hugh Dalton, a leading member of the Labour Party, came to the union in November 1937 to propose a motion approving the latest statement of Labour policies. Heath, chosen to oppose him, that evening produced his first notable success. Dalton was a crafty, portentous old Etonian. The grammar school boy from Broadstairs dissected each part of the Labour proposals in detail, and to an unusual extent also put forward his own alternatives. Dalton was defeated by 162 votes to 125 and left in a huff. A few weeks later Heath was elected secretary of the union.

Arguments about unemployment and social policy fell away as Hitler and Mussolini strengthened their grip on Europe. During these years Heath visited the continent three times. In the summer of 1937 his parents arranged an exchange with a German student, as part of which Heath visited Düsseldorf. He moved on alone to Bavaria, where he found himself casually invited to one of the Nazi rallies in Nuremberg. He literally brushed shoulders with Hitler as the Führer walked up to the platform; later at a party for foreign guests he met Goering and Goebbels and shook the soft wet hand of Heinrich Himmler. What impressed and depressed him was not the encounter with Nazi leaders but the extraordinary massed discipline and enthusiasm of their supporters. The next summer he saw fascism in action. He was part of a student delegation to the republican government in Spain, then in the last year of its doomed resistance to Franco's rebellion. In Barcelona the students stayed in their hotel rooms during an air raid, ignoring the advice of their hosts to go down to the basement shelter. A bomb went straight down the lift shaft, killing everyone in the shelter. A few days later their car was machine-gunned on the road south from Barcelona and they were forced to take refuge in a ditch. Heath returned to England unhurt and strongly anti-fascist.

A few weeks later Chamberlain's agreement with Hitler at Munich brought the whole argument to a head, not least in Oxford. All the Conservatives whom Heath admired denounced Munich. Naturally the Oxford Union would have its say. In the first debate of the autumn Heath and the future Labour minister Christopher Mayhew joined in proposing a motion deploring 'the Government's policy of Peace without Honour'. His speech was judged to be competent, though not as good as Mayhew's. What was more significant was the decision of Heath as the leading Conservative undergraduate to join forces with Labour against the Conservative government. Mayhew and Heath carried their motion by 320 votes to 266.

Almost at once the argument found a new focus. The Conservative member of parliament for the City of Oxford had died in August; the by-election was held in November. After much discussion the different camps that opposed appeasement persuaded Lindsay, the master of Heath's college, to stand as an independent candidate against Munich. The Labour and Liberal parties put forward no candidate. The official Conservative candidate was Quintin Hogg (later lord chancellor and Heath's colleague in cabinet). Heath threw himself into the battle on behalf of Lindsay, speaking, canvassing, and organizing. Few undergraduates then had the vote (the age limit being twenty-one) and the university's graduates were separately represented in the university seat; the city included the car workers of the new Morris factory at Cowley. Hogg won with a majority of 3434, roughly halved from the general election figure, but still reflecting the national sense of relief that war had been averted. The result gave the government some comfort, but its opponents encouragement and much publicity. Heath then moved on to his next and last Oxford campaign, for the presidency of the union. He was chosen for the following Lent term after a savage speech denouncing the Chamberlain government. He reorganized the union's flagging finances, attracted an exceptional range of speakers for the debates under his presidency, and for the first time ended the term with an evening party crowded with dons and their wives as well as undergraduates.

Meanwhile Heath tackled his academic work competently but without any dramatic success. His essays were praised and at the end of his four years, in 1939, he achieved what his tutor called 'a nice second' in philosophy, politics, and economics. He never set himself to achieve a second class in anything and was disappointed not to get a first. But he had not thought of following an academic career and his other achievements at Oxford were more important to him. His parents were divided on his future career. His father favoured accountancy, his mother the church. Neither appealed to Heath, whose favourite occupations were now politics and music, in that order. But neither of these careers in its early stages could sustain a young man without money of his own. On this as on other occasions Broadstairs showed solidarity. Heath received good advice and help from a local lawyer for whom his father had built a home; Gerald Moody arranged a scholarship for Heath at Gray's Inn. But the prospect of beginning a peaceful career must have seemed dim in the spring of 1939 when Hitler marched into Prague. Heath, with his friend Madron Seligman, chose for a summer holiday the hottest trouble spot he could find in Europe. Hitler made demands on Poland concerning the Baltic port of Danzig, so to Danzig the two young men travelled, to the dismay of the local British consular officials. They were advised to leave for home as soon as they could. As they hitchhiked westward they passed Polish and then German troops heading towards battle with each other. Peace held long enough for them to visit the galleries in Dresden before they caught a train across Germany and then hitchhiked across France. His relieved parents met Heath at Dover a week before the Second World War began.

Army officer, civil servant, and journalist Heath at once enlisted in the army, and was assigned to the Royal Artillery. But the number of men entering was so great that he was not wanted for several months. Indeed he was allowed to carry out an engagement he must have thought was doomed. Every year the Oxford Union sent two of its members across the Atlantic on a debating tour of the United States. Heath and a Liberal, Peter Street, had been chosen for 1939. When consulted, the Foreign Office agreed that the tour should go ahead but with a reservation that seemed bound to frustrate it: anxious not to be thought to interfere in American politics, it decreed that the two young debaters could discuss any subject except the war. This was ludicrous. The war was the only subject in which their audiences were interested. The debaters were rescued by the British ambassador in Washington, Lord Lothian. He suggested that they should debate the issue but even-handedly, one arguing each side of the argument about American entry. So on this bizarre basis Heath and Street toured the southern, eastern, and midwestern states, alternately taking each side of the argument. Heath was struck by the openness and egalitarianism of American society. Throughout his life he maintained a varying group of American friends unrelated to politics, whose company was for him a lively pleasure. He returned to England in January 1940 on a dismal and almost empty Cunard liner.

During that fraught summer of 1940, while his brother John fought with the British expeditionary force in France and was evacuated from Dunkirk, Heath stayed restless at Broadstairs, waiting for his call-up. Eventually in August he was sent to Sussex for anti-aircraft training, which that year included picking up wounded and dead British and German airmen, casualties of the battle of Britain. The next step was training for an officer's commission at Shrivenham in Wiltshire. Eventually in March 1941 he was allocated to the 107th heavy anti-aircraft regiment, whose immediate task was to defend part of Liverpool against German air attacks. The battle of the Atlantic was under way and Liverpool was the chief destination of the convoys that kept Britain going. For a fortnight in May 1941 Liverpool was bombed every night. Heath commanded a troop of four guns stationed just south of the city. The crews were in action all night and did their best to sleep in the day. During the next three years Heath and his anti-aircraft regiment travelled round the cities of England, deployed wherever attack was expected. For the first time he got to know the midlands and north of his own country. The closest he came to disaster had nothing to do with enemy action. In Northumberland he developed acute appendicitis and was rushed to hospital in Newcastle. He wrote a touching letter to his parents thanking them for all their sacrifices on his behalf. But the operation was successful. Heath often campaigned in Newcastle in later life, never without observing to his audience that as proof of his affection he had left his appendix in their care.

The three years on the move in England with his anti-aircraft regiment were tedious rather than heroic, but they provided Heath with experience. He showed himself highly competent in administration both as troop commander and on promotion to adjutant. He thought ahead, made a written plan for each exercise, and made sure that everyone knew about it. He was popular with the men under him, going out on exercise with them when he could have pleaded administrative work, and forming a five-piece band that played at dances and in the mess under the signature tune 'When you're smiling'. He formed a lifelong friendship with George Chadd, his battery commander.

On 5 July 1944, four weeks after D-day, the 107th heavy anti-aircraft regiment landed in Normandy. Its first battle task was to take part in the bombardment of Caen and in the stubborn fighting that eventually dislodged the Germans from Normandy and enabled the allied armies to sweep quickly through northern France and Belgium. After taking part in the liberation of Antwerp the regiment paused for a few days in the suburb of Wilrijk, where they received a memorable welcome from the Belgians. They took part in the unsuccessful action to relieve the British parachutists dropped at Arnhem in September 1944 and eventually crossed the Rhine at the beginning of April, a month before the German surrender. Heath had to supervise the execution of a young soldier of Polish extraction who had been found guilty of rape and murder; this experience confirmed his opposition to capital punishment. Later he had an opportunity to sit in the gallery during the Nuremberg trials. Around him in Germany lay the evidence of the ruin and death the Third Reich had caused its own people. The devastation of Germany shaped his views on Europe. He convinced himself that reconciliation between the peoples of Europe was essential if this tragedy was not to be repeated.

Heath was demobilized in August 1946 with the rank of major. Though in no way military in instincts, he had been deeply impressed by the army. His affection and respect for the institution was illustrated when in 1947, with the rank of lieutenant-colonel, he helped to form a territorial regiment of the Honourable Artillery Company, a connection that remained important to him through the rest of his life. He enjoyed the sense of comradeship based on discipline and the orderly taking of decisions. He paid careful attention to the views and interests of his men. He carried this concept of good order based on reasonable leadership into the world of peacetime politics. There was by now no doubt about the career of his choice; equally there was no doubt that he could not afford to pursue that career without income from another source. He looked in vain for a business employer so broad-minded that he could provide Heath with an income while allowing him to look round for a constituency. Eventually he applied for the civil service, passed in top, and was allocated to the planning directorate of the Ministry of Civil Aviation on a salary of £500 per year. To his army experience Heath now added knowledge of how the civil service worked. He developed a dislike for what he called 'bumbledom' but this did not undermine his belief that under proper leadership the civil service was capable of energetic and far-sighted administration.

The foreseen difficulty arose when after three unsuccessful attempts Heath was adopted as prospective parliamentary candidate for the Conservatives in Bexley. There was no way of combining this pursuit with his job in Whitehall; he had to resign and look elsewhere. From January 1948 he was the news editor at the *Church Times*. At £650 a year his salary was rather higher than it had been in the civil service but the job never caught his imagination and in October 1949 he was glad to move to a junior position in the small merchant bank Brown Shipley & Co. Ltd, which provided him with valuable experience of the world of finance. But the focus of his energies was Bexley, a traditional Kentish village swept up into suburban London by the surge of private house building in the 1930s. In the Labour landslide of 1945 the seat had been won handsomely for Labour by Janet Adamson, and subsequently (in a by-election in 1946) by Heath's contemporary at Oxford Ashley Bramall. It was the kind of seat the Conservatives had to win back if they were to form a government. Heath had to work hard to make himself known and described his progress in Bexley as 'not so much a Long March as an Interminable Dinner-Dance' (Heath, 126). Over the years he developed a strong personal relationship with the constituency based on mutual affection; this survived the alteration of the boundaries that in 1974 deprived him of Bexleyheath and changed the constituency name to Sidcup. (The name was changed again to Old Bexley and Sidcup in 1983.) Often commentators who took it for granted that Heath lacked the common touch were surprised to find this clearly contradicted in Bexley.

At that time it was no disadvantage to Heath that he remained a bachelor. This was no settled decision on his part. His friendship with Kay Raven had produced a general feeling which Heath evidently shared that one day they would get married. But he was slow, busy with other things, and, as he put it himself, took too much for granted. When she wrote to say that she was going to marry someone else, he never saw her again. Although he had many women friends he never seriously thought of marrying anyone else. Later there were occasional waves of speculation that Heath was homosexual. Those close to him never saw any evidence to support or justify such speculation.

MP and Conservative whip, 1950–1959 The general election of 1950 was tensely fought in Bexley as elsewhere. Election meetings were well attended and the technique of intensive canvassing probably more vigorously applied in the general elections of this decade than ever before or since. Heath was confident of victory but achieved it by the narrowest of margins, beating Bramall by 133 votes, thanks to the 481 votes siphoned away from Labour by a local electrician who stood as a communist and thus earned ironic thanks and compliments in Heath's speeches for many years to come. Though the Conservative Party failed by a narrow margin to dislodge Labour from power, the general election of 1950 strengthened its underlying position by bringing into the House of Commons an outstanding crop of new members, including Iain Macleod, Reginald Maudling, Enoch Powell, and Robert Carr. There was nothing to suggest that Heath would become prominent in this cohort but he benefited greatly from the habit that new members of parliament have of seeking each other's company. Out of this habit sprang the One Nation group of Conservative MPs who met over dinner, exchanged ideas, and planned a publication. The moving thought behind the group was that the Conservative Party could no longer afford a casual, amateurish approach to social and economic problems. Rab Butler had made a start in modernizing the party's thinking during the 1945 parliament, but its ideas now needed a harder edge. In later years the One Nation group was portrayed by many, including Heath, as a grouping of the centre left of the party. Initially, however, it included thinkers from both the left and the right, united mainly in the belief that serious and well-prepared thought was essential on such matters as trade union reform and the future of the welfare state. This emphasis on new ideas and thorough preparation suited Heath well. He had few other distractions at this time. He found himself simple accommodation in London, but Broadstairs was still his home and the family the centre of his limited social life.

For his maiden speech on 26 June 1950 Heath chose a European theme that flowed directly from his own experience before, during, and immediately after the war. He remained loyal to the theme of a united Europe for the rest of his life. In 1950 the Labour government decided not to take an active part in the Schuman plan, which led to the creation of the European Coal and Steel Community. Heath criticized this caution as a lost opportunity. Although he was at all times ready to argue the case for Europe on economic grounds, he never concealed either in this speech or later his own personal conviction that the essence of the case was political. In his memoirs he wrote that 'the *raison d'être* of the European Union is political, to integrate Germany into Europe, using its powerful geopolitical position for the benefit of our continent as a whole' (Heath, 144). Nearly fifty years earlier his maiden speech foreshadowed this emphasis.

Within months Heath was offered promotion as an opposition whip. He hesitated before accepting this offer. He could not have foreseen that he would spend the next eight years in the whips' office, first in opposition, then as a government whip, and eventually as chief whip to Anthony Eden and Harold Macmillan. But he knew that by agreeing to become a whip he was sentencing himself to almost complete silence in the House of Commons. For some whips this was no sacrifice. Heath by contrast remained intensely ambitious for government office. He would have liked to build up his reputation in debate. Yet for the ambitious it is a fairly safe general rule to accept whatever opportunities are actually offered. Moreover Heath saw how much experience could be gained from the close relationship between the whips' office and the leaders of the party.

Heath needed to fortify one weak point in his political prospects. His majority of 133 votes in Bexley made him vulnerable to the slightest swing of opinion against the Conservatives. He set himself to broaden and strengthen the local Conservative Association. By the standard of those times he was exceptionally assiduous in handling individual constituency cases. He was greatly helped by a loyal and efficient agent, Reg Pye, and by the acquisition as constituency headquarters of a modest house on Crook Log, with an upstairs flat where he could conveniently stay the night. These arrangements were only in their infancy when the next electoral test came in October 1951. Bramall fought to retake the seat but Heath achieved a slightly more comfortable majority of 1639. Gradually over the years that followed Bexley became more prosperous, the Conservative organization strengthened, and Heath, always well liked locally, made himself impregnable. Those who canvassed for Heath in later years felt that they were supporting a local institution rather than a party candidate.

For Heath the 1951 campaign was memorable for a sadder reason. His mother, the emotional focus of his life, was dying of cancer. He broke off his campaign each evening to go back to Broadstairs where he played her favourite music on the piano under the room where she spent her last days. She died ten days before polling day and as a sign of sympathy the Labour Party in Bexley suspended all campaigning. In later years Heath hardly ever spoke of his mother, but she was never replaced in his life.

In March 1952 Heath was appointed deputy chief whip under the easy-going leadership of Patrick Buchan-Hepburn. He set about reorganizing the whips' office as if he were once again adjutant of a regiment. At this stage of his life he became known for tact and patience. These qualities were crucially required after he was promoted to be Anthony Eden's chief whip in December 1955. This change transferred him from the narrow parliamentary stage to a position of national importance. The test came in the months of crisis between Nasser's nationalization of the Suez Canal in July 1956 and the resignation of Eden in January 1957. Although not a member of the cabinet he was invited to attend all the crucial meetings that led up to the invasion of Egypt at the end of October. He was one of the few to be told at the beginning of the prime minister's acceptance of a plan agreed at Sèvres by which Britain and France would connive at an Israeli attack on Egypt as an excuse for their own invasion. He later claimed that he had made clear to the prime minister in private his own misgivings about the invasion, but he did not believe that it would be right for him to express such views to the cabinet or indeed anywhere else. Nor did he believe that resignation was a choice open to him any more than it was open to an officer in the field. Only by adhering to these rules could he carry out the job he had accepted, namely that of keeping the parliamentary party to the greatest possible extent united behind the policy on which the government had agreed. His handling of the crisis helped to steady the government and save the parliamentary party from disintegration. He was probably the only substantial figure in the government whose reputation was actually enhanced by the crisis.

Heath as chief whip had to be outwardly impartial in the contest for the leadership that followed Eden's resignation, but his own view, expressed to the queen's private secretary, was firmly in favour of Harold Macmillan as opposed to Rab Butler. Butler had opened up the Conservative Party to modern thinking in a way that Heath strongly approved. But earlier memories prevailed; Butler had been an appeaser and a supporter of Munich whereas Macmillan had been staunch against fascism. Heath rightly judged that Macmillan was the more decisive character. The new era was characteristically ushered in by a dinner with oysters at the Turf Club at which the new prime minister and Heath happily planned the composition of the new government.

For two and a half years Heath continued as chief whip but the nature of the job had changed. Heath had liked and respected Eden but to Macmillan he was something between a comrade and a chief of staff. In retrospect Heath's attitude fell well short of idolatry. In private he criticized quite harshly two of Macmillan's main decisions as prime minister, namely his desire to appease Khrushchov during the Cuba missile crisis in 1962 and his deal with the Americans on the British nuclear deterrent at Nassau in the same year. In spite of this he judged that Macmillan had the most constructive mind of any politician whom he knew. The temperaments of the two men differed greatly. Heath had nothing of the actor in him and his knowledge of history and literature was limited. Macmillan allowed his scholarship and his stagecraft too large a place in his premiership. Heath saw through the trappings and recognized an intelligent and patriotic leader to whom he owed much.

Cabinet minister and shadow chancellor, 1959–1965 In October 1959, following his general election victory, Macmillan appointed Heath to succeed Iain Macleod as minister of labour. Heath was not a man to rush to conclusions on a new subject. He made no dramatic impression on the Ministry of Labour during his seven months as its head, but his apprenticeship in industrial relations strongly influenced his attitudes later as prime minister. Under successive Conservative ministers since 1951 it had functioned as a ministry of conciliation. The Conservative Party under Churchill, Eden, and Macmillan was anxious to distance itself as quickly as possible from the memories of mass unemployment and industrial disputes between the two wars. Heath would have been well aware of growing disquiet in sections of the Conservative Party about a policy that put industrial peace ahead of the competitiveness of industry, but these worries had not yet come to a head.

As minister of labour Heath had to deal with a serious dispute about pay in the nationalized railway system. British Railways was offering an increase of 4 per cent and the unions were holding out for 5 per cent. In the background an independent committee was brooding over the whole question. Believing, as it turned out correctly, that the committee would recommend a much more substantial increase, Heath persuaded the cabinet and British Railways to accept an increase to 5 per cent, and thus averted a damaging strike. A few commentators, notably *The Economist*, criticized what they regarded as a surrender, but the mood of the moment, emphatically shared by the prime minister, was to congratulate Heath on a skilful piece of diplomacy. Heath prided himself on the good personal relationships he established with the main trade union leaders, in particular the senior TUC figures Sir Vincent Tewson and Vic Feather. In their company he showed the qualities of tact and quiet reasonableness that had served him well as chief whip. He later tried to use the reputation thus gained to implement a very different policy.

In July 1960 Macmillan moved Heath to the Foreign Office as a second cabinet minister, with particular responsibility for European affairs and the official title lord privy seal. The European Economic Community had by then existed for two and a half years. Macmillan had not yet decided that Britain should apply for membership but by 1960 his thoughts were on the move. The foreign secretary, the earl of Home, was primarily interested in the Commonwealth and in relationships with the Soviet Union and the communist world. He would not be the man for intricate institutional and economic negotiations with the European Community. It is always tricky to place two cabinet ministers in the same department but this particular experiment was successful. For fifteen years in different capacities the two men, wholly dissimilar in background and outlook, worked smoothly together, each developing a genuine though sometimes humorous respect for the other's abilities.

Heath made a slow start as the spokesman for the Foreign Office in the House of Commons. He was not a man to improvise knowledge he did not possess, and it took him time to master the briefs. But during this period he developed a marked ability to handle the foreign politicians with whom he increasingly came in contact. Gradually the government edged forward towards Europe. In May 1961 Heath set out before the House of Commons the different options. At the end of July the government decided to apply for membership of the European Community and announced this decision to the House of Commons. In the middle of August Heath was appointed to take charge of the negotiations. Their substance was largely economic since that was the character of the community Britain wanted to join. But neither Macmillan nor Heath concealed the fact that their motives for joining were essentially political. In August 1961 Heath talked openly about the arguments for pooling sovereignty. That summer marked a turning point in his political career. Until then he had been dealing without passion or personal commitment with the different problems laid before him. The effort to get Britain into Europe was a different matter.

The European negotiations opened in Brussels in October 1961 and lasted for thirteen months. Heath was helped by a team of able officials, led by Sir Pierson Dixon, British ambassador in Paris, and Sir Eric Roll, from Whitehall. Heath quickly established himself as their leader in substance as well as name. The negotiations did not consist simply of sessions with the representatives of the six member states and the commission in Brussels; they included also the handling of the press and of the House of Commons. Heath mastered all three elements of his task. He possessed little natural wit or eloquence, but gained a dominant position by the ability to master a difficult subject and explain it in clear terms without subterfuge or prevarication.

There were three main obstacles to British entry. First, and least important, was that Britain had put together as a half-hearted rival to the European Community a group of like-minded countries on the periphery of Europe committed to free trade. Once it became clear that there was no chance of the European Free Trade Association (EFTA) as such negotiating its inclusion in the European Community, Britain had to detach herself from EFTA on terms that were reasonable to her former partners. Second, and more important, was the Commonwealth. The old white dominions had fought alongside Britain with great courage in two world wars; the emotional bonds could not be forgotten. The newer members of the Commonwealth in Africa, Asia, and the Caribbean were also worried about the economic effects of British membership. Finally there were the domestic issues. The Conservative Party, beguiled by the skills of the prime minister, was at this stage remarkably passive, though at party conferences in 1961 and 1962 Heath had to deal with principled opposition led by Sir Derek Walker-Smith. Much would depend on the detailed outcome of the negotiations, particularly as regards agriculture. Since the Agriculture Act of 1947 British farmers had settled comfortably into a system of deficiency payments by which the taxpayer in effect guaranteed them an income regardless of the market. The common agricultural policy, taking shape in separate discussions while Heath was negotiating for Britain, was likely to involve a completely different system. The inevitable complexity of the negotiations made it easy for any one country to achieve delays. Heath found that five of the six wanted to make good speed. The French, however, contrived delay after delay out of a general reluctance to see

Britain challenge French dominance of the community, and in particular because they were anxious not to let Britain take part in the community's own discussions about agriculture until these were buttoned up in a way that suited the French farmer.

Heath and his team had hoped to finish the negotiations before the summer holidays of 1962, but the French made this impossible. During the months that followed the prospects darkened. The Labour Party under Hugh Gaitskell, which had until then equivocated, came down firmly against British entry. A separate argument developed about the future of the British nuclear deterrent. At Nassau Macmillan negotiated with President Kennedy the supply of American Polaris submarine-based missiles to replace the cancelled Skybolt as the basis of the British nuclear deterrent. President de Gaulle of France interpreted this as evidence of Britain's commitment to Atlanticism ahead of Europeanism. Macmillan had a difficult session with de Gaulle at Rambouillet in December. In spite of this souring of relations between Britain and France, Heath and his team, strengthened by the support of the other five EEC member states, believed that there was a good chance of finishing their negotiations in January 1963. They were frustrated by the press conference given by President de Gaulle on 14 January in which, ignoring all the progress made in the negotiations, he claimed that Britain was unsuited to enter Europe. Heath tried to keep the negotiations going but despite the willingness of the other five the French were in the end able to prevent this. Heath made a dignified farewell to Brussels in a speech that was long remembered. He repeated that Britain was a part of Europe by geography, history, culture, tradition, and civilization, and that the British were not going to turn their backs on Europe. Nevertheless de Gaulle's veto was a savage blow to Heath and the Macmillan government. Heath continued unhappily as a Foreign Office minister until the autumn. But he had established a reputation in Europe as a man of real substance, and his place as a leading figure in national politics was now secure.

Heath was not a major actor in the dramatic events within the Conservative Party that followed the retirement of Macmillan in October 1963 and ended in the appointment of Sir Alec Douglas-Home (formerly the earl of Home) to succeed him. Heath was already on good personal terms with the new prime minister and it came as no surprise that he was promoted to become president of the Board of Trade and secretary of state for industry, trade and regional development. One result of the struggle for succession was, however, important to Heath two years later. Two able members of his political generation, who might have been natural rivals with him for the leadership, virtually excluded themselves by refusing to take part in Douglas-Home's government. With Iain Macleod and Enoch Powell out of the way Heath's main rival in his own generation was Reginald Maudling, chancellor of the exchequer. Although Maudling held this senior position he lacked the energetic ambition that drove Heath forward in his new post.

Heath now began to speak about the need for change with a sense of urgency he had not felt as minister of labour four years earlier. He pressed forward on two fronts that might have seemed contradictory, but for him were part of the same policy. He used the authority and funds of the government to promote a strong regional policy, with incentives to industry to create jobs in areas of unemployment. He always rejected the argument that this kind of regional policy was a distortion of the market; he believed that the government should work with both sides of industry to guide the creation of wealth into channels that were not only profitable but helpful to the wider public good. His other more controversial measure was to remove an important obstacle to the free market in Britain, the system of retail price maintenance that kept prices high and uncompetitive across a wide range of goods and services. The politics of this proposal were hotly contested within the Conservative Party, many of whose MPs relied for support, as they thought, on the small businessmen who might be swept away by competition in the high street. Heath made some concessions at the outset but sternly refused to consider further concessions when the bill ran into difficulty in the Commons. One important amendment was defeated by only a single vote, but Heath held firm and kept the cabinet with him. The episode established Heath's reputation as a convinced reformer, but also as a man who expected his followers to follow and had only limited time for listening to their objections to a policy on which he was determined.

On the whole success came to Heath through hard work rather than good fortune, but in the months after the Conservative defeat in the general election of 1964 luck turned sharply on his side. Douglas-Home had lost the election more narrowly than had been generally expected; it could not therefore be assumed that he would give up the leadership of the party. But as the months passed and the Wilson government established itself it became less and less likely that the Conservatives could succeed under him in the next election, which, given the government's narrow majority, could not be far off. The favourite to succeed him was Maudling, whom everybody liked, but who suffered from Wilson's success in pinpointing his chancellorship as responsible for the balance of payments crisis that the Labour government inherited. By accepting a large number of directorships immediately after the election Maudling appeared more keen on the good life than on political success. Heath by contrast took up only one directorship, with his former employer Brown Shipley, and flung himself into the two roles Douglas-Home gave him as shadow chancellor of the exchequer and director of party policy. By his aggressive attacks on the 1965 Finance Bill he fleetingly built himself a reputation as a formidable Commons debater. This was the skill that the parliamentary party felt it lacked when confronted with the quick wit and sharp tactics of the new prime minister.

Leader of the opposition, 1965–1970 When Douglas-Home announced in July 1965 that he was stepping down as leader of the party, Heath immediately entrusted a thrusting new back-bencher, Peter Walker, with the direction of his own campaign. Despite the efforts of the third candidate, Enoch Powell, the contest (under a new procedure, whereby the leader was chosen by a ballot of Conservative MPs) was not about ideas but essentially between two well-qualified candidates with similar 'one nation' philosophies. In the ballot held on 28 July Heath polled 150 votes, against 133 for Maudling and 15 for Powell. The parliamentary party thus narrowly backed what they believed to be the more able and energetic candidate. The fallacy in this argument immediately became clear when Heath was consistently worsted by Wilson in House of Commons debates. Setting a pattern that persisted for several years Heath recovered ground at the party conference in October 1965, but his personal ratings in the opinion polls began to fall behind those of the Conservative Party as a whole. An overseas event made things worse. The unilateral declaration of independence in 1965 by the white Rhodesian government under Ian Smith produced a deep rift within the Conservative Party. Heath struggled to keep the party together but on the question of sanctions against Rhodesia it split into three sizeable contingents, voting for, abstaining, and voting against the government's proposal on sanctions. When Wilson called a general election in March 1966 it was generally expected that Labour would win again. Heath fought a courageous campaign and earned personal credit for himself, but was disappointed with Labour's gain of forty-seven seats, giving Wilson an absolute majority of ninety-six.

Heath settled into a long slog as leader of the opposition, the most thankless task in British politics. By this time he had moved into a comfortable and well-placed bachelor flat in The Albany, just north of Piccadilly. He equipped himself with a small staff who had to work hard in return for small praise, but who became strongly attached to him through admiration for his energy and integrity. His two parliamentary private secretaries, Jim Prior and Anthony Kershaw, had the difficult task of keeping him on reasonable terms with the parliamentary party. Another group handled his relationships with the media, and in particular his broadcasts. All these supporters had to cope with a new tension that had built up inside Heath once he became leader of the party. The affable and understanding chief whip, the patient good-humoured negotiator in Europe, had become less easy in his dealings with most of the world. Those who knew him best enjoyed his sardonic humour and admired his far-sightedness. Others, including many on whose support he relied, glimpsed only an edgy, defensive man, sparing of those small politenesses that lubricate political life.

Heath divided his work into two parts, namely opposition to the Labour government and preparation for the government he would one day lead. There was no doubt that he found this second task more congenial. No leader of the opposition had ever spent so much time equipping himself and his colleagues for a task that often seemed distant or even out of reach. The party's policy work covered the whole field, but Heath interested himself particularly in three aspects. In March 1966 he set the Conservative Party on a new path as regards industrial relations. Under the mild but thorough leadership of Robert Carr the party planned the scheme that became the Industrial Relations Act 1971. For Heath, Carr, and the others concerned this was emphatically not an attack on the trade unions. It was an effort, based largely on American experience, to bring employers, unions, and government into a relationship compatible with a more competitive British economy. Second, Heath was determined to achieve British entry into the European Community. He kept the threads of policy closely in his own hands. The Foreign Office at the time played with ideas of isolating the French, and building a relationship with the remaining five members. Heath rightly thought that this was a doomed policy and that the main British effort should go into persuading the French to reverse de Gaulle's veto. Third, Heath concentrated on the machinery of government itself. In his view the government would have to shed the bureaucratic habits and prejudices that had been encouraged by the post-war Labour administration and left in place under Churchill and Macmillan. For this purpose he mobilized a team of businessmen who would be ready to come into government to help ministers. The very centre of government, namely the cabinet office and 10 Downing Street, should be organized to accept criticism and change. Heath believed that Wilson was polluting the integrity of government with practices of patronage that verged on the corrupt. The stable should be cleansed of partisanship and a more effective government established on the basis of national consensus.

While he directed his enthusiasm to the task of preparing for government, Heath had to carry out day by day the duties of leader of the opposition. He tried to do this by turning to effect his genuine indignation against Wilson and his government. There was a sharp contrast between the cool objectivity with which Heath set about preparing for power and the heated partisanship with which he ran the opposition. Of the two models set in the nineteenth century, namely Peel's carefully selective opposition and Disraeli's opposition for opposition's sake, Heath chose the second. This led him sometimes into arguments that appeared to run contrary to his fundamental beliefs. One example was his furious broadcast condemning the decision of the government to devalue the pound in November 1967. Another was his almost equal indignation against the government's decision in July 1967 to end British military deployment east of Suez. It is hard to see how the competitive, modernized Britain closely linked with Europe which Heath was planning to create in government could be founded on an overvalued pound or on indefinite commitments to a global military presence.

At this time Heath's relationships with most of his colleagues in the shadow cabinet were cool but correct. Their loyalty meant that there was no conspiracy to dethrone him even at times when his standing in the opinion polls sank dangerously low. The one exception was Enoch Powell; this exception led to a crisis that could have been fatal to Heath's career. Heath regarded Powell as a strange man whose natural intelligence was distorted by a reluctance to allow facts to prevail over political ideas. Powell's 'rivers of blood' speech about immigration delivered in Birmingham in April 1968 brought their strained relationship to breaking point. Heath at once dismissed Powell from the shadow cabinet and faced the consequences in the form of a backlash, particularly in London and the west midlands, in favour of Powell and against Heath personally. In the months that followed Heath had to spend what he regarded as an inordinate amount of time working out and proclaiming a detailed Conservative policy on immigration. Powell remained an explosive force within the Conservative Party, willing and able to detonate against its leadership in the two following general elections.

During these years Heath developed quickly a new personal interest, more surprising than the devotion he retained to music. His career as a sailor developed with extraordinary speed, culminating in the purchase of the yacht *Morning Cloud* and his entry in the Sydney–Hobart race in December 1969. This was emphatically not a leisure activity. Heath never cruised; he sailed to race and to win. His successes, and in particular his triumph in the Sydney–Hobart race, were not designed as public relations events to boost his political career. He kept his sailing distinct from his politics. He did not talk politics among the sailors or sailing among the politicians; indeed he relished the distance and difference between the two activities.

At the beginning of 1970 Heath decided that the time had come to draw together the threads of the Conservatives' preparation for government. The shadow cabinet were summoned to a meeting at the Selsdon Park Hotel in Sanderstead, Surrey. The event was unexciting, almost routine. Concepts by then well known were rehearsed and refined; some of the shadow cabinet wondered about the point of it all. At the end it was necessary to say something to the press. It was agreed to announce that a new Conservative government would make a serious effort against crime and this emphasis on law and order policies was duly reported. Wilson, who as prime minister spent much time analysing and exploiting the weaknesses of his opponents, quickly invented the concept of 'Selsdon man'. He argued that the Conservative leadership had decided to abandon the consensus policies of Churchill and Macmillan and to launch a savage right-wing policy aimed against the welfare state. Wilson was wrong, but his allegation stirred up a debate that in retrospect showed a gap in Conservative thinking. The economic debate of the day focused on incomes policy as a means of checking inflation. The Conservative leadership rejected the concept of a compulsory incomes policy. On the other hand they were far from believing that strict monetary policy would be enough in itself to curb inflation. But if there was to be no compulsory incomes policy and no reliance on monetarism, how would inflation be kept under control? To Heath the answer lay in his underlying trust in reason. He believed that given honest leadership and effective explanation the British people would accept the need to behave sensibly.

The pattern of the general election campaign in May and June 1970 followed closely the plan devised by the prime minister. No great policy issue dominated the debate. Seizing a moment of relative calm in the British economy and in international affairs, Wilson wished to present a contrast between a seasoned and moderate Labour government and an opposition being clumsily led by Heath towards hard right-wing policies. Helped by weeks of continuous sunshine the prime minister chatted his way around the country, in a low-key and confident campaign. By contrast the Conservative campaign seemed to suffer from an excess of professionalism. This produced an effect of stilted awkwardness in contrast to the informality of the prime minister. The opinion polls supported the impression that most political commentators formed, that Wilson was heading for a third victory and Heath for his second defeat. In the middle of the campaign Heath agreed to switch his tactics. He began to add informal walkabouts to the televised meetings. These went well, for example in the Medway towns and in Edinburgh, surprising those who were not familiar with the relaxed way in which he had for many years built up his personal position in Bexley. In the last few days of the campaign bad trade figures disfigured the sunny portrait of the British economy that Wilson was painting.

The policy content of the debate was slight. The Conservatives emphasized rising prices under Labour, though they remained vague about how a Conservative government would improve the position. Heath hammered away at his two main themes, which went beyond the ordinary run of policy issues. In his personal foreword to the election manifesto and throughout the campaign he continued to attack the shifty and second-rate quality of the Wilson government. He also set out his own idea of a Britain in which the good things of life, going beyond material prosperity, became much more widely available. These were themes on which he felt strongly from his own experience. In Australia at the time of the Sydney–Hobart race his driver had recently emigrated from Britain and found, as he explained to Heath, that in Australia the average citizen knew tomorrow would always be better than today. This phrase struck Heath forcibly and became the title of his election manifesto, *A Better Tomorrow*.

Three days before polling day a key opinion poll still put the Conservatives twelve points behind. Some in the Conservative leadership, though emphatically not Heath himself, began to prepare for defeat and the inevitable change of leadership that would result. Heath himself went to Bexley where he had to wrestle with the oddity of a rival candidate who had changed his name to Edward Heath. On the late evening of 18 June it became apparent from the first results that there had been an upset. Having achieved a substantially increased majority in Bexley, Heath was driven to London. By the time he arrived at Conservative central office it was clear against all the odds that he had won. He received this news calmly as something he had always expected. For his supporters the satisfaction was all the greater because the commentators as well as the Labour Party had been confounded. The Conservative Party gained an overall majority of thirty-one including the Ulster Unionists, and the following day Heath became prime minister.

Prime minister, 1970–1974 Much confused explanation followed. One opinion poll had at the last minute produced a finding favourable to the Conservatives. Only by postulating a dramatic late swing could the opinion pollsters and commentators find a justification for their predictions. To those who had followed the actual campaign on the ground this was an unconvincing theory. The tactical change in the Conservative campaign and the incident that worked against Labour in the last few days were not sufficient to produce such a sudden change in public attitudes. Local evidence suggested that the electorate had been steadily moving to an unfavourable verdict on the Wilson government and a willingness to give Heath a chance, even though this conclusion found no definite expression before polling day.

At his first party conference as prime minister in October 1970 Heath proclaimed that he had set in hand 'a quiet revolution' (*The Times*, 27 Oct 1970). The phrase achieved temporary fame and was then forgotten. One of Heath's difficulties throughout his premiership stemmed from his inability to convey to the public the enthusiasm and determination with which he approached his task. It was remarkable that a man with such an acute sense of musical harmony should fail to grasp the possibilities of the English language, with its reservoir of rich vocabulary and resonant phrases. To a young audience Heath could speak informally to great effect; but to the public as a whole, particularly on the set-piece occasions when stakes were high, the prime minister's phrases appeared clumsy and wooden.

Heath was not content with the instruments of government he inherited. He believed that under Wilson the machinery of government had lost its effectiveness and its integrity. At number ten he put an end to the warfare between civil servants and political advisers by giving clear primacy to the former. After a few weeks he was fortunate in finding as his principal private secretary Robert Armstrong, who served him first as an official and then as a friend with formidable loyalty for the rest of Heath's life. He cleansed the government's information machine by putting at its head a career Foreign Office official, Donald Maitland. To the dismay of some of his supporters he was puritanical in recommending honours for political services. But he was not content simply to rid the system of abuses; he believed that it deserved fundamental reform. Not all the initiatives he undertook prospered under his premiership, though some of them were carried forward by Margaret Thatcher ten years later. The most imaginative and significant reform was the creation of the central policy review staff and the appointment of Lord Rothschild to be its head. This small team of highly intelligent people, operating at the heart of government without loyalty to any particular department, looking with stylish courage but without preconceptions at the main problems of the day, acted as a valuable stimulant—though also occasionally as an embarrassment, which explains why it was emasculated and finally abolished by his successors.

If in some respects Heath was puritanical, in other ways he showed his own intense enjoyment of the office of prime minister. He maintained his active interest in sailing throughout the next decade and a half, even when prime minister, going down to Cowes to prepare or to race most weekends during the sailing season in a succession of yachts each in turn named *Morning Cloud*, competing in the Admiral's cup races that were held every other year, and captaining the British team to victory in 1971. To a man with no home of his own and with a tiny and distant family, it was a huge pleasure to live and entertain at 10 Downing Street and at Chequers. Both houses were dramatically redecorated. Heath was an excellent host and spread his hospitality to people of talent and achievement in different professions to an extent that went far beyond any calculation of political benefit. By bringing music into most of these occasions he gave notable pleasure to the performers and to his guests. One Thursday morning in November 1971 the cabinet was summoned to its regular meeting earlier than usual in order that the prime minister could go to the Royal Festival Hall to conduct a rehearsal with the London Symphony Orchestra of Elgar's overture *Cockaigne*. He answered prime minister's questions and held meetings that afternoon, and returned to the Festival Hall at 7.30 p.m. in full evening dress to conduct the performance.

Heath was fortunate in the talent and loyalty of his colleagues. It was not in his nature to be on easy terms with all of them but a small group were joined to him by loyalty and affection. Sir Alec Douglas-Home, William Whitelaw, Lord Carrington, and Jim Prior formed a relationship with him based on teasing, hard work, and mutual respect. It was a great misfortune that his chosen chancellor of the exchequer, Iain Macleod, died in July 1970 within weeks of taking office. Macleod was not close personally to Heath, but he had an outstanding intellect and grasp of political reality. He was also the most eloquent parliamentary speaker of his time. The last gift in particular was something the Heath cabinet sorely missed.

It was clear from the outset that one of Heath's priorities would be to negotiate Britain's entry into the European Community. But this was not the first foreign policy issue to come to the boil during his premiership. The Conservative Party in opposition had undertaken to remove the ban on the sale of British arms to the apartheid government in South Africa. When Douglas-Home as foreign secretary announced that this promise would be honoured a noisy argument developed inside the Commonwealth, which overshadowed the Commonwealth conference that Heath attended in Singapore in January 1971. It was resolved by an opaque compromise by which Britain joined her Commonwealth partners in a declaration against racism, retained her right to sell arms to South Africa, but did not in practice do so. In the margins of the same conference an answer was found to another problem that arose from promises made in opposition. Heath had fiercely denounced the Labour government's intention to remove British forces from east of Suez. It proved too late to reverse the withdrawal from the Gulf; but as regards the Far East a five-power agreement was worked out for regional defence involving Britain, Australia, New Zealand, Singapore, and Malaysia.

Meanwhile negotiations had been renewed in Brussels for British entry into the EEC. After Macleod's death Heath appointed Anthony Barber as chancellor of the exchequer. In Barber's place as chief negotiator in Europe he selected Geoffrey Rippon. Rippon was not a politician of the first rank, nor was he by temperament devoted to detail; but his shrewdness and knowledge of human nature served him well in a role that was bound to be subordinate to the overriding interest of the prime minister. Detailed negotiations opened in Brussels on 29 October 1970. The main briefs were already well thumbed. They included questions relating to Commonwealth suppliers, particularly of sugar from the Caribbean and Mauritius and butter from New Zealand. The EEC itself was at the time working out a fisheries regime that was obviously of great interest to the British applicant. The main difficulties emerged over the contribution Britain would have to make to the EEC budget, and the whole question of the role of the sterling area as a currency centre.

By February 1971 it looked as if negotiations were in danger of stalling, and this pessimism was renewed in March when the French tabled a plan that would have brought an early end to the sterling area. At this point Heath's grasp of the fundamental strategy asserted itself. There was no sense in trying to mobilize the five against France; the French had to be persuaded before negotiations in Brussels could succeed. Secret bilateral discussions began in Paris, with Christopher Soames, British ambassador and a seasoned politician, and Robert Armstrong in the lead on the British side, talking to the Elysée rather than the Quai d'Orsay. On 20–21 May the British prime minister and the French president met in Paris. Having persuaded himself that Britain under Heath's leadership would play a wholehearted part in the work of the European Community, President Pompidou on the last day of the meeting revoked publicly de Gaulle's veto on British entry. Negotiations in Brussels were then quickly concluded and on 7 July the British government issued a white paper setting out the terms on which entry had been negotiated.

It remained to achieve parliamentary approval. Against a background of public scepticism the Labour leadership began to move towards opposing entry on the terms set out. Given the existence of a substantial body of Conservative MPs opposed to entry, the parliamentary prospects were precarious. Under the skilful guidance of the chief whip, Francis Pym, the government postponed a vote until the autumn. In his speech on the second reading of the bill on 21 October Heath set out his vision of Britain in Europe. He hardly concerned himself with the terms of the negotiation; his emphasis was almost entirely political. Pym had persuaded Heath to allow the Conservatives a free vote, and Labour was compelled to follow suit. This tactic maximized the number of Labour pro-Europeans ready to support the government against the advice of the leadership. The sixty-nine Labour rebels outweighed the thirty-nine Conservative rebels who voted against the government, and the majority for entry, 112 votes, exceeded expectations. The bill ran into difficulties later because the Labour pro-Europeans did not feel able to repeat their heroic stand on second reading. The government's majority fell more than once into single figures but eventually the bill became law and Heath signed the treaty in Brussels on 22 January 1972. Britain duly joined the European Community on 1 January 1973. This was the greatest single achievement of Heath's premiership, and indeed of his political career.

Heath had not taken a close interest in Irish matters before he became prime minister; nor was it clear in the first few months that he need do so. Civil rights marches had started in 1968 and British troops had been sent to help maintain order by the Wilson government in the following year. Northern Irish matters remained under the supervision of the home secretary, a post to which Heath appointed his former rival Maudling. After Brian Faulkner became prime minister of Northern Ireland in March 1971 he struck up a good relationship with Heath, which he used in August 1971 to urge the prime minister and cabinet to agree to support mass internment in Northern Ireland as a solution to the deteriorating security situation. Heath and his colleagues reluctantly agreed, not least because Faulkner made it clear that if they did not he would be obliged to resign. But the security forces were operating on out-of-date and inaccurate lists, and the Provisional IRA had advance warning, with the result that the operation was botched. So, far from improving the security situation, it led to a fresh outbreak of violence.

The situation deteriorated even further after 'bloody Sunday' on 30 January 1972, when the British army shot dead thirteen demonstrators in Londonderry. Heath examined with colleagues all the possible options and came to the conclusion that the British government would have to exercise direct rule over the province, including in particular responsibility for security. Faulkner had no inkling of this change of heart and was amazed and angry when he was confronted with a *fait accompli* on 22 March. As part of the change a new Northern Ireland Department was created in London and Whitelaw was appointed the first secretary of state. During the next two years he, with steady support from Heath, set about the double task of reducing IRA violence and building a dialogue between the Unionist and nationalist political leaders in the province. It proved possible to hold assembly elections in June 1973 and to form a power-sharing executive under Faulkner's leadership at the end of November. From 6 to 9 December 1973 Heath presided over the Sunningdale conference, which was attended by the Irish government as well as the main parties in the north. Agreement was reached, the Irish accepting the power-sharing arrangement in the north in return for the establishment of a Council of Ireland with vague terms of reference. Faulkner agreed to this reluctantly, but the hostile reaction among his supporters began to undermine his authority. Heath's decision to call a general election in February 1974 prejudiced even further Faulkner's chances of winning through on the basis of the Sunningdale agreement. The last chance that the agreement might stand was swept away when the incoming Labour government in London yielded to the Ulster workers' strike organized by Ian Paisley. The whole structure painstakingly erected by Whitelaw and Heath then collapsed.

When he became prime minister Heath knew his government would have to deal with unexpected challenges, even disasters, such as those in Northern Ireland. But his underlying determination, passionately held though in the end frustrated, was that untoward events should not push the government away from its underlying purpose. The most clearcut of these was the proposal for an industrial relations act. Alongside this came the first budget of the new chancellor of the exchequer, Anthony Barber, on 27 September 1970, in which taxes were cut and economies made in public spending. At the same time the government made clear its intention to disengage from the management of industrial policy. Unfortunately for Heath all these policies began to run into difficulties. At the same time the absence of a practical policy in the most central of all areas, namely the control of inflation, was cruelly revealed.

The Industrial Relations Bill was at all times popular with public opinion. The government had received a clear mandate in its favour. The bill received its second reading in the House of Commons on 15 December. Its main aim was to reduce the number of strikes, in particular unofficial strikes, by making collective agreements legally binding and by removing immunity from a number of unfair industrial practices. The bill provided for a sixty-day cooling-off period and for a secret ballot before strike action. It created a national industrial relations court to administer its provisions. Heath and his secretary of state, Robert Carr, argued throughout the passage of the bill that it was not intended to penalize the unions but to bring up to date the framework of industrial relations in a way that would benefit the unions, the employers, and the public. Nevertheless the majority of the trade union leadership joined the Labour Party in the House of Commons in trying to block the bill, which took up more hours of parliamentary time than any bill since 1945. It eventually received the royal assent on 5 August 1971, but by this time had acquired a reputation as a union-bashing measure. The act was still supported by the general public but defeated its own purpose so far as the unions were concerned. Given the strong opposition of the unions, employers were reluctant to use it.

The government's intention to stand aside from industrial management and rely on private industry to stand on its own feet also came to grief when the prestigious firm Rolls-Royce ran into financial trouble as a result of miscalculating the cost of its aircraft engine contracts with Lockheed. Rather than allowing the company to go bankrupt, the cabinet eventually agreed in February 1971 that it should be taken over by the government in a form in which it could in due course be returned to the private sector. A year later, and without any of the justifications that could be urged for Rolls-Royce, the government rescued the collapsing firm Upper Clyde Shipbuilders with a scheme designed to avert the loss of jobs and possible violence on Clydeside.

The essential issue for the management of the economy was inflation. It was generally accepted by the political establishment that the main inflationary threat arose when wages pushed up costs. The Labour government in 1969 had abandoned the apparatus of incomes policy and the Conservative manifesto of 1970 had rejected statutory control of wages. How then were wages to be restrained? Heath believed that, in the new political situation he had created, an appeal to common sense and reason would fill the gap. Wage restraint was in the common interest of both employers and unions, since inflation was a common enemy. But he did not possess the skills of persuasion to overcome the traditional perception of opposed classes and economic interests. Wilson, more effective as leader of the opposition than as prime minister, consistently mocked the idea of a tory 'one nation'. He was helped in this by the clumsy handling of the Industrial Relations Bill and the resentment it created in the trade union movement.

The obvious and in the end fatal weakness in the government's position concerned public sector wages. The first serious challenge came from the power workers, who began a work-to-rule on 7 December 1970. Power cuts followed, the government declared a state of emergency and appointed a judge, Lord Wilberforce, to hold a court of inquiry. Wilberforce recommended an award of no less than 15 per cent. A postal strike in January 1971 was easier to deal with. At the end of the year, however, the National Union of Mineworkers, deeply anxious and resentful about the running down of the coal industry, put forward a wage claim far in advance of the norm. At first few people supposed that the miners would prevail but stocks at the power stations were inadequate and the miners used flying pickets to prevent coal reaching the power stations. The government felt obliged to refer the dispute to arbitration. Surprisingly Wilberforce was again chosen as arbitrator and in February 1972 he again produced an award highly favourable to the strikers. There was no doubt in anyone's mind that Heath and his colleagues had suffered a serious reverse.

In January 1972 the unemployment figure reached one million. For all those who remembered the mass unemployment of the 1920s and 1930s this was a dramatic event. Certainly Heath had always believed that the Conservative defeat in the 1945 election had been the result of a perceived link between the tory party and unemployment, and for him full employment or something close to it was an inescapable part of his concept of 'one nation'. During the summer and autumn of 1972 he set himself to overcome the challenge created by the two events of the preceding winter, the miners' strike and the unemployment figures. The budget of 1972 was largely his work. It once again cut taxes but also provided for a range of regional incentives to investment. The government aimed to expand the economy by 10 per cent between the first half of 1971 and the first half of 1973. The 'dash for growth' in the budget was supplemented in June 1972 by the ambitious Industry Act, providing a wide range of assistance to industry.

These initiatives were followed late in the summer by an energetic effort to work out a voluntary incomes policy with the trade unions. Heath chaired a series of meetings at Chequers with the TUC and the Confederation of British Industry. On 26 September he put to them a plan for economic growth, prices, pay, and pensions in the next twelve months. For the first time under a Conservative government the unions were invited to discuss, not just industrial relations but the core subjects of economic management. Although Heath had a good personal relationship with Vic Feather, the TUC general secretary, the plan came up against the firm insistence of the left-wingers of the TUC, Jack Jones and Hugh Scanlon, that there must be a statutory control of prices without a similar control on wages. When the tripartite talks finally collapsed on 2 November there was a fairly general acceptance that the government would be obliged to introduce statutory controls. On 6 November Heath announced to the Commons plans for a complete short-term freeze on all forms of income and the price of all goods and services except imports and fresh food. This 'stage one' would be the preliminary to a long-term counter-inflationary policy. The legislation both on industrial policy and on the wage and price freeze attracted strong criticism from a small minority of Conservative back-benchers, though not enough to put the government at risk. Both aspects of the revised policy were adequately supported by the press and public opinion.

These changes, though certainly dramatic, did not mean a reversal of Heath's personal views about the role of the state in economic affairs. While in opposition he had criticized from time to time the concepts of state aid for industry and, more directly, of the statutory regulation of wages, let alone prices. However, these criticisms were not fundamental to his beliefs. He had a strong respect for the intelligence and ability of the British civil service. He failed to see anything ridiculous or unreal in the notion that for a short exceptional period the government, through competent agencies, could assess the right price for a tube of toothpaste or the right level of reward for a small group of workers. He often spoke with admiration of the way in which France under the Fifth Republic seemed able to plan its economy and look to the long term. Throughout these twists and turns Heath did not alter his underlying purpose, which was to provide through steady economic growth a new range of opportunities for millions of workers with modest backgrounds such as his own.

During the early months of 1973 it seemed just possible that the dash for growth might succeed. In January Heath announced stage two of the statutory incomes policy, which came into effect in April and ran until the end of the year. Stage two allowed increases of £1 plus 4 per cent in ordinary wage settlements and was generally well received. Barber's budget in March further reduced taxation but did not cut government spending. Conservative back-benchers and some of the press began to show alarm at this policy of rapid expansion. Heath took no notice of these protests and was scornful of the critics. He was handicapped by his own determination; it prevented him giving a civil hearing to serious criticism. For the bulk of the Conservative Party in the House of Commons and elsewhere the test was success.

During the summer of 1973 the pressure against the policy mounted. The money available for investment tended to find its way into property rather than industry. Barber's policy of abolishing credit controls removed a piece of machinery on which previous governments had relied to check excess. In August 1971, when the American administration abandoned the fixed dollar price of gold that had been the linchpin of the international financial system since 1945, the British government had been forced to abandon the fixed exchange rate of sterling and let the pound float. The steady decline in the sterling exchange rate thereafter added to inflationary pressure. Stage two of the incomes policy was generally respected; stage three was announced on 8 October on the eve of the Conservative Party conference. At the conference Heath could point to falling unemployment, a rising standard of living, improved pensions, school building, and better social services, financed out of economic growth. But almost at once the internal and external pressures on the policy began to mount and became overwhelming. World commodity prices were already rising when the Arab–Israeli War broke out in October as Egypt and Syria attacked Israel. The price of oil rose rapidly. More immediate was the threat to supplies from Arab sanctions against Western friends of Israel. Britain, not yet benefiting from North Sea oil production, relied on imported oil for half its energy needs.

Against this background the unions were tempted to oppose stage three of the incomes policy even more strongly than its predecessors. The miners in particular found their hand much strengthened; with oil supplies under threat and by the end of the year quadrupled in price, the government could not effectively respond to industrial action by switching the power stations to oil. In July the conference of the National Union of Mineworkers had instructed its executive to table a claim for a 35 per cent increase in 1974. Unfortunately for Heath the National Coal Board decided to table an offer that at one bound went to the limits of what stage three could accommodate. The miners sensed weakness and expected to gain more in negotiations. They announced an overtime ban on 8 November; by then the oil crisis was in full swing. The effect on industry was immediate. Within a few days coal output was cut by 40 per cent. Peter Walker, the secretary of state for energy, announced a state of emergency and restrictions on lighting and heating. The government had been manoeuvred into another contest on the same battlefield where it had met a humiliating defeat in 1972. But in 1973 there could be no Lord Wilberforce to fix the terms for surrender. This time surrender would mean a fatal breach in the incomes policy and collapse of the authority of the government and in particular of the prime minister.

Heath had no desire for confrontation; his whole instinct was for negotiation, so that reason could prevail. He summoned Whitelaw back from Northern Ireland to use his well-known talent for conciliation as employment secretary. At the same time the government had to show firmness. On 13 December, immediately before flying to a European summit in Copenhagen dominated by the oil crisis, Heath announced that industry would operate on a three-day week after Christmas. The miners regarded this as a provocation. On 17 December Barber announced public expenditure cuts of £1200 million, which meant the end of the dash for growth. The nation was in full crisis.

The search for a settlement continued in the new year. Ministers were operating in an atmosphere of fatigue and confusion. The three-day week bought a little time in terms of coal stocks, but at a heavy political price. Some of Heath's advisers began to raise with him the possibility of an early general election. They argued that a fresh mandate from the electorate would strengthen the hand of the government in achieving the best possible settlement. The polls suggested that there was a chance of success. Heath disliked this advice. He saw that an election would become an angry confrontation between the government and the unions. Such a confrontation was the reverse of what his 'one nation' Conservative government should aim at. Different ideas were examined and found wanting. On 9 January the TUC produced a formula suggesting that the miners were a special case, so that a settlement with them would not be used by other unions as a precedent for their own claims. The government concluded that the TUC had in practice no means of carrying out this undertaking. The impasse continued.

There still seemed a chance that the government might win through. The three-day week had held coal stocks steady despite the overtime ban; oil supplies, though expensive, had been secured; spring was coming; it might soon be possible to move to a four-day week. But this prospect induced the National Union of Mineworkers to increase the stakes. On 23 January the executive called a ballot on strike action and on 4 February it was announced that 81 per cent of the miners had voted to strike. On 7 February, driven into a corner with no other answers to the prospect of a ruinous strike, Heath announced that a general election would be held on 28 February.

The general election campaign of February 1974 came as something of an anticlimax to those who had lived close to the events of the preceding three months. Heath concentrated doggedly on his theme about the fairness and crucial importance of the incomes policy. He was reasonably well received, and the polls suggested that he might win. The media and candidates on both sides understandably summarized the issue as 'who governs Britain?', but Heath's mood was stubborn rather than combative. He had to contend again with the destructive effort of Enoch Powell, who was not himself a candidate, but announced that he had voted Labour by post as a vote against the EEC. More damaging was the publication of a set of figures by the Pay Board, which suggested that miners' pay had been overstated. This turned out to be a statistical misunderstanding, but for a few hours it looked as if the government had blundered. Heath in his final very personal broadcast on 26 February sought to turn in his favour the argument that he was stubborn—'is not "stubborn" another way of saying "determined"?' But not enough people agreed. The Conservatives won more votes than Labour, but fewer seats. The Labour Party won 301 seats, the Conservatives 297, the Liberals 14. Over the following weekend Heath discussed with Jeremy Thorpe, leader of the Liberal Party, the possibility of a tory–Liberal coalition. This was an undignified manoeuvre that quickly collapsed. On Monday 4 March Heath drove to Buckingham Palace and resigned the premiership.

Leader of the opposition, 1974–1975 Heath remained leader of the Conservative Party, and therefore leader of the opposition, for another eleven months. For him the summer of 1974 was notable for his first visit to China. When prime minister he had accepted this invitation, and after his defeat the Chinese renewed it. It was far from clear when he set out what the character of the visit would be. He had been given no programme and the position of leader of the opposition was not one familiar in the people's republic. However, from the first hour it was clear that the Chinese government intended to treat him as if he were still prime minister. A huge array of schoolchildren sang and danced for him on the tarmac of the Peking (Beijing) airport; he had a long conversation with Mao in the last year of the chairman's life; welcoming crowds were assembled in Shanghai and Canton; and on the last day he was given a panda. The Chinese government made a shrewd investment; for the rest of his life Heath was a devoted student and admirer of the people's republic.

In the autumn Wilson called an early election to improve his precarious position in the House of Commons. This was held on 10 October 1974. The campaign centred on the question whether Britain needed a coalition government of national unity to cope with its acute economic difficulties. The concept was popular and at one level Heath was attracted by it. But it clashed with his own stubborn self-confidence. Heath could not envisage a successful government which was not led by himself. Despite pressure from advisers he would not use any words that committed him to more than an invitation to people from outside the Conservative Party to help solve the nation's problems. Against his own wishes and resolve, Heath was now widely seen as the man who a few months earlier had chosen confrontation with the miners, and lost. He was not credible as the leader of a government of national unity. He fought a courageous campaign. The Conservatives lost another seventeen seats to Labour. Their share of the vote was 35.8 per cent compared to Labour's 39.2 per cent, a rather better result than was generally expected. Nevertheless, it was another defeat, this time decisive.

Heath did not draw the natural consequences for his own position as party leader. Indeed from 1974 on he seemed to detach himself from the ordinary calculations of everyday politics at which he had once been expert. His courage never failed, but he repeatedly reached conclusions that made no sense, even to his friends. One of these was the decision to persevere as party leader after October 1974. He could then have stepped down with dignity, and retained respect. Instead he resisted in futile defiance. The most likely challenger to Heath was expected to be Sir Keith Joseph. But Joseph was a modest man, and was generally agreed to have scotched his chances by an ill-considered speech at Edgbaston in October, which appeared to advocate eugenic controls; he announced in November that he would not be a candidate. The name of Margaret Thatcher began to be canvassed; but she was comparatively little known compared to other possible candidates, Prior, Howe, and in particular Whitelaw. But these three found it impossible to stand against Heath. Thatcher's cause was much advanced when she asked the subtle and well-known back-bencher Airey Neave to manage it. To some he pressed Thatcher's case hard; to others he explained that she was unlikely to win, and the main purpose must be to teach Heath a lesson. This argument was powerful among the many back-benchers who had never had a comfortable relationship with Heath. The party in the constituencies showed continued support for Heath, but it was the Commons that counted. On the first ballot, held on 4 February 1975, Thatcher scored 130 votes, Heath 119 (and Hugh Fraser another 16). Under the new rules, which required a margin of 15 per cent for success, a second ballot was needed. Even Heath could see that there was no point in contesting that. On 11 February 1975 Thatcher was elected leader of the Conservative Party.

Back-bencher The European referendum campaign of 1975 provided the last happy episode in Heath's political career. He was not one of the organizers of the successful 'yes' campaign, but he was glad to speak at many meetings up and down the country. No longer needing to use a text or choose his words with care, he found a spontaneous way of explaining, especially to young audiences, why he believed in Britain's role in the European Community. He was particularly passionate and effective in his old debating ground at Oxford. The added advantage for him was that Thatcher, though leader of the Conservative Party, played a minor part in the affair, echoing orthodox pro-European sentiments but at this stage adding nothing distinctive of her own.

Heath's resentment against Thatcher prevented him from playing a useful political role during the rest of his life. He strongly disapproved of her monetarist policies, which in his view led to the destruction of British manufacturing. He had many opportunities, at party conferences, in the House of Commons, and in the country outside, to voice his complaints. But his personal feeling against the woman who had ousted him from political leadership was dominant. From time to time while the Conservative Party was still in opposition well-wishers tried to reconcile him with the new leadership, but all these attempts failed. Equally doomed was the suggestion that he should stand for the European parliament when it was for the first time directly elected in 1979. There was never a serious likelihood of Heath joining the Conservative government after Thatcher won power in May 1979. Both he and she knew that he could not have worked satisfactorily as foreign secretary under her as prime minister. He rightly regarded her suggestion that he might become ambassador in Washington as a means of getting him out of the way. She never regarded him with the resentment that governed his attitude to her. He had no rational ground for alleging that she had behaved badly when challenging him for the leadership in 1975, except on the untenable argument that since he had appointed her to her first cabinet post she owed him loyalty in all circumstances thereafter. Heath's hostility towards her faded somewhat in the last years of his life, along with his interest in politics as a whole. He never conspired or tried to rally friends against her; nor did he ever contemplate leaving the Conservative Party.

Heath's main interests during these years lay overseas. He was a member of the Brandt commission in 1977, which made recommendations for bridging the gap between north and south in the world. His taste in foreign leaders became somewhat bizarre. His unquestioning affection for the People's Republic of China led him into difficulties at the time of the shootings in Tiananmen Square in 1989. He visited and spoke up for Fidel Castro in Cuba and Saddam Hussein in Iraq, from whom he managed to extract thirty-three detained British subjects after the invasion of Kuwait in 1990. As consultant to the American firm Arthur Andersen he was able to make frequent visits to the United States.

Heath's activities as a yachtsman and as an orchestral conductor gradually subsided, and were replaced by authorship. His copiously illustrated books on sailing, music, and travelling were successful. He was determined to write his memoirs, but for many years it seemed doubtful whether he could achieve this. There were contractual complications and some confusion in the team assembled to help him. Eventually, however, he rallied his energy. As earlier when he had been prime minister, those working with him found that while he would not originate a chapter himself he was stirred to constructive effort when confronted with a draft by someone else. Eventually when published in 1998 the memoirs achieved a greater success than some had thought likely.

Heath found his greatest pleasure during his last years in Arundells, the house in the cathedral close at Salisbury that he bought in 1985. It was the first and last house he had ever owned: he used to say that it was the only home of his own that he had ever had. He filled it with his collection of paintings and memorabilia and thoroughly enjoyed entertaining his friends and after lunch walking them down through the garden to the River Avon. He was always a more successful host than guest. He regularly attended services in the cathedral, and was an active supporter of activities to raise funds for its restoration, among other things organizing and conducting concerts to support the cause.

Another great pleasure was the award of the garter in 1992, whereupon he became Sir Edward. He became father of the House of Commons the same year, and in that capacity oversaw the procedure for electing a new speaker in 2000. He never considered taking a peerage, preferring the choice of Winston Churchill to remain a commoner to the end of his days. He retired from the Commons at the 2001 election. He died at Arundells on 17 July 2005, of bronchopneumonia. His funeral was held in Salisbury Cathedral on 25 July, and his ashes were buried in the south crossing there. A memorial service was held at Westminster Abbey on 8 November 2005. He left an estate valued at more than £5 million; after small legacies to his sister-in-law and his housekeeper, the bulk of it was left to the Sir Edward Heath Charitable Foundation, to conserve Arundells as a museum in his memory.

DOUGLAS HURD

Sources G. Hutchinson, *Edward Heath* (1970) • M. Laing, *Edward Heath, prime minister* (1972) • D. Hurd, *An end to promises: sketch of a government, 1970–1974* (1976) • J. Campbell, *Edward Heath: a biography* (1993) • S. Ball and A. Seldon, eds., *The Heath government, 1970–1974: a reappraisal* (1996) • J. Ramsden, *The winds of change: Macmillan to Heath, 1957–1975* (1996) • M. Holmes, *The failure of the Heath government* (1997) • E. Heath, *The course of my life* (1998) • *The Times* (18 July 2005) • *Daily Telegraph* (18 July 2005) • *Financial Times* (18 July 2005) • *The Guardian* (18 July 2005) • *The Independent* (18 July 2005) • Burke, *Peerage* • *WW* (2005) • personal knowledge (2009) • private information (2009) • b. cert. • d. cert.

Archives Bodl. Oxf., papers • TNA: PRO, papers relating to Common Market, FO 800/887–893 | Bodl. Oxf., William Clark MSS • NL Scot., Tweedsmuir (Buchan) MSS • NL Wales, Desmond Donnelly MSS • TNA: PRO, various departments including PREM • U. Birm., Avon (Eden) MSS • U. Leeds, Bottomley MSS | FILM BFINA, 'Edward Heath: the man who went to the country', D. Rea (director), Channel 4, 16 March 1985 • BFINA, 'Heath at the helm', *Writing on the wall*, B. Shepard (producer), Channel 4, 10 Nov 1985 • BFINA, 'A very singular man: a film portrait of Ted Heath', M. Barrett (producer), BBC2, 27 Sept 1998 • BFINA, 'Sir Ted: a film portrait of Sir Edward Heath', M. Cockerell (director), BBC2, 18 July 2005 • BFINA, current affairs footage • BFINA, documentary footage • BFINA, party political footage • BFINA, performance footage | SOUND BL NSA, interview with D. Rowan, Nov 1986, C1037/2071 • BL NSA, *The tingle factor*, interview with J. Nicholas, c.1993, H1772/02 • BL NSA, *Music: a joy for life*, interview with S. Heath, Classic FM, 5 May 1997, H8917/1 • BL NSA, current affairs recordings • BL NSA, documentary recordings • BL NSA, parliamentary recordings • BL NSA, party political recordings • BL NSA, performance recordings • BL NSA, recorded speeches • BL NSA, recorded talks

Likenesses photographs, 1938–2004, Getty Images, London • photographs, 1947–2002, Photoshot, London • photographs, 1959–2003, PA Photos, London • J. Lee, watercolour on paper, 1965, House of Commons, Westminster, London • J. Gilroy, oils, 1971, priv. coll. • R. Spear, oils, exh. RA 1971 (*Brightly shone the moon that night*), priv. coll. • J. Bown, photograph, 1978, Guardian News and Media Ltd [*see illus.*] • J. Mendoza, group portrait, 1986–7, House of Commons, Westminster, London • M. Jennings, bronze bust, 1991, Oxford Union Society; two casts, priv. coll. and House of Commons, Westminster, London • D. Greenham, portrait, Carlton Club, London • photographs, repro. in Heath, *My life* • photographs, Rex Features, London • photographs, Camera Press, London • thirty-eight portraits, NPG

Wealth at death £5,362,240: probate, 18 Jan 2006, *CGPLA Eng. & Wales*

Heath, Roy Aubrey Kelvin (1926–2008), novelist, was born on 13 August 1926 in Georgetown, British Guiana, the second son and youngest of the four children of Melrose Arthur Heath (*d.* 1928), head teacher of a primary school, and his wife, Jessie de Weever (*d.* 1991), music teacher. His father died before Heath's second birthday, leaving his mother to bring him up with his two sisters, Avis and Lynette, his elder brother, Sonny, being cared for by his maternal grandfather. They lived in the coastal village of Agricola until Heath was eight, when they moved back to Georgetown. Although living in a working-class area of the city in straitened circumstances the mother maintained the family's respectability, and believed strongly in the importance of her children's education. Heath himself became fascinated by the seething variety of human life in the close-packed community, and by the folklore and storytelling that were to influence his own later writing. While still attending Georgetown Central High School, he made surreptitious excursions to the city's billiard saloons and low-life dives.

Heath left school at sixteen for a career in the civil service, becoming a clerk in the treasury in 1944. In 1950 he arrived in Britain to further his education, from 1952 reading modern languages, part-time, at London University, while a clerk at Allen and Hanbury's factory in London. He gained a BA in French in 1956. On 10 January 1953 he had married Emilia (formerly Aemilia) Oberli, then an au pair to the Jewish arts benefactor George Rapp, who became Heath's patron. They had two sons and a daughter. From 1959 he taught at primary schools for the inner London education authority, and from 1968 French and German at Christ's College grammar school, Finchley. He was later to study law, being called to the bar at Lincoln's Inn in 1964, and to the Guyana bar in 1973, but never practised as a lawyer.

Guyana's achievement of independence in 1966 prompted Heath's ambition to chronicle the social history of his homeland in the twentieth century. Beginning in 1972 he contributed short fiction to periodicals, to the Guyanese literary annual *Firebird*, and to the BBC. His first novel, *A Man Come Home*, followed in 1974. Its haunting narrative inspired by folk myth and its Guyanese setting heralded a distinctive talent confirmed by *The Murderer* (1978), a dark, intense tragedy set among the alleys and canals of Georgetown, which won that year's *Guardian* fiction prize. Seven novels followed, focusing on different aspects of Guyanese life and culture, all receiving high critical praise, as well as an autobiography of his early life, *Shadows Round the Moon* (1990).

Heath's Georgetown trilogy, *From the Heat of the Day* (1979), *One Generation* (1980), and *Genetha* (1981), reissued as *The Armstrong Trilogy* in 1994, chronicled the epic of a Guyanese middle-class family. The tragic protagonist in *Orealla* (1984) was poised between the frustrations of Georgetown society and the allure of a vanishing village culture. *The Shadow Bride* (1988), which he considered his finest work, re-created the life of the *déraciné* east Indian immigrants, with the conflicts between social idealism and individual passions accentuated by the country's divisions and corruption. Village life was the setting of *Kwaku* (1982), a picaresque novel of an incompetent fake healer, whose story was given a political turn in Heath's last novel, *The Ministry of Hope* (1997), in which Kwaku moved to Georgetown and ironically found himself becoming successful in a world of endemic fraud and corruption.

Proficient in French and German, Heath was conversant with contemporary European literature and ideas. He had a great love of classical music. At the heart of his work lay a fascination with psychology and the dark workings of the psyche. He was influenced in particular by Freud, and by Jung, whose theories of the archetypes and the collective unconscious shaped both the content and method of his writing. But if his interests were cosmopolitan, he remained resolutely and, as he put it, 'intensely Guyanese' (*The Independent*, 27 June 2008). For him psychology was inseparable from anthropology and history. The personal traumas central to his fiction were set in the context of Guyana's history of slavery, colonialism, and post-colonialism; the fragmentation of cultures imported from Africa, Asia, and Europe; and the powerful, distinctive presences of the country's towns and landscapes.

Heath refused British nationality, and eschewed publicity as a writer. He kept contacts with the immigrant working classes, teaching some of them English in adult evening classes. Until his mother's death he made regular return visits to Guyana. His one play, *Inez Combray*, won the Guyana Theatre Guild prize when produced in Georgetown in 1972. He gave the prestigious Edgar Mittelholzer lectures, 'Art and History', in 1984, and received the Guyana literature prize in 1989. Towards the end of his life he became increasingly debilitated by Parkinson's disease. Yet he never lost his interest in life. 'Perhaps the greatest truth', he wrote, 'is the elusiveness of truth' (*Shadows Round the Moon*, 124). He died on 14 May 2008 at Northwick Park Hospital, Harrow, London, of multiple causes, leaving behind a unique body of writing distinguished by its deep human insight and haunting evocation of place. He was survived by his wife, Emilia, and their three children.

LOUIS JAMES

Sources R. Heath, *Art and history*, Edgar Mittelholzer memorial lectures (1984) · M. McWatt, 'Roy A. K. Heath', *Fifty Caribbean writers*, ed. D. C. Dance (1986), 207–16 · R. Heath, *Shadows round the moon: Caribbean memoirs* (1990) · R. Heath, 'In memory of my father', *Arts Journal* [Guyana], 4 (March 2008), 77–80 · 'Arts Forum saddened at passing of Roy Heath', *Stabroek News*, 16 May 2008, www.stabroeknews.com/2008/archives/05/16/arts-forum-saddened-at-passing-of-roy-heath/, 21 July 2011 · *The Guardian* (20 May 2008) · *The Independent* (27 June 2008) · L. W. Brown, 'Roy A(ubrey) K(elvin) Heath: biography', biography.jrank.org/pages/4414/Heath-Roy-ubrey-K-elvin.html, 21 July 2011 · private information (2012) · m. cert. · d. cert.

Likenesses V. Wilmer, photograph, 1984, repro. in R. Heath, *Orealla* (1984), jacket · K. Wynn, photograph, repro. in R. Heath, *The Ministry of Hope* (1997), jacket · obituary photographs

Wealth at death £505,445: probate, 5 Dec 2008, *CGPLA Eng. & Wales*

Heilbron, Dame Rose (1914–2005), barrister and judge, was born on 19 August 1914 at 27 St James Road, Abercromby, Liverpool, the younger daughter of Max Heilbron and his wife, Nellie, *née* Summers. She was originally named Rosie, but this was later changed to Rose. Her father, described as an emigration agent on her birth certificate, ran a boarding house for Jewish emigrants *en route* to the United States, and then took over a small hotel, in which his daughters were expected to help. But it is said that Rose was allowed to get on with her studying while her elder sister, Annie, did much of the work. Her parents clearly thought it important that she be properly educated. She was sent to the Girls' Public Day School Trust's Belvedere School, Liverpool. There she regularly won prizes in history and drama. She also took elocution lessons, becoming a licentiate of the Guildhall School of Music and Drama at the age of sixteen. Her 'mellifluous voice' was a great asset to an advocate, although she never entirely lost a 'faint tang of the Mersey' (Rose, memorial oration). Another great asset was her intelligence. From Belvedere she went to Liverpool University, graduating LLB with first-class honours in 1935 and LLM in 1937. Meanwhile she joined Gray's Inn and in 1936 was the first woman to be awarded a Lord Justice Holker scholarship.

Heilbron was called to the bar on 3 May 1939. She joined the chambers of her pupil master, Richard Trotter, at 43 Castle Street in Liverpool and was elected to the northern circuit on 2 February 1940, proposed by the recorder of Liverpool, Edward Hemmerde. She rapidly built up a substantial criminal defence and personal injury practice. Like Elizabeth Lane, she may have found it easier to get started, despite the ingrained prejudices of clients, solicitors, clerks, and other barristers, because so many of the men were away during the Second World War. But by the time they returned she had proved her worth and her practice continued to grow apace. She was known as 'a persuasive advocate who gave her all in the preparation of a case and the mastery of detail' (Lynch, 'Mrs Justice Heilbron', 159). She worked extremely hard, no doubt because she 'always loved her work' (private information), but also because she had to support herself.

Heilbron was junior counsel in some notable reported cases: *Constantine* v. *Imperial Hotels Ltd* (1944), establishing that a common innkeeper could not refuse a room to the famous West Indian cricketer Leary Constantine; *Christie* v. *Leachinsky* (1947), establishing that an arrested person must be told the reason for his arrest at the time; and *Braddock* v. *Bevins* (1948), in which the Liverpool MP Bessie Braddock sued a Conservative candidate for saying that she had a tacit deal with the Communists. Heilbron appeared alone before the House of Lords in *Adams* v. *Naylor* (1946) representing two boys who were injured (one fatally) in a minefield on the sandhills between Crosby and Southport. The wind had blown the sand to cover the warning sign and most of the barbed wire fence. They lost the case for technical reasons but Heilbron was commended by the lord chancellor for her 'excellent argument', and the case led directly to the reform of civil proceedings against the crown in the Crown Proceedings Act 1947.

Dame Rose Heilbron (1914–2005), by Elliott & Fry, 1949

Heilbron's personal life also prospered. She met Nathaniel (Nat) Burstein (1905–2010), an Irish-born Liverpool general practitioner, at a VE-day party. They were married on 9 August 1945 at the Harrogate synagogue (because the rabbi was a distant relative of the bride). Their daughter, Hilary, was born on 2 January 1949 (and in due course also became a successful barrister). Not only was Heilbron the first woman to achieve spectacular success at the bar, she was also a pioneer in combining her career with a happy family life, helped by a live-in nanny and other domestics, as well as her husband, who as a GP could stay at home when she had to travel. She continued to use her maiden name.

Three months after Hilary's birth Rose Heilbron and Helena Normanton became the first women to be appointed king's counsel in England and Wales. Their careers had been very different. Normanton was then aged sixty-six, of twenty-seven years' call, and had had to struggle to build up a practice in the difficult years between the wars. Heilbron was aged only thirty-four (younger than anyone since Thomas Erskine, who took silk in 1783 at the age of thirty-three) and had built up the practice to justify it in only ten years. At that time northern circuit silks were not allowed to live within fifty miles of any assize town on the circuit. Heilbron had to ask permission to go on living in the family home with her husband and baby, a request which was 'somewhat grudgingly' granted (Glidewell, 88).

Once she had taken silk Heilbron's practice really took off and she became one of the most famous and successful defence advocates of the day. In the 1950s the broadsheet newspapers covered sensational trials in great detail and she became a household name. In 1949 she defended George Kelly, accused with George Connolly of shooting the manager and deputy manager of the Cameo Cinema in a bungled robbery. Kelly protested that 'I want no Judy defending me', but later praised her for her prodigious efforts on his behalf (*Daily Telegraph*). She should have won. The prosecution knew that its case was weak. It depended on the evidence of two people, who were rightly treated as accomplices, but they were corroborated by Robert Graham, who said that he had heard Kelly and Connolly confess in prison. The jury could not agree a verdict. Quite inexplicably a judge ordered that Kelly and Connolly be retried separately. Kelly was tried first, convicted and sentenced to death. Connolly was then persuaded to plead guilty to robbery and sentenced to ten years' imprisonment. After losing his appeal Kelly was hanged on 28 March 1950. But in 2003 both convictions were quashed by the Court of Appeal (*Kelly and Connolly* v. *R*, 2003). The prosecution had failed to disclose to the defence that Graham had earlier told the police that another man, Donald Johnson, had confessed to the murder months before, ironically just after Heilbron had successfully defended him on a charge of helping to dispose of the murder weapon.

In 1951 Heilbron defended three Liverpool dockers accused at the Old Bailey of conspiracy to incite an illegal strike. The attorney general, Sir Hartley Shawcross, withdrew the case shortly before it was to go to the jury. Among her other clients were Harold Winstanley, the Knowsley Hall footman found guilty but insane of murdering the butler, after her bold decision to call only a psychiatrist in his defence; Louis Bloom, the Hartlepool solicitor found guilty of manslaughter rather than murder of his mistress in his office; Violet Clark, also known as Vicky Wright, found guilty of manslaughter rather than murder when her twin sons died in a fire on the houseboat *Windmill*; and Jack 'Spot' Comer, acquitted of stabbing in a Soho affray, who called her 'the greatest lawyer in history' (*Daily Telegraph*). This, she felt, was 'something of an exaggeration' (Rose, 3).

Heilbron was a good lawyer as well as a good advocate. She continued to feature in the law reports as well as the press reports. Among the cases which she argued as leader were *Ormrod* v. *Crossville Motor Services Ltd* (1953), *Attorney-General* v. *Harris* (1961), *Gore* v. *Van Der Lann* (1967), and *S (an Infant)* v. *Recorder of Manchester* (1971). The most important was probably *Sweet* v. *Parsley* (1970), where the House of Lords held that *mens rea* (a guilty mind) was required for every criminal offence created by statute unless parliament had expressly said that it was not. A landlord was not guilty of 'being concerned in the management of' premises used for smoking cannabis if she did not know and had no reason to know that cannabis was being smoked there.

By then Heilbron was also established in a judicial career. In 1956 she was appointed recorder of Burnley, a post she held until it was abolished by the Courts Act 1971, when she became a recorder of the crown court and honorary recorder of Burnley. The first woman to hold salaried judicial office was Sybil Campbell (appointed a metropolitan stipendiary magistrate in 1945), the first woman to preside over a jury trial was Dorothy Dix (as deputy recorder of Deal in 1946), but Heilbron can properly be claimed as the first woman to be appointed judge. In 1957 she also became the first woman commissioner of assize, and in January 1972 the first woman to sit as a judge at the Old Bailey.

Despite (or perhaps because of) her success with juries and the public Heilbron's profession was slow to give her the recognition she had earned. In 1968 she was elected a bencher of Gray's Inn, nineteen years after she had taken silk, and long after her standing at the bar would have merited it. In 1973 she was elected leader of the northern circuit, the first woman to be leader of any circuit; by rights she should have been leader long before. Customarily this honour went to the most senior silk on the circuit, but, as a senior barrister said in 1970, 'with a certain amount of care to avoid Rose Heilbron' (personal knowledge). The northern circuit was in many ways more open and progressive than the London bar, but it was not until 1970 that women were admitted as full members of the bar mess, the dining club of which all male members of the circuit were automatically members. Heilbron always refused to take part in the circuit's 'ladies' nights' because they treated women barristers as second-class citizens.

In 1974 Heilbron became the second woman High Court judge. As a criminal and personal injuries practitioner of such repute she might reasonably have expected to be assigned to the Queen's Bench Division. There was a vacancy, but Sir Tasker Watkins was transferred from the Family Division to fill it, while Heilbron took his place in the Family Division. However, from 1979 to 1982 she was presiding judge on the northern circuit, again the first woman to be a presider. While on circuit she tried mostly criminal or civil cases. These included the six-month-long trial at Lancaster in 1981 of an international drug trafficker and his associates for the murder of the 'handless corpse' found in a flooded quarry. In 1980 the *Daily Mail* reported that 'Heilbron rules her courtroom with a rod of silk—smooth and elegant, but very tough' (*Daily Mail*).

Heilbron's expertise as a criminal lawyer was also put to good use in 1975, when she was appointed by the home secretary, Roy Jenkins, to chair the advisory group on the law of rape. This was prompted by the outcry raised after the decision in *DPP* v. *Morgan* (1975) that a man was not guilty of rape if he believed that the woman was consenting, no matter how unreasonable that belief might be. In its report (*Parl. papers*, Cmnd 6352 of 1975) the advisory group accepted that principle, but recommended that, among other things, it should be made clear that absence of consent (and not violence) was the crux of the offence; that questions should not be asked about the previous sexual history of the complainant with men other than the accused without leave of the judge; and that complainants should be and remain anonymous.

Heilbron showed a similar sensitivity to the realities of sexual politics in her most famous decisions as a judge in the Family Division. In *Re D (a Minor) (Wardship: Sterilization)* (1976) she made an eleven-year-old girl a ward of court at the invitation of an educational psychologist in order to prevent the sterilization which her mother had agreed with her paediatrician and gynaecologist. The child suffered from a rare congenital syndrome but it was common ground that she had sufficient intellectual capacity to marry in due course. Heilbron held that it was neither medically necessary nor in her best interests to perform an operation which would involve 'the deprivation of a basic human right, namely the right of a woman to reproduce'. On the other hand in *C* v. *S* (1988) she held that the putative father of an unborn child could not prevent the mother having an abortion, either on his own behalf or on behalf of the unborn child; the question was whether the proposed termination would have been a crime and she held that on the particular facts it would not. She was upheld by the Court of Appeal and the House of Lords swiftly refused leave to appeal so that the abortion could be performed before it was too late.

When Heilbron was appointed to the High Court bench her husband had retired from his medical practice. Their daughter was practising at the London bar. So they left their home in the Wirral to live in the flat at 2 Gray's Inn Square which was to be their home for the rest of her life. In 1985 she was elected treasurer (leader for a year) of Gray's Inn, the first woman to be treasurer of any of the four inns of court. It was the final accolade in a life full of firsts. But the recognition which she eventually achieved should not obscure the prejudice and discrimination which delayed it for so long.

Damned with faint and patronizing praise by some of the men, Heilbron was a beacon to all the women who joined the northern circuit in her wake. In 1994 there were six women High Court judges, five of whom (Dame Joyanne Bracewell, Dame Ann Ebsworth, Dame Janet Smith, Dame Heather Steel, and Dame Brenda Hale) were members of the northern circuit (and the sixth, Dame Mary Arden, came from a family of Liverpool lawyers). However slow the circuit had been to acknowledge one of its most successful practitioners, others had been able to follow where she had led.

Heilbron retired from the High Court bench in 1988. On appointment to it in 1974 she had become a DBE. Other honours included being an honorary colonel in the Women's Royal Army Corps (TA); an honorary fellow of Lady Margaret Hall, Oxford (1976), where her daughter had been a student, and honorary doctorates from the universities of Liverpool (1975), Warwick (1978), and Manchester (1980). Along with 'strength of mind and tenacious industry' she also had 'striking good looks' (Cowper, 182). The portrait by June Mendoza which hangs in Gray's Inn shows a woman of great beauty. She died at Highgate Nursing Home, Hornsey Lane, Islington, after some years there, on 8 December 2005, of pneumonia and cerebrovascular ischaemia. She was survived by her daughter, Hilary, and her husband, Nat, who was still living in Gray's Inn at the age of a hundred.

BRENDA HALE

Sources *Daily Mail* (15 July 1980) · F. Cowper, *A prospect of Gray's Inn*, 2nd edn (1985) · D. Lynch, 'Mrs Justice Heilbron', *A century of Liverpool lawyers*, ed. N. Fagan and others (2002), 159–62 · P. Polden, 'Portia's progress: women at the bar in England, 1919–1939', *International Journal of the Legal Profession*, 12/3 (2005), 293–338 · D. Lynch, *Northern circuit directory, 1876–2004* (2005) · *Daily Telegraph* (10 Dec 2005) · *The Times* (13 Dec 2005); (19 Jan 2006) · *The Guardian* (13 Dec 2005) · *Liverpool Daily Echo* (13 Dec 2005); (7 Jan 2006) · *Daily Post* [Liverpool] (13 Dec 2005); (19 Dec 2005) · *Burnley Express* (16 Dec 2005) · C. Rose, memorial service oration, Temple Church, London, 20 March 2006 · I. Glidewell, 'Master Heilbron', *Graya*, 70 (2007), 86–90 · press cuttings, Gray's Inn library · *WW* (2005) · Burke, *Peerage* · Constantine v. Imperial Hotels Ltd, *Law Reports: King's Bench Division* (1944), 693 · Adams v. Naylor, *Law Reports: Appeal Cases* (1946), 543 · Christie v. Leachinsky, *Law Reports: Appeal Cases* (1947), 573 · Braddock v. Bevins, *Law Reports: King's Bench Division* (1948), 1.515 · Ormrod v. Crossville Motor Services Ltd, *Weekly Law Reports* (1953), 1120 · Attorney-General v. Harris, *Law Reports: Queen's Bench Division* (1961), 1.74 · Gore v. Van Der Lann, *Law Reports: Queen's Bench Division* (1967), 2.31 · Sweet v. Parsley, *Law Reports: Appeal Cases* (1970), 132 · S (an infant) v. Recorder of Manchester, *Law Reports: Appeal Cases* (1971), 481 · Home Office, 'Report of the advisory group on the law of rape', *Parl. papers* (1975), Cmnd 6352 · DPP v. Morgan, *Law Reports: Appeal Cases* (1976), 182 · Re D (a minor; wardship: sterilization), *Law Reports: Family Division* (1976), 185 · C v. S, *Law Reports: Queen's Bench Division* (1988), 135 · George Kelly and George Connolly (both deceased) v. R., transcript, neutral citation: [2003] EWCA Crim. 2957 · personal knowledge (2009) · private information (2009) [Hilary Heilbron, daughter] · b. cert. · m. cert. · d. cert.

Likenesses Elliott & Fry, photograph, 1949, NPG [*see illus.*] · Elliott & Fry, three photographs, 1949, NPG · D. Miller, group portrait, photograph, 1949, Getty Images, London · photographs, 1949–58, Photoshot, London · J. Mendoza, portrait, exh. Royal Society of Portrait Painters, London 1987, Gray's Inn, London · obituary photographs

Wealth at death under £129,000: administration with will, 18 Jan 2006, *CGPLA Eng. & Wales*

Henshaw, Alexander Adolphus Dumphries [Alex] (**1912–2007**), aviator, was born on 7 November 1912 in Peterborough, Northamptonshire, one of four children of Albert Henshaw (1888–1964), a wealthy entrepreneur in agriculture, property, and the holiday industry in Lincolnshire. He was educated at Lincoln grammar school and King Edward VI Grammar School, Stratford upon Avon. While still a boy he received a Royal Humane Society award for saving another boy from the River Witham. Although his first interest was in engineering, he opted instead to join the family agricultural business.

Henshaw first became attracted to flying early in 1932 when captivated by Royal Air Force aircraft performing low-level aerobatics. After an intensive flying course that year with the Skegness and East Lincolnshire Aero Club, and first flying solo on 7 May, he gained his private pilot's licence on 6 June, and his air-minded father bought him a second-hand de Havilland Moth biplane for £300. He soon aspired to aerobatics himself, and this led to the purchase of a new Comper Swift single-seat monoplane with which, after only thirty-five hours of flying, he became one of the youngest ever competitors in the prestigious

Alexander Adolphus Dumphries Henshaw (1912–2007), by unknown photographer, 1938

1933 king's cup air race. He was also the youngest pilot to win the Siddeley challenge trophy—awarded to the light aeroplane club whose representative pilot in the race was the first to complete the 831 mile course—having averaged 128 m.p.h. He purchased a larger, passenger-carrying de Havilland Leopard Moth for the 1934 race, but was not placed. Together with his father, he also honed his skills in dead reckoning navigation and blind flying around Europe before replacing the Swift with the one and only prototype Arrow Active I light racing biplane in May 1935.

For the 1935 royal jubilee year king's cup race Henshaw purchased a specially built Miles Hawk Major monoplane. However, a crankshaft failure forced him to ditch in the Irish Sea and he was fortunate to be rescued by the steamer *Manx Queen*. Then, while he was aerobatting the Arrow Active later that year, the engine caught fire, forcing him to bale out, using the parachute that his father had bought him for his birthday only four weeks earlier. After flying the Leopard Moth in the 1936 king's cup race, and having had to retire with low oil pressure, he swapped it for a much faster Percival Mew Gull single-seat monoplane G-AEXF. He entered the 1937 king's cup race but suffered from oiled-up plugs. Nothing daunted, in 1938 he finally won the trophy with the suitably modified Mew Gull, setting an average speed of 236.25 m.p.h., the fastest time then recorded, over a course of 1012 miles—a record which still stood at the time of his death.

Henshaw then set his sights on the formidable objective of setting a new record flight to Cape Town and back. With his father he surveyed the route in the spring of 1938, checking routings down both sides of Africa. Opting to fly the western side, with the further modified Mew Gull, he departed from Gravesend on 5 February 1939. Without radio or navigation aids, he made fuel stops in Algeria, the Belgian Congo, and Angola before reaching Cape Town in just under forty hours, having flown 6377 miles. After only twenty-eight hours there, he followed a similar return route, landing completely exhausted at Gravesend on 9 February—four days, ten hours, and sixteen minutes after his original departure. He had broken the homeward record, established in November 1937 with a twin-engined aircraft flown by two pilots, by seven hours, and the out-and-back time by almost thirty-one hours. However, this truly epic achievement was overshadowed by the imminence of war and Henshaw received no public recognition at all.

Volunteering for war service with the RAF as a fighter pilot on the outbreak of the Second World War in 1939, Henshaw accepted an invitation to join Vickers-Armstrongs as a test pilot. In June 1940 he was posted to the newly opened Vickers-Supermarine Spitfire shadow factory at Castle Bromwich, near Birmingham, becoming chief production test pilot for the huge output of Spitfire fighters, and later Avro Lancaster heavy bombers, built there between 1940 and the end of the war in 1945. With a production rate rising to ten Spitfires a day in 1943, he often flight-tested twenty aircraft in a single day. In one instance in 1943, while ferrying a Spitfire from the satellite unit at nearby Cosford in bad weather, and suffering engine failure over the outskirts of Coventry, his hurried forced landing largely demolished a small house but fortunately he suffered only minor injuries and no one else was hurt. On another occasion he was forced to abandon his aircraft when the engine exploded: despite his badly torn parachute, he still managed to land safely. Often called upon to demonstrate the Spitfire to groups of visiting VIPs, he notably made a virtuoso display before the highly air-minded wartime prime minister, Winston Churchill. The authorities were less pleased when he flew a Spitfire (inverted) down Birmingham's Broad Street. He also test-flew Lancasters and was reputed to be the only pilot able to barrel-roll the bomber.

Altogether 11,694 Spitfires and Seafires (the naval sibling) and 305 Lancaster bombers were built and repaired at Castle Bromwich and the local dispersal factories at Cosford and Desford. Under Henshaw's intensely active leadership together with twenty-five short-stay RAF officers, 37,023 test flights were logged there. Henshaw himself test-flew some 2360 individual Spitfires and Seafires, amounting to more than 10 per cent of the overall total of 22,749 of these aircraft built anywhere.

On 17 February 1940 Henshaw had married Countess Barbara Maude de Chateaubrun (1916–1996), the widow of Count Guy de Chateaubrun, who had been killed in an air accident. She was the daughter of Sidney Harris Denman. They had one son, also named Alex. After the war, and a period in South Africa as a director of Miles Aircraft, in 1948 Henshaw rejoined his family's farming and holiday business, giving up flying in deference to his wife and the loss of her first husband. He then developed six miles of the Lincolnshire coastline, which had been requisitioned during the war, incorporating a residential estate at Sandilands, Sutton-on-Sea, with the main avenue bearing his name and all the streets and roads being named after the various aircraft he had flown. Yet despite his preoccupation with his diverse business interests, his abiding passion was for aviation and he remained in great demand at aviation functions for the rest of his life.

After his only national recognition with the somewhat meagre award of the MBE in 1944, in 1953 Henshaw was awarded the queen's commendation for bravery for his rescue work during the great floods of that year. Always taking great interest in promoting 'airmindedness' in young people, in 1997 he was awarded the Air League's Jeffrey Quill medal. In 2003, the centenary of flight year, the duke of Edinburgh invested him as a companion of the Air League. He became an honorary fellow of the Royal Aeronautical Society the same year. He captured his aviation life for posterity in four graphically descriptive books, and in many lectures and magazine articles. In 2005 he donated his papers, photographs, trophies, and specially commissioned aviation art collection to the RAF Museum at Hendon. He died on 24 February 2007 at his home, Arborfield, Fordham Road, Newmarket, of heart disease. He was survived by his son, Alex.

NORMAN BARFIELD

Sources A. Henshaw, *Sigh for a Merlin* (1979) • A. Henshaw, *The flight of the Mew Gull* (1980) • J. Quill, *Spitfire: a test pilot's story* (1983) • A. Henshaw, *Wings across the great divide* (2004) • A. Henshaw and M. Turner, *Alex Henshaw: a flying legend* (2009) • *Daily Telegraph* (28 Feb 2007) • *The Guardian* (1 March 2007) • *Daily Express* (2 March 2007) • *The Times* (7 March 2007); (20 March 2007); (23 March 2007) • *Aerospace Professional* [Royal Aeronautical Society] (July 2007), 22–3 • personal knowledge (2011) • private information (2011) • m. cert. • d. cert.

Archives RAF Museum, Hendon | Air League, London • Royal Aeronautical Society, National Aerospace Library, Farnborough • Solent Sky Museum, Southampton

Likenesses photograph, 1938, priv. coll. [*see illus.*] • portrait, 1939, Getty Images, London • photograph, 1957, Photoshot, London • photographs, 1996–2006, PA Photos, London • photographs, 2006, Rex Features, London • obituary photographs • photographs, RAF Museum, Hendon, Henshaw archive collection

Henshaw, Michael Noel (1930–2007), accountant, was born on 11 October 1930 in the Queen Mary Nursing Home, Derby, the son of Reginald Henshaw (1899–1985), railway clerk, and his wife, Noelle, *née* Kitley (1899–1988). At the time of his birth registration his parents lived at Kynance, Uttoxeter Road, Mickleover. He was educated at Bemrose Grammar School, Derby, and after doing his national service in the King's Royal Rifle Corps moved to London and joined the Inland Revenue as a tax inspector. On 12 September 1959 he married Irene Evelyn Myatt (*b.* 1935), a fellow civil servant, daughter of Edward Thomas George Myatt, engineer; they had one son and two daughters.

In London, in the company of his old friend John Dexter, the theatre director, Henshaw began to frequent the Partisan coffee bar in Carlisle Street, Soho. Opened in 1958, this was becoming the haunt of left-wing writers and intellectuals, and it was there that he met the playwright Arnold Wesker. When Wesker founded Centre 42, in 1961, Henshaw accepted his invitation to become its administrator, and left his job at the Inland Revenue. Centre 42 was set up in response to TUC resolution 42, which said that more attention should be paid to bringing the arts into the life of the community. After organizing several arts festivals for trades councils around the country, in 1964 Wesker acquired the remaining lease on the Roundhouse, a disused locomotive shed in Chalk Farm, London, intending to turn it into a permanent home for Centre 42. Although Henshaw lacked any formal accountancy qualification, as a former tax inspector he was able to help those with whom he came into contact through Centre 42 to fill in their tax forms, including Wesker himself. He became company secretary of several 'underground' ventures, including Lovebooks Ltd, founded in 1965 to publish alternative poetry and underground texts, and the Indica Gallery and bookshop in Masons Yard, St James's, Piccadilly (where John Lennon first met Yoko Ono, at a show of her work). The Indica Bookshop moved to 102 Southampton Row in 1966, and it was in its basement that the *International Times*, published by Lovebooks, had its office. Henshaw was the accountant for the paper, launched at an all-night event at the Roundhouse in 1966; after several police raids on the office he helped to organize the 14-Hour Technicolor Dream, a fund-raising concert at Alexandra Palace with bands including Pink Floyd. The Arts Lab in Drury Lane, Covent Garden, which started in 1967 as a multi-media arts collective with an all-night cinema in the basement and mattresses instead of seats, also benefited from his financial advice.

By now Henshaw had become 'the first money man of the underground' (Fountain, 20). At one time he was in charge of the tax affairs of film directors such as Ken Loach, the actors Michael Palin and Anthony Hopkins, playwrights including David Hare, the poet Ted Hughes, broadcasters like Humphrey Burton, and the painter Tom Phillips. He was 'the charming, untidy bohemian … a legend in the creative community … He was well-informed and took a real paternal interest in your career. Filling in tax forms was way down his agenda, something he took care of off-stage' (Birt, 361–2). Henshaw took the view that tax inspectors did not appreciate the contribution that creative people made to society, and he was famed for devising ingenious ways of minimizing the tax liabilities of his clients. Although his working methods were often chaotic his clients were happy to leave things to him.

In 1993, as the accountant handling the tax affairs of John Birt, director-general of the BBC, Henshaw became known to the public when it was revealed in the press that Birt was not an employee of the BBC but was paid through his company, John Birt Productions Ltd, thereby reducing his tax burden; it was Henshaw who had set up this scheme. Although it emerged that this was a continuation of a scheme set up when Birt was working at London Weekend Television, and that it was not illegal, it seemed at one point that Birt might have to resign, and Henshaw endured much adverse publicity. Shortly after this, in 1994, he was pursued by the family of the novelist Jean Rhys over funds missing from her trust fund. At the height of his popularity Henshaw lived in style in a large house overlooking Regent's Park, but a number of his clients left him in the 1980s, and he was declared bankrupt in 1990. His first marriage having ended in divorce in 1980, on 20 June 2003 he married Penelope Austin (*b.* 1936), a retired accountant's administrator, daughter of Frederick George Austin, artist. He lived latterly in Norley Wood, Lymington, Hampshire. He died on 22 September 2007 at Southampton General Hospital, of heart failure, and was survived by his wife, Penelope, and his children, Rachel, Bryony, and Ben. ANNE PIMLOTT BAKER

Sources N. Fountain, *Underground: the London alternative press, 1966–74* (1988) • *Independent on Sunday* (14 March 1993); (8 May 1994) • J. Birt, *The harder path* (2002) • B. Miles, *In the sixties* (2002) • *The Guardian* (4 Oct 2007) • b. cert. • m. certs. • d. cert.

Wealth at death under £265,000: probate, 14 Sept 2007, *CGPLA Eng. & Wales*

Herbert, Sir Walter William [Wally] (**1934–2007**), polar explorer, was born on 24 October 1934 at 41 Neville Street, York, the son of Walter William Joyce Herbert (1905–1972), a sergeant (later captain) in the army, and his wife, Helen, *née* Manton (*d.* 1982). The family moved to Egypt when he was three, and then to South Africa for nine years. At the age of seventeen he was persuaded to join the army by his father, who claimed that 'every male on his side of the family since Sir Harry Hotspur had been soldiers' (*Daily Telegraph*, 13 June 2007). He signed on for twenty years with the Royal Engineers, which trained him as a surveyor and sent him to Egypt. However, after three years' service he left the army in search of a more adventurous life, and wandered back to England through the Middle East and Mediterranean countries, drawing portraits for his board and lodging.

In 1955, with a humdrum job as a surveyor in Shoreham by Sea—the only nine-to-five job he ever held—Herbert noticed an advertisement for surveyors to work in Antarctica with the Falkland Islands Dependencies Survey. His successful application for such a post set his course for twenty-five years. He spent the next two and a half of them at the Hope Bay station, near the north-eastern end of the Antarctic peninsula, mapping the region on long journeys by dog sledge. In his most exciting journey, with a party of four, he crossed the Antarctic peninsula to link up with a survey party from the west coast. The last part of the journey involved travelling 100 yards along a narrow snow-covered ridge, there being steep drops of 1500 feet on either side. His name the Catwalk for the ridge and the name Herbert Plateau later appeared on official maps of the area and commemorated his party's achievement.

Herbert returned to England in 1959, having spent nearly a year hitch-hiking alone from Montevideo northwards through the Americas. He had lived and travelled rough, but 'failed to get the Antarctic out of my system' (*Polar Record*, 94). In England, lecturing on his experiences gave him a modest income until, the following year, he

Sir Walter William [Wally] Herbert (1934–2007), self-portrait, 1991

joined a summer expedition to Svalbard. There he received a cable inviting him to go to Greenland to acquire sledge dogs for the New Zealand Antarctic expedition, and to transport them by the American military transport service through the United States, Hawaii, Fiji, and Christchurch, New Zealand, to McMurdo Sound in the Antarctic, where the New Zealanders maintained their Scott base. He hurried from Svalbard to West Greenland, accomplished his mission, and, towards the end of 1960, found himself at Scott base in charge of a New Zealand field survey party for two summers and a winter.

In the first season Herbert's party with dog teams were airlifted to a partly explored region on the west side of the Ross ice shelf, where they mapped an area of about 10,000 square miles. In the following season, looking for a more exciting challenge, he had his party airlifted further south to the head of the Beardmore glacier. He then set about surveying the mainly unexplored Queen Maud Mountains, lying to the east, through which in 1911 Roald Amundsen with great daring had forced a new route to the south pole, to forestall Captain Scott, travelling up the Beardmore glacier. Herbert's party succeeded in mapping an area of about 26,000 square miles, and in making the first ascent of the 13,000 foot Mount Fridtjof Nansen, used as a survey station. Towards the end of the season they descended from the polar plateau down the very steep Axel Heiberg glacier, with its icefalls, the ascent of which had been the key to the success of Herbert's hero Amundsen, the master sledge traveller. Herbert is commemorated in this region by Herbert Range. He recorded his Antarctic years in his book *A World of Men* (1968).

By the time he returned to England in 1962 Herbert had decided that the era of Antarctic dog sledging was coming to an end and that the romance of Antarctic travel would soon disappear. The Antarctic was becoming too populated for his taste. Aircraft and tracked vehicles were being deployed more and more in support of major scientific projects in which he had no desire to take part. He now switched his sights to the Arctic, where the idea of a trans-Arctic expedition took shape in his mind, soon to be billed in the fashion of adventurers as 'the last great journey on earth'.

Late in 1966 Herbert and two companions undertook a training journey from Qanaq, in the Thule district of north-west Greenland, where they wintered. After adapting to the Inuit style of dog driving, in the early spring the party set out westward for Ellesmere Island, with Inuit support for the first part of the journey. Lack of judgement and disregard for Inuit advice caused Herbert to cross Ellesmere Island by a pass mostly windswept clear of snow, instead of crossing by way of the ice cap. The dogs were forced to drag the sledges over bare rocks. The crossing took four weeks instead of the standard four days. Men and dogs were in a starving condition when they reached the west coast on Eureka sound, leading north to Eureka weather station. In the sound Herbert swallowed his pride and accepted an airlift of food for the men and dogs from the station, which was eventually reached two months after leaving Qanaq. The party rested for ten days, and then continued its 1400 mile journey north around Axel Heiberg Island to the west and south towards Resolute on Cornwallis Island. The imminent break up of the sea ice forced them to abandon the journey at a point 100 miles short of Resolute, whence they were brought out by air. No doubt the hard-won experience served Herbert well on his next epic journey.

Herbert's greatest exploit was crowned on 29 May 1969, when two of his companions on his four-man trans-Arctic expedition made a touch-and-go landing in the European Arctic after a journey of 3620 miles across the Arctic Ocean from Point Barrow, Alaska, via the north pole. The party had left Point Barrow on 21 February 1968, and the land they eventually reached was Vesle Tavleøya, a small rocky island off the north coast of Svalbard. They had travelled with four dog teams acquired in north Greenland, had spent periods of encampment on the sea ice during mid-summer and mid-winter conducting scientific work, and had reached the north pole on 5 April 1969. During the journey they had benefited from the direction of drift of the Arctic Ocean pack ice.

Herbert had spent four years, mainly in England but partly in North America, meticulously planning and preparing for his expedition, and seeking financial support. No item of equipment and food escaped his careful selection, in particular the very robust dog sledges. The sledges were built to his specifications, based on the design of Robert Peary, whose claim to have reached the north pole in April 1909 was later disputed by some, including Herbert himself.

For so long a journey, both in distance and in time, massive air support was essential. Herbert rightly judged that this could only be obtained through a personal approach to the chief of the Canadian defence staff, General Jean Allard, whom he visited in Ottawa late in 1967. The expedition appealed to the general's sense of adventure and love of the outdoors, and long-range Hercules aircraft of the Royal Canadian Air Force were duly assigned to make airdrops over the summer and winter camps on the ice.

After touching land, Herbert had hoped to drive all four of his dog teams alongside HMS *Endurance*, sent to pick up his party in Svalbard waters. But this was not to be for, in deteriorating sea-ice conditions, stalked by polar bears and still forty miles from the ship, he was forced to accept a helicopter pick-up of his party, with all the dogs, sledges, and equipment. For Herbert it was an anticlimactic ending to his expedition, especially as it was at the time when man first landed on the moon. In the aftermath, following a civic reception on the ship's return to Portsmouth, further anticlimax came when Herbert was billed by the mayor's office for the sherry consumed. His *Across the Top of the World* (1969) was, in his words, 'a book of eloquent omissions'. On Christmas eve 1969, at Chelsea register office, Herbert married Marie Rita McGaughey (*b.* 1940/41). The daughter of Charles Angus McGaughey, professor of veterinary science, she was then working as a public relations librarian. She later worked as a personal growth and development therapist. They had two daughters. Marie and their first daughter accompanied Herbert on his next expedition to Greenland, to film the Inuit of the Thule district. From 1971 to 1973 they made their home and base of operations near Qanaq on the coincidentally named Herbert Island. Their sojourn there was described by Marie in her book *The Snow People* (1973), and led to Herbert's prize-winning book *The Eskimos* (1976).

Meanwhile, Herbert had been maturing plans for another ambitious expedition—the circumnavigation of Greenland by dog sledge and skin boat. In the spring of 1978 he and one companion were landed at Alert, the Canadian weather station at the north-eastern corner of Ellesmere Island, whence they planned to cross the channel to Greenland at the start of a journey of several seasons. After a long delay waiting in vain for solid sea-ice conditions, they were eventually airlifted to the north coast of Greenland too late in the season to cover by sledge more than a few hundred miles clockwise around the coast, before abandoning the expedition in that year. Lack of financial support in succeeding years finally scuppered Herbert's plans.

In these years Herbert was invited by the National Geographic Society to examine Robert Peary's records of his north pole journey, and to write an article for the *National Geographic Magazine*. He took up this task with enthusiasm, to the extent that he expanded his article into a full-length book, which occupied three years of his time. His *The Noose of Laurels* (1989) was a well-researched and scholarly study of Peary's life, in which he became totally absorbed. To his friends he virtually claimed psychic insight into the mind of Peary and a special affinity with the man, having discovered many coincidences between Peary's life and his own. Many disagreed with his conclusion that Peary reached no nearer than sixty miles at best from the north pole. Herbert could not be considered an unbiased critic for, had Peary not reached the north pole, he himself would have been the first to reach by traditional methods that elusive point on the drifting pack ice—an achievement that he coveted. His book was not a commercial success, but as a spin-off Herbert was invited to lead a filming expedition to north-west Greenland, Ellesmere Island, and the north pole in the summer of 1987, to obtain footage for a successful television documentary on the journeys of Peary and his rival American Frederick Cook.

In 1980 Herbert and his family moved to Devon. For two years he was installed in Buckfast Abbey, the home of Sir Francis Drake, as curator of a museum of exploration, which Plymouth city council proposed to establish there. His plans for the museum proved too ambitious, and he parted company with the city council and the abbey. With his expedition days over and with pressing personal financial and health problems, he turned to painting as a means of livelihood. It had been a recreation in which he had shown great talent, notably for his portraits of polar explorers and Inuit hunters. At the same time, he accompanied Arctic and Antarctic cruise ships as a guest lecturer, and in a similar capacity on trans-Atlantic voyages of *Queen Elizabeth II*, in which (and elsewhere) he staged one-man shows of paintings.

For his achievements in the polar field, Herbert's awards included the polar medal (with Antarctic and Arctic clasps), the founder's medal of the Royal Geographical Society, the Livingstone medal of the Royal Scottish Geographical Society, the French Geographical Society's medal, and the New York Explorers' Club's medal. He was offered appointment as CBE for his leadership of the trans-Arctic expedition but, clearly in expectation of higher recognition, turned down the award, acting with typical impetuosity and thus leaving doubt that his name would ever come up again. However, Sir Ranulph Fiennes campaigned to get him a knighthood, with eventual success in 2000. Herbert is commemorated in the Antarctic place names Herbert Plateau and Herbert Range.

Wally Herbert was one of the toughest travellers the polar regions have known, but he had not cultivated the ability in public relations needed by the handful of people in this country to have made a living as adventurers. True to himself, he did nothing by halves, and overstretched himself physically, mentally, and financially on his expeditions. Although heart problems did not quench his indomitable spirit, it was fortunate that, in his later years, he could fall back on the gentler pursuit of painting in the family home at Rowan Cottage, Catlodge, Laggan, Inverness-shire. He died at Raigmore Hospital, Inverness, on 12 June 2007, and was survived by his wife, Marie, and his elder daughter Kari, both authors of books on their time in north Greenland. A younger daughter, Pascale, had died, aged fifteen in a tragic accident at the family home in Devon.

G. HATTERSLEY-SMITH

Sources W. Herbert, *A world of men* (1968) • W. Herbert, *Across the top of the world: the British trans-Arctic expedition* (1969) • W. Herbert, *Across the top of the world: the last great journey on earth* (1971) • M. Herbert, *The snow people* (1973) • W. Herbert, *The third pole* (2003) • K. Herbert, *The explorer's daughter* (2006) • *Daily Telegraph* (13 June 2007) • *The Times* (14 June 2007) • *The Guardian* (15 June 2007) • *The Independent* (16 June 2007) • *Polar Record*, 44 (2008), 93–5 • Burke, *Peerage* • *WW* (2007) • personal knowledge (2011) • private information (2011) • b. cert. • m. cert. • d. cert.

Archives FILM BFINA, documentary footage | SOUND BL NSA, documentary recordings

Likenesses photographs, 1966–9, Photoshot, London • photographs, 1968–2000, PA Photos, London • R. Case, photographs, 1969, Getty Images, London, Hult. Arch. • self-portrait, scalpel and pencil, 1991, repro. in www.sirwallyherbert.com [*see illus.*] • F. Hanson, photograph, 2000, Camera Press, London • J. Finlay, photographs, 2006, Getty Images, London, Hult. Arch. • obituary photographs

Herlie, Eileen [*real name* Eileen Isobel Herlihy] (**1918–2008**), actress, was born on 8 March 1918 at 6 Marlborough Gardens, Clarkston, near Glasgow, the daughter of Patrick Herlihy, customs and excise officer, and his wife, Isobel, *née* Cowden. Her father was an Irish Catholic, her mother a Scottish protestant; both opposed her theatrical ambitions. After being educated at Shawlands Academy in Glasgow she worked briefly for an insurance company before making her stage début with the Scottish National Players in 1938 in *Sweet Aloes*. She then joined the Rutherglen Repertory Company, with whom she stayed for three years, which she later described as 'good, glad days, with plenty of work and the satisfaction of building' (*Daily Telegraph*, 11 Oct 2008). She made her London début in 1942 as Mrs de Winter in *Rebecca*, and subsequently toured in the powerhouse role of Regina Giddens in *The Little Foxes*, before joining the Old Vic Company at the Playhouse, Liverpool, during its wartime sojourn there (1944–5). She married a fellow actor, (Sidney) Philip Barrett (son of John Richard Barrett, woollen goods merchant) in Blythswood on 21 August 1942 but the marriage ended in divorce by the end of the decade. She then married Witold Kuncewicz, a tannery manager five years her junior, son of Jerzy Kuncewicz, lawyer, on 12 April 1951, but that marriage too ended in divorce.

In Liverpool Herlie played imposing leads in such diverse plays as *The Second Mrs Tanqueray* and *Hamlet* (as Gertrude), and as the eponymous prostitute in *Anna Christie*. Back in London, after the war, she won mixed notices for her majestic Andromache in *The Trojan Women* (1945) and the disfavour of Kenneth Tynan's acid-dipped pen for her playing of the half-mad monarch in *The Eagle Has Two Heads* (1947). Tynan described her performance in the title role of *Medea* (1948) as 'transparently pretentious'. In *The Eagle*, however, she won plaudits elsewhere for her 'epic tirade of a speech lasting more than 20 minutes' (*The Independent*, 14 Nov 2008). The play brought her to notice as a major new talent, and by this time she had established her versatility.

Herlie's first film role was in the Two Cities melodrama, *Hungry Hill* (1947), derived from Daphne Du Maurier's tale of two Irish families locked in conflict over ownership of a copper mine. The film starred Margaret Lockwood, Britain's top box-office star, but Herlie, looking rather more matronly than her twenty-eight years, made her mark as Lockwood's daughter-in-law, married to one son but not above embracing the other. Perhaps it was the result of her looking both sensually attractive and older than she was that led Laurence Olivier to cast her in her most famous screen role—that of Gertrude, mother to his Hamlet (1948), though she was eleven years his junior. The disparity in ages actually worked in favour of the film, and of Olivier's Freudian reading, and the feeling between mother and son acquired a resonant sexual charge, particularly in the closet scene.

After her success as Gertrude, Herlie's screen career might have been expected to accelerate but she never quite became a film star. Alexander Korda, failing to persuade Orson Welles to feature her in a projected but unrealized version of *Salome*, built *The Angel with the Trumpet* (1950) round her. However, this English-language version of a German multi-generation saga was generally heavy going, and Herlie had not quite the star presence to bring it to life. In a curious way she always seemed headed for character roles in films, rather than as a conventional leading lady, though she was a graceful and gracious presence as Helen D'Oyly Carte in *The Story of Gilbert and Sullivan* (1953). By her mid-thirties she was playing mother roles in such films as *Isn't Life Wonderful!* (1953), and was the heroine's mother in the enjoyable light comedy *For Better, For Worse* (1954), starring Dirk Bogarde. In both of these her husband was played by the cherishably polished Cecil Parker, who was twenty-two years older than she was. She was a handsome, rather than a pretty, woman and seems to have slid prematurely into middle-age roles. In the 1958 comedy *She Didn't Say No* she played the mother of seven children by five different fathers. One writer summed up the film thus: 'Comedy of embarrassment has some charm, is occasionally moving' (Quinlan, 373). Another described it as 'mediocre as well as mildly offensive' (*Monthly Film Bulletin*, 92). It marked the end of her British film career.

But the stage was another matter. Without the intense scrutiny of the cameras Herlie played a series of leading roles. In 1955 she appeared on Broadway, repeating her title role in *The Matchmaker*, having first had a hit with it at London's Haymarket. Subsequently most of her career was American-based. She played Paulina in *The Winter's Tale* and Beatrice in *Much Ado about Nothing* at Stratford, Ontario, in 1958, and on Broadway there was evidence of striking versatility in such plays as Peter Ustinov's *Photo-Finish* (1963) and *Halfway Up the Tree* (1967), as Gertrude again in *Hamlet* (1967), in Pirandello's *Henry IV* (1973), as Queen Mary in *Crown Matrimonial* (1973), and, in Chicago, as Martha in Edward Albee's *Who's Afraid of Virginia Woolf?* (1971).

There were two more films—John Huston's *Freud* (1962) and Sidney Lumet's *The Seagull* (1968)—but neither of these strongly cast titles did much for either their directors or for Herlie. Long since settled in America, she was most widely remembered as the boutique-owning matriarch Myrtle Fargate in 692 episodes of the American soap series *All My Children* (1976–2008). She spent the latter part of her life as companion to the actor Louis Edmonds (1923–2001), her co-star in the series. She also starred in the spin-offs of the series, *Loving* (1993) and *One Life to Live* (2000). She died in New York, still in harness, on 8 October 2008. She had no children. BRIAN MCFARLANE

Sources *Monthly Film Bulletin* (July 1958) • D. Quinlan, *British sound films: the studio years, 1928–1959* (1984) • 'John Justin', B. McFarlane, *An autobiography of British cinema* (1997) • C. Drazin, *Korda: England's*

only movie mogul (2002) • B. McFarlane, *The encyclopedia of British film*, 3rd edn (2008) • *Daily Telegraph* (11 Oct 2008) • *New York Times* (11 Oct 2008) • *The Times* (14 Oct 2008) • *The Guardian* (5 Nov 2008) • *The Independent* (14 Nov 2008) • www.imdb.com/name/nm0379047, 4 Feb 2010 • J. Parker, ed., *Who's who in the theatre*, 15th edn (1972) • *WW* (2008) • b. cert. • m. certs.

Archives FILM BFINA, performance footage | SOUND BL NSA, performance recording

Likenesses C. Beaton, bromide print, *c.*1946, NPG • photographs, 1946–84, Getty Images, London • photographs, 1947, PA Photos, London • photographs, 1948–2003, Rex Features, London • A. Buckley, bromide prints, 1950–53, NPG • double portrait, photograph, 1964 (with Richard Burton), Photoshot, London • obituary photographs

Hermon, Sir John Charles (1928–2008), police officer, was born at 28 Ardenvohr Street, in the Willowfield area of Belfast, on 23 November 1928, the son of William Rowan Hermon, slater, and his wife, Agnes, *née* Brown, both Presbyterians. His formative years were spent in the rural townland of Castletown, near Islandmagee, co. Antrim. His father, a veteran of the Ulster division in the First World War, built up a small building business but it never really prospered because of what his son described as his 'despotic and intemperate' ways (Hermon, 1). Hermon was the youngest of four children but his childhood, he said, was not a particularly happy one and he lived in some fear of his father's 'aggressive temperament' (ibid.) So too did his religiously inclined mother, to whom he said he owed more, for her 'protection, church-going, various sports, and such formal education as I achieved' (ibid.).

After Whitehead public elementary school, Hermon spent three years at Larne grammar school. His father then insisted he leave school and take a placement at an accountancy firm in Belfast. From the outset Hermon was unhappy and after several job changes he was accepted into the police and reported to the Royal Ulster Constabulary depot at Enniskillen for training on 2 February 1950. His first posting was to the rural village of Eglinton, near Londonderry, where he quickly gained notoriety for putting a ticket for obstruction on the car of a local magistrate after several warnings went unheeded. On 15 June 1954, at St Peter's Church of Ireland Church, Belfast, he married Jean Webb (1926/7–1986), daughter of Roy Webb, electrician. They had a son and a daughter.

Hermon soon overcame what he described as his early introspection, shyness, and gaucheness, and his police career quickly flourished. In 1957 he was promoted sergeant and posted to Coalisland, co. Tyrone, to replace a colleague murdered by an IRA booby-trap bomb. Soon afterwards he demonstrated great personal courage by successfully defusing a similar device. Policing the divided community in Northern Ireland had long been difficult. There were only about 250 Catholics in the 3000 strong RUC, which was seen as 'our' police by the protestant Unionist majority and 'their' police by the Catholic nationalist minority. In these difficult political circumstances Hermon early on became irrevocably committed to the concepts of impartiality and even-handed application of the law, and made what were to prove lasting friendships with influential members of both the protestant and Catholic communities.

Sir John Charles Hermon (1928–2008), by Bobbie Hanvey, 1989

Clearly marked out as a high-flyer, in 1963 Hermon became the first RUC officer sent for advanced training to Bramshill Police Staff College in Hampshire. On his return he was promoted to be head constable and posted to Hastings Street police station on the western fringe of Belfast city centre. His tenure there was dominated by the Divis Street riots of 1964, which erupted after extreme Unionist pressure, volubly stimulated by the emerging Revd Ian Paisley, forced the police to remove a tricolour from an Irish republican election headquarters. The incident had a profound effect on Hermon's thinking. Apart from initiating an enduring hostility to Paisley, it led him deeply but silently to resent what was then the customary Unionist political manipulation of the police force, especially in facilitating provocative Orange order processions. More important, he warned his superiors that the Stormont government's unwillingness fundamentally to address Northern Ireland's social inequalities would ignite the simmering sectarian and political tensions with unhappy consequences for the community but above all for the RUC, which was under-strength and neither trained nor equipped for the coming challenge.

Hermon's foresight proved all too accurate. Between October 1968 and August 1969 the RUC was driven to breaking point by a series of civil rights marches and Paisley-led counter-demonstrations, which resulted in sustained civil disorder. As the British army was deployed to restore public tranquility, the British government established a commission chaired by Lord Hunt, which recommended long overdue reforms of the RUC. Hermon, newly promoted to chief superintendent and training officer, was put in charge of the transformation but the aim of an unarmed, community-based police service had to be hastily abandoned as the community conflict intensified. Over the next few years, against a background of worsening civil disorder and escalating terrorist violence, Hermon played a pivotal role. The police were reluctantly rearmed while he masterminded the retraining of existing officers and supervised a huge recruiting intake as the RUC rapidly doubled in size to some 6000. Hermon's was an awesome task and his dedication to endless hours of work became legendary. He also set himself the most exacting standards and was ruthless in expecting the same of his colleagues, even at the cost of friendship and popularity.

Hermon's career steadily advanced and he became first assistant and then deputy chief constable, serving in a number of administrative and operational roles, before being appointed chief constable in 1980. His overriding objective as chief constable was to continue the policy of 'Ulsterization', expanding the capability and acceptability of the RUC to enable the British army to be taken off the streets. He was also deeply concerned to defend the independence of the police from political direction and assert the RUC's lead in the undercover war with the terrorist organizations, involving covert surveillance and sensitive work with informers cultivated among the terrorist ranks. In particular he wanted to contain the rivalries within his own force between the special branch and other departments and bring an end to the subservience of his officers to their military and security service counterparts. On one occasion, to his intense frustration, he was told that as 'need-to-know' goes up as well as down even he could not be told the details of a secret security operation. However, the intensity of the ongoing terrorist violence blunted his efforts and instead he was constantly forced to deal pragmatically with what became known as 'the politics of the latest atrocity'.

The first test of Hermon's leadership came in 1981 when Bobby Sands and nine other republican terrorists successively starved themselves to death in support of a demand for prisoner-of-war status in the Maze prison. Each death prompted serious rioting, tense funeral processions, and gun and bomb attacks on the police and soldiers, but despite the high emotions generated by the situation on both sides of the divided community the RUC was widely judged to have acquitted itself efficiently in handling the repercussions.

Not long afterwards Hermon was plunged into a fresh and debilitating controversy. On 27 October 1982 three of his officers perished near Lurgan, co. Armagh, when a roadside bomb was detonated as their patrol car passed by. The RUC's hitherto top-secret headquarters mobile support unit, trained by the British army's special forces in 'firepower, speed and aggression', according to subsequent court testimony, was then involved in three ambushes over the span of a month in which five unarmed terrorist activists were shot dead. The hotly disputed circumstances of the incidents prompted accusations that the police were operating a 'shoot-to-kill' policy, a proposition Hermon vigorously and consistently denied. In order to clarify the precise course of events, John Stalker, the deputy chief constable of Greater Manchester, was brought in to conduct an independent investigation. The two officers clashed from the outset. Stalker judged Hermon held the line by 'clumsy autocracy' and resented outside interference. Hermon believed that conventional policing standards, as represented by Stalker, were wholly inappropriate in the extraordinary circumstances then prevailing in Northern Ireland.

Although the RUC retreated behind a wall of silence and partial truths about the episode, embarrassing revelations gradually emerged. The explosives that killed the three police officers had supposedly been under covert observation but despite this the terrorists were able to carry out the fatal attack. Stalker discovered that the hide had actually been 'bugged' by the British security service, MI5, and that there was a tape recording of the second 'shoot-to-kill' incident at this location. However at this point, with his work threatening to come to an embarrassing political climax, Stalker was abruptly removed from the investigation after dubious allegations that he was corruptly involved with a cadre of flamboyant Manchester criminals known as the Quality Street Gang. In time Stalker's reputation was totally vindicated but even before then the lack of clarity about the incidents and his hasty removal from the investigation clung to the reputation of the RUC.

The signing of the Anglo-Irish agreement in November 1985 created another serious problem for the RUC. The treaty's provision to give the Irish republic an oversight role in the governance of Northern Ireland triggered great hostility among Unionists, a feeling shared by many individual police officers. Fearing a revolt in the ranks after the Unionist leaders, Ian Paisley and James Molyneaux, publicly encouraged the RUC to mutiny, Hermon issued a stark public warning to his officers that it was their clear duty to defend the democratic process whatever their own political opinions. Privately he said that the RUC was a mighty oak and he was determined that even if it lost some branches, it would go on upholding the law as before. In the event police discipline was maintained but after the RUC took vigorous action to break up Unionist protests about the agreement a wave of attacks was mounted on the homes of police families in previously safe protestant areas, forcing many to flee their homes. Hermon's wife was herself attacked during one of several morale-boosting visits to police families in what was one of the most testing periods for the RUC. Largely owing to Hermon's strong and clear leadership, the force emerged from the episode with a new sense of impartiality and confidence. In what was clearly his finest hour he rightly believed that the RUC had broken free from its controversial history and demonstrated an unprecedented impartiality. Although he remained a bullish, autocratic, and combative figure in public, the stress of his job had a profound emotional effect on him in private. After his wife died of cancer in 1986 he declined to attend the funerals of his murdered officers because of the constant emotional strain. Altogether 135 RUC officers died on his watch.

Even though the RUC was fighting a debilitating terrorist campaign it was not immune from the effect of the ongoing changes in society, one being the gender equality laws. As the number of women in the police ranks expanded, Hermon's old-fashioned notions dictated that they should not be armed like their male counterparts. The decision was challenged and overturned, earning him widespread criticism. Among his critics was Sylvia Eileen Paisley (*b.* 1955), a law lecturer at Queen's University, Belfast (and daughter of Samuel Robert Paisley, farmer), but after an initial meeting to discuss their differences, a relationship developed and the two married at Shore Street Presbyterian Church, Donaghadee, on 31 December 1988. They had two sons.

Hermon (who was appointed OBE in 1975, knighted in 1982, and awarded the Queen's police medal in 1988) retired as chief constable in May 1989. By firmly sticking to his belief that the police must be even-handed, drawn from all sections of the community, and acceptable to everyone, he had helped create the conditions that stimulated the protracted 'peace process' and culminated in the ground-breaking Belfast agreement in 1998. A subsequent commission, chaired by Chris Patten, recommended that the police should be reformed and renamed the Police Service of Northern Ireland. Hermon played a prominent role in the unsuccessful campaign to save the RUC name. His wife, Sylvia, was elected as the Ulster Unionist MP for North Down on 7 June 2001 and afterwards he played a highly supportive role as her political career advanced. However he subsequently developed Alzheimer's disease and was taken into care. After a threat to his life from breakaway IRA elements, he had to be moved to another location. He died on 6 November 2008 at Seaview House, a nursing home in Seacliff Road, Bangor, co. Down, and was buried in Ballyvester cemetery, Donaghadee. He was survived by his second wife, Sylvia, and his four children.

CHRIS RYDER

Sources Sunday Times Insight Team, *Ulster* (1972) · J. Stalker, *Stalker* (1988) · C. Ryder, *The RUC: a force under fire* (1989) · *Sunday Times* (2 July 1989) · J. Hermon, *Holding the line: an autobiography* (1997) · C. Ryder, *The fateful split: Catholics and the Royal Ulster Constabulary* (2004) · *Belfast Telegraph* (7 Nov 2008); (8 Nov 2008) · *The Times* (8 Nov 2008) · *Daily Telegraph* (8 Nov 2008) · *The Guardian* (8 Nov 2008) · *Irish Times* (8 Nov 2008) · *The Independent* (10 Nov 2008) · Royal Ulster Constabulary George Cross Foundation, oral history archive, including interview with Sylvia Hermon MP · *WW* (2008) · Burke, *Peerage* · personal knowledge (2012) · private information (2012) · b. cert. · m. certs. · d. cert.

Likenesses B. Hanvey, photograph, 1989, Boston College, Massachusetts, John J. Burns Library [*see illus.*] · obituary photographs · photographs, repro. in Hermon, *Holding the line*

Hetherington, Sir Thomas Chalmers [Tony] (**1926–2007**), lawyer and civil servant, was born on 18 September 1926 at 4 Francis Street, Langholm, Dumfriesshire, the elder son and eldest of three children of William Maxwell Hetherington, medical practitioner, and his wife, Alice Mary Cooper, *née* Booth. After Rugby School he was commissioned into the Royal Artillery from 1945 to 1948. He enjoyed his army service and remained in the Territorial Army until 1967. In 1948 he entered Christ Church, Oxford, and graduated with a second-class degree in jurisprudence in 1951. He was called to the bar by the Inner Temple the following year. On 23 May 1953 he married June Margaret Ann Catliff, a secretary three years his junior, daughter of Frank Ivor Catliff, chartered surveyor. They had four daughters.

In 1953 Hetherington joined the legal department of the Ministry of Pensions and National Insurance. Nine years later he moved to the law officers' department, as part of a small team assisting the attorney-general and solicitor-general in their wide-ranging remit. In 1966 he became legal secretary, that is head of that department. The department's work included significant involvement in criminal prosecutions, many of them of considerable public interest. The experience was to serve him well. In 1970 he was appointed CBE.

The Treasury solicitor is the most senior government lawyer. Hetherington was his deputy for two years from 1975, with an expectation of assuming the top post when it became vacant. In the event Sir Norman Skelhorn retired unexpectedly as director of public prosecutions in 1977 and Hetherington was appointed his successor. Criminal cases of particular importance or difficulty were reported to the director's department. It was seen as requiring reform to cope more expeditiously and reliably with its increasing caseload. Hetherington had established a reputation in government circles for administrative skills combined with sound legal judgement. On assuming office he took immediate steps to bring the workload under control. The prosecution of offences regulations, detailing the cases to be referred to his office, were rewritten. Greater flexibility was introduced into the reporting mechanism, allowing the submission of abbreviated reports in some cases. At Hetherington's request the home secretary appointed more assistant directors—the level at which most prosecution decisions were taken. Only cases of the utmost public interest reached Hetherington personally. The prosecution of the Liberal Party leader Jeremy Thorpe for attempted murder, eventually resulting in acquittal, was an early example. He concerned himself, too, in a succession of terrorist and espionage prosecutions and allegations of corruption in the police service.

At the outset of his tenure Hetherington announced that the invariable response of 'no comment' to media inquiries must change; information that could be given would be given. He maintained the friendly relations with legal journalists formed in the law officers' department. In 1981 he allowed the BBC broad access to the department to prepare a *Panorama* programme. In 1983 he authorized

Sir Thomas Chalmers [Tony] **Hetherington** (**1926–2007**), by Howard Lloyd

a 'warts and all' study of the department's workings by the Oxford Centre for Criminological Research. He, his staff, and departmental files were made freely available. The research was influential in the code for crown prosecutors, published in 1986 when the crown prosecution service came into existence. Hetherington's approach to openness, and much else in his style of management, permeated the service during the tenure of each of his several successors.

After Hetherington's early reforms there followed a several-year period of calm before the storm. He was appointed KCB in 1979. In 1981 the royal commission on criminal procedure, chaired by Sir Cyril Phillips, presented its report. Its most radical recommendation was that locally appointed, independent crown prosecutors should take over the conduct of most prosecutions from the police. A Home Office working party, including Hetherington, was established to advise on the government's response. The working party's report was annexed to a white paper published in October 1983. Instead of the locally based structure advocated by the royal commission the government accepted the working party's recommendation of a national service, with offices throughout England and Wales. The Prosecution of Offences Act 1985 laid the foundations of that service. Conveniently sized areas of England and Wales were each to be headed by a chief crown prosecutor reporting to the director of public prosecutions. The establishment of the crown prosecution service was Hetherington's major preoccupation for the remainder of his term of office.

There were concerns that a nationally structured service would create an unwieldy bureaucracy, with decisions of any moment concentrated at the service's headquarters in London. These concerns were comprehensively dispelled by the publication in December 1984, during the passage through parliament of the Prosecution of Offences Bill, of a white paper reflecting Hetherington's determination that the overwhelming bulk of casework, of all degrees of complexity and gravity, should be handled in local offices. He believed, then and in his earlier senior positions, that if people could demonstrate an appetite and aptitude for responsibility they should have it. Staff found this a motivating stance. Hetherington was a popular first head of the crown prosecution service, despite the burdens created by the initial acute shortages of funding and staff. Through the considerable personal loyalty thus engendered, a service with thirty-one area offices, about ninety branch offices, and several thousand staff could be launched in 1986, remarkably soon after the government announced its proposals three years earlier, and only one year after the enabling legislation was passed.

During his term as director of public prosecutions Hetherington was a member of the Criminal Law Revision Committee. The reports of the committee underlay various statutes of central importance in the criminal justice field. He wrote of his time as director in *Prosecution and the Public Interest* (1989). Meanwhile, shortly after his retirement in 1988, he and William Chalmers, his Scottish counterpart, were appointed to inquire into the feasibility of prosecuting persons then resident in the UK for German war crimes in the Second World War. Their report led to the highly contentious War Crimes Act 1991. The advanced ages and infirmity of potential defendants meant that only two prosecutions were practicable.

Tony Hetherington was a tall man of genial appearance, entirely consistent with his warm and wholly unstuffy personality. He had a lively sense of humour reflected in an infectious chuckle. A journalist said he 'made a well-cut suit look lived in'. Whatever the cares of office, any mention of his four daughters brought a twinkle to his eyes. His private office had standing instructions that calls from his family must be put through immediately, whatever his commitments. He took a genuine interest in the families and concerns of his staff, irrespective of their seniority. He and his wife lived at Lingfield in Surrey throughout their married life. He was much involved in the development of a fine community centre there. In his latter years he suffered from a gradually more debilitating neurological illness. His wife, June, cared for him with total commitment until his death, following a stroke, at Tandridge Heights Memorial Care Home, Oxted, Surrey, on 28 March 2007. MICHAEL CHANCE

Sources G. Mansfield and J. Peay, *The director of public prosecutions: principles and practice for the crown prosecutor* (1987) • J. Rozenberg, *The case for the crown: the inside story of the director of public prosecutions* (1987) • T. Hetherington, *Prosecution and the public interest* (1989) • *The Times* (30 March 2007); (5 April 2007) • *Daily Telegraph* (30 March 2007) • *The Guardian* (2 April 2007) • *The Independent* (6 April 2007) •

Burke, *Peerage* • *WW* (2007) • personal knowledge (2011) • private information (2011) • b. cert. • m. cert. • d. cert.

Archives FILM BFINA, 'Police complaints', *The London programme*, D. Featherstone (director), ITV, 6 Feb 1981 | SOUND BL NSA, documentary recording

Likenesses photographs, 1977–86, Photoshot, London • photographs, 1978, Rex Features, London • obituary photographs • H. Lloyd, photograph, priv. coll. [*see illus.*]

Wealth at death £774,482: probate, 24 July 2007, *CGPLA Eng. & Wales*

Hezlet, Sir Arthur Richard (1914–2007), naval officer and submariner, was born on 7 April 1914 in Pretoria, South Africa, of Ulster protestant descent, the only son (there were two daughters) of Major, later Major-General, Robert Knox Hezlet (1879–1963), army officer, and his wife, Josepha Dorothy, *née* Arter. His father's distinguished military career culminated in his being made director of artillery at the War Office (1930–34) and then in India (1934–8). From 1928 Hezlet was educated at the Royal Naval College, Dartmouth; he went to sea in 1932 and served in the destroyer *Daring* in the Far East before transferring to the submarine *Regulus*. By the outbreak of the Second World War he was second in command of the submarine *Trident*, operating against the German invasion of Norway, and was mentioned in dispatches. Having commanded the coastal submarine H44 from December 1940, he joined the renowned 10th submarine squadron in Malta and commanded the *Unique* and *Ursula*, being awarded the DSC for sinking the 11,000 tonne Italian troopship *Esperia*. On returning home he commanded the submarine *Trident* in the Arctic, on one occasion undertaking a rare task for a submarine of escorting mainly on the surface the large convoy PQ16 to north Russia, being again mentioned in dispatches.

In September 1942 Hezlet joined the midget submarine and 'chariot' development establishment HMS *Varbel* on the Clyde, where he made valuable and innovative contributions to the engineering, training, and tactics that were to be used in this new form of undersea warfare. This appointment led to his command of the *Thrasher*, one of six submarines that towed the midgets to the Alten Fjord, where the powerful German battleship *Tirpitz* was put out of action; for this strategic success lieutenants Donald Cameron and Godfrey Place were awarded the VC, and Hezlet gained another mention in dispatches.

In command of the *Trenchant*, based at Trincomalee, Ceylon, Hezlet took part in a number of operations that earned him his first DSO, notably the sinking of the German submarine U-859 in September 1944, the sinking by torpedo or gunfire of a number of Japanese minor war vessels, and the launch and recovery of the only successful 'chariot' attack in the Far East, the two 'human torpedoes' having entered Phuket harbour and sunk two large supply ships. In June 1945, in the Banka Strait off Sumatra, Hezlet carried out one of the most exceptional torpedo attacks of the war, intercepting as a result of Enigma intelligence the Japanese heavy cruiser *Ashigara* in dangerously flat, calm weather, having taken his submarine into mined and shallow water. To ensure success Hezlet fired ten torpedoes, scoring an unusual five hits and sinking the largest Japanese warship to fall to British submarines in the Far East theatre. He was ordered immediately to Subic Bay in the Philippines to receive the American legion of merit from the commander of allied submarines in the south-west Pacific, Admiral James Fife junior, and was subsequently awarded a bar to his DSO.

After the war Hezlet had a tour in the Admiralty and attended the naval and tri-service staff colleges. On 29 December 1948 he married (Anne Joan) Patricia Clark, the 23-year-old daughter of George Wallis Newport Clark, of Carnabane, Upperlands, co. Derry; they adopted two daughters. In the year following his marriage he was appointed to his first surface ship command, the destroyer *Scorpion*, which was fitted with a prototype anti-submarine attack system that was an acknowledged British success for the next twenty years. Promoted captain, the navy's youngest at that time, Hezlet was appointed chief staff officer to the flag officer, submarines (1953–4), commander of the *Battleaxe* and the 6th destroyer squadron (1955–6), director of the Royal Naval Staff College (1956–7)—where his students recalled the course as being not nearly as restful as expected—and commander of the cruiser *Newfoundland* (1958–9).

In July 1959 Hezlet was promoted rear-admiral (again the navy's youngest) and appointed flag officer, submarines, at a time of important developments: Britain's first nuclear-propelled submarine was launched in 1960 and decisions were being made about Britain's future nuclear deterrent based on the American Polaris missile, and these projects required radical provision. He was appointed CB in 1961 and promoted vice-admiral in 1962. His final tour was as flag officer, Scotland and Northern Ireland; he retired in 1964, when he was appointed KBE.

Widely nicknamed Baldy, Hezlet was always regarded by the Royal Navy's submarine fraternity with a mixture of affection and awe, as a man who, with an almost obsessive concentration, devoted his powerful intellect to the promotion of the submarine as an instrument of naval strategy. His first book, *The Submarine and Sea Power* (1967), forcefully set out his views but also foresaw the continuing invulnerability of the seaborne nuclear deterrent. Other publications were *Aircraft and Sea Power* (1970), *The 'B' Specials* (1972), regarded by many as too uncritical an account of the Ulster Special Constabulary, which had been disbanded two years previously, *Electron and Sea Power* (1975), and *The Trenchant at War* (2001). His *British and Allied Submarine Operations in World War II*, published by the Royal Navy Submarine Museum, Gosport, in 2001 as a boxed two-volume limited edition, provided an authoritative account of every patrol undertaken, awards, casualty statistics, and many other facts, displacing the official Admiralty staff histories by its level treatment of failures and unique strategic overview of all the theatres of war.

After inheriting the family home, Bovagh House, Aghadowey, co. Londonderry, Hezlet served on the general synod of the Church of Ireland, was chairman of the search and rescue committee of the Royal National Lifeboat Institution, and for twenty-five years was Northern Irish president of the Royal British Legion. He was an original council member of the University of Ulster. A keen yachtsman, he sailed frequently off the coasts of Scotland and Northern Ireland. He died of bronchopneumonia at Bovagh on 7 November 2007 and was survived by his wife and their two daughters. GUY LIARDET

Sources S. W. Roskill, *The war at sea, 1939–1945*, 3 vols. in 4 (1954–61) · J. Wingate, *The fighting tenth: the tenth submarine flotilla and the siege of Malta* (1991) · A. Hezlet, *British and allied submarine operations in World War II* (2001) · *The Times* (9 Nov 2007) · *Daily Telegraph* (9 Nov 2007) · *The Guardian* (20 Dec 2007) · Burke, *Peerage* · *WW* (2007) · personal knowledge (2011) · private information (2011) · m. cert. · d. cert.
Archives PRONI
Likenesses obituary photographs

Hibbert, Arthur Raymond [Christopher] (**1924–2008**), historian, was born on 5 March 1924 at the vicarage, Enderby, Leicestershire, the younger son and second of three children of the Revd (Harold) Victor Hibbert (1890–1972), vicar of Enderby from 1923 to 1951 and canon of Leicester Cathedral from 1947 to 1959, and his wife, (Catherine) Maud, *née* Doar (1892–1984). He was educated at Radley College, and in 1942 went to Oriel College, Oxford, to read history. His education was interrupted, however, when he joined the London Irish Rifles in 1943 where, on his first day in uniform, the sergeant-major saw Hibbert (who looked even younger than his eighteen years) and asked, 'Who we got here, then? Christopher fucking Robin?' The name stuck (private information). He served as an infantry officer with the Eighth Army during the Italian campaign, and was awarded the Military Cross during the attack on the German fortification on the River Senio in the winter of 1944–5. He was wounded twice while fighting with the partisans in the battle of Lake Comacchio in April 1945. In military hospital, he met another soldier, Terence Alexander, the character actor. They became lifelong friends.

After resuming his studies at Oxford in 1946 Hibbert rubbed shoulders with Kingsley Amis and Kenneth Tynan. He also met Susan Fay Primrose (Sue) Piggford (*b*. 1924), an undergraduate at St Anne's College reading English, and daughter of Raynor Hugh Piggford, engineer. So distracted was he in wooing her that he failed Latin (then a compulsory subject) five times, and achieved only a third-class degree in modern history, in 1948. They married at St Peter's Church, Harrogate, soon after he graduated, on 12 August 1948. (Sue took her degree the following year.) They had two sons, James (*b*. 1949) and Tom (1952–2011), and a daughter, Kate (*b*. 1956).

After his marriage Hibbert began an unloved career as a land surveyor in a firm of land agents, auctioneers, and surveyors. He wrote in his spare time, and became television critic of *Truth* magazine. His wife entirely supported his desire to make a living from writing even though the future, financially, would be insecure. He might have had a career in fiction, but was disappointed when a radio play was rejected by the BBC. He persevered, however, now with non-fiction, and his first book, *The Road to Tyburn* (1957), was accepted by Longmans, Green, where John Guest was his editor, and remained so for the majority of his books. In 1959 he was able to give up his job as a land surveyor. His fourth book, *The Destruction of Lord Raglan* (1961), won the Heinemann award for literature in 1962. Meanwhile he had acquired a literary agent, the author of *The Raj Quartet*, Paul Scott, of David Higham Associates, with which agency Hibbert remained his entire life.

Hibbert went on to write over fifty books. He covered a vast range of subjects: Africa, China, India, America, France, England, and Italy, being able quickly to master fields of which he might hitherto have known very little. He wrote biographies of great English figures (he was particularly proud of his two-volume biography of George IV, published in 1972–3), a huge social history of England (1987), and, with Ben Weinreb, conceived and edited the monumental *Encyclopaedia of London* (1983). Perhaps surprisingly for one whose war experiences were unhappy he was an Italophile and wrote a number of books on Italian history.

Some of Hibbert's best books were the result of detailed archival research on unpublished material, while others were based solely on printed sources. But his greatest gift was for narrative. His 'main aim' was 'to entertain and tell a good accurate story without attempting to … change historical opinion in any way. You've got to make the reader want to know what's going to happen next' (*Sunday Times*, 8 July 1990). He was described by J. H. Plumb as a 'writer of the highest ability', by the *New Statesman* as 'a pearl of biographers', and by the *Times Educational Supplement* as 'perhaps the most gifted popular historian we have'. The *Sunday Times* wrote, 'Among the most versatile of living historians, [Hibbert] combines impeccable scholarship with a liveliness of style that lures the reader from page to page', and *The Independent* described him as 'one of England's greatest living historical writers' (book jackets). Bruce Hunter, Hibbert's literary agent following Scott, wrote that he

> was the most amazingly productive author I ever came across … He always met his deadlines; in fact he was usually early, very rare. He took on more work than I ever thought anyone could handle and always seemed to have leisure for holidays and walks. (private information)

Having written a biography of one of his heroes, Samuel Johnson (1971), Hibbert was elected president of the Johnson Society in 1980. He was a fellow of the Royal Society of Literature and of the Royal Geographical Society, and was awarded an honorary DLitt by the University of Leicester in 1996. His manuscripts (he never used a typewriter, let alone a computer) were later deposited at the Howard Gotlieb Archival Research Center, Boston University.

Hibbert was a most amusing and stimulating companion: generous, hospitable, playful, and much loved by his numerous friends. He loved cats and gardening. He was, in his own words, uxorious and philoprogenitive. He enjoyed sixty years of an extraordinarily happy marriage, and was proud of his children. He died of bronchopneumonia at Townlands Hospital, York Road, in Henley-on-Thames, his home since 1954, on 21 December 2008. He was cremated after a humanist ceremony in Oxford on 2 January 2009, and was survived by his wife and their three children. F. H. W. SHEPPARD

Sources *Daily Telegraph* (24 Dec 2008) · *The Times* (29 Dec 2008) · *New York Times* (6 Jan 2009) · *The Guardian* (27 Jan 2009) · *WW* (2008) · personal knowledge (2012) · private information (2012) · b. cert. · m. cert. · d. cert.
Likenesses obituary photographs
Wealth at death £864,756: probate, 16 Nov 2009, *CGPLA Eng. & Wales*

Hibbert, Sir Jack (1932–2005), statistician and civil servant, was born at the Huddersfield Municipal Maternity Home, Huddersfield, Yorkshire, on 14 February 1932, the only child of William Collier Hibbert, a grocery branch manager, later master baker, and his wife, Ivy Annie, *née* Wigglesworth. After education at Leeds grammar school (1942–9) he gained entry to the civil service in 1950. He spent the next two years on national service with the Royal Air Force, then worked with the Exchequer and Audit Department in London and, from 1955, at the War Pensions Office near Blackpool. On 27 April 1957, in Selby, Yorkshire, he married Joan Clarkson (*b.* 1933), also an assistant auditor in the Exchequer and Audit Department, and daughter of Francis Clarkson, railway storeman. They subsequently had two sons and a daughter.

To improve his prospects Hibbert joined the Central Statistical Office (CSO) in London on 2 October 1960. His talents were quickly recognized, but a suitable university degree was needed for the top posts. Studying part-time and then full-time in 1965–6, Hibbert graduated BSc (Econ) at the London School of Economics. Returning to the CSO as a statistician, he enhanced further his already considerable reputation in national accounting, a subject that fascinated him. He became a chief statistician in 1970 and an assistant director in 1977.

Hibbert also came to be highly regarded in national accounting circles beyond the United Kingdom. He made a favourable impression at the 1975 conference of the International Association of Research in Income and Wealth. Participating frequently in later conferences, he served on the association's council from 1985 to 1992. In 1981, when high inflation had led to concerns about accounting conventions, the OECD and Eurostat commissioned Hibbert to examine the treatment of inflation in national accounts. The problems highlighted in his report, *Measuring the Effects of Inflation on Income, Saving, and Wealth* (1983), were among those addressed later in the review of the international system of national accounts. Hibbert might have been expected to make a major contribution to the review, but, following a period as under-secretary in the Department of Trade and Industry (1982–5), in 1985 he succeeded Sir John Boreham as director of the CSO and head of the Government Statistical Service, holding the post until 1992. He did, though, help to ensure that the review was brought to a conclusion when differences threatened to prolong it unduly. The outcome then provided the basis also of the EU's own system.

Hibbert became head of the Government Statistical Service when cuts had weakened it and there was mounting criticism, particularly of the reliability of unemployment statistics—revised following changes to benefit rules. In 1987 and 1988 discrepancies within the national accounts became so large that it was unclear how the economy was developing. The Treasury and civil service select committee called for an investigation. The Pickford review, launched in June 1988, resulted in the transfer of more responsibilities to the CSO and the establishment of the much enlarged CSO as a separate department. The major changes introduced in 1989 under Hibbert's leadership provided the basis for subsequent improvements to the quality of economic statistics, and were also the first of several involving greater centralization in UK official statistics.

The changes were, however, not those sought by critics outside government. In November 1989 the Royal Statistical Society established a working party on official statistics. In December 1989 the society and the Institute of Statisticians convened a meeting about public confidence in official statistics. Hibbert's written reply to the criticisms, published in the *Journal of the Royal Statistical Society* (1990), reveals especially clearly his thinking about the issues. The society's working party 'found no evidence of a lack of integrity among government statisticians', but considered that 'the organisational and operational framework' had to be changed ('Official statistics: counting with confidence', *Journal of the Royal Statistical Society*, series A, 154, 1991, 23–44). Its recommendations had little impact on the Conservative administration, but had more appeal to the Labour Party, which gained power in 1997. Hibbert was a member of the Royal Statistical Society's council for the sessions 1989–93 and a vice-president in 1990–91.

Hibbert was made KCB in 1990. He possessed integrity as well as technical expertise. Colleagues did not doubt that he would have resigned if required to do something he thought improper. He supported people facing difficulties. He was always calm, and in private had a friendly, sympathetic manner. He was less at ease with publicity and with press briefings, preferring to confine himself to issues he had considered carefully beforehand. In an address before he retired in 1992 he reflected on his experience and achievements (Hibbert, 'Official statistics').

In retirement Hibbert retained his interest in statistics. Comments in 2005 on the Atkinson report about measuring government output and productivity, and frequent letters to the press, demonstrated that he had lost little of his incisiveness. Nevertheless retirement allowed more time for other interests. Bridge had long been a passion and he became a national master. He and his wife, Joan, were members of Beckenham Bridge Club, whose *Newsletter* carried a warm tribute after his death. In major competitions he partnered primarily Tim Lloyd-Williams and Marie Horlock, devising with Lloyd-Williams a bidding system called 'compromised club'. Hibbert and Robbie Kingston won the English Bridge Union senior pairs at Eastbourne in 2003. He was a member of the Reform Club; he and Joan enjoyed particularly meetings of the Thackeray Society, and they joined Hever Castle Golf Club, where in 1995 he won the seniors' cup. To Hibbert's amusement, his gambling successes provoked one national bookmaker to refuse his bets.

Joan Hibbert supported her husband throughout his career, and he valued her opinions. For several years after retirement, Hibbert found himself caring increasingly for her, with support from their family, as Alzheimer's disease developed. Care in a nursing home eventually became essential. In later years he enjoyed the company of a circle of friends, with his last few years enriched by a close friendship with Ann Ramsay. Sporadic Creutzfeldt-Jakob disease caused Hibbert's startlingly rapid decline and then death, on 23 August 2005 at the Princess Alice Hospice in Weybridge Hospital. His funeral, which was non-religious, took place on 6 September at Randalls Park crematorium, Leatherhead. He was survived by his wife, whose condition gradually deteriorated further, and by their three children. DAVID WROE

Sources J. Hibbert, 'Official statistics in the UK: is there cause for concern?', *Statistical News*, 96 (1992) [extracts; full text at Office for National Statistics, Newport] • R. Ward and T. Doggett, *Keeping score: the first fifty years of the Central Statistical Office* (1991) • A. Vanoli, *A history of national accounting* (2005) • *The Independent* (12 Sept 2005) • R. Lynch, *Journal of the Royal Statistical Society: ser. A*, 169/2 (2006), 382–3 • R. Lynch, *Review of Income and Wealth*, 52/3 (Sept 2006), 487–8 • *Beckenham Bridge Club Newsletter* (Feb 2006) • personal knowledge (2009) • private information (2009) [John Hibbert, son; R. Lynch; T. Griffin; J. Walton; A. Croxford; B. Sanders; P. Allin; R. Kingston; M. Horlock; T. Lloyd-Williams; J. Steel; National Audit Office; Leeds grammar school; Hever Castle Golf Club] • *WW* (2005) • Burke, *Peerage* • b. cert. • m. cert. • d. cert.

Likenesses photograph, 1985, Photoshot, London; repro. in *The Independent* • photograph, repro. in Ward and Doggett, *Keeping score*

Wealth at death £268,228: probate, 4 Jan 2006, *CGPLA Eng. & Wales*

Hickox, Richard Sidney (1948–2008), conductor, was born in the vicarage, Stokenchurch, Buckinghamshire, on 5 March 1948, the only son of the Revd Sidney Edwin Hickox (1913–1988), vicar of Sts Peter and Paul, Stokenchurch, and his wife, Jean Macgregor, *née* Millar, a keen amateur pianist and teacher. He had an older sister, Charmian (*b*. 1943). Soon after his birth his father moved to the nearby St Paul's, Wooburn Green, where Hickox could be heard playing the organ for services at the age of seven. From 1959 to 1966 he attended the Royal Grammar School in High Wycombe, after which he studied organ, piano, and composition at the Royal Academy of Music for a year, before going up to Queens' College, Cambridge, as an organ scholar (1967–70). Even before leaving university he established an enviable reputation for tireless energy and enthusiasm, not least by founding the Wooburn festival (1967) in his home village. His ambition was manifest when he formed the Richard Hickox Singers and Orchestra in 1971, and it was as a choral trainer that the musical world took immediate note of him. The following year he became organist at the parliamentary church of St Margaret's, Westminster, and made his first commercial recording, with its choir. Significantly this was of unaccompanied settings of the mass by Edmund Rubbra,

Richard Sidney Hickox (1948–2008), by Nigel Luckhurst, 1995

for the music of English composers was to remain the bedrock of his work and reputation.

Hickox's rise was swift. In 1973 he became the youngest conductor ever to appear at the BBC Proms. He took over the Spitalfields festival in 1974, but perhaps more significant was his decision two years later to accept directorship of the ailing London Symphony Chorus. Through skilful application he re-established the choir's fiscal and artistic credibility, taking full advantage of the chance to work at first hand with such world-famous conductors as Claudio Abbado, André Previn, and Sergiu Celibidache. A plethora of appointments followed, including conductorship of the Bradford Festival Chorus (from 1978) and directorship of the City of London festival. In 1979 the Richard Hickox Orchestra was renamed the City of London Sinfonia. From 1982 to 1990 he was artistic director of the Northern Sinfonia, meantime working as associate conductor of the London Symphony Orchestra and forging links with numerous other orchestras throughout Europe and the USA. In 1990 he responded to changing tastes by founding yet another ensemble, Collegium Musicum 90, dedicated to playing baroque and classical repertoire in 'period' instrumental style. His tenure as chief conductor of the BBC National Orchestra of Wales (2000–6) and association with the Philharmonia Orchestra were specially fruitful, bound in as they were with a long-term contract for Chandos Records, with which he recorded over 300 works including symphonic cycles by Ralph Vaughan Williams, Michael Tippett, and many other English composers, as well as a complete set of Haydn's masses.

Perhaps closest to Hickox's heart was his leadership from 1974 of the St Endellion festival on the Cornish coast—not least for the opportunity it gave him to indulge what was, given his ample frame, an unlikely passion for surfing. The operas he performed in concert there provided cherished memories for all involved, and his springboard into stage music. From debuts at English National Opera (1979) and Covent Garden (1985) he moved to directorship of the Italian Spoleto festival from 1997 to 2002. None the less his appointment in 2005 as director of Opera Australia surprised many. The Australian job was to prove contentious and personally hurtful for Hickox when the local press seized on accusations of falling standards and lack of respect for native artists. A vote of confidence from the board did much to calm the situation, but the resultant stress may have played its part in bringing about Hickox's sudden death from a dissecting thoracic aneurysm on 23 November 2008 in the Marriott Hotel, Swansea Marina, shortly after a recording session.

The frenetic pace of his engagements (hundreds of performances every year) combined with his public reticence and lack of showy podium technique led some critics and orchestral players to regard Hickox's conducting as competent but slightly dull. This was never the view of the many singers inspired by his personal warmth and generosity, combined with punctilious attention to vocal technique and phrasing. In the final year of his life, thanks not least to a spiritually luminous reading of Vaughan Williams's opera *The Pilgrim's Progress* at Sadler's Wells (2008), his evident mastery of large forces won over sceptical critics; and his early death robbed the British musical world of one of its most recognizable icons.

Hickox was married three times: first on 4 July 1970 to Julia Margaret Smith; second on 9 July 1976 to Frances Ina Sheldon-Williams (*b.* 1950), timpanist; and third on 17 July 1995 to the Scottish operatic mezzo-soprano Pamela Helen Stephen (*b.* 1964), daughter of William Hay Stephen, marketing manager, with whom he worked frequently in Europe and Australia. He had one son, Tom, by his second marriage, and two children, Adam and Abigail, by his third. He was appointed CBE in 2002; other honours included numerous awards from within his profession, as well as an honorary doctorate from Durham University in 2003. He was survived by his wife, Pamela, and his three children. CHRISTOPHER WEBBER

Sources *The Times* (25 Nov 2008); (28 Nov 2008); (29 Nov 2008); (3 Dec 2008); (10 Dec 2008); (14 April 2009) • *Daily Telegraph* (25 Nov 2008); (29 Nov 2008) • *The Guardian* (25 Nov 2008); (8 Dec 2008) • *The Independent* (25 Nov 2008) • *New York Times* (25 Nov 2008) • *The Age* [Melbourne, Australia] (25 Nov 2008); (26 Nov 2008) • *Sydney Morning Herald* (26 Nov 2008) • *Western Briton* [Australia] (27 Nov 2008) • *Courier Mail* [Australia] (27 Nov 2008) • *The Australian* [all-round country edition] (27 Nov 2008); (20 Jan 2009) • www.richardhickoxfoundation.com, 5 May 2011 [includes biography and discography] • *WW* (2008) • personal knowledge (2012) • private information (2012) [Simon Joly, Stephen Lumsden] • b. cert. • m. certs. [1976, 1995] • d. cert.

Archives FILM BFINA, performance footage | SOUND BL NSA, current affairs, documentary, interview, and performance recordings

Likenesses N. Luckhurst, photograph, 1995, Lebrecht Music and Arts Photo Library, London [*see illus.*] • photographs, 1996–2007, Getty Images, London • obituary photographs • photographs, Lebrecht Music and Arts Photo Library, London

Wealth at death £396,154: administration, 10 Feb 2009, *CGPLA Eng. & Wales*

Higgs, Sir Derek Alan (1944–2008), banker, was born on 3 April 1944 at 19 Sherbourne Road, Acocks Green, Birmingham, the only son of Alan Edward Higgs (1912–1979) and his wife, Freda Gwendoline, *née* Hope (1914–1984). At the time of his birth his father was employed as the branch manager of a building society, but an entrepreneurial flair led him into the building business, where he profited considerably from the rebuilding of Coventry after the immense damage done to the city during the Second World War. The young Derek and his sister Marilyn enjoyed a comfortable childhood in the west midlands. He was sent to the private Solihull School and went on to read economics at Bristol University, and graduated in 1965. But although he received a somewhat privileged upbringing and education, his father had always made it clear to him and his sister that they would not inherit his wealth, since he believed that inherited wealth took away pride and self-motivation. When Alan Higgs died his £25 million estate was used to set up the Alan Edward Higgs Charity, the objectives of which were to benefit disadvantaged children and fund other socially progressive projects in the Coventry area. Derek and Marilyn Higgs became trustees of the charity.

From university Higgs went to work for the accountancy firm Price Waterhouse, but after four years decided that merchant banking would be a more interesting career. Answering an advertisement that declared 'no experience necessary', in 1969 he joined the blue-blooded Baring Brothers as a corporate finance executive. On 30 May the following year he married an economist, Julia Mary Arguile (*b.* 1945), daughter of Robert Thomas Arguile, civil engineer. They had two sons and one daughter.

Higgs soon realized that family connections rather than merit paved the way to the top at Barings, and he sought a place to work where skill and commitment mattered more than birthright. This led him, in 1972, to join S. G. Warburg & Co. The bank was already running rings around some of its more establishment competitors, and the culture was entirely suited to both Higgs's nature and his meritocratic instincts. His attention to detail, affable nature, and keen intelligence brought swift promotion, and he soon established himself as one of the most notable deal-makers and trusted advisers in the City of London. He guided many of Warburg's clients through the boom years of corporate finance in the 1980s, where he was the key banker in such high-profile deals as Burton group's contested takeover of Debenhams. By 1986, still in his early forties, he was made head of corporate finance at the bank, a position he held until, in 1994, he was appointed chairman.

One deal, however, eluded Higgs. In 1994 he was one of a number of investment bankers who recognized that their banks needed to increase their capital base if they were to prosper as truly global businesses. He set about negotiating a merger with the American bank Morgan Stanley. After weeks of negotiations, without making public its reasons, Morgan Stanley backed out of the deal. The failure of the merger caused significant damage to Warburg's reputation, from which the bank never fully recovered. In 1995 Warburg was acquired by Swiss Bank Corporation, its standing as the doyen of the investment banking business lost for ever.

After this débâcle Higgs resigned to become a director of the Prudential and chairman of its fund management business, a position he held for four years, until 2000. He then joined the boards of several companies as a non-executive director. They included British Land, Egg plc, and Allied Irish Banks. He was also in 2001 appointed senior adviser in the United Kingdom to UBS Warburg (as Warburg's had been renamed, following the merger of the Swiss Bank Corporation and the Union Bank of Switzerland in 1998), and subsequently to UBS Investment Bank (as it was once again renamed, in 2003), thus re-establishing a relationship with the firm with which he had spent the greater part of his working life.

It was for his work as head of a government inquiry into the role and effectiveness of non-executive directors in 2002–3 that Higgs came to widest notice, and for which he was given a knighthood in 2004. His report into what had become known as 'corporate governance' unearthed compelling evidence of the ineffectiveness of many existing governance arrangements and proved controversial, mostly because he recommended the separation of the roles of chairman and chief executive, and other measures to strengthen the powers of non-executive directors. By the time of his death, however, most of his recommendations were seen as good practice and generally accepted and adhered to.

After the publication of his report Higgs became chairman of the Alliance and Leicester Bank in 2005. In his latter years he was also pro-chancellor of Bristol University (from 2002), a director of various bodies, including the Financial Reporting Council (1996–2004), the City Arts Trust (1995–2001), and the Scott Trust (from 2008), and the owner of *The Guardian* newspaper, of which he was a lifelong reader. He was also a supporter of Coventry City Football Club, of which he was a director (from 1996 to 2008), and for whose Ricoh Arena he persuaded his father's trust to provide crucial funding. He attended his last Coventry City match two days before suffering a fatal heart attack in London on 28 April 2008. He was declared dead at Charing Cross Hospital the same day, and was survived by his wife, Julia, and their three children. DAVID BREWERTON

Sources *Evening Standard* (29 April 2008) · *The Times* (30 April 2008) · *Daily Telegraph* (30 April 2008) · *The Guardian* (30 April 2008) · *The Independent* (30 April 2008) · *Coventry Telegraph* (30 April 2008) · *Birmingham Post* (30 April 2008) · *Bristol Evening Post* (2 May 2008) · *WW* (2008) · b. cert. · m. cert. · d. cert.

Likenesses H. Borden, archival digital c-type print, 2002, NPG · photographs, 2003, Rex Features, London · photograph, 2004, Getty Images, London · photographs, 2004, Photoshot, London · obituary photographs

Wealth at death £3,382,898: probate, 8 Jan 2009, *CGPLA Eng. & Wales*

Higman, Graham (1917–2008), mathematician, was born at 18 Lee Street, Louth, Lincolnshire, on 19 January 1917, the second of three sons of Joseph Higman (1876–1954), Methodist minister, and his wife, Susan Mary Ethel, *née* Ellis (1885–1951). His grandfather William Higman (1830–1907) was also a Methodist minister, and president of the United Methodist Conference in 1890.

Higman was educated at Sutton Secondary School, Plymouth, and at Balliol College, Oxford, where his undergraduate tutor and later (after he had taken firsts in both his mathematical moderations and his finals) his DPhil research supervisor was J. H. C. (Henry) Whitehead. Although Whitehead was best known as a topologist the work that Higman did developed into pure algebra, and his later famous, and famously unpublished, thesis was written on the subject of units in group-rings. During the Second World War as a conscientious objector he worked first as a lecturer at a technical college in Essex, and then as a meteorologist. On 29 July 1941 he married Ivah May Treleaven (1917–1981), a secondary school teacher, and daughter of a Methodist minister; his father, Joseph Higman, and her father, Woodman Treleaven, officiated at the marriage at the Methodist Chapel in Keswick. They had five sons and one daughter.

After the war Higman was recruited as a lecturer at Manchester University by the great department-builder M. H. A. (Max) Newman. There he met many like-minded colleagues, in particular B. H. Neumann, with whom and with whose wife Hanna he wrote a much-cited paper about infinite groups. This was the paper that introduced the Higman–Neumann–Neumann (HNN) extension, and used it to spectacular effect to solve a number of open problems in what was then still the infant theory of infinite groups. At Manchester he also got to know Alan Turing, whose ideas about logic and computability he later used in a beautiful way to identify the finitely generated subgroups of finitely presentable groups (groups that can be described using finitely many generators and finitely many relations between those generators). His result was later widely known as Higman's embedding theorem.

In 1955 Higman returned to Oxford as reader in pure mathematics and tutor at Balliol in succession to Henry Whitehead, who had been elected to the Waynflete chair of pure mathematics. In 1958 he was elected a fellow of the Royal Society, and on Whitehead's death in 1960 he was again elected his successor and moved from Balliol to a fellowship of Magdalen: 'brewed in Balliol, matured in Magdalen', as Whitehead said of himself, and Jack de Wet, tutor at Balliol, extended to Higman. He supervised innumerable research students, gave innumerable lectures on algebra, and introduced mathematical logic into the Oxford curriculum. He was a demanding lecturer in the classical style (with rapid delivery, small writing on the blackboard, his back to the audience, and fluent and elegantly grammatical sentence construction), who, however, ensured that the content of what he had to say was always of such importance that for those who learned how to understand his lectures there were great mathematical riches to be gained. He was awarded the London Mathematical Society's Berwick prize (1962) and De Morgan medal (1974), and the Royal Society's Sylvester medal (1979).

Higman was one of a trio of three great British group-theorists. They inhabited the London–Oxford–Cambridge triangle, albeit at different times: William Burnside (1852–1927) worked in London (at the Royal Naval College, Greenwich), Philip Hall (1904–1984) in Cambridge, and Higman in Oxford. There is a direct connection in that one of Higman's most influential papers about finite groups was written jointly with Hall on the so-called Burnside problem. Not only did their contribution make a major step forward in the study of the problem but also, serendipitously, the techniques of the Hall–Higman paper turned out to be of very great importance in the study of finite groups and, in particular, in the search for finite simple groups.

Higman had a long and successful life. He was a complex character. As a colleague he was capable of treating mathematicians less able than himself with disdain or with direct and hurtful comments on their work. As a supervisor of research students he was frightening until the student discovered that, when bearded in his den and asked direct questions, he would treat the student with great respect and provide detailed advice tailored to the ability of the student. Although himself quite a difficult man to have an easy friendship with, he was a great success in his work for the Samaritans; he was also a great success in the congenial post-seminar meetings in the pub, where his astonishing grasp of ornithology, his deep love of poetry (especially that of Yeats and R. S. Thomas), and his gift for solving devilish crosswords emerged perhaps against his will. He owned neither a radio nor a television.

Higman remained true to his Methodist roots. He was admitted a local preacher in 1936 and served the Methodist community for sixty-five years, giving his last address in 2001. He was not always well understood by his congregation. In the 1960s his mathematical research students, many of whom called him Uncle Graham in a friendly way (but never in his earshot), had a story that he had preached a Christmas day sermon in one of the villages near Oxford and had omitted to make any mention of the Christmas story. His address at the memorial service for Ivah was, however, a model for what such sermons should be. He survived her for another twenty-seven years, continuing to live in Oxford, though latterly at the Albany nursing home in Headington, following the onset of Parkinson's disease. He died of aspiration pneumonia at the John Radcliffe Hospital, Oxford, on 8 April 2008.

PETER M. NEUMANN

Sources *The Independent* (8 May 2008); (14 May 2008) · *Daily Telegraph* (27 May 2008) · www-history.mcs.st-and.ac.uk/Biographies/Higman.html, 18 March 2011 · *WW* (2008) · personal knowledge (2012) · private information (2012) · b. cert. · m. cert. · d. cert.
Likenesses obituary photographs
Wealth at death £844,781: probate, 29 Oct 2008, *CGPLA Eng. & Wales*

Hill, Albert Edwin [Bertie] (**1927–2005**), equestrian and farmer, was born on 7 February 1927 at Birch Farm, Swimbridge, Devon, the son of Hubert Hill, farmer, and his wife, Margery Evelyn, *née* Thorne. His involvement with horses began at an early age. He is said to have followed the Devon and Somerset staghounds as a four-year-old, ridden his pony to Swimbridge primary school from the age of five, and competed regularly in local gymkhanas and showjumping classes throughout his childhood. He attended secondary school at West Buckland. He left full-time education during the Second World War, at the age of fifteen, and thereafter helped his father on the family farm. Wartime conditions meant that all available land was under the plough and Bertie (as he was always known) took charge of the shire horse team. The war impinged on the young man in other ways: as a member of the Home Guard he undertook night patrols of Exmoor on horseback. An accomplished horseman, he became an amateur jockey when the war ended, riding successfully in local point-to-point races.

Hill's exploits on the race field brought him to the attention of Captain Tony Collings, owner of the Porlock Vale Riding School in north Devon and the man charged with assembling and training the British three-day event team for the Olympic games in Helsinki in 1952. Originally a discipline closely associated with the cavalry, eventing, or combined training as it was then known, had finally been opened to British civilian riders. Bertie Hill already had the riding skills to compete in the cross-country and showjumping phases and an intensive schooling in dressage enabled him to join the Olympic team, one of the first two civilians to do so (the other was Reg Hindley). Riding Sir John Miller's Stella, he finished seventh.

The next four years established Hill as one of the top equestrians in Europe. With Major Laurence Rook and Major Frank Weldon he formed the British team that won gold medals at the European championships in 1953 and 1954, picking up the individual gold at Basel on Crispin on the latter occasion. In the same year he began to compete in events on Countryman, the horse with which he became most closely associated. Purchased for £90 in 1952 as an ostensibly unbreakable Irish-born colt, Countryman proved to be a good hunter and point-to-pointer under Hill's patient tuition, and made his international eventing début in 1955. Once again the British team of Hill, Weldon, and Rook won gold at the European championships held at Windsor, their third consecutive triumph: Hill and Countryman won individual bronze. The horse was then sold to a syndicate that included the queen, the queen mother, and the tenth duke of Beaufort, but Hill continued to partner him, gaining fourth place at the Badminton horse trials in spring 1956. The pair then became part of the British team that won gold at the Olympic games, the equestrian events of which took place in June at Stockholm.

During this period Hill began to farm in his own right at Great Rapscott, South Molton, less than 10 miles from his childhood home; he is said to have purchased half of his stock with the proceeds from the sale of Countryman. On 3 February 1954 he married (Clarice) Mary Holland, a 22-year-old farmer's daughter from the nearby parish of Fremington. They had a son, Antony, and a daughter, Sarah. In between major international events Hill continued to hunt, to exhibit horses at shows, and to compete in national horse trials. He never won at Badminton, a surprising omission from such a fine equestrian career.

In 1960, when the Olympics were held in Rome, Hill was again selected for the eventing team, the first British rider to compete in three Olympiads. Partnering Wild Venture, he rode a clear round in the showjumping but bad luck and misjudgements in the earlier cross-country phase left the British competitors 0.5 points outside the bronze medal position. Errors in the preparation and management of the British team in 1960 would provide valuable experience for Hill during a later stage of his life.

Following his retirement from international competition Hill, with his wife, set up the Rapscott School of Equitation at their farm. The first of its kind in north Devon, it became the training ground for countless British riders, sometimes to the detriment of his own equestrian success. Lying second after the cross-country in his final three-day event at Badminton in 1970, he was so concerned with supporting the ten students he had brought with him that he jumped the wrong fence and was eliminated. Among those who benefited from his tuition were Princess Anne, the princess royal, and Mark Phillips. In 1967 he was appointed official trainer to the British international eventing team, bringing to the post his experience gained through competition at the highest level. Major successes under his guidance included the European championships of 1967 and 1969, the world championships in 1970, and, most significantly, the Olympic games of 1968 in Mexico, where the British team of Derek Allhusen, Jane Bullen, Ben Jones, and Richard Meade won gold.

Bertie Hill—a horseman, a racing enthusiast, and a countryman who was passionate about traditional rural pursuits—lived his entire life on and around Exmoor. From 1975 to 1997 he was master of the Dulverton West foxhounds. A continued involvement with horses also led to judging classes at the same local shows in which he had competed as a young man. Having handed over the running of Great Rapscott to his son Antony, he died of heart disease on 5 August 2005 at Eastleigh, 91 East Street, South Molton, after a long battle with Parkinson's disease. He was survived by his wife and children. In June 2006 he was inducted into the British Horse Society's equestrian hall of fame. JOYCE KAY

Sources D. Williams, ed., *The horseman's year* (1961) · C. Stratton, *Encyclopaedia of show jumping* (1973) · D. Sly, *Badminton horse trials* (1999) · *North Devon Journal* (18 Aug 2005) · *Daily Telegraph* (30 Aug 2005) · *Western Morning News* (9 Sept 2005) · b. cert. · m. cert. · d. cert.

Likenesses photograph, 1956, Getty Images, London · photographs, 1956–60, PA Photos, London · obituary photographs

Hill, Sir John McGregor (1921–2008), nuclear physicist and public servant, was born on 21 February 1921 at Westminster Nursing Home, 50 Liverpool Road, Chester, the son of John Campbell Hill (1888–1982), a science teacher at Chester College of Scottish background who later became a schools inspector, and his wife, Margaret Elizabeth, *née* Park (1893–1984). The family moved to Richmond upon Thames in Surrey and he was educated at Richmond county grammar school and King's College, London, where he gained a first in physics. In 1941 he joined the Royal Air Force and spent the rest of the Second World War working in radar development, ending with the rank of flight-lieutenant. On demobilization in 1946 he returned to academic physics at the Cavendish laboratory and St John's College in Cambridge. After gaining a PhD in 1948 for work on radioactive substances with short half-lives, he became a lecturer in physics at the University of London. Meanwhile, on 25 October 1947, at All Saints' Church, Cambridge, he married Nora Eileen Hellett (*b.* 1927), a nurse at Addenbrookes Hospital, and daughter of Henry John Hellett. They had two sons and a daughter.

In the late 1940s the Labour government led by Clement Attlee initiated the development of nuclear weapons, with Christopher Hinton in charge of fissile materials. Technologically complex factories were required, the largest being the reactors (or 'piles') at Windscale, Cumberland, which would produce plutonium. Expertise in relevant fields was in desperately short supply and in 1950 Hill was recruited as a member of Hinton's team overseeing the completion of Windscale, working partly on site and partly at Risley in Lancashire. The targets were met and plutonium was delivered in time for Britain's first nuclear test in October 1952.

Starting in 1953, Hill, working with J. C. C. Stewart, produced a series of important reports on the future of the industrial side of the nuclear project, and in particular its costs and efficiency. It was the beginning of an involvement with nuclear energy strategy which dominated the rest of his life. He also participated in the design of Calder Hall, the more advanced reactors built next to the Windscale site which were celebrated in 1956 as the first in the world to deliver nuclear-generated electricity to a civil supply system. In that year Britain's nuclear project reached a peak in public esteem, appearing to be a leader in a field of remarkable promise, but the descent soon began. In October 1957 fire in one of the Windscale reactors caused a release of radioactive contamination into the atmosphere, which in turn made necessary the dumping of milk from Cumberland dairy herds. It was the world's worst reactor accident and remained so for another twenty-two years, and there was considerable public alarm. Hill, by now deputy director of technical policy at Risley, was closely involved in the aftermath. Sir William Penney conducted a swift official inquiry but the government statement which followed, though it calmed external concerns, left staff at Windscale and Risley unsatisfied and aggrieved. Hill was asked to review the evidence on the key early stages of the accident and his report in January 1958 blamed faulty instrumentation more than human error. His account was given considerable credit in the official history of the accident, published in 1992.

Hill was by now a rising star. A slight man of medium height, quick-moving and active, he combined a certain modesty with a confidence founded on deep scientific knowledge. He was an exceptional committee chairman with a gift for getting disparate people to work together, and was known for always asking incisive questions. Hinton, a difficult man to please, rated him highly for his judgement and willingness to show the courage of his convictions. Hill soon became manager of the production group, overseeing the full range of factories supporting the industry as well as Windscale (which had been renamed Sellafield after the accident), Calder Hall, and a further reactor site at Chapelcross. He would later say this was the job he most enjoyed, but he did not stay long. In

1964 he became a member of the UK Atomic Energy Authority (UKAEA) and three years later he succeeded Penney as chairman, a post he held until retirement in 1981.

Hill's vision, which altered little, was of a strong British nuclear industry supplying a substantial proportion of the country's electricity needs well beyond the time when North Sea oil ran out. At its heart would be fast-breeder reactors with uniquely efficient fuel consumption, producing relatively little waste. Prototypes were in development at Dounreay in Caithness. This vision, he argued, promised a balanced, sustainable, economical, and independent energy future, as well as one with strong export potential. The state had an essential enabling role to play in delivering it, with UKAEA conducting the research and development. Though Hill made his case eloquently and persistently, and from a position of authority, it was not to be.

The 1970s were exceptionally difficult years for the country and the nuclear industry, in which successive governments found it impossible to make strategic choices. They had to weigh factors such as the oil price shock of 1973, the discovery and landing of North Sea oil, turbulence in the coal industry, and spells of economic difficulty that brought declines in electricity consumption and demands for government stimulus. At the same time public distaste for matters nuclear was growing, encouraged by Sir Brian Flowers's report of 1976, on 'Nuclear Power and the Environment' (which emphasized the risks and uncertainties of nuclear energy and called for a halt to further reactors until the problem of disposing the waste safely could be solved), and the Three Mile Island accident in the USA in 1979. Worse still, the British nuclear industry seemed unable to fulfil the promise of cheap energy that in earlier years had dazzled politicians and public alike.

The first-generation civil reactors, known as Magnox stations, though safe and often described as workhorses, proved expensive and troublesome to operate, and UKAEA's successor design, the advanced gas-cooled reactor (AGR), soon ran into problems. These difficulties were not of UKAEA's making but flowed in large measure from a government policy of entrusting plant construction to a number of weak and ill-equipped private industry consortia. Hill declared that this policy did 'more damage to the British nuclear industry than any other decision … more damage than all the other decisions put together' (*New Scientist*, 17 July 1975). Besides the AGR the UKAEA also offered another design, the steam-generating heavy water reactor, as a possible technology to fill the gap until fast-breeder reactors became available, but neither attracted the principal customer, the Central Electricity Generating Board, which preferred the pressurized water reactor made by the American Westinghouse corporation. Ministers, buffeted by events and under pressure from vested interests, could not choose, and meanwhile UKAEA's long-term case was undermined as the fast-breeder reactor began to take on mirage-like properties (always seeming to need a few more years in development).

Through it all, Hill (who was knighted in 1969) remained a patient and persistent advocate for the UKAEA. Though he was sometimes at odds with ministers, notably the Labour energy secretary, Tony Benn, it is a measure of his standing that he was twice reappointed UKAEA chairman and that his fourteen-year tenure was unusually long in a public service post at such a high level at this time. His talents, however, were sometimes less obvious to the public. He was uncomfortable on television and for years maintained a brisk, almost dismissive tone about nuclear anxieties that could be seen as condescending. In 1977 he made international headlines by describing as 'science fiction' claims (later largely vindicated) by the Soviet exile Zhores Medvedev about a nuclear waste accident in Russia in 1957. Hill later explained that his remark had related to the alleged scientific causes, rather than the fact, of the explosion, but the damage was done. By the end of the 1970s, facing an increasingly informed and sophisticated anti-nuclear lobby, he had recognized the need to give higher priority to winning public trust.

From 1971, alongside his role at UKAEA, Hill was chairman of British Nuclear Fuels Ltd, a state-owned corporation created from his old northern production group, with Sellafield at its heart. His hope was to build a global business in nuclear fuel reprocessing, but again he was defeated by the combination of changing public attitudes, technical difficulties, rising costs, and political hesitation. Dogged by questions about health risks at Sellafield and about the prospects for safe disposal of nuclear waste, he was dismayed to find his reassuring arguments undermined by accidents and mistakes at the site. Nor was his firm conviction that future generations would solve the long-term storage problem enough to win that argument.

Hill retired from UKAEA on reaching sixty, but remained chairman of British Nuclear Fuels for a further two years, and of Amersham International plc, the former radiochemical centre which produced radioactive materials for industry, from its inception in 1975 until 1988. From 1984 to 1992 he was president of the British Nuclear Forum. His vision for the British nuclear energy industry may not have been realized (the fast-breeder programme was shut down in 1994), but some of his warnings were by the end of his life judged by some to be prescient. As early as the 1970s he argued that the long-term danger to the environment from burning fossil fuels was being underestimated, and he repeatedly stressed the need to have viable alternative energy sources available when British oil and gas supplies began to run out.

Though regarded as an approachable man by his colleagues, Hill liked to keep his private life private. He enjoyed gardening, the occasional glass of malt whisky, and golf. He served as captain and president of the Royal Mid-Surrey Golf Club in Richmond (he lived latterly at Dominic House, Sudbrook Lane, Petersham) and in his UKAEA days he used to say that one of the tests of his management ability and his powers of delegation was whether, once in a while, he could be spared to play eighteen holes on a Friday afternoon. He died on 14 January

2008 at the Royal Star and Garter Home, Richmond upon Thames, of a chest infection and Alzheimer's disease. He was survived by his wife, Nora, and their three children.

BRIAN CATHCART

Sources M. Gowing and L. Arnold, *Independence and deterrence: Britain and atomic energy, 1945–1952*, 2 vols. (1974) · *The Times* (24 Oct 1978); (30 Jan 2008) · W. Patterson, *Going critical: an unofficial history of British nuclear power* (1985); www.waltpatterson.org/goingcritical.pdf, 10 Aug 2011 · L. Arnold, *Windscale, 1957: anatomy of a nuclear accident* (1992) · *The Independent* (30 Jan 2008) · *The Guardian* (20 Feb 2008) · *Daily Telegraph* (27 Feb 2008) · *WW* (2008) · Burke, *Peerage* · private information (2012) [L. Arnold, A. Hills] · b. cert. · m. cert. · d. cert.

Archives CAC Cam., papers, 1946–94 | Institute of Mechanical Engineers Library, Lord Hinton papers | FILM BFINA, current affairs footage | SOUND BL NSA, current affairs recordings

Likenesses obituary photographs

Wealth at death £883,027: probate, 2 June 2008, *CGPLA Eng. & Wales*

Hill, Mary Eglantyne [Polly] (**1914–2005**), economic anthropologist, was born on 10 June 1914 at 35 Park Side, Cambridge, the eldest child of Archibald Vivian *Hill (1886–1977), physiologist, and his wife, Margaret Neville, *née* Keynes (*d.* 1970), social reformer. She was the progeny of a formidable Cambridge academic dynasty. Her father won a Nobel prize in 1922. Her maternal grandparents were (John) Neville *Keynes, logician and economist, and Florence Ada *Keynes, social reformer and local politician, while her uncles were John Maynard *Keynes, the founder of macroeconomics, and Sir Geoffrey *Keynes, surgeon and literary scholar.

Polly Hill read economics at Newnham College, Cambridge, but her scholarly ambitions were thwarted by the rule that only those with a first were eligible to do doctoral research. Her first employment was as an editorial assistant for the Royal Economic Society, and then as a researcher for the Fabian Society between 1938 and 1939. During the Second World War she worked successively for the Treasury, the Board of Trade, and the statistics department of the Colonial Office. Given her artistic and literary aspirations—she knew Henry Moore, and had a book of poetry published in 1945—she felt she 'languished' during these eleven years. In 1951 she was employed as commercial editor of the weekly publication *West Africa*, and her life was 'forever changed' by her posting to the Gold Coast in 1952 (Macfarlane). Back in England, at Hampstead register office on 20 July 1953, she married Kenneth Albert Curwood Humphreys (*d.* 1985), registrar of the West African Examinations Council, based in the Gold Coast, and son of Arthur Curwood Humphreys, schoolmaster. He was two years younger than Polly, and a widower.

The year following her marriage Polly Hill (who always published under her maiden name) finally entered academia, taking up a research fellowship in economics at the University College of the Gold Coast, and beginning research into the lives and economic strategies of migrant cocoa farmers. While her marriage lasted only eight years, she had the 'extraordinary good fortune' to give birth, aged forty-two, to her only daughter, Susannah, an event that she felt 'profoundly' improved the quality of her work (Macfarlane). She gradually abandoned the traditional social survey techniques that informed *The Gold Coast Cocoa Farmer: a Preliminary Survey* (1956), and crafted a pioneering new role as an engaged, empirical 'field economist'. She began to conduct village-level studies, painstakingly collecting life-histories, reconstructing inheritance patterns, and relating them to documentary and archival sources (especially nineteenth-century land maps). She remained in the Gold Coast following its independence (as Ghana) in 1957 and the re-naming of the University College of the Gold Coast as the University of Ghana in 1961.

In 1961–2, at the invitation of Meyer Fortes, Hill spent a year as a Smuts fellow at the department of social anthropology at Cambridge, analysing her data and writing her seminal work *The Migrant Cocoa-Farmers of Southern Ghana* (1963). She was awarded a PhD in 1967 for this work, and it was republished in 1997. Eschewing economic abstractions or Marxist generalizations, the book carefully documented how some migrant farmers formed collectives (called 'companies') to purchase parcels of farmland for subsequent investment and redistribution, while others relied on the wealth of their matrilineal group to purchase 'family' land as individuals, over which descendants had use-rights. The particular accumulation strategies of these dynamic rural entrepreneurs demonstrated the different economic rationalities they deployed. Her empiricism, and her sensitivity to geography, history, and social structure, led her to challenge homogenous depictions of an African subsistence 'peasantry', and the notion that the west African cocoa industry had been created by the colonial authorities, rather than the farmers themselves. The quality of her field research was visible in the rich narrative case-studies appended to each chapter. The approach defined all her subsequent work.

On returning to Ghana, Hill moved to the Institute of African Studies and began work on cattle rearing in northern Ghana, publishing *Rural Capitalism in West Africa* (1970). Concerned about her daughter's health, she left Ghana in 1965 for a non-stipendiary fellowship at Clare Hall, Cambridge. Ever independent and just as resourceful, she eked out a series of research grants to continue field research in Hausaland, northern Nigeria, and later in Kano, publishing the acclaimed *Rural Hausa: a Village and a Setting* (1972) and *Population, Prosperity and Poverty: Rural Kano 1900 to 1970* (1977).

Recognition for Hill's contribution to an emergent field of economic anthropology came eventually, with her election in 1973 as Smuts reader in Commonwealth studies at Cambridge. A sabbatical in 1977 took her to Karnataka in India, which led to *Dry Grain Farming Families: Hausaland (Nigeria) and Karnataka (India) Compared* (1982). In all she completed thirteen years of field research, more than most anthropologists. Her reputation grew with the expansion of development studies and the waning hold of structural Marxism on anthropology. Mounting frustration at the economists' 'ignorance' of the realities of rural poverty led her to write what she called a 'constructive' polemic (Macfarlane). *Development Economics on Trial: the*

Anthropological Case for the Prosecution (1986) went into six editions.

After what she called her 'slow start' Polly Hill's commitment to scholarship (which resulted in nine books and some fifty articles) continued into her eighties, along with her passion for poetry, sculpture, and modern art. Yet her last project on the history of female students at Cambridge was rejected by publishers. This reinforced her sense that, as a woman living for much of her career in the academic 'hinterland', her contributions had been overlooked. Undaunted, she wrote *The History of the Isleham Fens* (1990), and co-edited *Lydia and Maynard: Letters between Lydia Lopokova and John Maynard Keynes* (1989). Cared for by her daughter and her family in her last years, she died at 4 Coates Drove, Isleham, Ely, Cambridgeshire, on 21 August 2005, of bronchopneumonia. A memorial celebration was held at Clare Hall on 28 May 2006. DAVID MILLS

Sources A. Macfarlane, video interview with Polly Hill, DSpace, U. Cam., 20 July 1996, www.dspace.cam.ac.uk/handle/1810/269, 12 July 2008 • *The Independent* (25 Aug 2005) • *The Guardian* (26 Aug 2005) • K. Hart, 'Memorial celebration for Polly Hill', *Anthropology Today*, 22/5 (Oct 2006) • C. A. Gregory, 'Polly Hill', *The Elgar companion to development studies*, ed. D. A. Clark (2006), 223–6 • *WW* (2005) • personal knowledge (2009) • private information (2009) • b. cert. • m. cert. • d. cert.

Archives Northwestern University, Herskovits Library of African Studies, papers, fieldnotes, corresp. | FILM U. Cam., DSpace, interview with A. Macfarlane, 20 July 1996, www.dspace.cam.ac.uk/handle/1810/269

Likenesses obituary photographs

Hiller, Erwin [*known as* Erwin Hillier] (**1911–2005**), cinematographer, was born on 2 September 1911 in Berlin, of mixed Anglo-German parentage; his father was Robert Hiller, described by Erwin as 'of independent means'. He grew up in Germany and as a result his English retained a continental inflection for the rest of his life. After attending art school, he made his first contacts with the German film industry, working on a number of productions, including Fritz Lang's first sound film, the classic *M* (1931), where he assisted the principal cameraman, Fritz Arno Wagner. Although he often referred to having known and worked with various luminaries of Weimar cinema, the full extent of his cinematic apprenticeship in the German film industry is difficult to assess, as nearly all his contributions were uncredited. Nevertheless, his training in Germany had a marked effect on the style of his later work in Britain, especially in its emphasis on atmospheric lighting, visual fluidity, and unusual angles and movements.

Following Hitler's rise to power in 1933, Hiller relocated to London, briefly working as a press photographer, and joining Gaumont British's camera department. On 27 May 1933, at Kensington register office, he married Helen Yates, the twenty-year-old daughter of Joseph Southgate; they had one daughter, Shirley. Meanwhile, at Gaumont British's Shepherd's Bush studios Hiller became a camera operator on productions including Alfred Hitchcock's *Waltzes from Vienna* and *The Man Who Knew Too Much* (both 1934), assisting the established cinematographers Glen MacWilliams and Curt Courant respectively. He also worked on the Jessie Matthews musical *Evergreen* (1934), directed by Victor Saville and once again with MacWilliams as principal photographer, and on two Walter Forde films, *Jack Ahoy!* (1934) and *Brown on Resolution* (1935), in both cases working under Bernard Knowles. For most of these films Hiller received no screen credits. In the mid-1930s he moved on from Gaumont to work on such cheaply made 'quota quickies' as the Warner Brothers comedy *The Girl in the Crowd* (1935), shot at Teddington Studios, which marked his first film with the director Michael Powell. The two were reunited working for Joe Rock Studios at Elstree on the mystery drama *The Man Behind the Mask* (1936), and on Powell's first collaboration with the Hungarian screenwriter Emeric Pressburger, the spy thriller *The Spy in Black* (1939).

Following the outbreak of the Second World War, Hiller (by now known professionally as Erwin Hillier) became principal photographer on a number of propaganda shorts commissioned by the Ministry of Information; these included *Men of Tomorrow* (1942), produced by Sydney Box, which showcased the contributions from boy scouts to the war effort. The same year Hiller shot his first feature film as principal cinematographer, the comedy *The Lady from Lisbon* (1942), a British National production, followed by *Rhythm Serenade* (1943), a patriotic musical starring Vera Lynn. *The Silver Fleet* (1943), a drama about Dutch wartime resistance, marked the beginning of his association with Powell and Pressburger's production company The Archers. The richly allegorical *A Canterbury Tale* (1944) combined Hiller's predilection for chiaroscuro compositions with a perceptive way of photographing the English countryside.

In *I Know Where I'm Going!* (1945), for which he was credited by now unusually as Erwin Hiller, not Hillier, he devised a sublimely lyrical visual backdrop for the film's romantic drama set in Scotland's Western Isles. By now acclaimed primarily as an expert in black and white photography, he was replaced by Jack Cardiff in The Archers' subsequent colour films, *A Matter of Life and Death* (1946) and *Black Narcissus* (1947), while his own début on a colour production, the musical *London Town* (1946), proved a flop. Roy Ward Baker's atmospheric black and white *film noir The October Man* (1947), starring John Mills as an amnesiac accused of murder, played much more to Hiller's strengths, as did Brian Desmond Hurst's Gothic melodrama *The Mark of Cain* (1947), and Lawrence Huntington's *Mr Perrin and Mr Traill* (1948), set in a gloomy boarding school.

The whimsical war comedy *Private Angelo* (1949), starring Peter Ustinov as a cowardly Italian soldier, marked the beginning of Hiller's long association with the director Michael Anderson. In the 1950s their collaborations encompassed comedies (*Will Any Gentleman …?*, 1953), thrillers (*The House of the Arrow*, 1953; *Chase a Crooked Shadow*, 1958), and the acclaimed *Shake Hands with the Devil* (1959), set in Dublin in 1921, but their biggest success was the iconic war drama *The Dam Busters* (1955), about the legendary 'bouncing bomb' attacks on the Ruhr dams.

The film was a success not least thanks to Hiller's breathtaking and authentic aerial photography, once again showcasing his mastery of black and white photography.

During the 1960s Anderson and Hiller collaborated on a series of increasingly international productions, including the thrillers *The Naked Edge* (1961), *Operation Crossbow* (1965), and *The Quiller Memorandum* (1966), the latter scripted by Harold Pinter. Their last collaboration was the papal drama *The Shoes of the Fisherman* (1968). Hiller worked occasionally with other directors, and was nominated for a BAFTA award for *Sammy Going South* (1963), directed by Alexander Mackendrick. His last film was *The Valley of Gwangwi* (1969), directed by Jim O'Connolly, which mixed cowboys with dinosaurs. He died of ischaemic heart disease at his home, 7 Baronsmede, Ealing, London, on 10 January 2005, and was survived by his wife and daughter.

TIM BERGFELDER

Sources M. Powell, *A life in movies* (1986) • M. Powell, *Million dollar movie* (1992) • K. Macdonald, *Emeric Pressburger* (1994) • D. Petrie, *The British cinematographer* (1996) • P. Cook, *I know where I'm going* (2002) • B. McFarlane, ed., *The encyclopedia of British film* (2003) • *The Independent* (3 Feb 2005) • *The Guardian* (8 Feb 2005) • *The Times* (18 March 2005) • m. cert. • d. cert.

Likenesses R. Hawkins, two photographs, c.1952, Getty Images, London • obituary photographs

Hobbs, John Raymond [Jack] (**1929–2008**), pathologist and clinical immunologist, was born on 17 April 1929 at the Louise Margaret Hospital, Aldershot, the third of four sons of Frederick Walter Haydn Hobbs (1900–1975), a sergeant-major in the Duke of Cornwall's light infantry, and his wife, Anna Helena, *née* Froseler (1899–1960). At the time of his birth his family was living at 45 West Square, Marlborough Lines, Farnborough. He had a peripatetic early childhood, but the family eventually settled in Plymouth, where Hobbs's father became a civil servant on leaving the army. During the Second World War he and his brothers, Frederick, William, and Dennis, were evacuated to Penzance, before returning to Plymouth later in the war. He left school at sixteen, then trained as a pathology laboratory assistant at Plymouth Hospital.

Hobbs did his national service with the Royal Army Medical Corps in Britain and Egypt, and was promoted sergeant. Having saved his pay, on his return he attended Plymouth and Devonport Technical College, where he passed the external inter BSc (a qualification for entry to university) in nine months. With a state scholarship he went on to study medicine at the Middlesex Hospital in London. There he took his BSc in 1953, qualified MB BS in 1956, and won seven prizes. On 7 August 1954 he married Patricia Lilian (Paddy) Arnott (1930–2011), a teacher, children's writer, and radio playwright, and daughter of James Arnott, civil servant. They had three daughters, Wendy, Lucy, and Trudy.

After house jobs at the Middlesex, Central Middlesex, and Brompton hospitals, Hobbs returned to the Middlesex Hospital as a registrar in 1959. There he was much influenced by the work of Joe Humble, a haematologist at the Westminster medical school, who was interested in the possibility of bone marrow transplantation curing a range of genetic and other diseases. During this time he donated, under anaesthetic, half a litre of his own bone marrow for research purposes. He was awarded his MD in 1963 for a thesis on the diagnosis of thyroid diseases, which he wrote under the supervision of Richard Bayliss. Also in 1963 he was appointed a consultant at Hammersmith Hospital, where he developed his interest in protein biochemistry, particularly the role of serum immunoglobins and the pathology of myeloma.

In 1970 Hobbs was appointed professor of chemical pathology at the Westminster medical school, where he built up a department renowned for its skills in diagnostic biochemistry, and where he was also able to pursue his interest in the potential of bone marrow transplantation. The first successful human bone marrow transplant had been carried out by Robert Good in America in 1968. In 1971 Hobbs, together with Joe Humble and David James, a tissue-typing expert, carried out the first bone marrow transplant in the UK, in a seven-month-old baby with severe immunodeficiency. This transplant used, as Good's had, a sibling donor. Later the same year Hobbs's team performed the world's first parent-to-child transplant, and in 1973 they performed the world's first transplant using an unrelated donor. By 1992 the Westminster team had completed 285 transplants, with the highest success rate (measured by survival for over 100 days) in the world, both with family donors and with unrelated donors.

As a by-product of their work, in 1974 Hobbs and David James set up the first unrelated bone marrow donor register. This was later named after Anthony Nolan, a young patient of Hobbs's with Wiskott-Aldrich syndrome. Anthony died in 1979 before a donor could be found, but by the time of Hobbs's death the register included more than 400,000 potential donors, had enabled more than 4000 successful matches to be made, and had led to the creation of similar registers around the world. Following pioneering work in his department on serum proteins which showed that abnormal levels or types of such proteins provided good indicators for the diagnosis of disease, he was also instrumental in setting up the nationwide Supra-regional Assay Service, which co-ordinated the work of laboratories specializing in diagnostic biochemistry. Among Hobbs's other achievements at Westminster were developing the first non-invasive test for cystic fibrosis, and establishing standard reference levels for immunoglobins.

Bone marrow transplants were expensive treatments, particularly because of the need for isolation cubicles for patients. In the late 1970s Hobbs joined forces with Iris Burton, the editor of *Woman's Own* magazine, and Emma Nicholson, the director of the Save the Children Foundation (and later a Conservative and Liberal Democrat politician), to launch an appeal which raised more than £3 million to build isolation cubicles and facilities for parents at the Westminster Children's Hospital. In 1991 this fund became the Cogent Trust (named from Correction of Genetic Diseases by Transplantation). Hobbs was devastated when the Westminster bone marrow unit was closed in 1992 ahead of the amalgamation of five central London hospitals to create the Chelsea and Westminster Hospital the following year. He continued with his immunological research until his retirement in 1994, and remained closely involved in the Cogent Trust until shortly before his death. By that time the trust had raised some £13 million to sponsor research and clinical work in the field of transplantation for genetic diseases, including paying for a new transplant unit at Bristol Royal Hospital for Children and funding training and other activities both there and at the Royal Manchester Children's Hospital.

Hobbs wrote or co-authored more than 600 papers on a wide range of topics in pathology, clinical immunology, and protein biochemistry; the last was published in 2007. He was an excellent lecturer and was repeatedly invited to give lectures and presentations at a wide range of universities and medical schools in Europe, the USA, and elsewhere, and he also advised the governments of Russia, Poland, China, Peru, and Uruguay. It was calculated that 134 of his students achieved MDs or other higher university degrees, 70 went on to become members or fellows of the Royal College of Pathologists, and 48 to hold university chairs in chemical pathology, immunology, or related disciplines.

According to two of his colleagues, Hobbs 'could appear to strangers as a challenging person', but those who got to know him better discovered 'a moral, compassionate person who took delight in scientific achievement, gave unbending support to all those who trained in his department, and held an absolute belief in his work and the sanctity of every human life' (*The Guardian*, 5 September 2008). He enjoyed stamp collecting, and going to the theatre and opera. His activities were curtailed in the last year of his life by the onset of lung cancer, from which he died at Hayes Cottage Nursing Home, Grange Road, Hayes, London, on 13 July 2008. He was survived by his wife, Paddy, and their three daughters. ALEX MAY

Sources *BMJ* (27 June 1970), 804; (26 Aug 2008), 1934 · J. R. Hobbs, 'The achievements of the Westminster children's bone marrow team for some genetic diseases', and 'The Westminster contribution to the correction of thalassaemia major and other inborn anaemias', *Correction of genetic diseases by transplantation*, ed. C. G. Steward and J. R. Hobbs, 3 (1995), 1–15 and 80–89 · *The Guardian* (5 Sept 2008) · b. cert. · m. cert. · d. cert.

Likenesses photograph, 2007, repro. in en.wikipedia.org/wiki/John_Raymond_Hobbs

Wealth at death under £312,000: probate, 28 Oct 2008, *CGPLA Eng. & Wales*

Hobsbaum, Philip Dennis (1932–2005), poet and literary scholar, was born on 29 June 1932 at 24 Underwood Street, Whitechapel, London, the son of Joseph Hobsbaum, telephone engineer, and his wife, Rachel, *née* Sapera. His parents were both first-generation eastern European Jewish immigrants. In 1939 his father's job took the family to Yorkshire. They settled in 1942 in Bradford, where Hobsbaum obtained a place at Belle Vue Grammar School. Ronald Bradshaw, a perceptive English teacher, recognized ability in the bullied, physically awkward pupil, and moved him from the C to the A stream, encouraging him to try for a Cambridge scholarship. During his schooldays Hobsbaum participated in theatricals at the local Civic Theatre (at one point he toyed with the idea of becoming a professional actor) and debated at the local Jewish society. Both helped form his clear diction and well-modulated readings of verse and prose. Following school he worked for two years as a Ministry of National Insurance clerk. Poor eyesight meant that he failed the national service physical test. During this period he wrote many poems, short stories, and plays, and attended lectures given by the eminent Shakespearian critic G. Wilson Knight and others.

In 1952 Hobsbaum gained an exhibition to Downing College, Cambridge, where his teachers included F. R. Leavis, whom he subsequently described as 'the greatest man I ever met … an amazing teacher' (*The Guardian*). At Cambridge he edited the student literary magazine *Delta* (1954–6). As editor he displayed his acumen in recognizing talent, publishing early work by, among others, Ted Hughes and Peter Redgrove, and forming the foundations of what became important connections within the London literary establishment. Continuing to write poetry, he also created the first of many writing group meetings, at which poets read new work aloud and received criticism from their peers. He gained upper seconds in both parts of the English tripos, graduating in 1955.

On leaving Cambridge Hobsbaum moved to London, and became a licentiate of the Royal Academy of Music in 1956 and of the Guildhall School of Music in 1957. In London he worked in television and for a theatrical agent, and taught at various schools, including Tulse Hill comprehensive, where Ken Livingstone, subsequently mayor of London, was one of his students. Livingstone later said that if Hobsbaum hadn't left, in 1958, 'I would have probably stayed on for higher education' (*Independent on Sunday*, 28 Feb 1993). Meanwhile, at Brixton Synagogue on 7 August 1957, Hobsbaum had married Hannah Kelly, a nineteen-year-old dictaphone typist and poet; there were no children of the marriage. In their basement flat in Stockwell, south London, Hobsbaum convened a writing group known as the Group. Those attending included poets of the calibre of Martin Bell, George Macbeth, Peter Porter, Peter Redgrove, and Edward Lucie-Smith. Hobsbaum's own poetry also began to attract attention, being published in small magazines like *Extra Verse*, *Gemini*, the *Oxford and Cambridge Magazine*, *Universities' Poetry*, and elsewhere.

In 1959, supported by his wife, Hobsbaum enrolled at Sheffield University for a PhD, since the poet and critic William Empson, whom he greatly admired, taught there. Hobsbaum's essays for Empson had 'very wide margins, so he could scribble abuse' on them—a device Hobsbaum's subsequent students also found to be useful (*The Times*). Hobsbaum's relationship with Empson, his supervisor, was complex, intense, and at times hostile. His account was later published in his memoir, 'Empson as teacher: the Sheffield years', in *William Empson: the Critical Achievement* (ed. C. Norris and N. Mapp, 1993), and partially documented in the second volume of John Haffenden's biography of Empson. Empson nevertheless supported Hobsbaum's search for an academic position and in 1962 he was appointed lecturer at Queen's University, Belfast, where he taught for four years before moving to the University of Glasgow in 1966. The professor who appointed him to the Belfast English department was Peter Herbert Butter, known for his critical and editorial work on the Anglo-Scottish poet Edwin Muir. Hobsbaum moved to Glasgow University a year after Butter's appointment to the regius chair of English there. He spent the rest of his career at the Glasgow English department, where he formed the creative writing programme and moved progressively through the academic ranks, from lecturer to senior lecturer in 1972, from 1979 to 1985 as reader, and then to a personal chair until retirement in 1997.

Hobsbaum's PhD was eventually awarded in May 1968. Entitled 'Some reasons for the great variety of response to literature among modern literary critics', his dissertation subsequently appeared in various journal articles and as a monograph under the title *A Theory of Communication* (1970). Reflecting the influence of both Leavis and Empson, Hobsbaum argued that words depend on their context for meaning: 'One's approach to a poem must necessarily be governed by what is available to the reader' (*A Theory of Communication*, 58). During this period several volumes of Hobsbaum's poetry were published. His *Poems in the Place's Fault, and Other Poems* (1964), in the words of Heather Clark, 'emphasize Hobsbaum's feelings of marginalization in a class-obsessed culture that makes little room for a Jewish scholarship boy from Yorkshire' (Clark, 59); *Snapshots* appeared in 1965, a year later *Retreat and Other Poems*, and in 1969 *Coming Out Fighting*, and *Some Lovely Glorious Nothing: a Poem*. In 1972 *Women and Animals* was published. Peter Lawson observed that in such poems as 'Testimony' and 'Watching and Waiting', and 'animal poems' like 'The Sick Lion', 'together with his accomplished craft and ironic humour, Hobsbaum's quasi-Judaic faith redeems his poetic voice and saves it from disappearing into the silence of despair' (P. Lawson, *Passionate Renewal: Jewish Poetry in Britain since 1945, an Anthology*, 2001, 14). Hobsbaum's 'A Lesson in Love' was included by Philip Larkin in his selection *The Oxford Book of Twentieth Century English Verse* (1972).

Hobsbaum edited, with Edward Lucie-Smith, *A Group Anthology* (1963), a collection of poetry discussed at his writing workshops, and, as sole editor, an anthology, *Ten Elizabethan Poets* (1969), directed at sixth-formers. In his later years his publications focused on literary criticism and the clear exposition of the work of individual writers, although he continued to write poetry and dramatic sketches. *A Reader's Guide to Charles Dickens* appeared in 1972, *A Reader's Guide to D. H. Lawrence* in 1981, and *A Reader's Guide to Robert Lowell* in 1988. Hobsbaum wrote forewords to S. K. Hassan's *Philip Larkin and his Contemporaries: an Air of Authenticity* (1988) and Phil Moore's *Alasdair Gray: Critical Appreciations and a Bibliography* (2002). Gray attended Hobsbaum's Glasgow lectures and writer's workshops, as did Liz Lochhead and James Kelman, to name but a few of the significant creative talents encouraged by him. Gray's *Book of Prefaces* (2000) was dedicated to Hobsbaum, 'poet, critic, and servant of the servants of art'. In addition to many articles and reviews Hobsbaum's critical work included *Tradition and Experiment in English Poetry* (1979), *Essentials of Literary Criticism* (1983), and *Metre Rhythm and Verse Form* (1996). His stated aim was 'to get things clear. In poetry this means being true to one's experience, whatever that experience may be. In criticism it means trying to get across to the reader a sense of the text as verbal entity' (Chapman and Jorgenson, 209). He was sceptical of the kind of critical theory fashionable in academic circles at the close of the twentieth century. He believed that 'you should master the basic works of English Literature' rather than read criticism (*Daily Telegraph*).

Hobsbaum was perhaps most notable, to use the words of his *Times* obituarist, as a 'servant' to the 'makers' (the poets). The impact of his workshops in London, Belfast, Glasgow, and elsewhere was acknowledged by the Nobel prizewinner Seamus Heaney, who commented that Hobsbaum 'emanated energy, generosity, belief in the community, trust in the parochial, the inept, the unprinted' (Clark, 60). Others acknowledging their indebtedness to Hobsbaum during the Belfast years included such distinguished talents as Bernard MacLaverty, Derek Mahon, and Michael Longley. Hobsbaum's prominent role in fostering talent was reflected in the pages of Heather Clark's *The Ulster Renaissance: Poetry in Belfast, 1962–1972* (2006).

Hobsbaum's first marriage ended in divorce in 1968, but in 1976 he married, as his second wife, Rosemary Singleton, *née* Phillips, a teacher. He thereby acquired two stepdaughters. In spite of suffering from increasingly severe diabetes, in his last years he travelled, especially enjoying a visit to the Galapagos Islands. He also loved Handel, Bach, and the *EastEnders* soap opera. Bearded and heavy of stature, he was capable of great kindness and sympathy. During his final illness his satiric, puckish sense of humour did not desert him in spite of a leg amputation. Visited by an American dramatist whose work he had championed, he is reputed to have said as his last words, 'You see me' (in a broad Western drawl) 'in the Last Chance Corral' (*Daily Telegraph*). He died in Glasgow on 28 June 2005 from complications of diabetes, and was survived by his wife, Rosemary, and his two stepdaughters. Patrick Reilly in an obituary observed that 'wherever Philip went, literature flourished … To be the sponsor of three great movements of poetry—in London, Belfast, and Glasgow … is no small achievement. To be praised by giants like Heaney and Gray is an accolade given to few' (*The Herald*).

WILLIAM BAKER

Sources *Independent on Sunday* (28 Feb 1993) · C. Norris and N. Mapp, eds., *William Empson: the critical achievement* (1993) · J. Chapman and J. D. Jorgenson, eds., *Contemporary Authors* [new revision series], 56 (1997) · *Daily Telegraph* (1 July 2005) · *The Herald* [Glasgow] (4 July 2005) · *The Times* (6 July 2005) · *The Independent* (6 July 2005) · *The Guardian* (7 July 2005) · H. Clark, *The Ulster renaissance: poetry in Belfast, 1962–1972* (2006) · J. Haffenden, *William Empson: against the Christians* (2006) · *Who's who in Scotland* (2005) · personal knowledge (2009) · private information (2009) [Rosemary Hobsbaum, widow; A. Hook; P. Millett] · b. cert. · m. cert. [1957]

Archives priv. coll. · Ransom HRC, MS collection, poems · U. Glas. L., books and papers · U. Reading L., corresp. and literary papers · Victoria University, British Columbia, Canada, McPherson Library, literary MSS | FILM BL NSA, current affairs footage

| **sound** BL NSA, British Council tapes, *The poet speaks*, interview with P. Orr, 3 May 1970, 1CDR0003964 • BL NSA, current affairs recording • BL NSA, documentary recording • BL NSA, performance recordings

Likenesses L. Hobsbaum, portrait, repro. in V. B. Sherry, ed., *Poets of Great Britain and Ireland since 1960*, DLitB, 40 (1985), pt 1, 216 • obituary photographs

Wealth at death £29,006.55: confirmation, 9 Sept 2005, *CCI*

Hockley, Sir Anthony Heritage Farrar- (1924–2006), army officer, was born on 8 April 1924 at the Nursing Home, St Nicholas Street, Coventry, the son of Arthur Farrar-Hockley, journalist, and his second wife, Agnes Beatrice, *née* Griffin. He was named after his godfather, Heritage Peters. He had an elder sister, Pamela, and two half-sisters and a half-brother from his father's first marriage. At the time of his birth registration his parents lived at Newland, Palmerston Road, Coventry. He inherited a strong literary bent from his father but this did not emerge until his late twenties. His formal education was patchy. Latterly he attended Exeter School in Devon until he ran away in September 1939 aged fifteen to join the Gloucestershire regiment; he was discovered to be under age and returned home but could not resist the allure of the military life.

The Second World War In 1941 Farrar-Hockley re-enlisted and served in the ranks of the 70th young soldiers' battalion; a sergeant at seventeen, he was not yet eighteen when in November 1942 he was commissioned into the 6th battalion of the Parachute regiment. In August 1944 his battalion was parachuted into southern France, north of Fréjus; 'One by one, hanging below the sailing silk or nylon, they floated down quietly', as he described such landings twenty-five years later (*Airborne Carpet*, 1969, 81). Its mission was to hold ground in order to permit the untrammelled advance of the American Seventh Army northwards. Once this was accomplished an elated Farrar-Hockley noticed some nearby peasants and announced their liberation 'in my best French'. They stood impassively before a 'woman nudged one of the men and said … "Tell him to shove off"'. The young Farrar-Hockley was thus introduced to the humorous absurdities of war to which he thereafter usually responded with gusto and self-deprecating wit.

In December 1944 Farrar-Hockley landed in Greece, near Thebes, got food for its starving inhabitants, rounded up Germans, and pushed on to Athens. During a skirmish with communist guerrillas, his company commander was wounded, and Farrar-Hockley, aged twenty, found himself in charge of C company. For outstanding leadership he was awarded an MC. Even before his coming of age he had demonstrated that he was a natural leader and an instinctive commander. Back home, on 7 July 1945, at St Peter's Church, Ealing, he married Margaret Bernadette Wells (1919–1981). They had three sons, (Charles) Dair (*b.* 1946), Kerin (*b.* 1950), who survived only a week, and Hilary (*b.* 1954).

Korea and other conflicts By the war's end Farrar-Hockley had set his mind on a career as a professional soldier. After serving in Palestine in 1945–6 with the Parachute regiment he transferred back into the Glosters in 1948 with the substantive rank of captain. He served as adjutant of the 1st battalion in the Korean War, most notably in April 1951 during the defence of Hill 235 at the battle of the Imjin. The Glosters, part of the British 29th infantry brigade, became surrounded by a large Chinese force estimated at 10,000 troops. In his later recollections of this famous action Farrar-Hockley stressed how much he had been inspired by the conduct of his commanding officer, Lieutenant-Colonel Fred Carne, who was awarded the VC for his part in this epic defence against the odds. Farrar-Hockley realized that he was of little use at battalion headquarters and went forward to take command of A company. He placed himself in the very front trench and mounted a furious defence, striking the Chinese hard with grenades and machine gun fire as they tried to turn his left flank. He encouraged others by his determination, bravery, and quick-wittedness. Several years later he reflected on why men stand and 'continue an action which, for them, is almost certainly lost … Being the men they are, no other course is open to them' (*Edge of the Sword*, 1954, 43). On receiving orders to fall back he attempted to cover the withdrawal with fire and a smoke-screen, but to no avail, as the Chinese overwhelmed the position and Farrar-Hockley and his men became prisoners of war.

Sir Anthony Heritage Farrar-Hockley (1924–2006), by Hay Wrightson

Farrar-Hockley had imbibed the Christian faith that had directed his upbringing, and his spiritual beliefs were developed by the only padre to survive the prison camps, Sam Davies (author of *In Spite of Dungeons*, 1954). It is not an exaggeration to suggest that he survived the ordeal of imprisonment (including torture and solitary confinement) because of the growing strength of his Christian faith. This important facet of his life was a recurring theme throughout the challenges of a long professional life and his twilight years. (Much later Farrar-Hockley became a member of the Prayer Book Society, and a judge for the Cranmer awards.)

Farrar-Hockley described the battle and his 'uneasy leisure' as a prisoner in *The Edge of the Sword*, his most powerful and moving book. He escaped from prisoner-of-war camps no less than six times, though each bid for freedom came to grief; on one occasion his guards hurried him back to captivity minus his boots. This frustrating experience brought out the inner strength in Farrar-Hockley's not always comfortable personality: he was irrepressible, not easily intimidated, incorrigibly stubborn, defending what he thought was right tenaciously in interminable debates with his interrogators; his treatment was often brutal and he was tortured callously. On 31 August 1953, defiant to the last, he was released after the signing of the armistice that ended the Korean War. He may not have been a humble man, but he was an indomitable figure, and one who earned respect and admiration for the remainder of his life.

Farrar-Hockley was awarded the DSO for his part in the Imjin battle. By the time of his return to England he had a seven-year-old son in need of a boarding education, given the vicissitudes of service life, and he looked around for means of paying the fees. A friend (a literary agent) suggested writing about his experiences. The publisher, Frederick Muller, initially provided a ghost writer but this proved unnecessary. On its publication in 1954 *The Edge of the Sword* was an immediate success—an impressive literary début. In its strong human tone, wonderful felicity of style, and narrative gift, combined with a cool, clear-eyed understanding of the harsh realities of military life, *The Edge of the Sword* ranks among the finest British soldiers' memoirs of the twentieth century. Despite a literary success, however, Farrar-Hockley's appetite for soldiering remained undiminished. In 1955 he attended the Staff College, Camberley, finding time on a demanding course to edit the final papers of General Sir Ian Hamilton, *The Commander* (1957). On graduating he was appointed deputy assistant quartermaster-general of the 16th Parachute brigade, and subsequently served as brigade major (that is chief of staff). He served in Cyprus, operating against EOKA terrorists, and in 1956 at Suez; he was appointed MBE for his part in the planning of the Suez airborne landings. Two years later he participated in the intervention in Jordan.

In February 1959 Farrar-Hockley transferred finally back to the Parachute regiment, which before the late 1950s lacked a permanent cadre of officers. When this was created Farrar-Hockley decided to return to serve with his wartime comrades despite good prospects with the Glosters. He found his time as chief instructor of cadets at the Royal Military Academy, Sandhurst, militarily less fulfilling because he thought his career becalmed; but he made friendships among the Sandhurst historians, and their head, another older decorated Second World War veteran of adventurous inclinations, Brigadier Peter Young, became his mentor; he guided Farrar-Hockley towards the First World War as a profitable field of study. Farrar-Hockley's impatience resulted from frustrated ambition, but in 1962 he gained command of the 3rd battalion, Parachute regiment (3 Para) serving in the Persian Gulf. In 1964, during the revolt of the Radfan tribes in the western Aden protectorate, he was in his element. He overcame intense heat and inhospitable terrain and seized the Radfan stronghold by ordering two companies of 3 Para to abseil down ropes from above, gaining complete surprise. Farrar-Hockley received a bar to his DSO for this exploit. His military repertory was extended in 1965 in another direction when he served as chief of staff to the director of operations in Borneo during the 'confrontation' with Indonesia, planning and organizing special forces' operations that disrupted the Indonesian build-up. In 1966–8 he commanded the 16th Parachute brigade.

Military history TFH or Tony F-H, as Farrar-Hockley was known to his friends, Farrar the Para to the army at large, was a strong, powerfully made man, not tall but physically imposing, with a large round head and receding hairline and searching, enquiring pale blue eyes. He had a deep, almost stentorian, as he would put it himself, 'carrying voice' (*Edge of the Sword*, 115). Intensely competitive, he enjoyed unquenchable physical and mental energy. He had displayed toughness as a commander, more than able to instil fear into those who served under him in his relentless search for military efficiency. Yet his abrupt, decisive, commanding manner concealed a very kind man. He was very forgiving of military failure, for his long and varied experience had taught him that men would always make mistakes and that they should be given the chance to learn from them. He once erupted in fury and literally threw an unkempt young subaltern off the parade square and confiscated his sword. Yet he recognized his fundamental talent, and this bumbling, disorganized young man would eventually rise to equal him in rank.

Farrar-Hockley's formidable intellectual powers were already evident: an extraordinarily retentive memory, a very quick mind and sturdy synthetic intelligence, always alert, sceptical, and not inclined to accept received wisdom just because it was voiced by his superiors. Yet he was not a radical in thought or deed, and on many controversial issues he took a rather conservative line—a tendency that became more marked as he grew older.

In 1968–70 Farrar-Hockley attended Exeter College, Oxford, one of the second group of defence fellows, in a scheme established in July 1967 to permit senior officers to conduct research and write up their findings. He chose as his theme 'National service and British society'. He submitted his thesis for the degree of BLitt, and was very proud when it was awarded, as the army at that date had very few university graduates among its officers. By this time he had already entered that select company of soldier–historians and analysts who dominated the post-war British army: Michael Carver, John Hackett, W. G. F. Jackson, and Richard Clutterbuck. Early on he had befriended Sir Basil Liddell Hart, who opened the door to many connections in the world of publishing. In 1959 he published a short history of the Second World War in the Frederick Muller True Books series. His first major historical work was *The Somme* (1964), published in time for the fiftieth anniversary of the start of the First World War. This was a first-rate, accomplished piece of work, concise and well-shaped; a good starting point many years later even though it had been superseded by later archival research. The book also revealed Farrar-Hockley's independence of judgement. He did not accept Liddell Hart's hypercritical view of Douglas Haig's generalship or the fashionable notion that the Somme battle should be lamented as an unmitigated catastrophe. *The Death of an Army* (1967, about the first battle of Ypres, in 1914) followed, a superb piece of narration, as Farrar-Hockley was unrivalled in evoking the atmosphere and terrain of a battlefield. He was essentially a popularizer, making military history accessible to the lay reader, a skill revealed in *The War in the Desert* (1969) and *Airborne Carpet: Operation Market Garden* (1969), both written while at Oxford. The latter, thanks to Liddell Hart's patronage, was a contribution to the Purnell's History of the Second World War stable of books and magazines that catered to the massive revival of interest in the war that began in the mid-1960s.

Higher commands On returning from his scholarly labours in 1970 Farrar-Hockley became director of public relations (army) and did not mince his words in describing the expanding terrorist threat in Northern Ireland. He could not dissemble and always had to say what was in his mind. When promoted commander land forces, Northern Ireland, he thought it foolish to deny that the army faced an IRA-inspired guerrilla campaign and said so—an uncomfortable truth that members of Edward Heath's cabinet did not wish to hear so soon after taking office. In July 1971 he went to command the 4th armoured division in Germany, with his residence in the symmetrical elegance of Taurus House, near Herford. He could not have chosen a better place to read and write history. Having discharged his administrative tasks and reports, on long drives to inspect his formations he would read important books, and write long-hand drafts; his wife, Margaret (always known as Pat), was an enthusiastic collaborator and research assistant and would prepare the ground for him, and helped complete the final drafts; but no matter who helped, all Farrar-Hockley's books expressed his authentic voice in a distinctive, fluent, and luminous style.

By the mid-1970s Farrar-Hockley's professional challenges and historical work began to commingle. The latter began to shape his approach to the former. In *The Death of an Army* he had already shown that regimental spirit, quality of training, and sheer determination could throw back a numerically superior foe, but unwittingly contribute to the smaller army's incremental destruction. Would the British army of the Rhine (BAOR), to which Farrar-Hockley was a comparative outsider, succeed at the first and escape the second? He had his doubts. He explored these defensive conundrums from different angles in his two biographies from these years. *General Student* (1973, German translation 1983) was a study of a brilliant breaker-in of defensive lines, General Kurt Student. His best and most substantial book on the First World War, *Goughie: the Life of General Sir Hubert Gough* (1975), was a sustained defence of the Fifth Army commander attacked by overwhelming force on the western front during the German spring offensive in March 1918. Gough did well, Farrar-Hockley argued, in holding his line though driven back, before being made the scapegoat for an overall humiliation. The historical approach breathed new life into current military challenges. Farrar-Hockley concentrated on improving the training, readiness, and tactical proficiency of his division in defence before switching to the offensive.

Farrar-Hockley took perspectives derived from his historical research into his work as director, combat development (1974–7). He ploughed a lonely furrow, for whatever the preferences of individuals, army policy generally shifted away from historically based study over the next decade. Many of its premier staff and training courses stressed technical proficiency and technological solutions. Initially this reflected a preoccupation with nuclear issues and the downgrading of 'conventional' strategy and operations. Farrar-Hockley remained a consistent supporter of stable deterrence, but to him war was first and foremost a human activity. In 1976 he produced a short introduction, *Infantry Tactics, 1939–1945*, and ended it with a simple but profound truth: 'The greater the risk of injury or death, the greater the need for leadership.' Soldiers follow not because they have been ordered to do so. 'They obey only because they have confidence in the judgment and courage of the leader to carry them through the crisis' (p. 70).

In 1977 Farrar-Hockley was promoted lieutenant-general, appointed general officer commanding south-eastern district, and knighted KCB. Two years later he was given a NATO job in Oslo as commander-in-chief, allied forces northern Europe, in the rank of general (1979–82). He threw himself into it with his customary zeal and diligence. His command was about to be 'rediscovered, rather like an ageing Hollywood star', during that final tense phase of the NATO–Warsaw Pact confrontation when 'conventional operations' were assuming increased importance. In March 1983 Farrar-Hockley looked back at the strategic problems he had faced. The defence of Hamburg and Schleswig-Holstein was one of his highest priorities, vital for the reinforcement of the central region and the exploitation of any open flank should the Soviets mount an envelopment of the central region south of the Elbe (echoes of the failed Schlieffen plan in 1914 recounted in *Death of an Army* ring loudly). North Norway guarded the approaches to the bases of the Soviet northern fleet in the Murmansk area; south Norway and Denmark lay astride the narrow waters the Soviet Baltic fleet would need to seize to gain egress to the Atlantic sea lanes to prevent massive NATO reinforcement from the United States. Any third world war could not be won there, 'But my belief is … it could equally be lost there' ('Dynamic defence: the northern flank', *RUSI Journal*, 128/4, 1983, 5, 7, 11). Farrar-Hockley's enjoyment of his responsibilities was blighted in 1981 by Margaret's death, but he soldiered on.

Final years, and assessment Farrar-Hockley was aide-de-camp general to the queen and was appointed GBE in 1982, before retiring the following year. He had acquired a number of colonelcies appropriate to his rank, including the Glosters (1978–84) and the Parachute regiment (1977–83), but retirement demanded something more cerebral than looking over young cadets anxious to join either regiment. Indeed, he had already accepted an invitation to join the cabinet office historical section as official historian of the British part in the Korean War. Margaret had begun research in earnest on this project before her death, and on 10 December 1983 Farrar-Hockley married his other research assistant, the 33-year-old Linda Wood (daughter of George Leslie Wood, credit manager). The result of much concentrated effort, over 1000 pages in two volumes, subtitled *A Distant Obligation* (1990) and *An Honourable Discharge* (1995), *The British Part in the Korean War* stood as his *magnum opus* as a historian. The work constituted an attempt to 'comprehend the political as well as the military aspects of participation' (1.viii) and was therefore broader in scope than his earlier works.

Farrar-Hockley's last years were marked by some controversy and ill-fortune. A rumpus developed over his participation in the creation of an embryonic anti-communist resistance movement in the event of Soviet military occupation—which some hinted had more sinister motives. His robust television interviews defending the traditional ethos of the army were dismissed by young officers as old-fashioned and 'out of touch'. In 1990 an IRA assassination attempt was foiled by chance. Unrelatedly his house, Pye Barn, which he had bought in 1968, was damaged in a serious fire that destroyed an entire wing, but as a do-it-yourself enthusiast he and his former orderly, Sergeant Olive, substantially rebuilt the house. Through it all his buoyant, pugnacious spirit emerged unshaken, sustained by his sense of humour and love of history. In 2002–6 he served as president of the Army Records Society. He had looked exactly the same for twenty-five years but his physical decline after 2004 was precipitate. He died at the John Radcliffe Hospital, Oxford, on 11 March 2006, of bronchopneumonia and Lewy body disease, and was survived by his wife, Linda, and two sons, both of whom served in the forces.

Farrar-Hockley was a man of redoubtable character and impressive achievement. He demonstrated extraordinary courage and tenacity in adversity, and proved a born leader—an inspiration to all his men. As a small-unit and regimental commander he evinced brilliant skills; these were not to be put to the ultimate test at the higher level, but his drive, calm articulacy, and clarity of vision suggest that he would have made a fine wartime commander-in-chief. All his historical works were informed by keen powers of exposition and description, but they were not (with the exception of his official history of the Korean War and, perhaps, *Goughie*) very analytical. But this was compensated for by his acute soldier's insight. He modestly believed that being 'shot at in a battle' was at best 'a subsidiary advantage' for the military historian (*The Somme*, 1964, 5). In Farrar-Hockley's case it gives his books a singular appeal. His long career as a historian is crucial to understanding him as a soldier and vice versa; the two cardinal features of his life interlocked. His verdict on Sir Ian Hamilton serves as a suitable epitaph for himself: 'Sir Ian was agin backward-looking officers, and pompous officers, and officers who paid no heed to their profession. He loathed people without a sense of humour. He loved soldiers' (*The Commander*, 1957, viii). So did Farrar-Hockley, and he loved soldiering and writing about the campaigns of soldiers. BRIAN HOLDEN REID

Sources *The Times* (14 March 2006); (23 March 2006) · *Daily Telegraph* (14 March 2006) · *The Guardian* (15 March 2006) · *The Independent* (16 March 2006) · Burke, *Peerage* · *WW* (2006) · personal knowledge (2010) · private information (2010) · b. cert. · m. certs. · d. cert.

Archives priv. coll. | King's Lond., Liddell Hart C., Liddell Hart MSS | FILM BFINA, current affairs footage | SOUND BL NSA, documentary recordings

Likenesses T. Spencer, photograph, 1964 (with Anthony Ward-Booth), Getty Images, London, Time and Life pictures · photograph, 1977, Photoshot, London · photograph, 1977, PA Photos, London · D. Hartley, photograph, 1990, Rex Features, London · H. Wrightson, photograph, NPG [*see illus.*] · obituary photographs

Wealth at death £660,313: probate, 1 Sept 2006, *CGPLA Eng. & Wales*

Hoddinott, Alun (1929–2008), composer, was born on 11 August 1929 at 3 The Avenue, Gilfach, near Bargoed, at the head of the Rhymney valley in Glamorgan, the son of Thomas Ivor Hoddinott (1899–1974), elementary school teacher, and his wife, Gertrude, *née* Jones (1901–1966). His father was a teacher in Bargoed but moved to a post in Penlle'r-gaer, near Swansea, where Hoddinott grew up and received his early education. By all accounts his was not a very musical family but his innate gift soon showed through so that by the age of four he was already taking violin lessons and exhibiting a fine command of that instrument, along with the viola, which he later played with equal virtuosity as a first-generation member (from 1946) of the National Youth Orchestra of Wales. These talents had been nurtured at Gowerton grammar school, where he also displayed a very marked aptitude for composition and an evident will to make this the main focus of his efforts rather than pursuing a career as a performing musician.

That decision set the course of his later years at Gowerton and led to the award of a composition scholarship at University College, Cardiff, where he graduated in 1949. His time there had witnessed the production of numerous apprentice scores, among them some large-scale orchestral, concertante, choral, and chamber works. A good number of these were performed locally and some received national broadcast premières. However, Hoddinott later withdrew most of them and re-assigned their opus numbers, feeling that these were indeed apprentice pieces and not representative of his mature style. It was during this period also that he developed the capacity for sheer hard work under pressure—often in response to specific commissions or demands of circumstance—that added to his later (not entirely welcome) reputation for working to very tight deadlines.

The one notable exception to Hoddinott's veto on those early works was his 1949 clarinet concerto, written and given its first (BBC studio) performance during his third year as a student at Cardiff. A revised version of this piece enjoyed wider success and critical acclaim at its first concert performance at the Cheltenham festival five years later, with Gervase de Peyer as soloist and the Hallé Orchestra conducted by Sir John Barbirolli. Still Hoddinott thought himself in need of further expert guidance and therefore, on completing his undergraduate studies, took a series of private lessons with the Australian composer and pianist Arthur Benjamin. At the same time he continued to establish his institutional and academic home base in Cardiff, having been appointed first to a post at the Welsh College of Music and Drama in 1951 and then, in 1959, to a lectureship at University College, where he remained until his retirement (and the conferment of emeritus status) in 1987.

Hoddinott's marriage on 2 April 1953 to (Beti) Rhiannon Huws (*b.* 1928), a schoolteacher (daughter of Llewellyn Caradog Huws, minister of Carmel Independent Chapel, Gwauncaegurwen) and Welsh speaker, was undoubtedly the single most important event in his personal life and another clear mark of Hoddinott's attachment to the formative culture of his youth. This was despite the fact (a source of friction at times) that he never came out as a Welsh nationalist composer and was apt to make a fairly polemical point of not subscribing to any strongly nationalist—folk-based or other—version of the Welsh musical renaissance. Indeed he later accepted a commission for Prince Charles's investiture as prince of Wales in 1969 and produced a brief fanfare for the marriage in 2005 of Charles and Camilla Parker-Bowles. On the other hand his music often took inspiration from Anglo-Welsh and Welsh-language sources, whether by way of texts to be set or material for treatment in dramatic or extended song-cycle form. Later he was often highly vocal in his criticism of funding agencies and cultural bodies, Welsh National Opera among them, that he saw as failing in their important (if not primary) task of promoting native Welsh music.

From the late 1950s Hoddinott's music began to lose something of the jaunty high spirits, jazzy inflections, and at times hard-edged neo-classicism that had marked his earlier style. Thereafter that style was increasingly displaced by elements of the sombre, predominantly dark-hued (some called it Celtic) character that typified his music of the next four decades, and which found its first expression in his orchestral piece *Nocturne* of 1955. Not that he ever lost touch completely with the temperamental sources of that previous, more extrovert manner, retaining as he did a craftsman's pride in creating various 'occasional' works of a none the less inventive and technically resourceful kind. Like his close friend Alan Rawsthorne, Hoddinott combined an impressive versatility of style, language, and technique with a genuine capacity to produce music of a powerful and sometimes emotionally disturbing character.

This duality became something of a hallmark and continued to characterize his music throughout the long period of Hoddinott's tenure in Cardiff. Academically that period was punctuated by his promotion from lecturer to reader (in 1965) and then to professor and head of department in 1967, a sequence of advancements due in large part to his now well-established reputation as one of the most significant British composers of his generation. His university teaching was never a sinecure but continued to occupy a large part of his working day, so that much of his composing was done at night or during what time he could take off from an otherwise demanding workaday routine.

Despite this Hoddinott remained highly productive and diversified his output across the whole range of genres including symphonies, concertos, choral works, chamber music, piano sonatas, and operas. Though sensitive to any imputation of over-facility he was a fluent and highly professional composer who saw no sense in the romantic idea that the artist must choose between authentic self-expression or responding to commissions from soloists, orchestras, or funding bodies. The recording companies Argo, Lyrita, and Nimbus played a major role in promulgating Hoddinott's music from the mid-1960s on, as did the various festivals and annual events—chief among them the Cardiff festival of music, co-founded in 1967 by Hoddinott with his friend the pianist John Ogdon—where his own compositions often received a first performance. Through its offshoot, the Cardiff festival of twentieth-century music, which he launched in 1976, Hoddinott sought to acquaint audiences with developments across a wide range of present-day 'conservative' and 'modernist' idioms, as well as steering a middle course between the claims of nationalist and cosmopolitan allegiance. His more than twenty concertos—inventively scored for a range of solo instruments and orchestral forces—likewise reflect his capacity to work within broadly traditional forms while putting them to new and imaginative ends.

In the best-known works of his 'middle' period, from the early 1960s to the late 1970s, Hoddinott's music combines an exploration of complex formal devices (such as double palindromes and occasional twelve-note rows) with a continuing adherence to tonality, albeit often deployed in adventurous and ear-stretching ways. Like Bartók—undoubtedly a strong influence, along with others as varied as Hindemith, Stravinsky, Sibelius, and (most revealingly in this connection) Berg—Hoddinott put tonality to use not only as a source of vivid local contrasts but also as a means of sustaining long-range structural coherence. Nowhere is this more evident than in the cycle of ten symphonies—in many ways his crowning achievement—where Hoddinott progressively refined and extended his techniques for integrating long-breathed, arching melodic lines with tightly organized thematic and motivic development. The best-known, nos. 3, 4, and 5, were products of Hoddinott's intensely creative middle years and exhibit his keen sense of formal proportion, along with his sharp ear for subtle shifts of harmonic and rhythmic emphasis.

Hoddinott composed over six hundred works ranging across every major musical genre—among them, not least, six operas of a diverse and often decidedly heterodox character. As the work of a Cardiff-based (as well as more broadly Welsh) composer, Hoddinott's music, in conjunction with his other activities, academic, scholarly, performance-related, and administrative, did much to establish the existence of a distinctive musical culture in south Wales, possessed of a genuine national character but none the less open to wider sources of inspiration. These aspects of Hoddinott's achievement and legacy were recognized by, among many other honours, appointment as CBE in 1983 and the Glyndŵr award for outstanding contribution to the arts in Wales in 1997. A further accolade in 2008 was the naming of the Hoddinott Hall, an extension to the Millennium Centre in Cardiff Bay, the home base for the BBC National Orchestra of Wales. Hoddinott underwent a heart-valve operation in November 2007. He died of multi-organ failure at Morriston Hospital, Swansea, on 11 March 2008, and was survived by his wife, Rhiannon, and their son, Ceri.

CHRISTOPHER NORRIS

Sources L. Foreman, *British music now* (1975) · B. Deane, *Alun Hoddinott* (1978) · S. R. Craggs, *Alun Hoddinott: a bio-bibliography* (1993) · R. Matthew-Walker, *Alun Hoddinott on record* (1993) · L. Davies, *Bywgraffiadau cyfansoddwyr Cymru: Alun Hoddinott* (2004) · *South Wales Evening Post* (12 March 2008); (14 March 2008) · *Western Morning News* (13 March 2008) · *Western Mail* (13 March 2008); (22 Sept 2008); (25 Sept 2009) · *The Times* (14 March 2008); (15 March 2008); (18 March 2008); (24 March 2008); (2 April 2008) · *The Guardian* (14 March 2008) · *The Independent* (14 March 2008) · *Daily Telegraph* (15 March 2008) · *The furnace of colours: remembering Alun Hoddinott* (2009) · *WW* (2008) · personal knowledge (2012) · private information (2012) · b. cert. · m. cert. · d. cert.

Archives NL Wales, music manuscripts, letters, papers | FILM BFINA, light entertainment and performance footage. | SOUND BL NSA, current affairs, documentary, and interview recordings

Likenesses photographs, 1980–2004, Getty Images, London · K. Wilson Smith, bromide fibre print, 1984, NPG · B. Batchelor, photographs, 2004, PA Photos, London · photograph, 2004 (with the prince of Wales), Camera Press, London · D. Legakis, photographs, 2006, Rex Features, London · obituary photographs · photographs, Lebrecht Music and Arts Photo Library, London

Wealth at death under £18,000: probate, 28 April 2009, *CGPLA Eng. & Wales*

Hodges, Sir Lewis Macdonald [Bob] (**1918–2007**), air force officer, was born at 6 Ormond Road, Richmond, Surrey, on 1 March 1918, the son of Arthur Macdonald Hodges (1879–1940), decorative artist and later antiques dealer, and his wife, Gladys Mildred, *née* Lewis (1891–1975). He was educated at St Paul's Boys' School in Barnes and at the RAF College at Cranwell, which he entered in 1937. Known as Bob, he was commissioned into the RAF as a pilot officer in December 1938 and joined Bomber Command. Based at RAF Finningley in Yorkshire, he began flying Vickers Wellesleys with 78 squadron, moving to 49 squadron in 1940, flying Handley Page Hampdens.

Hodges's Hampden was damaged returning from a raid on Stettin on 4 September 1940 and he was forced to crash-land in Brittany. An eight-month sojourn on the run ensued. After setting fire to the plane Hodges and his air gunner (who had not heard the order to bale out) set off southwards to escape to Spain. With the help of farmers they reached Marseilles, where they were arrested by the Vichy authorities. Hodges managed to escape and stowed away on a cargo boat but was captured again in Oran and returned to Marseilles. Sent to the Vichy-controlled camp for British prisoners at St Hippolyte du Fort, near Nîmes, he escaped for a second time and made his way to Perpignan and across the Pyrenees. Arrested by Spanish customs officials, he spent some weeks in the prison camp at Miranda de Ebro before the British embassy secured his release. He returned to England in June 1941 and rejoined 49 squadron. He was awarded the DFC in May 1942 for operations that included attacks in the English Channel on the German battlecruisers *Scharnhorst* and *Gneisenau* in February 1942.

Later in 1942 Hodges was chosen by Wing-Commander Charles Pickard to join 161 squadron, based at RAF Tempsford, Bedfordshire, which was one of two squadrons detailed to support the Special Operations Executive on secret missions. Flying Halifax bombers, Hodges dropped agents and supplies all over occupied Europe. Awarded a bar to his DFC and promoted to commander of 161 squadron in May 1943, with the rank of squadron leader, he then flew Hudsons and Lysanders on six dangerous missions to pick up leading figures in the French resistance, landing on each occasion in remote and difficult places in rural France. Among the passengers he brought to Britain were two future French presidents, Vincent Auriol and François Mitterand. The former appointed him a commandeur of the Légion d'honneur in 1950; the latter advanced him to grand officier of the Légion in 1988. In October 1943 he received the DSO.

Hodges attended the RAF Staff College in 1944 and was briefly attached to Bomber Command's operations staff. Selected to serve in the Far East as staff officer to Air Chief Marshal Sir Trafford Leigh-Mallory, he requested a return to active duties after the death in action in Burma of his younger brother. It was another narrow escape, as Leigh-Mallory's plane and all its crew were lost over the Alps. Hodges then took command of 357 squadron at RAF Jessore near Calcutta in December 1944, flying four-engine Liberators, twin-engine Dakotas, and Lysanders. This was another special duties squadron supporting the Special Operations Executive, this time in Burma, with additional responsibilities assisting groups resisting Japanese occupation in Thailand and Malaya. The vast scale of these operations entailed sorties in Liberators of up to twenty hours. For his service in the Far East Hodges was awarded a bar to his DSO in October 1945.

After the war Hodges was a member of the directing staff at the staff college in Haifa and then joined the new Joint Services Staff College at Latimer in 1947. He was attached to the Air Ministry from 1949 to 1952 as staff officer to the deputy chief of air staff and then in the directorate of plans. He returned to Bomber Command in 1952 and commanded the team of three RAF Canberras that entered the London–New Zealand air race in 1953: they finished fourth after engine trouble, but set a new London–Colombo record in the process. On 17 June 1950, at St Saviour's Church, Walton Street, Chelsea, he married Elisabeth Mary Blackett (*b.* 1925), daughter of Geoffrey Herbert Blackett, stockbroker. They had two sons, David (*b.* 1952) and Nigel (*b.* 1955).

For the next two decades Hodges held a succession of highly responsible positions in the RAF and Air Ministry that took him to the very top of the service. From 1954 to 1959 he was involved in the development of Britain's V-bomber nuclear force. He began as chief instructor at the new operational training unit at Gaydon, training crews on Vickers Valiants. In 1956 he moved to command one of the largest RAF bases, at Marham, where the Valiants were being introduced in place of Canberras. He received there the two visiting Soviet leaders, Nikita Khrushchov and Nikolai Bulganin. He was promoted group captain in 1957 and appointed CBE the following year. After two years as assistant commandant at Cranwell between 1959 and 1961, now an air commodore, he was sent to Aden to oversee British air operations there. In 1963 he attended the Imperial Defence College, was promoted air vice-marshal and appointed CB, and was then posted to supreme headquarters, allied forces in Europe, as air executive to the nuclear deputy.

In 1965 Hodges returned to the Air Ministry as assistant chief of air staff (operations): for three years he was focused on the Indonesian emergency and the British withdrawal from Aden. In 1968 he was promoted air marshal and advanced to KCB. As commander-in-chief of air support command he was responsible for RAF transport aircraft worldwide for the next two years. Then in 1970 he became air member for personnel for three years, in which role he was involved in the reorganization of the RAF and reductions in its manpower. In 1971 he became air chief marshal. From 1973 to 1976 his final position was within NATO as deputy commander-in-chief, allied air forces, central Europe. During this final period of his career he was also air aide-de-camp to the queen.

After retiring from the RAF in 1976 Hodges was active in business and benevolence. He was a director of Pilkingtons from 1979 to 1983 and of the British United Provident Association (BUPA) from 1987. Active on behalf of the RAF Benevolent Fund—he chaired its education committee from 1979 to 1986—he was also president of the Royal Air Force Association from 1981 to 1984 and directed the successful refurbishment of the RAF Club in Piccadilly. Unsurprisingly he was especially committed to the RAF Escaping Society, a charity that gave assistance to those French who helped on the escape lines that conveyed aircrew out of occupied Europe, and to the Tempsford reunions, which brought together those who had been involved in the wartime Special Operations Executive operations from the base. A record of his wartime service was published in 1983 by the RAF Benevolent Fund in *Royal Air Force at War*. He retained a lifelong affection for France.

Bob Hodges died of a stroke at his home, Cob Orchard, Tree Lane, Plaxtol, near Sevenoaks, Kent, on 4 January 2007. He was survived by his wife and their two sons. A service of thanksgiving for his life was held at St Clement Danes, London, on 15 March 2007.

LAWRENCE GOLDMAN

Sources M. R. D. Foot, *SOE in France: an account of the work of the British Special Operations Executive in France, 1940–1944* (1966); rev. edn (2004) • C. Foxley-Norris, ed., *Royal Air Force at war* (1983) • M. R. D. Foot, *SOE: an outline history of the Special Operations Executive, 1940–1946*, new edn (1999) • *Daily Telegraph* (5 Jan 2007) • *The Independent* (6 Jan 2007) • *The Times* (8 Jan 2007); (16 March 2007) • www.rafweb.org/Biographies/Hodges.htm, 13 Aug 2010 • Burke, *Peerage* • *WW* (2007) • b. cert. • m. cert. • d. cert.

Archives RAF Museum, Hendon, log books

Likenesses photographs, 1970–91, Getty Images, London • Ministry of Defence, bromide print, NPG • obituary photographs

Wealth at death £415,047: probate, 3 Aug 2007, *CGPLA Eng. & Wales*

Hodgson [*née* Rosenthal]**, Miriam Ann** (**1938–2005**), editor of children's books, was born on 10 December 1938 at Denison House, Denison Road, Rusholme, Manchester, the only daughter of Erwin Isak Jacob Rosenthal (1904–1991), Hebrew scholar and orientalist, and his wife, Elisabeth Charlotte, *née* Marx (1907–1996). She had one older brother, Thomas Gabriel (Tom) Rosenthal (*b.* 1935), later chairman and chief executive of Andre Deutsch Ltd. Her parents, of Jewish descent, had fled Germany in 1933 and at the time of her birth her father was lecturer in Semitic languages and literature at the University of Manchester. In 1948 the family moved to Cambridge when her father was made a lecturer (later a reader) in oriental studies at the University of Cambridge. He published widely on both Judaism and Islam.

Miriam Rosenthal was educated at the Perse School for Girls, Cambridge, and then at St Anne's College, Oxford; she graduated with a third in modern history in 1960. She began her career working as an editor of adult books at Ernest Benn, which later became Associated Book Publishers. There she met her husband, Julian Russell Hodgson, then head of the education department, and son of John Hodgson, minister of religion. They married on 28 November 1969 at St Pancras register office. After the birth of her only child, Elinor, she returned to work in a new role working part-time as a children's books editor, which led to her becoming editorial director of publishing at Methuen Children's Books in 1986.

Passionate about the craft of writing, on which she said, 'I never cease to be in awe not only of my authors' achievements but also of the creative process of writing' ('On being an editor'), she was a gifted editor who inspired great loyalty from her authors. One of them, Annie Dalton, described her 'rare ability to befriend her authors whilst continuing to challenge us on every level. Her respect for the creative process is unique in my experience and her sensitivity is downright supernatural' (*The*

Times, 6 Dec 2005). Hodgson herself defined the ideal relationship between editor and author as 'the touching of minds … The editor is the servant of the writer. He never dictates' ('On being an editor'). But there was one principle on which she felt that an editor could dictate to a children's author: 'The only condition an editor should impose is to remind the author that he is writing for children, who deserve to keep a belief in good defeating evil' (ibid.).

Following this principle, Hodgson guided many of the best children's writers of her time, including Anne Fine, Caroline Pitcher, Michelle Magorian, Michael Morpurgo, Carlo Gebler, Theresa Breslin, Jamila Gavin, Bel Mooney, Jenny Nimmo, and many others. The importance of her role in shaping these authors' books was evident in their tributes to her. 'It was her ability to see the gold among the dross; it was her ability to recognise talent: big talent, small talent, fragile talent; to see the one seed she felt she could nourish like a gardener' that made her an outstanding editor, according to Jamila Gavin (Gavin, 'Miriam Hodgson'). Robert Westall dedicated *The Kingdom by the Sea* (1990) to 'Miriam, who understood', while a more robust editorial hand was revealed in Jean Ure's dedication of *Plague 99* (1989) 'To Miriam, who fought me womanfully every inch of the way'. Under her guidance and nurture Hodgson's authors went on to win the Carnegie medal, the Nestlé Smarties prize, the *Guardian* children's book prize, and the Whitbread award.

In addition to editing the novels of others, Hodgson compiled anthologies of stories for teenagers, mostly by her own authors. These included *Heartache* (1991), *Mother's Day* (1992), *Mixed Feelings* (1997), and *Sisters* (1998). Following the sale of Methuen's children's book division to Egmont in 1998, she remained chief editor of Egmont's children's books for a further year before her formal retirement. (In fact she continued editing until shortly before her death.) In 1999 she was made editor of the year at the British book awards and in 2003 she won the Eleanor Farjeon award, presented by the Children's Book Circle for outstanding services to children's literature. She died of ovarian cancer at St George's Hospital, Tooting, London, on 14 November 2005, and was survived by her husband and daughter. Her life has been honoured by the launch on 23 November 2006 of the Miriam Hodgson perspective series, a lecture series to be run in conjunction with Seven Stories in Newcastle.

JULIA ECCLESHARE

Sources M. Hodgson, 'On being an editor', *Books for Keeps*, 144 (Jan 2004), www.booksforkeeps.co.uk/issues/144/245, accessed 9 July 2008 • *The Independent* (18 Nov 2005) • *The Guardian* (23 Nov 2005) • *The Bookseller* (25 Nov 2005) • *The Times* (6 Dec 2005); (19 Dec 2005) • J. Gavin, 'Miriam Hodgson', *Armadillo*, 7/4 (winter 2005), www.siliconhedge.com/armadillo • G. Pollinger, 'The touching of minds', unpub. lecture, Seven Stories, Newcastle, 23 Nov 2006 • *International Research in Children's Literature* (winter 2006) • *WW* (2005) • b. cert. • m. cert. • d. cert.

Likenesses obituary photographs • photograph, Egmont Press, London; repro. in *The Times* (6 Dec 2005)

Wealth at death £241,000: probate, 28 Nov 2006, *CGPLA Eng. & Wales*

Hoffenberg, Sir Raymond [Bill] (**1923–2007**), physician, was born at Brema, a house near Fort Frederick in Port Elizabeth, South Africa, on 6 March 1923, the third child and only son of Benjamin Hoffenberg, produce merchant, born in Germany of Jewish parents, and his wife, Dora, *née* Kaplan, born in London, daughter of Simon Kaplan, later tobacconist of Grahamstown, South Africa. Bill Hoffenberg (he was never called Raymond) was a scholar and athlete at Grey High School, Port Elizabeth, leaving in 1939, aged sixteen, to study medicine at the University of Cape Town.

At the outbreak of the Second World War, Hoffenberg, under age, doubted his father would give permission for him to join up and so forged the necessary signature. He became a stretcher bearer in the 6th South African armoured division, serving in Egypt and Italy (in Rome, Florence, and Bologna). On return to Cape Town he lived the classical medical student life to the full. A convivial man, and one who never neglected the opportunity to have a party, he had a formidable reputation as a host and could, if challenged, drink others under the table, yet was always up early the following morning to put in three hours of work before breakfast, a habit he kept throughout his life. He excelled in both academic work and sport, representing his university at golf, tennis, squash, and water polo, while being no mean performer at rugby and boxing. He graduated MB ChB in 1948.

From the beginning of his career as a physician Hoffenberg was passionate about the skills of bedside clinical medicine, skills in which he himself excelled and which he taught so well to others. In 1951 he arrived in London to attend the postgraduate course at Hammersmith Hospital. He then became registrar in endocrinology at New End Hospital in Hampstead and achieved membership of the Royal College of Physicians, before returning in 1955 to the University of Cape Town as a senior lecturer, soon to begin research into intersex, gonadal dysgenesis, Sheehan's, and Turner's syndromes. Later a Carnegie fellowship took him to America to learn about the use of isotopes in endocrinology, but research was never his first love or his greatest talent. He once confessed that he had only dabbled and could not lay claim to any outstanding contribution.

In the early 1950s Hoffenberg was uninterested in politics, but after witnessing policemen beating up a lone innocent black man and seeing the result of such beatings in his patients, he joined Peter Brown, Leo Marquand, and Alan Paton in the Liberal Party. There he led the campaign against the solitary confinement of political prisoners and became a key supporter of the National Union of South African Students, but it was his chairmanship of the Defence and Aid Fund (which provided for the defence for those accused of political crimes) that led to the imposition of a banning order in 1967, which meant that he could not continue in the medical school. He, his wife Margaret, *née* Rosenberg, a social worker whom he had married in 1949 and who had done much to alleviate malnutrition in the poor, and their two adopted sons, Derek and Peter, left Africa early in 1968, sent off by a crowd of more than two thousand, to join the National Institute of Medical Research in London. There animal experiments on albumin metabolism were not to his taste ('I don't want to be a dog-doctor'; autobiographical notes), but he found solace with clinical work at New End Hospital and teaching at the Royal Free Hospital. In 1970 he moved to the clinical research centre at Northwick Park, where research continued to fail to inspire him, so that he was delighted to accept the William Withering chair of medicine at Birmingham in 1972.

At Birmingham Hoffenberg's major aim was to preserve excellence in clinical work and teaching, which he extended to involve the consultants in general hospitals in the region; but his own endocrine unit was to do distinguished work and chairs were created in cardiology, rheumatology, neurology, and geriatric medicine. He pioneered medical audit—the assessment of doctors' or a team's performance by colleagues, an innovation he fostered further at the Royal College of Physicians. He was a natural leader, charming, articulate, yet determined. His expert chairmanship of committees led to increasing demands for his services, for instance by the British Heart Foundation, the Mental Health Foundation, the UK Coordinating Committee on Cancer Research, the Medical Research Society, the Medical Research Council, the Committee on the Safety of Medicines, and in a number of local committees of the regional health authority.

Such was his personality and reputation that it was no surprise when Hoffenberg was elected president of the Royal College of Physicians in 1983, an office he filled until 1989 with particular distinction. He led the college, among other things, into concern about ethical issues in medicine, particularly about organ transplantation, brain death, issues at the end of life, research fraud, and relations between doctors and the pharmaceutical industry. Successful in almost all that he did, Hoffenberg nevertheless failed in trying to persuade the prime minister, Margaret Thatcher, that the introduction of the 'internal market' in the NHS might be a serious mistake. He referred to its rapid and untried introduction as an occasion on which instead of 'Get ready, take aim, fire' the government had preferred 'get ready, fire, take aim' (*The Times*, 4 Aug 1994). On another occasion, when he visited 10 Downing Street with other presidents of royal colleges to express concern about the state of the NHS, they were told by Thatcher that she would deal with them as she had with Arthur Scargill and the miners. Hoffenberg's last years as president of the Royal College of Physicians overlapped with his presidency of Wolfson College, Oxford (1985–93). There he continued his reputation for benign, yet firm, leadership. His concern for students, his and Margaret's hospitality in the lodgings, and his efficient conduct of committee work were legendary. The college looked back at his presidency with affection and admiration.

Hoffenberg had considerable personal charm and an infectious zest for life. He was a man of absolute integrity, determined, self-confident, and ambitious, characteristics which were abundantly evident in his opposition to apartheid in South Africa and in his leadership in medical affairs in England. He was widely held in great respect and admiration. He was appointed KBE in 1984 and received honorary degrees from Imperial College, London, from the universities of Leicester, Bristol, Cape Town, the Witwatersrand, and from City University, London. He became a fellow of the Royal College of Physicians (1971), the Faculty of Occupational Medicine and the Faculty of Pharmaceutical Medicine (both 1990), and the Royal College of Psychiatrists (1991), and an honorary fellow of learned societies in Australia, Canada, Malaysia, and the USA. He was posthumously awarded the (South African) order of the Baobab in silver in 2008.

On retirement in 1993 the Hoffenbergs followed their sons to Australia where, ever active and finding idleness unacceptable, Hoffenberg was appointed to the chair of medical ethics at the University of Queensland. Margaret Hoffenberg died after a long illness in 2005, and in December 2006 Hoffenberg married Gräfin Madeleine Charlotte Louise Douglas (*b.* 1939), an art consultant, who nursed him devotedly throughout the early months of the illness that ultimately caused his death. They had met and become close in Oxford during Hoffenberg's presidency of Wolfson College.

One of the issues Hoffenberg felt passionate about was that of assisted suicide. He wrote persuasive and logical refutations of the arguments put forward against such assistance and was a strong supporter of Lord Joffe's proposals on the matter to the House of Lords. Indeed, when his own death, from carcinoma of the stomach, was approaching, he asked who might give him morphine. Such treatment being denied, he accelerated his own death by taking no food and only enough water to moisten his mouth, until he died in Bletchingdon, Oxfordshire only a few weeks later, on 22 April 2007. He was deeply regretful that what he had sought for others was denied him in the end. He was cremated in Oxford on 3 May, and his ashes were buried at Schloss Langenstein, Germany, on 14 July; a memorial service was held at Wolfson College, Oxford, on 17 November 2007. He was survived by his wife, Madeleine, and his sons, Derek and Peter.

JOHN G. G. LEDINGHAM

Sources *The Independent* (24 April 2007) • *The Times* (25 April 2007) • *The Star* [South Africa] (25 April 2007) • *Daily Telegraph* (9 May 2007) • *The Courier Mail* [Australia] (23 May 2007) • *The Guardian* (29 May 2007) • *The Lancet*, 369/1854 (2–8 June 2007) • L. R. Humphreys, *Hoffenberg: physician and humanitarian* (2010) • munksroll.rcplondon.ac.uk/Biography/Details/5775, 22 June 2010 • R. Hoffenberg, autobiographical notes, priv. coll. [in possession of Madeleine Hoffenberg] • 'Celeberation of the life and work of Sir Raymond (Bill) Hoffenberg', CD, Wolfson College • Burke, *Peerage* • *WW* (2007) • personal knowledge (2011) • private information (2011) [Madeleine Hoffenberg, widow; J. Driver; J. Stallworthy] • d. cert.

Archives SOUND BL NSA, documentary recording

Likenesses N. Sinclair, bromide print, 1996, NPG • E. Frink, bronze bust, RCP Lond.; repro. in G. Davenport, I. McDonald, and C. Moss-Gibbons, eds., *The Royal College of Physicians and its collections, an illustrated history* (2001), 135 • obituary photographs

Hogg, Richard Milne (1944–2007), historian of the English language, was born on 20 May 1944 in the Simpson Memorial Maternity Pavilion, Edinburgh, the son of

Charles Milne Hogg, a linotype operator then serving as a lance-corporal in the Royal Corps of Signals, and his wife, Norenne, *née* Young. He grew up in Edinburgh and attended the Royal High School there and later Edinburgh University, where he graduated with first-class honours in 1967. In the same year he met his future wife, Margaret Kathleen White (*b.* 1947), at a party in the flat of Robin Cook, then the secretary of the university Labour Club. She was the daughter of Ronald Ernest White, civil servant. They were married at Emmanuel Church, Cheltenham, on 20 September 1969 and had two sons, Daniel and Robert.

Hogg remained at Edinburgh for his PhD which, at a time when the linguistic ideas of Noam Chomsky were especially influential, was a Chomskian analysis of current English syntax. He was also a research assistant on a project on Middle English dialects, established by the leading scholar of the English language at Edinburgh, Angus Macintosh. As this suggests, Hogg was soon at home in all periods of the language and could apply the most sophisticated theoretical constructs to its analysis.

Hogg's first academic position was as a lecturer in English between 1969 and 1973 at the University of Amsterdam. He then moved to the University of Lancaster, publishing in 1977 the book of his doctorate, *English Quantifier Systems*. In 1980, at a relatively young age, he was elected to the Smith chair of English language and medieval literature at the University of Manchester, the position he held for the rest of his career. From 1990 to 1993 he was dean of the arts faculty at Manchester, in which capacity he successfully administered a merger with the theology faculty. For a scholar of such wide interests and detailed knowledge, his lecturing style was notably easy and relaxed. But in this way he could reach all levels and all interests among his audiences and share with listeners his passion for language.

Over time Hogg came to specialize in Old English and its linguistic changes in the period up to the Norman conquest. He was also interested in phonological theory and co-wrote a textbook, *Metrical Phonology* (1987), with his former student and colleague Chris McCully. Five years later he published the first volume of his authoritative *A Grammar of Old English*, the second volume of which was nearly complete at the time of his death.

The first volume of the work for which Hogg became best known, the *Cambridge History of the English Language*, was also published in 1992. In six volumes and more than four thousand pages this multi-author work, published by Cambridge University Press over a period of nine years, charted the development of English from its provincial beginnings to the global language it had become by the late twentieth century. Hogg was the general editor of the *History*, a task that required very careful planning and much diplomacy, and also the editor of its first volume, to which he contributed a major essay on the morphology and phonology of Old English. The Cambridge *History* was more than a landmark in the study of English; it not only brought together the work of a generation of scholars in English but set a standard for the historical study of languages in general. It also helped to maintain the strong public interest in the development of English that was a notable feature of cultural life in Britain and other English-speaking countries in the 1990s and beyond.

Assisted by his Manchester colleague David Denison and Bas Aarts from University College, London, in 1997 Hogg went on to establish what rapidly became the leading academic journal in the field of English language scholarship, *English Language and Linguistics*. With Denison he also edited a *History of the English Language* (2006). His interests in the development of English dialects and in the way in which they had been studied resulted in a history of English dialectology, based on research carried out while Hogg was a Leverhulme senior fellow in 2000–02, but which was unfinished at his death.

Hogg was elected a fellow of the British Academy in 1994. He was due to give the biennial Sir Israel Gollancz lecture at the academy in 2008. In 2004 he became a fellow of the Royal Society of Edinburgh: such recognition in his home city gave him special satisfaction. He shared his passion for Altrincham Football Club with his family; he also enjoyed the cinema, fine wines, and holidays in France, and he remained devoted to Scotland and its culture. He died of a heart attack on 6 September 2007 at Wythenshawe Hospital, Manchester, and was survived by his wife and sons. In 2008 the International Society for the Linguistics of English established the Richard M. Hogg prize for the best paper by a young scholar on a research-related topic in the fields of English language or English linguistics. LAWRENCE GOLDMAN

Sources *The Guardian* (20 Sept 2007) · *The Independent* (10 Dec 2007) · www.royalsoced.org.uk/fellowship/obits/obits_alpha/hogg_richard.pdf, 13 Aug 2010 · *WW* (2007) · b. cert. · m. cert. · d. cert.
Wealth at death under £10,000: probate, 16 Nov 2007, *CGPLA Eng. & Wales*

Holland, Joan Mary Crossley- [*née* Joan Mary Cowper] (**1912–2005**), potter and gallery owner, was born on 3 April 1912 at Peatling Magna, Lutterworth, Leicestershire, the daughter of Claude Marriott Lovell Cowper, medical doctor, and his wife, Mary Bourne, *née* Collard, a nurse who was also a gifted amateur artist. Unusually she was educated at a Plymouth Brethren boys' school before going to Wycombe Abbey and the Central School of Arts and Crafts. She became a gifted potter, designed for Doulton, and was exhibited at Heal's and Liberty. Following her marriage on 10 September 1939 to the composer Peter Charles Crossley-*Holland (1916–2001) she resigned her career in favour of full-time housewifery and parenting of their son and daughter. The marriage lasted several decades and after its painful dissolution with marvellous improbability Joan Crossley-Holland through the introduction of a friend managed the fabulous Lake Palace Hotel in Udaipur for the maharana of Mewar. India is a country where art and craft are indissolubly linked and the experience also led to a store of wonderful stories with which her colleagues were later entertained.

With both administrative and art experience, Joan

Crossley-Holland became the manager of the Bear Lane Gallery in Oxford after her return to England in the mid-1960s. The gallery had held pioneering exhibitions in the 1950s and 1960s of contemporary British art, often with the help of the Arts Council and the brightest of critics and art historians, an achievement continued under Crossley-Holland's stewardship; but the trustees baulked at Crossley-Holland's idea of exhibiting craft, denouncing potters as the producers of (mere) casseroles. Crossley-Holland therefore struck out independently, founding in 1968 the Oxford Gallery at 23 High Street. She was backed with a minimum of capital from dons and enthusiasts who believed in the worth of the cause.

The Oxford Gallery was one of the first commercial craft and art galleries to be professionally designed for its purpose, by the architect Michael Brawne, a specialist in museums. In the face of high college rents, impossible parking, and initially an indifferent or even unsympathetic environment and without public subsidy, the gallery carried on as a genuine pioneer (and indeed long outlived the Bear Lane Gallery). Its tone was set by Crossley-Holland's robust and implacable perseverance, commitment, and belief in the work she exhibited. In her eighteen years as managing director, the work of artists was shown in more than 180 exhibitions; the judicious mingling of the known and unknown was authoritative, and visits to all the graduating shows of the leading art colleges led to many a discovery. The gallery's mix of fine art, notably prints and occasionally paintings, and the crafts in all media was unique and unexpected.

Crossley-Holland's extraordinarily well-developed aesthetic sense, immense knowledge, and commitment often turned window shoppers into collectors. However her occasional bossiness, fussiness, frankness, and even determination not to charm could at times alienate rather than soothe; her staff were used to picking up the pieces. Happy to educate, she was nevertheless intolerant of mental dullness. She believed with passion that an appreciation, even better ownership, of fine contemporary pieces enhanced life; the standards of the gallery were, for the time, outstanding. Some of the more rarefied artists objected to the creative jumble that at times characterized the gallery's displays, but the intention to be more of a shop than a gallery was designed to disarm those potential clients who might be intimidated by the typically austere art gallery displays that mimicked the museums of the day and could seem unapproachable.

The Oxford Gallery antedated by several years the Crafts Advisory Council and its successor the Crafts Council, and no one at the time could have foreseen the expansion of interest in contemporary applied arts and in contemporary craft and design on the part of both museums and the major auction houses. The genuine transformation of the climate for craft in Britain by the early twenty-first century, the proliferation of museum collections and of dedicated galleries within museums, and the growth of public and private collections owed a great deal to Crossley-Holland's robust character and determined advocacy. In 1984 and 1985 the gallery held innovative exhibitions outdoors in the gardens, designed by William Peto, of High Wall in Headington, Oxford (owned by Brian Beynon Lloyd, first director of Oxford Polytechnic and chairman of the board of the Oxford Gallery), which mixed everything from wicker baskets to fountains to huge outsize pots. These exhibitions illustrated magnificently the possibilities for objects displayed and integrated into the man-made landscape. In tribute to Crossley-Holland after her retirement to Suffolk in 1986, the Oxford Gallery staged another indoor–outdoor show in the conservatory at the Barbican. The Oxford Gallery continued as a significant and important outlet for ceramics, glass, textiles, furniture, jewellery, and artists' prints for another fifteen years after her retirement. Moreover, a number of her fellow directors and assistants went on to influential careers in the promotion of contemporary craft in public and private contexts. Not only did the Contemporary Art Society purchase from the gallery but the Ashmolean Museum benefited directly from gifts and bequests from collectors nurtured by Crossley-Holland and by donations of craft in her honour and in that of her successor, Valerie Stewart.

Crossley-Holland was always impeccably and neatly dressed with an old-fashioned approach to fashion, looking more like a bustling headmistress than a gallery owner. Beautifully made up, and with a preference for subdued colours from sludge green to rust red, she did however sport the unexpected piece of avant garde jewellery. Her artists attested to her loyalty; it was on their behalf that she was such a formidable figure. She had a surprisingly gentle descent into the classic ailments of old age, ending her days at Pinford End House nursing home, Hawstead, Suffolk, near her son, the poet and children's author, Kevin Crossley-Holland, whose own professed delight was devotion to East Anglia. She died at Pinford End House on 12 January 2005, of Alzheimer's disease; both her son and her daughter survived her.

MARINA VAIZEY

Sources *The Independent* (20 Jan 2005) • *The Guardian* (25 Jan 2005) • *The Times* (14 Feb 2005) • personal knowledge (2009) • private information (2009) • b. cert. • m. cert. • d. cert.
Likenesses obituary photographs

Holme, Richard Gordon, Baron Holme of Cheltenham (**1936–2008**), politician and businessman, was born on 27 May 1936 at 19 Bolingbroke Drive, Battersea, London, the only son of Jack Richard Holme, a detective constable in the Metropolitan Police, and his wife, Edna May, *née* Eggleton. His father, a lieutenant in the intelligence corps, was killed in action in 1940. As a son of a freemason, Holme boarded at the Royal Masonic School in Bushey, Hertfordshire. His national service was spent with the 10th Gurkha rifles in Malaya between 1954 and 1956. At St John's College, Oxford, he read jurisprudence, and joined the Liberals in 1959. On 4 July 1958, while still a student, he had married Kathleen Mary (Kay) Powell (*b.* 1938), daughter of Vincent Tom Powell, surgeon. They had two daughters followed by twin sons.

Holme had a varied and successful business career. After graduating with a second-class degree in 1959 he took marketing posts with Lever Brothers and then Cavenham Foods. He then moved into publishing, a lifelong interest, becoming a director first at Penguin Books and then at the British Printing Corporation's books division, of which he become chief executive in 1969. In the same year he moved to San Diego, California, as vice-president of a publishing company. In 1974 he decided to return to Britain, having accumulated enough money to concentrate on seeking a seat and advancing the Liberal cause. He fought Braintree in the general election of October that year. He had already fought East Grinstead for the Liberals in the general election of 1964 and in a by-election the following year.

Holme was a distinctive Liberal activist, becoming a day-by-day unpaid key adviser to the party leaders, David Steel then Paddy Ashdown. He had more influence than perhaps any other Liberal front-bench spokesman and was almost a permanent part of the party power structure. He had been vice-chairman of the Liberal executive in 1966 and became president of the party in 1980–81. He worked patiently for the party to exercise influence rather than be a debating society. He had joined the party when Jo Grimond was leader in the 1950s and had held out the hope of a centre-left realignment. This was a guiding theme in Holme's political life. In large part because of his role as a 'fixer', broker, and spin doctor, he was often distrusted by some party activists, who were suspicious of the leadership's attempts to work more closely with Labour and feared that such tactics would compromise Liberal principles. He usually had to prompt Steel to overcome his natural caution but had to urge patience on the more headstrong Ashdown. It was Holme who drafted the Königswinter compact in 1981 between the leaders of the Social Democratic Party and the Liberals, an initiative that led to the formation of the alliance and eventually, in 1988, the Liberal Democrat Party.

Not becoming an MP was a disappointment to Holme. He had good prospects as the Liberal and then the Liberal Democrat candidate in the general elections of 1983 and 1987 at Cheltenham. After his narrow failure in 1987 he decided after five attempts to retire from the fray. Ironically, a Liberal Democrat candidate won the seat in 1992. Having been appointed CBE in 1983, he became a life peer, as Baron Holme of Cheltenham, in 1990, and between 1992 and 1999 he was the party's Northern Ireland spokesman.

Having managed the Liberal Democrat general election campaign in 1997, which brought a third party its largest number of MPs since the 1920s, and having taken part in the pre-election coalition talks with Tony Blair, Holme was one of the five-strong Liberal Democrat team that sat on the Liberal Democrat–Labour joint cabinet committee between 1997 and 1999. He had long been an advocate of wide-ranging constitutional reform. Indeed he established his own think-tank, the Centre for Constitutional Reform, in 1985. He was able to see many of his hopes for constitutional reform fulfilled in the first years of the Blair government. When Ashdown resigned the party leadership in 1999, to be succeeded by Charles Kennedy, Holme thought it wise to step back from his leadership-counselling role.

Holme had an enormous range of contacts in business and in politics and was widely trusted and respected for his judgement. His political activities spanned the political divide, although they were always progressive in direction. He played an important role in founding the Green Alliance (though his post as a director of Rio Tinto Zinc between 1985 and 1988 upset some of his 'green' friends), and Charter 88. He served as chairman of the Hansard Society between 2001 and 2007 and held a number of visiting academic appointments, including that of chancellor of Greenwich University from 1988. He wrote a number of books and pamphlets, including *No Dole for the Young* (1975), *A Democracy Which Works* (1978), and *The People's Kingdom* (1987), and he was a joint editor of *1688–1988: Time for a New Constitution* (1988). He was deputy chairman of the Independent Television Commission and then became chairman of the Broadcasting Standards Commission, from which he resigned in 2000 after tabloid revelations about an extramarital affair.

Holme was immediately recognizable with his military moustache, tall and erect bearing, good looks, elegant attire, and warmth. Many eagerly sought his company because of his charm, quick mind, and enthusiasm for new ideas. Despite being diagnosed with terminal brain cancer early in 2007 he carried on with some of his activities. These included the chairmanship of GlobeScan, a market research company specializing in environmental issues, and of the House of Lords constitutional committee until his term ended in October of that year. He died on 4 May 2008 at his home, Hazards, Lurgashall, Sussex, and was survived by his wife and their four children.

DENNIS KAVANAGH

Sources *The Times* (6 May 2008) · *Daily Telegraph* (6 May 2008) · *The Guardian* (6 May 2008) · *The Independent* (7 May 2008) · A. Holmes, ed., *A liberal mind in action* (2008) · Burke, *Peerage* · *WW* (2009) · b. cert. · m. cert. · d. cert.

Archives FILM BFINA, current affairs footage | SOUND BL NSA, current affairs recordings

Likenesses photographs, 1998–2003, Photoshot, London · obituary photographs

Wealth at death £1,400,014: probate, 30 Oct 2008, *CGPLA Eng. & Wales*

Honeycombe, Sir Robert William Kerr (1921–2007), metallurgist, was born on 2 May 1921 in Elsternwick, Melbourne, Victoria, Australia, the son of William Honeycombe (1881–1962), accountant, and his wife, Rachel Annie, *née* Kerr (1886–1952). Both parents were born in Melbourne but their origins can be traced back to Devon and Edinburgh respectively. When Honeycombe was three the family moved to Geelong, Victoria, where his father became company secretary of the Valley Worsted Mills. Honeycombe was educated at Swanston Street state school, Geelong, and Geelong College. The family background was not associated with science but Honeycombe's father seems to have encouraged him into the subject through his interest in astronomy and by facilitating simple experiments in chemistry. He enrolled for a BSc degree in chemistry at Melbourne University, but was encouraged there by such scholars as Walter Boas to think about metal physics, and he graduated in 1941 with a degree in chemistry and metallurgy. His first research, on hard carbides, part of his work for the degree of MSc at Melbourne (awarded in 1942), helped alleviate the wartime shortage in Australia of tool tips for the machining of metals.

The next few years were formative in many respects. Honeycombe took up an appointment at the lubricants and bearings section of the Council for Scientific and Industrial Research, an agency of the commonwealth of Australia, located on the Melbourne University campus. His attempts with Walter Boas to understand the role of thermal cycles on tin-based bearing alloys revealed the development of distortions whose origins could be traced back to the fact that expansivity of tin crystals varies with direction. This work was later to have consequences for the safety of nuclear power plants, where uranium fuel rods undergo potentially unacceptable changes in shape due to repeated fluctuations in temperature.

It was during his time at the Council for Scientific and Industrial Research that Honeycombe met June Collins (*d.* 2006), who was a laboratory assistant pursuing a part-time BSc degree. They married on 8 December 1947, and shortly afterwards sailed for England so that Honeycombe could conduct research in Cambridge under the auspices of an ICI fellowship. (They had two daughters, Juliet and Celia, both born in the UK.) In Cambridge Honeycombe met some of the giants of the subject, in an environment that was thrilling and utterly conducive to creativity. It was a period of enormous excitement with new and challenging concepts emerging with remarkable regularity. Honeycombe did some outstanding work on the deformation of crystals, which led to the award of a PhD; this research was later the inspiration for his book *The Plastic Deformation of Metals* (1968), a self-contained tome that greatly influenced the development of the subject.

Honeycombe moved to Sheffield University in 1951 as senior lecturer in physical metallurgy, and his interest shifted gradually towards teaching and research on steels, in many ways a much more versatile and challenging material than the non-ferrous alloys he was used to. The scale and variety of the structures that could be generated by solid-state phase transformations required detailed characterization and Honeycombe embraced this challenge by implementing the emerging technique of electron microscopy, including thin foil studies where the crystallographic relationships between phases could be explored and unravelled. The explosion of knowledge that resulted from these studies had a lasting influence on steel metallurgy, both in terms of the fundamental mechanisms of crystal structure changes in the solid state, and in the way that the work was exploited in industry. The achievements led in 1955 to Honeycombe's appointment as professor of physical metallurgy at Sheffield. Throughout his adventures in steel there, he contributed to the well-being of the faculty of metallurgy, particularly in the development of graduate teaching.

Honeycombe moved from Sheffield to the Goldsmith's chair of metallurgy at Cambridge, with a fellowship at Trinity Hall, in 1966, and by the time he formally retired he had served the department of metallurgy and materials science for some eighteen years, the longest service in the history of the department. As the sole professor in the department he bore the major administrative burdens with what seemed like grace. The department thrived during his tenure, to become the leading centre for materials research. He was able to achieve this by recognizing that it was the relationship between structure and properties that underpinned the subject and that the approach required was interdisciplinary. It was this latter point that enabled the department to distinguish itself from materials activities in the much larger and better entrenched subjects of physics, chemistry, engineering, and earth sciences. Meanwhile Honeycombe took a full part in university life, and from 1973 to 1980 was the second president (and thereafter fellow and emeritus fellow) of Clare Hall, Cambridge.

The years of Honeycombe's professorship at Cambridge were a period in which the experimental techniques available for the characterization of materials advanced at a breathtaking pace, in terms both of spatial and of chemical resolution. Indeed, in some cases, individual atoms could be observed and analysed. Honeycombe and his team vigorously applied these methods to steels with great success. One particular phenomenon where the 'steel group' led the world in new discoveries was the subject that came to be known as interphase precipitation, in which particles of a third phase precipitate at an advancing interface as ferrite grows from austenite. This precipitate phase may be cementite, alloy carbides, or other crystals which have limited solubility in the majority phases at the transformation temperature. Honeycombe wrote a thoroughly readable review on the subject, which formed the basis of his Hatfield memorial lecture at Sheffield in 1979, published in *Metal Science* the following year. By the time of Honeycombe's death there were millions (possibly billions) of tons of steel quietly serving humanity that relied on interphase precipitation for their properties.

Honeycombe published numerous papers in scientific journals, as well as a leading textbook, *Steels: Microstructure and Properties* (1981, third edition with H. K. D. H. Bhadeshia 2006). He was elected a fellow of the Royal Society in 1981 and knighted in 1990. He was president of the Institution of Metallurgists in 1977 and of the Metals Society in 1980–81, and vice-president of the Royal Institution in 1977–8 and of the Royal Society from 1986 to 1992. He received many other honours both in Britain and abroad, including France, Japan, India, and his native Australia. He listed his recreations as gardening, photography, and walking. He had a wonderful and loving family, including latterly grandchildren whom he often chaperoned to school. But he also left a remarkable legacy of a large academic family: he earned the lasting gratitude of his former students and colleagues, whom he nurtured and who came to permeate every aspect of the science of materials in the subsequent generation. He lived latterly in Hardwick, near Cambridge, and died at Fulbourn Hospital, Cambridge Road, Fulbourn, Cambridgeshire, on 14 September 2007, of complications of chronic lymphocytic leukaemia. He was survived by his two daughters.

H. K. D. H. Bhadeshia

Sources www.admin.cam.ac.uk/news/dp/2007091903, 13 Aug 2010 · *Memoirs FRS*, 55 (2009), 91–106 · H. K. D. H. Bhadeshia, 'Personal perspective on microstructure of steels: 25th anniversary of MST and collection of papers in honour of Sir Robert Honeycombe', *Materials Science and Technology*, 26/4 (April 2010), 379–85 · V. Randle and J. F. Knott, 'Professor Sir Robert William Kerr Honeycombe KBE FRS FREng: an appreciation', *Materials Science and Technology*, 26/6 (June 2010), 633–5 · Burke, *Peerage* · *WW* (2007) · personal knowledge (2011) · private information (2011) · d. cert.

Likenesses obituary photographs · photograph, repro. in www.admin.cam.ac.uk/news/dp/2007091903

Wealth at death £405,984: probate, 11 Feb 2008, *CGPLA Eng. & Wales*

Hornby, Richard Phipps [Dick] (**1922–2007**), politician and building society chairman, was born on 20 June 1922 at the Old House, Upper Rawcliffe Road, St Michael's-on-Wyre, Lancashire, the oldest of the four sons of Hugh Leycester Hornby (1888–1965), vicar of St Michael's-on-Wyre (later rector of Bury and bishop-suffragan of Hulme), and his wife, Katharine Rebecca (1894–1979), daughter of C. G. May. He came from a clerical family: his paternal grandfather, the Ven. Phipps John Hornby, was archdeacon of Lancaster. From Winchester College, where he was a scholar, he won a scholarship to Trinity College, Oxford, but left to serve in the King's Royal Rifle Corps from 1941 until 1945. Landing in France six weeks after D-day, he saw fierce action in the Low Countries and Germany, and was involved in liberating concentration camps. He rarely spoke of these experiences. He returned to Oxford after the war and was awarded a second in modern history in 1948, and a soccer blue. He remained a lifelong supporter of Bury Football Club. He taught history at Eton College for two years before joining Hudson and Light, a Unilever subsidiary, in 1951. On 7 April the same year he married Stella Hichens (*b*. 1927), an opera singer, and daughter of Lionel *Hichens. Among the witnesses were Marmaduke Hussey and the countess of Waldegrave. Hornby and his wife had three sons and one daughter. He moved to the advertising agency J. Walter Thompson in 1952 as a copywriter.

Hornby was increasingly attracted by a career in politics, and stood as the Conservative candidate for Walthamstow West against Clement Attlee, leader of the opposition, in the 1955 general election, considerably reducing the Labour majority. In March 1956 he fought the by-election caused by Attlee's elevation to the House of Lords, again unsuccessfully, but in a by-election in June 1956 he won in Tonbridge, Kent. He remained MP for Tonbridge until 1974, continuing to work part-time for J. Walter Thompson. As a liberal Conservative he came into conflict with the more right-wing members of his party almost immediately, in June 1956, when he supported Sidney Silverman's private member's bill to abolish the death penalty. Although this was thrown out by the House of Lords, pressure from abolitionists including Hornby led the home secretary, R. A. Butler, to introduce a compromise bill abolishing the death penalty for certain types of murder in 1957. Silverman's bill was not revived until Labour took office, and in 1964 the death penalty was abolished. Later in 1956 Hornby joined the anti-Suez group, which put pressure on the prime minister, Eden, to cease military action against Egypt, and he was one of the Conservative MPs who abstained in the vote of confidence in Eden on 8 November 1956.

In 1959 Hornby was appointed parliamentary private secretary to Duncan Sandys, briefly minister of aviation but soon moved to become secretary of state for Commonwealth relations. For the last year of the Conservative government, from October 1963 to October 1964, he served as parliamentary under-secretary of state for the Commonwealth and the Colonial offices, with particular responsibility for Africa and for Commonwealth education. He continued to take an interest in Africa while in opposition, and in 1965 wrote a pamphlet, *The Changing Commonwealth*, for the Conservative Political Centre. He was also a member of the editorial board of *The Round Table*, the Commonwealth journal, from 1964 to 1981. In 1966 he supported the Labour government when it imposed oil sanctions on Rhodesia, nearly losing his seat as a result after pressure from his constituency party to stand down. He was deputy to Sir Edward Boyle, Conservative spokesman on education, but he did not share the views of the new Conservative leader, Edward Heath, and when Heath became prime minister in 1970, Hornby did not get a government post. As the Conservative Party moved to the right with the departure of such leading liberal figures as Iain Macleod, who died in 1970, and Edward Boyle, who was given a life peerage, and facing increasing hostility from his constituency party, Hornby decided not to stand in the general election of February 1974, despite having been selected for the new seat of Royal Tunbridge Wells.

After leaving parliament Hornby became director of personnel at J. Walter Thompson, and also accepted a seat on the London board of the Halifax, the largest of the building societies. In 1976 he became a member of the main board, and served as vice-chairman from 1981 to 1983 and chairman from 1983 to 1990, at a time of major changes in the financial services industry. Following the 1984 report of the Spalding committee, chaired by John Spalding, the chief executive of the Halifax, the government passed the 1986 Building Societies Act, allowing the building societies, which up to then had functioned mainly as mortgage providers, to engage in a wider range of financial activities. This was intended to enable them to compete with the banks, which were encroaching on the mortgage and savings markets. Building societies were also given the right to convert from mutual status into public limited companies. After much research and deliberation, in 1988 the Halifax board decided against conversion. Hornby believed in the ethos of the building societies, which were owned by their members, and at the meeting of the board on 20 July 1988 he said 'I am reluctant to take an irreversible step in present conditions that might deprive members of an institution which has served them well and which is not under immediate threat' (Pugh, 67). He also said later that while profit mattered, it did not matter 'so much as serving faithfully the interests of our customers' (*Daily Telegraph*, 28 Sept 2007). It was not until 1997, following its merger with the Leeds Permanent Building Society, that the Halifax Building Society was converted into a public limited company. The Halifax meanwhile remained the leading mortgage provider, and expanded its activities to include credit cards, loans, cheque books, insurance, and estate agency, opening new branches and increasing its staff. Hornby later claimed that his years as chairman of the Halifax were the happiest years of his working life.

Dick Hornby, as he was universally known, lived in retirement at Bowerchalke, near Salisbury, Wiltshire, where he was able to indulge his love of country pursuits, including shooting, fishing, riding, and walking. He died at his home, Ebble Thatch, Bowerchalke, on 22 September 2007 of heart failure, and was survived by his wife, Stella, and their three children. ANNE PIMLOTT BAKER

Sources M. Reid, *Abbey National conversion to plc* (1991) • R. Lamb, *The Macmillan years, 1957–1963* (1995) • P. Pugh, *The strength to change* (1998) • *The Times* (28 Sept 2007) • *Daily Telegraph* (28 Sept 2007) • *The Independent* (28 Sept 2007) • *The Guardian* (1 Oct 2007) • *Report* [Trinity College, Oxford] (2007) • *WW* (2007) • b. cert. • m. cert. • d. cert.

Likenesses Elliot & Fry, quarter-plate glass negative, 1953, NPG • photographs, 1963–86, Photoshot, London • W. Bird, photograph, 1964, NPG • Bassano, half-plate film negatives, 1965, NPG • obituary photographs

Wealth at death £629,401: probate, 19 Dec 2007, *CGPLA Eng. & Wales*

Hudson, John Pilkington (1910–2007), horticultural scientist and bomb disposal officer, was born on 24 July 1910 at Allethwaite, 15 Heath Grove, Buxton, Derbyshire, the only son of (William) Arthur Hudson (1884–1976), a sorting clerk and telegraphist for the Post Office, and his wife, Bertha, *née* Pilkington (1877–1969). He had a younger sister, Molly. After some years as a boarder at a dame school in West Kirby he gained a scholarship to New Mills secondary school. He left at sixteen with no qualifications and, surprisingly, no clear ambitions. He admitted to an interest in physics, though his teacher dissuaded him from pursuing avenues in this direction, on the grounds that 'everything in physics will shortly be known' (J. Hudson 'Obituary drafted by himself', Richard Hudson website). Later it was his ready grasp of physics that subsequently saved his life and those of many others. Initially he worked on a garden nursery venture begun by his energetic father, who was by now primarily a postmaster and shopkeeper at Chapel-en-le-Frith, Derbyshire. Almost by chance rather than ambition he enrolled on a one-year horticultural course at the Midland Agricultural and Dairy College, Sutton Bonington, near Nottingham. He passed with distinction. Having then gained the entry qualifications for a degree he took a BSc in horticulture at Sutton

John Pilkington Hudson (1910–2007), by unknown photographer, 1985

Bonington, at that time an external degree of the University of London. In 1935 he was briefly a lecturer at Plumpton School of Agriculture, Sussex. While a student he had met (Mary) Gretta Heath (1910–1989), a dairy chemist, sister of a lecturer at Sutton Bonington, and daughter of William Nathaniel Heath, farmer. They married on 11 July 1936 and lived in Plumpton for three years while he was a county council horticultural adviser. They had two sons, Colin and Richard.

Shortly before the outbreak of the Second World War Hudson joined the Territorial Army. He was soon serving with the British expeditionary force in Normandy and was evacuated from Dunkirk. He was assigned to the Royal Engineers bomb disposal unit and was in charge of a group during the blitz on Sheffield. Later, owing to his scientific background and keen observation, and his *ad hoc* reports on his experiences, he was summoned to London to lead a team working on a neutralizing mechanism for unexploded bombs, with promotion to the rank of major. He also liaised with his opposite numbers in the navy and air force and in 1942 spent several months in the United States sharing his experience with bomb experts there. He was awarded a military MBE in 1943 and, in the same year, the George Medal for disabling the first Y bomb fuse. In 1944 he received a bar to his George Medal for defusing the first V1 ('flying bomb' or 'doodlebug') that landed intact. New generations of fuses were being introduced in such devices and Hudson and his colleagues devised ingenious ways of overcoming these challenges. He later wrote, 'There was no real training, we learned by experience' (*University of Nottingham Magazine*, 2001). He never mentioned his war exploits to his friends and students after the war and many learnt about them only from a subsequent television series on unexploded bombs, broadcast in 2001.

In 1945 John and Gretta Hudson and their two young boys went to New Zealand. He worked in the department of agriculture at Wellington and in this period initiated experiments on the transportation of a new fruit to the UK, the Chinese gooseberry, later known as the kiwi fruit. He also helped to establish the experimental station at Levin. In 1948 he returned to the school of agriculture in Sutton Bonington, now a faculty of the new University of Nottingham, as a lecturer in the horticulture department. He became head of department in 1950, gained two research degrees, MSc in 1952 and PhD in 1954, and was appointed professor of horticulture in 1958 and dean of the faculty of agriculture and horticulture in 1965. He was justly proud to have occupied the first chair of horticulture at Nottingham, where he had graduated. He demonstrated his flair for organization; things had to go to plan and, generally, they did. He undertook research on plant propagation and carried out pioneering studies with his research students on environmental factors affecting plant growth. Partly as a result of his work on plant-water relations and his interest in tropical horticulture he was seconded, part-time, to found the department of horticulture at Khartoum University and was visiting professor of horticulture there from 1961 to 1963. He was able to spend six months of each year in Sudan and to share his time successfully between the two universities.

Hudson left Nottingham in 1967 to become director of Long Ashton Research Station, with a chair of horticultural science at the University of Bristol. Directing the station in the late 1960s was a testing time since there were shadows of research budget reductions on the horizon. Initially he undertook some vigorous reorganization, which he felt was desirable for the institute and the horticultural industry. He introduced essential changes while retaining the confidence of staff. He thoroughly enjoyed the job and the friendship of his colleagues. He had the rare gift to see the obvious and to cut through unnecessary detail; to an extent he brought a military approach to the direction of scientific endeavour. He initiated the successful annual national meeting known as the Under 40s Conference, enabling younger research workers, advisers, and growers to interact.

Hudson edited *Control of the Plant Environment* (1957), and a journal, *Experimental Agriculture*, between 1965 and 1982. He also served on the editorial boards of the *Journal of Horticultural Science* and *SPAN* (published by the Soil Association). He chaired the government's joint advisory committee on agricultural education, which reported in 1973, and served on the Royal Horticultural Society's examinations board. He was a good communicator and could present scientific information clearly; although he spoke with apparent ease he would always be thoroughly prepared. His lectures were ordered and delivered with precise timing. He tried to instil this latter attribute into his students, and had the unfortunate habit of bringing to seminars an alarm clock that rang noisily when the forecast time of the presentation was exceeded. Among his many awards was an associateship of honour of the Royal New Zealand Institute of Horticulture, in 1948. He was a president of the Horticultural Educational Association, and a founder member and honorary fellow of the Institute of Horticulture. In 1975 he was appointed CBE, for services to horticulture, and in the following year received the prestigious Victoria medal of honour in horticulture from the Royal Horticultural Society.

Hudson's career embraced research, teaching, and advisory spheres. Peter Waister, a former graduate student of his, said he excelled in all aspects: 'I was impressed by his ability to balance the three areas and to be inspirational in them all, a rare achievement' (funeral oration, 17 Dec 2007). In *Who's Who*, under the heading 'Recreations', Hudson listed 'Talking with my friends'. He was an extraordinarily modest man; he always seemed genuinely interested in the person with whom he was talking. He had a remarkable influence on many people's careers, lifestyle, and behaviour.

In retirement John and Gretta Hudson lived in the village of Wrington, near Bristol, where they developed a splendid large garden. With the exception of the lawns and hedges he managed all himself well into his nineties. In 1986 Gretta had a major stroke and he cared for her at home until her death in 1989. Hudson had a long and busy retirement; he served as a volunteer with the Samaritans, sang in the village choral society and church choir, took lessons in gliding, and enjoyed long walks. He died at his home, The Spinney, Ladywell, Wrington, Somerset, on 6 December 2007, of kidney failure. His elder son, Colin, an accomplished tropical agronomist, had died in Barbados in 2004. He was survived by his younger son, Richard, a professor of linguistics at University College, London.

BRIAN SELF

Sources *Daily Telegraph* (12 Dec 2007) · *The Times* (21 Dec 2007) · *The Independent* (8 Jan 2008) · *The Guardian* (8 Feb 2008) · *Experimental Agriculture*, 44 (2008), 141–4 · *The Horticulturist*, 17/2 (2008); 17/4 (2008) · www.phon.ucl.ac.uk/home/dick, 26 March 2010 · richardhudson.byethost2.com/family/jph, 26 March 2010 · *WW* (2007) · personal knowledge (2011) · private information (2011) · b. cert. · m. cert. · d. cert.

Likenesses photograph, 1985, priv. coll. [*see illus.*] · obituary photographs · photographs, repro. in richardhudson.byethost2.com/family/jph/johnhudson.htm

Wealth at death £503,443: probate, 19 June 2008, *CGPLA Eng. & Wales*

Hughes, David John (1930–2005), novelist, was born on 27 July 1930 at 6 Park Close Road, Alton, Hampshire, the only child of Gwilym Fielden Hughes (1899–1989), schoolmaster, writer, and broadcaster, and his wife, Edna Frances, *née* Cochrane (1903–1996). His father was the Yorkshire-born son of a Congregational minister from Caernarvonshire, and his mother was born in Lancashire. He was observant of his roots, perhaps the more so as his childhood was disrupted by the Second World War. In 1937 his father had moved from the headmastership of Alton senior boys' school to that of Queen's Road senior boys' school, Wimbledon, but two years later the family was evacuated to Chichester, and then back to Alton. They did not return to London until the war was over.

Hughes was educated at Eggar's Grammar School, Alton, and then at King's College School, Wimbledon. As an Alton choirboy he reported sermons for the *Hampshire*

Herald; at the age of seventeen he offered poems to John Lehmann's *Penguin New Writing*. During national service at RAF Warrington (1948–50) he read J. B. Priestley under his desk. At Oxford, where he read English at Christ Church and edited *Isis*, he kept in touch with Lehmann, giving him the idea for a BBC programme, *New Soundings*, and in 1953, when Lehmann was setting up his new title, the *London Magazine*, he took on Hughes (who had graduated with a second-class degree earlier that year) as his assistant editor. Lehmann, an autocrat, liked Hughes, whom he described as 'sweet-tempered and able', though he noticed 'grim psychological struggles in his relations with his family' (Wright, 212). Nevertheless Hughes left in 1955 to work for another autocrat, Rupert Hart-Davis, in publishing. (The *London Magazine* soon followed to the same address; Alan Ross, who succeeded Lehmann as editor from 1961, became one of Hughes's closest friends.) Hart-Davis, recognizing Hughes's ambition, gave him a paid half-day off a week to write and in 1957 his first novel was published, *A Feeling in the Air*.

It was as 'a young poet' (Zetterling, 152) that, the same year, he was introduced by Patrick Woodcock to the Swedish film star Mai Elisabet Zetterling (1925–1994), newly parted from Tyrone Power. Woodcock mischievously introduced Mai Zetterling as 'a middle-aged Latvian refugee who speaks only German' (*The Independent*, 19 June 2002). Hughes was tall and dark, Zetterling was tiny, elfin, blonde. They married in Oxford on 23 April 1958, in which year Hart-Davis published Hughes's second book, *J. B. Priestley: an Informal Study of his Work*.

Hughes's second novel, *Sealed with a Loving Kiss*, followed in 1959, but for the next sixteen years his career—apart from a stint as editor of Michael Heseltine and Clive Labovitch's magazine *Town*, 1960–61—was largely allied to Zetterling's. Hughes left his damp basement in Bayswater, Zetterling her smart flat in Kensington, and they bought and restored a tumble-down old rectory, Berry Grove, at Liss in Hampshire. Zetterling, determined to be more than a decorative studio actress, gave herself five years to get established as an independent film-maker. Hughes collaborated with her, whether as co-writer, sound man, or stills photographer, on the short *The War Game* (1962; nominated for a BAFTA award), *Loving Couples* (1964; nominated for the palme d'or at Cannes), the controversial *Night Games* (1966; nominated for the leone d'oro at Venice, but banned from public performance there), *Dr Glas* (1968; based on the novel by Hjalmar Söderberg), *The Girls* (1968; based on Aristophanes' *Lysistrata*), and *Vincent the Dutchman* (1972; a BAFTA award-winning drama-documentary about Van Gogh).

In 1964, the year he published *The Road to Stockholm and Lapland*, a relaxed account of a drive through northern Europe in Zetterling's Sunbeam Rapier convertible (most of her films were shot in Sweden), Hughes made his mark with a fourth novel, *The Major*. Brief, spare, impressively violent, it told the story of the mundane Major Kane's vicious campaign to reclaim his family house from an aged tenant. In 1968 came *The Man Who Invented Tomorrow*, a tease of H. G. Wells. But exile did not suit Hughes. Unhappy in the remote house near Uzès, in Languedoc, that Zetterling had fallen in love with four years before, deracinated and unable to write, he returned in 1974 to London. They divorced in 1976.

Hughes lived in Pimlico, then for a period in New York, teaching, before marrying, at Lambeth register office on 1 November 1980, Elizabeth Jane Booth, *née* Westoll (*b.* 1947), daughter of James (Tim) Westoll, landowner and ornithologist. He and Elizabeth settled down in contentment to live in London, finally at 163 Kennington Road, with a second home at a farmhouse in the hills above Llandovery in Carmarthenshire, and then in Aldington, Kent; they had a son, Merlin, and a daughter, Anna Rose. After the subtle, well-crafted novels *Memories of Dying* (1976), *A Genoese Fancy* (1979), and *The Imperial German Dinner Service* (1983), Hughes scored his most notable success with *The Pork Butcher* (1984). A haunting tale of a German ex-soldier returning to France to the site of a Second World War massacre in which he had participated, it displayed all Hughes's finest characteristics as a writer: wit, economy, sensuality, and a brutal power of surprise. The book won the W. H. Smith literary award and was turned in 1989 into a film, *Souvenir*, that Hughes deplored. His last work of conventional fiction was the light-hearted *But for Bunter* (1985), published in America as *The Joke of the Century* (1986), in which twentieth-century history was taken over by the Fat Owl of Frank Richards's remove.

J. B. Priestley liberated Hughes, he said, by his 'insistence on being his own man' (*Himself and Other Animals*, 6); by unbending frankness, Priestley achieves a direct relationship with his reader. In *J. B. Priestley* (defined, tellingly, as 'a chapter of autobiography'; p. 220) the 28-year-old Hughes asserted the duty of an author as 'clearly and honestly and in the round' to expose his personality: 'I have often felt that the difficulty of conveying oneself on paper, pleasantly and without falsehood, is something a writer must conquer before his images of other people can satisfactorily pass that way' (p. 48). One of his earlier books, the decidedly experimental *The Rosewater Revolution* (1971), exploring the margins of fiction and non-fiction, was initially subtitled 'aspects of myself'. 'Conveying oneself', conveying David Hughes in the full round, became the purpose of his later books, often to the discomfiture of reviewers.

All the characters in *The Little Book* (1996; half fiction, half not, and written almost as a love letter to his wife, Elizabeth) were 'aspects of myself', from Dave Higgs, Davis Fielden, and Hugh Dickinson to D. J. House and Davina Darley. After a brush with cancer he imagined a 'book to end books', 'the unwritable bible', 'the little book that said it all' (*The Little Book*, 8, 10). *Himself and Other Animals* (1997), a revision of the life of his friend (and sometime Hart-Davis author) Gerald Durrell that he had undertaken on his return to England in 1974, was as much about the author as his subject, the zookeeper in his several habitats, lunching in Jersey, drinking in the Midi. *The Lent Jewels* (2002), an explicitly personal, slyly inconclusive investigation of religious faith, purported to be about the death from scarlet fever of five out of the six daughters of Archibald

Campbell Tait (a future archbishop of Canterbury) in one month in 1856. Hughes's last book, *The Hack's Tale* (2004), a journey by autoroute, autostrada, and pilgrims' way into the worlds of Froissart, Boccaccio, and Chaucer, was a cry of frustration at the twenty-first-century media.

Benign, solicitous, clubbable, with an air of the bohemian schoolmaster, Hughes seemed never happier than at the lunch table, glass in hand, full board before him, and a long afternoon ahead. Mai Zetterling called him 'a sensualist *par excellence*' (Zetterling, 160). But he was a writer of the utmost seriousness, a painful perfectionist and a scrupulous critic. A man of appetites, he concealed his difficulties with art. Handsome, romantic, 'positively Byronic', for Zetterling he was 'a secretive person, even to himself' (ibid., 154, 157).

Elected a fellow of the Royal Society of Literature in 1986, Hughes served on its council from 1989 to 1996, edited its journal from 1992 to 1996, and in 1998 became a vice-president. He was editor of the New Fiction Society, 1975–8 and 1981–2, film critic of the *Sunday Times*, 1982–3, and fiction critic of the *Mail on Sunday*, 1982–99. From 1986 to 1995, with Giles Gordon, he edited an annual, *Best Short Stories*, for Heinemann. A brilliant technician who strove for 'good words exactly positioned' (*The Little Book*, 36), he was as diligent in encouraging younger writers as he was in keeping old friendships in spruce repair. He died on 11 April 2005 at St Thomas's Hospital, Lambeth, London, of sepsis and infective arthropathy (in his bad ankle) accompanied by liver and kidney failure. He was survived by his wife and their two children, and buried on 19 April in Bonnington, Kent, by the church of St Rumwold of which he had written vividly in *The Hack's Tale* (p. 63)—dedicated to 'a saint so holy he only lived a day'.

JAMES FERGUSSON

Sources D. Hughes, *J. B. Priestley: an informal study of his work* (1958) · *The Times* (24 April 1958); (20 April 2005); (27 May 2005) · M. Zetterling, *All those tomorrows* (1985) · D. Hughes, *The little book* (1996) · D. Hughes, *Himself and other animals* (1997) · A. Wright, *John Lehmann: a pagan adventure* (1998) · D. Hughes, *The Independent* (19 June 2002) [obit. of P. Woodcock] · D. Hughes, *A hack's tale* (2004) · *The Independent* (12 April 2005) · *Daily Telegraph* (13 April 2005) · *The Guardian* (13 April 2005) · *WW* (2005) · personal knowledge (2009) · private information (2009) · b. cert. · m. cert. [1980] · d. cert.
Archives SOUND BL NSA, documentary recordings
Likenesses two photographs, 1958, Getty Images, London · C. Garnham, bromide fibre print, 1985, NPG · obituary photographs
Wealth at death £764,558: probate, 6 March 2006, *CGPLA Eng. & Wales*

Hughes, Margaret Patricia (1919–2005), writer on cricket, was born on 1 October 1919 at 5 Beach Houses, Margate, Kent, the daughter of Arthur Hubert Hughes (*d.* 1944), pianoforte ironmonger, and his wife, Dorothy Maud, *née* Townsend. She had three brothers and it was from them that she was infected by the cricket virus during games played in the back garden of their house. She does not appear to have sought to play more seriously as an adult, perhaps slightly surprisingly since the 1930s saw a growth in interest in playing the game among young middle-class women. After leaving school at seventeen she took a job in the advertising department of the *Star* newspaper in London, the only woman in the company of a number of men who, as she later wrote, 'were as amusing as they were difficult to deal with' (*All on a Summer's Day*, 37). At least she got to see the cricket scores before the general public. During the MCC tour of Australia in 1936–7 she and her brothers took turns to find out the latest test scores broadcast on BBC radio from 3 a.m. and tuned in to the ball-by-ball commentary that began from 7.30 a.m. before catching their trains into London. Walter Hammond and Patsy Hendren were her cricketing heroes and Lord's her Valhalla. She saw Hendren's last appearance for Middlesex—he was forty-eight—and found it an emotionally powerful experience.

In 1941 Hughes joined the Women's Royal Naval Service (the Wrens), and spent a good part of 1944–5 on a posting to the United States. She found herself impressed both by the east coast and by the 'marvellous hospitality' but puzzled by the national fetish for hygiene and hot water. Demobilized at the end of April 1946, she spent much of her two months' leave at Lord's, her one disappointment being that it was one of the coldest and wettest summers on record. She later wrote that her passion for cricket was so intense that she determined to make it her central life interest. She would mark time through each winter and save enough money to see her through the cricket season. 'I wouldn't be hurting anyone … the country wasn't having to bear the brunt of my unemployment and I wouldn't be fretting in an office from May to September, wondering how events were shaping up at Lords' (*All on a Summer's Day*, 69). She found a job on the editorial staff of *Queen* magazine; she was one of three, her appointment assisted by the fact that the editor's secretary had also been in the Wrens.

It is not clear how or when Hughes met the music critic and cricket correspondent of the *Manchester Guardian*, Sir (John Frederick) Neville *Cardus (1888–1975), but there is no doubt that they became intimate friends, so much so that she became known as his 'cricket wife', as distinguished from his 'music wife', Else Mayer-Linsman. It was to Hughes that Cardus turned in 1949 when he was suffering from writer's block and he also wrote the foreword for her semi-autobiographical *All on a Summer's Day* (1953), possibly the first book on cricket not written by a man. Cardus must have helped her to obtain a place at cricket's exclusively male table. But that she was not lacking in self-belief is shown by her success in persuading the tough proprietor of the *Sydney Daily Telegraph*, Frank Packer, to allow her to cover the 1954–5 test series between Australia and England. She was rewarded by a stunning English victory which had seemed unlikely after defeat by an innings in the first test. She wrote about the series in her second book, *The Long Hop* (1955), described by John Arlott in his *Wisden* review as 'the book of an enthusiast' (*Wisden*, 1954, 976). She did not write another book but after the death of Cardus in 1975 became his literary executor and edited several anthologies of his writings, including *What is Music* (1977), *A Cardus for all Seasons* (1985), and *Cardus on the Ashes*

(1989). She took upon herself the role of guardian of his reputation.

Cricket is a game in which style is often thought more important than effectiveness. Cardus valued players for their style and character as much as their ability, and Hughes seems to have shared this preference. On the nawab of Pataudi, for example, 'you could look forward for weeks' to an innings by him, 'knowing you would see a true stylist' (*All on a Summer's Day*, 60). Lala Amarnath bowling off the wrong foot had 'the same effect on me as the scraping of a rusty file' (ibid., 62), while Joe Hardstaff was a 'Cyrano de Bergerac at the crease, erect and lithe and quick of foot, with his bat as a rapier, he makes exquisite poetry as he thrusts and parries' (ibid., 63). Grace and charm were important to her in cricketers, especially batsmen, and she spotted it in the eighteen-year-old Colin Cowdrey, whose '45 runs in that style is good enough for me' (ibid., 65).

Hughes was a true pioneer in a very male world and by the time of her death few others had followed where she led. She never lost her passion for cricket. Only in the final two years of her life did she stop going to watch cricket at Lord's. Having lived latterly at Melcombe Regis Court, Weymouth Street, London, she died on 30 January 2005 at St Mary's Hospital, Westminster, of pneumonia. She never married. Her brother David survived her.

TONY MASON

Sources M. Hughes, *All on a summer's day* (1953) · M. Hughes, *The long hop* (1955) · *Wisden* (1955) · *The Guardian* (9 Feb 2005) · *The Times* (19 Feb 2005) · b. cert. · d. cert.

Likenesses obituary photographs

Wealth at death £316,494: probate, 10 May 2005, *CGLPA Eng. & Wales*

Hughes, Selwyn (1928–2006), evangelical minister and devotional writer, was born on 27 April 1928 at 4 Tunnel Terrace, near Fochriw, Glamorgan, the elder of the two children of John Wyndham Hughes (1906–1986), an underground colliery electrician, and his wife, Lily, *née* Marshallsea (*b.* 1906), a former domestic servant. At the time of his birth his parents were sharing with his maternal grandparents their spartan two-roomed accommodation in a remotely situated terrace of four unprepossessing cottages perched on a hillside in the highest inhabited location in south Wales, overlooking the mining village of Fochriw. Despite the austerity of his upbringing in the great depression some of Hughes's most vivid childhood memories were of his relatives enthusiastically recounting tales of religious revival from the extraordinarily influential Welsh revival of 1904–5 and the more recent Pentecostalist ministry of Stephen Jeffreys. Dedicating his nephew shortly after his birth, David Thomas, the pastor of the Assemblies of God mission hall at Fochriw, a former ambulance station where most of the tightly knit congregation were members of Hughes's extended family, prayed that Selwyn, whose name in Welsh signified the attribute of a clear voice, might one day become a great preacher of the gospel.

The continuing economic depression forced Hughes's father in the mid-1930s to seek work at the Metropolitan Vickers factory at Saltley in Birmingham. The sudden experience of displacement suffered by Hughes induced a sense of alienation and introversion for the next three years until his father's failing health necessitated a return to his native Wales on the eve of the outbreak of the Second World War. An avid reader and devoted radio listener, Hughes developed an early love of language, and at the age of twelve he joined the local youth dramatic society, which provided his earliest experience of public speaking. However, his theatrical career ended when his father, a strict teetotaller, took exception to his over-enthusiastic portrayal on stage of a commercial traveller enjoying a convivial glass of whisky, and resolutely walked out of the public performance, much to his son's embarrassment.

After securing a coveted scholarship to Bargoed grammar school in 1940 he left, unusually, after two years, with a special dispensation to undertake an engineering course at Bargoed Technical College. This was followed by a five-year apprenticeship in the Guest, Keen and Nettlefolds steelworks in Dowlais, where he loved 'the whirr of the machinery' and 'the heavy acrid smell of burning steel' to such an extent that he believed he had found a career that would offer him complete fulfilment in life (Peters, *Selwyn*, 24). Within a few months he was running the apprentices' football pool. For all his family's experience of spiritual revival, he acknowledged in his autobiography that he had been a rebellious teenager, smoking, swearing, chasing pretty girls, and even going through a phase of petty pilfering. However, in February 1944 he experienced a dramatic religious conversion. Passing the open door of the mission hut *en route* for the dance hall, he heard his father praying fervently for his son's salvation, and when he eventually arrived at the dance hall he found its lure less appealing. He believed that God was calling him and shortly afterwards committed his life to Jesus Christ. On a bitterly cold March morning he was baptized by total immersion in the open air at Fochriw, with crowds watching from the hillside above, followed later by baptism in the Holy Spirit at a Pentecostal convention. He then trained successively as a Sunday school teacher and lay preacher, teaching himself to play the piano accordion to conduct open-air evangelistic campaigns. In 1946–8 he undertook national service at Bedlinog colliery, where the loss of a workmate in a catastrophic roof fall generated a sense of urgency to train for the ordained ministry, which he undertook at the Bristol Bible College, where his uncle had also trained.

After ordination Hughes served in a succession of Assembly of God churches in Cornwall, west Wales, and south Yorkshire. In his first appointment, at Helston, Cornwall, his frugal meal budgeting included a diluted daily penny beef cube for lunch. On 10 April 1951, at the Methodist church in Helston, he married Enid Mary Osmand (1929–1986), manageress of the NAAFI canteen at HMS *Culdrose*, who considerably enriched both his diet and his ministry through her faithful support for the next thirty-five years.

Hughes's desire to find new ways of communicating the gospel led him to operate outside denominational structures from 1958, when he resigned from the Assemblies of God following official opposition to a new urban mission he had started in Sheffield, near to an established Assemblies of God mission hall. After broadening his experience as a preacher and evangelist in the United States, and declining an offer to remain there, he went to London, where he launched a campaign for spiritual revival in 1963. This developed into the Crusade for World Revival, an international organization founded in 1965 for training Christian counsellors, leaders, and workers throughout the world and disseminating Christian resources. These included the daily devotional *Every Day with Jesus*, a bimonthly publication of themed reflections on the Bible modelled on the accessibility of the *Reader's Digest*, which ultimately won Hughes a global influence and respect from Christians of every denomination. When the Crusade for World Revival moved to Waverley Abbey House, near Farnham, Surrey—a Georgian mansion, purchased with donations from his supporters, situated alongside the site of the first English Cistercian abbey—Viscount Tonypandy, the former speaker of the House of Commons and a Welsh Methodist lay preacher, declared at its official opening in 1987 that it would become 'a powerhouse for the Lord Jesus Christ in the unfolding years' (Hughes, *My Story*, 2007, 328). It rapidly became Europe's largest centre for training in Christian counselling and pastoral care, introducing a biblical model of understanding people developed by Hughes, and linked to Hughes's international ministry of evangelistic discipleship and seminar programmes that spanned five continents. He also developed an innovatory style of ministry and was one of the first Christian leaders to utilize overhead projectors and later data projectors in his professionally presented teaching seminars. He was awarded an honorary doctorate of divinity in 2004 by Brunel University, when Lord Carey described him as 'a giant of the faith', and he delighted that year in preaching in Cardiff at the centenary of the Welsh revival.

Recordings of Hughes's sermons reveal a quietly spoken, measured delivery, with no pronounced Welsh accent (a consequence of his childhood years in Birmingham), but occasionally rising in volume and quickening in pace to emphasize key points or to challenge his congregation to a deeper spiritual commitment. His appearance, which one observer described as rather dapper, was characteristically modest, with neatly backcombed hair, greying in later portraits, longish sideburns, and lightweight spectacles framing a kindly, expressive face. His sermons, like his Bible reading notes, were engagingly titled, carefully crafted, graphically illustrated, lightened by humorous anecdotes, and enhanced by carefully selected quotations and examples from his vast reading and his wealth of personal experience.

The death of Hughes's wife after a debilitating, painful struggle with cancer, followed by the tragic loss within the space of ten months of their two sons, David and John, and Hughes's own protracted struggle with prostate cancer, enhanced his empathy with others experiencing suffering. He died at the Phyllis Tuckwell Hospice in Farnham on 9 January 2006, having assured those around him that 'he was looking forward to meeting his Lord' (*Idea*, March–April 2006, 14). His funeral at Farnham Baptist Church on 17 January was followed by cremation at Aldershot crematorium. A memorial service was held at Methodist Central Hall, Westminster, on 9 September 2006. The evangelical press pronounced him 'one of the UK's most influential post-war Christian leaders' while obituaries in the secular press paid tribute to his 'extraordinary achievement' in developing 'some of the most popular daily Bible study tools in the world, with nearly a million readers an issue' (*Daily Telegraph*, 23 Feb 2006; *The Times*, 4 March 2006). His ministry, combining the roles of counsellor, evangelist, pastor, preacher, teacher, and writer, had spanned six decades. His personal authorship of every issue of *Every Day with Jesus* had made him one of the most influential Christian devotional writers of any time. Indeed his influence through his preaching and writing in the twentieth century was comparable with that exercised by Spurgeon in the nineteenth century or Wesley in the eighteenth century. JOHN A. HARGREAVES

Sources S. Hughes, *Walking with destiny* (1965) · J. Peters, *Selwyn: every day with Jesus* (1990) · S. Hughes, *My story*, rev. edn. (2007) [with additional chapters by J. Peters] · S. Hughes, *Spoken from the heart*, 2 vols. (2005–6) · *Daily Telegraph* (23 Feb 2006) · *The Times* (4 March 2006) · *CWR Today*, 1 (Jan–March 2006); 2 (April–June 2006); 4 (Oct–Dec 2006); 13 (June–Sept 2009) · *Evangelicals Now* (March 2006) · *Idea* (March–April 2006), 14 · M. Ashford, 'A life lived every day with Jesus', *Headline* (spring 2006), 25 · J. Peters, *Great revivalists* (2008) · private information (2010) [J. Barwick; A. Lloyd] · b. cert. · m. cert. · d. cert.

Archives CWR, Waverley Abbey House, Farnham, Surrey, personal papers | SOUND BL NSA, performance recordings · BL NSA, documentary recordings · CWR, *40 years of Every Day with Jesus*, CD, 2005 · CWR, *He's just a carpenter*, CD, 2005 · CWR, *The Christ of burning, cleansing flame*, CD, 2006

Likenesses photograph, repro. in *Order of service, thanksgiving service, Methodist Central Hall, Westminster* (2006) · photographs, repro. in *CWR Today*, 2 (2006) · photographs, repro. in Hughes, *My story*

Wealth at death £408,717: probate, 20 April 2006, *CGPLA Eng. & Wales*

Hunt, Edgar Hubert (1909–2006), musician, was born on 28 June 1909 at 2 Upper Byron Place, Clifton, Bristol, the only son and elder child of Hubert Walter Hunt (1865–1945), organist and master of the choristers at Bristol Cathedral, and his wife, Clara Harriett Clements, teacher and singer, daughter of James Clements, village schoolmaster, of Haddenham, Buckinghamshire. On his father's side he came from a long line of church musicians: his grandfather had been a tenor lay clerk at St George's, Windsor. He was educated at Bristol grammar school, and in 1927 he took up a flute scholarship at Trinity College of Music, London. He was awarded the college's diploma in 1930, but remained at Trinity until 1933, having more lessons while unsuccessfully attempting a MusB degree of Durham University. In 1933 he was apprenticed to the music reader in the music printing factory of Novellos, and remained there for a year after finishing his apprenticeship in 1936.

It was at Trinity that Hunt became interested in the recorder, through the director of studies, Joseph Cox Bridge, the former organist at Chester Cathedral who in 1886 had discovered the 'Chester recorders' in the vaults of the cathedral. Hunt first heard recorders played in 1928, at a recital by the German Singers in Bristol, and fell in love with the pure sound of the instrument. He bought a treble recorder made by Oskar Dawson, and after teaching himself to play from *The Modern Music Master* (1731) he visited the Haslemere festival for the first time in 1930. Wanting to teach schoolchildren the recorder (he already taught the flute and the clarinet), but finding there was no recorder tutor available in England, he wrote his own, *A Concise Tutor for Descant, Treble and Tenor Recorders for Use in Schools* and *A Practical Method for the Recorder* (both 1935). There were no inexpensive recorders available either, unlike the situation in Germany, where recorders had been mass-produced since the early 1930s. But Hunt discovered that these recorders had a simplified fingering system, which meant that they had a limited range, poor sound quality, and were out of tune in most keys. In 1934 he persuaded one German maker, Wilhelm Herwig, to produce recorders with what he called 'English fingering', based on eighteenth-century fingering. He passed the Herwig agency on to a Liverpool firm, and recorder playing began to be introduced into elementary schools. Hunt was supported in this by Cyril Winn, chief inspector of schools. With his ensemble, Old Music with Old Instruments, he gave concerts in schools around the country so that the children could see and hear the instruments. But although he wanted every child to play the recorder, he fought all his life against the notion that the recorder was just something to play before moving on to a 'real' instrument.

Already teaching flute at Trinity, Hunt started recorder evening classes in 1935, and it was thanks to him that in 1937 Trinity started setting external recorder examinations, the first examination board to do so. In 1938 he was responsible for Trinity establishing the school of old music at Old Devonshire House, Bloomsbury; this was the first early music department in a music college in Europe. It closed at the outbreak of the Second World War, but was revived in 1947 as the department of sixteenth- and seventeenth-century music, with Hunt as head—he taught recorder, baroque flute, and viola da gamba—and Trinity became the first music conservatory in the world to award recorder diplomas.

In 1937 Hunt began to work for Schott & Co., the music publisher. He had been publishing recorder music since 1934, and in 1938 Schotts published the first of many collections of music arranged for recorder by him, *Twelve National Airs* and *Twelve Christmas Carols*. In 1937, with his friends Max and Stephanie Champion, and with Carl Dolmetsch, he founded the Society of Recorder Players. He started, and from 1937 to 1941 co-edited, *Recorder News*, the journal of the society. In the first months of 1940 he produced *Edgar Hunt's Recorder News-Letter*, and broadcast illustrated talks on the recorder. He was also invited to direct the first summer school for recorder players at Downe House, near Newbury, in 1939; these continued until 1960. On 11 June 1938 he had married Elizabeth Willingham Voss (*d*. 1966), daughter of Edward George Voss, an industrial chemist who worked in the oil industry before becoming a schoolmaster; they had one daughter. Elizabeth Voss had founded the quarterly *The Amateur Musician* in 1935, for which Hunt started to write soon after it began, starting a 'Home music supplement' in which he published recorder music.

As the outbreak of the Second World War became imminent, and the supply of cheap wooden recorders from Germany was no longer available, Hunt, in collaboration with Mark Barnes of Barnes and Mullins, began to design plastic recorders. These were manufactured by Schotts throughout the war. From 1941 to 1946 Hunt served in the Royal Artillery in India and was commissioned into the Inter-Services Broadcasting Unit in New Delhi, but after the war he returned to Trinity and to Schotts, where he was in charge of recorder music and recorder marketing, and had a workshop where he tested and repaired Schott recorders. He and Walter Bergmann built up the recorder catalogue and Schotts became the leading publisher of music for the recorder. His many editions included Anthony Holborne's *Pavans, Galliards, and Almans* (1599) arranged for recorder consort, a complete edition of John Dowland's consort music, and the four Handel recorder sonatas. He spent much time in the British Museum discovering a previously unknown repertoire for the recorder. The Society of Recorder Players was revived in 1946, and Hunt was elected chairman; he retired from this position in 1972. In 1948 he was one of the founders of the Recorder in Education Summer School; he was chairman until 1989, having been a tutor every year since the beginning. From 1962 to 1968 he collaborated with Jean Henry in organizing Anglo-French recorder courses, and from 1975 to 1995 he taught at Jean Henry's Rencontres Internationales de Musique Ancienne et Danses du Cour. He also ran courses on Renaissance music and dance at Missenden Abbey for many years.

Although he had first become interested in the recorder as a historical instrument, Hunt also encouraged contemporary composers to write for it. His favourite modern solo work for the recorder was Rubbra's *Meditazioni sopra 'Coeurs désolés'*, commissioned by Dolmetsch at Hunt's suggestion for his Wigmore Hall recital in 1949.

Hunt published *The Recorder and its Music* in 1952. This became the standard work in English, and was revised and updated in 1977. He also edited the *Recorder and Music Magazine* from 1974 until 1991, writing extensively for it, and although he was not a harpsichordist, in 1974 he started and until its demise in 1986 edited the *Harpsichord Magazine* (latterly the *English Harpsichord Magazine*). He wrote tutors for the bass recorder (1974) and the crumhorn (1975), and in 1977 brought out *Robert Lucas Pearsall, 'the compleat gentleman', and his Music* (1795–1856), based on a lifetime's research by his father, Hubert Hunt. He was a founding member of the Galpin Society, started in 1946 to further the study of the history of musical instruments.

Hunt retired from Schotts in 1974, and from Trinity in 1981. Despite his enormous influence on the revival of recorder playing in England he was a modest and unassuming person who preferred to keep out of the limelight, while working quietly behind the scenes. Described by many as the perfect English gentleman, he was good-humoured, tactful, patient, and generous with his time. A dedicated teacher, he wanted to make the recorder and its music available to as many people as possible. He died on 16 March 2006 at Wycombe Hospital, High Wycombe, Buckinghamshire, of bronchopneumonia. He was survived by his daughter, Rosemary. As a tribute Colin Hand wrote *Quartet in Memoriam Edgar Hunt* (2006); a memorial concert was held on 11 November 2006 at the Old Royal Naval College chapel, Greenwich.

ANNE PIMLOTT BAKER

Sources J. M. Thomson, *Recorder profiles* (1972), 36–8 · H. Rutland, *Trinity College of Music: the first hundred years* (1972) · E. Hunt, *The recorder and its music*, 2nd edn (1977), 132–42 · E. O'Kelly, *The recorder today* (1990) · *Recorder Magazine*, 11/1 (March 1991), 15–18; 26/2 (2006), 44–50 · A. Martin, *Musician for a while* (2002) · A. Mayes, *Carl Dolmetsch and the recorder repertoire of the 20th century* (2003) · A. M. Williams, 'The dodo was really a phoenix: the renaissance and revival of the recorder in England, 1879–1941', PhD diss., University of Melbourne, 2005 · private information (2010) · b. cert. · m. cert. · d. cert.

Archives priv. coll.

Likenesses drawing, 1932, repro. in *Recorder Magazine* (March 1988) · photograph, repro. in Thomson, *Profiles* · photograph, repro. in *Recorder Magazine* (2006), 44

Hunt, John Joseph Benedict, Baron Hunt of Tanworth (**1919–2008**), civil servant, was born at Northcote, Queens Road, Minehead, Somerset, on 23 October 1919, the elder son of Lieutenant (later Major) Arthur Lionel Hunt (*d.* 1959), an officer in the Royal Artillery, and his wife, Daphne Winifred, fifth of the six daughters of Captain Henry Ashton-Case. His only sibling, his younger brother, Ronald Francis, died in infancy. His mother's family home was at Beckford Hall, Warwickshire, where the private chapel had been a centre for parish Roman Catholics for over 200 years, and which in 1936 was acquired by the Salesian order as a novitiate.

Education, war service, and first marriage At the age of nine Hunt was sent to Avisford Roman Catholic preparatory school, near Arundel, whence he passed, four years later, to the strict tutelage of the Benedictines at Downside School. He won the school history prize and was president of the debating society. He also played in the school cricket, hockey, rugby, and squash teams. In 1938 he went as an open exhibitioner to read history at Magdalene College, Cambridge, where, after two years, he was awarded a second-class war degree. His extra-curricular activities included college cricket and hockey and membership of the committees of the Cambridge Union Society and the Footlights Club.

John Joseph Benedict Hunt, Baron Hunt of Tanworth (1919–2008), by Bassano, 1971

In common with many undergraduates Hunt joined the Royal Naval Volunteer Reserve on the outbreak of the Second World War and immediately after leaving Cambridge he was deployed on convoy escorts in the western approaches, earning exemplary appraisals for his organization and application. He qualified as a signals officer and in 1944 was transferred to Far Eastern sea duties serving in HMS *Taff* under Lieutenant-Commander Michael Impey, who judged him more suited to a staff job than front-line command. Nevertheless, Hunt's front-line experience included seagoing command at the age of twenty-four and taking the surrender of a Japanese garrison, receiving the general's samurai sword of command. He was released from the Royal Navy in March 1946. Meanwhile, on 16 August 1941, at the Roman Catholic chapel in Hale House (his parents' home) in Churt, Surrey, he married Magdalen Mary Lister Robinson (1921–1971), younger daughter of Roy Lister *Robinson, later Baron Robinson, forester. They had three children: Michael (*b.* 1942), Charlotte (*b.* 1947), and Martin (*b.* 1962).

Ascending the ladder, and second marriage In February 1946 Hunt joined the Dominions Office as a temporary administrative assistant and in April that year he took the administrative grade examination. At first put on a reserve list for successful candidates, by the end of the year he had been offered a permanent position in his first-choice department, the Dominions Office. It was not long before his organizing skills brought an appointment as private secretary to an up-and-coming parliamentary under-secretary, Patrick Gordon-Walker. The appointment proved seminal in that it gave Hunt an early experience of ministerial work (the partition of India and the dispute between India and Pakistan over Kashmir were dominant issues). Hunt also benefited from Gordon-Walker's advice to aim for pivotal postings in the central machine of government. On leaving Gordon-Walker's private office Hunt went as second secretary to the British high commission in Colombo, Ceylon, where he was promoted principal, before returning in 1951 to join the teaching staff of the Imperial Defence College for two years.

It was during a subsequent posting, as first secretary in the British high commission in Ottawa, that Hunt's adaptability in getting things done was spotted by the cabinet secretary, Sir Norman Brook. As a result, in 1956 Hunt found himself in the cabinet office for the first time, as private secretary to Brook. Brook was the secretary of the Egypt committee and one of the few civil servants privy to Anthony Eden's thoughts during the Suez crisis. Nevertheless, Hunt maintained in later life that Brook kept things so close to his chest that his private secretary knew little of what was happening.

After a further short spell in London with the Commonwealth Relations Office, in April 1960 Hunt was back again in the cabinet office, as secretary to the joint intelligence committee. When he left in May 1962 the committee recorded their 'warmest thanks for the magnificent work Mr Hunt had done which had extended well beyond what was normally regarded as the scope of the Secretary, and upon which [the chairman, Sir Hugh Stephenson] had greatly relied' (JIC minutes, 10 May 1962, TNA: PRO, CAB 159/37). Thereafter he spent six years (1962–7) on mainstream economic work at the Treasury.

From 1968 to 1971, as a deputy secretary, Hunt served as first civil service commissioner, responsible for the integrity of fair and open competition for appointment to the civil service. He took particular objection to the Fulton committee's damning judgement on civil service recruitment, believing it to be prejudice without a sound basis of evidence. He defended the civil service commission against the committee's strictures and sought the backing of Sir William Armstrong, the head of the home civil service, asking him to intervene to attempt to redress the balance of view. During this same period he was influential in reducing the archaic class barriers that inhibited the effective use of all civil servants, whatever their social origins. From 1971 to 1972 he was a third secretary in the Treasury, where his duties included chairmanship of the committee charged with running programme analysis and review. He later described this initiative (intended to ensure that departments presented clear statements of objectives before any resources were allocated) as a system which 'created a great deal of work but not much in the way of results' (Plowden, 67), but it convinced him of the need for central initiatives to handle cross-cutting issues, driven by a departmentally neutral body like the cabinet office or the new Central Policy Review Staff (also established in 1971).

In 1971 Magdalen, Hunt's wife of thirty years, died, leaving Hunt to bring up their younger son (then aged nine). He was remarried two years later, at the Carmelite church in Kensington on 15 September 1973, to Madeleine Frances Charles (1919–2007), the widow of Sir John Charles, a former chief medical officer, daughter of Sir William Errington Hume, cardiologist, and sister of Basil Hume (later cardinal and archbishop of Westminster). He became stepfather to her son and daughter.

Cabinet secretary Hunt succeeded Sir Burke Trend as cabinet secretary in October 1973 and remained in post until the end of 1979, serving four prime ministers (Edward Heath, Harold Wilson, James Callaghan, and Margaret Thatcher). It is not known whom Trend had favoured as his successor, nor if he offered advice on the matter. But early in 1972 William Armstrong had commended Hunt to Heath as outstanding among his contemporaries and marked out by 'his personal qualities of drive, energy and leadership. He combines a strong and stable personality with the ability to get on with other people both inside the Service and in public life generally' (W. Armstrong to R. Armstrong, 2 March 1972, cabinet office papers). The result was a further posting (1972–3) as second permanent secretary in the cabinet office and heir apparent to Trend, during which time his managerial drive helped establish two new bodies: a European unit to support ministers in managing the United Kingdom's new membership of the European Communities; and a civil contingencies unit to replace the Home Office emergencies organization, with which Heath had been dissatisfied during the 1972 miners' strike.

The 1970s were years of domestic economic decline, poor industrial relations (known as 'the English disease'), and precarious governments. Internationally it was a time of upheaval in the Middle East and in world economic power as oil price rises triggered recession in the West. In 1976 the government of James Callaghan was forced to seek funds from the International Monetary Fund as the markets lost confidence in sterling, resulting in a public expenditure crisis that threatened to split the cabinet irrevocably. Hunt's great contribution was that he so managed the flow of cabinet business and the advice on handling cabinet members that cabinet government never ceased to function. During the nine cabinet meetings on the loan Hunt passed manuscript notes to Callaghan with advice on handling the participants and keeping the discussion in play to the point where collective responsibility could prevail. At the same time he was working with Sir Kenneth Berrill of the Central Policy Review Staff to prepare a most sensitive doomsday scenario, of which only four copies were made; and he went to Germany on a secret mission for the prime minister to solicit the help of the federal government in securing the necessary financial support to calm the markets.

Internationally Hunt created the 'sherpa' role as the prime minister's personal representative preparing for the biannual economic summits of Western leaders. He maintained a strong relationship with successive American national security advisers, patiently engaging in the diplomacy around the 1974 defence review and later helping Callaghan secure the agreement of Jimmy Carter to supply Trident missiles to upgrade the Polaris deterrent. He worked successfully behind the scenes to preserve the intelligence 'special relationship' between the two countries, while domestically he revived and revitalized oversight of the intelligence agencies on behalf of the prime minister, notably in the aftermath of the United States Watergate scandal.

Constitutionally there were important innovations. The general election of February 1974 produced a hung parliament; this outcome had been foreseen and plans developed accordingly—mainly by Heath's principal private secretary, Robert Armstrong, but with contributions from Hunt on precedents. The incoming Harold Wilson created a policy unit under Bernard Donoughue to work exclusively for him. It was not universally welcomed by permanent secretaries but Hunt wisely set out to implement Wilson's intentions, negotiating a protocol with Donoughue covering the relationship between the new unit and civil servants which smoothed the way forward. A further innovation was preservation of collective responsibility through the cabinet's 'agreement to differ' over the 1975 referendum on whether to remain a member of the European Community, the work being driven by the European unit in the cabinet office, which was led by Sir Patrick Nairne and reported to Hunt. The fourth innovation was the establishment of a constitution unit in the cabinet office to handle the Callaghan government's proposals for devolution of powers to Scotland and Wales. Hunt was himself sceptical of the ideas, being one of the first to point up the 'West Lothian' problem that Scottish and Welsh MPs would continue to have powers to vote on issues that would only concern England (whereas English MPs would lose their powers over similar matters affecting Scotland or Wales).

There were also defeats. Neither Hunt nor ministers were quite ready for the ruthless and single-minded pursuit of its shareholders' interests by the Chrysler Corporation when it sought $32 million of UK government aid and threatened to close its UK operations (which employed 26,000) by the spring of 1976. On another occasion Callaghan took some delight in reading out a letter from Cardinal Hume stressing a moral imperative not to sell armed vehicles to El Salvador—which Hunt had briefed in favour of doing. But the greatest defeat was when Harold Wilson put Hunt forward to prevent the publication of Richard Crossman's diaries, which drove a coach and horses through the then conventional interpretation in Whitehall of cabinet confidentiality. Hunt himself undoubtedly thought that publication would be wrong but he was also the front man for ministers and struggled to convince the lord chief justice, Lord Widgery, of the government's case. Public opinion was shifting towards greater openness about government actions in its name and government was lagging behind. The case to prevent publication was lost, leading to new rules of behaviour about ministerial memoirs, including a fifteen-year moratorium before revealing cabinet discussions.

Contemporaries spoke with reverence of Hunt's skill at chairing meetings. A fellow permanent secretary described it as knowing where he wanted to get to—and getting there. He captured the essence of his approach in a short guide, 'The dos and don'ts of chairmanship', published in the civil service journal, *Management Services in Government*, in 1977. He was made a CB in 1968, knighted KCB in 1973, and promoted GCB in 1977. He was made a life peer, as Baron Hunt of Tanworth, in 1980.

Retirement and character In retirement Hunt was greatly in demand. His directorships included the Prudential Corporation (of which he was chairman from 1985 to 1990), IBM (UK) Ltd, and the UK arm of the Banque Nationale de Paris (of which he was chairman from 1980 to 1997). In 1982 a committee under his leadership produced an influential and notably liberal report supporting the widespread expansion of cable broadcasting. He was chairman of the House of Lords subcommittee on European trade and industry in 1992–5 when it investigated fraud in the European Union; the subcommittee's report, published in 1994, estimated the cost of such fraud at £5 billion a year. Other chairmanships included the Disasters Emergency Committee (1981–9), the Ditchley Foundation (1983–91), and the European Policy Forum (1992–8). But perhaps the achievement he was most proud of was his chairmanship (from 1984 to 1996) of the trust that published *The Tablet*, and his oversight of the financial rescue of that publication.

The dominant influence in Hunt's life was his Roman Catholic faith. In later life he carried with him a prayer by Cardinal Newman which begins: 'God has created me to do Him some definite service'. To colleagues he was unfailingly courteous and often kind, though at first sight he could appear forbidding and unapproachable. He was supremely able to compartmentalize the formidable array of issues crossing his desk. He had the gift of making younger colleagues feel that there was no one else he would rather be speaking to at the time. By contrast, some senior colleagues never felt that they got close to him, but as one of them said, 'He made the Cabinet Office into a real Department' (private information).

Hunt died on 17 July 2008 at his home, 8 Wool Road, Wimbledon, of cancer. A requiem mass was held in Westminster Cathedral on 29 October. He was survived by his two sons and his two stepchildren, his daughter having predeceased him in 1995. IAN BEESLEY

Sources C. R. Elrington, ed., *History of the county of Gloucestershire*, 8 (1968) • J. J. B. Hunt, lecture to RCDS, 1979 • J. J. B. Hunt, 'Reflections', lecture to Sunningdale Conference, 1983 • W. Plowden, ed., *Advising the rulers* (1987) • P. Hennessy, *Whitehall* (1989) • *Patrick Gordon Walker: political diaries, 1932–1971*, ed. R. Pearce (1991) • R. Chapman, *The Civil Service Commission, 1855–1991* (2004) • B. Donoughue, *Downing Street diary* (2006) • *The Times* (18 July 2008); (22 July 2008); (24 July 2008); (29 July 2008) • *Daily Telegraph* (18 July 2008) • *The Guardian* (18 July 2008) • *The Independent* (21 July 2008); (24 July 2008) • I. Beesley, 'Governing the ungovernable', PhD diss., U. Lond. • TNA: PRO, CAB PREM T and BA series • Civil service commission application, cabinet office • *Royal Navy Record* • Burke, *Peerage* • *WW* (2008) • personal knowledge (2012) • private information (2012) [family] • b. cert. • m. certs. • d. cert.

Archives SOUND BL NSA, current affairs and documentary recordings
Likenesses Bassano, half-plate film negative, 1971, NPG [*see illus.*] · photograph, *c.*1975, repro. in Hennessy, *Whitehall* · J. Stanton Ward, group portrait, oils, 1984, NPG · group portrait, photograph, 1988, PA Photos, London · N. Sinclair, bromide print, 1992, NPG · group portrait, photograph, 1998, Photoshot, London · obituary photographs
Wealth at death £930,903: probate, 11 Sept 2009, *CGPLA Eng. & Wales*

Hunter, George Kirkpatrick (1920–2008), literary scholar, was born at 77 Cuthbertson Street, Govanhill, a tenement district of Glasgow, on 7 October 1920, the only child of Samuel George Hunter, a journeyman electrician, and his wife, Mary Scott, *née* Currie. He developed both his love of books and his prodigious memory early. At elementary school in Cupar, Fife, given the run of the minister's library, he devoured the works of Sir Walter Scott from *Waverley* to *Woodstock*. On holidays in Moniaive, when his grandfather, the village schoolmaster, rashly challenged him to a wager designed to keep the over-talkative lad quiet, he flummoxed the old man and pocketed a schoolboy-sized fortune by learning psalms off by heart at sixpence each. Winning a bursary to Allen Glen's School, a science- and engineering-focused selective secondary school where his education was grounded (also) in the classics, he proceeded to Glasgow University in 1936 to read English literature. The importance of philosophy in the syllabus there gave him a breadth of reading unknown to most English humanities undergraduates, and shaped his understanding of what should constitute a university education.

Pre-empting call-up, and instead of starting his final year at university (though still having earned a university degree), Hunter joined the Royal Navy in 1939 and, assigned to convoy duties aboard HMS *Ulster Queen* in the Baltic, taught himself basic Russian so that he could serve as an interpreter. Later he trained as a code breaker in Japanese at Bletchley Park and was posted to Ceylon in 1944. He was reassigned, after Japan's surrender in August 1945, to Hong Kong as interpreter for a war crimes tribunal.

On demobilization in 1946 Hunter enrolled at Balliol College, Oxford, where he was awarded a DPhil in 1950 for a thesis whose title—'A comparison of the use of the sententia, considered as a typical rhetorical ornament, in the tragedies of Seneca, and in those of Gascoigne, Kyd, Heywood, Jonson, Marston, Dekker, Webster and Greville'—could serve as an epitome of his work in Renaissance studies, signalling its attention to the classical tradition's survival in early modernity, to language, rhetoric, cultural inheritance, comparativism, and, always, aesthetic effect, what the writing meant to the reader. Indeed the title signalled something more: that for Hunter no Elizabethan writer would be 'obscure', would forgo his attention. It was at Oxford that he met Shelagh Kathleen Edmunds (*b.* 1924), later a distinguished Victorianist (daughter of Christopher Montague Edmunds, principal of Birmingham School of Music); they married at the parish church in Solihull, Warwickshire, on 16 December 1950. Theirs was a partnership based as much on intellectual as domestic productivity, hers the editorial eye that had to be satisfied before anything he wrote was finished. They had three children, Mary, Andrew, and Ruth, who remembered lives full of books and conversation, and a father, passionate about football, theatre, family singsongs, and games, who regularly trounced them at Scrabble by putting vowel-less Anglo-Saxonisms on the board.

Hunter had in 1948, even before completing his DPhil thesis, been appointed an assistant lecturer at University College, Hull; this was converted to a full lectureship in 1950. Appointments followed at Reading (1955–8), where he worked alongside Frank Kermode and J. B. Trapp developing a programme of comparative Renaissance studies in the English department, and at Liverpool (1958–64), where Kenneth Muir was collecting a group of brilliant Shakespeareans. Hunter's first major publication, a superb *All's Well That Ends Well* (1959) for Arden Shakespeare, distinguished him as a meticulous editor, interested in the play's textual problems, but equally theatre-savvy, paying shrewd attention to what interested him as much: its performance possibilities. In 1962 appeared *John Lyly: the Humanist as Courtier*. Wry, witty, immensely learned, and positioning itself 'as part of the unceasing tug-of-war by which opinion comes to feel like understanding' (foreword, viii), this book effected a radical paradigm shift, establishing humanism (not, as C. S. Lewis had argued, medieval anti-secularism) as the defining Renaissance habit of mind.

In 1964 Hunter was among those pioneering academics recruited to the government's policy of expanding opportunity with the founding of seven new universities. Offered a professorship at the University of Warwick and free rein to develop the curriculum, he created a department of English and comparative literary studies that was socially diverse and based on an innovative programme that saw the European epic (from Homer to Milton) as its foundation and Shakespeare (taught as a jobbing playwright, writing for performance) as its climax. He head-hunted the brightest and best: among them Bernard Bergonzi, Claude Rawson (with whom he edited the *Modern Language Review*), William Righter, and Germaine Greer. On a bulldozer-scarred campus under construction that looked more like Wilfred Owen's Somme than Blake's New Jerusalem, he built a department on intellectual excitement: engaged not just in reading literature but in imagining what a university could be.

Hunter crossed the Atlantic in 1976, leaving Warwick for Yale, as a professor of English. Landing there in the middle of the 'deconstruction wars', this once-radical humanist found himself cast, ironically, as a reactionary in battles between 'tradition' and 'theory'. Disenchanted with the academic posturing of both sides, in 1985 he accepted the chairmanship of the PhD programme in Renaissance studies, an appointment he found challenging and rewarding. Given more time for writing, he brought to completion the Oxford History of English Literature, a series begun in 1935, producing the final volume, *English Drama, 1586–1642* (1997). At Yale, Hunter was appointed

Emily Sanford professor of English in 1987, and elected a fellow of the American Academy of Arts and Sciences (1978) and a corresponding fellow of the British Academy (1988). He nevertheless remained thoroughly unpretentious, and unimpressed by status and honours; on the occasion of Shakespeare's quatercentenary in 1964 his seven-year-old son Andrew had recorded in his school diary that 'This morning my Mum and Dad had an invitation to tea with the Queen. They are not going as Dad says it will be ded boring' (Rawson, 2).

Hunter's brilliance as a teacher and a scholar was an ability to ask disarmingly simple questions, such as wondering what the theatrical purpose of Othello's blackness might have been, that, answered, conducted students on astonishing journeys through history and myth, across maps, looking at etymology, demographics, visual and print culture, Elizabethan playhouse practice, all brought to focus on close readings of the text. His essays, collected in *Dramatic Identities and Cultural Tradition* (1978), demonstrate a mind scaled to Falstaff's girth. Properly combative, suffering no fool gladly, Hunter disdained academic cant and pretence (though the acerbity of his wit cutting some young Turk down to size was mollified by the voice, the burr of the Glasgow accent that never abandoned him). He taught students that the values and humanity that are expressed in great literature are worth fighting for.

Hunter retired in 1991, and (having lived since 1976 in New Haven) in 2007, with his wife, Shelagh, moved to Topsham, Maine, where he died after complications arising from Alzheimer's on 10 April 2008. He was cremated at Gracelawn Memorial Park, Auburn, Maine. Memorial services were held on 12 May 2008 at St Martins-in-the-Field Church, Finham, Coventry, and on 13 September 2008 at Davenport College, Yale University. His wife and their three children survived him.

CAROL CHILLINGTON RUTTER

Sources C. Rawson, 'George Hunter: a personal memoir', *The arts of performance in Elizabethan and early Stuart drama: essays for G. K. Hunter*, ed. M. Biggs and others (1991), 1–15 · 'In memoriam: George K. Hunter, Shakespeare scholar', 18 April 2008, opac.yale.edu/news/article.aspx?id=2260, 1 July 2011 · *The Independent* (21 April 2008) · *The Guardian* (23 April 2008) · *The Times* (2 May 2008) · *Balliol College Register* · personal knowledge (2012) · private information (2012) · b. cert. · m. cert.

Archives U. Birm. L., special collections, corresp. relating to *English drama, 1586–1642*

Likenesses obituary photographs

Hunter, Muir Vane Skerrett (1913–2008), barrister, was born on 19 August 1913 at 1 The Park, Mitcham, Surrey, the son of Hugh Stewart Hunter, civil servant, and his wife, Matilda Angela Antonia, *née* Williams (1878–1960), novelist (as George Lancing, Basil Hunter, and Bluebell M. Hunter). He was educated at Westminster School and Christ Church, Oxford, where he read *literae humaniores*. After graduating with a second-class degree in 1936, he accompanied his mother to China to research materials for a book she was writing on the empress Tzu Hsi. On his return home in 1937 he travelled to Spain to help evacuate children endangered as a result of the civil war. He was also selected as prospective Labour candidate for East Hampshire, though he never stood. Meanwhile he chose to pursue a legal career and was called to the bar by Gray's Inn in 1938. On 29 July 1939 he married Dorothy, otherwise Dorothea Eason, Verstone (1909–1986), daughter of Philip Eason Verstone, journalist. They had one daughter. Hunter was called up in 1940. He joined the Royal Armoured Corps, in which he rose to the rank of acting lieutenant-colonel, serving latterly in India as a military judge. In 1946 he returned to England to practice at the bar. In 1949 he was appointed standing counsel (bankruptcy) to the Board of Trade. He retained this position until he took silk in 1965.

Hunter appeared in more than 100 reported cases during his career at the bar. His most famous case concerned the bankruptcy of the corrupt architect John Poulson. Poulson had built up a substantial architectural practice in the 1950s and 1960s, but he became insolvent and was made bankrupt in 1972. The principal method of investigating the affairs of a bankrupt at that time was at his examination in public before the court. Hunter was instructed to conduct Poulson's examination by Poulson's trustee in bankruptcy, acting for the creditors. He was a tenacious cross-examiner with an eye for financial detail. Assisted by his junior, David Graham, he cross-examined Poulson in public on ten occasions over an eleven-month period in 1972–3 in the Wakefield county court. The hearings were attended by considerable publicity and public interest. As a result of the bankruptcy and of Hunter's cross-examination of Poulson there was a very substantial recovery for creditors. But on the wider stage Hunter's cross-examination exposed the extent of Poulson's corruption, and the bankruptcy led to a raft of criminal prosecutions of public figures and civil servants. Over twenty people were convicted, including Poulson himself, T. Dan Smith, Andrew Cunningham, and George Pottinger, all of whom received substantial custodial sentences. The Poulson prosecution has been described as the biggest corruption trial of the twentieth century. There was also one notable resignation of a senior politician, not attended by a prosecution. Reginald Maudling had to resign as home secretary in July 1972. He was cross-examined by Hunter in private before the bankruptcy court in July 1973. It was, perhaps, the only time in the Poulson bankruptcy proceedings when Hunter met his match. The Poulson bankruptcy also led directly or indirectly to three separate public inquiries, the departmental committee on local government rules of conduct, chaired by Lord Redcliffe-Maud, the royal commission on standards of conduct in public life, chaired by Lord Salmon, and a House of Commons select committee on the conduct of MPs who were involved in the Poulson affair.

Hunter was a principal contributor to all the leading bankruptcy and insolvency textbooks of the day. The title of the principal work on bankruptcy, *Williams on Bankruptcy*, was changed to *Williams and Muir Hunter on Bankruptcy* in 1979 to recognize Hunter's enormous contribution to the subject. From 1987 he was senior editor of *Muir Hunter on Personal Insolvency*. He was also a leading member of the EEC bankruptcy advisory committee (1973–6) and the Insolvency Law Review Committee (1977–82). The recommendations of these committees transformed insolvency law and practice in the UK and led to insolvency becoming a mainstream legal subject.

Hunter had extremely wide interests outside his practice at the bar. He was a founder of the North Kensington Neighbourhood Law Centre in 1969. He was an Amnesty International Court of Justice observer at human rights trials in Burundi in 1962, Rhodesia in 1969, and Turkey in 1972. He was a governor of the Royal Shakespeare Theatre between 1964 and 1983 and thereafter an honorary life governor. His poems were published in *Tears in the Fence* (1994) and *The Grain of My Life* (1997). He was chairman of Polish Hospices Fund between 1989 and 2002. In 1997 he was appointed a visiting professor in insolvency law at the University of Bournemouth, where he received an honorary LLD degree in 2000. He also became a visiting professor at the University of Kingston in 2007. The Muir Hunter Museum of Bankruptcy at the University of Kingston was named after him.

Following the death of his first wife, on 4 July 1986 Hunter married Gillian Victoria Joyce (*b.* 1929), company director and charity administrator, daughter of Alfred Alexander Webster Petrie, medical practitioner, and former wife of Ian W. Mountain. He died at his home, Hunterston, Barkers Hill, Donhead St Andrew, Wiltshire, on 18 October 2008, of cancer, and was survived by her and his daughter, Camilla. MICHAEL CRYSTAL

Sources L. Baston, *Reggie: the life of Reginald Maudling* (2004) • *Daily Telegraph* (23 Oct 2008) • *The Times* (27 Oct 2008) • *Yorkshire Post* (1 Nov 2008) • *The Guardian* (26 Nov 2008) • University of Kingston, Muir Hunter Museum of Bankruptcy, archives • *WW* (2008) • personal knowledge (2012) • private information (2012) • b. cert. • m. certs. • d. cert.

Archives University of Kingston, Muir Hunter Museum of Bankruptcy

Likenesses photograph, 1970, Photoshot, London • obituary photographs

Wealth at death £173,998: probate, 15 April 2009, *CGPLA Eng. & Wales*

Hurley, Susan Lynn (1954–2007), philosopher, was born in New York City on 16 September 1954, the daughter of Roy Hurley, an aeronautical industry executive, and his wife, Esther, a first-generation Armenian immigrant, who was a secretary. Her parents moved shortly afterwards to Santa Barbara, California. She had a younger brother, Jim. Although she never lived in Santa Barbara again after graduating from Marymount Convent School, this prosperous and pleasant town on the Pacific coast exerted a strong tug on her emotions for the rest of her life. This was due not just to the presence of her family; she also felt that in leaving first for the east coast and then for Europe she had run the risk of choosing a life of rational reflection rather than of the emotions and the senses. Ever afterwards the tuberoses and lotuses of California beckoned all the more persuasively when philosophy in the Oxford style—linguistically focused, highly cerebral, sometimes incapable of seeing the trees for the twigs—seemed just too unrewardingly hard. Colleagues who felt the cold grey skies of Britain were somehow the right setting for philosophy could feel enviously disapproving of her gravitation towards sunshine, fragrance, and an absolute reverence of the aesthetics of flowers and cats. Others found her incomprehension of the English puritan style of academic life a revelation.

After undergraduate studies at Princeton, Hurley went to St Catherine's College, Oxford, where she graduated BPhil in philosophy in 1979 and began a complex and lifelong attachment to Oxford—to the city, the university, the idea; but after the BPhil she returned to the USA to go to Harvard law school, which she claimed to have hated, though her legal studies were to exercise a powerful influence on her approach to philosophy. (She was eventually awarded the degree of JD *cum laude* in 1988.) Searching for a way to return to the Oxford that had so charmed her, she caused something of a sensation when in 1981 she was elected as the first woman fellow of All Souls College. This event provoked an avalanche of press comment and even a request (for she was as beautiful as she was clever) for a photo spread in *Vogue*, a request she declined. Fears on the part of some more traditional fellows that civilization as they knew it was now under threat were finessed with a mixture of diplomacy, charm, and firm conviction, and she remained a popular and loyal member of the college community for the rest of her life. However, she did not remain a full-time fellow, and (having completed her DPhil in 1983 with a thesis entitled 'Practical reason: deliberation, coherence, disagreement') took up successively a tutorial fellowship at St Edmund Hall from 1985, a professorship in the department of politics and international studies at the University of Warwick from 1994, and a chair in the department of philosophy at the University of Bristol from 2006 until her death. She was offered chairs at Harvard, the University of California at Riverside, and elsewhere, but declined primarily for family reasons: in 1986 she had married (John) Nicholas Pepys Rawlins (*b.* 1949), neuroscientist and later Watts professor of psychology at Oxford, and they had two sons, Alasdair (*b.* 1989) and Merryn (*b.* 1994).

Hurley made her philosophical reputation with *Natural Reasons*, published in 1989. This was a remarkable and ambitiously cross-disciplinary work that sought to undermine fashionable notions about the metaphysical shakiness of moral values with an appeal to material from law and economics as well as from traditional metaphysics and moral philosophy; it is a tribute in part to her quiet influence that such notions were less straightforwardly fashionable by the time of her death. Two later books, *Consciousness in Action* (1998) and *Justice, Luck and Knowledge* (2003), tackled other large themes in a similarly bold way. *Consciousness in Action* disposed convincingly of a version of the dominant Cartesian picture of the conscious mind as situated in some kind of observatory distinct from the world it observes, as having beliefs and desires about that world, and seeking to influence it by the psychic equivalent of pulleys and levers. Consciousness for her was embodied in a quite literal sense in the physical universe ('the mind goes all the way out into the world', as she liked to say), and there simply was no set of facts about someone's inner life that could be straightforwardly separated from what they said and how they behaved. *Justice, Luck and Knowledge* drew far-reaching consequences from this philosophy of mind for questions of personal and political responsibility of the individual in the world. Common to all three works was a rejection of such tidy dualisms as the fact-value distinction and the distinction between the mind and the world it observes. These dualisms, she felt, often failed to do justice to the sheer messiness of the challenges to human understanding posed by a world whose complexity outruns the concepts applied to it.

Hurley was diagnosed with breast cancer in her early forties and opted for aggressive chemotherapy that earned her remission for a decade. She died at her home, 13 St Margaret's Road, Oxford, on 16 August 2007 of secondary tumours in the bones and liver. She was survived by her husband and their two sons. A casket containing some of her ashes was placed facing the Pacific Ocean in the Santa Barbara cemetery; other portions of her ashes were buried in Kauai, Hawaii, Moorea, French Polynesia, and Zermatt, Switzerland, places she and her family greatly loved. PAUL SEABRIGHT

Sources www.bristol.ac.uk/news/2007/5587.html, 28 July 2010 · *The Times* (6 Sept 2007) · *The Guardian* (14 Sept 2007) · *Princeton Alumni Weekly* (24 Sept 2008) · www.bristol.ac.uk/philosophy/hurley/papers/cv.rtf, 28 July 2010 · personal knowledge (2011) · private information (2011) · d. cert.

Likenesses obituary photographs · photograph, repro. in www.bristol.ac.uk/philosophy/hurley_html/

Wealth at death £26,146: probate, 27 Oct 2009, *CGPLA Eng. & Wales*

Hussey, Joan Mervyn (1907–2006), Byzantine scholar, was born on 5 June 1907 at 35 Avenue Road, Trowbridge, Wiltshire, the daughter of William Hussey, master plumber and house decorator, and his wife, Grace Mildred, *née* Sawyer. She was taught privately at home and at Trowbridge High School for Girls. Her education expanded at the Lycée Victor Duruy, Paris, and she read history at St Hugh's College, Oxford, graduating with a second-class degree in 1929. Her postgraduate research was first encouraged by (William) David Ross, the provost of Oriel College, in classical moral philosophy, but her London PhD thesis of 1935 was supervised by Norman H. Baynes, whom she regarded as her prime mentor. She developed it into her first book, *Church and Learning in the Byzantine Empire, 867–1185* (1937). Religion and scholarship in the Byzantine empire remained her central research concerns. She accumulated skills in teaching and placing students and staff in what she conceived their most appropriate context; though always a very private person she was a formidable networker.

After an international travelling fellowship of the Federation of University Women in 1934, a Pfeiffer research fellowship at Girton College, Cambridge, took Hussey to work with Franz Dölger in Munich on the eleventh-century rhetorician John Mavropous and manuscripts in Vienna, the Vatican, and the monastery of St Stephen in

Joan Mervyn Hussey (1907–2006), by unknown photographer

the Meteora. Formidable she may have been, but the common story that the monks of Mount Athos, forbidden to women, would lower manuscripts to Hussey in a boat below, is certainly apocryphal. Hussey passed on her further research on the challenging Byzantine mystic St Symeon the New Theologian (949–1022) to Archbishop Basil Krivocheine, who published it, with others, from 1980. In Britain she was appointed assistant lecturer at the University of Manchester in 1937 and from 1943 lecturer and then from 1947 reader at Bedford College, London. From 1950 she was professor of history at Royal Holloway College, London, where she remained head of department until her nominal retirement in 1974.

Besides her own lucid textbook, *The Byzantine World* (1957), and her substantial *The Orthodox Church in the Byzantine Empire* (1986), Hussey promoted the teaching of her subject at many levels in the English-reading world, translating George Ostrogorsky's standard *History of the Byzantine State* (1956), which, as he recognized, became better known than his original German version. As a chief examiner of the Cambridge local examination board Hussey had much experience of developing syllabuses for schools and universities in Malaysia and Africa (especially Uganda and the Sudan). She took on from Norman Baynes the editing of two fresh Byzantine volumes of *The Cambridge Medieval History* (1966–7) and was a convenor of the thirteenth International Byzantine Congress held in Oxford in 1966 and co-editor (with Dimitri Obolensky and Steven Runciman) of its proceedings. This numerous polyglot assembly brought Hussey's scholarly network to life. Her contacts were deep but discrete. Few of her London students were aware that she was also an honorary fellow of St Hugh's College, Oxford, and of the Sicilian Institute for Byzantine Studies. She was welcome in Belgrade, East Berlin, Beirut, and particularly Prague, where she supported the revived journal *Byzantinoslavica* and a cultural exchange programme at a time when it was not politically conventional.

After her 'retirement' Hussey took on the editing of the

papers of the historian George Finlay (1799–1874), companion of Byron, held at the British School at Athens, as *The Finlay Papers: a Catalogue* (1973) and two volumes of *The Journals and Letters of George Finlay* (1995). She did much of this work on the island of Naxos, in a house below the historic Roman Catholic cathedral on the acropolis. She was received into the Roman Catholic church by the noted Jesuit theologian John Coventry—yet another surprise to many, when revealed at her funeral. In 1988 she was presented with a Festschrift, entitled *Kathegetria* ('Lady Professor'), edited by a former student, Julian Chrysostomides. She died at Merlewood nursing home, Virginia Water, Surrey, on 20 February 2006, of bronchopneumonia. She never married and had no children.

ANTHONY BRYER

Sources J. Chrysostomides, foreword, *Kathegetria: essays presented to Joan Hussey for her 80th birthday* (1988), 7–9 · *The Independent* (17 March 2006) · *The Times* (30 March 2006) · *SALON*, 136 (2006), www.sal.org.uk · *WW* (2006) · personal knowledge (2010) · private information (2010) · b. cert. · d. cert.

Likenesses photograph, repro. in *Kathegetria*, frontispiece [*see illus.*]

Wealth at death £1,156,849: probate, 1 Nov 2006, *CGPLA Eng. & Wales*

Marmaduke James [Duke] **Hussey, Baron Hussey of North Bradley (1923–2006)**, by Gemma Levine, 1985

Hussey, Marmaduke James [Duke], **Baron Hussey of North Bradley (1923–2006)**, newspaper and broadcasting executive, was born at Lychwood, Worplesdon Hill, Woking, Surrey, on 29 August 1923, the only son and elder child of Eric Robert James *Hussey (1885–1958), then a Sudan colonial servant, later director of education in Uganda and Nigeria, and his wife, Christine Elizabeth Justice, *née* Morley (1892–1977). He was educated at Rugby School, from where he gained an open scholarship to Trinity College, Oxford. Surrounded by sportsmen on both sides of the family, he too excelled. At Rugby he was in both the cricket eleven and the rugby fifteen. At Oxford he won a cricket blue as a left-arm slow bowler in 1942, and that autumn was selected for the varsity rugby match. However, since he was due to report to the Grenadier Guards the following Monday, he decided not to risk any delay, and so sacrificed—as he put it—'my life's ambition to play … against Cambridge' (*Chance Governs All*, 27).

Anzio and early career in newspaper publishing Hussey deemed the most critical impact on his life the five-year struggle to recover from fearful wounds suffered four days after the allied landing at Anzio, Italy, in January 1944. For forty years he reproached himself for his short war, but later was persuaded that the story might inspire. Machine-gunned at close range, hit in the right hand, right leg, and spine, he had his right leg amputated below the knee at a German field station. In great pain, he was transferred to Rome, then by hospital train northwards. His life's turning point came when he fought off the temptation to sleep. 'I knew I could conquer this, whatever it was, the belief never left me' (*Chance Governs All*, 44). That self-belief was tested repeatedly. From a prisoner-of-war hospital near Fulda, where the nuns were so certain he would not survive they added his name to those who died there, he was one of a handful repatriated in wartime by the Red Cross. Once he was back in Britain the ensuing five years saw treatment and surgery to the unhealed spinal wound, which had turned to the then incurable osteomyelitis. Finally an unorthodox operation at the Radcliffe Infirmary in Oxford produced a healing, though leaving him permanently crippled. For the rest of his life Hussey, with his cane and distinctive gait, publicly made light of his suffering, appearing invariably ebullient, with a hearty laugh. Back at Oxford in 1946, sport now only a memory, he resumed his history studies and in 1949 completed his final BA paper with distinction—although he did not get the first he had earlier hoped for.

On leaving Oxford in 1949 Hussey joined Associated Newspapers Ltd as a trainee. He started at the bottom—in the advertising department of the *Daily Mail* as a copy clerk—and finished at the top. He described his approach thus: 'I like a ladder to climb as fast as I can, not worrying too much on whom I step on the way up' (*Chance Governs All*, 74). A protégé of the owner, Esmond Harmsworth, second Viscount Rothermere, he climbed steadily: manager of the *Evening News*, manager of the *Scottish Daily Mail* (which he closed), director in 1964, and managing director in 1967. He knew more about newspaper production than journalism but he took credit for recruiting David English in 1969 from the *Daily Express* to be editor of the *Daily Sketch*, and eventually editor of the *Daily Mail*. Meanwhile, on 25 April 1959, in Bath Abbey, he married Lady Susan Katharine Waldegrave (*b.* 1939), fifth daughter of Geoffrey Noel Waldegrave, twelfth Earl Waldegrave. They had one son and one daughter. Lady Susan Hussey was a lady-in-waiting to the queen from 1960.

Showdown at Times Newspapers During his time at Associated, Hussey, with responsibility for labour relations, had become spokesman for the Newspaper Proprietors Association, where he first made Rupert Murdoch's acquaintance. At the association he learned much both of the unions' obduracy in defending their ruinously expensive restrictive practices, and of the owners' fecklessness in taking advantage of any rival title with union trouble rather than standing together. Both were to colour his approach to the eventual showdown at Times Newspapers Ltd (TNL), into which *The Times*, a chronic loss-maker, had been merged in 1966 with the Thomson-owned money-spinning *Sunday Times*. Hussey joined TNL in 1971, at the point when Roy Thomson, first Baron Thomson of Fleet, notwithstanding his 'open-ended' commitments to *The Times*, was expecting its losses to be trimmed to at least break-even point. Hussey was appointed chief executive in place of Thomson's lieutenant, Sir Denis Hamilton, who assumed the lesser job of chairman. The two men never got on. Hussey was also rarely comfortable with Gordon Brunton, the parent Thomson Organisation's chief executive, and this was fateful. It was a calamity for Hussey that Hamilton and Brunton had already initiated moving *The Times* from Blackfriars into a building next door to the *Sunday Times* on Gray's Inn Road. The aim was integration but its unintended consequence was that the ruinous malpractices of the latter's mostly casual labour force—whose disruption was such that the paper was dubbed the *Sunday Sometimes*—were to infect the whole operation. Also a setback for Hussey was the death in 1976 of Roy Thomson and his succession by his son Kenneth, whose interests always were more in Canada, and who made clear that his own commitment not to sell *The Times* was dependent on the introduction of the new computer typesetting technology by the end of that decade.

Hussey's approach to the unending labour problems was to act like an officer dealing with good NCOs. The trouble in this case, as with much of the then turbulent industrial relations besetting the Heath, Wilson, and Callaghan governments, was that the NCOs, the union general secretaries, might mean well but had mostly lost control of the more militant shop stewards. In print unions these were the branch officials known as 'chapel fathers', and Hussey had to deal with fifty-six separate bargaining units at TNL. The accusation that he ignored the chapels is not the whole truth; his plan was to get the general secretaries on his side in the hope that they could help restore union discipline, and then proceed to dot the *i*s and cross the *t*s with each chapel father. In the event he could hardly have done worse had he proceeded the other way round, and he might have done better.

The crunch came in 1978, with the Thomson interests prospering in North Sea oil, television, and travel, but haemorrhaging in TNL. Unofficial stoppages cost the group 7,337,000 copies overall in 1977. In the new year's first three months there were twenty-nine failures to complete the print run of *The Times*, and nine on the Sunday. At a TNL executive board meeting on 16 March chaired by Hussey, with William Rees-Mogg, editor of *The Times*, as his fellow 'hawk', there was a unanimous decision to go for the 'big bang', a shutdown if the unions failed to agree wholesale reforms by 30 November.

> Basically, if we were going to have a row we might as well have a bloody big row and throw in the kitchen sink … Yes I did feel a sense of mission in attacking what I saw as the canker of irresponsible trades union activity at the heart of the industry, and, indeed, the country. (*Chance Governs All*, 148)

Brunton, he reported, was 'absolutely delighted' (ibid.). However, little thought had been given to practicalities. Not until October did TNL's management produce detailed proposals for negotiation, and the November deadline arrived with only two chapels having reached agreement. Despite much attempted negotiation the general secretaries predictably failed to deliver. Hussey lamented later that 'I placed too much faith in those printing princes' (ibid., 154). Both papers and all supplements closed, a shutout if not a complete lockout (Hussey later incorrectly labelled it 'a strike'; ibid., 159). The trial of strength was on but there had been a miscalculation of the balance of forces. The unions proved to have alternative resources. Many of the sacked workers were opportunistically re-employed at other titles like *The Observer*, *The Guardian*, and the *Financial Times*, which put on extra pages and even sections. 'Almost magically, an industry that was already notoriously over-manned absorbed the staff of *The Times* and the *Sunday Times* as it came off the company's payroll' (Jacobs, 72).

To break the deadlock Michael Mander, whom Hussey had brought from Associated as advertising director, got the board to agree to a secret scheme to outflank the unions, involving printing abroad and selling round the world a weekly edition of *The Times*. Rees-Mogg was a fervent supporter. Timed for the eve of the British general election, the first edition, written by journalists who remained on the payroll, was to be computer-set in Darmstadt and printed in Frankfurt at a Turkish-owned plant. Alerted by the London unions at the last minute, German pickets and agitators demonstrated outside the plant. After petrol-soaked material was found in an apparent bid to sabotage the main presses the police advised that with the May day holiday imminent they could no longer guarantee the safety of the operation. The full print run of 80,000 was abandoned, though 10,000 copies with the date of 30 April 1979 were run off and distributed around the world. That feat of eluding pickets, albeit with a limited edition, convinced Hussey, supported by Rees-Mogg and his deputies at *The Times*, that they at last had the unions on the ropes. But even ahead of Frankfurt there had been some wobbling by Brunton, Hamilton, and Harry Evans, editor of the *Sunday Times*. They wanted contacts with the chapels, which Hussey saw as a stab in the back. Treating Frankfurt as a fiasco rather than a partial success, Brunton now reversed his approval and, seeking compromise, ordered no more international adventures. To Hussey this 'robbed us of what was our strongest card' (*Chance Governs All*, 164).

Hussey was even more dismayed when he got wind that Ken Thomson was also giving up, 'not prepared to foot the bill any longer' (Grigg, 491). Thomson came over in June and met the unions. With Hussey cut out of the negotiations, the final surrender still took another five months. Publication resumed on 13 November 1979, virtually on the chapels' terms, or terms they had no intention of implementing, after total TNL losses of £46 million. By the following summer Hussey was moved out and given the non-job, under Hamilton, of vice-chairman of a new TNL holding company. Suddenly, viewing the *Times* journalists' strike over pay as the last straw, Ken Thomson had had enough; in 1981 he put the papers up for sale, and they were bought by Rupert Murdoch. Significantly Murdoch cleaned out the TNL management but retained the holding company board with Hussey as consultant. Although not involved in Murdoch's successful showdown with the unions at Wapping in 1986, Hussey took some credit for advice he gave the new owner. Rees-Mogg later asserted that Hussey's defeat was Dunkirk to Murdoch's D-day.

Turmoil at the BBC By September 1986 Hussey was mixing various business chairmanships and directorships with good works: he was, among other things, a Rhodes trustee from 1972 to 1991, a member of the board of the British Council from 1983 to 1996, a member of the government working party on artificial limbs and appliance centres in England from 1984 to 1986, chairman of the Royal Marsden Hospital from 1985 to 1998, and in 1985–6 joint chairman of Great Western local radio in Bristol. On the death of Stuart Young, the BBC chairman, he was asked by the head of Margaret Thatcher's number 10 policy unit, Brian Griffiths, to suggest some candidates to replace Young. When they conferred Griffiths threw out that his wife, Rachel, had suggested Hussey do it, but Hussey laughed it off. In fact Griffiths was serious; he discreetly gained Denis Thatcher's approval, and that of the former home secretary William Whitelaw, and moved Hussey to the top of the list. By some Hussey was seen as an old-fashioned Liberal, but by others as a Thatcherite who would stand up to BBC management the way Murdoch had stood up to the unions at Wapping. Hussey was duly phoned by Douglas Hurd, the home secretary, offering the chairmanship, and further persuasion was added by William Waldegrave, a junior minister and Hussey's brother-in-law.

Even before getting to Broadcasting House (he had to check the address in the telephone directory) Hussey judged the corporation to be 'out of control with some pretty unreliable characters there' (*Chance Governs All*, 193). A state of war was reckoned to exist between management and the governors, with Alasdair Milne, director-general, and Rees-Mogg, outgoing vice-chairman, leading the opposing forces. Hussey found most of the BBC's top managers out of touch, 'marooned … like a couple of Boer contingents in a laager' (ibid., 202), and he threw himself into the fray with a hands-on approach not hitherto associated with his more supervisory predecessors. Within days he had gone behind the director-general's back in strictly management matters, and four months later he and the new vice-chairman, Lord Barnett, stealthily gained the consent of their fellow governors to dismiss Milne, the first director-general to be so treated. Hussey considered him 'unbalanced and irresponsible' (ibid., 213). With only cursory explanation that the governors wanted change, Hussey and Barnett told Milne that either he could resign or he would be dismissed. They had a letter ready for his signature. 'What terrible people, I thought' (Milne, 202).

Dismissal was one thing, appointment another, and there were fateful unintended consequences. Hussey then failed to get the governors to agree to his choice of successor, David Dimbleby, a leading television presenter who had little experience of BBC management. They chose instead Milne's deputy, Michael Checkland, an accountant expert in BBC finances. Hussey asked Checkland if he would accept Dimbleby as his deputy. Checkland demurred, and, at Paul Fox's suggestion, with Michael Grade's approval, invited John Birt, who came 'expensive', as Hussey put it (*Chance Governs All*, 271), from London Weekend Television.

Turbulent times ensued, over policy, appointments, and programmes. Hussey was firm in repulsing the attacks on the BBC from Norman Tebbit, the chairman of the Conservative Party, but he did not oppose the government's ban on direct interviews with Sinn Féin spokesmen—who, comically, were shown with their words spoken by actors. Throughout this time Thatcher had the BBC firmly in her sights. She had always anathematized the licence fee, asking why people who only watched ITV should pay it. She and her supporters were also incensed by current affairs coverage both of the Conservative Party and of Northern Ireland (although it was Thames TV that felt the heaviest blow). Hussey had well-grounded fears that she intended breaking up the corporation with part-privatization, stripping it of TV and radio channels in the projected Broadcasting bill, but her efforts in cabinet committee were talked out by ministers like William Whitelaw, David Mellor, and Hurd himself. The work was incomplete by the time she resigned. Under John Major, who was less aggressive, the BBC's new charter and licence fee settlement were reached.

Much china was broken on the way, however. Birt was no sooner made deputy director-general than he fell out with Grade, who left for Channel 4. Checkland worked mightily to trim spending and reform management practices, but Hussey harassed him for more, and finally schemed with Birt, and Patricia Hodgson, the one open high tory among top BBC executives, to replace him with Birt. In a messy compromise that pleased no one, Hussey made Birt director-general designate, while Checkland was to serve another year, itself foreshortened. Most unusually the post was not advertised for a competitive appointment board, which brought a protest from John Tusa, the managing director of the BBC World Service. In appointing Birt, Hussey had offended against his own axiom: 'appoint only a man who has the support and confidence of a good portion of the staff' (*Chance Governs All*, 218). Birt, after five years in charge of news and current affairs, was already seen as the most hated man in broadcasting. Whether in spite of or because of this he launched further rounds of reforms and manning reductions, relying massively (and expensively) on management consultants. Hussey was at first staunchly behind his protégé. In a public furore prompted by revelations that Hussey had allowed Birt a tax-efficient contract to be paid not as a BBC employee but by Birt's private company, which allowed his Armani suits and his wife's secretarial services to be tax-deductible, Hussey stood firm. *The Observer* called in vain for the resignations of both Birt and Hussey. Hussey later inaccurately and unfairly claimed that Birt's contract was identical to that of others—such as John Tusa. This was untrue, since Tusa and others were paid as self-employed freelances.

Yet by the time of the broadcasting white paper of 1994 Hussey and Birt's disenchantment was mutual. Hussey questioned Birt's lack of judgement, while Birt believed that Hussey was ageing and jealous of all the plaudits Birt got for the new licence-fee settlement. In their respective memoirs each claimed total credit for the latter, while Checkland pointed out, in a letter to *The Times* (22 Oct 2002), that the groundwork had been done under his aegis. Hussey and Birt's relationship finally foundered in 1996 on Birt's decision to withhold from Hussey the fact that Diana, princess of Wales, had recorded a TV interview with *Panorama*. Birt did not trust Hussey not to sabotage the planned scoop, through his wife's connection to the queen. Hussey was not told until one week before the scheduled transmission, the same day that Diana personally informed the queen, and the BBC publicized the interview. Hussey felt betrayed. All the reinforced procedures for referral of contentious matters to the governors had been defied. Hussey, who maintained that he never previewed programmes and in any case kept his wife's royal duties out of his business, would have been justified in calling for Birt's dismissal, but the interview drew a record audience and was hugely popular. Instead it was Hussey who departed shortly afterwards, after the longest spell of any BBC chairman. He was made a life peer, as Baron Hussey of North Bradley, on John Major's recommendation. His parting shot at Birt in a House of Lords debate in 1999 was seen by some as a belated conversion: 'There is too much bureaucracy, over-bloated policy units, and too much spent on expansion and management', he lamented (*Hansard 5L*, 597.1686, 3 March 1999).

Hussey's final years were clouded by the onset of dementia, and he died on 27 December 2006 at 3 Beatrice Place, Marloes Road, Kensington, London, a nursing home for the elderly. He was survived by his wife and their two children. At the time of his death, his legacy was deeply contested. He bestrode three careers, but perhaps relied too much on instinct rather than deepening knowledge. Yet had he, like Murdoch, had the benefit of Thatcher's laws curbing union power, he could well have saved the Thomson papers. At the BBC his engineering of Birt's appointment backfired on both of them in the end, with considerable fallout for the institution. Michael Grade scoffed in 2002 that all Birt (and Hussey) 'paraphernalia … has come apart and been hastily dismantled' (*The Guardian*, 26 Oct 2002). FRED EMERY

Sources E. Jacobs, *Stop press* (1980) · A. Milne, *DG: the memoirs of a British broadcaster* (1988) · J. Grigg, *The history of The Times*, 6 (1993) · M. Hussey, *Chance governs all* (2001) · J. Birt, *The harder path* (2002) · *The Times* (28 Dec 2006) · *Daily Telegraph* (28 Dec 2006) · *The Guardian* (28 Dec 2006); (4 Jan 2007) · *The Independent* (28 Dec 2006); (1 Jan 2007) · *WW* (2006) · Burke, *Peerage* · personal knowledge (2010) · private information (2010) · b. cert. · m. cert. · d. cert.
Archives SOUND BL NSA, documentary recording
Likenesses photographs, 1978–2004, PA Photos, London · photographs, 1979–2002, Camera Press, London · G. Levine, photograph, 1985, Hult. Arch., London [*see illus.*] · photographs, 1986–94, Rex Features, London · photographs, 1987–99, Photoshot, London · T. Graham, photographs, 1996 (with Lady Susan Hussey), Getty Images, London, Tim Graham photo library · obituary photographs
Wealth at death £4,359,502: probate, 28 March 2007, *CGPLA Eng. & Wales*

Hutchison, Terence Wilmot (1912–2007), philosopher and historian of economics, was born in Bournemouth on 13 August 1912, the son of Robert Langton Douglas (1864–1951), art historian, and Grace Hutchison (1870–1935). He was not aware of his father's identity until his teens. He was brought up as a Christian Scientist by his Australian mother (in his forties he was confirmed in the Church of England) and developed a lifelong interest in cricket, attending, at the age of fourteen, the entire Ashes test at the Oval, about which he was interviewed on Channel 4 almost eighty years later. He attended a preparatory school in Hampstead, Tonbridge School (1927–31), and Peterhouse, Cambridge (1931–4), where he started reading classics before switching to economics, in which he graduated with a first. He was tutored by Joan Robinson, and attended lectures by, among others, A. C. Pigou and J. M. Keynes (later rueing the loss, during the war, of his notes on the latter). In his final year he encountered Ludwig Wittgenstein's philosophy through two friends, to whom Wittgenstein was dictating his lectures.

After graduating Hutchison studied at the London School of Economics, as an occasional student, living with his mother in Golders Green. Having had his interest in philosophy aroused at Cambridge, he encountered Lionel Robbins and Friedrich Hayek at the London School of Economics, and attended lectures by Rudolf Carnap. He was one of the first economists to read Karl Popper's *Logic der Forschung* in 1934, and soon achieved his first publication in the *Review of Economic Studies*, the journal recently established by a group of young economists. During this time his political views were moving away from a socialism inspired by George Bernard Shaw, and he was repelled by the activities of the Marxists he encountered. However, he never swung as far as the free-market liberalism of Robbins and Hayek. He maintained his contacts with the London School of Economics during the 1930s, later recalling that a particularly important influence had been the philosopher Felix Kaufmann.

After his mother's death Hutchison decided to pursue his interest in the German methodological literature by working in Germany, and obtained a position of *Lektor* at the University of Bonn, where his duties were to deliver lectures that could be on any subject, so long as they were in good English. Intending to stay six months, he remained for three years, returning periodically to the London School of Economics. In Germany he met Loretta Hack (1910–1981), a philosophy student, and daughter of Wilhelm Hack, the socialist mayor of Traben-Trarbach and a vineyard owner. They married within three months of meeting, at Hendon register office on 23 December 1935, and had two daughters and a son. Hutchison continued to publish on methodology while in Bonn, his first book, and most important work on economic methodology, *The Significance and Basic Postulates of Economic Theory*, being published in 1937. Early in 1938 Kaufmann invited him to Vienna to help with some translation, but given the *Anschluss* it was fortunate that he did not go.

With an interest in the Middle East, Hutchison took a position at a teacher training college in Baghdad in 1938. There, during wartime, he responded to a lengthy critique of his book by the eminent Chicago economist Frank Knight, the exchange, in the *Journal of Political Economy*, publicizing his work. In 1941, with the advent of a pro-Nazi regime in Iraq, he and his family left for India, where he joined the Indian army as an intelligence officer, and served in India and the Middle East. He was lucky in being able to pursue his interest in cricket in Egypt.

Hutchison's British academic career started in 1946 with a one-year temporary lectureship at Hull, at the end of which he obtained a post at the London School of Economics, continuing his association with Robbins. He was promoted to a readership in 1951. This was when he turned to the history of economic thought, and wrote *A Review of Economic Doctrines, 1870–1929* (1953). In 1956 he was appointed Mitsui professor of economics at the University of Birmingham, a post he held until his retirement in 1978. He continued to teach the history of economic thought until 1980. After the death of his first wife, in 1983 he married an American academic, Christine Donaldson (1917–2003), and subsequently divided his time between Birmingham and Connecticut.

During the post-war period Hutchison established himself as one of the leading writers on economic methodology and the history of economic thought. In methodology he held to many of the ideas in his first book, emphasizing the need for economic theories to be testable and relevant to policy. He was a controversialist, clearly enjoying the accusation in the *New Statesman* that his *Economics and Economic Policy in Britain, 1946–1966* (1968) constituted 'the publishing outrage of the year' on the grounds that he held economists to account for what they said in the correspondence columns of *The Times*. Neither was he afraid of controversy in the history of economic thought. He held a lifelong antipathy to David Ricardo and those on the left who found inspiration in his work, and in *Before Adam Smith: the Emergence of Political Economy, 1662–1776* (1985) he challenged the view that the eighteenth century was a fallow period in economic thought. He vigorously criticized the interpretation of history of his Cambridge teachers Joan Robinson and Maurice Dobb, linking this to their political stance.

Hutchison was at various points a visiting professor at universities in the USA, Canada, Australia, Japan, and Germany. He was elected a distinguished fellow of the History of Economics Society in 1984, a fellow of the British Academy in 1992, and an honorary member of the European Society for the History of Economic Thought in 2003. He continued writing almost to the end of his life, publishing *On the Methodology of Economics and the Formalist Revolution* in 2000. At the age of ninety he was working on his final manuscript, a reflection on the 'formative decade' of the 1930s, published posthumously in 2009 as part of a special issue of the *Journal of Economic Methodology* examining his views on economic methodology. He died at the Royal Hampshire County Hospital, Winchester, Hampshire, of heart failure on 5 October 2007 and was cremated at Basingstoke crematorium on 16 October. He was survived by his three children. ROGER BACKHOUSE

Sources A. W. Coats, *Methodological controversy in economics: historical essays in honor of T. W. Hutchison* (1983) • K. Tribe, ed., *Economic careers: economics and economists in Britain, 1930–1970* (1997), 126–39 • J. Hart, 'A conversation with Terence Hutchison', *Journal of Economic Methodology*, 9/3 (2002), 359–77 • *The Independent* (22 Oct 2007) • *The Guardian* (30 Nov 2007) • *The Times* (5 Dec 2007) • R. E. Backhouse, 'Terence Hutchison', *New Palgrave dictionary of economics online* (2008); www.dictionaryofeconomics.com/article?id=pde2008_H000190, 5 Aug 2010 • *PBA*, 161 (2009), 179–203 • D. W. Hands and others, 'Symposium on Terence Hutchison and economic methodology', *Journal of Economic Methodology*, 16/3 (2009), 287–350 • *WW* (2007) • personal knowledge (2011) • private information (2011) • m. cert. [1935] • d. cert.

Archives U. Birm. L.

Likenesses Elliott & Fry, quarter-plate glass negative, 1951, NPG • obituary photographs • photograph, repro. in *PBA*

Wealth at death £296,633: probate, 6 May 2008, *CGPLA Eng. & Wales*

Ingilby, Joan Alicia (1911–2000). *See under* Hartley, Marie (1905–2006).

Ingpen [*née* Williams], **Joan Mary Eileen** (1916–2007), musicians' agent and opera administrator, was born on 3 January 1916 at 5 Beverley Gardens, Golders Green, London, the daughter of John Hamilton Williams, civil engineer, and his wife, Daisy, *née* Howe. In 1919 her father was sent to Russia, reputedly to try to help the tsar and his family, but he disappeared without trace and was presumed dead.

Joan Williams studied at the Royal Academy of Music in London, becoming an excellent pianist, but she did not feel good enough for a professional career. Instead she learned to type and worked in marine insurance. During the Second World War, however, she became assistant to Walter Legge, the classical music director of ENSA, which provided entertainment for British troops. On 7 March 1942 she married Noman Edward Ingpen (1918–1961), a lieutenant in the Royal Horse Artillery (and son of Norman Cecil Ingpen, also an army officer). After the end of the war she helped Legge found the Philharmonia Orchestra, then in 1946 she founded her own concert agency, Ingpen and Williams. She divorced Ingpen (but kept his name professionally) and on 5 February 1948 she married Erich Alfred Diez (*b.* 1895/6), also a concert agent (and son of Friedrich Leo Diez, master tailor). The great German bass-baritone Hans Hotter was a witness at their wedding. This marriage also ended in divorce, and in 1958 Ingpen began a relationship with the actor Sebastian Lewis Shaw (1905–1994), son of Geoffrey Shaw, music teacher, which lasted until his death. She had no children.

Ingpen worked very hard to build a strong list at her agency. The singers she represented included Joan Sutherland and Geraint Evans, as well as Hotter, while among the conductors were Rudolf Kempe and Georg Solti. In 1961 Solti became music director of the Royal Opera House, Covent Garden, and asked Ingpen to join him as controller of opera planning. She accepted, sold her agency to Howard Hartog, and in 1962 moved to Covent Garden, where her knowledge of singers and their roles was soon put to good use. The tenor Giuseppe di Stefano was due to give six performances as Rodolfo in Puccini's *La Bohème* in 1963; as he was not in good health she engaged as cover the then unknown tenor Luciano Pavarotti, whom she had heard in Dublin; in the event di Stefano sang one performance, Pavarotti the other five, and she was credited with launching the latter's rise to fame.

Ingpen worked very closely with Solti during the decade he was at Covent Garden, and when he left so did she, taking up a new post as director of planning at the Paris Opéra in July 1971. As always, she began planning the season two years ahead, but though Ingpen got on well with the new managing director, the composer Rolf Liebermann, she found the bureaucracy of the state-funded Opéra extremely difficult to deal with. When, therefore, in 1978 she received a summons from the Metropolitan Opera in New York, she accepted immediately. In New York she had to work exceptionally hard, as the Met, unlike Covent Garden or the Paris Opéra, performed opera seven nights a week, with no evenings of ballet. She calculated that she had to cast 3000 singing roles a season, as well as covers of sufficient stature to go on in an emergency. She had a good working relationship with James Levine, the Met's musical director, but her insistence on planning so far ahead and her sometimes abrasive manner made her unpopular with the management. She stayed in New York for three seasons, until 1981.

For several years after her return, Ingpen became a talent spotter for the Met in Britain and continental Europe. She lived latterly in Hove and until his death with Sebastian Shaw, taking his name. She died at the Royal Sussex County Hospital, Brighton, on 29 December 2007, of bronchopneumonia and chronic obstructive pulmonary disease. ELIZABETH FORBES

Sources *The Times* (9 Jan 2008) · *Daily Telegraph* (9 Jan 2008) · *Washington Post* (9 Jan 2008) · *The Guardian* (14 Jan 2008) · *The Independent* (23 Jan 2008) · personal knowledge (2011) · private information (2011) · b. cert. · m. certs. · d. cert.
Likenesses obituary photographs
Wealth at death £745,530: probate, 9 June 2008, *CGPLA Eng. & Wales*

Ingram, Vernon Martin (1924–2006), molecular biologist, was born Werner Adolf Martin Immerwahr on 19 May 1924 in Breslau, Germany, the younger son and youngest of three children of Kurt Immerwahr, timber merchant, and his wife, Johanna, *née* Freund. He had a brother, Heinrich (later Henry), and a sister, Hilde (later Hilda), who were respectively eight and four years older than him. The children were brought up as Christians, although their parents were of Jewish descent.

'I knew from the age of 10 that I was interested in science, in how things work', Ingram later said (Davis, 14323). He constructed his own radio receiver in order to listen to foreign broadcasts, despite this being banned in Nazi Germany. In 1939 he, his sister, and his parents fled Germany for Britain; his brother, Heinrich, who was studying in Italy, left separately for the United States, via Greece. On the outbreak of the Second World War Kurt Immerwahr was briefly interned as an enemy alien before being released. Vernon escaped this fate, and from 1941 to 1945 worked for Thomas Morson and Son Ltd, a pharmaceutical company based in north London, manufacturing drugs such as amphetamines for the war effort. At the same time he studied chemistry, mathematics, and zoology part-time at Birkbeck College, University of London, where he was particularly impressed by the animal physiologist Graham Jackson, whose teaching 'made the dinosaur walk in front of your eyes' (ibid.). He graduated BSc in 1945, and was immediately offered a post as demonstrator in chemistry, and an assistant lectureship in 1947. In 1949 he completed a PhD in physical organic chemistry under Fred Barrow. At Birkbeck he was also influenced by Desmond Bernal, the professor of physics there. In 1950 Ingram married Margaret Young, with whom he had a son, Peter, and a daughter, Jennifer.

In 1950–52 Ingram spent two years as a postdoctoral fellow in the United States, the first as a Rockefeller Foundation fellow at the Rockefeller Institute, New York, studying protein preparation with Moses Kunitz, and the second as a Coxe fellow at Yale, working on peptide chemistry with Joseph Fruton. Looking for a post in England, he heard from Freddie Gutfreund, a newly arrived postdoctoral student from England, about a vacancy for a protein biochemist at Max Perutz's Medical Research Council Unit for the Study of the Molecular Structure of Biological Systems at Cambridge; he applied for the post and was duly appointed.

In Cambridge it did not take long for Ingram to produce a derivative of haemoglobin with two atoms of mercury attached (one in each half-molecule), the isomorphous replacement needed to solve the phase problem and therefore the protein's crystal structure. At Perutz's suggestion he then set about comparing the molecular structure of normal haemoglobin and sickle-cell haemoglobin. Perutz had already identified the peculiar one-dimensional, crystal structure of sickle-cell haemoglobin (which deforms red blood cells, thereby causing sickle-cell disease, which can be fatal). The haemoglobin in sickle-cell disease had previously been investigated in the laboratory of Linus Pauling at the California Institute of Technology, where Harvey Itano and S. Jonathan Singer, two postdoctoral fellows, had shown that sickle-cell haemoglobin differs in electrophoretic mobility from normal haemoglobin. Building on methods for separating peptides developed by Fred Sanger in Cambridge in his studies of the amino acid sequence of insulin, Ingram employed a two-dimensional method to separate the peptides derived from haemoglobin: a combination of chromatography and electrophoresis, a technique he called 'fingerprinting'. As a result he was able to show that in each half-molecule of haemoglobin, consisting of nearly 300 amino acid residues, there is only a single amino acid difference between the normal and sickle forms, sickle-cell haemoglobin having valine whereas normal haemoglobin has glutamic acid. This result agreed closely with the prediction from the Pauling laboratory, based on electrophoretic properties, that sickle-cell haemoglobin has two to four more net positive charges than normal haemoglobin. Ingram's discovery showed for the first time that a change in a single amino acid, the consequence of a mutation in a single base pair, can be the cause of a specific disease. The results, published in *Nature* in 1956 and 1957, provided important support for the 'one gene, one protein' hypothesis of George Wells Beadle and Edward Lawrie Tatum. They also led Ingram to be widely known as the 'father of molecular medicine'.

Ingram continued to work for many years on the evolution, abnormalities, and embryology of haemoglobin (adult haemoglobin differing from foetal haemoglobin), and published *Haemoglobin and its Abnormalities* (1961) and *The Hemoglobins in Genetics and Evolution* (1963). By this time he had moved to the Massachusetts Institute of Technology (MIT), in Cambridge, Massachusetts, USA, having in 1958 accepted a one-year assistant professorship, which was extended (Ingram having decided that he liked the atmosphere at MIT and in the USA) and in 1961 converted into a full professorship.

The biology department at MIT had recently decided to focus on the new field of molecular biology and Ingram was a natural fit. Also, from 1961 to 1973, he lectured part-time in medicine at Columbia University in New York, where he collaborated in research on haemoglobin with Paul Marks. His first marriage ended in divorce, and in 1984 he married Elizabeth (Beth) Hendee, and with her he served as a much-loved housemaster at Ashdown House, an MIT graduate residence hall. In 1988 he succeeded John M. Buchanan as the John and Dorothy Wilson professor of biology. From 1989 to 1999 he served as director of the MIT experimental study group, initiating annual teaching seminars for student instructors and contributing to innovative teaching methods. He never retired, and continued working in the laboratory until his death.

Ingram's later research shifted to thalassaemia (he discovered that thalassaemia has two variants, alpha and beta), and thence to Alzheimer's disease. His interest in the latter was sparked by his second wife, Beth, who worked with people with Down's syndrome. (Nearly all people with Down's syndrome develop Alzheimer's disease by the age of forty.) His research focused on trying to identify compounds that obliterate the plaques composed of mis-folded β-amyloid protein that form in the brains of patients with Alzheimer's disease. Although he was unable to reach any definite conclusion by the time of his death, his research opened up several fruitful lines of enquiry, and had important implications for the study of Alzheimer's and of such other protein-based diseases as Huntington's disease and prion diseases (including Creutzfeldt-Jakob disease). They also provided tools for the investigation of a new class of functional amyloid proteins. These final papers capped a history of publication spanning more than fifty years.

Ingram was an extremely modest man, who always acknowledged the work of others, and described himself as simply a lucky link in the chain of human discovery. He nevertheless received many honours, including election as a fellow of the Royal Society in 1970, fellow of the American Association for the Advancement of Science in 1987, and member of the (American) National Academy of Sciences in 2004. In 2002 a former Ashdown House resident successfully petitioned to have an asteroid named 6285 Ingram, after Vernon and Beth Ingram. He was an accomplished pianist, an active supporter of the Rockport (Massachusetts) chamber music festival, and a talented photographer, specializing in close-up photographs of plants and flowers. He died at Massachusetts General Hospital, Boston, on 17 August 2006 after surgery for injuries sustained in a fall, and was survived by his wife, Beth, and the two children of his first marriage.

LISA A. STEINER

Sources V. Ingram, 'Sickle-cell anemia hemoglobin: the molecular biology of the first "molecular disease"—the crucial importance of serendipity', *Perspectives on genetics: anecdotal, historical, and critical commentaries*, ed. J. F. Crow and W. F. Dove (2004) · T. H. Davis, 'Biography of Vernon M. Ingram', *Proceedings of the National Academy of Sciences*, 101/40 (5 Oct 2004), 14323–5 · MIT press release, 22 Aug 2006 · *The Independent* (9 Sept 2006) · *Boston Globe* (10 Sept 2006) · S. Pincock, *The Lancet*, 368/9542 (30 Sept 2006), 1148 · *The Times* (24 Oct 2006) · *MIT Faculty Newsletter*, 19/1 (Sept–Oct 2006) · *WW* (2006) · personal knowledge (2010) · private information (2010) [Beth Ingram, widow; Henry Immerwahr, brother; S. Lindquist; R. Doolittle; H. Itano; S. J. Singer]

Archives Massachusetts Institute of Technology, Cambridge, Massachusetts

Likenesses J. Gross, photograph, RS · obituary photographs · photographs, Massachusetts Institute of Technology

Ingrams, Leonard Victor (1941–2005), banker and opera impresario, was born on 1 September 1941 at Stoneycrest Nursing Home, Hindhead, Surrey, the fourth and youngest son of Leonard St Clair Ingrams (1900–1953), banker, and his second wife, Victoria Susan Beatrice, *née* Reid (1908–1997). His father served in the Ministry of Economic Warfare during the Second World War, and was managing director of Continental Assets Realization Trust Ltd thereafter. Richard Ingrams (*b.* 1937), editor of *Private Eye* and *The Oldie*, was an elder brother. Wartime took the brothers to live with their grandmother, Lady Reid, in Ellon, Aberdeenshire. She had been a lady-in-waiting to Queen Victoria and had married the queen's doctor, Sir James Reid of Ellon, first baronet. Ingrams's mother encouraged her sons to play music: he learned the violin and met Vaughan Williams, Benjamin Britten, and Charles Münch, and played in the British Youth Orchestra under Sir Malcolm Sargent.

Ingrams went to Stonyhurst College and in 1959 won a scholarship to Corpus Christi College, Oxford. In 1961 he met Rosalind Anne Moore, the daughter of a diplomat, Antony Ross Moore, who was about to go to Oxford. They married on 19 September 1964 when she was twenty-one, and later had four children, three daughters, Lucy Sarah (*b.* 1965), Elizabeth (*b.* 1971), and Catherine (*b.* 1976), and a son, Rupert Antony (*b.* 1967). Meanwhile, with firsts from Oxford in classical moderations (1961) and *literae humaniores* (1963), a Derby scholarship (1963), and a senior scholarship (1964), in 1964 Ingrams took up a post as assistant lecturer in classics at Queen Mary College, London, but after two years gave up teaching and decided to enter Barings, the family bank. He and his family were then sent on a number of successful postings in Paris, Cologne, Hamburg, and Vienna between 1968 and 1969.

In 1974 Barings sent Ingrams as British adviser to the newly created Saudi Arabian Monetary Agency in Jiddah, together with David Mulford, later American ambassador in New Delhi. The agency required external expertise to manage the increasing assets generated by the kingdom's sudden oil wealth and Ingrams with his team implemented major government investment programmes. There he also pioneered the Jiddah (and later Riyadh) concert committee that by courtesy of the British embassy invited international professionals to sing or play in concerts. In 1980 he was appointed OBE for 'services to the British community' in Saudi Arabia. Meanwhile he served simultaneously as a managing director (one of a large number) of Baring Bros (1975–81). A series of employments followed: as chief financial adviser to the Saudi government (1981–4), a director of Robert Fleming Holdings (1985–96), and senior vice-president of the Arab Banking Corporation (1996–8). He was also a director of the Deutschland Investment Corporation (1990–99; chairman, 1990–96), and of the Czech and Slovak Investment Corporation (1992–2005; chairman, 1992–6). In 1998 he set up his own financial enterprise, L. V. Ingrams & Co. Ltd.

In 1982 Ingrams bought Garsington Manor, near Oxford, celebrated for the literati invited there by Lady Ottoline and Philip Morrell between 1915 and 1927. In 1988 an excellent acoustic was discovered from the loggia and in 1989 two nights of *The Marriage of Figaro* (in aid of the reopening of the Oxford Playhouse) brought in scores of fan letters. The following year Garsington Opera Ltd was formed. For six weeks each year the loggia became the stage, an orchestra pit held sixty, and a temporary auditorium held an audience of 500.

Ingrams immediately began to explore little-known repertory, beginning with Haydn's *Orlando Paladino*, a British première, in 1990. He introduced seven Haydn operas to the stage between 1990 and 1997. He pursued known and little-known works by Rossini (nine in total) and Richard Strauss (eight in total), as well as the entire Mozart repertory, including the little-known *Philosopher's Stone*. Only a fraction of Rossini's and Strauss's work was familiar to the British opera public: Ingrams's introduction of these forgotten works brought a new understanding to audiences and conductors alike and, eventually, also to the critics. Other 'discoveries' included Schumann's *Genoveva*, Strauss's *Die Ägyptische Helena* and *Die Liebe der Danae*, Tchaikovsky's *Cherevichki*, Janáček's *Šárka*, and Rimsky-Korsakov's *Mayskaya Noch*—whose first British professional productions were all at Garsington. During the first ten years the opera company suffered various prosecutions and refusals of planning permission until in 1995 an appeal by Ingrams at Oxford crown court found in his favour, and eventually, after a public inquiry, planning permission was granted.

In September 2000 Leonard and Rosalind Ingrams received from the queen of Denmark the European Culture Project award for performing arts on behalf of Garsington Opera, for their 'innovative and successful initiative in the performing arts and their exemplary nurturing of young talent'. Ingrams always sought and encouraged rising young artists, attending end-of-term performances at the music academies, and many of those he cast went on to take major roles. In his search for voices, character, and musicianship he explored widely: among other venues he travelled to Drottningholm in Sweden, le Théâtre de la Monnaie in Brussels, Pesaro and Palermo in Italy, as well as extensively in Britain. Orla Boylan, Juanita Lascarro, Melanie Diener, and Johannes Manov all made their British débuts in Garsington. The London Barbican's *Mostly Mozart* summer series invited four semi-staged Garsington Mozart productions, *Don Giovanni* (2002), *La finta giardiniera* (2003), *Così fan tutte* (2004), and *Le nozze di Figaro* (2005).

On 27 July 2005, while driving back from Glyndebourne, Ingrams died of a heart attack at the wheel, with his wife beside him. He was pronounced dead on arrival at Ashford Hospital, Stanwell, Surrey. His four children survived him. Two years later, the Metropolitan Opera House, New York, re-produced the director–designer David Fielding's 1997 Garsington production of Strauss's *Die Ägyptische Helena* (starring Deborah Voigt), a fitting tribute to Ingrams and his creation, Garsington Opera.

GRAHAM C. GREENE

Sources *The Independent* (2 Aug 2005) · *The Times* (4 Aug 2005) · *Daily Telegraph* (4 Aug 2005) · *The Guardian* (10 Aug 2005) · *WW* (2005) · personal knowledge (2009) · private information (2009) · b. cert. · m. cert. · d. cert.

Likenesses obituary photographs

Wealth at death £1,008,332: probate, 13 Dec 2006, *CGPLA Eng. & Wales*

Inman, William Howard Wallace [Bill] (**1929–2005**), medical researcher and pharmaco-epidemiologist, was born on 1 August 1929 at Braehead, Higher Drive, Cuddington, near Epsom, Surrey, the eldest of three sons of Wallace Mills Inman, industrial chemist, and later chairman of ICI's alkali division, and his wife, Maude Mary, *née* Andrews. He was educated at Ampleforth College, where he excelled at sports and broke the school junior mile cross-country record. He went to Gonville and Caius College, Cambridge, to read medicine, but at the age of twenty-one, just as he was about to start his clinical training, he contracted poliomyelitis, which left him in hospital for three years and in a wheelchair for the rest of his life. Cambridge had no medical clinical school at that time, the usual arrangement being to move to a London hospital for clinical training. Sensitive to Inman's disability, the university arranged for him to have individual tuition and training at Addenbrooke's Hospital in Cambridge, and so he became the first Cambridge medical graduate. After qualifying he spent three years as a junior hospital doctor at Addenbrooke's, before moving to his father's old company, ICI, but in the pharmaceutical division as a medical adviser. On 21 July 1962 he married June Evelyn Halfpenny, a 35-year-old shorthand typist, daughter of Stewart Arthur Maggs, electrical engineer, and widow of Douglas Halfpenny. Friends carried him in his wheelchair up the steps to the registry office in style. They had four daughters, one of whom died in infancy.

In 1964, in the wake of the thalidomide disaster in which many thousands of children were born deformed as a result of their mothers taking thalidomide in pregnancy, Inman joined the Department of Health, to work with the newly formed committee on safety of drugs, chaired by Sir Derrick Dunlop. Inman's remit was to develop an early warning system to recognize adverse reactions to medicines. His solution was what came to be known as the 'yellow card scheme', so called because of the yellow forms on which doctors reported any problem experienced by patients suspected to be caused by taking a drug. This scheme stood the test of time as a means of generating signals of drug safety, and Inman used its database to investigate, among other problems, the relationship between oral contraceptives and venous thromboses, and that between the anaesthetic halothane and liver damage. But the yellow card system also suffered drawbacks, the main one being under-reporting. One of the most important examples of this was with the 'beta blocker' practolol, which caused severe eye complications, including blindness, in several hundred patients, but there was no signal of this from yellow cards.

Inman believed that a second drug safety alert system was needed to supplement the yellow card scheme, but he found little support for his proposals in the Department of Health. So in 1980 he left the department to set up the Drug Safety Research Unit in Southampton, affiliated to the university there, with Inman as its first professor of pharmaco-epidemiology. He established a new monitoring system for recently introduced drugs, known as prescription event monitoring, in which general practitioners' prescriptions were used to generate a questionnaire to be completed by doctors on some 10,000 or more patients prescribed a new drug, thus providing information on adverse effects. This scheme proved to be complementary to the yellow card scheme, as Inman had hoped, and both formed important parts of the UK's programme to monitor drug safety. His concern for drug safety had an international dimension too. With collaborators he was influential in persuading the World Health Organization to set up its own drug safety monitoring programme.

Perhaps predictably, Inman did not have a comfortable relationship with the industry whose products he was monitoring. He regarded many of its post-marketing safety schemes as being no more than promotional exercises, and he was very critical of the involvement of industry with post-graduate medical education. Equally, his contacts with the Department of Health were not always easy, as he saw the relationship between government and the pharmaceutical industry as being too close. Thus he frequently had problems raising funds for his projects, since both the usual sources were unhelpful.

Inman's immobility from his poliomyelitis did not interfere with a range of physical activities that would have been daunting to an able-bodied person. He learned to fly gliders, continued his earlier passion for fowling, and drove motor cars both in the UK and abroad. He travelled extensively and was in great demand both nationally and internationally on lecture platforms, where he commanded great respect and affection. He retired from the Drug Safety Research Unit in 1994, and became medical vice-president of Remap, a charity run by engineers and physiotherapists that supplied free customized equipment to disabled people. In later years he developed post-polio syndrome, an affliction resembling motor neurone disease, and this led to his death at Southampton General Hospital on 20 October 2005. He was survived by his wife and three daughters. ALASDAIR BRECKENRIDGE

Sources *Daily Telegraph* (28 Oct 2005) · *The Guardian* (4 Nov 2005) · *BMJ*, 331 (17 Dec 2005), 1477 · *Pharmacoepidemiology and Drug Safety*, 15 (2006), 279–80 · W. H. W. Inman, *Feeling better, doctor?* (2006) · personal knowledge (2009) · private information (2009) · b. cert. · m. cert. · d. cert.

Archives SOUND BL NSA, 'Contraceptive pill interviews', interview with L. Marks, 13 Dec 1994, C1241/24

Likenesses obituary photographs

Wealth at death £454,103: probate, 13 Jan 2006, *CGPLA Eng. & Wales*

Inwood, Christiane Sourvinou- (1945–2007), Greek scholar, was born in Volos, Greece, on 26 February 1945, the daughter of Spyros Sourvinos, a colonel in the Greek army, and his wife, a teacher of economics and eventually a headmistress. The family moved from their home in Corfu to Athens and in 1962 she came first in the entrance exam to the 'philosophical' (classics) section of the university there; she was a star pupil of the excavator of Santorini, Spyridon Marinatos, and graduated in 1966 with the only first-class degree awarded that year. She then spent time attached to the Institute of Mycenaean, Aegean and Anatolian Studies in Rome, working on Linear B; she also participated in excavations in this period, and was briefly married to the specialist in Linear A and B, Jean-Pierre Olivier.

In 1969 Christiane Sourvinou came to the United Kingdom to write a doctoral thesis. After spending the autumn term at Birmingham supervised by Franz Tritsch, she moved to Oxford where she lived for the rest of her life. On 13 March 1971 she married Michael James Inwood (*b.* 1944), philosopher and fellow of Trinity College, Oxford, and son of William Inwood. Her thesis, 'Minoan and Mycenaean afterlife beliefs and their relevance to the Homeric underworld', supervised by John Boardman, was completed in 1973. From 1976 to 1978 she was a lecturer in classical archaeology at the University of Liverpool; she resigned after two years because of the strain of travel (always a torment to her). For similar reasons, compounded by health problems and tensions with certain colleagues, in 1998 she left the readership in classical literature created for her in Reading in 1995; from 1990 to 1995 she had been a senior research fellow of University College, Oxford. Despite her acknowledged brilliance as a scholar and teacher, no electoral committee for a tenured post in Oxford ever considered her, interdisciplinary as she was and un-Oxonian in intellectual style, quite right for its particular requirements. But for many undergraduates who encountered her during her fragmented teaching career she was the supreme teacher of their experience, challenging them, believing in them, and passionately committed to their well-being.

Intellectually Christiane Sourvinou-Inwood's most obvious characteristic was a concern for methodology. She waged ceaseless war on what she termed 'culturally determined' interpretations, which their proponents regarded as grounded in 'common sense' but which derived in fact, she insisted, from assumptions specific to their own culture and not that of the Greeks. Ernst Gombrich's studies of the different ways in which different cultures see and represent the world influenced her powerfully; and she spoke of all the other approaches that she deployed—structuralism, social anthropology, social history, the psychology of perception, semiology, cognitive studies, literary theory—as weapons that she learnt to use in the central battle against 'commonsense empiricism'. She believed that, with sufficient methodological rigour, subjective readings could be largely avoided, and she was a fierce critic of extravagant post-structuralist assertions (which she judged to be themselves culturally determined) of the indeterminacy of meaning. Though she may have been right on that issue, in her later works in particular she perhaps overestimated the amount of knowledge of the ancient world that it is possible for modern scholars to recover.

Sourvinou-Inwood's insistence that cultural products—texts, images, myths, rituals—need to be decoded was obviously much indebted to various strands of continental thought. But the synthesis was her own, and what made it so influential was the skill and energy with which she applied it to specific problems. Almost all her works argued a case about particular documents; her two longest books, *'Reading' Greek Death* (1985) and *Hylas, the Nymphs, Dionysos and Others: Myth, Ritual, Ethnicity* (2005), were investigations as wide-ranging as their titles suggest, but were provoked, respectively, by a two-line epigram and the image on a single Greek vase. Her chronological range extended from Minoan to (at least) late classical Greece, and she was equally at home discussing a tragedy or a vase, a site plan, or a myth. It was the combination of methodological rigour, attention to specifics, and breadth of expertise that gave her work its power.

Though Sourvinou-Inwood published two further short books and one long one, *Tragedy and Athenian Religion* (2003), in her lifetime, and another (*Athenian Myths and Festivals*, 2010) was rescued from work left unfinished at her death, her ideal mode was the article. Several of the most provocative and controversial sought to respond to the women of Greek tragedy as Athenian males might have done: Sophocles' unamiable Creon found in Sourvinou-Inwood an unexpected defender against Antigone. The articles collected in *'Reading' Greek Culture: Texts and Images, Rituals and Myths* (1991) showed her at her best. They included a powerful argument that the myth that Apollo's oracle at Delphi had been preceded by an oracle of earth was just that, a myth; an illustration from certain Locrian votive tablets of how a panhellenic myth could assume a new meaning in a local context; and a rigorous demonstration of the need to set images on vases, in this case those depicting erotic pursuit, in a series in order to understand any single member of the series. Her article 'What is polis religion?' (published in Oswyn Murray and Simon Price, eds., *The Greek City*, 1990) was probably the most widely quoted and discussed contribution to the study of Greek religion published in the last quarter of the twentieth century.

Christiane Sourvinou-Inwood was a warm-hearted, affectionate, impulsive, and vulnerable person, too thin-skinned to cope easily with criticism or perceived slights, intensely loyal to her many friends. She alternated academic work with creative writing, initially plays, later detective novels set in ancient Greece, always with *mises en scène* closely reflecting her current academic concerns. Three were published in English: *Murder Most Classical* (2007), under the pseudonym Christiana Elfwood, and in her own name *Murder at the City Dionysia* and *Murder near the Sanctuary* (both 2008). She died of cancer at what had for many years been her home, 10 Jericho Street, Oxford, on 19 May 2007, and was survived by her husband. She had no children. R. C. T. Parker

Sources *The Guardian* (31 May 2007) • *Daily Telegraph* (1 June 2007) • *The Independent* (2 June 2007) • *The Times* (8 June 2007) • C. Sourvinou-Inwood, curriculum vitae, priv. coll. • personal knowledge (2011) • private information (2011) • m. cert. [1971] • d. cert.

Likenesses obituary photographs • photograph, repro. in pegasuspublishers.com/authors.php?letter=I

Jack, Ian Robert James (1923–2008), literary scholar, was born on 5 December 1923 at 5 Cambridge Street, Edinburgh, the only child of John McGregor Bruce Jack (1888–1943), writer to the signet, and his wife, Helena Colburn (Lena), *née* Buchanan (1892–1932). He was afflicted with asthma from an early age and was never entirely free of this complaint. Nevertheless he was happy at his father's old school, George Watson's College, from 1931 to 1942. He was especially proud of having learned Latin and Greek there, and of winning the John Welsh classical scholarship. Despite his asthma he also played cricket for the second eleven for three years.

Exempted from military service (to his regret), Jack won a scholarship to Edinburgh University, where he read English. Among very much else he had a special interest in the poetry of John Clare. He was an enthusiast for the theatre, and for outdoor recreation, and walked in the Pentland Hills with his friend John McCann. During his time at

Edinburgh he persuaded Sir William Beveridge, author of the Beveridge report and one of the founders of the modern welfare state, to stand as lord rector of the university. Jack campaigned for him vigorously but failed in the end. Graduating from Edinburgh with a first, he went to Merton College, Oxford, of which he was in his later years elected an honorary fellow. There he worked on later seventeenth-century and eighteenth-century English literature under Nichol Smith and Helen Gardiner. He was awarded his DPhil in 1950 and in the same year became lecturer in English literature at Brasenose College. In 1955 he became a senior research fellow there. Meanwhile, he had married, in Oxford on 8 July 1948, Jane Henderson MacDonald (*b.* 1924/5), a fellow student, from Elgin, daughter of Charles MacDonald, civil servant. They had two sons and one daughter. Jane Jack became a scholar in her own right, and the two continued to collaborate after their marriage was dissolved some twenty years later.

In 1961 Jack successfully applied for a lectureship in the faculty of English at Cambridge, becoming also a fellow of Pembroke College. His early years at Cambridge may not have been his happiest. Difficulties of adjustment were made more sad by the break-up of his marriage to Jane. It was not long, however, before he met (Margaret) Elizabeth Crone (*b.* 1937), a schoolteacher, and daughter of Edward Rowland Crone, insurance broker. They married at the register office in Scarborough on 12 August 1972, and soon after bought Highfield House, Fen Ditton, a spacious and comfortable home which could accommodate Jack's great and growing collection of antiquarian and modern books. Pupils, colleagues, and friends enjoyed the unfailing hospitality of the house. They had one son.

While still at Oxford Jack had published *Augustan Satire* (1952), a successful study, ranging from Samuel Butler to Samuel Johnson. There were at least two decisive moves forward in his subsequent work. Having published in 1963 *English Literature, 1815–32*, he next published a book of an entirely different kind, *Keats and the Mirror of Art* (1967). Its focus was on a single author, and its approach, not conventional literary history, was a critical mode which brought poetry, painting, and sculpture together in an illuminating way. This book also betokened a final move through the earlier nineteenth century into the Victorian period. Jack had for some time been general editor of the Clarendon edition of the Brontë novels. *Jane Eyre*, the first volume, edited by Jane Jack and Margaret Smith, was published in 1969. In this series Jack published with Hilda Marsden a new edition of *Wuthering Heights* (1976). His part of the introduction (beginning at page xxv) showed his decisive grip on the notorious textual problems of that novel. Turning away from the conventionalized text produced for Charlotte Brontë by Smith Elder, he determined that the difficult first edition by T. C. Newby was, despite obvious errors, likely to have preserved more closely what Emily Brontë had wanted.

In 1970 Jack had published a one-volume edition of Browning's *Poetical Works, 1833–64*, followed up by a new critical work, *Browning's Major Poetry* (1973). At this point Jack may have reconsidered the direction of his research, but finally decided to build on his recent work and embark on a Clarendon Press edition of the whole *Poetical Works of Robert Browning*, consisting of text with full commentary. This was a remarkable decision. He was now nearing his sixties. Even with the collaboration of other editors, on the model of the Clarendon Brontë edition, he could hardly have hoped to see the project completed. He expected at least to see the edition reach Browning's famous collection, *Men and Women*. With the assistance of Rowena Fowler, Robert Inglesfield, and Margaret Smith, his expectation was fulfilled in 1995 and well displayed Jack's own full, learned, and meticulous annotation. During the course of this ambitious work on Browning, Jack's final critical work, *The Poet and His Audience*, published in 1984, discussed Dryden, Pope, Byron, Shelley, Tennyson, and Yeats.

While from his Oxford days Jack always pressed ahead with his publications, he was active in other ways too. He was Pembroke College librarian from 1965 to 1975. He was a frequent lecturer for the British Council, and between 1960 and 1989 held visiting lectureships and professorships at Alexandria, Chicago, California at Berkeley, British Columbia, Virginia, Tsuda College in Tokyo, New York, and Otago. He was guest speaker at the Nichol Smith seminar at the Australian National University in 1976, and at the Literary Society of Japan in 1978. He gave the British Academy Warton lecture on English poetry in 1967. He was reader in English poetry at Cambridge from 1973 to 1976 and professor of English literature from 1976 to 1989 (thereafter emeritus). He was elected a fellow of the British Academy in 1986. He listed his recreations in *Who's Who* as 'collecting books, travelling hopefully, thinking about words'. He died of a chest infection at his home in Fen Ditton on 3 September 2008 and was survived by his wife, Elizabeth, and his four children. A memorial service was held at Pembroke College chapel, Cambridge, on 15 November 2008. HOWARD ERSKINE-HILL

Sources *Daily Telegraph* (13 Sept 2008) • *The Times* (22 Sept 2008) • *Evening News* [Edinburgh] (23 Sept 2008) • *The Independent* (24 Sept 2008) • *The Guardian* (27 Oct 2008) • H. H. Erskine-Hill, *PBA* [forthcoming] • *WW* (2008) • personal knowledge (2012) • private information (2012) • b. cert. • m. certs. • d. cert.

Archives SOUND BL NSA, documentary and performance recordings

Likenesses obituary photographs

Wealth at death £430,575: probate, 7 Oct 2009, *CGPLA Eng. & Wales*

Jackson, Michael (1942–2007), journalist and writer on beer and whisky, was born on 27 March 1942 at Stockeld Park maternity home, Spofforth, Wetherby, Yorkshire, the son of Isaac (Jack) Jackson, First Aid Party member and commercial traveller, and Margaret Duff, *née* Millington, the wife of William Duff. At the time of his birth his mother lived at 29 Colwyn Road, Beeston, Leeds, and his father at 21 Artillery Street, Leeds. Jackson's Jewish grandfather, Chaim Jakowitz, had emigrated to Leeds from Kaunas, Lithuania, aged fifteen. Chaim's son, Isaac, had met Margaret, a gentile originally from Redcar, at a local dance hall while serving in the army during the Second World War. He had Anglicized his name to Jack Jackson (though

Margaret called him John), apparently unaware of the band leader and disc jockey of the same name. Nor can he be held responsible for giving his son names that were to be made famous across the globe by another Michael Jackson, the pop singer—though humorous references to his namesake were an advantage to Jackson later in his career as a writer and lecturer. He had a twin brother who died shortly after birth; he also had a sister, Heather (*b.* 1950). His parents married in 1946, after his mother's divorce.

Jackson was brought up in Leeds and, after the war, in Huddersfield. Isaac Jackson was variously the manager of a television shop, a bookmaker, and a lorry driver. For a time the family lived over a fish and chip shop. The tastes and smells of Jewish and east European cuisine, and of rich meals with his grandparents, were the background to Jackson's childhood. He was to write extensively and colourfully about the pairing of beer and whisky with food. Later he described himself as a 'pale-faced kid, whose gloomy Slavic features were not wholly softened by my bubbly dark curls. The lugubrious countenance disguised a child happy in his inner world, which had grown greatly since I learned to read' (*The Independent*, 3 Sept 2007).

Jackson was educated at King James's Grammar School, Almondbury, Huddersfield, leaving at sixteen to work as a trainee journalist on the *Huddersfield Examiner*. It was at this early stage in his career—no doubt stimulated by sessions in local pubs waiting for a story to materialize—that he began to develop his taste for, and interest in, beer. A period working in Amsterdam in 1969 allowed him to travel to Belgium where he discovered the remarkable range of tastes and styles of Belgian beer. Further trips to Germany and Austria sampling the brews to be found along the Rhine, Main, and Danube only increased his fascination with beer.

After he moved to London Jackson worked on the *Daily Herald* and then helped to transform a relatively obscure journal called *World's Press News* into the highly successful *Campaign*, a weekly magazine for a readership in the expanding worlds of advertising and marketing which was notable for its arresting design. On 23 December 1967, at Fulham register office, he married Margaret Teresa (Maggie) O'Connor (1943–1981), daughter of John O'Connor, bricklayer. There were no children of the marriage.

Jackson's first book on beer, *The English Pub* (1976), was almost an accident: he wrote it after another author let down the publisher. The book coincided with the growth in Britain of the Campaign for Real Ale (CAMRA), which raised public awareness of the intrinsic qualities of good beer, and fought for something better than the fizzy, pasteurized, mass-produced liquid that increasingly passed for ale at this time. Jackson was always at pains to explain that he was not a founder of the organization (which had originally been founded as the Campaign for the Revitalization of Ale in 1971), but his instincts and tastes made him an early supporter.

Jackson's second book, *The World Guide to Beer* (1977), made his reputation and is probably the most representative among the many books of a man known widely as 'the beer hunter'—the title of his television series in 1990. The work explored the different geographical and cultural traditions in brewing across the world, and described brews that most devotees, let alone occasional beer drinkers, had never encountered or even imagined. After it was published he turned to writing about beer full-time, enjoying further success with his *Pocket Guide to Beer* (1986), a compendium of world brews. Jackson did not hide his personal predilection for Belgian beers, and his later book *The Great Beers of Belgium* (1991), which went into five editions, was one of his most successful publications.

Jackson's range, influence, and reputation were all worldwide. He was published in eighteen languages, from Estonian to Japanese, and made television programmes on beer for Channel 4 in Britain and the Discovery Channel in the United States that were shown internationally. In the United States, indeed, he was credited with helping stimulate the development from the 1980s of microbreweries, whose excellent products he championed. One American cartoon, captioned *Michael Jackson in Hell*, depicted him being offered a can of Miller Lite—a popular American drink—by the Devil (*Daily Telegraph*, 1 Sept 2007). An entertaining lecturer whose quick wit and direct remarks were seemingly at odds with his shaggy looks and baggy style, he frequently held the attention of an audience of a thousand or more.

The transition to writing about whisky, which began with Jackson's *World Guide to Whisky*, published in 1987, and led to his *Malt Whisky Companion*, the world's best-selling book on the subject, two years later, was natural for a man who loved both drinks equally. Again, Jackson was part of a popular movement rediscovering the qualities of traditional tastes and methods, and his books contributed to the remarkable growth in sales of single malt whiskies from the 1980s. *Scotland and its Whiskies* (2001) encouraged drinkers to visit their favourite distilleries in the highlands and islands; Jackson's last book, simply entitled *Whisky* (2005), had already won five international awards by the time of his death.

Jackson was showered with honours: they included five Glenfiddich awards for writing about drinks; three gold tankards from the British Guild of Beer Writers; the literary medal of the German Academy of Gastronomy; the Mercurius award for services to Belgian brewing (presented to him by Crown Prince Philippe); and membership in 1997 of the Confederatie der Brauwerijen van België—the first person not to be a brewer to have been accorded this particular honour. Jackson was recognized for a remarkable set of books and articles, based on careful but evidently enjoyable research, which helped millions of people appreciate the diversity and flavour of two drinks that have shaped cultures throughout the world.

Michael Jackson did not disclose that he had been suffering from diabetes and Parkinson's disease until their symptoms led some to think he was drunk, a professional hazard he had scrupulously avoided throughout his career. In explaining his condition he made it clear that 'I do not have, and never have had, a drink problem' (*Daily Telegraph*, 1 Sept 2007). His partner for the last twenty-six years of his life was Patricia Medway (Paddy) Gunningham. He died at his home, 23 Nasmyth Street, Hammersmith, London, on 30 August 2007, following a heart attack. He was survived by Paddy, his stepdaughter Sam, and his sister, Heather. LAWRENCE GOLDMAN

Sources *Daily Telegraph* (1 Sept 2007) · *Washington Post* (1 Sept 2007) · *The Independent* (3 Sept 2007) · *The Guardian* (4 Sept 2007) · *The Times* (5 Sept 2007) · www.camra.org.uk, 13 Aug 2010 · michaeljacksonthebeerhunter.blogspot.com, 13 Aug 2010 · b. cert. · m. cert. · d. cert.
Archives Oxford Brookes University | FILM BFINA, performance footage
Likenesses obituary photographs
Wealth at death £688,237: probate, 11 March 2010, *CGPLA Eng. & Wales*

Jacobs, Louis (1920–2006), rabbi, was born on 17 July 1920 at 23 Penrose Street, Cheetham, Manchester, the only child of Harris (Harry) Jacobs, tailor, and his wife, Lena, *née* Myerstone. His traditional, but by no means ultra-Orthodox, parents enrolled him in Manchester central high school. He showed particular promise in his studies for his bar mitzvah and, on the encouragement of his teacher, transferred to the Manchester *yeshiva*, a college for intensive Torah and Talmudic education, where he was to remain, with the exception of a short period at the Gateshead *yeshiva*, for the next few years. He was exposed to the study of the full range of traditional Jewish texts, including the Talmud, legal codes, and pietistic and mystical literature. He formed a particular love for the latter, and a picture of his teacher in Hasidism, Rabbi Dubov, hung outside his study until the end of his life. He quickly gained a reputation as an *illui*, a prodigy with an outstanding intellectual grasp and extraordinary powers of concentration and memory. His plans to study at the *yeshiva* of Tels, home of the acute Lithuanian school of Talmudic analysis, and from where his mother's family originally hailed, were mercifully ended by the outbreak of the Second World War. He received ordination from the head of the Manchester *yeshiva*, Rabbi Moshe Segal, in 1943.

During the course of his teaching duties Jacobs met Sophie (Shulamit or Shula) Lisagorsky, daughter of Israel (Isser) Lisagorsky and his wife, Jane, both of Lithuanian origin; they were married in Manchester on 6 January 1944 and enjoyed sixty years of happy marriage until her death in 2005. She complemented his congregational work with her warm manner and lively interest in everybody. Their eldest child, Ivor, was born in 1945, followed by Naomi in 1947 and David in 1952.

In 1945 Jacobs took up a post as assistant to Dr Munk in his north London synagogue. The encounter with this branch of German Jewry, scrupulously Orthodox yet engaged in the intellectual and professional concerns of the wider world, was to have a great effect on Jacobs. But that was secondary to the impact of his studies at University College, London, where, enrolled for the BA honours degree, he was exposed for the first time to the historical-critical method of biblical criticism. Morris Steinschneider's witty reformulation of the verse from Psalm 111 into the adage 'The beginning of wisdom is bibliography' aptly articulated the tension that was henceforth to govern Jacobs's thinking, between the empirical evidence of a century and a half of research into the literary and cultural background to the Pentateuch on the one hand, and 'the fear of heaven' and the assumptions of orthodox Judaism on the other, based on belief in the divine authorship of the Torah.

Louis Jacobs (1920–2006), by John R. Rifkin

Appointed rabbi of Manchester Central Synagogue in 1948, Jacobs returned to his home city (he always retained both affection for it and the accent) and immersed himself in community life. He engaged in what he termed 'an orgy' of public speaking (*Helping With Inquiries*, 95), at which he excelled; learned, humorous, and unafraid of contentious issues, he would preach, to the end of his days, without a note in sight. He was awarded his doctorate in 1952 for his thesis on economic life in Babylon in the Talmudic period.

Jacobs's abilities attracted the attention of the chief rabbi, Israel Brodie, and in 1954 he was invited to become minister at the prestigious New West End Synagogue in London, where the congregation included some of the key figures of the Anglo-Jewish establishment. Jacobs was by now a rising star in the community, tipped to be its future leader.

In 1957 Jacobs published *We Have Reason To Believe*, dubbed by the *Jewish Chronicle* almost fifty years later, 'that small book that detonated modern British Jewry's biggest religious crisis' (*Jewish Chronicle*, 10 March 2006), and which ran through five editions in his lifetime. The opening paragraph set out the intellectual quest in which its author was to be engaged for the rest of his days: the need to face the issues posed by modern thought and scholarship honestly, neither rejecting them 'as of the devil', nor confining them to a discrete corner of the mind where they could 'exist side-by-side with tradition in water-tight compartments' (p. 9). The central issue was the nature of revelation. Jacobs argued that the facts made available by careful research meant that the classic concept of the dictation of the Torah by God to Moses, 'Torah from heaven', could no longer be understood literally and required reinterpretation. As he was often to say later, 'It all depends on what one means by "from"'.

Surprisingly, the book attracted little immediate attention. Meanwhile Jacobs was appointed moral tutor at Jews' College, Anglo-Jewry's key institution for the training of Orthodox ministers, with a clear view to his succeeding Isidore Epstein as principal upon the latter's retirement. However, when in late 1961 the time came for his promotion, the chief rabbi, Brodie, who was required to confirm the position, demurred, claiming alternatively that Jacobs lacked the scholarship, a preposterous assertion, or the beliefs necessary for the post. Jacobs resigned, together with the honorary officers of the college and the affair, with the *Jewish Chronicle* staunchly on Jacobs's side, reached the national press. The chief rabbi, who refused to confirm Jacobs's reinstatement at the pulpit of the New West End Synagogue in 1964, subsequently justified himself on the grounds of Jacobs's 'published views'. A further uproar followed, and the whole sequence of events, widely aired once again in the media, came to be known as the Jacobs affair. Though his Orthodoxy was challenged, at no point was Jacobs's learning, courage, or intellectual integrity called into doubt.

Jacobs's followers, who included many of the leaders of Anglo-Jewry, founded the Society for the Study of Jewish Theology in September 1962, a platform from which Jacobs, never shy of polemics, was able to bring his views to wide audiences throughout the country. His argument was clear; the empirical evidence made it impossible to hold the traditional position by which Orthodoxy had come to be defined, that the Torah was literally the word of God. Instead, revelation had to be seen as not just to, but through, human beings. The Torah retained its divinity, but as a sublime record of human beings and God reaching out to each other, not as a literal record of what God dictated to Moses. He maintained, elaborated, and argued this position and its consequences for the authority of Jewish law and religious life throughout his life, notably in his *Principles of the Jewish Faith* (1964), a rigorous analysis of the thirteen Maimonidean articles of belief in the light of modern knowledge, and *Beyond Reasonable Doubt* (1999), a resumption, forty years later, of the arguments begun in *We Have Reason To Believe*. At the same time Jacobs maintained, both in his preaching and in his personal practice, that the laws and traditional structures of Judaism retained their validity. In this he differed sharply from Reform Judaism, from which, despite his years of teaching at its seminary, Leo Baeck College, he took pains to distance himself. He argued, rather, that Jewish law had never been static—hence the subtitle of his seminal work on the subject, *A Tree of Life: Diversity, Flexibility, and Creativity in Jewish Law* (1984)—and that what was needed was a re-engagement with this spirit of dynamic interaction with the intellectual, theological, and social challenges of the times. Despite his stance on revelation, Jacobs's beliefs about God, prayer, and life after death remained deeply traditional, reflecting the pious world in which he was educated and for which a part of him yearned until the end of his life.

In 1964 Jacobs's followers created the New London Synagogue, where a large number of by now deeply disaffected members of the New West End Synagogue joined him. (Ironically, it was housed in an abandoned Orthodox synagogue.) It quickly became a thriving congregation; from his pulpit, where Jacobs remained until his retirement in 2001, he repeatedly challenged orthodoxy for its rejection of what he forthrightly called truth, for its drift towards ever more right-wing (fundamentalist) attitudes, and for the stance of its rabbinical court on such issues as conversion. Particularly popular were his Monday night lectures on the Talmud, in which he combined immense erudition and effortless recall with the skills of a superb raconteur. In spite of his international reputation as a theologian and scholar, Jacobs always considered himself at heart a communal rabbi. He never forgot anyone and had a pleasant personal word for all. He and Shula enjoyed the social life of the community and Anglo-Jewry.

Jacobs had an ambivalent relationship towards the nascent Assembly of Masorti Synagogues, which was formed in 1991 as new congregations were founded that shared his traditional but non-fundamentalist theology, and which regarded him as their spiritual leader. He accepted that he could no longer belong to Orthodoxy, given its self-definition, but he often said that what he wanted to create was 'a mood, not a movement'. What, perhaps, he really sought was vindication by the very community that had rejected him, together with its recognition that it was indeed possible to embrace new knowledge without weakening or abandoning traditional Judaism and that this was in truth the only course for a person of integrity to adopt. That was never forthcoming and Jacobs was subjected to persistent attacks and sporadic insults throughout his career. His knowledge of Jewish sources was acknowledged to be unrivalled, and Orthodox Jews would consult him in private at his home in Clifton Hill, St John's Wood. But there was no public apology for the treatment he received.

Throughout his forty years of ministry at the New London Synagogue, Jacobs wrote prolifically and lectured widely. He was the author of over fifty books, as well as more than 500 published articles, across the whole spectrum of Jewish theology, law, Talmudic methodology, philosophy, and mysticism. His academic appointments included a year at Harvard Divinity School in 1985–6, and he was appointed visiting professor at Lancaster University in 1987. He was appointed CBE in 1990.

In December 2005, to mark 350 years since the return of Jewry to England under Oliver Cromwell, the *Jewish Chronicle* conducted a poll to find 'the greatest British Jew of all time'. Jacobs won by a huge margin, afterwards good naturedly describing the whole competition as 'daft' (*The*

Times, 30 Dec 2005). But some of the comments which accompanied readers' votes were revealing. One stated:

> As an Orthodox rabbi, it is a sad state but I have to keep my identity confidential for obvious reasons. Without Rabbi Jacobs's inspiration I, and I am sure many others, would have lost our sanity having to work within the intellectual boundaries imposed on us … His contribution to Anglo-Jewry is immense and will be recognised for centuries to come. (*Jewish Chronicle*, 30 Dec 2005)

Jacobs was never the same after Shula died on 12 November 2005. He became ill not long afterwards, though he was formally diagnosed as suffering from oesophageal cancer only a few weeks before his death. He faced his end with faith in God and in life after death. He donated his vast library to the Centre for Hebrew Studies at Yarnton, near Oxford. He died on 1 July 2006, a sabbath, at the London Clinic, Devonshire Place, Westminster, and was survived by his three children.

Jacobs was often described as the greatest chief rabbi Anglo-Jewry never had. A man of few hobbies (he described them in *Who's Who* as 'reading thrillers, watching television, hill walking'), he devoted his life to his scholarship and his congregation. His unique place in Anglo-Jewish history, assured by his extensive and brilliant publications, will always also be defined by the 'Jacobs affair'. No doubt the argument had other causes and was in part a battle between modernists and traditionalists waiting to be joined. But it was Jacobs's position, that of a believer in love with tradition, but of a believer nonetheless open to evidence and convinced by reason, that, in the long fight against religious fundamentalism, earned him the greatest respect.

JONATHAN WITTENBERG

Sources L. Jacobs, *We have reason to believe* (1957); 3rd edn (1965) · L. Jacobs, *Helping with enquiries* (1989) · *The Times* (4 July 2006) · *The Guardian* (5 July 2006) · *Daily Telegraph* (7 July 2006) · *The Independent* (11 July 2006) · *WW* (2006) · personal knowledge (2010) · private information (2010) · b. cert. · m. cert. · d. cert.
Archives SOUND BL NSA, documentary recording
Likenesses photograph, 1964, PA Photos, London · S. Malin, pen and ink with Chinese white, 2007, NPG · J. R. Rifkin, photograph, priv. coll. [*see illus.*] · M. Wallach, photograph, NPG · obituary photographs · photograph, Photoshot, London
Wealth at death £316,452: probate, 8 March 2007, *CGPLA Eng. & Wales*

Jauncey, Charles Eliot, **Baron Jauncey of Tullichettle** (**1925–2007**), judge, was born on 8 May 1925 at 18 Walker Street, Edinburgh, the only child of Captain John Henry Jauncey (1889–1958), naval officer, and his wife, Muriel Charlie (*b.* 1898), eldest daughter of Admiral Sir Charles Hope Dundas of Dundas. At the time of his birth registration his parents lived at 30 Regent Terrace, Edinburgh. He was educated at Radley College and, after war service in the Royal Naval Volunteer Reserve (1943–6) in Egypt and then India (from where he was invalided home after contracting polio, which left him with a slight limp), at Christ Church, Oxford (where he took a second in jurisprudence in 1947) and Glasgow University (where he graduated LLB in 1949). He married on 11 September 1948 Jean Cunninghame Graham (*b.* 1928), daughter of Admiral Sir Angus Edward Malise Bontine Cunninghame Graham of Gartmore. That marriage was dissolved in 1969, and on 27 April 1973 he married Elizabeth Ann Ballingal (*b.* 1928), widow of Major John Ballingal, and daughter of Captain Robert Henry Vivian Sivewright, naval officer. That marriage was dissolved in February 1977, and on 6 May 1977 he married (Sarah) Camilla Cathcart (*b.* 1946), schoolteacher, and youngest daughter of Lieutenant-Colonel Charles Frederick Cathcart. With his first wife he had two sons and a daughter; there was also a daughter from his third marriage.

Work was in short supply when Jauncey joined the Scottish bar as an advocate in 1949, but he soon established a substantial practice. Reserved and very much a gentleman by nature, he was more suited to drafting and opinion work than to run of the mill advocacy. He was employed mainly in the more specialized areas of civil practice, notably those to do with the law of trusts and with company and planning law. He became standing junior counsel in Scotland to the Ministry of Works in 1953 and to the Admiralty in the following year. In 1955 his considerable interest in and knowledge of genealogy led to his appointment as Kintyre pursuivant of arms. He held this position, in right of which he appeared as an advocate in peerage cases in the Lyon court, until his first judicial appointment in 1971. He took silk in 1963. In 1971 he was appointed sheriff principal of Fife and Kinross, a part-time appointment. In 1972 he accepted another part-time judicial appointment as a judge of the Courts of Appeal of Jersey and Guernsey. He resigned from his office as sheriff principal in 1974 when it became a full-time judicial office so that he could remain in practice at the bar.

In 1979 Jauncey received the recognition that had long been expected when he was elevated to the bench in the Court of Session as a senator of the College of Justice. After his appointment he was chosen to preside over two of the longest running and most complex cases ever to be heard in that court: the Glasgow fluoride case and a patent case involving an alleged infringement by a heavy lifting crane barge operating in the North Sea. He conducted them with conspicuous patience, fair-mindedness, and attention to detail. He gave way to his strong sense of the ridiculous when he described the pursuer in his judgment in the fluoride case as an elderly edentulous female, but the judgment itself was a model of fairness and brevity. He was spared the huge task of preparing a judgment in the patent case when it was settled after 183 days of evidence.

In 1988 Jauncey was chosen to fill the vacancy for a Scots judge on the appellate committee of the House of Lords that had been created when Lord Mackay of Clashfern was appointed lord chancellor. He was sworn of the privy council in the same year. He sat as a lord of appeal in ordinary until he retired from that appointment in 1996. He continued to sit occasionally on the appellate committee as a retired law lord until he reached the compulsory retirement age in May 2000. As he himself would have been the first to admit, he was not among the intellectual giants during his time as a member of the appellate committee. But he was thorough, reliable, and hard working, and well suited to life on the law lords' corridor, which was heavily dependent on mutual trust and respect among colleagues. His judgments both in the House of Lords and in the judicial committee of the privy council, of which as a lord of appeal he was also a member, were well balanced, succinct, and eminently readable. After his retirement he was appointed to hear an appeal by Martin Neary, dean of Westminster, who had been dismissed from his office for financial misconduct. Although he upheld the dismissal he subjected the abbey's handling of the case to severe criticism. He chaired a House of Lords committee that absolved from blame the two pilots of a Chinook helicopter that crashed on the Mull of Kintyre in 1994. He continued to play an active part in the work of the House of Lords and its committees after his retirement as lord of appeal until 2004, when he suffered a severe stroke from which he never fully recovered. He was a member of the Royal Company of Archers (the queen's bodyguard for Scotland) from 1951 and of the Historic Buildings Council for Scotland from 1971 to 1992.

Tall, handsome, and patrician in appearance, Jauncey brought a quiet dignity to everything that he did. He was widely respected as an advocate and as a judge. But he had many interests outside the law too. They brought him into contact with a wide circle of friends with similar connections to the areas of Scottish life in which he was interested, especially genealogy, historic buildings, fishing, and the countryside. He was the author of a booklet on the law pertaining to fishing, *Fishing in Scotland* (1952), the second edition of which was published in 1984. For most of his professional life he commuted each week between his flats in Edinburgh and later in London and the family home at Tullichettle, near Comrie in Perthshire. He died at Tullichettle on 18 July 2007 from causes attributed to his stroke three years earlier. His third wife and his four children survived him. DAVID HOPE

Sources *Daily Telegraph* (21 July 2007) · *The Independent* (23 July 2007); (28 July 2007) · *The Times* (24 July 2007); (1 Aug 2007) · *The Guardian* (25 July 2007) · *The Herald* [Glasgow] (25 July 2007) · Burke, *Peerage* · *WW* (2007) · personal knowledge (2011) · private information (2011) · b. cert. · m. certs. · d. cert.
Likenesses photograph, 1978, Camera Press, London · photographs, 1995, Photoshot, London · obituary photographs

Jay [*née* Garnett], **Margaret Christian** [Peggy] (**1913–2008**), local government politician, was born on 28 January 1913 at 2 Anson Road, Rusholme, Manchester, the eldest of three daughters of (James Clerk) Maxwell *Garnett (1880–1958), principal of the Municipal School of Technology, Manchester, later general secretary of the League of Nations Union, and his wife, Margaret Lucy, *née* Poulton (1887–1965). When she was seven her parents moved to Hampstead, where she would live for the rest of her life. She was educated at Malvern Girls' College, St Paul's Girls' School, and Somerville College, Oxford, where she took a diploma in economics in 1933, before marrying, on 30 September 1933, Douglas Patrick Thomas *Jay, later Baron Jay (1907–1996), then a fellow of All Souls College, Oxford, later a journalist and politician. They had been neighbours in Well Walk, Hampstead, and he had tutored her for her Oxford entrance examinations. She married him despite his warning her that he regarded monogamy as a sin. They had two sons and two daughters. She shared his political commitment, and served as a Labour member of London county council (LCC) for Hackney from 1938 to 1949, and then for Battersea from 1952 to 1964, continuing as a member of the Greater London council until 1967. She chaired the schools and arts and leisure committees, and was noted for her advocacy for the poor and marginalized. She and Audrey Callaghan formed a particularly effective partnership on the LCC children's committee. Among the causes she was associated with were the alleviation of homelessness, the welfare of children in homes and in hospitals, the provision of play facilities, and the rights of patients in psychiatric hospitals. She was devoted to Hampstead, and from 1968 to 1989 served as a singularly successful chairman of the Heath and Old Hampstead Society, campaigning against transport planners' and property developers' designs on Hampstead Heath, estate agents' signs in Old Hampstead, the encroachment of supermarket and fast food chains, and lap dancing clubs. She was dubbed 'the uncrowned Queen of Hampstead' by the local paper (*Camden New Journal*, 30 Jan 2003). She enjoyed passing on her campaigning skills to younger generations, and her position as matriarch of a talented and ever-expanding family. More pro-European than her former husband (they divorced in 1972), she joined the Social Democratic Party in 1983, but rejoined the Labour Party when Gordon Brown became prime minister in 2007. She died in Hampstead on 21 January 2008, and was survived by her four children with Douglas Jay: Peter (*b.* 1937), an economist, diplomat, and broadcaster, Martin (*b.* 1939), a yacht designer, and Catherine and Helen (*b.* 1945), the celebrated 'Jay twins' of the swinging sixties.

Sources *The Guardian* (22 Jan 2008) · *The Times* (23 Jan 2008); (30 Jan 2008); (1 Feb 2008); (7 Feb 2008) · *Daily Telegraph* (23 Jan 2008) · *The Independent* (29 Jan 2008); (30 Jan 2008) · *Camden New Journal* (31 Jan 2008) · b. cert. · m. cert.
Likenesses obituary photographs

Jeger [*née* Chivers], **Lena May**, **Baroness Jeger** (**1915–2007**), politician and journalist, was born on 19 November 1915 at 14B Northbrook Road, Wood Green, Middlesex, the daughter of Charles Chivers, a sorter for the Post Office, and his wife, (Eugenie) Alice, *née* James (*d.* 1965). She attended Southgate county school in Middlesex and went on to study English and French at Birkbeck College, London, during which period she became vice-president of the National Union of Students. She joined the civil service on graduation and her first job in 1936 was at a relatively junior level in the customs and excise department. She then moved to the Ministry of Information and later joined the Foreign Office, where her linguistic skills were

Lena May Jeger, Baroness Jeger (1915–2007), by unknown photographer, 1980

recognized and she learned Russian. At the end of the Second World War she became the deputy editor of the newspaper *British Ally*, which was produced for propaganda purposes for circulation in the Soviet Union, and she spent some months in the British embassy in Moscow.

In 1945 Lena Chivers was elected as a Labour councillor for St Pancras in London and she served in this capacity until 1959, chairing the borough housing committee. Between 1952 and 1955 she was also an elected Labour member of London county council. Her political work brought her into contact with the popular local MP for St Pancras South East, elected in the 1945 general election, Santo Wayburn Jeger (1898–1953). He was a Jewish medical practitioner, a founder of the Socialist Medical Association, a staunch advocate of the new National Health Service, and a well-respected and experienced figure in the Labour Party in London. They were married at St Marylebone register office on 19 March 1948; there were no children. A year later Lena Jeger left the civil service, and from 1951 to 1954 she worked as a journalist on the London staff of the *Manchester Guardian*. She retained her links to *The Guardian* (as it was renamed in 1959) for the rest of her life, working for it as a columnist during the period when she was out of parliament, and writing articles for it thereafter when she was a member of the House of Commons and subsequently of the House of Lords. Some of these pieces were portraits of her political colleagues, others were political obituaries.

Santo Jeger died unexpectedly in 1953 and Lena Jeger was selected as the Labour candidate for the consequent by-election in the marginal constituency of Holborn and St Pancras South (as it had been renamed in 1950). It was widely expected that the seat would be taken by the Conservative candidate but Jeger fought a good campaign, local sentiment in her favour was strong, and she retained the seat for Labour, increasing the majority to 1976 votes. One of her stories from this campaign was often repeated as an example of the problems to be met in canvassing: when Jeger was trying to persuade a constituent from Camden Town who lived at the top of a block of flats of the dangers of German re-armament the woman replied, 'If you can't stop them pissing in our lift, how can you expect me to believe you can stop the Germans re-arming?' (*Camden New Journal*, 8 March 2007).

In the 1955 general election Jeger's majority fell to only 931 votes and in 1959 she lost to the Conservative candidate by 656 votes. Yet her deep identification with the constituency and her local popularity helped her to win back the seat in the general election of 1964 and retain it in four subsequent elections (in 1974 it changed to Camden, Holborn and St Pancras South). She was universally admired for her political courage and honesty and widely liked for her personal warmth and humour. In 1960–61 and from 1968 to 1980 she was a member of the Labour Party's national executive committee, then a more influential body than it subsequently became.

Jeger was generally perceived as a left-wing Labour MP, a so-called Bevanite in the 1950s. She was personally close to Aneurin Bevan and his wife, Jennie Lee, was a friend of Barbara Castle, and was a devoted neighbour of the socialist thinker and historian R. H. Tawney during his latter years before his death in 1962. She was against British development and possession of nuclear weapons, criticized the Vietnam War, disagreed with restrictions on immigration, and opposed the attempt by Labour governments in the 1960s and 1970s to control the economy by prices and incomes policies and legislation. She was against continued British membership of the EEC in the 1975 referendum on that issue. She also opposed cigarette smoking, and wrote a section of *Common Sense about Smoking* in 1963, republished in 1965 as a Penguin Special.

Jeger was a prominent supporter of the reforming legislation of the 1960s that ended capital punishment and legalized homosexuality. A passionate campaigner for the legalization of abortion, she was a sponsor of the Abortion Law Reform Act of 1967. In 1951 she had edited a pamphlet for the National Council for the Unmarried Mother and her Child entitled *Illegitimate Children and their Parents*, which summarized the relevant law and the social support available for one-parent families. On the issue of women's rights she played a role in securing the Equal Pay Act of 1970. She also campaigned successfully against rules that reduced widows' pensions if they worked. She long favoured the separate taxation of married women, a reform eventually introduced by Margaret Thatcher's Conservative administration. Her constituency included a substantial community of Greek Cypriots and she was persuaded by their arguments in favour of self-determination for Cyprus, and for the exclusion of Turkish influence in Cypriot affairs. She became a notable exponent of their cause whose advocacy shaped Labour Party policy on the future of the island.

As a committed campaigner drawn to some unfashionable and controversial causes Jeger was not considered ministerial material by either of the Labour prime ministers of the 1960s and 1970s, Harold Wilson and James Callaghan. She made her mark in other and sometimes unglamorous ways, not least as the admired chairman in 1969–70 of the government's working party on sewage disposal, which made a good case for increased investment in, and better management of, the disposal of sewage and the improvement of water quality.

In 1979 Jeger stood down as MP for Camden, Holborn and St Pancras South, which she had made a safe seat for Labour, passing it on to Frank Dobson. She was made a life peer by James Callaghan in his resignation honours in that year. With Labour divided over ideology and personalities after the 1979 election defeat Jeger, as chairman of the Labour Party in 1979–80, had the almost impossible task of chairing the party's annual conference in Blackpool in 1980, where she tried valiantly to prevent the sessions descending into personal attacks and procedural confusion. She was remembered for a characteristic peroration to her opening speech there: 'We have to take the poetry of our ideals and translate it into the prose and policies of everyday life.'

In the House of Lords Jeger, with a front-bench brief as opposition spokesman on health (1983–6) and also on social security (1983–90), proved an able and fluent defender of the collectivist values she had always believed in. She retired to the back benches of the Lords in 1990. She continued to attend and participate in Lords' debates in the last years of her life, never wavering in her long-held convictions. She died on 26 February 2007 at Ashton House nursing home, Bolnore Road, Haywards Heath, West Sussex, of breast cancer and multi-systems failure. Speaking in the month after her death at a graduation ceremony at Birkbeck College, the historian Eric Hobsbawm paid tribute to her life and social contribution: 'She didn't make millions or have a glittering ministerial career. But she served her cause and the people of London as well as she could. It was a good life, lived by a good person' (Hobsbawm, 'She served her cause').

LAWRENCE GOLDMAN

Sources *The Times* (2 March 2007) • *BBC News* (2 March 2007); news.bbc.co.uk/1/hi/england/london/6413313.stm, 4 Aug 2010 • *The Guardian* (3 March 2007) • *The Independent* (3 March 2007) • *Camden New Journal* (8 March 2007) • *Daily Telegraph* (16 March 2007) • E. Hobsbawm, 'She served her cause', *BBK* [Birkbeck College, London], 22 (summer 2007); bbk.ac.uk/about_us/publications/bbk/bbk22/cause, 4 Aug 2010 • Burke, *Peerage* • *WW* (2007) • b. cert. • m. cert. • d. cert.

Archives JRL, Manchester Guardian papers • London School of Economics

Likenesses photographs, 1953–60, Rex Features, London • photographs, 1966–80, Photoshot, London • M. Webb, photograph, 1972, Getty Images, London • T. Blau, bromide print, 1979, Camera Press, London • photograph, 1980, Photoshot, London [*see illus.*] • obituary photographs

Wealth at death £391,393: probate, 13 Sept 2007, *CGPLA Eng. & Wales*

Jellicoe, George Patrick John Rushworth, second Earl Jellicoe and Baron Jellicoe of Southampton (1918–2007), army officer, politician, and businessman, was born on 4 November 1918 at Holwell House, Hatfield, Hertfordshire, the only son of John Rushworth *Jellicoe, Viscount Jellicoe of Scapa, later first Earl Jellicoe (1859–1935), naval officer, and his wife, Florence Gwendoline (1877–1964), daughter of Sir Charles Cayzer, founder of the Clan Line shipping firm. Born into a family of national prominence and into a life of privilege, he was conscious from his early years of the expectations and responsibilities this entailed. George V was his godfather, the king and queen regularly stayed with his family on the Isle of Wight for Cowes week, and he was a page of honour at the coronation of George VI. He became Viscount Brocas at the age of seven, when his father was made an earl. He was educated at Winchester College and while still at school inherited his father's earldom. He won an exhibition to Trinity College, Cambridge, and before taking this up spent a year in Germany learning the language with a view to a diplomatic career. At Cambridge he achieved a first in history and—in the vacations—developed an enthusiasm for the Cresta run and for challenging skiing.

At the outbreak of the Second World War in 1939 Jellicoe surprised many people by opting for the Coldstream Guards rather than the navy with which his name was so closely associated. He was seconded to a guards commando unit and after training in Scotland saw active service in 1941 in north Africa, where he was wounded while leading a patrol behind enemy lines. In 1942 he was recruited by David Stirling for the newly formed Special Air Service (SAS) and the following year became commander of the Special Boat Squadron (SBS), which was deployed on dangerous sorties against the German-occupied Greek islands. In June 1942 he led a raid on Heraklion airfield on Crete, which was being used by the Germans to harass shipping convoys in the eastern Mediterranean. After being dropped off in rubber boats from a submarine his party cut the perimeter wire around the airfield and when they were challenged by sentries managed to convince the Germans that they were merely drunken Greek peasants. In the event they managed to place time-bombs on some twenty-one German aircraft and a munitions supply dump, eventually escaping to a rendezvous with another submarine. For this escapade Jellicoe was appointed DSO.

Other adventures followed thick and fast. In 1943, after the Italians had signed an armistice with the allies, he was parachuted into Rhodes to try to persuade the Italian governor to hand the island over to the allies rather than to the Germans. He landed off course and, fearing he would be captured, ate the letter he was carrying from General Maitland Wilson to the Italian commander. When

George Patrick John Rushworth Jellicoe, second Earl Jellicoe and Baron Jellicoe of Southampton (1918–2007), by Elliott & Fry, 1962

he managed to reach the latter he was frustrated by his lack of the swallowed credentials and the Italian's reluctance to antagonize the 10,000-strong German garrison. This setback did not prevent him from arranging for various other islands to be successfully occupied by British troops. For this operation he was awarded the MC. In the course of his campaigning he was also mentioned three times in dispatches and awarded the Légion d'honneur, the Croix de Guerre, and the Greek war cross. When the allied forces were eventually closing in on Athens and the Germans were evacuating the city it was Jellicoe (on a borrowed bicycle) who arrived first in the capital and announced to an ecstatic Greek population that they were liberated. Before demobilization he had reached the rank of colonel, although still only twenty-seven.

Jellicoe married on 23 March 1944 the Canadian-born Patricia Christine (Patsy) O'Kane (daughter of Jeremiah O'Kane, of Vancouver), whom he had met in Beirut while they were both engaged in sensitive operations; they had two sons, Patrick and Nicholas, and two daughters, Alexandra and Zara. He also made many enduring friendships during his special operations, notably with Patrick Leigh Fermor, who was engaged in activities similar to his own and with whom he remained on close terms until the end of his life.

With the war over Jellicoe achieved his original ambition of joining the foreign service. He served in Washington and Brussels as well as in the northern department of the Foreign Office (responsible for Soviet affairs) in London, and was widely considered (like his Washington colleague Nicko Henderson, later ambassador in Germany, France, and the USA) to be a rising star. However, by the time he was posted to Baghdad as deputy secretary-general of the Baghdad pact his marriage had run into difficulties and he set up house with Philippa Anne Bridge, a highly attractive young divorced woman (the former wife of Christopher Charles Cyprian Bridge, and the daughter of Phillip Rushwell Rendell Dunne, of Gatley Park, Herefordshire) he had met in London in 1955. The Foreign Office felt that this arrangement was not sustainable, and he was offered the choice of parting with Philippa or resigning from the diplomatic service. Without hesitation he chose the latter, although it was to be more than ten years before he obtained a divorce from Patsy and was free to marry Phillipa, which he did on 4 April 1966. They had a son, John, and two daughters, Emma and Daisy.

Long before his second marriage Jellicoe had embarked on a successful new career, this time in politics. He had already demonstrated an interest in political—particularly foreign—affairs with speeches in the House of Lords, and his first appointment, notwithstanding the scandal of his leaving the diplomatic service, was as a lord-in-waiting to the queen. He was promoted as a member of successive Conservative governments through a variety of junior posts until in 1963 he was appointed first lord of the Admiralty, in 1967 deputy leader of the opposition in the House of Lords, and in 1970 lord privy seal, minister for the civil service, and leader of the House of Lords. He played a major part in promoting government legislation in a number of fields including European affairs, industrial relations, public service conditions, and the handling of emergencies. He was widely respected as a prodigiously energetic minister who was popular with politicians and civil servants alike.

Given Jellicoe's steady ascent up the ministerial ladder it came as a serious shock when in 1973 Scotland Yard inquiries into a call-girl ring revealed his name. When questioned by the cabinet office about the accusations, he admitted to having had relations with call-girls, and although there was never any implication that national security had been compromised by his involvements, the simultaneous and more serious allegations—involving drugs and prostitutes—against Lord Lambton, and the vivid recollections of the embarrassment caused by the Profumo affair of a few years before, persuaded the prime minister, Edward Heath, to accept Jellicoe's promptly offered resignation. There were many who felt that his departure from the political scene was unnecessary as well as unfortunate, and there was a general consensus that he had acted honourably in not attempting to hang on to office. But it was now the second time that his promising career in public service had been undone by extra-matrimonial affairs.

Jellicoe immediately embarked on yet another successful career, this time in business. He became, among other things, chairman of Tate and Lyle, the Davy Corporation, and the British Overseas Trade Board, president of the

London chamber of commerce and industry, a director of Sothebys, Smiths Industries, Morgan Crucible, and Warburgs Bank, and governor of the Centre for Environmental Studies. In 1995 he became involved with Hakluyt, a confidential intelligence company. He also took on the chancellorship of Southampton University and the presidency of the Royal Geographical Society. All these bodies benefited from his energy and leadership skills. He was appointed KBE in 1986, elected a fellow of the Royal Society in 1990, and created a life peer (to enable him to remain a participant in the House of Lords), as Baron Jellicoe of Southampton, in 1999. He remained an active and highly sociable figure until his death. He had always been well off financially. He had bought Tidcombe Manor in Wiltshire soon after he left the diplomatic service, and this estate became a convivial and happy centre for his extended family. He died there on 22 February 2007 of a heart attack. He was survived by his wife, Philippa, their children, and his first family. He was succeeded as third earl by his son Patrick (*b.* 1950).

A biography of Jellicoe (published by Lorna Windmill in 2005) was entitled *A British Achilles*, and made clear that his Achilles heel was his susceptibility to women, to whom he had always been a very attractive figure on account of his dash, humour, and generosity of spirit. But he was also dearly loved by almost all who met him on account of his life-enhancing ebullience. The *Daily Telegraph* obituary of Jellicoe described him as 'by consensus … one of the nicest men in public life' and few contemporaries would have disagreed with the verdict. JOHN URE

Sources L. A. Windmill, *A British Achilles* (2005) · *The Independent* (24 Feb 2007) · *The Times* (26 Feb 2007) · *Daily Telegraph* (26 Feb 2007) · *The Guardian* (26 Feb 2007) · Burke, *Peerage* · *WW* (2007) · personal knowledge (2011) · private information (2011) · b. cert. · m. cert. [1966] · d. cert.

Archives Bodl. Oxf., William Clark MSS

Likenesses Lenare, cellulose acetate negatives, 1953, NPG · W. Stoneman, photograph, 1955, NPG · Elliott & Fry, half-plate negative, 1962, NPG [*see illus.*] · Elliott & Fry, half-plate negatives, 1962, NPG · photographs, 1963, Getty Images, London, Hult. Arch. · photographs, 1963–73, PA Photos, London · G. White, photographs, 1973, Rex Features, London · photographs, 1986–90, Photoshot, London · M. Ferguson, photographs, 2002, Rex Features, London · J. Merton, photograph, Courtauld Inst. · D. Moore, photograph, Camera Press, London · obituary photographs

Wealth at death £2,811,906: probate, 15 Sept 2008, *CGPLA Eng. & Wales*

Jenkins, (John) Robin (1912–2005), novelist, was born on 11 September 1912 at Burnside Terrace, Flemington, near Cambuslang, Lanarkshire, the son of James Jenkins, spirit salesman, and his wife, Annie, *née* Robin. His father died in 1919, after serving in the trenches during the First World War; his early death, which Jenkins attributed to the war, meant his mother had to work in domestic service to maintain her children. He was educated (on a bursary) at Hamilton Academy and then at Glasgow University, where he graduated MA in English in 1936, going on to become a teacher in Glasgow in 1937. On 30 June the same year he married Mary McIntyre (May) Wylie (1915–1988), hospital nurse, and daughter of John Wylie, shipyard

(John) Robin Jenkins (1912–2005), by Jennifer McRae, 2000

worker. They had two daughters, Helen and Ann, and a son, Colin.

Pacifism, brought about by powerful memories of his father's death, led Jenkins to become a conscientious objector in the Second World War, and he worked for six years for the Forestry Commission in Argyll. After the war he taught abroad, in Afghanistan (at the Ghazi School, Kabul, 1957–9), Spain (at the British Institute, Barcelona, 1959–61), and Malaysia (at Gaya College, Sabah, 1961–5), before returning to teach at Dunoon grammar school. He left teaching to take up a full-time career as a writer in 1970, producing a prodigious number of novels, not all of which were published before his death.

Jenkins's impressive body of work drew heavily on the distinctive and colourful elements of his personal experience. A clutch of early novels focused on childhood and poverty, clearly determined by his position as a scholarship boy (as in *Happy for the Child*, 1953), and his life as a teacher in Glasgow; he returned to such themes throughout his career, as in the striking *Just Duffy* (1985). *The Cone-Gatherers* (1955), one of his most successful novels in its wider public recognition and his personal favourite, used conscientious objectors in a forest setting as its subject; *A Would-be Saint* (1978) and *The Pearl-fishers* (published posthumously in 2007) also drew on Jenkins's Forestry Commission experience. A number of mid-career novels depicted situations made familiar to him by his teaching experience overseas; again he was interested in cultural conflicts and the misunderstandings they produce, through ethnicity as well as class. *Dust on the Paw* (1961) was one of his best and most ambitious works from this period but he also returned to these settings in later years in *Leila* (1995). The focus of all his novels, however, remained the same: the difficulty of goodness, both in the sense of being good, and the complicated responses that apparent goodness in an individual produces in others. Childhood, and the dynamic between innocence and experience, were consistently a basis for these explorations, from the early novel *The Changeling* (1958) to *Matthew and Sheila* (1998), although some later novels also explored the idiosyncrasies of old age (for instance *Willie Hogg*, 1993, and *Childish Things*, 2001). The particular implications of goodness, perceived or real, in a Scottish context were addressed through contemporary settings in *A Very Scotch Affair* (1968) and *Fergus Lamont* (1979), and with a historical backdrop in *The Awakening of George Darroch* (1985) and *Lady Magdalen* (2003). He also made forays into the short story with *A Far Cry from Bowmore* (1973) and *Lunderston Tales* (1996).

While Jenkins eschewed the vernacular and the visceral espoused by younger Scottish writers, his moral realism, the desire to confront the uncomfortable and unspeakable, can be seen recurring in such novelists as Iain Banks and A. L. Kennedy, whose subject matter might initially appear very different from his own. Jenkins himself cited Evelyn Waugh as an influence, and praised Robert Louis Stevenson's south sea fiction, but his interest in characters who represent fantastic or grotesque personalities might also be linked with earlier writers like James Hogg and Sir Walter Scott. Although he was described as 'the Scottish Thomas Hardy' because of the bleakness of his perspective, and while some of his novels might be aligned with Scottish working-class fiction of the 1950s, Jenkins saw himself as a blackly comic moralist, 'a mixture of dour Presbyterian realism and another part of me which says to hell with all that' (Norquay, 'Moral absolutism', 439), returning to the same concern with goodness and hypocrisy in all his novels.

Scottish literary critics frequently argued that Jenkins never fully achieved the commercial success his novels deserved. He may have failed to attract a wider readership and critical acclaim because his novels initially appeared to offer social realism but were concerned with much wider metaphysical explorations: they were uncomfortable to experience but profound in impact. As a writer he saw himself as very much working on his own. Although he attributed critical neglect to his time living in (and writing about) foreign parts, in later years he gained recognition for his contribution to Scottish literature, being appointed OBE in 1999 and receiving the Andrew Fletcher of Saltoun award in 2001, for services to Scottish life and culture. In 2003 he was given a Saltire Society lifetime achievement award. He died on 24 February 2005 at Inverclyde Royal Hospital, Greenock, following a stroke. He was survived by his daughters, Helen and Ann; his wife, May, and his son, Colin, predeceased him.

GLENDA NORQUAY

Sources G. Norquay, 'Moral absolutism in the novels of Robert Louis Stevenson, Robin Jenkins and Muriel Spark: challenges to realism', PhD diss., University of Edinburgh, 1985 · G. Norquay and others, 'Robin Jenkins: special feature', *Cencrastus*, 24 (1986) · *EdinR*, 106 (2001) [R. Jenkins issue] · *The Herald* [Glasgow] (25 Feb 2005); (26 Feb 2005); (27 Feb 2005) · *The Times* (26 Feb 2005) · *The Scotsman* (26 Feb 2005); (1 March 2005) · B. Morton, 'A personal appreciation', *Northings: Highlands & Islands Arts Journal* [online journal] (March 2005) · I. Murray, *Scottish writers talking* (2006) · *WW* (2005) · Robin Jenkins archive, NL Scot., acc. 12645 · personal knowledge (2009) · private information (2009) · b. cert. · m. cert. · d. cert.

Archives NL Scot. | SOUND BL NSA, documentary recording

Likenesses J. McRae, oil on linen, 2000, Scot. NPG [*see illus.*] · N. Ross, sculpture, Benmore Botanic Garden, Argyll · obituary photographs · photograph, repro. in Murray, *Scottish writers*, 102 · photograph, repro. in *Edinburgh Review*

Wealth at death £323,381.01: confirmation, 9 Aug 2005, *CCI*

Jennett, (William) Bryan (1926–2008), neurosurgeon, was born on 1 March 1926 at Finglas, Waldegrave Road, Twickenham, the only son of Robert William Jennett (1884/5–1956), a civil servant of Irish descent in the Ministry of Labour, and his Scottish wife, Jessie Pate, *née* Loudon (1892–1975). Through his mother he was related to at least fifteen medical practitioners. He had two sisters, Jean (*b.* 1923) and Sheena (*b.* 1929). He was educated at King's College, Wimbledon, and King George V School, Southport. At Liverpool medical school he was the top graduate of his year, in 1949, and was president of the British Medical Students' Association. He married his classmate Sheila Mary Pope (*b.* 1926) at Liverpool South register office on 15 September 1950 followed the next day by a service at Liverpool Anglican Cathedral. She was the daughter of Robert Herbert Pope, professional tenor and tea merchant, and went on to have a distinguished career as a respiratory physiologist. They had three sons, Peter, Martin, and John, and a daughter, Hilary.

Jennett's neurosurgical training and his abiding interest in head injuries began when he was house surgeon to Sir Hugh Cairns in Oxford and then, during national service, surgical specialist at the Royal Army Medical Corps hospital in Wheatley. Training posts followed in Cardiff and Manchester. He gained the fellowship of the Royal College of Surgeons of England in 1952, and in 1961 he gave a Hunterian lecture there on post-traumatic epilepsy. A Rockefeller fellowship in 1958/9 with the neurophysiologist Horace Magoun at the University of California, Los Angeles, produced the work on experimental brain compression for which he was awarded an MD by the University of Liverpool in 1960.

In 1963 Jennett was appointed to a combined NHS and university consultant neurosurgical post in the West of Scotland unit at Killearn Hospital and then became the first holder of the chair of neurosurgery at the University of Glasgow, from 1967 to 1991. He found a supportive, multidisciplinary collaborative environment in the Institute of Neurological Sciences, developed by J. Sloan Robertson, and in the university under the leadership of Sir Charles Illingworth. He was able to express his commitment to applying laboratory and clinical research to the care of patients and his philosophy of bringing scientists from other fields to apply their expertise to the solution of neurosurgical problems. The understanding gained in the 1960s and 1970s of relationships between brain blood flow and intracranial pressure changed the practice of neuroanaesthesia and advanced the treatment of patients with acute brain damage. During this time he co-directed with A. Murray Harper the Medical Research Council's cerebral circulation research group.

In the 1970s, in order to support rational decision-making, Jennett's focus turned to assembling information on the prognosis of severe injury. He addressed the social, ethical, and philosophical issues arising in the care of very severely brain damaged people and, in 1972, along with Fred Plum, a leading American neurologist, he first described the 'persistent vegetative state' in an article in *The Lancet*. He later contributed influentially to the debate that clarified legal aspects of the management and decisions about limitation of treatment of such people. The Glasgow coma scale, described with Graham Teasdale in 1974, and the Glasgow outcome scale, described with Michael Bond in 1975, established an international common language to assess brain damage, and over the next thirty-five years the papers in which they were presented, again published in *The Lancet*, became the two most frequently cited neurosurgical publications. International collaborative studies of prognosis and treatment followed, unique in their scale and continuity, which became the foundation of a critical search for improved treatments. Identification of risk factors for complications after mild injuries led to neurosurgeons under his leadership developing the first national guidelines for head injury care. Meanwhile the outstanding department that he created in Glasgow attracted trainees from many countries whom he inspired and supported enthusiastically and generously throughout their careers. Through them he advanced the academic approach to neurosurgery throughout the world.

Jennett (known to friends and colleagues as 'B.J.') was an outstanding communicator: lucid, rational, and convincing. He wrote almost 300 papers, the last in December 2007, and the clarity of his writing produced several influential books: *Epilepsy after Head Injuries* (1962, revised edn, 1975), *Introduction to Neurosurgery* (1964, running to five editions by 1994), *Management of Head Injuries* (with Graham Teasdale, 1981), *High Technology Medicine: Benefits and Burdens* (1984, revised edn, 1986), and *The Vegetative State: Medical Facts, Ethical and Legal Dilemmas* (2002). In 1980, in the face of great public controversy and concern caused by a *Panorama* documentary questioning the criteria used to establish brain death in potential organ donors, he courageously led a robust, effective defence both of the concept of brain death and of the criteria and codes of practice used to identify it; this proved pivotal in sustaining and then increasing the number of organs available for transplantation.

Between 1981 and 1986 Jennett served as dean of medicine at Glasgow University. His expanding breadth of interest and interactions with economists and policy makers led to his intellect and instinct for rigorous analysis being increasingly applied to issues across medicine and its interface with society. Ahead of his time, these included influential reports on the appropriate use of high-cost technology and the organization, with Barbara Stocking of the King's Fund, of a novel series of consensus conferences on clinical practice. He held many leadership roles in professional and public bodies including presidency of the neurology section of the Royal Society of Medicine (1986–7), the International Society for Technology Assessment in Health Care (1987–9), and Headway, the national head injury patients' group (1988–95). On retirement in 1991 he was appointed CBE and in 1993 he was awarded an honorary DSc by St Andrews University. In September 2007 he was the first recipient of the medal of the Society of British Neurological Surgeons.

Jennett's main recreation after settling in Scotland was sailing, a pastime shared with his wife, Sheila, and all his family. He died at his home, 3/3 Lauderdale Mansions, 47 Novar Drive, Glasgow, on 26 January 2008 from complications of multiple myeloma, diagnosed in 2002. He was survived by his wife and their four children.

GRAHAM TEASDALE

Sources *Surgical Neurology*, 10 (1978), 213–15 • *The Herald* [Glasgow] (29 Jan 2008); (30 Jan 2008); (2 Feb 2008); (5 Feb 2008) • *Evening Times* [Glasgow] (31 Jan 2008) • *The Independent* (16 Feb 2008) • *The Times* (21 Feb 2008) • *Times Higher Education Supplement* (21 Feb 2008) • *The Lancet* (23 Feb 2008) • *BMJ*, 336 (1 March 2008), 512 • *The Guardian* (19 March 2008) • *Brain Injury*, 22/4 (April 2008), 293–4 • *Neurology*, 71 (1 July 2008), 13 • N. Stocchetti and others, 'Bryan Jennett and the field of traumatic brain injury: its intellectual and ethical heritage in neuro-intensive care', *Intensive Care Medicine*, 34/10 (2008), 1774–8 • F. Ponce and A. Lozano, 'Measuring excellence in clinical translation: what are the top works in the field of neurosurgery?', *Clinical Neurosurgery*, 57 (2010), 94–6 • www.societyns.org/society/bio.aspx?MemberID=14741, 1 June 2011 • www.universitystory.gla.ac.uk/biography/?id=WH2474&type=P, 1 June 2011 • *WW* (2008) • personal knowledge (2012) • private information (2012) • b. cert. • m. cert. • d. cert.

Archives Royal College of Physicians and Surgeons of Glasgow, personal papers | SOUND BL NSA, documentary recording

Likenesses obituary photographs • photograph, repro. in *Surgical Neurology*, 213 • photograph, repro. in www.societyns.org/society/bio.aspx?MemberID=14741 • photograph, repro. in www.universitystory.gla.ac.uk/biography/?id=WH2474&type=P

Johnson, Douglas William John (1925–2005), historian, was born at 43 Pitt Street, Leith, Edinburgh, on 1 February 1925, the son of John Thornburn Johnson, land surveyor and town planner, and his wife, Christine Douglas, *née* Mair. His parents had married in Edinburgh in 1916, but at the time of his birth lived at 1 Seward Road, Hanwell, London. From his Scottish mother he may have drawn an understanding of the auld alliance between Scotland and France. He was educated at the Royal Grammar School, Lancaster, and was fifteen when on 18 June 1940 he heard General Charles de Gaulle's appeal to the French on the BBC to ignore the armistice requested by Marshal Pétain and continue the war against Germany. Often at school he wore the cross of Lorraine, a symbol of his support for the Free French. In 1942 he won a scholarship to read history at Worcester College, Oxford. He was called up for military service in the Northamptonshire regiment in 1943–4, but was invalided out. He returned to Oxford, graduating with a second-class degree in modern history in 1946, then continued with graduate studies, writing a BLitt thesis on Sir James Graham, home secretary to Robert Peel in the 1840s.

In 1947 Johnson was one of the first cohort of foreign students to be awarded a scholarship to the prestigious École Normale Supérieure in the rue d'Ulm, Paris, the training ground of France's academic and intellectual élite. He encountered a post-liberation Paris that was divided by powerful animosities inherited from the occupation. He was inspired by the Marxist philosopher Louis Althusser, and met the left-wing, Catholic, former resister and future historian François Bédarida. This was also, however, post-liberation Paris of some gaiety. At a joint ball with the women students of the École Normale Supérieure of Sèvres he met Madeleine Rébillard, whom he married in 1950. They had one daughter.

While Madeleine taught at Rouen to fulfil the terms of her government scholarship Johnson was appointed a lecturer at the University of Birmingham in 1949. In Paris he had studied nineteenth-century French history with Charles Pouthas, and in 1963 (the year in which he was promoted to a professorship at the University of Birmingham) he published *Guizot: Aspects of French history, 1787–1874*. Organized thematically, it explored the career of an austere Calvinist politician who sought to reconcile the gains of the French Revolution with ordered government, wrote 'whiggish' histories setting the French and European struggle for liberty in a millennial context, and as sometime ambassador at the court of St James was a great admirer of the English constitution of 1688, which French liberals had tried to imitate in 1830.

In 1968 Johnson succeeded Alfred Cobban as professor of French history at University College, London, a post he held until his retirement in 1990. He was head of the department of history (1979–83) and dean of the faculty of arts (1979–82). In London he continued his research into French history; his publications included *France and the Dreyfus Affair* (1966), *The French Revolution* (1970), and *Michelet and the French Revolution* (1990), and he was general editor of the Fontana History of Modern France. He also developed a new role, as an ambassador of Franco-British relations, at a time when de Gaulle's successive vetoes of British entry into the Common Market had done much to damage them. In 1965, on the invitation of Paul Barker of *New Society*, Johnson gave a lecture at Chatham House entitled 'The political principles of General de Gaulle'. After 1976 Johnson became a pillar of the Franco-British Council, set up in 1972 by Edward Heath to improve understanding between the two countries. With François Bédarida and the economic historian François Crouzet he edited *France and Britain: Ten Centuries of History* (1980), attracting contributions from a galaxy of historians, journalists, novelists, politicians, and diplomats. Under the auspices of the Franco-British Council he co-edited *A Day in June: Britain and de Gaulle, 1940* (2000) and *Cross-Channel Currents: a Hundred Years of the Entente Cordiale* (2004). From 1993 Johnson sat on the scientific council of the Fondation Charles de Gaulle. The French government showered him with honours. He was made a commandeur des Palmes Académiques in 1987, and chevalier (1990) then commandeur (1997) of the Légion d'honneur. Although he advised Margaret Thatcher on French matters the British government neglected to recognize his services.

Less formally Johnson provided benign but decisive support to a wide range of academics and graduate students who were studying French society, politics, and culture. As president of the Association for the Study of Modern and Contemporary France, founded in 1980, he used his contacts to invite a wide range of French figures to its conferences. He was instantly recognizable in his béret basque and cashmere scarf. His geniality, generosity, witty interventions, and deadpan humour endeared him to a wide field of lovers of France. In 2000 Martyn Cornick and Ceri Crossley edited a *Festschrift* in his honour, *Problems in French History*. The occasion was marked by 'an evening with Douglas Johnson' at the French Institute in London, when he did what he did best, telling stories about his encounters with French people and situations over more than half a century. He died of cancer of the oesophagus at the Royal Free Hospital, Camden, London, on 28 April 2005. He was survived by his wife, Madeleine, and their daughter. ROBERT GILDEA

Sources M. Cornick and C. Crossley, eds., *Problems in French history* (2000), xvii–xix · *The Guardian* (29 April 2005); (12 May 2005) · *The Independent* (30 April 2005); (9 May 2005) · *The Times* (5 May 2005) · *Daily Telegraph* (16 May 2005) · M. Evans, *History Today*, 55/7 (1 July 2005), 6–7 · S. Reynolds, *Modern and Contemporary France*, 13/4 (2005), 583–7 · J. Hoppit, 'Remembering Professor Douglas Johnson', symposium, 2 Dec 2005, UCL · *WW* (2005) · personal knowledge (2009) · private information (2009) · b. cert. · d. cert.
Likenesses obituary photographs

Johnson, Frank Robert (1943–2006), journalist, was born on 20 January 1943 at Hackney Hospital, London, the only son and first child of Ernest Johnson, baker and pastry cook, and his wife, Doreen Elizabeth, *née* Skinner, of 68 Belgrade Road, Stoke Newington. The family was close, and Johnson did not fully leave home until he was thirty-two. Until then, his mother would bring him a cup of tea in bed every morning.

Johnson failed the eleven-plus examination, and was educated at Chartesey and Shoreditch secondary schools. His school career was undistinguished, and he left at sixteen. By that time he had developed a love of opera that was to prove lifelong. At the age of fourteen he had appeared in *Norma* at Covent Garden, alongside Maria Callas, in the silent role of one of her sons. He later described the first night:

> I could not forget that when Callas bore down on us with the knife, her nostrils flared; that when, dropping the knife, she repentantly clasped me to her bosom, her perfume smelt like that of an aunt who was always kissing me; and that … there penetrated, into my left eye, the tip of the diva's right breast, which partnership remained throughout the subsequent duet with Stignani … there are few men who can truthfully say that their eye made contact with the right nipple of Maria Callas. (*Out of Order*, 246–7)

After leaving school Johnson took a bus to Fleet Street, and asked for and got a job as a messenger-boy at the first office he came to, that of the *Sunday Express*. In 1960 his talent was spotted and he joined the *Walthamstow Post* as a reporter. He moved to the *Walthamstow Guardian* the following year, and worked briefly in Barrow in Furness for the *North-West Daily Mail* from 1965 to 1966. In the latter year he joined the press gallery of the House of Commons as a reporter for the *Nottingham Evening Post*, soon becoming a lobby correspondent for the *Liverpool Daily Post*. He joined the political staff of *The Sun* in 1969.

It was during these early years in parliament that Johnson built up the habits of observation that were to stand him in such good stead when, in 1972, he became a leader writer for the *Daily Telegraph*, whose 'unfashionably right-wing views', as he put it, he shared 'before they became fashionably unfashionable' (*Out of Order*, 8). His working-class toryism was attracted by the rise of Margaret Thatcher. He began to write the paper's parliamentary sketch. It was in this role that he was the master. His comic gift was based on the effect of inverting expectations: 'exemplary cowardice'; 'Such is his [James Callaghan's] deviousness that he always knows the right moment at which to be straightforward'; 'If the Government bales out the C of E, all Heaven will break loose'. It was always deployed with a lightness of touch, and hit the right note with a public that wanted irreverence about the political situation of the 1970s, but not nastiness. He was a virtuoso, easily outclassing all others in the field. Amusing and handsome, with large quantities of wavy hair, Johnson was by this time considered one of the most eligible bachelors in London.

Johnson was so successful as a sketch-writer that he feared being trapped in the role. In 1979 he left the *Daily Telegraph* for much higher pay as the political columnist of Sir James Goldsmith's new weekly magazine *Now!*, but shortly before the magazine folded in 1981, he joined *The Times*, the paper that, as a young autodidact, he had most respected. There, too, he became the sketch-writer, but cast this off in 1984 in favour of being the paper's Paris diarist and then its correspondent in Bonn from 1985 to 1986, hoping through these posts to gain the education in European civilization his school had not provided. He returned to London, however, as the sketch-writer once more.

In 1987 Johnson became associate editor of *The Times*, but was at war—as was quite often the case in his career—with his editor, and left the paper in 1988 to become associate editor and political columnist of the *Sunday Telegraph* under the editorship of Peregrine Worsthorne, whom he much admired. There Johnson created what he called Worsthorne College, the mischievous, intellectually original comment pages that, despite endless skirmishing, survived the replacement of Worsthorne as editor (though not as the 'comment editor') by Trevor Grove, in the following year. In 1994 Johnson was promoted deputy editor by Grove's successor, Charles Moore. In 1995, after Moore's departure to edit the *Daily Telegraph*, Johnson hoped to succeed him at the Sunday paper. In fact, however, the owner, Conrad Black, made Johnson editor of *The Spectator* instead. Although Johnson brought to the job all his qualities of subversive humour, intellectual curiosity, and encouragement of the young, his time at the magazine was not very successful. His lack of organizational power was marked, and he fell out irrevocably with the business management of the paper. In 1999 he was removed from his post by Black, who appointed Boris Johnson in his stead. Johnson was hurt by Black's failure to give him this decision in person.

Despite his eviction from the editor's chair at *The Spectator*, Johnson continued to work for the Telegraph group, returning yet again to his most popular role as sketch-writer for the *Daily Telegraph*. But in 1999 he developed cancer, of which, after a long struggle, he died at the Chelsea and Westminster Hospital on 15 December 2006. He was lovingly cared for by Virginia Mary Fraser, *née* Grose, the widow of Simon Fraser, the master of Lovat; they had married on 23 December 1998. (Johnson's first marriage, which he omitted from *Who's Who*, had ended in divorce.) He had no children. Although Johnson was an Anglican his funeral took place at the Roman Catholic church of the Most Holy Redeemer and St Thomas More, Cheyne Row, on 22 December. He was cremated at Mortlake crematorium, and his ashes were scattered in the Languedoc region of France, where he and his wife had a house.

CHARLES MOORE

Sources F. Johnson, *Out of order* (1982) · *The Times* (16 Dec 2006) · *Daily Telegraph* (16 Dec 2006) · *The Independent* (16 Dec 2006) · *The Guardian* (18 Dec 2006) · *WW* (2006) · personal knowledge (2010) · private information (2010) · b. cert. · m. cert. [1998] · d. cert.
Archives FILM BFINA, current affairs footage
Likenesses N. Garland, cartoon, priv. coll. · obituary photographs
Wealth at death £153,547: probate, 24 May 2007, *CGPLA Eng. & Wales*

Johnson, Henry James [Jim] (1924–2008), army officer and businessman, was born on 21 December 1924 at 36 Royal Avenue, Chelsea, London, the son of Paul Manuel Johnson and his wife, Dorothy Maud, *née* Bird. His father was a Ceylon tea planter who was rumoured to have worked in intelligence in Italy in the 1930s and later at Bletchley Park during the war. His mother was Australian, and came from the family who owned H. & S. Bird & Co., provisioners based in Sydney. He was named after his paternal grandfather, Sir Henry James Johnson, solicitor. After a boyhood in Ceylon and Florence, he returned with his family to Britain in the late 1930s, living first in London and then in Letchworth Garden City. He attended St Edmund's School in Hindhead, Surrey, and later Westminster School, where his time was said to have been 'undistinguished' (Hart-Davis, 2). He had little interest in sport and did not make it to university despite wanting to.

While at Westminster, in the early stages of the Second World War, Johnson joined the Home Guard. On call-up he attended Sandhurst and was commissioned into the 2nd (armoured) battalion of the Welsh Guards. A series of unfortunate events spoiled his war and left him feeling that he had missed the action. He could not participate on D-day after falling off his tank and breaking his leg in the spring of 1944. He also later missed the crossing of the Rhine after succumbing to jaundice and spending months in hospital. He did see some action, though, being involved in the liberation of Brussels and the bitter fighting across north-west Germany. With the war in Europe drawing to a swift conclusion he quickly volunteered to join a guards division that was to be sent to the Far East and would fight in American uniform alongside the Americans themselves. Once again Johnson's plans to see more action were thwarted by the abrupt conclusion of the campaign against Japan.

After the war Johnson resigned his commission, feeling that he did not have enough money to be a regular peace-time officer. He then embarked upon a career as a marine broker at Lloyd's in which he was reportedly rather successful. A life in high finance did little to satisfy his adventurous side, however, and he missed army life. When he heard about the establishment of the Territorial Army 21st regiment of the Special Air Service (SAS) by Lieutenant-Colonel Brian Franks, he immediately volunteered. He was told that there were more than enough former special forces officers around and no room for any more, and that he would only be allowed to join if he entered the regiment as a regular trooper. This he did, working his way up to command the regiment from January 1960 to December 1962, whereupon he retired from the service and devoted himself full-time to his work at Lloyd's. Meanwhile, on 23 June 1950, at St Mary's Church, Cadogan Street, Chelsea, he had married Judith Hazel Lyttelton (1925–1979), daughter of Lieutenant-Colonel Archer Geoffrey Lyttelton, army officer. They had a son, Rupert (*b.* 1954), and a daughter, Charlotte (Lottie; *b.* 1959).

Johnson barely had a chance to settle himself fully back into civilian life after retiring from the Territorial Army before events thousands of miles away in North Yemen ended up giving him more of the adventure he clearly craved. The Middle East was in turmoil following Nasser's propaganda victory at Suez. Ahmed bin Yahya, the hereditary imam of the Mutawakkilite kingdom of Yemen, having faced considerable Arab nationalist pressure, had signed a defence pact with Egypt in 1956 and in 1958 had joined Nasser's United Arab States (UAS), a confederation with the United Arab Republic (UAR) of Egypt and Syria. The collapse of the UAS in September 1961 had led to deteriorating relations with Nasser, whose dreams of Arab unity had come to little with the collapse of both the UAS and the union with Syria in the UAR the same year. The death the following September of Imam Ahmed, who was succeeded by his son, Crown Prince Muhammad al-Badr, presented an opportunity that was seized upon by Egyptian-trained officers. The new imam was overthrown and a republic declared. This led to a civil war which in turn quickly led to large-scale Egyptian intervention on the side of the new republic and to a direct threat to Britain's interests in Aden and the protectorates of South Yemen, and potentially the wider region.

The British government was divided over recognition of the new regime, creating a vacuum that led to a number of individuals working unofficially as a network to support the forces of Imam al-Badr through the supply of weapons and French mercenaries. On 7 September 1963 key leaders of the network, including the founder of the SAS, David Stirling, met with the imamate's foreign minister and established a 'new organisation formed on a military basis … to assist the legal Government of the Yemen in every practical way to remove the invaders from their country' (Jones, 136–7). Johnson was approached to 'put something together' (*Daily Telegraph*, 13 Aug 2008) and recruit the necessary men with particular skills, especially command of Arabic, to make up the new British Mercenary Organization (BMO). Soon afterwards Johnson was also asked to organize a team to blow up the Egyptian MiG fighters that were causing such problems for the supporters of the imam. He flew into the Yemen after the main team, which went via Libya, had arrived. He travelled on a Canadian passport, 'with a pocketful of gold sovereigns' (ibid.). Over the next three years a resistance campaign against Nasser's forces in Yemen was conducted, funded mostly by the Saudis. This small, entirely unofficial, operation was successful out of all proportion to its size, causing Nasser to become bogged down in the Yemen, with many of his best units stationed there rather than in Egypt during the Arab–Israeli Six Day War of 1967.

After 1965, as the mercenary operation became more complex, lines of responsibility became blurred and some tensions began to emerge between those who had been regular members of the SAS and those who had been territorials. This, coupled with personality clashes and the difficult and often chaotic nature of the campaign, led to the diminishing effectiveness of the BMO. Indeed, by the autumn of 1966 'the BMO had become a shell of its former self' (Jones, 214). In the spring of 1967 the tensions came to a head with a split between the BMO leaders. Johnson tendered his resignation. The campaign was coming to an end at this point anyway and all Nasser's troops left Yemen by October 1967.

Johnson's experiences in Yemen and his army background led him to establish with a fellow former SAS officer, David Walker, Britain's first post-war private military company, KMS, in 1975. The company trained the sultan of Oman's special forces in the late 1970s and later operated in Sri Lanka and Afghanistan, in addition to providing diplomatic and commercial protection services in Latin America and the Middle East.

Johnson was appointed military OBE in 1963 'for classified reasons' (Hart-Davis, 1). He was later an ADC to the queen. Following the death of his first wife he married, on 18 September 1982 at St George's, Preshute, Wiltshire, Janet Carol Gay (*b.* 1946), photographer, daughter of Richard Michael Gay, farmer. He died after a long illness, on 20 July 2008, and was survived by his wife Janet and the two children of his first marriage. JAMES WORRALL

Sources A. Kemp, *The SAS: savage wars of peace, 1947 to the present* (1994) • K. Connor, *Ghost force: the secret history of the SAS* (2002) • C. Jones, *Britain and the Yemen civil war, 1962–1965: ministers, mercenaries and mandarins — foreign policy and the limits of covert action* (2004) • *Daily Telegraph* (13 Aug 2008) • *Sydney Morning Herald* (30 Jan 2009) • D. Hart-Davis, *The war that never was: the true story of the men who fought Britain's most secret battle* (2011) • www.specialoperations.com/Foreign/United_Kingdom/SAS/TA_SAS.htm, 4 Aug 2011 • www.sasspecialairservice.com/jim-johnson.html, 4 Aug 2011 • b. cert. • m. certs.

Wealth at death £3,979,444: probate, 10 July 2009, *CGPLA Eng. & Wales*

Johnson, William Henry [Peerie Willie] (**1920–2007**), musician, was born on 10 December 1920 at Upperhouse in Bouster, a small valley on Yell, the second largest of the Shetland Islands. Only his mother's name, Divina Johnson (1895–1990), shawl knitter, appeared on his birth certificate when she registered his birth the following February. His sister Evelyn (*b*. 1942) was from Divina's marriage (subsequently annulled) to Alexander Reid Milne, marine stoker.

As a boy Johnson attended school irregularly because of poor health exacerbated by where he grew up in Lerwick—'two dark damp rented rooms in the rather grandly named "Royal Buildings"' (Leask, *Willie's World*)—and lengthy convalescence after scarlet fever. Being short for his age, he acquired the nickname Peerie (meaning little) that stuck with him for the rest of his life. Trapped indoors in isolation and with visitors rationed, he saw a picture of a cowboy playing the ukulele and new vistas of the imagination opened. His mother, who herself played fiddle and melodeon, tracked down a ukulele for 10*s*. 6*d*. so he could pass the time. After a while, frustrated by the instrument's limited range, he graduated to guitar. His cousin John Henry Leask, the second of two sons born to Mary, the eldest of his mother's ten siblings, made his first guitar.

Johnson left school without any qualification and seemed set to drift into unskilled work. Indeed for much of his life he was a general labourer. In a Lerwick music shop in 1936, however, he met the innately competitive violinist Tom Anderson, his opposite both in temperament and musically. Always 'a history of love–hate friction and rivalry' (Clark, 145), theirs was the lengthiest musical relationship of his life. By a quirk of radio reception Johnson had been listening to jazz broadcasts from the other side of the Atlantic, enabling him to discover that the American jazz guitarist Eddie Lang and the violinist Joe Venuti were taking the guitar—hitherto an instrument relegated to supporting, rhythmic roles or, as in Al Bowlly's case, as crooner accompaniment—to new places. The Dundee-based songwriter Michael Marra later turned Johnson's shortwave radio experience into his song 'Schenectady Calling Peerie Willie Johnson' (1994). (In 1979, while touring with the Scottish folk group the Boys of the Lough, Johnson found himself in the very hall in Schenectady from where Venuti and Lang had broadcast.)

With the Nazi occupation of Norway in 1940 Johnson joined the Royal Air Force and was posted as ground crew to the strategically important Sullom Voe airbase on Shetland's Mainland. The base had its own full-time dance band composed of RAF bandsmen, most of whom had been professional or semi-professional musicians before the war. Johnson would sit in and jam, a habit he never lost down the decades. Although he never learned to sight-read, he developed a remarkable skill at playing by ear. After demobilization he resumed playing with Anderson in the Islesburgh Dance Band. On 2 July 1953 at St Columbus manse, Lerwick, he married Ethel Annabel Johnson

William Henry [Peerie Willie] **Johnson** (**1920–2007**), by Billy Fox, 2006

(1927/8–1997), daughter of Marjory Ann Johnson and stepdaughter of John Armstrong, garage assistant, of Lerwick. There were no children of the marriage.

Johnson's fame soon spread beyond the Shetland Islands. He recorded with the fiddler Willie Hunter at Abbey Road Studios in London in 1958, but most of his recordings were made in the Shetlands. His playing was included in such compilation albums as *Scottish Violin Music* (1963), *Shetland Fiddling* (1978), and *Silver Bow: the Fiddle Music of Shetland* (1995). Some of his performances—'Da North Road' / 'Robertson Crescent' being one example—were preserved on *Willie's World* (2007).

Self-taught as a guitarist, Johnson devised musical solutions when it came to shaping chords, runs and bass lines from what he heard that bear comparison with the music and achievements of Lang, Venuti, Stéphane Grappelli, and Django Reinhardt. He later picked up other instruments, including piano and double bass, in much the same way. His totally unschooled, utterly intuitive mind grasped guitar chords and melded jazz and Shetland folk idioms in ways that would impress generations of musicians, including Humphrey Lyttelton, Archie Fisher, and Martin Taylor. Fisher's memory of Johnson was of him

> sitting in his favourite haunt, The Lounge [Bar] in Lerwick. It was at a folk festival, and there were guitarists from all around the world. He was holding court with an old, battered acoustic guitar. They were all very good guitarists. They probably knew what all the chords were that he didn't know [the names of]. They were all sitting there like disciples. (*The Guardian*, 29 June 2007)

To the end of his life Johnson was happier as the soul-of-the-party and a supporting musician, for example, with the Shetland fiddler Aly Bain or the Boys of the Lough. Enormously approachable and open-handed, he would share his knowledge generously and across the generations. In one of his most memorable recordings he collaborated with the fiddler Debbie Scott on *The Selkies' Song* (made in 1985 and released in 2008). Scott also wrote a tribute to him, 'The Bousters Boy'. He died of chronic obstructive pulmonary disease at Taing House, Lerwick, on 22 May 2007 and was buried with his wife in Knab cemetery, Lerwick, on 30 May. On 22 May 2010 a memorial, provided by his sister Evelyn Leask, commemorating him and the two previous generations of the family, was unveiled in Bouster. Built of stones from his derelict birthplace, it is fashioned in the shape of a 'plantie crub'—a traditional windbreak for sheltering and growing young plants—and included his image and the logotype of the Peerie Willie guitar festival, inaugurated in 2005.

KEN HUNT

Sources A. Clark, *Aly Bain: fiddler on the loose* (1993) · *The Herald* [Glasgow] (26 May 2007) · *The Independent* (29 May 2007) · *The Scotsman* (30 May 2007) · *The Guardian* (29 June 2007) · *The Times* (3 July 2007) · D. Gardner, 'Musicians pay fitting tribute to isles' guitar wizard Willie', *Shetland Times* (28 Sept 2007) · E. Leask, *Willie's World*, (2007) [CD booklet notes] · E. Leask, 'Fame, family and friends' · private information (2011) [Evelyn Leask, sister; A. Fisher; O. Tierney] · b. cert. · m. cert. · d. cert.

Archives FILM BFINA, performance footage

Likenesses B. Fox, photograph, 2006, priv. coll. [*see illus.*] · C. Reinking, pastel on paper (after C. Reinking, photograph, 1992), repro. in Willie's World · obituary photographs · photograph, repro. in www.tradmusichall.com/PeerieWJohnson.htm · stone memorial, Bouster, Yell, Shetland Islands

Johnston, Sir John Baines [Jack] (**1918–2005**), civil servant and diplomatist, was born on 13 May 1918 at 8 The Ghyll, Ellenborough, Maryport, Cumberland, the son of Andrew Smith Johnston, Baptist clergyman, and his wife, Nora Agnes, *née* Baines, schoolteacher, and daughter of a blacksmith. When he was two the family moved to Derby; later they moved to Banbury in Oxfordshire. They were poor and family life revolved around the church. The First World War made his father a pacifist and he brought up his son in the same way. Johnston was educated at Banbury grammar school, where he was captain of cricket and rugby, and then, thanks to two scholarships, at Queen's College, Oxford, where he read modern history. When the Second World War began he was accepted as a conscientious objector and, after graduating with a second-class degree in 1940, was posted to the Pioneer Corps, a non-combatant unit, in Devon. There his views about the war changed and later in 1940 he enlisted. He joined the infantry and was commissioned as a second lieutenant in the Oxford and Buckinghamshire light infantry. He took part in the D-day landings and was then attached, as adjutant, to the Gordon Highlanders during the British advance into Holland. He was demobilized in 1946 with the rank of major.

In 1947 Johnston joined the Colonial Office. He was in Ghana in 1950–51 as assistant secretary to the West African Council and was then, until 1956, principal private secretary to Oliver Lyttelton and Alan Lennox-Boyd, two Conservative secretaries of state for the colonies. He was assistant secretary and head of the Far Eastern department at the Colonial Office when Malaya became independent in 1957. Transferred to the Commonwealth Relations Office the same year, from 1959 to 1961 he was in South Africa as deputy high commissioner, a formative period from which he emerged with a strong distaste for apartheid. He was there in February 1960 when the prime minister, Harold Macmillan, addressed both houses of the South African parliament at Cape Town during his African tour. No one assumed Macmillan's 'wind of change' speech would change South African minds and South Africa left the Commonwealth a year later. But it was still hailed as a success, because it was a statement of British policy about accommodating African nationalism within a Commonwealth context made in the heartland of apartheid. A number of individuals were involved in drafting the speech, among them Johnston, who was consulted by Sir John Maud, the high commissioner. After South Africa Johnston was high commissioner to Sierra Leone, 1961–3, during which time he was appointed CMG, in 1962.

In 1963 Johnston became high commissioner to the Federation of Rhodesia and Nyasaland. When he arrived in Salisbury, the capital of Southern Rhodesia and seat of the federal government, the federation was on the point of breaking up. Britain's efforts to reconcile the conflicting aspirations of the minority white populations in Northern and Southern Rhodesia with those of the black majorities in all three territories ended in failure. The Central African Federation, as it was known, was dissolved in December 1963. Nyasaland and Northern Rhodesia were set on course for separate independence which they achieved in July and October 1964 respectively, as Malawi and Zambia. This left Southern Rhodesia, internally self-governing under white rule since 1923, to which territory Johnston was now high commissioner alone. One of Johnston's earliest observations was that the Europeans in Rhodesia lived 'in a state of mental insulation from the outside world only surpassed by South Africa'. Persuaded there were no 'good solutions' to the Rhodesian problem, only 'difficulties and dangers', the high commissioner was clear there could be no long-term future for the Europeans in Southern Rhodesia 'through a policy of white supremacy and African suppression' (Hyam and Louis, 2.525).

In April 1964 the ruling Rhodesian Front in Rhodesia split. Winston Field was ousted as leader and replaced by Ian Smith. Johnston was one of the first to realize that Smith was a prisoner of the right wing of the party, which had engineered Field's downfall. In June 1964 he described Smith as dour and reserved, giving the impression of 'stubbornness of will and purpose, not entirely offset by his boyish appearance'. He believed Smith led a government with which there was no prospect of a negotiated settlement, so determined was it to maintain white supremacy and 'so impregnably armoured in self-righteousness' (Murphy, 2.382). But it was not in Johnston's view irrevocably set on a course of rebellion. However bleak the prospects, he argued that Britain had little option but to 'sit out the present situation', in the hope ultimately that Smith's government would alienate its own followers.

Two resounding by-election victories for the Rhodesian Front in October 1964 strengthened Smith's position. Considering Smith's intentions, Johnston now thought he was set on either 'independence at all costs', or exploiting his poll success to acquire additional leverage to find an acceptable way out because he still feared the consequences of an illegal declaration. The first hypothesis appeared to Johnston nearer the truth. 'We shall know very soon', was his verdict (Murphy, 2.400). He also wondered if pressure could be applied through Rhodesia's neighbours, South Africa and colonial Portugal, but officials in London thought this would make matters worse. Prime Minister Harold Wilson's personal intervention during a visit to Rhodesia in November 1965 failed to resolve the impasse. Smith made his unilateral declaration of independence on 11 November 1965. Johnston was withdrawn the next day.

In 1966 Johnston was knighted KCMG and for the next two years he was in London as assistant under-secretary of state at the Commonwealth Office. His areas of responsibility covered the Indian subcontinent and Nigeria at the time of the civil war. When the Commonwealth Office merged with the Foreign Office in October 1968 he was appointed deputy under-secretary of state in charge of the Far Eastern group of departments. On 17 May 1969 he married Elizabeth Mary Crace (*d.* 2004), a 37-year-old teacher, daughter of John Foster Crace, and niece of Lord Redcliffe-Maud, who as Sir John Maud had been high commissioner in South Africa when Johnston was his deputy. They had one son, John (*b.* 1970). Johnston's diplomatic career ended with two senior Commonwealth postings, as high commissioner to Malaysia (1971–4), and to Canada (1974–8). He was made KCVO in 1972 and GCMG in 1978.

Johnston was professional to a fault. His dispatches, especially from Salisbury, were eloquent and perceptive. Unassuming in character, he was instantly recognizable by a trademark rose in his buttonhole. The empire during his career became the modern Commonwealth. Influenced by his experiences in South Africa and Rhodesia, he believed that the Commonwealth played an invaluable role in promoting international co-operation and fostering interracial harmony. The creation of the Foreign and Commonwealth Office in 1968 was an uncomfortable period for those, like Johnston, who came from the Commonwealth side of the new department. They feared the merger might become a takeover by the Foreign Office. Their concerns were not without foundation.

In retirement Johnston settled in Oxford. He was a governor of the BBC (1978–85), chairman of the ARELS (Association of Recognised English Language Schools) Examinations Trust (1982–94), and a member of the Disasters Emergency Committee (1985–92). His wife died in December 2004 after a long illness during which Johnston nursed her. He died of lung cancer at 5 Victoria Road, Oxford, on 16 October 2005. His son survived him. S. R. Ashton

Sources E. Windrich, *Britain and the politics of Rhodesian independence* (1978) • J. S. Garner, *The Commonwealth Office, 1925–1968* (1978) • K. Flower, *Serving secretly: an intelligence chief on record, Rhodesia into Zimbabwe, 1964–1981* (1987) • R. Hyam and W. R. Lewis, eds., *British documents on the end of empire: the Conservative government and the end of empire*, 2 pts (2000) • R. Hyam and P. Henshaw, *The lion and the springbok: Britain and South Africa since the Boer War* (2003) • S. R. Ashton and W. R. Louis, eds., *British documents on the end of empire: east of Suez and the Commonwealth, 1964–1971*, 3 pts (2004) • P. Murphy, ed., *British documents on the end of empire: Central Africa*, 2 pts (2005) • J. T. R. Wood, *So far and no further: Rhodesia's bid for independence during the retreat from empire, 1959–1965* (2005) • *The Times* (21 Oct 2005) • *Daily Telegraph* (25 Oct 2005) • *The Guardian* (15 Nov 2005); (21 Nov 2005) • Burke, *Peerage* • *WW* (2005) • b. cert. • m. cert. • d. cert.

Archives TNA: PRO, CO, CRO, FCO papers
Likenesses obituary photographs
Wealth at death £486,065: probate, 12 Jan 2006, *CGPLA Eng. & Wales*

Johnston, (David) Russell Russell-, Baron Russell-Johnston (1932–2008), politician, was born David Russell Johnston on 28 July 1932 at 39 Palmerston Place, Edinburgh, the son of David Knox Johnston, a customs and excise officer, and his wife, (Georgina) Margaret Gerrie, *née* Russell. At the time of his birth his parents lived at Lews, Portree, Isle of Skye. He was brought up on Skye and was educated at Carbost public school and Portree high school. He then went to Edinburgh University, where he refounded the Liberal Club, became its president, and quickly earned a reputation as an excellent debater, winning the coveted *Observer* mace in 1961. After national service in the intelligence corps in 1958–9 he trained as a history teacher at Moray House College of Education, and briefly taught at Liberton secondary school near Edinburgh before becoming a paid research assistant for the Scottish Liberals in 1963. A year later he stood successfully for Inverness at the first attempt, a seat he held continuously until his retirement in 1997. On 5 August 1967, at St Andrew's Cathedral, Inverness, he married Joan Graham Menzies, a 23-year-old bank clerk and daughter of Donald Menzies, railway clerk. They had three sons.

Johnston (always known as Russell Johnston) was a passionate advocate of Scottish home rule, long before that cause became fashionable: in 1966 he introduced a private member's bill advocating a devolved Scotland, and he worked closely with John Smith in the late 1970s during the Liberal–Labour pact in an effort to establish a Scottish assembly. Although that project fell by the wayside, he also played a key role with Willie Ross, the secretary of state for Scotland, in setting up the Highlands and Islands Development Board (a body he had called for in a pamphlet published in 1964), which, with the support of European structural funds, contributed greatly to the economic development of the region.

Throughout his career Johnston remained a powerful advocate of Liberalism. Young Liberals were inspired to join the party by his pamphlet *To Be a Liberal* (1972). His closing speeches to Scottish Liberal Party conferences enthralled his audience, but his tendency to speak his mind occasionally landed him in trouble. After two visits to Greece in 1968 to inspect the conditions in which political prisoners were held he raised the ire of the Labour left by describing the colonels in the military government as 'officers and gentlemen' (*Daily Telegraph*, 29 July 2008). In 1970 he became the chairman of the Scottish Liberal Party, and its leader from 1974 to 1988, sparking a modest revival in the fortunes of the party north of the border. He was a keen supporter of the merger between the Liberals and the Social Democratic Party, and became deputy leader of the Scottish Liberal Democrats from 1988 to 1989 and deputy leader of the Liberal Democrats from 1988 to 1992, serving as the Scottish Liberal Democrat president from 1988 to 1994.

Johnston's greatest passion, however, was furthering

the cause of European integration. He was an unashamed European federalist, once remarking: 'I would much prefer to be ruled by a gentleman named Helmut Schmidt than one named Anthony Wedgwood Benn' (*Daily Telegraph*, 29 July 2008). He had the honour of being the first British Liberal member of the nominated European Assembly, and, wearing his kilt and sporran, made his maiden speech in French when he took his seat in 1973. He was devastated to lose twice to Winnie Ewing in 1979 and 1984 in the Highlands and Islands constituency, in the direct elections to the European parliament. He sought consolation as a member of the parliamentary assembly of the Council of Europe, to which he increasingly devoted nearly all his attention. Critics at home in Scotland were heard to remark, 'Where's Russell? Russell's in Brussels' (although in fact the Council of Europe met in Strasbourg). The neglect of his constituency nearly cost him his Westminster seat, now renamed Inverness, Nairn, and Lochaber, in 1992, when he squeaked home by 458 votes after three recounts, just ahead of the other three main Scottish parties, all four polling over 20 per cent of the vote. Thereafter he spent nearly all his time in Europe, becoming president of the parliamentary assembly of the Council of Europe from 1999 to 2002, a post he regarded as the pinnacle of his career, boasting to a friend that he was 'president of an assembly representing 830 million people' (*The Herald*, 12 Aug 2008). During his presidency he spoke out against ethnic cleansing in Kosovo, and championed the cause of human rights and internationalism across Europe.

Having been raised on the Isle of Skye as a bilingual Gaelic and English speaker, Johnston developed an interest in shinty, serving as vice-chief of the Camanachd Association, the sport's governing body. He was also a great lover of whisky, once remarking to his fellow Liberal Democrat MPs during a tour of the highlands, 'Isn't it time this meeting finished, so we can all go for a "toot"?' (*The Independent*, 30 July 2008). One of his personal traits was to send postcards to all his friends during his frequent trips to Europe and beyond. He was knighted in 1985, and, on becoming a life peer in 1997, he changed his name by deed poll to Russell-Johnston. Perhaps fittingly, he died on the continent, in his favourite hotel in Paris on 27 July 2008, succumbing to the effects of bone marrow cancer. He was cremated in Paris on 4 August 2008, and was survived by his wife and three sons, Graham, David, and Andrew.

MARK STUART

Sources *The Guardian* (28 July 2008); (29 July 2008); (2 Aug 2008) · *The Times* (29 July 2008); (12 Aug 2008) · *Daily Telegraph* (29 July 2008) · *The Independent* (29 July 2008); (30 July 2008) · *The Scotsman* (12 Aug 2008) · *The Herald* [Glasgow] (12 Aug 2008) · Burke, *Peerage* · *WW* (2008) · b. cert. · m. cert.

Archives Highland Council Archives · NL Scot.

Likenesses group portrait, photograph, 1988, Rex Features, London · photographs, 1997–2005, Photoshot, London · photographs, 1999, Camera Press, London · obituary photographs

Johnstone, James Connelly [Jimmy, Jinky] (**1944–2006**), footballer, was born on 30 September 1944 at 647 Old Edinburgh Road, Viewpark, Lanarkshire, the youngest of five surviving children (three had died in infancy) of Matthew (Matt) Johnstone, coalminer, and his wife, Sarah, *née* Crawley. He had an elder brother, Patrick, and three elder sisters, Theresa, Ann, and Mary. He was educated at St Columba's Roman Catholic primary school in Viewpark and St John's Roman Catholic secondary school in Uddingston. He became a Celtic 'ball boy' aged thirteen before playing for the club he, his family, and most of his local Catholic community of mainly Irish extraction supported. On leaving school aged fifteen he worked at Glasgow's meat market, then acquired a job in a clothing factory, and subsequently began an apprenticeship as a welder. From the latter two jobs he travelled two evenings a week to train with Celtic, the club for which he had recently signed, despite the close interest of the Manchester United manager Matt Busby. The red-haired Johnstone was later farmed out to a local junior club, Blantyre Celtic, for experience, and to add to his 5 feet 2 inch, six stone frame. He eventually settled at 5 feet 4 inches and weighed under ten stone throughout his playing days. On 11 June 1966 he married Agnes Docherty, a nineteen-year-old coil winder from Uddingston, and daughter of John Docherty, joiner. They had three children, James, Marie, and Eileen.

Johnstone had made his début for Celtic in March 1963 but only began to thrive and fully develop with the arrival of Jock Stein as manager in 1965. Johnstone went on to play 515 times for Celtic, scoring 129 goals. Although renowned as a small 'jinking' winger who mesmerized his opponents by dribbling the ball by and around them (sometimes repeatedly), he was an exceptionally rounded footballer. He was an outstanding passer of the ball and had dynamic speed, superb control, and exceptional spatial awareness. Despite his diminutive size a number of his goals were scored with his head. Although a brilliant individual, he was also a team player.

Between 1965 and 1974 Celtic won a then world record nine consecutive national league titles and numerous other trophies. In those years the team also played in four European champions cup semi-finals and two finals. In 1967 Celtic's 'Lisbon lions' became the first northern European club to win the European champions cup, beating Inter Milan 2–1 in the Portuguese city of Lisbon. Celtic again reached the final in 1970, but lost to Feyenoord. Johnstone was an outstanding member of the Celtic team during this period: a team that remains Scotland's most successful in European football. In the year Celtic won Europe's most prestigious football trophy Johnstone finished third in the voting for the European footballer of the year.

Johnstone made his full international début in 1964. He went on to play twenty-three times for Scotland. Among the reasons for such a small number of international caps (given his exceptional talent) were his fear of flying abroad for games, his occasional disciplinary problems (sometimes striking back at the brutal play of less skilful opponents), and a poor relationship with the Scottish football authorities, who were certainly affected by the anti-Catholic, anti-Irish, and anti-Celtic prejudices then prevalent in Scottish football and society. These manifested themselves in the way Johnstone was sometimes booed by home fans while playing for Scotland in Glasgow. The booing was compounded by the massive presence of Glasgow Rangers supporters among the Scotland fans, many of whom also preferred Willie Henderson, the Rangers winger.

On the field Johnstone was not inhibited by his lack of height and weight. In years of ball work and practice he had honed skills that were often beyond taller and more athletic looking footballers. As a youngster, after reading *Feet First* (1948), Stanley Matthews's autobiography, he had taken to dribbling around milk bottles every day in his hallway for three hours to perfect his skills. These were matched by a good deal of bravery, which was often required as 'Jinky' was frequently booted by less skilful players.

Johnstone's fear of flying was so intense that in November 1968 he arranged with the manager, Jock Stein, that he would be spared the flight to Yugoslavia for the return match of a European cup tie against Red Star Belgrade if he helped Celtic acquire a three-goal lead from the first match in Glasgow. Johnstone duly tore one of Europe's leading teams apart, scoring twice and laying on three other goals in a 5–1 victory: he didn't travel to the away tie. Johnstone said about Jock Stein, 'Jock was good with tactics, but his real talent was with people … He knew if you had a problem' (*The Independent*, 14 March 2006). Johnstone was uncomfortable with fame and ended up too often in bars. Stein used his network of Celtic-supporting informants to let him know whenever Johnstone was out drinking, and Johnstone would often receive a reprimanding call at the pub from Stein. Stein said:

> people might say I will be best remembered for being in charge of the first British club to win the European Cup or leading Celtic to nine league championships in a row, but I would like to be remembered for keeping the wee man, Jimmy Johnstone, in the game five years longer than he might have been. That is my greatest achievement.
> (*Daily Telegraph*, 14 March 2006)

Johnstone was eventually let go by Celtic in 1975. Thereafter he played briefly for San Jose Earthquakes, Sheffield United, Shelbourne, and Elgin City, before finishing his playing days back at Blantyre Celtic. He also briefly returned to Celtic Park in the mid-1980s to coach youth players. He had made no plans when he finished playing football and soon found himself in considerable difficulties—drinking too much, working as a navvy, and piling up debts. But the love of his family, his strong religious faith, and his infectious personality and sense of humour pulled him through those dark days. In Johnstone's latter years the actor Robert Duvall, who consulted him when making a football film, declared 'Wee Jinky Johnstone' the most remarkable character that he, in a lifetime in Hollywood, had ever come across. In a similar recognition, in 2005 Johnstone was immortalized on a limited-edition Fabergé egg, the only living person since the tsars and tsarinas of Russia to have been honoured in that way.

Celtic continued to be Johnstone's passion long after he stopped playing and he could often be seen at Celtic Park as a match-day host until he was diagnosed with motor neurone disease in 2001. To raise funds for the Motor Neurone Disease Association, together with Jim Kerr of the pop group Simple Minds, he launched a new version of the classic song 'Dirty Old Town', also a Celtic supporters' favourite. 'Jimmy was among the greatest players this game has seen', said Billy McNeill, the former Celtic captain. 'However, I have as much respect for him as a man and the courageous way in which he handled his illness as I have for him as a footballer' (*The Independent*, 14 March 2006). In 2002 Johnstone was voted Celtic's greatest ever player. A statue of him was unveiled outside Celtic Park in December 2008.

Johnstone died on 13 March 2006 at his home in Mossgiel Gardens, Uddingston, only a few hundred yards from where he was born. His funeral mass was held on St Patrick's day 2006 at St John the Baptist Church in Uddingston, concelebrated by numerous priests led by the bishop of Motherwell, Joseph Devine; thousands attended as his funeral cortège passed by. He was buried in Bothwell Park cemetery, near Uddingston. He was survived by his wife and children. JOSEPH M. BRADLEY

Sources J. Johnstone, *Fire in my boots* (1969) · T. Campbell and P. Woods, *The glory and the dream: the history of Celtic F.C., 1887–1986* (1986) · J. M. Bradley, *Celtic minded: essays on religion, politics, society, identity and football* (2004) · *Evening Times* [Glasgow] (13 March 2006); (14 March 2006); (18 March 2006) · *The Herald* [Glasgow] (14 March 2006); (15 March 2006); (17 March 2006); (18 March 2006) · *Daily Record* (14 March 2006); (16 March 2006); (18 March 2006) · *The Times* (14 March 2006); (24 March 2006) · *Daily Telegraph* (14 March 2006) · *The Guardian* (14 March 2006) · *The Independent* (14 March 2006) · *The Scotsman* (15 March 2006); (18 March 2006) · *Sunday Times* (19 March 2006) · b. cert. · m. cert. · d. cert.

Likenesses photographs, 1960–2003, Camera Press, London · photographs, 1963–2004, PA Photos, London · B. Thomas, photograph, 1964, Getty Images, London, Bob Thomas Sports · photograph, 1967, Hult. Arch., London · photographs, 1967–74, Photoshot, London · M. l'Anson, mixed media on paper, 2003, Scot. NPG · statue, 2008, Kerrydale Street, Glasgow · obituary photographs · photographs, Rex Features, London · photographs, repro. in Johnstone, *Boots*

Jolliffe, Peter Benedict (1947–2007), antiquarian bookseller, was born on 26 October 1947 at Hillbury Nursing Home, Hilperton Road, Trowbridge, Wiltshire, the son of Michael Jolliffe (1916–1977), librarian, and his wife, (Eleanor) Jeanne, *née* Pitt (1923–1949). His maternal great-grandfather was Henry Baston Pitt, ironmonger, founder of the shop H. B. Pitt in Trowbridge, which celebrated its centenary in 2000. At the time of Jolliffe's birth registration his parents lived at 120 Bradley Road, Trowbridge. His father was then chief assistant in Wiltshire County Library, but in December 1947 he was appointed librarian at Gordon Memorial College, Khartoum (from 1956 the University of Khartoum). The family followed him to Khartoum, where, on 8 October 1949, Peter's mother died giving birth to twin daughters, neither of whom survived. His father, thinking it would be kinder, sought to eradicate all trace of her.

A Roman Catholic convert, later a Benedictine oblate,

Michael Jolliffe sent his son to a convent school in Khartoum and, at the age of seven, back to Trowbridge to attend St Mary's Convent and live with his grandparents. In 1956 he went to St Mary's Hall, Stonyhurst, graduating to Stonyhurst College, Clitheroe, Lancashire, from which he won a place, in 1966, to read classics at Merton College, Oxford. Two years later he changed to English, but in his fourth year one of his lungs collapsed. After contriving a third-class degree, he was diagnosed with pulmonary fibrosis and diabetes insipidus. He was told he was unlikely to reach the age of thirty.

Jolliffe's first job was at Blackwell's paperback shop in Broad Street, Oxford, where he rose to be deputy manager. But his interest was less in new than in second-hand books, specifically modern first editions. At lunchtime he frequented Blackwell's antiquarian department, round the corner in Ship Street, and became a collector of poetry, notably R. S. Thomas. In Byron Rogers's biography of Thomas, *The Man Who Went into the West* (2006), he is simply the Collector, the man who, when asked by Thomas's son Gwydion what he was after in the way of personal copies and manuscripts, said 'Everything' (Rogers, 57). Meanwhile his father, from 1970 head librarian at Royal Holloway College, retired early after four years, after a serious bicycle accident. When he died, in 1977, his son and principal legatee set himself up on his own as a bookseller, operating from his house at 37 Bartlemas Road, Oxford. He had defied medical predictions, and, fortified by disfiguring steroids, would live to deal for another thirty years, an instantly recognizable figure, heavy, bald, rather monkish in appearance, stoically balancing several carrier bags of books wherever he went.

Jolliffe took stands at the fairs of the Provincial Booksellers Fairs Association, but his principal vehicle for sales was the series of idiosyncratic book catalogues that first issued from Bartlemas Road and continued until the month he died. He moved outside Oxford, to 2 Acre End Street, Eynsham, but gravitated to London, sharing an office in Fulham Road and then a shop in Soho; finally, in 1991, as Ulysses, in partnership with three other booksellers, he took premises in Museum Street, where he remained, latterly alone at number forty. He retained his house at Eynsham, but went for long periods without staying there, sleeping instead in his shop, upright in a chair.

The British book trade had tended to look down on modern first editions, as fit only for the novice collector and *parvenus*. Jolliffe, by a combination of obsessive scholarship and benign evangelism, raised their profile and their prices. His own prices were extravagant, even deliberately prohibitive. His critics protested that the collector in him never died: a habitual pessimist, he worried more if customers did buy his books than if they didn't. He was known to go and buy a book back (at a premium) the moment after he had sold it. He was, therefore, not easy to work with. But there was no doubting his learning; his enthusiasm was transparent, if occasionally doleful, and his stock inspiring. His lengthy, often autobiographical, catalogue notes, with their brutally deprecatory accounts of condition, were the stuff of anecdote. His catalogues, unlike those of almost any of his peers, bear repeated rereading.

A poet of competence himself (he printed several pamphlets in collectably diminutive editions), he had a particular sympathy for poets, collecting and promoting the works of Elizabeth Bishop, Seamus Heaney, and Derek Mahon, among many others, before they had universal currency. Of his own poems the most poignant is 'Survivor', written in his fifties on finding a single 'mundane' letter that his mother had written to his father the month before she died:

sometimes I ask myself
will they wonder why
I kept so close to me
a letter so dry,
how she missed the train at
Wadi Halfa—so had to fly

Jolliffe's last years were hampered by ill health and oxygen cylinders. Yet he remained stoical, acquisitive, productive, and a regular at book fairs and pub quizzes (where he deployed an encyclopaedic knowledge of music and cricket), the centre of a loyal circle of friends and booksellers. He died on 27 December 2007, at University College Hospital, London, shortly after publishing Ulysses catalogue number 102; the causes of death were given as bronchopneumonia, pulmonary fibrosis, and histiocytosis X lung fibrosis. His funeral was held at Islington and St Pancras crematorium on 10 January 2008, followed by a wake at the pub of his quizzes, The Plough in Museum Street, and his ashes were scattered on the Westbury white horse, near Trowbridge. He never married.

James Fergusson

Sources B. Rogers, *The man who went into the west: the life of R. S. Thomas* (2006) · *The Independent* (11 Jan 2008) · *The Times* (26 Jan 2008) · *Bookdealer* (Feb 2008) · personal knowledge (2011) · private information (2011) · b. cert. · d. cert.

Likenesses S. Gelberg, photograph, repro. in *Rare Book Review* (April–May 2008) · J. Nangle, photograph, repro. in *The Independent* (11 Jan 2008)

Wealth at death £528,779: probate, 17 June 2008, *CGPLA Eng. & Wales*

Jones, David Hugh (1934–2008), theatre, film, and television director, was born on 19 February 1934 at Devonport, 77 Longfleet Road, Poole, Dorset, the son of the Revd John David Jones, Congregational minister, and his wife, Gwendolen Agnes Langworthy, *née* Ricketts (1898–1987). He was educated at Taunton School and (with an interruption for national service as a second lieutenant in the Royal Artillery) Christ's College, Cambridge, from where he graduated with a first-class degree in English. At Cambridge he was much influenced by the work of F. R. Leavis, and in particular by his insistence on close attention to the text of any book or play.

In 1958 Jones joined the BBC, and was assigned by the formidable Grace Wyndham Goldie to work on *Monitor*, the BBC's first television arts programme, launched and produced by Huw Wheldon. Colleagues there included John Schlesinger, Ken Russell, Humphrey Burton, Patrick Garland, and Melvyn Bragg. Jones made a number of films for the programme, especially on literary subjects; in 1958 he scored a notable coup by persuading the usually camera-shy E. M. Forster to agree to an interview for a programme to mark his eightieth birthday the following year. In 1962 Jones succeeded Burton as editor of the programme. Meanwhile he also began directing for the London stage, beginning with a triple bill of plays by T. S. Eliot, W. B. Yeats, and Samuel Beckett at the Mermaid Theatre in 1961. In the following year he produced Boris Vian's *The Empire Builders* for the Royal Shakespeare Company (RSC), at the Arts Theatre. On 18 October 1964, at the parish church in Yeovil, Somerset, he married the actress Sheila Marion Essex Allen (*b.* 1932), daughter of William George Allen. They had two sons, Jesse and Joseph.

In the same year as his marriage Jones left the BBC in order to work full-time for the RSC under Peter Hall. Among his early productions were David Mercer's *The Governor's Lady* and Peter Weiss's *The Investigation* at the Aldwych, and John Whiting's *Saint's Day* at the Theatre Royal, Stratford East. When Trevor Nunn succeeded Hall as the RSC's artistic director in 1968, Jones's role expanded; he formed a quadrumvirate with Nunn, Terry Hands, and John Barton, responsible for the vast majority of the RSC's productions, and was given particular responsibility for the Aldwych, where he was director of the company from 1968 to 1972 and artistic director from 1973 to 1977. He directed an acclaimed revival of Maxim Gorky's *Enemies* in 1971, starring Alan Howard, Helen Mirren, Patrick Stewart, John Wood, and Ben Kingsley; this was followed by a number of other Gorky plays, including *The Lower Depths* (1972), *Summerfolk* (1974), and *The Zykovs* (1976). Other productions included Graham Greene's *The Return of A. J. Raffles* and Harley Granville-Barker's *The Marrying of Ann Leete* (both 1975), and Chekhov's *Ivanov* (1976), as well as several further plays by David Mercer. In 1972 he found himself in the media spotlight when John Arden and Margaretta D'Arcy attacked and subsequently picketed his production of their play *The Island of the Mighty*, claiming that he had imbued the production with an 'imperialist' slant. Matters were perhaps not helped when Jones and Nunn claimed that the RSC was 'a basically left-wing organization' (*The Times*, 5 Dec 1972), provoking the tory MP Angus Maude to resign from the RSC's governing body, much to the delight of some sections of the press.

Jones's work for television, which continued in tandem with his work at the RSC, included a portrait of the poet John Clare (1969), adaptations of Hardy and Chekhov short stories (1972 and 1973), and (after he had left the RSC to become producer of the BBC's *Play of the Month*) Harold Pinter's screenplay, *Langrishe, Go Down* (1978). His association with Pinter continued with his first feature film, Pinter's *Betrayal* (1983), starring Ben Kingsley, Jeremy Irons, and Patricia Hodge. Other feature films he directed included *84 Charing Cross Road* (1987), starring Anthony Hopkins and Anne Bancroft, which was chosen for a royal film performance, *Jacknife* (1989), starring Robert de Niro as a troubled Vietnam veteran, Kafka's *The Trial* (1993), and *The Confession* (1999), based on the novel by Sol Yurick and again starring Ben Kingsley.

Meanwhile, in 1979 Jones had moved to the USA, initially as artistic director of the Brooklyn Academy of Music Theatre Company, then from 1981 as an adjunct professor of drama at Yale University. Although he returned to the UK regularly, most of his work from this point was based in America, including acclaimed productions on Broadway of Pinter's *No Man's Land* (1994), Ronald Harwood's *Taking Sides* (1996), Pinter's *The Caretaker* (2003), Edna O'Brien's *Triptych* (2004), and Jean-Claude Carrière's *The Controversy of Valladolid* (2005). His work for American television was less remarkable, but included *A Christmas Carol* (1999), starring Patrick Stewart, Richard E. Grant, and Joel Grey, and *Custody of the Heart* (2003), based on a book by Barbara Delinsky, as well as numerous episodes for popular American television series. In 2004 he became 'masterclass' film professor at Columbia University.

In appearance Jones was rather Byronic; there was a sense of brooding about him, enhanced by a deep reverberant voice and a smoulder which was easily provoked into laughter. He was a resolute intellectual in a world in which instinct was too often rated too highly. But his unaffected charm tempered the rigour of his opinions.

David Jones's passion was for great literature, founded on a vast knowledge of English poetry. This gave him an indestructible inner confidence and a balance that enabled him to deal with the inevitable alarms and neuroses of world-class actors and writers. It was good to see him work: part explaining, part coaxing and encouraging, but also—the most effective part—very tough in his insistence on the truth of the play or the script or the subject. He wore his great talent and his relentless intelligence very gracefully. Those who worked with him felt they were working with a very fine mind.

Jones's marriage ended in divorce, and his partner for the last nineteen years of his life was the photographer Joyce Tenneson (*b.* 1945). He lived latterly in Manhattan and Rockport, Maine, and died in Rockport on 19 September 2008 following a heart attack. He was survived by Joyce Tenneson and by the two sons of his marriage.

MELVYN BRAGG

Sources *The Guardian* (23 Sept 2008) · *The Times* (24 Sept 2008) · *Daily Telegraph* (26 Sept 2008) · *The Independent* (26 Sept 2008) · *New York Times* (30 Sept 2008) · *WW* (2008) · personal knowledge (2012) · private information (2012) · b. cert. · m. cert.
Archives FILM BFINA, documentary footage
Likenesses obituary photographs

Jones, Sir (John) Derek Alun- (1933–2008), industrialist, was born John Derek Jones on 6 June 1933 at 88 Loraine Mansions, Widdenham Road, Islington, London, the only son of Thomas Alun Jones, later Thomas Alun-Jones (*d.* 1951), solicitor and managing clerk, and his wife, Madge Beatrice, *née* Edwards (*d.* 1986). He was educated at Lancing College, Sussex, and St Edmund Hall, Oxford. In 1955 he graduated with a third-class degree in jurisprudence, and in 1958 he passed his bar examinations. It was in the business world, however, that he decided to apply his skills, joining Philips Electrical in 1957 and then H. C. Stephens Ltd in 1959 as company secretary, thus initiating a career lasting sixteen years in the oil-related sector. On 16 July

1960 he married Gillian Palmer (*b.* 1937), a receptionist, and daughter of Ian Hamilton Palmer, businessman. They had a son, Jeremy (*b.* 1961), and a daughter, Casella (*b.* 1963), followed by triplets, Nicholas, Sophie, and Emma (*b.* 1968).

In 1960 Alun-Jones moved to Expandite Ltd, where he was appointed managing director when Expandite was acquired by Castrol in 1966. In turn, Castrol was acquired by Burmah Oil, providing him with an opportunity to join Burmah Industrial Products as managing director from 1971 to 1974. In the latter year he secured a seat on the main board of Burmah Oil, just at the point when it was experiencing severe financial difficulties, largely caused by the tanker division's inability to cope with the spillover from the 1973 oil price crisis. He was consequently deeply involved in handling not only the consequences of multiple mergers, but also the challenges associated with monitoring performance across divisionalized business organizations. It was experience that would stand him in good stead in the next phase of his business career.

At the same time that Burmah Oil, like many other British firms, was struggling in the economically difficult mid-1970s, Ferranti Ltd was experiencing a severe liquidity crisis. Although this family-owned electronics firm had become a major player in various defence markets, especially avionics and naval computer systems, the chairman and managing director, Sebastian de Ferranti, had refused to stem the losses made in the power transformers division, creating acute financial problems in 1974. Given Ferranti's major role in various military aircraft and Royal Navy projects, as well as being a major employer in some depressed parts of Lancashire, the incumbent Labour government used its newly created National Enterprise Board (NEB) to bail out the ailing firm. In return for £15 million, however, not only did the NEB take a 65 per cent stake in Ferranti Ltd, but Sebastian de Ferranti was obliged to stand down as chief executive (though he was able to retain his position as chairman).

On taking over as managing director of Ferranti in 1975, Alun-Jones immediately set about reorganizing the firm's financial and decision-making structures, bringing his previous experience to bear in making Ferranti Ltd much more profitable. Even though the working relationship with Sebastian de Ferranti proved difficult, eventually resulting in the former owner's resignation in 1982, to be replaced as non-executive chairman by his brother, Basil de Ferranti, by 1978 Ferranti had been refloated on the London stock exchange. When in 1980 the NEB sold its holding in Ferranti to a large number of financial institutions, the latter's willingness to buy shares in the company reflected the trust they placed in the management skills of Alun-Jones and the team he had by then assembled.

Having secured its independence of government, Alun-Jones successfully sustained his aim of building Ferranti into a highly profitable defence contractor, using the slogan 'Creating wealth from technology' to depict his core strategy. Ferranti shareholders certainly benefited from their investment, with dividend payments and share values increasing significantly up to 1987. This precipitated strong rumours that Ferranti would be targeted by a predator, given its profitability and strong product range. Alun-Jones's reputation was also significantly enhanced, leading to board appointments at Royal Insurance (1981–96), Throgmorton Trust (1978–84), Reed International (1984–90), Guest, Keen and Nettlefolds (1986–8), and Consolidated Gold Fields (1988–9). He was also chairman of governors (1986–99) at his old school, Lancing College, and a fellow of its owners, the Woodard Corporation (1986–2003). In 1987 he was knighted for services to British business.

An essential component in Alun-Jones's strategy for Ferranti was creating a stronger presence in the world's largest defence market, the USA, resulting in a host of acquisitions of American firms between 1978 and 1987. The largest of these purchases, however, International Signal and Control Inc. (ISC), of Lancaster, Pennsylvania, proved to be calamitous. This merger, in 1987, resulted in Alun-Jones's appointment as executive chairman, Basil de Ferranti having been elevated to company president, while ISC's majority owner, James Guerin, became deputy chairman. Unbeknown to not only the Ferranti board, but also a small army of advisers and auditors, Guerin had built hundreds of millions of dollars' worth of phoney missile contracts into the accounts. It also transpired that he had been supplying armaments to South Africa and other countries on the United Nations embargo list, acting as the CIA's agent in regions that were regarded as strategically important. When these phoney contracts and illegal transactions eventually came to light in September 1989, Ferranti shares were immediately suspended and Alun-Jones was obliged to request a massive bailout from a syndicate of twenty banks. Although he had led Ferranti into the ISC merger for all the right reasons—to build a stronger presence in the USA, as well as forestalling a predatorial bid—it destroyed his reputation. He was obliged to resign as chairman of Ferranti in 1990. There was considerable controversy over the £491,000 package he received on leaving Ferranti, but not only did he have two years of his contract to run, he successfully negotiated the bank rescue package and the sale of the avionics business to the General Electric Company for £300 million, keeping the firm afloat. Guerin was subsequently sentenced to a fifteen-year prison term in the USA, for fraud and money-laundering.

Alun-Jones effectively retired in 1990, having given up all his other directorships to concentrate on helping to look after an increasing number of grandchildren, play golf, and fish. (In 1993 there was again controversy when it emerged that he had bought Ferranti's fishing rights on the River Test at a knock-down price.) He lived for much of his married life at The Willows, Effingham Common, Leatherhead, Surrey. He died on 19 January 2008, of bronchopneumonia, at the Royal Surrey County Hospital, Guildford. He was buried in Effingham, and a memorial service was held at Chelsea Old Church, London, on 24 April 2008. He was survived by his wife, Gillian, and their five children.

JOHN F. WILSON

Sources J. F. Wilson, *Ferranti: a history. The emergence of a family business, 1882–1975* (2000); *From family firm to multinational, 1975–1987* (2007); *Management, mergers and fraud, 1987–1993* [forthcoming] · *Daily Telegraph* (7 Feb 2008) · www.lancingclub.org, 1 June 2011 · Museum of Science and Industry, Manchester, Ferranti archives · Burke, *Peerage* · *WW* (2008) · personal knowledge (2012) · private information (2012) · b. cert. · m. cert. · d. cert.

Likenesses E. Millner, bronze bust, repro. in commissiona portrait.com/media_viewer.asp?id=3357&true · obituary photographs

Wealth at death under £84,000: probate, 10 June 2008, *CGPLA Eng. & Wales*

Jones, Emrys (1920–2006), geographer, was born on 17 August 1920 at 81 Gadlys Road, Aberdâr, Glamorgan, the younger son of Samuel Garfield Jones (1893–1965) and his wife, Annie, *née* Williams (1895–1984). His father had started his working life as a coalminer; after being wounded in the First World War he was successively a police officer and civil service clerk (although his occupation on his younger son's birth certificate is given as newsagent). Theirs was a Welsh-speaking home, a tradition that Jones later followed. Educated at Aberdâr Grammar School for Boys, in 1938 he followed his elder brother Alun to the University College of Wales, Aberystwyth, where he was later joined by their close cousin Alwyn Williams. He obtained a first-class degree in geography and anthropology in 1941 and then, as a Peace Pledge Union member, was a voluntary hospital worker in Cardiff. He returned to Aberystywth in 1943, obtaining the degrees of MSc (1945) for work on rural settlements in the Teifi valley and PhD (1947) for a thesis on its main town, Tregaron, supervised by Emrys Bowen and Alwyn Rees. Jones's Aberystwyth studies provided a firm and enduring foundation for his geographical scholarship. The physical environment is a 'geographical circumstance' within which human activities are shaped by and impressed on the evolving landscape. Group culture expressed in family, religion, and language—to which he later added ethnicity—is central to that continual reshaping, creating the contexts within which explanations for a phenomenon under study are sought. There can be no general laws, however, because of each situation's particularity. Jones was especially critical of law-like statements based on economic reasoning.

In 1947 Jones was appointed assistant lecturer in the department of geography at University College, London. He married 23-year-old Iona Vivien Hughes, a fellow student at Aberystwyth who became a schoolteacher, in the Calvinistic Methodist chapel at Gaerwen, Anglesey, on 7 August 1948; she was the daughter of Richard Hywel Hughes, local government officer. They had two daughters, Rhianon (*d.* 1980) and Catrin. The academic year 1948–9 was spent in the United States with a Rockefeller Foundation fellowship. Jones intended to study rural sociology at Cornell but was inspired by the urban ecology of the Chicago school, soon abandoning research into rural settlements and becoming instead a pioneer urban social geographer. After a further year at University College, London, clouded by uncertainty about his future, in 1950 he accepted a lectureship in geography at Queen's University, Belfast (being promoted to senior lecturer in 1958). He edited the handbook for the 1952 British Association meeting, *Belfast in its Regional Setting: a Scientific Survey*, which included his first essay on the city's urban geography. Over the subsequent decade detailed field mapping and pioneering analyses of small-area census data generated several highly original papers and a major monograph, *A Social Geography of Belfast* (1960)—a classic study that established Jones's reputation and opened up a new field of investigation for geographers.

The year before *A Social Geography* appeared Jones had moved to the London School of Economics as reader in social geography; he was appointed to a vacant chair two years later, and remained happily there, attracting a large number of research students, until retiring slightly early in 1984. He followed three main research interests during this period. The first focused on London's social geography, with his pioneering *Atlas of London and the London Region* using small-area census data (1968); maps were his foundation for studying social patterns. Second, with Richard Llewelyn Davies he co-directed the Joint Unit for Planning Research at University College, London, for twelve years: their consultancies included preparing plans for Milton Keynes, Caracas, and Swindon. Jones attended several of the Delos international planning symposia organized by Constantinos Doxiadis, interacting with such scholars as Buckminster Fuller, Margaret Mead, and Arnold Toynbee. He incorporated the built environment into his philosophy as a further geographical circumstance, arguing for planning procedures that allowed communities freedom to create their own milieux with as few constraints as possible. Third, he wrote widely about cities and urbanization. Alongside an influential textbook, *Introduction to Social Geography* (1977), written with a former student, John Eyles, he produced two widely read and much translated overview volumes, *Towns and Cities* (1969) and *Metropolis: the World's Great Cities* (1990), and (with Eleanor van Zandt) the sumptuously illustrated *The City: Yesterday, Today and Tomorrow* (1974). These books sustained his core argument that although general tendencies may influence how people create, and act in, urban milieux, each city is unique and should be treated as such.

Jones was heavily involved in other activities. He chaired the panel whose argument resulted in the overturning of the decision to exclude his discipline from the Social Science Research Council's original portfolio, and in 1967 he became a founding member of its human geography and planning committee. He played a major role chairing the new Regional Studies Association between 1968 and 1970, when it established itself as an extremely successful society bringing together academics and planning practitioners. He also chaired the Council for National Academic Awards' geography panel, and was a council member of both the Institute of British Geographers and the Royal Geographical Society. He chaired the latter's research committee and then served a five-year term as vice-president (1978–83).

After Jones's retirement he and his wife remained in Hertfordshire, where they had lived since 1959. He was active locally as a school governor, and in local music and arts societies; music and books—he was a bibliophile with many first editions—were important leisure interests. He was also active in Hertfordshire's expatriate Welsh community, and continued his close involvement with London's Honourable Society of Cymmrodorion, which he joined in 1947 and where he much enjoyed the convivial company of his compatriots; an elected member of its council from 1978 to 2002, he served as chairman (1983–9) and president (1989–2002), receiving its gold medal from the prince of Wales in 2001. His last major research project generated an edited volume published by the society, *The Welsh in London, 1500–2000* (2002), with Jones contributing two-thirds of the contents; a wide range of sources was used to explore in considerable detail the lives of a largely invisible yet culturally distinct community.

Jones retained close ties with Wales throughout his life—Aberystwyth rather than Aberdâr—and was a frequent visitor. A Rockefeller Foundation official noted in the record of an interview in 1950 that 'His greatest handicap, however, is that he is Welsh and I am afraid he wants to go back to that harsh, foreboding and mystic environment' (Johnston, *PBA*, 256). He was a member of the college council at Aberystwyth from 1978 to 1985 and led much-enjoyed field excursions for alumni into its hinterland; he was made a fellow of the college in 1991. Honorary degrees were awarded by Belfast (1978) and the Open University (1990). He received the Royal Geographical Society's Victoria medal in 1977; was elected a fellow of the British Academy in 2002; and was received into the Gorsedd of Bards in 2005. He died of hepatocellular cancer in the Hospice of St Francis, 27 Shrublands Road, Berkhamsted, on 30 August 2006; he was survived by his wife and one of their two daughters. His funeral was at St Mary's Church, Hemel Hempstead; some of his ashes are retained there, alongside his daughter Rhianon's, and the remainder were scattered on the family plot of his wife, Iona, in Brynsiencyn, Anglesey. RON JOHNSTON

Sources *The Guardian* (15 Sept 2006) • *News and Views* [LSE] (16 Oct 2006) • R. Johnston, *GJ*, 172 (2006), 348–9 • R. Johnston, F. W. Boal, and J. Eyles, 'Makers of modern geography: Emrys Jones (1920–2006)', *Progress in Human Geography*, 31 (2007), 551–62 • R. Johnston, *PBA*, 153 (2008), 243–92 • *WW* (2006) • personal knowledge (2010) • private information (2010) • b. cert. • m. cert. • d. cert.
Likenesses photograph, repro. in *PBA*
Wealth at death £380,267: probate, 29 Nov 2006, *CGPLA Eng. & Wales*

Jones, Grenfell [Gren] **(1934–2007)**, cartoonist, was born at 1 Brynglas, Hengoed, in the Rhymney valley, Glamorgan, on 13 June 1934, the youngest son of Henry (Harry) Jones, a coalminer who was also an amateur oil painter, and his wife, Violet Lilian, *née* Glover. He had two older brothers, Raymond and Kelvin. In 1938 the family moved to 11 Brynavon Terrace, Hengoed, where he attended the local primary school before studying at Lewis Boys' School, Pengam. At the age of eight he began drawing pocket cartoons in the style of the *Daily Mail*'s Neb (Ronald Niebour), who had been at school in Barry near Cardiff and had grown up in Wales; 'Neb was responsible for my first interest in cartoons', he later said (G. Jones to M. Bryant, 6 July 1998). His first published drawing was a joke cartoon for the adult pocket pin-up magazine *Spick and Span*. He sold his first news-related cartoon to the *Birmingham Mail* with the help of the former *Western Mail* cartoonist (then working for the *News Chronicle*) William John Philpin Jones (Jon), whom he greatly admired and to whom he had earlier sent some drawings.

After school Jones served an apprenticeship as an engineering draughtsman for Welsh Metals in Caerphilly. He spent his national service in the RAF in Penang, Malaya (1957–8), where in his spare time he was lead guitarist in a skiffle group, the Venoms, and drew cartoons for the *Penang Gazette*. After returning to his parents' house in Hengoed he resumed work as a draughtsman for Welsh Metals in Caerphilly. On 5 April 1958 he married, in the Tonyfelin Baptist Chapel, Caerphilly, (Sarah) Ann Morgan (*b*. 1934), an invoice clerk and typist at Welsh Metals, and daughter of David Rees Morgan, foreman carpenter. After their marriage they moved into a rented house in Railway Terrace, Caerphilly. In 1962 they bought 78 Brynnau Road, Castle Park, Caerphilly, and while living there they had two sons, Darryl (*b*. 1964) and Christopher (Chris; *b*. 1970). In 1970 the family moved to 16 Watford Close, Caerphilly. During this time Jones continued to work as a freelance cartoonist and also became one of the founder members of the Knights of the Round Table pop group. He had already left the group by October 1960 when it was transformed into the successful satirical pop group the Barron Knights, named after Tony Osmond (the Barron), an old RAF friend from the Venoms, who was a co-founder of the new band.

Jones later left Welsh Metals and worked as a sales representative for Phillips machine tools and Marley ceramic tiles before becoming a full-time freelance cartoonist and illustrator in 1963, contributing to *Whizzer and Chips* and other publications. In November 1968 he joined the staff of the Cardiff-based *Western Mail* group of newspapers (itself part of the Thomson Group), where he met and was encouraged by the group's long-standing sports and political cartoonist J. C. Walker. At first he drew topical single-column 'pocket' cartoons for the *Mail*'s evening sister paper, the *South Wales Echo*, but when Geoff Rich became editor in 1971 his daily news-related cartoon appeared over five columns (Rich occasionally appeared in the cartoons himself). He also produced a strip, 'Big Deal' (later renamed 'Threadneedle'), about business and office life, which ran for thirty-five years and was widely syndicated, and contributed pocket cartoons to *Wales on Sunday*.

In the 1970s Jones began his best-known creation, the weekly strip 'Ponty an' Pop', which appeared in the Saturday sports edition of the *South Wales Echo*. Based in the fictional Welsh rugby-playing village of Aberflyarff in Scrumcap Valley on the River Efflew, its colourful main characters were Ponty (chairman of Royal Aberflyarff RFC, whose motto was 'Ifyer gerit kickit') and his smaller, older friend, the cloth-cap-wearing, moustached Pop (an unemployed former miner with an encyclopaedic knowledge of sport) and his mongrel dog Bleddyn. Other frequently seen figures included Deuteronomy Jones ('the village moaner'), Bromide Lil (the tattooed barmaid of the Golden Dap Hotel), Arnold Nutstrampler (captain of Royal Aberflyarff RFC), Ronald the Ref, Erotica Jenkins (club physiotherapist), Cyclops Llewellyn (a Llanelli fan), and Dai the Dap (official streaker). The strip led to three books, *Ponty and Pop and the Sporting World of Aberflyarff* (1974), *Ponty and Pop: the Aberflyarff Story* (1979), and *Ponty an' Pop: the Continuing Story of Aberflyarff Folk* (1996), and the characters also appeared on BBC Wales radio and television.

Though Jones usually signed his cartoons simply GREN in capitals, he sometimes also worked as Jones. Neville and Nigel, two message-bearing sheep, often appeared in both his editorial cartoons and the strip 'Ponty an' Pop', as did the famous Hengoed viaduct. He preferred to work in line and wash and, as well as cartoons, also enjoyed sketching harbour scenes and painting landscapes in watercolours. As well as his annual volumes of collected cartoons from the *South Wales Echo* (from 1982) he produced a great many books, including eight titles in Exley Publishing's the Duffer's Guide series (from 1985). Others included *My Wales* (1971), *Portrait of a Rugbyholic* (1986), *Portrait of a TV Addict* (1987), *How to be a Welshman* (1990), *We'll Keep a Welcome: a Guide to Wales for the Visitor and the Welsh* (1994), *Gren's Guide to Rugby* (1996), and *It's Gren Again: a Collection of Some of his Favourite Cartoons* (2001). In addition he illustrated Tom Bellion's *'And the Tanker Spent a Comfortable Night': a Collection of Rugby Stories* (1979); books by the comedian Max Boyce, including *Max Boyce: his Songs and Poems* (1979); *Boots, Balls and Banter: Welsh Rugby in the 70s* (1980) by the broadcaster and sports writer David Parry-Jones; and Roy Noble's *Noble Expressions* (1992) and *Welsh Nicknames* (1998). He also received a gold disc from EMI (the first one ever awarded to a cartoonist) for the cover design of Max Boyce's album *We All Had Doctors' Papers* (1975). After his death his son Darryl produced a board game, *Rugby Addicts*, based on his father's drawings, and all kinds of Gren merchandise were made available through his official website.

In appearance Gren Jones was about 5 feet 9 inches tall, clean-shaven, with light brown hair and blue eyes; he wore spectacles in later life. He spoke with a soft Welsh accent. A keen rugby fan (he played for Caerphilly in his twenties), he was also a member of the Caerphilly Golf Club and enjoyed sailing. After his divorce in 1990 he bought a house at 19 Rookwood Avenue, Llandaff, Cardiff, and on 11 June 1993, at South Glamorgan register office, he married Ann Maureen Hayes (1942–2006), daughter of George Jack Lewis, electrician. He was appointed MBE in 1989 for his services to the newspaper industry, was voted provincial cartoonist of the year four times by the Cartoonists' Club of Great Britain, received a Variety Club award, and was given an honorary degree by the University of Glamorgan in 2004. He retired from the *Echo*'s newsroom in 1999, but continued to provide a daily cartoon from his home in nearby Llandaff. After he was taken ill he even drew from his hospital bed, and his last cartoon was published the day he died, 4 January 2007, of chronic renal failure and ischaemic cardiomyopathy at the University Hospital of Wales, Cardiff. He was cremated at Thornhill crematorium after a funeral at Llandaff Cathedral on 16 January. He was survived by his sons, both of whom had become policemen. His drawings have been exhibited at St David's Hall, Cardiff; there was a Welsh Arts Council touring exhibition of his work in 1985–6; and examples of his cartoons are held in the collections of the Welsh Tourist Board, the Welsh Arts Council, the National Library of Wales, and the British Cartoon Archive at the University of Kent. In November 2008 Prince William unveiled a large (40 feet by 12 feet) ironwork monument to

Grenfell Jones [Gren] (**1934–2007**), by unknown photographer, 2003

Jones by Nia Wyn Jones. Featuring Ponty and Pop, it was installed on the wall of the Media Wales building in Park Street, Cardiff. MARK BRYANT

Sources M. Bryant and S. Heneage, *Dictionary of British cartoonists and caricaturists, 1730–1980* (1994) • M. Bryant, *Dictionary of twentieth-century British cartoonists and caricaturists* (2000) • *Western Mail* (2 March 2004) • *South Wales Echo* (25 March 2004); (4 Jan 2007); (9 Jan 2007); (1 Nov 2008) • *South Wales Evening Post* (5 Jan 2007) • *The Independent* (6 Jan 2007) • *Daily Telegraph* (9 Jan 2007) • *Press Gazette* (12 Jan 2007) • *The Guardian* (13 March 2007) • letters to M. Bryant, priv. coll. • personal knowledge (2011) • private information (2011) [Darryl Jones, son] • b. cert. • m. certs. • d. cert.

Archives Media Wales, cartoons • NL Wales, cartoons • University of Kent, British Cartoon Archive, cartoons • Wales Tourist Board, cartoons • Welsh Arts Council, cartoons

Likenesses obituary photographs • photograph, 2003, Media Wales, Cardiff [*see illus.*] • photographs, University of Kent, Canterbury, British Cartoon Archive • photographs, Media Wales, Cardiff

Wealth at death £438,588: probate, 19 July 2007, *CGPLA Eng. & Wales*

Jones, Sir John Henry Harvey- (1924–2008), industrialist, was born at 2 Queensdown Road, Hackney, Middlesex, on 16 April 1924, the son of Mervyn Stockton Harvey-Jones (1893/4–1968) and his wife, Eileen Margaret, *née* Wilson (1894/5–1963). His father had served in the Indian army during the First World War, leaving with the rank of captain. At the time of his son's birth he was working for a bank in London, but he was later appointed tutor and guardian to the maharaja of Dhar, a state within the central India agency. Harvey-Jones spent his early childhood in India, returning to England at the age of six. He was educated at Tormore preparatory school at Deal in Kent, an unhappy period which ended in 1937 when he went to the Royal Naval College at Dartmouth. This was the starting point for a naval career which lasted until he joined Imperial Chemical Industries (ICI) in 1956. Appointed a midshipman in 1941, he served at first on HMS *Diomede*, which was engaged in patrol duties in the North America and West Indies station, and later joined the submarine service, in which he remained for the rest of the Second World War. After the war he went to Cambridge University to learn Russian and later served as an interpreter and liaison officer in naval intelligence, principally in Germany; he rose to the rank of lieutenant-commander and was appointed MBE in 1952. On 26 July 1947 he married Mary Evelyn Atcheson (*b.* 1921), daughter of Francis Felix Bignell, 'gentleman'. (She had changed her name by deed poll before her marriage.) They had one daughter, Gaby.

Harvey-Jones's decision to leave the navy was taken mainly for family reasons. His daughter had contracted polio, and since the treatment was likely to be difficult and lengthy he needed a job where he could be sure of getting home in the evenings. Two of his navy colleagues had recently started work at ICI, and their enthusiasm for the company encouraged him to join them. In 1956 he was taken on as a work study officer at the Wilton works near Middlesbrough, the newest of ICI's complex of factories on Teesside.

ICI was the giant of the British chemical industry, and it was expanding rapidly, especially in petrochemicals, plastics, and fibres, with much of the new investment going

Sir John Henry Harvey-Jones (1924–2008), by Gemma Levine, 2002

into the Teesside factories. It was also beginning to embrace modern management techniques, a process that accelerated after the appointment of Sir Paul Chambers as chairman in 1960. Chambers, who had held senior posts in the Inland Revenue, was the first non-scientist to head ICI. Among his innovations was to bring in McKinsey, the American management consulting firm, to advise on changes in the organization of the company.

As a work study officer Harvey-Jones obtained a useful insight into factory management at the shop-floor level, and his contacts with shop stewards proved valuable in his subsequent dealings with trade unions. After two years in work study he was appointed supplies manager at Wilton, then sales manager, and later personnel director within the heavy organic chemicals division (later renamed the petrochemicals division), which embraced both Wilton and its sister plant at Billingham. In 1970, to his own surprise and that of colleagues, he was made chairman of the division, in preference to two deputy chairmen who had the technical qualifications that Harvey-Jones lacked and longer service in ICI. Three years later he was appointed to the ICI main board and moved to London.

The 1970s were difficult years for ICI. The post-war boom was over, and several of the products that had driven the chemical industry's growth in the earlier post-war decades, such as plastics and fibres, had acquired the status of commodities, subject to bouts of overcapacity and falling prices. As a main board director Harvey-Jones was given oversight responsibility for the fibres division, and he presided over a drastic contraction of this business, including withdrawal from Terylene, the polyester fibre that had been a big profit earner in the 1950s and 1960s.

While the problems in fibres were extreme, the chemical industry as a whole was entering a period of maturity, and as a junior member of the board Harvey-Jones was frustrated by ICI's sluggish response to what had become a much more competitive environment. As he wrote later, he began to feel 'that the whole way in which we operated was wrong and needed fundamental change' (Harvey-Jones, *Getting It Together*, 327). In 1974 he and two colleagues suggested some organizational reforms, aimed at enabling the board to set clearer objectives and to communicate them more effectively to the divisional heads, but their proposals won no support. As Harvey-Jones saw it, there was no vision on the board of what the company should be, and little discussion of strategy. There was an inertia about decision making at the Millbank head office, which meant that investment funds were allocated across the divisions in line with established practice instead of going to the areas that offered the best prospects of profitable growth. ICI was a 'rather self-satisfied institution' (ibid., 326), doing just well enough not to be forced to change its ways. It would take a major crisis to shatter this complacency.

That crisis came with the severe recession of 1980–81, precipitated by the anti-inflationary policies of the new Conservative government under Margaret Thatcher. A combination of high interest rates and increasing oil production from the North Sea led to a sharp increase in the exchange rate, which had a devastating effect on the profitability of exporters such as ICI. ICI reported a loss in the third quarter of 1980—the first loss in its history—and to the consternation of its investors the dividend was cut. Sir Maurice Hodgson, who had taken over the chairmanship in 1978, set in train a fierce cost-cutting drive; nearly 30,000 jobs in the UK were eliminated between 1979 and 1983. The biggest losses were in the petrochemicals and plastics division, and there were fears that some of these businesses might have to be closed. Fortunately ICI had bought a stake in the Ninian oilfield in the North Sea some years earlier, and profits from this source partially offset losses in other parts of the group.

Harvey-Jones had been made one of ICI's three deputy chairmen in 1978 and was thus a potential successor to Hodgson. His appointment to the chairmanship in 1982 came as something of a surprise, and probably reflected the board's view that he was the most likely of the three candidates to challenge the *status quo* and to give ICI the new sense of direction that was needed. Whereas previous chairmen had stayed in post for only three or four years, Harvey-Jones was asked to serve for a minimum of five years.

Harvey-Jones's priorities when he took on the top job were to lighten the bureaucracy at the centre, to speed up decision making, and to strengthen the board's ability to provide strategic direction. The size of the head office staff in Millbank was cut from 1200 to 400 and two-thirds of the space was sold. The number of executive directors was reduced from sixteen to eight, and within this smaller, more collegiate board the directors were required to focus on the group as a whole, without the distraction of having special responsibility for particular divisions and overseas companies. On strategy, Harvey-Jones believed that ICI should shift away from commodity products towards higher margin and less cyclical 'effect' businesses—that is, chemicals that sold on the basis of the effect they produced, such as paints, dyestuffs, and pharmaceuticals. While ICI already had some businesses of this type, he looked to acquisitions as a means of speeding up the transformation. Since the failure of Chambers's attempt to take over Courtaulds in 1962, there had been a lack of enthusiasm in Millbank for takeovers, especially if they were likely to be resisted by the target company. Harvey-Jones was determined to be bolder, and set up an acquisitions unit to study takeover opportunities. Three of the largest acquisitions involved American companies: Beatrice, bought for its expertise in advanced materials; Glidden, a decorative paints maker, which complemented ICI's strength in the UK through its Dulux brand: and Stauffer, which had a strong position in agricultural chemicals. These takeovers also helped to reduce ICI's dependence on its traditional markets in the UK and the Commonwealth. Some investments had been made in continental Europe and the USA during the 1970s, but most of them had taken the form of large chemical complexes similar to those that ICI operated in the UK. ICI had been seeking to compete across the board against local companies that were already well established in these markets. The new approach was more selective, aimed at sectors where ICI, through superior technology, should have a competitive advantage.

Within the UK, Harvey-Jones was willing to pull out of businesses that had been part of ICI's heritage but no longer generated an acceptable return. This policy had been started by his predecessor—a notable event was the sale of ICI's polythene business to British Petroleum—and several other divestments took place during Harvey-Jones's chairmanship. Towards the end of his term of office he put forward a more radical plan, to sell all ICI's heavy chemicals businesses, which by then had been grouped together in a free-standing subsidiary, ICI Chemicals and Polymers, to one of the oil companies. Detailed discussions were held with British Petroleum and Shell, but no deal was done. Another missed opportunity was the failure to clinch what might have been an attractive acquisition in pharmaceuticals. By the 1980s ICI's pharmaceutical division had emerged after a long period of low returns as one of the company's biggest profit earners; one of its drugs was the heart disease treatment Tenormin, which became the world's most successful beta blocker. There was a strong case for expanding this division, and ICI came close to acquiring Beecham, the consumer products company that had been outstandingly successful in antibiotics. These negotiations advanced a long way, and ICI made a provisional agreement to sell

Beecham's branded consumer products to Unilever. However, senior executives in the pharmaceutical division were unenthusiastic—they preferred organic growth—and the ICI board decided not to proceed.

By the time of Harvey-Jones's retirement in 1987 ICI's portfolio had been partially reshaped, though not as radically as he had hoped. In terms of profits, the company was in a much healthier state than it had been five years earlier. Pre-tax profits had risen from less than £400 million to over £1 billion, an increase in the return on assets from 7 per cent to 18 per cent. A large part of the improvement reflected the recovery in the British economy, and Harvey-Jones was also the beneficiary of the painful decisions taken by Hodgson in 1980 and 1981. Nevertheless, his five years at the helm marked a break with the past, making ICI less stuffy, more agile, and more responsive to the changes that were taking place in the world chemical industry. The fact that he was a late entrant to ICI, and not a scientist or engineer, gave him a perspective on the company that was different from that of his predecessors. Although relations with his board colleagues were uneasy, his approachable style and lack of pomposity won him great affection among ICI employees, and helped to lift morale after a period in which the company had been in retreat.

Harvey-Jones was an unusual chairman in other respects. While previous chairmen had mostly shunned the limelight, he did not hesitate to speak out on controversial policy issues. In particular, he criticized what he saw as Margaret Thatcher's indifference to the damage her policies were doing to manufacturing industry. (He thought this criticism—and his decision to join the Social Democratic Party in the early 1980s—might make him the only ICI chairman not to be given a knighthood; but he was given this honour in 1985.) He also attacked the City for its persistent undervaluation of industrial companies, and for what he saw as the vastly inflated salaries earned by City practitioners. He set out these views in his Dimbleby lecture in 1986, which was entitled 'Does industry matter?'

With his long, unruly hair and his garish ties, Harvey-Jones cut an unconventional figure among Britain's business leaders, and enjoyed considerable attention in the media. After he left ICI he was asked by the BBC to participate in a series of programmes—entitled *Troubleshooter* (1990)—in which he visited British companies, assessed their strengths and weaknesses, and advised them on what they should do next. This advice was presented in a trenchant style, and not much appreciated by some of the managers who were on the receiving end of Harvey-Jones's sarcasm, but it made for entertaining television. Through these programmes, which were watched by an audience of more than 3 million, Harvey-Jones became the country's best-known industrialist. With his down-to-earth, self-deprecating manner, he gave a human face to business. Such was the success of the programmes that further series were broadcast in 1991, 1992, 1995, and 2000.

During his time at ICI, Harvey-Jones was a non-executive director at Reed International and Grand Metropolitan; the former gave him valuable experience in the handling of acquisitions, while the latter gave him an insight into a service-based business, closer to the customer than most parts of ICI. After his retirement, in addition to his television career, he served as chairman of *The Economist* for several years, and he took on several other directorships. Outside business the two appointments that gave him most satisfaction were as chancellor of Bradford University (1986–91) and as president of the Multiple Sclerosis Research Charitable Trust (1999–2008). He also wrote several books, of which the most successful were *Making It Happen: Reflections on Leadership* (1988) and the largely autobiographical *Getting It Together: Memoirs of a Troubleshooter* (1991). He suffered two minor strokes in the mid-1990s and lived quietly thereafter with his wife and daughter in Hay-on-Wye. He died in Hereford County Hospital of multiple causes after a long illness, on 10 January 2008. A memorial service was held in Hereford Cathedral on 17 April.

GEOFFREY OWEN

Sources A. Pettigrew, *The awakening giant: continuity and change in ICI* (1985) · M. Goold and A. Campbell, *Strategies and styles* (1987) · J. Harvey-Jones, *Making it happen: reflections on leadership* (1988) · J. Harvey-Jones, *Getting it together: memoirs of a troubleshooter* (1991) · G. Owen, *From empire to Europe: the decline and revival of British industry since the Second World War* (1999) · *Daily Telegraph* (11 Jan 2008) · *The Guardian* (11 Jan 2008) · *The Times* (12 Jan 2008) · *The Independent* (14 Jan 2008) · *WW* (2008) · Burke, *Peerage* · private information (2012) · b. cert. · m. cert. · d. cert.

Archives FILM BFINA, 'The Richard Dimbleby lecture', P. Morpurgo (director), BBC1, 3 April 1986 · BFINA, current affairs footage | SOUND BL NSA, current affairs, documentary, interview, and performance recordings

Likenesses photographs, 1978–2003, Photoshot, London · photographs, 1983–2002, Getty Images, London · photographs, 1988–2003, Rex Features, London · photographs, 1991–2, PA Photos, London · G. Levine, photograph, 2002, Camera Press, London [*see illus.*] · N. Higton, caricature, 2004, repro. in P. Wynter Bee and N. Higton, *People of the day* (2004) · G. H. Byrom, miniature, repro. in commissionaportrait.com · A. Fox, repro. in *The Independent* (13 March 2000) · H. Mee, oils, repro. in *British eminencies* (1990) [exhibition catalogue, London Hop Exchange, 23 May–13 June 1990] · G. Wilson, oils, repro. in commissionaportrait.com · obituary photographs · photographs, Camera Press, London

Wealth at death £29,486: probate, 19 May 2009, *CGPLA Eng. & Wales*

Jones, Karen Ida Boalth Spärck (1935–2007), computer scientist, was born on 26 August 1935 at the Huddersfield municipal maternity home, the only child of Alfred Owen Jones, a lecturer in chemistry at the local technical college, and his Norwegian wife, Ida, *née* Spärck, both of 18 Gledholt Road, Huddersfield. They were on one of the last boats to leave Norway after the German invasion in 1940. Karen spent much of the war with her mother (who worked for the Norwegian government in exile) in London, but apart from that passed her childhood in Yorkshire. She attended the grammar school in Huddersfield, went to Girton College, Cambridge, in 1953, where she graduated BA in history in 1956, and then stayed on to do the final year of the moral sciences tripos, as philosophy was then called. As an undergraduate she met Roger Michael *Needham (1935–2003), whom she married on 10

June 1958; he was the son of Leonard William Needham, also a chemistry lecturer. There were no children of the marriage.

In 1962, after a brief spell teaching, Karen Spärck Jones (as she continued to be known after her marriage) accepted Margaret Masterman's invitation to join the Cambridge Language Research Unit. There, under the supervision of Masterman's husband, the philosopher Richard Braithwaite, she wrote her doctoral thesis, 'Synonymy and semantic classification'. It was the first application of statistical clustering methods to lexical data—in her case, the data was the whole of Roget's Thesaurus on IBM punched cards—and was an ambitious attempt to create a notion of primitive concepts for machine translation, a technology then in its infancy. Far ahead of its time, the work was not published until twenty years later, at which time Spärck Jones had to be persuaded it was still relevant. The historian in her added an extraordinary appendix on artificial languages for coding meaning. The work used the 'theory of clumps' algorithms, which her husband Roger Needham developed and used in his work for his own thesis on automatic classification.

In 1968 the need for more serious computer facilities took Spärck Jones from the Language Research Unit to the University of Cambridge Computer Laboratory. The director at the time would not allow work explicitly on natural language processing, though he deemed information retrieval to be respectable and scientific. Spärck Jones, who had completed three years as a research fellow of Newnham College, then became a research fellow of the Royal Society. She again used the 'theory of clumps' algorithms in her new career in information retrieval, a subject on which she became a world authority, and she was the originator of the tf/idf algorithm, which underlies almost all internet searching in some form.

Spärck Jones's academic promotion was slow: most of her career was as an assistant director of research funded by grant money, a post made permanent only in 1988. She was appointed reader in computers and information in 1994, the year in which she became president of the worldwide society on computational linguistics, the Association for Computational Linguistics. It was only in 1999 that she was awarded a personal professorship. Masterman remained an inspiration to her, and she thanked her warmly, along with Needham, at the end of her acceptance speech for the lifetime achievement award of the Association for Computational Linguistics (2004). She gained many other honours, some of which she did not live to receive (although she recorded video acceptance speeches): fellowships of the American and European artificial intelligence societies, fellowship of the British Academy in 1995 (she served as vice-president in 2000–02), the Special Interest Group on Information Retrieval's Salton award (1988), the American Society for Information Science and Technology's award of merit (2002), the Association for Computing Machinery and the Association for the Advancement of Artificial Intelligence's Allen Newell award (2007), and the Lovelace medal of the British Computer Society (2007).

Unlike Needham, Spärck Jones did not become involved in local or university politics, but she played a strong role in national technology policy, starting with her role in the management of the UK's Alvey programme (a government-sponsored research programme in information technology) in 1985. She also campaigned hard for more women to enter computing and was conscious that she, like Masterman before her, had a husband with a more powerful formal role. She had almost no small talk in public gatherings and often omitted formal greetings and farewells. She was, with Needham, an accomplished sailor, and they had an Itchen Ferry cutter; they built their house themselves as research students, along with a flat for her mother, who lived with them for many years. When the house became too small, they bought another across the road for their books. She was an avid traveller, and her collections included a large one of African baskets that she willed to the Archaeology and Anthropology Museum at Cambridge University. She herself made wonderful things from *objets trouvés*. She and her husband moved to 9 Long Lane, Willingham, when the noise from the M11 became oppressive. He died there of cancer in 2003 and she also died there of cancer on 4 April 2007.

YORICK WILKS

Sources *Daily Telegraph* (12 April 2007) · *The Independent* (12 April 2007) · *The Times* (22 June 2007) · www.cl.cam.ac.uk/misc/obituaries/sparck-jones/, 19 July 2010 · *WW* (2007) · personal knowledge (2011) · private information (2011) · b. cert. · m. cert. · d. cert.

Likenesses photograph, 2002, repro. in en.wikipedia.org/wiki/Karen_Sparck_Jones · obituary photographs · photograph, repro. in www.cl.cam.ac.uk/misc/obituaries/sparck-jones/

Wealth at death £3,216,434: probate, 26 July 2007, *CGPLA Eng. & Wales*

Jones, Kenneth Jeffrey [Ken] (**1921–2006**), athlete and rugby union player, was born at 36 Greenfield Place, Blaenafon, Monmouthshire, on 30 December 1921, the son of John Jones, coalminer, and his wife, Ella Caroline, *née* Burland. He attended Blaenafon Church of England Boys' School and west Monmouthshire grammar school, Pontypool, winning selection for the Welsh secondary schools rugby team in his final year, 1939–40. He trained as a teacher at St Paul's College, Cheltenham, before joining the Royal Air Force. Three years of war service in Burma and India saw him rise to sergeant and develop his athletic talents, winning the 100 yards title at the 1945 All-India championships.

After demobilization Jones taught at Bathwick primary school, Bath, and played rugby for Blaenafon and Pontypool, before joining Newport in September 1946. In the same year he won his first Welsh athletics titles at 100 and 200 metres. He was chosen on the right wing for Wales's first official post-war international, against England at Cardiff in January 1947. Wales lost, but Jones retained his place for a decade. On 30 December 1947, his twenty-sixth birthday, he married Irene Augusta Edmunds (*b.* 1923), a childhood sweetheart (daughter of Arthur Thomas Edmunds, engineer), who made shaving off his moustache a condition of the marriage, at Blaenafon parish church. They had one son, Philip Jeffrey.

In 1948 Jones set a Welsh 100 yards record of 9.8 seconds at the Olympic trials and was selected for the London games, which he reckoned the highlight of a remarkable sporting life. A semi-finalist in the 100 metres, he was part of Britain's silver medal winning team—awarded gold before America's disqualification was reversed—in the sprint relay. Studying at Loughborough College in 1948–9 earned him the specialist physical education qualification that enabled his appointment in 1950 as a teacher at Newport high school.

Jones's rugby career peaked in the early 1950s as the best winger in Europe, perhaps the world. He was the leading scorer in the five nations championship, with four tries in each season, when Wales won grand slams in 1950 and 1952, and he was chosen as one of the five players of the year by the *Rugby Almanac of New Zealand* following the British Lions tour in 1950, during which he scored sixteen tries in sixteen matches. At 5 feet 11 inches with 'the long tapering legs of a classical sprinter' (Thomas, *Great rugger players*, 184), weighing 12 stone 4 pounds, and 'with his jet-black hair, his head slightly forward from his angular, bony frame, and his stamina and streamlined grace of movement, Ken Jones in flight resembled nothing as much as a jaguar' (Smith and Williams, 335). In a low-scoring, defence-dominated era he scored thrilling long-distance tries; the journalist Terry McLean called his score for the Lions against New Zealand at Auckland in 1950 'the greatest try of all' (McLean, 131–8), while the Welsh reporter J. B. G. Thomas admitted to breaching press-box etiquette by thumping his desk and shouting 'Go on Ken!' (Smith and Williams, 335) as Jones scored against Ireland in 1952. He was much more than a mere sprinter. His Newport and Wales team-mate Bryn Meredith recalled 'a tremendous tackler … his defence was out of this world' (*South Wales Argus*, 20 April 2006). The New Zealand full-back Bob Scott rated him 'the complete wing three-quarter' (Scott and McLean, 108).

Most famous of all Jones's tries was the winning try for Wales against New Zealand—at the time of his death Wales's last victory over the All Blacks—at Cardiff in December 1953, after he beat his opposite number Ron Jarden to a cross-kick. It was his last try for Wales, although he played thirteen more matches. Wales's inability to supply opportunities led A. A. Thomson to suggest he wear plates reading 'running in, please pass' (Thomson, 37). When his team-mate Gareth Griffiths tried to break the pattern of neglect by passing to him several times in the early stages of the match against Scotland in 1954 he was however told 'either kick it or have a go yourself' (Richards, 178). Jones captained Wales in that match, in which he equalled Dickie Owen's previous Welsh record of thirty-five caps. He overtook George Stephenson's world record of forty-two caps in 1956, winning his forty-fourth and last a year later. He was surpassed in turn by Jack Kyle of Ireland in 1958, but remained the most-capped Welshman and also Wales's highest try-scorer—jointly with Reggie Gibbs and Johnnie Williams on seventeen—until Gareth Edwards took both records in 1976. He played his final match for Newport, totalling 146 tries in 294 matches, in 1958.

In athletics Jones retained his Welsh 100 and 200 metres titles until 1953, missing out only in 1950 because of the Lions tour, which also prevented him from competing in that year's empire games. In 1954 he won an empire and Commonwealth bronze for Wales in the 220 yards at Vancouver and, as Great Britain's team captain, a silver in the sprint relay at the European games in Berne. In 1958 he managed the Wales team at the empire and Commonwealth games in Cardiff and carried the baton with the queen's message into the opening ceremony. Mistaking the bemedalled lord lieutenant of Glamorgan for the intended recipient, the duke of Edinburgh, he was rebuked by the duke while a spectator shouted 'forward pass' (Smith and Williams 358).

Jones left teaching to start his own car tyre business and worked from 1958 to 1995 as a rugby and athletics writer for the *Sunday Express*. In 1960 he was appointed MBE. He was president of Newport rugby club before resigning in protest at the game's acceptance of professionalism in 1995. A stroke left him largely wheelchair-bound after 1998. He died from a cerebral haemorrhage and atrial fibrillation at his home, Tregarth, Pillmawr Road, Malpas, Newport, on 18 April 2006. His funeral was held at St Peter's Church, Blaenafon, on 25 April and he was buried in Varteg Road cemetery, Blaenafon. He was survived by his wife, Irene, and their son, Philip.

Huw Richards

Sources *Rugby Almanac of New Zealand* (1951) · J. B. G. Thomas, *Great rugger players* (1955) · R. W. H. Scott and T. P. McLean, *The Bob Scott story* (1956) · B. Williams, *Rugger, my life* (1956) · A. A. Thomson, *Rugger my pleasure* (1957) · T. McLean, *Great days in New Zealand rugby* (1959) · J. Davis, *Newport Rugby Football Club, 1875–1960* (1960) · *Rothman's Rugby Yearbook* (1975–6); (1976–7) · D. Smith and G. Williams, *Fields of praise: the official history of the Welsh Rugby Union, 1881–1981* (1980) · W. Thomas, *A century of Welsh rugby players, 1880–1980* (1980) · J. M. Jenkins, D. Pierce, and T. Auty, *Who's who of Welsh international rugby players* (1991) · D. Parry-Jones, *The Gwilliam seasons* (2002) · H. Richards, *Dragons and All Blacks* (2004) · *South Wales Argus* (19–27 April 2006) · *The Independent* (21 April 2006) · *The Times* (22 April 2006) · *Daily Telegraph* (25 April 2006) · *Rugby guide: français et international* (2009) · www.wru.com, 5 May 2009 · www.blackandambers.co.uk, 5 May 2009 · private information (2010) · b. cert. · m. cert. · d. cert.

Likenesses photograph, 1950, repro. in Scott and McLean, *Bob Scott*, facing p. 131 · photograph, 1950, repro. in Williams, *My life*, facing p. 49 · photographs, 1950, Getty Images, London, Hult. Arch. · photograph, 1953, repro. in Richards, *Dragons* · photograph, 1954, repro. in Smith and Williams, *Fields of praise* · photograph, 1958, repro. in www.rugbyrelics.com/SW/info/co/1958-co.htm · photographs, repro. in www.historyofnewport.co.uk

Wealth at death under £226,000: probate, 9 Nov 2006, *CGPLA Eng. & Wales*

Jones, Philip James (1921–2006), historian, was born on 19 November 1921 at 232 Queen's Road, Peckham, London, the son of John David Jones, schoolteacher, and his wife, Caroline Susan, *née* Davies. He was educated at St Dunstan's College, Catford, and Wadham College, Oxford. His studies were interrupted by call-up to the army during the Second World War, but he was discharged early (he saw no service abroad and claimed to have learned mainly how to clean shoes), returned to Wadham, and graduated with first-class honours in modern history in 1945, having been tutored by the agrarian historian Reginald Lennard. Over the next five years he won various scholarships that enabled him to complete his DPhil at Magdalen College. His thesis, on the Malatesta lordship of Rimini in the late middle ages, supervised by the distinguished historian of Italy, Cecilia Ady, was his first serious venture into the field that he later was to make his own—medieval and Renaissance Italy. About this time he also came under the influence of K. B. (Bruce) McFarlane, the leading Oxford medievalist of the day, from whom he acquired an abiding interest in the study of aristocratic power.

In 1949 Jones obtained his first university post, as an assistant lecturer at Glasgow University, before moving shortly afterwards to the University of Leeds, where for the next thirteen years he worked as lecturer (1950–61) and reader (1961–3) in medieval history. His doctoral researches in the late 1940s naturally took him to Italy, where he met his future wife, Carla Marianna Rosalia Susini (*d.* 2004). They were married in 1954 and had a son, Simon, and a daughter, Tessa. Through her translations Carla Jones played an important part in making her husband's work available to an Italian academic audience, among whom it was to have a tremendous impact. In his time at Leeds Jones published a series of pioneering articles on the agrarian history of Italy, which were later published in Italian as a book. He returned to Oxford in 1963 as a fellow and tutor of Brasenose College and spent the rest of his academic career there, also serving as college librarian (1965–89). Brasenose was a short step away from his main place of work, the Bodleian Library, where he became a familiar figure in the upper reading room—tall, angular, forbidding, wrapped in a large dark coat in all seasons, seated at a desk surrounded by towers of books, an image that gave substance to the opinion expressed by many who reviewed his work that he must have read everything that there was to read on medieval Italy.

Although he conducted meticulous archival work in the early stages of his career when working on the Malatesta, overall the most striking characteristic of Jones's work was an almost superhuman command of secondary literature, which was daunting and awe-inspiring in equal measure; his characteristic footnoting style, which many found infuriatingly cryptic, was designed to condense the sheer volume of reading that lay behind every point he made and that would have run for pages if rendered in a more expanded form. This encyclopaedic knowledge was far from deadening: on the contrary it allowed him to approach his subject in a highly revisionist—not to say controversialist—spirit. His tendency to formulate new interpretations of classic problems was based on profound learning and reflection, as is clearly evident in two pieces of work that defined him as a historian and guaranteed his lasting reputation. The first was a paper published in the *Transactions of the Royal Historical Society* in 1965 under the title 'Communes and despots: the city-state in late medieval Italy', in which he demonstrated that the transition from commune to lordship (*signoria*) was more complex and variable from city to city and region to region than had hitherto been believed. He convincingly rejected the widely held view that 'despotism', that is the rule of cities by a single dynastic family, represented a decline from the 'liberty' enjoyed under the commune. Rather, it was simply the reappearance of an overly aristocratic style of rulership that had been present also—if less visible—in the oligarchic regimes of the communes. 'In an age when, even in Italy, most governments were seigneurial or royal', he wrote, 'what is remarkable is not the return to monarchy but rather its interruption' (P. J. Jones, 'The city state in late medieval Italy', *TRHS*, 5th ser., vol. 15, 1965, 72).

This ability to alter scholarly orthodoxy resurfaced on a grander scale with the publication, in Italian, of the second of his two contributions to Einaudi's monumental Storia d'Italia series in 1978 (the first was published in 1974). In this long interpretative essay, provocatively titled 'Economia e società nell'Italia medievale: la leggenda della borghesia' (in R. Romano, ed., *Dal feudalismo al capitalismo*), he challenged the traditional view that medieval Italy was a land of great commercial cities run by merchants for merchants. This was mistaken, he argued, first because of the assumption that cities like Florence and Venice were typical when in fact they were exceptional, and second because it underestimated the integration of city and countryside and the power and influence wielded by the 'feudal' aristocracy. For Jones, the key to understanding why the cities flourished and ultimately why the Renaissance occurred in Italy lay in economic history, and particularly the history of landholding. Although his conclusions were shared by some of his contemporaries (mainly non-Italians), this so-called 'return to the land' was at first greeted with vociferous opposition and hostile reviews in many Italian journals. Jones did not directly participate in the long-running and at times heated scholarly debate that his 'Leggenda della borghesia' essay stimulated, but over time most of what he had proposed became generally accepted. In 1997 he published *The Italian City State: from Commune to Signoria*, the fruit of a lifetime's work in which he largely restated the conclusions he had reached twenty years earlier, though nuanced by further reflection. As it turned out, this was his last major publication; a planned second volume remained incomplete at his death.

Jones was an excellent teacher and an attentive supervisor of doctoral students. Many of his former pupils went on to become distinguished historians themselves in the field of Italian history. He also translated the work of Italian historians, notably Gino Luzzatto's as *An Economic History of Italy from the Fall of the Roman Empire to the Beginning of the Sixteenth Century* (1961). He was an assiduous reviewer, but despite his deep engagement with the writing of others and his penchant for scholarly debate he rarely gave papers himself and never attended conferences, preferring to let his published works speak for themselves.

He laboured unstintingly over these, not only in marshalling arguments to support his grand theories, but also in the selection of precise words and phrases. The opening of a discussion with an arresting paradox as in his 'Leggenda della borghesia' essay ('To begin an examination of the Italian Middle Ages through courts and estates (*curtes*) may seem at first sight out of place, appropriate for the history of transalpine Europe—monarchical, feudal and agrarian—but completely inappropriate for Italy'; p. 187), the use of alliteration, and other forms of word-play, were as recognizably Jonesian as the detailed dissection of the nature of complex economic and social structures. This 'ludic joy in the choice of words' as one of his former students put it (*The Independent*, 3 May 2006), may have stemmed in part from a lifelong passion for literature, particularly that of the nineteenth century; 'in history as in fiction,' he once wrote, 'the first problem is always that of choosing the point of departure' (Storia d'Italia).

Jones was made a fellow of the British Academy in 1984 and was awarded its Serena medal for Italian Studies in 1988. Having lived latterly at 167 Woodstock Road, Oxford, he died of a stroke at the John Radcliffe Hospital, Oxford, on 26 March 2006. He was survived by his son and daughter. EDWARD COLEMAN

Sources T. Dean and C. Wickham, eds., *City and countryside in late medieval Italy: essays in honour of Philip Jones* (1990), pp. vii–xv · *The Independent* (3 May 2006) · *The Guardian* (3 May 2006) · *PBA*, 161 (2009) · *WW* (2006) · personal knowledge (2010) · private information (2010) · b. cert. · d. cert.
Likenesses photograph, repro. in Dean and Wickham, *City*, xi
Wealth at death £825,328: probate, 5 Oct 2006, *CGPLA Eng. & Wales*

Juda [*née* Brauer], **Anneliese Emily** [Annely] (**1914–2006**), art dealer and gallery owner, was born on 23 September 1914 in Kassel, Germany, the eldest of the two daughters of Kurt Brauer (*d.* 1951) and his wife, Margarete, *née* Goldmann. Her father was an industrial chemist who moved with his wife from Berlin to Kassel to purchase a laboratory that had previously belonged to an associate of Goethe's; there, in addition to his research work, Brauer privately studied Goethe's theories of colour after a discovery of papers in the laboratory. Annely's mother, having trained with the Austrian artist Oskar Kokoschka in Berlin, worked as a fashion and typeface designer. As a child Annely enjoyed a rich cultural life encouraged by her parents and also gained a love of sports, including skiing, which remained a favourite recreation. She attended the Meysenberg School, Kassel, and at sixteen began a course in art history at Kassel University. However, the family's fortunes changed when the Nazis took control of the city in 1932. As a Jew, Annely was forbidden to attend the university, and in the following year her father was imprisoned for several months and his library confiscated. Warned of a second impending arrest Kurt Brauer left Germany for Palestine, to be followed by Annely in July 1934 and her mother and sister, Eva, in November. In their adopted country Annely travelled selling custard powders manufactured in her father's new factory at Jaffa.

Anneliese Emily [Annely] **Juda** (**1914–2006**), by unknown photographer

The work was hard and she found Palestinian society restrictive and excessively provincial.

In 1937, with no associates and only £1 to her name, Annely Brauer moved to London, where she initially worked at a Hampstead lodging house for German refugees in return for her keep. With money saved from additional work as a maid she took classes in art history and fashion design at the Reimann School of Art and Design, which had relocated from Berlin to London. At the lodging house she met a fellow German exile who was then studying law, Paul Arthur Juda (*b.* 1912/13), son of Adolf Juda. Assistance from the Juda family enabled Annely to study full-time for a year at the Reimann School and, on 15 November 1939, the couple married at the synagogue in Richmond-upon-Thames. Paul Juda also helped to bring Annely's parents to England; her father later died in London while her mother returned to Palestine. During the war Annely worked as a driver for the Women's Voluntary Service, delivering food to bomb-damaged areas of the capital. The couple lived in Richmond, and the first of their three children, Carol, was born in 1942, followed by David in 1946 and Susan in 1951. In 1949 the family went to Germany with the hope of reclaiming confiscated property in Cologne belonging to Paul Juda's family. Initially they prospered but by 1955 Paul Juda's business had failed and the couple divorced. Annely Juda now moved back to London with her children. In her first year she took on several menial jobs and lived again at the Hampstead lodging house where she was supported by the nanny of her youngest child, who accompanied her to England.

In 1956 Juda began work as a secretary and translator for the London-based art collector and dealer Eric Estorick, whose wife, Salome (Sal), she had met at the Reimann

School. Though the post was short-lived—she was sacked by Estorick at Christmas 1957—it convinced her of her future career and, after a spell at the Kaplan Gallery, she set up on her own at Molton Street, London, in 1960. There she achieved note as a pioneering sponsor of British abstraction by hosting solo exhibitions by members of the situation school, including William Turnbull (1960 and 1961), Robyn Denny and Bernard Cohen (both 1961), and Gillian Ayres (1962). In the following year—with the support of Nika Hulton, wife of the magazine publisher Sir Edward Hulton—she established the Hamilton Galleries on St George Street, where she exhibited American abstract expressionists, including Jackson Pollock, in 'Trends and Movements' (1966).

While working for Estorick, Juda had shown the Italian section of his collection in Berlin and had there established important connections with the German and central European art world. An exhibition of works by Paul Klee (1961) was one of Juda's first of continental modernism and was followed by a series of shows by which she introduced British audiences to Russian and east European modernism, Bauhaus, and such pioneers of west European abstraction as Piet Mondrian. Juda's considerable contribution to the understanding and appreciation of these movements was particularly evident in a series of exhibitions held from 1970 under the title 'The Non-Objective World' at 11 Tottenham Mews, Fitzrovia, the premises to which she had moved two years earlier. The first exhibition, covering the period 1914–24, included works by Wassily Kandinsky, Aleksandr Rodchenko, and Vladimir Tatlin, and was followed by three further summer shows (1971–3) which extended the period covered to the mid-1950s. A fifth, and particularly important, exhibition was held in 1978, while a sixth 'Non-Objective' show in 1988 featured a number of younger American and British artists. These exhibitions challenged established categorizations and chronologies by juxtaposing artists from different generations, as well as works by established and lesser-known painters and sculptors. Her 'Dada–Constructivism: the Janus Face of the Twenties' (1984) was a notable example of this interest and ability to inform an audience through exhibitions that were as much intended to serve intellectual as commercial ends. These exhibitions had an enormous impact on art historians and critics, curators, and the educated art public. As a consequence Juda gained a reputation as an extremely knowledgeable and trusted authority on Russian modernist art, for which in many cases accurate provenance was notoriously difficult to establish. At the same time her success in introducing non-figurative art to an often sceptical British audience revealed her dedication, stoicism, and determination. Courage was a quality many associated with her.

Other examples of Juda's innovation included her successful promotion, from the early 1960s, of modern Japanese artists in Britain (in contrast to other dealers' primary interest in simply selling Western art in Japan) and her undiminished appetite for new ideas, be they in formal exhibitions or student shows. In 1971 she presented the first British exhibition of the conceptual artist Christo, for whom, as for many of her artists, she developed a fierce, and reciprocated, loyalty: exhibitions of Christo's work were held on eleven occasions to 2005, while her professional association with Michael Michaeledes lasted for forty years from 1966. By the late 1980s she had added Prunella Clough and Anthony Caro to her list. They were joined in 1997 and 2000 respectively by David Hockney and Leon Kossoff (two of the very few figurative artists whom she represented). From 1982 Juda worked in partnership with Alexander Gregory-Hood (1915–1999), a fellow specialist in abstract art, who moved his collection from the Rowan Gallery, Knightsbridge, to 11 Tottenham Mews to create the Juda Rowan Gallery. The joint venture—in many ways a partnership of opposites between a diminutive Jewish émigrée and a tall, former British army colonel—worked well until it was amicably dissolved after five years.

Juda's final move, in 1990, was to custom-built premises at 23 Dering Street, off New Bond Street, once more as Annely Juda Fine Art. Eight years later she became the first contemporary art dealer to be appointed CBE; at the ceremony she was accompanied by Wilma Kuvecke, her child's nanny, who had accompanied her to England in 1955 and with whom she remained associated until her death. Her charity work included support, in London, for the Camden Arts Centre and the Air Gallery, and overseas for the British Friends of the Art Museum of Israel. After a year-long deterioration in her health, she died on 13 August 2006 at Nightingale House residential care home, 105 Nightingale Lane, Balham, London. A commemorative exhibition, organized by her son, David, with whom she had worked since 1967, was held at 23 Dering Street between May and July 2007. PHILIP CARTER

Sources *Masterpieces of the avant-garde*, exhibition catalogue, 1985 · *The Times* (17 Aug 2006) · *The Guardian* (17 Aug 2006) · *The Independent* (17 Aug 2006) · *Daily Telegraph* (25 Aug 2006) · *New York Times* (30 Aug 2006) · *Art Monthly* (1 Oct 2006) · N. Lynton, *Annely Juda: a celebration* (2007), 9–14 · *WW* (2006) · private information (2010) [M. Gooding] · m. cert. · d. cert.

Archives SOUND BL NSA, documentary recordings · BL NSA, National Life Story Collection, artists' lives, interviews with M. Petzal, 2002, C466/151

Likenesses D. Hockney, pencil, 1999, repro. in *Annely Juda* · photograph, Annely Juda Fine Art, London [*see illus.*] · photographs, repro. in *Annely Juda*

Wealth at death £551,891: probate, 20 Dec 2006, *CGPLA Eng. & Wales*

Kalman, Andras (1919–2007), art dealer, was born into a Jewish family in the small town of Mátészalka in north-eastern Hungary on 24 May 1919, the youngest of three sons of Ernest Kalman and his wife, Maria, *née* Laufer. His father was a prosperous pharmacist, and for a time the children had an English governess. His mother taught him to play tennis, and was encouraging when he proved highly gifted at the game; she, prophetically enough, told him it could prove an extremely useful skill in the future. He later collected nineteenth-century British naïve paintings: one picture—depicting maids on a balcony, ogling newcomers to a market town—reminded him of the often charmingly parochial atmosphere of the Mátészalka of his youth. He recalled:

> When the coach arrived in my little Hungarian village, the great thing was to watch who came in and who came out. We lived on a street corner where you could see everything. We had no memorable pictures in our small village. But when I was 13 or 14, my ambition was to be another Alexander Korda. How I ended up with silent pictures instead of moving ones I don't know! (Vann, 51)

He acknowledged that his later interest in both modernist and naïve art may, in part, have been unconsciously inspired by the still relatively vital Hungarian folk art tradition he had known in his early years.

At the age of nineteen Kalman came to England first to study English, then chemistry at Leeds University. In the summer of 1939, on the eve of Britain's declaration of war with Germany, he cut short a holiday in Normandy with his brother Gabor, and returned to England. His brother went home to Hungary. At the end of the war a message reached him that Gabor, ill with typhoid, had been rescued by the Americans from Dachau; he died shortly afterwards. In 1948 Kalman returned to Hungary to discover that his parents had perished in the concentration camps, and that, at the beginning of the war, his eldest brother, Tomas, had been kicked to death in the town square. The family home with its balcony and geraniums remained, but he found nothing left for him there. He later said: 'I had been a happy child, but after this I was lonely and unhappy for 20 years … Not till I married and had children did I begin to feel whole again' (*The Guardian*, 14 Sept 2007).

With the imposition of communism imminent in Hungary, Kalman returned to England with some family silver, saved by his mother's maid. Over the next fifty years he regularly sent money to this courageous woman. In 1949, having settled in Manchester, where he earned a living as a weekend tennis coach (he was by then a tennis player of professional standard, proud of the fact that he played three times at Wimbledon, in 1949, 1950, and 1951, albeit losing in the first round each year), he opened up a small art gallery there in a basement in a former air raid shelter. His Mancunian tennis doubles partner and friend Joseph Braka, a textile merchant, initially paid the rent. With a young man's chutzpah, Kalman set his sights high, writing to Ben Nicholson, Henry Moore, Jacob Epstein, Matthew Smith, Lucian Freud, and others, requesting works on a sale or return basis. Most responded well, but not so the public, none of whom turned up for the first private view. A *Manchester Guardian* typesetter misread Kalman's cursive script for 'new gallery opening' as 'Crane Gallery opening'. So he simply adopted this singular name, the gallery thereafter being known as the Crane Kalman Gallery. Towards the end of this first show the local painter L. S. Lowry came in and, sensing that Kalman was struggling, bought a small painting. So began a lifelong friendship.

In 1957 Kalman moved to London and set up the Crane Kalman Gallery at 178 Brompton Road. He showed many artists from the École de Paris, in 1963 putting on a show titled 'Soutine–Modigliani' (with a characteristically phrased subtitle: 'A modest complement to the Tate Gallery exhibition'). On 24 April 1961 he married Dorothy May Wareing (1935–2001), daughter of Harold Wareing, paint manufacturer, from a Quaker family of Bolton. They had three children, Sally, Andrew, and Richard. For over twenty years Kalman was significantly assisted in the running of the gallery by Sally and Andrew. Robin Light, who initially had come to the gallery aged eighteen for a month's internship, also played a key role in helping Kalman run the gallery for twenty-two years.

Kalman had a rare, discerning eye for the fresh, original impulse underlying the best modern art—a pristine, non-academic quality evident too in his collection of antique, naïve British paintings with their beautifully awry perspectives. Visitors to his gallery were invariably enchanted by his courteous charm, flair, and wittily, sometimes uproariously, perceptive stories about artists whose works he showed, including L. S. Lowry, Ben Nicholson, and Graham Sutherland. He felt strongly that art should intimately move and nourish the viewer, saying that when he visited Henry Moore he was 'aware of the humanity of the person. Moore would have a small sculpture on a table, some so beautiful you want to caress them, and that is the sort of art I like' (personal knowledge). Kalman's own collection of intuitively sophisticated evocations of ordinary daily life by self-taught painters (from about 1750 to 1900) also gave him persistent delight. This collection, acquired in 1993 by the Peter Moores Foundation, is now on permanent public display in the attic galleries at Compton Verney House in Warwickshire.

Kalman staged many exhibitions of works by artists he felt were critically underrated: Nicholson's first wife, Winifred, the maker of sensuous yet transcendent flower paintings; Alan Lowndes, the self-taught but far from naïve painter of ruggedly poignant scenes of northern English urban life; and Celso Lagar, the spirited Spanish painter of the bohemian circus, pre-eminent among them. He also liked to highlight neglected aspects of artists. He was, for example, infuriated by the growing popular myth of Lowry as a grumbling misanthrope, saying he found him 'warm, friendly, generous though lonely' (personal knowledge). In 1968 he put on a revelatory show, 'The Loneliness of L. S. Lowry', which included poignant oil sketches of ostracized down-and-outs, a man searching a dustbin for food, a bearded woman. He also showed what he called 'lonely Lowrys' (personal knowledge), bleak yet awe-inspiring moor scenes and nearly all-white seascapes. Kalman's warmth and erudition attracted many writers, actors, and film and theatre directors. Yet, ironically, what often brought them to his gallery was a subtle, unsensational, contemplative quality announced in the title of an exhibition in 1999, 'Silence in Painting'. This resounding quietness manifested itself here in landscapes by Giorgio Morandi, abstracts by Nicholson, and the spacious, luminous rural paintings of Mary Newcomb, the East Anglian painter Kalman had discovered and successfully exhibited.

Kalman's beloved and devoted wife, Dorothy, died in

2001. He responded stoically, towards the end of his life, to a fire at his home, which destroyed many cherished paintings. He was a regular, lively, loquacious presence in the gallery until a few months before his death, at the Royal Marsden Hospital, Chelsea, on 26 July 2007, of cancer. He was survived by his children, Sally, Andrew, and Richard. The latter ran a photographic gallery in Brighton.

PHILIP VANN

Sources J. Ayres, *English naive painting, 1750–1900* (1980) [preface by A. Kalman] · P. Vann, 'The Crane Kalman collection', *Antique Collector* (Oct 1988) · M. Gayford, 'The first pop art', *Telegraph Magazine* (16 Jan 1993) · A. Lambirth, *LS Lowry conversation pieces: Andras Kalman in conversation with Andrew Lambirth* (2003) · *The Independent* (30 July 2007) · *Daily Telegraph* (9 Aug 2007) · *Manchester Evening News* (10 Aug 2007) · *The Times* (11 Aug 2007); (30 Aug 2007) · *The Guardian* (14 Sept 2007) · personal knowledge (2011) · private information (2011) [Andrew Kalman, son] · m. cert. · d. cert.

Likenesses obituary photographs

Wealth at death £2,518,901: probate, 16 July 2008, *CGPLA Eng. & Wales*

Kavanagh, Patricia Olive [Pat] (**1940–2008**), literary agent, was born on 31 January 1940 in Durban, South Africa, the daughter of Christopher (Chris) Kavanagh (*d.* 1966), a journalist and ostrich farmer, and his wife, Olive Nellie (Mysti), *née* Leroux (1916–2002), a health inspector. Her father, who was of Irish origin, was the author of *Timid Eagle* (1962), about a Second World War pilot. Her parents separated when she was a child, and both remarried. At home she felt unloved; at Durban High School for Girls she felt an outsider for being the only girl with divorced parents, and—because they were poor—without servants. At eleven she acquired a half-sister (the dance biographer Julie Kavanagh) from her father's second marriage; at sixteen a half-brother (Michael F. O'Brien, a geologist) from her mother's. She spent the academic year 1957–8 at Cape Town University, but left to tour with a theatre group. Much later, in England, she was cast in a film of *Under Milk Wood*, in a sexy scene with Richard Burton. (Her performance as Louise Colet in the recording of Julian Barnes's *Flaubert's Parrot* gives a hint of her acting skills.) But she disliked life as an actor and life in South Africa. She left for England in 1964, and retained the lifelong émigré's mixed feelings for her homeland and edge-on view of her adopted country.

Kavanagh worked at the J. Walter Thompson advertising agency for two years, until, after answering an advertisement in the *New Statesman*, she was hired by A. D. Peters. She joined the agency on 1 January 1966, and stayed there for forty-two years. The firm had been established in 1924 by Peters, a literary agent who, according to Arthur Koestler (one of the clients Kavanagh took over and to whom she became very close) conferred upon the profession an aura of integrity, humanity, and dignity that it had not possessed before. Kavanagh rapidly became indispensable to Koestler and to others of A. D. Peters's writers, among them, then and later, S. J. Perelman, Laurie Lee, Auberon and Alec Waugh, and Tom Wolfe. Rebecca West, Kingsley Amis, and John Mortimer were also clients of the agency. Peters died in 1973; his firm merged with

Patricia Olive [Pat] **Kavanagh (1940–2008)**, by Derek Thompson

Fraser and Dunlop, which represented theatre and film clients, in 1988. The larger firm of Peters, Fraser and Dunlop, known as PFD, continued independently until 2001, when it was bought by CSS Stellar, a takeover leading eventually to the splitting-off of most of the agents and clients at PFD to form United Agents in 2008.

Kavanagh, supported by her assistant Carol MacArthur, developed and nurtured a distinguished list, including William Trevor, Brian Moore, Margaret Drabble, Robert Harris, Ruth Rendell, Joanna Trollope, Posy Simmonds, Julian Barnes, Michael Dibdin, Clive James, John Irving, Blake Morrison, Sally Beauman, Prue Leith, Leslie Kenton, and Adam Mars-Jones. She was an especially sympathetic agent to poets (such as Andrew Motion, Douglas Dunn, Craig Raine, John Fuller, James Fenton, and Wendy Cope). She worked equally well with scholarly academics and popular journalists (including Peter Conrad, Redmond O'Hanlon, Russell Davies, Duncan Campbell, Bee Wilson, Francis Wheen, and Jane Stevenson). She had warm relationships with performers-turned-authors, notably Dirk Bogarde, Emma Thompson, Deborah Bull, and Sandi Toksvig. She particularly liked discovering and helping young writers, with no necessary prospect of financial gain, and was as passionately concerned for her authors whether they had written a book that was likely to sell 1000 copies, or 1,000,000. She supported Joanna Trollope, for instance, when she was a struggling single mother with no popular following; she negotiated dazzlingly high advances early in the careers of women writers such as Sally Beauman and Ruth Rendell. Kavanagh's eye for promising talent can be seen in the careers of Helen Simpson, Emma Brockes, Sean and Nikki French, and Alice

Oswald. (If she could terrify old hands in the publishing business, she was always kindness incarnate to younger, more vulnerable people, such as her Raine godchildren, or her junior colleagues.) Most of her clients stayed with her for life and went with her to United Agents. Those who moved elsewhere—such as Marina Warner, Howard Jacobson, and Diane Johnson—remained friends. Martin Amis's widely reported defection to Andrew Wylie in 1995 was an exception to her steady relations with her clients.

Kavanagh was trusted and respected because she was a formidable negotiator (Peters taught her the art of silence in bargaining), had excellent judgement, was humorous, witty, and charming in her dealings with people, and told the truth. Dan Franklin, of Random House, said of her: 'She did not say anything that she did not mean; she did not indulge in hyperbole or special pleading; she never submitted a manuscript that was flawed' (*The Guardian*, 11 Dec 2008). She was succinct in her praise ('bloody good'), concise on the telephone ('Pat called'), and direct and discerning in her advice. She did not nanny her authors or raise false hopes—Howard Jacobson admired her 'melancholy pessimism' (*The Guardian*, 22 Oct 2008)—but was completely loyal and committed to them. Peter Conrad called her 'more of a conscience' than an agent (*The Observer*, 26 Oct 2008). She felt that a literary agent should be like an old-fashioned family doctor: discreet, anonymous, dedicated, and reliable.

In her personal life Kavanagh was funnier and warmer, and less confident, than she could sometimes appear in public. Her beauty and poise—the flaming hair, the wide green eyes, the small delicate bird-like uprightness, the wonderful cheekbones, the alluring smile—could be daunting, but she was also shy and vulnerable. She had talents and interests that she did not boast about: gardening, travelling, cooking, elegant clothes, bird-watching, art, music, piano-playing, Italian, tennis, collecting (especially pictures of women reading), dancing, walking, patchwork, writing, painting. Many of these interests centred on and flourished in her marriage to the novelist Julian Barnes (*b*. 1946), in the fine house in north London where they generously entertained their friends. They had married at Camden register office on 1 September 1979. He used her name for his Dan Kavanagh books, and continued to dedicate his books to her after her death.

Though much talked about, Kavanagh was a reserved, private, and modest person. She liked to be with chosen and well-loved friends, disliked large glitzy gatherings, eschewed publicity, did not talk much about herself, was often quiet in company, and never gave away her clients' secrets. The gossip and scandal that arose from Amis's defection, from her short-lived and turbulent affair with the novelist Jeanette Winterson in the late 1980s, and from the toxic meltdown at PFD in 2007–8, were none of her seeking, and caused her pain.

Kavanagh developed a cancerous brain tumour in the summer of 2008; her fatal illness, which she endured with great dignity, courage, and stoicism, progressed with horrifying rapidity. She died on 20 October 2008, to the grief and shock of all who knew her. She was buried in Highgate cemetery on 29 October, and was survived by her husband. A secular 'remembering' was held at the Almeida Theatre, Islington, London, on 10 December 2008.

Pat Kavanagh was a scrupulous, potent, and deeply respected literary agent. She attracted, and kept, a remarkable stable of writers, from established names to new discoveries. With publishers and editors she did business with legendary determination and cool resolve. With her authors, many of whom became her good friends, she was an attentive and generous adviser. In the often malicious and cut-throat environment of the marketing of books, she carried out her work with notable integrity and straightforwardness, for which she was greatly admired. She was identified with a tradition of honourable business dealings and close personal care for clients, which she derived from her first employer, A. D. Peters. She was also a strikingly beautiful, stylish, magnetic, and generous person, whose life was remarkable for her professional influence and stature, her varied friendships and interests, and her long and devoted marriage.

HERMIONE LEE

Sources *The Times* (21 Oct 2008) • *Daily Telegraph* (21 Oct 2008); (22 Oct 2008) • *The Guardian* (21 Oct 2008); (22 Oct 2008); (23 Oct 2008); (11 Dec 2008) • *The Independent* (21 Oct 2008); (22 Oct 2008); (23 Oct 2008) • *New York Times* (23 Oct 2008) • *The Observer* (26 Oct 2008); (14 Dec 2008) • United Agents files [C. MacArthur] • personal knowledge (2012) • private information (2012) • m. cert.

Archives FILM BFINA, current affairs footage • *Under Milk Wood* (1972) | SOUND BBC, *Flaubert's Parrot* • BL NSA, documentary recording

Likenesses T. Blackbrow, photograph, 1972, Rex Features, London • A. Gorgas, bromide print, 1978 (with Kingsley Amis), NPG • A. Gorgas, bromide print, 1978 (with Julian Barnes), NPG • A. Gorgas, group portrait, bromide print, 1978, NPG • J. Edelstein, bromide print, 1991 (with Julian Barnes), NPG • J. Edelstein, photographs, 1991–4, Camera Press, London • D. Thompson, photograph, repro. in 'Pat Kavanagh: a remembering' • D. Thompson, photograph, priv. coll. [*see illus.*] • obituary photographs

Wealth at death £3,862,603: probate, 17 March 2009, *CGPLA Eng. & Wales*

Keatinge, William Richard [Bill] (**1931–2008**), physiologist, was born on 18 May 1931 at 30 Beaufort Mansions, Chelsea, London, the only son of Sir Edgar Mayne Keatinge (1905–1998), land agent, later politician and businessman, and his wife, Katharine Lucile, *née* Burrell (1907–1990). His father was briefly Conservative MP for Bury St Edmunds from 1944 to 1945, and was later active in local government; he was knighted in 1960.

Keatinge was educated at Upper Canada College, Toronto, Canada (1940–44), and at Rugby School (1944–9), from where he won a scholarship to read medicine at Pembroke College, Cambridge, and St Thomas's Hospital medical school in London. On 15 October 1955 he married (Margaret Ellen) Annette Hegarty (1932–2000), daughter of David Hegarty, civil servant. They had a son and two daughters. He completed his national service as a naval surgeon-lieutenant in Cambridge (1956–8) before becoming director of studies in medicine and junior fellow at Pembroke College, Cambridge (1958–60). He then spent a year in the Cardiovascular Research Institute, San Francisco, as a Fulbright scholar before returning to England to a Medical Research Council post at the Radcliffe Infirmary and a fellowship of Pembroke College, Oxford (1961–8).

Keatinge joined the department of physiology at the London Hospital Medical College as reader in physiology in 1969 and was promoted to a personal chair in physiology in 1971. He was appointed head of the department of physiology in 1981. Following the merger of the college's basic medical sciences departments with that of St Bartholomew's Hospital and the move to Queen Mary and Westfield College in 1990, he became head of physiology in the joint school. He held this post until his retirement in 1996 when he became an emeritus professor at Queen Mary, University of London (as the newly integrated institution was known from 1995).

Bill Keatinge, as he was always known, ran an active and successful research group, highly rated and supported by the Medical Research Council for many years. Among his many publications were important articles on survival in cold water and local mechanisms controlling blood vessels. His lifelong interest in the effects of heat and cold on mechanisms controlling blood vessels stemmed from his time with the navy while completing his national service. The navy had lost about 30,000 people from cold immersion in the Second World War and needed to know how to reduce deaths from cold. During the 1980s there was much concern regarding excessive deaths among the elderly in the UK during winter. In a series of experiments Keatinge showed that both cold and heat stress caused alterations in blood composition that promoted arterial thrombosis and subsequently death from strokes and heart attacks.

Keatinge wrote many chapters in textbooks and journals and published more than 200 research papers, principally on temperature regulation and the control of blood vessels. In 1969 he published *Survival in Cold Water: the Physiology and Treatment of Immersion, Hypothermia and of Drowning* and in 1980 *Local Mechanisms Controlling Blood Vessels*. He was elected to membership of the Physiological Society (1968), was a member of its committee (1977–81), and was a member of the editorial board of the *Journal of Physiology* (1979–86). He was elected FRCP (1991) and was a fellow of the Cardiovascular Research Institute, San Francisco. He had numerous international collaborations, developed especially close links with Russia, and led a large EU Eurowinter project that co-ordinated research in eight European countries. After the break-up of the Soviet Union it became possible for him to extend his Eurowinter project to Siberia. He made full use of being part of a multi-faculty environment at Queen Mary and Westfield College by forging a link with the Russian department and learning to speak the language well enough to be understood on his visits to the Russian Federation.

Keatinge served as preclinical dean at the London Hospital Medical College at a time of considerable change and uncertainty. After the move to Queen Mary and Westfield College, a new building and a new curriculum were initiated and Keatinge played a leading role in designing and implementing these changes. He was elected dean of basic medical sciences at Queen Mary and Westfield in 1991. He took up the reins of authority when student numbers were being rapidly increased and staff appointments reduced. His term as dean ended in 1994 and he left administration behind, to concentrate on research. After his formal retirement in 1996 he continued to attract grants and to pursue his research interests. He retained an office at Queen Mary and concentrated on environmental problems, including global warming and the fact that cold caused far more deaths than heat. He was frequently the expert, interviewed by the media, at times of extreme cold and during heatwaves. He also made substantial contributions to the teaching of human physiology to undergraduates and postgraduates throughout his career.

In addition to his lifelong interest in physiology, Keatinge had interests in classical archaeology, history, and poetry. He enjoyed travel, especially dinghy sailing in the waters of the Aegean. He had an enduring love for his home in Teffont Evias, Wiltshire, and had a keen interest in forestry. After the death of his first wife, on 11 November 2005 he married Lynette Margaret Nelson, a widow six years his junior, and daughter of Phillip Anthony Browne, police officer. Although he became ill with prostate cancer he faced his illness with considerable courage and dignity. He continued to work until a few weeks before his death and completed his final projects. He died on 11 April 2008 at his home, Rose Cottage, Teffont Evias, and was buried in the churchyard at Teffont Evias on 19 April 2008. He was survived by his wife, Lynette, and the three children of his first marriage. MARGARET M. BIRD

Sources W. R. Keatinge, 'Researching unexpected hazards of cold and heat', *Physiology News*, 68 (autumn 2007), 9–11 · *The Times* (8 May 2008); (15 May 2008) · *Times Higher Education Supplement* (15 May 2008) · *BMJ*, 337 (5 Aug 2008), 1150 · www.physoc.org/site/cms/contentviewarticle.asp?article=778, 7 May 2010 · *Pembroke College Record* (2008–9), 105–7 · *WW* (2008) · personal knowledge (2012) · private information (2012) [Lynette Keatinge, widow] · b. cert. · m. certs. · d. cert.

Likenesses obituary photographs

Wealth at death £1,955,327: probate, 2 Sept 2008, *CGPLA Eng. & Wales*

Keatley, Patrick Crawford (1920–2005), journalist, was born in Vancouver, British Columbia, Canada, on 28 October 1920, the son of William Mahaffy Keatley, and his wife, Hilda Maud, *née* Sinclair. His parents were from Northern Ireland. His father, a schoolteacher, was visiting Canada when the First World War broke out and fought throughout with the Canadians in Europe before returning to Canada. His mother taught gymnastics. Keatley remained a Canadian citizen throughout his life.

Keatley was educated at Upper Canada College in Toronto and then took a degree in history and English at the University of British Columbia. He developed an interest in the Commonwealth from one of his lecturers, the English constitutional lawyer Ivor Jennings, who held a visiting professorship at the University of British Columbia in 1938–9. After graduating Keatley worked for the *Vancouver Sun* and the Canadian Broadcasting Corporation. Then, in 1952, he went to Britain as a Commonwealth Press Union fellow. The experience transformed his life. He was attached to the *Manchester Guardian* and scored early journalistic fame with a story on the trade in live horses shipped from Britain for slaughter in mainland Europe. He disguised himself as an American meat trader, strapped a camera to his leg, and travelled with the animals. His articles were reprinted as a pamphlet. The prime minister, Winston Churchill, summoned him to his presence and said: 'You have caused me a lot of trouble, young man' (private information). He returned briefly to the *Vancouver Sun*, but soon went back to *The Guardian*, which posted him to London. On 10 September 1955, at Chelsea Old Church, he married (Prudence) Eve Burgess, a 23-year-old BBC producer and later press secretary to the archbishop of Canterbury, Robert Runcie. She was the daughter of Henry Burgess, manufacturer. They had a son and two daughters.

Keatley served for more than thirty years as Commonwealth correspondent, then diplomatic correspondent, of *The Guardian*. All the time he remained a regular broadcaster. He was never lost for words, and his work for the Canadian Broadcasting Corporation, continued over forty years, soon led him to become a favourite with the BBC World Service. He took part almost daily in one programme or another, gave a weekly Commonwealth commentary on the World Service, and for thirty years broadcast for Canadian radio a newsletter about Britain.

Keatley began his career in London at a time when independence movements were gathering pace and the empire was transforming itself into the Commonwealth. Events in southern Africa—the front line in the struggle for black rule—occupied the front pages almost daily. Keatley was not just an astute reporter of the diplomatic developments in London; he covered the fast moving changes on the spot. The dominance in the 1960s of African coverage meant that he came to know especially well liberation leaders like Julius Nyerere, Kenneth Kaunda, and Joshua Nkomo, as well as British ministers involved, including Iain Macleod, David Owen, Alan Lennox-Boyd, and Sir Alec Douglas-Home. He made a special study of the unfolding fiasco of the Central African Federation and in 1963 produced what became a standard book on it, *The Politics of Partnership*.

In early 1965, a few months after China had conducted its first nuclear weapons test, Keatley caused a stir by writing about the possibility of India's becoming a nuclear power. He described the growing anxieties in key ministries in the Pakistan government, whose foreign minister was then Zulfikar Ali Bhutto. He quoted Bhutto as saying that if India got the bomb then Pakistan would have to get, or buy, one, 'even if we have to eat grass' (*The Guardian*, 11 March 1965). These were tense times. In August–September that year India and Pakistan were at war. Sometimes the danger was more personal. In the 1970s on a visit to Uganda during Idi Amin's rule Keatley stood in a crowd listening to a police band concert when the president spotted him, seized the conductor's baton, and announced: 'My friend Patrick will do the next number.' Keatley pretended a coughing fit and managed to slip away. Later that day the queen's counsel who led the Uganda bar advised him to leave the country at once.

Keatley was a likeable and always chatty man, finding it easy to connect with people of every station. He was inquisitive, as becomes a good journalist, and engaged with prime ministers and heads of state as matter-of-factly as with junior ministers, MPs, and diplomats. Punctuality was not his strong point. He was rarely on time for an appointment. Radio producers, interviewers, and news editors often came near to despair. He would appear before them moments before he was due on air or deliver his copy for *The Guardian* right up against the deadline. He was even late for appointments with cabinet ministers. No one knew how he got away with it, but he always did.

Keatley was hugely energetic and throughout his career was also an activist in helping fellow journalists. More than that, he was profoundly interested in raising their professional competence and status. He was a founder and first president of the Diplomatic and Commonwealth Writers Association in 1960, and co-founder of the Commonwealth Journalists Association and the Zambia Society. In London he was a wise and committed member of the Royal Commonwealth Society's library committee, offering much support to its librarians. He also served on the society's central council for several years. He was an eager attender and speaker at academic conferences until near the end of his life. He retired from *The Guardian* in 1985 and in 1996 moved with his wife to Somerset. He died on 9 May 2005 at his home, Manor Farm House, Lower Street, West Chinnock, Somerset, of fibrosing alveolitis and was buried on the 17th at West Chinnock. He was survived by his wife, Eve, and two of their children, Mark and Charlotte, his younger daughter, Victoria, having predeceased him. DEREK INGRAM

Sources *The Guardian* (12 May 2005) • *Globe and Mail* (20 May 2005) [Toronto] • *The Times* (9 June 2005); (22 June 2005) • personal knowledge (2009) • private information (2009) • m. cert. • d. cert.
Archives SOUND BL NSA, current affairs recordings
Likenesses photograph, repro. in *The Guardian*
Wealth at death £413,696: probate, 21 Feb 2006, *CGPLA Eng. & Wales*

Keeble, Sir (Herbert Ben) Curtis (1922–2008), diplomatist, was born on 18 September 1922 at St Kilda, The Avenue, Chingford, Essex, the only son and oldest of four children of Herbert Keeble (1886–1949), municipal accountant, and his wife, Gertrude Agnes Frances, *née* Hardy (1886–1969). The family moved to Clacton when he was young, and he attended Clacton County High School before proceeding to Queen Mary College, London, to read modern languages. However, in 1941 he volunteered for war service and the following year was commissioned into the Royal Irish Fusiliers. In 1944 he was accepted for translation duties, and despite little knowledge of Russian (having, as he put it, 'never progressed beyond Lesson 9' of Anna Semenova's *New Russian Grammar*; BDOHP, 3), was posted as sole translator on a ship repatriating 2000 unruly Russians, many of whom had fought with the Germans and were returning to an uncertain fate. After several further round trips, repatriating Russians who had been captured serving with the Germans and returning with British prisoners of war who had been liberated by the Russians (he was in Odessa on VE-day) he was stood down when his ship was sent to the Far East. He ended his 'singularly unheroic war' in a transit camp near Liverpool (ibid., 5).

Demobilized in 1947, Keeble returned briefly to Queen Mary College before learning of his success in the special entrance examination for former servicemen wishing to enter the Foreign Service. While awaiting a posting to Batavia as vice-consul he married, at St Matthew's Church, Cluny Gardens, Edinburgh, on 2 April 1947, Margaret Ellen Stephenson Stuart Fraser (*b.* 1922), whom he had met during wartime army service, and who was (until her marriage) working as an employment clerk for the Ministry of Labour. She was the daughter of John Stuart Fraser, tailor, of Edinburgh. They had three daughters, Suzanne (*b.* 1949), Sally (*b.* 1951), and Jane (1955–1998).

In Batavia Keeble and his wife witnessed the early stages of the independence struggle against the Dutch, which largely confined them to the city itself. After two years (1949–51) back in London, in the south-east Asia department, he was posted to Berlin, where among other things he was charged with receiving East German defectors; he later thought it 'remarkable that the Russians waited until 1961 before erecting the Berlin Wall, the symbol of failure of a state which had to lock up its citizens to prevent them from running away' (BDOHP, 20). Four years in Washington as a second secretary in the commercial department (1954–8) were followed by a further seven (1958–65) in London, where in 1961 he was put in charge of the Foreign Office department co-ordinating the negotiations for Britain's entry into the European Economic Community. He later regarded Britain's failure to join from the outset as 'arguably the biggest mistake in post-war foreign policy' (ibid., 30). After General de Gaulle's veto of the British application in 1963 he spent two years as head of the European Economic Organizations department of the Foreign Office. There followed two further postings abroad, as commercial counsellor in Berne (1965–8) and minister and deputy high commissioner in Canberra, responsible for economic and commercial matters (1968–71), then two years (1971–3) as an assistant under-secretary of state at the Foreign and Commonwealth Office (as the Foreign Office had become in 1968), in which post he was responsible for handling the negotiations with Iceland during the second 'cod war' of 1972.

In 1974 Keeble was appointed the first British ambassador to the German Democratic Republic. He found his embassy was thoroughly bugged and he was followed everywhere, but he travelled widely. He was particularly interested in the way the planned economy worked in East Germany: 'after all, if anyone could make sense of a socialist state-run economy, it ought to be the Germans'. But instead he found a 'great bureaucracy, a kind of reverse Midas, turn[ing] everything it touched to clay' (BDOHP, 59–60). From 1976 to 1978 he was a deputy under-secretary of state and chief clerk at the Foreign and Commonwealth Office, responsible for all administrative and personnel matters during a difficult period of financial cutbacks and turbulent relations with the service's political masters.

Keeble's final posting was as ambassador to the Soviet Union, from 1978 to 1982. This was a time of increasing East–West tensions, particularly after the election of a Conservative government led by Margaret Thatcher in Britain, and then the Soviet invasion of Afghanistan, at the end of 1979. In response to the latter, Keeble was instructed to keep his contacts with the Soviet regime to a minimum, and he felt at times like 'a kind of diplomatic "black hole"' (BDOHP, 105). Nevertheless he enjoyed warm personal relations with Andrei Gromyko and other senior Russian politicians, and was reckoned on both sides to have played a difficult hand well. Having been made a CMG in 1970 and knighted KCMG in 1978, he was promoted GCMG on retirement in 1982. For their part the Russians gave him the singular honour of a tour of the innermost parts of the Kremlin, which no Westerner had previously been allowed to see under the Soviet regime.

In retirement Keeble acted as the Foreign and Commonwealth Office's chief negotiator in the protracted negotiations with the Soviet Union to build new embassies in London and Moscow, and was a special adviser to the House of Commons foreign affairs committee in 1985–6. He was chairman of the Great Britain–USSR Association (which, following the collapse of the Soviet Union in 1991, was renamed the Britain–Russia Centre) from 1985 to 1995, and of the Foundation for Accountancy and Financial Management (set up to help former Soviet bloc countries develop their accounting and auditing professions) from 1993 to 2000. From 1985 to 1990 he was a member of council of Chatham House and the School of Slavonic and East European Studies at the University of London, and a governor of the BBC. He edited *The Soviet State* (1985), wrote *Britain and the Soviet Union, 1917–1989* (1990; revised and reissued as *Britain, the Soviet Union and Russia* in 2000), and contributed to other books on British–Russian relations.

Small in stature (Leonid Brezhnev told him that 'my modest five feet and nine inches did less than justice to the stature of my country'; BDOHP, 55), self-effacing, and with a wry sense of humour, Keeble was much loved by those who worked with him, and respected by those politicians both British and foreign with whom he negotiated. He enjoyed sailing (his ancestors had worked on Thames barges) and painting. He was a devoted family man, and was much affected by the death of his daughter Jane and her husband in a road accident in Australia in 1998. He lived for many years in Thames Ditton, Surrey. He died at the Royal Brompton Hospital, Chelsea, on 6 December 2008, of heart failure, and was survived by his wife, Margaret, and their daughters Suzanne, a medical practitioner, and Sally, Labour MP for Northampton North from 1997 to 2010.

ALEX MAY

Sources C. Keeble, memoir, British Diplomatic Oral History Programme, *c.*1993, www.chu.cam.ac.uk/archives/collections/BDOHP/Keeble.pdf, 15 Aug 2011 • *The Times* (12 Dec 2008); (16 Dec 2008); (18 Dec 2008); (7 Jan 2009) • *Daily Telegraph* (12 Dec 2008) • *East–West Review*, 8/1 (spring 2009), 13–14 • Burke, *Peerage* • *WW* (2008) • private information (2012) • b. cert. • m. cert. • d. cert.
Archives SOUND current affairs recording
Wealth at death £690,625: probate, 21 May 2009, *CGPLA Eng. & Wales*

Keen, Douglas Henry George (1913–2008), publisher, was born on 27 October 1913 at 1 Hillworth Hall Road, Cheltenham, Gloucestershire, the son of Henry Frederick James Keen (1889–1965), a butcher's assistant and later a market gardener, and his wife, Ellen May, *née* Short. His father soon left the matrimonial home, leaving Keen to be brought up by his mother. Working at home as a dressmaker she had little money to spare. Always ambitious to better his circumstances, Keen won a scholarship to Pate's Grammar School in Cheltenham. After leaving he studied commercial art and marketing at evening classes before working in advertising as a sign-writer. By this time he had acquired strong socialist beliefs.

In 1936 Keen moved to Wills and Hepworth, a printing firm based in Loughborough that mainly produced catalogues. But to use up 'machine time' between larger commercial commissions the firm also printed some nondescript children's story books, advertised as 'pure and healthy literature for children' and printed in two colours on cheap paper. Keen was not initially involved in the book side of Wills and Hepworth's business; as head of the firm's Birmingham office he dealt with commissions for printing in the west midlands. In 1940, the year the first book with the Ladybird imprint and format, *Bunnikins Picnic Party*, was produced by Wills and Hepworth (twenty-five years after the Ladybird name had first been registered as a trademark), Keen was called up into the RAF, though he continued to be paid a small retainer on the understanding that he would return to the firm after the war. He served with a mobile radar unit in Britain, France, and Belgium for the duration of the war. On 17 July 1941 he married an ARP telephonist, and fellow commercial artist, (Dorothy) Margaret Jones (1917–1999), daughter of William Henry Jones, railway stationmaster. They had two daughters.

On demobilization Keen returned to Wills and Hepworth and was given the job of making the firm's books more profitable. Visiting shops and schools over a wide area, he saw that while books to be read for pleasure were always designed to look attractive, educational books, with their soft covers, tired texts, and dreary illustrations, lagged behind. There seemed an obvious gap, therefore, for some short, lavishly illustrated, and properly researched factual books on approachable subjects that would also fit into a child's stocking. Unable at first to convince his firm, in 1948 he produced a mock-up with a text written by himself with watercolour pictures by his mother-in-law and line drawings of nests and eggs by his wife. This prototype, with the title *British Birds and their Nests*, was shown to the firm's chairman, Jim Clegg, who gave it the go-ahead. The final hard cover version, with a text by Brian Vesey-Fitzgerald and pictures by Allen Seaby, appeared in 1953, selling out almost immediately, with a second print-run of 50,000. Made up of fifty-two pages with twenty-four full-page colour illustrations, it laid down a marker for all future Ladybird books. It was sold for half a crown, a price that was to remain for nearly thirty years.

More nature books followed and were later joined by series including People at Work, Junior Science, and How It Works. Each of these books included clear technical drawing and texts commissioned from educationists and other experts. They were illustrated by a stable of post-war artists that included John Berry, Harry Wingfield, and Frank Hampson, many of whom became Keen's lifelong friends. There was also a large number of other titles for younger children, like retold fairy tales or the more factual *Shopping with Mother*, with its background of an affectionately idealized suburbia full of smiling tradesmen and immaculate lawns. This vision of post-war prosperity had particular significance for Keen and those of his artists who had known poverty when young.

One of Keen's greatest successes came with the launch in 1964 of the Ladybird Key Words Reading Scheme. Starring the brother and sister Peter and Jane, with texts written by William Murray, these books concentrated on the 100 most common words in the English language. Their picture of a cosy domestic life in the company of a smartly dressed young mother contentedly at home with her children attracted some satirical comments in the years to come. But these books were enormously successful, selling over 85 million copies and leading to Keen joining his board of directors. By the 1960s the firm had given up the commissioned side of its printing business in order to concentrate solely on the Ladybird books. Much amusement was had in the press when it was revealed that 100 copies of *The Computer* had been bought by the Ministry of Defence in order to introduce its employees to higher technology after it had requested—in vain—that the copies should come in a plain cover. Another title, *How It Works: the Motor Car*, was acquired in bulk by the Thames Valley police force driving school.

Keen worked mainly from home, commissioning writers and artists and then seeing each title to completion. With the help only of a part-time secretary he did most of his work in an extension to his purpose-built house (finished in 1953) in Stratford upon Avon. His wife was principal proof-reader, and there were many visits from his artists and writers, often ending with a trip to the local pub. But in 1973, when sales of Ladybird books had reached 20 million copies a year, Wills and Hepworth was taken over by Longman Pearson. Keen left the company that same year, out of sympathy with proposed changes that would see Peter and Jane reinvented in jeans and sweatshirts, and other rebranding of Ladybird books. Living quietly at home with easy access to his daughters, grandchildren, and later great-grandchildren, he retained until his death his commitment to socialism and his belief in the necessity of building a better world for all. A handsome man, on occasion mistaken for Kirk Douglas, he was predeceased by his beloved wife, Margaret, before dying of pneumonia at his home in Loxley Road, Stratford upon Avon, on 6 November 2008. He was survived by his daughters.

NICHOLAS TUCKER

Sources *Boys and girls: a Ladybird book of childhood* (2007) · *The Guardian* (29 Nov 2008); (1 Dec 2008); (9 Dec 2008) · *The Times* (17 Dec 2008) · *The Independent* (17 Dec 2008) · www.ladybirdflyaway home.com/keen.htm, 8 Dec 2010 · interview with Douglas Keen, www.theweeweb.co.uk/ladybird/douglas_keen.php, 8 Dec 2010 · b. cert. · m. cert. · d. cert.

Likenesses J. Wiseman, photograph, 1930–39, Rex Features, London · obituary photographs

Wealth at death £707,725: probate, 13 May 2009, *CGPLA Eng. & Wales*

Keenan, Brian Paschal (1941–2008), Irish republican activist, was born on 17 July 1941 in Dysert, Draperstown, co. Londonderry, the son of Henry Keenan, an accountant then serving as a warrant officer in the RAF and stationed at RAF Pocklington, Yorkshire, and his wife, Jane, *née* McAlea. Keenan's Roman Catholic family were from Belfast's New Lodge Road area, but evacuated to co. Derry following the Belfast blitz. The family returned to Belfast at the end of the war. At sixteen Keenan began an apprenticeship as an electronics engineer, joining the Electrical Trade Union. He later observed that 'from a young age my political outlook was shaped by my interest in trade unions' (*An Phoblacht*, 27 March 2008). In 1958 he moved to England, continuing his training at a Luton firm making guided missiles. Keenan also worked for a time in partnership with his brother as a television repairman in Corby, Northamptonshire. During his time in Corby he damaged a cigarette machine, leaving his fingerprints in the process. On 19 October 1960 he married, at St Mary's Roman Catholic Church, Luton, Christine (Chrissie) Campbell, a machinist in a clothing factory, daughter of Frank Campbell, labourer. They had two sons and four daughters. They returned to Belfast in 1963.

Keenan spent two weeks in Belfast's Crumlin Road prison in 1964, after being arrested during the Divis Street riots. He was asked to contribute a document on trade unionism to the 1966 IRA army convention but did not join the IRA until 1968. He saw 'republicanism [as] an ideology which should be firmly fixed socially and economically'. His view was that 'the enemy was capitalism and the system of exploitation', and he believed that 'the national question was always a class question' (*An Phoblacht*, 27 March 2008). The 'trigger for my generation to get involved in violent confrontation with the state was not the IRA, not republican politics, nor republican ideology. The trigger was the Civil Rights movement' (*An Phoblacht*, 3 April 2008).

By August 1971 Keenan was quartermaster of the IRA's Belfast brigade. His search for armaments included visiting Libya in 1972, establishing a contact which would prove highly valuable to the IRA. He was appointed IRA quartermaster-general the following year. In mid-1974 he was sentenced to one year's imprisonment in the Republic of Ireland for membership of the IRA. He was wounded during an escape attempt on 17 March 1975 but was released that July. Sean Callaghan, a former IRA member

Brian Paschal Keenan (1941–2008), by Martin McCullough, 1999

turned police informer, later claimed that Keenan wanted the IRA to retaliate severely for increasing sectarian attacks on Catholics by loyalist paramilitaries in the south Armagh area. Keenan argued (Callaghan claimed) that the only way 'to put the nonsense out of the Prods [Protestants] was to just hit back much harder and more savagely than them' (Harnden, 134). This led to the Kingsmill massacre of 5 January 1976, in which ten Protestant workmen were murdered. The atrocity was claimed by the 'South Armagh Republican Action Force', believed to have been a cover name for the local IRA unit. In the wake of Kingsmill sectarian attacks ended locally, allegedly owing to an agreement reached by local units of the IRA and the Ulster Volunteer Force. However, the attack had been carried out without the knowledge of the IRA army council and proved highly controversial within the republican movement itself. Gerry Adams insisted that there must 'never again be another Kingsmill' (ibid.).

By 1977 Keenan had become IRA director of operations and a supporter of Gerry Adams on the IRA army council. Together with Martin McGuinness, Keenan travelled the country speaking in support of Adams's 'long war' plan to reorganize the IRA. The IRA's English bombing campaign of the 1970s was run by Keenan. His fingerprints, on file since the incident in Corby, were found on a list of bomb parts discovered in follow-up raids after the December 1975 Balcombe Street siege. Arrested in Northern Ireland in March 1979, Keenan was sentenced to eighteen years' imprisonment on 25 June 1980, for conspiracy to cause explosions. Ironically part of this sentence was served in HMP Long Sutton, which had been constructed on the former RAF station Long Sutton, where his father had once served. Despite being in prison Keenan continued to wield influence within the IRA, supporting republican electoral participation and Adams's candidacy in the 1982 Northern Ireland assembly elections, in the face of doubts by the IRA's army council.

Keenan was released from prison in June 1993, and by 1996 was back on the IRA army council. He was a member of the army council that authorized the Docklands bombing of 9 February 1996, which ended the first IRA ceasefire, but this was probably a tactical necessity at this point to avoid a split within the IRA. Similarly, at the IRA general army convention in October 1996 Keenan adopted an anti-Adams line, only to switch sides once he had been elected to the IRA army executive. He supported the calling of a second ceasefire during a meeting between the IRA army council and the IRA army executive on 16 July 1997. Peter Taylor, in *Brits* (2002), interpreted anti-decommissioning speeches made by Keenan as a strategy to prevent IRA volunteers from defecting. Adams later asserted that there 'wouldn't be a peace process if it wasn't for Brian Keenan' (*The Independent*, 22 May 2008).

Once described as 'the biggest single threat to the British state' (*An Phoblacht*, 3 April 2008), Keenan was a militarist, but was also highly political. The choice between the bomb or the ballot box was likely tactical and dictated by pragmatic, rather than ideological, considerations. His last years were blighted by cancer, and he resigned from the army council in 2005. He died at 52 St Patricks Park, Cullyhanna, co. Armagh, on 21 May 2008. An atheist by the end of his life, he was cremated on 24 May at Roselawn crematorium, Belfast, following a secular service. SEAN SWAN

Sources P. Bishop and E. Mallie, *The Provisional IRA* (1988) · R. Christenson, ed., *Political trials in history: from antiquity to the present* (1991), 171 · T. Harnden, *'Bandit country': the IRA and south Armagh* (1999) · E. Moloney, *A secret history of the IRA* (2002) · P. Taylor, *Brits: the war against the IRA* (2002) · R. English, *Armed struggle: a history of the IRA* (2003) · *An Phoblacht* (27 March 2008); (3 April 2008); (22 May 2008) · *Daily Telegraph* (22 May 2008) · *The Guardian* (22 May 2008) · *The Independent* (22 May 2008) · *Irish News* (23 May 2008); (27 May 2008); (29 May 2008) · *The Times* (23 May 2008) · *Irish Times* (24 May 2008) · *Irish Independent* (24 May 2008); (26 May 2008) · *The Observer* (25 May 2008) · *Sunday Times* (25 May 2008) · b. cert. · m. cert. · d. cert.

Archives FILM BL NSA, documentary recordings | SOUND BFINA, current affairs and documentary footage

Likenesses photographs, 1998–9, Rex Features, London · M. McCullough, photograph, 1999, Rex Features, London [*see illus.*] · obituary photographs

Kelly, Barbara (1924–2007), performer and television personality, was born on 5 October 1924 in West Vancouver, British Columbia, Canada. Her father was an Irishman who worked as a lorry driver; her mother originally came from Manchester. Her childhood was not happy, and she hated the ballet and elocution classes forced on her by her stage-struck mother. Leaving school early, she nevertheless took up modelling, and joined an amateur dramatic company, performing at the Vancouver Little Theatre. It

Barbara Kelly (1924–2007), by unknown photographer, 1961 [with her husband, Bernard Braden]

was during a performance there in 1940 that she was spotted by a cast member then rehearsing for a Canadian Broadcasting Corporation (CBC) radio production of the York and Chester mystery plays. She was cast as the Virgin Mary, and it was while working on this production that she met her future husband, **Bernard Chastey Braden** (1916–1993), actor and broadcaster. Braden, also from Vancouver, was born on 16 May 1916, the son of Edwin Braden, a nonconformist minister, and his wife, Mary, a music teacher. After an education at local schools he began work in 1935 as a radio singer, then an announcer and engineer. After contracting tuberculosis, which interrupted his career for a year, he returned to radio, writing and performing for the CBC.

Recalling his first meeting with Kelly during rehearsals, Braden wrote that it was not only her outstanding beauty that drew attention: 'It was the voice that caused a hush. The range was incredible … I thought it phenomenal. So did everyone else' (Braden, 16). Her precocious talent and microphone technique led to her gaining a permanent place in the CBC's radio repertory company, while continuing her work as a fashion model. She and Braden were married on 13 April 1942, after which the couple moved to Toronto, where Braden continued to write and perform for the CBC; together they starred in a highly successful radio serial, *John and Judy*. They had three children between 1943 and 1948, Christopher, Kelly, and Kim.

In 1947 CBC sent Braden to Britain to make a series of documentaries on post-war recovery. It was a short working trip, but the material gathered for these programmes formed the basis of a book, *These English* (1948). In 1949 he was back in the UK, this time with Kelly. The couple quickly established themselves as popular entertainers on stage and radio, their bright, lively personalities, attractive accents, and warm humour endearing them to British audiences. Braden played the part of Harold Mitchell in Laurence Olivier's production of *A Streetcar Named Desire*, which opened at the Aldwych Theatre later the same year. Both Braden and Kelly were in demand separately in radio dramas, and Kelly became a hit in the West End show *Male Animal*, also in 1949. Although she appeared in a number of stage shows subsequently, she confessed that she never liked the medium, being much happier on radio, and later television. In May 1949 the couple appeared in a one-off situation comedy about two Canadians living in London, called *Leave Your Name and Number*. The show was so successful that the BBC developed it as a full series, starting in April 1951.

By this time Braden had established himself with the hugely successful *Breakfast with Braden*, a Saturday morning comedy and music series that was first aired in January 1950. The format was preserved when the programme moved to an evening slot in September 1950, becoming *Bedtime with Braden*, when Braden was joined by Kelly. In June of that year the couple appeared on the cover of the *Radio Times*. Braden's impact on British radio audiences of the time may be judged by an article in the 1951 edition of the *BBC Year Book*:

> One of the more mobile, quick-firing units in the current Canadian invasion of British entertainment is a one-man blitz named Bernard Braden … So far nobody has explained whence Braden derives the energy that has rocketed him to stardom in only a year. (*BBC Year Book*, 92–3)

In 1951, the still-young BBC Television featured *An Evening at Home with Bernard Braden and Barbara Kelly*.

Bedtime with Braden continued to run for a further four series, but in 1953 Kelly left the show to join the television panel game with which she was to become most associated, *What's my Line*. Chaired by Eamonn Andrews, and featuring the panellists David Nixon, Gilbert Harding, Isobel Barnett, and Kelly, the format was a simple one: members of the public would perform a short mime, from which the panel attempted to guess their occupation. Broadcast on Sunday evenings on the only television channel available until the launch of ITV in 1955, *What's my Line* was almost compulsory viewing for those families possessing a television set. It ran until 1963, and in 1984 it was revived, running for a further three years, with Kelly and Andrews the only survivors of its original cast.

During the early 1950s Kelly also appeared in a number of films, among them *A Tale of Five Cities* (1951), *Glad Tidings* (1953), and *Love in Pawn* (1953). These were undistinguished works, but they helped to subsidize the Bradens' flamboyant lifestyle, with a large flat in Knightsbridge and a fine house in Hampstead. By the start of the 1960s Kelly was one of the best-known personalities on British radio and television. Over the next decade, however, her career was eclipsed as her husband's moved into the ascendant. From 1962 to 1968 Braden presented the programme for which he is best remembered, *On the Braden Beat*, for ATV. With this programme and its BBC successor, Braden created a new genre; the programme, a pioneering example of consumer television, won a BAFTA award in 1964, and Braden became the Variety Club's personality of the year in 1965. In 1968 he presented a BBC version in a similar format, *Braden's Week*, which ran until 1972, when Braden was sacked, allegedly for presenting a margarine commercial on ITV. The broadcaster Esther Rantzen, a researcher on the show, later went on to present *That's Life*, a television programme much like *Braden's Week* in style and format. Although Rantzen always acknowledged her debt to Braden, Kelly remained bitter about the chain of events.

From the 1970s onwards the careers of both Kelly and Braden were in decline; despite some further occasional radio, television, and stage work, they were never again to reach the remarkable heights of popularity and public acclaim they had enjoyed during the 1950s and 1960s. During this time they developed Adanac Productions (Adanac being Canada spelt backwards), specializing in presentations at business conferences. Kelly also started an agency offering advice on career development to celebrities and, through her company Prime Performers, supplied the services of entertainers and broadcasters as after-dinner speakers.

In May 1987 Kelly was operated on for throat cancer. This was successful, but it left her face scarred and from this time she became more reclusive. In 1990 Braden published his memoirs, *The Kindness of Strangers*, and in 1992 the couple celebrated their golden wedding anniversary. Despite being in poor health herself, Kelly nursed her husband through a series of strokes. At the time of his death, at the Royal Free Hospital, Hampstead, London, on 2 February 1993, following a heart attack, Braden was working on a second volume of autobiography. In 2000 Kelly set up a new company, Speakerpower, 'specialising in personal training for everyone who has to speak in public', and utilizing the services of successful broadcasters and performers as trainers. Suffering from cancer, she died of chronic obstructive pulmonary disease at the Marie Curie Hospice, Camden, London, on 15 January 2007. She was survived by her two daughters, her son Christopher having predeceased her. By the time of their deaths, radio and television trends had changed out of all recognition, and Kelly's and Braden's last years were spent in relative obscurity. Nevertheless they had had a remarkable influence on post-war British media over a period of nearly thirty years. Kelly, vivacious, charming, attractive, was a breath of fresh air and a household name on both radio and television, while Braden deserves recognition not only for his extreme versatility, but for his major contribution to broadcasting by pioneering consumer television.

SEAN STREET

Sources *BBC Year Book* (1951) · D. Gifford, *The golden age of radio* (1985) · B. Braden, *The kindness of strangers* (1990) · *The Guardian* (4 Feb 1993); (17 Jan 2007) · *The Independent* (6 Feb 1993); (16 Jan 2007) · A. Briggs, *The history of broadcasting in the United Kingdom*, rev. edn, 5 (1995) · A. Foster and S. Furst, *Radio comedy, 1938–1968* (1996) · S. Street, *Historical dictionary of British radio* (2006) · *Daily Telegraph* (16 Jan 2007) · d. certs.

Archives BBC WAC | FILM BFINA, performance footage · BFINA, documentary footage · BFINA, light entertainment footage | SOUND BL NSA, performance recordings · BL NSA, documentary recordings

Likenesses Vivienne, photographs, 1950–56 (Bernard Braden), NPG · photographs, 1951–64 (with Bernard Braden), Getty Images, London · photographs, 1951–90 (with Bernard Braden), Photoshot, London · photographs, 1951–92 (Bernard Braden), PA Photos, London · photographs, 1953–92 (with Bernard Braden), PA Photos, London · photographs, 1953–97, PA Photos, London · photograph, 1954 (Bernard Braden), Photoshot, London · photographs, 1954–63, Getty Images, London · photograph, 1960, Photoshot, London · photograph, 1961 (with Bernard Braden), Getty Images, London [*see illus.*] · A. Messer, photograph, 1969, Rex Features, London · obituary photographs (Bernard Braden) · photographs (Bernard Braden), repro. in Braden, *Kindness*

Wealth at death £534,262: probate, 21 Dec 2007, *CGPLA Eng. & Wales* · £173,322—Bernard Braden: probate, 17 March 1993, *CGPLA Eng. & Wales*

Kelly, Sir (John William) Basil (1920–2008), judge, was born on 10 May 1920 in Clones, co. Monaghan, Ireland, the only son of Thomas William Kelly (*d.* 1955) and his wife, Emily Frances, *née* Donaldson (*d.* 1966). His father was a protestant farmer and small businessman in co. Monaghan, his mother a baker, but the family emigrated to Belfast in 1925 after they were burnt out in the bitter atmosphere of the time. They surmounted difficult economic circumstances with sufficient success to be able to send Kelly to Methodist College, Belfast, from which he went on to Trinity College, Dublin. Northern Ireland was exempted from conscription during the Second World War, and Kelly acceded to his mother's wish that he, an only son, should not enlist.

Kelly was called to the bar of Northern Ireland in 1944 and commenced a general common-law practice that took him to courts all over the province. He faced stiff competition when numbers of former servicemen returned to commence practice, but by 1958 he had made sufficient progress to be able to take silk. Over the next ten years he built up a varied practice, both civil and criminal, and became sought after on all sides of the community as a criminal defender. In 1957 he married Pamela, only daughter of Thomas Colmer and Marjorie Colthurst. There were no children of the marriage, but he became stepfather to her daughter.

When he was established in silk Kelly branched out into politics, at that time still regarded as a route to preferment. He was adopted for the safe Unionist seat of Mid-Down, to which he was elected in 1964 by a substantial majority and subsequently re-elected unopposed. In 1968 he was appointed attorney-general for Northern Ireland. Until the office of director of public prosecutions was established the attorney-general was responsible for the initiation and oversight of prosecutions, and Kelly worked hard and effectively to discharge this function, along with other legal work for the government. His advice was always shrewd and balanced, and it is thought that if the government of the day had consulted him earlier some of the unfortunate errors in putting internment into effect in 1971 might have been avoided.

Kelly returned to private practice in 1972 when the parliament of Northern Ireland was prorogued, but in the following year he was appointed a judge of the High Court of Northern Ireland and commenced a long judicial career spanning some twenty-two years. He served in the Queen's Bench Division until 1984, when he was promoted to the Court of Appeal, in Northern Ireland; he was knighted, and sworn of the privy council (he had become a member of the privy council of Northern Ireland in 1969).

Kelly proved to be a careful and thorough judge, who earned respect for his handling of many difficult criminal trials. His long experience of criminal law and practice and his unruffled demeanour enabled him to preside calmly and effectively in cases of all kinds—many of them non-jury 'Diplock' trials of terrorist offences—and to impose appropriate sentences on those convicted. Although he was a useful and industrious member of the Court of Appeal, he was at his best in trials at first instance, in which in accordance with the prevailing practice he continued to be constantly engaged when not sitting on appeals. He conducted a number of celebrated trials, but one of the most taxing was an important 'supergrass' case in 1983, in which almost forty defendants were charged with a large number of terrorist offences. The atmosphere in court was tense and hostile and the judge was guarded by armed police officers and wore a flak jacket under his robes. The trial lasted for many months, at the end of which Kelly retired to a secret address to write his judgment. He convicted on most of the counts, but the convictions were largely set aside by the Court of Appeal.

The terrorist threat and the need for personal security dominated judges' lives during the whole of Kelly's tenure of judicial office. Throughout this time he had guards on his home and was accompanied by armed escorts wherever he went, as several of his friends and colleagues were murdered and others attacked. For him, as with other judges, it became an established part of life, which he endured with equanimity and good humour. He had many Catholic friends. As one nationalist lawyer commented, he 'had a great sense of justice and he was very independent. He was old-style, liberal, paternalistic' (*The Independent*, 12 Dec 2008).

In his personal life Kelly liked to present a stylish appearance. He was an accomplished jazz pianist and claimed to have heard Fats Waller play in Chicago when he was a young man. He was interested in cultural matters, maintaining friendships in the arts world, and had a good collection of paintings. He played football for his university and was a regular golfer in later life. He did not, however, have much spare time to devote to leisure pursuits, for he continued during his whole career to be engrossed in legal work, at which he put in long hours every day. On his retirement in 1995 he moved to England, where he lived quietly until his death from cancer on 5 December 2008, at his home in Gerrards Cross, Buckinghamshire. His wife died in 2009. They were survived by her daughter.

ROBERT CARSWELL

Sources *The Independent* (12 Dec 2008) · *The Guardian* (16 Dec 2008) · *The Times* (18 Dec 2008) · *Daily Telegraph* (2 Jan 2009) · *Sunday Independent* [Ireland] (4 Jan 2009) · Burke, *Peerage* · *WW* (2009) · personal knowledge (2012) · private information (2012) · b. cert. · d. cert.

Likenesses T. Halifax, oils, 1995, Royal Courts of Justice, Belfast · R. Friers, cartoon, Parliament Buildings, Stormont · obituary photographs

Wealth at death £334,279: probate, 4 Feb 2009, *CGPLA Eng. & Wales*

Kelvedon. For this title name *see* Channon, (Henry) Paul Guinness, Baron Kelvedon (1935–2007).

Kemp, Sir (Edward) Peter (1934–2008), civil servant, was born on 10 October 1934 at Broadmead, Beech Road, Haslemere, Surrey, the elder son and eldest of three children of Thomas Kemp, company director, and his wife, Nancie, *née* Sargent. He was educated at Millfield School and the Royal Naval College, Dartmouth, following which he entered the Royal Navy as a midshipman. With his restless energy and love of the sea he was clearly destined for a promising naval career, but this was cut short when he contracted rheumatic fever. He was invalided out of the navy and became articled as a chartered accountant. A colourful period of his life then followed with accountancy work at home and abroad, notably in Paris and in British Guiana. He married at Kensington register office on 25 November 1961 Enid van Popta, a 24-year-old secretary, and daughter of Walle Melis van Popta, psychologist. They had three sons and a daughter.

In 1967 Kemp joined the civil service as a direct-entry principal, under a scheme designed to secure mature entrants to the administrative class of the service. It was a stiff competition and successful entrants were expected to progress to at least under-secretary level. In his relatively short civil service career Kemp far exceeded this expectation. He initially joined the finance department of the Department of Transport, where his accountancy training, capacity for hard work, and personal application saw him rise rapidly to assistant secretary. He also attracted the attention of the Treasury, and he moved there in 1973. Promoted to under-secretary in 1978 and deputy secretary in 1983, he became the Treasury's main negotiator with the civil service unions on pay and conditions of service. This was in the aftermath of the prolonged civil service strike of 1981, occasioned when the government arbitrarily scrapped the service's pay agreement which had lasted, despite vicissitudes, since 1956. Attempts to secure a new pay agreement proved to be abortive and, in the meantime, annual pay negotiations were conducted on an ad hoc basis. In these negotiations Kemp was always courteous and as fair and flexible as his rigid constraint of predetermined cash limits would allow. His atypical Treasury approach was well described in the admission he made in 2006: 'I was at the Treasury, probably doing my best not to help it too much' (Witness seminar, 2006). He was an unusual senior civil servant, far removed from the cool detachment normally associated with the typical Whitehall 'mandarin'. It is, however, a significant tribute to his skill as a negotiator that in the five-year period in which he was in charge of pay there was no serious industrial relations problem in his area of responsibility.

In February 1988, following the publication of Sir Robin Ibbs's report on civil service efficiency, *Improving Management in Government: the Next Steps*, the government launched a radical programme designed to separate the two distinct parts of the civil service—the administrative/policy work and the day-to-day delivery of direct public services. The idea was to create operational agencies of the latter, with a designated chief executive whose powers over the budget, including pay and staffing numbers in these essentially labour-intensive areas, would go far beyond what had traditionally been allowed. This idea was not new: the Fulton committee (1968) had recommended setting up 'accountable management units', but the intervening twenty years had seen little progress in this direction. The new initiative was christened 'Next Steps', and Kemp was the brilliant choice to be its director, with the rank of second permanent secretary in the Cabinet Office.

On the face of things, 'Next Steps' posed immense potential difficulties by stirring up hostilities in the centre of the service and in the departments affected. At the centre the Treasury could see its powerful position under threat, while the unions, still well organized and capable of obstruction, were suspicious that this initiative was a possible precursor to the privatization or contracting-out of the services concerned. In the departments some of the permanent secretaries (but not all) were resentful at losing control of functions for which they had been traditionally responsible. Kemp's approach, a blend of enthusiastic drive, cajolery, and endless perseverance, overcame all these potential problems. In this he had the crucial support of a dominant prime minister. With the unions he worked hard to secure at least their tacit support, involving them at each stage in consultation in an open-handed and frank way that sought to allay their misgivings. In the event this approach was successful. So far as the Treasury was concerned he was less successful. As he later remarked, 'It turned out, as you would expect, that the trade unions were far easier to deal with than the Treasury' (Witness seminar, 2006). Nevertheless, after four years of unremitting hard work, and in a nautical analogy that he would have liked, a 'Next Steps' armada of large ships (such as the Benefits Agency) and some cockleshell ones (such as the QE II conference centre) was successfully launched. By the time of his death about 75 per cent of the 600,000-strong civil service would eventually be in the agencies which, notwithstanding political and economic interventions, was a notable achievement in management terms. In recognition of this Kemp was knighted KCB in 1991, having been made CB in 1988.

Kemp's career ended abruptly in 1992, and in a surprising fashion. The reason given for his dismissal was a clash with his recently appointed minister, William Waldegrave. There were, however, other reasons, notably the enemies that he had created among some of his peer permanent secretaries in his zealous pursuit of creating agencies. He was bitterly disappointed at his cavalier treatment and had an arguable case for constructive unfair dismissal. In the event, and like the good sailor that he had trained to be, he took his departure with dignity and not too much fuss. Perhaps he was mindful that, to some extent, he was the architect of his own downfall.

In retirement Kemp worked for the Foundation for Accountancy and Financial Management, a charity encouraging higher standards of accountancy in the former communist countries of central and eastern Europe. He also served on the Audit Commission (1993–9), did the accounts for his local church in Sydenham, and was a governor of his old school, Millfield. He died on 24 June 2008 at King's College Hospital, Denmark Hill, London, after a short illness, and was survived by his wife and four children. PETER JONES

Sources Witness Seminar, Oct 2006, www.ccbh.ac.uk/witness_civilservicereforms_index.php, 25 March 2011, Churchill College, Cambridge · *The Times* (2 July 2008) · *The Guardian* (3 July 2008) · *Daily Telegraph* (11 July 2008) · *The Independent* (18 July 2008) · *WW* · personal knowledge (2012) · private information (2012) · b. cert. · m. cert. · d. cert.

Archives SOUND BL NSA, documentary recordings

Likenesses photographs, 1995, Photoshot, London

Wealth at death £739,151: probate, 6 Oct 2008, *CGPLA Eng. & Wales*

Kendall, David George (1918–2007), mathematician and statistician, was born on 15 January 1918 at 11 Ure Bank, Ripon, Yorkshire, the only son of Fritz Ernest Kendall (1888–1970), a ladies' outfitter then serving as a mechanic in the Royal Naval Air Service, and his wife Emma, *née* Taylor (1892–1985). He had a younger sister, Muriel (Betty; *b.* 1921). Both sides of the family had lived in the North Riding of Yorkshire for many generations. In 1926 he entered Ripon grammar school, a famous and venerable foundation where, as he later said, the teachers were 'fantastic, dedicated scholars every one of them' ('DGK: early days', Kendall papers). In particular George Viccars, the senior mathematics master, encouraged him to work on his own from the age of thirteen, lending him his Cambridge lecture notes and G. H. Hardy's *Pure Mathematics*.

Kendall's maternal grandfather George Taylor had been a merchant seaman, and had an interest in the stars that he transmitted to his grandson. A family friend lent Kendall a small telescope, but his more serious interest in astronomy was aroused by radio talks by Sir James Jeans on astrophysics. The school advised him that, if he wanted to be a professional astronomer, he should first take a degree in mathematics. He was entered for the scholarship examination at Gonville and Caius College in Cambridge, and was awarded an exhibition. But the family finances were such that he needed a full scholarship, and he had to refuse the Cambridge place. Fortunately Ripon was one of the schools whose pupils were eligible for the closed scholarships on the foundation of Lady Elizabeth Hastings at Queen's College in Oxford; Kendall was awarded one of these, and entered Queen's in 1936. In that year the college acquired a new tutorial fellow in Ughtred Haslam-Jones, a pupil of Hardy and an enthusiast for the sort of rigorous hard analysis that Hardy had introduced to Oxford before returning to Cambridge in 1931. This wind was not tempered to the shorn Yorkshire lamb, and indeed Haslam-Jones introduced him to the even more formidable E. C. Titchmarsh. But Kendall did not forget his astronomy, and had enough initiative to contact H. H. Plaskett and E. A. Milne. His first publication was a short note in *Zeitschrift für Astrophysik* in his second undergraduate year, and the next year he won the Skynner senior studentship at Balliol College, to enable him to undertake research in astronomy after his first degree. Many of his fellow students at Queen's were from Yorkshire, but he does not seem to have made friends easily, and for a time he fell prey to the Buchmanite Oxford Group. This phase passed, and he became more sociable, resolving his religious beliefs into a quietly devout Anglicanism, to which he remained loyal all his life.

Kendall graduated with first-class honours in mathematics in 1939, uncertain whether to devote himself to astronomy or pure mathematics. The outbreak of the Second World War swept aside his dilemma, and he was posted to the projectile development establishment at Aberporth, Cardiganshire. There he joined a group of mathematicians solving problems both about the trajectories of rockets and about ways of detecting the arrival of hostile projectiles. Inevitably these were not purely deterministic, and statistical advice was given by Maurice Bartlett, later to be recognized as one of the greatest statisticians of the twentieth century. All went well until Bartlett was sent to London, and a volunteer was sought to replace his essential expertise. The lot fell to Kendall, who was allowed a week to learn the subject, which had not been part of the Oxford curriculum. Thus was Hitler responsible for introducing a classically trained analyst to real problems of random variation, which Kendall was to make his own. He stayed in contact with Bartlett throughout the war, and when it ended and he returned to Oxford he pursued Bartlett's interest in stochastic processes, phenomena evolving randomly in time, but with a degree of mathematical rigour and sophistication that Bartlett did not attempt.

Kendall's work at Aberporth had come to the attention of Sir Henry Tizard, who had been throughout the war a leader of Britain's scientific efforts, but then returned to Oxford as president of Magdalen College. In 1946 Tizard recruited Kendall as the tutorial fellow in mathematics, a post he was to occupy until 1962. He had to teach across the whole range of the (by then very old-fashioned) Oxford syllabus, but his own work was in the theory of probability and its applications. He discovered that in France and Russia, and later in the USA, this had been developed as an elegant and rigorous study, notably by the Moscow mathematician A. N. Kolmogorov. Gradually, so as not to frighten the horses, he introduced this theory into Oxford mathematics, and by his activities in the London Mathematical Society and the Royal Statistical Society to the wider UK community.

Although he was a devoted and charismatic teacher,

Kendall sometimes scared his students, by the high standards he demanded and by the way his warm and caring nature was to some hidden behind a mask of austerity. He came to be referred to by his initials DGK, and to be spoken of with awe as for a time the only man in Britain who really understood Kolmogorov. Yet in Oxford he found many congenial social activities, and he met, and on 9 August 1952 married, Diana Louise Fletcher (1924–2008), schoolteacher, and daughter of Donald Vernon Fletcher. They had a long and happy marriage, and brought up six children (two sons and four daughters) in their house on Cumnor Hill. Their elder son, Wilfrid, followed his father into probability theory, and became a professor of statistics at Warwick, while the eldest daughter, Bridget, gained acclaim as an intrepid foreign reporter for the BBC.

For the first decade after the war most of Kendall's papers were in what came to be called applied probability, using the calculus of probability to construct and analyse models of random phenomena. Of particular importance to his work were Markov processes, in which the state of a random system at any time is specified in sufficient detail that probability statements about the future depend only on the present state. Such processes are natural for instance in areas of biology, and Kendall applied the theory to models of population growth and cancer. In 1951 he published a seminal paper on queueing theory, a subject originating in the study of telephone traffic but later becoming one of the enabling techniques of operational research. He spent the academic year 1952–3 in the USA, mainly at Princeton. There he discovered that mathematicians were building on the work of Kolmogorov, and of Paul Lévy in Paris, to produce a general theory of Markov processes in which there were some very deep problems. On his return to England, he teamed up with the Durham mathematician Harry Reuter to solve some of these by applying new results in abstract analysis (essentially, calculus in infinite-dimensional spaces) to explore the surprising possibilities of the general theory. The series of papers by Kendall and Reuter, and later their student David Williams, proved to be an essential foundation for the modern theory of random processes.

While all this was happening beside the Cherwell, the shores of the Cam remained in blissful ignorance. At last Cambridge awoke to the need to teach modern statistics and probability and created a chair of mathematical statistics, to which Kendall was inevitably appointed (with a fellowship of Churchill College) in 1962. He rapidly earned the respect of his fellow mathematicians, who allowed him to turn the small statistical laboratory into a thriving centre for both probability and statistical data analysis. It soon became filled with research students and visitors from overseas universities, inspired by Kendall's unassuming leadership. Perhaps because of his wider remit covering statistics as well as probability, his own research changed direction. He had always shown a broad curiosity, and in Oxford had tried to reconstruct data of Flinders Petrie on predynastic graves in Upper Egypt. This proved to be the first of a series of diverse studies whose common feature was the analysis of data with special structure, such as alleged ley lines, prehistoric stone circles, towns on Otmoor, and even the flight of homing birds. These special studies led him to a general theory of random shape, which proved to be a fruitful area of mathematics combining probability and geometry.

By the time of his translation to Cambridge Kendall was in great demand across the world, but his particular concern was to visit countries whose scientists were not allowed to travel, in eastern Europe and later in China. He collaborated with mathematicians in Romania, Poland, Hungary, and China, and encouraged international bodies that exchanged ideas across national barriers. He was in 1975 the first president of the Bernoulli Society for Mathematical Statistics and Probability. In Britain he inspired a rapid development of pure and applied probability, and was properly honoured as its leader. He was elected to the Royal Society in 1964, and received its Sylvester medal in 1976. The Royal Statistical Society twice awarded him its Guy medal, in silver in 1955 and in gold in 1981. The London Mathematical Society, of which he was president (1972–4), gave him its Whitehead prize in 1980 and its highest honour, the De Morgan medal, in 1989.

Kendall retired in 1985, but continued to live in the family home in Barrow Road, Cambridge, and remained active mathematically for many years. He was co-author of what became the standard book on its subject, *Shape and Shape Theory* (1999). Although his mental powers faded after that, he was physically active, striding the streets of Cambridge, throughout his ninth decade. He died at Addenbrooke's Hospital of prostate cancer on 23 October 2007, and was survived by his wife, Diana, and their six children. He was accurately described at his memorial service as the father of British probability theory. He was a powerful and scholarly mathematician, equally adept at abstract theory and in diverse applications, and his influence was profound and lasting. J. F. C. KINGMAN

Sources N. H. Bingham, 'A conversation with David Kendall', *Statistical Science*, 11 (1996), 159–88 · *The Independent* (1 Nov 2007) · *The Times* (22 Nov 2007); (29 Nov 2007) · *Memoirs FRS*, 56 (2009), 121–38 · D. Kendall, papers, CAC Cam., GBR/0014/KNDL · *WW* (2007) · personal knowledge (2011) · private information (2011) [Wilfrid Kendall, son] · b. cert. · m. cert. · d. cert.

Archives CAC Cam.

Likenesses obituary photographs · photograph, repro. in Bingham, 'A conversation with David Kendall' · photograph, repro. in *Memoirs FRS* · photograph, repro. in www.statslab.cam.ac.uk/kendall/index.html · photograph, repro. in www.analyticquest.com/gallery

Wealth at death £903,024: probate, 8 Aug 2008, *CGPLA Eng. & Wales*

Kenrick, Bruce Henderson (1920–2007), Presbyterian minister and housing campaigner, was born on 18 January 1920 at 14 Poulter Road, Walton, Liverpool, the son of John Ernest Drury Kenrick (1890–1968), incorporated accountant's clerk, later accountant, and his wife, Sarah Mabel, *née* Barber (1891–1962). He was brought up in Liverpool, educated at Merchant Taylors' School there and, until called up for military service in the Second World War, was training to be an accountant. During the war he served as a stretcher bearer in the Royal Army Medical Corps in the Gold Coast and later with both the Eighth Army and the Parachute brigade in Italy. Although he planned to be a doctor and went to Edinburgh University to study medicine after demobilization, he became involved in mission work with the Christian Union and subsequently switched to divinity. He graduated in 1954, the same year that he married Isabel Howland Witte (1926/7–2010), an American historian whom he met in Edinburgh where she was on a Fulbright scholarship.

After ordination as a Presbyterian minister Kenrick continued his studies at the Princeton Theological Seminary in New Jersey and it was when he was there that he became involved in the East Harlem protestant parish in New York. This was a ministry of social action, working cheek by jowl with the urban poor, drug addicts, and the homeless, and it made a deep impression on him. For three years thereafter (1956–9) he lived in Bengal, where he worked as a missionary and supported movements for land reform. However, typhoid forced him back to Britain and he and his wife, now with three daughters (the fourth child, a son, was born later), moved to the Scottish island community of Iona to recuperate. While he was there he wrote *Come Out the Wilderness* (1962) advocating a fully socially engaged and active church. 'The point of the Gospel', he wrote 'is not just to patch up society's wounds; it is also to grapple with the wills of the men who have inflicted those wounds, and who might well inflict them again.' This was his most influential book, although he also wrote *The New Humanity* (1956) and *A Man from the Interior: Cuba's Quest* (1980).

In 1962 Kenrick and his family moved to London's Notting Hill, into a house in Blenheim Crescent purchased with his father's legacy. The area then was far from the desirable location of later in the century, with large numbers dependent on an often exploitative private rented sector. Kenrick quickly involved himself in finding ways to improve what he described as 'damnable housing conditions'. Working in a team ministry, he was part of a campaign to persuade the Conservative-controlled council to take action, but struck out on his own in December 1963 when he called a meeting that led to the establishment of the Notting Hill Housing Trust, designed to do what the council would not do, namely to buy and renovate property for rent at affordable prices for those in need. Displaying the flair for publicity for which he would become renowned, he took the risk of spending large sums of money on hard-hitting advertising, including a photograph of a family of six in one room under the headline 'Heartbreak Notting Hill and you'. The result was that the trust in its first year was able to buy five houses and house fifty-seven people. Within five years it had become a significant presence in west London, housing nearly 1000 people. By then, though, Kenrick had moved on.

Although he had done much to raise the problem of poor housing into a political issue—Harold Wilson's Labour government that came to power in 1964 was committed to action—Kenrick struggled with the limitations of an essentially local organization, believing that the campaign for better housing had to be national if it were to be fully effective in forcing local councils to take their housing responsibilities seriously. This the committee of the Notting Hill Trust was not prepared to do, so Kenrick took on the task himself. The result was Shelter, which became a reality in 1966, thanks to Kenrick's tireless energy, lobbying, and promotion. Described as Shelter's founder, Kenrick wrote,

> The most exhilarating fact about the launching of Shelter's National Campaign for the Homeless is that it brings fresh hope of good, low-rent homes to many of Britain's three million families who now live in slums, in near slums, or in grossly overcrowded conditions. (*The Times*, 2 Dec 1966)

Shelter was given an enormous boost by the coincidence of its launch with the screening ten days earlier by the BBC of the film *Cathy Come Home*, which provoked a public outcry over homelessness. However, while Shelter established itself quickly as a major player on housing issues, Kenrick soon fell out with his colleagues and left the organization after it appointed Des Wilson, a talented organizer, as its director. This is perhaps not surprising for a man decribed by his daughter as a 'crusader' (*The Guardian*, 2 March 2010), by a former colleague at Notting Hill Housing Trust as a 'marvellous one man band' (*The Times*, 24 Jan 2007), by a former chief executive of Shelter as 'a founding member of the awkward squad' (*The Times*, 20 Jan 2007), and by a Glasgow *Herald* obituarist as a 'thrawn maverick' who 'could have raised a fight in a quiet cathedral, and indeed often did' (*The Herald*, 27 Jan 2007). His successor in the chair at Shelter acknowledged, though, that 'it was Bruce Kenrick who started Shelter and without him it would never have existed' (*The Guardian*, 19 Jan 2007). Later he was described by the chief executive of the Association of Chief Executives of Voluntary Organizations as one of the 'sector heroes' of social enterprise ('Bubb's blog', 10 February 2010, http://bloggerbubb.blogspot.com).

Kenrick remained in Notting Hill until 1980, and after further assignments in parishes in Bayswater and Hackney, moved again to Iona. Divorced from his wife in 1983 (though they remained close) and increasingly plagued by illness, he remained in Iona for the last twenty years of his life, sustained by his membership of the Iona Community. Although he lived quietly, he was writing another book at the time of his death, at the Lorn and Islands District General Hospital, Oban, of a gastro-intestinal haemorrhage, on 15 January 2007. He was survived by his four children. SAM YOUNGER

Sources *The Times* (2 Dec 1966); (20 Jan 2007); (24 Jan 2007); (27 Jan 2007) • *Daily Telegraph* (19 Jan 2007) • *The Guardian* (19 Jan 2007) • *The Herald* [Glasgow] (27 Jan 2007) • www.shelter.org.uk, 10 May 2010 • www.nottinghillhousing.org.uk, 10 May 2010 • www.richardhall.co.uk, 10 May 2010 • socialenterpriselive.com, 10 May 2010 • private information (2011) • b. cert. • d. cert.

Likenesses obituary photographs • photograph, repro. in www.nottinghillhousing.org.uk/news.aspx?id_Content=731

Kerr [*née* Newland], **Antonella Reuss** [Tony], **marchioness of Lothian** (**1922–2007**), journalist and charity founder, was born in Rome on 22 May 1922, the only child of Major-General Sir Foster Reuss Newland (1862–1943),

Royal Army Medical Corps doctor and director of Middle East medical services, and his wife, Donna Nennella (Agnes), *née* Salazar y Munatones, daughter of Count Michele Salazar, a lieutenant-general in the Italian army. Her parents were married in 1918 when her father was fifty-six, her mother twenty; the marriage was dissolved in 1928. Her mother then married William Greenwood Carr, a young army officer who later became a brigadier and lieutenant of the king's bodyguard of the yeomen of the guard. They had one further daughter, Annabel (*b.* 1930), who later married the thirteenth Earl Ferrers.

As an army officer's daughter Tony Newland had a peripatetic childhood, the more so after her parents divorced. She divided her life between Rome and San Remo in Italy, and Suffolk. She was home-educated with a group of cousins; unusually, this was in the liberal teaching methods of the Parents' National Education Union movement. Like many young women of her class and generation she was sent to Munich to be 'finished' in 1936. There she came across the horrors of fascism and master-race eugenics, political ideologies that provoked in her a lasting care and concern for 'the voiceless weak' and a determination to help those in trouble.

In 1940 a brief time at Oxford was interrupted by wartime duty as a nursing auxiliary. She always regretted not finishing her education, but it was at Oxford that she met up again with a childhood friend, Peter Francis Walter Kerr, twelfth marquess of Lothian (1922–2004). He was serving in the Scots Guards when they married on 30 April 1943 at the Brompton Oratory in Knightsbridge, London. After the war they lived in one of the remaining Kerr family properties, Melbourne Hall in Derbyshire, which they renovated and opened to the public in 1951. (Peter's predecessor as marquess of Lothian had bequeathed Blickling Hall in Norfolk to the National Trust, and Newbattle Abbey to the Scottish universities.) In 1950 they moved to the Scottish borders and began the restoration of Monteviot, the family's 18,000 acre country estate near Jedburgh, into which they eventually moved in 1962. But she was most proud of their rescue of Ferniehirst, a 'frontier castle' in the borders dating back to the seventeenth century, to which they retired in 1986. While she was proud of her husband's ancestral inheritance in the Scottish borders, she was unimpressed by the pomp of the aristocracy: 'I suddenly assumed an identity that had nothing to do with me' (Paton, 58–9). But she managed to pull off the trick of being both establishment and anti-establishment throughout her life.

Between 1944 and 1957 Tony and Peter Lothian had six children. They were active parents; he the quiet one, fond of jazz and playing the piano, she more outgoing and flamboyant. In 1949 she was asked to edit *Catholic Mother*, the quarterly magazine of the Catholic Mothers' Union. The circulation rose from 2000 to 20,000 by the time she left in 1961. She delighted in commissioning articles from friends such as Elizabeth Pakenham and Evelyn Waugh. In 1960 she was offered a weekly column in the *Scottish Daily Express* by its editor, Ian McColl (who is reputed to have said that if she could increase his readership too by 20,000 she was hired). Her trial article on trade sanctions against Rhodesia made the centre spread. For fourteen years she wrote (on the floor at home, in longhand and surrounded by children) on the critical social issues of the 1960s and 1970s, from working women to sex education, drugs, and youth. Balanced comment was her aim on all subjects, but as she later said, balance was not fashionable at the time. 'This', she said, 'gave me profound respect for the media men and women who told the truth' (Paton, 42). Her respect for those journalists who did fearlessly tell the truth led to her setting up, in 1974, the Valiant for Truth award with her good friends the American Marxist editor Mikki Doyle and the actress Renee Goddard.

Long before then, in 1955, came the project for which Tony Lothian was best remembered. In that year she persuaded Odette Hallowes, the former Second World War resistance fighter, and Lady Georgina Coleridge, the formidable 'Lady G', a magazine editor and publisher, and subsequently also Violet Attlee, wife of the former prime minister, to help her launch a Luncheon to celebrate women of achievement from all walks of life. The post-war achievements of women in business, academe, the trades, and professions were at the time generally ignored. Men had their clubs, their exclusive dinners, and established structures for status and recognition; women, for the most part, had nothing remotely similar. The Women of the Year Luncheon, held annually at the Savoy Hotel in London, set out to fill this gap. Artists might sit next to hospital matrons; a thatcher next to a station master, racing driver, or pop singer; Marxists next to high tories.

Every woman who attended the lunch was a 'woman of the year'. They came by invitation only, each guest paying for her ticket. Any profits went to charity, originally the Greater London Fund for the Blind, but later the foundation set up by the Women of the Year Luncheon to fund entrepreneurial projects for women around the world. There was a certain irony about the original choice of charity: Hallowes, Coleridge, and Lothian all subsequently had eye problems (Tony Lothian lost an eye to cancer), and from 1970 onwards each wore an eye-patch at the lunches. In her own style of red or white shirt, black waistcoat, and black skirt, Lothian cut 'a rakish, piratical-looking figure with a cockatoo shock of dark hair, a black eye-patch and what looks suspiciously like an Irish shillelagh' (Paton, 5). Guests included Valentina Tereshkova, who became a good friend and received Tony Lothian on several visits to Moscow for international conventions, and about whom she later wrote a book, *Valentina, First Woman in Space* (1993). Other notable national and international guests included Margaret Thatcher, Queen Noor of Jordan, Princess Margaret, Princess Diana, Coretta King, Jung Chang, and Simone Weil. Tony Lothian met many of the guests through her work as vice-president of the Royal College of Nursing (1960–80), court patron of the Royal College of Gynaecologists, patron of the National Council of Women, and president of the Institute of Journalists.

Tony Lothian was appointed OBE in 1997 for services to

women and blind people, and became a dame of St Gregory in 2002 for her work in interfaith understanding. She was the first president of the Order of Unity, which later became the Scottish Order of Christian Unity. She said that her major inspirations were Emmeline Pankhurst and Hildegard of Bingen. She died at Ferniehirst Castle on 6 January 2007, after a stroke. Her funeral and requiem mass were held on 15 January at St David's Roman Catholic Church, Dalkeith. A memorial service was held at Westminster Cathedral on 11 June 2007. She was survived by all six children. Her elder son, Michael, known as Michael Ancram (*b.* 1945), Conservative politician, had succeeded his father as thirteenth marquess of Lothian. In honour of her life and work, in 2009 her daughter Elizabeth, countess of Dalkeith, set up the Tony Lothian Biographers' Club prize for uncommissioned first-time writers of biography. JANE REED

Sources M. Paton, *The best of women: the history of Women of the Year* (2000) • *The Times* (8 Jan 2007); (12 Jan 2007) • *Daily Telegraph* (26 Jan 2007) • *Southern Reporter* [Selkirk] (11 Jan 2007) • *The Herald* [Glasgow] (12 Jan 2007) • *Daily Post* [Liverpool] (29 Jan 2007) • Burke, *Peerage* • *WW* (2007) • personal knowledge (2011) • private information (2011) [Elizabeth, countess of Dalkeith, daughter] • d. cert.
Archives SOUND BL NSA, documentary recording
Likenesses photograph, 1943 (with Peter Kerr, twelfth marquess of Lothian), Photoshot, London • Bassano, half-plate glass negative, 1946, NPG • obituary photographs • photograph, repro. in www.biographersclub.co.uk/prize.htm • photograph, repro. in thepeerage.com/p1140.htm • photographs, repro. in Paton, *The best of women*

Kerr, David Allan (1945–2008), theologian and scholar of Islam, was born at Poplar Hospital, London, on 16 May 1945, the son of Wilfred Allan Kerr (1915–1991), a Congregationalist minister who cultivated an interest in international development, and his wife, Agapé Jean, *née* Maclachlan, who was from a Scottish missionary family with a history of service in China. The background of his parents combined with the cosmopolitan character of London where he grew up sparked Kerr's interest in the world beyond the British Isles just as immigration was diversifying Britain's demographics and the rise of America and the Soviet Union was reducing Britain's global influence.

Kerr attended Mill Hill School, a boarding institution that had historically catered to families with nonconformist backgrounds. At Mill Hill the suggestions of a teacher, augmented by his own curiosity and a touch of whim, led him to study Arabic at the School of Oriental and African Studies in London. This decision would prove pivotal. At the School of Oriental and African Studies (from 1963 to 1966) reading as well as friendships with Muslim fellow students propelled him on a quest to comprehend the implications of Islam's existence for the Christian. One book in particular unsettled his confidence in both Christianity and 'Western' culture, posing problems he would spend the rest of his life addressing: *Islam and the West* (1960), by Norman Daniel, a Roman Catholic scholar committed to exposing the medieval Christian origins of Europe's false image of Islam. Another book, *The Arab Awakening* (1938) by George Antonius, an Arab Christian, deflated Kerr's erstwhile pride in Britain's imperial history. These works left Kerr deeply troubled by the polemical strategies of past Christian outreach as well as the self-interested nature of imperial politics.

In the wake of this personal intellectual awakening, Kerr left London to read theology at Mansfield College, Oxford, with the aim of ordination but with burning questions in his mind about Christian–Muslim relations. At Oxford (from 1966 to 1968) he came under the influence of two very different figures who would push him to broaden his inherited Calvinist outlook in different ways. From the revered Congregationalist biblical scholar G. B. Caird he learned to exercise caution against reading contemporary inter-faith concerns into the ancient historical world of the biblical text. Biblical exegesis alone, in the absence of serious theological and philosophical reflection, would not suffice. From the daunting and difficult Roman Catholic scholar of 'Eastern' religions R. C. Zaehner, Kerr discovered the mystical traditions of Christianity and Islam and came to appreciate their common interest in transcendence. Zaehner's singular pedagogical style also provided him with ample practice in the art of holding one's liquor amid exhausting and occasionally disturbing intellectual debate—a lesson Kerr was only too happy to forget.

While Kerr did not pursue formal theological or biblical studies any further after 1968, he did remain convinced that theological thinking was fundamental to every other intellectual pursuit. He took this conviction with him to St Antony's College, Oxford, where he had earned a scholarship to pursue research for a DPhil in oriental studies. At St Antony's he found an ideal supervisor in the person of Albert Hourani. Like Kerr, Hourani was an Old Millhillian who had grown up in a reformed, nonconformist household. Hourani also maintained a lively personal interest in both the theological and historical dimensions of Christian–Muslim relations. Under Hourani's guidance, Kerr explored church–state relations in twentieth-century Lebanon. The genuine interest in Arab Christianity Kerr cultivated during this period made him more sensitive than the majority of his peers to the important contributions 'non-Western' Christians could make to their 'Western' brethren on a number of issues, not least the challenge of Islam. In 1970 Kerr married Gun-Marianne Holmstrom, a Finnish nurse whom he had first met at his father's church in London. They had two children, Simeon and Anna.

After finishing his DPhil thesis Kerr worked briefly for the BBC World Service, focusing on Arab issues. During this time he encountered the theological reflections of the bishop of Mount Lebanon, George Khodr, whose view of the Trinity would prove foundational for Kerr's approach to Islam over the next thirty years. Since Kerr, like Khodr, came to believe that the Holy Spirit worked outside the historic Christian church in religions such as Islam, he was more open to acknowledging the efficacy of Muslim faith than those Christians who built their theology on a Christological rather than a pneumatological base.

In 1973 Kerr succeeded John B. Taylor as lecturer in Islamic studies at the Selly Oak Colleges in Birmingham. In 1976 he founded the Centre for the Study of Islam and Christian–Muslim Relations there. The new centre, under Kerr's direction until 1988, distinguished itself early on for its unique emphasis on 'study-in-dialogue' and its pioneering concern for the growing importance of Islam in Britain and Europe. Also in 1976 Kerr co-drafted the influential Chambesy statement on 'Christian mission and Islamic da'wah'. This pattern of activities would mark the rest of his career as he became more an accomplished teacher, administrator, institution builder, and practitioner than a scholar.

With his success at Selly Oak, Kerr became a sought-after scholar-administrator, enjoying productive stints from 1988 to 1996 at Hartford Seminary in Connecticut (as director of the Duncan Black Macdonald Center for the Study of Islam and Christian–Muslim Relations and editor of the Hartford journal, *Muslim World*) and from 1996 to 2005 at the University of Edinburgh (where he was professor of world Christianity and director of the Centre for the Study of Christianity in the Non-Western World). His last appointment, a chair in missiology at Lund University in Sweden, recognized his unique grasp of the global dimensions of the Christian–Muslim encounter and his contributions to the redefinition of Christian mission.

In the wake of the terrorist attacks of 11 September 2001 Kerr remained a determined advocate of peaceful dialogue between Christianity and Islam and did not mince words when fellow Christians or the British government seemed to threaten this endeavour. While at Edinburgh he was invited to a meeting with the prime minister, Tony Blair, to advise on fostering inter-faith relations, but, according to his son, 'left convinced that the government's interest did not extend beyond PR' (*The Guardian*, 23 June 2008). Soon after arriving in Sweden, he was diagnosed with motor neurone disease, which progressed rapidly. A person of extraordinary commitment, he supervised and mentored his PhD students into his last days. He died on 14 April 2008 and was survived by his wife, Gun-Marianne, and their two children.

TODD M. THOMPSON

Sources *Church Times* (25 April 2008) • *The Times* (5 June 2008) • *The Guardian* (23 June 2008) • b. cert.
Likenesses photograph, repro. in *Church Times* (25 April 2008)

Kerr [*née* Trimmer], **Deborah** (**1921–2007**), actress, was born Deborah Jane Trimmer on 30 September 1921 at 7 St James Terrace, a nursing home in Hillhead, Glasgow, twenty miles from Helensburgh, where her parents were living at the time. She was the daughter of Captain Arthur Charles (Jack) Trimmer (1893–1937), civil engineer and former army officer, and his wife, Kathleen Rose (Colleen or Col), *née* Smale (1893–1950); they had married in Gloucestershire in August 1919. Her father had had a leg amputated after being wounded at the battle of the Somme, and later developed tuberculosis. In her earliest childhood her two strong-minded grandmothers were a dominant influence. In 1924 the family moved to Alfold, Surrey, where Deborah's brother Edmund Charles (Teddy) was born in

Deborah Kerr (**1921–2007**), by Davis Boulton, 1948

1925. At some point during her childhood her father changed the family surname to Kerr-Trimmer. Her first school (1928–32) was St Martha's Kindergarten, Bramley, Surrey, after which she was sent as a boarder to Northumberland House School, Clifton, Bristol, in 1933, where she had a largely unhappy time, before entering the drama school in Bristol run by her aunt, Phyllis Smale. She early showed an interest in dance, which took her to the Sadler's Wells ballet school, but quite soon realized that her real passion was for acting. She had some experience of radio in Bristol, and first appeared on stage at Weston-super-Mare in 1937 as Harlequin in a mime, but her acting career really took off in Shakespearean productions at the Open Air Theatre in Regent's Park, London, where she was spotted by the agent John Gliddon, who later signed her up. This was followed in 1940 by a season at the Oxford Playhouse.

Though she would later enjoy some major successes in the theatre, Kerr's real pre-eminence belonged to the screen, where her characteristic poise and reserve seemed always to be hinting at undercurrents of strong feeling. Her first film role, in Michael Powell's *Contraband* (1940), was cut before the film's release, but Powell subsequently became a major influence in her career, and, indeed, her lover. Before this she established herself as a screen presence in Gabriel Pascal's *Major Barbara* (1941), in which she was touching as the Salvation Army girl Jenny Hill, and in three films for Lance Comfort, whom she 'enjoyed working with … enormously' and whom she considered 'very underrated' (McFarlane, *British Cinema*, 343). The three films were the socially rigorous *Love on the Dole* (1941), co-directed by John Baxter and Comfort; the somewhat ponderous biopic *Penn of Pennsylvania* (1942), as William Penn's wife; and *Hatter's Castle* (1942), as Robert Newton's cruelly used daughter.

The firmness of purpose and moral authority Kerr brought to these early roles were confirmed in 1943 when Michael Powell daringly cast her in *The Life and Death of Colonel Blimp* in the roles of the three women over four decades in the life of the protagonist, played by Roger Livesey. Technicolor highlighted her auburn-haired beauty as she subtly discriminated between these three women. It was clear that a new star was abroad in British cinema, honing a persona that was variously crisp, ladylike, and determined. There was an ineradicable freshness about all her British work in this decade, whether as the dowdy housewife who blossoms under wartime experiences in Alexander Korda's romance *Perfect Strangers* (1945), or as the British-hating Irish girl whose animosity is undermined by her falling for Trevor Howard in Frank Launder's delectable comedy thriller *I See a Dark Stranger* (1946), or, above all, in Powell's sublime *Black Narcissus* (1947). This latter film, in which she played Sister Clodagh, a nun sent to establish an Anglican convent in the Himalayas (filmed in Surrey), epitomized much of her image. The surface is poised, watchful, and controlled, but the altitude and the wind, the district officer (David Farrar), and the unstable Sister Ruth (Kathleen Byron) work on her suppressed memories and sexuality, evoking in the Christmas scene in the chapel a recollection of her Irish girlhood and the fiancé who left her. In one of the cinema's greatest flashbacks, she is utterly transfixing as present and past mingle (almost literally so, in the editing of the sequence). Meanwhile, on 28 November 1945, at St George's, Hanover Square, London, she married Squadron Leader Anthony Charles Bartley (1919–2001), an RAF fighter ace (credited with fifteen wartime kills), and son of Sir Charles Bartley, a judge in India. They had met at a film studio where she was filming *Hatter's Castle* and he was advising on an Air Ministry film, *The First of the Few* (1942). They had two daughters, Melanie and Francesca.

For the early part of her film career Kerr had been under contract to Pascal, but he sold the contract to MGM when she made *Perfect Strangers*. Hollywood soon beckoned and with her husband she set off for America in November 1946. (There he made a career in film and television production.) Hollywood brought her to international stardom, a status she maintained for the next forty years, but her first few films there were not very promising, and could not be said to have extended her. Her first American film, *The Hucksters* (1947), co-starred her with Clark Gable, so that in a sense she was starting at the top. She went on to star with many of Hollywood's leading male stars, including Cary Grant, Robert Mitchum, Robert Taylor, and Stewart Granger, with whom she had worked on stage in England, and who with characteristic non-gallantry later claimed that she had tried to seduce him. But most of her early American films simply confirmed her serenely ladylike image, and her beauty became somewhat homogenized to conform to the prevailing Hollywood standards. 'I came over to act', she later said, 'but it turned out all I had to do was to be high-minded, long-suffering, white-gloved and decorative' (*The Independent*, 19 Oct 2007).

There is not a lot of dramatic interest in the roles Kerr played in such films as the old-fashioned romantic melodrama *If Winter Comes* (1947), or the feeble comedy of *Please Believe Me* (1950). When she graduated to big-budget films like the African-set adventure *King Solomon's Mines* (1950), with Granger, or the Ruritanian romantic swashbuckler *The Prisoner of Zenda* (1952), with James Mason and Granger again, she was not able to be much more than decorative in the approved Hollywood leading-lady manner. She was never less than proficient in these films, but *Edward, my Son* (1949), the one film that gave her the opportunity for serious acting (as the young wife of an obsessive husband, played by Spencer Tracy, whose life turns sour and who ages as an alcoholic wreck) failed with the public, despite her poignant and compelling performance.

The 1950s, though, saw Kerr established firmly as one of the most versatile film actresses. She dyed her hair blonde to play opposite Burt Lancaster as the nymphomaniac army wife in *From Here to Eternity* (1953); one of the film's scenes, one of the most famous in all cinema, portraying an illicit sexual interlude on the beach, was considered daringly frank at the time, and all the more shocking given Kerr's previously fragile and ladylike film persona. This kind of dichotomy was at work again in *The End of the Affair* (1955), for which she returned to England, and in the governess who may or may not be sexually obsessed in Jack Clayton's brilliant ghost story *The Innocents* (1961), adapted from Henry James's *The Turn of the Screw*. Perhaps, too, in *The King and I* (1956), under the gracious guise of Mrs Anna Leonowens, governess to the royal children, a romantic yearning may be detected. This was a hugely popular success, as were several other films of this time: John Huston's island romance *Heaven Knows, Mr Allison* (1957), in which she again played a nun, opposite Mitchum as a marine; the classic romantic melodrama *An Affair to Remember* (1957), co-starring Cary Grant; and the Australian-set adventure *The Sundowners* (1960), one of the films of which she was proudest, with Mitchum again. While filming *The Journey* (1959), a drama of post-war tensions set on the Hungarian border, she met the screenwriter and novelist Peter Viertel (1920–2007), whose credits included Alfred Hitchcock's *Saboteur* (1942) and John Huston's *The African Queen* (1951). Kerr's marriage to Anthony Bartley had broken down, partly on the grounds of their frequent enforced separations, and ended in divorce in 1959. She and Viertel married on 23 July 1960.

Kerr returned to the stage from time to time, scoring a considerable success as the teacher's wife seducing a schoolboy who believes himself to be gay in *Tea and Sympathy* (New York, 1953). She reprised the role in the inevitably temporizing film version (1956), which could not touch on the idea of homosexuality. There were other stage performances of varying distinction, and several television roles, including *Witness for the Prosecution* (1982), as the starchy Nurse Plimsoll, and Emma Harte in the television adaptations of Barbara Taylor Bradford *A Woman of*

Substance (1984) and *Hold the Dream* (1986); she was also Helen, the widow of a tea planter, in *The Assam Garden* (1985), but by the 1980s she was withdrawing from the limelight. She and Viertel had houses in Los Monteros, Spain, and Klosters, Switzerland. Having been nominated six times for an Oscar, she was awarded an honorary one in 1994, 'in recognition of the "perfection, discipline and elegance" of her film work' (*Hollywood Reporter*, 22 March 1994). She had received other awards, including a BAFTA special award in 1991. She was appointed CBE in 1998. In 2004 she was much saddened by the death of her brother Edmund Trimmer, a television news editor, following a 'road rage' attack. She died at 30 Back Hills, Botesdale, Suffolk, on 16 October 2007, after a long struggle with Parkinson's disease, and was survived by her husband, Peter (who died less than three weeks later, on 4 November), and the two daughters of her first marriage.

BRIAN MCFARLANE

Sources E. Braun, *Deborah Kerr* (1977) · S. Granger, *Sparks fly upward* (1981) · M. Powell, *A life in movies* (1986) · B. McFarlane, *An autobiography of British cinema* (1997) · *The Times* (19 Oct 2007) · *Daily Telegraph* (19 Oct 2007) · *The Guardian* (19 Oct 2007) · *The Independent* (19 Oct 2007) · B. McFarlane, *The encyclopedia of British film*, 3rd edn (2008) · www.imdb.com, 10 Nov 2009 · http://ftvdb.bfi.org.uk/sift, 10 Nov 2009 · *WW* (2007) · b. cert. · m. cert. [1945] · d. cert.

Archives BFI, corresp. · JRL, corresp. with Robert Donat | FILM BFINA, 'From here to Hollywood', *Limited edition*, D. Clark (producer), ITV, 22 July 1996 · BFINA, documentary footage · BFINA, light entertainment footage · BFINA, performance footage | SOUND BL NSA, documentary recordings · BL NSA, performance recordings

Likenesses photographs, 1930–94, Getty Images, London · Baron, photographs, 1940–47, Getty Images, London · photographs, 1941–2004, Rex Features, London · C. Coffin, photograph, 1947, Conde Nast PL/Vogue · M. Rosher, photograph, 1947, National Film Archive · C. Beaton, bromide print, 1948, NPG · D. Boulton, photograph, 1948, Getty Images, London [*see illus.*] · photographs, 1949–94, PA Photos, London · photographs, 1956–94, Camera Press, London · Lichfield, photographs, 1980, Getty Images, London · J. Bown, photograph, 1984 (with Madhur Jaffrey), repro. in J. Bown, *Women of consequence* (1986) · D. Boulton, bromide print, NPG · B. S. Jordan, painting, repro. in *Woman's Journal* (Oct 1957) · T. Purvis, pastel; Christie's, 21 Sept. 1995, lot 295 · bromide print, NPG · obituary photographs · photographs, Photoshot, London

King, Alexander [Alex] (**1909–2007**), chemist, international civil servant, and environmentalist, was born on 26 January 1909 at 5 Battlefield Avenue, Langside, Glasgow, the eldest child of James Mitchell King, a cashier in the Nobel Explosives Company, later a director of ICI, and his wife, Janet, *née* Dale. He was educated at Albert Road Academy, Pollokshields, and then, after the family had moved to London, at Highgate School and the Royal College of Science (part of Imperial College), London, graduating in chemistry. While an undergraduate he edited the college's literary magazine, *The Phoenix*, and was president of the literary and debating society. He also attended Edith Sitwell's Saturday afternoon salons in Bloomsbury. After graduate research at the University of Munich, in 1932 he was appointed a demonstrator in physical chemistry at Imperial College, where he also pursued research on surface chemistry and emulsification, and wrote three chemistry textbooks. On 27 March 1933 he married, at the Presbyterian church in Falstone, Northumberland, Sarah Maskell Thompson (1909–1999), a talented pianist whom he had met in Munich, daughter of John Charles Read Thompson, solicitor, and niece of the Liberal politician Walter Runciman. They had three daughters. In 1938 King led the Imperial College expedition to Jan Mayen; he received the Gill memorial prize of the Royal Geographical Society in 1938, and served on the society's council from 1939 to 1940.

At the outbreak of the Second World War King was a senior lecturer in physical chemistry at Imperial College. After a short period investigating sabotage techniques, in 1940 he was recruited as assistant director of scientific research at the Ministry of Supply. One of his tasks was to examine intercepted communications containing scientific information that might be of use to the war effort. One such communication, from the Geigy company in Switzerland to its Manchester subsidiary, contained details of an organochlorine, dichlorodiphenyltrichloroethane (DDT), that one of Geigy's chemists, Paul Müller, had identified as an effective mothballing agent, harmless (as he thought) to humans. King recognized the chemical's potential as an insecticide, particularly against lice and mosquitoes, and its usefulness in limiting the spread of typhus and malaria. Within months he had arranged for the mass production of the chemical, which was later credited with saving thousands of servicemen's lives, particularly in the Far East. (He later expressed regret at the indiscriminate use of DDT as an agricultural pesticide in the post-war period.) In 1942 he was transferred to the Ministry of Production on its formation, as deputy scientific adviser, and then in 1943 was sent to Washington to share knowledge of DDT's properties with the Americans. In Washington he was made head of the British scientific mission, and scientific attaché at the British embassy; he was awarded the American medal of freedom in 1946.

King returned to the UK in 1947 to become secretary of the Advisory Council on Scientific Policy and scientific adviser to the lord president of the council, Herbert Morrison, who was charged with the co-ordination of economic planning. He was appointed CBE in 1948. In 1950 he moved to the Department of Scientific and Industrial Research as chief scientific officer, in which post he played an important role in deciding which research programmes would be funded by the government. He also served as chairman of the productivity and industrial research committee of the Organization for European Economic Co-operation (OEEC).

In 1956 King became an international civil servant, as deputy director of the European Productivity Agency, a semi-autonomous agency within the framework of the OEEC, which aimed to increase industrial and agricultural productivity in western Europe by encouraging the adoption of American technological and managerial techniques. When the OEEC was transformed into the Organization for Economic Co-operation and Development (OECD) in 1961 King became its director (from 1968 director-general) for scientific affairs, again concerned with promoting technological and scientific innovation in order to underpin and sustain economic growth.

While working at the OECD, which he later described as the 'high tabernacle of economic growth' (King, 293), King became concerned about the long-term social and environmental consequences of the untrammelled pursuit of industrialization. In 1966 he came across the transcript of a speech given in Argentina by the president of Olivetti, Aurelio Peccei, in which Peccei voiced his concerns about population growth, environmental degradation, and the misuse of technology, and predicted (if humanity failed to change its ways) a future of environmental crisis, food shortages, conflicts over energy and other resources, and a catastrophic decline in standards of living. King wrote to Peccei, the two met to discuss their concerns, and in April 1968 they organized a two-day meeting at the Accademia dei Lincei in Rome, bringing together some forty high-ranking scientists, industrialists, politicians, civil servants, and others, to explore future scenarios. The participants agreed to continue to meet regularly, choosing to name their organization the Club of Rome, under which name it was incorporated as a non-profit organization, with permanent headquarters in Switzerland. The club achieved a spectacular success with the publication of *The Limits to Growth* in 1972, based on research the club had commissioned from the Massachusetts Institute of Technology, modelling the impact of future population growth and economic activity on the environment, and making clear the need for a more sustainable approach. Published just before the oil crisis ushered in a period of acute economic turbulence across the developed world, the book sold some twelve million copies in the first few years, and was translated into thirty-seven languages. King developed many of the concerns raised by the Club of Rome in his own writings, which included *The International Stimulus* (1974), *The State of the Planet* (1980), and, with Bertrand Schneider, *The First Global Revolution* (1991). He also travelled indefatigably on behalf of the club, which he served as its second president from 1984 to 1991, following the death of Peccei.

King retired from the OECD at the age of sixty-five, in 1974. For the next ten years he served as chairman of the International Federation of Institutes of Advanced Study. He was a visiting professor at Brandeis and Montreal universities, an associate fellow of the Center for the Study of Democratic Institutions at the University of California, Santa Barbara, and an adviser to the government of Ontario. He was awarded honorary doctorates by the National University of Ireland, the Open University, and Strathclyde, Guelph, and Bucharest universities, the Erasmus prize in 1987, and the great medal of Paris in 1998. He was appointed CMG in 1975.

Both physically and mentally agile, King (known to friends and colleagues as Alex) was described by one obituarist as 'a man of engaging impatience' (*Daily Telegraph*, 26 March 2007). Ricardo Díez-Hochleitner, his successor as president of the Club of Rome, described him as 'a peace-searching, wise world citizen', and 'a real humanist because a solid scientist' (King, v). He published an engaging autobiography, *Let the Cat Turn Round: One Man's Traverse of the Twentieth Century*, in 2006. He enjoyed literature and music, but above all liked to keep in touch with global affairs. He kept a flat in London (in Chartwell House, Ladbroke Terrace, Hammersmith) and also a house in Callian, Fayence, Provence. He died at Hammersmith Hospital on 28 February 2007, of sepsis following a urinary tract infection, and was survived by two of his daughters (one having died in a climbing accident in the Swiss Alps).

ALEX MAY

Sources P. Moll, *From scarcity to sustainability: futures studies and the environment, the role of the Club of Rome* (1991) · A. King, *Let the cat turn round: one man's traverse of the twentieth century* (2006) · *The Times* (15 March 2007) · *Daily Telegraph* (26 March 2007) · *The Independent* (26 March 2007) · *The Guardian* (2 May 2007) · *Irish Times* (5 May 2007) · *WW* (2007) · b. cert. · m. cert. · d. cert.

Likenesses obituary photographs · photograph, repro. in www.clubofrome.at/news/index2007_1.html · photographs, repro. in King, *Let the cat*

Wealth at death £1,362,635: probate, 1 Nov 2007, *CGPLA Eng. & Wales*

King, John Leonard, **Baron King of Wartnaby** (**1917–2005**), businessman, discouraged enquiries about his early years and gave no birth date in his *Who's Who* entry, but in his *Burke's Peerage* entry he claimed to have been born in August 1917, the son of Albert John King and his wife, Kathleen. No birth certificate for a John Leonard King, son of Albert and Kathleen King, born in England in 1917, has yet been found; the only John Leonard King born in England that year was born on 21 June 1917 in Farnborough, Cropredy, near Banbury, Oxfordshire, the son of Jane King, a domestic servant, and an unnamed father. It is possible that his origins contributed to what one obituarist described as his 'deep insecurity about himself and his early life' (*The Independent*, 13 July 2005).

King's schoolmates in Dunsfold, Surrey, described him as a 'dunce' in school, but bold and lively out of it (*The Independent*, 15 July 1990). He left at sixteen without qualifications and found manual employment in engineering and motor workshops locally. Noted as a 'natty dresser' (ibid.), he graduated to be a car salesman for Coombs Garage in Guildford, run by Arthur Sykes, whose daughter, Lorna Kathleen (*d.* 1969) he married in 1941 (they had three sons and one daughter, born between 1943 and 1950). King's duties included the uncomfortable task of repossessing cars—the beginnings of his reputation as a tough man not to be trifled with. At the age of nineteen he started his own business, Whitehouse Motors, with finance from some local builders and the help of a Ford sub-agency from Sykes. He was aggressive enough to be chosen as a Ford salesman of the year. Following the outbreak of the Second World War the motor business failed but an engineering sideline, manufacturing components for aero engines, continued and expanded. Crucially King managed to secure access to modern American machine tools provided through the lend-lease programme. These gave him a major advantage when the war ended.

After the war King chose to switch production to Yorkshire, establishing Whitehouse Industries at Ferrybridge,

John Leonard King, Baron King of Wartnaby (1917–2005), by Chris Hay, 1987

in a depressed mining area, bringing skilled engineers from the midlands to train his workforce. It is not clear whether this move was because of access to scarce labour, or his friendship with the Yorkshireman James Hanson and his friend Gordon White, the founders of Hanson Trust. He later called it a social experiment; 'the Beveridge report was kicking around and the idea of doing something appealed' (*Financial Times*, 7 May 1983). At first he turned out miscellaneous products, from ballpoint pens to steel ladders, but he soon moved into manufacturing ball-bearings, 'one of the most basic things you can make' (ibid.). He took over Pollards, which made self-lubricating bearings. He and his wife, Lorna, were a dedicated partnership, working twelve-hour days on tight margins. Both learned to fly and at one critical moment Lorna took their aircraft to Dublin to raise vital funds.

King also played hard, socializing with Hanson and White. The company's move to Yorkshire began an obsession with hunting; he was master of the Badsworth foxhounds in 1949 and of the duke of Rutland's foxhounds in 1958, and chairman of the Belvoir hunt in 1972. Gordon White described him as 'the bravest fellow I have seen in the hunting field' (*The Guardian*, 13 July 2005). In the 1960s business success enabled him to buy a 2000 acre estate at Wartnaby, Leicestershire, prime hunting country, and the country boy relished his place among the landed gentry. He also joined the Conservative Party. 'I wondered whether one was grand enough for the Tories', he later said. 'I was certainly too grand for the Labour party. So I had a look at the Liberal party and when I discovered it was nothing more than a convenient attitude of mind, I got on with being a Tory' (*Financial Times*, 7 May 1983). He developed formidable networking skills, adept at finding ways to secure newspaper attention for his businesses. He moved further into political circles, in part with the help of the ubiquitous John Poulson, the corrupt architect and developer married to his wife's sister.

King built Pollards into the country's third largest ball-bearing manufacturer and sought a merger with the Swedish SKF company, but Labour's Industrial Reorganization Corporation intervened in 1969 to compel a merger of the three British companies. King walked away with a personal profit of £3 million but was struck by tragedy when his wife, Lorna, died. He placed a £20,000 pearl necklace in her coffin and was furious when his private gesture was publicized in a newspaper. At his dying wife's request King tried, but failed, to rescue the Poulson business, but in the process met Reginald Maudling, deputy leader of the Conservative Party. Maudling attended King's second wedding, on 21 September 1970, to the Hon. Isabel Cynthia Monckton (*b.* 1926), the third daughter of George Vere Arundel Monckton, eighth Viscount Galway. They had met while hunting.

King swiftly re-entered business after losing Pollards, returning to Surrey to buy into Dennis, the fire engine and dustcart manufacturer, and becoming its chairman. But it was as chairman of Babcock and Wilcox (1970–94), a prime manufacturer of power station boilers, that he really broke onto the national scene. He was an energetic chairman and began a necessary, but ultimately only partially successful, policy of diversification. His appointment brought an office in St James and a seat at the top tables of the Confederation of British Industry. By the mid-1970s he was a ubiquitous networker in his converted London taxi, with its own phone. From 1973 he chaired the Conservative Party's city and industrial liaison council; he sat on the review board for government contracts, and was knighted in 1979. He was marked out as a potential nationalized industry chairman. He was offered the British Steel Corporation but rejected it, saying he wanted 'something do-able'.

After Margaret Thatcher's election victory in 1979 King was appointed to the National Enterprise Board, Labour's mechanism for restructuring industry, and became chairman (1980–81), delighting in his brief to run it down, dismissing it as 'a reluctant provider of funds of last resort' (*The Guardian*, 13 July 2005). Cabinet ministers noted the prime minister's imprimatur. Nigel Lawson described King as a 'rugged, astute and politically aware industrialist … rightly one of Margaret's favourite businessmen' (Lawson, 227). Then in 1981 came the job he had lobbied for: chairman of British Airways. Norman Tebbit, the secretary of state for industry, acknowledged King's forcefulness. Interviewing him with John Nott as a possible candidate, he said:

> the impact was extraordinary. He is a man full of controlled, sometimes concealed, brute power with a razor-sharp brain often masked by his apparently naïve and simple questions … Our conversation, far from being a gentle probing exercise … ended with King agreeing to accept the job. (Tebbit, 168)

British Airways (BA) was in need of new direction. Formed by a merger between the British Overseas Airways Corporation and British European Airways years before, it still suffered their rivalries, and customer service was dreadful; cabin staff grudged passengers even a glass of water on flights from Heathrow to Paris. The airline had plummeted into loss against a budget promising rising profits. The key to King's appointment was the brief to bring in private capital—in essence to privatize the airline—the kind of project that King and other Thatcher advisers had been mulling over for years. It was by no means obviously possible; one city banker commented, 'I suffer the service. Don't say I have got to buy shares as well' (*Financial Times*, 7 May 1983).

King (who was made a life peer, as Baron King of Wartnaby, in 1983) worked a revolution with the help of smart branding and advertising, a dedication to customer service, and powerful financial engineering that took early write-offs to facilitate rising profits and later privatization. He commissioned a report from the accountants Price Waterhouse on which he based much of his strategy. He cut jobs at all levels including the boardroom. Executive perks were reduced and managers had to be more modest in their choice of company car. Overall staff numbers shrank from 52,000 to 37,500 in two years. The key to his success was to appoint good subordinates—first Gordon Dunlop as financial controller and then Colin Marshall as chief executive. Marshall's remorseless attention to detail and commitment to customer service combined well with King's determined vision and contacts. Though there were strains, it remained a winning combination. King dealt with the politicians, and negotiated some major aircraft deals. Marshall ran operations. Though never soulmates, they spoke regularly at 7:30 every morning.

King switched BA's advertising to Saatchi and Saatchi, the Conservative Party agency. A brilliant slogan, 'The world's favourite airline' (based on research showing that while BA did not have the largest overall number of customers it had the widest international spread), was allied to an unflagging drive to put customers first. On one far-flung press trip, King was accused of letting some journalists slum it in club class while others went first class. 'Club Class in British Airways', he returned acidly, 'is not slumming it' (private information). He was demanding, basing action on careful research, but not always close to the details. At an early press conference he gave a recorded television interview. At its conclusion, a public relations assistant leant over. 'Please don't use any of the figures', he said. 'He has got them all wrong' (personal knowledge). In 1985 he hired David Burnside, a combative Ulster Unionist, who had aggressively promoted free enterprise at the Institute of Directors. Under Burnside the BA public relations machine, with a potent mixture of good staff work and free flights for journalists, won over a sceptical press and helped the successful privatization that, delayed by an airline slump, eventually came in 1987.

During King's chairmanship of BA the airline's turnover more than doubled, from just over £2 billion in 1981 to over £5 billion in 1992. Over the same period a loss of £140 million was turned into a profit of £434 million, though profits fell back in 1993 to £185 million. The improvement was matched by a huge change in perception. BA became a symbol of the success of Thatcherite privatization, and a business school model of corporate turnaround. King saw it in patriotic terms, 'The message is the Union Jack … It's an interesting business, and it's British, and it's the best. And there's nothing wrong with that' (Corke, 136). His belligerent attitude to critics of Margaret Thatcher was typified by his resignation from the Confederation of British Industry in 1980 after its director-general, Sir Terence Beckett, threatened a 'bare-knuckle fight' with the government. But he could use strong-arm tactics with the tories too, cancelling political donations over a dispute on Heathrow landing slots.

King's acerbic, pigeon-chested, but always immaculately suited style embroidered the myth. He could be a bully with a 'beagle stare', but employees at BA saw him as their champion and he was popular with the shop floor at Babcocks. He enjoyed a good party and relished the company of celebrities. While confrontational with some journalists, he was particularly close to the *Daily Telegraph*, where he became a director.

Competition from other airlines was fierce and King used his links with the Conservative government remorselessly. In 1984 he was able to stop plans to hand some of BA's treasured Heathrow landing slots to British Caledonian and other airlines, and in 1987 he won an even sweeter victory when BA took over British Caledonian in spite of concerns about competition. But he was less successful internationally; key strategic aims of links with airlines in the United States and Belgium were thwarted. Competition from Richard Branson's Virgin Atlantic and its readiness to tease BA as monopolistic were persistent irritants, particularly when some of BA's routes were handed to Virgin. In 1991 rivalry broke into open warfare when Branson accused BA of a dirty tricks campaign. King, who had described Branson as 'a grinning sweater', made the mistake of publishing his reply, counter-accusing Virgin of a public relations campaign against BA. It precipitated a libel suit by Virgin in January 1993, alleging the spreading of smear stories, the poaching of passengers, and the shredding of documents. BA had to plead guilty and pay damages. In the storm that followed Burnside left and King, though probably ignorant of exactly what had gone on, agreed to bring forward his retirement, due later in the year. His consolation was to be appointed BA's president and, more strikingly, the standing ovation he received at BA's annual general meeting, when he entered the hall, from the small shareholders to whom he was a hero.

King retired to Wartnaby and his country interests, but

continued to use his BA office until 2001. He stepped down as chairman of Babcocks in 1994, again becoming president. In 1994 he briefly became chairman of the engineering group Aerostructures Hamble but this flotation was not a success and it was soon taken over. He died of heart failure on 12 July 2005 at his home, Friars Well, Wartnaby. He was survived by his second wife and the four children of his first marriage. His estate was valued for probate purposes at more than £27 million. MARTIN ADENEY

Sources *Sunday Times* (7 Oct 1984) · *Financial Times* (7 May 1983) · *Sunday Telegraph* (28 Sept 1980); (6 Jan 1985); (7 Jan 1990) · A. Corke, *British Airways: the path to profitability* (1986) · *Sunday Express* (19 July 1987) · N. Tebbit, *Upwardly mobile* (1988) · N. Lawson, *The view from no. 11: memoirs of a tory radical* (1992) · *Independent on Sunday Magazine* (15 July 1990) · *The Times* (13 July 2005) · *Daily Telegraph* (13 July 2005) · *The Guardian* (13 July 2005) · *The Independent* (13 July 2005) · *WW* (2005) · Burke, *Peerage* · personal knowledge (2009) · private information (2009) · b. cert. · m. cert. · d. cert.

Archives SOUND BL NSA, current affairs recording

Likenesses photographs, 1950–83, PA Photos, London · G. Levine, photographs, 1985–95, Getty Images, London · photographs, 1985–98, Photoshot, London · C. Hay, bromide print, 1987, NPG [*see illus.*] · N. Sinclair, bromide print, 1992, NPG · I. Nuttall, cartoon drawing; Bonhams, 2 Oct 1999, lot 318 · obituary photographs

Wealth at death £27,389,882: probate, 10 Feb 2006, *CGPLA Eng. & Wales*

King, Dame Thea (**1925–2007**), clarinettist and pianist, was born on 26 December 1925 at The Maples, Hitchin, Hertfordshire, the daughter of Henry Walter Mayer King, agricultural engineer and company director, and his wife, Dorothea Louisa, *née* Hass, both of 9 Balmoral Road, Hitchin. Her mother was a gifted amateur musician who taught her the piano from the age of four. In her last year at Bedford high school during the Second World War she made friends with Elizabeth Thurston, daughter of Frederick John (Jack) *Thurston (1901–1953), principal clarinet of the BBC Symphony Orchestra, then stationed nearby. Borrowing a clarinet from a schoolteacher she studied a fingering chart and joined the school orchestra, a few months later playing the andante of Brahms's F minor sonata in a competition adjudicated by Herbert Howells. She also had some lessons from the BBC orchestra's second clarinet, Ralph Clarke. In 1943 she won a piano scholarship to the Royal College of Music, where she studied with Arthur Alexander and, as second study, the clarinet with Thurston. She played both instruments in concerts and recitals, also acting as accompanist to Thurston's other pupils, who included Colin Davis and Gervase de Peyer.

Having graduated from the Royal College of Music in 1947 with the Tagore gold medal for the outstanding student of the year Thea King embarked on a career on both instruments, accompanying some of Thurston's recitals and also playing second clarinet at Sadler's Wells from 1950. An increasingly warm friendship with the widowed Thurston led to their living together and, on 22 January 1953, marrying. She withdrew from playing so as to look after him, but he died of lung cancer on 12 December the same year. There were no children, and she never remarried.

Dame Thea King (1925–2007), by Suzie Maeder

Returning to professional music Thea King found the clarinet beginning to dominate her work. She was one of the originators of the all-woman Portia Wind Ensemble, which did much for the status of women musicians, and also played with the Vesuvius and Robles ensembles. In 1955 she succeeded Gervase de Peyer as principal clarinet of the London Mozart Players, remaining for eighteen years, and was principal clarinet of the English Chamber Orchestra from 1964 to 1999. She also joined the Melos Ensemble, playing with them until 1993, and appeared with a number of other ensembles and as a soloist. She always preferred the greater freedom of working with chamber groups or small orchestras rather than accepting a post as principal of one of the major British symphony orchestras. She also taught at the Royal College of Music from 1961 to 1987, and at the Guildhall School of Music from 1988 to 2007. Her students included Colin Bradbury, David Campbell, and Michael Collins.

Unlike Thurston, who never liked recording, Thea King took to the studio with enthusiasm. The long list of her recordings includes music by composers from the earliest days of the instrument in the eighteenth century, such as Stamitz and Kramar, by way of the standard classics by Mozart, Weber, Spohr, and Brahms, to neglected English works by Holbrooke, Somervell, and Stanford, and her contemporaries Malcolm Arnold, Arthur Bliss, Benjamin Britten (with whom she worked at Aldeburgh in the 1950s and 1960s), Arnold Cooke, Benjamin Frankel, Gordon Jacob, Elizabeth Maconchy, Alan Rawsthorne, and Robert Simpson. Her recording of the concertos by Stanford and Gerald Finzi helped to launch the Hyperion label, and Ted Perry, the company's imaginative founder, acknowledged her contribution by designing colourful covers that often included a picture of her favourite animal, a cow (she was a talented artist, and made many cow drawings and caricatures). Several composers dedicated works to her; Benjamin Frankel's quintet (first performed by Gervase de Peyer in 1956) was inscribed 'For Thea Thurston—to Jack'.

Though Thea King took an interest in the early music movement she chose not to adapt her technique to authentic historical instruments, feeling that the reconstruction of the sound of past eras was probably impossible. However, she was one of the first to play Mozart's clarinet concerto and quintet on a basset horn, the then half-forgotten clarinet with an extension to allow extra low notes. 'Playing the basset horn in Mozart's divertimenti convinced me that the concerto was written for a clarinet with an extended lower compass', she said (*The Independent*, 29 June 2007). The subsequent discovery of manuscript material proved the case, and she was one of a number of clarinettists to record the works in this form. She also used her skills on both clarinet and piano to take advantage of studio techniques to record Brahms's F minor clarinet sonata, playing both instruments, and Mendelssohn's Konzertstück op. 114 for clarinet, basset horn, and piano, playing all three parts.

Thea King inherited Jack Thurston's clarinets and also much of his style of playing, including the particular charm of his musicianship in chamber music as well as in the orchestra. But though she always cherished his memory, and supervised the transfer of his few recordings to CD, she did not merely imitate his distinctive manner. She cultivated her own version of his warm, flexible tone, and her fluent technique was always used to illuminate music from within rather than to flash a brilliant superficial light upon it. She was always quick to learn new music, and if she did not possess the assertive temperament of many virtuosi, being determined but modest by nature, she could dominate and lead as a concerto performer as well as blend with colleagues and match their phrasing when sitting in the orchestra or in a chamber ensemble. Her warmth and generosity of personality infused her playing, and made her much loved in her profession. As an adjudicator and teacher she was kindly and encouraging while also imposing the highest standards of musicianship, insisting to students that making music involves 'putting ourselves in the shoes of the creator, rather than using the art for our own purposes' (*The Independent*, 29 June 2007).

Latterly Thea King tended to return to the piano as her first instrument, expressing her gratitude for this being possible when deteriorating health made clarinet playing a problem. She started attending piano master classes and having lessons again, and took pleasure in exploring the piano duet repertory and working as an accompanist and chamber musician. At a centenary concert for Thurston in 2001 she played the taxing piano part in John Ireland's *Fantasy Sonata*, written for him fifty-eight years previously. She had earlier made a record playing the clarinet part. She remained active to the end of her life, touring and making chamber and solo appearances but also giving her time to work with the young and to support local music-making: she was president of the Letchworth Music Club. She was made a fellow of the Royal College of Music in 1975, an OBE in 1985, and an honorary member of the Royal Academy of Music in 1998. In 2001 she was appointed DBE, the first wind player to earn such a distinction. She died in London on 26 June 2007. JOHN WARRACK

Sources *The Independent* (29 June 2007) · *The Times* (30 June 2007); (7 July 2007) · *Daily Telegraph* (30 June 2007) · *The Guardian* (2 July 2007) · *WW* (2007) · Burke, *Peerage* · personal knowledge (2011) · private information (2011) · b. cert. · m. cert.
Archives SOUND BL NSA, documentary recordings
Likenesses photograph, 1947, PA Photos, London · S. Maeder, photograph, priv. coll. [*see illus.*] · obituary photographs
Wealth at death £1,559,578: probate, 12 March 2008, *CGPLA Eng. & Wales*

Kington, Miles Beresford (1941–2008), humorist, jazz critic, and broadcaster, was born on 13 May 1941 at Down County Infirmary, Downpatrick, co. Down, the elder son of William Beresford Nairn Kington (1909–1982), a brewer then serving as a captain with the 4th Royal Welch Fusiliers, and his first wife, Jean Ann, *née* Sanders (1912–1973). His brother, Stuart, was two years younger. They grew up in north Wales, where their father was a director at Border Breweries, and Kington was educated at Trinity College, Glenalmond, in Scotland. Nevertheless, he saw himself very much as an Englishman (although to complicate matters further, he was actually half American, his mother being an American citizen).

'From an early age', Kington later wrote, 'perhaps confused by my shifting geography, I knew I wanted to be a humorous writer and a jazz musician.' At school he started his own jazz band and set up a humorous magazine in opposition to the official school magazine. While at Trinity College, Oxford, where he read French and German, he played the double bass in jazz groups and wrote humorously for undergraduate magazines. No doubt because of his extracurricular activities, he graduated with a third-class degree in 1963. 'When I left university I was almost entirely unfitted for life,' he later said, 'and consequently went to London to try my luck as a free-lance humorous writer, where I nearly starved to death.' To stave off hunger, he took up part-time gardening. Meanwhile, on 29 February 1964, he married Sarah (Sally) Paine (*b*. 1941), a museum research assistant, and daughter of Robert William Paine, architect. They had a daughter, Sophie, and son, Thomas (Tom). The marriage ended in separation in 1980, and subsequently divorce in 1987. In 1981 Kington met (Hilary) Caroline Maynard (*b*. 1948), a theatre and television director, and daughter of Bryan Carter, writer. They married on 6 June 1987. Through this

Miles Beresford Kington (1941–2008), by unknown photographer, 2006

marriage Kington gained a stepdaughter, Isabel, and then another son, Adam. He lived latterly in Limpley Stoke, near Bath.

Music was always important to Kington and he played a number of instruments, particularly the piano (always classical music) and the double bass (always jazz). Jazz was a passion and he acquired his first professional writing job, in 1965, at *The Times*, having lobbied the arts editor to employ him as the paper's jazz reviewer, a job he did for fifteen years. Similarly, in 1965 he set his sights on joining *Punch* and bombarded the editor with articles until he gave in and allowed him to join the staff. In 1970 he became the literary editor, recruiting a stable of talented reviewers. He was perhaps best known for his column, 'Let's Parler Franglais', described by Michael Bywater as 'a macaronic jeu d'esprit in which he dissected the vagaries of the British from behind the screen of a crazed bilingualism' (*The Independent*, 1 Feb 2008). So successful was the column that four volumes of Franglais were published between 1979 and 1982, followed by a fifth, *The Franglais Lieutenant's Woman*, in 1986. With characteristic self-deprecation, Kington described them as 'probably the most popular bilingual lavatory books of the 1980s' (*Le Bumper Book of Franglais*, 2010, book cover). His first book had been *The World of Alphonse Allais* (1977, republished in 1983 as *A Wolf in Frog's Clothing*), translations of the work of a nineteenth-century French poet and humorist. The book led to a broadcast on Radio 3 and was the beginning of a long association with the BBC as a broadcaster and writer.

In 1970 Kington joined Instant Sunshine, a popular cabaret group, all doctors excepting Kington himself. 'I always travel with three physicians in tow', he would quip (personal knowledge). He was the bass player, and wrote most of the introductions to their songs as well as wry, witty monologues. This gave him a taste for audiences and was a good training ground for developing his skills as an accomplished public speaker. He was a regular at the Edinburgh fringe festival and wrote his only full-length play, *Waiting for Stoppard* (1995), to première there. He also performed a one-man show, *A Rough Guide to the Fringe* (1992), and co-wrote and acted in *Bizarre* (1995) and *The Death of Tchaikovsky: a Sherlock Holmes Mystery* (1996), both with actor–musician Simon Gilman.

By the 1980s Kington was making regular appearances on British television and radio. Television programmes included *Three Miles High* (1980), about a railway journey in Peru, *Steam Days* (1986), *The Burma Road* (1989), *In Search of the Holy Foreskin* (1996), in which he searched for holy relics, and *Fine Families* (1998), in which he interviewed eccentric members of the Welsh aristocracy, all for the BBC; *Jazz at the Albert* for HTV; *Let's Parler Franglais* for Channel 4; and numerous guest appearances on *Call My Bluff* and other shows. But he eschewed a potentially glittering television career, turning down, among other things, the offer to present *Around the World in Eighty Days*. Television, he said, got in the way of writing. Radio, however, gave him the opportunity to exercise his considerable broadcasting skills. His light, witty touch, and his ability to look at life's experiences in a different, tangential, and oblique way meant he was much in demand. He presented various radio series, including *In the Archives*, *Double Vision*, *Reading Music*, *The Miles Kington Interviews*, and *It's a Funny Old World*. He was a regular guest on a wide variety of programmes including *The Write Stuff*, *Quote, Unquote*, *It's a Good Read*, and *The News Quiz*, and made over sixty documentaries on subjects as diverse as General de Gaulle, Brezhnev, Franco, John Betjeman, Jean-Paul Sartre, Django Reinhardt, Kansas City Jazz, and teaching English as a foreign language.

In 1980 Kington parted company with *Punch*. He wrote to Harold Evans, editor at *The Times*, offering himself as a humorous columnist. When Evans did not reply, Kington sent him copy daily until Evans relented. Kington's column, 'Moreover', appeared until 1987 when he switched to *The Independent*, where he continued to write on a daily basis, the last copy appearing the day he died; he also wrote a column for *The Oldie*. In all he wrote over 4500 columns, described by Simon Kelner as 'witty, topical, erudite, acutely observed' (*The Independent*, 1 Feb 2008). 'As with the very best in any sphere of endeavour,' Simon O'Hagan asserted, 'Miles's trick was to make it look easy. His lightness of touch amounted to a kind of genius. But behind the conversational prose lay craftmanship of the highest order. His standards never wavered' (*The Independent*, 8 Feb 2008). What struck his colleagues was his intense curiosity about everything, and his ability to wring humour from the most mundane object or situation. As Terence Blacker wrote, 'He had an excellent eye for a funny story but also had a great ear, presenting the column in a wide variety of registers and voices while retaining the particular personality of his writing' (*The Independent*, 1 Feb 2008).

Kington's later books included *Miles and Miles* (1982), *Nature Made Ridiculously Simple* (1983), *Vicarage Allsorts* (1985), *Welcome to Kington* (1989), *Jazz: an Anthology* (edited, 1992), *Motorway Madness* (1998), *Someone Like Me: Tales from a Borrowed Childhood* (2005), and the posthumously published *The Best by Miles* (2009) and *Le Bumper Book of Franglais* (2010).

Kington was diagnosed with pancreatic cancer in 2007 but continued working until his death, at his home, on 30 January 2008. His funeral was held on 11 February at St Mary's, Limpley Stoke, where he was buried; a memorial service followed on 25 June 2008 at St Martin-in-the-Fields, London. His hilarious response to his final illness, totally lacking in self-pity, formed the basis of the posthumously published *How Shall I Tell the Dog?* (2008). He was survived by his wife, Caroline, his three children, and his stepdaughter. GILL COLERIDGE

Sources *The Independent* (31 Jan 2008); (1 Feb 2008); (2 Feb 2008); (8 Feb 2008); (12 Feb 2008) · *The Times* (1 Feb 2008) · *Daily Telegraph* (1 Feb 2008) · *The Guardian* (2 Feb 2008) · C. Kington, afterword, in M. Kington, *How shall I tell the dog?* (2008) · *WW* (2008) · personal knowledge (2012) · private information (2012) · b. cert. · m. certs. · d. cert.

Archives priv. coll. | FILM BFINA, light entertainment footage · priv. coll. | SOUND BBC Radio Archives, 28 Oct 1980 and 14 June 1982 · BL NSA, current affairs, documentary, interview, light entertainment, and performance recordings · priv. coll. · *The last word*, BBC Radio, 1 Feb 2008 · 'Kington's last tapes', *The Archive Hour*, BBC Radio, 26 April 2008

Likenesses photographs, 1969–70, Punch Archive, London · photographs, 1970–81, Getty Images, London · photographs, 1973–2006, Rex Features, London · photograph, 1981, Photoshot, London · photograph, 2006, Rex Features, London [*see illus.*] · S. Muir, oils, priv. coll. · J. Owen Edmonds, photographs, priv. coll. · A. Roth, cartoon, priv. coll. · W. Rushton, cartoon, repro. in *The Oldie* · R. A. Smith, photographs, priv. coll. · obituary photographs · photograph, repro. in *The Times* (1 Feb 2008) · photographs, Independent Picture Library, London

Kirkwood, Patricia [Pat] (**1921–2007**), actress and singer, was born on 24 February 1921 at 6 Seedley Terrace, Pendleton, Salford, Lancashire, the elder child and only daughter of William Kirkwood, a shipping clerk of Scottish descent, and his wife, Norah, *née* Carr. Her mother had theatrical ambitions for Pat, who left Levenshulme high school to make her professional stage début billed as the Schoolgirl Songstress at the Royal Hippodrome, Salford, in 1935. She was immediately propelled into the rough and tumble of northern and London variety halls, honing her ability to grab an audience and 'sell' a number with gusto. She was spotted while performing at the Metropolitan, Edgware Road, by the impresario Prince Littler, who cast her in *Jack and the Beanstalk* (New Theatre, Cardiff, 1936), and she made her West End début as Dandini in *Cinderella* (Princes, 1937). She regularly appeared in variety shows,

Patricia [Pat] **Kirkwood** (**1921–2007**), by Anthony Buckley

including the royal variety (1952 and 1955) and two royal command performances, and fourteen Christmas pantomimes in the West End and the provinces. In *Humpty Dumpty* at London Coliseum (1943) she attracted great acclaim for her thigh-slapping principal boy, Prince Rupert, and her last pantomime role was Aladdin in Newcastle (1973). Solo cabaret performances—she was a great success at the Desert Inn in Las Vegas (1954) and at the Savoy Hotel, London (1957)—and plays were also part of her stage career. More significant were Kirkwood's star roles in revues and musical theatre between 1939 and 1959. She had her big break in Robert Nesbitt's successful revue *Black Velvet* (playing for two years at the London Hippodrome from 1939), which introduced Cole Porter's 'My Heart Belongs to Daddy'. Other revue appearances included *Starlight Roof* (Hippodrome, 1947) and *Fancy Free* (Prince of Wales, 1951). West End musical shows included *Top of the World*, with Tommy Trinder (Palladium, 1940), and *Let's Face It*, with Bobby Howes (Hippodrome, 1942), in which she sang Cole Porter's 'Just One of Those Things'. Noël Coward created the role of Pinkie Leroy for her in *Ace of Clubs* (Cambridge, 1950), which provided a hit number, 'Chase Me Charlie'. In *Wonderful Town* (Princes, 1955) she played Ruth in the Leonard Bernstein musical. She co-starred with her third husband (the actor and songwriter Hubert Gregg) in her last West End musical, *Chrysanthemum* (1958–9). Most critics praised the show, but it ran for only three months (at the Prince of Wales and Apollo theatres) owing to a chaotic management, and the two stars missed many later performances through illness. A highlight was Kirkwood's song 'Saturday Night'.

The success of Gracie Fields meant that British film producers were looking for more of the same, and regional voices such as Betty Driver and Pat Kirkwood were signed up, the latter to provide glamour and a song or two in *Save a Little Sunshine* (1938), *Me and My Pal* (1939), *Come on George!* (1939, with George Formby), and *Band Waggon* (1939, with Arthur Askey). Later films included *Flight from Folly* (1945) and the dramatic *Once a Sinner* (1950). Her one Hollywood film, *No Leave, No Love* (1946), in which she co-starred with Van Johnson, flopped, and medication prescribed by MGM's doctors caused her severe problems, leading to a nervous breakdown and several months in a sanatorium in Westchester county, New York, before she returned to London in 1947. Her two final films, *Stars in Your Eyes* (1956) and *After the Ball* (1957), were co-scripted by Gregg.

On television the *Pat Kirkwood Show* (BBC, 1954) was claimed to be the first variety show hosted by a female star. Her affinity with the music hall was displayed in *Our Marie* (BBC, 1953), a highly successful tribute to Marie Lloyd, followed by *The Great Little Tilley* (BBC, 1956) with Kirkwood starring as another great music-hall artist, Vesta Tilley. *After the Ball* was a colour film adaptation of this television production, providing Kirkwood with her last starring film role, opposite Laurence Harvey. Radio appearances included *Monday Night at Seven* (1938), *A Date with Pat Kirkwood* (1942), and (with Gregg) *My Patricia* (1956). She also made commercial recordings of over forty songs.

Between 1939 and 1958 Kirkwood was a leading star of the golden age of British revues and musical comedy, with a stage presence matching that of Ethel Merman (who also introduced Cole Porter songs to theatre audiences). Kenneth Tynan called Kirkwood's legs 'the eighth wonder of the world' (*The Guardian*, 29 Dec 2007), and publicists called her Britain's Betty Grable, a personification of 1940s glamour. At a time when leading ladies in British musical theatre tended to be genteel sopranos from the world of operetta, she had an easy, glorious command of the stage, and could not only sing sweetly but sell a song when necessary. Her natural home was the theatre—those who saw her on stage referred to her 'ebullient', 'exuberant', and 'vivacious' theatrical personality. She was a seasoned trouper with style, energy, charm, and spirit. She also remained true to her northern roots in her accent and her 'down to earth' quality. Apart from *After the Ball*, films did not convey her magnetism well.

Kirkwood and Gregg were a celebrity show business couple on stage, television, film, and radio from 1956 into the 1960s. With Gregg she starred in the traditional farce *Pools Paradise*, which attracted negative reviews (Phoenix, London, 1961), but after their move to Portugal in 1963 (she was to retain a property there for twenty years) Kirkwood became a less familiar name to the mass public, appealing to a more specialized theatrical crowd. She starred in nostalgia shows, touring productions of Somerset Maugham's *The Constant Wife* (1967) and *Lady Frederick* (1971), and the Rodgers and Hart musical *Pal Joey* at the Edinburgh Festival (Royal Lyceum, 1976), winning critical plaudits for her portrayal of Vera Simpson. She had the ability 'not so much to sell a song as to inhabit it and make it her own', wrote John Barber in the *Daily Telegraph* (Kirkwood, 236). Her final stage appearance was in *Noel / Cole: Let's Do It* for a ten-week run at the Chichester Festival Theatre (1994), in which she sang Cole Porter's 'You're the Top'.

Kirkwood married first, on 10 August 1940, at St Stephen on the Cliffs, Blackpool, John William Atkinson Lister, a theatrical manager fifteen years her senior. They were separated from 1943 and divorced in 1950, and on 22 February 1952, at St Marylebone register office, she married Spiro (Sparky) de Spiro Gabriele (*b*. 1903/4), a Russian-Greek emigré shipowner who died from a coronary thrombosis in 1954. On 4 May 1956, at St Columba's Church of Scotland Church, Pont Street, Chelsea, she married Hubert Robert Harry Gregg (1914–2004), author, actor, and songwriter, six years her senior. They were divorced in 1979, and on 3 March 1981 she married, in Gibraltar, her fourth husband, (James) Peter Knight, a retired solicitor and former president of the Bradford and Bingley Building Society. She had no children. For many years she was dogged by rumours of an affair with Prince Philip, centring on an evening in 1948 when, introduced and accompanied by the court photographer Baron Nahum (known as Baron), the recently married prince had visited her in her dressing-room, and taken her to dine at Les Ambassadeurs in Mayfair and then to the Milroy supper club, where they danced into the early hours before heading back to Baron's flat for breakfast. Kirkwood always denied the rumours of an affair, but complained that 'A lady is not normally expected to defend her honour publicly. It is the gentleman who should do that' (*The Express*, 27 Dec 2007). Her last years were clouded by Alzheimer's disease, and she died from a chest infection on Christmas day 2007 at her home, Glen Rosa, 24 Grove Road, Ilkley, Yorkshire. She was survived by her husband, Peter.

ROGER PHILIP MELLOR

Sources P. Kirkwood, *The time of my life* (1999) · K. Ganzl, *The British musical theatre*, 2: *1915–1984* (1986) · R. Seeley and R. Bunnett, *London musical shows on record, 1889–1989* (1989) · S. Bradford, *Elizabeth: a biography of Britain's queen* (1996) · C. Larkin, *The encyclopedia of stage and film musicals* (1999) · R. P. Mellor, 'Pat Kirkwood', in B. McFarlane, *The encyclopedia of British film*, 3rd edn (2008) · *Daily Mail* (23 Nov 2007) · *The Times* (27 Dec 2007) · *The Independent* (27 Dec 2007) · *Daily Express* (27 Dec 2007) · *The Guardian* (29 Dec 2007) · *Daily Telegraph* (29 Dec 2007) · H. Palmer, *Pat Kirkwood: 'Miss Show Business'*, CD booklet notes, BSLV 001 · T. Havers-Scott, *Chrysanthemum*, CD booklet notes, MCSR 3044 · M. Thornton, *The unforgettable Pat Kirkwood*, CD booklet notes, AVID AMSC966 · b. cert. · m. certs. [1940, 1952, 1956] · d. cert.

Archives FILM BFINA, performance footage · BFINA, *This is your life*, M. Aspel (presenter), ITV, 20 July 1994 · footage, 1951 and 1953, www.britishpathe.com | SOUND BL NSA, documentary recordings · BL NSA, performance recordings

Likenesses photographs, 1939–62, Getty Images, London · photographs, 1939–99, Camera Press, London · Baron, photograph, 1948, repro. in picasaweb.google.co.uk/edward.farley/PatKirkwoodImages# · photographs, 1948–99, Photoshot, London · photographs, 1950–57, Rex Features, London · Roye, bromide print, 1950–59, NPG · A. Buckley, modern bromide print,

1952, NPG • Barratts, photograph, 1953, PA Photos, London • Vivienne, photograph, 1957, repro. in picasaweb.google.co.uk/edward.farley/PatKirkwoodImages# • A. Buckley, photograph, Camera Press, London [*see illus.*] • T. Pilston, photograph, repro. in *Independent on Sunday* (4 April 1993) • photographs, repro. in picasaweb.google.co.uk/edward.farley/PatKirkwoodImages#
Wealth at death under £171,000: probate, 11 March 2008, *CGPLA Eng. & Wales*

Kitaj, Ronald Brooks [Ron] (1932–2007), painter and essayist, was born Ronald Brooks Benway on 29 October 1932, in Chagrin Falls, near Cleveland, Ohio, the son of Sigmund Benway and his wife, Jeanne, *née* Brooks (*d.* 1995), a steel mill worker and teacher. His father was born in Hungary, his mother in America, of Russian-Jewish parents. His parents separated when he was two and he was raised by his mother. While he would later stress his Jewish identity in much of his painting and writing, during his childhood he had 'only a consciousness of a Jewish-American milieu, of a Jewishness I would ponder only much later' (Bohm-Duchen, 17).

Early life and career When Ron was nine his mother married the research chemist Walter Kitaj (pronounced 'Kit-eye'), a Jewish refugee from Vienna whose surname he later adopted. In 1941 the family moved to rural upstate New York, where Kitaj attended Troy high school and spent his adolescence immersed in baseball and popular cinema, both themes he would return to frequently in his painting. Soon after finishing school he signed on as a merchant seaman, sailing throughout the Caribbean and South America. In 1951 he enrolled at the Akademie der Bildenden Künste in Vienna, followed by a year back in the United States studying at the Cooper Union in New York. After marrying Elsi Roessler (*d.* 1969) in 1953, he began a two-year stint in the United States army, stationed in Germany and later France. Sponsored by the GI Bill, upon discharge he matriculated at the Ruskin School of Drawing and Fine Art at the University of Oxford, and it was there—attending lectures by the noted art historian Edgar Wind—that he developed his enduring fascination with obscure, even recondite, iconography.

After leaving Oxford, in 1959 Kitaj entered the Royal College of Art in London, where he struck up a lasting friendship with the younger artist David Hockney, who often acknowledged Kitaj's shaping influence on his early work. Kitaj's association with Hockney and Patrick Caulfield at the Royal College of Art led some critics to categorize him as a pop artist, an identification he was at pains to disavow throughout his life. In his first solo exhibition in 1963, 'Pictures with Commentary, Pictures without Commentary' at Marlborough Fine Art in London, he showed a series of collage-based paintings with explanatory texts pasted directly onto the canvas, such as *The Murder of Rosa Luxemburg* (1960). These inscriptions progressively faded from Kitaj's canvases, although his self-declared bibliophilia later resurfaced in various ways, often to the chagrin of critics. In the mid-1960s he began to operate in a style defined by thinner brushwork and more complex compositional structures, fusing together often disparate imagery drawn from the history of art and film stills. *The Ohio Gang* (1964) was an early masterpiece from this period, but the *pièce de résistance*, and Kitaj's best-known work, was *If Not, Not* (1975–6). A large tapestry version of this modest-sized canvas was later hung in the British Library, an appropriately literary setting for a work inspired by T. S. Eliot's *The Waste-land*. In the upper left of the painting, the gaping mouth of the gatehouse of Auschwitz seems poised to inhale the contents of the picture. Amid a swirl of imagery culled from Matisse, Gauguin, and Giorgione, Kitaj seems to suggest that all the fruits of Western culture have—in the face of the holocaust—become unmoored.

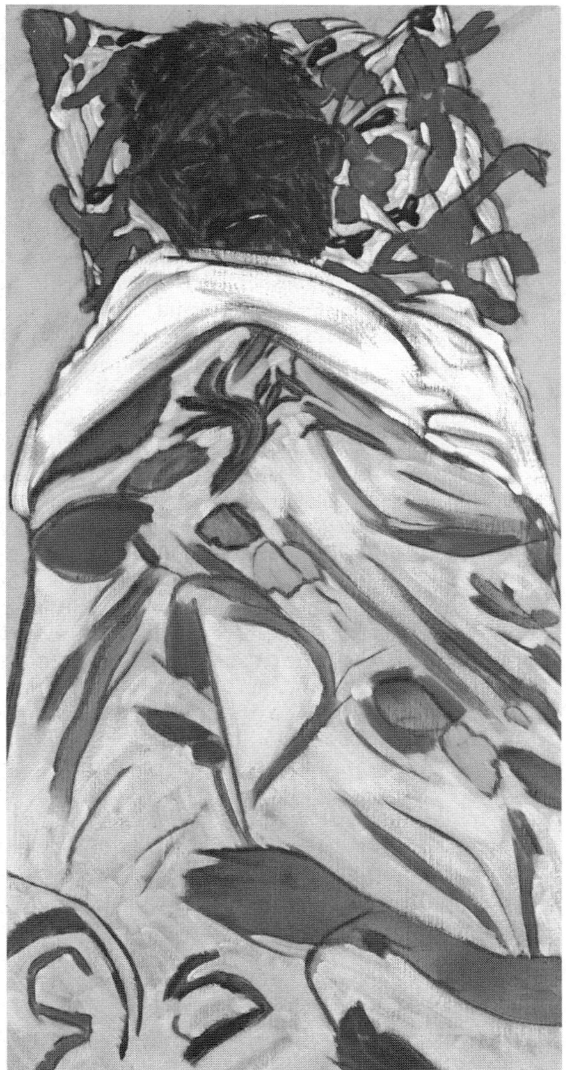

Ronald Brooks Kitaj (1932–2007), self-portrait, 1993–4

After the suicide of his first wife, with whom he had had a son, Lem (*b.* 1959), and adopted a daughter, Dominie, in 1964, Kitaj met the American painter Sandra Maureen *Fisher (1947–1994), whom he married on 15 December 1983 at the Bevis Marks Synagogue in London (with Hockney as best man). At Fisher's urging, and stimulated by the

Degas pastels that he saw in Paris in 1975, Kitaj began to reimmerse himself in drawing from life; the first of what he called his 'two beautiful obsessions' of the mid-1970s (Morphet, 50). His interest in the human figure, evinced in his sensitively observed pastel *Marynka Smoking* (1980), was reinforced by the company of other figurative painters working in England at the same time. In 1976 he drew many of these artists together for the Hayward Gallery exhibition 'The Human Clay', in which he proposed the existence of a 'School of London', including—among others—himself, Sandra Fisher, Michael Andrews, Frank Auerbach, Francis Bacon, Lucian Freud, David Hockney, and Leon Kossoff. While this group included several Jews—Auerbach, Freud, Kossoff, and Fisher—for Kitaj alone Jewishness constituted the second of his great 'obsessions'.

A Jewish 'diasporist' During these years Kitaj recalled that 'relative silence about the Holocaust began to break into print and my head would spin. I slowly decided I wanted to be some kind of new Jew' (Bohm-Duchen, 18). Essentially beginning his Jewish education in middle age, he travelled to Israel for the first time in 1980 and to the concentration camp at Drancy, France, in 1982, which inspired a series of sketches. Reading intently about the holocaust at the time and discovering 'that it didn't matter if you thought you were a Jew or not … they'd kill you anyway', Kitaj came to see the shoah as the central experience uniting modern Jews, and the centre of gravity for his painting (Amishai-Maisels, 320). Rephrasing Paul Cézanne's desire to 're-do Nicolas Poussin over again after nature', in 1980 Kitaj commented that it was his own ambition 'to do Cézanne and Degas and Kafka over again, after Auschwitz' ('Jewish art', 46).

Through the 1980s, stimulated in particular by conversations with Philip Roth, his London neighbour during the latter half of the decade, Kitaj began to see 'diasporism'—with the lurking sense of danger he read into the word—as the defining quality of post-holocaust Jewish life. In his *First Diasporist Manifesto* of 1989 Kitaj defined a diasporist work of art as 'one in which a pariah people, an unpopular, stigmatized people, is taken up, pondered in their dilemmas', resulting—in Kitaj's characteristically elliptical language—in 'views wrapped around … the contradictions of Diasporic life, apotheoses of groundlessness' (*First Diasporist Manifesto*, 73–5, 99). Casting a wide net, he insisted that there could be African-American, Palestinian, and other diasporist artists. Jews 'are not the only Diasporists by a long shot', he wrote, 'They are merely mine' (ibid., 21, 27, 75).

As he began to fix his diasporist vision in paint, Kitaj's brushwork loosened, and his application of paint became thicker. In *The Jewish School (Drawing a Golem)* (1980) the change is palpable in the figure of the *golem*, which a Jewish schoolboy attempts to summon into existence on a blackboard. According to popular legend, the *golem* of Prague, an automaton made of clay, was created to protect the Jews from the 'blood libel'. Here the *golem* remains unfinished, while a wary glance from a figure above, and tumbling bricks below, portend disaster. In his reimagining of the golem story Kitaj leaves it unclear whether the modern Jewish artist—symbolized by the sketching schoolchild—can spare his people from trauma, or only give shape and texture to their destruction. As in *The Jewish Rider* (1984–5), where the eponymous figure (based on Kitaj's friend the art historian Michael Podro) sits pensively in a railcar, oblivious to the chimney visible through his window, Kitaj's vision arcs towards inevitable tragedy.

In the year in which his manifesto was published Kitaj suffered a minor heart attack, hastening his sense that he was approaching a final chapter in his art. He had just begun to define what he called his 'old-age style'—exposing under-drawings beneath thin, sweeping strokes of vibrant colour—when the Tate mounted a retrospective of his work in 1994. Following his election as a Royal Academician in 1991, the Tate exhibition was intended to confirm Kitaj as one of the greatest painters of his generation in Britain. When the show opened, however, critics from several of the major broadsheets took sharp aim at what they perceived to be a contrived obscurantism in Kitaj's numerous references to artistic and literary idols, both in the paintings themselves, and especially in the 'prefaces' that Kitaj wrote to accompany them. Writing in *The Independent*, Andrew Graham-Dixon bemoaned Kitaj's 'unenlightening footnote[s]', concluding that instead of 'the T. S. Eliot of painting … Kitaj turns out, instead, to be the Wizard of Oz: a small man with a megaphone held to his lips' (*The Independent*, 28 June 1994). To James Hall, writing in *The Guardian*, Kitaj was 'a supreme dilettante … [who] comes off best when he and we leave his books behind' (*The Guardian*, 20 June 1994).

Return to the USA Detecting a stench of antisemitism in these charges of bookishness, Kitaj fired back at his critics. At the height of these skirmishes—which the artist rather grandly referred to as his 'Tate War'—his wife Sandra died suddenly from an aneurysm, leaving behind their nine-year-old son Max (*b.* 1984). Blaming his detractors for her death, Kitaj declared that England, too, was now dead for him. Barely disguising his antipathy, in an interview in the spring of 1997, he noted acerbically, 'The thing I'll miss most about England is Holland' (*The Independent*, 27 May 1997). After exhibiting his ferocious painting *The Killer-Critic Assassinated by His Widower, Even* (1997) at the Royal Academy summer exhibition in 1997, he boarded a plane for Los Angeles with Max, moving into a house close to his son Lem, by now a Hollywood screenwriter (under the *nom de plume* Lem Dobbs). The move to America also brought Kitaj into closer proximity to other members of his family, including Dominie and his sisters Karma and Madeleine.

On the one hand Kitaj was certain that his return to his native country was a step closer to the grave. In 2000 he entitled an exhibition of his work at Marlborough Gallery in New York 'How to Reach 67 in Jewish Art'. In 2005, seemingly surprised at having sustained himself through another half-decade of creative life, he unveiled 'How to Reach 72 in a Jewish Art'. Yet if his last decade in America was spent preparing to die the death of a misunderstood artist, the works that he produced in these final years—largely ignored by British critics—were also vibrant expressions of life. Even more accurately, they were the fruits of an afterlife that the artist had begun to live out in art; an American dream set in motion in the City of Angels.

'In the end', Kitaj wrote in his *First Diasporist Manifesto*, 'the Diasporist knows he is one, even though he may one day settle down and sort of cease to be one' (p. 29). This insistence on diasporism as a state of mind found an even greater relevance for the artist back in his native country. Returning to the United States felt like as much of an exile to Kitaj as it did a homecoming, and in his late writings and interviews he frequently alluded to Jewish narratives of expulsion. Immersing himself in the study of traditional Jewish texts—he kept the volumes of Adin Steinsaltz's Talmud translation stacked beside his easel—Kitaj came to identify his second wife with the figure of the shekinah, the female presence of God. Where, according to the Talmud, the shekinah followed the Jewish people into exile after the destruction of the first temple, Kitaj believed that Sandra had similarly accompanied him to his own personal Babylon: Los Angeles.

From his yellow studio behind his new home, Kitaj—by this point revelling in the reputation he had cultivated as a hermit—began the master works of his old age, the nearly three dozen paintings of his Los Angeles series (2000–07). Rather than descriptive views of the metropolis he now inhabited, the city he painted was a more intimate haven, an imagined dwelling place he set out to create afresh for himself and Sandra in each new canvas. While several artistic forebears provided models for the angelic figures that swoop through these light, breezy canvases, the central inspiration for the series came from the late bather paintings of Paul Cézanne, in particular Kitaj's 'favourite painting in London', Cézanne's *Large Bathers II* (*c*.1900–06) in the National Gallery (Morphet, 206).

London, and the loss that the city signified for Kitaj in his last years, clung to the artistic past from which he sought to fashion his imagined paradise. At its heart Kitaj's Los Angeles is inscribed with the memory of his displacement. As happened so often in his painting, however, what began as the depiction of a personal narrative ended by gesturing towards a vision of the wider Jewish condition. The hazy frontier he depicts between a remembered home and an imagined one is ultimately not merely a tension between London and Los Angeles, but a more fundamental description of the diasporist's wayfaring. The home left behind leaks into the vision of a home never fully attained. Jews may have invented Hollywood, as Kitaj claimed, but for the diasporist—his last paintings insist—there can never be a true Hollywood ending, even when you live in Los Angeles.

Kitaj lived just long enough to see his *Second Diasporist Manifesto: a New Kind of Long Poem in 615 Free Verses* into print in the autumn of 2007. An eccentric text—part diary, part rant, part compendium of quotations, from Franz Kafka to Ludwig Wittgenstein—this sequel manifesto cannot be distilled to any single message, except perhaps that of its final maxim: 'JEWISH ART IS OK to do without consulting your Rabbi, so do it! It's good and universal!' (*Second Diasporist Manifesto*, verse 615). The irony, of course, is that this statement figures the artist himself as a sort of rabbi, able to pronounce upon what is 'good and universal'. If there is a hint of heresy here, it is intentional. Above all else—in his writing, art, and life—Kitaj strove to play the part of the noble heretic. So long as the right people loved him—and Kitaj cared deeply for his friends, invariably signing his personal letters 'love, Kitaj'—vituperation was welcome. As he said in a late interview, with characteristic self-awareness, belied by nonchalance: 'There are only two types of people I hate: Nazis and people who hate me' (*The Independent*, 27 May 1997).

Kitaj (who nearly always signed his name R. B. Kitaj, and unusually did not give his forenames in *Who's Who*) received a number of honours, including honorary doctorates from the University of London (1982), the Royal College of Art (1991), California College of Art (1995), and Durham University (1996), the golden lion for painting at the Venice Biennale (1995), and the Wollaston award for the most distinguished work in the Royal Academy's summer exhibition (1997). He was elected to the American Academy of Arts and Letters in 1982, and nominated chevalier de l'ordre des Arts et des Lettres by the French government in 1996. On 21 October 2007 he took his own life by suffocation with a plastic bag in his Los Angeles home. He was survived by his children.

AARON ROSEN

Sources *The human clay: an exhibition selected by R. B. Kitaj* (1976) • R. B. Kitaj, 'Jewish art: indictment and defence, a personal testimony', *Jewish Chronicle* [colour magazine supplement] (30 Nov 1984) • M. Livingstone, *Kitaj* (1985); 3rd edn (1999) • R. B. Kitaj, *First diasporist manifesto* (1989) • M. Bohm-Duchen, 'The tribal passion: R. B. Kitaj', *Jewish Quarterly*, 146 (1992), 17–23 • Z. Amishai-Maisels, *Depiction and interpretation: the influence of the holocaust on the visual arts* (1993) • R. Morphet, ed., *R. B. Kitaj: a retrospective* (1994) • *The Independent* (28 June 1994); (27 May 1997); (25 Oct 2007) • *The Guardian* (20 June 1994); (23 Oct 2007) • J. Rios, *Kitaj: pictures and conversations* (1995) • J. Aulich and J. Lynch, eds., *Critical Kitaj: essays on the work of R. B. Kitaj* (2000) • A. Rudolf and C. Wiggins, *Kitaj in the aura of Cézanne and other masters* (2001) • A. Lambirth, *Kitaj* (2004) • *R. B. Kitaj: how to reach 72 in a Jewish art* (2005) • R. B. Kitaj, *Second diasporist manifesto: a new kind of long poem in 615 free verses* (2007) • *The Times* (23 Oct 2007) • *Daily Telegraph* (24 Oct 2007) • *New York Times* (24 Oct 2007) • *The Economist* (3 Nov 2007) • *Los Angeles Times* (5 Dec 2007) • *R. B. Kitaj: little pictures* (2008) • A. Rosen, *Imagining Jewish art: encounters with the masters in Chagall, Guston, and Kitaj* (2009) • *WW* (2007) • personal knowledge (2011) • private information (2011)

Archives SOUND BL NSA, documentary recordings • BL NSA, performance recordings

Likenesses Snowdon, bromide print, 1962 (with his wife and son), NPG • D. Hockney, india ink on paper, 1975; Christie's, 7 Feb 2008, lot 327 • J. Dine, drypoint in brown, 1976; Christie's, 7 Feb 2008, lot 353 • F. Auerbach, etching, 1980, NPG • S. Fisher, oils, 1980 (*Kitaj in San Feliu*), priv. coll. • self-portrait, lithograph, 1981; Christie's, 8-10 Feb 2006, lot 476 • self-portrait, crayon on tracing paper, 1982 (with Greta Prozor); Sotheby's, 18 Oct 2006, lot 635 • self-portrait, intaglio softground etching, 1982 (*Self-portrait, reading*), National Gallery of Australia • self-portrait, pastel on handmade paper, 1982; Christie's, 7 Feb 2008, lot 321 • self-portrait, intaglio softground etching, 1983 (*Self-portrait, cold in Paris*), National Gallery of Australia • self-portrait, oils, 1983–4 (*Cecil Court, London W.C.2, the refugees*), Tate collection • self-portrait, oils, 1983–4

(*Amerika, baseball*), priv. coll. • self-portrait, oils, group portrait, 1989–93 (*The Wedding*), Tate collection • self-portrait, oils, 1993–4 (*Self-portrait: Hockney pillow*), NPG [*see illus.*] • self-portrait, charcoal with red pastel, 1994 (*Self-portrait as a Cleveland Indian*), Cleveland Museum of Art, Ohio • F. Greer, bromide fibre print, 1998, NPG • self-portrait, drawing, 2000–4 (*Self-portrait after Freud's first painting of me*), Cleveland Museum of Art, Ohio • self-portrait, oils, 2004 (*Freud paints me twice*), Marlborough Gallery, New York • self-portrait, oils, 2006 (*Radiant turquoise self-portrait*), Marlborough Gallery, New York • self-portrait, oil and charcoal on canvas, 2007, Tate collection • L. Friedlander, photographs, repro. in L. Friedlander, *Kitaj* (2002) • D. Hockney, pencil, repro. in *The Royal Academy illustrated* (1997) • H. Hodgkin, oil on wood with painted frame; Sotheby's, 18 June 1997, lot 20 • M. Leonard, pencil, priv. coll. • R. Perry, photograph, repro. in *Sunday Times* (26 May 1980) • P. Sayer, photograph, repro. in *The Times* (7 Nov 1985)

Wealth at death £189,353: probate, 30 Dec 2008, *CGPLA Eng. & Wales*

Knatchbull, John Ulick, seventh Baron Brabourne of Brabourne [*known as* John Brabourne] **(1924–2005)**, film and television producer, was born on 9 November 1924 at 7 Upper Belgrave Street, London, the younger son of Michael Herbert Rudolf Knatchbull, formerly Knatchbull-Hugessen, fifth Baron Brabourne of Brabourne (1895–1939), and his wife, Lady Doreen Geraldine, *née* Browne (*d.* 1979), third daughter of George Ulick Browne, sixth marquess of Sligo. Part of his childhood was spent in India, where his father was governor successively of Bombay (1933–7) and of Bengal (1937–9). He was sent to Eton College, which he did not enjoy, before going to Brasenose College, Oxford, where he passed his military exam after nine months and immediately joined the Coldstream Guards. He became seventh baron, and sixteenth baronet, in September 1943, when his elder brother, Norton (*b.* 1922), an officer in the Grenadier Guards, was shot by the Germans after his escape from a train in northern Italy. Brabourne was wounded himself in combat near Brussels, and later became aide-de-camp successively to General Sir William Slim and Admiral Lord Louis *Mountbatten, when supreme allied commander south-east Asia. He was demobilized with the rank of captain in 1946. On 26 October that year, at Romsey Abbey, Hampshire, with princesses Elizabeth and Margaret acting as bridesmaids, he married Mountbatten's elder daughter, Lady Patricia Edwina Victoria Mountbatten (*b.* 1924). The marriage was happy, and they had five sons and two daughters.

Brabourne was fascinated by cinema. At Oxford he had visited the cinema twice a day, and three times on Sunday. With Mountbatten's assistance he obtained an introduction to the producer Ian Dalrymple, who employed him as a production assistant under the name John Brabourne. During the next seven years Brabourne worked his way up the production ladder, principally under Herbert Wilcox and Daniel Angel. Well aware that Brabourne's father-in-law was now the first sea lord, Michael Powell and Emeric Pressburger employed Brabourne as production manager on *The Battle of the River Plate* (1956), for which the Royal Navy's Mediterranean Fleet agreed to recreate the movement of ships off wartime Uruguay.

Brabourne's début production was *Harry Black* (1958). Backed by Twentieth Century Fox, it starred Stewart Granger as a professional hunter who tracks down a Bengal tiger that has been menacing an Indian village. Brabourne's next two films, both directed by Lewis Gilbert, had naval themes: *Sink the Bismarck!* (1960), starring Kenneth More and Dana Wynter, and *HMS Defiant* (1962), starring Alec Guinness and Dirk Bogarde.

In 1960, together with Anthony Havelock-Allan, Brabourne formed British Home Entertainment, a cable television service that, as a partner in 'pay-TV', offered quality productions to discerning audiences on a pay-per-view basis, starting in 1966. Brabourne produced film versions of Laurence Olivier's National Theatre productions of Shakespeare's *Othello* (1965) and Strindberg's *Dance of Death* (1968). Other productions included *The Mikado* (1967). British Home Entertainment's biggest success, however, was its live transmission of the heavyweight boxing match between Cassius Clay and Henry Cooper, when subscribers sold their neighbours ringside seats in their sitting rooms. This early venture into cable television closed in 1968 when, under pressure from the BBC, the government refused to allow the 'pay-TV' experiment to expand. Brabourne's and Havelock-Allan's next venture was a Paramount-backed production of *Up the Junction* (1967), Nell Dunn's tale of a Chelsea girl's discovery of the gritty realities of working-class life across the river in Battersea. Starring Suzy Kendall and Denis Waterman, it was the top money-maker for 1968 in British cinemas. Brabourne and Havelock-Allan went on to produce Shakespeare's *Romeo and Juliet* (1968), in which the director Franco Zeffirelli infused Shakespeare's verse with the teenage lovers' physical passion. Starring the newcomers Leonard Whiting and Olivia Hussey, it was backed by Paramount and the Italian public service broadcaster RAI. Financially it was very successful, grossing over $14.5 million in North America alone.

For several years Brabourne had enjoyed a close working relationship with his production manager, Richard Goodwin. In 1971 he acted as executive producer on *Tales of Beatrix Potter*, a musical starring members of the Royal Ballet, which Goodwin produced and scripted from an idea by his wife, Christine Edzard. The same team produced a follow-up in 1979: *Stories from a Flying Trunk*, based on the fairy tales of Hans Christian Andersen. Brabourne and Goodwin turned to fairy tales of another genre with their adaptations of four Agatha Christie mysteries: *Murder on the Orient Express* (1974), *Death on the Nile* (1978), *The Mirror Crack'd* (1980), and *Evil under the Sun* (1982). They distanced the narratives of all four films from Christie's original stories by adding period elements to her formal plot structures, and camp sensibilities to her sparse characterization. Three featured the Belgian detective Hercule Poirot, while *The Mirror Crack'd* was a Miss Marple story. For *Murder on the Orient Express* Brabourne carefully packaged a Hollywood director, Sidney Lumet, with a raft of British and Hollywood stars, and for twenty years it held the record as the British film industry's most profitable film. The other three were less successful, however. During the 1970s Brabourne also turned to children's films, acting as executive producer on three projects backed by the Children's Film Foundation: *Smokey Joe's Revenge* (1974), *The Copter Kids* (1976), and *Seal Island* (1977).

In 1979 one of Brabourne's sons, Nicholas, was murdered by the Provisional IRA, along with Brabourne's mother, the dowager Lady Brabourne, and father-in-law, Lord Mountbatten, and their Irish boat boy, Paul Maxwell, when it blew up their fishing boat off the west coast of Ireland. Brabourne, his wife (who became Countess Mountbatten of Burma by special remainder on the death of her father), and Nicholas's twin brother, Timothy, were all seriously wounded. Brabourne courageously returned to film production, and scored a success with *A Passage to India* (1984), which was scripted and directed by David Lean, after Brabourne's long struggle to persuade the fellows of King's College, Cambridge (the author's literary executors), to allow him to film E. M. Forster's book. His final film for the cinema was a third collaboration with Goodwin and Edzard, *Little Dorrit* (1987), which ran for nearly six hours. As a producer Brabourne's main interests lay in the story, the script, and the editing. Although the director was in charge on the studio floor, for Brabourne it was the producer who chose the story and ensured that the film actually reached the screen. His films were well regarded by his colleagues, and he received two Oscar nominations, as the co-producer of *Romeo and Juliet* and *A Passage to India*.

As cinema audiences declined Brabourne became increasingly involved in television. In 1969 Mountbatten refused to allow Associated Rediffusion to make the *Life and Times of Lord Mountbatten* unless Brabourne became the associate producer for the series. Brabourne also used his contacts with the royal family to persuade the queen to donate the substantial fee that she received from the BBC documentary *The Royal Family* (1969) to the embryonic British Academy of Film and Television Arts (BAFTA), which he and others were attempting to establish with suitable west London premises. He produced three television series, *Romantic versus Classic Art* (1973), *The National Gallery: a Private View* (1974), and *Leontyne* (1987), as well as *A Much-Maligned Monarch* (1976), a television programme about George III, in which Alistair Cooke interviewed Prince Charles.

From the mid-1970s Brabourne became more widely involved in industry matters. He was a director of the Copyright Promotions Group, Euston Films, Thorn EMI, and Thames Television (becoming chairman of the latter in 1991–3), and a governor of the British Film Institute (of which he was also made a fellow), the National Film School, the British Screen Advisory Council, and the National Museum of Photography, Film and Television. In 1975 Harold Wilson appointed him a member of his working party on the British film industry, and its successor, the interim action committee; and in the same year Brabourne became a trustee of BAFTA. He also served on many committees in the fields of education, science, charitable work, and Kentish matters, some of which he also chaired. He was particularly attached to the Caldecott Foundation, a therapeutic community for disturbed children, of which he was chairman from 1961 to 1992. His chairmanship was always scrupulously fair and his interventions were few, but always incisive, and finely calibrated. He was appointed CBE in 1993.

Brabourne was almost universally liked, although his polite and diffident manner masked a steely mind that understood the values of discretion and, on occasion, silence. He died on 22 September 2005 at his home, Newhouse, Mersham, Ashford, Kent, of heart and kidney failure. He was survived by his wife, Countess Mountbatten of Burma, four sons, and two daughters, and was succeeded as eighth baron by his son Norton (*b.* 1947).

VINCENT PORTER

Sources A. Walker, *Hollywood, England: the British film industry in the sixties* (1974) · A. Walker, *National heroes: British cinema in the seventies and eighties* (1985) · M. Powell, *Million dollar movie* (1992), 281, 292–5, 301–311 · *The Times* (24 Sept 2005); (4 Oct 2005) · *The Guardian* (24 Sept 2005); (30 Sept 2005) · *Daily Telegraph* (24 Sept 2005) · *The Independent* (26 Sept 2005) · *The Herald* [Glasgow] (24 Sept 2005) · *Yorkshire Post* (24 Sept 2005) · *University of Kent Newsletter*, 27/1, Oct 2005, www.kent.ac.uk/campusonline/newsletter/2005-10.txt, 23 Feb 2008 · Lord Crathorne, funeral address, www.lordbrabourne.com/page.php?id=12, 23 Feb 2008 · private information (2009) [J. Craven, vice-chancellor, University of Portsmouth]

Archives CKS, corresp. and papers | FILM BFINA, *This is your life*, B. Klein (director), Thames Television, 17 Oct 1990 · BFINA, news footage | SOUND BFI, BECTU history project, interview by A. Sapper, 2 March 1995, tape 346

Likenesses Bassano, group portrait, whole-plate glass negative, 1925, NPG · O. Birley, oils, 1944, priv. coll. · Madame Yevonde, group portrait, bromide print, 1946 (wedding party), NPG · photographs, 1946–79, Getty Images, London · group portraits, two photographs, 1947–65, PA Photos, London · Madame Yevonde, group portraits, two bromide prints, 1960, NPG · Levine, oils, 1960–61, priv. coll. · G. Argent, bromide print, 1969, NPG · J. Mendoza, double portrait, oils, exh. Royal Society of Portrait Painters, London 1984 (with Countess Mountbatten of Burma) · obituary photographs

Wealth at death £3,028,110: probate, 9 May 2006, *CGPLA Eng. & Wales*

Kneale, (Thomas) Nigel (1922–2006), television dramatist, was born on 28 April 1922 at Risedale Maternity Home, Barrow in Furness, Lancashire, the elder son of William Thomas Kneale (1896–1963), journalist, and his wife, Lilian, *née* Kewley (1889–1979). Both parents were natives of the Isle of Man, in exile at 74 Market Street, Dalton in Furness, while Kneale's father gained experience locally as a reporter. When Kneale was five they returned to the island capital, Douglas, in 1927, for William Kneale to join *Mona's Herald*, the newspaper that he would edit and eventually own. From junior school in Murray's Road, he went to Douglas High School for Boys, leaving at seventeen to be articled to an advocate. He found this uninteresting, and also rather limiting in that Manx law is not applicable elsewhere in Britain. And though he loved the island, especially the coast around Peel where his grandfather had a farm, its combination of wind and sun was already causing him discomfort. 'The sun and I are enemies', he would say. Whether or not this aversion was a factor, he was found medically unfit for military service in the Second World War.

In his spare time Kneale—known to family and friends as Tom, but more widely as Nigel—was writing stories. In 1942 he had his first magazine acceptance, and on a visit to London the following year was invited by Collins to assemble a collection for a book, though in the end it was six years before they published it. Meanwhile he failed to sit his final law exam, 'for fear of passing it,' he claimed, and enrolled at the Royal Academy of Dramatic Art (RADA). This was partly because he fancied being an actor, but also with a view to writing for the theatre or the screen. Next came two years carrying a spear at the Shakespeare Memorial Theatre in Stratford upon Avon, while continuing to pursue his writing ambitions. His volume of short stories for Collins, *Tomato Cain*, finally emerged in 1949. They were terse, imaginative, even weird: a wartime airman lost in the desert wanders into the palace of the Sleeping Beauty, or (in the title story) an island vegetable grower seeks to prohibit the cultivation of alien tomatoes, only to succeed in ridiculing himself. The book earned its author the Somerset Maugham award of 1950, but his earnings remained irregular, with spells back in the Isle of Man whenever he was hard up.

Then in 1951 came a lucky meeting with Michael Barry, who had been one of Kneale's tutors at RADA, and was now head of drama for the BBC's fledgling television service. Anxious to improve on the worn-out stage plays that accounted for much of the output, Barry hired Kneale as a staff writer. As there was no provision for such a post, he had to be paid out of the petty cash. Finally, authority was given to set up a script unit, 'although most of the money made available', the BBC's historian Asa Briggs acidly recorded, 'went to one man, Nigel Kneale' (Briggs, 689).

Much of the work that came Kneale's way was still adaptation from established sources, along with furnishing dialogue for children's puppet series. When, however, at a department meeting to make plans for 1953, he urged a venture into science fiction, not only was this accepted, but he was assigned to write it. The producer would be Rudolph Cartier, which was ideal casting. Viennese by birth, Cartier had worked with Max Reinhardt and at the Universum Film studios in Berlin before fleeing from the Nazis. His creed for television was to disregard the limitations of a tiny studio, cumbersome cameras, and live transmission, and attempt the impossible. *The Quatermass Experiment* (1953), a six-part serial about an astronaut returning to earth infected with the spores of a disease that would turn him into a human vegetable, held the nation agog. Yet the backdrop to the macabre climax in Westminster Abbey (chosen because it would be familiar to viewers from the coronation coverage earlier in the year) was simply a giant enlargement of an illustration in the abbey guidebook. Poking through it were Kneale's own hands in wash-leather gloves strung with noisome bits and pieces to represent the gruesome monster. Two further serials, *Quatermass II* (1955) and *Quatermass and the Pit* (1958–9), pursued the theme of advances in science whose implications only Kneale's hero, Professor Bernard Quatermass, seemed to grasp.

Meanwhile, in 1954, Kneale and Cartier had also collaborated on a brilliant realization of George Orwell's *1984*. A torture scene with live rats raised an outcry and a foolish demand in parliament that the customary repeat performance be cancelled, but the BBC held firm, and Michael Barry personally introduced the broadcast. On 8 May the same year Kneale married (Anne) Judith Kerr (*b.* 1923), daughter of a refugee German critic, Alfred Kerr, and sister of the lawyer Sir Michael Kerr. She became a lauded children's author and illustrator. They had a son, Matthew, a writer, and a daughter, Tracy, a painter.

Kneale's own career was, however, advancing a little uncertainly. Cinema versions of his Quatermass epics from Hammer (1956, 1957, and 1967) were low-budget, and looked it. Moreover, in the first two a 'tough guy' American, Brian Donlevy, was cast as the supposedly wise and cerebral professor. Only *Quatermass and the Pit*, with the Scottish actor Andrew Keir replacing Donlevy, had much of the force of the original. Kneale, ironically, was winning plaudits at this time with his screenplays for films far removed from his usual flights, including John Osborne's *Look Back in Anger* (1958) and then *The Entertainer* (1960). But worlds to come or latent terrors from the past were still the stuff of his striking original works. In *The Road* (1963) eighteenth-century dwellers by a country lane are haunted by the future victims of a disaster on the motorway that the lane will one day become. *The Stone Tape* (1972) offered the opposite proposition, present-day researchers beset by spirits trapped in the fabric of an old building. Another pair was prompted by the prospect of a grossly overpopulated planet. In *Wine of India* (1970) human beings earn a contract to dwell on earth, the span depending on each one's usefulness, and agree to euthanasia when their time is up. In the earlier but extraordinarily prescient *The Year of the Sex Olympics* (1968) the natural urge to make love and have children has been deliberately corrupted by non-stop pornography on all television channels, in particular a peep-show anticipating the 'reality television' that actually manifested itself within twenty years.

A temporary set-back was the BBC's decision not to go ahead, on cost grounds, with a four-part epilogue to the Quatermass canon. Thames Television took over the project and in 1979 brought the concerns of the now aged professor, played by John Mills, to a respectable and rather touching conclusion—or what would have been so had not a new channel, BBC4, mounted a foolhardy live performance, in 2006, of the original *Quatermass Experiment* scenario. Kneale watched it in dismay. The deepest disappointment of all was when, back in the 1970s, and again because of costs, Associated Television (ATV) abandoned production of his only major script rooted in Manx history. This was *Crow*, derived from the exploits of a notorious pirate and slave-runner. The consolation here came when Kneale's son, Matthew, drew on his father's researches for the background to his *English Passengers*, which won the Whitbread award in 2001.

From 1962 Kneale and his family lived on Barnes Common, London, where Kneale's friend and mentor Rudy

Cartier had also settled. He continued to contribute to such popular television series as *Kavanagh QC*, and he and his wife, Judith, enjoyed travel within the limitations of his aversion to sunlight. He died at the Chelsea and Westminster Hospital, London, on 29 October 2006 of multiple organ failure. He was cremated at Mortlake cemetery, Surrey, on 6 November and his ashes were scattered on Barnes Common, where also a tree was planted in his memory. He was survived by his wife, his son, and his daughter, Tracy. PHILIP PURSER

Sources A. Briggs, *The history of broadcasting in the United Kingdom*, 4 (1979), 689 · *The Times* (2 Nov 2006); (21 Nov 2006) · *The Guardian* (2 Nov 2006); (3 Nov 2006) · *The Independent* (2 Nov 2006) · *Daily Telegraph* (3 Nov 2006) · personal knowledge (2010) · private information (2010) · b. cert. · m. cert. · d. cert.

Archives Manx Museum, Douglas, Isle of Man | SOUND BL NSA, performance recording · BL NSA, documentary recording

Likenesses J. Kneale, sketch, 1956, priv. coll. · obituary photographs

Wealth at death £354,133: probate, 21 June 2007, *CGPLA Eng. & Wales*

Knowles, Jeremy Randall (1935–2008), chemist, was born on 28 April 1935 at 1 Murray Road, Rugby, Warwickshire, the younger son of Kenneth Guy Jack Charles Knowles (1908–1988), schoolmaster, and his first wife, Dorothy Helen, *née* Swingler. His father subsequently taught economic history at University College, Nottingham, before taking a post at the Institute of Economics and Statistics in Oxford; while there he published seminal statistical works on strikes and on wage patterns in industry in the UK.

From 1948 to 1953 Knowles was educated at Magdalen College School, Oxford. For the next two years he did national service as a pilot officer in the Royal Air Force, working primarily as a radar controller. He was the Sir Louis Stuart exhibitioner at Balliol College, Oxford, where he read chemistry from 1955 to 1959 and was taught by R. P. Bell, W. A. Waters, and R. J. P. Williams, all fellows of the Royal Society. He was awarded a first-class degree, having written his undergraduate thesis on the role of hyperconjugation in aromatic substitution. He continued his research in the Oxford laboratory of the physical organic chemist Richard O. C. Norman, receiving his DPhil degree in 1961 for a thesis on intramolecular effects in aromatic systems. This work was completed while Knowles was a Harmsworth senior scholar of Merton College and lecturer at Christ Church, Oxford. On 30 July 1960 he married Jane Sheldon Davis (*b.* 1938), daughter of Herbert John Davis, professor of English literature at Oxford and a noted authority on Swift. They had three sons, Sebastian (*b.* 1961), Julius (*b.* 1963), and Timothy (*b.* 1965).

In 1961–2 Knowles took leave for six months to work with the organic photochemist George S. Hammond at the California Institute of Technology. There extensive discourse with J. Bryan Jones, who like Knowles was an Oxford DPhil and who was doing postdoctoral work on enzymes, made the allure of these biological catalysts overwhelming. On returning to Oxford as a fellow of Wadham College, Knowles focused his attention on the glycolytic enzyme triosephosphate isomerase. He realized that the simple reaction that it catalysed facilitated detailed characterization. In the early 1970s he subjected triosephosphate isomerase to sixteen experiments, each employing isotopes of hydrogen in a distinct but incisive manner. The ensuing data, which were interpreted in collaboration with the Oxford physical chemist W. John Albery and reported in a series of eight papers in 1976, led to the elucidation of the first free energy profile for an enzyme-catalysed reaction. Surprisingly the energy of each enzyme-bound intermediate was comparable, as was the energy of each flanking transition state. This equanimity led Knowles and Albery to anoint triosephosphate isomerase as a 'perfect' enzyme and led to penetrating insights about the evolution of enzymatic catalysis.

Extended time at Illinois in 1962, Yale in 1969 and 1971, and Harvard in 1973 enticed Knowles to move to the United States. He joined the faculty at Harvard University in the autumn of 1974. Along with his Harvard colleagues Konrad E. Bloch and Frank H. Westheimer he established the roots of biological chemistry on that campus. In 1979 he was named the Amory Houghton professor of chemistry and biochemistry. At Harvard he continued to make broad and seminal contributions to chemical enzymology. His work on β-lactamases, their inhibition, and their localization spanned the realms of organic chemistry and microbiology. Fascinating enzymatic mechanisms were revealed in the shikimic acid pathway of plants and microbes, and intellectual seeds were planted for 'green' chemistry. Phosphoryl groups, chiral by virtue of oxygen isotopes, were synthesized, and the stereochemical consequences of their transfer were discerned by clever mass spectrometric and phosphorus-31 NMR spectroscopic methods. This work provided the first direct evidence (in 1982) for pseudorotation in the reaction of a phosphate monoester and (in 1988) of monomeric metaphosphate, which had long been sought as a solvated species.

A decade after triosephosphate isomerase, proline racemase provided a coda, along with more notable discoveries. In a series of seven papers in 1986 Knowles and Albery revealed the consequences of 'oversaturation', a regime in which catalysis is limited by the interconversion of distinct unliganded forms of the enzyme. They also described an elegant kinetic isotope experiment that reveals, without ambiguity, whether a reaction proceeds in a stepwise or concerted manner. By 1991 thirty years of rigorous analyses had convinced Knowles that enzymic catalysts were 'not different, just better'. Though most renowned as an enzymologist, he made landmark contributions to other aspects of biological chemistry. In 1968 he and Frederic M. Richards deduced the mechanism and products of chemical crosslinking by glutaraldehyde. In 1972 he developed the method of photoaffinity labelling.

These accomplishments led to Knowles becoming a fellow of the Royal Society (1977), the American Academy of Arts and Sciences (1982), and the American Philosophical Society (1988); a foreign associate of the National Academy of Sciences (1988); and a trustee of the Howard Hughes Medical Institute (1988). He was awarded the Davy medal of the Royal Society (1991); the Prelog medal of the Eidgenössische Technische Hochschule in Zürich (1989); the Bader award, Repligen award, and Nakanishi award of the American Chemical Society (1989, 1993, and 1999 respectively); and the Robert A. Welch award in chemistry (1995). He was an honorary fellow of Balliol and Wadham colleges, Oxford, and a recipient of honorary degrees from the University of Edinburgh and the Eidgenössische Technische Hochschule. He was the Newton–Abraham visiting professor at Oxford in 1983–4. He was appointed CBE in 1993. In 2008 the Royal Society of Chemistry established the Jeremy Knowles award 'to recognise and promote the importance of inter- and multi-disciplinary research between chemistry and the life sciences'.

In 1991 Knowles accepted an offer to become the dean of the faculty of arts and sciences, one that he had declined in 1983, and he closed his research laboratory. Intellectual sensitivity, born of genuine appreciation for the full spectrum of academic disciplines, made him especially well suited for this new challenge. Integrating extraordinary intellectual acuity with polished charm, eloquence, and wit, he was able to restore financial equilibrium to Harvard while renewing its expansion and renovation. He served in University Hall until 2002, and returned again as interim dean from 2006 to 2007, following a period of turbulence in the university.

Having transformed both chemical enzymology and Harvard University, Knowles died on 3 April 2008 at his home in Cambridge, Massachusetts, following a prolonged struggle with prostate cancer. On 12 April he was buried in the Mount Auburn cemetery on a hillside that affords a panoramic view of Harvard. On 30 May, a memorial service filled the Memorial Church on the Harvard campus. He was survived by his wife, Jane, and their three sons. RONALD T. RAINES

Sources *Chemistry in Britain* (1973), 283–4 · J. R. Knowles, 'Enzyme catalysis: not different, just better', *Nature*, 350/6314 (1991), 121–4 · *The Harvard Crimson* (16 Oct 1991); (3 June 1997); (4 April 2008) · D. E. Hansen, 'Jeremy R. Knowles: the evolution of an enzymologist', *Bioorganic Chemistry*, 23/4 (1995), 303–39 · *Boston Globe* (6 April 2008) · *Daily Telegraph* (9 April 2008) · *The Times* (22 April 2008) · *ACS Chemical Biology*, 3/5 (May 2008), 262–4 · *The Biochemist*, 30/3 (June 2008), 46–7 · *Nature Chemical Biology*, 4/6 (June 2008), 325 · *Harvard Magazine* (July–Aug 2008) · *Harvard Gazette* (14 May 2009) · *Memoirs FRS*, 56 (2010), 171–87 · *WW* (2008) · personal knowledge (2012) · b. cert. · m. cert.

Archives Bodl. Oxf., papers relating to Oxford Enzyme Group

Likenesses obituary photographs

Koerner, Roy Martindale [Fritz] (1932–2008), glaciologist and polar explorer, was born at 40 Kimbolton Road, Portsmouth, Hampshire, on 3 July 1932, the youngest of three sons of Bernard William Koerner (1898–1974), an electrical wireman at Portsmouth Dockyard, and his wife, Minnie, *née* Martindale (1897–1984). He attended Portsmouth Southern Grammar School and Sheffield University from where he graduated with a degree in geography in 1954. He taught for a spell, then in 1957 joined the Falklands Islands Dependencies Survey, and was posted for two years as a meteorologist to Hope Bay (later the Argentine station of Esperanza) at the northern tip of the Antarctic peninsula. There he learned to drive dogs and also developed a deep interest in glaciers.

In 1961 Koerner joined the Arctic Institute of North America's Devon Island expedition, as a glaciologist, working on the island's ice cap (covering roughly 3600 square miles). After wintering at the expedition's base-camp at Truelove Inlet he set out a radial network of mass-balance transects stretching for hundreds of miles and reaching every corner of the ice cap. Mass balance studies are aimed at discovering the budget of a glacier or ice cap, that is, whether it is growing, shrinking, or stable. Koerner repeated these transects annually for over forty-five years, and initiated similar studies on the Agassiz ice cap on Ellesmere Island and the Meighen Island ice cap in later years. Having enrolled in the PhD programme at the London School of Economics, he wrote his dissertation on the results of his work on Devon Island and was awarded the degree in 1968. While in London he met his future wife, Anna Kowalczyk, a Polish au pair. They were married in 1964. Thereafter she accompanied Koerner and assisted him on the Devon Island ice cap for several seasons. They had three daughters, Eva, Davina, and Kristina, and a son, Justin.

In 1966 Koerner joined the Institute for Polar Studies at Ohio State University in Columbus, Ohio, and in 1966–7 spent the southern summer at the Plateau Station near the summit of the Antarctic ice sheet at a height of 12,000 feet. There he concentrated on snow stratigraphy. From 1967 to 1969 he was a member of the four-man British transarctic expedition led by Walter (Wally) Herbert, whom Koerner had first met at Hope Bay. A 'practice run' took the expedition from Qanaq, north-west Greenland, across Ellesmere Island and around Axel Heiberg Island in the spring of 1967. Travelling by dog-sledge, the group left Point Barrow, Alaska, on 21 February 1968, reached the north pole on 5 April 1969, and Vesle Tavleøya, an islet off the north coast of Svalbard, on 29 May 1969. The party was supplied by air-drops by the Royal Canadian Air Force, which allowed them to camp for the period of winter darkness. This crossing, a distance of 3620 miles, was the first surface crossing of the Arctic Ocean and theirs was only the second expedition undisputedly to have reached the north pole (the first being the expedition led by the American Ralph Plaisted, which reached the north pole by snowmobile in April 1968). For Koerner it was more than just an adventure; he made a detailed study of the weather and sea ice and his was the first detailed, continuous survey of sea-ice thickness and characteristics on a complete transit of the Arctic Ocean. His data provided crucial baseline data for subsequent studies of the thinning and shrinkage of the sea ice of the Arctic Ocean.

In 1969 Fritz and Anna Koerner moved to Ottawa, where he joined the Polar Continental Shelf Project, an Arctic research and logistics arm of the Canadian government, to continue his glacier studies in the high Arctic. He became head of the project's ice core laboratory, which later came under the umbrella of the geological survey of

Canada. While continuing his work on Devon Island, he made oxygen-isotope studies of ice cores from the Agassiz ice cap, the cores extending from the surface down to bedrock. A study of the cores revealed summer temperatures back to 9000 BC. The late twentieth- and early twenty-first-century discourse on global climate change relied heavily on his ice core data. Koerner's publications included more than seventy scientific papers and chapters, many of them seminal.

Koerner's wife, Anna, died in 1989 after a prolonged illness which for long periods had effectively left Koerner as a single parent to his four children. After formally retiring in 1999 he continued his glaciological research as an emeritus scientist with the geological survey of Canada. He missed only two field seasons in the Canadian high Arctic between 1961 and 2008. In retirement he assumed a second role, that of guide, mentor, and instructor to school children on cruises to the Arctic and Antarctic with 'Students on Ice'. He could be hilariously funny and his wickedly irreverent, iconoclastic sense of humour appealed enormously to his young charges. A marathon-runner, a jogger in later life, and a regular competitor in the Ottawa–Montreal ski race, he was always very fit. None the less, feeling unwell during his 2008 Arctic field season, he cut short his field work and returned to Ottawa. He died of colon cancer on 26 May, only a few weeks after his return from the field; from his hospital bed he consulted with colleagues to ensure that his research projects would be continued. He was survived by his four children. WILLIAM BARR

Sources W. Herbert, *Across the top of the world: the British trans-Arctic expedition* (1969) • International Glaciological Society website, 26 May 2008, www.igsoc.org/news/fritzkoerner/index.html, 27 April 2011 • *Daily Telegraph* (30 May 2008) • *Ottawa Citizen* (1 June 2008) • *Gazette* [Montreal] (1 June 2008) • *Edmonton Journal* [Alberta] (1 June 2008) • *The Times* (4 June 2008) • *Globe and Mail* [Toronto] (14 June 2008); (30 June 2008) • *The Guardian* (13 Aug 2008) • personal knowledge (2012) • private information (2012) • b. cert.

Likenesses group portrait, photographs, 1968–9, Photoshot, London • group portrait, photograph, 1969, Rex Features, London • photographs, 1969–2006, Getty Images, London • obituary photographs

Kogan, Maurice (1930–2007), civil servant and scholar of education and public policy, was born Maurice Cohen on 10 April 1930 at 48 Stephens Road, West Ham, London. He and his identical twin, Philip, were the youngest of five boys and one girl of Barnett Cohen, born Barnett Kogan (1884/5–1935), and his wife, Hetty, *née* Vicker (1893–1978). The family was Jewish; his father, who had fought for Britain in the First World War, came from Russia, his mother from Poland. Though the birth certificates of the twins were in the name Cohen, their passports were always in the name Kogan, the story being that Barnett, arriving in England as Kogan, assumed the Anglicized form Cohen under family pressure, but the family reverted to the Russian form Kogan after 1945. When Maurice and Philip were four their father died and their mother ran a sweet-shop to make ends meet.

The young Maurice Kogan won a place at Stratford grammar school in east London. Hard working, politically minded, he typified the clever grammar school pupils given a chance by the Education Act of 1944. He won an exhibition to read history at Christ's College, Cambridge, and went on to gain a first in the historical tripos in 1953. In the same year he also achieved first place in the home civil service administrative grade examinations. Preferring, as he put it, the hands-on intrigues of Whitehall to the archival intrigues of medieval popes, he chose the Ministry of Education, where he was to remain for fourteen years.

On 11 August 1960 he married Ulla-Britta Astrid Svensson, daughter of Vilehard Svensson, florist. The marriage took place in Stockholm, the city in which she had been born and brought up. The newly married couple immediately set off for the United States on the Harkness fellowship that Kogan had been awarded for 1960–61, which gave him visiting status at Harvard, Chicago, and Stanford. On their return they settled in a terrace house in Islington decades before the area became fashionable, and had two sons, Tom and Peter. After the children started school Ulla became a social worker. Later they bought a house in Suffolk.

Kogan stayed in the Ministry of Education (from 1964 the Department of Education and Science) until 1967. He had been identified early as a high-flyer. From 1957 to 1959 he was private secretary to Sir Edward Boyle, at the time an influential parliamentary secretary. From 1963 to 1966 he was secretary to the Central Advisory Council (England) which, under the chairmanship of Bridget, Lady Plowden, produced a ground-breaking report on child-centred primary education. He was rewarded with promotion to assistant secretary status in 1966. During his time at the Central Advisory Council he and his superiors had hoped he would have a spell in the prime minister's office, another marker of his civil service career potential. But Lady Plowden, a forceful chairman, would not let him go.

In 1967 Kogan, convinced he had missed his civil service chance, moved into academia, joining Brunel University as director of the Hospital Organisation Unit. Brunel was a former college of advanced technology which had become a university in 1966, following the 1963 Robbins report on higher education. Though the former colleges of advanced technology did not have the cachet of Oxford and Cambridge, the major civic universities, or the new campuses like Sussex and York, Brunel stood out as attracting some very distinguished social scientists who believed that 'the new map of knowledge' of the 1960s should include technological institutions. They included Elliott Jaques, Keith Hopkins, Dan Miller, and John Vaizey. In 1969 Kogan became professor of government and social administration. In 1970 he was made head of department, a post he held for twenty years. From 1971 he was dean of the faculty of social sciences. In 1989 he became acting vice-chancellor for nine months, following the sudden death of the incumbent. By that time he was such an internationally acclaimed scholar of public policy, and particularly higher education, that full-time academic politics and management did not tempt him—other than 'their bloody great cars and their salaries' (personal knowledge).

In 1990 Brunel established the Centre for the Evaluation of Public Policy, which he directed until 2004.

Kogan produced many notable publications over forty years. Four books came out in 1971 alone, built around the public policy contracts he had won for Brunel and his experience at the Ministry of Education. By the end of his life he had produced almost forty books and about seventy articles. Their themes were power, politics, policies, and the processes of change, with a focus on public policy and the way in which forms of knowledge, the governance of knowledge, and professional values interacted with institutional change. There were important books on health but the majority were on education, especially higher education, and latterly on issues of evaluation. A hallmark was what came to be called evidence-based research (a revealing comment on social-science research of the 1970s and 1980s). Illuminated by empirical evidence, the conclusions of Kogan and the collaborators with whom he regularly worked (including Tony Becher, Mary Henkel, Ivar Bleiklie, and Stephen Hanney) were major contributions in conceptualizing the shift that was taking place from government to governance, and in particular how conflicts of values, beliefs about knowledge, and institutional pressures work out within political and administrative systems.

Notable among these 'evidence-based' books were *The Politics of Education* (1971), an analytic conversation guided by Kogan between politically opposed ministers of education; *County Hall* (1973), on the inner London education authority; *Directors of Education* (with Tony Bush, 1982); *Government and Research: the Rothschild Experiment in a Government Department* (with Mary Henkel, 1983; second edn, 2006), a study of the Department of Health (unravelling the issue of how government and scientists interacted on policy gave Kogan great satisfaction and continued to illuminate his thinking); *Reforming Higher Education* (with Stephen Hanney, 2000); and *Transforming Higher Education* (with Marianne Bauer, Ivar Bleiklie, Mary Henkel, and others, 2000; second edn, 2006). In parallel were Kogan's works that were destined to become standard social-science texts exploring policy-making theory: *Educational Policy-Making* (1975), *The Politics of Educational Change* (1978), and, most important, *Process and Structure in Higher Education* (with Tony Becher, 1980; second edn, 1992).

A third group of publications reflected Kogan's passionate engagement in political issues. Notable among these were the two books he co-wrote with his journalist nephew David Kogan. The first was *The Battle for the Labour Party* (1982). Horrified by the advance in London politics of the so-called Outside Left—the unlikely alliance of Trotskyists, Communist Party members, and supporters of Tony Benn MP—they uncovered the process by which the Outside Left's preferred candidate, Ken Livingstone, was able to seize the leadership of the London Labour Party and the Greater London council in 1981. *The Attack on Higher Education* (1983) followed, chronicling the undermining of the collegial tradition in the management of universities. Both reflected Kogan's passionate beliefs as much as his rigour.

Kogan was much in demand for national and international public-policy inquiries; his public service included membership of the Davies committee on hospital complaints procedure (1971), the Houghton committee on teachers' pay (1974), the education sub-committee of the University Grants Committee (1972–5), and the Social Science Research Council (1975–7). He undertook reviews for the Organization for Economic Cooperation and Development of education or higher education policy in the USA, Finland, Greece, Sweden, and Norway, and for many years edited its journal *Higher Education Management and Policy*. In 1988 he was one of the founders of the academically respected Consortium of Higher Education Researchers. In 2000 he became a founding fellow of the Academy of Social Sciences. He received honorary doctorates from two universities (Hull, 1987; Brunel, 1991).

The respect, affection, and gratitude in which Maurice Kogan was held was demonstrated on his birthday in 2005, when leading scholars of higher education came from around the world to offer him a Festschrift devoted to themes on which he had provided inspiration and leadership. Edited by his long-time collaborators Mary Henkel and Ivar Bleiklie, *Governing Knowledge* showed how much his rigorous and humane work had permeated scholarship and public-policy thinking. Although already diagnosed with a cancer that doctors expected to carry him off before then, he lived almost two years more. He died on 6 January 2007, survived by his wife, Ulla, and their sons.

ANNE CORBETT

Sources *The Times* (12 Jan 2007) · *The Independent* (13 Jan 2007) · *The Guardian* (10 Jan 2007) · *WW* (2007) · personal knowledge (2011) · private information (2011) · b. cert.
Likenesses obituary photographs
Wealth at death £653,388: probate, 13 April 2007, *CGPLA Eng. & Wales*

Kossoff, David (1919–2005), actor and broadcaster, was born on 24 November 1919, at the Mothers' Hospital, Clapton, London, the son of Lewis (Louis) Kossoff, tailor, and his wife, Annie, *née* Shaklovich. At the time of his birth registration his parents, Russian Jewish immigrants, lived at 104 Amhurst Road, Hackney. He was educated at an elementary school in east London and the Northern Polytechnic, London, which he left in 1937. The poverty of his parents, and those he saw around him, made him determined to do something better with his life. He spent a year as a draughtsman, took up interior design, especially of furniture, and was working on aircraft design when he told his appalled parents that he wanted to become an actor, reasoning that this was a good way of meeting attractive women. Years later he joked that his parents were so disturbed about the insecurity of an actor's life that they must have been the only parents of a son of call-up age in Britain who were relieved when the Second World War broke out. In the event he spent the war as a technical illustrator. On 3 October 1940, at Hackney register office, he married Elizabeth Kennedy, a 22-year-old member of the Women's Auxiliary Fire Service, and daughter of Richard McLeod Kennedy, civil engineer.

Kossoff made his début as an actor in 1943; he had joined

David Kossoff (1919–2005), by unknown photographer, 1987

the left-wing Unity Theatre at the end of the previous year, and at twenty-three played the part of Juan Rojo in *The Spanish Village*, a play about the Spanish Civil War. He remained with the Unity Theatre for three years, directing as well as acting in plays that were specially selected to entertain people who had had to spend night after night in air-raid shelters. When the war ended in 1945 he joined the BBC Drama Repertory Company, staying with it for six years. During this time he combined his radio acting with illustrating and designing. His first marriage having ended in divorce, on 25 September 1947 he married Marjorie Eileen (otherwise Margaret or Jennie) Hunt, the thirty-year-old daughter of Francis Jenkins, scientific instrument maker, and former wife of John Hunt. They had two sons.

It was his first major West End success, in Peter Ustinov's sometimes surreal play *The Love of Four Colonels*, that convinced Kossoff that he could become a full-time actor. At Wyndham's theatre in 1952 he took over the part of the Russian colonel, Alexander Ikonenko, one of four colonels representing the four victorious post-war powers in Berlin—the Russians, the Americans, the British, and the French. Despite his youth Kossoff gave a convincing and much praised performance of a Russian of narrow materialist vision who is incredulous and alarmed when things occur that do not follow his logic. He later again played a Russian—a KGB spy—in the film *The Iron Petticoat* (1956), starring Katharine Hepburn and Bob Hope. But although it was in 1953 that he made his film début in *The Good Beginning*, it was in Wolf Mankowitz's *The Bespoke Overcoat* at the Arts Theatre in 1953 (as in Jack Clayton's 1956 film version), in which he played the sympathetic and philosophizing tailor Morry, and *A Kid for Two Farthings* (1955), in which he played the same sort of role and gained a British Academy award, that he established his reputation as a 'natural' for playing Jewish men, often elderly and certainly philosophical, benevolent, and sympathetic. In *A Kid for Two Farthings* he was the elderly confidant of a boy who believes that his goat with only one remaining horn is really a unicorn.

In the late 1950s Kossoff was best known for playing the vulgar but endearing old scalliwag Alf Larkin in the television series *The Larkins* (1958–60 and 1963–4), based on the novels of H. E. Bates. To those who suggested that Alf the amiable oaf did not fully extend Kossoff's powers, the latter was apt to reply, as he did to one journalist:

> Alf earns ten times as much as Kossoff, mate. He helps Kossoff choose the parts he wants in straight plays and to say 'No' to the others. I like Alf. A lot of hard work went into creating him. He's probably the best thing I've ever done. (*The Guardian*, 24 March 2005)

The fact that his Alf was to record cockney songs on several records and star in a film spin-off, *Inn for Trouble* (1960), added to his satisfaction.

In 1961 Kossoff started reading his own idiosyncratic versions of Bible stories on BBC Home Service's 'Lift Up Your Hearts'. They became so popular that before long he had several radio series built around him as biblical raconteur, leading to the publication of pamphlets that in turn led to books, which then featured in television series. In the latter his square beard, heavy spectacles, and thoughtfully furrowed brow became his instantly recognizable trade mark. The stories were his own interpretations of incidents in the Old Testament, such as Jonah and the whale. Possibly because he would now be dealing with Christian beliefs, and might be thought to be mocking people other than himself, he was less at ease when he moved on from the Old Testament to the New Testament, admitting that he had done so only after numerous requests by the BBC. His play, *Big Night for Shylock*, was produced in 1968. His prayer book, *You Have a Minute, Lord?* (1977), was more characteristic, a logical extension of his flair for inoffensive humour. One of the texts was 'Must a person suffer fools, Lord?', which addressed the biblical injunction to make time for other people:

> But *all* people, Lord? *All?*
> The bigoted, the ignorant, the intolerant,
> the small-minded, the envious, the
> self-centred, the vain, the patronising,
> the phoney, the wicked?
> *Must I, Lord?*
> (*You Have a Minute, Lord?*, 31–2)

Kossoff's other books included *Bible Stories Retold by David Kossoff* (1968), *The Book of Witnesses* (1971), *The Three Donkeys* (1972), *The Voices of Masada* (1973), *The Little Book of Sylvanus* (1975), *A Town is a World* (1979), based on nineteenth-century Russian Jewish folk tales, *Sweet Nutcracker* (1985), and *The Old and the New* (2002). He wrote many of them, or corrected their proofs, while waiting in his theatre or studio dressing room to make his entry in plays, and claimed that his passion for writing was helped by the fact that he had never had a rejection slip. He was also highly popular in his one-man show based on reflections about religious matters, 'As According to Kossoff', which toured from 1970. Once his show consisted of him in a real restaurant, joining diners at their various tables, talking to them, and ultimately involving them in the act. This particular run was comparatively short.

Kossoff's second son, Paul *Kossoff (1950–1976), guitarist with the rock group Free, died at the age of twenty-five of a heart attack as the result of drug addiction. Kossoff had abandoned much of his other work to campaign against drugs when his son had had an earlier heart attack and appeared to have successfully given up drugs. When the withdrawal was not after all a success and Paul died Kossoff travelled widely, performing *The Late Great Paul* as a memorial to him, taking no money for himself. He could laugh at himself for usually being more financially minded. After he had made many lucrative commercials, he pointed out that Bible stories didn't pay extraordinarily well, but commercials did—and anyway 'it just occurred to me that God might have guided my hand to J. Walter Thompson' (*The Guardian*, 24 March 2005). He lived latterly at 45 Roe Green Close, College Lane, Hatfield, Hertfordshire. His wife predeceased him in 1995 and he died of cancer of the colon at St Christopher's Nursing Home, Drakes Way, Hatfield, on 23 March 2005. He was survived by his son Simon. DENNIS BARKER

Sources *The Times* (24 March 2005) · *Daily Telegraph* (24 March 2005) · *The Guardian* (24 March 2005) · *The Independent* (25 March 2005) · *WW* (2005) · personal knowledge (2009) · private information (2009) · b. cert. · m. certs. · d. cert.

Archives U. Southampton L. | FILM BFINA, 'The book of witnesses', W. Cartner (director), 16 June 1972 · BFINA, 'David and Paul', *Anno domini*, P. Armstrong (producer), BBC1, 19 Sept 1976 · BFINA, *Time to talk*, H. Raggett (director), Channel 4, 12 March 1992 · BFINA, documentary footage · BFINA, performance footage | SOUND BL NSA, AIRC programme sharing collection, broadcast LBC, 4 Dec 1989, C100/014/89/1 · BL NSA, documentary recordings · BL NSA, performance recordings

Likenesses photographs, 1954–79, Getty Images, London · photographs, 1955–91, Rex Features, London · J. Ayling, miniature, 1982, priv. coll. · photograph, 1987, Rex Features, London [*see illus.*] · obituary photographs

Wealth at death £905,708: probate, 18 Nov 2005, *CGPLA Eng. & Wales*

Kwok, Sui King [Lily] **(1918–2007)**, restaurateur, was born Sui King Leung in rural Guangdong (Kwangtung) province near Guangzhou (Canton), China, on 26 September 1918, the third of six daughters (there were no sons) of Leung, businessman, and his wife, Tai Po. She grew up in poverty. Her family survived primarily through subsistence farming and some work at a silk factory in Guangzhou. Her father eventually established a soy sauce factory processing surplus soya beans from the family farm into soy sauce, which was then sold on to restaurants in Hong Kong for a premium. His business became profitable and in 1925, at the age of seven, Sui King and her family migrated to Hong Kong. Rival producers took note of the booming enterprise and murdered Leung in his Guangzhou factory. Inheritance laws in China prohibited women from owning property, and the business passed to his nephew, leaving his widow and daughters penniless.

Sui King and her sisters picked up odd jobs sewing restaurant tablecloths, delivering letters, and collecting parcels to make ends meet. She eventually found stable employment working as a maid for expatriate families. It was during this period that she learned to cook a variety of Chinese and international dishes, catering for the tastes of her employers. Two of her classic dishes were developed at this time: her claypot chicken twice baked with shiitake mushrooms, and a savoury sauce for serving alongside Chinese lap cheong sausages.

Sui King met her husband, Kwok Chan, as a teenager. They were married in 1946. The first of their children, Ah Dar (Arthur), was born in 1947, and Bo Yee (Mabel) was born in 1950. A third child, Ah Bing, was born in 1953. By then estranged from her alcoholic and debt-ridden husband and unable to provide for an additional child, Sui King gave Ah Bing up for adoption by the Lees, a childless Chinese couple. Shortly after the birth of Mabel she had nevertheless found permanent employment with the Woodmans, an expatriate English family who lived on Robinson Road, Hong Kong. She cared for the children and was companion to the elder Mrs Woodman, who gave her an English name, Lily, which she adopted.

In 1953 Lily Kwok left Hong Kong with the Woodmans, leaving behind her children and estranged husband. Travelling aboard the P&O-owned SS *Canton* she developed what would become her signature chicken curry by the addition of a coconut base, self-raising flour for a light texture, and a secret mixture of spices. She continued her employment with the Woodmans upon arrival in Somerset. An inheritance following the death of the elder Mrs Woodman enabled her to return to Hong Kong in 1959 to collect her children. A loan from the Woodman family that same year also provided her with the funds to start her first restaurant in Manchester.

A site in Middleton, located eight miles from Manchester, was chosen as the location of Lily Kwok's new restaurant, Lung Fung, one of the first Chinese restaurants in the greater Manchester area. It opened in 1959 at the corner of Taylor Street and Oldham Road. Lung Fung served a mixture of English and Chinese dishes and soon developed a local following. The restaurant opened until 3 a.m. on Friday and Saturday evenings and became a popular after-hours haunt for musicians and celebrities like the Hollies and Cliff Richard. In 1960 Kwok Chan, the estranged husband whom Lily had left behind in Hong Kong, scraped together enough funds to travel to Middleton. Suffering from the effects of years of heavy drinking, he died less than a year later. Lily Kwok never remarried after his death.

The culinary and financial success of Lung Fung in the 1960s enabled Lily Kwok to expand her business to two takeaways in Bury and Blackburn. But in the 1970s a gambling habit and large debts led her to sell the takeaways and eventually Lung Fung. She later established a new takeaway, Lung Fung Too, but its business never matched the popularity of the original restaurant. She retired in 1993, leaving other members of her family to continue in the restaurant business. Her granddaughters Lisa, Helen, and Janet Tse became the third generation of restaurateurs in 2004, as co-owners of Sweet Mandarin in Manchester. Lily Kwok's chicken curry and other signature dishes, first served at Lung Fung in the 1950s, were featured as regular menu selections in honour of her work as one of Britain's pioneering Chinese restaurateurs and her dedication to Chinese cuisine. In 2007 her granddaughter Helen Tse published her biography, *Sweet Mandarin*. Lily Kwok died on 8 December 2007 at Springfield Park Nursing Home, Rochdale, of cancer. She had been reunited with her daughter Ah Bing, and was survived by all three children. WILLA ZHEN

Sources H. Tse, *Sweet Mandarin* (2007) · *Manchester Evening News* (2 Feb 2007); (19 Dec 2007) · *Evening Standard* (21 April 2007) · www.dimsum.co.uk/community/sweet-mandarins-lily-kwok–a-chinese-icon-dies.html, 5 May 2010 · *The Times* (27 Dec 2007); (1 Jan 2008); (7 Jan 2008) · *Daily Express* (29 Dec 2007) · www.sweetmandarin.com, 5 May 2010 · d. cert.

Likenesses photograph, repro. in www.timesonline.co.uk/tol/system/topicRoot/Food_and_Drink/ · photographs, repro. in Tse, *Sweet Mandarin*

Wealth at death under £218,000: probate, 21 July 2008, *CGPLA Eng. & Wales*

Kyle, (John) Keith (1925–2007), journalist, broadcaster, and historian, was born at the nursing home in Sturminster Newton, Dorset, on 4 August 1925, the only child of William Ernest Kyle (1890–1969), land agent, and his wife, Elsie Mary, *née* Maule (1895–1972). His parents were then living in nearby Iwerne Minster. He led a relatively solitary childhood as his parents feared that too close an association with the village children would leave him with an indelible west-country accent. In his early years he was taught at home by his mother, a qualified schoolteacher, who was determined that her son should be the first member of her family to go to both public school and university. At the age of nine he was sent to a nearby preparatory school, Chafyn Grove in Salisbury, from where he won a scholarship to Bromsgrove School in Worcestershire. A delicate boy, never any good at games, he found himself fully at home in the school library. His reward was to win an exhibition to Magdalen College, Oxford. By then the Second World War was well under way but those under the call-up age of eighteen were encouraged to spend two or even three terms at university before being required to join the forces. Kyle spent the Hilary and Trinity terms of 1943 being tutored by the already celebrated Oxford don A. J. P. Taylor, with whom he was to form a lifelong friendship.

Summoned to the colours in November 1943 Kyle at first joined the infantry but later transferred to the Royal Artillery, into which he was commissioned in 1944. Not released from the army until 1946—he spent most of the intervening period serving in India, where he reached the rank of acting captain—he returned to Oxford in the Michaelmas term of 1947, continuing his studies in modern history under Taylor and embarking on medieval history with another celebrated Magdalen don, Bruce McFarlane, as his tutor. A promising pupil, who was also able to play a full part in the university Liberal club (of which he became chairman) and the Oxford Union, he seems to have hoped to become an academic. A disappointing second-class degree in 1950 effectively put an end to that ambition, though Magdalen generously renewed his exhibition, allowing him to spend his last term as secretary of the Oxford Union.

At this time there were real anxieties about Kyle's health. He appears to have suffered from an undiagnosed version of myalgic encephalomyelitis (probably the cause of his relative failure in his degree examinations) and it was with some trepidation that he took up his first job in London. This was at the English Speaking Union headquarters in Mayfair, where he helped to run the organization's publications and meetings. It had not, in fact, been his first choice of employment as he had previously applied for a talks producer's job with the North American service of the BBC. The corporation, though, had taken so long to respond that, despairing of getting a positive answer, Kyle went to the English Speaking Union instead. He was rescued, however, when Bush House (its grant-in-aid from the Foreign Office having finally come through) offered him employment at double the salary he was receiving from the English Speaking Union.

In 1953 Kyle's experience in dealing with North American topics prompted him to apply for a Commonwealth Fund travelling fellowship in the United States. On the awards panel sat Geoffrey Crowther, the editor of *The Economist*, who—according to Kyle's account—gave him a particularly hard time. There was, however, a reason for that, Crowther having decided that the gangling youth in front of him (Kyle stood 6 feet 3 inches in his socks) would make an admirable correspondent for his own paper in Washington. Although it meant sacrificing the Commonwealth fellowship, which Crowther was kind enough to tell him he had already been awarded, Kyle had no hesitation about accepting the *Economist* offer. That autumn he arrived in Washington to take up his post as the first-ever British resident correspondent for the weekly. It was a glittering opportunity, and Kyle seized it with both hands. He was to spend five years working for *The Economist* in the United States, years that saw the formal desegregation of the nation's schools, the bus boycott in Montgomery, Alabama, the 1956 presidential election, and the emergence of the young John F. Kennedy as a potential White House contender. Reporting latterly also for the *News Chronicle* (which had a New York but not a Washington correspondent) Kyle—although his contributions to *The Economist* were necessarily anonymous—effectively made his reputation as a commentator on the American scene.

It was no surprise to his expatriate journalistic colleagues in Washington when Kyle was summoned home in the autumn of 1958 to become *The Economist*'s political and parliamentary correspondent. Again he dazzled and shone. From his first report on a particularly ill-fated Liberal assembly held at Torquay through his coverage of the 1959 general election to his vivid evocation of the gradual disintegration of the Macmillan government, he set a new standard in political reporting. He also became a familiar face on the BBC, appearing regularly on the early evening *Tonight* programme and accepting globe-trotting assignments for a variety of television projects. He left *The Economist* in 1961 but continued to work as a newspaper journalist (notably for *The Observer* and *The Spectator*) as well as a broadcaster (for both the BBC and independent television). His coverage for both media of decolonization in Africa and the Israeli–Palestinian conflict was highly regarded by his fellow professionals.

By now, however, Kyle's own sphere of interest had become the domestic political arena itself. After the 1959 election he shook off the remnants of his Liberal allegiance and joined the Labour Party. On 29 September 1962 he married Susan Mary (Suzy) Harpur, a television current affairs producer eleven years his junior, and daughter of Douglas George David Harpur, vicar of St Michael's Church, St Albans, and it was at St Albans, in the 1966 general election, that he first stood for parliament. Having lost there he did not find a seat for the 1970 general election, but in 1974 he contested the new constituency of Braintree in both the February and the October general elections. Narrowly losing there the first time, just before the second election he suffered a stroke and, though he managed to appear at the eve-of-poll rally, he was still a thousand votes short of victory. That marked, he declared, the end of his parliamentary aspirations and, while he fought one further election—this time for the Social Democratic Party at Northampton South, where he managed to come second in 1983—that proved in effect to be the case.

The rest of Kyle's career, which included eight years, from 1982 to 1990, on the staff of the Royal Institute of International Affairs (Chatham House), could be dismissed as being an anti-climax. But that would be unfair—for in 1991 came his lasting claim to fame, his definitive account of the Suez crisis of 1956. Entitled simply *Suez*, it was easily the best twentieth-century book on that whole bizarre diplomatic and military episode, owing a good deal to the ringside seat that its author occupied in Washington at the time. His other books included *Whither Israel?* (1993), *The Politics of the Independence of Kenya* (1999), and an engaging and remarkably candid volume of autobiography, *Reporting the World*, published posthumously in 2009, but none was to match and certainly not to surpass this model volume of contemporary history which led, quite properly, to his being invited to take up a visiting professorship at the University of Ulster, which he held from 1991 to 1998. He died from an abdominal aortic aneurysm at University College Hospital, Camden, London, on 21 February 2007. His funeral was held at his local church of St Mary, Primrose Hill, on 14 March 2007 and he was cremated at Golders Green crematorium. His wife, Suzy, and two adopted sons survived him.

ANTHONY HOWARD

Sources *Daily Telegraph* (22 Feb 2007) · *The Guardian* (27 Feb 2007) · *The Times* (7 March 2007) · *The Independent* (13 March 2007) · K. Kyle, *Reporting the world* (2009) · personal knowledge (2011) · private information (2011) · b. cert. · m. cert. · d. cert.

Archives Bodl. Oxf. | FILM BFINA, performance footage | SOUND BL NSA, current affairs recordings · BL NSA, documentary recordings

Likenesses J. Chillingworth, photograph, 1950, Getty Images, London, Hult. Arch. · photographs, 1971–83, Photoshot, London · obituary photographs · photograph, repro. in www.guardian.co.uk/books/2009/sep/27/keith-lyle-reporting-the-world · photographs, repro. in Kyle, *Reporting*

Wealth at death £1,017,330: administration with will, 15 July 2009, *CGPLA Eng. & Wales*

Laddie, Sir Hugh Ian Lang (1946–2008), barrister, judge, and legal scholar, was born on 15 April 1946 at 34 Eaton Rise, Ealing, London, the elder son and second of three children of Bertie Daniel Laddie (1915–1987), a solicitor then serving as a captain in the Royal Army Ordnance Corps, and his wife, Rachel, *née* Cohen (*b.* 1917). He was educated at Aldenham School, Hertfordshire, and St Catharine's College, Cambridge, where he originally read medicine but switched midway to law. Called in 1969 to the bar by the Middle Temple, he received a Blackstone pupillage award and joined T. A. Blanco White's chambers (later 8 New Square), a set specializing in intellectual property law. Shortly afterwards, on 2 April 1970, he married, at the New West End Synagogue, London, Stecia Elizabeth Zamet (*b.* 1948), a speech therapist whom he had known from his early teens. She was the daughter of Nathan Zamet, pharmacist. They had two sons and a daughter.

Intellectual property law was not then taught at Cambridge (or most other law faculties) and was widely regarded as rather arcane and fusty, but Laddie, with his interest in science, brought to it an ability to master complex technologies, combined with flair, wit, and impressive research and advocacy skills. At that time right holders felt powerless to prevent their work being freely copied and distributed without authority by small traders, who would dispose of the evidence as soon as they smelled detection. Drawing on old case law about preserving evidence that was in danger of being lost Laddie devised a type of order as close to a search warrant as one could come and set about persuading judges to grant it. Since the order was granted in camera and without notice, the first the suspect knew was finding a solicitor banging on his door with a court order requiring him to allow entry for the purpose of having copying equipment and infringing material seized. Once the order was executed the infringing activity was effectively closed down since few defendants would insist on a full court hearing unless some serious mistake had occurred. Laddie managed to have six such orders made during 1974 and 1975 but was denied one in a case where an English company was suspected of peddling secret drawings and knowhow to the competitors of Laddie's client, a large German electrical manufacturer called Anton Piller KG. Laddie promptly appealed and, in granting the order, the Court of Appeal confirmed the legality of the procedure, and simultaneously the need for stringent safeguards to prevent abuse.

Lord Denning noted that Laddie could 'claim the credit—or the responsibility' for this new procedure and later praised him for his 'enterprise' (*Anton Piller* v. *Manufacturing Processes*, 1975; *Ex parte Island Records*, 1978).

The significance of Laddie's invention of what became universally known as the *Anton Piller* order was profound. Lawyers and judges throughout the Commonwealth embraced it and scholars later identified the case as one of the most significant decisions in intellectual property law ever. Indeed the procedure became a victim of its own success as orders started being made and executed by the thousand well beyond intellectual property cases, sometimes in egregious circumstances and on flimsy evidence. Laddie himself came to argue for better safeguards, and his proposals were largely adopted in a practice note issued in 1994 by the lord chief justice, and given statutory footing as a search and seizure order in the Civil Procedure Act 1997 and the European directive on intellectual property enforcement of 2004.

When Laddie first went to the bar textbooks on intellectual property law were, with a few notable exceptions, tedious and uncritical works. Laddie saw the need for a fresh approach that took full account of rapid advances in technology and the progressive remapping of UK law resulting from Britain's entry into Europe. Collaborating with like-minded members of his chambers—Anthony Walton on patent law, and Peter Prescott and Mary Vitoria on copyright and design law—he co-authored two impressive books that came out in rapid succession: *The Patent Law of Europe and the United Kingdom* (1978) and *The Modern Law of Copyright* (1980). Legal scholars praised *Patent Law* for its 'detailed and stimulating' commentary (Sally Woodward, review of *Terrell on the Law of Patents*, *Cambridge Law Journal*, 42, 1983, 161), and *Copyright Law* as a 'most excellent book' with 'controversial views … supported by rigorous arguments that would be well received if they appeared in learned academic periodicals' (P. J. Russell, book review, *Cambridge Law Journal*, 40, 1981, 372).

Laddie's writing seemed barely to interfere with his legal practice, which had taken off especially after his *Anton Piller* successes, and he became in great demand for all sorts of litigation involving intellectual property. By the time he took silk in 1986 his name was associated with many leading cases, including those in which he had appeared as a junior counsel to the crown. So it continued until 1995, when he accepted an appointment to the High Court as a judge of the Chancery Division and Patents Court and received the usual accompanying knighthood.

Over the next decade Laddie brought to his decisions on patents, copyright, trade marks, designs, and associated common law and equity cases the enthusiasm, directness, clarity, and vigour which had characterized his practice and writing. The speed at which business was conducted in his court caused an observer to comment that '[i]f Laddie had been around in Dickens' day, Jarndyce and Jarndyce would have been over by lunchtime' (*The Guardian*, 24 June 2005). Faced with a notorious House of Lords decision (*American Cyanamid* v. *Ethicon*, 1975) that allowed pretrial injunctions to be granted on merely a 'seriously arguable' case, Laddie wrote (in *Series 5 Software* v. *Clarke*, 1995) a scholarly judgment confining it to cases where difficult questions of law or fact arose. In another case he had to wrestle with an unclear European directive on trade marks and the new English legislation it had spawned. He set out the approach that should be taken towards construing such laws: '[W]hat justifies the monopoly is not the monopoly itself but the extent to which it gives, or is hoped to give, a benefit to commerce which compensates for the temporary restraint on competition … Monopolies are the exception, not the rule … They need to be justified' (*Wagamama* v. *City Centre Restaurants*, 1995).

What justified a particular monopoly may of course strike different judges differently, but Laddie's views were broadly in line with most of his fellow English judges. When Elvis Presley Enterprises Inc. applied to register the late singer's name and signature as UK trade marks to foil an English trader who had long been selling Elvis memorabilia under his own registered Elvis marks Laddie denied the claim, stating that 'Even if Elvis Presley was still alive, he would not be entitled to stop a fan from naming his son, his dog or goldfish, his car or his house "Elvis" or "Elvis Presley" simply by reason of the fact that it was the name given to him at birth by his parents' (*Elvis Presley Trade Marks*, 1997). Laddie's judgment was later upheld in the Court of Appeal.

Laddie's views had more difficulty meshing with the increasingly protectionist stance of the European Court of Justice. When the Arsenal football club adopted a policy of shutting down sellers of unauthorized merchandise bearing Arsenal marks and colours his sympathies clearly lay with the traders who had long sold such merchandise without complaint from Arsenal. He found no public confusion in the case before him but referred some unsettled questions of European trade mark law to the European court for interpretation. When that court delivered a judgment for Arsenal that Laddie thought disregarded his findings of fact at trial, he ruled that the European court had exceeded its jurisdiction and dismissed the action. This time the Court of Appeal would have none of it and reversed Laddie on the basis that the European court was entitled to make the findings it did (*Arsenal FC* v. *Reed*, 2002, 2003).

It is unclear whether such setbacks contributed to Laddie's growing disenchantment with the job of judge, but other things certainly did. He enjoyed accepting the frequent lecturing invitations he received but met resistance from the vice-chancellor to his taking engagements outside the UK, particularly in developing countries, where he thought his expertise was needed. Dealing with his fair share of unfamiliar chancery business, such as taxation and landlord and tenant matters, also started taking its toll. In 2005, loath to let such irritations affect his judicial performance, Laddie abruptly resigned his judgeship (amid newspaper reports claiming he had said he was 'bored', a misquotation that privately upset him), and took a position as a consultant, arbitrator, and mediator for a London firm of intellectual property solicitors and patent and trade mark attorneys. No English judge had resigned quite like this since Sir Henry Fisher in 1970 and, while the public seemed sympathetic, professional and judicial reaction was generally adverse (as evidenced in Ministry of Justice, *Return to Practice by Former Salaried Judges: Response to Consultation*, 2007).

Laddie had one more surprise left. In 2006 University College, London, elected him to a chair in intellectual property law and at his behest established an Institute of Brand and Innovation Law, of which he became director. Once more throwing himself into the job he organized a set of popular seminars on current issues and established academic links with India and China. The critical freedom and intellectual stimulation offered by university life, combined with his consultancy work, clearly suited him. He could also more easily indulge his interests in fly-fishing, music, and theatre.

Shortly after taking up his chair, however, Laddie was diagnosed with prostate cancer, which despite treatment and early signs of remission eventually proved unrelenting. He none the less soldiered on as if nothing was amiss, chairing a public lecture with his usual humour just a few weeks before he died at his home, 1 Heathgate, Hampstead Garden Suburb, on 29 November 2008. He was survived by his wife and children. Friends quickly established at University College an annual lecture series in his name, and also the Sir Hugh Laddie chair in intellectual property, the first incumbent of which was, appropriately enough, his close friend and judicial colleague Sir Robin Jacob.

DAVID VAVER

Sources *The Guardian* (24 June 2005); (2 Dec 2008) • *The Lawyer* (10 Oct 2005) • *The Times* (16 May 2006); (5 Dec 2008) • *Law Society Gazette* (14 Sept 2006) • *UCL News* (6 Dec 2007); (3 Dec 2008) • *Daily Telegraph* (4 Dec 2008) • Burke, *Peerage* • *WW* (2008) • personal knowledge (2012) • private information (2012) • b. cert. • m. cert. • d. cert.
Likenesses photographs, 1986–96, Photoshot, London • photographs, 2006, Getty Images, London • obituary photographs
Wealth at death £349,093: probate, 14 Jan 2010, *CGPLA Eng. & Wales*

Laing, Sir (John) Maurice (1918–2008), industrialist, was born on 1 February 1918 at 42 St James's Road, Carlisle, the younger son of Sir John William *Laing (1879–1978), builder and civil engineering contractor, and his wife Beatrice, *née* Harland (1885–1972). He was brought up in an evangelical Christian household, both parents belonging to the Brethren movement, and educated at St Lawrence College, Ramsgate. He joined John Laing & Son Ltd in 1935, initially as a costing clerk and then an apprentice builder, but took his first managerial role in 1938 and became a director of the business in 1939. On 20 March 1940 he married Hilda Violet Richards (*b.* 1918), a library assistant, and daughter of William Tom Steeper Richards, schoolmaster; they had one son, John (*b.* 1959). Meanwhile in 1941 (against his father's wishes, and despite being in a reserved occupation) he enlisted in the RAF, with which he served for the remainder of the Second World War, including as a glider pilot during the crossing of the Rhine. On demobilization he returned to the family firm, becoming deputy chairman in 1966 and succeeding his brother, Kirby, as chairman in 1976, holding that position until his retirement in 1982. He and Kirby formed an effective partnership, with Kirby concentrating on international projects and Maurice on domestic ones, which ranged from motorway building through the construction of nuclear power stations to house-building. In 1978, concerned by the possibility of the nationalization of construction companies should the Labour Party win the next election, he restructured the company into separate property and construction divisions; Laing Properties was subsequently, in 1990, the victim of a hostile takeover by P&O, which made a good deal of money for the family's charitable trusts but which he saw as destroying the Laing heritage. Though he left the Brethren for the Church of England, he was deeply influenced by his Christian faith, served as president of the London Bible College (1993–9), and continued his father's policies of benevolent paternalism in employee relations. He undertook a wide range of outside appointments, most notably as a director of the Bank of England (1963–80) and as president of the British Employers' Confederation (1964–5), and, following the latter's merger with the Federation of British Industries and the National Association of British Manufacturers, first president of the Confederation of British Industry (1965–6). He was knighted in 1965. He was a keen sailor, serving as admiral of the Royal Ocean Racing Club (1976–82) and president of the Royal Yachting Association (1983–7), and was deeply interested in complementary medicine, funding the Centre for Complementary Medicine at the Peninsula Medical School in Exeter, founded in 1993. He also gave extensively to environmental and development projects in the developing world. He died in London on 22 February 2008 and was survived by his wife and son.

Sources *The Guardian* (25 Feb 2008) • *The Independent* (26 Feb 2008) • *The Times* (29 Feb 2008); (5 March 2008); (11 March 2008); (24 March 2008); (24 May 2008) • *Daily Telegraph* (19 March 2008) • *Times Higher Education Supplement* (19 May 2008) • Burke, *Peerage* • *WW* (2008) • b. cert. • m. cert.
Likenesses obituary photographs

Laker, Sir Frederick Alfred [Freddie] (1922–2006), aviation entrepreneur, was born on 6 August 1922 at 52 New Ruttington Lane, Canterbury, Kent, the son of Frederick Henry Laker, an able seaman in the Royal Navy, later builder, and his wife, Hannah, *née* Todd. His father deserted the family when Freddie was five, and he was brought up by his mother, a shopkeeper and cleaner who later ran a successful scrap metal business.

Education and early working life While attending Simon Langton School in Canterbury, at the age of fourteen Laker is said to have been determined to 'be a millionaire'. His passion for aviation was kindled in 1936 when he saw the German airship *Hindenburg* and an Imperial Airways Handley Page 42 biplane airliner flying over the city. This inspired him to join the Short Brothers flying-boat factory at nearby Rochester, shortly before the outbreak of the Second World War. Although his initial duties were little more than sweeping the floor and making tea, he demonstrated an embryonic entrepreneurial streak, inherited from his mother, by negotiating a bulk price for the tea

Sir Frederick Alfred [Freddie] **Laker** (**1922–2006**), by Ashley Ashwood

from the factory canteen before selling it on to the workers at a profit. Thereafter, he pursued both his aspiration to succeed financially and his passion for aviation, enjoying the high life afforded by the former while always regarding the well-being of his 'everyman' clientele as paramount in the latter.

After the Shorts factory was bombed in 1941 Laker spent a brief period working as a fitter with General Aircraft at Feltham, Middlesex. Despite being in a reserved occupation, to satisfy the urge to fly himself he inveigled his way into the Royal Air Force Air Transport Auxiliary, becoming a qualified flight engineer and pilot and ferrying aircraft from the production factories to service squadrons. Meanwhile, on 10 May 1942 he married Joan Mavis Smallwood, a 25-year-old publisher's clerk, and daughter of Owen Smallwood, accountant. They had a daughter, Elaine, and a son, Kevin, who was killed in a car crash in 1965, aged seventeen.

Laker spent three months with the newly created British European Airways in 1946, but was unable to relate to the state-owned culture, and with his war-ending gratuity of £40 switched to a succession of 'trading' ventures. Buying and selling a wide variety of mechanical items, he achieved his primary objective of establishing his own aviation business a year later. The names he adopted for his first two companies set up to provide a self-supporting independent air transport business—Aviation Traders and Air Charter—effectively described his chosen vocation and his distinctive personal credo. Initially operating Aviation Traders (Engineering) Ltd (ATEL) out of a small garage in Streatham, south-west London, he purchased huge stocks of government-surplus equipment. Also offering his personal service as a consultant, he was given a cheque for £38,000 by a Scottish client, in return for an earlier favour, which he used as starting capital to set up Air Charter Ltd to operate his expanding passenger and cargo charter business—basing both companies at Southend, Essex.

In June 1948 the extraordinary opportunity arose for Laker to gain a very lucrative share in the year-long, round-the-clock Berlin airlift—one of the most expeditious humanitarian logistical operations in modern times. This was desperately needed to frustrate the precipitate Soviet blockade of West Berlin by providing a massive air transport capacity to supply virtually every conceivable kind of consumable material of daily life. Accordingly he deployed a fleet of six Handley Page Haltons (converted war-surplus Halifax bombers), making 2577 round trips and carrying 17,131 tons of supplies—11.6 per cent of the total tonnage delivered—as well as supporting numerous other aircraft types and their operators.

Reverting to large-scale war surplus bomber aircraft conversion and resale for troop carrying and civil use, spare parts, and scrap (thereby long anticipating the vogue for large-scale recycling), in 1951 Laker began flying operations again in what he called his 'little Berlin airlift' to meet the continuing need for supply support and the evacuation of refugees. Another profitable venture came his way in 1952 in the form of a long series of government trooping flights to all parts of the British empire. ATEL also purchased a fleet of Avro Tudor airliners formerly owned by the British Overseas Airways Corporation, which he fitted with large cargo doors, five becoming 'Super Traders', and operated as far afield as Christmas Island in the mid-Pacific.

Laker's next major venture with ATEL was the design and construction of the innovative 28 seat, twin Rolls-Royce Dart propeller-turbine powered, Aviation Traders 'Accountant' airliner, as his own solution to the much-vaunted American Douglas DC-3 Dakota replacement market. Adopting the complete Dart powerplant of the highly successful Vickers Viscount, and a novel tensioned-skin construction concept, the prototype was first flown in July 1957. Laker regarded this project as his greatest achievement—although it also turned out to be his biggest commercial failure. Launching series production was well beyond ATEL's resources. Unable to secure government backing, he sought support from the major British aircraft manufacturers. However, serious negotiations with Avro proved unfruitful and, after spending about £750,000 on the project, he was forced to abandon it in January 1959—whereupon Avro proceeded with its own equivalent, the best-selling 748.

Meanwhile, after Laker bought a Bristol Freighter, his first brand new aircraft (for which type ATEL also built the centre sections), Air Charter began its pioneering Channel Air Bridge service in April 1954, carrying motor vehicles, passengers, cargo, and livestock between Southend and Lympne (Kent), and Calais. Four years later he conceived a most imaginative replacement with his ATL-98 Carvair (car-via-air) conversion of the Douglas DC-4 airliner. This incorporated a completely new front fuselage section with a raised cockpit enabling straight-in nose loading, long before the same concept was applied to the Boeing 747. ATEL produced twenty-two such conversions at Southend, which were distributed throughout the world, eventually operating with seventy-five airlines, transporting cars, royalty, rock groups, refugees, whales, rocket cases, gold, and even nuclear materials. Two were known to be still in service fifty years later.

British United Airways Laker sold ATEL and Air Charter to Airwork, another British independent operator, and in 1960 became managing director of the Gatwick-based British United Airways (BUA), formed by the merger of the Airwork and Hunting Clan empires. It soon acquired Silver City Airways, and thus became the biggest British (and European) independent rival to the state-owned British European Airways and British Overseas Airways Corporation, and hence the UK's third largest airline. Under his commanding leadership BUA operated scheduled services, charters, and government trooping contracts and, significantly, became the launch customer for the newly formed British Aircraft Corporation's BAC One-Eleven (the world's first 'tailored-for-the-job' regional twin-jet airliner), ordering ten 'off the drawing board' with a substantial influence in its design conception. BUA also operated the world's first scheduled hovercraft service, inaugurated on 20 July 1962 with the Vickers SRN2 plying across the five-mile estuary of the River Dee to link Merseyside and north Wales, and operated the world's first city-centre rail–air terminal at its London, Victoria, offices to serve its operating base at Gatwick airport.

By now a formidable figure on the world air transport stage, Laker was also a strong supporter of the Rolls-Royce Conway-powered Vickers VC10 intercontinental airliner, acquiring two of his own version incorporating a large main deck freight loading door. Always flaunting his patriotism, he launched the first aircraft into service by loading Rolls-Royce's Silver Cloud demonstration car into it at the 1964 Farnborough air show to fly direct to east and central Africa, thereby symbolizing the Britishness of the whole operation. This version of the aircraft was particularly suitable for the Royal Air Force, which ordered a fleet of fourteen similarly fitted multi-role military transports.

Laker Airways and Skytrain In October 1965 Laker expressed his firm belief in private enterprise in British air transport by stating that:

> The competitive stimulus that [the independent airline operators] have provided is in the interests of civil aviation and they should be encouraged to participate more in all kinds and in all spheres of scheduled international and domestic passenger and freight services, vehicle ferries and inclusive tours. ('Private enterprise in British air transport')

This was the ethic that prompted him to fulfil the long-held objective of setting up his own airline. Leaving BUA in November 1965, he formed his own 'wholesale' airline, Laker Airways. Launched on the back of the expanding UK inclusive tour holiday market, and using two turbo-prop Bristol Britannias and four newly ordered BAC One-Elevens, this became the largest individually owned airline in the world. After Laker replaced the Britannias with Boeing 707 jetliners it also became Britain's first all-jet airline. Travellers could arrive without booking and buy a cheap flight, and in-flight meals were paid for separately. In 1973 he also operated the world's first advanced booking charter (ABC) flight, between Manchester and Toronto (offering low-cost flights when booked more than four weeks in advance).

Setting himself up as the champion of 'the forgotten man' (*The Times*, 11 Feb 2006), in 1971 with his characteristically bold entrepreneurial style and vision, Laker took another significant pioneering step by acquiring a fleet of Douglas DC-10 intercontinental tri-jets specifically intended for the launch of his most ambitious project, the transatlantic Skytrain, aimed at breaking the dominance of the existing primary carriers. Conceived as a self-generating, no-reservation, walk-on, single-class, low-cost, no-frills operation to succeed his so-called 'affinity charter' transatlantic operation, it heralded the beginning of a veritable revolution in international air travel. The inspiration came in 1971 when the UK government cracked down on 'affinity groups', which had until then been a way of providing reduced fares for parties of supposedly like-minded people (the condition set by the International Air Transport Association, IATA, for allowing charter flights at fares below the agreed minimum fare), but was a system that had inevitably become abused. However, such was the serious competitive threat that Skytrain was seen to pose to the established members of the rigidly regulated IATA that it took him six years of complex and unflagging legal and political battles—through the American presidential terms of Nixon and Ford, and a high court action against Peter Shore, the British secretary of state for trade, earning him incalculable free publicity and goodwill in the process—to win a permit to launch the venture. Ultimately the permit was granted by President Carter's administration and Skytrain was inaugurated on 26 September 1977 with flights between Gatwick and New York Kennedy airports, carrying 272 passengers, paying £59 each one way. Laker was knighted in the queen's birthday honours in 1978.

By 1981 Skytrain had grown to encompass nine scheduled routes from three British airports to New York, San Francisco, Miami, Los Angeles, and Tampa, carrying one in seventeen transatlantic passengers. It was the fifth largest transatlantic carrier and was a revolutionary success. From 1976 to 1982 Laker also operated International Caribbean Airways for the Barbados government. He then envisaged an around-the-world Globetrain service via Los Angeles to Hong Kong and back to Britain to achieve the ultimate extension of his low-cost concept—also applying for licences to operate 140 routes to open up the intra-

European market to low fares, ordering ten European Airbus A300 twin-jets with which to do so.

However, in February 1982 (a year before the introduction of American air transport deregulation) Skytrain was peremptorily forced into receivership and liquidated. The airline, then operating twenty jet aircraft including eleven DC-10s, was part of the vertically integrated Laker Group of sixteen companies—which included aircraft maintenance and handling companies, wholesale tour operators, and retail travel companies in the UK, West Germany, Spain, Canada, and the USA. In fact Laker and his airline were never declared bankrupt. Although he had been consistently profitable for thirty-five years, he had an overdraft of £9 million with the Clydesdale Bank and was simply shut down by a bank foreclosure in unprecedented circumstances involving the predatory practices of his monopolistic competitors, the six largest transatlantic carriers, who combined to plot his downfall. Struggling with this debt—the year 1981–2 was also one of rising oil prices, recession, and a falling pound—it was Pan American's decision to cut its economy class fares by 66 per cent that finally killed off Skytrain. Laker filed a $1.5 billion anti-trust action in the USA, claiming that twelve major international and American airlines and others had conspired to force him out of business. In the event political intervention resulted in the lawsuit being settled out of court in 1985 for $56 million, with $48 million provided for refunds to an estimated 14,000 disenfranchised ticket holders, travel agents, and other small creditors, and all his staff were fully compensated. Despite the failure of Laker Airways, Laker had created a visionary template that inspired a later generation of aviation entrepreneurs, and transformed the air transport world.

Laker's first marriage ended in divorce in 1968, and on 22 July the same year he married Rosemary Belfrage Black, formerly Rosemary Belfrage Shanks, a 33-year-old South African divorcee, and daughter of David Belfrage Black, wool spinner. The marriage was dissolved in 1975, and on 18 July the same year Laker married Patricia LaVerne Gates, a 36-year-old American widowed public relations officer, and daughter of Robert Bowden, storekeeper. They had one son, Freddie Robert, who died four hours after birth, and another, Freddie Allen, who survived being shot in the stomach in Miami at the age of twelve. This marriage also ended in divorce, in 1982, and Laker married fourthly and finally, on 6 August 1985, Jacqueline Ann Harvey, a divorced 42-year-old airline hostess and public relations officer, and daughter of Horace Audley Harvey, engineer.

Final years and assessment Disillusioned but undaunted after the loss of Laker Airways, Laker refounded his business interests in the USA in 1983. There he set up his final air transport ventures in 1992: Laker Airways Inc., flying transatlantic services until 1998, and Laker Airways (Bahamas), flying affluent gamblers between Florida and the casinos on Grand Bahama island (where he lived latterly) until 2005. Diagnosed with prostate cancer in 1993, he campaigned vigorously for greater awareness of the condition. He died in Miami on 9 February 2006 following complications from cardiac surgery to implant a pacemaker. He was survived by his wife, Jacqueline, one daughter, and one son.

One of the most colourful, inspirational, and accomplished individuals to appear on the British and international aviation scene, and a national icon, Freddie Laker was self-assured, free-spirited, and patriotic; his company's motto was 'Strong, independent, British'. He faced opportunities and obstacles with equal fortitude. Promoting his many and diverse ventures with his own name, face, and outstretched arms, flying-fashion, he excitedly proclaimed his ever-popular slogans, 'Fly me, I'm Freddie' and 'Take a Laker', while adorning his aircraft with his own horse-racing colours and the national flag to flaunt his staunch patriotism. He was one of the few airline leaders who could tackle any job in the business himself—from comprehending and negotiating the complexities of a multi-million dollar aircraft purchase deal to flying and maintaining his own aircraft. The depth of his experience, professional ability, and flair, without dependence on adepts, was the foundation of his outstanding success as a private enterprise airline owner and industrial leader. Surviving and thriving through the arduous evolution of post-war British air transport, he was the true pioneer of low-cost air travel in the relentless pursuit of his 'dream of carrying ordinary people all over the world at prices they can afford' (Monckton and Fallon).

At the time that Richard Branson (who regarded Laker as a mentor) launched his low-cost Virgin Atlantic transatlantic flights Laker was reported as saying that the twentieth century had largely belonged to the traditional, high-cost airlines, but that the twenty-first century would be the preserve of the no-frills airlines. The global proliferation of such carriers had even by the time of his death validated his business model. Dubbed 'the people's champion', and the epitome of a self-made man, his profusely variegated six-decade aviation career was characterized by vision, fervour, astuteness, and patriotism.

NORMAN BARFIELD

Sources M. Pearson, *The millionaire mentality* (1961) · F. A. Laker, 'Private enterprise in British air transport', lecture at Royal Aeronautical Society, 14 Oct 1965 · R. Eglin and B. Ritchie, *Fly me, I'm Freddie* (1980) · C. Monckton and I. Fallon, *The Laker story* (1982) · H. Banks, *The rise and fall of Freddie Laker* (1982) · R. E. G. Davies, *Rebels and reformers of the airways* (1987) · J. Tegler, '"A over S": an interview with Sir Freddie Laker', *Airways USA* (Oct 1999) · 'The Laker Airways Skytrain', *Airliner World* (July 2005) · *BBC News*, 10 Feb 2006 · *The Times* (11 Feb 2006) · *Daily Telegraph* (11 Feb 2006) · *The Guardian* (11 Feb 2006) · *The Independent* (11 Feb 2006) · *Miami Herald* (11 Feb 2006) · *WW* (2006) · Burke, *Peerage* · b. cert. · m. certs.

Archives FILM BFINA, current affairs footage · BFINA, *Person to person*, R. Chapman (director), BBC1, 19 July 1979 | SOUND BFI NSA, *Trouble at the top*, BBC2, 8 Jan 1997 · BFI NSA, *The John Bull business*, BBC2, 18 Aug 1989

Likenesses photographs, 1963–2004, PA Photos, London · photographs, 1965–80, Getty Images, London, Hult. Arch. · photographs, 1975–96, Photoshot, London · A. Newman, bromide print, 1978, NPG · photographs, 1978–2001, Getty Images, London, Popperfoto · photographs, 1978–2005, Rex Features, London · P. Vicente, photographs, 1997, Getty Images, London, AFP · T. O'Neill, photographs, 2000, Getty Images, London, Premium Archive · A. Ashwood, photograph, Camera Press, London [*see* *illus.*] • B. Fantoni, pencil and gouache, NPG • G. Scarfe, cartoon, repro. in *Sunday Times* (7 Feb 1982) • obituary photographs • photographs, Royal Aeronautical Society, London • photographs, Camera Press, London

Lambert, Joyce Mildred (1916–2005), botanist and ecologist, was born on 23 June 1916 at 50 Oakbank Grove, Herne Hill, London, the daughter of Loftus Sidney Lambert, clerk for an electrical supply company, and later estate agent, and his wife, Mildred Emma, *née* Barker. She was brought up in Brundall, Norfolk, her family's ancestral county, to which she was devoted. She was educated at Norwich High School for Girls and then, in 1939, graduated in botany from the University College of Wales, Aberystwyth. After a short period as a schoolteacher in Norwich she was appointed lecturer in botany at Westfield College, London. In this formative period she fell under the influence of some of the outstanding botanists and naturalists of her time, each of whom helped shape her career and destiny in different ways. It was the Norfolk naturalist A. E. (Ted) Ellis and the botanist A. R. Clapham (then at Oxford) who encouraged her in the 1940s to study the ecology of the fens bordering the River Yare in the Surlingham–Rockland area of Norfolk.

In 1948 Lambert moved to Cambridge University and began working with the geomorphologist J. N. Jennings on the Bure valley. They published their collaborative work in three classic papers. In 1952 Jennings published the results of his own extensive research in the area, which concluded that most if not all of the great pattern of lakes known as the Broads were of natural origin. In her study Lambert used a similar basic stratigraphical technique: removing core samples of peat with a borer. Significantly however, she used a borer with a narrower diameter and took vast numbers of very closely spaced samples. These revealed, to her own and the scientific community's astonishment, that the sides of the lakes were almost vertical. The conclusion was inevitable—the Broads were artificial. But how could such vast excavations have been undertaken in an area so subject to inundation—and for what purpose? Further historical and archaeological studies backed by Cambridge University revealed that there had once been digging of peat for fuel on a monumental scale—the residents of each fenland parish had had turbary rights entitling them to dig within a certain area, but the practice had been abandoned by the end of the fourteenth century as the area became increasingly prone to flooding. These multidisciplinary studies were published in 1960 in a further book, *The Making of the Broads*, with Lambert and Jennings as the senior authors.

In 1950 Lambert had been appointed lecturer in botany at Southampton University. Her contributions there, in research and teaching, though overshadowed by her East Anglian studies, were significant. Known to everyone at Southampton as Bloss (an abbreviation of Blossom), she became one of the most inspiring teachers of plant ecology Britain has produced. She coined what is probably the most elegantly simple definition of this often overcomplicated subject: 'What grows where, and why?' (personal knowledge). She inspired her students by example and experience. She described working under Sir Harry Godwin at Cambridge and once being given a huge ecological tome one Friday and told to read and distil it into a 3000 word presentation by the following Tuesday. 'But Professor Godwin', she had complained, 'it's by Braun-Blanquet and I don't speak German.' 'Then I suggest you learn it' was Godwin's reply. She did (personal knowledge). At Southampton, too, Lambert made a pioneering contribution to the use of computers in botanical science in her collaboration with her head of department, Bill Williams, on the multivariate analysis of plant communities. Their elegant publications on association analysis, a statistical procedure that determines the frequency of association of different species in the same habitat, became among the most widely cited papers in the history of plant ecology.

Joyce Lambert was of striking appearance, short and almost spherical, with close-cropped silver-grey hair embroidered with a yellowish fringe at the front where the smoke from her ever-present Kensitas cigarettes curled upwards. She was a most companionable woman with inimitable enthusiasm and spirit, and rich good humour, quick talking, and with a deep mischievous laugh enhanced by a smoker's throatiness. She was also delightfully opinionated; she never, for instance, saw the point of installing an internal telephone system in the small Southampton botany building, saying that standing at the top of the stairs and shouting had always been perfectly satisfactory. She was an ardent supporter of Norwich City football club and after her retirement in 1980 returned to the house in Brundall that her grandfather had built in the 1920s. She spent some years looking after her ageing mother and enjoying her garden and then, because of increasing infirmity, for the last three years of her life was confined to a nursing home, Oakwood House, Old Watton Road, Colney, Norfolk. She died there on 4 May 2005 of bronchopneumonia. She received no significant award and was mystifyingly denied the formal recognition her remarkable work merited. She never married.

STEFAN BUCZACKI

Sources *The Guardian* (28 May 2005) • *The Times* (24 May 2005); (2 June 2005) • *Daily Telegraph* (17 May 2005) • personal knowledge (2009) • private information (2009) • b. cert. • d. cert.
Archives Norfolk RO, papers, incl. papers rel. to Norfolk Broads, MC 2442
Likenesses obituary photographs
Wealth at death £605,323: probate, 4 Oct 2005, *CGPLA Eng. & Wales*

Lambert, Verity Ann (1935–2007), television and film producer, was born on 27 November 1935 at 63 Fitzjohns Avenue, Hampstead, London, the only child of affluent Jewish parents, Stanley Joseph Lambert, a chartered accountant, and his wife, Ella Corona, *née* Goldburg. At the time of her birth registration her parents lived at 145 Nether Street, North Finchley, London. She was educated at Roedean School until the age of sixteen, studied at the Sorbonne for a year, and then returned to attend secretarial school in London for eighteen months.

Lambert began work in television as secretary to the

Verity Ann Lambert (1935–2007), by unknown photographer, 1965

press officer at Granada in 1956, then moved to ABC Television, working her way up from shorthand typist to production secretary in the drama department. At this point in her television career she wanted to move away from secretarial roles and into drama production, spending a year working for Talent Associates in New York, primarily as assistant to the producer and talk-show host David Susskind. After her return to the UK, and ABC, she became bored and frustrated by the lack of opportunities for women working in television production until Sydney Newman (the former producer of ABC's *Armchair Theatre*, who had been poached as head of drama by the BBC) invited her to work as producer on his new series, *Doctor Who*, in November 1963. At twenty-eight, she became the youngest producer at the BBC and the drama department's only female producer, known for her no-nonsense approach and for refusing to be overawed by more senior contributors. After the overnight success of *Doctor Who* (which Lambert produced for its first eighteen months) she produced other long-running series for the BBC, including another cult science fiction series, *Adam Adamant Lives!* (1966–7), and the W. Somerset Maugham series, which won the BAFTA award for the best drama series of 1969.

Lambert left the BBC in 1969 and went on to produce drama for London Weekend Television, initially working on *Budgie* (1971–2), a vehicle for the pop singer Adam Faith. Around this time she met the camera operator (later director) Colin Michael Bucksey (*b.* 1946), son of George Edward Bucksey, town hall attendant. They married at Kensington register office on 18 July 1973. After a brief return to the BBC—where she produced *Shoulder to Shoulder* (1974), a series of plays about the suffragette movement—Lambert moved to Thames Television in 1974 as controller of drama, and oversaw a prodigious period of 'quality drama' for the company: *Rock Follies* (1976), the musical drama series about an all-female rock group; *Bill Brand* (1976, Trevor Griffiths's study of a Labour politician); *The Naked Civil Servant*, starring John Hurt in an award-winning 'biopic' of Quentin Crisp, written by Philip Mackie under Lambert's *ITV Playhouse* umbrella in 1975; and *Rumpole of the Bailey* (1978–9). Lambert was also responsible for Thames's subsidiary company, Euston Films, which produced gritty comedies and drama for television, including *Minder* (1979–85) and *Widows* (1983), about a group of four women who pull off an armed robbery (its sequel, *She's Out*, was produced by Lambert's own company, Cinema Verity, in 1995). While she had initially juggled her work as head of drama at Thames with her work at Euston Films, she eventually switched to become the latter's full-time chief executive.

For three years, from 1982, Lambert was the director of productions for Thorn EMI Screen Entertainment, responsible for film series for television and cinema films, with varying success: in 1985 she oversaw Mel Smith and Griff Rhys Jones's *Morons from Outer Space*, but also Dennis Potter's Alice in Wonderland fantasy *Dreamchild*. She remained on the board at Thames, as a director (1982–5), and kept her post at Euston Films until 1983. (This period is surely evidence of Lambert's workaholism.) Unhappy at Thorn EMI, she established her own production company, Cinema Verity, in 1985. The company produced a wide range of material including *A Cry in the Dark* (1988, the 'dingo baby' film starring Meryl Streep), two sitcoms for BBC1, *May to December* (1989–94) and *So Haunt Me* (1992–4), and the critically acclaimed drama series *GBH* (for Channel 4, 1991). She also produced two BBC comedy dramas: *Jonathan Creek* (from its second series in 1998 to 2004) and *Love Soup* (2005–8). Cinema Verity's single (expensive) flop was *Eldorado* (1992–3), a soap opera filmed for the BBC on a purpose-built set in Spain that failed to gain audiences and was cancelled after only a year.

Verity Lambert was a hard-working, pioneering woman in a doggedly masculine industry, a highly successful populist with a prodigious talent for producing stories that gripped the nation and earned wide-reaching critical acclaim. She produced a huge range of drama that had an enormous impact on the British television industry. She was appointed OBE in 2002. She died of breast cancer on 22 November 2007 at the Royal Marsden Hospital, Chelsea, London. Her marriage had ended in divorce in 1987, and she had no children. HELEN WHEATLEY

Sources J. Tulloch and M. Alvarado, *Doctor Who: the unfolding text* (1983) · M. Alvarado and J. Stewart, *Made for television: Euston Films Limited* (1985) · R. Dickinson, 'Verity Lambert', *Museum of Broadcast Communications encyclopedia of television*, ed. H. Newcomb, 3 vols. (1997) · C. Brunsdon, *Screen tastes: soap opera to satellite dishes* (1997) · L. Cooke, *British television drama: a history* (2003) · J. Hallam, *Lynda La Plante* (2005) · *The Times* (24 Nov 2007) · *Daily Telegraph* (24 Nov 2007) · *The Guardian* (26 Nov 2007); (28 Nov 2007) · *The Independent* (26 Nov 2007) · www.screenonline.org.uk/people/id/550923/index.html, 10 May 2010 · *WW* (2007) · b. cert. · m. cert. · d. cert.

Archives Strathclyde University, Glasgow, papers | FILM BFINA, current affairs footage · BFINA, light entertainment footage | SOUND BL NSA, documentary recording

Likenesses M. Seymour, resin print from original negative, 1961, NPG · photographs, 1963–97, PA Photos, London · photographs, 1965–85, Getty Images, London, Hult. Arch. · G. Miller, archival inkjet print, 1984, NPG · A. McGuinness, C-type colour print, 1988,

NPG · L. Cendrowicz, photograph, repro. in *Independent on Sunday* (17 June 2001) · N. Libbert, photograph, repro. in *The Observer* (26 Aug 1990) · obituary photographs · photograph, 1965, BBC [*see illus.*]

Wealth at death £2,588,516: probate, 2 Oct 2008, *CGPLA Eng. & Wales*

Lambton, Ann Katharine Swynford [Nancy] (**1912–2008**), orientalist and Persianist, was born at Mesnil Warren, Bury Road, Exning, Newmarket, Suffolk, on 8 February 1912, the elder daughter and second of the four children of George *Lambton (1860–1945), racehorse trainer, and his wife, Cecily Margaret, *née* Horner (1882–1972). She was the granddaughter of George Frederick D'Arcy Lambton, second earl of Durham, and of Sir John Francis Fortescue Horner of Mells Park, Somerset. Her father was an outstanding racehorse trainer and manager from the 1890s to the 1930s. One of her middle names, Swynford, commemorated her father's 1910 St Leger winner and she won acclaim aged fourteen for skill in the saddle at Newmarket Heath. She roller-skated in her teens and, later, commuted by bicycle from Maida Vale to teach and thrash varsity squash opponents at Russell Square.

A family friend, Sir Denison Ross, persuaded Lambton's parents to allow her to study Persian, initially as a student unregistered for a degree course, at the School of Oriental Studies, London, of which he was the founding director. On matriculation with a certificate in Persian in 1932, she began her Persian honours, with a subsidiary in classical Arabic, plus German, geology, and Latin studied at King's College. Her teachers were Ross, and professors Hamilton Gibb, Arthur Tritton, Vladimir Minorsky, and Hasan Taqizadeh. Conferred the Ouseley memorial scholarship in Persian in 1934, and her BA degree in 1935, along with the Aga Khan travelling scholarship, she commenced her doctorate in the latter year on Persian Seljuq administration and submitted it in 1939 despite spending thirteen months in Tehran and major provincial centres recording dialects (published as *Three Persian Dialects*, 1938, from the Furlong scholarship, Royal Asiatic Society); studying craft guilds as well as Persian and Arabic with local scholars; and teaching history in Persian in a girls' high school in Isfahan. She returned to Persia in July 1939 for further research and was there when the Second World War broke out. Appointed press attaché at the British legation, she made her mark interpreting at press conferences, summarizing local papers for a weekly digest, combating axis propaganda, and preparing news commentaries on allied efforts. She was appointed OBE in 1943. Links with Persians across all classes, predicated on a solid philological training, afforded her an extraordinary insight into local life.

The Ministry of Information reluctantly released Lambton to accept Arthur Arberry's offer of a post at the School of Oriental and African Studies (SOAS, as the School of Oriental Studies had become in 1938). London University could not afford the proposed readership and Lambton came after VJ day as senior lecturer in October 1945. A readership, three years later, was swiftly followed by a professorship in 1953, a signal year when her landmark *Landlord and Peasant in Persia: a Study of Land Tenure and Land Revenue Administration* and *Persian Grammar* appeared, for which London University awarded her a D.Lit. Both rapidly became standard works, even in Persian editions. Subsequently she published *Persian Vocabulary* (1964) and *The Persian Land Reform: 1962–66* (1969), which incisively analysed the mixed results of the shah's 1963 white revolution. Lambton's headship of the Near and Middle East department at SOAS (1972–8) spoke for her ability even as articles and profoundly meticulous studies appeared in the *Cambridge History of Islam* (co-edited with another Gibb protégé, Bernard Lewis), *The Cambridge History of Iran*, *Encyclopaedia of Islam*, and *Encyclopædia Iranica*. Her *Theory and Practice in Medieval Persian Government* (1980) and *State and Government in Medieval Islam* (1981)—both published after her retirement from SOAS in 1979 (whereupon she became a professor emerita)—were indispensable for comprehending Muslim statecraft. Her Columbia University lectures, *Continuity and Change in Medieval Persia: Aspects of Administrative, Economic and Social History, 11th–14th century* (1988) crowned her output.

Among the litany of failures enumerated by James Bill in *The Eagle and the Lion: the Tragedy of American–Iranian Relations* (1988) was that only 10 per cent of American diplomats posted to Iran spoke and read fluent Persian compared with almost 45 per cent of British diplomats. He attributed this to Lambton's 'stiff exams', describing her as one of 'the West's leading Iran specialists', and noting that all senior British diplomats had been her SOAS students (Bill, 392). She possessed 'remarkable first-hand knowledge of Persians & their mentality', Anthony Eden declared, as did Whitehall's mandarins, who routinely sought her counsel and scrutiny of bilingual treaties. Lambton, unsurprisingly, in a Foreign Office brief during the 1951 oil crisis concluded that Americans 'lack our experience or the psychological insight' of Iran. She correctly concluded that 'it was impossible to do business' with Mohammed Mossadegh's cabinet, which would renege on any agreement—eastern erraticness was a familiar bane to the British—and recommended toughing it out during the deadlock by co-opting equally alarmed, reasonable Persians whose otherwise explicit denouncement of the 'stupidity, greed and lack of judgement of the ruling classes' would be seditious. Lambton also baldly forewarned that the Anglo-Iranian Oil Company 'could not hope to return in any shape' thanks to the '10 years that A.I.O.C. were making a psychological mess of their relations with Persia' (TNA PRO, FO 371/91609). Revisionists and sensationalists later seized upon her advice as the genesis of the 1953 coup, which led indirectly to the 1979 Islamic revolution. Nevertheless, as William Roger Louis argued, Lambton's suggestions were misappropriated by London, whose diplomatic dénouement stemmed from the disastrous cupidity of the Anglo-Iranian Oil Company and particularly its belligerent chairman, Sir William Fraser.

More embarrassed than even the shah's Western allies were those experts watching Iran implode in 1978–9. Save Lambton nobody prognosticated in 1964 that 'the tendency to look for the establishment of the kingdom of

God upon earth … if pressed to its conclusion is likely to lead either to political quietism or violent revolution' (Lambton, 'A reconsideration of the position of the *Marja' al-Taqlīd* and the religious institution', *Studia Islamica*, XX, 1964, 135). Published the very year Ruholla Khomeini was exiled to Turkey, its oracular import cannot be gainsaid. If such insights were revelatory they were only a bonus given Lambton's unrivalled breadth and stamp covering Persian grammar and dialectology; medieval and early modern Islamic political thought; Seljuq, Mongol, Safavid, Qajar, and Pahlavi administration; tribal and local history; and Iranian land tenure and agriculture.

Lambton received numerous honours: the Sir Percy Sykes memorial medal of the Royal Central Asian Society (1960); fellowship of the British Academy (1964); honorary doctorates from Durham (1971) and Cambridge (1973); honorary fellowships of New Hall, Cambridge (1973) and SOAS (1983); honorary life membership of the Middle East Studies Association of North America; and the triennial gold medal of the Royal Asiatic Society (1991). An annual A. K. S. Lambton honorary lecture series was established in 2001 at Durham University, which housed her library and papers. The British Institute of Persian Studies, of which she was an honorary vice-president, hosted her ninetieth birthday reception at Carlton House Terrace, in 2002. In 2004 she was awarded the British Society for Middle Eastern Studies' outstanding service award and the Cross of St Augustine by Archbishop Rowan Williams. Both, in a sense, were the ultimate recognition of her life's work. Lambton led morning prayer, preached on Sundays, and delivered Lent talks, even into her nineties, in the Newcastle diocese. In his *laudatio* the archbishop cited her voluntary work in Iran, assistance on inter-faith matters, and attempts to prevent the church's persecution after the Islamic revolution. He also commended her exceptional theological erudition, in comparison with churchmen, and particular devotion to Pope Gregory I, the namesake of her residence, Gregory Cottage, in East Kirknewton, Wooler, Northumberland, where she died on 19 July 2008. She was unmarried. BURZINE K. WAGHMAR

Sources *The Economist* (6 Oct 1945); (31 Oct 1970) · *The Observer* (17 March 1946) · *The Times* (22 Aug 1951); (23 July 2008); (19 Aug 2008) · A. Lambton, *Islamic society in Persia* (1954) · R. Bullard, *The camels must go: an autobiography* (1961), 219 · *The Guardian* (6 Feb 1970); (15 Aug 2008) · W. R. Louis, *The British empire in the Middle East, 1945–1951* (1984), 659–61 · J. Bracken, 'Preface: Professor A. K. S. Lambton', *Bulletin of the School of Oriental and African Studies* [in honour of Ann K. S. Lambton], 49 (1986), 1–4 · A. Lambton, 'Recollections of Iran in the mid-twentieth century', *Asian Affairs*, 19 (Oct 1988), 273–88 · J. Bill, *The eagle and the lion: the tragedy of American–Iranian relations* (1988), 392 · J. Colville, *Those Lambtons! a most unusual family* (1988), 100–02 · R. Bullard, *Letters from Tehran: a British ambassador in World War II Persia* (1991), 6–7, 18, 67, 96, 190 · B. Waghmar, 'The vice-regency of the jurisconsult: sacred politics in the Islamic Republic of Iran', diss., Boston University, 1996, 39 · *Women in diplomacy: the FCO, 1782–1999* (1999), 11–12 · S. Dorril, *MI6: inside the covert world of her majesty's secret intelligence service* (2000), 560–78 · A. Lambton, *Local particularism and the common people in pre-modern Iran*, Durham Middle East Papers, 67 (2001) · W. R. Louis, 'How Mussadeq was ousted', *TLS* (29 June 2001), 13 · C. E. Bosworth, *A century of British orientalists, 1902–2001* (2001), 27 · B. Waghmar, 'Ann Lambton at 90', *Circle of Inner Asian Art Newsletter*, 15 (June 2002), 31 · A. Lambton, 'Remembering Seyyed Hasan Taqizadeh', *Irān Nāmeh: a Persian Journal of Iranian Studies*, 21 (spring–summer 2003), 109–11 · 'BRISMES award for services to Middle Eastern studies: Professor Ann Lambton', *British Society for Middle Eastern Studies Newsletter*, 19 (Nov 2004), 11 · R. Williams, 'Award to Professor Lambton', *Bible Lands: Magazine of the Jerusalem and Middle East Church Association*, Pentecost (2005), 31–2 · Sam Falle interviewed by Mike Thomson, 'A very British coup', BBC Radio 4, 22 Aug 2005 · C. de Bellaigue, 'Where Said was wrong', *TLS* (19 May 2006), 6 · R. Irwin, *For lust of knowing: the orientalists and their enemies* (2006), 207, 258 · W. R. Louis, *Ends of British imperialism: the scramble for empire, Suez and decolonization* (2006), 732–57 · D. Morgan, 'Orientalism and after', *TLS* (2 June 2006), 17 · *Evening Chronicle* [Newcastle] (22 July 2008) · *The Independent* (1 Aug 2008) · *Daily Telegraph* (9 Aug 2008) · *The Chronicle* [Newcastle] (16 Aug 2008) · V. Stock, 'Sermon: Professor Ann Lambton', memorial address · *Journal of the Iran Society*, 2 (2008), 37–40 · *British Institute of Persian Studies Newsletter*, 34 (2008), 21 · *Bible Lands: Magazine of the Jerusalem and Middle East Church Association*, advent (2008), 11 · *The Middle East in London*, 5 (Sept 2008), 19 · *Iranian Studies*, 42 (2009), 139–43 · *Iran: Journal of the British Institute of Persian Studies*, 47 (2009), vii–x · *Middle East Studies*, 45 (2009), 161–3 · *Journal of the Royal Asiatic Society* (2011), 99–109 · D. Morgan, 'Hollow crown', *TLS* (21 Oct 2011), 32 · J. Gurney, 'Ann K. S. Lambton', *PBA* [forthcoming] · D. Morgan, 'Ann K. S. Lambton', *Encyclopædia Iranica* [forthcoming] · *WW* (2008) · Burke, *Peerage* · personal knowledge (2012) · private information (2012) · b. cert. · d. cert.

Archives SOAS · U. Durham, Palace Green Library | TNA: PRO, FO 371 | SOUND interview, 'Persian Studies in Britain', BBC World (Persian) Service, 2001

Likenesses J. Colville, photograph, repro. in Colville, *Those Lambtons!* · obituary photographs · photograph, repro. in *The Guardian* (6 Feb 1970) · photograph, repro. in 'BRISMES award' · photograph, repro. in 'Award to Professor Lambton' · photographs, SOAS · photographs, priv. coll.

Lambton, Antony Claud Frederick, styled **Lord Lambton (1922–2006)**, politician and writer, was born on 10 July 1922 at West Marden Hall, Emsworth, Sussex, the younger son of John Frederick Lambton, fifth earl of Durham (1884–1970), and his first wife, Diana Mary (1901–1924), only daughter of Granville Frederick Richard Farquhar, of Dalton Hall, Beverley, Yorkshire. After attending Harrow School, in 1941 Antony Lambton became heir to the family earldom in tragic circumstances, when his elder brother, John, shot himself. Lambton joined the Hampshire regiment in the same year, but was soon invalided out of the army due to eye trouble. (This affliction led him in later life always to wear sunglasses.) He went to work in a munitions factory, where he met the spirited Belinda Bridget (Bindy) Blew-Jones (1921–2003), daughter of Major Douglas Holden Blew-Jones, of Westward Ho!, Devon. The couple married on 10 August 1942 and had five daughters followed by a son.

Lambton belonged to an illustrious political family. The first earl of Durham, John George Lambton, a radical whig MP, cabinet minister, ambassador to Russia, and governor-general of Canada, was famous for the Durham report of 1838, which led to self-government in the Canadian and subsequently other colonies. Several other ancestors had served as MPs, usually for their native co. Durham. Lambton's first cousin was Lord Dunglass, later Sir Alec Douglas-Home (prime minister in 1963–4). It was therefore not surprising that Lambton embarked on a political career after the Second World War. Defeated in the general election of 1945, when he fought Chester-le-Street for the Conservatives, he served as a somewhat controversial councillor in Durham for two years before suffering a second parliamentary defeat, at Bishop Auckland in 1950. Refusing to rest on the fame of his family, he had worked hard within the Conservative organization in the north-east, becoming area president of the Young Conservatives. His reward was selection for the Conservative-held seat of Berwick upon Tweed, which he won in the general election of 1951. Although he was far from being an assiduous constituency MP, he held the seat until 1973.

As the scion of such a notable family, Lambton's prospects for advancement should have been bright. However, he was not universally popular among his colleagues. Even before he had entered parliament an astute Conservative colleague, the diarist Cuthbert Headlam, regarded him as 'an irritable and impatient man who does not suffer fools gladly' (Ball, 595). Lambton's maiden speech, delivered on 13 March 1952, was more controversial than the usual offering, and included a prescient warning about the likely effect of an ageing population on the social security budget. The next speaker, Labour's Harold Wilson, offered his congratulations; years later (during a speech in the House of Commons on 26 April 1966) Lambton joked that this was the only time that Wilson had ever spoken about him in civil terms.

In 1954 Lambton became parliamentary private secretary to the minister of supply, Selwyn Lloyd. This appointment took on greater significance in April 1955, when Lloyd was elevated to the cabinet as minister of defence, winning further promotion to foreign secretary in December. Yet Lambton's connection with Lloyd turned out to be a mixed blessing. Lloyd was foreign secretary during the Eden government's ill-fated Suez intervention, and although Lloyd stayed in his post after the humiliating British retreat, Lambton resigned. He was disgusted by the aftermath of Suez, and never forgave Eden's successor, Harold Macmillan. The ill feeling was reciprocated, which did little to help Lambton's hopes of promotion while Macmillan remained party leader.

During the next decade Lambton devoted much of his energy to cross-party back-bench initiatives. For example he played a key role in the passage of Roy Jenkins's Obscene Publications Act in 1959. This was not the only respect in which Lambton deviated from the stereotype of a right-wing Conservative; for example he also advocated the decriminalization of cannabis. Lambton's idiosyncratic ideas—often expressed in pungent contributions to the Beaverbrook press—helped to debar him from preferment even when his cousin, Alec Douglas-Home, succeeded Macmillan as prime minister in 1963. His parliamentary career seemed fated to end in futility. He could, though, continue to raise issues close to his heart; in April 1969 he introduced a Bill of Rights into the House of Commons, and although the measure failed its supporters included Home and Margaret Thatcher.

Towards the end of 1969 Home's successor as Conservative leader, Edward Heath, gave Lambton official responsibility to speak for the party on foreign affairs. The appointment signalled that Heath was willing to promote talented right-wingers—even those, like Lambton, who disagreed with him on the key issue of Britain's relationship with the European Economic Community. Lambton had also worked for Heath's opponent, Reginald Maudling, in the Conservative leadership election of 1965. However, there was no question of Lambton's securing a cabinet position when his party unexpectedly won the general election of 1970. Instead, he was made an under-secretary within the Ministry of Defence; his area of special responsibility was the Royal Air Force.

It might have been better for Lambton if Heath had left him out of the government. Foreign affairs—especially the politics of the Middle East—continued to be his main interest, and he later confessed to being bored by his duties at the Ministry of Defence. His most notable contribution to political life in this period was his decision to renounce the earldom of Durham, which he inherited on his father's death in February 1970. Lambton had consistently argued that heirs should be able to renounce their peerages in order to stay in the House of Commons. However, he combined this view with a firm attachment to hereditary honours, and continued to insist (against the objections of procedural experts) that he should be known by the courtesy title of Lord Lambton for parliamentary purposes.

After three years of unremarkable service in junior office, Lambton suddenly created unwelcome headlines by resigning from the government in May 1973. Thanks to a concealed camera and microphone, a tabloid newspaper had secured evidence of Lambton's dealings with more than one prostitute; particularly damaging was a photograph of Lambton in bed with two prostitutes, smoking marijuana. Eventually this material was handed to the police, and Lambton was investigated by the secret services in case his activities had constituted a security risk, like those of John Profumo a decade earlier. Although there was no basis for this suspicion, it was impossible for Lambton to continue in office. He resigned his parliamentary seat and was later convicted of possession of cannabis. The lord privy seal, Lord Jellicoe, resigned shortly afterwards because of his own involvement with prostitutes.

After his resignation Lambton gave a television interview to Robin Day in which he frankly admitted to his relations with prostitutes, offering the explanation that 'people sometimes like variety. I think it's as simple as that and I think that impulse is understood by almost everybody' (*The Independent*, 2 Jan 2007). After leaving public life he retired to the magnificent seventeenth-century Villa Cetinale, near Siena in Italy, taking a keen personal role in the restoration of the house and gardens. Although he never divorced his wife, his companion in this voluntary exile was Claire Ward, a noted society beauty. In the ensuing years his villa was visited by numerous politicians and pop stars; it was rumoured that Lambton presided over many dissolute parties, and he enjoyed playing practical jokes on his guests.

Apart from his love of women and gardening, Lambton wrote several books in retirement. A volume of short stories published in 1983 was followed by two novels, *Elizabeth and Alexandra* (1985) and *The Abbey in the Wood* (1986). These productions confirmed the impression that Lambton had considerable talents, but lacked the consistency of application that might have created a lasting legacy. Ironically his next and best-known book, *The Mountbattens* (1989), accused the late Lord Louis Mountbatten of exaggerating his own achievements. It could be countered that Lambton himself, for all his abilities, had few tangible achievements to exaggerate. More sympathetically, the erratic career of Antony Lambton could be used to exemplify the dilemmas that faced members of the aristocracy during a supposedly 'meritocratic' era. His six children (who included the noted author and broadcaster Lady Lucinda Lambton, born in 1943) displayed enough ability, dynamism, and eccentricity to suggest that they would have become prominent people even if they had lacked social advantages. When he died at Villa Cetinale, Sovicille, on 30 December 2006, Lambton's obituarists concentrated on the sexual scandal that had ended his political career. He was cremated in his adopted home of Siena, and the ashes were buried in a specially restored chapel at his villa. His son Edward (Ned; *b.* 1961) became seventh earl of Durham and inherited his father's entire estate, valued at £11,800,360 net in England and Wales.

MARK GARNETT

Sources *Parliament and politics in the age of Churchill and Attlee: the Headlam diaries, 1935–1951*, ed. S. Ball, CS, 5th ser., 14 (1999) • *The Times* (2 Jan 2007) • *Daily Telegraph* (2 Jan 2007); (7 May 2007) • *The Guardian* (2 Jan 2007) • *The Independent* (2 Jan 2007) • *Sunday Times* (7 Jan 2007) • *WW* (2006) • Burke, *Peerage* • private information (2010) [Lucinda Lambton, daughter] • b. cert.

Archives priv. coll. | Bodl. RH, Welensky MSS • Parl. Arch., Beaverbrook MSS • U. Birm. L., Avon MSS | FILM BFINA, current affairs footage

Likenesses photographs, 1952–74, Rex Features, London • Bassano, half-plate film negatives, 1964, NPG • Elliott & Fry 1955, vintage prints, NPG • obituary photographs

Wealth at death £11,800,360: probate, 1 March 2007, *CGPLA Eng. & Wales*

Lane, Geoffrey Dawson, Baron Lane (1918–2005), judge, was born on 17 July 1918, at Crantock, Farley Road, Derby, the only son and youngest of the four children of Percy Albert Lane (1880–1964), manager of Smith's Bank in Lincoln, and his wife, Polly, *née* Dawson (1880–1961), who had graduated in classics from Royal Holloway College, London.

Education, war service, and marriage Lane was educated at Shrewsbury School, where he was head of school and a keen cricketer. He was awarded a scholarship to Trinity College, Cambridge, where he achieved a first in part one of the classical tripos, when his education was interrupted by the Second World War. He joined the Royal Air Force and served throughout the war, initially as a pilot in

Geoffrey Dawson Lane, Baron Lane (1918–2005), by unknown photographer, 1980

Bomber Command, flying Wellington aircraft. His experiences were varied and highly dangerous. Apart from missions over Germany and occupied France his skills as a pilot were recognized when he was chosen to set up the RAF's first dedicated air postal services, using first the notoriously unstable Albermarle aircraft, and later the C47 Dakota. The purpose of the service was to ensure that British soldiers serving under General Montgomery in north Africa would receive their mail from home, an important contribution to morale. In February 1943, as a young squadron leader, he was entrusted by Winston Churchill with correspondence to be taken and flown south-west out over the Atlantic and then south-east, via Gibraltar, to Montgomery in north Africa. After Montgomery had read the documents he explained to Lane that the German army would attack the following morning at a specific time and place. It was only many years later that Lane realized that this intelligence must have been gathered through allied code-breaking achievements at Bletchley Park. Next morning Lane flew out of north Africa carrying Montgomery's hand-written response to Churchill, which Lane duly delivered, personally, to 10 Downing Street. For his work in Transport Command flying long-range aircraft to north Africa he was awarded the Air Force Cross in 1943.

On D-day and subsequent operations in 1944 Lane flew paratroops and supplies behind enemy lines, and once the bridgehead was established he flew supplies into and serious casualties out of France and back to England for treatment at the Radcliffe Hospital in Oxford. In September 1944 he towed gliders on the Arnhem expedition and thereafter flew supplies in to support that doomed force. By 1945 he was stationed in India as part of the RAF contingent preparing for the invasion of Japan. He never spoke about his wartime experiences but those who served with him remembered him as an inspirational leader. His experiences were later put to good use when, as a QC, he led the investigation into the Vanguard crash at Heathrow in 1965 and, as a High Court judge, he was the chairman of the public inquiry into the Trident crash at Staines in 1972.

On 25 January 1944 Lane married, at North Wraxall church, Wiltshire, Jessie (Jan) Macdonald (1914–2006), daughter of Donald Macdonald, farmer, of Tulloch, Aviemore. They had met in 1942 when Lane was a patient in an RAF hospital in Buckinghamshire and she was a nurse responsible for his care. Thus began a wartime romance that, for both of them, lasted a lifetime. They had one son.

The bar, and early judicial career After demobilization Lane returned to Cambridge, again taking firsts, this time in parts one and two of the law tripos. He was called to the bar by Gray's Inn in 1946, became a pupil to Richard Elwes, and joined the midland circuit. Before his practice developed he supplemented his income by giving tutorials at Cambridge. However, his skills as an advocate, allied to his robust common sense, were immediately and obviously attractive, and he developed a huge and varied junior practice. A little unusually at that time he believed that however busy he was, the service to solicitors should be rapid. As his handwriting was always legible and tidy he dealt with relatively routine papers almost immediately, in handwriting, by return of post whenever possible.

One of Lane's last cases before he took silk in 1962 was the notorious trial of James Hanratty at Bedford assizes. Lane was junior counsel to the crown. After many years of controversy and passionate contention that Hanratty had suffered the supreme penalty when he was innocent it was a relief to Lane that in 2002 the development of DNA demonstrated beyond question that Hanratty was indeed guilty and rightly convicted of murder. In 1965 he acted for the Metropolitan Police in the inquiry conducted by Sir Daniel Brabin into the conviction and execution of Timothy Evans for a murder committed by the main prosecution witness against him, John Christie. These two cases reinforced Lane's strongly held views about capital punishment, to which he was opposed.

In 1965 Lane addressed a constitution of five judges on the vexed and complicated problem of joint enterprise by defendants resulting in death. His encapsulation of authorities from 1830 onwards was summarized in a single sentence, and his analysis of the principle was adopted virtually verbatim in the judgment of the court given by the lord chief justice, Hubert Parker, Baron Parker of Waddington. What is more, over forty years later this principle remained the source to which the courts dealing with the problem of joint enterprise returned time and again when doubt and uncertainty appeared to have crept into the law (*R.* v. *Rahman*, 2008).

Those who knew Lane as a barrister remembered in particular his generosity with his own limited time. Advice and help were always available. He was not prone to indulge younger barristers, or to allow them to be self-indulgent. His advice was always clear, and the language never left any doubt about his meaning. He then expected his interlocutors to consider what he had said, wished them luck, and left them to make up their own minds. Thereafter, throughout his judicial career, Lane was always tolerant of the young and the inexperienced, but he had no time for the idle and those who failed to prepare their cases properly. They were failing both their clients and their responsibility to the court. He had huge faith in the jury system, and confidence in the ability of the jury to decide when it was appropriate to convict and when to acquit. This loyal adherence to the constitutional primacy of the jury in criminal matters was later to expose him to vituperative and often ill-informed criticism.

Lane's first judicial appointment was as deputy chairman of Bedfordshire quarter sessions, in 1960. He was later deputy chairman of Lindsey quarter sessions and Rutland quarter sessions (becoming chairman of the latter when the previous incumbent stood down), and recorder of Bedford (1963–6). After a glittering career at the bar, and only four short years in silk, and no doubt in part because of the extraordinary quality of his submission to Lord Parker in 1965, he was appointed as a judge of the High Court of Justice, Queen's Bench Division, in 1966. He was knighted the same year.

One memorable observation by Lane when, as a judge of the Queen's Bench Division, holding that quite considerable force was justified to prevent an obstruction of the highway by a violent and abusive driver, was that 'one did not use jewellers' scales to measure reasonable force' (*Reed* v. *Wastie*, 1972). This provided an early demonstration that his capacity as an advocate to capture the essence of a complicated legal problem in a few short words was undiminished by the assumption of his new office.

In 1974 Lane was promoted to the Court of Appeal and sworn of the privy council. Within a few months he identified the principle that applied when drunkenness and its possible effect on the defendant's state of mind was in issue: 'A drunken intent is nevertheless an intent' (*R.* v. *Sheehan and Moore*, 1975). More than thirty years later this simple, unequivocal direction continued to be used to direct juries whenever this issue arose.

Five years later, in 1979, Lane was appointed a lord of appeal in ordinary, taking the title Baron Lane, of St Ippollitts in the county of Hertford. In 1980, after only six months as a law lord, he was appointed lord chief justice. Many had thought that his elevation to the House of Lords might preclude this appointment, and his return to the Court of Appeal was enthusiastically welcomed. One wit summed up the general mood, 'Geoffrey Dawson, Baron Lane, nice to have you back again' (personal knowledge).

Lane had not sought office as lord chief justice. He and his wife were a private couple, hugely happy with each other and content with the company of friends. Neither wished for limelight. They realized that he was exchanging the low-key, intellectually stimulating, but essentially peaceful life of a law lord for a high-profile office. It was only his sense of public duty that led him to accept the appointment. He was, and for the rest of his life remained, modest, unpretentious, and unassuming. In a speech to his old circuit, at a dinner when his appointment was honoured, he explained that he had discovered that the first holder of the office of chief justiciar was Odo. With his marvellous ability to explode pomposity and bring his audience down to earth he continued, 'now you have got Thicko!' (personal knowledge). With his characteristic moral courage he went on to declare that the bar could not shuffle off responsibility for the inefficiencies of the criminal justice system, which he, as lord chief justice, would now have to address.

Lord chief justice Lane was lord chief justice for twelve years. Two principles guided his own approach to the extra-judicial problems of his office. The maintenance of the independence of the judiciary was an absolute. In a speech in Malta in February 1990 he spoke of judicial independence as the 'foundation stone of freedom' and 'something which it is never prudent to take for granted'. He spoke of the judge as a 'vital part of the constitutional jigsaw puzzle'. He continued:

> And what is the nature of that puzzle? It is surely this: how best to balance the rights and duties of the individual against the powers which the State must necessarily have if it is going effectively to govern … the duty of upholding the balance, in civilised communities passed on the judges, is of no value unless the judge is in a position to act according to his conscience without fear or favour, affection or ill-will.

In his speech he made clear that he was 'truly', indeed 'avidly', non-political, 'both by reason of my profession and by reason of my own inclination' (*Sunday Times of Malta*, 11 Feb 1990). By then he had expressed himself in trenchant terms on the separate but equally critical principle of individual liberty for which so many of his generation had fought and died. He once said that

> loss of freedom seldom happens over night … oppression does not stand on the doorstep with a toothbrush moustache and a swastika armband. It creeps up step by step, and all of a sudden the unfortunate citizen realises that freedom has gone. (*The Guardian*, 23 Aug 2005)

This particular observation, reflective of his own deeply held personal commitment to the principle of individual freedom, was made in response to proposals to reform the legal profession advanced by the then lord chancellor, Lord Mackay of Clashfern. Treated as a reaction to intended legislation this was, and at the time was regarded as, intemperate and over-blown language. As a warning against the insidious effect of what appear at first to be only small encroachments on individual freedom it was salutary.

Lane's commitment to these overarching principles had some important practical consequences. He limited his contacts with politicians to the absolute minimum necessary to enable the business of the courts to be done. Shortly after his appointment he rejected attempts by the Home Office to involve the judiciary in the administrative aspect of sentencing policy and strategy on the basis that, in the long term, it would undermine the independence of the sentencing judge. In his last speech as lord chief justice, at the lord mayor's banquet on 9 July 1991, he drew attention to the vast increase in applications for judicial review which had taken place during his period of office and which, he suggested, demonstrated the need for an independent judiciary to resolve disputes between the individual citizen and the increasingly mighty executive. Without an independent judiciary the rights of the citizen would evaporate.

Within three months of his appointment Lane addressed the problem of dangerously overcrowded prisons and identified the principles that were subsequently repeated and continued throughout a plethora of statutes which addressed sentencing issues. His very first suggestion, in the context of dangerously overcrowded prisons, attempted 'to ensure, if an immediate custodial sentence is necessary, that the sentence is as short as possible, consistent only with the duty to protect the interests of the public and to punish and deter the criminal' (*R. v. Bibi*, 1980). This principle was repeated by successive lord chief justices. The decision in *R. v. Bibi* (1980) foreshadowed another of Lane's reforms of the sentencing process. 'We are not aiming at uniformity of sentence; that would be impossible. We are aiming at uniformity of approach' (ibid.). The sentencing decision was for the trial judge, but in Lane's view an endeavour to achieve a coherent approach to sentencing did not constitute an interference with judicial independence. This led to a series of new 'guideline' cases, designed to address sentencing problems whenever what Lane described as a 'divergence' of judicial approach had become apparent. Such cases included cases involving breach of trust, drugs, death by dangerous driving, incest, and rape. It became commonplace for the Court of Appeal criminal division to provide guidance to sentencers, and in 2003 the Criminal Justice Act created the Sentencing Guidelines Council, which represented the logical conclusion of Lane's belief that there should be a consistency of approach to similar sentencing problems throughout the country. The Criminal Justice Act 1988 granted the attorney-general the power to refer 'unduly lenient' sentences to the Court of Appeal. Subsequent legislation significantly increased the types of case to which these powers applied. Again it was Lane who identified the applicable principles and commented: 'that mercy should season justice is a proposition as soundly based in law as it is in literature' (*Attorney-general's reference no. 4 of 1989*).

In short, from the beginning to the end of his period in office one of Lane's continuing concerns and major achievements within the criminal justice system was to keep the hugely complex issue of sentencing in individual cases constantly in mind, and to achieve a cohesive series of guiding principles which remained the foundation for subsequent legislative changes and judicial decision.

Another troublesome feature when Lane took office was that a number of serving judges did not appear to understand the difference between acting robustly and behaving discourteously and unfairly. Lane's sense of fairness was innate, and he well understood the importance of ensuring that the trial process should not only be fair, but should be perceived by the defendant, the jury, and anyone who happened to be in court, to be fair. He was quick to criticize judges who were unfair to defendants:

> however distasteful the offence, however repulsive the defendant, however laughable his defence, he was entitled to have his case fairly presented both by counsel and by the judge. Where the cards seemed to be stacked most heavily against a defendant, the judge should be most scrupulous to ensure that nothing untoward occurred. (*R.* v. *Marr*, 1989)

Not least because Lane made clear that judicial misconduct taking the form of bullying and unfairness would not be tolerated it became very rare indeed.

A more intractable problem that Lane sought to address was the problem of unprepared, discursive summings up that confused rather than elucidated the issues. This type of summing up was described by him as 'hornswoggle'. No judge hearing a summing up of his own described in this way would have regarded it as a compliment. Subsequent developments of the criminal law after his retirement meant that the lengthy summing up was not eradicated, but Lane's objective, that the summing up should be as short as possible consistent with the judge's duty, was universally understood.

It was in relation to the substantive criminal law that the brilliance of Lane's mind can best be appreciated. When dealing with appeals against conviction said to have arisen from errors of law his technique was to gather together all the relevant statutes and decided cases and to reduce huge and often difficult, sometimes irreconcilable, judicial statements into a sentence or two that encapsulated the essence of the principle. The technique that had served him so well as a QC in 1965 was revived time and again. Examples of these landmark judgments abound. They include dishonesty throughout the criminal law, duress, and mistake, where Lane expressed 'the utmost sympathy' for the 'unfortunate recorder' because the case 'raised issues of law which have been the subject of debate for more years than one likes to think and the subject of more learned academic articles than one would care to read' (*Gladstone Williams*, 1984). Typically, Lane's judgment covered a few brief pages. As a result of his determination to establish principle in easily understood English innumerable summings up were made more understandable and more readily understood.

Perhaps the most remarkable judgment produced by Lane involved the examination and discarding of the fiction that a husband who had sexual intercourse with his wife without her consent could not be guilty of rape:

> The idea that a wife by marriage consents in advance to her husband having sexual intercourse with her whatever her state of health and however proper her objections … is no longer acceptable. It can never have been other than a fiction, and fiction is a poor basis for the criminal law … where the common law rule no longer even remotely represents what is the true position of a wife in present day society, the duty of the court is to take steps to alter the rule if it can legitimately do so … the time has now arrived when the law should declare that a rapist remains a rapist subject to the criminal law, irrespective of his relationship with his victim … this is not the creation of a new offence, it is the removal of a common law fiction which has become anachronistic and offensive. (*R.* v. *R.*, 1992)

Lane was distinctly media-unfriendly. In his view communication skills outside the terms of the judgment in court were unnecessary. Everything appropriate for a judge to say should be said in court. He would not accept that a less rigid (he would have contended, a less principled) approach would not have undermined the independence of the judiciary but rather would have produced a better understanding of what judicial independence means and why it matters. One consequence of his rigid self-denying ordinance never at any time, even after his retirement, to answer personal criticism was that he came to be known most widely as one of the three judges who, in January 1988, dismissed the appeals of the six men convicted of a terrorist bombing attack in Birmingham in 1975.

The judgment in this notorious case was massive, running to well over 150 pages of typescript. At the very end the judgment observed that, 'as with many cases referred by the Home Secretary to the Court of Appeal, the longer this case has gone on, the more convinced this court has become that the verdict of the jury was correct' (*R.* v. *Callaghan and others*, 28 Jan 1988). An analysis of the judgment shows that the court dismissed the appeals on the basis of the evidence available to it during the course of the lengthy hearing in late 1987, disregarding the campaigning and out-of-court comments by supporters and opponents of the appellants. The observation at the end of the judgment was no doubt intended to address and bring the controversy the case had generated to a conclusion. It was an uncharacteristic mistake for Lane to make, not least because one of the constant refrains throughout his judicial career was that allowance should always be made for the unforeseen and the unforeseeable. When, in 1991, the case returned to the Court of Appeal, although the issues before that court were not the same as those before the court in the first appeal, attention naturally focused on the last sentence in the judgment, which had attracted much attention at the time when it was spoken. The decision of the court in the second appeal demonstrated that the convictions were unsafe and unsatisfactory, and accordingly they were quashed. The criticism of Lane was immediate and personal. A hundred and forty MPs signed an early day motion, in effect urging that the lord chief justice should resign immediately. The royal commission on criminal justice, chaired by Viscount Runciman, was appointed, not least because public confidence in the administration of criminal justice was inevitably undermined by concern that six men had been imprisoned for so many years before their convictions were eventually quashed. Lane was the focal point for these criticisms and concerns, and in the immediate aftermath he was treated as if he were the embodiment of all the perceived deficiencies in the criminal justice system. History will lend a kinder perspective, and Lane's many remarkable achievements as lord chief justice will come to be more widely appreciated.

It was later suggested that, as a result of the second Birmingham six appeal, Lane retired early. He did not. Despite the hostility of the personal criticism directed against him he remained in office, continuing to provide judgments of the highest quality and offering encouragement and support to his colleagues. In one of his very last judgments, Stefan Kiszko's appeal against his conviction for murdering a young girl, after he had served many years in prison, was quashed. Later scientific advances led to the conviction of another man for this murder. Lane's fortitude during this difficult period reinforced the warm admiration and respect of his judicial colleagues. When, at his valedictory, in April 1992, Lord Donaldson, the master of the rolls, spoke of giving voice 'to the anger and disgust which we have felt at the campaign of calumny waged against you in recent months' (personal knowledge), he was accurately reflecting the views of the judicial bench as a whole that an outstanding lord chief justice had been unfairly traduced.

Lane was made an honorary bencher of the Inner Temple in 1980 and an honorary fellow of his old college in 1981, and was made an honorary LLD of Cambridge in 1984. After his retirement to Hitchin, Hertfordshire, he became a trustee of the Prison Reform Trust, and chaired the committee on the penalty for homicide, which in 1993 urged the abolition of the mandatory life sentence for murder. He died at the Lister Hospital, Stevenage, on 21 August 2005, of heart failure, and was survived by his wife and son. After his death Sir Louis Blom-Cooper QC, who in his time represented many clients associated with unpopular causes, observed that 'by common consent of the legal profession, Lane was a very great Lord Chief Justice of England and Wales' (*The Guardian*, 23 Aug 2005). Perhaps in Lane's case truth may indeed be the daughter of time. IGOR JUDGE and COLIN COLSTON

Sources *The Guardian* (23 Aug 2005) · *The Times* (24 Aug 2005) · *Daily Telegraph* (24 Aug 2005) · *The Independent* (25 Aug 2005) · Burke, *Peerage* · *WW* (2005) · personal knowledge (2009) · private information (2009) · b. cert. · m. cert. · d. cert.

Likenesses photographs, 1972, Getty Images, London · photographs, 1979–80, Photoshot, London · photograph, 1980, Photoshot, London [*see illus.*] · photographs, 1980–89, PA Photos, London · G. J. D. Bruce, portrait, exh. Royal Society of Portrait Painters, London 1983, Gray's Inn, London · obituary photographs

Wealth at death £575,964: probate, 3 Aug 2006, *CGPLA Eng. & Wales*

Large, Sir Peter (1931–2005), civil servant and campaigner for the rights of disabled people, was born on 16 October 1931 at 100 Hawkeys Lane, Tynemouth, the son of Rosslyn Victor Large (*d.* 1955), bank clerk, later a principal at the Bank of England, and his wife, Ethel May, *née* Walters (*d.* 1981). At the time of the registration of his birth his parents lived at 34 Chase Court Gardens, Enfield, London. He was educated at Enfield grammar school and University College, London where he graduated BSc in civil engineering. His love of sport and his ability on the football field earned him a trial with Arsenal Football Club. During his national service (1953–5) he served on submarines and was the first national serviceman to be appointed a submarine engineer officer. He left the navy as a sub-lieutenant.

Sir Peter Large (1931–2005), by unknown photographer

In 1956 Large joined Shell International Petroleum as an engineer. Initially posted to Nigeria, he served also in Ghana and the Persian Gulf before being posted to Indonesia in 1962. There he contracted poliomyelitis, which left him paralysed. He was flown back to the UK by the Royal Air Force and spent fourteen months in hospital. He was unable to use his legs or arms and was totally dependent on others. Had it not been for his determination and intellectual vigour he could well have been consigned for life to an institution. On 27 April 1962, while still an in-patient at the Royal Free Hospital, London, he married Susy Baber, a 33-year-old divorcee (through whom he acquired a stepson and two stepdaughters), and daughter of Bernard Fisher, medical practitioner. With her assistance he was able to leave hospital. In 1966 he joined the Board of Trade and in 1976 he became a senior scientific officer.

Although he remained a civil servant until 1991, Large's main impact was elsewhere. Also in 1966 he joined the board of the British Council for Rehabilitation of the Disabled, and when this merged with the Central Council for the Disabled in 1977, to form the Royal Association for Disability and Rehabilitation (RADAR), he became a member of the executive committee of the new organization, a position he held until 2001. This gave him a pivotal role in the world of disability politics. Meanwhile he had noticed that services for disabled people were geared towards those of non-managerial status and, together with Mary Greaves, he established the Association of Disabled Professionals in 1971. He became its first chairman, a post he retained until 1993 when he became its parliamentary adviser.

Large quickly became a superb lobbyist who won the respect of those he worked with as well as of the ministers and civil servants whose minds he had to change. In the

1960s there were no social security benefits to meet the particular needs of disabled people who had not been in the military. Large campaigned for a disability benefit in two parts. One part would be taxable and would compensate for loss of earnings and the other, which would be tax free, would meet the extra costs that disability inevitably imposed. Although this was never achieved in the form Large wanted, his efforts bore fruit in social security benefits such as the disability living allowance and incapacity benefits. For twenty years Large was the parliamentary adviser to the Disablement Income Group and from 1985 to 1993 was its vice-chairman.

Large also made a major contribution to the mobility of disabled people. In the 1960s the assistance disabled people received towards their mobility was, apart from wheelchairs, an invalid tricycle that had only one seat; passenger carrying was forbidden. A number of disability organizations campaigned to have these tricycles replaced by a small car. Large, who could not drive because he could not use his arms, argued that the existing scheme helped those who already had the most mobility and ignored those with greater impairments. Against considerable opposition he won the argument and the government introduced the mobility allowance, a cash payment intended to enable disabled people to purchase a car. However, as the allowance was not enough for that purpose Large joined a working group set up by the Central Council for the Disabled. The government accepted its main recommendation that a new organization should be established to enable disabled people to lease a car for the value of their allowance. The charity Motability was the result and Large was a trustee from its inception in 1978 until his death. By that time it was supplying cars to 440,000 disabled people and was responsible for 5 per cent of all new car sales in the UK. Large also worked to make public transport accessible. His main platform was his chairmanship of the Joint Committee on Mobility for Disabled People (1971–97) but he also advised the Department of Transport through his membership of the influential Disabled Persons Transport Advisory Committee (1986–2002). He promoted accessible air travel but his diffidence seemed to prevent him taking advantage of the services he won for other people. He rarely travelled further than London.

Perhaps Large's greatest contribution was his successful fight for legislation outlawing discrimination against disabled people. The world's first minister for disabled people, Alfred (Alf) Morris, invited Large to chair the Silver Jubilee Committee on Improving Access for Disabled People (1977–9) to investigate the extent to which disabled people were prevented from getting around by the structure of the built environment. His report, *Can Disabled People Go Where You Go?* (1979), prompted the response 'no'. Also in 1979 Morris invited Large to chair another committee, the Committee on Restrictions Against Disabled People, which reported in 1982. The new (Conservative) minister was less responsive to meeting the needs of disabled people than Morris had been. Large pointed out that discrimination was not only about employers and service providers treating disabled people unjustly because of their disability. It also occurred when buildings were designed with features such as steps that prevented wheelchair users getting into them. Hotels routinely turned disabled people away, as did cafés, restaurants, and shops. He argued that seeking to tackle discrimination by persuasion was a waste of time; legislation was needed to make it unlawful. He argued that he did not care what people thought about him, what was important was the way they treated him. Jack Ashley introduced a Disability Discrimination Bill into parliament. It was defeated, as was every other attempt until 1995, when a Disability Discrimination Act was finally passed. This legislation provided inadequate means to enable disabled people to enforce their rights, but in 2000 the Disability Rights Commission was established. A twenty-year battle had been won.

Large's wife, Susy, developed a kidney disease in 1979 and was advised to stop smoking. Large, who was a heavy smoker, supported his wife and gave up overnight, another example of his remarkable willpower. Susy died in 1982. Large needed help for all physical activity and hired a number of carers to support him. Eventually he employed Sheenah McCaffrey (the daughter of Joseph James McCaffrey, hospital boiler stoker), who moved into his home to provide the twenty-four-hour care he needed. They married on 16 October 1992. With her support he was able to continue attending countless meetings in London to press the cause of disabled people. In later years he used artificial respiration during the day as well as at night. He was drafting a response to a government document on behalf of the Association of Disabled Professionals the day before he died.

Large was appointed MBE in 1974 and CBE in 1987, and knighted in 1993. Those who knew him were struck by his intelligence and determination, and his endless ability to support any disabled person who sought his help. He was always courteous and modest. His favourite entertainments were talking to his cats and listening to jazz. He died of respiratory failure on 23 January 2005 at his home, 14 Birch Way, Warlingham, Surrey, and was survived by his wife, Sheenah. BERT MASSIE

Sources J. Ashley, *Acts of defiance* (1992) · *The Independent* (26 Jan 2005) · *Daily Telegraph* (27 Jan 2005) · *The Guardian* (27 Jan 2005) · *The Times* (27 Jan 2005); (1 March 2005) · D. Kinrade, *Alf Morris: people's parliamentarian* (2007) · *WW* (2005) · Burke, *Peerage* · personal knowledge (2009) · private information (2009) · b. cert. · m. certs. · d. cert.

Likenesses obituary photographs · photograph, priv. coll. [*see illus.*]

Wealth at death £675,949: probate, 3 Sept 2007, *CGPLA Eng. & Wales*

La Rose, John Anthony (1927–2006), trade unionist, publisher, and poet, was born on 27 December 1927 at Arima, Trinidad, the younger son of Ferdinand La Rose, a cocoa trader, and his wife, Emily, a teacher. He had five siblings: four sisters, Lillia, Maura, Teresa, and Xysta (Zita), and a brother, Boysie. He was born into a staunchly Roman Catholic family, very active in the life of the local church in Santa Rosa. He attended the church's primary school,

John Anthony La Rose (1927–2006), by Julian Stapleton

where he distinguished himself as a very bright student, winning a scholarship at the age of nine to the prestigious St Mary's College in Port of Spain. On finishing secondary school he taught Spanish at St Mary's before working as an insurance executive with the Colonial Life Insurance Company. His father wanted him to be a doctor, his mother and the staff at St Mary's a priest. He aspired to be neither.

The West Indian colony into which La Rose was born had a history of working-class struggle dating back to the latter decades of the nineteenth century. There were those to guide the young La Rose who had themselves lived through the 'water riots' of 1903 and the massive upsurge of working-class and peasant revolts throughout the 1930s. Neville Giuseppi and Arnold Thomasos introduced him to Marxist thought and ideology, deepening his already clear sense of the need for social transformation and the rebalancing of power to the benefit of workers and peasants in Trinidad and the West Indies, and of working people everywhere. He was an executive member of the Youth Council in Trinidad and produced its fortnightly radio programme, *Voice of Youth*, for Radio Trinidad. He helped to form the Workers' Freedom Movement in Trinidad in the 1940s and edited its journal, *Freedom*. He became an executive member of the Federated Workers' Trade Union, and then general secretary of the West Indian Independence Party, under which banner he unsuccessfully contested a seat in the general election of 1956 in Trinidad. Through his involvement in radical politics he also became an activist in the Oilfields Workers' Trade Union, helping to build and democratize the union. He was later (in 1962) made its European representative, a role he filled until his death.

La Rose developed a keen interest in music, literature, and art, and in the link between cultural expression and politics, a connection that for him was as evident in the so-called high art of the élite as in the folk language, stories, and art forms of the workers and peasants. At a time, therefore, when steel band music, stick fighting, calypso singing, and other such popular arts were being frowned upon by high society, he was finding deeper meanings in popular forms of expression like these and in their revolutionary potential among the masses of the people. Thus it was that in the mid-1950s he co-wrote with the calypsonian Raymond Quevedo (Attila the Hun) the first study of calypso, originally entitled 'Kaiso, a review', and subsequently published as *Attila's Kaiso* (1983). He married the Venezuelan-born Irma Hilaire in 1954 and they had two sons, Michael and Keith. In 1958, as a result of the repression he suffered on account of his political activism and his ideological beliefs, he moved to Venezuela with his family, working as a secondary school teacher and becoming active in the Venezuelan Communist Party. In Caracas he was reunited with his friend and comrade Rafael Cadenas, who had been exiled to Trinidad by the dictator Perez Jimenez.

In 1961 La Rose moved with his family to England, where he found work as a manager of a pig farm in Norfolk before studying law. He then settled in north London, where he lived for the remainder of his life. He and Irma separated, and his partner from 1965 until his death was the science historian Sarah Swinburne White. They had one son, Wole.

La Rose's fundamental belief in the integral relationship between culture and politics led him to be as concerned about writers, visual and performing artists, footballers, cricketers, musicians, and storytellers, and their art in the context of human endeavour and social transformation, as about political activists in the struggle for social liberation and against political repression. It was this belief that inspired the formation in 1966 of the Caribbean Artists Movement by La Rose, Andrew Salkey, and Edward Kamau Brathwaite. Also in 1966, La Rose and Sarah White founded New Beacon Books, the first specialist Caribbean publisher, bookseller, and international book service in the United Kingdom. This aimed to remedy the difficulty of obtaining Caribbean literature in the UK, but also published Caribbean-oriented educational materials at a time when most educational publications were unashamedly Eurocentric and even racist. Concerned by the low expectations and achievements of Caribbean children in the UK, in 1969 he founded the George Padmore Supplementary School, which sought both to improve the learning and skills of Caribbean children and to instil in them a sense of pride in their own history and culture. He was later a co-founder of the Caribbean Education and Community Workers' Association, and a co-founder and first chairman of the National Association of Supplementary Schools. In 1971 New Beacon, with the Caribbean Education and Community Workers' Association, published Bernard Coard's groundbreaking work *How the West Indian Child is Made Educationally Sub-Normal in the British School System*, which highlighted the shocking incidence of placing Caribbean children in schools for the educationally sub-normal in the UK. La Rose campaigned on this and many other educational issues.

La Rose was involved in many other movements for social and racial justice. In 1975, after a black schoolboy was assaulted by police outside his school in Haringey, La Rose provided much of the impetus for the founding of the Black Parents Movement, which agitated for non-discriminatory treatment of young black people. Together with the Black Youth Movement and the editorial collective of *Race Today* (an offshoot of the Institute of Race Relations, which La Rose had chaired in 1972–3), the Black Parents Movement was instrumental in forming the New Cross Massacre Action Committee in response to what was perceived as the poor police response to an arson attack that had resulted in the deaths of thirteen young black people attending a birthday party in January 1981; the committee held weekly vigils and mobilized an unprecedented 20,000 black people to take part in a 'black people's day of action' in March 1981. In 1989, in response to the rise of the far right across Europe, he co-founded, with others from France, Germany, Italy, and Belgium, European Action for Racial Equality and Social Justice. He was also involved in various international solidarity movements, including Africa Solidarity, which supported those struggling against dictatorships in Africa, and (with his friend the Kenyan novelist Ngugi wa Thiong'o) the Committee for the Release of Political Prisoners in Kenya.

A deeply cultured and impressively knowledgeable man, La Rose edited several issues of the *New Beacon Review*, which covered literature, music, and the arts, as well as politics and history. He published two volumes of poetry, *Foundations* (1966) and *Eyelets of Truth Within Me* (1991). From 1982 to 1995 he played the major role in organizing the International Book Fair of Radical Black and Third World Books, initially as co-director with Jessica Huntley and then as sole director; the book fair soon attracted writers, publishers, artists, film-makers, musicians, and others from across the globe to attend its annual meetings in London. In 1991 he founded and was the first chairman of the George Padmore Institute, an archive, educational resource, and research centre relating to the black community in Britain and Europe, dedicated to the memory of the pan-Africanist and global campaigner for political freedom George Padmore.

There were few aspects of black British politics and culture with which La Rose was not involved. The poet Linton Kwesi Johnson described him as 'the elder statesman of Britain's black communities', and 'the most remarkable human being I have ever known' (*The Guardian*, 4 March 2006). In person he was modest, erudite, and gentle, but his easy-going manner hid a steely determination and an acute sense of justice. He was an inspiration to generations of black British people. He was decorated with the labour star, the union's highest honour, by the Oilfields Workers' Trade Union in 1986, and awarded honorary doctorates by Leeds Metropolitan University in 1994 and by the University of Trinidad and Tobago, posthumously, in 2006.

La Rose lived for the last forty years of his life in Albert Road, Finsbury Park, a short distance from his New Beacon Bookshop and the George Padmore Institute. It was from there that he was taken to Whittington Hospital, Islington, on 28 February 2006 after suffering a heart attack. He died shortly after arrival. He was buried in Islington and St Pancras cemetery on 13 March, after a service at the New Testament Church of God, Wood Green. A memorial celebration in Trinidad was organized by the Oilfields Workers' Trade Union in April 2006, and an all-day celebration of his life held at the South Bank Centre in February 2007 drew writers, artists, and intellectuals from Africa, the Caribbean, and North America as well as Europe and was heavily over-subscribed. He was survived by his partner, Sarah, and his three sons. GUS JOHN

Sources R. Harris and S. White, eds., *Foundations of a movement: a tribute to John La Rose* (1991) • A. Walmsley, *The Caribbean Artists Movement, 1966–72* (1992) • *Americas* (1 Sept 1996) • B. W. Alleyne, *Radicals against race: black activism and cultural politics* (2002) • S. White, R. Harris, and S. Beezmohun, eds., *A meeting of the continents: the International Book Fair of Radical Black and Third World Books* (2005) • E. A. Markham, *At home with Miss Vanesa* (2006), 3–14 • *The Guardian* (4 March 2006); (28 March 2006) • G. John, 'John La Rose in the cause of social liberation across the continents', address at Oilfields Workers' Trade Union memorial celebration, Trinidad, 8 April 2006 • *The Independent* (22 April 2006) • *ABC Magazine* (18 Feb 2007) • George Padmore Institute, www.georgepadmoreinstitute.org, 20 Aug 2009 • Institute of Race Relations, www.irr.org.uk, 20 Aug 2009 • New Beacon Books, www.newbeaconbooks.co.uk, 20 Aug 2009 • personal knowledge (2010) • private information (2010) • d. cert.

Archives FILM BFINA, light entertainment footage • *Dream to change the world*, H. Ové (director) | SOUND BL NSA, performance recordings • BL NSA, documentary recordings

Likenesses H. Ové, group portrait, giclée print, 1974, NPG • E. Lloyd, bronze bust, 2002, priv. coll. • J. Stapleton, photograph, George Padmore Institute, London [*see illus.*] • obituary photographs • photographs, George Padmore Institute, London

Latham, John Aubrey Clarendon (1921–2006), artist, was born on 21 February 1921 in Livingstone, Northern Rhodesia, the second of three children and only son of Geoffrey Chitty Latham (1887–1980), colonial official, and his wife, Kathleen Anne Clarendon, *née* Godfrey (*d.* 1970), widow of Captain Aubrey E. Coulton, and daughter of Dr H. J. C. Godfrey, of Bridlington. Latham's father had fought in east Africa during the First World War and was a devout Christian. At the time of Latham's birth he was a native commissioner, but he soon after became director of native education for Northern Rhodesia. Latham and his sisters spent their early years in a house overlooking the Victoria Falls. In 1927–8 Latham attended boarding school in Livingstone and Bulawayo. From 1929 he was a boarder at a preparatory school in England before following his father to Winchester College from 1934 to 1940. He later said he hated school and academically he was undistinguished.

In 1940 Latham volunteered for the armed forces and joined the Royal Navy as an ordinary seaman serving on the battleship *King George V*, which became the flagship of the Home Fleet after the sinking of HMS *Hood* in May 1941. Having been made a lookout, it was from the ship's crow's nest that, three days later, he observed the battle in the Atlantic during which *Hood*'s opponent, the *Bismarck*, was sunk. Promoted to temporary acting sub-lieutenant, Latham transferred to motor torpedo boats carrying out night patrols in the English Channel. Subsequent service in the Mediterranean provided the opportunity of studying the art and architecture of ancient Greece and Rome. While in Rome he encountered for the first time paintings by El Greco, whose fusion of natural and metaphysical elements fascinated him and later became something of an inspiration. Eventually he commanded minesweepers in the North Sea, operating from the port of Flushing. During this final phase his boats were twice blown up, although Latham came through without injury.

Encouraged by the example of the artist and ornithologist Peter Scott, whom he befriended, Latham began to make paintings of birds and motor torpedo boats. In 1946, while on leave in London, he extended this emerging artistic interest by attending art classes at the Regent Street Polytechnic. After demobilization he studied full-time at Chelsea School of Art from 1946 to 1950. During this time his tutors included the painters Robert Medley, Robert Buhler, and Ceri Richards; among his fellow students were the sculptors Robert Clatworthy and Elizabeth Frink. By 1948 he was sufficiently advanced to hold his first exhibition, which he shared with fellow student John Berger, at the Kingly Gallery in Soho. Latham's début comprised paintings encompassing a range of subjects and approaches, from observation to allegory.

At Chelsea Latham met Barbara Mary Lesley Steveni, then a student on the foundation course, and they were married on 7 February 1950. Seven years his junior, she was the daughter of Leo Steveni, Indian army officer. They later had three children: Noa, John-Paul, and Xenia. Following their wedding the Lathams moved to a flat in Fleet, Hampshire, where they remained until 1955. Of crucial significance during this time was his contact with Clive Gregory and Anita Kohsen, who lived nearby. Gregory was a respected astronomer, previously director of the University of London observatory. Kohsen was a parapsychologist who taught philosophy and psychology at the Polytechnic of North London. Their respective backgrounds in science and philosophy underpinned a shared dissatisfaction with a perceived fragmentation of knowledge into disparate disciplines and beliefs. Both sought a coherent world view, which they called 'psychophysical cosmology'. These ideas profoundly influenced Latham's thinking.

At Gregory's and Kohsen's invitation, in October 1954 Latham made a mural for a halloween party at their house. Using a spray gun he applied a cloud of black paint to a white ceiling, creating fields of tiny spots which he then developed figuratively. For Latham the minuscule marks resulting from a short burst of spray suggested the way that existence comes into being from a state of nothing via a 'least event': 'an occurrence of not-nothing on a state of nothing, for a least instant' (*Time-Base and Determination in Events*, 1976, 4). He now saw that a fundamental unit of time formed the basis for a unified theory of reality. This realization was the genesis of the complex fusion of scientific, philosophical, and artistic ideas that united all Latham's subsequent work. Soon after, Gregory and Kohsen, with Latham as honorary founder member, formed the Institute for the Study of Mental Images, a society that published papers ranging from physics and the natural sciences to metaphysics and the paranormal. About the same time Latham commenced what would become an expansive artistic output in various media, including paintings, sculpture, relief assemblages using a range of found objects, films, and installations.

From 1958 Latham used books as primary material: burnt, dissected, and animated. In the same year the Lathams left Hampshire and moved to London, which heralded a period of exceptional activity. In addition to making works of art, during the 1960s Latham staged events and held exhibitions in Britain, Europe, and the United States. Increasingly, destruction became a theme. Between 1964 and 1967 he created columns of old books—'skoob towers'—which were then burnt or exploded in public areas. In 1966 and 1968 he participated in the Destruction in Art Symposium, two events held in London and New York respectively. In August 1966, while teaching part-time at St Martin's School of Art, he staged *Still and Chew Event* in which Latham and a group of students shredded and chewed a library copy of *Art and Culture* by Clement Greenberg. The resulting pulp was then fermented and stored in a glass tube. As a result Latham was dismissed from the teaching staff. Alongside these developments, from 1966 Latham was actively involved with Steveni and other founder members in the Artist Placement Group, renamed O + I (Organization and Imagination) in 1989, which aimed to place artists, acting as consultants, within a range of industries, businesses, and institutions.

By the end of the 1960s Latham was using the term 'event structure' to describe his time-based theories. While his output of artwork was sustained, during the 1970s he increasingly employed text, diagrams, and other methods to explain and disseminate his ideas. These included manifestos, papers, reports, and statements; performances and mixed-media events; experimental films; installations; and seminars, lectures, and interviews. Throughout he continued to mount regular exhibitions internationally and in Britain, including those with Lisson Gallery, Latham's only dealer after 1970. In 1975 his first retrospective exhibition was held at the Städtische Kunsthalle, Düsseldorf. The following year an exhibition at the Tate Gallery provided the first British overview of his work.

As a result of this far-ranging activity and exposure,

from the 1980s and throughout the 1990s Latham consolidated an international reputation as a complex, obscure, controversial, avant-garde, and deeply unconventional artist and thinker. At the same time his distinctive contribution to British art, and to contemporary art in general, became recognized. In addition to solo exhibitions in London, Edinburgh, Berlin, and New York, and inclusion in numerous international group shows, in 1994 the Tate Gallery devoted a room to a display of the gallery's holdings of his work. Despite this attention, Latham continued to work and live modestly in his terraced house in Peckham, London, which doubled as a studio. Gentle by nature and softly spoken, he could also be roused to considerable ire, not least when one of his sculptures, *God is Great*, was deemed too controversial for inclusion in an exhibition held at Tate Britain in late 2005 and he accused the gallery of censorship. He failed to recover from a chill caught while visiting the De La Warr Pavilion at Bexhill with his wife, and died of pneumonia on 1 January 2006 in King's College Hospital, Denmark Hill. He was survived by his wife and their three children. PAUL MOORHOUSE

Sources J. Latham, *Time-base and determination in events* (1976) · R. Hamilton, in *John Latham: early works* (1987) · J. A. Walker, *John Latham, the incidental person: his art and ideas* (1995) · P. Moorhouse, 'Insights from afar: the art of John Latham', *John Latham in focus* (2005) · P. Moorhouse, 'And the word was made art', *Tate Etc*, 5 (2005), 102–4 · *The Independent* (5 Jan 2006) · *The Guardian* (7 Jan 2006) · *The Times* (10 Jan 2006) · personal knowledge (2010) · private information (2010) · m. cert. · d. cert.
Archives Tate collection, letters to Lady Norton | SOUND BL NSA, performance recordings · BL NSA, documentary recordings
Likenesses I. Kar, photographs, *c*.1960, NPG · F. Monteforte, photograph, 2005, Getty Images, London, AFP · P. Wardle, red chalk, 2005, NPG · obituary photographs
Wealth at death £529,878: probate, 29 Sept 2006, *CGPLA Eng. & Wales*

Law, Sir Horace Rochfort (1911–2005), naval officer, was born on 23 June 1911 at 46 Merrion Square, Dublin, the younger son of (Samuel) Horace Law (1873–1940), ear, nose, and throat surgeon, and his wife, Sybil Mary (1878–1952), daughter of Sir George Clay, first baronet. Though intent on a naval career (he traced his descent back to Lord Nelson's elder brother, William) he was unable to enter the Royal Naval College on account of ill health and spent four years at Sherborne School before joining the Royal Navy as a special entry cadet at seventeen. Throughout the 1930s he served in surface ships and specialized in gunnery, achieving advanced or 'dagger' qualifications.

The outbreak of the Second World War found Law as gunnery officer of the cruiser *Cairo*, in which he served through the ill-fated Norway campaign of 1940. His experience in fighting off air attacks and dodging bombs delivered both in dives and level flight was a notable baptism of fire, and resulted in a mention in dispatches. His ship was damaged off Narvik and he moved on to HMS *Coventry*, in which he went through the Greece and Crete campaigns in the Mediterranean in 1940–41. These involved intensive attacks by Italian and German aircraft in which Law distinguished himself, earning the DSC. He returned to the United Kingdom at the end of 1941 and on 13 December that year married Heather Valerie Coryton (*d.* 1996), the 24-year-old daughter of Henry Haworth Coryton, rector of Merrow, Surrey. The wedding cake had been made by Groppi's in Cairo—a rare sight in wartime Britain. There were two sons and two daughters of the marriage. Law's wartime naval service continued with trials of an American anti-aircraft gunnery system in the cruiser *Delhi*. His enthusiasm for this did not endear him to the Admiralty authorities. In 1942 he joined the cruiser *Nigeria*, in which he served for the remainder of the war.

Law was promoted commander in 1946. His first command was the frigate *Modeste*, the gunnery training ship. Thereafter, after an Admiralty appointment in the gunnery division, he moved on to be fleet gunnery officer in the Far East. During the Korean War he was closely involved in the intricate business of naval gunfire support for the UN forces and particularly the South Korean army. For this work he was appointed OBE in 1950. Promotion to the rank of captain followed, with command of the new and powerful destroyer *Duchess*. After further staff appointments he assumed command of HMS *Centaur*, then employed as the training carrier, and then moved on to be captain of the Royal Naval College, Dartmouth, in 1960–61. There he oversaw the introduction of a new scheme of entry and training, with the ability to manage change effectively that was increasingly a feature of his career.

On promotion to rear-admiral in 1961, Law became flag officer sea training, in charge of working-up ships from Portland, then flag officer submarines, an unusual appointment for a non-submarine officer. Promoted vice-admiral in 1965, he became controller of the navy, responsible for all aspects of the service's material development. Tenure of this gruelling post coincided with the navy's battle to keep alive the project for a new generation of fixed-wing aircraft carriers, ultimately lost with its cancellation under Denis Healey in 1966. Law, who had some doubts (never voiced in public) about the project, remained in post as controller and oversaw the subsequent evolution of the 'through deck cruiser', eventually to become the Invincible class. His final appointment, from 1970 to 1972, was as commander-in-chief, naval home command, in charge of all shore establishments in the United Kingdom, serving simultaneously as first and principal naval aide-de-camp to the queen. He was appointed CB in 1963, knighted KCB in 1967, and promoted GCB in 1972.

Law's most striking characteristic, among senior officers of his generation, was his devout Christianity. He underwent two deep religious experiences, one as a midshipman and one during the Second World War; and, strikingly, he sought divine guidance during the successful installation, in action conditions, of new gun barrels in a twin 4 inch mounting. He demonstrated his faith in an address given at the empire youth service in Westminster Abbey on 26 April 1942. In later years he was president of the Officers' Christian Union (1976–86) and chairman of the Church Army Brigade (1980–87). This aspect of his life was generally acknowledged and respected throughout the navy—he said, wryly, that he was 'known as a God-botherer' (interview with J. Parsons)—but his unfailing fairness and professional judgement ensured that it did not cloud his views of those with differing opinions.

After his retirement in 1972 Law was chairman of the shipbuilding firm R. and W. Hawthorn Leslie & Co. (1973–81), a member of the security commission (1973–82), and president of the Royal Institute of Naval Architects (1975–7). As a governor of Sherborne School he had to handle a difficult matter of staff succession, which he did with skill. He lived during his retirement at Cowpers, West Harting, near Petersfield, Sussex, and died there of bronchopneumonia on 30 January 2005. He was survived by his four children. RICHARD HILL

Sources H. R. Law, address, Westminster Abbey, 26 April 1942, priv. coll. • interview recorded by grandson, Jonathan Parsons, c.2003, priv. coll. • *The Times* (1 Feb 2005); (17 Feb 2005); (21 Feb 2005) • *Daily Telegraph* (2 Feb 2005) • TNA: PRO, ADM 1/28644; DEFE 24/387 • Burke, *Peerage* • *WW* (2005) • private information (2009) [Jonathan Parsons, grandson; T. S. Sampson; M. B. Casement; J. Blackham; A. Welch; P. Haddacks; Leigh Merrick; naval secretary] • personal knowledge (2009) • b. cert. • m. cert. • d. cert.

Archives SOUND priv. coll., interview with J. Parsons

Likenesses group portrait, photograph, 1971, PA Photos, London • obituary photographs

Wealth at death £639,480: probate, 2 June 2005, *CGPLA Eng. & Wales*

Lawther, Patrick Joseph (1921–2008), physician and medical researcher, was born at 15 Victory Avenue, Gretna, Dumfriesshire, on 9 March 1921, the son of Joseph Lawther, marine engineer, and his wife, Winifred, otherwise Winefride, *née* Mulholland. He went to school in Carlisle and then in Morecambe. His undergraduate career began at King's College, London, in 1939 where he read chemistry but did not take a degree. He returned to Morecambe and taught at Apperley Bridge, Yorkshire, for a year. In 1941 he was appointed as a chemist with Hickson and Welch Ltd, where he stayed for the remainder of the Second World War. In 1944 he decided to study medicine, read for the first MB examination while at work, and, after preclinical studies at Cambridge, proceeded to St Bartholomew's Hospital medical school and graduated MB BS in 1950. He became a member of the Royal College of Physicians in 1954. Meanwhile he married Kathleen May Wilkowski (1917–1998), daughter of Vincent George Wilkowski, accountant, on 4 November 1944. She also became a doctor. They had two sons, Anthony and Christopher, and one daughter, Judith (*d.* 2003).

The London smog of December 1952, which killed at least 4000 people, had a great effect on Lawther's career. He had been a house physician at St Bartholomew's Hospital between 1950 and 1951 and was a Cooper and Coventson research scholar at the time of the smog. In 1955 the Medical Research Council established the MRC Group for Research on Atmospheric Pollution (later the Air Pollution Unit, and later still the Environmental Hazards Unit) at St Bartholomew's Hospital, and Lawther was appointed director. This was a remarkable step for a young physician and a brilliant appointment by the Medical Research Council. Lawther recruited a number of scientists to his unit, including Brian Commins, in charge of analytical work, and Robert Waller, who had read physics at Imperial College, moved to statistical work, and worked on cancer producing compounds with Sir Ernest Kennaway. Thus began a remarkably productive association and a series of seminal research programmes on the effects of air pollutants on health. The focus of the work was on the effects of particulate matter and of sulphur dioxide, the main pollutants of the coal-smoke era. Lawther adopted a characteristically broad approach: he measured concentrations of pollutants in the air, studied panels of patients suffering from chronic bronchitis and related their symptoms to ambient levels of pollution, and undertook experimental studies on himself and his staff. With Waller he was one of the first to apply the electron microscope to the examination of particles collected from the air. The work led to a series of publications and established the reputation of the unit as perhaps the world's leading centre for air pollution research. The Clean Air Act of 1956 led to the progressive reduction of levels of air pollutants in London and other British cities, and Lawther's group followed the declining effects on health. By the 1970s London air pollution was much reduced and in 1977 the unit was closed with Lawther's agreement, its work being seen as essentially complete. In retrospect this was an error: research on the effects of air pollutants on health dried up in the UK and did not recover until the early 1990s. This soured relations between Lawther and his North American colleagues, and only later did UK research workers regain a leading position in the field. It was later discovered that levels of air pollution that Lawther would have regarded as trivial have a significant effect on health. After the closure of the unit Lawther moved to the Medical Research Council's toxicology unit at Carshalton and led the clinical section there. He retired in 1981. In addition to his work for the Medical Research Council he had been honorary consultant and physician in charge of the department of environmental and preventive medicine at St Bartholomew's Hospital from 1962 to 1981, and had held the chair in environmental and preventive medicine there from 1968 until 1981. In the latter year he was appointed an emeritus professor of London University.

Lawther's distinction as a medical research worker led him into a good deal of committee work. He served as chairman of the Department of Health and Social Security's committee on the medical aspects of contamination of air and soil (1973–85), the same department's working party on lead and health (1978–80), and the Royal Navy's underwater medicine committee, and as a member of the medical committee of the Ministry of Defence's Chemical Defence Establishment at Porton. This work took up a good deal of his time: he was an excellent chairman and committee member. His wide range of knowledge and infectious wit enlivened all discussions. He was advanced to fellowship of the Royal College of Physicians in 1963, made DSc by London University in 1971, and appointed CBE in 1978. His distinction was also recognized by the award of the silver medal of the Royal Society of Arts (1964), the bronze medal of the Académie Nationale de Médicine (1972), the Bissett Hawkins medal of the Royal College of Physicians (1974), and the Edwin Stevens gold medal of the Royal Society of Medicine in 1975.

Lawther's interests extended far beyond medicine. He was a keen fisherman, and excellent shot, an enthusiastic cricketer (in his younger days), and a bibliophile of note. He founded the Lawther Library at his old school in Morecambe and donated a splendid Golden Cockerel edition of the King James gospels (designed and edited by Eric Gill) and the Gegynog Press edition of the Arabic romance *The Stealing of the Mare* to the library of the Royal College of Physicians. He was interested in music, played the recorder, and presented a rare piccolo to the Victoria and Albert Museum. He was widely read, especially in poetry, and knew many of the poems of W. B. Yeats by heart. He died at Dawson Lodge nursing home, Botley Road, West End, Southampton, on 6 June 2008, of sepsis, and was survived by his two sons. ROBERT MAYNARD

Sources *The Times* (25 June 2008) · *The Lancet* (23 Aug 2008) · *WW* (2008) · personal knowledge (2012) · private information (2012) · b. cert. · m. cert. · d. cert.
Likenesses photograph, 1969, Getty Images, London · photograph, repro. in *The Lancet*
Wealth at death £1,310,258: probate, 3 Nov 2008, *CGPLA Eng. & Wales*

Lawton, Harold Walter (1899–2005), soldier and French scholar, was born on 27 July 1899 at 28 Grove Street, Burslem, Staffordshire, the son of William Thomas Coates Lawton, potter's tile fixer, and later owner of a tile-laying and mosaics business, and his wife, Alice, *née* Hill. He attended Newcastle-under-Lyme middle school, and then Rhyl grammar school, after a family move to north Wales. In 1916 he enlisted as a private, initially with the Royal Welch Fusiliers. He was sent to the western front with the Manchester regiment in 1917. In March 1918 he was dispatched to Béthune to help the 4th battalion, East Yorkshire regiment, hold the line against a major German offensive. The German army redoubled its attack on 8 April. Lawton's battalion was sent to reinforce Armentières. The enemy outflanked Lawton and six companions as they attempted to reoccupy a trench that had just been abandoned. They were cut off for several days, with limited supplies and no officer support, before the Germans came to take them prisoner. At first incarcerated in a cage in a field, Lawton next spent a brief period in the fortress at Lille known as the Black Hole, where conditions were intolerable. He was transferred to Germany, eventually to a prisoner-of-war camp at Minden, where, as a better-educated prisoner, he spent the rest of the war peeling potatoes.

After this 'interruption' Lawton began to study for a degree in French at the University College of North Wales in 1919. He graduated BA in 1921, and MA in 1923, with a dissertation on Roman Gaul. In 1923 he embarked on doctoral research in Paris under Henri Chamard, one of the first French scholars to specialize in Renaissance French literature. Lawton was awarded his doctorate in 1926 for a thesis on the dissemination and influence in sixteenth-century France of the Roman comedies of Terence. It was a massive undertaking. Terence was a major school author and a formative influence on French writers brought up, as almost all were at that period, to imitate the elegance of classical Latin. Lawton was working as something of a pioneer in a body of literature that was only just being opened up to scholarly investigation, but his valuable expertise in Latin enabled him to underpin his research with the methodological rigour associated with classical studies. The result was a two-volume study entitled *Térence en France au XVIe siècle*, of which the first part was devoted to Latin editions and French translations of the plays and the second to imitations by French playwrights. The first volume was published in Paris in 1926, but it was not until 1970 and 1972 that both volumes appeared in print. The work set a standard for research into early printed editions of an ancient author and for study of the impact of the classical tradition on vernacular culture.

In 1926 Lawton was made lecturer in French at University College, Southampton, where he was promoted to the chair of French in 1937. In 1950 he was appointed professor of French at Sheffield University, remaining in that post until his retirement in 1964. His far-sighted administrative skills, spiced by a subversive sense of humour that manifested itself in witty limericks and deft caricatures, were widely appreciated. As pro-vice-chancellor of Sheffield from 1961 to 1964 he was active in preparing the university for the student expansion of the 1960s.

Lawton's main academic publications, apart from the magisterial work on Terence, were an extremely well-received anthology of texts (*Handbook of French Renaissance Dramatic Theory*, 1949) and an annotated selection of the poems of Joachim du Bellay (1961). But Lawton had other strings to his bow. A committed Anglican, he composed numerous sermons. Perhaps as a side-effect of this aspect of his life he was asked by the archbishop of Canterbury to produce a typescript of W. E. Gladstone's vast daily journal, held at Lambeth Palace, which he completed between 1933 and 1936. A happy consequence of this commission was that he was helped in the task by Bessie Pate (*d.* 1991), daughter of Thomas Coates Pate. They married on 8 July 1933, and had two sons and a daughter.

Already a recipient of the Médaille d'Argent de la Reconnaissance Française (1946) and named officier d'Académie (1948), Lawton was made a chevalier of the Légion d'honneur in 1999. This was not a belated tribute to his promotion of French studies, but to his position as a surviving veteran of the First World War. Indeed in his last years Lawton enjoyed considerable fame as Britain's only remaining former prisoner of war from that conflict. He himself became a rather amused object of historical research, providing lucidly recalled information for interviewers who came to visit him at his last address, Oak House residential home, Pond Lane, Greetham, Rutland. He died there on 23 December 2005 and was cremated on 3 January 2006. He was survived by his daughter, his sons having predeceased him. ANN MOSS

Sources J. C. Ireson, I. D. McFarlane, and G. Rees, eds., *Studies in French literature presented to H. W. Lawton* (1968) • R. van Emden, *Britain's last Tommies* (2005) • *The Times* (26 Dec 2005) • *Daily Telegraph* (26 Dec 2005) • *Daily Post* [Liverpool] (27 Dec 2005) • *Yorkshire Post* (31 Dec 2005) • *Birmingham Post* (4 Jan 2006) • *Peterborough Evening Telegraph* (11 Nov 2005); (4 Jan 2006) • *The Sentinel* [Stoke] (4 Jan 2006) • *The Independent* (31 Jan 2006) • *WW* (2005) • personal knowledge (2009) • private information (2009) • b. cert. • m. cert. • d. cert.

Likenesses Elliott & Fry, three photographs, 1949, NPG • obituary photographs • photograph, repro. in Ireson, McFarlane, and Rees, *Studies*

Wealth at death under £129,000: probate, 2 Aug 2006, *CGPLA Eng. & Wales*

Leach, David Andrew (1911–2005), potter, was born on 7 May 1911 in Japan, the elder son of Bernard Howell *Leach (1887–1979), potter and writer, and his wife and cousin (Edith) Muriel, *née* Hoyle (1885–1955). With the exception of a brief interlude with his parents in China he spent the first nine years of his life in Japan, until the family settled in St Ives. He originally hoped to study medicine, but his family could not afford the fees. In 1930 he joined his father's Leach Pottery, but recognizing his own technical ignorance spent two years studying ceramics at Stoke-on-Trent, much to the disapproval of his father, who referred to it as 'the industrial devil'. Luckily David Leach inherited his father's passion for ceramics but not his lack of business sense. He was instrumental in establishing the pottery on a firm financial footing, particularly through the introduction of repetition tablewares, and such other innovations as mail-order catalogues. On 23 April 1938 he married the 25-year-old (Mary) Elizabeth Facey, daughter of Surgeon Commander Samuel Henry Facey RN of Harting, Sussex. They had three sons.

During the Second World War David Leach served with the Duke of Cornwall's light infantry. He then returned to the Leach Pottery, whose growth he continued to nurture. He also helped establish potteries in Norway and at Aylesford in Kent (the latter for the Carmelite friars, in 1954). He began to acquire a reputation for his own pots, particularly after an exhibition at a St Ives art gallery in 1949. In 1955 David and his younger brother Michael left to start their own potteries, David founding Lowerdown Pottery at Bovey Tracey, Devon. There he produced many acclaimed examples of earthenware, and more especially stoneware and porcelain. He was an excellent thrower, and made some beautiful, and often very large, stoneware pots. His development in 1967 of a light, translucent porcelain (later widely used by other potters) enabled him to produce some exquisitely delicate, fluted pots and bowls. His work was acquired by more than forty public collections in Britain alone, and was exhibited in many countries.

David Leach was chairman of the Craftsmen Potters Association of Great Britain in 1967 and won the gold medal of the International Academy of Ceramics the same year. He was also a committed and talented educator. Having spent the year 1953–4 running the pottery department at Loughborough College of Art, he continued teaching there until the mid-1960s. In 1963 he advised Harrow School of Art on its new two-year diploma in studio pottery, and in 1976 he was a key figure in the establishment of the Dartington pottery training workshop. He continued living in Bovey Tracey until his death, on 15 February 2005, at Torbay Hospital, Torquay, of a lower respiratory tract infection. He was survived by his wife of sixty-six years, Elizabeth, and their three sons.

Sources E. Cooper and K. Niblett, *David Leach: a biography* (2003) • K. Niblett and T. Andrews, 'David Leach: a potter's life', *Ceramic Review*, 200 (2003), 18–23 • *The Times* (25 Feb 2005) • www.studiopots.com/davidleach.htm, 26 Sept 2008 • www.ceramike.com/LowerdownPottery/Lowerdown1.asp, 26 Sept 2008 • www.cornwall.gov.uk/index.cfm?articleid=29050, 26 Sept 2008 • m. cert. • d. cert.

Likenesses N. Kurtz, photograph, 1998 • photograph, repro. in *The Times* (25 Feb 2005) • photographs, Leach Pottery, St Ives, Cornwall • photographs, repro. in Cooper and Niblett, *David Leach* • photographs, repro. in www.ceramike.com/LowerdownPottery/Lowerdown1.asp

Wealth at death £18,314: probate, 18 Oct 2005, *CGPLA Eng. & Wales*

Legum [*née* Roberts], **Margaret Jean** (1933–2007), economist, journalist, and political activist, was born on 8 October 1933 in Pretoria, South Africa, the daughter of Andrew Henry Roberts, civil engineer, and his wife, Margaret (Peggy), *née* Mackenzie. Her father was the founder of one of South Africa's largest construction companies, but a greater influence was her mother, a member of Black Sash (the white women's group set up to campaign against apartheid). She was educated at Rhodes University, Grahamstown, South Africa, and Newnham College, Cambridge. She then spent a couple of years lecturing in economics at Rhodes University before returning to England as a research assistant at the London School of Economics. On 27 July 1960, she married in London, the South African-born journalist Colin *Legum (1919–2003). After her marriage she worked briefly for the Fabian Society and co-wrote with her husband *South Africa: Crisis for the West* (1964) before becoming a full-time housewife and mother. She returned to work in 1984 for Voluntary Service Overseas, organizing health and social development programmes abroad, mainly in Africa. She was a long-standing member of the Iona Community, and sought to bring a Christian perspective to bear on political and economic questions. After her and her husband's return to South Africa in 1996 (they had been banned by the apartheid regime in 1962) she was a notable supporter of the African National Congress (ANC), but not an uncritical one. She was a founder of the South African New Economics Network, and her most notable book, *It Doesn't Have to Be Like This* (2002), based on a series of lectures at the University of Cape Town, argued for the introduction of a basic income grant (a policy rejected by the ruling ANC). In 2007 she published a well-received book of poems, *Learning to Saunter*. Living at Kalk Bay, near Cape Town, she died in Cape Town on 1 November 2007, after surgery for cancer. She was survived by her three daughters, her son David having died in Israel in 1994.

Sources *Sunday Times* [South Africa] (4 Nov 2007) • *Business Day* [South Africa] (5 Nov 2007) • *The Independent* (9 Nov 2007) • *The*

Guardian (16 Nov 2007) · *The Times* (21 Nov 2007) · personal knowledge (2007) · private information (2007) · m. cert.
Likenesses obituary photographs

Leslie, Sir Peter Evelyn (1931–2007), banker, was born on 24 March 1931 at the Acland Nursing Home, Oxford, the son of Patrick Holt Leslie (1900–1972), bacteriologist and research statistician, and his wife, Evelyn (1905–1988), daughter of Major George John Lewes de Berry, of the Royal Artillery. At the time of his birth his parents lived at 97 Bainton Road, Oxford. He was educated at the Dragon School in Oxford, followed by Stowe School, and then completed his national service with the Argyll and Sutherland Highlanders—in which he was commissioned in 1951—before going to New College, Oxford, to read modern history. He graduated with a second-class degree in 1954.

Leslie's original ambition was to enter the diplomatic service, but he failed the Foreign Office entrance examination. Determined, despite the rejection, to pursue a career overseas, he joined Barclays Bank in 1955, choosing the Dominions, Colonial and Overseas (DCO) subsidiary, which at that time was managed separately from the parent bank in the UK and had minority shareholders owning 45 per cent of its shares. Starting in the Sudan he was posted over the next eighteen years to various other exotic locations including Algeria, Zaire, Kenya, and the Bahamas. In Africa he met Charlotte Wenban-Smith (*b.* 1938), daughter of the British diplomat Sir Edwin Chapman-Andrews, and wife of William Nigel Wenban-Smith. They married on 20 December 1975 in Aylesbury after her divorce from her first husband; Leslie acquired four stepchildren.

By the early 1970s Barclays had decided to reorganize and expand. As part of this process the DCO minority stake was bought in and the name of the overseas operations changed to Barclays Bank International. Leslie was brought back to London in 1973 as general manager in charge of planning for both the domestic and international operations. He developed great skills as an administrator and progressively worked his way up the promotional ladder in what was at that time a rather old-fashioned organization still dominated by members of the 'founding families', such as the Tukes and the Bevans, who had formed Barclays through a complex merger of regional banks in 1896. He was appointed to the Barclays board in 1980 and became chief general manager of Barclays Bank International in 1982. This global role placed him in the middle of one of the great international banking crises, the Latin American financial collapse, which began in Mexico in 1982. His political talents were employed as a negotiator on behalf of British banks, and he was co-chairman of a key meeting of international bankers held at Ditchley Park.

In 1985 the Barclays group developed a scheme to merge its domestic and international divisions and Leslie, at the peak of his career, was appointed the overall chief general manager. Two years later, however, he suffered the second of his career near-misses: when Barclays searched for its first non-family chairman, to succeed Sir Timothy Bevan, he was passed over in favour of John Quinton, whose domestic experience was considered to have given him an advantage over Leslie at a period of intense competition among high street banks in the UK. Leslie was made managing director and deputy chairman but after more than thirty years his career in Barclays was essentially over. He retired from his executive role in 1988 and stepped down as deputy chairman on reaching the age of sixty in 1991. At this point he was knighted.

Even before leaving Barclays, however, Leslie was becoming a considerable resource for the broader financial industry. He was a member of the Bank of England's board of banking supervision from 1989 to 1994. This made him well qualified to join the troubled Midland Bank as deputy chairman in 1991: Midland was still suffering from the effects of its ill-judged takeover of Crocker National Bank in California in 1981. The next year, however, Midland was acquired by the Hongkong and Shanghai Banking Corporation and Leslie's role ended. He also had important positions on the Export Credits Guarantee Advisory Council, at different periods, including as chairman from 1987 to 1992. Other banking industry involvements included chairmanships of the executive committees of the British Bankers' Association and the London and Scottish Clearing Bankers. From 1989 to 1995 he was chairman of the Commonwealth Development Corporation, a government body that developed a role in venture capital funds, mainly in Africa, and from 1995 to 1998 he was chairman of a privatized offshoot, NCM Credit Insurance.

In later retirement Leslie embarked on a personal project that brought together strands from his early experiences in reading history, living in Africa, and seeking a diplomatic career, and in 2005 he published *Chapman-Andrews and the Emperor*, a study of the long relationship between his father-in-law, Sir Edwin Chapman-Andrews, and Emperor Haile Selassie of Ethiopia, dealing in particular with the British-aided reinstatement of the emperor in 1941. Other retirement activities included the chairmanship of the governors of Stowe School from 1994 to 2001, while he was chairman of the audit committee of Oxford University from 1992 to 2001 and a curator of the university chest from 1990 to 1995. He died on 27 September 2007, of a brain tumour, at his home, 22 St John Street, Oxford, about a mile from where he had been born. He was survived by his wife, Charlotte, and his four stepchildren. BARRY RILEY

Sources *The Times* (1 Oct 2007); (26 Nov 2007) · *Daily Telegraph* (12 Oct 2007) · *WW* (2007) · Burke, *Peerage* · *Barclays fact sheet*, Barclays Group Archives · b. cert. · m. cert. · d. cert.
Likenesses N. Norrington, photographs, 2001 (with Joan Collins), Camera Press, London · obituary photographs
Wealth at death £4,559,229: probate, 11 Dec 2007, *CGPLA Eng. & Wales*

Levey, Sir Michael Vincent (1927–2008), art historian and gallery director, was born at 90 Kenilworth Avenue, Wimbledon, on 8 June 1927, the only child of Otto Lemuel Herbert Levey (1893–1961) and his wife, Gladys Mary, *née* Milestone (*b.* 1892). His father, of Irish descent, was a civil servant working in the Air Ministry. His mother came from a rural community in the North Riding of Yorkshire, very different from her husband's urban background. They had met during the First World War, when he was nursed by her in hospital in St Omer. They were disparate in character and temperament; he was open and jovial, she shy and withdrawn. Levey's close relationship with his parents and his childhood experiences, both at home and at school, were delightfully described in his memoir, *The Chapel is on Fire: Recollections of Growing Up* (2000).

Levey was educated at the Oratory School in Berkshire. In 1945, faced with national service, he volunteered and the following year was commissioned into the King's Shropshire light infantry. He was subsequently attached to the Royal Army Education Corps in Egypt, where he reached the rank of acting major in a very short time. After leaving the army in 1948 he went to Exeter College, Oxford, where he read English, and had the good fortune to be tutored by Nevill Coghill. Recognizing Levey's exceptional ability, Coghill persuaded him to take his degree after two years; he got a first. When he accidentally left his unfinished BLitt thesis in a café in Oxford he decided it was time to leave Oxford. He was undecided what to do, until a girlfriend asked for help in completing an application form for a vacant post of assistant keeper in the National Gallery in London. Immediately recognizing the attractions of the job, he also put his name forward and was duly appointed in 1951.

The situation in the National Gallery in 1951 was very different from that when Levey left it thirty-five years later, when with a hugely increased staff there were specialists covering every field of activity. The director, at that time Sir Philip Hendy, and a staff of five keepers virtually ran the whole operation. All attention was given to curation and acquisition. There were almost no exhibitions and only minimal low-key public programmes. Levey speedily completed two catalogues, *The Italian Eighteenth Century School* (1956), later expanded to *The Seventeenth and Eighteenth Century Italian Schools* (1971), and *The German School* (1959), and wrote a large number of more popular publications, effortlessly covering the whole field of the gallery's holdings. Almost as a sideline he compiled a catalogue for the Royal Collection (*The Later Italian Pictures in the Collection of her Majesty the Queen*, 1964; 2nd edn, 1991).

At a new year's eve party in 1953 Levey met Brigid Antonia *Brophy (1929–1995), an up-and-coming writer, and daughter of the writer John *Brophy. Love was instantaneous and less than six months later, on 12 June 1954, they were married. They lived from then until 1991 in a flat in the Old Brompton Road. He said of her: 'Blondes appealed to me. I was struck by her blondness and the unmissable diamond-like quality of her mind.' She said of him: 'He is a natural creature. He's like a cat. I prefer animals to people, which is why I married Michael' (*Daily Telegraph*, 11 Aug 2000). Her novel *Flesh* (1962) was said to have been inspired by their courtship. Their union was loving but unconventional. They greatly rejoiced in sharing the experience of their blossoming writing careers, stimulating one another in the process. They had many interests in common, and were both keen vegetarians with an inbuilt love and respect for animals. Although their marriage took place according to the Roman Catholic rites Levey abandoned Catholicism shortly afterwards; their refusal to have their daughter, Kate, baptized led to the break-up of his close relationship with his father, whom Levey later described as 'unyielding, merciless almost, in the pressure he put upon me to bend to his wishes' (*Louth Leader*, 12 July 2000). Both Leveys entered wholeheartedly into the spirit of the 1960s and became part of the public scene, appearing on television quiz shows. The manner was extravagant. The clothing was flamboyant and trendy. He was not averse to personal publicity. There was a much remarked on dichotomy between the life of a civil servant in Trafalgar Square and a follower of the swinging sixties.

In 1968 Levey overtook a more senior colleague to become keeper, in 1970 deputy director, and finally in 1973 director, unusually without a public competition and against the wishes of the prime minister, Edward Heath, who would have preferred Sir John Pope-Hennessy. There was a change in Levey's attitude towards authority and his behaviour became less extrovert, but the wit, charm, and warmth was not diminished. His clothing remained distinctively personal if less flamboyant; he wore red shoes for one trustees' meeting. He was a masterly and efficient administrator; any visitor from mid-morning onwards would be confronted by a completely clear desk and an empty in-tray. He was treated by his staff with some awe but much affection. Feeling that he himself had been deprived of responsibility as an assistant keeper, he was generous in giving his younger colleagues freedom of action.

Levey left the gallery a very different place from what it had been when he took over. His fervently held wish that the collections should be more widely known and enjoyed was realized by the greatly increased number of visitors over the period. At the beginning of his directorship he expressed the wish that Nicholas Poussin's dictum 'The purpose of art is pleasure', with which he fully concurred, should 'be written up in letters of gold over the entrance to the Gallery'. Exhibitions became a major part of the gallery's programme, and varied from such manifestations as 'Art in Seventeenth-century Holland' (1976), pioneering in its display of sculpture and the decorative arts with paintings, to the series entitled Painting in Focus, which concentrated on a single masterpiece. He created a professional education department, with a fully developed programme with manifold activities, as well as an artist-in-residence programme. Within the building there was much activity in refurbishing and rehanging galleries, but he was not someone caught up in the movement for the restoration of historic interiors. For him it was the experience of the individual painting that counted. Aiming for a feeling of intimacy rather than for the overall space of a gallery, he introduced suspended ceilings, screens, and changes of level, all of which were later removed. He added new galleries within the existing building and also played, after living through the débâcle of the Ahrends Burton Koralek design of 1982 for the Hampton site (described by the prince of Wales as a 'monstrous carbuncle'), a major role in the long and controversial planning of what eventually became the Sainsbury wing, opened in 1991.

Ultimately Levey's greatest achievement was the addition of no less than fifty-five paintings to the collection, including a substantial number of masterpieces, such as Altdorfer's *Christ Taking Leave of his Mother*, Rubens's *Samson and Delilah*, and Monet's *Gare St Lazare*. One of his favourites, J.-L. David's coolly beautiful portrait of Jacobus Blauw, involved extended negotiations in Paris and New York over a number of years before the French authorities agreed to its export. Yet his out-and-out favourite acquisition was a simple and straightforward picture; *Still Life with Oranges and Walnuts* by Luis Meléndez. With works by Klimt, Matisse, and Picasso he brought the collections well into the twentieth century for the first time. Having so brilliantly enriched the collection, his appeal for more funds was answered, not by a parsimonious and uncaring government, but by a private individual, not even a national of this country. In 1985 J. Paul Getty junior made the munificent gift of £30 million, later increased to £50 million, to serve as an endowment fund, which went on to play a significant part in the gallery's acquisitions. Overall Levey can claim to have been one of the most distinguished and effective directors in the National Gallery's history. He was appointed LVO in 1965, knighted in 1981, and elected a fellow of the British Academy in 1983. In 1986 he was made a foreign member of the Ateneo Veneto, and an honorary fellow of the Royal Academy.

Levey had an unusual intensity of emotion and conviction, which informed personal relationships and public polemics in every area he touched. On his own terms he was a very warm friend, capable of great generosity, both material and spiritual. He was exquisitely polite and considerate to everyone he had dealings with, whatever their station in life. But he had a complex personality and, as he himself acknowledged, he could be difficult to deal with. Underneath his carapace of courtesy lurked a will of iron, and once his mind was made up he was immovable. His likes and dislikes, usually very strongly expressed, were unpredictable, and could sometimes seem perverse. The negative side can be seen in *Fifty Works of English Literature We Could Do Without* (1967), written with his wife and a friend, Charles Osborne. It was meant to irritate the *bien pensants*, and it did. In music Bellini and Puccini were 'in', whereas Bach, Beethoven, and Verdi were 'out'. In art Rembrandt was definitely 'out', although Levey bought a major painting by him for the National Gallery.

Living with his wife in an environment dedicated to writing, Levey's output was remarkable for its diversity of subject matter and its quantity, maintained even during the period when he was director of the National Gallery, and at the same time looking after his sick wife. In an unusual tribute to an art historian he was elected a fellow of the Royal Society of Literature in 1980. He had a beautifully crafted style, which owed something to Walter Pater, whom he greatly admired and wrote about (*The Case of Walter Pater*, 1978). With an impeccable choice of words he conveyed a highly personal and sensuous appreciation of works of art. As a colleague wrote, 'Almost any page of any of his writings will reveal insights which no one had shown before, felicities both of thought and phrase' (Gould, 369).

Levey's first love was Venice; he wrote about eighteenth-century painting there (*Painting in 18th Century Venice*, 1959; rev. edn, 1980) and much later he produced a monograph on his favourite artist, Giambattista Tiepolo (1986), which won the Banister Fletcher prize. Of his two volumes for the Penguin Style and Civilization series, *The Early Renaissance* (1967) and *The High Renaissance* (1978), the first won the Hawthornden prize, never previously awarded to a work of non-fiction. Dealing with that elusive, much written about subject, he perhaps produced his most distinguished study of the art and culture of an individual period. *Painting and Sculpture in France, 1700–1789* (1992), which, perhaps unexpectedly, displayed a wonderful sensitivity towards the sculpture of the period as well as a sensuous understanding of painting, became a standard work. More out of his recognized field was an evocative book on Ottoman art (1976). In the field of music he wrote a deeply felt biography of his favourite composer, Mozart (*The Life and Death of Mozart*, 1971). His three novels never received the same admiration. He delivered the Slade lectures at both Cambridge (1963–4, published as *Rococo to Revolution*, 1966) and much later Oxford (1994–5), and the Wrightsman lectures in New York (1968, published as *Painting at Court*, 1971). At his death he was engaged in writing a biography of Ellen Terry.

In 1986 Levey took early retirement from the National Gallery in order to look after his wife, who was increasingly suffering from the debilitating effects of multiple sclerosis. Eventually in 1991 he decided to leave London and move permanently to what was essentially a workman's cottage in the attractive small Lincolnshire town of Louth, where his daughter lived, and he could attend to his wife in a nursing home there, where she died in 1995. Finding the peace of mind he sought, he continued to write vigorously, and communicate with a wide range of friends in letters full of wit and erudition lightly worn; he was exceptionally well-read. With his sharp eye for human traits and foibles, his remarks about friends and colleagues were delightfully piquant. His flowing conversation was marked by sparkle and great charm of manner. On 23 December 2008 he was taken ill and he died of a stroke in the county hospital at High Holme Road, Louth, five days later. He was cremated and his ashes were scattered in Somersby churchyard. He was survived by his daughter, Kate. CHRISTOPHER WHITE

Sources *The working of the National Gallery* (1974) · M. Levey, *Director's choice: selected acquisitions, 1973–1986* (1986) · *National Gallery News* (Dec 1986) · C. Gould, 'Michael Levey: a tribute', *Apollo*, 135 (1986), 369 · M. Levey, *The chapel is on fire* (2000) · *Daily Telegraph* (30 Dec 2008) · *The Guardian* (30 Dec 2008) · *The Independent* (30 Dec 2008) · *The Times* (31 Dec 2008) · *New York Times* (3 Jan 2009) · *PBA*, 153 (2009), 234–56 · Burke, *Peerage* · *WW* (2008) · personal knowledge (2012) · private information (2012) · b. cert. · m. cert. · d. cert.

Archives King's Cam., Annan papers | SOUND BL NSA, current affairs recording

Likenesses D. Miller, double portrait, photograph, 1965 (with Arthur Lucas), Getty Images, London · J. Twine, double portrait, photograph, 1965 (with Arthur Lucas), Rex Features, London · D. Montgomery, group portrait, photograph, 1974, repro. in *Sunday Times* (10 March 1974) · obituary photographs · photograph, repro. in *Daily Telegraph* (1 July 2000)

Wealth at death £634,366: probate, 17 June 2009, *CGPLA Eng. & Wales*

Lewis, Geoffrey Lewis (1920–2008), Turkish scholar, was born at 13 Abersham Road, Hackney, London, on 19 June 1920 (the date was incorrectly recorded on the birth certificate as 14 June). He was the second of the three children, and the only son, of Jewish parents, Ashley Lewis (1887–1971), foreman at a clothing factory, and his wife, Jeanne Muriel, *née* Cohen Sintrop (1892–1960). He was educated at University College School, London, and went up to St John's College, Oxford, in 1938 as an exhibitioner, to read classics. He gained a second in classical honour moderations in 1940 (subsequently qualifying for a BA degree by war decree, which was conferred *in absentia* in 1942), and then joined the Royal Air Force, in which he spent five years, mostly serving in Egypt and Libya as a radar operator. At Epping register office on 26 July 1941, six months before being posted abroad, he married Rhoda, otherwise Raphaela Rhoda Bale (Raff), Seideman (1920–2004), whom he had known since they were classmates in London at the age of four. The daughter of Reuben Seideman, civil engineer, she was then working as a shorthand typist; later she was a teacher, author, linguist, and renowned cook. They had one son and one daughter.

It was during his wartime service in north Africa that Lewis found the opportunity to teach himself Turkish, an undertaking inspired by a half-joking suggestion by his Latin tutor in 1939 that he take up the language 'as a hobby'. Because of the almost complete absence of textbooks on Turkish at that time he made use of local Turkish contacts that he cultivated in the places where he was posted. Another resource was such Turkish translations of English classics as his wife was able to find by scouring the bookshops in Charing Cross Road. She would send these out to him together with the English originals.

On his return to Britain in 1945 Lewis, who had now set his heart on an academic career in Turkish studies, consulted the Laudian professor of Arabic, H. A. R. Gibb, who said that he had long wished to see Turkish added to the syllabus of the Oriental studies faculty, but that a sound knowledge of Arabic and Persian was necessary for a scholarly understanding of the language, especially in its only recently abandoned Ottoman form. Lewis thereupon embarked on a second BA course, in Arabic and Persian, which he completed with first-class honours only two years later, in 1947, and was awarded the James Mew Arabic scholarship. Before commencing his doctoral studies he visited Turkey for the first time, spending six months immersing himself in the language and culture. This laid the foundations of a lifelong relationship with Turkey and its people that was to be as strong as his love of the language. Before beginning to make his distinctive mark in the relatively virgin territory of Turkish studies Lewis established his academic credentials as an Arabist. He gained his DPhil degree in 1950 for a translation (published in 1959) of an important but problematic medieval Arabic philosophical text, based on the Greek writings of the neo-Platonist Plotinus.

With his doctorate completed, in 1950 Lewis was appointed as the first lecturer in Turkish at Oxford. In the early years of his academic career his involvement in Arabic and Islamic studies continued alongside his pioneering work in the Turkish field, and this was recognized by his promotion, in 1954, to senior lecturer in Islamic studies. The next change of title, in 1964, to senior university lecturer in Turkish, reflected the fact that Turkish had now been recognized as a 'main language' in the Oriental studies syllabus at Oxford, supported by the creation of a second (history) post in the Turkish studies field. Lewis was elevated to a personal chair in Turkish in 1986, a year before his retirement. From 1961 he was a fellow (and from 1987 emeritus fellow) of St Antony's College.

In the course of his teaching career at Oxford, Lewis held a number of visiting professorships, notably at Princeton (1970–71, 1974), the University of California at Los Angeles (1975), and as British Academy Leverhulme visiting professor in Turkey in 1984. A particularly remarkable association was that with Robert College in Istanbul (later Boğaziçi University), where as visiting professor in 1959–60 and with annual follow-up visits in the period down to 1968 he set up and ran a 'Bicultural Humanities Programme' providing an introduction to Eastern and Western history and culture for students of engineering.

Lewis's name became widely known through his first publication, *Teach Yourself Turkish* (1953), which provided, for a whole generation of post-war Turcophiles, precisely the tool that he himself had found missing when he needed it. Two years later *Turkey* (1955) provided a similarly lucid presentation of the country itself and its modern history. Both these works went into revised editions. Lewis's *Turkish Grammar* (1967) saw him established as a world authority in the analysis of the language. After his retirement *The Turkish Language Reform: a Catastrophic Success* (1999) presented a devastating dissection of the linguistic 'purification' that was an integral part of the process of modernization in Turkey. Among Lewis's other publications, translations figured prominently. In the field of classical Arabic studies apart from the Plotinus text there was the masterly *Albucasis on Surgery and Instruments* (1973), a definitive edition as well as translation of a major work of Arabic medicine, on which he collaborated with a consultant pathologist. In the Turkish field his translations included, in addition to a number of modern works, *The Balance of Truth* (1957), an Ottoman work on disputed issues in Islamic religion, and *The Book of Dede Korkut* (1974), a work of medieval Turkish epic literature. Both these translations were amply provided with scholarly annotation, yet presented in a form that was highly accessible to the general reader.

Throughout his career Lewis worked tirelessly in a number of ways, both formal and informal, to enhance Turco-British relations, especially at the cultural level. He was a member of the British–Turkish Mixed Commission (1975–95) and vice-president (1972–2003) then president (from 2003) of the Anglo-Turkish Society. His advice was frequently sought by Turkish as well as British diplomats, and in the 1960s he even worked for a time in the Turkish prime minister's office. Much later, in 1991, he was asked by prime minister Turgut Özal to write the preface to the document setting out the case for Turkish membership of the European Community.

Lewis was elected a fellow of the British Academy in 1979, and an honorary fellow of St John's College, Oxford, in 2000. His service to the cause of British–Turkish relations was recognized by his appointment as CMG in 1998. Honours came from the Turkish government also, in 1973, 1991, and finally in 1998, when he received the Order of Merit of the Republic of Turkey for his contributions to Turkish studies. Described by his son as 'quietly Jewish' (private information), he was a kind and gentle person, always ready to see the best in others, and much loved by colleagues and students alike. His ready sense of humour was evident in most of his writings, as well as in his legendary capacity for telling anecdotes. Another personal hallmark was the ubiquitous pipe, which he would puff on before answering questions. The remarkable strength of his marriage was demonstrated in the fact that, after the death of their daughter in 1976, the couple took upon themselves a major role in the upbringing of her two small children. His wife's sudden death in 2004 was a great blow to Lewis. He himself died following a heart attack in Oakthorpe Road, Summertown, Oxford, on 12 February 2008, and was buried in Wolvercote cemetery, Oxford, on 19 February. He was survived by his son, Jonathan. CELIA KERSLAKE

Sources introduction, 13–16; A. Mango, 'Geoffrey Lewis *Âbi*', in Ç. Balım-Harding and C. Imber, *The balance of truth: essays in honour of Professor Geoffrey Lewis* (2000), 17–22 • *The Times* (21 Feb 2008) • *Oxford Mail* (27 Feb 2008) • *The Guardian* (12 March 2008) • *Anatolian Studies*, 58 (2008), v–vi • *PBA*, 166 (2010), 215–24 • *WW* (2008) • personal knowledge (2012) • private information (2012) [Jonathan Lewis, son] • b. cert. • m. cert. • d. cert.
Archives Bodl. Oxf. | SOUND BL NSA, current affairs recording
Likenesses photograph, St. Ant. Oxf, Middle East Centre • photograph, repro. in Balım-Harding and Imber, *Balance of truth* • photograph, Oxford Mail and Times Library • photograph, repro. in G. Lewis, *Modern Turkey* (1974), jacket
Wealth at death £881,204: probate, 21 July 2008, *CGPLA Eng. & Wales*

Lichfield. For this title name *see* Anson, Thomas Patrick John, fifth earl of Lichfield (1939–2005). For other subjects who held this title name *see Oxford DNB*, 33.719.

Lings, Martin (1909–2005), scholar of Islam, was born on 24 January 1909 at Barciecroft, Burnage Lane, Burnage, Lancashire, the son of George Herbert Lings, cotton spinner and ornithologist, and his wife, Gladys Mary, *née* Greenhalgh. After spending much of his childhood in the United States he returned to England to finish his studies. He became head boy at Clifton College, Bristol, and matriculated at Magdalen College, Oxford, in 1929 to read classics, but soon switched to English. At Oxford he came under the influence of C. S. Lewis, who encouraged the cultivation of his literary gifts. Throughout childhood Lings had experienced 'nostalgia for the past' (Lings, 'Frithjof Schuon', 15), and Lewis's compelling evocation of the 'surpassing greatness of the Middle Ages' (Lings, *The Elements*, 9) provided him with a fixed point from which to judge other epochs. Though Lewis awakened in Lings a love for Old English poetry and Dante's *Divine Comedy*, Lings did not follow Lewis into Christian faith. Before coming to Oxford he had forsaken corporate worship. Though he had not abandoned private prayer he focused instead on the search for beauty in literature, nature, and art. When he left Oxford with a second-class degree in English in 1932 the composition of poetry was his sole aspiration.

In 1935 Lings accepted a lectureship in Anglo-Saxon and Middle English at Vytautas Magnus University in Kaunas, Lithuania, where he remained until 1939. During this period he discovered the writings of the French traditionalist René Guénon. In his encounter with Guénon Lings felt he had come 'face to face with the truth' (Lings, 'Frithjof Schuon', 15). Guénon criticized the marginalization of religion in modern civilization and argued for the existence of a common core of esoteric truth in all of the world's great faiths. But Guénon believed esoteric truth was best pursued through the adoption of a valid form of religious ritual under the guidance of a spiritual master. After corresponding with Guénon Lings looked first to Hinduism, but soon turned to Islam. In 1938, with the approval of Guénon, he visited Frithjof Schuon, another traditionalist thinker who lived in Switzerland. Schuon had been initiated into the Shadhiliyyah Sufi order by the celebrated Algerian Sheikh Ahmad al-ʿAlawi in 1932 and under Schuon's guidance Lings embraced Islam and took the name Abu Bakr Siraj ad-Din.

Adrian Patterson was a close friend of Lings from Oxford and shared his literary tastes and spiritual interests. Patterson had taken up a position at Cairo University and become an intimate of Guénon's household. In 1939 Lings went to Cairo to visit both Patterson and Guénon and the outbreak of the Second World War prevented him from leaving. In a fateful turn of events in the coming months Patterson died tragically in a horse riding accident and Lings took his place as a lecturer in English literature at the university. He also replaced Patterson as Guénon's personal assistant. During these years Lings temporarily abandoned his poetic ambitions and focused on his spiritual pursuits. He concentrated on learning Arabic and writing a manuscript later published as *The Book of Certainty: the Sufi Doctrine of Faith, Wisdom and Gnosis* (1952), which reflected the maturation of his new-found convictions. On 14 August 1944, while on leave back in England, Lings married Lesley Smalley, a childhood friend with whom he had kept in touch over the years. Aged thirty-one at their marriage, she was a chartered physiotherapist, and daughter of Edgar Smalley, cotton waste merchant. There were no children of the marriage.

Guénon's death in 1951 and the Egyptian revolution of 1952 signalled the end of Lings's Egyptian sojourn. When the new government dismissed British staff from Cairo University he returned to England. There he resumed his education at the School of Oriental and African Studies, University of London, where he graduated BA in Arabic in 1954 and PhD in 1959. He also secured a job as assistant keeper (1955–70), deputy keeper (1970–71), and finally keeper (1971–3) of oriental manuscripts and printed books at the British Museum.

Though Guénon had become estranged from Schuon before his death and Schuon had distanced himself from Islam, Lings remained loyal to his mentors. He also remained committed to Islam, becoming a leading expositor of the Sufi vein of traditionalist thought. Through a series of publications including *A Muslim Saint of the Twentieth Century* (1961), the revised version of his PhD dissertation, on Sheikh Ahmad al-ʿAlawi, Lings earned a reputation as a sympathetic and incisive commentator on Sufi mysticism. In 1976 he was closely involved with the World of Islam festival in London and wrote the festival's companion volume on Koranic calligraphy. However, his most highly acclaimed work was undoubtedly *Muhammad: his Life Based on the Earliest Sources* (1983), for which he received commendations from the governments of Pakistan and Egypt. In this work Lings followed the earliest traditions and utilized his own considerable literary abilities to produce a vivid narrative of the Prophet's life from a believer's perspective. His other published works included studies of the esoteric meanings in Shakespeare's plays, and a volume of *Collected Poems* (1987, revised and expanded 2002).

Lings was a diminutive man. Lewis once likened his movements about Magdalen College to those of a 'furtive mouse' (*Collected Letters*, 2.24). He was also a gentle, serious individual who gave generously of his time to those seeking spiritual guidance. He died of heart failure at his home, 3 French Street, Westerham, Kent, on 12 May 2005, and was buried beneath the garden he had so lovingly tended. A memorial service was held in the chapel of Magdalen College, Oxford, on 24 September 2005. He was survived by his wife, Lesley. TODD M. THOMPSON

Sources M. Lings, *The elements and other poems* (1967) • M. Lings, 'Frithjof Schuon: an autobiographical approach', *Sophia*, 4/2 (1998), 15–16 • C. W. Ernst, 'Traditionalism, the perennial philosophy, and Islamic studies', *Middle East Studies Association Bulletin*, 28/2 (1994), 176–81 • M. Sedgwick, *Against the modern world: traditionalism and the secret intellectual history of the twentieth century* (2004) • J.-B. Aymard and P. Laude, *Frithjof Schuon: life and teachings* (2004) • C. S. Lewis, *Collected letters*, ed. W. Hooper, 2: *Books, broadcasts and war, 1931–1949* (2004) • C. S. Lewis, *Collected letters*, ed. W. Hooper, 3: *Narnia, Cambridge and Joy, 1950–1963* (2006) • *The Independent* (21 May 2005) • *The Times* (25 May 2005) • *The Guardian* (27 May 2005) • *New York Times* (29 May 2005) • *Sevenoaks Chronicle* (2 June 2005) • *Q News* (June 2005) • *Sophia: the Journal of Traditional Studies*, 11/1 (2005) • *WW* (2005) • b. cert. • m. cert. • d. cert.

Likenesses K. Backer, photograph, 2004, priv. coll. • obituary photographs

Wealth at death £166,684: probate, 7 Nov 2005, *CGPLA Eng. & Wales*

Lipstein, Kurt (1909–2006), jurist, was born on 19 March 1909 in Frankfurt am Main, Germany, the son of Alfred Lipstein, a distinguished physician from Königstein, East Prussia, and his wife, Hilda, *née* Sulzbach, who belonged to a prominent banking family in Frankfurt. Both parents were of Jewish descent. After attending the Goethe Gymnasium in Frankfurt he spent a year at the University of Grenoble (1927), before undertaking juristic studies at the University of Berlin (1927–31). Once the National Socialists gained power in 1933 he saw his hopes of entering the German judicial service dashed. Within a year he emigrated to England (he had an English great-grandfather and his grandmother had grown up there). Having secured a place at Trinity College, Cambridge, he set to writing a thesis on the Roman law of suretyship, which he defended successfully in 1936. He was then helped through a difficult financial period by his mentor, Harold Gutteridge, professor of comparative law at Cambridge. Gutteridge paid him personally to supervise students, thus securing him a small foothold in Cambridge law teaching. In 1940 this was interrupted by internment, from which the university rescued him. He stayed on in Cambridge, sustained by membership of Clare College, secretaryship of the law faculty, and his informal but central place in the Squire Law Library. On 23 June 1944, at the register office in Wheatley, Oxfordshire, he married Gwyneth Mary Herford (1909/10–1998), the daughter of Henry John Robberts Herford, civil servant. At the time of their marriage she was serving as a subaltern in the Auxiliary Territorial Service. They had two daughters, Eve and Diana.

In 1946 Lipstein obtained a lectureship in the faculty, and eventually in 1956 a fellowship at Clare. Meanwhile he was called to the bar by the Middle Temple in 1950. In 1962 his scholarly achievements led to a university readership in conflict of laws and in 1973 he became professor of comparative law. He retired in 1977, but continued teaching and writing until his final year. This was a period in which the value of his scholarship gained further recognition: a doctorate of laws from Cambridge in 1977, a Festschrift in 1980, election to the exclusive Institut de Droit International in 1993, and appointment as honorary queen's counsel in 1998 (he had been made an honorary bencher of Middle Temple in 1966).

He made a striking impression on his many pupils (some of whom became highly distinguished), on those from the European continent and elsewhere who visited him in the faculty, on the many students who attended the summer school in English legal method, and on the scholars who collaborated with him in his kaleidoscopic work in international law, comparative law, and European Community law. The warmth of his personality, his readiness to offer help, and his love of intellectual discussion became legendary. Only weeks before his death members of the law faculty gathered to celebrate the acceptance of his doctoral thesis seventy years before and to listen raptly to his account of why he came to England to undertake the work for it.

Lipstein brought to England a considerable knowledge

of European legal systems and the languages in which they were conceived. The subject most crucial to him proved to be private international law, that set of rules that strives to identify how the courts of one jurisdiction should deal with foreign factors in civil litigation before them: determining whether they should hear the case, deciding upon which law to apply, and settling whether to recognize or enforce a foreign judgment. English lawyers of the time had come to treat these issues in a rather insular fashion. Lipstein and other fugitive jurists sought to highlight comparisons between the solutions reached in different legal systems—a thread running through his voluminous writings on the subject. At crucial points of his career he was able to tackle such basic dilemmas as the need to categorize the legal character of a dispute (on which he concentrated in his Hague lectures of 1973); and likewise the need to determine whether a choice of foreign law to govern the substance of a dispute also entailed adopting the private international law rules in that foreign system for making the choice of law. On this perplexing question of *renvoi* he at least secured for the Institut a basic resolution that had eluded it for a century. His writings took up difficult or neglected fields, such as the private international law of restitutionary claims, intellectual property, trusts, and interpersonal conflicts. The last two topics were among his own chapters in volume 3 of the *International Encyclopedia of Comparative Law*, which is devoted to private international law. Of this volume he was editor-in-chief from its outset in 1972.

Lipstein contributed to aspects of international law, seeking to show both the public and private sides as part of a greater whole. Noteworthy here was his work on private international law issues before international tribunals; also his appearance as an advocate before the International Court of Justice in the *Nottebohm case*, *Liechtenstein* v. *Guatemala* (1955, concerning the right of a country to determine its own citizenship, and of another country not to recognize that citizenship). He advanced knowledge of European Community law, writing a full and commodious textbook for a controversial discipline. It was published in 1974, the year after Britain became a member state, its coherence establishing a model for subsequent literature. The death of Lipstein's wife, Gwyneth, in 1998 was a serious blow to him, filling with loneliness the last years before his own death, at Addenbrooke's Hospital, Cambridge, of aspiration pneumonia on 2 December 2006. He was survived by his two daughters.

W. R. Cornish

Sources P. Feuerstein and C. Parry, eds., *Multum non multa: Festschrift für Kurt Lipstein auf Anlass seines 70 Geburtstages* (Heidelberg, 1980), vii–x • R. Zimmermann, 'Happy birthday, Kurt Lipstein', *Praxis des Internationalen Privat- und Verfahrensrecht*, 4 (1998), 296–7 • C. Forsyth, *Jurists uprooted*, ed. J. Beatson and R. Zimmermann (2004), 463–81 • C. von Bar, *Jurists uprooted*, ed. J. Beatson and R. Zimmermann (2004), 749–60 • K. Lipstein, *Jurists uprooted*, ed. J. Beatson and R. Zimmermann (2004), 761–70 • *The Times* (18 Jan 2007) • *The Guardian* (29 Jan 2007) • Squire Law Library, Cambridge, Kurt Lipstein papers • Kurt Lipstein in conversation with Terry Moore and Colin Turpin, Clare College, Cambridge, oral history series, no. 2 • www.squire.law.cam.ac.uk/eminent_scholars, 1 July 2009, Squire Law Library, eminent scholars archive • *WW* (2006) • personal knowledge (2010) • private information (2010) • m. cert. • d. cert.

Archives Squire Law Library, Cambridge | sound Clare College, Cambridge, oral history series, no. 2

Likenesses photographs, 1998, Photoshot, London • B. Humphreys, portrait, 2003, U. Cam., Squire Law Library • obituary photographs • photographs, repro. in Feuerstein and Parry, eds., *Multum* • photographs, repro. in www.squire.law.cam.ac.uk/eminent_scholars/professor_kurt_lipstein_gallery.php

Wealth at death £1,840,749: probate, 26 April 2007, *CGPLA Eng. & Wales*

Lister, Moira (1923–2007), actress, was born on 6 August 1923 in Cape Town, South Africa, the youngest of the three daughters of Major James Martin Lister, army officer and property developer, and his wife, Margaret Winifred (Molly), *née* Hogan. Her mother, whose own chances as an actress had been frustrated, encouraged her daughters to pursue the arts. Lister's first stage appearance was with the Johannesburg University Players in Ibsen's *The Vikings of Helgeland* when she was six. In England in the early 1930s she studied voice production with Henry Hulbert (father of actors Jack and Claude), but her decisive break came back in South Africa when the actor–manager Sir Seymour Hicks, presenting three plays there, cast her in *Vintage Wine* (1935). He persuaded her mother to take Lister from Johannesburg's Parktown Convent, where she was being educated, to London to appear in a film he was writing; the film was cancelled, but she stayed in London and made her first appearance there in *Post Road* (Golders Green Hippodrome and Queens Theatre, 1937).

Lister returned to South Africa, where she did nine plays by night and a variety of unrewarding jobs by day, but she became obsessed with the idea of a stage career in England, and finally made her way back there during the latter stages of the Second World War. Turning nothing down, she quickly found radio and film work (a small role in *The Shipbuilders*, 1943), and, after several small roles in the West End, auditioned successfully for the 1945 season at Stratford upon Avon, in which she had six major roles, including Juliet and Desdemona. Then came John Clements's season of two plays, *The Kingmaker* and *Marriage à la Mode*, at the St James's Theatre in 1946, followed by the role that probably established her true métier, as Joanna Lyppiatt in Noël Coward's *Present Laughter* (Haymarket, 1947). She showed herself most adept at witty, sophisticated comedy, to which she brought her shapely blonde beauty and an upper-class demeanour. In the later 1940s she met Jacques de Gachassin-Lafite, vicomte d'Orthez (1905–1989), a French cavalry officer and, later, champagne producer; they married in London in 1951 and had two daughters, Chantal and Christobel. By her own account she always needed to combine her acting career with domesticity.

While the stage was her first allegiance as an actress, Lister also forged a substantial film career at this time. She had a brief flirtatious moment with Stewart Granger in the popular *Love Story* (1944) and was Ray Milland's bitchy mistress in the brilliant melodrama *So Evil My Love* (1948). In the latter she exploited a persona suggestive of malice and duplicity that she brought to several other film roles, including the society girl with her eye on Dirk Bogarde in *Once a Jolly Swagman* (1949), the con-girl out to fleece a Welsh innocent abroad in London in the Ealing comedy *A Run for Your Money* (1949), Denholm Elliott's faithless wife in another Ealing film, *The Cruel Sea* (1953), the *soignée* insider contact for a gang of thieves in the Norman Wisdom comedy *Trouble in Store* (1953), and conniving Babs who meets a bad end in *Grand National Night* (1953). In the often anodyne British cinema of the 1950s she was injecting something spikier.

There were *ingénues* aplenty in contemporary British films but, even when not playing someone downright wicked or deceitful, Lister could be counted on to provide a sense of texture in her characterization. She seemed not to play for sympathy and, if never a major film star, made her presence felt in key supporting roles in such upmarket productions as *White Corridors* (1951), as a nurse whose brittle personality contrasts with Googie Withers's dedicated doctor, *The Deep Blue Sea* (1955), in which she played second fiddle to Vivien Leigh, and *Seven Waves Away* (1957), in which she clung to a lifeboat with Tyrone Power and Mai Zetterling. She appeared intermittently in films until 1989, including a cameo in Anthony Asquith's all-star vehicle *The Yellow Rolls-Royce* (1964), but increasingly stage and television commanded her chief attention.

Lister's first great success on stage was in *The Love of Four Colonels* (Wyndham's, 1951), by and co-starring Peter Ustinov, and for the next twenty or so years she was rarely off the stage. She toured Europe and the English provinces (and later appeared at the Palace Theatre, London) with the Shakespeare Memorial Company, led by John Gielgud, playing Regan in *King Lear* and Margaret in *Much Ado about Nothing* (1955), and she began a congenial partnership with Ian Carmichael in *The Gazebo* at the Savoy Theatre in 1960, their comedic styles meshing happily and leading to five further collaborations. There were more tours—of Africa and Australia—and she continued to act on stage into her seventies and eighties. In *The Aspern Papers* (Wyndham's, 1996), she was described as 'still arrestingly lovely' as Henry James's ancient spinster (*The Guardian*, 30 Oct 2007), and in 2004 she toured with her one-woman show about Noël Coward. She won a Variety Club best actress award for her role in the comedy *Move Over Mrs Markham* (Vaudeville, 1971), and other honours included freedom of the City of London in 2000, and the Naledi award for services to theatre in South Africa in 2006.

Lister had a great deal of experience of popular television, in series, single dramas, and 'specials' of various kinds, becoming a household name in two BBC series devised by Alan Melville, *The Whitehall Worrier* (1967) and *The Very Merry Widow* (1967–9), written specially for her. Her last film was *Flood* (2007), released just a few months before her death. Her character was simply listed as Grandma, a title hard to accommodate to the elegant image she maintained over so many decades. She died in Cape Town on 27 October 2007 and was buried with her husband at St Edward's Roman Catholic Church, Sutton Green, Surrey; she was survived by her two daughters.

BRIAN MCFARLANE

Sources M. Lister, *The very merry Moira* (1969) · J. Parker, ed., *Who's who in the theatre*, 15th edn (1972) · D. Quinlan, *British sound films: the studio years, 1928–1959* (1984) · *The Independent* (29 Oct 2007) · *The Times* (30 Oct 2007) · *Daily Telegraph* (30 Oct 2007) · *The Guardian* (30 Oct 2007) · B. McFarlane, *The encyclopedia of British film*, 3rd edn (2008) · A. Goble, *The complete index to British film*, CD Rom · imdb.com, 10 Nov 2009

Archives FILM BFINA, performance footage | SOUND BL NSA, documentary recordings · BL NSA, performance recordings

Likenesses photographs, 1948–72, Getty Images, London · photographs, 1949–2001, Rex Features, London · photographs, 1951–80, PA Photos, London · A. Buckley, modern bromide print from original negative, 1956, NPG · R. Westwood, bromide print, NPG · obituary photographs · photographs, Photoshot, London

Litvinenko, Aleksandr Valterovich (1962–2006), intelligence officer and dissident, was born on 30 August 1962 in Voronezh, Soviet Union, the son of Valter Litvinenko, physician for the Interior Ministry, and his wife, Nina, *née* Belyavskaya. He attended secondary school in Nalchik, in the Caucasus. His early career was as an exemplary soldier of the Soviet order. On leaving school in 1980 he was drafted and assigned to the internal security forces. Choosing to enlist as an officer cadet, he served in the élite Dzerzhinsky special designation division. In 1986 he also became an informant for the KGB's third chief directorate, responsible for monitoring the loyalty of the armed forces. In 1988 he made a sideways career move, transferring full-time into the KGB. After training at the Novosibirsk military counter-intelligence school he became a full operational officer. On the dissolution of the USSR he remained within the KGB's successor agency, eventually renamed the Federal Security Service (FSB). Within the FSB his duties became increasingly varied and increasingly troubling. He served in a counter-intelligence role and operated in Chechnya during the first Russo-Chechen war (1994–6). After Chechnya he began also to moonlight as part of the security detail of the wealthy and politically well-connected businessman Boris Berezovsky. Meanwhile, he was married twice. First, in 1981, to Nataliya (*b.* 1963), an accountant, with whom he had a son, Aleksandr, and a daughter, Sonia. This marriage was dissolved in 1994 and in the same year he married Marina (*b.* 1962), a ballroom dancer and fitness instructor, with whom he had a son, Anatoly.

In 1997 Litvinenko became a senior operational officer within the FSB's organized crime directorate. This proved a life-changing experience. He found himself navigating the murky post-Soviet underworld in which politics, business, and crime seamlessly interconnected. For a professional investigator he seems to have remained in some ways naïve, and the corrupt behind-the-scenes deals taken for granted within political circles—and even within the FSB and police—shocked and horrified him. He tried to bring them to the attention of his superiors, to no avail, and then went up the chain of command, eventually even drafting a report for Boris Yeltsin which either did not reach the president or was ignored.

According to Litvinenko, in December 1997 he was ordered to assassinate Berezovsky, who had since fallen from Kremlin favour. This proved the catalyst for Litvinenko's break with the FSB and the post-Soviet system altogether. He warned Berezovsky and when the latter publicized the plot, Litvinenko and four other colleagues gave a press conference in support. Litvinenko was the only one of the officers who did not conceal his identity and thus inevitably took the lion's share of the authorities' wrath. He was dismissed from the FSB by its director, Vladimir Putin, and although Berezovsky found him a position within the executive secretariat of the Commonwealth of Independent States—which the businessman headed at the time—he was a marked man. In 1999 the FSB accused him of abusing his position while in its ranks. He was arrested twice and although cleared still spent a total of seven months in the FSB's Lefortovo prison. He realized that there was no real future for him in Russia, not least as Putin was now president.

In breach of a written undertaking not to leave the country, in June 2000 Litvinenko fled for Britain via Ukraine and Turkey, followed by his wife and son. He was sentenced *in absentia* by a Russian court to three and a half years in prison. He was granted political asylum in 2001 (becoming a naturalized British citizen in 2006) and drifted into the court of Berezovsky, who had also taken up voluntary exile in London. Berezovsky began supporting him, in return for a steady stream of revelations and allegations directed against Putin. Litvinenko became an outspoken and intemperate critic of the Kremlin, claiming in his book *Blowing Up Russia* (2002) that it masterminded terrorist attacks to justify the war in Chechnya. His allegations became increasingly controversial, as he blamed the Kremlin for everything from supporting al-Qaeda to murdering inquisitive journalists. While his zeal could not be questioned, his portrayal of the Putin regime verged on conspiracy theory and it became difficult to know quite how seriously he deserved to be taken. Someone did take him seriously, though. In the final controversy of his life, on 1 November 2006 he suddenly fell ill, poisoned by the rare radioactive material Polonium-210. He died at University College Hospital, London, on 23 November, characteristically using his last statement to blame Putin for his death. British investigators sought to question two former FSB officers he had met, but Moscow refused extradition, leaving his murder unsolved and inevitably the subject of speculation. Praised as a martyr by some, vilified as a muckraking traitor by others, he was buried on 7 December in a lead-lined coffin in Highgate cemetery, attended by a heterogeneous mix of family, friends, anti-Kremlin agitators, Chechen émigrés, and journalists. According to his father he had converted to Islam a few days before his death, and Muslim prayers were said over the coffin. He was survived by his wife, Marina, and his three children.

MARK GALEOTTI

Sources A. Litvinenko, *Lubyanskaya prestupnaya gruppirovka* (2002) • A. Litvinenko and Y. Felshtinsky, *Blowing up Russia* (2002) • *The Times* (25 Nov 2006); (8 Dec 2006) • *Daily Telegraph* (25 Nov 2006); (8 Dec 2006) • *The Guardian* (25 Nov 2006); (8 Dec 2006) • *The Independent* (25 Nov 2006) • A. Litvinenko, *Allegations* (2007) • A. Goldfarb and M. Litvinenko, *Death of a dissident* (2007) • M. Sixsmith, *The Litvinenko file* (2007) • M. Dejevsky, 'The Litvinenko files', *The Independent* (2 May 2008) • 'Alexander Litvinenko: complete profile', www.axisglobe.com/article.asp?article=1137, 20 July 2009

Likenesses obituary photographs

Lloyd, Christopher [Christo] (1921–2006), gardener and author, was born on 2 March 1921 at Great Dixter, Northiam, Sussex, the fifth son and sixth child of Nathaniel Lloyd (1867–1933), printer, architect, and architectural historian, and his wife, Daisy, *née* Field (1881–1972). His father had been a successful printer and in 1909 sold his share of Nathaniel Lloyd & Co. (founded by his grandfather, also Nathaniel Lloyd) to his brother Robin Wiley Lloyd, in order to devote himself to his architectural interests. Having bought Great Dixter, a ruined fifteenth-century timber-framed house and its estate, he employed the arts and crafts architect Edwin Lutyens to develop it into a family house. Lutyens re-erected alongside Dixter the timber shell of another hall house and added his own new service wing; he also designed the bones of the 6 acre garden, later given further architectural details by Nathaniel Lloyd. The planting was developed by his wife, Daisy, and son Christopher over the next ninety years.

Daisy Lloyd was proud to trace her ancestry back to Oliver Cromwell and saw motherhood as the object and duty of female existence; she instilled atheism and a puritanical, intellectual ethic in all her children. A persuasive and domineering woman, she was a massive influence on Christopher, known to family and friends as Christo, who lived with his mother at Dixter until her death; he then lived there alone until his own death. His siblings included Selwyn Lloyd (*d.* 1935), Oliver Cromwell Lloyd (*d.* 1985), Patrick Lloyd (who was stoned to death in Aden in 1956), Quentin Lloyd (*d.* 1995), and Letitia Lloyd (who committed suicide in 1974).

Lloyd's mother was passionate about letter writing, botany, and the kind of gardening promulgated by William Robinson in his seminal book *The Wild Garden* (1870). Even as an infant Lloyd took earnestly to all her interests. Schooled at Wellesley House, Broadstairs, and later at Rugby, he became a skilled field botanist and gardener and, under the tutelage of an enlightened music master, Kenneth Stubbs, also a family friend, he became an accomplished pianist and oboe player, able to read an orchestral score like a novel. Daisy Lloyd regularly travelled Europe with her children, to study alpine plants and to introduce them to her friends in Jewish musical circles, especially the family of Walter Hirsh in Frankfurt.

In 1939 Lloyd left Rugby to study modern languages at King's College, Cambridge, having reluctantly set aside architectural ambitions, but he was called up in 1941 before he could complete his course. Serving as a gunner in the Royal Artillery, he was an incompetent soldier, spending much of his war in English army camps, writing

Christopher Lloyd (1921–2006), by Jonathan Buckley

long lonely letters, and botanizing wherever he went. In 1945 he was sent to east Africa but saw no military action. Demobilized in 1946, he returned to Great Dixter, humiliated by army life and considering himself without any skill but gardening.

After receiving a deferred degree from Cambridge, Lloyd studied horticulture at Wye College in Kent (part of London University), staying on to become an assistant lecturer and feeling he had found his métier at last in teaching. During the week he lived at Wye, but he came home at weekends, now very much the master of the garden with his mother acting as clerk of works. His determination always to be right led to friction with the college authorities and he left Wye in 1954, returning full time to Dixter, where his mother was pleased to have her gardening soulmate close to hand. His homosexuality was unspoken between them, neither approved nor condemned.

Lloyd now set out to make Great Dixter itself his occupation, and established a small specialist nursery, concentrating initially on clematis, and opened the house and garden more frequently to the public (it had always been opened for the Queen's Fund). In effect, writing as a plantsman about gardening at Dixter filled the remaining sixty years of his life. Over those years the garden waxed and waned in quality, but it was never better than in the last fifteen years of his life, when he employed Fergus Garrett to be his head gardener. Garrett gradually became Lloyd's best friend and adjutant in all things, and the garden became an icon for gardeners the world over. Like Lloyd, Garrett was a graduate of Wye College, and one of many young people whom Lloyd launched into the gardening world; for many he developed platonic infatuations.

Lloyd's reputation as an author was made with *The Well-Tempered Garden* (1970); this and *Foliage Plants* (1973) were generally considered his best and most influential books. At a time when gardening books were ponderous and dour, Lloyd's elegant, engaging, intelligent, precise, and witty prose was quite new. As well as books about Great Dixter he produced *Clematis* (1977), *Gardener Cook* (1998), *Dear Friend and Gardener* (1998, an anthology of correspondence between himself and his friend the nurserywoman Beth Chatto), and *Other People's Gardens* (1995), his only foray beyond his own territory of Dixter. At the end came three highly illustrated and popular books with which he increasingly needed help from Garrett and his editors, *Colour for Adventurous Gardeners* (2001), *Meadows* (2004), and *Succession Planting for Adventurous Gardeners* (2005). He wrote on an occasional basis for many magazines, including *American Horticulture*, but the column for which he was best known was in *Country Life*, for which he wrote without missing a week, even after a triple bypass operation, from 1962 to 2005. He also wrote for *The Observer* and, from 1989 to 2006, for *The Guardian*. In later years he despaired over diminishing word lengths and ignorant sub-editors, but maintained a mercilessly large output right to the end, in order to help fund Great Dixter and the garden.

Lecturing was another way in which Lloyd promoted Great Dixter and he began it straight after the war, his mother sitting at the back and constantly chipping in. As he became better known and ultimately the grand old man of British gardening, he was asked to speak in Australia, New Zealand, South Africa, and frequently in the USA, alongside such luminaries as James Van Sweden, John Brookes, Penelope Hobhouse, Rosemary Verey, and Helen Dillon. Often he took no fee in return for a fortnight's tour of local gardens and wild flowers, staying with knowledgeable gardeners who often joined the legion of people he invited to stay at Great Dixter. Occasionally he would lecture on his annual holiday in the highlands and islands of Scotland (every year from 1963), where he regularly stayed with Alan Roger at Dundonnell House in Wester Ross. In his last years he became a television guru, making occasional appearances in his outrageously colourful shirts to express youthfully vigorous opinions. In recognition of his services to horticulture he was appointed OBE in 2000 and was awarded the Royal Horticultural Society's Victoria medal of honour (1979), an honorary doctorate of the Open University (1996), and the lifetime achievement award of the Garden Writers' Guild.

After his mother died in 1972 Lloyd made Great Dixter a social hub for gardening; it was always full of guests who were charmed by Dixter's antiquated plumbing, and by his excellent cooking, irascible dachshunds, and gifts of tickets for the opera at Glyndebourne. He died on 27 January 2006 of a stroke as a result of an operation on an arthritic knee, at the BUPA Hospital, Hastings, but not before he had reluctantly set up a trust to manage Great Dixter's future. STEPHEN ANDERTON

Sources *Country Life* (1962–2005) · *The Guardian* (1989–2006); (30 Jan 2006); (31 Jan 2006) · *The Times* (30 Jan 2006); (7 Feb 2006) · *Daily Telegraph* (30 Jan 2006) · *The Independent* (30 Jan 2006) · *Daily Mail* (31 Jan 2006) · S. Anderton, *Christopher Lloyd: his life at Great Dixter* (2011) · Great Dixter archive · archives, Royal Horticultural Society, London · *WW* (2006) · personal knowledge (2010) · private information (2010) · b. cert. · d. cert.

Archives Great Dixter archive, Great Dixter, Northiam, East Sussex | Royal Horticultural Society | FILM BFINA, *Mavis on 4*, C. Bould (director), Channel 4, 18 Aug 1988 · BFINA, light entertainment footage · *Gardener provocateur*, BBC2, 22 Dec 2006

Likenesses A. Hasson, 1996–2003, Camera Press, London · T. Traeger, silver gelatin print, 2001, NPG · J. Buckley, photograph, priv. coll. [*see illus.*] · B. Moody, photograph, repro. in *Country Life*, 185/17 (25 April 1991) · obituary photographs · photograph, repro. in *Country Life* (9 Feb 2006)

Wealth at death £2,104,277: probate, 5 Dec 2006, *CGPLA Eng. & Wales*

Lloyd, June Kathleen, **Baroness Lloyd of Highbury** (**1928–2006**), paediatrician, was born on 1 January 1928, in Gilgit, Kashmir, India, the elder child of Arthur Cresswell Lloyd (*d.* 1955), a major in the Royal Indian Army Service Corps, and his wife, Lucy Bevan, *née* Russell (*d.* 1990). The family returned to England when she was eight, shortly after the birth of her brother, Philip. She was enrolled at the Royal School in Bath, where she excelled and became head girl. She then studied medicine at the University of Bristol, graduating MB ChB with a gold medal in 1951, and took the degree of MD in 1966. She became one of the youngest female members of the Royal College of Physicians of London in 1954. But it was difficult for women to make their way in a competitive male environment and she was advised to try public health. She therefore undertook a course at Newcastle (then part of the University of Durham) while working in South Shields and was again told that paediatrics was not for women. But she was undaunted, and after further training in Bristol she went to Birmingham, where she became research assistant to Otto Wolff. Her friendship with him and his family was probably the most important of her life.

While teaching at the University of Birmingham from 1958 to 1965 Lloyd developed her research interests in obesity, inherited disorders of fat metabolism, and other metabolic diseases. Her chief contribution was the recognition of the fat-soluble vitamin deficiencies that occur in children with abetalipoproteinaemia. She also took an interest in the early diagnosis of familial disorders of fat metabolism where parents died of coronary heart disease at a very young age. She followed Wolff to Great Ormond Street and the Institute of Child Health in 1965, becoming senior lecturer (and in 1973 professor of paediatrics), and there she further developed her research interests. During this time she was very active in teaching, travelling widely to lecture, and began to serve on major national committees, including the Medical Research Council. In 1975 she was appointed to establish a new department of

June Kathleen Lloyd, Baroness Lloyd of Highbury (1928–2006), by unknown photographer

paediatrics at St George's Hospital medical school and, despite many inconveniences—the clinical facilities were far away from the Portakabin housing the academic offices—the department flourished. Many of the young doctors whom she appointed went on to become professors and leaders in paediatrics. Lloyd also developed close associations with biochemists and geneticists, which enabled her research to flourish.

In 1985 Lloyd returned to Great Ormond Street as the Nuffield professor of child health. This second period at the Institute of Child Health was not as enjoyable as her first, because she did not really fit well into the new, highly scientific atmosphere in which laboratory science took precedence over clinical matters. She continued to assume national responsibilities, however, and was the first woman president of the British Paediatric Association from 1988 to 1991. She retired in 1992 but continued to work for the promotion of paediatrics and children's health. She served as paediatric vice-president of the Royal College of Physicians from 1992 to 1995, and many tipped her to be the first non-physician to be president of that ancient institution. For many years she was civilian adviser to the Royal Navy, and she took this responsibility very seriously, showing special concern for the dependent children of isolated service families. She would often tell colleagues that although the position of adviser was honorary she was really an admiral. By this stage her brother, Philip, was a commander in the Royal Navy, and he took great pleasure in seeing both their names in the same navy list.

A determined advocate of children's health, Lloyd was instrumental in the establishment of the Royal College of Paediatrics and Child Health. Founded in 1996, this assumed the responsibilities for the training and standards of paediatricians that had previously rested with the Royal College of Physicians. Such a redrawing of professional boundaries did not go uncontested, and it was thanks to the persistence of Lloyd, by then the honorary secretary of the British Paediatric Association, and others, including Wolff, by then president of the association, that royal college status was finally granted after half a century of agitation by physicians interested in children. Lloyd's contribution was commemorated in the college's coat of arms, which featured her as one of the supporters, along with Thomas Phaer—the author of the first book on paediatrics in the English language, published in 1545—and a baby, adapted from the coat of arms of the Foundling Hospital in Coram Fields. Lloyd was depicted holding the staff of Aesculapius, but instead of a serpent it was intertwined with a double helix, representing DNA and the importance of science—of which Lloyd was a powerful proponent.

Lloyd had a fiery temper to match her red hair. She had a steely eye, and attention to detail was impressed on all who worked for her, including the keeping of meticulous charts of every facet of any child who was a patient under her care. She was much in demand for committee work, thanks to her thoroughness, conscientiousness, and reliability. She was an excellent chairman who had a rare ability to conduct meetings without a hint of tension, and she could sum up in a calm, fair, reflective, and authoritative manner. She used words sparingly but when she did speak little more needed to be said. Her quietness was associated with warmth and practicality.

Although she was always accessible to colleagues, if she was concentrating on papers at her desk it could take many minutes before a visitor at the open door could gain her attention. She was probably most comfortable in the company of her younger male colleagues. Despite her formidable public persona she had a great sense of fun—which she kept for special occasions—and was capable of great kindness. She was good with children, although she did not find close personal contact easy. She was engaged to be married soon after qualifying as a doctor but this was called off at a late hour and she never married.

In 1990 Lloyd was appointed DBE and in 1997 she was made a life peer, as Baroness Lloyd of Highbury. When informed that she was to enter the House of Lords and that it was the best club in town, she said: 'But I am not a clubbable person' (personal knowledge). Shortly before she was due to be introduced into the House of Lords, while she was chairing a meeting on alcohol at the Ciba Foundation, she suffered a massive stroke that left her disabled and unable to speak. With the help of lords Walton and Kilpatrick she did eventually take her seat in 1998, but her disability prevented her from playing an active part. She spent the last few years of her life at Chilton House nursing home, near Aylesbury, Buckinghamshire, where she died on 28 June 2006 following a further stroke. Her funeral service was held in Chilton parish church. A memorial service was held at the church of St George the Martyr in Queen Square, London, on 17 January 2007. She was survived by her brother. ALAN W. CRAFT

Sources *The Times* (10 July 2006) · *The Guardian* (11 July 2006) · *BMJ*, 333/7562 (5 Aug 2006), 306 · *The Lancet*, 368/9535 (12 Aug 2006), 574 · Burke, *Peerage* · *WW* (2006) · personal knowledge (2010) · private information (2010) · d. cert.

Likenesses photographs, 1997, Photoshot, London · obituary photographs · photograph, Royal College of Paediatrics and Child Health, London [*see illus.*]

Wealth at death £949,160: probate, 17 Sept 2007, *CGPLA Eng. & Wales*

Lloyd, (Hugh) Russell (1916–2008), film editor, was born on 16 January 1916, at Maes-yr-haf, Sketty Road, Swansea, Glamorgan, the son of Captain Lionel Robert Lloyd (1881–1947), a solicitor then serving in the 50th provisional battalion, and his wife, Eleanor Caroline, *née* Llewellyn (1887–1971). He claimed that he was destined for the film industry because his mother's labour pains began one Saturday evening at a local cinema and he arrived the following morning. He was educated at Bradfield College, Berkshire, was fascinated by cinema from his earliest recollections, and worked for nearly a year as a projectionist in Swansea. Nothing in his family background inclined him towards the cinema, except that an uncle arranged an interview for him with Norman Loudon, who owned Sound City Film Studios. He didn't get the job he had been interviewed for, but 'it started me writing to all sorts of film companies, and finally it was from London Films I got a telegram asking me to report Monday' (personal knowledge).

Lloyd originally wanted to be a cinematographer, but from the 1930s on he found his niche as a film editor, starting at Alexander Korda's Denham Studios early in 1933 after an interview with the production manager David Cunynghame. His first job was as 'numbering boy', synchronizing film rushes, but he was quickly promoted to assistant cutter on such classic films as *Sanders of the River* (1935), *Rembrandt* (1936), and *Things to Come* (1936). After he filled in—and covered up—for the American Jack Dennis ('a wonderful man but he did like his drink and his socialising'; McFarlane, *Autobiography*, 367) as editor on *The Squeaker* (1937) Dennis generously insisted on Lloyd's having the editor credit on the film.

The Second World War interfered, as for so many of Lloyd's age, with a career that was gathering momentum at Denham and Pinewood. He served in the Royal Naval Volunteer Reserve, but was seconded in 1943 to the Crown Film Unit to edit a documentary on submarines, *Close Quarters*. Just after D-day he was again recalled to Pinewood to edit a documentary about Mulberry harbours, commissioned by the Admiralty. On 31 August 1943 he married Nora Rosamund Jones, the actress Rosamund *John (1913–1998), but they divorced in 1949. On 26 April 1950 he married (Jean) Valerie Cox (*b*. 1929), a model, and daughter of Vincent Herrick Cox, accountant. He had a son by his first marriage, and three sons and a daughter by his second.

Following demobilization Lloyd quickly found work editing Peter Ustinov's *School for Secrets* (1946), about the role of radar during the war. He also had some directing experience on two London Films productions—*Anna Karenina* (1948), as second-unit director, and *The Last Days of Dolwyn* (1949), in which he shared the directing credit with Emlyn Williams—and also did second-unit direction on Disney's *Treasure Island* (1950). He said in 1994 that, though the cutting room was not his first goal, he came to believe that it was 'the most interesting department' in film-making, because it involved dealing with performances, with lighting, with covering up mistakes, with continuity:

in fact, with the whole production process (personal knowledge).

After cutting a further half-dozen films in various genres (including the thriller *I'll Get You for This*, 1951, and the 'naughty' compendium *Decameron Nights*, 1953) and working for American directors and with Hollywood stars, Lloyd took a major career step in 1956. He heard that the American director John Huston was looking for an editor for his British-based film version of *Moby Dick* (1956), went to meet Huston in Milford Haven, where the director was working with model whales, and the two got on so well that Lloyd was hired. He subsequently edited a further nine films for Huston, culminating with *The Man Who Would Be King* (1975), for which Lloyd was nominated for an Oscar. The other intervening films included such diverse pieces as *The Roots of Heaven* (1958), set in French Equatorial Africa, *The Unforgiven* (1960), a western starring Burt Lancaster with whom Lloyd enjoyed playing golf, and the bizarre *Reflections in a Golden Eye* (1967), about some very strange goings-on in an American army camp. Explaining how he and Huston worked together, Lloyd said,

> John had a method of shooting which I liked … He would do an opening shot, usually of some [importance], then maybe you'd go into favouring shots over one shoulder and then the other, and then you'd have close-ups for the same thing … John's shots were all well designed; he didn't just do a lot of shots and hope they would come together in the cutting-room. (McFarlane, *Autobiography*, 369–70)

Lloyd was articulate about the challenges posed by various directors, including Henry Hathaway, who quit *Of Human Bondage* (1964) after differences with its star, Kim Novak. The replacement director, Ken Hughes, asked Lloyd to piece together a missing scene of necessary explanation: 'I got lines and words from all sorts of places and fitted them to the faces, making an entirely new scene with new dialogue' (McFarlane, *Autobiography*, 370). He enjoyed working for Lindsay Anderson on *In Celebration* (1975), though he wished Anderson had stayed out of the cutting room, and there were a couple of duds in 1979—the ill-advised remake of *The Lady Vanishes* and the unspeakable *Caligula*. He went on working until the late 1980s, his last British credit being on the calamitous musical *Absolute Beginners* (1986). He survived unscathed, his reputation utterly secure as one who had always exercised his craft creatively. He died at Cedar Court Care Home, Elmbridge Road, Cranleigh, Surrey, on 21 January 2008, of bronchopneumonia. After cremation his ashes were interred at the churchyard of St Peter and St Paul, Ewhurst. He was survived by his wife, Valerie, and his children. BRIAN MCFARLANE

Sources 'Prime cut: 75 editors' filmographies', *Film Comment* (March–April 1977) • B. McFarlane, *An autobiography of British cinema* (1997) • B. McFarlane, *The encyclopedia of British film*, 3rd edn (2008) • *The Independent* (25 Jan 2008) • *The Times* (5 Feb 2008) • uk.imdb.com/name/nm0516125/, 26 March 2010 • personal knowledge (2012) • private information (2012) • b. cert. • m. certs. • d. cert.

Archives SOUND University of the West of England, Bristol, interview with Brian McFarlane

Likenesses group portrait, photograph, 1940–49, Rex Features, London • C. Hewitt, photograph, 1949 (with Emlyn Williams), Getty Images, London • obituary photographs

Wealth at death £141,433: probate, 26 March 2008, *CGPLA Eng. & Wales*

Lockhart, Alexander John [Sandy] **Bruce-, Baron Bruce-Lockhart (1942–2008)**, politician, was born at Woodthorpe Lodge, Wakefield, Yorkshire, on 4 May 1942, the younger son of John MacGregor Bruce *Lockhart (1914–1995), army officer, later a distinguished public servant who ended his career as deputy director of MI6, and his wife, Margaret Evelyn (1916–2000), daughter of Campbell Richard Hone, bishop of Wakefield. After being educated at the Dragon School, Oxford, Sedbergh School, and the Royal Agricultural College, Cirencester, he left Britain to become manager of a substantial farm in Rhodesia. Repelled by that country's racist regime, he moved briefly to Australia before returning to Britain early in 1966. The homeward journey was fortunate for Lockhart; Tessa Dorothy (Tess) Pressland (*b.* 1944), daughter of Edward Frank Pressland, businessman, was on the same boat, and after a whirlwind romance they married at the Church of the Transfiguration, Canford Cliffs, Dorset, near her family home in Branksome Park, on 12 March the same year. After marriage they settled at Headcorn, Kent, and had two sons and a daughter.

In Kent, Bruce Lockhart established himself as a fruit farmer and became devoted to his adopted county. Until the mid-1980s he showed little interest in a political career, either locally or at national level; he did not join the Conservative Party until 1984. However, he became chairman of the Weald of Kent Preservation Society, strongly opposed to the proposed route of the channel tunnel rail link—a stand that ultimately prevailed. It was suggested that he should stand for election to Kent county council, which he did, successfully, in 1989 in the ward of Maidstone Rural East.

Initially Bruce Lockhart was sceptical about the value of local government, and he assumed that his new position would make minimal demands on his weekly routine. As it turned out he soon became immersed in council business. His charm, combined with a cool head in negotiations, made him a natural leader for Kent's Conservatives, and he took over the leadership of the group in 1993. The Conservatives had lost control of Kent county council for the first time, and given the travails of the party at the national level the prospects of a recovery looked bleak. However, in 1997 the Kent Conservatives bucked the national trend, and Bruce Lockhart became leader of the council. His first decisions suggested that, having come to the Conservative Party fairly late in life, he had fully imbibed its prevailing 'Thatcherite' ideology. The council's £1 billion budget was cut, along with a workforce that numbered about 45,000 when the Conservatives regained control, and more business-friendly methods were introduced. Yet Bruce Lockhart could never be labelled as an unreflecting ideologue, and from his new vantage point he soon developed a positive view of local government that marked him out from hard-line Thatcherites.

Although the Conservatives were unable to make significant progress against Labour in Westminster elections over the decade after 1997, the party gradually rebuilt its strength in local government. Bruce Lockhart won many admirers within the Local Government Association, becoming vice-chairman in 2002. Two years later he became chairman, succeeding Labour's Sir Jeremy Beecham. He was knighted in 2003. By this time he had become well known on the national stage, not least because Kent was the geographical focus of a passionate debate about asylum seekers. Kent was affected by this problem in part because of the channel rail link, which had brought Bruce Lockhart into politics. Unlike some contributors to the debate on asylum seekers, he was difficult to accuse of racist motivations; his sour memories of apartheid made him a warm admirer of Nelson Mandela. The main reason for his strongly expressed views on asylum was his anxiety to defend the interests of local government. He was determined that coastal counties like Kent should not suffer unduly from the fact that they were obvious access points for people who hoped to find in Britain refuge from oppression.

It was, perhaps, Bruce Lockhart's misfortune to become a national figure thanks to his views on the sensitive issue of asylum seeking. He also courted negative publicity in some quarters through his support for section 28 of the Local Government Act, the unenforceable legislation that prevented local authority schools from presenting homosexuality in a positive light. In other respects, though, he held views that owed more to 'one nation' Conservatism than to Thatcherism. In particular he was well aware that Kent, 'the garden of England', was a county that contained pockets of poverty as well as affluence. It was no surprise that he was a prominent supporter (and trustee) of the Centre for Social Justice, set up by Iain Duncan Smith.

As chairman of the Local Government Association Bruce Lockhart proved a robust champion of the argument that, given the poor reputation of central government, effective power in key areas should be devolved to the localities. While this approach was generally approved in principle by the two main political parties, previous experience suggested that they were unlikely to put it into practice. Nevertheless, Bruce Lockhart was treated with considerable respect by the Labour government after 1997; and on receiving a life peerage in 2006 (as Baron Bruce-Lockhart; he changed his surname to match his hyphenated title) he became an ideal candidate to speak for the Conservative Party on local government issues. Instead, when he stepped down from his duties at the Local Government Association in 2007 he became chairman of the government quango English Heritage. Whatever the reasons for this choice, it was an appropriate position for Bruce-Lockhart, who had always loved history and the natural environment. Within a few months of the appointment cancer was diagnosed. He kept up his contributions to debate, through the media and speeches in the House of Lords, until a short period before his death, in Maidstone, on 14 August 2008. He had shown himself to be a man who learned very quickly, and one can only speculate about his likely achievements had he enjoyed a more protracted political career. As it was, for someone who arrived relatively late and left early, his impact on British politics must be counted a remarkable achievement. He was survived by his wife and children.

MARK GARNETT

Sources *The Times* (15 Aug 2008) · *Daily Telegraph* (15 Aug 2008) · *The Guardian* (16 Aug 2008) · *The Independent* (16 Aug 2008) · Burke, *Peerage* · *WW* (2008) · b. cert. · m. cert.
Archives FILM BFINA, current affairs footage
Likenesses P. Searle, photographs, 2001, Camera Press, London · photograph, 2005, Getty Images, London · photograph, 2005, PA Photos, London · obituary photographs
Wealth at death £651,545: probate, 23 Dec 2008, *CGPLA Eng. & Wales*

Lothian. For this title name *see* Kerr, Antonella Reuss, marchioness of Lothian (1922–2007). For other subjects who held this title name *see Oxford DNB*, 34.471.

Luke, Frederic Davey [David] (**1921–2005**), German scholar and translator, was born at Emsworth, Linden Road, Clevedon, Somerset, on 13 June 1921, the son of Thomas Davey Luke, a doctor, and his wife, Jane Thompson, *née* Pattison. His father died young, and Luke (known in the family as Derek, to everyone else as David) was brought up by his mother and an elder sister. He was educated at Sedbergh School and at Christ Church, Oxford, where, exempted from military service, he took a first in modern languages in 1944, and a DPhil on the French symbolist poet Rimbaud in 1947. His career was shaped by a bizarre chance, when in 1947 his application for a French lecturership at Manchester was pre-empted by the offer of a less obviously relevant post in German. He occasionally expressed regret at the diversion. In 1959 he returned to Oxford to become student (fellow and tutor) in German at Christ Church.

In these early years Luke published only the occasional article—on Kafka, or Nietzsche. He was confessedly inhibited by the formal requirement to assimilate all previous scholarship on a topic before advancing one's own views. He made a pilgrimage to Zürich to ask Emil Staiger, author of an authoritative three-volume study of Goethe, how he had come to terms with 150 years of secondary literature. Meantime he was a devoted and effective tutor and a much appreciated, idiosyncratic lecturer, as recorded by a review for the undergraduate journal *Isis* of his Nietzsche course by the later *Private Eye* humorist John Wells (never published, since the proctors put a stop to the series). Though occasionally driven to despair at the deficient motivation of some students, and to positive rage at basic failures of comprehension, he conscientiously helped the lame dog while inspiring the talented. He would spend evenings rereading texts for the next day's tutorials so as to give full value.

University teaching was then regarded as a respected activity for its own sake, with or without a research 'output'. Yet it would have been sad if, apart from teaching, Luke's literary sensitivity and European breadth of reading had gone to waste. The riches were released when he turned to translating, especially verse. Goethe's *Roman Elegies* (1977), metrically simple and rhymeless, were followed by the immensely stiffer challenge of his *Faust* (part

1 1987, part 2 1995), whose variety of verse forms exhausts the repertoire: a challenge triumphantly met, as was that of Goethe's equally protean lyrical poetry (*Selected Poems*, 1999). Stephen Spender's notion that Luke had improved on the originals was nonsense; but here indeed were poetic recreations that allowed English readers to experience direct the quality of one of Europe's greatest poets. The care and elegance of the introductions and notes fully measured up in the end to what is expected of 'secondary literature'. Luke also translated narrative works by Kleist, Stifter, the brothers Grimm, and Thomas Mann, whose *Death in Venice* he, as a homosexual, regarded virtually as a sacred text. His achievements were recognized by German and European prizes. British research evaluation, however, discounted literary translation in favour of learned articles. Yet quite apart from the social and international value of opening windows on otherwise inaccessible cultures, and the much broader audience for foreign literary works as against the narrow readership of specialized journals, translation is at least as rigorous an activity as secondary writing, calling for all a scholar's capacities and more: a precise and loving understanding of the original, a highly developed stylistic judgement, and a delicate, often ingenious feel for the resources of English.

Luke's devotion to poetry made him a friend of W. H. Auden during the latter's tenure of the Oxford professorship of poetry in the late 1950s, and it was Luke's doing that Auden was allowed to live out his last years in the 'south brewhouse' (later called the Auden cottage) in the shadow of his alma mater. Luke's other great love was music, especially opera, more especially Mozart and Wagner. He was also (in this respect a typical bachelor don) a lover of the table and of travel. He was a generous and delightful host, witty and wrily self-ironizing, inclined to half-comic rage when a new piece of the technical equipment to whose acquisition he was addicted could not be made to behave. He kept animals, first a cat (dogs being forbidden in colleges, unless, in one legendary instance, pragmatically renamed 'the dean's cat') then in retirement dogs. When his in-college cat Mowgli died, he drove to his cottage in the Scottish borders to bury him.

Luke stood at a mildly eccentric angle to the outside world. To go shopping with him was to witness cross-purposes over the simplest transaction. He could be awkward in academic matters too, but not by ill will, and in ways that did not lessen colleagues' affection. His closest colleague, the Christ Church French tutor Alban Krailsheimer, when asked why he put up with Luke's eccentricities without divorcing, answered: 'For the sake of the children'. The humorous parallel hits off the educational values to which, under a sometimes blasé exterior, Luke too was committed. Variously influenced by Nietzsche's atheism, Goethe's secular humanism, and years of psychoanalysis, Luke went through phases of religious belief, the last being Russian Orthodox, it too finally abandoned. He died of pneumonia at the John Radcliffe Hospital, Oxford, on 5 December 2005. T. J. REED

Sources *The Times* (9 Dec 2005) · *The Independent* (9 Dec 2005) · personal knowledge (2009) · private information (2009) · b. cert. · d. cert.
Archives SOUND BL NSA, documentary recording
Likenesses Ramsey & Muspratt, photograph · obituary photographs
Wealth at death £760,693: probate, 20 April 2006, *CGPLA Eng. & Wales*

Lusher, Gordon Douglas [Don] **(1923–2006)**, trombonist and bandleader, was born in Providential Place, Nelson Street, Peterborough, Northamptonshire, on 6 November 1923, the only child of Gordon Clayton Lusher (1889–1973), hardware salesman and shop assistant, and his wife, Annie Ethel, *née* Briggs (1889–1964). Both parents were Salvation Army officers with the Peterborough Salvation Army corps, his father a trombonist and his mother a songster leader. Educated at Deacon's Grammar School, Peterborough, Lusher started playing the trombone at the age of six. At fifteen he joined his father and grandfather in the senior Salvation Army band.

Being a Salvationist, it never entered Lusher's mind that he might earn a living from music. When he was called up at the age of eighteen his request to audition for the Royal Artillery band was rejected. With the approach of D-day his unit found itself awaiting transportation in West Ham football stadium when they were treated to a concert by Geraldo, one of Britain's top dance bands. It was an evening that was to change his life as he vowed that he too would play in a band one day. He did not know that the lead trombone in Geraldo's band was Ted Heath, whose bandleader Lusher eventually became. There was, however, little opportunity for him to play trombone until VE-day, when he volunteered to join a twelve-piece band for a concert party. He remained in the army for another six months, during which time he learned to read bass clef and improvise from chords.

Following his demobilization Lusher answered an advertisement in *Melody Maker* and successfully auditioned for Joe Daniels and His Hotshots. A stint with Lou Preager at Hammersmith Palais followed, where he met the band's vocalist, Eileen Mary Orchard (1924–1981), daughter of Ernest James Orchard, butcher's cutler. They married on 7 March 1948. They had two sons.

After a stint in the Squadronaires, in 1951 Lusher joined Geraldo on fourth trombone, but the following year he was poached by the band that was to make his name, Ted Heath and His Music. Tours to Australia and New Zealand in 1955 preceded Ted Heath's first visit to America in 1956 and the band's much acclaimed appearance at Carnegie Hall. Lusher was also a member of the orchestra that accompanied Frank Sinatra on all his European tours and was first call on the session scene in the UK, being heard on the sound tracks of all the James Bond and Pink Panther films.

In 1975, at the request of Ted Heath's widow, Moira, Lusher took over the Ted Heath band, leading it for twenty-five years alongside his own band. In 1975 he gave the first performance of Gordon Langford's *Rhapsody for Trombone* at London's Royal Albert Hall, and subsequently performed it on numerous occasions all over the world. Other premièred works included Gareth Woods's *Dance Sequence* and Gordon Carr's *Concerto for Trombone*. He was also an accomplished composer himself, writing *DL Blues*, his band's signature tune, and *Carnaby Chick*, adopted for television commercials and sports programmes. He also wrote for and recorded with the country's top brass bands. In 1979 BBC television presented him with the ultimate musical accolade, an hour-long show entitled *The Musical World of Don Lusher* with the Don Lusher Big Band, Black Dyke Mills Band, and special guest Nelson Riddle, who later (at the Grosvenor House Hotel, London, on 2 September 1981, when Riddle was conducting for Ella Fitzgerald) described Lusher as 'a consummate craftsman and one of England's national treasures' (private information).

Lusher's first wife died in March 1981, and on 28 September that year he married Diana Marjorie Kevin, *née* Bramwell (*b*. 1937), a television production assistant, and daughter of Leslie Kirkham Bramwell, civil servant. After their marriage they moved to Cheam in Surrey. He was a professor at the Royal College of Music during the 1990s, coaching their big band, and was made a fellow of the college in 1992. For seven years he taught at the Royal Marines School of Music in Portsmouth, and received an honorary doctorate of music from the University of Portsmouth in 2005. He continued to tour with his own band until the end of that year and was a founder member of the Best of British Jazz, with whom he appeared until a few weeks before he died.

Frequently topping the *Melody Maker* poll throughout the 1950s, Lusher received many awards, including the British Academy of Songwriters, Composers, and Authors' gold badge of merit for services to British music in 1987. He was given the freedom of the City of London in 1993 and appointed OBE in 2003. The International Trombone Association award for 2006 would have been presented to him at the end of July 2006, but he died on 5 July that year following an operation for carcinoma of the bowel at St Anthony's Hospital, North Cheam. He was cremated at the north-east Surrey crematorium after a funeral service at St John's Church, Belmont, Surrey, on 12 July. His memorial concert at the Salvation Army's Regent Hall, Oxford Street, London, on 25 September 2006 attracted an audience of more than 600. He was survived by his second wife, a stepson, and the two sons of his first marriage. SHEILA TRACY

Sources *The Independent* (7 July 2006) · *The Guardian* (10 July 2006) · *The Times* (11 July 2006) · *Daily Telegraph* (17 July 2006) · personal knowledge (2010) · private information (2010) · b. cert. · m. certs. · d. cert.

Archives SOUND BL NSA, documentary recording

Likenesses Associated Newspapers, photograph, 1956, Rex Features, London · A. Mcdougall, photograph, 1998, Rex Features, London

Wealth at death £627,580: probate, 3 Nov 2006, *CGPLA Eng. & Wales*

Lympany [*née* Johnstone], **Dame Moura** (**1916–2005**), pianist, was born Mary Gertrude Johnstone at Greenbank

Dame Moura Lympany (1916–2005), by Felix Man, 1944

Villa, Saltash, Cornwall, on 18 August 1916, the daughter of John Johnstone, then serving as a captain in the Australian infantry, and his wife, Beatrice Mary, *née* Limpenny. Her father, later an insurance agent, was frequently absent. The greatest influence was her mother, who spoke seven languages, had been a governess in Russia before her marriage, and taught piano and cello. From her Mary inherited a sharp business acumen and a keen sense of adventure. The latter quality stood her in good stead when she left England for a convent school in Belgium at the age of six. Any sense of loneliness or isolation was countered by her growing awareness of her instinctive talent. Cherished but occasionally chided by the nuns (her exuberance was sometimes viewed as a product of 'the sin of pride') she astonished all who heard her with a performance of Liszt's ultra-virtuoso E major polonaise. Her return to England (where she attended Our Lady of Sion convent school in Kensington) was marked by her début in Harrogate where, aged twelve, she played the Mendelssohn G minor concerto, a work for which she retained a lifelong affection. It was the conductor of that performance, Basil Cameron, who suggested she change her name to Moura Lympany, an ingenious alteration reflecting her mother's love of all things Russian and her Cornish origins (Limpenny being an old Cornish name).

After her triumph in Harrogate, Lympany studied at the Royal Academy of Music for three years (winning the Challen gold medal), then for a year in Vienna under Paul Weingarten. After a creditable performance in the first Liszt competition in Budapest, she returned to the Royal Academy of Music, where she studied under Mathilde

Verne (who had taught Solomon Cutner, otherwise Solomon) and, most importantly, Tobias Matthay, whose influence was at the heart of her legendary fluency and musicianship. Maxims like 'never play faster than you can think', a quiet but firm insistence on relaxation, and, above all, naturalness of line, impetus, and phrasing became central to her musical outlook.

Always enterprising and wide-ranging in her choice of repertory, Lympany followed a performance of the Grieg concerto in 1932 with one of the Delius concerto and Vincent d'Indy's *Symphonie cévenole* and also gave a triumphant Wigmore Hall début recital in 1935. She achieved international acclaim when she won second prize in Belgium's Queen Elizabeth competition in 1938, a time when competitions were few and mattered supremely. The youngest of seventy-nine competitors, she gave a performance of the Liszt E flat concerto that was of such freshness and agility that it deflected the jury's interest from other already celebrated pianists including Yakov Flier and Arturo Michelangeli. Only Emil Gilels excelled her in the final result. Her Proms début quickly followed, and in 1940 she commenced her long association with the Khachaturian concerto, an exotic showpiece initially offered to Clifford Curzon who, daunted by the amount of time needed to master both its character and its intricacy, reputedly said, 'send it to Moura, she learns so quickly' (private information). Recorded for Decca with Anatole Fistoulari conducting, this concerto was an outstanding item in Lympany's discography, as was the first of three recordings of the complete Rachmaninov preludes. Performances of Rachmaninov's first three concertos, the Paganini rhapsody, and the second sonata (in the 1931 revision) became part of her stock-in-trade, but so too were her performances of English music, with premières and appearances in works by Benjamin Dale, Richard Arnell, Benjamin Britten, Frederick Delius, John Ireland, Alan Rawsthorne, and Cyril Scott.

During the Second World War Lympany played regularly at the National Gallery lunchtime concerts, and toured throughout Britain; she was later described as an 'indispensable part of wartime musical life' (*Daily Telegraph*, 31 March 2005). She was reputedly the first British musician to perform in Paris after the liberation, playing Rawsthorne's first concerto, though she was at this time particularly known for her interpretations of Russian music. On 30 May 1944 she married, as his second wife, Colin Defries, an aircraft engineer and amateur pianist thirty-two years her senior, and son of Daniel Colman Defries, mechanical engineer. The marriage was short-lived, and ended in divorce in 1950. On 10 August the following year she married Bennet Henry Korn (*d.* 1989), a 37-year-old American radio advertising, later television, executive, and son of Samuel Korn, hat manufacturer. She suffered two miscarriages, one of twins, before giving birth to a premature son who lived for thirty-five hours. There were no surviving children. The marriage ended in divorce in 1961.

In contrast to her private life, Lympany enjoyed triumph after triumph in her post-war musical career. She built up a considerable following not only in Britain but in Europe and the United States, where she made her début in 1948, South America, Australia, and New Zealand. For much of her life she was constantly on the move. She nevertheless found time to refine her technique (taking lessons with Eduard Steuermann, the pupil and interpreter of Schoenberg, in the 1950s) and to expand her repertory. She remained particularly associated with Russian music, but also became known for her interpretations of Beethoven, Brahms, and Schumann, as well as of the contemporary British composers whom she championed. Her recordings were both numerous and popular.

Constantly clarifying and refining her art, Lympany had little use for exaggeration and surplus display, or for lurid bursts of speed. She aimed, she said, 'to play straight, nothing chichi, not what I call powdered rubato. And never to bang the keys' (*Daily Telegraph*, 31 March 2005). In the words of one American critic, she was 'a virtuoso of dreaming' (*The Independent*, 30 March 2005). Energy born of single-mindedness and an iron will to succeed were central to her success, and she rarely sacrificed her daily stint of four hours' practice even when interrupted by her incessant travels. Resilience was in the broadest sense the keynote to her life. Beset with serious illness and personal unhappiness, she resolved never to look back. Returning to the Wigmore Hall after a mastectomy in 1970 she regaled her audience with the story of her invitation to her music-loving surgeon to her Royal Festival Hall performance of Ravel's left-hand concerto only to receive an anxious letter asking her to confirm which part of her he had removed.

Moura Lympany was never easily tolerant, and could sometimes be surprisingly vain: when invited to be a castaway on *Desert Island Discs* she chose eight of her own recordings. Yet her warmth and sympathy were proverbial and she always showed the keenest interest in younger generations. Her autobiography, published in 1991, was more fluffy than substantial. She was appointed CBE in 1979 and DBE in 1992. Among many other awards both British and foreign, she was made a commander of the order of the Crown in Belgium in 1980, a chevalier de l'Ordre des Arts et des Lettres in France in 1992, and a member of the order of Prince Henry the Navigator in Portugal in 1996. Latterly she divided her time between London, Monaco, and Rasiguères in Languedoc, where she owned a vineyard and between 1981 and 1992 ran an annual festival of music and wine that attracted artists of the calibre of Victoria de Los Angeles and Elizabeth Harwood. She continued playing until her eighties, and was much acclaimed in the United States as well as in Europe. She died in Menton, France, on 28 March 2005. A service of thanksgiving was held at the church of the Immaculate Conception, Farm Street, London, on 7 June.

BRYCE MORRISON

Sources M. Lympany, *Moura Lympany: her autobiography* (1991) · B. Morrison, 'Moura Lympany', *Moura Lympany: Decca recordings 1951–1952* (2004), 2 CDs, 4756368 [DC 2] · *The Independent* (30 March 2005) · *Daily Telegraph* (31 March 2005) · *The Guardian* (31 March

2005) • *WW* (2005) • Burke, *Peerage* • personal knowledge (2009) • private information (2009) • b. cert. • m. certs.

Archives FILM BFINA, documentary footage • BFINA, performance footage | SOUND BL NSA, *Kaleidoscope*, interview with P. Vaughan, B1190/3 • BL NSA, interview with D. Manildi, Minnesota Public Radio, 1CDR0022864 • BL NSA, documentary recordings • BL NSA, performance recordings

Likenesses F. Lion, portrait, exh. Royal Society of Portrait Painters, London 1942 • F. Man, photograph, 1944, Getty Images, London [*see illus.*] • F. Man, photographs, 1944–5, Getty Images, London • G. Watson, crayon drawing, 1948, priv. coll. • bromide print, 1950–59, NPG • B. Schwartz, dye transfer print, 1978, NPG • M. Goddard, photographs, 1979, Rex Features, London • T. Mercer, C-type colour print, 1985, NPG • D. Wimsett, photograph, 1991, Photoshot, London • S. Markeson, photograph, 1998, Camera Press, London • obituary photographs

Lynton, Norbert Casper (1927–2007), art historian and critic, was born on 22 September 1927 in Berlin, the son of Paul Loewenstein Basevi von Truenberg, a musicologist who worked for the family's retail business, Hirsch Brothers, and his wife, Amalie Christiane (Mally), *née* Lippert. The family name was changed by deed poll in 1948 when the family was naturalized as British. The youngest child, Norbert had two older brothers, Nicholas (*b.* 1923), who kept the family name of Loewenstein, and Rolf (*b.* 1924). The household was formal and middle-class, with Norbert confined to the nursery while his brothers were at school. His father, a cultured man with extensive knowledge and love of music, was often absent; his mother, domineering, showed little affection for her children. Although their father was Jewish the children were brought up in their mother's Catholic faith.

As a young child Norbert, with his mop of blond, curly hair, was a photographic model, and recalled seeing his photograph on an advertising hoarding in Berlin. A self-confessed timid and well-behaved child, he attended the local Volkschule from 1932, but by 1934 he had a growing awareness of the political situation in relation to his father's Judaism, reinforced by his father's move to London for work. The family joined him in 1936, but the children were soon sent back to Germany because his father developed diabetes and lost his job. Norbert, separated from his brothers, was lodged with his mother's half-brother in Berlin, unhappy at being dumped and suffering physical abuse. A short, miserable period at a boarding-school on the Rhine followed, but he finally left Germany with his brothers in 1938, joining his parents at a boarding house in Willow Road, Hampstead, where his mother was housekeeper.

From this unsteady start, after Easter 1938 Norbert was placed in Douai School, a small boarding-school near Reading run by Benedictine monks. He was happy there, in contrast with his continuing unhappiness at home. He initially spoke no English, but found he could learn rapidly, and soon excelled academically. He also developed physical confidence through sports and won many prizes. The monks were kind and paternalistic, and the headmaster, Father Ignatius Rice, taking a great interest in his development, invited him to train as a novice at the end of his schooling in 1945. Lynton considered the proposal seriously, but instead took a part-time job with Low Fox Printing and Laurence Printing in a small office in High Holborn while studying for a BA in English, history, and art history at Birkbeck College, London, under Nikolaus Pevsner. Impressed with Norbert's acute perception and ability to analyse and interpret, Pevsner encouraged him to study for a second BA in the history of art at the Courtauld Institute, then under the directorship of Anthony Blunt.

At the Courtauld, Lynton's career in the history of art was placed on a firm path. Blessed with an excellent memory, a profound ability to look closely and compare intelligently, and with his knowledge of religious iconography through his Catholic faith, he was well equipped for his studies. While at the Courtauld he met and on 1 October 1949 married Janet Mary (Jan) Irving (1925–2004), a fellow student, and daughter of Henry Braid Irving, a senior principal scientific officer at the Ministry of Supply. Lynton was desperate to leave home; his mother thoroughly disapproved of the marriage and neither parent, nor his brother Rolf (for religious reasons), attended the register office wedding.

On graduating from the Courtauld, Lynton was supported by Blunt in his successful application to the school of architecture at Leeds College of Art, where he taught the history of architecture course from 1950 to 1955, moving on to the art school, where he added the history of contemporary art to the curriculum until his departure in 1961. Jan accompanied him to Leeds, but her lack of personal direction put a strain on their relationship. In Leeds he saw the beginning of his writing career when W. A. Eden passed on to him the task of rewriting the parts on English, French, and Dutch Renaissance architecture for F. M. Simpson's *History of Architectural Development* (1962). He also enjoyed the company of practising artists, including Harry Thubron, Tom Hudson, Hubert Dalwood, Martin Froy, Victor Pasmore, Gregory Fellows, Terry Frost, and Alan Davie. On a visit to the painter Trevor Bell in Cornwall he developed polio. Isolated in a Truro hospital and supported by letters from friends and colleagues in Leeds and by visits from Jan, he recovered slowly. But the emotional impact of his illness had taken its toll, and he felt distant from his wife; eventually reconciled, they had two sons, Jeremy (*b.* 1957) and Oliver (*b.* 1959).

Paradoxically, given the difficult relationship with his mother, Lynton loved women. He embarked on a series of affairs when his marriage failed in 1960, leaving home when his youngest son was one year old. He experienced great joy through parenthood, but was prevented from gaining regular access to his children, a situation made worse by a serious affair with a student at Leeds School of Art, Sylvia Anne Towning (*b.* 1939). In 1961 he moved to London, lecturing weekly at Regent Street Polytechnic at the invitation of Lawrence Gowing. He was also receiving commissions to write articles, his first on an exhibition of work by Hubert Dalwood, commissioned by the critic Jasia Reichardt for *Art News and Review*. In 1962 he published a booklet on Kenneth Armitage, and his first full-length book, *Klee*, was published in 1964. He was London correspondent for *Art International* from 1962 to 1966 and wrote regularly for *The Guardian* from 1965 to 1970. In his later years he expressed regret that critics rarely wrote about shows in commercial galleries, concentrating largely on museum exhibitions. His direct and continuing contact with artists led to his abiding love and deep understanding of abstract art, which gradually broadened to embrace figurative contemporary work. Having gained the position as head of history of art at Chelsea College of Art in 1963 he built a strong department, reserving Fridays for studio visits. Sylvia joined him from Leeds, and they married on 23 May 1969, producing two sons, Tom (*b*. 1971) and Peter (*b*. 1973).

From Chelsea Lynton moved in 1970 to the Arts Council, where he was head of exhibitions, with responsibility for the Hayward Gallery, which had opened in 1968. His exhibition programming was strong, pioneering, wide-ranging, and sometimes controversial. Among his successes were the Hayward Annual series, Art and Revolution (1971), 11 Los Angeles Artists (1971), in which Newton Harrison's work involved showing catfish that were killed and eaten in the gallery, causing uproar in the press, and Pioneers of Modern Sculpture (1973). In 1975 Lynton returned to teaching, becoming professor of art history at Sussex University, and from 1985 dean of the school of European studies until his retirement in 1989. He transformed the teaching of art history at Sussex, introducing the study of contemporary art.

In retirement in Brighton, Lynton, now professor emeritus, wrote some of his most important books and regularly contributed essays to artists' exhibition catalogues. The second edition of *The Story of Modern Art* was published in 1989 and substantial volumes followed on Victor Pasmore (1992), Ben Nicholson (1993), Ken Kiff, written with Andrew Lambirth (2001), William Scott (2004), and David Nash (2007). *The Yale Dictionary of Art and Artists*, compiled with Erika Langmuir, was published in 2000. His last book was *Tatlin's Tower: Monument to Revolution*, published posthumously in 2009. He served on a number of committees, including the British Council's visual arts advisory group and the Arts Council. He was a trustee of the National Portrait Gallery (1985–99) and a chairman of the Charleston Trust (1998–2006). In 2006 he was appointed OBE for services to arts and heritage.

In 1989 Norbert and Sylvia Lynton separated but they never divorced, remaining on friendly terms. He was in regular and close contact with his children from both marriages until his death from cancer at his home, Flat 4, 14 Clifton Terrace, Brighton, on 30 October 2007. His legacy to the cultural life of Britain was forged from the inside, teaching how to look at art through conversation, his teaching, and his writings. He would say 'we British', but his warm, attractive, persuasive, courteous, and charismatic personality remained entirely European.

ANN ELLIOTT

Sources *The Guardian* (3 Nov 2007) · *The Times* (6 Nov 2007) · *The Independent* (7 Nov 2007) · *Daily Telegraph* (13 Nov 2007) · interview with M. Petzal, 12 Feb 2004–24 Oct 2007, BL NSA, National Life Story Collection, artists' lives, C466/108/xx · *WW* (2007) · personal knowledge (2011) · private information (2011) · m. certs. · d. cert.

Archives Tate collection, research papers | SOUND BL NSA, National Life Story Collection, artists' lives, interviews with M. Petzal, 12 Feb 2004–24 Oct 2007, C466/108/xx · BL NSA, documentary recording

Likenesses Snowdon, bromide print, 1963, NPG · K. Kiff, charcoal and pastel, *c*.1991–1993, NPG · obituary photographs · photograph, repro. in www.brighton.ac.uk/news/2003/030717 honorarygrads.php?PageID=804

Wealth at death £531,007: probate, 20 May 2008, *CGPLA Eng. & Wales*

Lyons, (Isidore) Jack (1916–2008), businessman, philanthropist, and convicted fraudster, was born in Leeds on 1 February 1916, the fifth of six children of Samuel Henry Lyons (1883/4–1959), businessman, and his wife, Sophie, *née* Niman (1885–1971). His immediate elder brother, **Bernard Lyons** (1913–2008), businessman and philanthropist, was born on 30 March 1913 at 60 Grange Avenue, Leeds. Their father was an Orthodox, music-loving Jew who had emigrated from Poland as a child, and had set up a prosperous clothing manufacturing and retailing business. Both boys attended Leeds grammar school until the age of sixteen, when they joined the family firm, initially in the cutting room. It was soon clear that both brothers, like their father, had heads for business. Both were extraordinarily successful, and gifted with enormous energy and a prodigious appetite for work that served them well throughout their lives.

Alexandre Ltd, the family firm that the brothers joined, already had a substantial factory and a chain of several dozen shops. Soon both brothers were made directors, Bernard concentrating on the manufacturing side of the business while Jack was put in charge of sales and marketing. In 1938 Jack went to New York to study business at Columbia University, where it was hoped he would gain useful knowledge of American retailing methods. On the outbreak of the Second World War, with the United States at that time uninvolved, he enlisted in the Canadian army, but because of poor eyesight was not considered fit for active service. Instead he put his expertise and knowledge of the clothing industry to work to organize the supply of uniforms for the forces. In 1944 he was made assistant director of the Canadian wartime Prices and Trade Board, with responsibility for textiles, partly to prevent the development of a black market during wartime rationing. In Canada he met a classically trained singer, Roslyn Marion Rosenbaum, whom he married in 1943; they later had two sons and two daughters. Jack Lyons and his wife shared a passion for music, and it was this joint interest that later led to Lyons's generous patronage of the arts. Bernard Lyons had remained in Britain, also contributing to the war effort. He had on 18 December 1938 married Lucy Hurst (1916–2001), daughter of Wilfred Hurst, of Leeds; they had three sons and a daughter.

After the war Jack and Bernard Lyons took over the management of the family firm. As joint managing directors, under the chairmanship of their father, they expanded the branch network and set up a flourishing export business. The Lyons' flair for clothes retailing had not gone

(Isidore) **Jack Lyons (1916–2008)**, by unknown photographer

unnoticed in the business world. In 1954, by which time Alexandre Ltd had eighty-eight shops, the vast conglomerate United Drapery Stores (UDS) was experiencing troubled times. The UDS managing director, Joseph Collier, lacked sufficient expertise in the menswear industry to pull round a recent acquisition, Price's Tailors (another Leeds-based multiple tailoring firm trading under the Fifty Shillings Tailors brand), and turned to the Lyons. An agreed takeover of Alexandre by UDS saw the brothers join the board of the much bigger UDS. Jack Lyons continued to focus on the selling side of the business, and found himself in charge of more than 500 retail outlets while still in his forties, while Bernard continued to focus on manufacturing. Under their stewardship the UDS business continued to grow. Over the next decade the conglomerate became one of the country's largest retailers, with over 1300 branches. Its interests embraced men's and women's clothing (including Alexandre Stores, John Collier, and Richard Shops), departmental stores (notably Allders of Croydon), shoe shops, mail order, consumer credit, and duty-free shops at airports. The group was selling over a million men's suits a year by the mid-1960s. In 1967 the group's attempt to take over its rival, Burtons, was only prevented by the intervention of the Monopolies and Mergers Commission.

The personal wealth generated by the business enabled both Jack and Bernard Lyons to become very significant philanthropists. Encouraged by his wife, who feared Leeds becoming a cultural desert, Jack Lyons helped to save the Leeds music festival when it was threatened with closure in 1955. He served as chairman of the festival for the next seventeen years. He was particularly generous to York University, to which he first donated £150,000 to establish a music school. The chancellor at the time was Lord Harewood, whom Lyons had earlier brought in as artistic director of Leeds music festival. Lyons funded the construction of the university's campus concert hall, which bears his name, the music research centre, and music scholarships. He also donated large sums to the Royal Academy of Music, which named its theatre in his honour, and to the London Symphony Orchestra, where he was chairman of the trust from 1963 until 1991. In Leeds he jointly founded (in 1961) and bankrolled the Leeds International Pianoforte Competition. In 1964 he chaired the Shakespeare exhibition, celebrating the quatercentenary of Shakespeare's birth, and three years later he became a life trustee of the Shakespeare Birthplace Trust. In 1973 he was deputy chairman of the Fanfare for Europe programme, to mark Britain's entry into the European Communities, and in 1976 he was chairman of the Bicentennial Committee for the Arts, to celebrate the bicentenary of American independence. Lyons also actively participated in Jewish community and charitable affairs: he chaired the Federation of Jewish Relief Organisations from 1958 to 1986 and was president of the Joint Israel Appeal from 1972. He was appointed CBE in 1967 and knighted (on the recommendation of his friend and fellow music enthusiast Edward Heath) in 1973.

Bernard Lyons was also a prominent and generous supporter of Jewish and educational causes. He served for twelve years as president of the Jewish Representative Council in Leeds; he was also at various points chairman of the Leeds branch of the Council of Christians and Jews, chairman of the Yorkshire and north-east conciliation committee of the Race Relations Board, and a member of the Community Relations Commission. The University of Leeds was one of the main beneficiaries of his generosity: he funded a substantial expansion of the law library, a lectureship in community and race relations, and (reflecting his own love of rare books) a research award in bibliography and textual criticism. He was also a significant donor to the Conservative Party (having sat as a Conservative member of Leeds city council from 1951 to 1965). He was appointed CBE in 1964.

In 1983 UDS was the subject of a hostile takeover by the Hanson Trust, which proceeded to break up the group and sell its best-known retail chains in order to finance the acquisition. Bernard Lyons (who had been chairman of UDS from 1972) retired to concentrate on his family's investments, his philanthropy, and writing: having published a memoir of his time in the textile business, *The Thread is Strong*, in 1981, he published two novels, *The Narrow Edge* (1985) and *Tombola* (1996).

Jack Lyons had resigned from UDS in 1980, three years before the Hanson takeover. By then his business interests were more in the financial area than in retailing. He joined the American management consultants Bain & Co.

as a senior adviser, and it was that connection which ultimately led to his downfall and conviction in 1990 as one of the 'Guinness four' (the others being Ernest Saunders, Anthony Parnes, and Gerald Ronson) for theft, false accounting, and conspiracy. It was argued in his defence that the £3 million he had received from Guinness was a payment for his advice during the bid by Guinness for the drinks business Distillers in 1986. Indeed, Lyons had written to the prime minister, Margaret Thatcher, urging her to dissuade the government from referring the controversial bid to the Monopolies and Mergers Commission. Ten days later it was announced that the bid would not be referred. But the nub of the Guinness affair was the illegal share support operation in which Lyons was a participant. Unlike his co-conspirators Lyons was spared a custodial sentence because of his past philanthropy and his frail health. However, he was fined £3 million (in addition to having to return his £3 million fee) and the following year was stripped of his knighthood and CBE (though the concert hall at York University and the theatre at the Royal Academy of Music continued to bear the name Sir Jack Lyons). Subsequently he sold his London home and retired to Switzerland, where he engaged in prolonged legal appeals to have his convictions overturned, claiming that share support operations were widespread in the City and that he and his co-defendants had been singled out in order to be made examples. One conspiracy count was reversed, and in 2000 the European Court of Human Rights ruled that the trial had been unfair, since the defendants had been compelled to provide self-incriminating information to the Department of Trade and Industry inspectors that was then used as evidence against them. Eventually, however, in 2002 there was a final decision in the House of Lords that the remaining convictions should stand.

Bernard and Jack Lyons died within weeks of each other in the early months of 2008, Jack in Geneva, Switzerland, on 18 February, and Bernard (who played no part in the Guinness affair) at his home in Fulmer, Buckinghamshire, on 12 April. Jack Lyons was survived by his wife and four children, and Bernard Lyons by his four children.

DAVID BREWERTON

Sources B. Lyons, *The thread is strong* (1981) • N. Kochan and H. Pym, *The Guinness affair: anatomy of a scandal* (1987) • J. Saunders, *Nightmare: Ernest Saunders and the Guinness affair* (1988) • A. Milne and J. Long, *Guinness scandal: biggest story in the City's history* (1990) • J. Guinness, *Requiem for a family business* (1997) • G. Ronson and J. Robinson, *Gerald Ronson: leading from the front* (2009) • *The Times* (20 Feb 2008); (22 April 2008) • *The Guardian* (20 Feb 2008) • *The Independent* (20 Feb 2008) • *Daily Telegraph* (21 Feb 2008) • *Yorkshire Post* (21 Feb 2008); (23 Feb 2008) • *York Press* (23 Feb 2008) • *Jewish Chronicle* (8 May 2008) • *WW* (2008) • b. cert. [Bernard Lyons] • m. cert. [Bernard Lyons] • d. cert. [Bernard Lyons]

Likenesses photographs, 1987–90, Rex Features, London • photographs, 1987–97, PA Photos, London • photograph, 1990, Photoshot, London • S. Mark, photograph, Camera Press, London • obituary photographs • obituary photographs (Bernard Lyons) • photograph, Telegraph Media Group, London [*see illus.*]

Wealth at death £8,483,852—Bernard Lyons: administration, 23 July 2008, *CGPLA Eng. & Wales*

Lyth [*née* Menzies], **Isabel Edgar Punton** [*known as* Isabel Menzies Lyth] (**1917–2008**), psychoanalyst and social scientist, was born at the manse, Dysart, Fife, on 12 September 1917, the only child of the Revd Hugh Menzies, minister of Dysart, and his second wife, Sarah Curran, *née* Ness. Her father's first wife had died ten years previously, following the death in infancy of their only son, leaving two daughters, Margaret and Jennie. He was the minister of one of the largest churches in Scotland. His second wife, Sarah, was the daughter of a local factory manager.

Isabel Menzies was educated at the local primary school, and at the first comprehensive school in Kirkcaldy. At the age of sixteen she won a scholarship to Madras College, a grammar school in St Andrews. She went on to St Andrews University, graduating in 1939 with a double first-class degree in economics and experimental psychology. She stayed on at the university from 1939 to 1945 as a lecturer in economics. One of her tutors in the psychology department at St Andrews was Eric Trist, and he arranged for her to do war work in the long vacations, joining the newly established War Office selection boards for officer selection. There she met future colleagues, including John Bowlby and Hugh Murray. In 1945 she resigned from her lectureship and joined the civil resettlement headquarters of the British army, at Hatfield House, Hertfordshire, which was established to help British former prisoners of war to settle back home. This work was influenced by earlier experiments in individual and group work at Northfield Military Hospital in Birmingham, led by psychiatrists and psychoanalysts who were to be significant in post-war years, including John Rickman, Wilfred Bion, Harold Bridger, and Tom Main.

In 1946 Menzies was the only woman among the group of psychiatrists and social scientists who founded the Tavistock Institute of Human Relations. She moved to live in London, where her mother joined her. In 1954 she qualified as a psychoanalyst and then in 1957 as a child analyst. In 1960 she became a training analyst at the London Institute of Psychoanalysis. She worked as a researcher and consultant at the Tavistock Institute until 1975. Her commitment to the application of psychoanalysis to everyday life was such that she could apply it to firemen ('the public think that we just squirt water'), to central heating systems (allowing 'affectionate freedom' in the family), and to the maternal role in contemporary society ('birth is a reminder of death').

In 1960 Menzies published, in the journal *Human Relations*, the paper for which she was to be most remembered, 'A case-study in the functioning of social systems as a defence against anxiety', based on research that she was doing with the nursing staff of a London teaching hospital. Her account of the defensive ways that the nursing task was organized, both formally and informally, to defend against the anxieties associated with intimacy and death proved to be hugely influential for subsequent generations of researchers and practitioners in human service organizations, and a powerful theoretical contribution to the understanding of unconscious processes in organizational life.

Menzies continued to develop her consultancy approach, applying the theories of John Bowlby about the need for attachment in early life, demonstrated by James and Joyce Robertson in their ground-breaking films observing young children separated from their mothers. Her later Tavistock work included two major initiatives addressing the psychological needs of young children in hospital and in day nurseries. She took an active and powerful role also as a group relations consultant, in particular at the Tavistock Institute's international 'Leicester conferences' on the dynamics of authority and leadership in organizations. She was influenced in this work by Wilfred Bion (who was also her second analyst) and brought an understanding of psychotic processes in groups to her consultancy practice.

On 23 May 1975, at the register office in Hampstead, Isabel Menzies married a fellow psychoanalyst, Oliver Lyth (1908/9–1981), and left London to live in Oxford with him. Following his death she remained in their home in Church Way, Iffley, where she continued her private practice in psychoanalysis and her organizational consultancy with educational and therapeutic services. Known after her marriage as Isabel Menzies Lyth, she travelled extensively and for some years was an adviser to the 'socio-analysis' movement in Australia, directed by a former colleague from the Tavistock Institute, Alistair Bain. Her papers were collected in two volumes, *Containing Anxiety in Institutions* (1988) and *The Dynamics of the Social* (1989). In 1997 she received a doctorate from the Tavistock Clinic and University of East London. She died at the John Radcliffe Hospital, Oxford, on 13 January 2008, of heart failure. She had no children. TIM DARTINGTON

Sources *The Scotsman* (23 Jan 2008) • *The Independent* (4 Feb 2008) • *The Guardian* (20 Feb 2008) • *The Times* (26 Feb 2008) • *British Journal of Psychotherapy*, 24/4 (2008), 522–8 • www.acsa.net.au/articles/Isabel%20Menzies%20Lyth.pdf, 3 April 2011 • personal knowledge (2012) • private information (2012) • b. cert. • m. cert. • d. cert.

Archives Wellcome L., papers and corresp., 1950–2008 | FILM interview by A. Fraher (http://webcasts.ispso.org)

Likenesses obituary photographs

Wealth at death £1,342,058: probate, 22 July 2008, *CGPLA Eng. & Wales*

Lyttelton, Humphrey Richard Adeane [Humph] **(1921–2008)**, jazz musician and broadcaster, was born on 23 May 1921 at St Christopher, Eton College, Buckinghamshire, the only son of the Hon. George William Lyttelton (1883–1962), schoolmaster, and his wife, Pamela Marie, *née* Adeane (1889–1975), a keen amateur musician. He had four sisters. One of his distant relatives, Humphrey Littleton, had been hung, drawn, and quartered for his role in the Gunpowder Plot. His maternal grandfather, Charles Adeane, had been lord lieutenant of Cambridgeshire while his paternal grandfather, the eighth Viscount Cobham, according to Lyttelton, 'owned half of Worcestershire'. Among his relatives was the politician Oliver Lyttelton, Lord Chandos.

Lyttelton was educated at Sunningdale preparatory school and Eton College. As a boy, he considered following in the steps of his father, described as 'a great oak tree of a man who had delightfully little in common with most people's idea of a schoolmaster' (*The Times*, 28 April 2008). A plan for him to work with an uncle in the City came to nothing and he was sent to spend eighteen months at the steel mill in Port Talbot to see if he had the makings of an industrialist. He did not, and the experience turned him into a lifelong left-winger. Then the Second World War came and he joined the Grenadier Guards; he once danced with the thirteen-year-old Princess Margaret at a ball at Windsor Castle. He had already fallen in love with jazz, initially playing the harmonica and then graduating to trumpet in a band at school in which the future writer and broadcaster Ludovic Kennedy played the drums. He acquired his first trumpet in Charing Cross Road when visiting London with his mother to watch the annual Eton–Harrow cricket match. He took the instrument with him during his war service, even at the landing on the beach at Salerno where he went ashore carrying a pistol in one hand and his trumpet in the other. On VE-day he played *Roll Out the Barrel* standing on the back of a handcart that was pulled to Buckingham Palace. He had also developed a strong interest in art and on demobilization enrolled at Camberwell School of Art and Crafts as well as joining a traditional jazz band, the Dixielanders, a fairly rough and ready aggregation led by the pianist George Webb which played at a pub in Bexley, Kent. At the same time, he drew cartoons for the *Daily Mail*, and supplied story lines for the popular strip, 'Flook', drawn by his friend and fellow jazz musician, Wally Fawkes.

Humphrey Richard Adeane Lyttelton (1921–2008), by Triad Studios, 1954

In 1949, Lyttelton, who was also a good clarinet player, formed his own band which earned considerable success playing traditional jazz mainly in the 100 Club in a basement in Oxford Street. At the Nice jazz festival, he was delighted to learn that in referring to him, his hero, Louis Armstrong, had said, 'That boy's comin' on'. The idea of an old Etonian leading a group playing the music of New Orleans was a great novelty and its sessions at the 100 Club attracted a smart audience as well as jazz fans; however, he recalled appearing at debutante dances at which the mothers would ask the musicians to play quietly, so the horn men put in mutes and turned to face the wall. In the following years, he moved into mainstream swing, stopping short of 'bop' modern jazz but dropping the banjo and adding a fine saxophonist, Bruce Turner, to the horror of diehard enthusiasts for his original New Orleans style; when Turner soloed at one concert in Birmingham traditionalists stood up waving a banner inscribed, 'Go Home Dirty Bopper'. 'People accused us of going commercial when we wore uniforms for the first time rather than moth-eaten turtle-necked sweaters', Lyttelton recalled. Meanwhile, on 19 August 1948, he married Patricia Mary (Pat) Braithwaite (*b.* 1929), daughter of John Wellesley Gaskell, engineer, and stepdaughter of John W. C. Braithwaite. They had one daughter, Henrietta (*b.* 1949), but the marriage was dissolved in 1952, and on 1 November the same year he married (Elizabeth) Jill Richardson (1933–2006), daughter of Albert Edward Richardson, civil servant. They had two sons, Stephen (*b.* 1955) and David (*b.* 1958), and a daughter, Georgina (*b.* 1963).

Lyttelton's band's records did well, and in 1956 its version of a simple riff tune, *Bad Penny Blues*, produced by Joe Meek, became the first jazz record to get into the Top Twenty. The same year Humphrey Lyttelton and his band were chosen to support Louis Armstrong and his All Stars at a series of concerts in London. In the late 1950s the band expanded with the presence of three top-rate saxophonists, Tony Coe, Jimmy Skidmore, and Joe Temperley. It incorporated Caribbean rhythms and was joined by visiting American stars, including the blues singer Jimmy Rushing and the trumpeter Buck Clayton, with whom Lyttelton had a strong friendship and whose style influenced his playing. As well as his trumpet work (always with his eyes closed) and his leadership of a series of top-class bands, Lyttelton was a prolific composer with more than 200 tunes to his credit. As one of Britain's best-known jazz musicians, he performed all over the country and abroad; his *Who's Who* entry listed jazz festival appearances at 'Nice, Bracknell, Zurich, Camden, Montreux, Newcastle, Warsaw, Edinburgh, and Glasgow'. He also founded his own record label, Calligraph, and his own music publishers, Humph Music.

Lyttelton gained a national audience for his BBC Radio 2 programme, *The Best of Jazz*, which became a Monday night fixture for forty years from 1967 and on which, as well as playing an eclectic range of music, he honed his skills as a broadcaster, erudite and wryly amusing at the same time, constructing programmes built around often quite arcane themes in which he took a special delight. He had also presented a shorter-lived television series, *Jazz 625* (1964–6), which featured the best visiting American musicians. In 1972 his skill as a broadcaster led to his becoming chairman of the long-running radio quiz game, *I'm Sorry I Haven't a Clue*, in which his deadpan but sharp wit and perfect timing marked him out as a true original presiding over a seemingly anarchic cast of top comedians whom he set 'silly things to do' in what was billed as 'an antidote to panel games'. His own contribution was peerless in the role of a somewhat absent-minded schoolmaster innocently reading out smutty *double entendres* about the ever-absent, mythical, and beauteous hostess, Samantha, guiding the rest of the cast through an impossibly arcane game dubbed 'Mornington Crescent' whose rules were, he claimed, a secret he kept to himself, and periodically exclaiming 'you couldn't make it up, could you?'

Lyttelton's laconic, urbane style hid great industry. He appeared to be the epitome of the classic upper-class Englishman who moved seamlessly through life never taking anything too seriously and charming all around him, but he was a deeply committed craftsman, always open to new ideas and fired by enthusiasm. As the poet and jazz enthusiast Philip Larkin put it, 'One musn't be misled by the amiable, bumbling persona … He is a toughly intelligent man moving confidently in any kind of surroundings from Windsor Castle to Birdland [the New York jazz club]'. As he approached his seventy-fifth birthday, a member of his band described him as 'the world's oldest teenager' (*The Observer*, 19 May 1996). He himself wrote that, when he was shopping in a supermarket at Barnet, he looked as though he was 120, a 'stooping, shuffling human wreck clearly wishing he was dead', but when he was on the bandstand he felt as if he were still forty (*Last Chorus*, 4).

'Humph', as he was known, was a man of many parts. As well as leading his band for six decades, broadcasting, and cartooning, he was an accomplished calligrapher (presiding over the Society for Italic Handwriting), a restaurant critic for *Harper & Queen*, an occasional do-it-yourself enthusiast, and an excellent writer as shown in his many newspaper articles, two books on the history of jazz, *The Best of Jazz* (1978) and *The Best of Jazz 2* (1981), and six volumes of memoirs, notably *It Just Occurred to Me* (2006) and *Last Chorus* (published posthumously in 2008). Despite his fame, he was an intensely private man. He designed his house in Arkley, Hertfordshire, with blank walls on the outside and the windows opening onto an internal courtyard. He hated using the telephone and kept his number ex-directory, changing it if anybody else discovered it—though he relented in later life after acquiring a mobile handset which he guarded less closely. Given his dislike of the telephone, he communicated by post, including letters to hire and fire members of his band. He also developed a striking ability to read backwards at high speed and delighted in inappropriate juxtapositions of letters read one way and then the other.

Lyttelton received honorary degrees from Warwick, Loughborough, Durham, Hertfordshire, and De Montfort universities as well as Keele, where he was an honorary professor of music, and was given the Walpole medal of excellence in 2007. He was honoured with lifetime achievement awards in jazz in 2000 and 2001 and with a

Sony gold award in 1993 for his broadcasting. He was reported to have been offered a knighthood twice but to have turned it down on principle. On 21 April 2008 he was operated on at Barnet General Hospital for an acute abdominal aortic aneurysm. Awaiting the operation, he told his son, Stephen: 'This is a win-win situation for me. If the operation goes to plan, then I will wake up with you all around me. If it doesn't then I will know no different but you will all be OK' (*Last Chorus*, foreword). He died four days later. Announcing his death, his website carried his last thought: 'As we journey through life, discarding baggage along the way, we should keep an iron grip, to the very end, on the capacity for silliness. It preserves the soul from desiccation'. JONATHAN FENBY

Sources H. Lyttelton, *I play as I please* (1954) • H. Lyttelton, *Second chorus* (1958) • H. Lyttelton, *Take it from the top* (1975) • H. Lyttelton, *Why no Beethoven?* (1984) • H. Lyttelton, *It just occurred to me* (2006) • H. Lyttelton, *Last chorus: an autobiographical medley* (2008) • *The Independent* (26 April 2008); (28 April 2008) • *The Times* (28 April 2008) • *Daily Telegraph* (28 April 2008) • *The Guardian* (28 April 2008) • www.humphreylyttelton.com, 11 Aug 2011 • *WW* (2008) • Burke, *Peerage* • personal knowledge (2012) • private information (2012) • b. cert. • m. certs. • d. cert.

Archives FILM BFINA, current affairs, documentary, and light entertainment footage | SOUND BL NSA, current affairs, documentary, interview, light entertainment, and performance recordings

Likenesses photographs, 1948–2007, Getty Images, London • photographs, 1949–2007, Rex Features, London • H. Hammond, bromide print, 1954, NPG • W. Hanlon, double portrait, photographs, 1954 (with Jill Lyttelton), NPG • W. Hanlon, photograph, 1954, NPG • Triad Studios, cream-toned vintage press print, 1954, NPG [*see illus.*] • Triad Studios, cream-toned vintage press prints, 1954, NPG • photographs, 1955–2005, PA Photos, London • J. Hedgecoe, photograph, 1956, repro. in J. Hedgecoe, *Portraits* (2000) • photographs, 1956–2005, BBC • S. Samuels, bromide print, 1968–70, NPG • J. Kennington, bromide fibre print, 1987, NPG • obituary photographs • photographs, Camera Press, London • photographs, repro. in *Independent Magazine* (2007)

Wealth at death £1,157,714: probate, 28 April 2009, *CGPLA Eng. & Wales*

Macarthur, Arthur Leitch (1913–2008), Presbyterian and United Reformed Church minister, was born on 9 December 1913 at 14 Ilford Road, Newcastle upon Tyne, the son of Edwin Macarthur (1881–1929), a linotype operator for the *Newcastle Chronicle* and session clerk for the local Presbyterian church, and his wife, Mary, *née* Leitch. He was educated at Rutherford College, Newcastle, and Armstrong College, University of Durham (located in Newcastle), before proceeding to Westminster College, Cambridge, in 1934. He was ordained a minister of the Presbyterian Church of England at Alnwick, Northumberland, in 1937.

Macarthur's first pastorate was at Clayport Street Presbyterian Church, Alnwick, from 1937 to 1944. Being in a reserved occupation he was not obliged to declare his pacifism during the Second World War, but he worked for the Young Men's Christian Association with a detachment sent to France just before the German invasion, and was evacuated from St Nazaire in 1940. Further postings elsewhere were impossible because of the German occupation and he returned to Alnwick. In 1944 he became minister of St Augustine's Church, New Barnet, north London, which brought him closer to the Presbyterian national offices. From 1944 to 1947 he was a member of the negotiating committee which tried but failed to achieve a union between the Presbyterian and Congregational churches; in 1948, after sharing in an international project to build a youth centre for the Waldensian Church in the Italian Alps, he travelled to Amsterdam as an alternate representative of his church at the first World Council of Churches' Assembly. While in New Barnet he met (Doreen) Esmé Muir (*b.* 1924), an executive officer at the Board of Trade, a member of his congregation, and daughter of Thomas Muir, a civil servant at the Post Office. They married in New Barnet on 4 March 1950. Soon after Macarthur was called to be minister of St Columba's Church, North Shields. With a congregation of more than 600, and 400 children attending the church's Sunday school, he also developed a new church at Chirton, assisted by Ella Gordon, whom he proposed for ordination as the first woman minister in the church. The Macarthurs' own four children—Donald, the twins Colin and Ian, and Janet—were all born in North Shields.

After serving as convener of the Presbyterian inter-church relations committee Macarthur was appointed general secretary of the Presbyterian Church of England in 1960; his principal concern rapidly became the support of renewed moves towards its union with the Congregational churches. This was eventually achieved, not least through his efforts, in 1972, and Macarthur became joint general secretary, with the Congregational minister John Huxtable, of the resultant United Reformed Church, from 1972 to 1974; thereafter he served as sole general secretary until 1980. He was also the last moderator of the Presbyterian Church of England in 1971–2, moderator of the United Reformed Church in 1974–5 and of the Free Church Federal Council in 1980–81, and a vice-president of the British Council of Churches from 1974 to 1977. While general secretary of the United Reformed Church he was involved in a number of wider ecumenical initiatives: in 1972 he was invited to visit South Africa to try to build bridges between black and white Christian leaders from the Dutch Reformed and Presbyterian churches; and in 1974 as chairman of the Irish Advisory Group of the British Council of Churches he and the group met members of the army council of the Provisional IRA in Feakle, co. Clare, in the Irish Republic, to try to bring about a ceasefire in Northern Ireland—a meeting suddenly ended by the hurried departure of the IRA leaders and the arrival of the Irish police.

Macarthur's whole life was devoted to evangelism, from his early open-air speaking as a student on depression-ridden Tyneside, through imaginative initiatives in New Barnet during post-war reconstruction, to his successful pastorate at North Shields in the 1950s. But it was also concerned with the unity of the church, sparked by the realities of the Nazi menace he experienced during a walking tour in Bavaria in 1938, his presence at Amsterdam ten years later, and his subsequent involvement in both successful and unsuccessful unity efforts from the 1940s until his retirement in 1980. He later reflected on 'the strange quirk of fate' that led him to become the chief executive of the United Reformed Church: 'no academic, with no training in the skills of organisation and with no passionate vision of how things should be done' (undated draft memoir, Macarthur papers). It was a characteristic piece of self-deprecation, for he had learned more than many PhDs, he knew how to relate to people, and the clarity of his vision inspired others. Tall, and severe at first sight, but always with a twinkle in his eye and a Northumbrian accent that remained with him until his dying day, Macarthur was a man of craggy humour, shrewd judgement, and absolute integrity.

After retirement in 1980 Macarthur became part-time minister at Christ Church, Marlow, Buckinghamshire. He was appointed OBE in 1984. In 1986 he moved to Gloucestershire, first to Chalford Hill and then to Cirencester, where he remained active in local church life and wrote his memoirs, *Setting up Signs: Memories of an Ecumenical Pilgrim* (1997). He died in Cirencester on 1 September 2008 and was survived by his wife, Esmé, and their four children. DAVID M. THOMPSON

Sources A. Macarthur, *Setting up signs: memories of an ecumenical pilgrim* (1997) • *The Independent* (9 Sept 2008) • *The Times* (10 Sept 2008) • *Daily Telegraph* (11 Sept 2008) • *The Guardian* (23 Sept 2008) • Macarthur papers, United Reformed Church History Society, Westminster College, Cambridge • *WW* (2008) • personal knowledge (2012) • private information (2012) • b. cert. • m. cert.

Likenesses obituary photographs

McClelland, Ivy Lilian (1908–2006), scholar of Spanish literature, was born on 18 May 1908 at 64 Sheil Road, West Derby, Liverpool, the only daughter and elder child of William Henry McClelland, insurance agent, and his wife, Selina, *née* Foxall. With her brother, Leslie (*d.* 1980), two years her junior, she grew up in Liverpool, where she attended Holly Lodge School, which gave her the academic yet liberal secondary education to which she was always indebted. She had planned to study English literature at Cambridge, but went instead to the University of Liverpool, where she specialized in Spanish studies, taught by Edgar Allison Peers, the scholar who inspired her own lifelong dedication to Spain. She graduated BA in 1930 with first-class honours in Spanish, then after two years of research under Peers's supervision, MA in 1932. Her MA thesis was to provide the basis for her first book, *The Origins of the Romantic Movement in Spain* (1937), a pioneering investigation into eighteenth-century aesthetic uncertainties during Spain's previously undervalued 'age of reason', which thus emerged as her principal field of research.

In 1930, at a time when, for a woman, an academic career was almost unattainable, McClelland was appointed, with Peers's backing, to an assistant lectureship in Spanish at Glasgow University, within the department then under the headship of William Entwistle. Scotland became, by adoption, her homeland, and she spent her professional career entirely at Glasgow University, always living in or near its precinct. During the Second World War, while the head of department, William Atkinson, was on secondment to the Foreign Office, she had charge of Hispanic studies at Glasgow, doing most of the teaching, and fire-watching besides, keeping the department going, and ensuring its future. Her colleagues down the years remained her friends for life, even when their careers took them far from Scotland. One of them, in the early 1940s, was the Spanish poet Luis Cernuda. Homesick for Spain and an introvert, Cernuda was ill at ease in Scotland, and particularly with women, but, always pleased to speak to him in Spanish, McClelland gained his trust and friendship.

Generations of students—to whom she was, affectionately, 'Ivy', though rarely to her face—owed McClelland a permanent debt. She was adept at drawing out bright but diffident undergraduates, many from working-class Scottish homes, often the first in their families to obtain a university education. A surprising number went on to become academics, forming a veritable 'Ivy League' of Hispanists in universities in Britain and worldwide. Throughout the 1950s she acted, too, as a tutor to women undergraduates at Glasgow University's Queen Margaret Hall of Residence. This was a time when staff were expected to keep aloof from students, but McClelland stepped discreetly in to help these future teachers, lawyers, doctors, and scientists over exam nerves and other personal troubles. Her unpublished memoirs provide important insights into the attitudes and experiences of women undergraduates in Glasgow University during a period of impending change.

Gifted teacher though she was, research was McClelland's favourite work. She would spend every summer based in Madrid, carrying out research in Spanish archives and libraries, producing, as a result, numerous important publications on pre-twentieth-century Spanish culture. She published in 1948 a ground-breaking monograph on Tirso de Molina, a major seventeenth-century dramatist. Repaying her debt to her professor, after his death she edited and completed the final volume (1960) of Peers's monumental three-part *Studies of the Spanish Mystics*, a task that, characteristically, she carried out anonymously. There followed nearly four more decades of scholarly activity, during which she demonstrated the breadth and depth of her knowledge of the Enlightenment in Spain through her books and other studies. These included *Benito Jerónimo Feijoo* (1969), *Ignacio de Luzán* (1973), *Diego de Torres Villarroel* (1976), her two-volume *Spanish Drama of Pathos, 1750–1808* (1970), which stands as her *magnum opus*, and her final monograph, *Ideological Hesitancy in Spain, 1700–1750* (1991). Robert Johnson aptly described her as 'supreme amongst those who have written on the eighteenth-century Spanish stage; she can excite the mind' (Johnson, 420).

McClelland gained her international reputation as a leading authority on Spain's age of reason at a time when women might hope for, but were not expected actually to occupy, positions as professors in British universities. At Glasgow University promotions were, to put it mildly, slow in coming her way. She did not get her senior lectureship until 1956, and it was 1966 before she was promoted to reader, the title she still held when she retired in 1973.

After her retirement, however, honours and awards were bestowed in abundance. In 1986 a volume of *Studies for I. L. McClelland*, edited by David T. Gies, was published in the United States. A British initiative followed in 1991: *The Eighteenth-century in Spain: Essays in Honour of I. L. McClelland*, edited by Ann L. Mackenzie, appropriately issued from Liverpool University and sponsored by the British Academy. But it was the post-retirement honours from the University of Glasgow that she prized above all. In 1981 an annual Ivy McClelland lecture was set up. In 1989 Glasgow University made her an honorary doctor of letters, and in 1995 the university established the Ivy McClelland research chair of Spanish in her honour, the first holder of which was one of her former students. At long last, in 1997, the university elevated McClelland herself to a university chair, which, as honorary professor, she occupied with distinction until her death.

Even when she retired, after more than forty years' service, it had never occurred to McClelland to leave Glasgow. Until the late 1990s her small, upright figure was familiar in University Gardens, in the university library, or in the College Club, her favourite place for meeting friends. Though she never married and outlived her close relatives, she was blessed with a devoted family of friends. A devout Anglican, she attended church twice weekly, even when her failing eyesight made the short walk from her flat in Glasgow's elegantly Victorian West End to St Bride's in Hyndland Road a perilous excursion. Her poetry, influenced by Lewis Carroll, which she called her 'nonsense rhymes', reflected her fondness for the countryside and for all animals, wild or domestic, though references to universities, or Spain, were sometimes worked in. Her mind was acute until the end, but in 2002 her frailty obliged her to enter a nursing home, Balmanno House, Cleveden Road, Glasgow, where she died from a heart attack on 2 April 2006; she was cremated on 11 April at Clydebank crematorium, North Dalnottar. A volume of essays, contributed by Hispanists from the UK, Spain, and beyond, entitled *Hesitancy and Experimentation in Enlightenment Spain and Spanish America: Studies on Culture and Theatre in Memory of I. L. McClelland* (2009), confirmed the enduring influence of her work internationally. Her research advanced scholarly understanding of a critical epoch of transition—cultural, ideological, and scientific—within the history not only of Spain but of Europe and the world. ANN L. MACKENZIE

Sources R. Johnson, *Bulletin of Hispanic Studies*, 52/4 (1975), 414–20 • D. T. Gies, *Diechiocho: Hispanic Enlightenment, Aesthetics and Literary Theory*, 9/1–2 (1986), 3–6; 29/2 (autumn 2006), 309 • A. L. Mackenzie, *Bulletin of Hispanic Studies*, 68/1 (1991), 1–11 • *The Herald* [Glasgow] (2 May 2006) • *The Independent* (28 April 2006) • *The Times* (29 May 2006) • A. L. Mackenzie, *Bulletin of Spanish Studies*, 86/7–8 (2009) • C. Byrne, *Bulletin of Spanish Studies*, 86/7–8 (2009) • I. L. McClelland, 'Nonsense rhymes', *Bulletin of Spanish Studies*, 86/7–8 (2009) • I. L. McClelland, 'The University of Glasgow's Queen Margaret Hall, *c*.1950–60', U. Glas. • U. Glas., I. L. McClelland papers • U. Lpool, I. L. McClelland papers • personal knowledge (2010) • private information (2010) • b. cert. • d. cert.

Archives U. Glas., Archives and Business Research Centre, corresp. and papers, including lecture and research notes • U. Lpool, papers, including undergraduate lecture notes

Likenesses photograph, repro. in *The Herald* (2 May 2006) • photograph, repro. in *Bulletin of Hispanic Studies*, 68/1 (1991) • photograph, repro. in *Bulletin of Spanish Studies*, 86/7–8 (2009)

Wealth at death £371,043: confirmation, 19 June 2006, *CCI*

McCrum, Michael William (1924–2005), classicist, headmaster, and college head, was born at 3 Ashburton Road, Alverstoke, Hampshire, on 23 May 1924, the third of the four sons of Captain Cecil Robert McCrum (1892–1976), naval officer, and his wife, Ivy Hilda Constance (1891–1990), daughter of William Nicholson, fruit farmer and sugar planter. He won scholarships from Horris Hill, Newbury, to Sherborne School in Dorset (1937–42), where he was head of school and a member of the first fifteen, and from Sherborne to Corpus Christi College, Cambridge. Naval service delayed his arrival at Corpus until 1946. Having enlisted as an ordinary seaman, he was commissioned as a sub-lieutenant in the Royal Naval Volunteer Reserve in December 1943. He served on Arctic convoys and off Sicily in 1943, and subsequently in the Far East on the aircraft carrier HMS *Victorious*, which was subjected to kamikaze attacks in 1945. He observed VJ-day gratefully thereafter.

At Corpus (1946–8) McCrum gained a double first in the classical tripos (with distinction in part two) and played rugby for the LX Club. In 1948 he was appointed assistant master at Rugby School, where he took charge of part of the classical sixth and found time to play rugby for Warwickshire. Lasting consequences of his time there were a love of teaching and his marriage on 6 September 1952 to Christine Mary Kathleen fforde, the 23-year-old daughter of the head master, Sir Arthur Frederic Brownlow *fforde (whose entry in the *Dictionary of National Biography* McCrum later wrote). They had three sons and a daughter, and the closeness of the bond between them was central to their official, as to their private, lives.

In 1950 McCrum returned as a fellow to Corpus with a view to becoming tutor, responsible for the admission and wellbeing of students. From 1951 to 1962 he was both tutor and director of classical studies. Appointed university lecturer (1952–62), he dealt in detail with the Athenian constitution. In 1961 he and his Corpus colleague A. G. Woodhead published *Select Documents of the Principates of the Flavian Emperors, including the Year of Revolution, AD 68–96*. As tutor, he loomed large in the lives of undergraduates, taking a close interest in them and entertaining them with apparent relish. He urged Corpus to respond to problems identified by a university committee on which he sat and arising from the growing numbers of research students, for whom colleges made limited provision, and of academics holding university posts who had no college affiliation. In 1962 an attractive graduate campus was established at Leckhampton House and eleven new fellows were elected on a single day.

In 1962 McCrum was invited to become headmaster of Tonbridge School. He was immediately seen to be 'a vastly energetic headmaster' (*The Tonbridgian*, 1963). Tall and upright, he was a commanding presence—more of 'a personage than a person' as Vikram Seth supposed, until he was invited to lunch (*Two Lives*, 9). He had a formidable knowledge of boys and supported their activities tirelessly, but did not seek their good opinion. He doubled as housemaster of School House, recognition on his part that he still had school business to learn. He was remembered for his 'insatiable desire for constructive activity' and for his readiness to submit 'practically everything' to 'methodical scrutiny' (*The Tonbridgian*, 1970). He stressed, and raised, academic standards, and modified curriculum and timetable. He made a point of tidiness and punctuality (a fetish, some thought, of the latter), but permitted informal clothes in the evenings, visits to the cinema, and pub meals for prefects. He abolished practices he thought outmoded, including fagging and beating by boys. A committed worshipper and regular preacher, but aware of the challenge of securing a response from boys, he modified services and required chapel attendance just once on Sundays. The cadet corps became voluntary. By 1967 *The Tonbridgian* was writing: 'Never have there been so many changes in so short a time.' One view was that during his eight years as headmaster he had transformed 'a good public school in Kent [into] one of the top schools in the United Kingdom' (*The Tonbridgian*, 1970). The process was variously remembered, some judging that a determined headmaster had imposed his views, others that he had wanted nothing so much as to engage the common room in collegial review.

McCrum was pressed to become head master of Eton College, where his predecessor's time had been cut short, in 1970. He quickly demonstrated 'exceptional ability to master issues and to make decisions' (Card, 268). He dealt firmly, but consistently, with matters of discipline, retaining his right to administer corporal punishment, which had brought criticism upon his predecessor. He made a sustained attempt to improve academic standards, and adjusted entry procedures to reduce what could be considered an academic tail. Aware that implementing changes at Eton would prove complex, he made effective use of its apparatus of committees, though he did not always succeed in disarming criticism or resistance. Beating by boys and personal fagging were abolished, and more relaxed dress was permitted out of school hours, as was occasional weekend leave for senior boys. McCrum visited in his turn questions about the Eton curriculum originally raised by the public schools commission in the 1860s, and modified arrangements in the lower school, reserving a prominent place for Latin and Greek, but dismantling classical divisions, in which English and divinity had also been taught, and making extended time available for artistic subjects. Senior boys were given a choice between weekday chapel services and assemblies intended to promote open enquiry. McCrum made time to serve as chairman of the Headmasters' Conference in 1974, and was particularly keen to open Eton to a wider world. He brought large numbers of visitors to the school (the McCrums viewed the end of an Eton half as the closing of their hotel). As at Tonbridge, he strongly supported community service, and introduced junior scholarships that brought boys from maintained primary schools, via preparatory schools, to Eton. In the opinion of one historian of Eton he had brought to 'the basic management of Eton … greater skill than any Head Master since Dr Warre in his prime' (Card, 283).

In 1980 McCrum returned to Corpus as master, and held that office until 1994. In 1982 he persuaded the college to admit women as students and fellows, and he admitted twice as many new fellows as any one of his predecessors. A building programme and appeal were launched to accommodate expanding numbers. He resumed an active part in the counsels of the university, and in 1987 became vice-chancellor, the last college head to take the two-year turn that had been customary. He stressed the importance of a measure of financial independence for the university, and the Cambridge Foundation was established in his time. In demand as a governor, he maintained his involvement with schools, and chaired both the Governing Bodies Association (1989–94) and the Oxford and Cambridge Schools Examination Board (1981–7). He also became the first chairman of the Cathedrals Fabric Commission (1991–9), and in 1996 was appointed CBE for his work in that capacity, his contribution to education, curiously, going unremarked.

McCrum had run the institutions entrusted to him with conspicuous efficiency, but he had never been content merely to run them. Committed to them as places of learning, communities, and Christian foundations, he had taken up with enthusiasm the task of refitting them for changing, and challenging, times. Two late published works pointed to convictions and attitudes that had shaped a lifetime: *Thomas Arnold, Head Master: a Reassessment* (1989) and *The Man Jesus: Fact and Legend* (1999). He was tried late in life by Parkinson's disease and cancer of the prostate, but was determined not to be diminished by them. He died suddenly of cardiac arrest at his home, 32 Clarendon Street, Cambridge, on 16 February 2005. He was buried in the churchyard of St Andrew and St Mary at Grantchester, and was survived by his wife, Christine, and their four children. JOHN E. LEWIS

Sources J. Roach, 'Michael McCrum', *School and College Management* (June 1963) · 'Sic transit gloria McCri: Michael McCrum, 1962–1970', *The Tonbridgian* (Nov 1970) · D. H. Macindoe, 'Michael McCrum: a farewell', *Eton College Chronicle* (4 July 1980) · B. Orchard, *A look at the head and the fifty: a history of Tonbridge School* (1991) · T. Card, *Eton renewed: a history from 1860 to the present day* (1994) · M. E. Bury and E. J. Winter, eds., *Corpus: within living memory* (2003), 181–3 · V. Seth, *Two lives* (2005), 9–10, 13, 19 · *Daily Telegraph* (23 Feb 2005) · *The Guardian* (23 Feb 2005) · *The Independent* (23 Feb 2005) · *The Times* (24 Feb 2005); (3 March 2005); (11 March 2005) · *The Scotsman* (28 Feb 2005) · 'Michael McCrum, 1924–2005', www.admin.cam.ac.uk/news/dp/2005022302, 23 April 2008 · CCC Cam., funeral and memorial service addresses; 1949 note regarding McCrum as prospective tutor · *WW* (2005) · *Sherborne register* · personal knowledge (2009) · private information (2009) · b. cert. · m. cert. · d. cert.

Archives FILM BFINA, current affairs footage | SOUND BL NSA, current affairs recording

Likenesses R. Foster, pencil drawing, 1982, Eton College · E. Nelson, portrait, repro. in Orchard, *Tonbridge School*, 100 · obituary photographs · photograph, repro. in *Eton College Chronicle* · photographs, repro. in *School and College Management* (June 1963) · photographs, repro. in *The Tonbridgian* (Sept 1962–Nov 1970)

Wealth at death £863,003: probate, 25 Aug 2005, *CGPLA Eng. & Wales*

McDonald, (William) Ian (1933–2006), neurologist, was born on 15 March 1933 at Ngaio Road, Wellington, New Zealand, the son of William Allan Chapple McDonald, insurance manager, and his wife, Helen, *née* Leithead. Both parents had been born in New Zealand. McDonald and his sister, Leithe, younger by three years, grew up in Christchurch, where he was educated at St Andrew's College, subsequently matriculating at Knox College, Otago, in 1951 and graduating in medicine in 1957. He worked first as a research officer of the New Zealand Medical Research Council with Archie Macintyre, obtaining the degree of PhD with a thesis entitled 'The effects of experimental demyelination on conduction in peripheral nerve: a histological and electrophysiological study' (1962), having already written a dissertation on ascending long spinal reflexes (1955); he then worked as lecturer in medicine at Otago. But academic life in New Zealand, and occasional work as a jackaroo fixing fences on his father's property, had its limitations; in 1963 McDonald moved to London, where his aesthetic interests were cultivated and his personality was more easily expressed.

Although the National Hospital for Nervous Diseases, Queen Square, was an intimidating place to work in the 1960s, McDonald's talents were quickly recognized there, and he was appointed proleptically to the consultant staff in 1966 before working for three years in Boston, USA, with another New Zealander, Derek Denny-Brown, to whom the brightest neurologists training at Queen Square were usually sent at that time to broaden their experience of experimental neurology. The remainder of McDonald's career was spent at Queen Square, as consultant neurologist and consultant physician at Moorfields Eye Hospital from 1969 and as professor of neurology in the University of London from 1974. He rapidly honed the traits that characterized his professional style; sought after for his clinical opinions and renowned for his expertise and knowledge of multiple sclerosis and neuro-ophthalmology, he trained by example, lifting less gifted colleagues, and reflecting with generosity and uncomplicated pride on their achievements. Apparently easy performance, in his lectures and in writing, concealed meticulous preparation and attention to detail. McDonald was adept at synthesizing a complex story, with perspective and modesty concerning his own achievements set in the context of the illustrious predecessors he so much admired.

In the 1960s McDonald was one of very few neurologists active in laboratory work who transferred the rigorous discipline of descriptive clinical neurology into the modern era of mechanistic studies. Working at that time with Tom Sears, he characterized the physiology and morphology of demyelination and remyelination in the central nervous system, work that leaned on classical studies and anticipated the era of limiting and repairing the damage in multiple sclerosis. In the 1970s, with Martin Halliday, he pioneered laboratory methods for supplementing the clinical diagnosis of multiple sclerosis. The observations brought objectivity to the diagnostic process, and the techniques became the definitive markers of what happens physiologically when the myelin sheath is lost from nerve fibres in the brain and spinal cord. In the 1980s McDonald realized that magnetic resonance imaging and spectroscopy could be used to illuminate the nature of inflammatory brain disease; his work provided laboratory measures for charting the efficacy of the first wave of disease-modifying treatments introduced in the mid-1990s.

McDonald understood better than others the contribution made to the evolution of modern neurology in the UK by his mentor Roger Gilliatt, foundation professor of neurology in the University of London and chairman of the department at Queen Square from 1962, whom he expected to succeed in 1987. But it was not until 1995, following David Marsden and Anita Harding, that McDonald was appointed, and then for only a short period before his own retirement in 1998. He edited *Brain* from 1991 to 1997, having earlier brokered the financially successful move of that journal, established in 1878, from Macmillan to Oxford University Press, achieving financial security in the process and thereby allowing the guarantors subsequently to distribute significant resources in support of young people training in the neurosciences. He was elected a fellow of the Royal College of Physicians in 1972, of the Royal College of Ophthalmologists in 1989, and of the Academy of Medical Sciences in 1999. He co-founded the European Neurological Society and served as its president in 1994–5; he also served as president of the Association of British Neurologists (1994–5) and the World Congress of Neurology (2001). Among many international prizes was the Charcot award of the International Federation of Multiple Sclerosis Societies (1991); and, being in love with the city, he was particularly pleased to be elected a foreign member of the Venetian Institute of Science, Arts, and Letters.

In retirement, McDonald served as Harveian librarian at the Royal College of Physicians of London, editing Munk's *Roll*, seeing through to publication the final volume of the *History of the Royal College of Physicians of London* (by Asa Briggs, 2005), and with others editing an illustrated history of *The Royal College of Physicians and its Collections* (2001). When the sale of important items such as the Wilton psalter was mooted, he was a staunch defender of the responsibility that the college had to preserve the legacies of those fellows who had built up the collection. The item that gave him most pleasure—for professional and historical reasons—was the manuscript diary of Augustus d'Este, grandson of George III, who first wrote a personal account of multiple sclerosis.

McDonald's partner from the early 1980s was Stanley Joseph Hamilton (1951–2011), with whom he entered into a civil partnership in 2006. They had many friends among people active in music, dance, the visual arts, literature, and history; and these friendships outside medicine provided a counterpoint to McDonald's professional work and a rich source of information and anecdote that he used in conversation, and in his writings and lectures. His passion was music. He considered himself to be of average competence as a pianist, being a useful accompanist in lieder and chamber music from the baroque classical and easier Romantic repertories; but others judged that, as a member of a trio, he was exceptional—certain in rhythm, intensely musical in his ability to see a long phrase within a theme, and with the fingers led by the ear. It was poignant that a small stroke in 2004 removed, for a while, his ability to understand music, read a score, or play the piano. Later he published, in *Brain*, a characteristically erudite account of this intensely personal episode. He died suddenly of a heart attack at home, 15 St Peter's Street, Islington, London, on 13 December 2006. He was survived by his civil partner, Stanley Hamilton.

ALASTAIR COMPSTON

Sources *The Independent* (19 Dec 2006) • I. Oransky, *The Lancet*, 369 (2007), 364 • C. Richardson, *BMJ*, 334 (2007), 160 • D. A. S. Compston, *Bulletin of the Royal College of Physicians of London* (Jan–Feb 2007), 9 • D. A. S. Compston, *World Neurology*, 22 (2007), 13 • D. A. S. Compston, *Harvey's keepers: Harveian librarians through the ages*, ed. L. G. Fine (2007), 50–54 • personal knowledge (2010) • private information (2010) • b. cert. • d. cert.

Archives priv. coll. | RCP Lond. | FILM BFINA, documentary footage

Likenesses F. Topolski, portrait, *c.*1976, priv. coll. • W. Bowyer, portrait, 1998, Institute of Neurology, Queen Square, London • photographs, 1998, Photoshot, London • photographs, RCP Lond. • photographs, Association of British Neurologists, London

Wealth at death £1,348,464: probate, 9 March 2007, *CGPLA Eng. & Wales*

McEwen, Alexander Dundas [Alex, Eck] **(1935–2008)**, folk singer, was born on 16 May 1935 at Marchmont House, Polwarth, Berwickshire, the fourth of six sons and fifth of seven children of Sir John Helias Finnie McEwen of Marchmont and Bardrochat, first baronet (1894–1962), poet and politician, and his wife, Bridget Mary (1904–1971), eldest daughter of Sir Francis Oswald Lindley, diplomat. His brother **Roderick (Rory) McEwen** (1932–1982), botanical artist and folk singer, the third son, was born there on 12 March 1932. Both parents were Roman Catholics. The two brothers were brought up at Marchmont. Its contours, folkways, and natural history would profoundly affect them both. 'I was born in an eighteenth-century house', Rory wrote, 'brought up, truth to tell, in the eighteenth century' ('An autobiographical fragment', in Rix, Hall and McEwen). Their father was Conservative MP for Berwick and Haddington from 1931 to 1945, and president of the Scottish Unionist Association in 1949–50; he passed on his passion for Scottish history and genealogy to all his children. His daughter (the brothers' sister), Christian Mary (Kirsty), later Lady Hesketh (1929–2006), was a notable hostess, public servant, and historian, and author of a definitive guide to Scottish tartans.

All six McEwen brothers were educated at Eton College, from where Rory, like all his brothers except Alex and the oldest, Jamie, went on to Trinity College, Cambridge (where he appeared in Footlights shows along with Jonathan Miller). Both did terms as commissioned officers in their father's regiment, the Queen's Own Cameron Highlanders, Rory serving in Tripoli and Egypt and Alex in Germany. Both emerged trilingual (in English, French, and Scots) from their upbringing and life experiences. They switched naturally between the English of the upper classes and royalty and the Scots of the borders.

The brothers' interest in music was shaped in part by their father's love of Scottish ballads and by French songs taught them by their governess, and in part by their brother Jamie's passion for blues and jazz. Both learned to play the guitar while teenagers, and developed a repertoire including Scottish ballads, traditional French songs, sea shanties, and their own versions of southern American blues songs. The American folklorist Kenneth S. Goldstein, who recorded two of their albums, described them as 'seemingly tireless globetrotters' whose 'present repertoire is a virtual international songbag' (Goldstein, *Great Scottish Ballads*, 3).

After completing his national service in 1955 Alex McEwen turned down a place at Cambridge to travel with his brother to the United States, intending to seek out some of their musical heroes. The brothers' privileged background and connections allowed them to travel there at a time of currency exchange control restrictions. However, it was their talents as musicians that opened doors. They had already supplied one track, 'Bonnie George Campbell', to Peter Kennedy's anthology, *Folk Song Today: Songs and Ballads of England and Scotland* (1955), before they arrived in the USA. There they befriended and were befriended, appearing, for example, on the *Ed Sullivan Show* (on consecutive nights) and the *Arthur Godfrey Show*. They also recorded two LPs, *Great Scottish Ballads* (1956) and *Scottish Songs and Ballads* (1957). The first concentrated on so-called Child ballads such as 'The Wife of Usher's Well', 'Binnorie' (a variant of 'The Twa Sisters'), and 'Clerk Saunders'; the second was lighter fare including 'Peerie Fairies', learned from the folk singer and actress Isla Cameron, 'A Lum Hat Wantin' a Croon', learned from the Glasgow Kelvingrove MP Walter Elliot, and 'Palworth on the Green', a piece by Allan Ramsay, the so-called 'restorer of Scottish poetry', celebrating Palworth. In New York they stayed initially with the four-times-married socialite Alice Astor. Later, on 15 April 1958, Rory married her daughter by her second marriage, Romana von Hofmannsthal (*b.* 1935), daughter of Raimund von Hofmannsthal and granddaughter of the Austrian man of letters Hugo von Hofmannsthal and of John Jacob Astor IV (who perished on the *Titanic*). There would be four children of the marriage: Flora (*b.* 1959), Samantha (*b.* 1960), Christabel Mary (*b.* 1962), and Adam (*b.* 1965). Meanwhile, Rory had returned to Britain in 1957 while Alex stayed on to take guitar lessons from the Revd 'Blind' Gary Davis, a blues and gospel singer and finger-picking-style guitarist—anticipating later students such as Bob Weir of the Grateful Dead and the guitarist Stefan Grossman.

Alex McEwen returned to Britain and rejoined his brother in 1958. The brothers' name now had cachet. They had appearances on domestic and American records, had connections, and they soon found themselves blazing musical trails. Their slots on the BBC's teatime television magazine programme *Tonight*, presented by Cliff Michelmore, incorporating both Scottish ballads and original topical material written with Bernard Levin, led the way for later appearances by the likes of Cy Grant, Noel Harrison, and Robin Hall and Jimmie Macgregor. They also appeared at the Edinburgh Festival and the Royal Festival Hall. As early as 1958, on their 10-inch LP *Folksong Jubilee*, they included bouzouki in a folk context outside Greek music—pre-dating Anne Briggs and Sweeney's Men 'introducing' the instrument to British and Irish folk music (as was sometimes claimed) by a decade. In 1962 the brothers met the American picaresque writer and singer Richard Fariña and his first wife, the folk singer Carolyn Hester, in Edinburgh. This led to them recording a four-track EP together. *Four for Fun* included Hamish Henderson's 'Banks o' Sicily', a bluesy 'Salty Dog', and the lusty faux-Elizabethan ballad 'Chastity Belt'. Through Fariña the brothers met Bob Dylan, and Rory in turn introduced Dylan to the poet and novelist Robert Graves. Of Dylan, Rory later said, 'He can walk into a room and give the impression that he knows just a little more about the world than anyone in that room. He probably does, but it rankles a little that he should act as he does' (Shelton, 180). Meanwhile, in 1958 Alex had met Cecilia Leontine Marie, Gräfin von Weikersheim (*b.* 1937), daughter of Franz Maria Joseph Antonius Benedicta, Prince Weikersheim. They married on 30 June 1960 in London. There were three children of the marriage: Sophie Cristina (*b.* 1961), Alexander Francis Charles (*b.* 1962), and Hugo Gabriel (*b.* 1965).

On the back of the brothers' television success Alex McEwen got his own show, *Alex Awhile*, on Scottish Television (1961–5), a platform for blues, calypso, Scottish traditional ballads, and folk songs of several nations. Rory also continued a career in television. A 1964 recording of 'My Girl' (a folk-friendly version of Leadbelly's 'In the Pines'), preserved on Martin Carthy's *The Carthy Chronicles* music boxed set (2001), captured him, Lisa Turner, Martin Carthy, and Davey Graham performing on the late-night ATV series *Hullabaloo*, which he also presented. The brothers mixed in several strata of society. Rory, in an equerry role, escorted Princess Margaret to functions. At the other extreme the brothers performed in folk clubs in London pubs such as the Ballads and Blues with Ewan MacColl, and at fairgrounds. Rory's home in Tregunter Road, near to London's Fulham Road, became something of a hub for visiting musicians. Sometimes he held musical soirées known as *mehfils* or 'cushion concerts' for guests invited from his extensive address book of musicians, actors, writers, artists, and nobility. Those who performed included Hindustani maestros of the calibre of the vocalist Salamat Ali Khan, the sarodist Ali Akbar Khan, the tabla player Alla Rakha, and the sitarist Ravi Shankar. Indeed such was McEwen's role in this promulgation and appreciation of Indian classical music that he was nicknamed Rory Khan in Indian circles.

With folk music now eclipsed by the rise of rock 'n' roll, the McEwens largely gave up performing about 1965. Rory pursued his interest in art. His interest in botanical illustration had first been encouraged by his French governess, and by his art teacher at Eton, Wilfrid Blunt, who described him as 'perhaps the most gifted artist to pass through my hands' (Kress and Sherwood, 95). McEwen's early paintings of carnations and pinks, auriculas, and tulips—published in *Old Carnations and Pinks* (1955) and *The Auricula* (1964)—were fine works in a stylized antiquarian representational style. After 1965 he also worked in abstract forms, with glass and acrylic sheet, 'table-sculptures' in clear plastic and refractive glass, and a series of 'veils', 'exhibited for the sheer pleasure of their folds' (C. McEwen, 30). In another venture he collaborated with the American artist Jim Dine on *Songs Poems Prints* (1969), a package that contained a long-playing record of songs and poems written and performed by the two of them, and an original silk-screened print by each. Later studies might focus on fritillary or tulip specimens, a single chilli or persimmon, dead violets, a tulip petal, or, in a series called True Facts from Nature (1972–3), wilting, diseased, or fallen leaves. Terminally ill with two brain tumours, one of which was pressing on the optic nerve causing him to see double, Rory McEwen took his own life by throwing himself under a London underground train on 16 October 1982 at South Kensington station. He was survived by his wife, Romana, and their four children.

Alex McEwen, meanwhile, after studying agriculture at Moulton College, Northamptonshire, took up both farming—first at Whiteside, on the Marchmont estate, then at Bardrochat, Ayrshire, and finally at Colmonell, Ayrshire—and business. In 1965 he joined the Edinburgh-based newsagent and bookseller John Menzies (run by a Berwickshire neighbour), becoming for many years the group's personnel director. He also sculpted and carved, and in his latter years acted as an art dealer. He died at Dalreoch, Colmonell, on 4 December 2008, of a heart attack. He was survived by his wife, Cecilia, and their three children.

KEN HUNT

Sources K. Goldstein, *Great Scottish ballads*, booklet notes, 1956 • K. Goldstein, *Scottish songs and ballads*, booklet notes, 1957 • *The Times* (20 Oct 1982); (16 Dec 2008) • C. McEwen, 'Music hiding in the air: a memoir of Rory McEwen (1935–1982)', *Archipelago*, 4/3 (autumn 2000); www.archipelago.org/vol4-3/mcewen.htm, 30 April 2011 • M. Rix and D. Hall, *Rory McEwen, 1932–1982: the botanical paintings* (1988) • *The Scotsman* (16 Dec 2008) • *Daily Telegraph* (9 Jan 2009) • *The Guardian* (6 March 2009) • W. J. Kress and S. Sherwood, *The art of plant evolution* (2009) • R. Shelton, *No direction home: the life and music of Bob Dylan*, ed. E. Thomson and P. Humphries (2011) • Burke, *Peerage* • personal knowledge (2012) • private information (2012) [M. A. Aulia, A. Briggs, A. A. Khan, D. Suff] • b. cert. [A. McEwen] • d. cert. [A. McEwen]

Archives BL • FM Cam., paintings [Rory McEwen] • priv. coll., paintings [Rory McEwen] • Scottish National Gallery of Modern Art, Edinburgh, paintings [Rory McEwen] • Tate collection, paintings [Rory McEwen] | SOUND BL NSA, performance recordings • Museum of Modern Art, on Atlantic Records, New York, *songs poems prints*, 1969, MM 020 [Rory McEwen] • Smithsonian Folkways, Washington D. C., *Great Scottish ballads*, 1956, FW 6927; *Scottish songs and ballads*, 1957, FW 6930 • Waverley Records, Edinburgh, *Four for fun*, 1963, EP 113, reissued by Waverley Records, Hayes, Middlesex, *Folk favourites*, 1966, ZLP 2067 • *Folk song today: songs and ballads of England and Scotland*, 1955 HMV DLP 1143; *Folksong jubilee*, 1958, HMV CLP 1220

Likenesses photographs, 1950–59, BBC • photographs, 1950–59 (Rory McEwen), BBC • L. Friedlander, photograph, 1978 (Rory McEwen), Museum of Modern Art, New York • obituary photographs

MacEwen [*née* Radford], **Ann Maitland** (1918–2008), architect and town planner, was born on 15 August 1918 at Saxtead, Marshalls Road, Sutton, Surrey, the daughter of Maitland Radford (1884–1944), doctor and medical officer of health for St Pancras, and his wife, Muriel Ann, *née* Lloyd (1889–1983), a doctor working in public health. She was educated at Howell's School, Denbigh, and in 1935 entered the Architectural Association, before graduating in 1940.

Ann Radford was born into a family tradition of socialism. Her grandparents had been members of the Socialist League alongside William Morris, and her parents were committed socialists also. She continued this tradition, and her commitment to left-wing politics coloured the choices she made throughout her career. It was only natural, therefore, that her time at the Architectural Association saw her participation, alongside a group which included Anthony Cox, Richard Llewellyn Davies, Elizabeth Chesterton, and Leo de Syllas, in the student rebellions that sought the modernization of the school's curriculum in order that architects might be better equipped to design for the needs of a modern age. Importantly for her later career, she gained an early introduction to town planning through her assistance on a collaborative project, known as Tomorrow Town, which the students who formed Unit 15 submitted as their thesis project in 1938. Based on extensive research, and designed by group work, the scheme presaged the sort of techniques which she would practise in her post-war work for the London county council (LCC).

Ann Radford married one of the Tomorrow Town team, John Wheeler (1916–1945), son of Walter James Wheeler, bank manager, on 21 December 1940 and, like him, became a member of the Communist Party of Great Britain (CPGB). As she wrote later,

> one reason for joining the party was … the conviction that without radical changes in society the skills of the architect could not be used to benefit ordinary people … one had to work politically as well as professionally and for some of us Marxism and the Communist Party seemed to offer the way forward. (letter to Anthony Cox, December 1989, Cox papers)

The Wheelers' two daughters were born in 1941 and 1943. John Wheeler, who, despite the CPGB's official neutrality between 1939 and 1941, had joined the RAF shortly before their marriage, was killed in a plane crash in September 1945 while out testing a new plane at high altitude. By this date the family had been living in a communal household at 6 Keats Grove, Hampstead, with Ann's brother and sister-in-law, and she had begun work for the architect–planner Judith Ledeboer, assisting her work on neighbourhood planning. Between 1946 and 1947 she then took on a similar role with Geoffrey Jellicoe, assisting on the master plan for the new town at Hemel Hempstead. She married for a second time, on 22 May 1947, the journalist Malcolm MacEwen.

After her marriage Ann MacEwen decided to focus her career on town planning and, following discussions with Jacqueline Tyrrwhit, head of the School of Planning and Regional Reconstruction in Gordon Square, London, it was agreed that she could take its planning diploma in two terms, while pregnant with her third child (a daughter), who was born in September 1948, two months after she completed the course. This allowed her to qualify for work at the LCC and she joined Percy Johnson Marshall's team in 1949, working for the head of planning, Arthur Ling, on the reconstruction of Stepney and Poplar. Despite the progressive politics of many of her colleagues who, like her, were CPGB members, her refusal to work on Saturdays in order to be with her family initially caused her to be denied pension rights and promotion. The repeal of this mode of institutional sexism allowed her to win establishment and promotion, which culminated in her taking on responsibility for the detailed planning of the reconstruction of north-east London. At the LCC she, and her co-workers, reflecting the influence of the pre-war thesis projects of the Architectural Association, brought to their planning schemes a desire to address both the physical and social needs of the rehoused, but budget cuts thwarted their visions for social and health centres, nursery schools, parks, and recreation grounds alongside the new housing estates.

From the LCC Ann MacEwen (who had left the CPGB in 1956, in protest at its response to the Hungarian uprising of that year) went to the Ministry of Transport in 1961, to form part of the team working under Colin Buchanan on what became the *Traffic in Towns* report (1963). The report was significant for forming part of a nascent movement against the unquestioned dominance of the motor car and the power of the traffic engineer in post-war planning. The team sought to balance the demands of traffic and commerce with existing historic urban infrastructure and while it retained a fondness for comprehensive redevelopment, its stress on managing the impact of the car, the maintenance of environmental standards, the safety and well-being of pedestrians, and the need for good public transport, represented an important challenge to the contemporary orthodoxy. MacEwen became a partner in Colin Buchanan and Partners from 1964 to 1973, where she produced planning and transport studies of Bath, Edinburgh, and Canterbury, as well as Bergamo, Italy. She succeeded in Edinburgh in getting plans to build a motorway-scale bridge between the Old and New towns abandoned. She also pursued an academic career as a researcher in the transport section of the department of civil engineering at Imperial College, London (1963–4), and later as senior lecturer at the school of advanced studies at Bristol University (1974–7).

In the late 1970s the focus of MacEwen's attention turned to national parks, then under threat of redevelopment, working in close collaboration with her husband. Based at University College, London, where they were both honorary research fellows from 1977, and funded by the Nuffield Foundation, they were early pioneers of sustainable planning. In particular they advocated the continued validity of national parks, not as nostalgic acts of preservation, but as what they called 'greenprints' for the future. Their two books, *National Parks: Conservation or Cosmetics?* (1982) and *Greenprints for the Countryside? the Story of Britain's National Parks* (1987), provided the intellectual rationale for the campaign. The MacEwens had moved to the Manor House, Wootton Courtenay, Somerset, in 1968, the shift from Hampstead to the west country being a key factor in their interest in environmental politics. In retirement Ann MacEwen learned to weave silk and also set up a local branch of the University of the Third Age. She spent much of the 1990s caring for her husband, who had suffered a series of strokes before his death in 1996.

Ann MacEwen's significance lay not just in her status as the pre-eminent woman town planner of her generation and her ongoing attempts to strike a balance between heritage and modernity in the age of the car. It may also be attributed to her presence among that generation of architect–planners who sought to develop a people-centred mode of planning, however thwarted their intentions may ultimately have been. In 2004 she moved into sheltered accommodation and died at Springdene Nursing Home, 55 Oakleigh Park North, Whetstone, Barnet, of bronchopneumonia on 20 August 2008.

Her second husband, **Malcolm MacEwen** (1911–1996), journalist and environmentalist, was born on 24 December 1911 at Brangan, Lower Drummond, Inverness, the son of Sir Alexander Malcolm MacEwen (1875–1941), lawyer and Scottish nationalist, and his wife, Mary Beatrice, daughter of Surgeon-Major George Henderson of the Indian Medical Service. Educated at St Salvator's preparatory school, Inverness, Inverness Academy, and Rossall School, Lancashire, he initially embarked on a degree in forestry at Aberdeen University in 1929, abandoning this after two years for the study of law at Edinburgh University. There he met his first wife, Barbara Mary Stebbing (1910–1944), a geology student, and daughter of George Stebbing, stockbroker. They married on 2 April 1937 and had one daughter. His political engagement began as a young man. Following an initial flirtation with the Scottish nationalism of his father, he turned next to the Labour Party, a conversion he attributed to the loss of his leg in a motorcycle accident in 1933, when the costs of his care convinced him of the need for a free public health service. Between 1938 and 1940 he served as Labour councillor in Ross and Cromarty but his instincts were towards communism and he joined the party in 1939. In 1940 he joined the staff of the *Daily Worker*, becoming its parliamentary correspondent in 1943. He left the post, and the party, in 1956, for the same reasons as his second wife. In this period he was involved in the establishment of the *New Reasoner* and the *New Left Review*.

In 1956 MacEwen entered a second phase of his career, as an architectural journalist and administrator. On the recommendation of Leo de Syllas, he joined the staff of the *Architects' Journal*. In 1960 he moved to the Royal Institute of British Architects as head of its information services (1960–66), later taking the role of editor of its *Journal* (1964–71), head of its publishing services (1966–70), and director of public affairs (1971–2). This period saw him become heavily involved in critiques of contemporary urban and transport planning resulting, first in 'Motropolis', a special issue of the *Architects' Journal* in October 1959, analysing the social and economic disadvantages of the car. This early sign of a concern for the compromising of the promise of post-war reconstruction culminated in his book, *Crisis in Architecture* (1974), a critique of the RIBA. The move to Exmoor in 1968 inaugurated the final phase of his career and what he called (in the title of his autobiography) 'the greening of a red'. As a nominee of the Ramblers' Association, he became a member of the Exmoor National Park committee and fought from within its support of the ploughing up of moorland. A long and bitter campaign finally succeeded, in 1977, in saving the land. In his later years he worked closely with his wife to advocate sustainable conservation. He died on 11 May 1996 at the Winsor Nursing Home, The Avenue, Minehead, following a series of strokes. His first daughter had predeceased him; he and Ann were survived by their daughter, and by her two daughters with John Wheeler.

ELIZABETH DARLING

Sources M. MacEwen, *The greening of a red* (1991) • *The Guardian* (15 May 1996); (6 Sept 2008) • *The Herald* [Glasgow] (16 May 1996) • *The Independent* (17 May 1996); (11 Sept 2008) • *The Times* (20 May 1996); (15 Sept 2008) • E. Darling, *Re-forming Britain: narratives of modernity before reconstruction* (2007) • *Western Morning News* (10 Oct 2008) • *WWW* • *WW* (2008) • Anthony Cox papers, V&A, RIBA Library Drawings and Archives collection • b. cert. [M. MacEwen] • b. cert. [A. Radford] • m. certs. • d. cert. [M. MacEwen] • d. cert. [A. MacEwen]

Archives RIBA, Malcolm MacEwen papers [Malcolm MacEwen] | Architectural Association, student work • V&A, RIBA Library Drawings and Archives collection, Anthony Cox papers | SOUND BL NSA, documentary recordings [Malcolm MacEwen]

Likenesses obituary photographs • obituary photographs (Malcolm MacEwen)

Wealth at death £675,800: probate, 29 April 2009, *CGPLA Eng. & Wales* • £110,349—Malcolm MacEwen: probate, 19 Aug 1996, *CGPLA Eng. & Wales*

Macfadyen, Donald James Dobbie, **Lord Macfadyen** (**1945–2008**), judge, was born at 10 Clairmont Gardens, Glasgow, on 8 September 1945, the elder son of Donald James Thomson Macfadyen (1915–1985), solicitor, and his wife, Christina Dick, *née* Dobbie (1916–1996). His parents were both Scottish. At the time of his birth they lived at 5 Waverley Drive, Wishaw. He attended Wishaw primary school (where in his final year he was school dux) and then Hutchesons' Boys' Grammar School, Glasgow. In 1963 he entered the law faculty at Glasgow University from which he graduated LLB with first-class honours in 1967. In the course of his university career he received many marks of distinction and won a number of prizes. These included the Gillies memorial prize (for civil law), the Cunningham bursary (for conveyancing), and the William Whyte bursary. On 29 July 1971 he married Christine Balfour Gourlay Hunter, a schoolteacher, and daughter of John Hunter, linotype operator. They had two children, Catherine (Katie) (*b.* 1975) and Donald (Donnie) (*b.* 1979). Donnie later played rugby football for Glasgow Warriors and was for several seasons a member of the Scottish international team.

Having graduated from Glasgow University, Macfadyen

undertook a bar apprenticeship with Messrs Simpson and Marwick, an Edinburgh firm of solicitors, and thereafter devilled, principally to David Edward, and for some time to John Murray (later Lord Dervaird). He was admitted to the Scots bar on 6 June 1969. He quickly built up a successful practice. At that time personal injury work was a significant part of first instance business in the court of session. Macfadyen regularly appeared in such cases on behalf of members of the National Union of Mineworkers. However, his talents were also deployed elsewhere. He was frequently instructed in the outer house and in the inner house of the court of session. From 1977 to 1979 he was standing junior counsel to the Department of Agriculture and Fisheries for Scotland and from 1982 to 1983 standing junior counsel to the Scottish Home Department. Between these appointments he served as an advocate depute, prosecuting in trials and appearing for the crown in appeals in the high court of justiciary.

In 1983 Macfadyen took silk. Again his practice, which was principally in civil business, flourished. As counsel he contributed significantly to a number of leading decisions. He was appointed by Lord Clyde, the chairman of the Orkney inquiry, to be counsel to that inquiry. This involved delicate and difficult issues arising from the removal from their families of nine children resident in the Orkney Islands. The report of that inquiry, to the quality of which Macfadyen undoubtedly contributed, was of enduring importance in the field of the compulsory care of children in Scotland. In 1992 he was elected vice-dean of the Faculty of Advocates, an office he held with distinction until his appointment to the court of session bench in 1995.

While a judge of the outer house of the court of session, Lord Macfadyen (as he now was) discharged a range of duties, being particularly highly regarded for his work as a commercial judge. He was latterly the principal commercial judge. He was appointed one of the five senior judges who comprised the bench which heard and rejected in the Netherlands the appeal *Megrahi* v. *HM Advocate* (2002) (a case involving Abdelbaset Ali Mohmed al-Megrahi, a Libyan convicted of involvement in the bombing of Pan Am flight 103 over Lockerbie in 1988). In 2002 he was advanced to the inner house of the court of session and appointed a privy councillor. In his final years he regularly chaired extra divisions of that house as well as appellate benches of the high court of justiciary. He contributed to legal literature, being general editor of the loose-leaf publication *Court of Session Practice*, a regular source of reference by practitioners. He was for many years a judicial member of the Scottish Council for Law Reporting. After his death that body instituted an annual lecture in his memory.

Macfadyen was a judge of true distinction and highly popular. He always showed patience and courtesy to those who appeared before him but had an acuteness of mind which allowed him readily to identify the true issues. His judgments were both profound in content and elegant in expression. As vice-dean of faculty he was a regular attender at the conferences of the International Bar Association. On his appointment to the bench he joined the association's judges' forum, rising to be chair of that forum. His thoughtful and well-researched presentations at its sessions were highly regarded. He was from 1993 a fellow of the Chartered Institute of Arbitrators.

Macfadyen was much interested in the built environment. In 2001 he became chairman of the Cockburn Association (the Edinburgh Civic Trust) and remained in that office until his death. He was held in affection and high regard by all those with whom he had dealings in that field. He was diagnosed with cancer in 2006 but continued to perform judicial duties until very shortly before his death, at St Columba's Hospice, Edinburgh, on 11 April 2008. He was survived by his wife and their two children.

A. C. Hamilton

Sources *Evening News* [Edinburgh] (15 April 2008) • *The Herald* [Glasgow] (16 April 2008); (19 April 2008); (29 Sept 2008) • *The Scotsman* (18 April 2008) • *The Times* (10 June 2008) • *The Firm*, 28 April 2008, www.firmmagazine.com/features/377/OBITUARY%3A_Lord_Macfadyen_1945-2008.html, 25 April 2011 • International Bar Association website, www.ibanet.org/ENews_Archive/IBA_May_2008_ENews_MacfadyenObituary.aspx, 25 April 2011 • *WW* (2008) • personal knowledge (2012) • private information (2012) • b. cert. • m. cert. • d. cert.

Likenesses obituary photographs

Macfarlane, Sir George Gray (**1916–2007**), engineer and public servant, was born on 8 January 1916 at Deanston, Victoria Place, Airdrie, Lanarkshire, the youngest child of John Macfarlane (*d.* 1938) and his wife, Mary, *née* Knox (*d.* 1933). His father, a prosperous grocer, was a strict Presbyterian, an elder of the church, the provost, and a JP, and took his family to church twice every Sunday with prayers morning and evening. He also took them rowing, sailing, and hill walking. Macfarlane became fascinated by the ships on the Clyde and in particular the mystery of wireless telegraphy on a cargo boat.

At Airdrie Academy Macfarlane initially did so poorly that his mother arranged a year of rigorous personal tuition and no play. He did better, obtained a higher leaving certificate in classics and was advised to go straight to university for an arts degree. Against his father's wishes and all advice he was determined to become an engineer and after acrimonious discussions he was allowed to remain at the academy for a further year to attempt higher leaving certificates in physics and chemistry, not previously studied, and advanced mathematics. He gained distinctions in all three but still was advised by the dean of engineering at Glasgow University that as he had no family connections with engineering there was no future for him in it. He persisted and in 1933 was accepted, specializing in electrical engineering. He did outstandingly well, was top of his year, and obtained a first-class degree. On the advice of George Howe, professor of electrical engineering at Glasgow, he accepted a scholarship at the Technische Hochschule in Dresden. He completed his thesis within two years and was granted a doctorate for his research on electric wave filters. He left hastily in mid-August 1939 two weeks before Germany invaded Poland.

Following the outbreak of the Second World War, Macfarlane applied for a commission in the Royal Navy. At his interview he was told that because of his specialist training in electronics he could not be accepted but was to join the Air Ministry research establishment in Dundee. On arrival there he was initiated into the secrets of radio direction finding (RDF, or radar) and given the task of assessing the capabilities of different types of equipment from first principles. In May 1940 the team (now renamed the Telecommunications Research Establishment) moved to Worth Matravers in Dorset, and in May 1942 to Malvern, on Prime Minister Churchill's direct instructions. Throughout the war Macfarlane was involved in a great variety of theoretical studies, especially on radio wave propagation and reflection, basic to all systems. He made major contributions that greatly enhanced the effectiveness of the ground radars used to direct British fighters in the night blitz and the airborne equipment used to detect and attack U-boats and to bomb land targets accurately. These had a major effect on the allies avoiding defeat and ultimately achieving victory. In 1945 he was put into RAF uniform as a squadron leader, sent to south Germany as an intelligence officer attached to the American G-force advancing eastwards, and charged with collecting information on German radar and communications. He was in Paris on VE-day and witnessed the victory parade down the Champs Elysées. Meanwhile, on 23 July 1941, he married, in Glasgow, Barbara Grant Thomson (*b.* 1916), a schoolteacher from Airdrie, and daughter of Thomas Thomson, solicitor and town clerk. They had one son and one daughter.

Macfarlane was convinced that basic science and engineering had to advance together, particularly in electronics, and at the end of the war refused lucrative offers in industry and remained with the Telecommunications Research Establishment to help develop a pioneering research centre to serve civil as well as defence interests. During the next fifteen years he played a leading role in building this up into one of the most prestigious centres of electronics research in Europe. He published over twenty significant research papers on electronics and semiconductors, including a much cited study of the optical properties of germanium and silicon, central to the development of infra-red detectors. He designed and developed the first digital computer, RREAC, using transistors instead of valves, worked on new computer languages, and initiated the Advanced Computer Techniques Project, a programme of research and development between government and industry to strengthen the British computer industry.

In 1960 Macfarlane was appointed deputy director of the National Physical Laboratory, which maintained the national standards for time, length, weight, and all measurable quantities used in industry. It also provided a wide range of testing facilities, including wind tunnels, ship tanks, radioactive chambers, metallurgical test rigs, and noise monitoring equipment. The new laser research programme he introduced thrived. After two years, however, he returned to the Royal Radar Establishment (as the Telecommunications Research Establishment had been renamed, in 1957) as director. He made its outstanding work better known and appreciated by arranging lectures and open days for ministers, service chiefs, senior civil servants, captains of industry, and the local population. In 1965 he was appointed CB and in 1967 was awarded the degree of LLD by Glasgow University. He received a number of medals and prizes from professional institutions—the Heaviside medal of the Institution of Electrical Engineers, the Glazebrook gold medal of the Institute of Physics, and a gold medal for services to the McRobert Award Trust.

In 1967 Macfarlane moved to London to fill the post of controller of research in the Ministry of Technology under Tony Benn. He set up an effective means of bringing together and controlling the work of all the research and development establishments formerly in the Ministry of Aviation, the Department of Scientific and Industrial Research, and the non-nuclear work of the United Kingdom Atomic Energy Authority. Of the 23,000 staff involved over 9000 were qualified scientists and engineers. As well as continuing defence work for the Ministry of Aviation the objective was to give technological support to manufacturing industry to drive forward the 'white heat' of technological revolution sponsored by Harold Wilson. When Edward Heath became prime minister in 1970 the Ministry of Technology was split up and the Ministry of Aviation became part of the Ministry of Defence. Macfarlane was appointed controller of establishments and research programmes to reorganize the twenty-four research and development establishments of the three services into a single research and development function without disruption of essential work. He persuaded the reluctant staff to accept his plans. In the further reorganization of the Ministry of Defence in 1971 by Derek Rayner as procurement chief executive, the service chief scientists, who had been advisers, were given full management responsibility for their service groups of establishments under Macfarlane. He was knighted in 1971.

Macfarlane retired from the civil service in 1975 and served on the Carter committee to review the Post Office. It recommended hiving off telecommunications as a separate business but the government decided to embark on an 'experiment in industrial democracy' in which unions filled half the seats on the board with the other half divided between management and independents. In 1977 Macfarlane agreed to join the board to take responsibility for engineering policy. Post Office engineers were in the forefront of research into digital computer-based switching and optical fibre networks but the telephone system was still based on old Strowger mechanical exchanges and copper wire lines. The UK was losing out both as a supplier and user of communication services. In 1980 Margaret Thatcher's Conservative government split the Post Office into postal and telecommunication corporations and the industrial cartel and union resistance to change was overcome. Macfarlane remained on the board of the British

Telecommunications Corporation until its privatization in 1984, and of its successor, British Telecom (as corporate director), until 1987.

Macfarlane served on the National Enterprise Board from 1980 to 1985 and was a trustee of the Imperial War Museum (1978–86). He was deputy president of the Institution of Electrical Engineers twice (1972–4 and 1976–8) but twice refused the presidency in protest at the institution's refusal to admit physicists. He was a founder member of the Fellowship of Engineering (and vice-president, 1983–6), and helped transform it into the Royal Academy of Engineering (in 1992). He died on 20 May 2007 at Kingston Hospital, Kingston upon Thames, Surrey, of aspiration pneumonia following a stroke. He was survived by his wife, Barbara, and their two children, John and Anne.

W. H. Penley

Sources autobiography, priv. coll. • *Malvern Gazette* (23 May 2007) • *The Times* (31 May 2007) • *The Guardian* (30 July 2007) • *The Herald* [Glasgow] (7 Aug 2007) • Burke, *Peerage* • *WW* (2007) • personal knowledge (2011) • private information (2011) [John Macfarlane, son] • b. cert. • m. cert. • d. cert.
Likenesses obituary photographs
Wealth at death £320,752: probate, 6 Aug 2007, *CGPLA Eng. & Wales*

McGeoch, Sir Ian Lachlan Mackay (1914–2007), naval officer, was born on 26 March 1914 at Durie House, Helensburgh, Dunbartonshire, the son of Lauchlan Alexander Mackay McGeoch, ironmonger (his own second name was originally spelt Lauchlan), and his wife, Margaret Sayers, *née* Wilson. He was educated at the Nautical College, Pangbourne, and entered the Royal Navy in 1931. After sea experience in surface ships as a midshipman, sub-lieutenant, and lieutenant he entered the submarine service in 1936. In 1937 he married (Eleanor) Somers Farrie, daughter of the Revd Canon Hugh Farrie. They had two sons and two daughters.

The outbreak of the Second World War found McGeoch in the submarine *Clyde*, from which he progressed rapidly to the commanding officers' qualifying course (the 'perisher') and command of the submarines H43 and *Ursula*. His first operational patrol was unsuccessful and, recovering from a stomach ulcer, he most unusually applied to requalify for command. This accomplished, he took command of the submarine P228, subsequently renamed *Splendid*. In this vessel he conducted five successful war patrols in the central Mediterranean between November 1942 and April 1943. During this period the *Splendid* sank more tanker and supply-ship tonnage than any other British submarine, as well as two destroyers. Allied land and air forces were then occupied, in the period after the battle of El Alamein and the Torch landings, in their north African offensive against axis forces, in which denial of enemy supplies from Europe was crucial. He was gazetted DSC and DSO for these exploits.

On 21 April 1943, however, the *Splendid* was detected and attacked by the German (formerly Greek) destroyer *Hermes*, depth charged, and forced to the surface out of control. McGeoch gave the order to abandon ship, opened the main vents himself to ensure the boat sank, and was the last to leave. He was wounded in the right eye. He and the other survivors—over half the *Splendid*'s company—were taken on board the *Hermes* and later incarcerated in a succession of Italian prisoner of war camps. Escape was in his mind from early on, but he was hampered by lack of knowledge of Italian and by the risk to his remaining eye. However, in a train bound for Rome he and another prisoner saw an opportunity and jumped, wearing improvised Afrika Korps caps. They were at large for two days before being recaptured. They were transferred to a more secure camp near Gavi, reserved for 'very dangerous prisoners'. Plans for further escapes were halted when McGeoch, his eye still giving trouble, was transferred in September 1943 to a military hospital in Bergamo. This coincided with the departure of Italy from the war, but many German troops were still about and McGeoch decided to abscond on foot into Switzerland.

With the help of local people, by now largely sympathetic to the allies, McGeoch made his way to Bern and there first managed treatment for his eye—a steel splinter from *Splendid*'s periscope standard was skilfully withdrawn by a magnet—and then arrangements for his passage through occupied France to Spain. This adventurous and often arduous journey, helped by many sympathizers both official and from the resistance, was completed in March 1944. From Spain, with the British consular staff now well used (in spite of the leanings of the Franco regime) to the passage of allied service people towards repatriation, McGeoch returned, sailing from Gibraltar in the old battleship *Centurion*, to the United Kingdom. His war service was completed in the Far East on the staff of the 4th cruiser squadron.

Much of McGeoch's post-war career was in submarines, culminating in the post of flag officer, submarines (1965–7), but he also commanded the cruiser *Lion* (1962–4) and was admiral president of the Royal Naval College, Greenwich (1964–5). His final appointment, as vice-admiral, was as flag officer, Scotland and Northern Ireland (1968–70), where at the height of the cold war his submarine experience and operational judgement were of critical importance. Having been made CB in 1966, he was knighted KCB in 1969.

On the retired list McGeoch was active particularly in academic fields, achieving an MPhil degree at the University of Edinburgh and editing the *Naval Review* for eight years (1972–80). He wrote *An Affair of Chances* (1991), a memoir of his war experiences, and *The Princely Sailor* (1996), a biography of Lord Mountbatten, and contributed to a 'future history' of *The Third World War*, edited by Sir John Hackett (1978). He was a proponent of merchant ship identification systems, though not in the form in which they eventually emerged, and contributed to the work of the Royal Institute of Navigation, the Nautical Institute, the Honourable Company of Master Mariners, and the Greenwich Forum. He was a member of the Queen's Bodyguard for Scotland, the Royal Company of Archers (1969–2003), the Royal Yacht Squadron, and the Royal Naval Sailing Association (of which he had been commodore, 1968–70). A man of deep cultivation, humanity, and humour behind a sometimes austere manner, he was a revered figure in the naval service. He died of cancer of the bladder at West Suffolk Hospital, Bury St Edmunds, on 12 August 2007 and was survived by his wife, Somers, and their four children.

RICHARD HILL

Sources I. McGeoch, *An affair of chances* (1991) · *Daily Telegraph* (17 Aug 2007) · *The Times* (20 Aug 2007); (30 Oct 2007) · *The Independent* (25 Aug 2007) · *The Guardian* (26 Oct 2007) · Burke, *Peerage* · *WW* (2007) · private information (2011) · b. cert. · d. cert.

Likenesses photograph, 1942, PA Photos, London · obituary photographs

Macgregor [*née* McPherson], (**Janet**) **Elizabeth** [Betty] (**1920–2005**), cytologist, was born at 11 Lynedoch Place, Glasgow, on 12 January 1920, the daughter of Andrew McPherson (1884–1946), company secretary, and his wife, Jean (Jennie), *née* Craig (1886–1929). She had an elder brother, Andrew (1917–1940), later an RAF pilot who was awarded the first DFC of the Second World War, in 1939, and two younger sisters, Agnes Jean (1922–2005) and Margaret (1924–1984). When she was nine years old her mother died of tuberculosis. The family lived in Glasgow where she attended Bearsden Academy and then studied medicine during the Second World War. She qualified in 1943, after which she served in the Royal Army Medical Corps, reaching the rank of captain. She and her future husband, Alastair Goold Macgregor (1919–1972), met as medical students. They married at the University memorial chapel, Glasgow, on 13 October 1944, and their four children were born between 1946 and 1953. After working in both Edinburgh and Sheffield they moved to Aberdeen, where Alastair Macgregor was appointed regius professor of materia medica in 1958 and Betty (as she was known to friends and family) became a research assistant to Sir Dugald Baird, professor of midwifery, in the department of obstetrics and gynaecology. She was awarded the degree of MD with honours in 1963 and later became senior lecturer and consultant in the department of pathology.

In Aberdeen, Betty Macgregor initiated, as early as 1960, and then managed and evaluated, the first successful population-based cervical cancer screening programme in the UK. Working with the wholehearted support and collaboration of Sir Dugald Baird, she was motivated by what she had seen of the clinical manifestations of this devastating disease, which most often affected women in their forties at a vital stage of life when they were bringing up their children. Macgregor and Baird, in an article in the *British Medical Journal* in 1963, said that 'cervical cytology has now passed beyond the experimental stage' and that cervical cancer could largely be prevented by cytological detection and treatment of a pre-invasive stage (J. E. Macgregor and D. Baird, 'Detection of cervical carcinoma in the general population', *BMJ*, 22 June 1963, 1631). She kept meticulous records of her practice and, having the courage of her convictions, combined research with action. In the absence of computers she and her colleagues kept records in books and card indexes. Clinical and screening histories were coded on punch cards and sorted with knitting needles. But Macgregor did not spend all her time in the laboratory and applied a holistic approach to her work. She talked to and gradually won round general practitioners, convincing them that their patients should be screened. She visited women in their homes, giving balloons to the children to occupy them while she took their mothers' smears. She paid a great deal of attention to cytology training and quality control. Importantly, she collaborated with epidemiologists and statisticians to evaluate the effectiveness of screening.

Although there were centres of excellence elsewhere in the UK where cytology screening was practised and promoted, there was considerable apathy and even antipathy to its development and some evidence that its effectiveness might have been overstated. A rather poorly funded NHS programme was started in 1967. Its inadequacy was foretold in a letter that year to the *BMJ* by Stanley Way, chairman of the British Society for Clinical Cytology, of which organization Macgregor later became chairman and president. The failure of the first NHS programme was reported in a *Lancet* editorial in 1985 entitled 'Cervical cancer: death by incompetence'. Meanwhile, the Aberdeen programme became internationally recognized with the publication in the *BMJ* in 1985 of a case-control study demonstrating its effectiveness. This provided key evidence for the International Agency for Research on Cancer publication *Screening for Cancer of the Uterine Cervix* (1986), which was influential in the development of cervical screening throughout the world, including the successful NHS programme that was implemented in 1988. Macgregor was invited to speak at a conference celebrating the silver jubilee of the Royal College of Pathologists in 1987 and was presented to the queen and duke of Edinburgh. Always tactful and diplomatic, she was also honest and straightforward. When the duke asked her what caused cervical cancer she replied, 'Sexual intercourse, Sir' (private information). From her research she had always suspected there was an infective cause, which during her lifetime was proved to be high-risk types of human papillomavirus. This led to the development of a vaccine, which ironically was announced in the UK in a press release on the very day she died.

There was much more to Betty Macgregor than her successful career, which she combined, at a time when it was difficult to do so, with a rewarding family life as wife, mother, grandmother, and finally great-grandmother. As one of her granddaughters later said, 'She was a remarkable woman, a much-respected colleague, an admired friend, a devoted mother, a generous, fun-loving and strong-willed grandmother' (private information).

Macgregor was awarded fellowships of the International Academy of Cytology (1963), the Royal College of Pathologists (1982), and the Royal College of Obstetricians and Gynaecologists (1986), and appointed OBE in 1984. After retirement, she became director of the Harris Birthright Research Centre in Aberdeen, commuting from a house she had bought on the Isle of Seil. Her husband predeceased her in 1972 as did her eldest son, Andrew, in 1995. She died of cerebrovascular disease on 8 October 2005 at the Lynn of Lorne Nursing Home, Benderloch, near Oban, having spent her final days on the west coast of Scotland enjoying the beautiful views that she loved so much. She was survived by a daughter, Elisabeth, and two sons, Alastair and Roy. AMANDA HERBERT

Sources *Aberdeen Press and Journal* (11 Oct 2005) • *The Herald* [Glasgow] (28 Oct 2005) • *The Times* (21 Nov 2005) • C. Richmond, 'Janet Elizabeth Macgregor', *BMJ*, 331 (10 Dec 2005), 1410 • E. Logan, 'Janet Elizabeth Macgregor', *Bulletin of the Royal College of Pathologists* (Jan 2006) • P. A. Trott, *Cytopathology*, 17 (2006), 403–4 • personal knowledge (2009) • private information (2009) [Elisabeth Logan, daughter; Roy Macgregor, son] • b. cert. • m. cert. • d. cert.
Likenesses obituary photographs • photograph, repro. in *BMJ*
Wealth at death £212,359.24: confirmation, 8 May 2006, *CCI*

McGregor, Sir Ian Alexander (1922–2007), malariologist, was born on 26 August 1922 at 12 Church Street, Cambuslang, Lanarkshire, the son of John McGregor (*d.* 1945), tailor, and his wife, Isabella Chapman Greig, *née* Taylor (*d.* 1974). He had two older half-brothers, his mother's first husband having died in an industrial accident. He was educated at Rutherglen Academy, Lanarkshire. Uncertain as to whether to pursue a career in medicine or veterinary medicine, he was too late to gain a place in medicine at the University of Glasgow. He elected instead to study at the extramural St Mungo College and Glasgow Royal Infirmary, and graduated in 1945, having secured the class medals in anatomy, physiology, surgery, obstetrics and gynaecology, and public health, with certificates of merit in seven other subjects, a record McGregor himself described simply as 'good' (autobiographical notes).

McGregor was conscripted into the army in 1946. Before the end of the year he was posted to a field ambulance at Suez, by the side of the canal, relocating after only a few weeks to al-Sarafand in Palestine. He was ordered to train as a malariologist at the Middle East School of Hygiene at Dimra, near Gaza, and then assumed the post of command malariologist, spending his time travelling through Palestine and Transjordan inspecting the seven malaria control units that were in his charge and organizing training courses for other regimental medical officers.

Having completed his military service in 1948, McGregor enrolled to study for the diploma in tropical medicine and hygiene at the London School of Hygiene and Tropical Medicine and in 1949 was persuaded by Benjamin Stanley Platt, professor of human nutrition at the school, to join the Medical Research Council (MRC)'s human nutrition research unit that had been established in the Gambia. He was asked to investigate the possible contributory role of parasitic infections on protein malnutrition and began by assessing the incidence of splenic enlargement and anaemia in children under ten years of age in the village of Keneba, in the remote Kiang West district. It was during this period of relative isolation in Keneba that his lifelong interest in acquired malarial immunity and the mechanisms responsible for it developed. He had observed a reduction in the incidence of malaria in residents of Keneba as a result of the use of insecticide and periodic drug treatment but even when used in combination these interventions failed to eliminate the disease. Repeated serious episodes of malaria in young children stood in stark contrast to the infrequent cases in adults, leading McGregor to question the view that immunity to malaria was ineffective.

McGregor published the results of his preliminary but detailed observations in 1952, as 'A nutritional assessment of the results of the control of parasitic diseases in Keneba, a rural Gambian village' in the *Transactions of the Royal Society of Tropical Medicine and Hygiene*. This led to the MRC's invitation to him to develop his research on diseases that were important in the Gambia, as director of the Gambian unit, later termed the MRC Laboratories, in 1954. Meanwhile, on 30 January that year, at Mapledurham, Oxfordshire, he married (Nancy) Joan Small (*b.* 1922), an executive officer in the MRC, and daughter of Frederick Herbert Small, company director. They had two children, Alistair (*b.* 1956) and Lesley (*b.* 1957).

As director of the MRC's Gambian unit, McGregor embarked on the seminal field studies of malaria immunity that led to the demonstration that antibodies from adult Gambian serum had the capacity to reduce both the levels of malaria parasites in the blood and the clinical effects of the infection in the recipients, who were young Gambian children suffering acute clinical *Plasmodium falciparum* or *Plasmodium malariae*. This was the first reliable experimental data showing that humans repeatedly exposed to malaria infection could develop an immunity that was capable of restricting clinical illness and the density of parasites in the blood. Since this acquired immunity could be transferred by antibodies from immune serum, vaccination against malaria was at least theoretically possible. Subsequent experiments demonstrated that adult Gambian serum had the same therapeutic effect when used in children from Tanzania who had *Plasmodium falciparum* malaria, suggesting that west and east African strains of the malaria parasite had common features and that a vaccine against parasites from one region of Africa might be effective in protecting against parasites from other regions.

Many other important contributions followed. McGregor's work at the MRC Laboratories, Gambia, on malaria immunology and epidemiology underpinned the global effort to combat malaria. The quest for an effective vaccine, essentially triggered by McGregor's passive transfer of immune serum, continued at his death. His nutritional studies from Keneba provided demographic and health data that was also still being used by researchers at the time of his death.

McGregor served as chair or rapporteur on several important World Health Organization committees on malaria. He gave generously of his time, and his encyclopaedic knowledge of malaria, gleaned from his many years of practical experience in the field, ensured that the epidemiological features of malaria immunity were paramount when decisions on policy and planning of malaria research and control activities were being made by the World Health Organization in Geneva. McGregor was one of the very few scientists who had a complete mastery of malariology, amply demonstrated in his publication, with

Walter Wernsdorfer, of *Malaria: Principles and Practice of Malariology* in 1988.

McGregor finally left the Gambia in 1980, becoming a professorial fellow at the Liverpool School of Tropical Medicine. He continued to write about malaria and was particularly supportive of younger researchers at the school until he retired in 1994. He received many prizes and other honours. He was appointed OBE in 1959 and CBE in 1968, and knighted in 1982. He became a fellow of the Royal Society in 1981 and of the Royal Society of Edinburgh in 1987, and was president of the Royal Society of Tropical Medicine and Hygiene from 1983 to 1985. He died at Salisbury District Hospital, Salisbury, on 1 February 2007, following a heart attack suffered at home in Homington, Wiltshire, and was survived by his wife, Joan, and their two children. PAUL HAGAN

Sources *The Times* (14 Feb 2007) • *The Independent* (14 Feb 2007) • *The Herald* [Glasgow] (17 Feb 2007) • *The Guardian* (9 March 2007) • *BMJ*, 334 (19 May 2007), 1062 • www.royalsoced.org.uk/fellowship/obits/obits_alpha/mcgregor_ian.pdf, 28 July 2010 • *Liverpool School of Tropical Medicine Annual Report*, 2006/7, www.lstmliverpool.ac.uk/about/communications/documents/annual_report0607.pdf, 28 July 2010 • www.who.int/tdrold/publications/tdrnews/news78/in_memoriam.htm, 28 July 2010 • I. McGregor, autobiographical notes, Royal Society of Edinburgh • Burke, *Peerage* • *WW* (2007) • personal knowledge (2011) • private information (2011) • b. cert. • m. cert. • d. cert.

Likenesses obituary photographs

Wealth at death £486,667: probate, 9 July 2007, *CGPLA Eng. & Wales*

McIntosh of Haringey. For this title name *see* Sargant, Naomi Ellen, Lady McIntosh of Haringey (1933–2006).

McIntosh, Angus (1914–2005), linguistic scholar, was born on 10 January 1914 at Healeyfield, Whitburn Road, Cleadon, co. Durham, the elder son of Kenneth McIntosh, accountant and insurance broker, and his wife, Mary, *née* Thompson. He was educated at Ryhope grammar school and Oriel College, Oxford, graduating in 1934 with first-class honours in English language and literature. A Harmsworth scholarship at Merton College led in 1936 to a diploma in comparative philology. He spent 1936 to 1938 at Harvard University as a Commonwealth Fund fellow, graduating (in 1937) AM in comparative literature, before taking up a lectureship in the department of English at University College, Swansea. In 1939 he married Barbara Bainbridge (1917–1988), a New Englander. They had two sons and a daughter. His academic career was interrupted by the Second World War. From 1940 to 1945 he was in the army, beginning as a trooper (private) in the tank corps and ending as a major in military intelligence. His most significant war work was at Bletchley Park where, with other academics turned code-breakers, he contributed to the Ultra operation that followed the decryption of the Enigma cipher. His time at Bletchley strongly influenced his thinking about problems in the history of the English language. In particular he foresaw the potential of computers as a tool to aid linguistic analysis.

From 1946 to 1948 McIntosh was lecturer in medieval English at the University of Oxford: after tutoring at Jesus College and Wadham College he was lecturer then student (fellow) at Christ Church. In 1948 he was appointed Forbes professor of English language and general linguistics at the University of Edinburgh and thereafter his academic career was based in Edinburgh. After the establishment of a separate chair in general linguistics in 1964, he held the new Forbes chair of English language until 1979. From then on, as emeritus professor, he became full-time director of the Middle English Dialect Project, which he had initiated in 1952 and which was the source of his most important work. He had been joined at an early stage of the project by Michael Samuels (later professor of English Language at the University of Glasgow) and subsequently also by Michael Benskin (later professor of older English at the University of Oslo). The culmination of this work came in 1986 with the publication of *A Linguistic Atlas of Late Mediæval English*.

During his long academic career in Edinburgh, McIntosh displayed a tremendous breadth of interest, and a creative energy that led to the inception of a number of major enterprises. As well as setting up the Middle English Dialect Project (later the Institute for Historical Dialectology) he was a prime mover in the establishment of the Linguistic Survey of Scotland and of the university's school of Scottish studies and school of applied linguistics. He was a key supporter of the *Scottish National Dictionary* and the *Dictionary of the Older Scottish Tongue*. After his retirement in 1979 he was honoured by two separate Festschriften, celebrating the main areas of scholarship that he fostered in his teaching and research. The first focused on philology and historical linguistics: the dialectology of medieval English, Scots, and Hiberno-English, codicology, textual studies and scribal orthographies, word-geography, onomastics, and the rise of standard English. The second reflected his general linguistic interests in language structure, syntax, style, and metre. In both areas McIntosh not only published himself but was also an inspirational and generous motivator of research.

McIntosh's intellectual vision led him constantly to forge connections between the disciplines with which he was engaged, and he never lost this capacity for flexible cross-disciplinary thinking. Indeed it was McIntosh's involvement with the modern language Linguistic Survey of Scotland that provided the context for one of his most important insights in the historical study of language. It was already well known that Middle English in its written forms exhibited high degrees of linguistic variation, which had broad correlation with the regional geography of England. What had not been attempted before was the application of the methodology of modern dialect surveys to past stages of the language. McIntosh experimented with the Linguistic Survey data, discovering that it was possible to localize material from informants purely on the evidence of their linguistic forms. The method McIntosh devised became known as the 'fit-technique', and it revolutionized dialect research in historical linguistics.

McIntosh served on numerous academic councils, committees, and editorial advisory boards, and was awarded many honours. From 1977 to 1989 he was president (and thereafter honorary president) of the Scottish Text Society. He was a member of the council of the Early English Text Society and a foreign member of the Finnish Academy of Sciences and Letters. He held honorary doctorates from the universities of Poznan (1972), Durham (1980), Glasgow (1994), and Edinburgh (2004). He was a fellow both of the British Academy (which awarded him its Sir Israel Gollancz prize in 1989) and of the Royal Society of Edinburgh. After his death in 2005 his name was added to the Institute for Historical Dialectology annual lecture, and in 2007 the Scottish Text Society also established an annual lecture in his name. His academic legacy included a corps of active researchers, at the University of Edinburgh and elsewhere, pursuing work in the tradition whose foundation he laid.

McIntosh was inspirational not just as an academic. He combined charm, wit, and determination with the capacity for making others feel the possibility of success. He led by example and his interests were always translated into action. His entry in *Who's Who* listed as his recreations gardening, painting, and music, in all of which he was, at one time or another, a proficient practitioner. He was also an accomplished and published poet. If the size of his academic projects was on a monumental and serious scale, his poems tended towards economy—haikus, tankas, limericks, and clerihews—delighting in the whimsical nature of language. Following the death of his first wife, in 1988 he married Karina Williamson, *née* Side (*b.* 1928), the widow of Colin Williamson, a fellow of Jesus College, Oxford. In the last years of his life McIntosh continued to enjoy the company of his friends and large, far-flung, extended family. He died peacefully at Liberton Hospital, Edinburgh, on 26 October 2005 of kidney failure and renovascular disease. His funeral in the kirk of the Canongate, Edinburgh, on 3 November 2005 was a glorious celebration of his life, character, and achievements. He was buried in the Grange cemetery, Edinburgh. He was survived by his second wife, Karina, and the three children of his first marriage. MARGARET LAING

Sources M. Benskin, 'The Middle English dialect atlas', *So meny people, longages and tonges: philological essays in Scots and mediaeval English presented to Angus McIntosh*, ed. M. Benskin and M. L. Samuels (1981) · M. Benskin, 'A biographical note', *So meny people, longages and tonges: philological essays in Scots and mediaeval English presented to Angus McIntosh*, ed. M. Benskin and M. L. Samuels (1981) · *The Herald* [Glasgow] (31 Oct 2005) · *The Independent* (1 Nov 2005) · *The Scotsman* (1 Nov 2005) · *The Guardian* (2 Nov 2005) · *WW* (2005) · personal knowledge (2009) · private information (2009) · b. cert. · d. cert.

Archives University of Edinburgh, Institute for Historical Dialectology, academic papers and corresp. | SOUND BL NSA, documentary recording

Likenesses obituary photographs · photograph, U. Edin., school of informatics

Wealth at death £830,209.58: confirmation, 27 Feb 2006, *CCI*

Macintosh, Farquhar (1923–2007), educationist and promoter of the Gaelic language, was born on 27 October 1923 at 1 Elgol, near Broadford, Skye, Inverness-shire, the eldest of eight children of John Macintosh, crofter, ghillie, and seaman, and his wife, Katie Ann, *née* MacKinnon, also from Elgol. He was brought up in a Gaelic-speaking home and did not learn English until he went to Elgol primary school, where he was taught through the medium of English. His secondary education was at Portree high school, where he was an excellent all-round scholar. After leaving in 1942 he went to Edinburgh University to follow a course in mathematics and science, but like many of his contemporaries he was called up at the end of his first academic year and opted to join the Royal Navy. He served from 1943 to 1946 and became a commissioned officer in 1944. After demobilization he continued his studies at Edinburgh University, where he graduated MA in history in 1950. He was offered a place at Balliol College, Oxford. Because of the financial situation at home he was not able to accept the offer and the following year he took a diploma in education from Glasgow University.

Macintosh began his professional career as a history teacher at Greenfield junior secondary school, Hamilton, and then taught at Glasgow Academy before becoming the principal teacher of history at Inverness Royal Academy in August 1959. On 19 December 1959, at Leckie Memorial Church, Peebles, he married Margaret Mary, a 23-year-old teacher from Peebles, daughter of James Inglis, shoemaker. They had four children, John, Kenneth, Ann, and Ailsa.

It was in school education that Macintosh first made an impression on Scottish public life. He became the rector (head teacher) of three noted Scottish schools. In 1962 he returned as rector to his alma mater, Portree high school, before moving to Oban high school in 1967. He took over the headship of the Royal High School, Edinburgh, in 1972, and remained there as rector until his retirement in 1988. From early on it was apparent that he would not be the kind of rector who would spend his life sitting behind his desk. He was very much involved in a wider educational world, with an extensive knowledge of Scottish and international education. He was a visionary and a man of ideas. He was the first of a new kind of school leader in Scotland, who wanted to change the experience of pupils and was not afraid of curricular reform. In Portree and Oban he introduced leisure activities into the curriculum. Former pupils talked fondly of his impact on their lives. As rector of the Royal High School in Edinburgh he introduced the international baccalaureate, believing that this would help solve the curricular challenges of the Scottish senior school. Many public appointments in education followed. Perhaps the most important and influential was his chairmanship of the Scottish Examination Board, which began in 1977. It was not an easy time, as industrial problems threatened to disrupt the examination system. He skilfully chaired the board through that period and went on to manage the introduction of standard grade examinations throughout secondary schools in Scotland. When he left the board in 1990 he had served an unprecedented third term.

Macintosh was always aware of his roots in the Isle of Skye, in the Gaelic language, and in the culture and life of the highlands and islands. For seventeen years, from 1965 to 1982, he served on the Highlands and Islands Development Consultative Council and was convener of its education subcommittee. In 1973, when Stirling was preferred to Inverness as a new Scottish university, it was Macintosh who articulated the idea of a university based on a federal model, founded on the existing further education colleges in the highlands and islands. It was that inspired idea that Sir Graham Hills adopted in his report of 1992 which led to the creation of the UHI Millennium Institute, which was granted higher-education institution status in 2001 and powers to award taught degrees in 2008. Macintosh's interest in higher education and the Gaelic language came together in his chairing of the board of trustees of Sabhal Mòr Ostaig, the Gaelic college in Skye (1991–2007). He believed that the survival of the language relied heavily on the progress of Gaelic-medium education, and he was convinced that Gaelic schools would have to appear in the traditional heartlands and especially in the islands.

Macintosh was one of the great public servants in Scotland in the second half of the twentieth century. He served on, among others, the Broadcasting Council for Scotland (1975–9), the court of Edinburgh University (1975–91), and the board of governors of Aberdeen College of Education (1961–6), Jordanhill College of Education (chairman, 1970–72), and the Royal Blind School of Edinburgh (1990–2006); he was an active Rotarian, an elder at St Giles's Cathedral, and a faithful supporter of the former pupils' club of the Royal High School of Edinburgh. He became, variously, chairman of the School Broadcasting Council for Scotland (1981–5), the Highlands and Islands Educational Trust (1988–97), and the Scottish European Movement (1996–2004). His public service was recognized with his appointment as CBE in 1982 and by honorary doctorates from Heriot Watt University in 1980 and the University of Edinburgh in 1992. Fellowships were bestowed on him by the Educational Institute of Scotland, the Scottish Vocational and Educational Council, the Scottish Qualifications Authority, and the University of the Highlands and Islands Millennium Institute. Having lived latterly in Rothesay Place, Edinburgh, he died on 18 November 2007 at St Columba's Hospice, Edinburgh, of cancer, and was buried on 24 November in Elgol, Skye. He was survived by his wife and four children. His son Kenneth was the Labour member of the Scottish parliament for Eastwood, and an education spokesman for his party.

MATTHEW MACIVER

Sources *The Scotsman* (23 Nov 2007) • *The Independent* (27 Nov 2007) • *Times Educational Supplement* (30 Nov 2007) • www.royalcelticsociety.org.uk/socinfo.htm, 30 April 2010 • *WW* (2007) • personal knowledge (2011) • private information (2011) [Margaret Macintosh, widow] • b. cert. • m. cert. • d. cert.

Likenesses photograph, repro. in www.uhi.ac.uk/home/about-uhi/uhi_news/dr-farquhar-macintosh-cbe • photograph, repro. in www.smo.uhi.ac.uk/smo/naidheachd/fiosan/oraid2004_b.html

Mackay, Eric Beattie (1922–2006), newspaper editor, was born at 41 Balmoral Place, Aberdeen, on 31 December 1922, the younger son and youngest of three children of Lewis John Johnstone Mackay, a printer and compositor, and his wife, Agnes, *née* Johnston, a staunchly Conservative Aberdonian who lived to the venerable age of ninety-six. Brought up in the traditions of a Scottish middle-class family, where children were not expected to question authority, his was, nevertheless, a happy childhood, and though throughout his life he tended towards a reserve bordering on taciturnity his memories of Aberdeen between the wars were warm ones.

Educated at Aberdeen grammar school, where a classically based curriculum was still employed, Mackay proceeded to Aberdeen University, but his studies were interrupted by the outbreak of the Second World War. He joined the 1st Fife and Forfar yeomanry, equipped with flamethrowing Churchill Crocodile tanks, and forming part of the British Second Army after the invasion of Normandy. In October 1944, with the rank of corporal, he was travelling in a scout car from Antwerp to Bergen op Zoom, across the Dutch border, when it was hit by a stray artillery shell. The driver was killed outright, and Mackay was severely injured. He spent two years in hospital, where it was feared that he would lose a leg. He recovered eventually, though for the rest of his life he walked with a pronounced limp.

After resuming his university course Mackay graduated MA in 1948, and joined a small Aberdeen paper, the *Bon-Accord*, from which he went to the *Elgin Courant*. In 1950 he joined *The Scotsman* as a downtable sub-editor, and deputy chief sub-editor, before moving to London and a brief stint with the *Daily Telegraph*. He returned to *The Scotsman* in 1953, and on 26 June the following year, at St Peter's Roman Catholic church, Falcon Avenue, Edinburgh, married Moya Margaret Myles Connolly, aged nineteen, whose mother, Brigid Connolly (widow of Thomas Myles Connolly, a technical officer with the GPO), ran a boarding house in which Mackay was lodging. Beautiful and vivacious, Moya was a hospital nurse, who, on her marriage, had to give up her career since the rules governing the profession at that time specified that nurses must be single. They had four children.

In 1957 Mackay was appointed London editor of *The Scotsman*, and moved to live in Bromley, Kent. His contacts with Church of Scotland missionaries in Africa led to a series of front-page stories from the Federation of Rhodesia and Nyasaland about the repression of black protesters by British security forces. These disclosures greatly annoyed the Foreign Office, and Mackay was summoned to see the foreign secretary, Sir Alec Douglas-Home, who appealed to him to desist in the national interest. Mackay brusquely refused. After returning in 1961 to Edinburgh he became deputy editor under Alastair Dunnett. The two made an ideal team, Dunnett outgoing and gregarious, Mackay detached and enigmatic. As Dunnett became more involved in management, so Mackay increasingly took on direct editing responsibilities, and in 1972 he was appointed editor.

Mackay's early period in charge of a publication regarded by both its readers and its editorial staff as Scotland's national paper coincided with a critical time for the political process in that country. In the general election of

October 1974 the Scottish National Party returned eleven members to Westminster, winning over 30 per cent of the national vote, and the pressure for political change became seemingly unstoppable. *The Scotsman* had long argued the case for devolution, and now it led the debate in the run-up to the 1979 referendum, throwing its weight behind a Scottish assembly within the union, and taking the circulation close to the magic figure of 100,000. Mackay may himself have been intellectually drawn to the notion of independence, but he was acutely aware that Scots in general were not, and he was well tuned to his readership.

During his tenure Mackay recruited a distinguished team of journalists that included Neal Ascherson, Magnus Magnusson, Gus Macdonald, James Naughtie, and Andrew Marr. He also trained two journalists who went on to become editors of the *Herald* in Glasgow, Arnold Kemp and Harry Reid, and two of his own successors, Chris Baur and Jim Seaton.

Mackay was not an articulate man, his sentences often left half-finished, his ideas open to interpretation rather than being spelled out. But he had a sure sense of what worked in a newspaper, and he was content to appoint writers who were more fluent than he was; the fact that his journalists understood that he was on their side meant that he commanded great loyalty. This was never more important than in the aftermath of the failure of the 1979 referendum bill, when morale dropped and several of the paper's star writers left. Mackay was called on to settle a damaging industrial dispute, and in 1981 he suffered a personal blow when his wife, Moya, died at the age of forty-six. However, he continued to edit the paper until 1983, holding the circulation at well over 90,000. After his retirement he played no further part in public life in Scotland and never revisited the paper (though he did revisit the paper's old building on North Bridge, after it had been converted into a hotel).

In later life Mackay suffered a mild stroke, and later angina and diabetes. He was greatly saddened by the death of his eldest son in 2005. He died at the Royal Infirmary in Edinburgh on 16 May 2006, from lung cancer, and was cremated at the Mortonhall crematorium, Edinburgh. He was survived by a daughter and two sons.

MAGNUS LINKLATER

Sources [M. Magnusson and others], *The glorious privilege: the history of The Scotsman* (1967) · A. Dunnett, *Among friends* (1984) · *The Scotsman* (17 May 2006) · *The Independent* (18 May 2006) · *The Herald* [Glasgow] (20 May 2006) · *The Times* (22 May 2006) · *The Guardian* (24 May 2006) · *Press Gazette* (26 May 2006) · *WW* (2006) · personal knowledge (2010) · private information (2010) · b. cert. · m. cert. · d. cert.

Likenesses A. Morrocco, portrait, The Scotsman, Edinburgh · obituary photographs

Wealth at death £373,662.94: confirmation, 15 Nov 2006, *CCI*

MacKeith, James Alexander Culpin [Jim] **(1938–2007)**, forensic psychiatrist, was born at Priors House Nursing Home, Leamington Spa, Warwickshire, on 29 October 1938, the eldest child in the family of three sons and three daughters of Stephen Alexander MacKeith (1906–1995), medical practitioner, and his wife, Frances Millais, *née* Culpin, only daughter of Millais *Culpin, psychologist and psychotherapist. At the time of his birth registration his parents lived at Thistley Hill, Hill Farm Road, Hatton, Warwickshire. His father was a psychiatric hospital medical superintendent, who contributed to military psychiatry in the Second World War, during which he served with the Royal Army Medical Corps, while Jim MacKeith spent most of the war years with his mother and sister in Australia (where his mother had been born). After the war the family moved to Norwich, where his father worked as a psychiatrist.

MacKeith was educated at King Edward VI Grammar School in Norwich and Epsom College in Surrey. He qualified in medicine in 1965 from Trinity College in Dublin and held a number of junior medical posts between 1965 and 1971, which included being an exchange fellow at Johns Hopkins Hospital, Baltimore. It was while studying in Dublin that he developed a long-lasting affection for Ireland and an interest in Irish affairs. He gained a diploma in psychological medicine in 1971 and became a member of the Royal College of Psychiatrists in 1972. On 27 July 1973, at Conway Hall, South Place Ethical Society, London, he married Cornelia (Keesje) van Erkelens (*b.* 1946), a social worker and later psychoanalyst, and daughter of Cornelius Hendrikus van Erkelens, geophysicist. They had two sons and one daughter.

Between 1972 and 1974 MacKeith was employed as a medical officer at Brixton prison. In 1974 he became a consultant forensic psychiatrist at Broadmoor Hospital and worked there until 1977, when he took up a forensic psychiatry post at the Bethlem Royal Hospital, where he worked until his retirement in 1999. He became a regional adviser for forensic psychiatry at the South East Thames Regional Health Authority, which involved setting up five medium secure units in the south of England, developing forensic psychiatry regional training, working as a consultant on one of the units, the Denis Hill Unit, and enthusiastically supporting the operation and management of the other units. In 1992 he was elected a fellow of the Royal College of Psychiatrists. He was chairman of the forensic psychiatry faculty of the Royal College of Psychiatrists between 1992 and 1994. Between 1992 and 2006 he was an expert medical adviser to the European Committee for the Prevention of Torture and made fourteen inspection visits to twelve different countries.

In 1997 MacKeith became one of the founding members of the Criminal Cases Review Commission and acted as a commissioner until the year before his death, initially working for the commission two days a week, which he extended after his retirement from the National Health Service in 1999. The commission took over from the Home Office responsibility for reviewing alleged miscarriages of justice in England, Wales, and Northern Ireland. MacKeith played a large part in the success of the commission, and his clinical insight and diplomatic skills made an impact on numerous applications to it.

MacKeith's contribution to the criminal justice system

was twofold: first, his unique contribution as a commissioner of the Criminal Cases Review Commission, and second, but probably more important, his contribution as a forensic psychiatrist and expert witness in several key cases of miscarriages of justice, including the Guildford four, the Birmingham six, and the case of Judith Ward. His interest in false confessions and the potentially deleterious effects of interrogation had developed in the late 1970s and early 1980s. After presenting a paper at an international conference in Sweden on witness psychology in 1982 MacKeith joined forces with a psychologist, Gisli Gudjonsson, to investigate the psychological and psychiatric factors associated with false confessions. The work involved extensive research and expert testimony in England, Northern Ireland, and the USA. In 2006 Charles Patrick Ewing and Joseph T. McCann reviewed the 'great cases in law and psychology' and concluded that the case of the Guildford four 'is one of the most infamous occurrences of wrongful conviction based on false confession and was one of the worst miscarriages of justice in recent history' (Ewing and McCann, 54). MacKeith played a major part in the successful appeal of the Guildford four, as also of the Birmingham six. He was appointed OBE in 2007 for services to the criminal justice system, the secretary of state for justice, Jack Straw, writing to congratulate him on having 'changed the landscape in criminal justice and human rights' (*The Independent*, 9 Aug 2007).

For most of his working life MacKeith lived in Dulwich, south London. He was immensely proud of his wife and children and they were always a priority in his life. Within about a year of his retirement from the NHS he was diagnosed with cancer of the upper jejunum. He survived seven years of active and fruitful life before he died of the disease at his home, 27 Woodwarde Road, Dulwich, on 5 August 2007. He was survived by his wife, Keesje, his daughter, Gwen, a scholar and translator of Latin American literature, and his sons, Sam and Peter, both medical doctors. GISLI GUDJONSSON

Sources C. P. Ewing and J. T. McCann, *Minds on trial: great cases in law and psychology* (2006) • L. Elks, *Righting miscarriages of justice? ten years of the Criminal Cases Review Commission* (2008) • *The Independent* (9 Aug 2007) • *The Times* (10 Aug 2007) • *The Guardian* (13 Aug 2007) • *Daily Telegraph* (24 Aug 2007) • curriculum vitae, priv. coll. • personal knowledge (2011) • private information (2011) • b. cert. • m. cert. • d. cert.

Archives Wellcome L., corresp. and case files

Likenesses photographs, 1992, PA Photos, London • obituary photographs

Wealth at death £475,345: probate, 4 Aug 2008, *CGPLA Eng. & Wales*

McLaren, Dame Anne Laura Dorinthea (1927–2007), geneticist, was born on 26 April 1927 at 38 South Street, Mayfair, London, the younger daughter and fourth of five children of Henry Duncan *McLaren, second Baron Aberconway (1879–1953), politician and industrialist, and his wife, Christabel Mary Melville, *née* Macnaghten (1890–1974). Her father was Liberal MP for West Staffordshire from 1906 to 1910, and for Bosworth from 1910 to 1922; he was also a wealthy industrialist with interests in the coal, iron and steel, and engineering industries, and a distinguished horticulturist (creator of the gardens at Bodnant, Denbighshire, which he handed over to the National Trust with an endowment in 1949).

McLaren (who gave an early indication of her quiet self-confidence when appearing alongside Raymond Massey and Ralph Richardson in the film *Things to Come* in 1936) was educated at Longstowe Hall, Cambridgeshire, and Lady Margaret Hall, Oxford. She had intended to read English, but later claimed that she decided instead to read zoology when she found the entrance papers for English too hard. She was taught by Alister Hardy and Willy Holmes and the geneticist E. B. Ford, and graduated with a first-class degree in zoology in 1949, also winning the Christopher Welch scholarship the same year (the first woman to do so). After working on mite infestation in drosophila (fruit flies) under J. B. S. Haldane at University College, London, and studying the inheritance of acquired characteristics in rabbits under Peter Medawar, she embarked on research on neurotropic viruses in mice (a topic of relevance to poliomyelitis) under the supervision of Kingsley Sanders for her DPhil, awarded in 1953. One of her fellow students was Donald *Michie (1923–2007), son of James Kilgour Michie, East India merchant. In 1952 she and Michie both obtained research posts at University College, and on 6 October, at St Columba's Church House, Chelsea, married. They had two daughters, Susan (*b.* 1955) and Caroline (*b.* 1959), and a son, Jonathan (*b.* 1957). The marriage ended in divorce in 1959, but she and Donald Michie remained close friends. They also continued to share political beliefs: they had both joined the Communist Party of Great Britain at the height of the cold war, and although Michie resigned in 1956 (McLaren remained a member until the party's dissolution in 1991) they collaborated on a variety of left-wing causes, and frequently took part in marches, demonstrations, and fund-raising events together.

McLaren did not let marriage, the arrival of three children, or her political involvements deflect her from her scientific career. She continued to work at University College until 1955, when she moved to the Royal Veterinary College, London. There she worked on aspects of the reproductive biology of mice. In 1958, with John Biggers of University College, she produced the first litter of mice grown from eggs that had developed as embryos in tissue culture and then been transferred to a surrogate mother. This work was crucial in the later development of *in vitro* fertilization and embryo transfer in humans (which led to the birth of the first 'test tube baby' in 1978).

In 1959, following her divorce, McLaren moved to Edinburgh, where she joined the staff of the Agricultural Research Council's unit of animal genetics at Edinburgh University. She remained there for fifteen years, continuing her work on reproductive biology and embryo transfer (including refining techniques for the latter), but expanding also into research on mammalian fertility, immunocontraception (with Alan Beatty), DNA hybridization (with Peter Walker), and chimeras, organisms consisting of genetically different kinds of tissue produced by the fusion of different embryonic cells (with Hans Grüneberg). She also acted as both supervisor and mentor to a large and subsequently very successful group of graduate students. Unusually at that time she did not insist on adding her name to their publications, despite her sometimes important contributions. (She nevertheless published more than 300 scientific papers in her lifetime.)

In 1974 McLaren moved back to London, where she became director of the Medical Research Council's mammalian development unit at University College. In this post, specifically created for her, she continued her research on all aspects of reproduction, but focused increasingly on the development and differentiation of germ cells—the cells from which eggs and sperm derive. She was particularly interested in how these developed into stem cells, crucial to understanding how cells may generate other cells (with important implications for future health treatments, for instance the replacement of human cells damaged by injury or by degenerative diseases). It was while she was in London that she published her two books, both quickly regarded as classics, *Mammalian Chimæras* (1978) and *Germ Cells and Soma* (1980).

In 1992, while continuing to live in London, McLaren was appointed a principal research associate at the Wellcome–Cancer Research Campaign Institute (later the Wellcome Trust–Cancer Research Institute, and later still the Gurdon Institute) in Cambridge, where she also became a fellow of King's College. Her research in Cambridge added still further to knowledge about germ cells, the roles of sex chromosomes, and other aspects of the very early stages of reproduction.

A sceptic in religious matters, McLaren was nevertheless acutely aware of the ethical issues surrounding her area of research, and was willing to provide leadership in discussing and resolving them. She was a member of the Warnock committee on human fertilization and embryology, which led to the Human Fertilization and Embryology Act of 1990 and the establishment of the Human Fertilization and Embryology Authority to regulate *in vitro* fertilization and the use of human embryos. She was a member of the authority from 1990 to 2001. She was also a member of the Nuffield Foundation's bioethics council, and of the European Group on Ethics in Science and New Technologies, an advisory group to the European Commission. She appeared frequently on radio and television to put the scientific case for carefully regulated research on early mammalian and human embryos. (She was an extremely fluent and clear speaker as well as writer.) She was also a long-term and active council member of the Pugwash conferences, which sought to ensure that scientific advances were put to peaceful uses, and which won the Nobel peace prize in 1995.

McLaren was made a fellow of the Royal Society in 1975, and became closely involved in its affairs, as a member of its council from 1985 to 1987, its foreign secretary from 1991 to 1996, and a vice-president from 1992 to 1996. She was the first woman to hold office in the society. During her vice-presidency she travelled widely on its behalf, and in particular sought to promote the attractions of a scientific career for women, and to ensure equal opportunities for them. Bearing in mind her own experience as a young mother she often spoke in favour of improved government help for childcare (not only for scientists). She took on responsibilities in many other professional and scientific bodies: she was a member of the committee of managers of the Royal Institution from 1976 to 1981 (and Fullerian professor of physiology there from 1990 to 1995), president of the British Association for the Advancement of Science in 1993–4 and of the Association for Women in Science and Engineering from 1995, chairman of the governing body of the Lister Institute of Preventive Medicine from 1994 to 2002, and a trustee of the Natural History Museum from 1994 to 2003. She received

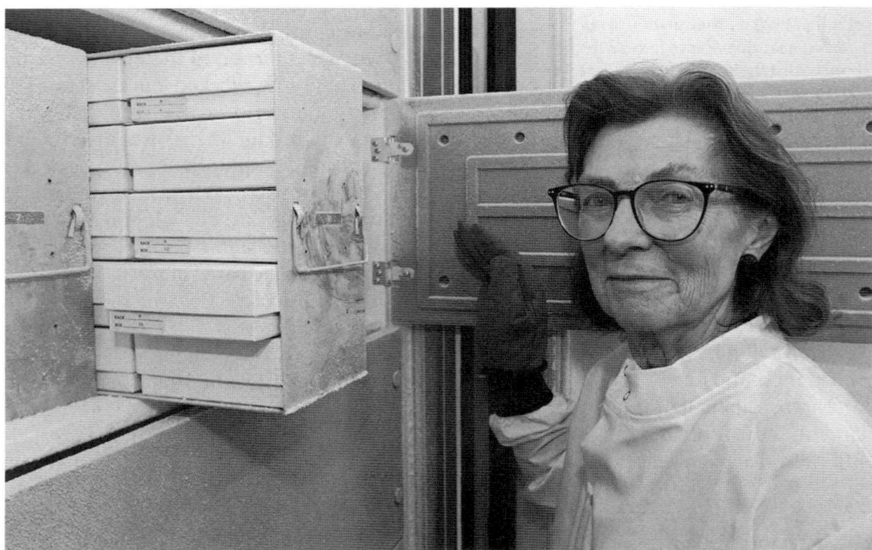

Dame Anne Laura Dorinthea McLaren (1927–2007), by Fiona Hanson, 2004

many honours. She was a founding member of the Academia Europaea in 1988 and a founding fellow of the Academy of Medical Sciences in 1998, an honorary fellow of University College, London, and of King's and Lucy Cavendish colleges, Cambridge, and she received the scientific medal of the Zoological Society of London (1967), the Marshall medal of the Society for the Study of Fertility (1985), the royal medal of the Royal Society (1990, the society's highest award), the Japan prize of the Science and Technology Foundation of Japan (2002), and the March of Dimes prize in developmental biology (2007). She was appointed DBE in 1993.

Despite her achievements and eminence McLaren remained an essentially modest person; she insisted on being called Dr McLaren even after being made a professor and then dame. Her colleagues and students much appreciated her kindness, courtesy, and interest in others, as well as her razor-sharp intellect. She loved parties, children, and football. One of her colleagues later said that 'when any international match was on television it was a waste of time trying to talk to her' (*The Guardian*, 10 July 2007). She died in a car crash on the M11 motorway in the parish of North Weald Bassett, Essex, on 7 July 2007, while travelling back from Cambridge to London; Donald Michie, who was travelling with her in the car (and with whom she had recently begun to cohabit again), was also killed. They were survived by their three children, and their lives were jointly celebrated at a memorial meeting at the Zoological Society of London on 19 July. She was also commemorated by separate annual memorial lectures held under the auspices of the International Society for Stem Cell Research, the UK National Stem Cell Network, and Lady Margaret Hall, Oxford, by Anne McLaren fellowships at the University of Nottingham, and by various activities in the fields of science education and genetic research sponsored by the Anne McLaren Fund.

ALEX MAY

Sources B. Hogan, 'From embryo to ethics: a career in science and social responsibility, an interview with Anne McLaren', *International Journal of Developmental Biology*, 45 (2001), 477–82 • M. Skipper, 'Research highlights: an interview with Anne McLaren', *Nature Reviews Genetics*, 8 (June 2007), 412 • www.admin.cam.ac.uk/news/dp/2007070902, 16 Aug 2010 • www.gurdon.cam.ac.uk/anne-mclaren.html, 16 Aug 2010 • *Daily Telegraph* (9 July 2007) • *The Guardian* (10 July 2007); (11 July 2007); (28 July 2007) • *Morning Star* (11 July 2007); (18 July 2007) • *The Times* (12 July 2007) • *The Independent* (12 July 2007) • *New York Times* (23 July 2007) • Burke, *Peerage* • *WW* (2007) • private information (2011) • b. cert. • m. cert. • d. cert.

Archives BL, Add. MSS 83830–83981 | SOUND BL NSA, documentary recording

Likenesses photograph, 1998, Photoshot, London • F. Hanson, photograph, 2004, PA Photos, London [*see illus.*] • obituary photographs • photograph, repro. in www.gurdon.cam.ac.uk/mclaren.html

Wealth at death £52,095,843: probate, 28 April 2008, *CGPLA Eng. & Wales*

McLean, (John David) Ruari McDowall Hardie (**1917–2006**), typographer and author, was born on 10 June 1917 at Herouncroft, Minnigaff, Newton Stewart, Kirkcudbrightshire, the only child of John Thomson McLean, a customs and excise officer, whose own father had been a shoemaker from Stranraer, and his wife, Isabella Mary (Isabel), *née* Ireland, a publisher's editor and primary school teacher. A childhood spent in Oxford, where his father had been posted, was a happy one. His parents had artistic and literary leanings and sent him to the Dragon School and Eastbourne College. After failing to gain a classical scholarship to Oxford and unsure of his future, at the suggestion of a family friend, Basil Blackwell, he entered the Shakespeare Head Press to learn printing. At the Shakespeare Head he was guided by the distinguished book designer Bernard Newdigate, who helped him to obtain work experience in a German printing firm. After attending Edinburgh School of Printing he undertook further training at *The Studio* and Percy Lund Humphries, a forward-looking Bradford printing firm, where he discovered his lifelong influence, Jan Tschichold, whose book *Die neue Typographie* (1928) trumpeted a revolutionary style of asymmetric design. For the rest of his life McLean retained a receptiveness to modern influences.

Despite pacifist leanings, at the outbreak of the Second World War McLean volunteered for the Royal Navy, serving first in submarines as a liaison officer on the Free French submarine *Rubis* (which, he was delighted to find, carried few torpedoes because of the space required for 900 litres of red wine), and then as a naval intelligence officer, becoming a member of COPP (combined operations pilotage parties) conducting dangerous reconnaissance surveys of Japanese-held beaches in the Far East. He was awarded the Croix de Guerre in 1942 and the DSC in 1943. Much later he wrote a memoir of his wartime career, *Half Seas Under* (2001). On 24 January 1945 he married Antonia Maxwell Carlisle (1919–1995), a 25-year-old history teacher (and daughter of Henry George Carlisle, medical practitioner), with whom he had two sons and one daughter.

In 1946 McLean, who had been in touch with Allen Lane before the war when he was sharing a flat with Edward Young, designer of the Penguin emblem, became responsible for the design of the lively Puffin Picture Books series, which introduced him to many artists who became his friends. He was one of the small band after the war making typography a new profession. In 1947 Tschichold, now embracing a classical approach, had been brought in to advise on design. McLean was able to cement his friendship with him and was later to translate his writings and write two books about him, *Jan Tschichold, Typographer* (1975) and *Jan Tschichold: a Life in Typography* (1997).

McLean left Penguin in 1949, and, besides teaching for a period at the Royal College of Art, became involved in the planning and design of the children's magazine *The Eagle*, the brainchild of the clergyman Marcus Morris, whose parish magazine for Colnbrook, near the Penguin headquarters, McLean had initially redesigned. In 1951 he joined George Rainbird to found Rainbird, McLean, a pioneering firm devising 'package' books, where McLean's skill designing complex illustrated books with Rainbird's business acumen produced, notably, the About Britain guides, edited by Geoffrey Grigson, and reproductions of flower and bird books. Always helpful to others, he gave work to Rowley Atterbury, whose printing firm the Westerham Press grew to become the major printer of illustrated books in the country. These books were widely copied and changed the face of illustrated book publications. Through the influence of Robert Harling, who had published and written a series of influential journals including *Typography* and *Alphabet and Image*, McLean founded his own periodical, *Motif*. Its lively and original thirteen issues, published between 1958 and 1967, added modern sculpture and painting to its typographical content.

McLean maintained that to survive a book typographer needs to write. Books soon poured from his pen: *Modern Book Design* (1951, updated 1958) was followed by the pioneering *Victorian Book Design and Colour Printing* (1963), *Victorian Publishers' Bookbindings in Cloth and Leather* (1973), and *Victorian Publishers' Bookbindings in Paper* (1983). His influential *Thames and Hudson Manual of Typography* (1980) was widely translated and much reprinted. From the early 1960s he enjoyed being an assessor of graphic design at art schools all over the country. He gave the Sandars lectures in bibliography at Cambridge in 1983. He also wrote monographs on the contemporary illustrators Joan Hassall, Edward Bawden, and Nicolas Bentley, as well as on the pioneering Victorian publishers and printers Joseph Cundall and Benjamin Fawcett. He amassed a huge collection of magazines, besides his collection of Victorian coloured books, useful when writing the first book on the subject in 1969, a practitioner's manual, *Magazine Design*. The appeal of the balance of illustration and type to McLean probably originated in a childhood spent in bed with recurring tonsillitis, when he preferred reading magazines to books.

Leaving Rainbird in 1958, McLean had formed Ruari McLean Associates in partnership with Fianach Jardine, daughter of the England cricket captain Douglas Jardine, setting up an office with their corgi, Slocum, in Villiers Street, London. Besides being consultant to the new *Observer* magazine and the *New Scientist*, he became honorary adviser to the Stationery Office in 1966, for which he was appointed CBE in 1973.

Also in 1973 McLean and his wife moved to Dollar, Clackmannanshire. The *Concise Scots Dictionary* and Lorimer's *New Testament in Scots* were two of the many books he designed there. Eight years later, at the time he was appointed a trustee of the National Library of Scotland, they moved to a row of fishermen's cottages at Carsaig on the Isle of Mull. A large Scandinavian log cabin was constructed to accommodate his 10,000 volumes, some of which were later housed in the University of Toronto. There he wrote his autobiography, *True to Type* (2000), 'anecdotal, engaging, laddish and sometimes a bit chaotic', as James Fergusson aptly put it (*The Independent*, 8 April 2006). Courageous, a lover of humour, fine wine, and the company of beautiful women, McLean had above all the capacity to enjoy life to the full. In his autobiography are reproduced his witty line drawings. He delighted his friends with his skilfully drawn Christmas cards, and his godchildren with rebuses. He could have been a cartoonist, as evidenced by his illustrations for *McLean's Silly Diving Signals*, published by the Scottish Sub-Aqua Club in 1990. Following the death of his wife, Antonia, in 1995 he moved to Tillicoultry, near Dollar. He died at the Royal Infirmary, Stirling, on 27 March 2006, of bronchopneumonia and acute kidney failure due to rhabdomyolysis. He was survived by his three children.

HUMPHREY STONE

Sources R. McLean, *True to type* (2000) • R. McLean, *Half seas under* (2001) • *The Times* (30 March 2006) • *The Guardian* (7 April 2006) • *The Independent* (8 April 2006) • *WW* (2006) • personal knowledge (2010) • private information (2010) • b. cert. • m. cert. • d. cert.
Archives BL, Edward Bawden MSS • NL Scot., corresp. • U. Reading L., business corresp. and designs
Likenesses obituary photographs

McManners, John [Jack] (**1916–2006**), historian and Church of England clergyman, was born on 25 December 1916 at 14 Lanark Terrace, Ferryhill, co. Durham, the second of three sons of Joseph (Joe) McManners, a miner, and his wife, Annie, *née* Marshall, a schoolteacher. He grew up in an Anglican vicarage after his father was ordained, and was educated at the Alderman Wraith Grammar School, Spennymoor. In 1936 he won an exhibition to St Edmund Hall, Oxford, and graduated with first-class honours in modern history in 1939.

Abandoning plans for a research degree on the outbreak of the Second World War, McManners at once volunteered for officer training in what he saw as a just and necessary conflict. Joining the Northumberland Fusiliers, a machine-gun regiment, in 1940, he was posted to Egypt and almost immediately found himself in the besieged garrison of Tobruk. The first sight of dead Germans strengthened a hitherto weak vocation to be ordained after the war ended. Subsequently he was wounded, but served throughout the north African campaign, rising to the rank of major and adjutant of his battalion. He ended the war, vividly chronicled in his memoir *Fusilier* (2002), as a liaison officer with the Greek army in exile, and was made an officer of the order of King George of the Hellenes.

Once more unsure of his vocation, McManners was nevertheless persuaded on demobilization to take a theology course at St Chad's College, Durham. In 1948 he was finally ordained. At Durham he also met his wife, Sarah Carruthers, a 31-year-old geographer, and daughter of William Isaac Errington, farmer. They were married by McManners's father at St Oswald's Church, Durham, on 27 December 1951, and had two sons and two daughters. By the time of his marriage McManners had returned to his old Oxford college as chaplain and tutor in modern history, remaining until 1956. In that year, perhaps inspired by wartime memories of Australian comradeship, he took a chair in history at the University of Tasmania. His years in Hobart were scarred by disputes not of his making, but they brought the completion of *French Ecclesiastical Society under the Ancien Régime: a Study of Angers in the Eighteenth Century* (1960), which instantly established his reputation. The result of summer vacations in the early 1950s spent in

French archives, it painted a lively picture of a provincial church on the eve of violent disruption by the revolution. It was unpartisan, but showed an empathetic understanding of pre-revolutionary ways seldom found in French historiography. All its author's subsequent work was imbued with the same spirit.

From 1959 McManners spent happier years at the University of Sydney, but a sabbatical leave in 1965–6 as visiting fellow at All Souls College, Oxford, reminded him of how distant Australia was from the best scholarly resources, not to mention his ageing parents. He returned to England in 1967 to become professor of history at the University of Leicester. From there he published the 'harvest of that delightful year' back in Oxford, a brilliant short distillation of current knowledge, *The French Revolution and the Church* (1967), and a fuller discussion of later relations between Catholicism and the Third Republic, *Church and State in France, 1870–1914* (1972). When in the latter year the regius chair of ecclesiastical history at Oxford fell vacant, requiring as it did a holder in orders, he was an obvious candidate. He hesitated before accepting an offer that took him by surprise, but his appointment was widely welcomed in the university. It entailed a canonry at Christ Church, and membership of two faculty boards. He served as a very popular and successful chairman of that of modern history from 1978 to 1981. It seemed the peak of his career, with election as a fellow of the British Academy in 1978, and the publication in 1981 of *Death and the Enlightenment*, which won the Wolfson prize for history. But when he reached the customary retirement age in 1984 he was invited to return to All Souls as chaplain. He remained there for seventeen years, which he described as the happiest of his life. They saw the publication of the best-selling *Oxford Illustrated History of Christianity* (1990), which he had edited, and culminated in his eighty-second year in the magnificent, two-volume *Church and Society in Eighteenth Century France* (1998). Condensing a lifetime's learning, it avoided what its author called 'morbid analysis' (*Church and Society*, 1.1), making points with teeming examples and anecdotes, 'no good story' as he put it, 'knowingly left out' (*The Independent*, 16 Nov 2006). It offered a vast panorama of the church first encountered in microcosm in Angers, with all its idiosyncrasies, inconsistencies, and vices, but also many humble virtues, comforts, and decencies, all doomed to perish tragically in a largely unexpected revolution. No Englishman had ever written better, or with more insight, about the *ancien régime*.

Invested as a commander of the Ordre des Palmes Académiques in 1991 and the Ordre National du Mérite in 2001, and appointed CBE in 2000, McManners was an accomplished lecturer and preacher, invited to give many endowed lectures outside his own institutions. Widely respected for his integrity, common sense, and quiet generosity of spirit, he was unfailingly good-humoured, a lover of puns, and an assiduous reader of the popular press for its human interest stories. Wiry in build, he was also a lifelong sportsman, playing football when younger, and tennis almost daily well into his eighties. He died of chronic obstructive airways disease at his home, 71 Cunliffe Close, Oxford, on 4 November 2006, and was survived by his wife, Sarah, and their four children.

WILLIAM DOYLE

Sources N. Aston, 'John McManners, man and historian', *Religious change in Europe, 1650–1914: essays for John McManners*, ed. N. Aston (1997), 1–21 • J. McManners, *Fusilier: recollections and reflections, 1939–1945* (2002) • *Daily Telegraph* (8 Nov 2006) • *The Times* (14 Nov 2006) • *The Independent* (16 Nov 2006) • *Northern Echo* (23 Nov 2006) • *The Guardian* (14 Dec 2006) • *WW* (2006) • personal knowledge (2010) • private information (2010) • b. cert. • m. cert. • d. cert.

Likenesses A. Newman, group photograph, 1978 (*Regius professors*), NPG • obituary photographs • photograph, repro. in Aston, ed., *Religious change*, frontispiece • photographs, repro. in McManners, *Fusilier*

Wealth at death £404,082: probate, 13 Feb 2007, *CGPLA Eng. & Wales*

Macquarrie, John [Ian] (**1919–2007**), theologian, was born on 27 June 1919 at 9 Inchinnan Road, Renfrew, the second son of John Macquarrie, pattern maker, and his wife, Robina Lindsay, *née* McInnes. John, known to his family and friends as Ian, was educated at Renfrew high school where he won a gold medal, and at Paisley grammar school from 1934 to 1936. He won a bursary to Glasgow University, where he graduated MA with first-class honours in mental philosophy in 1940. Although he had wanted to study theology at the Episcopalian College in Edinburgh, he remained at Glasgow out of loyalty to his father, taking his BD degree in 1943. He commented that 'the three years I spent in the formal study of theology were not the happiest in my life'. For the following seven years he claimed not to have opened a book of theology, regarding the subject as 'systematic superstition' ('Pilgrimage', xii).

As a theological student Macquarrie gained pastoral experience at Dumbarton, followed by a period after ordination in 1944 as assistant minister in Paisley. From 1945 to 1948 he served as an army chaplain, in which post he organized services and gave lectures to German prisoners of war in the Middle East (enabling him to perfect his abilities in German). This was followed by a period as parish minister of St Ninian's, Brechin. After an engagement of eight years he married Jenny Fallow, *née* Welsh, a secondary school teacher, in 1949. They had one daughter and two sons. From 1953 he was lecturer at Trinity College, University of Glasgow, where he was encouraged by John Riddell, professor of divinity, to work with Ian Henderson on Rudolf Bultmann. He completed his PhD in 1954, publishing it the following year as *An Existentialist Theology: a Comparison of Heidegger and Bultmann*. Never entirely happy with what he called Bultmann's 'almost pure existentialism', he drew on the thought of Paul Tillich and Karl Rahner ('Pilgrimage', xiv). This fusion led him to adopt a panentheist theology, along with a high view of religion: 'With me,' he noted, '"religion" is not a bad word' (ibid., xi). He retained an interest in existentialism (though without much personal angst), translating (with Edward Robinson) Heidegger's *Being and Time* in 1962. At the invitation of the publishers Harper and Row he began work on *Twentieth-Century Religious Thought* (1963), and gave the Hastie lectures in 1962 (published in 1967 as *God-Talk*).

John [Ian] **Macquarrie (1919–2007)**, by unknown photographer, *c*.1970

His 1960 lectures at Union Theological Seminary in New York were published as *The Scope of Demythologizing* by SCM Press, a publisher with which he retained a close link throughout his life. He became professor of systematic theology at Union Theological Seminary in 1962, finding the process of emigration 'painless' (*On Being a Theologian*, 30).

Even as a Church of Scotland minister Macquarrie considered himself catholic, having been influenced by George MacLeod and Govan parish church. Encouraged by his colleague John Knox, a Methodist who had become an Episcopalian in 1962, he joined the American Episcopal church and was ordained deacon in June 1965, and priest a year later. This denominational change gave him what he called a sense of 'spiritual renewal' (*On Being a Theologian*, 39), although he remained proud of his Celtic roots: he was fluent in Gaelic, preaching his last Gaelic sermon in London in 2005. At the invitation of the publishers Charles Scribner's Sons he published his widely used systematic theology *Principles of Christian Theology* in 1966. Adopting an 'existential–ontological' approach, it was one of the few comprehensive systematic statements of the Christian faith by an Anglican theologian.

Having acted as a consultant to the 1968 Lambeth conference of the bishops of the Anglican communion, Macquarrie was approached by Henry Chadwick to be Lady Margaret professor of divinity at the University of Oxford, which carried with it a canonry at Christ Church. Taking up his post in September 1970, he busied himself in graduate supervision and lecturing. He also undertook administrative duties in the cathedral, becoming canon treasurer. His range of interests spanned the whole compass of modern theology, including ecumenism, spirituality, and ethics, and he was prepared to address audiences well beyond the academy. His inaugural lecture in 1970 was on creation and the environment (published in *Thinking about God*, 1975), and he gave the Firth lectures at Nottingham (published as *The Concept of Peace*, 1972), and the prestigious Gifford lectures at St Andrews in 1983–4 (published as *In Search of Deity*, 1984). Although he was a man of catholic spirituality—he had published on benediction of the blessed sacrament—he was never a party man, even though he became a governor of the Anglo-Catholic Oxford institutions, St Stephen's House and Pusey House. He took a moderately conservative but always eirenic line in the debates over the incarnation following the publication of *The Myth of God Incarnate*, edited by John Hick (1977). His overseas invitations took him to Rome, where he met Pope Paul VI, as well as Denmark, Japan, and India. He was made an Oxford DD in 1981, and elected a fellow of the British Academy in 1984. He gained a large number of academic distinctions, including honorary degrees from five of the Episcopal seminaries in the United States.

On retirement in 1986 Macquarrie was presented with a Festschrift (*Being and Truth*, edited by Alistair Kee and Eugene Long), and in 1999 marked his eightieth birthday with the publication of a set of autobiographical reflections edited by John Morgan (*On Being a Theologian*). He and his wife moved to Headington, Oxford, where he preached regularly at St Andrew's Church. In retirement he maintained an active academic life, accepting overseas invitations, including to Russia and to China, where he gave the first theological lecture since 1948. 'The life of the theologian,' he wrote, 'will always be a pilgrimage with no stopping place that he or she can consider final. In what time remains to me, I shall carry on my quest for a Christian theology truly catholic and truly critical' ('Pilgrimage', xviii). A second Festschrift was edited in 2006 by Robert Morgan to mark the fiftieth anniversary of his association with SCM Press (*In Search of Humanity and Deity*). Despite serious surgery after the diagnosis of stomach cancer in 2002 he continued to write until very shortly before his death, from a recurrence of the cancer, at Sobell House, Oxford, on 28 May 2007. His funeral service was at St Andrew's, Headington, on 6 June. He was survived by his wife, Jenny, and their three children.

MARK D. CHAPMAN

Sources E. T. Long, *Existence, being, and God: an introduction to the philosophical theology of John Macquarrie* (1985) · J. Macquarrie, 'Pilgrimage in theology', *Being and truth*, ed. A. Kee and E. Long (1986) · D. E. Jenkins, *The scope and limits of John Macquarrie's existential theology* (1987) · J. Macquarrie, *On being a theologian: reflections at eighty*, ed. J. H. Morgan and others (1999) · O. F. Cummings, *John Macquarrie: a master of theology* (2002) · R. Morgan, *In search of humanity and deity* (2006) · *Daily Telegraph* (30 May 2007) · *The Times* (1 June 2007) · *The Independent* (1 June 2007); (9 June 2007) · *Church Times* (1 June 2007) · *New York Times* (3 June 2007) · *The Guardian* (5 June 2007) · *PBA* (2009), 161, 259–77 · *WW* (2007) · personal knowledge (2011) · private information (2011) · b. cert. · d. cert.
Archives Bodl. Oxf.
Likenesses photograph, *c*.1970, Christ Church Oxf. [*see illus.*] · obituary photographs · photograph, repro. in *PBA*
Wealth at death under £217,000: probate, 15 April 2008, *CGPLA Eng. & Wales*

McRae, Colin Steele (1968–2007), rally driver, was born on 5 August 1968 at the William Smellie Memorial Hospital, Lanark, the second of three children of James Steele (Jimmy) McRae (*b.* 1943), haulage contractor, later plumber, and rally driver, and his wife, Margaret Ritchie, *née* Mayes. At the time of his birth his parents were living at 21 Vere Road, Kirkmuirhill, Lanarkshire. By the time he was eight he was riding off-road motorbikes and in his early teens he became the Scottish schoolboy motor-cross

Colin Steele McRae (1968–2007), by Fabian Gredillas, 2001

champion. Yet his real passion was cars and after a number of preliminary events he entered his first formal rally, the Kames stages, in 1985, driving a borrowed Talbot Avenger 1600, coming fourteenth and first in his class. His enthusiasm for fast cars was nurtured by his father, a highly successful driver in his own right, who came to hold the British rally championship five times (in 1981, 1982, 1984, 1987, and 1988). McRae's brother Alister (*b.* 1970) was also a successful rally driver.

By his own admission Colin McRae had little interest in formal education but after leaving school he joined a mechanical engineering course at a local college and worked part-time at a garage in Lanark. Combining the two activities proved difficult and his father suggested that he join the family business, which he did, training successfully as a plumbing and heating engineer. He believed that his ability to drive a rally car at high speed was instinctive rather than the product of formal instruction. Nevertheless he must have benefited from his father's advice and support, including the loan of his own co-driver, Ian Grindrod, for the 1986 season of the Scottish championship. McRae was also soon joined by Derek Ringer, who remained his co-driver during the most successful period of his career. With the support of the British junior rally team, he took part in his first world championship event, the Swedish rally, in 1987. He completed the course and achieved a highly creditable third in class. In 1988 he succeeded in winning the Scottish championship. In the following year he switched to larger cars and, driving a Ford Sierra XR 4x4, came fifteenth in the Swedish rally and, in another Ford, fifth in New Zealand.

For many years McRae had to rely on short-term financial support, which, he felt, forced him to concentrate 'on being careful and avoiding mistakes rather than relaxing, driving naturally and showing what I could really do' (McRae and Allsop, 33). The problem was resolved in 1991 when he signed a contract with Prodrive, the start of a relationship that lasted eight years and brought him his greatest triumphs. David Richards, founder of Prodrive and former rally co-driver, had known the McRae family for many years and was well acquainted with Colin's driving skills. However, his decision was also strongly motivated by Prodrive's link with the car maker Subaru, who were anxious to evaluate McRae at close quarters. McRae's success with Prodrive was immediate. In 1991 he achieved victory in the British rally championship, a feat he repeated in the following year. In 1993 he graduated full-time to the world rally championship (WRC) and in the same period achieved his, and Subaru's, first success in the competition by winning the New Zealand rally. The pinnacle of his professional career was reached in 1995 when, driving a Subaru Impreza, he became the first Briton, and the youngest ever competitor, to win the world rally championship. He was runner-up in 1996 and 1997 and his partnership with Subaru was also pivotal in enabling them to win the WRC constructors' title three years in succession. On 14 July 1997 he married Alison Jane Hamilton (*b.* 1968), one of his earliest co-drivers (and daughter of Gavin Leggate Hamilton, farmer). They had two children.

A lucrative contract attracted McRae to Ford in 1999. Although at times frustrated with the unreliability of the Ford Focus, McRae went on to achieve another nine WRC victories and towards the close of the 2001 season was well placed to win the drivers' championship, only to crash on the final round in Great Britain and finish second to the eventual winner, Richard Burns. McRae's final WRC victory was in the Safari rally of 2002, bringing his total to twenty-five, a record at that time. A switch to Citroën in 2003 proved a disappointment and he was left without a sponsor for the following season. Yet his love of motor sport remained undiminished. In 2004 he rejoined Prodrive for the Le Mans twenty-four-hour race, finishing ninth overall, and the following year made one-off appearances in the WRC for Škoda. His final drive in the WRC was in Turkey in 2006.

McRae was widely liked and respected by his colleagues within motor sport. He contributed greatly to the popularity of rallying since his success was achieved through a style of driving that thrilled spectators, including television audiences. In 1996 he was appointed MBE for services to motor sport. His autobiography, *The Real McRae*, was published in 2001. He died in a helicopter crash a mile north of Lanark, near his Scottish home, on 15 September 2007; all four occupants on board were killed, including his young son, Johnny. His funeral took place at Daldowie crematorium on 26 September, and a thanksgiving service took place at St Nicholas's Church, Lanark, on 30 September. He was survived by his wife, Alison, and their daughter, Hollie. DAVID THOMS

Sources C. McRae and D. Allsop, *The real McRae* (2001) • H. Hope-Frost and J. Davenport, *The complete book of the world rally championship* (2004) • A. Henry, *Driven man: David Richards, Prodrive and the race*

to win (2005) • *The Times* (17 Sept 2007); (1 Oct 2007) • *Daily Telegraph* (17 Sept 2007) • *The Guardian* (17 Sept 2007) • *The Independent* (17 Sept 2007) • www.colinmcrae.com, 19 March 2010 • b. cert. • m. cert.
Likenesses photographs, 1988–2003, Camera Press, London • photographs, 1991–2007, PA Photos, London • photographs, 1992–2006, Rex Features, London • photographs, 1999–2002, Photoshot, London • F. Gredillas, photograph, 2001, Getty Images, London [*see illus.*] • photographs, 2001–6, Getty Images, London • obituary photographs • photographs, repro. in www.colinmcrae.com • photographs, repro. in McRae and Allsop, *McRae*

Macsween, John Angus (1939–2006), haggis manufacturer, was born on 17 October 1939 at Queen Mary Maternity Home, Edinburgh, the eldest of three children of John Charles (Charlie) Macsween (*d.* 1975), butcher, and his wife, Jean Maguire, *née* Muir. His father was the manager of William Orr, butchers, poulterers, and game dealers, with a large emporium at 130 George Street in the west end of Edinburgh, where he had met his wife, Jean, who worked in the accounts department. Orr was ahead of his time in separating raw and cooked meats, and in having his own slaughterhouse, engineers, workshops, and a fleet of vans. When Orr died in 1942 Charlie Macsween managed the business very successfully for his widow and after her death in 1949 his daughter Esther Gooderham. She sold the shop in 1952 and loaned the Macsweens £5000 to help them open their own business at 126 Bruntsfield Place in June the following year. This was a bold decision as rationing was still in place and the public had to register for a period of twelve months with the butcher of their choice. They very quickly established a successful enterprise and offered a wide range of home-made products, such as pies, sausages, and haggis. Charles Macsween & Son, as it later became known, created a reputation for high quality, attention to detail, excellent personal service, and a wide range of meats and game.

John Macsween was educated for two years at James Gillespie's School before moving to George Heriot's School at the age of seven. On the day he left school in 1957 he became apprenticed to his father. They developed an excellent relationship both in and out of the workplace, and had a mutual respect and regard for each other. On 29 August 1964, at Cramond parish church, Edinburgh, Macsween married Katherine Sheila (Kate) McKay, the daughter of Sir James Wilson McKay, a prominent Edinburgh businessman, who served as lord provost of the city of Edinburgh from 1969 to 1972. They had four children, Karen, Johanna (Jo), James, and Katharine. After her marriage Kate Macsween joined her mother-in-law in the family firm's office, enabling Charlie and John Macsween to concentrate on expanding and developing the business.

In 1966 Charlie Macsween made John a partner in the business. Following Charlie's death in 1975, with Jean in poor health, John and Kate took full charge. The retail market, particularly in towns and cities, was undergoing immense change with the emergence of the first supermarket chains. John and Kate Macsween far-sightedly expanded the manufacturing side of the business and placed greater emphasis on the potential of the export market for their haggis to exiled Scots both south of the

John Angus Macsween (1939–2006), by unknown photographer

border and overseas. In 1976 John was given the opportunity to take part in a Scottish food promotion week at Selfridges in Oxford Street. At the end of the week he was complimented by the buyer for producing the best promotion ever experienced by the store. A contract to supply Selfridges was immediately forthcoming and orders from the other premium stores in London, such as Harrods and Fortnum and Mason, followed rapidly. About the same time what had started as a very small national mail order business expanded into an international market supplying Scottish societies and British embassies throughout the world.

In 1984 the poet Tessa Ransford invited Macsween to sponsor the opening of the new Scottish Poetry Library on 25 January, Burns night, and challenged him to make a vegetarian haggis for the event. At first he was very sceptical, but with Ransford's help and encouragement he began experimenting with different concoctions, and Macsween's meat-free haggis was born, containing lentils, mushrooms, kidney beans, carrots and oatmeal, and using a plastic casing instead of the traditional ox-bung. Many thought a vegetarian haggis to be an oxymoron, but it caught the mood of the times and came to account for some 25 per cent of the turnover of the business. The firm's growing reputation for their haggis earned Macsween the nickname of Great Chieftain of the Pudding

Race, after Robert Burns's ode. Being a bit of a joker, when requiring a taxi to take him to the shop, he would not give the address but asked to be taken to the best haggis shop in Edinburgh. He was never let down.

John and Kate Macsween built their business by adhering to the traditional values of excellent personal service, attention to detail, and good value for money. They were always willing to offer advice and assistance, particularly for the organization of Burns suppers. The growth in popularity of Burns night celebrations throughout the world owed much to their industry and inspiration. John Macsween was passionate about the business and in particular the Scottish heritage and traditions associated with haggis. In 1996 the business was relocated to the first all-purpose, custom-built factory at Loanhead, but retained a retail presence in Bruntsfield until 1998. By the end of the decade the business had expanded and had customers throughout Britain, as well as supplying countries across the globe where import regulations allowed. Macsween was an outspoken critic of the British government's failure to deal effectively with the concerns over BSE that had serious repercussions for exports. He won many accolades, including a Scottish Food lifetime achievement award in 1996 and in 2001 the Sir Alistair Grant award for outstanding small business. The family as a whole had undertaken executive succession planning with the Caledonian Family Business Centre. In 1999, as part of the programme, John and then Kate started to wind down and hand over the reins to their daughter Jo and son James.

During their later years John and Kate Macsween travelled extensively and John spent many happy hours with another of his passions, the beautiful garden he created at their home, Preston Dene House, near Pathhead in Midlothian. He died there on 12 July 2006 after a two-year battle with cancer, which he fought with tremendous courage and dignity, and was buried at Crichton collegiate church, Midlothian. He was survived by his wife, Kate, and their four children. MICHAEL S. MOSS

Sources *The Herald* [Glasgow] (15 July 2006) · *The Independent* (20 July 2006) · *Daily Telegraph* (22 July 2006) · *The Times* (25 July 2006) · *Daily Record* (8 March 2007) · *Daily Mail* (8 March 2007) · private information (2010) [Kate Macsween, widow; John Macsween, son] · b. cert. · m. cert. · d. cert.

Likenesses obituary photographs · photograph, priv. coll. [*see illus.*]

Wealth at death £2,157,106.33: confirmation, 14 Feb 2007, *CCI*

Maddox, Conroy Ronald (1912–2005), artist, was born on 27 December 1912 at 8 The Homend, Ledbury, Herefordshire, the only son and elder child of Albert George Maddox (1886–1958), rate collector and Territorial Force volunteer, and his wife, Eleanor Annie, *née* Ballinger (1884–1975). His sister, Eleanor Joan, was born on 29 December 1913. His earliest memory, which was to influence his mature paintings, was of travelling to a Manchester hospital in August 1915 with his sister and mother to visit his father, who had been wounded at Gallipoli. His elementary education began in 1918 at the Court House School, where he was singled out for an art prize. From there he went in 1924 to Ledbury grammar school and then the

Conroy Ronald Maddox (1912–2005), by unknown photographer, 1938

newly opened Chipping Norton county school, when the family moved to Chipping Norton in 1928 to take proprietorship of the Blue Boar inn. He spent his free time painting landscapes in one of the inn stables. In 1933 the Maddox family moved again, to Birmingham, where Maddox's father became a representative in the wine and spirits trade. Aged twenty, Maddox started work as a clerical assistant in a solicitor's office. He went on to be an assistant in an analytical laboratory and then a designer in a car mascot casting firm. By 1935 he was working more permanently as a designer of trade fair exhibition stands.

The year 1935 also coincided with Maddox's discovery of surrealism, which he regarded as a turning point. He visited the International Surrealist Exhibition in London in 1936 and spent the summer of 1937 in Paris, attending classes at the art academy in the rue de la Grande Chaumière, where he experimented with 'invented surrealist transformations of the model'. On his return he exhibited at the Birmingham Group exhibition at the Lucy Wertheim Gallery in September 1937. By this time he had met the painter John Melville and his brother Robert, a writer and art critic, with both of whom he formed the nucleus of the surrealist group in Birmingham, which was to include Eric Malthouse, Desmond Morris, Emmy Bridgwater, Oscar Mellor, Stephen Gilbert, and William Gear. In the summer of 1938 Maddox again stayed in Paris, where he associated with William Gear, Reinhart Kalnine, and Georges Hugnet, and met Marcel Duchamp and Man Ray, the last of whom influenced his *Onanistic Typewriter*

(1940), a typewriter that sports vertical nails on each of its keys. In January 1939 he participated in the 'Living Art' in England exhibition at the London Gallery, the nerve centre of surrealism in Britain, and had a page devoted to him in *London Bulletin*, the surrealist journal edited by E. L. T. Mesens. Maddox's artistic production at this time was diverse: his lyrical, colourful gouaches depicting biomorphic, semi-abstract figures contrasted with collages containing violent and erotic surrealist juxtapositions. His object-mannequin *Cloak of Secrecy* (1940) was suggestive of severed limbs and a dismembered female body.

At the outbreak of the Second World War Maddox entered a reserved profession with the Birmingham firm Turner Brothers, manufacturers of aircraft parts. He continued to flourish as an artist and played a key role in the Zwemmer Gallery's 'Surrealism Today' exhibition, for which, as well as exhibiting, he designed a window display in which a child's cot containing rumpled sheets was transfixed by a dagger. His collages were equally disconcerting and, at the height of the war, several were seized by the special branch during a raid on the home of Simon Watson Taylor, on suspicion of being coded messages to the enemy or anarchist propaganda. Ironically, Maddox's war work had intensified at this time with a posting to British Thomson–Houston in Rugby for secret work on the stereopticon projector used by Rank Studios. In that year he met Wilhelmina Nancy (Nan) Burton (1924–1996) and entered a relationship even though Nan was married to Wilfred Sullivan Bruce Burton. Two children were born outside wedlock, Stefan (1945–1971) and (Wilhelmina) Lee (*b.* 1947). The couple had settled at 29 Speedwell Road, Edgbaston, in 1946, but it was not until 14 February 1948, following Nan's divorce, that they married, at Birmingham register office. The choice of a register office was significant. Maddox maintained that organized religion was corrupt and he repeatedly attacked the clergy in his work. At times this attitude resulted in irreverent humour, particularly evident in a series of staged photographs, *Entertaining a Nun* (1946), in which Maddox progressively inebriates and plays pranks on a young woman dressed as a nun. At this time he also invented the semi-automatic procedure of 'écrémage', which ranks alongside coulage, fumage, grattage, and decalcomania as a surrealist painting technique.

In 1954 Maddox and his family moved to London but he and Nan soon separated, and were living apart in 1955. A new relationship began with Pauline Drayson (*b.* 1935) in 1957 and, with her financial help, Maddox settled at 17A Lambolle Road, Belsize Park, in 1965. There he developed a more representational style of painting, as well as experimenting with pop art techniques. The 1967 surrealist festival, The Enchanted Domain, involved Maddox both as exhibitor and organizer, and served to renew his friendship with E. L. T. Mesens, with whom he collaborated on collages. The early 1970s saw great productivity and regular exhibitions in London, as well as regular contact with the Chicago surrealist group. The premature death of Maddox's son, Stefan, in 1971 prompted a stream of unsettling, grief-ridden paintings, such as *Residue of the Day* (1971). A fascination with hysteria and the nineteenth-century Parisian neurologist Jean-Martin Charcot led to works depicting madness and mayhem at the Pitié-Salpêtrière hospital, which was in keeping with the defamiliarization of the commonplace that underpinned all his work. When the Hayward Gallery mounted the Dada and 'Surrealism Reviewed' exhibition in 1978, Maddox felt that surrealism had not been properly represented and promptly organized a protest exhibition, 'Surrealism Unlimited'.

In 1979 Maddox met Deborah (Des) Mogg (*b.* 1963), who became his final companion. A retrospective was held at the Stoke-on-Trent City Art Gallery in 1995, and the last of some twenty one-man exhibitions was held at Whitford Fine Art in 2002. During his seventy years as an active surrealist, Maddox produced over 2000 works and constantly championed the theoretical purism of the surrealist movement. He died on 14 January 2005 in the Royal Free Hospital, Camden, London, of bronchopneumonia and was cremated in Finchley, north London, on the 21st. His ashes were scattered in the garden of his home. He was survived by Des, Pauline, and his daughter, Lee.

SILVANO LEVY

Sources S. Levy, ed., *Conroy Maddox: surreal enigmas* (1995) · S. Levy, *The scandalous eye: the surrealism of Conroy Maddox* (2003) · *The Independent* (15 Jan 2005) · *The Times* (17 Jan 2005) · *The Guardian* (19 Jan 2005) · *Daily Telegraph* (21 Jan 2005) · personal knowledge (2009) · private information (2009) · b. cert. · m. cert. · d. cert.
Archives FILM BFINA, documentary footage | SOUND BL NSA, National Life Story Collection, artists' lives, interviews with R. Dutt, 1996,1997, 1998, F6321–F6328
Likenesses photograph, 1938, priv. coll. [*see illus.*] · T. Evans, bromide print, 1985, NPG · M. Gerson, cibrachrome print from original transparency, 1987, NPG · C. Maddox, self-portrait, oils (after Moreau); Phillips, 14 Jan 1992, lot 120 · Z. Roboz, charcoal drawing, repro. in Z. Roboz and others, *British art now: a personal view* (1993), 49 · Z. Roboz, oils, repro. in Z. Roboz and others, *British art now: a personal view* (1993), 95 · obituary photographs
Wealth at death £571,880: probate, 20 Oct 2005, *CGPLA Eng. & Wales*

Magnusson, Magnus (1929–2007), Icelandic scholar, broadcaster, and environmentalist, was born on 12 October 1929 in Reykjavik, Iceland, the son of Sigursteinn Magnússon (1899–1982), European export manager of the Icelandic Co-operative, and later Icelandic consul-general for Scotland, and his wife, Ingibjörg Sigurðardóttir (1905–1983). The second youngest of four children, he had a brother, Sigurður (1927–1985), and two sisters, Margrét (1928–1996), and Snjólaug (*b.* 1935). With this nationality and parentage he should have been called Magnús Sigursteinsson, but this was regarded as too difficult for non-Icelanders to pronounce in the family's newly adopted country of Scotland, where they moved when Magnus was nine months old. So, Magnús Magnússon he became, and remained, although he Anglicized the spelling by removing the accents. He was educated at Edinburgh Academy, where he was dux (he later wrote the school's history, *The Clacken and the Slate*, 1974), and, having

Magnus Magnusson (1929–2007), by unknown photographer, 1987

won an open scholarship, at Jesus College, Oxford, where he graduated with a second-class degree in English in 1951.

Journalist and broadcaster Forsaking the academic life, Magnusson began his long and distinguished career in the media. He started as a staff writer and was later assistant editor (1953–61) of the *Scottish Daily Express*. He was sought out by Alastair Dunnett, the editor of *The Scotsman*, to be chief features writer and rose to become assistant editor. It was in these jobs that he honed his skills as an investigator and writer of repute. Meanwhile, on 30 June 1954, at Wardlawhill parish church, Rutherglen, Glasgow, he married Mary Ian (Mamie) Baird (daughter of John Baird, janitor, and his wife, Sarah), a fellow journalist and chief feature writer on the *Scottish Daily Express*. They had five children, Sally, Margaret, Anna, Siggy, and Jon. Siggy was killed in a motor accident aged eleven. The other children followed their father into radio or television broadcasting. Magnusson was a true family man, being described by his daughter Sally as 'the most generous, steadfast, loving and loved of husbands and fathers' (*The Times*, 8 Jan 2007).

Magnusson began his television career as a presenter and producer of current affairs and documentaries on BBC Scotland in the mid-1960s. This was followed by two years as a presenter on the late evening current affairs programme *Tonight*. A long-running archaeological programme, *Chronicle* (1966–80), followed; Magnusson was creator, researcher, and presenter, displaying his mastery of gathering knowledge and communicating it to a wider audience.

Magnusson was best known as the 'interrogator' in the television quiz series *Mastermind* which he fronted for twenty-five years, from 1972 to 1997. This programme suited his approach to knowledge: he described his hobbies in *Who's Who* as 'digging and delving'. He had a mellifluous voice and deep humanity, always putting contestants at their ease behind the scenes with a smile and a joke. The phrase he made famous, 'I've started, so I'll finish', had special significance as Magnusson was the consummate finisher of everything he started. The final programme, recorded in St Magnus Cathedral, Kirkwall, Orkney, brought together three facets of his interests: broadcasting, the Nordic world, and outstanding national heritage.

Icelandic scholar Magnusson was deeply attached to his native country in mind and soul, although he never lived there permanently. 'My hearth is in Scotland, but my heart is in Iceland', he often said. He was a master of Iceland's history and folklore, an expert on Icelandic literature, could read Old Norse and modern Icelandic with ease, and could speak and translate the Icelandic language fluently. He studied Old Norse literature at Oxford University and in Copenhagen. With his colleague and collaborator Hermann Pálsson, he translated five of the Sagas: *Njál's Saga* (1960), *Eirík's Saga* (1965), *The Vinland Sagas* (1965), *King Harald's Saga* (1966), and *Laxdæla Saga* (1969). Such was his meticulous approach to translation, the sign of a true scholar, that he revised his translations for a new publisher late in life. He was a consummate interpreter and teller of Iceland's history. Those fortunate enough to hear him give a recitation from Lögberg (the Law Rock at the world's first democratic parliament, the Althing, in Thingvellir) felt they had experienced the drama and significance of the original proceedings. He led tours telling the stories set out in the sagas. Listening to him telling the story behind the name of each hummock in the landscape was to attend a master class in cultural history. He translated five of the novels of Iceland's nobel laureate in literature, Halldór Laxness, bringing to the English-speaking world otherwise inaccessible novels of the highest quality. His services to Iceland were recognized by his being made a knight of the order of the Falcon in 1975 and knight commander in 1986, and also by an Edda (equivalent to a BAFTA award) for his contribution to television.

Magnusson was immensely passionate about Iceland's natural environment, had little time for conserving just a few special places, and argued that the whole of the Icelandic highlands should be a national park. This was not achieved in his lifetime. He acted as the environmental guide and mentor to his great friend, the former president of Iceland, Vigdís Finnbogadóttir, who later said of him 'no one has matched the scale on which Magnus presented Iceland to the English speaking world' (funeral oration). He was revered throughout the Nordic world and he was warmly welcomed whenever he visited those northern realms. His daughter Sally's account of visiting Iceland with her father in *Dreaming of Iceland: the Lure of a*

Family Legend (2005) told of the handing on of the love affair with his native country and provided insights into her father's character.

Writer and speaker Magnusson was a wordsmith of the highest calibre. He wrote some fifteen books, translated another ten, and wrote many speeches and articles. What began as a small task might end as a well researched and highly readable book. A talk on the Hebridean island of Rum ended with a book on its history (1997). The series of broadcasts entitled *Tales of a Grandfather* (after Sir Walter Scott's classic book) ended as a 700-page *tour de force*, *Scotland: the Story of a Nation* (2001), which was described by a reviewer as 'so well written, so well researched, so well understood'. Erudition, scholarship, rigour of research, vigour and determination in the execution, along with elegant phrasing, were hallmarks of his approach. Quotations from many sources peppered his talks and books. He was particularly fond of Gerard Manley Hopkins. He published a book of quotations collected over his lifetime of reading, *Keeping my Words* (2004). He devoured dictionaries and was a severe grammatical taskmaster. It was said about working with him, 'to unforgivably split an infinitive ... was a serious offence' (Smout).

Magnusson investigated each subject meticulously, whether for a book, a speech, or a broadcast. He prepared for every event as if all of life depended upon it, whether a meeting with a government minister, a parliamentary committee, or a board meeting. He recorded briefings on his trusty pocket recorder, listened to them assiduously, and typed them into his notes. His preparation of a lecture or talk was equally detailed. He wrote all of his speeches and declaimed them word for word, although few realized this as his delivery was so accomplished. Giving a speech from notes left too much to chance, he believed, but he admired those who could do it.

Heritage and environmental campaigner Magnusson's contribution to heritage and the environment was also very significant. The starting point was bird watching as a schoolboy at Edinburgh Academy. At the age of fourteen he won the Royal Society for the Protection of Birds' public schools essay competition on the mating rituals of blackbirds. Later in life he became president of the society (1985–90) and loved to focus the lens of his precious Bausch and Lomb binoculars on a bird and identify it by its 'jizz'.

Magnusson was chairman of the Scottish Churches Architectural Heritage Trust (1978–85), and of the Ancient Monuments Board for Scotland (1981–9). His work on national heritage, particularly in Scotland, in increasing the public's understanding through broadcasting, writing and committee work was recognized with the award of an honorary KBE (he retained his Icelandic nationality), and the Medlicott medal of the Historical Association, both in 1989. Sir Malcolm Rifkind, the secretary of state for Scotland, surprised many and silenced critics by appointing him chairman of the newly created Scottish Natural Heritage (1992–9). In preparation for this role he was appointed by Rifkind successively as chairman of the Scottish advisory committee of the Nature Conservancy Council (1989–91), and chairman of the Nature Conservancy Council for Scotland (1991–2). He worked tirelessly and with enormous determination to resolve many inherited conflicts in pursuit of his vision of bringing people and nature together.

Magnusson never avoided difficult tasks, but sought to bring opposing factions together, both in Iceland and in Scotland. Some very knotty problems were what he called 'a two pipe job'. Debates about the future of the Cairngorms Mountains in Scotland (he chaired a government working party in 1991–3), about geese and farmers on Islay, or about access over sporting estate land in Scotland, were addressed, along with a foray into the conservation battles around Lake Mývatn in Iceland. To all of these, and many other contentious issues in the environmental field, he applied his intellect and humanity alongside his ability to ensure that opponents began to see the sense of a different approach. The title of his report on the Cairngorms, *Common Sense and Sustainability*, echoed his whole approach.

Educationist Magnusson devoted a great deal of effort to the education of younger generations, and being with children gave him great delight. He was chairman of the Scottish Youth Theatre (1976–8). He was a very effective rector of Edinburgh University (1975–8), bridging the gap between the student and teaching communities. He later devoted his boundless energy to the chancellorship of Glasgow Caledonian University (2002–7). He would have been delighted with the Magnus Magnusson awards established by the university in 2007 to promote the ideas of young people, the Magnus Magnusson fellowships to stimulate discussion of issues of major concern to society, and the Magnus Magnusson PhD studentship, first awarded by Scottish Natural Heritage in 2008. His contributions to the life and heritage of Scotland were recognized by the honorary degrees awarded by seven universities (Edinburgh, Glasgow, Glasgow Caledonian, Napier, Paisley, Strathclyde, and York).

Character and assessment Magnusson was a brilliant, charismatic man of many parts who graced public life, literature, and the media in Scotland, Britain, and Iceland. He achieved more in one lifetime than most would achieve in three. He was the archetypal polymath and, as he liked to say, an opsimath: a learner late in life. He was also one of the most kindly and humane of people, with a great sense of humour. He had his favourites, people whom he trusted and who shared his visions, took action, and were not bowed down by bureaucracy. A favourite phrase was 'I like the cut of his jib', of someone he had just met and was keen to work with. He could use his personality and knowledge to gain the upper hand, for example, in meetings with government ministers, much to the chagrin of their officials. To others about whose views he was sceptical he would respond enigmatically, 'You may well be right'. He was by nature an optimist and always wished to find solutions. He despised humbug and arrogance, and was intolerant of negativity. He was very demanding and expected everyone to work as long and as hard as he did; he could not tolerate missed deadlines. His daughter Sally summed her father up exquisitely: he 'did everything to excess: drank hard, smoked fervently, loved deeply, gave generously, worked furiously, committed himself passionately to the things he cared about and drove himself relentlessly. Mediocrity was anathema. Political correctness never got a look in' (*Sunday Herald*, 11 March 2007).

Magnusson died of pancreatic cancer on 7 January 2007 at his family home, Blairskaith House, in Balmore, Torrance, north of Glasgow. He was buried ten days later at Baldernock parish church near his home and beside his son Siggy, perhaps reflecting where his heart ultimately lay. By the time of his death he had raised the standard of television broadcasting to new heights through his research and communication skills, and through the most famous quiz programme of his generation. In her funeral oration for Magnusson, Vigdís Finnbogadóttir said that 'he transformed the way the world saw Icelandic culture and civilisation' and that 'he was a cultural icon in both Britain and Iceland'. He demonstrated that a combination of intellect, hard work, meticulous preparation, and a winning smile could result in significant movement from entrenched positions. He galvanized a new approach to dealing with environmental conflicts in Scotland. And he made a more comprehensive contribution to communication and broadcasting than almost anyone of his generation. ROGER CROFTS

Sources T. C. Smout, 'Magnus', *Scotland's Natural Heritage*, 14 (1999), 16 · *The Times* (8 Jan 2007); (9 Jan 2007); (11 Jan 2007); (18 Jan 2007); (25 Jan 2007); (16 Feb 2007) · *The Guardian* (8 Jan 2007); (9 Jan 2007) · *Daily Telegraph* (9 Jan 2007) · *The Independent* (9 Jan 2007) · *The Herald* [Glasgow] (9 Jan 2007) · *Sunday Express* [Scotland] (11 March 2007) · *Sunday Herald* [Scotland] (11 March 2007) · *Review of the Session, 2005–2006* [Royal Society of Edinburgh] (2007), 328–32 · *WW* (2007) · V. Finnbogadóttir, funeral oration, 17 Jan 2007 · personal knowledge (2011) · private information (2011) · m. cert. · d. cert.

Archives FILM BFINA, documentary footage · BFINA, light entertainment footage · BFINA, performance footage | SOUND BL NSA, documentary recordings · BL NSA, performance recordings · BL NSA, light entertainment recordings

Likenesses Lenare, cellulose acetate negatives, 1953, NPG · photographs, 1964–2002, PA Photos, London · photographs, 1978, Getty Images, London · photographs, 1981–2006, Photoshot, London · photographs, 1985–2006, Rex Features, London · photograph, 1987, BBC [*see illus.*] · photographs, 2002–6, Camera Press, London · obituary photographs

Maizels, Alfred [Alf] (**1917–2006**), economist, civil servant, and international civil servant, was born on 17 January 1917 at 100 Newark Street, Whitechapel, London, the third son of Israel Maizels, a master tailor who had immigrated from Poland in 1905, and his wife, Rebecca, *née* Levy, a seamstress whom he had married in 1910. His parents were Jewish, and he attended Raine's Foundation School, in Bethnal Green, learning economics in the sixth form. He then entered the London School of Economics to study statistics, graduating in 1937 with a first-class degree and the Farr medal and prize in statistics. The LSE immediately hired him as a research assistant. While there he met (Edith) Joan Sidey, a sociologist, whom he married in 1942. They had two sons and a daughter.

In 1941 Maizels—known to friends and colleagues as Alf—became a temporary civil servant at the Board of Trade. There he helped to devise a successful clothing rationing scheme to a very tight timetable, 'a remarkable feat of administration' according to the official war historians (Hancock and Gowing, 333). After the war he moved from the statistics division of the Board of Trade to the commercial relations and exports division. His first foreign posting was his secondment in 1950–51 to the United Nations Economic Commission for Europe in Geneva. His research on the European timber and wood products industries laid the basis of future co-operation among European timber producers.

When the Board of Trade became concerned about the impact on Britain's post-war trade of the industrialization of underdeveloped countries Maizels transferred to the National Institute for Economic and Social Research in 1955, as a senior research officer. There, with a small team, he began research that became increasingly ambitious as he realized that the effect of overseas industrialization on Britain was just one aspect of the changing economic relations between all industrial countries and countries that produced mainly primary commodities. The research was published as *Industrial Growth and World Trade* (1963), which was rapidly recognized as a classic. It demonstrated that in many underdeveloped countries—probably the majority—industrialization was the key to economic progress, and that this would require the already industrialized countries to reduce their trade barriers, and to increase capital flows to developing countries.

Dissatisfaction with the existing international trade regime led in 1964 to the calling of the United Nations Conference on Trade and Development (UNCTAD), of which Raúl Prebisch was the secretary-general. Prebisch recruited Maizels to the secretariat of UNCTAD in 1966, as deputy director of the commodities division. He produced a new UNCTAD strategy for commodities in October 1966, which set the policy trajectory of UNCTAD for the next decade and a half. The new strategy paper envisaged a significant increase in the number of international commodity agreements (ICAs). It also advocated the establishment of a new source of finance for these agreements, a common fund, to facilitate this increase. In May 1974 the United Nations general assembly proclaimed a new international economic order. Gamini Corea, the new UNCTAD secretary-general, attempted to make UNCTAD the central negotiating forum of the new order, with the integrated programme on commodities and the common fund proposal as its centrepiece. Corea brought Maizels into his own office, as director of the economic policy evaluation and coordination unit. Drawn into the project, Maizels had an awkward role to discharge. He became Corea's speech writer and the principal draughtsman and editor of all major UNCTAD documents, defending UNCTAD negotiating positions. Though formally a technical appointee, he had to play an essentially political role. Ultimately the new international economic order negotiations failed. Maizels rightly thought it a landmark that UNCTAD had succeeded in establishing the first international non-aid financial institution that was not dominated by the developed countries. At the same time he acknowledged the emasculation of his original proposals.

After his retirement from the United Nations in 1980 Maizels held a number of academic appointments—at University College, London, and then at the World Institute of Development Economics, Helsinki. In 1987 the School of Oriental and African Studies made him an honorary professorial research fellow. From 1991 to 2004 he was also a senior research associate at Queen Elizabeth House, Oxford. In all these positions he published important contributions to commodity policy and cognate topics (including aid and disarmament). His *Commodities in Crisis* (1992) was later described as 'the definitive work on the subject' (*The Guardian*, 25 Aug 2006).

Maizels was averse both to neo-classical economic theory and to neo-Marxism. His open-minded and strongly empirical style of economics was much appreciated in Britain. He diagnosed economic dependence on primary commodities as the cause of poor countries staying poor, but his scheme for releasing developing countries from commodity dependence could not be squared with intractable diplomatic realities. He died at his home, 42 Llanvanor Road, Childs Hill, Barnet, London, on 10 May 2006, following a stroke, and was survived by his wife and three children. After his death Manmohan Singh, prime minister of India, lauded him as 'a brilliant economist who devoted his life to promoting the development of poor countries' (Rayment). JOHN TOYE

Sources W. K. Hancock and M. M. Gowing, *British war economy* (1949) • L. Jayawardena, 'Alfred Maizels: an appreciation', *Economic crisis in developing countries: new perspectives on commodities, trade and finance*, ed. M. K. Nissanke and A. Hewitt (1993) • *The Guardian* (25 Aug 2006) • J. Toye, 'Alfred Maizels (1917–2006): challenging economic dependence on commodities', *Oxford Development Studies*, 34/3 (2006), 293 • P. Rayment, *UN Special*, 654 (Sept 2006) [www.unspecial.org/UNS654/t33.html] • personal knowledge (2010) • private information (2010) • b. cert. • d. cert.

Archives UNCTAD, Geneva

Likenesses photograph, repro. in *UN Special*, www.unspecial.org/UNS654/t33.html

Wealth at death £285,045: probate, 29 Aug 2007, *CGPLA Eng. & Wales*

Mander, Noel Percy (1912–2005), organ builder and restorer, was born on 19 May 1912 at The Laurels, Crouch, near Wrotham, Kent, the son of Percy Mander, who worked in publishing, and his wife, Constance Emmie (Emily), *née* Pike. With the onset of the First World War the family moved to Brockley, south London, where Mander was introduced to the stimulus of music (he sang in the local choir at St Peter's, Brockley) and to organ-playing, his mother receiving lessons from Frederick Bridge, organist at Westminster Abbey. In 1925 the family moved to East Sheen and Mander attended Haberdashers' Aske's School, Hatcham, but found the classroom constricting and left as soon as he could.

Mander's first employment was with the publishers A and C Black, where he delighted in the books; but office life was not to his taste and he quickly looked elsewhere, to find his life's devotion: organs, especially organs in Anglican churches. After a period working with a self-employed organ restorer (Ivor R. Davies), Mander set up his own business, N. P. Mander Ltd, in 1936 by renting a nave at Christ Church, Jamaica Street, Stepney, from

Noel Percy Mander (1912–2005), by unknown photographer, c.1969

where he carried out repair work, notably at St Peter's, Bethnal Green, and, because of closure or upgrading, also oversaw the relocation of several organs for use elsewhere. But the first bombing raid of the Second World War on London destroyed the church and his workshop, and in October 1940 he joined the Royal Artillery, serving in north Africa (where he repaired an organ in Algiers) and southern Italy. An injury and some later illness took him out of active service, but during recuperation at Naples he wrote to every clergyman in the London diocese to solicit work on his return to England. It was an initiative that in both employment opportunities and professional standing was to be richly rewarded.

Indeed, when Mander returned to London (having been regularly consulted throughout his absence by officials of the diocese about the worth of organs in many war-damaged churches) he assisted the London Reorganisation Committee by identifying organs at churches across the diocese that merited storing, ready for later repair and reconditioning, and, it was hoped, later use in fresh venues. This commitment provided Mander with an unrivalled knowledge of needs and opportunities, and from a works that he established in 1946 in the former St Peter's School at Bethnal Green he was soon ruffling feathers at several firms of standing. In part this can be attributed to his establishing new methods of working for his staff—by, for instance, providing tuners with vans which enabled them to move from job to job much more easily and efficiently than if restricted to public transport. There was also a certain resentment that Mander was unwilling to adhere to the 'rules of the trade'; although invited, he refused to join the Federation of Master Organbuilders. A good example of his stance arose in connection with a historic seventeenth-century organ at Adlington Hall in Cheshire. Defunct for a century and more, it had been inspected and judged as beyond repair, but for Mander, influenced in part by knowing that a maternal ancestor, George Pyke England (1765?–1815), was an organ builder, the task was a challenge not to be ducked. Although many of the pipes were crushed and soundboards split Mander was able to restore them, in

1958–9, and an instrument of its size, rated as one of the earliest unaltered organs in Britain and one on which Handel played, was rescued for later generations. Meanwhile, on 2 June 1948, at St Peter's, Bethnal Green, he married Enid Watson (*b.* 1921), daughter of James Watson, education officer; they had three sons and two daughters.

Mander restored many other historic instruments, including those at St Mary's, Rotherhithe; St John's, Upper Norwood; St Mary's, Finedon; and St Philip's, Salford, and undertook major reconstructions, as well as the creation of entirely new instruments. Especially notable was the work done at St Pancras, Euston Road; St Michael's, Croydon; St Lawrence Jewry; St Vedast, Foster Lane; Peterhouse, Cambridge; the Livery Hall of the Worshipful Company of Merchant Taylors; St Giles, Cripplegate; Corpus Christi, Cambridge; Sheffield Cathedral; St Paul's School; Canterbury Cathedral; and the Ulster Hall, Belfast. He also restored an instrument from the bombed Wren church, St Mary Aldermanbury, which was transported stone by stone from London to Westminster College, Fulton, Missouri, to form part of a memorial (dedicated in 1969) to Winston Churchill, his 'iron curtain' speech having been delivered there in 1946.

If a single instrument had to be chosen to demonstrate the pinnacle of Mander's career, it was that at St Paul's Cathedral. He was approached in 1970 to rebuild (and provide a new case for) an 1881 organ known as the 'Willis-on-wheels', and his success ensured he was a natural candidate to modernize Henry Willis's 1872 chancel organ. The instrument, originally of fifty-two stops, had grown over the years to a 'ninety-sixer', and owing to somewhat piecemeal repairs and additions had lost its musical integrity. Much debate ensued, but Mander was able to begin work in 1972. The task was immensely complicated and the finished instrument sported 107 stops, grouped in a chancel section (great, north choir, pedal, swell, south choir, and solo organs), a dome section (fifth manual, and a pedal organ), and, on Mander's initiative, an entirely new west section incorporating a diapason chorus (to lead congregational singing) and three reed trumpets for ceremonial use. Work was completed in time for the queen's jubilee service of thanksgiving on 7 June 1977, Mander himself being recognized by his being made an MBE in 1979.

Within a few years of this triumph Mander judged his professional contribution was complete, and in 1983 he passed the firm to his eldest son, John Pike Mander, and promptly retired to Hawthorns, The Street, Earl Soham, Woodbridge, Suffolk, a house purchased in the early 1960s. There, as well as maintaining friendships at Westminster College, Fulton, from whom he received an honorary doctorate in 1984, and pursuing much neglected reading (except about organs), he became sensitive to the needs of the rural community. He relished the opportunity to help elderly villagers with the mundane tasks of life, such as carrying coal buckets, or helping with shopping, much in the spirit of his wife who, as well as being the resident nurse at the family business, had extended her firm gaiety and compassion to children in Bethnal Green by taking them on educational trips across the city.

In a volume of essays published to mark his achievements, *Fanfare for an Organ-builder* (1996), Mander's principal contributions were described as his initiative in saving and restoring many historic British organs, his insistence on high-quality materials and workmanship, and his promotion (where possible) of tracker action (that is, a mechanical, rather than electronic or pneumatic, linkage between organ key and organ pipe). But his interests were wider than that summary suggests: he was active in the Council of Christians and Jews (in several churches he worked happily alongside the muralist Hans Feibusch); was master of the Worshipful Company of Parish Clerks (1970); a fellow of the Society of Antiquaries (1974); and a loyal supporter of many causes in the East End of London. He remained active into his nineties, and died on 18 September 2005 at his home in Earl Soham, of heart disease. He was survived by his wife, Enid, and their five children. He was accorded a full set of obituary notices in the national press, as well as a fulsome notice in the *New York Times*, which was the first to be published.

PAUL FOSTER

Sources *Fanfare for an organ-builder: essays presented to Noel Mander to celebrate the sixtieth anniversary of his commencement in business as an organ-builder* (1996) • *New York Times* (24 Sept 2005) • *Daily Telegraph* (27 Sept 2005) • *The Guardian* (29 Sept 2005); (1 Oct 2005) • *The Times* (3 Oct 2005); (2 Dec 2005) • *The Independent* (10 Oct 2005) • archives, Manders Organs, St Peter's Square, London • *WW* (2005) • private information (2012) [Polly Mander, daughter; John Pike Mander, son] • b. cert. • m. cert. • d. cert.

Likenesses obituary photographs • photograph, *c.*1969, priv. coll. [*see illus.*]

Manning, Bernard John (1930–2007), comedian, was born Bernard Manning on 13 August 1930 at 15 Mitchell Street, Manchester, the second child of John Manning, greengrocer, and his wife, Mary Ellen (Nellie), *née* Barnes (*d.* 1995). He adopted the middle name John in later life. He was the second of five children, being preceded by Jack, who was seven years his senior (and who died at the battle of Arnhem in 1944), and followed by Alma, Cathrine (Rene), and Frank. At the time of his birth his parents lived at 183 Great Ancoats Street, Manchester. On his father's side he traced his ancestors back to a Jewish family named Blomberg, from Sevastopol, but he was brought up a strict Catholic. Growing up in a working-class district of Manchester in the depression of the 1930s, he was educated at the Roman Catholic Mount Carmel School in Ancoats, leaving school at fourteen to work at the Senior Service cigarette factory. He was called up for national service in 1948, and it was while he was on leave shortly before finishing this that he met Veronica (Vera) Finneran (1929–1986), a clerk in a textile factory, and daughter of Fred Finneran, fish salesman. They later married, at Our Lady of Mount Carmel Roman Catholic Church, Manchester, on 27 June 1956.

By the age of twenty Manning had started earning extra money singing in local clubs. This led to a variety theatre engagement at the Manchester Palace, where he was billed as 'Britain's newest singing thrill'. After a few months of singing for Oscar Rabin's band in London he left Rabin and moved back to Manchester, where he got a

Bernard John Manning (1930–2007), by Harry Goodwin, 1970s

job as the resident compère at the Northern Sporting Club. Gradually he began to introduce comic patter between the songs, and as the jokes became more important than the tunes he became a stand-up comedian. About this time he also became an impresario, buying the Temperance Billiard Hall in Harpurhey and converting it into the Embassy Club, which opened in December 1959 and continued to thrive for the rest of his life. A decidedly family business, it was set up with money lent to him by his father, and staffed by his parents and some of his siblings. Manning compèred the shows, and Jimmy Tarbuck, Matt Monro, and the Beatles were among the acts he introduced. Much later his only child, Bernard (*b.* 1960), took over the management of the club.

In 1971 the Granada TV producer Johnnie Hamp launched *The Comedians*, a showcase for club comics, and Manning was one of the first comedians he booked. The success of the series saw Manning's fees for live performances rise from £15 to £2000 or £3000 per night. He was one of the comedians from the show who appeared in a successful season at the London Palladium in 1972, leading to an appearance in the royal variety performance later that year. His television career continued throughout the 1970s, as the regular compère on *The Wheeltappers and Shunters Social Club*, and later in one-off specials. One of these was a documentary that followed his progress as he was taken to appear at the MGM Grand in Las Vegas, where he received a standing ovation.

Manning had a fearsome work ethic. Initially he would perform at the Embassy seven nights a week, as well as getting involved with the running of the club. After each show he would often go on to perform at one or more venues elsewhere, always travelling back home to Manchester afterwards, no matter how far away he was. As a result of this, he became a very wealthy man. His style was typical of the comedians who thrived in working men's and sporting clubs, in that it was heavily based on packaged jokes, with no pretentions to originality. He happily admitted, 'Sometimes I steal a gag because I can tell it much better than the other fellow who is putting it over' (Margolis, 166). His was an aggressive strain of stand-up comedy, with jokes told at the expense of women, homosexuals, and particular ethnic groups. He claimed to draw the line at jokes about the disabled, 'sick gags, cripples and all that carry on', as he put it, but it was not too difficult to find exceptions to this rule, as when he described the veteran comedian Tommy Trinder as being 'about as funny as woodworm in a cripple's crutch' (ibid., 65–6, 155). It was the racism of his act that made Manning increasingly notorious. Asians in his audience—whom he referred to as Pakis—and people of black descent would be picked out for ridicule, and he would cheerfully tell the rest of the audience that they would lynch his unfortunate victim after the show. When he appeared on the *Mrs Merton Show* on BBC television on 19 March 1998 he said of black Britons 'They think they're English because they're born here. That means if a dog's born in a stable it's a horse'. At an engagement at the Pennine Hotel in Derby in 1995 he comically abused two black waitresses, who successfully sued their employer for subjecting them to discrimination.

Manning's notoriety meant that videos of his act sold extremely well in the 1980s and 1990s, but the racism and his frequent use of expletives made television executives increasingly wary of booking him. When he did appear on television he was often shown in a less than flattering light. In 1995 a *World in Action* documentary caused a furore when it secretly recorded him telling racist jokes at a police function, and in 2003 Channel 4 took him to India to play to an audience of the type of people who were normally the butt of his jokes—with humiliating results for the comic. Perhaps most tellingly, on the *Mrs Merton Show* Caroline Aherne's comic character skilfully turned an audience of elderly Manchester folk—his core constituency—against him by challenging his racism. On the other hand Manning had a bewilderingly varied set of admirers, including the novelist Howard Jacobson, the celebrity chef Marco Pierre White, and Mark E. Smith, the lead singer of the Fall, and he was noted for his generosity, which did not discriminate between people of different races. He also ridiculed the far-right political parties, who reportedly loathed him.

Manning was always overweight, as his critics often pointed out, and towards the end of his life he increasingly suffered from ill health, having been diagnosed with angina and type 2 diabetes. He died of renal failure in North Manchester General Hospital on 18 June 2007, and was survived by his son. OLIVER DOUBLE

Sources J. Margolis, *Bernard Manning* (1996) · *The Times* (19 June 2007) · *Daily Telegraph* (19 June 2007) · *The Guardian* (19 June 2007) · *The Independent* (19 June 2007) · b. cert. · m. cert. · d. cert.

Archives FILM BFINA, *This is your life*, M. Aspel (presenter), Thames Television, 27 Nov 1991 · BFINA, documentary footage · BFINA, light entertainment footage · BFINA, performance footage | SOUND BL NSA, documentary recordings · BL NSA, performance recordings · BL NSA, light entertainment recordings

Likenesses H. Goodwin, photograph, 1970–79, Rex Features, London [*see illus.*] · H. Goodwin, photographs, 1970–99, Rex Features, London · photographs, 1972–95, Rex Features, London · photographs, 1972–98, Photoshot, London · photographs, 1972–2003, PA Photos, London · photographs, 1985–2000, Getty Images, London · T. R. Hart, C-type colour print, 1997, NPG · obituary photographs · photographs, Camera Press, London · photographs, repro. in www.bernardmanning.com

Manton, Sir Edwin Alfred Grenville (1909–2005), insurance underwriter, art collector, and philanthropist, was born on 22 January 1909 at Burrows Road, Earls Colne, Essex, the eldest of three children of John Horace Manton, bank clerk, later bank manager, and his wife, Emily Clara, *née* Denton. His father was descended from a miller in Grantham, Lincolnshire, two of whose brothers were the celebrated gunsmiths John and Joseph Manton. At the time of Manton's birth his parents lived in Stoke Newington, but a few months later the family moved to Westcliff-on-Sea, at the mouth of the Thames estuary, a location that gave him a lifelong affection for expanses of water and sky. Eight years later, while his father was temporarily serving in the army in Egypt, his uncle Edwin, alarmed by the number of German air raids on the Thames, moved the family including his younger sister, Phyllis, and brother, Paul, to the safety of Shaftesbury, Dorset. On his father's demobilization the family moved again to Hampstead, London, but Manton was by then enrolled at Shaftesbury grammar school and stayed on as a boarder. At school he excelled at languages, and being a tall and athletic figure played for the school in both the cricket and football teams.

In 1926 Manton won a scholarship to Cambridge University, but decided in favour of adventure and financial security and followed his uncle's introduction to B. W. Noble, the Paris agent of the Caledonian Insurance Company. Years later, in his late eighties, Manton would continue to astonish young executives with his command of idiomatic French. By 1933 he had been spotted by George Moskowski and the legendary Cornelius Vander Starr and had been invited to join the small American International Underwriters Corporation, then employing thirteen staff, as a casualty underwriter. In rapid succession he gained an American wife, Florence Vivian (Gretchen) Brewer (1911–2003), whom he married on 20 January 1936, a daughter, Diana Harborough (*b.* 1938), and a swift series of promotions within the company. He became a vice-president in 1938 and served as president (1942–69), chairman (1969–75), and finally as a senior adviser to the parent group, American International Group Inc. (AIG), until his death. During his most influential years the company grew to a force of 50,000 people and Manton became a leading figure in the American insurance business. He was devoted to the 'firm', as he called it, and to its employees, frequently declining invitations to society events so that he could attend company retirement parties or the annual company picnic. He continued to work well into his nineties and was still walking to the office every day until shortly before his death. His tall, spare frame made him an impressive figure, even at an advanced age, but his acute mind and deep curiosity coupled with a twinkling smile won the affection of generations of his colleagues.

Although Manton had moved to New York in 1933, he retained his British citizenship until his death and throughout his life he retained a strong affection for the country and in particular the county of his birth. In 1939 he had returned to London and volunteered for service but was rejected on medical grounds, having suffered from Stokes-Adams disease. He was unable to return for a further eight years, but during the war he developed an interest in the paintings of John Constable and in 1949 he acquired at auction in New York his first 'Constable', *View on the Stour*. Over the next twenty years he slowly assembled one of the best collections of early nineteenth-century British paintings and drawings in private hands, buying in New York and on regular visits to London, but facing stiff competition from the dominant buyer in the market at that time, Paul Mellon. Shortly after the 1976 bicentenary Constable exhibition in London, Manton was introduced to Leslie Parris, deputy keeper of the British collection of the Tate Gallery. During the 1970s Constable scholars had begun to distinguish between the works of John Constable, his son Lionel, and followers, and when Parris informed Manton that many of his works, including his first purchase, were not by the master himself Manton characteristically accepted that this had been a small price to pay for the pleasure and education that his collection had brought him, and he renamed his 'mistakes' as 'Constabiles'.

In 1987 his growing friendship with Parris encouraged Manton to make a generous contribution to an appeal for funds to acquire Constable's *The Opening of Waterloo Bridge* for the Tate Gallery. Shortly afterwards he made a gift of AIG shares that established the American Fund for the Tate Gallery with an endowment of $6.5 million in 1988. In creating a fund that would respond to the Tate's wish to strengthen its collection of American art, he was giving expression both to his affection for his birthplace and to his enthusiasm for the culture and values of his adopted country. By the time of his death the fund had grown to nearly $30 million and with his encouragement had broadened its remit to acquire major works by three generations of American artists and had laid the ground for a serious collection of Latin American art in London. Manton's further gifts to the Tate in 1992 and 1997 were the cornerstones for the centenary development which opened on Millbank in 2001 with a new entrance, named the Manton Entrance in his honour. Taken together, Manton's benefactions were by far the most generous gift in the history of the Tate. Manton (known by his friends in England as Jim and in America as Jimmy) was knighted for his services to art and to the Tate Gallery in the new year's honours of 1994.

Following Manton's death in New York on 1 October 2005 the majority of his considerable wealth, estimated by the press as £260 million in 2004, passed to the Manton Foundation, which he and Gretchen had established in 1991 in order to support institutions and causes in the church, medicine, and the arts that were the preoccupations of the Mantons in their lifetime. The Manton collection of early nineteenth-century British art was given by his family to the Sterling and Francine Clark Art Institute, Williamstown, Massachusetts, in June 2007.

NICHOLAS SEROTA

Sources *Daily Telegraph* (6 Oct 2005) · *The Independent* (8 Oct 2005) · *The Times* (14 Oct 2005) · *The Guardian* (17 Oct 2005) · *WW* (2005) · Burke, *Peerage* · Tate archives · personal knowledge (2009) · private information (2009) · b. cert.

Likenesses photographs, 1997, PA Photos, London · J. Wonnacott, oils, 2000, Tate collection · obituary photographs

Mark [*née* Brisland], **Janet Marjorie** [Jan] (**1943–2006**), children's writer, was born on 22 June 1943 at Brocket Hall Maternity Hospital, Lemsford, near Welwyn, Hertfordshire, the only daughter and elder child of Colin Denis Brisland, a research director in the film industry, and later an advertising executive, and his wife, Marjorie Léa, *née* Harrow. At the time of her birth her parents lived at 52 Sandringham Gardens, North Finchley. Although she spent an 'unsettled childhood in and around London' until the family moved to Ashford in Kent (*The Independent*, 18 Jan 2006), she was able to read by the time she was three, was writing by the age of four, and always understood that writing was for writing books. She was educated at Ashford grammar school and at Canterbury School of Art (1961–5), where she began as a sculptor and stone carver, was told that she was not 'a natural scholar' (*The Guardian*, 24 Jan 2006), and gained a national diploma in design. Evidence of her artistic ability, delicate and detailed sketches, can be seen in her Canadian travel book, *Great Frog and Mighty Mouse* (1992). She taught English and art at Southfields School, Gravesend (1965–71), and on 1 March 1969 married Neil John Morrison Mark, a computer operator six years her junior. They subsequently moved to Ingham, Norfolk, and had two children, Isobel and Alexander (Alex).

Jan Mark had been runner-up in a *Daily Mirror* literary competition when she was fifteen and later said that while never actually planning to become a writer she assumed she would write 'a book, or three' (Stephenson, 'Working from home', 23). In the event, she wrote more than eighty books of rare quality: novels of all lengths and for most ages (including one written under the pseudonym Leah Harrow, an approximation of her mother's maiden name), short stories, picture books, plays, television scripts, and non-fiction. For adults, she published poetry and a complex, witty novel, *Zeno was Here* (1987), winner of the Angel award.

Mark's first book, *Thunder and Lightnings* (1976), won the Kestrel–Guardian prize for a children's novel by a previously unpublished writer and, like the later *Handles* (1983), the Carnegie medal. More concerned with the interplay of character than plot, it was written 'to meet the demands of myself as an adult, not those of the child I once was' (*The Independent*, 18 Jan 2006). While this and her second novel, *Under the Autumn Garden* (1977), were imbued with her characteristic humour, she was never afraid to invoke a darker picture. *The Ennead* (1978), *Divide and Rule* (1979), and *Aquarius* (1982), winner of the Rank–Observer prize, were science fiction novels set in bleak future worlds that explored the pressures brought to bear on free-thinking individuals. This strain of controlled fantasy, the ability to create coherent alternative social structures, continued throughout her career, alongside her more realistic work, generating powerful books such as the millennium novel *The Eclipse of the Century* (1999), *Useful Idiots* (2004), *Riding Tycho* (2005), and *Voyager* (2006), the closest she came to a sequel. The wildly inventive *They Do Things Differently There* (1994) straddled both the fantastic and the real, with its satirical portrait of an English village under imagined Martian control.

Some of Mark's most incisive writing was in her short stories, a form in which she excelled. Volumes like *Feet and Other Stories* (1982), winner of the Angel award, *Enough is Too Much Already* (1988), a sequence of stories told in dialogue about a single group of schoolmates, and *Eyes Wide Open* (2003), exemplified her definition of the modern children's short story as 'a sharply focused examination of an illuminating moment' (*Oxford Book of Children's Stories*, 1993, introduction, xix).

A perceptive critic, for *The Guardian*, the *Times Educational Supplement*, and *Carousel* among others, Mark cared deeply about what she reviewed. Ruthless in her condemnation of any book she considered sub-standard, she delighted in discovering a writer she admired. Her brilliance as an inspiring and tireless teacher of writing was widely recognized. She was an Arts Council writing fellow at Oxford Polytechnic in 1982–4, a lecturer in creative writing at Reading University (1999–2000), and a frequent tutor for the Arvon Foundation, the Taliesin Trust at Tŷ Newydd, Llanystumdwy, Caernarvonshire, and the KATHO polytechnic in Torhout, Belgium, with whose students she enjoyed an affectionate and creative relationship.

When it came to the actual business of writing, Mark was very much a down-to-basics craftswoman: first drafts handwritten, second and subsequent ones hammered out on a typewriter. Her response to the suggestion that a computer would save time was swift and unequivocal: 'Writing is not about saving time' (Stephenson, 'Remembering Jan', 4). Dissembling was not in her nature. The black looks, directed from beneath a bush of hair, could be off-putting; but behind the occasional awkwardness of manner there was a shyness, a girlishness, and a capacity for gaiety. An insatiable curiosity prompted her accumulation of all sorts of knowledge: the superiority of Heathrow airport's trolleys over the supermarket model (*Heathrow Nights*, 2000); the precise weight of a particular edition of the Saturday *Guardian* (*Turbulence*, 2005); and electromagnetic waves, induction rings, and the books of the Bible (*The Electric Telegraph*, 2005).

Mark's marriage ended in divorce in 1989, though she and Neil Mark remained on good terms, after which she moved to a book-crammed house in Howard Street, east

Oxford, a geographical distinction she was keen to stress, contrasting 'the people's republic of East Oxford' with 'the kingdom of Oxford' over Magdalen Bridge (*The Guardian*, 24 Jan 2006). There she wrote, looked after her cats, and gardened. In 2005 she donated her manuscripts and working papers to Seven Stories, the Centre for Children's Books in Newcastle upon Tyne. She died suddenly, at home in Oxford, on 16 January 2006, of meningitis-related septicaemia, and was buried at Holy Trinity Church, Ingham, Norfolk. Her son Alex died later the same year.

CHRIS STEPHENSON

Sources C. Stephenson, 'Jan Mark: working from home', *Carousel*, 25 (autumn 2003), 22–3 · *The Independent* (18 Jan 2006) · *The Times* (23 Jan 2006) · *The Guardian* (24 Jan 2006) · C. Stephenson, 'Remembering Jan', *Carousel*, 33 (June 2006), 4 · N. Tucker, 'Jan Mark: the writer', *Carousel*, 33 (June 2006), 5 · P. Pullman, www.writersinoxford.org/janmark.htm, 10 Oct 2008 · *WW* (2006) · personal knowledge (2010) · private information (2010) · b. cert. · m. cert. · d. cert.

Archives Seven Stories (Centre for Children's Books), Newcastle upon Tyne, MSS and working papers | FILM BFINA, documentary footage

Likenesses S. Druce, photograph, repro. in J. Mark, ed., *The Oxford Book of Children's Stories* (1993) · obituary photographs · photographs, repro. in www.janmark.be

Wealth at death £394,145: probate, 31 July 2006, *CGPLA Eng. & Wales*

Markham, Edward Archibald [Archie] (**1939–2008**), poet and novelist, was born on 1 October 1939 in Harris, Montserrat, the youngest in a family of four children. Montserrat, a small volcanic island, was a British possession with a population of fewer than 6000 people. His educated and prosperous parents had returned there from the Dutch West Indies so that their child could be born British. He attended the only grammar school on the island, but in 1956, when his parents parted company, his mother brought him to England. Within a short time he was studying philosophy and English at St David's College, Lampeter. He continued his academic career at the University of East Anglia, researching seventeenth-century comedy, then became a lecturer at Kilburn Polytechnic. For the rest of his life he was never far from a campus or a theatre, with the notable exception of two years, from 1983 to 1985, when he was based as a media co-ordinator in Papua New Guinea. This period of his life was recalled years later in his memoir, *A Papua New Guinea Sojourn: More Pleasures of Exile* (1998).

Markham (who published as E. A. Markham when not using a pseudonym) began his writing career as a playwright, but he never had much success in this role. His best work on stage was not as a dramatist but as a director and administrator. In 1969 he formed the Caribbean Theatre Troupe and then for several months ran the Caribbean Theatre Workshop in the eastern Caribbean. A theatrical ability to assume disguises was evident in some of his poetry and throughout his fiction. He was a writer with the facility to adopt different voices and other personae. Indeed he sometimes wrote under various *noms de plume*, the best known being Paul St Vincent. This allowed the moderate and erudite E. A. Markham to transmogrify into an angry working-class product of another Caribbean island, St Vincent. Under this name he created the character of Lambchops, an alienated poet. Later he wrote as Sally Goodman, a feminist Welsh woman, and he created a representation of himself in his fiction, the intelligent but sometimes barely coherent Pewter Stapleton.

Edward Archibald Markham (1939–2008), by Kathy de Witt, 2003

In the early 1970s Markham started to appear as a poet in a variety of small magazines and pamphlets. His first collections were *Crossfire* (1972) and *Mad and Other Poems* (1973), followed by *Love Poems and Maze* (1978), *Masterclass* (1979), and several others, all published by independent small presses. They were not the kinds of publications to be widely reviewed or distributed, but Markham's was a slow burn reputation. By 1984 he had amassed enough work and begun to be sufficiently esteemed for Anvil Press, a respected publishing house funded by the Arts Council of Great Britain, to bring out *Human Rites*, a volume that brought together the best of his poems so far. Further collections followed, including *Living in Disguise* (1986), *Towards the End of a Century* (1989), *Misapprehensions* (1995), and *Fragments of Memory* (2003). His poetry was never predictable, though it was unified by a determination to avoid, except when in deliberate pastiche, any sort of Caribbean stereotyping. He wrote long and short poems, in standard English and with nuanced localism, personally and politically. In one of his best poems, 'Late Return', he was both 'the juvenile not yet exiled' and a 'professional migrant/eyeing the landscape'.

This diversity characterized Markham's subsequent career. He was an excellent editor—of *Artrage*, for example, a London-based literary journal for which he was responsible between 1985 and 1987. He also edited *The Penguin Book of Caribbean Short Stories* in 1996. Without abandoning poetry he expressed himself increasingly in prose, establishing himself in the short story form first, but then in 1999 producing a novel, *Marking Time*. In the 1970s and 1980s he held writing fellowships at the universities of

Humberside, Ulster, and Newcastle, as well as at Trinity College, Dublin. The academic side of his life blossomed when he was appointed to a lectureship in English literature at Sheffield Hallam University in 1991. There he not only ran courses for aspirant writers, becoming professor of creative writing in 1997, but undertook research and founded a journal, *Sheffield Thursday*, a droll allusion to the local football team. He directed the biennial Sheffield literature festival and was frequently heard on the radio or seen in print as an advocate of moderate radicalism in race relations.

Markham was one of the Caribbean's outstanding poets in the English language. As a dramatist, novelist, editor, and teacher he was a significant contributor to debates about the changing ethnic and social composition of his adopted country, Britain. Although he lived mainly in Europe from 1956 onwards, he never lost his island identity. When hurricane Hugo devastated his homeland in 1989 and again when Plymouth, the capital of Montserrat, was destroyed by an eruption in 1997, Markham responded by writing some of his best poetry and by feverish fund-raising. *The Hugo Poems* (1993) and *A Rough Climate* (2002) recorded these epic events, but in a way that linked them with larger concerns and with the writer's own development: 'hurricane and volcano and the carelessness/of migration have destroyed evidence of a life/before this life'.

In manner Markham was eager, gentle, and courteous, qualities perhaps derived from his old-fashioned British-style education and fairly privileged family background in Montserrat. He inspired great affection among his friends, who shared countless anecdotes about his minor mishaps and plans gone wrong. He was capable, however, of articulate and focused anger where he perceived social injustice.

Markham had a particular appreciation of France and owned a house there for many years. After retiring from Sheffield Hallam University in 2005 he went to live in Paris and it was there that on 23 March 2008 he died suddenly of a heart attack while in a pharmacy. His passing was marked by a packed memorial service in London a few weeks later. In 2009 Anvil brought out a well-received posthumous selection of his poems, *Looking Out, Looking In*, the editing of which he had nearly completed.

ALASTAIR NIVEN

Sources E. A. Markham, *A Papua New Guinea sojourn: more pleasures of exile* (1998) • F. Volans and T. O'Rourke, eds., *A Festschrift for E. A. Markham* (1999) • *The Independent* (12 April 2008) • *Daily Telegraph* (23 April 2008) • *The Guardian* (26 April 2008)

Archives SOUND BL NSA, documentary and performance recordings

Likenesses K. de Witt, photograph, 2003, Lebrecht Music and Arts Photo Library, London [*see illus.*] • obituary photographs

Marland, (Peter) Michael (1934–2008), headteacher and educationist, was born at 2 Nightingale Lane, Clapham, London, on 28 December 1934, the only child of James Albert (Bert) Marland (1904–1976), professional pianist, and his wife, Margaret Veronica, *née* Conley (1904–1972). At the time of his birth registration his parents lived at 55 Cavendish Road, Clapham. His father, from whom he inherited a great love of music, was the pianist for Henry Hall's dance band. Marland was educated at Christ's Hospital, Horsham, where he founded the Christ's Hospital Players, and devised an Elizabethan musical and dramatic entertainment that was performed in the ruined St Anne's Church, Soho, and around the country. He read English and history at Sidney Sussex College, Cambridge, from 1954 to 1957, where he was president of the University Amateur Dramatic Club and a founder member of the Musical Comedy Association. On his twenty-first birthday, 28 December 1955, he married the 21-year-old Eileen Lim at Chelsea Old Church. The daughter of John Lim, barrister, she was a bookseller at the time of their marriage, and lived in Cheyne Walk. They had five children, Edgell, Folly, Oliver, Tim, and Ben.

After graduating Marland taught English at schools in Germany, Canterbury, and Abbey Wood, Greenwich (where he was head of English), before being appointed in 1964 head of English and subsequently director of studies at the 2000-pupil Crown Woods School in Eltham. In the 1960s his love of music and particular admiration for the works of Benjamin Britten (Marland himself wrote a play entitled *Peter Grimes* in 1971) led to the purchase of the Green Farmhouse at Walsham-le-Willows in Suffolk. This served several purposes—as family and holiday home, writing retreat in a study increasingly awash with papers and proofs, and venue for staff seminars and conferences. In 1968 tragedy struck when Eileen died in a car crash. In 1971 Marland was appointed headteacher of Woodberry Down School in Hackney and on 4 March the same year married Rosemary Jean (Rose) Studdert-Kennedy (*b.* 1931/2), daughter of Edwin Arnold Hallett, electrical engineer, and former wife of William G. Studdert-Kennedy. This marriage was dissolved in 1977.

In 1980 Marland became the first headteacher of the three-site North Westminster Community School, a post he held until retirement in 1999. His vision and leadership as headteacher of North Westminster encompassed local, national, and international communities. Thus the Studio Theatre provided not only a venue for school and community performances but also attracted professional artists of international repute, for example Jessye Norman and Willard White. Eminent writers including Margaret Drabble, Keith Waterhouse, and Fay Weldon came to the school to judge short-story competitions and to talk about their work. Marland led from the front in matters of pedagogy and curriculum, for example by initiating and teaching a core course in the area of 'science, technology, and society'. He insisted that the curriculum should be designed by beginning with those things that sixteen-year-olds needed to know, understand, and experience, and then deciding how best to achieve these aims. Thus subject departments had to bid for contact time in order to teach various aspects of the curriculum. Marland's basic aim was to unlock and develop the potential of everyone at North Westminster, and all pupils and staff were treated as full members of the community. Staff development included regular discussion of educational issues both at school and at his Suffolk home. There, over some excellent mulled claret, he would share his own cogent views on each and every educational topic that might arise. On 11 February 1989 Marland, by this time a grandfather, married 37-year-old Linda Susan Marsh (*b.* 1951), a teacher at the school, and daughter of Derrie David Marsh, civil servant. Their son, Matthew, was born in the following year.

Marland's energy found numerous outlets and his *Who's Who* entry listed more than twenty organizations in which he played a leading role. Major committee service included the Bullock committee on the teaching of English (1972–5) and the Finniston committee on technology in education (1985–8). Public honours included a CBE in 1977, an honorary professorship at the University of Warwick (1980–92), honorary doctorates from the universities of Kingston (2000) and Surrey (2001), and honorary fellowship of the Institute of Education, University of London (2002). Books were an essential part of Marland's life and he served as chair of the Books in the Curriculum Research Project (1982–2008) and the National Textbook Reference Library Steering Committee (1984–92). He was general editor of the Heinemann Organization in Schools series, the Student Drama series, and Longman Imprint Books, which brought the works of such writers as Stan Barstow, Doris Lessing, Bill Naughton, and Alan Sillitoe into secondary school classrooms.

Marland was himself a prolific author. Pioneering publications in the field of English language and literature, frequently located within a multicultural and multilingual context, included *The Experience of Colour* (1969), *The Practice of English Teaching* (1970), and *Multilingual Britain* (1987). Similarly, *Head of Department* (1971), *Pastoral Care* (1974), and *School Management Skills* (1986) helped to define these fields. These books were widely used by teachers, but Marland's most influential work was *The Craft of the Classroom: a Survival Guide to Classroom Management in the Secondary School*. First published in 1975, this slim volume immediately became an essential guide for prospective and practising teachers alike. Its final paragraph provides the key to understanding both the personality of a man who enriched the lives of everyone he met, and the reasons for his success:

> The craft won't work without a spirit compounded of the salesman, the music-hall performer, the parent, the clown, the intellectual, the lover and the organizer, but the spirit won't win through on its own either. Method matters. The more 'organized' you are, the more sympathetic you can be. The better your classroom management, the more help you can be to your pupils.

Charming, erudite, witty, and immaculately clad with trademark bow tie, Michael Marland was a staunch champion of comprehensive secondary schools and one of the most inspirational, innovative, and influential educational figures of his day. Imbued with boundless energy, even when walking (his preferred mode of transport) between North Westminster's three sites, he would talk endlessly into his trusty dictaphone, producing masses of material for his secretaries to type. His ever-inquiring mind devoured educational research and tried to implement its findings in schools. He believed passionately that all children, whatever their backgrounds, should have access to the arts. He was a fine example of Matthew Arnold's men of culture—'true apostles of equality' imbued with 'a passion for diffusing, for making prevail, for carrying from one end of society to the other, the best knowledge, the best ideas of their times'. His principles, that schools are about people not systems, that children come first, and that the school curriculum is not essentially concerned with discrete subjects but with making connections across all aspects of knowledge and across cultures, flourished most readily in the 1970s and 1980s when he was a doyen among London headteachers. The demise of the inner London education authority, the advent of a new Westminster education authority, the national curriculum, national testing, league tables, and stringent accountability were less conducive to his style of leadership and frequently inimical to his concept of education.

Marland died of cancer on 3 July 2008 at St John's Hospice, St John's Wood, London. A private funeral was held on 14 July at St Mary's Church, Walsham-le-Willows. Marland's international influence was evident as candles were simultaneously lit in London, Greece, India, New Zealand, and Spain, while some 600 people attended a memorial service and celebration of his life at the Union Chapel, Islington, on 15 September 2008. He was survived by his wife, Linda, and five of his children, his son Edgell having died in a car crash in 1990. RICHARD ALDRICH

Sources R. Aldrich, *Lessons from history of education* (2006), 118–20 · *The Guardian* (4 July 2008) · *The Independent* (7 July 2008) · *The Times* (8 July 2008) · *Camden New Journal* (11 July 2008) · *Journal of Educational Administration and History*, 41/1 (2009), 7–10 · *WW* (2008) · www.facebook.com/group.php?gid=20693707790, 10 May 2011 · personal statement, Nov 2005, U. Lond., Institute of Education · personal knowledge (2012) · private information (2012) · b. cert. · m. cert. · d. cert.

Archives Institute of Education, U. Lond. [deposited May 2011]

Likenesses obituary photographs

Wealth at death £934,845: probate, 2 Jan 2009, *CGPLA Eng. & Wales*

Marre [*née* Gilling], **(Romola) Mary, Lady Marre (1920–2005)**, voluntary worker and public servant, was born on 25 April 1920 at 2 High Street, Chelmsford, Essex, the eldest child in the family of two sons and two daughters of Aubrey John Gilling, bank manager, and his wife, Romola Marjorie, *née* Angier, the daughter of a sailmaker in Brightlingsea, Essex. She was educated at Chelmsford County High School for Girls, and went on to Bedford College, University of London, graduating with a second-class degree in philosophy in 1941. During the war London University was evacuated to Cambridge, where along with many other students she was attracted to communism, and may have joined the Communist Party. After leaving university she worked as a civil servant in the Ministry of Health for a year before joining the Auxiliary Territorial Service in 1942. On 24 December 1943 she married Alan Samuel *Marre (1914–1990), son of Joseph Moshinsky, a Russian Jewish immigrant who ran a tobacconist's shop in the East End of London. Marre was a civil servant: he was knighted in 1970 and was appointed parliamentary ombudsman in 1971. They had one son and one daughter.

While her children were young Mary Marre did voluntary work locally in north London, and in 1962 she became the organizer of the West Hampstead Citizens' Advice Bureau. In 1965 she was appointed deputy general secretary of Camden Council of Social Service, and through her work there became known to those working in the voluntary sector as an excellent committee chairman. From 1974 to 1984 she served as chairman of the London Council of Social Service (renamed in 1978 the London Voluntary Service Council), which provided advice for local councils of social service, which co-ordinated links between voluntary organizations and the local authorities. She was founder president of Barnet Voluntary Service Council from 1979. Among the many other voluntary organizations and committees she was involved with were the Prince of Wales's Advisory Group on Disability, of which she was a member from 1982 to 1984. She was also deputy chairman of the Royal Jubilee Trusts from 1981 to 1988. As a trustee from 1975 and vice-chairman from 1989 to 1993 of the City Parochial Foundation, which funded charities which were tackling poverty in London, she was particularly closely involved with the work of the Trust for London. Set up by the government in 1986, after the abolition of the Greater London council, with the City Parochial Foundation as trustee, the Trust for London concentrated on making small grants to locally based community groups, especially to black and ethnic minority organizations, refugee committees, and women's groups, at a time when there were very few other sources of money for such groups: these included the Haringey Muslim Women's Council, the Centre for Armenian Information and Advice, the Tamil Action Committee, and the Kurdish Charitable Association. She was instrumental in the awarding of grants to supplementary schools, run by minority ethnic groups outside school hours to help children keep up with their school work, and mother-tongue schools, which helped children to remain fluent in their original languages. She was appointed CBE in 1979.

When the Law Society and the Bar Council set up the Committee on the Future of the Legal Profession in 1986 they appointed Lady Marre as chairman. As a lay person, but a former member of the Lord Chancellor's Advisory Committee on Legal Aid (1975–80), and with her reputation as an efficient chairman, she was a good choice to head the committee of six barristers, six solicitors, and six independent members, whose object was to look at the changes necessary to improve the legal profession and its ability to meet the needs of the public. The Marre committee presented its report, *A Time for Change*, two years later, with a note of dissent attached from five of the barristers and one independent member. Its main conclusion was that it was not in the public interest that the crown courts should continue to be the exclusive preserve of the bar, and it recommended that solicitors should be able to plead in the crown courts, and should be eligible for appointment as High Court judges: it was over these encroachments on the traditional preserve of the bar that the committee could not agree. Because the committee had failed to find a solution acceptable to both sides, and because of the acrimonious public debate that followed publication of the report, the lord chancellor, Lord Mackay, introduced three green papers on the future of the legal profession. These led to the introduction of the Courts and Legal Services Act, which became law in 1990 and implemented many of the proposals of the Marre committee.

After the death of her husband in 1990 Mary Marre found great happiness in her relationship with Alan Lipfriend (1916–1996), a retired crown court judge, with whom she lived in Edmunds Walk, East Finchley, from 1991 until his death. Lipfriend was a practising Jew, a member of the New London Synagogue in St John's Wood. Mary Marre had converted to the Jewish faith before her marriage, but neither she nor her husband was a practising Jew: she now reconverted, and became very interested in and committed to Judaism, and involved in Jewish charities. This continued after Lipfriend's death.

A lively, intelligent woman, Mary Marre was rooted in the voluntary sector, and saw that it was no use giving money for projects unless there were good people there to run them. She had a deep understanding of London and its needs. Astute and shrewd, with a terrier-like mind, she was greatly respected by her colleagues and staff, who listened to and valued her advice, and she in turn was a conduit for other people's ideas. Alongside her serious concern for disadvantaged people she had a sense of humour and a light touch, and with a very wide network of friends and contacts she was extremely effective in getting things done. Having moved to Kingsbarns, near St Andrews, Fife, she died of heart disease on 6 March 2005 in St Andrews Care Home, 1 James Foulis Court, St Andrews. She was survived by her son and daughter.

ANNE PIMLOTT BAKER

Sources 'Thursday people: 12 fast talkers facing a listener—Lady Marre', *The Guardian* (14 July 1988) • 'The Marre report', *Sunday Times* (17 July 1988) • F. Cownie, 'The reform of the legal profession or the end of civilisation as we know it', *The changing law*, ed. F. Patfield and R. White (1990) [ch. 12] • 'The bar's defining decade', *The Lawyer* (10 June 1997) • *The Times* (21 March 2005); (23 March 2005) • *Jewish Chronicle* (13 May 2005) • 'Trusting in the community: a report on the first ten years of the Trust for London', www.trustforlondon.org.uk, 15 July 2008 • *WW* (2005) • private information (2009) • b. cert. • m. cert. • d. cert.

Likenesses photograph, repro. in Association of Lipspeakers website, www.lipspeaking.co.uk/feature_mary_marre

Wealth at death £395,831.97: confirmation, 19 July 2005, *CCI*

Marshall, Sir Arthur Gregory George (1903–2007), aviator, pilot instructor, and industrialist, was born at Gregory Villa, De Freville Avenue, Chesterton, Cambridge, on 4 December 1903, the eldest of the eight children of David Gregory Marshall (1873–1942), college servant, later steward of the Pitt Club, Cambridge, and independent businessman, and his wife, Maude Edmunds, *née* Wing (1879–1931). He was born thirteen days before the Wright brothers' first powered flights. In 1909 his father launched the Brunswick Motor Car Company, initially with two

Sir Arthur Gregory George Marshall (1903–2007), by unknown photographer [far right]

chauffeur-driven cars. In 1914 he renamed the business Marshall's Garage. During the First World War the garage undertook war work and David Marshall ran canteens for the army, Woolwich arsenal, and the Ministry of Munitions; he was appointed MBE for his services.

Arthur Marshall was educated at the Perse School, Cambridge, Tonbridge School, and Jesus College, Cambridge, where he obtained a first-class degree in engineering. Cambridge became the centre of his life, particularly in his efforts to diversify the economy of the city away from the university-centred structure that his father had known. A Cambridge blue for running, he was selected as a reserve member of the British team (which included Harold Abrahams and Eric Liddell) for the 1924 Olympic games.

In 1926 Marshall joined his father's garage business. However, he was already an enthusiast for aviation: in 1911 he and his father watched the *Daily Mail* round Britain air race and in 1912 he carried petrol and oil to the army airship Beta II, which had made a precautionary landing at Cambridge near his father's garage in Jesus Lane (Beta II's engine was repaired in the Marshall workshop). Then came a visit to William Rhodes-Moorhouse's aircraft workshop and hangar at Huntingdon (Rhodes-Moorhouse, later the first airman to be awarded the Victoria Cross, had made several landings on Cambridge Commons near the Marshall garage). After the First World War the family's home on Newmarket Road was renamed Aviation Hall following his father's purchase of a war-surplus Handley Page bomber for £5 and a Bessoneau canvas hangar, in which it was stored in a paddock behind the house. His first flight came in July 1919 as a joy-ride with his father in a Fairey seaplane at Brighton (there were no seat-belts so Marshall stood for part of the flight); his first commercial flight was in August 1922 when he flew to Paris in a Handley Page airliner (wicker seats for the passengers and an open cockpit for the pilots).

In 1928 Marshall obtained his B (private) pilot licence; the aviation journal *Flight* reported that his first solo was a 'splendid show' and that the landing was 'a treat to watch' (*Flight*, 12 July 1928). In 1929 father and son established the first civilian aerodrome within the city boundaries of Cambridge in a field behind the family home. There they founded the Marshall Flying School with a de Havilland Gipsy Moth biplane and Arthur Marshall as chief instructor. The first three Marshall pupils were Norman de Bruyne (later inventor of the Redux bonding process), Bill Humble (later chief test pilot at Hawker Aircraft), and H. G. Barrington (later a test pilot at de Havilland). Later in the 1930s Peter Masefield was a Marshall pupil. At this time separate Marshall companies were incorporated to run the garage and flying school activities. Marshall qualified for his commercial pilot's licence in March 1930; he was admitted an upper freeman of the Guild of Air Pilots and Air Navigators in 1931 and liveryman in 1958 (at his death he was by far the longest serving member of the guild; in September 2003 he delivered the guild's Sir Frederick Tymms lecture). On 22 April 1931 he married Rosemary Wynford Dimsdale (1908–1988), daughter of Marcus Southwell Dimsdale, fellow of King's College, Cambridge, and granddaughter of the sixth Baron Dimsdale. She was his constant companion and staunchest supporter for the next fifty-seven adventurous and exciting years, as he later described them. They had three children, Michael, David, and Judy.

In 1936 the family bought land that subsequently formed the core of the Marshall aerodrome, which became Cambridge airport. Marshall was always immensely proud that the aerodrome provided the region with a fully licensed airport at no cost to central or local government. The fully engineered runway, the hangars, and other facilities were also company-funded. In February 1938 the Air Ministry established No. 22 Elementary and Reserve Flying School at Cambridge under the management of Marshall's Flying School, to train Royal Air Force aircrew; the company rapidly established the school's reputation as the country's most productive. In all over 20,000 RAF pilots, instructors, and navigators were trained by Marshall; Johnnie Johnson and Leonard Cheshire were among those who learned to fly with him. Marshall developed a revolutionary programme for training *ab initio* candidates as pilots and flying instructors; despite initial resistance Marshall persuaded the RAF in 1941 to accept his training method, which subsequently became the basis of RAF training. In 1939 Marshall and his father founded the Cambridge squadron of the Air Defence Cadet Corps, later named 104 (City of Cambridge) squadron, Air Training Corps; he served as chairman of the squadron's civilian committee from 1939 until 1976 despite the pressures of his wartime and post-war business duties, and subsequently wrote its history.

During the Second World War Marshall was a test pilot for his company's work, which included the repair or modification of more than 5000 military aircraft. The heaviest type in his log-book was the B17 Flying Fortress, and he was always proud of his permit to fly the Typhoon fighter–bomber. During the battle of Britain, by deft management of the production schedules, he ensured that there were always available two overhauled and armed Gladiator fighters so that he, and his chief test pilot, might fly in defence of the airfield. The pair 'scrambled' frequently but were never called upon to engage the enemy; for lack of radio their signal to return to base was seeing the Cambridge buses running again after the all-clear siren. Marshall's management style imbued his workforce with the same 'can-do' spirit. He was appointed chairman of the Marshall companies after the death of his father in 1942.

In the immediate post-war years the garage business was expanded beyond its original base in Cambridge into a regional business with twenty depots throughout the south-east of England, selling cars and commercial vehicles. Aircraft skills were held together by branching out into building vehicle bodies (including those for buses) as a further diversification of Cambridge's economy and by the maintenance of commercial aircraft; then came the demands of maintaining RAF aircraft for the Berlin airlift in 1948–9. In the cold-war era Marshall supported the RAF's nuclear strike force with work on the Valiant and Canberra bombers and on the Blue Steel missile. Additionally Venom jet fighters were assembled at Cambridge and ejector seats were fitted to Vampire jet training aircraft. The company also became a centre of excellence for the repair and modification of aircraft for major airlines.

The Marshall company was involved in practically every major post-war British aircraft project including the Concorde supersonic airliner, for which the company designed and built the droop nose and visor (Marshall secured that contract himself within hours of an invitation to join the project; he also secured for his company design authority for the task, the sole delegation of authority for structural design granted to a United Kingdom contractor for Concorde). He then demonstrated a stroke of genius when the Ministry of Defence decided in 1965 to acquire the Lockheed Hercules for the RAF. Recognizing that the Hercules fleet would require technical support, he was successful in persuading the ministry and Lockheed that the Marshall company was ideally qualified. The first Hercules landed at Cambridge in December 1966, marking the start of a continuing Hercules business with the RAF and overseas services. During the Falklands conflict in 1982 he supervised the design and installation of a flight refuelling capability into batches of RAF Hercules; the first aircraft was delivered within three weeks of a telephoned instruction to proceed. The modified type proved vital to the liberation of the islands. After the conflict the Ministry of Defence accepted Marshall's proposal to modify a batch of TriStar airliners into a long-range trooping and air refuelling role for the RAF.

The first contribution to space travel was made in the 1950s when, under the sponsorship of the National Research Development Corporation, Francis Thomas (Tom) Bacon developed his fuel cell at the Marshall works with the assistance of Marshall staff. Bacon recalled, 'I wanted a practical works atmosphere in which we could get things done … Arthur Marshall is a man who takes instant decisions and, after we had talked about it for a little while, he said "Yes—we'll do it." I am very glad he did' (P. Fairley, *Project X*, 1970, 120). Marshall was always proud that electrical power and drinking water generated by Bacon cells made possible the United States' Apollo programme of lunar exploration. President Nixon acknowledged that, without the cells, 'we wouldn't have gotten to the Moon' (K. R. Williams, 'Francis Thomas Bacon', *Memoirs FRS*, 39, 1994, 13). Space work continued in the 1980s with the design and build of a space sled to investigate space motion sickness on behalf of the European Space Agency. The sled was flown in the space shuttle *Challenger* for 121 orbits over seven days in 1985.

Marshall remained an active pilot of the corporate executive jet until 1988, having upgraded his licence ten years earlier. He retired as chairman of the Marshall Group at the end of 1989, when he was succeeded by his son Michael, who had joined the family business in 1955. Retirement was, however, a concept foreign to Marshall. Elected honorary life president by the shareholders, he moved his office to a company-owned farmhouse on the edge of the aerodrome where, seated at his father's old desk, he continued to take a keen interest in the company's well-being and in the fortunes of his wide circle of friends and acquaintances. He was able to devote more time to his charitable activities; he was an active fundraiser for the Royal Air Force Benevolent Fund and, for many years, he was president of the Cambridge 'chariots of fire' charity run. He was a governor of Cranfield University between 1979 and 1997.

Marshall was knighted in 1974; it is typical of the man that he chose for his motto the words *Felix qui laborat* ('Happy is he who works'), for he was known to be in his office even on Christmas day. He had been made an OBE in 1948 and a deputy lieutenant of Cambridgeshire in 1968, and served as high sheriff of Cambridgeshire and the Isle of Ely in 1969–70. He was a member of the Air Cadet Council (1951–9 and 1965–76); chairman of the Aerodrome Owners Association (1964–5); and a member of the Advisory Council on Technology (1967–70). Among many other honours he was made an honorary member of the Royal Air Force Club (1969); an honorary old Cranwellian (1978); a companion of the Royal Aeronautical Society (1980) and of the Air League (1997), which gave him its founders' medal in 2003; an honorary fellow of Jesus College, Cambridge (1990) and of the Royal Aeronautical Society (2001); and an honorary freeman of the City of Cambridge (2004). He received honorary doctorates from Cranfield and Cambridge universities (in 1992 and 1996). In 1990 he was awarded the order of Istiqlal, first class, by King Hussein of Jordan (the country's highest award for a non-Jordanian other than a head of state).

A quiet, unassuming man (but a shrewd businessman whose watchwords were 'price, delivery, quality'), Marshall took his flying club of the 1920s into supersonics and the space age, served his country well in both war and peace, and created an internationally recognized aerospace engineering company, which at the time of his death was one of the largest family-owned companies in the country. He was not active politically but he took pride in a compliment paid him by Prime Minister Margaret Thatcher during a factory visit: 'It's men like you who should be running this country, not us politicians' (*The Times*, 5 April 2010). Marshall bore with stoicism the frailties of advancing years but he always retained an inquiring mind and unquenchable cheerfulness: he closed his autobiography, *The Marshall Story: a Century of Wheels and Wings* (1994), with the words that he had been 'a lucky fellow' (p. 360). He died at his home, Horseheath Lodge, Linton, Cambridgeshire, on 16 March 2007, of cerebrovascular disease. He was buried at Horseheath parish church beside his wife, Rosemary; following the committal Tiger Moth training aircraft of the Cambridge Flying Group flew past in salute. A service of thanksgiving for his life was held in 17 hangar, Cambridge airport, his last, and largest, building project at Cambridge. He was survived by his three children. He was commemorated by the Sir Arthur Marshall trophy of the Air Training Corps, established to recognize achievement by individual squadrons. Cambridge University established the Sir Arthur Marshall Institute for Aeronautics in 2001, and in 2009 established the Sir Arthur Marshall chair in sustainable urban design. The Royal Aeronautical Society established a Marshall lecture, and in 2008 unveiled an aeronautical heritage plaque in his honour at Cambridge airport. There are Sir Arthur Marshall memorial rooms at the engineering department and the athletics pavilion at Cambridge University, at Jesus College, Cambridge, and at the Imperial War Museum, Duxford. His running medals are on loan to the Hawks Club, Cambridge. GORDON BRUCE

Sources A. Marshall, *The Marshall story: a century of wheels and wings* (1994) • A. Marshall, *No. 104 (City of Cambridge) Squadron air training corps: the first fifty-six years, 1939–1994* (1994?) • *Daily Telegraph* (17 March 2007) • *The Times* (21 March 2007) • *The Independent* (24 March 2007) • *The Guardian* (26 March 2007) • *Teamwork* [Marshall Group house magazine] (spring 2007), 8 • Marshall Group archives • priv. coll., Marshall papers • Burke, *Peerage* • *WW* (2007) • personal knowledge (2011) • private information (2011) • b. cert. • m. cert. • d. cert.

Archives priv. coll. | CAC Cam., Francis Bacon MSS • Marshall Group archives

Likenesses M. Noakes, portrait, Marshall Group • M. Richards, bust, Marshall Group • obituary photographs • photograph, Marshall Group [*see illus.*] • photographs, Marshall Group • stained glass window, All Saints' Church, Horseheath, Cambridge

Wealth at death £4,830,699: probate, 2 Aug 2007, *CGPLA Eng. & Wales*

Marshall [*née* Edwards], **Sybil Mary** (**1913–2005**), educationist and author, was born on 26 November 1913 at Lotting Fen, Ramsey, Huntingdonshire, the daughter of William Henry Edwards, farmer, and his wife, Kate Mary, *née* Papworth. She grew up in the black fens of Huntingdonshire in Lotting Fen, a village three feet below sea level, without electricity or running water, in one of the poorest parts of the country. She was educated at Ramsey Heights elementary school (1919–23) and Ramsey grammar school (1924–32). She left at the height of the agricultural depression to become an unqualified, uncertificated teacher, first at South Woodham Ferrers, Essex (1933–6), then in Huntingdon (1936–9). On 27 August 1939 she married Francis Charles (Frank) Marshall, a 26-year-old local farmer then serving in the RAF. A son (*b.* 1940) died in childbirth, but the following year she gave birth to a daughter, Prue. In 1942 she became headteacher of Kingston county primary school, Cambridgeshire, a one-room, single-teacher school containing some twenty-six pupils aged between four and eleven. In 1948–9 she attended Exhall Grange Emergency Training College, Coventry, before returning to Kingston county primary school, now as a qualified teacher. There she developed what she called her 'symphonic method', whereby subjects were integrated rather than being taught separately—so that lessons, for instance, on the Romans might combine elements of literature, art, music, and home economics, as well as history. Meanwhile Frank Marshall found it difficult to keep up with such a brilliant wife, and eventually left her for another woman. They divorced in 1948.

When Kingston county primary school was closed by the government in 1960 Sybil Marshall won a bursary to New Hall, Cambridge, to read English as a mature student. (She had already, while still a teacher, attended a Cambridge University extramural class in English at Bassingbourn Village College.) She completed her degree in two years, graduating in 1962. She was immediately appointed a lecturer in primary education at Sheffield University under Boris Ford, who had heard her speak on the arts in education at a residential course for primary school teachers. While at Sheffield she published *An Experiment in Education* (1963), a highly influential account of her teaching methods at Kingston, which became known as 'the teacher's bible', and which clearly influenced the 'child-centred' approach of the Plowden report, 'Children and their primary schools', of 1967. Also while at Sheffield, in 1963 she met a dapper little man, Ewart Oakeshott (1916–2002), an accomplished commercial artist and an international authority on arms and armour, with whom she formed a close and loving relationship. They married in 1995 after the death of his first wife.

In 1967 Sybil Marshall had followed Boris Ford to the University of Sussex, where she was reader in primary education until her retirement in 1976. Among her publications on education during this period was *Adventure in Creative Education* (1968), a hilarious account of headteachers learning the Sybil Marshall method in a disused Rotherham warehouse. She was also educational adviser to the successful Granada Television series for children *Picture Box*, from 1965 to 1978. A short, round, jolly woman with a strong fenland accent, she was much loved by those who trained under her, or who worked with her.

In 1967 Sybil Marshall had published an engaging account of her fenland upbringing, and of local history and folklore, *Fenland Chronicle*. In retirement this was followed by *Everyman's Book of English Folk Tales* (1981), for which she won the Angel prize for literature in 1982, and *Once upon a Village* (1979), *The Silver New Nothing* (1987), and *A Pride of Tigers* (1992), containing further stories of fenland life. She published her first novel, *A Nest of Magpies*, in 1993. This and its sequels, *Sharp through the Hawthorn* (1994), *Strip the Willow* (1996), *A Late Lark Singing* (1997), and *Ring the Bell Backwards* (1999), was thinly disguised autobiography, the characters Fran and William being based on Sybil and Ewart Oakeshott (the latter providing the illustrations). She also published a collection of short stories, *The Chequer Board* (1995). She died of cerebrovascular disease on 29 August 2005 at her home, 40 St Mary's Street, Ely, and was survived by her daughter, Prue Atmore, a headmistress. DAVID HOLBROOK

Sources S. Marshall, *Fenland chronicle* (1967) • S. Marshall, *Once upon a village* (1979) • S. Marshall, *The silver new nothing* (1987) • S. Marshall, *A pride of tigers* (1992) • *The Guardian* (31 Aug 2005) • *The Independent* (5 Sept 2005) • *The Times* (28 Sept 2005); (3 Oct 2005); (4 Oct 2005) • *Daily Telegraph* (3 Oct 2005) • curriculum vitae, www.oakeshott.org//SMBio.html, 26 Feb 2008 • personal knowledge (2009) • private information (2009) • b. cert. • m. cert. [1939] • d. cert.
Archives FILM BFINA, current affairs footage; performance footage | SOUND BL NSA, performance recordings
Likenesses obituary photographs
Wealth at death £296,971: probate, 18 Jan 2006, *CGPLA Eng. & Wales*

Marwick, Arthur John Brereton (1936–2006), historian, was born on 29 February 1936 at the Elsie Inglis Maternity Hospital, Edinburgh, the younger son of William Hutton Marwick (1894–1982), economic historian, and his wife, Maeve Cluna, *née* Brereton. His parents, who lived at 5 Northfield Crescent, Edinburgh, were Quakers, caring and earnest intellectuals, but also austere. Marwick was educated at George Heriot's School, Edinburgh, and at Edinburgh University, where he won the gold medal for being the outstanding history student of his year. He moved to Balliol College, Oxford, where he undertook research on the Independent Labour Party. His thesis was awarded a BLitt instead of a doctorate but, undeterred, in 1959 he moved back to Scotland to take up an assistant lectureship at Aberdeen. After a year he returned to the history department at Edinburgh, where he taught for most of the 1960s, and where he built a reputation as a prolific author and an inspirational tutor. In 1969 he was appointed the first professor of history to the newly established Open University. He remained there until his retirement in 2001, serving as dean and director of studies of the arts faculty from 1978 to 1984. He also spent sabbatical leave as a visiting scholar at various American and European universities.

Marwick's move to the Open University in 1969 was a bold one. The new institution was designed to offer a university education to those who had missed the opportunity on leaving school. It was expected that many students would be in full-time jobs and that all would study in their own time through correspondence texts and educational broadcasts transmitted by the BBC. Marwick seized the opportunity to develop ideas that he had formulated at Edinburgh about the skills of the historian and the analysis of primary source material. In this he pre-empted ideas that were to become central to the teaching of history in both schools and universities later in the century, and he did so with much more humanity than many of those that followed. He also saw the Open University's link with the BBC as providing the opportunity for demonstrating the value of film as a historical source.

For many years Marwick's research interests focused on the relationship between war and social change. *The Deluge: British Society and the First World War* (1965) argued that war fostered domestic, as much as international change; by implication it was critical of the traditional perspective that saw war as an interruption to social and political development and a topic best reserved for military historians. It became a seminal text, going through many editions, and was still in print at the time of his death. Other work in this area was less successful, notably *War and Social Change in the Twentieth Century* (1974), which compared the impact of the two world wars on Britain, France, Germany, Russia, and the United States: this book made much of a conceptual model for the study of war and society which seemed rooted in the unique British experience. There were to be more books on British history, the most successful of which was *British Society since 1945* (1982); this also went through several editions. But, curiously for a solid empiricist, Marwick was also keen to develop international comparisons about perceptions and understandings. *Class in the Twentieth Century* (1986), *Beauty in History: Society, Politics and Personal Appearance since c.1500* (1988), and *It: a History of Human Beauty* (2004) were not well received. More successful was *The Sixties: Cultural Revolution in Britain, France, Italy and the United States* (1998), a 900 page discussion of what he saw as the revolution in attitudes, living standards, and relationships during the period from roughly 1958 to 1974.

Running throughout Marwick's teaching and publications was his fervent belief that history was a social necessity, enabling individuals and societies better to appreciate and understand their present. This went together with his insistence that historians eschew meta-narratives and take particular care over their analysis of source material and the presentation of their findings. These ideas underpinned *The Nature of History* (1970), the one book that he significantly rewrote for successive editions, becoming increasingly strident in his condemnation of what he understood as post-modernism. He took a similar combative line when he became co-editor of the *Journal of Contemporary History* in 1995, first with an article (1995) and then with a manifesto (1997). At the same time he changed the direction of editorial policy to include many more articles dealing with the period since 1945.

Marwick reflected his parents' earnestness and commitment to hard work; he also rebelled against them by indulging in lively hedonism when the day's work was over. He was an enthusiastic football and tennis player well into his fifties. He wore long hair and a beard and had a flamboyant style of dress. He enjoyed fine wine, and could be an embarrassment to friends and colleagues when in his cups. He never married, but had a daughter, Louise, on whom he doted, and was extremely proud when he became a grandfather. From the 1960s he lived in Fitzjohn's Avenue, Hampstead. In 2006, following a stroke, he was forced to move to Devon, to be close to his daughter. He died of a further stroke in the Royal Devon and Exeter Hospital, Exeter, on 27 September 2006. His daughter survived him. CLIVE EMSLEY

Sources *Daily Telegraph* (4 Oct 2006) • *The Independent* (4 Oct 2006) • *The Guardian* (7 Oct 2006) • *The Times* (10 Oct 2006) • C. Emsley, *Journal of Contemporary History*, 42/2 (2007), 181–4 • *WW* (2006) • personal knowledge (2010) • private information (2010) • b. cert. • d. cert.
Archives FILM BFINA, documentary footage • Open University, course materials archive | SOUND Open University, course materials archive
Likenesses obituary photographs
Wealth at death £701,525: probate, 29 May 2008, *CGPLA Eng. & Wales*

Masefield, Sir Peter Gordon (1914–2006), aeronautical engineer, journalist, and industrialist, was born at Tolima, Albert Road, Trentham, Staffordshire, on 19 March 1914, the son of William Gordon Masefield (1885–1974), a doctor specializing in mental health, and his wife, Marian Ada (1885–1976), daughter of Edmund Lloyd-Owen of New York. He was a cousin of John Masefield, the poet laureate from 1930 to 1967. Educated at Brentwood School, Essex (1925–6), Westminster School (1926–9), and Chillon College, Montreux, Switzerland (1929–32), he gained his engineering degree at Jesus College, Cambridge, in 1935. On 9 May 1936 he married Patricia Doreen Rooney (1912–2006), commercial artist, and daughter of Percy Harold Rooney, company director. They had a daughter, Victoria, and three sons, Charles, Richard, and Oliver.

After graduating Masefield had joined the design office of Fairey Aviation at Hayes, Middlesex, as an aeronautical engineer, supplementing his income by writing articles for *The Aeroplane* magazine, before being invited by the founder editor, the formidable C. G. Grey, to join the staff in 1937 as assistant technical editor. Initially learning to fly at Marshalls of Cambridge, and gaining his private pilot's licence in 1939, he was accredited as the journal's war correspondent and spent time with the Royal Air Force in France until early 1940. Later that year he also contributed authoritative articles on the air war to the *Sunday Times* and the London *Evening Standard*. In December 1940 he persuaded Temple Press, the magazine's publishers, to launch, and to allow him to edit, a new magazine, the *Aeroplane Spotter*, which was published from January 1941 until July 1948, its fortnightly circulation soaring to 200,000 copies. In 1942 he was also invited to chair a committee to produce *Aircraft Recognition: the Inter-Services Journal* for the Ministry of Aircraft Production.

As a war correspondent and RAF Bomber Command liaison officer, in August 1942 Masefield visited the United States Army Air Force (USAAF) base at Bovingdon, Hertfordshire, to interview Boeing B-17 bomber crews after the base's first European mission, against Rouen in northern France. There he also sought permission from the USAAF commander-in-chief, General 'Hap' Arnold, whom he had escorted on a British industry tour in 1938, to fly on operational missions with the 'Mighty 8th'. After a two-week combat course to qualify for this assignment, he flew his first mission on 14 July 1943 to bomb the German-occupied Paris Le Bourget airport and was lucky to escape with his life when his aircraft was hit. At Arnold's invitation, two months later he also undertook a comprehensive seven-week, top-level tour of the American aircraft industry and USAAF facilities, which also included broadcasts to American audiences.

Sir Peter Gordon Masefield (1914–2006), by J. Russell & Sons

Masefield's dispatches to the *Sunday Times* were soon spotted by Lord Beaverbrook, the ebullient minister of aircraft production and lord privy seal, who recalled him to become his personal adviser on civil aviation and secretary of the war cabinet committee considering post-war civil air transport. His duties included liaising with the Brabazon committee, originally formed in 1942 to recommend the types of wholly new civil aircraft with which the British industry should proceed after the war. He also participated in the intergovernmental negotiations in Chicago in 1944 that led to the formation of the International Civil Aviation Organization.

After a further visit to the USA with a British aviation delegation in July 1944, Masefield was appointed the first civil air attaché in the British embassy in Washington in July 1945. He then played a key role with the British delegation in securing British interests in the Bermuda agreement of February 1946, which governed air traffic rights between the United States and Britain and its colonies and dependencies (and stood for the next thirty-one years until it was overtaken by the Bermuda II agreement of 1977). He also advised on the procurement and introduction into airline service of the Lockheed Constellation and Boeing Stratocruiser with the British Overseas Airways Corporation. Returning to Britain in December 1946, he was appointed director-general of long-term planning and projects in the newly created Ministry of Civil Aviation.

In July 1949 Masefield left the civil service to join the struggling British European Airways, formed three years earlier, as chief executive. He revitalized the airline's operations by inducting a modern fleet of British aircraft, notably the then revolutionary Brabazon type IIB propeller turbine Vickers Viscount. On 29 July 1950 he enabled the airline to operate the original prototype Viscount 630 G-AHRF on the world's first scheduled fare-paying passenger service by gas turbine power, between London and Paris. It then inaugurated the world's first sustained turboprop service with the enlarged Viscount 701 on 18 April 1953. In October of that year he was manager of the team leading the prototype of this initial production model, the Viscount 700 G-AMAV, specially named Endeavour, in the London–Christchurch, New Zealand, air race. He also formed a pioneering commercial helicopter unit in British European Airways and on 1 July 1950 the airline began the world's first scheduled helicopter passenger service, between Cardiff and Liverpool.

In November 1955 Masefield accepted an apparently attractive offer to become managing director of Bristol Aircraft to accelerate the protracted development of the Brabazon type III turboprop Britannia. Ironically, shortly afterwards he was offered the chairmanship of the British Overseas Airways Corporation, which he honourably but regretfully declined, only to find that he was not afforded the full authority that he needed at Bristol. With the absorption of Bristol Aircraft into the newly formed British Aircraft Corporation in January 1960, the Pressed Steel company invited him to create and head a new light aircraft manufacturing company formed in October 1960—British Executive and General Aviation Ltd, which became Beagle Aircraft, and which also took over Auster Aircraft a month later. But when Pressed Steel withdrew its support due to a downturn in the motor industry, its core business, Beagle was forced into receivership in 1969. Its Bulldog military trainer aircraft was taken over by Scottish Aviation in 1970 for successful quantity production.

During his Beagle tenure Masefield was also part-time chairman of the newly formed British Airports Authority from 1965 to 1971, reinvigorating the expanding operation of Heathrow, Gatwick, Stansted, and Prestwick airports. He was deputy chairman of British Caledonian, then Britain's largest independent airline (1975–8), and chairman and chief executive of London Transport (1980–82). His final professional appointment was as a director of Air Bristol (1993–6). He also held high office in more than thirty other organizations, notably the presidency of the Royal Aeronautical Society, the Chartered Institute of Transport, the British Association of Aviation Consultants, the Institute of Road Transport Engineers, and the International Federation of Airworthiness; he was chairman of the Royal Aero Club, the Royal Society of Arts, the Imperial War Museum, and the Brooklands Museum Trust. Knighted in the 1972 new year's honours list, he also received many professional and academic awards in recognition of his hugely accomplished professional career and his outstanding leadership and personal qualities.

A lifelong author and lecturer on civil aviation matters of wide compass and import, in his latter years Masefield also became a consummate aviation historian. His publications included his major work, *To Ride the Storm* (1982), which recounted the definitive story of the ill-fated government-sponsored R101 airship, and his autobiography, *Flight Path* (2002). His career had embraced aircraft design; aviation journalism and publishing; war reporting and broadcasting; wartime government service and the formulation of post-war British and international civil aviation regulatory organisms and statutes; service as the first civil air attaché in the British embassy in Washington, DC; airline management and operation; large-scale and light aircraft manufacturing management; and airport and public transport systems management. He was throughout a most erudite and prodigious chronicler of contemporary aviation matters. He died of bronchopneumonia on 14 February 2006 at his home, Kitley Lodge, Lewes Road, Laughton, Sussex. His wife, Patricia, died just sixty days later and only three weeks before what would have been their seventieth wedding anniversary. They were survived by their four children. Charles and Oliver had followed their father into the aviation industry, and Charles, a former president of BAe Commercial Aircraft and head of the Defence Export Services Organization, had been knighted in 1997. NORMAN BARFIELD

Sources P. Masefield and B. Gunston, *Flight path* (2002) • *The Times* (16 Feb 2006) • *Daily Telegraph* (17 Feb 2006) • *The Guardian* (17 Feb 2006) • *The Independent* (23 Feb 2006) • *Aerospace Professional* [Royal Aeronautical Society] (June 2006) • *WW* (2006) • Burke, *Peerage* • private information (2010) • b. cert. • m. cert. • d. cert.

Archives British Airways • Brooklands Museum, Weybridge, Surrey • IWM • Royal Aeronautical Society | RAF Museum, Colindale, Constance Babington Smith MSS | FILM British Airways • Brooklands Museum, Weybridge, Surrey • Royal Aeronautical Society | SOUND BL NSA, *Any questions*, BBC light programme, 13 Jan 1961, B3023 C7 • BL NSA, documentary recordings • BL NSA, recorded lecture • British Airways • Brooklands Museum, Weybridge, Surrey • Royal Aeronautical Society

Likenesses M. Noakes, oils, 1972, priv. coll. • S. Dack, photograph, 1980, Getty Images, London, Hult. Arch. • G. Turner, photograph, 1981 (with Peter Parker), Getty Images, London, Hult. Arch. • photograph, 1995, PA Photos, London • Elliott & Fry, vintage print, NPG • J. Russell & Sons, photograph, Royal Aeronautical Society [*see illus.*] • obituary photographs • photographs, priv. coll. • photographs, Brooklands Museum, Weybridge, Surrey • photographs, Royal Aeronautical Society • photographs, British Airways Archive • photographs, IWM

Wealth at death £18,678: probate, 26 April 2006, *CGPLA Eng. & Wales*

Mason, Stephen Finney (1923–2007), chemist and historian of science, was born on 6 July 1923 at 11 Prebend Street, Leicester, the son of Leonard Stephen Mason, motor bus proprietor, and his wife, Crissie Harriette, *née* Finney, both of 24 Leicester Road, Anstey, four miles from Leicester. The family ran a general store and garage in Anstey with Crissie's father, Sam Finney, a former farm worker. Mason's father ran a bus service to Leicester but left the family and business in 1927. Mason won a scholarship to Wyggeston Grammar School, Leicester, and an open scholarship to study chemistry at Wadham College, Oxford. He took a first in 1945 and completed his DPhil in 1947, on the biological activity of antimalarials—then a key topic because of the wartime Japanese occupation of the cinchona plantations of Java—under Dalziel Llewellyn Hammick.

Mason's interest in the history of science was awakened by the connection between Wadham College and Bishop John Wilkins in the Commonwealth period. As a result of an essay he wrote on the proto-chemistry of Robert Boyle, Robert Hooke, and John Mayow for a junior research fellowship at Magdalen College he was invited by Frank Sherwood Taylor, the curator of the Museum of the History of Science at Oxford, to join his staff as a departmental demonstrator (junior lecturer) in 1947. He had been blocked from any further progress in the university chemical hierarchy by the hostility of Robert Robinson (towards Hammick rather than Mason). Taylor also prevailed on Mason to become the secretary and treasurer of the Society for the Study of Alchemy and Early Chemistry, which was then in a rather parlous state as a result of the death of its patron, Sir Robert Mond, and the war. The close relationship between Taylor and Mason was surprising in some ways. Taylor was a Catholic apologist while Mason became a member of the Communist Party. He joined Christopher Hill's Communist Party Historians Group, but left the party with Hill in 1957 after the Soviet invasion of Hungary. Another member of the group was Bridget Sutton [*see* Hill, Bridget Irene (1922–2002)], and they were married on 31 December 1949. This marriage did not endure (she subsequently married Christopher Hill), and on 1 October 1955 Mason married Joan Banus (1923–2004), an assistant lecturer in chemistry at University College, London, and daughter of Mark Banus, accountant. She went on to have a distinguished career as a chemist, at the University of East Anglia and the Open University, specializing in particular in nuclear magnetic resonance spectroscopy. They had three sons, Oliver (*b.* 1957), Andrew (*b.* 1959), and Lionel (*b.* 1960), who became respectively an electronics engineer, a professor of gastroenterology at the University of Alberta, and a professor of mathematics at the University of Oxford.

As a result of teaching the university course on the history of scientific ideas Mason became interested in the relationship between the scientific revolution of the seventeenth century and the voyages of discovery on the one hand and the agricultural and industrial revolutions on the other. He also worked briefly with Joseph Needham in Cambridge in 1950 on the history of Chinese science, which broadened his interests to the relationship between science and non-Western civilizations. Soon afterwards, however, his career reached a watershed when Hammick retired in 1952 and Mason no longer had access to a chemical laboratory. By this time Taylor had left Oxford to become director of the Science Museum at South Kensington. His position at the museum had been taken by Kurt Josten, a historian of alchemy and astrology who was a German Catholic monarchist. Under him Mason's prospects as a historian of science were not good and he decided the best course of action was to become a professional chemist and an amateur historian of science.

In 1953 Mason joined Adrien Albert at the medical chemistry department of the Australian National University, which was then based at the Wellcome Institute in London, while Albert waited for the completion of the department's laboratories in Canberra. In the course of his work with Albert, Mason took up spectroscopy and theoretical chemistry—partly under the influence of Charles Coulson—which became his major field of research. In 1956 Albert and his group moved to Canberra, but facing opposition from conservative elements in the university Mason took up a lectureship in chemical spectroscopy at the University of Exeter, where he developed his interest in the technique of circular dichroism (the absorption of polarized light across the spectrum). He benefited from the explosion of new universities in the early 1960s when he was offered a chair in chemistry at the new University of East Anglia in 1964. His acceptance by the scientific establishment was sealed by a chair at King's College, London, in 1970 and his election as a fellow of the Royal Society in 1982. He served on the council of the Chemical Society (from 1980 the Royal Society of Chemistry) in 1964–9 and 1978–81.

At King's College, London, Mason worked on ligand polarization theory and the relationship between the weak nuclear force and the origin of bimolecular homochirality. Ligand polarization theory is based on the assumption that the physical properties of transition metal complexes (such as their spectra) can be explained by the electronic influence of the transition metal ion on its ligands (the species bound to the metal ion) in contrast to the older and more conventional crystal field theory which emphasizes the influence of the ligands on the metal ion. Mason's work in this field led to his last major publication, *Chemical Evolution: Origins of the Elements, Molecules and Living Systems* (1991). In this widely praised book he combined his understanding of spectroscopy, biochemical systems, and the history of science to explain the evolution of 'handedness' (chirality) in the universe and hence the origin of life, a topic that had been of longstanding interest to Marxists, stemming from the materialist ideas of Friedrich Engels and the research of the Soviet biochemist Alexander Oparin in the 1920s.

Despite all this scientific activity Mason never lost his interest in the history of science. He had published a ground-breaking work, *A History of the Sciences: Main Currents of Scientific Thought*, which arose out of his teaching on the scientific revolution at Oxford, in 1953. In sharp contrast to the orthodox Marxist view—established by Boris Hessen in the 1930s and faithfully followed by J. D. Bernal—that science had been shaped by economics and capitalist society, Mason argued that both economic and intellectual factors had been important in its development. He also continued to publish papers on the history of science. In 1974, through the pages of *Chemistry in Britain*, he invited his fellow members of the Chemical Society to join him in setting up a historical group. The first meeting of the group was held at King's College, London, in 1975, with Mason in the chair; he left the leadership of the group in 1980, but it remained active.

When he retired in 1988 Mason moved to Cambridge, where his wife, Joan, had academic links. He became an honorary research associate in the department of history and philosophy of science, and a fellow of Wolfson College. He died of cancer at his home, 12 Hills Avenue, Cambridge, on 11 December 2007. He was survived by his three sons. PETER J. T. MORRIS

Sources www.rsc.org/Membership/AboutRscMembership/Obituaries/SMason.asp, 19 March 2010 • *Ambix*, 55/2 (July 2008), 97–8 • S. F. Mason, memoir, March 2007, RS • *WW* (2007) • private information (2011) [Lionel Mason, son] • b. cert. • m. certs. • d. cert.

Archives King's Lond., papers and corresp.

Likenesses photograph, repro. in www.rsc.org/Membership/AboutRscMembership/Obituaries/SMason.asp

Wealth at death £855,198: probate, 1 April 2008, *CGPLA Eng. & Wales*

Massingberd, Hugh John Montgomery- (1946–2007), genealogist, obituaries editor, and author, was born on 30 December 1946 at Rondels, Cookham Dean, Berkshire, the only son of John Michael Montgomery, later Montgomery-Massingberd (1913–2004), temporary administrative assistant in the Colonial Office, later head of personnel central services for the BBC, and his wife, Marsali Mary (1912–2004), daughter of Francis Joseph Seal, stock jobber, and widow of Roger de Winton Kelsall Winlaw, cricketer and RAF officer, killed in action in 1942. He had two older stepbrothers, an older stepsister, and a younger sister. Originally Montgomery, the family assumed the name Montgomery-Massingberd by deed poll in 1964, in compliance with the will of Diana, Lady Montgomery-Massingberd, widow of Field-Marshal Sir Archibald Montgomery-Massingberd. At one point the family lived at Gunby, a fine William and Mary house in Lincolnshire, but were unable to afford to keep up the tenancy.

Montgomery-Massingberd was educated at Harrow School, and, after a restless phase as a solicitor's articled clerk, turned down a place at Selwyn College, Cambridge, to become an editorial assistant of the Burke's series in 1968, rising to be editorial director of Burke's Peerage Ltd, which he ran from 1971 to 1983. He was a man with an encyclopaedic memory, the full force of which he brought to his ambitious publishing programme at Burke's. He edited many books for the firm, including a new edition of *Burke's Landed Gentry* (1969–72), *Burke's Guide to the Royal Family* (1973), *Presidential Families of the USA* (1975), *Burke's Irish Family Records* (1976), *Burke's Family Index* (1976), two volumes of *Burke's Royal Families of the World* (1977 and 1980), and three volumes of *Burke's Guide to Country Houses* (1978–81). These were monumental works of reference, which Montgomery-Massingberd enriched with vivid biographical additions. At that time his love was for the squirearchy of Britain—those county families who (as his parents had aspired but failed to do) maintained their estates, cared for their inherited houses, and sought to pass them on to future generations. He was caricatured in *Private Eye* as Hugh Montgomery-Massivesnob.

Meanwhile, Montgomery-Massingberd embarked on a parallel career as an author of a prodigious number of popular, frequently illustrated, books, mainly on the British monarchy, aristocracy, and gentry. These included *The Monarchy* (1979), *The British Aristocracy* (also 1979), *The London Ritz* (with David Watkin, 1980), and a number of biographical studies—of Diana, princess of Wales (1982), the queen (1986), and Queen Elizabeth, the queen mother (1999). There was a series on great houses (England and Wales, 1994, Scotland, 1997, Ireland, 1999, and English manor houses, 2001), with photographs by Christopher Simon Sykes. He wrote and later revised *Blenheim Revisited* (1985), an enjoyable history of the palace and its inhabitants. He also reviewed many books, always perceptively and usually with generosity, though his scathing review in *The Times* of Noble Frankland's biography of Prince Henry, duke of Gloucester, caused long-term reverberations.

Montgomery-Massingberd married first, on 19 February 1972, Christine Anne Martinoni (*b*. 1948/9), a colleague at Burke's, and daughter of Jacques Georges Martin Martinoni, businessman, of Paris and Ridge, Hertfordshire. They had a son and a daughter, but were divorced in 1979. He married on 22 February 1983 his second wife, (Dorothy) Caroline Ripley (*b*. 1947), researcher, and daughter of Sir Hugh Ripley, fourth baronet. There were no children of this second marriage.

In 1986 Montgomery-Massingberd took over the editorial chair of the obituaries department of the *Daily Telegraph*, and, in friendly rivalry with James Fergusson at *The Independent*, brought the art of the obituary to lasting new heights. The moribund atmosphere of the obituary department changed to one of vibrancy, and his pages were eagerly read. He saw no reason not to be outspoken. His obituaries (always anonymous) were read with glee, not least because they celebrated eccentricity. He enjoyed understatement and was a master of the art of litotes. Occasionally he caused outrageous offence. His success as obituaries editor led the *Telegraph* to give him further responsibilities, including as a restaurant critic and, from 1992, editor of the Peterborough column.

After a serious heart attack in 1994 Montgomery-Massingberd was briefly the *Telegraph*'s television critic, but in 1996 he resigned. He then edited five anthologies of obituaries, which proved popular and encompassed the deceased by type. These were followed by *The Very Best of the Daily Telegraph Obituaries* (a compilation drawn from the five). The fifth volume (*Twentieth-Century Lives*) was shortlisted for the inaugural Bollinger Everyman Wodehouse prize for comic writing in 2000. Montgomery-Massingberd was also a seasoned broadcaster and an occasionally mischievous lecturer, and as his confidence grew there were occasions when he burst into song. He wrote, produced, and staged *Ancestral Voices* (2002), a one-man show, starring Moray Watson, based on the life of James

Lees-Milne, which played for 100 performances, almost all of which he witnessed. He also devised and performed in *Love and Art*, based on Anthony Powell's *Dance to the Music of Time*, produced at the Wallace Collection in 2005.

Montgomery-Massingberd (who latterly dropped the first part of his surname, becoming Hugh Massingberd) had a capacious appetite for food, bordering on gluttony. He broke King Farouk of Egypt's record of eating the largest-ever breakfast at the Connaught Hotel. Indeed, it was said that when a waiter reeled off the menu for breakfast he simply nodded. Not surprisingly he magnified from a willowy youthful figure into a man sometimes pressing twenty stone. His generosity was legendary and quixotic. Though never well off financially, he invariably seized the bill in restaurants, or would entertain his friends for a weekend of racing. He was modest, self-effacing, hard working, inspired, and confident of his knowledge, which encompassed the aristocracy, the turf, cricket, and soap operas. He loved the theatre, and saw *The Phantom of the Opera* over fifty times. More important, he was a huge morale booster who kick-started the careers of a great number of writers, and he enhanced and corrected the texts of innumerable books. From shy beginnings he ended his life with a host of admiring friends, many of whom paid him the compliment of considering themselves his best friend. In 2001 he published his memoirs, *Daydream Believer: Confessions of a Hero-Worshipper*, a masterpiece of self-deprecatory comic writing.

Massingberd's last years were dogged with ill health, though he rose from many setbacks and was a calm, articulate patient. Eventually the treatment proved too onerous and he retreated to a hospice in London. He died there of cancer on Christmas day 2007. He passed through life unhonoured, but his death was celebrated globally as obituarists vied to pay homage, the *Daily Telegraph* assigning him a full page. The headline in one Australian paper, 'Obituary editor in grave condition', was one he would have greatly enjoyed. He was survived by his wife, Caroline, and by his children, Luke and Harriet.

Hugo Vickers

Sources H. Massingberd, *Daydream believer* (2001) • *Daily Telegraph* (27 Dec 2007) • *The Independent* (27 Dec 2007) • *The Times* (28 Dec 2007) • *The Guardian* (31 Dec 2007) • Burke, *Gen. GB* • personal knowledge (2011) • private information (2011) • b. cert. • m. certs.

Archives FILM BFINA, documentary footage

Likenesses D. Wimsett, photographs, 2004, Photoshot, London • E. Bentall, photographs, repro. in www.telegraph.co.uk/news • obituary photographs • photographs, repro. in Massingberd, *Daydream believer*

Wealth at death under £118,000: probate, 29 May 2008, *CGPLA Eng. & Wales*

Mathias, Roland Glyn (1915–2007), poet and literary critic, was born on 4 September 1915 at Ffynnon Fawr, a farmhouse in the parish of Llanddeti and the valley of Glyn Collwn, above Tal-y-bont ar Wysg in Brecknockshire, the eldest of the three children of Evan Mathias (1885–1962), a Congregational minister and chaplain with the South Wales Borderers then serving in the Dardanelles, and his wife, Muriel (1891–1979), daughter of Joseph Morgan and his wife, Rachel, who farmed Ffynnon Fawr. The valley was subsequently flooded to make Tal-y-bont reservoir and the house was demolished.

Both of Mathias's parents were Welsh but only his father was Welsh-speaking and the language of the boy's home and education was English. He first became aware of his Welsh identity while reading an adventure novel by Owen Rhoscomyl (Owen Vaughan), but it was to be many years before he could immerse himself in the history and English-language literature of Wales. At the end of the First World War Evan Mathias was pressed to remain with the army in Cologne where, in 1920, his family joined him, his son receiving his early schooling at British military schools in Germany and subsequently at camps on Salisbury Plain and at Aldershot. His mother's Christian pacifism and antipathy to her husband's career in the army created tension in the home that was never properly resolved.

Educated at Caterham School, Surrey, which he entered in 1925, and at Jesus College, Oxford, where he took a first in modern history in 1936, Mathias began teaching at Cowley Boys' Grammar School, St Helens, Lancashire, and then at the Bluecoat School in Reading, Berkshire. In 1941 he served a term of three months in prison, with hard labour, for refusing to be conscripted or do any kind of war work but, on his release, was intransigent in this regard; in the year following he received another three-month sentence but was released after his pupils and colleagues at the Bluecoat School collected money to pay his fine. On 4 April 1944, at the Baptist chapel in Chipping Norton, Oxfordshire, he married Mary Annie (1916–1996), schoolteacher, daughter of Sidney Hawes, a farmer from Enstone. They had a son and two daughters.

At the war's end Mathias was given a part-time post at Carlisle Boys' Grammar School and in 1946 he took a full-time post at St Clement Dane's School in London. In 1948 he returned to Wales as headmaster of the grammar school at Pembroke Dock. In the year following, and in collaboration with Raymond Garlick, whom he had appointed to the teaching staff, he was a prime mover in the foundation of the periodical *Dock Leaves*, which in 1957 was renamed the *Anglo-Welsh Review*. Further headships followed: at the Herbert Strutt School, Belper, Derbyshire (1958–64), and at King Edward VI Five Ways School in Birmingham (1964–9), after which (with the help of a bursary from the Welsh Arts Council) he settled in Brecon to become a full-time writer; there he remained for the rest of his life.

Mathias's verse showed but little change in its preoccupations over the fifty years of its composition. The poems in his first collection, *Days Enduring* (1943), were written at a time when he was suffering the consequences of his pacifist convictions. Almost all his work drew its strength from the nonconformist tradition and his staunch Christian beliefs. Even the famous sense of guilt associated with that tradition did not inhibit him as a writer: 'it shows me a particular vision, a measurement', he once commented. 'Out of it I can write' (*Contemporary Poets of the English Language*, ed. R. Murphy, 1970, 719). He went on to publish seven more collections: *Break in Harvest* (1946), *The*

Roses of Tretower (1952), *The Flooded Valley* (1960), *Absalom in the Tree* (1971), *Snipe's Castle* (1979), *Burning Brambles: Selected Poems* (1983), and *A Field at Vallorcines* (1996). His *Collected Poems*, edited by Sam Adams, appeared in 2002. Very much to do with Wales and its history, and with specific Welsh landscapes, particularly along the border with England, his poetry was sometimes considered difficult, obscure even, usually because of its allusions and erudition, but it was marked by its engaging honesty, vivid language, and meticulous craftsmanship. The same qualities went into the making of his short stories, published as *The Eleven Men of Eppynt* (1956) and *The Collected Short Stories of Roland Mathias* (edited by Sam Adams, 2001).

As an editor and critic Mathias made a major contribution to an understanding of the English-language literature of Wales, helping to define and develop it more than any of his contemporaries, so that by the end of his life he enjoyed a reputation as the founding father of this discipline. His work on the origins of this literature, from about the fifteenth century, drew its substance and accuracy from his training as a historian, and his literary criticism blazed a trail down which many others have since ventured. As editor of the *Anglo-Welsh Review* between 1961 and 1976 he continued this work with a flair and commitment that was admired by his compatriots, and not only those in Welsh academe. With a deep sense of mission and insisting that English-speakers had a vital part to play in the cultural life of Wales, he sought to strengthen the attachment of writers to the national heritage, his professional interest as a historian clearly reflected in the magazine's contents, notably in the many substantial reviews, articles, and editorials that he contributed. His literary criticism had a breadth of outlook, a high seriousness, and a concern with issues rather than with personalities. His most important books were *Whitsun Riot* (1963), a study of Catholic recusancy in Herefordshire; a monograph on Vernon Watkins in the Writers of Wales series (1974); a study of the poetry of John Cowper Powys (1979); and an illustrated history of Welsh writing in English (1987). He also edited (with Sam Adams) an anthology of short stories by Welsh writers, *The Shining Pyramid* (1970), the collected short stories of Geraint Goodwin (1976), a collection of essays on David Jones as writer and artist (1976), and, with Raymond Garlick, an acclaimed anthology of Welsh poetry in English from 1480 to 1980 (1984). A selection of his criticism appeared under the title *A Ride through the Wood* in 1985.

After settling in the old county town of Brecon in 1969 Mathias threw himself into the literary life of Wales that he had done so much to foster. He served as a member of the Welsh Arts Council from 1970 to 1979 and as chairman of its literature committee; he also chaired the English-language section of the Welsh Academy, the national society of writers in Wales. For *The Oxford Companion to the Literature of Wales* (1986) he wrote several hundred entries and acted as consultant to its editorial board, saving it from many an error of fact and judgement. In the same year he suffered a stroke from which he never fully recovered, though he remained jovial, convivial, and approachable to the last. He also remained a staunch member of the Plough Chapel (United Reformed church) in Brecon (he is commemorated by a plaque in the chapel's porch). He died on 16 August 2007 at the War Memorial Hospital, Brecon, of bronchopneumonia and heart failure, and was buried on 23 August at Aber Chapel, Tal-y-bont ar Wysg. He was survived by his three children.

MEIC STEPHENS

Sources autobiographical essay, in M. Stephens, *Artists in Wales*, 1 (1971) · S. Adams, *Roland Mathias* (1995) · *The collected poems of Roland Mathias*, ed. S. Adams (2002) · *The Independent* (17 Aug 2007) · *The Times* (26 Sept 2007) · *The Guardian* (17 Oct 2007) · personal knowledge (2011) · private information (2011) · b. cert. · m. cert. · d. cert.

Archives Buffalo State College, State University of New York, papers and letters · NL Wales, corresp. and papers | NL Wales, Emyr Humphreys papers · NL Wales, Harri Webb papers · U. Reading L., Bodley Head archives | SOUND BL NSA, documentary recordings · BL NSA, performance recordings · *Poets of Wales*, Argo, 1975, PLP 1201

Likenesses L. Bewsey, portrait (posthumous), priv. coll.; repro. in www.lorrainesartstudio.co.uk/5.html · obituary photographs

Wealth at death £348,909: probate, 19 Nov 2007, *CGPLA Eng. & Wales*

Matthews, Sir Peter Alec (1922–2006), engineer and businessman, was born on 21 September 1922 on Vancouver Island, British Columbia, Canada, the son of Major Alec Bryan Matthews, a steel engineer, and his wife, Elsie Lazarus, *née* Barlow. Brought up on a farm at Westholme, Vancouver Island, he was educated at Shawnigan Lake School, Vancouver Island, and Oundle School in England. He joined the army in 1940, and was commissioned in the Royal Engineers, serving in north Africa, Sicily, Italy, and Greece, and reaching the rank of major. In 1946 he was demobilized, and on 29 November the same year he married Sheila Dorothy Bunting, a 25-year-old flying officer in the WAAF, daughter of John Henry Bunting, electrical engineer; they had four sons and one daughter.

After the war Matthews joined Stewart & Lloyds Ltd, manufacturers of iron and steel tubes, at their Glasgow works, and during the 1950s travelled all over the world for the company, including a three-year stint building a steel and pipe mill in Canada. In 1962 he was appointed to the board of Stewart & Lloyds as director of research and technical development, based in Corby, Northamptonshire. Following the renationalization of the steel industry in 1967 he was invited to join the board of the British Steel Corporation as member for research and development, a position he held until 1970. Under the chairmanship of Lord Melchett, the corporation faced the task of modernizing the fourteen nationalized companies, and creating a unified structure. Matthews was influential in the drawing up of a development plan to rationalize the industry, unveiled in 1970. Steelmaking was to be concentrated into fewer but larger plants, in five coastal areas, with the closure of many smaller, inland plants, involving the loss of up to 50,000 jobs. Although the strategy was accepted with the publication of a government white paper in 1972, the Labour government elected in 1974, worried by the unemployment implications of the plan, demanded a review of all the proposed closures. By the time the corporation began to implement the strategy there had been a dramatic slump in world demand for steel, and a deepening recession in the United Kingdom brought the British steel industry close to the point of collapse. Matthews was appointed as a non-executive deputy chairman of the corporation in 1973, under the new chairman, Monty Finniston, and served until 1976.

In 1970 Matthews moved from the British Steel Corporation on his appointment as managing director of Vickers, which had been founded in Sheffield in 1867 as a steel manufacturer but had grown into a huge engineering conglomerate embracing the production of aircraft and guided weapons, naval shipbuilding, and nuclear submarines. When Matthews took over, Vickers was facing a crisis, with the engineering group deeply in debt. One of his first decisions was to sell the Vickers-Zimmer chemical engineering business in Frankfurt, which had been a drain on the resources of the group, and by the end of 1971 recovery was under way. Another crucial decision, at the end of 1972, was to buy a further 10 per cent share in the British Aircraft Corporation, bringing Vickers's share to 50 per cent: from 1973 profits from the British Aircraft Corporation were to increase dramatically. Matthews had been appointed because many of the shareholders wanted a more dynamic management style. He made a number of good appointments, recruiting younger men from outside the company, including J. R. Hendin as chief executive of the engineering group. Believing that managers should have closer contact with the workforce, Matthews set an example by spending at least one day a week out of the office visiting factories and offices. When the government nationalized the aviation and shipbuilding industries in 1977, the loss of the British Aircraft Corporation and Vickers Ltd Shipbuilding Group cut Vickers's revenue by over half, and reduced its annual profits by two-thirds; Vickers was left with only the engineering group. Its fortunes revived following the merger of Vickers and Rolls-Royce Motors in 1980, when Rolls-Royce was on the verge of financial collapse. Matthews succeeded Lord Robens as chairman of Vickers in 1980, remaining until 1984.

Matthews had many other business interests: he was chairman of the Pegler Hattersley engineering company in Doncaster from 1979 to 1987, and on the boards of Lloyds Bank, British Electric Traction plc, Sun Alliance and London Insurance, Lead Industries Group, Hamilton Oil GB, and Lloyds and Scottish. He was also in demand to serve on national councils and committees, and his many offices included the chairmanship of the Armed Forces Pay Review Body from 1984 to 1989; the presidency of the Sino-British Trade Council from 1983 to 1985 and of the Engineering Employers Federation from 1982 to 1984; and membership of the Top Salaries Review Body from 1983 to 1986, the National Research Development Council from 1974 to 1980, and the Export Guarantees Advisory Council from 1973 to 1978. He was chairman of the council of University College, London, from 1980 to 1989, a period in which the college faced government cuts in university funding. Matthews and the provost, Sir James Lighthill, turned to non-government sources, including research councils, charitable foundations, and industry, to make up the shortfall in funding, and despite the government cutbacks the 1980s was a decade of expansion, culminating in the amalgamation of the University College Hospital and Middlesex Hospital medical schools.

Matthews was knighted in 1975 for services to exports, and in 1980 was one of the first foreigners to be appointed to the Order of Australia, for his help to the Australian heavy engineering and shipbuilding industries while at Vickers. Having suffered for many years from Parkinson's disease, he died on 20 May 2006 at his home, Chalkwell, Nether Wallop, Stockbridge, Hampshire. He was survived by his wife and their five children.

Anne Pimlott Baker

Sources J. Vaizey, *The history of British Steel* (1974) • H. Evans, *Vickers against the odds, 1956–1977* (1978) • J. J. Richardson and G. F. Dudley, 'Steel policy in the UK', *The politics of steel: western Europe and the steel industry in the crisis years (1974–1984)*, ed. Y. Mény and V. Wright (1986), 308–67 • G. F. Dudley and J. J. Richardson, *Politics and steel in Britain, 1967–1988: the life and times of the British Steel Corporation* (1990) • *Daily Telegraph* (6 June 2006) • *The Times* (8 June 2006) • *WW* (2006) • Burke, *Peerage* • m. cert. • d. cert.

Archives CUL, Vickers archive

Likenesses photograph, repro. in Evans, *Vickers*, facing p. 217

Wealth at death £250,164: probate, 27 Sept 2006, *CGPLA Eng. & Wales*

Mawer [*née* Entwistle], **(Elizabeth) Barbara (1936–2006)**, biochemist, was born on 6 March 1936 at 82 Sandy Lane, Blackburn, Lancashire, the elder daughter of Thomas Entwistle, schoolmaster, and his wife, Gladys Mary, *née* Cornall. She was educated at Blackburn High School for Girls and Queen Mary School, Lytham St Anne's. She realized from the age of ten, following a visit to a chemistry lab with her father, that she wanted to follow a career in chemistry. She received her undergraduate education in the biochemistry department at Edinburgh University, where she was inspired by the professor of chemistry in relation to medicine, Guy Marrian, and was awarded a PhD in 1961 for a thesis entitled 'The metabolism of cholesterol in the animal body'. In 1957 she had married George Mawer, a doctor and clinical pharmacologist. They had three daughters, Deborah, Vanessa, and Rebecca.

In 1967, after a period as an assistant lecturer in biochemistry at Edinburgh University (1958–63) and a short break to care for her young children, Mawer joined the University of Manchester as a research associate to pursue research into vitamin D metabolism and metabolic bone disease with William Stanbury. Vitamin D, produced in the skin by the action of sunlight, is converted into the hormonal form (1,25-dihydroxyvitamin D) by successive hydroxylation in the liver and kidneys. The signals it sends to the intestines increase the absorption of calcium and phosphorus; calcium absorption leads to the formation and maintenance of strong bones. Stanbury and Mawer were among the first clinical researchers to show that patients with renal disease were unable to make 1,25-dihydroxyvitamin D, and were thus unable to absorb enough calcium from the gut to make their bones mineralize properly.

In Manchester, Mawer was promoted successively to senior research fellow (1974), a north-west regional health authority senior research fellow (1983–93), reader in medicine (1993), and eventually to a personal chair as professor of bone and mineral metabolism in 1995. After Stanbury's retirement in 1983, she applied for funding to the Medical Research Council, indicating that she had been supported by it for many years. The council claimed never to have heard of her, as funding had gone to the professor. Mawer, a fine role model for women scientists working in clinical medicine, overcame this obstacle with her usual grit and determination. Subsequently she enjoyed considerable funding success with her friend and colleague Mike Davies, enabling them to study basic and clinical aspects of vitamin D metabolism. The realization that 1,25D receptors in cell nuclei are to be found all over the body, including muscle and the brain, expanded the scope of their research. They were the first in the UK to demonstrate that macrophages from patients with pseudovitamin D deficiency rickets lack any detectable 1-hydroxylase activity when compared to unaffected individuals, owing to novel mutations in their P450c1 gene. Further work led to the development of clinical assays for the measurement of vitamin D metabolites, and Mawer's laboratory became renowned for its contributions to the assay field. From 1994 to 2001 she was director of the supra-regional assay service for the measurement of vitamin D metabolites, providing this service for the whole of the UK.

Mawer was a highly influential figure in the calcium homoeostasis field in the UK. She was an outstanding secretary, then president (1992–4) of the Bone and Tooth Society, and deputy director of the Bone Disease Research Centre at Manchester for its first three years (1994–7). She was honoured with a career achievement award from her colleagues at the Eleventh International Vitamin D Workshop in Nashville in 2000. She retired from the university in 2001.

In her life outside science Mawer was active in local politics, serving as a parish councillor and chair of school governors at Thelwall, near Warrington. On Warrington borough council, to which she was elected in 1987, she became leader of the Liberal Democrat opposition group (1991–2004). She was greatly concerned with education, the environment, planning, regeneration, and protecting the rights of individuals, and represented Warrington council on the north-west regional assembly. Her first marriage ended in an amicable divorce, and on 2 May 1981 she married Clifford Gordon (Cliff) Taylor, a research chemist ten years her junior, and son of William Harold Taylor, grocer.

To the community of researchers around the globe studying bone and mineral metabolism Mawer was an elegant figure with a quiet, unassuming, but firm demeanour. Those who worked with her learned to fear her no-nonsense style, but appreciated her sense of humour and unconditional support. Shortly before her death the Bone Research Society established an annual travelling fellowship in her name to support laboratory work by its members. She died in the Christie Hospital, Manchester, on 7 March 2006, after a brave battle with liver cancer. She was survived by her husband, Cliff, and by the three daughters of her first marriage. JACQUELINE BERRY

Sources *Orbit News* [Warrington] (10 March 2006) · *The Times* (2 May 2006) · *The Guardian* (16 June 2006) · *The Endocrinologist*, 81 (autumn 2006), 6 · *The Biochemist* (Oct 2006), 60 · personal knowledge (2010) · private information (2010) · b. cert. · m. cert. [1981] · d. cert.

Likenesses obituary photographs

Wealth at death £263,674: probate, 18 Jan 2008, *CGPLA Eng. & Wales*

Mawer, June Knox- [*née* June Ellis] (**1930–2006**), writer and broadcaster, was born on 10 May 1930 at 27 Acton Rise in Acton Garden Village in rural Denbighshire, the only daughter and elder child of Frank Ellis (*c.*1898–1970), accountant, and his wife, Mary Irene, *née* Renfrey (1902–1971), teacher. She attended Grove Park Grammar School for Girls in Wrexham. 'We were in Wales all right', she wrote of that time, 'but only by the skin of our teeth' (*A Ram in the Well*, 2). She was later to describe lying in bed on early winter mornings listening to the sounds of the miners walking past the house on their way to Gresford colliery; she could clearly hear 'the iron ring of their boots and the harsh sound of coughing' (ibid.). After school she was offered, at the age of seventeen, a job as cub reporter on the *Chester Chronicle*, just across the border, where to her great delight her £4 a week duties included covering the local races, allowing her to wear fashionable 'new look' frocks and hats. With the pale skin and thick dark hair that marked her as a true Celt, she was considered exceptionally good-looking. On 30 June 1951, after a five-year courtship, she married the young barrister Ronald (Ronnie) Knox-Mawer (1925–2009), the son of George Robert Knox-Mawer, businessman. They had a daughter, Vanessa, and a son, Howard. In 1952 Ronald Knox-Mawer was appointed chief magistrate and acting chief justice in Aden, and June Knox-Mawer found herself transported into an exotic world, with a retinue of servants and a whirl of social duties. She made friends with local Arab people, an exciting experience about which she wrote later in *The Sultans Came to Tea* (1961). From Aden the Knox-Mawers moved in 1958 to the south Pacific, where her husband acquired an impressive portfolio of responsibilities including senior magistrate, puisne judge, justice of appeal, and acting chief justice of Fiji, as well as joint chief justice for Nauru and Tonga. This was a life that June Knox-Mawer was to describe in *A Gift of Islands* (1965), comparing her own experience with that of two Victorian women travellers visiting when ritual murder and even cannibalism were by no means unknown in Fiji. The south sea islands were also the setting for her first novel, *Marama* (1972), and later *The Shadow of Wings* (1995). In Fiji Knox-Mawer first acquired her radio broadcasting skills: Chris Venning, subsequently a senior BBC radio drama producer, employed her on the local *English by Radio* transmissions and later as an announcer and interviewer. Her time in Fiji was also to provide material for broadcasts on BBC radio's *Woman's Hour* in the 1970s.

The Knox-Mawers returned to Britain in 1971 on Ronald's retirement from the colonial service. He took up magisterial duties in the north of England and subsequently London, where he was metropolitan stipendiary magistrate and a deputy circuit judge until 1984. This enabled June to renew her broadcasting career, working first in Liverpool for BBC Radio Merseyside and then in Manchester, where she became the presenter of the north of England edition of *Woman's Hour*. Her warmth of manner and effective interviewing technique led to regular engagements in the 1970s and into the 1980s as both a presenter of and contributor to *Woman's Hour* from London; her radio partnership on that programme with Edward Blishen, talking knowledgeably and enthusiastically about the paperback books they had recently enjoyed, was a particularly popular contribution. She fronted for BBC Radio 4 a series of illustrated interviews with musicians, *Concerto*, while a documentary programme about a National Trust property close to her childhood home, Erddig, near Wrexham, was memorably atmospheric. Erddig was the rather forbidding property once owned by a series of eccentric and reclusive squires called Yorke; her guide on the radio broadcast was the last squire, Philip Yorke. She also took her microphone along the hills and valleys of Radnor and Brecknockshire to follow the footsteps of the Victorian parson and diarist Francis Kilvert. The intelligence and care she brought to all her broadcasting made hers a versatile and reliable radio voice.

June Knox-Mawer continued to write books as she pursued her radio career. Her last novel, *Sandstorm*, in which she returned to an Arabian milieu, won the romantic novel of the year award in 1992. *A Ram in the Well* (2001), her final book, concentrated on life in the family's Welsh cottage, Fron Fawr, perched halfway up a mountainside in Denbighshire. The Knox-Mawers had found Fron in the early 1970s ('access is difficult but views are panoramic', said the estate agent) in a terrible state, but they successfully restored it. Despite its isolation and propensity to be cut off by snow in severe winters—one Christmas the turkey was brought by a neighbouring farmer by tractor and eventually on the end of a pitchfork—it enabled them to divide their time between Wales and their small flat at the top of a house near Grosvenor Square in London. She died of cancer on 19 April 2006 at St John's Hospice, St John's Wood, London, and her ashes were scattered at Fron. She was survived by her husband and their two children.

SUE MACGREGOR

Sources J. Knox-Mawer, *The sultans came to tea* (1961) · J. Knox-Mawer, *A gift of islands* (1965) · J. Knox-Mawer, *A ram in the well* (2001) · *The Times* (26 April 2006) · *Daily Telegraph* (28 April 2006) · *The Guardian* (3 May 2006) · obituary, British Yemeni Society, www.al-bab.com/bys/obits/knox_mawer.htm, 1 Oct 2008 · personal knowledge (2010) · private information (2010) [Ronnie Knox-Mawer, husband; Vanessa Knox-Mawer, daughter; C. Venning; A. Howells] · b. cert. · m. cert.

Archives SOUND BL NSA, current affairs recordings · BL NSA, documentary recordings · BL NSA, performance recordings

Likenesses obituary photographs

Wealth at death under £64,000: probate, 2 Nov 2006, *CGPLA Eng. & Wales*

May, Pamela [*real name* Doris Maud May] (**1917–2005**), ballet dancer, was born on 30 May 1917 in San Fernando, Trinidad, the daughter of Reginald Henry May, civil engineer. She moved to England with her parents when she was four. After local schooling and some early ballet lessons, then courses at the Royal Academy of Dancing, she was admitted, aged sixteen, to the ballet school founded by Ninette de Valois as a feeder for her newly formed company at Sadler's Wells Theatre in London. De Valois was always on the lookout for new talent, and never more so than when her young company lost its prima ballerina, Alicia Markova, who left in 1935 to lead a new company with the dancer Anton Dolin. During her training May caught the eye of de Valois, who first thought to groom her as Markova's successor. That distinction was bestowed instead on Margaret Hookham, later known as Margot Fonteyn. May became Fonteyn's close associate and lifelong friend, usually alternating with her in the principal roles in the main ballet classics, and sharing accommodation with her on tour.

May was already getting her first experience of solo roles, dancing the Prelude in *Les sylphides* while still a student paying her course fees at the Royal Academy of Dancing. Her formal début from the *corps de ballet* was in the prominent *pas de trois* in *Swan Lake* in its first production by the Sadler's Wells Company in 1934. Up to this point she had been billed in programmes as Doris May, but de Valois, who liked her solo dancers to have mellifluous names, decreed that Doris should choose a different first name. According to Mary Clarke's history of the company, 'after weeks of indecision', Doris decided that she would call herself Angela May and went to de Valois to announce her great decision, only to be told cheerfully, 'It's too late, dear. The programmes have been printed and you are down as Pamela' (Clarke, 80). So Pamela May she became for the rest of her long professional career. In her *Invitation to the Ballet* (1937), de Valois described her as 'beautifully made, a graceful and talented handful'. May quickly captivated audiences with her lyrical gaiety, stunning glamour, and immense charm.

From the first May was especially admired in ballet's equivalent of theatrical soubrette roles, notably the spirited and wily Swanilda in *Coppélia*. Indeed, Sir Peter Wright, director laureate of the Birmingham Royal Ballet, said that it was her performance in this role that motivated him to become a dancer: 'She always made dancing so exciting and such fun that I longed to be up there on the stage with her' (*The Stage*, 16 June 2005). Conscious of her femininity, she projected immense vitality across the footlights. According to several reports she favoured relaxation from the stage by engaging in strip-poker with her fellow players including, on occasion, Frederick Ashton, the dancers Robert Helpmann and Michael Somes, and the music director Constant Lambert. Yet at the same time May developed a purity of classical line and style that led Mary Clarke, in her account of the Sadler's Wells Ballet, to describe her as 'the most purely classical of English dancers' (Clarke, 204). Some of this quality no doubt derived from an interlude in Paris in 1935 when Fonteyn's

Pamela May (1917–2005), by Gordon Anthony, 1946

mother, prompted by friendship rather than potential rivalry, escorted her daughter, with May and June Brae (another prominent teenage ballerina in the company, with whom May had been paired as the Red Girls in Ashton's *Les patineurs*), to Paris to take classes with eminent émigré Russian ballerinas from the former St Petersburg Maryinsky company, Lubov Egorova, Mathilde Kschessinskaya, and Olga Preobrazhenska. This the girls managed to do without exceeding their very limited funds.

Another aspect of May's accomplishment was her skill in responding to new choreography. She had already shared with Fonteyn the role of the voluptuous Creole Girl in Ashton's *A Day in a Southern Port* (1931, later called *Rio Grande*) and he featured her again in *Le baiser de la fée* (1935) and *Apparitions* (1936). De Valois cast her in a solo role in *The Gods go a-Begging* (1936) and the next year gave her a created role as the warmly supportive Red Queen in her new ballet, *Checkmate*. Also that year May was praised for her appealing account of the forlorn Violet forever pursuing the timidly elusive Ernest in Ashton's *A Wedding Bouquet*. In his *Horoscope* (1938) the poetry of her curving *ports de bras* in the role of the Moon made a lasting impression. Other roles that brought her to wide attention included that of the eighteenth-century coquette Mlle Théodore in de Valois's *The Prospect before Us* (1940), a title of some irony as the shades of the Second World War closed in. Also in 1940 Ashton created his barefoot *Dante Sonata*, where May was given a memorably anguished solo, 'rocking back and forth in frustration and grief' (Anderson, 70). This wartime ballet was successfully revived with Pamela May's help by Birmingham Royal Ballet in 2001. Meanwhile the Sadler's Wells Company had in 1937 paid one of its regular visits to the Arts Theatre, Cambridge, where the prettiest girls were often invited to stay on to attend the May balls and where that year, by coincidence, both May and June Brae met future husbands at the same party. On 25 May 1940 May married, at All Souls' Church, Marylebone, Painton Sidney Cowen (1917/18–1942), a lieutenant in the Royal Marines, and son of Walter Painton Cowen, mining engineer. After her marriage May danced the beautiful Euridice in de Valois's *Orpheus and Euridice* (1941) and a sensuous duet, startling for its time, with Somes (a former lover) in Ashton's *The Wanderer* (1941). May took leave from the company to have a son, also named Painton, whose father was reported killed in action three weeks after the baby was born.

Eventually May felt again the call of the stage and returned to Sadler's Wells, first with the opera company, dancing in the circus divertissement of Smetana's *The Bartered Bride*. She subsequently responded to an invitation from de Valois to rejoin the ballet company, but found a lack of stamina inhibited her attempt at the full-length *Swan Lake*, which she then split instead with a newly rising young star, Moira Shearer. As May regained her strength she was once more cast in ballerina roles, and when the company reopened the Royal Opera House, Covent Garden, in 1946 with its production of *The Sleeping Beauty* in a run of continuous performances, May alternated night after night with Fonteyn as Aurora (as she did again during the company's groundbreaking first season in New York in 1949). Ashton too was keen to involve her in his new plans, and he took May to possibly the peak of her career when he cast her with Fonteyn and Shearer as the three ballerinas in his *Symphonic Variations* (1946), his first new ballet after his return from war service, which many consider his greatest work. His celebrated designer, Sophie Fedorovich, took May aside during rehearsals and said to her, 'Margot is dark, Moira is red and you are … mouse!' (Anderson, 93), persuading her to become blonde for more effective contrast at the first performance, a colouring May then retained. Ashton followed up May's success in this role by creating for her the role of the Fairy Godmother in *Cinderella* (1948), Ashton's first three-act ballet.

On 3 August 1946 May married Charles Howard Gordon, a civil servant, the host of the Cambridge party for the dancers six years previously. They had a daughter, Caroline, and May found lasting happiness in her marriage and in family life. After her marriage she enjoyed continuing success in the Royal Ballet for several years more as she moved into mature character roles like the Princess-Mother in *Swan Lake* and the Queen in *The Sleeping Beauty*. To all of these she brought an impressive dignity and forceful presence, and she was highly praised for preserving the style of traditional classic mime.

In 1954, after her retirement from the stage, May was a teacher at the Royal Ballet School until 1977. Her students respected and admired her authority and her meticulous care in the preparation of roles, which she liked to explore in depth, as well as her assurance of technique. She received the highest distinction in the British dance profession, the Queen Elizabeth II coronation award from the Royal Academy of Dancing, in 1976, and became a governor of the Royal Ballet companies and vice-president of the Royal Academy of Dancing. She was appointed OBE in 1998. She was a close and sympathetic companion to de Valois in the latter's failing health. She herself moved from London to Birmingham to be near her daughter. She died on 6 June 2005 at Selly Oak Hospital, Birmingham following a stroke. A service of thanksgiving was held at St Paul's Church, Covent Garden, on 19 September 2005. She was survived by both children. NOËL GOODWIN

Sources G. Davidson, *Ballet biographies* (1952) • M. Clarke, *The Sadler's Wells Ballet: a history and an appreciation* (1955) • G. Anthony, 'Pioneers of the Royal Ballet: Pamela May', *Dancing Times* (Jan 1971), 204 • A. Bland, *The Royal Ballet: the first 50 years* (1981) • *Daily Telegraph* (8 June 2005) • *The Times* (13 June 2005) • *The Guardian* (18 June 2005) • *The Independent* (20 June 2005) • Z. Anderson, *The Royal Ballet: 75 years* (2006) • personal knowledge (2009) • private information (2009) • m. certs. • d. cert.

Archives FILM BFINA, documentary footage; performance footage | SOUND BL NSA, documentary recordings

Likenesses Baron, photographs, 1940–46, Getty Images, London • G. Anthony, photogravure, 1946 (as Aurora in *The sleeping beauty*), NPG [*see illus.*] • G. Anthony, photographs, V&A • obituary photographs • photographs, Royal Opera House

Wealth at death £518,672: probate, 31 Aug 2005, *CGPLA Eng. & Wales*

Mayne, Michael Clement Otway (1929–2006), dean of Westminster, was born on 10 September 1929 at the rectory, Harlestone, Northamptonshire, the only son of Michael Ashton Otway Mayne, rector of Harlestone, and his wife, Sylvia Clementina Lumley, *née* Ellis. Reduced to penury by the sudden suicide of the father when Mayne was aged three, the family moved to London and then to Torbay, whence his mother was enabled by clergy charities to send him to King's School, Canterbury. There he disclosed his gift and enthusiasm for acting, and indeed stayed for an extra year in order to be able to play Hamlet in a school production. After national service in the RAF, in 1951 he went to Corpus Christi College, Cambridge, where his passion for the theatre found abundant scope, though to the detriment of a good class in English and theology. In fact he would have followed a career on the stage had not his former headmaster, Canon John Shirley, steered him towards ordination. Accordingly Mayne went to Cuddesdon Theological College in 1955 and was ordained priest in 1957.

After a curacy at the church of St John the Baptist, Harpenden, Mayne was appointed domestic chaplain to Mervyn Stockwood, who had recently become bishop of Southwark. There he encountered some of the progressive movements that were seeking to revive the parochial life of the Church of England. There too he met 28-year-

Michael Clement Otway Mayne (1929–2006), by unknown photographer

old Alison Geraldine McKie, daughter of Henry E. McKie, whom he married at Southwark Cathedral on 16 October 1965 and with whom he had a son and a daughter. In the same year he was appointed vicar of Norton, near Letchworth, Hertfordshire. In 1972 he was offered the post of head of religious programmes, BBC Radio. To this he brought his love of poetry and English literature, his enthusiasm for drama, and an instinctive concern for quality of editing and production. This experience in religious broadcasting made him a favoured candidate to be the vicar of Great St Mary's, the university church in Cambridge, where he worked from 1979 to 1986, developing a significant ministry, not just to undergraduates but to his clerical and lay colleagues in the university. He also compiled and published a small book for clergy, *Prayers for Pastoral Occasions* (1982).

The end of Mayne's time at Cambridge was deeply affected by the onset of chronic fatigue syndrome (ME), which forced him to take a year's leave, but which was also to inspire his first substantial book, *A Year Lost and Found* (1987), in which he chronicled the spiritual journey he had been forced to travel during this time. Meanwhile he had been offered appointment as dean of Westminster, and the ME was sufficiently in remission for him to be able to take it up in 1986, just in time to conduct the marriage of the duke and duchess of York.

Mayne's predecessor at Westminster, Edward Carpenter, had made the abbey well known for (sometimes controversial) ecumenical and inter-faith events. The changes Mayne made were, by contrast, primarily to do with the worship and pastoral ministry of the abbey: he devoted much attention to strengthening the 'family' sense of the large community of paid and unpaid workers, and he rearranged Sunday morning services so as to make the sung eucharist the principal service, conducted at a moveable altar below the sacrarium steps with (eventually) full eucharistic vestments. He also used to the full the opportunity the abbey offered to exploit and strengthen his ties with members of the acting profession, not only through their contributions as readers at memorial services, but by inviting them to choose and read their favourite poems at evening gatherings in the Jerusalem Chamber, thereby raising large sums of money for AIDS charities, a cause to which Mayne was deeply committed, along with work for refugees and the promotion of human rights. Shortly before his retirement he brought to completion the project that had been closest to his heart, the creation of a monument outside the west front of the abbey to all innocent victims of oppression, violence, and war, which was unveiled by the queen in 1996 in the presence of a poignant group of surviving victims.

While at Westminster Mayne had written another book, *This Sunrise of Wonder* (1995), in the form of reflective letters to his grandchildren. After his retirement in 1996 (when, as was customary, he was appointed KCVO) he moved to Salisbury, where he continued to raise money, often through theatrical ventures, for the Medical Foundation for the Care of Victims of Torture and other charities. He also wrote *Pray, Love, Remember* (1998), Lenten reflections based on experiences at the abbey, *Learning to Dance* (2001), the metaphor of dancing applied to literature, the natural world, and religion, and *The Enduring Melody* (2006), a deeply spiritual chronicle of his struggle with terminal cancer of the floor of the mouth, which was published shortly before his death at his home, 37 St Mark's Road, Salisbury, on 22 October 2006. The funeral was held at Salisbury Cathedral, and he was cremated at Salisbury crematorium on 3 November 2006, and survived by his wife and children. A memorial service was held on 1 February 2007 at Westminster Abbey. A. E. HARVEY

Sources *Daily Telegraph* (24 Oct 2006); (28 Oct 2006) · *The Times* (25 Oct 2006); (4 Nov 2006) · *The Independent* (28 Oct 2006) · J. Huffstetler, *Gratitude and grace: the writings of Michael Mayne* (2009) · Crockford (1957–2006) · *WW* (2006) · personal knowledge (2010) · private information (2010) · b. cert. · m. cert. · d. cert.

Archives Westminster Abbey Muniment Room, corresp. | SOUND BL NSA, current affairs recording · BL NSA, documentary recording · BL NSA, news recording · BL NSA, performance recording

Likenesses M. Noakes, oils, *c.*1993, Westminster Abbey, London, deanery · obituary photographs · photograph, Great St Mary's, Cambridge [*see illus.*] · photographs, PA Photos, London · photographs, Photoshot, London

Wealth at death under £206,000: probate, 13 April 2007, *CGPLA Eng. & Wales*

Mc. Names starting Mc— are alphabetized as though they started Mac—.

Meadows, Bernard William (1915–2005), sculptor, was born at 354 Unthank Road, Norwich, on 19 February 1915, the son of William Arthur Frederick Meadows, a solicitor's clerk, and later insurance clerk, and his wife, Ethel Maud, *née* Blowers. He attended the City of Norwich School, where he remembered art as 'the only thing I could do' (Woollcombe, tape 7). When he left school at the age of sixteen in the middle of the great depression he was persuaded by his father to take a secure job in an accountants' office. Finally, in 1934, he was allowed to enrol at Norwich School of Art.

In 1936, through a friend of his wood-engraving teacher, Meadows was introduced to the sculptor Henry Moore. As a result he was invited to become Moore's studio assistant, and worked for him during the holidays in Kent and Hertfordshire, on and off until the late 1940s, assisting with his carvings and early experiments in lead casting. They developed a strong relationship that lasted for fifty years. Through this connection, Meadows was introduced to avant-garde artistic circles, and was able to exhibit at the International Surrealist Exhibition held in London in 1936, alongside Moore and Pablo Picasso. Meadows was drawn to surrealism, a thread that underlies his entire oeuvre, but he preferred the work of Picasso, with 'its flickering nervousness', to that of Moore (Woollcombe, tape 103).

Later in 1936 Meadows moved from Norwich to London to study painting at Chelsea School of Art (1936–7), and then at the Royal College of Art (1938–40), where his education was interrupted soon after the outbreak of the Second World War. On 11 October 1939 he had married the 23-year-old Marjorie Winifred Payne, whom he had met at Norwich School of Art. She was the daughter of Albert Carswell Payne, schoolmaster. They made their first home in Moore's former studio in Hampstead, continuing to live in the area all their married life. They had two daughters.

Meadows had joined the Communist Party in the 1930s and, at the beginning of the war, declared himself a conscientious objector. However, he changed his mind in 1941, when Germany invaded Russia, and joined the Royal Air Force as part of the air–sea rescue squad. He saw little action, and suffered rather from boredom, though it was a formative period for his art. He was posted to India, Ceylon, and the Cocos Islands, in the Indian Ocean, where he spent his spare time painting and sketching. He became fascinated with the creatures of the Cocos Islands, particularly the giant crabs, which paraded menacingly along the beach, creating a 'sort of set up of fear', analogous in his eyes to human society (Woollcombe, tape 47). The crab, with its armoured exterior and soft interior, became a recurring theme in his work.

Meadows returned to the Royal College of Art in 1946, joining the sculpture course for his last year. Afterwards, he taught at Chelsea College of Art (1948–60), and occasionally at the Bath Academy of Art, Corsham Court (1955–7). In the 1950s and 1960s he made a series of sculptures of 'cocks', 'crabs' and dead birds, which he described as 'human substitutes … vehicles expressing my feelings about human beings', appearing variously as 'hysterical' and 'domineering' (Robertson). Together with his Chelsea students Elizabeth Frink and Robert Clatworthy he was important in the revival of interest in animal sculpture in post-war Britain. He was an accomplished and prolific draughtsman, who developed his sculpture through his drawing. However, after his student days he never drew from life. Throughout his career he almost obsessively worked and reworked a few chosen themes, allowing the forms to emerge through the drawing process.

Meadows rose to fame at the Venice Biennale of 1952, where he was selected to represent Britain alongside his contemporaries Eduardo Paolozzi, William Turnbull, Robert Adams, and Kenneth Armitage, as well as Moore. Though ultimately a disparate group, the younger artists were heralded as the successors to Moore and Hepworth by the art critic Herbert Read, who described their work as depicting 'excoriated flesh, frustrated sex, the geometry of fear' (Read, introduction to *New Aspects of British Sculpture*, British Council, 1952). Meadows went on to have a series of solo shows at Gimpel Fils, London, and Paul Rosenberg, New York, in the late 1950s and 1960s, and produced a massive bronze, *The Spirit of Trade Unionism*, for the entrance to the Trades Union Congress's headquarters, Congress House, in Great Russell Street, London.

The turning point in Meadows's career came when he was appointed professor of sculpture at the Royal College of Art (1960–80). Under his direction, sculptors as diverse as Nigel Hall, Martin Naylor, William Pye, and Tony Cragg graduated from the department. Meadows became a leader of his profession, serving on public bodies such as the Arts Council's art panel and the royal fine art commission, and acting as governor for schools of art at Norwich, Chelsea, Corsham, and Bristol. Nevertheless, he remained a modest and retiring man: a sceptic and not fundamentally 'a joiner in' (Woollcombe, tape 93). The 1960s and 1970s were also a productive period for Meadows's own work, as he had studio space at the Royal College and established an in-house foundry. He preferred bronze casting to carving, though he often worked over the surfaces of his plaster models. He was closely involved in the casting of his work and almost always patinated and polished it himself, as he became increasingly interested in qualities of surface.

In the early 1960s, following a visit to Florence, Meadows turned to the human figure in his work with a series of 'armed' figures and busts. These were images of bullies, inspired by Renaissance statues of Roman emperors and military leaders, with such titles as *Augustus*, *Brutus*, and *Personnage très important*. He described them as 'armoured, aggressive, protected, but inside the safety of the shell, completely soft and vulnerable' (Bowness, 15). He developed the seated 'armed' figures into pointing figures, inspired by a photograph of the film director Luchino Visconti. These became the vehicle for another change: from the dark, craggy surfaces of his earlier bronzes, to the bright, smooth finishes of his later works, like *Help* (1966) and *Lovers* (1980). From the mid-1960s his sculpture had a more erotic charge, with soft, bulbous forms, appearing as fruit, eyes, and other body parts, encased within or squeezed between other harder, more angular shapes. In 1967 he executed thirty-four etchings and a box for an edition of Samuel Beckett's *Molloy* (1951), sharing the author's interest in existentialism.

Meadows was the only British sculptor at the Venice Biennale in 1964, and in the 1970s he had solo shows in Paris, London, and Tokyo. He was selected for key group shows including 'Sculpture of the 1970s', at the Royal Academy, London, in 1972. Throughout his career he accepted relatively few commissions, preferring to concentrate on his own work. His major public sculpture of this period was for the new headquarters of Eastern Counties Newspapers in his native Norwich in 1969–70.

After retiring from the Royal College in 1980 Meadows became closely involved with the Henry Moore Foundation, serving as acting director from 1983 to 1988. In this late period he focused mostly on drawing. He had a major retrospective at the Yorkshire Sculpture Park in 1995. He lived latterly in Belsize Grove, Hampstead, and died at the Royal Free Hospital, Camden, on 12 January 2005, of an internal haemorrhage. He was survived by his wife and daughters. SOPHIE RAIKES

Sources B. Robertson, *Recent sculpture by Bernard Meadows* (London, Gimpel Fils, 1959) • *Bernard Meadows: recent sculpture, February–March, 1963* (London, Gimpel Fils, 1963) • G. Fils, *Bernard Meadows: recent works* (London, Gimpel Fils, 1967) • W. Strachan, *Bernard Meadows: drawings for sculpture* (Taranman, London, 1975) • F. Giacomoni and others, *Meadows* (Paris, Galanis, 1977) • *Bernard Meadows at the Royal College of Art, 1960–1980* (1980) • A. Bowness, *Bernard Meadows: sculpture and drawing* (1995) • P. Curtis, *Bernard Meadows* (1995) • *The Times* (14 Jan 2005); (19 Jan 2005) • *The Guardian* (15 Jan 2005) • *Daily Telegraph* (15 Jan 2005) • *The Independent* (17 Jan 2005) • *WW* (2005) • BL NSA, National Life Story Collection, artists' lives, interview with Tamsyn Woollcombe, 1992 • b. cert. • m. cert. • d. cert.

Archives SOUND BL NSA, National Life Story Collection, artists' lives, interviews with T. Woollcombe, 3, 10, 17, 20, 26 Nov, 15 Dec 1992, F2999–F3010 • BL NSA, documentary recording

Likenesses Snowdon, photograph, 1964, Camera Press, London • A.-K. Purkiss, bromide fibre print, 1994, NPG • obituary photographs

Wealth at death £233,892: probate, 24 June 2005, *CGPLA Eng. & Wales*

Medawar [*née* Taylor], **Jean Shinglewood**, **Lady Medawar** (**1913–2005**), campaigner for family planning, was born the single survivor of twins on 7 February 1913 at 36 Earls Court Square, Kensington, London, the first of three surviving children of Charles Henry Shinglewood Taylor (1882–1935), general practitioner, and his wife, Katherine Leslie, *née* Paton, who came from a family of cotton traders based in Liverpool and Washington, DC. She was brought up in Cambridge. Her father had a distinguished military record as a medical officer at Gallipoli. Her mother had been deaf since childhood and was described as reclusive yet suffering periods of hyperactivity. Jean's aunt, Mary (her mother's elder sister), had inherited a large part of the Paton cotton fortune, and was a dominant influence on Jean's family and her upbringing and paid for her schooling: middle-class Edwardian values were inculcated and adhered to. After attending Benenden School in Kent she won a scholarship to read zoology at Somerville College, Oxford, where Solly Zuckerman was her tutor. She graduated with a third-class degree in 1936.

At Oxford Jean Taylor met Peter Brian *Medawar (1915–1987), a brilliant, good-looking zoology student, the

Brazilian-born son of a Lebanese commercial agent and his English wife. Jean's declared intention to marry him evoked strong, prejudiced resistance: Peter had neither 'background' nor money, and would not be received into society; her mother warned of the danger of having 'coloured' babies; Aunt Mary stopped her personal allowance. They nevertheless married in Oxford on 27 February 1937, and during the war Jean kept house in Banbury Road, where the first of their four children was born. In the summer of 1940 a twin-engine bomber crashed into their neighbour's garden, a devastating experience for the whole family. The pilot survived with 60 per cent burns and Peter, who was then working in Howard Florey's laboratory, was asked to see the patient, to offer any bright ideas to save his life. He later admitted that this striking event turned him towards transplantation biology. That sudden change of academic direction permanently changed Jean's life too: until his illness in 1969 her husband's compulsive commitment to research in immunology and to science (which won him a Nobel prize in 1960 and a knighthood in 1965, besides many other honours) gave him relatively little time for his family. His promotion to professor at Birmingham in 1947 and University College, London, in 1951 brought Jean a busy social life among a rapidly expanding circle of scientists who came to work with him, and she undertook many foreign visits with him.

Following an insightful tour to Russia in 1955 Jean Medawar started work in a family planning clinic in Islington and subsequently as public relations officer for the Family Planning Association (FPA). She got to know Margaret Pyke, the chairwoman, and her son David Pyke, intimately, the latter a productive relationship that continued for more than forty years. On Margaret Pyke's death in 1967 Jean Medawar succeeded her as the second chairwoman of the FPA. Influenced by her friend Barbara Ward, she brought to the field a new emphasis on sustainable development, conservation, and population control in the face of 'the natural conspiracy in favour of fecundity' (P. Medawar and J. Medawar, *Aristotle to Zoos*, 1983, 218). Her primary message was that exponential population growth would cause overcrowding, drought, and starvation, that people had to act responsibly to control birth rates, and that this message had to be taught at all levels of society, starting with the children.

Jean Medawar had unusual skill in enlisting famous and influential supporters of the FPA. One vote of thanks began, 'As all of you know, Jean is remarkably good at letting other people get her own way' (private information). By 1967 she and David Pyke had set up the Margaret Pyke Centre for Training in Family Planning. In 1981 she founded Common Ground International, 'a group of leaders who work … towards keeping a balance between people and resources' (*The Guardian*, 10 May 2005), which hosted a major exhibition in the Natural History Museum. For *Lifeclass*, an audio-visual pack based on Ward's *Only One Earth* (1972), she quickly persuaded a galaxy of bishops, scientists, artists, and naturalists to back the project, and the commentary was spoken by Sir Peter Scott, David Bellamy, and David Attenborough. On a trip abroad, while planning an updated videotape for *Lifeclass*, she 'accidentally' tripped over the outstretched legs of John Cleese, whom she then persuaded to support the production of the tape, and to appear as lead actor in it. She retired from the chair of the FPA in 1975.

In 1969 Peter Medawar suffered a physically incapacitating stroke, the first of several which eventually caused his death in 1987. For nineteen years she supported him and fought for him as he continued writing a series of seminal books and lectures on immunology and the philosophy of science. At international conferences and in their large circle of friends the pair were revered for their tenacious determination, he a tall figure, bent but dignified, she a graceful yet resilient helpmate, always clearing his path, organizing his transport, and helping him prepare and deliver his lectures. They both continued to enjoy the company of many leading intellectuals and musicians at their home in Hampstead and abroad. Together they wrote several publications, including *Aristotle to Zoos: a Philosophical Dictionary of Zoology* (1983). Jean Medawar described her life with Peter in her remarkable autobiography, *A Very Decided Preference* (1990), which complemented his own life history, *Memoir of a Thinking Radish* (1986). Together the stories described a rare personal and intellectual synergism. They were united by a conviction of the need for progress (a theme that recurred constantly in their writings) and a steadfast refusal to bow to adversity.

After her husband's death Jean Medawar continued to write, and in 2000 published, with David Pyke, *Hitler's Gift: Scientists Who Fled Nazi Germany*, which illustrated vividly the loss to Germany and gain to Britain and other countries that resulted from Hitler's antisemitic policies. She died at the Royal Free Hospital, Camden, London, on 3 May 2005, of bronchopneumonia following a stroke, and was survived by her four children (two sons and two daughters). She was buried at Alfriston churchyard, Sussex, on 17 May. ROBERT SELLS

Sources P. B. Medawar, *Memoir of a thinking radish* (1986) • J. Medawar, *A very decided preference: life with Peter Medawar* (1990) • *The Guardian* (10 May 2005) • *The Independent* (12 May 2005) • *Daily Telegraph* (13 May 2005) • personal knowledge (2009) • private information (2009) • b. cert. • d. cert.

Likenesses obituary photographs • photograph, repro. in *BMJ* (11 June 2005)

Wealth at death £189,413: probate, 17 Oct 2005, *CGPLA Eng. & Wales*

Megarry, Sir Robert Edgar (1910–2006), judge and jurist, was born on 1 June 1910 at 25 Woodstock Road, Croydon, Surrey, the elder son of Robert Lindsay Megarry (*d.* 1952), civil servant, and his wife, Irene Marion Edgar, *née* Clark (*d.* 1929), daughter of Major-General Edgar Gibson Clark of the Bengal staff corps. His father, whose family came from Belfast, read law at Trinity Hall, Cambridge, was called to the bar by the Inner Temple, and briefly practised as a barrister in Lincoln's Inn before becoming a civil servant, first at the Board of Education and then in the Air Ministry, ending his career as an assistant secretary.

Megarry, known to his friends as Ted, was educated at Lancing College, to which he remained devoted throughout his life, later serving as president of the Lancing Club and long-standing chairman of the Friends of Lancing Chapel. Before going to Trinity Hall in 1929 he taught briefly at a preparatory school, where he discovered his liking for teaching and innovatively required his pupils to answer questionnaires about his effectiveness as a teacher. He read law at Cambridge, but found the course dull and uninspiring, gaining only a third in part one, a lower second in part two of the law tripos and a third in the LLB, preferring such wider pursuits as playing football and tennis for his college, learning to fly, and being *Varsity*'s first music critic (writing under a pseudonym to hide his activities from his supervisor). In 1935 he qualified as a solicitor after studying with the law 'crammers' Gibson and Weldon, who took pride in the quality of their teaching and whose staff he joined as a lecturer. In 1939 he published his first book, *An Introduction to the Rent Acts*, in later much expanded editions (eleven were published) renamed *The Rent Acts*. In 1939–40 he taught undergraduates as a member of the Cambridge law faculty. Rejected for military service on medical grounds he spent the Second World War as a civil servant, rising to assistant secretary in the Ministry of Supply. On 14 November 1936 he had married Iris Davies, a local government official, and daughter of Elias Lawson Davies, wholesale clothing merchant, of Neath, Glamorgan. They had three daughters.

In 1941 Megarry chose a new career. He had his name removed from the roll of solicitors and joined Lincoln's Inn. In 1944 he was awarded a certificate of honour in his bar finals and was called to the bar. From 1946 (when he left the civil service) until 1967 he practised as a chancery barrister, acquiring a substantial practice in new areas of the law such as town and country planning. However, he also continued teaching and writing. From 1944 to 1947 he was director of the Law Society's refresher courses. In 1946–7 he was a sub-lector at Trinity College, Cambridge, and from 1946 to 1967 he taught bar students as reader in equity for the Council of Legal Education. He lectured solicitors and civil servants on planning law. He was a visiting professor and lecturer at numerous universities in the USA and Canada. Among his many lectures in England, in 1962 he gave the Hamlyn lectures, published as *Lawyer and Litigant in England*. In 1946 he had produced *A Manual of the Law of Real Property*. It was primarily intended for 'the examination candidate whose main anxiety is not whether he will head the list but whether he will appear in it at all'. It was popular with students: by 2002 eight editions had been published. His other writings reached a wider readership. In 1947 he became the editor of the twenty-third edition of *Snell's Equity*. Having never seen a book on equity bring a happy smile to a reader's lips, he hoped to 'smooth away some frowns' by reorganizing and enlivening that standard textbook. He co-edited (with Paul Baker) five further editions. Even the index grabbed attention, with entries such as 'Fornication, pre-marital' and 'O.K., meaning of'. In 1957 he produced with William Wade his most famous textbook, *The Law of Real Property*. As was explained in the preface this attempted to state the English law of real property in a form both intelligible to students and helpful to practitioners. The book was user-friendly: it contained a glossary and stated clearly the principles on which the law had developed. It was an immediate success, frequently cited forensically in the authors' lifetimes, despite the rule that books only become authoritative after their authors' deaths. They produced four further editions before relinquishing responsibility for the sixth edition. From 1939 Megarry wrote numerous articles and case notes, many brilliant in their succinct analysis, for the *Law Quarterly Review*, of which he was assistant editor and book review editor. One critical review of a Court of Appeal decision in *Hankey* v. *Clavering* (1942) was relied on more than fifty years later by a law lord, Lord Steyn, to overrule that decision. All his writings were distinguished by their scholarly exposition and their comprehensibility. Such was his reputation as a legal scholar that in 1965 he was elected president of the Society of Public Teachers of Law and in 1970 a fellow of the British Academy.

Megarry's overbusy life nearly led to his professional ruin. He was prosecuted in 1954 for making false income tax statements, having omitted to declare some of his sources of income. This was a high-profile case, with the solicitor-general leading for the prosecution, Megarry's defence counsel being Gilbert Paull. The Old Bailey judge directed the jury that the case should be stopped unless they were certain that Megarry had known that the returns were false. The case was duly stopped and Megarry acquitted.

This brush with the law did not stop Megarry's progress in the profession. In 1956 he was appointed queen's counsel and in 1967 he was elevated to the High Court bench as a chancery judge, receiving the traditional knighthood. He had no qualms about hearing cases involving points on which he might have expressed views as an author. He was always prepared to be persuaded. As he put it, 'argued law is tough law'. In 1976 he became the vice-chancellor of the Chancery Division, and was sworn of the privy council in 1978. In the late 1970s he was offered promotion to the Court of Appeal but declined. By reason of a statutory rearrangement of the courts in 1982 he became the vice-chancellor of the Supreme Court and an *ex officio* member of the Court of Appeal, but chose not to sit in that court. He retired in 1985 on reaching the statutory retirement age but sat in the judicial committee of the privy council until he reached the age of eighty.

As a judge Megarry dealt with many of the important cases of the day brought in the Chancery Division. In addition to the standard fare for chancery judges of that time relating to trusts, tax, company law, bankruptcy and property, he resolved disputes involving trade unions (for example *Chappell* v. *Times Newspapers*, 1975), the domicile of Errol Flynn (*Re Flynn deceased*, 1968), equitable remedies for breach of confidence (*Coco* v. *Clark*, 1969), telephone-tapping before the incorporation into English law of the

European convention on human rights (*Malone* v. *Metropolitan Police Commissioner*, 1979), the exercise of investment powers by the National Union of Mineworkers' pension fund trustees (*Cowan* v. *Scargill*, 1985), and land rights of the Banaban inhabitants of Ocean Island, from which phosphate was extracted (*Tito* v. *Waddell, no. 2*, 1977). His conduct of the hearing of the Ocean Island case, which lasted a then record 206 days, exemplified his patience as a judge and his belief that the most important person in court was the litigant who would leave the court unsuccessful. At the islanders' request he went on a gruelling journey to the Pacific to view Ocean Island. He delivered his judgment, written in his small, neat hand, orally for two and a half days. It occupies over 240 pages of the law reports and is a repository of erudite learning. A traditionalist by nature, he was no bold innovator in the law. Thus, in *Uppal* v. *Home Office* (1978), he was resistant to the logic of the procedural rules relating to judicial review that required the Chancery Division to relinquish its jurisdiction as an occasional forum for administrative law cases. However, in one case, *Ross* v. *Caunters* (1980), his strong instinct for justice led him to fashion a remedy for a testamentary beneficiary, the gift to whom was defeated through the negligence of the testator's solicitor; the House of Lords in a subsequent case (*White* v. *Jones*, 1995) was to support the result but by a different route. He sought by his judgments to bring clarity and order to the law. Written in a style commanding attention, they were notable for their lucidity, their scholarly treatment of precedent, their meticulous findings of the facts, and their careful analysis of the arguments. He was rarely reversed.

Lord Scarman, in introducing Megarry delivering the 1977 Child & Co. lecture (on judges and judging), described him as 'the legal universal man', being a 'teacher … a writer … a judge, and above all … a wit'. A humorous man, Megarry enjoyed collecting legal anecdotes to produce in 1955 *Miscellany-at-Law*, 'a diversion for lawyers and others'. A *Second Miscellany* followed in 1973 and in 2005 he produced a third in the series, *A New Miscellany-at-Law* (with the help of Bryan Garner). In 1969 he also published *Arabinesque-at-Law*, containing utterances of the eccentric Serjeant Arabin at the Old Bailey in the 1840s. In 1972 for the Selden Society he wrote *Inns Ancient and Modern*. Of particular delight to him in the Ocean Island case was the chance discovery of a judgment of Sir Salathiel Lovell, to whose judicial career Megarry enjoyed referring; Lovell, when appointed a baron of the exchequer in 1708, was nearly eighty.

Megarry's professional distinction led him to be appointed a member of the lord chancellor's law reform committee from 1952 to 1973 and a consultant to the BBC's *Law in Action* series from 1953 to 1966, his broadcast talks evidencing his ability to communicate to the ordinary man. He was chairman of the Notting Hill Housing Trust in 1967–8, treasurer of Lincoln's Inn in 1981, and, as an enthusiastic and knowledgeable oenophile, chairman of the inn's wine committee for over twenty years. His inn's affection for him was demonstrated by the commissioning (from Anthony Morris) of a portrait of him in 2001. His high standing in and services to the law were recognized by the University of Cambridge in making him an LLD in 1959 and by his college in appointing him an honorary fellow of Trinity Hall in 1973. He also received honorary doctorates from London and several other universities. He died at the Royal Free Hospital, London, of heart failure, on 11 October 2006 at the end of a career described by a reviewer of his last book as 'unmatched in its distinction, breadth and diversity' (S. Cretney, *Law Quarterly Review*, 123, 2007, 165). He was survived by his three daughters, his wife, Iris, having predeceased him in 2001. PETER GIBSON

Sources *The Times* (16 Oct 2006) • *Daily Telegraph* (17 Oct 2006) • *The Guardian* (19 Oct 2006) • *The Independent* (26 Oct 2006) • M. Nourse, memorial service address, Lincoln's Inn chapel, 12 March 2007 • S. Cretney, 'Sir Robert Megarry', *PBA*, VII (2008) • Burke, *Peerage* • *WW* (2006) • personal knowledge (2010) • private information (2010) • b. cert. • m. cert. • d. cert.

Likenesses W. Dring, group portrait, oils, 1981, Lincoln's Inn, London • A. Morris, oils, 2001, Lincoln's Inn, London • obituary photographs

Wealth at death £1,796,330: probate, 4 May 2007, *CGPLA Eng. & Wales*

Megaw, Arthur Hubert Stanley [Peter] (1910–2006), architectural historian and archaeologist, was born on 20 July 1910 at Portobello House nursing home, South Richmond Street, Dublin, the second of the four sons of Arthur Stanley Megaw (*d.* 1961), solicitor, of Ternanage, Castle Park, Belfast, and his wife, Helen Isabel Bertha (Mimi), *née* Smith (1877–1962). He was educated at Campbell College, Belfast (1924–8), and read architecture at Peterhouse, Cambridge (1928–31). After graduating, with no immediate professional prospects, he moved in 1931 to the British School at Athens to work on Byzantine architecture. His early publications on particular churches (for example 'The chronology of some middle Byzantine churches', published in the *Annual of the British School at Athens* for 1931–2) remained well regarded many years later. Unexpected responsibilities in the school brought out his administrative gifts; for a time in 1936 he became acting director. Later that year he was appointed director of antiquities, Cyprus. In 1937 he married the artist Elektra Elena Mangoletsi (1905–1993), daughter of Helias Mangoletsi, of Koritsa, Albania. There were no children of the marriage.

In 1935 the British administration in Cyprus enacted a new antiquities law, creating a government department of antiquities to replace the former museum committee and curatorship of antiquities, largely to ensure improved care of the island's standing monuments. The first director found ambivalent support, and soon resigned. Megaw, who succeeded him, was either more robust, or better treated, or both. An embryonic department was already in place. He developed it to administer the museums, excavations, monuments, publications, private collections, and dealers across the whole island. Leaving pre-Christian archaeology and museums to the capable Porphyrios Dikaios, curator of the Cyprus Museum, Megaw concentrated on early Christian and later antiquities, including virtually all standing monuments. Helped initially by an expert from the Ancient Monuments Board in London, he assembled and trained a permanent monuments staff for the repair and consolidation needed by so many buildings. Much of the necessary extra funding had been raised by Lord Mersey's Cyprus Committee. Besides work on many churches—re-roofing, consolidating masonry, and conserving wall paintings, for which years later, in 1995, he received the Society of Antiquaries' Frend medal—his major concerns were Lusignan and Venetian monuments, including the fortifications of Nicosia and Famagusta and the buildings within them, the northern mountain castles, the fortress of Kyrenia, and Bellapais Monastery. He repaired their fabric, improved their ambience, and secured them from future development. This, his greatest achievement, was barely chronicled outside the official *Annual Report of the Director of Antiquities*. He was appointed CBE in 1951.

Megaw's administration was too good for him to be left undisturbed. There was secondment during the Second World War, involving visits to Palestine. In 1950 he was loaned to Egypt to report on an excavated fifth- to seventh-century basilican church at Hermopolis Magna, in the ruins of a Ptolemaic shrine. (The resulting report, written with A. J. B. Wace, was published in 1959.) Following the earthquake of 1953 he worked for the Paphos Earthquake Reconstruction Committee, resiting villages and designing earthquake-resistant homes. He had other duties during some of the EOKA insurgency (1955–8). In 1956 came military occupation of Famagusta's monuments during the Suez crisis.

The early 1950s brought two young Cypriot graduates to new curatorial posts. They lightened both Megaw's and Dikaios's workloads. Megaw could begin his own projects. He became expert in Byzantine and medieval ceramics. With A. I. Dikigoropoulos in 1952–6 he cleared three early Christian basilicas at Cape Drepanon in west Cyprus. In 1956 and 1958 at Kourion he revived the excavation of an early Christian episcopal church and its ancillary buildings, discontinued twenty years before by an American expedition. In 1957–9, at Saranda Kolones, Paphos, he started the excavation of an early Lusignan castle, destroyed by earthquake in 1222.

In 1960 Cyprus became independent and Megaw retired from his department. After a short spell at Dumbarton Oaks in Washington, DC, and working at the Byzantine Institute in Istanbul he became director of the British School at Athens. His directorship, lasting from 1962 to 1968, was a happy and successful period for the Megaws, and for the school. He found the company of young postgraduates stimulating and the regular presence of his academic peers congenial, providing an atmosphere that had been largely missing in Cyprus. He travelled widely to visit the school's field projects, and some of his architectural haunts of the early 1930s. He completed studies initiated then (including 'The Skripou screen', published in the *Annual of the British School at Athens* in 1967), pursued his ceramic interest (resulting in articles such as 'Zeuxippos ware', published in the *Annual* in 1968), and supervised building additions in Athens and the completion of the Stratigraphic Museum at Knossos. He experienced the early months of the Greek military government of 1967–74. He did not forget Cyprus: in 1966–7 he returned, with sponsorship from the British School at Athens, to the Paphos Castle excavation.

After Megaw's unexpectedly early retirement from the British School at Athens in 1968, he and Elektra moved between Athens (in the winter), Cyprus (in spring and autumn), and Hampstead (in high summer). He wrote, continued his Kourion and Paphos excavations, and studied his material. While director of antiquities in Cyprus, he had preserved and closely studied the mosaic-decorated apses of two early Christian basilicas, the greater part of both of which had been reconstructed much later. In 1977, with E. J. W. Hawkins, he published a magisterial study of one of them, *The Church of the Panagia Kanakaria of Lythrankomi … its mosaics and frescoes*. (He failed to see a similar volume on the church of the Panagia Angeloktistos at Kition through to publication before his death.) Funded by Dumbarton Oaks (in 1970 and 1971) and Boston College (in 1981–4), he finished work on Paphos Castle. After preliminary reports (for example 'Excavations at Saranda Kolones, Paphos', published in the *Report of the Department of Antiquities, Cyprus* in 1971) he entrusted publication to a younger colleague.

The Kourion excavation was completed in 1974–9. Though from 1985 Megaw was free to prepare the final publication, progress was slowed by his need to care for his wife. When she died in 1993 his own health was deteriorating. On his ninetieth birthday he was presented with a Festschrift, *Mosaic* (2001), edited by Judith Herrin, Margaret Mullett, and Catherine Otten-Froux. He collapsed soon afterwards, never fully recovering. A close family friend helped him with the proofs of *Kourion* and (up to 2004) visits to Cyprus. He died of cancer in his London home, 27 Perrins Walk, Hampstead, on 28 June 2006, and was cremated on 20 July at Golders Green crematorium. His *Kourion* appeared the following year. H. W. Catling

Sources *Annual Report of the British School at Athens* (1932–68); H. W. Catling and G. B. Waywell (2005–6), 60–62 · *Annual Report of the Director of Antiquities, Cyprus* (1948–59) · H. Waterhouse, *The British School at Athens: the first hundred years* (1986) · J. Herrin, M. Mullett, and C. Otten-Froux, eds., *Mosaic: Festschrift for A. H. S. Megaw* (2001) [introduction; bibliography] · *The Times* (4 May 2006) · J. Rosser, *American Journal of Archaeology*, 111 (2007), 151–4 · H. W. Catling, 'A. H. S. Megaw: a memoir', *Annual Report of the British School at Athens*, 102 (2007), 1–10 · *WW* (2006) · personal knowledge (2010) · private information (2010) [Ted Megaw, nephew; S. Meade; H. Hughes Brock; Peterhouse, Cambridge] · b. cert. · d. cert.

Likenesses photograph, 2002, repro. in http://www.qub.ac.uk/schools/ByzantineStudies/NewsandEvents/OpeningoftheBenefactorsLibrary · N. Clarke, pencil sketch, repro. in Catling, *BSA* (2007), 2 · photograph, repro. in *The Times* (4 Aug 2006) · photograph, repro. in Waterhouse, *British School*, 45 · photograph, repro. in Herrin, Mullett, and Otten-Froux, *Mosaic*, frontispiece · photograph, repro. in *Americal Journal of Archaeology* (2007), 151

Wealth at death £1,607,175: probate, 27 April 2007, *CGPLA Eng. & Wales*

Mellers, Wilfrid Howard (1914–2008), composer and musicologist, was born on 26 April 1914 at Leamington

Spa, Warwickshire, the only child of Percy Wilfrid Mellers (1880/81–1947), schoolteacher, and his wife, Hilda Maria, *née* Lawrence (1881–1965). He attended Leamington College and in 1933 went to Cambridge as a scholar at Downing College, where he read English, before graduating with a first-class degree in 1936. He took a second degree in music while also studying composition with Egon Wellesz and Edmund Rubbra at Oxford. He taught at Dartington Hall from 1938 to 1940 and on 26 September 1940 married Vera Muriel Hobbs (*b*. 1913), daughter of Augustus Herbert Hobbs, rating officer. During the Second World War he was a conscientious objector, and worked on the land.

Mellers returned to Downing College as supervisor in English and college lecturer in music in 1945. At Cambridge he had come under the influence of F. R. Leavis and contributed to his hard-hitting literary periodical *Scrutiny* as author and (from 1942) board member. For some years he also lodged with the Leavises. From 1948 to 1964 he was staff tutor in music in the extramural department at Birmingham University. On 18 March 1950, following a divorce, he married the singer Peggy Pauline Lewis (*b*. 1922), daughter of William Lester Lewis, coachbuilder. They had two daughters; he also had another daughter by an earlier relationship.

Mellers was visiting Andrew Mellon professor of music in the University of Pittsburgh from 1960 to 1962, which gave him the impetus to write his classic study of American music, *Music in a New Found Land* (1964). In the same year as the book was published he was recruited to launch the music department at York University. As professor of music and head of the music department at York until 1981 he exerted an enormous influence on several generations of British musicians. His department was a beacon of enlightenment as new universities were being founded and it was necessary to redefine the teaching of music. Unlike most British university music departments, then dominated by musicologists, York started with a faculty of young composers including Peter Aston, David Blake, Bernard Rands, and Robert Sherlaw Johnson, later joined by John Paynter. The curriculum also gave performance a high place. Mellers's starting point was that music was not music until it was heard and so there should be no separation between theory and practice. He put contemporary ideas at the centre of his new department; brought music for young people into the curriculum; and was open to all kinds of musical expression, anticipating the pluralism and multi-culturalism of the twenty-first century rather than the inherited distinctions between highbrow and lowbrow. The centre of all this was Mellers himself, whose lecturing technique was charismatic. Some of his early articles for *Scrutiny* were criticized for their excessively enthusiastic tone. Mellers retorted that a reputation for critical rigour was more easily gained through a negative approach than his own positive and inclusive attitude. For more than sixty years afterwards everything he did was characterized by his affirmative outlook. He developed a technique based on applied historical knowledge often derived from the study of literature, using the context to inform understanding of the work itself. To him, music was not just notes to be played, but emanated from people.

Throughout his career and long into his retirement Mellers produced a steady stream of books and articles which made him one of the most readable and stimulating writers on music in the second half of the twentieth century. He published the first study of François Couperin in 1950; he recognized the seminal significance of Erik Satie; and was the first British writer to consider American music of all kinds. He raised eyebrows when, as a British university professor, he wrote *Twilight of the Gods: the Beatles in Retrospect* (1973). Undeterred, he followed it with *A Darker Shade of Pale: a Backdrop to Bob Dylan* (1984) and *Angels of the Night: Popular Female Singers of our Time* (1986). His mainstream interests were represented by books on music and society as well as monographs such as *Bach and the Dance of God* (1980), *Beethoven and the Voice of God* (1983), *Vaughan Williams and the Vision of Albion* (1989), *Percy Grainger* (1992), and *Francis Poulenc* (1993), as well as studies of less familiar figures such as Frederic Mompou (1989). *Between Old Worlds and New* (1997) was an anthology of his critical writings from some of the leading periodicals, selected by John Paynter; it was followed in 2002 by *Celestial Music: Some Masterpieces of European Religious Music*.

Another dimension of Mellers was always his own music, though it was sometimes overshadowed by his other activities. As a result of his American experience, he saw music whole, incorporating jazz, pop, and ethnic traditions. A major landmark from this point of view was his extravaganza, *Yeibichai*, commissioned by the BBC for the 1969 Proms. It was vintage 1960s, with a coloratura soprano, a scat singer, an improvising jazz trio, orchestra, and tape.

Mellers's honours included a DMus from Birmingham in 1960 and an honorary DPhil from City University in 1982, the year he was appointed OBE. He was made an honorary fellow of Downing College in 2001. After his second divorce in 1975 he met Robin Stephanie Hildyard (*b*. 1931), former wife of Robert C. T. Hildyard and daughter of Robert Henry Scanes Spicer, businessman; they married on 17 July 1987, which gave him the security he needed in his final years. He died on 16 May 2008 at The Granary, Plaster Pitts Farm, Scrayingham, Malton, Yorkshire, of heart disease. He was survived by his wife, Robin, and his three daughters. PETER DICKINSON

Sources *New Grove*, 2nd edn, 16 (2001), 349–52 · *The Guardian* (19 May 2008) · *The Independent* (19 May 2008) · *The Times* (20 May 2008) · *Daily Telegraph* (23 May 2008) · *WW* (2008) · personal knowledge (2012) · private information (2012) · b. cert. · m. certs. [1940, 1950, 1987] · d. cert.

Archives Borth Inst., papers | FILM BFINA, documentary footage | SOUND BL NSA, documentary recordings

Likenesses obituary photographs · photographs, Lebrecht Music and Arts Photo Library, London

Wealth at death £343,604: probate, 24 Oct 2008, *CGPLA Eng. & Wales*

Melly, (Alan) George Heywood (1926–2007), writer and singer, was born on 17 August 1926 at The Grange, St Michael's Hamlet, Toxteth, Liverpool, the elder son and eldest of three children of Francis Heywood Melly (1900–

(Alan) **George Heywood Melly** (1926–2007), by Maggi Hambling, 1998

1961), wool broker, and his wife, Edith Maud (Maudie), *née* Isaac (1891–1983). At the time of his birth registration his parents lived at 26 Linnet Lane, Liverpool. His father was a businessman who would rather have been a hunter and an angler. He later advised his son: 'Always do what you want to. I never did' (*The Times*, 17 Dec 2003). Melly's Jewish mother, to whom he owed his early love of theatre and music hall, was aspirational on her son's behalf. 'She wanted me to be Noël Coward, which may be why I imitate him so much' (*The Independent*, 8 Nov 1997).

Sent as a boarder to Stowe School, Melly came home 'spouting Eliot and Auden and raving about Picasso and Matisse'. He also discovered surrealism in a magazine reproduction of René Magritte's *Le viol* (a female face with breasts for eyes and pudenda for a mouth). 'For me', he later said, 'Surrealism was a revelation, the key to a magic kingdom where misery and regression were banished for ever and poetry reigned supreme' (*Daily Telegraph*, 8 Nov 1997). It was an aesthetic that would rule his life. But he also found the release of jazz, in the person of Bessie Smith singing 'Gimme a Pigfoot (and a Bottle of Beer)': 'This woman roaring around, singing that line made me think, "Well, this is what I want!"' (*Daily Telegraph*, 5 June 2004).

In 1944 Melly enlisted in the Royal Navy, in and out of whose uniform he pursued a series of homosexual encounters. But it was art that truly caught his subversive instincts. At a surrealist 'séance' in the Barcelona restaurant in Soho he met E. L. T. Mesens, Magritte's friend and editor of the *London Bulletin*. Melly was engaged at Mesens's London Gallery in Beak Street, and became involved in a love triangle with Mesens and his wife, Sybil. Melly found he preferred women to men: 'It was just a matter of taste … not a moral decision. Suddenly, I just liked girls' legs better than boys' arses' (*The Independent*, 8 Nov 1997).

Back in civilian life Melly turned to performance as a new means of expression. Joining Mick Mulligan's Magnolia Jazz Band, he sang 'revivalist' 1920s jazz classics, using Benzedrine to stay up all night and occasionally sleeping in brothels. Soho was his adoptive, nocturnal home, 'a scruffy, warm, belching, argumentative, groping, spewing-up, cadging, toothbrush-in-pocket, warm-beer-gulping world' (*Owning Up*, 284–5). Melly met his first wife, Elizabeth Victoria (Vicky) Vaughan, a fashion model, in a Soho club. She was the daughter of Henry Owen Vaughan, radio dealer. They married in Edinburgh on 26 April 1955 and had one daughter, Pandora, but within a year she had left him for a man with whom Melly himself had already had an affair, and the marriage ended in divorce in 1962. In that year he met Diana Margaret Campion Dawson (*b.* 1937) at the Colony Room, his favoured Soho dive. She was the daughter of Geoffrey Campion Dawson, railway clerk, and the former wife of Michael H. St George Ashe. She had changed her surname to Melly by deed poll by the time they married on 7 May 1963, two days before their son, Tom, was born.

By now Melly's jazz career—he had recorded for Decca—was overshadowed by a new pop culture that he would address in his influential survey *Revolt into Style* (1970). For the first time a writer took pop culture seriously, applying historical perspective and examining its post-war eruption from Colin MacInnes to the Rolling Stones. 'Pop in this country evolved from its primitive beginnings (1956–7), through its classic period (1963–6) towards its noisy and brilliant decadence (1969–?)', Melly wrote. 'It lit up the contemporary landscape as if by a series of magnesium flares … the evolution of a new kind of culture, neither "popular" nor mandarin' (*Revolt into Style*, 123).

Revolt into Style both reflected and was mirrored in Melly's music criticism of the period. Typically his journalism was unconstrained, and ran from lucrative speech balloons for the *Daily Mail*'s 'Flook' cartoon to film and television criticism for *The Observer*. He lectured most passionately on his beloved surrealists; and turned to scriptwriting with 'swinging London' screenplays like *Smashing Time* (1967) and *Take a Girl Like You* (1970), the latter based on Kingsley Amis's novel, directed by Jonathan Miller, and starring Hayley Mills and Oliver Reed.

The sixties suited Melly. He was arrested at a 'Ban the bomb' march, and in 1971 testified at the infamous *Oz* trial, when the magazine was prosecuted for obscenity. The trial judge, Michael Argyle, asked Melly: 'For those of us who don't have the benefit of a classical education, what do you mean by the word "cunnilinctus"?' (*New Statesman*, 14 Aug 2008).

Melly also returned to jazz, singing with John Chiltern's Feetwarmers, and in 1972 recorded an album, *Nuts*, of Fats

Waller and Count Basie classics. The follow-up, *Son of Nuts* (1973), included his signature tune, 'Good Time George', written by Chiltern. In 1974 Melly resigned from *The Observer* and joined Chiltern's band full time, adopting his trademark razor-sharp 1930s suits and outrageous fedoras. It was a pop cultural silhouette, ironic and self-referential. Nor did age abate his sense of anarchy. He fell out with Roland Penrose, surrealist and founder of the Institute of Contemporary Arts, when Penrose invited the duke of Edinburgh to open a Picasso exhibition. He subsequently turned down a CBE: 'I didn't see the point of accepting an honour from a Hanoverian sovereign of a former empire' (*The Guardian*, 18 Feb 2004).

Melly had published his first volume of memoirs, *Owning Up*, in 1965. A rumbustious, picaresque account of his town and provincial jazz tours, the book was both filthy and hilarious. It was followed by a prequel in the shape of *Rum, Bum and Concertina* (1977), which dealt with his disreputable naval service and offered such memorable scenes as Melly, the put-upon rating, being defended below decks by a tough seaman: '"Anyone who says a word against fucking Picasso", he murmured gently, "gets fucking done over"' (*Owning Up*, 320). A third volume, *Scouse Mouse* (1984), retold his Liverpudlian upbringing and underlined, in a wonderfully unsentimental yet nostalgic manner, how far he had travelled. In all three books he was at pains to strike a deliberately outrageous tone, one that enhanced rather than concealed his essentially humane and affectionate personality.

Melly also wrote a witty account, with Barry Fantoni, of his milieu in *The Media Mob* (1980). His sensitive biography of the outsider artist Scottie Wilson, *It's All Writ Out for You*, appeared in 1986—a theme pursued in *Tribe of One: Great Naïve and Primitive Painters of the British Isles*, with Michael Wood, in 1991. He edited Edward James's *Swans Reflecting Elephants: My Early Years* (1982), an evocation of the great surrealist patron; and in 1997 published *Don't Tell Sybil: an Intimate Memoir of ELT Mesens*. *Hooked!* (2000) was enlivened with a passage about masturbating over a trout. 'I put that bit in early because not many people are interested in reviewing a fishing book unless something startles them' (*Scotland on Sunday*, 1 July 2001).

In later years Melly remained a man about town despite being arthritic and quite deaf, sporting a hearing aid that gave him the air of a portly Johnny Ray. In 2005 the publication of his wife Diana Melly's frank memoir, *Take a Girl Like Me*, reminded the public of the bohemian nature of their lives together, and apart. Melly's own *Slowing Down* (2005) examined his own decrepitude with unerring honesty and lack of reticence. Despite ill health he performed into his old age, and remained steadfastly in the public eye. In a late interview for the *Daily Telegraph* he declared 'I'm still a surrealist in the way that I'm still an anarchist. I don't mock the naivety of my youth. I only envy it' (*Daily Telegraph*, 8 Nov 1997). He died on 5 July 2007 at his home, 81 Frithville Gardens, Shepherd's Bush, London. He had refused treatment for lung cancer, and his wife Diana arranged for four of his mistresses to visit him on his deathbed. He was carried to the West London crematorium in a white cardboard coffin, decorated with paintings, drawings, and poems from his family and friends.

PHILIP HOARE

Sources G. Melly, *Owning up: the trilogy* (2006) · *Daily Telegraph* (8 Nov 1997); (5 June 2004); (6 July 2007) · *The Independent* (8 Nov 1997); (6 July 2007) · *Scotland on Sunday* (1 July 2001) · *The Times* (17 Dec 2003); (6 July 2007) · *The Guardian* (6 July 2007) · *Evening Standard* (13 July 2007) · *WW* (2007) · personal knowledge (2011) · private information (2011) · b. cert. · m. certs. · d. cert.

Archives Tate Gallery archive | FILM BFINA, light entertainment footage · BFINA, documentary footage · BFINA, performance footage | SOUND BL NSA, documentary recordings · BL NSA, performance recordings · BL NSA, light entertainment recordings

Likenesses photographs, 1950–2007, Getty Images, London · L. Morley, bromide print, 1960–69, NPG · photographs, 1960–2004, Camera Press, London · photographs, 1961–2007, Rex Features, London · Snowdon, bromide print, 1964, NPG · J. S. Lewinski, bromide print, 1968, NPG · B. Flanagan, intaglio prints, 1972, Tate Collection · photographs, 1974–2005, PA Photos, London · J. Edelstein, C-type colour print, 1989 (with Ronnie Scott), NPG · J. Eckersley, bromide print, 1992, NPG · photographs, 1994–2004, Photoshot, London · M. Hambling, oils, 1998, NPG [*see illus.*] · J. Bown, photograph, 2000 (with Maggi Hambling), Guardian News and Media Ltd · obituary photographs

Wealth at death £635,180: probate, 16 Oct 2007, *CGPLA Eng. & Wales*

Melrose, Denis Graham (1921–2007), physiologist, was born on 20 June 1921 in Cape Town, South Africa, the son of Thomas Robert Gray Melrose, medical practitioner and former naval doctor, and his wife, Floray, *née* Collings. The family came to England in the 1930s and he was educated at Sedbergh School in Yorkshire. He then went to University College, Oxford, with a history bursary but found that his father had enrolled him as a medical student. On the outbreak of the Second World War in 1939 he ran away from college to enrol in the navy but the proctors brought him back to study for his medical degree. His clinical work was done at University College Hospital medical school, London, and he graduated BM BCh in 1944. At college a fellow student fired a gun at students as they left the refectory. Melrose was seriously injured (a bullet being deflected from his heart by a pen in his chest pocket) and his best friend was killed. On 18 April 1945 he married Ann Meredith Warter (*b.* 1922), daughter of Henry Warter, of Portway House, Kirtlington, Oxfordshire; they had two sons.

After junior hospital posts Melrose was in the Royal Naval Volunteer Reserve from 1946 to 1948. He then had the good fortune to obtain a lecturer's post in the department of surgery at the Postgraduate Medical School of London, at Hammersmith Hospital, whose head was Ian Aird. Aird was a surgical visionary and he enthusiastically supported Melrose in his ambition to design a heart–lung machine that would enable the surgeon to operate on a bloodless heart with cardio-pulmonary bypass. At that time cardiac operations were done with instruments passed through the walls of the beating heart without the actual lesion being visualized. The Medical Research Council refused support but help came from a Hungarian refugee, Francis Kellerman, who had established a medical instrument firm called New Electronic Products (the initials NEP being deliberately selected as an ironic memory of the disastrous New Economic Policy of the Soviet Union). Kellerman bravely borrowed a large sum of money and his firm engineered what came to be known as the Melrose NEP heart–lung machine.

Even with cardio-pulmonary bypass there was still a big problem, namely that the heart continued to beat, causing difficulty for the surgeon who was presented with a moving target. Melrose solved this problem by inventing a method of stopping the heartbeat by injecting a solution of potassium citrate into the heart once the patient was safely on bypass. Elective cardiac arrest became a routine procedure in open heart surgery and a modification of the Melrose method remained in worldwide use at the time of his death. Several other centres in the world had invented a heart–lung machine, but Melrose's potassium arrest method was unique.

The cardiac surgeon responsible for the clinical development of open heart surgery at Hammersmith Hospital was William Paton (Bill) Cleland, and the first publication came in the *British Medical Journal* in 1953. A full programme of operations on patients with congenital heart disease started on 17 April 1957 when a thirty-year-old woman had a hole in the heart (atrial septal defect) closed with success. She was still well twenty-five years later. By 1968 some 1200 patients had been operated on at Hammersmith Hospital with the Melrose NEP machine. The Melrose NEP machine was also used in other British centres and in New Zealand and Australia, and a special recognition of its value came in 1959 when the Institute of Cardiovascular Surgery in Moscow obtained one. The Hammersmith team went to Moscow for two weeks and operated with success on four children with severe congenital heart disease. This invitation came at the height of the cold war and the team was congratulated by the Soviet deputy prime minister, Anastas Mikoyan, who said, 'Doctors are clean but politicians are dirty. The strongest friendship is between medical men, nothing on the political side can interfere with this friendship. We wish you the best of success' (*Daily Mail*, 16 May 1959).

Melrose worked at the Postgraduate Medical School of London (from 1974 the Royal Postgraduate Medical School) from 1948 to 1983, being successively lecturer, reader, and professor: initially he was professor of clinical rheology and then became professor of surgical science, being made an emeritus professor on retirement. He extended his work on cardio-pulmonary bypass as a Fulbright fellow at Stanford University in 1957–8. After 1962 he undertook research on the development of a membrane-type oxygenator for use in heart surgery, and then started what was in fact a second career in sports medicine inventing a type of legging to prevent deep vein thrombosis in the leg, which was reckoned to have saved hundreds of lives by the time of his death.

Denis Melrose had an exceptionally friendly and outgoing personality, which enabled him to guide other units through the early stages of starting open-heart surgery even though he was not himself a surgeon. He became a fellow of the Royal College of Surgeons of England but it was said that his maverick tendencies prevented his being awarded public honours for his work. After retirement he and his wife, Ann, went to live in Ibiza so that they could enjoy the sun and indulge their joint passion for sailing. Their house overlooked San Antonio harbour. His last few years were sadly clouded by dementia and he died on 2 July 2007 at Santa Eulalia. He was survived by Ann and their two sons. ARTHUR HOLLMAN

Sources *Daily Mail* (11 May 1959); (16 May 1959) · *Daily Express* (11 May 1959) · *Komsomolskaya Pravda* (15 May 1959) · W. P. Cleland and others, 'A decade of open heart surgery', *The Lancet*, 1 (1968), 191–8 · *Daily Telegraph* (16 July 2007) · *Imperial College Reporter* (19 July 2007) · *The Independent* (10 Sept 2007) · *Perfusion*, 22/3 (May 2007), 152 · W. S. Stoney, 'Evolution of cardiopulmonary bypass', *Circulation*, 119 (2009), 2844–53 · *WWW* · personal knowledge (2011) · private information (2011) · m. cert.

Likenesses group portrait, photograph, 1959, priv. coll.; repro. in www.oxforddnb.com/view/article/6674 · photograph, repro. in *Daily Telegraph* (16 July 2007)

Meneghello, Luigi [Gigi] (**1922–2007**), Italian scholar and author, was born on 16 February 1922 in the small Italian town of Malo, near Vicenza, the son of Cleto Meneghello (1892–1963), a car mechanic who also ran a small firm of local buses, and his wife, Giuseppina (Pia), *née* Canciani (1894–1949), who came from the Friulian city of Udine and was a schoolteacher. He had two younger brothers, Bruno (*b.* 1925), who became a judge, and Gaetano (1930–2006), an engineer. A sister, Ester Elisa, born in 1935, died as a baby. Meneghello's grandfather Piero was a broker for land and cattle sales, but according to his grandchildren his main avocation was contraband. Meneghello's father had several siblings, who frequently appeared (together with many other relatives, and people from the same town, sometimes under different names) in Meneghello's books: Antonia (Zia Nina), Francesco (Zio Checco), Ermenegildo (Zio Ernesto), Elvira (Zia Adele), Candida (sometimes called antiphrastically Zia Mora), and Ubaldo (Baldo; Zio Dino), the youngest and most important of the uncles, 'a great wooer of females, [who] for me … was the boyfriend of all the most beautiful women in the world' (Meneghello, lxxxviii).

Meneghello received his elementary and secondary education in Malo and in Vicenza, obtaining his school leaving certificate (*maturità classica*) at the Lycée Pigafetta in July 1939. In October 1939 he enrolled at the faculty of letters and philosophy of the University of Padua. In May 1940 he took part, as a member of the Gruppo Universitario Fascista (GUF) in the *Littoriali della Cultura* at Bologna, and came first in the competition on *dottrina fascista*. The winners of the *littoriali* were offered employment as journalists, and Meneghello worked at the Padua newspaper *Il Veneto* between 1940 and 1942. In January 1943 he was called up for military service, and after a period of training at Merano was sent to Tarquinia, to contribute to the defence of the Tyrrhenian coast against possible allied landings. He was there on 8 September 1943 when the Italian army collapsed. In the general chaos he, with a group of comrades and friends, managed to move north to the Veneto, where (having renounced fascism) they set up a resistance group inspired by the liberal-socialist Partito d'Azione. From March 1944 until the liberation in April 1945 the group fought in the area of Belluno, Vicenza, and Padua, in partisan actions against fascists and Germans (Meneghello later published a striking account in *I piccoli maestri*, 1964). In December 1945 he graduated with distinction, submitting a dissertation (presented orally, as was permissible in those exceptional immediate post-war circumstances) on modern culture in Benedetto Croce's journal *La Critica*. In the brief biographical notes on the back cover of one of his books he later wrote:

> My studies, at Vicenza and Padua, were absurdly 'brilliant', but useless and partly damaging. I was exposed, as a youth, to the effects of a fascist education, and then somehow was re-educated during the war and the civil war, under the small, protective wings of the Partito d'Azione. (Meneghello, lxxxvii)

After the liberation the intoxicating hopes for a radical renewal were quickly disappointed and Italian society passed from being subjected to fascist dictatorship to being politically controlled by the opposing, oppressive apparatuses of the Christian Democrat and Communist parties. Meneghello began to feel the need for a freer intellectual atmosphere and in 1947 was successful in obtaining a British Council scholarship to spend a year in Britain, based at the University of Reading. On 23 September 1948, in Milan, he married, with a civil rite, Katia Bleier (1919–2004). All their friends were struck by her penetrating intelligence and by Meneghello's reliance on her judgement even in his literary and academic choices. She was a Hungarian-speaking Yugoslav, a Jew from Vojvodina, who had been deported to Auschwitz with her family, who were mostly murdered after the selection on arrival at Birkenau. Her sister Olga, with her husband, Geza (Eugenio) Varnai, having had the good fortune of being captured by the Italians and not by the Germans, had been deported to Malo in 1941. Katia, liberated by the British in April 1945, managed to reach her sister in Malo, where she met Meneghello in 1946, at a local cultural club. According to his account, when he asked her, 'Miss Bleier, do you believe in God?', and she answered 'No', he told himself: 'I am going to marry this one. A fine girl, lively, foreign, culturally attractive (because we are also xenophile), from a family of orthodox Jews, and she does not believe in God.' He added: 'This is the way I have told the story many times, and it has become true. Katia has never contradicted it' (Meneghello, cxxiv). In December 1948 Katia joined him in Reading.

Meneghello's scholarship at Reading developed into an appointment to teach aspects of the Italian Renaissance in the university's English department. This led in 1955 to an Italian section being formed and in 1961 to an independent department, headed by Meneghello until he retired in 1980 to devote himself full-time to his writing. The Reading English department in the 1950s and early 1960s included such other distinguished figures as Philip Brockbank, Donald Gordon, Frank Kermode, Jo Trapp, and John Wain. The professor of French was A. G. (George) Lehmann, while the vice-chancellor in Meneghello's first few years there was the eminent medieval historian Sir Frank Stenton. Meneghello took advantage of the 1960s expansion of universities to plan the direction of his young department. With his own wide interests, which came partly from his Italian academic training, and with the support of like-minded colleagues, the department was probably the first in the country to offer an Italian studies syllabus rather than a more traditional language and literature course. A full-time historian and a professional linguist were recruited, while Warburg and Courtauld Institute colleagues provided part-time teaching in art history. A little later film studies were added. This innovative pattern spread to other universities.

Meanwhile Meneghello pursued his vocation as a writer, and became one of the most interesting, and according to some critics perhaps the most accomplished Italian writer of the twentieth century. His first book was *Libera nos a malo* (1963). The title page called it a novel (*romanzo*) but it belonged to no traditional genre and was simultaneously an autobiography, an essay about the life and culture of his village, and a penetrating reflection on literature, language, and the human mind. The viewpoint was both that of the protagonist as a child, growing up in a Veneto village, and that of the adult author, an academic in an English university, familiar with European cultures, and writing in a strikingly crisp literary Italian. The title was borrowed from a Latin phrase in the Lord's prayer ('deliver us from evil'), playing on the name of the author's village (Malo). The structure of the book is an apparently random sequence of chapters devoted to aspects of the life of the village, but is in fact an extremely well-constructed account of the language, religion, culture, education, and society of an Italian town at the beginning of the twentieth century. There is naturally also the universal aspect of a great literary work, so that readers, not only from other parts of Italy but also from other countries, are faced with the shock of recognition. Meneghello used a mix of sophisticated literary Italian, of current spoken Italian, and of Veneto dialect. The result was a prose of extraordinary beauty and efficacy.

After *Libera nos a malo* Meneghello published many other books, which often provided rich autobiographical information. These included *I piccoli maestri* (1964), translated as *The Outlaws* (1967), on his experience as a partisan; *Pomo pero* (1974), on his family and childhood; *Fiori italiani* (1976), on his schooling; *Bau-sète!* (1988), on the post-war period; and *Il dispatrio* (1993) and *La materia di Reading* (1997), which dealt with his reactions to England and his absorption of a new culture that was decisively to transform his attitude towards his Italian background. Particularly relevant in this context were the three volumes of *Le carte* (1999–2001), which collected his working notes over three decades. A collection of selected works, *Opere scelte* (2006), was published in the Meridiani Mondadori.

When he left Reading, in 1980, Meneghello moved with his wife to London, where they were often seen working in the north library of the British Museum. In Italy they had a house in Thiene (near Malo) where they regularly went during their holidays. It was mainly in the last fifteen years that Meneghello's fame in Italy spread. He was in great demand at literary festivals, such as those of Mantua and Pordenone, and was the recipient of honorary degrees from Reading, Turin, Perugia, and Palermo universities. Just before his death he was due to receive from the president of the Italian republic the coveted Feltrinelli–Lincei prize. After Katia's death he left his Bloomsbury flat and moved permanently to Thiene, where he died on 26 June 2007. He was buried in Malo, together with Katia, in the Meneghello family tomb. He had no children. He left his possessions, together with his papers, to the Fondo Manoscritti of the University of Pavia (Fondazione Corti).

GIULIO LEPSCHY

Sources L. Meneghello, *Opere scelte* (2006) • *The Times* (1 Aug 2007) • *The Guardian* (17 Aug 2007) • personal knowledge (2011) • private information (2011)

Likenesses obituary photographs • photograph, repro. in www.reading.ac.uk/internal/italian/meneghello2.htm

Menter, Sir James Woodham [Jim] (**1921–2006**), physicist, industrialist, and university administrator, was born at Oxford House, Lynsted, near Sittingbourne, Kent, on 22 August 1921, the only son of Horace Menter, railway signalman, and his wife, Jane Anne, *née* Lackenby, nurse. He had two older sisters, Barbara, who died at the age of six months, and Jean. Having only a modest income, and in order to give the children a better education, the family moved to Deal. Menter attended Deal parochial school and, later, Dover county school, to which he had won a scholarship, thereby relieving the financial burden on his parents. He came from a loving, caring family, which was later reflected in his own marriage and family life.

Jim Menter (as he was always known) excelled academically, participating in all school activities and becoming head boy in 1939. With the outbreak of the Second World War the school was evacuated to Ebbw Vale, but that did not disrupt his scholastic progress. Under the influence of his physics teacher, W. E. Pearce, he found physics the most interesting subject and, having won an open scholarship to Peterhouse, he went to Cambridge in October 1940 to read natural sciences. However, his studies were foreshortened after part one, and in 1942 he was sent as an experimental officer to work at the Anti-submarine Experimental Establishment at Fairlie in Ayrshire. This was his first encounter with the application of science, which probably influenced the way his career developed in later years from basic scientific research to the industrial exploitation of science. The experience of working as a member of a team during sea trials of various underwater detection devices on board destroyers, involving voyages to the Atlantic and the Mediterranean, must also have shown him the importance of being able to work with others in achieving the successful planning and accomplishment of a project.

After returning to Cambridge in 1945 to complete part two of his degree course in physics, Menter worked for the degree of PhD in the research laboratory for the physics and chemistry of rubbing solids under the direction of Philip Bowden and supervised by David Tabor. It was at this time that he met (Marjorie) Jean Whyte-Smith (daughter of Thomas Stodart Whyte-Smith, writer to the signet), then a student at Girton, later a schoolteacher, whom he married in Edinburgh on 1 November 1947. This was a wonderfully happy marriage. Jean's constant support was there in everything he subsequently achieved. Their first son, Ian, was born in 1949, followed by their second son, Will, in 1951 and their daughter, Frances, in 1953. In later years Jim and Jean always expressed great pride and joy in their family.

Menter's work as a research student and then, after he was awarded his PhD in 1949, as a research fellow in the physics and chemistry of rubbing solids, was largely concerned with the study of various surface layers on metals and the way these influence their frictional behaviour. The work was highly innovative in the use of the electron microscope and electron diffraction, techniques in their infancy at that time, to reveal the micro-crystalline structure of the surfaces. He was awarded the prestigious Beilby medal in 1954 in recognition of his achievement. This early recognition of the potential of the electron microscope as a tool was to have an even greater importance in the direction of Menter's later work.

In 1954 the Tube Investments (TI) Group of companies, all concerned with the production and fabrication of metal alloys, established a research laboratory, Tube Investments Research Laboratories (TIRL), at Hinxton Hall, near Cambridge. Menter was one of the first senior scientists to be appointed. He was attracted by the opportunity to pursue work of a fundamental nature on materials of practical importance. This coincided with a major technological development, the production by the Siemens company of the Elmiscop 1, a new breed of transmission electron microscope capable of very high resolution. Menter was able to persuade TIRL to purchase one of these and within a few weeks after delivery he had shown how it was possible to adapt the instrument to reveal for the first time the atomic layer structure of crystalline materials. His early observations were made on crystals in the form of thin flakes of the compound platinum phthalocyanide, but the implications of this for the study of more practical materials were quickly realized after the publication of his classic paper 'The direct study by electron microscopy of crystal lattices and their imperfections' in the *Proceedings of the Royal Society*, series A, in 1956. There followed many further advances in these studies in a wide range of applications by Menter and his colleagues at TIRL and by materials scientists in laboratories worldwide, with major consequences for the improved understanding of the relationship between structure and the physical properties of materials. Menter also recognized the importance of developing these structural probes in other ways. He gave strong support and encouragement to David Melford and Peter Duncomb, his colleagues at TIRL, who designed and built the first scanning electron probe X-ray microanalyser (EPMA), an instrument capable of mapping the composition of metal alloys. This was subsequently manufactured and sold worldwide by the Cambridge Instrument Company.

Menter became director of TIRL in 1961. He saw that it was important that the laboratory, which had by now achieved a high scientific reputation, should build on this with a more active programme of support for the manufacturing components of the TI Group. New methods of financing the work of the laboratory were introduced to encourage this, which led directly to the launch of a number of successful new production methods and the establishment of several new and profitable companies.

Menter's scientific contributions and his technical and managerial abilities were becoming recognized in many ways. In 1966 he was elected a fellow of the Royal Society, and he became a fellow of Churchill College, Cambridge, in the same year. In 1965 he had become director of research and development for the whole of TI and a director of the TI Group, and in 1968 he relinquished his position as director of TIRL in order to concentrate on these posts. His managerial abilities were soon realized and he became a member of a small, select group of directors making up the group's executive committee. He was knighted in 1973. As a director of TI he became involved in major aspects of company policy at a time when very significant changes were occurring in the manufacturing area. His scientific background, his careful assessment of all the relevant facts before making decisions, and his inherently straightforward approach earned him the respect of others and his opinion and judgement were much sought after.

When in 1976 Menter was invited to become principal of Queen Mary College he saw this as a big new challenge. Queen Mary College was an institution with a long history of providing higher education for working people and was proud of its history as the 'People's Palace', but it was relatively small and lacked a strong research profile. Menter became totally committed to the task of building on this. With the support of an equally committed wife he set about ensuring that the college was a happy environment in which to work, for staff and students alike. He was much respected for his integrity and straightforward approach in management and, despite the difficult times of diminishing resources and the very significant changes occurring in the university system during the period of his principalship, he was able to lead the college in an expansion of a wide range of academic development. Not surprisingly, given his experience in the engineering profession, the college grew to become a major provider of engineering education, supported by a strong research profile. It grew in other ways: in computational science, in science following a merger with smaller colleges in the University of London and, very significantly, a merger between Queen Mary College, the Royal London Hospital's Medical College, and St Bartholomew's Medical College, giving a new integrated approach to medical education. His final big achievement was to secure the funding for a new library. He left the college in very good shape when he retired in 1986.

Menter's experience in research and development and in management, and a reputation for sound judgement, were widely recognized and sought after by professional bodies, industry, and government. He was president of the Institute of Physics (1970–72) and of the Metals Society (1976); a vice-president (1971–6) and treasurer (1972–6) of the Royal Society; and a manager (1982–4), a vice-president (1983–5), and chairman of the council (1984–5) of the Royal Institution. He was a member of the Science Research Council (1967–72), and a member and deputy chairman of the Advisory Council for Applied Research and Development (1976–9). After moving to Queen Mary College he retained his association with TI as a non-executive director and also joined the board of BP (1976–87). Among many honours and awards he received the Bessemer gold medal of the Iron and Steel Institute in 1973 and the Glazebrook medal and prize of the Institute of Physics in 1977. He was made a Cambridge ScD in 1960 and received honorary doctorates from Brunel and Stirling universities (in 1974 and 1995 respectively).

Widely acknowledged as a scientist with the distinction of being able to recognize the importance of linking scientific research with technological advances, Menter was also remembered by many as a gentleman, at times serious and thoughtful, but usually kindly, approachable, and with a wry sense of humour. Following his retirement he and Jean moved to live at Carie on Loch Rannoch in Perthshire, where they already had a holiday home. There they enjoyed many happy years, participating actively in the local community and welcoming regular visits by their many friends from past associations. Menter very generously gave time to the University of Stirling where he was a member of the court (1987–95) and chairman of the audit committee. He never lost the ability to take on a big project and his final endeavour was the building of a spectacular gazebo in the grounds of Carie. In 2001 he and Jean moved to Aberfeldy, a few miles from Carie, to be closer to their daughter Frances. He died in Aberfeldy Cottage Hospital on 18 July 2006, of uraemia, kidney failure, and cancer of the kidney and prostate, and was survived by his wife, Jean, and their three children.

A. J. Forty

Sources *The Independent* (28 July 2006) · *The Times* (3 Oct 2006) · P. Hirsch and D. Pashley, *Memoirs FRS*, 54 (2008), 193–214 · A. J. Forty, www.rse.org.uk/fellowship/obits/obits_alpha/menter_james.pdf, 12 Aug 2009 · Burke, *Peerage* · *WW* (2006) · personal knowledge (2010) · private information (2010) · b. cert. · m. cert. · d. cert.
Likenesses W. Bird, RS · photograph, repro. in *The Independent* (28 July 2006) · photograph, repro. in *Memoirs FRS*
Wealth at death £365,309: confirmation, 16 Oct 2006, *CCI*

Meyer, Laverne Ignatius Henry (1935–2008), dancer and choreographer, was born on 1 February 1935, in Guelph, Ontario, Canada, one of seven children of Lincoln Meyer, farmer, and his wife, Cora, *née* Voll. A childhood enthusiasm for dancing from watching films starring Fred Astaire and Ginger Rogers led to his choice of career. Beginning with tap dance lessons, he went on to ballet training in Toronto with the Russian teacher Boris Volkov, touring with the Volkov Canadian Ballet. After coming to Britain in the 1950s he attended Sadler's Wells Ballet School and also took classes in London with Cleo Nordi and Anna Northcote and in Paris with Lubov Egorova. He first danced professionally with the Welsh National Opera in 1956.

At Northcote's studio Meyer met the remarkable Elizabeth West, artistic director of the recently founded Western Theatre Ballet, and joined her company in 1957. Western Theatre Ballet was a lively, experimental group with a very talented and exciting team of dancers. The repertory was initially choreographed mainly by Peter Darrell and West herself. The Darrell ballets had great appeal for young audiences as they broke away from familiar ballet traditions. His 1957 *Non Stop* was spirited, up to the moment, and set to jazz music, while *The Prisoners*, a grim drama about escaped convicts, became a signature piece for the company. In the ensuing years Western Theatre Ballet flourished both in Britain and abroad (in Belgium they had a fruitful collaboration with Maurice Béjart and the Théâtre de la Monnaie). West commissioned Meyer's first ballet. Choosing as music Webern's *Five movements for string quartet* (he was the first choreographer in Britain to create ballets to scores by Webern and Berg) he staged *The Web* on 4 September 1961. Its theme was of a girl saved from suicide and her relationship with her rescuer.

On 2 October 1962 West died in a climbing accident on the Matterhorn. Darrell was named director but had other commitments as well, so Meyer stepped in very successfully as ballet master and associate artistic director and from this point only danced one or two special roles. He knew that West intended to link up more with American modern dance and in July 1963 the company appeared at Jacob's Pillow, Massachusetts, and in Central Park, New York, where it was welcomed wholeheartedly; Walter Terry called it 'a highly auspicious debut' (*New York Herald Tribune*, 18 July 1963). On 28 September 1963 Meyer's second ballet, *Reconciliation*, was premiered. Set to Berg's string quartet, it dealt with a wife trying to mend the damage caused by her affair with another man. Meyer now spent some weeks in New York, studying with Martha Graham and José Limon, and in February 1964 he took over as sole artistic director of Western Theatre Ballet. In late May he choreographed *Sextet*, to Hindemith's *Kleine Kammermusik*. John Percival wrote that 'the sense of contact or alertness between dancers ... gives heightened interest to a series of fluent and musical dance patterns' (*New Daily*, 24 June 1964). Meyer's next ballet (premiered on 4 July 1966) was *Trial*, set to Berg's *Lyric suite for string quartet*, about a young woman destroyed by a conflict between reality and fantasy.

In January 1968 Meyer launched a workshop venture to discover new talent, and the company toured in Belgium, Germany, Switzerland, and Holland. Then an offer was accepted from Scottish Opera for WTB to become a new ensemble, Scottish Theatre Ballet, with Darrell as artistic director. A joint production of Scottish Opera and Scottish Theatre Ballet in 1969 was an historic staging in its entirety of Berlioz's *The Trojans*, in which a notable series of celebratory dances was imaginatively choreographed by Meyer.

Meyer, however, decided not to move to Scotland. He thought the north of England deserved its own dance company and after researching the situation in depth he put forward an admirable feasibility study for such a project. Three pilot programmes in March 1969 at the University Theatre, Manchester, were outstandingly successful and on 28 November 1969 Northern Dance Theatre was launched with Meyer as founder-director and choreographer and Freda Steel as administrator. He recruited a group of ten versatile and keen young dancers and over the next half-dozen years created a diversified repertory that included significant revivals (such as Kurt Jooss's *The Green Table* and Andrée Howard's *Death and the Maiden*) and new works by Peter Wright, John Chesworth, Charles Czarny, and Clover Roope, as well as finding a good new choreographer in one of his dancers, Jonathan Thorpe. Other leading dancers included Cecilia Barrett, Suzanne Hywel, Ursula Hageli, and John Fletcher. In the 1970s the board of directors decided to enlarge the company and reduce its experimental character. Meyer met their wishes by choreographing three longer ballets (*Schubert Variations*, *Cinderella*, and *Aladdin*), but in 1975 matters came to a head. Elizabeth Conran later described how the board's chairman, Simon Townley, ordered Meyer to resign there and then—'It was brutal ... and unappreciative of what he had achieved' (*The Guardian*, 25 June 2008).

After this severe shock, Meyer concentrated on international teaching for companies in Israel, Canada, Portugal, and New York, and in London at Pineapple Dance Centre. From 1991 to 1995 he was director of the Legat School (Sussex), and senior lecturer at the Laban Centre (London), establishing its classical ballet syllabus. He retired in 2000. A modest man of great artistic integrity, he had a special ability for creating and sustaining small classically based companies. He lived latterly in Lorne Road, Richmond, Surrey, and died at Kingston Hospital, Kingston upon Thames, on 25 April 2008, of pneumonia. He never married. After his death, Northern Ballet acknowledged him as its founder, and its artistic director, David Nixon, dedicated a performance to his memory, writing 'We are extremely grateful to his pioneering spirit and passion for dance' (*Yorkshire Post*, 10 May 2008).

KATHRINE SORLEY WALKER

Sources *Yorkshire Post* (10 May 2008) · *The Independent* (13 May 2008) · *The Times* (18 June 2008) · *The Guardian* (25 June 2008) · *Dancing Times* (June 2008) · personal knowledge (2012) · private information (2012) · d. cert.

Likenesses obituary photographs

Wealth at death £535,773: probate, 7 Oct 2008, *CGPLA Eng. & Wales*

Miall, (Rowland) Leonard (1914–2005), broadcaster and television executive, was born on 6 November 1914 at 73 Corringham Road, Golders Green, London, the elder son of Rowland Miall (1879–1955), scientific instrument maker, and his wife, Sara Grace, *née* Dixon (1885–1975). He was a scholar at Bootham School, York, and went on first to Freiburg University, where he studied German, and then to St John's College, Cambridge, where he read economics and law. In 1936 he was president of the Union and editor of the *Cambridge Review*. In a profile of Miall, *Granta* predicted that he would end up in the BBC.

After lecturing in the United States and serving for two years as secretary of British-American Associates, in 1939 Miall joined the BBC's newly formed German Service as its first talks producer. His colleagues then included Hugh Greene, the future director-general of the BBC, Patrick Gordon Walker, the future foreign secretary, and Marius Goring, the actor. There were tensions over what should be broadcast to Germany in wartime: the BBC sought editorial independence, while the government's black propaganda units sought control. Miall honed his diplomatic skills during those years. In 1942 he was seconded to the political warfare executive and sent to the United States, first as director of news in San Francisco and then as head of the office in New York. His affection for America never ceased. After returning to Europe in 1944, he worked as personal assistant to the deputy director-general of the political warfare executive and then, briefly, in the psychological warfare division of the Supreme Headquarters, Allied Expeditionary Force in Luxembourg. On 18 January 1941 he had married Lorna Barbara Rackham (1916–1974), the 24-year-old daughter of George John Rackham, mechanical engineer. They had three sons and one daughter.

Miall rejoined the BBC in 1945 and, after a brief spell as special correspondent in Czechoslovakia, became the corporation's Washington correspondent. He was a skilled broadcaster, reporting on American affairs with authority. He knew the powerful people in Washington, and he was on good terms with opinion formers like Edward R. Murrow and James Reston. He had a gift for spotting the importance of a story. Never was this more true than in 1947, when he heard of General George Marshall's speech at Harvard on reconstruction in war-ravaged Europe. Americans were sympathetic to Europe's plight, Marshall said, and he urged the European nations to set up a concerted plan. Because Ernest Bevin, the British foreign secretary, heard Miall's broadcast, diplomatic action followed swiftly and the Marshall plan was born. Years later Dean Acheson, by then the secretary of state, said: 'It was a good thing that Leonard did not lose his voice that night' (private information).

In 1954 Miall returned to London and was appointed head of the quaintly named television talks, a department which under his leadership went on to be responsible for such programmes as *Panorama*, *Tonight*, *Monitor*, *Zoo Quest*, *Gallery*, *The Sky at Night*, *Face to Face*, and many other documentaries and programmes ranging from science to gardening. It was a heady time for television and for those who worked in the shabby offices in Lime Grove studios, London. Miall was in charge of a group of talented people who went on to command the heights in broadcasting, Huw Wheldon, David Attenborough, Donald Baverstock, and Alasdair Milne among them. On screen the reporters—who included Richard Dimbleby, James Mossman, Robert Kee, and Alan Whicker—showed craftsmanship of the highest order. Miall encouraged them with a friendly nod usually; a gentle admonition occasionally. Egos were pushed to one side, pressure from Broadcasting House as well as the political parties was fielded deftly. But it was too good to last.

One Friday morning in 1962 (the year after he was appointed assistant controller, current affairs and talks, and appointed OBE) Miall was summoned by the director-general, Hugh Greene, his wartime colleague, and told that he would be replaced by his deputy, Grace Wyndham Goldie, fourteen years his senior. Greene offered him a post in Scotland, but such was the affection in which Miall was held in the television service that a job was created for him within forty-eight hours. By the Monday morning Miall had an office in Television Centre as special assistant to the director of television (Kenneth Adam), with the task of planning the start of BBC2, then three years away. So well did he buckle down to this administrative job that within a year he was promoted to assistant controller, programme services.

In 1966 the BBC showed its wisdom by sending Miall back to New York as its American representative. For the next four years he was a fine ambassador for the BBC and for Britain. He had always cared for the United States, he had many friends in the television networks there and in Washington, and he entertained stylishly, but modestly. Back in London, Miall spent the last three years of his BBC career as controller of overseas and foreign relations, a roving job that took him around the world, advising foreign broadcasters on what the BBC was all about. Because he was such a likeable person with a natural charm, he opened many doors and made new friends.

With the exception of war service Leonard Miall's entire working life was spent in the BBC and even after his formal retirement in 1974 he continued to work for the corporation part-time as its research historian. He prepared the material for three of Asa Briggs's books about the BBC, and in 1994 he published *Inside the BBC*, a book of profiles of twenty-five personalities from Lord Reith to Sir Robin Day. These were short but witty essays, reflecting the urbanity of the author. He continued to write, because it was his hobby, and his name was often seen under obituaries in *The Independent*.

Of middling height, slightly stooped, Miall had a visual resemblance to Alastair Sim, and his stories were illuminated by his genuine enjoyment in telling them. His first wife, Lorna, having died in 1974, on 10 October 1975 he married Sarah Greenaway (Sally) Bicknell (1918–2010), rally driver and novelist, former wife of Nigel Bicknell, RAF officer, and daughter of Gordon Leith, architect. He died at his home, Maryfield Cottage, High Street, Taplow, Buckinghamshire, in the Chiltern hills, on 24 February 2005, of bronchopneumonia and cerebral vascular disease. He was survived by his wife, Sally, and the four children of his first marriage.

PAUL FOX

Sources *Daily Telegraph* (25 Feb 2005) · *The Guardian* (25 Feb 2005) · *The Independent* (25 Feb 2005) · *The Times* (26 Feb 2005); (1 March

2005) · *WW* (2005) · personal knowledge (2009) · private information (2009) · b. cert. · m. certs. · d. cert.
Archives FILM BFINA, documentary footage · BL NSA, news footage | SOUND BL NSA, documentary recordings
Likenesses obituary photographs · photographs, BBC
Wealth at death £790,592: probate, 19 July 2005, *CGPLA Eng. & Wales*

Michie, Donald (1923–2007), geneticist and computer scientist, was born on 11 November 1923 in Rangoon, Burma, the eldest of three sons of James Kilgour Michie (1887–1967), East India merchant, and his wife, Marjorie, *née* Crain (1898–1986). His brother James *Michie (1927–2007) achieved fame as a publisher, poet, and translator. Donald was educated at Rugby School. In 1942 he won an open scholarship in classics to Balliol College, Oxford. There he tried to enrol on a Japanese language course for intelligence officers, but because the course was full he opted for instruction in cryptography instead. In the summer of 1942 he was assigned to Bletchley Park, the wartime code-breaking centre. His most important contribution to the war effort came in the spring of 1944. At that time an electronic code-breaking computer, the Colossus, had been operating for some months. Michie made improvements to the machine that led to a several-fold increase in the rate at which intercepted messages were decrypted. At Bletchley he developed a friendship with Alan Turing, a founder of the emerging field of computing. Michie was intrigued by Turing's conception of self-learning, intelligent machines, although he was also aware that computer technology would have to mature before it would be possible to pursue the idea. In the meantime he decided to become a geneticist.

Michie returned to Oxford in 1946, graduating MA in human anatomy and physiology in 1949 and taking a doctorate in mammalian genetics in 1953. On 10 January 1948, at Oxford register office, he married Zena Marguerite Davies (*b.* 1916/17), librarian, and daughter of Frederick Davies, master draper. They had one son, but the marriage was dissolved soon after, and on 6 October 1952, at St Columba's Church House, Chelsea, he married Anne Laura Dorinthea *McLaren (1927–2007), a fellow genetics research student, and daughter of the second Baron Aberconway. They had two daughters and one son. Michie and McLaren took up research positions at the University of London, where they made pioneering genetic studies of mice that laid the foundations for *in vitro* fertilization techniques. In 1958 Michie took up a senior lectureship in the department of surgical science at Edinburgh University. McLaren also obtained an appointment at Edinburgh, but they divorced in 1959. Michie was married for a third time, on 1 March 1971, to Jean Elizabeth Hayes (1928–2002), psychologist, and daughter of Charles Henry Crouch, army officer. There were no children of this marriage.

About 1960 Michie's interest in intelligent machines was rekindled, and he designed a programme that would learn the game of noughts and crosses. Lacking access to a real computer he simulated the programme's behaviour by a device consisting of matchboxes and glass beads. The contraption proved his point, and this led to an invitation to programme the system for real at Stanford University, which owned a large IBM computer. After returning to Britain Michie was concerned by the lack of comparable computing facilities. He discovered he had an aptitude for lobbying, and through personal appeals, lectures, and newspaper articles he argued for the provision of better computing facilities in British universities. His message began to get across and he earned a reputation as an authoritative academic voice. He was promoted to a readership in 1962, but dissatisfaction with surgical science and his growing interest in computing induced him to break away to form an experimental programming unit. The unit was given official recognition by the University of Edinburgh in 1965.

In 1965 Michie organized the first biennial machine intelligence workshop in Edinburgh. The workshops, and the published proceedings, *Machine Intelligence*, which Michie edited, became the major forum for British artificial intelligence (AI) researchers. Michie attracted to the unit the psychologist R. L. (Richard) Gregory and the theoretical chemist H. C. (Christopher) Longuet-Higgins. With Longuet-Higgins he established an influential programme of industrial robotics. In 1967 he was given a personal chair in machine intelligence and the unit was given departmental status as the department of machine intelligence and perception, with chairs for the senior staff. This turned out to be a mixed blessing, as it put his department into conflict with the recently formed department of computer science. Michie also had disputes over the direction of research with his senior colleagues, as a result of which Gregory left for the University of Bristol in 1970 and Longuet-Higgins broke away to form his own research unit.

The conflicts in the Edinburgh research community, which were mirrored elsewhere, provoked the UK Science Research Council to commission a report on the state of AI research from Sir James Lighthill. Lighthill's report, published in 1973, was critical of the lack of progress in the field and the result was a massive drop in funding that cast a pall over AI research for a decade. Within Edinburgh University there was concern at the academic infighting and a restructuring was imposed. A new department of artificial intelligence was established, while Michie was given his own independent machine intelligence research unit; however, he had been sidelined. He continued his personal research and still organized the machine intelligence workshops. He accepted several prestigious visiting professorships, took up scientific journalism, and continued to be a prominent advocate for his field. But, from the mid-1970s, his star was on the wane.

In the early 1980s AI began to recover its prestige, partly from the perceived economic importance of Japanese industrial robots and Japan's so-called fifth generation computer initiative, as well as the blossoming of 'expert systems' that mimicked the decision processes of human experts. Michie turned to expert systems research. He became professor emeritus in 1984 and remained fully active if less influential. Until 1997 he was chair of the Turing Trust, which he had set up in 1975 to establish an archive for Turing's papers and a series of memorial lectures. He founded the Turing Institute at Glasgow in 1984, which conducted industrially oriented machine intelligence research, and was its director of research (1984–6) and then chief scientist (1986–92), during those years also holding a visiting professorship at the University of Strathclyde. In 1994 he established the Human-Computer Learning Foundation, a charitable educational trust. He was the recipient of numerous honorary degrees and awards from learned societies in computing and AI. He and Anne McLaren (from 1993 Dame Anne McLaren) had remained close friends after their divorce, and they started to live together again (at 21 Dunollie Road, Camden Town, London) from 2005. They were both killed in a motoring accident on the M11 near North Weald Bassett, Essex, while returning from Cambridge to London on 7 March 2007. Michie was survived by all four of his children. A memorial service was held at the Zoological Society of London on 19 July 2007. MARTIN CAMPBELL-KELLY

Sources *Daily Telegraph* (9 July 2007) · *The Guardian* (10 July 2007) · *The Times* (12 July 2007) · *The Independent* (12 July 2007) · cv, www.aiai.ed.ac.uk/~dm/dmcv.html, 4 July 2010 · *WW* (2007) · personal knowledge (2011) · private information (2011) · m. certs. · d. cert.

Archives FILM www.aiai.ed.ac.uk/~dm/ | SOUND www.aiai.ed.ac.uk/~dm/

Likenesses P. Stobart, photographs, 1984, Rex Features, London · obituary photographs · photographs, repro. in www.aiai.ed.ac.uk/~dm/

Wealth at death £346,221: probate, 27 March 2008, *CGPLA Eng. & Wales*

Michie, James Crain (1927–2007), poet and publisher, was born on 24 June 1927 at South Lodge, March Road, Weybridge, Surrey, the second of the three sons (there were no daughters) of James Kilgour Michie (1887–1967), East India merchant and later banker (chairman of National and Grindlay's Bank Ltd, 1946–63), and his wife, Marjorie Crain, *née* Pfeiffer (1898–1986). His elder brother, Donald *Michie, became an expert on artificial intelligence. His younger brother, Ian, followed his father into banking.

Michie was educated at Marlborough College, where he was captain of squash: despite an owlish demeanour and large horn-rimmed spectacles, he remained a surprisingly sporty figure, excelling at tennis, squash, and golf, and given to long walks in the Pyrenees. He won an exhibition in classics to Trinity College, Oxford: he took a second in classical moderations in 1947 but switched to English, in which he gained a second-class degree in 1949. He began to make his mark as a poet while at Oxford: he compared poems with Kingsley Amis, with whom he co-edited *Oxford Poetry* (1949). Amis later admitted that Michie's efforts were 'embarrassingly better' (Amis, 109).

A conscientious objector, Michie abjured national service, working instead as a porter at Guy's Hospital, and for the International Voluntary Service for Peace in Bavaria and Jamaica. In Jamaica he met Daphne Segre (*b.* 1927/8), pianist, and daughter of Ralph Segre, industrial chemist. They went through a form of marriage in Jamaica on 5 April 1952. She subsequently moved to London to study at the Royal College of Music, and they were formally married at Chelsea register office on 1 April 1955. The marriage was dissolved in 1960; there were no children.

Michie had contributed poems to John Lehmann's *Penguin New Writing* before it was closed down in 1950. In 1954 Lehmann founded the *London Magazine*, and Michie was included on its editorial board. He combined this with teaching for the Workers' Educational Association, but in due course he opted for regular employment and joined Heinemann as a commissioning editor. Despite a languid manner and easygoing ways, he soon made a reputation as a shrewd talent spotter. He took on Sylvia Plath's first collection of poems, *The Colossus* (1960), and her first novel, *The Bell Jar* (1963); he encouraged Anthony Burgess to write his Malaysian trilogy of novels; and he commissioned Michael Holroyd to embark on his biography of Lytton Strachey (1967–8). Nor did he neglect his own gifts. In 1959 Rupert Hart-Davis published *Possible Laughter*, his first collection of poems. It was a very slim volume, but all Michie's qualities as a poet were in evidence: intellectual and stylistic elegance, wit, craftsmanship, a classicist's sense of the sad absurdity of life. He also made his mark as a translator, into verse, of Greek, Latin, and French writers: W. H. Auden so admired his version of Horace's odes that he decided to abandon his own attempt; it was followed by translations of Martial, Catullus, Euripides, Virgil, Ovid, Aesop, and La Fontaine.

In 1962 Graham Greene defected from Heinemann to the Bodley Head. Greene thought so highly of Michie that he urged Max Reinhardt, the managing director of the Bodley Head, to 'steal James Michie from Heinemann' (Lewis, 421). Once installed at the Bodley Head, Michie soon made his mark. He encouraged William Trevor, persuaded Muriel Spark to move to the firm, published Solzhenitsyn's *Cancer Ward* (1968), knocked Charlie Chaplin's memoirs into shape, and found a cult best-seller in Robert Pirsig's *Zen and the Art of Motorcycle Maintenance* (1974). But Michie's heart was no longer in publishing. He fell out with Graham Greene, who moved to another editor within the Bodley Head; he turned down Paul Theroux's *The Black House*, so losing the firm one of its most promising writers; his lunches grew longer and his hours shorter, and Reinhardt complained that 'I don't in the least mind James doing the crossword in my time, but I do wish someone would ask him to keep his door closed while he's doing it' (*The Independent*, 21 Nov 2007). On 2 October 1964 he had married Sarah Louise Courtauld (*b.* 1943), secretary, and daughter of Walter Pierre Courtauld, businessman. They had two sons and a daughter, and until their divorce in 1982 Michie enjoyed a rare period of financial security. Over the years he gradually faded out as a publisher, much to the regret of his authors.

But Michie was not done with the literary life. His *New and Selected Poems* had been published in 1983. His *Collected Poems* were published in 1994, and won the Hawthornden prize the following year (the jury felt, rightly, that Michie had never had the recognition he deserved); he co-edited, with P. J. Kavanagh, *The Oxford Book of Short Poems* (1985:

Kingsley Amis had started on the book with him, but had pulled out on the grounds that there were not enough short poems worth publishing); he proof-read *The Spectator* every week and, as Jaspistos, indulged his love of puzzles and word play by setting its weekly competition; he was the only poet Richard Ingrams allowed to appear in the pages of *The Oldie*, and *Last Poems*—a collection of his rueful ruminations on the depredations of old age and the imminence of death—was published by the magazine in 2008, after his death.

An amused habitué of Soho pubs and seedy Greek restaurants, Michie also enjoyed a reputation as a ladies' man, employing wit, charm, and a degree of determination. He had a daughter with Tatiana Orlov; and while working on *The Spectator* he met Clare Asquith (*b.* 1955), the companion of his later years, with whom he had a son. He died of carcinoma of the larynx on 30 October 2007, at his home, 45 Okehampton Road, Kensal Rise, London. As he wrote in one of his later poems

I used to fancy crabmeat as a treat:
Now crab's the epicure, and I'm the meat.
(*Last Poems*, 2008, 110)

He was buried in Kensal Green cemetery on 9 November, and was survived by Clare Asquith and by his five children. JEREMY LEWIS

Sources K. Amis, *Memoirs* (1991) • P. Theroux, *Sir Vidia's shadow* (1998) • J. Lewis, *Shades of Greene* (2010) • *Daily Telegraph* (3 Nov 2007) • *The Guardian* (5 Nov 2007) • *The Times* (8 Nov 2007) • *The Independent* (21 Nov 2007) • *RSL: Royal Society of Literature Review* (2009) • personal knowledge (2011) • private information (2011) • b. cert. • m. certs. • d. cert.
Archives SOUND BL NSA, performance recordings
Likenesses obituary photographs
Wealth at death £663,178: probate, 21 Feb 2008, *CGPLA Eng. & Wales*

Michie [*née* Bannerman], **(Janet) Ray, Baroness Michie of Gallanach (1934–2008)**, politician, was born on 4 February 1934 at the Old Manse, Balmaha, Stirlingshire, the third of four children of John Macdonald *Bannerman, Baron Bannerman of Kildonan (1901–1969), politician and rugby player, and his wife, Jenny Murray (Ray), *née* Mundell (*b.* 1906/7). She was born and brought up on Loch Lomondside, where her father was farm manager to the duke of Montrose. Native highland culture provided the backdrop for a happy childhood. Educated at Aberdeen High School for Girls and Lansdowne House school, Edinburgh, she later trained at the Edinburgh College of Speech Therapy. On 11 May 1957, at Buchanan parish church, Stirlingshire, she married Iain Michie (1932–2006), a medical practitioner then serving as a lieutenant in the Royal Army Medical Corps. He was the son of Malcolm Michie, crofter; they had met at the Edinburgh Highland Society. They had three daughters.

After their marriage Iain and Ray Michie spent the next sixteen years in Germany and eastern Asia, where Iain continued to work with the Royal Army Medical Corps. After returning to Scotland, Iain Michie became a consultant at the county hospital in Oban, where thereafter they settled. Ray was then able to pursue her own professional career, becoming area speech therapist for the Argyll and

(Janet) Ray Michie, Baroness Michie of Gallanach (1934–2008), by unknown photographer

Clyde Health Board in 1977. She was later (from 1991 to 2001 and from 2002 again) vice-president of the Royal College of Speech and Language Therapists.

Although Ray Michie made a career in speech therapy, as the daughter of John Bannerman, a frequent parliamentary candidate, politics was in her blood. All her political instincts came from him, as did her campaigning style; she insisted on holding public meetings until well into the 1990s. Unlike her father, however, Michie achieved what had eluded him on eight occasions—election to the House of Commons.

Michie became involved in politics immediately after her return to Scotland, serving as chairman of the Argyll Liberal Association (1973–6), and from 1977 to 1979 vice-chairman of the Scottish Liberal Party (her father had been chairman), as which she fought the Argyll constituency (which John Bannerman had contested in 1945) for the first time in 1979. In 1983 she came second, finally gaining it from the Scottish education minister John Mackay in 1987.

Initially the Liberals' only female MP, Michie increased her majority at two general elections and built an energetic if low-profile Commons career. She combined front-bench duties on transport, Scotland, and women's issues with tenacious pursuit of constituency matters, including the loss of the fishing vessel *Antares* in 1990, and the fatal Chinook crash on the Mull of Kintyre in 1994. A member of the Scottish Affairs select committee for five years (1992–7) and, in her final parliament, one of the speaker's panel of chairmen, Michie chaired the Scottish Liberal Democrats in 1992–3. She also pursued what internal and external critics considered rather dated causes like crofting (she encouraged a local buy-out when the island estate of Gigha came up for sale), the Gaelic language (although she herself was not fluent), and, more fashionably, Scottish devolution, which she always spoke of as 'Home Rule'. On this she exceeded the Liberal (and later Liberal

Democrat) party line, promoting a multi-option referendum bill (which included independence) in the Commons. Shortly before the general election of 1997 she published, with Malcolm Bruce (the Liberal Democrat MP for Gordon), a pamphlet on Scottish devolution that called for, among other things, a new national anthem and a new union flag.

Had the Scottish parliament been established prior to 1999 Michie might have ended her political career as an MSP, but her husband's long illness and the suicide of her daughter Joanne led to her retirement from the Commons in 2001. Again she echoed her father's career by joining the House of Lords the same year with a life peerage, as Baroness Michie of Gallanach; she took her oath in Gaelic, the first peer to do so. Despite having waited so long to enter parliament, however, she never developed any affection for either house, disliking the late hours and gruelling commute from rural Argyllshire. She also lacked any interest in internal political positioning. As Jim Wallace, the former leader of the Scottish Liberal Democrats, remarked at her funeral, 'Ray was too straightforward to be classed as a wily operator but she would always state her case with passion and sincerity'. Often blunt and less than liberal on social issues, she proved 'you could be a good Liberal and not care a whit about political correctness' (Wallace, funeral eulogy, 10 May 2008).

A good boss and a generous host, Michie was tall and striking in appearance and possessed of a wicked wit. She shared her father's love of rugby (he had been capped thirty-seven times), rarely missing a Scottish fixture, as well as tennis, swimming, and golf. Her range of political interests was reflected in honorary positions in An Comunn Gaidhealach, the Scottish National Farmers' Union, the Scottish Crofting Foundation, the Clyde Fishermen's Association, and the National Council for Women. Towards the end of her life she chaired the West Highland Health Services Solutions Group, which sought to reconcile the demand for care in remote areas with NHS resources. She was also appointed to the Scottish first minister Alex Salmond's Scottish Broadcasting Commission, although illness prevented her taking an active part. She died at Tigh an Eas, Glenmore Road, Oban, on 6 May 2008 following a long battle with cancer of the colon; she was survived by two daughters. DAVID TORRANCE

Sources *Bannerman: the memoirs of Lord Bannerman of Kildonan*, ed. J. Fowler (1972) • R. Michie, 'John Bannerman', *Dictionary of liberal biography*, ed. D. Brack and M. Baines (1998) • *Daily Telegraph* (7 May 2008) • *The Guardian* (9 May 2008) • *The Times* (11 May 2008) • *The Independent* (12 May 2008) • J. Wallace, eulogy, Oban Old Parish Church, 10 May 2008 • *WW* (2008) • Burke, *Peerage* • private information (2012) • b. cert. • m. cert. • d. cert.

Likenesses photographs, 1993–2001, Photoshot, London • photographs, 1996–2001, PA Photos, London • obituary photographs • photograph, BBC [*see illus.*]

Mill, Robert Duguid Forrest Pring- (1924–2005), scholar of Catalan, Spanish, and Latin American literature, was born on 11 September 1924 at Talbot House, Stapleford Tawney, Essex, the son of Captain (later Major) Richard Pring-Mill, an officer in the Royal Field Artillery, and his wife, Nellie Morton Turner, *née* Duguid. He was educated at the Jesuit school of Montesión, Palma de Mallorca, before enlisting in 1941 and serving in the Far East as an intelligence officer in the Black Watch, rising to the rank of captain and being mentioned in dispatches. His first published work, improbably in view of what he would go on to achieve, was entitled *Chinese Triad Societies* (1946), and arose out of his post-war military service. He was demobilized in 1947 and graduated with a first-class degree in modern languages (French and Spanish) from New College, Oxford, in 1949. A visit to South America earlier that year under the auspices of Sir Eugen Millington-Drake kindled a lifelong interest in the continent. In 1950 he was elected to a senior demyship at Magdalen College, Oxford, and on 19 August the same year, at the Roman Catholic chapel of Our Lady and St Paulinus, Dewsbury, married (Maria) Brigitte Heinsheimer, a 28-year-old undergraduate, and daughter of Ludwig Heinsheimer; they had a son, Francis, and a daughter, Monica. He was appointed university lecturer in Spanish in the University of Oxford in 1952, from which post he retired in 1988. He was simultaneously a lecturer at New College (1956–88) and Exeter College (1963–81), and tutor at St Catherine's College (1965–88). He was a fellow of St Catherine's College until his death.

Pring-Mill was one of the most distinguished British Hispanists of his generation, with an unusually wide range of interests, reflected in a series of published works that achieved international critical recognition. His fascination with interlocking patterns of language and ideas found particular expression in his work on medieval Catalan and golden age Spanish literature. His interest in the medieval Catalan polymath Ramón Llull was sustained throughout his working life; his earlier studies, for which he was awarded the Premi Crítica 'serra d'or' de Recerca (Barcelona), were collected in *Estudis sobre Ramón Llull (1956–78)* in 1992. Golden age Spanish drama also claimed his attention from an early stage. His introduction to Jill Booty's translation of five plays by Lope de Vega (1961) proved very influential, while his extensive writing on Calderón culminated in his *Calderón: estructura y ejemplaridad* (2001). His fascination with the intellectual currents of golden age poetry and prose, especially *conceptismo*, led to other important articles.

Pring-Mill was also closely involved in the study of Latin American literature. He was instrumental in bringing the Chilean poet Pablo Neruda to Oxford in 1965 to be awarded a DLitt. He was proud that for some years Neruda, who would go on to win the Nobel prize for literature in 1971, was the only living author studied in a major paper in the final honour school of modern languages in Oxford. Pring-Mill's epic, year-long journey across the Americas in 1967, from Montreal to Puerto Montt, which Brigitte and their children shared in part, brought him new contacts with emerging trends in Latin American culture, most notably the poetry of the Nicaraguan Ernesto Cardenal, with whom he worked on the Solentiname islands in Lake Nicaragua in 1972, and of whose work he published editions, translations, and pioneering studies. Cardenal was minister of culture in the Sandinista government from

1979 to 1987, which brought Pring-Mill into contact with liberation theology (of which, as a practising Roman Catholic, he approved) and political revolutionary movements in Latin America (about which he became more sceptical). He also acquired a deep interest in the protest poetry and songs arising out of the political ferment of the continent, and devoted considerable scholarly attention to these. But it is probably for his work on Neruda, as editor, translator, and commentator, that he was best known. His *Pablo Neruda: a Basic Anthology* (1975) quickly established itself as a standard work. He left his substantial collection of recorded and published material concerning protest poetry to the Institute of Popular Music at Liverpool University, and a significant archive of material relating to Neruda to the Taylor Institution in Oxford.

Pring-Mill served as president of the Anglo-Catalan Society from 1973 to 1976. He was made an Oxford DLitt in 1986, and elected a fellow of the British Academy two years later. His work was recognized abroad in a series of honours and prizes: he became a corresponding member of the Institut d'Estudis Catalans in 1966 and of the Reial Acadèmia de Bones Lletres, Barcelona, in 2002. He was awarded the Premi Pompeu Fabra (1956) and the Premi Catalònia (1991). He received the Creu de San Jordi from the Generalitat de Catalunya in 1990, and the same year was made a Comendador de la Orden de Isabel la Católica by the Spanish government. The Chilean government honoured him twice, as an officer of the order of Bernardo O'Higgins in 1992, and with the Medalla Presidencial de Honor in 2004.

Alongside his many contributions to scholarship, and in no sense for him less important or deserving of his full attention, was Pring-Mill's commitment to the teaching of undergraduates. As an assiduous and devoted tutor he won the respect and affection of generations of them. He was a man of innate courtesy and deep charity, and possessed a real gift for sustaining friendships, most memorably through the generous hospitality he and Brigitte provided in their home. Having lived latterly in Brill, Buckinghamshire, he died at the John Radcliffe Hospital, Oxford, on 6 October 2005, following an internal haemorrhage brought on by a duodenal ulcer. He was survived by his wife, Brigitte, and their two children.

COLIN THOMPSON

Sources N. Griffin and others, eds., *The discerning eye: studies presented to Robert Pring-Mill on his seventieth birthday* (1994), preface · *The Independent* (15 Oct 2005) · *The Guardian* (17 Oct 2005) · *Taller de Letras* (1 Nov 2005) · *The Times* (3 Nov 2005); (7 Nov 2005) · *WW* (2005) · personal knowledge (2009) · private information (2009) · b. cert. · m. cert. · d. cert.

Likenesses obituary photographs

Wealth at death £341,877: probate, 4 April 2006, *CGPLA Eng. & Wales*

Millar, George Reid (1910–2005), special operations officer, author, and farmer, was born on 19 September 1910 at Boghall, Baldernock, Stirlingshire, the younger son (there was no daughter) of Thomas Andrew Millar (*d.* 1921/2), architect, and his wife, Mary Reid, *née* Morton (*d.* *c.*1938). As a small boy he shared his cot with the family

George Reid Millar (1910–2005), by C. Woods, 1946

Airedale, which had to be put down in 1917 as there was no meat to spare for it; this did not make him pro-German. He went from Loretto School, which he rather disliked, to St John's College, Cambridge, where he read architecture and enjoyed himself. He tried work as an architect, between 1930 and 1932, but soon gave it up for journalism. The *Glasgow Herald* sent him to investigate the wreck of the *Lusitania*, which led to a lifelong fascination with the sea. In 1934 he moved on to the *Daily Telegraph*, and once scooped the *Daily Express*, which captured him with a larger salary. He was unusually good-looking, and made his first marriage on 2 December 1937 to Annette Rose Forsyth, the 25-year-old daughter of Brigadier-General Clifton Inglis Stockwell, and the former wife of Michael Noel Forsyth; she abandoned her first husband for him. She joined him in Paris when he became one of the *Express*'s Paris correspondents shortly before the outbreak of war in 1939. By June 1940 he was the only one left, and made a hazardous escape from the advancing German forces by motor car south-westwards, managing to get out to England just in time. She had been driving an ambulance at the front, and escaped separately.

Millar at once threw up his profession to join the army, and was soon commissioned into the rifle brigade and sent to north Africa. In the confused fighting round Gazala in June 1942 his platoon got separated from the 1st battalion and he was taken prisoner, lightly wounded. He was packed off to a prisoner-of-war camp in southern Italy, where he soon ran a black market in food with the local peasantry. When this was discovered he was moved to a punishment camp near Genoa, from which he was abruptly transferred to Germany in September 1943. He escaped from the train, made friends with some French forced labourers, got into France, stumbled on a British escape line, and crossed the Pyrenees with difficulty. On the way he met a Special Operations Executive (SOE) organizer, Richard Heslop, who refused to recruit him, but mentioned his name to his SOE commander. SOE interviewed and recruited him when he reached London. During his escape, which earned him a military cross, he had been buoyed up by thoughts of rejoining his wife; she had not waited for him.

Millar plunged into SOE training and, on the rebound, into a new love affair, with Isabel Beatriz Hardwell, the wife of Charles George Hardwell, and daughter of Montagu Bentley Talbot Paske-Smith, diplomat, and his Spanish wife. He was parachuted into eastern France on the night of 1–2 June 1944, a few days before the Normandy landings, to set up a new sabotage circuit called Chancellor; his personal codename was Emile. He went to work in the Ourcq valley, north of Besançon, where Georges Molle, the leading local poacher, proved a tower of strength to him. From a very late start, he was able to assemble groups of saboteurs devoted to him, whom he made skilled at their tasks and kept supplied with explosives. They disrupted traffic on the local railway, which was of some strategic importance to the Germans, and made a substantial distraction of German effort away from the main fighting fronts, at a price in casualties. His powers of leadership and sheer charm were such that, fifty years later, elderly women who had worked for him as teenage couriers would lay hand on heart and cry 'Ah! Emile!' if his codename was mentioned. He was appointed to the DSO by the British and to the Légion d'honneur by the French, who also awarded him a Croix de Guerre.

After the liberation of France Millar put an account of his escape into a book, *Horned Pigeon* (1946), and of his SOE adventures into another, *Maquis* (1945). He wrote them fast, but well, and secured clearance for their publication. The latter sold extensively: it gives a matchless account of how to live hour by hour, never knowing whether you will see the next through. De Gaulle told him in a private interview that his was the best account of life in the maquis, though he could not say so in public.

Millar divorced his first wife, and on 11 May 1946 married Isabel as soon as she was free of her first husband. After a protracted honeymoon sailing round the Mediterranean, they leased a farm of 1500 acres in west Dorset, where he settled down to breed cattle, hunt, shoot, and write. The best of several travel books were *Isabel and the Sea* (1948), on their honeymoon, and *Oyster River* (1963), on SOE's sea link between Cornwall and Brittany. He also wrote *Road to Resistance* (1979), a memoir of his war years. In 1989 Isabel emerged unconscious from a road accident, from which she died in 1990 without ever having recognized him again. He gave up the farm, and moved to Uploders Place, a house near Bridport, where Venetia Ross-Skinner looked after him as he went blind and old age crept up on his still undaunted spirit. He died at Warmwell House, Dorchester, on 15 January 2005, of bronchopneumonia. Venetia Ross-Skinner arranged an annual prize in his memory at Bridport literary festival. He had no children. M. R. D. Foot

Sources G. R. Millar, *Maquis* (1945) · G. R. Millar, *Horned pigeon* (1946) · G. R. Millar, *Road to resistance* (1979) · M. R. D. Foot, *SOE in France: an account of the work of the British Special Operations Executive in France, 1940–1944*, 3rd edn (2004) · *Daily Telegraph* (18 Jan 2005) · *Daily Mail* (19 Jan 2005) · *The Times* (20 Jan 2005); (25 Jan 2005) · *Sunday Telegraph* (23 Jan 2005) · *The Independent* (26 March 2005) · *WW* (2004) · personal knowledge (2009) · private information (2009) · b. cert. · m. certs. · d. cert.
Archives priv. coll. | TNA: PRO, HS 9, SOE personal file; SOE report
Likenesses C. Woods, photograph, 1946, Getty Images, London [*see illus.*] · obituary photographs
Wealth at death £807,812: probate, 29 April 2005, *CGPLA Eng. & Wales*

Millar, Sir Oliver Nicholas (1923–2007), art historian, was born at Standon House, Standon, Ware, Hertfordshire, on 26 April 1923, the elder son of Gerald Arthur Millar (1895–1975), publisher, and his wife, Ruth Gwendolen Mary (1900–1971), daughter of Charles Hornblower Cock, of Mainstone Court, Ledbury. From an early date Millar had an instinctive love of history and literature. Attendance at Rugby School was followed by study at the Courtauld Institute of Art, University of London, where he obtained an academic diploma. Not being eligible for war service during the Second World War owing to a heart condition, he retained close professional links with the Courtauld Institute for several years thereafter. Not least this was because one of those who attended his lectures was his future wife, Delia Mary Dawnay (1931–2004), daughter of Cuthbert Henry Dawnay, farmer. They married at the Queen's Chapel, Marlborough Gate, London, on 21 January 1954 and had one son and three daughters.

Millar's early connections with the Courtauld Institute coincided with its growing reputation in the art historical life of the nation and on a personal basis two staff members were to feature strongly in his later career: Anthony Blunt (later director of the Courtauld Institute) at the Royal Collection and Margaret Whinney (later reader), who was his co-author in 1957 of *English Art, 1625–1714* in the Oxford History of English Art series.

Millar's long association of some forty years with the Royal Collection began in 1947 when he was appointed assistant surveyor of the king's pictures under Anthony Blunt, who had succeeded Kenneth Clark as surveyor two years previously. The rest of Millar's career was spent in the Royal Collection, where he rose to the positions of deputy surveyor in 1949 (following Benedict Nicolson), surveyor in 1972 (following Anthony Blunt), and ultimately the first director in 1987, one year before his retirement, when he was appointed surveyor emeritus. In line with these promotions was his advancement within the Royal Victorian Order: CVO in 1963, KCVO in 1973, and GCVO in 1988.

Millar's immense contribution to the Royal Collection can be summarized under two headings, administrative and scholarly. When he joined the royal household the

Royal Collection operated under the aegis of the lord chamberlain's department, which meant in effect that one of the greatest art collections in the world was, in Millar's words, 'to a large extent in the hands of a succession of charming retired Lieutenant-Colonels of the (generally 1st) Foot Guards' (Millar, 17). Some other members of the royal household, including superintendents of royal palaces and even housekeepers, also claimed (and sometimes demonstrated) a proprietorial interest in the works of art in their various fiefdoms. Millar quickly realized that this was no way to run such an important collection, particularly one that was so freighted with history. Through diplomacy, tact, and perseverance he gained the support of his colleagues and dragged the Royal Collection into the modern era. He published specialist catalogues, organized exhibitions in the Queen's Gallery at Buckingham Palace (from 1963), and pursued an active conservation policy. All these developments were officially acknowledged at the time of the Peat Marwick report on the royal household commissioned by the queen through the lord chamberlain, which proposed that the Royal Collection should be made into a sixth department within the royal household and administered independently. As the first director of the modern Royal Collection (1987–8) Millar gained full responsibility for all the works of art throughout the royal residences—a phenomenal number of items including paintings, miniatures, drawings, prints, books, photographs, and manuscripts, as well as every conceivable aspect of the decorative arts. Symbolizing this new-found status was the setting up of a proper office for the surveyor of pictures and the surveyor of works of art in Stable Yard House in St James's Palace, which was a considerable advance on the two cramped rooms off a corridor in the state apartments, where for many years the surveyors were uncomfortably situated with a skeleton staff.

The concern that Millar showed for the practical needs of the Royal Collection was matched and even surpassed by his scholarly activities. His own personal contribution was three major catalogues of the British pictures: *The Tudor, Stuart and Early Georgian Pictures in the Collection of Her Majesty the Queen* (1963), followed by *The Later Georgian Pictures* (1969) and *The Victorian Pictures* (1992). The strength of these volumes lay principally in the extensive research done in the royal archives on the early provenances and picture movements within the palaces and the listing of the various versions or copies. Not much attention was paid to stylistic or iconographical matters. Millar also edited a series of catalogues of paintings by artists of the continental schools and of the miniatures, written at his invitation by distinguished scholars from outside the Royal Collection. In addition he wrote catalogues of the numerous exhibitions organized for the Queen's Gallery at Buckingham Palace on different wide-ranging themes.

Millar's highly compressed method of cataloguing did not do justice to the elegance of his prose, which was seen at its best in the introductions he wrote to his own catalogues of the British pictures. Describing the portraits of the duke and duchess of Cumberland by Thomas Gainsborough, for example, he wrote that 'the vicious little Duke, nervously fingering his George as he steals across the stage, and his raffish Duchess with her lovely eyes, are the most intelligent and amusing of all portraits bounded by the conventions of the state portrait'. *The Queen's Pictures*, published in 1977 to mark the silver jubilee of Elizabeth II's reign, and dedicated 'To all my colleagues in the Royal Households, 1947 to 1977', was a masterly and at the time of his death unsurpassed account of the pictures in the Royal Collection.

Millar's main area of expertise was seventeenth-century British art. Notable were his transcriptions of the inventories and documents recording Charles I's collection in two volumes of the Walpole Society (1960 and 1972). A leading authority on Sir Anthony Van Dyck, although regrettably he never found the time to write a definitive monograph, he organized the exhibition 'Van Dyck in England' (1982) at the National Portrait Gallery, and wrote about that part of the artist's life for *Van Dyck: a Complete Catalogue of the Paintings* (2004). This last was in some ways the summation of his own scholarly career as the book was a long-running project only brought to a close in the same year as the death of his wife, to whom he dedicated his section. They were a devoted couple, and mutual support had always been accorded their various independent undertakings, culminating in Millar's encouragement of his wife's monumental two-volume publication *The Victorian Watercolours and Drawings in the Collection of Her Majesty the Queen* (1995).

A series of pioneering exhibitions complemented Millar's work on Van Dyck: 'William Dobson' (1951), 'The Age of Charles I' (1972), and 'Sir Peter Lely' (1978). Yet, however much he favoured the seventeenth century, he was able to widen his focus to incorporate the achievements of such other artists as Johann Zoffany in the eighteenth century and Richard Redgrave (a former surveyor of the royal pictures) in the nineteenth. Overall his commitment to British art was of the greatest significance for the development of the subject. The high quality of the volume of essays published in his honour, *Art and Patronage in the Caroline Courts*, edited by David Howarth (1993), was testimony to the importance of his contribution.

Outside the Royal Collection Millar held a number of important positions, including those of trustee of the National Portrait Gallery (1972–95), visitor of the Ashmolean Museum (1987–93), trustee of the National Heritage Memorial Fund (1988–92), chairman of the Patrons of British Art at the Tate Gallery (1989–97), and president of the Walpole Society (1998–2007). He also served on the Reviewing Committee on the Export of Works of Art (1975–87) and the executive committee of the National Art Collections Fund (1986–98). He was elected a fellow of the British Academy in 1970.

A tall man with a slightly stooping gait, Millar never ceased to wonder at the beauty of the world surrounding him, whether it was manifested in art, music, or nature. His unalloyed pleasure on seeing beautiful pictures was expressed by sharp intakes of breath or a variety of short exhalations accompanied by a shrugging of the shoulders, a flapping of the elbows, and a shuffling of the feet with an almost childlike response of chuckles and snortles. A torch and a tape measure were his essential tools, together with an overcoat to offset the often freezing temperatures characteristic of royal palaces. Music, ornithology, and sport (particularly cricket and also golf) were engrossing passions matched by a love of Pope's poetry, Byron's letters, and novels by Dickens and Trollope.

The tendency to judge people by his own high standards often caused Millar to make sharp and sometimes wounding criticisms (occasionally retracted overnight) which to some made him seem like a bully when in fact he was a man capable of great sympathy and generosity of spirit, with a marked fondness for the young. There was an occasional air of snobbery in his conversation about the owners of those houses he visited in search of pictures by Van Dyck and Lely, but then this was no more than a characteristic of those of his generation. He was also by no means an unskilful artist in his own right, regularly designing and often making his own Christmas cards. His spidery handwriting, done with the finest of nibs and often embellished with the most elegant of paraphs, presented something of a challenge, to the extent that one of the queen's private secretaries (Sir Michael Adeane) once politely but firmly instructed him in a memorandum, 'Could you please use a typewriter' (private information).

Millar was a long-serving and remarkably effective surveyor of pictures, acutely aware and forever proud of the historical tradition in which he worked. He was always conscious of the standards and requirements of the queen, whom he referred to as 'the employer'. At all times he avoided sycophancy and some of his assessments of certain royal collectors were surprisingly hard-hitting. His essay entitled 'Surveyors past and present' in *The Queen's Pictures: Royal Collectors through the Centuries* (1991), the catalogue accompanying an exhibition in the National Gallery, ended with a meditation on the unique role that the surveyor still had in the British art world.

Millar, who lived latterly in Penn, Buckinghamshire, died on 10 May 2007 of a heart attack in St James's Square after inspecting a picture by Lely at Christies and while on his way to luncheon with two former colleagues at the National Gallery restaurant; he was declared dead at University College Hospital, Camden. Most appropriately, his *Portrait of Princess Mary (1631–1660), Princess Royal and later Princess of Orange* by Van Dyck was allocated after his death to Hampton Court Palace through the acceptance in lieu scheme. He was survived by his four children.

CHRISTOPHER LLOYD

Sources K. Rose, *Kings, queens and courtiers: intimate portraits of the royal house of Windsor from its foundation to the present day* (1985), 210 • O. Millar, 'Caring for the queen's pictures: surveyors past and present', in C. Lloyd, *The queen's pictures: royal collectors through the centuries* (1991), 14–18 [exhibition catalogue, National Gallery, London, 1992] • R. Allison and S. Riddell, eds., *The royal encyclopedia* (1991), 342 • *The Times* (12 May 2007) • *Daily Telegraph* (14 May 2007) • *The Independent* (16 May 2007) • *The Guardian* (17 May 2007) • *Burlington Magazine*, 149 (2007), 554–5 • Burke, *Peerage* • *WW* (2007) • personal knowledge (2011) • private information (2011) • b. cert. • m. cert. • d. cert.

Archives priv. coll. | Royal Arch., surveyor's papers

Likenesses photographs, 1983, Photoshot, London • L. A. Dickens, C-type colour print, 2001 (with Delia Mary, Lady Millar), NPG; repro. in *The Guardian* (17 May 2007) • R. Slade, photograph, repro. in Rose, *Kings*

Wealth at death £4,237,890: probate, 9 Jan 2008, *CGPLA Eng. & Wales*

Mills, Sir John Lewis Ernest Watts (1908–2005), actor, was born at Watts Naval Training School for Boys (a branch of Dr Barnardo's Homes) in Bintree, North Elmham, Norfolk, on 22 February 1908, the son of Lewis Mills (1867–1953), schoolmaster, and later headmaster of the village school at Belton, Suffolk, and his wife, Edith Catherine, *née* Baker (1868–1935). He had one sister, Edith Mabel, who later changed her name to Annette [*see* Mills, Annette (1894–1955)]. Fourteen years older than John, Annette was a dancer and it was she who first encouraged his desire to be an actor. He was educated first at his father's school in Belton, then at Balham grammar school, London, followed by Sir John Leman High School, Beccles, Suffolk, and finally Norwich High School for Boys, where at first, being small for his age, he was bullied. On leaving school, where he had distinguished himself more on the playing field than in the classroom, he was forced to supplement family finances by taking a job as a clerk in Ipswich. During this time he joined both the Felixstowe Players and the local amateur dramatic society. With limited support from his father, now separated from his mother (who, like Annette, was enthusiastic about his chances in the theatre), he set off for London and what eventually became one of the longest careers in British show business; not, however, before a brief, unsuccessful stint as a door-to-door salesman for Sanitas Company, toiletry suppliers.

Mills began his stage career as a dancer, first appearing at the New Cross Empire with Frances Day, then in the chorus of *The Five O'Clock Girl* at the London Hippodrome in 1929. (Over forty years later, in 1973, he delighted theatre audiences with a complicated tap routine in a production of *The Good Companions*.) Joining a travelling company called The Quaints, he embarked in the same year on a tour of the Far East that would introduce two very influential people into his life. In Tientsin, China, he met Mary Hayley Bell [*see below*], his doubles partner at tennis and, twelve years later, his second wife. The other meeting was professionally crucial: in Singapore, Noël Coward saw the company's performance of *Journey's End*, and was impressed enough with the young actor playing Raleigh to have him in mind for roles in *Cavalcade* (1931) and the musical revue *Words and Music* (1932).

Mills retained a lifelong love of the theatre and returned to it throughout his career, but it is as a film actor that he made a greater mark. It is scarcely an exaggeration to say that he became the quintessential British film star. In the 1930s he appeared in twenty films, starting with the Jessie Matthews musical *The Midshipmaid* (1932), and perhaps most notably including *Brown on Resolution* (1935; reissued

Sir John Lewis Ernest Watts Mills (1908–2005), by Cornel Lucas, 1950s

as *Forever England*), a naval adventure derived from C. S. Forester, and Mills's first major starring role in films. Most of his other films of the decade were unmemorable, though he was a likeable hero in *The Ghost Camera* (1933), drew engagingly on his song-and-dance skills in *Car of Dreams* (1935), and touchingly partnered Nova Pilbeam in the historical drama *Tudor Rose* (1936). On 12 March 1932 he had married the actress Aileen Cynthia Raymond (1910–2005), with whom he had acted on the Far East tour. She was the daughter of George Raymond, medical practitioner. By the late 1930s the marriage had failed, and Mills re-met Mary Hayley Bell, now in England and recovering from a broken romance. They eventually married on 16 January 1941, after Mills and his first wife had divorced.

The Second World War made Mills a star. He had been coming along quite agreeably in the 1930s without making a great impression: pleasant-looking rather than handsome, shorter (at about 5 feet 6 inches) than most leading men, adept across several genres rather than a compelling hero in any particular one. Invalided out of the Monmouthshire regiment with an ulcer in 1941, he was lucky enough to be in a series of popular, prestigious films in which he established a new sort of Everyman hero in British cinema. He may have lacked the dash of Robert Donat or the suavity of David Niven or the sensual menace of James Mason, but what he did convey was an essential decency and loyalty, a reliability in crisis that was especially reassuring in the early 1940s, a modesty of bearing (making his slight frame work for him), and a courage that was the more impressive for being so understated. There was a chap-next-door ordinariness about his persona that struck some very responsive chords.

Noël Coward, whom Mills claimed to have dubbed the Master, wrote the role of Shorty Blake with Mills in mind when he was preparing *In Which We Serve* (1942), a tribute to Lord Mountbatten's ship the *Kelly*, which had been sunk in the eastern Mediterranean. Mills's working-class boy who becomes a hero struck a true note in a film whose restraint later came to seem somewhat theatrical, and this was also true of his Billy Mitchell, who becomes a naval officer in the film of Coward's *This Happy Breed* (1944). Mills co-starred to convincing effect in both with Kay Walsh, then the wife of David Lean, who directed both and who would be a continuing influence in Mills's career. There were several other wartime films for Mills, including the submarine adventure *We Dive at Dawn* (1943) and the air force drama *The Way to the Stars* (1945), both for the director Anthony Asquith. The latter film, in production during the last months of the war but not released until after its end, was one of the most affecting films of the period, with Mills's reading of John Pudney's poem 'For Johnny' to a comrade's widow (Rosamund John) a quietly emotional highlight. In *Waterloo Road* (1945), he played a soldier who goes absent without leave to protect his wife from the unwelcome attentions of a spiv-like lothario and cemented his reputation as the ordinary man who can rise to the occasion. In a very cleverly staged fight, short, slight Mills convincingly dealt with the much taller and heavier Stewart Granger.

It was as though these wartime roles had been preparing Mills for the post-war British cinema in which a new realism would predominate, at least in those films that brought most prestige to the industry. Mason and Granger would shortly defect to Hollywood but Mills remained a British star, only rarely venturing into American films. In his first post-war role, he was a definitive Pip in Lean's classic version of *Great Expectations* (1946). When, at the film's end, he rips down the curtains in Miss Havisham's decaying mansion, this can be seen as symbolic of shedding new light on ossified traditions—and announcing a new sort of hero, not merely one who has risen in society but also one who will not be satisfied merely to perpetuate the past. In his next (and contrasting) post-war role, in *The October Man* (1947), Mills played Jim Ackland, a brain-damaged man who fears he may have killed someone: the murder inquiry is secondary to the 'internalised battle involving Jim's psychological problem' (Mayer, 102). Mills's versatility was being subtly confirmed in such roles, which allowed mutations on the Everyman persona without obliterating it. He might have made *Scott of the Antarctic* (1948) a less ponderous paean if he had been allowed to explore Scott's character in more human detail, but it was a high-profile film of its day and chosen for the royal film performance of the year. He was more interesting as Bassett, the groom, in *The Rocking Horse Winner* (1950), and as the meek little protagonist in *The History of Mr Polly* (1949), both of which he produced. Years later he said, 'I wasn't a very good producer because I was always trying to get on the floor and I didn't really like the office work' (McFarlane, *British Cinema*, 415).

The 1950s are often regarded, perhaps unfairly, as a dullish decade in British cinema, with too many films dealing in *Boy's Own* fashion with the war. Certainly Mills came in for his share of these, but he nevertheless brought his effortless-seeming authority to bear in such wartime adventures as *The Colditz Story* (1955), *Above Us the Waves* (1955), *I Was Monty's Double* (1958), and *Dunkirk* (1958). During this period he was unobtrusively shading into character roles, in such films as *The Long Memory* (1952), as a man released after twelve years in prison for a murder he didn't commit; *The End of the Affair* (1955), as a shabby private detective; *Tiger Bay* (1959), the film that made an instant star of his younger daughter, Hayley, and in which he played the police superintendent; and, best of all the war-based adventures, *Ice Cold in Alex* (1958), as the captain battling alcoholism and north African minefields. Earlier in the decade his association with David Lean reached another peak with his perfect incarnation of the bootmaker Willie Mossop in *Hobson's Choice* (1954): in this Mills most effectively married the twin aspects of his screen image, as both little man and hero of a kind.

The British 'new wave' of the late 1950s and early 1960s passed Mills by, but he managed to give some of his most subtly honed performances in the character roles that prolifically did come his way. Two studies in resentful military types further attested to his protean abilities: his twitchy by-the-book lieutenant-colonel who clashes with the boisterous extrovert played by Alec Guinness in *Tunes of Glory* (1960) was a masterly study of neurotic repression; and two years later he mined some of this neurosis for social comedy in *Tiara Tahiti* (1962). His daughter Hayley's career was burgeoning rapidly and he directed her, though not with much success, in *Sky West and Crooked* (1966), from a screenplay by Mary Hayley Bell. Much more successful was *The Family Way* (1966), in which he played Hayley's father-in-law, and most movingly suggested that no relationship in his life had meant as much to him as that with his long-lost friend Billy.

Mills was in some poor films (with appearances in more than 100 films this was inevitable) and was sometimes miscast, as he was in *War and Peace* (1956), as a Russian peasant, or as an Australian cane-cutter in *Summer of the Seventeenth Doll* (1959). Some would also say that his Oscar-winning turn as the village idiot in Lean's Irish-set romance, the tedious *Ryan's Daughter* (1970), was a triumph that owed more to cosmetic than to histrionic art. Nevertheless, he could give stature to such modest films as *The Vicious Circle* (1957) and could imbue cameo roles in 'big' films with a momentary presence, as he did in Kenneth Branagh's *Hamlet* (1996), as Old Norway, for whom Shakespeare had carelessly failed to provide dialogue. In his last film, *Bright Young Things* (2003), at the age of ninety-five, he was briefly vivid as a coke-snorting socialite. Throughout his long career in the British film industry he also continued to act on stage. Most memorably he and John Gielgud caused both outrage and hilarity with the profanities of their roles in Charles Wood's *Veterans* in 1972, the reactions to which he amusingly described in the television talk shows in which he frequently appeared in the 1990s and 2000s. No physical infirmity, including near-blindness towards the end, was allowed to stand in his way.

'The family way' might well describe the other path by which John Mills came to occupy such a secure place in filmgoers' affections and esteem. Both daughters, Juliet (*b.* 1941) and Hayley (*b.* 1946), went on to notable acting careers; his son Jonathan (*b.* 1949) was a screenwriter; while **Mary Hayley Bell** (1911–2005) continued to write, though she largely subordinated her aspirations to those of her husband and children. Born in Shanghai on 22 January 1911, the daughter of Francis Hayley Bell, an army officer and commissioner for maritime customs in China, and his American wife, Agnes (1878–1960), she was educated first by a governess, then at Malvern Girls' College and the Royal Academy of Dramatic Art. She first appeared on stage in Shanghai in *The Barretts of Wimpole Street* (1932) and subsequently in several roles on Broadway and in the West End. She stopped acting following her marriage to Mills and turned her attention to writing. Her first performed play, *Men in Shadow* (1942), with Mills starring, had a substantial success at London's Vaudeville Theatre, as did her most famous play, *Duet for Two Hands* (1945, at the Lyric), in which Mills played a maimed poet on whom a surgeon unwittingly grafts a murderer's hands. She gradually lost interest in writing plays when they proved difficult to place, and turned her attention to other forms. Her most acclaimed work was the novel *Whistle Down the Wind* (1958), which was attractively filmed in 1961 by Bryan Forbes, with Hayley as one of the children who mistakes an escaped convict for Jesus Christ. She also wrote an autobiography, *What Shall We Do Tomorrow?* (1968), and a book about the family dog in 1981. Above all she concentrated her attention on domestic matters, raising three children and maintaining a marriage of legendary happiness and longevity. She suffered from vascular dementia in later years, and like Mills she also lost her sight, but they managed to walk down the aisle in a renewal of their marriage vows in 2001. She died on 1 December 2005 at their home, Four Gables, Village Road, Denham, Buckinghamshire, of heart failure.

Mills had predeceased his wife on 23 April 2005, also at Four Gables, following a stroke. He had been made a CBE in 1960 and knighted in 1976; his memoir, *Up in the Clouds, Gentlemen Please*, was published in 1980, followed by *Still Memories* in 2000; but his greatest achievements are fortunately preserved in the films in which he made his name and on which he conferred such distinction.

BRIAN MCFARLANE

Sources M. H. Bell, *What shall we do tomorrow?* (1968) · *Who's who in the theatre*, 15th edn (1972) · B. McFarlane, *An autobiography of British cinema* (1997) · J. Mills, *Up in the clouds, gentlemen please* (1980) · S. Granger, *Sparks fly upward* (1981) · J. Mills, *Still memories* (2000) · B. McFarlane, ed., *The encyclopedia of British film* (2003) · G. Mayer, *Roy Ward Baker* (2004) · B. McFarlane, *Sight and Sound* (June 2005) · *The Times* (25 April 2005) · *Daily Telegraph* (25 April 2005) · *The Guardian* (25 April 2005) · *The Independent* (25 April 2005) · *The Times* (3 Dec

2005) [Mary Hayley Bell] • *The Guardian* (5 Dec 2005) [Mary Hayley Bell] • *The Independent* (5 Dec 2005) [Mary Hayley Bell] • *WW* (2005) • Burke, *Peerage* • personal knowledge (2009) • private information (2009) [Hayley Mills, daughter] • b. cert. • m. certs. • d. cert. • d. cert. [Mary Hayley Bell]

Archives Boston University, Massachusetts, USA, plays etc. [Mary Hayley Bell] • priv. coll. | FILM BL NSA, 'John Mills: eighty years on', with C. Frayling, BBC 1, 19 Feb 1988, V5195/1 • BL NSA, *The South Bank show*, 'Sir John Mills', LWT, 22 Sept 1996, V3799/2 • BL NSA, documentary footage • BL NSA, performance footage | SOUND BL NSA, documentary recordings • BL NSA, performance recordings

Likenesses photographs, 1931–2003, Getty Images, London • Stage Photo Company, group portrait, glossy bromide print, 1934, NPG • photographs, 1935–2005, Rex Features, London • photographs, 1941–2004, PA Photos, London • photographs, 1941–2004, Camera Press, London • F. W. Daniels, bromide print, 1945, NPG • photographs, 1946–2002, Photoshot, London • C. Lucas, bromide print, 1950–59, NPG [*see illus.*] • photograph, *c.*1951, Kobal Collection, London • H. Mee, oils, 1984, priv. coll. • N. Sinclair, selenium-toned silver print, 1990, NPG • obituary photographs

Wealth at death £399,685: probate, 20 July 2005, *CGPLA Eng. & Wales* • £91,820—Mary Hayley Bell: probate, 20 April 2006, *CGPLA Eng. & Wales*

Milton, (Clement) Arthur (1928–2007), cricketer and footballer, was born on 10 March 1928 in Bristol General Hospital, the son of William Clement Milton (1898–1980), a mechanic in a cardboard box factory, and his wife, Violet May, *née* Cryer (1897–1985). At the time of his birth registration the family lived at 6 Maple Avenue, Fishponds, Bristol. William Milton was a keen club cricketer and introduced his son to the game as a boy. Arthur was a pupil at Hillfields Park infants and junior school between 1933 and 1939 and then attended Cotham grammar school in Bristol, where he showed considerable ability in mathematics: later in life he regretted not taking his education further. At school he was known as Archie and, a natural games player with a dramatic turn of speed, he captained the cricket, rugby, and football teams. He also played cricket for his local club, Stapleton. He was encouraged by an English master at Cotham, Bert Crew, who at one time served as the scorer for Gloucestershire County Cricket Club. During Milton's time at the school two other future players for Gloucestershire and England, David Allen and John Mortimore, were also pupils there.

Milton's skill and speed on the right wing brought him to the notice of Arsenal, for whose reserve team he played before being called up for national service in the army in 1946. By 1948, in his other chosen sport, he had graduated from Gloucestershire's second eleven to play two matches for the county side. His first-class début came in June of that year in a county match against Northamptonshire. He then made 58 runs not out against the combined services, enough to secure him a contract with Gloucestershire for the next summer. He scored his first century for his county in the 1951 season and in the following year achieved national prominence when he aggregated 1992 runs at an average of 43.68.

By this stage Milton was already an England international at football. He had played only twelve first-division matches on the right wing for Arsenal when an injury to Tom Finney led to his late inclusion in the England team for a match at Wembley—his one and only international cap—against Austria in November 1951. He shone at first but did not contribute much thereafter to a 2–2 draw. Picked for England at the last moment—he had to collect his boots and take a bus across London to join the England team at their hotel—he was perhaps mentally unprepared to play at this level. Meanwhile at Arsenal his highly talented team-mates included Eddie Hapgood, Ted Drake, and the Compton brothers, Denis and Leslie. Among such players he struggled to hold his place and was not picked for the 1952 cup final against Newcastle. But he appeared twenty-three times for the championship-winning team of 1952–3 and a further twenty-nine times for Arsenal over the next two seasons.

In February 1955 Milton was transferred to his local team, Bristol City, for a fee of £3000. He played fourteen times for them in the remainder of the season and helped Bristol to the third division title. But at this point he decided that the strain of all-year sport was too much and that cricket was his game, so retired from professional football. In all he had made eighty-nine senior club appearances, and scored a creditable twenty-one goals. Meanwhile, on 22 August 1953 he had married Joan Anita Gore (*b.* 1933), bank clerk, and daughter of Robert Frederick Gore, electrical engineer. Joan's mother was Milton's first landlady as an Arsenal player. They had three sons, Robert, David, and Richard.

Milton was the twelfth man in the cricket home series against Australia in 1953 and in the first test against South Africa in 1955, though he withdrew from the latter match through injury. His international début came in the third test against New Zealand at Headingley on 3 July 1958. He opened the batting there with another double international (though in rugby and cricket), the future England captain M. J. K. Smith, and scored 104 not out—the first Gloucestershire player to score a century on his test début since W. G. Grace. Remarkably Milton contrived to stay on the pitch throughout the match, fielding through New Zealand's first innings, carrying his bat as an opener throughout the England innings, and then fielding again through the New Zealand second innings in a match England won by an innings and 71 runs. He played again in the fifth test at the Oval and then toured Australia during the following winter, when he played in the tests at Brisbane and Sydney. An injury to a finger forced him to return home early, but he had not been playing at his best in any case. Two further tests followed against India in 1959, but the second match of this series, at Lord's, was his last international appearance. In all he had played six test matches for England in 1958 and 1959.

Milton was one of the Wisden cricketers of the year in 1959. He was a gifted batsman, but never quite in the very highest class. In six tests he made 204 runs at an average of 25.50. His career in county cricket continued to flourish, however, and he became a much-loved senior professional for Gloucestershire who was admired far beyond the county. Usually an opening batsman, he played 620 first-class matches for his county, and amassed 32,150 runs at an average of 33.73, including more than fifty centuries. Playing largely off the back foot he was noted for his ability to cut and pull the ball. Fast between the wickets, he was also the master of the quick single. He took 79 wickets with his right-arm medium pace bowling and 758 catches in the field, one of the highest totals ever in first-class cricket: his fitness and speed made him a notably fine fielder and he freely admitted that as a cricketer he enjoyed fielding the most. His sharp mind and facility with numbers made him a very good judge of the tempo of an innings and the balance of a match.

The statistics for his batting were not outstanding, but it was his dependability and consistency, alongside his modesty and west-country charm, that endeared him to his many admirers. Fair-haired, of medium height, and boyish in appearance, he made more than a thousand runs in sixteen seasons, enjoying some of his best performances towards the end of his career when, in 1967, aged thirty-nine, he passed 2000 runs in a season in which he scored seven centuries. He captained Gloucestershire in the following year, finally retiring after twenty-six years of playing for the county in 1974. His total of 1017 innings for Gloucestershire was still at the time of his death the record for the county.

Milton's inclusion in the England football team was undoubtedly fortunate; on the other hand, with better luck he might well have played in more test matches for his country. As the last man to have played both cricket and football for England, he was one of a celebrated band of twelve double-internationals, including such figures as C. B. Fry and Milton's contemporary Willie Watson, who represented their country at both sports. In retirement he coached the University of Oxford's cricket team during the mid-1970s. He enjoyed talking to the players about their studies as much as their cricket. For ten years between 1978 and 1988 he was a postman attached to the Westbury-on-Trym sorting office and in retirement he delivered newspapers around his home on the Bristol downs. Valuing academic life as he did he was especially gratified by the award of an honorary degree in 2002 by the University of Bristol. He died on 25 April 2007 at Southmead Hospital, Bristol, of ischaemic heart disease, and was survived by his wife and three sons.

LAWRENCE GOLDMAN

Sources *Wisden* (1959) · *Gloucestershire cricketers, 1870–1979*, Association of Cricket Statisticians (1979) · D. Hayes, *Gloucestershire cricketing greats* (1990) · 'Milton's sporting paradise', *The Cricketer* (Sept 1991); www.cricinfo.com/england/content/story/139120.html, 3 Aug 2010 · K. Gerrish, *Gloucestershire County Cricket Club first-class records, 1870–1997* (1998) · D. Hayes, *Gloucestershire County Cricket Club* (1998) · G. Hudd, *Arthur Milton* (2000) · www.cricinfo.com/england/content/story/292360.html, 3 Aug 2010 · *Daily Telegraph* (27 April 2007) · *The Guardian* (27 April 2007) · *The Independent* (27 April 2007) · *The Times* (28 April 2007) · www.cricinfo.com/wisdenalmanack/content/story/353626.html, 3 Aug 2010 · b. cert. · m. cert. · d. cert.

Likenesses photographs, 1946–51, Rex Features, London · S & G, photographs, 1951–68, PA Photos, London · photograph, 1954, Photoshot, London · D. Davies, photograph, 2006, PA Photos, London · obituary photographs · photograph, repro. in www.cricinfo.com/england/content/player/17037.html

Wealth at death under £244,000: probate, 11 Feb 2008, *CGPLA Eng. & Wales*

Minghella, Anthony (1954–2008), playwright, screenwriter, and film director, was born on 6 January 1954 at 76 Pellhurst Road, Ryde, Isle of Wight, the second of five children of Edward Minghella (*b.* 1921) and his wife, Gloria Alberta, *née* Arcari (*b.* 1930), both second-generation offspring of Italian immigrants. He grew up in a bustling household with three sisters, a younger brother, and a spirited maternal grandmother, where everyone was expected to lend a hand to make a success of the family business, the manufacture and sale of quality ice cream at a high-street café. Prophetically enough, his main contribution as a child was to sell ices from a tray in the cinema next door. Enrolled at eleven as a day boy at St John's College, a Catholic boarding school in Southsea, he became rebellious and took to playing truant. He fared better after moving in 1969 to Sandown grammar school, especially in the sixth form, where a dynamic English teacher involved him in performances with a local dramatic society and urged him to apply to university.

A gifted pianist who played keyboards with teenage rock bands, Minghella had seemed destined for a career in music, but in 1972 he was offered a place to read drama at Hull University. There, the balance in the degree course between formal academic study, practical tuition, and hands-on experience of production work on stage or in television and radio studios precisely answered his needs and served to develop his latent talents. On gaining a first in 1975, he embarked on postgraduate research into the work of Samuel Beckett and was engaged initially as a part-time tutorial assistant in the drama department, before being appointed to a lectureship in 1978. It was during this period that he wrote and directed his earliest plays, *Mobius the Stripper* (a musical based on the story by Gabriel Josipovici) and *Whale Music*, both first performed by students in the department's theatre, and made his first film, *A Little Like Drowning* (later rewritten as a stage play). Through the department he also met the Hull-based playwright Alan Plater, who gave him encouragement and commissioned another piece, *Child's Play*, for presentation at Hull Arts Centre, of which Plater was chairman. Subsequently Minghella always acknowledged his debt to the intellectual and creative stimulus he derived from his nine years at Hull University, and returned there to give master classes and to receive an honorary DLitt in 1997.

On 20 September 1975 he married Yvonne Allport, a 22-year-old psychologist, and daughter of Rex Allport, technical sales representative; they had one daughter, Hannah (*b.* 1979), but the marriage soon ended in separation and ultimately divorce, and in 1981 Minghella abandoned both teaching and research to make his way in London as a full-time writer. Later that year *Whale Music* was staged professionally at the Leicester Haymarket, and was soon followed by two new plays, *Two Planks and a Passion* at the Northcott Theatre, Exeter, in 1983, and *Love Bites* at Derby Playhouse in 1984. Together these earned him the Critics' Circle award in 1984 for most promising playwright, and at London's Aldwych two years later he took the award for best play with *Made in Bangkok*, a sardonic

Anthony Minghella (1954–2008), by Wyatt Counts, 1996

commentary on the interface between economic and sexual exploitation. He had already secured a foothold in television in 1981 as co-author, with Jim Hawkins, of the BBC drama series *Maybury*, set in a hospital psychiatric unit. He maintained a regular low-key presence during the mid-1980s as script editor of *Grange Hill* before establishing his reputation in 1986 on Channel 4 with *What If It's Raining?*, a dramatic trilogy, dedicated to his daughter, poignantly recounting the breakdown of a marriage and its impact on a parent–child relationship, in which the prevailing mood of autobiographical hurt is undercut by irony and occasional slapstick. In the meantime he had remarried, on 2 March 1985, to the Hong Kong-born dancer–choreographer (and former fellow student a year his junior) Carolyn Jane Choa (formerly Lunn), daughter of George Choa, medical practitioner. Their son, Max Giorgio, was born in the same year.

In the late 1980s Minghella contributed episodes to ITV's crime series *Inspector Morse* and *Boon*, and, in contrast, scripted Jim Henson's live action/puppet programmes for children, *The Storyteller* (1988) and *Living with Dinosaurs* (1989). Switching media, he proved equally responsive to the possibilities of radio drama with *Hang Up* (1987), which won the Prix Italia, and *Cigarettes and Chocolate* (1988), which picked up Giles Cooper and Sony awards.

A watershed that largely determined Minghella's creative future was reached in 1990 with *Truly, Madly, Deeply*, a dark fantasy, interlaced with wry comedy, about a traumatic bereavement and the regenerative power of love, which Minghella both wrote and directed. Initially commissioned for BBC television, it was released as a feature film and met with critical as well as popular acclaim on both sides of the Atlantic, collecting a BAFTA and a Writers' Guild award for best original screenplay, and giving him a directorial entrée to Hollywood. His first film there, *Mr Wonderful* (1993), a low-budget romantic comedy about a divorced couple rediscovering mutual attraction, was affecting but unremarkable, whereas its successor, *The English Patient* (1996), which he adapted from the novel by Michael Ondaatje and shot on location in Italy and Tunisia, caused a sensation. Ambitious in narrative structure and emotional intensity alike, this saga of adulterous grand passion and tragic redemption dominated the industry's trophy ceremonies, amassing nine Academy awards (including those for best picture and best director), two Golden Globes, and six BAFTAs. His adaptation, too, of Patricia Highsmith's *The Talented Mr Ripley* (1999) was commended by reviewers for its subtle handling of the homoerotic infatuation and class envy underlying the action and leading inexorably to multiple homicide. In the following year he joined the American director Sydney Pollack as partner in the independent production company Mirage Enterprises, but a disappointingly ambivalent reception was accorded to his expansive screen version of Charles Frazier's novel *Cold Mountain* (2003), an *Odyssey*-like tale of doomed romantic love set against a backdrop of the American Civil War, which emblematically counterpointed sequences of battlefield carnage and lawless marauding against images of restoring a moribund farm to fruitful life.

As a mark of the professional esteem in which he was now held, Minghella was appointed CBE in 2001, and awarded further honorary doctorates by the universities of Southampton (2000), Bournemouth (2001), and Reading (2006). In 2003 he identified himself with the cause of cinema in the UK by becoming chairman of the British Film Institute, redefining its purview to attract a more inclusive public and promote a broader, better informed film culture. To this end he oversaw a major expansion of the facilities at BFI Southbank and raised additional funding to restore and digitize the institute's unique film archives for wider access. Off duty he demonstrated his political affiliation by producing an election broadcast for the Labour Party in 2005 and his sporting allegiance as a lifelong supporter of Portsmouth FC, memorabilia of whose exploits shared domestic shelf space with his own.

In 2005 Minghella returned triumphantly to the London theatre with an imaginative production for English National Opera of Puccini's *Madam Butterfly*, featuring choreography by his wife and a life-size, bunraku-style puppet as Butterfly's child, which, save for die-hard traditionalists, enthralled audiences at the Coliseum and won an Olivier award, before being restaged at the Metropolitan Opera in New York. There was applause, too, at The Place for his witty 'text for dance', *Self Assembly*, but his return to present-day London for *Breaking and Entering*

(2006) aroused little excitement: his attempt to encompass in one film issues of divided loyalty, conflicting value systems, and personal accountability in a multi-ethnic King's Cross was seen as overly contrived and unconvincing.

Minghella's last film, an adaptation with Richard Curtis of Alexander McCall Smith's *The No. 1 Ladies' Detective Agency*, shot in Botswana, was shown on BBC television in March 2008 to a mixed critical reaction overshadowed by a sense of shock at his untimely death. He had died suddenly at Charing Cross Hospital five days earlier, on 18 March, of a haemorrhage following an apparently successful operation for cancer of the tonsils. He was cremated at Golders Green crematorium, and survived by his wife, Carolyn, and his children. Obituaries were suffused with profound regret for an outstanding talent denied the opportunity to attain his full potential; equally regrettable in retrospect is that so much creative energy which could have been reserved for his own highly original writing was expended on adapting that of others.

Of the work that Minghella did complete, perhaps the most remarkable quality is its sheer versatility: with a resourcefulness evident in his early writing for the stage, he quickly adjusted to the demands of radio or television drama before mastering those of film-making, and proceeded to achieve international recognition in each. No less striking is its range of tone. Minghella's enterprise in tackling story-lines of epic grandeur, with locations to match, and in which the musical score plays an organic part, prompted comparisons with David Lean, yet alongside the great vistas of desert sand or spectacles of Confederate bloodshed he crafted scenes of compelling tenderness and intimacy, in which the precise rhythmical texture of his writing elicited performances of exquisite sensitivity and nuance from his actors. At the heart of virtually his entire body of work lay a deep-seated thematic preoccupation with the various complexions of love (and its vulnerability to separation, estrangement, and loss), together with a predilection for confronting audiences with a problematic situation viewed from multiple angles, in line with his belief that films should function as 'some kind of moral gymnasium' (*The Independent*, 12 December 2003). He was well served by his empathetic rapport with actors, several of whom chose to work with him on more than one film, as did key members of his production team. While ostensibly an auteur, intent on realizing his own screenplays, he was certainly no autocrat: his closest associates invariably described his approach as that of a born collaborator, unpretentious, even-tempered, funny, with a warm generosity of spirit that brought out the best in others, and, above all perhaps, a lucid intelligence. He remained at bottom an intellectual, unwavering in his devotion to Beckett, of whose *Play* he directed an incisive production for Channel 4's Beckett on Film cycle in 2000 and whose inventive command of language he singled out as the most potent influence on his own writing. A new drama studio was named in his honour at Hull University, as were a departmental building at Southampton University and a theatre at the Quay Arts Centre in Newport, Isle of Wight, of which he was made a freeman in 1997 and where an annual film festival was instituted in his memory. Both his children went on to pursue active film careers in America. DONALD ROY

Sources *The Independent* (26 March 1997); (12 Dec 2003); (19 March 2008) · *Hull Daily Mail* (4 July 1997) · D. Argent, 'The talented mister', *Creative Screenwriting* (Jan/Feb 2000) · E. Cochrane, interview, *Empire* (March 2000) · *The Observer* [review section] (19 Jan 2003) · *Screen International* (16 April 2004) · J. Davis, 'Breaking and entering', *Creative Screenwriting* (Nov/Dec 2006) · *The Times* (19 March 2008); (20 March 2008) · *Daily Telegraph* (19 March 2008) · *The Guardian* (19 March 2008); (20 March 2008) · *Sunday Times* (23 March 2008) · *Screen International* (28 March 2008) · R. Stayton, 'The talented Mr Minghella', *Written By* (April 2008) · *Sight and Sound* (May 2008) · www.screenonline.org.uk/people/id/497858/index.html, 25 April 2011 · *WW* (2008) · personal knowledge (2012) · private information (2012) [Edward and Gloria Minghella, parents; J. Lunn; J. Stevenson; R. Cooper; A. Nevill; J. Daish] · b. cert. · m. certs. · d. cert.

Archives U. Hull, archives [drafts etc.] | FILM BFINA, 'Anthony Minghella talks to Mark Lawson', *Mark Lawson talks to...*, M. Lawson (interviewer), BBC4, 27 Dec 2003 · BFINA, 'Love, loss and Anthony Minghella', *Imagine*, M. Springford (director), BBC1, 8 July 2008 · BFINA, current affairs and documentary footage · *A life in pictures: Anthony Minghella*, www.bafta.org · *Media Masterclass: Anthony Minghella*, http://youtu.be/-ihVndJm_yM · interview at Starz Denver Film Festival, http://youtu.be/KaeK8Nvrank | SOUND BL NSA, documentary recordings

Likenesses P. Tozer, bromide fibre print, 1990, NPG · photographs, 1993–2007, Rex Features, London · W. Counts, photograph, 1996, PA Photos, London [*see illus.*] · photographs, 1996–2007, Getty Images, London · photographs, 1996–2007, PA Photos, London · P. Dawes, photograph, 1997, repro. in *Hull Daily Mail* (4 July 1997) · photograph, 1997, repro. in *Daily Mail* (26 March 1997) · photographs, 1997–2007, Photoshot, London · F. Greer, bromide print, 1998, NPG · photograph, *c*.1999, repro. in *The Guardian* (15 Dec 2001) · G. Calton, photograph, repro. in *The Observer* (19 Jan 2003) · J. Evans, photograph, repro. in *The Independent* (12 Dec 2003) · N. Turner, photograph, repro. in *Times Higher Education Supplement* (14 March 1997) · obituary photographs · photograph, repro. in *The Independent* (26 March 1997)

Wealth at death £6,581,238: probate, 28 Oct 2009, *CGPLA Eng. & Wales*

Mishcon, Victor, **Baron Mishcon** (**1915–2006**), solicitor and politician, was born on 14 August 1915 at 1 Helix Road, Brixton, London, the son of Rabbi Arnold Mishcon (1879/80–1935), who had emigrated from Poland, and his west-country wife, Queenie, *née* Osler (1878/9–1949), who was a teacher at an elementary school. His father had become a rabbi at the age of twenty-two, and four years later became rabbi at the United Synagogue in Brixton, of which he was the founder. He was an authority on Jewish liturgy and one of the compilers of the English translation of the Babylonian Talmud.

Legal practice As a boy Mishcon attended Dulwich College preparatory school, but its senior school was ruled out because it had Saturday morning classes which, because of his religion, he could not attend, so he went to the City of London School. He said later that he would have liked to have become a barrister but, not having the wealthy parents or independent income necessary for the early years at the bar, he instead became an articled clerk, undertaking the five years of articles that at that time could lead to

Victor Mishcon, Baron Mishcon (1915–2006), by Carolyn Djanogly, 2000

qualification as a solicitor. Through his father's connections he was articled to Walter D'Arcy Hart, a partner at Gilbert, Samuel & Co., a firm based in the City of London. He was offered a position there on completing his articles but decided he would be better off starting his own firm. In the 1930s there was no period of supervised practice for the newly qualified solicitor, so in 1937, at the age of twenty-one, he established Victor Mishcon & Co., at 463–5 Brixton Road, above Barclays Bank. At that time Brixton was an important shopping centre in south London, with department stores such as Morleys, a thriving market, a cinema, and a theatre.

During the Second World War Mishcon served in the Royal Fusiliers. He became a major, but did not see active service. The firm was meanwhile continued by his managing clerk, Leon Simmons. By the early 1950s Mishcon had founded another firm, specializing in trade-union work, Blatchfords, in Norwich House, Southampton Place. It was in that building that by the late 1950s Victor Mishcon & Co. had established a central London office. In 1961 the firm moved around the corner to 125 High Holborn and Mishcon acquired his first partner. The Brixton branch was closed shortly after. Before the move to central London, Victor Mishcon & Co. had a mixed practice, some commercial work, with company formation and liquidation, property, estates, and litigation, including proceedings for personal injury, property compensation claims, and family law. By the late 1950s the firm was also conducting litigation in the field of consumer credit for what was one of its important commercial clients at the time, Lombard Banking Ltd. By the late 1960s Victor Mishcon & Co. had five partners. That had not increased by the mid-1970s, although there were as many assistant solicitors again. Even by the late 1980s the firm had fewer than ten partners, fifteen lawyers in all. It was a typical small central London firm, with commercial work and private clients. But by this time other law firms were growing substantially. A merger thus made sense. In 1988 the merger with some of the partners of Bartletts de Reya, a firm based in Fleet Street, to form Mishcon de Reya, created a firm employing eighty staff. In 1992 Mishcon retired as senior partner of the firm, although he remained as a consultant and attended the firm regularly, almost until his death. His personal charm and judgement made him immensely attractive to private clients. His style was to seek to avoid litigation if possible. He had a reputation, however, as a tough negotiator. His success turned on his extraordinary sense of judgement, tact, and shrewdness.

Mishcon's first celebrity client was Ruth Ellis, whose hanging in 1955 was an important catalyst in the abolition of capital punishment in Britain. Mishcon had acted for Ellis for her divorce, but had declined to defend her on the murder charge, on the grounds that he was not qualified. However, after her conviction for murder she wished to make a will, especially so that arrangements were in place for her two young children. Mishcon and his clerk, Leon Simmons, visited her in prison. In the course of the consultation she revealed that Desmond Cussen had supplied her with the loaded revolver and driven her to Hampstead to confront David Blakely. Mishcon persuaded her to allow him to apply for a reprieve. He visited the Home Office, but Cussen could not be found in time to corroborate her story, and she was hanged the following day.

In the 1960s Mishcon was solicitor to Donald Campbell, who broke world speed records, at a time when Campbell was in dispute with one of his backers, Sir Alfred Owen. Jeffrey Archer was another client when, as the MP for Louth in 1974, judgment was obtained against him for some £172,162 owed to Anthony Bamford, which Archer had borrowed to buy shares. Subsequently the firm acted for Archer in his successful defamation action in 1987 against the *Daily Star*, when the newspaper alleged that Archer had slept with a prostitute. Fourteen years later Archer was imprisoned on charges of perjury and perverting the course of justice for the evidence he gave in that case. Lord Palumbo, the property developer, was also a client, and Mishcon de Reya represented him most notably in the litigation that went to the House of Lords over the controversial development, number 1 Poultry, in the City of London.

It was Palumbo who introduced the firm's most famous client, Diana, princess of Wales. She first used the firm in actions against the *Sunday Mirror*, which published photographs of her exercising at a gym in 1993. Then the firm acted for her in her divorce from Prince Charles. Mishcon recorded a note of what the princess told him and two of his partners at a meeting at Kensington Palace in October 1995, to the effect that

> efforts would ... be made if not to get rid of her, be it by some accident in her car, such as pre-prepared brake failure or whatever ... at least to see that she was so injured or damaged as to be declared 'unbalanced'. (www.scottbaker-inquests.gov.uk/evidence/docs/INQ0006335.pdf)

Mishcon noted that he could not accept that this was credible. None the less, when the princess died in a car accident in Paris less than two years later, he handed over the note to the Metropolitan Police. The note became public at the inquest conducted into Diana's death in 2007–8 by Lord Justice Scott Baker.

Politics From 1945 to 1949 Mishcon was a Labour member of Lambeth borough council for Angell ward, and chaired its finance committee for two years. In March 1946 he was elected to London county council (LCC), representing Brixton, and served until the abolition of the council in 1965. During his time on the LCC he chaired various committees, and was appointed chairman of the council in 1954–5. Along with others, he strongly opposed the Conservative government's proposals to abolish the LCC. When the Greater London council (GLC) finally replaced the LCC, he became Lambeth's representative until he was swept from office in the swingeing defeat the Labour Party suffered in the 1967 local elections. Until then he was chairman of the general purposes committee. Along with others, including Isaac Hayward and Reginald Goodwin, he was one of the 'inner cabinet' of the LCC and GLC during the 1950s and 1960s. London government brought him into contact with national political leaders and enabled him to speak authoritatively on a range of subjects. In 1954 he was appointed a member of the Wolfenden committee, which recommended that homosexual behaviour between consenting adults should no longer be a criminal offence.

While always extolling the virtues of local government, Mishcon tried a number of times to enter the House of Commons. He was the Labour Party candidate for Leeds North-West in 1950 and for Bath in 1951. In 1955 he was a candidate in Gravesend, Kent. Sir Richard Acland, the Labour MP, had resigned his seat in protest against the party's policy on nuclear weapons and intended to fight a by-election as an independent on the issue. Mishcon was selected to fight as the Labour candidate. But a general election intervened, and the seat was won by the Conservatives with a majority of 2909 votes, Acland splitting the Labour vote. Mishcon was re-endorsed for Gravesend in 1959, but this time the Conservatives made much of his legal work for his cousin Maxwell Joseph, a hotelier and property developer, who was engaged in taking over a hotel group at a time when the Labour Party was running a campaign against takeovers. The Conservative majority was increased. In singling Mishcon out in a series of stories the *Daily Express* 'managed to combine xenophobia, implicit anti-Semitism, and malice' (D. Butler and R. Rose, *The British General Election of 1959*, 1960, 113). There was a final foray for a parliamentary seat in 1963, when Mishcon's name was added to those already on the Labour Party shortlist for the vacancy caused in Leeds South by the death of the party leader, Hugh Gaitskell. But Merlyn Rees was narrowly chosen and became the MP at the by-election.

In March 1978 Mishcon's name was among the all-party list of sixteen new working peers announced. In his maiden speech he addressed reform of the *ex gratia* scheme for compensating victims of crime, to increase the level of awards and extend it to those like battered wives. He also recommended that legal aid be available to those seeking compensation: it was Gilbertian that the offender readily obtained criminal legal aid but victims were denied any assistance. In his early years on the back benches he spoke mainly on legal issues, family policy, local government, and education. Then in 1983 he was appointed an opposition spokesman on home affairs and, as a result, became even more active in the Lords. With Lord Elwyn-Jones's death in late 1989, he became shadow lord chancellor. In 1992 Lord Mackay of Clashfern, the lord chancellor, appointed Mishcon an honorary QC, the first practising solicitor to hold that rank. But it was at that point that the Labour Party lost the 1992 election and its new leader, John Smith, appointed the younger Lord Irvine of Lairg as shadow lord chancellor.

Mishcon continued to attend and speak in the House of Lords on a regular basis. When Labour was elected in 1997, he supported the government, but not uncritically. Though he had served on the Wolfenden committee in the 1950s he now cautioned against repeal of so-called clause 28, which had provided that local authorities should not promote homosexuality. He was also critical of what were seen as attempts to limit the right of trial by jury and to reduce the coverage of legal aid. During the debates on significant changes to the latter in 1999 he acted as an intermediary for the Law Society with the government to defend the current arrangements.

The Middle East Like his father, Mishcon was a Zionist. He was active in Jewish affairs from an early age, founding with Abba Eban a youth movement, Ha Etid. Among his roles were president of the Association of Jewish Youth, vice-president of the Board of Deputies of British Jews, chairman of the Institute of Jewish Studies, University College, London, and vice-chairman of the Council of Christians and Jews. In 1976 he was a co-signatory with four others, including Saul Bellow, of a public letter protesting at the harassment by the Soviet authorities of those attending a symposium on Jewish culture in Moscow.

In his memoirs Shimon Peres told of how, as Israel's minister of foreign affairs in 1987, he wanted to cut through necessarily slow-moving diplomacy:

> I approached a common friend of mine and of King Hussein's, the prominent London attorney Mr (now Lord) Victor Mishcon, who is a model of wisdom, tact and discretion, and asked him to set up a meeting. The time and place were fixed: Saturday, 11 April 1987, at Mishcon's home in central London. (S. Peres, *Battling for Peace*, 1995, 305)

After lunch King Hussein suggested that the two assist with clearing the dishes and the washing-up. Then in the afternoon a seven-hour discussion ensued, leading to a draft of agreements and understandings between Israel and Jordan that became known as the London agreement. That came to nothing, as a result of internal Israeli politics, but there were further bilateral discussions in the following years, which ultimately led to the 1994 peace treaty between Israel and Jordan.

Mishcon's friendship was initially with Peres, through his Jewish background and the Labour Party. The friendship with Hussein dated from the late 1960s and came through Mishcon's daughter, Jane, who attended Benenden School with the king's only sister, Princess Basma bint Talal. In a programme for Israeli television in 2004 Mishcon told how before the London meeting there had been other meetings at his home in Hampshire involving the king. Subsequently he crossed the Allenby Bridge between the two states many times, carrying secret messages from one side to the other. Once the peace agreement was signed the deputy foreign minister of Israel, Yossi Beilin, told the Knesset that nobody else could have done what Mishcon had done. In 1995, as a mark of appreciation, King Hussein and Queen Noor invited Mishcon and his family to Jordan to celebrate his eightieth birthday. In 1998 Mishcon facilitated a gift of $1 million from the king to the families of Israeli schoolgirls shot by a rogue Jordanian solicitor. Mishcon had unbounded admiration for the king.

Public service, private life Mishcon was active in other aspects of public life. Thus he was chair of governors at Stockwell Manor School, a comprehensive school in south London, an experience he used in debates in the House of Lords. In 1965 Jennie Lee, Labour's minister for the arts, appointed him to the board of the National Theatre. He was also a member of the South Bank Theatre Board and the London Orchestra Board.

Mishcon's manner was charming and courteous, but also formal. Even his law firm partners were addressed by title, rather than first name. His secretary of some forty years was always Miss Hymans. His judgement and persistence were legendary. He took a long-term view of problems and tried to ensure that those on the other side of negotiations always thought they had achieved something. Despite his many achievements he was self-effacing. He had enormous powers of concentration. His religion meant a great deal to him, in a traditional way.

While he had a very active public life, Mishcon was a private man. He married four times. His first wife was Jean Marie Hydleman, the nineteen-year-old daughter of Louis Jules Hydleman, hardware merchant, whom he married at Brixton United Synagogue on 21 July 1940, when she was already terminally ill; she died in 1943. He married second, on 17 October 1945, at the New West End Synagogue, St Petersburgh Place, 21-year-old Beryl Honor Posnansky, daughter of Jacob Posnansky, businessman. They had two sons, Peter (*b.* 1946) and Russell (*b.* 1948), and a daughter, Jane (*b.* 1950), but divorced in 1959. He married as his third wife, in 1967, Doreen Segal, *née* Hayden. This marriage also ended in divorce, in 1972. His fourth marriage, on 21 September 1976, at the Central Synagogue, Great Portland Street, was to Joan Estelle Conrad, the 44-year-old proprietor of a shop selling *objets d'art*, and daughter of Bernard Monty, businessman. This marriage ended in divorce in 2001. Mishcon died at his flat in 15 Hyde Park Gardens, London, on 27 January 2006, after a stroke; he was survived by his three children.

ROSS CRANSTON

Sources F. Elwyn-Jones, *In my time* (1983) · R. Mendick, 'The royal Victor', *The Lawyer* (8 March 1999) · M. Crick, *Jeffrey Archer: stranger than fiction* (1995) · *The Times* (30 Jan 2006) · *Daily Telegraph* (30 Jan 2006) · *The Guardian* (30 Jan 2006) · *The Independent* (1 Feb 2006) · *Jewish Chronicle* (2 Feb 2006) · G. Langdon-Down, 'Lord of the manor', *Law Society Gazette* (16 Feb 2006) · Burke, *Peerage* · *WW* (2006) · personal knowledge (2010) · private information (2010) [R. Goode] · b. cert. · m. certs. [1940, 1945, 1976] · d. cert.

Archives FILM appears in *Shalom, Jordan*, D. Gil-Har, Israeli TV, 2005

Likenesses Elliott & Fry, photographs, 1951–9, NPG · photograph, 1954, PA Photos, London · photographs, 1954–2001, Photoshot, London · Snowdon, photographs, 1984, Camera Press, London · N. Sinclair, bromide print, 1992, NPG · B. Beirne, photograph, 1995, Rex Features, London · C. Djanogly, photograph, 2000, Camera Press, London [*see illus.*] · obituary photographs

Wealth at death £2,704,857: probate, 7 Sept 2006, *CGPLA Eng. & Wales*

Mitchell, Adrian Christopher (1932–2008), poet, was born on 24 October 1932 at 16 Hocroft Avenue, Cricklewood, London, the son of James Gibb (Jock) Mitchell, a research chemist then working in the chemical research laboratory of the Department of Scientific and Industrial Research in Teddington (later the National Physical Laboratory), and his wife, Kathleen Emily, *née* Fabian, a nursery schoolteacher. His father had grown up in Cupar, Fife, and had fought in the First World War as a captain in the 9th Argyll and Sutherland highlanders. His mother had lost two brothers in the conflict. Their experiences shaped their son, who was always best known for his very public pacifism.

Educated first at a boarding-school, Monkton Combe School, near Bath, where he was bullied, Mitchell was sent in 1940 to Greenways preparatory school, which had been evacuated from Bognor Regis to Ashton Gifford House in Wiltshire, and which was run by a friend of his mother. He enjoyed his time there and then moved on to Dauntsey's School, another private boarding-school nearby in Wiltshire. He wrote his first play, 'The Animals' Brains Trust', aged nine at Greenways, and continued to write and perform drama as a teenager. He did two years of national service in the RAF, which, he said, 'confirmed my natural pacifism' (Adrian Mitchell website), before entering Christ Church, Oxford, where he read English, edited *Isis*, the Oxford student magazine, and became chairman of the university poetry society. On 6 August 1955, while still at Oxford, he married, at Barnes parish church, (Daphne) Maureen Bush (*b.* 1933), daughter of Alfred Trevor Bush, schoolmaster. She had been a secretary to W. H. Auden. They had two sons, Alistair and Danny, and a daughter, Briony. The marriage was dissolved in 1963.

On leaving the university Mitchell first became a journalist on the *Oxford Mail*, moving to the *Evening Standard* in London where he worked on the 'Londoner's Diary'. He continued to write for several newspapers as a freelance in the 1960s, including the *Daily Mail*, *The Sun* (before it was

Adrian Christopher Mitchell (1932–2008), by Brian Shuel, 1963

purchased by Rupert Murdoch), and the *Sunday Times*. He was sacked from the *Sunday Times* for reviewing the infamous film by Peter Watkins, *The War Game* (1965), which visualized the aftermath of a nuclear attack and which was withdrawn without being broadcast by the BBC under pressure from Harold Wilson's Labour government.

By this time Mitchell had found a place in the literary counter-culture. With Christopher Logue he was a pioneer of live poetry readings in the late 1950s. The mixture of poetry and jazz that these events included—often, in Mitchell's case, the recitation of his own poetry to a jazz backing—led to his being termed a 'jazz poet'. He had always wanted to be a writer and with the help of a small legacy from his mother he wrote and published a first novel, *If You See Me Comin'* (1962), which was about a judicial execution. He published two more novels, *The Bodyguard* (1970) and *Wartime* (1973).

1964 proved to be Mitchell's annus mirabilis. First he came to public attention when he read his poem 'To Whom It May Concern (Tell Me Lies About Vietnam)' at an anti-Vietnam War protest in Trafalgar Square in that year:

I was run over by the truth one day.
Ever since the accident I've walked this way
So stick my legs in plaster
Tell me lies about Vietnam.

Also in 1964 Mitchell's lyrics were shown to the theatre director Peter Brook, who was looking for someone to adapt the translation of Peter Weiss's play *Marat/Sade* for the Royal Shakespeare Company. Mitchell thus found himself at work on the text of one of the seminal plays for one of the seminal productions of the modern theatre. The play's themes of madness and political revolution were neither unfamiliar nor unwelcome to him, and the result was a remarkable if darkly controversial success which began his long association with the mainstream and alternative theatre in Britain. He also met Emily Cecelia (Celia) Hewitt (*b*. 1933) in 1964. She was an actress, later a bookseller, and the daughter of John Hewitt, schoolteacher. They were married on 22 January 1965 at St Marylebone register office and had two daughters, Sasha and Beattie.

In 1965 Mitchell appeared in Michael Horovitz's Poetry Olympics at the Royal Albert Hall where he again read 'To Whom It May Concern'. It marked the start of a long relationship with Horovitz, the literary entrepreneur largely responsible for the promotion of alternative poetry in the 1960s and 1970s. Horovitz edited the famous anthology *Children of Albion: Poetry of the Underground in Britain* (1969) in which Mitchell's work—a selection of his most notable early poems including 'Veteran with a Head Wound', 'Lullaby for William Blake', 'To the Statues in Poet's Corner, Westminster Abbey', 'To a Russian Soldier in Prague', and 'To Whom It May Concern'—was given pride of place. Horovitz also published Mitchell's poetry in his magazine, *New Departures*, which featured experimental work in many genres and held the poetry underground together. Mitchell himself was often bracketed with the three poets who constituted the 'Mersey Sound' as published in the Penguin Modern Poets series in 1968, Adrian Henri, Roger McGough, and Brian Patten.

Another of Mitchell's long-term collaborators was the jazz composer and orchestrator Mike Westbrook. In 1971 Mitchell and Westbrook worked together on Mitchell's study of William Blake, *Tyger*, written for the National Theatre, which was hailed by the drama critic Kenneth Tynan as 'one of the most dazzling debuts by a playwright that I have read' (*Daily Telegraph*, 14 Jan 2009). They collaborated again in 1977 on a life of Mark Twain, *White Suit Blues*, in a production for the Nottingham Playhouse.

Mitchell spoke for many left-wing and counter-cultural causes and liked to shock. He was one of twenty-two writers and entertainers who sent a wreath to the funeral of Stephen Ward, the well-connected osteopath embroiled in the Profumo affair who committed suicide, with the message 'To Stephen Ward, a victim of British hypocrisy'. He spoke in favour of the legalization of cannabis before a crowd of five thousand people at Speakers' Corner, Hyde Park, in 1967. When asked to compose a poem about the special relationship between the prince of Wales and the Welsh people he wrote simply 'Royalty is a neurosis. Get well soon'. In 1972 at a concert in Southwark Cathedral to celebrate Shakespeare's birthday he publicly rebuked the prime minister, Edward Heath, who was in the audience: 'I wish you would stop your killing. I wish you would stop your germ warfare. I wish you would stop sending your terrorists to Northern Ireland'. The imprecision of the attack and his abuse of the occasion undermined Mitchell's impact (*The Times*, 26 April 1972).

In all Mitchell wrote more than thirty plays, adaptations, and librettos for some of the most innovative companies in Britain including 7:84 and the Everyman Theatre, Liverpool. He adapted *The Lion, the Witch and the Wardrobe* (1998) and *Alice in Wonderland* (2001) for notably successful productions by the Royal Shakespeare Company; for the National Theatre he adapted, among other plays, Calderon's *The Mayor of Zalamea* (1981), Gogol's *The Government Inspector* (1985), and Lope de Vega's *Fuente Ovejuna* (1989). His *Man Friday* (1972) was one of the most memorable plays in the celebrated strand of 'Plays for Today' on BBC1: in Mitchell's version of the famous story the roles were reversed as Crusoe was instructed and civilized by the resourceful Friday.

Mitchell published fifteen volumes of poetry, beginning in 1964 with *Poems*: if he was most famous for his political poetry and verses he wrote many love lyrics as well. He also gave hundreds of readings of his own work in the attempt to spread an interest in poetry far and wide, though in a characteristic gesture of opposition to the literary establishment (which he always criticized for taking the joy out of literature) he refused to allow his poetry to be used as school examination set texts. Nevertheless his poems were often read and studied in schools and helped provide an introduction to poetry and modern creative writing for generations of schoolchildren.

Mitchell was a central figure in the counter-culture which emerged in the 1960s. His ironic, satirical, iconoclastic, witty, and caustic lyrics made him its house poet and one of its leading spokesmen. His opposition to war, social and political hypocrisy, greed, inequality, and exploitation captured the mood of that movement and that age. Often he hit his target in clever, simple phrases whose impact was the greater because they were so memorable. Sometimes his lack of restraint and the absence of form and discipline in his verse led to self-indulgence, and encouraged merely crude and blunt complaints about all the ills of the world. Mitchell loved Hampstead Heath and spent most of his life in its vicinity. He died of pneumonia and atherosclerosis at the Royal Free Hospital, Hampstead, London, on 20 December 2008. Memorial events were held for him in several places including at Shoreham on 18 June 2009 (organized by the performance poet Attila the Stockbroker) and at the Queen Elizabeth Hall, London, on 9 December 2009. He was survived by his wife, Celia, and his five children. LAWRENCE GOLDMAN

Sources 'Afterwords', *Children of Albion: poetry of the underground in Britain*, ed. M. Horovitz (1969) • *The Guardian* (22 Dec 2008); (24 Dec 2008); (29 Dec 2008); (12 Jan 2009) • *The Times* (23 Dec 2008); (29 Dec 2008); (26 Sept 2009) • *The Independent* (23 Dec 2008) • *New York Times* (24 Dec 2008) • *Morning Star* (6 Jan 2009) • *Irish Times* (10 Jan 2009) • *Daily Telegraph* (14 Jan 2009) • www.adrianmitchell.co.uk/#/biography/4538662557, 4 Aug 2011 • *WW* (2008) • b. cert. • m. certs.

Archives SOUND BL NSA, documentary, interview, and perfomance recordings

Likenesses B. Shuel, modern bromide print, 1963, NPG [*see illus.*] • B. Shuel, photographs, 1963–8, Getty Images, London • C. Cutner, bromide fibre print, 1986, NPG • T. Phillips, pencil drawing, 1987; Bonhams, 3 Oct. 2005, lot 13394 • photographs, 1997–2004, Rex Features, London • P. Noble, photographs, 2001, PA Photos, London • C. Barker, photograph, repro. in C. Barker, *Portraits of poets*, ed. S. Barker (1986) • obituary photographs • photographs, Camera Press, London

Wealth at death £320,183: probate, 27 April 2009, *CGPLA Eng. & Wales*

Mitchell, John [Mitch] (**1947–2008**), drummer, was born on 9 July 1947 in Ealing, London, the son of Jack and Phyllis (Phyl) Mitchell. His parents enrolled him in drama school at the age of ten. He first entered show business as a teenage actor in children's television films such as *Jennings at School* and *Whack-O!*, also taking parts in *Emergency Ward 10*, and in television commercials. He took up drums after seeing a Premier kit in the window of a music shop on the Uxbridge Road, playing it without permission, running away, and then returning a few days later to ask Jim Marshall (owner and amplifier designer) if he could work there on Saturdays. He turned professional in 1965 on joining the Riot Squad, playing also with the Pretty Things and Georgie Fame and the Blue Flames, among others.

Mitchell became Jimi *Hendrix's drummer early in October 1966, apparently on the toss of a coin, with Aynsley Dunbar as the losing candidate. Another factor may have been that Dunbar wanted £30 a week, whereas Mitchell had been offered £20. A 'perm' and some psychedelic-dandy clothes soon gave him the requisite image to match that of Hendrix and Noel Redding. By the end of 1966 the Jimi Hendrix Experience had their first hit single, 'Hey Joe', on which Mitchell made a powerful entrance. In addition to classic singles such as 'Purple Haze', Mitchell's drumming contributed much to the albums *Are You Experienced* (1967), *Axis: Bold As Love* (1967), and *Electric Ladyland* (1968).

In the flamboyance and power of his style Mitchell bore comparison with Ginger Baker and Keith Moon. He was influenced by drummers such as Max Roach, Elvin Jones, and Joe Morello. His busy style suited the power trio format, filling musical space when Hendrix was soloing and adding interest when Hendrix played chords. He combined elements of jazz and rock drumming into a 'fusion' style that supercharged the former with the energy of the high-volume rock sound of the late 1960s, and extended the latter from simple beat-marking. He was perfectly equipped to cope with songs in challenging rhythms, such as the triple time of 'Manic Depression' and the fox-trot verse of 'House Burning Down', and to respond creatively to the opportunities presented by the more experimental tracks on *Electric Ladyland* (1968). His jazz influences offered additional musical avenues to Hendrix, whose background was in blues, soul, and rhythm and blues. Mitchell's style suited instrumentally extended songs and jams (and it is said that this is a reason why he later failed a 1974 audition for Paul McCartney's Wings).

After the break-up of the Jimi Hendrix Experience in 1969 Hendrix was sufficiently well disposed to Mitchell (in contrast to Redding) to invite him to be his drummer both at Woodstock that August and in the 1970 line-up of the

John [Mitch] **Mitchell** (**1947–2008**), by Gered Mankowitz, 1967

Experience with Billy Cox on bass. In the late 1960s Mitchell also took part in the Rolling Stones' film *Rock and Roll Circus* (1968), and played with Jack Bruce and Friends, and with Miles Davis during sessions for *Bitches Brew*, though he is not heard on the issued album.

Hendrix's death in September 1970 was a devastating shock, and after it Mitchell's life was never the same. He assisted engineer Eddie Kramer in finishing some of the unfinished songs that the guitarist had left. These tracks were initially released on *The Cry of Love* and *Rainbow Bridge* (1971) and later on CDs such as *First Rays of the New Rising Sun*. In 1972 he recorded one album as the group Ramatam with two musicians from the American group Iron Butterfly, the outfit touring as support for Emerson, Lake and Palmer. He also briefly worked with the Jeff Beck Group and Jack Bruce, and many years later with Billy Cox in the Gypsy Sun Experience group. Financial difficulties drove him to sell his rights to income from future Hendrix recordings in the 1970s, and in 1990 he sold a Fender Stratocaster guitar that had been Hendrix's at Sothebys for £180,000. In 1994 he expensively lost a libel case brought against the publishers of a Hendrix book. In later years he worked on various Hendrix tribute projects. With John Platt he co-authored a memoir, *The Hendrix Experience* (1990). He had completed a four-week, eighteen-date 'Experience Hendrix' tour of America only five days before he died in his sleep in the Benson Hotel in Portland, Oregon, of natural causes, on 12 November 2008. He was survived by his wife, Dee, and a daughter.

RIKKY ROOKSBY

Sources M. Mitchell and J. Platt, *The Hendrix experience* (1990) · N. Redding and C. Appleby, *Are you experienced?: The inside story of the Jimi Hendrix Experience* (1990) · H. Shapiro and C. Glebbeek, *Jimi Hendrix: electric gypsy* (1990) · J. McDermott, *Jimi Hendrix sessions: the complete studio recording sessions, 1963–1970* (1995) · *The Times* (14 Nov 2008) · *Daily Telegraph* (14 Nov 2008) · *The Guardian* (14 Nov 2008) · *The Independent* (14 Nov 2008)

Archives FILM BFINA, documentary and performance footage

Likenesses H. Goodwin, photographs, 1960–69, Rex Features, London · photographs, 1960–2008, Getty Images, London · G. Mankowitz, photograph, 1967, Getty Images, London [*see illus.*] · O. Noel, group portrait, photograph, 1967, Lebrecht Music and Arts Photo Library, London · I. Wright, group portrait, bromide print, 1967 (*The Experience*), NPG · photographs, 1967–9, PA Photos, London · photographs, 1967–2005, Rex Features, London · photographs, 1967–2008, Photoshot, London · photographs, 1968–2007, Camera Press, London · obituary photographs · photographs, repro. in Mitchell and Platt, *Hendrix experience* · photographs, repro. in Redding and Appleby, *Are you experienced?* · photographs, repro. in Shapiro and Glebbeek, *Electric gypsy* · photographs, repro. in McDermott, *Sessions*

Mobbs, Sir (**Gerald**) **Nigel** (**1937–2005**), property developer and businessman, was born on 22 September 1937 at 38 Wake Green Road, Moseley, Birmingham, the only son of Lieutenant-Colonel Gerald Aubrey Mobbs (1911–1976), property developer, and his wife, Elizabeth, younger daughter of Frank Lanchester, of Kenilworth, Warwickshire. He was born into considerable wealth, the family fortunes being based on the 600 acre Slough trading estate to the west of London, which had been founded by his grandfather Sir (Arthur) Noel Mobbs (1880–1959), a Northamptonshire businessman who had amassed his first fortune in the motor trade. His father, Gerald Mobbs, served with the airborne division during the Second World War, and was wounded and taken prisoner at Arnhem in 1944. (He became managing director of Slough Estates in 1956 and chairman in 1971.) Mobbs's great-uncle, Edgar Mobbs, was a legendary rugby player, killed at Passchendaele in 1917.

Mobbs was educated at Marlborough College and Christ Church, Oxford, where he failed to obtain a degree in his chosen subject, engineering. He attributed this failure to engineering being 'extremely boring', and to being himself no more than 'academically average' (*The Times*, 29 Sept 1990). On leaving college he was given a job at Hillier Parker, the Mayfair estate agents, to learn the ropes of the property business, and after nine months was brought into the family firm, in 1960. The previous year his grandfather died, and he inherited his grandfather's secretary, an experience he later described as 'very frightening' (ibid.). He was always destined to reach the top, despite starting, as he admitted, 'with no qualifications whatsoever' (ibid.). In 1963 he was made a director, and in 1971 he became managing director. Five years later, on the death of his father, he became both chief executive and chairman, and continued in both roles for the next twenty years, and as chairman until shortly before his death.

The Mobbs family combined hard business with a country lifestyle, and a year after starting at Slough Estates, on 14 September 1961, Mobbs married (Pamela) Jane Marguerite Berry (*b.* 1937), the second of four daughters of (Geoffrey) Lionel Berry, second Viscount Kemsley, the newspaper baron whose family at that time owned both the *Daily Telegraph* and the *Sunday Times*. The two had met at a hunt. They had a son, Christopher, and twin daughters, Virginia and Penelope.

The origins of the Mobbs family's fortune lay in an area of some 600 acres of land, originally farmland, which had been used by the War Office as a depot for repairing and ultimately dumping government vehicles used during the First World War. In 1920 it was put up for sale and was bought for £7 million by a group of motor trade entrepreneurs headed by Sir Percival Perry (who later set up Ford's UK operations) and Mobbs's grandfather Noel, who initially invested just £20,000 in the venture. The former government vehicles were gradually repaired and sold off, releasing land and funds to begin developing the huge buildings on the estate for letting to various manufacturers. By 1960 the Slough estate was one of Britain's first and largest industrial parks, with some 240 manufacturers represented. It even boasted its own power station.

Mobbs was said to show more of the entrepreneurial spirit of his grandfather than his father, and when he took control of the company in 1976 he pursued a policy of direct and active management of the Slough estate alongside the acquisition of other property in order to diversify the group's assets outside the Slough area, which had by then become known as the popular 'M4 corridor'. By the time he stepped down as chief executive, Slough Estates' properties were worth an estimated £1.8 billion. He was a man of robust opinions and convictions, straightforward and decisive, who did not take kindly to being either crossed or criticized. He managed down to matters of detail that in most other companies of the size of Slough Estates would have been delegated. Few, however, questioned his undoubted 'feel' for business, and he became sought after to fill non-executive roles in other major boardrooms. He had a thirty-year association with Barclays Bank, of which he became a director in 1979 and served as chairman for two years. He was chairman of Charterhouse Banking Group from 1977 to 1983 and deputy chairman of the retailer Kingfisher (owner of Woolworths, Superdrug, and B&Q) from 1990 to 1995, in the latter year playing the leading role in demoting the then chairman Geoff Mulcahy, who had fallen out with his chief executive, and (after an interim period in which he himself served as chairman) bringing in a replacement. He was chairman of Bovis Homes for nine years until the year of his death. At various times he was a director of Cookson, the electronics group, and of the Howard de Walden estate, one of London's largest commercial and residential landowners.

A convinced free-marketeer, Mobbs served Margaret Thatcher's government as an adviser on property affairs from 1980 to 1986. He was chairman of the libertarian pressure group Aims of Industry from 1985 until 2002, and a member of the advisory panel on deregulation at the Department of Trade and Industry from 1988 to 1994. He was variously chairman of the Conservative Party (1993–6), vice-president of the Association of British Chambers of Commerce (1976–90), and lord lieutenant of Buckinghamshire (1997–2005). He was chairman of the Historic Royal Palaces from 2003. He was knighted in 1986.

Despite all his public commitments, Mobbs maintained a determined grip on the management and affairs of Slough Estates, and this led to a split in 1996 with Roger Carey, who had been Slough's managing director for eighteen years, and who resigned in protest at Mobbs's controlling manner. Under pressure from investors Mobbs reluctantly agreed to split the roles of chairman and chief executive, but continued as executive chairman until he was forced, through ill health, to retire in August 2005.

Although Mobbs's skills as a businessman were widely sought after in industry and the City, and he accepted boardroom posts at several other substantial businesses, he was said to be happiest when at what he described as his 'modest' Buckinghamshire estate near Princes Risborough, surrounded by his family, horses, dogs, and sheep. He was an imposing man, more than 6 feet tall, an accomplished fox-hunter, skier, and golfer. He was once compared by a City journalist to 'a slightly lumbering but affectionate and appealing Great Dane' (*The Times*, 29 Sept 1990). He died of cancer of the kidney at his home, Widmer Lodge, Pink Road, Parslows Hillock, Princes Risborough, Buckinghamshire, on 21 October 2005. A memorial service held on 16 February 2006 at the chapel of the Royal Hospital, Chelsea, of which he was a commissioner, was attended by numerous representatives of government, the royal family, and business. He was survived by his wife, Jane, and their three children.

David Brewerton

Sources *The Times* (29 Sept 1990); (24 Oct 2005); (17 Feb 2006) · *Daily Telegraph* (22 Oct 2005) · *The Independent* (1 Nov 2005) · Burke, *Peerage* · *WW* (2005) · personal knowledge (2009) · private information (2009) · b. cert. · m. cert. · d. cert.

Likenesses photographs, 1994–8, Photoshot, London · photograph, 1996, Rex Features, London · K. Breeden, oils, exh. Royal Society of Portrait Painters, London 2007 (posthumous) · obituary photographs · photograph, repro. in *The Times* (15 Sept 1961)

Wealth at death £7,775,814: probate, 20 April 2006, *CGPLA Eng. & Wales*

Mogotsi, Pearl Cynthia Connor- [*née* Pearl Cynthia Nunez; *other married name* Pearl Cynthia Connor] (**1924–2005**), actress and theatrical agent, was born Pearl Cynthia Nunez in Diego Martin, Trinidad, on 13 May 1924, the ninth of twelve children of Albert Antonio Nunez, a headmaster, and his wife, Georgina Agnes, *née* Fitt, a teacher. Her father was of Portuguese and African descent; her mother 'was a white woman with red hair but she had some Carib in her' (*The Guardian*, 2 March 2005). She had 'a lovely, magical, folklore-based childhood', but 'I was terribly rebellious', she later recalled (*The Independent*, 14 Feb 2005). In Trinidad her greatest influence was Beryl McBurnie, a woman dedicated to promoting the culture and arts of the island and the founder of the Little Carib Theatre, where Pearl Nunez gained her first acting experience.

Soon after the Second World War Pearl Nunez travelled to London, where she enrolled at King's College to study law. In London, on 26 June 1948, she married the popular Trinidadian folk-singer, actor, and broadcaster Edric Esclus *Connor (1913–1968), whom she had met in Trinidad. He was looked upon as a father figure in Britain's post-war black community. After her marriage Pearl Connor gave up her law studies in order to assist in the management of her husband's career, and also to bring up their two children, Geraldine and Peter. From 1956 until 1976 she ran the Edric Connor Agency, which later became known as the Afro-Asian Caribbean Agency: 'the need of the people [on our books] always remained our first priority', she later said:

> We struggled along for years because the pay for artistes was not a lot. We didn't have named artistes on our books, we didn't have people with great reputations, we were building reputations. And that was our pioneering work. We were breaking stones and it was very tough. (Pines, 36)

The Jamaican actor Lloyd Reckord, who arrived in Britain in the early 1950s, described her as a guardian angel to all young black actors in Britain:

> Her house was always a home for people like us. And she just worked continually, pushing black actors, quarrelling with the powers-that-be, arguing 'Why can't black actors get this sort of part?', and generally working for us. (ibid., 53)

Meanwhile Pearl Connor studied at the Rose Bruford Training College of Speech and Drama and worked as a broadcaster for BBC radio, making appearances on their Caribbean Service. She also acted in BBC radio plays, including *The Barren One* (1958), *My People and Your People* (1959), and Jan Carew's *The Riverman* (1968). There were occasional appearances on the stage, including in Barry Reckord's *You in Your Small Corner* at the Royal Court in 1960, and in such films as Lindsay Anderson's *O Lucky Man!* (1973). In 1961 she helped launch the Negro Theatre Workshop at the Lyric Theatre in London with a production of *A Wreath for Udomo*, written by the black South African Peter Abrahams. The company also presented Wole Soyinka's *The Road* (1965), staged at the Theatre Royal, Stratford East, for the Commonwealth Arts Festival, and *The Dark Disciples* (1966), a jazz version of the St Luke passion, which was chosen to represent Britain at the first World Festival of Black and African Arts in Senegal. *The Dark Disciples* was also produced for BBC television in 1966.

Edric Connor died in 1968, and on 26 March 1971 Pearl married, in London, Joseph Kully (Joe) Mogotsi, the 46-year-old South African lead singer of the Manhattan Brothers. Together they planned and organized tours throughout the world for black South African singers, dancers, musicians, and actors. In 1977 she represented Trinidad and Tobago at the second World Festival of Black and African Arts in Lagos, Nigeria. In 1995 she opened the twelfth International Book Fair of Radical, Black and Third World Books in London, and took part in *A Brighter Sun: a Celebration of the Life and Work of Sam Selvon* at the Royal Festival Hall. In 2003 she introduced a screening of Edric Connor's 1960 film *Carnival Fantastique*—which had been thought lost—at the National Film Theatre. Occasionally she was called upon to contribute to television and radio documentaries, including BBC2's *Black and White in Colour* (1992), BBC Radio 2's *Salutations* (a profile of Edric Connor; 1993), *Alex Pascall's Caribbean Folk Music* (1995), and two productions in the BBC's 1998 *Windrush* season, *Their Long Voyage Home* (Radio 2) and *Black Firsts: Edric Connor* (BBC2). She was also seen in Channel 4's *Songs From the Golden City* (1997), the story of Joe Mogotsi and the Manhattan Brothers.

In 1972 the government of Trinidad and Tobago awarded Pearl Connor-Mogotsi the Humming Bird silver medal for 'outstanding services to the immigrant community in the United Kingdom', and in 1992, in Britain, she received the national black women's achievement award. She died in Johannesburg, South Africa, on 11 February 2005, and was survived by her husband Joe and the two children of her first marriage. Her funeral service was held in London at St Martin's Church, Kensal Green, on 26 February. On 13 October 2007 family, friends, and colleagues paid tribute to her with a celebration of her life and career at the church hall, Church of the Ascension, Wembley Park.

STEPHEN BOURNE

Sources J. Pines, ed., *Black and white in colour: black people in British television since 1936* (1992) • J. Robeson, 'Reflections', *Weekly Journal* (c.1992) [undated clipping, priv. coll.] • P. Connor-Mogotsi, 'Our olympian struggle', 23 March 1995, www.black-history-month.co.uk/articles/pearl.html, 28 May 2008 • S. Bourne, *Black in the British frame: the black experience in British film and television*, 2nd edn (2001) • *The Independent* (14 Feb 2005) • *The Guardian* (2 March 2005) • *The Times* (22 March 2005) • J. La Rose, 'Eulogy for Pearl Connor-Mogotsi', St Martin's Church, Kensal Green, 26 Feb 2005, www.onepaper.com/caribiadigest, 28 May 2008 • S. Whyte, 'Connor-Mogotsi, Pearl', www.screenonline.org.uk/people/id/499408, 28 May 2008 • personal knowledge (2009) • private information (2009) • m. certs.
Likenesses obituary photographs

Monro, Hector Seymour Peter, Baron Monro of Langholm (1922–2006), farmer and politician, was born at 18 Walker Street, Edinburgh, on 4 October 1922, the younger child and only son of Ian Alastair Seymour Hale Monro (*d.* 1943), a lieutenant and later captain in the Cameron Highlanders, and his wife, Marion Frances, *née* Ewart. He came from a military family: he was the maternal grandson of Lieutenant-General Sir John Spencer Ewart of Craigcleuch, whose own father, General Sir John Ewart, had been a lieutenant-colonel in the 93rd highlanders at the siege of Lucknow during the Indian mutiny of 1857. His paternal grandfather was Brigadier-General Seymour Monro, who served in the Afghan and South African wars, and on India's north-west frontier. Monro was also proud of being a direct descendant of General Sir Thomas Brisbane, an astronomer who mapped the southern skies, and gave his name to the city of Brisbane when he became governor of Queensland.

Monro was brought up at Craigcleuch, near Langholm, in Dumfriesshire, but his father's military service meant several postings abroad. Educated at Upland House preparatory school in Sussex, then Canford School in Dorset, he went to King's College, Cambridge, but only spent a year there, leaving the university air squadron in 1941 for a commission flying in RAF Coastal Command. For the remainder of the Second World War he took part in Atlantic patrols in Sunderland flying boats, and Far East missions on Catalinas. He was demobilized with the rank of flight lieutenant in 1946 but continued flying at weekends with the Royal Auxiliary Air Force until 1953, when he received the air efficiency award. On demobilization he took up farming at Craigcleuch, and on 4 March 1949 he married (Elizabeth) Anne (*d.* 1994), daughter of Major Harry Welch of Longstone Hall, Derbyshire. They had two sons, Seymour (*b.* 1950) and Hugh. In 1955 Monro bought a 300 acre beef and grain farm at Williamwood, Kirtlebridge, in Dumfriesshire, where he lived for the rest of his life.

Monro embarked on a political career in 1952, when he became a councillor on Dumfries county council, holding this position until 1967. He served as chairman of the planning committee and the police committee, and from 1958 to 1963 was chairman of the Dumfriesshire Unionist Association. In 1964 he was elected the Conservative and Unionist MP for Dumfries, which he went on to represent, devotedly, for the next thirty-three years. Ian Lang, the secretary of state for Scotland from 1990 to 1995, later recalled that Monro was 'deeply rooted in the area—there was no other seat that he wanted to represent more' (*The Times*, 31 Aug 2006).

Monro's ministerial career spanned three decades, but with large gaps in between. In 1967 he was made an opposition Conservative whip, a post he maintained into government on Edward Heath's victory in 1970. A year later he was made parliamentary under-secretary of state at the Scottish Office, a post he held for the remainder of Edward Heath's government. In opposition he continued as Scottish affairs spokesman until 1975, when Margaret Thatcher appointed him shadow minister for sport, a portfolio he held until 1979, when he was made parliamentary under-secretary of state within the Department of the Environment, with special responsibility for sport. It was the perfect ministerial job. Monro loved sport, especially rugby union (he served as president of the Auto-cycle Union from 1983 to 1990 and of the Scottish Rugby Union in 1976–7). In government he was embroiled in controversy when he opposed the South African Barbarians' rugby tour of Britain in August 1979, and the British Lions' tour of South Africa the following January; he also opposed Thatcher's proposal that the British team boycott the Moscow Olympics, following the Russian invasion of Afghanistan. Within the Department of the Environment he also had responsibility over planning matters, and piloted the Wildlife and Countryside Bill, overcoming opposition in his own party to push through the 'Sandford amendments' (named after John Edmondson, second Baron Sandford), which created the concept of sites of special scientific interest (SSSI).

Whether because of his independent-mindedness or his One Nation views, Monro was returned to the back benches in 1981, though he received the compensation of a knighthood the same year. He chaired the Scottish Conservative members' committee (1983–92) and the Conservative parliamentary committee on sport (1984–5), and also served as a member of the Nature Conservancy Council (1982–91) and the council of the National Trust for Scotland (1983–92). He was a stout defender of Scottish agriculture, having been a long-term member of the area executive committee of the National Farmers' Union of Scotland: in 1986, following the Chernobyl nuclear disaster in the Soviet Union, he publicly urged the secretary of state for Scotland, Malcolm Rifkind, to pay Scottish farmers (then suffering financial losses as a result of the ban on marketing lambs) £1 million in compensation and to send the bill to the Kremlin. In 1988 his reputation as a constituency MP was sealed when, in the aftermath of the Lockerbie disaster (when Pan-Am flight 103 was blown up by a bomb over the town), he went straight to the scene, spending many hours comforting the victims. He again served as parliamentary under-secretary of state at the Scottish Office under John Major, from 1992 to 1995. On his retirement from the Commons in 1997 he was raised to the peerage as Baron Monro of Langholm.

Monro took a keen interest in all country sports, especially shooting, and was president of the National Small Bore Rifle Association (1987–92). He was a particular enthusiast for antique cars and enjoyed driving round his constituency in an open-top Bentley, showing off the old county number plate, SM4. Following the death of his first wife, on 23 December 1994 he married one of her friends, Doris Louise Kaestner, *née* Schuchhardt, a widow from Baltimore. After a short illness he died of cancer of the pancreas at the Royal Infirmary, Dumfries, on 30 August 2006. He was survived by his second wife and the two sons from his first marriage, both of whom had followed the earlier family tradition of army service, Seymour rising to the rank of major-general and Hugh to the rank of brigadier.

MARK STUART

Sources I. Lang, *Blue remembered years: a political memoir* (2002) · *The Times* (31 Aug 2006) · *Daily Telegraph* (31 Aug 2006) · *The Guardian* (1 Sept 2006) · *The Independent* (1 Sept 2006) · *WW* (2006) · Burke, *Peerage* · b. cert. · d. cert.

Likenesses photographs, 1995–8, Photoshot, London · obituary photographs

Wealth at death £1,312,863.93: confirmation, 26 March 2007, *CCI*

Montefiore, Hugh William (1920–2005), bishop of Birmingham, was born on 12 May 1920 at 35 Palace Court, Bayswater, London, the third son of Charles Edward Montefiore Sebag-Montefiore (1884–1960), senior partner of the family stockbroking firm, a former lieutenant in the Royal Artillery, and a noted philanthropist, and his wife, Muriel Alice Ruth, *née* de Pass (1891–1977), eldest daughter of Charles de Pass, also a stockbroker. Though his parents used the surname Sebag-Montefiore, in adult life he always used the abbreviated surname, Montefiore.

Early life Montefiore's Sephardi Jewish parents were ill matched: his father energetic, bold, and practical; his mother artistic, romantic, and reticent. (Later in life she was diagnosed with manic depression and after her husband's death converted to Christianity.) In 1925 the family moved to 2 Palace Green, Kensington. They had eight servants and attended the Lauderdale Synagogue in Paddington. Hugh went to two preparatory schools before entering Rugby School in 1933. A comment in an early school report—'careless, slapdash and takes no pains' (Peart-Binns, 20)—stung him into becoming a lifelong workaholic. His social conscience was awakened when he visited the Rhondda valley and Durham, where the dire situation of unemployed miners affected him. He joined the officers' training corps, gained his rugby colours, and loved etching and painting. He had to work hard to achieve success. His final school report contains a clue to a character trait: 'Enterprising and fluent—occasionally rather too much of both—but always interesting' (ibid., 26).

Montefiore had thought of becoming a rabbi until one wintry afternoon, aged sixteen, when his life was abruptly and indelibly changed: 'I suddenly became aware of a figure in white whom I saw clearly in my mind's eye. I heard the words "Follow me". Instinctively I knew that this was Jesus' (*Oh God, What Next?*, 1). He had not even read the New Testament. His parents were devastated but continued to show him affection. For his brothers and the wider Jewish community it was apostasy.

Montefiore went to St John's College, Oxford, in 1939 to read a shortened one-year 'war' version of classics, before enlisting for army service. He served with the Royal Buckinghamshire yeomanry (99 field regiment RA). Rigid discipline and a vigorous sense of duty were implanted. At 6 feet 3 inches he was imposing, with a large, mobile, sharp, and intelligent face. He was promoted to captain and served in India and Burma, where he was fearless in leading his men. During the battle of Kohima he narrowly escaped death when a Japanese bullet nicked the sleeve of his pullover, killing the colonel lying next to him. There were two momentous changes in Montefiore's own life during the war. First, he made the decision to be ordained in the Church of England. Second, he had always felt shy and awkward with girls until he was attracted by the brains and beauty of Elisabeth Mary Macdonald Paton (*d.* 1999) of Lady Margaret Hall, Oxford, who was to take a first in English, and whom he met at Student Christian Movement meetings. Her father, William *Paton, was a Presbyterian and one of the great figures of ecumenism. They became engaged as Montefiore joined the army and were married in St Albans Cathedral on 1 December 1945, a fortnight after his repatriation, when she was twenty-six. They had three daughters.

After returning to St John's College Montefiore achieved a first in theology in 1947 and proceeded to Westcott House Theological College, Cambridge. For ordination in 1949 he went to welcoming, warm-hearted Newcastle, serving his curacy at St George's, Jesmond. 'He got things done' was his vicar's verdict (private information). And it was done with vivacity, verve, boldness, and imagination. Two years later he made a wrong decision by returning to Westcott House as chaplain and tutor, then vice-principal. He felt himself a *tertium quid* with the regime of Kenneth Carey, Alan Webster, and later Robert Runcie. The immense teaching load of New Testament doctrine with twenty-seven supervisions a week was endangering his marriage and led him to the verge of a breakdown. He suffered a ruptured disc that affected him spasmodically for the rest of his life. He was invited to be chaplain of St John's College, Oxford, but Carey held him to his contract by refusing to release him, and when he was able to resign, in 1954, it was without a job to go to.

Cambridge Charles Raven, an old Caian and former vice-chancellor of the university, came to the rescue by recommending Montefiore as fellow and dean of Gonville and Caius College, Cambridge, to which was added in 1959 a lectureship in the faculty of divinity. He made himself available to undergraduates and ensured that the well-attended chapel had an 'open' table to all who presented themselves for holy communion. Another characteristic, already well developed, was now immense, namely his insatiable lust for activity—lecturing, writing, preaching, thinking, reading, endless pastoral calls, and much travelling. In personality he moved from ebullience to depression, was adversarial and vulnerable, self-confident and guilt-ridden, and always 'driven' beneath a cloud of self-doubt.

Montefiore was on the top of Mount Carmel during a sabbatical in 1963 when a telegram arrived offering him the living of Great St Mary's, Cambridge, in succession to Mervyn Stockwood and Joe Fison, who were respectively elevated to the bishoprics of Southwark and Salisbury. Montefiore did not have Stockwood's magnetism nor the fire for God of Fison, a prophet who disturbed with affection. He rather saw this as an opportunity to bring academic learning to the service of pastoral ministry. With the help of two curates, a Roneo machine spluttering out sermons, and a red mini driven Jehu-like, the parish was organized for up to seven services on a Sunday as well as weekday celebrations. There were criticisms of Montefiore for being too donnish in the pulpit, and for being brusque with people. Nevertheless Great St Mary's continued to draw 'town' and 'gown' and attracted capacity congregations to hear the outstanding preachers and leaders of the age.

Montefiore's arrival at Great St Mary's in 1963 coincided with the publication of John Robinson's *Honest to God*. It was a fertile time for radical thinking. Montefiore contributed with *Truth to Tell* (1966) and an essay in *Soundings* (1967). He was too much of a whirlwind, courageous, and full of enthusiasms to be in the academic top rank of theological thought, but there was a distinctive legacy in *The Probability of God* (1985), on the support that science could give to theistic belief, and *Credible Christianity* (1994). He regarded his major contribution as the essay *What I Believe*, which he wrote for the doctrine commission report, *Christian Believing* (1976). He had been appointed to the new commission in 1967.

Montefiore appeared to enjoy deliberately provoking controversy, sometimes with unintentional consequences. He read a paper at the annual conference of modern churchmen at Oxford in July 1967 in which he speculated about whether Jesus was homosexual in nature. He did not describe Jesus as a homosexual, but the use of the word was sufficient to cause a conflagration. Ian Paisley charged him with 'diabolical blasphemy' (Peart-Binns, 127), and many erstwhile supporters were hostile. There was a clamour for him to resign. The prime minister's appointments secretary, John Hewitt, was determined that he should never be a diocesan bishop and, until Hewitt retired, he was effectively blocked.

In 1969 Montefiore published *The Question Mark: the End of Homo Sapiens*, about the terrifying results of man's obsession with growth and rapid and easily acquired prosperity. This book, praised by U Thant, Arthur Koestler, and Gordon Rattray Taylor, led to Montefiore's notable involvement with environmental and technological concerns. He chaired commissions on population control, reprocessing nuclear waste at Windscale, cultural pluralism, management accountability, and designing for survival. In 1972 he organized and chaired an independent commission on transport, which, in less than a year, produced *Changing Directions*, which stopped just short of advocating the restriction of car ownership. In 1976, as president of the Heathrow Association for the Control of Aircraft Noise, he went to America for a one-day hearing on Concorde and criticized the way in which the United Kingdom government had measured noise levels and subsequently misled parliament. Labour and Conservative MPs tried to lampoon him but failed because his arguments were based on hard evidence.

At Cambridge the pace and self-inflicted pressures were unsustainable, resulting in absence from duties for three months. How long could he keep the Great St Mary's circus on the road? John Robinson, then dean of Trinity College, Cambridge, may not have looked like God's messenger, but he was Bishop Mervyn Stockwood's forerunner when, in the late autumn of 1969 over lunch, he slipped into the conversation, 'Oh, by the way Hugh, would you like to be Bishop of Kingston?' The approach was sanctioned by the archbishop of Canterbury and the appointment was announced on 7 January 1970.

Kingston upon Thames The suffragan see of Kingston upon Thames covers an area from Brixton and Clapham to Wimbledon and Richmond. Dissatisfied with proposals of where he should live, Montefiore's mother lent him the money to buy White Lodge in Wandsworth, which would be his home again when he left Birmingham. David Sheppard was his fellow suffragan at Woolwich. Led by Stockwood, Southwark was at the time the most exciting diocese in the Church of England. Intellectually a radical socialist and emotionally a high-church tory with friends in high places, Stockwood had a sense of theatre. He knew how to perform and needed a strong supporting cast. The imprint of Stockwood was unmistakable in Montefiore, who was perhaps unwise to learn his bishoping from him. Gradually Montefiore made his own way and revealed great pastoral concern and care for people.

Montefiore was not ideally suited to a secondary position. Archbishop Donald Coggan endeavoured to place him into the deanery of St Paul's Cathedral, to no avail. The Church of England was waiting to see who would be Birmingham's new bishop in 1977, the first appointment under the new Crown Appointments Commission. When fifty-seven-year-old Montefiore was named there was an immediate campaign to reject him, orchestrated by the *Birmingham Evening Post* and some local Conservative MPs, notably Anthony Beaumont-Dark. How could such a bishop come to the home of the motor car and British Leyland? The 'welcomers' were those who recognized his extraordinary combination of intellect, moral passion, and concern for the underprivileged.

Birmingham After the calm, reassuring, and uneventful episcopate of Laurence Brown, Montefiore swept in on his episcopal chariot like an imperial Caesar come to administer justice. He bullied, cajoled, and annoyed to get his way. Yet in his study he was superb at listening, caring, and encouraging. If he unintentionally caused pain he was distraught. He bore no malice and his flashes of temper were soon forgotten. He visited all the clergy and their families and photographed them, not merely as a memory aid but so that he could hold them and their needs in prayer in his private chapel. Hours of time were spent with sad cases of moral failure, scandal, or breakdown, and, although he could be fierce, he searched for practical solutions.

Temperamentally Montefiore was a hierarchical person with a dash of the patriarch. He inaugurated *The Bishopric*, a periodical to further his teaching ministry. His presidential addresses to the diocesan synod were on matters of public moment in church and state. His style was usually animated and often adversarial. He was a 'loner' in his intellectual work, rapidly formulating with precision what he wanted to say. He was always in danger of unwarranted dogmatism, and because he fly-whisked criticism aside it required very determined alertness to challenge him. Examples of his endless initiatives were: a 'vision' (a favourite expression) for lay education and training in the parishes directed by himself; an appeal in 1984 for bicycles and mattocks to be sent to the battered church in Uganda; and a diocesan pilgrimage of 3000 people to Canterbury in 1986. He energetically sought good relations with the Islamic and Hindu faiths and the Afro-Caribbean community.

In 1982 Montefiore succeeded Graham Leonard, bishop of London, as chairman of the Church of England's board for social responsibility. It was a daring appointment of someone who could be unpredictable and volatile. The major time-consuming topics were the Church of England's response to the Warnock report, *Human Fertilization and Embryology* (1984), and the welfare state and social diversity in an ever-changing Britain. However, Montefiore's greatest triumph in the general synod came earlier, in 1983, when he was unexpectedly eirenic on the controversial report *The Church and the Bomb*, which opted for unilateral disarmament. He was neither dove nor hawk, and his speech and its accompanying successful amendment were a *tour de force*, saving the day. It required the government to provide adequate defence, urged it to negotiate disarmament urgently, and insisted that nuclear weapons could only be held on the basis of 'no first use'.

None the less, Montefiore's demeanour did not make him one of the synod's most persuasive speakers. He was considerably better on his feet in the House of Lords, where he made his maiden speech on 23 January 1985. For the next two years he was a frequent speaker. When the Shops Bill (1986), which would have ended the regulation of Sunday trading in England and Wales, occupied the house for eight long days, Montefiore strenuously opposed total or extensive deregulation. On one occasion he was supported by twenty spiritual peers, a near record for the twentieth century. The bill was later unceremoniously thrown out by the House of Commons.

Montefiore almost made history when he introduced his own bill—the Infant Life (Preservation) Bill—on 17 December 1986. Its simple and single aim was to change the twenty-eight week limit for abortions to twenty-four weeks. During the debate on 29 January 1987 there was much passion, noticeably from opponents. However, it passed its second reading. Afterwards Lord Whitelaw, leader of the house, informed Montefiore that three peers, violently against the bill, threatened to filibuster it out of existence. It went to a select committee whose members were largely hostile. By the time the committee reported Montefiore had retired and his bill lapsed.

Montefiore's energies were consumed in principles and causes to which he tenaciously clung like a limpet, until he reversed his position, which was then equally vociferously defended. In 2004 he was forced to resign from his twenty-year trusteeship of Friends of the Earth when he switched from opposing nuclear power to advocating its use. Similarly, he continually re-examined his own beliefs. He was agnostic on the virgin birth but did not doubt the empty tomb or the physical resurrection of Jesus. He was a vocal critic of the views of David Jenkins, bishop of Durham.

Retirement and final years Montefiore was the most remarkable bishop of his time. He wrote twenty-eight books (twelve of them in retirement) and edited or contributed to a further forty-five works, including important pamphlets. In 1987, still at the height of his powers, he resigned to care for his wife, who was suffering from Alzheimer's disease. Montefiore never realized the respect and affection in which he was held until 7000 people attended a farewell eucharist at the National Exhibition Centre in Birmingham on 31 March.

Retirement brought Montefiore an inner emptiness, which was assuaged with writing books, lectures, exhortations, and a weekly column in *Church Times*. He chaired Transport 2000 and a charity for the homeless. He was taken ill on his eighty-fifth birthday, while dining with one of his daughters, and died the following day, 13 May 2005, at St George's Hospital, Tooting, of an aortic aneurysm. At his funeral at St Mary Magdalene, Wandsworth Common, on 21 May the congregation were invited to clap the man they loved. There was thunderously charged applause. Private cremation followed. For all Montefiore's achievements there was an underlying melancholy about this engaging and sensitive man, a living tornado with a human face. He said: 'I was deraciné; an exile from the Jewish community and, I felt, not really accepted in the Christian community' (*Oh God, What Next?*, 240).

JOHN S. PEART-BINNS

Sources J. S. Peart-Binns, *Bishop Hugh Montefiore* (1990) • H. Montefiore, *Oh God, what next?* (1995) • *The Times* (14 May 2005) • *Daily Telegraph* (14 May 2005) • *The Guardian* (14 May 2005) • *The Independent* (16 May 2005) • LPL, Hugh Montefiore archive • *WW* (2005) • personal knowledge (2009) • private information (2009) • b. cert. • m. cert. • d. cert.

Archives LPL, corresp. and papers | CUL, Joseph Needham MSS • Girton College, Cambridge, D. M. M. Needham MSS • University of Bradford, J. B. Priestley Library, Peart-Binns episcopal biography archive | FILM BFINA, 'Rt Rev Hugh Montefiore', *Face the press*, J. Goldby (director), Channel 4, 26 Feb 1984 • BFINA, current affairs footage [also BL NSA] | SOUND BL NSA, current affairs recordings

Likenesses I. Showall, group portrait, photograph, 1971 (London bishops), Getty Images, London • O. Campion, oils, 1982, Bishop's Croft, Birmingham • D. Girouard, double portrait, oils (with his wife), priv. coll. • M. Yeoman, portrait, Birmingham Diocesan Offices • obituary photographs • photograph, Birmingham Diocesan Offices

Wealth at death £2,547,630: probate, *CGPLA Eng. & Wales*

Moore, Sir (John) Jeremy (1928–2007), Royal Marines officer, was born at the Cottage Hospital, St Mary, Lichfield, Staffordshire, on 5 July 1928, the son of Charles Percival Moore (*d.* 1959), a captain in the King's Liverpool regiment, later a lieutenant-colonel, and his wife, (Alice Hilda) Mary, *née* Bibby (1898–1994). His parents were at the time living at Whittington Barracks, Lichfield. Jeremy Moore was educated at Brambletye School, East Grinstead, and Cheltenham College, before being commissioned into the Royal Marines in 1947.

After training and a short tour of duty in the cruiser *Sirius*, Moore was posted to 40 commando, Royal Marines, where, like so many Royal Marines officers of his generation, he found his real military home. When he joined 40 commando it was engaged in anti-communist terrorist operations in Malaya. While following up information from a terrorist who had surrendered, he was responsible for mounting a highly successful snap ambush. This action, and other successes, resulted in his being awarded the military cross, in 1952, and established his reputation as a first-class commando soldier. From 40 commando he was sent to instruct at the Royal Marines non-commissioned officers' school (1955–7), where his Malayan experience was put to good use teaching leadership and tactics to potential corporals, perhaps the most important level of junior leadership in a commando or infantry battalion. A tour as adjutant of 45 commando in the Near East and Mediterranean followed in 1957–9, including operations in Cyprus against EOKA guerrillas. From there he went to instruct at the Royal Military Academy, Sandhurst, for two and a half years, before being posted to command a company in 42 commando in the Far East.

Moore was soon in action again during the 1962 Brunei uprising. Rebels had seized the town of Limbang and taken a number of hostages, including the British resident, Richard Morris, and his wife. Moore was ordered to free them. He devised a bold plan, which involved motoring up river by night in two commandeered public works department lighters, and landing at dawn. Supported by two Vickers medium machine guns, Moore's company assaulted the town, and after a brisk fight freed all the hostages unharmed. The action cost the company five dead and eight wounded. Out of the enemy force of 350 rebels

Sir (John) Jeremy Moore (1928–2007), by S. & G. Barratts, 1982

at Limbang, fifteen were killed and fifty captured: the remainder escaped into the jungle. Moore was awarded a well-deserved bar to his military cross. Following graduation from the Australian army staff college he became the general staff officer, grade 2 (operations) in the 17th Gurkha division in 1965, under Major-General Walter Walker, then responsible for the prosecution of the 'confrontation' campaign against Indonesia in Borneo. From the Far East Moore was sent to almost his only job in the Ministry of Defence as one of the team of assistant secretaries to the chiefs of staff committee (1966–8). He was then sent to the commando carrier HMS *Bulwark* as amphibious operations officer (1968–9). Meanwhile, on 3 September 1966, at the parish church of Chobham, Surrey, he married Veryan Julia Margaret Acworth (*b.* 1942), daughter of Oswald Roney Acworth, vicar of Chobham (who married them). They had two daughters, Helen and Sarah, and a son, Andrew.

After only sixteen months in the *Bulwark* Moore was appointed to command the officers' wing at the commando training centre (1969–71). There, in the third of his training jobs, he was responsible for the selection and training of Royal Marines young officers. Thus during his career he had a hand in influencing the military education of non-commissioned officers in the Royal Marines, and officers in the Royal Marines and British army. Next he was given command of 42 commando, Royal Marines (1972–3). During his time in command he completed two tours in Northern Ireland, including participating in Operation Motorman, the reclamation of the IRA's self-proclaimed 'no-go areas', in his case in Belfast. The commando flourished under his command, and they became known throughout the commando brigade, and by all with whom they came in contact, for their 'can do' attitude and style. For his service in Northern Ireland he was appointed OBE in 1973. From 42 commando he went to be commandant of the Royal Marines School of Music (1973–5). After a short spell at the Royal College of Defence Studies he was given command of the 3rd commando brigade (1977–9). In this post he had the task of expanding the Royal Marines' commitment to the northern flank of NATO from just 45 commando group to a brigade-sized force. Bringing a fresh eye to the task, and leading from the front by example, he quickly assimilated what had been a fiercely independent commando group into his brigade. In August 1979 he was promoted major-general and appointed to command commando forces, from which post he was due to retire, when Lieutenant-General Sir Steuart Pringle, commandant general, Royal Marines, was severely injured by an IRA bomb under his car, in October 1981. Moore, as senior major-general in the corps, took over temporarily, still spending the majority of his time in his own command, while the chief of staff, Major-General Michael Wilkins, who should have relieved Moore in April, remained in Whitehall.

Moore was still in command of commando forces and handing back command of the Royal Marines on the day before Argentina invaded the Falkland Islands, on 2 April 1982. Having dispatched the 3rd commando brigade, Royal Marines, to the South Atlantic, the cutting edge of the force that would ultimately repossess the islands, Moore transferred with most of his staff to Northwood in London, the headquarters of Admiral Sir John Fieldhouse, the Falklands task force commander. There, deep underground, he found a headquarters totally unprepared for commanding the war it was about to fight, a series of sea–air–land battles, as opposed to the one for which it was staffed: an all-maritime affair against the Soviet northern fleet in the North Atlantic. With only one Royal Marines major permanently on his staff, the task force commander was neither best placed to advise the war cabinet on the intricacies of that most complicated operation of war, an amphibious landing, nor on the land war that would follow. Moore and his staff soon injected some realism into the headquarters.

Moore remained at Northwood until 20 May 1982, one day before the initial landings on the Falklands by the 3rd commando brigade, at which point he flew south to Ascension Island to join the liner *Queen Elizabeth II*, carrying the 5th infantry brigade which, with 3rd commando brigade, would form his division, also known as land forces Falkland Islands. The communications in the liner were faulty, and Moore was unable to keep abreast of events in the Falklands until he arrived ten days after land operations had begun. Later he was to express regret that he had not arranged to arrive ahead of the *Queen Elizabeth II* by parachute, being a qualified parachutist. Having stepped ashore at the beachhead at San Carlos, he endorsed all tactical moves that were already in progress, and took command of the land forces to complete the final repossession of the islands. His command style was to give his subordinates their mission, and leave them to decide how they would carry it out. He spent most of each day forward, visiting all the units under his command so that they could acquaint themselves with him, and he with them. Having worked at Northwood, and seen the pressure under which the task force commander was placed almost daily by the prime minister and members of her war cabinet, Moore knew that one of his many duties was to be as up-beat as possible, within the constraints of veracity, in his reports sent back by signal each day. His signals, chatty in style, and full of optimistic predictions, which he privately dubbed the 'daily rubbish', did the trick; Northwood, the chiefs of staff, and, presumably, the war cabinet, were well satisfied. The high point of Moore's distinguished military career came on 14 June 1982, when he accepted the surrender of the Argentinian commander, Brigadier-General Mario Menendez, along with that of all enemy forces on the Falkland Islands. His contribution to victory was recognized by his being knighted KCB in 1982 (he had been made a CB earlier that year). He spent the last year of his service (1982–3) at the Ministry of Defence.

On retiring from the Royal Marines, Moore worked as the director-general of the Food and Drink Federation. This was not to his liking, and he left after a year. Following this, he undertook a number of part-time activities, including lecturing on leadership, three non-executive directorships, some consultancy work, and a period spent advising the House of Commons select committee on defence. During his retirement he did some broadcasting, notably presenting a Radio 4 series, *The Savage Wars of Peace*. He also found time to qualify as a guide to take visitors round Bath, and Wells Cathedral (near his home in Norton St Philip, Somerset), which he much enjoyed. He was colonel commandant of the Royal Marines between 1990 and 1993. He developed prostate cancer, which he bore bravely and uncomplainingly, but in the end this did not cause his death: he died on 15 September 2007 at the Royal United Hospital, Bath, having suffered a stroke. He was survived by his wife, Veryan, and their three children.

Moore was a soldier's soldier, far preferring to be out in the field, especially with his beloved Royal Marines, than sitting in his headquarters. As well as being a fine operational soldier, he was a consummate trainer of troops. He was at his best as a regimental officer. The sub-units and units he commanded were always highly successful, and thanks to his style of leadership, all who served in them felt that they were special. JULIAN THOMPSON

Sources J. Thompson, *The Royal Marines: from sea soldiers to a special force* (2000) • J. Thompson, *3 commando brigade in the Falklands: no picnic* (2007) • *The Times* (17 Sept 2007) • *Daily Telegraph* (17 Sept 2007) • *The Guardian* (18 Sept 2007) • *The Independent* (26 Sept 2007) • Burke, *Peerage* • *WW* (2007) • personal knowledge (2011) • private information (2011) • b. cert. • m. cert. • d. cert.

Archives FILM BFINA, 'General Sir Jeremy Moore', *The other side of me*, Independent Television, 20 Feb 1983 | SOUND BL NSA, documentary recording

Likenesses S & G Barratts, photograph, 1982, PA Photos, London [*see illus.*] • photographs, 1982–2007, Photoshot, London • photographs, 1982–2007, PA Photos, London • photographs, 2007, Rex Features, London • C. Leeds, portrait, Royal Hospital Chelsea, London • obituary photographs

Wealth at death £393,945: probate, 18 Dec 2007, *CGPLA Eng. & Wales*

Morgan, Philip (1930–2005), United Reformed minister and promoter of Christian unity, was born on 22 June 1930 at 64 Curzon Street, Maryport, Cumbria, the son of David Lewis Morgan, a Welsh minister of the Churches of Christ, and his wife, Pamela, *née* Hutchinson. The Churches of Christ (Disciples of Christ in the USA) was a group of congregational churches with a strong emphasis on the baptism of believers and the weekly celebration of the eucharist. Thomas Campbell, one of the founding fathers of the denomination, voiced his deep conviction in 1809 that 'the Church of God is essentially, intentionally and constitutionally one' (T. Campbell, *Declaration and Address of the Christian Association of Washington*, 1809, 16), a conviction Morgan was to make richly his own.

Morgan went for training as a Churches of Christ minister to Overdale College, part of the Selly Oak Colleges federation, and received the degree of BA in theology from Birmingham University. In 1952 he was sent to a post in the south Wales valleys and he was ordained there in 1953, serving a group of churches around Merthyr Tudful (which included Aberfan, whose sufferings in 1966 were to move him deeply). On 17 July 1954 he married Greta Mary Hanson, a 25-year-old grammar-school teacher, and daughter of Frederick Oliver Hanson, drapery shop superintendent. They had two children, Ghislaine and Jonathan. Morgan often later spoke of his five years in the valleys, along with subsequent ministries in Avery Hill, south-east London (1958–62), and twin churches in Saffron Lane and South Wigston, Leicester (1962–6), as very happy and rewarding.

In 1967 Morgan was appointed assistant general secretary of the Association of the Churches of Christ, and a year later became its general secretary. This post he held in Birmingham, combining his national responsibilities until 1980 with ministry in a joint church experiment with a parish of the Church of England in Balsall Heath, a somewhat run-down area not far from the city centre. His travelling ministry took him throughout the British Isles. Already in 1958 he had been chosen to represent the Churches of Christ on the assembly of the British Council of Churches (BCC), so he was a long-respected participant in its life when he became chairman of its division of ecumenical affairs in 1978 and then general secretary in 1980, serving until 1990.

Following the definition of unity in Christ reached by the New Delhi assembly of the World Council of Churches in 1961, a senior pastor in the Churches of Christ, James Gray, had published an article challenging his fellow members to take active steps to unite with at least one other denomination. That stirred Morgan to discuss with his friends and colleagues a far-reaching plan to work in this direction, strongly encouraged both by the 1964 British Faith and Order Conference's call to the churches to achieve unity by Easter day 1980, and then by the beginnings of discussions between the Presbyterian and Congregational churches for the unity they eventually achieved in the United Reformed church (URC) in 1972. His plan was built around a pattern of frequent consultation with every local Church of Christ, two rounds of which he carried through with his colleagues in his early years as general secretary. Resistance in a number of local churches was encouraged by the promise of money and manpower from like-minded circles in the USA, so eventually he arranged for the dissolution of the existing national association in order to allow those churches supporting union with the URC to establish a new national body and pursue that goal without in any way forcing the others. The unity of the majority of Churches of Christ and the URC was thus celebrated in 1981. In 1983 Morgan was elected to serve as the year-long moderator of that whole church, which he combined admirably with his BCC post.

Meanwhile the invitation of the URC's founding assembly to the other churches to consider closer unity had led to the establishment of the Churches' Unity Commission, involving (unlike the BCC) the Roman Catholic church. This published a set of 'ten propositions' on 'visible unity' in 1976. These, with the Catholic and Baptist churches accepting only observer status, then led to the Churches' Council for Covenanting, which produced its proposals for a far-reaching covenant in mid-1980. Morgan had shared in drawing up the appendix on 'Joint decision making for common obedience under the covenant', and under his chairmanship the board of the BCC division of ecumenical affairs presented to the assembly just before Easter 1980 a paper, 'Unity: why not yet', surveying the movements towards unity among the British and Irish churches. Meanwhile the BCC had been in careful discussion with a group appointed by the Roman Catholic bishops' conference for England and Wales in the light not only of the Second Vatican Council's text on Christian unity but still more of the recommendation of their national pastoral congress in May 1980 that the bishops reconsider the question of the entry of the Catholic church into the BCC. This was the single most important goal that Morgan set for himself and the council in the 1980s. It was joyously achieved by means of the dissolution of the former BCC and the founding of the new Council of Churches for Britain and Ireland (CCBI), with the Catholic church and a number of black-led churches as incoming members, in a memorable service spanning both the Anglican and Catholic cathedrals in Liverpool in September 1990. Morgan's patience, determination, pastoral insistence on full consultation at every stage, and above all prayer-filled passion to be, as he saw it, pursuing God's path of unity for the whole of Christ's church, were crucial throughout these ten years.

There were plenty of other matters to fill Morgan's agenda during his time as general secretary of the BCC. He eagerly led a group in considering the possibility of a British and Irish conference on church and society, whose inconclusive debates none the less provoked Lesslie Newbigin to write his worldwide best-selling *The Other Side of 1984* (1983). Morgan admirably followed through the courage of his predecessor, Harry Morton, in engaging in secret conversations with certain men of violence in Northern Ireland in the hope of finding an agreed path to peace. He also followed Morton in interpreting the policy of the World Council of Churches to support those struggling against the violence of the apartheid regime in South Africa. He encouraged those who had collaborated with their colleagues in the conservative evangelical world to initiate a 'nationwide initiative in evangelism', and was founding chairman of the Centre for Black and White Christian Partnership at the Selly Oak Colleges from 1978 onward. Most startlingly, he led a small group from the BCC executive to the Falkland Islands after the war there, on the way to the World Council of Churches central committee in Buenos Aires.

Morgan was delighted, on leaving the BCC as it transmuted into the Council of Churches for Britain and Ireland, to take up a local pastorate at St Andrew's United Reformed church in Frognal, Hampstead, north London, for five years up to retirement. He enjoyed a happy family life with his wife, Greta, who also became a minister in the URC. He died of aspiration pneumonia following a stroke, at Barnet General Hospital, London, on 17 October 2005, and was survived by Greta and their two children. A thanksgiving service was held on 2 November in St Andrew's, Frognal. MARTIN CONWAY

Sources *The Independent* (21 Oct 2005) · *Daily Telegraph* (21 Oct 2005) · *The Times* (28 Oct 2005) · *The Guardian* (3 Nov 2005); (7 Nov 2005) · *WW* (2005) · personal knowledge (2009) · private information (2009) · b. cert. · m. cert. · d. cert.

Likenesses obituary photographs

Wealth at death under £21,000: probate, 22 May 2006, *CGPLA Eng. & Wales*

Morley, Sheridan Robert [Sherry] (**1941–2007**), theatre critic and biographer, was born on 5 December 1941 at Five Trees nursing home, overlooking Ascot racecourse, Berkshire, the elder son of the actor, writer, and producer Robert Adolph Wilton *Morley (1908–1992), and his wife, the actress Joan North, *née* Buckmaster (1910–2005), daughter of Dame Gladys *Cooper. His birth coincided with the first night in London of *The Man Who Came to Dinner*, in which his father was playing the outrageous Sheridan Whiteside, after whom he was named.

As a child of the theatre, with which he fell deeply in love at a very early age, Morley was never going to enjoy a traditional English childhood. His formal education began at Rupert House preparatory school in Henley-on-Thames. 'Hopeless at art and handiwork', read his autumn term report in 1947. 'Avoids sport whenever possible … Imitates teachers well. Totally unable to catch or throw balls' (*Asking for Trouble*, 42). The following year he left for America with his mother and younger sister, Annabel. They stayed first with Gladys Cooper in California. After a year in New York, where his father's hugely successful play *Edward, My Son* was playing on Broadway, and an eighteen-month tour of Australia and New Zealand, the family returned to England and his father set about finding a suitable school for him. To this end he inserted an advertisement in the personal column of *The Times*: 'Father with horrible memories of his own schooldays at Wellington is searching for a school for his son where the food matters as much as education, and the standards are those of a good three-star seaside hotel' (ibid., 81). A number of headmasters were interviewed, and the job finally went to a Dutchman called Harry Tuyn who ran Sizewell Hall, an eccentric school on the Suffolk coast near Aldeburgh where the forty or so children decided what they wanted to learn. The star-struck teenager spent his school holidays wherever his father happened to be filming—most memorably in Ravello with Humphrey Bogart and Gina Lollobrigida shooting John Huston's *Beat the Devil*.

Given that Sizewell was not an ideal preparation for anything else—'more of a total once-in-a-lifetime experience' (*Asking for Trouble*, 84)—it says a lot for Morley's determination that he managed to gain a place at Merton College, Oxford, in 1960 to read French. An immediately recognizable figure in Oxford, large, exuberant, with an enormous gift for friendship, for three years he roamed the theatrical and journalistic landscape, cultivating his many skills—as a trenchant critic for *Isis*, assistant producer to Peter Dews who came to direct *Henry IV*, parts 1 and 2, at the Playhouse, secretary of the Oxford University Dramatic Society, and, given half a chance, actor. But he always knew that, however else he might emulate his father, it would not be on the stage.

Morley graduated with a third-class degree in 1963 and, having landed a job with ITN, first enjoyed a year in the drama department of the University of Hawaii in Honolulu, where he met Margaret Gudejko from Boston, who in 1965 became his first wife and with whom he had three children. Meanwhile, in the autumn of 1964 he took up his job at ITN as a newscaster, reporter, and scriptwriter. Three years later he moved to the BBC where he spent four happy years on the pioneering, open-ended discussion programme *Late Night Line-Up* alongside Joan Bakewell, Denis Tuohy, Michael Dean, and Tony Bilbow.

Nevertheless Morley yearned to be a drama critic and began to realize his ambition when *The Times*'s revered arts editor John Lawrence employed him as third-string reviewer. When John Higgins took over from Lawrence he commissioned Morley to write a series of profiles, 'Great Exiles'. One of his first subjects was Noël Coward, who not only agreed to be godfather to Morley's son Hugo, but also that Morley should be his first biographer. The publication of *A Talent to Amuse* in 1969 coincided with Coward's seventieth birthday celebrations and launched Morley on a long and distinguished career as an author of theatrical biographies. His next subject—while still working as monthly reviewer for *The Tatler* and London drama critic of the *International Herald Tribune*—was Oscar Wilde (1976), chosen not least because his father had been the first actor to play him on stage and screen. Ever since childhood Morley had been susceptible to star quality, and his books reflected his passion. A biography of Sybil Thorndike (1977) was followed by *Marlene Dietrich* (1977), which concentrated on her hitherto unchronicled post-war stage life.

For the next thirty years Morley juggled drama criticism, journalism, television and radio broadcasts, and book writing. In 1973 he joined *The Times* as deputy features editor under Margaret Allen, and in 1975 he moved to *Punch*, where he was at his happiest for the next fourteen years as arts editor and drama critic under the editorships of William Davis and Alan Coren. It was a matter of great pride to him that he and Robert Morley were the only father and son to have been made members of the *Punch* table (other than members of the Agnew family). While at *Punch* he continued to celebrate the lives of such legendary stars as his grandmother Gladys Cooper (1979), Gertrude Lawrence (1981), Katherine Hepburn (1984), Ingrid Bergman (1985), Elizabeth Taylor (1988), and James Mason (1989). In 1983 he published *Tales from the Hollywood Raj*, a glorious account of the heyday of the British acting colony, whose denizens included Sir C. Aubrey Smith, Ronald Colman, Leslie Howard, Nigel Bruce, Basil Rathbone, the Oliviers, and David Niven, whose biography, *The Other Side of the Moon* (1985), he wrote at the request of Niven's sons after their father's death.

It was inevitable that, sooner or later, Morley would start writing for the stage, which he did in 1983 with *Noël and Gertie*, a highly entertaining and at times touching account, compiled from their letters and diaries, of the loving friendship of Noël Coward and Gertrude Lawrence. By the time of Morley's death more than fifty productions had been mounted all over the world. Other musical shows devised by Morley included *Spread a Little Happiness*, an anthology of the songs of Vivian Ellis (King's Head and Whitehall, 1992), and the *Jermyn Street Revue* (2000). He made many cabaret appearances, notably at Pizza on the Park with the nostalgic American pianist Steve Ross, and with Michael Law, with whose Piccadilly Dance Orchestra he appeared as the narrator in a programme of songs by Coward, Cole Porter, and Irving Berlin.

Despite bouts of depression, Morley's appetite for work was undiminished. His marriage to Margaret was dissolved in 1990. He moved from Waltham St Lawrence, Berkshire, to London and in 1995 married the television producer and writer Ruth Lucille Leon, with whom he wrote four books: *Gene Kelly* (1996), *Marilyn Monroe* (1998), *Hey, Mr Producer: the Musicals of Cameron Mackintosh* (1999), and *Beyond the Rainbow: Judy Garland* (1999). When his father died in 1992 he immediately sat down and wrote an affectionate biography, *Robert, My Father* (1993). He followed this with *Audrey Hepburn* (1993), *Ginger Rogers* (1995), and, much against his subject's will, *Dirk Bogarde: Rank Outsider* (1996). Meanwhile, to his great and lasting sadness, *Punch*, as he knew and loved it, was dying on its feet and in 1990 he joined *The Spectator*, where he enjoyed ten years as its drama critic, followed by several rather less happy ones at the *New Statesman* and the *Daily Express*. In 2001 he completed the book that stands alongside *A Talent to Amuse* as a major theatrical biography, *John G: the Authorised Biography of John Gielgud*. The following year he published his own memoirs, *Asking for Trouble*.

His health failing, Morley still managed to direct Vanessa and Corin Redgrave in a revival of Coward's *A Song at Twilight* (King's Head and Gielgud, 1999). In 2002 he was invited to play a corrupt judge in the BBC series *Judge John Deed*. Following a long hot day in court, he removed his robe to find printed on the label: 'Outsize Judge. Robert Morley. 1968'. He died in his sleep of heart failure on 16 February 2007. His ashes were buried next to his parents' in the churchyard of St Mary's, Wargrave. He was survived by his wife Ruth and the three children of his first marriage, Hugo, Alexis, and Juliet.

CHRISTOPHER MATTHEW

Sources S. Morley, *Asking for trouble* (2002) · *The Times* (17 Feb 2007) · *Daily Telegraph* (17 Feb 2007) · *The Guardian* (19 Feb 2007); (22 Feb 2007) · *The Independent* (19 Feb 2007); (21 Feb 2007) · *New York Times* (19 Feb 2007) · *WW* (2007) · personal knowledge (2011) · private information (2011) · b. cert. · d. cert.

Archives Kingston University, Ontario, archives and special collections | FILM BFINA, performance footage | SOUND BL NSA, documentary recordings · BL NSA, performance recordings

Likenesses photographs, 1950–54, Getty Images, London · photographs, 1957–2002, PA Photos, London · photographs, 1957–2006, Rex Features, London · photographs, 1971–98, Photoshot, London · G. Levine, photographs, 1980–85, Getty Images, London · obituary photographs · photographs, repro. in Morley, *Trouble* · photographs, Camera Press, London

Wealth at death £303,732: probate, 10 May 2007, *CGPLA Eng. & Wales*

Morrice, Norman Alexander (1931–2008), choreographer and ballet director, was born on 10 September 1931 in Agua Dulce, Mexico, the younger child of British parents, his father being an oil engineer. Brought up from the age of six by his grandmother at Aboyne, Scotland, he first saw a ballet, *Swan Lake*, in nearby Aberdeen and his schoolboy interest was heightened because the young ballerina's shoulder strap revealingly broke. Morrice (pronounced Morris) intended to follow his father's profession and studied geophysics at Nottingham University, then worked for Anglo-Iranian Oil before deciding to study ballet. So he was late, already twenty-one, before joining the Ballet Rambert School and then graduating to its company. But his personality soon won roles not only in modern works but in two big classics: *Coppélia* as the eccentrically amusing doll-maker Dr Coppélius and *La Sylphide* as the hero James, a role demanding both technique and romantic style. Hilarion in *Giselle* and the Poet in George Balanchine's *Night Shadow* also came his way.

The Ballet Rambert's associate director, David Ellis, noting that Morrice worked on new choreography with his friends, invited him to make a ballet. The outcome was *Two Brothers* (1958), a modern-dress drama about two brothers' murderously jealous rivalry, cinematic in treatment, starring Morrice with John Chesworth and Gillian Martlew. The success of this won him the offer to produce more ballets. The next, *Hazaña* (also 1958), was even more unusual, about a workman (played by Chesworth) struggling alone to raise a heavy cross into position outside a newly built church, variously helped and hindered by other characters. These early ballets also revealed Morrice's liking to work with designers—including Ralph Koltai and Nadine Baylis—who brought a new three-dimensional look to dance and theatre.

A television showing of *Two Brothers* brought Morrice a grant from the Ford Foundation to visit New York for five months in 1961–2, enabling him to see what was happening there in dance and also to study at the Martha Graham School, where he established a warm relationship with that pioneer of American dance, and with the émigré British choreographer Antony Tudor. This experience, combined with Morrice's admiration for the practice of the Netherlands Dance Theatre in presenting almost only specially made works, prompted him to suggest that Ballet Rambert's financial difficulties could be overcome by dispensing with the corps de ballet and concentrating on a modern repertory with a troupe of only sixteen to eighteen dancers, all of soloist quality. This plan was adopted in 1966 and Morrice was appointed co-director with Marie Rambert. He put on a wide range of new works himself, the most striking of them being *That is the Show* in 1971, which—inspired by the words and music of Luciano Berio's *Sinfonia*—succeeded in combining the legend of Tristan and Isolde with suggestions of the assassination of John F. Kennedy. Morrice encouraged dancers in the company to tackle choreography: they included Chesworth, Jonathan Taylor, and—most significantly—Christopher Bruce, who went on to enjoy international success. Morrice also brought in American choreographers, including Anna Sokolow and above all Glen Tetley, who put on a whole series of much admired works, both revivals and creations, including Tetley's acknowledged masterpiece, *Pierrot Lunaire* (1967), inspired by the score by Arnold Schoenberg and providing first-rate roles for its cast of two men and one woman. Morrice himself, besides his many productions for Rambert, worked busily elsewhere. He made several works for the Batsheva Dance Company in Israel, and at Sir Frederick Ashton's invitation created *The Tribute* for the Royal Ballet's touring company, with carnival characters enacting old fertility rites. There were also productions in Australia, Germany, and Canada.

Wanting more time for his creative work, Morrice resigned from Rambert's directorship in 1974, and was surprised in 1977 to be the first outsider invited to direct the Royal Ballet. Although reluctant, he was persuaded by Marie Rambert to accept. However, his contract stipulated no choreography, so his only productions were revised versions of *Swan Lake* and *Giselle*. He resigned after nine years (a longer spell than either Ashton or Kenneth MacMillan) but continued teaching choreographic studies in the company until 1996 and in the school until 2000. Choreographers who later acknowledged his encouragement and guidance included David Bintley and Christopher Wheeldon. His attempts to develop young dancers had only limited success, however.

A man renowned for his modesty, courtesy, and helpfulness to others, Morrice received the Royal Academy of Dancing Elizabeth II Coronation award in 1974. All former Royal Ballet directors had appeared in the honours lists on retirement, and it was widely thought that he was offered a knighthood but declined it. He lived latterly in Kensington, having rented a flat in Marie Rambert's home. He never married. After his retirement he lived quietly, still attending the theatre regularly and seeing his many friends, though he ventured out less frequently after being mugged near his home. Early in 2008 (after spending Christmas with his sister) he complained of feeling unwell. He died in his sleep in the early hours of 11 January; the diagnosis was chronic obstructive pulmonary disease. He was cremated. JOHN PERCIVAL

Sources *Daily Telegraph* (15 Jan 2008) · *The Times* (16 Jan 2008) · *The Independent* (16 Jan 2008) · *New York Times* (16 Jan 2008) · *The Guardian* (21 Jan 2008); (16 Feb 2008) · *WW* (2008) · personal knowledge (2012) · private information (2012) · d. cert.
Archives FILM BFINA, performance footage | SOUND BL NSA, documentary recordings
Likenesses obituary photographs
Wealth at death £683,073: administration, 24 Nov 2008, *CGPLA Eng. & Wales*

Morris, Max (1913–2008), headteacher and trade unionist, was born at 10 Overdale Gardens, Glasgow, on 15 August 1913, the second of three sons of Nathan Morris, Hebrew scholar, and his wife, Annie, née Moselowsky. His elder brother was Jerry Morris (1910–2009), epidemiologist. From a poor Russian Jewish family, he attended Hutchesons' grammar school, noted for its traditionalist methods, but when he was sixteen the family moved to north London, where he attended Kilburn grammar school. He won a scholarship to University College, London, to read history, from which he graduated with a first-class degree. At University College, influenced by Harold Laski and the socialist society established by Hugh Gaitskill, he developed his lifelong passion for politics. But it was the Communist Party, which was seen by many of his generation as the most effective vehicle for achieving a just society, that he initially joined, rather than the Labour Party.

Having received his diploma in education from London's Institute of Education, and after exhaustively seeking a post at a time when jobs were being cut, Morris was appointed a teacher at Willesden technical college in 1936. Though himself of a more academic bent, he valued immensely the technical and practical intelligence of his colleagues, realizing that such a wider vision of learning was central to secondary education for all. On 12 September 1939 he married Barbara Joyce Trotman (1918–2009), daughter of Leonard Harry Trotman, dairy engineer; she was then working as a copywriter for the advertising agency J. Walter Thompson, but was later a distinguished arts and crafts scholar and curator at the Victoria and Albert Museum. During the Second World War he served with the Royal Army Service Corps in Europe and India (rising to the rank of captain).

Demobilized in 1946, Morris returned to teaching, initially at a college of education and then in a secondary school. After what he described in his *Who's Who* entry as 'nine years of political discrimination' by the Conservative-controlled Middlesex county council, which had banned communists from headships and deputy headships (a policy overturned when the Conservatives lost control of the council to Labour), he was appointed a deputy head in Tottenham in 1960. He became headmaster of Chamberlayne Wood secondary school, Kensal Rise, in 1962, and finally first headmaster of Willesden high school (a large comprehensive formed from the amalgamation of grammar, secondary modern, and technical schools) from 1967 until his retirement in 1978. Meanwhile, his first marriage having been amicably dissolved, on 18 February 1961 he married Margaret Saunders, *née* Howard (*b.* 1930/31), historian and adult education lecturer, and daughter of Reginald Louis Howard, executive officer for the National Assistance Board. There were no children from either of Morris's marriages.

The philosophical and political vision which drove Morris was encapsulated in his books *The People's School* (1939) and *Your Children's Future* (1953). In these he set out the vision of a comprehensive system, which would finally, though not universally, be achieved in the 1960s and 1970s. He had witnessed first-hand as a boy the low expectations and poor quality of education for those who came from impoverished backgrounds and who were excluded from the kind of secondary education he had received. He took on those who had provided the evidence for selection at eleven—those, like Cyril Burt and Charles Spearman, who believed that intelligence was an innate capability, independent of nurture and education, which could be accurately measured at the age of eleven. His understanding of the issues and his powers of persuasion were an important factor in propagating the comprehensive ideal.

Morris believed that argument was not enough, however. His immediate academic interests had been devoted to a history of the Chartist movement, resulting in *From Cobbett to the Chartists* (1948). But, no doubt influenced by his studies, he never saw theory as being divorced from practice. It was a matter of not just understanding society, but changing it in the light of that understanding. Hence he chose not to pursue an academic career as a historian but to teach in the sort of school he envisioned in *The People's School* and at the same time play a larger political role in seeking to make that vision universal.

As a political activist, Morris became a power in the National Union of Teachers, and took a lead in changing it from a talking shop into a campaigning organization. He became the most influential teacher politician of the 1960s and 1970s. He was a key figure in the negotiations leading to the creation of the schools council in 1964 (working closely with the government's assistant secretary in charge of the curriculum study group, Derek Morrell). In 1973–4 he was president of the union at a time when Margaret Thatcher was secretary of state for education; the two developed a mutual respect despite their profound political differences. Between 1976 and 1979 he chaired the union's action committee, one feature of which was to persuade members not to supervise school meals in the campaign to get better conditions of service.

Morris was closely involved with many school examining bodies, including as chairman of the Middlesex regional examining board (1975–9) and its successor, the

London regional examining board (1979–90). He was also a member of the Burnham committee (1970–79), the Schools Broadcasting Council (1972–80), and the national advisory committee on the supply and training of teachers (1973–8). He resigned from the Communist Party in 1976, disillusioned by its support of the views of some 'progressive' teachers and sociologists which, in Morris's view, endangered the comprehensive ideal that he had fought for. Despite his justified reputation as a 'firebrand politician', a 'left-wing radical', and an antagonist to Margaret Thatcher's reforms when she was secretary of state, he was in many respects traditional as far as educational standards were concerned. He objected to many of the so-called progressive educationists, because, in his view, equality and justice for the many required access to the culture and opportunities hitherto available only to the few. He was briefly a Labour councillor, on Haringey borough council from 1984 to 1986, where he was an opponent of the more left-wing policies embraced by the majority of his Labour colleagues.

Morris was committed to an active pursuit of a more equitable society, based upon a decent education for all young people. That pursuit lasted, with a remarkable coherence and passion, for seventy years. He was for a long time an active member of the Socialist Educational Association, of which he was chairman from 1995 to 1998, and vice-president thereafter. His final battles included his trenchant criticisms of the creation of academies under the Labour government in 2002. He was especially unhappy when Willesden high school was turned into Capital City Academy the following year. He listed among his recreations in *Who's Who* 'baiting the Department for Education and Science', later changed to 'baiting the bigwigs of educational policy', as well as 'ridiculing Trotskyists and trendies'. He died in Menton, France, on 27 August 2008, and was survived by his second wife, Margaret.

RICHARD PRING

Sources *Daily Telegraph* (6 Sept 2008) · *The Independent* (6 Sept 2008) · *The Guardian* (9 Sept 2008); (10 Sept 2008) · *The Times* (10 Sept 2008) · *WW* (2008) · personal knowledge (2012) · private information (2012) · b. cert. · m. certs.

Likenesses photographs, 1972–8, Photoshot, London · Bassano, half-plate film negatives, 1974, NPG · obituary photographs

Morris, Sir (James) Richard Samuel [Dick] (1925–2008), engineer and industrialist, was born on 20 November 1925 at Upper Heath, Hampstead, London, the son of James John Morris (*d.* 1976), banker, and his wife, Kathleen Mary, *née* McNaughton (*d.* 1976). At the time of his birth registration his parents lived at 86 Lichfield Grove, Finchley. Known to his friends as Dick, he was a chorister at All Souls, Langham Place, and educated at Ardingly College in Sussex. He joined the Welsh Guards in 1944 and served as a captain in Palestine at the time of the creation of the state of Israel. After a brief period at Guest, Keen, and Nettlefolds, in 1950 he joined Courtaulds who arranged for him to study chemical engineering at Birmingham University. He returned in 1955 with a first-class degree plus the vice-chancellor's prize but minus an ear which he had lost in a riding accident—replaced by a 'trademark' prosthetic. After returning to Courtaulds he married Marion Reid Sinclair (*b.* 1930), a hospital almoner, and daughter of James Denny Sinclair, general practitioner, on 13 September 1958; they had two sons and two daughters. His career took off and from 1959 to 1964 he was managing director of the Courtaulds subsidiary National Plastics Ltd. In 1967 he became the youngest main board member at Courtaulds and chaired several of their subsidiaries including British Celanese Ltd (1970–72), Northgate Gp Ltd (1971–6), and Meridian Ltd (1972–6). He became group technical director in 1976.

In 1978 Morris left Courtaulds to become the deputy chairman of the National Enterprise Board, the Labour government's instrument for industrial intervention. There, in addition to helping to try to resolve the problems with British Leyland and others, he encountered the large American engineering company Brown and Root, a major player in the field of pipelines and offshore platforms. In 1980 the company made him chairman of its British subsidiary, in which position he was instrumental in upgrading the company's technology and guiding it through the problems of the 1980s recession. His influence even extended to helping the upgrading of the parent company in the USA. He was subsequently also given responsibility for north Africa where Brown and Root had discovered substantial underground water reserves while drilling for oil in the Sahara Desert. Consequently Morris led the design and management of one of the world's largest engineering projects, the Great Man-Made River pipeline. This involved taking water from wells in the desert and transporting it over 1200 kilometres in massive underground pipes to irrigate large tracts of land on the north coast of Libya. At that time the British and American relationships with Libya were very difficult, particularly after the United States bombed Libya in 1986. There were even occasions when the Libyan government withheld payments to Brown and Root. As a British engineer leading an American contractor at that time, Morris had to demonstrate considerable degrees of diplomacy and courage in addition to engineering leadership. Indeed, following his meetings with Colonel Gaddafi his efforts were also responsible for a degree of *rapprochement* between Libya and the UK at that time.

Morris's next challenge arose when the British government decided to privatize the royal dockyard in Devonport. The contract was won by a consortium led by Brown and Root and Morris became chairman of Devonport Management Ltd and Devonport Royal Dockyard plc from 1987 to 1991. This involved significant upgrading of facilities to service the British fleet of nuclear-powered submarines and delicate negotiations with the board of the Admiralty.

Having previously served as a non-executive director of British Nuclear Fuels (from 1971 to 1985), in 1989 Morris took on an even more challenging role when he was appointed chairman of Nirex (the nuclear industry radioactive waste executive). This body was charged with solving the storage issues for the growing quantity of nuclear waste. Apart from the scientific and engineering issues there were many different stakeholders with strongly held commercial, environmental, and political views. His report proposed an underground laboratory to understand better the technical problems and evaluate the way forward. After a lengthy public inquiry, his proposals were eventually turned down by the environment secretary, John Gummer (just before the 1997 election), on the grounds of scientific uncertainty—the very uncertainties that the experimental laboratory was intended to resolve. Consequently Morris chose to stand down as chairman. Now into his seventies, he again made a change of direction. In 1997 he became chairman of M40 Trains Ltd, the company that ran the Chiltern railway operating out of Marylebone Station, which became one of the more successful train operating companies. He subsequently also joined the boards of Spectron Ltd in 1999 and Lang Rail Ltd in 2000, prior to retirement in 2003.

Despite his successful career in business, Morris also found much time for many professional and advisory roles in government and education. He was a transformational president of the Institution of Chemical Engineering in 1977 and vice-president of the Fellowship of Engineering (later the Royal Academy of Engineering) in 1986–91, as well as chairman of its education committee. He developed a long association with Loughborough University, becoming pro-chancellor in 1982 and chairman of the university's council from 1986 to 1995. His impact on the university was substantial, and included two key appointments of vice-chancellor. He also persuaded Sir Dennis Rooke to become its chancellor. During his period as chairman the university grew significantly in size and reputation. This experience also led him to become the first chairman of a group comprising all the chairs of university councils, which produced a report on improved university governance.

Morris had been a member of the Advisory Board of the Research Councils since 1981 and was deputy chairman in 1988–9, when he produced the Morris report on the structure of research councils which was influential in their subsequent reorganization. He was also a governor of Repton School from 1987 and chairman of governors from 1997 to 2003. He was chairman of Derby Cathedral Council in 2000–03 and a room there was named after him. He was an ardent fund-raiser for both Derby Cathedral and the Royal School for the Deaf in Derby. He was elected a fellow of the Royal Academy of Engineering in 1977 and of the Royal Society of Arts in 1986. He was appointed CBE in 1985 and knighted in 1992. He received honorary degrees from the universities of Leeds (1981), Bath (1981), Birmingham (1985), and Loughborough (1991).

Morris was a brilliant chairman: energetic, determined, and robust, but also kind. He knew how to get the best out of people. He operated with vitality and humour; no meeting would proceed far without bursts of laughter. His final retirement enabled him to enjoy his farm in Breadsall, Derbyshire, where he designed and built his last home, planted 13,000 trees, and grew his own fruit and vegetables. He died of cancer on 1 July 2008 at Derby City General Hospital and was survived by his wife and their four children. A memorial service was held in Derby Cathedral on 4 September 2008. D. E. N. DAVIES

Sources R. Dale, 'A decade of success', *Latitude* [magazine of Brown and Root UK Ltd] (Nov–Dec 1990), 5–9 • *The Times* (24 July 2008) • *Daily Telegraph* (24 July 2008) • *The Independent* (7 Aug 2008) • *Chemical Engineer* (Nov 2008), 66 • records, Institution of Chemical Engineering • records, Royal Academy of Engineering • Burke, *Peerage* • *WW* (2008) • personal knowledge (2012) • private information (2012) [Marion Morris (Lady Morris), widow] • b. cert. • m. cert. • d. cert.

Likenesses obituary photographs

Wealth at death £670,064: probate, 20 Jan 2009, *CGPLA Eng. & Wales*

Morrow, Sir Ian Thomas (1912–2006), accountant and businessman, was born on 8 June 1912 in Park Road, Crumpsall, Manchester, the elder son of Thomas George Morrow (*d.* 1973), an expatriate manager of a jute mill in Brazil, and his wife, Jamesina, *née* Hunter (*d.* 1919). He was born while his mother was en route from Brazil to the family home in St Andrews, arriving before she could complete the journey. He came from a family of engineers on his father's side, while his mother, who died when he was seven, was a granddaughter of Old Tom Morris, a golf champion of the 1860s.

Morrow was sent to the Dollar Academy in Clackmannanshire, Britain's oldest co-educational boarding school, which began an association that remained with him all his life (at the time of his death he was still a governor, a post he held from the 1950s). When the decision had to be made about his further education he clashed with his father. He wanted to go to Oxford, but his father wanted him to remain in Scotland. It was finally agreed that he would follow his father into the textile industry, but as an accountant rather than an engineer. After two years and with a burgeoning interest in cost accounting, he took articles with Dewar and Robertson, a small accounting firm, and in 1936 qualified as a chartered accountant at the Scottish Institute of Chartered Accountants. A year after qualifying he joined the Macclesfield silk weaving company Brocklehurst-Whiston Amalgamated, and it was during his time there that he worked to become an associate of the Institute of Cost and Management Accountants. He was admitted to membership of the institute (later renamed the Chartered Institute of Management Accountants) in 1939 and served on its council from 1952 to 1970.

On 15 June 1940, at St James's Episcopal Church, Dollar, Morrow married Elizabeth Mary Thackray, a 32-year-old secretary (and daughter of Ian Kershaw, electrical engineer), with whom he had one son and one daughter. In the same year he left the textile industry, and he spent the years 1940–42 with the New York management consultants Stevenson, Jordan, and Harrison, mastering the techniques of cost and budgetary control. In 1942 he set up his own management consultancy, Robson, Morrow & Co., with Lawrence Robson. During the ensuing nine years he built up the consultancy and by 1950 was sufficiently recognized in management circles to lead the Anglo-

American Council on Productivity management accounting team on a trade mission to the United States. At the beginning of the 1950s he formed what was to be a thirty-year association with the banker Jocelyn Hambro, who had previously provided Morrow with office space from which to run Robson, Morrow & Co. Under the patronage of Hambros Bank, in 1951 Morrow returned to industry with the Brush Electrical Engineering Company, steadily working his way up from financial director to managing director. He lost that job when Brush was taken over by Hawker Siddeley in 1958.

Bringing together his consultancy skills with his hands-on manufacturing experience, in the late 1950s Morrow turned his hand to becoming a corporate troubleshooter, largely working with companies associated in some way with Hambros, and concentrating on restoring the fortunes of businesses going through difficult times. He became involved in industries as diverse as whaling and the manufacture of kitchen appliances, optical equipment, fire alarms, and road trailers. Among many other directorships he was on the board of UK Optical and Industrial Holdings (1959–86), Crosfield Electronics (1963–72), and the Kenwood Manufacturing Company (1961–8).

In 1971 this quiet Scottish accountant came to the notice of the public when he was called in to sort out Rolls-Royce, the aero-engine and motor car manufacturer, which was teetering on the brink of insolvency. At the time Rolls-Royce was a minnow in the aero-engine business, which was dominated by two American giants, General Electric and Pratt and Whitney. Nevertheless the company had secured a contract to develop a technologically advanced engine for a new airliner, the Lockheed Tristar. In order to win the business from its powerful rivals Rolls-Royce had agreed to a fixed price, but development costs for the engine, the RB-211, had spiralled out of control and were crippling the company. Rolls-Royce urgently needed capital, but there was no chance of raising it in the financial markets at the time. He presented the Conservative government of Edward Heath with a stark choice: let Rolls-Royce collapse or reverse its 'no lame ducks' policy and take the company into public ownership. It chose the latter and Morrow was appointed managing director. Under his direction Rolls-Royce was stripped of its motor manufacturing business to concentrate on jet engines; he renegotiated the Lockheed contract and laid the foundations for its eventual return to the private sector as Britain's foremost technology company. His association with the company ended abruptly in 1973 when he disagreed with the minister for aerospace and shipping, Michael Heseltine, over the choice of his successor as managing director. Instead of becoming chairman, as planned, he resigned rather than compromise. However, the clash did him little harm. He was knighted the same year, and was later able to take up the presidency of the Institute of Chartered Accountants of Scotland, which had been delayed by the Rolls-Royce assignment.

Picking up the relationship with Hambros, Morrow became a director of the bank and continued his troubleshooting career, where he became known for his maxim 'where there's cash there's hope'. Among others, he sorted out the secondary or so-called 'fringe' bank J. H. Vavasseur, and then, well into his seventies, took on the challenging role of managing a Lloyds insurance syndicate that was facing debts of £130 million.

Morrow was a man of quiet charm, whose ready sense of humour could hide a steely determination and fierce intellect. He did things his own way and listened less to the excuses of the directors of troubled companies than to the workers on the shop floor. His activities made him a wealthy man. He was an expert golfer and skier. His first marriage was dissolved in 1967, and on 6 October the same year he married Sylvia Jane Taylor, a 37-year-old beauty therapist, and daughter of Arthur Frederick Taylor, farmer. They had one daughter. Morrow died at his home, Broadacres, Seven Devils Lane, Saffron Walden, Essex, on 19 April 2006, of bronchopneumonia. He was survived by his second wife and his three children. A memorial service was held at St Paul's Cathedral on 6 September 2006.

DAVID BREWERTON

Sources *The Guardian* (31 Dec 1994); (18 May 2006) · *Daily Telegraph* (10 May 2006) · *The Times* (24 May 2006) · *The Independent* (29 May 2006) · *WW* (2006) · Burke, *Peerage* · b. cert. · m. certs. · d. cert.
Archives SOUND BL NSA, documentary recordings
Likenesses photograph, 1976, Photoshot, London · photograph, 1989, Photoshot, London · obituary photographs
Wealth at death £363,376: probate, 2 Aug 2006, *CGPLA Eng. & Wales*

Moss, Patricia Ann [Pat] (1934–2008), showjumper and rally driver, was born on 27 December 1934 at Greentrees, Queens Drive, Thames Ditton, Surrey, the younger child and only daughter of Alfred Ethelbert Moss (1896–1972), dentist, and his wife, (Nora) Aileen, *née* Craufurd (1900–1980). When she was two years old the family moved to a house called Long White Cloud on a backwater of the River Thames at Bray, Berkshire, and it was there that she spent her 'wonderful' childhood with her older brother, a governess, and a succession of pets including piglets, lambs, and ponies (*The Story so Far*, 11). Her parents were keen rally drivers and owned a number of cars including a Lagonda and an Alfa Romeo, but at this stage the children were more interested in four-legged modes of transport. Pat was given a Shetland pony, Queenie, on her fourth birthday and she competed regularly at local horse shows from the age of eight. By the time she went to Wings boarding school in Gloucestershire, aged eleven, she had amassed nearly 350 prizes in show and jumping classes. Five years later, in 1950, she was juvenile jumper of the year at the Horse of the Year show.

After the family moved to a farm in Tring, Hertfordshire, Pat Moss's parents and brother became members of the Harrow Car Club and continued to be enthusiastic competitors in car trials and rallies. It therefore seemed inevitable that Pat, presented with her own car on her seventeenth birthday, would also be drawn towards motor sport but she described herself as initially a nervous driver, unwilling to tackle the heavy traffic of London. She started rallying in the early 1950s as a navigator but, with growing confidence, graduated to driving at a time

Patricia Ann Moss (1934–2008), by Frank Hudson, 1953

when her brother Stirling Moss (*b.* 1929) was making his way to the top of international motor racing. Horses, however, remained her paramount interest. She briefly tried her hand at point-to-point racing but withdrew from the sport after her horse was killed in a fall during their third race. In 1952 she was chosen for the British showjumping team and her skill as a showjumper brought her three runners-up rosettes in the Queen Elizabeth cup (the blue riband event for female riders), twice on Danny Boy in 1952 and 1956 and later on Geronimo. Ironically it was her continued achievements in jumping events that enabled her to buy her first sports car, a Triumph TR2, in 1954, and led to her competitive rallying career.

Over the next eight years Moss and her regular co-driver, Ann (Wiz) Wisdom, competed in rallies throughout Europe with increasing success. She obtained her first works drive with the British Motoring Corporation in the 1955 RAC rally; by 1962 she had won three European ladies' touring car championships driving BMC Morris Minors, Austin Healeys, and Mini Coopers. More significantly, perhaps, she took on and beat the best male drivers, with outright victory in the arduous Liège–Rome–Liège event (1960)—the first time a woman had won an international rally—and second places in the Coupe des Alpes (1960) and the RAC rally (1961). She was voted joint winner of the 1960 driver of the year award by the International Guild of Motoring Writers, the first woman to receive this accolade. Alongside her successful rallying career she continued to enter showjumping classes during the summer months.

In 1962 Moss drove a new works Mini Cooper to victory in the Netherlands Tulip rally and was third in the gruelling east African Safari rally, driving her own Saab, a car recommended to her by her Swedish fellow rally driver, Erik Hilding Carlsson (*b.* 1929), son of Hilding Carlsson, store proprietor. The purchase of the Saab heralded a new chapter in her life. She and Carlsson married at Westminster register office on 9 July 1963 and, after a year with Ford, she joined the Saab team in 1964. That season, with Liz Nystrom as her navigator, she was third in the Acropolis rally, fourth in both the Liège–Sofia–Liège and RAC, and fifth in the Monte Carlo. In 1965 a third place in the Monte Carlo helped her carry off a second European ladies' championship in successive years. She and her husband also co-wrote *The Art and Technique of Driving* (1965), a manual for the ordinary motorist.

In 1967 Moss switched to the Lancia team and published a memoir, *The Story so Far*. She won the Sestriere rally in 1968 and continued to achieve top-ten finishes, but after the birth of a daughter, Suzy, in 1969, she made fewer competitive appearances. She drove briefly for Renault Alpine and Toyota in the early 1970s before finally retiring in 1974, having successfully combined prize-winning careers in two dangerous sports over nearly twenty-five years. She maintained an involvement with horses throughout her life. She died of cancer at her home, 60 Totternhoe Road, Eaton Bray, Bedfordshire, on 14 October 2008 and was survived by her husband and daughter.

JOYCE KAY

Sources P. Moss, *The story so far* (1967) · *The Times* (18 Oct 2008) · *Daily Telegraph* (18 Oct 2008) · *The Guardian* (27 Oct 2008) · *The Independent* (13 Nov 2008) · b. cert. · m. cert.

Likenesses F. Hudson, photograph, 1953, Rex Features, London [*see illus.*] · Lenare, cellulose acetate negatives, 1953, NPG · photographs, 1953–63, Rex Features, London · obituary photographs · photographs, repro. in Moss, *Story so far*

Wealth at death £980,529: probate, 15 June 2009, *CGPLA Eng. & Wales*

Moule, Charles Francis Digby [Charlie] (**1908–2007**), New Testament scholar, was born on 3 December 1908 in Hangchow (Hangzhou), China, the third son of Henry William Moule (1871–1953), a missionary, and his wife, Laura Clements, *née* Pope (1870–1972). Educated by his parents in China until he was ten, he received his formal education at Weymouth College, Dorset, and proceeded from there to Emmanuel College, Cambridge, in 1927. After gaining first-class honours in both parts of the classical tripos, along with several university prizes, he moved to Ridley Hall, Cambridge, in 1931 to study theology and prepare for ordination in the Church of England. He was ordained deacon in 1933 and priest in 1934, exercising his ministry as a tutor of Ridley Hall and part-time curate of St Mark's, Cambridge. After a curacy at St Andrew's, Rugby, in 1934–6, he returned as vice-principal to Ridley Hall, where he remained (for five years combining the post with a curacy at Great St Mary's) until his appointment as dean of Clare College, Cambridge, in 1944. He soon became an assistant lecturer, and then lecturer, in the faculty of divinity, and in 1951 was elected Lady Margaret's professor of divinity.

Trained initially as a classical scholar, and soon adding to this an expert knowledge of the biblical languages,

Moule approached the New Testament profoundly convinced that detailed scrutiny of possible meanings of the original words and phrases was an essential under-girding of any interpretation placed upon them. In his first major publication, *An Idiom Book of New Testament Greek* (1953), he brought his linguistic knowledge to bear on many instances where exact definition of the meanings of words in their grammatical contexts shed light on disputed interpretations. But for him such expertise, though highly technical, was never of purely academic interest. He came from a family of distinguished evangelical clergy (George Evans *Moule, bishop of mid-China, was his grandfather, and Handley *Moule, bishop of Durham and founder of Ridley Hall, was his great-uncle), and his approach led him to seek textual confirmation of the structure of faith he had inherited, and if necessary to modify it. This faith remained unshaken throughout his life; but his scrupulous attention to the details of the text led him to reformulate it in ways that he often hoped would facilitate a *rapprochement* with other traditions.

Moule's subsequent publications, besides numerous and often influential articles, included only a small number of really substantial books, but these were widely read and respected. His *The Birth of the New Testament* (1962) became a standard introduction to the results of recent scholarship, setting the origin of the texts firmly in the life and worship of the early Christian communities. The book was translated into a number of languages, and was rewritten for a third edition in 1982. *The Origin of Christology* (1977) was a notable contribution to theological debate, and was awarded the Collins theological book prize. It argued strongly that Christology did not 'evolve' through assimilation to Jewish and pagan conceptions, but 'developed' through reflection upon an experience of Jesus that was there from the beginning; and Moule characteristically rested part of his argument on the precise meaning of the Greek preposition in the crucial phrase used by St Paul, 'in Christ'. The same preoccupation with textual precision was evident in his work as one of the translators of the New English Bible, both for the New Testament and for the Apocrypha (published in 1961 and 1970 respectively), an ecumenical project he hoped could further promote unity among the churches. Along the same lines, he believed research into the scriptural evidence for the earliest forms of Christian worship, which he summarized in his short book *Worship in the New Testament* (1961), would help to overcome historic confessional differences in matters of worship.

Moule (known throughout his life as Charlie) was a bachelor and his entire academic career was spent in Cambridge in the service of his college and the university. He was chairman of the influential senior New Testament seminar, and his lectures on the theology and ethics of the New Testament, which he constantly revised over many years, were invariably crowded, and seldom ended without an invitation to anyone who wished to visit him in his rooms for further discussion. His surname (pronounced 'Mole'), his diminutive stature, and his upwardly peering manner inevitably invited reference to *The Wind in the Willows*; but he made a far more persistent impression by his quite exceptional courtesy, modesty, and humble respect for the views of others. The journalist Matthew Parris (an undergraduate at Clare) wrote that he was 'unbelievably generous with his time', and that his 'patient willingness to talk over doubts, beliefs and difficulties … seemed unlimited' (*The Times*, 11 Oct 2007).

Later described as 'probably the most influential British New Testament scholar of his time' (*PBA*, 281), Moule was elected a fellow of the British Academy in 1966, was awarded the British Academy's Burkitt medal for biblical studies in 1970, was an honorary DD of St Andrew's and Cambridge universities, and was made a CBE in 1985. On retirement from his professorship in 1976 he returned to live and teach at Ridley Hall until he moved to Sussex in 1980 and a retirement home, the Old Vicarage, Leigh, near Sherborne, Dorset, in 2003. He died there on 30 September 2007. His funeral took place in Yetminster, and his memorial service (at which the archbishop of Canterbury was the preacher) in Great St Mary's, Cambridge, on 9 February 2008. A. E. HARVEY

Sources G. Hunt, *About the New English Bible* (1970), 2 · B. Lindars and S. S. Smalley, eds., *Christ and spirit in the New Testament* (1973), viii · *Daily Telegraph* (2 Oct 2007) · *The Independent* (2 Oct 2007) · *The Times* (5 Oct 2007); (11 Oct 2007); (13 Oct 2007); (22 Oct 2007) · *Church Times* (12 Oct 2007) · *The Guardian* (24 Oct 2007) · *Letter of the Corpus Association*, 86 (2007), 64–7 · *PBA*, 161 (2009), 281–310 · *WW* (2007) · personal knowledge (2011) · private information (2011) · d. cert.
Archives FILM BFINA, documentary footage
Likenesses Elliott & Fry, quarter-plate negative, 1961, NPG · Bassano, half-plate film negatives, 1963, NPG · E. Leigh, photograph, repro. in *PBA* · obituary photographs · photograph, repro. in www.admin.cam.ac.uk/news/dp/2007100202 · photograph, repro. in www.churchtimes.co.uk/content.asp?id=45888
Wealth at death £486,786: probate, 27 Dec 2007, *CGPLA Eng. & Wales*

Mowlam, Marjorie [Mo] **(1949–2005)**, politician, was born on 18 September 1949 at 43 King Street, Watford, Hertfordshire, the second of three children of Frank William Mowlam, Post Office worker, and his wife, Bettina Mary (Tina), *née* Rogers, telephonist. She described her parents as 'classic lower-middle class' (personal knowledge). When she was eleven the family moved to Coventry, where her father became an assistant postmaster. He was an alcoholic, and his behaviour at home was a constant trial for her. Her mother, however, was very different, and a source of strength and friendship.

After a short spell at Chiswick Girls' Grammar School in London Mowlam went to Coundon Court comprehensive school, Coventry, where she excelled. She went on to become head girl, as well as being an outstanding netball player and winning a duke of Edinburgh's award. In 1968 she progressed to Durham University, where she read social anthropology. She became a student leader and had a number of boyfriends, including one whom she followed to Iowa University in 1973. While there she gained her PhD (on referenda in Switzerland). She then went to Florida State University in 1977. Two years later she

Marjorie Mowlam (1949–2005), by John Keane, 2001

returned to Britain and became a politics lecturer at Newcastle University. Shortly afterwards, her former boyfriend, from whom she had parted in 1976, died in a drowning accident.

In Newcastle Mowlam became very politically active, chairing Tyne Bridge constituency Labour Party, joining the Campaign for Nuclear Disarmament, and playing a part in getting Neil Kinnock elected as Labour Party leader. She left Newcastle University in 1983 and took an administrative job at Northern College, Barnsley. She was unsuccessful in finding a parliamentary seat to fight at that time. Shortly before the general election of 1987, however, James Tinn, MP for Redcar, announced, at the last minute, that he was not going to seek re-election. From a shortlist of four Mowlam was chosen to contest the seat for Labour, beating the strong local candidate, Richard Lewis, by the narrow margin of seven votes in the selection process. Lewis and his wife, Ruth, remained steadfast friends of Mowlam for the rest of her life.

Mowlam was thirty-eight when she entered the House of Commons. In her maiden speech she paid special tribute to Ellen Wilkinson, the Labour MP of the 1920s, and made particular mention of the problem of low-paid women. She was soon a member of the influential public accounts committee, before Neil Kinnock made her a junior spokesperson on Northern Ireland, only ten months after her entry to the house. Her new job gave her an initial insight into the complicated politics of Northern Ireland. In 1989 she moved to become Labour's spokesperson on the City of London and corporate affairs, working with Gordon Brown. Their relationship was not a warm one. She was elevated to the shadow cabinet in 1992, becoming the party's spokesperson on women and the 'citizens' charter', a post she neither wanted nor enjoyed. She was elected a member of Labour's national executive committee, pleasing some party members with her decidedly republican views.

On John Smith's death Mowlam took a major role in the election of Tony Blair as the party's new leader. She would have liked to have been Blair's campaign manager, but the job went to Jack Straw. Blair made her shadow secretary of state for Northern Ireland, which she felt was a demotion. It proved to be nothing of the sort. The Labour Party's position on Northern Ireland needed an overhaul, if there was to be a settlement under a Labour government, changing from one that was seen to be very 'pro-green' to one of consensus and even-handedness. Mowlam soon got to know all of the main players in Northern Ireland, drawing on her previous experience as a shadow Northern Ireland minister.

In 1995 Mowlam's personal life changed dramatically when on 24 June she married Jonathan Paul (Jon) Norton (*d.* 2009), a forty-year-old Labour-supporting merchant banker whom she had met when she had been Labour's City spokesperson. She acquired two stepchildren, Henrietta and Freddie, as well as a new home in Islington. In 1997 her life was transformed in a very different way. She was diagnosed with a brain tumour and had to undergo difficult radiotherapy treatment. She kept this news very much to herself and a close circle around her, including her able adviser Nigel Warner, the speaker Betty Boothroyd, and Tony Blair. When newspapers started to comment unfavourably on her increased weight and new wig, she felt she had to make her condition public. As a result she received tremendous public support for her courage. In meetings, she would often astound people by taking her wig off and continuing as if nothing had happened.

After the general election of 1997 Mowlam became the first woman secretary of state for Northern Ireland. She immediately went to Belfast to meet people in the street. Her style was a complete contrast to that of any previous secretary of state. She was very much a 'people person'—'touchy feely' was a phrase often used about her—and also used robust language and was very plain-speaking. With her attractive and charismatic personality she had no difficulty in relating to ordinary people, especially women. She carried little religious or political 'baggage', believing that the 'principle of consent' was the only way ahead for Northern Ireland. Her style did not appeal to all. Many Unionists, in particular, did not quite know what to make of her. Relations between her and David Trimble, the Ulster Unionist Party leader, were never good.

Mowlam's immediate task in Northern Ireland was to revive a flagging peace process. Working closely with the senior American politician Senator George Mitchell, the chairman of the talks, and prime ministers Blair and Ahern, she started her job by overseeing a new ceasefire by the Irish Republican Army, which was necessary before inclusive negotiations could start. This succeeded, and Sinn Féin re-entered the process; but Ian Paisley and his

Democratic Unionist Party left it. During the autumn of 1997 little progress was made, and by the winter it looked as if the peace process was nearing collapse. In January 1998 Mowlam spectacularly and controversially visited loyalist prisoners in the Maze. This kept loyalism on board, and helped revive the process.

Although, inevitably, 10 Downing Street took the lead on Northern Ireland issues, with Tony Blair playing a very important role, the day-to-day business of the process was handled by the indefatigable Mowlam. The Belfast, or 'Good Friday', agreement of April 1998 led eventually to the establishment of a power-sharing executive, an elected assembly, the release of prisoners, major changes to human rights and policing, and, especially significantly, an agreed and settled status for Northern Ireland. Properly, Mowlam was given much credit for the outcome of the talks. By contrast, it was sometimes also said that Mowlam was marginalized in the process, especially during the final negotiations. This was not the case—she played a vital part, along with the two prime ministers and the Northern Ireland politicians. She was, however, the first to say that the politicians and people of Ireland, north and south, were the real creators of the new arrangements. It would take a decade before the agreement was implemented in full, but the Good Friday agreement was the key to the success of the peace process.

Mowlam had, many argued, become the most popular politician in Britain. Indeed, a Gallup poll for the *Daily Telegraph* revealed that she was the most popular member of the cabinet. During the Labour Party conference of 1998, in the middle of Tony Blair's speech, the prime minister's reference to 'our one and only Mo' resulted in a unique and heartfelt standing ovation. It has been claimed that this was to work to her disadvantage, and that her eventual departure from Northern Ireland to a lower-profile cabinet job stemmed from this occasion. Certainly, her future was now to be controversial. She refused the offer of standing as the Labour candidate for the London mayoralty (the eventual winner, the then independent Ken Livingstone, later said that she would have won had she stood), and the job of secretary of state for health. She would have preferred to become foreign secretary or defence secretary, but in the end she was appointed minister for the cabinet office and chancellor of the duchy of Lancaster, in October 1999. She was replaced in Northern Ireland by Peter Mandelson. She did not much like her new job, although she worked particularly hard on issues relating to the international drugs trade. She became increasingly disaffected with the direction of the government and was not in favour of the invasion of Iraq.

Mowlam retired from the government and from the Commons in 2001, publishing her autobiography, *Momentum*, the following year. She took part in television programmes, toured the country in 'An audience with Mo Mowlam', and was still very much the darling of the Labour Party, gaining recognition and admiration wherever she went. She and her husband retired to a farmhouse in Sittingbourne, Kent, where she worked on a book about drugs policy. Her health problems, however, continued. She died on 19 August 2005, in the Pilgrim's Hospice, 56 London Road, Canterbury, of bronchopneumonia and astrocitoma of the brain. She was survived by her husband, Jon, and her two stepchildren.

Mowlam's name will always be associated primarily with Northern Ireland and the Good Friday agreement—rightly so, since the impetus she gave to a flagging peace process was very real. She was seen as someone who was genuinely different from previous Northern Ireland secretaries. She was inevitably overshadowed by Tony Blair, and she could antagonize people, especially Unionists. But her achievements were genuine, her bravery unquestioned, and her popularity in the country, among people of all political persuasions, unrivalled.

PAUL MURPHY

Sources J. Langdon, *Mo Mowlam: the biography* (2000) • M. Mowlam, *Momentum* (2002) • D. Godson, *Himself alone: David Trimble* (2004) • *The Times* (20 Aug 2005) • *Daily Telegraph* (20 Aug 2005) • *The Guardian* (20 Aug 2005) • *The Independent* (20 Aug 2005) • *WW* (2005) • personal knowledge (2009) • private information (2009) • b. cert. • m. cert. • d. cert.

Archives FILM BFINA, 'The rise and fall of Mo Mowlam', T. Stark (director), Channel 4, 6 May 2000 • BFINA, current affairs footage • BFINA, documentary footage • BFINA, performance footage | SOUND BL NSA, Harman-Shepherd interviews, interview with L. Fairbrother and B. Sones, 20 July 2004, 1CDR0032678

Likenesses photographs, 1988–2004, PA Photos, London • photographs, 1991–2004, Rex Features, London • S. Humphrey, drawing, 1995, priv. coll. • photographs, 1995–2004, Getty Images, London • photographs, 1997–2004, Camera Press, London • V. Carew Hunt, bromide fibre print, 1998, NPG • J. Giles, colour photograph, 1998, priv. coll. • J. Keane, oils, 2001, NPG [*see illus.*] • S. Amery, clay model, priv. coll.; bronze cast, U. Durham • obituary photographs • photographs, repro. in *Momentum* • photographs, repro. in Langden, *Mo Mowlam*

Wealth at death £316,163: probate, 21 Nov 2005, *CGPLA Eng. & Wales*

Muir, (Isabella) Helen Mary (1920–2005), biochemist, was born on 20 August 1920 at Naini Tal, India, the daughter of G. B. F. (Basil) Muir, a member of the Indian Civil Service, and his wife, Gladys Helen Mary, *née* Stack. Always known as Helen, she was educated by her mother in India up to the age of ten and then at boarding schools in Montreux, Switzerland, and in England, including Downe House in Berkshire. She gained entry to Somerville College, Oxford, to read medicine in 1940. Influenced by her tutor, Dorothy Hodgkin, she switched to study chemistry, and graduated with a second-class degree in 1943 then DPhil in 1947 for a thesis supervised by Sir Robert Robinson on the chemical synthesis of penicillin. After a year at the Dunn School of Pathology in Oxford (1947–8) she moved to the National Institute of Medical Research in Mill Hill, where she worked in the biochemistry department with Albert Neuberger from 1948 to 1954, on the metabolic origin of carbon and nitrogen atoms in haem and later in collagen. Her work on collagen led her to develop an interest in connective tissues and arthritis, and she moved to the department of medicine headed by Stanley Peart at St Mary's Hospital, Paddington, from 1954 to 1966, where her work on cartilage identified the link between chondroitin sulphate and protein and established the basic structure of proteoglycan, which is a major component of joint cartilage. This area of research formed the focus of her scientific career.

Muir was of striking appearance and matched the description of a fiery redhead. She had many male admirers, but was never married. In addition to scientific research the other strong interest of her life was horse riding. She was a member of the Bedale hunt in Yorkshire, where her parents had an estate and had built a house, Langlands, near Bedale. She suffered a bad riding accident in the 1950s, but this never detracted from her enthusiasm for riding and she continued until ill health forced her to stop when she was seventy-five. In London, where she worked for most of her career, she lived for many years in East Sheen and rode in nearby Richmond Park.

Much of Muir's career was spent at the Kennedy Institute of Rheumatology in Hammersmith, which was the world's first specialist rheumatology institute, funded by the Arthritis Research Campaign. She was recruited as head of the biochemistry division in 1966 and went on to become director from 1977 until her retirement in 1990. Her group at the Kennedy carried out fundamental work on cartilage function, with novel work on the supramolecular organization of proteoglycans and studies on cartilage degeneration in experimental osteoarthritis. This work was fundamental in establishing that degenerative joint diseases were not just the product of 'wear and tear' associated with old age, but involved an active disease process. Muir's major achievement was thus in moving research in joint diseases from an era of observational descriptive pathology to the molecular and cellular analysis of the processes underlying these diseases.

Muir's work at the Kennedy Institute on cartilage degeneration and osteoarthritis was internationally recognized. She was elected a fellow of the Royal Society in 1977 and a foreign member of the Royal Swedish Academy of Sciences in 1989. She was appointed CBE in 1981 for her contribution to medical research. She also received many other prestigious awards, including the Heberden medal of the British Society for Rheumatology (1976), the Feldberg Foundation award (1977), the Bunim medal of the American Rheumatism Association (1978), the Neil Hamilton Fairley medal of the Royal College of Physicians (1981), the Ciba medal of the Biochemical Society (1981), and the Steindler award of the American Orthopaedic Research Society (1982). She was also made a DSc of Oxford in 1973 and received honorary degrees from Brunel and Strathclyde universities and the University of Edinburgh, where her great-grandfather Sir William Muir had been principal.

Muir was well known for speaking her mind in a clear and objective way and she became the first woman member of the council of the Medical Research Council (1973–7). She was also later appointed a trustee of the Wellcome Trust (1982–90) and played a major part developing the trust's role in the support of UK biomedical research. She was able to promote the development of research on the role of extracellular matrix in health and disease, including the formation of the Wellcome Trust Centre for Cell-Matrix Research at the University of Manchester, which she opened in 1995.

Muir continued her interest in science and medicine into her retirement in Yorkshire, where ecological and environmental concerns led her to fit solar panelling to her house and to work to conserve the habitats of local wildlife. She suffered from spinal stenosis later in life, which restricted her mobility, and she survived breast cancer over several years before succumbing to it on 28 November 2005, at her home, Langlands House, Hornby, near Bedale, Yorkshire. She was buried in the local church at Hornby. TIM HARDINGHAM

Sources *Daily Telegraph* (15 Dec 2005) · *The Guardian* (4 Jan 2006) · T. Hardingham, 'Helen Muir', *The Biochemist*, 28/3 (June 2006), 62–4 · *WW* (2005) · personal knowledge (2009) · private information (2009) · d. cert.

Archives FILM BFINA, 'Our brilliant careers', *Sex and the scientists*, F. Adams (director), Channel 4, 19 Aug 1996 · Biochemical Society, interview with T. Hardingham

Likenesses Bassano, six half-plate film negatives, 1975, NPG · obituary photographs · photograph, RS

Wealth at death £2,561,429: probate, 25 April 2006, *CGPLA Eng. & Wales*

Mumford [*née* McFarland], **Enid Mary** (**1924–2006**), social scientist, was born on 6 March 1924 at Iona, Groveland Avenue, Wallasey, Cheshire, the daughter of Arthur McFarland (1893–1966), a hospital secretary, and later a prominent barrister and chief stipendary magistrate of Liverpool, and his wife, Dorothy, *née* Evans, a headteacher. Her family and intellectual heritage were in the north-west of England. She attended Wallasey high school before joining the social sciences department at Liverpool University, where she took a special interest in social psychology and graduated BA in 1946. She then went to work in industry, first with Rotol Ltd, aeronautical engineers, as a personnel manager responsible for industrial relations strategy for a large number of female staff, and subsequently with the Liverpool clock and watch maker J. D. Francis as a production manager. The experience of working in industry close to the shop floor proved invaluable for her later academic work as a teacher and researcher. On 28 July 1947, at the parish church of St Nicholas, Wallasey, she married James Muir (Jim) Mumford, a dental surgeon one year her senior (son of James Montgomery Mumford), who was later to become professor of operative dental surgery at Liverpool University. They made their home at 4 Windmill Close, Appleton, Warrington, Cheshire, situated conveniently between the universities of Liverpool and Manchester. They had two children, Michele and Colin.

Much of Enid Mumford's intellectual development and identity was forged in the social science department of Liverpool University which she joined as a research associate in 1948, working with some of the key figures then

Enid Mary Mumford (1924–2006), by unknown photographer

making Liverpool University one of the foremost centres in the world for the study of industrial sociology, including Joan Woodward, Olive and Joe Banks, A. H. Halsey, and Tom Lupton. She became interested and involved in research on technical change and its impacts in a variety of industries including coalmining, steelmaking, and the Liverpool docks. In particular, one of the problems faced by the UK after the Second World War was that, despite heavy investment in machinery to make industry more efficient, productivity did not get the expected boost. Mumford discovered that researchers at the Tavistock Institute were at this time developing an understanding of the importance of a socio-technical approach: that investment in technology alone was not sufficient to gain the benefits of new technology, social factors being as important as technical factors. But what equally attracted her to the approach espoused by the Tavistock Institute researchers was their insistence that the object of technical change was more than financial benefit, and had to include the enhancement of the quality of working life. She was also influenced by the writings of Mary Parker Follett, the pioneering American management teacher of the early twentieth century, whom she regarded as having helped to inform her own thinking and values. Follett's ideas on negotiation, power, and employee participation became a critical component of Mumford's own methodologies. Throughout her life as an academic and researcher she placed her values and beliefs at the centre of her work. This was reflected most clearly in one of her last books, *Systems Design: Ethical Tools for Ethical Change* (1996). Her work with the Tavistock Institute led to her becoming a council member of the institute.

From her experience of working in industry Mumford realized that if she were to understand properly how technical change in industry could be made to achieve its objectives she had to immerse herself in the workplace, to soak up the attitudes, preconceptions, capabilities, and desires of the workforce at all levels. Thus when she studied the coalmining industry to analyse why the investment in mechanization by the National Coal Board had not yielded the expected increases in productivity, she went down the mines for several months to watch and talk to the face workers as well as to the deputies who acted as supervisors. Again, when studying industrial relations at Liverpool docks in the context of changing work practices in the 1950s, she first enrolled as a catering assistant in order to get closer to the stevedores without her becoming suspect as a management spy. Her account of these experiences in her later book *Redesigning Human Systems* (2003) made fascinating reading.

A year at the University of Michigan followed in 1956–7, when Mumford studied at the university's bureau of public health economics. On returning to England she took up a lectureship at Liverpool and graduated PhD at the University of Manchester, before in 1966 joining the staff of the new Manchester Business School (initially as a lecturer, then as a senior lecturer, reader, and from 1979 as professor of organizational behaviour and director of the computer and work design research unit). In the 1950s and 1960s computers began to be used to support and automate business processes. Once again there were questions about the impact of these new technology-based systems, and this was a problem Mumford set out to address. In 1967 she published, with Olive Banks, *The Computer and the Clerk*, their study of the impact of computers on the workforce of an Irish bank. This was one of the first studies of the way computer systems affected work practices, and crucially also of the response of the workforce at all levels to the use of computers. *Computers: Planning for People* (1968), co-written with Thomas Ward, demonstrated the values she held to all her life.

More studies followed, at Turner and Newall, the asbestos manufacturers, Rolls-Royce, ICI, and many other places. Mumford's earlier studies had convinced her that the accepted methods of introducing computer systems were oriented towards the technology rather than the people who had to use that technology as part of their everyday jobs. She turned her attention to devising an improved methodology for introducing computer systems into organizations. Her methods were based on the socio-technical approach espoused by the Tavistock Institute and the ideas she had inherited from Mary Parker Follett. They included the conviction that if computer systems were to deliver both financial value and improved working conditions and job satisfaction, all those involved, and in particular those who had to work with the new systems, had to participate in the design process.

Her experience in industry and her earlier research studies had convinced her that the capability for designing systems was not confined to 'experts' but could be learned by employees at all levels, and that often design ideas stemming from members of the workforce were more radical (and realizable) then those put forward by the experts.

These new ideas for design were encapsulated in Mumford's book *Effective Systems Design and Requirements Analysis: the ETHICS Approach* (1995), a restatement of work first published in 1979 with her co-author Mary Weir. The acronym ETHICS stood for Effective Technical and Human Implementation of Computer-based Systems. Her ETHICS approach evolved through its use in many action research studies, mainly in the UK but also including a major study with the Digital Equipment Corporation in the USA. In the evolution of ETHICS Mumford drew on many sources. Thus she took on the different notions of 'job satisfaction', re-examined all of them, and synthesized her own, more comprehensive model. To test the validity of new designs emerging from the ETHICS approach she adopted the 'viable systems model' developed by the cybernetician Stafford Beer and the notion of 'requisite variety' from Ross Ashby. She was a scholar who quickly got to the heart of practical concerns, but at the same time never forgot the humanistic values she espoused. Each of her many action research studies was carefully documented in a monograph or a paper in a journal. These provided examples of her participative approach, its rationale, and a narrative that included the voices of the participants themselves. At the same time difficulties encountered were recorded and the lessons that could be derived from their analysis were spelled out. Nevertheless most of the action research projects had successful outcomes. She was a superb facilitator. Her charisma, her smile, and her arguments persuaded hardened managers of the old, more authoritarian, top-down school to give her methods a chance.

Mumford retired in 1988, with the title of emeritus professor. But retirement did not end her contributions as a scholar, and a stream of articles and books followed, including, in 2003, *Redesigning Human Systems*, in which she provided a reprise of her most important studies. Her work was recognized internationally, and she received many honours, including the J. D. Warnier prize for her contribution to information science, the Association for Information Systems top prize, the LEO award for her lifetime contribution to the study of information systems in 1999, and an honorary doctorate from the University of Jyvaskyla in Finland in 1996. She was also made a companion of the Institute of Personnel Development, and a fellow of the British Computer Society. Perhaps the clearest indication of her reputation was the publication in 2006 of 'Enid Mumford: a tribute', with contributions from leading scholars from many parts of the world, in the *Information Systems Journal*, followed in 2007 by a special edition of the *Journal of the Association for Information Systems* devoted to analysing her contributions.

Throughout her career and into retirement Mumford worked for the improvement of the position of women in a variety of situations. She was affronted by the treatment of women in her local golf club, which led to a long campaign to gain recognition and culminated in her appointment as club captain. She was interested in modern art and became an accomplished artist herself. She died at Riverbank Nursing Home, Egerton Street, Howley, Warrington, Cheshire, on 7 April 2006, after a massive stroke, and was survived by her husband, Jim, their daughter, Michele, a businesswoman based in Australia, and son, Colin, a consultant neurologist in Edinburgh.

FRANK LAND

Sources *The Guardian* (3 May 2006) · 'Enid Mumford: a tribute', *Information Systems Journal*, 16 (2006), 343–82 · *Journal of the Association for Information Systems* (Sept 2007) [special Mumford edition] · www.enid.u-net.com, 5 May 2009 · *WW* (2006) · personal knowledge (2010) · private information (2010) · b. cert. · m. cert. · d. cert.

Likenesses photograph, repro. in www.enid.u-net.com · photograph, University of Manchester, Manchester Business School [*see illus.*]

Wealth at death £378,774: probate, 27 July 2006, *CGPLA Eng. & Wales*

Munro [*née* Donald], **Dame Alison** (**1914–2008**), civil servant and headmistress, was born on 12 February 1914 at Dean Place, Liskeard, Cornwall, the fourth of five children (the first of whom died in infancy) of John Donald, a medical doctor, and his wife, Helen Barrow, *née* Wilson, concert pianist. In the mid-1920s the family emigrated to South Africa, a move dictated by the father's ill health. Eighteen months afterwards, in 1927, Helen Donald died, and her husband's death followed a few months later. The four orphans, who included Ian *Donald (1910–1987), the pioneer of ultrasound, were left in the care of a housekeeper to whom they became devoted, but, in order to remain together in South Africa, the children had to fight the trustees of their mother's will: it was the inheritance she left that provided for their education. The aggression and tenacity needed for this fight remained strong in Munro always; another South African legacy was her enthusiasm for the free and open air life she experienced there.

In South Africa, Alison Donald attended Wynberg Girls' High School, but by 1930 it had become clear to the young Donalds that they must move to London to realize their educational ambitions. The advice of a local headmistress who had taught at St Paul's Girls' School led Alison Donald to Hammersmith. From St Paul's she went to St Hilda's College, Oxford, in 1933, graduating in 1936 with a third in philosophy, politics, and economics. She had met Alan Lamont Munro (two years her junior, son of James Watson Munro, professor of entomology at Imperial College, London) in Oxford and they married at Chelsea Old Church on 3 September 1939. After twins were stillborn she was carrying her son, Alan, when her husband (an RAF flying officer and test pilot) was killed in an air crash in 1941.

Through the intervention of her father-in-law, Alison Munro went in 1942 to work for Sir Robert Watson-Watt at the Ministry of Aircraft Production. She worked closely and travelled extensively with him, his powerful personality and fights with the civil service making a deep impression. She moved after the war, in 1945, to the newly formed Ministry of Civil Aviation, where Watson-Watt was chief telecommunications adviser to the minister. The deputy secretary, Sir George Cribbett, became another influence. His 'encyclopaedic knowledge of the workings of international air transport agreements' and his 'somewhat formidable' presence at a conference table (*The Times*, 24 June 1974) were strengths Munro was to make her own. Often described as a legendary figure in negotiation, first about airfields, then about flying routes, Munro relished verbal jousting and the discomfiture of opponents, and was swift with her put-downs. She became under-secretary at the Ministry of Transport and Civil Aviation in 1958 and at the Ministry of Aviation in 1960.

In 1964 Munro abandoned her civil service career to take up the post of high mistress of St Paul's Girls' School. She was made a CBE the same year. She certainly missed the collegiality of civil service work when she discovered the isolation of the headmistress's study. She commented later on her move into education: 'It was crazy and I dropped money to do it' (*Evening Standard*, 17 May 1973). She enjoyed the myth of having been head hunted for the post, just as she relished (and polished) many of the widely circulated anecdotes about her life. In fact the move was a considered one, the Mercers' Company (the governors of St Paul's) noting drily that her lack of experience 'does not deter her from asking to be considered for the appointment'. They also noted 'her detailed enquiry as to the value of the emoluments'. It was Munro's predecessor, Margaret Osborn, who commented to the governors that 'SPGS has a brilliant but pigheaded staff who are quite capable of maintaining the high academic standards in the school, even with a High Mistress who was new to the teaching world, but it would need to be a very strong personality to hold the reins under such circumstances' (Mercers' Company Archives, SPGS 100 Mrs A Munro 3/1405). Of Munro's strength of personality there could be no doubt. The Mercers' decision to make 'a notable departure from tradition and conventional practice' proved to be a good one—they were prepared for it to be either 'an outstanding success or a complete failure' (ibid.).

In her decade of tenure, Munro moved St Paul's Girls' School into the late twentieth century in terms of resources and organization. Her tough frankness and robustness meant that departmental fiefdoms and procedures unaltered over decades presented little by way of problem to her. Indeed her trenchancy, self-confidence, and energy made her formidable to her governors—and to any who answered to her. Her pupils certainly respected a force to be reckoned with. Re-entering the school in the 1960s meant that she had to contend with sex, drugs, and rock 'n' roll: there were a number of expulsions. Probably a majority of Paulinas both observed her coolly while recognizing her capacity to help students; they especially relished her refusal to accept commonplace assumptions and expectations regarding appearance and ambitions. Her achievements at the school were extensive: new reporting requirements; abolition of the prefect system; creation of a full school council; new buildings, extensions, and refurbishments. It was hard for her after 1974 to admit that any genuine innovation had been created following her departure.

Shortly before she left St Paul's, Munro was invited to become chairman of the newly-constituted Merton, Sutton and Wandsworth health authority. After eight years she then chaired the Chichester health authority for another six. Both alongside her headship and in the years afterwards, she chaired various public enquiries and boards ranging from a committee of enquiry into children's footwear (1972) to the Central Transport Committee (1980–85). She was a member of the board of the British Library (1973–9) and of the British Tourist Authority (1973–81). She was made a DBE in 1985.

Among Munro's papers only one personal piece of writing was found—an unpublished memoir of her South African childhood. Everything else was to do with her public life and administrative roles. The status and prestige attached to these were enormously important to her. Developed early in her orphanhood and strengthened later by her husband's death and her subsequent work in the company of competitive and towering personalities, her carapace of self-protection seemed impenetrable. Norman Blamey's portrait, commissioned by St Paul's, was a good likeness: he caught well a slightly forbidding, somewhat isolated, and faintly vulnerable character. It was a portrait Munro hated. Certainly it had no trace of the energetic enthusiast for sailing (she was commodore of West Wittering Sailing Club in 1986–8) and Scottish dancing. She died on 2 September 2008 at Heathfield Nursing Home, West Wittering, Sussex, and was cremated at Chichester crematorium. She was survived by her son, Alan.

JANET GOUGH

Sources *The Times* (25 Feb 1960); (25 May 1964); (24 June 1974); (5 Sept 2008); (19 Sept 2008) • *Catholic Herald* (19 Oct 1969) • *Daily Telegraph* (22 Jan 1972); (31 Aug 1985); (4 Sept 2008) • *Evening Standard* (17 May 1973) • D. M. Greenwood, *Holy Terrors* (1983), 2, 5, 70, 71 • *British Medical Ultrasound Society Bulletin* (Sept 1989) • *The Independent* (5 Sept 2008); (10 Sept 2008) • *Sunday Times* (7 Sept 2008) • *The Scotsman* (9 Sept 2008) • *The Guardian* (22 Sept 2008) • A. Munro, 'The Donalds in South Africa', priv. coll. • Mercers' Company Archives, SPGS 100 Mrs A Munro 3/1405 • St Hilda's College, Oxford, archives • *WW* (2008) • Burke, *Peerage* • private information (2012) [Alan Munro, son; P. Shovelton; M. Ward] • b. cert. • m. cert. • d. cert.

Archives Mercers' Company Archives • St Hilda's College, Oxford, archives • St Paul's Girls' School, archives

Likenesses N. Blamey, oils, St Paul's Girls' School, London • obituary photographs

Wealth at death £1,056,151: probate, 13 Feb 2009, *CGPLA Eng. & Wales*

Murphy, Sir Leslie Frederick (1915–2007), banker and industrialist, was born at 27 Dudley Road, Norwood, London, on 17 November 1915, the son of Frederick Charles Murphy, a labourer at a margarine factory, and his wife, Lillian Annie, *née* Bradshaw. After education at Southall county school (where he was remembered as 'a very clever, modest person, firmly based in his [Anglican] faith'; *The Times*, 10 Oct 2007) he became a clerk to help support the family. But he studied at Birkbeck College,

London, in the evening for a maths degree, taking a first before joining the civil service, marking himself out by coming top in the national entry examination. On 15 June 1940, at St John's, Southall, he married Marjorie Iris Cowell (1910–1991), daughter of Robert Charles Cowell, clerk. They had a son and a daughter.

After work on bomb designs during the Second World War as a scientific officer, Murphy became private secretary to Hugh Gaitskell, the minister of fuel and power in the testing year of 1947, when power supplies were disrupted by a savage winter. His ability and Labour sympathies commended him to Gaitskell, and when he left Whitehall as an assistant secretary in 1952 to join the rapidly expanding oil industry, Gaitskell sought a promise that he would return to Whitehall if requested. He was chairman of Mobil Supply and Mobil Shipping from 1955 to 1959 and then finance director of the Iraq Petroleum Company, a union of the major western oil companies that controlled Iraq's oil reserves before nationalization.

In 1964 Murphy was recruited to become a director of Schroders merchant bank by Gordon Richardson, later governor of the Bank of England, and became deputy chairman in 1972, as the bank expanded internationally. He was successful, particularly in raising finance for British subsidiaries of American companies, although his modest background and direct manner did not always sit well in the establishment milieu of the City, where family and school connections counted heavily and support of the Conservative Party was assumed. He was an obvious candidate in 1975 when Tony Benn as industry minister put together a range of interests from trade unionists to captains of industry on the new National Enterprise Board (NEB) under Lord Ryder of Eaton Hastings, former head of the Reed publishing empire. The board, flagship of Labour's interventionist industrial policy, was an uncomfortable mixture of intensive-care ward for ailing industries and nursery for fledgling technologies.

Murphy, appointed deputy chairman, called the NEB 'a bridge between state ownership and private entrepreneurial activity'. He saw it filling a gap left by private investors' unwillingness to provide risk capital and the reluctance of investment institutions to intervene in management (Sampson, 390). But the new board's agenda was hijacked before it was even formally constituted, by a crisis over British Leyland, the motor company that was the sickest patient in the NEB's intensive-care ward, which also nursed Rolls-Royce Aero Engines, Ferranti electronics, and Herberts machine tools. British Leyland's approach to the government for urgent funds resulted in an inquiry by Ryder, a hopelessly optimistic report, and a proposed injection of £1.4 billion. Under Ryder's autocratic chairmanship the NEB was drawn into disastrous and time-consuming micro-management of the company. Murphy was appalled both by Ryder's discouragement of debate and by the lack of information from the company.

In 1977 Ryder resigned as chairman of the NEB and Murphy was appointed to pick up the pieces. He selected an NEB colleague, Michael Edwardes of Chloride, to run British Leyland and initial results were positive, with new models and a major change in industrial relations as a result of a tough and often confrontational policy. The refusal of Murphy and the new industry minister, Eric Varley, to intervene in disputes contrasted with Ryder's earlier intervention. Edwardes described Murphy as 'competent and decisive', remarking that the situation was 'made palatable by [his] goodwill' (Edwardes, 208–9). Murphy was knighted in 1978.

Murphy monitored new opportunities closely and supported the NEB's investment in Inmos to give the UK a stake in the emerging silicon chip market. He had plans for consortia to take advantage of international business opportunities. His more inclusive handling of the board was praised. But pressures escalated in the run-up to the 1979 election. As British Leyland sought to close factories making refrigerator components, Murphy refused urging from Varley to take them over. He had been closely involved with Rolls-Royce, which was particularly resistant to the NEB's oversight. He criticized their disastrous assumptions about the exchange rate, and tried unsuccessfully to get them to renegotiate contracts. But now its chairman, the City grandee Sir Kenneth Keith, was increasingly vociferous about removing the company from the NEB's supervision. The 1979 Conservative election victory marked the end. With the free-market Sir Keith Joseph as industry minister, Keith prevailed, and Murphy and his board who had, perhaps unwisely, made it a point of principle, resigned. It only hastened the inevitable. The NEB was steadily wound down and merged with the British Technology Group, its businesses moved out and sold.

Murphy resumed his directorship at Schroders and took on others, including Simon Engineering Ltd (1980–85), Folksam International Insurance (UK) Ltd (1980–90), and Petroleum Economics Ltd (1980–94, chairman 1980–87). He was one of the 100 people who signed the letter to *The Guardian* supporting the Limehouse declaration, which led to the founding of the Social Democratic Party in 1981, becoming a party trustee from 1981 to 1990, a choice, he said, which owed much to his experiences of a Labour government. A keen organist and an active Anglican, he was on the Church Army board for thirty years (1964–94) and was chairman of its housing arm (1973–82). An enthusiastic golfer, he led a successful campaign to redevelop the golf course at his home in Barton-on-Sea, Hampshire. After the death of his first wife, on 23 January 1993 he married Dorothy Anne Murray (1928–2002), widow, and daughter of Charles Frederick Walker, editor. He died of heart failure and bronchopneumonia following a fracture of his femur on 29 September 2007 at Christchurch Hospital, Christchurch, Dorset. He was survived by his son and daughter. MARTIN ADENEY

Sources *The Economist* (21 April 1979); (5 May 1979) · A. Sampson, *The changing anatomy of Britain* (1982) · M. Edwardes, *Back from the brink* (1983) · M. Adeney, *The motormakers* (1989) · *The Times* (8 Oct 2007); (10 Oct 2007) · *Daily Telegraph* (8 Oct 2007) · *The Guardian* (10 Oct 2007) · Burke, *Peerage* · *WW* (2007) · b. cert. · m. certs. · d. cert.

Archives SOUND BL NSA, current affairs recording

Likenesses obituary photographs · photograph, repro. in www.dailymail.co.uk/sport/othersports/article-483708/Former-athletics-chief-Norman-dies.html

Wealth at death £1,018,782: probate, 3 April 2008, *CGPLA Eng. & Wales*

Neal, Sir Leonard Francis [Len] (**1913–2008**), trade unionist and industrial relations adviser, was born on 27 August 1913 at 60 Peacock Street, Newington, London, the youngest son of Arthur Henry Neal (*d.* 1939), meat porter, and his wife, (Emma) Mary, *née* Cahill (*d.* 1947). His father was a Smithfield porter who rose to become chief meat salesman at the historic London meat market, where his four eldest sons were also employed. When, at fourteen, Len Neal left his local elementary school, Southwark central, he preferred to break family tradition to train as an apprentice wood carver. Yet this proved a short-term interruption of the family routine and after two years of wood-carving apprenticeship he joined his father and brothers at Smithfield meat market as a trainee meat porter. He also followed the family tradition of attachment to the local Methodist community by attending the church's boys' club before moving on to the Methodist theological college at Richmond upon Thames, where, after a day's work in the meat market, he studied for a life in the ministry.

Yet it wasn't the church that eventually captured Neal's sustained interest but rather his trade union, the Transport and General Workers' Union (TGWU), which represented meat market workers. By his late teens he had decided that it was the trade union movement that offered a more effective ministry for his ideals, and on reaching the age of twenty-one he became the first secretary of the new Smithfield branch of the TGWU. By the outbreak of the Second World War he had progressed to butcher's cutter, and remained active in the TGWU. On 23 December 1939, at Walworth Methodist Church, Southwark, he married Mary Lilian Puttock (*b.* 1916), a ledger clerk at Harrods, and daughter of Thomas Puttock, carpenter, of Orpington, Kent. They had a son, Geoffrey, and daughter, Susan.

During the war Neal was employed by the Ministry of War Transport principally to help allocate workers to various key depots in south London where rationed food distribution, including meat from Smithfield, was organized. In that role he came to the notice of Ernest Bevin, then minister of labour in Churchill's war cabinet and former general secretary of the TGWU. When the war ended Neal returned to his union as a full-time official—clearly benefiting from Bevin's influence—and with help from his union he won a scholarship for a three-year course in industrial relations at the London School of Economics from where, aged thirty-nine, he went on to secure an award at Trinity College, Cambridge. He graduated with a good degree in economics and felt obliged to return to the TGWU to continue his career as a full-time official. But that was not easy. The post-war mood created an atmosphere in which some of his union colleagues regarded the Cambridge graduate with some scepticism—as more academic than trade union campaigner. After two years back with the union he applied, in 1955, for the post of assistant general secretary of the TGWU. He was one of eight candidates but came near the bottom of the list. The winner was Frank Cousins, who went on to become general secretary and one of the most dominant figures in post-war British trade unionism. Neal felt this was time for him to move on.

In 1956 he resigned from the TGWU to become an instructor in management and supervision at the Esso oil company's training centre in Abingdon, Berkshire. In 1961 he was appointed employee relations manager at the Esso refinery at Fawley, Hampshire, where he introduced major reforms in the company's industrial relations policy—opening shots in what developed into a crusade to improve Britain's industrial climate. At Fawley, alongside a groundbreaking wages and productivity agreement, he launched a new culture of joint consultation over working practices, bringing top management into discussion with the shop floor. He also ensured that management and workers shared common dining and canteen facilities, with everyone starting work at the same time—revolutionary concepts at the time. Some of Esso's top brass were shocked, even alarmed, by Neal's crusade, yet had the courage to let him continue with what became known nationally as the Fawley plan.

The success of Esso's industrial relations strategy at Fawley led to Neal's advice being sought by industries in both public and private sectors and in 1967 he landed the job of industrial relations director at British Rail. This was a huge challenge since the nationalized railways and their three rail unions had a record of constant conflict. Neal began where he left off at Esso by transforming pay negotiations across the system and then insisting that the railway chiefs and trade union leaders sit at a round table for their discussions rather than face each other across a long table, in trench-warfare style. It was a simple but brilliant psychological move—and succeeded, despite the scepticism of British Rail's top management. As at Esso Neal continued to press for changes in managerial, and union, attitudes. However, after four years, and some considerable achievements across the rail network, Neal's luck began to fade, chiefly because of a collapse in the Wilson government's pay policy.

A new Conservative government in 1970 under Edward Heath introduced a programme of legislative reform for industrial relations and Neal was appointed chairman of a revamped commission on industrial relations, originally created by the Wilson government. Also in 1970 he was appointed part-time professor of industrial relations at Manchester University. Two years earlier, along with Andrew Robertson, he had published *The Manager's Guide to Industrial Relations*. He was appointed CBE in 1971 and knighted in 1974. In 1974 the new Labour government abolished the Commission for Industrial Relations, and Neal joined the boards of several large private companies including Pilkingtons, the glass group. He later became a strong supporter of Margaret Thatcher and agreed with her legislation to curb trade union power and influence. He effectively came full circle from his early days as a trade union idealist. Experience had convinced him that the unions could not be reformed without strong legislation. Nevertheless even into his late seventies he continued his modified crusade to reform industrial relations and joined the Conservative party think-tank, the Centre for Policy Studies. He died at Ashby House care home, Eaglestone, Milton Keynes, of heart failure on 4 May 2008. He was survived by his wife and children.

In the 1960s Neal acquired a national reputation for pioneering a more imaginative and creative relationship between management and workers. When this aspiration foundered it was not due to a flawed concept, but arguably because he was ahead of his time. Despite subsequent disillusionment with the trade unions he never lost his early missionary zeal nor a conviction that relations between shop floor and management required fundamental reform, above all of attitudes on both sides. He was in many respects a pivotal figure in the post-war attempt to find a more rational and equitable formula to ease, if not cure, the blight of industrial conflict that had become an endemic problem in post-war Britain.

GEOFFREY GOODMAN

Sources H. Pollins, *Britain's railways: an industrial history* (1971) · P. S. Bagwell, *The railwaymen: the history of the National Union of Railwaymen*, 2 (1982) · *Daily Telegraph* (9 June 2008) · *The Times* (10 June 2008) · *The Guardian* (24 June 2008) · *WW* (2008) · Burke, *Peerage* · personal knowledge (2012) · private information (2012) · b. cert. · m. cert. · d. cert.
Likenesses obituary photographs
Wealth at death £456,436: administration, 10 Oct 2008, *CGPLA Eng. & Wales*

Needham, Rodney (1923–2006), anthropologist, was born Rodney Needham Green on 15 May 1923 at The Limes, Belle Grove Road, Welling, Bexley, Kent, the only son and eldest of three children of Horace Edward Green, a clerk in the War Office (later an official in the Ministry of Supply), and his wife, Mary Elizabeth, *née* Needham. After a year of schooling at Haileybury College he enlisted in the Scots Guards in 1941. In 1942 he was posted to India, where he transferred to the 1st Gurkha rifles. He was commissioned second lieutenant that year, and promoted temporary captain in 1943. In 1944, just before the battle of Kohima, he was severely wounded in the leg while attempting to light a flame thrower; his subahdar, Narang Ghal, was awarded an MC for rescuing him under heavy enemy fire. Demobilized in 1947, he changed his name to Rodney Needham (a change confirmed by deed poll in February 1951), apparently because of disappointment that his father had not once written to him while or after he recovered from his battle injuries in Burma. In 1947 he enrolled at the School of Oriental and African Studies in London to learn Chinese, and on 10 April 1948 he married (Maud) Claudia Walch, *née* Brysz (1919/20–1989), a translator for the BBC. She was the former wife of Frederic Alfred Walch and daughter of Stanislaw Brysz, a university professor. They had two sons, Tristan and Guy.

After completing his studies at SOAS in 1949 Needham went to Merton College, Oxford, for graduate training in social anthropology. In 1951–2 he carried out fieldwork among the nomadic Penan of Sarawak, Borneo, for which he received a doctorate. In 1954–5 he conducted fieldwork on the Indonesian island of Sumba. In 1956 he was appointed lecturer in social anthropology at Oxford and later became a fellow of Merton College. In 1976 he was elected professor of social anthropology and made a fellow of All Souls College, Oxford. He held numerous visiting fellowships and professorships in universities in the USA, Australia, and Japan.

Needham's reputation rested primarily on his early championing of Lévi-Strauss's version of structuralism, which, together with Edmund Leach and Mary Douglas, he brought across the channel, Anglicizing it in the process. He used to say he had found a copy of Lévi-Strauss's *Les structures élémentaires de la parenté* (1949) in an Oxford bookshop the week before going on fieldwork in Borneo. Primed by his knowledge of Dutch structural anthropology, he immediately recognized its significance and its concern with conceptual structure over social organization. Structuralism gave Needham a radically new approach to the study of kinship systems, the template for social structure in small-scale societies. An industrious scholar, he applied this new style in a series of brilliant papers in which he stressed the importance of alliance, through marriage, over that of descent. He established his reputation in 1962 with the publication of *Structure and Sentiment*, a highly polemical short work in which he argued convincingly for the power of structuralist approaches in the study of kinship systems over psychological ones, as advocated by the American anthropologists George Homans and David Schneider.

However, Needham's promotion of a strict Lévi-Straussian structuralism ended abruptly in 1969 when the French anthropologist somewhat unfairly attacked Needham's assiduous editing of the translation into English of his *Structures élémentaires*. Needham, ever the painstaking scholar, wanted to restrict Lévi-Strauss's ideas to those societies where they could be fruitfully applied. Lévi-Strauss would have none of this: he wanted his ideas to be generally applicable, not ethnographically restricted. This attack, alongside Needham's realization in the course of the translation that the power of Lévi-Strauss's approach owed as much to the rhetoric of his prose as to the incisiveness of his thought, led him to pursue and develop his own version of structuralism. From then on he only made reference to Lévi-Strauss in a critical vein, cutting through his oratorical excesses and moulding structuralism into a more exact practice. At one point he even suggested that Lévi-Strauss, who in wartime New York had participated in André Breton's circle, should be regarded not as the famed exponent of structuralism but as 'the greatest Surrealist of them all' ('The birth of the meaningful', *TLS*, 13 April 1984).

From the early 1970s onwards Needham published a stream of important books and articles on systems of classification, cognitive universals, indigenous psychologies, and kinship theory, in particular *Percussion and Transition* (1967), where he pointed out the global use of percussive sound in rites of passage, *Polythetic Classification* (1975), in which he contended that most terms used for cross-cultural comparison will not have simple definitions but are more akin to Wittgenstein's idea of family-resemblant concepts, *Skulls and Causality* (1976), where he argued against the unnecessary imposition of intermediary terms when trying to understand the causal reasoning of other peoples. He also edited the highly influential *Rethinking Kinship and Marriage* (1971) and *Right and Left: Essays on Dual Symbolic Classification* (1973). He was perhaps proudest of *Belief, Language and Experience* (1972), in which he performed a cross-cultural, cross-disciplinary investigation to argue that belief is not a human universal.

In the 1960s structuralism was viewed by its supporters in almost messianic terms as offering a new vision of the world. Thanks to the work of Lévi-Strauss, his champions, and his popularizers, the anthropological version of this approach gained a renown far beyond its usual disciplinary boundaries. Thanks to Needham, Oxford became a world centre for structuralist anthropology and attracted students from all over the globe. He was an exacting but kindly tutor who drilled his students both to take imaginative risks and to be ever sceptical. He regarded it as his academic duty to be exceptionally generous with his time for his students, and to be a forever loyal supporter of most of them. Many of those he had supervised regarded him as the greatest single academic influence in their lives, and an almost inimitable exemplar of dedicated, inspiring scholarship.

Needham, ever the polemicist, frequently enjoyed taking a contrary path to most of his colleagues. Thus he took particular pains to revive interest in anthropologist predecessors whose work, he felt, had been undervalued or overlooked. He and, at his behest, some of his protégés translated and edited books by, among others, Arnold van Gennep, A. M. Hocart, and Robert Hertz. But these re-editions sold badly. His students quietly confessed that they bought copies only to read his extended introductions. In his later years much of his most powerful work was published as series of essays, especially *Against the Tranquility of Axioms* (1983), *Exemplars* (1985), and *Counterpoints* (1987). Their individual chapters were models of elegant scepticism and have continued to serve as powerful cautionary tales for fledgeling anthropologists. By adopting an increasingly sceptical style in later life Needham's work echoed that of two of his heroes, Ludwig Wittgenstein and Lucien Lévy-Bruhl, both of whom spent the second half of their intellectual lives systematically questioning the positions they had advanced in the first half.

Needham's experience of the Second World War and his time with the Gurkhas were central to his life. He learnt Gurkhali and even in old age was able spontaneously to sing wartime songs in the language. It was important to him that, in his last years, he achieved reconciliation with Japanese veterans of a battle he had participated in. Several of them paid him visits in Oxford, some repeatedly. But, above all, Needham was a self-made Oxford man. He revelled both in its great traditions and in its petty ceremonies. As he was ready to admit, he created and lived a dream of Oxford. Many of his students, especially from abroad, were happy to join him in this. Though inclined towards atheism, he enjoyed attending the weekly ritual of the university sermon. At Sunday lunchtimes he would sit in the 'don's bar' of the King's Arms, ready to hold court to whoever might turn up. This, he felt, was the way an Oxford don should comport himself. He loved classical music and painting. He was enchanted by form and was more interested in clarifying the conceptual structures underlying the nitty-gritty of daily life than examining their political manipulation. He would often lament that when attending a seminar in theoretical physics or mathematics he knew anthropology could not withstand comparison with such logically grounded subjects.

Uninterested in the analysis of power, Needham was ready to acknowledge that he was not very skilled at its deployment. In 1972 he was not chosen to succeed his mentor Sir Edward Evans-Pritchard in the Oxford chair, though many saw him as the leading candidate. He was finally awarded the post four years later. But some of his departmental colleagues soon came to regard him as over-eager to revitalize their centre. When, towards the end of the first year of his incumbency, senior members of the university overruled an administrative decision of his, he packed his books and moved into college rooms. He never returned to the department, though he remained in post until his retirement in 1990.

Needham was enamoured of many aspects of the United States, especially its landscape. In middle age he would often speak of his desire to abandon academia and run a ranch in Montana. After his retirement he took pleasure in repeated visits to New Mexico and Arizona. He cherished friendship and assiduously kept up a voluminous correspondence. Maintaining an almost military discipline to the end, he bore his long, final illness, the result of colonic cancer, with composure and good humour. In his last week he refused to enter a hospice as he did not wish to lose contact with his friends. He died from pulmonary fibrosis at his home, a Merton College flat at 56 Holywell Street, Oxford, on 4 December 2006. He was survived by his two sons. JEREMY MACCLANCY

Sources *Daily Telegraph* (13 Dec 2006) · *The Independent* (13 Dec 2006) · *The Guardian* (16 Jan 2007) · *The Times* (19 Feb 2007) · personal knowledge (2010) · private information (2010) · b. cert. · m. cert. · d. cert.

Likenesses obituary photographs

Wealth at death under £15,000: probate, 2 May 2007, *CGPLA Eng. & Wales*

Nerina, Nadia [*real name* Nadine Judd] (**1927–2008**), ballerina, was born on 21 October 1927 in Cape Town, South Africa, the daughter of Frank Lawrence Judd, a car company executive, and his wife, Nerina, whose name (from nerine, a South African flower) became part of Nadine's Russianized stage name. She had a younger brother, Lee. The family lived in Bloemfontein, where she began dance classes at the age of eight. After moving to Durban in 1939 she trained with two exceptional teachers, Eileen Keegan, who had danced with Anna Pavlova's company, and Dorothea McNair. A government appointment for her father

Nadia Nerina (1927–2008), by unknown photographer

meant living in Johannesburg, but she was allowed to stay in Durban, finding solace in long days of training when her mother suddenly died. In October 1945, although the Second World War was barely over, her father managed to secure a boat passage for her to England, where she joined other outstanding Commonwealth dancers reinforcing British ballet. In London, she went straight to the Mercury Theatre, Notting Hill, home of the school and company led by Marie Rambert, with whom her teacher McNair had worked. Soon after, however, at her father's urging, she switched to the school attached to Ninette de Valois's Sadler's Wells Ballet.

As Nadia Nerina, she made her British stage début at the company's historic opening night on 20 February 1946 in its new home, the Royal Opera House. She was a supernumerary nursemaid in the premiere of a definitive production of *The Sleeping Beauty*. The company she subsequently joined, however, was de Valois's new touring ensemble, the Sadler's Wells Theatre Company. Her first newspaper review was for her performance in Mikhail Fokine's *Les Sylphides* in Bath; her first created role was the Circus Dancer in Andrée Howard's *Mardi Gras* on 26 November 1946. Although she had been anxious beforehand, working alone after rehearsals and crying on the avuncular shoulder of the theatre's fireman, Howard's ballet established her with the public. In December 1947 she was transferred to the senior company and three days later danced the lead in *Les Sylphides*, partnered by Alexis Rassine. At the other extreme, she had to dance in the *corps de ballet*, a new experience. At first, the other dancers, not realizing how petrified she was and feeling she needed taking down a peg, would answer 'find out' whenever during a performance she would whisper 'which way do I turn?'

Nerina will be especially remembered for creating the role of Lise, the enchanting and delinquent daughter in Frederick Ashton's masterpiece *La Fille mal gardée* (1960). However, the first role he made for her was that of the Spring Fairy in his *Cinderella* of 1948. He started by asking her what her role's music sounded like. When she answered 'the bursting of buds', he translated that phrase into a beautiful pattern of small jumps and hand movements. Although very different from Ashton's muse, the lyrical Margot Fonteyn, Nerina was chosen by him for other new roles—in *Homage to the Queen*, *Variations on a Theme of Purcell*, and *Birthday Offering*—and for the leads in his *Cinderella*, *Sylvia*, and *Ondine*. She also excelled in Fokine's ballets: among them, *The Firebird*, *Carnaval*, and *Petrushka*. Leonid Massine chose her to dance the title role in his *Mam'zelle Angot* and the Can-Can Dancer in his *Boutique Fantasque*. In 1954 de Valois cast her as Swanilda, a heroine not unlike Ashton's Lise, in her new production of *Coppélia*, dancing with David Blair, who would become a frequent partner. If many of these were demi-caractère roles, Nerina could also rise to the challenge of the grand classics, as she showed with her luminous geometric perfection as *The Sleeping Beauty*'s Aurora. Nerina was notable for reaching a larger public beyond the opera house, but found time to marry Charles Gordon (*b.* 1926/7), an export company director (and son of Shollom Gordon, also a businessman), on 11 October 1955 in London.

During the 1950s Nerina made regular television appearances, when ballet broadcasts were still an infant art. Rassine was often her partner in these, but in 1964 she danced with Rudolf Nureyev in his televised production of the *Laurencia pas de six*. From 1952 to 1955, again with Rassine, she toured parts of Africa in concert performances. From 1956 to 1960 they performed similar programmes around Britain and appeared at London's Palace Theatre in a variety bill alongside Frankie Vaughan and Petula Clark. As a guest artist with many companies abroad, she became in 1960 only the second dancer from a British company to be invited to Russia. She performed *Swan Lake* with Moscow's Bolshoi, partnered by the great Nikolai Fadeyechev (with whom she had danced *Giselle* on British television), and *Giselle* in Leningrad, opposite the Kirov Ballet's even more illustrious Konstantin Sergeyev. The Russians were fascinated by the stylistic differences and greeted her as an old friend when she returned the following year with the Royal Ballet. On that tour she performed *La Fille mal gardée*. 'One thing was fully realized', the Russian critic Natalia Roslavleva commented, 'he [Ashton] could not have done it without the brilliance of Nerina's special talent' (Crisp).

La Fille mal gardée had been an immediate success at its London premiere on 28 January 1960. The rehearsals were gloriously happy, Ashton cajoling Nerina and David Blair to surpass themselves, and exploiting Nerina's lightness and bubbling personality. The ballet was televised in 1962, with the same cast. In 1965 she performed the lead in

Home, created for her and Western Theatre Ballet by Peter Darrell. The playwright John Mortimer's darkly realist scenario about life in a psychiatric home was against type, but she fitted in well. Her last created role was Clorinda in a danced production of Monteverdi's *Il Combattimento di Tancredi e Clorinda* for the 1967 Aldeburgh Festival.

Nerina was the most virtuosic ballerina of her British generation, with a daring speed, impeccable line, and crisp footwork. 'Nerina's elevation', Rassine wrote, 'could be the envy of many a *premier danseur*' (Crisp). This, along with a natural flow of movement, gave her dancing a Russian quality. She only once succumbed to the temptation to show off. Seeing Nureyev insert no fewer than sixteen *entrechat-six* jumps into *Giselle*, she performed twice as many one night when she knew he was in the audience, as a substitute for the famous thirty-two *fouettés* of *Swan Lake*. Yet her dancing was not mere bravura display. In South Africa she had also studied drama, and always made a wholehearted identification with character and style central to her performance.

In 1969 Nerina retired and moved to the south of France; but her wish to start a family was not fulfilled. She organized charity galas, sat on ballet juries, and in 1972 donated *Zemran*, a sculpture by William Pye that stands outside London's Queen Elizabeth Hall. She died in Beaulieu-sur-Mer, France, on 6 October 2008 and was survived by her husband. NADINE MEISNER

Sources C. Crisp, ed., *Ballerina: portraits and impressions of Nadia Nerina* (1974) · *Daily Telegraph* (8 Oct 2008) · *The Guardian* (8 Oct 2008) · *The Times* (10 Oct 2008); (25 Oct 2008) · *New York Times* (11 Oct 2008) · *The Independent* (14 Oct 2008) · *WW* (2008) · m. cert.

Archives FILM BFINA, performance footage | SOUND BL NSA, documentary recording

Likenesses photographs, 1951–63, PA Photos, London · photographs, 1952–63, Getty Images, London · photographs, 1956–69, Rex Features, London · C. Beaton, bromide print, 1966, NPG · obituary photographs · photograph, Getty Images, London [*see illus.*] · photographs, repro. in Crisp, *Ballerina* · photographs, Lebrecht Music and Arts Photo Library, London

Nevill, James Francis [Jim] (**1927–2007**), police officer, was born on 20 February 1927 at Queen Charlotte's Hospital, Hammersmith, London, the son of John Archibald Nevill (1893–1964), a ladies' tailor's manager, of 2 Radipole Road, Fulham, and his wife, Charlotte Helen, *née* Lynn (1889–1969). He was originally named Francis James (and his father later also reversed his own forenames). After leaving school he worked in a munitions factory before enlisting in the Royal Fusiliers in 1945 and serving in the Middle East driving armoured cars.

Nevill joined the Metropolitan Police in 1948, based at Rochester Row in Victoria. He soon moved to detective work, initially as an aide to CID, the term for a uniformed officer on secondment to test potential as a detective. In 1954 he was appointed a detective constable working in the criminal records department at Scotland Yard. He remained a CID officer for the rest of his career. On 17 March 1955, at St Andrew's Church, Deal, he married Marion Edith Newton (*b.* 1932), also a police officer, whom he had first met at Rochester Row. She was the daughter of Joseph Newton, miner. They had a son and a daughter.

Nevill, commended three times for outstanding work, became a sergeant in 1959 and a member of the flying squad, regarded as the élite CID unit in London, in 1963. He was one of the team that formed the special train robbery squad investigating the great train robbery, in which a team of London robbers had stopped the night mail train near Lechlade in Buckinghamshire and stolen £2.5 million. Promoted detective inspector in 1965, he moved to West End central and rose through the ranks, recognized as a tenacious, unflappable, and capable detective.

By the early 1970s Nevill was detective chief superintendent for A division, based at Cannon Row. His case book now included banknote forgeries, the first karate murder in Britain, a murder at the RAC Club, and the organization of security for Princess Anne's wedding in 1973. But the Provisional IRA's growing mainland campaigns plucked him from routine CID work. On 17 June 1974 the IRA bombed the annexe to Westminster Hall in the houses of parliament. Nevill, whose office was a few hundred yards away, arrived at the scene to be awarded a battlefield promotion to second in command of Scotland Yard's growing bomb squad. As the IRA intensified their attacks on London, many of them launched by a highly successful unit responsible for forty incidents, Nevill became a familiar figure at bomb scenes.

In the autumn of 1975 Scotland Yard, desperate to catch the unit, set a trap using 700 detectives and uniformed officers deployed in a massive undercover operation across central London to watch potential targets. The trap was sprung on 6 December as the IRA unit fired shots at a Mayfair restaurant. Chased by police, the unit drove into a cul-de-sac, abandoned their car, and took shelter in the flat of an elderly couple, John and Sheila Matthews, in Balcombe Street, near Marylebone Station. After police cut phone lines to the flat, Nevill, who was the senior officer on the scene, began negotiations with the IRA men by loudhailer from the street. When they accepted a field telephone he sat for twelve hours a night by a handset at his temporary headquarters nearby waiting to talk to them. In time he managed to build a rapport. When the frustrated terrorists threw their telephone out of the window Nevill went back to the street with his loudhailer and resumed contact. The gang wanted £20,000 and safe passage to Dublin. Nevill remained firm that the only option was surrender. The gang finally released their hostages after police leaked news to the media that the SAS was on standby to attack. The bloodless conclusion after more than five and a half days owed much to Nevill's calm patience and dedication. With the surrender of the gang Nevill, despite the long hours he had already given, took part in another thirty-three hours of questioning.

In the aftermath of Balcombe Street, Nevill was promoted in 1976 to commander, as the first head of the newly created 100-strong anti-terrorist branch. London was now a battlefield for Middle East politics and over the next three years Nevill headed investigations into the murder of two former Middle Eastern premiers, the machine-gunning of an El Al bus, and the murder of an official of the Palestine Liberation Organization. His diplomatic skills honed in these investigations were tested again in his last major police inquiry, when he was asked to assess the disastrous, stalled hunt for the Yorkshire Ripper. His findings were only revealed publicly in 2006 and showed that he had clearly identified the central flaws of the investigation: he criticized the failure to make greater use of forensic science, questioned the over-reliance on an alleged tape-recording by the Ripper to eliminate suspects, and attacked poor management. His key recommendations were ignored.

In 1980 Nevill underwent heart surgery and left the police at the age of fifty-three, young for a man of his rank. Awarded the queen's police medal in 1978, he worked as security adviser for Barclays and Securicor before finally retiring in 1995. A qualified police marksman for much of his career, he developed a passion for shooting and was at one time president of Bisley Gun Club. He lived latterly in St James's Avenue, Hampton Hill, London. He died of heart disease and vascular dementia on 12 December 2007 at Emberbrook Care Centre, Thames Ditton, Surrey. He was survived by his wife, Marion, and their two children.

STEWART TENDLER

Sources *The Times* (12 Oct 1963); (6 Jan 1978); (18 Feb 2008) · B. Huntley, *Bomb squad: my war against the terrorists* (1977) · R. Mark, *In the office of constable* (1978) · N. Darbyshire and B. Hilliard, *The flying squad* (1993) · M. Fido and K. Skinner, *The official encyclopedia of Scotland Yard* (1999) · B. Reynolds, N. Reynolds, and A. Parker, *The great train robbery files* (2000) · *Daily Telegraph* (25 Jan 2008) · Metropolitan Police archives · b. cert. · m. cert. · d. cert.
Archives FILM BFINA, documentary footage
Likenesses obituary photographs
Wealth at death £517,751: probate, 6 Oct 2008, *CGPLA Eng. & Wales*

Newby, (George) Eric (1919–2006), travel writer and adventurer, was born at 3 Castelnau Mansions, Barnes, Surrey, on 6 December 1919, the son of George Arthur Newby, a partner in a firm of wholesale dressmakers, and his wife (Minnie) Hilda, *née* Pomeroy, a former dress model at Harrods. A strain of adventure ran in the family: his father had run away to sea as a boy before settling into his career as a couturier, and Newby himself was influenced at an early age by hearing a lecture at school about Scott's expedition to the south pole and reading about exotic foreign places. He was educated at St Paul's School in London, and left at sixteen—having already established himself as something of a school joker—to join an advertising agency; but after two years (inadvertently following his father's footsteps) he signed on to join a four-masted Finnish barque that was setting out on a 30,000 mile round trip carrying grain between Ireland and Australia. He was later to write an account of this in *The Last Grain Race* (1956), in which he described the hazards of climbing masts 'as high as Nelson's column'.

With his taste for adventure already awakened, it was not surprising that at the outbreak of the Second World War in 1939 Newby promptly enlisted in the London Scottish regiment, being later sent to the Royal Military College, Sandhurst, and after a spell in the Middle East being transferred to the Special Boat Section (later to become the Special Boat Service). It was with them that he was sent in 1942 on a commando-type raid against a military airfield in Sicily that was proving a serious menace to allied convoys attempting to supply and reinforce Malta. The operation was ill-prepared, and Newby was landed at night with a party of six men on an unreconnoitred coastline to attack a heavily defended position; almost inevitably the intruders were discovered and forced to retreat to the beach where they had landed. They failed to make the rendezvous with their submarine, were decanted into the water from their fragile canoes, and were eventually picked up by some Italian fishermen who handed them over to the authorities.

(George) Eric Newby (1919–2006), by Fergus Greer, 2003

Newby then began a series of escapades and escapes. He was initially in a prisoner-of-war camp in Italy (having survived threats of being shot as a saboteur), but when the Italians surrendered in 1943 he was smuggled out of the camp hospital—where he was suffering from a broken ankle—to a more sympathetic hospital run by Italian nuns. It was there that he met Wanda Skof, a Slovene girl, who taught him some Italian, brought him treats in hospital, and encouraged him to escape before the Germans arrived. When writing about these experiences many years later in *Love and War in the Apennines* (1972) he compared her to the gaoler's daughter who befriends Toad in *The Wind in the Willows* and confessed, 'I had begun by thinking her a very good-looking girl … then I had begun to admire her courage and determination … now I was in love with her' (p. 65). She arranged for him to be sheltered by Italian peasants in the Apennines, but he was eventually betrayed and sent to a prisoner-of-war camp in Germany. At the end of the war he was awarded a belated Military Cross for his part in the Sicily raid and—more importantly—managed to return to Italy and propose to Wanda. They were married in Florence in 1946 and had two children, Sonia and Jonathan.

Returning to civilian life Newby entered his father's profession and worked in the family business and later with the couture house Worth Pasquin. He appreciated the humorous side of the fashion industry and later recorded this in his book *Something Wholesale* (1962). But his heart was not in it, and he dreamed of returning to his wartime days of adventures abroad. He brought these dreams into reality in 1956 when he sent a telegram to his friend the diplomat Hugh Carless, enquiring 'Can you travel Nuristan June?' The prompt reply—'Of course, Hugh'—resulted in the hilarious and seminal travel book, *A Short Walk in the Hindu Kush* (1958), in which he recounted his amateurish exploits, first in a brief attempt to come to terms with mountaineering in Wales and later in attempting serious climbing in northern Afghanistan. Carless is presented as a solemn and responsible foil to Newby's own fecklessness. The book ends with the report of a memorable encounter with the veteran explorer Wilfred Thesiger who, on seeing the intrepid couple inflating mattresses before sleeping on the bare rocks, allegedly declared, 'God, you must be a couple of pansies' (Newby, *A Short Walk*, 2008 edn, 248). The book, for which Evelyn Waugh had been persuaded to write an introduction, was an instant success, and following this Newby—after a few years as a fashion buyer for the John Lewis group—changed the course of his life to one of literature and travel.

In 1964 David Astor was expanding the scope of *The Observer* and Newby was appointed as travel editor. During the decade in which he held this appointment he brought imagination and a high standard of writing in the travel pages, but he had little interest or aptitude for the administrative side of the job, for which he leaned heavily on his colleagues. He deplored the degeneration of independent travel and exploration into tourism and tried to resist this in the columns of *The Observer*. It was said that without the dedication of his staff to the day-to-day routine of producing this section of the paper the travel pages might sometimes have failed to appear altogether. This was partly because much of Newby's energy and concentration during these years was on planning and carrying out further adventurous travels himself. Many of his trips were made in the company of Wanda, and they resulted in such books as *Slowly Down the Ganges* (1966). It was during these years that he wrote of his wartime experiences and also a number of less celebrated titles. None of his later books received, or warranted, quite the acclaim of his Hindu Kush and Apennine books.

Newby and his wife had always maintained their affection for Italy, and in 1967 they acquired a derelict farmhouse near Lerici in Liguria, which over the years they restored to a degree of comfort; he wrote about the experience in *A Small Place in Italy* (1994). They spent part of the year there and part at their home in Dorset; they subsequently moved to Surrey. He continued writing travel books until well into his eighties, but the quality of his later work (he wrote some twenty-five books in all) inevitably reflected his diminishing energy. He was appointed CBE in 1994 and had long been a fellow of the Royal Society of Literature and of the Royal Geographical Society. In his last years Wanda supported him as actively and loyally as she had done during their first encounters in wartime Italy. He died at Birtley House care home, Birtley Road, Bramley, near Guildford, Surrey, on 20 October 2006 following a stroke, and was survived by his wife and their two children.

Eric Newby did for travel writing after the Second World War a service similar to that which Peter Fleming had performed for the genre between the wars. He brought a genuinely daring spirit of adventure to his travels, but he wrote about them in a light-hearted and self-deprecating way—often including passages of riotous joking. His sense of fun infected his readers. In this way he inspired younger travellers to seek out remote corners of the world on their long vacations and gap years, in the same way as his near-contemporary—and fellow war hero—Patrick Leigh Fermor inspired them to explore the remoter corners of Europe. His distinctive mixture of courage in the face of danger, irreverence in the face of authority, and good humour in the face of discomfort and adversity, appealed to a whole generation as being quintessentially British.

JOHN URE

Sources E. Newby, *A short walk in the Hindu Kush* (1958) · E. Newby, *Love and war in the Apennines* (1972) · E. Newby, *A small place in Italy* (1994) · *The Times* (23 Oct 2006) · *Daily Telegraph* (23 Oct 2006) · *The Guardian* (23 Oct 2006) · *The Independent* (23 Oct 2006) · H. Carless, 'Eric Newby, the Hindu Kush and the Ganges', *Asian Affairs*, 38/3 (Nov 2007), 357–70 · *WW* (2006) · personal knowledge (2010) · private information (2010) · b. cert. · d. cert.

Archives Guardian News and Media Archive, corresp. with *The Observer* | FILM BFINA, 'Quickly up the Thames', *Omnibus*, N. Williams (director), BBC, 19 July 1985 · BFINA, *The South Bank show*, T. Knox (director), LWT, 22 May 1994 | SOUND BL NSA, documentary recording

Likenesses S. Doherty, photographs, 1986, Getty Images, London, Time and Life Pictures · U. Anderson, photographs, 1992, Getty Images, London · F. Greer, Lambda print, 2003, NPG [*see illus.*] · E. McCabe, photographs, Camera Press, London · V. Watts, photographs, Rex Features, London · obituary photographs · photographs, repro. in Newby, *Love and war* · photographs, repro. in Newby, *A short walk* · photographs, repro. in Newby, *A small place* · photographs, repro. in Carless, 'Eric Newby'

Wealth at death £355,218: probate, 16 July 2007, *CGPLA Eng. & Wales*

Nicholson, David (1939–2006), jockey and racehorse trainer, was born on 19 March 1939 at Filey Lodge, Worple Road, Epsom, Surrey, one of three children of Herbert Charles Denton (Frenchie) Nicholson, jockey and racehorse trainer, of 42 Woodcote Hurst, Epsom, and his wife, Diana, *née* Holman. As with many in racing he was bred for the turf. His maternal great-great-grandfather saddled three Grand National winners; his maternal grandfather was a trainer at Cheltenham; and his father was a champion National Hunt trainer and joint champion rider. Ironically Nicholson himself was allergic to horses and suffered from asthma throughout his life, an affliction that allowed him to avoid national service.

Nicholson attended Oakley Hall preparatory school at Cirencester and then Haileybury College, but had no academic pretensions and was determined to enter racing. In 1951, to allow him to race in public while still at school, he was apprenticed to his father, who later gained a reputation for his tutelage of flat-race jockeys. In the yard his haughty attitude gained him the sobriquet the Duke, which followed him through life. After leaving Haileybury he rode his first winner in April 1955 when he piloted home Fairval, one of his father's charges, in a selling hurdle at Chepstow. By the time he retired from the saddle he had accumulated 583 winners, though he never finished higher than third in the National Hunt riders' championship. His most notable victory was on Millhouse in the 1967 Whitbread gold cup. In 1974 he retired from racing after a winning ride at Hereford; by his own admission he had lost his nerve. He combined the last six years of his riding career with training at Cotswold House, Condicote, Gloucestershire, which he had purchased six months before his marriage, on 31 May 1962 at St Mary's Church, Temple Guiting, Gloucestershire, to Dinah Caroline Pugh, the 22-year-old daughter of John Geoffrey Pugh, managing director of a major lawnmower manufacturing company. They had two sons, Philip and John, neither of whom followed their father into racing.

Nicholson's early training career, with Dinah as his head 'lad', was patchy, partly owing to the inadequate facilities at Condicote and also because Nicholson at that time was prejudiced against horses that had come to jumping from the flat. Later he recognized that, if they were schooled well, the natural speed of such horses gave them an advantage. He was generally resistant to change but eventually began to work his horses harder, though he continued to place conformation before pedigree in choosing animals for his owners. Between 1980 and 1984 he sent out 228 winners and every box in the yard was occupied. Unfortunately Nicholson had more horse sense than business acumen and the enterprise faced insolvency with debts of nearly £250,000; it was rescued only by a group of friends and owners who transformed the business into a company, David Nicholson Racing. Its early operations were hit badly by a virus running through the stables, but with Peter Scudamore and then Richard Dunwoody as stable jockey, it began to flourish. It was becoming profitable by 1992 when Nicholson was invited by Charles Smith, a retired engineering contractor and a part-owner of Charter Party, the Nicholson-trained 1988 Cheltenham gold cup winner, to move to the purpose-built, eighty-box Jackdaws Castle in Temple Guiting, a project on which Nicholson had advised. He went as a salaried trainer and, by leaving the business side to Smith and focusing solely on the horses, he immediately sent out over a hundred winners, at the time only the fifth jumps trainer to achieve that in a season since the Second World War. In the next season, 1992–3, he became the champion National Hunt trainer, a feat that he repeated the following season, during which he secured a treble on one afternoon at the Cheltenham festival. After a reported disagreement with Smith he retired from training in 1999, one short of 1500 winners, and worked for the Thoroughbred Breeders Association, promoting British bloodstock.

Nicholson had a reputation for being difficult and outspoken. Yet he engendered loyalty from his stable staff. He excelled as a teacher of riding skills, even coaching Princess Anne to become a winning National Hunt rider. He was proud that almost a hundred riders gained their first win under his guidance: out of his stables came some outstanding riders including Dunwoody, Richard Johnson, Robert Thornton, and Adrian Maguire. He generally recruited inexperienced, young stable staff who could be taught his ways, including good manners and the wearing of collar and tie in the saddling enclosure. Recognizable at any race meeting with his commanding presence, trilby hat, sheepskin coat, red socks, and often a large brandy, he was a convivial man, given to celebrate with a 'serious glass', and at times he drank too heavily. His humour was of the boisterous schoolboy variety. He raised substantial sums for charity by devising the idea of a stable open day, begun at Condicote in 1975. His competitive streak even entered the many charity cricket and soccer matches in which he participated. As captain of the National Hunt jockeys' cricket team for twenty-seven years he was prone to sharp practice and challenging umpires' decisions; as a footballer he was a hard, some would say dirty, player.

Perhaps surprisingly for such an opinionated individual, Nicholson was deeply superstitious. Following his first Cheltenham festival victory with Solar Cloud in the 1986 triumph hurdle—after eighteen years of trying—he thereafter always wore red socks when going racing, as he had on the day of the breakthrough. He sought to win races not money, and became a non-betting trainer, as by early experience he found the strain of watching races on which he had gambled too much to take. He died on 27 August 2006 at Cheltenham General Hospital following a heart attack aggravated by his asthma. Ten years before his death he was asked how he would like to be remembered. His chosen epitaph was 'a good tutor of jockeys, a good schooler of horses, and a hard bastard' (*Daily Telegraph*, 29 Aug 2006). He was survived by his wife, Dinah, and their two sons. WRAY VAMPLEW

Sources D. Nicholson and J. Powell, *The Duke: the autobiography of a champion trainer* (1995) · W. Vamplew and J. Kay, *The encyclopedia of British horseracing* (2005) · *The Times* (29 Aug 2006) · *Daily Telegraph* (29 Aug 2006) · *The Independent* (1 Sept 2006) · *The Guardian* (5 Sept 2006) · *WW* (2006) · b. cert. · m. cert. · d. cert.

Likenesses S & G, photographs, 1967–74, PA Photos, London · D. Hartley, photographs, 1986–2003, Rex Features, London · J. Nicholson, photographs, 1992, Rex Features, London · J. Bareham, photograph, 1993, Rex Features, London · J. Herbert, photographs, 1997–9, Getty Images, London · photographs, 1997–

9, Photoshot, London · M. Fearn, photographs, 1999, PA Photos, London · T. Marshall, photographs, 1999, PA Photos, London · N. French, photograph, 2003, PA Photos, London · obituary photographs

Wealth at death £85,387: probate, 3 Nov 2006, *CGPLA Eng. & Wales*

Nixon, Sir Edwin Ronald (1925–2008), computer industry executive, was born at 4 Grace Road, Leicester, on 21 June 1925, the son of William Archdale Nixon, a bookbinder and later printer, and his wife, Ethel, *née* Corrigan. He was educated at Alderman Newton's School, Leicester, and Selwyn College, Cambridge, where he read mathematics. He began his business career in 1950 as an accountant at Deixon Ltd. On 28 June 1952, at St Barnabas's Church, Kensington, he married Joan Lilian Hill (1925–1995), daughter of Albert Richard Hill, clerk. They had one son and one daughter.

Nixon joined IBM (UK) Ltd (the British subsidiary of the American company International Business Machines) in 1955, initially as a salesman. Although IBM was the world's largest manufacturer of punched-card machines and later computers, at the time of Nixon's joining it had a very small operation in the UK, consisting of headquarters in London and a first plant in Greenock, Scotland. Initially he had to explain to clients who his employer was. But by 1965, when (having rapidly worked his way up) he became managing director, the company had begun to expand at breakneck speed. That same year the 6000th employee joined the company and a second extension to the plant in Greenock was opened. Research activities had been developed in Hursley and began to be developed at the Havant plant. 1965 was also the year in which the first System/360 computer was installed in Britain. This was IBM's most important product at the time and a turning point in the computer industry, with its introduction of modular architecture, and its use of integrated circuits, remote terminals, and compatible software applications.

By 1968 IBM was the third biggest American investor in the UK. That year a merger took place between British indigenous computer manufacturers, resulting in the creation of International Computers Limited (ICL). As the only large-scale British computer manufacturer, ICL received preferential treatment in government contracts. Nixon consistently claimed that IBM products could undercut ICL's in price and performance. Nevertheless the favourable treatment proved to be a major obstacle to securing a large share of public sector contracts for many years. That was not the case in the private sector. Between 1965 and 1969 IBM doubled its workforce in the UK. This reflected how successful, under Nixon, the British subsidiary (and its European sister organizations) was in migrating American computer power across the Atlantic. At this point, ICL and IBM enjoyed roughly the same share of the British computer market. In 1969 Nixon decided to move the company's headquarters out of London. As on several other occasions, Nixon furthered government objectives through the location of IBM facilities, this time into reclaimed land in Portsmouth, where naval support facilities had declined. Nixon referred to this event as 'probably my most important decision since becoming Managing Director of IBM UK' ('The Nixon years', 7).

Although IBM brought its distinctive American corporate culture and demanding targets to the British subsidiary, Nixon also put his personal mark on it. For instance, under him IBM UK actively supported education and the arts, and also in 1970 introduced an innovative secondment programme. During the following sixteen years a total of 150 employees were posted to charitable or not-for-profit organizations, professional organizations, or government departments. According to Nixon there were about twenty-five people on secondment at any one time, the most senior of whom went to the National Health Service as personnel director. As Nixon pointed out, this was 'probably the largest personnel job in the U.K.' ('Edwin Nixon'; *Think*, 43). Another senior manager went to the cabinet office to help find ways to improve the efficiency and effectiveness of the civil service. Nixon also promulgated innovative business methods, such as those that tore down barriers between managers and workers (including the former eating at the canteen and forgoing reserved parking spaces). He sought opportunities for employees to be heard. He read all the suggestions made through the company's 'Speak up' programme and offered financial incentives for worthwhile ideas. In 1973 a pilot programme for a system of flexible working hours, called 'selective work schedule', was introduced at six locations in the UK. Nixon's management style reflected IBM's policy of being protective of and loyal to staff. Some argued that IBM UK's work practices were to stiffen the company and result in loss of competitiveness in the decades ahead. But in 1977 this same loyalty resulted in staff almost unanimously voting down an offer for pay and employment conditions to be negotiated with IBM by a trade union on their behalf.

In March 1971 the Hursley-developed System/370 model 135 mainframe computer was released. This was the most important product announcement since the System/360. Production was assigned to Havant, making this the first product to be developed and manufactured in Britain. The standards of sophistication and flexibility of use set by the System/360 and System/370 were instrumental in their wide acceptance by the business community. Thanks to them IBM secured more than 40 per cent of the British computer market throughout the 1970s. The highlight of 1974 was the queen's visit to the Havant plant. That year Nixon was appointed CBE for services to export. The honour reflected the very active role of IBM's British subsidiary in developing and manufacturing products for the global market, as part of IBM's co-ordinated operations in Europe and beyond.

In 1975 Nixon began his involvement with the National Westminster Bank, where he was appointed non-executive director. Also in 1975 he announced IBM's new marketing strategy, with an emphasis on office products and general-purpose computer systems. In 1979 he was named chairman of the board and chief executive of IBM

UK Holdings Ltd, while plans for a new headquarters on London's South Bank were announced. During the following twelve months a number of major product announcements signalled IBM's move towards low-cost terminals and the company's commitment to text and information processing. These technological developments were to characterize the early 1980s and provided a platform for sustained growth in the context of high unemployment and adverse economic conditions in the UK. Indeed, in 1981, when the company celebrated thirty years at Greenock and Nixon twenty-five years of employment by the company, the total group revenue exceeded £1000 million for the first time.

In 1981 Nixon presided over the launch of the groundbreaking IBM personal computer. In the same year, and in light of new rules on open tendering of government contracts under the General Agreement on Tariffs and Trade, he threatened to lodge an international complaint against the British government for its continuing support of ICL. The government backed down and discontinued its support of the latter. Not long after this ICL lost its independence to Fujitsu, the Japanese electronics conglomerate. In 1983 the *Financial Times* ranked IBM UK as one of the 100 top British exporters for the first time. The following year, 1984, Nixon received a knighthood and launched a number of academic-related programmes. These included two IBM institutes, joint projects with Cambridge University and Imperial College, London, and the introduction of personal computers to schools and higher education. In 1985 he was named businessman of the year. By the time of his retirement as chief executive of IBM UK in 1986 the company had 18,798 employees and recorded annual gross revenues of £3043 million, a 203.7 per cent increase from the annual turnover in 1981. It was the largest British-based supplier of computer and office systems.

Nixon retained his post as chairman of IBM UK until 1990 while, at the same time, serving in a number of executive and charitable roles. These included deputy chairman of NatWest (1987–96), chairman of the medical research company Amersham International (1988–96), and chairman of the board of trustees of the Royal Opera House, Covent Garden (1984–7). He was a member of the selection panel for the Harkness Fellowships of the Commonwealth Fund of New York, and served on the governing bodies of several educational outlets and universities, including Manchester Business School, Westfield College, London, the Oxford Centre for Management Studies, and the Open University; he was chairman of the council of Leicester University from 1992 to 1998. He received honorary doctorates from Aston, Stirling, Brunel, Manchester, and Leicester universities, and was an honorary fellow of Portsmouth and Leeds polytechnics. Approachable and good-humoured, he was nevertheless a perfectionist who liked things done well. He was renowned for his clear analysis, relentless drive for targets, and attention to detail. After the death of his first wife, on 22 November 1997 he married Bridget Diana Rogers (*b.* 1942), an educational administrator, and daughter of Reginald Charles Rogers, teacher. He lived latterly at Starkes Heath, Rogate, near Petersfield, Hampshire, and died on 17 August 2008. He was survived by his second wife, Bridget, and the two children of his first marriage.

BERNARDO BÁTIZ-LAZO

Sources 'Edwin Nixon', *Think* [IBM magazine], 2 (1986), 42–5 · J. H. Dunning, *The role of American investment in the British economy* (1969), 165, 177 · N. Hood and S. Young, *Multinationals in retreat: the Scottish experience* (1982), 161–2 · 'The Nixon years', *IBM UK News* (Dec 1986), 6–7 · *The Times* (22 Aug 2008); (27 Aug 2008); (9 Oct 2008) · *Daily Telegraph* (27 Aug 2008) · *The Guardian* (17 Sept 2008) · *WW* (2008) · Burke, *Peerage* · b. cert. · m. certs.

Likenesses photographs, 1995, Photoshot, London · obituary photographs

Wealth at death £4,445,281: probate, 10 Oct 2008, *CGPLA Eng. & Wales*

Noakes, George (1924–2008), bishop of St David's and archbishop of Wales, was born on 13 September 1924 at Pen-y-gaer, Nancwnlle, Cardiganshire, the eldest of three sons of David John Noakes, colliery labourer and later farmer, and his wife, Elizabeth Mary, *née* Lewis. The family was bilingual, the father's first language being English and the mother's Welsh. He worshipped in the morning at his local parish church, and in the evening at Bwlch-llan Calvinistic Methodist chapel. After education at Tregaron grammar school he was called up into the RAF and towards the end of the Second World War was a navigator with Bomber Command.

Noakes saw his future in the ordained ministry of the Church in Wales. After graduating in philosophy at University College, Aberystwyth, and training at Wycliffe Hall, Oxford, he was ordained in 1950. He spent his ministry in St David's diocese apart from nine years (1967–76) as vicar of Dewi Sant, Cardiff, serving the Welsh-speaking population; before then he was curate of Lampeter (1950–56), then vicar of Eglwyswrw (1956–9), then Tregaron (1959–67). By nature and inclination he was a moderate evangelical, making an impact by pastoral attentiveness and brilliance in simple, direct, and relevant preaching. His skill in communication developed in radio and television broadcasts. He played a role in the negotiations that led to the passing of the Welsh Language Act 1967. In 1976 he was appointed rector of Aberystwyth, and three years later he became archdeacon of Cardigan. He was also a canon of St David's Cathedral (1977–9) and vicar of Llanychaearn, Cardiganshire (1980–82). On 23 April 1957 he married Jane Margaretta Davies (*b.* 1927/8), daughter of Samuel Richard Davies, engineer. There were no children of the marriage.

In 1982 Noakes was elected bishop of St David's, the largest diocese in Wales, where two-thirds of the parishes were Welsh in culture and language. He saw his episcopate as an extension of his work as a parish priest ministering to a rural diocese. He rose at 5.30 a.m., always said his prayers in Welsh, and never retired before 11 p.m. Living in Carmarthen, fifty miles from St David's Cathedral, was not ideal. He drove over 30,000 miles a year, often on narrow mountainous roads, bewailing that he spent more time in his car than in his study and more in committees than in preaching. He had a deep desire to 'show Jesus' to the people of west Wales, and mission and evangelism were his primary concerns. He saw himself as a fisher-of-men, not an ecclesiastical aquarium keeper. Apathy, local Welsh rivalries, and the innate conservatism of some people were his enemies. A diocesan mission in 1988 culminated in a morale-boosting service at Stradey Park rugby ground in Llanelli, though some parishes were unready or unwilling to hoist their sails to the wind of the spirit. Confirmation services were momentous occasions.

Some doubted whether it was wise to elect Noakes, a sixty-three year old and unambitious 'people's bishop', as archbishop in 1987. He was solidly built and dressed immaculately; his inability to say 'no' to invitations resulted in a mild heart attack in 1990. Under his presidency the governing body changed from a legalistic assembly to a family gathering. Capable, respected, and affable, he steered meetings quietly but firmly when the ordination of women priests, remarriage in church after divorce, and the grouping of parishes were on the agenda. The Church in Wales had a reputation for failing to grasp nettles and for back-tracking. The 'archbishop's state of the church study' was a great project which hatched three significant reports (1990, 1991, and 1993), though with few results: a proposal that a future archbishop should live in or near Cardiff, either in a separate archiepiscopal see or as bishop of Llandaff, was stalemated. Noakes was prominent in the 400th anniversary of Bishop William Morgan's translation of the Bible into Welsh (1988), the publication of the new Welsh Bible (also in 1988), and the 1400th anniversary of the death of St David in 1989. His deep commitment to ecumenism was reflected in his appointment as the first president of the newly formed Churches Together in Wales. There were also congenial Anglican communion benefits for Noakes, with visits to Singapore, Cape Town, and Cyprus for meetings of primates, and the Anglican Consultative Council, whose assembly he hosted in Cardiff in 1990.

Noakes was the best loved archbishop since disestablishment. He regarded himself as a consolidator, acknowledging that the great archbishops were Glyn Simon and Gwilym Williams. He was instrumental in persuading the young Rowan Williams to abandon Oxford and become a candidate for the vacant see of Monmouth in 1991. A spiritual and humble man, by following the precept of St David 'to do little things' he gave the Church in Wales new confidence and kept it united. He retired in 1991. He enjoyed angling and watching cricket and football. He died at West Wales General Hospital, Carmarthen, on 14 July 2008 and was survived by his wife, Jane. She had been closely involved in his ministry. After a funeral service in St Peter's Church, Carmarthen, on 22 July, he was cremated in Parc Gwyn crematorium, Narberth.

JOHN S. PEART-BINNS

Sources *South Wales Evening Post* (14 July 2008) • *Western Telegraph* (15 July 2008) • *Daily Telegraph* (16 July 2008) • *The Times* (22 July 2008); (26 July 2008) • *The Independent* (25 July 2008) • *Carmarthen Journal* (30 July 2008) • *The Guardian* (13 Aug 2008); (21 Aug 2008) • *WW* (2008) • personal knowledge (2012) • private information (2012) [Tudor Noakes, brother; W. Gladstone] • b. cert. • m. cert. • d. cert.

Archives NL Wales • University of Bradford, J. B. Priestley Library, Peart-Binns episcopal biography archive

Likenesses photograph, 1988, Photoshot, London • A. Davies, photograph, priv. coll. • D. Griffiths, portrait, Provincial Offices of the Church in Wales, 39 Cathedral Road, Cardiff • obituary photographs

Wealth at death £153,000: administration with will, 19 Feb 2009, *CGPLA Eng. & Wales*

Nolan, Michael Patrick, **Baron Nolan** (**1928–2007**), judge and first chairman of the Committee on Standards in Public Life, was born on 10 September 1928 at 2 Woodside Avenue, North Finchley, Middlesex, the younger son and youngest of three children of James Thomas Nolan (1895–1955), motor engineer, later estate agent, and his wife, Jane Agnes, *née* Walsh (1894–1954). His siblings were Elizabeth (Betty; 1923–1940) and James (Jim; 1925–2001). The branch of the Nolan family from which he was descended had been living in co. Kerry, Ireland, until they were driven out by the potato famine of the mid-nineteenth century. His grandfather took the family to England.

Education, national service, and early career Michael Nolan was brought up first in North Finchley and then at Bexhill-on-Sea, Sussex, where his parents went to live to look after his father's ailing parents in the mid-1930s. Nolan regarded his own parents, who were devout Roman Catholics, as the first and foremost influences on his life. By 1940 the family was back in their North Finchley home. He was educated at Ampleforth College. When he was studying there for the higher certificate his main subjects were Latin, Greek, and ancient history, with German and Spanish as further options. One other discipline he learned there from one of the monks was the art of fly-fishing. The passion for this remained with him throughout his life. It seems legitimate to infer that his devotion to the Roman Catholic faith was also firmly settled by the time he left school. This gave him the unshakeable personal integrity that was such a prominent feature of his adult character. He later said that although the teaching at Ampleforth was excellent, the most important things he learned there were self-confidence and the proper use of authority. Ampleforth with its wide Yorkshire landscape filled the gaps created by earlier years spent in towns and cities. He enjoyed Yorkshire village cricket as the captain of a school team called the Optimists and excelled at rifle shooting.

After Ampleforth Nolan spent his two years' national service in the army (1947–9), ending with a commission in the Royal Artillery and duties in Germany. (His first preference had been the Irish Guards, but on interview the regimental colonel told him that there were vacancies only for those seeking a regular commission; his second choice, the Royal Inniskilling Fusiliers, also never became a possibility.) He maintained his military links after national service with some six years of service in the Territorial Army (1949–55). Meanwhile in 1949 he went to Wadham College, Oxford, as a commoner. The original intention had been that he would read Greats under the watchful eye of Sir Maurice Bowra, the distinguished classical scholar who was warden of the college. But Greats took four years and Nolan was by then more attracted by a

Michael Patrick Nolan, Baron Nolan (1928–2007), by Bassano, 1968

three-year course. It seems that the suggestion that he should select law as his subject came from his Ampleforth headmaster, Paul Nevill. Whatever the source of this selection it undoubtedly suited Nolan admirably, both intellectually and temperamentally. In his first term at Wadham, Peter Carter became the law tutor of the college. He had won the Croix de Guerre (with silver star) in Normandy, and subsequently developed a great reputation as a legal scholar and teacher. (He became an honorary bencher of the Middle Temple in 1981 and an honorary QC in 1990, no doubt with Nolan's backing.) Nolan graduated with a second in jurisprudence in 1952.

After graduating Nolan went as a pupil into the chambers of Melford Stevenson (later a High Court judge). His pupil-master was Alan Orr (later a High Court judge and thereafter a lord justice of appeal). He was called to the bar by the Middle Temple in 1953. On 9 April the same year he married Margaret Mary Noyes (*b.* 1932), the younger daughter of the poet Alfred *Noyes and his second wife, Mary, *née* Mayne. In his uncompleted memoirs he related how he had gone to a ball without a partner. He was asked to look after a girl whose partner was smitten by flu and had to go home early. Nolan was not very pleased with the idea of looking after an unknown girl, his preference being to be a free agent.

> But then I saw Margaret, smiling at me across the room. As she will be the first to confirm, I have no gift at all for romantic words, in speech or in writing, so I simply state as a fact that I knew at once that I had found the love of my life. Margaret has the most beautiful smile in the world, and it has never ceased to gladden my heart, nor to remind me of the first time I saw her. (Michael Nolan, memorial address)

They had five children: Patricia (*b.* 1954), Michael (*b.* 1955), Sheila (*b.* 1957), Anne (*b.* 1959), and Clare (*b.* 1965).

At the time Nolan qualified as a barrister it was notoriously difficult for a beginner to make much of an income at the common-law bar. He had to wait seven years before he could bank his first cheque. Even then he had a problem in deciding whether to frame it or bank it. This paucity of common-law work caused him to think that he might do better by joining one of the specialist bars. His reflections led him to choose the tax bar. He approached Cyril King, who was the head of a leading set. King invited him to tea in his chambers while making it clear that the decision must rest with the juniors. Nolan had tea with three of them. He was invited to have a second cup of tea. This was the moment of decision. Number 4 Pump Court became Nolan's chambers for the rest of his time at the bar.

Nolan's career started slowly but he gradually built up a formidable tax practice. He became a wholly persuasive advocate with a calm and measured style, and with the habit of making the main points once and once only. He would have nothing to do with schemes for the avoidance of tax. His approach was invariably ethical and principled. His exceptional grasp of accounting fundamentals led to his appointment as a member of the Sandilands committee on inflation accounting (1973–5).

Nolan took silk in 1968. When his work involved litigation in Northern Ireland he joined the bar there too in 1974. He also became a serious performer in Singapore and Hong Kong, fortuitously starting his career in each territory with a win on behalf of the Inland Revenue. These successes naturally stimulated further briefs from both sides of the line. He was made a bencher at the Middle Temple in 1975 and took an active part in the life of the inn and its committee work. He would have been an obvious choice to become treasurer of the Middle Temple had not the volume of his public duties rendered this impossible.

Judicial office In his practice Nolan had had no experience of dealing with the criminal law. To gain such experience he tried first to be appointed as a JP in Kent in order, as he put it, to see the criminal justice system from the bottom rung of the ladder. But no such appointment was forthcoming. So in 1975 he took the somewhat surprising step of applying to be appointed a recorder of the crown court. This would involve him annually in sitting for two to four weeks as a judge in a criminal court, trying cases, summing up the evidence to the jury, and sentencing those found guilty. His application was accepted and he duly sat for some seven years as a recorder. He trained himself diligently for the role by studying and sitting alongside colleagues who were recorders. He was given every assistance by both branches of the profession and by the officials who serviced the courts of the western circuit. He may have wanted to be appointed as a recorder in order to share the experience of his contemporaries at the bar. Moreover it may be that he contemplated the possibility that his name might one day come up for consideration as a candidate for a High Court judgeship and he did not want that possibility to be destroyed by the revelation that he had no knowledge of the substance and procedures of the criminal law.

Nolan was indeed appointed as a judge of the Queen's Bench Division of the High Court of Justice in 1982. He sat as a judge for many years. Much of the work was routine but some high-profile cases came before him which provided the opportunity for the display of his cool and independent judgement. In 1984 he granted the National Coal Board injunctions against the use of flying pickets by the National Union of Mineworkers. The following year he awarded injunctions in favour of Westminster council restraining the Greater London council from using posters to persuade Londoners to back the fight against its own abolition. In 1989 he awarded Muslim leaders the right to challenge a JP's refusal to issue blasphemy summonses against Salman Rushdie, author of *The Satanic Verses*. In another case he, controversially, sentenced a man who had raped his daughter to only three years in prison. No doubt Nolan believed that there were special circumstances that justified a more lenient sentence than would have been normal. But the appeal judges took a different view, and his sentence was set aside. In 1984 he was asked by the lord chief justice, Lord Lane, whether he would like to take on the job of being presiding judge on the western circuit. Nolan had never himself belonged to a circuit and had no idea what was involved. Lane explained: 'It is very simple. It means that if anything goes wrong on the Western Circuit you get the blame' (Mackay of Clashfern, memorial address). With this encouragement Nolan accepted.

In 1991 Nolan was promoted to the Court of Appeal. He had caught the eye of the lord chancellor, Lord Mackay of Clashfern, when they had both served on a committee set up to simplify the tax system, in the early 1970s. As a lord justice of appeal he was involved in many cases that hit the headlines. He decided that an anorexic girl could be forcibly treated against her will. In another case he agreed with the court's decision to reject compensation claims for nervous shock brought by relatives of those who died in the Hillsborough football stadium disaster. In a case arising out of the deaths of fifty-one people in the *Marchioness* riverboat disaster he refused to overturn the decision of the director of public prosecutions to bring no criminal charges. In an important case it was alleged against Kenneth Baker, the home secretary, that he had acted in contempt of court in failing to secure that a Nigerian citizen was brought back to the UK from Nigeria, since he had been aware of but had ignored an order made by a High Court judge that barred any attempt to return the would-be immigrant to Nigeria. Nolan was one of the majority in the Court of Appeal who upheld the finding of contempt against Baker, naming him personally. In the House of Lords the law lords accepted an argument to the effect that the contempt order should not name Baker personally but should be issued against the secretary of state for home affairs.

In 1992 Nolan was a member of a Court of Appeal panel that decided in Judith Ward's case that the prosecution had failed in its duty to share with the defence evidence that tended to show weaknesses in the prosecution's case or which revealed that the defendant's mental state was such as to make her supposed confessions intrinsically unlikely to be true. The extent of the non-disclosures and the number of persons in the prosecution team who were guilty of reprehensible conduct led the court in its judgment to state that 'a grave miscarriage of justice had occurred' (*The Independent*, 5 June 1992). This decision had a very significant effect on the manner in which all prosecutions were thereafter handled.

The Committee on Standards in Public Life In 1994 Nolan was promoted to the House of Lords as a lord of appeal in ordinary, with the title Baron Nolan. He took as his motto to accompany his shield the three words *Fides, familia, lex*, which aptly summarized his philosophy. Much of his time as a law lord was, however, taken up by his duties as the first chairman of the Committee on Standards in Public Life (1994–7). The lord chancellor, Lord Mackay of Clashfern, had recommended to the prime minister, John Major, that Nolan was the best lawyer to take the chair of this new committee. The prime minister asked Mackay to ascertain whether Nolan would accept the appointment. His telephone response was immediate: 'If the Prime Minister wants me to do it, I certainly shall' (Mackay of Clashfern, memorial address).

The prime minister had established the committee to deal with numerous charges of misconduct being made by members of the public and by the media against members of parliament. Most, but not all, charges were against Conservative MPs. One group of charges involved allegations that MPs took money in exchange for asking questions. A committee of nine members was appointed under Nolan's chairmanship with secretarial support. Three members represented the three major political parties, each being a serving MP or member of the House of Lords. The committee worked with extraordinary efficiency and collegiality. As Nolan insisted, all the reports produced by the committee during his term of office were unanimous. It took evidence from the public, from the media, and from experts. Evidence was taken orally in many parts of the country. The committee's hearings were held in public. There had been an episode soon after it was first appointed when a spokesman for the prime minister announced that the committee would probably sit in private. This led at once to a statement by Nolan that his committee would sit in public. That was what he was trained to do as a judge, he said, and he had no intention of altering his practice.

Over a period of three years the committee worked on and took evidence leading to the publication of four reports: *Standards in Public Life* (Cm 2850, 2 vols., May 1995); *Local Public Spending Bodies* (Cm 3270, 2 vols., May 1996); *Standards of Conduct in Local Government in England* (Cm 3702,

2 vols., July 1997); and *Review of Standards of Conduct in Executive Non-Departmental Public Bodies, NHS Trusts and Local Public Spending Bodies* (no command paper number, 1 vol., Nov 1997). As its title indicated, the fourth report reviewed what had been the response by late 1997 to the first two reports. The report indicated that considerable and welcome progress had been made, though more needed to be done.

It is clear that the first report was the most important. A striking feature was the promulgation in it of what were called the 'Seven Principles of Public Life', namely selflessness, integrity, objectivity, accountability, openness, honesty, and leadership. The report stated that 'these principles apply to all aspects of public life. The Committee has set them out here for the benefit of all who serve the public in any way' (*Standards in Public Life*, 14). Each principle had an explanatory text. For example, selflessness, which was the first principle, was described as follows: 'Holders of public office should take decisions solely in terms of the public interest. They should not do so in order to gain financial or other material benefits for themselves, their family, or their friends' (ibid.). The other reports produced when Nolan was chairman all repeated the seven principles in a prominent position. The principles became well known and widely reproduced, sometimes with additions.

The prime minister had when appointing the committee asked that it should produce its first report within six months. Nolan responded to this by saying that the available time did not permit the committee to cover the entire field in six months, so it confined its first report to the three subjects which appeared to be giving rise to the greatest public concern, namely issues relating to members of parliament; ministers and civil servants; and executive quangos and NHS bodies. As Nolan reported in a letter of May 1995 to the prime minister, published at the front of the report, the public consultation which the committee undertook confirmed that it had correctly chosen the three areas which gave rise to the greatest public concern. The experienced parliamentarians and other eminent persons who were the nine members of the committee admired the calm and gentle style of their chairman. Without making any fuss he managed to steer the debate towards his own conclusions. As one member put it, 'he was endlessly gentle and courteous in his handling of the committee, allowing everyone to have their say, never showing any sign of impatience' (private information). Another member confirmed that Nolan gave excellent leadership and deserved the fullest credit for the respect the committee enjoyed and for the standing that its reports subsequently had: 'Certainly I found it a matter of pride but also something which did command wide respect—the simple statement that "I was a member of the Nolan Committee"' (private information).

When the first report was published it was well received by the public. But some of those who were criticized in the report (such as members of parliament) were highly critical. They claimed that they were represented as acting like criminals. Sir Edward Heath, the former prime minister, declared that Nolan seemed to lack a certain 'worldliness' (*The Times*, 19 May 1995). Nolan, however, was quite impervious to such criticism and simply carried on with his work on the next three reports. The public was impressed. The House of Commons decided to implement the recommendations that concerned it; and the omnipresent sleaze that had been gaining ground in the early 1990s suffered a serious check (albeit to resurface in the form of the abuse of parliamentary expenses in the following decade).

Retirement, honours, and final years Nolan retired as a lord of appeal in ordinary in 1998, having reached the age of seventy. He seldom spoke in debates on the floor of the house. When he did so the speech or intervention tended to be linked to matters of which he had personal knowledge from his time on the bench. He remained an interception of communications commissioner until 2002, having been appointed in 1994. The last task he undertook in relation to the setting of standards was carried out at the request of the archbishop of Westminster, Cardinal Cormac Murphy O'Connor. Many cases had been reported in the media in the 1990s where Catholic priests were charged with sexual abuse of children. In some instances the abuse had continued over a period of years and had resulted in grave trauma for the children. In 2000 the cardinal asked Nolan to investigate child protection in the Catholic church in England and Wales and to report, giving his recommendations for cleansing the stables. He immediately undertook the task with a committee. His first report was published in 2001. The tone was set by an early paragraph in this report:

> Child abuse is a great evil. It can leave deep scars on victims and their families. It is particularly abhorrent when a child or young person is abused by someone in a position of trust and responsibility. It is most abhorrent when that position of trust is held by a member of the clergy or a lay Church worker. The care of children is at the forefront of the teachings of Christ and is, therefore, one of the primary responsibilities of all members of the Church led by their priests and bishops.

The report made some fifty recommendations, including fundamental provisions to the effect that there should be an investigation into the background of every person who wanted to serve the church in any capacity who might come into contact with children. All with doubtful backgrounds should be denied employment and all contact. Those who appeared innocent but who were subsequently alleged to have transgressed should be debarred from contact subject to a full investigation of the allegations.

Nolan was a member of the Bar Council for 1973–4 and a member of the senate of the inns of court and the bar for seven years (1974–81), for two of which (1977–9) he held the office of treasurer. He was a member of the governing body of the Convent of the Sacred Heart, Woldingham (1973–83), and a governor of Combe Bank School (1974–83). He was an honorary fellow of Wadham College from 1992, chairman of the board of the Institute of Advanced Legal Studies from 1994 to 2000, and from 1997 to 2002 he was chancellor of Essex University, well known for his 'hands-on' approach in the role. He received honorary doctorates from the universities of Essex (1996), Surrey (1996), Warwick (1998), Exeter (1998), Middlesex (1999), and Bournemouth (2000). In 2002 he was made a knight of St George. In 1996–7 he and Sir Stephen Sedley gave between them six Radcliffe lectures (three each) at the University of Warwick. The series was entitled 'The making and remaking of the British constitution'. Geoffrey Wilson delivered a postscript and the entire collection was published.

A contemporary from Oxford (not himself from Ampleforth or on the Nolan committee) observed: 'I think what characterised Michael was always a quiet and courteously managed certainty in all that he undertook'. While lacking proof he was inclined to identify Nolan's time at Ampleforth as providing the engine for this. 'Michael was a very faithful Roman Catholic, and one became aware of this and—I think—of an inner strength of mind and purpose deriving from it—the better one got to know him' (private information). Lord Lloyd of Berwick wrote that 'Michael was a marvellous judge to sit with. Like Denning, he had a clarity of mind, and simplicity of language which few have equalled. Of all the judges I have known, he was the least ostentatious' (*The Guardian*, 26 Jan 2007).

Nolan died at his home, Old Farm Cottage, Scords Lane, Toys Hill, Westerham, Kent, on 22 January 2007 of bronchopneumonia and multi-system atrophy, having had to endure a progressive degenerative disease that ultimately took away even his capacity to speak, leaving only the ability to smile. It was appropriate that a splendid memorial service should have been held on 22 March 2007 at Westminster Cathedral with Cardinal Murphy O'Connor presiding. In his homily he expressed his 'great admiration, esteem and gratitude for someone who did the Church a great service, but did it in such a way that it seemed the most natural thing for him to do'. The congregation was asked by the cardinal to 'remember and pray for the repose of the soul of this good man, Michael Nolan' (Cardinal Murphy O'Connor, homily). Nolan was survived by his wife, Margaret, and their five children, three of whom followed careers in the law. PATRICK NEILL

Sources *The Times* (25 Jan 2007) · *Daily Telegraph* (25 Jan 2007) · *The Guardian* (26 Jan 2007) · *The Independent* (26 Jan 2007) · C. Murphy O'Connor, homily at celebration of the life of Lord Nolan, Westminster Cathedral, 22 March 2007, www.rcdow.org.uk/cardinal/default.asp?library_ref=1&content_ref=1256, 21 July 2010 · M. Nolan and Lord Mackay of Clashfern, addresses at celebration of life of Lord Nolan, Westminster Cathedral, 22 March 2007 · Burke, *Peerage* · *WW* (2007) · personal knowledge (2011) · private information (2011) · b. cert. · m. cert. · d. cert.

Archives FILM BFINA, current affairs footage

Likenesses Bassano, half-plate film negative, 1968, NPG [*see illus.*] · Bassano, half-plate film negatives, 1968, NPG · photographs, 1968–97, Photoshot, London · P. O'Connell, bromide print, 1995, NPG · obituary photographs

Wealth at death £42,139: probate, 19 June 2007, *CGPLA Eng. & Wales*

Norman, Andrew John [Andy] (1943–2007), athletics administrator and agent, was born on 21 September 1943 at 95 Council House, Parish Road, Bramford, Suffolk, the son of Russell William Norman, a sheet metal worker then serving as a leading aircraftsman in the Royal Air Force, and his wife, Nora Alice, *née* Goodall. He was educated in Ipswich, where he developed an interest in athletics, then moved to south London in 1962 to join the Metropolitan Police. He became involved in athletics while a policeman, first as a middle distance runner, and then as an administrator. Through his work with the Metropolitan Police's athletics team he took on roles for the Amateur Athletic Association southern counties, including the organization of events at Crystal Palace.

Athletics was an amateur sport at this time, with no prize money or appearance fees and tight controls on competitors' expenses, but the enforcement of these rules was inconsistent. In this setting Norman became an agent for a number of athletes, renowned for finding loopholes in the rules and ensuring appearance fees for his athletes. He became well known within the sport for his dynamism and his ability to make things happen, but also for his abrasive personality. His kindest critics described him as 'no-nonsense' (*The Times*, 26 Sept 2007), but less charitable commentators described him as 'bombastic' and 'bullying' (*The Independent*, 26 Sept 2007).

Norman was part of a modernizing trend within athletics. He saw the sport's enormous commercial and media potential, but he recognized that its modernization would have to include the professionalization of athletes. Supported by Primo Nebiolo, president of the International Amateur Athletics Federation (IAAF), he helped to bring this change about in 1982 when he made a key speech (co-written with the journalist John Rodda) to the IAAF which called for open payments. The IAAF accepted the idea, and professionalism—officially through trust funds—replaced under-the-counter 'shamateurism'.

Norman thrived in this new environment. In 1984 he left the Metropolitan Police to devote himself full-time to athletics as promotions director at the British Amateur Athletics Board, which was reconstituted as the British Athletics Federation (BAF) in 1991. However, the sport's new economy did not have enough regulations in place to control Norman's ambitions, and he developed a number of roles within the sport that created conflicts of interests. He continued to represent some of the best British athletes of the period, including the runners Linford Christie, Brendan Foster, and Steve Ovett, the hurdlers Sally Gunnell and Colin Jackson, the triple jumper Jonathan Edwards, and the javelin throwers Steve Backley and Fatima Whitbread. As the BAF's promotions officer, he was responsible for organizing events and booking athletes, which put his athletes at an advantage over those who were not on his books, and enabled him to get the best packages for his stars. He was also highly successful in attracting television coverage of athletics, notably through his deal with ITV, which helped both the sport and the athletes he was representing. On the international stage he was involved in marketing for the rebranded IAAF (International Association of Athletics

Federations) from 1984, and for the European Athletics Association from 1992. These clashes of interest also spilled into his private life, as he divorced his Norwegian wife, Gerd, with whom he had had a son and a daughter, in 1986 and had a relationship with Fatima Whitbread (*b.* 1961) while representing her. Norman and Whitbread set up Chafford Hundred as an élite marketing club for athletes, which extended Norman's patronage further. They married on 24 May 1997, at the parish church in Capthorne, Sussex, and had one son, although they became estranged in 2005.

Allegations of malpractice started to build up against Norman, and between 1987 and 1994 he underwent three formal investigations by the British athletics authorities. The first, in 1987, came after hammer thrower Martin Girvan alleged that Norman rigged drug tests by planting clean urine samples for his athletes. No evidence was found to incriminate Norman, but many involved were convinced of his guilt. Two years later his friend and protégé Steve Ovett spoke out against Norman's management of appearance fees for athletes. The BAF took financial affairs out of Norman's formal remit after this, and the Amateur Athletics Association recommended that he should not combine his post as promotions officer with his work as an agent, although this was not enforced. The most controversial crisis started in August 1993, when the athletics coach and journalist Cliff Temple wrote a critical piece on Norman, 'British athletics out of control', in the *Sunday Times*. The article slated the BAF for allowing Norman to become 'a one-man cartel, the Mr Big of athletics', and drew attention to Norman's methods (*Sunday Times*, 1 Aug 1993). In response Norman spread unfounded rumours that Temple had sexually harassed the middle distance runner Shireen Bailey, whom Temple coached. Temple was already suffering from depression, and these allegations contributed to his breakdown and, in January 1994, his suicide. After the coroner at Temple's inquest cited Norman's behaviour as a factor in the tragedy, the BAF sacked him from his post as promotions officer. The journalists Stephen Downes (whom Norman had also threatened) and Duncan Mackay included an exposé of Norman's record in their book *Running Scared* (1996).

Despite the damage that this incident did to Norman's reputation, he stayed in athletics, working as a consultant on promotions and events in various countries, including South Africa and Hungary, and remained active in the IAAF. He died of a heart attack at Birmingham International Airport on 24 September 2007 while travelling home from an athletics meeting in Stuttgart.

Norman's posthumous reputation has been mixed. He was one of the key modernizers in athletics, partially responsible for the sport's development since the 1980s. His organizational and networking skills were admired, as was his ability to negotiate high sums from media companies and sponsors, and his technical knowledge of the sport. However, these positive attributes were coloured by the controversies he created, and by his dictatorial management style, his excessive use of patronage, and his record as a bully. As the *Sunday Times* put it after his sacking in 1994, 'Athletics may be a little poorer without Norman. But it will be much healthier' (*Sunday Times*, 10 April 1994). MARTIN POLLEY

Sources *Sunday Times* (1 Aug 1993); (16 Jan 1994); (6 Feb 1994); (27 March 1994); (10 April 1994); (24 April 1994) · *The Independent* (6 March 1994); (26 Sept 2007) · S. Downes and D. Mackay, *Running scared: how athletics lost its innocence* (1996) · M. Polley, '"The amateur rules": amateurism and professionalism in post-war British athletics', *Amateurs and professionals in post-war British sport*, ed. A. Smith and D. Porter (2000), 81–114 · *The Times* (26 Sept 2007) · *Daily Telegraph* (27 Sept 2007) · *The Guardian* (28 Sept 2007) · *WW* (2007) · b. cert. · m. cert. [1997] · d. cert.

Likenesses photographs, 1998 (with Fatima Whitbread), Rex Features, London · obituary photographs · photograph, repro. in www.dailymail.co.uk/sport/othersports/article-483708/Former-athletics-chief-Norman-dies.html

Wealth at death under £2000: probate, 16 Sept 2008, *CGPLA Eng. & Wales*

Norris, (George) Leslie (1921–2006), poet and short-story writer, was born on 21 May 1921 at 11 Hankey Terrace, Merthyr Tudful, Glamorgan, the eldest son of George William Norris (*b.* 1898), electrician and milkman, and his wife, Mary Jane, *née* Jones (*b.* 1900). His father's family were from Buckinghamshire and his mother's from Cynghordy in Carmarthenshire. His father worked at Plymouth colliery in Merthyr Tudful but, after an accident underground, found work delivering milk. The family had relatives who owned Y Wern, a small farm on the mountain between Merthyr and Aberdâr, which was to appear in several of Norris's poems and stories.

Norris attended Georgetown primary school, where he came under the influence of a gifted teacher who introduced him to the pleasures of poetry, and, from the age of eleven, Cyfarthfa Castle Grammar School, housed in the former home of the Crawshays, the local ironmasters, which he found a dismal experience. He nevertheless became an avid reader, began writing verse, boxed, and played football and rugby; he also attended Bethel, a Welsh Baptist chapel, despite his lack of Welsh, and later Market Square English Presbyterian Church. The town where he had been born was economically depressed but still socially vibrant, and he was to write movingly about the poverty and colourful characters he encountered there. Curiously, the radical history of his home town, which had been the setting for the workers' rising of 1831, seems to have held no interest for him and barely figures in his writing: he remained indifferent to politics for the rest of his life. Much more influential was the splendid countryside a little to the north of the town, in particular the hills, fields, and streams of the Brecon Beacons where he was able to observe the flora, fauna, and avi-fauna that appear so often in his poems and stories.

Leaving school in 1938, Norris took his first job as a clerk in the rates department of Merthyr Tudful council, where he stayed for two years. He was then called up for service with the Royal Air Force Volunteer Reserve, training as an airframe fitter in Blackpool and Little Rissington, but served for little more than a year on account of severe blood poisoning contracted from handling steel ropes; he then returned to his old job in the town hall. About this time he discovered the work of such modern English and American poets as Gerard Manley Hopkins, Edward Thomas, W. H. Auden, and Ezra Pound. In 1943 some of his early poems were published by the Favil Press as a pamphlet, *Tongue of Beauty*, which was reprinted as *Poems* three years later. On 31 July 1948 he married Catherine Mary (Kitty) Jennings (1920–2008), the former wife of Norman Verdun Jennings, and daughter of David John Morgan, school caretaker. She was from Dowlais, and a colleague at Merthyr town hall. There were no children of the marriage.

In 1948 Norris enrolled as a student at the City of Coventry Teacher Training College; he was never to live permanently in Wales again. His first teaching post was at Grass Royal School in Yeovil, Somerset, where he taught English, and he subsequently held posts at Southdown junior school in Bath, where he was deputy head, and Westergate School in Chichester, Sussex, where he was headmaster. The Norrises settled in the village of Aldingbourne, becoming acquainted with the poets Andrew Young and Ted Walker, who lived in the same district. In 1958, the year in which he completed an MPhil thesis on the poetry of Vernon Watkins at Southampton University, he obtained a lectureship at the college of education in Bognor Regis (later the West Sussex Institute of Higher Education), where his wife also taught. In 1967 a booklet of his poems was published by Meic Stephens as *The Loud Winter* in the Triskel Poets series and, later in the same year, encouraged by the interest of Cecil Day-Lewis at Chatto and Windus, he brought out his first book, *Finding Gold*, in the Phoenix Living Poets series. His second book, *Ransoms* (1970), won the Alice Hunt Bartlett prize in the year of its publication. The years Norris spent in southern England were crucial to his development as a poet, if only on account of his reading of Edward Thomas, whose melancholy he shared and whose reponse to the rural scene was similar to his own.

Having tried for several years to give up teaching in order to become a full-time writer, in 1973 Norris accepted an invitation to be visiting professor at the University of Washington in Seattle. On his return to England he found himself so unsettled by his experience of America that he resigned his principal lectureship in degree studies at the West Sussex Institute and resolved to earn a living by his pen. His book *Mountains Polecats Pheasants* appeared in 1974 and he began publishing poems and stories in the *Atlantic Monthly* and the *New Yorker*. A number of writer's fellowships followed, notably at Eton College in 1976. Between 1975 and 1980 he served as chairman of the Southern Arts Association's literature panel. He wrote two books of poems for children, *Merlin and the Snake's Egg* (1978) and *Norris's Ark* (1988). His first collection of short stories, *Sliding* (1982), won the David Higham prize for fiction. In 1982 he read the poem 'Fern Hill' at the unveiling of the plaque commemorating Dylan Thomas at Poets' Corner in Westminster Abbey; he was also a consummate reader of his own verse. In 1983 he was invited to become visiting poet at Brigham Young University in Provo, Utah, and so began a long association with the Mormon university, which was to end only with his death. He was appointed Christiansen professor of poetry and head of the creative writing section of the department of English in 1985 and humanities professor of creative writing four years later. The Norrises lived in Orem, not far from Provo.

Norris's other published works included *Water Voices* (1980), *Sequences* (1988), and *A Sea in the Desert* (1989); a volume of translations of poems by Rainer Maria Rilke, *The Sonnets to Orpheus* (in collaboration with Alan Keele, 1989); and a second volume of stories, *The Girl from Cardigan* (1990), for which he was awarded the Hay literature festival prize. His monograph on Glyn Jones, another Merthyr man, appeared in the Writers of Wales series in 1973, and a Festschrift of essays on his work, *An Open World*, edited by Eugene England and Peter Makuck, was published in 1994, the year in which he was awarded the honorary degree of DLitt by the University of Glamorgan. His *Selected Poems* was published in 1986 and his *Collected Poems* and *Collected Stories* in 1996; his *Complete Poems* was published posthumously in 2008.

Norris was a complex man, easily hurt, ambivalent towards his native Wales, proud of his calling as a poet, staunch in his friendships, fond of thoroughbred terriers, and generous towards younger writers. Among his most anthologized poems were 'The Ballad of Billy Rose', about a boxer whom he had seen blinded in the ring, the delicately evocative 'Water', set at Y Wern, and 'Elegy for David Beynon', in memory of a teacher who, after the coal tip's slide onto the Pant-glas School at Aberfan in 1966, had been found dead at his desk and, under his arms, the bodies of four children whom he had been trying to protect from the slurry. From such local incidents Norris made poems of universal significance and great emotional power. If some critics saw him as essentially a poet writing in the English Georgian tradition, and others complained about his lack of social awareness and his preoccupation with the vanished world of his youth, he stuck steadfastly to his last, content to remain 'at the edge of things', that mysterious land where the familiar and the unfamiliar meet, and where his poems and stories had their abundant source. He died on 6 April 2006 in Provo, Utah, of a cerebral haemorrhage, and was survived by his wife, Kitty. MEIC STEPHENS

Sources J. A. Davies, *Leslie Norris* (1991) · E. England and P. Makuck, eds., *An open world: essays on Leslie Norris* (1994) · *Deseret Morning News* [Utah] (17 April 2006) · *The Independent* (10 April 2006) · *South Wales Echo* (11 April 2006) · *Western Morning News* (13 April 2006) · *The Herald* [Glasgow] (28 April 2006) · *The Times* (24 June 2006) · personal knowledge (2010) · private information (2010) [Kitty Norris, widow] · m. cert.

Archives Brigham Young University, Provo, Utah · NL Wales, corresp. and literary papers | FILM Brigham Young University, Provo, Utah | SOUND BL NSA, *The poet speaks*, British Council tapes, recorded 19 Oct 1965, M1474B BD 1 · BL NSA, current affairs recording · BL NSA, performance recordings · Brigham Young University, Provo, Utah

Likenesses J. Elwyn, oils, 1972, priv. coll. · B. Kershisnik, oils, 2001, Capitol, Salt Lake City, Utah

North, John David (1934–2008), historian, was born at 61 Kipling Road, Cheltenham, Gloucestershire, on 19 May 1934, the son of John Ernest North (1901–1987), wool buyer, and his wife, Gertrude Annie, *née* Lobley (1902–1989). Both parents were born in Bradford. After attending the grammar school at Batley in Yorkshire, where he distinguished himself in science and literature, North entered Merton College, Oxford, in 1953, as a postmaster in mathematics. He soon took up the broader challenge of philosophy, politics, and economics, in which he graduated in 1956. Halfway through his undergraduate career he met Alistair Crombie, then newly arrived as lecturer in the history of science, and also Marion Jean Pizzey (*b.* 1935), the daughter of James Herbert Pizzey, electrical engineer, to whom he became engaged after a brief courtship.

North postponed his move to Crombie's domain until he had a solid credential in science. He obtained it, an external London BSc degree in physics and astronomy, in 1958. Meanwhile he and Marion married, at Aylestone parish church, on 6 April 1957, and North began to study for a doctorate in the history and philosophy of science at Oxford while teaching full time at Magdalen College School. The work eased in 1963 when he won a five-year Nuffield research fellowship. Marion, who had experience as a librarian, was the perfect collaborator. She acted as sounding board, initiator, encourager, research assistant, and typist. In addition to the books and articles, three children (two daughters and a son) came from their partnership.

Fresh from his studies of modern physics and astronomy, North chose the development of cosmology during the first half of the twentieth century as his thesis topic; faithful to his interest in philosophy, he extracted an epistemology from the history he constructed. The thesis, published as *The Measure of the Universe* (1965), was not for readers unacquainted with tensors. It had a qualitative philosophical part, however, which tended toward the conventionalism of Henri Poincaré. Fortunately, North was not to follow Poincaré's dismissal of history as a sequence of unique and, consequently, uninteresting events. North grew to give priority to the individual and the 'sequence of unique and unrepeatable events' that constitute history (*The Universal Frame*, 353).

In 1968, his fellowship having lapsed, North became assistant curator and librarian at the Museum of the History of Science, Oxford, then directed by Francis Maddison. The museum's scholarly work centred on its outstanding collection of astrolabes and early modern navigational equipment. Led by Maddison into a 'medieval maze from which there was to be no escape' (*God's Clockmaker*, xvii), North mastered these instruments while continuing to help run Crombie's seminar and to teach throughout the growing programme in the history and philosophy of science. A professor was needed to pull it all together. In 1973, a board of electors chaired by the vice-chancellor, Sir Alan Bullock, and including Sir Rudolf Peierls, Hugh Trevor-Roper, and others whose interests did not align with Crombie's and Maddison's, chose one. The appointment—of Margaret Gowing, an economic and political historian who had written widely on atomic energy—stunned the inbred community of historians and philosophers of science.

Meanwhile, while exploring manuscripts in the Bodleian Library, North had discovered the oldest detailed description of a mechanical clock. This was the work of Richard of Wallingford (*c.*1292–1336), the leprous Benedictine abbot of St Albans. Richard designed several astronomical instruments and wrote about mathematics. North's transcription, translation, and elucidation of all the known treatises by him ran to three volumes, published in 1976. Only everything would do: 'the need for [completeness] in such a work as this should be as evident as the need to include uninteresting people in telephone directories' (*Richard of Wallingford*, 1.vii–viii). While working on *Richard of Wallingford* and at the museum, North also served as editor of the *Archives* of the Académie Internationale d'Histoire des Sciences, to which he was elected in 1967. For eleven years ending in 1978 he polished the English of papers submitted from remote places and, by printing them in the *Archives*, brought their authors to international attention. In 1983 he became the academy's permanent secretary and in 1989 its honorary permanent secretary with an everlasting seat on its executive council. His balance and fairness were frequently in demand.

In 1977, realizing that his hard work and growing reputation would not be rewarded at Oxford, North applied for and immediately obtained the chair of the history of philosophy at the University of Groningen. Determined to function fully in his new environment, he mastered Dutch and rose to be dean of the philosophical faculty (1990–93). Finding little else to do in the northern Netherlands, he became more productive than ever.

No one interested in the intellectual history of the middle ages and the Renaissance can avoid astrology. In 1986 North issued a guide to the subject, *Horoscopes and History*. It could not be recommended, as Chaucer did his treatise on the astrolabe, as 'bread and milk for children'. It systematized in unprecedented detail the various dissections of the ecliptic employed by astrologers in their house systems and demonstrated how adepts as ingenious as North could recover information of historical interest from technical minutiae in surviving horoscopes. His *Chaucer's Universe* (1988), which a reviewer in the *Times Literary Supplement* (2 Dec 1988) ranked as 'one of the century's monuments of scholarship', exemplified this recovery. It identified largely hidden astronomical and astrological references in Chaucer's poems, some of which give important insights into plot and narrative while others are so subtle that perhaps only North could see them.

North judged it important to bring the fruits of his scholarship to wider audiences. He began to review books for the *Times Literary Supplement* in 1964. Soon the editors listed his speciality as 'everything'. He contributed compulsively to general reference works: 27 articles in the *Dictionary of Scientific Biography* (1970–80), making him its most prolific collaborator, and 184 in the *Oxford Companion to Chaucer* (2003). He was a major contributor to the *Storia della scienza* (2001), the second volume of the *History of the University of Oxford* (1992), and the *Oxford DNB* (2004). At Marion's suggestion he took on the entire history of astronomy at a level accessible to all readers 'in a historical frame of mind'. These, he now decided, were his chief audience: 'No professional historian ever admits of being pleased by universal history, but then, the sort of history that can only satisfy professional historians of science is hardly worth writing.' *The Fontana History of Astronomy and Cosmology* (1994, published in the USA as *The Norton History of Astronomy and Cosmology*) ran from 'pre-history' through many cultures up to the end of the twentieth century. It did not have the reception North professed to expect. The professional historians of astronomy immediately recognized his book as a classic.

While his general history was moving through the press, North was finishing another tour de force, *Stonehenge: Neolithic Man and his Cosmos* (1996), which began with a long analysis of long barrows. North worked out that a neolithic astronomer's eye would sight stars over the artificial horizon of the barrow's roof if he stood in the ditch surrounding it. Applying similar analyses to Stonehenge, he concluded that in its first version it served to sight stars and only in later versions the sun: not the midsummer sunrise as is commonly believed, but midwinter sunset. Like *Chaucer's Universe*, North's *Stonehenge* was a bold reworking of a well-ploughed field; and, also like the earlier book, its general approach is likely to stand although, as North conceded, some of its special interpretations may not. During his stay in Groningen he also published two thick volumes of reprinted essays, *The Universal Frame* and *Stars, Minds and Fate* (both 1989).

On retirement in 1999 North returned to Oxford. He had hoped to do so earlier, but had been disappointed in his bid to succeed Gowing after her retirement in 1986. He had time in retirement for three more books, one of them a new departure. This was *The Ambassadors' Secret* (2002), inspired by the restoration of Hans Holbein's masterpiece and a suggestion by Marion. North established that the astronomical instruments featured in the painting point to 4 p.m. on Good Friday, 1533, exactly a millennium and a half after the Crucifixion. The sun then stood 27° above the horizon, which is also the angle at which the viewer must look down at the anamorphosis in the foreground to see it as a human skull. Looking upward from the same position, again at 27°, the viewer sees a crucifix half hidden behind a curtain. Trinity taken three times is 27. More controversially, North determined that certain items, which can be read as planetary symbols, fall within a virtual horoscope in a standard format imagined superimposed over the middle of the picture. Most reviewers judged *The Ambassadors' Secret* to be a fascinating tour through Renaissance culture, and, in places, an exciting mystery. However, the mystery and the technical arguments met resistance from connoisseurs disquieted by the transformation of a familiar painting into a puzzle. *The Ambassadors' Secret* became the most controversial of North's books. It was the one of which he was fondest.

God's Clockmaker: Richard of Wallingford and the Invention of Time (2006) presented what little is known about the man against a detailed rendering of the political and social circumstances in which his abbey operated. With it and *Cosmos* (2008), an updating of *Astronomy and Cosmology*, North returned to less adventuresome topics. He had not lost his touch. *Cosmos* was probably the best single-volume survey of astronomy ever written. It improved on its earlier version at both ends and in many interspersed addenda, including 200 new illustrations. Naturally, North favoured certain topics. Responding in advance to the criticism that he had slighted astral religions, he wrote what might be taken as his historiographical credo: 'astrology and cosmic religion are commonplace, viewed as symptoms of the human condition. The long record of achievement in astronomy, on the other hand, has very few intellectual parallels in the whole of human history' (*Cosmos*, 3).

North received his share of ordinary high academic honours—made a DLitt of Oxford (1993), he was elected to the British Academy (1992), the royal academies of science of Denmark and the Netherlands (both 1985), and the Academia Leopoldina (1992), and received a knighthood in the Orde van de Nederlandse Leeuw (1999) and unstinting admiration from his colleagues. His technical mastery and playful inventiveness, learning, and wit, and his willingness to serve his profession and to share his knowledge, made him formidable as a scholar, admirable as a man, and a treasure as a colleague. With Marion's constant help, he made a smooth join between his work and his family. He died of cancer at the John Radcliffe Hospital, Oxford, on 31 October 2008. He was survived by Marion, their three children, and several grandchildren, for whose use and amusement he had liked to cannibalize old computers. J. L. HEILBRON

Sources *Oxford University Calendar* (1973) · A. V. Simcock, ed., *Robert T. Gunther and the Old Ashmolean* (1985), 93–4 · *Oxford Gazette* (17 Jan 1972); (8 June 1972); (21 Jan 1988); (24 June 1988) · *PBA*, 97 (1998), 257–70 · A. Bullock, 'Margaret Gowing, an appreciation', *Science, politics and the public good: essays in honour of Margaret Gowing*, ed. N. A. Rupke (1988), 1–66 · J. D. North, *The universal frame* (1989), 61–2 · A. C. Crombie, *Science, optics and music in medieval and early modern thought* (1990), 453–64 · *Directory* [Académie Internationale d'Histoire des Sciences] (2002) · *The Times* (12 Nov 2008) · *The Guardian* (22 Nov 2008) · *The Independent* (24 Nov 2008) · *Daily Telegraph* (28 Nov 2008) · *WW* (2008) · personal knowledge (2012) · private information (2012) [Marion North, widow] · b. cert. · m. cert. · d. cert.

Wealth at death £677,161: probate, 22 April 2009, *CGPLA Eng. & Wales*

Norwood [*née* Sirnis], **Melita Stedman** [Letty] (**1912–2005**), spy, was born on 25 March 1912 at 402 Christchurch Road, Bournemouth, the elder daughter of (Peter) Alexander Sirnis (1881–1918), estate manager, and his wife, Gertrude Elizabeth Gurney, *née* Stedman (1878–1967), cobbler. An elder brother, Wilfrid, had died in infancy, and she had a half-brother, Alfred, from her mother's first marriage. Her father had been born in Lemsal, Latvia, and was a follower of the Russian writer Lev Tolstoy. After Tolstoy had been banished to his estates at Yasnaya Polyana his literary executor, Vladimir Chertkov, was exiled overseas and settled in the small Hampshire village of Tuckton. He brought with him Tolstoy's manuscripts and occupied a large Victorian mansion, Tuckton House, on behalf of the Tolstoy Fund. Chertkov initially invited Alexander Sirnis, then living in America, to Tuckton to work as a translator. On arrival he took over the duties of estate manager, and joined the Marxist British Socialist Party. During his stay at Tuckton he translated Tolstoy's diaries, several short stories by Maxim Gorky, and Lenin's *The Collapse of the Second International*, and met Melita's English mother, Gertrude, then a young widow, who worked as the community's cobbler. Her first husband, Carl Brandt, had died of influenza in Spain in 1902. Melita's parents married in 1909. Her sister Gerty was born in 1914 in Davos, where her father was undergoing treatment for tuberculosis. The family returned to England in 1915. By this time the First World War had reached a bloody stalemate and Alexander Sirnis discarded Tolstoyism for Bolshevism. He died of tuberculosis in November 1918.

In 1923 Melita Sirnis (or Letty, as she was known to friends and family) won a scholarship to Itchen School, a mixed secondary school near Southampton, where in 1928 she became school captain. In 1930 she went to Southampton University College to study Latin and logic. She was a poor student and failed to complete her course. In 1931, accompanied by her mother and sister, she went to Heidelberg for ten months, where she became involved in anti-fascist activities. Back in England she joined the Independent Labour Party, and in 1932 started work as a secretary with the British Non-Ferrous Metals Research Association (BN-FMRA), where she became an organizer for the Association of Women Clerks and Secretaries. At the time she was living in the same house as her future husband, Hilary Nussbaum (1911–1986), and his parents, Bronislau and Dora, Russian Jews who had emigrated from Russian Poland in the 1900s. Letty and Hilary shared the same politics, and sold the *Daily Worker* and *Labour Leader* on Saturday mornings outside Golders Green underground station. Both were members of the Friends of the Soviet Union and in 1934, after a meeting on the shortage of tractor parts on collective farms, she was recruited to the NKVD, the forerunner of the KGB, by Andrew Rothstein. She joined the British Communist Party the following year. In November 1935 Hilary Anglicized his name to Norwood, and on 14 December the couple married, at Barnet register office.

Norwood's spying career began in 1938 when she was involved with a spy ring operating inside the Woolwich arsenal. On the outbreak of the Second World War BN-FMRA was evacuated to Berkhamsted, Hertfordshire, a fortunate choice as the Norwoods had earlier moved to Cheshunt following Hilary's employment as a mathematics teacher at Cheshunt School. In 1943 Norwood gave birth to her daughter, Anita, returning to work the following year. She was then working for the director of BN-FMRA, G. L. Bailey, who was a member of the advisory committee of Tube Alloys, Britain's atomic bomb project. In March 1945, after BN-FMRA won a contract from Tube Alloys, Norwood (codenamed Hola, or Tina) gained access to documents that Moscow Centre described as being 'of great interest and a valuable contribution to the development of the work in this field' (*The Times*, 11 Sept 1999). Arguably the information she supplied on the behaviour of uranium metal at high temperatures permitted the Soviet Union to test an atomic bomb four years earlier than British and American intelligence thought possible.

At the end of the war the Norwoods moved to Bexley in Kent. In 1958 she joined the Campaign for Nuclear Disarmament, and was awarded the order of the Red Banner by the KGB. In 1960 the KGB offered her a pension of £20 a month which she declined. In 1967 she recruited a civil servant codenamed Hunt, who for fourteen years provided extensive scientific, technical, and other intelligence on British arms sales. She retired from both the

Melita Stedman Norwood (1912–2005), by Chris Harris, 1999

BN-FMRA and the KGB in 1973, and became involved in local politics. In 1986, following her husband's death, Bexley Trades Union Council established the Hilary Norwood trophy, to be awarded for the best piece of writing on trade-union history in local schools. She was exposed as a spy by *The Times* newspaper on 11 September 1999, shortly before the publication by Christopher Andrew and Vasily Mitrokhin of *The Mitrokhin Archive*, based on KGB documents smuggled out of Russia by Mitrokhin. She remained utterly unrepentant. The home secretary, Jack Straw, claimed that the information she had provided could only have been of marginal significance for the Russian atomic weapons programme, though the documents in the Mitrokhin archive suggested otherwise; in the event she was never prosecuted. She died of cancer and heart disease at New Cross Hospital, Wolverhampton, on 2 June 2005, having moved in 2003 to Wombourne, Staffordshire, to be near her daughter, who survived her.

DAVID BURKE

Sources C. Andrew and V. Mitrokhin, *The Mitrokhin archive* (1999) · *The Times* (11 Sept 1999); (28 June 2005) · *The Independent* (14 June 2000); (6 July 2005) · *The Guardian* (28 June 2005) · *Daily Telegraph* (29 June 2005) · *The Observer* (3 July 2005) · D. Burke, *The spy who came in from the Co-op* (2008) · personal knowledge (2009) · private information (2009) · b. cert. · m. cert. · d. cert.

Archives U. Leeds, Brotherton L., Tuckton House papers, MS 1381

Likenesses S. Bell, photograph, 1999, PA Photos, London · C. Harris, photograph, 1999, Rex Features, London [*see illus.*] · C. Harris, photographs, 1999, PA Photos, London · photographs, 1999, Rex Features, London · obituary photographs · photograph, repro. in *The Times* · photographs, repro. in Burke, *The spy*

Wealth at death £177,000: probate, 10 Aug 2005, *CGPLA Eng. & Wales*

Nuttall, Anthony David [Tony] (**1937–2007**), literary scholar, was born on 25 April 1937 at 150 Whitecross Road, Hereford, the younger son of Kenneth Nuttall, schoolteacher, and his wife, Hilda Mary, *née* Addison. His brother, Jeff *Nuttall (1933–2004), was a celebrated figure in the 1960s counter-culture—poet, artist, musician, and author of *Bomb Culture* (1968). The two boys enjoyed childhood together in rural Herefordshire, but if Jeff strayed far from his origins, Anthony, known as Tony, was always spiritually close to his roots, and remained devoted to long walks in the countryside until his death. He was educated at Hereford Cathedral School and Watford grammar school, and went to Merton College, Oxford, in 1955. There he formed a lifelong friendship with his fellow undergraduate Stephen Medcalf. Both read for classical moderations (in which both took seconds) before switching to study English (in which both graduated with firsts), both became literary scholars and critics, both taught at the University of Sussex, and both died in the same year. Nuttall's handsome, classical features and dark curly hair, coupled with his wit and charm, made him the heartthrob of 'half the girls at Oxford' (*The Independent*, 8 Feb 2007). On 1 July 1960, at Leeds register office, he married Mary Donagh (*b.* 1933), a fellow student, later a secondary school teacher, daughter of Ernest Percy Donagh, engineer's toolmaker. They had a son and a daughter.

Nuttall retained strong interests in classics and philosophy, which he applied throughout his career to the analysis of English literature. His BLitt thesis (1963) was on the philosophical implications of Shakespeare's *The Tempest*, and formed the basis of his second book, *Two Concepts of Allegory* (1967). (His first was a short study of *The Winter's Tale*, published in Edward Arnold's Studies in English Literature series in 1966.) He had appreciative supervisors of his work in the philosopher and novelist Iris Murdoch and later the philosopher Tony Quinton. Indeed Murdoch described Nuttall and Medcalf as the most brilliant students she ever taught. But it was said that his path to a doctorate was blocked by the traditionalism of another well-known Oxford figure, Helen Gardner, who objected to the combination of philosophy with literary criticism.

Nuttall had begun lecturing at the University of Sussex in 1962, a year after its foundation, in an institution where interdisciplinarity, the mark of his early work, was embedded in the very structure and ethos of the university. He was appointed to a readership and chair at Sussex in 1970 and 1973 respectively, and to the horror of some colleagues took on the administrative role of a pro-vice-chancellor between 1978 and 1981. But growing responsibilities did not blunt the extraordinary range of his interests or the abundance of his publications. *A Common Sky: Philosophy and the Literary Imagination* (1974) examined the relationship between literature and the reality of the external world—one of Nuttall's distinctive interests—in Locke, Hume, Sterne, Wordsworth, and others. A study of *Crime and Punishment* in 1978 considered the murder committed by Raskolnikov as an experiment in philosophy. The book grew out of a course on the modern European mind that Nuttall had helped to devise and teach at Sussex. Two years later *Overheard by God*, a study of the devotional poetry of George Herbert, Milton, and Dante, considered how God could be made the subject of literature. *A New Mimesis: Shakespeare and the Representation of Reality* (1983) was published when the vogue for literary theory was especially intense and was an eloquent defence of traditional ways of thinking and writing about literature in opposition to the then rising tide of discourse analysis and Jacques Derrida's 'deconstructionism'. Much of it was based on Nuttall's close reading of Shakespeare, but in its appreciative use of structuralism it was never merely traditional or reactionary. Nuttall's last book written at Sussex was his study *Pope's Essay on Man* (1984).

Nuttall seems to have grown weary of Sussex, perhaps as a result of disenchantment with student radicalism and some ignorant criticism of his work in a local student newspaper. His wife noticed that a fellowship in English at New College, Oxford, had just been advertised and Nuttall was duly elected in 1984, though he was much older than the norm for an appointment as a college tutorial fellow. He explained the reasons for his return to Oxford with a characteristic mix of truth and humour: 'I want to spend the morning in a library which has every book I could possibly want, and then have lunch in a pub not designed by Basil Spence' (*PBA*, 315). Though it entailed more teaching and a cut in salary as compared with his previous position,

Nuttall thrived in collegiate life. The breadth of his interests and publications were well suited to the range of undergraduate teaching he now undertook and he was an inspiring, generous, indiscreet, and always entertaining tutor. In 1992 he was appointed to a personal chair at Oxford.

Despite Nuttall's new responsibilities, publications on the most diverse subjects, all written with his blend of philosophical rigour and playful, witty criticism, continued as before. A brilliant study of *Timon of Athens* (1989) was followed by a collection of his essays, *The Stoic in Love* (1989). *Openings: Narrative Beginnings from the Epic to the Novel* (1992) explored how works of literature start; his next work, *Why Does Tragedy Give Pleasure?* (1996), first delivered as the 1992 Northcliffe lectures at University College, London, analysed how tragic heroes come to their end and why we find that compelling. In his study of gnostic heresy in Marlowe, Milton, and Blake, *The Alternative Trinity* (1998), he returned to his earlier theme of the relations between literature and theology. A quite different subject then formed the basis of his penultimate book, *Dead from the Waist Down: Scholars and Scholarship in Literature and the Popular Imagination* (2003). It cleverly wove together the life and work of Isaac Casaubon, the Renaissance classical scholar; Mark Pattison, the nineteenth-century Oxford don who spent many years studying Casaubon, though he never completed and published his great work on the man; and the dessicated pedant Edward Casaubon, supposedly based on Pattison, who appears in George Eliot's *Middlemarch*. The book was dedicated 'to Oxford'. Nuttall's final work, published posthumously, was *Shakespeare the Thinker* (2007), and in it he returned to his first theme and abiding interest: the place of philosophy in Shakespeare's works. In between his first and this last work Nuttall had followed his remarkably broad interests across four centuries of English literature, exemplifying the best traditions of humane criticism and close reading.

Nuttall was elected a fellow of the British Academy in 1997. When he retired in 2004 he had to vacate his rooms in New College. The college bursar looked the other way when Nuttall found himself another room elsewhere in the college and began to 'squat'. He was found there on 24 January 2007, having died from a heart attack. A Festschrift entitled *Thinking with Shakespeare*, composed of essays by his colleagues and friends and including 'The last word' by Nuttall himself, was published shortly after his death. He was survived by his wife and children.

LAWRENCE GOLDMAN

Sources *Daily Telegraph* (3 Feb 2007) · *The Independent* (8 Feb 2007) · *The Times* (9 Feb 2007) · *The Guardian* (27 March 2007) · *New College Record* (2007), 74–9 · *PBA*, 161 (2009), 313–30 · *WW* (2007) · b. cert. · m. cert. · d. cert.

Likenesses R. Hamilton, oil on montage, New College, Oxford; repro. in *New College Record* · R. Hamilton, photograph, repro. in *PBA* · obituary photographs

Wealth at death under £53,000: probate, 18 Sept 2007, *CGPLA Eng. & Wales*

Nuttall, Geoffrey Fillingham (1911–2007), Congregational minister and church historian, was born at Bryn-y-graig, Conway Road, Colwyn Bay, Denbighshire, on 8 November 1911, the younger son and second of three children of Harold Nuttall (1871–1950), general medical practitioner, and his first wife, Muriel Fillingham, *née* Hodgson (1880–1931). He was a delicate, sensitive child, who was often ill. Although he later learnt Welsh he always regarded himself as English. Deeply conscious that he was descended from generations of Congregational ministers on both sides of his family, he determined at an early age to become a minister. From Baswich House School, near Stafford (where his uncle was headmaster), he won a scholarship to the Quaker Bootham School, York, which confirmed him as a lifelong pacifist. Though one of his masters, A. Neave Brayshaw, was an important influence he was poorly taught, studying mainly through his own efforts. On the advice of W. B. Selbie, principal of Mansfield College, Oxford, another strong influence, he entered Balliol College, Oxford, in 1929 to read *literae humaniores*, but only obtained a third in 1933. This was partly explained by his pursuit of other scholarly interests, including assisting the Erasmus scholar Percy Allen with his *Opus epistolarum*. Nuttall retained a lifelong interest in Erasmus, and similarly in Dante, for which he learnt Italian. At Oxford he made two important friendships, with the medieval historian Richard Southern, and the educationist Roy Niblett. Their correspondence is now at Dr Williams's Library.

Nuttall was a ministerial student at Mansfield College between 1933 and 1936, but was out of sympathy with the new principal, Nathaniel Micklem. He spent a year (1936–7) studying in Marburg, where he attended the lectures of Rudolf Bultmann and met Theodor Sippell, the scholar of puritanism, but he also saw Nazism at first hand. In 1938 he graduated BD, and the same year, on 4 May, he was ordained minister of the Congregational church at Warminster, Wiltshire. It was not easy being a pacifist in a military town, and he did not enjoy pastoral work, though he discharged it faithfully. In October 1943 he became a research fellow at Woodbrooke, the Quaker college in Selly Oak, Birmingham. There he wrote what became *The Holy Spirit in Puritan Faith and Experience* (1946), writing a chapter a week, drawing on research begun at Warminster. In January 1945 he submitted his thesis. He was one of the youngest, and only the second nonconformist, to be awarded an Oxford DD degree. On 5 September 1944, at the Friends' meeting house in Colthouse, Lancashire, he married Mary Powley *née* Preston (1901–1982), secretary of Woodbrooke. The widow of George Philip Powley, and daughter of William Preston, a merchant, she was a former Congregationalist who had become a Quaker. They had no children.

In 1945 Nuttall was appointed lecturer in church history at New College, London, part of the faculty of theology in the University of London, which trained Congregational ministers. He remained until the college closed in 1977, when he oversaw the transfer of its historic collections to Dr Williams's Library, where he served as a trustee for fifty years until 1997. As New College librarian he had devoted a great deal of time to identifying the books that had belonged to the earlier dissenting academies and their tutors. Dr Williams's Library lay at the heart of his interests.

During his years at New College Nuttall's reputation as an exacting and severe scholar and critic developed. Gordon Rupp advised his successor at Manchester, Basil Hall, never to allow Nuttall to be an external examiner. Certainly his criticism could seem severe, but it was a measure of his own very high standards and scholarly integrity. Some of his students at New College found him terrifying. He in turn was disappointed that not one of them undertook a research degree. A man who ate his breakfast cereal without milk, but who enjoyed sharing a Cadbury's chocolate cake with his visitors over tea, a scholar whose concern for the books in his care was evident, but whose own (many now at Dr Williams's Library) contain his annotations and corrections in ball-point, a committed Congregationalist and Christian who numbered Catholics and Unitarians among his friends, might seem a paradox. What resolved the paradox was his consistently warm, generous, and painstaking help of those he thought serious, including many younger scholars. He maintained a regular and extensive handwritten correspondence (much of which was preserved by its recipients for its content), which often overflowed into the margins, and even onto the envelope. An increasingly isolated figure in his own denomination, in 1972 he reluctantly sided with the Congregationalists and Presbyterians who formed the United Reformed church.

Nuttall was the outstanding historian of the puritan tradition. Much of his work focused on people and was characterized by a concern with evangelical Christianity; his subjects included notably Richard Baxter, George Fox, and John Bunyan in the seventeenth century, Isaac Watts and Philip Doddridge in the early eighteenth, and Whitefield, Wesley, and the countess of Huntingdon in the late eighteenth. His calendars of the Quaker Swarthmore letters, the correspondence of Baxter (with N. H. Keeble) and of Doddridge, his introduction to George Fox's *Journal*, and his analysis of the surviving manuscript of *Reliquiae Baxterianae*, were invaluable contributions to historical knowledge. Besides *Holy Spirit* his most influential studies were *Visible Saints: the Congregational Way, 1640–1660* (1957; second edn, 2001), *The Welsh Saints, 1640–1660* (1958; second edn, 1971), *Richard Baxter* (1965), and *The Puritan Spirit* (1967). Wider interests included Benedictine monasticism, Swiss and Dutch church history, and Welsh poetry. The Benedictine David Knowles proved a crucial influence in the development of his ideas. Astonishingly productive, Nuttall published over 600 items, much after he retired. So long was his publishing career (his first book, *The Letters of John Pinney, 1679–1699*, was published in 1939) that in 1992 Chicago University Press republished *Holy Spirit* without permission, certain he was dead. The republication demonstrated the rediscovery of Nuttall's work by a new generation of scholars appreciative of his insights, though generally neglecting the subject closest to his heart, religious faith itself.

Nuttall never obtained a university chair, despite at least three attempts, but he received many of the honours of a leading academic. He gave the F. D. Maurice lectures at King's College, London (1970), and the Charles Gore lectures in Westminster Abbey (1968). He was made honorary DD by the University of Wales (1969), was made a vice-president of the Honourable Society of Cymmrodorion (a rare tribute for an Englishman) in 1978, and in 1972 was president of the Ecclesiastical History Society. He had served as president of the Friends' Historical Society in 1953, the Congregational History Society from 1965 to 1972, and the United Reformed Church History Society from 1972 to 1977. He was elected a fellow of the British Academy in 1991. On his retirement King's College, London, made him a visiting professor, and he received a Festschrift, *Reformation, Conformity and Dissent* (1977), with essays from such leading scholars as Owen Chadwick, Patrick Collinson, A. G. Dickens, and Christopher Hill. He was invited to preach university sermons at Oxford (twice), Cambridge, London, and Leeds.

In 1979 Nuttall moved from Hampstead Garden Suburb to Bournville, Birmingham, with a small but carefully chosen library. After suffering a stroke in 2000 he entered a nursing home, Burcot Grange, Burcot, near Bromsgrove, Worcestershire. He died there on 24 July 2007 of bronchopneumonia. He left his residual estate to support the New College collection at Dr Williams's Library.

David L. Wykes

Sources T. Liu, 'A bibliography of the writings of Geoffrey F. Nuttall', *Reformation, conformity and dissent: essays in honour of Geoffrey Nuttall*, ed. R. Buick Knox (1977) · *Journal of the United Reformed Church History Society*, 5 (1996), 511–43 [includes bibliography, 1977–1996] · C. Binfield, 'Profile: Geoffrey Nuttall, the formation of an Independent historian', *Epworth Review*, 25 (1998), 79–106 · *Daily Telegraph* (14 Aug 2007) · *The Independent* (14 Aug 2007) · *The Times* (29 Aug 2007) · *The Guardian* (12 Sept 2007) · N. H. Keeble, 'Geoffrey F. Nuttall (1911–2007): puritan scholar', 16 Nov 2007, dspace.stir.ac.uk/dspace/bitstream/1893/1459/1/GFN.pdf, 21 July 2010 · E. Duffy, 'Geoffrey Nuttall: a friendship in letters', *Congregational History Magazine*, 5/4 (2008), 212–20 · A. P. F. Sell, 'Geoffrey Nuttall in conversation', *Journal of the United Reformed Church History Society*, 8/5 (2009), 266–90 · *Balliol College Register* · Nuttall papers, DWL · *WW* (2007) · personal knowledge (2011) · private information (2011) · b. cert. · m. cert. · d. cert.

Archives DWL

Likenesses obituary photographs

Wealth at death under £282,000: probate, 15 Nov 2007, *CGPLA Eng. & Wales*

Obote, (Apolo) Milton (1925–2005), prime minister and president of Uganda, was born on 28 December 1925 at Akokoro in Lira district, Lango, northern Uganda, the son of Stanley Opeto Anyanga, a farmer who eventually became a minor chief, and his second wife, Priscilla Acen Eyer.

Education and early political career Obote was educated in Church of Uganda (Anglican) schools. Starting his schooling in 1936 at Ibuje elementary vernacular school for boys, he went on to an elementary school at Boroboro, thence to Gulu high school, and finally to Busoga College, Mwiri, where he took his school certificate. At each stage he strove, almost obsessively, to come top of the class. From Mwiri he gained entrance to Makerere College, Kampala,

(Apolo) **Milton Obote** (1925–2005), by Peter Kemp, 1983

where he wanted to study law, which Makerere did not then teach. He therefore took a general arts course studying English, geography, and general studies. He was at Makerere for the years 1948 and 1949, but he then left after an apparent mix-up over an offer of a place to study law abroad that the protectorate government would not fund. This left him with a grudge against the colonial authority. He went to Kenya briefly before returning to Uganda and finding employment with the construction company Mowlem, and in 1952 joined the newly formed Uganda National Congress. When sent to Kenya for the second time by Mowlem he was active in the Kenya African Union.

There was less popular pressure for independence in Uganda than in Kenya and Tanganyika: there were hardly any white settlers and protectorate rule had been relatively benign. The country faced two main problems on the road to independence. The first was the ambition of the Buganda kingdom to retain the privileged status it had enjoyed under protectorate rule, even if that meant secession. The second was the religious divide between the Roman Catholics and the protestants (the Anglican Church of Uganda). There were virtually no other Christian denominations in Uganda. A plethora of political parties emerged, fissured, and merged again until only two remained: the Democratic Party, identified with the Roman Catholics, and the protestant Uganda People's Congress (UPC), of which Obote emerged as the leader. The parties strove to overcome this sectarian identification but in the pre-independence elections of 1961 the Democratic Party defeated the UPC largely because the mainly protestant Ganda boycotted the election. Benedicto Kiwanuka then became Uganda's first prime minister. When new national elections were held in April 1962 Obote forged an alliance with the royalist Kabaka Yekka ('the king alone') party of Buganda, in order to win, and succeeded Kiwanuka as prime minister. At independence on 9 October 1962 Obote remained prime minister, as he did following the declaration of a republic exactly a year later, when the *kabaka* of Buganda, Frederick Mutesa, became president. On 11 November 1963 Obote married Miria Kalule (*b.* 1936), with whom he had four sons.

Prime minister and president In January 1964 Obote faced his first challenge in the shape of a mutiny in the over-rapidly expanded army at the main barracks at Jinja, Uganda's second city and the site of the only bridge over the Nile. No one has ever fully explained why the armies of all three east African countries should have mutinied in the same month, though dissatisfaction with pay and promotion were issues. The presidents of all three countries called in British troops to quell the mutinies. Before these could arrive in Uganda, Obote sent Felix Onama, minister of defence, to negotiate with the mutineers. He was taken captive by them and gave in to most of their demands, including huge pay rises and rapid promotions. A contingent of 450 British soldiers then put down the mutiny without a shot being fired. Obote made the mistake that neither of the other east African presidents did, of failing to discipline the mutineers, for which he was later to pay dearly. Among those too rapidly promoted was Idi *Amin, who had escaped court martial for a massacre committed under his command. He was one of only two Ugandan commissioned officers and neither the governor nor Obote felt it would be wise to court-martial him on the eve of independence. Obote came to regret this decision. The following April, Obote set up the General Service Unit, dedicated to countering insurgency and under the command of Akena Adoko, a close associate.

Having used the Kabaka Yekka to gain power Obote now worked to render this alliance unnecessary and establish a one-party state. By July 1964 sufficient Democratic Party and Kabaka Yekka members of the national assembly had been induced to cross the floor and join the UPC to render the alliance unnecessary. The pretext for Obote to take over the presidency occurred two years later. He was secretly aiding the Simba rebels against President Moise Tshombe of Congo on the grounds that Tshombe was a puppet of Western capitalist interests. Obote kept this secret, even from his cabinet, not all of whom would have approved. Amin was entrusted with gold and ivory by the rebels to be used in payment for arms; he later deposited the equivalent of £24,000 sterling into his personal bank account. Early in 1966, when Obote was away from Kampala, an MP, Daudi Ocheng, who was dying of cancer and knew he would therefore be secure against victimization, accused Amin in the national assembly of embezzling the money and called for an inquiry into the actions of Amin, Obote, and two other government ministers who, he claimed, had taken their share of the proceeds. This call had the overwhelming support of MPs and provided a focus for their distrust of Obote. On his return to Kampala, Obote detained five ministers whom he suspected of plotting to overthrow him, and appointed a judge of the court of appeal of eastern Africa, Sir Clement Nageon De Lestang, to hold an inquiry, whose findings, however, were not published until after Obote had been ousted from power. Obote then introduced a new constitution, which he forced the national assembly to accept unseen (it was known as the 'pigeonhole constitution': MPs were told they could collect it from their pigeonholes after the debate was over). Obote went on to declare himself president with full executive powers and appointed Amin head of the army, which was recruited mainly from the supposedly warlike peoples of northern Uganda, as had been colonial practice.

The *kabaka* refused to accept Obote's usurpation of power, and on 20 May the Buganda parliament ordered the Ugandan government off Bugandan soil within ten days. Obote's response was to impose a state of emergency and on 24 May he ordered the army under Amin to investigate reports that there was a cache of arms in the *kabaka*'s palace. The troops overran the palace in a day-long bloody battle in which many Ganda were killed or wounded. The *kabaka* escaped over the back wall, eventually finding refuge in Britain. The Ganda elsewhere rose in the *kabaka*'s defence, and were violently suppressed: the army high command had difficulty in restraining the troops. These events left the Ganda with a lasting hatred of Obote. A state of emergency was imposed in Buganda that remained in force as long as Obote remained in power. In September 1967 Obote abolished all the pre-colonial kingdoms of southern and western Uganda. Because the army had been used to resolve a political matter, Obote and all successive Ugandan governments became dependent on it.

In the next two years Obote moved to restrict the Asians who dominated the import–export trade (this was a popular move), and towards the end of 1969 announced the 'move to the left', to be expounded in five documents. The first, announced in October, was the 'National service proposal', and the second in December was 'The common man's charter'. A few days later, on 19 December, an assassination attempt was made on Obote in Lugogo stadium. There was no one but soldiers in the area of the stadium from which the shots were fired. Obote was not seriously hurt, but was rushed to hospital through streets where his army escort shot at bystanders. Responsibility for the attempt was never firmly placed, but Amin fled Kampala and was believed to be implicated. Throughout 1970 further policy initiatives were taken to implement the 'move to the left'. In April and May many companies were nationalized, investors took fright, and an economic crisis followed, with imported goods ceasing to be available and supermarket shelves emptying while the value of the Ugandan currency fell against both sterling and the dollar. In November 1970 Obote expelled 33,000 Kenyan workers, which damaged the economy further, though some began filtering back fairly soon.

The Amin regime While Obote was attending a Commonwealth heads of government meeting in Singapore, Amin seized power in a coup on 25 January 1971. The immediate cause seems to have been an attempt by Obote to curb military expenditure. His failure to exert control over the army now proved to be his undoing. It had been a disastrous mistake not to court-martial Amin for the pre-independence massacre and then to promote him. Obote had other shortcomings as well. He lacked the charisma of the other east African leaders, Jomo Kenyatta of Kenya and Julius Nyerere of Tanzania. He was a tactician and manipulator rather than an orator and populist. Uganda lacked any common language in which he could address the nation, nor did Uganda have any slogan around which support could focus, like Kenya's *Harambee* ('togetherness') and Tanzania's *Ujamaa* ('familyhood'). The 'move to the left' and 'The common man's charter' were attempts to fill this gap, but they came too late and failed to capture the popular imagination.

Throughout the period of Amin's rule Obote was given sanctuary in Tanzania by President Julius Nyerere, who shared his socialist views. The chance of making a comeback occurred in 1978–9 when Amin tried to divert attention away from the murderous factions forming within his army by invading Tanzania's Kagera salient, a triangle of land adjacent to south-west Uganda, in response to alleged provocations by Tanzanian troops. Tanzanian forces, together with a small contingent of Ugandan exiles loyal to Obote, counter-attacked. Finding no serious resistance, they fought their way on foot to Kampala, which they reached on 10 April 1979, and thence pushed through to the Sudan border. Obote had been sidelined at the Moshi unity conference held in March 1979 by exiled Ugandan leaders to plan their next moves. His return to fight elections in early 1980 was engineered by Paulo Muwanga, who had emerged as the strong man, after the two disastrous, but short-lived, presidencies of Yusufu Lule and Godfrey Binaisa. The 1980 elections were shamelessly rigged after the Commonwealth observer group had left so as to return Obote and the UPC to power, a result that was not accepted by a large part of the Ugandan population.

Second presidency Obote's second presidency was marked, not mainly by what he did, but by what he omitted to do. His overriding failure was shared with Muwanga: between them they failed to bring the largely untrained Uganda National Liberation Army under control or to prevent tribal factionalism developing within it. Acholi and Langi troops, who had suffered most from Amin, took early revenge against West Nile, the district from which Amin and many of his followers had come. By mid-1983 there were nearly 100,000 refugees from West Nile in Zaire and Sudan. By 1984 a few had returned under a scheme operated by the United Nations High Commission for Refugees, but many remained in exile until Obote had been overthrown.

In order to halt the economic decline Obote's government dropped all pretensions to socialism, accepting World Bank and International Monetary Fund advisers. As a result the West, and Britain in particular, turned a blind eye to reports of atrocities. In the context of the cold war, Yoweri Museveni, whose well-disciplined Uganda Resistance Army and Movement was winning popular support in western Uganda, was seen as dangerously left-wing, whereas Obote's new dedication to capitalism aligned Uganda with Western interests in this part of Africa and helped provide a bulwark against socialist Tanzania and Sudan.

The undisciplined forces of the Ugandan army having driven many Ugandans into exile, Obote now turned against those who had taken refuge in Uganda, blaming them for atrocities committed by Uganda's unruly troops. The Rwandese were popular targets, accused of taking land. In 1982 members of the UPC youth wing in Ankole in south-western Uganda turned on those who had been settled on land near the border with Rwanda, and eventually against all Rwandese, no matter how long they had been in Uganda or whether or not they were Ugandan citizens—and many of them were. Many were driven back into Rwanda, where they were not permitted to leave the border areas, or were trapped on the border. All speakers of Kinyarwanda who remained in Uganda were eventually moved to refugee camps elsewhere, whether they were refugees or not. The expulsion of Rwandese and their subsequent mistreatment had long-term consequences. Rwandese naturally turned to support Yoweri Museveni's insurgency and joined the National Resistance Army, which eventually ousted Obote from power. These were the people who subsequently defected from the National Resistance Army and invaded Rwanda in 1990, and it was in the context of this invasion that the Rwandan genocide of 1994 was sparked off.

When Museveni's forces moved to the Luwero Triangle to the north-west of the capital in 1982–3, the Uganda National Liberation Army responded by rounding up the civilian population, placing them in camps, and shooting them as insurgents if they ventured out to find food or water. The Uganda government eventually had to call in the international aid agencies to deal with what the agencies considered an emergency of the government's own making, but one so acute that they felt bound to assist. The atrocities committed by the Uganda National Liberation Army alienated the civilian population and provided support for the well-disciplined National Resistance Army soldiers. Torture was documented by Amnesty International in a report dated 18 June 1985, which shook Britain and Uganda's Western allies. This included a report of the totally unprovoked massacre at Namugongo, not even in the conflict area, of 100 persons including the principal and students of a theological college, and the imam of a nearby mosque.

Exile and final years Divisions within the army were Obote's eventual undoing. In 1985, in a belated attempt to exercise control over the army, he promoted a clan-relative, Brigadier Smith Opon Acak, as commander-in-chief over the heads of more experienced generals. This act precipitated a putsch led by Bazilio Olara-Okello and Tito Lutwa Okello in which he was ousted from power for the second time. In January 1986 Yoweri Museveni captured Kampala and was proclaimed president.

No neighbouring country would give Obote sanctuary: he eventually found refuge in Zambia, where he was forced to live in semi-isolation but was politically active in supporting the UPC. He only resigned from the chairmanship of his much depleted party early in 2005. His wife, Miria, succeeded him. He died of kidney failure in a Johannesburg hospital a few months later, on 10 October 2005. He was given a state send-off from South Africa when his body was returned to Uganda, and a controversial eight-day lying-in-state and state funeral at All Saints' Cathedral in Kampala, on the order of his old foe, Museveni; he was, after all, the person who had finally led Uganda to independence. His body was then taken to Lango and buried on 22 October at Akokoro, where he had been born.

M. Louise Pirouet

Sources A. G. Macpherson, ed., *Makerere College Register, 1922–1953* (1955) • kabaka of Buganda, *Desecration of my kingdom* (1967) • S. R. Karugire, *A political history of Uganda* (1980) • *Uganda elections, December 1980: report of the Commonwealth observer group* • J. J. Jorgensen, *Uganda: a modern history* (1981) • T. Avirgan and M. Honey, *War in Uganda: the legacy of Idi Amin* (1982) • *Uganda and Sudan: north and south*, Minority Rights Group (1984) • J. W. Clay, *The eviction of Banyarwanda: the story behind the refugee crisis in southwest Uganda* (1984) • *Uganda: evidence of torture*, Amnesty International (18 June 1985) • A. Omara-Otunnu, *Politics and the military in Uganda, 1890–1985* (1987) • D. A. Low, 'The dislocated polity', *Uganda now: between decay and development*, ed. H. B. Hansen and M. J. Twaddle (1988), 36–53 • S. Karugire, *The roots of instability in Uganda* (1988) • C. Watson, *Exile from Rwanda: background to an invasion* (1991) • P. Mutibwa, *Uganda since independence: a story of unfulfilled hopes* (1992) • K. Ingham, *Obote: a political biography* (1994) • H. B. Hansen and M. J. Twaddle, eds., *From chaos to order: the politics of constitution-making in Uganda* [1994] • M. L. Pirouet, 'Chronology', *Historical dictionary of Uganda* (1995), xxiv–xxxix • *New Vision* [Kampala] (12 Oct 2005) • *The Times* (12 Oct 2005) • *Daily Telegraph* (12 Oct 2005) • *The Guardian* (12 Oct 2005) • *The Independent* (12 Oct 2005) • *New York Times* (12 Oct 2005) • 'State funeral for Uganda's Obote', BBC news, 12 Oct 2005, http://newsvote.bbc.co.uk/1/hi/world/africa/4333618.stm/, 19 Sept 2008 • *WW* (2005)

Archives Amnesty International, Uganda Co-ordinating Group • Uganda government archives • US State Department archives | SOUND BL NSA, party political recordings • BL NSA, recorded speeches

Likenesses photographs, 1962–8, Camera Press, London • photographs, 1962–9, Photoshot, London • photographs, 1962–80, Getty Images, London • photographs, 1962–83, PA Photos, London • two photographs, 1981, Rex Features, London • P. Kemp, photograph, 1983, PA Photos, London [*see illus.*] • obituary photographs

O'Brien, Conor Cruise (1917–2008), diplomatist, politician, and author, was born Donal Conor David Dermod Donat Cruise O'Brien at 44 Leinster Road, Dublin, on 3 November 1917, the son of Francis Cruise O'Brien (*d.* 1927), journalist, and his wife, Kathleen (Katherine), *née* Sheehy (*d.* 1938). Everything about the time of his birth—the year after the Easter rising, the day after the Balfour declaration, a few days before the Bolshevik revolution—had political implications, and the place was almost too suffused with literary associations. His father, a genial if eccentric and needy journalist, from 'the lower end of the educated middle class', in his son's words, was a friend of W. B. Yeats; his mother, a Gaelic language enthusiast, was

Conor Cruise O'Brien (1917–2008), by unknown photographer, 1968

the model for Miss Ivors in James Joyce's story 'The Dead'; and her father was the Mr David Sheehy MP whose wife converses with Father Conmee in *Ulysses*. Even the obstetrician who delivered Conor has a fleeting mention in *Finnegans Wake*.

Despite the fact that Francis, and later his son, would be accused of excessive Anglophilia, the family were unmistakably 'green Irish'; O'Brien is indeed a pre-Celtic surname, from the aboriginal inhabitants who preceded the invasion, and O'Brien liked to joke (at the expense of linguistic and sporting nationalists) that he resented those Gaelic incomers, with their barbarous tongue and foreign games. At the same time the differences and tensions within Irish life were exemplified by the family. One of O'Brien's uncles was Francis Sheehy-Skeffington, a radical nationalist and pacifist, who was murdered by a British officer during the rising; another was the barrister and home rule MP Tom Kettle, who was killed months later on the Somme while serving as a captain in the Royal Dublin Fusiliers.

Education and early writings Although Conor's mother brought him up as a Catholic, his agnostic father, who died on Christmas day 1927 in his son's presence, had insisted that the boy should go to Sandford Park, a non-denominational school, where he largely mixed with protestants. So he did at Trinity College, Dublin, founded under Elizabeth I to promote the protestant Church of Ireland, still in O'Brien's time a Unionist bastion, and a place Catholics could attend only in defiance of episcopal ban. That mattered little to O'Brien, who had ceased to be a practising or believing Catholic by the time he came of age, and who would one day become the first proclaimed agnostic to sit in the Irish Dáil. His detachment from Irish nationalism took much longer, although one early experience was formative. On a vacation job from Trinity teaching at Belfast Royal Academy he met Christine Foster, daughter of the headmaster, Alexander Roulston Foster. They married at Dublin register office on 22 September 1939; he was twenty-one and she was twenty. As well as producing a son and two daughters, marriage into a liberal Ulster Presbyterian family opened up a new perspective for O'Brien.

O'Brien's undergraduate career was bibulous but brilliant, with sundry prizes, and first-class honours in French and Irish and then again in history. He began work on a doctorate, and academic life might have beckoned, but 'I found no welcome' at Trinity. Instead he joined the department of finance, the senior branch of the Irish civil service, transferring to the department of external affairs in 1944.

For all his remarkable later careers in three continents, and his intellectual cosmopolitanism, O'Brien was formed more than he realized by the sheer insularity, in every sense, of Ireland in the first half of the twentieth century. At the time he finished his education the greatest war in history began, but that war passed southern Ireland by completely, and it was inconceivable that someone of O'Brien's age and background could have done as his uncle had in the previous war and served in the British army. As it was this natural European barely set foot outside Ireland until his thirties.

He first escaped through books, when he began to write literary essays, under the pen-name Donat O'Donnell because of his position as a public servant. One of them, 'The pieties of Evelyn Waugh', published in the Dublin magazine *The Bell* in 1946, drew a clever response from its subject ('I think perhaps your reviewer is right in calling me a snob', before insisting that this had nothing to do with his Catholic faith). A collection of these essays on Catholic writers was published as *Maria Cross* in 1952, with an unlikely consequence. O'Brien had also continued his work as a historian: his doctoral dissertation was published in 1957 as *Parnell and his Party*, a learned, penetrating, and original work of scholarship with unusually witty footnotes. (During the divorce suit which ended Parnell's career, his supporters' 'addiction to the *tu quoque* would not have helped the cause much either. In a London church when a clergyman at this time condemned Parnell's moral lapse, an interrupter loudly asked, "What about the Prince of Wales?"' (*Parnell*, 294).)

Diplomacy: Paris, New York, and the Congo In 1955–6 O'Brien was counsellor at the Irish embassy in Paris, where one of his colleagues was Máire MacEntee (Máire Mhac an tSaoi), who, apart from her official work, was a notable poet in the officially revived but in truth imperilled Gaelic language. She was the daughter of a very different kind of Ulsterman, Seán MacEntee, a militant republican who had fought with the Irish Republican Army before the free state was born, served as a minister under de Valera and his successors until the age of seventy-six, and sat in parliament until eighty. O'Brien's marriage was petering out, and he and Máire began a clandestine attachment.

From 1956 to 1960 O'Brien served in New York as a member of the Irish delegation at the United Nations, to which Ireland had just been admitted. This proved to be the turning point of his life. Ireland had been neutral to a fault between allies and axis during the war; O'Brien wished it to be neutral also in the cold war, on the model of Sweden, and he courted American wrath by favouring the admission of Communist China to the United Nations. Improbably enough it was less his public work than his writing which caught the admiring eye of Dag Hammarskjöld: the introverted and cerebral Swede who was secretary-general of the United Nations was, as O'Brien drily said, 'one of the very few people who had read' *Maria Cross*.

In 1960 the Belgian Congo became independent. Violence erupted, with malign forces working from outside, as the southern province of Katanga, rich in minerals and effectively controlled by the Belgian Union Minière, seceded from the new state. This was condemned at the United Nations, where a Security Council resolution authorized measures to 'prevent the occurrence of civil war in the Congo', including 'the use of force, if necessary'. Hammarskjöld picked O'Brien as his representative in Katanga, where he served from May to December 1961. It was a disastrous episode. Hammarskjöld was killed when his flight from Northern Rhodesia to Katanga crashed in suspicious circumstances, and O'Brien was recalled to New York. He resigned from the United Nations and the Irish service under duress.

Much obloquy was heaped on him in the London popular press. Displaying what O'Brien elsewhere called their 'cockiness, ignorance, carelessness, prurience, innuendo, and lip-service to the highest moral standards', those papers leapt on the fact that Máire joined him in Africa (they had been writing to each other in Gaelic to avoid interception). Unmarrying and remarrying was tricky. Divorce had been abolished by the free state, but since Conor and Christine had not been married in a Catholic church their marriage was null in canon law. In 1962 they divorced in Mexico on the amicably agreed ground of '*assoluta incompatibilidad*', and in the same year O'Brien and Máire married in New York in a Catholic church, at her wish; they would marry again quietly in Dublin on 23 February 1999, after Irish law had been changed at last.

This eventful period produced a clutch of books. *Katanga and Back* in 1962 lucidly set the record straight, and settled some scores. It was followed by *Conflicting Concepts of the UN* in 1964, *The United Nations: Sacred Drama* in 1967, *Murderous Angels*, O'Brien's one play, about the death of Hammarskjöld, in 1968, and a long essay on Camus in 1969. *Writers and Politics* (1965) was a collection of essays, some written for the London weeklies, and he was now also writing for the newborn *New York Review of Books*.

Academia: Ghana and America If Katanga had made O'Brien a villain to the right it made him a hero to the anti-colonialist and anti-Western left, a gallery to which he played happily enough at the time. He wrote admiringly about Frantz Fanon, and quoted with approval his namesake the Irish nationalist William O'Brien, who said that 'Violence is the only way of ensuring a hearing for moderation', a view he would come very much to repudiate. His sympathy with anti-colonialism led to his next appointment, as vice-chancellor of the University of Ghana, which proved another unhappy experience.

He had been invited by Kwame Nkrumah, who had led Ghana as the first of the African colonies to become independent. But O'Brien's time there from 1962 to 1965 saw a descent into despotism, with Nkrumah proclaiming himself life president of a one-party state, accompanied by economic decline and rampant corruption. O'Brien later described a session of the Ghanaian parliament he had witnessed, where Nkrumah had solemnly averred that assets illegally held abroad by politicians must be repatriated, to an audience 'rocking with laughter'. The only positive consequence of these years was that the O'Briens adopted a part-Ghanaian son and daughter.

Rescue came from America, though not without irony. O'Brien had described Albert Schweitzer as 'a tragic anachronism' who personified 'the most irritating, if not the most noxious, aspects of the white man in Africa'; in 1965 he became Albert Schweitzer professor of humanities at New York University. He plunged into the thick of what might fairly be called radical-chic life, which included demonstrating against the Vietnam War (and being kicked hard by an Irish-American policeman). He was also engaged in a running battle, literary and sometimes legal, with the magazine *Encounter*. It accused him wrongly of being a fellow-traveller, though he was at the time very much an 'anti-anti-Communist' and exponent of 'moral equivalence' between East and West, and he accused it, correctly as events proved, of being supported by the CIA.

Politics: Eire and the north Now at the height of his literary powers, O'Brien began to engage again with his own country. His brilliant essay on Yeats, 'Passion and cunning', was a backhanded centennial tribute in 1965, showing how close the writer's affinity with fascism had been, and that at the time of some of his greatest poetry. Then another change of course saw another irony. O'Brien had an ill-concealed disdain for domestic Irish politicians and parties, including the Irish Labour Party, whose leaders he had called 'dismal poltroons, on the lines of O'Casey's Uncle Payther'; in 1969 he returned to stand as a Labour candidate in the general election. He won, and sat in the Dublin parliament for eight years.

After he had witnessed so much violence far from Europe, O'Brien came home just as violence had erupted in Northern Ireland. This would dominate his life for many years to come. He had been brought up and long remained a nationalist; in the early 1950s he had worked, with no lack of enthusiasm, on the Dublin government's 'anti-partition' campaign; and on the fiftieth anniversary of the Easter rising in 1966 he wrote about it as a high aspiration as yet unfulfilled. Moreover he knew 'the North' better than most southern Irishmen, and wrote at length in 1969 about the discrimination Catholics there had suffered, up to the brutal repression of the civil rights movement. Nevertheless he was appalled by the murderous savagery of the new Provisional IRA, and by the way that it had been clandestinely armed by ministers in the Dublin government, notably Charles Haughey. The two became deadly rivals, a situation made more piquant by the fact that, under the proportional multimember system, they represented the same constituency in north-east Dublin.

After the February 1973 election a coalition government was formed between Fine Gael and Labour, with Liam Cosgrave as prime minister, and O'Brien became minister for posts and telegraphs. This plunged him into bitter controversy when he preached unremitting hostility to the IRA, as its terrorist atrocities became bloodier, and banned representatives of their front organization, Sinn Féin, from appearing on RTE, the Irish public service broadcaster. This was censorship by any name, and O'Brien did not deny it, though even some of those who disagreed with him conceded that he had not followed the ignoble tradition of some Irishmen of hypocritical condemnation of terrorists whose aims they shared.

All this was a practical demonstration of the change of heart—or coming to terms with reality—which O'Brien had already expressed brilliantly in *States of Ireland* (1972), a book which influenced a generation. He saw that partition, while scarcely desirable in itself, recognized the reality of two different communities in the island, and that the Dublin state's formal irredentist claim on Northern Ireland was undemocratic and even imperialistic, as well as insincere. The republican ideology to which most Irish people paid lip service was a shirt of Nessus, he later wrote: 'it clings to us and burns'.

But O'Brien's years of ministerial office were not a success, and came to an abrupt end. At the general election in June 1977 the coalition was defeated and O'Brien lost his own seat. He was bitter about this, though attributing his personal eviction, perhaps rightly, less to his stand against the IRA than to the pitiful Irish telephone service for which his department was responsible. He did not entirely turn his back on Ireland, and served as an appointed member of the senate in 1977–9, but his sense of alienation was increased when the gun-runner Haughey became prime minister.

The Observer, and flirtation with Unionism By then O'Brien had been appointed editor-in-chief of *The Observer*, the London Sunday newspaper, itself going through a turbulent period. In that role from 1979 to 1981 he contributed some turbulence himself, attempting to stop Mary Holland, whom he correctly saw as a republican sympathizer, from writing about Northern Ireland. He then attempted to resist the acquisition of the paper by Roland ('Tiny') Rowland, a disreputable businessman. When Rowland did buy the paper O'Brien's days there were numbered.

O'Brien was liked and admired by colleagues—Anthony Howard, the deputy editor, said that he was an excellent team player, who 'covered the 1983 election brilliantly' (*The Guardian*, 12 July 2003)—but much the happiest feature of his *Observer* years was his own column, for which he won a What the Papers Say award. Sometimes it was directly topical, on one occasion with unfortunate timing. O'Brien had become a strong supporter of Zionism and Israel, perhaps as a form of transference while his Irish nationalism faded. In 1986 he published a long and well-researched book, *The Siege: the Saga of Israel and Zionism*, but in 1982 he had defended the Israeli incursion into Lebanon, in a column which appeared on a Sunday when the news had broken overnight of the massacre by Christian Phalangists at two Palestinian refugee camps, Sabra and Shatila, with Israeli forces looking on. Much better in every way was 'Dead Cat Calwell Meets Arctic Dev', an exquisitely funny column describing a meeting years before between de Valera and a horny-handed Australian politician.

After his departure from *The Observer*, O'Brien found other fields, including American universities. He had already in the 1970s been a visiting fellow at two Oxford colleges, Nuffield and St Catherine's, and now sojourned at Dartmouth College in 1984–5, and at the National Humanities Center of the University of North Carolina in 1993–4. But this proved to be anything but a retreat into the ivory tower. Out of office O'Brien became a still more vehement foe of the republicans, in the columns of the London *Times* for some years and the *Irish Independent* for longer.

Playing Cassandra, O'Brien regularly predicted a full-scale civil war which never came, or insisted that the IRA had gone beyond the pale and would never be touched by the Irish and British governments, at a time when those governments were secretly talking to the IRA. All of this led to a strange finale. After the Belfast agreement had been concluded in 1998, providing for devolution on the basis of consociationalism, this was put to referendum in both parts of Ireland. It overwhelmingly passed in the south, much more narrowly in Northern Ireland, with only a bare majority of protestants in favour. O'Brien had joined a campaign against the agreement, sharing a platform in Belfast with Robert McCartney, the leader of the UK Unionist party, which O'Brien now joined, but also with Ian Paisley, whose intransigence was legendary. This octogenarian turn dismayed younger Irish people like the Dublin writer and commentator Fintan O'Toole, for whom O'Brien's 'influence had once had enormous value' (*The Guardian*, 12 July 2003). Instead of following 'the duty of a public intellectual to be equally critical of both sides, he was explaining himself away with the kind of argument he'd have torn to shreds if it'd come from some Provo fellow-traveller' (ibid.). O'Brien was characteristically impenitent—'I have no regrets' (ibid.)—although his intervention made little difference, except to emphasize his singularity.

Even if O'Brien's prognosis was wrong his diagnosis was

correct: the natural human longing for peace was the terrorists' strongest weapon, since only they could deliver peace by desisting from violence; and the claim, so widely made, that the final settlement, with the IRA leader Martin McGuinness as minister of education, was a 'defeat for terrorism', was intellectually absurd, when what had happened was patently a victory for 'the men of violence'. Against that, O'Brien lived to see the final humiliation of Haughey, when his years of gross corruption finally became undeniable.

Later years Well-built and rubicund, O'Brien was fitter than he sometimes seemed, since he lived to be ninety-one. But his last years saw a physical and mental decline. He had always been convivial, with a tendency, as his *Observer* colleague Alan Watkins put it, to drink heavy red wine as though it were lemonade shandy on a summer afternoon; even Donald Harman Akenson, his semi-official biographer, wrote that in later years he had become an alcoholic. And those years were blighted by financial difficulties, as well as a deeper sorrow, the sudden death of his daughter Kate, a short-storywriter and publisher, at the age of fifty-nine. By the new century his journalism was repetitious, and few of his later books, *Ancestral Voices* (1994), *On the Eve of the Millennium* (1996), and *Memoir: My Life and Themes* (1998), were truly memorable. *The Long Affair: Thomas Jefferson and the French Revolution* (1996) was better, though an eccentric polemic. O'Brien's last pinnacle had in truth come in 1992 with *The Great Melody: a Thematic Biography and Commented Anthology of Edmund Burke*, an idiosyncratic but masterly work. He died on 18 December 2008 at his home, Whitewater, Howth Summit, Dublin, of a chest infection, and was survived by his second wife, Máire, two of the children of his first marriage, and the adopted children of his second marriage. He was buried at Glasnevin cemetery, Dublin, after a funeral at the Church of the Assumption, Howth, on 22 December.

For much of his life O'Brien was an acutely controversial figure, who inspired hatred and abuse as well as affection and esteem, and in some quarters contempt was not stilled by his death. His public life saw plenty of misjudgements, follies, and failures; his personality, marked by vanity more than ambition, was more that of a scholar than of a statesman; and he was remembered not for his political career but for what he was as a man and for what he wrote. Just the same had been true of Burke, of whom Samuel Johnson famously said that 'You could not stand for five minutes with that man beneath a shed while it rained, but you must be convinced you had been standing with the greatest man you had ever seen'. Reviewing *The Great Melody*, this 'wonderful book—learned, passionate, nobly written, and true to the spirit of Burke even where they both seem wrong', the Oxford political philosopher Alan Ryan recalled Johnson's tribute, and said that it could, 'without absurdity, have been paid to the latest of Burke's innumerable commentators and biographers' (*New York Review of Books*, 3 Dec 1992).

GEOFFREY WHEATCROFT

Sources C. Cruise O'Brien, *To Katanga and back* (1962) • D. H. Akenson, *Conor: a biography of Conor Cruise O'Brien* (1994) • A. J. Jordan, *To laugh or to weep: a biography of Conor Cruise O'Brien* (1994) • C. Cruise O'Brien, *Memoir: my life and themes* (1998) • *Irish Times* (19 Dec 2008); (20 Dec 2008); (23 Dec 2008) • *Irish Independent* (19 Dec 2008); (20 Dec 2008); (23 Dec 2008) • *Daily Telegraph* (19 Dec 2008) • *The Times* (20 Dec 2008) • *The Guardian* (20 Dec 2008) • *The Independent* (20 Dec 2008) • *New York Times* (20 Dec 2008) • *Sunday Independent* [Dublin] (28 Dec 2008) • *Sunday Times* (1 Feb 2009) • *New York Review of Books* (26 March 2009); (2 July 2009); (13 Aug 2009) • D. Whelan, *Conor Cruise O'Brien: violent notions* (2009) • *WW* (2008) • personal knowledge (2012) • private information (2012) • b. cert. • m. certs. • d. cert.

Archives TCD, Hubert Butler MSS | FILM BFINA, current affairs footage | SOUND BL NSA, current affairs, documentary, and performance recordings

Likenesses photograph, 1961, Photoshot, London • photographs, 1961, Rex Features, London • photographs, 1961–73, PA Photos, London • photographs, 1961–78, Getty Images, London • photograph, 1968, Getty Images, London [*see illus.*] • E. McCabe, photographs, Camera Press, London • obituary photographs

Odell, John William [Jack] **(1920–2007)**, businessman and toy manufacturer, was born on 19 March 1920 at 736 Holloway Road, Islington, London, the elder son of William John Odell, bus driver, and his wife, Alice Esther, *née* Williams. Expelled from council school at the age of thirteen for what he later described as rebelliousness, he failed to find regular employment, drifting from Simms Motor Units into van driving, menial work with an estate agent, and a spell as a cinema projectionist. In 1939 he joined the Royal Army Service Corps and, when it was created in 1942, the Royal Electrical and Mechanical Engineers. He adapted well to military life, serving in north Africa and Italy and rising to the rank of sergeant. Charged with vehicle maintenance, he used his spare time to mend primus stoves, thereby building up savings that allowed him to marry Joan Marguerite Carter (*b.* 1919/20), daughter of Sydney Carter, transport driver, at the church of St Peter le Poer, Friern Barnet, on 24 March 1945. They had two daughters, Anne and Elizabeth.

Demobilized, Odell found work with Die-Cast Machine Tools, a small north London firm where he learned die-casting from one of the partners, Sidney Ambridge. Deciding that the firm's products were of poor quality, Odell bought some tools of his own but the local council refused him permission to manufacture from his own home. Subsequently he accepted an invitation from a fellow employee at Die-Cast, Rodney Smith, to join Lesney, which Smith had set up in partnership with an unrelated namesake, Leslie *Smith, to manufacture die-cast parts for the electrical and motor industries.

An order for a toy gun part appears to have turned the partners' thoughts to diversification and model vehicles were among the first Lesney toys appearing after 1948. Rodney Smith left the firm in 1951 but Odell found ample scope for his own engineering and design skills. When his daughter Anne complained that she was not allowed to take to school anything that would not fit into a matchbox, he cast a miniature steamroller which proved instantly appealing to her classmates. Odell's miniaturized souvenir model of the 1953 coronation coach was

John William [Jack] **Odell** (**1920–2007**), by Chris Ware, 1968 [right, with Leslie Smith]

equally appealing and a commercial success, selling 1 million in 1953 alone. Packed into small matchbox-like containers, the subsequent Matchbox range of model vehicles proved irresistible, not least because they were cheap and stocked by a huge variety of shops.

In 1960 Lesney became a public company, making millionaires of both remaining partners—an ambition that Odell said he had always intended to realize by the age of forty. The fourth largest toy company in Europe, Lesney had numerous plants in and around London and ultimately employed some 6500 workers producing over 5 million units a week, 80 per cent of which were exported to over 130 countries, thereby winning the company five queen's export awards.

This success rested jointly on Smith's commercial acumen and Odell's artistic flair and engineering expertise, which enabled him to design intricate miniatures and often the requisite tooling as well. These included a machine to make the plastic interiors that helped keep Matchbox models well ahead of the established market leader, Dinky. Odell was also responsible for the tooling behind the Superfast range, a response to Mattel's fast running Hot Wheels models whose success from 1969 so threatened Matchbox sales that, as Odell himself put it, 'All of a sudden we were arguing over whether we could afford a new typewriter' (*Daily Telegraph*, 10 July 2007). With the company returned to profitability, he retired as joint managing director in 1973. On 16 September 1980, a year after his first marriage had ended in divorce, he married, at Barnet register office, Patricia Maud (formerly Maud Patricia) Cochrane (*b.* 1929), daughter of George Hilsden, railway clerk, and former wife of Donald H. Cochrane.

In 1981 Odell returned to Lesney as joint vice-chairman. By now the company was struggling, the consequence of sustained losses brought about by the strength of sterling, ill-judged overseas expansion, and crippling interest rates on significantly increased borrowing. The task, which Odell likened to assuming command of the *Titanic* 10 minutes before she sank, was beyond him and in 1982 Lesney went into receivership, giving Odell more time to devote to his beloved golf. By 1983, however, he had acquired some old Matchbox moulds and set up Lledo (an inversion of his own name), which produced historical models and ultimately secured a niche market, making limited editions of die-cast vehicles carrying promotional liveries. He sold this firm in 1996.

Jack Odell was a gifted raconteur and host who enjoyed the fruits of his business success, building a large house on an extensive site in north London and establishing a trust fund to support local and national charities. However, he had no sense of self-importance. At Lesney he preferred being on the factory floor and for years had no office or secretary of his own. Nor was he a self-publicist: he boasted that his was one of the shortest entries in *Who's Who* and, unlike his partner Leslie Smith, he took little part in the wider affairs of his industry, though none disputed the validity of his desire to be remembered as 'a damn good engineer' (*Daily Telegraph*, 10 July 2007). He was appointed OBE in 1969. Suffering from Parkinson's disease, he died of bronchopneumonia at Arkley Nursing Home, Barnet, on 7 July 2007. He was survived by his second wife, Patricia, his two daughters from his first marriage, and three stepchildren. KENNETH D. BROWN

Sources M. Fawdry, *British tin toys* (1990) · K. D. Brown, *The British toy business: a history since 1700* (1996) · C. Mack, *Encyclopedia of Matchbox toys* (2002) · *The Independent* (9 July 2007) · *The Times* (10 July 2007) · *Daily Telegraph* (10 July 2007) · *Daily Mail* (10 July 2007) · *New York Times* (17 July 2007) · *Boston Globe* (18 July 2007) · *The Herald* [Glasgow] (20 July 2007) · www.matchbox.com, 1 May 2010 · private information (2011) · b. cert. · m. certs. · d. cert.

Likenesses C. Ware, photograph, 1968, Getty Images, London [*see illus.*] · photograph, *c.*1968, repro. in www.fcarnahan.com/pg/jodell.html · obituary photographs · photographs, repro. in homepage.ntlworld.com/d.jones7317/public_html/factory.htm

Wealth at death £8,619,431: probate, 22 Jan 2008, *CGPLA Eng. & Wales*

Oliver, Peter Raymond, **Baron Oliver of Aylmerton** (**1921–2007**), judge, was born on 7 March 1921 at 51 St Barnabas Road, Cambridge, the younger son of David Thomas *Oliver (1863–1947), jurist, and his wife, Alice Maud, *née* Kirby. He was educated in Cambridge at the Leys School and Trinity Hall, the college of which his father was a fellow. He went there in 1939, but the Second World War interrupted his university education. He saw military service from 1941 until 1945, serving in the 12th battalion of the Royal Tank regiment in north Africa and Italy. He was mentioned in dispatches and left the army with the rank of captain. He returned to Trinity Hall in 1946 and graduated in 1947 with a first in both parts of the law tripos. On 4 July 1945 he married Mary Chichester Rideal (1922–1985), whom he had known since childhood. She was the daughter of Sir Eric Keightley *Rideal, professor of colloid science at Trinity Hall. Fittingly the marriage was celebrated in Cambridge in the university church of St Mary the Great. Mary graduated in English and then law from Newnham College. They had two children, David (*b.* 1949) and Sarah (*b.* 1951).

In 1948 Oliver was called to the bar by Lincoln's Inn. He practised as a Chancery barrister from chambers at 13 Old Square. In the aftermath of the war, work was scarce. But at the bar, as elsewhere, the outstandingly able succeed. Peter Oliver was one of these. With unremitting hard work he gradually built up a fine Chancery practice and took silk in 1965. In 1973 he was elected a bencher of his inn.

Oliver's appointment as a judge of the Chancery Division of the High Court in 1974 (followed by the customary knighthood) came as no surprise to his contemporaries. He was a member of the restrictive practices court from 1976 to 1980. In 1979 he was appointed chairman of a review body of the practices and procedures of the Chancery Division. In 1980, while still conducting this review, he was elevated to the Court of Appeal and sworn of the privy council.

Oliver's report was published in 1981. Chancery judges and practitioners had long smarted under jibes about *Bleak House* and *Jarndyce* v. *Jarndyce*. Oliver set himself to put matters right once and for all. The report was comprehensive and thorough. It identified the continuing problems. The practices of the division were 'archaic and confusing', and there was 'no facile method of unravelling the results of many years of painstaking entanglement' (*Report of the Review Body on the Chancery Division of the High Court*, Cmnd 8205, 1981). The report made eighty-eight recommendations, and was welcomed by the lord chancellor, Lord Hailsham, with approbation as 'the most searching inquiry into chancery for over 100 years' (*Daily Telegraph*, 23 Oct 2007). Virtually all the recommendations were eventually adopted.

In 1986 Oliver was further promoted to be a lord of appeal in ordinary. He was created Baron Oliver of Aylmerton, this being the place of his country retreat in Norfolk. With his Welsh roots he adopted as his armorial motto *Trwy weithred y dysgir* ('we learn through experience'). Meanwhile, following the death of his first wife, Mary, who had herself become a distinguished academic lawyer and law teacher, on 3 January 1987 he married Wendy Anne Jones, *née* Harrison (*b.* 1925), widow of (Ivon) Lewis Lloyd Jones and daughter of Walter Harrison, merchant. Oliver's retirement in 1992 was hastened by the onset of macular degeneration, an affliction leading ultimately to his becoming blind. He was made an honorary fellow of Trinity Hall in 1980 and received honorary doctorates in law from the City of London Polytechnic in 1989, the University of East Anglia in 1991, and the University of Cambridge in 1995. He was commissary of Cambridge University from 1989 to 2002. Then, by special grace, he was given the personal titular appointment of emeritus commissary. Lincoln's Inn accorded him its highest honour by electing him treasurer for the year 1993.

Oliver was one of the outstanding practitioners and judges of his generation. Notable among his personal characteristics was his kindly humanity. He was a delightful man. He always had time to listen to other people, whoever they might be, and give them his full attention. He combined a brilliant legal mind with an imperturbable temperament and unassuming manner. In practice as a barrister he was immensely popular with clients and judges alike. They warmed to him and respected him. So did his colleagues, always the acid test in such a highly competitive profession. As an advocate he presented his cases simply. He did not overstate his arguments. This endeared him to judges, who welcomed being shown the way through the problems confronting them. His opinions were written in his own distinctive felicitous style.

On the judicial bench Oliver was impressive: good humoured, courteous, perceptive, intolerant of bullies, totally lacking in pomposity, well versed in the law. With his light touch his judgments were clearly reasoned and a delight to read, even when they were a trifle prolix. Above all he had the essential attributes of a good judge: a huge fund of common sense and an innate sense of the requirements of fairness, both in the conduct of a case and in its outcome. Those who appeared before him invariably left his court feeling they had received a fair hearing.

With typical modesty Oliver was apt to say he had enjoyed his work in the Court of Appeal but counted himself among those who had not settled so well as a lord of appeal. In saying this he did less than justice to his contribution to the development of the law by the House of Lords. He held his high judicial office in changing times. By nature he was not a radical reformer. But his analysis of legal problems was penetrating. He added much strength to the appellate committee of the House of Lords and the judicial committee of the privy council in his comparatively short time there. One instance was the *Spycatcher* case. Peter Wright, formerly a senior officer of MI5, had disclosed internal workings and activities of MI5 and MI6 in his book *Spycatcher*. In 1987 the law lords upheld a temporary ban on further newspaper publication of this confidential material in the UK. They did so, even though the book had been published in the United States and copies were readily obtainable here. Oliver joined the dissenting minority. The defendant newspapers could not properly be prevented from making use of information which every other newspaper in the western hemisphere was free to use:

> Ideas, however unpopular or unpalatable, once released and however released into the open air of free discussion and circulation, cannot for ever be effectively proscribed as if they were a virulent disease. 'Facilis descensus Averno' and to attempt, even temporarily, to create a sort of judicial cordon sanitaire against the infection from abroad of public comment and discussion is not only … certain to be ineffective but involves taking the first steps upon a very perilous path. (*Attorney-General* v. *Guardian Newspapers*, 1987)

Subsequent events showed how right his common-sense approach was.

Oliver (who lived latterly in Wimbledon) died on 17 October 2007 at St George's Hospital, Tooting, London, from ischaemic heart disease and multiple injuries following a fall. He was survived by his second wife, Wendy, and the two children of his first marriage. His son, David, followed him to Trinity Hall and as a practising QC in the Chancery Division. NICHOLLS OF BIRKENHEAD

Sources *Daily Telegraph* (23 Oct 2007) • *The Times* (29 Oct 2007) • *The Independent* (31 Oct 2007) • Burke, *Peerage* • *WW* (2007) • C. Rimer, funeral tribute • personal knowledge (2011) • private information (2011) • b. cert. • m. certs. • d. cert.
Likenesses photographs, 1986–90, Photoshot, London • T. Ward, pastel portrait, Lincoln's Inn, London • obituary photographs
Wealth at death £632,890: probate, 20 March 2008, *CGPLA Eng. & Wales*

O'Malley [*née* Hickey], **Mary Margaret** (1918–2006), theatre founder, was born on 28 July 1918 at West End, Mallow, co. Cork, the younger child of Daniel Hickey (1878–1918), asylum attendant, and his wife, Ann Margaret, *née* Lysaght (1875–1959). Her father died four months before she was born and she was brought up in Youghal, co. Cork, by her mother, a boarding-house landlady who—with the help of a scholarship—managed to send her to the Loreto convent boarding school, St Michael's, in Navan. There, at the age of thirteen, she wrote and directed her first play, *The Princess*. University was a step too far financially, so she took a secretarial course, which led in the late 1930s to office jobs in Dublin, where she lived with her brother Gerard (1909–1961), a civil servant and stage designer at the Abbey Theatre, to whom she was always close. She had an active cultural life, joining the left-wing New Theatre Group in 1941, encountering Maud Gonne and Jim Larkin, and becoming politically aware. In 1943 she met a young psychiatrist, (Patrick) Pearse O'Malley (1918–2004), son of Patrick O'Malley, farmer. He was from south Armagh and after she married him on 16 September 1947 they moved north, where he took up an appointment as a consultant at the Mater Hospital in Belfast.

Mary O'Malley found Belfast an alien environment where, culturally, semi-desert conditions prevailed. But she saw living in 'the bitter, black north' (Yeats, *On Baile's Strand*) as a challenge. At first she sought involvement as a Catholic socialist and nationalist in the politics of a sharply divided, protestant-dominated city. As a Republican Labour councillor she won a seat on the Belfast corporation, which she held from 1952 to 1954. She spoke out fearlessly (her husband often helped with the speeches) but hated the duplicities of the political world. In fact her attention had already turned to the theatre: she produced a highly successful Christmas entertainment for the Newman Society at Queen's University in 1950. This led to more productions at an interesting venue—starting in March 1951 with three short plays, including Yeats's *At the Hawk's Well*, presented in the large window bay of her husband's consulting rooms in their home, Ulsterville House, in Lisburn Road, Belfast. This was 'the birth of the Lyric Players' Theatre, although it had not, as yet, taken a name' (O'Malley, 23). This political and theatrical activity ran concurrently with the bearing and raising of three sons, Kieran (*b*. 1949), Donal (*b*. 1951), and Conor (*b*. 1954).

By 1952 the O'Malleys needed a larger home, so they moved to a sizeable detached mid-Victorian house in Derryvolgie Avenue, on the fringes of the affluent (and largely protestant) suburb of Malone Road. The house had an old stables with a loft that they converted into a fifty-seat theatre with a tiny stage, twelve feet deep by ten feet wide. Once she was established in this cramped, but strangely attractive, environment, the Lyric, as it was soon called, took off. It was for its first twenty years a 'poets' theatre'—putting on not just verse drama but plays with poetic qualities or, as Yeats put it, 'a base of reality and an apex of beauty'. There were seven productions in the 1952–3 season—still mainly short plays like Yeats's *Dreaming of the Bones*. By the mid-1950s full-length works by, among others, Garcia Lorca, Shakespeare, T. S. Eliot, and Aristophanes came into the repertory, but the bedrock remained Yeats.

The Lyric had an implicit political stance. Mary O'Malley was operating a mid-century cultural version of what later became 'the peace process'. She put before a Belfast audience some of the artistic heritage of the whole island of Ireland and strove mightily to reduce the insularity of a community that had found the simplicities of sectarianism so seductive. Chekhov, O'Neill, Ibsen, Beckett, O'Casey (particularly the later plays), and Schiller were all produced to a very high standard as the theatre hit a bigger stride in the early 1960s. Later in the decade more new Irish writing was presented, including works by Brian Friel, John B. Keane, James Plunkett, and G. P. Gallivan.

O'Malley's energy and drive were extraordinary. She personally directed 140 of the 180 plays produced in the theatre's first twenty-five years. But she also founded and ran the Lyric drama school in 1956, and started a distinguished literary magazine, *Threshold*, in 1957 (which was to publish notable contributions from Thomas Kinsella and the young Seamus Heaney). In the early 1960s she added an Academy of Music, an Irish handicrafts shop, and an art gallery to the Lyric's cultural portfolio. She had a lot of domestic help, but her organizational capacity was remarkable. In her theatre she was both producer and director; in the latter role she was excellent at casting, gave the actors very considerable freedom (although she was stern with those who drank before they played), was surprisingly good at fight scenes, and sought simplicity in design—imaginatively implemented by distinguished artists like Alice Berger Hammerschlag, Colin Middleton, Terence Flanagan, and Rowel Friers. Her son Conor later described a childhood spent in this theatrical maelstrom as 'like living in a public space' (private information), although he loved the backstage excitement during performances.

By the end of the 1950s O'Malley had begun to chafe at the limitations of the converted stables and by 1960 plans were afoot for expansion into a larger theatre. Fund-raising turned out to be a long and tortuous process—sometimes hampered by the perceived political unreliability of a theatre that did not play the British national anthem at its performances. Finally, with the last-minute donation of a flat roof from the builders McAlpine (who later constructed the National Theatre in London) and a hesitant contribution from the Northern Ireland Arts Council, a new 300 seat theatre in Ridgeway Street, overlooking the River Lagan, opened in October 1968.

The new Lyric did not have an easy beginning. Some of the busy bees from the warm-hearted theatrical beehive at Derryvolgie Avenue found adjustment to the spacious new theatre difficult. The Arts Council's annual grant of £8000 was inadequate. The transition from an amateur or part-professional theatre to a fully professional one pushed up costs enormously; Equity, the actors' union, was inflexible in its attitudes. The problems multiplied quickly and, not long after the opening, the theatre had to close briefly. Next, the 'troubles' aggravated the Lyric's own difficulties. The result was that O'Malley—who had given up her role as artistic director—came back to direct productions, including notably Patrick Galvin's enormously successful ballad opera about the troubles, *We Do It for Love*. In the new theatre she and others continued to do the classics, but also began to put on plays by local writers who bravely dissected sectarian attitudes. The wide open spaces of the new stage enabled her to deliver superlative productions of the whole Yeats canon, aided by such high-calibre Derryvolgie stalwarts as Louis Rolston and Sam McCready. She nurtured many young professional actors, among them Liam Neeson, who recalled her with affection: 'She gave me my professional start at the Lyric and believed in whatever raw talent I had. Her love and pride in the Lyric Theatre was infectious and she became a sort of mother to us all' (*Irish News*, 25 April 2006).

Mary O'Malley stayed on at the Lyric until 1976, when she and her husband returned to Dublin. Inevitably some of the consistency and continuity which she brought went with her. Nevertheless, there were highlights, like Marie Jones's *Stones in his Pockets* (1999) and hard-hitting new works by Tom Murphy, Graham Reid, and Martin Lynch, among others. At the time of her death the theatre was embarking on an £18 million rebuilding programme.

In retirement Mary O'Malley enjoyed life in her beloved Dublin until the early 1990s, when heart trouble and mini-strokes led eventually to dementia. She died of heart failure at Clonskeagh Hospital, Dublin, on 22 April 2006. She was survived by her three sons. BERNARD ADAMS

Sources C. O'Malley, *A poets' theatre* (1988) • *Irish News* (25 April 2006); (1 June 2006) • *Belfast Telegraph* (25 April 2006) • *The Independent* (29 April 2006) • *The Times* (20 May 2006); (29 May 2006) • private information (2010) [Conor O'Malley, son] • b. cert. • m. cert. • d. cert.
Archives Linen Hall Library, Belfast, Lyric Theatre archive • National University of Ireland, Galway, Lyric Theatre archive

O'Neill [*née* Whitaker], **(Katharine) Jean, Lady O'Neill of the Maine (1915–2008)**, horticulturist, was born on 16 January 1915 at 41 Upper Brook Street, Mayfair, London, the fourth daughter and youngest of five children of (William) Ingham Whitaker (1866–1936), and his wife, Hilda Guilhermina, *née* Dundas (1877–1971), daughter of Charles Saunders Melville Dundas, sixth Viscount Melville. She grew up at Pylewell Park, near Lymington, Hampshire, which had been bought by her paternal grandfather with a fortune derived from the import of Marsala wine. Her father, who inherited the estate in 1893, was a keen horticulturist and traveller, who brought back various Asian and Australian plants and created a renowned garden at Pylewell. She was educated at home, but most enjoyed helping the head gardener, and mucking about on a small sailing boat. In 1937 she toured Europe with a friend in a Ford V8, and met Unity Mitford and Joseph Goebbels, neither of whom impressed her. During the Second World War she served as a Voluntary Aid Detachment nurse. On 4 February 1944 she married Terence Marne *O'Neill, later Baron O'Neill of the Maine (1914–1990), politician, and prime minister of Northern Ireland from 1963 to 1969. After her marriage, as well as bringing up her two young children and acting as a dutiful politician's wife, she cultivated a five acre garden at Glebe House, Ahoghill, near Ballymena, advised the National Trust on the restoration of its gardens at Rowallane, Mount Stewart, and Castle Ward, and served as the first president of the Rose Society of Northern Ireland. On the family's return to the mainland in 1970 she created a new garden of rare plants at Lisle Court (in the grounds of Pylewell Park), near Lymington, Hampshire, many of them collected on her travels, particularly to Australia, where her son had settled. She also researched horticultural history, publishing many articles in *Country Life*, the *Garden History Journal*, and the *Journal of Natural History*. Her biography of Peter Collinson, the eighteenth-century collector, written jointly with Elizabeth McLean, was published posthumously in 2008. She was a fellow of the Linnean Society and in 2000 was awarded the Veitch memorial medal of the Royal Horticultural Society. Her last expedition, undertaken at the age of eighty-eight, was a two-week excursion down the Amazon. She was a devout Christian and had disliked the sectarian atmosphere of Northern Ireland. She died of a stroke on 15 July 2008 and was survived by her two children.

Sources T. O'Neill, *The autobiography of Terence O'Neill* (1972) • *Daily Telegraph* (4 Aug 2008) • *Belfast Telegraph* (7 Aug 2008) • *Irish Times* (9 Aug 2008) • *The Times* (23 Aug 2008); (11 Sept 2008) • *Sydney Morning Herald* (25 Aug 2008) • b. cert. • m. cert.
Likenesses obituary photographs

Oranmore and Browne. For this title name *see* Gray, Sally [*née* Constance Vera Stephens; *married name* Constance Vera Browne, Lady Oranmore and Browne] (1915–2006).

Orgel, Leslie Eleazer (1927–2007), theoretical chemist and molecular biologist, was born on 12 January 1927 at 17 St Kildas Road, Stoke Newington, London, the son of Simon Orgel, a boot and shoe-lace dealer, and his wife, Deborah, *née* Grivisch. He was educated at the Dame Alice Owen School in London and Magdalen College, Oxford; he graduated with first-class honours in chemistry in 1949. In 1950 he was elected a fellow of Magdalen College and in 1951 was awarded his DPhil in chemistry. He was married on 30 July 1950 at the Adath Yisroel Synagogue in Stoke Newington to Hassia Alice Levinson, a medical student at

Lady Margaret Hall, Oxford, and daughter of Leopold Levinson, merchant. They had two sons, Richard and Robert, and a daughter, Vivienne.

Orgel's early passion was theoretical inorganic chemistry, which he pursued first at Oxford, then at the California Institute of Technology and the University of Chicago, before returning to the UK in 1955 to join the department of chemistry at Cambridge University as assistant director of research and in 1963 as reader. He was a fellow of Peterhouse from 1957. At Cambridge he helped develop ligand field theory, a very elegant approach to describing chemical bonding in metals. The Orgel diagram reflects his contributions, showing how the energy levels of a transition-metal atom split when the metal is placed in the field of a ligand. In the Orgel diagram the energy is shown on the vertical axis and the strength of the ligand field on the horizontal, with zero ligand field strength at the centre. This is one of the most attractive aspects of transition-metal chemistry, providing insights into spectroscopic, optical, and magnetic properties of octahedral, tetrahedral, and other symmetrical complexes of transition metals. In 1960 Orgel published *An Introduction to Transition-Metal Chemistry: the Ligand Field Theory*, a beautifully written monograph that made the life of many generations of chemistry students a lot easier.

Orgel had a broad interest in science; he was always attracted by 'the new and the different'. In 1953, together with others in the department of chemistry in Oxford, including Dorothy Hodgkin, Sydney Brenner, Jack Dunitz, and Beryl Oughton, he had travelled to Cambridge to see the model of DNA constructed by Francis Crick and James Watson. This clearly impressed them; indeed both Brenner and Orgel subsequently worked with Crick. Moreover, during his time in Cambridge, Orgel joined with Brenner, Crick, Watson, and sixteen others to form the RNA Tie Club, each of whose members took a nickname from one of the twenty amino acids and wore a tie representing the chemical structure of RNA. The role of RNA was to prove a long-term focus of Orgel's research.

In 1964 Orgel was appointed senior fellow and research professor at the Salk Institute for Biological Studies in La Jolla, California, where his research interests were largely in nucleic acid chemistry and molecular biology, and their applications to prebiotic evolution and the origin of life. The then current dogma that the flow of information in living organisms was from DNA to RNA to protein had led to a paradox: there can be no proteins without DNA, and there can be no DNA without proteins. Orgel knew that DNA is more stable than RNA and that ribonucleotides of RNA are more readily synthesized than are the deoxyribonucleotides of DNA. He also understood the difficulty of proposing a prebiotic scenario in which proteins could replicate in the absence of nucleic acids. He therefore suggested a way out of the chicken-and-egg conundrum, as did Crick and the microbiologist Carl Woese, each publishing their ideas independently. They proposed the existence in prebiotic evolutionary time of the 'RNA world' in which RNA catalysed all the reactions necessary for a precursor of the last common ancestor of living organisms to survive and replicate. Once living organisms were established the more stable DNA could then have taken over RNA's role as the guardian of heredity, while RNA took on a more supporting role. Orgel presented these ideas in two influential books, *The Origins of Life: Molecules and Natural Selection* (1970) and *The Origins of Life on the Earth* (1974), the latter written with Stanley Miller.

In the following years Orgel focused his laboratory of chemical evolution on non-enzymatic polymerization reactions that depend on the formation of double-helical complexes between a preformed polynucleotide template and complementary mononucleotides or polynucleotides. He supported his hypothesis of the RNA world by demonstrating that selected templates could facilitate synthesis of complementary RNA sequences. Further strong evidence for the hypothesis came in 1983 when Thomas R. Cech of the University of Colorado at Boulder and Sidney Altman of Yale University discovered the first known ribozymes, enzymes made of RNA.

Nevertheless doubts about the RNA world remained. It was suggested that ribose might not have been stable enough to survive the low-oxygen and high-radiation conditions of the early earth. Moreover, attempts to form RNA under laboratory conditions mimicking the primordial earth were not fully successful. Orgel began to think that RNA probably took over from a peptide nucleic acid (PNA), and showed that this could be copied in the test tube. There were also questions about how a universal genetic code could have evolved. In 1973 Orgel and Crick even put forward the idea of 'directed panspermia'—the seeding of life on other worlds by a guiding intelligence, although they qualified their suggestion by saying that the evidence was so inadequate that no one could say anything about the probability.

Thoughts about seeding of life—particularly from other planets—led to Orgel's long association with the American government's National Aeronautics and Space Administration (NASA). He was one of the principal investigators in the NASA-sponsored programme in exobiology, among other things designing the gas chromatography mass spectrometer instrument for the exploration of chemicals on other planets. In 1998 he was the chair of the US National Research Council task group on analysis of small solar systems bodies, and served on the NASA astrobiology oversight committee. He was also a member of a strategic planning group for the Search for Extra-Terrestrial Intelligence Institute, Mountain View, California, for the study of life in the universe.

Like all good scientists Orgel recognized unintended outcomes. His chemical evolution laboratory synthesized cytosine arabinoside, a compound that is one of the most commonly used anticancer agents, and this synthesis became widely used in the pharmaceutical industry.

Orgel's research interests were multidisciplinary, including chemistry, molecular biology, prebiotic evolution, and the origin of life. His achievements were recognized by the award of many prizes, and by election as a fellow of the Royal Society in 1962 and (having taken American citizenship in the 1980s) a member of the

National Academy of Sciences in 1990. He will be remembered for what Crick called Orgel's second rule: 'Evolution is cleverer than you are', meaning that the trial-and-error processes of evolution can produce better results than centralized planning. He was a major contributor to some important concepts that have challenged our understanding of life on this planet. He died at a hospice in San Diego, California, on 27 October 2007, of pancreatic cancer, and was survived by his wife, Alice, and their three children.

TOM L. BLUNDELL

Sources R. Lewis, 'Scientists debate RNA's role at the beginning of life on earth', *The Scientist* (31 March 1997) • 'Salk chemical evolution scientist Leslie Orgel dies', Salk Institute press release • *Boston Globe* (1 Nov 2007) • *New York Times* (5 Nov 2007) • *The Scientist* (Nov 2007) • *The Times* (6 Dec 2007) • *WW* (2007) • U. Cal., San Diego, Geisel Library, Leslie Orgel papers • nobelprize.org/educational/medicine/gene-code/history.html, 19 Jan 2010 • www.seti.org/csc/index.php, 19 Jan 2010 • personal knowledge (2011) • private information (2011) • b. cert. • m. cert.

Archives U. Cal., San Diego, Geisel Library | Bodl. Oxf., C. A. Coulson papers | SOUND BL NSA, documentary recording

Likenesses obituary photographs • photograph, repro. in www.salk.edu/insidesalk/article.php?id=53

Orme, Stanley [Stan], **Baron Orme (1923–2005)**, politician, was born on 5 April 1923 at Sale Memorial Hospital, Sale, Cheshire, the son of Sherwood Orme, corn miller's bookkeeper, and later clerk at a cotton mill, and his wife, Nellie, *née* Drew. He was brought up in difficult financial circumstances. He left elementary school at fourteen, and worked as an instrument maker's apprentice at the Metropolitan–Vickers plant in Trafford Park industrial estate. In 1942 he enlisted in RAF Bomber Command as a warrant officer and navigator. His fellow airmen had a great regard for his skill as a Pathfinder navigator, and his sheer courage as an aircrew leader. Throughout his life he felt that in view of the number of sorties that he undertook, and his repeated postings, he was lucky to be alive, and to have survived the war.

On demobilization in 1947, Orme returned to the Metropolitan–Vickers factory at Trafford Park. Having joined the Labour Party in 1944, he worked hard to improve his education in classes at the National Council of Labour Colleges and in night classes organized by the Workers' Educational Association. He became a powerful convener of shop stewards for the Amalgamated Engineering Union (working closely with Hugh Scanlon) and sat on Sale borough council from 1958 to 1965. On 20 January 1951 he married Irene Mary Harris, a 27-year-old solicitor's clerk, of Sale, and daughter of Vernon Fletcher Harris, musician. It was a close marriage, but there were no children.

Orme was disappointed to be defeated in his attempt to win Stockport South in the 1959 general election. He won Salford West in 1964, and worked closely with a political soul-mate, the Labour MP for Salford East, Frank Allaun. His maiden speech, devoted to industrial issues from the point of view of a skilled engineer, instantly identified him as a politician to watch. As a back-bencher he supported the Campaign for Nuclear Disarmament, criticized Harold Wilson's refusal to condemn America over the Vietnam war and his dithering over Ian Smith's unilateral declaration of independence in Rhodesia, and opposed Barbara Castle's white paper *In Place of Strife* of 1969. He was firmly identified with the Labour left and occasionally made a great deal of trouble for the government, but most ministers realized that he never made trouble for the sake of it: he was far too intense and serious about his politics and the interests of working-class people.

Increasingly concerned by the civil rights situation and then the outbreak of the 'troubles' in Northern Ireland, Orme was made a junior spokesman on the province by Wilson in 1972. Along with Jock Stallard and Kevin McNamara, he organized the vote against internment in the Commons. However, when he became minister of state for Northern Ireland following the first general election of 1974, under Merlyn Rees, he started by signing detention orders, which caused a breakdown in relations with some of his former allies without fully endearing him to the Unionist leadership. He subsequently felt humiliated by the protestant working class spurning the attempts by the general secretary of the TUC, Len Murray, and others to reach a compromise. He was loyal to Rees, but perhaps misread the situation. Nevertheless he did do a considerable amount of good work at the Northern Ireland Office, in particular by piloting through a bill outlawing religious discrimination in employment, and by arranging subsidies to keep the great shipyard of Harland and Wolff in existence.

Orme was no doubt thankful to wash his hands of Northern Ireland and move on to being minister of state at the Department of Health and Social Security in April 1976, in Jim Callaghan's government. Five months later he was promoted to be minister for social security and a member of the cabinet, but his time in that post was again unhappy, given the need for tight curbs on government expenditure. Following Labour's defeat in the 1979 election he served successively as opposition spokesman on health and social services (1979–80), industry (1980–83), and finally energy (1983–7). He held the latter post through the miners' strike of 1984–5, when he publicly supported but privately criticized the intransigent leader of the miners, Arthur Scargill, and then through the subsequent decimation of the British coal industry and the privatization of the gas industry. Complex, deep-thinking, more than a little secretive, often suspicious of his colleagues, prone to respond to questions by posing another question in reply, he was a fair-minded if sometimes irascible chairman of the Parliamentary Labour Party, basically loyal to but not uncritical of Neil Kinnock, from 1987 until 1992.

Orme, who had held Salford West until the 1983 election, and Salford East thereafter, retired from the House of Commons at the 1997 election, and was immediately made a life peer, as Baron Orme, of Salford. A keen and lifelong supporter of Manchester United Football Club and of the Lancashire cricket team, he lived his final years in Northwood Grove, Sale. He died on 28 April 2005 at Trafford General Hospital, Davyhulme, following a stroke, and was survived by his wife, Irene.

TAM DALYELL

Sources *Daily Telegraph* (2 May 2005) · *The Times* (3 May 2005) · *The Guardian* (3 May 2005) · *The Independent* (3 May 2005) · Burke, *Peerage* · *WW* (2005) · personal knowledge (2009) · private information (2009) · b. cert. · m. cert. · d. cert.

Archives LSE | FILM BFINA, current affairs footage · BFINA, documentary footage · BFINA, party political footage | SOUND BL NSA, current affairs recording · BL NSA, documentary recording · BL NSA, parliamentary recordings · BL NSA, party political recordings

Likenesses photographs, 1980–86, Getty Images, London · J. Mendoza, group portrait, oils, 1986–7, House of Commons, Westminster, London · photographs, 1991–5, Photoshot, London · obituary photographs

Wealth at death £149,169: probate, 12 July 2005, *CGPLA Eng. & Wales*

Orr, Sir David Alexander (1922–2008), businessman, was born on 10 May 1922 at 2 Temple Terrace, Dalkey, a few miles south-east of Dublin, the third of the four children of the Revd (later Canon) Adrian William Fielder (Billy) Orr (*d.* 1964), Church of Ireland clergyman, and his wife, Grace, *née* Robinson (*d.* 1967). His father held the living in several parishes in and around Dublin until he became the rector of Taney parish, Dundrum, in 1935, where he stayed until his retirement in 1958; he became a canon of Christ Church Cathedral, Dublin, in 1946.

David Orr was educated at the High School, Dublin, before going on to Trinity College, Dublin, where he began by reading classics. He was a keen sportsman, being a noted rugby player who captained the Trinity team as well as a champion boxer. (Rugby was a lifetime interest; in the early 1950s when he lived in London he played rugby for London Irish, captaining the club from 1951 to 1954, and in later life he was its president, from 1986 to 1988.) Before the outbreak of the Second World War, he joined the Territorial Army (Royal Ulster Rifles) and in 1941 he left Dublin to enlist in the British army. He was commissioned into the Royal Engineers and served with distinction, especially in the Burma campaign of 1944–5, being awarded the military cross and bar in 1945. He returned to Trinity College in 1946, and graduated with a first-class degree and an LLB in 1948. He then joined the Anglo-Dutch multinational corporation Unilever as a graduate trainee, a scheme then widely recognized for its quality *per se* as well as that of the senior managers who emerged from it. In the following year he married Phoebe Rosaleen Davis, daughter of Harold Percival Davis, of Dublin; they had three daughters.

Unilever's businesses were spread across the world and Orr spent five years (1955–60) with Hindustan Lever in India and two years in New York (1965–7) as president of Lever Brothers in the USA. When he returned to London he was made a director, followed three years later by appointments as vice-chairman of Unilever plc and a member of the three-man special committee, then the decision-making body for both the UK and the Dutch Unilever companies. In 1974 he became chairman of Unilever, a post he held for eight years. His abilities as well as his personal charm had 'facilitated an almost seamless upward rise through the Unilever hierarchy' (Jones, 55).

For much of Orr's time as chairman multinational corporations like Unilever faced not only public criticism of their activities but also an exceptionally turbulent economic environment. Orr worked 'to maintain the cohesion of Unilever and to protect the jobs of its employees' (Jones, 92). He was personally involved with Unilever's significant acquisition of the American company National Starch in 1977, seen as part of a more focused approach to strategic thinking. He was knighted in 1977 and, two years later, was appointed a commander of the Dutch order of Orange Nassau. Outside Unilever he was a member of the Wilson committee which reviewed the functioning of financial institutions (1977–80). While the survival and success of Unilever under his watch were no mean achievement in the face of the difficult conditions, in the judgement of Geoffrey Jones, Unilever's historian, the strategic thinking and a correction of the balance of power between the English and Dutch partners in the running of the company were his principal achievements.

In the two decades after he left Unilever in 1982 Orr was busy with corporate and public activities until poor health dictated his retirement in 1998. In the early 1970s he had been a member of the Confederation of British Industry committee chaired by Harold Watkinson, whose report recommended more use of non-executive directors, and he became a non-executive director at a number of companies, including Rio Tinto Zinc (1981–92) and Shell (1982–92). He was chairman of the Inchcape group (1983–6), deputy chairman (1986–91), and chairman again (1991–2). Beyond corporate life he served on both the top salaries review body for the civil service (1982–5) and the Armed Forces Pay Review body (1982–4), and was involved in a wide range of charitable, educational, and cultural organizations, including the London School of Economics (of which he was a governor, 1980–96), the Liverpool School of Tropical Medicine (of which he was president, 1981–9), and the College of Speech Therapists (of which he was also president, 1992–6). He was chairman of the Leverhulme Trust (1982–92) and of the British Council (1985–92); his Irish connections had always been important to him and he was a member of the court of the Bank of Ireland (1983–9), chairman of the cultural think tank Anglo-Irish Encounter (1983–7), and chancellor of the Queen's University, Belfast (1992–8). For all of these he exercised what *The Times* described as 'his silver-tongued powers of persuasion' (1 June 1992), but the most public legacy of this may be the Globe Theatre, on London's South Bank, which opened in 1997. As chairman from 1982 of the trust established to build the theatre, he acted as principal fundraiser for Sam Wanamaker's project. A bust of Orr at the theatre commemorates his work. He died at his home, Home Farm House, Shackleford, near Godalming, Surrey, on 2 February 2008, of cancer of the bladder, and was survived by his wife, Phoebe, and their three daughters.

JUDY SLINN

Sources C. Wilson, *Unilever, 1945–1965: challenge and response in the post-war industrial revolution* (1968) · D. K. Fieldhouse, *Unilever overseas: the anatomy of a multinational, 1895–1965* (1978) · W. J. Reader, *Fifty years of Unilever* (1980) · *The Times* (1 June 1992); (12 March 2008) · G. Jones, *Renewing Unilever: transformation and tradition* (2005) · *Daily Telegraph* (29 Feb 2008) · *Irish Times* (8 March 2008) · *The*

Independent (13 March 2008) · *Irish Independent* (16 March 2008) · *WW* (2008) · Burke, *Peerage* · b. cert. · d. cert.
Archives SOUND BL NSA, documentary recording
Likenesses bust, Globe Theatre, London · obituary photographs · photograph, repro. in Jones, *Renewing Unilever*, 56
Wealth at death £1,496,706: probate, 19 Nov 2008, *CGPLA Eng. & Wales*

Orr, Robert Kemsley [Robin] (**1909–2006**), composer and musical administrator, was born on 2 June 1909 at Glebe House, Trinity Road, Brechin, Forfarshire, the elder child of Robert Workman Orr, linen manufacturer, and his wife, Florence Mary, *née* Kemsley, who came from a farming family in Essex. His sister Kirsteen was born in 1911. Both his parents were amateur musicians and Orr's first taste of music was in regular family musical evenings in the home. After a few years at Brechin high school he was sent to a preparatory school, Hurst Grange, in Stirling. There he was taught music by J. W. Kinnear, who encouraged his first attempts at composition. From Stirling he went to Loretto School, on the outskirts of Edinburgh. At that time there was little to encourage the young musician there, so he left early and studied privately before entering the Royal College of Music, in London, at the age of sixteen. There he studied organ with Walter Alcock, piano with Arthur Benjamin, and composition with Henry Moule. In 1929 he became organ scholar at Pembroke College, Cambridge, where he came under the influence of Cyril Rootham and Edward Dent. Later he studied with Alfredo Casella in Siena and with Nadia Boulanger in Paris. From 1933 to 1936 he was director of music at Sidcot School in Somerset. He was then an assistant lecturer in music at the University of Leeds (1936–8) before becoming organist and director of studies in music at St John's College, Cambridge. On 29 December 1937 he had married Margaret Ellen Mace, the 24-year-old daughter of the Egyptologist Arthur Cruttenden Mace. They had three children, twins, Alison and David (*b.* 1940), and Jean Kirsteen (*b.* 1945).

During the Second World War Orr served as a photographic intelligence officer in the RAF. On demobilization with the rank of flight lieutenant in 1945 he returned to Cambridge, where he was appointed university lecturer in music (1947–56) and became a fellow of St John's in 1948. It was during those post-war years that he began to devote more of his time to serious composition. Professorships followed at the Royal College of Music (1950–56), at the University of Glasgow (1956–65), and at Cambridge (1965–76). He was also founder chairman of Scottish Opera (1962–76), director of the Cambridge Arts Theatre (1970–75), and a director of Welsh National Opera (1977–83). He was elected to honorary fellowships at St John's and Pembroke colleges, Cambridge, and was appointed CBE in 1972. His first marriage ended in divorce in 1979, and on 14 July the same year he married Doris Ruth Winny-Meyer, a 56-year-old art historian from Switzerland, and daughter of Leo Meyer, watch manufacturer.

Notwithstanding Orr's gifts as a musical administrator and the consequent demands on his time and energies, he still found time to produce a formidable output of interesting and assured works in a language very much his own. Although marked by a passing resemblance to other composers, which makes his music quite difficult to categorize, there is an innate sense of lyricism and Scottish grittiness that runs through many of his important works. He had a certain success with his first orchestral venture, the overture *The Prospect of Whitby* (1948), but the orchestral work that brought him into prominence was the *Symphony in One Movement* (1963) which, although modelled on Sibelius's seventh symphony, was in no way a mere shadow of this work. It has drama and a lucid compactness which appealed to audiences of the time. Championed by Sir Alexander Gibson and the Scottish National Orchestra (as were so many of Orr's orchestral works) it had several performances by this orchestra. Two more symphonies were to follow, also both in one movement, in 1970 and 1978.

Orr's first opera, *Full Circle*, in one act, to a libretto in Scottish dialogue by Sydney Goodsir Smith, was commissioned by Scottish Television and premièred by Scottish Opera in 1968. It shared a double bill with Stravinsky's *The Soldier's Tale*, and had a similar sparse orchestration. It also broke new ground by being set in the Scots vernacular, which few composers had attempted before. A more ambitious three-act opera, *Hermiston*, followed in 1975. The libretto was by Bill Bryden, after Robert Louis Stevenson's *The Weir of Hermiston*, and it was premièred at the Edinburgh international festival. Its bleak drama and scenes of a hanging, rape, murder, madness, and suicide, probably contributed to its failure to find a regular place in the repertoire. Nevertheless it showed Orr's growing mastery of the operatic genre. His next opera, an adaptation of Tom Stoppard's comic *On the Razzle* (1988), was brilliantly produced by the students of the Royal Scottish Academy of Music and Drama in Glasgow, and enjoyed a greater success.

Orr excelled in music for the church, much of it written for St John's College. For its 450th anniversary he wrote a fine anthem 'Come and let yourselves be built' (1961). In addition there were songs and chamber and instrumental music, as well as a *Rhapsody* (1956) for string orchestra, and a delightful song cycle, *From the Book of Philip Sparrow* (1969), for mezzo-soprano and strings, which was premièred by Janet Baker and the Scottish National Orchestra.

Orr's approach to teaching and administration was the opposite of didactic. His generous nature and open-mindedness made him much sought after as a champion of new music and as someone who could get things done. During his nine years in Glasgow he teamed up with the young Alexander Gibson, who had just taken over as musical director of the Scottish National Orchestra, and assisted him with his Musica Viva concerts. These concerts brought Stockhausen, Schönberg, Stravinsky, and several Scottish composers including Iain Hamilton, Thea Musgrave, and Orr himself into prominence with the Scottish public. When Gibson approached him for support with the formation of Scottish Opera in 1960, Orr enthusiastically agreed. The company became highly successful and at the time of his death, in spite of government cuts, was still one of the most successful of British opera companies.

Robin Orr was a man who had time for many other interests besides music. After an article he wrote for the *Glasgow Herald* concerning a visit to the Wexford festival, and mentioning at length its gastronomic and liquid delights, he was invited by the editor to write a weekly food column. This was followed by other invitations from gastronomical journals eager to share his knowledge and experience. His reputation as a bon vivant was legendary and he endeared himself to many as a perfect and generous host, as well as a delightful raconteur. To those who didn't know him well, he often gave the impression of being a little vague, but beneath this he was the shrewdest of men who had a rare gift for dealing quite quickly with the poseur and the bore. In later life he enjoyed walking in the Swiss Alps (he took Swiss nationality in 1995) near his second home in Klosters. There he composed his last orchestral work, *Sinfonietta Helvetica* (1990), to mark the 700th anniversary of the Swiss confederation. His musical autobiography, *Musical Chairs*, was published in 1998. He died at the Cambridge Nursing Centre, 5 High Street, Chesterton, Cambridge, on 9 April 2006, of a urinary tract infection, and was survived by his wife, Doris, and the three children of his first marriage. Orr's funeral was held at Pembroke College, Cambridge, and a memorial service took place at St John's College, Cambridge, on 4 November 2006.

JOHN MCLEOD

Sources R. Orr, *Musical chairs* (1998) · *The Herald* [Glasgow] (12 April 2006) · *The Independent* (13 April 2006) · *The Guardian* (14 April 2006) · *The Scotsman* (14 April 2006) · *The Times* (17 April 2006) · *Daily Telegraph* (15 May 2006) · I. Kemp, *The Eagle* [St John Cam. magazine] (2006) · papers of Robin Orr, 1946–96, CUL · papers of Robin Orr, 1946–96, Pembroke Cam. · papers of Robin Orr, 1946–96, St John Cam. · www.scottishmusiccentre.com, 10 April 2009, Scottish Music Centre, catalogues and holdings · *WW* (2006) · personal knowledge (2010) · private information (2010) · b. cert. · m. certs. · d. cert.

Archives CUL, corresp., music MSS, papers · Pembroke Cam. · St John Cam.

Likenesses J. Bown, bromide fibre print, 1990–99, NPG · obituary photographs · photographs, repro. in Orr, *Musical chairs*

Wealth at death under £82,000: probate, 28 Nov 2006, *CGPLA Eng. & Wales*

Orton, Peter Charles (1943–2007), television executive and businessman, was born at Collyers Steep, Petersfield, Hampshire, on 17 June 1943, one of four sons of Herbert Charles Orton (1887–1953), an aircraft fitter and former cruise liner steward, and his wife, Eva Lilian, *née* Dallas (1904–1995). At the time of his birth the family lived at 2 The Spain, Petersfield. He was brought up in Portsmouth then Brighton, and attended Portsmouth Technical College and Westlain Grammar School, Brighton. He left at the age of sixteen to become a salesperson for a naval tailor's. He moved to the specialist footwear company Scholl Medical in 1962, with responsibility for the west country, then Scotland. In Scotland he met Susan Virginia (Sue) Stevenson (*b.* 1950), daughter of Anthony Ronald Guy Stevenson, insurance broker, of Seton House, Longniddry, East Lothian. They married in Seton Chapel, Longniddry, on 12 August 1972. They had one son, Jamie.

In 1967 Orton joined Television International Enterprises (a business run by David Stirling, founder of the SAS), as a buyer of programmes to be shown in the Middle East, Africa, and the Caribbean. He was particularly successful in negotiating the rights for those countries to screen the 1970 world cup, which earned the company a profit of £350,000. The marketing of *Sesame Street*, the pioneering programme for pre-school children, featuring Muppet characters created by Jim Henson, was another of his successes, resulting in its producer, the Children's Television Workshop, appointing Orton its international director of programming in 1969. He left three years later to found Sport on TV, a television sports packaging company, but returned in 1972 as vice-president of the Children's Television Workshop's worldwide distribution arm, responsible for international sales.

In 1982 Henson launched Henson International Television, and Orton became its chief executive officer, expanding the Muppets into feature films and building up those characters and the programme *Fraggle Rock* as international brands. When Henson sold the company to the Walt Disney Company in 1989 Orton set up his own business, taking the previous company's initials and forming the British-based HiT Entertainment as a distributor of pre-school children's shows, with the rights to *Alvin and the Chipmunks* and *Postman Pat*. Programmes it later sold around the globe included *Angelina Ballerina* and *Fireman Sam*. 'I was extremely lucky with my timing', said Orton. 'There was very little competition and most of it worked in big companies who weren't working to survive as I was' (*Daily Telegraph*, 10 Dec 2007).

HiT Entertainment began trading on the alternative investment market in 1996, receiving a full listing on the London stock exchange a year later, which made it one of the first independent television companies to be floated. In 1998 it formed the HOT Animation studio, based in Manchester, making such television series as *Brambly Hedge*, *Pingu*, *Rubbadubbers*, and, most successfully, *Bob the Builder*, and creating employment for hundreds of British-based animators, producers, directors, and musicians. HiT Entertainment bought Lyrick Studios, the producer of *Barney and Friends*, in 2001 and, a year later, Gullane Entertainment (formerly the Britt Allcroft Company) for £139 million, giving it the rights to the Thomas the Tank Engine brand and ownership of the animated television series *Thomas the Tank Engine and Friends*, which had begun in 1984. Ninety per cent of HiT Entertainment's income—which reached £168 million in 2003—came from licensing and merchandising; indeed, Orton liked to joke that he should be paying the BBC and ITV to screen his programmes rather than the other way round, as they acted in effect as advertisements for the company's products. He was chief executive of the company from 1989 to 2001, executive chairman from 2001 to 2002, and non-executive chairman from 2003 to 2005. In the latter year he negotiated the sale of the company to the private equity group Apax Partners for £489 million. The following year he organized the children's party at the palace, featuring characters from children's literature, to mark the queen's eightieth birthday.

Softly spoken, unpompous, and self-deprecating, Orton was extremely shrewd, though he ascribed much of his success to luck. He worked very long hours and could be demanding of his employees, but he was also generous, and liked to point out that he had made at least ten of his employees millionaires. He also funded scholarships, courses, and work placements for those trying to enter the children's television industry. He received BAFTA's lifetime achievement award in 2002 (when he was also presented with an honorary doctorate by De Montfort University) and another from the Marché Internationale des Programmes de Télévision (MIP-TV) in 2005. He was appointed CVO for his contribution to children's literacy two years later. For the last ten years of his life he suffered from cancer, and he was president of, and a generous donor to, the Head and Neck Cancer Research Trust. He died at his home, Lower Greenhill Farm, Wootton Bassett, Wiltshire, on 5 December 2007, and was survived by his wife, Sue, and son, Jamie. ANTHONY HAYWARD

Sources *The Guardian* (7 May 2005); (12 Dec 2007) • *Daily Telegraph* (10 Dec 2007) • *The Times* (12 Dec 2007) • *The Independent* (12 Dec 2007) • *WW* (2007) • peterorton.com, 1 Feb 2010 • hitentertainment.com, 1 Feb 2010 • randomhouse.com/kids/thomas/authors.html, 1 Feb 2010 • SIFT database, BFI • www.uk.imdb.com • b. cert. • m. cert. • d. cert.

Likenesses photographs, 2001, Photoshot, London • G/M, photograph, Camera Press, London • obituary photographs

Wealth at death £21,268,633: probate, 19 May 2008, *CGPLA Eng. & Wales*

Osgood, Peter Leslie (1947–2006), footballer, was born on 20 February 1947 at 26 East Crescent, Clewer Without, near Windsor, Berkshire, the son of Leslie Frank Herbert Osgood, bricklayer, and Ivy Lillian Rose Ashley, *née* Cowley. He attended Clewer Green primary school in Hatch Lane, Windsor, and Dedworth secondary modern school. On leaving school he followed his father into the building trade. He had played schoolboy football for the Slough and district team and for the local youth club at Spital. He applied for a trial at Reading Football Club but heard nothing from them. When offered a trial by Arsenal FC he turned them down. His uncle Bob then wrote a letter about his nephew to Chelsea FC, who duly signed up the young Osgood as an amateur in 1964. Osgood scored a hatful of goals for the reserves and Chelsea's manager, Tommy Docherty, soon offered him a professional contract. His first team début followed on 16 December 1964 at Stamford Bridge, the Chelsea ground, in a fifth round tie of the league cup against Workington Town. Osgood scored both the Chelsea goals in that match, which they won 2–0, and his career was launched. Three days later he married his first wife, Rosemary Heather Snow, an eighteen-year-old bank clerk from Windsor, and daughter of Eric Randolph Snow, gardener. They had two sons, Anthony (*b.* 1965) and Mark (*b.* 1967).

Tall (at 6 feet 2 inches) and lean (he weighed only 12 stone), Osgood had remarkable control with both feet, strength, positional sense, and personal courage. In an era when football was a notably physical game and centre-forwards could expect to suffer for their skills, centre halves rarely got the better of him. Osgood—known to everyone as Ossie—moved with elegance and speed on the pitch; off it there was always something of a swagger to his style. Whether remonstrating with referees or conducting an interview with journalists, his face was always likely to break into a knowing, mischievous grin. He was admired almost as much for his jack-the-lad cheek and bravado around the pubs and boutiques of the King's Road in Chelsea as for his panache on the ball.

Peter Leslie Osgood (1947–2006), by unknown photographer, 1972

So impressive were his performances in his early matches that, though only nineteen, Osgood was named in the forty-man squad picked in April 1966 by Alf Ramsey, the England manager, for the forthcoming world cup. In the event Osgood was not a member of the final squad of twenty-two. He suffered a broken leg after a tackle from Emlyn Hughes, then playing for Blackpool, in October 1966, and missed the rest of the 1966–7 season, including Chelsea's FA cup final defeat by Tottenham Hotspur. When he returned to the first team he was probably slightly slower on the ball but also more guileful; what he had lost in pace he made up for in skill. There followed the best years of his career, when he was the spearhead of a Chelsea team of all the talents between 1967 and 1971. In 1969–70 he was the first division's top scorer, with thirty-one goals. Chelsea won the FA cup in that season, defeating their close rivals Leeds in the first final ever to have gone to a replay after a 2–2 draw at Wembley stadium.

Osgood scored a brilliant diving header to equalize the scores at 1–1 in the second match at Old Trafford, which Chelsea eventually won 2–1. In the following year, again after a replay, Chelsea brought home the European cup winners' cup after defeating an ageing Real Madrid side 2–1 in Athens. Osgood scored in both matches.

Osgood's success as a player cannot be separated from the talents around him. Several Chelsea players of that era, including the goalkeeper Peter Bonetti, the defender and club captain Ron Harris, the midfielders John Hollins and Alan Hudson, and Osgood's partner in the Chelsea attack, Ian Hutchinson, were on the fringes of the England team. Two more, the full-back Eddie McCreadie and the midfielder Charlie Cooke, were regular choices for Scotland. Together the team played some of the most attractive football of the age, though their relatively modest achievements in the Football League were evidence of their inconsistency: Chelsea were a team for the big occasion rather than the weekly challenge of first division combat. They were also the team that most closely mirrored the style of the age: situated close to the fashionable parts of west London, the Chelsea team were the 'kings of the King's Road', celebrities who attracted the support of other celebrities in turn. Osgood apparently charmed Raquel Welch, the Hollywood film goddess then at the height of her fame, and she is said to have once run along the touchline waving to him. When he scored his hundredth goal for Chelsea he returned to the dressing room to find Steve McQueen, the most charismatic film actor of the era, awaiting him.

Osgood had played for England at youth and under-twenty-three level but he only won four caps as a full international and only started the match in the first and last of those games, against Belgium in February 1970 and Italy in November 1973. He was a member of the 1970 Mexico world cup squad and came off the bench in the games against Czechoslovakia and Romania. That Osgood was overlooked in this way has been put down to the caution and conservatism of Ramsey, who liked obedient, respectful, and hard-working players and was instinctively mistrustful of flair, especially when displayed fitfully and with a confident and defiant attitude. But it was also owing to the plethora of good forwards of different styles who graced the English game in the late 1960s and early 1970s: Geoff Hurst, Jeff Astle, Francis Lee, Martin Chivers, Allan Clarke, and later Malcolm Macdonald were a formidable clutch of competitors for the centre-forward's jersey.

Osgood scored in Chelsea's 2–1 defeat by Stoke City at Wembley in the 1972 league cup final. The match marked the beginning of Chelsea's decline. A series of disputes between several crucial players and the Chelsea manager, Dave Sexton, marred the next two years and eventually the team was broken up. Osgood was placed on the transfer list and sold to Southampton for £275,000, a club record, in March 1974. He spent three years there, scoring thirty-six goals in 157 games, and helped the Saints to victory in the 1976 FA cup final against Manchester United, the firm favourites. While at Southampton he enjoyed a brief stint on loan to Norwich City. He then played for the Philadelphia Furies in the United States, where he managed only a single goal in twenty-three matches. Finally, at the end of 1978 he returned to play ten more matches for Chelsea but neither he nor they were the forces they had once been and a year later he retired. In all he played 376 games for Chelsea and scored 152 goals for them.

Like many former footballers Osgood went into the pub business, teaming up with his former partner in the Chelsea attack, Ian Hutchinson, but was declared bankrupt in 1985. He then turned back to football and was variously youth team coach at Portsmouth, in public relations for Southampton FC, a match day host at Chelsea, and a popular after-dinner speaker who evoked the nostalgia of his audiences for the players and games of their youth. His first marriage having ended, on 17 October 1980 he married Philippa (Pippa) Cooke-Smith, a 29-year-old airport stewardess, and daughter of Richard Anthony Wellwood Cooke-Smith, civil aviation director. The marriage ended in divorce, and on 1 June 1987 Osgood married, as his third wife, Lynnette Ann Finlay, a 34-year-old airline receptionist, and daughter of Raymond Noël Thorogood, contracts engineer. They had one son, Darren (*b.* 1989). Osgood overcame alcoholism but died of a heart attack after collapsing at the funeral of a family member in Slough on 1 March 2006; he was declared dead at Wexham Park Hospital. A memorial service, including the band of the Coldstream Guards, was held for him at the Shed End of the Stamford Bridge stadium on 1 October 2006. His ashes were buried under the penalty spot. He was survived by his three sons and by his third wife, Lynnette, who served as the director of the Peter Osgood Trust, helping disadvantaged children to fulfil their potential through football. LAWRENCE GOLDMAN

Sources *The Times* (4 Feb 1966); (2 March 2006) • P. Osgood, *Ossie the wizard* (1969) • P. Osgood, M. King, and M. Knight, *Ossie: king of Stamford Bridge* (2002) • C. Batty, *Kings of the King's Road* (2004) • R. Glanvill, *Chelsea FC: the definitive story of the first 100 years* (2006) • T. Matthews, *Who's who of Chelsea* (2005) • *Daily Telegraph* (2 March 2006) • *The Guardian* (2 March 2006) • *The Independent* (2 March 2006) • www.peterosgood.co.uk, 30 July 2009 • www.thepeterosgoodtrust.org, 30 July 2009 • b. cert. • m. certs. • d. cert.

Archives FILM BFINA, documentary footage | SOUND BL NSA, documentary recording

Likenesses photographs, 1965–2006, PA Photos, London • photographs, 1966–8, Photoshot, London • photographs, 1966–2005, Rex Features, London • photographs, 1966–2005, Getty Images, London • photograph, 1972, Hult. Arch., London [*see illus.*] • obituary photographs

Osmond, Sir Douglas (1914–2006), police officer, was born at 40 Stewart Road, Bournemouth, on 27 June 1914, the son of Ernest Herbert Osmond (*d.* 1914), blacksmith, and his wife, Eliza, *née* Mitchell, schoolteacher. His father joined the Royal Navy and was killed in action in October 1914, leaving Osmond and his brother William to be brought up by their mother and educated locally. In 1932 he was awarded a scholarship from the Kitchener Memorial Fund (to help the children of members of the armed services) to read mathematics at University College, London. In 1935, after graduating, he joined the Metropolitan

Police under the new fast-track promotion scheme recently introduced by Lord Trenchard, Metropolitan Police commissioner and former head of the Royal Air Force. He was one of only a few university-educated recruits to have entered the police service as a constable. The Trenchard scheme, as it was colloquially known, symbolized the contemporary shift in organizational thinking from a command to a managerial approach: the scheme was designed to improve the quality of Metropolitan Police management by identifying potential managers early in their careers and promoting them directly into the middle ranks at the level of inspector. From there onwards they would rise through the ranks on their own merits. After graduating from the Metropolitan Police College at Hendon Osmond quickly became inspector. On 23 July 1938 he married Doris Evelyn (Eve) Finnemore (*d.* 1995), daughter of Walter Finnemore, manufacturer, at the parish church in Northchurch, Hertfordshire. They had two daughters, Nicola and Joanna.

Osmond joined the Royal Navy in 1943 and from 1944 to 1945 was seconded to the Allied Control Commission for Germany. As deputy assistant inspector-general in the public safety division he worked on plans for the post-war reorganization of the German police. After military service he returned to the police and in 1946 was appointed as the chief constable of Shropshire. He was not the youngest chief constable: Richard Dawnay Lemon was twenty-seven when made chief constable of the East Riding in 1939, and Eric St Johnston was twenty-nine when made chief constable of Oxfordshire in 1940. He was, however, one of a cohort of young Trenchard scheme graduates who left the Metropolitan Police to take command of provincial (mainly county) police forces. The reason for this drift was local pragmatism. Prior to the 1939 wartime regulations giving the home secretary the final approval over chief officer appointments, the provincial police authorities had successfully resisted the Home Office regulation that all chief constables must have prior police experience, preferring instead to maintain their long-standing tradition of appointing chief constables with social standing and military rather than police experience. Following the change in practice the graduates of the Metropolitan Police College conveniently provided county and large city police authorities with a pool of chief officers whom they deemed both professionally and socially suitable to command their police forces. Consequently Osmond and his youthful cohort formed a select group of modern career chief officers who came to dominate the police service until the late 1970s and shape its structure.

During his sixteen years as chief constable of Shropshire Osmond sought to improve the conditions of his police officers and also their efficiency. Not only did he campaign for better housing and conditions, but he also took an innovative approach to crime prevention by introducing a poster campaign that used cartoon characters and comic verse. He left Shropshire in 1962, to head the larger Hampshire and Isle of Wight constabulary, and presided over its amalgamation with the Portsmouth and Southampton city forces in 1967. He remained as chief constable of Hampshire until his retirement in 1977. Always forward thinking, he oversaw the building of new police headquarters at Winchester and campaigned for more police officers. He also took the innovative step of introducing crime prevention officers into each division at a time when policing was almost wholly reactive. During his time as chief constable he also had to manage some major local events, which included policing the Isle of Wight pop festivals (which he attended) and also the aftermath of the 1972 IRA bombing of the Aldershot barracks.

Osmond's contribution to policing was not confined to Hampshire. Between 1967 and 1969 he served as president of the Association of Chief Police Officers of England and Wales. In the late 1960s he and the Metropolitan Police deputy commissioner, Robert Mark, reviewed the policing of Northern Ireland. Their highly critical report almost led the home secretary, James Callaghan, to replace the senior management of the Royal Ulster Constabulary, although the eventual action was the installation of an advisory committee. After retirement Osmond joined the Phillips commission (the royal commission on criminal procedure), whose report led to the Police and Criminal Evidence Act 1984.

Osmond was awarded the Queen's Police Medal in 1962. He was appointed OBE in 1958 and CBE in 1968. In 1971 he became an officer of the order of St John of Jerusalem and was knighted in the same year. In 1981 he became deputy lieutenant of Hampshire. Having lived latterly in Shaftesbury, Dorset, he died at Sutton Veny House nursing home, Sutton Veny, near Warminster, Wiltshire, of cerebrovascular disease, on 20 April 2006. He was survived by his two daughters. DAVID S. WALL

Sources *Daily Telegraph* (28 April 2006) · Burke, *Peerage* · *WW* (2006) · private information (2010) · b. cert. · m. cert. · d. cert.
Wealth at death £152,289: probate, 12 Oct 2006, *CGPLA Eng. & Wales*

Page, Sir Frederick William (1917–2005), aircraft designer and industrialist, was born on 20 February 1917 in Wimbledon, Surrey, the only child of Richard Page, a chauffeur then serving in the army, and his wife, Ellen Sarah, *née* Potter (*d.* 1960). His father was killed on active service in France during the First World War shortly before his birth. Brought up in humble circumstances by his widowed mother, he won a scholarship to Rutlish Grammar School at Merton, Surrey, before gaining a Surrey county major scholarship and entrance to St Catharine's College, Cambridge, in 1935. Reading mathematics and aeronautics, he achieved the rare distinction of starred first-class honours in the mechanical sciences tripos. Ambitious from his mid-teens to design aircraft, in 1938 he joined Hawker Aircraft at Kingston upon Thames, working under Sydney Camm, designer of the famous Second World War Hurricane fighter. There he worked during the war on the Hurricane, Typhoon, and Tempest aircraft, designing structures, control systems, and high-speed aerofoil sections. On 6 July 1940 he married Kathleen Edith de Courcy (1916–1993), a 24-year-old ARP warden, and daughter of Albert Edwin de Courcy, post office official. They had three sons, Gordon, Stephen, and Alan, and a daughter, Jennifer.

Such were Page's demonstrated abilities that in 1945 he was invited to join W. E. W. (Teddy) Petter's newly created aircraft design team at English Electric in Preston, Lancashire. Over the next thirty years Page was to play a leading role in both design and management in the very advanced military combat aircraft programmes emanating from what, largely under his inspired direction and guidance, became the most accomplished military aircraft organization in Europe. The initiating project there was a jet bomber replacement for the wartime de Havilland Mosquito, in the conception of which he was centrally involved and which was realized as the highly successful Canberra, Britain's first jet bomber. First flown in May 1949, it proceeded swiftly through development and into production.

Now located at nearby Warton, Page was appointed assistant chief designer later in 1949 and, after the resignation of Petter, he was made chief engineer in 1950 at the age of only thirty-two, and played a major role in bringing the Canberra into operational service. Serving with the Royal Air Force from May 1951 and with fourteen overseas air forces in twenty-one variants, and capturing twenty-two world distance and altitude records, the total production of this aircraft ran to 1376 units, including licensed production in the United States and Australia, the last example continuing in service with the RAF until 2007. In parallel Page guided Petter's first studies of the P-1A twin-engined supersonic research aircraft initiated in August 1948, incorporating a 60° wing sweepback. The P-1A was first flown in August 1954, becoming the first British (and European) aircraft to achieve sustained supersonic speeds. His team then went on to evolve this aircraft into the Lightning supersonic fighter for the RAF. First flown in April 1957, the Lightning became the first British aircraft to exceed Mach 2 (twice the speed of sound, i.e. 1400 m.p.h.) in level flight. No other aircraft design team anywhere in the world made the transition from subsonic to bisonic flight in one leap (while also incorporating a complex weapons system). The Lightning entered operational service in June 1961, and a total of 340 were produced in six variants for the RAF and for export. Most significantly, the Lightning formed the basis of a series of major contracts in the Middle East, notably for Saudi Arabia, and the starting point for the huge exports of military equipment to that country that followed.

In 1957 Page's team began studies to meet the RAF's general operational requirement GOR339 for a supersonic successor to the Canberra—the bisonic tactical, strike, and reconnaissance TSR2—also intended as a 'golden welding flux' in facilitating the concentration of the UK's then twenty-two airframe and six engine companies into three and two large units respectively. The eventual government contract was placed in March 1959 with Vickers–Armstrongs at Weybridge, Surrey, with English Electric as a 50 per cent partner. Accordingly, when English Electric Aviation was formed that year Page was appointed chief executive. The TSR2 programme was effectively the means for the creation of the government-enforced merger of the two companies, together with Bristol Aircraft, to form the British Aircraft Corporation (BAC) in January 1960. However, this very advanced and complex programme was dogged by excessively demanding equipment changes and performance increases that also meant it was beset by corresponding delays and cost escalation that in turn greatly exacerbated its political vulnerability. Although the first example had flown successfully in September 1964, and essentially demonstrated its formidable performance capability, and Page had belatedly been given overall programme responsibility, it was precipitously cancelled by the incoming Labour government in the budget of April 1965, just as quantity production was about to begin. What would have constituted around half the forward military aircraft workload of the new joint company until well into the 1970s was thus lost at a stroke, presenting Page with the daunting management challenge of reconstructing the seriously depleted Warton workforce to maintain its nationally essential core competence.

By mid-1965 an inter-governmental agreement with France was sealed to give the go-ahead to a joint programme with Dassault–Breguet and a management company, Sepecat, for a new supersonic fighter-bomber and advanced trainer, later named Jaguar and first flown in France in September 1968; Page was appointed co-chairman of Sepecat, with a French counterpart. A total of 200 aircraft each was produced for the RAF and for the French air force, and ninety-four for export by BAC to Ecuador, Oman, and India, where Page also played a leading part in the establishment of the licenced production of an initial batch of seventy-six Jaguars, which was subsequently augmented by further large batches. He later also became chairman of Panavia, the Anglo-German-Italian joint company formed in 1969 in Munich with Messerschmitt–Bölkow–Blohm and Fiat to produce the supersonic, variable wing sweepback, multi-role combat Tornado. First flown by BAC in August 1974, 872 were jointly produced for the three home countries, with a further 120 exported to Saudi Arabia in the al-Yamamah programme.

In 1967 Page had become chairman of the BAC military aircraft division. Five years later he was appointed BAC's managing director (aircraft), with the added responsibility as chairman of BAC's commercial aircraft division of rationalizing the company's then struggling commercial aircraft portfolio and rebalancing the company's overall aircraft work loading. In this, his perceptive and imaginative industrial management strategies and techniques in financial and risk management, as well as technical and multiple programme management, were a key ingredient in the run-up to the long-threatened government edict nationalizing the aircraft industry. In particular, his earlier developed 'matrix' management structure—wherein the corporate functional control lines were meshed with the multiple programme operational lines—proved to be consistently effective. Eventually implemented in 1977, bringing together BAC, Hawker Siddeley Aviation, and Scottish Aviation, nationalization resulted in the creation of British Aerospace, of whose aircraft group Page was appointed chairman and chief executive. His final appointment, this presented him with a further substantial managerial challenge in initiating the progressive return of the company to private ownership in 1982.

Appointed CBE in 1961 and knighted in 1979, Page was also made a fellow of the Royal Society (1978), the Fellowship of Engineering, later the Royal Academy of Engineering (1977), an honorary fellow of the Royal Aeronautical Society (1980), and received numerous other honours, including the British gold medal for aeronautics in 1962 for his 'outstanding practical contribution to aircraft design', and the gold medal of the Royal Aeronautical Society in 1974. Formally retiring from the board of British Aerospace in June 1983, he then served on the councils of the Royal Society and the Royal Academy of Engineering, which included a two-and-a-half-year study of acidic emissions, and the council of the Royal Institution, before fully retiring in 1990. He died of myelodysplasia on 29 May 2005 at Avon Reach nursing home, Farm Lane, Mudeford, Dorset. He was survived by his four children, the eldest of whom, Gordon, also became an aeronautical engineer and chairman of Cobham plc, a specialist aerospace and defence equipment company.

Of outstanding ability and integrity, Page—affectionately known to his professional colleagues as Freddie—was one of the most highly accomplished and highly regarded British aircraft designers and industrial leaders of his generation. Entering the industry during the extreme pressures of wartime expediency, and in the immediate post-war years becoming centrally engaged in the pioneering of the jet age and the supersonic era of military aircraft, his forty-five-year aviation career spanned some of the most demanding times and situations in British and world affairs and for the aeronautical industry in particular—and throughout which he lived out his teenage ambition to the full. Pioneering and inspiring a generation of leading-edge aviation technologies and a progressive and innovative industrial management style and techniques that in many respects were well ahead of his contemporaries, he went on to become one of the key figures in the large-scale integration of the British aircraft industry and in international collaboration in Europe. All of this also resulted in the provision of hugely valuable high-calibre employment and commercial and export benefits for Britain and Europe.

NORMAN BARFIELD

Sources memoir, Royal Aeronautical Society, London • *Daily Telegraph* (7 June 2005) • *The Times* (10 June 2005) • *Aerospace Professional* (Sept 2005) • I. R. Yates, *Memoirs FRS*, 52 (2006), 231–50 • *WW* (2005) • Burke, *Peerage* • personal knowledge (2009) • private information (2009) • b. cert. • m. cert. • d. cert.

Archives BAe Systems, Warton, Lancashire, heritage department

Likenesses R. Coleman, photograph, 1978, RS; repro. in *Memoirs FRS* • obituary photographs • photographs, BAe Systems, heritage archive, Farnborough, Hampshire • photographs, BAe Systems, communications department, Warton, Lancashire

Wealth at death £520,274: probate, 5 Oct 2005, *CGPLA Eng. & Wales*

Page, Sir John Joseph Joffre (1915–2006), businessman, was born on 7 January 1915 at 7 Wymond Street, Putney, London, the second of four sons of William Joseph Page (*d.* 1935), successively a soldier, a milkman, and an insurance agent, and his wife, Frances, *née* Blyth (*d.* 1977). He attended St Mary's, the local primary school, and then gained a scholarship to Emanuel School, Wandsworth, the first child from St Mary's to do so. Highly intelligent, he excelled also in rugby, boxing, athletics, and cricket. In 1933, leaving Emanuel School, he joined the RAF on a short service commission, and was posted to Iraq to serve with an armoured car unit engaged in combined land and air operations. His abilities soon showed, and by 1936 he was a flying officer. In 1937 he gained the influential post of personal assistant to Air Vice-Marshal Courtney, the air officer commanding in Iraq, and soon was promoted flight lieutenant. He was already in a position where he needed to be able to ride a horse on ceremonial occasions, and his teacher was Cynthia Swan (*d.* 2003), whose father, Lionel Swan, was a financial adviser to the Iraqi treasury. They had more in common than a liking for horses and were married in Iraq in 1939; they subsequently had two sons.

In 1938 Page had resigned from the RAF to take up a post with the Iraq Petroleum Company (IPC), which controlled the whole Iraqi oil industry, but he rejoined the RAF at the outbreak of the Second World War. He served in the administrative and special duties branch, where he was a liaison officer with General Montgomery, with the rank of squadron leader. He was mentioned in dispatches in 1943, and was demobilized with the rank of group captain in 1946, when he returned to IPC.

During the Second World War, Page had become used to the company of the powerful, and this experience stood him in good stead as he held a string of increasingly senior positions in IPC. In 1961 the new Iraqi government nationalized all IPC's concessions (about 99.5 per cent) that were not being actively exploited at the time, which might explain Page's move to Bahrain as chief representative and general manager. Trouble still followed him, for as IPC's chief representative in Syria from 1965 he had to try to preserve supplies via the Tripoli pipeline through and after the Six Day War of 1967. He served in key appointments around the Middle East and in London, usually roles where his diplomatic manner was particularly needed. (In Syria, during a break in diplomatic relations, he at one point served as unofficial British ambassador, signified by a large Swiss flag outside his house—Switzerland being then technically responsible for looking after British interests.) He was appointed OBE in 1959 and retired in 1970, and indulged his love of fly fishing and watching cricket for two years.

In 1972 Page was brought out of retirement to become chairman of the Mersey Docks and Harbour Company. The finances of the Mersey docks were, like those of all

Britain's older general cargo ports, in deep trouble. Heavily in debt, the company's predecessor, the Mersey Docks and Harbour Board, knew that the future lay in bulks and containers, but with interest rates at up to 9.75 per cent was unable to raise the funds for the necessary investment in specialist berths, originally estimated at £15 million and eventually reaching about £50 million. Some key decisions had already been made, including one that when the new berths became available more than 300 acres of obsolete docks would be closed and sold. The port had other problems too, including a reputation for an unusually alienated and strike-happy workforce and the obligation imposed by the national dock labour scheme to employ men made redundant by the closure of private master porterage firms. In 1971 the board lodged a bill in parliament to authorize a writing-down of its debt, a moratorium on repayment of bond debts, and reorganization of the board as a statutory company. The bill was passed, and the Mersey Docks and Harbour Company first met in August 1971, under the chairmanship of John Cuckney, who had been 'parachuted in' the previous year to solve the port's problems. Thus when Page was appointed chairman in April 1972 he was to face two massive problems, as well as a host of minor ones, and had to do so, like his predecessor, with no previous experience of the ports industry. The first was to get the stockholders to accept a write-down of at least 30 per cent on an investment that was supposed to be low-to-zero risk. This involved much careful preparation and some stormy public meetings, in which he was defeated; the issue went to the high court and the eventual write-down was 60 per cent. The second was to get the dockers to accept new working practices at the new berths, in which success did not come quickly. Page was also chief executive from 1975 to 1977, leaving in order to chair the National Ports Council, in which role he was knighted in 1979, the same year the council was wound up. A reappointment to the chairmanship of the Mersey Docks and Harbour Company in 1980 saw the end of a run of unprofitable years, though the cargo tonnage figures revealed that the improvement was for some further years a purely financial one. Nevertheless, by the time Page retired a second time in 1984, the mechanism of recovery was in place.

Page served as chairman of the Chester district health authority in 1981–2, of the north-west regional health authority from 1982 to 1988, and of the Christie Hospital NHS Trust in 1991–2. He was made an honorary fellow of Manchester Metropolitan University in 1993. After the death of his wife he moved from Tarvin, Chester, to live with a son in Farnham, Surrey. He died on 5 February 2006 at Frimley Park Hospital, Frimley, Surrey, after a spontaneous intracerebral haemorrhage, and was survived by both sons. ADRIAN JARVIS

Sources A. Lynch, *Weathering the storm: the Mersey docks financial crisis* (1994) • *Daily Telegraph* (20 Feb 2006) • *Daily Post* [Liverpool] (21 Feb 2006) • *The Times* (23 Feb 2006) • *The Guardian* (3 March 2006) • Burke, *Peerage* • *WW* (2006) • b. cert. • d. cert.

Archives Merseyside Maritime Museum, Liverpool, Mersey Docks and Harbour Board collection • University of Warwick, BP archive

Likenesses obituary photographs

Pagel, Bernard Ephraim Julius (1930–2007), astrophysicist, was born on 4 January 1930 in Berlin, the only surviving child of Walter Traugott Ulrich *Pagel (1898–1983), medical historian and pathologist, and his wife, (Maria) Magdalene E. (Magda), *née* Koll (1894–1980). His grandfather Julius Leopold Pagel had also been an eminent medical historian and physician. When Walter Pagel was dismissed from his post in 1933 as Nazi persecution of the Jews increased, the family moved briefly to Paris, and then to England. They initially lived in Papworth village settlement, near Cambridge, but moved to London just before the Second World War.

Bernard Pagel was educated at Merchant Taylors' School and, resisting pressure to follow a medical career, won an open scholarship to read natural sciences at Sidney Sussex College, Cambridge, from 1947. After graduating in 1950 with first-class honours in physics he remained in Cambridge as a research student at the university and solar physics observatories, also studying at the University of Michigan. From 1953 to 1956 he was a research fellow at Sidney Sussex; he graduated PhD in 1955, and for a short period in the same year he was Radcliffe student at the Radcliffe Observatory in Pretoria, South Africa. His early research was mainly on the determination of the variation of temperature with height in the solar atmosphere, and the investigation of the variation of the strength of spectral lines from the centre to the limb of the solar disk. The influence of the future Nobel laureate Willy Fowler (who was visiting Cambridge in 1954–5) inspired him with an interest in the relative abundances of the chemical elements in the universe, and what they could reveal about the origin of elements and the evolution of galaxies, themes that were to dominate his subsequent research. On 11 July 1958, at Hampstead register office, he married Annabel Ruth Tuby (*b.* 1932), then a student of French, daughter of Edmund Tuby, civil engineer. They had a daughter, Celia, and two sons, David and Jonathan.

In 1956 Pagel had been appointed a principal scientific officer at the Royal Greenwich Observatory at Herstmonceux Castle in Sussex. It remained his scientific home for most of his career, and he progressed to the grades of senior principal scientific officer (1961–71) and deputy chief scientific officer (1971–89). In 1960 he held a visiting position at Sacramento Peak Observatory, New Mexico. His search for more reliable and accurate estimates of the abundances of chemical elements in stars led him to develop new methods of analysing stellar spectra. The methods were not used as widely as might be expected, partly because of a policy that restricted employees to the observatory's own publications, rather than international journals, and because the methods were largely overtaken by the introduction of digital computers. Nevertheless he established himself as a major figure, and was already becoming known for his extraordinarily astute critical abilities. It was this critical ability, as well as his encyclopaedic knowledge of research worldwide, that was to become so valuable for the development of all areas of the study of astronomical chemical abundances.

The establishment of an MSc programme in astronomy at the nearby University of Sussex led to Pagel becoming a visiting reader in 1966, and visiting professor from 1970. In the 1970s he began to collaborate more widely, and to develop simple but elegant theoretical models describing the way in which chemical abundances evolve in galaxies. The advent of the Anglo-Australian telescope in 1975 led to a long series of collaborations on the analysis of the spectra of glowing interstellar gas regions in nearby spiral and irregular galaxies, starting with an extensive study of the Magellanic clouds. A particularly important and subsequently much used development was a method for analysis of spectra for abundances where only a few strong lines could be seen. The work continued in the northern hemisphere with the availability of the Isaac Newton telescope in the Canary Islands from 1984, and Pagel became postgraduate supervisor to several Spanish students who went on to successful academic careers.

A compulsory retirement age of sixty meant that Pagel had to leave the Royal Greenwich Observatory in 1990, but he was appointed professor of astrophysics at the Nordic Institute for Theoretical Physics in Copenhagen. He became highly respected throughout Scandinavian astronomy, assisted by his great facility with foreign languages. A programme of research to determine the cosmologically important abundance of the element helium in the early universe, published in 1992, set a benchmark for subsequent investigations. It was during this period that he completed his definitive book, *Nucleosynthesis and the Chemical Evolution of Galaxies* (1997).

Pagel served for periods as vice-president and foreign correspondent of the Royal Astronomical Society and for fourteen years on the editorial board of its *Monthly Notices*, and was awarded its gold medal in 1990. In 1992 he was elected a fellow of the Royal Society. He was always in demand for his astute and clear summaries of specialist conferences, the syntheses he achieved acting as acknowledged guides for the field. He was an enthusiastic amateur pianist, a cyclist, in later life a keen skier, and an appreciator of good red wines. He retired back to Sussex in 1998, but remained active scientifically until his death on 14 July 2007, at his home, Groombridge, Lewes Road, Ringmer, Sussex, from a sudden and rapid onset of pancreatic cancer; he was buried at Brighton and Hove Port Slade cemeteries on 20 July. He was survived by his wife, Annabel, and their three children. MIKE EDMUNDS

Sources *Bulletin* [University of Sussex] (27 July 2007) • *The Independent* (22 Aug 2007) • *Astronomy and Geophysics*, 48/6 (2007), 6.37; 49/6 (2008), 1.06 • *WW* (2007) • personal knowledge (2011) • private information (2011) [Annabel Pagel, widow; D. Lynden-Bell] • m. cert. • d. cert.
Archives CUL
Likenesses photograph, 1992, RS • photograph, repro. in obs.carnegiescience.edu/ociw/symposia/symposium4/photos.html • photographs, repro. in www.astro.virginia.edu/~rtr/photos/camb74/pagel.jpg • portrait, repro. in *Astronomy and Geophysics*, 51/1 (2010) • portrait, repro. in M. G. Edmunds and R. J. Terlevich, eds., *Elements and the Cosmos* (1992), frontispiece
Wealth at death £383,906: probate, 7 Dec 2007, *CGPLA Eng. & Wales*

Painter, George Duncan (1914–2005), biographer and bibliographer, was born on 5 June 1914 at 23 Galton Road, Oldbury, Worcestershire, near Birmingham, the son of George Charles Painter, schoolmaster and singer, and his wife, Minnie Rosendale, *née* Taylor, artist. He was educated at King Edward's School, Birmingham, and at Trinity College, Cambridge, where he was a Bell exhibitioner, attaining first-class honours in classics and the second chancellor's classical medal in 1936. In 1938, after a year working as a lecturer in Latin at Liverpool University, he joined the British Museum printed books department. During the Second World War he was a conscientious objector, serving in the Pioneer Corps. On 1 August 1942 he married (Isabel) Joan Britton, a 29-year-old state registered nurse, and daughter of Samuel Morley Britton, inspecting engineer. They had two daughters. After the war Painter returned to the British Museum. In 1954 he was appointed assistant keeper in charge of fifteenth-century books. He remained in that post until his retirement twenty years later.

In 1951 Painter published *The Road to Sinodun*, a volume of poetry written more than ten years earlier, which tells of the suffering and anxious self-scrutiny provoked by a failed relationship. The book was not a success and was Painter's only foray into that genre. His penetrating vision was focused thereafter on the lives of others, and on documents and textual sources, the assessment, analysis, and translation of which he performed with great skill, as testified by his short life of André Gide, also published in 1951. He published translations of two of Gide's novels (*Marshlands* and *Prometheus Misbound*) in 1953, and, in 1956, Proust's *Letters to his Mother*. Nevertheless it was the two volumes of his *Marcel Proust: a Biography* (1959–65) that made his name.

Painter's life of Proust is a hugely accomplished piece of scholarship, albeit flawed in the assumptions upon which it is founded (that Proust's characters in *À la recherche du temps perdu* each had one or more 'originals' among his real-life acquaintances, and that understanding the novel, a 'creative autobiography', was largely a matter of mapping one set of individuals onto the other) and in its overly simplistic Freudian interpretations of many events in Proust's life. Notwithstanding such criticisms—and there are others, for instance that Painter did not carry out any interviews with Proust's living relatives or acquaintances—his biography formed a landmark in an exceedingly crowded field, remained in print throughout his life, and contributed invaluably to an understanding of the socio-historical circumstances of the novel's production. The second volume of Painter's *Proust* received the Duff Cooper memorial prize in 1965, the same year he was elected a fellow of the Royal Society of Literature. The first volume of his life of Chateaubriand (1977)—in fact the only one to appear—although less critically acclaimed than his *Proust* won the James Tait Black memorial prize.

As with his biographies, Painter's work in the field of

bibliography and fifteenth-century printing was meticulous, although never without humour. This is evinced by his essay 'Caxton through the looking-glass' (1963), his account, combining technical expertise, rigorous scholarship, and admirable analytical clarity, of how, using a mirror in analysing a fragment of printer's waste, he identified otherwise unknown editions of a text probably printed by Caxton. Painter's great depth of knowledge of his subject, something that exudes from the pages of his *Proust*, was no less evident in his bibliographical essays and reviews, the pick of which were collected in his *Studies in Fifteenth-Century Printing* (1984). His talents were seen at their most adventurous in his contributions to *The Vinland Map and the Tartar Relation*, a contribution to the debate over the authenticity of the Vinland map, a supposed fifteenth-century copy of a much earlier Norse map of the North American coast, which he published in collaboration with R. A. Skelton and T. E. Marston in 1965. Painter introduced, edited, translated, and commented on the 'Tartar relation', the Latin text from which, he argued, much of the controversial map's annotations were drawn. He was repeatedly challenged by scholars sceptical of his claims for the map's authenticity and showed great tenacity in fighting his corner; the debate, nevertheless, remained open at the time of his death. His description of his remarkable undertakings as the efforts of a 'well-meaning layman' was characteristic of his humility.

Painter published *The Chelsea Way, or, Marcel in England*, a translation of André Maurois's Proustian pastiche, the year after *The Vinland Map*, an antidote, perhaps, to the rigours of his recent immersion in the Mongol conquests of the thirteenth century. This easy to-and-fro between the literary productions of the twentieth century and the medieval and early modern worlds is testimony to the remarkable amphibiousness of Painter's mind. He was appointed OBE in 1974, the year of his retirement. He published an exhaustive quincentennial biography of Caxton in 1976 and three years later received an honorary doctorate from the University of Edinburgh. From 1970 he lived with his wife in Hove, Sussex, where he enjoyed gardening and playing violin to his wife's piano accompaniment. He died at the Victoria Highgrove Nursing Home, 59 Dyke Road Avenue, Hove, on 8 December 2005. He was survived by his wife, Joan, and their two daughters.

Adam A. Watt

Sources J. M. Cocking, 'The perils of the biographer', in J. M. Cocking, *Proust: collected essays on the writer and his art* (1982) • D. E. Rhodes, preface, in G. D. Painter, *Studies in fifteenth-century printing* (1984) • *The Times* (21 Dec 2005) • *The Independent* (21 Dec 2005) • *The Guardian* (30 Dec 2005) • *Daily Telegraph* (5 Jan 2006) • *WW* (2005) • b. cert. • m. cert. • d. cert.

Likenesses C. Beaton, two bromide prints, 1966, NPG • D. Fraser, bromide print, 1982, NPG • J. Painter, acrylic, *c.*1990, priv. coll. • obituary photographs

Wealth at death £269,697: probate, 22 May 2006, *CGPLA Eng. & Wales*

Pallo, Jackie [*real name* Jack Ernest Gutteridge] (**1926–2006**), wrestler, was born at 33 Britannia Row, Islington, London, on 12 January 1926, the son of Ernest Harold Gutteridge, french polisher, also boxing instructor and gymnasium owner, and his wife, Annie Elizabeth, *née* Lovelock. His grandfather, also Ernest Harold Gutteridge, had been knucklefight lightweight champion of England and one of the first to wear gloves in the ring. Jackie's father boxed under the name of Bob Wilson and taught boxing at Arnold House School, St John's Wood, for over a quarter of a century. (Jackie took over from him in 1943, teaching there until 1973.) Jackie's cousin Reg Gutteridge was a well-known boxing writer.

Jackie Pallo (1926–2006), by unknown photographer, 1961

At the age of fourteen Jackie started work in a butcher's shop and was then apprenticed as a motor mechanic. Three years later he met his future wife, Georgina Preston (Trixie) Wilson, daughter of Robert William Wilson, building labourer; they married on 9 August 1950, when Trixie was twenty-five. After the war he wrestled as an amateur at the Ashdown Club in Islington, which had provided the whole British team at the 1936 Olympics, and it was to supplement his earnings that he decided to become a professional wrestler. With around twelve promotions weekly in London alone a wrestler could make about £30 a week, double the salary of a newly qualified solicitor. He approached the promoters Dale Martin but after being badly beaten in a trial bout was told to become a ring second to learn the tricks of the trade. It was not until 1952, aged twenty-six, that he made his début, at Eltham against Young Atlas. He then had two years of hard apprenticeship, being scuffed round the ring by his superiors, before he was allowed a win. Not wanting to embarrass his boxing family he took his ring name Pallo from his American brother-in-law.

By the 1960s Jackie Pallo had become one of the most

recognizable figures in British wrestling. Although weighing less than 12 stone at a time when heavyweights generally ruled the ring, the bombastic Pallo (known also as Mr TV) topped the bills around the country. He may not have been the best shooter (or technician) in the business but, wearing candy-striped Y-front trunks and gold boots, and with his peroxided hair in a black velvet bow, he had an unerring ability to 'heat' or work a crowd into a frenzy (usually against him)—which was what the spectators had paid their money for. He was particularly unpopular with elderly ladies who watched him avidly and from time to time hit him with handbags or jabbed him with hairpins. His speciality move, which pleased them greatly, was seemingly to mistime a dropkick and land in apparent agony astride the top rope.

Pallo was best remembered for his drawn matches on television with another 'villain', Mick McManus, watched before the cup finals of 1963 and 1965 by audiences said to have exceeded those of the match itself. Pallo claimed that he received a maximum of £80 for one such bout, but at a subsequent match with McManus at the Royal Albert Hall he received £600. He wrestled Johnny Kwango at the same venue before the duke of Edinburgh, tipping Kwango out of the ring in defiance of strict instructions, almost into the duke's lap. Again at the Albert Hall in 1969 he won the British middleweight title from the technically superior Bert Royal. He was only allowed to keep it for a fortnight, losing it again to Royal in Paisley. Driving thousands of miles a month, he was known as exceptionally reliable and prided himself on not missing a bout even when injured or unwell.

In the 1970s the face of wrestling began to change. The impresario Jarvis Astaire bought up various promoters and Pallo and his son, Jackie junior (JJ), who had his first bout in tag with Pallo in 1971, quarrelled with the new general manager of Dale Martin. In 1975 they set up their own venture promoting in small halls around the country. Overall it was not a success. Pallo claimed to have over half the wrestlers in the country on his books, but he found that printers refused his work, posters were never distributed, and halls suddenly became unavailable; if he had a promotion booked, a rival organization would work the town two nights before. At the time promoters were getting a 70 per cent share of the gate money but hall owners began to demand an equal share. When the ITV contract came up for renewal in 1982 Pallo failed to secure even a modest share. He also failed to realize that wrestling was dying as a popular entertainment. In 1985 he hastened its death when, a bitter man, he published *You Grunt, I'll Groan*, an exposé of the game, explaining the 'soft holds' employed, the choreographed matches, and the fixed results. He claimed that in his career, 'I can hardly remember fighting a straight fight, and I have seldom heard of a straight pro fight' (*You Grunt, I'll Groan*, 9). Three years later ITV took wrestling off its Saturday afternoon programmes, which at their height had been watched by 15 million viewers. Pallo finally retired to his home in Kent in his sixties, having suffered for some time from arthritic hips.

Pallo's success in the televised sport led to other acting roles. His first acting part was as an injured wrestler in the television soap *Emergency Ward 10*. He appeared again as a wrestler in *Are You Being Served?* (in 1979), but in *The Avengers* (1964) he was a gravedigger, knocked out accidentally by Honor Blackman. His first pantomime appearance was at Norwich in 1969 as Bad Baron Hardup in *Goldilocks and the Three Bears*. It remained his favourite role. He appeared with Barbara Windsor both in pantomine and in the film *Not now Darling* (1973). He narrated *Peter and the Wolf* at the Royal Albert Hall and also appeared in Gerry Cottle's circus. A racehorse was named after him.

For a considerable time after the publication of his book, which broke the *omerta* code of the professional wrestler, Pallo was in disgrace in the profession. He claimed ingenuously that his target was the promoter rather than the wrestler but, although he attended the annual southern area reunions, he was no longer completely comfortable with his former colleagues. It was, however, his old rival Mick McManus who, when hearing Pallo was suffering from oesophageal cancer, suggested that the other wrestlers should support him and, whatever reservations they may have once had, they rallied around him. He died at his home, Ozengell Farm House, Haine Road, Ramsgate, Kent, on 10 February 2006, and was survived by his wife and son. On hearing of Pallo's death, Dickie Davies, the former presenter of *World of Sport*, is said to have remarked that it was 'an unprecedented example of Pallo not faking it' (*The Independent*, 18 Feb 2006). JAMES MORTON

Sources J. Pallo, *You grunt, I'll groan* (1985) · S. Garfield, *The wrestling* (1996) · R. Gutteridge and P. Batt, *Uppercuts and dazes* (1998) · *The Times* (16 Feb 2006) · *Daily Telegraph* (16 Feb 2006) · *The Independent* (16 Feb 2006); (18 Feb 2006) · *The Guardian* (17 Feb 2006) · personal knowledge (2010) · private information (2010) · b. cert. · m. cert. · d. cert.

Archives FILM BFINA, *This is your life*, M. Baker (director), ITV, 18 April 1973 · BFINA, light entertainment footage | SOUND BL NSA, documentary recording · BL NSA, performance recordings

Likenesses photograph, 1961, Rex Features, London [*see illus.*] · photographs, 1961–9, Rex Features, London · photograph, 1968, Getty Images, London, Hult. Arch. · photographs, 1968–74, PA Photos, London · J. Curtis, photographs, 1970–79, Rex Features, London · obituary photographs · photographs, repro. in Pallo, *You grunt*

Paolozzi, Sir Eduardo Luigi (1924–2005), sculptor and printmaker, was born on 7 March 1924 at 6 Crown Place, Leith, Edinburgh, the only son and elder child of Alfonso Rudolfo Armando Antonio Paolozzi (1901–1940), confectioner, and his wife, Carmela Maria, *née* Rossi (1902–1955), daughter of Pietro Rossi and his wife, Margherita Coletta. He was baptized at the Roman Catholic church of St Mary Star of the Sea, Leith, on 20 March.

Family, internment, and art studies Paolozzi's parents were born in Viticuso in the province of Frosinone, Italy, his mother's family emigrating to Scotland in the early years of the twentieth century, his father following in 1920, after service in the Italian army. In 1925 Paolozzi's father rented a confectionery shop at 10 Albert Street, off Leith Walk, and the family moved into the flat above it, where

Sir Eduardo Luigi Paolozzi (1924–2005), by Ida Kar, 1959

Paolozzi's sister Yolanda Margherita was born in 1932. Paolozzi attended Leith Walk primary school and Holy Cross Academy, Leith, and from the ages of nine to fifteen spent summers at the Italian youth camp, Colonia Marina XXVIII Ottobre a Cattolica. After the outbreak of the Second World War in 1939, when Paolozzi was in his last year at school, his father tried to find him a position in an engineering works, but without success. When Italy declared war in June 1940 the family shop was one of several Italian shops looted by an angry mob. Paolozzi, his father, grandfather, and other male kin were arrested under the emergency powers of the Enemy Aliens Act, and interned in Saughton gaol, Edinburgh. His father and grandfather subsequently lost their lives with 800 other Italians and Germans when the *Arandora Star*, transporting them to Canada, was sunk by a German U-boat. On release from prison Paolozzi took casual jobs, but in October 1941 joined the general evening class at Edinburgh College of Art, an essentially craft-based course that included 'designs for all commercial purposes with special reference to the processes of reproduction' (*Edinburgh College of Art Prospectus, 1940–1941*, 55). He initially envisaged a career in commercial art, but his ambitions changed on transferring to the full-time course.

In June 1943 Paolozzi's art training was interrupted by service in the pioneer corps, during which he discovered a copy of Amédée Ozenfant's book, *Foundations of Modern Art* (1931), the modernist spirit of which remained a lifelong inspiration. On leave in London in 1943 he met his future wife, Freda Madge Elliott (*b.* 1925), the daughter of Ernest George Elliott, journeyman tiler. After fifteen months' service he successfully convinced an army medical board that he was mad by invoking the spirit of Donatello. His discharge enabled him to study at the Ruskin School of Drawing and Fine Art, Oxford, in October 1944, but within a year he knew he 'wanted to make things' (interview, BL NSA), so in 1945 he transferred to the Slade School of Fine Art, London, to study sculpture, and lived in the Slade hostel in Cartwright Gardens. At the Slade Paolozzi's friends included William Chattaway, Richard Hamilton, Nigel Henderson, Raymond Mason, and William Turnbull. Like them Paolozzi enthusiastically embraced European modernism, especially the art of Picasso and the surrealists, developments disapproved of by his teachers, including the Slade sculpture master, A. H. Gerrard, with whom Paolozzi clashed. Paolozzi's first sculptures, two casts, *Horse's Head* and *Fisherman*, were roughly modelled in red, white, and blue concrete respectively, and exhibited with similarly Picasso-inspired ink and collage drawings of Newhaven fishing subjects, at the Mayor Gallery early in 1947, and praised by Robert Melville in *Horizon*.

The success of his first sculptures persuaded Paolozzi to abandon his Slade diploma, and in June he left for Paris, living there for the next two years, first in an attic room in the rue Budé on the Île St Louis, previously occupied by Raymond Mason, where Freda Elliott joined him, and then in a *chambre de bonne* where they lived on the rue de Chanaleilles. He worked in a studio on the rue Visconti belonging to the artist Grégoire Michonze, and mixed with British and American artists and writers, including Peter Rose-Pulham (who encouraged him to meet Francis Bacon, of whose art he became a lifelong admirer), Saul Bellow, Stanley Geist, and Jesse Reichek. He exhibited twice with the international artists' group known as 'Les mains éblouies' at the Galerie Maeght, Paris, and had two further one-man shows at the Mayor Gallery, one of Paris fair and lottery drawings (1948), and a second which included bas-relief sculptures (1949). He met, among others, Arp, Braque, Brancusi, Dubuffet, Hélion, Léger, and Tristan Tzara, but the artist who impressed him most in Paris was Giacometti.

Redefining sculpture When Paolozzi returned to London as instructor in textile design at the Central School of Arts and Crafts in 1949 the sculpture he brought back included 'Forms on a Bow' in plaster, which the Contemporary Art Society commissioned in bronze for the Tate Gallery. Giacometti's surrealism of the 1930s also influenced other sculpture Paolozzi made in 1951 such as *Cage*, commissioned by the Arts Council, *Fountain*, designed for the Festival of Britain, and his short-listed entry for the Unknown Political Prisoner international sculpture competition (1952–3). On his return to London he lived briefly with Lucian Freud and the Hendersons in Chisenhale Road, while working in a studio in Bunsen Street, before moving into a flat in Holland Road. On 7 July 1951 Paolozzi and Freda Elliott married at Kensington register office. They set up home in a flat in Kathleen Raine's house in Paultons Square, Chelsea. With the birth of their first daughter in 1954 the Paolozzis moved to Gull Cottage, Thorpe-le-Soken, Essex, which remained the family home until 1988, and where their second and third daughters were born in 1957 and 1960.

At the Institute of Contemporary Arts (ICA), early in 1952, Paolozzi gave a lecture illustrated with his own collages, magazine advertisements, and images from the cinema and science fiction, but for which he provided little or no commentary. Their sources were almost entirely American. The audience included the artists Richard

Hamilton and Nigel Henderson, and the critics Lawrence Alloway and Reyner Banham, who with Paolozzi and others became founder members of the Independent Group later that year. The images themselves were overlooked until 1972, when they were published as facsimile prints entitled *Bunk!*, and Paolozzi was recognized as a formative influence on pop art. Also in 1952 Paolozzi exhibited three sculptures and three drawings at the Venice Biennale. The following year he was awarded the British critics' prize. In 1953 he collaborated with his fellow Independent Group members Nigel Henderson, the architects Peter and Alison Smithson, and the engineer Ronald Jenkins, on 'Parallel of Life and Art', an exhibition at the ICA that used photography to examine visual relationships between art and science in the modern world. In 1954 he created Hammer Prints with Henderson, to supply the trade with original designs for ceramics, textiles, and other domestic products. In 1955 he played the part of the deaf mute in the film *Together* (directed by Lorenza Mazzetti) alongside the artist Michael Andrews. In 1956 Paolozzi worked again with Henderson and the Smithsons on another exhibition, 'This Is Tomorrow', at the Whitechapel Art Gallery. Their *Patio and Pavilion*, which consisted of an ordinary lean-to garden shed, expressed the 'fundamental necessities of the human habitation', and was 'furnished with symbols for all human needs', including a bicycle wheel and other odds and ends. In 1956 Paolozzi received a William and Noma Copley Foundation award.

Between 1955 and 1956 Paolozzi taught sculpture at St Martin's School of Art, and afterwards developed a process of making sculpture which he called 'the metamorphosis of rubbish' (*The Times*, 2 May 1958). It involved pressing obsolete found objects in plaster, and casting the impressions in wax sheets, from which heads and figures were assembled for recasting in bronze. The resulting sculptures, some larger than life, have a distinctly mechanized look, and others, with such titles as *Icarus* and *St Sebastian*, ironically assume a mythological or religious identity. In an interview in 1959 Paolozzi said he was interested, 'above all, in investigating the golden ability of the artist to achieve a metamorphosis of quite ordinary things into something wonderful and extraordinary that is neither nonsensical nor morally edifying' (Roditi, 160). The new sculpture was shown in London at the Hanover Gallery (1958), and in 'New Images of Man' at the Museum of Modern Art, New York (1959), as well as at the Venice Biennale (1960), by which time the British Council and the New York dealer Betty Parsons were promoting Paolozzi's sculpture abroad. The robotic pathos of the sculpture was often seen as a commentary on the uncertainties of the cold war, and from this period dates Paolozzi's international reputation; he won the David E. Bright Foundation award for best sculptor under forty-five, in New York (1960) and the Watson F. Blair prize in Chicago (1961). In 1960 he met the heiress Gabrielle Keiller who acquired a large collection of his work, some of which is now in the Dean Gallery, Edinburgh, together with examples from her collection of surrealist art, which Paolozzi helped form.

In 1960 Paolozzi bought a studio in Dovehouse Street, Chelsea, later acquiring three more adjacent studios, where he worked for the rest of his life. In 1960–62 he taught a course he called 'The translation of experience' at the Hochschule für Bildende Künste in Hamburg, which was based on surrealist methods and made extensive use of James Joyce's *Finnegans Wake*. In 1961 he began to make more abstract sculpture referenced by, among others, German architecture and expressionist cinema. He welded it from pre-fabricated aluminium units on the shop floor of an engineering works, a process based on the aesthetic pioneered by the American sculptor David Smith, which was illustrated in Paolozzi's two books *Metafisikal Translations* (1962) and *The Metallization of a Dream* (1963). With his machine-age sculptures Paolozzi captured the mood of post-war Germany, and the collages he made in Hamburg for the film *The History of Nothing* (1962) poetically evoked its pre-war past. In 1964–5 he made As Is When, a set of ten screen prints based on the life and philosophy of Ludwig Wittgenstein, with whose love of 'low' culture and unhappy experience of living in a foreign land Paolozzi identified. Part figurative, part abstract, As Is When was a milestone in the history of screenprinting, and questioned the limits of visual language to describe things and ideas. Meanwhile Paolozzi's sculpture, which in 1964 he began to paint with bright colours to resemble his prints, questioned the necessity of the third dimension to represent solid form. In 1964 Paolozzi's 'Wittgenstein' prints and sculpture were exhibited at the Museum of Modern Art, New York, and the following year he told Richard Hamilton, 'Some people need, perhaps, [the American art critic Clement] Greenberg, I need Wittgenstein' (Spencer, *Writings and Interviews*, 128). In 1967 he won the purchase prize for international sculpture at the Solomon Guggenheim Museum, New York, and first prize for sculpture at the Carnegie International Exhibition, Pittsburgh.

In 1968 Paolozzi was made a CBE, and became tutor in ceramics at the Royal College of Art, a post he held until 1989. In the late 1960s he assembled elaborate novels from 'cut-up' texts in the manner of Raymond Roussel and William Burroughs, but only the briefer *Kex* (1966) and *Abba Zaba* (1970) were published as books. In 1969 he published a chapter of his illustrated anti-war novel *Why We Are in Vietnam* in the magazine *Ambit*, of which, with the novelist J. G. Ballard, he was contributing editor. Although a regular visitor to America, including California, where he was visiting lecturer at Berkeley in 1968, Paolozzi became increasingly disillusioned with the 'American dream', which he parodied in a pop idiom in two sets of prints, Moonstrips Empire News (1967) and General Dynamic F.U.N. (1970), the second with an introduction by Ballard. In 1969 he visited Japan to make the sculpture *Osaka Steel* for the World Expo, Osaka (1970). In 1970 he supplied designs for Lanvin's spring collections in Paris. In his one-man exhibition at the Tate Gallery in 1971 Paolozzi criticized the links between Vietnam, big business, and the art world: the cover of the catalogue illustrated an American soldier's boot, and a gold ingot was reproduced on the back.

In the 1970s Paolozzi's graphics substituted Mickey Mouse for an abstract language that was distinctly European. In his sculpture he worked mainly in relief. In 1972 he was commissioned by the architect Michael Spens to design tapestries and nine ceiling panels for Cleish Castle in Scotland (now in the Dean Gallery, Edinburgh), which led to the commission from Glasgow University for aluminium doors for Whitfield Partners' new Hunterian Art Gallery (installed in 1980 but later unsympathetically rehung). In 1972 he was elected an associate member of the Royal Academy, and gave part of his collection of popular culture, 'The Krazy Kat Arkive', to St Andrews University for research (now in the archive of art and design, V&A). In 1974 he began a lifelong association with the model maker Ray Watson as his principal assistant. In 1974–5 he worked as guest of the German academic exchange service in Berlin, where retrospective exhibitions of his art were held at the Nationalgalerie, and Kupferstichkabinett. The abstract language of his reliefs, which evoked the Bauhaus, was developed synaesthetically in Calcium Night Light (1974–7), a suite of nine prints dedicated to the American modernist composer Charles Ives. In the later 1970s Paolozzi was briefly represented by the Marlborough Gallery, London. Between 1977 and 1980 he was professor of ceramics at the Fachhochschule, Fachbereich Kunst und Design, Cologne. In 1977 a large cast-iron sculpture *Hommage à Anton Bruckner* was commissioned for the grounds of the Brucknerhaus, Linz, and in 1978 a similar outdoor sculpture *Camera* was made for the European Patent Office, Munich.

Late work and public recognition In 1980 Paolozzi won first prize in a competition to redevelop the banks of the Rhine in Cologne, and by 1986 twenty-seven of his bronze sculptures were installed in conjunction with stones and water. Between 1980 and 1986 he also designed the mosaic decorations for Tottenham Court Road underground station, and made the sculpture *Piscator* outside Euston Station, London. By this time Paolozzi began to speak of such public works as 'social sculpture', and of 'placing objects in a culture, not to present objects as culture' (private information). He was professor of master class at the Internationale Sommerakademie für Bildende Kunst, Salzburg (1981–2), and in 1981 appointed professor of sculpture at the Akademie der Bildenden Künste, Munich, a post he held until retiring in 1991. In Munich he made a close study of the antique sculpture in the Glyptothek, which led to a return to the figure in his art, and arranged for his students to draw in the museum when the building was closed. In 1982 he received further commissions for public sculpture in Germany, and was also consultant for Richard Rogers and Partners' unsuccessful competition entry for the National Gallery extension, London. In 1983 he received the grand prix d'honneur at the Fifteenth International Print Biennale, Ljubljana, Yugoslavia.

By the mid-1980s Paolozzi's fragmented imagery began to reflect the ecological and global issues that were of increasing concern to him. In 1984 he exhibited cut and fractured heads, the fruits of his Munich studies, in his large exhibition 'Recurring themes', at the Edinburgh International Festival. In the early 1980s he selected material from the collections of the Museum of Mankind of the British Museum, to explore post-modern attitudes to Africa and third-world cultures, for his exhibition 'Lost magic kingdoms and six paper moons', which toured widely in England and Wales between 1985 and 1989. In 1984–5 he designed the sets for Percy Adlon's film *Herschel und die Musik der Sterne*, and played the part of the archbishop. In 1986 his sculpture *For Leonardo* was installed outside the Alte Pinakothek, Munich, and the large relief *On This Island* in the Queen Elizabeth II Conference Centre, London.

In 1986 Paolozzi was appointed her majesty's sculptor in ordinary for Scotland. The National Portrait Gallery appointed him a trustee in 1988, and in the new year honours of 1989 he was knighted. In 1991 he was presented with the Goethe medal in Frankfurt. He was also a Royal Academician (1979); honorary member of the Architectural Association (1981); honorary member of the Royal Scottish Academy (1987); visiting professor, Royal College of Art (1989); corresponding member of the Bayerische Akademie der Bildenden Künste, Munich (1990); cavaliere officiale, ordine al Merito della Repubblica Italiana (1991); honorary professor of the Akademie der Bildenden Künste, Munich (1991); honorary fellow of the Royal Incorporation of Architects in Scotland (1991); and the holder of nine honorary degrees and fellowships from British universities.

In 1991 *The Manuscript of Monte Cassino*, a large three-part bronze sculpture to commemorate the Italian community in Scotland, was unveiled outside St Mary's Cathedral, Edinburgh. In 1992 a twelve-foot high bronze version of 'Newton after Blake' was commissioned for the courtyard of the new British Library, and unveiled by Cherie Booth (wife of the prime minister, Tony Blair) in 1997. In 1993 the queen unveiled *The Wealth of Nations*, in front of the Royal Bank of Scotland, Edinburgh. In 1995 he gave a large collection of his work to the National Galleries of Scotland, for exhibition in the Dean Gallery, which opened in 1999. Included in the permanent displays are Paolozzi's *Vulcan*, a 27 foot tall stainless steel figure, and a reconstruction of his studio. In the late summer of 2000, shortly after completing a suite of prints about the cryptologist Alan Turing, he collapsed in his London studio. Although in intensive care and not expected to survive, he made a partial recovery, and visited Edinburgh in October 2002 for the inauguration of his three stained glass Millennium Windows in St Mary's Cathedral, and again in 2004 for a party in honour of his eightieth birthday. He remained in care in a London nursing home until his death from a pulmonary embolism at the Hammersmith Hospital on 22 April 2005. He was cremated on 13 May at West London crematorium, Kensal Green, and was survived by his three daughters (his marriage having ended in divorce in 1988).

Assessment The recurring subject of Paolozzi's art was the relationship between man and machine, and the role of artificial intelligence in the post-industrial age. He also made several animated films on related themes and was a prolific writer of novels and poetry. His innovatory sculptural language was based on the cut, a process derived from making collage, which became his signature style. His role as an initiator of avant-garde exhibitions, and the ideas behind his Wittgenstein sculpture and prints, were of significance for concept-based art movements. His art became part of the postmodern urban landscape of Europe, when the influence of American art and theory declined, and narrative and decoration were no longer considered incompatible with the modernist spirit of art and architecture. He once said that artists, like the early Italians and Russians, 'should be able to embrace rather complex and broad-ranging content, from designing a pullover to painting their mother, and all in one week' ('Conversations', 5).

From his teenage experience in Scotland, of cigarette cards and the cinema, Paolozzi believed that popular culture (the dynamism of which is present in his best work) was innately superior to much fine art, a belief he still upheld in the salons of Hampstead when he was a Royal Academician and the holder of several honorary degrees. Herein lies the paradox of Paolozzi's humble beginnings and his later social and professional life, as well as his equivocal attitude to the intensely capitalized commodity known as pop art, of which he was unquestionably a founding father, but about which he felt uncomfortable, saying: 'I don't want to go down in history as a pop artist. I would much rather go down, perhaps [as] an observer about something, [which] I would have thought, had much deeper European roots' (interview, BL NSA). To remain independent of the reductive fashions of the art market, and to make only what he wanted to, he avoided dealers; his few involvements with them were brief and generally unproductive. To compensate he assiduously cultivated social contacts, and from an early period was familiar with architects and architectural practice, knowledge which was useful when he made models and entered competitions. He also controlled his work by publishing his prints and sculpture in unique or very small editions, often with different colourways or minor variations, thus bringing an innovative approach to the reproductive conventions of graphics and sculpture.

Paolozzi's generosity was legendary, and he gave his work away liberally, to both friends and institutions. But his psychology was complex, and he could manipulate people as skilfully as he did objects. He was an amusing and challenging conversationalist, and loved the theatre as well as the cinema, but music moved him most as a spur to creativity. He remained an art school teacher all his life, his longest attachment being to the Royal College of Art, where he channelled the fees he received from Wedgwood and Rosenthal for his stylish designs into student scholarships. Of Paolozzi's legacy his friend the novelist J. G. Ballard said: 'if the entire twentieth century were to vanish in some huge calamity, it would be possible to reconstitute a large part of it from Paolozzi's sculpture and screenprints' (Grigor and Grigor). He left behind a vast archive of work in progress, comprising valuable ephemeral material collected over a lifetime, which will remain an important tool for art and cultural historians of the twentieth century for generations to come.

Robin Spencer

Sources *Edinburgh College of Art prospectus, 1940–1941* (1940) • R. Melville, 'Eduardo Paolozzi', *Horizon*, 16 (Sept 1947), 212–13 • *The Times* (2 May 1958); (23 April 2005) • E. Roditi, *Dialogues on art* (1960), 156–68 • M. Middleton, *Eduardo Paolozzi* (1963) • D. Kirkpatrick, 'Eduardo Paolozzi: a study of the artist's art, 1946–1968', PhD thesis, University of Michigan, 1969 • D. Kirkpatrick, *Eduardo Paolozzi* (1970) • F. Whitford, *Eduardo Paolozzi* (1971) [exhibition catalogue, Tate Gallery] • R. Spencer and others, *Eduardo Paolozzi: recurring themes* (1984) [exhibition catalogue, Royal Scottish Academy] • *Eduardo Paolozzi: private vision–public art* (1984) [exhibition catalogue, Architectural Association] • W. Konnertz, *Eduardo Paolozzi* (1984) • C. Jencks, *Towards a symbolic architecture: the thematic house* (1985) • 'Conversations between Eduardo Paolozzi and Alvin Boyarsky, May 1984', *Eduardo Paolozzi Underground Designs* (1986), 5–13 • M. Grigor and B. Grigor, 'EP sculptor: five themes and variations in the work of Eduardo Paolozzi', film, 1987 • E. Paolozzi, 'Wonderful world', *Cities of childhood: Italian colonies of the 1930s*, ed. S. de Martini and A. Wall (1988), 10 • *Unter Helden und Göttern: Eduardo Paolozzi und junge Bildhauer der Münchner Akademie in der Glyptothek* (Glypthothek, 1989) [exhibition catalogue] • D. Robbins, ed., *The Independent Group: postwar Britain and the aesthetics of plenty* (1990) [exhibition catalogue, MIT and ICA] • A. Massey, *The Independent Group: modernism and mass culture in Britain, 1945–1959* (1995) • E. Cowling and others, *Surrealism and after: the Gabrielle Keiller collection* (1997) [exhibition catalogue, Scottish National Gallery of Modern Art] • F. Pearson, *Eduardo Paolozzi* (1999) • R. Spencer, ed., *Eduardo Paolozzi: writings and interviews* (2000) • *Daily Telegraph* (23 April 2005) • *The Guardian* (23 April 2005) • *The Independent* (23 April 2005) • *WW* (2005) • Burke, *Peerage* • BL NSA, National Life Story Collection, artists' lives, interviews, 1993–5 • personal knowledge (2009) • private information (2009) • b. cert. • m. cert. • d. cert.

Archives NL Scot., acc. 11632 • Scottish National Gallery of Modern Art, GMA A40 • Tate Gallery, London, archives, papers and corresp., TGA 9411 • V&A, archive of art and design, the Krazy Kat Arkive of twentieth-century popular culture, AAD/1985/3, 1989/5, 1994/17, 1997/15 | FILM BFINA, *South of Watford*, J. Carlaw (director), ITV, 7 Feb 1986 • BFINA, 'EP sculptor: five themes and variations in the work of Eduardo Paolozzi', M. Grigor and B. Grigor (dirs.), Channel 4, 6 Dec 1987 • BFINA, documentary footage • BFINA, performance footage • 'Eduardo Paolozzi', H. Cokliss (dir.), 1971 • 'Eduardo Paolozzi', A. Kettelhack (dir.), 1971 • 'Maltamour', M. Grigor (dir.), 1972 • 'The Paolozzi Story', A. Lauder and C. Waldebauer (dirs.), 1980 • 'Euston Head: the making of *Piscator*', M. Grigor (dir.), 1982 • 'Top casting: the making of *The wealth of nations*', M. Grigor and B. Grigor (dirs.), 1993 • 'Paolozzi', L. Wardle (dir.), 2000 | SOUND BL NSA, *Private Passions*, BBC Radio 3, 6 Dec 1997, H9517/1 • BL NSA, National Life Story Collection, artists' lives, F4988–F4999 • BL NSA, current affairs recording • BL NSA, documentary recording • interview with Richard Cork, BBC Radio 3, March 1986 • *Desert Island Discs*, BBC Radio 4, 2 Dec 1990

Likenesses L. Miller, modern archival-toned silver gelatin print from original negative, 1948, NPG • J. Deakin, bromide print, 1952, NPG • C. Mann, oil on canvas, 1952, NPG • I. Kar, bromide print, 1959, NPG [*see illus.*] • I. Kar, two bromide prints, 1959, NPG • L. Morley, bromide print, 1959, NPG • Lord Snowdon, bromide print, 1964, NPG • H. Diamond, bromide fibre print, 1975, NPG • J. Kennington, bromide print, 1987, NPG • E. Paolozzi, self-portrait, bronze, 1987, High Holborn, London • E. Paolozzi, self-portrait, bronze statuette, 1987, NPG • E. Paolozzi, self-portrait, plaster and polystyrene statue, 1987 (*The artist as Hephaestus*), NPG • E. Paolozzi, self-portrait, plaster bust, 1987, NPG · F. Thurston, toned bromide print, 1988, NPG · J. Hedgecoe, photograph, 1989, priv. coll. · E. Andersen, C-type colour print, 1998, NPG · N. G. Henderson, group portrait, vintage bromide print (*Four artists included in the exhibition This is Tomorrow*), NPG · obituary photographs · photographs, repro. in Spencer, *Paolozzi*

Wealth at death £2,415,951: probate, 3 Oct 2005, *CGPLA Eng. & Wales*

Papadakis, Andreas Constantine (1938–2008), publisher, was born on 17 June 1938 in Nicosia, Cyprus, the son of Constantine Papadakis, a pharmaceuticals trader, and his wife, Nathalia, *née* Christou, a teacher and amateur painter. Educated at the Pan-Cyprian Gymnasium in Nicosia, he moved in 1956 to London, where he studied physics first at Imperial College and subsequently at Brunel University, which awarded him the degree of PhD in 1971. He published a number of papers in scientific journals, but by the mid-1960s his interests increasingly lay in the visual arts. The house in Holland Street, Kensington, which he bought in 1964 had a shop attached. This soon became the Academy Bookshop. From selling books Papadakis quickly moved to publishing them. The first book which appeared under the Academy Editions imprint was a collection of drawings by Aubrey Beardsley, which ran to many editions. Books on Alphonse Mucha and Charles Rennie Mackintosh followed, reflecting the 1960s fad for art nouveau. In 1971 Papadakis acquired the respected art publishing company Tiranti, expanding the Academy list to embrace contemporary architecture.

In 1975 Papadakis bought *Architectural Design*, a long-established magazine with a reputation, established by its long-serving editor, Monica Pidgeon, for championing avant-garde design. Papadakis gave *Architectural Design* the financial underpinning it desperately needed but, personally assuming the editorship, quickly turned its emphasis away from hardline modernism to a more pluralistic approach. Under his direction the magazine championed the cause of post-modernism and the work of architects such as Michael Graves, Robert Stern, Leon and Rob Krier, Piers Gough, and Terry Farrell. (The latter was responsible for the vivid colour scheme applied to the exterior of the large Victorian house at 42 Leinster Gardens, Bayswater, into which Papadakis moved his offices in 1974.) A long association with the architect and critic Charles Jencks began in 1977 with the publication of Jencks's *The Language of Post-modern Architecture*, which became a best-seller. Academy's list was, however, catholic in its content: Papadakis published the first monograph on the work of the arch-traditionalist Quinlan Terry (1981) but also the first extended study of the architecture of Richard Rogers (1985) and monographs on the work of Norman Foster and James Stirling.

From the mid-1980s, doubtless encouraged by the advocacy of the prince of Wales, *Architectural Design* focused increasingly on the work of the new school of classical architects, including the Krier brothers, Demetri Porphyrios, and John Simpson. This made its publisher unpopular in some modernist circles. Papadakis had no difficulty, however, in attracting such rising stars of the avant-garde as Daniel Libeskind, Zaha Hadid, and Peter Eisenman to the forum on deconstruction in architecture held at the Tate Gallery in 1988. The Academy forums, sponsored by Papadakis, which soon relocated to the Royal Academy, became an important focus for architectural discourse in London. Papadakis also sponsored an annual architecture lecture at the academy, attracting a series of distinguished speakers.

In 1990 Papadakis sold what had become the Academy Group Ltd to the German academic publisher VCH. He became managing director of the Academy subsidiary but two years later the arrangement ended acrimoniously. Under the terms of his agreement with VCH he had to refrain from publishing for five years. He found the period of enforced inactivity frustrating but it gave him scope to pursue his passion for restoring old buildings: Kilbees Farm in Berkshire, several London houses, and Dauntsey Park House in Wiltshire, where his plans to rebuild a missing wing as part of a major restoration programme fell foul of local planners.

In 1997 Papadakis launched a new publishing venture, Papadakis Publisher, as part of the New Architecture Group Ltd. Architecture again featured strongly on its list but particularly successful was a series of lavishly illustrated books published in conjunction with the Royal Botanic Gardens, Kew; the association led to Papadakis's election in 2006 as a fellow of the Linnean Society. In 2007, ever astute in his property dealings, he acquired Monkey Island Hotel at Bray, Berkshire, planning its restoration as an ideal retirement project.

It was probably Papadakis's association with post-modernism and classicism which led the architectural profession to disregard his contribution: he was proposed for an honorary fellowship of the RIBA but failed to be elected. He never married, but a ten-year relationship with Josette Gerlier (whom he had met in the Academy Bookshop) led to the birth of a daughter, Alexandra, in 1979. He subsequently formed a lasting relationship with Sheila de Vallée, whom he had met as a student. A lifelong member of the Greek Orthodox church, he was appointed archon pronotarios of the Ecumenical Patriarchate in 2003 and was actively involved in the development of London's Hellenic Centre and the Hellenic Institute at Royal Holloway College, London. He died of prostate cancer at the Princess Margaret Hospital, Windsor, on 10 June 2008, and was survived by his daughter, Alexandra, who took over the running of Papadakis Publisher and of the Monkey Island Hotel. KENNETH POWELL

Sources G. Broadbent, 'Pioneer of PoMo', *Building Design* (13–20 Dec 1990), 14–15 · K. Powell, 'Publisher with a cause', *Architects' Journal* (9 July 1998), 24–5 · *Daily Telegraph* (29 Jan 2005); (19 Aug 2008) · *Building Design* (18 July 2008) · *The Times* (30 July 2008) · personal knowledge (2012) · private information (2012) [Alexandra Papadakis] · d. cert.

Likenesses obituary photographs

Parker, Sir (Arthur) Douglas Dodds- (1909–2006), colonial administrator, special operations officer, and politician, was born on 5 July 1909 at 2 Holywell Street, Oxford, the younger child and only son of Arthur Percy Dodds-

Parker, formerly Parker (1867–1940), surgeon, and lecturer (later reader) in applied anatomy at the University of Oxford, and his wife, Mary (*d.* 1934), daughter of Joseph Alexis Patrick Wise JP, of Belleville Park, co. Waterford. At Winchester College he was captain of boats and at Magdalen College, Oxford, president of the Boat Club. He loved both places with passion for the rest of his life, and in old age would enjoy the look of astonishment on the faces of interlocutors when remarking casually 'Of course, I have known every President of Magdalen who has held office in the twentieth century' (private information).

After taking a second-class degree in modern history in 1930 Dodds-Parker joined the Sudan political service, and found himself exercising wide powers in Kordofan at the age of twenty-two. He loved the country and the people, rose in the service, and within a few years found himself assistant private secretary to the governor-general in Khartoum, and then assistant district commissioner in the Blue Nile province. Always putting his annual leave to good use, by the age of thirty he had travelled extensively in Africa, Europe, and (in 1937) America. He also worked with refugees fleeing from Nazism in 1938–9, organizing their safe passage to Britain and Canada.

Convinced that war was coming, and told that members of the Sudan political service would not be released for military service, early in 1939 Dodds-Parker resigned his post with regret, returned to London, and was commissioned at once in the Grenadier Guards, again a connection in which he retained a lifelong pride. His experience in the Sudan and neighbouring territories and his work with anti-Nazi refugees marked him out as a man who might contribute much to irregular warfare and clandestine operations. Recruited to the Special Operations Executive (SOE), he served with distinction for five years in several theatres: London and the Middle East, at one stage with Orde Wingate in east Africa, and the Mediterranean. In 1941–2 he was involved in planning the operation to assassinate Reinhard Heydrich. After the allied landings in north Africa towards the end of 1942 he faced turbulent times with resolution and good humour. It was he who issued a pistol to one of SOE's French instructors, who on Christmas eve shot dead Admiral Darlan. Whether SOE's pistol or another weapon was used has been much disputed. Dodds-Parker immediately confessed to his military superiors, American and British, his own role in the affair, and the crisis passed. He made no secret at the time or afterwards of his belief that Darlan had to be disposed of, by one means or another. By the summer of 1943 his work had attracted the attention of the minister resident, Harold Macmillan, who judged him 'a very fine man' (Macmillan, 144). As the tide of war turned, Dodds-Parker's SOE responsibilities extended over a large part of the Mediterranean. In accordance with strict instructions, little was recorded on paper, and what remained was largely destroyed. All the same it is clear that SOE under his guidance played a vital part in the negotiation of the Italian surrender in 1943, and in the crescendo of French resistance before and after the allied landings.

The activities of SOE were naturally overtaken by military campaigns of a more orthodox nature. When Dodds-Parker went to bid farewell in the autumn of 1944 to Macmillan, the latter wrote in his diary, 'He is an excellent fellow and I think would like to get into the House of Commons. He would certainly be a great addition to that body, as he is young, earnest and attractive. And he loves talking' (Macmillan, 534). Promoted colonel in 1944, he was appointed to the Légion d'honneur and awarded the Croix de Guerre, but received no British recognition beyond a mention in dispatches.

In the general election of 1945 Dodds-Parker won the seat at Banbury, in his beloved Oxfordshire. Churchill's invitation to become his parliamentary private secretary he declined with regret, explaining that after fifteen years as a modestly paid public servant he must build up a career in business. On 6 April 1946 he married Aileen Beckett Woods, ten years his junior, widow of his second cousin, Captain Ellison Murray Woods, of the Irish Guards, and daughter of Norman Beckett Coster, civil engineer, of Grand Detour, Illinois, USA. Through his marriage Dodds-Parker acquired a stepson; he and Aileen had a son, and shared a partnership of unalloyed happiness for sixty years.

When Churchill returned to power Dodds-Parker was chosen to move the address in response to the speech from the throne on 6 November 1951. He spoke about the Sudan and the Middle East, praying that a way would be found to restore traditional friendship between the British and Arab worlds and remarking that in the grave economic crisis then threatening Britain the country must earn its own living if it were to regain its standing in the outside world. Both Attlee and the new prime minister congratulated him warmly.

With his wide knowledge of foreign and Commonwealth affairs he was in 1953 fittingly appointed as one of the parliamentary under-secretaries at the Foreign Office; in the following year he moved to the Commonwealth Relations Office; and then returned to the Foreign Office at the end of 1955 when Selwyn Lloyd became secretary of state. Dodds-Parker, who found Lloyd edgy and unwelcoming, had to bear much of the brunt in the House of Commons the following autumn, during the Suez crisis. Like other junior ministers he had no part in the military planning, and disapproved when at a late stage he learned something of the collusion between Israel, France, and Britain. Nevertheless he felt it would be wrong to resign in the middle of the imbroglio. When Macmillan succeeded Eden, Dodds-Parker was not reappointed to his post. He never held ministerial office again, and retired to devote himself to business in 1959.

However, the attractions of public life remained strong, and within five years Dodds-Parker had come back to parliament, this time representing Cheltenham. From 1970 to 1973 he was chairman of the Conservative parliamentary foreign and Commonwealth committee. Believing that there was nothing incompatible between devotion to the Commonwealth and a strong British impetus in Europe, he served as a member of the British delegation to the European parliament at Strasbourg from 1973 to 1975. He was knighted for his public services in 1973. Soon after he left the Commons in the autumn of 1974 one of his Labour opponents observed 'It can now be revealed, as it cannot possibly do him any political damage, that Sir Douglas had as many friends on this side of the House as he had on his side' (*Hansard 5C*, 11 Dec 1974, 569).

During a long retirement Dodds-Parker travelled widely, supported innumerable good causes, sustained contacts with friends in every part of the globe, laboured with success for the Special Forces Club in London, and watched with dismay unfolding tragedies. 'My beloved Sudan', he wrote: '2 MILLION said to have perished since I was sent out to haul down the Flag' (Dodds-Parker to Sir Richard Wilson, 3 March 2000, Dodds-Parker papers). He published *Setting Europe Ablaze*, an account of SOE's exploits, in 1983 and *Political Eunuch*, a wry record of his public life, in 1986. Immensely tall, with a grace of manner and amiability that caused many to overlook his shrewdness, he retained to the end a memory of exceptional power, gladly put at the service of historians. He died at his London home, 9 North Court, Great Peter Street, Westminster, on 13 September 2006, a few days after putting forward one set of proposals to increase rail travel between Britain and continental Europe, and another to find a means whereby the three faiths to which the site is sacred might live more harmoniously in Jerusalem. He was survived by his wife, son, and stepson.

DAVID DILKS

Sources D. Dodds-Parker, *Setting Europe ablaze: some account of ungentlemanly warfare* (1983) · H. Macmillan, *War diaries: politics and war in the Mediterranean, January 1943 – May 1945* (1984) · D. Dodds-Parker, *Political eunuch* (1986) · B. Richards, *Secret flotillas: the clandestine sea lines to France and French north Africa, 1940–1944* (1996) · M. Thomas, 'The Massingham mission: SOE in French north Africa, 1941–1944', *Intelligence and National Security*, 11/4 (Oct 1996), 696–721 · T. C. Wales, 'The "Massingham mission" and the secret "special relationship"', *Intelligence and National Security*, 201 (March 2005), 44–71 · *The Times* (14 Sept 2006) · *Daily Telegraph* (15 Sept 2006) · *The Independent* (21 Sept 2006) · *The Guardian* (26 Oct 2006) · *WW* (2006) · Burke, *Peerage* · Burke, *Gen. GB* · Magd. Oxf., Dodds-Parker papers · personal knowledge (2010) · private information (2010) · b. cert. · m. cert. · d. cert.

Archives Magd. Oxf.

Likenesses photographs, 1946–67, Photoshot, London · Elliott & Fry, vintage prints, 1955, NPG · obituary photographs

Wealth at death £1,827,822: probate, 26 Feb 2007, *CGPLA Eng. & Wales*

Parkes [*née* Parr], **Margaret**, **Lady Parkes** (**1925–2007**), educationist, was born on 26 September 1925 at Camberley House, Seaton, Devon, the eldest of the three daughters of (Arthur) John Parr, schoolmaster, and his wife, Dorothy Ann, *née* Roberts, also a teacher. At the time of her birth registration her parents lived at 27 St Leonards Avenue, Exeter. John Parr moved as headmaster to Balsham and then Histon schools in Cambridgeshire, before being appointed in 1939 by Henry Morris, education secretary for Cambridgeshire, as warden of the new Impington Village College, where he worked on the design with the Bauhaus architect Walter Gropius.

Margaret Parr was educated at the Perse School for Girls, Cambridge, and after service as a nurse at St Thomas's Hospital in London during the latter stages of the Second World War she qualified as a domestic science teacher at Leicester College of Domestic Science. After returning to Cambridge she taught at Cambridge High School for Girls. On 4 November 1950 she married Edward Walter Parkes (*b.* 1926), a research student in structural engineering at the University of Cambridge. He was the son of Walter Frederick Parkes, jeweller. They had one son and one daughter.

After moving to Leicester in 1960 on her husband's appointment as head of the new university engineering department Margaret Parkes embarked on research into how young children learn technological skills, and received the degree of MEd, but she became increasingly interested in the work of the sociology department under its head, Ilya Neustadt. In 1965 she and her husband moved back to Cambridge, where he was professor of mechanics, and for nine years she was principal lecturer in the sociology of education at Homerton College, a teachers' training college.

In 1974 Edward Parkes became vice-chancellor of City University, London, and in 1978 chairman of the University Grants Committee. They moved to London, and it was at this point that Margaret Parkes began to take part in public life. In 1976 she was asked by the bishop of London to chair the London diocesan board of education, and she succeeded in separating the London and Southwark boards, setting up a separate director of schools for Southwark, as the existing board had too wide a remit. In 1977 she became a JP for inner London, and in 1978 was appointed a member of the Press Council. Already gaining a reputation as a good chairman, she was appointed to chair the Radio London Advisory Council, from 1979 to 1983. BBC Radio London had been set up in 1970 as the local radio station for London, and she guided its relaunch in 1981 as an FM station. Her experience dealing with the problems facing a local radio station serving a very large audience led to her being invited to Beijing in 1980 to advise on similar problems there. She had a lifelong passion for radio, and was delighted to be appointed a governor of the BBC in 1984, a position she held until 1989. Another appointment in these years, from 1981 to 1987, was as chairman of the governors of Whitelands College, a teachers' training college in Putney, part of the Roehampton Institute of Education since 1975. She was also chairman of the colleges advisory committee of the general synod board of education from 1982 to 1986. These appointments may have led to her inclusion in the new Secondary Examinations Council, set up in 1982, which in 1984 recommended the abolition of the GCE O-levels and the CSE and their replacement with a single system of examinations at sixteen, the GCSE. She also chaired the council's committee for craft, design, and technology.

When Margaret Parkes and her husband moved to Leeds, in 1983, on his appointment as vice-chancellor of the university (he was knighted the same year), she kept her commitments in London, but began to take on local responsibilities, mainly connected with the church. She was chairman of the Ripon diocesan board of education from 1988 to 1991, and chaired the Leeds parish church commission in 1988, which drew up proposals for the reorganization of the Leeds parishes: she recommended a Leeds city centre parish to include five existing parishes. She was also president of the Leeds Marriage and Personal Counselling Service.

It was as chairman of the design and technology working group for the national curriculum, from 1988 to 1999, that Margaret Parkes was to make the most impact. Already known for her support for design and technology through her work on the Secondary Examinations Council, she was appointed by the secretary of state for education, Kenneth Baker, following the passage of the 1988 Education Reform Act, which established a national curriculum for five- to sixteen-year-olds. The working group was asked to draw up the curriculum for the new compulsory subject of design and technology. The report, published in June 1989, brought together a number of subjects already taught in British schools, including craft, art, design, business studies, and information technology. Children were no longer to be assessed just on what they knew, but also on what they could do. It was not enough just to acquire knowledge; children must learn to use their knowledge to solve problems, and it was proposed that all children should learn how to design, make, and market a product. The report stressed the importance of involving businesses through work experience and industrial visits. The rationale behind the report was that the introduction of design and technology as a compulsory school subject would reverse a century of neglect of practical skills in British schools, and thus reverse Britain's industrial decline in the twentieth century. The report was hailed as 'a blueprint for the 21st century pupil' (*Daily Telegraph*, 6 July 1989). It was welcomed by Kenneth Baker and by teachers, but she was disappointed when the National Curriculum Council rewrote it, making many changes. Design and technology nevertheless became part of the national curriculum in 1990, making England the first country in the world to introduce technology education for all children at state-funded schools.

Margaret Parkes was a formidable chairman. Very clever and astute, she was forceful and energetic, and sometimes intimidating. She kept discussions to the point, and could be ruthless in exposing sloppy thinking. She was described as like a 'down to earth Shirley Williams' (*Daily Telegraph*, 6 July 1989), although she described herself as a 'wet Conservative'. She was appointed CBE in 1990. In her later years in retirement in Oxford (her husband retired as vice-chancellor of Leeds University in 1991) she kept her interest in education as president of the Christian Education Movement from 1992 to 2000. She also continued to support Festival Arts, a youth drama organization in St David's, Pembrokeshire, with which she had been involved since it was founded in 1969. She and her husband had bought land overlooking St David's Cathedral and had asked James Gowan, architect of the Leicester engineering building, to design a holiday house for them: the Round House, completed in 1967, later became a listed building. She died on 23 August 2007 at her home, The Cottage, Headington Hill, Oxford, of respiratory arrest. She was survived by her husband and their two children.

ANNE PIMLOTT BAKER

Sources *Yorkshire Evening Post* (19 May 1987), 9 ['Women's world' section]; (19 Sept 1989) • *The Times* (21 June 1989); (30 Aug 2007) • *Financial Times* (21 June 1989) • *Times Educational Supplement* (23 June 1989) • 'A blueprint for the 21st century pupil', *Daily Telegraph* (6 July 1989) • K. Baker, *The turbulent years: my life in politics* (1993), 204 • M. Parkes, 'Why technology in the schools curriculum', *Technology, Innovation and Society* (winter 1993–4), 12–14 • V. Wilson and M. Harris, 'Creating change? A review of the impact of design and technology in schools', *Journal of Technology Education*, 15/2 (spring 2004) • *WW* (2007) • private information (2011) • b. cert. • m. cert. • d. cert.

Likenesses photograph, repro. in *Daily Telegraph* (6 July 1989)

Wealth at death £513,147: probate, 11 Jan 2008, *CGPLA Eng. & Wales*

Parrinder, (Edward) Geoffrey Simons (1910–2005), Methodist minister and scholar of comparative religion, was born into a Methodist family on 30 April 1910 at Walpole, Hadley Road, New Barnet, Hertfordshire, the second of three sons of William Patrick Parrinder (1877–1944), warehouseman and commercial traveller, and his wife, Florence Mary, *née* Bellamy (1880–1976). His father worked for glove firms in the City of London, eventually setting up his own business. Parrinder went to school in Leigh-on-Sea where his family had moved in 1919, before leaving at sixteen to work as a booking clerk at the local railway station. While working as a railway clerk he qualified as a local preacher and then trained for the Wesleyan Methodist ministry at Richmond College, London (1929–32).

Responding to a call from the Methodist Mission House to serve in French west Africa, Parrinder left for Dahomey in 1933, after studying some theology and French in Montpellier. From that time he worked on and off in Africa for nineteen years. In 1936 he returned to England to be ordained. On 25 July 1936, at the Wesley Central Hall in Hendon, he married Esther Mary Burt (1909–2007), a nurse whom he had met some years earlier at a Methodist meeting. She was the daughter of Frank Burt, farmer. Mary and Geoffrey Parrinder were deeply devoted to each other throughout sixty-nine years of married life. They had one daughter and two sons.

When on leave in England in 1940 the Parrinders could not return to Dahomey because it was under Vichy collaborationist rule. Parrinder then worked in the Methodist circuit in Redruth, Cornwall (1940–43) and in the French circuit in Guernsey (1946–9), with another spell in west Africa in between. During this time he first took external London BA and BD degrees, then worked for the degrees of MA, MTh, and PhD, using empirical research into the indigenous religious beliefs of west Africa. This prefigured his subsequent career as a pioneering scholar and teacher of comparative religious studies. His first book, *West African Religion* (1949), was soon followed by more research on religion in Ibadan, published as *Religion in an African City*

(1953), which gained him the London University degree of DD. Other important publications were *African Psychology* (1951), *African Traditional Religion* (1954), and *Witchcraft* (1958).

In 1949 Parrinder was appointed to the highly innovative department of religious studies at University College, Ibadan, Nigeria, first as a lecturer (1949–50) and then as senior lecturer (1950–58), influencing many African students, including the Nigerian novelist and poet Chinua Achebe, and making lasting friendships. On a six-month sabbatical and a grant from the Carnegie Trust in 1956 he travelled to east and south Africa, India, Pakistan, Burma, and Ceylon. The resulting book, *An Introduction to Asian Religions* (1957), helped him to obtain in 1958 the new post of reader in the comparative study of religions at King's College, London. Awarded a personal chair in 1970, he became dean of the faculty of theology (1972–4), and retired in 1977.

Parrinder was a founding member of the British Association for the Study of Religions, its honorary secretary (1960–72) and president (1972–7), and later a life member. He was active in the London Society for the Study of Religion, of which he was president (1980–82), and in the London Society of Jews and Christians, which elected him president (1981–90) and then honorary life president (1990). Other important activities included participating in the World Congress of Faiths and the Shap Working Party on World Religions in Education, of which he was a founding member in 1969 and co-president until 1987. He served on the editorial boards of several journals and gave many prestigious lectures, among others the Charles Strong lectures in Sydney (1964), the Wilde lectures in natural and comparative religion at Oxford (1966–9), and the Westcott Teape lectures in India (1973). He was also a visiting professor at the International Christian University in Tokyo (1977–8) and a visiting lecturer at the University of Surrey (1978–82). He was made a fellow of King's College, London, in 1972 and an honorary DLitt of Lancaster University in 1975.

Parrinder's publishing output was phenomenal, including thirty-four single-author and seven edited books, one jointly written book, and two anthologies between 1949 and 2000, as well as numerous shorter and revised works, published under new titles. His pioneering work on African religions probably ranked highest among his academic achievements, but his wide influence was largely due to his works on Indian religions, Islam, and comparative themes that appealed to a large public. The widely used textbook *What World Religions Teach* (1963) was a best-seller, and his first work, *West African Religion*, remained in print for forty years. Among his well-known comparative works were *Worship in the World's Religions* (1961), *Avatar and Incarnation* (1970), *Mysticism in the World's Religions* (1976), and *Sex in the World's Religions* (1980), republished as *Sexual Morality in the World's Religions* (1995). Parrinder went on writing until January 2003, producing after forty-five years his last report, 'Religion', for the *Annual Register of World Events*.

Through his numerous writings, lectures, radio and television talks, and his work with educational bodies and academic associations, Parrinder exercised a wide influence on the study of world religions in schools and universities in Britain and abroad. A towering academic figure with an impressive career, he always remained humble and kind, even a little shy, and never boasted about his academic achievements. A tall, gaunt figure with a mass of hair and erect bearing, he always had a welcoming gesture towards guest and stranger. Family and friends knew him as a spirited, witty raconteur with a great love for stimulating conversation, whether pursuing an intellectual or political argument, or just small talk about the latest academic affairs. He was a man of great compassion, kindness, and a large heart who flourished as a human being and made others flourish around him. He ceaselessly worked for closer collaboration between members of different faiths and cultures, and for the advancement of the study of religions as a significant subject area in all educational institutions, from schools to universities. Former students, colleagues, and friends published a Festschrift for his eightieth birthday (with a bibliography of his works), *Turning Points in Religious Studies* (1990), for which Archbishop Desmond Tutu, once his student, wrote the foreword.

Parrinder died of heart failure on 16 June 2005 at 31 Charterhouse Road, Orpington, Kent, where he had lived since his return from Africa. He was survived by his wife, daughter, and one son, one son having predeceased him. During a service of thanksgiving at Orpington Methodist church, where he and his wife had worshipped for more than forty years, he was fondly remembered as a distinguished scholar, a close friend, and a happy family man.

URSULA KING

Sources J. Hinnells, 'A personal tribute to an outstanding career', *Turning points in religious studies: essays in honour of Geoffrey Parrinder*, ed. U. King (1990), 3–6 • M. Wiles, 'Some personal recollections of a colleague', *Turning points in religious studies: essays in honour of Geoffrey Parrinder*, ed. U. King (1990), 7–9 • J. Ferguson, 'A personal tribute: an unfinished piece by John Ferguson', *Turning points in religious studies: essays in honour of Geoffrey Parrinder*, ed. U. King (1990), 10–11 • M. Forward, *A bag of needments: Geoffrey Parrinder and the study of religion* (1998) • A. Hastings, 'Geoffrey Parrinder', *Journal of Religion in Africa*, 31/3 (2001), 354–9 • *The Times* (6 July 2005) • *The Guardian* (5 Aug 2005) • U. King, 'Professor Geoffrey Parrinder', *British Journal of Religious Education*, 28/2 (2006), 115–18 • *WW* (2005) • personal knowledge (2009) • private information (2009) [Catharine Boston, daughter; Steve Parrinder, son] • b. cert. • m. cert. • d. cert.

Archives SOUND BL NSA, current affairs recording

Likenesses obituary photographs

Wealth at death £391,898: administration, 23 Dec 2005, *CGPLA Eng. & Wales*

Partridge [*née* McMain], **Monica Agnes** (1915–2008), Russian and Slavonic scholar, was born on 25 May 1915 at 64 Cedar Road, Northampton, the daughter of John McMain, elementary schoolmaster, and his wife, Florence Emma Marjorie, *née* Roberts. She grew up in Northampton, attending Northampton School for Girls before reading French, with Latin, at University College, Nottingham, where she graduated in 1936. While there she met Maurice William (Bill) Partridge (1913–1973), a student of chemistry, and they married on 29 June 1940. In the same year she began to expand her knowledge of languages by taking up Russian at the School of Slavonic and East European Studies in London. From 1943 to 1947 she pursued postgraduate studies in the department of phonetics at University College, London. In 1947 she won the Laura Soames prize for original research on the phonetics of a language and was appointed part-time assistant lecturer at University College. She had begun to acquire teaching experience by giving lessons in Russian to civil servants visiting the Soviet Union on official business during the war.

In 1947 Partridge was appointed tutorial assistant in the department of Slavonic languages at University College, Nottingham (which the following year became the University of Nottingham). She began work on her doctoral thesis on Alexander Herzen and in 1949 she was appointed to a lectureship in Russian. Her head of department was Janko Lavrin, a Slovene, and he encouraged Partridge to establish links with Slovenia. Later, the contacts she made in both Ljubljana and Zagreb led to a steady flow of Yugoslav postgraduate students to the English department at Nottingham. She graduated PhD in 1953.

While she continued to work on Russian topics, publishing articles on Russian phonetics in addition to several on Herzen, Partridge's interest in Serbo-Croat was growing. In 1964 she published the first edition of her *Serbo-Croatian: Practical Grammar and Reader*. (A second, revised and improved edition was published by Izdavački zavod in Belgrade in 1972, and a third edition, published by Prosveta, appeared there in 1988.) This work filled a conspicuous gap in available works in English for students of the language and proved a valuable tool for learners for many years.

In 1967 Partridge was appointed to the chair of Slavonic studies at Nottingham—the first woman professor to be appointed by the university. Through her contacts with the universities of Zagreb and Ljubljana a series of language teachers in Serbo-Croat and Slovene came to Nottingham from the 1970s onwards. Through the intergovernmental cultural agreement, administered by the British Council, she was also able to use these contacts to place Nottingham students of Serbo-Croat and Slovene in Zagreb and Ljubljana. In the early 1970s she became a member of the British committee of the Association Internationale des Études Sud-Est Européennes.

While her professional career flourished Partridge suffered a severe blow in 1973, when her husband, by then professor of pharmaceutical chemistry and deputy vice-chancellor of Nottingham University, died suddenly of a heart attack. Her reputation for tough-mindedness was borne out by the way she continued to develop her professional life. She played an active part in helping to establish the Dubrovnik International Postgraduate Centre and became a member of the executive committee of its council. In recognition of her work in promoting Yugoslav studies in Britain she was awarded the order of the Yugoslav Flag with a gold star in 1980, the year of her retirement.

Throughout her career, Partridge maintained her interest in Herzen, publishing articles regularly and collecting material for a proposed book, which was intended to revise widely held views of his life and work. In 1983 she had the distinction, possibly unique for a British scholar, of receiving an honorary doctorate from the University of Kiev. A short biography of Herzen appeared in 1984 and a collection of her essays on him in 1988 (with a second, revised edition in 1993). In 1990, to mark her seventy-fifth birthday, a group of colleagues and professional associates presented her with a Festschrift, *The Bell of Freedom*, edited by Peter Herrity. At about this time she was elected an honorary fellow of Fitzwilliam College, Cambridge, to which she gave a selection of her late husband's paintings. Later she was made a member of Pembroke College, Cambridge, where she endowed an academic travel scholarship, and to which she eventually bequeathed the fine collection of watercolours that she and Bill had assembled during his lifetime.

Monica Partridge had a forceful personality and was not always an easy colleague. But her students remembered her ready support for them with appreciation and fondness, as former colleagues and friends did her sometimes prickly determination. She continued to live in the Nottingham area until her death, at the Queen's Medical Centre, Nottingham, on 19 March 2008. Her will included a substantial endowment to support Slavonic studies in Nottingham. She had no children.

CELIA HAWKESWORTH

Sources *The Times* (21 April 2008) · M. Jones, *Slavianskii Mir: the story of Slavonic studies at the University of Nottingham in the twentieth century* (2009), 71–96 · personal knowledge (2012) · private information (2012) [M. Jones] · b. cert. · m. cert. · d. cert.

Wealth at death £711,445: probate, 17 June 2008, *CGPLA Eng. & Wales*

Pattinson, Sir (William) Derek (1930–2006), church administrator and Church of England clergyman, was born on 31 March 1930 at Risedale Maternity Home, Barrow in Furness, Lancashire, the only child of Thomas William Pattinson (*d.* 1970), a clerk in the Ministry of Labour and later a tax inspector, and his wife, Elizabeth, *née* Burgess (*d.* 1986), a schoolmistress. He was educated at Whitehaven grammar school; this was followed by national service in the Royal Air Force, where he did not distinguish himself, staying in the lowest rank. He won an exhibition to Queen's College, Oxford, and was awarded the Stanhope historical essay prize in 1951. After graduating with a second-class degree the following year he entered the home civil service and served in the inland revenue department at Somerset House in London from 1952 until 1970. During that time he was seconded on two occasions (1962–5 and 1968–70) to the Treasury.

Pattinson (who always used the name Derek rather than William) was a prominent member of the William Temple Association, serving for a time as its chairman, and in that capacity he came to the notice of Archbishop Michael Ramsey, who in 1966 invited him to become a member of the church and state commission chaired by Owen Chadwick. Pattinson was one of the more radical members of the commission, pressing for the church rather than the prime minister to have the final say in episcopal appointments.

When in 1970 it was decided to replace the church assembly with a general synod Pattinson was an obvious candidate to follow Sir John Guillum Scott as secretary-general. He was persuaded to apply for the post much against the advice of his mother, who considered that he would become a permanent secretary if he stayed in the civil service. He did not heed her advice and was appointed associate secretary-general in 1970, becoming secretary-general on Scott's retirement in 1972. It proved to be an inspired appointment. Pattinson devoted all his energies to establishing the new general synod, ensuring that it had a high profile with the media. Without doubt he was the most influential layman in the church during his period of office. In its first twenty years the synod dealt with many controversial matters that often put the synod—and the church—at odds with the government of the day; *The Church and the Bomb* (1982) and *Faith in the City* (1985) were two reports that placed the general synod in the media spotlight and caused annoyance to the administration of Margaret Thatcher.

During James Callaghan's time as prime minister the synod resolved to tackle the question of bishops' appointments and, with Pattinson as part of the negotiating group, concessions were made by Downing Street on the lines of the proposals of the Chadwick report. This gave satisfaction to Pattinson, who was now seen as a skilful political operator, but within the church he had critics who considered that he had too much power. Ramsey's successor at Canterbury, Donald Coggan, relied to a large extent on his own staff at Lambeth and consultation with Pattinson and his colleagues at Church House was kept to a minimum. This caused difficulties for Pattinson but a better relationship developed when Robert Runcie became archbishop in 1980.

One of the most difficult events in Pattinson's career occurred in 1987 when Canon Gareth Bennett of New College, Oxford, was commissioned by Pattinson and his opposite number in the church commissioners to write the anonymous preface to *Crockford's Clerical Directory*, published annually by Oxford University Press. The preface contained paragraphs that were highly critical of Runcie's appointment of liberals to bishoprics and deaneries. The media clamoured for the author's identity. Pattinson refused to name him but others pointed the finger at Bennett, who denied authorship. Media attention became too much for Bennett and he committed suicide. Some called for Pattinson's resignation over the affair but the archbishop stood by him and he weathered the storm. Speaking in the general synod when Pattinson retired in 1990, Runcie said 'Where the Synod is, there is Derek; where Derek is, there is the Synod. It is not too much to say that Derek has been married to the Synod, and has loved and cherished it even in its most unpopular moments' (*Report of Proceedings of the General Synod*, July 1990). Pattinson was knighted on retirement.

In the early 1980s Pattinson's widowed mother moved to London and he was very attentive to her needs; there was a close bond between them. She died suddenly and Pattinson was much affected. Always a person who enjoyed the good things of life—he was a City liveryman and a freemason—it was noticed that he was drinking more and keeping questionable company. However, he followed his vocation to the priesthood and was ordained deacon by the bishop of London, Graham Leonard, in 1991. He became an honorary assistant curate at St Gabriel's, Pimlico, and was ordained priest the following year by Leonard's successor, David Hope. Unusually, he was allowed to call himself the Revd Sir Derek Pattinson, since he had been knighted before being ordained priest. He proved to be an excellent preacher and a good pastor although his liturgical sense was not so well developed. About this time a gay rights activist and former member of the general synod, Barnaby Kemp Graham Miln, moved into Pattinson's Westminster flat, causing some scandal when this was revealed by the newspapers. Miln later nursed Pattinson when the latter's health deteriorated, until it was necessary for him to have professional care. He died on 10 October 2006 at St Johns Wood Care Centre, Camden, London, of dementia and obstructive hydrocephalus, and was cremated on 7 November. He was survived by Barnaby Miln, who was described in Pattinson's final *Who's Who* entry as his partner.

BRIAN J. T. HANSON

Sources *Report of Proceedings of the General Synod* (1972–90); (July 1990) · H. Carpenter, *Robert Runcie: the reluctant archbishop* (1996) · *The Times* (14 Oct 2006) · *Daily Telegraph* (14 Oct 2006) · *The Guardian* (16 Oct 2006) · *The Independent* (17 Oct 2006) · *Church Times* (20 Oct 2006) · *Yorkshire Post* (21 Oct 2006) · *WW* (2006) · personal knowledge (2010) · private information (2010) · b. cert. · d. cert.

Likenesses photographs, 1985–6, Photoshot, London · obituary photographs

Wealth at death £134,241: probate, 6 Sept 2007, *CGPLA Eng. & Wales*

Peacocke, Arthur Robert (1924–2006), biochemist and theologian, was born on 29 November 1924 at 221 Chester Road, Watford, Hertfordshire, the son of Arthur Charles Peacocke, butcher, and his wife, Rose Elizabeth, *née* Lilly. He was educated at Watford grammar school and Exeter College, Oxford, where he gained a first-class degree in chemistry in 1946 before undertaking research for the degree of DPhil (awarded in 1948) under the supervision of Sir Cyril Hinshelwood. He then lectured in biophysical chemistry at Birmingham University from 1948 to 1959. His early scientific interests focused on the physical chemistry of DNA, but later in his long scientific career he concentrated on the study of the general thermodynamics of biological systems. On 7 August 1948 he married Rosemary Winifred Mann, a 22-year-old schoolteacher, later an inspector of schools, and daughter of Edgar Mann, jeweller. They had a son and a daughter.

Peacocke had been attracted to Christianity in his youth, but as an undergraduate he became an agnostic. However, a sermon preached in Oxford by William Temple persuaded him that religious belief could be approached with intellectual openness and scrupulosity. He also began to feel that the order and fruitfulness of the world, revealed by science, intimated the possibility of there being a divine mind and will behind the history of the universe. Influenced by the liberal theologian Geoffrey Lampe, a colleague at Birmingham University, he returned to religious belief and took first a diploma in theology (1960) then a degree in theology (1971), both from Birmingham. Later he was to have the unusual distinction of being both a DSc (1962) and a DD (1982) of Oxford University.

In 1959 Peacocke returned to Oxford as university lecturer in biochemistry and a fellow of St Peter's College, combining this from 1964 with a lectureship in chemistry at Mansfield College. In 1971 he was ordained to the Anglican priesthood and began to make a name for himself as a careful and insightful writer on science and religion. His first book on this subject, *Science and the Christian Experiment*, was published in 1971. In 1973 he made a decision, which he subsequently described as not having been easy, to move to Cambridge to become the dean of Clare College. At Cambridge he gave lectures both in chemistry and in theology. The invitation to give the Bampton lectures at Oxford in 1978 led to a major work, *Creation and the World of Science* (1979), which was widely influential on both sides of the Atlantic. In 1984 he returned again to Oxford to be the first director of the Ian Ramsey Centre, established in St Cross College for the interdisciplinary study of the relationship between theology and contemporary culture. He relinquished the directorship in 1988, but returned in 1996 for a second spell until 1999, in order to help in the establishment of an international programme of workshops in science and religion. In between he served as catechist at his old college, Exeter (1989–93), an appointment he greatly enjoyed. He was made an honorary chaplain at Christ Church, Oxford, in 1988, and an honorary canon in 1995.

The invitation to give the Gifford lectures at St Andrews University in 1993 afforded Peacocke the opportunity to survey his mature position on the relationship between science and religion. The lectures formed the basis of his most important book, *Theology for a Scientific Age* (1993). It was followed by *From DNA to Dean* (1996), which contains a particularly interesting autobiographical chapter outlining the spiritual pilgrimage of his life. He continued to write on these matters right up to the time of his death, displaying, if anything, an increased anxiety that theology should have the boldness to take scientific insight seriously and be prepared in response to modify its own discourse in the ways that he believed had proved to be necessary. As a biologist he was able to give a positive theological interpretation of evolution, emphasizing that God is no cosmic despot keeping tight control of creation, but one, who in Charles Kingsley's phrase, allows creatures to be themselves and to 'make themselves'. The history of the world is to be understood theologically as an unfolding exploration and unending improvisation of great and continuing fruitfulness, in which creator and creatures both participate. Peacocke delighted to illustrate these insights with metaphors drawn from music, which meant much to him in his personal life.

Although Peacocke quite often spoke in a revisionary mode about the need for modifications in theological discourse, he also had respect for the insights of the past, taking with great seriousness the importance of the New Testament witness and expressing his admiration for the truth-seeking stance taken by such thinkers as Origen, Augustine, and Anselm. He was robustly critical of scientistic reductionism, remarking that 'atoms and molecules are not more real than cells, or populations of cells, or human communities, or human persons' ('From DNA to Dean', *Zygon*, 26/4, Dec 1991, 491). Like many scientist-theologians, he took a critical realist view of the nature of human knowledge, both in relation to science and to theology, a position that he defended in *Intimations of Reality* (1984).

In addition to his many personal contributions to the dialogue between science and religion Peacocke played an important part in founding a number of organizations that went on to play significant roles in facilitating that dialogue. In the early 1970s he was a leader in the discussions that led to the formation of the Science and Religion Forum in the United Kingdom, and he served as the forum's first chairman (1972–8). Later he participated in moves to found the European Society for the Study of Science and Theology. His most imaginative and fruitful achievement of this kind was the conception and foundation of the Society of Ordained Scientists, a kind of 'dispersed religious community', prayerfully linking together clergy with serious scientific concerns. He was the society's first warden (1987–92). A friendly and modest person, he was a courteous participant in many debates. Throughout his life he manifested a sincere desire to seek for truth without reserve. He received much international recognition for his achievements in the field of science and religion, including honorary degrees from DePauw University, Indiana, and Georgetown University, Washington. He was appointed MBE in 1993 and in 2001 was awarded the Templeton prize for progress in religion. He died of cancer of the prostate at the Westminster Beaumont Nursing Home, Bayworth Lane, Boar's Hill, Oxford, on 21 October 2006, and was survived by his wife, son, a professor of philosophy, and daughter, an Anglican priest. JOHN POLKINGHORNE

Sources *Zygon*, 26/4 (Dec 1991) [Peacocke issue] · A. Peacocke, *From DNA to dean* (1996) · *Daily Telegraph* (25 Oct 2006) · *The Independent* (6 Nov 2006) · *The Times* (15 Nov 2006) · A. R. Peacocke, *All that is* (2007) · *WW* (2006) · personal knowledge (2010) · private information (2010) · b. cert. · m. cert. · d. cert.
Archives Bodl. Oxf., Sir Rex Richards MSS
Likenesses obituary photographs
Wealth at death £49,480: probate, 13 July 2007, *CGPLA Eng. & Wales*

Pearce, (Ann) Philippa (1920–2006), children's writer, was born on 23 January 1920 at Crofters, Woodlands Road, Great Shelford, Cambridgeshire, the younger daughter and youngest of four children of Ernest Alexander Pearce, master flour miller and corn merchant, and his wife, Gertrude Alice, *née* Ramsden. Brought up in the Mill House in Great Shelford, a handsome early nineteenth-century dwelling set in the upper reaches of the River Cam, Pearce suffered so badly from the kidney disease nephritis that she started school only at the age of eight. Despite this she was still able on occasion to enjoy fishing, swimming, and skating. From the Perse Girls' School in Cambridge she won a state scholarship to read English and history at Girton College, Cambridge. Employed as a civil servant from 1942 to 1945, she then moved to the BBC to work as a producer and scriptwriter in its schools broadcasting department.

During a long period in hospital in 1951 recovering from another bout of nephritis Pearce helped pass the time by recreating every moment of a favourite canoe trip taken many years previously on the river next to her childhood home. These memories led to her first novel, *The Minnow on the Say* (1955). Illustrated by Edward Ardizzone, this outwardly conventional story of two boys finding lost treasure in time to save the family home was also a sensitive exploration of mood, friendship, and the power of place. It was runner-up for that year's prestigious Carnegie medal for excellence in children's literature. Her next novel, *Tom's Midnight Garden* (1958), was an instant success and soon took on classic status. Inspired by the fact that her father had decided to sell the family home before retiring, Pearce wrote a story based on the walled garden that she, her father, and her grandfather had all once enjoyed as children. She also drew on J. W. Dunne's *An Experiment with Time* (1927), and its central notion that different periods of time are able to co-exist and blend together. The story describes how Tom, a schoolboy from the modern suburbs, somehow has regular meetings with Hatty, a child orphan living in Victorian times. It won the 1959 Carnegie medal and was televised three times, turned into a play, and made into a film.

In 1958 Pearce moved to work in publishing, first at the Clarendon Press and then, from 1960, for André Deutsch. Meanwhile she provided the text for her only picture book, *Mrs Cockle's Cat* (1961), illustrated by Antony Maitland. Her next novel, *A Dog So Small* (1962), was rejected by her preferred publisher on the grounds that it was too depressing. This was a sad misreading of a fine novel that describes how a bored and lonely child slowly discovers that living in a fantasy world provides no long-term alternative to embracing reality to the full. Finally published by Constable, it was another critical success.

On 9 May 1963, at Hampstead register office, Pearce married Martin James Graham Christie, a fruit farmer and researcher seven years her senior, son of James Christie, businessman. He died in 1965 just after the birth of their daughter Sally, never having recovered fully from his time as a Japanese prisoner of war. Bringing up her child single-handed, Pearce found less time for writing. But in *The Children of the House* (1968) she expertly fictionalized the poignant but tangled childhood memoirs of Major Sir Brian Fairfax-Lucy, who had been brought up in the stately home of Charlecote in conditions of severe emotional and physical neglect. This outstanding joint publication was reissued in 1989 as *The Children of Charlecote*. Pearce's next publications, *The Elm Street Lot* (1969) and *What the Neighbours Did* (1972), were both genial collections of short stories, some of which had been televised on the BBC's children's programme *Jackanory*. Returning to her previous prize-winning form, *The Battle of Bubble and Squeak* (1978), an account drawn from her own experience of a family's up-and-down adventures with a couple of lively gerbils, won the Whitbread children's book award for that year.

Leaving London, where she had been working as a freelance for the previous six years, Pearce moved in 1973 with her daughter to Ashton, a small cottage built by her grandfather opposite the Mill House in Great Shelford, which she had immortalized in fiction as 'Great Barley'. Among her later books were *The Way to Sattin Shore* (1985), once again runner-up for the Carnegie medal, and *The Little Gentleman* (2004), an affectionate tale about a talking mole whom she imagined living beneath an old log visible from her window and on which she liked to sit. With her daughter Sally, by then a writer and publisher herself, and her two grandsons living next door, and with a pony, goat, dog, cat, and hens for additional company, Pearce remained a much loved figure at home and at meetings and conferences, whose audiences were always charmed by her wit, wisdom, and inherent sense of grace. Elected a fellow of the Royal Society of Literature in 1993 and appointed OBE in 1997 for services to children's literature, she died of a stroke at the University Hospital of North Durham, in Durham, on 21 December 2006, having just addressed a meeting at Seven Stories, the centre for children's books in Newcastle upon Tyne. She was survived by her daughter. NICHOLAS TUCKER

Sources S. Pendergast and T. Pendergast, eds., *St James guide to children's writers* (1999) • *The Independent* (23 Dec 2006) • *The Times* (27 Dec 2006) • *Daily Telegraph* (27 Dec 2006) • *The Guardian* (2 Jan 2007) • *WW* (2006) • b. cert. • m. cert. • d. cert.

Likenesses H. Craig, bromide fibre print, 2000, NPG • obituary photographs

Wealth at death £697,246: probate, 26 June 2007, *CGPLA Eng. & Wales*

Pearson, Colin James (1923–2007), potter, was born on 14 September 1923 at 21 Ramsden Road, Friern Barnet, London, the son of James Edward Pearson, a clerical officer in the Ministry of Health, and his wife, Mabel Clara, *née* Lake. There was little in his background to suggest a career in art. During war service in the RAF he gained a knowledge of mathematical instruments that served as the basis for an ingenious glaze calculator that he later developed with Denis Healing. With an aptitude for drawing, he used his war service grant to study painting at Goldsmiths' College, University of London, followed by teacher training. While at Goldsmiths' he met his future wife, Leslie Heathcote Thomas (*b.* 1930), daughter of Reginald Vaughan Thomas, aircraft pattern maker. They eventually married at Chelsea register office on new year's eve 1955. They had three children, Julian, Clare, and Daniel.

It was also at Goldsmiths' that Pearson was introduced to clay. Fascinated by the magical transformation that took place in the kiln, he approached pottery as a series of surfaces to be adorned, producing slip-cast or moulded platters decorated in a bright Picassoesque style. Very much of their time, they were later described by Pearson as in a 'comparatively bizarre maiolica style' (personal knowledge). Following advice from Charlotte Bawden (who had worked at the Leach Pottery) to learn to make 'proper pots', he approached Ray Finch at Winchcombe Pottery, where he was accepted primarily for his enthusiasm. Under Finch's watchful eye he learned professional production throwing, which, with its economy and precise movements, proved a sound training. In 1954–5 he worked at the Royal Doulton factory, where he was taught professional mould-making and other semi-industrial processes.

After a spell as a teacher Pearson resumed his career as a potter when he was invited by David Leach to join him in setting up a pottery workshop producing tableware for the Carmelite friars at Aylesford, Kent. Father Malachy Linch, a firm supporter of arts and crafts ideas, was keen to extend creative activity for the friars. When Leach left Pearson took over, building a new kiln and replacing the slipware with tougher stoneware. All was well until Linch discovered, and disapproved of, Pearson's left-wing views. Pearson left the friars but remained in Aylesford, setting up the Quay Pottery in a picturesque but cramped old stable on the banks of the Medway, later acquiring the adjacent property. With the help of his wife, Leslie, and various assistants he developed a range of nearly 100 items of well-designed, functional, unfussy tableware covered with quiet buttery creams, lightly speckled pinky-whites, and rich temmoku glazes, work that perfectly fitted the counter-cultural, anti-consumerist mood of the times.

Pearson became involved in the studio pottery course at Harrow College of Art, where a revolutionary syllabus was devised to teach students to become working potters. Among other skills he taught production and repetitive throwing, introducing a workshop ethic that was based on real experience. It was a revelation not only for the students but also for other members of staff, including Michael Casson and Walter Keeler. Later Pearson became an influential teacher at Camberwell and Medway schools of art.

Perhaps inspired by his involvement with the creative art school atmosphere, Pearson began exploring more individual forms. These were based on cylinders onto which were added 'wings' that recalled the formality of early Chinese bronzes, particularly when covered with a metallic, bronze-like finish. The wings, made by piercing a block of clay with a stick and slicing it with a wire, produced a random, lace-like quality. Working with porcelain and with a black clay body, Pearson created visually exciting forms that had lightness and verve. Later other shapes and types of wing decoration were explored, but always with a view to how they would work within the whole form. Pearson's individual forms in black stoneware and pale blue porcelain, dubbed 'angels and devils', shown at the British Craft Centre in 1971, were an instant success, signalling a breakthrough for his work as a potter.

In 1971 Pearson moved to Islington, London, where he focused entirely on individual pieces. Without a kiln for reduction firing, techniques had to be reassessed for the electric kiln. He devised slips saturated with fluxes like zinc oxide, and a range of softly toned glazes that were perfectly in tune with the forms. Exhibitions in this country and abroad affirmed his standing as a distinguished potter.

As a testament to the soundness of an apprentice-based training, it would be difficult to match the work and achievement of Pearson as one of the leading potters of the post-war period. Affable and approachable, he was an active member of the potters' community, working tirelessly for the Craft Potters Association and encouraging young potters. The gradual onset of progressive extra pyramidal syndrome, a form of Parkinson's disease, limited his output, but with the help of assistants he continued to produce work. With roots deep in the studio pottery movement of Bernard Leach and Michael Cardew, he brought his own vision to bear, often playful and joyous but always with a deep seriousness and respect for his chosen material. He died at Homerton University Hospital, Hackney, London, on 3 December 2007, of heart failure, and was survived by his wife, Leslie, and their three children. EMMANUEL COOPER

Sources *The Times* (5 Dec 2007) · *The Independent* (11 Dec 2007) · *The Guardian* (20 Dec 2007) · personal knowledge (2011) · private information (2011) · b. cert. · m. cert. · d. cert.

Archives SOUND BL NSA, documentary recording

Likenesses D. Neame, bromide fibre print, 1988, NPG · obituary photographs · photograph, repro. in www.merrynlloyd-pottery.com/biographypage.html · photographs, repro. in *Ceramic Review*

Wealth at death under £11,000: probate, 14 Jan 2009, *CGPLA Eng. & Wales*

Pennington [*married name* Tutin], **Winifred Anne** (**1915–2007**), botanist and palaeolimnologist, was born on 8 October 1915 at 73 Ramsden Street, Barrow-in-Furness, the daughter of Albert Roger Pennington, Post Office supervisor, and his wife, Margaret (Maggie), *née* Elliott. She was educated at Barrow-in-Furness grammar school and the University of Reading, where she graduated in botany in 1938. While an undergraduate she showed early promise and wide interests in botany, undertaking and later publishing research on algae and the ecology of mosses. Her determination was recognized by her supervisor, Thomas Maxwell Harris, who balanced her joint interests in algology and what was to become her main area of research, the natural history and sediments of freshwater lakes. This latter interest was fired by her undergraduate vacation visits to the Wray Castle laboratory of the Freshwater Biological Association at Windermere, accessible from her home town, where she became a field assistant. The common ground between these two areas gave Pennington an unrivalled knowledge of palaeolimnology, which supported her throughout her career of research and formed a basis of the thesis for which she was awarded her PhD degree by the University of Reading in 1941.

While at Wray Castle in 1936–8 Pennington became embedded in the research activities of the laboratory, and notably was asked by Clifford Mortimer to help with his pioneer attempts to sample the lake sediments in Low Wray Bay. The resulting samples were examined by Pennington, and led her into the world of diatoms, pollen grains, and macroscopic plant remains, as well as the nature and chemistry of the sediments that contained these fossils. In 1938 she attended the British Association's annual meeting, held in Cambridge, where she listened to a lecture by Harry Godwin on pollen analysis and vegetation history; she wrote that as a result she 'was hooked on pollen for life' ('What I did'). On 25 February 1942 she married a fellow botanist, Thomas Gaskell *Tutin (1908–1987), whom she had met at Wray Castle. After their marriage she joined him in Cambridge, where he was working for the naval intelligence division of the Admiralty. There she worked in the botany school on her samples until 1944, in association with Godwin.

At the time Pennington began her research knowledge of British post-glacial vegetation history was mostly obtained from the study of peat deposits. Pennington, having looked at the Low Wray Bay cores, fully realized the potential of lake deposits. The first sentence of her paper on Windermere sediments proclaimed her life's work: 'The deposits of lakes are as interesting as those of bogs in the study of post-glacial history' (*New Phytologist*, 42, 1943, 1). With her background of work at Wray Castle and her association there with pioneers in limnology, especially B. M. Jenkins, F. J. H. Mackereth, and Clifford Mortimer, who were inventive and knowledgeable about coring lakes and lake chemistry, she was ideally placed to develop palaeolimnology and palaeoecology in Britain. This she did with an extended and planned programme of research, much of it collaborative with the Freshwater Biological Association. After the original Windermere cores of the 1930s further cores were obtained from the north basin of Windermere. The results from these early studies (published in 1943 and 1947) were an important milestone in the understanding of late- and post-glacial history in Britain, providing detailed analyses of fossils and sediments and the associated interpretations of the lake's history in terms of the sediments, diatom flora, and record of vegetation history in the Lake District, with an estimated time-scale covering the time since the end of the last glaciation some 10,000–12,000 years ago.

After Cambridge Pennington's studies continued at University College, Leicester, where her husband had been appointed head of the botany department in 1944. A year later, after the arrival of her first baby, she 'retired' until 1947 when she became a demonstrator and special lecturer in the botany department at Leicester, at the same time bringing up her family of three daughters and one son, later becoming honorary reader (1971–9) and honorary professor (1980–2007). During the period at Leicester from 1947 to 1967 she maintained a close connection with the Freshwater Biological Association's research at Windermere. She widened her field of research to studies of the sediments of upland tarns in the Lake District, relating changes of sediment to environmental changes within the catchment of the tarns, aided by the development of improved corers by Mackereth. This led to further study of catchment characteristics, the significance of erosion and weathering in the catchments and their connection with vegetation history as indicated by pollen diagrams, and the recognition of anthropogenic factors that governed change.

In 1967 Pennington became a member of the scientific staff of the Freshwater Biological Association (as a principal scientific officer) and worked with a very active multidisciplinary group on lake sediments and their chemistry and biology. The following twenty years saw a succession of research projects that greatly enlarged the approaches to palaeoecology, the use of absolute pollen diagrams, new applications of dating methods, regional syntheses of vegetational history in England and Scotland, and resolution of Quaternary geological problems. In 1979 Pennington was elected a fellow of the Royal Society in recognition of these fundamental contributions.

Pennington (who published as Winifred Pennington but was known to friends and family as Anne) was an active and determined field scientist, generous with her time, and ready for analytical discussions of the progress of her research and that of colleagues. She started research in the 1930s in a field waiting to be explored and requiring both laboratory and field expertise, and her resolution was matched by her achievement as a leading scientist in a field that by the time of her death had come to be seen as of increasing importance in understanding the environment. Pennington died in Basingstoke, Hampshire, on 1 May 2007, and was survived by her four children. R. G. West

Sources J. W. G. Lund, 'Winifred Tutin: a personal note', *Lake sediments and environmental history*, ed. E. Y. Haworth and J. W. G. Lund (1984), 1–10 · J. Talling, 'The development of freshwater science in Britain, and British contributions abroad', *Freshwater Forum*, 22 (2004), 22–80 · *The Independent* (23 May 2007) · *FBA News* (autumn 2007), 16–18 · *Journal of Palaeolimnology*, 38 (2007), 601–5 · W. Pennington, 'What I did: publications, 1937–2003', Freshwater Biological Association archives · *WW* (2007) · personal knowledge (2011) · private information (2011) · b. cert. · m. cert.
Archives Freshwater Biological Association
Likenesses photograph, repro. in Haworth and Lund, *Lake sediments*, frontispiece · photograph, repro. in *FBA News*
Wealth at death £454,297: probate, 24 Aug 2007, *CGPLA Eng. & Wales*

Perkins, Geoffrey Howard (1953–2008), comedy writer and radio and television producer, was born on 22 February 1953 at the maternity hospital in Bushey, Hertfordshire, the son of Wilfrid John Perkins, electronic engineer, and his wife, Peggy, *née* Patterson, of 1 Manor House Cottages, Elm Park, Stanmore, Middlesex. He first revealed his talent for comedy in the sixth form at Harrow County School for Boys, a grammar school that boasted a particularly gifted year. In his class were Michael Portillo, who became a Conservative cabinet minister, Nigel Sheinwald, who became the UK's ambassador to Washington, Francis Matthews, who became a theatre director under the stage name Matthew Francis, and the future television presenter Clive Anderson, with whom Perkins produced the school's Christmas revue *Happy Poison*. Perkins won an exhibition to read English at Lincoln College,

Geoffrey Howard Perkins (**1953–2008**), by Richard Kendal, 2001

Oxford, where he joined the Oxford Theatre Group Revue as a writer and director. When he left university his career took a somewhat aberrant turn when he and Portillo, on the advice of the university careers service, took jobs at a Liverpool commercial shipping company, Ocean Transport and Trading. So disruptive were Perkins's continual anarchic comic interjections that a corner of the open-plan office was boxed off to contain him.

A year later, in 1976, Perkins returned to London to join BBC Radio light entertainment. His potential was immediately evident to his radio trainers. During a quiz programme he devised during training, a long pause was followed by the presenter saying, 'This is a question in two parts. Was this pause by Harold Pinter or Samuel Beckett? And the second part is, which line of dialogue preceded it?' (private information, B. Maxwell). Over the next six years he produced more than twenty different programmes and 200 individual shows. He managed to cajole the famously procrastinating Douglas Adams into completing the scripts for *The Hitch-Hiker's Guide to the Galaxy* (1978 and 1980), turning it into a cult classic. He made creative use of the BBC's Radiophonic Workshop in devising unusual sounds for actors playing aliens. At this time he met his future wife, Lisa Charlotte Braun (*b.* 1951), a studio manager on the series, and daughter of Rudolph Herbert Braun, accountant. They married on 18 January 1986. Their first-born, Jack, died a cot death. They had two more children, Charlotte and Arthur.

Perkins co-wrote with Angus Deayton the popular *Radio Active* series (1981–7), a spoof on local radio. It was later turned into television, as *KYTV* (1990–93), for once putting him in front of the camera as the character Mike Flex. The series won the silver rose of Montreux in 1992. Meanwhile, after a brief stint with Thames TV, Perkins had in 1988 co-founded Hat Trick Productions, whose successes included *Drop the Dead Donkey* (1990–98), *Father Ted* (1995–8), and *Have I Got News for You* (1990–). By now he had acquired a reputation as a brilliant script editor with a meticulous line-by-line approach, and had developed an acute sense of what was or could be made funny. For *Father Ted*, for example, he persuaded the writers to transform their draft mock documentary into a highly successful sitcom.

In 1995 Perkins was appointed head of comedy at BBC Television to bolster a department criticized for its stale sitcoms. The job enabled him to work with performers and writers who had previously been unavailable to him and he introduced a new generation of edgier, more irreverent series to the corporation's output. Perkins described himself as a 'nurturer' of comedies and comic dramas. He was well aware that past classics like *Fawlty Towers*, *Only Fools and Horses*, and *One Foot in the Grave* had taken time to be accepted, so he was prepared to stay loyal to shows that didn't make an immediate impact. He was responsible for such popular fare as the *Harry Enfield* programmes, *The Fast Show*, *The Thin Blue Line*, and *My Family*. He nurtured performers too, particularly emerging talent like Catherine Tate and Harry Enfield, giving them the confidence to realize their potential. He kept traditionalists happy by continuing such stalwarts as *Last of the Summer Wine*, while ensuring that the scripts remained fresh. He made the occasional error of judgement. He was lukewarm about *The Royle Family*, a sitcom about a northern working-class family of couch potatoes. But the views of the writers Caroline Aherne and Craig Cash prevailed and the series, launched in 1998, became very popular.

For his outstanding contribution to the industry Perkins was made a fellow of the Royal Television Society in 1999. In 2001 he left the BBC to become an executive producer with Tiger Aspect Productions. In an interview with *The Independent* in October that year he criticized the BBC's director-general John Birt for hindering the creative process through an obsession with budgets and bureaucracy. His Midas touch continued at Tiger Aspect with such series as *Gimme Gimme Gimme* (1999–2001), *The Catherine Tate Show* (2004–6), and another series teaming up Harry Enfield and Paul Whitehouse called simply *Harry and Paul*. On 29 August 2008, only days before this series was broadcast, he suffered a heart attack before falling under a lorry in London's Marylebone High Street (it was at first thought he had died in a road accident). He was survived by his wife, Lisa, and his children, Charlotte and Arthur.

Bob Chaundy

Sources *The Times* (1 Sept 2008) · *Daily Telegraph* (1 Sept 2008) · *The Guardian* (1 Sept 2008); (6 Sept 2008) · *The Independent* (4 Sept 2008) · *Sunday Times* (7 Sept 2008) · private information (2012) [C. Anderson, P. Bennett-Jones, B. Maxwell, F. Matthews, J. Plowman, G. Linehan, M. Portillo] · b. cert. · m. cert. · d. cert.

Archives FILM BFINA, *Comedy connections*, K. McMunigal (director), BBC2, 8 Nov 2008 | SOUND BL NSA, documentary and performance recordings

Likenesses photographs, 1987, Rex Features, London · group portrait, photograph, 1989, PA Photos, London · photographs, 1992–3, Photoshot, London · photographs, 1995–2001, BBC · R. Kendal, photograph, 2001, BBC [*see illus.*] · obituary photographs

Wealth at death £1,627,525: probate, 3 Dec 2008, *CGPLA Eng. & Wales*

Peyton, John Wynne William, **Baron Peyton of Yeovil** (**1919–2006**), politician, was born on 13 February 1919 at 6 Berkeley Street, Mayfair, London, the elder son of Ivor Eliot Peyton, of independent means, a farmer and captain in the South Nottinghamshire hussars, and his wife, Helen Dorothy, *née* Elphinstone. He was educated at Eton College, and went to Trinity College, Oxford, in 1937 to read jurisprudence. At Oxford he met Edward Heath, and had a minor interest in university politics and the union. From 1936 onwards he was convinced that war was inevitable, and in 1939 he suspended his studies to enlist in the 15th/19th hussars, in which regiment an uncle had once been a general. Stationed in York, he met and fell in love with Mary Constance (*b.* 1921), daughter of (Everard) Humphrey Wyndham, an army officer then serving as aide-de-camp to George VI, and granddaughter of the second Baron Leconfield of Leconfield (and niece of the third, fourth, and fifth barons).

A member of the British expeditionary force, Peyton was captured during the invasion of Belgium in 1940, and spent the next five years as a prisoner of war. This was undoubtedly a formative period in his life, and several of his fellow prisoners became lifelong friends. He discovered an interest in music (he later became a friend of William Walton), and under the tutelage of Jack Hamson (before the war a Cambridge academic lawyer) studied for his bar exams. In 1941 he was part of an unsuccessful escape attempt that included Desmond Llewelyn among its participants. Peyton spent several months handcuffed during daylight hours in 1942, and was devastated by news of his brother Tommy's death that year. He wrote later of the 'bottomless misery of war' (Peyton, 42).

Liberated in 1945, Peyton at first found it difficult to adjust to freedom; to compound matters, on return to London he discovered that Mary Wyndham was about to marry Ralph Hamilton Cobbold. Called to the bar in 1945, in 1946 he approached Walter Monckton to secure a place in chambers, and was invited to become his personal assistant as constitutional adviser to the nizam of Hyderabad and Berar (then believed to be the richest man in the world) during the preparation for Indian independence. He spent two periods in India, allowing him to observe at first hand events surrounding independence. He returned to the country in the 1980s and 1990s. In 1947 he survived a serious plane crash near Basrah. In December 1947, in Johannesburg, South Africa, he married Diana Clunch, whom he had met a few months before. She was the daughter of Douglas Clunch of Durban. By this time Peyton had become a Lloyds broker, but quickly decided to enter politics. He stood unsuccessfully as Conservative candidate for Bristol Central in the general election of 1950, then won the seat of Yeovil in October 1951. In 1950 he and his wife had moved to Odcombe near Yeovil; they had three children, a daughter and two sons.

In parliament Peyton soon became reacquainted with Edward Heath (then deputy chief whip). In 1951 he became parliamentary private secretary to Nigel Birch (also educated at Eton), a junior minister at the Ministry of Defence. His membership of the regional health board both shaped his view of the limitations of state bureaucracy and allowed him to campaign successfully for a new hospital in Yeovil. During the 1950s he became an opponent of capital punishment, a stance that did not always find favour with his constituents. He was nevertheless a strong advocate of free market economics, and was a member of the right-wing Monday Club by the early 1970s.

In 1960 Peyton's younger son died during a routine operation; this led to a period of great unhappiness in his life. In 1962 he renewed his acquaintance with Mary Cobbold (*née* Wyndham). He and she were both divorced in 1966, and married on 27 July that year; it was a happy marriage that lasted the rest of his life. He became a stepfather to her son and daughter by her marriage to Ralph Cobbold.

In June 1962 Harold Macmillan asked Peyton to become parliamentary secretary at the Ministry of Power. Peyton saw poor industrial relations and management of nationalized industries as the two key issues, and embarked on a programme of visiting coalmines. He found the paperwork associated with ministerial life frustrating. He was not invited to join Heath's shadow team in 1965, but was asked to develop a policy for the west country before the general election of 1970. This identified developing transport links as being the priority for the region; following Heath's victory Peyton was surprised to be invited to become minister of transport. Industrial relations and poor infrastructure were again key themes, and he began developing good links with trade union leaders, including Jack Jones. His two most important decisions during this period were the introduction of compulsory helmets for motorcyclists and the signing of the treaty agreeing the channel tunnel in 1974. He viewed the latter as an important physical symbol of Britain's commitment to Europe; it also enabled him to strengthen his friendship with Christopher Soames, then British ambassador in Paris. In 1971 Peyton was responsible for the sale of British Rail's travel agency, Thomas Cook.

After the Conservative defeat in the general election of February 1974 Peyton began to develop his business interests, becoming chairman of the British subsidiary of Texas Instruments. He was also a director of Alcan Aluminium and of the London and Manchester Assurance Society. In November 1974 Heath invited him to become shadow leader of the House of Commons. Following Heath's defeat in the first round of the leadership election of 1975 (after which Peyton advised him to resign), Peyton stood in the second ballot, a move he later regretted. He received eleven votes. The victor, Margaret Thatcher, subsequently asked him to continue as shadow leader of the house, moving him sideways to become shadow minister of agriculture in 1976, a post he never really enjoyed.

Peyton had admired Heath; his relations with Thatcher were less strong. In 1979 he was disappointed at being the only opposition spokesman not to be offered a cabinet post. His relationship with Thatcher never recovered; she offered him a life peerage at the next election, and he requested she confirm this in writing. He expressed misgivings at her divisive policies and treatment of the miners, but admired the way in which the Falklands conflict was handled in 1982.

In 1983 Peyton was appointed to the House of Lords, as Baron Peyton of Yeovil; his sponsors were the former prime minister Alec Douglas-Home, Lord Home of the Hirsel, and Lord Zuckerman, a longtime government scientific adviser. Zuckerman persuaded Peyton to become involved with the Zoological Society of London, and he quickly became treasurer, securing much funding during the 1980s. A well-received autobiography was published in 1997, and a biography of Zuckerman in 2001. In retirement he remained a highly regarded figure in his former constituency and could often be seen walking near his home in Hinton St George, wearing a distinctive black beret. He was a master of mischievous retort, a skill that made his writing attractive but did not always endear him to contemporaries; John Biffen once remarked, 'I wonder what quip John will make when he meets God' (*The Independent*, 25 Nov 2006). He died at St George's Hospital, Tooting, London, on 22 November 2006, of multi-organ failure. He was survived by his second wife, his daughter, one son, and his stepchildren. A bequest was used for a memorial screen in Hinton St George church.

M. A. BRYANT

Sources A. Sampson, *The new anatomy of Britain* (1971) · H. Young, *One of us: a biography of Margaret Thatcher* (1989) · J. Peyton, *Without benefit of laundry* (1997) · A. Clark, *The tories: Conservatives and the nation state, 1922–1997* (1998) · *The Times* (24 Nov 2006) · *Daily Telegraph* (24 Nov 2006) · *The Independent* (25 Nov 2006) · *The Guardian* (27 Nov 2006) · *WW* (2006) · Burke, *Peerage* · b. cert. · m. cert. [1966] · d. cert.

Likenesses Bassano, photographs, 1959–65, NPG · photograph, 1966, PA Photos, London · photograph, 1971, Getty Images, London, Hult. Arch. · photographs, 1971–2002, Photoshot, London · G. W. Hales, photograph, 1972, Getty Images, London, Hult. Arch. · obituary photographs

Wealth at death £1,667,964: probate, 28 March 2007, *CGPLA Eng. & Wales*

Philips, Sir Cyril Henry (1912–2005), historian, university administrator, and public servant, was born on 27 December 1912 at 57 Church Road, Worcester, the only son and elder child of William Henry Philips (*b.* 1884), a railwayman from Glamorgan, and his wife, Mary Elizabeth, *née* Kimberley (*b.* 1888), a Londoner. His sister, Margaret (Peggy), was born in 1921, the year in which his father became employed as an engine driver in Bihar in British India, where Philips spent the following four years. Living conditions were hard and in 1925, leaving his father in India, his mother brought the children back to live in Birkenhead, where financial struggles continued. Philips had begun primary school at Mersey Park and in Bihar had attended Asansol College, and now continued his education at Rock Ferry high school. Supported by a teacher training grant, he went on to read history at Liverpool University in 1931, graduating in 1934 with a first-class degree. After completing his teacher training requirements he went in 1935 to the School of Oriental Studies (from 1938 the School of Oriental and African Studies, or SOAS) in London, where he wrote his PhD thesis, subsequently published in 1940 as *The East India Company, 1784–1834*. By that time he had been appointed to the academic staff of the school as an assistant lecturer in Indian history and had married (in September 1938 in Wallasey) Dorcas Rose, a teacher whom he had met as a fellow student in Liverpool. She was the daughter of John Rose, of Wallasey. Philips's marriage, which gave him great happiness, also contributed to an estrangement from his mother. He and Dorcas had a son and a daughter.

The quiet progress of Philips's life was greatly changed by the outbreak of the Second World War in 1939, his service in the army from 1941 to 1945, and his rise to the rank of lieutenant-colonel in the Army Education Corps and commandant of the Army School of Education, where he revealed considerable talent not only as an innovative teacher but also as an organizer. At the end of the war he received attractive offers of employment in industry and in the civil service but, after a short spell in the Treasury, as chief instructor in the department of training, he chose to return to academic life and SOAS, where he was in 1946 appointed professor of oriental history and head of the department of history. He never regretted the decision and the school benefited greatly from it because during the next thirty years (including twenty years, 1957–77, as director) he transformed that institution into the leading academic centre in the Western world for the study of classical and modern Asia and Africa.

In 1947 SOAS began a period of substantial, but haphazard, expansion in the wake of the report of the Scarbrough commission of 1947. Many academic posts were created but few undergraduate students came to SOAS; by 1957 the institution looked expensive and vulnerable. With the aid of money from American foundations Philips as director launched a major programme of expansion. What was later named the Philips Building (formally opened in 1976 and housing the school's magnificent library) was essentially his creation: it was his passionate speech at a meeting of the University of London convocation on 20 February 1969 that narrowly defeated the strong opposition of conservationists to the Bloomsbury development. Philips also expanded modern studies in the school, established departments of economics and politics and of geography, and endeavoured to attract more students to SOAS by developing new and attractive programmes of study. One distinctive instrument by which he sought to bring students to SOAS was a department of extramural studies, which also served another of his aims, namely to spread the study of the societies of Asia and Africa more widely throughout Great Britain. His membership of the University Grants Committee (1961–71) further enabled him to promote the growth of Asian and African studies in other universities in the United Kingdom.

From 1971 to 1976 Philips served as vice-chancellor of the University of London, of which SOAS was a constituent college. The post was part-time and had been largely ceremonial, but Philips found himself in troubled waters when he was obliged to deal with the fallout from the Murray report, which recommended a strengthening of the central organization of the university, a proposal that ran counter to the long-standing and irresistible movement within the university towards the decentralization of power to the colleges. With little help from the university administration and in the face of discordant voices within the colleges, Philips strove to find a way forward. Overburdened with work as he was, personal tragedy also struck when his wife, Dorcas, died in August 1974. Philips, who had been knighted earlier that year, struggled on with his customary determination and eventually found a formula that commanded general support within the university, although the details could not be settled for some years as parliamentary legislation was required. On the personal front he found new support and happiness with Joan Rosemary Marshall, an officer of the university, seven years his junior, and daughter of William George Marshall, landscape gardener. They married on 30 August 1975.

In 1976 Philips gratefully gave up the vice-chancellorship and returned full-time to SOAS. Times had, however, changed: the expansionist mood of the 1960s and early 1970s had been replaced by financial caution in the governing body under its new chairman, Lord Gore-Booth. A clash between Gore-Booth and Philips, an unrepentant expansionist, was inevitable and in 1977 Philips decided he had had enough and resigned. But others had seen something of his outstanding abilities and an invitation soon came to chair the royal commission on criminal procedure (1978–80), setting him on a new career in public service. The royal commission was concerned with pre-trial procedure, that is to say with the role of the police in investigating and prosecuting crime, and therefore was an extremely sensitive subject with political ramifications. Philips's handling of the commission was masterly and set new standards for royal commissions by his insistence on commissioning basic research on which conclusions were founded, by setting out clear principles, and by the strongly practical emphasis of the report (*Parl. papers*, Cmnd 8092 of 1981), surprisingly signed by all the members. The report led to subsequent legislation regulating police procedures and establishing an independent prosecution service, although not the local service Philips had wanted. Further public service work followed as chairman of the Police Complaints Board (1980–85), monitor of the Prevention of Terrorism (Temporary Provisions) Act of 1984 (1985–6), and chairman of the Council of Tribunals (1986–9).

Philips, who was always known as Phil even to his wives, was small in stature, wiry in build, hard-working and abstemious by disposition, companionable enough but essentially private by inclination, fond of walking alone or with someone close to him. In short he was a serious man, a liberal whom experience had left mistrustful of the claims of authority. As monitor of the anti-terrorism act he did not hesitate to challenge the conduct of the police. He was very much a historian: in the royal commission report Philips may be recognized in the remark that 'it is the British tradition to assume that institutions can best be understood by the manner in which they are seen to emerge from their history'. His own career as a historian, despite all his efforts to keep it alive through seminars and publications, eventually suffered from the demands of administration. As an academic administrator he stood in the first rank, combining as he did several talents: to see clearly the nature of a problem, to devise a solution, to create the structures required to implement that solution, to assemble the necessary resources, and to drive the work through to a successful conclusion.

In 1991 Philips and his wife retired to live in Swanage, Dorset. He died at their home, 77 D'Urberville Drive, on 29 December 2005. His health had been declining for many years. He was survived by his wife, Joan, and his daughter, Margaret (Meg). His son had died in 1957 following an accident at school. M. E. Yapp

Sources *School of Oriental and African Studies: annual reports, 1935–1978* • C. H. Philips, *Problems, policies and progress, 1957–1961* (1961) • C. H. Philips, *The School of Oriental and African Studies, University of London, 1917–1967* (1967) • *University of London Bulletin*, 32 (March 1976) • C. Philips, *Beyond the ivory tower: the autobiography of Sir Cyril Philips* (1995) • D. Arnold and C. Shackle, eds., *SOAS since the sixties* (2003) • *The Times* (9 Jan 2006) • M. Yapp, 'Tribute to Professor Sir Cyril Philips', *SOAS Information Sheet* (16 Jan 2006) • *The Independent* (19 Jan 2006) • *The Guardian* (2 Feb 2006) • proceedings at a memorial service, DVD, 22 Feb 2006, SOAS • *WW* (2005) • Burke, *Peerage* • personal knowledge (2009) • private information (2009) • b. cert. • m. cert. [1975] • d. cert.

Archives LSE, papers relating to royal commission on criminal procedure • SOAS

Likenesses obituary photographs • photograph, SOAS; repro. in *The Independent*

Wealth at death £138,745: probate, 14 Aug 2006, *CGPLA Eng. & Wales*

Phillips, Dewi Zephaniah (1934–2006), philosopher, was born on 24 November 1934 at 56 Lan Street, Morriston, near Swansea, Glamorgan, the youngest of three sons of David Oakley Phillips, a labourer in a steelworks, and his wife, Alice Frances, *née* Davies. He was educated at Swansea grammar school and the University College of Wales, Swansea, where he graduated with first-class honours in philosophy in 1956. He had intended to be ordained as a Congregational minister, but decided in 1958 to study for a BPhil in Oxford. Disillusioned with philosophy there, he changed to a BLitt (awarded in 1961), writing on 'The language of talking to God'. Meanwhile, on 2 September 1959, at Peniel Green English Congregational Church, Swansea, he had married (Margaret) Monica Hanford, a 22-year-old secretary to the chief clerk at a hospital, and daughter of Frederick John Hanford, process worker. They had three sons.

After teaching briefly in Dundee (1961–3) and Bangor (1963–5) Phillips returned to Swansea as a lecturer in philosophy in 1965, and became professor and head of department in 1971. He held visiting professorships at various American universities, and in 1992 was appointed

Danforth professor of the philosophy of religion at Claremont graduate school, California, a post he combined with his professorship at Swansea until 1996, when he became Rush Rhees research professor at Swansea. In 2003 he became emeritus professor at Swansea.

Phillips's first and perhaps most influential book was *The Concept of Prayer* (1965), based partly on his Oxford BLitt thesis. The philosophy of religion started to make a comeback in British philosophy in the 1950s, after a period when it had been neglected because of the logical positivists' attack on the meaningfulness of metaphysics and theology (popularized in A. J. Ayer's *Language, Truth and Logic* in 1936). The posthumous publication of the later work of Ludwig Wittgenstein, starting with his *Philosophical Investigations* in 1953, played an important role. Phillips's *The Concept of Prayer* was the first book fully to apply Wittgenstein's work to the philosophy of religion. It showed both philosophical acumen and religious sensitivity, reflecting the influence not only of Wittgenstein but also of Kierkegaard and Simone Weil (this trio of thinkers influenced him deeply throughout his life).

Phillips published over twenty other books, mostly in the philosophy of religion, but also in ethics, and in philosophy and literature. *Faith after Foundationalism* (1988) showed most clearly his aims in the philosophy of religion and why he found so much philosophy wrong-headed. In his work in the philosophy of religion he was often fighting on two fronts: against sceptics who dismissed religious beliefs as meaningless, false, or based on insufficient evidence; and against some of his fellow Christian philosophers who sought to buttress their religious beliefs by giving them a philosophical foundation, for example by demonstrating the existence of God or by constructing theodicies to answer the problem of evil. He thought that the latter philosophers were in danger of reducing the philosophy of religion to apologetics and so introducing an impurity into the subject, whereas he thought that its primary goal was to help to understand religion. It seemed to him that both sceptics and apologists often misunderstood the reality of God and the nature of religious belief, because they relied on too uniform concepts of existence, evidence, reality, and so forth. Not surprisingly, he was attacked from both sides. Sceptics accused him of begging the question by resorting to what one critic called 'Wittgensteinian fideism' (K. Nielsen, 'Wittgensteinian fideism', *Philosophy*, 42, July 1967, 191–209), while some of his fellow Christian philosophers accused him of denying the reality of God by reducing him to a concept, and of rejecting some central religious beliefs, like the possibility of life after death in his *Death and Immortality* (1970). Certainly his own position could be elusive: at times it seemed clearer what he was rejecting than what he believed. This is especially true perhaps of his discussions of the idea of divine creation. But he was a doughty controversialist, quick-witted, and ready to take on his critics verbally at conferences and in writing.

Phillips was proud of his roots: he published professionally in Welsh as well as in English, and wrote a book on the poet R. S. Thomas, subtitled 'poet of the hidden God' (1986). That book exemplified his interest in the arts and literature, also manifested in his books *Through a Darkening Glass* (1982) and *From Fantasy to Faith* (1991), which discussed the religious and ethical issues raised in a wide range of literary works. He became well known in the USA, especially after taking up his chair at Claremont, and also on the continent of Europe through his enthusiastic participation, intellectually and socially, in the European philosophers of religion conferences. He served as president of the British Society for the Philosophy of Religion from 2001 to 2003. His combination of intelligence, warmth of personality, and sense of humour endeared him to many people, including those who usually disagreed with him. He was generous in supporting his fellow scholars, including some of his critics, and he devoted much of his later time at Swansea to editing and publishing the work of his former teacher and colleague, Rush Rhees. It was while he was working in Swansea University Library that he died of a sudden heart attack on 25 July 2006. He was survived by his wife, Monica, and his sons Aled, Steffan, and Rhys. PATRICK SHERRY

Sources I. Lloyd, 'A personal tribute', *The possibilities of sense*, ed. J. H. Whittaker (2002), 1–8 • *The Independent* (9 Aug 2006) • *The Times* (18 Aug 2006) • *The Guardian* (21 Aug 2006) • *Proceedings and Addresses of the American Philosophical Association*, 81/2 (2007), 180–81 • *WW* (2006) • personal knowledge (2010) • private information (2010) • b. cert. • m. cert. • d. cert.

Likenesses obituary photographs

Wealth at death £221,000: probate, 27 Nov 2006, *CGPLA Eng. & Wales*

Pimlott, Steven Charles (1953–2007), opera and theatre director, was born at 332 Wellington Road North, Stockport, Cheshire, on 18 April 1953, the younger child of Arthur Pimlott, a fire insurance assessor, and his wife, Marian, *née* Whittaker. At the time of his birth registration the family lived at 42 Preston Road, Levenshulme, Manchester. In 1955 they moved to Brooklands, a quiet residential area of Sale; and from 1964 Pimlott attended Manchester grammar school. He went to Sidney Sussex College, Cambridge, in 1971, and graduated three years later with a degree in English literature. His school years set the tone for much of his later work. A gifted adolescent actor excelling in middle-aged female roles—his Mother Courage in Bertolt Brecht's play and what he described as a 'definitive' Gertrude (aged twelve) in a school production of *Hamlet* were specially thrilling—he also found time to indulge a love for the oboe, and lifelong obsessions with board games, rollercoasters, and the operas of Gilbert and Sullivan. At Cambridge, as a member of a set that included his younger schoolfriend Nicholas Hytner, he added directing to this portfolio. Vivid university society stagings of *Don Giovanni* and *HMS Pinafore* demonstrated his talent, not for fashionable conceptual or intellectual readings, but for theatrical bravura and sensual immediacy.

In 1976 Pimlott became a staff producer at English National Opera, collaborating notably with the director John Copley, before joining the newly formed Opera North in 1978. Of his many Leeds productions *Nabucco* (1979), *Der Freischütz* (1980), and the British stage première

Steven Charles Pimlott (1953–2007), by Clare Park, 2004

of Borodin's *Prince Igor* (1982) were representative in their darkly powerful mastery of theatrical effect. On the strength of this success Pimlott swiftly amassed a long list of operatic credits throughout Europe and beyond. A spectacular, bullring *Carmen* starring Maria Ewing at Earls Court (1989, revived with José Carreras as Don José in Tokyo and elsewhere) was the most monumental of these; the much revived production of *La Bohème* for English National Opera (1993) captured perfectly the youthful high spirits of the piece, while charting the sadness at its heart. His sensuous, lucid *Coronation of Poppea* for the same company (2000) was another career highlight.

Yet Pimlott's honest admission of the directorial limitations proper to opera led him to spend increasing time in 'straight' theatre, starting with a stint as associate director under Clare Venables at the Sheffield Crucible (1987–8). Productions there of *Twelfth Night* and Botho Strauss's *The Park*, added to a spiritually luminous cycle of *The Mystery Plays* for the city of York (1988), marked him out as a rising star of the mainstream. About this time, too, his collaborations with the stage designers Tom Cairns and Stefanos Lazaridis led to a sea change in Pimlott's working method, away from minutely detailed pre-planning towards a more intuitive, organic approach.

Pimlott's National Theatre début with Stephen Sondheim's *Sunday in the Park with George* (1990, nominated for an Olivier award) and *The Miser* (1991) were less sure-footed than usual, but his work with the Royal Shakespeare Company (RSC), latterly as associate director (1996–2002), proved much more congenial, with new writing as well as classic revivals. A mordant *Richard III* (1995) and sexually graphic *Antony and Cleopatra* (1999) were memorable, his work in Stratford's more intimate spaces especially so. Working without the visual trappings available to the large auditorium freed him up as an 'actor's director', and *Richard II* (The Other Place, 2000, with Samuel West) was a milestone. This RSC period was capped by a *Hamlet* (2001, again with West) bound by bleak searchlights from lowering watchtowers.

Pimlott's forays into commercial theatre were artistically as well as financially lucrative. He brought the same brilliance to the blockbusters *Joseph and his Amazing Technicolor Dreamcoat* (London 1991, Broadway 1993), *Doctor Dolittle* (1998), and *Bombay Dreams* (2002) as to his work in the subsidized sphere, admitting no contradiction between the two. For Pimlott, good theatre was good theatre, whether it came from Aeschylus or Agatha Christie—another of his extramural passions.

Of his late projects, one in particular enjoyed signal artistic success. As part of a triumvirate (with Martin Duncan and Ruth Mackenzie) coming together to run the Chichester festival, reduced by 2003 to its nadir, Pimlott breathed some fresh life into the once great space with boldly spiritual productions of Shakespeare, Chekhov, and Gotthold Lessing's *Nathan the Wise* (2003), as well as introducing strong new writing and a wondrous staging of Bulgakov's novel *The Master and Margarita* (2004). Chichester's educational and rehearsal building was named after him following his death.

As a personal turning point, the most important of all Pimlott's productions was Paul Dukas's rarity *Ariane et Barbe-Bleue* (Krefeld, 1986), in which he directed the German soprano Daniela Christina Bechly (*b.* 1956), daughter of Adolf Friederich Bechly, whom he married at Holy Trinity, Clapham, on 27 July 1991. They had three children, one daughter preceded by two sons. Pimlott was appointed OBE in 2007, and died of lung cancer on 14 February that year, at his home, Old House, Old House Road, Great Horkesley, Essex. He was survived by his wife and their children. His gift for conveying the relish of the moment, whether in opera, drama, or the musical, marked him out as a rare theatrical magician of his time.

CHRISTOPHER WEBBER

Sources *The Times* (16 Feb 2007) · *Daily Telegraph* (16 Feb 2007) · *The Guardian* (16 Feb 2007) · *The Independent* (16 Feb 2007) · *WW* (2007) · personal knowledge (2011) · private information (2011) [Marian Pimlott, mother; Daniela Bechly, widow; Rafael Pimlott, son; A. Wickes] · b. cert. · m. cert. · d. cert.

Archives SOUND BL NSA, documentary recordings · BL NSA, performance recordings

Likenesses C. Park, photograph, 2004, priv. coll. [*see illus.*] · T. Larkin, photograph, 2005, Rex Features, London · obituary photographs · photograph, PA Photos, London · photograph, repro. in www.pimlottfoundation.org/steven-pimlott.php · photographs, repro. in www.stevenpimlott.org

Wealth at death £3,947,881: probate, 25 Jan 2008, *CGPLA Eng. & Wales*

Pinter, Harold (1930–2008), actor, playwright, and director, was born on 10 October 1930 at Tudor House, Newington Green, London, the only child of Hyman (Jack) Pinter (1902–1997), ladies' tailor, and his wife, Frances, *née* Moskowitz (1904–1992). At the time of his birth his parents lived at 8 Ashtead Road, Springhill, Hackney, but later moved to 19 Thistlewaite Road, where he was brought up. For many years it was assumed that his family were Sephardic Jews of Spanish or Portuguese origin. In fact his paternal grandfather, Nathan, was born in Russian Poland in 1870 and fled to England in 1900 with his wife and family to escape the pogroms. Meanwhile Pinter's maternal grandfather, Harry Moskowitz, arrived in London from Odessa also in 1900 and settled in the East End with his Polish-born wife. Both sides of the family were Ashkenazi Jews importing from eastern Europe a love of culture, a memory of suffering, and an extraordinary resilience.

Early years and formative experiences Although Pinter grew up in a large extended family—his father had four siblings and his mother three—he was, by his own admission, a somewhat solitary child: at the age of eight he would sit under a lilac tree in the family garden and conduct imaginary conversations with invisible friends. But, although that is not uncommon among only children, a number of factors in Pinter's early life helped to shape his theatrical imagination. One was the Second World War. In 1939 he was evacuated to Cornwall for a year and experienced an acute sense of separation, loneliness, and loss: after returning to London at the height of the blitz, he was confronted every day with the reality of death. 'People really felt', he said, 'their lives could end tomorrow' (Billington, 8). Pinter's precocious awareness of mortality was complemented by a voracious appetite for reading, easily satisfied at Hackney Public Library where he devoured works by Dostoyevsky, Virginia Woolf, D. H. Lawrence, T. S. Eliot, and Ernest Hemingway. At Hackney Downs Grammar School from 1944 to 1948 he shone at sports, setting a school record for the 100 yard sprint. He also came under the influence of an inspirational English teacher, Joe Brearley, who fostered his love of poetry and introduced him to great drama. Brearley cast Pinter as Romeo and Macbeth in school plays and, on their walks together through Hackney, would declaim passages from the plays of John Webster. Alongside Brearley, Pinter also acquired a circle of teenage, predominantly Jewish, friends who shared a love of intellectual adventure and an ironic sense of humour. They talked avidly about their latest literary discoveries, new European movies, and the relative merits of Bach and Beethoven: it was a world of shared passions, and occasional sexual betrayals, that Pinter captured in an autobiographical novel, *The Dwarfs*, on which he worked throughout the 1950s, dramatized in 1960, and finally published in 1990. It was a measure of the importance to Pinter of this teenage camaraderie that he kept in close touch with many of his Hackney friends, including Henry Woolf, Mick Goldstein, and Morris Wernick, for the rest of his life.

Harold Pinter (1930–2008), by Justin Mortimer, 1992

As young Jewish intellectuals the friends were keenly aware of the resurgence of fascism in London's post-war East End: Pinter, of necessity, became skilled in the use of verbal evasion to defuse menacing situations. But the need to counter local fascist violence, after a war that had been waged against Nazism, fuelled Pinter's rage against any form of injustice. From his earliest days he had shown an instinctive resistance to authority. At thirteen, after his barmitzvah, he renounced religion for good. And when, at eighteen, he received his national service call-up papers he declared himself a conscientious objector. He was summoned before two military tribunals to explain his case and twice asked to appear before a civil magistrate. Expecting to go to prison, he was instead asked to pay two substantial fines (which his father paid for him) and his case was dismissed. But for Pinter it was a formative experience. Basing his initial hostility to conscription on the absurdity of preparing for another world war, he found himself at the centre of a web of Kafkaesque bureaucracy in which statements he had never made were formally attributed to him. 'I really smelled a rat', he said later (Billington, 24). And, although he was fortunate to escape prison, the experience reinforced his natural suspicion of the established order.

Acting, and first plays By the age of twenty Pinter was already aware of the precariousness of human existence, of the tactical possibilities of language, and of society's injustice: all qualities that would feed into his plays. He also in 1950 appeared in print for the first time when two of his poems were published in the magazine *Poetry London*. But, needing to earn a living, he had already decided to become an actor. After a brief, unhappy spell as a drama student at the Royal Academy of Dramatic Art and a more productive one at the Central School of Speech and Drama, in 1951 he joined the company of the touring Irish actor–manager Anew McMaster (known to everyone as

'Mac'). This proved a vital theatrical education. It gave Pinter the chance to play increasingly important Shakespearian roles including Bassanio, Macduff, Iago, and even Hamlet for a single matinée ('Very good', said Mac afterwards, 'but next time be a bit nicer to your mother' (Billington, 39)). It also gave him the chance to witness at first hand Mac's ability to impose himself on an audience and instil silence in an unruly crowd through the isolation of a single word. But Pinter's year with Mac also led to a major personal discovery. Riffling through a magazine called *Poetry Ireland*, Pinter came across a fragment of a novel, 'Watt', by Samuel Beckett. Stunned by Beckett's humour and his ability to create his own unique world, Pinter on coming back to London borrowed a copy of *Murphy* from a public library that, to his dying day, he never returned.

For much of the 1950s Pinter led a curious double life. On the one hand he was a closet writer, working on poems, prose-sketches, and *The Dwarfs*. But he was also a jobbing actor, slogging round the English weekly repertory theatres and often living in unpalatable digs. After a brief spell in Donald Wolfit's classical company he spent 1954 to 1958 on the repertory circuit appearing under the name of David Baron. Far from being time wasted Pinter's years in repertory provided a vital theatrical apprenticeship. Specializing in sinister roles, he learned a lot about the mechanics of structure and about the achievement of dramatic effects: in one play, *The Uninvited Guest*, he played a runaway mental patient who stands with his back to the audience while being vehemently interrogated. It was an idea Pinter was later to deploy in *The Birthday Party* (1957). That play was also based on Pinter's memory of staying in seedy seaside digs in Eastbourne in 1954, where one of his fellow lodgers was a former concert party pianist who was always being goosed by his landlady. It was while in repertory in Bournemouth in 1956 that he met a darkly voluptuous actress named Vivien Merchant (whose real name was Ada Brand Thomson (1929–1982) and who was of Irish-Catholic origin, the daughter of William Thomson, personnel manager for a precision engineers). She was already well established on the provincial circuit. After a brief affair they got married at Bournemouth register office on 14 September 1956: when Pinter rang his parents to tell them there was a certain amount of dismay since he had not only married a non-Jewish girl but had unwittingly chosen Yom Kippur (the most solemn religious fast of the Jewish year) for the day of the wedding. Although constantly struggling to make ends meet, Pinter and his wife were delighted when they had a son, Daniel, in January 1958.

What transformed Pinter's life professionally was an invitation in the autumn of 1956 from his old friend Henry Woolf, now doing a postgraduate year in Bristol, to write a play for the university's drama department. Over four days and nights Pinter came up with *The Room*, which was eventually performed in May 1957. What was fascinating was how Pinter instantly staked out his own particular theatrical territory. The play's heroine, Rose, is an anxious recluse who finds the bedsit she occupies with her largely silent husband subject to constant invasion: first by her talkative landlord, then by a young married couple, and finally by a blind black man called Riley bearing a message from Rose's father bidding her to come home. The play ends with Rose's husband beating Riley to death and with Rose herself suffering temporary blindness. Cryptic, mysterious, and comic, the play not only showed Pinter's ability to create eerie suspense but also his preoccupation with society's demands on those who seek to withdraw to sequestered rooms. Filled with promise, *The Room* quickly became Pinter's calling card. It attracted the attention of an agent, Jimmy Wax; and, when it was revived at the 1957 National Student Drama Festival, a glowing notice from Harold Hobson in the *Sunday Times*, invoking Beckett, Ionesco, and Henry James, prompted a young impresario, Michael Codron, to set up a crucial meeting with Pinter at which he agreed to stage the dramatist's next play.

That was *The Birthday Party* (1957) which, after a short, highly successful provincial tour, opened at the Lyric Hammersmith on 19 May 1958 but closed at the end of the week. The notices weren't just bad. They were, with the exception of Harold Hobson's in the *Sunday Times*, which appeared the day after the play closed, disastrous. It is not immediately easy to see why the play aroused such hostility. It has a traditional three-act structure. It has a naturalistic surface. And the sequence of events is not, in itself, obscure. We know that Stanley, an ex-pianist hiding away in a seaside town, is sought out by two men, Goldberg and McCann, who intimidate him and finally take him away to the headquarters of the organization they represent. What, however, seemed to annoy critics was Pinter's reluctance to spell out who precisely his twin abductors represented. Some years later it seemed blindingly obvious that Goldberg and McCann, a Jew and an Irishman, stood for the West's two most autocratic religions and its two most persecuted races. But, although the play came to be seen as a political work about the need for active resistance to conformity, at the time it was myopically dismissed for its 'puzzling surrealism' and 'inconsequential gabble' (Billington, 86).

Having turned down a lucrative acting job Pinter had staked everything on the success of *The Birthday Party*. But, although rocked by the reviews, he survived, thanks partly to a series of commissions from BBC radio, partly to the German theatre's willingness to produce another early piece, *The Dumb Waiter* (1957, staged 1960), and partly to his own strong self-belief. Pinter, from the beginning, possessed the capacity to see the significance of his own life. Recalling an earlier experience when he had enrolled as a guinea-pig at a London psychiatric hospital and been subjected to shock treatment he wrote a play about a state-run 'rest-home' designed to turn obstinate nonconformists into model citizens. An abiding personal memory was turned into a powerful political metaphor; and had *The Hothouse*, as the play was called, been staged shortly after it was written in 1958, it might have changed the public perception of Pinter and seen him designated a political, rather than absurdist, writer. Instead he put *The Hothouse* in a bottom drawer, only to retrieve it for its London première in 1980.

Unaware of the existence of *The Hothouse* critics and public began to discover in Pinter a skilful purveyor of comic menace. Short plays such as *A Slight Ache* (1958, produced on radio 1959), *A Night Out* (1959, produced on radio and television 1960), and *Night School* (1960, produced on television the same year) appealed both to the select audiences that listened to the BBC's Third Programme and to the mass audience that watched Sunday night television. At the same time Pinter was writing sketches for the intimate revues that Michael Codron regularly produced in the West End. But what linked all Pinter's work was his distinctive use of language. He was clearly alert to the banalities of everyday speech. He also showed how such language could become poetic through its echoes, symmetries, and repetitions. Above all he seemed highly conscious of the way words could be used as either strategic weapons of domination or a tactical means of evasion. A highly idiosyncratic writer was emerging but one who had still to write a universally popular stage play.

The Caretaker* and *The Homecoming That gap was repaired with *The Caretaker*, which Pinter wrote in 1959 and which opened at the Arts Theatre, London, on 27 April 1960. The critics who had dismissed *The Birthday Party* two years earlier now found in the new play a mastery of popular speech and a rich store of potential meaning. It was not that *The Caretaker* was a staggeringly better play than its predecessor. What had happened, in the intervening two years, was that Pinter had imposed himself on the public consciousness: he had acclimatized audiences, and critics, to a new form of demotic theatrical poetry concealing an intense battle for power. And power lies at the very heart of *The Caretaker*, in which a homeless tramp, Davies, is given shelter by the kindly, brain-damaged Aston. In seeking to drive a wedge between his host and his sharp-witted brother Mick, the unscrupulous Davies ends up alienating both and facing expulsion from his temporary Eden. What Pinter grasps is that life, apart from being mired in self-delusion, is an endless series of negotiations for advantage, and that a contest between three men in a shabby west London room can become an infinitely extendable metaphor. In 1960, and ever since, the play has been subject to every possible interpretation: psychological, political, theological, ethological. But in the end it is a closely observed study of the way, in any social context, there is a constantly shifting balance of power. Boasting a memorable performance from Donald Pleasence, as a blustering, belligerent, but ultimately vulnerable Davies, the original production transferred to the West End, where it ran for 444 performances. The play was also taken up by major European theatres and filmed in 1963 with Pleasence and Alan Bates, as the fly, nimble Mick, repeating their stage performances, and with Robert Shaw as Aston. With the success of *The Caretaker* there was no doubt that Pinter had finally arrived.

The suddenly fashionable Pinter was now in demand in every medium. He enjoyed success on television with *The Collection* (1961) and *The Lover* (1963): the latter, dealing with the erotic games a husband and wife play in order to refresh their stale marriage, was both a popular hit and a persistent prize-winner. In the early 1960s Pinter also started out on a long, highly productive career as a screenwriter. His first film was *The Servant* (1963), which was adapted from a Robin Maugham novella and which dealt with a predatory manservant who brings about his master's downfall by exploiting his infantile dependence and sexual ambivalence: brilliantly directed by Joseph Losey, and starring Dirk Bogarde and James Fox, the film showed Pinter's ability to transfer his preoccupation with hermetic power-battles and the intricacies of human speech directly to the screen. He quickly followed this with screenplays for *The Pumpkin Eater* (1964, directed by Jack Clayton) and *The Quiller Memorandum* (1966, directed by Michael Anderson), which brought the same lapidary skill to a domestic drama and an espionage thriller.

Matching his cinematic partnership with Losey, Pinter forged an even more crucial theatrical relationship with Peter Hall, a young director who founded the Royal Shakespeare Company (RSC) in 1960 and who understood the precise musicality of Pinter's dialogue, his ironic Cockney humour, and his ability to explore the insecurity and passion that lurked beneath the mask of everyday speech. In 1962 Hall invited Pinter to collaborate on a stage version of *The Collection* at the Aldwych: one that whetted Pinter's appetite for directing and revealed his obsessive concern with textual rhythm and the weight that should be given to any pause. At one point Pinter gave a note to the actor Michael Hordern in which he said, 'I wrote dot, dot, dot and you're giving me dot, dot': far from being bemused, Hordern instantly grasped the difference between a long and short pause (Billington, 141). As a director Pinter also revived *The Birthday Party* for the RSC in 1964; but it was with his new play, *The Homecoming* (written in 1964 and staged in 1965), that he was to provide the RSC with one of its most prestigious successes and bring the naturalistic side of his playwriting career to a rich climax.

What is startling about *The Homecoming* is its ability, over the years, to change its meaning without any loss of its power to shock and disturb. Like many of Pinter's plays it had its origins in recollected experience: Pinter's memory of a Jewish friend from Hackney who had married a Gentile girl, emigrated to Canada, and kept his marriage a secret from his family. This was the springboard for Pinter's imagination but the play itself is a fiction: one which Pinter fiercely resisted being seen as a specifically Jewish family drama. The play's real provocation lies in the way Ruth, the wife of an academic who returns to his family home, chooses to stay with her boisterous in-laws rather than go back to the sterility of American campus life. Even more unsettling is the way the patriarchal Max, his pimping son Lenny, and the dumb-witted brother Joey invite Ruth to pay her way in her new family by working as a high-class prostitute.

The Homecoming can be seen as a Freudian family drama, a territorial struggle, or an enactment of some ancient ritual in which the old king is replaced by the new fertility goddess. But what unnerved audiences, and critics, was the absence of any conventional moral framework and

Ruth's apparent willingness to submit to the family's outrageous sexual demands. Close study of the text, however, reveals that Max and Lenny are rendered impotent and ineffectual at the end and that Ruth is securely in charge. With the advance of feminism, indeed, it became possible to see the play as a study of Ruth's empowerment rather than her humiliation. Even in Peter Hall's immaculate 1965 production, with Vivien Merchant as a memorably silky Ruth, there were strong hints of that; and when Hall revived the play in 1991, with Cherie Lunghi as an insidiously determined Ruth, the play seemed even more clearly about Ruth's triumphant territorial and sexual takeover.

Withdrawal from naturalism While *The Homecoming* was a great success it marked a watershed in Pinter's playwriting career. After that play he abandoned conventional theatrical naturalism. As he put it, 'I couldn't any longer stay in the room with this bunch of people who opened doors and came in and went out' (Billington, 181). Pinter was still active after *The Homecoming*: he wrote the movie script of *Accident* (1967) for Losey, a television play called *The Basement* (1966, broadcast 1967), and directed Robert Shaw's *The Man in the Glass Booth* (1967) at St Martin's Theatre in the West End. But there were no stage plays until the double-bill of *Landscape* and *Silence*; and even these had their première on BBC radio in 1968 because Pinter refused to accede to the request of the theatrical censor, the lord chamberlain, to remove several four-letter words. When the plays finally appeared in a Peter Hall production for the RSC in 1969 they clearly marked a decisive formal shift. *Landscape* is a deeply moving two-hander about marital isolation and the power of emotional memory; *Silence*, written for three characters, was a less successful, more opaque variation on the theme of loss of love.

What led to this withdrawal from naturalism was partly the influence of Beckett, whose own work showed a similar rejection of conventional structures. Having worked in film and television Pinter was also fascinated by the stage's potential for exploring characters' inmost thoughts. In addition the circumstances of Pinter's own life were changing: if he dwelt on the memory of lost happiness it may have been because his marriage to Vivien Merchant was slowly deteriorating. But Pinter was clearly conscious that, for all the poetic beauty and imagistic power of *Landscape*, he was in danger of drying up. He made his fears public in a speech at Hamburg in June 1970 when he accepted the prestigious Shakespeare prize. He spoke of the irony of accepting the prize at a moment when he was creatively fallow, adding, 'When you can't write, you feel banished from yourself' (Billington, 205).

For Pinter, however, the 1970s were to prove a decade both of considerable public activity and of private disruption. In 1971 *Old Times* had its première in a Peter Hall production at the Aldwych. What it did was to take Pinter's abiding preoccupation with memory to a new level. In the play Deeley and his wife Kate welcome one of the latter's oldest friends, Anna, into their home. But what follows is a verbal, psychological, and even musical battle between Deeley and Anna over possession of the stoically unclaimable Kate: in the process memory becomes a weapon as if to demonstrate that the past is no more fixed or certain than the present or future. Having wrestled with the fallibility of memory in *Old Times* Pinter then spent a whole year working on a screen version of Proust's *A la recherche du temps perdu* for Joseph Losey. Although the project never reached the screen it led to a published screenplay (1972), later adapted for both radio and the stage. Pinter's total immersion in Proust also had many beneficial effects. It reinforced his own convictions about the power of art, stimulated further experiments with time and memory, and drove him still further away from representational realism.

That imaginative freedom was immediately apparent in *No Man's Land*, which had its première at the Old Vic in April 1975 in a Peter Hall production for the National Theatre, an institution of which Pinter had become an associate director two years earlier. Set in the home of a wealthy and immured man of letters, Hirst, the play shows Spooner, a temporary guest and minor poet, seeking to rescue his host from the spiritual and physical no-man's-land into which he is slowly retreating. Although not easily subject to rational analysis the play's dynamic depends on the tension between death and life, resignation and resistance, the sterile affluence of Hirst's home and a remembered world of sunlit lawns and bucolic gaiety. As performed by Ralph Richardson and John Gielgud the play combined a tragic trajectory with a comic vivacity and was an instant, popular success, eventually transferring to the West End and Broadway. Unfortunately the play's London opening coincided with the news that Pinter's marriage to Vivien Merchant had broken up and that he was engaged in a passionate relationship with Lady Antonia Fraser (*b.* 1932), a historian and biographer, wife of a Conservative MP, Sir Hugh Fraser, and daughter of a Labour peer, Francis Aungier (Frank) Pakenham, seventh earl of Longford. Throughout the summer of 1975 Pinter and Fraser were pursued by the tabloid press; and the endless hullabaloo about their affair meant that, for both of them, a prolonged period of work became intensely difficult.

For two years Pinter largely confined himself to acting and directing. In September 1978 his screenplay, *Langrishe, Go Down*, adapted from a novel by Aidan Higgins, and originally written in 1970, was shown on BBC television. Two months later his new play, *Betrayal*, directed by Peter Hall, had its première at the National's Lyttelton Theatre. At the time the play was widely misunderstood: it was myopically seen as a variation on the all-too-familiar theme of middle-class adultery. But the play, with its ingenious reverse chronology and symmetrical structure, was infinitely more than that. In tracing the course of a seven-year-long affair between a literary agent and the wife of his oldest friend it explored a whole series of interlinked betrayals: betrayal of one's marital partner, of one's lover, of the high idealism of youth, and ultimately of one's self. Peter Hall in his *Diaries* was even moved to compare the play to Mozart: 'there's the same precision of means, the same beauty, the same lyricism and the same sudden descents into pain which are quickly over because of a healthy sense of the ridiculous'. Although ostensibly triggered by Pinter's memories of his own seven-year affair with the television presenter Joan Bakewell, the play transcended the autobiographical impulse to achieve a universal resonance.

Privately Pinter had achieved a new-found happiness with Antonia Fraser but the break-up from his first wife still consumed much of his energy. It was not until the autumn of 1980 that Vivien finally granted him a divorce. As soon as that came through Pinter and Fraser were married, at Kensington register office, on 27 November. During a difficult time when Pinter was wrestling with the legal entanglements of divorce he had devoted himself to other activities than playwriting. He co-edited two poetry anthologies. He directed a number of plays including Simon Gray's *The Rear Column* (Globe, 1978), *Close of Play* (National, 1979), and *Quartermaine's Terms* (Queen's, 1981). He also struggled with, and eventually conquered, the problem of turning John Fowles's *The French Lieutenant's Woman*, with its shifts of perspective and alternative endings, into a film (released in 1981).

Pinter's return to the theatre came in October 1982 with 'Other Places', a triple bill of short plays at the National Theatre. *Family Voices*, originally written for radio (and broadcast in 1981), concerned the fear that, whether as parents or children, we never express the depths of our love. *Victoria Station* seemed a macabre throwback to the Pinter of the 1950s revue-sketches. But it was the third play, *A Kind of Alaska*, that seemed an outright masterpiece. Unusually for a Pinter stage-play it was inspired by an existing work: Oliver Sacks's *Awakenings* (1973), which dealt with the victims of a sleeping sickness that spread through Europe and the world in the winter of 1915/16. But, although inspired by Sacks's work, *A Kind of Alaska* had all the Pinter trademarks. As his heroine, Deborah, awakes from a twenty-nine-year sleep she feels her past as vividly present: indeed the whole play depends on the contrast between the inner subjective reality of Deborah's world and the outer objective reality of the doctor and his wife, Deborah's sister, who have lovingly tended her. As played initially by Judi Dench, Deborah became a living testament to the unassailable power of memory.

Political engagement and public recognition After the success of 'Other Places' Pinter had a creatively quiet period but one that was marked by an increasing sense of engagement with the public world and human rights abuses. His early work had shown his instinctive resistance to authority. But even if the plays of his middle period explored private worlds his concern with politics had been re-ignited by a number of factors. One was his friendship with the Marxist playwright David Mercer and the militant actress Peggy Ashcroft: it was partly at the latter's prompting that in 1973 he voiced his opposition to the American government's involvement in the overthrow of President Allende of Chile. Pinter's relationship with, and eventual marriage to, Antonia Fraser also meant that political discussion was part of their daily life: both were highly active members of PEN, an organization devoted to writers imprisoned and abused by authoritarian regimes. And it was while on a trip to Turkey with Arthur Miller in 1985 on behalf of PEN that Pinter made his anger at US support of the Turkish regime palpably evident at an American ambassadorial dinner, in an episode subsequently much publicized.

Pinter's increasing engagement with politics bore fruit in his work. In 1984 his short, viscerally powerful play *One For The Road* made its début in a lunchtime production at the Lyric Hammersmith. The piece was triggered by an encounter at a London party with two young Turkish women who shrugged off stories about their country's use of torture in military prisons. Although conceived in anger, the resulting play is a skilful examination of the psychology of a man responsible for state torture. Instead of making his hero, Nicolas, a stereotypical sadist out of a bad spy movie Pinter showed him as a man motivated by a belief in the family, the state, and religion: indeed when Pinter himself played the role in a 2001 revival, seen in London and in New York, he even suggested that Nicolas was a lonely, troubled figure who needed several shots of whisky in order to boost his public persona.

Inspired by his 1985 visit to Turkey, and by his anger at Turkish suppression of the Kurdish language, Pinter also started to write a play about that particular subject. But he put it aside and only resumed work on it in 1988 when it was premièred at the National Theatre as *Mountain Language*. By then the play was informed by Pinter's conviction that freedom of expression was under threat in Britain. His conclusion rested on a number of factors: restrictions on a suspect's right to silence, extension of the Official Secrets Act, and raids on BBC offices to remove all material relating to a television series, *Secret Society* (1987). The fact that a private discussion group founded by the Pinters, the June 20th Society, had to be terminated after it became the subject of media derision also fuelled Pinter's belief that Britain was no longer a place of liberal tolerance.

Although commissioned rather than personally chosen Pinter's work for film and television in the late 1980s reflected his political concerns. In 1988 he wrote, and Christopher Morahan directed, an adaptation for television of Elizabeth Bowen's *The Heat of the Day* (1989). Set in 1942 Bowen's story concerns a divorced woman who learns, through an espionage agent, that her War Office lover is passing secret information to the Germans. In the hands of Pinter, and Morahan, the film offers not just a masterly evocation of wartime but also an infinitely subtle study of the corrosive effect of fascism on human relationships. Pinter explored the same theme, in a different historical setting, in the film *Reunion* (1989). Based on a novella by Fred Uhlman, the film deals with a rich Jewish Manhattan lawyer's search for his own past in the Stuttgart of the 1930s, and in particular his passionate schoolboy friendship with a civilized scion of the German aristocracy who seemingly endorses the antisemitism of the period. As so often with his screen adaptations Pinter's work becomes a vehicle for exploring his own abiding concerns: memory, betrayal, and the power of the past over the present.

Now in his sixties Pinter found himself occupying a dual role in British life: admired senior playwright and combative public figure often mocked for his opinions. But Pinter stuck to his guns and formed a fruitful relationship with London's Almeida Theatre. It was there that in 1991 he staged the première of *Party Time*, a powerful portrait of a heedless group of socialites so concerned with their own well-being that they remain blithely indifferent to the erosion of civil liberties. In 1992 he played Hirst in a striking Almeida revival of *No Man's Land*. And in September 1993 his play *Moonlight* had its première. A deeply moving tone-poem about love, loss, separation, and mortality, the play had its roots in Pinter's own experience. It sprang partly from Pinter's guilt that he had never fully had time to mourn his mother, Frances, who died while he was rehearsing *No Man's Land*. In its portrait of two sons, estranged from their dying father and their mother, it also reflected his own sadness at his isolation from his son, Daniel, who had come to a mutual agreement with Pinter that they were better off not seeing each other, and who indeed had adopted his maternal grandmother's maiden name, Brand. Yet, although rooted in personal experience, *Moonlight* is a haunting, elegiac play that addresses the universal theme of unexpressed familial love.

Frequently revived in London, Pinter was positively fêted in Dublin. In May 1994 Michael Colgan, the dynamic director of Dublin's Gate Theatre, produced a celebratory Pinter Festival in which six works were staged over a three-week period. And it was the Gate Theatre that provided the bulk of the productions for another two-week Pinter celebration that took place at New York's Lincoln Center in July 2001. If Pinter's work was honoured abroad, he also received periodic recognition on home soil. As early as 1966 he had been made a CBE. In 1995 he received the prestigious David Cohen award for a lifetime's achievement in literature. And, although Pinter rejected the offer of a knighthood from the Conservative government in 1996, in 2002 he was happy to be appointed a Companion of Honour.

But what mattered most to Pinter was his continuing activity as playwright, director, and occasionally actor, as well as his use of his right as a citizen to protest about abuses of power. The two activities came together in *Ashes to Ashes*, which Pinter wrote and directed for the Royal Court, during its temporary exile in the West End, in 1996: the result is a mesmerizing play that starts as a domestic inquisition and opens up to admit the horrors of twentieth-century history. Even *Celebration*, which turned out to be Pinter's final play and which was staged in tandem with *The Room* at the Almeida in 2000 in celebration of his seventieth birthday, was less benign than it first seemed: ostensibly a comic account of restaurant bad manners it offered a sharp satire on the moral coarseness and spiritual bankruptcy of the super-rich.

Later years and the Nobel prize Pinter's later years were marked by an extraordinary concatenation of circumstances: a series of progressively debilitating illnesses; a growing public recognition that his eloquent anger about US foreign policy was amply justified; and the bestowal of an impressive series of public honours. The first sign of the gravity of his illness came after Pinter directed a revival of *No Man's Land* at the National Theatre in December 2000. Shortly after the play's opening he was diagnosed with cancer of the oesophagus. After a five-year struggle with cancer he then developed a rare skin disease called pemphigus, which was followed by a form of septicaemia consisting of an ulcer in the foot. For the last eight years of his life he rarely enjoyed a day of good health.

Yet as far as was humanly possible Pinter kept on working and campaigning. He wrote and performed a short piece, *Press Conference* (2002), for the National Theatre, satirizing media collusion with the state. He published a volume of poems under the title *War* (2003). He wrote the script for a new film of Anthony Shaffer's *Sleuth* (2007), starring Jude Law and directed by Kenneth Branagh. And he seized every opportunity to attack a belligerent American and British foreign policy. In 2003 he addressed 150 peace campaigners at the houses of parliament, spoke at a mass anti-Iraq War rally in Hyde Park, and read his poems at a City Hall demonstration hosted by Ken Livingstone. Once derided for his political stance, he now seemed in touch with the public mood.

The ultimate recognition came with the award of the Nobel prize for literature in 2005. Pinter received the news shortly after he returned from a celebration of his seventy-fifth birthday at the Gate Theatre in Dublin: an event that had ended in his sustaining head injuries through a bad fall. Greeting the world's news media on the morning of 13 October in a jaunty cap to disguise his head wounds, he resembled a veteran sailor just returned from an exhausting round-the-world trip. The award of the prize generated an overwhelming response from writers around the world. He was soon summoned back to hospital. He refused to go, however, until he had completed his Nobel lecture, 'Art, truth and politics'. What it argued, with polemical vigour, is that while art is driven by a remorseless search for truth, politics, as currently practised, was driven by rhetorical evasions and downright lies. Although Pinter was too ill to attend the Nobel ceremony in December his speech was recorded for television and shown, to considerable excitement, in Stockholm itself. It was some compensation that in March 2006 he was able to travel to Turin to receive the European theatre prize. Even more remarkably in October 2006 he gave ten brilliant performances in Beckett's *Krapp's Last Tape* at the Royal Court Theatre Upstairs. In 2007 he also received the Légion d'honneur at the French embassy and recorded the role of Max in *The Homecoming* for Radio 3.

The final years of Pinter's life were marked by a constant struggle against physical incapacity. But his work offers its own testament to a remarkable career. As a dramatist he redefined the nature of theatrical poetry, helped to strip theatrical dialogue of much of its rhetorical fat, and mapped out a theatrical country that possessed its own distinctive topography: a place haunted by the ambivalence of memory, flecked by uncertainty, reeking of sex, and echoing with a strange, mordant laughter. His work for film and television was characterized by a similar verbal tautness and an ability to fuse perfectly word and image. As a director he was revered by actors for the no-nonsense clarity of his approach and his scrupulous attention to textual detail. His unstinting campaigning fervour also received a glowing testament from Kofi Annan, the former UN secretary general, who wrote to him after the award of the Nobel prize that 'throughout your career you have had the courage to be honest and outspoken on some of the most important and difficult issues facing humanity, from the personal and domestic to the global' (Billington, 425).

As a private man Pinter belied his sometimes forbidding public image. He was a man of passionate enthusiasms: for cricket, poetry, wine, good talk, and the company of beautiful women. He had an almost sacerdotal belief in friendship and a profound loyalty to those whom he trusted. Through the latter half of his life he was sustained by his love for his second wife, Antonia. He died at the Hammersmith Hospital, London, on 24 December 2008, of gastrointestinal bleeding and cancer of the liver, and was buried at Kensal Green cemetery on 31 December. He was survived by Antonia and his son, Daniel, and by three stepsons and three stepdaughters. He left behind a host of cherished memories for his friends and colleagues and a body of work that, in its poetic precision, savage humour, and understanding of the insecurity that haunts our daily existence, radically changed the theatre of his time. MICHAEL BILLINGTON

Sources *The Pinter Review*, passim • M. Esslin, *Pinter the playwright* (2000) • M. Billington, *The life and work of Harold Pinter*, updated edn (2007) • *The Times* (26 Dec 2008) • *Daily Telegraph* (26 Dec 2008) • *The Independent* (26 Dec 2008); (27 Dec 2008) • *New York Times* (26 Dec 2008) • *The Guardian* (27 Dec 2008) • A. Fraser, *Must you go?* (2010) • *WW* (2008) • personal knowledge (2012) • private information (2012) • b. cert. • m. certs. • d. cert.

Archives BL • Indiana University, Lilly Library | BBC WAC • BFI, Joseph Losey MSS • V&A, Theatre Museum Archive, Christopher Fry MSS | FILM BFINA, *Face to face*, J. Birkett (producer), BBC2, 21 Jan 1997 • BFINA, *South Bank show*, D. Thomas (director), ITV, 29 Nov 1998 • BFINA, 'Harold Pinter, part one, the room', *Arena*, N. Williams (director), BBC2, 26 Oct 2002 • BFINA, 'Harold Pinter, part two, celebration', *Arena*, M. Rosenbaum (producer), BBC2, 26 Oct 2002 • BL, videos | SOUND BL NSA, current affairs, documentary, interview, and performance recordings

Likenesses M. Gerson, bromide prints, 1960, NPG • J. Hedgecoe, group portrait, bromide print, 1960 (*Playwrights*), NPG • R. Mayne, bromide print, 1960, NPG • B. Brandt, photographs, 1961–81, NPG • photographs, 1961–2008, Getty Images, London • photographs, 1961–2008, PA Photos, London • C. Beaton, bromide prints, 1962, NPG • N. Libbert, bromide print, 1963, NPG • photographs, 1965–2007, Photoshot, London • D. Kasterine, modern bromide print from original negative, 1977, NPG • A. Newman, double portrait, bromide print, 1978 (with Tom Stoppard), NPG • photographs, 1980–2008, Rex Features, London • J. Mortimer, oils, 1992, NPG [*see illus.*] • B. Ryan, bromide print, 1994, NPG • L. Douglas-Menzies, double portrait, bromide fibre print, 2002 (with Ronald Harwood), NPG • A. Shuckburgh, pastel and acrylic on wood, 2006, repro. in *The Times* (1 Jan 2009) • L. Clapham, caricature, *c.*2007, repro. in P. Wynter Bee and L. Clapham, *People of the day*, 3 (2008), 48 • J. Hill, portrait, priv. coll.; repro. in *The Times* (24 March 2009) • K. Lathigra, photograph, repro. in *The Independent* (6 May 1999) • obituary photographs • photographs, Camera Press, London • photographs, repro. in Billington, *Harold Pinter* • photographs, repro. in Esslin, *Pinter* • photographs, repro. in Fraser, *Must you go?* • photographs, Lebrecht Music and Arts Photo Library, London • photographs, repro. in *Observer Magazine* (27 Oct 1991), 7

Wealth at death £4,335,984: probate, 23 Dec 2009, *CGPLA Eng. & Wales*

Pippard, Sir (Alfred) Brian (1920–2008), physicist, was born at 41a Penywern Road, Earl's Court, London, on 7 September 1920, the younger son of (Alfred John) Sutton *Pippard (1891–1969), civil and aeronautical engineer, and his wife, (Frances Louisa) Olive, *née* Field (1892–1964). His father was professor of civil engineering at Bristol University from 1928 to 1933 (he was later professor of civil engineering at Imperial College, London, from 1933 to 1956, and was elected a fellow of the Royal Society in 1954). It was in the Bristol area that Pippard received his schooling. After junior school at Westbourne House, Penarth, from 1925 to 1928 and Bristol grammar school until 1930, he attended Clifton College preparatory school. He was then awarded an entrance scholarship to Clifton College, which he attended from 1934 to 1938.

Pippard had begun learning the piano at the age of five and became an excellent pianist, a passion which remained with him all his life. His teacher at Clifton, Douglas Fox, seriously suggested that he should consider a career in music but he realized his own limitations as a pianist and musician when compared with his contemporary at Clifton, David Willcocks. He thoroughly enjoyed physics and chemistry at school but believed he could not compete with the best students in mathematics. Rumour had it that mastering the new physics of quantum mechanics demanded high mathematical ability and so he considered physical chemistry a more appropriate career choice. He won a minor entrance scholarship to Clare College, Cambridge, and in his first year read physics, chemistry, physiology and mathematics with outstanding academic success. The Second World War broke out in his second year and his tutor informed him that the country did not need chemists but that there was a demand for physicists. Pippard soon found that physics was indeed what he had always wanted to do. In 1941 he graduated with first-class honours in part two of the natural sciences tripos.

In the spring of 1941 Pippard was interviewed by C. P. Snow to judge his suitability for research in support of the war effort and was assigned to work on radar. The four-year period during which he was employed as a scientific officer at the Radar Research and Development Establishment (from 1941 to 1945) was devoted to mastering and developing microwave radar techniques. Magnetrons and klystrons provided powerful new sources of microwave radiation which, combined with parabolic antennae, provided higher angular resolution than the existing radar arrays, which operated at much longer wavelengths. Pippard made numerous contributions to the development of radar techniques. These four years of war work provided an ideal training in research techniques. Specifically, he developed the discipline of carrying out experimental work with economy and imagination.

Sir (Alfred) Brian Pippard (1920–2008), by Godfrey Argent Studios

The immediate postwar years provided many opportunities for innovative research. Basic physics had been on hold for six years while a vast array of new experimental capabilities had become available. In 1945 Pippard was awarded a Stokes studentship at Pembroke College and became a member of the Royal Society Mond laboratory, which was the centre of low temperature physics research in Cambridge. He was already familiar with the skin effect, the restriction of microwave fields to a thin surface layer when radio waves are incident on a metallic surface, and began investigations into this phenomenon in superconducting metals (materials which lose all electrical resistance below a transition temperature close to absolute zero). He built microwave resonant circuits of superconducting materials such as tin and mercury and successfully observed a dramatic reduction in microwave absorption when the materials were cooled through their transition temperatures.

Pippard's doctoral work contained the seeds of two further developments. First, he noticed that he could obtain an unambiguous value for the complex conductivity of his samples. Second, he reaffirmed Heinz London's observation in 1940 that in normal metals the surface resistance did not continue to decrease with falling temperature as the direct current resistance did, but reached a limit. Pippard developed a theory of this 'anomalous skin effect' using a simplified model in which he regarded as 'effective' only those electrons moving at such a small angle to the surface that they remained within the skin depth between scatterings. To develop the theory further, he found he had inadequate mathematical tools and so sought help from Ernst Sondheimer, who formulated the problem more precisely using three-dimensional Fermi statistics and the Boltzmann equation. With the assistance of G. E. H. Reuter, these equations were solved and the full theory of the anomalous skin effect was published, fitting all Pippard's data remarkably closely. An important feature of this work was the understanding that the anomalous skin effect was a 'non-local effect': the current depended not only on the electric field at a particular point, but also on the field at neighbouring points through which the electrons had travelled since last being scattered.

In 1947 Pippard was appointed a university demonstrator, and returned to Clare College as a research fellow and director of studies in physics. After his doctorate (in 1949) he became interested in the geometry and dynamics of normal–superconducting boundaries, and introduced the idea that their stability was determined by whether the magnetic penetration depth was larger or smaller than a characteristic 'coherence length', which, like the penetration depth, diverged at the transition temperature. A phenomenological theory of superconductivity was proposed by Lev Landau and Vitaly Ginzburg in 1950 and, unknown to Pippard, their theory also contained a coherence length. They had come to similar conclusions about the normal–superconducting interface energy. At about the same time, Pippard (who was appointed a university lecturer in Cambridge in 1950) made two significant new observations on the penetration depth. First, he measured the skin depth of tin alloyed with indium to reduce the electron free path. The alloying not only increased the normal state skin depth as expected, but also increased the superconducting penetration depth. Second, he measured the anisotropy of the penetration depth in pure tin, and found that it varied with surface orientation in a manner that was in conflict with Heinz London's equations of superconductivity, but was very similar in form to the anisotropy of the normal state skin depth, governed by Chambers's non-local equation.

Pippard drew the bold conclusion that non-local effects were being observed in the supercurrent, and in a celebrated paper of 1953 proposed that the local London relation should be replaced by a non-local equation analogous to Chamber's formula. He solved the penetration depth analysis exactly, the new theory fitting the data remarkably well. In early 1957 Pippard made a short visit to Moscow with a delegation of British scientists, where he encountered Landau, Ginzburg, and Alexey Alexeyevich Abrikosov. Landau strongly rejected Pippard's proposal, partly because the Ginzburg–Landau theory led to no non-locality of the supercurrent. Later that year, John Bardeen, Leon Cooper, and John R. Schrieffer published their revolutionary pairing theory of superconductivity and in it they were at pains to demonstrate that their new theory confirmed Pippard's model almost exactly, the coherence length being interpreted as the scale over which pairs of electrons are correlated. The Moscow theorists generously sent Pippard a private message conceding that he had been right; indeed they regarded his brilliant insights as of Nobel prize standing.

Meanwhile, Pippard's interests had shifted to the Fermi surface, a theoretical three-dimensional boundary in momentum space within which the conduction electrons of a metal were thought to be contained at absolute zero. In 1952 Onsager had interpreted the de Haas–van Alphen effect, the oscillations of the magnetization of metals with applied magnetic field, in terms of the Fermi surface. The shape of this surface determines many of the properties of the metal but there was no experimental determination of its shape for any metal. In 1954 Pippard first showed that in the extreme anomalous limit the surface resistance provides a measure of one component of the curvature of the Fermi surface. By making sufficient observations of the surface resistance in different orientations, the geometry of the Fermi surface in a fairly simple case, such as that of copper, could be determined. He planned to carry out these experiments during the sabbatical year he was about to take in Chicago. In the meantime, through his musical connections, he had met Charlotte Frances Dyer, who was studying calligraphy at the art college. Two years his junior, she was the daughter of Francis Gilbert Dyer, a professional musician. They were married at St Edward's Church, Cambridge, on 2 July 1955, and had three daughters, Corinna (*b.* 1957), Deborah (*b.* 1960), and Eleanor (*b.* 1962).

After their marriage Brian and Charlotte Pippard left almost immediately for Chicago. Morrel Cohen had arranged for the Institute for the Study of Materials to grow a very large single crystal of copper. The data were taken successfully and Pippard was able to map out the Fermi surface of copper, a widely recognized tour de force. This was the first time any Fermi surface had been measured experimentally. Pippard was elected a fellow of the Royal Society in 1956, the same year as his return to Cambridge. In 1959 he became a university reader and was awarded the Royal Society's Hughes medal. He was appointed John Humphrey Plummer professor of physics in 1960. Among his first programmes was the development of a magnet laboratory which provided the physicists with very strong steady magnetic fields. The complex subject of magnetoresistance remained a major preoccupation, culminating in his definitive text, *Magnetoresistance in Metals* (1989). In 1961 his graduate student Brian Josephson developed a new theory of quantum tunnelling between superconductors which subsequently earned him a Nobel prize for physics.

From 1966 to 1973 Pippard was the first president of the newly founded college Clare Hall, which offered hospitality to distinguished academic visitors and their families in Cambridge. He was responsible for overseeing the design of the college by the architect Ralph Erskine. He succeeded in making the college an informal and happy home for graduates, visitors, and their families. His humanitarian instincts came to the fore when the college provided a home for Rudi Dutschke, a left-wing German student activist who had been shot by a maverick right-winger after a campaign against him in the German press.

During the late 1950s Neville Mott had become convinced of the need to move the Cavendish Laboratory to new buildings in west Cambridge, and Pippard quickly became the protagonist in promoting this enterprise. He was deeply involved in all aspects of the planning of the new buildings and successfully oversaw the move of the Cavendish to the new site. In 1971 he was elected Cavendish professor of experimental physics. He was president of the Institute of Physics from 1974 to 1976 and knighted in 1974. During his tenure as head of the physics department, he took a strong interest in the teaching programme. The role of the teaching committee was strengthened and he was proactive in the reform of undergraduate physics teaching. There were some subjects that he abhorred—four-vectors, operator formalism, and the grand canonical ensemble, to mention but a few. His horror was of mathematical formalism that obscured what he considered to be the underlying physics content.

When the University of Cambridge offered a generous early retirement package in 1982, Pippard took that opportunity. In retirement, he maintained an active interest in the areas of physics he found absorbing. He investigated in considerable detail the perturbations of the Foucault pendulum and designed and had built a drive and mount that eliminated many of them. His parametrically driven Foucault pendulum was displayed in the Science Museum, London. His books *The Physics of Vibrations*, vol. 2 (1983; he had published a first volume in 1978) and *Response and Stability* (1985) were published during this period. A major undertaking was his editorship of the three-volume work *Twentieth-Century Physics* (1995).

Brian Pippard was a brilliant experimental physicist who made numerous pioneering contributions to condensed matter physics. The particular achievements for which he will be remembered were the first determination of the Fermi surface and his non-local theories of electrical conduction in metals and superconductors. He was capable of great kindness and he was always intellectually stimulating. But he also had an enormous boyish relish in simply being clever. In April 1994 he suffered a serious accident when he was knocked off his bicycle after a walk with his wife at Wandlebury county park. He suffered a mildly fractured skull and a broken shoulder, as well as losing the sight of his left eye. Nevertheless he made an excellent recovery and was soon back playing the piano. He died of a stroke at the Hope Residential and Nursing Care Home, Cambridge, on 21 September 2008, and was survived by his wife, Charlotte, and their three daughters. MALCOLM S. LONGAIR

Sources *Daily Telegraph* (24 Sept 2008) · *The Guardian* (24 Sept 2008) · *The Times* (25 Sept 2008); (27 Sept 2008); (1 Oct 2008); (10 Oct 2008) · *The Independent* (7 Oct 2008); (10 Oct 2008) · *Nature*, 455 (30 Oct 2008), 1191 · *Memoirs FRS*, 55 (2009), 201–20 · *WW* (2008) · Burke, *Peerage* · personal knowledge (2012) · private information (2012) · b. cert. · m. cert. · d. cert.

Archives CUL, scientific and personal papers | SOUND interview with A. Macfarlane, 31 March 2008, www.dspace.cam.ac.uk/handle/1810/197074
Likenesses obituary photographs • Godfrey Argent Studios, photograph, repro. in *Memoirs FRS* [*see illus.*] • photograph, U. Cam.; repro. in http://physicsworld.com/cws/article/news/35962
Wealth at death £342,148: probate, 23 Jan 2009, *CGPLA Eng. & Wales*

Pitt, Sir Harry Raymond (1914–2005), mathematician and university administrator, was born on 3 June 1914 at 212 Oldbury Road, West Bromwich, Staffordshire, the only son of Harry Pitt, iron turner, and his wife, (Florence) Harriet, *née* Draper. His father, who had left school at thirteen, later became an engineer in the motor industry; his ancestors were small farmers and craftsmen. Pitt received an excellent education at King Edward VI School, Stourbridge, and went as a state scholar to Peterhouse, Cambridge (1932–5), where he took first-class honours in parts one and two of the mathematics tripos, and a distinction in part three. His undergraduate tutor was J. C. Burkill. He went on to do research at Peterhouse under the supervision of G. H. Hardy, becoming a bye-fellow (1936–9) and spending the year 1937–8 as a Choate memorial fellow at Harvard University.

At Hardy's suggestion Pitt made a deep study of the then new general Tauberian theory of the pre-eminent American mathematician Norbert Wiener. Tauberian theorems (which stem from the work of the Slovak mathematician Alfred Tauber, published in 1897) deal with the passage from the average, or some other smoothed version, of a function or sequence, back to the function or sequence itself. Taking an average typically improves mathematical properties, and so the reverse operation typically makes them worse, but this may not happen under suitable auxiliary conditions, known as Tauberian conditions. Such results had been studied in special cases by Hardy and his collaborator J. E. Littlewood—the term Tauberian theorem is due to Hardy and Littlewood—but it was Wiener's work, and powerful new methods based on the Fourier transform, that changed the whole area by making it possible to work generally. Pitt wrote two papers in collaboration with Wiener during his year at Harvard; he wrote eight papers altogether in 1938, including much of his best work.

Pitt was a lecturer at Aberdeen University from 1939 to 1942, before being seconded to the Air Ministry to work with RAF Coastal Command on the then new area of operational research. His war work concerned the most efficient use of RAF resources, including fuel. On 5 April 1940 he married (Clemency) Catherine Jacoby (*d.* 2004), a 21-year-old secretary, and daughter of Henry Charles Edward Jacoby, engineer. They had four sons.

Pitt was appointed professor of mathematics at Queen's University, Belfast, in 1945, at the age of thirty-one. He moved in 1950 to be professor of pure mathematics at Nottingham University. During this time he continued his work on Tauberian theory, and other areas of mathematical analysis such as Fourier analysis. He worked on the connection between Tauberian theory and number theory, in particular the then newly discovered elementary proof of the prime number theorem (which says that the number of primes up to a large number x is approximately $x/\log x$, where $\log x$ is the natural logarithm of x). He summarized his work on Tauberian theory in his book *Tauberian Theorems* (1958). He also developed new interests, in probability theory, statistics, and ergodic theory. At Nottingham he supervised the doctorate of Clive Granger, later a Nobel laureate in econometrics. He also performed a number of senior administrative duties, including those of deputy vice-chancellor (1959–62).

In 1964 Pitt made a career switch from academic mathematics to academic administration, and became vice-chancellor of Reading University, a post he held until his retirement in 1978. During this time Reading University expanded from a small institution in the centre of the town to a much larger one on the parkland campus of Whiteknights. Pitt's time as vice-chancellor included the student disturbances of the 1960s. His strategy for dealing with these was one of masterly inactivity, and forethought: at one time he and his registrar were locked in by protesting students, but escaped by using a spare key.

As a mathematician Pitt is best remembered for a result of his from 1938, Pitt's form of Wiener's Tauberian theorem (still the basis of textbook accounts), and as the author of the first book on Tauberian theorems. As a vice-chancellor he was notable for his leadership of Reading University for fourteen years during a period of expansion, and for his consensual style of leadership. He was a kind and a religious man, and was described as a 'communicator extraordinaire'. He combined great intelligence with personal humility; it was said of him that 'his power was only equalled by his modesty' (private information). He was widely honoured. He was elected a fellow of the Royal Society in 1957, and received several honorary doctorates. He was knighted on retirement as vice-chancellor of Reading in 1978. He died on 8 October 2005 at St Mary's Nursing Home, Ednaston, near Brailsford, Derbyshire, of vascular dementia and atrial fibrillation. He was survived by his four sons, his wife, Catherine, having predeceased him. N. H. BINGHAM

Sources J. C. Holt, *The University of Reading: the first fifty years* (1977) • M. Sewell, 'Tribute to Sir Harry Raymond Pitt, FRS', *Mathematics Today*, 42 (2006), 10–13 • *The Times* (19 Oct 2005); (21 Oct 2005); (24 Oct 2005) • J. D. M. Wright, 'Sir Harry Raymond Pitt', *LMS Newsletter*, 343, www.lms.ac.uk/newsletter/343, 18 June 2008 • N. H. Bingham and W. K. Hayman, *Memoirs FRS*, 54 (2008), 257–74 • Burke, *Peerage* • *WW* (2005) • private information (2009) • b. cert. • m. cert. • d. cert.
Likenesses N. Blamey, oils, 1978, U. Reading • photograph, repro. in *The Times* (19 Oct 2005)
Wealth at death £108,420: probate, 16 March 2006, *CGPLA Eng. & Wales*

Plaschkes, Otto (1929–2005), film producer, was born on 13 September 1929 in Grinzing, a suburb of Vienna, the second child and elder son of Jewish parents, Heinrich Plaschkes (1899–1970), butcher, and his wife, Gertrude, *née* Grosz (1901–1964). His father was born in Bratislava and his mother in Budapest. Plaschkes always suspected that his mother may have added a year to his age to facilitate his escape to Britain from the invading Nazis by the

Kindertransport. His parents also managed to escape, and they were reunited in Salisbury, where his father established a sausage-casing business. At Bishop Wordsworth's School the English master, William Golding, allegedly based the character of Piggy in *Lord of the Flies* upon the young Plaschkes. After reading history at Peterhouse, Cambridge, he did his national service with the Royal Army Service Corps, before taking a diploma in education at Wadham College, Oxford.

Plaschkes discovered cinema through the Cambridge Film Society, and in 1955 Sir Michael Balcon agreed to employ him as a runner at Ealing Studios, where he embraced his employer's vision of an indigenous British cinema. When Ealing closed, Plaschkes worked his way up the production ladder at other studios, through a series of uncredited jobs as assistant director. In 1961, with an Australian, Jim Jeffreys, he set up Jimar Pictures (Pty) Ltd to produce television commercials. Plaschkes persuaded the Children's Film Foundation to allow him to produce a one-hour film in Australia, *Bungala Boys* (1961), and in order to secure a passage there Jeffreys persuaded P&O Lines to commission them to make a documentary about life on its England–Australia liner. *Bungala Boys* was a baptism of fire, for the production ran out of money, and Plaschkes had to work for his ticket home. Nevertheless, the film won a special award at the Venice film festival.

After working as production assistant on David Lean's acclaimed *Lawrence of Arabia* (1962) and as production manager for *Tarzan's Three Challenges* (1963) Plaschkes was engaged to advise Robert Goldston, the American co-producer of *The Uncle* (1964). They co-produced three feature films together: *Georgy Girl* (1966), *The Bofors Gun* (1968), and *A Separate Peace* (1972). *Georgy Girl*, which starred James Mason and Alan Bates, with Lynn Redgrave as the eponymous Georgy, was a 'swinging London' fairy tale, intermittently accompanied by a popular, relentlessly up-tempo title song, sung by the Australian pop group the Seekers. The film grossed over £13 million worldwide, and garnered four Academy award (or Oscar) nominations. *The Bofors Gun* was a commercial failure, although Ian Holm won a BAFTA award as best supporting actor. The Paramount-backed *A Separate Peace*, filmed in America, also failed to match the success of *Georgy Girl*. Ely Landau then engaged Plaschkes as the executive producer for four of his American Film Theatre productions, which were designed to introduce London and New York stage plays to a wider American audience: *The Homecoming* (directed by Peter Hall), *Butley* (directed by Harold Pinter), *Galileo* (directed by Joseph Losey), and *In Celebration* (directed by Lindsay Anderson). On 9 May 1975 Plaschkes married Louise Stein, a 36-year-old art gallery assistant, and daughter of Barnet Glickler, architect. They had one daughter.

As cinema audiences declined, Plaschkes sought, along with other members of the Association of Independent Producers, to persuade the government to assign all the revenues from the British Film Fund to the National Film Finance Corporation, but to no avail. However, in 1976 he was appointed to the National Film Development Fund to advise the National Film Finance Corporation on which scripts appeared to be the best projects in which to invest development money. He returned to Vienna to work as line producer on Elliott Kastner's *A Little Night Music* (1977) and then, back in England, persuaded the Thames Television subsidiary Euston Films and the National Film Finance Corporation to back *The Sailor's Return* (1978) which, in his view, 'celebrated the English character in its best and worst form' (Downs, 17). In 1980 he worked again for Ely Landau and his second wife, Edie, to produce *Hopscotch*, a cloak-and-dagger comedy starring Walter Matthau and Glenda Jackson.

Plaschkes and the American producer Sy Weintraub planned to produce six Sherlock Holmes films, starring Ian Richardson as Holmes. But Weintraub reduced this to two—*The Hound of the Baskervilles* and *Sign of Four* (both 1983)—when he discovered that the British rights to the Conan Doyle stories were already in the public domain, thus allowing Granada Television to produce its own rival series. Plaschkes next began to produce the offbeat *Shadey*, backed by Channel 4's Film Four International, in which Anthony Sher played a transsexual car repairer able to transmit telepathic images. But the production had to be postponed when Ely Landau, who had had a stroke, suddenly asked Plaschkes to take over the production of *The Holcroft Covenant* (1985), directed by John Frankenheimer and starring Michael Caine. Plaschkes finally completed *Shadey* in 1985.

Menachem Golan and Yoram Globus appointed Plaschkes as head of creative affairs when their Cannon Film Company took over EMI. 'The way to make a project happen', asserted Golan, 'is to excite the lovely Mr. Otto Plaschkes, who will excite me' (Walker, *Icons in the Fire*, 47). But Plaschkes only managed to authorize two co-productions with Channel 4 Television, *Business as Usual* and *The Kitchen Toto*, and to produce *In Search of Hanna*, a documentary in which he interviewed Golan about the making of *Hanna's War*. Between 1986 and 1988 Plaschkes acted as chief executive of the British Film and Television Producers' Association, after which he produced *Doggin' Around* (1994), directed by Desmond Davis, for the BBC's *Screen One* series.

Intellectually a pessimist, but temperamentally an optimist, Plaschkes was highly regarded by his creative colleagues and fellow producers. An Austrian by birth, he always struggled to make authentically British films, although he often had to rely on American money to keep his career afloat. He died from a heart attack on 14 February 2005 at University College Hospital, Camden, London, after attending a screening of *As It Is in Heaven*, a Swedish film which had been nominated for an Academy award as the best foreign-language film. He was survived by his wife, Louise, and their daughter. VINCENT PORTER

Sources *The Times* (20 Aug 1968); (3 Dec 1973); (29 Sept 1977); (30 Aug 1983); (7 March 2005) • A. Walker, *Hollywood, England: the British film industry in the sixties* (1974) • C. Downs, 'Profile: Otto Plaschkes', *AIP & Co.*, 21 (Oct 1979), 17–18 • I. F. McAsh, 'Films: around the studios and on location', *Films on Screen and Video*, 5/2 (Feb 1985), 4–5 • B. Beghani, 'The Plaschkes profile', *AIP & Co.*, 67 (summer 1985), 26–7 • D. Gifford, *British national film catalogue, 1895–1985* (1986) • O. Plaschkes, 'Is this the end of our film industry?', *Mail on Sunday*

Review (21 April 1991), 3 • A. Walker, *Icons in the fire: the decline and fall of almost everyone in the British film industry, 1984–2000* (2004) • *The Guardian* (16 Feb 2005) • *Daily Post* [Liverpool] (18 Feb 2005) • *The Scotsman* (21 Feb 2005) • *The Herald* [Glasgow] (1 March 2005) • *The Independent* (5 March 2005) • *Los Angeles Times* (13 March 2005) • private information (2008) [Louise Plaschkes, wife; G. Fisher] • BFI film and TV database, www.bfi.org.uk/filmtvinfo/ftvdb/, 15 April 2008 • internet movie database, www.imdb.com/search, 15 April 2008 • I. Richardson, www.sherlock-holmes.org.uk/world/irichardson.php, 15 April 2008 • m. cert. • d. cert.

Likenesses obituary photographs

Wealth at death £225,928: probate, 28 Nov 2005, *CGPLA Eng. & Wales*

Plowright, David Ernest (1930–2006), television producer and executive, was born on 11 December 1930 at the Maternity Home, Scunthorpe, Lincolnshire, the youngest of three children of William Ernest Plowright, editor of the *Scunthorpe and Frodingham Star*, and his wife, Daisy Margaret, *née* Burton. At the time of his birth registration, the family lived at 1 Central Square, Brigg, near Scunthorpe. With the lively encouragement of their mother, whose artistic aspirations had found an outlet in the formation of a local drama group, all three children were to become high achievers. The career of Plowright's elder brother, Robert, was to lead to a professorship at the Trinity College of Music, London, while his sister, Joan (*b.* 1929), would go on to enjoy a distinguished career as an actress leading, in 1961, to her marriage to Sir Laurence Olivier (later Baron Olivier) and eventually to her appointment as DBE in 2004.

Plowright was educated, like his sister, at Scunthorpe grammar school, where his main interest lay in sport. It was not until he did his national service in Germany with the Royal Corps of Signals and was offered a special course in journalism that he realized his true aptitude was for news reporting. Having gained experience on his father's newspaper, in 1954 he joined the *Yorkshire Post*, where he worked as reporter, feature writer, and occasionally equestrian correspondent, a role in which he would attend local gymkhanas impressively mounted on his own horse. On 27 June 1953 he had married Brenda Mary Key, a hairdresser two years his senior, whom he had met through his mother's drama group. She was the daughter of Harry Benson Key, fitter. They had three children, Nicholas, Kathryn, and Charlotte.

Within a year of the founding of Granada Television by the brothers Sidney and Cecil Bernstein, Plowright was recruited, in 1957, as a researcher in current affairs before becoming, soon afterwards, the fledgeling company's first news editor. His journalistic flair and sharp eye for a news story immediately made him a broadcasting asset. His early assignments, which included outside broadcasts and Granada's pioneering election programme *Marathon*, also enabled him to develop Granada's favoured multitasking working method. This would require him to act simultaneously as producer, reporter, and presenter. In these various roles he also helped establish Granada's distinctively terse and witty northern voice.

In 1966 Plowright truly came into his own when he took over the company's flagship current affairs programme, *World in Action*, first broadcast in 1963. To this much admired model of television investigative journalism he brought a renewal of energy and some bold editorial judgements, frequently taking the programme into dangerous political waters and constantly honing its formidably sharp-edged style. In 1968 he became head of current affairs, from which position he rapidly ascended the Granada managerial ladder. From 1969 to 1979 he was Granada's controller of programmes and, from 1975 to 1981, joint managing director with Sir Denis Forman, Plowright's blunt northern canniness making him a good foil to the subtle, patrician Forman. During this period he also displayed an old-fashioned sense of showmanship when he promoted the development of Granada Tours, a television theme park where, on a site close to the studios, the public could tour the sets of their favourite television shows, visiting Sherlock Holmes's rooms in Baker Street, sitting on the front benches in the House of Commons, or downing a pint in the Rover's Return. More important, he discovered a new passion for drama. Largely responsible for steering the somewhat turbulent production of Evelyn Waugh's *Brideshead Revisited* into safe harbour and ensuring its ultimate worldwide success, it was Plowright who had taken the brave decision to relaunch the production after the ITV technicians' strike had brought the show to an untimely stop in August 1979. He also fostered Granada's pioneering efforts to take television drama out of the confines of the electronic studio and into the freer and more creative realms of location filming.

When Plowright's brother-in-law, Laurence Olivier, with whom he had formed a close bond, was recuperating in the early 1970s after a long period of debilitating illness Plowright believed he could best speed Olivier's recovery by engaging him to produce a television series of six great twentieth-century plays. These included Harold Pinter's *The Collection* (1976), *Cat on a Hot Tin Roof* (1976) by Tennessee Williams, and William Inge's *Come Back Little Sheba* (1977), in all three of which Olivier played a starring role. After Olivier played a leading role as Lord Marchmain in *Brideshead Revisited* (1981) Plowright invited him to star in three other Granada dramas, Shakespeare's *King Lear* (1983), *The Ebony Tower* (1984) by John Fowles, and *Lost Empires* (1986) by J. B. Priestley. Olivier's monumental performance as Lear led to an invitation from President Reagan to the White House, a visit on which Plowright accompanied him together with his sister, Joan.

From 1981 to 1987 Plowright was sole managing director of Granada Television, and from 1987 to 1992 chairman. In 1991 he pulled off a characteristically daring coup. Under new rules largely promoted by the prime minister, Margaret Thatcher, parties competing in the new television franchise round were instructed to submit sealed bids. Plowright, who had lobbied diligently behind the scenes for the establishment of a quality threshold, had shrewdly reckoned that Granada's output was so strong that no regulator would dare to remove its right to broadcast. His bold assumption proved correct. Plowright secured the renewal of Granada's franchise with the low bid of just £9 million. The rival broadcaster had bid almost four times as much.

A year later, however, events were to move swiftly against Plowright, leading to his rancorous ousting from the company. This occurred when the board of Granada Group, worried by declining revenues, appointed as chief executive Gerry Robinson, a determined young businessman from the world of mass catering, who swiftly embarked on a strategy of aggressive cost-cutting. Plowright believed the measures proposed were too draconian and were being too swiftly applied, particularly when they were likely to include the sacrifice of creative staff and a decline in programme quality. His response was to comply with Robinson's demands where he could, but to give only a limited degree of co-operation when he felt they might damage the integrity of Granada's programming. Robinson argued that he could not work alongside a reluctant partner and moved quickly to force Plowright's resignation. After thirty-five years of distinguished service Plowright's virtual dismissal was greeted in the media with a chorus of anguished protest. His supporters included Harold Pinter, Alan Bennett, and John Cleese, who were among a hundred signatories to a letter in *The Guardian*. Protests also came from the cast of *Coronation Street*, the actors' union Equity, and the Directors' Guild of Great Britain. John Birt, Plowright's former protégé as a young producer on *World in Action* and at this time director-general designate of the BBC, gave a farewell party for him at Broadcasting House where old colleagues presented him with a BBC microphone as a memento of his contribution to broadcasting. For many in the industry Plowright's departure from Granada was seen as a symbolic turning point in the fortunes of independent television.

Although his abrupt severance from Granada had wounded him, Plowright did not repine but threw himself into numerous public activities. In a single year, 1992, he was appointed deputy chairman of Channel 4 Television, visiting professor of media studies at Salford University, and chairman of the Manchester City of Drama committee. Also in that year he was made a fellow of BAFTA. When he was not engaged in a continuous round of public duty he found solace in his favourite recreation, 'messing about in a boat' (*Who's Who*) and sailing the coastal waters of Britain, sometimes with his friend the physician, broadcaster, and Liberal peer Michael Winstanley. In 1996 he was appointed CBE for services to television. He retired from Channel 4 in 1997.

Plowright, a ruggedly handsome man with a somewhat dour and shy exterior, liked to present himself as a blunt northerner. Strongly aware of his roots, he had always lived with his family in the north of England. But beneath his bluff exterior colleagues often found deep funds of sensibility and warmth, and although he always disclaimed the more flamboyant aspects of leadership he had a remarkable capacity for getting the best out of those who worked for him. The respect he commanded from creative people derived as much from his instinctive understanding of their problems as from the example of his own fierce integrity, perhaps the very quality that had so clouded the end of his career. His habitually reserved manner did not exclude a dry and insightful wit. After his forced resignation from Granada he wryly commented, 'I'm not an easy man to tell what to do. I was a difficult problem for Granada. I was quite a difficult problem for the rest of the industry, come to that' (*The Independent*, 17 June 1992). He died from a sudden heart attack on 24 August 2006 while working in his study at his home in Wilmslow Road, Mottram St Andrew, Cheshire. His funeral took place at St Peter's Church, Prestbury, Cheshire, on 5 September 2006, and was followed by cremation. He was survived by his wife, Brenda, and their three children.

DEREK GRANGER

Sources L. Olivier, *Confessions of an actor* (1982) · B. Sendall, *Independent television in Britain*, 1–2 (1982–3) · C. Moorehead, *Sidney Bernstein: a biography* (1984) · D. Granger, 'The Granada factor', *Olivier: in celebration*, ed. G. O'Connor (1987) · J. Potter, *Independent television in Britain*, 3–4 (1989–90) · P. Chippindale and S. Franks, *Dished! The rise and fall of British Satellite Broadcasting* (1991) · A. Davidson, *Under the hammer: the inside story of the 1991 ITV franchise battle* (1992) · D. Forman, *Persona Granada* (1997) · P. Bonner and L. Aston, *Independent television in Britain*, 5 (1998) · M. Tracey, *The decline and fall of public service broadcasting* (1998) · W. Kay, *Lord of the dance: the story of Gerry Robinson* (1999) · J. Plowright, *And that's not all* (2001) · J. Birt, *The harder path* (2002) · T. Coleman, *Olivier: the authorised biography* (2005) · P. Goddard, J. Corner, and K. Richardson, *Public issue television: World in Action, 1963–98* (2007) · R. Fitzwalter, *The dream that died: the rise and fall of ITV* (2008) · *The Guardian* (5 Feb 1992); (28 Aug 2006) · *The Times* (28 Aug 2006) · *The Independent* (29 Aug 2006) · *Daily Telegraph* (30 Aug 2006) · *WW* (2006) · personal knowledge (2010) · private information (2010) [Dame Joan Plowright, sister; Nicholas Plowright, son; R. Fitzwalter] · b. cert. · m. cert. · d. cert.

Archives FILM BFINA, current affairs footage · BFINA, documentary footage · Granada Television, Manchester, performance footage

Likenesses photographs, 1967–89, Rex Features, London, ITV archive · obituary photographs

Wealth at death £2,568,595: probate, 7 March 2007, *CGPLA Eng. & Wales*

Podro, Michael Isaac (1931–2008), art historian, was born Michael Isaac Podrushnik on 13 March 1931 at Gloucester Lodge nursing home, Golders Green, London, the son of Joshua Podrushnik, later Podro (1893/4–1962), who ran a press cuttings agency, and his wife, Fanny, *née* Klinghoffer. At the time of his birth registration his parents, who were both Jewish immigrants, lived at 21 Crespigny Road, Hendon, Middlesex. His father, originally from white Russia, was a noted Judaic scholar who collaborated with Robert Graves on the *Nazarene Gospel Restored* (1953–7). His mother came from Austria. Podro grew up within a highly cultured family in Hendon, and attended Berkhamsted School in Hertfordshire. After national service in the RAF he read English at Jesus College, Cambridge, where he was profoundly influenced by F. R. Leavis and William Empson.

In 1955 Podro enrolled as a part-time student at the Slade School of Fine Art, London, with the intention of

Michael Isaac Podro (1931–2008), by R. B. Kitaj, 1984–5

becoming a painter. At that time E. H. Gombrich was teaching art history at the Slade, giving the inspiring lectures that later became *Art and Illusion* (1960). Podro realized that if he wanted to emulate Gombrich he would have to study philosophy. After a preliminary year at University College, London, studying philosophy, he started his PhD thesis on the German neo-Kantian theorist of art, Konrad Fiedler, under the joint supervision of Gombrich, at the Warburg Institute, and Richard Wollheim at University College. He obtained his PhD in 1961. While at the Slade he met his fellow student Charlotte Booth (*b.* 1936), daughter of Norleigh Booth, solicitor. They married at Hampstead register office on 19 December 1961 and had two daughters, Sarah and Natasha.

Also in 1961 Podro took up his first job, as founder of the art history department at Camberwell School of Arts and Crafts in south London. There he made friends with R. B. Kitaj and Frank Auerbach. Podro wrote about their work and they depicted him. (Podro's very distinctive features can be seen in Kitaj's *Jewish Rider*, 1985.) In 1967 he became lecturer in the philosophy of art at the Warburg Institute. In 1969 he was appointed reader of art history at the University of Essex and was promoted to professor in 1973. Although Joseph Rykwert was the founding professor, it was Podro who was responsible for building up the department and establishing it as a beacon of philosophically informed art history.

Podro's time at the Warburg Institute and his doctoral research prepared him for the key role he played in mediating to an Anglo-American audience the writings of German-speaking art historians, particularly those in the post-Kantian and Hegelian tradition of art history that included Alois Riegl, Heinrich Wölfflin, Aby Warburg, and Erwin Panofsky. His teaching at Essex was dedicated to this end: students were struck by the sense of urgency he brought to his seminars on Kant's *Critique of Judgement*, Hegel's *Lectures on Fine Art*, or Schiller's *Letters on the Aesthetic Education of Mankind*. These texts were of more than academic interest to him; he understood them as models of a more fully human way of being in the world, intellectually, bodily, and emotionally.

The dissemination of Podro's research was also accomplished through the publication of three books. His first, *The Manifold in Perception: Theories of Art from Kant to Hildebrand* (1972), was an analysis of the late eighteenth- and early nineteenth-century philosophical and psychological theories of art that later informed the most ambitious art historical writing in German. His next and most important book, *The Critical Historians of Art* (1982), surveyed the work of those art historians. The book revived interest in the founders of art history as a discipline and demonstrated how philosophical ideas about the nature of beauty, knowledge, and morality could have purchase in writing about art. The overarching aim of the book was to show how a sense of the artist's freedom in constructing a work of art came to be seen as a means of achieving an ethical, inward sense of composure. In this way the role of the work of art became one of overcoming our ordinary relations with the world. This philosophical approach contrasted sharply with the sort of art history that prided itself on a purely empiricist form of scholarship. In his third and final book, *Depiction* (1998), Podro wrote about artists who had preoccupied him throughout his career, Donatello, Rembrandt, Chardin, and Hogarth, always attending carefully to the works while also bringing to bear his theoretical concerns. He was especially concerned with how these artists' handling of their materials brought out aspects of the subject depicted. His unusual sensitivity to the nature of an artist's achievement rested on his formation as both painter *manqué* and philosopher.

Podro's energies were mainly devoted to teaching, research, leading the department at Essex, and reading and commenting helpfully upon drafts of books and articles for friends and colleagues, but he did find time for extracurricular activities. He was a trustee of the Victoria and Albert Museum from 1987 to 1996 during a period of some upheaval. He served on numerous editorial boards in the UK and Germany and from 1998 to 2005 he was chair of the Squiggle Foundation, an organization set up to promote the teachings of Donald Winnicott, a psychiatrist interested in the importance of play in infantile development and in adults' sense of their connection with the world. This latter role attests to Podro's abiding interest in psychoanalysis, which also informed his understanding of art. Podro was elected a fellow of the British Academy in 1992 and appointed CBE in 2001. He died of cancer at his home, 1 Provost Road, Camden, London, on 28 March 2008, and was survived by his wife, Charlotte, and their two daughters. MARGARET IVERSEN

Sources *The Independent* (1 April 2008) · *The Times* (3 April 2008) · *The Guardian* (3 April 2008) · *Daily Telegraph* (25 April 2008) · *Jewish Chronicle* (9 May 2008) · *WW* (2008) · personal knowledge (2012) · private information (2012) · b. cert. · m. cert. · d. cert.
Archives SOUND BL NSA, documentary recording

Likenesses R. B. Kitaj, oils, 1984–5 (*The Jewish rider*), Marlborough Art Gallery, New York [*see illus.*] • F. Auerbach, etching, 1989–90, FM Cam. • L. A. Dickens, c-type colour print, 2001, NPG • obituary photographs

Wealth at death £3,194,544: probate, 17 July 2008, *CGPLA Eng. & Wales*

Polani, Paul Emanuel (1914–2006), geneticist, was born Paulo Emanuele Polani on 1 January 1914 in Trieste, the elder son of Enrico Polani (*b.* 1883) and his wife, Elsa, *née* Zennaro (*b.* 1889). Trieste was at that time part of the Austro-Hungarian empire (it was annexed by Italy after the First World War), and one of Polani's early memories was of helping at the royal stables, at the nearby village of Lipice, where he was allowed to exercise the mares, starting a lifelong interest in horses and equestrianism. After early schooling in Trieste he studied biology at the University of Siena, where his interest in genetics was stimulated by the teaching of Umberto d'Ancona. He then moved to the prestigious Scuola Normale Superiore at Pisa, qualifying in medicine in 1938.

After a year's internship, and disliking Italy's fascist government, Polani decided to pursue research in Britain, arriving on 1 September 1939, just as the Second World War broke out. It was immediately clear that there was no possibility of research, but fortunately his Italian medical degree was recognized in Britain and he obtained temporary work as a ship's doctor. During this voyage Italy entered the war and on his return Polani was interned as an 'enemy alien' and was due to be deported to Canada with many other Italians on the ship *Arandora Star*, which was torpedoed and sunk with heavy loss of life. At the last minute he was removed for medical duties, first to an internment camp on the Isle of Man, then to Evelina Children's Hospital in Southwark, London, where he remained throughout the war as the only resident doctor, performing over 1500 surgical operations. He also broadcast for the Italian service of the BBC, where he met Nina Sullam (*d.* 1999), whom he married in 1944. There were no children of the marriage.

The Evelina Hospital was linked with nearby Guy's Hospital, and the visiting Guy's paediatricians noted Polani's ability. After the war they encouraged him to take the examination for membership of the Royal College of Physicians (1948) and in the same year gave him a research fellowship at Guy's Hospital to work on animal models for brain damage in haemolytic anaemia (kernicterus), the start of his long-term interest in the mechanisms of developmental brain disability. The research fellowship led to a more substantive post, supported by the National Spastics Society, as a research physician at Guy's Hospital.

In 1950 Polani's interest in genetics as applied to medicine was rekindled by forming links with Lionel Penrose, who in 1945 had been appointed head of the Galton Laboratory at University College, London. Polani spent most of his spare time learning human genetics with Penrose, 'sitting at his feet', as Polani put it, since 'Penrose was not a man that was given to a great deal of effusion, so you had to pick pearls as they fell out of his mouth' (Polani, interview). The combination of this rigorous analytical genetic approach with the abundant clinical data from Guy's Hospital formed the basis of Polani's major study of the genetic basis of congenital heart disease, undertaken jointly with the cardiologist Maurice Campbell, which led to Polani's most important discoveries.

Adopting Penrose's insistence on subjecting the full raw data to detailed statistical and genetic analysis, Polani showed that one congenital heart defect, coarctation of the aorta, principally affected males, but contained a number of patients, all female, with Turner's syndrome, a wider disorder also affecting ovarian development. He wondered if this might represent a disorder of the sex chromosomes and was able in 1954 to prove, together with the Guy's Hospital pathologist Bernard Lennox, that Turner's patients showed no sex chromatin body, suggesting that they had only one X chromosome, not the two expected in a normal female. He also detected a frequency of red-green colour blindness comparable to males, a defect almost unknown in females. Polani's conclusion from this work was that Turner's patients might be lacking a Y chromosome, and have a single X chromosome, suggesting also that the Y chromosome played a vital role in sex determination. This view was contrary to that generally accepted at the time, which held the Y chromosome to have a negligible role, but Polani was vindicated when the detailed analysis of human chromosomes became possible and he was able to show in 1959, with the cytogeneticist Charles Ford, that there were only forty-five chromosomes, not the normal forty-six, in Turner's syndrome.

1959 marked the beginning of an exciting period in human genetics, not just for the discovery of sex chromosome abnormalities but also for the recognition of an extra chromosome as the basis for Down's syndrome. Here Polani and his colleagues were able to demonstrate that there was a distinct group of Down's patients, often familial and born to younger mothers, where the chromosome number was normal, but who had an extra copy of chromosome 21 joined to another chromosome—'translocation' Down's syndrome.

These and other important discoveries established Polani's scientific reputation, leading the National Spastics Society to decide in 1960 to fund the creation of a major research institute located at Guy's Hospital, to promote understanding of the causes of developmental disability, and to appoint Polani as its director and research professor. This institute, the Paediatric Research Institute, was the base for all of his later career and research, and was founded on the applications of a human genetic approach to human development. 'My detailed blueprint was for a multidisciplinary research unit with a genetic Leitmotif for both its basic research and its clinical service application' (Polani, interview). Polani's great ability as a leader and director of research soon became evident, in addition to his own originality of research and enthusiasm. He appointed to key positions people who were both talented as individuals and highly interactive, resulting in a medical genetics institute that was of a range and depth unequalled elsewhere in Europe, and at that time probably worldwide. Cytogenetics held a prominent place, with John Hamerton, subsequently professor of human genetics in Winnipeg, joined by Francesco Giannelli, who later introduced molecular genetics, and Mary Seller, whose studies increasingly moved to the field of neural tube defects. The whole unit had a particularly strong foundation of support services, including an outstanding library.

Polani's skill lay in fusing these different themes and in encouraging his staff to address the successive challenges that were rapidly appearing in human genetics: not just the technical and clinical aspects of cytogenetics, but the possibilities of prenatal diagnosis and the understanding and prevention of neural tube defects. A boost to this was provided by the institute's move to purpose-built laboratories and academic accommodation in the new Guy's tower block. Recognizing the need for service development in the field Polani was able to initiate a full genetic counselling service, attracting John Fraser Roberts when he retired from the Medical Research Council's clinical genetics unit, as well as Caroline Berry, who had previously worked with Hans Grüneberg at the Galton Laboratory. Polani's skill and foresight in attracting not only the people but NHS and university funding for these developments showed entrepreneurial flair as well as his organizational ability. This was also responsible for providing exceptionally sound foundations that helped to ensure that the unit continued to flourish.

Polani's widespread reputation internationally, at a formative time for medical genetics, meant that his ideas on its development were strongly influential across Europe, with the Guy's unit being looked to as a model for integrated research and service. He was a co-founder of the British Clinical Genetics Society. Perhaps surprisingly, though, he trained relatively few clinical geneticists among the following generation, most of those working with him being basic scientists, albeit often medically qualified.

Despite his widened interests and responsibilities Polani's own research focus continued to be principally on human cytogenetics, in particular the sex chromosomes. Through his long continued association with his former colleagues and department after his formal retirement in 1983 he was able to see the full development of molecular approaches in both research and service, and was particularly delighted to be able, in November 2005, to open the new laboratories that replaced the long outgrown original facility that he had founded. He received many accolades, including election as a fellow of the Royal Society (1973), the Sanremo international award and prize for genetic research (1984), the Baly medal of the Royal College of Physicians (1985), and the gold medal of the International Cerebral Palsy Society (1988). He lived latterly at Little Meadow, Clandon Road, West Clandon, Surrey, and died on 18 February 2006 at Mount Alvernia Hospital, Guildford, of acute myeloid leukaemia, following a brief illness. PETER S. HARPER

Sources P. Polani, autobiographical notes, RS • P. Polani and P. S. Harper, recorded interview, 12 Nov 2003, priv. coll. • *The Times* (28 Feb 2006) • *The Guardian* (17 March 2006) • P. S. Harper, *BMJ*, 332 (18 March 2006), 670 • *The Independent* (21 March 2006) • I. Oransky, *The Lancet*, 367 (8 April 2006) • F. Giannelli, *Cytogenetic and Genome Research*, 115 (2006), 2–4 • P. S. Harper, 'Paul Polani and the development of medical genetics', *Human Genetics*, 120 (2007), 723–31 • *WW* (2006) • personal knowledge (2010) • private information (2010) • d. cert.

Archives SOUND priv. coll., interview with P. S. Harper, 12 Nov 2003

Likenesses Kodak, photograph, RS • obituary photographs

Wealth at death £1,984,093: probate, 7 Aug 2006, *CGPLA Eng. & Wales*

Pollock, Sir Michael Patrick (1916–2006), naval officer, was born on 19 October 1916 at Downs House, Higher Downs, Dunham Massey, Altrincham, Cheshire, the son of Charles Albert Pollock (*d.* 1937), a civil engineer then serving as a lieutenant in the Royal Engineers, and his wife, Gladys, *née* Mason. He was educated at the Royal Naval College, Dartmouth, from the age of thirteen and joined HMS *Nelson*, flagship of the Home Fleet, as a midshipman in 1934. From then until the outbreak of the Second World War his appointments followed the standard series of training courses and service in surface ships, including a tour in the cruiser *York*, flagship of the West Indies station, from 1937.

Early in the war Pollock, by now a lieutenant, was appointed as second in command of the aged destroyer *Vanessa*, employed mainly in escorting convoys along the east coast. She was severely damaged by air attack in July 1940 and was towed back to Chatham for three months' repairs, followed by further patrol and convoy protection work. In January 1941 Pollock was selected for specialization in gunnery, and on qualification—after a course in Portsmouth frequently interrupted by bombing raids and anti-invasion measures—was appointed to the cruiser *Arethusa* in the Mediterranean. There, on one of the last of the convoys that ensured Malta's survival (operation Stoneage), the *Arethusa* was heavily damaged by an airborne torpedo; 155 men were killed and it was only with great difficulty that the ship was towed back to Alexandria. Pollock was mentioned in dispatches for his gallantry on this occasion. He was subsequently sent to the cruiser *Norfolk*, again as gunnery officer, and in this ship he took a leading part in the destruction of the German battle cruiser *Scharnhorst* on 26 December 1943. In near darkness and heavy weather *Norfolk* was one of three cruisers in Rear-Admiral Burnett's force charged with heading off the battle cruiser. She scored several hits, one on the *Scharnhorst*'s gunnery radar, and sustained two herself; Pollock's part in the action was recognized by a further mention in dispatches. This was followed in the birthday honours of 1944 by the award of the DSC for his good service throughout the war. He had, on 3 May 1940, married Margaret Mary (Peg) Steacy (*d.* 1951), the 24-year-old daughter of William Edward Steacy, a major in the Royal Canadian Artillery; they had two sons and a daughter. After her death he married, on 2 June 1954, Marjory Helen (Midge) Reece (*d.* 2001), a 36-year-old widow and daughter of Francis Herbert Bisset. By this marriage he acquired a stepdaughter.

During the later 1940s Pollock was employed in the appointments usual for a rising gunnery officer, culminating in service in HMS *Glasgow*, from which he was promoted commander in June 1950. After further duty ashore, he became executive officer of the cruiser *Newcastle*, where he saw action at the end of the Korean War and helped to mastermind a singularly happy commission. He was promoted captain in June 1955. In this rank he had his first taste of Whitehall, initially as an assistant director of plans and later as director of surface weapons. These appointments, however, were interleaved with sea duties, first as captain (D) Portsmouth and in command of HMS *Vigo* (1958–9) and then, more weightily, in command of the aircraft carrier *Ark Royal* (1963–4), then in her heyday as one of the two premier carriers of the fleet. His success in this command—never the easiest assignment for a non-aviator—culminated in his promotion to flag rank as rear-admiral in July 1964.

From 1964 to 1966 Pollock was assistant chief of naval staff, a position then devoted mainly to carrying out duties of responsibility but not of mainstream importance, often perhaps things that the authorities found difficult to allocate to anyone else. This was not to be so in any subsequent appointment. The first, as flag officer second in command, Home Fleet (1966–7), involved extensive seagoing, not indeed in the most dramatic part of the navy's work—that was still east of Suez, where the aftermaths of the Indonesian confrontation, the Arab–Israeli War in the Middle East, and the withdrawal from Aden all figured prominently—but in the essential task of generating forces capable of handling the ongoing problems. He also found himself, in his flagship *Tiger*, host to the talks on the future of Rhodesia between the prime minister, Harold Wilson, and Ian Smith, leader of the regime in that country. His next task was an unusual one for a non-submariner: flag officer, submarines (1967–9). In this post he witnessed the first firing of a Polaris missile from a British submarine and oversaw the opening of the submarine base in Faslane. He was much occupied with the provision of appropriate weaponry for the emerging generation of nuclear-powered attack submarines, which lagged behind the capabilities of the submarines themselves.

Pollock then, in 1970, became third sea lord and controller of the navy. This was a task particularly congenial to Pollock, who had the experience and mental capacity to handle detailed *matériel* planning and acquisition. It was, moreover, an exceptionally demanding time, following as it did the cancellation of the navy's projected class of fixed-wing aircraft carriers in 1966 and the planned contraction, in early 1968, of its activities largely into the NATO sea area. These developments had entailed a rapid evolution of both operational and *matériel* concepts, following initially from the studies of the future fleet working party, which envisaged a force built round a class of 'cruisers' capable of limited aircraft operations. Initially these were to be confined to anti-submarine helicopters, but as the capabilities of the Harrier jump jet were enhanced by improved technology, the operational benefits were plain to the navy and provision for them was included in the plans. At the same time escort vessels and nuclear-powered submarine building remained in the programme.

Pollock could have expected in normal circumstances a tour as controller that would have enabled him to carry these projects within sight of completion. However, the untimely death of Admiral Sir Michael LeFanu, the chief of defence staff, meant the elevation of Admiral Sir Peter Hill-Norton to that office; this left the post of first sea lord and chief of naval staff vacant, and Pollock was appointed to it. The record suggests that he was a safe pair of hands. During his tenure, which coincided with a Conservative administration but not with any relaxation of financial stringency on the defence budget, the design of the 'through-deck' cruiser was approved as it had evolved into the Invincible class, and provision for the Sea Harrier remained in the programme, although approval for acquisition of the aircraft was yet to come. He kept a close eye on the rest of the programme, restraining any efforts at radical initiatives at either the official or the political level. Inter-service difficulties he tended to deal with by encouraging contacts between his subordinates and counterparts in the other services they might find congenial, while remaining on polite but more distant terms with those colleagues likely to remain unbending. In the public role he visited many foreign countries and strengthened ties with their navies.

In early 1974, at the end of what had been an arduous and unlooked-for tour as first sea lord, Pollock was paid the unique compliment of a farewell by the fleet at a gathering at Virgin Gorda. Promoted admiral of the fleet in August 1974, he lived in retirement at Churchstoke, Powys. He had been appointed CB in 1966, knighted KCB in 1969, and promoted GCB in 1971, and was Bath king of arms from 1976 to 1985. In 2005 he moved into Hurst Manor residential and nursing home, Martock, Somerset, where he died of bronchopneumonia on 27 September 2006. A thanksgiving service was held at St Ann's Church, HM Naval Base, Portsmouth, on 15 December. He was survived by his three children and his stepdaughter.

RICHARD HILL

Sources *The Times* (29 Sept 2006) · *Daily Telegraph* (29 Sept 2006) · *The Guardian* (2 Oct 2006) · *The Independent* (10 Oct 2006) · Burke, *Peerage* · *WW* (2006) · Admiralty Board minutes, 1968–72, TNA: PRO · statement of service supplied by naval secretary, priv. coll. · personal knowledge (2010) · private information (2010) [D. G. Armytage; B. C. Foyston; E. Cassidy] · b. cert. · m. certs. · d. cert.
Archives SOUND BL NSA, current affairs recording
Likenesses obituary photographs · photographs, Getty Images, London, Hult. Arch.
Wealth at death £166,605: probate, 20 Sept 2007, *CGPLA Eng. & Wales*

Pomerans, Arnold Julius [Arno] **(1920–2005)**, translator, was born in Königsberg, Germany, on 27 April 1920, the son of William Pomerans, accountant. Antisemitism was a precipitating factor in the family's relocations during his childhood, first to Berlin and then to Yugoslavia. His father's profession meant he could practise wherever they settled. By the time Arnold was sixteen, this was South Africa. He remained there until the nationalist regime introduced apartheid (in 1948) and his militant opposition put him in direct danger.

On arriving in Britain in 1948, Pomerans became a science teacher for seven years, first at the Hasmonean Grammar School, Hendon, and later at the New Sherwood School, a progressive school in Epsom. His subjects were primarily physics and chemistry although students recalled him as a polymath with strong interests in the arts as well as the sciences. In 1955 he turned to full-time translation and on 28 July 1956 he married his second wife (his first marriage having been dissolved), Erica Mary Aubone White (*b.* 1937), daughter of Raymond Maurice White, fire brigade official. They had met while living in Hampstead, but moved out to Polstead Heath in Suffolk the year after their marriage, where their two sons were born. A lifelong working partnership developed, whereby Erica's literary role migrated from being his 'editor' to 'co-translator' and, in some instances, finally a translator in her own right.

Pomerans brought much more than basic translation skills to his profession. He always researched and annotated his translations in the most scholarly fashion: typically, that of Pieter Geyl's *Orange and Stuart, 1641–72* (1969) listed his contribution to the 'preface, references at the end of each chapter, conclusion, genealogical tables, list of abbreviations, index' (abebooks.co.uk). At least one author referred to the quality as well as the quantity of his contribution. Marianne Krull's foreword to the American edition of *Freud and his Father* (1986) opened:

> My special thanks go to Arno Pomerans, whose brilliant translation is a pleasure to the eye and to the ear. I only wish he had also been the translator of Freud's works, letters etc., in which case he would have saved us so much of the trouble we had to take in retranslating the Standard Edition. (p. xv)

That edition may, in Krull's opinion, 'have been totally incomprehensible to anyone not familiar with the German original' (ibid.). Pomerans's translated excerpts did indeed lead him to translate many more core psychoanalytic works, including Jean Piaget (from the French) on child psychology (1969), *The Sigmund Freud–Ludwig Binswanger Correspondence, 1908–1938* (2003), and Douwe Draaisma's *Why Life Speeds Up As You Get Older: How Memory Shapes Our Past*, from the Dutch (2004).

While veering consistently towards classic texts, the breadth of Pomerans's choices was phenomenal. Perhaps understandably, given his times and background, he appears to have been drawn to wars—and to the Second World War in particular. Histories such as *The History of Jews in the Netherlands*, edited by J. C. H. Blom (2001), or *The Great War and the French People* by Jean-Jacques Becker (1985) linked to period fiction, such as Hugo Claus's *The Sorrow of Belgium* (1990), almost a *War and Peace* for the Netherlands. The most daring variant was his translation of Rudi van Dantzig's *For a Lost Soldier* (1991), the tale of a Dutch boy seduced by a Canadian soldier at the close of the Second World War. The book caused a furore, with demands for the soldier to be prosecuted for rape, thirty years on, although the subsequent film softened the tale. Women's voices were foregrounded, particularly as Erica Pomerans collaborated for the Dutch translations. Together they translated Etty Hillesum's diaries (1983) and letters (1987) and the critical edition of Anne Frank's diary (1989), the latter a long-running global best-seller that underwent numerous re-editions. Other lives include George Grosz's autobiography, *A Small Yes and a Big No* (1982), and *The Life and Death of Leon Trotsky* (1975) by Victor Serge and Natalya Sedova Trotsky (also the collaboration of a married couple). Memory was a recurrent theme, presumably one of particular interest to Pomerans: not only Professor Draaisma's scientific investigations but also Grosz's ruminations fed into this. Grosz's self-styled 'attempt at an autobiography' freely admits that: 'I have forgotten a great deal, but that is not necessarily a sign of a poor memory: the veil drawn over the past is kind and well suited to the face of the times' (p. 9).

Pomerans declared his dislike for teaching, and was grateful to the publisher who recommended he put his linguistic skills to good use by getting paid 10*s.* per 1000 translated words. Yet he had started by translating mathematics and chemistry textbooks and always retained an interest in the sciences. In 1971 his translation of Werner Heisenberg's *Physics and Beyond* was published, and in 2005, the year of his death, that of Jelto Drenth's *The Origin of the World: Science and Fiction of the Vagina*. At the time of his death he was still working on the correspondence between Anna and Sigmund Freud. In total he translated nearly 200 works spanning a wealth of genres and languages, from fiction to biography, history to psychology, principally from his native German, then Dutch, French, and Italian—although he reckoned he could turn his hand to most European languages. Among such diverse interests it is hard to select one signature book; but few are more characteristic of his style and interest than the *Letters of Vincent van Gogh* (1996). He died at his home in Polstead Heath, Suffolk, on 30 May 2005, of cancer, and was survived by Erica. One obituary described him as 'a prolific translator of literary and non-fiction works' (*The Times*, 5 July 2005), and another raised the bar in hailing him as 'one of Britain's finest translators' (*The Independent*, 16 June 2005). AMANDA HOPKINSON

Sources *The Independent* (16 June 2005) · *The Times* (5 July 2005) · m. cert. [1956] · d. cert.

Pontefract, Ella (1896/7–1945). *See under* Hartley, Marie (1905–2006).

Porter, Sir Leslie (1920–2005), businessman, was born Leslie Posament on 10 July 1920 at Streatham Manor, Leigham Avenue, Streatham, London, the youngest child in the family of two sons and one daughter of Henry Alfred Posament, later Porter (*d.* 1955), textile merchant, and his wife, Jennie (*d.* 1983), daughter of Jacob Goldstein, owner of a chain of tailoring shops. His father had arrived in England from Łódź, Poland, shortly before the First World War, and his mother came from a Russian Jewish family who had settled in England five generations earlier; she

Sir Leslie Porter (1920–2005), by Robin Laurance, 1978

started and founded a clothing design academy. At the time of his birth registration they lived at 4 South Villas, Camden Square, London. He grew up in Camden Town, and was educated at Holloway county secondary school, leaving after matriculating to work in a garage, Sam Morris & Co. He moved to another car dealer, H. R. Owen, in the West End of London, in 1937. As a member of the Territorial Army he was called up at the outbreak of the Second World War, joining the 1st battalion, the Rangers, the King's Royal Rifle Corps, and served in Greece, Cyprus, north Africa, and Italy, ending the war with the rank of technical quartermaster-adjutant. In 1946 he joined his father's household textile business, J. Porter & Co., in Old Street, becoming managing director in 1955, the year of his father's death.

On 26 June 1949, at the New West End Synagogue, Paddington, Porter married Shirley Cohen (*b.* 1930), younger daughter of Sir John Edward (Jack) *Cohen, founder and chairman of Tesco Stores Ltd; they had one son and one daughter. Although his father-in-law tried to persuade him to join his other son-in-law, Hyman *Kreitman, at Tesco, Porter resisted for ten years, preferring to build up his own family business, and it was not until 1959, after Jack Cohen's illness, that he agreed to join the Tesco board as a part-time consultant. He became a full-time member of the board in 1960, and assistant managing director in 1964. Porter's experience had been in the marketing of textiles, and when in 1960 Cohen bought Harrow Stores, a drapery and furnishings business, he made Porter joint managing director. At the same time Porter began introducing household goods and furnishings into some Tesco stores, and by 1966 the sale of non-food items had reached nearly 10 per cent of the company's turnover. After the sale of Harrow Stores in 1967 the Tesco board decided to create Tesco Home'n'Wear Ltd to operate and expand the non-foods side of the company, and Porter took charge of that. By 1973 there were sixty-two separate Home'n'Wear stores, and floor space devoted to non-food items in many Tesco supermarkets. In the meantime, following the critical report on the Tesco management by McKinsey & Co. in 1969, there was a boardroom reshuffle, and in 1970 Porter became deputy chairman, Hyman Kreitman was elected chairman, and Cohen was given the title of life president. Porter was briefly managing director in 1972, and when Kreitman resigned in 1973 he became chairman, a position he retained until 1985.

While Jack Cohen was still running Tesco, he quarrelled constantly with his sons-in-law, but while Kreitman, a quiet and unassuming man, was intimidated by this, Porter, self-confident and tough, stood up to his father-in-law, their confrontations including one famous occasion when they were said to have pursued each other round the boardroom brandishing the ornamental Wilkinson swords that hung on the wall. But after 1973 Cohen was forced into the background, while Porter faced the growing crisis threatening Tesco, which in 1974 suffered a £20 million (19.8 per cent) fall in profits. Jack Cohen's policy of 'pile it high, sell it cheap' no longer attracted customers, who were moving to rival chains including Sainsburys and Asda. Cohen had failed to see that low prices alone were not enough, that the quality of the product mattered as well, and the Tesco stores appeared old-fashioned and cluttered, selling cheap and shoddy goods, unlike Sainsburys, which had a reputation for quality. At the same time the popularity of trading stamps was waning: a report commissioned by Tesco showed that customers would prefer price cuts to stamps. In 1977, after a bitter struggle on the board, Tesco terminated its agreement with the Green Shield Trading Stamp Company. This was followed by the launch of operation Checkout, with the slogan 'Check out at Tesco: prices that help keep the cost of living in check', the start of a new direction for Tesco, combining a price-cutting campaign made possible by the £20 million a year saved by abandoning trading stamps with a new look for the Tesco stores. At first they could not keep up with demand—in the first year Tesco's share of the grocery market rose from 7 per cent to 12 per cent—but a new centralized buying system replaced the autonomy of individual store managers, while many of the smaller stores were closed, and were replaced by fewer but larger supermarkets. Between 1977 and 1983, 371 stores were closed and 97 new ones opened, and between 1980 and 1985 the average size rose from 11,000 to 17,000 square feet. Tesco stores now had a reputation for offering quality products at affordable prices. One casualty was the Home'n'Wear division: all Home'n'Wear departments and stores were closed in order to concentrate on making Tesco Britain's leading food retailer, an objective that was realized in the 1990s. Although Porter was not responsible for all these changes, under his chairmanship a new management style based on collective responsibility developed, with Porter at the head of a team that he trusted and allowed to get on with the job. 'Sir Leslie was not a dictatorial executive chairman', according to David Malpas, managing director from 1983 to 1997. 'His style was more participative in that he "presided over" rather than "implemented" change' (Porter, 57). Whereas Cohen had been a wholesaler, Porter was a retailer whose aim was to find out what the customer wanted. Cohen concerned himself with short-term profits, while Porter planned for the future, realizing that short-term profit might need to be sacrificed for the sake of longer-term gains: for example, in the late 1970s Tesco invested £100 million in advanced information technology systems.

Porter was knighted in 1983, and in 1985 resigned as chairman. He was appointed president, a title he retained until 1990, but he did not interfere in the running of the company. He had hoped that a member of the Cohen family would join the Tesco board on his departure, but his successor, Ian MacLaurin, the former managing director, opposed the idea of having Porter's wife on the board. Porter later claimed that MacLaurin had promised his son John a seat, a claim MacLaurin denied. Among his public positions Porter was chairman of the Sports Aid Foundation from 1985 to 1988, and international vice-president of the Museum of the Diaspora from 1984.

Porter's wife, Shirley, had been elected to Westminster city council in 1974, becoming leader of the council in 1983; appointed DBE in 1991, she served as lord mayor of Westminster from 1991 to 1992. But in 1994, after the district auditor ruled that she and other members of Westminster city council had been engaged in gerrymandering, involving losses to public funds of some £21 million, and after the death of their grandson in Israel, the Porters settled in the seaside town of Herzliya Pituach, north of Tel Aviv. In 1993 Porter was elected chancellor of Tel Aviv University, where he and his wife founded the Cohen–Porter United Kingdom Building of Life Sciences and the Porter Super Centre for the Environment and Ecological Research, which became the Porter School of Environmental Studies. The Porter Foundation funded the Porter Institute for Poetics and Semiotics, the Shirley and Leslie Porter School of Cultural Studies, and the Cohen-Porter Family Swimming Pool.

Porter died in Tel Aviv on 20 March 2005, and was survived by his wife and their two children.

ANNE PIMLOTT BAKER

Sources M. Corina, *Pile it high, sell it cheap: the authorised biography of Sir John Cohen, founder of Tesco* (1971) • D. Powell, *Counter revolution: the Tesco story* (1991) • I. MacLaurin, *Tiger by the tail: a life in business from Tesco to test cricket* (1999) • A. Seth and G. Randall, *The grocers*, 2nd edn (2001), 23–51 • L. Porter, *Life according to Leslie* (2003) • J. Bevan, *Trolley wars* (2005) • A. Hosken, *Nothing like a dame* (2006) • *The Times* (19 May 1999); (23 March 2005) • *Daily Telegraph* (23 March 2005) • *The Guardian* (24 March 2005) • *The Independent* (25 March 2005) • *WW* (2005) • Burke, *Peerage* • private information (2009) • b. cert. • m. cert.

Likenesses R. Laurance, bromide print from digital scan, 1978, NPG [*see illus.*] • J. Bratby, oils; Bonhams, 21 June 2005, lot 126 • obituary photographs • photograph, repro. in Powell, *Counter revolution*, following p. 146 • photograph, repro. in Bevan, *Trolley wars*, following p. 138

Wealth at death £2,626,100—in England and Wales: probate, 14 Sept 2006, *CGPLA Eng. & Wales*

Posner, Michael Vivian (1931–2006), economist, was born on 25 August 1931 at Queen Charlotte's Hospital, Marylebone Road, London, the son of Jack Posner, millinery manufacturer, and his wife, Lena, *née* Buck. Both his parents were of Jewish descent. He was originally named Vivian Michael; at what point he reversed the order of his names is unclear. At the time of his birth his parents lived at 40 Mayfair Avenue, Ilford, Essex. The family moved from there to Croydon, where he attended Whitgift School. He won a scholarship to Balliol College, Oxford, where after enrolling as a student of modern history he switched to philosophy, politics, and economics. He graduated with first-class honours in 1953. On 7 August the same year he married a fellow student, Rebecca Reynolds (*b.* 1929), daughter of William Reynolds, a packer at a coal mine. A distinguished scholar, and professor of the Romance languages at the University of Oxford (1978–96), she remained his companion for the rest of his life. They had a daughter and a son.

After graduation Posner worked first as a research officer at the Oxford Institute of Statistics (1953–7) and then briefly in Wesleyan University in the USA (1957–8). He then joined Trinity College, Cambridge, from where he moved to Pembroke College, Cambridge, as a fellow in 1960, relinquishing his fellowship in 1983. Between 1958 and 1979 he also worked in the faculty of economics and politics of Cambridge University, successively as assistant lecturer, lecturer, and reader. He played an important role as secretary of the Cambridge economics faculty for ten years before serving as its chairman in 1974–5. He had the gift of getting the best out of his students with his friendly but firm guidance, and always came forward to help any student suffering from shyness or other difficulties.

Posner's life and work can be seen as a very active intertwining of three passions. First, he was committed to public service in which intelligent policy making in a highly imperfect world restrains unjust outcomes of the working of the market or malfunctioning governance. Second, he followed a Cambridge tradition of applied economics among the pupils of Marshall and Keynes in which theory plays an important but unobtrusive role in reasoned policy advice. In his books on public enterprise, fuel policy, or energy policy, he was careful to set out the possible alternative strategies, depending on changes in assumptions about the real world. His moderation, fair-mindedness, and firm adherence to a concept of public interest won him the loyalty of his co-workers but might have obscured the extent of his achievement in setting out the conceptual elements that would go into policy advice. Finally, he believed that research into real life issues in a world fraught with unexpected changes and uncertainty must accompany teaching of the social sciences in the universities. In his quest for the right mix of evidence and theory to guide policy, he wrote *Italian Public Enterprise* (1966, jointly with S. J. Woolf), *Fuel Policy* (1973), and *Energy Economics* (1981, with Richard Eden and others), as well as editing *Resource Allocation in the Public Sector* (1977) and *Demand Management* (1978). His advice to the government on matters of energy policy, railway electrification, and macroeconomic management in general was informed by research.

Posner's association with government policy making started in 1966 when he became director of economics at the Ministry of Power. He then served successively as economic adviser and economic consultant to the Treasury (1967–71), energy adviser to the National Economic Development Office (1973–4), economic adviser to the Department of Energy (1974–5), and finally deputy chief economic adviser to the Treasury (1975–6). In between he had a stint as consultant to the International Monetary Fund (1971–2). He was chairman of the Social Science Research Council (SSRC) between 1979 and 1983. In 1985–6 he was economic director of the National Economic Development Office. He was secretary-general of the European Science Foundation from 1986 to 1993. He also served the British Railway Board and the Post Office Board as member. He was appointed CBE in 1983.

As a public servant Posner's crowning achievement was the rescue of the Social Science Research Council from the destructive zeal of Sir Keith Joseph, education minister in the first Conservative government of Margaret Thatcher. Joseph was persuaded to choose Lord Rothschild, former chairman of the policy review committee, to report on the future of public funding for social science research, hoping that he would recommend outright abolition of the council. Posner mobilized all his political and intellectual contacts to convince Rothschild that public funding was essential for social science research, and Rothschild's report, submitted in May 1982, endorsed that view. Posner's strategy and hard work helped save the research council, though the word 'science', which offended Joseph's Popperian sensibilities, was expunged, and the council was renamed the Economic and Social Research Council.

In his monographs on fuel policy, public enterprise, and energy policy, and in his proposal of 1972 for a 'minimal reform programme' of the world monetary system, Posner provided for alternative scenarios and resulting solutions. But in 1973 the price of oil rose steeply and governments eventually turned to financial and economic liberalization, which conflicted with Posner's views. Even in that era, however, in his work at the European Science Foundation, Posner used his gifts as a leader who listened to others but was firm in his recommendations. At the foundation he emphasized the necessity of forward planning and of retaining the national councils to fund scientific research instead of shifting the entire responsibility to the European Commission.

The qualities of judiciousness and fair-mindedness that had earned Posner the loyalty of his co-workers in the government, the Social Science Research Council, and the European Science Foundation may have deprived him of the credit he deserved for being a pioneer in two interrelated areas of international trade theory: his 'International trade and technical change', published in *Oxford Economic Papers* in 1961, contained the germs of the theory of product cycles characterizing trade in manufactures and the signalling of the vastly increased role of intermediate products in global trade flows. In his later work he continued to analyse the effect of technical change on international trade and its policy implications. But he always tried to show that his theory was an outgrowth of received doctrine rather than a break with it. His very modesty in this respect diminished the recognition he deserved in a subject given to shouting of the cheerleaders.

Posner lived latterly at Rushwood, Jack Straw's Lane, Oxford, where he died on 14 February 2006, of heart disease. He was survived by his wife and their two children. A memorial service was held at Pembroke College, Cambridge, on 7 October 2006. AMIYA KUMAR BAGCHI

Sources *The Independent* (9 March 2006) · *The Guardian* (17 March 2006) · *The Times* (20 March 2006) · *ESRC Newsletter* (March 2006) · *Royal Economic Society Newsletter* (April 2006) · R. Matthews, I. Byatt, and C. Mühlberg, addresses at memorial service, Pembroke College, Cambridge, 7 Oct 2006 · *WW* (2006) · personal knowledge (2010) · private information (2010) · b. cert. · m. cert. · d. cert.
Likenesses obituary photographs
Wealth at death £171,000: probate, 8 May 2006, *CGPLA Eng. & Wales*

Postgate, (Richard) Oliver (1925–2008), children's television writer and producer, was born at 4 Elm Close, Hendon, Middlesex, on 12 April 1925, the second son of Raymond William *Postgate (1896–1971), an author and journalist who later founded *The Good Food Guide*, and his wife, Daisy, *née* Lansbury (1892–1971). His father was a pacifist who was imprisoned as a conscientious objector during the First World War. His mother, a suffragette, was the daughter of the Labour Party leader George Lansbury and an aunt of the actress Angela Lansbury.

Postgate attended Woodstock School and Woodhouse county secondary school, both in London, before being evacuated during the Second World War to Devon, where he was educated at Dartington Hall School. In 1942 he joined the Home Guard and studied at Kingston College of Art, with the aim of becoming a stage director. When, like his father, he refused to serve in the army he was sentenced to three months at Feltham juvenile prison. After the war he worked as a Red Cross stretcher bearer in the occupied ruins of Germany. In 1948 he began training as an actor at the London Academy of Music and Dramatic Art, and won the gold medal at the end of his first year, but he left before completing the course to work as an actor and stage director with a Brighton repertory company. He gave up theatre work after a short time and took jobs as a photographer and record-sleeve designer, as well as having an idea about a card pig that played the violin rejected by the BBC in 1950. A year later he worked as a freelance

(Richard) Oliver Postgate (1925–2008), by unknown photographer, 1969?

designer for a company that created displays for the Festival of Britain. He then worked for Kay's Industries. On 4 November 1957 he married Prudence Capell Myers (1922–1982), daughter of William Britton, clergyman. He became stepfather to her three children, and they had a further three sons.

Postgate's chance to enter television had come earlier, in 1957, when he joined the ITV London company Associated-Rediffusion as a stage manager working on children's programmes, creating props for productions including the science series *New Horizon*. Thinking he could make such programmes with more substance, he devised *Alexander the Mouse* (1958), about an animal character discovering his royal lineage. He also narrated the stories, which had characters and backgrounds drawn by Peter Firmin, an art-school lecturer with whom he would enjoy a professional partnership lasting almost thirty years. A crude system of animation was used whereby characters were moved by magnets positioned under the table that acted as their set. This was followed by a further ITV series, *The Journey of Master Ho* (1958).

When Postgate and Firmin went freelance and started their own production company, Smallfilms, they became pioneers in children's television and found their biggest successes, starting with *Ivor the Engine* (1959–64), about a Welsh steam engine that wanted to sing in a male-voice choir. The thirty-two black-and-white episodes, made for ITV, were followed a decade later by forty colour episodes on the BBC (1976–7). The pair's first BBC series was *The Saga of Noggin the Nog* (1959–65, revived in colour in 1982), which was Firmin's idea, based on Norse legends. Their other early series included *The Seal of Neptune* (1960), about sea horses in an undersea kingdom, and *Pingwings* (1961), featuring penguin characters. These programmes employed stop-motion animation—each character or object moved slightly, then photographed, with the frames then played as a continuous sequence—and were made in a studio established inside a disused cowshed at Firmin's home after he moved to Blean, near Canterbury. Postgate and his family also moved to Kent, first to Whitstable, and then to Broadstairs.

Postgate would come up with programme ideas for Smallfilms productions, write the scripts, direct and produce them, and provide the narration, while Firmin designed the characters—whether drawings, models, or puppets—and sets. Particularly popular were *Pogles' Wood* (1966–8), about a family living in the root of a tree; *The Clangers* (1969–74), the pair's first colour production, featuring small, pink, knitted, mouse-like creatures living on a blue moon, with neighbours such as the Soup Dragon and the Froglets; and *Bagpuss* (1974), whose pink-and-white-striped 'saggy, old, cloth cat' was seen in just thirteen episodes that were repeated regularly for thirteen years and voted number one in a BBC poll of the best children's television programmes in 1999. Postgate and Firmin's final series was *Pinny's House* (1986), about a race of tiny people.

In 2000 Postgate published his autobiography, in which he reflected on the allure of the programmes over a quarter of a century:

> They are simple, and they are well-founded in a safe place. They are full of fun and, like a good meal, they are rich and satisfying. They also stretch the mind and flex the imagination. And the songs and the pictures are marvellous. (*Seeing Things*)

In 2007 Postgate and Firmin were jointly presented with the Action for Children's Arts J. M. Barrie award 'for a lifetime's achievement in delighting children'. Without Firmin, Postgate worked as an animator on episodes of *Captain Pugwash* (1959–63). He was also a campaigner on environmental issues and for nuclear disarmament. In 1982 he published a pamphlet, *Thinking it Through: the Plain Man's Guide to the Bomb*, that was widely distributed. He also produced a film for the United Nations Association, *Life on Earth Perhaps* (1984). He had always enjoyed children's company, and entertaining them, and he thrived as a grandfather. Following the death of his wife, Prue, his partner for the last twenty years of his life was Naomi Linnell. He died of kidney failure at Carlton Lodge nursing home, 21 Victoria Parade, Broadstairs, on 8 December 2008 and was survived by her, his three children, and his three stepchildren. ANTHONY HAYWARD

Sources O. Postgate, *Seeing things: an autobiography* (2000) • *The Times* (10 Dec 2008) • *Daily Telegraph* (10 Dec 2008) • *The Guardian* (10 Dec 2008); (11 Dec 2008); (13 Dec 2008) • *The Independent* (10 Dec 2008); (13 Dec 2008) • *Morning Star* (10 Dec 2008) • *Daily Post* [Liverpool] (10 Dec 2008) • *Whitstable Times* (11 Dec 2008) • *Isle of Thanet Gazette* (12 Dec 2008) • *Sunday Times* (14 Dec 2008) • *Bristol Evening Post* (18 Dec 2008) • *Oliver Postgate: a life in small films*, 'Time Shift', BBC Four, broadcast 22 Dec 2009 • www.smallfilms.co.uk, 26 July 2010 • 'Oliver Postgate and Peter Firmin', *BFI Screenonline*, www.screenonline.org.uk/tv/id/562266/, 26 July 2010 • SIFT database, ftvdb.bfi.org.uk/sift/individual/469, 26 July 2010, BFI • www.imdb.com/name/nm0692927, 26 July 2010 • b. cert. • m. cert. • d. cert.

Archives FILM BFINA, 'Ivor the engine and the story of Small Films', P. Moss (director), BBC4, 2 May 2005 • BFINA, documentary and light entertainment footage | SOUND BL NSA, performance recordings

Likenesses photograph, 1969?, Smallfilms, Kent [*see illus.*] · photograph, 1974?, Smallfilms, Kent · photographs, 1974–2005, BBC · J. Styles, photograph, *c.*1985, priv. coll. · W. Conran, photographs, 2001, PA Photos, London · N. Jorgensen, photograph, 2001, Rex Features, London · T. Craig, photograph, repro. in *The Independent* (17 May 2001) · obituary photographs

Wealth at death £818,451: probate, 3 April 2009, *CGPLA Eng. & Wales*

Pounds, Norman John Greville (1912–2006), geographer, was born on 23 February 1912 at 13 Kensington Gardens, Walcot, Bath, one of three sons of John Greville Pounds (1883–1935), a type compositor, and his wife, Camilla Martha Minnie, *née* Fisher (1884–1963), a schoolteacher. From explorations of Bath and its environs on foot and by bicycle, from a growing awareness of the impact of the First World War even on Bath, and from reading his father's books on famous battles through the centuries, Pounds developed his lifetime enthusiasm for geography and history. Sensitive to the fundamental importance of education during early childhood, Pounds's parents sent him successively between the ages of five and eleven to three schools. The first two were Church of England schools: they underpinned his lifelong hostility to organized religion but not to its history. From 1923 to 1931 he was a scholarship boy at King Edward's, the local independent grammar school where he became head prefect and captain of rugby. Aside from development of his critical faculties, Pounds acquired from his parents an abiding passion for classical music and from King Edward's his enduring commitment to rugby as player, coach, referee, and spectator.

In 1931 Pounds went to Fitzwilliam House, Cambridge, then a non-collegiate institution of the university. After obtaining an upper second in part 1 of the historical tripos in 1933 he transferred to read part 1 of the geographical tripos, being placed in the first class in 1934. He had been able to attend lectures by distinguished historians (including the medievalists Helen Cam and G. G. Coulton) and geographers (including the historical geographers Bernard Manning and H. Clifford Darby). After graduating BA in 1934 he returned to Cambridge for a further year to acquire a diploma in education.

Pounds taught geography and history at Falmouth grammar school in Cornwall from 1935 until 1944. He married Dorothy Josephine Mitchell (1910–1989), daughter of Joseph Mitchell, cabinet-maker, on 30 July 1938: she was then said to be living in Bath and he in Falmouth. Unfit for war service because of poor eyesight, Pounds served as a fire-watcher but also used his time, registered as an external student of the University of London, to obtain in 1942 a first-class BA degree in geography and history and to write a dissertation on the historical geography of Cornwall, for which he was awarded the degree of PhD in 1945. Pounds returned to Cambridge in 1944, as director of studies in geography and tutor at Fitzwilliam House. Although not holding a university appointment, he lectured for the geographical tripos on economic and political geography, but not every year, and he was never a tripos examiner.

Disappointed at not being integrated fully into the university's department of geography, and despairing of constantly mediating between two disputatious colleagues at Fitzwilliam House, Pounds sought new pastures. For the Michaelmas term of 1949 he went as visiting professor to the University of Wisconsin-Madison, attracted there because its staff included Richard Hartshorne, whom Pounds revered as a political and historical geographer. While there he also visited, by invitation, Indiana University. He returned to Cambridge for two university terms before leaving to take up an offered appointment as professor of geography at Indiana. He held that post until 1968, when it was transformed into a professorship of geography and history, reflecting his teaching and research interests and his work with Indiana University's Institute of East European Studies.

Pounds was involved in university administration, as tutor at Fitzwilliam House (1944–50), as chairman of Indiana's Institute of East European Studies (1952), and as head of Indiana's department of geography (1962–5), but he derived little satisfaction from it. Instead he devoted his vitality and creative intellect to teaching and writing. He only stopped teaching when he was ninety-two (in 2004, after lecturing to audiences of more than 100 members of the University of the Third Age in Cambridge) and he was still writing at the time of his death (an unfinished book on postage stamps and politics). His beautifully structured lectures were full of information and anecdotes, made surprising connections, and paraded his profound enthusiasm for his subject. At Indiana University in 1961 he was voted 'the most popular professor' on campus; the class of 1969 presented him with the distinguished teaching award 'for his excellence in teaching as exemplified by mastery of his academic field, effective classroom presentation, and sensitivity to the needs of his students'; and in 1980 a survey of Indiana's graduates about the teaching of more than 1200 professors placed Pounds in the top 16. He was an outstanding and captivating lecturer.

Pounds's desire to communicate with large audiences also found expression in his writing of books—many, but not all of them, student textbooks—on economic geography, political geography, the historical geography of Europe, the history of material culture, medieval castles, and medieval cities. In addition he wrote books on the historical, economic, and political geographies of particular countries and regions, including Germany, Poland, the Soviet Union, the Ruhr, eastern Europe, North America, the Mediterranean, and Upper Silesia. For these he travelled widely and read publications in many European languages. He wrote and published his first book while teaching at Falmouth, in his thirties, but probably the most enduring of his writings were his two significantly original books published in retirement, in his late eighties and early nineties, on the history of church and parish in England as a whole and in Cambridgeshire in particular.

Pounds had no children. He was a workaholic, addicted

to lecturing and publishing. He retained affection for Cornwall and Cambridge. Royalties from his books enabled him during periods of his life to have homes in both places as well as in Bloomington, Indiana. Retired from Indiana University in 1977, he moved back to the United Kingdom, ultimately settling down in Cambridge. An active retirement led to his being elected a fellow of the Society of Antiquaries (1980), president of the Royal Archaeological Institute (1987–90), and president of the Cambridge Antiquarian Society (1992–4). He was elected to an honorary fellowship of Fitzwilliam College in 1990. He was generous in giving time to his students and friends, and money to his favoured institutions: he funded musical activity and a bronze statue, *The First Undergraduate, 1869*, at Fitzwilliam College (the college had been founded as Fitzwilliam Hall in 1869), and he established a development and welfare fund to support the staff of Cambridge University Library in recognition of the unstinting help they gave him during his declining years when increasingly confined by arthritis to a wheelchair. He died at his home, 189 Huntingdon Road, Cambridge, on 24 March 2006 of leukaemia, bronchopneumonia, and heart failure. His funeral service, held on 6 April at Fitzwilliam College chapel, was followed by burial at the woodland burial ground at Barton, near Cambridge. A memorial service was held at Fitzwilliam College on 4 November 2006. ALAN R. H. BAKER

Sources *Cambridge University Reporter*, 62–65 (1931–5); 75–80 (1944–50) • *Cambridge Historical Register Supplement, 1931–1940* (1942) • *The Guardian* (13 April 2006) • *Society of Antiquaries of London Online Newsletter*, 139, 8 May 2006, cms.sal.org.uk/salon, 30 July 2010 • W. Black, memorial resolution, Bloomington Faculty Council, Indiana University, www.indiana.edu/~bfc/docs/circulars/09-10/B22-2010.pdf, 30 July 2010 • *Indiana University Department of Geography Newsletter* (autumn 2006) • *Journal of the Fitzwilliam Society* (2007) • *Cambridge University Library Readers' Newsletter*, 35 (2007) • personal knowledge (2011) • private information (2011) [W. Black; R. A. Butlin; H. D. Clout; P. Searby; C. Spong; L. Wetton] • b. cert. • m. cert. • d. cert.

Likenesses B. Rubbra, portrait, pencil, 2002, Fitzwilliam College, Cambridge • photograph, repro. in *The Guardian* (13 April 2006)

Wealth at death £1,005,197: probate, 4 July 2006, *CGPLA Eng. & Wales*

Powell, Sir Richard Royle (1909–2006), civil servant, was born at Maythorn, Leigh Road, Walsall, Staffordshire, on 30 July 1909, the elder son of Ernest Hartley Powell, bank cashier, and his wife, Florence, *née* Royle. He attended the Blue Coat Elementary School and Queen Mary's Grammar School in Walsall and in 1927 went to Sidney Sussex College, Cambridge, with a major scholarship in classics. At Cambridge his intellectual ability was demonstrated in a sequence of awards and prizes. He graduated with a first-class degree in the classical tripos in 1930.

Powell was given a year's research scholarship by his college until he reached the age to sit the civil service examination in 1931. He came tenth. After higher-placed candidates had had their pick the only vacancy available was in the Admiralty. In 1934 he was appointed assistant private secretary to the first sea lord, Sir Ernle Chatfield,

Sir Richard Royle Powell (1909–2006), by Elliott & Fry

and two years later was posted to the office of the first lord of the Admiralty, first Viscount Monsell and then Sir Samuel Hoare, where he first gained experience of the wider range of affairs in which a cabinet minister was involved.

Leaving the private office in 1937 in the rank of principal, Powell was immediately plunged into emergency planning for the impending war. He was promoted in 1940 to assistant secretary to take charge of a new branch set up at Churchill's behest to deal with merchant shipbuilding. He was subsequently sent to Canada to set up the British Admiralty technical mission, then to New York to join the merchant shipbuilding mission under Cyril Thompson, negotiating the building and loan of ships. He later commented 'we were totally in the hands of the Americans, who were of course entirely financed by us on a cost plus basis' (interview by Seldon). He finally went to Washington to negotiate lend-lease arrangements; while there he made many lasting friends in the American administration. Recalled to London early in 1944, he was briefly immersed in the preparations for Operation Neptune (the initial phase of the Normandy landings). Then, in the autumn of 1944, he was dispatched to Australia as civil adviser to the commander-in-chief of the British Pacific Fleet, Admiral Sir Bruce Fraser, and also with an attachment to the commander-in-chief of the East Indies Station, Admiral Sir Arthur J. Power. Powell admired and liked these two high-ranking and battle-hardened naval officers. He drily described his duties as 'wide-ranging …

everything from financing airfields to securing duty-free gin' (ibid.).

With the dropping of the atomic bomb, the war in the Far East ended abruptly and Powell was recalled to London. In 1946 he was moved from the Admiralty into the peacetime Ministry of Defence on promotion to under-secretary. The Ministry of Defence as initially conceived was to be a tiny co-ordinating department, servicing the chiefs of staff committee, and dealing with finance, international relations, and so on. It sat alongside three vast service departments, each with its own cabinet minister, permanent secretary, and chief of staff. The system was dependent on negotiation and compromise. Powell was always a quietly skilful negotiator. The new department's first minister was A. V. Alexander and the permanent secretary was the formidable Sir Henry Wilson Smith. Powell's laconic assessment of Alexander was that 'he was probably the best available man, but that's not to say that he was necessarily any good' (interview by Seldon).

Powell was briefly recalled to the Admiralty for two years from 1948 on promotion to deputy secretary, but as the up-and-coming official in the defence field he was called back to the Ministry of Defence in 1950 at the instigation of the prime minister, Clement Attlee, to start up a rearmament programme in the wake of the Korean War. Powell found himself working closely with Sir Edwin Plowden and William Strath on consecutive multi-million pound defence programmes. Within the ministry he concentrated on high-level policy, and strategic and financial issues. He led the team of defence experts that supported Plowden in Paris in 1950 in NATO's Three Wise Men exercise. He was also a member of a small secret committee that worked under Strath in 1954–5 on the devastating implications of a hydrogen bomb attack. He was knighted in 1954.

Then came Suez. In the summer of 1956 the ministry, and Powell personally, were much involved with the military planning for dealing with Nasser. Powell was one of the small group of people who knew about Prime Minister Eden's collusion with France and the Israelis in the operation to seize the Suez Canal. He sat on the Egypt committee, was present at meetings with Christian Pineau and Guy Mollet, and in October was present at meetings at Chequers at the critical time when Eden dispatched first Patrick Dean and then the foreign secretary, Selwyn Lloyd, to Sèvres to conclude plans with the French. Eden found Powell easier to deal with than his minister of defence, Sir Walter Monckton, who made no secret of his reservations. At the height of the crisis Eden insisted that Powell install a scrambler telephone in his flat where he could take calls from the prime minister at any hour of the day or night. This should not be taken to imply that Powell himself was a hawk over Suez. On the contrary, interviewed in later life when the papers had come into the public domain he commented that:

> No civil servant from Norman Brook downwards was in favour of the operation … my philosophy was always that, as a civil servant, you give the Minister your advice and press it as strongly as you could but … then you went away and did it. It would never have occurred to me to have resigned over a thing like that. (interview by Gort and Scott Lucas)

Monckton vetoed a plan for Powell to move on promotion to the War Office as permanent secretary. Instead, the existing incumbent was retired from the Ministry of Defence and Powell took his place as permanent secretary in October 1956. He saw his role as permanent secretary as threefold. He was the central policy adviser to the minister; the administrative head of the department; and the representative on interdepartmental committees. He was also the *primus inter pares* of the three parts into which the department was divided: the civil service side, the scientific side, and the chiefs of staff committee. The post-Suez period was not a happy one for the Ministry of Defence, however. Powell found himself serving a sequence of mostly short-term defence ministers: Monckton, Antony Head, Duncan Sandys, and then Harold Watkinson. Early in 1957 Powell accompanied Sandys on a visit to Washington to try to rebuild bridges with the administration. He later recalled a lunch in Washington with Sir Pierson Dixon and Henry Cabot Lodge as 'one of the most awkward and tricky occasions that I ever took part in' (interview by Gort and Scott Lucas). Quite apart from the post-Suez fallout, this was a stressful time for the defence establishment. Within a reduced defence budget, defence strategy had to be reshaped to adjust to new threats and new technology. The ministry was grappling with such issues as the nuclear deterrent, its delivery systems, the issue of missiles against manned bombers, and the abolition of conscription. Powell was very closely involved in the drafting of the important 1957 defence white paper, which reshaped defence and nuclear policy. Sandys was not an easy minister to work for, but he respected Powell greatly, and the white paper was the joint production of the two men.

Towards the end of 1959 Powell was abruptly informed by Sir Norman Brook, the cabinet secretary, that he was to leave the Ministry of Defence and succeed Sir Frank Lee as permanent secretary of the Board of Trade. Later he was given to understand that this unexpected move had been designed to give him wider experience as a possible candidate in time for the top Treasury post. 'I swallowed hard and said, "All right" … It was the ethic of the Administrative Class … Higher authorities ask you to do something, you do it' (interview by Seldon). The Board of Trade, an enormous and diverse administrative department with thousands of staff, could hardly have been more different from the tight-knit, high-spending world of the Ministry of Defence. As any permanent secretary must, he focused on individuals and staffing issues, but he also took an interest in manufacturing industry and in matters involving overseas trade. This was the period in which Britain's first bid to join the Common Market was vetoed by de Gaulle and international trade policy had to be pursued through the European Free Trade Association and the General Agreement on Tariffs and Trade (GATT). The tariff negotiations were of considerable complexity. Powell's unassuming manner concealed a sharp mind and the ability to master a complex brief. In Geneva the lofty Roy

Denman was initially inclined to dismiss the modest figure of his permanent secretary, parachuted in from London, but quickly came to appreciate the value of Powell's decisive intervention in a particular GATT cliff-hanger, and the precision of the papers he drafted for cabinet on his return to London. Powell came to admire the senior staff of the Board of Trade and they him. During his time at the Board of Trade he was appointed KCB in 1961 (and advanced to GCB in 1967). Whatever may have been hinted to him on appointment, he was not offered the top Treasury post when Sir Frank Lee retired. This went as usual to one of their own (Sir William Armstrong) in 1962.

The return of a Labour government to power in 1964 imposed strains on relations between civil servants and ministers, who were suspicious that the service had been tainted by thirteen years of toryism. For the Board of Trade in particular it was a difficult period. The establishment of a new, interventionist Department of Economic Affairs was bound to diminish the status of the Board of Trade, where a not particularly distinguished minister (Douglas Jay) had to cohabit with two strong economic ministers in the Treasury (James Callaghan) and the Department of Economic Affairs (George Brown).

It is possible that this background made Powell more receptive to an approach from Kenneth Keith that offered him a second career after retirement from Whitehall. The service would have liked to keep him for a year or so more, but he decided that this opening was too good to miss. He therefore retired from the civil service in 1968 to join the board of the Philip Hill Investment Trust and in 1970 the main board of the Hill Samuel Group. He remained in these posts until 1981 and 1979 respectively. Transfers from Whitehall to the City do not always work out as planned. Powell's, however, worked exceptionally well. His colleagues appreciated his keen brain, his analytical approach, his judgement, and his ability to identify the right people to resolve problems. Between 1968 and his final retirement he was at various points on the boards also of GEC (1968–79), Albright and Wilson (1968–73, chairman 1969–73), Whessoe Ltd (1968–88), the Sandoz Group (chairman, 1972–87), Wilkinson Match (1973–80, chairman 1976–80), BPB Industries (1973–83), Ladbroke (1980–86), the Bridgewater Paper Company (1984–90), and Alusuisse Ltd (chairman, 1969–84). After retirement from the civil service he also continued a public service role, as deputy chairman of the Permanent Committee on Invisible Exports (1968–76), president of the Institute for Fiscal Studies (1970–78), chairman for a time of the British North America Committee, and member of a panel to hear appeals from civil servants in respect of security breaches. In 1987 he was invited by the financial services industry to chair the Campaign for Independent Financial Advice. Consistently with his personal interests, he was actively involved in the Königswinter conferences, an annual invitation-only gathering of high-ranking German and British delegates that had been established in 1949 to bring the two nations together.

Powell was a public servant of the old school, a model mandarin. In person he was unassuming and unpretentious. He did not set out to shape his own career; indeed he had no obvious personal agenda unless it were a personal commitment to European co-operation. Although he served loyally under ministers who were both pro-Europe (such as Edward Heath) and the reverse (like Douglas Jay), he is on record in old age as commenting that he believed personally 'that we had made a mistake in 1950 by not recognising that the future lay with Europe and we should have joined the Coal and Steel Community and EURATOM and accepted our destiny in that way' (Kandiah and Staerck, 19). He went where he was sent, mastered his brief, and performed there at the highest level. He was enormously respected both by politicians and by his staff. He was a skilful negotiator, a shrewd judge of people, calm and reassuring in a crisis. He once commented that the first requirement in a permanent secretary was 'monumental calm' (private information, P. Carey). He was entirely discreet, and never gossiped prematurely about such high affairs as he had been involved in.

Throughout his long life Powell made many friendships, especially with those who shared his passionate love of music. As a young man in the 1930s he made the acquaintance of Peter Pears and a group of young men and women who saw each other constantly for meals, the opera, concerts, or the ballet, and visited Switzerland together. In later life he would make up parties to Glyndebourne or the Royal Opera House. For much of his life he lived with his sister Mary, also unmarried, who was his companion in visits to opera and concerts. They shared a flat in Montagu Square, London, and when they found this flat too much to cope with they moved together to retirement accommodation in Ipswich, with the support of a nephew. He had a lasting love for his Cambridge college, which elected him to an honorary fellowship in 1972. In his own time as an undergraduate Sidney Sussex had nothing that could properly be described as a library for students. His first major donation was for the creation of the undergraduate library that carries his name. In his retirement he was a frequent visitor to the college. He gave his large personal collection of books and music to the college in his lifetime and left it almost his entire estate, valued at more than £2 million. He died at Ipswich Hospital on 30 March 2006. His memorial service was held in the chapel of Sidney Sussex College on 1 July 2006 and his ashes were buried in the college gardens.

ELIZABETH LLEWELLYN-SMITH

Sources A. Sampson, *Anatomy of Britain* (1962) · H. Macmillan, *Riding the storm, 1956–1959* (1971) · S. Lloyd, *Suez, 1956* (1978) · S. Foreman, *Shoes and ships and sealing-wax: an illustrated history of the Board of Trade, 1786–1986* (1986) · P. Hennessy, *Whitehall* (1989) · C. Headington, *Peter Pears: a biography* (1992) · P. Hennessy, *Muddling through* (1996) · R. Denman, *The mandarin's tale* (2002) · *Daily Telegraph* (15 April 2006) · *The Times* (23 June 2006) · transcript of interview with A. Seldon, 6 Aug 1980, BLPES, British oral archive of political and administrative history · transcript of interview with A. Gorst and W. Scott Lucas, 1993, King's Lond., Liddell Hart C., papers of the Suez oral history project · M. D. Kandiah and G. Staerck, eds., 'The move to the Sandys white paper of 1957' [transcript of seminar, King's College London, July 1988] · *WW*

(2006) • Burke, *Peerage* • personal knowledge (2010) • private information (2010) [D. Bailes; J. Blow-Darlington; P. Brown; P. Carey; V. H. E. Cole; R. Croft; Lord Croham; C. J. Farrow; E. Fergusson; F. Glaves-Smith; M. D. C. Johnson; R. Lloyd; P. Nairne; Neill Powell, nephew] • b. cert. • d. cert.

Archives FILM 'Sir Richard Powell for war and peace in the nuclear age: the education of Robert McNamara' [DVD-R] | SOUND BLPES, interview with A. Seldon, 1980

Likenesses E. Clark, photograph, 1957, Getty Images, London, Time and Life Pictures • W. Bird, photograph, 1959, NPG • Elliott & Fry, vintage print, NPG [*see illus.*] • obituary photographs

Wealth at death £2,299,648: probate, 8 Nov 2006, *CGPLA Eng. & Wales*

Prior, Allan (1922–2006), screenwriter and novelist, was born at 4 Fifth Avenue, Newcastle upon Tyne, on 13 January 1922, the son of Percy Prior, at the time a brewer's traveller, who went through a string of other jobs, and his wife, Martha Ann, *née* Henderson. When he was ten his father moved the family to Blackpool in search of work. Prior attended the town's grammar school before starting his working life as a clerk in a mail-order firm. He joined the RAF in 1942. In the following year, while serving with a fighter squadron in Northern Ireland, he won a forces magazine short story competition. He married Edith Adonia Playford at Sheppey register office on 13 July 1944. Then aged twenty-one, and serving in the Women's Auxiliary Air Force, she was the daughter of Henry Playford, a skilled labourer in a naval dockyard.

On being demobilized in 1946, Prior took a civil service job in the Ministry of Agriculture but left to pursue a writing career, which began with his first novel, *A Flame in the Air*, a tale of men returning from the Second World War to a northern town, eventually published in 1951. He also made documentaries for BBC radio, starting in 1948, before his first for television, *The Blackpool Story* (1954), which charted that town's growth as a resort.

After switching to drama Prior wrote plays for BBC radio, such as *The Prawn King*, based on the life of his grandfather, a Newcastle fishmonger, then the ITV series *Armchair Theatre*, beginning with *The Common Man* (1956), as well as contributing episodes to the BBC television soap opera *Starr and Company* (1958). Drawing on his family's music-hall background—his grandfather managed a hall in the north-east and his aunt Clara was part of a double act with her husband—he wrote many episodes of the BBC sitcom *The Two Charleys* (1959), featuring Charlie Chester and Eleanor Summerfield as a husband-and-wife act touring variety theatres. His first complete series was *Magnolia Street* (1960), about a Manchester community of Jewish and gentile residents in the early twentieth century, and he was one of the first scriptwriters to be hired by Granada Television in early 1961 for its new programme *Coronation Street*, after Tony Warren's initial episodes had proved popular enough to ensure its survival.

Prior was also one of the original writing team on *Z Cars*, the BBC series that revolutionized the portrayal of the police on television, with an air of gritty realism and featuring officers with flawed characters. With its co-creator, Troy Kennedy Martin, and script editor, John Hopkins, Prior was joint winner of the 1963 Writers' Guild of Great Britain best drama series or serial script award. He wrote seventy-eight episodes (1962–78), as well as almost thirty for the spin-offs *Softly Softly* (1966–70) and *Softly Softly: Task Force* (1970–71), and seven for two more spin-offs, *Barlow at Large* (1971, 1973) and *Barlow* (1974–5). He showed his versatility as a writer by contributing episodes to a wide range of other programmes, including *Dr Finlay's Casebook* (1965–7), the sitcom *Parkin's Patch* (1969–70), *The Onedin Line* (1972–7), *Sutherland's Law* (1974), *The Sweeney* (1975), *Blakes 7* (1979–81), and *Juliet Bravo* (1982).

With the producer Gerard Glaister, Prior later created the popular soap opera *Howards' Way* (1985–90), set in a boatyard on the south coast and starring Maurice Colbourne as a redundant aircraft designer, Tom Howard, who invests his pay-off in a failing boatyard, and Jan Harvey as his wife, Jan. He also adapted novels for two series starring Nigel Havers: *The Charmer* (1987), from Patrick Hamilton's 1930s stories about a conman who preys on women, and *A Perfect Hero* (1991), based on Christopher Matthew's book about a flying officer shot down and badly burned during the battle of Britain. Meanwhile Prior drew on his aunt's music-hall background again for the 1982 radio serial *Never Been Kissed in the Same Place Twice*, based on his 1978 novel of the same name. His last major play for radio was the two-part *Führer* (1995), adapted from his biographical novel about Hitler (published in 1991). His novel *One Away* (1961) had been shortlisted for a gold dagger award by the Crime Writers' Association, which in 1963 presented him with a special merit award for television crime screenplays.

Following the death of his wife, Edith, in 2004, Prior married Norma Ochs, *née* Vogan, a voice and acting coach, at Christ's Chapel of God's Gift at Dulwich, on 7 April 2005. A widow thirteen years his junior, she was the daughter of John William Herbert Vogan, prison governor. Prior died of bronchopneumonia at Lakeside Nursing Home, Auckland Road, Upper Norwood, London, on 1 June 2006. He was survived by his second wife, as well as the two children from his first marriage, Michael and the folk-rock singer Maddy Prior, as well as another daughter, Clara. His funeral took place at West Norwood crematorium. ANTHONY HAYWARD

Sources *The Times* (6 June 2006) • *The Guardian* (9 June 2006) • *The Independent* (10 June 2006) • BFI SIFT database, www.bfi.org.uk/filmtvinfo/ftvdb/, 28 Nov 2008 • internet movie database, www.imdb.com, 28 Nov 2008 • Crime Writers' Association website, www.thecwa.co.uk, 28 Nov 2008 • The Crime Writers' Association of Great Britain dagger awards, 1955–2002, www.hycyber.com/MYST/daggers.html, 28 Nov 2008 • b. cert. • m. certs. • d. cert.

Archives FILM BFINA, *Generation to generation*, M. Stewart (director), BBC1, 8 Aug 1976 • BFINA, documentary footage

Likenesses Ling, photographs, 1978, Rex Features, London • obituary photographs

Wealth at death £389,950: probate, 12 Sept 2006, *CGPLA Eng. & Wales*

Profumo, John Dennis [Jack] (1915–2006), politician and social worker, was born on 30 January 1915 at 28 Basil Street, Kensington, the second son (the elder had died in infancy) and fourth of five children of Albert Peter

Anthony Profumo (1879–1940), barrister, and fourth Baron Profumo of the kingdom of Italy, and his wife, Martha Thom, *née* Walker, an actress and dancer from Edinburgh. The Profumo family was Sardinian by origin, the barony having been bestowed on Antonio Profumo in 1843 by the king of Sardinia. It became an Italian barony in 1903. Antonio's grandson Joseph, the third baron, was educated in England and settled in London having married an Englishwoman. In 1885 he and his four children became British subjects. He had been a founder in 1877 of the Provident Life Association, which became the basis of a substantial family fortune. John Profumo succeeded his father as fifth Baron Profumo of the kingdom of Italy in 1940.

Early life John Profumo—known throughout his life as Jack—began his education at Mr Gibbs's School in Sloane Street, London, before going to preparatory school at Wellington House, Westgate-on-Sea, Kent, and thence in 1928 to Harrow School. He was not academically distinguished but made a mark on the rugby field, in the officer training corps (which he left in the rank of sergeant), and in amateur dramatics and cinematography: while still at school he built his own cinema in the converted laundry of his family's country house in Warwickshire. In 1933 he went to Brasenose College, Oxford, to read law, but this study came second to a very active sporting and social life; he won half-blues for polo, point-to-point riding, and pole-vaulting. He also became something of a ladies' man, an interest that would have ramifications later on. He became well-known as a well-dressed, well-groomed, and debonair socialite. In the long vacation before his final year at Oxford he took an extensive tour of Russia, China, and the Far East, returning via America, which greatly opened up his mind and seems to have stimulated an interest in politics. It did nothing to improve his academic record, and in 1936 he left Oxford with a pass degree. He had become active in the Conservative Party during his final year at Oxford, and conceived an ambition to enter the House of Commons; both his father and grandfather had tried and failed. He spent three months in early 1937 as an observer at the League of Nations in Geneva, and then became closely involved with William Waldorf (Bill) Astor's constituency Conservative association in Fulham. Astor (who later succeeded his father as third Viscount Astor, in 1952) became Profumo's patron, and by the end of 1937 Profumo was the youngest man on the Conservative Party's list of approved candidates. He soon became chairman of the East Fulham Conservative Association and head of the Warwickshire Junior Imperial League, the forerunner of the Young Conservatives. In March 1939 he was adopted as prospective candidate for Kettering in Northamptonshire, a safe Conservative seat whose MP, J. F. Eastwood, had chosen not to fight the next election, due within a year. That June he joined the Northamptonshire yeomanry, part of the 20th light armoured brigade, as a territorial.

War service The outbreak of the Second World War meant the indefinite postponement of a general election, and Eastwood decided to resign at once. Profumo felt his military duties should take precedence over political ones, but was summoned to Downing Street and implored by Neville Chamberlain to carry on. It was therefore in uniform that he fought a by-election on 6 March 1940. Labour did not contest the poll, and Profumo won by 11,298 votes on a small turnout to become the youngest MP in the House of Commons. His first vote in the house was on 8 May, when with considerable courage he was one of the thirty-three

John Dennis Profumo (1915–2006), by Jimmy Sime, 1960

Conservative MPs who sided against Chamberlain in the Norway debate and brought an end to his administration.

Stationed in England as a general staff officer, Profumo was able to attend the house reasonably regularly until the autumn of 1942, when he went to north Africa and took part in the battle for Tunis. He then participated in the invasion of Sicily and fought through Italy, including at Monte Cassino, specializing in liaison with the RAF and United States Army Air Force on Field Marshal Lord Alexander's staff. He was mentioned in dispatches. He returned to London in the autumn of 1944 after the fall of Rome, by special permission to attend a Commons debate on demobilization arrangements. He was awarded a military OBE in December 1944 and the following month was awarded the bronze star by the United States for his part in planning operations in Italy. His own demobilization was delayed, and he had the further frustration of losing Kettering in the Labour landslide of July 1945. However, that October he was promoted brigadier and offered the post of second-in-command of the British military mission in the Far East, based in Tokyo. In his eight months there he worked closely with the supreme commander of allied forces in the Pacific, General Douglas MacArthur.

Return to politics Once demobilized in the autumn of 1946 Profumo sought to resume a political career. He remained a candidate for Kettering, turning down at least one safe seat offered him. He worked for Conservative central office as the party's first broadcasting liaison officer, with a brief to monitor the BBC for signs of bias. A big boundaries change for parliamentary seats made it easier for him to extricate himself from Kettering, and in late 1948 he became the candidate for the safe seat of Stratford upon Avon. He got to know and be liked by Winston Churchill, which proved useful in his subsequent career; and he began to court the celebrated film actress (Babette Louisa) Valerie *Hobson (1917–1998), whose marriage to the producer Anthony Havelock-Allan was disintegrating. In February 1950 he won Stratford upon Avon, but was in opposition until the Conservatives' victory in October 1951. He had to wait another year for office, being appointed parliamentary under-secretary at the Ministry of Transport and Civil Aviation in November 1952. British aviation was in the doldrums at this stage and Profumo brought a typical burst of showmanship to his role, acting for instance as steward to the crew of a BEA Viscount in a London to New Zealand air race. Shortly after his return, in December 1953, he collapsed in the House of Commons with a burst appendix and was off duties for three months. During his convalescence he was visited often by Valerie Hobson, and on 31 December 1954 they were married at St Columba's, Pont Street, London. In 1955 they had their only child, David, later a successful journalist and author.

Although Profumo and his wife (who retired from acting almost immediately) were soon established as one of the most glittering couples in London society, his political career proceeded slowly. He moved sideways to become parliamentary under-secretary for the colonies in 1957, then for foreign affairs in 1958, being promoted to minister of state at the Foreign Office in 1959. In all three roles he and his wife spent much time in extensive foreign travel. In 1960 Harold Macmillan appointed him secretary of state for war, a senior post outside the cabinet. He was sworn of the privy council. In this post he had some notable challenges. He had to oversee the abolition of national service and the return to an all-regular army. There would later be criticism that he was over-promoted and unequal to the demands of this post; but he was initially popular with the army, not least because of his war record and his considerable charm.

The Profumo scandal The catastrophe of Profumo's political career was set in train on the evening of Saturday 8 July 1961 when, as a guest at Lord Astor's house at Cliveden in Buckinghamshire, he came across a naked Christine Keeler in the swimming pool after dinner. Keeler, an occasional prostitute, was the guest of Stephen Ward, an osteopath, who rented a cottage on Astor's estate. Also of the party was the Soviet naval attaché, Captain Yevgeny Ivanov. The next day Profumo met Keeler again and asked for her telephone number. An affair began quickly, but was over within a month. It finished because Ward, who was known to be close to Ivanov, had been boasting of the secretary of state for war's friendship. Profumo had been warned by Sir Norman Brook, the cabinet secretary, to steer clear of Ward and his circle. He dropped Keeler at once (though he made the mistake of doing so in writing, in a letter beginning 'Darling'), fearing the security services must know about their affair. Sadly, he could not rely on Keeler's discretion. One of her other inamorati, an Antiguan called Johnny Edgecombe, fired shots at Keeler in a lover's tiff in December 1962, and in the aftermath of this incident Keeler spoke to numerous people (including policemen, lawyers, and journalists) about whether what had happened might have an impact on Profumo. No one could imagine why, until Keeler enlightened them. When Edgecombe was put on trial the main witness against him, Keeler, had fled the country, so a minor irruption then became a much reported Fleet Street story. Some in the press and the police suspected that Profumo had spirited her away to avoid his name coming out in court. He had not. But he then acted recklessly. Macmillan had been alerted that there were rumours of Profumo's having had an affair with Keeler. Profumo then denied these to Tim Bligh, Macmillan's private secretary, Martin Redmayne, the chief whip, and Sir John Hobson, the attorney-general. It was decided to bother Macmillan no further with the matter. Profumo also instructed his solicitors to pursue for libel any publication that repeated the suggestions. However, on 21 March 1963, and under parliamentary privilege, the Labour MP George Wigg invited the home secretary to deny the rumours about Profumo and Keeler. The Ivanov connection was supposedly underpinning the question—this was the height of the cold war—but the Conservative government had lost some by-elections, was deemed to be exhausted and in trouble, and there had been another minor spy scandal involving William Vassall, a clerk at the Admiralty, the previous year, that had led to a ministerial resignation. Labour smelled political advantage and so pursued Profumo.

Redmayne immediately told Profumo that he must make a public denial along the lines of those already made privately. Profumo took a sleeping pill and went to bed. He was awoken in a drugged state at 3 a.m. and brought to the House of Commons, where several of his senior colleagues had decided a denial must be issued without delay in an attempt to ward off scandal. One of them, Iain Macleod, the leader of the house, said to Profumo: 'Look, Jack, the basic question is, "Did you fuck her?"' (Profumo, 181). Profumo continued to deny that he had. William Deedes, the minister without portfolio and a future editor of the *Daily Telegraph*, drafted a statement that Profumo agreed to deliver the next morning in the Commons. Profumo later told his son that 'I felt I couldn't tell the truth at that stage … it would have been beyond my political ability to own up to them—having got that far telling lies' (ibid., 182). Deedes, thirty years after the events, compared what had happened with Star Chamber. Thus it was that Profumo attended the house the next day and, having told the truth that he had had nothing to do with Keeler's disappearance, and had only seen Ivanov twice, and socially, then told the blatant lie—that there had been 'no impropriety whatever' in his relationship with Keeler—that would end his career and cement one of the most celebrated scandals in British political history.

The rumours would not go away. Profumo had his lawyers issue writs against two European magazines that continued to publicize them. A further complication was that the police were compiling a case against Stephen Ward for living off immoral earnings. Ward asked to see Bligh at Downing Street, claiming that he had been covering up for Profumo over certain security aspects of the case. On 29 May Macmillan finally acceded to a demand that he initiate an inquiry into the matter, and charged the lord chancellor, Lord Dilhorne, to conduct it.

On 31 May the Profumos left for a holiday in Venice, Profumo having maintained to Dilhorne before his departure that he was sticking to his story. However, once in Venice he confessed to his wife that he had had an affair with Keeler. She advised him to return home at once and own up, which he did. In his letter of resignation from the government to Macmillan on 4 June he admitted his lie, apologized, and said he had lied 'to protect, as I thought, my wife and family' (Profumo, 188). Too ashamed to ask for an audience of the queen to return his seals of office, he had them sent to Buckingham Palace by courier. He also resigned from the House of Commons. Various moral arbiters at Westminster and in Fleet Street, notably Lord Hailsham, in an over-emotional television appearance and an interview with *The Times* newspaper, got on their moral high horses, and Britain became convulsed by spasms of prurience and hypocrisy and the centre, for a time, of the world's focus. On 20 June the House of Commons formally censured Profumo, three days after a debate on the government's handling of the issue. In the course of that Macmillan had been turned on memorably by one of his backbenchers, Nigel Birch, who during a devastating attack on the prime minister quoted the lines 'never glad, confident morning again' from the poem *The Lost Leader* by Robert Browning. Macmillan did not recover, and resigned four months later. Profumo requested that he be allowed to resign from the privy council, and his resignation was accepted. Stephen Ward committed suicide in August 1963. An official report by Lord Denning was published in September, which exonerated the security service and refuted claims of any security breach. It sold 90,000 copies on the day of publication. Of Profumo, Denning said: 'His disgrace was complete' (*The Times*, 11 March 2006).

Redemption The remaining forty-three years of Profumo's life became, however, an epic of redemption. In the immediate aftermath he and his family retired to the country. After a few months of reflection and comparative isolation, and at the suggestion of a friend, the dowager marchioness of Reading, he rang Toynbee Hall in London's East End and offered his services as a volunteer. Named after the Victorian social reformer Arnold Toynbee, the hall had been founded in 1884 by a clergyman, Samuel Barnett, as the first of the university settlements, in which students were given subsidized lodgings in return for help with the local poor. It was now short of funds. When Profumo joined the band of helpers in April 1964 the worldwide publicity put Toynbee back on the map. He did a series of menial tasks, such as helping with the laundry and working in the kitchens. He danced with old ladies at tea parties and comforted meths drinkers. Conscious of his disgrace he kept a low profile even within the charity. He went in every day and soon developed a genuine affection for the place and for the East End. He slowly reintegrated himself into his former milieu too, made easier by the fact that many political friends stood by him, and that the royal family also took a lead in inviting him and his wife to social occasions.

Having established himself at Toynbee, Profumo used his contacts and experience to cause the charity to grow and to solicit money. The charity was often in the news, either because of Profumo's activities there, or because of the famous names from politics, society, and show business whom he managed to attract to visit it. In 1968 the government invited him to join the board of Grendon Underwood psychiatric prison in Buckinghamshire, which was taken as a mark of his official rehabilitation. He served until 1975. His success in securing a visit by the queen to Toynbee Hall in 1971 to open a new building there set the seal on his redemption. He was appointed CBE for services to charity in 1975. He rose through the ranks at Toynbee to become first chairman, from 1982 to 1985, and then president until his death in 2006. He was made an honorary life member in 2001, and in the same year was made an honorary fellow of Queen Mary College, University of London. Even in his seventies he was spending several days a week there. Over the four decades of his association with the charity its clients changed from the largely elderly poor and down-and-outs to impoverished immigrants, notably Bangladeshis. Profumo steered the charity successfully through the evolutionary process needed to cope with such changes, and never relaxed in looking for new volunteers or new sources of income. One of his fellow volunteers said: 'Everybody here worships him. We think he's a bloody saint' (*Daily Telegraph*, 11 March 2006). He and his family were distressed when, in 1989, his rehabilitation secure and his reputation restored, a feature film was made of the scandal, dragging the business up yet again.

Profumo's wife engaged in her own considerable charitable work, and he was profoundly affected by her death in 1998. He was close to his son and his son's family, and remained gregarious; but in his eighties his health began to fail. He had a series of minor strokes and endured increasing difficulties with his mobility. He never spoke in public of the events of 1963, and was reticent about them even with his son, who published a memoir of him and Valerie Profumo shortly after Profumo's death. He could have commanded a sizeable sum in return for an autobiography or even an interview at any time after 1963, but chose never to seek to justify himself or his conduct. His decades of devoted charitable work were the only statement he had to make, and were often cited as an example to other politicans who paid less of a price for far worse behaviour. He maintained an immaculate dignity in what he called 'my personal desire for privacy' (*The Times*, 18 March 2006).

Of just short of average height and with a receding hairline from an early age, Profumo was distinguished by his considerable courtesy and charm. He adored the company of women, but also enjoyed fishing and gardening. He had a natural line in self-deprecation, was generous and blessed with a well-developed sense of humour. Margaret Thatcher described him as 'one of our national heroes' (*Daily Telegraph*, 11 March 2006). It would have been hard to imagine, when he left politics in abject disgrace in 1963, that a Conservative prime minister would ever refer to him in such terms. Not long before he died he told his son: 'You know, I *have* enjoyed my life!' (Profumo, 5). Yet his friend Bishop Jim Thompson, with whom he had worked closely in the East End, said that 'No-one judges Jack Profumo more harshly than he does himself. He says he has never known a day since it happened when he has not felt real shame' (*The Guardian*, 11 March 2006).

Profumo died on 9 March 2006 in the Chelsea and Westminster Hospital, London, from pneumonia in the aftermath of a stroke. He was cremated after a funeral at St Paul's, Knightsbridge, on 20 March 2006. He was survived by his son, David Profumo, and his stepson by Valerie Hobson's first marriage, Sir Mark Havelock-Allan.

SIMON HEFFER

Sources D. Profumo, *Bringing the house down* (2006) • P. Knightley and C. Kennedy, *An affair of state: the Profumo case and the framing of Stephen Ward* (1987) • *The Times* (11 March 2006); (15 March 2006); (18 March 2006); (20 March 2006) • *Daily Telegraph* (11 March 2006) • *The Guardian* (11 March 2006); (15 March 2006) • *The Independent* (11 March 2006) • *Financial Times* (11 March 2006) • *Press Association Newsfile* (20 March 2006) • *WW* (2004) • personal knowledge (2010) • private information (2010) • b. cert. • m. cert. • d. cert.

Archives CAC Cam., P. G. Buchan-Hepburn papers • NL Wales, Desmond Donnelly papers

Likenesses Bassano, vintage print, 1938, NPG • photographs, 1947–71, Getty Images, London, Popperfoto • photographs, 1952–85, Getty Images, London, Hult. Arch. • photographs, 1952–2003, Photoshot, London • W. Stoneman, photograph, 1954, NPG • photographs, 1955–2005, Rex Features, London • Lenare, photograph, 1956, NPG • photographs, 1959–2005, PA Photos, London • J. Sime, photograph, 1960, Hult. Arch., London [*see illus.*] • photographs, 1960–63, Camera Press, London • Vivienne, photograph, 1960–69, Camera Press, London • photographs, 1960–71, Getty Images, London, AFP • W. Bird, photograph, 1962 • S & G Barratts, photographs, 1962–5, PA Photos, London • S. Mark, photographs, 1989, Camera Press, London • J. Veysey, photographs, 2003, Camera Press, London • D. Wimsett, photographs, 2003–5, Photoshot, London • D. Long, photographs, 2005, Camera Press, London • S. Ward, drawings, NPG • obituary photographs

Wealth at death £3,015,102: probate, 13 July 2006, *CGPLA Eng. & Wales*

Puxon [*née* Hale], **(Christine) Margaret** (1915–2008), gynaecologist, obstetrician, and barrister, was born at 15 High Street, West Bromwich, Staffordshire, on 25 July 1915, the daughter of Reginald Wood Hale (1884–1971), iron merchant, and his wife, Clara Lilian, *née* Poulton (1887–1948). She was brought up in Stourbridge, Worcestershire, and attended Abbey School, Malvern Wells, Worcestershire. She initially read veterinary medicine before switching to medicine at Birmingham University (she had turned down a place to read English literature at Oxford University). In her first year as an undergraduate she met Ralph Edward Goldsbrough Weddell (1913–1999), an engineering student whom she married on 4 September 1937 at Hagley parish church, Worcestershire. She had two children as a student. She graduated with honours in 1942 and was awarded the gold medal in obstetrics and gynaecology. She was then gynaecological registrar at the Queen Elizabeth Hospital, Birmingham; she took the degree of MD in 1944. She divorced her first husband and, having moved to Colchester, married François Edward Mortimer (Peter) Puxon (1907–1982), a solicitor, at Colchester register office on 29 August 1946. She gained membership of the Royal College of Obstetricians and Gynaecologists the same year. She was appointed consultant gynaecologist by Essex county council.

Margaret Puxon was off work while she was pregnant with her third child, born in 1949; during this period she started to study law, initially by a correspondence course. She was called to the bar by the Inner Temple in 1954. Her second marriage had by then broken down and she moved to London as a pupil barrister and obtained a tenancy in chambers at a time when professional advancement for women was still a challenge. Her interest in law overtook her interest in medicine. Always feminine but not a feminist, she was content to be better than the men in order to succeed. In the early 1950s she met her third husband, (Frederick) Morris Williams (1915–1986), also a solicitor; they married at Chelsea register office on 20 September 1955. She continued to use her second married name for professional purposes.

Puxon's practice initially concerned legally aided divorce cases for former servicemen; such work was not popular with other barristers. As her practice grew she became a sought after advocate for divorce, family, and children cases. She also developed a specialist practice in medical law. In 1963 she wrote *The Family and the Law*, a popular paperback published as a Pelican Original for 5 shillings. A second edition was published in 1971. In 1970 she acted in the landmark House of Lords case *J.* v. *C.*, which established the principle that the paramount consideration in family law cases was the welfare of the child, a principle later enshrined in legislation. Her medical law practice flourished, reflecting not just the growth of clinical negligence cases but also the developing interface between medical science and the law. The advances in biological technologies required a regulatory framework to apply ethical principles in novel situations. She advised in connection with such matters as assisted conception, and whether the prescription of the morning-after pill amounted to procuring an abortion.

In 1979 Puxon was elected a fellow of the Royal College of Obstetricians and Gynaecologists, and in 1982 she was appointed QC. She thus joined a very select club of persons who had both been elected to fellowship of a medical royal college and taken silk—the most famous being Sir Roger Ormrod. She was a deputy circuit judge from 1970 to 1980, and a recorder from 1986 to 1988. Among her other appointments she was a privy council member of the council of the Royal Pharmaceutical Society from 1975 to 1990, a member of the ethics committee of the Royal College of General Practitioners from 1981 to 1993, and chairwoman of the ethics committee of the Lister Hospital IVF unit from 1983. She contributed to leading textbooks, including *Progress in Obstetrics and Gynaecology* (1983); *In Vitro Fertilisation: Past, Present and Future* (1986); *Gynaecology* (1991); and *Safe Practice in Obstetrics and Gynaecology* (1994). She also wrote many articles for medical and legal journals.

Puxon was always interested in meeting people and exploring new ideas. In 1991 she met a group of younger lawyers who were predominantly former junior doctors to form the Society of Doctors in Law, a learned society that held dinner meetings. As chairwoman she was able to invite distinguished speakers from her circle of contacts who happened to be in the news. Her brother Norman Hale (1919–2008), well known as the rather autocratic and formidable headmaster of Milbourne Lodge, which he had transformed into a leading preparatory school, occasionally attended the dinners.

In 1993 Puxon retired as a barrister practising from chambers. However, she continued to pursue professional interests and provided advice on a consultancy basis. She was appointed consulting editor of *Medical Law Reports*, and her case commentaries demonstrated wisdom and humour. For example, she would comment critically on civil legal aid with an objectivity that often eluded even the cleverest lawyers. In advancing years she showed a remarkable facility for the personal computer and its associated technologies. She was fortunate that her lively intellect and sharp but humane wit were preserved. Her visitors were rewarded with her warmth, excellent company, and valuable insights into the human condition. She died of bronchopneumonia at the King Edward VII Hospital for Officers, Beaumont Street, Westminster, on 1 April 2008, and was survived by her three children.

ANTHONY BARTON

Sources *The Guardian* (30 April 2008) · *The Times* (19 May 2008) · *BMJ*, 336/7659 (25 June 2008), 1510 · *WW* (2008) · personal knowledge (2012) · private information (2012) · b. cert. · m. certs. · d. cert.

Likenesses photograph, 1982, Photoshot, London · photograph, repro. in *The Guardian* (30 April 2008)

Wealth at death £760,115: probate, 22 Oct 2008, *CGPLA Eng. & Wales*

Pym, Francis Leslie, **Baron Pym** (1922–2008), politician, was born on 13 February 1922 at Penpergwm Lodge, Llangattock, near Usk, Monmouthshire, the fourth and youngest child and only son of Leslie Ruthven Pym (1884–1945), land agent, and his wife, Iris Rosalind, *née* Orde (1892–1982). His family mixed politics with imperial service and churchmanship: his grandfather Walter Ruthven Pym was bishop of Mauritius then of Bombay, and his father was conservative MP for Monmouth from 1939 to 1945. Pym was educated at Eton College and Magdalene College, Cambridge, and at the age of twenty was commissioned in the 9th Lancers, just in time to take part in the battle of El Alamein. He served as adjutant of his regiment until the end of the Second World War, was twice mentioned in despatches, and in 1945 was awarded the Military Cross. The citation praised his efficiency and hard work in organizing the supplies of the regiment, at times in circumstances of great difficulty and under heavy fire. He was demobilized with the rank of captain in 1946 and returned to Cambridge to take his degree. Having done so, on 25 June 1949 he married Valerie Fortune Daglish (*b.* 1929), daughter of Francis John Heaton Daglish, company director, of Liverpool. They had two daughters and two sons.

After leaving Cambridge, Pym began a business career with a near-bankrupt firm of contractors, Holloway and Webb, which he built into a successful concern. He had also, in 1945, inherited Hazells Hall estate in Bedfordshire, which had been in the family since the eighteenth century, but which needed a lot of attention. Nevertheless, having achieved his immediate goals, his thoughts turned increasingly to politics. There was never any doubt about his political allegiance. He stood as a Conservative in the safe Labour seat of Rhondda West in the 1959 general election. Two years later there was a by-election in Cambridgeshire, conveniently close to his family's estate. He stood and was elected to the House of Commons in March 1961.

Pym quickly established himself as a safe pair of hands who could handle competently whatever job came his way. He began, like his father, in the whip's office, as an assistant government whip (unpaid) in 1962 and an opposition whip from 1964. Edward Heath appointed him deputy chief whip in 1967. After Heath's election victory in June 1970 Pym became chief whip and was sworn as a privy councillor. The Conservatives had a solid majority in that parliament, but their loyalty soon came under strain, partly because of divisions on Europe, and partly because

Francis Leslie Pym, Baron Pym (1922–2008), by Bassano and Vandyk Studios, 1978

Heath, under pressure, fell back on some of the policies which he had denounced in opposition, notably a statutory incomes policy and state aid to specific industries. Pym did not regard it as part of his job to probe the merits of the prime minister's foreign or economic policy and remained totally loyal in private as well as public. He always inclined to the pessimistic view of any parliamentary situation. Since the votes usually turned out better than his prediction he earned a reputation of sober reliability and (as in the war) steadiness under fire. Heath came to rely on his judgement, realizing that in Pym he had a chief whip who did not meddle but only gave sound advice when it was requested. A good example was provided in 1971 by the Commons vote on the second reading of the bill enabling Britain to enter the European Communities. Both the main parties were divided. No one knew in advance how many Conservatives would vote against the bill or how many Labour MPs would support it. If the government allowed a free unwhipped vote to its backbenchers it would be hard for the opposition to impose a whip. Yet the natural instincts of the prime minister (himself a former chief whip) was to impose a whip and order the whips to do their best to enforce it. To allow a free vote was risky, and the whole government policy was at stake. The argument rattled round the corridors of the party conference in Brighton that October. It gradually emerged that Pym was arguing for the riskier course of a free vote. The prime minister kept back his own opinion until the last minute. The announcement of a free vote took the press by surprise. Pym had won the argument, and on the night the gamble paid off. The government won the vote by a majority of 112. Pym's reputation for sound judgement was confirmed.

The prime minister badly needed this quality in Northern Ireland at the end of 1973. The province was under direct rule from London, and Heath relied on the political skill of the secretary of state, Willie Whitelaw, to prevent it from exploding. But he was forced to bring Whitelaw back to England to help deal with the crisis created by the miners' overtime ban. Heath knew he could rely on Pym's sense of duty and steadiness, and with much reluctance Pym accepted the appointment as secretary of state, in December 1973. The Sunningdale Agreement for power-sharing in Northern Ireland had been negotiated by Heath himself. Pym would have had the task of carrying it against the savage opposition of Ian Paisley and the intransigent Unionists, but his quality in this role was never tested, as Heath was defeated in the general election called in February 1974.

Back in opposition Pym held several shadow jobs in succession, beginning with agriculture, while Heath remained party leader. In early 1975 he supported Whitelaw in his unsuccessful leadership campaign after Heath stood down. Margaret Thatcher, the new party leader, asked him to continue as shadow spokesman on agriculture, but in 1975 he returned to the backbenches after a heart attack. He was fit again by the following year and Thatcher moved him from agriculture to take charge of the Conservative policy on devolution. This was an unhappy period because of division on the subject within the Conservative Party. It came to an end when Labour's devolution plan was defeated by the referenda in Scotland and Wales. Briefly Pym was made shadow foreign secretary but this too was unsatisfactory because it was widely and correctly thought that if Thatcher became prime minister, Peter Carrington would be her foreign secretary. So it turned out in May 1979.

Pym was compensated with the job of defence secretary for which he was well suited. He built a good working relationship with the United States and did his best to resist cuts in defence spending. He robustly defended the policy of stationing cruise missiles in Britain. In the reshuffle of January 1981 he became leader of the House of Commons and chancellor of the duchy of Lancaster. He became lord president of the council in October 1981 but continued as leader of the House of Commons. In April 1982 Carrington resigned as foreign secretary, taking responsibility for the loss of the Falkland Islands, and Pym took his place.

Pym was now a familiar and respected figure in the Conservative hierarchy. He had a forceful yet attractive speaking voice and a wide range of ministerial experience. He had survived the purge of the so-called 'wets' of the party in 1981 and was discussed as a possible successor if anything happened to Margaret Thatcher. But he was not at ease in her government and his time at the Foreign Office confirmed this unhappiness. While remaining strictly loyal, he was out of sympathy with the thrust of her domestic policy. In his time Carrington had established a good working relationship with the prime minister, partly because he took little interest in domestic affairs, but mainly because she respected his mastery of the foreign affairs brief. She made no secret that this respect was not transferred to his successor. Pym was accustomed to dealing with male colleagues of the same background as himself. Mrs Thatcher needed a frank and robust relationship with her foreign secretary, but Pym was reluctant to join in arguments with a forceful woman. He tended to retreat from the fray, and sit silent in his chair with hunched shoulders, her forceful arguments washing over him. He managed to keep the lines of British diplomacy open while the prime minister concentrated on mobilizing the task force which eventually retook the Falkland Islands. During the run-up to the election of June 1983 Pym made known his hope that the Conservatives would win with only a modest majority. It was an arguable case, but held no attraction for Thatcher. In the reshuffle which followed the election he lost his job. She tried to compensate him with the speakership of the House of Commons, a post which he did not want and which anyway was not in her gift.

Pym retired to the backbenches and in 1984 summed up his political views in his book *The Politics of Consent*. So far from being a liberal wet, he placed himself exactly in the centre of the Conservative Party and tried to rally those who shared his doubts about dogmatic Thatcherism. But he was not by nature a conspirator. The group which he formed and christened Centre Forward never really got going. It stood for loyalty and old-fashioned good manners. It was typical of Pym himself, but hardly of the tory party in Margaret Thatcher's heyday. Pym did not contest the 1987 election and was made a life peer in that year. He was chairman of the English-Speaking Union from 1987 to 1992 and took on other voluntary roles as well as City directorships, including as chairman of Christie Brockbank Shipton Ltd from 1994 to 1999 and Diamond Cable Communications plc from 1995 to 1999. In 1998 he published a family history, *Sentimental Journey*.

Pym was a good practical administrator and straightforward in his dealings with the House of Commons and the electorate. He enjoyed most of his political life but his qualities were perhaps better suited to a somewhat earlier age. Having sold Hazells Hall in the 1980s, he lived latterly at Everton Park, Sandy, Bedfordshire. He died there on 7 March 2008, of cerebrovascular disease, and was survived by his wife, Valerie, and their four children.

DOUGLAS HURD

Sources F. Pym, *Sentimental journey* (1998) · *The Times* (8 March 2008) · *Daily Telegraph* (8 March 2008) · *The Guardian* (8 March 2008) · *The Independent* (8 March 2008) · *WW* (2008) · Burke, *Peerage* · personal knowledge (2012) · private information (2012) · b. cert. · m. cert. · d. cert.

Archives priv. coll. | FILM BFINA, *The parliamentarians*, A. Thompson (producer), BBC2, 18 Feb 1979 · BFINA, current affairs and documentary footage | SOUND BL NSA, documentary and performance recordings

Likenesses photographs, 1961–83, PA Photos, London · Bassano, half-plate film negatives, 1964–8, NPG · photographs, 1976–85, Getty Images, London · Bassano and Vandyk Studios, colour transparency, 1978, NPG [*see illus.*] · Bassano and Vandyk Studios, half-plate film negatives, 1978, NPG · J. Blau, photographs, 1978–9, Camera Press, London · L. Cherrault, photograph, 1979, Camera Press, London · photographs, 1979–84, Rex Features, London · N. Sinclair, photographs, 1991–*c*.1993, NPG · photographs, 1997, Photoshot, London · Luck & Flaw, caricature, repro. in *Sunday Times* (5 April 1981) · Marc [M. Boxer], caricature, repro. in *The Observer* (11 April 1982) · Marc [M. Boxer], caricature, repro. in *The Observer* (1 July 1984) · M. Noakes, oils, repro. in www.michael-noakes.co.uk/gallery2.htm · group portraits, photographs, Camera Press, London · obituary photographs

Wealth at death £2,518,931: probate, 5 Nov 2008, *CGPLA Eng. & Wales*

Rae, John Malcolm (1931–2006), headmaster and author, was born at 2 Rutford Road, Streatham, London, on 20 March 1931, the son of (Lawrence) John Rae, radiologist, and his wife, (Annie) Blodwen, *née* Williams. He was educated at Bishop's Stortford College and, after national service as a second lieutenant in the Royal Fusiliers, at Sidney Sussex College, Cambridge, where he took a lower second-class degree in history. Competitive sport was the driving force that fuelled his already burgeoning ambition. He won half-blues for swimming and water polo, and narrowly missed a rugby blue. Swimming was a principal recreation to the end of his life.

After considering a career in the security services Rae decided to become a schoolmaster. During his teaching practice at Fettes College, Edinburgh, in 1955 he became a protégé of the headmaster, Donald Crichton-Miller, a powerful figure from whom he learned much about public school politics. Rae was advised by Crichton-Miller, a Cambridge blue and Scottish rugby international, to emphasize his sporting prowess, and in his first appointment as an assistant master at Harrow, from 1955, Rae was soon a successful coach of both swimming and rugby. At Harrow his lessons were remembered for their skilful organization. He had a commanding voice, and even then a physical presence that exuded authority. He was never a shrinking violet and the headmaster, Robert James, though an admirer, found him somewhat difficult to handle. When the first Wilson government set up the public schools commission in 1965, Rae suggested to the education secretary that he should represent the rank and file of the teaching profession. Although he was not appointed his opinions were canvassed and from this point his career and public profile blossomed. Meanwhile, on 17 December 1955, he had married Daphne Ray Simpson, the 22-year-old daughter of John Phimester Simpson, insurance manager. They had two sons and four daughters.

Rae's eyes were always on a leading headmastership and he knew the potential handicap of his nonconformist background, moderate degree, and minor public school education. In his revealing autobiography, *Delusions of Grandeur* (1993), he admitted that he became an Anglican partly for career reasons, and took a doctorate at King's College, London, to bolster his academic standing. His thesis, on conscientious objectors in the First World War, was published in 1970 as *Conscience and Politics*. His doctorate was awarded in 1965, the day after he learned of his appointment to his first headmastership, at Taunton School. But even then his iconoclastic side was not trimmed by propriety and he said that many people who had doctorates were actually very dull. This was an accusation never levelled at Rae himself.

As a student of Napoleon, Rae was always conscious of

John Malcolm Rae (1931–2006), by Bassano, 1973

the importance luck played in a career. He was one of the lucky generals in both of his principal appointments. When he had applied for the headmastership of Taunton School, three coincidental factors counted in his favour among the older governors: his father had practised briefly in Taunton in the 1930s; Crichton-Miller, his principal referee, had made his mark as a youthful head of Taunton before the war; and another admired predecessor, whom Rae somewhat resembled physically, had also been educated at Bishop's Stortford and Sidney Sussex.

Rae was always happiest when he had something big to tackle and he certainly found that at Taunton. The school was in need of a shake-up and under Rae it got it. When his wife attended the formerly all-male chapel on his first Sunday, the atmosphere, he recalled, was as though he had introduced a striptease dancer to the Athenaeum. He soon imposed his authority by expelling four senior boys, a necessary but courageous decision, as several private schools in Taunton fought over a diminishing market. Housemasters resented the weakening of their autonomy by his desire to build a sixth-form centre (opened by Princess Anne in his last term). In 1967 his pessimistic speech-day pronouncements on the future of the public school system caused much resentment. His address in 1969 on the failings of parents brought further trenchant publicity and the accusation that he was biting the hand that fed him. As a whispering campaign began, the fate of Crichton-Miller, whose headmastership of Stowe had recently been prematurely ended, was never far from Rae's mind.

Taunton had proved a baptism of fire and Rae had no qualms about moving on, indecently early even in the eyes of his opponents, when the opportunity of Westminster presented itself after four years. Once again luck played its part. His principal rival dropped out before interview, believing, mistakenly, that he was about to be appointed headmaster of Eton. Another contender accepted the headmastership of Christ's Hospital, for which Rae had also been a candidate. At his Westminster interview Rae was asked what he would do if rebellious pupils appeared at his door demanding a change to the rules. 'Invite them in for a sherry' was his reply (*Delusions*, 57). Such insouciance may have been too bold for some schools, but in the more urbane surroundings of Westminster it was a positive recommendation. Unexpected though his appointment was, it was a shrewd identification of the right man for the school at that time. He was exceptionally energetic and articulate, contributing widely to the national discourse on education policy. He was a regular contributor to the *Times Educational Supplement* and was frequently interviewed on television and radio, where he always made a sound and courteous impression.

Westminster, a centrifugal institution well suited to Rae's personal dynamism, was a school that appealed to the liberal-minded professional classes, who felt that country boarding schools were outmoded. His great achievement, in an era of social and cultural upheaval, was to treat intelligent sixth-formers not as recalcitrant adolescents, but as putative undergraduates, so that for some even Oxford or Cambridge seemed anti-climactic by comparison. Westminster pupils during his reign knew that they were there to work. His priorities were well focused; what mattered were the big issues, such as co-education, changing adolescent mores, or drugs, on which he was rigorous and uncompromising. Conscious that he was headmaster of a great school almost by accident, he felt that he had to play out that role. As a self-publicist, who needed to be the centre of attention, he had a masterful whiggish public manner and kept the school in the spotlight.

Rae's constant public exposure led many outsiders to think he was neglecting the school, but this was not true. His energy and work-rate were prodigious. His immense stamina, helped by his regular 2 mile swims in the RAC pool in Pall Mall, was always an asset. He skilfully varied the routine with imaginative appointments, for example signing up the former England cricket captain Mike Brearley on a short-term contract. Parents were at ease with him (even if not with the television cameras that Rae allowed in to film the life of the school in 1979) and he was always more controversial outside the school than within it. He knew all his pupils by name, and provided a sympathetic ear for their problems, although some felt he was uneasy in the presence of emotion.

In an era of rampant inflation Rae coped well with the financial pressures on the school, especially as only 3 per cent of the pupils were the sons or daughters of Old Westminsters (against a comparable figure of 40 per cent at

Eton). He undertook expansion on a limited site skilfully, with a new day house (Dryden's), a girls' boarding house in Barton Street, and a new Under School in Vincent Square. During his lengthy tenure girls became full members of the school for the first time and overall numbers rose from 464 to 640. The success of the school was in many ways compensation for his own academic record. In 1977 he proved a politically astute chairman of the Headmasters' Conference.

Rae's ultimate ambition was to move to Eton, but his failure in 1979 even to secure an interview was a watershed in his life. Westminster was not going to see him through to retirement and a change of career beckoned. Two factors hastened this process. His opposition to Margaret Thatcher's assisted places scheme in 1980, which he saw as subsidizing the cash-strapped middle classes, was at odds with the wishes of many of his governors. Characteristically he said 'You do not deal with a famine by sending a few lucky children to lunch at the Ritz' (*Delusions*, 174). Second, in 1983 his wife published a frank book on the public schools, *A World Apart*, criticism of which served as vicarious criticism of Rae himself. Rae supported his wife's freedom to publish what she wanted, but some felt that his authority had been undermined. Eventually his chairman, the dean of Westminster, felt it was time for a change. Rae had had a long innings and in 1984 he was privately given two years to find himself a new job. He left Westminster in March 1986. One of his last acts was to appoint a Barbadian girl as head of school, shocking those he called 'the croakers' in the common room, though it was an appointment that proved an outstanding success.

After leaving Westminster Rae found no shortage of interesting opportunities. He was adopted as a parliamentary candidate by the Social Democratic Party, became a director of *The Observer* (1986–93), and was appointed director of the Laura Ashley Foundation (1986–9), set up to foster educational opportunities for those who had left school without qualifications. From 1989 to 1996 he was the first director of the Portman Group, a trade body that promoted responsible use of alcohol. He was also a member of the National Board for Crime Prevention (1993–5).

As an author Rae had an early success with *The Custard Boys* (1960), a sensitive story of evacuee children living out the war in a remote corner of the English countryside. The novel was filmed by Columbia as *Reach for Glory* (1962), in which Rae appeared in a cameo role, and for which he received a United Nations award. He wrote several other successful novels, initially for his own children, as well as books on the challenges facing British education, notably *The Public School Revolution* (1981) and *Too Little Too Late* (1989). In 2001 he published a biography of Sister Genevieve O'Farrell, principal of St Louise's, a comprehensive school for Catholic girls in west Belfast. His last major work was 'The agnostic's tale', a rigorous examination of his own religious doubts, which he completed in 2004 but which remained unpublished at his death.

John Rae was at the heart of the revolution that transformed private education in post-war Britain and he was the best-known public school headmaster of his day, combining exceptional leadership skills with a capacity to influence public life. He understood clearly how boarding schools would have to adapt to reflect changing social expectations and the demands of a generation of parents who were new to the independent school world. The process was sometimes painful and with his strong personality he divided opinion. Some felt he was the breath of fresh air desperately needed, especially on co-education; others that he was something of a Trojan horse, rarely tempering unpalatable truths with discretion—he once observed, for example, that the tendency for Anglican priests to experience qualms of conscience about private schools stemmed from the time they could no longer afford them. He was never a bland figure, nor was he the traditional 'safe pair of hands'. In this lay his individual strength. His willingness to follow his own instincts and avoid prevarication, together with his deep commitment to the welfare of all his pupils, gave him a special place in both the educational and social history of his times. His final years were clouded by the onset of cancer, which he faced with the same courage and realism that had characterized his professional career. He died at his home, 2S Cedar Lodge, Lythe Hill Park, Haslemere, Surrey, on 16 December 2006, and was survived by his wife and their six children. In 2009 Rae's diaries, *The Old Boys' Network*, were published, which gave an insight into the pressures faced by a late twentieth-century headmaster.

D. R. THORPE

Sources J. Rae, *Delusions of grandeur: a headmaster's life, 1966–1986* (1993) · J. Rae, *The old boys' network: a headmaster's diaries, 1972–1988* (2009) · *The Times* (19 Dec 2006) · *Daily Telegraph* (19 Dec 2006) · *The Guardian* (21 Dec 2006) · *The Independent* (25 Jan 2007) · *WW* (2006) · personal knowledge (2010) · private information (2010) · b. cert. · m. cert. · d. cert.

Archives FILM BFINA, current affairs footage · BFINA, documentary footage | SOUND BL NSA, current affairs recordings · BL NSA, documentary recordings

Likenesses Bassano, half-plate film negative, 1973, NPG [*see illus.*] · R. Stone, oils, Westminster School, London

Wealth at death £386,554: probate, 13 July 2007, *CGPLA Eng. & Wales*

Raitt, Alan William (1930–2006), French scholar, was born on 21 September 1930 at 18 Olympia Gardens, Morpeth, Northumberland, the son of William Raitt, schoolmaster, and his wife, Mary Ann, *née* Davison. He was educated at King Edward VI Grammar School in Morpeth, and in 1948 went on to read modern languages (French and German) at Magdalen College, Oxford, graduating with a first-class degree in 1951. While an undergraduate Raitt won the Heath Harrison travelling scholarship in two successive years, first in French and then in German, and after graduating took up a prestigious Zaharoff travelling scholarship which he used to spend a year in France in 1952–3. His tutor at Magdalen was the distinguished nineteenth-century French scholar Austin Gill, author of important books on Mallarmé, and later professor of French at Glasgow. Raitt remained at Magdalen and began doctoral research under Gill's supervision on the playwright, poet, and prose writer Auguste Villiers de l'Isle-Adam.

Raitt was awarded his DPhil in 1957, but was publishing seminal articles in journals while still a graduate student. The book based on his doctoral thesis appeared in French from the publisher José Corti in 1965: *Villiers de l'Isle-Adam et le mouvement symboliste*. It quickly became what the French call an *ouvrage de référence*, an essential work in its field, but it also restored to serious critical attention an author whose significance and intrinsic interest had never been so fully explored. Also in 1965 Raitt published an important introduction to nineteenth-century French literature, *Life and Letters in France: The Nineteenth Century* (part of a series edited by Gill). Between them these two books, written while he was still in his early thirties, reveal the qualities that were to define Raitt's scholarship: on the one hand patient, precise, and exhaustive primary research, and on the other an ability to contextualize and communicate large swathes of a period's literature in stimulating but never reductive ways. His command of French nineteenth-century literature was unequalled, but he also knew a great deal about French art, music, and historical thought. A knowledge of German literature and culture ensured that he was able to approach literature from comparative and interdisciplinary angles too. Raitt's range was reflected in the work of the graduate students who worked under his guidance on subjects as diverse as avant-garde theatre, Swinburne and French literature, Wagnerism in France, and Flaubert and classicism.

Raitt was made a fellow by examination at Magdalen in 1953, and in 1955 became fellow and lecturer in French at Exeter College, Oxford. He remained there until 1966, when he returned to Magdalen to succeed Gill as fellow in French. In 1979 he was made reader, and in 1992, the same year he was made a fellow of the British Academy, he was given a personal chair. Though a prolific publisher and busy tutor, he was also a believer in contributing to collegiate and university work. At Exeter he was sub-rector for three years, and at Magdalen he was senior tutor (1974–7) and vice-president (1983–5). He was also chairman of the university's modern languages committee between 1969 and 1987. An active member of the Society for French Studies, he was the general editor of the journal *French Studies* between 1987 and 1997. As well as fellowships of the Royal Society of Literature (1971) and the British Academy, he won ample recognition in France for his services to French culture: in 1987 he received the grand prix du rayonnement de la langue française, and in 1995 was made a commander of the Ordre des Palmes Académiques.

Though Raitt remained at Oxford throughout his professional life, he was by no means confined to it. He held visiting professorships at the Sorbonne, the University of Georgia, Vanderbilt University, and the University of the South (Sewanee), and was frequently called upon to examine doctoral candidates or advise on research in universities across the world. Villiers remained a central focus of his research, and he published an English-language biography of Villiers in 1981 with Oxford University Press, and *Villiers de l'Isle-Adam: exorciste du réel* with Corti in 1987. In 1986, along with his friend the French scholar Pierre-Georges Castex, he produced the two-volume Pléiade edition of Villiers's *Oeuvres complètes*, a magisterial work of collaborative scholarly editing. Raitt followed this in 1993 with an edition of Villiers's novel *L'Ève future* for Gallimard. Among Raitt's other books were the Imprimerie Nationale edition of Flaubert's *Éducation sentimentale* (1979), a literary biography of Prosper Mérimée (1970), and a study of Flaubert's *Trois contes* (1991). After his retirement from Magdalen in 1997 he founded and edited a prestigious scholarly series for the publisher Peter Lang, Romanticism and After in France / Le romantisme et après en France. It was for this series that he wrote a further four books on Flaubert, culminating in his last book, a study of Flaubert's first (1845) *Éducation sentimentale*, the novel he left to one side before returning to it and transforming it into the *Éducation sentimentale* we know. *Flaubert's First Novel* was published posthumously in 2009.

Raitt taught and supervised generations of students and researchers, and his former pupils went on to distinguished careers in universities across the world. In 1998 Oxford University Press published a Festschrift in his honour, *The Process of Art*, with contributions by colleagues and former students, including the novelist Julian Barnes, who had studied Flaubert with Raitt and who remained in touch with his former tutor. For all his distinction, Raitt was a strict meritocrat, an approachable, unfussy man, who valued modesty, sincerity, and precision, not just in academic life but outside it. His passion for sport was matched by deep knowledge, and he held a season ticket to Oxford United Football Club, whose rosette had pride of place on his mantelpiece alongside his various medals, certificates, and embossed invitations. He rarely missed a home match, and his students knew better than to phone him during major sporting tournaments. Once put in charge of entertaining an important Soviet academician when Oxford United were due to play a major game, Raitt resolved the dilemma of clashing priorities by taking the visitor—along with his KGB minder—to the match. Aside from sport, Raitt was an accomplished pianist and loved music. Another area in which he could impress with wide knowledge and discriminating taste was the detective novel. His preference was for the harder-boiled examples of the genre, and students in his rooms in Magdalen (which had also been Gill's) might find their attention drawn by a bookcase in the corner full of well-thumbed thrillers and French *polars*. Raitt was typically generous about lending them to students he felt were working too hard or in need of diversion, and on one occasion he lent a student with an interest in American modernism a novel by Elmore Leonard in which Ezra Pound featured. The conjunction of knowledge and pleasure was characteristic of Raitt.

Raitt married another French scholar, Janet Suzanne Taylor (*d.* 2002), seven years his junior, on 30 July 1959. She was the daughter of Percy Strawson Taylor, chief education officer for Reading borough council. They had two daughters, Claire and Suzanne. They divorced in 1971 and on 16 December 1974 Raitt married Lia Noémia Rodrigues Correia, a Portuguese scholar two years his junior, and daughter of Vergílio Lopes Correia, naval officer. There were no children of the second marriage. Raitt died in Parede, Portugal, on 2 September 2006, and was survived by his wife, Lia, and the two daughters of his first marriage. PATRICK MCGUINNESS

Sources *The Independent* (6 Sept 2006) • *The Times* (21 Sept 2006) • *Oxford Mail* (28 Sept 2006) • *The Guardian* (5 Oct 2006) • M. Freeman, *French Studies*, 61/1 (Jan 2007), 133–5 • *WW* (2006) • personal knowledge (2010) • private information (2010) • b. cert. • m. certs.
Likenesses obituary photographs
Wealth at death £297,225: probate, 4 Jan 2007, *CGPLA Eng. & Wales*

Randle, Sir Philip John (1926–2006), biochemist, was born on 16 July 1926 at 99 Queen's Road, Nuneaton, Warwickshire, the son of Alfred John Randle (*d.* 1952), master baker, and his wife, Nora Annie, *née* Smith (*d.* 1968), music teacher. He attended King Edward VI Grammar School, Nuneaton, and went on to read natural sciences at Sidney Sussex College, Cambridge. He obtained a first-class degree in biochemistry in 1947 and then moved to University College Hospital medical school, London, where he completed his medical studies. On 27 September 1952, at the parish church in Nuneaton, he married Elizabeth Ann Harrison (*d.* 2004), a 21-year-old library assistant, and daughter of Dennis Arthur Harrison, local government officer. They had three daughters and one son.

After qualifying in medicine Randle returned to Cambridge to carry out post-graduate research on insulin under the supervision of Frank Young. He was awarded his PhD in 1955 for a thesis entitled 'Studies on the metabolic action of insulin'. This immediately led to his appointment as lecturer in biochemistry at the University of Cambridge, where in 1957 he was also appointed a fellow and director of medical studies at Trinity Hall. He established a research group in a basement laboratory in the Dunn School of Biochemistry in Tennis Court Road. The open drainage system for all the laboratory sinks in the building ran through Randle's laboratory, so that when, as often happened in those days, flammable organic solvents were poured down a sink somewhere in the building the Randle researchers had to beat a hasty retreat—not least because Randle would almost certainly be smoking his pipe.

In Cambridge Randle continued his studies of various aspects of insulin action and the control of metabolism, especially in muscle. These resulted in a series of highly influential papers published in collaboration with an outstanding group of talented young researchers, including Eric Newsholme, Nick Hales, Peter Garland, and Hal Coore. The papers focused on two distinct aspects of the control of mammalian fuel metabolism, both relevant to insulin-dependent diabetes. The first of these, the mechanisms involved in fuel selection by mammalian tissues,

Sir Philip John Randle (1926–2006), by Godfrey Argent Studio, 1983

was encapsulated in the 'glucose–fatty acid cycle' hypothesis (reported in *The Lancet* in 1963) often subsequently referred to as the Randle cycle; the second aspect, the way in which insulin-producing pancreatic β-cells respond appropriately to changes in blood glucose concentration, became known as the 'substrate-site hypothesis'. Validation of these two models and elucidation of the underlying biochemical mechanisms led to decades of research, not only by Randle and his colleagues but also by many other workers in diabetes.

The glucose–fatty acid cycle was based on a series of experiments showing that cardiac and skeletal muscle, when provided with both fatty acids and glucose as potential fuels, preferentially oxidized the fatty acids. This increased supply of fatty acids to muscle could, by diminishing glucose uptake, lead to hyperglycaemia and thereby be involved in the insulin resistance associated with type-2 diabetes and obesity. The fundamental importance of the glucose–fatty acid cycle in the normal physiology of muscle and other tissues soon became widely accepted.

The substrate-site hypothesis for the control of insulin secretion emerged from two ground-breaking advances by the Randle group. The first of these was the development, with Nick Hales, of the radio-immunoassay for insulin (reported in the *Biochemical Journal* in 1963), which permitted accurate and precise measurement of the concentration of insulin in biological fluids. The second was the introduction, with Hal Coore, of an *in vitro* technique for studying the control of insulin release from isolated pieces of rabbit pancreas (reported in the *Biochemical Journal* in 1964). Based on the specificity of the secretory response to various sugars and metabolic inhibitors, the novel hypothesis was proposed that rather than binding to some hypothetical cellular receptor, as had been supposed, glucose actually triggered insulin secretion through some product(s) of the metabolism of the sugar within the β-cell. At the time this hypothesis was put forward it was not possible to test it directly since the β-cells made up only a small part (roughly 1 per cent) of the pancreatic mass. However, when methods became available to separate islets of Langerhans (containing predominantly β-cells) from the rest of the pancreas, evidence to support the substrate-site hypothesis was soon forthcoming from studies, published from 1970 onwards, with Steve Ashcroft in the Randle laboratory. Many decades of work were required to elucidate the biochemical mechanisms involved, but the essential role of β-cell glucose metabolism in regulation of insulin secretion was firmly established.

In 1964 Randle was appointed to the newly established chair of biochemistry at the University of Bristol. This was a period of expansion in British universities, but even in that context the rapid development of the department of biochemistry under Randle's leadership was remarkable. Bristol had had medical, veterinary, and dentistry schools for some time, but, although there were a few biochemists working in the departments of physiology, biology, and chemistry, there was no biochemistry department. Within seven years the new department of biochemistry under Randle had become one of the strongest in the country, both for research and for teaching. There were several reasons for this achievement. In the first place Randle made a series of inspired appointments over the entire field of biochemistry including mitochondriology, protein structure, molecular enzymology, and mammalian metabolism. Further, he was highly successful in acquiring sufficient space and funding for the new department from the university. Needless to say his plans did not always meet with whole-hearted support from entrenched interests in existing departments. However, Randle's physical presence (he was well over six feet in height), intellect, and booming voice (accompanied by copious pipe smoke) ensured that his expansionist plans were fulfilled at the critical stage in the development of the department.

The rapidly growing Bristol department of biochemistry was an exciting place to work in during the twelve years that Randle headed it. His influence on the many research students he personally supervised there was immense. His intellectual rigour, his ability to identify and focus upon the essential aspects of important biochemical problems, and his quite remarkable memory for facts, left an indelible impression on all those who worked with him. The young department had a happy atmosphere and a flourishing social life. On Sunday mornings Randle and many of the department were often to be found at the then brand-new university swimming pool. This could occasionally prove hazardous for those who engaged in conversation with Randle while in the pool, since the conversation would usually take place in a part of the pool where he could comfortably stand but most others were required to swim round and round to avoid drowning.

Shortly after moving to Bristol, Randle was invited to give the British Diabetic Association's Banting lecture (1965), and was the first recipient of the prestigious Minkowski prize of the European Association for the Study of Diabetes (1966), in connection with which he wrote an important article, 'Carbohydrate metabolism and lipid storage and breakdown in diabetes', published in *Diabetologia* the same year. In 1975 he moved to Oxford to found another new department, the Nuffield department of clinical biochemistry. Of his two most long-standing associates, Dick Denton remained in Bristol to continue work on insulin action in adipose and other tissues, while Steve Ashcroft moved with Randle to Oxford to pursue further studies on the substrate-site hypothesis for the control of insulin secretion. In contrast to the large Bristol department, the Nuffield department remained small and highly focused on diabetes-related research, for which it gained an international reputation. Randle continued his own active laboratory research, mainly on the regulation of pyruvate dehydrogenase, a key regulatory enzyme in adipose tissue and muscle metabolism.

In addition to his university activities Randle took on many other tasks. He was chairman of a large number of research committees and boards for the British Diabetic Association, the Medical Research Council, and the British Heart Foundation; he played a large part in the founding of the European Association for the Study of Diabetes and served as its president from 1977 to 1980; he also was president of the Biochemical Society (1995–2000) and vice-president of the Royal Society (1988–9), of which he was made a fellow in 1983. In the early 1980s he took on an advisory role to the government on aspects of food policy, chairing the influential food policy panel on diet and cardiovascular disease (1981–4). This panel developed recommendations, published in 1984, on lowering intake of unsaturated fats, simple sugars, and salt—advice that remained highly relevant in subsequent years, when clinical obesity was on the increase. His work in all these spheres led to numerous further honours. He gave the Humphry Davy Rolleston lecture of the Royal College of Physicians in 1983, published in the college's journal the following year, was knighted in 1975, and became a founder fellow of the Academy of Medical Science in 1998.

Randle's physical and intellectual stature made him a formidable opponent in scientific debate and he was held in some considerable awe by his colleagues. Nevertheless, beneath a somewhat forbidding exterior he was a warm and generous man who gave great encouragement to those under his wing. He was capable of great kindness and provided real help to his associates if they were in need. Throughout his life he took great pleasure in his family, especially his grandchildren, with whom he spent many happy holidays. He loved opera and the theatre, eating out, and watching television detective series such as *Inspector Morse*. He was always a great traveller and made many trips with his wife, Elizabeth, usually when he was invited to give a keynote speech at a meeting in faraway, and often exotic, surroundings.

Randle retired from his Oxford post in 1993. The major international scientific meeting held in his honour that year in Oxford was eloquent testimony to the affection and esteem in which he was regarded throughout the world. His death on 26 September 2006 in Oxford, from a sudden massive intracerebral haemorrhage, marked the end of an era in British diabetes research. He left behind, however, an enormous legacy, both in the Bristol department of biochemistry, which continued to go from strength to strength, and in a worldwide network of researchers whose careers had been substantially enriched by time spent under his supervision. A permanent collection of his published work and other memorabilia was established at the Oxford Centre for Diabetes and Metabolism. He was survived by two daughters, Rosalind and Sally; his son Peter had died in 1971 while still a teenager, and his daughter Susan died in 2005.

STEPHEN J. H. ASHCROFT and RICHARD M. DENTON

Sources P. J. Randle, 'Regulatory interactions between lipids and carbohydrates: the glucose fatty acid cycle after 35 years', *Diabetes / Metabolism Reviews*, 14 (1998), 263–8 · *Daily Telegraph* (10 Oct 2006) · *The Times* (7 Nov 2006) · *The Lancet*, 368 (11 Nov 2006), 1644 · *The Independent* (2 Dec 2006) · S. Ashcroft and R. Denton, *The Biochemist* (Dec 2006), 60–61 · R. M. Denton and S. J. Ashcroft, 'A tribute to the life and work of Philip Randle', *Diabetologia*, 50 (2007), 1359–61 · M. C. Sugden, 'In appreciation of Sir Philip Randle: the glucose–fatty acid cycle', *British Journal of Nutrition* (2007), 97, 809–13 · Munk, *Roll* [www.rcplondon.ac.uk/heritage/munks-roll] · www.bristol.ac.uk/news/2006/5164.html, 20 Jan 2009 · Burke, *Peerage* · *WW* (2006) · personal knowledge (2010) · private information (2010) · b. cert. · m. cert. · d. cert.

Archives CUL, Peter Mitchell MSS

Likenesses Godfrey Argent Studio, photograph, 1983, RS [*see illus.*]

Wealth at death £884,944: probate, 21 Feb 2007, *CGPLA Eng. & Wales*

Rao, Raja (**1908–2006**), novelist, was born on 8 November 1908 in the small town of Hassan, in the princely state of Mysore, India. His mother Gauramma died when he was only four years old. Throughout much of his later writing he placed women on a platonic level of abstract purity, as though he was searching for this lost and idealized parent. He was mainly brought up by his Brahman but Anglicized schoolmaster father, H. V. Krishnaswamy (*d.* 1940), though it was more from his paternal grandfather that he received his spiritual instruction. He was encouraged to think independently and philosophically, outside the confines of orthodox Hinduism. Indeed, he was sent for his education to the Madrasa-i-Aliya, a famous Muslim school in Hyderabad. From there he went in 1925 to the Aligarh Muslim University in north India, progressing two years later to Nizam's College in Hyderabad, from where he graduated BA in English and history. In 1929 the government of Hyderabad awarded him its Asiatic scholarship for study abroad. He went to the University of Montpellier in France in order to develop the keen interest in French literature and language which he had first shown in Aligarh.

In 1931 Rao began writing professionally. He chose to do so in his mother tongue, Kannada, contributing to the periodical *Jaya Karnataka*. However, a commitment to undertake research at the Sorbonne on Indian influences in Irish drama meant that he was increasingly absorbed in French and English. Although there were many Kannada resonances in Rao's work, he subsequently only rarely used the language for creative purposes. In 1933 his first stories appeared, in French. He was invited to join the editorial board of a distinguished literary review, *Mercure de France*, on which he remained for four years. However, a return visit to India in 1933 inclined him increasingly to use English as his language of expression, because he wanted initially to write about his own country and he felt that it would be the more appropriate language in which to do this.

Rao's first full-length work, *Kanthapura* (1938), written in France, became one of the foundation stones of the newly named Indo-Anglian fiction that was emerging at the time. Critics immediately placed him alongside Mulk Raj Anand and R. K. Narayan in a triumvirate of literary pioneers. Though none of them much cared to be linked in this way, it was their fate to be so conjoined thereafter. There were two reasons for this. While all three novelists wrote in English, they did so in forms of the language that were heavily dependent on the rhythms, euphony, and metaphors of their indigenous tongues. Second, they enfranchised the poor as legitimate subject matter for fiction. *Kanthapura* has a village setting and in the course of it Rao examined contemporary Gandhian thought (though not the character of Gandhi himself) as a continuance of ancient spiritual truths to be found in the puranas. The manner of the telling recalled the oral tradition with which Rao had grown up in Hassan.

On his return to India in 1939 Rao lived for short periods, but with some frequency, in ashrams near Madras, imbibing the spiritual ambience of such places. It was clear by now that he was dedicating his life and art to the pursuit of truth and learning. Though the stories he wrote at this time often had rural settings, they became increasingly conjectural. In 1947 he published a collection of short stories, *The Cow and the Barricades*, in which the title itself united his current interests in religion (the cow being the sacred mother of India) and politics (the barricades of revolutionary protest). The presence of Gandhi imbued these stories, sometimes explicitly in the person of the mahatma, and there is no doubt that Rao associated himself with the rising nationalism of the anti-colonial movement.

Then, however, Rao's life changed direction. He had married a French schoolteacher, Camille Mouly, two years after his arrival in France in 1929; they were divorced in 1939, and by the time he returned to France in 1948, leaving India in the year of its independence, he regarded himself as a free agent. The relationships depicted in his next major work, *The Serpent and the Rope* (1960), were based on those he himself experienced in the 1950s, when he travelled widely in Europe, especially in France, and made his first visits to the United States, where he was eventually to settle. He never again lived permanently in India, though he continued to stay there almost annually, sometimes in the company of a distinguished foreigner. In 1958, for example, he travelled widely in the subcontinent in the company of the French writer André Malraux.

The Serpent and the Rope is the second of the books by which Rao's claim to greatness will always be measured. For some its exploration of themes of royalty, the feminine principle, religious heresy, the infusion of Indian philosophy in European civilization, and the pursuit of perfection, are inchoate or overstated, but for others there has simply been no other modern novel as comprehensive in its philosophical ambition. Its central character, Rama, is on a pilgrimage to find purity, in art, in metaphysics, and in his own personal development, but his quest is unfulfilled because Rao felt that the only aim human beings can set themselves in their lives is to search for what must by definition be unattainable.

In the early 1960s Rao moved to the United States, where he lived a quiet and frugal life. He was based mainly at the University of Texas at Austin, where from 1966 to 1983 he taught Indian religion and philosophy. In 1965 he married Katherine Jones, an actress, and, after a divorce, he married another American, Susan Vaught, in 1986. In his later years he was a prolific writer. Two novellas, *The Cat and Shakespeare* (1965) and *Comrade Kirillov* (1976), several collections of short stories, a biography of Gandhi entitled *The Great Indian Way* (1998), and many essays were published. The longest work of his career, *The Chessmaster and his Moves*, came out in 1988, coinciding with his winning the prestigious Neustadt international prize for literature. At the time of his death in Austin on 8 July 2006 he was very frail and no longer travelling, but he left behind a number of lengthy typescripts that scholars who have had access to them consider to be among his most important work. He was survived by his wife, Susan, and two sons.

Raj Rao, though honoured internationally, did not play a big part in public or literary affairs. He was a fastidious and private person who both liked to cultivate an air of enigma and was genuinely drawn to the silence and serenity of meditation. He was the most metaphysical of the generation of Indian novelists that emerged in the 1930s and secured for the subcontinent a place among the great literatures of the English language. Having come from the Brahman caste he maintained a patrician demeanour all his life, despite the fact that his first novel, *Kanthapura*, regarded by some as his masterpiece, was rural in setting and popular in its sympathies. Apart from *Kanthapura*, he never had a large readership, but there were many people who none the less regarded him as the greatest of twentieth-century Indian writers, not only among those who wrote in English. ALASTAIR NIVEN

Sources C. D. Narasimhaiah, *Raja Rao* (1973) · R. Rao, *The meaning of India* (1996) · M. Paranjape, ed., *The best of Raja Rao* (1998) · *The Guardian* (17 July 2006) · *The Times* (18 July 2006) · *Daily Telegraph* (18 July 2006) · *The Independent* (19 July 2006) · www.therajaraoendowment.org, 13 Aug 2009 · personal knowledge (2010) · private information (2010)
Archives Raja Rao Memorial Literary Foundation, Austin, Texas
Likenesses photograph, 1961, Camera Press, London · obituary photographs · portraits, repro. in www.therajaraoendowment.org

Ratcliffe, Derek Almey (1929–2005), ecologist and conservationist, was born on 9 July 1929 at 80 Crouch Hill, Islington, London, the only son of Frank Bernard Ratcliffe, a solo organist and cinema pianist, and his partner, Kathleen Marie Almey, who later taught English and French. His first experiences with nature were on his maternal grandfather's Jarvis Farm, south of Cromer, Norfolk, where he collected butterflies and moths, and later common birds' eggs. Nine years later his family moved to Carlisle, where he developed a passion for the wildlife of the Lake District and of the uplands beyond in south Scotland and the Pennines. He joined Carlisle's active Natural History Society, where he came under the tutelage of Ernest Blezard, the curator of natural history at Tullie House Museum. His first step on the literary ladder was a school essay on peregrines and ravens, for which he won a prize at Carlisle grammar school. Almost six decades later he published the New Naturalist book *Lakeland: the Wildlife of Cumbria* (2002), which contained a rich seam of original observations on the nature of that popular region.

In 1947 Ratcliffe won a city corporation scholarship to study zoology at Sheffield University. Bored by dull practicals and lectures, he switched to botany and found inspiration in the teaching of Roy Clapham and colleagues. He graduated in 1950 with first-class honours in botany, and won a Nature Conservancy studentship at the University College of North Wales, Bangor. There he studied mountain vegetation under the supervision of Paul Richards, completing his PhD in 1953. There followed a year's national service in the Royal Army Education Corps at Catterick. In 1956 he was appointed scientific officer in the Nature Conservancy in Edinburgh, where he worked on the Scottish Highlands Vegetation Survey, and was promoted to senior scientific officer in 1958. With Donald McVean he made a pioneering description and classification of upland vegetation in the Scottish highlands, published in *Plant Communities of the Scottish Highlands* (1962). Many of the areas he visited had not been formally studied before, and some of the fieldwork entailed bicycle and foot journeys of more than thirty miles in successive days. By the late 1950s he was one of the best-travelled naturalists in the UK, with a keen eye for nesting birds and rare plants.

During 1961–2, on behalf of the British Trust for Ornithology, Ratcliffe led the first national survey of peregrine falcons. The Home Office, which wanted facts and figures to address concerns from pigeon fanciers alleging that peregrines were ruining their sport, had instigated this. The upshot of the survey was a milestone in environmental science: Ratcliffe found that numbers of peregrines were in decline, and in some parts of Britain they had ceased to breed. The cause of the decline was persistent

Derek Almey Ratcliffe (1929–2005), by Des Thompson, 1989

pesticides, notably DDT, which caused eggshell thinning and catastrophic breeding failure. Ratcliffe published a classic paper on eggshell thinning in the journal *Nature* in 1967, and a more detailed paper in the *Journal of Applied Ecology* in 1970, both of which were among the most frequently cited ornithological scientific publications.

Ratcliffe had transferred to the Nature Conservancy's Monks Wood experimental station in 1963, where he continued his work on peregrines and other raptors, and in 1966 he was promoted to principal scientific officer. A year later he was appointed scientific assessor to the Nature Conservancy's nature conservation review, which developed into a major inventory of Britain's best sites for wildlife and habitats. At the heart of this work was the exposition of a philosophy for nature conservation founded on the use of such concepts as 'diversity', 'fragility', and 'naturalness', which enabled scientists systematically to compare sites and even regions. This became, and remained, the cornerstone of nature conservation, culminating in the publication of the two-volume book edited by Ratcliffe, *A Nature Conservation Review* (1977). In 1970 Ratcliffe had been appointed deputy director (scientific) of the Nature Conservancy, based at Belgrave Square, London, and on new year's day 1974 he became chief scientist of the newly established Nature Conservancy Council. During the late 1970s and 1980s, until his retirement in 1989, Ratcliffe effectively led the science base of the statutory nature conservation movement, providing leadership for the designation of hundreds of sites of special scientific interest (SSSIs) and the opposition to the large-scale afforestation of upland areas in the 1980s. On 22 March 1978 he married (Marie) Jeannette Chan-Mo, a 33-year-old personal secretary and daughter of the late Emmanuel Chan-Mo, clerk.

During six decades, from his early encounters with wildlife through to difficult and sometimes strained relations with politicians and senior civil servants, Ratcliffe earned himself the status, according to the *Sunday Times*, of one of the people who had most influenced the twentieth century. His publications were remarkable for the breadth of subjects in which he had expert knowledge. He published two classic bird monographs, *The Peregrine Falcon* (1980, revised in 1993) and *The Raven* (1997), and a highly original book, *Bird Life of Mountain and Upland* (1990). He enjoyed writing about his travels and experiences, and captured these first in *Highland Flora* (1977), later in his memoir of early years in the field, *In Search of Nature* (2000), and finally in *Galloway and the Borders* (2007), published after his death. He also wrote many scientific papers, chapters in books, and articles, which all had the hallmark of first-hand observation, clarity, clear analysis, and fluent writing. He was an outstanding photographer, with some of his pictures becoming conservation icons, such as the wave of conifers breaking over the uplands of Kirkcudbrightshire, Rannoch Moor with its relict pine stumps exposed, and the great beeches of the New Forest. He received several awards, including the degree of DSc from Sheffield University (1970), an honorary doctorate from Lancaster University (1991), and in 1983 appointment to the order of the Golden Ark, of the Netherlands, for his 'pioneering work on the effects of pesticides on birds of prey, and his major contribution to the science of nature conservation'.

Ratcliffe was a shy, modest, determined, scholarly, and kindly man, who corresponded by hand with hundreds of friends and associates. In retirement, he remained active in conservation, and developed a keen interest in the wildlife of northern Scandinavia, spending six to eight weeks in a dormobile each spring with his wife, Jeannette, observing wild nature; this culminated in the publication of *Lapland: a Natural History* (2005). He died in his sleep, on 23 May 2005, at the Pembroke Caravan Park near Leeming Bar, Northallerton; he had just set out from Cambridge on his fifteenth annual expedition to Fennoscandia. The cause of death was heart failure. He was survived by his wife.

Des Thompson

Sources D. Ratcliffe, *In search of nature* (2000) • *The Independent* (26 May 2005) • *Daily Telegraph* (27 May 2005) • *The Times* (28 May 2005) • *The Guardian* (31 May 2005) • D. Ratcliffe, foreword, *Galloway and the borders* (2007) • personal knowledge (2009) • private information (2009) • b. cert. • m. cert. • d. cert.
Archives Royal Botanical Gardens, Edinburgh, botanical notes
Likenesses photograph, 1952, repro. in *In search of nature* • D. Thompson, photograph, 1989, Joint Nature Conservation Committee, Peterborough [*see illus.*] • obituary photographs
Wealth at death under £24,000: probate, 3 Nov 2005, *CGPLA Eng. & Wales*

Rawlinson, Peter Anthony Grayson, Baron Rawlinson of Ewell (**1919–2006**), barrister and politician, was born on 26 June 1919 at 6 Beresford Road, Oxton, Birkenhead, Cheshire, the younger son of Lieutenant-Colonel Arthur Richard (Dick) Rawlinson (1894–1984) and his wife, Ailsa Margaret Harrington, *née* Grayson, daughter of Sir Henry Grayson, Conservative MP for Birkenhead from 1918 to 1922. His father, who had served in military intelligence during the First World War, was working as a master ship repairer at the time of Rawlinson's birth; later he became an author and playwright for theatre, film, radio, and television, and served as deputy director of military intelligence during the Second World War.

Rawlinson, whose childhood was spent in Sussex, was educated at Downside School in Somerset, which confirmed his lifelong Catholic faith, and whence he won an exhibition to Christ's College, Cambridge. He was there reading law (and co-starring with Jimmy Edwards in the Footlights) when the Second World War broke out in 1939. Straightaway—already tall and strikingly handsome—he was commissioned in the Irish Guards, with whom he served throughout the war, while continuing his legal studies, and publishing *War Poems and Poetry Today* (1943). Wounded in battle and mentioned in dispatches in north Africa, he was demobilized in 1946 with the rank of major, and in the same year called to the bar by the Inner Temple. (His elder brother, Michael, did not survive the war, having been killed in action in 1941 while serving as a pilot officer in the RAF.) On 29 June 1940, Rawlinson had married his first wife, Annie Adelaide Genevieve (otherwise Haidee McMorrough) Kavanagh (1917/18–1982), daughter of Jeremiah Michael Kavanagh, wholesale merchant of Dublin; they had three daughters. This marriage was annulled and on 27 December 1954 he married his cousin, the sensationally beautiful Elaine Angela Dominguez (*b.* 1935), daughter of Vincent Luis Dominguez, of Newport, Rhode Island, with whom he had two sons and a daughter.

That second, lifelong marriage took place eight years after the start, in the chambers of that most distinguished barrister Walter Monckton, of Rawlinson's own career at the bar. This was always his first love, despite his fascination with politics from university days. As a powerful, but always balanced, advocate, he quickly built up a good practice, initially on the criminal side, with several headline-hitting cases: for example the defence of the so-called towpath murderer, Alfred Whiteway, and later Ruth Ellis, the last woman to be hanged in Britain. Less visibly he was, on Saturday nights, the duty libel lawyer at the *Sunday Express*.

Rawlinson was able too to find the time to advance his political career. In the general election of 1951 he cut his teeth by contesting the Labour stronghold of Hackney South. Four years later, however, in the rock-solid Conservative seat of Epsom he 'inherited' a majority of 20,000 from the outgoing MP, David Maxwell-Fyfe, on the latter's appointment as lord chancellor. Rawlinson was to retain this seat (renamed Epsom and Ewell in 1974) until his acceptance of a life peerage in 1978. His political views gradually moderated during that time. Initially he spoke in defence of capital punishment and against reform of divorce, abortion, and homosexual law. But by the time he took silk in 1959 he spoke, for example, on the Wolfenden report (on homosexual law reform) with compassion and common sense, and was serving on the council of Justice and as a trustee of Amnesty International. He came out too in support of the accused (including Nelson Mandela) in the 1958–61 treason trial in apartheid South Africa.

About the same time Rawlinson was fortunate enough to join the chambers of the eminent QC Gerald Gardiner, a future Labour lord chancellor. From this relationship Rawlinson was able to learn a good deal, and to inherit some important clients as well. His reputation, as advocate and parliamentarian alike, deservedly continued to grow. So it was no surprise when, in June 1962, as a consequence of the cabinet upheaval known as 'the night of the long knives', Rawlinson was invited by the prime minister, Harold Macmillan, to fill the vacancy of solicitor-general. He was given the customary knighthood on appointment. He quite soon found himself one of the five ministers who had to struggle with the crisis arising from the Profumo scandal (when the secretary of state for war, John Profumo, had to acknowledge that he had lied to parliament about his affair with a prostitute). Because it was (quite wrongly) thought that he might have connived in the falsehood Rawlinson gallantly offered his resignation—only for it to be refused, so that when Macmillan was replaced as prime minister by Sir Alec Douglas-Home in October 1963 he remained in office as solicitor-general.

Rawlinson's term as solicitor-general came to an end a year later, when Labour narrowly won the general election of 1964, installing Gerald Gardiner as lord chancellor and thus opening the way for Rawlinson to take Gardiner's place as head of his chambers. During the years of opposition that followed Rawlinson's practice resumed its strong growth. By 1968 he was back in place as the law spokesman in Edward Heath's shadow cabinet. And, with the Conservative electoral victory of 1970, he became attorney-general for the next four years. For those who worked with him it was a great privilege—and real pleasure—to observe him tackling the job with his customary zeal, while always managing to give the impression that it was all great fun. He insisted, for example, on leading for the crown in more criminal trials than any of his predecessors had done, on every circuit but the Welsh. These included not only the really notable cases but also many of the charges against IRA terrorists, particularly after the Aldershot and London bomb explosions. He was a tough prosecutor but, as defence counsel were quick to testify, fair to the point of magnanimity. Even in retrospect the diversity of the caseload he had to handle—before European and international courts of justice as well as British—looks daunting. It included the Icelandic fisheries dispute; Britain's duty to accept Asian refugees from Uganda; the possible repudiation of the Concorde contract; the consequences of the collapse of Rolls-Royce; the deportation of the West German student leader Rudi Dutschke; and the prosecution—or not—of the Palestine Liberation Organization terrorist Leila Khaled, while several airliners were being held hostage for her release. Rawlinson came to face an even graver challenge in March 1972, with the establishment of direct rule in Ulster, for the English (Roman Catholic) attorney-general thus became Northern Ireland's attorney-general as well, and so deeply immersed in Irish affairs.

Following the defeat of the Heath government in the general election of February 1974 Rawlinson and his party were in the political wilderness for five years. When, in

1979, the Conservatives returned to power under Margaret Thatcher, it was expected in many quarters that he might become Britain's first Roman Catholic lord chancellor since Sir Thomas More. A bill had been introduced, by none other than Lord Hailsham in 1974, to make this a lawful possibility. But it was not to be. Thatcher, with whom Rawlinson had never really been in tune, turned again to Hailsham himself—and the office of lord chancellor was to be the only important legal office that Rawlinson never held.

Rawlinson nevertheless appeared quite undismayed, for at least two reasons. First, because he genuinely had no overriding political ambition. The bar always had been his first, and truest, love. And so it remained, through eight more years of immensely busy practice, on behalf of his profession as much as himself: more than ninety major cases in the law reports, leader of the western circuit from 1975 to 1982, chairman of the bar council and the senate in 1975–6, treasurer of the Inner Temple in 1984, and president of the senate of inns of court and the bar in 1986–7. All the service he gave in those capacities, and others, was of immense value in steering the bar, indeed the profession as a whole, into a modern age. In every one of those roles he displayed real political skill—the ability to secure necessary change without conflict. That is why so many believed that it was the nation's great loss that he never did sit on the woolsack. Even so, and although he never thought of himself as such, he was for a generation of younger barristers an immensely kind mentor, and a perfect role model. This was recognized by the Inner Temple's establishment in his honour of the Peter Rawlinson memorial prize for advocacy.

Rawlinson's second reason for returning to the bar matters perhaps even more than the first. He had cause to measure the impact of political life on his wife and family: the life of perpetual tension, constant separations, of police guards, bomb scares, and actual attacks, all summed up in the title of his autobiography, *A Price too High* (1989). And, given his self-liberation, he was able to rejoin not just his family but the rest of the human race, and thus to blossom in many different ways. He was the author of seven well-reviewed novels, as well as two more serious books, about Sir Thomas More (1978) and the Jesuits (1990). He turned out too to be a truly talented artist, having been equipped—surprisingly by his second wife, Elaine, very early in their marriage—with a seaside anti-boredom kit of canvases, oils, and brushes. He was truly a man for all seasons.

Following his elevation to the House of Lords in 1978, as Baron Rawlinson of Ewell, Rawlinson continued to contribute incisively to the political life of the nation, perhaps most notably in 1993 when he supported John Major over ratification of the Maastricht treaty and criticized those Conservatives who sought to weaken Britain's position in Europe. He lived latterly in an apartment in Wardour Castle, near Tisbury, Wiltshire, and died on 28 June 2006 while on holiday near Avignon in France. He was buried in Wardour cemetery following a funeral service at Wardour Castle on 7 July, and a memorial service was held in the Guards' Chapel, Wellington Barracks, London, on 4 October. He was survived by his wife, Elaine, and by five children, one daughter from his first marriage having predeceased him. GEOFFREY HOWE

Sources P. Rawlinson, *A price too high: an autobiography* (1989) · *Daily Telegraph* (29 June 2006) · *The Times* (30 June 2006) · *The Guardian* (30 June 2006) · *The Independent* (30 June 2006) · Burke, *Peerage* · *WW* (2006) · personal knowledge (2010) · private information (2010) · b. cert. · m. cert.

Likenesses photographs, 1951–70, Hult. Arch., London · Elliott & Fry, photographs, 1962, NPG · Bassano, photographs, 1970, NPG · photographs, 1970–94, Photoshot, London · obituary photographs

Wealth at death £2,059,763: probate, 4 Sept 2006, *CGPLA Eng. & Wales*

Raymond, Paul [*real name* Geoffrey Anthony Quinn] (**1925–2008**), theatrical impresario, publisher, and property owner, was born at Brentwood, Rathmore Avenue, Mossley Hill, Liverpool, on 15 November 1925, the son of Francis Joseph, otherwise Francis William, Quinn, and his wife, Maud Aloysia, *née* McKeown (1894–1972). His father was a philandering Irish haulage contractor who left the family when the boy was five. He was brought up, shy and stuttering, as a Roman Catholic in Liverpool by his mother, grandmother, and three aunts. After his education at St Francis Xavier's College, his mother wanted him to take a 'safe' job as a railway clerk. When he left school at fifteen he worked for the Manchester Ship Canal as an office boy, filling his spare time as a drummer for dance bands. As a wartime conscript he was first a Bevin boy working down the mines, but soon fled and was brought back home by the police. When he joined the RAF instead as a bandsman and switchboard operator, he ingratiated his way into amateur theatricals. This led to him becoming a theatrical agent in Liverpool and a modest impresario in Manchester. He also ran a summer-season clairvoyant act on Clacton pier with Noreen O'Horan, with whom he had a son, Derry. In 1947 he adopted the name Paul Raymond. On 15 November 1952, at Westminster register office, he married Jean Mary Bradley (1931–2002), daughter of John Bradley, caretaker. They had a son, Howard, and a daughter, Debbie.

One theatre manager issued Raymond with an ultimatum: he said he would allow Raymond and his two female colleagues to appear on his stage only if the girls were prepared to strip. When the girls agreed to do so for an extra ten shillings a week Raymond embarked on a course that would reportedly lead him to be at one time the richest man in a Britain that was changing fast. He first began to be nationally noticeable when in 1957 he opened Raymond's Revue Bar in Soho, dodging the laws against indecency by making it a private club whose membership could be bought at the door. His early acts included Julie Mendez the Snake Girl, who appeared to swallow a snake onstage, and Bonnie Bell the Ding Dong Girl, whose bells members of the audience were invited to ring. Raymond was brought before the London sessions in 1961 for allegedly keeping a disorderly house at the Revue Bar, the

Paul Raymond (1925–2008), by unknown photographer, 1988

chairman calling the acts 'filthy, disgusting and beastly' and fining him £5000—an amount that was dwarfed by the value of the publicity.

Raymond's career in pornography continued when he took over the Whitehall Theatre in the early 1960s and in 1974 the Windmill Theatre, where under a previous proprietor the national moral climate had been such that 'nudes' could appear only on condition that they did not move. As the moral climate swung towards the permissive Raymond's approach was to go for full and mobile nudity but without the crudity that could have led to legal action. His shows included *Yes, We Have no Pyjamas*, *Let's Get Laid!*, and *Come into My Bed*. His commercially golden touch was extended to the magazines he began establishing in 1964 with one called *King*. He promised 'laughing haystack and sunshine girls, not grimacing plastic-mac and whiplash girls'—an indication that he had diagnosed that success lay in making nudity comfortable and almost respectable. *King* failed, but by 1971 Raymond had relaunched the magazine *Men Only*, whose pictures of girls in their underwear had ceased to be competitively beckoning in a permissive age. Raymond filled the magazine with photographs of his own Revue Bar artists, and eventually claimed a circulation of 500,000. *Razzle*, *Mayfair*, *Club International*, and *Club Pour Homme* were added to his magazine interests. By the late 1980s profits from his magazines and other interests were estimated at £6 million a year. He had a black Rolls-Royce with PR11 on the number plate. An admirer of Margaret Thatcher, he sent 30,000 copies of *Men Only* to be distributed to troops during the Falklands War.

Raymond's private life was not equally golden. After twenty-two years of marriage his wife, Jean, divorced him in 1974 following his admitted adultery with the star of many of his shows, Fiona Richmond (*b*. 1945). He took other girls out, but those close to him doubted whether he in fact slept with them. His son and presumed heir Howard developed drug problems, and in 1992 his daughter, Debbie, who had played a vital part in helping to run his businesses (after first appearing in them as a showgirl), died of a drugs overdose. Raymond, with dyed hair, an artificial tan, and his nails rarely cut, became a virtual recluse in his penthouse flat next door to the Ritz Hotel in London, one observer suggesting that he 'evoked Dracula lurking in the guise of an Oxford Street spiv' (*Daily Telegraph*, 4 March 2008). He claimed never to have read a book: 'Maybe I attempted to read the wrong sort of book', he said (*The Guardian*, 4 March 2008).

Raymond's financial success continued amid the years of his personal tragedy, though increasingly from his property empire rather than his pornographic enterprises. When in 1994 he bought for £15 million the Café de Paris, the Rialto cinema site, and shops and offices in Rupert Street and Coventry Street in Soho, he said: 'Years ago I queued up across the road at 5 o'clock in the morning at the kitchen entrance of Joe Lyons to work as a washer-upper for ten shillings a morning' (*The Times*, 2 July 1994). But it was rumoured that he had cancer, and in 1994 he appointed the banker Joe Daniel as his managing director. Two years later he bought the Queen's House leisure centre in Leicester Square for £12 million, but in 1997 he sold the Revue Bar to Gerard Simi, the man who for twenty-one years had been his chief choreographer. Raymond subsequently forced the closure of the bar by charging an astronomical rent. In 2000 Raymond brought his brother, Philip Quinn, and nephew, Mark Quinn, into the business, and gradually withdrew from the organization. In an interview shortly before her death, his former wife, Jean, said, 'Paul's fortune hasn't brought him any happiness. In his last call he said … people liked him only because of his money. He sounded so sad and lonely' (*Daily Mail*, 4 June 2004). Raymond died of prostate cancer and respiratory failure at Parkside Hospital, Wimbledon, on 3 March 2008, an entrepreneur not temperamentally constituted to enjoy his private life or the rewards of his commercial success. Often called the King or Godfather of Porn, and undoubtedly one of the significant faces of permissiveness of the post-war years, Raymond made watching female nudes entertaining rather than furtive, and later accidentally saved many London theatres from falling victim to property developers anxious to develop their sites into flats and offices. He was survived by his two sons.

DENNIS BARKER

Sources *The Times* (4 March 2008) • *Daily Telegraph* (4 March 2008) • *The Guardian* (4 March 2008) • *Daily Mirror* (4 March 2008) • *The Independent* (5 March 2008) • *New York Times* (8 March 2008) • *Irish Independent* (8 March 2008) • P. Willetts, *Members only: the life and times of Paul Raymond* (2010) • b. cert. • m. cert. • d. cert.
Archives FILM BFINA, 'The king of Soho', *Sex in the 70s*, L. Osmond (director), Channel 4, 2 Feb 2005 • BFINA, documentary and light entertainment footage
Likenesses photographs, 1955–85, Camera Press, London • photographs, 1955–89, Getty Images, London • photographs, 1960–95, Rex Features, London • photographs, 1960–97, PA Photos, London • photographs, 1964–88, Photoshot, London • G. Scarfe, caricature, pubd 1971, repro. in G. Scarfe, *Drawing blood: forty five years of Scarfe uncensored* (2005), 105 • G. Galvin, Lambda print, 1980, NPG • photograph, 1988, PA Photos, London [*see illus.*] • obituary photographs
Wealth at death £74,286,106: probate, 6 Nov 2008, *CGPLA Eng. & Wales*

Rayner, John Desmond (1924–2005), rabbi and liturgist, was born Hans Sigismund Rahmer, in Berlin, Germany, on 30 May 1924, the only son and younger child of Ferdinand Josef Adolf Rahmer (1887–1942?), chief French correspondent at Deutsche Bank, and his wife, Charlotte, *née* Landshut (1897–1942?). The Rahmers, entirely unobservant Jews, lived in the lower-middle-class Berlin suburb of Lindenhof, where Hans was the only Jewish child at the local school. After 1933, as antisemitism grew in Germany, his parents sent him to the Zionist Theodor Herzl Schule, where he learned excellent English, but his education was cruelly interrupted by the events of Kristallnacht, on 9 November 1938, after which his father was arrested by the SS. At that point the Rahmers hoped to emigrate. Hans's uncle, Kurt Landshut, was already in Uruguay, and promised to get them visas. The family was forced to leave its home in Lindenhof, which had been declared *Judenrein* (Jew free), and moved to a cramped shared apartment in Berlin's west end. It was to that home that Ferdinand Rahmer returned seven weeks after his arrest, with Hans unable to recognize as his father the man 'standing on the doorstep like a skeleton, with filthy clothes hanging loosely from him—he looked like a scarecrow' (*Before I Forget*, 19). Shortly afterwards the family heard that Kurt Landshut had been swindled over the visas, so the Rahmers made every effort to get their children out of Germany. Hans came to England to board at Durham School, arriving, on 11 August 1939, on one of the last 'kindertransports' that brought some 10,000 Jewish children to the UK.

Hans Rahmer went to live with the family of Robert William Stannard, rector of Bishopwearmouth, co. Durham, who soon became his family—Uncle Will and Aunt Muriel. They succeeded in getting a nursing place for his sister Erica at Sunderland Royal Infirmary, and she arrived on 25 August 1939. Hans attended Durham School, and, later, with restrictions in place for German refugees in case they were Nazi agents, was transferred to Giggleswick School, from which he won an open scholarship in modern languages to Emmanuel College, Cambridge. He took that up in 1947, after four years in the Durham light infantry, during which he changed his name from Rahmer to Rayner.

At some point in 1946 his hope against hope that his parents might have survived was finally dashed—he had received a last Red Cross note from them early in 1943, sending their love and asking him to 'pray to beloved God'. They had apparently been arrested on 13 December 1942 and deported the following day, by cattle-truck, with about 800 people, of whom none survived, to Auschwitz.

While staying with the Stannards and the Wilkinsons, another clergy family, John Rayner became increasingly attracted by their liberal, open-minded brand of Anglicanism. He began to think seriously about religion, and discovered Liberal Judaism, first in Liverpool and then in London, so that the young man whose parents had practised nothing, and who had had a bar mitzvah at his own request in the little synagogue of a Jewish old people's home in Berlin, became convinced that he wanted to be a religious leader. He changed from modern languages at Cambridge to moral sciences (gaining a first) and then to Oriental languages, specializing in Hebrew. He became president of the Cambridge University Jewish Society and founded the Cambridge Progressive Jewish group. From then on, his service to the Jewish community was in no doubt.

Rayner was ordained into the Liberal Jewish ministry by Rabbi Israel Mattuck in June 1953, and served the South London Liberal Synagogue in Streatham as their first full-time paid minister until 1957, when he received the 'call', as he described it, to the Liberal Jewish Synagogue in St John's Wood, to be associate minister to Rabbi Leslie Edgar. The south London years were happy times. On 19 June 1955 he married Jane Priscilla Heilbronn (*b.* 1931), a secretary, and daughter of Lionel Heilbronn, manufacturer's agent, and his wife, Pauline; they had two sons and one daughter. In the early years of their marriage they lived penuriously—the salary was minuscule—in Upper Norwood, and made many friends. Rayner was particularly remembered in the congregation not only for his brilliant sermons and his unfailing devotion to pastoral care, but for his car, which, due to his lack of money, was an old, failing Austin Seven named Gomer after the prophet Hosea's wife, who had been unfaithful but whom he loved just the same. The Liberal Jewish Synagogue, with its place at the heart of the Liberal Jewish movement at the time, suited John Rayner perfectly. All three Rayner children were born in the first few years of his time there (Jeremy in 1957, Benjamin in 1959, Susan in 1962), and, following Leslie Edgar's retirement on health grounds in 1961, he became senior minister, only agreeing to do so if the congregation would give him two years' absence to study for rabbinic ordination at the Hebrew Union College–Jewish Institute of Religion, in Cincinnati. He was ordained there privately in 1965.

Upon his return from America, Rayner's life's work in liturgy and teaching began. He produced, together with his great friend the American rabbi Chaim Stern, the sabbath, festival, and high holy day prayer books for the Liberal movement (in 1967, 1995, and 1973 respectively). He produced one passover Haggadah for the Liberal movement in 1962, with John Rich, and then in 1981 edited a wholly new Haggadah, with new material and detailed notes, as well as writing pamphlets, lectures, and articles. Among his books were *Judaism for Today* (1978) with Bernard Hooker, *The Jewish People* (1987) with David Goldberg, and three collections of sermons and lectures.

Rayner's sermons were beautifully crafted, often very moving, and always passionately felt. People often did not agree with him, but he was recognized as one of the country's greatest preachers, *inter alia* by *Harpers and Queen* magazine in 1976. He was also the foremost Jewish liturgist of the twentieth century. His knowledge and expertise were unparalleled, and his capacity to find words from the early versions of traditional prayers that fitted with modern Liberal Jewish theology was truly astonishing, such that his notes to each prayer book were consulted by scholars the world over. To add to that, though he was never fully acknowledged for it, his prayer books became the basis of modern American Reform liturgy as well. His collaboration with Chaim Stern was a felicitous one. Though Rayner wrote elegant prose, Stern had more of the poet in him; the combination of Rayner's learning and scholarship with Stern's own compositions created an excellent contemporary liturgy. Their prayer books received widespread approval, even from those not wholly sympathetic to their universalistic theology. Rayner used to quote with embarrassed amusement the letter he received from another great scholar, Jakob Petuchowski, after *Service of the Heart* was published (in 1967), that ended with 'all good wishes to you, your family, and all mankind' (Rayner, 'The liturgy of Liberal Judaism', lecture at Northwood and Pinner Liberal Synagogue, 17 Feb 2002, privately printed, 8). He also piloted the use of gender inclusive language, particularly in relation to God, and introduced a radical change when he substituted 'you' in addressing God for the 'Thou' of the old Liberal liturgy.

Rayner taught at Leo Baeck College, becoming honorary director of studies on his return from the United States. He lectured in rabbinic literature, codes, and liturgy for some thirty-five years, inspiring his students with his knowledge, and, perhaps even more, his devotion to the texts. All this, with his unrelenting schedule of pastoral and congregational duties, led to ill health. He underwent coronary bypass surgery in 1980 and again in 1995, and the after-effects of an aneurysm operation in November 2003 left him confined to a wheelchair. Yet he never stopped. He was life president of Liberal Judaism, a vice-president of Leo Baeck College, and president of the London Society of Jews and Christians. He was appointed CBE in 1993 for his inter-faith work. But, all the honours he received in his lifetime notwithstanding, it was his courage and integrity that marked him out. He never flinched when being attacked by fellow Jews for his views on the state of Israel, and his assertion that many of its policies were unethical and indefensible; and he was fearless in his sermons encouraging his congregation to strive for a truly ethical, socially aware, prophetically inspired Judaism. For him, Liberal Judaism was no easy way to be Jewish—it was harder than traditional Judaism. It required the informed and enlightened conscience, and it required enormous effort.

Rayner's courage and integrity were leavened with a playful sense of the absurd. He produced pastiche Shakespeare speeches on the burning Jewish issues of the day, wrote words to Christmas carol tunes to tease confirmation class students, and told joke after joke at dinner or at the end of a class. But he was a deeply serious scholar and religious leader, who truly believed that Judaism could be 'a major force for good and therefore for the survival of humanity' (*Before I Forget*, 185). He died of cancer of the liver and colon at his home, 37 Walmington Fold, Woodside Park, Barnet, London, on 19 September 2005, optimistic to the end, still working on a book, and was cremated at Golders Green crematorium four days later. He was survived by his wife and their three children.

JULIA NEUBERGER

Sources J. D. Rayner, *Before I forget: an illustrated chronicle of a twentieth century life* (1999) [privately published] · *The Independent* (22 Sept 2005) · *The Guardian* (26 Sept 2005); (29 Sept 2005) · *The Times* (29 Sept 2005); (5 Oct 2005) · M. Shire and others, 'In memoriam: John D. Rayner', *European Judaism*, 39/1 (spring 2006), 123–36 · A. Goldstein, *John Rayner: German, English and American liturgist* (2006) · Tributes at memorial service, www.ljs.org/rabbis.php?&id=1, 22 Jan 2008 · *WW* (2005) · personal knowledge (2009) · private information (2009) · m. cert. · d. cert.

Archives U. Southampton L., James Parkes MSS | SOUND BL NSA, recorded lecture

Likenesses obituary photographs

Wealth at death £51,276: probate, 12 May 2006, *CGPLA Eng. & Wales*

Rees, Charles Wayne (1927–2006), organic chemist, was born on 15 October 1927 in Cairo, Egypt, the son of a serving British soldier, later a civil servant, Percival Charles Rees, and his wife, Daisy Alice, *née* Beck. He was educated at Farnham grammar school. Working subsequently for the Royal Aircraft Establishment at nearby Farnborough as a laboratory technician, he developed a love for chemistry, obtained his higher school certificate (mainly by evening study), and became a chemistry undergraduate at the University College of Southampton. He gained a first-class honours degree in 1950 and then began work for a PhD under the supervision of Norman B. Chapman. Later studies under Adrien Albert (of the Australian National University, which had an outpost in London) led to the award of his PhD (Southampton) in 1953. On 19 December the same year he commenced a happy and enduring marriage to Patricia Mary (Tricia) Francis, the 22-year-old daughter of George Walter Francis, a representative of the tobacco manufacturers W. D. and H. O. Wills. They had three sons (David, George, and Michael). For years the family lived in Kensington after his appointment as assistant lecturer at Birkbeck College, London, in 1955.

After two years at Birkbeck, Rees moved to King's College, London, where he spent eight years (1957–65) in the department chaired by the pioneer of free radical chemistry, Donald Hey. Free radicals are transient intermediates in chemical reactions where each molecule has an odd unpaired electron. Rees's later interest in free radicals must have dated from those years, though he also worked with Hey on different aspects of a branch of chemistry that he was later to make specially his own, that of heterocyclic compounds. In 1965 he was appointed professor of organic chemistry at the University of Leicester, and in 1969 moved to become professor of organic chemistry at Liverpool, succeeding George Kenner as Heath Harrison professor of organic chemistry in 1977. After one year as Harrison professor he was translated to the chair at Imperial College, London, named after another great pioneer in organic chemistry, A. W. Hofmann. He succeeded the Nobel laureate Sir Derek Barton, and finally retired from the chair in 1993. He was appointed emeritus professor and thereafter spent much time in his laboratory, unrestricted by regular teaching commitments.

Charles Rees was a rare example of a distinguished organic chemist who was popular with a wide range of chemists and historians of chemistry. He was closely associated with the Royal Society of Chemistry, formerly the Chemical Society. He delivered the Tilden lecture in 1974 and the Pedler lecture (reported in *Chemical Society Reviews*) ten years later. He served on many of its committees, including as chairman of its publication and information board for four years, and in 1982 became president of the Perkin division of the society, concerned with organic chemistry. The ultimate token of esteem came with his election to the presidency of the Royal Society of Chemistry itself (1992–4). As president he went to great lengths to attend meetings of the smaller groups of the society and became widely known as a friend to all.

Rees's great preoccupation was with that sub-group of organic substances known as heterocyclic compounds. They are substances whose molecules contain a ring of atoms, one at least of these being other than carbon. He became familiar with the properties of many heterocyclic ring systems, not least the aziridines and azoles in their many forms. Many of the new compounds contained other elements in their rings as well as nitrogen, for instance sulphur or even selenium. He was particularly interested in the decomposition of heterocyclic compounds, including their responses to heating. For his work in this field he was awarded the Royal Society of Chemistry award in heterocyclic chemistry in 1980 and the International Society of Heterocyclic Chemistry senior award in 1995. This research frequently involved surprising reactions; they often seemed to proceed through a transient intermediate as a derivative of benzyne (C_6H_4). In 1965 Rees obtained evidence for benzyne in the oxidation of the heterocycle 1-aminobenzotriazine, and in the early 1970s he discovered a new route to benzynes using low temperatures. Sometimes other intermediates were identified, as free radicals like carbenes (by then well known elsewhere), or the less familiar nitrenes. He obtained these by pyrolysis of aziridines and showed their key role in many heterocyclic decompositions, employing them in several important syntheses.

Beyond the field of strict heterocyclic chemistry Rees was also concerned with aromaticity (a kind of stability, due to a number, usually six, of π-electrons in the molecule). In that connection he succeeded in preparing for the first time derivatives of [10]annulene (or cyclodecapentaene) and other non-heterocyclic compounds to put current theories to rigorous test. Other work was centred on derivatives of the 'square' molecule, cyclobutadiene, that showed the strange phenomenon of 'valence isomerism'.

Much of Rees's work was entirely academic, yet even basic research in heterocyclic chemistry is relevant to living systems. Occasionally this became obvious, as when he participated in the discovery of cimetidine, a synthetic drug once used widely in the treatment of gastric ulcers. He claimed that this discovery saved the National Health Service a billion pounds and showed that academic chemistry, pursued for its own ends, could sometimes have important industrial or social consequences. Several other compounds of biological importance were also isolated.

Rees published about 500 papers, generally in collaboration with his research staff and others, and the *Annual Reports* of chemical progress for many years rarely failed to report his research. Some of these references were to prove immensely important for others in their future work. He contributed to many books and was a co-author of the seminal *Organic Reaction Mechanisms* (three volumes, 1965–9), *Carbenes, Nitrenes and Arynes* (1969), the multi-volume *Comprehensive Heterocyclic Chemistry* (1984 and 1996), and *Organic Functional Group Transformations* (1995). Elected a fellow of the Royal Society in 1974, he became president of the chemistry section of the British Association for the Advancement of Science in 1984. He received honorary doctorates from the universities of Leicester (1994), Sunderland (2000), and London (2003) and was appointed CBE in 1995.

Rees's devotion to academic chemistry showed itself in his frequent impromptu remarks at heterocyclic conferences, where his interventions were nearly always helpful, and in his lecturing technique, which was brilliant and deeply appreciated. He was always approachable and given to generous hospitality. Rarely seen in public without his customary bow-tie, he had a great sense of humour and was highly regarded by all who met him. He appreciated excellence in wine, music, and theatre. He died at his home, 67 Hillgate Place, Kensington, London, from cardiac arrest on 21 September 2006, and was survived by his wife, Tricia, and their three sons. COLIN A. RUSSELL

Sources *Annual Report on the Progress of Chemistry* (1960–) · Royal Society of Chemistry press release, Sept 2006 · *Daily Telegraph* (29 Sept 2006) · *The Times* (9 Oct 2006) · *The Independent* (12 Dec 2006) · D. Phillips, *Chemistry World*, 3/11 (2006), 15 · W. Griffith, *Royal Society of Chemistry Newsletter* (Feb 2007), 9 · *WW* (2006) · personal knowledge (2010) · private information (2010) · m. cert. · d. cert.

Likenesses G. Argent, photograph, RS · obituary photographs · photograph, RS · portrait, Royal Society of Chemistry, London · portrait, repro. in *Chemistry World*

Wealth at death £787,141: probate, 6 Dec 2006, *CGPLA Eng. & Wales*

Rees, Merlyn Merlyn-, **Baron Merlyn-Rees** (**1920–2006**), politician, was born Merlyn Rees on 18 December 1920 at 30 Howell Street, Cilfynydd, near Pontypridd, Glamorgan, the son of Levi Rees, miner, and his wife, Edith Mary, *née*

Merlyn Merlyn-Rees, Baron Merlyn-Rees (1920–2006), by Bassano, 1965

Williams. He was the son and grandson of miners and at his birth had little to look forward to other than more of the same. On his birth certificate his father was described as a coalminer-hewer, that is, one who worked underground actually cutting the coal, the hardest and dirtiest job in the pit. Cilfynydd was, in many ways, an ordinary south Wales mining village, although it was perhaps atypical in that in the space of a few years it produced not only Merlyn Rees, but two singers of international renown, the baritone Sir Geraint Evans and the tenor, Stuart Burrows, as well as the Welsh rugby international Glyn Davies.

Wales, London, war, and marriage Rees's early life was to a large extent dominated by his father's experiences. An early supporter of the Labour Party, Levi Rees was sacked from his job because he had been distributing the *Daily Herald*, then regarded as Labour's newspaper. He found it impossible to get work in or near Cilfynydd. He therefore decided to try his luck in London. Unable to afford the train fare, he walked from south Wales, eventually finding work in Harrow. Merlyn Rees was then six years old. Soon thereafter, the whole family moved to London, but it proved hard to find suitable accommodation and Merlyn was sent back to Wales to live with his grandmother. He had much of his elementary schooling there. When things in London had improved somewhat, he rejoined his parents in Harrow and went to Harrow Weald grammar school.

Shortly after the outbreak of the Second World War, Rees went to Goldsmiths' College to train as a teacher. In this he followed many from the valleys. Teaching was a 'tidy' job. It had status, stability, and, just as important, a pension. Its attraction for many a valley parent was natural and obvious: it kept the boy out of the pit and gave him a secure future. Rees was soon evacuated to Nottingham, and there he joined the RAF.

Rees had what used to be called 'a good war'. Certainly it was brave and adventurous. He rose rapidly and became a squadron leader at the age of twenty-five. His main duty was as a ground controller for advanced units of the desert air force, and he saw action mainly in Italy. One of his fellow officers, whom he greatly admired, was Group Captain W. G. G. Duncan Smith, the father of Iain Duncan Smith, Conservative leader from 2001 to 2003. Another pilot he served with was Frank Cooper, who later became a distinguished civil servant and Rees's permanent secretary at the Northern Ireland Office.

Although Rees spent most of the war as a ground controller, the memory of war and its horrors never left him. It was certainly not that he had a quasi-pacifist reluctance to contemplate the use of force. He fully recognized that there were circumstances in which force was necessary, and indeed unavoidable. It was the consciousness of the waste that attends military conflict that deeply affected him. A close friend of his was killed in the early years of the war. The memory never left him even when he was an old man.

When the war ended Rees was offered a permanent commission in the RAF, but declined. Instead, he went to the London School of Economics, where he read economics under Harold Laski. Having taken a course at London University's Institute of Education, in 1949 he went back to his old school as a master. On boxing day 1949 he married Colleen Faith Cleveley, a 22-year-old secretary (and daughter of Henry Faith Cleveley, electrician), who had herself been a pupil at Harrow Weald. Her family was of Irish descent, which, together with the fact that his father had served in Dublin during the Easter rising of 1916, gave Rees an attachment to Ireland that lasted the whole of his life. Rees's marriage was the start of a partnership that lasted for fifty-five years. Together, they were one of the most successful teams in Westminster. The contribution Colleen made to his life, work, career, and personal well-being was immense. They had three children, Patrick, Gareth, and Glyn, to each of whom he was very close, and whom he talked about with pride.

Early career in politics Following his father, Rees was an active member of the local Labour Party. In the 1950s he fought the constituency of Harrow East no fewer than three times, once at the general election of 1955, once at a by-election in March 1959 caused by the resignation of Ian Harvey, the sitting MP, and finally at the 1959 general election. By then Rees had caught the attention of Morgan Phillips, the general secretary of the Labour Party, who was also a product of industrial south Wales. Phillips asked him to organize the Festival of Labour in 1960–62, which he did with considerable success. When Hugh Gaitskell died unexpectedly early in 1963 Rees (who since 1962 had been working as a lecturer in economics at Luton College of Technology) inherited his Leeds South constituency. He was duly elected in a by-election in June 1963, with a majority of 12,789, and held the seat (renamed Morley and Leeds South in 1983) until 1992.

Rees's allegiance to his constituency and his constituents was legendary. Even at the height of his career he regarded it as a natural part of being an MP that he should be available, in person if possible, to those of his constituents who needed his help. In return, he would get to hear what he often presented at Westminster as the authentic voice of the northern working class, usually gathered in his regular round of the working men's clubs in Leeds. 'They won't have it' was a familiar theme when the government or the party was engaged in a particularly difficult piece of political exotica—and usually he was right.

Rees gave his maiden speech in the Commons on 17 July 1963. No doubt he rose (as do all new MPs) apprehensive, nervous, and anxious. For Rees it was in some ways worse. He was following Hugh Gaitskell, the leader of the opposition and a man of national and international renown. Understandably, therefore, he asked for the 'traditional tolerance and indulgence of Honourable Members on both sides of the House'. The speech itself was on higher education but it contained some personal reflections that were revealing. Dealing with his background, he said:

> I am one of the Welshmen of the great dispersion of the 1920s and the 1930s, but although, as a consequence, I have spent the greater part of my life in an outer London suburb, to which I owe a great deal, my roots are firmly embedded in the mining valleys of South Wales where many of my family still live and where I was nurtured.

Later in the same speech he revealed some of his preoccupations:

> I have little patience with the argument that there is something noble about poverty. I know too much about it in whatever degree to believe this. I believe passionately that there is a case for using science and technology to raise the standard of living of the people of this country. If, concurrently, we not only think of that, but think also of the arts and social sciences, we shall be taking a step towards making eventually a better country. The key to it all is an expansion of higher education. (*Hansard 5C*, 681.574–7, 17 July 1963)

These were beliefs he held all his political life. He was a passionate advocate of higher education for as many young people as possible. Towards the end of his career in 1994 he became the first chancellor of the University of Glamorgan, whose campus was near the village where he had been born and brought up.

Shortly after he entered the Commons, Rees formed a lasting political and, for him, formative relationship with Jim Callaghan, and he soon became Callaghan's parliamentary private secretary. In his autobiography Callaghan referred to Rees in the following terms:

> Merlyn attracts such words as dependable, thoughtful, hardworking, but he is more than that. He is essentially a conciliator … He is [also] a very amusing raconteur who often lightened our proceedings, although he would fall into a typical celtic gloom from time to time. He had no side … and never pushed himself. If anything, he underrated his own strength. I have been fortunate to have him as a friend to whom I could always turn for advice and criticism, knowing that I had his understanding and support. (Callaghan, 234–5)

After a year as Callaghan's parliamentary private secretary, Rees became a junior minister. He was parliamentary under-secretary for the army from 1965 to 1966, then for the RAF from 1966 to 1968. He found these jobs fascinating and enjoyed dealing with the services, particularly the RAF. In 1968, however, he was moved (no doubt at Callaghan's behest) to the Home Office, Callaghan himself having resigned from the Treasury and become home secretary. There Rees found himself in charge of a large part of immigration policy, which was hardly popular in political terms. He again showed himself to be loyal in his attachment and moderate in his views and expressions. But it was not an easy or a particularly congenial post. He was once heard to say, 'The trouble with the Home Office is that things don't happen as they do in the MOD [Ministry of Defence]. There you ask for something to be done and it is. In the Home Office, you ask for something to be done, they agree and then it just doesn't seem to happen' (personal knowledge).

After the Labour defeat in 1970 there was a suggestion that Rees might become the general secretary of the Labour Party. He prudently declined, particularly when he realized that it meant exile from parliament. He therefore stayed on in the shadow Home Office team. In 1971 he was a member of the Franks committee set up to review section 2 of the Official Secrets Act, but more and more of his time was dominated by Northern Ireland. In October 1971 he visited some of the internment camps and went with Harold Wilson, leader of the opposition, to Dublin to a meeting, which appalled Unionists. He was also appointed by Wilson to head the Labour team in discussions with the Heath government over Northern Ireland matters. A result of all this was that in 1972, following his election to the shadow cabinet, he became the opposition spokesman on Northern Ireland. From 1972 to 1974 he shadowed Willie Whitelaw, a man whose expansive exterior belied his internal shrewdness. They got on well.

Northern Ireland and the Home Office In 1974, after the Labour Party was unexpectedly returned to office, Rees became secretary of state for Northern Ireland. At that point the situation in Northern Ireland was dire. The power-sharing executive envisaged in the Sunningdale agreement had just been established, but the composition of the assembly was ominous. Extreme Unionism was much stronger than had been expected, and the executive, led by Brian Faulkner, a moderate Unionist, was hardly bedded in. In his book on Northern Ireland, Rees wrote 'I was already beginning to learn that the Ulster loyalists were loyal to a Protestant Northern Ireland not to the UK' (*Northern Ireland*, 21). This heady brew soon resulted in a major confrontation. The Ulster workers' strike, a highly organized demonstration by extreme protestant elements, started very shortly after he assumed office. It aimed at the destruction of the executive and the death of Sunningdale. It succeeded.

Later Rees was widely blamed for indecision, it being argued that firm action at the outset might have succeeded in averting the strike. Whether anyone could have behaved differently is doubtful. A minister trying to placate the protestant parties, and at the same time showing a more liberal approach to the Catholic communities, was, given the atmosphere at the time, doomed to fail. It was not indecision but the inherent impossibility of conciliation that was to blame. The conditions for an agreement did not exist and they could not be invented.

Nevertheless, Rees ended detention without trial and the special status for political prisoners that he had inherited. He tried by means of a convention to lay down some ground rules for the governance of Northern Ireland. That, not unsurprisingly, failed as well. As Edward Pearce wrote, 'It failed, as such honourable, rational projects have tended to fail, given the irreconcilability of tribes hating each other, despising London and being, in the full, soaraway sense of the word, irresponsible' (*The Guardian*, 6 Jan 2006).

That Rees developed an acute sense of commitment to the problems of Northern Ireland is undeniable. Whatever he did in the future, those problems rarely left his mind. In his view it was a part of the obligation one owed to civilized behaviour that efforts at conciliation had to be undertaken. The unsettleable cannot be settled but an effort has to be made to improve the situation; time might produce a change for the better. He therefore concentrated on keeping the level of violence as low as he could and on trying to make life as bearable as possible for ordinary people living in Ulster.

In 1976 Roy Jenkins went to Brussels as president of the European Commission, and Rees left the Northern Ireland Office to become home secretary. His tenure there from 1976 to 1979 was somewhat quieter. It cannot be said that there was one predominant theme or one comprehensive set of associated issues. The Home Office is always a posting in which crises happen unexpectedly and quickly. One moment all is serene, then something happens that unless dealt with immediately, effectively, and sensibly can result in political consequences out of all proportion to the original event. Rees saw his job as essentially one of calming things down at difficult moments, making sure that the police were sufficiently and properly equipped, but also accountable. In addition, he had to administer immigration and asylum policies that generated intense political interest and scrutiny. The fact that he emerged from the Home Office with his reputation intact as a fair and compassionate minister is itself a tribute to his character. He recognized that, as compared to the 1960s, the era of great liberal reforms in home affairs was over, and that his function now was maintenance rather than innovation.

Rees caused some controversy, particularly on the left of the Labour Party, by deciding to deport Philip Agee and Mark Hosenball (respectively a renegade former CIA officer and an investigative journalist) on undisclosed grounds of endangering national security. This incident tended to reinforce the opinion that Rees was a stern figure when it came to upholding law and order. Perhaps his greatest achievement, however, was in establishing the review commission on criminal procedure. For too long police behaviour when interviewing suspects had been under criticism. The methods used were old. They ignored modern technology that was now available to provide an objective record of the interview itself, and the opportunity for dishonesty in the evidence given in court was great. The commission was the precursor of the major reforms of the 1980s, which resulted in police procedures and techniques being radically overhauled.

There was a distinct thread of the bi-partisan in Merlyn Rees. This was shown in his relationship with Willie Whitelaw. They shared rational and centrist views on law and order. They trusted and respected each other and the continuity of the two as home secretary and shadow home secretary was effective in lowering the political temperature. When Labour was defeated in 1979 Whitelaw became home secretary and the relationship continued when Rees was in opposition.

Later life When Michael Foot became leader of the Labour Party in 1980 Rees became shadow secretary of state for energy, but he retired from the shadow cabinet in 1983. His life was then considerably lightened. He survived with little difficulty the defection from the party of the 'gang of four' led by Roy Jenkins and the subsequent formation of the Social Democratic Party. It would never have occurred to him to take them too seriously, and even if he did it would never have been acceptable to him to join another political party. As he once said, he owed the Labour Party a very great deal. It was in his blood, and he was certainly not going to leave it.

Rees dealt with a number of disparate issues while in opposition. He was one of the principal activists in the campaign to free the wrongly convicted Guildford four and the Maguire seven. He gave evidence for the civil servant Clive Ponting, who was tried for breaches of the Official Secrets Act. One issue he pursued vigorously was that of war crimes. He was one of those most responsible for the passage of legislation that gave British courts the right to try Nazi war criminals for crimes committed outside the UK by non-British citizens. And always there was Ireland. He became an active member of the British delegation to the UK–Irish Parliamentary Council, and thus maintained his interest and connection.

In 1992 Rees left the House of Commons and was made a life peer. His title caused some disagreement with the relevant authorities. He was anxious to maintain the name Merlyn in his title. On being told that he could not do that because it was his Christian name, he changed his name from Rees to Merlyn-Rees. This was not exactly approved of by the powers-that-be, but nevertheless Merlyn-Rees he remained. The other problem was his 'territorial designation'. He had two intense and long-term loyalties, one to his birthplace and Wales and the other to his constituency and Leeds. Since the creation of every title cites a territorial attachment, he solved the problem by being created Baron Merlyn-Rees, of Morley and South Leeds, county of

West Yorkshire, and of Cilfynydd, county of Mid-Glamorgan.

Merlyn-Rees's time in the Lords coincided with a deterioration in his health. He suffered from Parkinson's disease and bore his gradual decline with good humour and little complaint. Chauffeured by Colleen, he managed to keep an attachment both to Leeds and to the House of Lords. His interest in Ireland remained. Three weeks before his death he made his final speech in the chamber on the issue of detention without trial, drawing on his experience that it had not been successful in Northern Ireland. Over Christmas 2005, after a fall outside his house in Southwark, he lapsed into a coma from which he never emerged, dying peacefully on 5 January 2006 at St Thomas's Hospital. He was survived by his wife, Colleen, and their three sons.

The words most often used to describe Merlyn-Rees's character and political career were balanced, measured, consensual, diplomatic, decent, and fair. He saw politics in terms of reaching a consensus and his own function—particularly in Northern Ireland—as trying to bring about a settlement that both sides could see as fair, or at least an agreement with which each side was equally dissatisfied and would accept even if not with enthusiasm. His great appeal as a senior politician lay in the ability to recognize that his own party had to persuade a majority of the electorate to trust them, and that this in turn meant that its appeal could never be extreme. It also meant that he recognized from time to time that the other side might have a point. His were not the politics of rancour—they were more the politics of reason. Like Lyndon Johnson he believed that a process of rational discussion between opposing views could produce a distillation of those views and an agreement—provided that the discussions took place with good will on both sides. IVOR RICHARD

Sources B. Faulkner, *Memoirs of a statesman*, ed. J. Houston (1978) · B. Castle, *The Castle diaries, 1974–1976* (1980) · B. Castle, *The Castle diaries, 1964–1970* (1984) · M. Rees, *Northern Ireland: a personal perspective* (1985) · J. Callaghan, *Time and chance* (1987) · R. Jenkins, *A life at the centre* (1991) · B. Castle, *Fighting all the way* (1993) · K. O. Morgan, *Callaghan: a life* (1997) · *The Times* (6 Jan 2006) · *Daily Telegraph* (6 Jan 2006) · *The Guardian* (6 Jan 2006) · *The Independent* (6 Jan 2006) · Burke, *Peerage* · *WW* (2006) · personal knowledge (2010) · private information (2010) · b. cert. · m. cert. · d. cert.

Archives London School of Economics and Political Science, papers 1949–2002 | FILM BFINA, current affairs footage · BFINA, documentary footage

Likenesses photographs, 1959–79, Hult. Arch., London · photographs, 1959–82, Rex Features, London · photographs, 1959–2005, PA Photos, London · Bassano, half-plate film negative, 1965, NPG [*see illus.*] · photographs, 1978–2001, Photoshot, London · N. Sinclair, bromide print, 1992, NPG · obituary photographs

Wealth at death £150,194: probate, 3 May 2006, *CGPLA Eng. & Wales*

Rees, Peter Wynford Innes, Baron Rees (1926–2008), politician, was born on 9 December 1926 at Pinewood, Gordon Road, Camberley, Surrey, the elder child and only son of Captain (later Major-General) Thomas Wynford (Pete) Rees (1898–1959), Indian army officer, and his wife, (Agatha) Rosalie (1905–1966), daughter of Sir Charles Alexander Innes, governor of Burma. His father had joined the army in 1916, serving during the First World War in Mesopotamia and Palestine, between the wars mainly in Waziristan, and during the Second World War in north Africa, Eritrea, and Burma, retiring in 1947 to live at Goytre Hall, near Abergavenny, the ancestral home that Rees eventually inherited.

Rees was educated at Stowe School, joined the Scots Guards for his national service in 1945 and in 1948 went to Christ Church, Oxford, to take a war-shortened course in history. After graduating with a third-class degree in 1949 he studied for the bar and was called by the Inner Temple in 1953. Specializing in tax law, he practised in London and on the Oxford circuit, becoming a QC in 1969. On 15 December of the same year he married Anthea Peronelle Wendell (*b.* 1931), daughter of Major Hugh John Maxwell Hyslop of the Argyll and Sutherland Highlanders, and former wife of Major Jack Wendell of the Grenadier Guards. There were no children of the marriage.

Rees was keen to enter parliament as a Conservative and had fought unpromising seats in south Wales and Liverpool at the general elections of 1964 and 1966. In 1970 he narrowly won Dover. Following reorganizations the seat became safer, as Dover and Deal in 1974 before reverting to Dover in 1983. He was a distinctive figure in parliament: short, bald, bespectacted, a fox-hunter, and almost Pickwickian in manner and appearance. He was soon made parliamentary private secretary to Sir Geoffrey Howe, the solicitor-general. The connection proved to be significant, for Howe became something of a patron. When Margaret Thatcher was leader of the Conservative opposition she appointed Rees to join the Treasury team under Howe in 1977. She and Howe appreciated his technical expertise and mastery of detail.

When the Conservatives returned to government in 1979 Rees was appointed a minister of state at the Treasury. He was part of the team that presented the remarkable budget in 1981 that deflated the economy at a time of high unemployment. But as a Treasury minister some of his earlier activities came back to embarrass him. He had earlier advised the Rossminster Financial Group about tax avoidance, and it subsequently lost a court battle with the Inland Revenue. Opposition politicians pointed to the conflict of interest as long as he was the minister responsible for the Inland Revenue. He was moved sideways as minister of state to the Department of Trade and Industry in 1981, but joined the cabinet in 1983 as chief secretary to the Treasury. His task was to control the level of public spending under the chancellor, Nigel Lawson. At first things went well. But he lacked the political weight or the persuasiveness in his dealings with spending ministers to keep public spending under control. Lawson lost patience with him and he was dismissed by Thatcher in September 1985.

Not expecting any further preferment, Rees quickly decided that he would stand down as an MP at the next general election. His last year in parliament was made uncomfortable because he reflected his Dover constituents' opposition to the proposed channel tunnel, a project supported by the government. He had, however, decided to develop his business career. He became deputy chairman of Leopold Joseph Holdings in 1985 and, out of parliament and ennobled as Baron Rees, after the general election of 1987, collected other directorships and chairmanships. He was a director of the Fleming Mercantile Investment Trust, one of three external members of Lloyds council, of which he had been a long-standing 'name', and chairman of London and Scottish Maritime Oil (later LASMO), an oil and gas exploring company, General Cable, CLM plc, and the Duty Free Confederation. His chairmanship of LASMO ended in tears as the fall in oil prices dented profits and the company suffered from its takeover of Ultramar.

As a minister and an MP Peter Rees had had a narrow range of interests, largely trade and finance. But at one time his star had seemed to be in the ascendant. He had a reputation as a combative and sharp-tongued figure. In a debate in 1975 Denis Healey, the Labour chancellor of the exchequer, called him 'an emotive little man'. But those who worked closely with him, including opposition Labour figures, paid tribute to his patience and mastery of his subject. He was also a cultured man, and as a peer was an active member of the all-party arts and heritage group. After a short illness he died of a spontaneous subarachnoid haemorrhage at St Thomas's Hospital, Lambeth, London, on 30 November 2008, and was survived by his wife. He was buried in the churchyard of St Peter's Church, Goytre, after a funeral service there on 9 December 2008. DENNIS KAVANAGH

Sources *Daily Telegraph* (3 Dec 2008) · *The Times* (4 Dec 2008) · *The Guardian* (4 Dec 2008) · *The Independent* (6 Dec 2008) · Burke, *Peerage* · *WW* (2008) · b. cert. · d. cert.

Likenesses G. Turner, photograph, 1979, Getty Images, London · group portraits, photographs, 1983, Rex Features, London · photographs, 1983–91, Photoshot, London · obituary photographs

Wealth at death £3,708,984: probate, 8 April 2009, *CGPLA Eng. & Wales*

Reeves, Christopher Reginald (1936–2007), merchant banker, was born on 14 January 1936 at 58 Penylan Road, Cardiff, the son of Reginald Raymond Reeves (1901–1989), bank accountant, and his wife, Dora Grace, *née* Tucker (*b.* 1901). He was educated at Malvern College. After national service with the rifle brigade in Kenya and Malaya in 1955–7, he entered the Bank of England in 1958. In 1963, aged twenty-seven, he became an aide to Kenneth Keith, who was putting together the new City powerhouse that, through a series of mergers, became Hill Samuel in 1965. On 12 June 1965 he married Stella Jane Whinney (*b.* 1940), air hostess, and daughter of Patrick Whinney, company director. They had three sons.

In 1968 Reeves joined Morgan Grenfell, another City merchant bank, becoming a director in 1970. He focused initially on professionalizing its human resources and information technology functions, but soon switched to banking and became head of the banking division. He was appointed group chief executive in 1980, and group deputy chairman and chairman of the British merchant bank (while remaining group chief executive) in 1984. 'He wears grey suits and is an uncharismatic man', commented the banking correspondent of the *Financial Times*, 'who has made Morgan what it is less through superhuman force than a well-developed ability to spot and harness human talent' (*Financial Times*, 18 June 1986). The barrister David Hood noted that 'Mr Reeves had preached the gospel that the City should not work by the old boy network but on true market sentiment and competition' (*Financial Times*, 27 Nov 1991). 'Merchant banking is all about innovation', Reeves himself observed; 'Innovation is the only response to competition and competition will always be with us' (*Financial Times*, 18 June 1986).

As chief executive Reeves pursued international expansion to take advantage of opportunities created by the removal of UK exchange controls by the recently elected Thatcher administration, looking to replicate the London merchant bank in overseas locations. International mandates flooded in, but Reeves's decision to establish a corporate finance subsidiary in New York led the American bank Morgan Guaranty to sell its long-standing one-third shareholding in Morgan Grenfell. Additional capital was raised by a rights issue and by the sale of a 4.9 per cent interest to Deutsche Bank in 1984. The funds were used to build a securities business as Reeves positioned the firm to take advantage of the City's 'big bang' deregulation measures of October 1986.

But the key to Morgan Grenfell's 'extraordinary success' (*Financial Times*, 11 March 1985) and its emergence as the City's foremost and most profitable merchant bank of the mid-1980s was its booming corporate finance business. Under Reeves the corporate finance team doubled in size and consciously sought pushy, fast-growing corporate clients that aimed to expand by acquisition, abetted by Morgan Grenfell's aggressive '"no-holds-barred" style of takeover' (*Financial Times*, 31 Dec 1986). 'Christopher Reeves, the chief executive of Morgan Grenfell, is sometimes referred to in the City of London as "superman"', observed a *Financial Times* profile. 'Apart from sharing the name of the actor who portrays the cape-clad hero, his bank's rate of growth has sometimes seemed to defy gravity. Almost everywhere you look in the world of high finance these days the men from Morgan are doing eye-catching deals … pursuing novel, even daring techniques' (*Financial Times*, 18 June 1986). Morgan Grenfell's profits soared 40 per cent in 1985, providing a launch-pad for its initial public offering in June 1986, a year in which it advised on 111 deals with an aggregate value of £15 billion, far outstripping its rivals.

The aggressive and innovative conduct that drove Morgan Grenfell's success was also the source of its downfall. As adviser to Guinness in its hostile bid for the whisky-maker Distillers, Morgan Grenfell's corporate financiers orchestrated a secret share support operation that clinched the deal. But an official investigation into the illegal share purchases was launched in the summer of 1986, ultimately resulting in criminal trials and prison sentences for several protagonists. In January 1987, under pressure from the Bank of England, Reeves and other senior executives resigned, the 'cowed and battered' firm being subsequently acquired by Deutsche Bank (*Financial Times*, 31 Dec 1986).

Barred from the City by the Bank of England, Reeves found himself 'left to hang out to dry', as he put it (*The Times*, 5 Dec 2007). But in New York, Merrill Lynch was keen to make use of his services, appointing him senior adviser to the president on capital markets strategy. In 1989 he was made vice-chairman of Merrill Lynch International and from 1993 executive chairman of Merrill Lynch Europe. The latter, London-based, appointment, which required the lifting of 'certain restrictions' by the Bank of England, was hailed by the *Financial Times* with the headline 'Reeves' rehabilitation complete' (*Financial Times*, 31 August 1993). Under Reeves's leadership Merrill Lynch built a substantial and successful business in London and Europe, a key move being its acquisition of Smith New Court, a major British brokerage firm, in 1995. It also developed a formidable mergers and acquisitions team, notably through hirings from Morgan Grenfell. Reeves stepped down as chairman in 1998, but continued as a senior adviser, focusing particularly on the Middle East and India. He held a number of directorships, and was chairman of MGM Assurance from 2000.

Outside the office Reeves's favourite pastimes were sailing, shooting, and opera. He was a long-standing member of the council of City University business school and of the Institute for Fiscal Studies, as well as assisting several schools and theatres. He received an honorary doctorate from City University in 2000. He lived in Chelsea and died at the Hammersmith Hospital of cancer after a short illness, on 20 November 2007. He was survived by his wife, Stella, and their three sons. RICHARD ROBERTS

Sources *Financial Times* (5 Dec 1979); (29 Dec 1979); (27 May 1981); (21 Sept 1981); (8 Nov 1984); (11 March 1985); (18 March 1986); (18 June 1986); (31 Dec 1986); (27 Nov 1991); (31 Aug 1993); (28 Nov 1997) • K. Burk, *Morgan Grenfell, 1838–1988: the biography of a merchant bank* (1989) • D. Hobson, *The pride of Lucifer: Morgan Grenfell, 1838–1988* (1990) • *The Times* (5 Dec 2007) • *WW* (2007) • b. cert. • m. cert. • d. cert.

Wealth at death £23,589,269: probate, 4 June 2008, *CGPLA Eng. & Wales*

Reger [*née* Phillips], **(Esther) Janet** (**1935–2005**), lingerie designer, was born in Jubilee Street, London, on 30 September 1935, the eldest daughter of Hyman Phillips, textile manufacturer, and his wife, Ray, *née* Levine. Both her parents were the children of Jewish immigrants; her paternal grandfather, Zaida Phillips, from the Ukraine, had established a textile business in London's East End. When the Second World War bombing of London began in 1940 she, with her sister Barbara (*b.* 1939) and her parents, moved to Reading, where many of her maternal relatives lived. By the time the family had moved to Caversham, north of Reading, she had two more sisters, Gloria (*b.* 1941) and Sandra (*b.* 1948). She attended Battle council primary school in Reading, and Kendrick Girls' Grammar School, Reading, where she excelled in art.

As the family textile business declined in the late 1940s Janet Phillips's parents developed a successful sideline making brassières, recycling textile factory offcuts. Realizing the underwear market had potential, her father persuaded Janet to study corsetry and underwear design at Leicester College of Art and Technology. She started the two-year diploma course in September 1951. She specialized in designing co-ordinated sets of lingerie, an innovation at that date, and the set she made for her diploma final gained much publicity in the end-of-year fashion show.

(Esther) Janet Reger (1935–2005), by John Stillwell, 1990

After leaving college in 1953 Janet Phillips worked for several established underwear and swimwear manufacturers, gaining experience and good salaries, but frustrated by the prevailing conservatism of underwear design, and lack of interest in her more adventurous ideas, she travelled to Israel in May 1958 to work on a kibbutz. In her first week there she met a fellow worker, Peter Reger, formerly Adolf Peter Reger (1940–1985), a German chemistry student from Munich, and the two were immediately attracted. By November, when Peter returned to Munich to complete his degree, they had decided to marry, and Janet planned a move to south Germany. In April 1960 she started work in Zürich for a lingerie and corsetry firm, and after graduation Peter found employment there also. Their future now looking secure, they married at Reading Synagogue on 1 January 1961. By April she became pregnant, and since her salary was essential she was persuaded by Peter to work from home as a freelance lingerie designer for firms throughout Europe. Her daughter Aliza, her only child, was born in London on 27 December 1961. Back in Zürich, Janet's freelance career developed with great success; Peter acted as her agent and secretary, and the couple enjoyed a luxurious lifestyle. However, by the mid-1960s it became difficult for foreign nationals to get Swiss work permits, and in December 1966 the Regers left Zürich for London.

Since freelance design work was scarce in Britain the Regers decided to manufacture as well as design garments. Their company, Janet Reger Creations Ltd, was registered in June 1967, Janet working as designer, cutter, and production manager, and Peter as business manager. Deliveries to shops started in August, and immediately the new company was inundated with orders, as Janet Reger's pretty, glamorous lingerie caught the current mood, appealing to young, self-confident, and increasingly affluent women, who found the products of established underwear firms dull and utilitarian. The Regers set up business premises in Southwick Mews, Paddington, with a small staff and outworkers. Reger products were sold to trendy London boutiques as well as department stores, and thanks to enormous media interest the name Janet Reger became widely known. By 1970 the business had expanded into three buildings in Southwick Mews, and Janet had added new lines inspired by Edwardian and 1920s lingerie, and introduced her dragonfly Reger trademark. To meet increasing demand a mail order catalogue was issued, *Bottom Drawer*.

The 1970s saw a period of constant expansion, financial success, and unprecedented publicity for Janet Reger Creations, owing to the high profile of customers, including royalty and the wives of pop stars. Needing to expand production, the Regers took over a small factory in Wirksworth, Derbyshire. They moved their London base to Beauchamp Place, Knightsbridge, opening a boutique there, followed by a second shop in Brook Street, to cater for a West End clientele. In 1976 the American market was opened up through sales to Saks, the New York store, and a further London shop opened in New Bond Street in 1978. The hard work involved to ensure this success, however, took its toll on the couple's marriage: Peter suffered from stress and depression and Janet became aware of his frequent extramarital affairs. From then onwards their relationship was soured by rows.

By the end of the 1970s the business was also facing difficulties. The high exchange rate deterred American customers, other lingerie firms were now offering competition, copying Janet's designs in cheaper materials, and the business had overexpanded. In 1982 the Regers signed a contract with the corset manufacturers Berlei, who proposed to market a 'Janet Reger collection', which proved a disastrous decision for the Regers. By the end of 1982 sales of luxury goods generally were in recession, and in January 1983 Janet Reger Creations Ltd went into liquidation. In the sale of the firm's assets Berlei bought the Janet Reger trademark, and attempted to prevent her from trading independently. Discovering that the contract referred to her company rather than to herself, Janet set up a new firm, Designs by Janet Reger, bought back the lease to the shop in Beauchamp Place, re-opening it in April 1983, and business flourished once more, a proof of her considerable entrepreneurial skills. The crisis of the liquidation ended the Regers' marriage, however. In 1984 Peter was bought out of the business, and in October 1985 he committed suicide.

In early 1986 Berlei went into receivership, and Janet bought back her Janet Reger trademark, at enormous cost. She recouped this through licensing deals with firms manufacturing bedlinen, soft furnishings, and accessories under the Janet Reger name, as well as producing a couture lingerie collection. Her daughter Aliza took an increasing role in the business, becoming chief executive in 1998. After developing breast cancer in 1991, which was successfully treated, Janet spent much of her time in Mauritius, where her products were manufactured. She wrote her autobiography, with Shirley Flack, in 1991, because, she said, 'my story seems to occupy a special place in the public's imagination' (*Janet Reger*, preface). She continued to be involved in her company until cancer returned and she died in the West Middlesex Hospital, Isleworth, London, on 14 March 2005.

Janet Reger said that she knew her name had become a household word in 1978 when Tom Stoppard included the line 'Don't get your Janet Regers in a twist' in his play *Night and Day* (*Janet Reger*, 73). Her designs introduced glamour, luxury, and sexiness into underwear at a time when the more liberated attitudes of the 1960s made the erotic acceptable, and by using sensuous fabrics and fine embroidery she turned underwear into 'lingerie', eagerly bought by women and their male partners. Her 1970s designs exactly accorded with the prevailing nostalgia for 1920s and 1930s Hollywood glamour, re-introducing garments such as French knickers, camisoles, and basques, for which an international fashionable clientele paid couture prices. Janet Reger's legacy was the large number of high street firms producing glamorous and erotic lingerie in the twenty-first century, satisfying a market she created. ANTHEA JARVIS

Sources J. Reger and S. Flack, *Janet Reger: her story* (1991) • A. de la Haye, ed., *The cutting edge: 50 years of British fashion, 1947–1997* (1996) • K. W. Bressler and K. Newman, *A century of lingerie* (1997) • *The Times* (16 March 2005) • *Daily Telegraph* (16 March 2005) • *The Guardian* (16 March 2005) • *The Independent* (16 March 2005) • m. cert. • d. cert.

Archives FILM BFINA, *Regrets?*, D. Heather (producer), Thames Television, 16 July 1986

Likenesses photographs, 1960x69–1998, Rex Features, London • photographs, 1983–90, PA Photos, London • J. Stillwell, photograph, 1990, PA Photos, London [*see illus.*] • photographs, 1992–2002, Camera Press, London • obituary photographs • photographs, repro. in Reger and Flack, *Janet Reger*

Wealth at death £296,522: probate, 30 Aug 2006, *CGPLA Eng. & Wales*

Reid, Sir Norman Robert (1915–2007), painter and gallery director, was born on 27 December 1915 at 244 Upland Road, Dulwich, London, the only son and second of three children of Edward Daniel Reid (1887–1956) and his wife, Blanche, *née* Drouet (1888–1961). His sisters were Blanche (*b*. 1913) and Hazel (*b*. 1930). The house in which he was born was one of a pair of semi-detached two-storey Victorian family houses. In 1932 the family moved to a similar house in Bromley. Reid's father owned a bespoke bootmaking business in Queen Victoria Street in the City of London. The boots were made by his partner in Northampton. Customers included successive lord mayors. The shop was destroyed in an air raid on the night of 29–30 December 1940, but the next morning Reid senior was outside the still smoking ruins with his order book, greeting customers. He shortly found new premises almost opposite. Family history had it that his wife was descended from Jean-Baptiste Drouet, the citizen who recognized Louis XVI on his flight from revolutionary Paris in 1791, leading to the king's arrest and eventual execution. If the story is true Reid may have inherited something of Drouet's spirit since all his life he was firmly left of centre in his politics.

Reid attended Wilson's Grammar School, Camberwell, where his artistic talent was spotted and he decided that his future lay somehow in art. His father accepted this only to the extent that he arranged Reid's entry into a commercial studio when he left school, and was horrified when Reid secretly applied for and won a scholarship to Edinburgh College of Art. Reid had chosen Edinburgh, he later said, because 'it was the furthest I could get from my family' (private information). From the school of art he went on to take a doctor of arts degree at Edinburgh University. An artistic presence in his background was his great-uncle John Robertson Reid (1851–1926), an interesting painter of rural social-realist scenes in an accomplished *plein air* style. Two of his paintings entered the Tate collection as part of Sir Henry Tate's original gift in 1894. John Robertson Reid's sister, Flora MacDonald Reid (1861–1938), was also a professional painter, exhibiting regularly at the Royal Academy in London between 1881 and 1932.

When the Second World War broke out Reid served initially in the Royal Engineers, where his artistic talents were thought to be of use, but underwent officer training and was commissioned into the Argyll and Sutherland highlanders, seeing action in Italy and reaching the rank of major. Meanwhile, on 1 August 1941, at Palmerston Place Church, Edinburgh, he had married Jean Lindsay Bertram, an art lecturer, also aged twenty-five, daughter of Alexander Taylor Bertram, manager of a cabinet-making business. They had met while both were students at Edinburgh College of Art. They had two children, John (*b*. 1944) and Katherine (*b*. 1946).

On demobilization in 1945 Reid joined the staff of the Tate Gallery and rose rapidly. The director (since 1938), Sir John Rothenstein, had established the Tate in the public consciousness as never before, but lacked the eye for detail that Reid supplied. The early 1950s was a period of intense internal turbulence at the Tate following the appointment to the staff in 1949 of the South African artist and art historian LeRoux Smith LeRoux. Reid soon spotted that he was seeking power. Systematic attempts by LeRoux over the next few years to topple Rothenstein for alleged financial misdemeanours traumatized the institution and nearly succeeded. Eventually, in 1954, the trustees, after conducting an inquiry, formally reprimanded Rothenstein and forced LeRoux to resign. Of Reid, who had held the fort throughout, the chairman of trustees, Sir Colin Anderson, noted that although he appeared to lack ambition he was 'gold all through' (Spalding, 128). In the wake of the affair he was promoted deputy director in 1954. The whole episode clearly left its mark, however, and perhaps accounted for Reid's occasional authoritarianism, and intermittent paranoia about the press, after he became director, notably during the media storm in 1976 over Carl Andre's brick sculpture *Equivalent VIII*.

Reid's appointment as director of the Tate Gallery was a classic case of a dark horse. When Rothenstein retired in 1964 one of the trustees, the flamboyant painter and critic Lawrence Gowing, proposed himself for the post and the board obsequiously agreed. The appointment was about to be announced when the Treasury (to which the Tate was then directly responsible) caused consternation by insisting on an open competition. This attracted several additional high-profile candidates, but Reid came from behind to beat them all. Although he had achieved much during his deputyship, including the creation of what became a world-standard conservation department, he was now able seriously to set about dragging the Tate into the modern age, putting what was still a relatively small and amateurish institution on the road to expansion, and professionalizing it. In respect of the Tate collection he made a dramatic change that at a stroke resolved a fundamental anomaly in the Tate's statutory collecting brief and laid the foundation for the creation of Tate Britain and Tate Modern in 2000.

The Tate Gallery had been founded in 1894 (and opened in 1897) as the National Gallery of British Art and was also (until 1954) administratively part of the National Gallery. In 1916, as a result of a strange combination of circumstances, and by means of a Treasury minute, it was suddenly given the additional responsibility of forming a national collection of modern foreign art, and was renamed the National Gallery Millbank. (It was renamed the Tate Gallery in 1932, but its remit remained the same.) This created huge tensions, both in collecting policy and in the display of the collection, which continued to torture the institution until Reid became director. Before then the modern foreign work had been ghettoized within the gallery. Reid's radical idea was that the Tate collection should be treated as a continuous chronological sequence simply divided into historic British and international modern, with the modern foreign blended into the modern British. The division was initially defined by artist's date of birth, before or after 1860. This was later changed to the date of the work of art, before or after 1900. On this basis he created two separate sets of displays, one of historic British art and the other of international modern art. Both began at the front of the Millbank building, so the visitor could turn left and process through four centuries of British art, or right and proceed through the modern collection. Administratively he created two curatorial departments, the historic British collection and the modern collection, and appointed a slew of bright young curators to reinforce two earlier appointments, of Martin Butlin and Ronald Alley, who became respective heads of the new sections (in the case of Butlin after a brief interim in which Gowing was given the post, possibly as a sop). The new appointments included most notably Michael Compton, Richard Morphet, and Anne Seymour (later D'Offay), and on the historic side the young Constable scholar Leslie Parris.

From 1968 the Tate took (from the Arts Council) responsibility for its own exhibition programme, and in 1970 Reid formally created the first Tate department of exhibitions with Compton at its head. Compton had a feel for the burgeoning pop culture of the 1960s and for the pop art that reflected it, but was equally attuned to the radical minimal and conceptual art movements of the decade. The results were spectacular, with exhibition after exhibition drawing huge numbers and a new youthful audience to the Tate. The historic side was not neglected, with dramatically staged and ground-breaking explorations of Elizabethan, Jacobean, and Caroline art among much else. It was a period of extraordinary dynamism, exuberance, excitement, and optimism. The Tate's success at this time was not hindered by Reid's warm relations with Jennie Lee, the Labour government's minister for the arts.

Meanwhile the young curators were pushing acquisitions in the avant-garde areas. This often caused battles with and among the trustees, who had the ultimate say, and Reid himself, who, while a committed modernist, found himself out of his personal aesthetic comfort zone with what was soon to become known as postmodernism. It is a tribute to him that he nevertheless backed his curators. This resulted, for example, in the acquisition, against bitter opposition from the trustees, of Roy Lichtenstein's iconic, and soon priceless, pop masterpiece *Whaam!*, and the formation of a pioneering collection of minimal and conceptual art virtually as it was being made. However, after the furore over the acquisition of the Andre brick sculpture in 1976 he became notably less willing to support adventurous acquisitions.

Reid, though, was in his element with the classic modernists of his own generation, and brought in important gifts from Barbara Hepworth, Henry Moore, and Ben Nicholson. When Alberto Giacometti came to London in 1965 for his retrospective at the Tate, Reid provided him with a studio in the basement (where he produced a major sculpture during his stay) and scraped together £20,000 to purchase work by him. Curators drew up a list of desirable pieces and presented it to Giacometti over lunch with the question, 'how many of these can we have for the money?' His reply was 'all of them and for ten thousand and I insist on presenting a further work' (private information). The group of sculptures thus acquired became, again, a priceless asset of the Tate collection.

The most famous of Reid's acquisitions was the nine huge canvases by the American abstract expressionist Mark Rothko that constitute the Tate's celebrated Rothko room. Reid had developed a friendship with the laconic artist and a gift was first mooted in 1966. Tortuous negotiations followed. Finally in 1969 Reid flew to New York with a model of the room in which the gift was to go, and the two of them finalized the choice of works and the arrangement. The paintings reached the Tate on 25 February 1970 and as the crates were being opened to reveal the dark, brooding presences within, news arrived from New York that Rothko had been found in his studio, dead by his own hand.

Development of the Tate building on Millbank to fill the whole of its large rectangular site had continued at intervals almost from the moment it opened, but had come to a halt in 1937. By 1968 pressure on space was such that Reid had to grasp the nettle of filling the remaining north-east quarter, about the size of a football pitch. For maximum flexibility it was decided to create a continuous space with a single roof span and movable internal walls. It was an extraordinarily bold concept and its engineering proved difficult. But it finally opened in 1979, the last year of Reid's directorship, and transformed the gallery.

Reid had begun his own artistic career as a portraitist, in the modern realist manner of the Euston Road School, and his gifts were apparent in highly sensitive portraits of his wife and daughter, for example. Painting inevitably took something of a back seat during his Tate directorship but in retirement he devoted himself to it with renewed energy. His cubist-influenced collages were a quiet but distinctive contribution to British abstract art. At the same time he practised landscape and still-life painting, in which a modernist sense of form and a rich sense of colour were married to a feel for nature that echoed and extended the English Romantic tradition. Works by him are in the Tate collection and that of the Scottish National Gallery of Modern Art. He was also a keen and knowledgeable gardener.

Norman Reid blended quiet competence and authority, and a clear vision of the future, with deep understanding of and empathy with art and artists. On his retirement his old rival Lawrence Gowing praised him generously in print, concluding, 'Norman Reid has left an instrument and a resource with an incomparable potential' (L. Gowing, 'The new Tate', *Encounter*, August 1979). It was Reid who set the Tate Gallery on course to become, in the hands of a later director, Sir Nicholas Serota, the massive museological phenomenon known from 2000 simply as Tate, with its single Tate collection feeding its four Tate galleries. Reid was knighted in 1970, and made an honorary LittD by the University of East Anglia the same year. His wife, Jean, was a strong support throughout his life, and it is perhaps unsurprising that he survived her by only a few months. He died on 17 December 2007 at the New Cavendish Club, 44–8 Great Cumberland Place, London, and was survived by his two children.

SIMON CASIMIR WILSON

Sources F. Spalding, *The Tate: a history* (1998) · *The Times* (19 Dec 2007) · *The Guardian* (19 Dec 2007) · *The Independent* (19 Dec 2007) · *Daily Telegraph* (20 Dec 2007) · Burke, *Peerage* · *WW* (2007) · personal

knowledge (2011) · private information (2011) [Katherine Reid, daughter; Hazel Reid, sister; R. Alley] · b. cert. · m. cert. · d. cert.
Archives SOUND BL NSA, performance recordings
Likenesses Snowdon, bromide print, 1964, NPG · L. Gowing, oil on canvas, 1980, Tate collection · obituary photographs · photographs, Tate archives
Wealth at death £1,081,250: probate, 27 Aug 2009, *CGPLA Eng. & Wales*

Renfrew, Glen McGarvie (1928–2006), journalist and news agency executive, was born at Aberdare, New South Wales, Australia, on 15 September 1928, the youngest of ten children of Robert Renfrew, a coalminer who became a lay preacher for a gospel church, and his wife, Jane Grey, *née* Watson. His parents could afford to give him a better education than many of his siblings. He attended Newcastle high school and the University of Sydney, where he studied English, history, and modern languages. After graduation he spent time as a labourer at a hydroelectric construction site where hard drinking and fisticuffs ruled. He was later to admit that when he first joined Reuters in 1952 'maybe I still had some of the manner of that place' (Read, 353). He was to be long remembered for his involvement in a fight at the Cogers public house, which (curiously) was part of the Reuters Fleet Street building.

Despite his bluff physical appearance—of medium height but broad shouldered, hair close cut—Renfrew was always much more than 'a wild colonial boy'. He was, for example, an enthusiast for literature and the arts. His cheery grin and engaging Australian accent helped him to relate to people of all sorts and nationalities. He liked a no-nonsense approach, preferring informal discussion (often over a drink) to set committee meetings.

Renfrew's recruitment to Reuters was decidedly informal. After travelling around Europe he arrived unannounced at Reuters' headquarters and asked at the desk for a job interview. He had no experience in journalism, but the head of Comtelburo (later Reuters Economic Services) was impressed by his command of French and Italian, as well as some German, and he was made a trainee. Two years later, on 20 February 1954, by then a fully fledged journalist, he married Daphne Ann, a 21-year-old Reuters secretary, and daughter of Harry Walter Hailey, clerk. They had a son and three daughters.

Renfrew eventually became Comtel manager for southern Africa, and then in 1960 manager for south-east Asia, based in Singapore. Next he became manager of the new Brussels office, which was taking over distribution of Comtelburo services from the Belgian news agency. In July 1964 he was made manager of the computer division of the newly named Reuters Economic Services (RES). In that role he quickly expanded the Stockmaster system—Reuters' first entry into the world of computers—which supplied stock market and commodity prices, and which he drove from small beginnings in Europe to a worldwide presence. Stockmaster had originally been introduced to Reuters by the RES manager, Michael Nelson, whose deputy Renfrew formally became in 1969. But Gerald Long, Reuters' general manager and chief executive, soon decided to give Renfrew his head by making him, in 1971, manager for all Reuters services in North America, where the agency was belatedly attempting to establish itself independently in competition with the American agencies, Associated Press, Dow Jones, and UPI. Opinion within the company was later to differ strongly about how far Renfrew succeeded in the United States. He claimed to have turned losses of $2 million per year into a profit; but this was doubted by Reuters' European staff whose successful Monitor services were making most of the company's money. In the United States Renfrew promoted 'row grabbing' as an alternative to Monitor, using cable television delivery. This led Reuters North America into the manufacture of its own hardware, something that had never been risked previously. For technical reasons row grabbing proved to be a non-starter outside North America.

In 1981 Renfrew succeeded Gerald Long as managing director and chief executive of Reuters. The board had been persuaded that Renfrew was now showing greater dynamism than Nelson. Thereafter Renfrew still spent more time in New York than in London. He quickly restructured the company's global organization so as to reveal more profit in the bottom line: 'Then I just beat the drum and said, "Let's get profits up. Let's get margins up"' ('Renfrew: reflections on a decade', 10). Annual profit before tax immediately quadrupled to nearly £17 million in 1981. By 1989 it was £283 million. Moneymaking was also very important for Renfrew personally. He introduced various executive share-option schemes, and in the process himself became a multi-millionaire. He also encouraged the editorial staff by opening fresh news bureaux worldwide. Throughout the decade he enthusiastically bought up a diversity of smaller businesses as 'strategic acquisitions', even though some of his senior colleagues doubted the wisdom of this policy. Nevertheless even his sharpest critics were to recognize that the acquisition of Instinet, an automated equity brokerage business, made much money for Reuters and put its name on the American business map. With Reuters now in huge profit, it went public in 1984. Whether the selection of Renfrew to lead Reuters through the 1980s was the right choice will remain debatable, however. Nelson would have made many fewer acquisitions, preferring organic growth. John Jessop, who worked for both men, in retrospect favoured Nelson's balance of enterprise with caution: 'he invariably picked winners' (Jessop, 490).

In 1991 Renfrew retired to Bermuda, where he pursued his love of sailing. He had reacted negatively to soundings about accepting a knighthood, emphasizing that Reuters was an international company independent of all governments. He returned to England when dementia set in, and died at Allington Court nursing home, Bricket Wood, St Albans, on 29 June 2006. He was survived by his wife, Daphne, his son, Barry (a senior executive with AP), and two daughters, one daughter having predeceased him.

DONALD READ

Sources J. Lawrenson and L. Barber, *The price of truth*, rev. edn (1986) · J. Fenby, *The international news services* (1986) · D. Hamilton, *Editor-in-chief* (1989) · 'Renfrew: reflections on a decade', *Reuters World* (March 1991), 10–11 · D. Read, *The power of news: the history of*

Reuters, 2nd edn (1999) · *The Times* (5 July 2006) · *The Guardian* (7 July 2006) · *The Independent* (7 July 2006) · *Daily Telegraph* (17 July 2006) · J. Jessop, *Tales from the south pier* (2008) · *WW* (2006) · personal knowledge (2010) · private information (2010) · m. cert. · d. cert.
Archives Reuters Archive, London
Likenesses photograph, 1984, PA Photos, London · obituary photographs · photographs, Reuters Archive, London
Wealth at death multi-millionaire

Rheinberg, Netta (1911–2006), cricketer and cricket administrator, was born on 24 October 1911 at 23 the Avenue, Brondesbury, Middlesex, the daughter of Jewish parents, Julius Rheinberg, export merchant, and his wife, Frieda, *née* Loewy. She was educated at South Hampstead High School for Girls and was afterwards sent to Europe to learn languages. She then attended secretarial college and was temporary secretary to J. F. Roxburgh, headmaster of Stowe School, in 1932, before becoming company secretary in her father's silk and textile business in the City. She began playing cricket while at school, and joined Gunnersbury Women's Cricket Club in 1932, becoming captain of the third eleven in only her second season. She went on to captain the first eleven and represent her county, Middlesex.

Rheinberg joined 'Gunns' at the start of what she regarded as a golden age in the women's game. The Women's Cricket Association (WCA), founded in 1926, encouraged a dramatic growth of female participation in the sport, and many young women who had enjoyed playing cricket at home with their brothers, fathers, and uncles grasped the opportunity to join one of the newly formed clubs: there were 10 sides nationally in 1927, 80 in 1934, and 123 by 1938. This activity reflected a degree of social emancipation for women, but it also challenged a male preserve, and did not go uncontested. As Rheinberg observed, the press reaction was mixed:

> the reputable correspondents … recounted what they saw, albeit sometimes with a smile. But the more lively journals, in their search for the sensational, were all too prone to happen on some graceless pose or some sartorial effrontery, which gleefully they splashed abroad as front-page news, and which took a deal of living down. (Joy, 36)

The WCA encouraged strict adherence to a dress code and took great care in staging its first public match, between London and District and the Rest of England at Beckenham in 1929. Progress thereafter was rapid and within a few years a 'women's ashes' series had begun with the Australians. Male acceptance, though, was neither quick nor universal. Rheinberg later commented that 'men thought we were really a bit ridiculous in those days', and Len Hutton once remarked to Brian Johnston: 'It's just like a man trying to knit, isn't it?' (*Fair Play*, 9). Johnston disagreed.

Rheinberg proved herself a capable batsman and slip for club and county, and helped to keep Gunnersbury in being during the Second World War as captain of the only eleven. She was never regarded as a first-rate player, but was selected for the England side that toured Australia in 1948–9. By then her administrative skills were well recognized—she was secretary of the Middlesex WCA, 1937–47, and assistant secretary of the WCA, 1938–47—and she doubled as tour manager. The party left Tilbury on the *Orient* on 14 October 1948 and reached Fremantle on 9 November, having defeated an All-Ceylon eleven in Colombo en route. Rheinberg made 97 against Queensland Country at Bundaberg on 14 December, her highest score of the tour, but she also had the misfortune to make a 'pair' during her only test appearance, at Adelaide in mid-January: she was stumped for nought in her first innings and clean-bowled by Betty Wilson on the first ball of her second. Australia won the match and, since the second and third tests were drawn, the series. It was England's only loss in nineteen matches in Australia. The tourists defeated New Zealand at Eden Park, on 26–9 March 1949, before returning home on 13 May. The seven-month tour had been an unforgettable experience, but Rheinberg estimated that it had cost each player around £300; they drew assistance from an appeal fund that was supported by the MCC and all of the first-class counties.

Netta Rheinberg (1911–2006), by S. & G. Barratts, 1948

Rheinberg's business background and bright persona made her an ideal team manager, and she accompanied the England side that toured Australia and New Zealand in 1957–8. She was secretary of the WCA from 1948 to 1958, and served as president of both Gunnersbury WCC and the Middlesex WCA. She was also membership secretary and vice-chairman of the Cricket Society, and ran the journal *Women's Cricket* from 1950 until 1967 when, under the pressure of inflation, it folded. Many in the cricket world mourned the title's passing—it was founded in 1930—and E. W. Swanton offered Rheinberg regular space in *The Cricketer* to compensate. She wrote for two years before handing over to Rachel Heyhoe-Flint, and the pair later co-wrote a history of the women's game, *Fair Play* (1976).

In December 1983 Rheinberg was made MBE in recognition of her services to women's cricket, and in 1999 she was one of ten women accorded honorary membership of the MCC in a symbolic dismantling of the club's men only rule. The admission of women to Lords came after years of campaigning, during which Rheinberg and her peers adopted an attitude of patient moderation: 'We decided', she said, 'to make our protest in a dignified fashion and wait' (*Daily Telegraph*, 7 July 2006). She had enjoyed representative honours as a player, but was foremost an administrator and a writer who helped nurture the game in the post-war era. Heyhoe-Flint described her as 'an action girl': 'We had very few people then, and she galvanised activity, partly just by having a great personality and a sense of humour' (*Wisden*). Rheinberg's mother had warned her that she would 'never meet nice men' if she played cricket, and she later reflected: 'She was quite right in a way. I won't say I didn't meet nice men, but I didn't marry' (*Daily Telegraph*). She enjoyed a lifelong friendship with Edna Golding, for many years treasurer at Gunnersbury WCC, and the two women shared a bungalow in Pinner, Middlesex, for almost forty years, until Golding's death in early 2006. Rheinberg then moved to Erskine Hall care centre in Northwood, where she died on 18 June 2006, of heart disease. MARK POTTLE

Sources N. Joy, *Maiden over: a short history of women's cricket and a diary of the 1948 to 49 test tour to Australia* (1950) · N. Rheinberg and R. Heyhoe-Flint, *Fair play: the story of women's cricket* (1976) · *LondG*, 49583 (30 Dec 1983) · J. L. Hawes, *Women's test cricket: the golden triangle, 1934–84* (1987) · *The Guardian* (17 March 1999) · *The Times* (27 June 2006) · *Daily Telegraph* (7 July 2006) · *Wisden* [2007] · Gunnersbury Women's Cricket Club website, www.gunnersburywcc.co.uk, 6 Oct 2008 · www.cricinfo.com, 6 Oct 2008 · b. cert. · d. cert.

Likenesses S & G Barratts, photographs, 1948–57, PA Photos, London [*see illus.*] · group portrait, photographs, 1999, Photoshot, London · photograph, repro. in http://content.cricinfo.com/england/content/player/53839

Wealth at death £1,021,410: probate, 4 Oct 2006, *CGPLA Eng. & Wales*

Richardson, Ian William (1934–2007), actor, was born on 7 April 1934 at 21 Duff Street, Edinburgh, the only son and eldest of three children of John Richardson (1909–1990), a manager at the McVitie and Price biscuit factory, and his wife, Margaret Pollock (Peggy), *née* Drummond (1910–1988). His parents had met at the McVitie factory, where, Richardson claimed, his father invented the Jaffa cake.

Richardson was educated at Balgreen primary school and Heriot's and Tynecastle high schools, all in Edinburgh. He felt he was 'a hopeless student' (*The Independent*, 6 Dec 1997) but showed some aptitude in art and piano playing, and his dramatic leanings manifested themselves early, when he was chosen to read Laurence Binyon's 'For the Fallen' at an armistice day service. 'It was my turn to say "They shall not grow old as we that are left grow old": I did it without looking at the paper and in front of the altar, not at the lectern' (ibid., 1 Nov 1995). He made his first visit to the theatre at fourteen, and his first appearance as an aristocratic boy in an amateur production of *A Tale of Two Cities*. The director told him that he needed to modify his accent to progress, so his mother arranged elocution lessons. Thereafter he took on stage-management jobs with the Edinburgh People's Theatre and with the visiting Wilson Barrett Company. His three years of national service were spent mostly in Libya, and involved locating and retrieving remains for burial in the Tobruk war cemetery. He then became a duty announcer with the British Forces Broadcasting Service, working on classical music programmes and directing dramas. Influenced heavily by the clipped tones of the chief announcer, he learned to suppress his Scottish accent still further, and determined to become an actor.

On returning to Scotland Richardson entered the College of Dramatic Art in Glasgow, and concurrently studied for a teaching qualification at Glasgow University. His father, an austere Presbyterian, had strongly disapproved of his son's choice of profession, but was won round on seeing him perform at college, and thereafter was supportive. Richardson left college in 1957, having won the James Bridie gold medal, and the following year joined the Birmingham Repertory Theatre, under the actor and director Bernard Hepton. His roles included John Worthing in *The Importance of Being Earnest*, and the title role in *Hamlet*, directed by Hepton. Among those who admired his youthful Hamlet was the critic J. C. Trewin, who wrote that he entered as 'a slight, sad-eyed figure of settled melancholy, earnest, sweet and boyish, who could suggest heartbreak in an inflection, a twist of the lip' (*Daily Telegraph*, 10 Feb 2007).

Richardson's performance was also seen by the Shakespearian scholar and director John Barton, who recommended him to Peter Hall, the newly appointed director of the Shakespeare festival in Stratford upon Avon. Richardson was offered a three-year contract, becoming one of the first in an ensemble that, a year later, was renamed the Royal Shakespeare Company (RSC). He stayed for fifteen years, fast becoming a cornerstone of the company. He gained attention even in minor roles. His somewhat inbred Prince of Aragon in Michael Langham's production of *The Merchant of Venice* (1960) was 'the last expiring flicker of an effete lineage—preceded by his own portrait which had evidently adorned the Academy at Saragossa, and escorted by a matriarch of "endless age"' (Speaight, 278). The matriarch was played by the actress Maroussia Frank (*b.* 1940), whom Richardson married on 2 February 1961. Six years his junior, she was the daughter of Alexei Frank, a Russian émigré, and his wife, Elizabeth (Betty) Scorer, a dancer, and later ballet and theatre critic for the *News Chronicle*. They had two sons, Jeremy (*b.* 1961), later a graphic designer, and Miles (*b.* 1963), who was to become an actor.

Richardson's other early roles at Stratford included a glittering and devilish Oberon opposite Judi Dench's Titania (1961), and a wonderfully flamboyant Antipholus of Ephesus in Clifford Williams's hugely inventive, and much revived, *Comedy of Errors* (1964). He played Malatesti to Peggy Ashcroft's Duchess in the *Duchess of Malfi*, the RSC's first production at the Aldwych Theatre (1960), which thereafter became the company's London home, and in 1964 toured the eastern bloc and America as Edmund in the legendary Peter Brook–Paul Scofield *King Lear*, and played the Herald in Brook's equally groundbreaking production of Peter Weiss's *Marat / Sade*. In 1965 he made his New York début playing Marat in *Marat / Sade*, causing something of a sensation, in that he was the first actor to appear naked on the Broadway stage. He first played Ford in *The Merry Wives of Windsor* in 1964 and repeated the role for a number of years. As a suburban man driven to distraction by his own suspicions of cuckoldry, his was a great comic performance, 'a study of obsessional jealousy as frightening as it was funny' (*The Independent*, 10 Feb 2007). In 1965 he gave what John Barton considered the definitive Chorus in *Henry V*, followed by, among others, a dazzling Vendice in Trevor Nunn's reclamation of Tourneur's *The Revenger's Tragedy* (1965 and 1969), a neurotic and patrician Coriolanus (1966), an ice-cold Cassius in *Julius Caesar* (1968), a wildly camp Proteus in *Two Gentlemen of Verona*, and a wonderfully despairing Prospero in *The Tempest* (both 1970).

In 1970 Richardson took time out from the RSC, and faced a year of unemployment when a television project was cancelled, and he and Maroussia were reduced to scouring Covent Garden for discarded fruit and vegetables. He was rescued by the Bristol Old Vic Theatre, and gave a touching performance as Tom Wrench, the sweet-natured playwright, in *Trelawny*, Julian Slade's and Aubrey Woods's musical version of Pinero's *Trelawny of the 'Wells'*, which then transferred to Sadler's Wells (1971–2). He returned to the RSC in 1973 to give one of his greatest performances, as Berowne in *Love's Labour's Lost*. Berowne remained his favourite role, exercising all his technical prowess. In John Barton's acclaimed production of *Richard II* (1974) he and Richard Pasco shared and alternated the roles of Richard and the usurper Henry Bolingbroke, Barton's intention being to show the King and Bolingbroke as mirror images. His Richard was (in Michael Billington's words) a performance of 'infinite sweetness, bruising irony and thunderous scorn' (*The Guardian*, 10 Feb 2007), in a production that redefined the play for years to come. Richardson's final roles with the company included Iachimo in *Cymbeline* (1974), and the title role in *Richard III* (1975). His Richard, in a highly conceptualized production set in a psychiatric ward, resembled a grotesque child unrestrained by social customs.

In the Americas Richardson proved himself a consummate Shavian. In 1976, as Henry Higgins in the twentieth-anniversary Broadway revival of *My Fair Lady*, he gave a dazzling performance of lightning speed and attack, winning the Drama Desk award and a Tony nomination, and the following year at the Shaw festival in Niagara on the Lake, Canada, he played Jack Tanner in *Man and Superman* and the Doctor in *The Millionairess*. In 1979 he returned to the British stage, on tour and at the Old Vic, as Mercutio, and, in another great comic performance, as Khlestakov, in Gorky's *Government Inspector*. Richardson was an astonishingly accomplished stage actor, combining physical grace, great energy, impeccable style, and quicksilver comic timing. As a man he was quite emotional and vulnerable, and often suffered sickness before going on stage. There was an inner turbulence that underscored his work. But it was his voice that finally marked him out. He was a masterful verse-speaker, of matchless clarity and dexterity, with formidable breath control. He seemed to take long speeches on one breath, his voice variously described as oboe-, trumpet-, and bell-like.

Richardson had made his television début in the early 1960s, repeating his performances in filmed RSC productions. In 1971 he played Anthony Beavis in Aldous Huxley's *Eyeless in Gaza*, and in 1979 Montgomery in *Churchill and the Generals* and *Ike: the War Years*. As Bill Haydon, the mole in MI6, in John le Carré's *Tinker, Tailor, Soldier, Spy* (1979) he gave a mesmerizing and mischievous performance. He later credited Sir Alec Guinness, the star of *Tinker, Tailor*, with teaching him to act for the camera. In 1981 he won the Royal Television Society's best actor award for his bravura performances as several characters—a Scottish crook, a 'dodgy' British agent, and a bungling Nazi officer—in *Private Schulz*. Other television roles included impressive performances as Sherlock Holmes in *The Sign of Four* and *The Hound of the Baskervilles* (both 1983), Nehru in *Mountbatten: the Last Viceroy* (1986), Anthony Blunt in *Blunt* (1987), the Master in Tom Sharpe's *Porterhouse Blue* (1987), Sir Robert Morton in *The Winslow Boy* (1989), and the Falkland Islands' governor Sir Rex Hunt in *An Ungentlemanly Act* (1992).

As Francis Urquhart, the Conservative Party chief whip who will stop at nothing, including murder, to get to Downing Street, in Michael Dobbs's *House of Cards* (1990), Richardson found his defining role as a screen actor, and was every bit as accomplished as he was on stage. The critic James Wolcott wrote that:

> Like the late Sir Laurence Olivier, [Richardson] is a master of the raised eyebrow, and he carries his head as if it belonged on a coin. His nose gleams like a dagger. His narcissism is cut so fine that he seems to be peeling off a personal supply of thin smiles. (*New Yorker*, 17 Jan 1994)

Richardson's Urquhart was a charming, sardonic, and wholly captivating creation, addressing the camera in direct asides he made the audience co-conspirators in his schemes, and coined a catchphrase ('You might think that: I couldn't possibly comment') that resonated long afterwards and was quoted by Prime Minister John Major in the House of Commons. Richardson won awards from the British Film Academy and the Broadcasting Press Guild, and received further nominations for his work in the two sequels, *To Play the King* (1993) and *The Final Cut* (1995). Later parts included Lord Groan in *Gormenghast*

(2000), and the voice of Death in Terry Pratchett's *Hogfather* (2006).

Although his television career brought him fame and reward, Richardson's cinema appearances were rare. Early roles included filmed versions of *Marat / Sade* (1967) and of Peter Hall's production of *A Midsummer Night's Dream* (1968). Other film work included the Priest alongside Peter O'Toole in *Man of La Mancha* (1972), an incisive Polonius in *Rosencrantz and Guildenstern Are Dead* (1990), and various mandarins or judges in *Brazil* (1985), *Cry Freedom* (1987), *M Butterfly* (1993), *From Hell* (2001), and *Becoming Jane* (2007). In America he was probably best known for his appearances in commercials for Grey Poupon mustard, 'a matter of infinite regret' (*New Yorker*, 13 Aug 2007).

Partly at the prompting of a young actor who confronted him with the irresponsibility of denying a younger generation the opportunity of seeing his work on stage, Richardson returned to the theatre to play the title roles in Molière's *The Miser* (1995) and Pinero's *The Magistrate* (1998), both at the Chichester Festival Theatre. He continued his association with the RSC, taking part in occasional all-star tours of *The Hollow Crown* from 2002 to 2004, alongside his fellow RSC alumni Sir Donald Sinden, Sir Derek Jacobi, and Dame Diana Rigg. It seemed wrong that Richardson, who had been appointed CBE in 1989, did not have a title himself. After another gap he played in a West End thriller, *The Creeper* by Pauline Macauley, in 2006, and rather more happily made his much belated National Theatre début the same year, voluptuous as Sir Epicure Mammon in Nicholas Hytner's production of *The Alchemist*. It was to be his last stage appearance.

Richardson had been about to start work on an episode of the popular television series *Midsomer Murders* when he died suddenly, in his sleep and at his home, 131 Lavender Sweep, Battersea, on 9 February 2007, of heart failure, with his wife by his side. They had been a devoted couple, Richardson having said that 'without Maroussia I cannot function. I don't know which bank my account is with, the name of my accountant or how to work the Aga' (*Daily Mail*, 25 Feb 2006). He was also survived by his two sons. A memorial service was held at St Paul's, Covent Garden, and his ashes were interred in row A in the stalls of the newly rebuilt Shakespeare Memorial Theatre, Stratford upon Avon, where he had given so many memorable performances. ALEX JENNINGS

Sources J. Goodwin, ed., *Royal Shakespeare Theatre Company, 1960–1963* (1964) • R. Speaight, *Shakespeare on the stage* (1973) • S. Beauman, *The Royal Shakespeare Company: a history of ten decades* (1982) • P. Hartnoll and P. Found, eds., *The concise Oxford companion to the theatre*, 2nd edn (1992) • *New Yorker* (17 Jan 1994); (13 Aug 2007) • *The Independent* (1 Nov 1995); (6 Dec 1997); (10 Feb 2007) • B. McFarlane, ed., *The encyclopedia of British film* (2003) • A. Dickson, *The rough guide to Shakespeare* (2005) • *Daily Mail* (25 Feb 2006) • *The Times* (10 Feb 2007) • *Daily Telegraph* (10 Feb 2007) • *The Guardian* (10 Feb 2007) • *New York Times* (10 Feb 2007) • S. Mail, *We could possibly comment: Ian Richardson remembered* (2009) • I. Herbert, ed., *Who's who in the theatre*, 16th edn (1977) • BL, theatre archive project, interview by A. Sikora, 29 Jan 2007; www.bl.uk/projects/theatrearchive/richardson.html, 6 Aug 2010 • www.imdb.com/name/nm0007183/, 6 Aug 2010 • *WW* (2007) • personal knowledge (2011) • private information (2011) • b. cert. • m. cert. • d. cert.

Archives FILM BFINA, documentary footage • BFINA, performance footage | SOUND BL, theatre archive project • BL NSA, documentary recordings • BL NSA, performance recordings

Likenesses photographs, 1967–2006, Getty Images, London • photographs, 1967–2007, Rex Features, London • photographs, 1994–2004, PA Photos, London • photographs, 1994–2006, Photoshot, London • photographs, 1999–2006, Camera Press, London • obituary photographs • photographs, repro. in Mail, *We could possibly comment*

Wealth at death £212,964: probate, 23 July 2007, *CGPLA Eng. & Wales*

Richardson, Joanna Leah (1925–2008), biographer, was born on 8 August 1925 at 36 West Heath Drive, Golders Green, London, the elder child of Fred Samuel (later Frederick Samuel) Richardson (1897–1978), leather merchant, and his wife, Charlotte Elsa, *née* Benjamin (1895–1978). Her parents were South African, of Jewish descent, and had married in London in 1924. Her father was an opera lover and an Italophile, who later interviewed Italian prisoners of war as a captain in the intelligence corps during the Second World War; from her mother she inherited a love of literature and the arts. She had one brother, Martin (1929–2001), who later became a successful architect.

Brought up in Hampstead Garden Suburb, Richardson was educated at the Downs School, Seaford, where she was unhappy, and at St Anne's Society, Oxford, which she enjoyed. Despite graduating with a third class degree in modern languages in 1946 she registered for graduate study under Enid Starkie, the flamboyant but sometimes brutal scholar of French literature. They had a difficult relationship, and Richardson's DPhil submission was rejected (it was sometimes rumoured on Starkie's advice); nevertheless Richardson was fascinated by Starkie's character, devilled for Starkie on her biography of Baudelaire (1957), and much later wrote a discreet official biography of her (1973).

Meanwhile, after working briefly as a research assistant to the illustrations editor of *Chambers's Encyclopaedia*, Richardson had embarked on a career as a freelance writer, becoming a correspondent for the *New English Weekly* and reviewing books for *The Listener*. She also translated French plays for the BBC, and began writing for newspapers and magazines, which later included regular contributions to the *Times Literary Supplement*, the *Modern Language Review*, and *French Studies*.

Richardson's first biography, published in 1952, of Fanny Brawne, the muse of the poet John Keats, was reputedly inspired by her discovery of an ambrotype of the subject, and involved extensive research in family papers and scattered libraries. Her fascination with Keats was an enduring one. Among her publications were *The Everlasting Spell: a Study of Keats and his Friends* (1963), *Keats and his Circle: an Album of Portraits* (1980), *The Life and Letters of John Keats* (1981), and numerous articles in the *Keats–Shelley Memorial Bulletin*. She was also closely associated with the Keats House Museum, near her home in Hampstead. An interest in nineteenth-century Britain was further pursued in biographies of Tennyson (1962), Edward Lear (1965), Thomas Creevey and Charles Greville (1967), and many writings on Victoria and Albert.

Richardson was best known for her studies of French, predominantly nineteenth-century, writers and other public figures, starting with Théophile Gautier (1958), and continuing with Princess Mathilde Bonaparte (1969), Paul Verlaine (1971), Stendhal (1974), Victor Hugo (1976), Émile Zola (1978), Judith Gautier (1987), Joseph-Napoléon Primoli (1987), and Charles Baudelaire (1994). Her biography of Judith Gautier, the talented and unconventional daughter of Théophile Gautier, was awarded the prix Goncourt for biography after its French translation was published in 1989; this was the first time either a woman or a non-Frenchman had won the prize. She was made a chevalier de l'Ordre des Arts et des Lettres in 1987.

Richardson was often attracted to complex characters, who might on a personal level have been difficult, egotistical, or disreputable (or all three), and she was sometimes at pains to point out her subjects' flaws. Among her favourite research projects were those that led to *The Courtesans: the Demi-Monde in Nineteenth-Century France* (1967) and *The Bohemians: la Vie de Bohème in Paris, 1830–1914* (1969). Her biographies were best described as fact-laden. She revelled in reviews which suggested that she knew (and was going to tell the reader) what her subject ate for breakfast. Some critics were less kind; A. S. Byatt observed of her *Baudelaire* that 'Some biographies glitter with the dead life of a world and a human being. Some, like this one, have a peculiar deadness—the spirit isn't raised, the ghost doesn't walk' (*Evening Standard*, 11 April 1994). She prided herself on her original research, but some academic critics in particular suggested that she at times owed rather too much to other people's findings. It was especially alleged that her *Baudelaire* owed too much to Starkie's, but it is probably truer to say that she was merely reclaiming some of her research, which Starkie had passed off as her own. For the most part she eschewed analysis or literary criticism, though sometimes she applied crude psychoanalytical concepts, as in her study of Baudelaire's supposed Oedipus complex. Her translations, which included Verlaine's and Baudelaire's poems (1974, 1975) and Gautier's *Mademoiselle de Maupin* (1981), similarly divided critics. Some praised her faithfulness to the French versions, while others thought she stuck 'too closely to the original, so that sharpness of image could be sacrificed to a cautious and clumsy fidelity' (*The Independent*, 18 March 2008).

A friend described Richardson as 'adamantine … determined, solitary, committed, and ruthless with herself and sometimes others' (*The Ship*, 56). A royalist, antique-collecting, high-church Anglican, high tory, she held unashamedly élitist views, and exhibited a degree of forthrightness and self-belief which frequently led her into combative situations. She sometimes seemed to relish, and indeed to nurture, feuds. Her time as a council member of the Royal Society of Literature from 1961 to 1987 was notable for several well-publicized spats. Nevertheless she had a circle of influential friends, mostly Oxford-based, among them Dame Janet Vaughan, Sir Isaiah Berlin, and A. L. Rowse. Berlin arranged for her to hold a visiting fellowship at Wolfson College, and Oxford belatedly awarded her a doctorate, making her a DLitt for her published work in 2004. Thereafter she liked to be known as Dr Richardson. She lived for many years at 55 Flask Walk, an early nineteenth-century terraced house in Hampstead. She died at the Royal Free Hospital, Camden, on 7 March 2008, and was cremated at Kensal Green crematorium on 19 March. At the time of her death she was working on a biography of Flaubert. She was unmarried.

ALEX MAY

Sources *Daily Telegraph* (12 March 2008) · *Camden New Journal* (13 March 2008) · *The Independent* (18 March 2008) · *The Times* (24 March 2008) · *The Ship* [St Anne's College, Oxford], 98 (2008–9), 56–7 · *WW* (2008) · private information (2012) · b. cert. · d. cert.
Archives Ransom HRC | Bodl. Oxf., Winfred Hamilton-Meikle papers | SOUND BL NSA, documentary recordings
Likenesses obituary photographs
Wealth at death £833,775: administration, 12 June 2008, *CGPLA Eng. & Wales*

Riddelsdell, Dame Mildred (1913–2006), civil servant, was born on 1 December 1913 at the Old Registry, Llandaff, Glamorgan, the second of the three daughters of Harry Joseph Riddelsdell (1866–1941), sub-warden of St Michael's College, Llandaff, and his wife, Maud, *née* Butt (*c.*1870–1943). Harry Riddelsdell later became rector of Wigginton and then vicar of Bloxham in Oxfordshire and it was there that Mildred and her sisters, Audrey and Yolande, grew up. She was educated at St Mary's Hall, Brighton, and then at Bedford College, the women's college of the University of London.

Riddelsdell passed the civil service examinations in 1936 and entered the Ministry of Labour, a revealing choice at a time of high unemployment and social distress, and one that shaped the whole of her career, which was to be focused on the administration of benefits for workers and families under the new welfare state. During the Second World War she was assistant private secretary to Ernest Bevin, the minister for labour and national service, a man she admired both for his personal qualities and for his ideals. At the war's end she became an assistant secretary in the new Ministry of National Insurance and was one of a small team charged with the introduction of family allowances and contributory benefits. In three years she and her colleagues drafted the necessary legislation and regulations, established departmental procedures, and set up hundreds of offices across the country through which the new system was administered. By 1950 she had become an under-secretary, a notable achievement for a 36-year-old woman in the civil service at that time.

Riddelsdell was seconded to the United Nations in New York between 1953 and 1956 to advise on pensions and national insurance, in which areas she was already a recognized expert. Appointed CBE in 1958, between 1962 and 1965 she was secretary of the National Incomes Commission. She returned to what was then the Ministry of Pensions and National Insurance for a year before transferring to the Ministry of Social Security as deputy secretary in 1966. In 1968 this was amalgamated into the Department of Health and Social Security under the new secretary of state, Richard (Dick) Crossman.

Crossman's controversial diaries, published in the mid-1970s after their author's death, and setting out in detail Crossman's experiences as a cabinet minister, provide revealing glimpses of Mildred Riddelsdell's work and style as a senior civil servant. Crossman evidently admired her as an exceptionally able and committed civil servant 'of deep personal integrity'. She was, he wrote, 'a terribly noble and nice woman' (16 Dec 1969, 8 June 1970, *Diaries*, 3.754, 940). Though generally suspicious of higher civil servants, when Riddelsdell wrote a paper that committed him to a position he had formerly rejected, Crossman accepted her explanation that it had been a genuine mistake without demur: 'I simply know Miss Riddelsdell assumed that I, being intelligent, would want what she wanted, and therefore she heard me say what she wanted me to say and misunderstood me' (4 Sept 1969, ibid., 2.625–6). She was adept at defending the interests of her ministry and dealing with Treasury ministers and their mandarins: on another occasion when Riddelsdell outwitted the latter Crossman recorded the 'naughty glint in her eye' with approval (8 Sept 1969, ibid., 3.633). She could be waspish in her judgement of others and also very funny: another of her ministers, Tam Dalyell, who was Crossman's parliamentary private secretary at the time, recalled her description of a meeting with the chancellor of the exchequer, Roy Jenkins, and his associates: 'It was like visiting Mussolini and his advisers' (*The Independent*, 29 July 2006; 4 Nov 1969, *Diaries*, 3.715). Following another meeting with the chancellor and his advisers, this time on occupational pensions, Crossman commented that 'Mildred Riddelsdell stood out as superior in intellectual content and mastery of the subject' (10 Nov 1969, *Diaries*, 3.722).

In December 1969 Crossman requested Riddelsdell's promotion to permanent secretary of the Department of Health and Social Security but the head of the home civil service, Sir William Armstrong, opposed the idea. However, in 1971 the next secretary of state at the department, Sir Keith Joseph, after consulting Crossman, ensured her final promotion to second (that is deputy) permanent secretary. She was appointed DCB in 1972, the first woman to join the order in the more than two hundred years of its existence. She retired the following year.

Riddelsdell became a member of the advisory committee on business appointments taken by civil servants and between 1974 and 1977 she was chairman of the Civil Service Retirement Fellowship. She enjoyed an active retirement herself over the next thirty years, during which she never lost touch with developments in her old department and in the provision of pensions and social security more generally. Her friendship with her older contemporary in the civil service, Dame Mary Smieton, who had been permanent secretary in the Department for Education, lasted long into her old age. Her father had been a botanist who contributed to many botanical publications and she was a keen gardener. Living in retirement in Witney, Oxfordshire, she regularly attended courses in history and literature at the University of Oxford's department for continuing education, where her lucid, insightful, and crystal-clear comments, delivered in her high, melodious voice and with the most exact pronunciation, were a feature of class discussions. In manner and attitude she was modest to a fault, making nothing of her former seniority in government.

Mildred Riddelsdell was one of the first women to reach the highest ranks of the civil service at a time when women were notably under-represented in them and before concerted efforts were made to equalize opportunities in central government. She was also a key figure in the construction and implementation of the welfare state in the generation following the Second World War. To that task she brought not only her formidable intellect and skills, but her personal commitment: there can be no doubt that she believed in the object of her career, the provision of security and social improvement through a contributory benefits system managed by the state. She died after a stroke at the Old Prebendal House nursing home in Shipton under Wychwood, Oxfordshire, on 25 July 2006, and her remains were buried at Oxford crematorium on 3 August 2006. She never married.

LAWRENCE GOLDMAN

Sources R. H. S. Crossman, *The diaries of a cabinet minister*, 3 vols. (1975–7) • *The Independent* (29 July 2006) • *The Guardian* (2 Aug 2006) • *Daily Telegraph* (8 Aug 2006) • *The Times* (8 Aug 2006) • Burke, *Peerage* • *WW* (2006) • personal knowledge (2010) • private information (2010) • b. cert. • d. cert.

Likenesses obituary photographs

Wealth at death £544,082: probate, 31 Oct 2006, *CGPLA Eng. & Wales*

Ridley [*née* Mosley], **Dame** (**Mildred**) **Betty** (**1909–2005**), church administrator, was born on 10 September 1909 at the rectory, Newby Place, Poplar, London, the daughter of Henry Mosley (1868–1948), rector of Poplar, later bishop of Stepney and then bishop of Southwell, and his wife, Mildred, *née* Willis (*d.* 1963). She was educated at the North London Collegiate School and Cheltenham Ladies' College. She won a place at the Royal College of Music (her love of music never left her and she sang with the Bach Choir for many years) but, aged nineteen, she fell in love with her father's chaplain, Michael Ridley (1899/1900–1953), and married him on 3 September 1929. After a brief spell in Hampshire (to which she returned in retirement) they moved to London where he became incumbent of St Gabriel's, Pimlico, and then rector of Finchley. She was an active vice-chairman of St Hilda's Settlement in Bethnal Green. Before her husband's untimely death in 1953 they had four children: Clare (*b.* 1930), Simon (*b.* 1933), Adam (*b.* 1937), and Giles (*b.* 1946).

Widowed at forty-four and with her three elder children moving into adult life, Betty Ridley directed her full energies toward the central councils of the Church of England, in which she had been moving with increasing confidence. She had been elected to the church assembly in 1945 and became vice-president of the British Council of Churches in 1954–6. She served on the central board of finance of the church assembly (from 1970 the general synod) for twenty-two years (1955–79). It was a mark of her rapidly won reputation that she was invited to assume the chairmanship of an important committee set up to rationalize the convoluted, politicized, and overlapping internal committee structure of the assembly. The committee had originally been chaired by Sir Peter Agnew MP, but he had found it impossible to combine the workload with his parliamentary duties. The Ridley report, which she introduced in a two-hour speech, carried the house and established a revised structure which lasted for many years both in assembly and general synod. She was made an honorary MA (Lambeth) in 1958.

Ridley served as a church commissioner from 1959 to 1981. She became the first chairman of the newly established redundant churches committee in 1968 and then, in 1972, was appointed by Archbishop Ramsey to be third church estates commissioner, the first woman to hold that post. In parallel she became, when the assembly metamorphosed into the general synod, a member of its highly influential (and highly political) standing and business committees, serving from 1971 to 1981. This decade, in which she held leading positions in both church commission and synod, saw her at the height of her reputation and powers. She was appointed DBE in 1975 and, upon retirement in 1982, was asked to chair the appointments committee that made recommendations leading to the appointment of John Habgood as archbishop of York.

Ridley's continuous and growing influence in the central structures of the Church of England sprang from a number of sources. Her personal qualities were many and formidable: maternal instincts, expressed through a warm and responsive manner, which attracted wide confidence; complete self-assurance and social ease; a good brain; common sense; keen perception and sound political judgement; and, although sometimes hidden, determination of purpose. Her energies were unflagging. Also of crucial importance was her familiarity with (by birth, education, and marriage), and her acceptance of, the prevailing customs, manners, and inherent assumptions of her (still largely male) colleagues in the assembly, synod, and commission at that time. By friends and opponents alike her gender was perceived as a source of strength (indeed comfort), never as a threat. It was no surprise that when the Reform Club elected women she should become the first woman to sit on its general committee.

These attributes informed Ridley's handling of her lifelong belief in and support for the ordination of women to the priesthood. Aged twenty she had expressed this view to the Council for Women's Church Work, of which her father was chairman. She was promptly invited to join them. When in 1950 the Lambeth conference of bishops reiterated the view that it was impossible for a woman to be ordained priest, she became a founder member of the influential Anglican Group for the Ordination of Women. The cause prospered and in 1992 when the general synod voted that there were no 'fundamental objections' to the principle of women's ordination, she heard the news, in retirement, 'with tears of joy' (*The Times*, 5 Aug 2005). Earlier, in 1975, her political judgement (characterized by some as too warm an attachment to the establishment) led her to urge some delay in the process; nevertheless, in 1979 she readily joined with other (more vociferous) colleagues in the foundation of the Movement for the Ordination of Women.

Her work as a leading church commissioner brought her, especially through her chairmanship of the houses and redundant churches committees, into close contact with the practicalities of dealing with much loved churches, often of historic and architectural value. They no longer had the congregations or patrons able to maintain them, to the distress of faithful parishioners faced with their 'redundancy'. Her understanding and personal experience of the economic realities of clerical family life made her uniquely effective in dealing with the commissioners' financial assistance for rectories and vicarages, and for their administration of the diocesan bishops' houses for which they were directly responsible. It was such qualities that marked her work as a leading figure in the life of the Church of England for over thirty years.

After her retirement in 1982 Ridley moved to St Swithun Street, Winchester. She was made an honorary DSC of Southampton University and served as a governor of King Alfred's College, Winchester (later Winchester University), and as chairman of the Hampshire Churches Preservation Trust. Her final years were spent at Brendon Nursing Home, Park Road, Winchester. She died at the Royal Hampshire County Hospital, Winchester, on 1 August 2005. She was survived by her four children.

PATRICK LOCKE

Sources *Daily Telegraph* (3 Aug 2005) · *The Guardian* (4 Aug 2005) · *The Times* (5 Aug 2005) · *The Independent* (10 Aug 2005) · *WW* (2005) · Burke, *Peerage* · personal knowledge (2009) · private information (2009) · b. cert. · m. cert. · d. cert.

Likenesses two photographs, 1975–7, Photoshot, London · obituary photographs

Wealth at death £465,853: probate, 14 Dec 2005, *CGPLA Eng. & Wales*

Ridley, Walter John [Wally] (**1913–2007**), songwriter and record producer, was born at 23 Medburn Street, St Pancras, London, on 28 February 1913, the eldest of five children of Walter Ernest Ridley, at the time a cloth worker's salesman, later a furniture dealer, and his wife, Edith Elizabeth Rose, *née* Sutton. He started piano lessons when he was six and was soon demonstrating the instruments his father sold in his furniture store in Camden Town. In 1926 he won a scholarship to the Northern Polytechnic, London, to study piano manufacture. When he was fifteen he joined the music publisher Feldmans to demonstrate songs to stage and radio performers. His first composition, written with the veteran music hall composer Harry Castling, 'One Little Hair on his Head', was recorded by Gracie Fields. By 1935 he was a manager at another publisher, Peter Maurice, and he promoted Michael Carr and Jimmy Kennedy, helping them without credit (according to his testimony) to write the standards 'Dinner for One Please, James' and 'Did Your Mother Come from Ireland?' He matched 'Home Town' with the Crazy Gang comedians Bud Flanagan and Chesney Allen, and he wrote 'My Way' for the Paul Robeson film *Jericho* (1937). On 15 April 1939 he married Libusé (Liba) Izerova (1918–1997), a secretary, born in Czechoslovakia, daughter of Cyril Izer, tailor. They had one son and two daughters.

Because of suspected tuberculosis Ridley was exempted from military service during the Second World War, but his contribution to the war effort was considerable. He coached a young singer, Vera Lynn, thereby expanding her range. He produced her radio series, *Sincerely Yours*, which made her the Forces' Sweetheart, and found her biggest success, 'We'll Meet Again'. He was impressed with a Canadian army captain based in Britain, Robert Farnon, and promoted his talent.

In 1948 Ridley persuaded the BBC to broadcast a radio series live from a theatre. The series starred Donald Peers, and his signature tune, again found by Ridley, was 'Powder Your Face with Sunshine'. Ridley expected the BBC to mock his suggestion of a radio series featuring a ventriloquist, but *Educating Archie* with Archie Andrews and Peter Brough captured twenty million listeners and made household names of Beryl Reid, Max Bygraves, Harry Secombe, and Tony Hancock. Later in 1948 Ridley joined EMI Records to establish a popular catalogue for the HMV label. The label, restricted by shellac shortages, only had regular releases from Joe Loss and George Melachrino and their orchestras. Soon Ridley was having success with Peers, Bygraves, Ronnie Hilton, and Malcolm Vaughan. There was also Alma Cogan, known as 'the girl with the giggle', another of Ridley's suggestions. In 1955 a tearful Jeannie Carson told Ridley that she needed a decent song, 'something like "The Trolley Song"' (made famous by Judy Garland), for a film she was making, *An Alligator Named Daisy*. Ridley wrote 'I'm in Love for the Very First Time'.

At EMI Ridley had to determine which records from America's RCA Victor label were right for release in the UK. In 1956 he released Elvis Presley's 'Heartbreak Hotel', and EMI nearly sacked him. However, the public bought the record and it went to number two. Although he tried with Don Lang and Bert Weedon, Ridley knew that British artists couldn't capture that sound and he had his main success with middle of the road ballads, producing 'St Therese of the Roses' for Malcolm Vaughan and 'No Other Love' for Ronnie Hilton. They fitted Ridley's maxim that if a song was well written, had a clear, clean message, and was delivered with sincerity with a good quality performance, good orchestra, and good sound, it would sell and sell. His first venture into rock 'n' roll was with Johnny Kidd and the Pirates, who topped the UK charts in 1960 with 'Shakin' All Over'. The British beat explosion of the mid-1960s was not for him but he did produce top ten hits by the Swingin' Blue Jeans, including 'Hippy Hippy Shake' (1963).

When a music publisher asked Ridley to cover an American song, 'Mad Passionate Love' (1958), he expected the song to be taken seriously, but Ridley placed it with the comic actor Bernard Bresslaw, whose lugubrious delivery made it a hit. Ridley worked with many comedians, finding Morecambe and Wise's signature tune, 'Bring Me Sunshine', and producing Max Bygraves's 'Gilly Gilly Ossenfeffer Katzenellen Bogen by the Sea' (1954), Benny Hill's 'Ernie (the Fastest Milkman in the West)' (1971), and Windsor Davies and Don Estelle's 'Whispering Grass' (1975). He also produced big-selling albums by the Black and White Minstrel Show as well as recording the Deep River Boys, Andy Stewart, Iris Williams, and the Mike Sammes Singers.

In retirement Ridley undertook occasional projects, producing, for example, *Love is Jose Carreras* (1984). He won two Ivor Novello awards for his contributions to the music industry. He died at his home, Vermala, Southlea Road, Datchet, Berkshire, on 23 January 2007, of a ruptured abdominal aortic aneurysm. He was survived by his three children. SPENCER LEIGH

Sources *The Times* (31 Jan 2007) • *The Independent* (1 Feb 2007) • *Daily Telegraph* (15 Feb 2007) • *The Guardian* (26 Feb 2007) • personal knowledge (2011) • private information (2011) • b. cert. • m. cert. • d. cert.
Archives SOUND BL NSA, performance recordings • BL NSA, documentary recordings
Likenesses obituary photographs
Wealth at death £663,888: probate, 21 May 2007, *CGPLA Eng. & Wales*

Rigby, Terence Christopher Gerald (1937–2008), actor, was born on 2 January 1937 at 8 Bretby Grove, Erdington, Birmingham, the son of Charles Rigby, who ran a small business making hydraulic packing products, and his wife, Teresa, *née* Byrne. He took an early interest in acting while he was a boy scout. After national service in the RAF he became bored with his training as a quantity surveyor and, after a series of unskilled jobs, studied at the Royal Academy of Dramatic Art for two years (1958–60). He was thrilled to be taken on at the Birmingham Repertory Company, which he regarded as 'one of the top four or five regional theatres' in the UK (McNiven, interview). For the next five years he underwent an arduous and very thorough apprenticeship, working in regional rep companies, where he had to learn parts very quickly in a bewildering variety of plays, and occasional touring productions, such as Joan Littlewood's production of *Fings Ain't Wot They Used T'Be*. He survived fallow patches by doing walk-on parts in television drama and clearing tables at the Royal Opera House, where he progressed to running the artists' bar. In 1964, while playing several roles in *Pickwick*, a musical starring Harry Secombe, he heard that the Royal Shakespeare Company was having problems casting the part of Joey in Harold Pinter's new play, *The Homecoming*. He auditioned by interpreting a role he had played in John Osborne's *Requiem for George Dillon* as if it had been written by Pinter. After some prevarication he won the part and began a long and productive relationship with Pinter and the director Peter Hall.

This was Rigby's breakthrough and he would continue to play strong supporting stage roles for the rest of his career. He also began to make his presence felt in film and television. Pinter recruited him to play a detective in *Accident* (directed by Joseph Losey, 1967), and in *Get Carter* (directed by Mike Hodges, 1971) he played the gangland boss Gerald Fletcher as a threatening figure capable of matching Michael Caine's Jack Carter in ruthless violence. On television too Rigby's ability to appear frightening but fascinating made him effective as both villain and policeman. His ideal role perhaps was as the dog handler PC Snow in *Softly, Softly* (1967–76). As Bryn Hughes put it in a letter to *The Guardian*, 'It was a brilliant notion to have this brutish-looking figure engaged in an openly caring and mutually respectful relationship, even with a four-legged colleague' (*The Guardian*, 16 Aug 2008).

Although Rigby never graduated to starring roles like his contemporaries at the Royal Academy of Dramatic Art Tom Courtenay and John Thaw, his appearances on stage, in film, and on television were always meticulously prepared and rivetingly effective. In BBC Television's adaptation *The Hound of the Baskervilles* (1982), he played a subtle and thoughtful Dr Watson, forging an effective partnership with Tom Baker's lightweight Holmes. In Alan Plater's *The Beiderbecke Affair* (1985) and *The Beiderbecke Connection* (1988) his truculent Big Al was similarly well matched with James Bolam's garrulous Trevor Chaplin. Rigby was rather less benevolent as Tommy 'Bomber' Lancaster, ruling dictatorially over the motel in the last days of *Crossroads* (1986–8), and in such film roles as Bond's villainous opponent General Bukharin in *Tomorrow Never Dies* (1997), as cruel Bishop Gardiner in *Elizabeth* (1998), and as the granite-faced bodyguard Henry Hobbs in *Essex Boys* (2000).

Rigby's deep voice and slow delivery were easier to recognize than his appearance, which his years in provincial rep had taught him to alter radically to fit the part. Perceptive directors realized that he could establish himself before he opened his mouth: in *Tinker, Tailor, Soldier, Spy* (1979), in which he played the Kremlinologist Roy Bland, he didn't say a word in his first scene, merely coughed, shuffled papers, and ostentatiously refused to look at the other characters; in *Our Friends in the North* (1996), as the disturbed policeman Berger, viewers saw only his massive back, which filled the screen, as he bombarded Daniel Craig with cryptic warnings. Tony Palmer, who cast Rigby as Stalin in *Testimony* (1988), later told a revealing anecdote of how the Russian writer Solomon Volkov, invited for supper with some of the cast and crew, suddenly 'dropped his glass of wine and began to tremble violently'. He had glimpsed Rigby, still dressed as Stalin, standing in the doorway; '20 years later when Volkov and I were together at a Shostakovich festival in Rome, Volkov told me that the image of Rigby standing in that Wigan doorway still haunted him'. Palmer added: 'the irony was that Rigby was one of the gentlest of men whose personal kindness knew no bounds' (*The Times*, 13 Aug 2008).

Rigby never married. In 1987 he told *The Sun*: 'I have always been a loner. When I was 16 I'd go walking in the rain with five Woodbines for company and be happy' (*The Sun*, 21 Feb 1987). A keen tennis player and a qualified umpire, he was occasionally tempted to switch careers; but there was never a long enough gap between parts for him to take up this option. In the early 1990s he moved to New York, though not to the luxury associated with the successful actor's life. Michael Billington reported that: 'He lived for a while in the apartment of a partying Puerto Rican family with a fire station underneath and a nightclub next door. Eventually Rigby got his own tiny New York studio but, even when off-Broadway work came in, life was still tough' (Billington, 'Rigby'). But Rigby was an actor who won and retained the admiration of directors and other actors, and he continued to work regularly on both sides of the Atlantic. Late roles as the tramp Davies in a Bristol Old Vic production of Pinter's *The Caretaker* (2003) and as Pozzo in Peter Hall's revival of *Waiting for Godot* (2006) showed Rigby's theatrical presence undimmed. He also made an indelible impression on screen as a philosophical nineteenth-century pub landlord in *Simon Magus* (directed by Ben Hopkins, 1999). At the end of the film the martyred Simon Magus delivers miracles to the film's good characters: Rigby's bald, genial Bratislav gets a half-full glass of beer that endlessly fills itself up—an appropriate metaphor for Rigby's optimism and good cheer.

Rigby became ill while touring America with *A Woman of No Importance* in March 2008. He returned to London, and died of lung cancer at his flat in Devonshire Court, Devonshire Street, Westminster, on 10 August.

ROBERT MURPHY

Sources *The Times* (12 Aug 2008); (13 Aug 2008) · *Daily Telegraph* (12 Aug 2008) · *The Guardian* (12 Aug 2008); (16 Aug 2008) · M. Billington, 'Remembering Terence Rigby', www.guardian.co.uk/stage/theatreblog/2008/aug/12/rememberingterencerigby1937, 21 March 2011 · *The Stage* (18 Aug 2008) · *The Independent* (20 Aug 2008) · K. McNiven, interview with Terence Rigby, www.bl.uk/projects/theatrearchive/rigby.html, 21 March 2011 · b. cert. · d. cert.
Archives FILM BFINA, performance footage | SOUND BL, theatre archive
Likenesses photographs, 1967–2005, Rex Features, London · photographs, 1986–98, Photoshot, London · photograph, 1987, PA Photos, London · N. Norrington, photographs, 2006, Camera Press, London · B. Glikas, photographs, 2007, Getty Images, London · obituary photographs
Wealth at death £377,237: administration (will), 13 Nov 2009, *CGPLA Eng. & Wales*

Ritchie, (Joseph) Murdoch (1925–2008), neuroscientist, biophysicist, and pharmacologist, was born on 10 June 1925 at 56 Commerce Street, Aberdeen, the elder son and second of three children of Alexander Farquharson Ritchie (1892/3–1967), grocer, and his wife, Agnes Jane, *née* Bremner (1897/8–1987). He was educated at Walker's Road Primary School, Aberdeen, and Aberdeen Central Secondary School, where he was named dux (as the student at the school with the top academic achievement). In 1942 he entered Aberdeen University to study natural philosophy (mathematics and physics); he took a war-shortened (unclassified) degree in 1944, and was then required to enrol for war service. Rather than enlisting in the armed forces he joined the Telecommunications Research Establishment at Malvern, where he worked for a little over a year, and where, importantly, he met one of the outstanding figures in British science, A. V. (Archibald Vivian) Hill.

Although Ritchie considered returning to Aberdeen to

study medicine after the war, instead he entered Hill's laboratory in the department of biophysics at University College, London, as a research assistant, despite having no previous biological training. This latter defect was subsequently rectified and Ritchie gained a BSc in physiology from University College, London, in 1949, followed by a PhD in biophysics and a DSc in biophysics from the same institution, in 1952 and 1960 respectively. Meanwhile in 1949 he became a lecturer in physiology at University College; on 28 July 1951, at the parish church of Chalfont St Giles, Buckinghamshire, he married a fellow physiologist, Brenda Rachel Bigland (*b.* 1927), daughter of Ranulf Aggs Bigland, farmer, with whom he subsequently had a son, Alasdair (*b.* 1953), and a daughter, Jocelyn (*b.* 1956); and in the same year, 1951, he became a research scientist in the division of physiology and pharmacology at the Medical Research Council laboratories at Mill Hill.

The switch from mathematics and physics to physiology was highly propitious, paralleled Hill's own inclinations and career path, and allowed Ritchie to apply the analytical skills attained in the physical sciences to biological problems. His background found expression in early work that included insightful and groundbreaking studies into the energy expenditure of muscle (in collaboration with his wife, Brenda, and others), and the mechanism of action of local anaesthetics. While he was at the Medical Research Council laboratories his interests moved from the properties of muscle to the properties of nerve. He collaborated with W. W. Douglas and the Swiss scientist R. W. Straub, and with Straub he provided a groundbreaking insight into the functioning of the Na^+ pump (Na/K-ATPase) in nerve, the findings later revisited with another long-standing collaborator, Humphrey Rang.

With a growing reputation Ritchie moved to America to take up a permanent position as an associate professor at Albert Einstein College of Medicine, New York, in 1958, and was subsequently joined on the faculty by a former collaborator from Mill Hill (and later Nobel prize winner), Paul Greengard, with whom he collaborated on the mechanism of action of local anaesthetics. In 1963 he became a full professor, and in 1968 he was appointed to the Eugene Higgins chair of pharmacology at Yale, and became the chairman of the department of pharmacology. The work of Rang and Ritchie was published in the *Journal of Physiology* in the same year, demonstrating that the Na^+ pump was electrogenic, and the expulsion of Na^+ ions from the inside of a nerve following impulse activity is accompanied by an outwardly directed electric current that impacts the membrane potential and hence nerve activity. Ritchie's subsequent work included studies on radiolabelled toxin techniques to count numbers of Na^+ channels in axons (with Richard Keynes, David Colquhoun, and others), voltage-clamp of the mammalian node of Ranvier (with Richard Rogart, Bill Chiu, and David Stagg), and the simulation of the nerve impulse in mammalian nerve using the technique of numerical integration (with S. Y. Chiu et al., the key article being published in the *Journal of Physiology* in 1979). This latter achievement was coupled with his early embracing of laboratory computing technology for data collection, analysis, and simulation in the 1970s, establishing a biomedical computing unit at Yale under the direction of David Stagg. He remained Eugene Higgins professor until retirement in 2003, when he was named a professor emeritus.

Ritchie, who was always known by friends and colleagues by his middle name, Murdoch, and professionally as J. Murdoch Ritchie, was a charismatic teacher and mentor, who loved life, and his science. He was unpretentious, and generous with his time and encouragement for younger colleagues. While he had a fondness for verbal word-play and the occasional limerick, he was also fastidious in the use of written English, and Fowler's *Modern English Usage* was keenly interrogated and a key resource for papers emanating from his laboratory. For younger colleagues he was an unforgettable figure who was interested in the energetic application of intellectual prowess, favouring wholeheartedly those who ran up the stairs to get to the laboratory, rather than those who took the more leisurely elevator ride. His innate dynamism was faithfully reflected in his love of skiing and in his choice of cars, which included a soft-top Ford Mustang and a soft-top BMW, both with the personalized Connecticut licence plate TTX.

Ritchie received many honours, including an honorary MA from Yale in 1968, and election as a fellow of the Royal Society in 1976. He received an honorary DSc from Aberdeen in 1987, an accolade of deep significance to him. In 1997 he was made a fellow of the Institute of Physics. He was a founder member of the Society for Neuroscience. He died in Hamden, Connecticut, USA, on 9 July 2008, and was survived by his wife and two children.

MARK BAKER

Sources *New York Times* (1 Aug 2008) · *The Times* (4 Aug 2008) · *The Herald* [Glasgow] (16 Aug 2008) · *Yale Bulletin* (29 Aug 2008) · www.sfn.org/index.aspx?pagename=memberObituaries_ritchie, 27 April 2011 · *Memoirs FRS*, 55 (2009), 241–55 · *WW* (2008) · personal knowledge (2012) · private information (2012) · b. cert. · m. cert.

Likenesses obituary photographs · photograph, repro. in *Memoirs FRS*

Roberts, Eirlys Rhiwen Cadwaladr (1911–2008), advocate of consumer rights, was born on 3 January 1911 at The Villas, Brynawel, Mynyddislwyn, Monmouthshire, the elder daughter of Ellis James Roberts, doctor, and his Scottish wife, Jane Tennant, *née* Macaulay. Brought up in Clapham, south London, she was educated at Clapham high school (a Girls' Public Day School Trust school) and went on to Girton College, Cambridge, to read classics. She was awarded second-class honours in both parts of the tripos, in 1931 and 1932.

In the summer of 1932 Eirlys Roberts and her Cambridge boyfriend, Jacob *Bronowski (1908–1974), later to become a well-known mathematician and writer, spent a month in Deyá, Majorca, at the invitation of the American poet Laura Riding. Riding and Robert Graves had gathered a group of writers around them to collaborate on literary projects, and Roberts and Bronowski were asked to work on *The Critical Vulgate* (later published as *Epilogue*), a literary periodical. They returned to Deyá at the end of 1933, and Roberts was put to work on checking the accuracy of the classical references in Graves's novel *I, Claudius* (1934), and also helped with *Claudius the God* (1935): the only mistake she could find concerned the colour of the hem of a prostitute's gown. She also helped Laura Riding on *The Word 'Woman'* (published posthumously in 1994), an exploration of the nature of women's identity.

On her return to England in the summer of 1934, Roberts worked on women's magazines as a sub-editor for Amalgamated Press. On 20 December 1941 she married the poet and artist John Douglas Cullen (1909–1977), son of Thomas Heatherington Cullen, a Wesleyan minister. Cullen had been a friend of Bronowski at Cambridge, whom he had introduced to Laura Riding and who had been for a time part of her circle in Deyá, contributing to *Epilogue*. At the time of their marriage he was working as a radio telephonist in the Royal Air Force. The marriage ended in divorce after the war. They had no children. Meanwhile, from 1943 to 1945 Roberts served in military and then political intelligence, and from 1945 to 1947 she worked in public relations for the United Nations Relief and Rehabilitation Administration mission in Albania, which had suffered widespread devastation when the occupying Germans retreated. The relief mission was hampered by the new Albanian government, suspicious of the motives of the mission, and, in addition to the economic crisis and shortage of food supplies, the mission had to deal with the problem of the Albanian refugees driven out of Greece by terrorist bands.

Roberts joined the civil service in 1947, and worked at the Treasury in the economic information unit, set up by the minister for economic affairs, Sir Stafford Cripps, to inform the public on the economics of everyday life. As well as writing reports and liaising with women's organizations, she wrote articles on consumer matters for *The Observer*. Through this work she became known to others interested in consumer affairs, and was one of a group round the sociologist Michael Young that founded the Consumers' Association in 1957 and launched *Which?* magazine in October of that year. Their aim was to protect consumers from exploitation by business by providing them with accurate information about consumer goods, thereby also (they hoped) raising the standards of British goods, and enabling them to compete better in foreign markets. From the start *Which?* was independent of government and business, and was funded by subscriptions from its members. After the publication of the first issue, 10*s*. subscriptions poured in, and within weeks there were 10,000 members; by the end of the first year there were 47,000, and at its peak, in 1987, the magazine had more than 1 million subscribers. The idea was that the magazine would buy, test, and compare consumer products, and then publish its conclusions.

When the Consumers' Association advertised for its first director, Roberts's application was turned down because she wanted to edit the magazine but not manage the Consumers' Association as well, but when the original director left after a few months, in 1958, she was appointed editor and head of research, while Young became the director. Described by Young as 'the most considerable figure thrown up by the British consumer movement' (Roberts, 5), Roberts was determined that the magazine should be written in language that could be understood by its readers. Clarity and brevity were important to her, and she later wrote that just as 'a good teacher will require that a Latin or Greek text shall be translated into Anglo-Saxon words' (ibid., 27), she wanted scientific and technical terms to be translated into plain English, with the emphasis on short words and short sentences, and the avoidance of abstract nouns. Thus she preferred 'shop' to 'retail outlet', 'prices going up' to 'inflation', and 'poor' to 'lower income group'. She wanted consumers to be able to make rational decisions based on accurate facts: talking of the founders of *Which?* she wrote, 'there are—they felt—spheres in which it is proper that emotion, and not reason, should operate—such as love and aesthetics—but that buying a refrigerator is not one of them' (E. Roberts, *Consumers*, 1966, 78–9).

As the membership increased, *Which?* became a monthly rather than a quarterly publication in 1959, and new magazines, supplements, and pamphlets were added. The first separate publication was *The Law for Consumers* (1962), followed by titles such as *What to Do when Someone Dies* (1967), *Avoiding Back Trouble* (1975), and *On Getting Divorced* (1978). In 1963 the *Which? Supplement on Contraceptives* appeared. Annual tax-saving and car-buying guides appeared; *Motoring Which?* started publication in 1965, followed by *Holiday Which?*, *Gardening Which?*, and others. The Consumers' Association bought the *Good Food Guide* in 1962. Roberts herself wrote *Consumers* (1966), a history of the consumer movement. In the early days of *Which?* there was a hope that as consumers became more influential they could transform British society, but the membership remained composed largely of middle-class professionals, who read *Which?* for purely practical reasons. By the time Roberts resigned as editor in 1973, she had built up a staff of over 300, with the headquarters in London, the subscription department in Hertford, and the research laboratories in Harpenden.

While remaining at the Consumers' Association as deputy director from 1973 to 1977, Roberts turned her attention to Europe, following Britain's entry into the Common Market in 1973. She was the first chief executive of the Bureau of European Consumer Organizations, based in Brussels, from 1973 to 1978, and a member of the economic and social committee of the EEC from 1973 to 1982, chairing its environment and consumer protection section from 1978 to 1982. In 1978 she set up the European Research Institute for Consumer Affairs, and chaired it until 1997, campaigning, among other things, for the use of plain language in European Commission publications. She was appointed OBE in 1971, and CBE in 1977.

Described by Peter Goldman, director of the Consumers' Association, as having 'toughly intelligent Celtic charm' (Roberts, 5), Eirlys Roberts lived for many years in a flat at 8 Lloyd Square in Clerkenwell, London, where she enjoyed gathering and entertaining her friends. Her interests included walking, skating, and reading detective novels. In the late 1990s she moved to live with her younger sister in Forest Hill, south-east London. Later she developed Alzheimer's-type dementia, and entered Cheverton Lodge nursing home, 30 Cheverton Road, Islington, London. She died on 18 March 2008 in the Whittington Hospital, Islington. ANNE PIMLOTT BAKER

Sources G. Woodbridge, *UNRRA: the history of the United Nations Relief and Rehabilitation Administration*, 2 (1950), 171–84 · E. Roberts, *Which? 25: Consumers' Association, 1957–1982* (1982) · *Thirty years of Which? 1957–1987* (1987) · J. Epstein, *The early days of the Consumers' Association* (1989) · R. P. Graves, *Robert Graves: the years with Laura Riding, 1926–1940* (1990) · A. Briggs, *Michael Young: social entrepreneur* (2001) · M. Hilton, *Consumerism in twentieth-century Britain: the search for a historical movement* (2003), 194–218 · E. Friedmann, *A mannered grace: the life of Laura (Riding) Jackson* (2005), 228–30 · *The Guardian* (22 March 2008) · *The Times* (7 April 2008) · *The Independent* (10 April 2008) · *WW* (2008) · b. cert. · m. cert. · d. cert.
Archives SOUND BL NSA, documentary recordings
Likenesses photograph, 1957, repro. in Roberts, *Which? 25*, 26 · obituary photographs · photograph, repro. in *Thirty years*, 8
Wealth at death £752,353: probate, 30 July 2008, *CGPLA Eng. & Wales*

Roberts, Sir Gareth Gwyn (1940–2007), physicist and university administrator, was born on 16 May 1940 at Craig Beuno Nursing Home, Bangor, Caernarvonshire, the son of Edwin Roberts (*d.* 1974), a wages clerk in the local granite quarry, and his wife, Meri, *née* Jones (*d.* 1959). He was brought up with his twin sister, Gwyneth, and younger sister, Enid, in the family home at 3 St David's Terrace, Penmaenmawr, where Welsh was the spoken language and weekly attendance at chapel compulsory. His mother was a considerable influence, engendering in him a steely determination to succeed that remained with him throughout his life. From John Bright Grammar School in Llandudno he progressed to the University College of North Wales, Bangor, where he gained a first-class honours degree in physics in 1961 and studied for a PhD in the rapidly developing field of semiconductor physics (his thesis was entitled 'A theoretical study of space charge currents in solids') before taking up a lectureship in physics there in 1963. A year earlier, on 15 August 1962, at George Street Congregational Church, Croydon, he had married Charlotte Standen (*b.* 1942), insurance clerk, and daughter of Albert John Williams Standen, shop manager. They had two sons and one daughter. The marriage ended in divorce in 1993.

In 1966 Roberts moved to the Xerox Corporation in Rochester, New York, working as a senior research scientist on selenium and other materials used in copying machines. The American culture of competitiveness and high expectation suited him admirably, but in 1968 he accepted an invitation from his PhD supervisor, Richard Tredgold, to join him at the New University of Ulster at Coleraine and help establish a department of physics. Roberts went on to become professor and head of the department of physics and dean of the school of physical sciences. His research in this period was aimed at modifying the properties of materials like gallium arsenide and

Sir Gareth Gwyn Roberts (1940–2007), by unknown photographer, 1997

indium phosphide by doping to produce improved semiconductor devices. After eight years at Ulster he took on a fresh academic challenge—the headship of the department of applied physics and electronics at Durham University, which provided the perfect setting for his research at the interface between science and engineering. Following his involvement in a successful visit to Durham by the University Grants Committee he was invited to join its equipment committee, which he subsequently chaired. It was the first of many public and professional bodies to seek his services.

Roberts believed that scientific research and its applications should go hand in hand, and each of his senior academic appointments was combined with a post in industry. During his time in Ulster he worked in ICI's corporate laboratory in Runcorn, with Geoffrey Allen as his mentor, and after the laboratory's relocation to Durham he developed even closer research links with the company. He had no thought of leaving Durham, but when the package of chief scientist (later research director) at Thorn EMI for four days a week and an Oxford visiting professorship in engineering science for one day a week (not to mention a fellowship at Brasenose College) was offered to him in 1985 he felt compelled to accept. Colin Southgate, chief executive of Thorn EMI, was engaged in a major programme of modernization and delegated to Roberts responsibility for reorganizing the company's Central Research Laboratories and devising technology strategies for each of its operating divisions.

At Oxford Roberts established a new research group in the field of molecular electronics, an area in which he had an international reputation. His particular interest was the physical behaviour of Langmuir-Blodgett films—ultra-thin films of organic material deposited sequentially on a solid substrate in layers one molecule thick. Roberts was among the first scientists to appreciate the versatility of these films. Working with ICI researchers in Durham he designed a new type of trough for precisely assembling the monolayers and extended the range of organic materials used in making them. He also investigated their applications in such electronic devices as field-effect transistors. In his Oxford laboratory he focused his energies on the unique sensing properties of Langmuir-Blodgett films and their potential use as heat sensors for security devices and vapour sensors for environmental monitoring. He was the author of over 200 publications and patents, and two books, *Insulating Films on Semiconductors* (1979) and *Langmuir-Blodgett Films* (1990). His membership of the prime minister's Advisory Council on Science and Technology (1989–92) gave him the opportunity to discuss Langmuir-Blodgett films with Margaret Thatcher, who had worked in this field during her time as a research chemist. Roberts was elected a fellow of the Royal Society in 1984 and received the Holweck gold medal of the Institute of Physics in 1986.

When the University of Sheffield's chancellor, Lord Dainton, sounded out Roberts for the post of vice-chancellor he faced competition from a number of other universities, but Roberts liked what he saw at Sheffield and moved there in 1991. His tenure was strikingly successful and the university rapidly ascended the league tables for research and teaching on the back of judicious appointments to chairs, which on occasion brought in entire research teams. He led from the front in a campaign of relentless initiative, though his urgency could sometimes offend the university's most collegiate instincts. However, his personal qualities of integrity and fairness, combined with his formidable powers of persuasion, enabled him to implement far-sighted policies (such as multidisciplinary research groupings) that won the support of the academic community. One of his great legacies at Sheffield was the early outreach scheme, lauded by the government, providing a route into higher education for underprivileged pupils in inner-city schools.

Roberts was the networker supreme, adept at founding national and international partnerships, such as the Russell group of leading UK universities; the White Rose University Consortium of Leeds, Sheffield, and York universities; and the Worldwide Universities Network, an alliance of pre-eminent universities in four continents. He was equally committed to the regeneration of Sheffield, serving on the boards of the Sheffield Development Corporation, the Sheffield Health Authority, and the Regional Development Agency for Yorkshire and the Humber, and co-founding the Sheffield First Partnership with the leader of the city council. Many of these enterprises had their origins in 'town and gown' dinners held at his formal residence, The Croft, which he shared with his second wife, Carolyn Mary Rich, *née* Butler (*b.* 1948), a health service executive and trained nurse (daughter of Albert Edward Butler, musician, and former wife of Stephen Rich), whom he married at Leeds register office on 18 February 1994. She had two daughters by her first marriage.

Roberts's election in 1995 as chairman of the Committee of Vice-Chancellors and Principals—the collective voice of the UK higher education system—marked his entry onto the national political stage and almost immediately he was plunged into conflict with the Conservative government over its latest round of cuts in university funding. His refusal to listen to a speech from the minister for higher education, coupled with a vigorous national campaign mounted alongside the unions to highlight the systematic underfunding of higher education, signalled a new way forward for the Committee of Vice-Chancellors and Principals. The outcome was the Dearing report of 1997 (named after the chairman of the national committee of inquiry into higher education, Sir Ronald Dearing), largely accepted by the incoming Labour government, which mirrored many of the recommendations made by the committee to alleviate the funding shortfall, including the introduction of means-tested tuition fees.

Roberts was knighted for his services to higher education in 1997. In the same year he joined the board of the Higher Education Funding Council for England and went on to chair its research committee. He had previously been a member of the Universities Funding Council (1989–92). In 1998 he was elected president of the Institute of Physics and two years later he became founding president of the Science Council, set up to promote the profession of scientist by the designation 'chartered scientist'. He also served a four-year term as chairman of the Defence Scientific Advisory Council (1993–7). As a chairman he was practical and pragmatic, always polite and charming, but above all incisive.

The presidency of Wolfson College, Oxford, to which Roberts was appointed in 2001, was described by *The Guardian* as 'one of the best post-VC jobs in the business' (30 May 2000). Importantly it afforded him sufficient time to pursue his many national and international initiatives. He was a driving force in the development of UK policy on university research, chairing a critical review of the research assessment exercise and addressing the urgent need for better career opportunities for the growing numbers of contract research staff in universities. In 2001 he was commissioned by the Treasury to investigate ways of increasing the numbers of skilled scientists, engineers, and technologists needed to support a competitive modern economy. His landmark report, 'SET for success: the supply of people with science, technology, engineering and mathematical skills', published in the following year, was commended by the prime minister and fully funded by the government at all levels, from schools through to universities and research councils. Stipends for PhD students were almost doubled and the 'Roberts money', as it became known, enabled universities to provide transferable skills training and career development programmes for all their graduate and postdoctoral researchers.

Throughout his career Roberts took a keen interest in the promotion of science to young people. In 1988 he presented the Royal Institution Christmas lectures, 'The home of the future', on BBC television, and in 2005 he was appointed chairman of SETNET, the government-sponsored body charged with enriching school science. In the following year he took on the presidency of the Association for Science Education and also became chairman of the Engineering and Technology Board. His expertise was sought overseas, most notably in Hong Kong, Singapore, and Australia, where he advised the government on the best way of assessing the quality of publicly funded research. He retained an active interest in the business community through his visiting professorship in the Saïd Business School at Oxford and his directorship of Isis Innovation, Oxford University's technology transfer company. He was also chairman of the healthcare and biotechnology company Medical Solutions. He received honorary degrees and fellowships from ten university institutions.

Roberts was a transformational leader, a man of extraordinary vision, energy, and determination who had a profound impact on science policy and higher education in Britain. At Wolfson College, as in all his other appointments, he was open and accessible to students and staff, and this in turn inspired great loyalty among those who knew him. He was admired as a public speaker and his dinner parties and attendant quizzes were legendary, as too was his warm personality and his support of Tottenham Hotspur Football Club. Conceding little to his final illness (and remaining president of Wolfson College), he died from cancer on 6 February 2007 at his home, 10 Chadlington Road, Oxford, and was cremated at Oxford crematorium on 16 February. He was survived by his wife, Carolyn, his two stepdaughters, and the three children of his first marriage. ROGER ALLUM

Sources *The Guardian* (30 May 2000); (17 March 2007) · H. Mathers, *Steel city scholars: the centenary history of the University of Sheffield* (2005) · *Daily Telegraph* (22 Feb 2007) · *The Independent* (5 March 2007) · *The Times* (20 March 2007) · *Journal of the Foundation for Science and Technology*, 19/4 (March 2007) · *Wolfson College Record* (2006–7) · *WW* (2007) · Burke, *Peerage* · personal knowledge (2011) · private information (2011) [Carolyn Roberts, widow; C. Hilsum; T. Richardson; H. Mathers] · d. cert. · m. certs. · d. cert.

Archives University of Sheffield Library

Likenesses photographs, 2001, Photoshot, London · I. Spooner, photograph, *c.*2002, RS · J. Mendoza, portrait, University of Sheffield · J. Mendoza, portrait, Wolfson College, Oxford · obituary photographs · obituary photographs · photograph, 1997, University of Sheffield [*see illus.*] · photographs, University of Sheffield · photographs, Wolfson College, Oxford

Wealth at death £630,207: probate, 18 Sept 2007, *CGPLA Eng. & Wales*

Robertson, Sir Lewis Findlay (1922–2008), industrialist and public servant, was born on 28 November 1922 at 1 Scotswood Terrace, Dundee, the second son of John Farquharson Robertson (*d.* 1976), jute merchant, and his wife, Margaret Eleanor, *née* Arthur. He was educated at Glenalmond College, Perthshire, and became an articled clerk in his grandfather's accountancy firm. Offered a wartime place at Cambridge, he chose instead (on hearing the news of his brother's death while serving in the Royal Navy) to enlist. He joined the RAF, spending much of the war at Bletchley Park, the code-breaking centre. Later on he became known as 'the most methodical man in Scotland' (*The Herald*, 27 Nov 2008), and this may have stemmed from the combination of his accounting and Bletchley Park experience.

On demobilization Robertson joined the family firm of J. F. Robertson, later Robertson Industrial Textiles. He married, on 10 June 1950, at St Andrew's Church, East Linton, East Lothian, Elspeth Margaret Dorothy Badenoch (1924/5–2001), a registered general nurse two years his junior, and daughter of Alfred Badenoch, medical practitioner; they had three sons and a daughter. In 1954 he became managing director of J. F. Robertson and guided the flotation of the company four years later. In 1965 he led the merger of his company with a larger, also family-owned, jute enterprise, Scotts. He was managing director of this merged company, Scott Robertson Ltd, from 1965 to 1970, and chairman from 1968 to 1970. However, the Scott family eventually rebelled against his strategy for the company, and he was deposed in 1970.

Beyond this involvement with his own jute company, Robertson also came to play a central role in the complex interactions between the jute industry as a whole and government that characterized the 1950s and 1960s. Jute had been granted protection in 1939, but in the post-war period there was continuous questioning of this policy, and the jute employers were forced into frequent negotiations with successive governments in London to try to defend the industry's interests against the competition of Calcutta. These negotiations were undertaken in the 1950s and 1960s by 'three wise men', consisting of the heads of the two biggest jute companies (Hugh Bonar and William Walker) and Robertson, a much younger man from a much smaller firm. In his role as strategist and spokesman for the jute industry, Robertson also played the key role in formulating the industry's defence against the case brought in the restrictive practices court in 1963 against price-fixing in jute. The case was lost, but it cemented his position as a leading figure in the industry, and no doubt also prepared him for his role as a member of the Monopolies and Mergers Commission (1969–76), and later (1983–96) of the restrictive practices court itself.

After leaving the jute industry Robertson developed a high-powered career which embraced both public appointments and executive roles in a wide range of industries. He was, for example, chief executive of Grampian Holdings from 1971 to 1976, and chairman of the Stakis hotel group from 1991 to 1995. The second of these was perhaps the most significant of the companies where he came in as a 'company doctor', taking over a failing firm and returning it to profitability. In the case of Stakis, this turnaround involved cutting head-office staff by a third and sacking the founder's son from his role as chief executive; the company was later sold to the Hilton group for £1.3 billion. Robertson had the commanding personality as well as the skills to take on the role of absolute controller of a company's fortunes, demanding this as the necessary price of rescue. In 1990 he set up the first specialist consultancy in company rescue, the Postern Executive Group. He countered criticism of his fees by saying, 'I am expensive. It is very foolish to pretend there could, or should, be a cheap corporate rescue service. Anything companies get for peanuts is fit for nothing but monkeys' (*The Guardian*, 3 Dec 2008). One of his last company rescues was in 2002–5, when he increased the market capitalization of the consulting engineers W. S. Atkins plc more than twelve-fold, to £700 million.

Robertson's involvement in public bodies was multiple and diverse. He was chair of the Eastern Regional Hospital Board (Scotland) from 1960 to 1970, and of the committee planning the new Ninewells Hospital in Dundee. He was a member of the court of the University of Dundee from 1967 to 1970, and had senior and long-term involvement with the synod of the Episcopal Church of Scotland, the Carnegie Trust for the Universities of Scotland (of which he was chairman from 1990 to 2003), and the Royal Society of Edinburgh (of which he was made a fellow in 1978, and as whose treasurer he served from 1994 to 1999). More directly linked to his experience as an industrialist was his position as first chief executive of the Scottish Development Agency from 1976 to 1981. In a newspaper article marking his retirement from this post, he stressed the need for such public bodies to encourage industrial expansion and reduce unemployment. He would probably have stayed on in this post if the election of the Thatcher government in 1979 had not made the role and even existence of development agencies a high-profile political issue.

While his background was that of a traditional family firm in a declining staple industry, Robertson recognized both the need for companies to change radically to respond to intensifying competition, and the positive role that government could play in offsetting the impact of industrial decline. In all his roles he brought to bear great intelligence and drive, though his approach did not always win friends. Another jute insider suggested that he was 'regarded with some suspicion in Dundee' due to his 'academic' and 'sarcastic' manner, generating a 'feeling that he is not only too clever, but rather anxious to show he is' (private information). He was appointed CBE in 1969 and knighted in 1991. He lived latterly in Inverleith Place, Edinburgh. He died at the Western General Hospital, Edinburgh, on 24 November 2008 of acute kidney failure. He was survived by two sons and a daughter, his wife and one son having predeceased him. JIM TOMLINSON

Sources D. N. Charlish, 'Report from the annual dinner of the UK Jute Goods Association', 31 May 1961, TNA: PRO, BT 258/834 · L. Robertson, 'Reversing economic decline', *Dundee Courier* (13 Jan 1981) · *Management Today* (1 July 1992) · *The Herald* [Glasgow] (27 Nov 2008); (1 Dec 2008) · *The Independent* (29 Nov 2008) · *The Guardian* (3 Dec 2008) · *Evening News* [Edinburgh] (4 Dec 2008) · *Daily Telegraph* (17 Dec 2008) · J. Tomlinson, C. Morelli, and V. Wright, *The decline of jute: managing industrial change* (2011) · Burke, *Peerage* · *WW* (2008) · private information (2012) · b. cert. · m. cert. · d. cert.

Archives NL Scot., Acc. 12517, 13065, 12345, 11679 | Dundee University archives, papers of Association of Jute Spinners and Manufacturers, MS 84

Likenesses photographs, 1980–2002, Getty Images, London · photographs, 1995, Photoshot, London · obituary photographs

Robinson, John Ebdon [*known as* John Ebdon] (1923–2005), planetarium director and broadcaster, was born on 22 December 1923 at Durham House, 102 Crouch Hill, London, the son of William Ewart Robinson, export and import merchant, of 109 rue du Relais, Ixelles, Brussels, and his wife, Yvonne Bertha, formerly Cryer, *née* Ebdon. He was educated at an English-language school in Switzerland and at Blundells School, which he did not enjoy. During the Second World War he served with the Royal Air Force; he twice survived having to bale out after being shot down, and suffered flash blindness as a result of a blast. After the war he planned to become an actor, and trained at the Royal Academy of Dramatic Art, but was advised against a career in the theatre since the bright lights affected his eyes. He took an external degree in English literature from the University of London while working as a buyer, and on 19 April 1952 married Angela Mary Knyvett (*d.* 2003), a 21-year-old occupational therapist, and daughter of John Seymour Knyvett, army officer; they had two sons and one daughter.

Uncertain about his career, from 1952 to 1957 Robinson lived in east Africa, working as a game warden and also buying and selling skins. He found time to master Swahili (languages always came easily to him) and founded a repertory company, the Nairobi City Players. When he returned to England he considered being ordained in the Anglican church, but rejected the idea on the grounds that he would find it hard to support his family on a clergyman's income. Nevertheless it had become clear that his real future lay in public speaking; he had what had been called a 'port-wine' voice, and as a lecturer he was helped by the fact that he was tall and good-looking.

London's first Planetarium had been opened at Madame Tussaud's in Baker Street but had not been quite the success originally expected, and soon after his return to England Robinson (who by now was known as John Ebdon) was invited to become its chief narrator. His arrival made all the difference; his lectures—he preferred to call them 'displays'—were immensely popular, and the Planetarium was soon presenting several shows each day. He devised a wide range of programmes besides those for the general public, including special 'displays' for primary schoolchildren, secondary schoolchildren, and students of astronomy; for children with learning disabilities, gifted children, and the blind; and for those interested in references to medieval astronomy and astrology in English literature. One of his main strengths was his sense of humour, and unlike his predecessor he was always ready to talk informally to his audience after the end of the official display. Quite apart from this, astronomy had always been one of his main hobbies, so that he was well equipped to answer questions about it. He became director of the London Planetarium in 1968, when the moon landings were imminent, and remained until ill health forced him to retire in 1989.

Long before then, Robinson had become established in a new career, that of a popular broadcaster (again using the name John Ebdon). A senior BBC producer, Denys Gueroult, heard him speaking at the Planetarium and was quick to appreciate his potential. He invited Robinson to compile a programme based on snippets from the BBC sound archives, adding his own comments between the excerpts; this was ideally suited to his rich voice, whimsical humour, and grasp of what was happening in Britain and abroad. The programme, *Archive Feature*, was broadcast on Radio 4 on the first Monday of each month, and ran uninterrupted for over a quarter of a century. Millions of listeners looked forward to his programme, which he always opened with 'How do you do?' and closed with 'Anyway, if you have been, thanks for listening'. Frequent references were made to his cat Perseus (to whom Robinson attributed some of his more controversial opinions), and the cat earned the unusual distinction of an obituary when he died in 1978. When the series came to an end in 1987 it was widely missed. He also appeared regularly on *Woman's Hour*, *Thought for the Day*, and *Any Questions*, and devised and presented other series, including *A World of Sound*, *Nonsense at Noon*, *April Foolery*, and *Near Myths* (the latter based on tales from Greek mythology).

Robinson's third career was as an author. *Ebdon's England* (1985) was perhaps the best of his books, but all were beautifully written and all were well received. He was a great traveller, and had a particular fondness for Greece; he spent many of his holidays there, and wrote three books about it—*Ebdon's Odyssey* (1979), *Ebdon's Iliad* (1983), and *Near Myths* (1989), the last based on his radio series. He mastered both ancient and modern Greek and often broadcast on Greek radio, one listener commenting that his command of the language was almost perfect.

Witty, good-humoured, and always urbane, Robinson was one of the most accomplished and popular broadcasters of the post-war BBC. His retirement was marred by the death of a son in a parachute accident, and by the death of his first wife, but he found happiness in a new relationship with Mary Elizabeth Lawson Light, a state registered nurse, and daughter of Albert Lawson Light, consultant surgeon. They married on 6 February 2004. Robinson died a year later, on 19 March 2005, at his home, 41 Hillside Road, Northwood, London, of cancer; he was survived by his second wife and two children of his first marriage. PATRICK MOORE

Sources *The Guardian* (21 March 2005) • *The Times* (24 March 2005) • *The Independent* (25 March 2005) • *Daily Telegraph* (1 April 2005) • personal knowledge (2009) • private information (2009) • b. cert. • m. certs. • d. cert.

Archives SOUND BL NSA, 'John Ebdon's silver archive', 1CDR0016748

Likenesses obituary photographs • photograph, BBC; repro. in *The Times*

Wealth at death £345,952: probate, 19 Jan 2006, *CGPLA Eng. & Wales*

Roddick [*née* Perella], **Dame Anita Lucia** (**1942–2007**), businesswoman, was born on 23 October 1942 in a bomb shelter at 32 New Road, Littlehampton, Sussex, one of the four children of Gilda (*b.* 1914/15), daughter of Domenico de Vito, farmer, and wife of Donato (Donny) Perella (1912–1973), caterer and restaurateur. Her biological father was Donato's cousin, Henry Perilli (1914–1953), ice-cream and soda bar proprietor. Her mother was divorced after the war, and married Henry Perilli in December 1951, but he

Dame Anita Lucia Roddick (1942–2007), by Gareth Davies, 2002

died sixteen months later of a heart attack. Anita's working life began as a small child in her parents' café and ice-cream and soda bar in a converted Methodist chapel opposite Littlehampton railway station. She quipped that her adored mother's formidable work ethic was tantamount to slave labour for the children. From her mother she learned the importance of personality in business. 'She made me realize that you can't be a nondescript person or you will have a nondescript product. "Be special," she would always say. "Be anything but mediocre"' (*Business as Unusual*, 33). She was educated at St Joseph's Convent and Maude Allen secondary modern school, both in Littlehampton, before training as a schoolteacher at Newton Park College of Education in Bath. She then taught history and English at Maude Allen school.

On 21 July 1965, at Worthing register office, Anita Perella married Larry Winston Cason (*b.* 1938/9), musician, son of David Cason, interior decorator. This marriage soon failed. She went abroad, working in the *International Herald Tribune* clippings library in Paris, in the women's rights department of the International Labour Organization at Geneva, and on an Israeli kibbutz before crossing the world to the Pacific. About 1968, in her mother's Littlehampton nightclub, she met (Thomas) Gordon Roddick (*b.* 1942), son of a Scottish grain broker. They had one daughter, Justine, before their marriage in Reno, Nevada, in 1970, and a second daughter, Samantha (Sam), in 1971. During the early 1970s the Roddicks ran a small hotel in Littlehampton.

In Polynesia Anita Roddick had admired women who achieved velvety skin by rubbing cocoa butter on their breasts and bellies. Back in Littlehampton she collected grandmotherly recipes for kitchen-made cosmetics. She became determined to open a shop in Brighton selling a range of fifteen skin preparations, soaps, and oils that she had devised from natural ingredients. After her application for a loan was rejected by a bank manager who mistrusted her Bob Dylan T-shirt, her husband negotiated a loan of £4000 before leaving to fulfil his longstanding ambition to ride a horse from Buenos Aires to New York. In 1976 she chose The Body Shop as the name for her first premises, from a notice at a garage specializing in panel-beating, and received free publicity when nearby undertakers protested at her shop sign.

Roddick concocted the early products in her kitchen, gave them exotic names, sold them in recycled urine sample bottles (initially to save money), and painted the interior of her shop dark green to hide the damp patches and mould. Dark green became the hallmark colour of her premises. In her shops she displayed photographs of the distant countries from which her raw materials came, and of their indigenous peoples, to accompany descriptive stories about them. Roddick knew the power of storytelling, and her shops came with a narrative as well as their products. Following her husband's return from his equine adventure he devised the methodical structures and franchise system that enabled her to expand the Body Shop chain. This proliferated swiftly, with the first overseas franchised Body Shop opening in Brussels in 1978.

It was Roddick's aim to run an ethical business. She cared not only how her profits were made, but how they were spent. The Quaker model of business responsibility for the common good appealed to her. Making profits and improving the world were not irreconcilable, she insisted. Long before ecological responsibility was fashionable, she embraced green politics. In 1986 Body Shops displayed posters supporting Greenpeace's anti-whaling campaign. By 1989 the shops were collecting signatures for a petition to save the Brazilian rain forest. Roddick's cosmetics had natural rather than synthesized ingredients; she opposed the testing of products on animals; she deprecated wasteful packaging, and encouraged customers to return bottles for refilling; and her ardour about ecological responsibility, third-world development, and human rights made her unique among retailers. Her products were distinctive, too, and included fuzzy peach shower gel, brazil nut hair-conditioner, raspberry shampoo, pineapple face-scrub, peppermint-oil foot lotion, and strawberry exfoliators.

Roddick taught that it was possible both to be a consumer and to retain ethical self-respect. It was permissible to prettify or coddle oneself, and yet not be selfish or thoughtless about the planet, human rights, warfare, third-world exploitation, and sexual injustice. She upheld the radical feminism of her generation, and was the first international cosmetics tycoon who could not be considered complicit in the subjugation of women or what was becoming known as 'body fascism'. Younger women who did not wish to doll themselves up to please men as their mothers had done, but still wished to feel good about their appearance, flocked to Body Shops. Roddick was a life-enhancing force, who brought harmless pleasure to millions of women, and intensified the political consciousness of many of them too. This fearsomely energetic woman made shopping a moral choice without being a prig.

Roddick, who was voted Veuve Clicquot businesswoman of the year in 1984, floated Body Shop on the stock exchange in 1985. This was at the height of Thatcherism, and Roddick as a child of the 1960s counter-culture who had built a business empire was an inspiringly subversive role model. Like Margaret Thatcher she was incapable of seeing both sides of a question, and frustrated by people who did. For her, too, there was right and there was wrong: temporizing values were for timewasters. Both women fought for what they thought was right. She was as much in earnest about her vision for the world as was Britain's first woman prime minister, but had the redeeming gift of raunchy, joyous humour. Her sultry Italian looks and curly unkempt hair, the laddered tights on her legs and the Doc Marten boots on her feet, as much as her denial of the primacy of profit, made her the antithesis of the style and ethos of Thatcherism.

Body Shop was valued at £8 million when it was floated in 1985. At times Roddick rued her decision to turn Body Shop into a publicly quoted company, feeling that her vision of an ethical company providing fair pay and good conditions to deprived communities was compromised, and that as a public company Body Shop's success was measured only in terms of profit. The Roddicks' 30 per cent stake in the company made her the fourth richest woman in Britain by 1990. By the end of the century there were 1800 Body Shops in forty-nine countries across twelve time zones. Roddick remained an inspiration for other women setting up their own companies. She scorned conventional advertising, but was a compulsive communicator: Body Shop deluged its customers and employees with posters, pamphlets, leaflets, flyers, and videos, on subjects from skin ageing to the extermination of tribes.

Body Shop opened its first stores in the USA in 1988, and started franchising outlets there in 1990. Body Shop's American sales grew by 47 per cent to $44.6 million in 1993 and profits rose by 63 per cent to $1.9 million. In that year Roddick opened a sumptuous, environmentally sound headquarters and distribution centre at Raleigh, North Carolina, anticipating a 30 per cent expansion of business annually. Raleigh became a deadly incubus when in 1994 Body Shop's growth faltered, and then receded. Some reasons for this greatest setback of Roddick's career redound to her credit, although others involved misjudgement.

Although Roddick disliked shopping malls, which she recognized had destroyed the community spirit of 'Main Street America', Body Shop opened franchises in many malls. Body Shop had always injected politics into retailing, but mall-owners were furious when Body Shop celebrated Martin Luther King day, and inveighed against

Body Shop's voter registration and human rights campaigns. She realized belatedly that Body Shop was antithetical to the suburban mall mentality: her outlets belonged in vibrant, teeming cities, and on main streets of urban areas.

Meanwhile the American religious right launched prurient attacks. When American Body Shop issued a Christmas poster depicting Santa Claus in a back-to-front baseball cap, listening to a walkman, it was accused of inciting gang violence. A poster for male deodorant was denounced for promoting homosexuality. A New Hampshire woman ignited nationwide hysteria after fainting in a shop when confronted by an image of a youth in speedos with a bottle of watermelon tanning lotion shoved in front of his crotch. The chief executive of Body Shop in America objected so strenuously when a banner promoting HIV prophylaxis was hung outside its premises in San Francisco, reading '2-4-6-8, use a condom or masturbate', that Roddick felt alien in her own company.

The business suffered, too, from copycat retailers led by Leslie Wexner, the mogul from Columbus, Ohio, who opened a hundred demotic cut-price Bath and Body Works stores in 1990–91, grossing $45 million a year. Roddick was told that the Bath and Body Works chairman had a mission statement displayed on his wall, 'Bury the Body Shop' (*Business as Unusual*, 155). Roddick was slow to understand American retailing's dependence on advertising, two-for-the-price-of-one promotions, and discount sales: American price promotions, she felt, made it hard to know the real value of anything.

In Britain, too, during the 1990s, Roddick faced unwelcome confrontations. When the Gulf War erupted in 1991, she displayed pacifist billboards and organized peace petitions in her British shops. While she was in America, Body Shop's UK managing director, fearful that the campaign would damage the company's marketability, obtained a board decision that the posters and petitions should be removed. She was, however, supported by her workforce, and the managing director who wished to normalize the business's core values left the business soon afterwards.

In 1992 Channel 4 broadcast a television documentary alleging that Body Shop lied about animal-testing of its products and presenting the Roddicks as hypocrites. Body Shop's share price plunged on the day after the broadcast, and sales also fell. Although the Roddicks were vindicated after a protracted libel action, trust in the Body Shop brand never completely recovered. It was suspected that the claims to ethical probity of some products were exaggerated and that her vaunted activism was a huckster's trick to create lucrative publicity. Thereafter, especially in the mid-1990s, Roddick was attacked by journalists who found it newsworthy to attack her integrity. Some coverage amounted to harassment. Roddick was a woman with deep self-belief, who was shaken by these assaults, and proved vulnerable to them.

Roddick was managing director of Body Shop from its foundation until 1994, when she became chief executive (1994–8), co-chairman (1998–2002), and non-executive director (2002–6). Body Shop was sold in 2006 to the French cosmetics conglomerate L'Oréal for £652 million. The Roddicks received about £118 million from the deal, which was deplored by some commentators. Roddick was so much a creature of the 1970s and 1980s, for whom the 1990s had often been bruising, that she could not hope to keep ahead of the game in the new century.

Roddick became a public legend when young, and remained so. There was an element of role-playing in 2000 when she described herself as a 'ballsy, truth-telling, free-thinking, heart-bleeding, myth-debunking, non-conforming and hell-raising activist' (*Business as Unusual*, v). There was, too, an element of stunt in press interviews when she spoke at full pelt about her motives, opinions, and experiences, and gave outspoken, emphatic voice to her beliefs on wars, globalization, slash-and-burn corporate greed, social justice, ethical responsibility, gender oppression, pubic hair, and cocoa-butter. Like other effective polemicists, she sometimes was awry in her facts while hammering at the right point. Journalists' presentation of her as a mouthy woman who defied convention, which had been a boost in the early years, became ultimately a baneful caricature. It was inevitable that her eloquent activism raised expectations that could not be fulfilled, indeed expectations that in some cases were unreasonable.

Roddick supported Amnesty International, Friends of the Earth, Greenpeace, the campaigning housing charity Shelter, and anti-nuclear groups. From 1987 she helped John Elkington to nurture SustainAbility, advising businesses on sustainable development. After visiting Romanian orphanages in 1990 she founded the Children on the Edge charity to support children in eastern Europe and Asia. Body Shop's £500,000 was decisive in the launching in 1991 of *The Big Issue*, a magazine sold on city streets by homeless people. From 2003 Roddick helped to support Crisis Action, a private company bringing together humanitarian activists and foreign policy analysts to respond strategically to armed conflict and human rights abuses. She supported the Hepatitis C Trust, having been infected by a blood transfusion at the time of her second daughter's birth. With her husband she became an eager, inveterate traveller in developing countries where she hoped to ameliorate poverty, injustice, and disease. In 2005 she endowed the Roddick Foundation with £51 million to support individuals and groups working to promote social, labour, and environmental justice, and human rights. Meanwhile, through its 'community trade' initiative, the Body Shop funded Romanian orphanages, an organic farm co-operative in Nicaragua, health and education initiatives in India, a brazil nut co-operative in Brazil, a cocoa butter initiative in Ghana, and much else. In 2007 Roddick became chairwoman of Reprieve, an organization opposed to the death penalty.

Roddick's memoirs, *Body and Soul*, were published in 1991. Her autobiographical business manifesto, *Business as Unusual*, followed in 2000. Both works have compelling vitality, disarming candour, and fertile ideas: if they are occasionally self-mythologizing, their purposive zest is inspiriting. Roddick's other books included *Mamatoto: the*

Body Shop Celebration of Birth (1991), and an activists' handbook, *Take it Personally: How Globalization Affects You and Powerful Ways to Challenge It* (2004). She was made an OBE in 1988 and DBE in 2003. She lived in a farmhouse at Slindon, near Arundel, Sussex, for almost thirty years until her death following a brain haemorrhage, on 10 September 2007, at St Richard's Hospital, Chichester. She was survived by her husband, Gordon, and their two children.

RICHARD DAVENPORT-HINES

Sources A. Roddick, *Body and soul* (1991) • A. Roddick, *Business as unusual* (2000) • *The Times* (11 Sept 2007) • *Daily Telegraph* (11 Sept 2007); (12 Sept 2007) • *The Guardian* (11 Sept 2007); (12 Sept 2007) • *The Independent* (11 Sept 2007); (12 Sept 2007) • *WW* (2007) • b. cert. • m. cert. [1965] • d. cert.

Archives FILM BFINA, party political footage • BFINA, documentary footage • BFINA, light entertainment footage | SOUND BL NSA, current affairs recordings • BL NSA, performance recordings • BL NSA, light entertainment recordings • BL NSA, current affairs recordings

Likenesses M. Reik, bromide print, 1980–89, NPG • photographs, 1980–2007, Rex Features, London • photographs, 1985–2007, PA Photos, London • photographs, 1986–2007, Getty Images, London • T. Leighton, photographs, 1989, NPG • Chen Yan Ning, oils, 1991, repro. in W. Mak Kai Wing, ed., *Chen Yan Ning: the selected oil paintings* (1997), 147, no. 53 • photographs, 1991–2007, Photoshot, London • M. Zinn, bromide print, 1993, NPG • S. Rossberg, watercolour, 1995, NPG • G. Davies, photograph, 2002, Getty Images, London [*see illus.*] • R. Campos, C-type colour print, 2006, NPG • C. Kent, photograph, repro. in *British Journal of Photography* (3 Dec 2003), 21 • J. Swannell, photograph, repro. in J. Swannell, *I'm still standing* (2002), 63 • obituary photographs • photographs, Camera Press, London • photographs, repro. in M. Baren, *How it all began up the high street* (1996), 22, 26

Wealth at death nil—net: probate, 11 April 2008, *GGPLA Eng. & Wales*

Rogers, Sir Frank Jarvis (1920–2005), journalist and newspaper executive, was born on 24 February 1920 at Holly Villas, Church Lawton, Cheshire, the son of Percy Rogers (*d.* 1960), an earthenware manufacturer, and his wife, Elsie Mary, *née* Jarvis (*d.* 1956). He was educated at Wolstanton grammar school, Staffordshire, leaving at the age of seventeen to become a trainee on the sports desk of the *Daily Mirror* in Manchester. Within three years he had become the newspaper's correspondent in Sheffield. In those first years as a journalist, as he would later recall, he stumbled across the kind of restrictive industrial practices that characterized the national press for decades, and that he would spend much of his later career attempting to control. The local chapel of the National Union of Journalists complained that, although designated a reporter, he had been carrying with him the equipment by which photographers transmitted their pictures, and so was effectively doing someone else's job.

In 1940 Rogers was conscripted into the Royal Army Service Corps, serving in north Africa and Italy. When the war ended in 1945 he returned to the *Mirror* and worked in several regional offices before applying in 1949 to be editor of the Nigerian *Daily Times*, recently acquired by the Mirror Group. On 23 July the same year he married Esmé Elizabeth Sophia (Esma) Holland (*d.* 1998), a 21-year-old receptionist and bookkeeper, and daughter of Arthur Edwin Holland, builder. They had two daughters. After two years in Lagos, Rogers decided that his talents were better suited to administration than journalism and he switched to being the paper's general manager. In 1952 he was sent to Melbourne to manage *The Argus*, the Mirror Group's most recent acquisition.

By now Rogers had caught the eye of Cecil King, the Mirror Group's chairman, who recalled him to London in 1955 as his personal assistant. Three years later he was made managing director of Overseas Newspapers, the division of the company that ran its west African publications, based in London. In 1960 he was appointed to the board of the *Daily Mirror*, then at the peak of its success with a circulation approaching 5 million—a sixfold increase in the twenty-three years since he had joined it. His particular responsibility was industrial relations, meaning that he spent many hours in negotiation with the print unions, whose power to halt production at will won them repeated concessions over pay and manning levels. Later he would characterize the employers' attitude at the time as 'a totally inexplicable syndrome of weakness and spinelessness and plain poor management', adding: 'Managements let themselves be tyrannized' (private information). He came to recognize that eventually the proprietors would have to engineer a showdown with the unions, but it would be another two decades before they were finally forced to abandon their resistance to change.

In 1961 the Mirror Group won a takeover battle with Robert Maxwell to acquire Odhams Press, and the combined group became the International Publishing Corporation (IPC). Apart from its portfolio of profitable magazines, Odhams published two national newspapers, *The People* and the failing *Daily Herald*. Rogers and Hugh Cudlipp, the *Mirror*'s editorial director, were the prime movers in transforming the *Herald* into *The Sun* in 1964, aiming to create a hybrid between a tabloid and a serious broadsheet that would appeal to the modern generation. It failed to do so and after five loss-making years King and Cudlipp decided to sell it cheaply to Rupert Murdoch, the young Australian who had recently bought the *News of the World*. Rogers, who had been appointed managing director of IPC in 1965, was opposed to the sale, foreseeing correctly that Murdoch would transform *The Sun* into a powerful competitor with the *Mirror*. He advocated closing *The Sun* down; but Cudlipp and King feared that this would antagonize the unions and provoke industrial trouble at the group's other publications.

In 1968 Rogers was intimately involved with Cudlipp in the palace coup by which King was ousted. The chairman, increasingly gloomy about the state of the nation, had promoted a scheme to replace Harold Wilson's Labour government with a national government led by Lord Mountbatten, in which he imagined he would play a role. The board were appalled by this and, when King refused to resign, they dismissed him and appointed Cudlipp as chairman. Later Rogers was to admit that, although King had to go, it was a mistake to choose Cudlipp as his successor: 'He had all the wrong skills', he said (Dudley Edwards, 415). King was allowed to address the company's annual general meeting and took the opportunity to denounce those who had engineered his dismissal. While he praised Rogers's handling of the print unions in his previous role, he criticized his performance as managing director. He proved right, in that IPC fared poorly after his departure and in 1970, on Rogers's initiative, it became a subsidiary of the Reed Paper Group. Very soon Rogers was dismissed by Reed's chairman, Don Ryder.

On leaving the company where he had until then spent his entire career Rogers's first appointment was as chairman of the National Newspaper Steering Group, a committee of employers and union leaders charged with improving the industry's labour relations. It was a measure of the respect in which he was held by his peers that he was chosen to serve for many years on other industry bodies, including the Newspaper Publishers' Association and the International Press Institute. In 1971 he was appointed to the board of East Midland Allied Press, becoming chairman in 1973. He held that position for seventeen years, overseeing the company's transformation from a small regional newspaper group to a powerful publisher of national magazines. He still found himself in regular confrontation with the print unions, having to endure a six-month strike by journalists on the *Northamptonshire Evening Telegraph* in Kettering, who were seeking to make union membership compulsory.

In 1985 Rogers moved back into the world of national newspapers. At the suggestion of Andrew Knight, editor of *The Economist*, the Canadian entrepreneur Conrad Black had bought a minority interest in the Daily Telegraph Group and invited Rogers to serve as one of his nominated representatives on the board. Some months later Black assumed full control, appointing Knight as his chief executive and Rogers deputy chairman, in which role he used his experience in negotiating with the print unions to pave the way for the introduction of computerized technology. By now he had come to be regarded as a hard-headed elder statesman of the industry, a status endorsed when he was knighted in 1988. As chairman of the Newspaper Publishers' Association he was a key figure in the establishment of the Press Complaints Commission in 1990, replacing the Press Council as the industry's self-regulatory body. Instances of intrusion by the media had fuelled demands for privacy legislation, which Rogers and most others in the industry opposed. By enforcing its code of conduct the commission sought to show that such legislation was unnecessary. He remained on the Telegraph board until he was eighty, stepping down in 2001, shortly before Black had to dispose of his newspaper empire to face charges of financial irregularities in the United States.

Following the death of his first wife, on 3 January 2001 Rogers married Sheena Phillips, a widowed, 52-year-old general nurse, daughter of Peter Mulvie, accountant. She nursed him through a long illness until on 19 July 2005 he died from cerebrovascular disease at his home, Greensleeves, Loudwater Drive, Rickmansworth, Hertfordshire. He was survived by his second wife and the two daughters of his first marriage. MICHAEL LEAPMAN

Sources C. H. King, *The Cecil King diary, 1965–1970* (1972) • H. Cudlipp, *Walking on the water* (1976) • G. Cleverley, *The Kettering standoff* (1978) • D. Hart-Davis, *The house the Berrys built: inside the 'Telegraph', 1928–1986* (1990) • R. Dudley Edwards, *Newspapermen: Hugh Cudlipp, Cecil Harmsworth King, and the glory days of Fleet Street* (2003) • *Daily Telegraph* (21 July 2005) • *The Times* (22 July 2005) • *The Independent* (23 July 2005) • *The Guardian* (5 Aug 2005) • *WW* (2005) • Burke, *Peerage* • personal knowledge (2009) • private information (2009) • b. cert. • m. certs. • d. cert.

Likenesses obituary photographs

Wealth at death £2,937,393: probate, 20 Feb 2006, *CGPLA Eng. & Wales*

Roll, Eric, Baron Roll of Ipsden (1907–2005), economist, public servant, and banker, was born Erich Roll on 1 December 1907 in Nowosielitza, near Czernowitz, in the duchy of Bukowina, Austria, the younger son (there were no daughters) of Mathias Roll (1872–1954), banker, and his wife, Fany, *née* Frendel (1878–1934), daughter of a grain trader.

Early years and academic career Roll was one of a remarkable group of men who emerged from the mayhem of pre-war central Europe to play key parts in Britain's economic and academic life after the Second World War. His parents were intellectuals and social democrats, who kept two huge German encyclopaedias in their dining room so that any argument over dinner could be instantly resolved. His early education was at the village school and at home; his mother was a trained teacher. Czernowitz, where the economist Joseph Schumpeter once taught, was at the meeting place of Austria, Romania, and Russia. It was to change nationality three times by the end of Roll's long life (finally becoming part of independent Ukraine in 1991). Roll's childhood was interrupted by the outbreak of the First World War, during which his parents fled to Vienna, where Roll's schooling continued, at the Piaristenschule then the Piaristengymnasium. Back in Czernowitz, now part of Romania, he attended the Liceul Emanoil-Grigoroviza, where the language of his education switched from German to Romanian. He also learned French at school and English privately, including large passages of Shakespeare by heart.

In 1925 Roll left for Birmingham University. His father particularly admired Britain's social and political system and cultural climate. Roll expected to work in Romania's thriving oil industry, and enrolled in the school of oil engineering and refining, then the only one of its kind. However, he discovered he had little enthusiasm for chemistry and quickly switched to economics. He graduated BCom in 1928, then PhD two years later, finding time to win both the Gladstone memorial prize and ballroom dancing competitions. In 1930 his thesis, on the manufacturing and marketing of steam engines in Britain, 1775–1800, became his first published book. His university days already revealed his enduring knack for accumulating a remarkable network of friends and acquaintances, many of whom either were or became distinguished figures in their field. Even before he had finished his first degree he took a motoring holiday with Hilary Marquand, a future

Eric Roll, Baron Roll of Ipsden (1907–2005), by Bernard Lee Schwartz, 1978

Labour cabinet minister, and met the economists Austin and Joan Robinson.

Meanwhile the economy in central Europe was growing bleaker. In the spring of 1931 Roll became a British subject. From then on he saw himself as English. When Sir Denis Hamilton, editor of *The Times*, once asked him which language he dreamed in, Roll promptly replied, 'English'. He later added, 'I make Shakespeare responsible for that. I've long concluded that the essence of national identity is language' (*Desert Island Discs*, Aug 2001). Roll's English was almost without accent—as indeed were his French and German.

In the autumn of 1930, and with the backing of John Maynard Keynes, Roll took a teaching post at the new University College of Hull under George Cyril Allen. When, three years later, Allen departed for University College, London, Roll was given the task of running the economics department, but it was two more years before he achieved the title (and salary) of professor of economics and commerce. Within his first few weeks at Hull he met Winifred (Freda) Taylor (1909–1998) at a bus stop. The daughter of Elliott Taylor, a Yorkshire railway official, she was president of the students' union at Hull. She later recalled that they had looked so similar, both with fair hair and blue-grey eyes, that they were occasionally mistaken for brother and sister—a confusion that occasionally proved useful during their four-year courtship. They married on 22 September 1934 at Sculcoates register office, and had two daughters, Joanna and Elizabeth.

In old age Roll still thought of himself as very much a product of the 1930s. As his parents had done in Czernowitz, he became part of a group of like-minded intellectuals in Hull. He was aghast at the economic impact of the depression. He and his wife organized relief work during the Spanish Civil War, and wrote and circulated a pamphlet attacking Britain's policy of appeasement. In the course of the 1930s he also produced two successful textbooks, one of which, *About Money* (1934), was extensively annotated by T. S. Eliot, one of the directors of Faber and Faber. He wrote his most famous book, *A History of Economic Thought* (1938), in the summer of 1938, dashing off the first draft in six weeks. He worked in the garden of a cottage in Wendens Ambo, near Cambridge, rented with Jacob Bronowski and Eirlys Roberts. With its accessible prose and its strong emphasis on Marx in the early editions, the book was initially disdained by other academic economists. However, it remained in print, in many languages and editions, earning good royalties throughout his life. Even in his mid-nineties Roll was wondering whether to write one more edition. In his final career, as a merchant banker, the book became his greatest passport to international eminence: finance ministers had frequently read the book and were flattered to meet its author.

In 1939, on a Rockefeller fellowship, Roll and his wife sailed for the United States, where they were to stay until 1946. He visited Harvard and Princeton and taught in Austin, Texas. 'You should have stayed,' Lyndon Johnson said to him many years later. 'We might have made something of you' (E. Roll, 36). He also met a galaxy of up-and-coming economists, including J. K. Galbraith, Wassily Leontief, Fritz Machlup, Gottfried von Haberler, Paul Samuelson, and Robert Triffin. Not only were they part of a great flowering of economic thought; most were or became deeply involved with public policy. But within two years Roll's first career, as an academic, was effectively at an end and he had embarked upon the second, as a public servant with the British food mission in Washington.

Public service J. K. Galbraith once described Roll as the most accomplished negotiator in public affairs in the post-war era (Stormonth-Darling, 97). He arrived in Washington just before the signing of the Lend-Lease Act. He was plunged into the international politics of food and agriculture, and the problems caused by the chronic shortage of dollars—two issues that were vital to the British war effort, and that continued to dominate the early years of the post-war era. Through them, Roll discovered the art that he later called 'alliance politics': how to conduct negotiations with a number of parties who shared the same basic objectives but operated under different constraints (E. Roll, 40–41). Linking international negotiations with the government machine was to be Roll's main task for the following two decades. It was the career of a diplomat, undertaken by an economist, working not in the Foreign Office but in one or another of Whitehall's economic ministries. He remained with the British food mission for five years, latterly as deputy.

In 1946, with his rather reluctant wife and two small daughters, Roll returned to Britain, which he had now come to regard as home. Urged by John Maynard Keynes, he decided to stay in the civil service. Almost immediately he was once more negotiating. This time it was the Marshall plan. Roll commuted to and from Paris initially as an assistant secretary in the Ministry of Food and later as an under-secretary in the Treasury, attached to the central economic planning staff, where he met many of those who were to dominate Whitehall in the 1960s and 1970s. He also became a close friend of Robert Marjolin, the first secretary general of the Organization for European Economic Co-operation, the body that would oversee the administration of Marshall aid.

Negotiations were sometimes hampered by a shortage of solid statistics. When this led Roll to complain to Whitehall about the difficulties of making bricks without straw, the reply was 'Goldman expert strawless brickmaker is on the way' (E. Roll, 54). On another occasion, delegates were requested at short notice to ask their capitals to fill out a detailed questionnaire on requirements for reconstruction. Roll found one delegate filling it out himself. 'I think I know better what to put in than they do back home', he said. Another delegate, scanning the elaborate document, exclaimed, 'On fera de la poésie' (ibid., 56). Roll subsequently became one of the so-called four wise men responsible for the initial allocation of aid. 'I cannot think of many operations I have been involved in, before or since, that equalled it in complexity' he later recalled (ibid., 61). Britain emerged with the largest tranche, a triumph for which Roll deserved much of the credit.

As these negotiations came to an end, Roll became part of the permanent British delegation to the Organization for European Economic Co-operation with the title of minister, and moved his family to France. In her autobiography Freda Roll calculated that she had moved at least sixteen times during her married life. The move gave Roll a close view of the institutions that shaped post-war European integration. In 1952 he became deputy head of the British delegation to NATO, with responsibilities for its economic work. He was one of Britain's observers at the Franco-German talks that led to the creation of the European Coal and Steel Community. In his autobiography he recounted a curious secret visit with Stafford Cripps, then chancellor of the exchequer, to the French finance minister to discuss the creation of an alternative to the steel community. That scheme got nowhere. Roll felt that Britain's early ambivalence towards European integration shaped long-term relations with Europe. Whitehall's search for a perfect solution, that would square the three circles of Europe, the Commonwealth, and the relationship with the United States, led to inaction or dangerous delay.

Roll's return to London in 1953 meant reduced living standards (deprived of duty-free tobacco, he gave up smoking). It also meant a return to the Ministry of Food, soon to be uncomfortably amalgamated with the Ministry of Agriculture. But in 1957 he was negotiating again, to create a new world sugar agreement. He was then for a year the executive director of the new International Sugar Council. The experience persuaded him that a 'realistic and pragmatic approach' was preferable to the unrestricted supremacy of the free market. Rather, government intervention could often be combined with market forces to secure 'politically accepted economic and social goals' (E. Roll, 94).

Back in London from 1959 as deputy secretary at the Ministry of Agriculture, Fisheries and Food, Roll was once more involved in Britain's tortured relationship with Europe. In 1960, as Britain dithered about an application to join the Common Market, he chaired a working party on the emerging common agricultural policy. It concluded that most of the problems were manageable, that the policy was not yet set in stone, and that a speedy application was therefore essential. Britain formally submitted a bid in 1961—but speed was not to be had.

Edward Heath included Roll (who was knighted KCMG in 1962, having been made CMG in 1949 and CB in 1956) in the high-powered group of civil servants—the 'flying knights'—who masterminded Britain's part in the Brussels negotiations. Roll's skills, Heath later recalled, included 'seven languages and the ability to lip-read in both French and German' (*The Times*, 1 April 2005). Roll later felt that those negotiations were perhaps the high point of his work as a public servant, in their complexity, technicality and 'the pressures to which I and my fellow negotiators were subjected' (E. Roll, 103). On holiday with Robert Marjolin before the talks began, he realized that the concessions available to Britain would be limited by the commission's desire not to undermine the community. In the event, the structure of the negotiations caused problems just as great as the substantive issues under discussion. The six countries of Europe, in the throes of reaching their own agreement on the common agricultural policy, insisted on negotiating as a bloc, and the British frequently found themselves facing a spokesman merely expounding a common position. When de Gaulle finally torpedoed talks in January 1963, Roll expressed surprise to Olivier Wormser, of the French Ministry of Foreign Affairs. 'Indeed', said Wormser, 'You don't know how close to success you were' (ibid., 128).

In 1963 Roll returned to the United States as economic minister at the embassy and head of the UK Treasury delegation in Washington. It was a vibrant time, with John Kennedy and then Lyndon Johnson in the White House and many of Roll's academic friends in public life. He built a new set of enduring friendships with America's bankers, many of them through Siegmund Warburg, who was to shape the final third of Roll's long career. But with the election in 1964 of a Labour government, Roll was recalled early for what proved to be his final stint in public life.

Before he had taken up his embassy post, Roll had lunched with George Brown, then in opposition. Brown had asked Roll whether he thought the economic work of government would be improved by having a Department of Economic Affairs. Roll had replied cautiously that it might be so, adding that the power of the Treasury was so great that such a department would find it hard to assert itself. Later that year, Roll bumped into Brown again, who urged him not to put down deep roots in America. In 1964 Roll reluctantly became permanent secretary of the new department. 'I was even at the time very sceptical about the exaggerated hopes for the DEA entertained by many others', Roll subsequently wrote (E. Roll, 164).

For much of the autumn Roll shuttled between London and Washington, where no successor was appointed for three months (Alec Cairncross having refused the post). It was a bad beginning. Douglas Allen, moved from the Treasury, had to handle recruitment for the new department and most organizational matters. Indeed, much of Roll's public service had been in international negotiations, in roles more typical of the Foreign Office than of the other parts of Whitehall. He had little effective experience of departmental management. He also had to cope with a floundering economy, a prime minister whose economic training reinforced his reluctance to relinquish control of economic policy, a hostile and entrenched Treasury, and a tempestuous minister.

One of Roll's most endearing characteristics was a desire always to emphasize the best in others. Even to George Brown, Roll was kindly in retrospect, despite Brown's inebriated bullying: within a month of taking office, Brown had already 'sacked' Roll once (Cairncross, 14). Much later, pressed by the broadcaster Sue Lawley to describe Brown's tantrums, Roll recalled Brown storming into his office shouting furiously at his permanent secretary to 'Find my car!' Roll demurred: 'I'm always ready to serve you, but not to find your car', and generously remembered that Brown had apologized the next morning, 'which he usually did after a row'. He was, reflected Roll, a highly intelligent man, with good instincts, frustrated by losing the battle for the party leadership to Harold Wilson (*Desert Island Discs*, Aug 2001).

When Brown moved to the Foreign Office in the summer of 1966 he tried to persuade Roll to follow him. Roll refused, pointing out that the Foreign Office would never accept an outsider. But Roll by then had decided to leave the civil service, two years before the official retirement age. There had been talk of making him governor of the Bank of England (he was later on the court), but in the end he embarked upon his third and—as it turned out—his longest career, as a merchant banker.

Banker at Warburgs In the spring of 1967, after spending the enforced six-month period of 'decontamination' at Harvard, writing *The World after Keynes* (1968), Roll joined S. G. Warburg & Co. Ltd as deputy chairman. He became a devoted admirer of Siegmund Warburg, one of the most influential figures in the post-war City. Other merchant banks had wooed Roll, but Martin Gordon, who also joined the bank in the 1960s, recalled that Warburg had told Roll that he would probably 'have more fun with us' (Gordon). He was to spend the next thirty-eight years at Warburgs. He became chairman in 1974, joint chairman with David Scholey from 1983 to 1987, president from 1987 to 1995, and finally senior adviser to what had by then become, first, part of Swiss Bank Corporation, and then part of UBS (Union Bank of Switzerland).

When Roll joined Warburgs the influence on financial markets of that middle-European intellectual hothouse was at its height. The merchant bank had created the eurobond market four years earlier by issuing the first eurodollar loan. It had also, thanks to Warburg's partner Henry Grunfeld, won the first great post-war British take-over battle, for British Aluminium in 1958, and now dominated the market.

Roll's first months were unpromising. Others resented the seniority Warburg conferred on his new deputy chairman, who clearly knew little of the banking business. Some, irritated by his transparent hero-worship of the charismatic Warburg, named him Sir Echo. Sometimes Warburg would tease Roll by unexpectedly changing his position and leaving him stranded. Ian Fraser, one of the inventors of the eurobond, described an occasion when Roll chaired the bank's morning meeting and refused to accept a majority view on whether to issue more bonds in a certain deal. 'There is someone whose opinion I particularly admire and whom I should like to consult before we minute this decision', he explained. There was a chorus of laughter: all knew that he wanted Warburg's clearance (Fraser, 277). However, Roll had a good teacher, and learned quickly. He and Warburg would walk at weekends round the silent squares of Belgravia, talking less about theory than practice: the quirks of particular companies, banks and, above all, people. When Warburg died in 1982 it was Roll with Grunfeld, dubbed the 'uncles', who handled Scholey's succession.

Warburgs were eager to extend their eurobond business, notably to Japan and then to China. Roll's greatest assets were his charm, his astonishing address book, and his instinctive internationalism. He embarked on a tremendous programme of travel on the bank's behalf, generally accompanied (until her death in 1998) by his wife. At his ninetieth birthday party, Scholey said that Roll had never knowingly passed an airport without going into it. Were someone from London to land on an iceberg in Antarctica, said Scholey on another occasion, one of the penguins would be likely to ask how Eric Roll was. He knew everyone by name; was not thrown by Japanese or Chinese names; and had a phenomenal memory for people and for what they had done. His ability to quote reams of Shakespeare endeared him to one head of the Bank of Tokyo, his experience in government to another. He was instrumental in encouraging his friend Yoshitoki Chino, chairman of Daiwa Securities, to set up the Daiwa Anglo-Japanese Foundation, of which he served as founding chairman from 1988 to 2001, and which soon became the major British charity supporting links between Britain and Japan. In cultivating Japanese financial institutions, his advancing years were often a positive advantage. He was also one of the first bankers to go to China, where he impressed his hosts with his knowledge of Marx. S. G. Warburg issued the first eurobond in London for the Bank of China.

In other areas of public life Roll's charm was also a continuing asset. He sat on the boards of several companies, mostly Warburgs' clients, including Times Newspapers and the Rootes car company. From 1971 to 1980 he was also on the National Economic Development Council. Ronald McIntosh, its director-general from 1973, found him a shrewd adviser on cabinet and Treasury machinations against the council. In his diaries McIntosh recalled a fraught lunch of politicians, industrialists, and trade unionists in the thick of a miners' strike that had reduced Britain to a three-day week, with 'Eric working hard to keep the conversation light and interesting … In fact, it was all quite enjoyable' (McIntosh, 31).

In the final decade of his life Roll continued to travel and to draw on his immense network. Like Grunfeld, who continued to work until his death at the age of ninety-five in 1999, Roll came regularly to work at about 10 a.m. until the week of his death. He would spend the morning in his office close to Scholey's, moving on after lunch to attend the House of Lords (he had become a life peer, as Baron Roll of Ipsden, in 1977 and was a reliable member of the economic affairs committee). Global financial leaders such as Alan Greenspan would ring him up, and he would knowledgeably quiz young colleagues and visiting journalists.

Roll also continued his prolific output of books, academic papers, and speeches. He wrote a rather bland autobiography, *Crowded Hours* (1985), with not a single harsh word or unkind revelation. His economic views remained essentially Keynesian and interventionist, although with some subtlety. In 1938, in the first issue of the *Modern Quarterly*, a journal whose editorial council included not just Roll but left-wing intellectuals such as Harold Laski and Joseph Needham, he had given warning of the danger that fascist regimes were misusing Keynes's precept of interventionism for militarist ends. Four decades later, in his Stamp memorial lecture of 1976, he chastised those who believed the myth that there had once been a golden age of the market economy. He spoke of the inevitability of more formal channels of intervention in managing the economy. But he also attacked the 'clichés of collectivism' coming from the other side of the political divide.

Roll also remained a committed European all his life. He deeply regretted the Thatcher government's refusal in 1979 to join the European exchange rate mechanism. Indeed, he had always been an enthusiast for a common currency, having toyed in the early 1960s with the idea of a unit called the *moneta*. 'I suppose it would have been the forerunner to the euro', he reflected (Moore). In the early 1990s he chaired a committee that examined the case for giving independence to the Bank of England. It came down strongly in favour of independence. It might seem surprising that a man with Keynesian leanings should have favoured the separation of authority for fiscal and monetary policy, but he was probably moved mainly by the desire to see Britain position itself to participate in the euro. He wrote two more books on political and economic matters: *Where Did We Go Wrong?* (1995) and *Where Are We Going?* (2000). In both cases, the main answer to the question lay in Europe. Roll feared that the Conservative government would become increasingly anti-European and xenophobic, with a 'disagreeable type of demagogic appeal to lower middle-class instincts' (*Where Are We Going?*, 163). Speaking privately of Margaret Thatcher, he abandoned his usual bonhomie: 'that terrible woman' was his phrase at a lunch in the 1990s (private information).

In one sense Roll's long life was a history of might-have-beens, and not just in terms of his long disappointment over Britain's half-hearted involvement with Europe. He was several times considered for, but never held, one of those offices at the head of an international organization like the World Bank, the General Agreement on Tariffs and Trade, or the Organization for Economic Cooperation and Development, for which his background would so ideally have prepared him. As an economist, he was a brilliant expositor but not an original theorist. Moreover, he came to believe that the 'limits within which economics can be relied on for precise guidance are very narrow indeed' (E. Roll, 239). But Roll was never a disappointed man. 'He had a sunny nature and a spontaneous gaiety which endeared him to many people', recalled his wife, looking back on their early years together (W. Roll, 35). Moreover, Roll also left monuments in all his three careers, any one of which would have been a life's achievement for most people. His *History of Economic Thought* continued to sell, seventy years after it first appeared; his success in the Marshall plan negotiations helped to set Britain on the slow path to post-war recovery; and he helped to hold Warburgs together in the years after Siegmund Warburg's death. He made more friends in each career than many do in one; and he had not an ounce of malice. He went to work at Warburgs for the last time in the week of his death, which occurred at King Edward VII's Hospital, Westminster, on 30 March 2005. He was survived by his two daughters. FRANCES CAIRNCROSS

Sources E. Roll, *Crowded hours* (1985) • R. Chernow, *The Warburgs: a family saga* (1993) • W. Roll, *My journey through the century* (1995) • A. Cairncross, *The Wilson years: a Treasury diary, 1964–1969* (1997) • P. Stormonth-Darling, *City Cinderella: the life and times of Mercury Asset Management* (1999) • I. Fraser, *The high road to England: an autobiography* (1999) • P. Moore, 'Founding fathers and 35-year olds', *Euromoney* (1 June 2004) • *The Times* (1 April 2005) • *Daily Telegraph* (1 April 2005) • *The Guardian* (2 April 2005) • *The Independent* (2 April 2005) • *The Spectator* (9 April 2005) • M. Gordon, *Lord (Eric) Roll of Ipsden (1907–2005) and S. G. Warburg and Shirasu Jiro* (2006) • R. McIntosh, *Challenge to democracy: politics, trade union power and economic failure in the 1970s* (2006) • *Desert island discs*, BBC Radio 4, Aug 2001 • private information (2009) • m. cert. • d. cert.

Archives SOUND BL NSA, National Life Story Collections, City lives, interviews with C. Courtney, 12 and 22 Oct 1992, 22 March and 24 April 1993, F3816–F3820 • BL NSA, recorded talk

Likenesses W. Bird, bromide print, 1962, NPG • Elliott & Fry, seven half-plate negatives, 1962, NPG • Elliott & Fry, quarter-plate negative, 1963, NPG • A. Rowdon, bronze, 1971, priv. coll. • B. L. Schwartz, dye transfer print, 1978, NPG [*see illus.*] • photograph, 1979, Photoshot, London • A. Tkachuk, oils, Japan House, Regent's Park, London

Wealth at death £2,894,847: administration, 2 Sept 2005, *CGPLA Eng. & Wales*

Rolt, Anthony Peter Roylance [Tony] (**1918–2008**), soldier, racing driver, and engineer, was born on 16 October 1918 at Forest Lodge, Hollywater, Alton, Hampshire, the fourth child and only son of Brigadier-General Stuart

Peter Rolt (1862–1933), army officer, and his wife, Evelyn Roylance, *née* Court. He grew up in St Asaph, Flintshire, and appears to have been destined from an early age for a career in the army. He was educated at Eton College and Sandhurst, and in 1939 was commissioned as a lieutenant in the rifle brigade. He was awarded the Military Cross for his gallantry during the hopeless defence of Calais by the British expeditionary force in May 1940. Captured at the end of that battle, he attempted many escapes from German prisoner-of-war camps (at one point almost reaching Switzerland) before being transferred to Oflag IV-C in Colditz Castle. He was closely involved in the celebrated plan to build and launch a glider from the castle, and was one of four men who would have drawn lots to form the craft's two-man crew, but the liberation of Colditz by the American army in April 1945 rendered the scheme unnecessary. He later said: 'Escaping was not a game. Nor was it fun. It was a duty' (*Daily Telegraph*, 8 Feb 2008). After his return home he was awarded a bar to his MC in recognition of his exploits during his period of incarceration. On 17 August 1945, at the parish church of St Miniver, Cornwall, he married Lois Valentine Blomfield (1922–2005), daughter of Captain Patrick Valentine Blomfield of the Indian army, and stepdaughter of Major Alexander Allan of the rifle brigade. They had two sons and two daughters.

Rolt's interest in motor sport had developed as a teenager when he competed in the Eton schoolboy trials, driving a Morgan three-wheeler. In 1936 he participated in the Spa 24 hour race in Belgium, finishing a creditable fourth in class and, in the same year, aged eighteen, he became a full member of the British Racing Drivers' Club. In 1937 he twice won coronation trophy races at Donington Park, and in 1939 he won the prestigious 200 mile British empire trophy, again at Donington.

The conclusion of hostilities permitted Rolt to resign his commission in order to indulge his love of motor sport. He raced a number of different vehicles including Nash-Healey and Jaguar sports cars and, with particular distinction, the Walker A-type Connaught. His success in endurance events attracted the attention of Jaguar and he was eventually given a permanent place with the works team, becoming one of the country's most respected amateur race drivers. He competed on three occasions in the British grand prix, including the 1950 event that inaugurated the official world championship. Although forced to retire from each of these races, Rolt and his co-driver, Duncan Hamilton, won the 1953 Le Mans in a C-type Jaguar at a record average speed of more than 100 m.p.h. In the following year the pair came close to another Le Mans win in the new Jaguar D-type before being narrowly beaten by a Ferrari after oil filter pit stops. Rolt and Hamilton also came second in the 1954 Reims 12 hours race, again in a Jaguar. Rolt retired from racing in 1955 to concentrate on his business interests, but his decision may have been influenced in part by the Le Mans disaster of 1955, a racing accident that resulted in more than eighty fatalities. This was particularly horrifying for Rolt—who had retired from the race owing to gearbox problems, and according to some accounts witnessed the disaster—since in the previous year he had expressed the view forcefully that parts of the Le Mans circuit were extremely dangerous and that near accidents were commonplace. The Le Mans tragedy highlighted a number of long-standing safety issues and helped to usher in a new culture of safety for both participants and spectators, for which Rolt was partly responsible.

Rolt's interest in the business aspect of motor vehicle technology began after the war, when he established Rolt Dixon Research with Freddie Dixon, a fellow pre-war racing driver. The firm became engaged in the development of four-wheel drive and other advanced automotive technology. Their success attracted the support of the tractor manufacturer Harry Ferguson, and led to the creation of Ferguson Research in 1950. After the departure of Dixon, Rolt and Ferguson continued to work on four-wheel drive systems, with perhaps their most notable achievement being Project 99. This was a four-wheel drive racing car, which, driven by Stirling Moss, won the international gold cup event at Oulton Park in 1961. This was a non-championship meeting but it was notable as the only time a car of its type won a formula one race. The application of four-wheel drive technology to formula one racing was short lived. However, in 1971 Rolt founded FF Developments, which became a world leader as interest grew in the general application of four-wheel drive technology. Partnerships were formed with a number of major motor firms, including Ford, Chrysler, Audi, Fiat-Lancia, and General Motors. Rolt's pioneering engineering work became an important part of motor sport through its incorporation into endurance racing, both in Europe and in the United States.

Rolt was a man of considerable charm, with a passion for motor racing but wary of personal publicity. He lived latterly in Stratford upon Avon, and died of pneumonia on 6 February 2008 at Warwick Hospital, Warwick. He was survived by his daughter Angela and his sons, David and Stuart, his wife, Lois, and his daughter Nikki having predeceased him. DAVID THOMS

Sources I. Rendall, *The chequered flag: 100 years of motor racing* (1993) · C. Hilton, *Le Mans '55* (2004) · P. Raby, *Grand prix: driver by driver* (2007) · *Daily Telegraph* (8 Feb 2008) · *The Times* (8 Feb 2008) · *The Guardian* (9 Feb 2008) · *The Independent* (11 Feb 2008) · en.wikipedia.org/wiki/Tony_Rolt, 21 Feb 2011 · b. cert. · m. cert. · d. cert.

Archives SOUND BL NSA, documentary recording

Likenesses photographs, 1953, Rex Features, London · obituary photographs

Wealth at death £1,538,414: probate, 8 July 2008, *CGPLA Eng. & Wales*

Rooke, Sir Denis Eric (1924–2008), engineer and industrialist, was born on 2 April 1924 at 42 Erlanger Road, New Cross, London, the younger son of Frederick George Rooke, printer and commercial traveller, and his wife, Ada Emily, *née* Brown. As a very young child he spent four years in and out of Great Ormond Street Hospital, and did not learn to read and write until he was seven. He was educated at Westminster City School and Addey and Stanhope School, New Cross, and in 1944 graduated from University College, London (evacuated to Swansea during the war), with a first-class degree in mechanical engineering. Commissioned into the Royal Electrical and Mechanical Engineers in 1944, he served in Britain and India, rising to the rank of major. After demobilization in 1948, he studied for a postgraduate diploma in chemical engineering at University College, London, which was awarded in 1949. On 22 January 1949 he married (Elizabeth) Brenda Evans (*b.* 1922), an investigator providing research services, and daughter of David Daniel Evans, chief clerk of the Miners' Federation, of Ystradgynlais, Brecon; they had one daughter, Diana.

After a temporary job with the South Metropolitan Gas Company, Rooke was appointed assistant mechanical engineer for the South Eastern Gas Board in 1949, the year of the nationalization of the gas industry, working at the coal tar by-products works in Greenwich; he was appointed deputy manager of the tar works in 1954. The gas industry had been searching for natural gas (methane) since 1952, and in 1957 Rooke was seconded to the North Thames Gas Board to explore the possibility of securing a supply of liquefied natural gas to replace 'town gas', manufactured from coal, which was dirty and smelly. He was invited in 1959 to join the team of technicians sailing on the first voyage of the experimental tanker *Methane Pioneer*, bringing liquefied natural gas across the Atlantic from Louisiana to Britain. The Gas Council set up a development and planning section to be responsible for planning new production and processes and to develop a new integrated supply system, and in 1960 Rooke was appointed development engineer to head the new organization. Following the successful trials of this method of transporting methane, the first natural gas terminal in Britain was built on Canvey Island, and natural gas began to be shipped from the United States and Algeria, and distributed through pipelines to the area gas boards.

In 1964 methane was discovered under the North Sea, the first licences were issued to oil companies to prospect for North Sea gas, and the Gas Council committed itself to the supply of North Sea gas. Rooke joined the board of the Gas Council in 1966 as member for production and supplies, responsible for exploration and controlling the delivery of gas from the gas fields to the consumer via the area boards. This entailed the design and construction of new onshore terminals on the east coast to receive the gas, and expansion of the gas grid throughout the mainland. The first supplies of gas began coming ashore at Easington in 1967. Over the next ten years Rooke played a leading role in the conversion of every gas appliance in Britain, in 12 million households, as natural gas did not burn satisfactorily in appliances designed to burn manufactured gas, and also oversaw the construction of a national pipeline system. When in 1977 he announced the completion of the appliance conversion programme, he described it as 'perhaps the biggest peacetime operation in the nation's history' (*The Times*, 2 Sept 1977). Meanwhile, appointed deputy chairman of the Gas Council in 1972, he was responsible for the reorganization of the distribution network, replacing the twelve area boards with a new regional structure for the British Gas Corporation (BGC), created in 1973.

Rooke was appointed chairman of the BGC in 1976. In 1979 a Conservative government led by Margaret Thatcher was elected, committed to reforming the nationalized industries (though not yet to their wholesale privatization). One of its first targets was the gas industry, and a few months after the election the government proposed the sale of the oil interests of the BGC. The latter had been building up its interests in North Sea gas exploration, and had developed onshore oilfields, the most important of which was at Wytch Farm, in Dorset, a collaboration with British Petroleum. Rooke, opposed to the break-up of the gas industry, as were many members of his board, also resisted the plan to part with its oilfield interests, continuing to battle with Nigel Lawson, the new secretary of state for energy, despite a government direction in October 1981 to dispose of Wytch Farm for the best price, and doing his best to frustrate the sale: 'The detailed information … had to be supplied by British Gas, and extracting this proved very much more difficult than extracting the gas itself' (Lawson, 214). This sale was concluded in 1984, by which time the government had sold all the other oilfield assets of the BGC.

Government intervention in fuel-price setting had already attracted Rooke's ire. In 1979 David Howell, the energy secretary, increased the price of domestic gas by ten percentage points more than the rate of inflation for the following three years. These large annual increases were attacked by Rooke in a leaflet which was enclosed with every household bill, blaming the government for the price rise. In 1981 Nigel Lawson took steps to weaken what he called 'Rooke's empire', including the abolition of the BGC's monopoly in the purchase of gas and its resale to industry, which had given it full control of the exploitation of North Sea gas fields and the volumes available to British industry. Lawson regarded Rooke's view that gas was too high quality a fuel to burn in power stations as a 'mystical doctrine', and accused the BGC of refusing to supply to customers of whom Rooke disapproved. The Oil and Gas (Enterprise) Act of 1983 enabled oil companies that produced gas as a by-product to supply large customers using the BGC pipeline network. However, Rooke's opposition prevented the sale of the 900 BGC gas showrooms, proposed in 1981.

After the 1983 general election, when the Conservatives were returned to power with the promise to accelerate privatization, the government turned to privatization of the BGC. Lawson, now chancellor of the exchequer, wanted to break the corporation up into separate regional companies. Rooke could see no case for structural change, and progress was slow. Peter Walker, the new energy secretary, was more sympathetic to Rooke's view that the company should be kept intact. Realizing what a formidable opponent she faced, and anxious to complete the privatization of gas during the life of the parliament, the prime minister agreed to the privatization of the British Gas Corporation as a whole. The Gas Act was passed in July 1986, and British Gas was floated in December 1986 as a regulated monopoly. After the successful 'Tell Sid' campaign to attract small investors, the offer was more than twice oversubscribed, with 4.5 million buying shares in the new company, netting the government £7.7 billion. Rooke remained chairman until his retirement in 1989. Successive subsequent regulatory measures resulted in 1997 in the break-up of British Gas plc into two new companies, Centrica/British Gas and Transco (later National Grid UK), and the opening of the market to competition.

Rooke, described by Peter Walker as 'the best nationalised industry chairman I met' (Walker, 192), spent his whole career in the gas industry, and played a large part in the switch from manufactured gas to cheap natural gas from the North Sea and the development of a national gas distribution network. Throughout his struggle against privatization he was driven by the conviction that a nationalized gas industry best served the needs of the consumers. He was knighted in 1977, and was appointed to the Order of Merit in 1997. Elected to the Fellowship of Engineering (later the Royal Academy of Engineering) in 1977, he was elected a fellow of the Royal Society in 1978 and was awarded the society's Rumford medal in 1986. Described by Nigel Lawson as 'a large, craggy overbearing man' (Lawson, 213), he had a direct and sometimes abrasive manner, and a powerful intellect. He had a strong commitment to engineering education, serving on many boards and advisory committees: he was chairman of the Council for National Academic Awards from 1978 to 1983. As chairman of the Royal Commission for the Exhibition of 1851, from 1987 to 1991, he overhauled the commission's award structure with the aim of focusing the awards on the needs of British industry. After his retirement from British Gas he devoted a lot of time and energy to raising the status of the engineering profession, helping to establish both the Fellowship of Engineering and the Worshipful Company of Engineers, which he served as president. He was chancellor of Loughborough University from 1989 to 2003, where a bronze bust (2004) by David Williams-Ellis was unveiled outside the new building named after him. He served as president of the Royal Academy of Engineering from 1986 to 1991 and was awarded its Prince Philip Medal in 1992. Two medals were named after him: the Rooke medal for the public promotion of engineering, awarded by the Royal Academy of Engineering, and the Sir Denis Rooke medal, a lifetime achievement award given by the Institution of Gas Engineers and Managers. Rooke loved listening to music and opera, and was a keen wildflower photographer. He died of cancer on 2 September 2008 in Greenwich and Bexley Cottage Hospice, 185 Bostall Hill, Abbey Wood, London, and was survived by his wife and daughter. A memorial service was held in Southwark Cathedral on 26 November 2008.

ANNE PIMLOTT BAKER

Sources T. I. Williams, *A history of the British gas industry* (1981) · *Daily Express* (12 Nov 1981) · K. Hutchison, *High speed gas: an autobiography* (1987) · P. Walker, *Staying power* (1991), 189–93 · N. Lawson, *The view from no. 11: memoirs of a tory radical* (1992), 171–5, 213–16 · M. Thatcher, *The Downing Street years* (1993), 680–81 · *Financial Times* (21 Sept 1996) · *Daily Telegraph* (6 Sept 2008) · *The Times* (8 Sept 2008); (13 Sept 2008); (23 Sept 2008) · *The Guardian* (8 Sept 2008) · *The Independent* (8 Sept 2008) · *Gas International* (Jan–Feb 2009) · D. Parker, *The official history of privatisation*, 1: *The formative years, 1970–1987* (2009) · Burke, *Peerage* · *WW* (2008) · private information (2012) · b. cert. · m. cert. · d. cert.

Archives Institution of Mechanical Engineers library, Lord Hinton MSS | SOUND BL NSA, documentary recording

Likenesses photographs, 1976–80, Photoshot, London · group portrait, photograph, 2002, Camera Press, London · D. Williams-Ellis, bronze bust, 2004, Loughborough University, Sir Denis Rooke Building · obituary photographs · photograph, repro. in Hutchison, *High speed gas*, following p. 152 · photograph, repro. in *The Times* (6 Nov 1981), 21

Wealth at death £2,206,672: administration with will, 21 Sept 2009, *CGPLA Eng. & Wales*

Rosen, Harold (1919–2008), educationist, was born on 25 June 1919 in Brockton, Massachusetts, USA, the only son and third child of Morris (Moshe) Rosen (1878–1950), shoe worker and trade unionist, and his wife, Rose, *née* Hyams (1882–1956), a disabled garment worker and communist activist. His parents were both Jewish; his father was born in Krośniewice (then in Russia, later in Poland), his mother in Whitechapel. On their separation Rosen moved back to London with his mother at the age of two but remained an American citizen. Mother and son lived in an overcrowded and poverty-stricken house, 14 Nelson Street, Whitechapel, with grandparents, uncles, aunts, and his sister Sylvia. In a largely observant Jewish neighbourhood the family was secular and left-wing and received a constant stream of socialist and trade union visitors.

Rosen attended Myrdle Street elementary school, the Foundation School (later renamed the Davenant Foundation Grammar School) in Whitechapel, and the sixth form of the Polytechnic Secondary School in Regent Street. While at school he joined the Young Communist League and met Connie Ruby Isakofsky, otherwise Connie Ruby Freedman (1919–1976), daughter of Friedman Isakofsky (later Frank Freedman), cap maker. Together they were present at the battle of Cable Street in 1936; their emotional partnership and intellectual collaboration lasted forty-one years, until her death from cancer in 1976. Politics informed their friendships, their family life (they married on 3 May 1941 and had two sons), and their work in education, though they left the Communist Party in 1957 (having decided it was no longer likely to help bring about the social change they desired and that its views conflicted with their own on education).

From school Rosen won a scholarship to study English at University College, London (1937–40), where, though disappointed with the course, he read widely and engaged energetically in politics, rugby, and middle-distance running. After graduating with a third-class degree he took his teacher's diploma in 1941 at the University of London Institute of Education (then evacuated to Nottingham). When his application to serve in the British forces was rejected because of his American citizenship, he spent the remainder of the Second World War teaching in Leicester and Middlesex, until finally called up to serve in the US Army education corps in Frankfurt and Berlin.

Rosen returned from military service in 1947 to teach in grammar schools in Middlesex and worked with his lifelong associates Nancy Martin and James Britton to set up the London Association for the Teaching of English (LATE). His last school post was as head of English (1956–8) at Walworth School, Southwark, one of five 'experimental' comprehensives established by London county council in 1946. This was perhaps the first comprehensive to develop, under his leadership, a distinctive pedagogy for English: the pupils' experiences, ideas, and vernacular speech were accepted in the classroom as the basis for development towards a more public and impersonal language giving access to the broader culture, while the literary offering included recent fiction and international classics. Rosen's methods of English teaching at Walworth pioneered approaches that were widely adopted ten years later.

From his thirteen years in schools Rosen moved into teacher education, initially at Borough Road Training College in Isleworth and then, from 1962 to 1984, in the English department of the London Institute of Education, where he gained the degree of PhD in 1969 and, from 1976, held the first chair in the teaching of English as a mother tongue. Over his career at the institute and into his retirement his work, typically collaborative, gained an international reputation and spanned a succession of themes. His work with LATE colleagues on 'language across the curriculum' led to the Penguin book, *Language, the Learner, and the School* (1969, with Douglas Barnes and James Britton); *The Language of Primary School Children* (1973) was the product of a collaboration with his first wife, Connie, by then an inspiring figure in primary education; and *The Development of Writing Abilities (11–18)* (1975) emerged from research with colleagues at the Institute of Education led by James Britton. A concern with language and class, and specifically with the character and potential of working-class language, led him to develop an influential critique of Basil Bernstein's theory of 'elaborated' and 'restricted' codes, in *Language and Class* (1972). A third phase concerned the under-researched issue of school students for whom English was not the mother tongue: with Tony Burgess he wrote *Languages and Dialects of London School Children* (1980). His later activity owed much to the long and happy relationship he enjoyed with his second wife, whom he married on 29 March 1978, Betty Anne Watson, *née* Bolton (*b.* 1935), daughter of William George Bolton, metallurgist, and former wife of Percy E. Watson. She was an English teacher whose work with traditional stories fanned his long-held interest in narrative and autobiography and led to theoretical studies (for example *Speaking from Memory*, 1998) and autobiographical writing (notably *Troublesome Boy*, 1993, and *Are You Still Circumcised?*, 1999). It also took him, with Betty, into storytelling in schools and work with the National Storytelling Society and the London Narrative Group, which he started.

Rosen's contributions to debates on language and education embodied a lifelong political aspiration that working-class (including immigrant) people should have the chance to realize their potential and reflected a deep knowledge of and respect for their intellectual, cultural, and moral resources. His work was central to advances in English teaching and internationally significant in thinking about language, literature, and culture. He was an educationist who lit up in the presence of children and knew how to be with them, a deeply read connoisseur of language and literature, a vigorous and subtle writer and speaker, and a warm, witty, and irreverent conversationalist. He lived in Pinner from 1945 to 1962, then in Rickmansworth, and finally from 1966 in Muswell Hill, first with Connie and then with Betty, who cared for him devotedly in his last illness. He died of a pulmonary embolism on 31 July 2008 in the Whittington Hospital, Islington, and was cremated at St Marylebone crematorium. He was survived by Betty and his two sons, Brian, a distinguished palaeontologist, and Michael, poet, author, and children's writer. His life and work were celebrated on 12 March 2009 at an event at the Institute of Education attended by over 200 family, friends, and admirers.

PETER MEDWAY

Sources H. Rosen, *Troublesome boy* (1993) • H. Rosen, *Are you still circumcised?* (1999) • *The Guardian* (4 Aug 2008) • *Socialist Worker* (9 Aug 2008) • *Jewish Chronicle* (10 Oct 2008) • *Changing English*, 16/1 (2009) • www.muswell-hill.com/muswell/people/haroldrosen.htm, 3 March 2011 • personal knowledge (2012) • private information (2012) [Betty Rosen, widow; Brian Rosen, son; Michael Rosen, son; J. Richmond; T. Burgess; J. Hardcastle; J. Miller] • m. certs. • d. cert.

Archives Institute of Education, U. Lond., interview with J. Hardcastle and P. Medway, research project 'Social change and English: a study of three English departments, 1945–1965' | SOUND BL NSA, documentary recording

Likenesses photograph, repro. in www.muswell-hill.com/muswell/people/haroldrosen.htm • portraits, repro. in *Changing English*, 3, 40

Wealth at death under £103,000: administration with will, 3 Feb 2009, *CGPLA Eng. & Wales*

Rotblat, Sir Joseph (1908–2005), scientist and peace activist, was born Józef Rotblat on 4 November 1908 in Warsaw, the eldest of five surviving children (two others died in infancy) of Zygmunt, otherwise Zelman, Rotblat, the owner of a haulage company specializing in the paper trade, and his wife, Sonia, otherwise Schaindl, *née* Krajtman. Both parents were of Jewish descent. His earliest years were spent in some comfort, but the First World War brought ruin to his father's firm, as business slumped and horses were requisitioned for the armed forces, and the family slipped suddenly into poverty. Rotblat later recalled that at one point they were reduced to distilling and selling illegal vodka to get by.

Childhood, education, and marriage Rotblat's childhood, he would later say, was 'a very unhappy one' (David Krieger, 'Joseph Rotblat and peace', in Braun and others, 43). At the age of twelve he was apprenticed to an electrician. One early job had him tearing up cobbles in Warsaw streets in the depths of winter to lay electrical cables. Though his parents had hopes that their thoughtful, intellectual eldest son would eventually become a rabbi he had other plans and, by studying at night, won a scholarship to the Free University of Poland to take a degree in physics.

After graduating with a master's degree in 1932 Rotblat landed a post as research assistant at the Radiological Laboratory of Warsaw, working under Ludwik Wertenstein. These were exciting times in physics, with a rush of discoveries about the nature of the atomic nucleus, and Rotblat was able to play a part. Though Wertenstein was a scientist of international reputation his laboratory was poorly resourced, and Rotblat's publications in the 1930s, mostly studies of nuclear bombardment, were a triumph over slender circumstances. One experiment involved a Geiger counter that he had to share with another scientist who worked on a different floor, so that at fixed intervals Rotblat would have to fling himself down two flights of stairs so as to take timely readings. In a paper from this period there was also a hint of the persuasiveness that was to become his hallmark, as he thanked the Bank of Poland for the loan of almost a kilogram of gold for use in an experiment.

Rotblat gained his PhD in 1938, by which time he was married to Tola Gryn, a young woman from Lublin whom he had met in 1930, when she was a student of Polish literature. He also had a new ambition: he wanted the Warsaw laboratory to have what was then the ultimate research tool in his field, a cyclotron, 'so we could start a proper school of nuclear physics' (Landau, 48). Cyclotrons accelerate subatomic particles to high speeds for use in experiments breaking down atomic nuclei. To gain the necessary experience Rotblat accepted an invitation to join a team that was building a cyclotron at Liverpool University, under James Chadwick. (He turned down an offer to work in Paris with Frédéric Joliot-Curie, Marie Curie's son-in-law.) His Polish government bursary, however, would not support two people, so he left for England alone in early 1939, intending that Tola should join him as soon as he could afford it. Sure enough, his circumstances in Liverpool swiftly improved—an impressed Chadwick found him a second bursary—so that summer Rotblat returned to Warsaw to collect his wife. Just as they were to leave, however, she fell ill with appendicitis and again he left alone, expecting her to follow in days. Before she recovered the Germans invaded. All Rotblat's desperate efforts to get her out of Poland over the months that followed came to nothing.

Tube Alloys These events in 1939 coincided with important developments in nuclear physics. First came the discovery of fission, a process by which very heavy radioactive elements can split when penetrated by neutrons, releasing large quantities of energy. Then came evidence (which Rotblat was one of the first to investigate) that each episode of fission was accompanied by the expulsion of stray neutrons. This raised the possibility of a fission chain reaction. While most physicists soon decided that a bomb exploiting this process remained impractical a few (again including Rotblat) were concerned enough to look further. It was two refugees working at Birmingham University, Rudolf Peierls and Otto Frisch, who first identified a way of making such a bomb and alerted the British government. The result was a secret feasibility study under the codename Maud, followed by the launch of a research and development programme, codenamed Tube Alloys directorate. Rotblat, who by now was also lecturing at Liverpool, played an important role. Rated by Chadwick as 'an extremely able man, one of the best I have come across in years' (Brown, 187), he took effective charge of the Liverpool cyclotron, which was much in demand for Tube Alloys work. From the outset he had reservations about working on an atomic weapon, which he shared with Wertenstein in the summer of 1939, but such feelings were outweighed in his mind by the fear that Nazi Germany might develop such a bomb first.

During 1942 and 1943 the Manhattan project, the

Sir Joseph Rotblat (1908–2005), by Dominick Tyler, 1995

American nuclear weapon enterprise, grew so vast that Britain's Tube Alloys became little more than a junior partner with the task of supplying any expertise that could help. Thus in March 1944 Rotblat was sent to Los Alamos, the secret weapons laboratory in the New Mexico mountains—though before going he displayed another of his lifelong characteristics, stubbornness, by refusing to swap his Polish nationality for British to please his American hosts. Los Alamos left a profound mark on him, even though, unlike some of his British colleagues, he made no important contribution to the weapon. He befriended Niels Bohr, the Danish philosopher–physicist who was an adviser at Los Alamos, and their conversations stirred in him an anxiety about a future world with atomic weapons, and the risks of an arms race with the Soviet Union and wholesale destruction. Such fears deepened, he wrote much later, when he heard a senior American military official say: 'You realise, of course, that the real purpose of making the bomb is to subdue our chief enemy, the Russians' (Szasz, 57).

A pivotal moment in Rotblat's life came in the autumn of 1944 when the allies learned that Germany had made only rudimentary progress in nuclear research and did not have a bomb. With this news, he wrote forty years later, 'the whole purpose of my being in Los Alamos ceased to be, and I asked for permission to leave and return to Britain' ('Leaving the bomb project', 18). He concluded, in other words, that since neither Germany nor Japan posed a credible nuclear threat there was no moral justification for continuing work on the atomic bomb. No other scientist at Los Alamos took this stance, and the British authorities were embarrassed by his request, but he insisted on leaving. A moment of black farce ensued when American security staff suddenly produced a dossier of evidence suggesting that Rotblat wanted to return to Europe so that he could deliver atomic secrets to Moscow. This was founded on some lurid gossip related to unauthorized visits he had made to an Englishwoman who lived near Los Alamos. Rotblat was able to show that many details in the dossier were wrong, and explained that he had visited the woman at the request of a mutual friend in Britain because she was becoming deaf and needed support. With this the last objections to his leaving were withdrawn, though he was told that the record would show that the grounds for his departure were that he wished to return to Europe to look for his family. This factor, indeed, must have been in his mind: he had heard nothing from his wife or the rest of his relatives since 1939.

The ASA and St Bartholomew's News of the atomic attacks on Hiroshima and Nagasaki in August 1945 reached Rotblat at Liverpool, where he had resumed his post. He was shocked: he had retained a hope that the weapon would not work, or that the Americans and British would scruple to use it against civilians. Free, finally, to make public his private anxieties, he joined the earliest calls in Britain for action to ensure that atomic weapons would never be used again. He urged fellow scientists to lead the way, favouring for a short time a moratorium on nuclear research. He joined efforts to harness scientific opinion through the Association of Scientific Workers but found the trade union's left-wing leanings divisive. Instead, in March 1946 he, along with Nevill Mott, Rudolf Peierls, Harrie Massey, and others set up the Atomic Scientists' Association (ASA), with the aims of informing the public about nuclear matters, advancing the case for international control of atomic energy, and influencing public policy. From the outset Rotblat was among its most dynamic activists and he took the lead in what proved to be its most notable public success, the Atom Train. This travelling exhibition toured Britain in 1947–8, putting before the public an engaging scientific account of the economic and military potential of atomic energy. Many thousands visited it, attended the supporting talks and debates, and bought the literature, and it was no less notable as a triumph both of organization, in what were economically hard times, and of diplomacy, for the Labour government was suspicious of the venture.

Although the ASA would survive another decade, events soon pushed it to the margin as the attempt to create United Nations control of atomic energy failed, the cold war set in, Britain pressed ahead with its own nuclear weapons programme, and the Soviet Union tested its first atomic bomb, in 1949. Rotblat remained active in the group, becoming its executive vice-president, and for all its frustrations the experience was to exert a strong influence on him. Through the ASA he forged international connections, not least with American counterparts at the *Bulletin of the Atomic Scientists*, based in Chicago. He also learned some of the hazards of attempting to be publicly active in the sphere of policy and politically neutral at the same time, and he gained experience both in motivating scientists and keeping a voluntary group afloat. These lessons would prove useful.

Rotblat's personal and professional life underwent upheaval in these post-war years. Soon after his return to Liverpool from Los Alamos he heard from his family in Poland. Remarkably, his mother, two sisters, and one brother had survived, having gone into hiding in the countryside. (His father had died before the war.) His wife, Tola, however, was dead—though there was no official record his family had learned that she died in Majdanek concentration camp, probably in 1942. Rotblat (who did not remarry) arranged for his surviving relatives to join him in Liverpool, in itself a feat of willpower, and in the process he finally abandoned Polish nationality and became a British subject. A few years later his remaining brother also made contact. He had fought the Germans as a partisan in Russia and remained in the Soviet Union after the war. Soon he too moved to England.

In 1949 Rotblat altered the direction of his scientific career by accepting the post of professor of medical physics at St Bartholomew's Hospital, London. This was a controversial move: some physicists, including Chadwick, felt he was abandoning a brilliant, important career for one of doubtful scientific value, while some senior hospital staff were horrified at the appointment of an outsider with no medical track record. Rotblat, as ever fully knowing his own mind, was undeterred, and from his perspective the move had clear ethical advantages. Experience had shown that it was impossible to anticipate the future uses of research of the kind he had pursued since 1932, but in health physics he felt certain he could do lasting good. Moving to London, he bought the house at 8 Asmara Road in West Hampstead which was to be his home for the rest of his life, as well as a hub for the wider Rotblat family and the depository for an ever-growing personal archive of papers.

Rotblat remained at Bart's until retirement in 1976, a talented teacher fondly remembered by generations of students, a gifted manager of research groups, and a dynamic administrator. From 1960 to 1972 he was editor-in-chief of the journal *Physics in Medicine and Biology*, whose reputation he did much to establish, and he conducted sustained research of his own in the use of radiotherapy in cancer treatment. His principal scientific achievements in these years, however, arose from a programme of experiments conducted in partnership with Patricia Lindop on the effects of radiation on healthy mice, which shed important light on the risks of human exposure to radiation.

Pugwash It was Rotblat's unusual mix of talents, experiences, and interests that placed him, in 1954–5, in the position to make a set of deductions that caused international uproar. In 1954 Japanese fishermen on a boat called the *Lucky Dragon 5* were showered with fallout from an American thermonuclear test. Several became ill and one died six months later. Rotblat, through a Japanese contact, learned details of the contamination, which led him to the conclusion that this had been a new, three-stage, fission-fusion-fission weapon, and he saw that this design must multiply many times the amount of radioactivity produced. After some hesitation he published his findings, prompting public alarm and official fury in London and Washington. This, and the focus it placed on the radiation hazards of nuclear weapons tests, eventually led to the break-up of the ASA.

About this time Rotblat was approached by Bertrand Russell, who was alarmed at the nuclear arms race and at the dangers of fallout from tests, and conceived the idea of issuing an international appeal for action. Rotblat lent his support, guidance, and, it seems, organizational flair. The result was the 'Russell–Einstein manifesto' of July 1955, which bore the signatures of Russell, Albert Einstein, eight other Nobel prizewinners, and Rotblat. Mentioning the fate of the *Lucky Dragon*, it declared that the human race was in peril and called for an international congress of scientists to review the options and make recommendations. The initiative won widespread support and led to the birth, two years later (once the crises of Suez and Hungary had passed), of the Pugwash conferences on science and world affairs, named for the small town in Nova Scotia where the first meeting was held.

Pugwash became the great work of Rotblat's life. In 1997 he presided over a fortieth anniversary gathering at Lillehammer in Norway. By then there had been 229 meetings and workshops in forty countries, attended by 3360 people of more than 100 nationalities. Pugwash had a ruling council, offices, thirty-eight national groups, and an international student branch. Its reports were widely read, and had influence in the world's most important capitals. Yet it was hard to pin down—a movement rather than an organization—and almost unknown to the general public. The paradox was deliberate, owing something to Russell's inspiration and a great deal to Rotblat's vision and experience. He co-chaired the first meeting in Canada and served successively over those forty years as secretary-general (1957–73), chairman of British Pugwash (1978–88), and then president of Pugwash worldwide (1988–97). He attended the great majority of meetings, often taking the chair, and by common consent was the guiding light and dynamo of the operation.

The mission of Pugwash was to bring together experts to seek ways of reducing the dangers to the world, initially from weapons of mass destruction and war but as time passed from such other threats as food and energy shortage and economic imbalance. Those who attended did so by invitation, and spoke only in a personal capacity. The spirit was of 'rational analysis and objective inquiry', and 'mutual trust and friendship' (Moore, 41–2). Conclusions and recommendations were often communicated personally to those intended to receive them, without public declaration. On this basis Pugwash was consistently able to bring together leading experts from many countries, notably from both sides of the iron curtain, even in the coldest periods of the cold war. Inevitably this excited suspicion, and Pugwash was sometimes denounced as a puppet of one side or another, but the dialogue continued.

The influence of such a process is difficult to measure, but Pugwash has been credited with contributing ideas and impetus to the partial test ban treaty of 1963, the nuclear non-proliferation treaty of 1968, the anti-ballistic missile treaty of 1972, the biological weapons convention of 1972, and the chemical weapons convention of 1993, as well as to longer-term East–West nuclear arms reduction processes and European confidence-building measures. In addition it had other impacts, notably in providing East–West channels of communication during the Cuban missile crisis and the Vietnam war. Mikhail Gorbachov, the last leader of the Soviet Union, said of Pugwash in 1990 that 'Through its activities, due to scientific and moral authority, Pugwash has contributed in a unique way to averting the military danger, has helped to stop the "Cold War" and to achieve profound positive changes in the development of the world' (J. Harris, 'Joseph Rotblat and Pugwash', in Braun and others, 11).

Rotblat was never alone in this work, but it was his extraordinary dynamism, charm, and single-mindedness that made it happen. A slim, handsome figure with old-world manners and a gentle, Polish accent even in old age, he had the gift of communicating easily with people of all kinds, and particularly with the young. He was also a brilliant, steely eyed committeeman and master of procedure, and he could be ruthless in the cause of peace. When an Israeli scientist late with a contribution to a Pugwash publication paid a social visit to Rotblat's office he found himself locked in a cellar until he finished the piece, with only the occasional bowl of soup passed in to sustain him. Rotblat's own energy was phenomenal. He wrote more than 300 books and articles and edited countless more, and he continued to write, lecture, and travel tirelessly even in his tenth decade. The story was told that some young men saw him rush past them at a London underground station and called out: 'What's the hurry, you're an old man!'. He answered: 'Don't you see? It's because I'm an old man that I'm in a hurry' (T. Milne, 'Joseph Rotblat', in Braun and others, 209).

Behind Rotblat's frenetic activity lay a very powerful moral sense, the sense that caused him to walk out of Los Alamos in 1944, and that perhaps led his parents, years before that, to think that he had the makings of a rabbi. In adulthood he had no religion besides the cause of peace (he described himself as an agnostic rather than an atheist, since he could not be certain that God did not exist), and he saw his particular mission as one of reaching out to scientists and engaging them in that cause. Scientists, he felt, must accept responsibility for their discoveries and must participate fully in the debates about their use, because they were human beings first and scientists second. He liked to quote a phrase from the Russell–Einstein manifesto: 'Remember your humanity'.

For most of his post-war life Rotblat was a respected figure though not a well-known one, even in his adopted country; but recognition, honours, and a certain fame came in a rush in his final years. In 1995, the fiftieth anniversary of Hiroshima and Nagasaki, he and Pugwash were jointly awarded the Nobel prize for peace (he donated every penny of his prize money to Pugwash) and in the same year he was elected a fellow of the Royal Society. In 1998 he was knighted and—a different sort of honour, but one he also relished—invited to appear on BBC Radio 4's *Desert Island Discs* programme. In 2004 he suffered a minor stroke, which finally put a stop to his travels, and his health declined from then until his death at the Royal Free Hospital, Camden, on 31 August 2005, of septicaemia. He outlived his siblings but two nieces survived him.

BRIAN CATHCART

Sources J. Rotblat, ed., *Scientists, the arms race and disarmament* (1982) • J. Rotblat, 'Leaving the bomb project', *Bulletin of the Atomic Scientists*, 41/7 (Aug 1985), 16–19 • F. M. Szasz, *British scientists and the Manhattan project* (1992) • S. Landau, 'Joseph Rotblat: the road less traveled', *Bulletin of the Atomic Scientists*, 52 (Jan 1996) • A. Brown, *The neutron and the bomb: a biography of Sir James Chadwick* (1997) • M. Moore, 'Forty years of Pugwash', *Bulletin of the Atomic Scientists* (Nov–Dec 1997) • *The Times* (2 Sept 2005) • *Daily Telegraph* (2 Sept 2005) • *The Guardian* (2 Sept 2005) • *The Independent* (2 Sept 2005) • P. Rowlands and V. Attwood, eds., *War and peace: the life and work of Sir Joseph Rotblat* (2006) • R. Braun and others, eds., *Joseph Rotblat: visionary for peace* (2007) • *Memoirs FRS*, 53 (2007), 309–26 • *WW* (2005) • Burke, *Peerage* • personal knowledge (2009) • private information (2009) • d. cert.

Archives CAC Cam., Sir James Chadwick MSS • CAC Cam., A. V. Hill MSS • Nottingham University Library, R. Peers MSS • Pugwash Office, 63A Great Russell Street, London, Pugwash archives | FILM BFINA, current affairs footage | SOUND BL NSA, 'Eureka', interview with B. Myers, BBC Radio 4, 22 Jan 1997, H8355/2 • BL NSA, *Desert island discs*, interview with S. Lawley, BBC Radio 4, 8 Nov 1998, 1CD0170595 • BL NSA, National Life Story Collection, interviews with K. Thompson (undated), F7208–F7209, F7411–F7412, F7541–F7542, F7652–F7653, F7665–F7666, F7858, F8060–F8061, F8314–F8315, F8690–F8691, F8694–F8694, F9240–F9241 • BL NSA, documentary recordings

Likenesses photographs, 1948–95, Getty Images, London • photographs, 1962–96, PA Photos, London • G. Argent, bromide print, 1969, NPG • photographs, 1986–2002, Camera Press, London • P. Cuming Associates, photograph, 1995, RS; repro. in *Memoirs FRS* • A.-K. Purkiss, bromide fibre print, 1995, NPG • D. Tyler, bromide fibre print, 1995, NPG [*see illus.*] • photograph, 1997, Photoshot, London • obituary photographs

Wealth at death £2,150,332: probate, 12 April 2006, *CGPLA Eng. & Wales*

Roth, Sir Martin (1917–2006), psychiatrist, was born on 6 November 1917 in Budapest, in the dying days of the Austro-Hungarian empire, the second of the three children of Samuel Simon Roth, cantor in a synagogue, and his wife, Regina. In 1925 the family moved to England, before settling in the East End of London. There Roth attended the Davenant Foundation School, where he excelled both academically and as a pianist. For a time he considered a career as a musician but decided instead on medicine. He obtained a place at St Mary's Hospital, London, but had to delay his studies because of illness. At St Mary's he worked hard, rowed for the hospital, and qualified in 1942. After a further period of ill health, he began work as a doctor at Park Prewett Hospital, then a military hospital. In 1943 he moved to Maida Vale Hospital to train in neurology under Russell Brain. In the following year he passed the examination for membership of the Royal College of Physicians of London, and in 1945 was awarded the London MD. On 18 August the same year, at Hampstead register office, he married Constance Heller, a 26-year-old civil servant, and daughter of Samuel Heller, businessman. They had three daughters.

At Maida Vale Roth gained experience in clinical neurology and also learnt the basics of neuropathology—knowledge that was to inform his later research. He enjoyed neurology and spent nearly three years at Maida Vale but found that he was increasingly interested in the psychological problems of his patients. Encouraged by Brain, he decided to specialize in psychiatry at the Maudsley Hospital. There he worked with Aubrey Lewis, Eliot Slater, and other leading psychiatrists of the day and was introduced to the renowned refugee German psychiatrist Willie Mayer-Gross. Mayer-Gross was impressed by Roth and offered him a post at the well-known Crichton Royal Hospital in Dumfries. Roth, who was not entirely happy at the Maudsley, accepted.

Roth moved to Dumfries in 1948 and soon set up a new laboratory where he began research into the changes in electroencephalography associated with electroconvulsive therapy. The research went well and Roth was awarded a prize by the Royal Medico-Psychiatric Association, at that time the professional organization for psychiatrists. In Dumfries he also became interested in the psychiatric disorders occurring in elderly people, which at that time were thought to be varied manifestations of a single ill-defined and untreatable condition known as

Sir Martin Roth (1917–2006), by Bassano, 1972

senile psychosis. At the same time he accepted an invitation from Mayer-Gross to collaborate on a new textbook that he was writing with Eliot Slater. However, neither the research nor the book was completed in Dumfries because in 1950 Roth was appointed director of research at Graylingwell Hospital, near Chichester, Sussex.

At Graylingwell Roth continued to investigate the psychiatric disorders of old age and, in a landmark follow-up study, produced evidence that they were not all of one kind, as had previously been supposed, and did not all have the same outcome. This work was the first of a long series of groundbreaking studies of the psychiatric disorders of late life which continued well into Roth's retirement years. The research laid the scientific foundation for the specialty of old age psychiatry and thereby to much-needed improvements in the care of elderly psychiatric patients. At the same time Roth continued work on the textbook with Mayer-Gross and Slater, which was eventually published in 1954. The book, *Clinical Psychiatry*, combined the scientific basis of psychiatry with vivid clinical descriptions and authoritative advice about treatment. It was immediately recognized as a major work of scholarship and a significant advance on other textbooks of the time and it soon became the standard British postgraduate textbook. It passed through three editions and was translated into Spanish, Italian, Portuguese, and Chinese. It was a turning-point in the teaching of psychiatry and its approach was the forerunner of what was to be known, much later, as evidence-based psychiatry. Following these successes Roth was the natural choice as director when, in 1956, the Medical Research Council established a clinical research unit at Graylingwell Hospital. However he did not take up the post because in the same year he was elected to the chair of psychiatry at King's College, Newcastle (then part of the University of Durham). He remained there after King's College became the independent University of Newcastle upon Tyne in 1963.

In Newcastle between 1956 and 1977 Roth built a world-class academic department with a wide-ranging research programme which included studies of the psychiatric disorders of old age, mood disorders, and child psychiatry. Among the important findings from Roth's own research were those showing the neuropathology of the psychiatric disorders of old age, carried out with Bernard Tomlinson, work which confirmed Roth's original classification based on clinical features and outcome. Other important studies used epidemiological and statistical methods to study paranoid disorders occurring in elderly people, and to investigate whether depressive disorders with different clinical features were distinct conditions or manifestations of a single basic disorder.

Roth's achievements in Newcastle went far beyond research. He was a skilful and caring clinician, and an inspiring teacher who drew to his department many talented young psychiatrists who went on to successful academic careers in Britain and elsewhere. Before long his growing reputation led to appointment to the committees of national and international organizations. In 1958 he joined the World Health Organization's expert committee on mental health problems of the aged. From 1964 to 1968 he served on the Medical Research Council, from 1968 to 1971 on the council of the Royal College of Physicians, and from 1968 to 1975 on the government's standing mental health advisory committee. In 1968 he was elected president of the section of psychiatry of the Royal Society of Medicine.

In 1971 Roth was elected as the first president of the newly established Royal College of Psychiatrists. Until this date the professional organization of psychiatrists had been the Royal Medico-Psychological Association. This organization, founded in the nineteenth century, and granted a royal charter in 1926, already carried out many of the functions of a medical royal college and many senior members of the profession of psychiatry saw no reason to abandon it, while many junior members feared that the entrance requirements for membership of a royal college would add yet one more obstacle to their already difficult career path. Thus the task of the first president was not easy: the college started life amid controversy and there were many doubters to convince. Roth dealt with these problems with great skill and outstanding success. He brought wisdom, dignity, diplomacy, and authority to the office of president, and worked tirelessly and with great determination. At the first full meeting of the college, he won over the doubters with a memorable address that combined a clear vision of the future, compassion for the problems of the younger members, and disarming wit. Another problem was that the new college had no permanent home. Roth set about raising the substantial funds needed to acquire suitable premises in central London and succeeded in a remarkably short time, impressing major donors with his clear plans and his ability to carry them through. During his presidency the college flourished: a rigorous system of training was established, a fair system of examination was implemented, and trainees were given a voice in the college's debates. Before long the views of the new college were being sought regularly by government. In 1972 Roth's outstanding achievements were recognized by the award of a knighthood.

In 1977 Roth was elected to the newly established chair of psychiatry at the University of Cambridge, and to a fellowship of Trinity College. Starting from very little, he soon established academic psychiatry as a major discipline within the university. His impressive scholarship and wide cultural interests quickly made him a respected figure in the wider academic community which he served in many ways, notably as a syndic of Cambridge University Press from 1980 to 1987. In Cambridge he soon established a new programme of research into the psychiatric disorders of old age. An important early product was the Cambridge mental disorders of the elderly examination (CAMDEX), a research tool that was quickly adopted by research groups worldwide. Roth's research so impressed the Nobel prizewinner Sir Aaron Klug that he embarked on a programme of collaborative research into the molecular pathology of Alzheimer's disease. This research was important not only for its immediate findings but also as a stimulus for studies by other scientists into the molecular basis of Alzheimer's disease, which led to a better understanding of the causes of disorder and pointed the way to possible treatments.

Roth cared deeply about the suffering of mentally ill people and was sympathetic to the problems of the most disadvantaged among them. He believed passionately that careful diagnosis of their conditions and scientific study of the causes could alleviate suffering. He grew increasingly concerned, therefore, about the status being given, in the 1970s and beyond, to the ideas of the anti-psychiatry movement based on the writings of R. D. Laing and Thomas Szasz. These authors argued that mental illnesses did not exist and that their clinical manifestations were the responses of healthy minds to unfavourable circumstances of life. For Szasz, a psychiatric diagnosis was a meaningless label that stigmatized but did not help, and often harmed, the person labelled. When Roth saw how much credence these ideas were gaining among the public, he determined to counter them through writing and public debate. He argued that they were founded on an incomplete understanding both of the experiences of people suffering from serious mental disorders, and of the scientific evidence about the nature and causes of these conditions. In 1986 he published, with Jerome Kroll, *The Reality of Mental Illness*, a sharply argued rebuttal of the ideas of the anti-psychiatry movement and a clear account for the general reader of the humanitarian and scientific foundations of modern psychiatry. The book was an important contribution to the public understanding of psychiatry.

Roth retired from his university post in 1985 but remained a fellow of Trinity College. As the years went by he lost none of his vigour, intellectual curiosity, and originality of mind, and he continued with a busy schedule of research and writing. By now he was recognized internationally as the founder of the academic discipline of old age psychiatry and in 1996 he was elected a fellow of the Royal Society. He received many other honours and prizes, among them fellowship of the Academy of Medical Sciences, and distinguished or honorary fellowship of the American, Canadian, Australian, and New Zealand psychiatric associations; the Anna Monika prize (1977); the Sandoz prize of the International Association of Gerontology (1985); the gold medal of the Max Planck Institute (1986); and the lifetime achievement award of the Society of Biological Psychiatry (1996).

Roth was devoted to his children and to his wife, who supported him throughout his career. He had an extensive knowledge of European and classical literature, the result of wide reading and a retentive memory. He enjoyed music and was an accomplished pianist, and had a well-informed appreciation of the visual arts. He enjoyed good company and lively conversation and was interested in new ideas and in other people. He possessed a seemingly boundless store of entertaining stories and wise sayings and was an accomplished public speaker. His health was in decline in his later years, and in August 2003 he was critically ill and spent three months in hospital, following which he never regained mobility. His wife, Constance, then cared for him until his death at his home in Hills Road, Cambridge, on 26 September 2006. He was also survived by their three daughters. M. G. GELDER

Sources *Daily Telegraph* (13 Oct 2006) • *The Independent* (19 Oct 2006) • *The Times* (24 Oct 2006) • *The Guardian* (27 Oct 2006) • *WW* (2006) • Burke, *Peerage* • transcript of interview with Katherine L. Bick, priv. coll. • personal knowledge (2010) • private information (2010) [Lady Roth, widow] • m. cert. • d. cert.

Archives FILM [NBL NSA has documentary footage] | SOUND BL NSA, Oral history of geriatrics as a medical specialty, interview with M. Jefferys, 18 May 1991, F3313-F3314 • BL NSA, recorded lecture

Likenesses Bassano, half-plate film negatives, 1972, NPG [*see illus.*] • M. Noakes, portrait, exh. 1976, Royal Society of Portrait Painters, London • M. Noakes, pencil drawing, exh. 1994, Royal Society of Portrait Painters, London • Prudence Cuming Associates, photograph, 1996, RS • obituary photographs • portrait, Royal College of Psychiatrists, London

Wealth at death £843,971: probate, 27 Feb 2007, *CGPLA Eng. & Wales*

Rothschild, Dame Miriam Louisa (1908–2005), naturalist, entomologist, and conservationist, was born on 5 August 1908 at Ashton Wold, Ashton, near Oundle, Northamptonshire, the eldest daughter of (Nathaniel) Charles *Rothschild (1877–1923), merchant banker, and conservationist, and his wife, Rozsika (1870–1940), third daughter of Colonel Alfred von Wertheimstein, a landowner and army officer from Nagyvárad, Austria-Hungary. Her three siblings included the zoologist Victor *Rothschild and the musical patron Nica de Koenigswarter. Miriam was taught at home by her father (who disapproved of examinations), and by governesses. Her father was immensely keen on

Dame Miriam Louisa Rothschild (1908–2005), by Tessa Traeger, 2001

natural history, and from an early age she helped him with his butterfly collecting. He was among the first to realize how important it is to preserve the habitat if a species is to survive. He founded the Society for the Promotion of Nature Reserves in 1912, and, after contacting the secretaries of all known natural history societies in England and Wales, in 1915 issued a list of sites worthy of protection. He was an expert on fleas and travelled widely, collecting specimens. He was the first to describe *Xenopsylla cheopsis*, later found to be the vector for bubonic plague. After the First World War he contracted a type of influenza, encephalitis lethargica, which left him with frequent attacks of severe depression. In the midst of one of these, he committed suicide. Miriam was only fifteen at the time. His work on setting up nature reserves had been making good progress, but when he died the impetus went. Miriam Rothschild later, in 1946, wrote a leader article in *Nature*, pointing out that of her father's list of 174 sites worthy of protection in England, only 150 had been re-selected by the Nature Reserves Investigation Committee in 1945. Later still she published *Rothschild's Reserves* (1997), co-written with Peter Marren.

Another important influence was her uncle Lionel Walter *Rothschild, second Baron Rothschild. The family frequently stayed at Tring Park, in Hertfordshire, where he had set up a natural history museum. He organized the collection worldwide of a range of animals. The museum had a vast collection of preserved animals. *Novitates Zoologicae*, the museum's journal, was published from 1894 to 1939. Miriam Rothschild was a co-editor for the last three years. She learnt a great deal from her uncle, and published *Dear Lord Rothschild* (1983) in his memory.

Rothschild initially thought of being a writer, and attended classes in literature at Bedford College, University of London. She soon decided, however, that she wanted to be a zoologist, and enrolled for evening classes in biology at Chelsea Polytechnic. At Whitsun 1931 her group went to the Marine Biological Association laboratories in Plymouth. When she was dissecting *Nucula*, a bivalve mollusc, she found the larval stage of a trematode flatworm that her tutor, Marie Lebour, had not seen before. As a consequence Rothschild decided to undertake research on trematodes. Her research centred on the parasites of *Hydrobia ulvae*, a gastropod snail abundant on tidal mud and salt marshes. From 1932 to 1935 she examined over 2700 specimens. Besides detailed observations of the behaviour and morphology of the parasites, she worked out their life cycles, partly by studying the local bird population. Her research was done mainly at Plymouth, but she also worked at the zoological station in Naples, where she was awarded a place at the London University research table.

In the late 1930s Miriam Rothschild worked with several organizations dedicated to helping Jewish children escape from Germany and Austria. Many of the children were given a safe refuge at Ashton Wold. When the Second World War broke out in September 1939 scientists were in reserved occupations so could continue with their research. In 1940 the Marine Laboratory in Plymouth was bombed and the main casualties were the aquarium and Rothschild's laboratory. Her jars of specimens, slides, and notebooks—seven years' work—were damaged or destroyed. She had already applied for a position with the War Office, so after three days she left Plymouth. She subsequently worked as a code-breaker at Bletchley, using her knowledge of German. Meanwhile her home in Ashton was used by the Red Cross as a convalescent hospital for military personnel. Among those billeted there was Captain George Lane, formerly Lanyi (1915–2010), a Hungarian-born but naturalized British writer and journalist. When war was declared he joined the British army and won the MC for his bravery. He and Miriam Rothschild were married on 14 August 1943. They had one son and three daughters, and adopted one son and one daughter, but separated in 1954 and were divorced in 1957.

After the war Rothschild managed the farm at Ashton. She was concerned for the welfare of the farmworkers and introduced tractors with cabs before this was a legal requirement. She was also concerned about the unnecessary suffering of farm animals. Many of her ideas for improving the wellbeing of animals were later accepted. She was increasingly interested in conservation and realized that there were relatively few different species of wildflowers. She decided to convert her lawns into wildflower meadows, and successfully managed some of her hay meadows so that they produced marketable quantities of wildflower seeds. One mixture she developed was called 'farmer's nightmare'. She arranged for many roadside verges to be sown with wildflowers and gave packets of seeds to local schools. In 1952 the family moved to Elsfield Manor, near Oxford, for the sake of the children's education, though Miriam Rothschild was still responsible for the farm and the estate at Ashton Wold (and moved back there permanently in 1970). The move to Oxford enabled her to embark on her research on aposematic insects, especially butterflies and moths. These are insects with warning colourations or markings to repel or warn predators. She pioneered research in ecological biochemistry. She showed that several insects can sequestrate and store cardiac glycosides, such as digitalin, from their food plants. Ragwort, *Senecio jacobaea*, contains pyrrolizidine alkaloids which harm cattle. Caterpillars of the cinnabar moth, *Tyria jacobaeae*, feed on ragwort and sequestrate and store the alkaloids. Their conspicuous colouring warns predators. With a range of laboratory experiments and field observations, starting in 1958, Rothschild and her collaborators published numerous papers in the field of chemical ecology. J. B. Harborne, in his preface to *Introduction to Ecological Biochemistry* (4th edn, 1993), wrote that 'by her own pioneering experiments with aposematic insects and equally her encouragements of other scientists' Rothschild had 'contributed more than anyone else to this new subject'.

Rothschild retained her interest in fleas throughout her life. In the early 1950s she decided to catalogue the vast collection of fleas that her father had given to the Natural History Museum. Working with G. H. E. Hopkins she published, in six volumes, *An Illustrated Catalogue of the Rothschild Collection of Fleas (Siphonaptera) in the British Museum (Natural History)* (1953–1983). With Theresa Clay she published *Fleas, Flukes, and Cuckoos: a Study of Bird Parasites* (1952), a volume in the Collins New Naturalist series. This was thoroughly researched and entertaining. In the early 1960s, when myxomatosis spread among the rabbit population in Britain, Rothschild thought that the disease was spread by fleas, rather than by mosquitoes as in Australia. She followed this up, and found that the reproductive cycle of the rabbit flea was linked to hormones from the newly born rabbits. This was the first example of the reproductive cycle of a parasitic insect being controlled by the reproductive cycle of the host. With her co-researchers she investigated the jumping mechanism of a flea, discovered the chemical involved in the flea's leap, and worked out the mechanism involved. She demonstrated this at the Royal Society on 10 May 1973. Later still, in collaboration with Yosef Schlein and Susumo Ho, she published *A Colour Atlas of Insect Tissues via the Flea* (1986). This included 200 of her photographs of flea tissues.

From her first publication in 1932 to her last in 2005 Rothschild had over 300 publications to her name, ranging from first-class scientific research to entertaining articles about her pets. She believed that art, literature, and natural history were linked, and *Butterfly Cooing Like a Dove* (1991) was a pioneering attempt to combine her observations and experience as a biologist with paintings and quotations from literature, mainly of butterflies and birds. She was always aware that she was part of the Rothschild dynasty and wrote about the family history, especially the women members, and about the Rothschild gardens. Latterly she wrote several introductions for books on subjects she was interested in.

Rothschild was the first woman to be a trustee of the British Museum (Natural History), a position she held from 1967 to 1974. She was visiting professor at the Royal Free Hospital, London, where she lectured to first-year medical students. She was the first woman to be president of the Royal Entomological Society and was one of the eight members of the Entomological Club, founded in 1826. She served on the councils, or as vice-president or patron, of several scientific societies, for example the British Dragonfly Society. In 1996 she opened on her estate the first dragonfly museum in Britain. In 1985 she was elected a fellow of the Royal Society. Her brother Victor was already a fellow, making them the first brother and sister to be fellows. She was awarded eight honorary degrees, by Oxford, Cambridge, and the Open University among others. She was appointed CBE in 1982 and DBE in 2000. She received many other awards in the various fields in which she worked, including the Victoria medal of honour of the Royal Horticultural Society (1991) and the Wigglesworth gold medal of the Royal Entomological Society (1982). She often helped with unpopular causes, and set up the Schizophrenia Research Fund in 1962 as her sister Elizabeth had had the condition. She was also involved in 1963 with the Wolfenden report, which looked at the legal situation regarding homosexuality.

Miriam Rothschild, who was a vegetarian, had a very strong empathy with her pets and with the wild animals she befriended. (Princess Alice, duchess of Gloucester, when invited to lunch was startled to find a tame fox sitting on the chair next to her.) She was very hospitable and cared about her employees on the Ashton estate. She believed in thanking everyone who helped her, whether in a minor or major capacity, and was a great encourager. Even in her nineties she had an excellent memory and worked immensely hard. She died on 20 January 2005 at her home (and birthplace), Ashton Wold, Northamptonshire, from heart failure. A private funeral took place on 21 January. A memorial service was held on 7 April 2005 at the Liberal Jewish Synagogue, St John's Wood, London. She was survived by a son and three daughters, two children having predeceased her. With funding from the Lisbet Rausing Charitable Trust, a Miriam Rothschild chair of conservation biology was endowed at the University of Cambridge in 2006. CATHARINE M. C. HAINES

Sources E. Irons, 'The lady chose fleas', *Evening Standard* (6 May 1952), 10 • M. Rothschild, 'A liberating aerial bombardment', *The Scientist*, 1 (1987), 17 • 'Desert island discs', M. Rothschild and S. Lawley, interview, 28 April 1989, BL NSA, ICDR 0027761 BD2 • 'Miriam Rothschild: self-taught naturalist and biologist', *Shell Times*, 72 (1980) • S. A. Ewing, ed., *Wendell Krull: trematodes and naturalists* (2001) • *International women in science: a biographical dictionary to 1950* (2004) • P. Marren, *The new naturalists*, 2nd edn (2005), 209–11 • *The Times* (22 Jan 2005); (4 Feb 2005) • *The Guardian* (22 Jan 2005); (9

Feb 2005) • *The Independent* (22 Jan 2005); (24 Jan 2005) • *Daily Telegraph* (24 Jan 2005) • E. Nevo, 'Miriam Rothschild: naturalist, conservationist, and protagonist (1908–2005)', *Israel Journal of Ecology and Evolution*, 52 (2006), 221–32 • H. F. van Emden and J. Gurdon, 'Dame Miriam Rothschild CBE', *Memoirs FRS*, 52 (2006), 315–30 • 'Miriam Rothschild', Rothschild archive, London, bibliography, 28 pp. 1932–2004, 2007 • G. Ireland, *Plutocrats: a Rothschild inheritance* (2007) • R. Fortey, *Dry store room no. 1: the secret life of the Natural History Museum* (2008) • M. Jolles, *The bibliographies of Hon. Nathaniel Charles Rothschild and Dame Miriam Rothschild CBE FRS* (2008) • M. L. Rothschild, bibliography, 11 pp., http://www.journals.royalsoc.ac.uk, 18 June 2008 • natural history archives, BM, DF files, 306/79, 306/80, 633/62, 633/63 • Rothschild, Dame Miriam Louisa, RS, EC/1985/33 • *WW* (2005) • Burke, *Peerage* • private information (2009) [M. Edmunds] • personal knowledge (2009) • b. cert. • m. cert. • d. cert.

Archives NHM • priv. coll. | Bodl. Oxf., Edmund Brisco Ford MSS • Bodl. Oxf., T. R. E. Southwood MSS • NHM, corresp. with G. R. de Beer; corresp. with keeper of entomology; corresp. with NHM directors • Wellcome L., Sir Ernest Chain MSS, corresp. • Wolfson College, Oxford, H. B. D. Kettlewell MSS | FILM BFINA, TV films | SOUND BL NSA, *Eureka!*, BBC Radio 4, 11 June 1987 • BL NSA, *Desert Island Discs*, 28 April 1989, 1CDR 0027761 BD2 • BL NSA, *The Natural History Programme*, 12 Nov 1989 • BL NSA, 'Down to earth', interview with L. Brodie, 24 Oct 2001

Likenesses photographs, 1956–85, Getty Images, London • photograph, 1980–86, Rex Features, London • photograph, 1983, Photoshot, London • N. Sinclair, bromide print, 1993, NPG • B. Robinson, oils, 1995, priv. coll. • T. Traeger, bromide print, 2001, NPG [*see illus.*] • M.-L. von Motesiczky, portrait, Goethe Institute, London • obituary photographs • photograph, repro. in M. Cook, *Faces of science* (2005), 136 • photographs, repro. in 'Miriam Rothschild: self-taught naturalist and biologist', *Shell Times*, 72 (1990) • photographs, repro. in van Emden and Gurdon, 'Miriam Rothschild'

Rothwell [*married name* Barbirolli], **Rosalind Alice** [Evelyn], **Lady Barbirolli (1911–2008)**, oboist, was born on 24 January 1911 at Elmhurst, Castle Street, Wallingford, Oxfordshire, one of three children of Richard Hornsby Rothwell (1863–1955), tea dealer, and his wife, Winifred Evelyn, *née* Hedges (1885–1965). She was known throughout her life as Evelyn. She was brought up in a loving environment in which music played a minor role. With a father who had only a limited interest in the arts and a mother who struggled with the piano, she considered her maternal aunts her early musical role models: her aunt Geraldine had been a pupil at the Royal College of Music and her aunt Margaret had taught piano and violin at Downe House School, near Newbury. It is probably no coincidence that the two institutions with which her aunts were affiliated later became central to Evelyn Rothwell's development as a musician.

For her secondary education Rothwell attended Downe House School, where she was persuaded by its violin teacher Marjorie Gunn to take up the oboe after two of the school orchestra's oboists left suddenly. In later life, she claimed that she 'had never seen nor heard an oboe before' (*Glorious John*, 25), but was fascinated by its sound. That fascination soon encouraged her to investigate the instrument's potential, and by combining hard work with a natural aptitude she won a scholarship to study oboe at the Royal College of Music. There she was taught by the doyen of oboists, Leon Goossens, who had done much to bring the instrument before the public and who was known for his beauty of sound and his secure musicianship, qualities that were also later associated with Rothwell.

Although a scholarship winner, Rothwell quickly realized that she would have to work as a freelance performer to supplement her meagre student income. Combining the roles of jobbing musician and student from 1929, she was soon engaged by many of the ad hoc ensembles that were a common feature of English musical life at the time. It is a testament both to her early skill and to her potential that she was able to survive in a profession heaving with unemployed musicians and that experienced players, whose livelihoods had evaporated with the demise of London's silent-movie-house orchestras, were willing to accept her as an equal. Nevertheless, she was aware that as a young, female oboist hoping to break into an already overcrowded, male-dominated market she needed to be versatile, and along with her work as a pit musician at some of London's leading theatres, she also trod the boards as a member of the male chorus for a production of Mussorgsky's *Boris Godunov* at Covent Garden. These early experiences quickly began to bear fruit and she was soon working under leading conductors such as Sir Thomas Beecham, who offered her a regular job in his (then all-male) London Philharmonic Orchestra to replace Goossens whenever he was away, an offer that she decided not to accept because of her inexperience.

In 1931 Rothwell received a 'letter from someone whose name [she] read as John Barkworth, asking [her] to give an audition, quite soon, in the Crush Bar of Covent Garden' (*Glorious John*, 32). As it turned out, the letter was not from 'John Barkworth' but from John *Barbirolli (1899–1970), who wanted her to join the Covent Garden Touring Company's orchestra for a six-week tour of the provinces. Her audition was far from easy, and although she found the sight-reading exacting she was offered the job. Her stint with the company must have been something of a baptism of fire, as the works that she performed included Wagner's *Die Walküre* and *Die Meistersinger von Nürnberg*, Strauss's *Der Rosenkavalier*, Gounod's *Faust*, Verdi's *Rigoletto*, and Johann Strauss the younger's *Die Fledermaus*. Nevertheless, she performed admirably and was later invited by Barbirolli to join him in Glasgow, where he had been appointed conductor of the Scottish Orchestra in 1933.

With the Scottish Orchestra, Rothwell was engaged as principal oboe. From the start it was clear to Barbirolli that he had discovered an exceptional talent that deserved nurturing. Consequently he invited Rothwell to perform Handel's oboe concerto in B flat major, Mozart's Sinfonia concertante for winds, Marcello's oboe concerto, and his own performing version of an oboe concerto based on the music of Pergolesi. But Rothwell's work in Scotland was only seasonal and during the summer months she returned to England to work as a freelance musician. The quality of the engagements that she was offered as a freelance was high. She played for the opening of the Glyndebourne Festival Opera with Fritz Busch in 1934, and on recordings of J. S. Bach's orchestral suites and

'Brandenburg' concertos with Busch's brother Adolf in 1935 and 1936.

It was during Rothwell's time with the Scottish Orchestra that she and Barbirolli became involved romantically. But their road to happiness was not without obstacles, as the conductor had married the singer Marjorie Parry in 1932. Barbirolli quickly realized that his marriage to Parry was a mistake and they soon went their separate ways. Nevertheless, they remained married until June 1939, when their divorce was decreed absolute. During that time, Barbirolli and Rothwell remained a devoted couple even after Barbirolli moved to America as music director of the New York Philharmonic in 1937. (Rothwell declined a proposal of marriage from his successor as the Scottish Orchestra's conductor, George Szell; she later recalled her Glasgow encounter with him with a twinkle in her eye, and said that 'he was a horrible man, but he always took me to the nicest restaurants' (personal knowledge).) With Barbirolli's career thriving in New York and with his divorce settled, he and Rothwell married at Holborn on 5 July 1939. Although she later described him as a 'good Christian but a bad Catholic' (personal knowledge), it must have been disappointing for him to be married without the blessing of the church.

The Barbirollis' hopes for an immediate future together were soon put on hold, because Barbirolli had to sail without her in September for New York to start the Philharmonic's 1939–40 season. Unable to gain an American visa until October, she occupied her time by helping to prepare Britain for war: driving evacuees, removing signposts, and packing medical supplies for the Red Cross. When she was finally reunited with Barbirolli in New York her life changed markedly. She no longer earned her living as an orchestral player but was the wife of one of America's leading music directors. Although her opportunities to pursue her career were reduced considerably, she associated with some of the greatest musicians of the age, including Arturo Toscanini, Vladimir Horowitz, Sergei Rachmaninoff, Fritz Kreisler, and Jascha Heifetz, and was able to pursue her passion for chamber music.

When Barbirolli returned to Britain as permanent conductor of the Hallé Orchestra in 1943, Rothwell once again adapted her career to accommodate his. Unlike in New York, where resources were plentiful, music-making in Manchester was often managed on a shoestring budget, resulting in Rothwell becoming Barbirolli's artistic 'girl Friday'. Not only did she act as his secretary and driver but also as his best critic. If a performance did not meet his usual exacting standards, she was the first to point this out and was the first to suggest ways in which it could be improved. This mutual artistic trust meant that they were also a formidable performing partnership. Where possible, Barbirolli engaged Rothwell as a soloist and, when possible, they recorded much of the repertoire that they performed together. Consequently, a substantial discography by the Barbirollis exists that documents oboe concertos by composers from the eighteenth to the twentieth centuries. Some of these works were in arrangements by Barbirolli, while others were edited or arranged by artists such as Arthur Benjamin and Charles Mackerras. A concerto with which Rothwell was particularly associated was that by Ralph Vaughan Williams, a work written in 1944 and performed first by Goossens.

Life with Barbirolli (who was knighted in 1949) was not always easy for Rothwell. He was a workaholic who suffered increasingly from health problems during the 1960s. Along with his activities at Manchester, he accepted the music directorship of the Houston Symphony Orchestra and was in great demand as a guest conductor around the world. Rothwell would accompany him on many of his foreign journeys and would attempt to make their often-transient existence as pleasant as possible. But Barbirolli's heart condition grew steadily worse as the decade progressed and it was clear that her final years would be those of a widow. As a devout Christian, Barbirolli was concerned that their marriage should receive the blessing of the Roman Catholic church before his inevitable early death. His wish was granted by his friend Father Andrew Griffith, who performed a private, religious marriage ceremony at Archbishop's House in Dublin on 9 May 1970. Less than two months later, on 29 July, Barbirolli died in London, the day before Rothwell's other admirer from her Scottish years, George Szell, died in America.

Throughout her marriage Evelyn was known professionally as Rothwell, but as a widow she was known as Evelyn Barbirolli. With the prospect of an uncertain financial future alone, caused by the dishonesty of a former manager, she set about rebuilding her life by working as a performer, teacher, and adjudicator. As a member of the Royal Academy of Music's professorial staff, she was admired and respected by colleagues and students alike. Her work as an adjudicator took her around the world and her disarming honesty meant that she often left those with little artistic potential in no doubt that their futures lay outside the music profession. Her three-volume treatise on oboe technique, *The Oboist's Companion* (1974–7), was one of the most authoritative books on the subject, and her candid autobiography, *Life with Glorious John* (2002), was one of the finest and wittiest books on a musical marriage. She was passionate about antique glass and gardening and continued to have an interest in all things musical.

Evelyn Rothwell was by the end of her life one of Britain's last links with its early twentieth-century musical past. Her cultured charm, her incisive wit, and her deep-rooted knowledge of music and music-making meant that she was a much-loved performer, teacher, writer, and friend. Throughout her long and colourful life she remained artistically honest and kept alive not only the skills that she had learned from some of her great musical antecedents but also the memory and achievements of her husband. Appointed OBE in 1984, she died of bronchopneumonia at the Hospital of St John and St Elizabeth, near her home in Belsize Park, on 25 January 2008. She had no children. RAYMOND HOLDEN

Sources M. Kennedy, *Barbirolli: conductor laureate* (1971) • H. Atkins and P. Cotes, *The Barbirollis: a musical marriage* (1983) • E. Barbirolli,

Life with glorious John: a portrait of Sir John Barbirolli (2002) • *Glorious John: a collection of Sir John Barbirolli's lectures, articles, speeches and interviews*, ed. R. Holden (2007) • *Daily Telegraph* (26 Jan 2008) • *The Times* (29 Jan 2008) • *The Guardian* (29 Jan 2008) • *The Independent* (29 Jan 2008) • Barbirolli archive, Royal Academy of Music, London • personal knowledge (2012) • private information (2012) • b. cert. • d. cert.

Archives FILM BFINA, documentary and light entertainment footage | SOUND BL NSA, interview and performance recordings

Likenesses photographs, 1948–69 (with Sir John Barbirolli), Getty Images, London • photographs, 1948–75, Rex Features, London • photographs, 1952–4 (with Sir John Barbirolli), Photoshot, London • B. Denington, oils, 1997, repro. in blog francisiles.wordpress.com/2011/02/18/how-brian-denington-got-to-paint-sir-john-and-lady-barbirolli • obituary photographs • photographs, Lebrecht Music and Arts Photo Library, London

Wealth at death £1,210,847: probate, 21 May 2008, *CGPLA Eng. & Wales*

Routh, John Reginald Surdeval [Jonathan] (**1927–2008**), television presenter, author, and painter, was born at Northwoods, Gosport Road, Bridgemary, near Gosport, Hampshire, on 24 November 1927, the only son of Captain (later Colonel) Herbert Charles Edric Routh (1894–1984), Royal Artillery officer, and his wife, Ella Margaret, *née* Whitehouse (1900–1987). His father claimed to be able to trace the family's history back to one of the knights who was with William the Conqueror during his invasion of England.

Routh went to Uppingham School, Rutland, as a scholar, and then read history at Emmanuel College, Cambridge, for only a year but he edited *Granta*, the university magazine, and was involved with the Footlights dramatic society. Helped by this he got a job on the national magazine *Everybody's* as its show-business editor. As the magazine specialized substantially in historical figures, he had energy to spare, and found relief in hoaxing. For the BBC's Third Programme he invented a fictional eighteenth-century poet, Jeremy Feeble, and he became a presenter for Radio Luxembourg's *Candid Mike*, which borrowed its format from Allen Funt's successful American radio series *Candid Microphone*. On 2 April 1949, at St Luke's Church, Chelsea, Routh married Renate Sophia (Nandi) Heckroth (1926/7–1972), a film costume designer, and daughter of Heinrich Heckroth, artist; they had two children.

Routh set about seriously selling himself as a practical joker when, in 1957, he put an advertisement in *The Times* saying, 'Practical joker with wide experience of British sad gullibility organises, leads and guarantees success of large-scale hoaxes.' The 'wide experience' included dispatching himself through the post to Wandsworth covered in £2-worth of stamps, and trying to take a tube journey with a grand piano.

Candid Camera was launched on BBC TV in 1960, based on Allen Funt's similarly named series, which had run on American television since 1948, and which consisted of pointing a hidden camera at innocent victims of hoaxes and practical jokes. It was presented by Bob Monkhouse, with the beetle-browed and intense Routh and Arthur Atkins as the troublesome characters who set up and appeared in the jokes. In the first programme they were in a car that ran downhill straight into a garage forecourt.

John Reginald Surdeval [Jonathan] **Routh** (**1927–2008**), by unknown photographer

The driver asked the attendant to fill up his oil. Raising the bonnet, the startled man found that the car had no engine. Later jokes included having Routh dress up as a tree and, while standing at a bus stop, asking disconcerted would-be passengers, as a bus arrived: 'Does this go to Sherwood Forest?' The humour in the ingenious and sometimes unkind jokes was in the always puzzled and sometimes horrified reaction of the victims as they were, for instance, asked to lean against Nelson's Column to prevent it falling down, or asked to allow a car park attendant to park their Rolls-Royces for them, when the 'attendant' had just been seen badly scraping and denting two previous cars as he parked them. The formula became so popular with viewers that they sent in 1000 ideas a week. It was rare for the victims not eventually to enter into the spirit of the thing, though Routh was once chased by a man wielding a crowbar, and the heavyweight boxer Sid Richardson gave him a black eye. Public taste and the fast-altering mores of society as a whole proved more formidable opponents. The increasing permissiveness of the 1960s resulted in contrived practical jokes not being regarded as so outrageous as they had once been, and *Candid Camera* came to an end in 1967. Routh subsequently joined Kenny Everett and Germaine Greer in a variation of the *Candid Camera* format called *Nice Time* (1968). Some of the production team wanted less victimizing of innocent members of the public, but as this was the essence of Routh's anarchic art the programme did not last long. An attempt to revive *Candid Camera* in 1976 was also brief.

In the troughs of his career Routh took to writing offbeat books reflecting his tastes. His autobiography, *The Little Men in My Life*, was published in 1953. His *Good Loo Guide* (1965) was subtitled *Where to Go in London*. Then came *The Good Cuppa Guide* (1966), the *Guide Porcelaine to the Loos of Paris* (1966), and *The Better John Guide* (1966), with Serena Stewart, extending the survey to New York. Among his other books were one on hangovers, one on disasters entitled *So You Think You've Got Problems* (1967), and the even more jokey *Leonardo's Kitchen Note Book* (1987), which was allegedly 'translated' with his second wife, Shelagh, and had the premise that all the machines in the drawings by Leonardo da Vinci were in fact illustrations of the making of pasta. In 1970 Routh began painting in the naïve style, and was to confess that he had never had any money, but spent his life staying in the homes of friends, in the UK and elsewhere, who did. He often bartered his paintings for restaurant meals and other living costs.

Routh's private life was as anarchic and bizarre as his professional life. Separated from his wife, in 1969 he began a relationship with Eileen (Bobbie) Hamlyn (*b.* 1926/7), wife of Paul Hamlyn, the publisher. She committed suicide two years later, after her husband had divorced her and Routh had left her for the heiress Olga Deterding (1926–1979). In 1972 his wife Nandi's car hit a tree and she died. In 1975 he married Shelagh Marvin, a film publicist, with whom he lived in Rome before they settled in Jamaica in 1980. There Routh shared a three-roomed hut with no electricity, rising with the sun to paint. He had a penchant for painting nuns. His oeuvre included nuns on trampolines, driving racing cars, picnicking in the jungle, and being shot from cannon. Some of his nuns found their way into a series of children's books, starting with *The Nuns Go to Africa* (1971). He also wrote and illustrated *Jamaica Holiday: the Secret Life of Queen Victoria* (1984). His Mona Lisa paintings showed the woman naked and holding a tin of spaghetti. He died in London on 4 June 2008 and was survived by his wife, Shelagh, and the two sons of his first marriage. DENNIS BARKER

Sources J. Routh, *The little men in my life* (1953) • *The Times* (6 June 2008) • *Daily Telegraph* (6 June 2008) • *The Independent* (7 June 2008) • *The Guardian* (9 June 2008) • b. cert. • m. cert. [1949]
Archives FILM BFINA, documentary and light entertainment footage | SOUND BL NSA, performance recordings
Likenesses photographs, 1960–99, Rex Features, London • photographs, 1962–87, PA Photos, London • obituary photographs • photograph, Rex Features, London [*see illus.*]

Rowlands, Sir John Samuel (1915–2006), airforce officer, was born in Stamford Way, Ewloe, Hawarden, Flintshire, on 23 September 1915, the son of Samuel Rowlands (*d.* 1919), general labourer and later mechanical engineer, and his wife, Sarah, *née* Evans. He was educated at Hawarden grammar school and the University of Wales, where he gained an honours degree in physics, was in the university officers' training corps, captained the football team, and played tennis. In April 1939 Rowlands joined the Royal Air Force Volunteer Reserve, and at the outbreak of the Second World War he was mobilized and posted to 2 School of Technical Training, then in July 1940 to 1 Armament School. In April 1941, while serving with Technical Armaments, his scientific training was put to the test when unusual features were discovered in an unexploded German bomb located at a depth of about 6 feet, with a fuse in the nose set to ignite within 72 hours, and an anti-handling device fitted with a trembler switch, which could be ignited by the slightest movement and detonate the bomb. Rowlands inserted a liquid fuel discharge in the nose fuse, neutralizing it after 30 minutes, then dealt similarly with the anti-handling device at the tail end of the bomb, which was subsequently raised up and taken away for examination. In the June 1942 birthday honours he was appointed MBE (military) in recognition of his cool courage, and on 27 June, at the Methodist church, Darlington Street, Wolverhampton, he married Constance Wight, a 22-year-old secretary in local government and daughter of Henry Rowe (Harry) Wight, a wing commander in the RAF. They subsequently had two daughters.

Rowlands's bravery was further dramatically exemplified when in June 1943, by then a wing commander, visiting a bomber station, he was told that eighteen men were missing after an explosion at RAF Snaith in Yorkshire, the result of the accidental detonation of a bomb, which damaged huge quantities of high explosive and incendiary weapons, many of them primed ready for use. Over the next ten days Rowlands and his team, working with delicacy and bravery, succeeded in making the site safe. Two months later he was awarded the George Cross for his 'conspicuous courage … in circumstances of great personal danger'. In 1943 he became superintendant of design at Fort Halstead, and during 1945 travelled to north Africa, Italy, and Germany, working just behind the allied front lines.

Rowlands was granted a permanent commission in the RAF in September 1945. He attended the Staff College course at Haifa in 1946 and in 1947 undertook pilot training at 28 Elementary Flying Training School. When the United Kingdom government decided that Britain should develop an atomic bomb William Penney was given overall control and Rowlands was appointed to lead the team at Fort Halstead in developing the device, which was successfully tested at the Monte Bello Islands on 3 October 1952, when he was senior RAF adviser. The atomic device then had to be translated into a bomb, designed by the Bomber Command Armament School which Rowlands commanded from its formation at Wittering on 1 August 1953—reversing the order of his heroic wartime disarming of weapons. The bomb was to be carried by the new generation of four-jet RAF V-bombers; all the development work was done at the school, where the first (Valiant) squadron, 138, was formed. The bomb was named Blue Danube, and weighed just under 10,000 lb. It was successfully test-dropped from a Valiant at Christmas Island on 15 May 1957.

In 1958 Rowlands was promoted group captain and posted to the Atomic Weapons Research Establishment at Aldermaston as senior RAF adviser on the thermonuclear (H-bomb) project. After some three years there he was sent to Washington, DC, as a special adviser at the British embassy. Then he took the Imperial Defence College course, and at its successful conclusion was promoted to air commodore and appointed director of technical training at the RAF College, Cranwell. In 1968, promoted air vice-marshal, he became director-general of training for the RAF. He was knighted KBE in 1971 (having been appointed OBE in 1954). His last RAF appointment was in charge of Maintenance Command, with the rank of air marshal, until his retirement in 1973.

Following a brief spell in university administration at Queen Mary College, University of London, Rowlands served as assistant principal of Sheffield Polytechnic from 1974 to 1980. He was a vice-president of the Aircrew Association and a committee member of the Victoria and George Cross Association. A keen photographer, he also kept up his lifelong enthusiasm for tennis.

John Rowlands was an exceptionally brave man, modest to a fault. His knowledge of bombs and their fiendishly intricate methods of fusing was matched by his cool courage in disarming them, when the slightest wrong move could spell disaster. Yet he never wrote, or spoke, about his heroic wartime achievements. He died of cancer of the oesophagus at Thornbury Hospital, Fulwood Road, Sheffield, on 4 June 2006, and was survived by his wife, Constance, and their two daughters. HUMPHREY WYNN

Sources *Daily Telegraph* (7 June 2006) · *The Guardian* (29 June 2006) · *The Times* (3 July 2006); (3 Aug 2006) · Burke, *Peerage* · *WW* (2006) · RAF record of service, RAF Cranwell, Sleaford, Lincolnshire · private information (2010) · b. cert. · m. cert. · d. cert.
Archives FILM [BL NSA has documentary footage]
Likenesses obituary photographs
Wealth at death £237,917: probate, 10 Aug 2006, *CGPLA Eng. & Wales*

Roza, Lilian Patricia [Lita] (**1926–2008**), singer, was born at 13 Upper Pitt Street, Abercromby, Liverpool, on 14 March 1926, one of seven children of Francis Vincent (Frank) Roza (1900–1979), a cook on a steamship, later a marine engineer, and his wife, Elizabeth Ann, *née* Fowles (1900–1973). Her exotic looks can be traced to her father's Spanish ancestry. Frank Roza played the piano-accordion in Liverpool clubs and Lilian and her sister Alma would sing with him. She attended Granby Street council school, but left during the early stages of the Second World War. She was a singer and dancer in pantomimes at the Liverpool Empire and in 1941 joined a touring variety show, *Black Velvet*, starring the Liverpool comedian Ted Ray. At her mother's request, she returned home when bombing intensified. She cut slabs of butter for domestic sale and then worked in a cycle shop, but after catching her leg on jagged glass in a storeroom she was left with a scar and knew any dancing ambitions were over.

When Roza was singing in a Southport restaurant the owner combined her Christian names as Lilita, which she shortened to Lita. When she had saved £16 she moved, very independently, to London. She joined Harry Roy's band as his vocalist, Réné Lester, was leaving. When the band went to Egypt to entertain the troops she was too young to go. She stayed in London and had two jobs, at the Albany and Embassy clubs, effectively singing from 8 p.m. to 4 a.m. A whirlwind courtship with James Shephard Holland, an American serviceman in the Royal Canadian Air Force (nine years her senior, a salesman for a petroleum company before the war, and son of James Shephard Holland, building contractor), led to their marriage, on 27 July 1944. After the war Roza moved with him to Miami. His job of spraying crops meant he rose early and went to bed early, while Roza was singing in nightclubs. When Roza returned to Liverpool for her twenty-first birthday she discovered she was diabetic. She returned to Miami but she and James Holland were divorced in 1950.

Lilian Patricia Roza (1926–2008), by unknown photographer, 1956

In February 1950 the bandleader Ted Heath invited Roza to become a vocalist with his orchestra, working with Dickie Valentine and then Dennis Lotis. In 1951 she recorded 'Allentown Jail' with Heath. Although record sales were not yet collated, it was undoubtedly her first hit, as the song rose high in the sheet music charts. After 'Allentown Jail' Dick Rowe, her recording manager at Decca, asked her to sing 'How Much is that Doggie in the Window?'. Roza demurred but Rowe insisted. Roza, famously, said that she would sing it once and never sing it again. With this song Roza became the first female to top the UK charts (in April 1953) and although proud of the fact she wished it had been with another song. In May 1954 Roza left Heath and worked as a solo act. The following year she had successes with 'Hey There' and 'Jimmy Unknown'. She recorded two albums of standards, *Listening in the Afterhours* (1955) and *Love is the Answer* (1956). She topped the *Melody Maker* poll for favourite female vocalist from 1951 to 1955, and a similar one in the *New Musical Express* from 1952 to 1955.

On 5 May 1956 Roza married a thirty-year-old trumpet player from Heath's band, Ronald (Ronnie) Hughes (the son of David Llewellyn Hughes, lorry driver). The marriage didn't last, although they remained friends. She acted as Digby Wolfe's girlfriend in the television sitcom *Sheep's Clothing* (1957), a role she duplicated in real life.

Hughes was featured on her best album (despite its appalling title), *Drinka Lita Roza Day*, recorded in 1960 at the Prospect of Whitby pub in Wapping. In the same year she recorded another fine album, *Me on a Carousel*, but after that she only recorded sporadically. Her sister Alma Warren recorded for EMI and became an assistant to the record producer George Martin.

Roza's stage career nevertheless lasted another four decades. In the 1960s she performed in nightclubs owned by the Kray twins, and their mother was keen for Ronnie to marry Roza to assuage doubts about his sexuality. Roza, courageously, declined the invitation. Her health was not an issue until she went to South Africa in the early 1970s. She had not adjusted her insulin for the high altitude in Johannesburg and collapsed on stage. There were erroneous rumours of drink or drugs. Ted Heath had died in 1969, but the orchestra was reformed in 1982 under the leadership of the trombonist Don Lusher. Roza sang with them until 2000 and appeared in a royal gala performance in 1985.

As the first person from Liverpool to have a number one hit Lita Roza unveiled the Wall of Hits, opposite the Cavern Club in Liverpool, in 2001. She made her final appearance, at the Liverpool Empire, the following year. She joked, 'My work was once considered middle of the road, but now you would say it was the end of the road' (personal knowledge). She died at her home, 14 Dents Road, Wandsworth, London, on 14 August 2008, of heart failure. Her ashes were scattered on the Mersey. It is unfortunate that her name came to be so linked with a children's novelty, 'How Much is that Doggie in the Window?' There were few to rival her talent as a sultry and sophisticated interpreter of romantic ballads and her 'Man in the Raincoat' was among the best British records of the 1950s.

Spencer Leigh

Sources *The Independent* (15 Aug 2008) · *The Times* (18 Aug 2008) · *The Guardian* (18 Aug 2008) · *Daily Telegraph* (19 Aug 2008) · personal knowledge (2012) · private information (2012) · b. cert. · m. certs. · d. cert.

Archives FILM BFINA, light entertainment and performance footage | SOUND BL NSA, interview and performance recordings

Likenesses photograph, 1956, BBC [*see illus.*] · obituary photographs · photographs, BBC

Wealth at death £992,836: probate, 23 Feb 2009, *CGPLA Eng. & Wales*

Rudduck, Jean (1937–2007), educationist, was born on 11 February 1937 at 41 Rushey Green, Catford, London, the daughter of Frank George Rudduck, analytical chemist and later RAF flying officer, and his wife, Dorothy Maud, *née* Harris (1904–1997). Her father was killed in action over the Netherlands in June 1944. Her mother (who never remarried) was later a legal secretary.

Rudduck was educated at Mary Datchelor Girls' School, Camberwell, and at Westfield College, University of London, where she read English literature and in 1958 took one of the top four first-class honours degrees in her cohort across the whole of the university. She then trained as a teacher at King's College, London, and in 1961 she began her career as a teacher of English and drama at Godolphin and Latymer School, Hammersmith.

In 1965 Rudduck took up her first research post, at the Schools Council, and it was there, in her involvement in the report *Enquiry 1: Young School Leavers*, that the seeds were sown of her later interest in and commitment to the importance of teachers and adults listening with care to the perspectives of young people. Research team contracts were short term and in 1967 she accepted a post as lecturer in English at Brighton College of Education. Always diffident about the move away from research, within a year she joined the ground-breaking Humanities Curriculum Project (1967–72) directed by Lawrence Alexander *Stenhouse (1926–1982) and based first at Philippa Fawcett College, London, and from 1970 at the University of East Anglia.

The move to East Anglia was to have a profound effect, both on Rudduck's academic development and on her personal life. Academically, the internationally acclaimed work of the Humanities Curriculum Project led in 1970 to John Elliott, Barry MacDonald, Jean Rudduck, and Lawrence Stenhouse setting up the Centre of Applied Research in Education, which had a remarkable influence on subsequent generations of teachers and academics in the English-speaking world. It also led to Rudduck's appointment, first to a lectureship and then to a senior lectureship, at the University of East Anglia. On a personal level, Rudduck and Stenhouse became partners in 1971 and remained together until his death.

In 1983 Rudduck moved to Sheffield University as professor of education, only the second female professor in the university at that time. It was there that she met her partner and future husband John Michael Gray (*b.* 1948), a fellow member of staff and subsequently professor in the same department. Arguably the most important book of her Sheffield years was *Innovation and Change* (1991), which established her own voice and her own identity in ways that looked forward to the work for which she became best known, namely, encouraging learners to be active partners with their teachers in the ongoing research process that lies at the heart of all good pedagogy. In 1994 Rudduck and Gray became joint directors of research at Homerton College, Cambridge, a position they held until 2001. In many respects it was at Cambridge that Rudduck reached the zenith of her work as a researcher, writer, and advocate of a generously conceived, humanely realized form of schooling that deserved the title of education.

Ironically the book that brought her to the attention of a wider public—*School Improvement: What can Pupils Tell Us?* (1996)—owed at least some of its fame to its subsequent adoption by those working in the field of school effectiveness. In her later work she objected strongly to the overly instrumental approach to schooling that this entailed. The many publications and the full-hearted, always warmly appreciated engagement with teachers, parents, young people, policy makers, and academics that were so characteristic of her time at Cambridge were understood and recognized by her peers as well as her wider public. In 1994 she gave the presidential address at the British Educational Research Association and in 2002 she was elected professor of education at Cambridge University, its first female professor in the subject. She retired in 2004 but remained a fellow of Homerton College and continued to publish books, most frequently with her colleague Julia Flutter, including *How to Improve Your School: Giving Pupils a Voice* (2004) and *Consulting Pupils: What's in it for Schools* (2004), as well as numerous articles in journals. She was, as ever, in great demand, both nationally and internationally, as a keynote speaker. She and John Gray married at Cambridge register office on 14 April 2005.

Despite suffering from ovarian cancer, Rudduck continued to write until the time of her death. *Improving Learning through Consulting Pupils* (2007), written jointly with Donald McIntyre, was published posthumously. Her writing was always elegant and occasionally beautiful. She believed that schools could be places of, and for, a generously conceived view of education, but only if adults and young people were able to listen to and learn with and from each other in what she often described as 'a communal venturing forth'. For that to happen schools needed to be transformed. Her work contributed significantly to that admirable possibility. She died at her home, Scales Barn, 1 Pearce's Yard, Grantchester, Cambridge, on 28 March 2007 and was buried on 11 April 2007 at the church of St Andrew and St Mary, Grantchester. She was survived by her husband and three stepchildren.

MICHAEL FIELDING

Sources *TES* (6 April 2007); (25 July 2008) · *The Guardian* (1 May 2007) · *Cambridge Journal of Education*, 37/3 (Sept 2007), 317–20 · M. Fielding, 'Jean Rudduck (1937–2007) "Carving a new order of experience": a preliminary appreciation of the work of Jean Rudduck in the field of student voice', *Educational Action Research*, 15/3 (Sept 2007), 323–36 · www.admin.cam.ac.uk/news/dp/2007040301, 25 June 2010 · www.educ.cam.ac.uk/people/formermembers/rudduck/, 25 June 2010 · *WW* (2007) · personal knowledge (2011) · private information (2011) · b. cert. · m. cert. · d. cert.

Likenesses photograph, repro. in *The Guardian* (1 May 2007) · photograph, repro. in www.admin.cam.ac.uk/news/dp/2007040301

Wealth at death £706,207: probate, 6 June 2007, *CGPLA Eng. & Wales*

Russell, John (1919–2008), art critic, was born on 22 January 1919 at Lochiel, Connaught Road, Fleet, Hampshire, the son of Violet Russell. His father was not named on his birth certificate. He was brought up by his grandparents, Isaac James Russell and Harriet Elizabeth, *née* Atkins, who lived in London. His grandfather was a wine merchant and licensed victualler, and the owner and proprietor of several pubs. Although his grandparents' home contained few books, Russell was sent to the highly academic and distinguished St Paul's School, and as an adolescent spent what pocket money he had on opera and the arts; when he was the only boy in his class able to define surrealism his schoolmaster told him he could make a career writing about the arts. He went on to Magdalen College, Oxford, where he read philosophy, politics, and economics, graduating in 1940 with a second-class degree. Almost immediately (while awaiting call-up) he joined the Tate Gallery as an unpaid assistant, and after the bombing of its London site he was evacuated in tandem with the art treasures to Worcestershire. He served in the Ministry of Information (1942–3) and then with naval intelligence (1943–6). By this time he was already publishing not only articles in the *Times Literary Supplement*, *Cornhill*, *Horizon* (edited by Cyril Connolly), and *The Listener*, but books as well: his first books were *Shakespeare's Country* (1942) and *British Portrait Painters* (1945). On 17 November 1945 he married Alexandrine Antoinette Maria Juliana Herberta Franciska Apponyi (*b.* 1919), daughter of Count Anton Apponyi, of independent means. They had one daughter, Lavinia (*b.* 1946). The marriage was dissolved in 1950, and on 21 December 1956 Russell married, second, Vera Barry, *née* Poliakoff (1911–1992), a Russian Jewish art critic, daughter of Vladimir Poliakoff, journalist, and former wife of Sir Gerald Reid Barry, journalist (and before that of Major Percy Basil Harmsworth Burton, army officer). There were no children of this marriage, which ended in divorce in 1971.

Russell first began writing for the *Sunday Times* in 1945, as a books and art critic, on the recommendation of Ian Fleming. When the paper's chief art critic, Eric Newton, was dismissed in 1949 for writing, in the eyes of the establishment, too negative a review of a Royal Academy exhibition Russell succeeded him, and over the following two and a half decades became the most influential art critic in Britain. He was a highly regarded supporter of contemporary British art, and *Private View* (1965), with its eloquent photographs by Lord Snowdon, was a major factor in initiating the emergence onto the international stage of various of the artists thus championed, from David Hockney, Bridget Riley, and Howard Hodgkin to Anthony Caro and Francis Bacon. He was also the curator for several revelatory and influential exhibitions, in the main for the Arts Council of Great Britain, including Modigliani (1964), Rouault (1966), and Balthus (1968), all held at the Tate, the last exhibition controversial because of what many perceived to be a perverted sexual attitude underlying some of Balthus's paintings. He also curated 'Pop Art Redefined' (1969) at the Hayward, by then the major outlet for Arts Council exhibitions, in collaboration with the American art historian Suzi Gablik, his partner at the time. Considering John Russell's penchant in the main not only for the beautiful but the agreeable, his interest in Bacon and Balthus (of whom he said, 'as a liar, he is without equal'; *Century Association Yearbook*) was surprisingly piquant. Equally surprising perhaps was his distaste for Rodin, whom he called 'an old rascal'; he thought that the crowds who appreciated Rodin's *Gates of Hell* would probably have equally appreciated a public hanging, the sculpture in question being to serious art what a disaster movie was to *King Lear* (*New York Times*, 18 July 1982).

In 1974 Russell left his job on the *Sunday Times*, which at the time had a circulation of over 1.5 million, making him by far the most widely read of all newspaper commentators on the visual arts, to join the *New York Times*, first as second art critic to the sharp-edged and conservative Hilton Kramer, then from 1982 to 1990 as chief art critic (and thereafter critic emeritus); he moved in part too to join the woman he regarded as the love of his life, the art historian and broadcaster Rosamond Bernier (*b.* 1917). In 1975 they married at the architect Philip Johnson's iconic glass house in Connecticut in a ceremony attended by leading lights of the American intelligentsia: Leonard Bernstein wrote the music for the ceremony, Aaron Copland gave the bride away, and Pierre Matisse, son of Henri, was the best man. One of Russell's most fascinating books was indeed *Matisse Father and Son* (1999), based on unpublished correspondence with which he was entrusted by the family; the book was dedicated to the memory of Pierre Matisse.

Russell regarded New York as the supreme art city of the post-war period: 'There are as many New Yorks as New Yorkers … a self-devouring, self-renewing city … one of the supreme subjects of our century: one for which we would wish Balzac, Dickens and Proust to have been born again' (*The Meanings of Modern Art*, rev. edn, 1991, 296). At the time he left London he spoke of the struggle to get the *Sunday Times* to take art seriously, and of his delight at the enthusiastic backing given to cultural writing by the *New York Times*. In both countries he was a newspaper editor's dream, writing with extraordinary rapidity, always to length and never needing editing; what he wrote was printed. In New York he also wrote for *The Criterion*, and published long essays in the *New York Review of Books*, which were regarded by many as the most thoughtful of his cultural journalism. Surprisingly clubbable, he became a prominent member of the Century Association and edited *The Centurion*, the club's monthly bulletin, for twenty-five years.

Russell was passionate about art: 'Art is there to tell us where we are, and it is also there to tell us who we are', he once wrote (*The Meanings of Modern Art*, rev. edn, 1991, 13). He regarded his career as being able to conduct his education in public. 'I wanted to teach, in an almost subliminal way. But I did not want to preach. That is still what I try to do', he told an interviewer for the *Art Newspaper* in 1999. At its worst Russell's journalism, while always stylistically flowing and almost compulsively readable, was anodyne, bland, and replete with the higher gush, as when he wrote of a Van Gogh exhibition in 1986 that 'there never was within living memory a Van Gogh exhibition that did not spread happiness' (*New York Times*, 16 Nov 1986). In the same article he also, surprisingly, claimed that Van Gogh the artist and Van Gogh the suicide had nothing in common with one another. Russell did not like distress, and preferred to ignore the unseemly, uncertain, and disorderly. This meant that the occasional ferocity that emerged from his silky prose was all the more powerful. At its best Russell's intensely erudite enthusiasm was contagious, illuminating, and informing, and appealed to a wide audience to come and understand for themselves. His substantial stutter (to which he attributed his fluency in writing) prevented a career as a lecturer, although Rosamund Bernier was one of the most celebrated lecturers of her day, and he wrote scripts for films on art that they made together.

Russell was one of the last genuine men of letters, surviving admirably by virtue of almost being a pen-for-hire in a variety of publications, and the author of some twenty books. His output was prolific and prodigious, literally thousands upon thousands of articles and more than half a dozen substantial catalogues: his books on Seurat (1965) and Vuillard (1971) were much admired. He was extraordinarily knowledgeable across a wide cultural spectrum, taking in all the arts, and in the course of a career that spanned well over sixty years was one of the most fluent writers on culture in general and the visual arts in particular. He was an almost unnervingly elegant commentator on art exhibitions in the major museums and galleries on both sides of the Atlantic as well as continental Europe. In person he was ruddy faced, slim, boyishly good-looking, even dapper, adored by women (his liaisons and attachments were invariably to exceptionally strong and strong-willed women), and utterly charming, with a beguilingly diffident manner, which was misleading as he was a man of very sharp opinions. In his published criticism he mostly praised, but occasionally was fiercely opinionated: the Austrian expressionist Egon Schiele showed us, Russell wrote, things we would rather not see, and one of his famous polemics was anger at the sounds of the cash register of the gallery shop ringing in the magnificently disturbing room in which Van Gogh's last paintings were hung in a special exhibition at the Metropolitan Museum in New York. Russell, however, was rarely negative and claimed to share John Updike's view that it was 'better to praise and share than blame and ban'.

Russell was appointed CBE in 1975; his other honours included the Austrian grand medal of honour (1972), appointment as an officier de l'Ordre des Arts et des Lettres, of Paris (1975), and a member of the Federal Republic of Germany's Order of Merit (1982), the Frank Jewett Mather award of the College Art Association (1979), and the Mitchell prize for art criticism (1984). He was made a chevalier of the Légion d'honneur in 1986, an honorary fellow of the Royal Academy of Arts in 1989, and a member of the American Academy of Arts and Letters in 1996. In 2004, along with Rosamond Bernier, he was named a 'National Treasure' by the Municipal Art Society of New York. In 2008 they were also named a 'Living Landmark' by the New York Landmarks Conservancy. He died in the Bronx, New York, on 23 August 2008 and was survived by his wife, Rosamond, and his daughter, Lavinia (who had married the architect Sir Nicholas Grimshaw).

MARINA VAIZEY

Sources J. E. Kaufman, interview, *Art Newspaper* (July–Aug 1999), 49 · *The Times* (25 Aug 2008) · *New York Times* (25 Aug 2008) · *The Independent* (30 Aug 2008) · *Art in America* (1 Oct 2008) · *Century Association Yearbook* (2009) · www.theartstory.org/critic-russell-john.htm, 5 Aug 2011 · *WW* (2008) · personal knowledge (2012) · private information (2012) · b. cert. · m. certs. [1945, 1956]

Archives Bodl. Oxf., Jack and Catherine Lambert MSS · Tate Gallery Archive, Lord Russell MSS | SOUND BL NSA, National Life Story Collection: Artists' Lives, interview

Likenesses Snowdon, photograph, 1963, Camera Press, London · obituary photographs

Russell, Sir Peter Edward Lionel (1913–2006), Spanish and Portuguese scholar, was born Peter Edward Lionel Russell Wheeler in Christchurch, New Zealand, on 24 October 1913, the elder son of Hugh Bernard Wheeler, a career officer in the Royal West Kent regiment, and his wife, Rita Muriel, the youngest of the three daughters of Thomas Gregory Russell. His father had been born in Halifax, Nova Scotia, while his maternal grandfather, Thomas Gregory Russell, barrister and accountant, had emigrated from Norfolk to Launceston, Tasmania, and thence to New Zealand, where he became a pioneer in the motor import business and acquired the ownership of a group of newspapers, including the *Christchurch Herald*. Before Peter's birth his grandfather's mansion had become associated with exploration and adventure, since in 1901 the naval officer Robert Falcon Scott and the Cheltenham physician and naturalist Edward Adrian Wilson had lived with the Russells while planning their first Antarctic expedition. As an infant Peter accompanied his mother in 1915 and early in 1917 on two dangerous wartime voyages on liners to England. Peter's younger brother, Hugh Bernard Langford Wheeler, born in Christchurch on 9 August 1916, accompanied them on the second voyage, when, half an hour after they disembarked at Plymouth, the liner was torpedoed by a German U-boat.

Both brothers were typical products of the outposts of the British empire, their childhood being imbued with talk of military exploits and dangerous expeditions. The family contacts with the two polar explorers may have accounted for the choice of Cheltenham College in 1925 for Peter's secondary education, and for his younger brother's enrolment at Pangbourne Nautical College in 1929. (Hugh later studied tropical medicine and became a distinguished epidemiologist at the World Health Organization.) Peter expressed his hatred of his years at Cheltenham, though the college gave him a useful grounding in Latin grammar and rhetoric. The divorce of their parents caused Peter and his brother to change their surname by deed poll in December 1929.

Russell's life changed much for the better in the golden inter-war Oxford years after he matriculated at Queen's College in 1931. During his study trip to Madrid in the summer of 1932 the street violence and burning of churches he witnessed made a deep impression on him. As the recipient of the De Osma studentship in 1934 he was for a time a guest at the Residencia de Estudiantes, where he observed from a distance the circle of Federico García Lorca, Pablo Neruda, and Luis Buñuel. He said that he holidayed that summer with a group of English poets and writers in huts on a deserted beach near Maspalomas, at the southern tip of Gran Canaria, which was later to develop into La Playa del Inglés. His teachers at Oxford included the philologist William J. Entwistle, the dilettante George A. Kolkhorst, and Dámaso Alonso, the Spanish poet and literary scholar.

After graduating with a first in Spanish and French in 1935 Russell began to study under Entwistle's supervision the chronicles of the important fourteenth-century Portuguese historian Fernão Lopes, and spent some time in Coimbra and Lisbon, working on the original documents. There he began to develop his future scholarly approach, which was to question the veracity of the medieval historian's text by cross-checking it with its possible sources and other contemporary accounts. As two articles Russell drafted before the Second World War attest, he had already embarked on the massive research required for his first major book, *The English Intervention in Spain and Portugal in the Time of Edward III and Richard II* (1955), under the somewhat erratic supervision of the regius professor of modern history, Maurice Powicke. He said that he spent the summer of 1935 at a Hitler Youth camp in the Black Forest, but any illusions he may have harboured about national socialism were soon dispelled when he witnessed the sadistic behaviour of Nazi youths towards the old and the frail, especially Jews, on the streets of German cities. He led small groups of Oxford undergraduates to Salazar's Portugal and to Franco's Spain in the summers of 1937 and 1938. During the first of these visits he lent a Portuguese scholar at Coimbra a copy of his draft dissertation on the sources of Fernão Lopes, and was much surprised, on his way to the Caribbean via Lisbon in March 1942, to find copies of an unauthorized Portuguese edition of it on sale. He may have been first approached by British intelligence in 1937–8, since he said he was arrested by the Spanish civil guard on the Cíes Islands at the mouth of the Vigo estuary in Galicia in August 1938 while photographing the cruiser *Canarias*, whence he was marched before two SS officers in the Hotel Atlántico in the port of Vigo. While Franco's provisional government at Burgos was being consulted, the German officers invited him to dine with them after learning of his summer in the Black Forest. Franco's order arrived for him to be deported to Portugal via the international bridge at Túy on 29 August 1938, a crossing he later recalled as the most traumatic of his career, though he was ever after grateful to Franco for saving his life.

At Oxford in the late 1930s Russell's lofty stature and aristocratic appearance marked him out as one of the most striking students of his time, and as a college lecturer at St John's he began to move in the circle of Maurice Bowra and Oliver Franks, and was in contact with exiled Spanish artists and intellectuals, including Gregorio Prieto, who sketched him, and the poet Luis Cernuda. The day after the fall of Paris to German forces on 14 June 1940 he went with other Oxford dons to the army recruiting office to volunteer. After some military training at Droitwich and at Cheltenham he was commissioned by MI5 with the rank of second lieutenant in the Intelligence Corps at its headquarters (then at Oriel College, Oxford) on 20 December 1940. After courses there and at Matlock, Derbyshire, he underwent the terrors of a brief training course at Lochailort in Scotland, soon returning to Oriel to prepare to go to Spain. As a passenger in a motorcar that crashed into the back of a lorry in the blackout between Burford and Oxford on 21 March 1941, he received serious facial injuries that ultimately required a series of reconstructive operations by the famous New Zealand plastic surgeon Archibald McIndoe at Basingstoke Hospital over a four-month period. These left two permanent scars on his brow and chin that later gave rise to numerous stories among his undergraduates. As he aged his noble features became more leonine, and his mane of white hair and his calm air of 'smiling granite' made him the object of admiration, one student commenting that 'he had obviously had a life outside the University' (*The Times*, 26 July 2006). His important lectures in the Taylor Institution on golden age thought and literature were delivered at a high intellectual pitch in his elegant Oxford drawl, which some phoneticians considered to be unique to Queen's in the 1930s. When fully relaxed on social occasions, at which he was the most generous of hosts, his infectious chortling laugh with an occasional George III-like 'w'hot, w'hot?'—half interrogative and half exclamatory—endeared him to students, colleagues, and friends alike.

Russell's first major posting in MI5 began on 18 March 1942 when he sailed from Newport, Monmouthshire, to become security co-ordination officer with the rank of captain in Jamaica. In the summer of 1943 he was reassigned to west Africa to monitor the naval activities of the Vichy French (he was issued with a driving licence in the Gold Coast in March 1944). There his intelligence activities and his historical research interlaced once more, as he acknowledged in the preface to his second major historical book, many years in the making, *Prince Henry 'the Navigator'* (2000), in which he expressed his debt to the RAF pilots who ferried him up and down the coast at low altitude in 1943–4. This second massive project revealed once again his penchant for debunking legends, in showing that the prince himself had never voyaged further than from the Algarve to Ceuta and back, though his captains were to encompass half the globe. With the rank of acting lieutenant-colonel, Russell's last and most important assignment for MI5 was in the Far East from mid-1944 to December 1945, when he was based in Colombo, Ceylon, and interrogated and 'turned' an Indian nationalist agent codenamed Carbuncle, in order to feed naval disinformation to the Japanese. This operation led to the sinking of the heavy cruiser *Haguro* off Penang by a British destroyer flotilla in May 1945.

Although offered a permanent position in MI5 after the Japanese surrender, on his return to Oxford on 24 January 1946 Russell accepted with alacrity appointment as university lecturer in Spanish and fellow of Queen's, where he tutored a series of distinguished future professors of Spanish and held numerous college offices. After the death of Entwistle in 1952 the electors for the King Alfonso XIII professorship chose Russell, the youngest candidate, who held the post from October 1953 until his retirement in 1981, when he took his Oxford DLitt. His most important literary publications were his biography of Cervantes (1985), his edition of Rojas's *Celestina* (1991), and his seminal articles on the dating and authorship of the *Poem of the Cid*, and his demolition of native myths about Spanish fifteenth-century humanism. In 1962 he did his best to stay in the background when playing host to the foundation congress of the International Association of Hispanists. His training in military intelligence was doubtless responsible for his preferred role as a lone scholar, working quietly in British and foreign archives, preparing the printer's copy in secret, and then surprising his colleagues with the published work. He made numerous contacts in continental Europe, as well as the USA, where he was visiting professor at the universities of Virginia in 1982, Texas in 1983 and 1987, Johns Hopkins in 1986, and Vanderbilt in 1987. He was James Bond-like in his enthusiasm for the latest inventions and gadgets, and his early hobbies included photography and use of a cine-camera. He invested in a personal computer for his research work as soon as they appeared in 1982, upgrading his system periodically, and became a keen user of the internet when it was introduced.

Probably the most influential Hispanist and Lusitanist of the second half of the twentieth century in Great Britain, Russell received many honours: he was made a corresponding member of the Acadêmia da História de Portugal (1956) and the Acadèmia de Bones Lletres de Barcelona (1972), a fellow of the British Academy (1977), an emeritus fellow of Exeter College, Oxford (1981), an honorary fellow of Queen's College (1990), the first laureate of the Antonio de Nebrija prize, Salamanca (1989), and a commander of the order of Isabella the Catholic (Spain, 1989) and of the Infante Dom Henrique (Portugal, 1993). He also received four Festschriften. He was knighted in 1995 for his services to Peninsular history and literature. He was not at all displeased at being the inspiration for a protagonist in four of Javier Marías's novels.

With the family wealth he and his brother inherited in the 1970s, Russell was always able to keep up an elegant bachelor lifestyle in a comfortable flat in north Oxford, and his hobbies in horticulture, philately, and collecting rare books and *objets d'art*. He revised his skilfully worded will from time to time, leaving the greater part of his fortune to his family, and generous bequests to the Bodleian and Taylorian libraries and to Queen's and Exeter colleges, with selected bibliographical items for his friends. Two years before his death he planned every detail of his cremation and funeral service, and he died quietly of heart failure at his home, 23 Belsyre Court, Oxford, on 22 June 2006 while taking coffee and reading the morning paper. His brother Hugh had predeceased him by six weeks.

IAN MICHAEL

Sources A. Deyermond and J. Lawrance, eds., *Letters and society in fifteenth-century Spain* (1993) · *The Independent* (5 July 2006) · *Daily Telegraph* (10 July 2006) · *The Times* (14 July 2006); (26 July 2006) · *El País* (15 July 2006) · J. Marías, 'Como un caballero bueno', *El País Semanal* (23 July 2006) · *The Guardian* (22 Aug 2006) · I. Michael, *Bulletin of Spanish Studies*, 83 (2006), 1134–44 · *Bulletin of Hispanic Studies*, 83 (2006) · *PBA*, 172 (2011), 275–89 · M. C. Pimenta, 'Sir Peter Russell and Portuguese history: the story of a great passion', *e-journal of Portuguese History* [Brown University], 5/1 (summer 2007); www.brown.edu/Departments/Portuguese_Brazilian_Studies/ejph/html/issue9/pdf/mpimenta.pdf, 5 July 2012 · diaries and travel documents, priv. coll. · Burke, *Peerage* · *WW* (2006) · personal knowledge (2010) · private information (2010) [B. Taylor] · d. cert.

Likenesses obituary photographs · photographs, U. Oxf., Taylor Institution

Wealth at death £2,381,961: probate, 7 Nov 2006, *CGPLA Eng. & Wales*

Russell, William Morris [Bill] (1920–2006), engineer and designer, was born on 22 July 1920 at 73 Oxford Road, Islington, London, the youngest in the family of two sons and two daughters of Albert Edward Russell, printer, and his wife, Agnes Mary, *née* Carrick (*b*. 1918). There were a number of artists in his mother's family; she was also a socialist and an enthusiast for the arts and crafts movement, which may explain her choice of names for him. In 1933 Russell won a scholarship to High Wycombe Technical Institute, leaving to take up an apprenticeship with the Rheostatic Company, manufacturer of electrical controls and switchgear, in Slough, where he completed a diploma in engineering. In 1943 he volunteered for the Royal Electrical and Mechanical Engineers, and was commissioned, spending the rest of the Second World War serving in an anti-aircraft battery. On 8 January 1944 he married Kathleen Annie (Anne) Swabey (*b*. 1918), a shorthand typist, daughter of James Swabey, a joiner and cabinet maker. They had two sons.

After the war Russell trained troops in India and Ethiopia. Demobilized with the rank of major in 1947, he joined the electrical appliance manufacturer Morphy Richards as a designer, and worked on their thermostatically controlled irons, toasters, and hair dryers. While he was working for them, Morphy Richards launched the first British automatic toaster, in 1949, and the Atlantic lightweight iron, 'the iron with the butterfly touch', in 1951. Their first electric hair dryer came on the market in 1953.

With the return of prosperity in the 1950s, the market for domestic electrical appliances grew, and in 1952 Peter Hobbs, the former managing director of the South African division of Morphy Richards, approached Russell about the possibility of developing an automatic coffee percolator. Hobbs had been working on an idea patented in Germany for installing electric elements in ceramic coffee pots: Russell saw how it could be done, and they decided to set up their own business, Russell Hobbs, in a disused factory in Croydon, Surrey. Russell was in charge of developing new products, Hobbs was the sales director, and at first much of the work was done at home, with Russell using Meccano to design the manufacturing tools. He always said that his final safety test for a new product was to pour half a pint of boiling gravy over it.

Russell Hobbs launched the world's first automatic coffee percolator at the end of 1952. The coffee was kept hot after it had dripped through by means of a temperature control similar to that on a thermostatic iron: this enabled the machine to turn itself off. There was also a device for controlling the strength of the coffee. The coffee percolator was followed by an automatic tea maker, which was switched on by an alarm clock, but it had to compete with the long-established Goblin Teasmade and did not sell well.

In 1955 the K1 kettle, the world's first automatic electric kettle, came on the market: this was the first kettle capable of switching itself off automatically when the water had boiled. Designed by Russell, the kettle worked through a bimetallic strip: when the water boiled, a jet of steam was forced through the lid of the kettle, which activated the strip, cutting the power supply and turning off the kettle. Although the electric kettle had been invented towards the end of the nineteenth century, designers had been unable to solve the problem of preventing the kettle from boiling dry if it had not been switched off manually. In 1960 the K2 appeared: a more elegant design, it was soon established as a classic, and was in demand all over the tea-drinking world. This model was not updated until the mid-1970s.

To enable the company to expand, Russell and Hobbs sold it to Tube Investments, a conglomerate based in Birmingham, in 1963, and production of Russell Hobbs appliances moved to Wombourne, near Wolverhampton, in Staffordshire. There they shared a factory with Creda, manufacturer of electric cookers, another subsidiary of Tube Investments. The partnership split up: Hobbs became a director of the Valor stove company and Russell was appointed technical director of Creda, before moving to Portsmouth as managing director of Turnright, another Tube Investments subsidiary.

Russell retired in 1985, and was able to devote more time to his two passions, the novels of Proust and the music of Wagner. The Russell Hobbs brand, which had become a household name, survived many changes of ownership. Regarded as a classic of British design, the K2 kettle is displayed in the Design Museum, in London, while the CPI coffee percolator and the K1 kettle are on show in the Science Museum. Having lived latterly at 72 The Maltings, Westgate, Chichester, Sussex, Russell died on 16 February 2006 in St Richard's Hospital, Chichester, of heart failure. He was survived by his wife and their two sons.

ANNE PIMLOTT BAKER

Sources 'Electric kettles', *Electrical Review* (24 Feb 1956), 308–13 • P. Sparks, *Electrical appliances* (1987), 62–5 • P. Linnell, *Simply switch on*, rev. edn (2000) • C. McDermott, *20th c design* (1997), 216 • *Daily Telegraph* (4 March 2006); (21 April 2008) • *Liverpool Daily Post* (7 March 2006) • *The Times* (23 March 2006); (3 May 2008) • private information (2010) • b. cert. • m. cert. • d. cert.

Likenesses photograph, repro. in *Daily Telegraph* (4 March 2006)

Wealth at death £318,222: probate, 11 Jan 2007, *CGPLA Eng. & Wales*

Sadie, Stanley John (1930–2005), musicologist and music critic, was born on 30 October 1930 at 57 Forty Avenue, Wembley, the only son of David Sadie, a silk manufacturer's agent, and his wife, Deborah, *née* Simons; he had one older sister. He was of Jewish descent. He was educated at St Paul's School, London, and at Gonville and Caius College, Cambridge, where he read music under Thurston Dart, Charles Cudworth, and Patrick Hadley; he graduated BA MusB in 1953, and PhD in 1958. His thesis was on eighteenth-century British chamber music, a subject about which little had hitherto been discovered. As a schoolboy he had played the clarinet in the RAF central band; he went on to become an accomplished and active bassoonist. On 10 December 1953, at the New West End Synagogue, Paddington, he married Adèle Bloom, formerly Simmons (1931–1978), a hospital committee clerk, and daughter of David Simmons, commercial traveller. They had two sons and a daughter.

Sadie taught at Trinity College of Music, London, from 1957 to 1965, and in 1964 joined *The Times* as a music critic, reviewing regularly for the paper until 1981. In 1966 he was appointed assistant editor of the *Musical Times*, two years later becoming its editor, a post he held until 1986. For forty years, from the mid-1960s, he also reviewed regularly for *The Gramophone* and made many broadcasts for the BBC. He wrote numerous programme articles and notes to accompany recordings.

Sadie's years with *The Times* coincided with a period of rich diversity in British musical life: performances of contemporary and new music were widespread and, at the same time, there was a growing interest in early music and the re-creation of historical styles of performance (a subject that fascinated him). He was a percipient and lively critic of a range of music-making and, though he expressed his views very directly, his notices were fair. When he became editor of the *Musical Times* it was the most widely read music journal in Britain and the only one of musical record. Under his editorship it published articles by leading scholars as well as a range of reviews of publications and performances; Sadie himself contributed numerous reviews, especially of opera (to which he was especially drawn throughout his life). In all his writings his prose was elegant and unpretentious, and revealing of his sharp and sometimes scathing wit. His trenchant views could lead to rifts with colleagues.

In 1970 Sadie began work on a sixth edition of *Grove's Dictionary of Music and Musicians*, published in 1980 as *The New Grove Dictionary of Music and Musicians*, in twenty volumes. His combination of encyclopaedic knowledge and experience of music's practicalities made him the obvious choice as editor of the new edition of the dictionary, his greatest achievement. Not only was it on an unprecedented scale, but it embraced topics new to musicology (including world music, ethnomusicology, ancient music, sources, analysis, popular music) and was written by an international team of specialists. No longer was the dictionary directed at the informed amateur. It set new standards of musical writing, scholarship, and bibliography.

This ground-breaking work of musical lexicography generated several other reference works with which Sadie was involved, notably *The New Grove Dictionary of Musical Instruments* (3 vols., 1984), *The New Grove Dictionary of American Music* (with H. Wiley Hitchcock; 4 vols., 1986), *The Grove Concise Dictionary of Music* (1988), *The New Grove Dictionary of Opera* (4 vols., 1992), and *The New Grove Book of Operas* (1996). Sadie was later co-editor, with John Tyrrell, of the seventh edition of the main dictionary (29 vols., 2001). In 2000, however, the publishers (Macmillan Holtzbrinck) suddenly stipulated that the dictionary be published later that year. Sadie protested that this would be impossible without compromising editorial standards; he was dismissed. (As it happened, the new deadline was still not met.) He was involved with the texts of these works at every level; he was a skilful editor who enjoyed teaching the art to his large team of young colleagues, in whom he inspired great loyalty; he launched the careers of numerous scholars, writers, and editors.

Sadie's writings and performing editions focused on the music of his two great loves: Mozart and Handel. He published a monograph on Mozart in 1956, another in 1966, an edition of Mozart's piano sonatas (1981), a revised edition of Emily Anderson's edition of Mozart's letters (1985), a book on Mozart's symphonies (1986), and a volume of essays on Mozart (1996). In spite of his lengthy final illness he completed the first of a projected two-volume study of Mozart, *Mozart: the Early Years, 1756–1791* (2006). His books on Handel were published in 1962, 1966, and 1972, and in 1987 he co-edited (with Anthony Hicks) the *Handel Tercentenary Collection*. From 1976 he was editor of Dent's Master Musicians series. He also published books of a less specialist nature, notably *The Cambridge Guide to Music* (with Alison Latham; 1985), and he edited a set of six volumes, *Man and Music* (1989–93), which were conceived alongside a series of television programmes, presented by Bamber Gascoigne and Alan Bennett among others.

On 18 July 1978, following the death of his first wife, Sadie married Julie Anne Vertrees, *née* McCormack (*b.* 1948), an American musicologist, bass-viol player, and cellist, and daughter of Walter Stewart McCormack, dentist. They had a son and a daughter, and lived initially in Hampstead. During their marriage they were involved in several joint projects, including *The New Grove Dictionary of Women Composers* (with Rhian Samuel; 1994). In 1993 Sadie founded the Handel House Trust, to create a museum and recital room in Handel's London house in Brook Street; his wife was also instrumental in establishing the Handel House Museum. Through this venture Sadie and his wife developed a wider interest in composers' memorials and birthplaces. They made some forty trips to Europe, gathering information for a projected guide. (It was on one of these journeys, in the Ukraine in 1999, that they were involved in a car accident in which Sadie was badly injured.) *Calling on the Composer* was published posthumously in 2005.

Sadie was at the centre of British musical life for nearly fifty years. He occupied a unique place: he was a distinguished scholar, but he possessed that rare gift of being able to communicate his knowledge and enthusiasms to the general reader and listener. He devoted passionate energy to his numerous projects, and usually worked long into the night. But he nevertheless had a strong sense of family and clear views on topical issues that affected everyday life. He listed his recreations in *Who's Who* as 'watching cricket, drinking (mainly wine and coffee), bridge, travel, reading'. In 1982 he was made a CBE. He was president of the Royal Musical Association (1989–94) and of the International Musicological Society (1992–7). He received several honorary doctorates.

Sadie and his wife moved to Cossington, Somerset, in 2000. There they established a series of chamber concerts. His last year was marked by a debilitating deterioration of his health; a diagnosis of motor neurone disease was made just a week before he died, of bronchopneumonia, at his home, The Manor, Cossington, on 21 March 2005. He was survived by his wife and five children. There was a private funeral in Cossington, followed by a woodland burial in the Quantock hills. A memorial service was held at Cossington on 4 April, and a memorial concert at the Royal Academy of Music on 1 November. Sadie lived long enough to see the publication a month before his death of a volume of essays in his honour, *Words about Mozart* (edited by Dorothea Link). In 2005 he was posthumously awarded the Handel prize by the city of Halle.

ALISON LATHAM

Sources D. Link, ed., *Words about Mozart: essays in honour of Stanley Sadie* (2005) [includes bibliography and biographical essays by A. Porter and L. Langley] • *The Guardian* (23 March 2005) • *The Independent* (24 March 2005) • *Daily Telegraph* (25 March 2005) • 'Sadie, Stanley', Grove Music online, www.grovemusic.com, 14 Aug 2008 • *WW* (2005) • personal knowledge (2009) • private information (2009) • b. cert. • m. certs. • d. cert.

Archives FILM BL NSA, documentary footage | SOUND BL NSA, documentary recordings

Likenesses photograph, 1981, Photoshot, London • obituary photographs • photographs, Oxford University Press

Wealth at death £867,313: probate, 12 July 2005, *CGPLA Eng. & Wales*

Saffman, Philip Geoffrey (1931–2008), applied mathematician, was born on 19 March 1931 at 47 Savile Road, Leeds, Yorkshire, the son of Sam Ralph Saffman (1904–1974), solicitor, and his wife, Sarah Rebecca, *née* Leviten. His parents were both Jewish, of Russian and Lithuanian descent. Saffman, one of three brothers, was educated at Roundhay, the premier grammar school of Leeds, from where, at the unusually early age of fifteen, he won an open entrance scholarship to study mathematics at Trinity College, Cambridge. Before doing so, he spent a year with relatives in Baltimore, USA, returning to England to carry out his national service with the Royal Air Force. At Cambridge he took his BA as a wrangler (first-class honours in mathematics) in 1953; he then engaged in research in fluid mechanics under the supervision of George Batchelor. On 2 September 1954, at the Chapeltown United Hebrew Synagogue, Leeds, he married Ruth Arion, also of Leeds, the 20-year-old daughter of Louis Arion, woollen merchant. They had three children, Louise, Mark, and Emma.

In 1955 Saffman was elected to a prize fellowship at Trinity College. His PhD thesis covered three related topics: the rise of small bubbles (as in a glass of champagne), the motion of small particles suspended in a viscous shear flow, and the coalescence of small water droplets in clouds to form raindrops. Part of the work was supervised by Sir Geoffrey Taylor, also of Trinity College. Following his PhD, which he completed in 1956, he continued to work with Taylor on a problem of great significance for the oil extraction industry, namely the manner in which one fluid such as water can penetrate another of greater viscosity such as oil. This celebrated work led to the discovery of what became known as 'Saffman–Taylor fingering', a prototypical phenomenon that underlies the formation of dendritic structures, arising in many branches of physics.

Saffman was appointed assistant lecturer in applied mathematics at Cambridge in 1958, where he lectured at graduate level on waves and gas dynamics. He moved to a readership at King's College, London, in 1960. His work in many aspects of fluid flow, both laminar and turbulent, flourished during this period. One particularly notable contribution concerned the interaction of convective and diffusive effects in turbulent flow, the start of a long interest in fundamental problems of turbulence and the closely related field of vortex dynamics. In these areas, Saffman brought great analytical skill to bear upon exceedingly difficult problems; he took particular delight in overturning the foundations of the subject, as for example in his investigation of the large-scale structures of turbulence, where he challenged a theory that had been promoted in the mid-1950s by his own supervisor and mentor, George Batchelor.

In 1964 Saffman emigrated to the USA to take up an appointment as professor of applied mathematics at the California Institute of Technology (Caltech), where he remained throughout the rest of his scientific career. He maintained his links with Britain, particularly through his long collaboration with D. W. Moore of Imperial College, London, on problems of vortex dynamics. Their paper 'Axial flow in trailing line vortices', published in 1973, had very practical implications for air-traffic control. Saffman served as a consultant to the aircraft industry during the 1980s. His analysis of the dispersion of turbulent vortices in the wake of an aircraft on take-off helped to establish new guidelines for the time that must be allowed to elapse before safe take-off of the following aircraft.

Saffman was preoccupied throughout much of his career with the great unsolved problems associated with the phenomenon of turbulence in fluid flow. He was sceptical, indeed scathing, concerning approaches that relied too heavily on mathematical abstraction, preferring himself to focus on the details of vortex interactions, and the inspired scaling and dimensional arguments to which this led. He could, however, be equally dismissive of his own results in this area, recognizing that a solution to the dynamical problem of turbulence was well beyond current analytical or computational capacity.

On the basis of his contributions in viscous flow theory, vortex dynamics, and turbulence, Saffman was elected a fellow of the Royal Society in 1988. His published output was prodigious; he summarized many of his contributions in his research monograph *Vortex Dynamics* (1992), which rapidly became a classic reference in this field. However, it is mainly for his earlier work in the field of viscous flow theory, and particularly his collaboration with Taylor in the 1950s, that he will be chiefly remembered. His analysis of such problems as the collision of drops in turbulent clouds (1956), the motion of small particles in shearing flow (1965), or (with Max Delbrück) Brownian motion in biological membranes (1975), showed profound originality, and established Saffman as one of the great twentieth-century contributors to theoretical fluid dynamics.

Saffman's achievements at Caltech were recognized by his appointment in 1995 to the Theodore von Kármán chair of applied mathematics and aeronautics, by the award of the Otto Laporte prize of the American Physical Society, and by his election as a fellow of the American Academy of Arts and Sciences (in 1978). By 2000 his health was beginning to fail. He continued in retirement at his home in Pasadena, California, where he died on 17 August 2008, survived by his wife, Ruth, and their three children.

H. K. MOFFATT

Sources *The Times* (29 Aug 2008) • *Yorkshire Post* (20 Sept 2008) • *Jewish Chronicle* (3 Oct 2008) • H. A. Stone, 'Philip Saffman and viscous flow theory', *Journal of Fluid Mechanics*, 409 (2000), 165–83 • D. J. Pullin and D. I. Meiron, 'Philip G. Saffman', *A voyage through turbulence*, ed. P. Davidson and others (2011) • *WW* (2008) • personal knowledge (2012) • private information (2012) • b. cert. • m. cert.
Likenesses obituary photographs

Sainsbury, Simon David Davan (1930–2006), businessman and philanthropist, was born on 1 March 1930 at 27 The Vale, Chelsea, London, the second of three sons of Alan John *Sainsbury, later Baron Sainsbury (1902–1998), grocer and businessman, and his first wife, Doreen Davan, *née* Adams (1904–1985), daughter of Leonard Adams. His early life was spent in Chelsea, and at Dorney, near Windsor, during the Second World War. He was educated at Eton College, where he became head of his house and president of Pop, the Eton society. He excelled at music and sport, scoring a century in the Eton–Harrow match at Lord's in 1947. After national service with the Life Guards (where he was made sports officer), he took a degree in history at Trinity College, Cambridge, before qualifying as a chartered accountant in 1956. He joined the family food retailing firm, J. Sainsbury Ltd, later the same year. Initially he worked closely with his uncle Robert *Sainsbury (1906–2000) on matters relating to personnel, finance, and general administration. He was appointed a director in April 1959.

Whereas previous generations of the Sainsbury family had largely been trained 'on the job', it was felt important, as the business grew in scale and complexity, that the fourth—Alan's sons John (*b.* 1927), Simon, and Timothy (*b.* 1932), and Robert's son David (*b.* 1940)—should be better equipped to manage different aspects of its strategy and direction. Thus while his elder brother John gradually assumed responsibility for trading and marketing and his younger brother, Timothy, became a chartered surveyor and subsequently director responsible for estates and store development (and also Conservative MP for Hove from 1973 to 1997, a government whip, and a junior minister), Simon Sainsbury built on his accountancy training and experience in administration to play a key role in updating the business's financial, administrative, and distributive infrastructure and in planning its future development. In particular he championed investment in the modernization of the company's antiquated distribution system and the introduction of an administrative structure that was reliant on professional managers. He was also responsible for the first application of computer technology to British food retailing.

In 1969 Simon Sainsbury succeeded his brother John as deputy chairman of Sainsbury's on John's appointment as chairman. Together with their younger brother Timothy, and subsequently also their cousin David, the brothers oversaw the company's growth from a medium-sized regional family firm to become Britain's most successful food retailer. A crucial aspect of this transformation was the company's flotation on the stock exchange. Simon Sainsbury, who took responsibility for this move, explained to readers of the company's house magazine that the timing of this decision was governed jointly by the Sainsbury family's desire to see the completion as a private company of the centenary in 1969 and by its decision to have 'largely completed' the replacement of the pre-war store portfolio with self-service shops and the updating of its supporting distributive and administrative infrastructure before going public. It was to be the biggest and most oversubscribed public flotation to that date; it was also the first to be advertised on television. The share offer opened at 10 a.m. on 19 July 1973. When it closed one minute later it was oversubscribed thirty-four-fold. Priority in allocation of shares was given to small investors, and to members of Sainsbury's staff, for whom a million shares were set aside.

In 1975 Simon Sainsbury began a gradual handover of his responsibilities as deputy chairman to Roy Griffiths, whom he had brought into the business in 1968. Roy Griffiths had succeeded him as personnel director and now became joint deputy chairman. The transfer of responsibilities lasted until 1979, when Simon Sainsbury finally retired. Subsequently his involvement with the business was confined to supervision of its arts sponsorship committee, of which he was chairman from the programme's inception in 1981 until 1990. He was thus responsible for establishing the company's reputation as one of Britain's most enlightened corporate arts sponsors through projects that included a mixture of existing arts programmes and 'own brand' events like the Sainsbury choir of the year competition.

At the same time Simon Sainsbury was conducting a much less publicized programme of private philanthropy, much of it anonymous. He possessed an exceptional eye for art and design, shared with his uncle Robert. In 1965 he set up the Monument Trust, which in its early days gave generous support to architectural charities, including the Georgian Society and the National Trust, funding the restoration for the nation of the interiors of a number of important country houses and enabling the trust to bid at auction for items that had been sold by their previous owners. His support included major donations to the British Museum, Royal Academy, the V&A, the Council for the Protection of (later Campaign to Protect) Rural England, the Landmark Trust, and Christ Church, Spitalfields. With his support the original Addenbrooke's Children's Hospital building at Cambridge was saved from demolition and transformed into the Judge business school.

The Monument Trust provided essential finance for HIV and AIDS sufferers before statutory funding was made available. It also supported projects to make the lives of prisoners more hopeful, and the regeneration of Meadow Well estate, north Tyneside, after the riots of 1991. It was characteristic of Simon Sainsbury's style of patronage that beneficiaries of his philanthropy received much more than money: he took a keen interest in their progress, often over a period of many years. He was a trustee of the Wallace Collection from 1977 until 1997, serving as its chairman for the last five years of that period, and a trustee of the National Gallery from 1991 until 1998.

Simon Sainsbury preferred his patronage to remain undisclosed, but when the high-profile funding of the National Gallery's Sainsbury wing by the three Sainsbury brothers (John, Simon, and Timothy) made it impossible to maintain anonymity he relented. 'Now that my name is in letters a foot high in Trafalgar Square, there doesn't seem much point', he told Martin Drury, director-general of the National Trust (*The Times*, 18 Oct 2006). Neil McGregor, the National Gallery's director, recalled that Simon Sainsbury's chairing of meetings with the gallery and the architects over an extended period provided 'masterclasses in running a project' (*The Independent*, 4 Oct 2006). After the gallery opened in 1991 it was Sainsbury who organized a party for the stonemasons and car-park attendants.

In his private life Simon Sainsbury was reticent almost to the point of reclusiveness. Friends reported his virtues correspondingly to be those of modesty: loyalty, persistence, understatement, and self-discipline, leavened with a dry sense of humour. Neil McGregor observed in his *Independent* obituary that Simon Sainsbury 'would … have hated to read this tribute' (*The Independent*, 4 Oct 2006). It was characteristic that he declined to appear in *Who's Who*, and was reported to have turned down public honours. His partner of over forty years was Stewart Grimshaw, restaurateur and bookseller, with whom he registered a civil partnership in January 2006; a fitting, very private, celebration for a couple who had campaigned over many years for disadvantaged same-sex couples (and had provided crucial funding for Stonewall, the group campaigning for lesbian and gay equality). His last years were marred by the progressive onset of Parkinson's disease. He died on 28 September 2006 at Southampton General Hospital following a fall, and was survived by his civil partner, Stewart Grimshaw. He left an estate valued at almost £300 million, and bequeathed eighteen paintings from his collection to the National Gallery and Tate, including works by Monet, Degas, Francis Bacon, and Lucian Freud. BRIDGET SALMON

Sources *JS Journal* • [J. Boswell], ed., *J. S. 100: the story of Sainsbury's* (1969) • B. Williams, *The best butter in the world* (1994) • *The Independent* (4 Oct 2006) • *The Times* (7 Oct 2006); (11 Oct 2006); (17 Oct 2006); (18 Oct 2006) • *Daily Telegraph* (9 Oct 2006) • Museum of London, Sainsbury archive • Burke, *Peerage* • private information (2010) [Lord Sainsbury of Preston Candover, brother; Stewart Grimshaw, civil partner] • b. cert. • d. cert.

Archives Museum of London, Sainsbury archive

Likenesses obituary photographs • photographs, Photoshot, London

Wealth at death £298,254,579: probate, 12 Feb 2007, *CGPLA Eng. & Wales*

Sandberg, Alexander Christer Edward [Alec] (**1923–2008**), civil and structural engineer, was born on 31 July 1923 at 3 Cadogan Place, Chelsea, London, the son of Oscar Fridolf Alexander Sandberg (1878/9–1940), civil engineer, and his wife, Audrey Maude Edward, *née* Furber (1899–1980). He was born into a Swedish rail engineering dynasty that was established in the 1860s after his grandfather, Christer Peter Sandberg, emigrated to England. The firm flourished for two generations by providing international consultancy services during the golden age of railway engineering.

Sandberg, usually known as Alec, progressed from Charterhouse School in 1940 to City and Guilds Engineering College, South Kensington, later part of Imperial College, London. In the early part of the Second World War he volunteered to work as an air raid warden and was subsequently involved in firefighting and ambulance driving. Although initially granted deferment from the armed forces for education he eventually joined the Royal Engineers in 1943 and a year later was sent to Burma, where he brought to bear his extensive knowledge of railways to assist in the reconstruction of its rail industry after the war.

In 1950 Sandberg joined the family firm at a time when its lucrative rail consultancy work had virtually ceased. Appointed senior partner in 1955, he remodelled the firm into a specialist materials testing organization, working closely and profitably with the Ministry of Transport on motorway contracts. On 19 October 1957, at St Michael's Church, Chester Square, Pimlico, London, he married Aline Isobel Duncan (*b.* 1929), daughter of William Edmonstone Duncan, army officer. They had three sons, Michael, Christopher, and Neil.

Under Sandberg's leadership the practice expanded to a staff of 400 with specialists in specific materials. The firm was able to play a leading role in the aftermath of the box-girder bridge difficulties (caused by the collapse of three bridges in 1970–71) and was able to advise design consultants for the Milford Haven (later Cleddau), Severn, Wye, Erskine, and Humber bridges. Expertise in testing for steel corrosion in reinforced or pre-stressed concrete was also developed about this time. In tandem with this development were additional contracts on suspension bridges, ports, railways, and other civil engineering projects in Hong Kong, China, Thailand, Bahrain, and Dubai. In particular he helped to resolve a dispute between designer and contractor over the quality of concrete used in the Tsing Ma bridge in Hong Kong. He was also much in demand as an expert witness in fraud cases centring around the alleged use of poor-quality concrete.

Sandberg's forward-looking approach ensured that the firm was always abreast of developments like the property boom of the late 1980s, which included the vast reconstruction of the old dock areas of Canary Wharf and the explosion of refurbishment schemes. He was involved in the restoration of Windsor Castle after the fire of 20 November 1992, Nelson's Column, Eros in Piccadilly, and the Albert Memorial in Hyde Park.

Sandberg was a founder member of the executive committee of the British group of the International Association for Bridge and Structural Engineering, and helped organize various Henderson symposia at Cambridge University, where his extensive overseas connections helped to recruit knowledgeable engineers from outside the UK to the meetings. He chaired the organizing committees of the colloquia on liability (1984) and rehabilitation and renovation (1987). He was subsequently appointed a member of honour in recognition of his achievements for the committee. In 1998 he was appointed OBE for his services to civil engineering. He was influential as a member and sometime chairman of the organization known colloquially as the French Civils. This was a group of Francophile British engineers who were affiliated to the Conseil National des Ingénieurs et des Scientifiques de France. A man with an irrepressible sense of humour, it is reported that on one occasion he had gone ahead to make arrangements for a visit of the group to France. He arranged for the coach driver to pick him up from the side of the road, posing as a Breton onion seller, complete with striped shirt, onions, and false moustache.

It was a characteristic of Sandberg that his jokes were usually at his own expense—rarely did he offend any of his associates or even his opponents. However, those who might be encouraged to take advantage of his easy-going manner could be surprised by his acute sense of business and the depth of his engineering knowledge. Behind his smile was a profound knowledge of his subject, whether it was engineering, contract bridge, or things of the heart. His calm and sensitive humour defused many a tense meeting where tempers were in danger of becoming frayed. Above all, he had the gift of making engineering seem fun. He died at his home, 16 Thames Quay, Chelsea Harbour, London, on 1 August 2008 after a long period of relatively poor health. He was survived by his wife, Aline, and their three sons. His well-attended memorial service was held at St Michael's Church, Chester Square, London, on 2 October 2008. DAVID DORAN

Sources *New Civil Engineer* (5 Aug 2008) · *The Times* (30 Sept 2008) · *IABSE News*, 27 (autumn 2008), 8 · personal knowledge (2012) · private information (2012) · b. cert. · m. cert. · d. cert.

Wealth at death £3934: probate, 11 May 2009, *CGPLA Eng. & Wales*

Sandbrook, (John) Richard (1946–2005), environmentalist and campaigner against poverty, was born on 13 August 1946 at Forbes Fraser Hospital, Bath, the second of five sons of John Peter Sandbrook, a lieutenant-commander, later captain, in the Royal Navy, and his wife, Ethel Joan Wakeham, *née* Sutton. He attended Dauntsey's School in Wiltshire, and went on to the University of East Anglia, where he took a degree in biology. After a year as president of the Students' Union he spent five years with the accountancy firm Arthur Andersen & Co. On 18 July 1970 he married, at the parish church of Earlham St Mary, Norfolk, Mary Wray, a 21-year-old economist, and daughter of George Arthur Wray, medical doctor. They had two sons.

While working as an accountant Sandbrook was already active in the environmental movement, helping to set up Friends of the Earth in the UK, and attending the United

(John) Richard Sandbrook (1946–2005), by unknown photographer

Nations conference on environment and human development in Stockholm in 1972, before taking over as managing director of Friends of the Earth in 1974. After just two years there (which included some 'iconic' campaigning moments, such as dumping thousands of bottles on the doorstep of Schweppes UK as part of the campaign to promote returnable bottles), he moved on to join Barbara Ward (Baroness Jackson of Lodsworth) at the International Institute for Environment and Development, where he spent the next twenty-three years of his working life.

The institute (established in 1973) is seen by many as the birthplace of the concept of sustainable development. Barbara Ward was a development economist and one of the first people to argue that environmental stewardship and the alleviation of poverty had to go hand in hand. Sandbrook rapidly became her favoured protégé as he took on different roles within the organization, eventually becoming executive director for Europe in 1986 and overall executive director in 1989. By then the so-called Brundtland report, *Our Common Future* (1987), had begun to popularize the idea that wealth should only be created in any one generation in ways that did not jeopardize the prospects of future generations—in a nutshell, sustainable development.

Sandbrook's tenure as executive director was later characterized by one close colleague as 'five parts inspiration, four parts perspiration and just one part administration' (private information). He was endlessly pursuing the next pot of money from donor governments or charitable foundations, but somehow there was always time to support other people's 'breakthrough initiatives' (such as Bob Geldof's Band Aid) and to establish enduring spin-offs such as Earthscan Books. It was for his services to the UK Overseas Development Administration that he was appointed OBE in 1990.

In its early years the institute had been very apprehensive about working with big business, but when Sandbrook returned from the 'earth summit' in Rio de Janeiro in 1992 he set out on a path to establishing and getting involved in a number of ground-breaking initiatives that brought the influence and resources of multinational companies to bear on a range of sustainability challenges. One of the first outcomes was the report *Towards a Sustainable Paper Cycle* (1996), which looked at ways of reducing the massive environmental and social impacts of the pulp and paper industry. This led on to a similar but more controversial project with the mining industry (from which the International Council on Mining and Metals emerged), and further work with the United Nations Development Programme as part of its 'growing sustainable business' initiative. But even Sandbrook's astonishing mediating skills were put to the test in projects with both BP and Shell International in 'hot spots' like Colombia and Nigeria. Radical environmental organizations looked on askance at his strategy.

The reason for Sandbrook's engagement with 'big business' was not so much ideological as tactical: he just couldn't see a way of making solutions work without the enthusiastic participation of the business community. Most of his new ventures after leaving the International Institute for Environment and Development in 1999 reflected that pragmatic urgency, including his activity as a founder trustee of Forum for the Future, as non-executive director of the Eden Project in Cornwall from 1999 to 2003, and as vice-chairman (and for a short while acting chief executive) of Plantlife, a conservation charity that gave full rein to his own personal passion for plants and gardening. The focus on British initiatives (together with his work as an adviser to the prince of Wales) helped him cut back on what had always been a punishing amount of international travel, which in turn generated an endless flow of amusing and often improbable anecdotes. Despite such adventures, he was never happier than when at home with Mary and their two sons—especially in their garden in Wimbledon. He died at St George's Hospital, Tooting, on 11 December 2005, of cancer. His wife and children survived him.

Sandbrook's interest in the environment had started in the early 1970s, and remained his abiding passion as the rest of the world gradually awoke to the seriousness of the environmental crisis. He had a profound influence both on the environmental movement and on the world of international development. He was a much-loved friend to countless people all over the world, and a man who understood the joy and the importance of constant conviviality. In July 2006 his life and work were celebrated at a gathering in central London. Many people commented at the time that it wasn't until they looked back over everything he had achieved that the real significance of his work became apparent. JONATHON PORRITT

Sources *The Independent* (13 Dec 2005) · *The Times* (14 Dec 2005) · *Daily Telegraph* (14 Dec 2005) · *The Guardian* (16 Dec 2005) · personal knowledge (2009) · private information (2009) · b. cert. · m. cert. · d. cert.

Likenesses obituary photographs · photograph, Eden Project; also PA Photos, London [*see illus.*]

Wealth at death £773,940: probate, 1 June 2006, *CGPLA Eng. & Wales*

Sapper, Alan Louis Geoffrey (1931–2006), trade unionist, was born on 18 March 1931 at 59 Bridge Avenue, Hammersmith, London, the youngest of three sons of Max Sapper, land surveyor and accountant, who would later die prematurely of wounds sustained during the Second World War, and his wife, Katie, formerly Williams, *née* Laketer. At the time of his birth registration his parents lived at 7 Beauclerk Road, Hammersmith. The family were secular Jews proud of the radical Jewish cultural tradition. Both parents were supporters of the Spanish republican cause, and Sapper's mother had been a suffragette. Both Sapper and his older brother Laurie were heavily influenced by their parents' radicalism and emphasis on active participation in politics. At the age of fourteen Laurie tried to cross the frontier into Spain to enlist with the International Brigades; he later joined the Communist Party and became general secretary of the University Teachers' Union.

Sapper won a scholarship from Brackenbury Road primary school to Latymer Upper School and left aged seventeen to work at Kew Gardens as a botanist. He subsequently obtained an external degree from London University. He joined the Labour Party at the age of seventeen and became a union shop steward at Kew. This inhibited his chances of promotion despite his successful work identifying (for example) numerous new classes of ferns.

In 1958 Sapper left Kew to become assistant to the general secretary of the Association of Cinematograph, Television and Allied Technicians (ACTT). While in this post, he married, on 19 April 1959 at Ohel Shem Beth Hamedrash (synagogue), Willesden Green, Helen Rubens, a 23-year-old medical practitioner, and daughter of John Rubens, general dealer. They had one son and one daughter. After three years as general secretary of the Writers' Guild (1964–7) Sapper returned to the ACTT as deputy general secretary and then, in 1969, became general secretary—the youngest in the trade-union movement. He held this post until the ACTT's merger with another union in 1991 (which he helped bring about) to form the Broadcasting, Entertainment, Cinematograph and Theatre Union (BECTU).

Although Sapper's union was small he reached the highest levels of position and influence in the trade-union movement because he was perceived as a man of total integrity and high intellect. He secured the respect of the leaders of the three biggest unions—Jack Jones (Transport and General Workers' Union), Hugh Scanlon (Amalgamated Engineering Union), and Alan Fisher (National Union of Public Employees). He was elected to the general council of the TUC in 1969, serving until 1984.

Sapper was a man of his times. His period of leadership in the trade-union movement coincided with its greatest size, strength, influence, and radicalism. Battles within the trade unions had a major influence on national politics. Thus the internal battles were often as bitter and personal as the battles with the employers and the government. The politics had three strands illustrated by differing attitudes to the anti-apartheid struggle in South Africa and the class struggle in Britain. There was the right wing, often described by the press as 'moderates', who regarded Nelson Mandela as a dangerous terrorist and shied away from confrontation over wages and conditions for British workers. Sapper often dubbed the extreme right as 'extreme moderates'. Exactly opposite were the extreme left—who sneered at the African National Congress and Mandela as merely bourgeois reformists and who regarded any form of settlement of industrial disputes as a betrayal. Sapper avoided both tendencies, adhering to what was known as the broad left position, which unequivocally supported the African National Congress and while fighting hard for wages and conditions recognized that there came a point when these struggles could not continue indefinitely and had to result in a settlement. The skill was to settle for the maximum that was realistically possible.

The intense antagonism towards Sapper from the right and extreme left meant that for two decades he was fighting battles in his back yard. For example in 1982 he was the natural candidate for chairman of the TUC, having served on the general council longer than any other member who had not held that office. The right wing tried to block him with the support of the extreme left, only failing by the narrowest margin. In 1986 there was an attempt to dismiss him from his post in the ACTT that involved the same unholy alliance. Sapper, refusing compromise, narrowly held on, at one point by a single vote.

Despite the allegations of the extreme left that he was too soft with employers Sapper was a thorn in the flesh of the commercial companies that ran the film and television industries. He saw no contradiction between on the one hand the high level of industrial militancy leading to an improvement in pay and conditions and on the other hand his profound concern for the health and success of the British film and television industries. He believed that good salaries and conditions of work improved the status and thus the professionalism of his members. This view brought him into conflict with the owners of the film and television companies, leading to several major strikes, like one in 1979 that took ITV off the air for ten weeks and resulted in pay increases for his members of around 45 per cent, and a less successful one against new working practices at TV-am in 1987, which failed to prevent a large number of redundancies. During such industrial disputes Sapper was regularly branded by the employers and by much of the press as a wrecker. At the same time he enjoyed cordial relations with creative leaders of the industry such as David Putnam, Richard Attenborough, and Alan Parker. The head of the National Film School, Colin Young, was a close personal friend. Sapper was a governor of the National Film School (1980–95) and the British Film Institute (1974–95). After his retirement from the ACTT in 1991 he founded Interconnect AV, a company supporting British film-making; he finally retired as its chief executive in 2000.

Even his bitterest enemies recognized that Sapper was a civilized, witty, and erudite man. In his early years he had harboured ambitions of becoming a television playwright; he wrote two unpublished plays for stage, 'On Licence' and 'Kith and Kin', and in 1961 his television play *The Return* was broadcast. He was known for his love of good food and wine, which he consumed without abandoning his left-wing principles. Ill-health dogged his later years and he died in London on 19 May 2006 after a long illness. He was survived by his wife and their two children, Simon, a trade-union official, and Sarah, a film producer.

MICHAEL SEIFERT

Sources *Daily Telegraph* (22 May 2006) • *The Times* (23 May 2006); (25 May 2006) • *The Guardian* (23 May 2006); (13 June 2006); (8 July 2006) • *The Independent* (27 May 2006) • *Morning Star* (29 May 2006) • *WW* (2006) • personal knowledge (2010) • private information (2010) • b. cert. • m. cert.
Archives FILM BFINA, current affairs footage | SOUND BL NSA, documentary recordings
Likenesses photograph, 1985, Getty Images, London, Hult. Arch. • photograph, 1997, Photoshot, London • obituary photographs
Wealth at death £652,223: probate, 23 Oct 2006, *CGPLA Eng. & Wales*

Sargant, Naomi Ellen, Lady McIntosh of Haringey (1933–2006), broadcaster and educationist, was born on 10 December 1933 at 42 Talbot Road, Hornsey, London, the younger daughter of Thomas (Tom) Sargant, then a bank clerk, later a metal merchant and later still first secretary of Justice, which campaigned for the rule of law and against miscarriages of justice, and his wife, Marie Anna, *née* Hloušková, a philologist, later active in the wartime Czech government in exile. At the time of her birth registration her parents lived at 93 Hornsey Lane, Highgate, London. She was educated at the Friends' School, Saffron Walden, and at Bedford College, London, where she was active in national student politics and took an honours degree in sociology. On 2 January 1954 she married Peter Joseph Kelly, a fellow student and educationist, later professor of education at the Chelsea College of Science and Technology; they had one son. The marriage ended in divorce, and Sargant married, as her second husband, on 15 May 1962, Andrew Robert McIntosh (1933–2010), then a market research executive, later a Labour politician on the Greater London council (where he was leader of the opposition in 1980–81) and in the House of Lords (having been made Baron McIntosh of Haringey in 1982). They had a further two sons.

After twelve years in market and social research Naomi Sargant (who reverted to using her maiden name in professional life following the ennoblement of her second husband) became a senior lecturer at Enfield College of Technology, where she was an enthusiast for the Robbins agenda of expanding access to higher education to all who might benefit from it, and notably those who, having missed an opportunity on leaving school, sought to return later. In 1970 she joined the Open University—the most important post-war innovation in increasing opportunities for adult education—at its inception, initially as a senior lecturer in research methods. There she later became Britain's first woman pro-vice-chancellor (for student affairs, 1974–8), then professor of applied social research (1978–81). As pro-vice-chancellor for student affairs she became the voice of students, fronting the Open Forum radio and television feedback programmes, and investigating their patterns of study, providing invaluable information with which tutors could improve learners' experiences, and earning her an international reputation for groundbreaking studies into mature students' learning.

In 1981 Sargant moved to help establish the educational role of a second major innovative institution when she was appointed as the founding senior commissioning editor for educational programming at Channel 4 television. There her unusual combination of skills, as an expert in adult education, in market research, and in the potential educational uses of broadcast technologies, opened a wealth of new opportunities for learning to adults. She commissioned a highly regarded body of programmes that were clearly educational yet spanned the full spectrum of the channel's programming—in the arts and sciences, environment, health, history, consumer advice, gardening (a lifelong passion), and food and wine, as well as in adult literacy and numeracy. There were programmes that addressed directly the interests of older people, people with disabilities, and people with more time than money; and she ensured that the educational possibilities of news and drama were exploited through the extensive range of back-up materials available to viewers wanting to follow up the programmes afterwards. She had a flair for finding the people who could turn ideas into popular, accessible programmes, was a powerful champion of women's opportunities in the media, and had a knack with titles, and an infectious if sometimes exhausting energy. In recognition of her work she was admitted to the Royal Television Society hall of fame in 1996.

Throughout her career Sargant had a focus on how to make lifelong learning accessible to all, and especially to those previously excluded. She wrote widely and contributed to a sequence of national inquiries into lifelong learning policy. For the Advisory Committee on Adult and Continuing Education (1976–82), chaired by Richard Hoggart, she was the principal author of its seminal report, *Continuing Education: from Principles to Practice* (1982). She made similar important contributions to the work of Helena Kennedy's report on widening access to further education, *Learning Works* (1997), and to Bob Fryer's report on lifelong learning, *Learning for the Twenty-First Century* (1997). After she left Channel 4 in 1989 she led the research of the National Institute of Adult Continuing Education, firmly establishing the importance of participation studies in identifying effective strategies for engaging adults who had previously missed out in education. She was awarded an honorary doctorate by the Open University in 2005.

Sargant was an indefatigable public intellectual, a lifelong socialist, and a passionate and brilliant advocate, active in a wide range of civil society organizations. She was, among other things, a trustee of the National Extension College (1975–97), pro-chancellor of the University of East London (1992–4), chair of the Great Ormond Street Hospital NHS trust (1997–2000), vice-chair (1998–2001) then president (2001–6) of the Open College of the Arts, a councillor on Haringey borough council (1964–8), and president of the Highgate Horticultural Society (listing gardening as her recreation in *Who's Who*). Her commitment to consumer interests was forged in an early association with Michael Young, the social entrepreneur. She chaired the National Gas Consumers' Council (1977–80), was president of the National Society for Clean Air (1981–3), and served on the National Consumer Council (1978–81), the Energy Commission (1978–9), the Commission on Energy and the Environment (1979–81), and as vice-chair of the National Council of Voluntary Organisations (1992–8). She died of cancer in London on 23 July 2006. A selection of her writings was published posthumously as *Lifelong Learning: a Brave and Proper Vision* (2009). She was survived by her husband, Lord McIntosh of Haringey, and her three sons. ALAN TUCKETT

Sources *Times Educational Supplement* (28 July 2006) · *The Guardian* (28 July 2006); (4 Aug 2006) · *The Times* (11 Aug 2006) · Great Ormond Street Hospital for Sick Children NHS trust press release, www.ich.ucl.ac.uk/pressoffice/pressrelease_00458, 20 March 2009 · Royal Television Society magazine, www.rts.org.uk, 20 March 2009 · NIACE, Leicester, N. Sargant MSS · *WW* (2004) · personal knowledge (2010) · private information (2010) · b. cert. · m. certs.

Archives NIACE, Leicester

Likenesses obituary photographs

Wealth at death £702,318: probate, 5 Dec 2006, *CGPLA Eng. & Wales*

Saunders, Dame Cicely Mary Strode (1918–2005), physician and founder of the modern hospice movement, was born on 22 June 1918 at Linden Lodge, Bedford Avenue, Barnet, Hertfordshire, the daughter of (Philip) Gordon Saunders (*d.* 1961), land surveyor, and his wife, Mary Christian, *née* Knight (*d.* 1968). She had two brothers, John (*b.* 1920) and Christopher (*b.* 1926). Her supportive father became a senior partner with the estate agents John D. Wood & Co. His children enjoyed all the material comforts of a prosperous family, although Saunders later spoke of having a very distant relationship with her mother. Tall and shy, she described herself as 'sadly unpopular' at school (Saunders and Swann, 58). At the age of fourteen she was sent to Roedean School. Initially unhappy, she eventually made friends and became head of house.

In 1938 Saunders went to St Anne's College, Oxford, to read philosophy, politics, and economics, her parents having disapproved of her earlier ambition to become a nurse. In 1940, after the outbreak of the Second World

Dame Cicely Mary Strode Saunders (1918–2005), by Carolyn Djanogly, 1999

War, she interrupted her studies to begin training as a nurse at St Thomas's Hospital in London. She described that period as 'the first time in my life I felt I really belonged and fitted in' (Saunders and Swann, 58). The friendships she made with her nursing set continued for the rest of her life and it was at this time that she deepened her love of music and enjoyed singing in a choir. Four years later, to her bitter disappointment, she was forced to leave nursing following the exacerbation of spinal problems that had troubled her since childhood. She returned to Oxford, gained a war degree, and in 1945 qualified with a diploma in public and social administration. She began training as a hospital almoner at St Thomas's Hospital.

It was while working as an almoner at London's Archway Hospital in 1947 that Saunders met the first of three Polish men who were to change the course of her life. David Tasma was a Jewish refugee from the Warsaw ghetto and she was drawn to his lonely suffering. A close relationship developed and they discussed the idea of creating a more home-like environment where those coming to the end of their lives could be offered hope and comfort. When Tasma died in 1948 he left her £500 'to be a window in your home' (du Boulay, 58). It was Tasma who told Saunders, 'I want only what is in your mind and in your heart' (ibid., 56). Saunders quoted this in speeches throughout her life, emphasizing that good care required both scientific rigour and loving compassion.

Saunders's life's work was now determined. Her vision to establish her own home for the dying was underpinned by her religious faith, discovered while on holiday in Cornwall with Christian friends. It was, she said, 'as if a switch had flipped' (du Boulay, 49). In order to understand more about the needs of the dying she began work as a volunteer at St Luke's, a home for the dying in Bayswater. Norman Barrett, a surgeon, told her that if she wanted to make an impact she must study medicine: 'It's the doctors who desert the dying', he said (ibid., 63). Saunders commenced medical training in 1951; she graduated MB BS in 1957 and took up a research fellowship at St Mary's School of Medicine in 1958.

To further her studies of pain management in the incurably ill Saunders started work at St Joseph's, a Catholic hospice for the dying poor in Hackney. She was well accepted by the nuns and began to encourage the regular use of oral opioids rather than pursue the standard hospital practice of inadequate and infrequent injections of morphine that left many patients abandoned to uncontrolled pain and ignored by doctors, who saw dying as failure. She began to formulate her concept of total pain: the need to pay attention to social, emotional, and spiritual needs, as well as delivering a systematic approach to symptom control. Her ideas were first published in 1958 in an article, 'Dying of cancer', in *St Thomas's Hospital Gazette*. She described 'a team who work together to relieve where they cannot heal, to keep the patient's own struggle within his compass and to bring hope and consolation to the end'. This was followed by an influential series of six articles for the *Nursing Times* in 1959, which received favourable reviews in *The Lancet*. Saunders began to lecture widely, using personal stories of patients' suffering based on over 1000 meticulously recorded case histories. These narratives were to have a huge impact on the increasing numbers of clinicians who came to hear her speak.

It was while she was at St Joseph's that Saunders met a second Pole, Antoni Michniewicz. They had a passionate, spiritual relationship confined to short meetings on the ward. She later said, 'I loved him very much … he taught me what it was like to be dying and to be bereaved' (*Daily Telegraph*). The deaths soon afterwards of 'Mrs G', another patient with whom Saunders had enjoyed a mutually supportive friendship for over seven years, and of her father in 1961, left Saunders prostrated by grief. None the less she continued to pour her energies into planning and fundraising for her own hospice, to be called St Christopher's, after the patron saint of travellers.

By the end of 1959 Saunders had drawn up a ten-page proposal for the hospice and St Christopher's was registered as a charity in 1961. In 1963 her brother Christopher found her a site on Lawrie Park Road in Sydenham and building began in 1965. Saunders worked tirelessly and discovered a remarkable talent for marshalling others to her cause, including major charitable trusts, London's merchant companies, and members of the British establishment. St Christopher's admitted its first patients in 1967, the opening ceremony being performed by Princess Alexandra, St Christopher's patron. Subsequently Saunders commented that it took '19 years to build the home around the window'. She had initially thought of creating an Anglican religious community but broadened her vision so that St Christopher's became a place that welcomed staff and patients of any faith or none, thus creating a model capable of wide adaptation. However, Saunders's strong Christian faith was a fundamental factor in her commitment to the dying and remained an anchor throughout her life. She was a long-standing opponent of the legalization of euthanasia and was an important influence on the report by the Church of England, *On Dying Well* (1975), which rejected the argument for euthanasia, asserting that everyone should have the right 'to die well', without pain and with dignity.

The opening of St Christopher's is widely recognized as the birth of the modern hospice movement and the next twenty years saw a surge of interest in Saunders's new approach to the care of the dying, particularly in the United States where she undertook lecture tours in 1963, 1965, and 1966. Inspired by meeting Saunders, Florence Wald, dean of the Yale University school of nursing, established the first hospice home care team in America at New Haven. Saunders was to be medical director of St Christopher's for the next eighteen years. She was primarily an outstanding bedside clinician but was determined to evaluate the new approaches to care and recruited a team of leaders in their fields to do so. The professor of pharmacology at St Mary's Hospital in London, Harold Stewart, was the chairman of St Christopher's research committee. He was supported by John Hinton, professor of psychiatry at the Middlesex, who wrote a widely influential Penguin paperback, *Dying*, in 1967, and undertook significant studies on the quality of the care that was being delivered. Robert Twycross worked as research fellow at St Christopher's and began the programme of studies on oral morphine and diamorphine which were to revolutionize the practice of the relief of chronic pain, demonstrating that morphine given orally in the right dose, at the right interval, could provide constant pain relief without addiction.

Saunders always believed that 'hospice' referred not to a building but to a philosophy of care that needed a sound academic footing in order to become an integral part of general healthcare systems. The fifty-four in-patient beds at St Christopher's were quickly followed by the development in 1969 of the first service to deliver care to patients in their own homes, led by Mary Baines, a local GP who had helped with weekend on-call cover for the hospice. Colin Murray Parkes from the Tavistock Institute supported the development of care for family and friends and the bereavement service was launched in 1970, followed by day care.

Saunders emphasized that the St Christopher's model should not be slavishly copied but needed adapting to local needs and cultures, as her voluminous correspondence supporting service developments across the world demonstrated. She enjoyed her increasing acclaim but was never too busy to respond to those with a genuine interest in care of the dying. She understood that hospices could never respond to the needs of all and that education would be vital in the drive to improve care of the dying in other settings. In 1973 a purpose-built study centre was opened. Gillian Ford, then deputy chief medical officer for England, was seconded to St Christopher's to oversee its development, and by the time of Saunders's death over 50,000 healthcare professionals had trained there. Ford was to be instrumental in achieving recognition of palliative medicine as a speciality by the Royal College of Physicians. Another friend from medical school days, Tom West, returned from work as a missionary doctor in Africa to become Saunders's deputy in 1973 and medical director in 1985, when Saunders retired from the role to become chairman of council.

Throughout her life Saunders wrote and taught, enjoying international lecture tours. In the eighteen years of her medical directorship, she was the author of over eighty-five publications, some of them translated into several languages; these included the edited volumes *Management of Terminal Malignant Disease* (1978) and *Living with Dying* (1983). She received prizes and honours from many countries including more than twenty-five honorary degrees. In 1977 she became the first person for more than 100 years to receive an honorary doctorate of medicine from the archbishop of Canterbury, and in 1987 she was awarded the British Medical Association's gold medal for services to medicine. Other honours included the Onassis prize for services to humanity (1989) and the Franklin D. Roosevelt four freedoms medal for worship (2000). She was made a DBE in 1980 and in 1989 received the rare honour of entry into the Order of Merit. In 2001 St Christopher's was awarded the Conrad N. Hilton humanitarian prize of $1 million, which Saunders received on behalf of the hospice from Kofi Annan, secretary-general of the United Nations, in New York.

On 31 January 1980, in the parish church of St Philip in Sydenham, Saunders married the third Pole in her life, Marian Bohusz-Szyszko (1901/2–1995). He was seventeen years her senior and the relationship was to provide the sense of personal joy and confidence she had sought all her life. Bohusz was an artist and the couple had met in 1963 when he was exhibiting in London. Saunders admired his intense religious works and bought one for the walls of the hospice. A long friendship began and Bohusz became artist in residence at St Christopher's, setting up a studio in the hospice. After the marriage his health became ever poorer and he died at St Christopher's in 1995. In Bohusz's later years Saunders became increasingly involved in his nursing care and more tied to the house they shared at 51 Lawrie Park Gardens, close to the hospice. After his death she once again began to lecture and travel. In 1998 her eightieth birthday was celebrated with a conference in her honour at the Royal College of Physicians, London. In 2000 she retired as chairman of St Christopher's to become founder-president and helped in the development of Cicely Saunders International, a new foundation to further international research in palliative care. She continued to go into her office in the hospice on most days.

Saunders's vision of holistic care, supporting family as well as patient, caught the imagination of the public as well as professionals. She was the subject of a biography, many articles in newspapers and popular magazines, television documentaries, and films for professional audiences. She was photographed on hundreds of occasions and her husband painted her portrait several times. Two images stand out: a bronze head, which captures her unflinching determination, completed by the sculptor Nigel Boonham in 2001; and the portrait commissioned from Catherine Goodman for the National Portrait Gallery, and unveiled there in April 2005 in Saunders's presence.

Saunders was an imposing and sometimes intimidating figure in whom personal motivation and professional aspirations combined to create a vision that changed the practice of medicine and transformed the care of the dying. People everywhere responded to Saunders's insistence that death must not be seen as failure, but as part of life and to her assertion that people should be able to live until they die. As she put it, 'You matter because you are you and you matter to the last moment of your life. We will do all we can to help you, not only to die peacefully but to live until you die' (*Nursing Times*, 1976, 72.1003–5). Her energy and enthusiasm were irrepressible; she often commented, 'There is still so much more to be done.' She was an inspirational leader. She also had a wonderful sense of humour and an inclination to gossip, and took pleasure in a daily 'whisky on the rocks'. By the time of her death there were some 200 hospices in the UK and similar programmes in 115 countries across the world. She died in St Christopher's Hospice of metastatic breast cancer on 14 July 2005. She continued to see visitors up to the end and remembered, close to her own death, to ask after the dying father of one of her nurses. Following cremation at Beckenham crematorium on 29 July her ashes were buried on 2 September, with those of her husband, in the garden of St Christopher's. Over 2000 people attended the memorial service held on 8 March 2006 in Westminster Abbey. BARBARA MONROE

Sources C. Saunders and Y. Swann, 'When I was a child', *Woman's Weekly* (17 Dec 1991), 58 [interview] • D. Clark, ed., *Cicely Saunders, founder of the hospice movement: selected letters, 1959–1999* (2002) • D. Clark and others, *A bit of heaven for the few? An oral history of the hospice movement in the United Kingdom* (2005) • *The Times* (15 July 2005) • *Daily Telegraph* (15 July 2005) • *The Independent* (15 July 2005) • *The Guardian* (16 July 2005) • *BMJ* (23 July 2005) • *The Lancet* (20 Aug 2005) • *Pain*, 118 (2005) • S. du Boulay, *Cicely Saunders: founder of the modern hospice movement* (1984) • D. Clark, introduction, in C. Saunders, *Cicely Saunders: selected writings, 1958–2004* (2006) • *WW* (2005) • Burke, *Peerage* • private information (2009) • personal knowledge (2009) • b. cert. • m. cert. • d. cert.

Archives King's Lond., personal memorabilia, diaries, photographs and other items [http://www.kcl.ac.uk/iss/archives/] • Lancaster University, End of Life Observatory, letters, writings and other archives [http://www.eolobservatory.net/history/index.htm] | FILM BFINA, *The Frost interview*, M. Catherwood (director), BBC2, 19 Sept 1974 • BFINA, 'A window in your home', *The light of experience*, J. Wilcox (producer), BBC2, 19 Sept 1976 • BFINA, 'St Christopher's Hospice', *Songs of praise*, S. Hammond (producer), BBC1, 31 Jan 1988 • BFINA, current affairs footage • BFINA, performance footage • Madison Deane Initiative, 'Pioneers of hospice: changing the face of dying', 2005 [www.pioneersofhospice.org] | SOUND BL NSA, *In the psychiatrist's chair*, with A. Clare, BBC Radio 4, 28 July 1985, NP9353/01 • BL NSA, *Profile*, 'Cicely Saunders', with B. Jackson, NP5168R • BL NSA, current affairs recording

Likenesses M. Bohusz, oils, 1970–79, St Christopher's Hospice, London • photographs, 1977–81, Photoshot, London • photographs, 1977–2001, Getty Images, London • photographs, 1977–2001, PA Photos, London • M. Bohusz, oils, 1980–89, St Christopher's Hospice, London • J. Bown, photograph, 1989–90, repro. in *The Observer* • A.-K. Purkiss, bromide fibre print, 1990, NPG • S. Amery, bronze bust, 1990–99, St Thomas's Hospital, London • G. Bruce, brush monochrome on prepared paper, 1992, Royal Collection • N. Sinclair, bromide print, 1995, NPG • C. Djanogly, bromide print, 1999, NPG [*see illus.*] • C. Djanogly, photographs, 1999, repro. in *Centurions: a photographic tribute to 100 men and women who have changed the face of 20th century Britain* (1999) • photographs, 1999–2003, Camera Press, London • N. Boonham, bronze head, 2001, St Christopher's Hospice, London • C. Goodman, oils, 2005, NPG • M. McCartney, photograph, repro. in *Good Housekeeping* (Oct 2002) • obituary photographs

Wealth at death £949,971: probate, 22 Dec 2005, *CGPLA Eng. & Wales*

Scannell, Vernon [*real name* John Vernon Bain] (**1922–2007**), poet and novelist, was born at his parents' home, 6 Tennyson Green, Skegness, Lincolnshire, on 23 January 1922, the second of the three children of James Bain, photographer's assistant, and his wife, Elsie Mabel, *née* Wrate. The family subsequently lived for periods in co. Roscommon in Ireland, in Beeston near Nottingham, and in Lancashire, before settling in 1931 in Aylesbury, Buckinghamshire, where James Bain had his own photography studio. With his elder brother, Kenneth, Vernon was admitted to Queen's Park Boys' School, which he attended from the age of eight until reaching school leaving age in 1936. (In 2009 the school became an arts centre, and a plaque is displayed in his memory at the main entrance.)

At Queen's Park, Vernon Bain received some minor encouragement from one teacher for his attempts to write stories. But his profound devotion to literature and music was developed mainly as a process of self-education shared with his brother Kenneth (the recipient of his first poems) in resistance to a cruel father. The latter, Vernon wrote later, created in the family home 'a background dark and heavy with fear, shame and hatred'. He later adopted 'Scannell', a name appearing on an identity card he bought from a merchant sailor, as 'an act of symbolic dissociation' (*Drums of Morning*, 7). Important in these early years was his talent for boxing, at which he became a national schoolboy champion, but by the age of seventeen he was convinced that he was destined to be a poet.

Scannell's principal employment in the years before the Second World War was as a clerk in an accountant's firm. Rejected when volunteering for flying duties in the RAF owing to colour blindness, he enlisted in the Argyll and Sutherland Highlanders in January 1940. He served in the Gordon Highlanders in north Africa and Normandy, and was wounded near Caen. He was initially reticent about his long war service, declaring in the first of his four volumes of autobiography, *The Tiger and the Rose* (1971), that he could 'only present it in a fragmentary way' (p. 84). Having experienced sheer terror and seen appalling carnage, he felt justified, at the end of the war in May 1945, in deserting, walking out on the army and warfare in general after his recovery from his severe personal injuries in a military hospital in Scotland.

Scannell's period on the run in London and in Leeds, where a lucky introduction to Bonamy Dobrée, professor of English at the university, enabled him to attend lectures and use student facilities, marked the beginning of his serious ambition to make a career as a writer. This period of wary freedom came to an end when he was arrested, court-martialled, and dispatched to a psychiatric hospital after his judges heard that he wrote poetry. Discharged after three months with no further obligation to the army, he started to place the poems he was producing in national journals and smaller magazines, notwithstanding what he described as his 'irreconcilable passions for boxing and literature' (*The Tiger and the Rose*, 81). In 1948 he published a first volume, which he later rejected as 'a woolly and wordy collection', and worked as a boxer in fairground booths. By 1953 he had finished and published a first novel, *The Fight*. A second, *The Face of the Enemy*, appeared one year later, but despite all this activity he lived a hand-to-mouth existence. Early in 1954, in London, he met Josephine Elspeth (Jo) Higson (*b*. 1924/5), painter, daughter of Claude Higson, company director. They married on 1 October 1954 at Kensington register office, and had three sons and two daughters.

Scannell's first widely recognized book of poems, *A Mortal Pitch*, appeared in 1957, at a time when he was working as a teacher of English in a preparatory school in Surrey. A characteristic note of rueful romanticism—how to balance life and love with the demands and disciplines of art—was immediately established. *The Masks of Love* (1960) added a recognizable urban world of streets, parks, and bars, although his family life in the country was a new and moving theme. With further volumes like *Walking Wounded* (1965), *Epithets of War* (1969), and *The Loving Game* (1975)—altogether seven books were represented in his *New and Collected Poems* (1980)—he became a poet of considerable formal skill and resource, confidently broadening his treatment of such subjects as personal memories of war, boxing, love (a more painful experience), drink and drinkers, the process of ageing, the fear of death.

Almost throughout his career Scannell continued to publish novels, notable among them *The Big Time* (1965) and *Ring of Truth* (1983), both concerned with boxing, and finally *Feminine Endings* (2000), a satirical comedy about a bibulous poet tutoring a residential creative writing course. His fiction showed a talent for vigorous narrative and convincing background detail, which reviewers readily acknowledged, but it failed to achieve the solid critical reputation of his poetry. On the other hand his four autobiographical books won much critical appreciation and enjoyed a wider readership. His method in each was to begin with his life in the present (in his 1977 volume, *A Proper Gentleman*, for example, when he was an incongruous writer-in-residence on a bleak council estate), then to break off to revisit the past. In *The Tiger and the Rose* (1971) he wrote comprehensively about his difficult childhood and his employment as a fairground pugilist; *Argument of Kings* (1987) extended his account of wartime experience; and *Drums of Morning* (1992) revisited his childhood and adolescence. All are compellingly readable, notable for their authenticity, candour, and humanity—and a sense of humour that survives the privations and the suffering.

For most of his post-war life Scannell's income came from the activities increasingly available to—and expected of—an outgoing professional writer: public readings (including poetry-and-jazz concerts), conducting writing courses, producing reviews and critical studies, providing fiction and verse for children. He was several times a writer-in-residence. He received the Heinemann award for *The Masks of Love*, and *The Loving Game* was a Poetry Book Society choice. He was given a Cholmondeley award for his achievement in poetry in 1974, and in 1981 he received a civil list pension for services to literature.

Later books like *Winterlude* (1982) and *A Time for Fires* (1991) confirmed Scannell's ability to master the craft of writing in virtually any verse form; the poems are consistently skilful, as well as serene and sharply observant. A large *Collected Poems* appeared in 1993, and he continued to write and publish numerous individual poems, booklets, and pamphlets right up to his death. During those years he maintained a warm and lively correspondence with his fellow poets and friends, always eager to give his views on the contemporaries about whom he felt strongly, whether the feeling was firm admiration or emphatic doubt.

Scannell and his wife drifted apart in the 1970s, and from 1979 to 1985 his partner was Angela Beese. From 1992 onwards he lived in Otley, Yorkshire, with Jo Peters, who looked after him until his death (from cancer and emphysema) in Otley on 17 November 2007. His marriage to Jo Higson was never dissolved; she survived him, as did his partner Jo Peters, and four of his children (one son having predeceased him). ALAN BROWNJOHN

Sources V. Scannell, *The tiger and the rose* (1971) • V. Scannell, *A proper gentleman* (1977) • V. Scannell, *Argument of kings* (1987) • V. Scannell, *Drums of morning* (1992) • *Daily Telegraph* (19 Nov 2007) • *The Guardian* (19 Nov 2007); (23 Nov 2007) • *The Independent* (19 Nov 2007) • *The Times* (20 Nov 2007) • *Yorkshire Post* (23 Nov 2007) • *TLS* (5 Dec 2007) • biography and recordings, www.poetryarchive.org/poetryarchive/singlePoet.do?poetId=35, 23 June 2010, Poetry Archive • biography, www.warpoets.org/conflicts/ww2/scannell/, 23 June 2010, War Poets Association • *WW* (2007) • personal knowledge (2011) • private information (2011) • b. cert. • m. cert.

Archives BL, notebook with poems • Ransom HRC • U. Leeds, Brotherton L., draft autobiography • University of Calgary | NL Wales, Dannie Abse papers • U. Reading L., Bodley Head papers | SOUND BL NSA, documentary recordings • BL NSA, performance recordings • Poetry Archive, http://www.poetryarchive.org/poetryarchive/singlePoet.do?poetId=35

Likenesses L. Silbert, bromide print, 1972, NPG • C. Harris, portrait, repro. in www.warpoets.org/conflicts/ww2/scannell/ • obituary photographs

Wealth at death under £189,000: probate, 23 July 2008, *CGPLA Eng. & Wales*

Schofield [*née* Smith; *other married name* Matheson], **Sylvia Anne Terry** (**1916–2006**), writer and traveller, was born on 28 May 1916 at 113 Ramsden Road, Balham, London, the elder daughter of William Horace Smith, architect and chartered surveyor, and his wife, Annie, *née* Terry, a Salvation Army officer. Her father took the name Terry-Smith when his office began sharing a building with the stationer W. H. Smith; she became known as Sylvia Terry-Smith. She left Wimbledon Technical College at the age of sixteen, but took evening classes at Wimbledon School of Art while working as a freelance journalist.

After the outbreak of the Second World War Sylvia Terry-Smith joined the monitoring service of the BBC, where she met Angus Matheson (1912–1962), son of Malcolm Matheson, a minister in the Outer Hebrides. They married at Kingston and Surbiton Presbyterian Church on 19 December 1941, and although the marriage ended in divorce in 1950 she later published all her non-fiction books under the name Sylvia A. Matheson. A monitor at the BBC at the time of their marriage, Angus Matheson went on to become professor of Celtic languages and literatures at the University of Glasgow. After her transfer to the political intelligence department of the Foreign Office, the cover name for the political warfare executive, Sylvia Matheson prepared news reports and wrote propaganda pamphlets to be dropped behind enemy lines. Shortly before the end of the war she went to Florence as a field correspondent attached to the headquarters of General Mark Clark, commander-in-chief of the allied forces in Italy, and in May 1945 she witnessed the unconditional surrender of all the German troops in Italy.

Interested in Asia ever since she was a child, Sylvia Matheson went to India after the war, working as a journalist and advertising copywriter, and in 1946 made her first visit to Baluchistan. After collecting potsherds and beads at a prehistoric site at Nushki, in the Chagai district of Baluchistan, she took her collection to Delhi to Mortimer Wheeler, director-general of the Archaeological Survey of India, and he suggested she take it to London, to the Institute of Archaeology and the British Museum. This led to a year's study of field archaeology at the Institute of Archaeology, before she took a job as a copywriter with the advertising agency J. Walter Thompson. But she never gave up the idea of going back to Asia, and in 1955 she accepted an invitation from the leader of the prehistoric section of the French archaeological delegation in Afghanistan to join an excavation of a site dating back to 3000 BC at Mundigak, near Kandahar, in Afghanistan. She described her five months in the high, bare, mountainous, desert area in *Time off to Dig* (1961), not so much an account of the excavations as a description of her travels, her French colleagues, and the Afghan workers and their families, the meals and parties, and the scorpions, beetles, and ants. As Wheeler wrote in his introduction to the book, 'all that the professional archaeologist ignores in his record is here chronicled with shameless gusto' (*Time off to Dig*, 9). She left Mundigak feeling that she had caught a glimpse of the lives of people who had lived there two or three thousand years before the birth of Christ. While still in Afghanistan she was asked by *The Times* to report on the visit of Bulganin and Khrushchov to Kabul: as part of the entertainment there was a performance of the ancient game of *buzkashi*—'dropping the goat'—a game so rough it had been banned in Russia. Involving teams of horsemen armed with whips, and a dead goat, the game is described in great detail in *Time off to Dig*.

Before returning to London in December 1955 Sylvia Matheson flew to the recently discovered Sui gas field, the first and largest natural gas field to be developed in Pakistan, in the Bugti tribal area, to prepare a talk for the BBC and a piece for *The Times*. There she met, and in 1956 married, Henry Beaumont Schofield (1916–1990), a petroleum engineer in charge of exploiting the gas field for Pakistan Petroleum Ltd. During her five years there, living in the middle of one of the world's hottest deserts, she travelled around Baluchistan accompanied by her personal bodyguard, Mohammed Mondrani of Mut, a famous murderer. As well as chronicling and photographing local tribal customs, she recorded ancient songs, and also songs commemorating recent events such as the discovery of the Sui gas field and the arrival of the company. She described these experiences in *The Tigers of Baluchistan* (1967).

Sylvia Schofield and her husband left Baluchistan in 1961, when he was posted to Burma, and after Burma nationalized the oil industry they moved to Assam for a year, before returning to England. During these years she published four Crime Club novels under the pseudonym Max Mundy (the name of her dog), adventure thrillers featuring a news photographer named Russell Jones. *Death is a Tiger* (1960) was based on her experiences in Baluchistan, *Dig for a Corpse* (1962) was set in the mountains of central Asia, *Pagan Pagoda* (1965) in Burma, and *Death Cries Olé* (1966) in Spain. From 1967 until 1979 they lived in Iran, leaving at the time of the revolution. She published *Persia: an Archaeological Guide* (1972), a guide to sites and excavations from prehistoric times to the end of Seljuk rule, most of which she had visited herself, followed by *Leathercraft in the Lands of Ancient Persia* (1978); she also travelled as a lecturer for the cruise company, Swan Hellenic. In 1979 they moved to Abu Dhabi.

Following Henry Schofield's retirement in 1981, he and Sylvia moved to a villa in Javea on the Costa Blanca in Spain. She continued to lead tours to India, Burma, and Afghanistan, and in 1984 published *Rajasthan, Land of Kings*, a big, glossy book about the history, art, handicrafts, costumes, and religion of Rajasthan, lavishly illustrated with photographs by Roloff Beny. At the end of her life she suffered from failing eyesight, and spent her final years in the Finca San Antonio nursing home near Sagra, Benissa, Alicante, Spain. She donated her collection of archaeological items from Baluchistan and Afghanistan to the Soler Blasco Museum in Javea. She died in the Finca San Antonio nursing home on 2 March 2006.

ANNE PIMLOTT BAKER

Sources S. Matheson, *Time off to dig* (1961) • S. Matheson, *The tigers of Baluchistan* (1967) • P. Titus, introduction, in S. Matheson, *The tigers of Baluchistan*, 2nd edn (1997), xi–xxvi • *Daily Telegraph* (5 April 2006) • private information (2010) • b. cert. • m. cert.

Likenesses photograph, repro. in Matheson, *Tigers*, 2nd edn, jacket • photograph, repro. in Matheson, *Time off*, facing p. 16

Schwarzkopf, Dame (Olga Maria) Elisabeth Friederike (1915–2006), singer, was born on 9 December 1915 in Jarotschin, near Posen, German Silesia, the daughter of

Dame (Olga Maria) Elisabeth Friederike Schwarzkopf (1915–2006), by Baron, 1956

Friedrich Schwarzkopf, classical scholar and teacher, and his wife, Elisabeth, *née* Fröhlich. Like others from similar backgrounds she enjoyed a cultured, middle-class upbringing and was introduced early to music with piano lessons. Having started to study that instrument from the age of seven, she then began to take lessons on the viola, and the organ from the age of ten. It seems that she also had an interest in vocal music during those formative years, because she sang the role of Eurydice in a school production of Gluck's *Orfeo ed Eurydice* at Magdeburg in 1928.

When the family moved from Silesia to Prussia in 1933 Schwarzkopf enrolled in the Augusta School in Berlin and, later, the Berlin Hochschule für Musik. There she had lessons with Lula Mysz-Gmeiner, Heinrich Egenolf, and Maria Ivogün-Raucheisen before being engaged to sing in the chorus for Sir Thomas Beecham's recording of Mozart's *Die Zauberflöte* for EMI in 1937. A member of the technical team at those sessions was Schwarzkopf's future husband, (Harry) Walter *Legge (1906–1979), who later recalled that 'I did not even notice her when Sir Thomas Beecham and I were recording *Die Zauberflöte* in Berlin in 1937. She was in the chorus … I must have been blind!' (Schwarzkopf, 138). Her relative obscurity was short-lived, however, because within twelve months of that recording she sang at the Deutsches Opernhaus Berlin, where she made her début as a flower maiden in Wagner's *Parsifal*. With striking good looks and a voice that indicated clearly her potential as a future operatic star, she then performed the role of Zerbinetta in Strauss's *Ariadne auf Naxos*. But it was her membership of the Nazi party, her involvement in a number of propaganda films for Josef Goebbels, and her appearance at Paris in 1941 in a production of Johann Strauss's *Die Fledermaus* for the German occupying troops that later came to dominate any discussion of this part of her career.

Having joined the Nazi party at the height of Germany's power in 1939, Schwarzkopf later tried to downplay her membership by arguing that 'Everybody at the opera joined … We thought nothing of it. We just did it … [it was something] akin to joining a union' (*New York Times*, 4 Aug 2006). Clearly aware that her argument was less than convincing, she tried to defuse the situation by stating that 'I applied for membership when I was 24, in my second year at the Deutsche Oper in Berlin … I was told that I must do so if I wanted to continue my career. The membership card never reached me' (BBC News website, 4 Aug 2006).

With an eye fixed firmly on her future Schwarzkopf turned her professional attention from Berlin to Vienna in 1943. That year she auditioned for the director of the Vienna Staatsoper, Karl Böhm, who engaged her to sing Zerbinetta in Strauss's *Ariadne auf Naxos*. She continued to perform for the company during the final years of the war and, after undergoing the denazification process, continued there in peacetime. She was eventually to give 222 performances of 22 roles in 19 operas by 10 composers at that house between 12 December 1945 and 3 February 1965. Nevertheless, her life in post-war Vienna must have been both challenging personally and uncertain professionally, so it was something of a relief when Legge, now EMI's talent scout, approached her about the possibility of a recording contract in 1946. While Schwarzkopf had made no personal impact on Legge as a member of the chorus for Beecham's recording of *Die Zauberflöte* in 1937, he was certainly aware of her professionally by the time of their meeting in Vienna. Benefiting from a network of contacts that spread across the globe like an artistically aware spider's web, Legge recalled in 1975 that 'In the later war years her name … seeped through to me in letters from young friends serving in the Mediterranean and North Africa who had heard her on German Services broadcasts.' Impressed by those second-hand reports, Legge added Schwarzkopf's name to his 'list of artists to be heard and perhaps engaged for EMI when the war was over' (Schwarzkopf, 138).

As EMI's principal representative in post-war Vienna, Legge was keen to draw on the city's rich musical past and to exploit some of its interpretative artists for the professional gain of the British company. Along with established performers, such as Herbert von Karajan, Legge wanted to engage some of the more talented younger artists. Many of those were beneficiaries of central Europe's highly integrated opera house system and were ideal fodder for the re-emerging gramophone market. Clearly Schwarzkopf was one such performer and, after an initial meeting at the Café Mozart, Legge 'first heard her … as Rosina in *Il barbiere di Siviglia*—a brilliant, fresh voice shot with laughter, not large but admirably projected, with enchanting high *pianissimi*'. But he had no intention of engaging her hastily, so he 'listened to her in two or three other roles, and once at a party at a friend's house ... before inviting her to discuss an exclusive recording contract' (Schwarzkopf, 138–9). Refreshingly for Legge, Schwarzkopf was not one of the 'singers internationally famous from prewar years [or] others yet to win renown, [who] pursued [him] with uncapped fountain pens ready to sign anything' (ibid., 139). Instead, 'Schwarzkopf was made of sterner stuff and insisted on "a proper audition [of] two or three hours"' (ibid.). It seems that she did not want him 'to buy a cat in a sack and regret it' or for him to offer her less than what he thought she was worth. Impressed by her businesslike manner he recognized in the young singer 'the firm will and guts necessary to make an exceptional career in what Toscanini described as "the primeval jungle we call the world of music"' (ibid.).

Having struck a deal, Legge and Schwarzkopf quickly set about making discs that were sure to capture the interest of record collectors around the world. With a well-honed understanding of how to maximize market share and with the ability to draw the best from the artists with whom he worked, Legge started recording works with Schwarzkopf that drew attention to her very obvious vocal strengths and that were attractive to connoisseur and dilettante alike. Moreover, by having her document Countess Almaviva in Mozart's *Le nozze di Figaro*, Gretel in Humperdinck's *Hänsel und Gretel*, and Die Feldmarschallin in Richard Strauss's *Der Rosenkavalier*, Legge consciously transformed Schwarzkopf from a talented young coloratura soprano into one of the most respected lyric sopranos of the mid-twentieth century.

But to suggest that Schwarzkopf's expertise was restricted to the world of opera would be to underestimate considerably the breadth of her interests. She was also passionate about *Lieder* and in the years directly following the Second World War she began to explore the songs of Hugo Wolf. Her interest in that composer was stimulated by Legge, who, as a junior member of the advertising staff of EMI in 1931, had championed this then largely unknown composer. To broaden Wolf's appeal and to secure sales for his employer Legge decided to target a small, but discerning, group of subscribers by creating the Hugo Wolf Society. The members of that society were then eligible to buy their discs in advance. By guaranteeing sales before manufacture Legge was able to make a commercial success of his passion and to further a musical cause about which he felt strongly. Wolf's music continued to fascinate Legge in the post-war years and when Schwarzkopf began to share his passion he quickly realized that she was a blank canvas on which he could paint his own interpretative picture. In formulating his Wolf style he began 'to work with her ... bar by bar, word by word, inflection by inflection' (Schwarzkopf, 139). Encouraged by Schwarzkopf's progress he decided to promote *Liederabende* at the Wigmore Hall at which she made her London début as a *Liedersängerin* in 1947. With a heavy emphasis on the music of Wolf, Mozart, and Strauss, the concerts were oversubscribed in advance and were an overwhelming financial and artistic success. Excited by the public's response and the box-office receipts Legge then explored the possibility of using the Royal Festival Hall as a venue for further *Liederabende*. These, too, were a success and in later life he recalled that it was 'one of the happiest and proudest days of my life when every one of the more than 3,000 seats [at that hall] was sold out to hear Hugo Wolf's complete *Italienisches Liederbuch* by Elisabeth Schwarzkopf, Dietrich Fischer-Dieskau, and Hermann Reuter' (ibid., 217).

Although she had shot to operatic stardom in post-war Europe, Schwarzkopf's American stage career was less meteoric. After making her American début in 1953 with a recital at Town Hall, New York, she performed at the San Francisco Opera the same year. (She and Legge married that year, on 19 October, in Epsom, Surrey. There were no children of the marriage.) But it was some eleven years later that she made her début at the Metropolitan Opera House, New York, the reasons for which were probably more political than musical. As a former member of the Nazi party she would almost certainly have been targeted by that city's anti-fascist protesters during the 1950s and was probably concerned that demonstrations against her would have damaged her long-term professional future in the United States. Her colleague and friend Herbert von Karajan was the subject of protests when he toured America with the Berlin Philharmonic in 1955 and had difficulty freeing himself from the tarnish of Nazi party membership, even though he had married a woman of Jewish extraction in 1942 and had been boycotted professionally by the German authorities because of that marriage.

Over the next two decades Schwarzkopf reduced her repertoire considerably and restricted herself to a handful of roles that included Fiordiligi, Donna Elvira, and the Countess Almaviva from Mozart's *Così fan tutte*, *Don Giovanni*, and *Le nozze di Figaro* respectively; Die Feldmarschallin and the Countess from Strauss's *Der Rosenkavalier* and *Capriccio*; and Alice from Verdi's *Falstaff*. Her decision to reduce her repertoire so drastically might have been influenced by the less than harmonious circumstances surrounding the world première of Walton's *Troilus and Cressida* at Covent Garden during the 1954–5 season. Having composed the role of Cressida 'with [Schwarzkopf's] voice in mind', Walton was devastated when she 'was not allowed to sing' the part by her husband, Walter Legge. Apparently the 'excuse was that her English was not good enough and her voice not suitable for the wide range that [Walton] required'. Nevertheless, 'Eight years after *Troilus*, [she] at long last premièred a work by [Walton], the *Song for the Lord Mayor's Table*, commissioned by the Worshipful Company of Goldsmiths', even though her English 'was no better than it had always been' (Walton, 144 and 146). Schwarzkopf's relationship with Covent Garden never recovered fully after the Walton incident and her work there came under increasing scrutiny over the next few years. Matters came to a head some years later, and after she was savaged critically because of her interpretation of Die Feldmarschallin in Strauss's *Der Rosenkavalier* in 1959 she never performed at Covent Garden again.

Schwarzkopf's performance style continued to divide

commentators for the rest of her career. B. H. Haggin complained of her 'excessively mannered and affected phrasing and expressive hamming, exaggerated pouting, archness, gasps and whispers' (*Washington Post*, 4 Aug 2006). J. B. Steane by contrast considered Schwarzkopf's 'thought and art' to be

> so marvellously exact that one wants to call them calculated, which immediately suggests something unfeeling and insincere; yet this is self-evidently absurd, for insincerity, like sentimentality, betrays itself by inexactness and distortion. What one has in Schwarzkopf is a high degree of awareness—of colours and styles, and of the existence of *choice*. (Steane, 349)

Most later writers on interpretation, looking at her on film or listening to her recordings, would probably agree with Steane's assessment of Schwarzkopf's performance style and would recognize that the ways in which she related to a score physically and emotionally were often more complex than some surface discussions suggest.

Schwarzkopf retired from the stage after a performance of *Der Rosenkavalier* in Brussels in 1971 and from the concert hall after three farewell recitals in London in 1976. Together with Legge until his unexpected death in 1979, and thereafter singly, she gave masterclasses and worked with many young singers, instilling in them some of the central tenets of their performance aesthetic. After her husband's death she published his memoirs, *On and Off the Record*, in 1982, and was a guest on BBC Radio 4's *Desert Island Discs*, where she shocked many listeners by selecting her own records. In 1992 she was made a DBE, a rare honour for a former member of the Nazi party, and after leaving Britain she lived for a period at Zumikon, Switzerland, before moving to Schruns, Austria, where she died in her sleep on 3 August 2006.

A formidable woman and a controversial figure, Elisabeth Schwarzkopf was a household name throughout the latter half of the twentieth century for all those interested in opera, oratorio, and art song. Although her career began in Germany her rise to international fame was a post-war phenomenon that was shaped by a Svengali-like figure who recognized her unique talents and marketed them in both an astute and an often ruthless manner.

RAYMOND HOLDEN

Sources H. Rosenthal, *Two centuries of opera at Covent Garden* (1958) · J. B. Steane, *The grand tradition: seventy years of singing on record* (1973) · F. Hadamowsky, *Die Wiener Hoftheater (Staatstheater), 1776–1966*, 2: *Die Wiener Hofoper (Staatsoper)* (1975) · E. Schwarzkopf, *On and off the record: a memoir of Walter Legge* (1982) · S. Walton, *William Walton: behind the façade* (1988) · A. Sanders and J. B. Steane, *Elisabeth Schwarzkopf: a career on record* (1995) · H. Hoyer, *Chronik der Wiener Staatsoper: 1945 bis 1995* (Vienna, 1995) · A. Jefferson, *Elisabeth Schwarzkopf* (1996) · BBC News, 4 Aug 2006 · www.bloomberg.com · *The Times* (4 Aug 2006) · *Daily Telegraph* (4 Aug 2006) · *The Guardian* (4 Aug 2006) · *New York Times* (4 Aug 2006) · *Washington Post* (4 Aug 2006) · *The Independent* (5 Aug 2006) · *Gramophone* (7 Aug 2006) · *WW* (2006) · Burke, *Peerage* · *Grove music online*, www.grovemusic.com · m. cert.

Archives FILM BFINA, *South Bank show*, A. Benson (director), LWT, 2 March 1986 · BFINA, documentary footage · BFINA, performance footage

Likenesses Lipnitzki, photographs, 1948–62, Getty Images, London, Roger Viollet · photographs, 1948–76, Getty Images, London, Hult. Arch. · photographs, 1951, Getty Images, London, Popperfoto · photographs, 1954–7, Getty Images, London, Time and Life Pictures · Baron, photograph, 1956, Hult. Arch., London [*see illus.*] · photograph, 1957, Photoshot, London · photographs, 1957–84, Getty Images, London, AFP · photographs, 1959–2002, Camera Press, London · photographs, 1962, Rex Features, London, GTV archive · M. Ward, photographs, 1967, Rex Features, London · obituary photographs · photographs, repro. in Sanders and Steane, *Schwarzkopf* (1995) · photographs, repro. in Jefferson, *Schwarzkopf* (1996) · photographs, PA Photos, London

Scofield, (David) Paul (1922–2008), actor, was born at 466 Gillott Road, Edgbaston, Birmingham, on 21 January 1922, the younger son and second of the three children of Edward Harry Scofield (1892–1976), schoolteacher and headmaster, and his wife, Mary, formerly Keyte, *née* Wild (1895–1996). His parents were married in 1919, his mother having previously been married to Joseph W. Keyte, who died at Arras, France, in 1917.

Early years: education, wartime, marriage Scofield's father was headmaster of the village elementary school at Hurstpierpoint, Sussex, which Paul attended until he was twelve. His childhood was a happy but divided one; his father was 'Sir' at school and 'Dad' at home, and his mother's Catholicism meant that on 'some days we were little protestants and on others devout little Catholics' (O'Connor, 14). He claimed that he was never a scholar, and that he only ever excelled in reciting poetry. Aged nine he delivered Portia's 'quality of mercy' speech in a school recitation of the trial scene from *The Merchant of Venice*, and more dramatic opportunities came when he transferred to Varndean School for Boys in Brighton, making the journey by bicycle and train. At Varndean he played Juliet, Rosalind, and, when his voice broke, Prince Hal. Playing Juliet was a turning point for the young Scofield, who found acting a tremendous release. Though rarely a boastful man, he said his performance 'was a sensation', and that 'thenceforward there was nothing else I wanted to do' (O'Connor, 15).

At fifteen Scofield made his first appearance on a professional stage as an unpaid volunteer, in a crowd scene, in Sir John Martin-Harvey's touring production of *The Only Way*, at the Theatre Royal, Brighton. He found Martin-Harvey an awe-inspiring figure. Excited by this experience, and disillusioned with his academic progress, he left Varndean in 1939, during his final term, and with the help of his headmaster and the manager of the Theatre Royal, gained a scholarship to the Croydon Repertory Theatre School.

At the outbreak of the Second World War Scofield was declared medically unfit ('They found I had crossed toes: I was unable to wear boots. I was deeply ashamed'; O'Connor, 19), and with the closure of the Croydon school, he began to study at the London Mask Theatre School where he made his professional début in January 1940, walking on in Eugene O'Neill's *Desire Under the Elms*, and subsequently speaking as the Third Clerk and First Soldier in John Drinkwater's *Abraham Lincoln*.

In the spring of 1941 some of the Mask School students, including Scofield, were evacuated to Bideford in north Devon, where Eileen Thorndike (the younger sister of

(David) **Paul Scofield (1922–2008)**, by Cornel Lucas, 1956

Sybil) and Herbert Scott, who had been teachers at the school, set up a semi-professional student repertory company. Scofield played a variety of leading parts, including the murderous Danny in Emlyn Williams's psychological thriller, *Night Must Fall*, a performance that elicited a prophetic review from 'Candidus', the local critic for the *Bideford Weekly Gazette*: Scofield

> played Dan very quietly, with a most nauseating charm and a combined simplicity that was quite horrible … One would hesitate to put any limit to what this actor is going to be able to do as he grows older. If he can keep the enthusiasm and capacity for hard work which he obviously has now, he will be a great actor before many years have passed. (O'Connor, 21–2)

Later in 1941 Scofield toured for the Entertainments National Service Association (ENSA) in Robert Atkins's production of *The Taming of the Shrew*, and in John van Druten's *Young Woodley*, which played for a week at the Birmingham Repertory Theatre, where he was spotted by Basil C. Langton, who was to be an important early influence on him. Langton had inaugurated the Travelling Repertory Theatre, intent on taking classical and modern drama to blitzed towns, army camps, and munitions factories, under the auspices of the Council for the Encouragement of Music and the Arts (the forerunner of the Arts Council). For the Travelling Repertory Theatre Scofield played Algy in *The Importance of Being Earnest*, and, returning to Birmingham, Horatio in a *Hamlet* which played over two nights. Langton both directed and played Hamlet, and the Ophelia was a young actress named Joy Parker. They toured together in Langton's productions of Shaw's *Arms and the Man*, in which Scofield was Sergius, 'the chocolate soldier', and in *The Moon is Down*, a rare play by John Steinbeck. Joy Mary Parker (*b*. 1922) was the daughter of Henry Edward Parker, a company secretary, and she and Scofield were married, during a week off between the tour and the London run of *The Moon is Down*, on 15 May 1943 at All Saints' Church, Weston, Surrey. They had a son, Martin (*b*. 1945), and a daughter, Sarah (*b*. 1951).

Birmingham, Stratford, London Scofield and Parker continued touring with Langton's company until the autumn of 1944. He was then offered his first season at the Birmingham Repertory Theatre, which, under the visionary management of Sir Barry Jackson, was one of the most dynamic and daring theatres in the country, famous for attracting many young actors who became leading figures in British theatre. Laurence Olivier, Ralph Richardson, and Peggy Ashcroft had all trained there, and contemporaries of Scofield included Donald Sinden, Eric Porter, and Margaret Leighton. Here, Scofield said, he achieved 'a certain amount of technical balance as an actor' (*New Yorker*, 26 June 1965), playing such roles as the Clown in *The Winter's Tale*, a memorably puffed up Mr Toad in *Toad of Toad Hall*, Young Marlow in *She Stoops to Conquer*, a highly praised John Tanner in *Man and Superman*, Dr Wangel in *The Lady from the Sea*, and Philip the Bastard in *King John*. These last three productions were directed by the very young Peter Brook, whose professional partnership with Scofield proved to be one of the innovative cornerstones of post-war British theatre. Of their first meeting, in Jackson's office, Brook wrote, 'I looked into a face that unaccountably in a young man was streaked and mottled like an old rock, and I was instantly aware that something very deep lay hidden behind his ageless appearance' (Brook, *Threads*, 31–2).

From early on Scofield commanded attention from public and critics alike. As a student in Devon he had become the star actor, the Thorndike family were early champions, and as the critic J. C. Trewin wrote of his time in Birmingham, echoing Peter Brook, 'the stage lay open before this striding actor with the sierra-voice of peak and valley, the tentative gestures, the face in which pensive age and extreme youth stood for ever on guard' (Trewin, *Scofield*, 29). Scofield's voice was already distinctively his own, and not without its detractors, who complained of a tendency to a mannered harshness and over rapidity, but it was clear that here was a born actor, with an original approach to every new role.

In 1946 Jackson left Birmingham to run the Shakespeare Memorial Theatre, taking the Scofields and Brook with him. In this first season Scofield played 'a miraculously brainless' Cloten in *Cymbeline* (Trewin, *Scofield*, 32), a Henry V that some thought lacked the necessary fire, a clear and sincere Malcolm in *Macbeth*, and, poles apart, a slippery and lascivious Lucio in *Measure for Measure*. The hit of the season, however, was *Love's Labour's Lost*, directed by Brook, who at twenty-one was the youngest director ever to have worked at Stratford. His sombre and elegiac production was noted for its visual evocation of the romantic, rococo paintings of Watteau, and for Scofield's quixotic and melancholic Don Armado, looking, thought the critic

Philip Hope-Wallace, like 'an over-bred and beautiful old borzoi' (Speaight, 242).

After a brief appearance in London, at the Arts Theatre Club, in Christopher Fry's *A Phoenix Too Frequent*, Scofield returned to Stratford for the 1947 season. Brook directed a controversial *Romeo and Juliet* on a sun-drenched, virtually empty stage. Taking his inspiration from a single line, 'these hot days is the mad blood stirring', Brook emphasized the violence of the play, with properly youthful lovers, and Scofield as a memorably intense and dangerous Mercutio, quietly delivering the Queen Mab speech stretched out on the ground, with torches flaming around him. In the same season he played Pericles, in a much-truncated version; froze the blood as Mephistopheles in Marlowe's *Faustus*; and as Sir Andrew Aguecheek was 'a knight made of pink blancmange' (Alan Dent, quoted in Trewin, *Scofield*, 46).

For the first time the Stratford Memorial Theatre transferred part of its repertory to London, including the *Romeo* and *Twelfth Night*, after which Scofield played Young Fashion in Anthony Quayle's revival of Vanbrugh's *The Relapse* (Lyric, Hammersmith, 1947), with Cyril Ritchard as the outrageous Lord Foppington. In the following year he returned to Stratford for his third season, again playing Philip in *King John* and the Clown in *The Winter's Tale*, and adding Bassanio, Troilus, Roderigo in *Othello*, and his first Hamlet, alternating in the role with the Australian ballet dancer Robert Helpmann. The staging was by Michael Benthall, in a Victorian Gothic setting. While some critics thought Helpmann the more technically assured, Scofield presented a romantic, spiritual, youthful Hamlet, of great fragility and tenderness, a performance that defined the role for his generation. Harold Hobson said he had 'never seen a Hamlet more shot through with the pale agony of irresolution' (Trewin, *Scofield*, 50), and the young Kenneth Tynan regarded it as the best he had ever seen, writing 'I know now that there is in England a young actor who is bond-slave to greatness' (*The Times*, 21 March 2008).

Scofield had his first starring role in London as Alexander the Great in Terence Rattigan's *Adventure Story* (1949), which was written for him, but this ambitious play met with hostility from a press who preferred their Rattigan firmly behind drawing-room doors. He then played Constantin in *The Seagull* (Hammersmith), and, reuniting with Brook, scored a great success in *Ring Round the Moon* (Globe, 1950), Jean Anouilh's 'charade with music'. Scofield played the double role of the twins, the heartless Hugo and the sweet-natured Frédéric, switching between the two with great subtlety and elegance, and with dazzling technique, leaving the stage as one twin and returning almost immediately as the other.

Ring Round the Moon, which ran for two years, began Scofield's ten-year association with the West End producer Hugh ('Binkie') Beaumont, who had long dreamed of a permanent London company, led by John Gielgud, in a repertory of classic plays. Scofield, who in 1952 had played Don Pedro in Gielgud's own production of *Much Ado about Nothing*, jumped at the chance to join this fledgling 'national theatre' company for a season at the Lyric, Hammersmith, in 1952–3. Gielgud, who had been the outstanding Richard II of his generation, directed Scofield as a constrained and chilly Richard, a performance that disappointed some, and for which Gielgud typically took some of the responsibility, feeling that he had been unable to help Scofield find his own way with the part; and as the ridiculously self-absorbed Sir Wilful Witwoud in an all-star revival of Congreve's *The Way of the World*, alongside Pamela Brown, Margaret Rutherford, and Gielgud himself. Tynan thought his Witwoud 'a beautifully gaudy performance, pitched somewhere between Hermione Gingold and Stan Laurel' (Tynan, *Curtains*, 38). The two actors were also brilliantly matched in Brook's classical production of Thomas Otway's *Venice Preserv'd*, a Restoration tragedy not seen since the nineteenth century, and the surprise success of the season.

In 1955 Scofield again played Hamlet, and found more irony and assurance in the role, in a production directed by Brook that opened in Birmingham, before travelling to Moscow, the first time a company from Britain had played in Russia since 1917. They were met at the airport by leading Russian actors, presented with bouquets of chrysanthemums, and received huge ovations. Scofield was congratulated by the critic of *Pravda* for presenting the prince as a dynamic rather than a passive figure.

When *Hamlet* moved to London, it was as part of a three-play season with Scofield and Brook as joint directors, although Scofield said that 'with Peter that meant he decided what to do and I agreed' (O'Connor, 122). While playing Hamlet, rehearsals were taking place for an adaptation of Graham Greene's *The Power and the Glory*, with Scofield as the whisky-sodden Mexican priest. Brook felt he wasn't getting near the role, but Scofield was biding his time, waiting to finish with Hamlet before transforming into Greene's 'trudging, wizened hero-victim … the authentic face of Mexico, flyblown and God-bitten' (Tynan, *Theatre Writings*, 105). It was another astonishing performance, lauded by Olivier as one of the greatest he had seen, and the 'season of sin and damnation' (ibid., 116) was rounded off with a revival of T. S. Eliot's *The Family Reunion*, with Scofield as Harry Monchensey, Eliot's Oresteian hero.

Triumphs: More, Lear, Salieri The director Peter Hall commented that when Scofield arrived 'he came as a real shock—you could suddenly feel this sulphurous passion. It was an entirely new note', and for some time Scofield had been talked of as the natural heir to Olivier, a suggestion he would characteristically dismiss. Brought up in 'the theatre of articulacy', on the plays of Shakespeare and Shaw, Scofield in a sense came between two schools, the classical style exemplified by Gielgud, an actor he greatly admired, and the 'Royal Court' school, represented by such actors as Albert Finney and Alan Bates. In truth Scofield always went his own way, maintaining something of the vagabond spirit of Langton and Jackson and the Thorndike-Cassons, staying outside the mainstream, and never allying himself to any particular institution or theatrical group.

Throughout the 1950s Scofield would successfully, and with a personal sense of relief, combine his classical work with forays into contemporary drama: playing an American in Charles Morgan's French resistance drama, *The River Line* (1952); a schoolmaster who discovers that his father has been hanged for murder in Wynyard Browne's *A Question of Fact* (1953); giving a brilliant character performance, as a man who is hanged for a murder he did not commit, in Rodney Ackland's *A Dead Secret* (1957); and, making his only appearance in a musical, *Expresso Bongo* (1958), he showed his versatility as Johnny Jackson, an unscrupulous and seedy Tin Pan alley agent. In 1960 he played the role that brought him the greatest international acclaim, as Sir Thomas More in Robert Bolt's *A Man for All Seasons*. Scofield found the steel in More through an apparent mildness of tone and manner, and captured all of More's moral strength and unflinching faith, his humour, sensuality, and wily grace. The play transferred to New York in 1961, and Scofield won the Tony award as best actor. It was to be his only appearance on the Broadway stage.

Prior to his New York run as More, Scofield played a Napoleonic Coriolanus and, once again, Don Armado, this time described by one critic as 'a loon among swans', both at the Shakespeare Festival in Stratford, Ontario, Canada. In 1961 Scofield had agreed to lead Peter Hall's first company as artistic director of the Royal Shakespeare Company, playing Shylock, Petruchio, and Thersites, but had withdrawn barely two months before rehearsals were due to start. He had simply realized that he didn't want to play those parts. Forgiven by Hall, whose respect for Scofield was limitless, he returned to England's Stratford in 1962 as King Lear, his final and most glorious stage collaboration with Peter Brook. Brook presented a godless and merciless Beckettian world, stripped of any sentimentality or hope of redemption, and Scofield's grizzled old king was equally severe and radical. His Lear was an arrogant, wilful, vain, and terrifying despot, with a voice 'made of granite which cracked and splintered under the pressure of inner dissolution' (Callow), his essential humanity revealed as he gave way under the intolerable elemental force of Shakespeare's (and Brook's) vision. The production travelled to London, Paris, Moscow, and eastern Europe, toured the USA, and opened the new Lincoln Center in New York. Scofield's revelatory performance, which many considered his greatest, defined the role for a generation.

Staying with the Royal Shakespeare Company, Scofield was electrifying as a 'titanically angry' Timon of Athens (1965), and showed his brilliance in comedy as Gorky's Government Inspector, in which 'every voice he has ever heard seems to have left an imprint on his memory and he tries to imitate them all simultaneously', and as an outrageously camp hairdresser in Charles Dyer's *Staircase* (both 1966). The following year he played Macbeth in Peter Hall's controversial production, but many were disappointed. Scofield himself felt that perhaps Macbeth should have come before his Lear, and he never really gelled with Vivien Merchant, who was his Lady. At the Royal Court he returned to form as Laurie, the waspish and self-loathing writer–hero in John Osborne's *A Hotel in Amsterdam* (1968), and was a heart-stopping Uncle Vanya (1970), his 'great thunder-sheet of a voice, muted by bitterness and disappointment' (C. Hampton, in National Theatre memorial programme), in Anthony Page's fine production.

There had been questions asked about Scofield's non-appearance at the National Theatre during Olivier's directorship. It was said that Olivier was envious of Scofield (he referred to his Lear as 'Mr Lear'). Projects including Coriolanus and *The Misanthrope* never materialized. However, he finally made his début there in 1971, in Carl Zuckmayer's picaresque tale, *The Captain of Köpenick*. Scofield played Wilhelm Voigt, an adenoidal, shabby vagrant and former jailbird, who successively transforms into a model prisoner and the ramrod captain of the title. It was a great comic performance, where even his moustache seemed to be acting. He also gave a 'fascinating lizard-like performance' in Pirandello's *The Rules of the Game*, opposite Joan Plowright (Irving Wardle, in *Theatre* 72). During the 1970s his career took unexpected turns. He returned to the Royal Court in Christopher Hampton's *Savages*, played Prospero at the Leeds Playhouse for his old friend from Birmingham days, John Harrison, and appeared at the Nottingham Playhouse in Athol Fugard's *Dimetos*, and at the Manchester Royal Exchange in Ronald Harwood's *A Family*.

On returning to the National Theatre in 1977, now under Peter Hall's direction, Scofield was a magnificently voracious Volpone, wonderfully ostentatious as Constantine Madras in Granville-Barker's *The Madras House*, and then in Peter Shaffer's *Amadeus* (1979) he enjoyed a popular success comparable to his Thomas More. As the composer Antonio Salieri, tormented by the genius of the puerile Mozart and the awareness of his own mediocrity, Scofield never left the stage. As the older Salieri he 'invented an extraordinary old geezer, wheezing and leering … who disappeared in the twinkling of an eye when the young Salieri stepped forward and the action of the play commenced' (Callow, 164). Scofield once again dazzled, and showed great generosity to the young Simon Callow as Mozart. He declined the chance to take the play to New York, and was not even asked to play Salieri on film, but a fragment of a recording shows the extraordinary power of his portrayal.

Film, television, and radio From the time of his first Hamlet Scofield had attracted the attention of the film studios. The Hollywood mogul Darryl F. Zanuck declared, on seeing an early screen test, 'That actor! The best I've seen since John Barrymore' (Trewin, *Scofield*, 75). He made his big screen début in 1955 in *That Lady*, a costume epic, in which he played a careworn Philip II of Spain opposite an eye-patched Olivia de Havilland as the Princess of Eboli. It was an auspicious début, a performance 'perfectly scaled for the camera's ruthless perception of thought', and he won the most promising actor prize from the British Film Academy. Thereafter Scofield would make only a handful of films, the stage continuing to dominate his career, and he claimed he didn't know what the cinema wanted of a classical actor. However, he was able to repeat his Thomas More in Fred Zinnemann's massively successful film of *A Man for All Seasons* (1966). The moguls had wanted Olivier, but Zinnemann held out, and Scofield won numerous prizes, including the British Academy award and the Hollywood Oscar. Typically he didn't attend the ceremony; the golden statuette was sent to him in the post, and when it arrived it was broken.

Despite his cinematic ambivalence, Scofield made distinguished appearances in *Carve Her Name with Pride* (1958), as the lover of Violette Szabo; as the fanatical German officer in *The Train* (1964); as the accountant in an adaptation of Herman Melville's *Bartleby* (1971); as *King Lear* (1971), in Brook's austere film, full of close-ups of Scofield's face, 'etched with inexpressible pain and bewilderment'; and as Tobias in Tony Richardson's film of Edward Albee's *A Delicate Balance* (1973), with Katharine Hepburn as his wife. He was off-screen for more than a decade. Later notable performances included an elderly eccentric in *When the Whales Came* (1989); the King of France in Kenneth Branagh's *Henry V* (1989); the Ghost in Franco Zeffirelli's *Hamlet* (1991), with Mel Gibson as the prince; the American writer and academic, Mark Van Doren, in Robert Redford's *Quiz Show* (1994), for which he was nominated as best supporting actor by the American and British academies; and Judge Danforth in Nicholas Hytner's film of Arthur Miller's *The Crucible* (1996), for which he won the BAFTA award as best supporting actor.

Scofield's work on the small screen was equally rare, first appearing in televised versions of *Hamlet* (1956) and *Expresso Bongo* (1958). His original television performances included Pirandello's Henry IV (1959), Strindberg's Captain in *Dance of Death* (1966), and a QC in *Emlyn* (1969), for which he won an Emmy award as best actor. Later roles included Lambert Strether in an adaptation of Henry James's *The Ambassadors* (1977), two of Noël Coward's old roles in *A Song at Twilight* and *Come into the Garden, Maud* (both 1981) with Deborah Kerr and Geraldine McEwan, Karenin in *Anna Karenina* (1985), Otto Frank in *The Attic: the Hiding of Anne Frank* (1988), and two gloriously contrasting performances as Dickens's Chuzzlewit brothers, the upright Old Martin and the amoral Anthony, in a splendid serialization of *Martin Chuzzlewit* (1994).

Scofield's work on radio was far more prolific, starting in 1948 with *Love's Labour's Lost*, this time as Berowne. He loved the medium, relishing its comparative anonymity, and he remained a loyal and prolific recording artist, sometimes playing roles one regretted he had never played on stage—Marlowe's Tamburlaine and Edward II, Chekhov's Vershinin, Coward's Garry Essendine and Elyot Chase, Melville's Captain Vere—and sometimes returning to a part he had played, or would play—a Macbeth with Peggy Ashcroft, an exhilarating Othello in a brilliant partnership with Nicol Williamson, Prospero, Don Quixote, Don Armado (yet again), Salieri, and, in 2001, a final Lear. He recorded classics and new plays, poetry and narrations. His readings of Eliot's *Four Quartets* and *The Waste Land* are extraordinary distillations of Scofield's art.

Later roles, private life, assessment After the triumph of Scofield's Salieri it seemed inevitable that there would be disappointments. Perhaps expectations were too high for his National Theatre Othello (1980), although it did gain stature during the run and acquired a heart-breaking tenderness in the final moments. In the 1980s he played Don Quixote and a silvery Oberon, both at the National, and was constantly pursued by the National's successive directors asking him to appear in play after play, but throughout his long career he never did anything he didn't want to do. He was extraordinarily discriminating, listening, he said, to an inner voice. But some of his later choices raised eyebrows. The Herb Gardner comedy *I'm Not Rappaport* (1986) and, more particularly, the Jeffrey Archer newspaper drama *Exclusive* (1989), hardly seemed worthy of such a titanic talent. However, in the 1990s it was a relief to see him again tackling the classical peaks of Shaw and Ibsen: playing a wildly eccentric Captain Shotover in Trevor Nunn's starry Haymarket revival of *Heartbreak House* (1992); and especially in the title role of *John Gabriel Borkman* (1996), in Richard Eyre's National Theatre revival, with Vanessa Redgrave and Eileen Atkins. As Ibsen's Borkman, a man trapped and frozen by the past, Michael Billington thought he gave 'his finest performance since King Lear … Scofield's greatness lies in the way he reveals the private turmoil behind the posturing facade' (*The Guardian*, 13 July 1996), and Peter Brook felt that there was a lot of '[Paul] in the character—proud, lonely and obsessed'. In 2001 he made his last stage appearance, at the Almeida Theatre, reading Anton Chekhov's letters to Olga Knipper, the actress who became Chekhov's wife, and whom Scofield had met when he played Hamlet in Moscow all those years previously. His co-reader was Irene Worth, who had been Goneril to his Lear at Stratford.

The Scofields lived a very private life at The Gables, Balcombe, Haywards Heath, Sussex, in the Edwardian house they had bought in 1951, barely a dozen miles from the Hurstpierpoint school where his father had been headmaster. They enjoyed a profoundly happy marriage for over sixty years. When working in the theatre Scofield would set off for the train to Victoria station, with the sandwiches his wife had made for him, and he would return after a performance, often to find her waiting on the doorstep. He was a countryman at heart, happiest when riding his horse, cycling, gardening, smoking his pipe, reading, baking bread, or walking his beloved dogs on the South Downs or at his summer retreat on the Isle of Mull. He protected his privacy, rarely giving interviews, and never appearing on television chat shows. He was quite shy socially; a man of sweet temperament, he could be gossipy and indiscreet, droll and acerbic. The critic Michael Billington said of him that 'if Scofield revealed himself it was through his work; and what we saw was a figure of rich humanity, wide-ranging compassion and unflinching integrity' (*The Guardian*, 21 March 2008).

After his return from playing Hamlet in Moscow in 1956,

Scofield was appointed CBE, an honour, he considered, 'with a hint of hard work about it'. He turned down a knighthood on several occasions, happy to be addressed as 'Mr' rather than 'Sir', but did accept his appointment as Companion of Honour in 2001. He won numerous awards throughout his career, for his work in theatre and on film, and he held honorary degrees from Glasgow, Kent, Sussex, St Andrews, and Oxford universities. He died of leukaemia at the Royal Sussex County Hospital, Brighton, on 19 March 2008, and his funeral was held nine days later at Balcombe church. He was survived by his wife and their two children. On the first anniversary of his death a service of thanksgiving was held at St Margaret's Church, Westminster Abbey, followed by a memorial performance at the National Theatre, attended by many of the leading actors, directors, and writers of the day. The service ended, fittingly and movingly, with Scofield's recording of Prospero's final speech from *The Tempest*.

Scofield was, said Simon Callow, 'a late flowering of that astonishing generation which included Olivier, Gielgud, Ashcroft, Evans, Redgrave and Richardson' (*The Guardian*, 24 March 2008). He was a towering actor, physically powerful and 'flamboyantly handsome'; he had, said Richard Eyre, 'the face of a medieval statue—half-saint, half-warrior' (National Theatre memorial programme). He approached every role he played with complete dedication and meticulous attention to the words of the writer, finding the character within himself, intuitively and imaginatively. His incomparable voice was variously described by Peter Hall as 'a magical oboe', by Simon Callow as 'an organ with limitless stops, from the mightiest of bass rumbles, through light tenorial lyricism to falsetto pipings' (Callow, 163), and by Richard Eyre as 'like walking through a wood, the top notes like wind through the branches, the low notes thick like timber' (National Theatre memorial programme). Sometimes known as Saint Paul, or more simply and affectionately as Sco, he was revered in his profession as an actor without equal.

ALEX JENNINGS

Sources J. C. Trewin, *Paul Scofield* (1956) · K. Tynan, *Curtains* (1961) · J. C. Trewin, *The Birmingham Repertory Theatre, 1913–1963* (1963) · *New Yorker* (26 June 1965) · S. Morley, ed., *Theatre 72* (1972) · R. Speaight, *Shakespeare on the stage* (1973) · *Peter Hall's diaries*, ed. J. Goodwin (1983) · J. C. Trewin, *Five and eighty Hamlets* (1987) · P. Brook, *The shifting point* (1988) · R. Huggett, *Binkie Beaumont: éminence grise of the West End theatre, 1933–1973* (1989) · P. Hall, *Making an exhibition of myself* (1993) · C. Duff, *The lost summer: the heyday of the West End theatre* (1995) · P. Brook, *Threads of time* (1998) · G. O'Connor, *Paul Scofield: the biography* (2002) · K. Tynan, *Theatre writings* (2007) · *The Times* (20 March 2008); (21 March 2008); (26 March 2008); (1 April 2008); (2 April 2008); (5 April 2008); (23 April 2008); (26 April 2008); (2 May 2008) · *Daily Telegraph* (20 March 2008); (21 March 2008) · *The Guardian* (13 July 1996); (20 March 2008); (21 March 2008); (24 March 2008) · *The Independent* (20 March 2008); (21 March 2008) · *The Stage* (20 March 2008) · *New York Times* (21 March 2008) · *The Observer* (23 March 2008) · *Paul Scofield: an actor for all seasons*, National Theatre memorial programme, 2009 · S. Callow, *My life in pieces* (2010) · *WW* (2008) · personal knowledge (2012) · private information (2012) · b. cert. · m. cert. · d. cert.

Archives FILM BFINA, *Arena*, D. Thompson (director), BBC2, 24 Dec 2008 · BFINA, documentary and light entertainment footage | SOUND BL NSA, current affairs, documentary, light entertainment, and performance recordings

Likenesses photographs, 1943–2003, Getty Images, London · C. Beaton, bromide prints, 1948?, NPG · N. Parkinson, group portrait, bromide print, 1955 (*Time Remembered*), NPG · photographs, 1955–2003, Rex Features, London · photographs, 1955–2004, PA Photos, London · C. Lucas, bromide print, 1956, NPG [*see illus.*] · A. Frueh, pen, brush, and ink with gouache, 1962, repro. in A. J. Frueh, *Theatre caricatures by Al Frueh: West End meets Broadway* (1990); priv. coll. · B. Willoughby, bromide print, 1966, NPG · photographs, 1966–97, Photoshot, London · Z. Dominic, photograph, *c.*1967, Camera Press, London · D. Bachardy, pencil and ink wash, 1968, repro. in D. Bachardy, *One hundred drawings* (1983) · E. Lucie-Smith, bromide print, *c.*1970, NPG · C. Beaton, bromide prints, 1972, NPG · B. L. Schwartz, dye transfer print, 1977, NPG · B. Brandt, bromide print, 1981, NPG · Snowdon, vintage bromide print, 1983, NPG · N. Sinclair, selenium-toned silver prints, 1990, NPG · I. Sedleck, resin bronze, 1992, repro. in G. Ashton, *Pictures in the Garrick Club*, ed. K. A. Burnim and A. Wilton (1997), 534 · R. Barton, toned silver print, 1994, NPG · P. Tozer, bromide fibre print, 1996, NPG · L. Knight, black chalk (*Hamlet*); Sothebys, 7 May 1975 · L. Knight, black chalk and watercolour; Sothebys, 26 Sept 1985 · L. Knight, chalk; Sothebys, 6 Nov 1974 · L. Knight, charcoal; Bonhams, 20 Nov 2007, lot 14952 · L. Knight, portrait, Royal Shakespeare Theatre, Stratford upon Avon · obituary photographs · photograph, repro. in R. Mander and J. Mitchenson, *A picture history of the British theatre* (1957) · photographs, Lebrecht Music and Arts Photo Library, London

Wealth at death £1,304,570: probate, 6 Oct 2008, *CGPLA Eng. & Wales*

Scott, Sir (William) David Stewart (**1921–2006**), submariner and naval officer, was born on 5 April 1921 at Dalhousie, Gordon Road, Camberley, Surrey, the son of Lieutenant-Colonel (later Brigadier) Henry St George Stewart Scott of the 4th Gurkha rifles, and his wife, Ida Christabel Trower, *née* Hogg. David Scott (as he became known) was educated at Tonbridge School and entered the Royal Navy as a special entry cadet in 1938. When the Second World War broke out he was serving in the battleship HMS *Revenge*, which played a key role in the defence of Britain from invasion in 1940 as well as protecting convoys from German capital ships.

Scott transferred to submarines in 1942 and, after a brief period as second-in-command of the old boat H33, was appointed in the same position to HMS *Seraph*, serving under N. L. A. (Bill) Jewell. *Seraph* found itself involved in clandestine operations of great significance, most famously Operation Mincemeat, when in 1943 a body purporting to be that of a Royal Marines officer was landed on the Spanish coast carrying papers to mislead the axis powers into believing the main allied blow was to fall on the Balkans, Sardinia, and Corsica rather than Sicily. Scott manned the conning tower of *Seraph* as the body was delivered into the water. *Seraph* and Scott had already distinguished themselves the previous year by transporting General Mark Clark to and from north Africa for talks with the Vichy French and, posing as an American submarine, picking up General Henri Giraud from the French coast near Toulon. In 1944 Scott got his first command, the small submarine HMS *Umbra*, which was used to train submarine commanders. He then transferred to command her sister HMS *Vulpine* in 1945 before moving in the same year to a sister of *Seraph*, HMS *Satyr*.

Scott was next appointed first lieutenant of the destroyer HMS *Volage* in the Mediterranean and soon found himself thrust into more notable events. He played a major part in the Corfu channel incident of October 1946. The British were exercising the right of passage through the straits that had been challenged by the Albanians. The destroyer HMS *Saumarez* had her bows blown off by a mine. *Volage* was ordered to tow the stricken ship but was mined herself. Forty-four men were killed, mainly on *Saumarez*. None the less, the two destroyers got back to Corfu, Scott being specially commended by the commander-in-chief for his courage and coolness in saving the ships. He next was put in charge of HMS *Meteorite*, a captured and rebuilt Walter U-boat, powered by highly volatile high test peroxide (HTP). The trials, while difficult and dangerous, led to Britain ordering HTP boats of her own design. In 1948 Scott went to the Far East as flag lieutenant to the commander-in-chief, Admiral Sir Patrick Brind. In April the following year the frigate HMS *Amethyst* became trapped by communist Chinese forces on the Yangtze (Yangzi) River. She had destroyed her codes to stop them falling into Chinese hands, so Scott devised a code system using the frigate's crew list to allow secure communications to and from the commander-in-chief. Eventually, more than three months later, *Amethyst* made it to safety.

The Royal Navy was pursuing midget submarine development as a possible means of nuclear delivery and Scott was put in charge of this unit in 1951 in command of HM trawler *Gateshead*. A more static life in the UK led to personal developments. On boxing day 1952 he married Pamela Dorothy Whitlock, a civil servant ten years his junior. They had one son and two daughters. Scott moved back to sea in 1953 in HMS *Andrew*. He took her all the way across the Atlantic submerged using her snort (schnorkel) to provide air for the diesels, a considerable pioneering achievement. His last submarine command was the heavily modernized HMS *Thermopylae* in 1955. He was then promoted to become training commander at Dartmouth in 1956.

Scott became fleet operations officer with the Home Fleet in 1958 before taking up command of the despatch vessel HMS *Surprise*, used by the commander-in-chief, Mediterranean Fleet. Promoted captain in 1962, he was sent to the US Naval War College before commanding the second submarine squadron from the depot ship HMS *Adamant*. He became deputy director of naval plans at the newly unified Ministry of Defence in 1965 before serving as chief of staff to the flag officer, submarines. He was then given command of one of the large guided missile destroyers, HMS *Fife*, in 1969. In 1971 he was promoted rear admiral and was sent to Washington as chief of British navy staff. He got on well with his American contemporaries, including the controversial chief of naval operations, Admiral Elmo Zumwalt. On his return in 1973 Scott was thrust into the highly secret Chevaline Polaris improvement programme, first as deputy controller Polaris until 1976 and then as chief of the Polaris executive (with responsibility for both scientific and naval aspects) until 1980, when he retired. The project was a troubled one (hugely exceeding its projected costs) and Scott's diplomatic skills were at a premium.

Scott was appointed CB in 1974 and knighted KBE in 1977. After retirement he became a director of Civil and Marine, a dredged aggregates company, with whom he maintained his connections until his death. His service career had been remarkable for its eventfulness and significance. He was a personally popular figure, gifted with gentlemanly charm towards both seniors and subordinates, although he retained the submariner's keen sense of humour. He died of a heart attack at Hammersmith Hospital, London, on 20 January 2006, and was survived by his wife, Pamela, and their three children.

ERIC J. GROVE

Sources E. Montagu, *The man who never was* (1953) · *The Times* (24 Jan 2006) · *Daily Telegraph* (9 May 2006) · Burke, *Peerage* · *WW* (2006) · b. cert. · m. cert. · d. cert.
Archives CAC Cam. | CAC Cam., incl. papers relating to *Amethyst* incident, GBE/1004 DKNS · Royal Naval Museum, Portsmouth, memoirs
Likenesses obituary photographs

Scott, Margaretta Mary Winifred (1912–2005), actress, was born at 6 Mandeville Place, Westminster, on 13 February 1912, the daughter of Hugh Arthur Scott (1878–1951), music critic, and his wife, Bertha Eugenie, *née* Casano (1878–1965). Her mixed Scottish, French, and Spanish ancestry may have accounted in part for the attractively exotic strain in some of her earlier work in particular. She was educated at the convent of the Holy Child Jesus, in Cavendish Square, London, and studied acting first with Rosina Filippi and then at the Royal Academy of Dramatic Art. She shared a scholarship there with Celia Johnson, who became a lifelong friend, and she was awarded the Kendal prize.

Scott's seventy-year career in the theatre began when, aged fourteen, she appeared as Mercutio's page in *Romeo and Juliet* at the Strand Theatre, London. This was followed by a season with the Repertory Theatre, Hull, before she started her West End career proper in *Her Shop* at the Criterion in July 1929. With her stunning dark beauty, eloquent voice, and versatility, she quickly established herself as a popular stage star with a wide emotional range, appearing in about fifty productions during the following decade. Though she graced many modern plays, such as *The First Mrs Fraser* and Emlyn Williams's *A Murder has been Arranged*, in which, one critic noted, she 'played the heroine with an emotional assurance beyond her 18 years' (*The Times*, 21 April 2005), she made her major impact in Shakespearian roles. For instance, at the Haymarket in 1931 she played first the Player Queen in *Hamlet*, and then succeeded Fay Compton as Ophelia, and in the following year was a notably fiery Viola in *Twelfth Night* at the Garrick. However, she was probably most tenaciously associated with the Open Air Theatre, Regent's Park, where, in four seasons (1933, 1934, 1936, and 1937), she played many leading roles, famously Olivia and Viola (in all four seasons) in *Twelfth Night*, Hermia in *A Midsummer Night's Dream*, Juliet in *Romeo and Juliet*, and Rosalind in *As You Like It*. She also played prolifically in the West End, had seasons at the Old

Vic and at Stratford, and during the Second World War, when she wasn't starring in *Major Barbara* for Birmingham Repertory Theatre or at the Aldwych in *Watch on the Rhine*, she was touring in *Quiet Weekend* for ENSA, as Marcia contemplating weedkiller for her golf-mad husband.

As she entered middle age Scott evinced a most commanding authority, allied to her still potent beauty, in a series of notable character roles including Katherine Parr in *The Young Elizabeth* at the New Theatre, 1952; Gertrude to Peter O'Toole's *Hamlet* at the Bristol Old Vic, 1958; Mrs Rossiter in the ripe drama of Victorian corruptions *The Right Honourable Gentleman* at Her Majesty's, 1965; Jocasta to Derek Jacobi's Oedipus in *Oedipus Rex* at Birmingham Rep, 1972; and Lady Bracknell in *The Importance of being Earnest* at the Old Vic, 1980. She was back at the Open Air Theatre in 1985 as the wheelchair-bound Madame Desmemortes in *Ring around the Moon*, and in her last role, as the imperious Mrs Hepworth, in the Chichester revival of *Hobson's Choice* (1995), she was grateful to have a week off in a very hot August because of the burden of her period costume. For someone aged eighty-three this seemed little to ask.

If there was some slight slackening of Scott's stage work in the 1950s this was due to the importance she attached to family life. On 14 September 1948 she married the composer of film scores and much decorated RAF flying ace John de Lacy Wooldridge (1919–1958), with whom she had two children, Susan and Hugh. Her marriage was cut tragically short by John Wooldridge's death in a car accident. In the late 1950s and early 1960s she also taught at the London Academy of Music and Dramatic Art, winning the respect of many students who went on to become famous.

Though the theatre was her first allegiance Scott also had distinguished careers in film and television. Apart from an uncredited part in Alexander Korda's *The Private Life of Don Juan* (1934) she made her film début in *Dirty Work* (1934), in which she and Basil Sydney played a pair of upper-class crooks, and in many of her films she vividly espoused a haughty aristocratic demeanour, often ruthless, sometimes merely opportunistic. Of her nearly thirty films, among the most memorable were *Things to Come* (1936), as Roxana, Ralph Richardson's mistress in this science-fiction classic; *The First Gentleman* (1948), as the prince regent's mistress helping him on with his boots; the snobbish Mrs Dixon in John Guillermin's excellent thriller *Town on Trial* (1957); and a mother-in-law from hell in *A Woman Possessed* (1958), an unusually classy vehicle for the infamous Danziger brothers. She was a less minatory presence as Marcia in *Quiet Wedding* (1941), a gracious heroine opposite Anton Walbrook in *The Man from Morocco* (1945), and the Empress Eugénie in the supremely idiotic *Idol of Paris* (1948), which she would later recall with a chortle of horror. But perhaps her finest work on film was as the coldly sensual, but humanly understandable Alicia in *Fanny by Gaslight* (1944), giving possibly the most stylish performance in any of the Gainsborough melodramas.

Scott embraced television early and played Beatrice in *Much Ado about Nothing* (1937); she later recalled playing Portia in *The Merchant of Venice* (1947) when Robert Adams, the first black actor to appear in Shakespeare on British television, playing the Prince of Morocco, dropped in a dead faint at her feet, and she was left improvising (this being live TV), 'Help, ho! the Prince!' (McFarlane, 517). Though she appeared in many popular series, the one for which she was perhaps most famous was *All Creatures Great and Small* (1978–90), in which she played the benign aristocrat, Mrs Pumphrey, owner of the pampered Pekinese, Tricky-Woo. There was, however, a great deal of more challenging work than this in all the acting media, and she left her mark in them all.

As well as devotion to her family and to a large circle of friends, to many of whom she was Peggy, Scott also gave tirelessly of her time to many theatrical charities, including service on the board of the Actors' Charitable Trust, which managed Denville Hall, the retirement home for former actors. Further, and—given her imposingly patrician acting persona—surprisingly, she was a founder signatory (and the last surviving one) of the actors' union, Equity, in 1934. Though she was known for playing malevolent mistresses and dangerous dowagers, she was a woman of great warmth, kindness, and good humour, enormously respected for both her professional and her personal qualities. She died at her home, 30 Molyneux Street, St Marylebone, London, on 15 April 2005, of pneumonia and breast cancer, and was survived by her daughter, Susan, an actress, and son, Hugh, a theatre director.

BRIAN MCFARLANE

Sources J. Parker, ed., *Who's who in the theatre*, 15th edn (1972) • B. McFarlane, *An autobiography of British cinema* (1997) • *The Guardian* (18 April 2005) • *Daily Telegraph* (20 April 2005) • *The Times* (21 April 2005) • *The Independent* (7 May 2005) • www.imdb.com, 26 Oct 2007 • Trinity College of Music, London, Mander and Mitchenson collection • private information (2009) [Hugh Wooldridge, son; Susan Wooldridge, daughter] • personal knowledge (2009) • m. cert. • d. cert.

Archives Trinity College of Music, Greenwich, Mander and Mitchenson collection, papers, corresp., signed photographs, theatre programmes | FILM BFINA, documentary footage • BFINA, performance footage | SOUND BL NSA, performance recordings • University of the West of England, Bristol, interview with B. McFarlane, 1990

Likenesses photographs, 1934–49, Getty Images, London • A. Wysard, group portrait, watercolour and pencil drawing, pubd 1937 (*Diners at Denham Studios restaurant*), NPG • F. Daniels, bromide print, 1940x49–1950x59, NPG • R. Westwood, matt bromide print, 1950–59, NPG • photographs, 1980, Rex Features, London • obituary photographs

Wealth at death £199,093: probate, 21 Nov 2005, *CGPLA Eng. & Wales*

Scott, Sir Nicholas Paul (1933–2005), politician and businessman, was born at the North Middlesex County Hospital, Edmonton, London, on 5 August 1933, the eldest son of Percival John Scott, a Metropolitan Police officer, and his Irish Catholic wife, Teresa Mary, *née* Murphy. At the time of his birth his father was a police constable, but he later rose to be a chief inspector. Scott was educated modestly, first at St Andrew's primary school in Streatham, and then at Clapham College. Later he studied part-time at the City of London College and the City Literary Institute, which allowed him to acquire a variety of executive posts and consultancies, principally in print, design, and publishing. After college he joined the RAF as a trainee navigator, but bad eyesight curtailed his career. On 7 August 1964, by then the personal assistant to the managing director of an advertising firm, he married Elizabeth Rosemary Merriell, a thirty-year-old divorcee, general secretary of an educational organization, and daughter of Robert Bissett Robinson, director of government contracts at the General Post Office. They had a daughter, and adopted a son and a daughter.

Scott was involved in Conservative politics from an early age, serving as a Conservative councillor on Holborn borough council in 1956–9 and 1962–5, and as national chairman of the Young Conservatives in 1963. He unsuccessfully contested Islington South-West in the general elections of 1959 and 1964 before being chosen as candidate for the safe Conservative seat of Paddington South, which he duly won in the general election of 1966. As a backbencher he spoke out against Enoch Powell's attack on Commonwealth immigrants in 1968, and in the same year repeatedly voted against James Callaghan's legislation to limit the entry into Britain of east African Asians. When the Conservatives returned to government in 1970, he was named parliamentary private secretary to Iain Macleod, the chancellor of the exchequer, just a month before Macleod died. Returning to the back benches, he stuck to his liberal views, opposing the sale of arms to apartheid South Africa. In 1972 he re-entered the government, this time as parliamentary private secretary to another liberal Conservative, Robert Carr, the home secretary. In January 1974, at the very end of Edward Heath's government, he became parliamentary under-secretary of state at the Department of Employment, under William Whitelaw.

Despite having been lauded by *Time* magazine as one of the 'future leaders of the world' (*Daily Telegraph*, 8 Jan 2005), Scott's political career suddenly stalled. First, he lost his Paddington seat at the election of February 1974. Second, although he made a swift return to the Commons in October 1974 via the safe seat of Chelsea, Margaret Thatcher, the new Conservative leader, removed him from his post as shadow housing minister when he refused a more junior post. Nor was he included in Thatcher's first government following the Conservatives' return to power in May 1979. Instead he was elected to the chairmanship of the Conservative back-bench employment committee, as well as serving on the executive of the back-bench 1922 committee. Once described by Richard Crossman as 'the most liberal Tory of them all' (*The Independent*, 10 Jan 2005), Scott had founded Nick's Diner, an informal club where like-minded tory 'wets', who had originally gathered, according to Kenneth Clarke, 'to prevent Ted Heath becoming too left-wing' (ibid.), now met up to criticize Margaret Thatcher's monetarist policies. Scott briefly flirted with the idea of joining the Social Democratic Party (SDP), but ultimately stayed loyal.

Scott's luck turned in September 1981, when James Prior, exiled to Northern Ireland, handpicked his own ministerial team. As parliamentary under-secretary of state, given responsibility for prisons, Scott was heavily criticized after a mass breakout from the Maze prison in September 1983, but Prior threatened to resign if Scott was dismissed. In the event, in September 1986, Scott was promoted to minister of state, returning in June 1987 to the mainland as minister of state at the Department of Health and Social Security, following the longest period in office in Northern Ireland by any post-war minister. In this new post his liberal tory instincts for higher public spending repeatedly jarred with Margaret Thatcher's constant desire for cutbacks. He continued at the trimmed-down Department of Social Security under John Major, taking on the additional title of minister for the disabled in 1990. His political career hit the buffers in May 1994, when he was found to have misled the House of Commons over government wrecking tactics that killed off a back-bench Civil Rights (Disabled Persons) Bill. His cause was not helped when his daughter, Victoria, herself a disabled rights campaigner, led the political attack against him. Two months later, he lost his post in a ministerial reshuffle.

In 1995 John Major recommended Scott for a knighthood—he had already been appointed MBE in 1964 and sworn of the privy council in 1989. Thereafter Scott suffered a series of personal misfortunes. Having survived a tough reselection battle for the redrawn seat of Kensington and Chelsea, his car shunted into another, trapping a three-year-old in a pushchair. Scott departed the scene, leaving his secretary to cope. He was later found guilty of drink-driving. Then, in 1996, he was photographed face down in a Bournemouth gutter, following an Irish embassy party at the Conservative Party conference. Few believed his story—that he had only had two glasses of wine, but that these had interacted with prescribed pain-killers—and especially disbelieving were many of the Eurosceptic members of his Kensington and Chelsea constituency association. They called a vote of confidence: Scott lost, making way for Alan Clark.

It is said that Scott only joined the Conservative Party because 'I was told the prettiest girls were in the Young Conservatives' (*Daily Telegraph*, 8 Jan 2005). His first marriage ended in 1976. There followed several high-profile alliances, including one with the black model Mynah Bird. On 18 April 1979 Scott married the Hon. Cecilia Anne Tapsell (*b*. 1943), dress designer, former wife of the Conservative MP Sir Peter Tapsell, and daughter of Bladen Wilmer Hawke, ninth Baron Hawke of Towton. They had one son and one daughter. Scott died on 6 January 2005, at Nazareth House, Hammersmith Road, Hammersmith, London, after suffering for a long period with Alzheimer's disease. He was survived by his second wife and four children, the adopted daughter from his first marriage having predeceased him. MARK STUART

Sources P. Norton, ed., *Dissension in the House of Commons: intra-party dissent in the House of Commons' division lobbies, 1945–1974* (1975) · J. Prior, *A balance of power* (1986) · A. Clark, *The last diaries* (2003) · D. Hurd, *Memoirs* (2003) · *The Guardian* (7 Jan 2005) · *The Times* (8 Jan 2005) · *Financial Times* (8 Jan 2005) · *Daily Telegraph* (8 Jan 2005) · *The*

Independent (10 Jan 2005) • Burke, *Peerage* • *WW* (2005) • private information (2009) • b. cert. • m. certs. • d. cert.
Archives FILM BFINA, current affairs footage | SOUND BL NSA, current affairs recordings; documentary recording
Likenesses photographs, 1959–96, Photoshot, London • J. Mendoza, group portrait, oils, 1986–7, House of Commons, London • photographs, 1994–6, PA Photos, London • photograph, 1996, Rex Features, London • E. McCabe, photograph, Camera Press, London • obituary photographs

Scott, Peter Graham (1923–2007), television director and producer, was born on 27 October 1923 at 25 Fitzgerald Avenue, Mortlake, Surrey, the son of Frederick George Scott, a bookmaker's clerk, formerly on the clerical staff of the Canadian army records office in London, and later a civil servant, and his wife, Constance, *née* Cornish. His father had lost a leg at Ypres, and the family's circumstances were sometimes hard. Scott won a scholarship to the county school, Isleworth, and encouraged by his mother, a keen amateur actress, also attended drama classes at the Italia Conti School. At the age of fourteen he played a small part in Alfred Hitchcock's *Young and Innocent* (1937) and was smitten with the ambition to become a film director himself.

On leaving school in 1942 Scott contrived to be taken on by the Ministry of Information's film division, headed by Sir Kenneth Clark and numbering such luminaries as Graham Greene and John Betjeman. A planned film with Dylan Thomas came to naught and Scott was called up for military service. He was commissioned into the Royal Artillery in 1943 and posted to the 145th field artillery (the Berkshire yeomanry), only to be invalided out after an accident in training. He reapplied himself to making a career in the cinema and became a skilled film editor, notably on *Brighton Rock* (1947), starring the young Richard Attenborough. In the meantime the BBC's pioneering television service had come back on the air after its wartime closure, and there was already talk of setting up a rival commercial system. In common with many contemporaries Scott was attracted by the possibilities of the new medium and in 1952 enrolled as a BBC trainee. He was soon making programmes of his own, notably a biography of the music hall star Marie Lloyd (1953), played by Pat Kirkwood. Meanwhile, on 10 June 1950 he married Eve Rosemary (Mimi) (*b.* 1929), production design assistant, and daughter of Herbert Raymond Martell, bank manager. They had two sons and two daughters.

When ITV was finally launched in 1955 Scott left the BBC to join the London weekday contractor, Associated Rediffusion, and it was there that his particular talents came into their own. Plays were still being broadcast live from the studio, with bits of outdoor action, if unavoidable, filmed in advance and cut into the transmission on cue. The switch would usually stick out like a sore thumb. Drawing on his film editing expertise, Scott directed two productions that defied such limitations. In *The Last Enemy* (1956), from Richard Hillary's memoir of war in the air, he slid seamlessly from studio to film and back again, while also hitting on such simple, effective studio ploys as a bare white wall to locate a scene in a hospital. The following year he deliberately restricted Brendan Behan's *The Quare Fellow* to cramped studio interiors, the better to bring out its enclosed prison setting. He had secured the television rights to the play after an evening's heavy drinking with Behan in a London pub.

As the fashion for drama series rather than single plays gained ground, Scott directed episodes of the racier examples that ITV were airing, including *Danger Man* (1960–61) and four episodes of *The Avengers* (1965–6). It was about this time that in order to avoid confusion with the naturalist and familiar face on the small screen Sir Peter Scott he inserted his middle name, Graham, into his credits. The change complemented his return to the BBC as a full-blown producer and, moreover, a producer of drama series that would be critically esteemed as well as being immensely popular. The archetype was *Mogul* (1965), set in the world of a giant oil company. Democratically, it would feature all ranks, from managing director down to workers on the rigs. But the audience preferred outsize characters, in this case the tycoon played by Geoffrey Keen and the financial wizard played by Philip Latham.

As the producer of a second series of *Mogul* in 1966 Scott astutely shifted the emphasis onto a couple of young executives, played by Ray Barrett and Robert Hardy, sent to sort out problems arising the world over. With a change of title to *The Troubleshooters*, it ran to a remarkable 123 episodes over six years, though latterly Anthony Read took over as producer. Scott was by then busy with *The Borderers* (1968–70), a kind of north-eastern western taking place on the Scottish borders in the seventeenth century, with Iain Cuthbertson as the warden trying to keep the peace between smugglers, rustlers, and plotters from both sides. Then came the most seductive series of all, *The Onedin Line* (1971–80), romanticizing the life and voyages of a nineteenth-century shipping owner and much helped by the dreamy strains of the accompanying Khachaturian score and the fortuitous sale of the show to West German television when the high costs of the maritime scenes threatened its survival. In the end it ran to ninety-one episodes.

Scott next moved to Harlech Television, the contractor for Wales and the west country, where he produced children's programmes as well as dramatizations of Daphne du Maurier's *Jamaica Inn* (1983) and Oscar Wilde's *The Canterville Ghost* (featuring John Gielgud, 1986). His career continued into the closing years of the century but he never quite mastered the vogue then for 'mini-series', which were in fact full-length stories—or movies—compressed into two or three outsize episodes. His was *Jenny's War* in 1985. He was elected a fellow of the Royal Television Society in 1979, and in 1984 won its Sir Ambrose Fleming award for outstanding services to television. His memoirs, *British Television: an Insider's History*, were published in 2000. He died at Frimley Park Hospital, Frimley, Surrey, on 5 August 2007, of heart disease, and was survived by his wife, Mimi, and their two daughters, his two sons having predeceased him. PHILIP PURSER

Sources P. G. Scott, *British television: an insider's history* (2000) • *Daily Telegraph* (11 Aug 2007) • *The Independent* (21 Aug 2007) • *The Times* (25

Aug 2007) • *The Guardian* (31 Aug 2007) • personal knowledge (2011) • private information (2011) • b. cert. • m. cert. • d. cert.
Archives SOUND BL NSA, current affairs recordings • BL NSA, documentary recordings • BL NSA, performance recordings
Likenesses obituary photographs

Seaton, Michael John (1923–2007), physicist and astronomer, was born on 16 January 1923 at 4 Arlington Villas, Clifton, Bristol, the son of Arthur William Robert Seaton (1892–1959), commercial traveller for a paper manufacturer, and later an advertising consultant, and his wife, Helen Amelia, *née* Stone (1893–1985). His primary education was interrupted by health problems and his secondary education at Wallington county grammar school, Surrey, by his political commitment. His opposition to fascism led him to join the Young Communist League in 1938 and he was expelled from school as a result of his political activities, though he was allowed to sit the matriculation examinations. Years later he was invited back to present the school prizes. His affiliation to the Communist Party ended in 1956 after the Soviet invasion of Hungary.

After leaving school Seaton worked for two years in a chemical factory before enlisting in the Royal Air Force as a navigator on Lancaster bombers during the Second World War. He flew many dangerous bombing missions, including some over Germany. There were numerous stories of how his skill with instruments and the precision of his calculations saved his crew from enemy action and even from a collision with Mont Blanc, which at the time was shrouded in clouds. On 10 June 1943 he married Olive May Singleton (1919–1959), who was then serving in the Women's Auxiliary Air Service. She was the daughter of Charles Singleton, and before her war service had worked as a shorthand typist. They had one son and one daughter.

After the war Seaton was admitted in 1946 to University College, London, as an undergraduate. This period marked a new era for atomic physics and astrophysics at University College. Harrie Massey had returned to his appointment as Goldsmid professor of mathematics and was joined by a number of colleagues including David Bates and Richard Buckingham. Seaton graduated with first-class honours in 1948 and began research under the direction of Bates. During his work on his PhD thesis he published six papers that significantly were equally distributed between astronomy and physics journals. The theme of his thesis became the basis of his subsequent scientific work. He received his PhD in 1951. In October 1950 Massey moved to the physics department at University College as Quain professor of physics, and Seaton was appointed as assistant lecturer, followed by promotions to lecturer in 1953, reader in 1959, and professor in 1963. Meanwhile, following the death of his first wife, on 20 October 1960 he married Joy Clarice Balchin (*b.* 1933), secretary, and daughter of Harry Albert Balchin, newsagent. They had one son.

Seaton made enormous contributions to both atomic physics and astrophysics. He was the author of nearly 300 journal articles as well as many other publications. He laid the foundations of the modern theory of electron–ion collisions, and established the crucial role that this theory and associated calculations play in the analysis of astronomical spectra. His work in astrophysics ranged from seminal papers on the central stars of planetary nebulae, density diagnostics using forbidden lines, the Seaton extinction curve, plasma diffusion theory, and many other topics. Of particular importance was his collaboration over some thirty years with Donald Osterbrock, which laid the foundation of later understanding of physical processes in planetary nebulae. Following his early work on electron–ion collisions, while on sabbatical in 1954–5 at the Institut d'Astrophysique de Paris, Seaton began a highly influential series of papers on quantum defect theory. Early applications of the theory were to resonance phenomena in electron–ion collisions and to photoionization. Later quantum defect theory was extended by other workers to ultracold two-body collisions and to molecules.

Seaton and his group at University College, London, were leaders in the development of general computer programmes for atomic structure, electron–atom and electron–ion collisions, and photoionization. This made possible the first accurate electron collision calculations for Fe II, iron being called the 'Rosetta Stone element' by Lawrence Aller. Seaton played a seminal role in 1978 in establishing the international journal *Computer Physics Communications*, and his support was crucial in the establishment of the UK Collaborative Computational Project on the 'continuum states of atoms and molecules' (CCP2), which became central to the development of state-of-the-art computer programs used in the analysis of laboratory and astrophysical plasmas. A major initiative that grew out of the availability of these general computer programs was the international Opacity Project proposed and led by Seaton, which was established in 1983 and involved about thirty collaborators from five different countries (France, Germany, UK, USA, and Venezuela). Knowledge of the opacity of stellar material is of fundamental importance to all studies of stellar structure and evolution and the *ab initio* calculations for atomic radiative processes, and the resulting stellar opacities solved several outstanding problems in astronomy. The Opacity Project was rightly hailed as the 'crowning achievement of computational atomic physics' (introduction to ITAMP workshop). Arising out of the Opacity Project, Seaton and David Hummer initiated the international Iron Project in 1992 to study collisional and radiative processes for iron and iron-peak elements. About seventy papers had been published in the Iron Project series by 2010.

Seaton was elected a fellow of the Royal Society in 1967 and received honorary doctorates from the Observatoire de Paris in 1976 and the Queen's University of Belfast in 1982. He was president of the Royal Astronomical Society in 1979–81 and awarded the society's gold medal in 1983. He was awarded the Guthrie medal and prize of the Institute of Physics in 1984 and the Hughes medal of the Royal Society in 1992. He was an honorary member of the American Astronomical Society, an honorary fellow of the American Physical Society, and a foreign associate, also known as an honorary foreign member, of the US Academy of Sciences. Although he retired to the Brecon Beacons he continued to carry out world-leading research up to the last few weeks of his life. He was an immense source of inspiration to all who knew him. He died of leukaemia and kidney failure at his home, Chatsworth, Bwlch, Brecknockshire, on 29 May 2007 and was buried on 7 June at the Usk Castle Chase Meadow natural burial ground in Monmouthshire. He was survived by his wife, Joy, and his children. PHILIP G. BURKE

Sources P. G. Burke and others, eds., *Atoms in astrophysics* (1983) • K. Kirby, A. Dalgarno, and A. Pradhan, introduction to ITAMP workshop in honor of Michael J. Seaton, Harvard-Smithsonian Center for Astrophysics, 7–9 Aug 2009, www.cfa.harvard.edu/itamp/HA06/seaton_page.pdf • *The Times* (7 June 2007) • *The Guardian* (31 Aug 2007) • *Bulletin of the American Astronomical Society*, 39/4 (2007), 1081 • P. Storey and P. Burke, 'Mike Seaton's legacy: an introduction', *News and Reviews in Astronomy and Astrophysics*, 49/6 (2008), 15 • *WW* (2007) • personal knowledge (2011) • private information (2011) [Mrs J. C. Seaton, widow] • b. cert. • m. certs. • d. cert.
Likenesses obituary photographs • photograph, repro. in www.phys.ucl.ac.uk/department/history/BFox4.html#Fox530 • photograph, repro. in www.ucl.ac.uk/silva/phys/seaton
Wealth at death under £19,000: probate, 13 Sept 2007, *CGPLA Eng. & Wales*

Seldon, Arthur (1916–2005), economist, was born on 29 May 1916 in London's East End, the son of Pinchas Margolis, merchant, and his wife, Masha. He was orphaned at the age of two when his parents, Russian Jewish immigrants, both died in the outbreak of Spanish flu in 1918. He was adopted by a cobbler and his wife, Mark and Eva Slabadain (later Anglicized to Seldon), also Russian Jewish immigrants. He was educated at Dempsey Street elementary school, Stepney, and Raines Foundation Grammar School. In 1934 he won a scholarship to the London School of Economics to read economics. Following a brief flirtation with the Fabian side of the school, he came under the influence of the classical liberal economists Lionel Robbins and F. A. Hayek. Small, slightly built, and cursed with a stammer, the young Seldon threw himself into his studies. He graduated with a first in 1937 and then became a research assistant to the economist Arnold Plant. Under the influence of these mentors he was converted to the merits of competitive markets, the rule of law, secure property rights, personal independence, and limited government. These values guided him for the rest of his life. He joined with others to found a student Liberal society. Following war service with the army in Africa and Italy, between 1942 and 1945, he became a tutor for the University of London Commerce Degree Bureau (1946–56), editor of *Store* (1946–9), and an economic adviser to the brewing industry. On 23 February 1948 he married the widowed (Audrey) Marjorie Perrott, a 28-year-old journalist and daughter of Lieutenant Wilford Willett, an officer in the London rifle brigade. They had three sons.

In January 1957 Seldon first met Ralph Harris, then director and sole employee of the Institute of Economic Affairs (IEA). Antony Fisher, a farmer, had established the IEA in 1955 from the profits of his Buxted Chicken Company. It was founded as 'a research and educational trust'; later it would be described as a think-tank. Seldon co-wrote the first IEA pamphlet, *Pensions and a Free Society* (1957), arguing the case for personal private pensions. The two men soon began a remarkable thirty-year collaboration. Harris was the public face of the IEA, a skilful networker and fund-raiser. Seldon, retiring but blessed with a fluent writing style, great energy, and tenacity, was soon made editorial director, a post he held until 1981, when he became consultant director until 1988. The two men challenged the post-1948 collectivist Keynesian assumptions about economic policy shared by leading politicians in both the Labour and Conservative parties. Seldon sought out authors, suggesting topics and badgering them to develop early drafts and to push inchoate ideas to a bold conclusion. He was fond of urging them to ignore warnings that their conclusions might be thought administratively impracticable or 'politically impossible'. His watchword was 'think the unthinkable'.

The IEA emphasized the importance of the pricing mechanism as a means of allocating resources, discovering alternative ways of providing services, and making comparisons between different goods and producers. It therefore opposed the state provision of 'free' public services, notably in health and education. It also promoted ideas from abroad (including a public choice school based in the University of Virginia, which argued that interest groups often shaped government policy and that interventions by vote-seeking politicians were often against the public interest) and the monetarist views of Milton Friedman and Hayek; the last two, both Nobel laureates, were IEA authors. It organized lectures and seminars and provided a congenial base for Friedman and Hayek's visits to the UK. Seldon's talent, apart from finding and marrying authors and topics, was in getting people to write in an accessible and jargon-free style and in using IEA media contacts to promote their ideas.

In contrast to some think-tanks, the IEA was more concerned to address the public than politicians. Seldon and Harris believed it was more effective to work indirectly, shaping the climate of opinion, which in turn would influence politicians. Although they provided encouragement for Margaret Thatcher's brand of Conservatism, Seldon in particular was concerned that the IEA should keep its distance from any political party. The IEA's publications successfully urged the case for privatization, the contracting out of services, deregulation, greater autonomy for schools (though it failed with school vouchers), trade-union reforms, an independent university, and student loans. The policy suggestions were designed to empower people, particularly the less well-off; why should the power to choose be confined to the wealthy? Producers and bureaucrats dominated the welfare state. Greater competition and consumer choice, and charging for services, were means of making public services more responsive to the public. The open market could be even more democratic than elections. The cash register operated as a referendum all day and every day.

Seldon was a prolific writer, although his skills were perhaps best demonstrated as a probing and sympathetic editor. Several of his twenty-eight books and over 200 articles were co-written or edited. The books, pamphlets, and collections of essays restated his commitment to the free society, the benefits of free markets and personal choice, and the negative effects of government intervention. They included *Corrigible Capitalism, Incorrigible Socialism* (1980), *Wither the Welfare State* (1981), *Socialism Explained* (1983), *The New Right Enlightenment* (1985), and *The Riddle of the Voucher* (1986). In retirement he also wrote *Capitalism* (1990), *The Dilemma of Democracy* (1998), and *The Retreat of the State* (1998). Colin Robinson, his successor as the IEA's editor, edited his collected works in seven volumes which were published by the Liberty Fund in 2004–5. Seldon was made a founder president of the IEA in 1990. He was also a founder trustee of the Social Affairs Unit, a vice-president of the Mont Pelerin Society, and an honorary fellow of the London School of Economics. He was appointed CBE in 1983. He died of cancer of the prostate at his home, Thatched Cottage, Godden Green, Sevenoaks, Kent, on 11 October 2005. His wife and their three sons survived him.

DENNIS KAVANAGH

Sources R. Cockett, *Thinking the unthinkable* (1994) • A. Seldon, *The making of the IEA* (2002) • *The Times* (12 Oct 2005) • *The Independent* (12 Oct 2005) • *Daily Telegraph* (13 Oct 2005) • *The Guardian* (13 Oct 2005) • *WW* (2005) • personal knowledge (2009) • private information (2009) • m. cert. • d. cert.

Likenesses obituary photographs • photographs, repro. in www.arthurseldon.org

Wealth at death £527,424: probate, 24 July 2008, *CGPLA Eng. & Wales*

Selwyn, Victor (1917–2005), journalist and literary editor, was born Victor Solomin at 19 Northcote Road, Battersea, London, on 11 January 1917, one of five children of Leon Solomin, later Selwyn, fur trader, and his wife, Sophia, *née* Melnick. His parents had emigrated from Lithuania. Educated in London, he graduated BSc from the London School of Economics shortly before the outbreak of the Second World War.

During the war Selwyn served in the Surrey regiment in north Africa and Italy as a navigation officer. But it was in Cairo in 1942 that he found his mission in life when, in Music for All, a meeting place for servicemen, he and two other men, David Burk and Denis Saunders—none of them with a higher rank than corporal—wondered why there seemed to be no poetry about the Second World War as there was about the First. Within four months, with the help of General Sir Henry Maitland (Jumbo) Wilson, the commander-in-chief in the Middle East, they appealed in newspapers and on the radio for poetry from men serving in the region. More than 3000 poems from 800 would-be contributors arrived, and a substantial selection was published under the title of *Oasis* by Salamander Productions in Cairo in 1943.

When he returned from the war Selwyn worked for a time as a market-research statistician. On 20 October 1946, at the synagogue in Singers Hill, Birmingham, he married Irene Rebecca Cohen, the 26-year-old daughter of Philip Cohen, tailor. They had two daughters, Trixie (*b.* 1949) and Louise (*b.* 1957). Selwyn's interest in writing eventually led to a successful career as a freelance journalist, and he wrote on a wide variety of subjects—including athletics, economics, and medical topics—for such newspapers as the *Daily Telegraph*, *The Guardian* and *The Times*. He also published several books, *Investment Guide Western Europe* (1972), *Guide to National Practices in Western Europe* (1973), and *Plan your Route: the New Approach to Map Reading* (1987). In 1955 the family moved from Acton to Hove and then in 1960 to 7 Lenham Avenue, Saltdean, where they remained until his death.

During the 1970s the idea of collecting and publishing the poetry of the Second World War was revived. Selwyn and several of the original Cairo poets established the Salamander Oasis Trust in 1976, and advertised for poetry from British servicemen everywhere. This appeal attracted thousands of poems and related items, and Selwyn and the trust began to seek publication. The first post-war anthology, *Return to Oasis: War Poems and Recollections from the Middle East, 1940–1946*, was published with an introduction by Lawrence Durrell in 1980. It was followed in 1983 by *From Oasis into Italy: War Poems and Diaries from Africa and Italy 1940–1946*, with a preface by Field Marshal Lord Carver. Both books were published by Shepheard-Walwyn. As more wartime writing was discovered, J. M. Dent published *Poems of the Second World War: the Oasis Selection* in 1985 and *More Poems of the Second World War: the Oasis Selection* in 1989. An anthology, especially edited (with Dennis Butts) for schoolchildren, *Schools Oasis: Poems of the Second World War*, was published by Nelson in 1992, and, fifty years after the end of the war in Europe, Penguin published *The Voice of War: Poems of the Second World War, the Oasis Collection* in 1995. Selwyn edited or co-edited all these works.

The Salamander Oasis Trust gradually expanded its interest during these years, trying to find, preserve, and, where possible, publish the poetry and diaries from all theatres of the war by men and women from the Commonwealth as well as Britain, including the famous, such as Keith Douglas's 'Elegy for an 88 Gunner' ('*Vergissmeinicht*'), as well as Elsie Cawser's less well-known comic 'Salvage Song' and the anonymous ballad 'The D-Day Dodgers'. There were poems about Dunkirk, Arnhem, and Belsen but also about air-raids, monotonous food, and missing letters. This was the stuff of a people's war. Selwyn, who eventually became editor-in-chief of the Salamander Oasis Trust, defined the character of its publications in his introduction to the *Schools Oasis*:

> In contrast to many anthologies, the *Oasis* series includes only poems by those serving in World War Two and written at the time. This gives the poems their immediacy. Poems, especially from the unknowns, smell of war, an authenticity ensured by the compilers having also been participants in that War, both serving and writing. That is how it was. We were there.

Apart from helping to collect and edit the material, Selwyn laboured tirelessly on behalf of the trust. Money had to be raised somehow, from charities and private donations, and often by public readings and the sale of books and audio-tapes. Hundreds of letters had to be written and numerous phone calls made. Selwyn called upon the support of former servicemen, including Ian Fletcher, Denis Healey, and Spike Milligan, and was also able to persuade gifted performers, like Dirk Bogarde, Barry Humphries, and Martin Jarvis, to help with public performances.

Selwyn's energy and (often stubborn) determination undoubtedly made him the driving force behind the Salamander Oasis Trust and all its works. He remained indefatigable, despite numerous ailments, and successfully resisted throat cancer in his later years. The trust lodged more than 17,000 poems and related documents in the Imperial War Museum, and thus made an invaluable contribution to an understanding of the Second World War. Selwyn was appointed MBE in 1996 in recognition of his contribution to Second World War literature. He died of aspiration pneumonia at Ireland Lodge, Lockwood Crescent, Brighton, on 26 October 2005, and his body was cremated at Woodvale crematorium, Brighton, on 4 November. He was survived by his wife and their two daughters. A memorial poetry reading held at the Imperial War Museum on 7 December ended with a spirited rendition of 'The D-Day Dodgers', led by Lord Healey.

DENNIS BUTTS

Sources *The Argus (Brighton & Hove)* (3 Nov 2005) • *The Guardian* (11 Nov 2005) • obituary on the Salamander Oasis Trust website, www.salamanderoasis.org/news/obituary-selwyn-victor.html, 10 July 2007 • personal knowledge (2009) • private information (2009) [T. Harmer, daughter] • b. cert. • m. cert. • d. cert.
Archives IWM
Likenesses photograph, repro. in *The Guardian* (11 Nov 2005)

Serpell, Sir David Radford (1911–2008), civil servant, was born at 3 Oakleigh Terrace, Plymouth, Devon, on 10 November 1911, the second son of Charles Robert Serpell (1870–1949), solicitor, and his wife, Elsie Leila, *née* Friend (1880–1958). Brought up in a strict nonconformist household, he was educated at Plymouth College and then at Exeter College, Oxford, where he graduated with a disappointing third in history in 1933. He subsequently took advantage of a wider intellectual canvas, obtaining a diploma from the University of Toulouse for a thesis on protestantism in France from 1650 to 1654. After a brief period as an assistant in Templin, Germany, in 1934, he studied at Syracuse University in New York state and then as a fellow at the Fletcher school of law and diplomacy of Tufts University. In 1937 he entered the British civil service, working first with the imperial economic committee. On 8 April 1938, at Maryfield Church, Torpoint, Cornwall, he married an American, Alice Ann Dooley, then aged twenty-one, daughter of Maurice Sylvester Dooley, professor of medicine. They had met during Serpell's stay in the USA, and had three sons, David, Peter, and Thomas.

On the outbreak of the Second World War Serpell joined the Ministry of Food and in 1941 became private secretary to Gwilym Lloyd George, the parliamentary under-secretary. When Lloyd George was appointed minister of fuel and power in June 1942 Serpell moved with him as his principal private secretary (1942–5). He spent the years 1945–60 at the Treasury, where he progressed to the rank of under-secretary in 1954. James Dunnett, permanent secretary at the Ministry of Transport, then secured his transfer at deputy secretary level in 1960. Responsible for inland transport, he assisted the minister, Ernest Marples, in dismantling the unwieldy British Transport Commission and establishing a more cost-effective railway industry. To that end a special advisory group was appointed under the chairmanship of Sir Ivan Stedeford to address the railways' mounting deficit, and Serpell was one of two civil servants who served as members. The outcome of a somewhat messy exercise in public policy was the demise of the British Transport Commission and the appointment of Richard Beeching as chairman of the commission and subsequently of the British Railways board, in 1961. Serpell also co-chaired an Anglo-French steering group that in 1963 produced the white paper on the channel tunnel.

From the Ministry of Transport Serpell moved to the Board of Trade as a second secretary (1963–6), then second permanent secretary (1966–8). A brief spell at the Treasury as a second secretary was followed by his return to the Ministry of Transport as permanent secretary in November 1968. This was another critical time, with Barbara Castle's Transport Act, 1968, in place, a determined minister, Richard Marsh, at the helm, and a McKinsey-inspired reorganization of British Rail in progress. On top of this the return of the Conservatives to power in 1970 resulted in the establishment of the giant Department of the Environment, which included transport, and Serpell served as its first permanent secretary until his retirement in August 1972. His career was characterized by a strong adherence to civil-service principles—an assiduous impartiality, appetite for hard work, emphasis on analysis, and a somewhat austere manner. He was described by *The Times* in May 1972 as 'a witty, subtle, moody, introverted man' who had 'the fire-breathing reputation of a man with extraordinarily high standards and little time for those who did not measure up to them' (*The Times*, 8 May 1972). His first marriage had ended in divorce in 1971, and on 30 May 1972, at Tonbridge register office, he married Doris May Farr (1919–2004).

Although British Rail had never appointed a former civil servant to its board, it was becoming more difficult to attract good part-time members with a modest salary of £1000, unchanged from 1958 to 1978, and Serpell, who was willing to put service before financial reward, was an obvious candidate. He was also expected to improve relationships between British Rail and its sponsoring department. As a board member from 1974 to 1982 his patient, understated contributions to policy became much valued, particularly in the strategy field, where he joined Michael Posner in formulating imaginative plans for investment. He resigned in May 1982 to undertake another fundamental review of railway finances, in light of the large and growing deficit in British Rail's accounts.

The *Review of Railway Finances* (1983), known simply as the Serpell report, was one of the most influential documents on the political economy of nationalized railways in Britain. It followed calls by Margaret Thatcher and her adviser Alan Walters for a cheaper railway and an end to union power, and exposed Serpell to the full rigour of media attention at the age of seventy-one. Ironically, his selection as chairman of the review committee had been completely unexpected, having followed numerous unsuccessful attempts to recruit someone else. As he later recalled, 'I was absolutely flabbergasted because all the talk had really been about getting a good neutral' (Gourvish, *British Rail*, 569). In accordance with its remit, the report rehearsed several options for a financially more robust railway network, ranging from retaining the existing 10,300 mile network to cutting it to 1630 miles, but opponents fastened onto the more draconian options and Serpell, who was clearly no political Machiavelli, was easily outmanoeuvred: by the minister, David Howell, who effectively changed the terms of reference at the eleventh hour to focus more on short-term considerations; by Alfred Goldstein, a maverick member sympathetic to Walters's views, whom Serpell sought to accommodate but who insisted on producing his own minority report; and finally by his former colleagues at British Rail, who leaked against the report, doing much to undermine it. Serpell, who had played a straight bat throughout, and had scrupulously refrained from making clear his own preferences (which were in fact in favour of retaining as extensive a network as possible), emerged visibly bruised by the affair. It was little consolation that many of the ideas for improving productivity and performance, particularly in operating and engineering, were taken up by Bob Reid, chairman of the British Railways board from 1983.

Serpell took on some more congenial tasks in retirement. A keen environmentalist, from 1973 to 1977 he was chairman of the newly created Nature Conservancy Council and a member of the council of the National Trust. He was also a member of the National Environmental Research Council in 1973–6 and chaired the Ordnance Survey review committee in 1978–9. He had been appointed OBE in 1944, CMG in 1952, and CB in 1962, and knighted KCB in 1968. He was elected an honorary fellow of Exeter College, Oxford, in 1992. He had a happy retirement in Crossparks, Dartmouth, Devon, where he enjoyed walking, golf, and reading crime novels, but with advancing years moved to a retirement home, Hyne Town House, in Strete, Dartmouth, where he died of prostate cancer and heart disease on 28 July 2008. He was survived by his three sons. TERRY GOURVISH

Sources P. Parker, *For starters: the business of life* (1989) • T. R. Gourvish, *British Railways, 1948–73: a business history* (1986) • T. Gourvish, *British Rail, 1974–97: from integration to privatisation* (2002) • C. Loft, *Government, the railways and the modernization of Britain: Beeching's last trains* (2006) • T. Gourvish, interviews with David Serpell, 27 Jan 1984; 12 March 1991, National Railway Museum • A. Whitehouse, interview with David Serpell, 'Back to Beeching', BBC, broadcast 27 Feb 2010 • *The Times* (7 Aug 2008); (13 Aug 2008) • *Daily Telegraph* (7 Aug 2008) • *The Independent* (8 Aug 2008); (2 Sept 2008) • *The Guardian* (11 Aug 2008) • *The Scotsman* (12 Aug 2008) • *British Imperial Calendar and Civil Service List* (1941–72) • *WW* (2008) • Burke, *Peerage* • personal knowledge (2012) • private information (2012) • b. cert. • m. certs. • d. cert.

Likenesses photographs, 1982, PA Photos, London • obituary photographs

Wealth at death under £145,000: probate, 19 Nov 2008, *CGPLA Eng. & Wales*

Shackleton, Sir Nicholas John [Nick] (**1937–2006**), earth scientist and palaeoclimatologist, was born on 23 June 1937 at 112 Cheyne Walk, Chelsea, London, the only son and eldest of three children of Robert Millner *Shackleton (1909–2001), geologist, and his first wife, Gwen Isabel (1906/7–2000), daughter of Alfred John Harland, schoolmaster. He also had a half-brother and sister by his father's second marriage. He was related to the Antarctic explorer Sir Ernest Shackleton (his grandfather being a second cousin). At the time of his birth his father was a lecturer in geology at Imperial College, London, who travelled widely for research and industry, which led to his spending 1940–45 in Kenya searching for gold and strategic minerals, thereby giving Nick an early childhood on the African plains, out of the way of wartime London bombing.

Shackleton attended Cranbrook School, Kent, as a boarder from 1949 to 1956. National service followed, in the Queen's Own Royal West Kent regiment, where, as Bandsman Shackleton, and already an accomplished clarinettist, he was secretary of the regimental band. He entered Clare College, Cambridge, in 1958 to read natural sciences. He found several outlets for his enthusiasms, including music, and his undergraduate career was academically undistinguished: he obtained lower seconds in parts one and two, and graduated BA in physics in 1961. In the first two years of his course he had split his time about equally between physics and maths and, perhaps following his father, geology and mineralogy. He then did physics for part two. Despite his poor degree, however, he stayed on at Cambridge to do research.

Shackleton's first, seminal, achievement was to modify a mass spectrometer so that it could measure the mass ratio of the isotopes of oxygen (O-18/O-16) in minute samples of calcium carbonate. Samples as small as 0.4 milligrams (representing about five to ten shells of the pinhead-sized fossil foraminifera, common in marine sediments) could be measured to an accuracy of one part in 10,000. He was set this task by the professor of botany (and director of the sub-department of Quaternary research), Harry Godwin, who had already set up a radiocarbon laboratory to make carbon-14 age measurements, and to whom Sir Edward Bullard, then reader in geophysics at Cambridge, had suggested that he add the determination of past temperature through oxygen isotopes, work pioneered in Chicago. Godwin was a fellow (and Bullard a member) of Clare College, where Shackleton was an undergraduate. The American Harold Urey (who had won the Nobel prize for chemistry in 1934) had shown in 1947 that there was a small change in the O-18/O-16 ratio in calcium carbonate from its value in (sea) water dependent on the water temperature from which it was precipitated (either inorganically or by organisms). Shackleton's task for his PhD ('The measurement of palaeotemperatures in the Quaternary era', awarded in 1967) was to exploit this.

Of course it was necessary first to know what was the isotopic composition of the seawater in which fossils lived. Cesare Emiliani of Chicago, who in the mid-1950s had used the method to estimate the glacial to interglacial sea temperature change, assumed that the corresponding seawater change was not great. Some change was to be expected because, when water evaporates, the light isotope comes off preferentially and the resulting snow that gets locked up in ice sheets is isotopically lighter (it has more O-16) than the ocean. Emiliani estimated that Caribbean surface waters were up to 6°C colder in the last glacial period, about 20,000 years ago. Shackleton made measurements on the same deep-sea sediment cores as Emiliani using the rare species of foraminifera that live on the sea bed where the temperature is now very low (less than 4°C), and thus unable to be very much colder in a glacial. Shackleton saw that the changes in surface- and bottom-dwelling foraminifera were rather similar and deduced that there was a large ice-volume effect and a much smaller temperature change than Emiliani had supposed. This had huge implications.

Working down sediment cores Shackleton was able to chart the growth and decay of ice sheets and specify the position of glacial maxima. This led to his pivotal position in the attempt to map the temperature of the glacial ocean using fossil plankton species composition (rather than the O-18/O-16 ratio) because he could say where the glacial level was in a core. The analysis of the down-core spectrum of ice-volume and temperature changes was shown to match the spectrum of changes in the amount of solar radiation received by the earth (insolation) due to changes in its orbit around the sun, a theory first expressed by James Croll in the 1870s but calculated by Milutin Milankovitch, a Serbian astronomer, in the 1930s. The demonstration that the Milankovitch theory of orbital climate change was correct and could be recognized in isotopic (and later many other physical) properties of rocks meant that an age scale based on astronomical calculation could be applied to rocks in which this cyclicity could be recognized. In this way Shackleton revolutionized the determination of ages and the field of stratigraphic geology. The calculated time-sequence of insolation values provided a template whose ages could be transferred onto the matching sequence of isotope values, a procedure known as 'orbital tuning'. This was later applied to sequences of rocks hundreds of millions of years old.

There were many other consequences of Shackleton's work. Most were worked out in numerous fruitful collaborations with other scientists around the world. Knowing ice-volume changes allowed him to establish glacial changes in sea level. He correlated climatic changes in the oceans with those on land through collaboration with pollen analysts, with Chinese specialists on wind-blown dust deposits, and with workers on Greenland and Antarctic ice-cores. He was one of the principal originators of the field of palaeoceanography, the study of marine sediments and their enclosed fossils to deduce past ocean conditions. In this he also used the stable carbon isotope ratio (C-13/C-12) in marine fossils, which provides insight into the cycling of carbon through the oceanic and terrestrial ecosystem. In particular the shifting of carbon from land to ocean and CO_2 between ocean and atmosphere, and its timing in relation to ice-volume and temperature changes, was his final seminal contribution. Between 1965 and 2007 he published over 300 papers and data reports, and edited six collections of papers, to which over 16,000 references had been made in the scientific literature by May 2009. This represents an enormous impact, rivalled by very few others in the earth sciences.

Shackleton married, on 10 June 1967, Judith Carola Murray (*b.* 1945/6), then an undergraduate at Newnham College, and daughter of Henry Murray, chemist. They were divorced in 1977, and on 25 September 1986 he married Vivien Anne *Law (1954–2002), a distinguished linguistic scholar, and daughter of John Ernest Law, engineer. Shackleton claimed to be in awe of her intellectual prowess and said she could learn a new language by reading a grammar over the breakfast table. As she knew over a hundred languages this seems entirely likely, though he had no reason to be in awe of anyone.

With many friends Shackleton shared a love of music; he was a brilliant clarinettist, and a collector and scholar of the instrument. In Cambridge he lectured and supervised in the faculty of music on the physics and acoustics of music and contributed articles to the *Galpin Society Journal* and to the *New Grove Dictionary of Music and Musicians* (1980 and 2001). He amassed the largest collection of clarinets in the world. When he bequeathed it to the University of Edinburgh (because it agreed to his stipulation that the instruments be available to be played) his collection numbered nearly 900 instruments, including 817 clarinets and basset horns, and was estimated to be worth around £1 million. He liked to remark, somewhat disingenuously, having had no children, that all this could be done on just a lecturer's salary.

Shackleton won numerous awards and prizes for his research. He was made a fellow of the Royal Society in 1985 and of the Academia Europaea in 1988, a foreign associate of the US National Academy of Sciences in 2000, and a foreign member of the Royal Netherlands Society of Arts and Sciences in 2001. His many medals included the Shepard medal (Society for Sedimentary Geology, USA, 1985), Carus medal (German Academy of Sciences Leopoldina, 1985), Lyell and Wollaston medals (Geological Society of London, 1987 and 1996 respectively), Huntsman medal (Canada, 1990), Crafoord Prize (Royal Swedish Academy of Science, 1995), Milankovitch medal (European Geophysical Society, 1999), Ewing medal (American Geophysical Union, 2002), Urey medal (European Association of Geochemistry, 2003), royal medal of the Royal Society (2003), Vetlesen prize (Columbia University, USA, 2004), and in 2005 the founder's medal of the Royal Geographical Society and the blue planet prize (Japan). In the earth sciences the Crafoord and Vetlesen prizes are considered of Nobel rank, there being no Nobel prize for these fields. Honorary degrees came from Dalhousie (Canada), Stockholm, and Padua universities. He was knighted in 1998. His last years were clouded by his lymphoma and then the death of his wife, Vivien. He died at his home, 12 Tenison Avenue, Cambridge, on 24 January 2006. In 2008 the Geochemical Society established the Nicholas J. Shackleton award in his name. I. NICHOLAS MCCAVE

Sources *Cambridge University Reporter*, 89–91 (1958–61) · *The Times* (31 Jan 2006); (3 Feb 2006); (9 Feb 2006) · *The Independent* (8 Feb 2006) · *New York Times* (12 Feb 2006) · *The Guardian* (13 Feb 2006) · G. H. Haug and L. C. Peterson, *Nature*, 439/7079 (23 Feb 2006), 928 · C. Tzedakis, *Quaternary Science Reviews*, 25/5–6 (March 2006), 403 · T. Crowley, *Eos*, 87/17 (25 April 2006), 167 · W. F. Ruddiman, *Science*, 312 (5 May 2006), 711 · D. B. Booth, *Quaternary Research*, 65/3 (May 2006), 353 · J. D. Hays, *Quaternary Science Reviews*, 25/23–4 (Dec 2006), 3090–91 · 'List of publications of Nicholas J. Shackleton', *Quaternary Science Reviews*, 25/23–4 (Dec 2006), 3463–75 · A. Myers, *Galpin Society Journal*, 59 (2006), 291–3 · H. Fricke and others, *Historic musical instruments in the Edinburgh University collection: catalogue of the Sir Nicholas Shackleton collection*, ed. A. Myers (2007) · E. Hoeprich, 'The Shackleton collection', *Early Music*, 36/1 (Feb 2008), 160–61 · 'Citation for the first Nicholas J. Shackleton award of the Geochemical Society', *Geochimica et Cosmochimica Acta*, 73/13, suppl. 1 (2009) · Clare College, Cambridge, archives · *WW* (2006) · Burke, *Peerage* · personal knowledge (2010) · private information (2010) · b. cert. · m. certs. · d. cert.

Archives RS

Likenesses obituary photographs · photograph, RS

Wealth at death £1,651,971: probate, 14 Aug 2006, *CGPLA Eng. & Wales*

Moira Shearer [Kennedy] (**1926–2006**), by Baron, 1948

Shearer, Moira [*née* Moira Shearer King; *married name* Moira Shearer Kennedy, Lady Kennedy] (**1926–2006**), ballet dancer, actress, and writer, was born on 17 January 1926 at Morton Lodge, Dunfermline, Fife, the only child of Harold Charles King, civil engineer, and his wife, Margaret Crawford Reid, *née* Shearer. Part of her early childhood was spent in Ndola, Northern Rhodesia. It was her mother who insisted on her learning to dance, initially with a former Diaghilev dancer in Ndola. After returning to Scotland and studying at Dunfermline high school and Bearsden Academy, Glasgow, she resumed her dance classes in London with Flora Fairbairn and subsequently Nadine Nicolaeva Legat, then at Sadler's Wells School. Her professional début came at the age of fifteen with Mona Inglesby's new International Ballet. Other dancers greatly admired the strong technique, classical style, and grace of her Swallow solo in Inglesby's creation *Planetomania*, not to mention her physical beauty, set off by the red hair that she kept throughout her life.

At the age of sixteen Moira Shearer joined the Sadler's Wells company, taking part in their wartime tours and London seasons. Soon she was given many standard solos besides taking roles specially made for her: by Frederick Ashton as Pride in his Faerie Queene ballet *The Quest*; by Ninette de Valois in a trio in her display ballet *Promenade*; by Andrée Howard as Butterfly in her *Festin de l'araignée*; and by Robert Helpmann as a young lover in his *Miracle in the Gorbals*. When Sadler's Wells moved to Covent Garden in 1946 Ashton cast Shearer as one of the three ballerinas in his immensely admired classic ballet *Symphonic Variations*, which would alone have been enough to make her name for all time. Soon afterwards Ashton made the role of the young wife for her in his *Don Juan*, and also chose her to replace the injured Margot Fonteyn at the première of his first full-evening ballet, *Cinderella*, with himself and Helpmann playing the ugly sisters. About this time Léonide Massine arrived as guest choreographer and dancer, and he picked Shearer to dance with him the can-can in *La boutique fantasque*, one of his most celebrated ballets. Thereafter he gave her the lead in the British première of his ballet *Mam'zelle Angot*, and followed that by creating a new work around her, *Clock Symphony*, to Haydn's music. Soon, in 1950, she had further roles she greatly enjoyed: in Georges Balanchine's classic *Ballet imperial* at Covent Garden and in Roland Petit's dramatic *Carmen* in Paris.

Shearer had, reluctantly, been persuaded to take the lead, as a ballerina who finally kills herself for love, in *The Red Shoes*, which proved to be the most popular ballet film ever made, constantly repeated on television after its première in 1948. Consequently, when the Sadler's Wells Ballet first visited New York, Shearer was its best-known member there and the American management wanted her to dance Princess Aurora on the opening night, but de Valois naturally and rightly insisted that that distinction had to go to Margot Fonteyn. Shearer was given the prominent although smaller Bluebird duet. Her début in that role at Covent Garden was booed by fans who thought it unfair to take it away from its usual interpreter, Violetta Elvin. *The Red Shoes* led to further ballet films: as both Olympia and Stella in *Tales of Hoffman* (1951) and the *Cyrano de Bergerac* section of Petit's *1-2-3-4 ou Les collants noirs* (1960). Having revealed acting skills in *Red Shoes*, she was cast in dramatic films like *The Story of Three Loves* (1953), *The Man who Loved Redheads* (1955), and *Peeping Tom* (1960).

Meanwhile, on 25 February 1950, at the Chapel Royal in Hampton Court Palace, Shearer had married Ludovic Henry Coverley Kennedy (1919–2009), author and broadcaster, and son of Edward Coverley Kennedy, naval officer. They had three daughters and a son between 1966 and 1971. She became Lady Kennedy when her husband was knighted in 1994.

Shearer left the Sadler's Wells Ballet in 1952 but did have a few further dancing roles: in Michel Fokine's *Le spectre de la rose* with the London Festival Ballet at Monte Carlo in 1952; in *Gold Diggers*, a gala number made for her as a Fred Astaire figure by Peter Darrell with the Scottish Ballet in 1980 (she also acted with lucidity and charm as commentator in their film of August Bournonville's three-act classic *Napoli*), and finally creating the mother in Gillian Lynne's film ballet about the painter Lowry, *A Simple Man*, for Northern Ballet in 1987, although she declined to repeat the role on its stage transfer.

From 1954, however, Shearer preferred acting, first as Titania in an Old Vic production of *Midsummer Night's Dream* at the Edinburgh festival and touring North America. There followed Sally Bowles in Isherwood's *I Am a Camera* in 1955. In the same year she joined the Bristol Old Vic, and was Shaw's Major Barbara there in 1956. She appeared in *A Man of Distinction* at the Edinburgh festival in 1957. Much later, when the Kennedys were living by the Water of Leith, she played Madame Ranevskaya in *The Cherry Orchard* (1977) and Judith Bliss in *Hay Fever* (1978), both at the Royal Lyceum, Edinburgh, and Juliana Bordereau in *The Aspern Papers* (1994) at the Citizens' Theatre, Glasgow.

Meanwhile Shearer had begun lecturing on ballet and giving poetry and prose recitals, often with her husband, including three tours on the liner *Queen Elizabeth II*. She also became a regular book reviewer (not only of dance books) for the *Daily Telegraph* and *Sunday Telegraph*; contributed articles on Ashton and Balanchine to the *Dictionary of National Biography*; and published two books of her own, *Balletmaster: a Dancer's View of George Balanchine* (1986), and a biography of Ellen Terry (1998). But after starting her memoirs she abandoned them, claiming that nobody would find the subject interesting. She was a member of the BBC's general advisory council (1970–77) and of the Scottish Arts Council (1971–3), and was a director of Border Television (1977–82).

In their later years the Kennedys moved to Avebury, Wiltshire, and later to Boars Hill, Oxford. In 2000 Shearer was diagnosed as suffering from viral encephalitis, which impaired her memory. About the time of her eightieth birthday she felt notably weak, was admitted to the John Radcliffe Hospital, Oxford, and died there of septicaemia and a urinary tract infection on 31 January 2006, surrounded by her family. She was survived by her husband, Ludovic, and their four children. JOHN PERCIVAL

Sources P. Noble, *British ballet* (1948) • H. Fisher, *Moira Shearer* (1952) • H. Koegler, *The concise Oxford dictionary of ballet*, 2nd edn, updated (1987) • *The Times* (2 Feb 2006) • *Daily Telegraph* (2 Feb 2006) • *The Guardian* (2 Feb 2006) • *The Independent* (2 Feb 2006); (3 Feb 2006) • Burke, *Peerage* • *WW* (2006) • personal knowledge (2010) • private information (2010) • b. cert. • m. cert. • d. cert.

Archives FILM BFINA, *Borderers*, N. Fraser (director), 1976 • BFINA, current affairs footage • BFINA, documentary footage | SOUND BL NSA, documentary recordings • BL NSA, performance recordings

Likenesses C. Beaton, bromide print, 1940–49, NPG • photographs, 1942–67, Getty Images, London, Popperfoto • photographs, 1943–67, Hult. Arch., London • R. C. Guthrie, oils, *c*.1946, NPG • C. Lucas, bromide fibre print, 1947, NPG • photographs, 1947–94, Rex Features, London • Baron, photograph, 1948, Hult. Arch., London [*see illus.*] • R. Westwood, cibachrome print, 1948, NPG • photographs, 1948–50, Getty Images, London, Time and Life pictures • photographs, 1948–91, PA Photos, London • Y. Karsh, bromide print, 1954, NPG • photographs, 1954–67, Getty Images, London, Popperfoto • photograph, 1957, Camera Press, London • A. Arikha, oils, 1993, Scot. NPG • M. Bishop, drawing, repro. in *Harpers and Queen* (Nov 1985), 33 • J. Bown, photograph, repro. in J. Bown, *Women of consequence* (1986) • Sir W. R. Flint, red chalk; Christie's, 24 Sept 1992 • J. Player, photograph, repro. in *New York Times* (10 Jan 1988) • P. Sayer, photograph, repro. in *Sunday Express* (4 Oct 1981) • obituary photographs • photograph, Kobal Collection, London; repro. in J. Kobal and J. Russell Taylor, *Portraits of the British cinema, 60 glorious years 1925–1985* (1985) • photographs, Photoshot, London • photographs, repro. in www.ballerinagallery.com

Wealth at death £398,661: probate, 11 Jan 2007, *CGPLA Eng. & Wales*

Sheppard, David Stuart, **Baron Sheppard of Liverpool** (**1929–2005**), cricketer and bishop of Liverpool, was born on 6 March 1929 at 86 Doods Road, Reigate, Surrey, the younger child of Stuart Morton Winter Sheppard, solicitor, and his wife, Barbara, *née* Shepherd. His father was a cousin of Tubby Clayton, the founder of Toc H, and his mother was the daughter of J. A. Shepherd, an artist who regularly drew for *Punch* magazine. The family lived comfortably in Chelsea, London, until Sheppard was eight, when his father died aged only forty-two. Before his death he had instilled a love of cricket in his young son, taking him to watch games at Hove and Lord's. Afterwards the family moved to Sussex, where his mother began rebuilding the family's life, and patiently encouraged Sheppard's cricketing prowess. As a young boy he would spend hours batting a tennis ball against the coal-shed door, imitating some of the great players like Wally Hammond. His mother and older sister, Mary, left him in no doubt that he was born 'on the right side of the tracks' and there were frequent family debates on the demerits of socialism.

England cricketer Sheppard became a weekly boarder at Northcliffe House School, Bognor Regis, before going to Sherborne School at the age of thirteen. His experiences of public school were mixed but he declared himself grateful for the foundations that were laid there: he gained a love of choral music, 'beautiful expressions of distant truths' (*Steps along Hope Street*, 12), which he maintained throughout his life and which he was able to indulge particularly in retirement, and he was encouraged to excel at cricket. It has been said that Sheppard was not a born cricketer, but one whose talent was nurtured through sheer application and hard work. He himself listed 'powers of concentration; determination to succeed; application and the need to review' among the qualities learned through cricket (ibid.).

David Stuart Sheppard, Baron Sheppard of Liverpool (1929–2005), by Sefton Samuels, 1980

Sheppard went to Trinity Hall, Cambridge, to read history in 1947. The pitches at Fenner's were ideally suited to his style of play. He excelled in the university team of 1950, scoring 227 in an opening stand of 343 against the West Indies. In August of that year he gained his first England cap against the tourists at the Oval, and the following winter he toured Australia. He went on to play a total of 22 test matches between 1950 and 1963, scoring a total of 1172 runs at an average of 37.80, including 3 centuries and 6 fifties. His top test score of 119 came in 1952 against India at the Oval. Meanwhile he played county cricket for Sussex, a team he joined while at university. Eventually he skippered them and brought them from bottom of the table to the position of runners-up in 1953, when he was named *Wisden* cricketer of the year. This success led him to the England captaincy on two occasions in 1954. In 1962 he toured Australia again, scoring 113 in the second test and 66 in the fifth. It was in one of those tests, when Sheppard, by now ordained, had a particularly bad day in the slips, that Fred Trueman commented, 'It's a pity t'Rev doesn't put his hands together more often in t'field' (*Daily Telegraph*). Sheppard's final three test match appearances followed in New Zealand early in 1963. His total first-class runs amounted to 15,838 at an average of 43.51 and 45 centuries.

Ordination, marriage, and suffragan bishopric During Sheppard's cricketing career came the two major life choices that together determined his future path: ordination in 1955 and marriage in 1957. In his first term at university Sheppard came into contact with evangelical Christianity, through a Christian Union mission conducted by the American evangelist Donald Grey Barnhouse. Subsequently realizing the difference between this and the formal religion learned from his family and public school, he underwent a profound conversion and so began the journey of faith that was to give him a very different public profile from that of a sportsman. Following national service in 1953 he wrote an 'appreciation of the situation', army-style, as he began to think about his future. He was thinking about how he could best serve God—perhaps reaching out to the many people who felt that the church and the Christian gospel were not for them—and was, later the same year, accepted for training as an ordinand by Bishop George Bell of Chichester. This was followed by two years' theological training at Ridley Hall, Cambridge, and ordination at St Paul's Cathedral, London, on 29 September 1955. His first post was as curate of St Mary's, Islington, where a future bishop of Norwich, Maurice Wood, was vicar. Cricket was almost a distant memory as Sheppard threw himself into parish life with a passion, and also took to writing, beginning a weekly column for *Woman's Own*, which continued for seventeen years. However, his cricketing career was not yet over: in 1956 Sheppard played a month's cricket for Sussex, and was surprised to find himself called up for England again for the fourth test against Australia. He was even more surprised to score 113 in this, the famous 'Laker test', when the legendary bowler took nineteen wickets.

While at Ridley Hall Sheppard met his future wife, (Eleanor) Grace Isaac, a student at Homerton College, and daughter of Bryan Raymon Isaac, clergyman. Their meeting led to marriage on 19 June 1957 (when Grace was aged twenty-two) and a partnership of forty-eight years. On honeymoon Grace became ill and the consequences of this were long-lasting. Her experience led to deep reflection, which after her recovery enabled her to take up a new vocation as a writer and speaker. She chronicled her story in her book *An Aspect of Fear* (1989), in which she told of Sheppard's faith, strength, and constancy. Indeed the book was dedicated to him 'for being there and sharing the risks'. The Sheppards' marriage became known for its strength and depth, with Grace strenuously supporting her husband, despite her personal problems, in both public and private ministry.

Six months after their marriage the Sheppards moved to Canning Town, and to the Mayflower Family Centre where, for twelve years, they immersed themselves in urban life, building the centre up to a congregation of 110 and a full-time staff of 10. In 1963 their daughter Jenny was born and their home became the very heart of the centre's work. Influenced by local people, notably George Burton, who 'left an indelible impression on [his] approach to inner-city mission', Sheppard began to understand what later became a central strand of his thinking: that social structures as well as human hearts need to change in order for God's kingdom of justice and peace to be seen (*Steps along Hope Street*, 12).

In 1960 Sheppard had refused to tour South Africa, because of the apartheid regime. In 1968 there was a much greater furore over the 'D'Oliveira affair', prompted by the South African government's refusal to allow an English cricket team to enter the country if Basil D'Oliveira, a 'coloured' South African, was a member. Initially the MCC was prepared to succumb, but after loud protests from prominent cricketers, including Sheppard, the tour was called off. Friendships were broken, and Sheppard was badly hurt by things said both in private and in the newspapers about him.

Later the same year the enigmatic bishop of Southwark, Mervyn Stockwood, having seen Sheppard on television arguing the anti-apartheid cause, and himself never one to avoid controversy, settled on Sheppard as his new colleague as suffragan bishop of Woolwich. They had never met. There followed six happy years as the Sheppards settled into their new home in Peckham—not, by their own request, in commuter-belt Surrey—and the life of a bishop. This period was a formative time for Sheppard as he began to bring together his experience and reflections on urban poverty with the influence and potential for change afforded him as a bishop. His second book, the substantial *Built as a City* (1974), covered a whole sweep of issues concerning both church and secular bodies, individual and organizational behaviours. Paramount among his concerns was the need for local people to be given more responsibility for their own lives, and the recognition that there could be no 'quick-fix' solutions for urban problems. He called for long-term investment of both human and material resources in urban areas, by church and state.

Bishop of Liverpool Woolwich was an episcopal apprenticeship for Liverpool as Islington had been a priestly one for Canning Town. In 1975 came Sheppard's appointment as bishop of Liverpool, following Stuart Blanch's translation to York. He was the youngest diocesan bishop in the country, and was installed on St Barnabas's day, 11 June. Soon a new Roman Catholic archbishop of Liverpool, Derek Worlock, was appointed, arriving in March 1976, and so began a profound and influential friendship that affected the lives of many on Merseyside. Within hours of his arrival Worlock received a visit from his Anglican counterpart and he became a regular visitor to Bishop's Lodge, where both Grace and Jenny received him with affection. Years later Jenny was to convert to Catholicism, inspired by Worlock and guided by Father Michael Hollings. It was a measure of the Sheppards' ecumenical spirit that this caused no disruption within the family.

Although Sheppard and Worlock faced many issues together as public figures, it was more than a working relationship. They would meet frequently, along with other Merseyside church leaders (notably John Newton, the Methodist chairman), and it was their custom to phone each other, wherever they were, each Good Friday to share their common faith. Inevitably, they were the butt of Liverpool humour, being referred to (among other things) as 'fish and chips', since they were always together and never out of the paper. Such humour, though, was always affectionate, as the two were credited with overcoming two major controversies in Liverpool. On the religious front, the city had a history of often violent clashes between Roman Catholics and protestants (especially the Orange lodge). Liverpool was sometimes called a 'mini-Belfast'. The two church leaders made it their business, wherever possible and appropriate, to appear together in public and demonstrate through their friendship the reality of reconciliation. Together they welcomed the queen to Liverpool in 1978 to celebrate the completion of the Anglican cathedral; together in 1982 they welcomed the pope who, like the queen, visited both cathedrals. They did not attempt to hide their differences, theological or otherwise, but proved that more could be achieved for the common good in partnership than in opposition. In testimony to this, the Anglican and Roman Catholic colleges of education, St Katharine's and Notre Dame, merged under their leadership to become, first, the Liverpool Institute of Higher Education and, subsequently, Liverpool Hope University. Its library, opened by Grace Sheppard in 1997, was named after them. Their leadership also brought into being the Merseyside and Region Churches Ecumenical Assembly (MARCEA) in 1984.

The 1980s were dark days for Liverpool, with seemingly endless conflict between the extreme left-wing city council dominated by Labour's Militant Tendency and the tory government of Margaret Thatcher. During the Toxteth riots of 1981 Sheppard and Worlock walked the streets together, at one point negotiating the loan of a police megaphone for black community leaders who were struggling to call for calm. Subsequently they represented the city to central government, despairing of the intransigence of the militants, and gained the confidence of cabinet members such as Michael Heseltine. This led to new inward investment resulting in, for example, the International Garden Festival in 1984. They jointly founded the Michaelmas group of business leaders who, meeting over breakfast, sought fresh ways of bringing regeneration to the city. Great public affection for Sheppard and Worlock was gained by their handling of two major soccer disasters, in a city where football is as much a religion as Catholicism and protestantism. After the Heysel stadium riot in 1985 Sheppard and Worlock took a leading role in healing relationships between Liverpool and Turin. When, in 1989, ninety-six Liverpool fans were crushed to death at Hillsborough stadium, Sheffield, both bishops were involved in publicly bringing comfort to the bereaved.

As an Anglican, and former England cricket captain, Sheppard was more of an establishment figure than Worlock and therefore potentially more influential. Liverpool was no longer a wealthy commercial city, with thriving docks. It had been deeply affected during the twentieth century by war and recession, and it desperately needed inward investment if it was to reinvent itself as a centre for culture and tourism. Unemployment was high and morale was low. With his understanding of urban poverty, of both spirit and wealth, Sheppard set about championing the 'left behind', those unable to 'get on their bikes' (to use the phrase of the cabinet minister Norman Tebbit) and find work. Such people also tended in Liverpool to be poorly educated members of ethnic minority groups, for whom Sheppard had a particular concern. For some years he chaired the area board of the Manpower Services Commission, which sought to provide employment opportunities for the jobless. The jibe was sometimes made that 'if you're not poor, black or unemployed, he's not interested' yet this was far from the truth (personal knowledge). In private at least Sheppard spent as much time with the wealthy and the powerful as he did in public with others. His philosophy was summed up well in his Dimbleby lecture of 1984, 'The other Britain', where he contrasted 'comfortable Britain' (which, of course, he represented) and the urban poor for whom he was an advocate. Many of the themes of *Built as a City* reappeared in the lecture and were developed further in his book *Bias to the Poor* (1983). Visiting London to deliver the lecture, Sheppard found, to his embarrassment, that he had failed to pack a suitable pair of shoes. After a few last-minute telephone calls, a pair of black size elevens was found, and he delivered the lecture suitably shod. He found this to be a poignant symbol of his call for the affluent to 'stand in the shoes' of the poor, to see the world from their viewpoint, and to empathize with their life experience.

As a diocesan bishop Sheppard was much loved, though sometimes misunderstood, for his public stances. Those who went to him in a crisis, particularly the clergy, found him to be a friend indeed. The home he and Grace made was always warm and hospitable. He was assiduous in carrying out his diocesan duties—spending time equally in both affluent and deprived parishes—and was known as a 'team player' among his colleagues. All those who worked with him knew that they had his trust. He would say that a highlight of his month was the day-long staff team meeting, which included particularly his closest colleague, suffragan bishop Michael Henshall. The role of his suffragan was unusually important because of Sheppard's national prominence. Sheppard was frequently pursued for comments by the media, but was discreet in how he responded: everyone received a reply but not necessarily anything for publication. He had a heavy postbag, and many invitations from home and abroad for speaking engagements. Most of these he had to decline.

Sheppard became a lord spiritual in 1980, and took an active part in the life of the House of Lords. From 1987 he was national president of Family Service Units—an organization with which Grace was heavily involved locally. From 1989 to 1993 he had the somewhat thankless task of chairing the central religious advisory committee for the BBC and IBA, and in 1991 he became chairman of the Church of England's board for social responsibility. Under his chairmanship two seminal reports were published: *Something to Celebrate* (1993), on family life, and *Unemployment and the Future of Work* (1997), a major study which Sheppard wanted to see completed before his retirement, and whose publication coincided with the election of a new Labour government under Tony Blair.

However, it was in 1985 that Sheppard's most controversial and ground-breaking work was completed. At the height of Margaret Thatcher's time as prime minister, Archbishop Robert Runcie had established a commission on urban priority areas, with Sheppard as vice-chairman. The ensuing report, *Faith in the City*, damned as 'Marxist' by one of Thatcher's ministers, gave a cogent, comprehensive, and compelling analysis of life in urban areas, highlighting the effects of government policies (or lack of them) in such places. One major outcome of the report was the Church Urban Fund which, more than twenty years later, continued to distribute hundreds of thousands of pounds annually to inner-city church and community projects nationwide.

Sheppard retired as bishop of Liverpool in 1997, and moved to his and Grace's retirement home in West Kirby on the Wirral, across the Mersey. He was made a life peer as Baron Sheppard of Liverpool in 1998, thereafter making frequent visits to London to participate in Lords debates. In retirement he continued to write and speak publicly, while pursuing his hobbies of gardening, painting, and choral singing. He also enjoyed immensely being a grandfather. In 2003 he was diagnosed with bowel cancer and received lengthy treatment, during which the courage, grace, and tenacity for which he had become famous as both cricketer and church leader were much in evidence. He died at his home, 11 Melloncroft Drive, West Kirby, on 5 March 2005. He was survived by his wife, Grace, and daughter, Jenny. His funeral took place at St Bridget's Church, West Kirby, and his ashes were interred in Liverpool Cathedral. The cathedral hosted a memorial service on 23 May 2005 attended by more than 3000 people. In May 2008 a sculpture by Stephen Broadbent was erected in Hope Street, in sight of both cathedrals, in tribute to Sheppard and Worlock. Consisting of life-size figures of the two men, set in two bronze doors 15 feet high, it includes a third space in which the viewer is invited to stand. That circle is inscribed with the words 'Better Together—We Meet in Hope'. This was a most fitting epitaph to Sheppard's life in cricket, marriage, church, and nation.

GODFREY BUTLAND

Sources D. Sheppard, *Steps along Hope Street* (2002) · *Daily Telegraph* (7 March 2005) · *The Guardian* (7 March 2005); (8 March 2005); (19 March 2005) · *The Independent* (7 March 2005) · *The Times* (7 March 2005); (16 March 2005) · *WW* (2005) · Burke, *Peerage* · personal knowledge (2009) · private information (2009) · b. cert. · m. cert. · d. cert.

Archives Lpool RO, corresp. and papers | FILM BFINA, current affairs footage | SOUND BL NSA, current affairs recordings · BL NSA, documentary recording · BL NSA, recorded lecture [Edward Boyle memorial lecture, 1995]

Likenesses photographs, 1950–81, Getty Images, London · photographs, 1950–98, PA Photos, London · photographs, 1950–2001, Photoshot, London · G. Argent, bromide print, 1970, NPG · S. Samuels, bromide fibre print, 1980, NPG [*see illus.*] · S. Samuels, two photographs, 1980, Rex Features, London · S. Shakeshaft, double portrait, C-type colour print, 1994 (with Derek Worlock), Liverpool Daily Post and Liverpool Echo · S. Broadbent, bronze figure, 2008, Hope Street, Liverpool · obituary photographs

Wealth at death £339,346: probate, 25 Oct 2005, *CGPLA Eng. & Wales*

Shepperd, Sir Alfred Joseph [Shep] (1925–2007), industrialist, was born on 19 June 1925 at 37 St Peter Street, Bethnal Green, London, the son of Alfred Charles Shepperd (1898–1939), printer, and his wife, Mary Ann, *née* Williams (1896–1975), milliner. His maternal grandmother, Amelia Williams (*née* Tucker), died when Shepperd was young and left £200 to each of her seven children. This allowed Shepperd's parents to buy a house in Thornton Heath, Croydon. Shepperd was educated at Archbishop Tenison's

School in Croydon, and at the outbreak of the Second World War he was evacuated to Crowborough in Sussex. This experience instilled a strong work ethic in Shepperd: he passed his school certificate and matriculated. In 1943 he enrolled in the Fleet Air Arm and was commissioned.

After his wartime service Shepperd read economics at University College, London, and began his business career in 1949 on the finance side of the entertainment group the Rank Organisation, where he rose to the post of senior accountant. On 26 August 1950, at St Bedes' Roman Catholic Church, Clapham Park, he married Gabrielle Yvette Marie Bouloux, a medical student three years his junior, and daughter of Joseph André France Bouloux, medical practitioner. They had two daughters. Meanwhile Shepperd continued to ascend the business ladder, transferring to Selincourt & Sons Ltd in 1963 and the Chamberlain Group in 1965. In 1967 he became managing director of Keyser Ullmann Industries Ltd and a director of Keyser Ullmann Ltd, and in 1971 finance director of Laporte Industries Ltd.

In 1972 Shepperd joined the Wellcome Foundation Ltd as finance director. He became chairman and chief executive of the foundation five years later. A major pharmaceutical business, the Wellcome Foundation traditionally placed a high priority on research (four of its scientists won Nobel prizes). This focus stemmed from its unorthodox ownership: all the foundation's shares were owned by—and were the sole asset of—the Wellcome Trust, the medical research charity established in 1936 on the death of the American-born pharmaceutical tycoon Sir Henry Wellcome. The relationship between the Wellcome Trust and the Wellcome Foundation was understandably very close, but their managements were kept totally separate.

Under Shepperd's leadership the Wellcome Foundation became a world leader in antiviral therapy, with the introduction of acyclovir (marketed as Zovirax), a treatment for herpes and cold sores, and zidovudine (later branded as Retrovir), the first anti-viral treatment for HIV and AIDS. Zidovudine was developed by Wellcome's American arm, Burroughs Wellcome, and patented in 1985. When its potential to extend the life expectancy of AIDS sufferers became apparent Wellcome came under great external pressures in relation both to the speed of commercialization—allowing very limited time for further testing and the establishment of production facilities—and to the price at which the drug would be made available. Shepperd weighed these issues and went ahead with the launch of the product in March 1987. The initial high price of Retrovir provoked demonstrations and accusations of unethical conduct. Shepperd's response was to point to Wellcome's massive investment in research, both in other drugs with far less market potential, and to wider medical research, through the portion of the company's dividends that passed to the Wellcome Trust.

In the 1980s the Wellcome trustees, under the chairmanship of Sir David Steel, came to the conclusion that the trust's income was less than might be expected from such a thriving company, and decided to convert some of its interest in the foundation into an investment fund rather than depend on one source of income. Accordingly in February 1986 the trust reduced its holdings in the foundation from 100 to 75 per cent, resulting in the flotation of the company as Wellcome plc. Reinvestment by the trust produced £211 million. The Wellcome Trust sold a further 288 million shares in Wellcome plc in 1992, doubling its income and making it the world's largest grant-giving charity. After the 1986 flotation Shepperd remained as chairman and chief executive of Wellcome plc. As he approached retirement he declared that the company, with the support of the trust, should remain independent, rather than following the drugs-industry fashion for mergers. After his retirement in 1990, however, Wellcome

Sir Alfred Joseph Shepperd (1925–2007), by unknown photographer, 1980s

merged with Glaxo (in 1995), eventually becoming part of GlaxoSmithKline (in 2000).

During his tenure Shepperd transformed the Wellcome Foundation, presiding over the greatest period of growth in the company's history. He was a formidable businessman—a combative and workaholic boss who maintained such a grasp of detail that he saw no need to appoint a finance director under him when he moved up to become chairman. If his sharp intellect and forceful opinions often made him difficult to work for, Shep (as he was universally known) also had a human touch, which came through in his dry sense of humour and in his dealings with junior staff. Shepperd, indeed, was recognized by his peers as being equally at home on the shop floor and in the boardroom.

Shepperd was chairman of Barts NHS Trust from 1991 to 1993, a member of the government's Advisory Council on Science and Technology (1989–93), and a governor of the National Institute of Economic and Social Research (1981–90). After his retirement from Wellcome he took on a number of directorships, including Isoscelles plc (1991–3), Oxford Instruments plc (1991–5), and National Transcommunications Ltd (1992–6), and was involved in fundraising for London Zoo. He was knighted in 1989 and was also honoured in Italy, Belgium, and Spain. He lived latterly in Guildford, Surrey, and died at Mount Alvernia Hospital, Guildford, on 15 October 2007, of bronchopneumonia following multiple strokes. He was survived by his wife and their two daughters. WILLIAM CASTELL

Sources 'Sir Alfred bids farewell', *Wellcome Journal* (July 1990) • *The Times* (22 Oct 2007); (23 Oct 2007) • *The Independent* (26 Oct 2007) • *Daily Telegraph* (31 Oct 2007) • P. O. Williams, *The story of the Wellcome Trust* (2010) • C. Reeves, 'The Wellcome Trust', *Encyclopaedia of life sciences*, www.els.net, 28 May 2010 • Burke, *Peerage* • *WW* (2007) • personal knowledge (2011) • private information (2011) • b. cert. • m. cert. • d. cert.

Likenesses photograph, 1980–89, Wellcome Library, London [*see illus.*] • obituary photographs

Wealth at death £918,218: probate, 15 Oct 2007, *CGPLA Eng. & Wales*

Sheridan, Bernard (1927–2007), solicitor, was born Bernard Chernoff at 150 Union Road, Leytonstone, London, on 7 March 1927, the son of Maurice Chernoff, shopkeeper, and his wife, Ada, *née* Slatkoff. He was of Jewish descent. His parents separated when he was young and, brought up by his mother, he was educated at Holloway county grammar school for boys and then the London School of Economics where he read economics. He had been offered a place at Cambridge but the London School of Economics offered a scholarship. His interest in the law was kindled when, during his national service, he took statements from soldiers seeking to petition for divorce. This was the era of the mid-tier firm led by a dynamic principal—others of the time included those of Lord Goodman and Sir David Napley—and after qualifying Sheridan set up his own firm, Bernard Sheridan & Co., in the oddly named 82 Z Portland Place building before moving to Parton Street, Holborn, and then in 1956 to nearby Red Lion Square, Holborn, setting up a mixed practice dealing with a wide range of cases, much of it legally aided, for the local community. On 21 May 1955, at St Mary the Boltons, West Brompton, he married Bethune Gladys (Bethin) Thomas (*b.* 1929/30), a teacher, and daughter of Stanley Carlton Thomas, importer. They had two sons and a daughter.

One major plank of Sheridan's practice was the music industry and he was one of the first of a generation of lawyers to challenge the standard agreements of the record companies; he improved the royalty agreements for such diverse clients as Matt Munro, Kate Bush, and Pink Floyd, whose manager he met every Monday morning. He also obtained damages for Johnny Dankworth when the *News Chronicle* said that the bandleader was prepared to play at a Wolverhampton ballroom in defiance of a Musicians' Union ban after the venue refused to admit non-whites. In another successful action he won damages for Christian Aid over allegations that donations made via the charity to the African National Congress were being used to buy hand grenades. One of his most celebrated criminal cases was his successful defence in 1979 at the Old Bailey of the comedian and film collector Bob Monkhouse, who had been charged with defrauding film companies over his collection of old films.

Sheridan's successes in these fields helped to finance what was often unremunerative work in the then unfashionable, indeed unknown and certainly unnamed, field of human rights. Over the years he continually fought on behalf of victims of racial discrimination and other injustices. Shortly before his death he had the satisfaction of hearing that the House of Lords had ruled that the orders prohibiting the return of the Chagos Islanders to Diego Garcia were an abuse of power. Sheridan had been battling on their behalf for over twenty-five years. Heavily involved in anti-apartheid campaigns, he also worked, often unavailingly, to save the lives of Africans sentenced to death in the former Rhodesia. In 1965 he took the case of Richard Mapolisa, sentenced to death for his involvement in a petrol bombing which failed to ignite, to the judicial committee of the privy council. Although the death sentence was upheld, the sentence was commuted. If Sheridan, a man who instinctively knew what was ethically right or wrong, never attained the high profile of some media lawyers it was because he never sought it, but also because he tried to keep his clients out of the vagaries of the legal system, preferring a timely settlement to a full-blown action. A supporter of both Justice and Amnesty International, he was also committed to the work of Toynbee Hall and Christian Aid, and for some years was secretary of War on Want.

When Sheridan attended a meeting for his clients he would often carry under his arm not the file, the contents of which he retained in his memory, but the *Evening Standard*. He was described by his first articled clerk and later partner, Cyril Glasser, as having 'perfected the art of walking out of a meeting in his own office' if he thought the moment was right (*The Independent*, 23 Aug 2007). His acumen was such, however, that he usually came away with what he and they wanted. 'No one could say Bernard was ever less than 100 per cent', remarked another former articled clerk (private information). In 1985 the name of the firm was changed to Sheridans and two years later Sheridan himself became a consultant. In 1997 he left the firm to become a consultant with Jacobs Allen Hammond, working seven days a week for a list of clients that included the artist Damien Hirst.

Always dressed immaculately, the tall and slim Sheridan had a great interest in all the arts, particularly in English music and twentieth-century art. A footballer at school, he was a lifelong supporter of Tottenham Hotspur. A man with a quick if not lasting temper and never over-interested in office administration—his desk was said to be awash with unpaid bills and unanswered letters—he had a short attention span when something ceased to interest him. He was a man who liked intellectual challenge, never happier than when someone would debate with him, although he tended to treat his partners as if they were articled clerks. On one occasion after he had bought himself a Rolls-Royce he took his partners for a drive around Red Lion Square as a 'treat' for them. He lived latterly in Stubhampton, Blandford Forum, Dorset, and died on 26 May 2007 at Salisbury District Hospital, of cancer. He was survived by his wife and their three children.

JAMES MORTON

Sources *Daily Telegraph* (6 June 2007) · *The Times* (27 June 2007) · *The Guardian* (2 July 2007) · *The Independent* (23 Aug 2007) · personal knowledge (2011) · private information (2011) · b. cert. · m. cert. · d. cert.

Likenesses obituary photographs

Wealth at death £833,620: probate, 21 Jan 2008, *CGPLA Eng. & Wales*

Sherman, Sir Alfred (1919–2006), journalist and political activist, was born on 10 November 1919 at the Mothers' Hospital, Clapton, Hackney, in London, the son of Jacob Vladimir Sherman, tailor, and his wife, Eva, *née* Goldental, both Jewish immigrants from Russia. He was brought up in extreme poverty, and in a politically aware family; his father was a Labour councillor. He was educated at Hackney Downs county secondary school until 1936 and briefly studied at Chelsea Polytechnic. At the age of seventeen he cut short his studies to fight in the International Brigade on the republican side in the Spanish Civil War, until captured by the Italians and repatriated. At the time he was a communist and felt betrayed by the tactics of the Russian commanders. A sense of betrayal was to be a recurring motif in his life. Sherman's service in field security during the Second World War took him to the Middle East and, because of his remarkable language skills (he was fluent in at least five languages), he then worked as an administrator in the enemy occupied territories after the war. On return to civilian life he enrolled at the London School of Economics and was president of the student branch of the Communist Party. In 1948, however, he was expelled from the party for 'Titoist deviationism' (his support for Yugoslavia in its disagreement with Stalin). Following his graduation in 1950 and a brief and unsatisfactory spell as a schoolteacher he became a journalist, working on the *Jewish Chronicle*. During the 1950s he developed his free market views while he was a member of the economic staff of the Israeli government. In Israel he met Zahava Levin, daughter of Dr Gideon Levin; they married in 1958 and had one son, Gideon. On his return to England he was recruited in 1965 to the *Daily Telegraph*. His *Telegraph* leader page articles, particularly on local government, showed his polemical talents. He was a vigorous critic of 'one-nation' Conservatism on the grounds that it was too ready to compromise with Labour and too accepting of the post-war consensus of welfarism and state ownership. He was particularly disillusioned with the Conservative government of Edward Heath (1970–74), not only for its support for British membership of the European Economic Community, but also its U-turns in 1972 to favour industrial intervention and incomes policies. He served as a Conservative councillor in Kensington and Chelsea from 1971 to 1978.

In the late 1960s Sir Keith Joseph had become a friend, attracted in part by Sherman's journalism. The two men grew apart when Joseph was a member of the Heath government and Sherman complained that he had been 'captured' by his civil servants. In opposition in 1974, however, Joseph came to regret his part in the government and the two men worked together to restate the case for economic liberalism. Sherman had a major hand in Joseph's Preston speech in September 1974 that urged that money supply was the main cause for inflation. It broke with the Heath government's reliance on incomes policy as an answer to inflation, and many looked to Joseph as a potential leader of the Conservative Party. But the controversy caused by Joseph's speech in October at Edgbaston, in which Sherman again played a major role, effectively ended his leadership prospects. It argued that poverty was caused by 'fatherless families' with 'mothers from classes IV and V'. The implication of his remarks was that steps should be taken to limit breeding among the underclass. The hostile reaction caused Joseph to decline to contest the party's leadership and opened the way for Margaret Thatcher to stand and eventually succeed Heath as party leader the following February.

In April 1974 Sherman had co-founded, with Joseph and Thatcher, the Centre for Policy Studies. Like the Institute of Economic Affairs it was intended to promote free-market ideas but also to influence Conservative thinking. He became its first director, researching and writing speeches for Joseph and Thatcher, whose aide and speech writer he became, until 1983. He had many gifts—great drive, independence of mind, originality, courage, and a flair for coining brilliant phrases. He supplied many of the phrases popularized by Joseph, such as the need to reverse the 'ratchet of socialism' or to distinguish between the 'common ground' (on which most voters agreed) and the 'middle ground' (a point midway between the parties' positions). In his drafts of speeches, and in his journalism, he provided many of the ideas that collectively became known as Thatcherism. These included the need to curb trade-union powers, cut taxes and public spending, restore control of the money supply, and reform the welfare system so that it reduced dependence. At his prompting the economist Alan Walters was brought back from the United States in 1981 to become an influential economic adviser to Thatcher.

Sherman's influence was at its height during the Conservative Party's period of opposition from 1974 to 1979. But his almost fanatical intolerance of alternative views and unwillingness to compromise hardly suited the role of an adviser. He was dismissive of what he regarded as the political establishment, particularly the higher civil service and much of the leadership of the Conservative Party—even though he would need their support or co-operation if he was to succeed. He was rarely comfortable with the socially advantaged or those he found 'smooth' or 'wet'. With the Conservatives in government after 1979, he attacked Thatcher's deviations from his advice, and she and her advisers tired of his persistent calls and public criticisms. At times his lack of tact, his vanity, and his divisiveness were self-defeating. As its research director Sherman wanted the Centre for Policy Studies to 'think the impossible' and not be too close to the Conservative government, but be a candid—and at times critical—friend of ministers. More influential figures disagreed and, always highly sensitive to slights, he was devastated when the centre's chairman, Lord Thomas of Swynnerton, abruptly sacked him from his position as research director in 1984. Sherman complained that he was being written out of accounts of the Conservative Party and that there was a process of 'de-Shermanization' underway. In 1986 he lost another platform when he was dismissed as a contributor to the *Daily Telegraph* by its new editor, Max Hastings. His knighthood in 1983 was scant consolation for the denial of continued access to number 10.

Sherman became a public adviser to the National Bus Corporation, advocating paving over railways. In 1987 he controversially invited the French National Front leader Jean-Marie Le Pen to the Conservative Party conference to address a fringe meeting and further embarrassments accompanied his racist remarks about 'coloureds' and the Irish. He also became an adviser to the Bosnian Serb leader Radovan Karadžić, later indicted for war crimes. Conscious of his contribution to the making of Thatcherism he eagerly studied the indexes of books on politics to see if he received appropriate recognition. He was particularly aghast that Thatcher in her 900-page *Downing Street Years* (1993) made just one perfunctory reference to him. His own memoir, *Paradoxes of Power: Reflections on the Thatcher Interlude* (2005), attempted to set the record straight. At its launch party Thatcher generously asserted that 'We could never have defeated socialism if it hadn't been for Sir Alfred' (*Evening Standard*, 28 July 2005).

Sherman's first wife died in 1993. On 3 December 2001 he married Angela Valentina Martins, a 49-year-old beautician, and daughter of Joachim Martins, farmer. He died on 26 August 2006 at the Chelsea and Westminster Hospital, of pneumonia. He was survived by his second wife and his son from his first marriage.

DENNIS KAVANAGH

Sources A. Sherman, *Paradoxes of power: reflections on the Thatcher interlude* (2005) • *Daily Telegraph* (28 Aug 2006) • *The Times* (29 Aug 2006) • *The Guardian* (29 Aug 2006) • *The Independent* (5 Sept 2006) • *WW* (2006) • Burke, *Peerage* • b. cert. • m. cert. [2001] • d. cert.

Archives Royal Holloway College, Egham, Surrey, papers | FILM BFINA, current affairs footage • BFINA, documentary footage | SOUND BL NSA, Communist Party of Great Britain Biographical Project, interview with K. Morgan, C1049/134/01 • BL NSA, current affairs recordings

Likenesses photographs, 1980, Photoshot, London • photograph, 1987, PA Photos, London • obituary photographs

Wealth at death £440,000: administration, 13 Nov 2007, *CGPLA Eng. & Wales*

Sherrin, Edward George [Ned] (**1931–2007**), film, theatre, and television producer and writer, was born on 18 February 1931 at Gawlers Farm, Low Ham, Somerset, the second son of Thomas Adam Sherrin (1889–1965), farmer, and his wife, Dorothy Finch, *née* Drewett (1895–1980). He was educated at Sexey's School, Bruton, where he staged a musical adaptation of Bernard Shaw's *Pygmalion* (years in advance of *My Fair Lady*) and persuaded the masters to establish an arts sixth form in which he was the only student. After two years of national service with the Royal Corps of Signals in Catterick and Aldershot, and in Austria, he took up a scholarship to read law at Exeter College, Oxford. At Oxford he distinguished himself in university theatre and revue, playing the Fairy Queen in an Oxford University Dramatic Society pantomime. The newly formed Oxford Theatre Group took a revue to the Edinburgh festival in 1953, and the actress Maggie Smith sang a song about a cinema usherette for which Sherrin had written lyrics ('It's my première tonight, and I'm scared as scared can be'). The item was recycled in a BBC television programme—marking the débuts in the medium of both Smith and Sherrin (who boasted his first credit as producer)—called *Oxford Accents* (1954).

A chance encounter with an Oxford friend the day after he was called to the bar (at Gray's Inn) in 1955 diverted Sherrin from both theatre and the law: he instantly became a backroom boy in the earliest days of commercial television, working in the ATV studios at Kensington and floor-managing there one of the first breakfast shows. Two years later he joined Grace Wyndham Goldie's exceptional current affairs department at the BBC and was soon directing the cameras on a ground-breaking early evening show, *Tonight*, which achieved immense popularity through its mixture of news-related 'human' stories and brilliant journalism; the star reporters included Cliff Michelmore, Geoffrey Johnson Smith, Derek Hart, Alan Whicker, MacDonald Hastings, and Fyfe Robertson.

Out of this programme came the idea for a weekly satirical look at the news. *That Was the Week That Was*, soon known as *TW3*, was launched, and aired live, in November 1962. Nothing like it had been seen on television before. Riding the wave of the new 'satire boom' both in print (*Private Eye* magazine had been launched in 1961) and in the theatre (*Beyond the Fringe* had made overnight stars of Jonathan Miller, Alan Bennett, Peter Cook, and Dudley Moore), *TW3* attacked politicians (mostly those in the ruling Conservative Party), organized religion, businessmen, trade unionists, the press, and show business celebrities. It had a field day with the Profumo affair, which involved high-

Edward George [Ned] **Sherrin** (1931–2007), by Patrick Jackson, 1997

ranking politicians, call-girls, and Russian spies. Sherrin's first stroke of luck, or genius perhaps, as producer, was to hire the unknown David Frost as chairman—the 24-year-old Cambridge graduate Frost had 'risen without trace', according to Kitty Muggeridge (H. Carpenter, *That Was the Satire That Was*, 2000, 208)—and surround him with other talented new performers like Roy Kinnear, Millicent Martin, Kenneth Cope, Lance Percival, and William Rushton.

TW3's material was provided by a hard-bitten team of writers including Keith Waterhouse and Willis Hall, the television dramatist Dennis Potter, the songwriter and journalist Herbert Kretzmer, and the future Labour MP Gerald Kaufman. The star prosecuting witness was Bernard Levin, who skewered his interviewees with a mixture of caustic wit and merciless abuse; he once described Charles Forte's catering company, to Forte's face, as 'lazy, inefficient, dishonest, dirty and complacent'. David Frost was equally irreverent. In one programme, he told viewers that Reginald Maudling, the chancellor of the exchequer, had ended a brief interview with a group of unemployed people with the words, 'Well, I've got work to do, even if you haven't.' Pubs and restaurants emptied on a Saturday night as people stayed at home to see what might happen next, which institution or bigwig might be lampooned or exposed. An unpopular home secretary, Henry Brooke, was lacerated as 'the most hated man in Britain', and a 'consumer guide to religion' caused predictable offence.

But *TW3*, which was attracting 13 million viewers, was short-lived; barely into its second year, it was dropped by an increasingly nervous BBC on the grounds that a forthcoming general election would necessitate a clamp-down on outspokenness in the interests of impartiality. Before then, and most memorably, the assassination of President John F. Kennedy caused Sherrin to scrap the planned schedule in favour of a hastily assembled, sombre memorial programme on 23 November 1963 in which Millicent Martin sang 'In the Summer of His Years' with tears in her eyes. The last show went out on 28 December 1963. Sherrin tried to keep the momentum going after the election of a new Labour government by producing *Not So Much a Programme, More a Way of Life*, notable for John Bird's impersonations of Harold Wilson and the African leader Jomo Kenyatta, and a third sketch and discussion show, *BBC3*, on which Kenneth Tynan uttered the first 'F-word' on television in a debate on censorship with Mary McCarthy and Robert Robinson. But, as the American playwright George S. Kaufman observed, satire is what closed on Saturday night, and Sherrin moved on.

Sherrin had begun a long collaborative association with a writer and critic thirty years his senior, Caryl Brahms, a small, intimidating woman who, with her (by then deceased) writing partner S. J. Simon, had written one of Sherrin's favourite books, *No Bed for Bacon* (1941). Sherrin had persuaded Brahms to work with him on a stage version of the book at the Bristol Old Vic in 1959. Their subsequent theatre pieces included Britain's first black pantomime, *Cindy-Ella, or, I Gotta Shoe* (1962), and a lively musical biography of Marie Lloyd, *Sing a Rude Song* (1970). He also produced nine or ten films in a hectic period in the late 1960s and early 1970s, including *The Virgin Soldiers* (1968), based on Leslie Thomas's best-selling novel; *Up Pompeii* (1971), starring the comedian Frankie Howerd; and, in 1972, a screen version of Peter Nichols's stage play *The National Health*.

Sherrin's finest post-*TW3* hour arrived in 1977, when he co-devised and presented *Side by Side by Sondheim*, a cabaret-style collage of the relatively unknown (in Britain) composer Stephen Sondheim's songs, performed by Millicent Martin, Julia McKenzie, and David Kernan, and linked with his own witty commentary, which he updated nightly in response to the news at home and abroad. The dinner-suited Sherrin sat on a bar stool at the side of the stage, delivering his lines with devastating, acidulous aplomb. The show ran in London for eighteen months and transferred to Broadway. With Brahms again he followed through with *Beecham* (1980), a solo show for the actor Timothy West about the eccentric British conductor Sir Thomas Beecham, and, just before Brahms died in 1982, a charming and nostalgic musical, *The Mitford Girls* (1981), with a score by Peter Greenwell, which opened at the Chichester Festival Theatre and transferred to the Globe in the West End.

In 1984 Sherrin won an Olivier award for his production of *The Ratepayers' Iolanthe*, a political skit based on Gilbert and Sullivan that he wrote with Alistair Beaton, paired with another on the same local government theme, *The Metropolitan Mikado*, at the Queen Elizabeth Hall. Beaton remained a collaborator for the rest of Sherrin's life, writing lyrics and sketches for him, as well as a lavish but unsuccessful musical about the great impresario *Ziegfeld*

(1988) at the London Palladium. But his theatre work really picked up again in a series of West End collaborations with Keith Waterhouse, two of them outstanding: an affectionate distillation of suburban Pooter-land in *Mr and Mrs Nobody* (1986), starring Judi Dench and her husband, Michael Williams, and *Jeffrey Bernard is Unwell* (1989), a brilliantly funny comedy based on Jeffrey Bernard's columns in *The Spectator*, in which Peter O'Toole gave a magnificent, Falstaffian performance as the chaotic and bibulous scribe of the Coach and Horses public house in Soho. Other West End productions he directed included Waterhouse's *Bookends* (1990), starring Michael Hordern and Dinsdale Landen; Kay Mellor's *A Passionate Woman* (1994), with Stephanie Cole; and *A Saint She Ain't* (1999) by Dick Vosburgh and Denis King, which transferred from the King's Head to the Apollo. He also toured with a solo show, *An Evening with Ned Sherrin*.

A tall, well-built man, with an imposing physical presence, Sherrin was an inveterate first-nighter, always enjoying a couple of stiff Martinis before the show and a good supper afterwards. His knowledge of theatre folk and lore was legendary and is preserved in two volumes of autobiography (the first, *A Small Thing—Like an Earthquake*, 1983, is an essential document, too, of his pioneering television career; the second is simply entitled *The Autobiography*, 2005), two collections of theatrical anecdotes, and a 'backstage' novel, *Scratch an Actor* (1996). Although he said that he had enjoyed two long-lasting relationships, he mostly lived alone in his Chelsea mansion flat, openly gay from the 1980s, Conservative in his politics, a monarchist, a churchgoer, and latterly 'memorial services correspondent' for *The Oldie* magazine, always sure, he said, to have sufficient money to pay for the bare necessities of life: food, wine, and taxis.

For twenty years, from 1986 until throat cancer affected his speech—a cruelly ironic development in one so brilliant in his conversation, both on and off the microphone—towards the end of 2006, he was a peerless chat show host on BBC Radio 4's *Loose Ends*, presiding wittily and imperiously over a babble of conversation, songs, and satirical sketches which, at its peak, was a latter-day *TW3*, with contributions from the likes of Stephen Fry, John Sessions, Emma Freud, and Arthur Smith, and live music from cutting-edge bands that were not necessarily to Sherrin's own taste. He bore the shock of the new with a patient shrug, much happier when celebrating those musical theatre giants he most admired, Noël Coward, Cole Porter, and, of course, Stephen Sondheim. He was appointed CBE in 1997. He died on 1 October 2007 at his home, 4 Cornwall Mansions, Ashburnham Road, Chelsea, London. His funeral was held on 9 October at Chelsea Old Church and was followed by a memorial service on 18 February 2008 at St Paul's, Covent Garden.

MICHAEL COVENEY

Sources N. Sherrin, *A small thing—like an earthquake* (1983) · N. Sherrin, *Ned Sherrin: the autobiography* (2005) · *The Times* (2 Oct 2007); (3 Oct 2007); (8 Oct 2007); (17 Oct 2007) · *Evening Standard* (2 Oct 2007) · *Daily Telegraph* (3 Oct 2007) · *The Guardian* (3 Oct 2007) · *The Independent* (3 Oct 2007); (6 Oct 2007) · *New York Times* (5 Oct 2007) · *WW* (2007) · personal knowledge (2011) · private information (2011) · b. cert. · d. cert.

Archives FILM BFINA, documentary footage · BFINA, performance footage | SOUND BL NSA, current affairs recordings · BL NSA, performance recordings · BL NSA, documentary recordings

Likenesses photographs, 1963–2004, Getty Images, London · photographs, 1963–2006, Rex Features, London · photographs, 1965–2006, PA Photos, London · photographs, 1980–2005, Photoshot, London · D. Waugh, C-type colour print, 1981 (with Caryl Brahms), NPG · J. Bown, photograph, 1985, priv. coll.; repro. in www.guardian.co.uk/media/2007/oct/02/bbc.radio · P. Jackson, bromide fibre print, 1997, NPG [*see illus.*] · obituary photographs · photograph, repro. in *TLS* (12 Oct 2007), 3 · photographs, repro. in Sherrin, *Sherrin* · photographs, repro. in Sherrin, *Small thing* · photographs, Camera Press, London

Wealth at death £1,127,929: probate, 9 Jan 2008, *CGPLA Eng. & Wales*

Shields, Sir Robert (1930–2008), surgeon, was born at 73 Lounsdale Drive, Paisley, Renfrewshire, on 8 November 1930, the only son of Robert Alexander Shields (*d.* 1947), electrical engineer, and his wife, Isabella McDougall (*d.* 1982), otherwise Isobel Dougall, *née* Reid. Educated at the John Neilson Institute, Paisley, and Glasgow University, his decision to become a doctor was inspired by the family doctor who treated his mother's compound ankle fracture. An outstanding undergraduate, he won the Macleod medal and Mary Margaret Isobel Ure prize (for surgery), the Asher-Asher memorial medal (for ear, nose, and throat disease), and the Captain H. S. Ranken VC memorial prize (for pathology).

Shields qualified in 1953 with distinction in pathology and was house officer in Sir John Macnee's and Sir Edward J. Wayne's medical and Sir Charles Illingworth's surgical units in the Western Infirmary. He saw national service (from 1954 to 1956) as a regimental medical officer in the Argyll and Sutherland Highlanders, rising to the rank of captain and serving in Berlin, where his responsibilities included care of war criminals in Spandau prison. While in Berlin he met (Grace) Marianne Swinburn, a Queen Alexandra nursing officer, and daughter of George Swinburn; they married on 19 January 1957 and had two daughters and a son. Shields maintained an association with the Territorial Army until 1962 and was honorary colonel of the Liverpool University officer training corps from 1994 to 2001.

Shields obtained fellowship of the Royal College of Surgeons in Edinburgh (1959) and England (1966) and rose rapidly in Illingworth's pre-eminent school of surgery. In 1959–60 he worked with the leading gastrointestinal physiologist, Charles Code, at the Mayo clinic in Rochester, Minnesota, USA. His MD thesis on intestinal absorption was awarded the Bellahouston gold medal by Glasgow University in 1965. In 1966 he won the Moynihan prize and medal of the Association of Surgeons of Great Britain and Ireland.

Meanwhile in 1963 Shields had become senior lecturer (later reader) at the Welsh National School of Medicine, Cardiff, with Patrick Forrest. In 1969 he was appointed professor of surgery at the University of Liverpool, a post he occupied with distinction until retirement in 1996. A small, demoralized department was soon transformed into one of the most successful in the UK, becoming a referral centre for patients with disease of the liver, gastrointestinal tract, and breast. In the first national Research Selectivity Exercise (1986), his was one of only two starred surgical departments (denoting 'international status'). Liverpool became a magnet for aspiring academic surgeons and developed an outstanding regional training programme. Shields's students included twelve who went on to be professors of surgery (including the first woman to chair a department of surgery in the UK). His loyalty to his department was total and he graciously but firmly declined invitations to move to prestigious positions elsewhere. His own contribution to the management of portal hypertension was a major achievement in a challenging field.

Shields was a superb administrator who carried colleagues with him. An excellent dean of medicine (1982–5), he promoted research rigour, interdisciplinary collaboration, and equitable resource distribution. He nurtured university–NHS relationships as a member of the Liverpool area health authority and the Mersey regional health authority, the Royal Liverpool Hospital Trust, Department of Health working parties, and the specialist training authority of the medical royal colleges. He advised the secretary of state for health on regional provision of acute services. In Scotland he chaired the committee of royal colleges, the advisory board on the roles and responsibilities of health boards (1996), and the quality assurance working party (1998) that established the clinical standards board. He was a visionary president of the Royal College of Surgeons of Edinburgh (1994–7), where he reorganized governance, improved training, and strengthened intercollegiate relationships. The college lecture at the Association of Surgeons meeting was named after him, as was the medal awarded by the Hong Kong College of Surgeons in the joint fellowship examination.

Shields's surgical and scientific standing was reflected in his extensive list of publications, lectures, visiting professorships, and membership of editorial boards. He was a member of the Medical Research Council (1987–91) and its cell board (1974–7), and advised universities and Commonwealth research councils. He was president of the Surgical Research Society (1983–5), the Association of Surgeons of Great Britain and Ireland (1986–7), and the British Society of Gastroenterology (1990–91). He treasured his honorary DSc from the University of Wales (1990) and his honorary fellowship of eleven surgical associations in nine countries.

Robert Shields had total integrity, a rigorous intellect, and a capacity for focused hard work. He was a gifted leader who inspired a generation of surgeons and his engaging personality encouraged friendship. His knighthood in 1990 was widely acclaimed while his appointment as deputy lieutenant of Merseyside in 1991 attested his regional standing. He was an active supporter of local and national charitable causes. He had a great zest for life, an abiding interest in military history, and a love of sailing and the family's second home in Argyll. He died of cancer at his home in West Kirby on 3 October 2008 after a long, trying illness that he bore bravely and with little complaint. He was survived by his wife and their three children.

DAVID CARTER

Sources *Daily Telegraph* (9 Oct 2008) · *The Times* (15 Oct 2008) · *The Independent* (31 Oct 2008) · *Daily Post* [Liverpool] (3 Nov 2008) · *WW* (2008) · Burke, *Peerage* · personal knowledge (2012) · private information (2012) [Lady Shields, widow] · b. cert. · d. cert.
Likenesses obituary photographs
Wealth at death £60,716: probate, 29 April 2009, *CGPLA Eng. & Wales*

Shivas, Mark (1938–2008), film and television producer, was born on 24 April 1938 at Stone Field, Kidbrooke Grove, Kidbrooke, south-east London, the only child of James Dallas Shivas (1904–1986), an English teacher, and his first wife, Winifred Alice Lighton, *née* Bristow (1904–1978), a librarian. He was educated at Whitgift School, Croydon, and at Merton College, Oxford, where in 1960 he took a third in jurisprudence. He was articled to a solicitor but could not resist the lure of what had always fascinated him, cinema and the romance of the Hollywood studios, so he left and in 1962 joined *Movie* magazine as an assistant editor.

In 1963 Shivas joined Granada Television and the industry proper. His placements—as an assistant in the story department under the veteran West End playwright Gerald Savory, directing studio news shows, and producing and presenting *Cinema*—suggested grooming for executive power, but it was not Granada which benefited. Savory became BBC Television's head of plays, and in 1968 poached his protégé and made him a producer. Shivas started at the top, with Savory's pet project, *The Six Wives of Henry VIII* (1970), and never looked back. He was, after all, in a studio world: different companies had individual identities, money came from increasing numbers of licence fees or from advertising, artistic power was devolved, and producers parlayed the talent. Of this system Shivas was a master. Slightly built, discreetly attired, courteous, considerate, witty, a good listener who kept his emotions to himself, he reassured managements and protected the artists. He was not so much a cutting edge person as an enabler. He did not impose his own taste, but used it to decide who was clever and could be trusted. If colleagues were congenial, so much the better, and for the audience he had respect. Were they not like Shivas himself in his cinema-going youth, seeking excitement, amusement, and a bit of glamour, but intelligent and curious for all that? The result was that for thirty years his projects, whether initiated or assigned, set the standard for quality in the vital middle ground.

From all these events, even when he was their mainspring, Shivas had an amused detachment, and the air somehow of a modest 1930s bachelor hero: a Morgan sports car, a cottage in Gloucestershire, a fondness for Italy and for faded (and not so faded) grand hotels. His homosexuality was evident but never an issue; his partner of many years was the artist and antiques dealer Karun Kumar Thakar, their relationship celebrated in a civil partnership ceremony on 5 December 2005.

In 1979 Shivas did become a film producer, as creative

director of Southern Pictures, but in 1981 the parent company, Southern Television, lost its licence, and for the next ten years he freelanced. Then in 1988 he was appointed head of BBC drama and from 1993 to 1997 he was head of BBC films—a movie mogul at last. But by this time television was under financial pressure and society had changed. Television's studio system crumbled. BBC power was centralized. Governments eased ITV's quality controls and insisted upon a quota of programmes from independent producers, not realizing, perhaps, that these would be puppets who depended for money and air-time on existing bureaucracies. Markets fragmented. New kinds of people had power. Shivas, who once again went freelance in 1997, won some independent commissions, but what he stood for was deemed old hat, and time between film festivals hung heavy.

Many television careers had a similar trajectory, but none sponsored such a diversity of personalities and creative agendas as Shivas's. Writers with whom Shivas worked included Hugh Whitemore, John Hopkins, Dennis Potter (*Casanova*, 1971), Alan Plater, David Hare, Christopher Hampton, Julian Mitchell, Henry Livings, Howard Brenton, Kingsley Amis, Jack Rosenthal (*The Evacuees*, 1975), Frederic Raphael (*The Glittering Prizes*, 1976, and *Rogue Male*, 1977, the latter based on a novel by Geoffrey Household), Brian Clarke (*Telford's Change*, 1979), Ian Curteis, Alun Owen, Tom Stoppard (*Professional Foul*, 1977), William Humble, Alan Bennett (*A Private Function*, 1984, and the second series of *Talking Heads*, 1998), Allan Scott (*Regeneration*, 1997), John Prebble, and Roddy Doyle (*The Snapper*, 1993). Directors included Alan Parker, Michael Apted, Alan Clark, Christopher Morahan, Clive Donner, Mike Newell (*Bad Blood*, 1982, and *Enchanted April*, 1992), Jan Skolimowski (*Moonlighting*, 1982), Nicholas Roeg (*The Witches*, 1990), Gillies Mackinnon (*The Grass Arena*, 1992, and *Hideous Kinky*, 1998), Anthony Minghella (*Truly Madly Deeply*, 1990), Jack Clayton, Stephen Frears, Michael Winterbottom (*Jude*, 1996), and Anthony Harvey.

Most of these people, and many actors, actresses, and others valued friendship with Shivas as a gift unique to themselves. Mischievous but discreet, and huge fun, he gave all his feelings to what was held in common but said little about his own problems. A 'concealed' man, the writer Ronald Harwood called him (*The Guardian*, 16 Oct 2008), and yet no one resented it. No one was surprised that his cancer was kept secret, or that beyond a certain point he refused treatment so that he could work on. He won a BAFTA television award (for *The Six Wives of Henry VIII*; he was nominated another five times), and an Emmy (for *The Storyteller*, 1988), but colleagues scarcely knew this, because his pride was in the work of others. In 2005 he formed Headline Pictures with Stewart Mackinnon and Kevin Hood, and he was working on a number of projects at the time of his death, at St John's Hospice, Westminster, on 11 October 2008, of melanoma. He was survived by his civil partner, Karun Thakar. KEITH DEWHURST

Sources *The Times* (16 Oct 2008) • *The Guardian* (16 Oct 2008) • *Daily Telegraph* (16 Oct 2008) • *The Independent* (16 Oct 2008) • *WW* (2008) • www.imdb.com/name/nm0794480/, 1 June 2011 • personal knowledge (2012) • private information (2012) • b. cert. • d. cert.
Archives BFI, Special Collections | SOUND BFINA, documentary footage
Likenesses photograph, 1979, PA Photos, London • obituary photographs
Wealth at death £1,391,817: probate, 13 May 2009, *CGPLA Eng. & Wales*

Simmons, John Simon Gabriel (1915–2005), librarian and Slavonic scholar, was born on 8 July 1915 at 2 Duchess Road, Edgbaston, Birmingham, the second of three children and elder son of Bernard Rintel Simmons (1868–1956), manufacturing jeweller, and his wife, Johanna, *née* Selig (1886–1940), the latter originally from Frankfurt am Main. He was educated in Birmingham, at West House School and at King Edward's School. At the age of seventeen he became a student-librarian at Birmingham University Library before beginning, in 1934, his BA in Russian and Spanish, awarded in 1937. Almost one-to-one tuition from the professor of Russian, Sergey Konovalov, made him fluent in the language, and his unofficial role as Konovalov's research assistant honed his research skills. After graduation, while working as an assistant librarian, he began a doctoral dissertation on the history of printing in Russia, cut short by the outbreak of the Second World War.

During the war Simmons served in the Royal Warwickshire regiment as an infantry regimental officer and as a staff officer in England and, from 1944, in France, Belgium, and Germany on the staff of Field Marshal Montgomery's twenty-first army group. In 1945 he was responsible for organizing the retrieval, cataloguing, and evacuation of the regimental war diaries of the German high command. He was mentioned in dispatches for 'gallant and distinguished services in North West Europe', and made a military OBE in October 1945. On 14 November 1944 he had married Fanny Elizabeth Lily Craven, otherwise Krebsman (*d.* 1999), a private secretary and personal assistant seven years his senior, and daughter of Joseph Krebsman, master hairdresser.

After demobilization Simmons returned to Birmingham University Library until 1949, when he moved to Oxford to take up the post of librarian-lecturer in charge of Slavonic books, created specially for him by Konovalov (by then professor of Russian at Oxford). His duties—building up the retrospective Slavonic (principally Russian) collections of the Taylorian and Bodleian libraries and giving thirty-six lectures a year—and his status as a member of the faculty of modern languages answerable principally to Konovalov, who gave him a relatively free rein, suited ideally his erudite, but deeply practical, inventive, and sometimes unorthodox approach. In 1953, when relations with the USSR were constrained by rigid bureaucracy and protocol, he made a private visit to Moscow, and, turning up unannounced at the Lenin State Library, armed with lists of Oxford University Press publications and Oxford desiderata, instigated a pioneering book exchange. Exchanges with other libraries in Moscow and Leningrad ensued, fed by his hundreds of lists of desiderata, drawn mainly from footnotes in scholarly publications. He considered, with justification, that the resulting comprehensive research collections, combined with the remarkable academic teachers recruited by Konovalov, Maurice Bowra, and Isaiah Berlin, led to Oxford's preeminence as a centre for Slavonic studies. His acquisitions also fed into seminars designed to enlighten 'bibliographically innocent' graduate students, on the basis of which he established in 1966 the Bodleian Library's unique Slavonic reading room, and published *Russian Bibliography, Libraries and Archives* (1973).

Although his first decade at Oxford was devoted principally to library activities, Simmons assisted with the editing of *Oxford Slavonic Papers* (becoming general editor in 1968), played an active role in Oxford bibliophile circles, and continued his own research. He compiled for *Oxford Slavonic Papers* a bibliography of British theses in Slavonic and east European studies, updated quinquennially. Over the years he published some 500 articles, reviews, translations, and collaborative works (listed in his *Autobibliography* of 1975, with supplements in 1985 and 1995). They reflected the wide scope of his interests—bibliography, Russian printing history, the dissemination of information about the book in eastern Europe, paper and watermark history, heraldry and genealogy, and Anglo-Russian relations—and exemplified his 'conviction that the mere intermediary, informant, and bibliographical recorder has an important part to play in the process whereby learning advances' (*Autobibliography*, 1975, viii). His 1974 Sandars lectures in Cambridge, 'Russian printing to 1917: a view from the West', drew on his uncompleted doctoral dissertation. A lifelong mission was the registration and description of all extant copies of early printed Cyrillic books. His groundwork, exhortations, and encouragement finally bore fruit in the publication of the *Union Catalogue of Cyrillic Books Printed before 1701 in British and Irish Collections* (2000) and international union catalogues by his Russian colleagues.

For many years Simmons acted as an information conduit through the iron curtain, exchanging letters, offprints, and books with scholars in the Soviet Union, many of whom became friends. He drew attention to their scholarship on the pages of professional journals, and celebrated their achievements in his self-published 'memorials' (obituaries with lists of publications). In 1985 he formalized this international brotherhood, founding the characteristically serio-comic 4Cs Club, presenting to scholars whom he deemed to share his attitude club ties bearing the interlocking 4Cs emblem, representing his four 'categoricals'—Conserve, Consider, Contribute, Co-operate. A world authority on the study of paper, he was general secretary of the Paper Publications Society from 1965 to 1994, and translated and edited the Russian classic watermark albums, culminating in *Likhachev's Watermarks* (1994). His professional achievements were recognized with the award of a civilian OBE in 1981 and the honorary degree of DLitt from Birmingham University in 1987.

All Souls College, Oxford, was an important part of Simmons's life, initially through his friendships with its warden, John Sparrow, and with Isaiah Berlin. As early as 1961 he was accorded the rare privilege of being made a member of the common room, and he was elected a fellow in 1965. Between 1970 and 1982 he was senior research fellow and Codrington librarian. After his retirement in 1982 and appointment as deputy archivist, he lectured and published on the history of the college, collaborating with Howard Colvin on a series of Chichele lectures which led to *All Souls: an Oxford College and its Buildings* (1989).

On retirement, with characteristic lack of sentimentality and regard for the useful, Simmons was at pains to ensure that his considerable working library was distributed among suitable libraries and individuals. After the death of his beloved wife, Fanny, in 1999, the Codrington Library became a second home. He died at the John Radcliffe Hospital in Oxford on 22 September 2005 after a heart attack. He left his body to science and stipulated that there should be no funeral or memorial service. A celebration of his life took place in the Codrington Library on 28 January 2006. He left part of his estate (valued at around £880,000) to All Souls College on condition that it move its sundial, designed by Sir Christopher Wren, from the wall of the Codrington Library to the south front of the college chapel (where it had originally been placed); the college declined the bequest. CHRISTINE G. THOMAS

Sources J. S. G. Simmons, *An autobibliography* (1975); suppl. (1985); suppl. (1995) · 'An address delivered by J. S. G. Simmons … in the great hall of the University of Birmingham on 9 July 1987' · Z. V. David, 'The Simmons Russica collection in the Kennan Institute Library', *Modern Greek Studies Yearbook*, 7 (1991), 473–93 · *The Independent* (23 Sept 2005) · *The Times* (17 Oct 2005) · 'J. S. G. Simmons (1915–2005)', *Slavonic studies at Oxford: a brief history*, ed. G. Stone (2005), 20–22; www.mod-langs.ox.ac.uk/files/docs/russian/slavonic_studies.pdf, 27 March 2009 · A. K. Gorfunkel, 'Zhiznennaia zadacha: znakomstvo i perepiska s Dzhonom Simmonsom', *Solanus: International Journal for Russian and East European Bibliographic, Library and Publishing Studies*, 19 (2005), 14–21 · V. Petritskii, 'Pobornik knigi i slavianskoi kul'tury', *Solanus: International Journal for Russian and East European Bibliographic, Library and Publishing Studies*, 19 (2005), 22–9 · A. Bell, *Information Update* [CILIP], 5/1–2 (Jan–Feb 2006) · 'The recollections of John Simmons (1915–2005), librarian–lecturer, bibliographer, buccaneer', *Solanus: International Journal for Russian and East European Bibliographic, Library and Publishing Studies*, 20 (2006), 5–30 · 'A chronological list of publications about J. S. G. Simmons', *Solanus: International Journal for Russian and East European Bibliographic, Library and Publishing Studies*, 20 (2006) · J. S. G. Simmons, 'Some autobiographical notes', *Solanus: International Journal for Russian and East European Bibliographic, Library and Publishing Studies*, 20 (2006), 30–33 · *Daily Telegraph* (13 June 2006); (20 June 2006) · personal knowledge (2010) · private information (2010) · b. cert. · m. cert. · d. cert.

Archives All Souls Oxf., Codrington Library · U. Leeds, Brotherton L., Leeds Russian archive | SOUND BL NSA, interview with C. Thomas

Likenesses photograph, 1967, repro. in Simmons, *Autobibliography*, (1975) · H. A. Freeth, watercolour, 1983, All Souls Oxf.; repro. in Simmons, *Autobibliography* (1985) · photograph, 1989, repro. in Simmons, *Autobibliography*, suppl. (1995)

Wealth at death £885,826: probate, 20 March 2006, *CGPLA Eng. & Wales*

Simon, Jocelyn Edward Salis [Jack], **Baron Simon of Glaisdale (1911–2006)**, politician and judge, was born on 15 January 1911 at 51 Belsize Park, Hampstead, London, one of five sons of Frank Cecil Simon, stockbroker, and his

Jocelyn Edward Salis Simon, Baron Simon of Glaisdale (1911–2006), by Elliott & Fry, 1952

wife, Claire Evelyn, *née* Mamelsdorf. His parents were Unitarians but he later became a practising Anglican. Educated at Gresham's School, Holt, Norfolk, and, as an exhibitioner, at Trinity Hall, Cambridge, he was called to the bar by the Middle Temple (where he was a Blackstone prizeman) in 1934 and was able slowly to build a practice. On 15 May 1934, at Hampstead register office, he married Gwendolen Helen Evans, a 29-year-old actress, and daughter of Edwin James Evans, shirt manufacturer. The marriage was cut short by her death from chronic pulmonary tuberculosis in 1937.

Simon had joined the inns of court regiment, and on the outbreak of the Second World War was commissioned in the Royal Tank regiment. In 1942, as an acting major in command of a special service squadron, he took part in Operation Ironclad (a combined forces' assault on the French island colony of Madagascar). Although this was eventually successful all Simon's tanks were at one stage disabled and he spent thirty-six hours as a prisoner of war of the defending Vichy French garrison. Mentioned in dispatches for his courageous part in this politically sensitive operation, he was posted to India as staff officer to Major-General Francis Festing, took part in the Burma campaign, and was demobilized in 1945 with the rank of lieutenant-colonel. His long war service gave him a personal and sympathetic understanding of the realities of life for many of his compatriots. He returned to practise at the bar, frequently acting as junior to Seymour Karminski (a KC with a distinguished and erudite practice, who was later to serve as a judge of the Probate, Divorce, and Admiralty Division for some eighteen years before being promoted to the Court of Appeal). On 12 November 1948 Simon married, at Holy Trinity Church, Brompton, Fay Elizabeth Leicester Pearson, a 22-year-old secretary at the BBC, and daughter of Brigadier Hugh Guy Astley Pearson. They had three sons, Peregrine (*b.* 1950), Mark (*b.* 1953), and Crispin (*b.* 1958).

Shortly after taking silk in 1951 Simon was approached to stand as the Conservative Party candidate for Middlesbrough West. He accepted, and in the general election held in October that year succeeded in wresting the seat from Labour with a majority of 2097. He was a conscientious constituency MP and his majority increased in the elections of 1955 and 1959. His outstanding talents were quickly recognized at Westminster: within two months he was appointed parliamentary private secretary to the attorney-general, Sir Lionel Heald, and he made his mark among reforming tories by contributing to *Change is Our Ally* (1954) and *A Giant's Strength* (published in 1958, this foreshadowed later Conservative trade-union legislation). In 1954 he was appointed to serve on the royal commission on the law relating to mental illness and mental deficiency chaired by Lord Percy of Newcastle, and was an active and influential member. The commission's report (1957) led to the enactment of the Mental Health Act 1959 which finally swept away much of the nineteenth-century law with its stigmatizing vocabulary of 'lunatic', 'idiot', and 'mental defective', and sought to substitute a medical and therapeutic approach to dealing with sufferers from mental illness, prioritizing out-patient treatment over institutional care. Ministerial office came to Simon in January 1957 with his appointment as parliamentary under-secretary of state at the Home Office under Rab Butler. A year later he was appointed to the demanding office of financial secretary to the Treasury in succession to Enoch Powell (who with the other Treasury ministers had resigned in protest against the refusal of the prime minister, Harold Macmillan, to countenance significant spending cuts). In October 1959 he was appointed solicitor-general, succeeding Sir Harry Hylton-Foster (who had been elected speaker of the House of Commons). He received the law officers' conventional knighthood.

This highly promising political career came to an end in February 1962 when Simon was appointed president of the Probate, Divorce, and Admiralty Division of the High Court. As president his judgments on technical issues ranging from the validity of 'marriages' between displaced persons in the chaos of post-capitulation Germany to the validity of divorce decrees granted by judges of the 'illegal' regime in Southern Rhodesia were marked by meticulous scholarship and scrupulous interpretation of legal sources. But even in these technical areas his compassion for the victims of circumstances was apparent—not least in his decision that a marriage ceremony between Professor Szymon Szechter and Nina Karsov (a young Polish student imprisoned for political reasons) was legally void because the two had never truly consented to be married. (As a result of the 'marriage' Nina

Karsov had been allowed to settle in England; and following Simon's decision the professor was freed to remarry his first wife.) But such cases were untypical: much of the president's time was taken up with hearing appeals from judgments of (usually lay) magistrates under the distinctive code of law then governing maintenance and custody matters. Simon was in fact well aware of the need for structural reform of the family justice system (for the administration of which the president had a responsibility) and as early as 1952 he had given evidence to the royal commission on marriage and divorce urging the creation of a new court structure. But the Family Division only became a reality in 1972 after Simon had demitted office as president.

In January 1971 Simon was raised to the peerage with the title Baron Simon of Glaisdale—taking his territorial designation from the village on the north Yorkshire moors where he had made his home and where he was able during legal vacations to indulge his taste for fishing and his enthusiasm for gardening. In April of that year he was appointed a lord of appeal in ordinary and for six years sat in the appellate committee of the House of Lords (in effect the country's ultimate appeal court, whose judges at the time included such juristic giants as lords Reid, Wilberforce, Diplock, and Scarman). The cases that came to the house on appeal often involved important issues of policy. Should duress be a defence to a murder charge? Should a man accused of rape be entitled to an acquittal if he could convince the court that he had, albeit unreasonably, believed the victim had consented? Should the court be empowered to override as 'unreasonable' a homosexual father's refusal to consent to his son's being adopted? Was the publisher of a gay contact magazine guilty of 'conspiring to corrupt public morals'? The fact that some of these questions could even be asked may indicate the extent to which attitudes changed in the decades following Simon's retirement from judicial office but his approach was entirely consistent: parliamentary and ministerial experience convinced him that it should be for parliament, not the judges, to effect changes in unsatisfactory laws. Thus the effectiveness of a statute, validly enacted, was not to be impugned (as he argued in *Pickin* v. *British Railways Board*, 1974), but equally the prevalence of 'horrifying acts of political terrorism' was not a justification for the judiciary to allow traditional immunities (such as that prohibiting extradition for crimes of 'a political character' to be eroded (*Cheng* v. *Governor of Pentonville Prison*, 1973). His opinions were of permanent value, not least for their careful and profound examination of often competing issues, but as decisions many were overtaken by subsequent legislative change.

Simon's belief in the importance of the distinction between the legislative and the judicial function did not mean that he thought judges should not hold, and in an appropriate forum express, views about legal policy in areas where their judicial experience was relevant. He had been appointed president of the Probate, Divorce, and Admiralty Division of the High Court at a time of growing dissatisfaction not only with the substance of a divorce law which denied dissolution and the possibility of remarriage to many whose relationships had undeniably broken down, but also with the legal procedures for dealing with family breakdown. He was an active participant in discussions on these matters, not least at the private seminar organized by the Law Commission in July 1966, which paved the way for the compromise about the ground for divorce eventually embodied in the Divorce Reform Act 1969. He made no secret of his concern that such reforming legislation might endanger the institution of marriage and in consequence harm the weak, especially children. He was also deeply concerned at the inadequacy and unfairness (especially to women) of the traditional 'separation of property' regime of English law, and in 1964 expressed those concerns and his views of the way forward in an outstandingly powerful address to the Birmingham University Holdsworth Club, 'With all my worldly goods'. He was also concerned by the ease with which the legal system itself could exacerbate domestic tensions: he saw no reason to allow an inappropriate application of the doctrine of the separation of powers to hinder the introduction of mediation as an element in resolving disputes. In these ways he had an important influence on the development of family law, significantly more than might be thought from a mere recital of his judicial decisions.

By judicial standards Simon's retirement from judicial office on 30 September 1977 was somewhat premature. The explanation is that surgical removal of a benign tumour some twelve years previously had caused visual impairment (he habitually wore a black eye-patch), partial facial paralysis, and some slurring of speech. Although he remained a sociable man whose sweet and tolerant personality was apparent to all who had regular dealings with him, his disabilities increasingly caused difficulties both to him and his interlocutors, and it was this which led him eventually to believe that he should retire. But he continued actively and effectively to participate in House of Lords debates (not least urging the introduction of a system of community of property as a method of removing the injustice of the marriage laws); years later the Conservative leader in the House of Lords, Lord Strathclyde, recalled 'the incisive rumblings from behind his eye patch of Lord Simon of Glaisdale', adding that when Simon spoke 'you knew you were doomed in a way that you were not doomed if a mere politician was probing your arguments' (*Hansard 5L*, 28 July 2009, 1510). His last appearance in the House of Lords was in December 2004 when he voted in support of the Constitutional Reform Bill that was to deny judges of the newly created Supreme Court the right to participate in parliamentary debates—a right he had exercised to very great public advantage. He was indeed a master of the English language: not for nothing had he read English (rather than law) at Cambridge. His judgments and lectures were impressive examples of clear and elegant exposition, enlivened by a wealth of apt literary allusions. A deeply cultured man with a fine sense of humour and a broad range of interests, he was, throughout his life—as clearly evidenced by the four scholarly and indeed encyclopaedic papers he contributed to the *Law Quarterly Review* between 1960 and 1965, 'English idioms from the law', and his erudite article published in the *Review* in 1968, 'Shakespeare's legal and political background'—an avid reader with a wide and profound knowledge of the English language and its literature.

Simon was the last exemplar of what had become a tradition of the English legal system: men who successfully practised at the bar, became MPs, held ministerial office, and were then appointed to the highest judicial office. (Indeed it was sometimes assumed that a man who had served as attorney-general or solicitor-general could expect to be offered appointment as lord chief justice or head of one of the divisions of the High Court, or might become lord chancellor.) Simon's career exemplifies some of the benefits of such a career pattern. As a Home Office minister he had, for example, developed his understanding of the practical workings of the criminal justice system (shouldering much of the burden of taking the Homicide Act of 1957 through the House of Commons); as financial secretary he had become a master of public finance, the technicalities of taxation law and policy, and the intricacies of the rigid exchange control regime in force at the time; and as solicitor-general he not only appeared in the courts as counsel in cases of special public importance but also saw significant law reform measures (such as the Trustee Investment Act 1961, which enabled trustees to invest in equities) onto the statute book. No doubt he also experienced at first hand the difficult and sensitive issues that from time to time arise when what is politically convenient may not be consistent with the application of the rule of law. He thus came to high judicial office with an experience of the realities of the law-making process much greater than could be expected of those whose professional experience had been gained exclusively in legal practice, and he was able to express influential views at the right time and in the right place. Over the years he did much to shape the family justice system.

Simon was a modest man, and a loyal colleague and friend. He died on 7 May 2006 at the Chelsea and Westminster Hospital, London, and was survived by his wife, Fay (to whom he was devoted), and their three sons (the eldest of whom, Sir Peregrine Simon, had been appointed a judge of the Queen's Bench Division of the High Court in 2002). S. M. CRETNEY

Sources *Law Reports* (1962–78) · J. L. J. Edwards, *The law officers of the crown* (1964) · J. Simon, 'With all my worldly goods', presidential address to the Holdsworth Club, Birmingham University, 1964 · minutes of law commissioners' meetings, July 1966, TNA: PRO, BC 3/3 · *The Times* (June 1983) [obituary note: Szymon Szechter]; (8 May 2006) · S. M. Cretney, *Law, law reform and the family* (1998) · S. Cretney, *Family law in the twentieth century: a history* (2003) · *Daily Telegraph* (8 May 2006) · *The Guardian* (8 May 2006) · *The Independent* (9 May 2006) · P. Simon, funeral oration, Temple Church, May 2006 · Burke, *Peerage* · *WW* (2006) · private information (2010) · b. cert. · m. certs. · d. cert.

Likenesses Elliott & Fry, quarter-plate glass negative, 1952, NPG [*see illus.*] · Elliott & Fry, photographs, 1952–5, NPG · W. Bird, photograph, 1959, NPG · photograph, 1971, Photoshot, London · obituary photographs

Wealth at death £170,000: probate, 11 April 2007, *CGPLA Eng. & Wales*

Singer, Aubrey Edward (1927–2007), broadcasting executive, was born on 21 January 1927 at 12 Mornington Villas, Manningham, Bradford, Yorkshire, the son of Louis Henry Singer (1894–1976), a technician in the textile industry, and his wife, Elizabeth, *née* Walton, head of music at Bradford Girls' Grammar School. He was educated first at Giggleswick School, then at Bradford grammar school, leaving at seventeen to become a trainee film editor at the British Gaumont film studios, where he directed instructional films for the armed forces. He then worked for a time in Africa and Austria, and in 1949 joined the fledgling BBC television service, where he was to spend most of his subsequent career. On 21 December the same year he married Cynthia Hilda Adams (*b.* 1924), a secretary, and daughter of Leslie George Adams, company director. They had three daughters and a son.

Singer's first job at the BBC was in outside broadcasts. Later postings took him in 1951 to Glasgow and in 1953 New York, from where he returned to London in 1956 as a producer, specializing in programmes about science—a field in which, in the following two decades, he made his greatest mark. In 1959 he took his first step on the executive ladder, becoming assistant head of outside broadcasts. Two years later he was appointed head of science and features, and in 1967 head of features group, a grander title for what was essentially the same job. That was also when he came closest to leaving the BBC. He had been part of the consortium that won the ITV franchise for Yorkshire and could have gone to Leeds as its director of programmes. He decided, though, that his future lay with the corporation, wedded as he was to the high moral principles laid down by Lord Reith, its first director-general.

Singer had made this commitment clear in 1960 when, five years after the launch of commercial television, the BBC was being accused of pushing too hard for mass audiences and neglecting its public service obligations. The controller of programmes canvassed senior staff for their views. Singer maintained that the order of priorities set down in the corporation's charter had been reversed: instead of trying to educate, inform, and entertain, it now seemed that entertainment had been placed first, compromising the social purpose of broadcasting (Briggs, 323). During his thirteen years in charge of most of BBC television's factual output (excluding news and current affairs) he adhered faithfully to his belief in education and information. He introduced many outstanding programme strands, notably the long-running *Horizon* (1964–) and *Tomorrow's World* (1965–2003), and commissioned Jacob Bronowski to write and present the groundbreaking series *The Ascent of Man* (1973). These programmes set a pattern for the popular science features that were to remain a staple of British broadcasting. They also reflected his remarkable fecundity: 'Aubrey has roughly 100 ideas every day', according to one colleague, 'of which 98 are quite useless. [But] the other two more than justify his salary' (*Daily Telegraph*, 28 May 2007).

In 1974 Singer was made controller of BBC2, and was by now one of half a dozen senior executives being spoken of as a possible future director-general. In 1978 he broadened his experience by moving away from television to become managing director of BBC radio. In this role he initiated plans to put all BBC radio on VHF and to introduce twenty-four-hour broadcasting, but he also became involved in a damaging dispute in 1980 when, as part of a drive to bring down the corporation's costs, it was decided to reduce the number of its house orchestras from eleven to six, involving the loss of 172 jobs. It fell to Singer to try to mollify the Musicians' Union, whose well-publicized demonstrations against the cuts had gained wide sympathy; but he was too stubborn to be a good negotiator and the dispute was settled by compromise only when he was persuaded to stand aside from the talks.

That defeat was a blow to his prospects for advancement, but Singer's fortunes improved when George Howard was appointed chairman of the BBC. The two men had much in common: both were plump and outgoing, appreciative of the good things in life, and sharing a fascination with China, where they travelled together on BBC business, with plenty of time for sightseeing. That interest was reflected in Singer's only published book, *The Lion and the Dragon* (1992), an exhaustively researched account of the first British embassy to Peking (Beijing) in the late eighteenth century. It was thanks to Howard that Singer returned to television in 1982 as managing director of BBC television, with the additional title of deputy director-general, even though the newly installed director-general, Alasdair Milne (with whom Singer had previously clashed), was opposed to the appointment. Singer presided over a decline in ratings at a time when Margaret Thatcher's administration was pressing for radical reforms at the BBC. After he had been in the post for less than two years, shortly after Howard stepped down as chairman, Milne persuaded him in early 1984 to retire. In the same year he was appointed CBE for services to broadcasting.

Some time earlier Singer had prudently registered the name of an independent production company, White City Films, and as part of his severance arrangements the BBC agreed to fund the development of its programmes for five years. The company flourished during the 1980s but later its output declined and it ceased to operate in 1996. That was also the year when Singer stepped down, after twelve years, from the council of the National Museum of Photography, Film, and Television in his native Bradford, one of a number of professional bodies with which he was involved. He received an honorary doctorate from the University of Bradford in 1984. He died from arterial vascular disease and complications at Wakefield Nursing Centre, Ravenscourt Gardens, Hammersmith, London, on 26 May 2007, and was survived by his wife and three of his children, one daughter having predeceased him. His son Adam also made his name as a television executive.

MICHAEL LEAPMAN

Sources A. Briggs, *The BBC: the first fifty years* (1985) • M. Leapman, *The last days of the Beeb* (1986) • A. Milne, *DG: the memoirs of a British broadcaster* (1988) • *Daily Telegraph* (28 May 2007) • *The Guardian* (28 May 2007) • *The Independent* (28 May 2007) • *The Times* (29 May 2007) • *WW* (2007) • personal knowledge (2011) • private information (2011) • b. cert. • m. cert. • d. cert.

Archives BBC WAC | SOUND BL NSA, current affairs recordings • BL NSA, documentary recordings

Likenesses obituary photographs • photograph, repro. in www.hometheaterforum.com/forum/thread/267249/the-htf-film-and-necrology-report-for-2007-part-ii • photographs, BBC Archives, London

Wealth at death under £121,000: probate, 24 June 2008, *CGPLA Eng. & Wales*

Singer, Sir Hans Wolfgang (1910–2006), development economist, was born on 29 November 1910 in Elberfeld in the Rhineland, Germany, the eldest of three sons of Heinrich Singer, a doctor with a large practice (and always available for sick people), and his wife, Antonia. He was brought up as a member of a minority within a minority within a minority—a Jewish community within a protestant enclave in a largely Roman Catholic area of a predominantly protestant country. This early experience, Singer often said, gave him a lifelong affinity with groups that were oppressed or discriminated against.

Singer's early education was in Germany, at the local Gymnasium, concentrating on classics, and then from the age of nineteen at Bonn University, where he studied medicine until, one day, he smuggled himself in to listen to Joseph Schumpeter and was immediately captivated by this brilliant and original economist. He never looked back; in 1931 he received his diploma in political economy and started working on a PhD dissertation, initially under Schumpeter's guidance. But Nazism was growing and in 1934, having married Ilse Lina Plaut (1911–2001), with whom he was to have two sons, Singer fled Germany. Shortly afterwards he received the offer of a scholarship from Cambridge: Schumpeter had written to John Maynard Keynes recommending Singer as one of his brightest students. He was soon enrolled at King's College, Cambridge, working on a thesis on urban land values, supervised by Colin Clark. He became one of a circle of graduate students, including Alec Cairncross and V. K. R. V. Rao, who were following with fascination the latest developments of Keynes's pioneering work *The General Theory of Employment, Interest, and Money* (1936).

Singer obtained his doctorate in 1936. Soon afterwards he was recruited for a major study of unemployment in the depressed areas of the United Kingdom, funded by the Pilgrim Trust and under the supervision of a committee chaired by William Temple, archbishop of York, and with William Beveridge as the main adviser. Singer and his two co-workers, Walter Oakeshott and David Owen, lived with poor unemployed families in six towns where they conducted a detailed sample survey of the lives and conditions of the unemployed. Their report, published as *Men without Work* (1938), became an important influence on William Beveridge for his later path-breaking study *Full Employment in a Free Society* (1944). In 1938 Singer obtained a lectureship in economics at the University of Manchester. Notwithstanding his high-level contacts and the circumstances of his fleeing Germany, Singer was interned as an enemy alien for about six weeks in the early months of the Second World War, until released at the personal intervention of Keynes. He taught at Manchester until 1944, then, after a brief interlude working in the Ministry of Town and Country Planning, at the University of Glasgow in 1946–7. During the war years he also prepared a series of twelve articles on the German war economy, published in the *Economic Journal* (1940–44).

From 1947 to 1969 Singer was employed as one of the first economists in the United Nations, beginning in the newly established department of economic affairs. He was recruited by David Owen, the first head of the department, and worked in a small section dealing with the problems of 'underdeveloped' (that is developing) countries. At that time the UN was acknowledged to have a leading role in international economic matters. The World Bank was preoccupied with reconstruction in post-war Europe, cautious on development, and mostly lacking in talented thinkers and analysts. Singer rapidly brought intellectual brilliance and exceptional creativity to the UN, becoming its working economist of choice, moving from new department to new department, and helping to initiate economic work in the UN's many new organizations, including the Africa Development Bank, UNICEF, the World Food Programme, the UN Research Institute for Social Development, and the UN Industrial Development Organization.

The third phase of Singer's career started in 1969, on his formal retirement from the UN, when he was appointed a professorial fellow at the newly created Institute of Development Studies at the University of Sussex. His prodigious output continued at the institute, and he could now publish in his own name, not anonymously under a UN institutional label. John Shaw, in his biography of Singer published in 2002, listed Singer's output to date: 107 books, 83 major reports, over 260 professional articles, and an almost uncountable number of book reviews, letters to the press, and other pieces. Singer even added a few more books and articles during his last four years.

Undoubtedly Singer's best-known work related to the declining terms of trade experienced by developing countries. Generally referred to as the Prebisch–Singer thesis, the original analysis underlying this important work was largely attributable to Singer himself, according to John and Richard Toye. (Raul Prebisch, of the UN Economic Commission for Latin America, nevertheless played an important role in promoting the thesis and its implications for policy.) The Prebisch–Singer thesis, developed while Singer was at the UN, was first published in 1949 and presented that year at the American Economic Association. It tracked the long-term decline in the terms of trade between developing and developed countries and analysed the underlying causes. At the time, when Keynesian preoccupations were directing most attention to short-term fluctuations in commodity prices, Singer's work attracted both attention and controversy. Many economists disputed the existence of a long-term secular decline but, more than fifty years later, dominant professional opinion had shifted in Singer's favour. Much of the countervailing action that Singer recommended had, however, not been taken, with the result that countries still dependent on coffee, cotton, and other primary commodities for the bulk of their export earnings continued to be at a disadvantage.

Over his lifetime Singer made many other fundamental contributions to development thinking. In the 1950s he was secretary to the committee that explored a proposal to create a soft-loan facility for poor developing countries and recommended the creation of a UN fund for economic development. The fund was about to be called by the acronym UNFED, until Singer pointed out how unfortunate such a name would be. So, as Singer used to delight in telling, it became SUNFED, the Special UN Fund for Economic Development. None the less, Eugene Black, the president of the World Bank at the time, did his best to keep it unfed, opposing the proposal for seven or eight years, and indeed referring to Singer as 'one of the wild men of the UN' (Singer, 'Terms of trade controversy', 299). But by the end of the 1950s the idea of concessional loans to poorer countries was accepted and became the basis for the International Development Association, established in 1959 as the World Bank's main mechanism for concessional lending to developing countries.

In 1961 the UN responded to the American president John F. Kennedy's call in the UN's general assembly to set up a 'development decade' focused on the reduction of world poverty. Singer was the main drafter of *The United Nations Development Decade: Proposals for Action* (1962), which brought together the contributions of the different parts of the UN and provided guidelines for implementation. Singer's ideas on aid and development always had a creative eye to policy applications. He was the first to write about the problems of 'fungability'—how development assistance provided for one purpose could in its broader effects be used to support quite another, since it eased general budget constraints. This was one of several reasons why Singer always opposed tough conditionality in the use of aid.

Singer fashioned many of the ideas underlying food aid and the creation of the World Food Programme, which bestowed on him its 'food for life' award in 2001. He was also one of the first economists to work in the Economic Commission for Africa and later served (in 1967–9) as the first director of research for the UN Industrial Development Organization. For UNICEF he wrote the first document on children and economic development, which he thought so important that for several months he set aside his work on the terms of trade. Indeed, there were few development agencies of the UN to which Singer did not at one time or another contribute, with such creativity and impact that many of their staff often thought that it was to them alone that Singer was giving such special attention.

Some of Singer's most significant contributions came after he had retired from the UN in 1969 and joined the Institute of Development Studies at the University of Sussex. He helped draft the *Sussex Manifesto: Science and Technology to Developing Countries during the Second Development Decade* (1972). He revisited his theory of the declining terms of trade for developing countries, to give more attention to the part played by technological advance in developed countries. He was appointed one of the two main advisers to the world employment programme of the International Labour Office. In 1972 he was co-leader of the mission to Kenya, which later that year produced the International Labour Office's highly influential report *Employment, Incomes, and Equality*. On this mission Singer originated the concept of redistribution from growth, which later became the theme of a seminal study, *Redistribution with Growth* (World Bank and Institute of Development Studies, 1974). The Kenya report was also the first international document to draw attention to the positive contributions of the informal sector, and it laid the foundation for the 'basic needs strategy' that for a few years after the World Employment Conference in 1976 became fashionable orthodoxy.

Singer's extraordinary energy and intellectual leadership issued from a small man, of modest appearance and mild-mannered stance, his head often cocked to one side, with bushy eyebrows and a friendly but questioning smile. He was loved and deservedly fêted by many for his visionary and creative thinking, which was bold, innovative, and positive, in contrast to his gracious and unassuming style and total disregard for outward appearances. In the UN he was widely known and admired for his outstanding professional qualities, his ready willingness to help, and his scrupulous avoidance of gossip and infighting. The old guard of the UN remembered him as one who had maintained his integrity even while he was singled out for personal attack by Senator McCarthy (for his work on SUNFED). Indeed, because of these pressures on him, he resigned from the UN in 1953 and was on the point of leaving when Dag Hammarskjöld, the newly appointed secretary-general, directly appealed to Singer to stay, which, fortunately for the UN, he did.

Singer's wife, Ilse, provided not only support but brought her own moral commitments and an incisive and independent perspective to their partnership. A lifelong supporter of the Women's League for Peace and Freedom, she also for many years held the British record for sales of UNICEF greeting cards. In the polarized politics of New York in the McCarthy era of the 1950s, it was Ilse Singer who explained to the teacher of their son's class that she must get used to UN children from other countries not being expected to pledge allegiance to the American flag. In her seventies she could be seen in Brighton, joining with the women's liberation movement to campaign against, among other things, female beauty contests.

Singer was awarded honorary degrees by the universities of Santa Fe (Argentina), Sussex, Glasgow, Innsbruck, and Kent, and the Universidade Tecnica de Lisboa in Portugal. He was awarded the Francis Wood memorial prize of the Royal Statistical Society in 1939, and received an honorary fellowship of the Institute of Social Studies in The Hague in 1975 and the Allan Shawn Feinstein world hunger award for research and education in 1994–5. In 1993 he was elected president of the Development Studies Association in the UK, which honoured him with a lifetime achievement award in 2004. He was knighted in 1994 for 'services to economic issues'. A Hans Singer memorial lecture was established posthumously in 2009 jointly by the University of Bonn, the German Development Institute, and the Institute of Development Studies at the University of Sussex.

Singer travelled widely throughout his career, both at the UN and at the Institute of Development Studies. Indeed, Sir Alec Cairncross, first head of the (UK) government economic service, once commented:

> there are few of the developing countries that he has not visited and still fewer that he has not advised. He must have addressed a wider variety of academics in a wider variety of places about a wider range of subjects than any other economist, living or dead. He has moved from continent to continent, expounding, advocating, and devising strategies of economic development. His influence has been felt as much by word of mouth in the succession of countries where he has lectured as through the pile of working documents and published reports that survive like spoor from his travels. (D. Sapsford and J. Chen, eds., *Development Economics and Policy: the conference volume to celebrate the 85th birthday of Professor Sir Hans Singer*, 1998, 13–14)

In the UN and in the Institute of Development Studies Singer was known as someone who always found time for others—for students as for colleagues—even while maintaining his prodigious output and an almost unbelievable range of correspondence, especially with friends at or formerly at the UN. His last lecture for graduate students was given a few days short of his ninety-fifth birthday. He lectured without notes—and without hesitation—pausing only to elaborate a point, or to explain his early calculations on how much aid would be needed if developing countries were to accelerate their growth and development. His memory and intellect were undimmed and his vision and international commitment were evident to all. He died at Hyman Fine House, Burlington Street, Brighton, on 26 February 2006, of bronchopneumonia and other complications following a fall four days earlier, and was buried in Brighton borough cemetery. He was survived by one son, his wife and his elder son having predeceased him. RICHARD JOLLY

Sources H. W. Singer, 'Early years (1910–1938)', *Employment, income distribution, and development strategy, problems of the developing countries: essays in honour of H. W. Singer*, ed. A. Cairncross and M. Puri (1976) · H. W. Singer, 'Terms of trade controversy and the evolution of soft financing: early years', *Pioneers in development*, ed. G. M. Meier and D. Seers (1984) · D. J. Shaw, *Sir Hans Singer: the life and work of a development economist* (2002) · J. Toye and R. Toye, *The UN and global political economy: trade, finance, and development* (2004) · T. G. Weiss and others, *UN voices: the struggle for development and social justice* (2005) [includes interview with Singer] · *The Times* (28 Feb 2006) · *The Guardian* (1 March 2006) · *The Independent* (4 March

2006) • *Daily Telegraph* (6 March 2006) • Burke, *Peerage* • *WW* (2006) • personal knowledge (2010) • private information (2010) • d. cert.
Archives U. Sussex, Institute of Development Studies
Likenesses C. Green, photograph, 1994, priv. coll. • obituary photographs • photographs, repro. in Shaw, *Sir Hans Singer*
Wealth at death £3,065,668: probate, 7 Aug 2006, *CGPLA Eng. & Wales*

Slade, Julian Penkivil (1930–2006), composer and playwright, was born on 28 May 1930 at 33D Eccleston Square, Westminster, London, the second of three sons and third of four children of Sir George Penkivil Slade (1899–1942), barrister, and his wife, Mary Albinia Alice, *née* Carnegie (1896–1988). He was educated at a preparatory school in Oxford and at Eton College, and he had a children's story book, *Nibble the Squirrel* (1946), published when he was only sixteen. Then, at Trinity College, Cambridge, his ability to write tuneful songs resulted in the undergraduate musicals *Bang Goes the Meringue* (1950) and *Lady May*, the latter for May week in 1951. Having ambitions as an actor, he also played Lady Macbeth opposite John Barton's Macbeth in an all-male Shakespeare production.

After graduating in 1951 Slade joined the Bristol Old Vic theatre school. He played small roles in Bristol Old Vic productions, but a future in music rather than acting was determined when the theatre's director, Denis Carey, asked him to supervise the musical side of the productions and appointed him musical director. He composed incidental music for *Two Gentlemen of Verona* (1952), and when volunteers were sought to create a Christmas musical in the same year he collaborated with the actors Dorothy Reynolds and James Cairncross on *Christmas in King Street*. He followed it with incidental music for Sheridan's *The Duenna* (1953), as well as another Christmas piece, *The Merry Gentleman* (with Reynolds, 1953), and music for a BBC television version of Shakespeare's *The Comedy of Errors* (1954).

Wider fame came when Slade and Reynolds collaborated on *Salad Days*, a small-scale, nostalgic, fanciful, and tuneful show written in six weeks as a Bristol Old Vic end-of-season celebration. Taking its title from Shakespeare's *Antony and Cleopatra*, it was built around a magical old street piano and portrayed an idealistically innocent world. It captured the hearts of a British public still welcoming relief from the deprivations of war, as well as offering a respite from more modern and sophisticated American musical shows. First produced at Bristol Old Vic in 1954, it then took up residence at the Vaudeville Theatre, London, where for the first eighteen months of its run Slade himself played one of the two pit pianos that served as orchestra. In all, *Salad Days* ran at the Vaudeville Theatre for five and a half years, its total of 2288 performances breaking the record for the longest-running musical show of the London theatre, which had been held for almost forty years by *Chu Chin Chow*. It subsequently enjoyed major West End revivals in 1976 and 1996. The similarly charming *Free as Air* (at the Savoy Theatre, London, in 1957) was perhaps a more polished work and used a fourteen-piece orchestra. However, it could not strike the same spark, and later works in similar style failed to capture the same freshness of invention. These included *Hooray for Daisy!* (Bristol, 1959), *Follow that Girl!* (a reworking of *Christmas in King Street* with Susan Hampshire; London, Vaudeville, 1960), and *Wildest Dreams* (London, Vaudeville, 1962).

Wildest Dreams was Slade's final collaboration with Dorothy Reynolds. Thereafter he sought to develop his style in such works as *Vanity Fair* (after Thackeray; London, Queen's, 1962), which starred Sybil Thorndike; *Nutmeg and Ginger* (after the Jacobean comedy *The Knight of the Burning Pestle*; Cheltenham, 1963); *Sixty Thousand Nights* (Bristol, 1966); and an adaptation of Nancy Mitford's *The Pursuit of Love* (Bristol, 1967). However, he would never again approach matching his success of the 1950s. In 1970 he composed songs for *As You Like It*, *A Midsummer Night's Dream*, and *Much Ado about Nothing*, the latter two for the Regent's Park Open Air Theatre. He provided additions to Harold Fraser-Simson's music for A. A. Milne's *Winnie-the-Pooh*, which was for some years performed annually at the Phoenix Theatre, and he also collaborated on two adaptations of A. W. Pinero. *Trelawney* (1972) starred Hayley Mills alongside Ian Richardson and moved from Bristol Old Vic to Sadler's Wells Theatre (with Gemma Craven replacing Mills). However, *Out of Bounds* (after *The Schoolmistress*; Bristol, 1973), for which Slade provided the book as well as lyrics and music, failed to make the transfer to London. In the era of Andrew Lloyd Webber's *Joseph and the Amazing Technicolor Dreamcoat* and *Jesus Christ Superstar* Slade's time was past.

Slade's later ventures included incidental music for Nancy Mitford's *Love in a Cold Climate* (Thames Television, 1980), a musical adaptation of J. M. Barrie's *Dear Brutus* (1985), and a musical play, *Now We Are Sixty* (1986), based on the works of A. A. Milne. Other ventures included revisions of, or backward looks at, earlier successes, including a recording in 1981 in which Slade played and sang numbers from musicals he had composed over a period of thirty years. His later years also saw occasional revivals. Besides *Salad Days* at the Vaudeville Theatre in 1996, *Nutmeg and Ginger* was performed at the Orange Tree Theatre, Richmond, in 1991, and *Vanity Fair* at the Covent Garden festival in 2001. At the Bristol Old Vic in 2004 Cameron Mackintosh mounted a celebration of the fiftieth anniversary of *Salad Days*.

Though he considered himself to be principally self-taught in music, Slade acknowledged the assistance provided by Belle Dunhill at Eton College in 1947, Cecil Belcher at the Guildhall School of Music in 1957, and his shows' musical directors, Grant Hossack (1966–7), Ed Coleman (1968), and Neil Rhoden (from 1971). In 1987 he was awarded a gold badge of merit by the British Academy of Songwriters, Composers, and Authors. Latterly he lived in some disarray in a ground-floor and basement flat in Beaufort Street, Chelsea, its walls covered by theatrical mementoes and his own drawings. He never married, but took great pleasure in the children of his two brothers, Christopher (*b.* 1927), who became a lord justice of appeal, and Adrian (*b.* 1936), a marketing consultant and Liberal

Party activist, and his sister Pauline. He died of cancer at the London Clinic, 20 Devonshire Place, Westminster, on 17 June 2006. ANDREW LAMB

Sources K. Gänzl, *The encyclopedia of the musical theatre*, 2nd edn, 3 vols. (2001) · *The Times* (20 June 2006) · *The Guardian* (20 June 2006) · *Daily Telegraph* (22 June 2006) · *The Independent* (23 June 2006) · *WW* (2006) · private information (2010) [Sir Christopher Slade, brother] · personal knowledge (2010) · b. cert. · d. cert.

Archives SOUND BL NSA, documentary recordings

Likenesses Fievez, photograph, 1976, Rex Features, London · obituary photographs

Wealth at death under £150,000: resworn probate, 30 March 2007, *CGPLA Eng. & Wales*

Smalls, Derek Crighton [Bertie] (**1937–2008**), bank robber and police informant, was born on 20 May 1937 at the Elizabeth Garrett Anderson Hospital, London, the eldest of four children of Sidney Crighton Ethelbert Smalls (1907–1959) and his wife, Iris Anne, *née* Fridgen (1909–1952). He drifted into crime at an early age, and at fifteen was sentenced to a period in an approved school for breaking into a railway restaurant car. On his release he progressed to more serious criminal activity, and received convictions for living off immoral earnings and possession of a loaded gun. By the early 1970s, a heavy drinker, prematurely balding with hair combed over, slightly overweight, and sporting a Mexican-style moustache, Bertie Smalls was well known in London's criminal fraternity, and reputedly at the forefront of the switch from coshes and pickaxe handles to handguns and sawn-off shotguns as a wave of armed robberies swept across London. By this time he had two young children, Adele (*b*. 1966) and Derek (*b*. 1971), with his partner, Diana Doris Wheeler, *née* Whates (*b*. 1939), the estranged wife of Francis J. Wheeler.

In August 1972 Smalls took part in an armed raid on a branch of Barclays Bank in Wembley, north London, which netted some £138,000. He and other gang members then lay low, Smalls spending time in Torremolinos before returning to the UK. His name had by then become linked to the robbery through a small-time police informant, and he also attracted attention by trying to buy a farm in Northamptonshire with cash. He was arrested in his underpants in a dawn raid on his brother's house. Faced with mounting evidence and the prospect of a substantial gaol term not only for the Barclays raid but also for an earlier violent robbery of a jewellers in Hatton Garden, he offered to tell the police everything he knew about not only those raids but many others, in return for immunity from prosecution. The director of public prosecutions, Sir Norman Skelhorn, agreed to a deal, and an eight-point agreement was drawn up and signed in his office, guaranteeing Smalls immunity from prosecution for the Barclays raid and all other previous criminal activity, and allowing him to keep the proceeds of his crimes. (He estimated that he had made about £300,000 from robberies, but insisted that he had by then blown most of it on living the high life.) He was also to receive police protection and to be paid a small retainer by the police for the rest of his life.

In all Smalls confessed to fifteen armed robberies, and named thirty-two of his associates. His evidence resulted in the successful prosecution of his six accomplices in the Barclays raid, who were handed sentences totalling 106 years, and over the next year and a half his evidence was crucial in securing the conviction of a further twenty-one men, who received sentences totalling 308 years. His partner, Diana, referred to in court as Mrs Bertie Smalls, was also called to give evidence but refused, saying, 'These are not bad people; they are not wicked people' (*The Times*, 15 June 1974). He also secured the release of Jimmy Saunders, wrongly imprisoned for a raid on a Barclays Bank in Ilford in 1970, after Smalls provided evidence that Saunders had taken no part in the raid. In the immediate aftermath of the trials, the number of bank robberies in London fell from sixty-five in 1972 to twenty-six in 1973, before rising again in the late 1970s as a new generation of armed robbers filled the niche. The deal offered Smalls was controversial. Chief Superintendent Jack Slipper, famous for his role in investigating the Great Train Robbery of 1963, said that Smalls was 'the greatest weapon the police have ever had against the underworld' (*Daily Mirror*, 11 Feb 2008). On the other hand, even the prosecution lawyer in one of the trials admitted that Smalls was 'a man with not only the worst possible character … but with a motive to lie' (*The Times*, 4 Sept 1974). Defence lawyers claimed that Smalls's evidence was inherently unreliable, since he was still likely to be influenced by continuing inducements. Sir Frederick Lawton, sitting in the Court of Appeal, rejected this argument, but criticized as 'distasteful' a deal which enabled Smalls to escape scot-free (*R.* v. *Turner* [1975], Cr. App. R 67). It was subsequently established as a principle that informants should first plead guilty to any charges against them, and that they should receive reduced sentences rather than complete immunity from prosecution. Smalls was thus the first and only police informant to have negotiated complete immunity.

Such was the scale of the information that he gave the police that Smalls was soon dubbed the UK's first 'supergrass' by the media, and the phrase 'do a Bertie Smalls' found its way into slang, to mean any form of informing. At one Old Bailey trial at which Smalls gave evidence, those in the dock began singing Vera Lynn's song, 'We'll meet again', making mock pistols directed at Smalls with their fingers. It was reputed that a price of £1 million was put on his head by leading underworld figures, including the Krays. Nevertheless, and despite his wife and children receiving death threats, Smalls refused the police's offers to pay for plastic surgery for him, or to assist his emigration to Australia. Indeed, he even sold his story to a newspaper in 1975, allowing himself to be photographed, and later started drinking in his old haunts. One of those convicted on his evidence, Bobby King, later recalled coming across Smalls in the street after his own release from prison, and quipped that it was a testament to the reforming power of prison that he had resisted the urge to take a swipe at him. On one occasion, though, Smalls was beaten up in a car park. The *Times* journalist Peter Watson began work on a biography of him, but 'we didn't get far—he drank triple vodkas and neither the meagre advance nor my liver could stand it' (*The Times*, 4 Aug 1981). Smalls lived latterly in Croydon, where he died of natural causes on 31 January 2008. ALEX MAY

Sources A. Ball, L. Chester, and R. Perrott, *Cops and robbers: an investigation into armed bank robbery* (1978) · *Daily Mirror* (11 Feb 2008) · *Daily Express* (13 Feb 2008) · *The Independent* (12 Feb 2008); (1 March 2008) · *The Times* (27 Feb 2008); (11 March 2008) · b. cert.

Smieton, Dame Mary Guillan (1902–2005), civil servant, was born at Brookside, Mountfield Road, Finchley, London, on 5 December 1902, the younger daughter of John Guillan Smieton (1839–1913) and his wife, Maria Judith, *née* Toop (1872–1943). There had been a name change, John Smeaton the lighthouse builder being among her forebears. Her father had independent means but served as librarian and bursar of London Presbyterian Theological College, which became Westminster College, Cambridge, in 1899. He and his much younger wife both suffered ill health, the two girls being cared for partly by aunts until their father died in 1913 and their mother set up home in Wimbledon.

Mary Smieton attended the Perse School, Cambridge, and Wimbledon Girls' High School, then travelled daily to read history at Bedford College, London. After a year she entered Lady Margaret Hall, Oxford, to read philosophy, politics, and economics, graduating with a second-class degree in 1925. She joined the administrative class of the civil service later that year, which was the first in which women became eligible. Having opted for the Ministry of Labour she was posted to the Public Record Office as its first ever female recruit. This proved mutually daunting and work on medieval Latin documents was not to her taste. She transferred to the Ministry of Labour in 1928 and so began her main career, just before the great depression, with its heavy unemployment and hunger marches. She was on personnel work at a time of great expansion in the staff and it was in dealing with people that her strengths developed.

In 1938 Smieton was chosen to help the dynamic Lady Reading create the Women's Voluntary Service, as its first general secretary (attached to the Home Office). Its almost immediate role after the outbreak of the Second World War was to assist with children's evacuation—arranging billeting and schooling, and keeping families in touch—as well as running canteens for troops on the move. The Women's Royal Voluntary Service (as it became) proved indispensable and was to continue in peacetime. Smieton returned in 1940 to the Ministry of Labour and National Service, and for the rest of the war was a senior aide to the minister, Ernest Bevin, in the recruitment of women for essential work in factories, on the land, and in the armed services. There were little-used powers to direct labour if necessary, but persuasion was all important. She helped organize such events as a major women's rally at the Albert Hall when the war was going badly, attended by Winston Churchill, with Bevin in the chair. She also succeeded in flying in a Lancaster bomber.

With the war in Europe over and priorities in place for demobilization and return to peacetime production, Bevin became foreign secretary and Smieton was from 1946 to 1948 seconded to the United Nations in New York as its first director of personnel. There she found the administration chaotic and political interference rife (for example the Soviets would not accept White Russian translators and others considered UN staff recruitment a matter for patronage rather than merit). Smieton was relieved to return to the Ministry of Labour (as an under-secretary) in 1948. She was made DBE in 1949 and became deputy secretary from 1955 to 1959, responsible to ministers for employment policy as the country sought to recover prosperity, repay debts to the USA, and come to terms with the end of empire.

In 1959 Smieton was appointed permanent secretary of the Ministry of Education, only the second woman (after Dame Evelyn Sharp) to hold this civil service rank. She had no experience of educational administration and faced an unfamiliar culture of working largely through local authorities rather than by central control. Education was rising rapidly in economic, social, and political importance, particularly as the space age gathered momentum, and among many urgent needs were those of science and technology, leading to the chartering of new universities and the establishment of the Department of Education and Science. Most education policy was bi-partisan but the political debate on comprehensive schools was already joined with the Labour opposition. In advising ministers Smieton did not want for able and energetic deputies. She was an arbiter rather than an expert—but a very able one, drawing on vast experience of people and situations. Her main minister was Sir David Eccles (her favourite after Bevin), followed in 1962 by Sir Edward Boyle (young enough to be her son), who was as charmed by her matronly approach as she was by his youth and erudition.

After retirement in 1963 Smieton continued to represent the UK on the board of UNESCO in Paris until 1968 and served on a number of cultural bodies, for example as a trustee of the British Museum (1963–73) and as a member of the Advisory Council on Public Records (1965–73) and of the Standing Commission on Museums and Galleries (1970–73). She took a particular interest in women's education, and from 1967 to 1970 chaired the council of Bedford College. Her private life was devoted to travel and entertaining friends in her large house and garden in St Margaret's-on-Thames and to attending the annual varsity rugby match at nearby Twickenham. She let out the house occasionally for film-making, though her policy (with a twinkle) was to refuse 'commercials'. Her garden was open annually to the public. Enjoying good health and living long enough for her pension to have exceeded her earnings (victory over the Treasury being a source of wry amusement), she revelled in life and was always game for new experience, such as chartering a helicopter to visit a distant friend when in her late nineties. She died, unmarried, on 23 January 2005 at her home, 14 St George's Road, St Margaret's-on-Thames, of pneumonia and heart failure, following a fall. A memorial service was held at Lady Margaret Hall. She left an estate valued at just over £3.6 million, mainly to charities, including her house, which was given to the Royal Society for Nature Conservation with a request to protect her garden from future building. GEOFFREY COCKERILL

Sources *The Times* (26 Jan 2005) · *The Independent* (27 Jan 2005) · *The Guardian* (28 Jan 2005) · *Daily Telegraph* (31 Jan 2005) · *WW* (2005) · Burke, *Peerage* · private information (2009) · personal knowledge (2009) · b. cert. · d. cert.
Archives SOUND IWM, recording, 7 March 1994
Likenesses W. Stoneman, bromide print, 1957, NPG · photographs, 1960–66, Photoshot, London · obituary photographs
Wealth at death £3,610,551: probate, 27 April 2005, *CGPLA Eng. & Wales*

Smith, Antony John (1934–2008), medical journalist, was born on 4 December 1934 at 10 Wren Street, Coventry, the elder son of Walter Harold Smith, a clerk for the public medical service, and his wife, Doris, *née* Searle. At some time both parents worked in Jaguar's Browns Lane car factory. Winning a scholarship to Bablake Grammar School and then to University College, Oxford, Smith initially read law, but—having decided not to become a professional bridge player—switched to medicine, qualifying at the London Hospital in 1959. Though he had edited its journal the hospital failed to offer him the usual house appointment; instead he worked in several dilapidated former workhouses around the capital. There began his lifelong challenge to the establishment, guaranteeing that he would not ascend the medical specialist ladder. Thus he refused to care for his consultants' private patients without being paid, or to accept the stratagems then needed to pass the MRCP examination. On 23 August 1958 he married Evelyn Mary Adey, a fellow medical student, daughter of Stanworth Wills Adey, chemical engineer; they had two daughters and a son.

Despite his lack of advancement within the profession Smith developed a lifelong profound knowledge of medicine. He used this well throughout his career, from 1965 to 1995 at the *British Medical Journal*, from 1971 to 1982 as the *Times* medical correspondent, and in freelance work. At the *BMJ* he successively edited every section, introducing successful new features widely copied by others, such as 'Minerva' (a miscellany of medical happenings). He initiated expert statistical appraisal of submitted articles; and the 'Hanging Committee', which decided whether to accept or reject refereed papers for publication (so called by analogy with the Royal Academy's judging panel). He also helped steer the journal's policy to a humane approach to difficult new issues such as abortion, organ transplantation, and euthanasia.

At *The Times* Smith continued this liberal attitude, widening the scope of its articles to subjects such as living with a colostomy, child abuse, and hormone replacement therapy. Writing quickly and fluently, he rarely altered his texts, though this reflected much thought and experience (his favourite saying was 'the first million words were the worst'). But he disagreed with the new editor, Harold Evans, who, he claimed, wanted medicine on the front page as often as possible, whereas Smith saw his duty in keeping unsubstantiated claims off it. Heartbroken at being sacked from the paper in 1982, he diverted his surplus energies to the British Medical Association's *Family Doctor* booklets. He had already written several books—two on contraception and, jointly, a prize-winning Penguin, *The Medical Risks of Life* (1977), and the *Reader's Digest Family Health Guide* (1972)—and in the next twenty-five years produced many others. A particularly fruitful relationship was with the publisher Dorling Kindersley, resulting in several beautifully illustrated books such as the *Guide to Healthy Living* (1993) and *Adolescence: the Survival Guide for Parents and Teenagers* (1994), which sold in their thousands. Hence, though he declined to take any credit, the vast change in medical and lay attitudes towards health and disease owed much to his efforts.

Such work made Smith rich, though with a comfortably off wife he had always lived well, as a student residing on a houseboat on the River Lea and subsequently in a detached house in Blackheath, a house near Regent's Park, and a palatial Suffolk rectory. Handsome and saturnine (his grandfather had been a Gypsy blacksmith before settling in Coventry), and immaculately dressed, he was attractive to women. He enjoyed good food and wine and would buy modern lithographs, also urging his friends to read fiction: though many novels were meretricious, one in ten might alter your world outlook, he maintained. He would read one in an evening and give it away.

Smith was shy and rarely smiled, but people went to him for advice, whether on health or personal problems. He was a lifelong socialist, though believing that New Labour had betrayed the cause. His father had been a shop steward and he argued that every citizen deserved a comfortable life. Thus Smith admired the Nordic countries with their generous social welfare and high happiness index, and after his divorce from Evelyn in 1981 he spent much time in Oslo with his partner, Inga Lunde, a pharmacist, sometimes sailing there in his boat. Unsurprisingly Smith also had the naïveté of the early socialists, echoing their pre-war enthusiasm for the Soviet Union when he went to Mao's China: it had, he alleged, not only abolished venereal disease but also flies and other pests.

In his last five years Smith developed Parkinson's disease, which became so severe that he returned to Britain and admitted himself to a nursing home in Woodbridge, Suffolk. Having gone for a solitary walk on 5 June 2008, he did not return and, despite an extensive search, his body was not found until 1 March 2009. He was survived by his three children. STEPHEN LOCK

Sources *The Times* (10 March 2009); (23 March 2009) · *BMJ*, 338 (10 March 2009), 983 · *East Anglian Daily Times* (16 March 2009) · *Newsletter of the Medical Journalists Association* (April 2009) · *The Guardian* (28 April 2009) · *The Independent* (27 May 2009) · personal knowledge (2012) · private information (2012) · b. cert. · m. cert.
Likenesses photographs, priv. coll.
Wealth at death £613,648: probate, 8 Oct 2009, *CGPLA Eng. & Wales*

Smith, Ian Douglas (1919–2007), prime minister of Rhodesia, was born on 8 April 1919 in Selukwe, Southern Rhodesia, the only son and third of the four children of John Douglas (Jock) Smith (1879–1956), butcher, mine manager, and horse breeder, and his wife, Agnes, *née* Hodgson (1891–1978), daughter of Thomas Hodgson of Cumberland. His father was Scottish, and had emigrated to Rhodesia in 1898.

Education, war service, and early career in politics Educated at Chaplin School in Gwelo, where he excelled at sport, Smith began studying for a bachelor of commerce degree at Rhodes University in Grahamstown, South Africa. His studies were interrupted in 1941 by his decision to join the Royal Air Force. After training he was posted to 237 (Rhodesia) squadron, at first in the Middle East and later in the western desert. In 1943 he was seriously injured when his Hawker Hurricane crashed on take-off. Following reconstructive surgery which left one side of his face immobile, he returned to active service, flying Spitfires as the allies ground their way up the Italian peninsula. Shot down over the Po valley in 1944, he was picked up by partisans, and spent three months with them behind enemy lines. Remembering those days as some of the 'most interesting months' of his life (*Great Betrayal*, 17), Smith learned Italian and read Shakespeare before crossing the maritime Alps into American-occupied France. His final posting was to 130 squadron, then based in Germany, and finally in Norway. Adopted by the maharaja of the Punjab, the squadron benefited from a generous discretionary fund to ensure that its pilots did not suffer 'unnecessary' hardships.

Once demobilized, Smith returned to Rhodes University in 1946. In the course of his final year he headed the student representative council, played cricket and rugby, and won an award for rowing. Back in Southern Rhodesia he set about acquiring farming experience, and in August 1948 leased land with an option to purchase, near his home town of Selukwe. That same month he married a local schoolteacher, Janet Duvenage, *née* Watt (*d.* 1994), a University of Cape Town history graduate and widowed mother of two children (a son, Robert, and a daughter, Jean), with whom he had a further son, Alec.

Earlier in 1948 Smith had been persuaded by the right-wing Liberal Party to stand for the Southern Rhodesia legislative assembly and was duly elected with a clear majority. Initially sceptical of moves to establish the Central African Federation (incorporating Northern and Southern Rhodesia and Nyasaland), he decided to work with rather than against the new dispensation, transferring his political allegiance to the United Federal Party led by Sir Godfrey Huggins and Roy Welensky. In 1953 he was elected to the federal assembly, serving as the party's chief whip from 1958 until his resignation in 1961. Objecting to new constitutional proposals for Southern Rhodesia, whose provision for African representation he claimed were 'racialist' because of the abandonment of the common roll, and realizing that the federation's days were numbered, Smith concentrated his energies on territorial politics. After discussions with Winston Field, leader of the opposition Dominion Party, and his close political friend and business partner, Douglas (Boss) Lilford, Smith emerged as one of the founding members of the Rhodesian Front (RF) in March 1962.

Appointed deputy prime minister and minister of the treasury after the RF came to power nine months later, and against a background of hardening attitudes on the part of white and black alike as Britain's retreat from empire gathered pace, Smith, together with Field, attended the Victoria Falls conference, called to wind up the affairs of the federation, in July 1963. With Southern Rhodesia awarded by far the greater part of the federal armed forces, and believing that they had understood

Ian Douglas Smith (1919–2007), by unknown photographer, 1965

R. A. Butler, Britain's minister for central African affairs, to have intimated that independence would soon follow, the Rhodesian delegation co-operated fully with the business to hand. But while Field was willing to take British assurances on trust, Smith, reserved and suspicious, on his own telling, warned Butler that if that trust was broken, he would 'live to regret it' (*Great Betrayal*, 54). Butler denied that any such assurances were given, and there is no documentary evidence in support of Smith and Field's recollection of the occasion. Subsequent negotiations between the two sides, however, were conducted in an atmosphere of mistrust. Determined to halt the wind of change on the Zambezi, Smith and nearly all of his cabinet colleagues lost patience with Field's inability either to secure or seize independence from Britain, the problem being London's reluctance 'to grant independence to Southern Rhodesia, at a point of time when the franchise is incomparably more restricted than that of any territory which has acquired independence in the last 50 years' (Sandys to Field, 22 Feb 1964, *Parl. papers*, Cmnd 2807). In April 1964 the RF parliamentary caucus ejected Field and chose Smith, the first prime minister to be born in Rhodesia. The latter's stated aim was negotiated independence, but he could 'visualise circumstances which could drive us to do something else' (Young, 107).

Prime minister of Rhodesia: the unilateral declaration of independence and the bush war Among Smith's first acts as prime minister of Rhodesia (as the colony was known after the dissolution of the Central African Federation and renaming of Northern Rhodesia as Zambia) was the detention without trial of the African nationalist leaders, Joshua Nkomo of the Zimbabwe African People's Union (ZAPU) and Ndabaningi Sithole and Robert Mugabe of the Zimbabwe African National Union (ZANU). He also bolstered his support among white Rhodesians, his deputy, Clifford Dupont, robustly seeing off in October 1964 a by-election challenge from Welensky. Visiting London in January 1965 to attend the funeral of Winston Churchill, Smith met the prime minister, Harold Wilson, whose Labour Party had narrowly won the British general election three months previously. The encounter was not a success. In May the RF swept the board in an election presented as a united demand for independence, even as preparations were made for more drastic action, something that the self-governing colony was uniquely placed to do. Further talks in London and in Salisbury during October 1965 ended in failure. Ignoring Wilson's televised appeal to 'think again' and a last-minute telephone call, Smith, with the full backing of his cabinet, unilaterally declared Rhodesia independent of Britain on 11 November 1965, safe in the knowledge that London had eschewed the use of force. 'We have struck a blow for the preservation of justice, civilisation, and Christianity—and in the spirit of this belief we have thus assumed our sovereign independence', he claimed (Wood, *So Far and No Further*, 390, 475).

When neither Smith's belief that Rhodesia's unilateral declaration of independence (UDI) would be a 'nine-day wonder' after which international acceptance would follow nor Wilson's claim that economic sanctions would end the rebellion in weeks rather than months showed any sign of happening, the search for a settlement was renewed. Smith rejected increasingly accommodating British proposals tabled at talks on HMS *Tiger* in December 1966 and on HMS *Fearless* in October 1968, before reaching agreement in November 1971 with Sir Alec Douglas-Home, foreign secretary in Edward Heath's Conservative government. Confident that Rhodesia had the 'happiest Africans in the world', Smith and his advisers, who had earlier endorsed a 'world-beater' republican dispensation confining African political ambitions to parity with the white minority, completely underestimated the degree of black hostility to continued settler rule. When the Pearce commission, appointed to test the acceptability of the proposed constitution, returned a 'no' verdict in May 1972, Smith was outraged, criticizing it for its 'naivety and ineptness' (Godwin and Hancock, 82).

Aware that the security situation was deteriorating, Smith was none the less taken by surprise in December 1972 when Zimbabwe African National Liberation Army forces, the military wing of ZANU, sheltered by local peasants, gave effect to new guerrilla tactics by attacking a white-owned farmstead. The ensuing armed struggle eventually engulfed the entire country at a cost of some 30,000 lives, with the Rhodesian security forces winning every battle but eventually losing the war. Before the military coup in Portugal in 1974 and South Africa's turn to a policy of détente with her black neighbours Rhodesia was able to circumvent sanctions and contain guerrilla incursions. Now exposed to unprecedented dangers, however, the authorities in Salisbury were gradually obliged to make concessions. Minor aspects of racial discrimination were pared back. Smith told a press conference in March 1976:

> I have said before, we are prepared to bring black people into our Government to work with us. I think that we have got to accept that in the future Rhodesia is a country for black and white, not white as opposed to black and vice versa … I don't believe in majority rule ever in Rhodesia … not in 1,000 years. I repeat that I believe in black and whites working together. If one day it is white and the next day black I believe we have failed and it will be a disaster for Rhodesia. (Godwin and Hancock, 152)

Six months later Smith was forced to concede the principle of majority rule within two years. Unable to resist the combined weight of American and South African pressure, he accepted a settlement package assembled by the United States secretary of state, Henry Kissinger. When Smith refused to accede to additional African nationalist demands, the deal fell apart. The war escalated, and by 1978 Rhodesian raids into Mozambique and Zambia were commonplace. Most casualties occurred in this period. An 'internal settlement' reached that same year with Bishop Abel Muzorewa's moderate United African National Council and other minor groupings conceded the appearance of black rule while preserving the substance of white control over the egregiously renamed Zimbabwe-Rhodesia, Smith relinquishing the post of prime minister. Lacking international recognition and with no end to the war in sight, the Salisbury government attended the Lancaster

House conference called by Britain in September 1979. Against Smith's advice, Muzorewa stepped down in favour of an interim British governor, Lord Soames, bringing the rebellion to an end, even as for the first time it placed the country under Westminster's direct control.

Final years and assessments At independence in April 1980 Zimbabwe came under the rule of Robert Mugabe, an outcome particularly opposed by Smith. Yet their initial meetings were cordial. As recorded in his autobiography, Smith's first impressions were positive. 'He behaved like a balanced, civilised Westerner, the antithesis of the communist gangster I had expected' (*Great Betrayal*, 342). But Smith soon clashed with the country's new rulers. In March 1981 his objection to the government's announced intention of creating a one-party state caused Mugabe never to see him again. Returned to parliament as leader of the opposition by the white electorate, Smith was expelled from the assembly in 1986, all such seats disappearing the following year with the expiry of the reserved clauses of the Lancaster House constitution. Holding on to his farm, Gwenoro, outside Shurugwi (as Selukwe was now called), Smith also maintained a modest, unguarded home in Harare, the former Salisbury. Although no longer active in politics, he entertained a regular flow of journalists and academics, losing few opportunities to justify his past actions or comment on present-day issues. His memoirs, published in 1997 as *The Great Betrayal*, and subsequently revised and reissued as *Bitter Harvest* (2001), enjoyed significant sales. The violent downwards trajectory followed by Zimbabwe as Mugabe tightened his grip on power was grist to Smith's mill. Calling Mugabe 'mentally deranged' for having embarked on the fast-track land reform programme, Smith was threatened in October 2000 with imprisonment and trial for genocide, but no action was taken. With police help, his own farm was initially spared occupation by the self-styled 'war veterans' operating at ZANU's behest. His health failing, Smith moved to South Africa for medical treatment in 2005.

As much condescended to by successive British governments as he himself patronized African nationalists, Smith's measure was not easy to take. A character assessment prepared in 1964 by the Commonwealth Relations Office described him as:

> a simple minded, politically naïve, and uncompromising character … He possesses a strong vein of schoolboy obstinacy and there is a mixture of schoolboy stubbornness, cunning and imperceptions about his speeches. Likewise there is a 'Boys Own Paper' ring about his patriotic utterances. Nevertheless his pedestrian and humourless manner often conceals a shrewder assessment of a particular situation than at first appears on the surface and he should not be under-rated. (TNA: PRO, DO 183/293, 'Visit of Mr I. D. Smith, prime minister of Southern Rhodesia, to London, September 1964')

Equally unflattering were the opinions of the old settler establishment whom Smith and the RF dislodged from office. To Huggins, Smith remained 'a farm boy from Selukwe, devious, parochial and suspicious' (Blake, 361); while Welensky, on hearing that Smith had replaced Field as prime minister, described Smith as 'the most rigid, inflexible and prejudiced man imaginable' (Evans, 43). His followers saw him very differently. According to the chairman of the RF in 1970, Smith had a

> certain mixture of characteristics of caution, obstinacy, dedication, vision, tenacity and toughness that have invoked rage in some, frustration in others, and admiration and loyalty in most … no other man … has the physical and mental toughness necessary to have led Rhodesia where it is today. (Godwin and Hancock, 67)

At the time UDI was declared, the Conservative peer Lord Salisbury believed Smith to be 'a man of outstanding rectitude and honesty' (Joyce, 265); and a few years later, the former American presidential candidate Barry Goldwater insisted that what the world needed was 'more men like Ian Smith. We have too few leaders and I'd like to see him multiplied a little bit, and spread around' (Lake, 118).

As the war escalated in the 1970s, Smith was increasingly reviled. In 1976 the British foreign secretary, James Callaghan, described Smith as 'leading his country on the path of death and destruction' (Evans, 251); and by the time of the Lancaster House constitutional negotiations in 1979 Lord Carrington was persuaded that Smith was 'a man who saw every tree in the wood but couldn't see the wood … he was a … bigoted, stupid man' (Holland, 64). Inside Rhodesia whites to the right of the RF regarded Smith's attempts to reach an internal settlement as treachery. Notable exceptions aside, assessments of Smith's political career at the time and subsequently were negative where they were not positively hostile. Where Kissinger detected courage and dignity in Smith's surrender to the inevitable, others were struck by his racism and intransigence. Smith's claims to uphold 'civilized standards of behaviour' were contrasted with his humiliation and oppression of Africans 'because he could afford to regard them as a beaten people' (Verrier, 157); his invocation of a communist threat to Rhodesia was dismissed as a self-serving ideological fantasy; and he was invariably criticized for the narrowness of his views. Smith understood his fellow whites, 'their fears, emotions and prejudices, largely because he shared those very feelings', concluded the historian Lord Blake in 1977:

> But the same quality is a defect in dealing with the outside world. He has frequently failed to foresee foreign reactions and had made bad miscalculations about the consequences of some of his own decisions … On a more fundamental issue too his parochialism betrayed him. No-one who understood the world of 1965 would have expected UDI to be, as Smith prophesied, a 'nine day wonder'. (Blake, 362)

Recognizing that Smith's 'deepest attachments were to his family, to his farm, and to the whole land of Southern Africa of which Rhodesia was a part', an earlier account noted that the Britain of the 1960s was:

> a foreign, and somewhat effete, land to Smith and most of the born Rhodesians. By the same token, he seems a foreigner in all but language to most British politicians—a man of convictions so outdated, of tastes so naïve, as to make mutual understanding almost impossible. (Young, 128)

If those same beliefs explained Smith's baffled regret at imperial decline, they occasionally served as bulwarks against the more extreme ambitions of his followers. The autonomy of the multiracial University of Rhodesia under renewed threat in the early 1970s found a champion of sorts in Smith. They were not convictions that permitted compromise with African nationalist leaders except those of his choosing, his later admiration for Nelson Mandela notwithstanding. Nor did they lend themselves to self-doubt. Asked in an interview in 1970 what his biggest mistake had been, Smith could not think of one. 'I'm not by nature a pessimist, and I don't brood over mistakes. I rather tend to look to the future and to what I'm going to do for the good of my country, than worry about past mistakes' (*Illustrated Life Rhodesia*, 24 March 1970). UDI had delivered 'fourteen great years', he asserted elsewhere (Godwin and Hancock, 279). His memoirs betrayed no hint of remorse. Insisting that the 'tragedy of Rhodesia hinged to a large extent on timing', he denied that independence was taken

> in order to ensure permanent white minority rule. History proves conclusively that this is a blatant lie. It was, of course, a continuation of the campaign of the communists, who all along had been trying desperately to frustrate our legitimate objective. (*Great Betrayal*, 408)

Where things had gone wrong, it had been the fault of others, South Africa and Britain in particular:

> And in all honesty, what had Rhodesia done to deserve all this treachery? Our opponents had great success in twisting the truth against us. They accused us of being racist, when in fact we were being realists, constantly planning ways and means to improve the lot of all our people, black and white. (ibid., 410)

If this was not a version of events that was widely recognized, elements of it were wryly acknowledged. In Harare news of his death elicited some predictable government responses:

> Smith will not be mourned or missed here by any decent person because he was an unrepentant racist whose racist stance and opposition to our independence caused a war, and he was responsible for a lot of deaths and suffering. (*Mail and Guardian*, 21 Nov 2007)

Less obviously, a measured obituary in a state-owned newspaper, while concluding that Smith's 'tragedy of being unable to break out of his own past and prejudices became a tragedy for his Rhodesian whites', noted mildly that:

> besides his exemplary family life, he had a group of intensely loyal friends whom he supported through thick and thin, and was also regarded as a good and progressive farmer, leading many to wish that he should have left politics alone and concentrated on this first-class private life. (*The Herald*, 21 Nov 2007)

More telling was the comment that while Smith 'was an oppressor … he was an efficient oppressor because there was no inflation during his time … and [no] destruction of the economy' (*The Independent*, 21 Nov 2007).

To his supporters Smith remained 'good old Smithy' to the very end. He died in St James, outside Cape Town, on 20 November 2007, his wife having predeceased him by thirteen years. His son, Alec, a supporter of black majority rule who was nevertheless later his father's business partner, also predeceased him, in January 2006.

IAN PHIMISTER

Sources K. Young, *Rhodesia and independence*, new edn (1969) · 'Ian Smith: riding the crest', *Illustrated Life Rhodesia* (24 March 1970) · J. Todd, *The right to say no* (1972) · L. W. Bowman, *Politics in Rhodesia: white power in an African state* (1973) · P. Joyce, *Anatomy of a rebel: Smith of Rhodesia, a biography* (1974) · H. Wilson, *The Labour government, 1964–1970: a personal record* (1971) · A. Lake, *The 'tar baby' option: American policy toward Southern Rhodesia* (1976) · R. Blake, *A history of Rhodesia* (1977) · P. Berlyn, *The quiet man* (1978) · A. Verrier, *The road to Zimbabwe, 1890–1980* (1986) · K. Flower, *Serving secretly: an intelligence chief on record, Rhodesia into Zimbabwe, 1964–1981* (1987) · P. Godwin and I. Hancock, *Rhodesians never die: the impact of war and political change on white Rhodesia, c.1970–1980* (1993) · M. Evans, 'The role of ideology in Rhodesian Front rule, 1962–1980', PhD diss., University of Western Australia, 1993 · I. Smith, *The great betrayal* (1997) · J. T. R. Wood, *So far and no further: Rhodesia's bid for independence during the retreat from empire, 1959–1965* (2005) · P. Murphy, ed., *British documents on the end of empire: central Africa*, 2: *Crisis and dissolution, 1959–1965* (2005) · J. R. T. Wood, *A matter of weeks rather than months: the impasse between Harold Wilson and Ian Smith: sanctions, aborted settlements and war, 1965–1969* (2008) · H. Holland, *Dinner with Mugabe* (2008) · *The Times* (21 Nov 2007) · *Daily Telegraph* (21 Nov 2007) · *The Guardian* (21 Nov 2007) · *The Independent* (21 Nov 2007); (22 Nov 2007) · *The Herald* [Zimbabwe] (21 Nov 2007) · *New York Times* (21 Nov 2007) · *Cape Times* (22 Nov 2007) · *WW* (2007) · personal knowledge (2011) · private information (2011)

Archives Rhodes University, South Africa, Cory Research Library | Bodl. RH, Welensky papers · South African foreign affairs archive, Pretoria · TNA: PRO, DO 183/293 | FILM BFINA, documentary footage · BFINA, 'Interview with Ian Smith', *The Frost programme*, ITV, 13 Feb 1972 | SOUND BL NSA, documentary recordings · BL NSA, current affairs recordings

Likenesses photographs, 1963–71, Getty Images, London · photograph, 1965, Getty Images, London, Hult. Arch. [*see illus.*] · photographs, 1965–98, Photoshot, London · photographs, 1965–2002, PA Photos, London · G. Scarfe, caricatures, 1968–76, repro. in G. Scarfe, *Drawing blood* (2005) · W. Fawkes, cartoon, 1970, repro. in *Punch* (17 Nov 1970) · G. Scarfe, caricatures, 1970–78, repro. in G. Scarfe, *Line of attack* (1988) · photographs, 1997–2000, Rex Features, London · G. Scarfe, caricature, repro. in *Private Eye* (26 Nov 1965), cover · obituary photographs · photograph, repro. in en.wikipedia.org/wiki/Ian_Smith · photographs, repro. in news.bbc.co.uk/1/hi/in_pictures/7104935.stm · photographs, repro. in Smith, *Great betrayal*

Smith, Sir John Lindsay Eric (1923–2007), banker, politician, and philanthropist, was born on 3 April 1923 at 83 Sloane Street, Chelsea, London, the eldest of three sons and second of four children of (Evan Cadogan) Eric Smith (1894–1950), a captain in the 9th lancers, and his wife, (Beatrice) Helen (1896–1988), daughter of Albert Williams. The family into which he was born was among the oldest banking dynasties, the firm dating back to 1658. Smith's parents occupied a spreading Victorian country house, Ashfold, Slaugham, Sussex. Works to reduce this pile from forty to twenty-four bedrooms gave the young Smith an early introduction to the practicalities of adapting a historic building to changed circumstances.

At Eton College, Smith became captain of the oppidans and won the Rosebery prize for history. In 1941 he joined the Fleet Air Arm. He served in the Mediterranean and the Atlantic, and was a navigator in the dive-bombing raid on the German battleship *Tirpitz* in Kvaenangen fjord in July 1944, before joining the aircraft carrier HMS *Indomitable* in the Pacific and a naval air squadron in the Far East. After the war, demobilized with the rank of lieutenant, he went to New College, Oxford, where he rowed for the college and read modern history. It was at Oxford that he met Christian Margaret Carnegy (*b.* 1927), a level-headed Scotswoman who read English at St Anne's. She was the younger daughter of Ughtred Elliott Carnegy, army officer, and sister of Elizabeth Carnegy, later Baroness Carnegy of Lour. They married on 5 January 1952 and had five children, Adam (*b.* 1953), Bartholomew (*b.* 1955), Emma (*b.* 1956), Serena (*b.* 1959), and Dido (*b.* 1962).

Although Smith had ideas of becoming an architect the pull of family tradition proved too strong, and after graduating with a third-class degree in 1948 he joined Coutts and Co., into which the family bank had been subsumed. In 1950 he became a director of Coutts and remained one until 1993, as well as serving on the boards of other financial and industrial concerns, including the Financial Times Ltd, Rolls-Royce (of which he was chairman for a time), and Royal Exchange Insurance.

In November 1965, at a by-election occasioned by the death of Sir Harry Hylton-Foster, the speaker of the House of Commons, Smith became the Conservative MP for the Cities of London and Westminster. He served as a member of the executive of the 1922 committee (1968–70) and of the public accounts committee (1968–9), but politics did not retain his interest. When a bill to introduce registration for chiropodists was presented to the House of Commons in 1969, he remarked:

> What are we to say when at the latter day, we are called to the dreadful bar of judgment and we are asked what we were doing in Parliament, at this colossal juncture in our national affairs, when there is civil unrest in Northern Ireland and industrial unrest in our own country … when the Russians and the Americans are … reaching out into space? What are we to say when we are asked what we, the heirs of Trafalgar, were doing in Parliament today, the anniversary of the Battle of Trafalgar? Are we to say, 'Well, actually, we were registering chiropodists'? (*Hansard 5C*, 788.964–5, 21 Oct 1969)

He retired from the Commons at the 1970 general election.

1965 was also the year that Smith and his wife founded the Landmark Trust. Perhaps Smith was conscious of the example of his maternal great-grandfather, Sir George Williams, who founded the Young Men's Christian Association, as well as his earlier forebear Thomas Cook, whose activity as a travel agent grew out of his crusades for Methodism and temperance. Indeed this would have seemed entirely credible to those who knew Smith, whose bearing, according to one obituary, was that 'of a great Victorian divine' (*The Independent*, 1 March 2007). With his passion for architecture Smith had, in 1952, joined the historic buildings committee of the National Trust; he was later a member of the trust's executive committee (1959–85) and its council (1961–95) and served as deputy chairman from 1980 to 1985, and was judged, by a former director-general, Martin Drury, to have been 'one of the handful of people' who transformed it 'from the small, inward-looking society it had become after the war into the great movement' it was by the time of his retirement (*The Guardian*, 10 March 2007). But not every building of note could be taken under the stewardship of the trust, whose finances allowed it to accept only those that came fully endowed, or could earn an income by being let to a tenant. There seemed to be no home for the smaller treasures—sometimes works of high architecture, sometimes documents of social history, but often just whimsical or highly flavoured—that contributed so much to the charm of Britain's countryside and towns. Many buildings of this kind were neglected and decaying because they were in remote situations, or because their owners had no use for them, or because, even if they were suitable for occupation, the cost of restoration would not give an economic return. Smith conceived the idea that such buildings could be restored, appropriately decorated with simple, old furniture (chosen by his wife), and rented for short holidays to a public that would not only benefit spiritually from the pleasure of staying in them, but provide the income that would put them beyond risk.

It was, of course, Smith's financial acumen that made the Landmark Trust's activities possible. Unlike many visionaries he was thoroughly practical about ways and means, setting up the Manifold Trust (with a loan from his friend Pat Gibson) to generate income for the charities he supported. The trust would buy up short, mainly commercial, leases that could be let at high rents for the remainder of their terms—a strategy that might have come unstuck in other hands, but which, managed by Smith, produced what he described as a 'cataract of gold' (*The Independent*, 1 March 2007).

Typical of the Landmark Trust's early projects was the Gothic Temple at Stowe, part of Lord Cobham's great landscape of ideas, which had been decaying since the 1920s. Initially suitable buildings had to be sought out, but as the trust's reputation grew it came to seem the natural and desirable owner of small buildings of personality but no means. By the time of Smith's death in 2007 the trust had rescued over 200 structures, principally in Britain but also in Italy and the United States. They included follies, fortifications, mills, gatehouses, hunting boxes, manor houses, an arsenic mine, interesting cottages, most of the buildings on Lundy, Palladio's Villa Sacaceno in the Veneto, A. W. N. Pugin's home in Ramsgate, and a Doric-fronted pigsty in Yorkshire. In 1991 Smith provided funds to launch the Landmark Trust USA as a separate entity, with properties that included Rudyard Kipling's house, Naulakha, in Vermont.

The Landmark Trust was, however, only one among many recipients of the Manifold Trust's bounty. Smith's generosity to numerous causes concerned with buildings or British history—particularly that of a watery nature—was immediate and open-handed. A believer in the therapeutic potential of waterways, through the Manifold Trust he gave £250,000 to help build an aqueduct over the M6 toll road near Birmingham, to further the restoration of the Lichfield canal. He championed the rescue of such ships as the Second World War cruiser HMS *Belfast*, Brunel's SS *Great Britain*, and the Victorian warship HMS *Warrior*. Churches and church bells, sea cadets, and libraries were among other beneficiaries of Smith's largesse.

At a time when it was generally assumed that listing and

state grants were the means by which Britain's fragile heritage of old buildings should be saved from destruction Smith showed that the man of taste could still perform a unique and valuable role. The organization that he left behind, the Landmark Trust, rightly became—like the much larger National Trust—the envy of conservationists around the world, for nothing quite like it existed elsewhere. Its peculiarly British character reflected Smith's own, in which rigorous standards and an understanding of how the world works were combined with a patrician's wit and an eye for architecture. He stood out for the scale of his generosity towards causes, often the product (as he said of the canal system) of 'English genius', which other donors might not have been tempted to support.

Smith was a member of the Standing Commission on Museums and Galleries (1958–66), the Inland Waterways Redevelopment Committee (1959–62), the Historic Buildings Council (1971–8), the Redundant Churches Fund (1972–4), and the National Heritage Memorial Fund (1980–82). He was high steward of Maidenhead from 1966 to 1975 and lord-lieutenant of Berkshire from 1975 to 1978. He was made an honorary fellow of the Royal Institute of British Architects in 1973 and of the Royal Incorporation of Architects of Scotland in 1983; he was also made a fellow of Eton College in 1974 and an honorary fellow of New College, Oxford, in 1979. He received honorary degrees from Exeter University in 1989 and Portsmouth University in 1994. Appointed CBE in 1975, he was knighted in 1988 and made a companion of honour in 1994.

Smith was a man of courtesy and charm whose wry sense of humour and fund of anecdotes made him an engaging companion, though he could sometimes be impatient, and indeed alarming to people who did not know his manner. He was described by Drury as relishing 'the odd and the absurd' (*The Guardian*, 10 March 2007), a taste that he was able to satisfy during epic travels around the globe. (He claimed to be the first person to have visited all the explorers' huts in Antarctica.) At home, however, he preferred to surround himself with elegance, a quality that both he and his wife seemed to epitomize. The background to his life was their country house, Shottesbrooke Park, Berkshire, inherited from a distant cousin and reduced to less than half its size, retaining only its eighteenth-century core. (One of his dicta was that 'buildings are seldom improved by additions but very often by subtraction'.) His London address was, with grand understatement, 1 Smith Square. He died at Thames Hospicecare, Windsor, on 28 February 2007 of duodenal cancer, and was survived by his wife and four of his children, his daughter Emma having predeceased him.

CLIVE ASLET

Sources *The Independent* (1 March 2007) • *The Times* (3 March 2007); (14 March 2007); (15 March 2007); (19 March 2007); (24 March 2007); (10 April 2007) • *Daily Telegraph* (3 March 2007) • *Architects' Journal* (6 March 2007) • *The Guardian* (10 March 2007); (16 March 2007) • Burke, *Peerage* • *WW* (2007) • personal knowledge (2011) • private information (2011) • b. cert. • d. cert.

Likenesses obituary photographs

Wealth at death £7,302,753: probate, 29 Feb 2008, *CGPLA Eng. & Wales*

Smith, Leslie Charles (1918–2005), industrialist and toy manufacturer, was born on 6 March 1918 at 26 Palace Gardens, Enfield, Middlesex, the son of Edward Arthur Smith, a journeyman joiner, and his wife, Elizabeth, *née* Niblett. After leaving Enfield central school at the age of fourteen he worked in London for J. Raymond Wilson, a die-casting company. On the outbreak of the Second World War in 1939 he and his three brothers were advised by their father (who had served in the trenches in the First World War) to join the Royal Navy. Initially a signals rating, he was commissioned, commanding a torpedo boat during the Dieppe raid and a minesweeper during the D-day landings.

Demobilized with the rank of lieutenant, Smith and a former schoolfriend and service colleague, Rodney Smith (no relation), pooled their demobilization gratuities to buy a second-hand die-casting machine in January 1947. Under the trade name of Lesney Products, an amalgam of the two founders' first names, early production, mainly in zinc, included car engine parts and components for electrical firms. Soon the Smiths were joined by Jack *Odell, an expert toolmaker with a penchant for model making. On 4 September 1948 Smith married Nancy Jackson-Moore (*d.* 1969), a 27-year-old secretary from Yorkshire, and daughter of Colin Trippett Jackson-Moore, maintenance worker. They had two sons and one daughter.

Shortages of zinc arising from the Korean War briefly threatened the fledgling company's existence, a particular worry for Leslie Smith in view of his recent marriage. Rodney Smith was equally alarmed, withdrawing from Lesney in 1951. One delayed project was a large model of the state coach, but with zinc becoming more freely available again after the conclusion of the Korean conflict, a miniaturized version was produced as a coronation souvenir. Packed into a matchbox-style box, and offering high quality engineering at the low price of 1*s.* 6*d.*, it sold a million units by the end of 1953.

With Odell providing the design and engineering expertise, additional miniature models were developed under the trade name Matchbox. Yet it was Leslie Smith's commercial skills as managing director responsible for sales and marketing that underpinned the astonishing success of this product range. By 1960 Matchbox accounted for 80 per cent of Lesney sales and the company's first listing on the stock exchange was oversubscribed fifteen times, making both Smith and Odell millionaires. By 1968 sales were worth £28 million worldwide, including in the United States, a market notoriously resistant to overseas penetration. In the same year *Management Today* placed Lesney at the top of its list of Britain's 200 most profitable companies, and Smith was appointed OBE. More aware, perhaps, than many contemporary toymakers of the importance of exports, he was a ready dispenser of advice on overseas marketing and, as sometime chair and president of the British Toy Manufacturers' Association, a consistent advocate of establishing a British international toy and hobby fair.

Smith's other major role at Lesney was in ensuring that

labour relations remained harmonious, no mean achievement with a labour force that ultimately grew to some 6000, working in thirteen different factories. Always mindful of his own modest background (he never left Enfield), Smith took a close interest in the workforce, providing dedicated transport and creating a family-like working environment. Consequently he was initially reluctant to countenance offshore manufacturing as the world toy market grew progressively more competitive through the 1970s. Matchbox's success had attracted significant competition, and the first check to progress occurred in 1969 when Mattel launched its best selling Hot Wheels range in the United States. Almost overnight exports of Matchbox to America collapsed from 40 to 10 per cent of annual output. Several hundred workers were laid off and Smith took a 75 per cent pay cut to help the company regain lost ground. Although new product lines did recoup sales, earning the firm a fifth queen's award for industry in 1977, the necessary retooling was funded from substantially increased borrowing at a time of rising interest rates. A concurrent strategy of product diversification proved relatively unsuccessful. The purchase of ATM, an American plastic kit manufacturer, was particularly miscalculated. With levels of debt soaring under the impact of escalating interest rates, and strong sterling adversely affecting the overseas markets that accounted for 80 per cent of sales, Lesney ultimately found the burden unsupportable. Losses of £3.6 million were recorded in 1980 and even the temporary return of Odell, who had retired as joint managing director in 1973, failed to halt the decline. In the summer of 1982 Lesney passed into the hands of the receiver, effectively ending Leslie Smith's industrial career.

In retirement Smith devoted himself to his three children and their families. Apart from his chairing two boards of school governors, the rest of his time was occupied with his garden and yachting. However, both the magnitude of his achievement in creating from scratch a world-leading die-cast toy company and his wider contribution to the British Toy and Hobby Manufacturers' Association were acknowledged in 1998 when he received the association's lifetime achievement award. He died at his home, 9A Broad Walk, Winchmore Hill, Enfield, on 26 May 2005, of pleomorphic liposarcoma. He was survived by his three children. KENNETH D. BROWN

Sources M. Fawdry, *British tin toys* (1990) · K. D. Brown, *The British toy business: a history since 1700* (1996) · *The Times* (2 June 2005) · *New York Times* (4 June 2005) · *The Independent* (7 June 2005); (9 July 2007) · *Daily Telegraph* (10 June 2005) · *Daily Mail* (9 July 2007) · Matchbox club website, www.matchbox.com, 19 May 2008 · *WW* (2005) · b. cert. · m. cert. · d. cert.

Likenesses photographs, 1966–8, Getty Images, London · obituary photographs

Wealth at death £3,679,270: probate, 13 Dec 2005, *CGPLA Eng. & Wales*

Smith, Sir Leslie Edward George (1919–2006), industrialist, was born on 15 April 1919 at 87 St John's Road, Deptford, London, the eldest son in the family of eight children of Edward Vinzenso or Vincenzo Smith, a fish salesman's clerk, later a sub-postmaster, and his wife, Doris Emma, *née* Browning. His father had served as a private in the 9th north Hampshire regiment during the First World War. Smith won a scholarship to Christ's Hospital in Horsham, Sussex, but the family could not afford to send him on to university and he embarked on accountancy studies. These were cut short by the outbreak of the Second World War. He served in the Royal Artillery from 1940 and, after being commissioned, in the Royal Fusiliers, with whom he saw action in Italy. On 11 August 1943, by then a lieutenant, he married, at Lewisham register office, Lorna Bell Pickworth, the 24-year-old daughter of George Boyes Pickworth, dentist. They had two daughters.

After the war, and a decade of what he called 'messing about' in which he failed to secure a grant to study at Cambridge and tried his hand at farming and as an auctioneer, Smith completed his accountancy qualifications and joined the British Oxygen Company as an assistant accountant in 1956. The business then had many of the worst characteristics of British imperial enterprises. It was hierarchical, hidebound, and dependent on a semi-monopoly position in the UK and protected markets in the British empire, with limited opportunity for expansion. Many of its managers still displayed their military ranks on their office doors. Smith found the deferential atmosphere of the company hard to take. But his ability was rapidly recognized and by 1960 he was effectively in charge of the finance department. He became a director in 1966 and managing director in 1969, and was chairman from 1972 to 1985.

Smith's achievement was to turn the British Oxygen Company into one of a select band of globally competitive businesses under British ownership. A large, ebullient man, with a keen strategic brain, he was an early pioneer of good corporate governance, introducing non-executive directors from outside for fixed terms and with the proviso that they spend a third of their time on the company. He restructured operations into divisions responsible for their own budgets and gave them a considerable degree of autonomy. He addressed the corporate culture with a new climate of openness—criticizing the old deferential habits with superiors addressed as 'sir' as 'bad business' and claiming with some hyberbole that 'anyone can walk into my office' (*The Times*, 17 July 2006). A corporate rebranding in 1975 brought not only a new name—BOC—and a new corporate logo, but also an attempt to have global corporate standards. His crucial achievement was to redirect the group's focus from stagnant imperial markets to the major international economies, the United States in particular. Against a background where even well-run British companies would regularly come to grief in attempts to expand in the USA in the late twentieth century, Smith was a spectacularly successful pioneer.

BOC had formed a joint venture with the American company Airco to develop and install air separation plants. When Airco was threatened with takeover in 1974, Smith bought 35 per cent of its shares. Then, four years later, after lengthy anti-trust battles in which he demonstrated his determination and persistence, BOC acquired the whole company. The takeover was fiercely contested and

Smith's ability to go without sleep and to drink others under the table gave him a telling advantage in the late-night negotiations. He underlined the change by appointing Airco's energetic chief executive, Richard (Dick) Giordano, who had opposed the takeover, as chief executive of BOC in his place, at the highest salary of any British chief executive—far exceeding his own remuneration as chairman. It was a virtually unheard-of initiative and not popular with Smith's British senior managers. He patiently heard them out, but refused to budge, and a number left. This move demonstrated both his strategic thinking and his willingness to subordinate personal interests to the good of the company. It also secured the allegiance of the acquisition. Giordano became a hugely influential management figure in the UK and their partnership brought BOC outstanding success.

In the face of the recession sparked by the oil price shocks of the early 1970s Smith and Giordano reshaped the company, selling off peripheral activities, including a pizza manufacturer and a trout farm left over from the days when the company was renowned for its executive perks, and aiming investment at fast-growing markets, with a major new plant in South Carolina. Both the workforce and senior executive numbers were drastically cut. By February 1982, still in recession, Smith was defending a 76 per cent increase in Giordano's salary—to £477,000—by pointing to a 50 per cent increase in pre-tax profits, 80 per cent from outside Britain. Smith himself was earning just £120,000. Under Smith's chairmanship BOC became the most international of industrial gas companies, with operations in fifty countries. Smith was knighted in 1977, before retiring as chairman in 1985. In retirement he finally fulfilled his thwarted ambition of academic study, taking an Open University degree in history.

Smith's strategic intelligence and determination were recognized by his contemporaries. In 1982 the minister in charge of energy, Nigel Lawson, appointed him to the board of British Gas as one of a trio of industrial heavyweights to challenge the dominance of the formidable chairman, Sir Denis Rooke. He was an active chairman of the British industry committee on South Africa, arguing strongly against disinvestment during the apartheid regime on the grounds that the continuing presence of British companies would encourage political reform. He was also instrumental in establishing the Industry and Parliament Trust, designed to give politicians experience of industry and commerce through a system of fellowships. An affable man with an enthusiasm for bridge, rarely seen socially without a cigarette and a gin and tonic, he described his recreations in *Who's Who* as 'unremarkable'. But a willingness to believe the best of everyone was accompanied by firm resolve. As one acquaintance put it, 'he was the most charming person to have dinner with, but no-one should confuse this good nature with softness' (private information).

Smith's first marriage ended in divorce, and in 1964 he married Cynthia Barbara (Cyndy) Holmes (*d.* 2005). They had a son and a daughter. Smith died on 4 July 2006 at his home, Woolstaplers' House, High Street, Chipping Campden, Gloucestershire, of bronchopneumonia and heart failure; he was survived by his four children. Later in 2006 BOC finally lost its independence after a take-over by its German rival, Linde. MARTIN ADENEY

Sources A. Sampson, *The changing anatomy of Britain* (1982) • N. Lawson, *The view from no. 11: memoirs of a tory radical* (1992) • *The Times* (17 July 2006) • *Daily Telegraph* (20 July 2006) • *The Guardian* (8 Aug 2006) • Burke, *Peerage* • *WW* (2006) • private information (2010) • b. cert. • m. cert. [1943] • d. cert.

Likenesses obituary photographs

Wealth at death £619,108: probate, 18 Dec 2006, *CGPLA Eng. & Wales*

Smith, Linda Helen (1958–2006), comedian, was born on 29 January 1958 at Hainault Maternity Home, Erith, Kent, the only child of Raymond Smith, railway track maintenance worker, and his wife, Elizabeth Evelyn (Bessie), formerly Boyce, *née* Locke. She had an elder half-sister, Barbara, from her mother's first marriage. She was still very young when her sister left home, leaving her as the only child of older parents whose marriage was blighted by her father's domineering and sometimes violent attitude. She found Erith dull and uninspiring, later describing it in her stand-up act as 'not exactly a city that never sleeps, more a town that lies awake all night staring at the ceiling' (Lakin and Parsons, 306). Escape from the grimness of her surroundings was found in books, television, and comedy, particularly Peter Cook and Dudley Moore. At Lessness Heath primary school and Bexleyheath School she acted out comedy sketches at playtimes and appeared in school productions, later being offered a place at the Royal Academy of Dramatic Art, which she could not take up due to lack of funding. Instead she went to Erith College of Technology to get the A-levels she needed to study English with drama at Sheffield University, which she attended from 1979 to 1982.

After graduating Smith helped to form a group that became known as Sheffield Popular Productions, and it was in this that she met her devoted lifelong partner, Warren Gary Lakin. They produced community theatre shows and ran numerous benefit gigs in support of the miners during the strike of 1984–5, reflecting her passionate political beliefs, which she once described as 'left wing, but not in an organised way' (Lakin, 200). Her stand-up career grew out of these activities, initially in sketches in new variety nights in Sheffield pubs, then in a double act with Anne Lavelle called Token Women (and later Tuff Lovers), and finally as a solo act, mainly on the fledgeling provincial comedy circuit, in which she found the audience 'not as jaded' as in London.

Smith's early routines were dominated by her imaginary boyfriend Clive, a parody of painfully feminist men. She rightly argued that it was 'quite reactionary' to judge her as a specifically female stand-up, instead of simply a stand-up like any other. Jo Brand described her as the 'only genuinely funny, female, political comedian' (Lakin and Parsons, ix), and the politics of her act meant that she had more in common with comics like her long-term friend Jeremy Hardy than with other women on the circuit. She joked about health cuts ('I don't like this new fun-sized National Health, do you?'), miscarriages of justice ('The Guildford Four. I don't know, I think that Jeremy Beadle goes too far, sometimes'), and her racist grandmother, whom she described as being 'personally twinned' with Birmingham, Alabama. Her disappointment with the Labour Party's lack of radicalism was a constant theme, as in a routine that sent up Neil Kinnock's line on the poll tax: 'You resist by paying. But when you pay—Oo, you give that town clerk such a look!' There were also routines about less political matters, including cricket, miserable British holidays, and a Saturday job at the Co-op, which she described as being 'like spending your youth in Poland under martial law' (*I Think the Nurses are Stealing my Clothes*, audio CD).

While based in Sheffield Smith collaborated with comedians including Henry Normal, Hattie Hayridge, and Steve Gribbin on various projects, as well as putting together the Chuffinelles (a left-wing comedy trio made up of working-class women who had never previously performed), and compèring Sheffield Popular Productions' comedy club, Route 52. In 1993 she moved to London, and became a regular at the Comedy Store's topical comedy show *The Cutting Edge*, where her fellow team member Mark Thomas described her as being 'completely at ease amidst the rising tide of testosterone and bad puns' (Lakin, 72). This led to appearances on BBC Radio 1's *Loose Talk*, and by the late 1990s she had moved away from the live comedy circuit to concentrate on radio work. She became a stalwart of those comedy panel game institutions *The News Quiz*, *Just a Minute*, and (from 2001) *I'm Sorry I Haven't a Clue*, and starred in her own self-penned radio sitcom, *A Brief History of Timewasting* (2001–2). A Radio 4 interview about her atheism led to her becoming president of the British Humanist Association in 2004. She appeared less frequently on television, albeit with appearances on programmes as varied as *Room 101* and *Question Time*. Her popularity allowed her to return to live work, touring her solo stand-up show, and in 2002 she was voted 'wittiest living person' by listeners to BBC Radio 4's *Word of Mouth*. In that same year she was diagnosed with ovarian cancer. She continued to work for several years, keeping her condition quiet, but treatment was eventually unsuccessful and she died at her home, 1 Park Road, Wanstead, London, on 27 February 2006, surrounded by close family members. She was survived by Warren Lakin.

OLIVER DOUBLE

Sources O. Double, 'An approach to traditions of British stand-up comedy', PhD diss., University of Sheffield, 1991 [includes transcript of interview, 7 Sept 1989, as appx] · 'Anarchist with attitude: Laurie Taylor interviews Linda Smith', *New Humanist*, 119/5 (Sept–Oct 2004) · *The Times* (1 March 2006) · *Daily Telegraph* (1 March 2006) · *The Guardian* (1 March 2006); (2 March 2006) · *The Independent* (1 March 2006); (2 March 2006) · *I think the nurses are stealing my clothes: the very best of Linda Smith*, ed. W. Lakin (2006) [audio CD] · *I think the nurses are stealing my clothes: the very best of Linda Smith*, ed. W. Lakin and I. Parsons (2006) · L. Smith, *Linda Smith live* (2006) [audio CD] · W. Lakin, *Driving Miss Smith: a memoir of Linda Smith* (2007) · personal knowledge (2010) · private information (2010) · b. cert. · d. cert.

Archives FILM BFINA, light entertainment footage · BFINA, documentary footage | SOUND BL NSA, performance recordings

Likenesses S. Dhanda, photograph, 2003, Camera Press, London · S. Barber, photographs, 2004, Camera Press, London [*see illus.*] · A. Cotterill, photographs, 2004, Camera Press, London · obituary photographs

Smith, Michael George [Mike] (**1943–2008**), songwriter and musician, was born on 6 December 1943 at North Middlesex County Hospital, Edmonton, the only child of George William Henry Smith, bus conductor, later interior decorator, and his wife, Maudie, *née* Willis. At the time of his birth his parents lived at 11 Alberta Road, Bush Hill Park. He began taking piano lessons at the age of five. At the age of thirteen he entered Trinity College of Music, London, but soon lost his interest in classical study when

Linda Helen Smith (1958–2006), by Simon Barber, 2004

he heard the fiery rock and roll piano of Little Richard and Jerry Lee Lewis.

Smith first met Dave Clark on the sports field; both were enthusiastic soccer players, and bonded over a shared enthusiasm for rock and roll. Smith kept his day job as a debt collector while playing in north London groups, until Clark invited him to join his own more successful outfit, the Dave Clark Five. While the group was named after its photogenic drummer, it was Smith's energetic piano playing and raw, rhythm-and-blues-style singing which helped establish its reputation. That early success was forged in the burgeoning Mecca ballroom circuit of the early 1960s, where groups played live music to audiences of enthusiastic teenage dancers. With over 200 venues nationwide, Mecca was a crucial part of the live UK circuit, so when Clark's group won Mecca's gold cup for best live group of 1963, record companies paid attention. Indeed, the success of the Dave Clark Five playing to 6000 enthusiastic fans at the Tottenham Royal ballroom landed them a record deal. But it was not until the fourth Dave Clark Five single, 'Glad All Over', a UK number one in January 1964, that they established themselves on disc. The follow-up, another Smith–Clark collaboration, 'Bits and Pieces', peaked at number two in March 1964, but established the drum-pounding popularity of the group.

The Dave Clark Five were the first group to make an impact on the American charts immediately after the Beatles. 'Glad All Over' hit the American charts in March 1964, barely a month after the Beatles' arrival. Such was the depth of the Beatles' American success, however, that any UK group was painted with the same brush—so the manifestly London-based Dave Clark Five were touted by a trade paper advertisement as 'the Mersey sound with the Liverpool beat' (F. Bronson, *The Billboard Book of No. 1 Hits*, 2003, entry 189). The group was summoned to capitalize on its stateside success with an appearance on the prestigious Ed Sullivan show. 'I'd never been on a plane before', Smith recalled later; 'On Friday I was told "pack up your job", on Saturday I flew to America and on Sunday I played in front of 70 million people' (*Daily Telegraph*, 1 March 2008). The group went on to notch up a further seventeen appearances on Sullivan's show, more than any other pop or rock act. Between 1964 and 1967 the Dave Clark Five landed eight American top ten and a further eight top thirty hits. Ironically, for all the group's American success, their only American number one was in December 1965, a cover version of Bobby Day's 'Over and Over'. In all, the total worldwide record sales of the Dave Clark Five were estimated at over 100 million. Even though the music scene changed in the late 1960s, the popularity of the Dave Clark Five's brand of breezy, energetic pop remained, registering four further UK top ten hits between 1967 and 1970.

Lagging only behind the Beatles and Rolling Stones in the pop charts, the Dave Clark Five might also have made a successful transition to cinema, but their only film was *Catch Us if You Can* (1965, released in the USA as *Having a Wild Weekend*). Unlike his beat contemporaries, Clark, a former film stuntman, was an astute businessman, and for the film he enlisted the fledgling director John Boorman (who went on to win acclaim with *Deliverance*) and scriptwriter Peter Nichols (later famous for *A Day in the Death of Joe Egg*). None of the group, however, was particularly enthusiastic about a cinematic career, and it remained their only film.

In 1970 Clark decided to disband the group, and proceeded to enjoy a successful career as businessman and entrepreneur. Although Mike Smith had, for six years, been the lead singer of the group, he was never happy with the cult of celebrity and on the disbandment of the group took up record production and session work. From then until his death he produced albums by artists including Shirley Bassey and Michael Ball, and recorded advertising jingles for clients including Volvo, British Airways, and McDonalds. In 1976 he appeared on the original album release of the musical *Evita*. In 2003, at the helm of Mike Smith's Rock Engine, he toured America for the first time since the heyday of the Dave Clark Five.

Smith was married first, on 24 June 1978, to Jill Carole Barker (*b*. 1944), a London hairdresser, and daughter of Ronald George Barker, estate agent; they had one son, James (Jamie). The marriage soon ended in divorce and he lived from 1980 to 1998 with Jane Geerts, who worked in artist management. In 2001 he married his second wife, Arlene Charles (Charlie) Gorek, a former Miss Indiana whom Smith had first met while on tour with the Dave Clark Five in 1964; she had re-established contact in 1999 after her own first marriage, to the heavyweight boxer Jerry Quarry, had ended in divorce. A long-time resident of Spain, Smith was paralysed in a fall at his home in 2003, which left him permanently confined to a wheelchair, and much of the remainder of his life was spent at Stoke Mandeville Hospital. Benefit concerts by his contemporaries Peter and Gordon, the Zombies, and Herman's Hermits helped defray the costs of his medical expenses. Bruce Springsteen was another fan, who personally invited Smith to his London concert in 2007. Smith died of septicaemia and pneumonia as a result of the spinal injuries caused by the fall, at Stoke Mandeville Hospital on 28 February 2008, a fortnight before he was due to be inducted by Tom Hanks into the Rock and Roll Hall of Fame with the Dave Clark Five. He was survived by his second wife, Charlie; his son, Jamie, had died in a scuba diving accident in 2003. PATRICK HUMPHRIES

Sources P. Doggett, 'Dave Clark: "Glad All Over Again"', *Record Collector*, 166 (June 1993) · *New York Times* (29 Feb 2008) · *The Times* (1 March 2008) · *Daily Telegraph* (1 March 2008) · *The Independent* (1 March 2008) · *The Guardian* (3 March 2008) · b. cert. · m. cert. [1978] · d. cert.

Likenesses N. Parkinson, group portrait, bromide print, 1964 (*The Dave Clark Five*), NPG · obituary photographs

Wealth at death under £66,000: probate, 21 Nov 2008, *CGPLA Eng. & Wales*

Smithers, Sir Peter Henry Berry Otway (1913–2006), intelligence officer, politician, and gardener, was born on 9 December 1913 at Donisthorpe House, Moor Allerton, Yorkshire, the only child of Captain, later Lieutenant-Colonel, Harry Otway Hirsch Smithers (1877–1941), an officer in the Bedfordshire regiment, and his wife, Ethel Maud Mary (*d.* 1952), daughter of Henry Berry, a Leeds hydraulic machinery manufacturer. At the time of his birth his parents lived at Penpergwm Lodge, near Abergavenny; they later moved to Itchen Stoke House, near Alresford, Hampshire. He was educated at Hawtrey's School, Thanet, Kent (1922–7), and Harrow School (1927–30). Finding the latter unpleasant, he left for a year's private cramming, won an open history demyship at Magdalen College, Oxford (1931), and achieved first-class honours in modern history (1934). Fourteen years of historical research resulted in an Oxford DPhil (1953), published as *The Life of Joseph Addison* in 1954.

Smithers was called to the bar at the Inner Temple in 1936 and joined chancery chambers in Lincoln's Inn the following year. Commissioned as a lieutenant in the Royal Naval Volunteer Reserve, he served on HMS *Radiant*, Lord Iliffe's yacht, testing anti-aircraft devices in the English channel, until he was recruited by Ian Fleming to MI6, and became naval member at MI6 headquarters in Paris. After the retreat from Dunkirk he worked in an MI5 section tracking and intercepting German spies who had parachuted into England. Later in 1940 he was appointed assistant naval attaché at the British embassy in Washington, responsible for intelligence liaison with the US Navy Department. In 1942 he became acting naval attaché in Mexico, the five central American republics, and Panama, and honorary aide-de-camp to the governor of British Honduras, charged with monitoring submarine warfare in the Gulf of Mexico and Caribbean. Colonel Smithers in Fleming's spy novel *Goldfinger* was named after him. After a courtship of three weeks, he married on 9 June 1943, in her home town of St Louis, Missouri, Dorothy Jean (Dojean) Sayman Lane (*d.* 2006), daughter of Dr Thomas Maycroft Sayman. In addition to her son by a previous marriage to Colonel Dennison Lane, of the US army, they had two daughters. Smithers's stepson, Charles Dennison Lane, was a counter-insurgency expert in the American army special forces, with special expertise in Thailand and the Balkans.

Demobilized in 1946 with the rank of lieutenant-commander, Smithers joined the boards of two family companies, Butterworth the publishers and Henry Berry, hydraulic engineers. The Berry business led to his serving as master of the Turners Company in 1955. Having served as a Winchester rural district councillor (1946–9), he was elected as Conservative MP for Winchester in 1950, and represented this constituency until 1964. In parliament he concentrated on colonial and international affairs. He was parliamentary private secretary first to Henry Hopkinson, minister of state for colonial affairs (1952–5) and then to Alan Lennox-Boyd, secretary of state for the colonies (1955–9). In addition he was chairman of the Conservative Overseas Bureau (1956–9), vice-chairman of the Conservative parliamentary foreign affairs committee (1959–61) and parliamentary under-secretary at the Foreign Office (1962–4).

Edward Heath's lobbying obtained for Smithers selection in January 1964 as secretary-general of the Council of Europe at a tax-free annual salary of £10,000. Smithers accordingly retired from the Commons. In Strasbourg, drawing on his previous experience as a delegate to the consultative assembly of the Council of Europe (1952–6 and 1960) and vice-president of the European assembly of local authorities (1959–62), he supervised a rationalization of intricate, confusing intergovernmental structures. Retiring from the secretary-generalship in 1969, he was disappointed in his hopes of a life peerage, having displeased Edward Heath, but was knighted in 1970.

Smithers had sold Itchen Stoke House, which he had inherited from his father, to Lord Ashburton in 1949, and in 1970 made the painful decision to sell Colebrook House, a fine house abutting Winchester Cathedral that he had inherited from his mother and where he had created a superb garden. Instead he bought one acre of abandoned vineyard in Vico Morcote in the Italian-speaking Ticino canton on the Swiss side of Lake Lugano. There he built a house overlooking the steep site. Subsequently he became a Swiss citizen.

From childhood Smithers had been a keen plantsman and gardener. He relished his wartime posting to Mexico as providing matchless opportunities for the study of tropical botany, and grew orchids in his garden at Cuernavaca. Dendrobiums were for twenty years his governing plant passion, and in 1964 he joined the Royal Horticultural Society's orchid committee. At Vico Morcote he laid out his grounds with exotic plants suited to the climate and soil that would mature into an ecosystem needing little maintenance as he grew older. An inveterate and ingenious plant-hunter who travelled widely in Asia to obtain rare specimens, he never attempted a complete collection of *genera*, but instead planted at Vico Morcote some 10,000 species and varieties, including collections of tree peonies, magnolias, lilies, and wisteria that were world-class. His most laudable work was to import numerous Japanese tree peonies unknown in Europe, devise a breeding programme, and produce such beautiful *Peony suffruticosa* Rock's variety hybrids as 'Dojean', 'Luella', 'Lydia Foote', 'Ambrose Congreve', 'Baron Thyssen-Bornemisza', and 'Ice Storm'. The seedlings he gave to Michel Rivière's historic peony nursery at Crest in the Rhône valley ensured that these glorious tree peonies became commercially available. Similarly the Swiss nurseryman Otto Eisenhut developed a worldwide business in propagations from Smithers's rare and extensive magnolia collection. Smithers revived the cultivation of nerines and planned an ambitious cross-breeding programme and bred and tested other plants.

Smithers, who made BBC television documentaries in the early 1950s, was a world-class plant photographer and was awarded the Royal Horticultural Society's gold medal for photography on five occasions after 1981 and the Grenfell medal for photography in 1984. He was also an armchair astronomer, a pioneer home-computer enthusiast, and in old age a devotee of the internet. His memoirs, *Adventures of a Gardener* (1995), are a classic of gardening history: in addition to many superb colour photographs taken by him they are full of shrewd advice and charming asides.

Smithers was senior fellow of the United Nations Institute for Training and Research (1969–72) and general rapporteur of the European conference of parliamentarians and scientists (1970–77). He received an honorary doctorate from Zürich University (1969), the Alexander von Humboldt gold medal for nature conservation (1970), the Council of Europe medal of honour (1984), and the Schulthess prize for best Swiss garden (2001). He died on 8 June 2006, at Vico Morcote, and was survived by his daughters and stepson, his wife having recently predeceased him. RICHARD DAVENPORT-HINES

Sources P. Smithers, *Adventures of a gardener* (1995) • *Daily Telegraph* (10 June 2006) • *The Times* (15 June 2006) • *The Guardian* (15 June 2006) • *The Independent* (15 June 2006) • *The Herald* [Glasgow] (22 June 2006) • *Western Morning News* (27 June 2006) • *WW* (2006) • Burke, *Peerage* • private information (2010) • b. cert.

Archives priv. coll. | CAC, Cam., Patrick Beesly papers • Lilly Library, Indiana University, Bloomington, Indiana, USA, Leonard Russell papers

Likenesses Elliott & Fry, quarter-plate glass negatives, 1949, NPG • Elliott & Fry, vintage print, 1949, NPG • photograph, 1962, PA Photos, London • K. Mathis, photographs, 2003, PA Photos, London • obituary photographs • photographs, repro. in *Adventures*

Southward, Alan James (1928–2007), marine biologist, was born on 17 April 1928 at 18 Delamore Street, Kirkdale, Liverpool, the only child of James Fisher Southward (1896–1964), an engineering fitter with Cunard and ultimately Meccano, and his wife, Mary Gertrude, *née* Aney (1893–1963). He won a scholarship to attend Liverpool Collegiate School. He lost his hearing and sense of balance (subsequently balancing by sight) as a result of contracting meningitis in his mid-teens, but passed his school certificate while learning to lip read. An interest in seashore organisms prompted entry to the University of Liverpool to read zoology, where he gained a first-class degree in 1948, a major achievement for a profoundly deaf student. His PhD thesis on the ecology of the seashore was completed in 1951 under the guidance of J. H. Orton at the marine biological station of the University of Liverpool at Port Erin on the Isle of Man. He was an early pioneer of experimental ecology. He then undertook a Department of Scientific and Industrial Research fellowship mapping geographic distributions of intertidal organisms and experimentally relating the patterns observed to climate. On the Isle of Man he met a fellow marine biologist, Eve Caroline Judges (*b.* 1930), daughter of Arthur Valentine Judges, educationist; they married in Plymouth on 15 July 1954.

In 1953 Southward moved to the laboratory of the Marine Biological Association in Plymouth, where he worked for the rest of his life, beyond formal retirement in 1987 and up until the day before he died. While consolidating his work on intertidal organisms he assumed responsibility for long-term studies of zooplankton and fish under the guidance of the association's director, Sir Frederick Russell, adding his own time series on intertidal barnacles. He soon realized that climatic fluctuations were responsible for changes in the English Channel ecosystem over the previous fifty years. Historical methods were subsequently used to show that fluctuations between cold-water herring and warm-water pilchards had been occurring since the middle ages. The long-term rocky shore surveys proved an invaluable baseline after the *Torrey Canyon* oil spill in 1967; Alan and Eve Southward charted the more than ten-year recovery of the shores from both the oil and the indiscriminate application of highly toxic dispersants, which they showed to be more detrimental to wildlife than the oil itself.

Southward also worked on the taxonomy of barnacles, revisiting Darwin's monograph and with the help of new biochemical and genetic approaches describing new species. The proofs for the definitive taxonomic work on British barnacles were sent to press for the Linnean Society a month before he died. While he was dredging for deepwater barnacles an interest in the distribution and nutrition of deepwater gutless pogonophore worms was stimulated. This joint work with Eve Southward became highly significant after the discovery of deep-sea hydrothermal vents with their spectacular large gutless vestimentiferan worms in the late 1970s.

Southward had a mastery of a diverse range of research topics: from barnacle taxonomy and experimental intertidal ecology, to his work with Eve Southward on deep and shallow water symbiosis-based sulphide-driven chemosynthetic ecosystems. He was always willing to embrace and learn new techniques. His greatest legacy was as an early champion of broad-scale and long-term studies of marine ecosystems and steward of the resulting data. With the growing realization that man-made climate change was occurring, these time series came to be seen as essential tools to help disentangle climate-driven change from such regional and local impacts as overfishing, habitat loss, and pollution. Southward was also well versed in the history of the Marine Biological Association, producing its centennial history in 1987.

Southward wrote lucidly and despite his deafness was an extremely amusing speaker, never shying away from controversy. He wrote well over 220 papers and book chapters including several seminal contributions to *Nature*. He also wrote semi-popular articles for the *New Scientist* and contributed to the environment pages of *The Guardian*. For over twenty years he was a meticulous editor of *Advances in Marine Biology*, taking particular care with manuscripts from overseas contributors, being especially helpful to Russian scientists as the cold war rapidly thawed.

As well as being a fine scientist in her own right, Eve Southward was a collaborator and source of support to Alan, helping with communication. Together they provided much hospitality, support, and encouragement to the British and wider European marine biological community. They were generous and unselfish collaborators and fine hosts, always taking much interest in young researchers of all nationalities. Southward had an impish sense of humour and a penchant for practical jokes. He was an outspoken critic of short-termism in British science in the 1980s. It was a surprise to many that he did not receive more formal recognition of his scientific achievements other than honorary professorships at Liverpool and the University of Victoria, Canada, and an honorary fellowship of the Linnean Society, in all of which he took great pride. He was one of the most influential marine biologists of his generation. He died on 27 October 2007 at his home in Plymouth, Devon, of heart disease; his body was cremated on 9 November at Plymouth crematorium. He was survived by his wife, Eve. STEPHEN J. HAWKINS

Sources *The Guardian* (17 Nov 2007) · *The Times* (29 Nov 2007) · *Daily Post* [Liverpool] (30 Nov 2007) · *Nature*, 451 (2008), 28 · *Advances in Marine Biology* (2008), xv–xxiv · personal knowledge (2011) · private information (2011) [Eve Southward] · b. cert. · m. cert. · d. cert.

Likenesses photograph, repro. in www.timesonline.co.uk/tol/system/topicRoot/Scientific_Pionerers/

Wealth at death £100,804: probate, 18 April 2008, *CGPLA Eng. & Wales*

Southwood, Sir (Thomas) Richard Edmund (1931–2005), ecologist and university administrator, was born at Marlborough Cottage, Old Perry Street, Northfleet, Kent, on 20 June 1931, the only child of Edmund William Southwood (*d.* 1984), dairy farmer, and his wife, Ada Mary, *née* Regg (*d.* 1949), jewellery designer and daughter of T. R. Regg, archdeacon of Newcastle, New South Wales, Australia. When he was four years old, the family moved from the farm where he was born and where the family business continued, more as a wholesale and retail dairy business than a farm, to Kingston House, Old Perry Street. Northfleet, near Gravesend, was still 'country' at that time, although changing with urban creep.

Entomologist and natural historian Southwood's interest in natural history, expressed in observing, identifying, and collecting specimens (mainly insects), began early, and by six he was resolved on a career as an entomologist. From the ages of five to eleven he attended the small and local Bronte School, where all ages were together in one class. He was thus ill prepared for Gravesend grammar school, but its headmaster's judgement in giving more importance to his eleven-plus result than to his formal learning at that point was validated by his performance there. He went on to study entomology at Imperial College, London (1949–52), and to complete his PhD there in 1955. His research was carried out at the Rothamsted experimental station, where he met his wife, Alison Langley Harden, secretary, and daughter of Arthur Langley Harden, hat manufacturer. They married on 10 September 1955, at the parish church in Harpenden, Hertfordshire, and had two sons, Mark (*b.* 1959) and Charles (*b.* 1960).

Southwood published five scientific papers—four entomological notes and an observation on sunbathing by pigeons in *British Birds*—while still at school. As an undergraduate at university he moved on to more serious publications in academic entomological journals. One of these was referred to in the leading ecology text of the day, giving him the unusual distinction of a textbook citation before he had completed his PhD. He was active in the Royal Entomological Society as a schoolboy, and as an undergraduate taught summer courses at the Field Studies Centre at Flatford Mill, in East Bergholt, Suffolk, showing early the flair and enthusiasm that generations of subsequent students at Imperial College's field station at Silwood Park, near Ascot, Berkshire, and elsewhere would appreciate.

After completing his PhD Southwood was appointed to a lectureship at Silwood Park in 1955. His story to this point had been one of a keen and precocious naturalist—a watcher, collector, and codifier, mainly but not exclusively of insects—moving on to become a professional entomologist. The broader discipline of ecology at this time was still primarily an observational and descriptive science. Although prefigured by some early mathematical models and by some penetrating questions about 'why is it so?', it was not until the 1960s that the subject began to acquire a substantial conceptual base, at the hands of such seminal figures as Evelyn Hutchinson (at Yale), David Lack and Charles Elton (at Oxford), Robert MacArthur (at Princeton), and others. This quest for deeper understanding was reinforced by growing needs to control insect pests and the effects of introduced alien species, and other environmental problems associated with an unprecedented growth in the human population. From his base as a consummate entomologist, Southwood became one of the influential pioneers in forming a vision of how ecology should develop across a broad front, fusing scientific natural history, applied biology, and the more theoretical, quantitative approaches to population biology.

Entomological ecologist Southwood's journey from classical entomologist to the newly emerging category of entomological ecologist was gradual; there was no Damascene epiphany. His first paper asking primarily ecological questions was 'The number of species of insect associated with various trees', published in the *Journal of Animal Ecology* in 1961. In this he used his encyclopaedic knowledge of insects to examine why different tree species harbour markedly different numbers of herbivorous insect species feeding on them. This paper anticipated important aspects of Robert MacArthur and E. O. Wilson's highly influential *Theory of Island Biogeography* (1967). His encyclopaedic knowledge of Heteropteran bugs led him to ask why they vary considerably in their dispersal abilities, with some being completely wingless and others strong fliers. The answer, he suggested, lay in the ways in which the spatial structure and scale of the environment influence the evolutionary strategies of species, affecting reproduction and dispersal in various ways. Beginning with his article 'The relationship of flight and habitat in some Carabidae', published in *The Entomologist* in 1962, this body of work was drawn together in his presidential address to the British Ecological Society in 1977, 'Habitat, the templet for ecological strategies', which, after publication in the *Journal of Animal Ecology*, became one of the most cited papers in the entire field of ecology. This paper was particularly notable for the way it linked traditional informal and descriptive approaches to studying life histories with the growing body of mathematical theory based on optimality arguments and trade-offs among different demands on an organism's limiting resources.

Ecology textbooks of the 1950s were almost wholly descriptive. The corresponding texts of the 1990s, by contrast, contained a blend of observation, field and laboratory experiment, and theory expressed often in mathematical terms. Southwood was one of the principal architects of this maturation of the subject. His strengths were an extraordinary knowledge of, and acute appreciation for, the natural world of plants and animals, coupled with an intuitive feeling for the major questions that population biologists and ecologists should be asking. His own mathematical talents were minimal, but when more explicitly mathematical elements were necessary in the assault on a question or problem he engaged fruitfully and happily with appropriate colleagues—many of whose own careers flourished under his aegis.

In addition to his primary research, on topics ranging from entomological systematics and taxonomy, through population and community ecology, to the practical control of particular agricultural pests or disease vectors, Southwood was also highly adept at consolidating and synthesizing in authoritative reviews. One such was his influential book with Don Strong and John Lawton, *Insects on Plants* (1989). One compendium surpassed all else in its comprehensiveness and influence on generations of ecologists: Southwood's *Ecological Methods* first appeared in 1966 and went through three editions by 2000, each extensively and conscientiously updated and otherwise revised. It was often referred to as the ecologist's bible.

Southwood had remarkable skills as an academic manager and leader. Imperial College recognized this early, appointing him head of the department of zoology and applied entomology, and at the same time, director of the field station at Silwood Park, in 1967. In the early 1970s he took on additional major roles, becoming the first chairman of Imperial College's newly formed division of life sciences in 1974. In 1979 he moved to Oxford University to become Linacre professor of zoology, head of the zoology department, and a professorial fellow at Merton College. At Imperial College he had built arguably the world's leading group of researchers in ecology and evolutionary biology. His arrival at Oxford closely followed the retirement or death of three of the twentieth century's major figures in these fields: David Lack, Charles Elton, and the Nobel laureate Niko Tinbergen. But under his skilful leadership the zoology department retained its status (as objectively evidenced by one quarter of all the prestigious Royal Society research professorships in the UK, four out of sixteen, being held in this one department). He did this helped by an extraordinary—almost uncanny—instinct for 'good people', matched by a clear vision of the needs, directions, and values of the department as a whole. Such good deeds do not go unpunished, and in 1989 he was appointed vice-chancellor of Oxford University (1989–93), the first since 1632 who was not head of a college. In this post he initiated several important developments, including the beginning of significant reforms of governance, and a major fund-raising campaign (which exceeded its initial target by more than 50 per cent).

Southwood was never one of those academics to whom teaching was a chore. As head of department at Imperial College and later at Oxford (including the period of his vice-chancellorship) he gave the introductory lectures for first-year students, illustrating his belief that the introductory courses were the most important in any academic department. These lectures were the basis for his trade book, *The Story of Life* (2003), which was a masterly overview of the origin and evolution of living things.

Wider fields Southwood's administrative skills were increasingly recognized in the wider world. Especially pleasing to him was his appointment in 1974 as a trustee of the British Museum (Natural History). During his four-year term as chairman of the trustees (1980–83) he initiated a series of changes, responding to challenges in funding and the need for closer public engagement: an appropriately more diverse array of distinguished trustees, more visitors attracted to the museum (including more school parties), and an extraordinary increase in funds gathered from marketing and outside sponsors.

Arguably Southwood's most important achievement and legacy was ensuring the removal of lead from petrol in the UK. The royal commission on environmental pollution was set up early in 1970; he joined it in 1974, and served as chairman from 1981 to 1986. His first act as chairman was to evaluate the effectiveness of the commission's work, and its possible future direction. The resulting decision was to concentrate on a study of lead in the environment, about which there was growing concern at that time, particularly in regard to lead additives in petrol. There was, however, fierce resistance to total elimination of lead from petrol by a combination of interests (motor manufacturers, oil refiners, and driving organizations). Southwood deployed his skills to good effect, producing an appropriately trenchant and urgent report, and steering through the political shoals, recommending the total removal of all lead additives from petrol. Within days of the publication of *Lead in the Environment* in 1983, the secretary of state for the environment announced that all the commission's recommendations had been accepted. Appropriate legislation soon followed. In contrast with earlier unsuccessful efforts, Southwood's success owed much to the way his careful management of relations with officials and ministers had smoothed the way for this dramatic and satisfactory outcome (catching the opposition on the hop).

In 1988 Southwood was asked to bring his committee skills and biological knowledge to chairing, for the Department of Health and the Ministry of Agriculture, Fisheries and Food, the working party on Bovine Spongiform Encephalopathy (BSE), in the wake of the outbreak of BSE or 'mad cow disease' in Britain. This committee was established two years after BSE had been identified in British cattle and thus after a large number of infected animals had already entered the food chain. The issue was obviously highly sensitive, with a risk to human health if the disease could jump the species barrier, but also with serious economic consequences for the British farming industry if such risks were overstated. From the start Southwood's group were strongly critical of the aggressive changes in 'rendering practice' that had resulted in the remains of cattle and sheep being fed to cattle. They regarded this as foolish on basic epidemiological and ecological grounds, and strongly recommended that such practices should stop forthwith. They further recommended that certain parts of the cow—brains and offal—should not enter the human food chain. Most of these recommendations were implemented in 1989, although not with the sense of urgency that Southwood wished. Southwood's study was, however, responsible for the changes in regulation of cattle feed that ended the epidemic in cattle, and for the changes in abattoir practices that kept infectious material out of the human food chain from then on.

At the time it was not known whether the BSE prion, if ingested by humans, could cause disease. By analogy with scrapie in sheep—a disease whose aetiology in sheep is similar to BSE in cattle, which has been around in sheep for centuries, and which has no known effect on humans—the best guess was that there would be no problem. This opinion was shared by essentially all informed scientists at the time. But this best guess was not a certainty, and Southwood's report was properly cautious, emphasizing the uncertainty and the need to address it. Unfortunately, the proper equivocation in Southwood's report was glossed over by ministers and civil servants anxious to reassure the public. When it became clear that indeed there was a connection between BSE in cattle and a new variant of the allied Creutzfeldt–Jakob disease (vCJD) in humans, some sought to suggest that Southwood had not sufficiently emphasized the uncertainty. A retrospective reading of the report does not support this attempt to shift the blame.

Another major contribution to public life was Southwood's chairmanship (from 1994 to 1997) of the government's Round Table on Sustainable Development, in the aftermath of the 1992 world summit on sustainable development. Building on the good start he gave it, this body later transmogrified into the Sustainable Development Commission. Looking beyond the UK, Southwood played a major role in helping establish the environment programme at the nascent Central European University, established in 1991 with funding from George Soros to help bring students from the former Soviet Union and central and eastern European countries into the mainstream. There was a crying need for such a programme in eastern Europe at this time. Southwood was subsequently invited to become rector of the Central European University, when he stepped down as Oxford's vice-chancellor. He declined, but did continue to play a strong role in this institution's successful growth.

Honours and final years Southwood had an extraordinary influence on ecological and environmental science in Britain and more generally, partly through his own work but even more through the successive generations of younger colleagues whose careers he fostered. Some contemporaries saw the academic world as an increasingly competitive one; his emphasis was always on co-operation, and he took genuine pleasure in the achievements of others. He was elected a fellow of the Royal Society in 1977 (serving as vice-president in 1982–4), and gave its prestigious Croonian lecture in 1995. He was also elected a foreign associate of the American National Academy of Sciences (1988), a member of the Pontifical Academy of Sciences (1992), an honorary foreign member of the Norwegian Academy of Science and Letters (1987), a foreign member of the Royal Netherlands Academy of Arts and Sciences (1995), and a member of the Hungarian Academy of Sciences (1998). He was knighted in 1984, and appointed a deputy lieutenant of Oxfordshire in 1993. Besides other honours, four major overseas universities and nine British ones awarded him honorary degrees. Major academic awards included Imperial College's Huxley medal (1962), the Zoological Society's scientific medal (1969), the Linnean Society's gold medal (1988), and the Maria Theresa medal of Pavia University (1997). He was a fellow (trustee) of Eton College (1993–2001), a member of the Rhodes Trust (1986–2002; chairman, 1999–2002), and an honorary member, member, or chairman of many other bodies, in the UK and elsewhere.

Southwood had earlier encounters with cancer, but had been in healthy remission for some time. The final recurrence came quickly, and he died peacefully at his home, April Cottage, 32 Upland Park Road, Oxford, on 26 October 2005. He was survived by his wife and their two sons.

ROBERT M. MAY

Sources *The Times* (1 Nov 2005); (17 Nov 2005); (18 Nov 2005) · *Daily Telegraph* (3 Nov 2005) · *The Independent* (9 Nov 2005); (17 Nov 2005) · *Nature*, 438/7070 (2005), 928 · Munk's Roll online, www.rcplondon.ac.uk/heritage/munksroll/munk_details.asp ?ID=5511, 5 Aug 2008 · *Entomologia Experimentalis et Applicata*, 118 (2006), 175 · *Memoirs FRS* [forthcoming] · *WW* (2005) · Burke, *Peerage* · R. Southwood, 'From natural history to biology: the foundations of a career', Bodl. Oxf., Southwood papers · personal knowledge (2009) · private information (2009) · b. cert. · m. cert. · d. cert.

Archives Bodl. Oxf., corresp. and papers | Oxford University Museum of Natural History, Dennis Leston MSS · Oxford University Museum of Natural History, G. C. Varley MSS

Likenesses Bassano, six half-plate film negatives, 1970, NPG · photographs, 1985–98, PA Photos, London · photographs, 1995, Photoshot, London · Bassano, photograph, Camera Press, London · obituary photographs · oils, Merton Oxf. · pencil sketch, Rhodes House, Oxford · photographs, RS

Wealth at death £643,499: probate, 24 May 2006, *CGPLA Eng. & Wales*

Spark [*née* Camberg], **Dame Muriel Sarah** (1918–2006), poet and novelist, was born on 1 February 1918 at 160 Bruntsfield Place, Edinburgh, the second child of Bernard (Barney) Camberg (1885–1962), mechanical engineer (fitter) at the North British Rubber Company, and his wife, Sarah Elizabeth Maud (Cissy), *née* Uezzell (1888–1974), daughter of Thomas (Tom) Uezzell, and his wife, Adelaide, *née* Hyams, of Watford. Muriel's father, a Scottish Jew whose parents had married in Kovno, Lithuania, was the

Dame Muriel Sarah Spark (1918–2006), by Frank Monaco

ninth child of eleven and the seventh to be born in Edinburgh. Her mother was brought up as a Christian but married Bernard Camberg in the East London Synagogue on 1 February 1911. Adelaide Uezzell, a huge influence on her granddaughter, always maintained that she was a 'gentile Jewess', and Muriel later used the phrase to describe herself, her mother, and her grandmother as the children of Jewish fathers and gentile mothers.

Early life and marriage: Edinburgh, Watford, and Southern Rhodesia, 1918–1944 Muriel Camberg grew up in a small, crowded flat with her brother, Philip (1912–2001), and various lodgers, amid a host of Jewish relations in Edinburgh. The extended family, however, extended rather to Watford, then a quiet market town, and to Cissy's Christian relations. At 288 High Street Adelaide and Tom Uezzell ran a 'shop-of-all-sorts' (later demolished). Nearby, Cissy's brother, (Thomas) Philip Uezzell (Uncle Phil), and his wife, Alice, lived with their six children. Uncle Phil was a railwayman turned tailor, Alice a cook for gentlemen's clubs in London. They were, like Muriel's father, of the skilled working class but there was always a sense, encouraged by Adelaide, that the Cambergs were socially superior. Tiny, brisk, and smart-tongued, Adelaide was dismissive of Alice and her more rough-and-tumble brood. The Cambergs visited Watford for Barney's fortnight's summer holiday from the factory, and the Uezzells frequently travelled to Edinburgh. When Tom died in 1926, Adelaide first lived with Phil's family but, quarrelling with them, was taken in by the Cambergs and installed in Muriel's bedroom. During the next six years, until Adelaide's death in 1933, Muriel's bed was a sofa in the kitchen. For the last three, Adelaide was crippled by two strokes, her speech scrambled by aphasia. Muriel, fascinated by the old lady, spent many hours in her company and remembered her warmly for her spirited defiance.

Muriel's autobiography, *Curriculum Vitae* (1992), depicts her mother as embarrassing, English, nervous, and showy, her father as Scottish, steady, and taciturn. She always found her brother dull. He was a rationalist, she imaginative and gifted. Both attended James Gillespie's, a small, fee-paying merchant school. It was there that Muriel flourished in the juniors under the wing of a charismatic teacher, Christina Kay, whose spirit was immortalized in her sixth and most famous novel, *The Prime of Miss Jean Brodie* (1961). Kay cherished the nascent writer in Muriel, as did two other teachers, her poems regularly appearing in the school magazine and in a book of Edinburgh schools' writing, *The Door of Youth* (1931). In 1932 she won the city's schools competition to mark the centenary of Sir Walter Scott's death.

Muriel matriculated in 1934 but her parents could not support further study for university. After a précis course at Heriot-Watt College and jobs teaching English and in a department store, she left on 13 August 1937 for Southern Rhodesia, aged nineteen, to marry Sydney Oswald Spark (Solly or SOS), a schoolteacher of Jewish origins. They had met at a dance at Edinburgh's Overseas Club and become engaged, and he had gone on ahead to take up a job in Fort Victoria. Thirteen years her senior, he seemed adventurous and mature, an intellectual. They married in Salisbury registry office (neither had religious faith) on 3 September 1937, a few days after her arrival, and on 9 July 1938 their only child, Samuel Robin, was born in Bulawayo after a long and agonizing labour. By then the marriage was already in ruins.

Solly, unstable and given to firing off his revolver in enclosed spaces, had lost jobs in Britain and was soon in trouble with the Rhodesian authorities. With the outbreak of the Second World War, all civilian passages to the UK were stopped. Nevertheless, Muriel Spark determined that she must escape, first setting up independently with Robin and supporting herself with secretarial jobs, then placing him in a Gwelo convent boarding school and making her way to South Africa, where in 1944 she took a troop ship to Liverpool.

Catholicism and fiction: London and New York, 1944–1966 Having three times won prizes for her poetry and prose in the Rhodesian eisteddfod, Spark headed for London to establish her literary career, but first worked as a telephonist for Sefton Delmer's black propaganda unit at Milton Bryan, near Woburn Abbey. Memories of this scenario figure in her New York novel *The Hothouse by the East River* (1973), memories of her tortured time in Africa in a series of brilliant short stories written in the 1950s and 1960s, particularly 'The Go-Away Bird' and 'Bang-bang You're Dead'. Her son Robin returned in 1945 and went to Edinburgh, where he was brought up by her parents. From 1947 to 1949 she was editor of the Poetry Society's *Poetry Review* and became the society's general secretary. In these circles she met and began a tempestuous affair with the poet and editor of *Outposts*, Howard Sergeant (1914–1987), introduced payment for published work, and generally irritated the old guard (particularly Marie Stopes) so much that first there was a mass resignation from the council and then Spark was sacked. Setting up a counterblast magazine, *Forum: Poetry and Stories*, she began an affair with the poet Derek Stanford (1918–2008), her closest companion for almost a decade.

Spark and Stanford edited four books together—on Wordsworth (1950), Emily Brontë (1953), Mary Shelley (1953), and Cardinal Newman (1957)—while she produced her own work: poems and essays; biographies of Mary Shelley (1951) and John Masefield (1953); and a selection of Emily Brontë's poetry (1952). The relationship began to collapse with her reception into the Roman Catholic church on 1 May 1954. About January 1954, while she was starting instruction, she suffered terrifying hallucinations, detecting coded, threatening messages in T. S. Eliot's writing. This was due to her overdosing on Dexadrine (later known as 'speed') prescribed as slimming pills. Suffering the depression common to withdrawal from dextro-amphetamine poisoning, she left London for The Friars, a Carmelite retreat in Kent, moving on to a cottage in the grounds of the Carmelites' nearby Allington Castle, to write her first novel. The young Alan Maclean, brother of the traitor Donald Maclean, had commissioned it for Macmillan on the basis of her short stories (she had won the *Observer* Christmas story competition in 1951 with 'The Seraph and the Zambesi') and on the recommendation of Graham Greene, who, along with David Astor and A. J. Cronin, supported her financially.

Throughout this difficult period, 1954–5, Stanford was Spark's chief ally: organizing the 'plight fund', and acting as her agent and go-between. She would often travel to London to visit him and for regular consultations with her lay psychoanalyst and spiritual counsellor, the Jungian Father O'Malley. It was O'Malley who introduced her to Tiny Lazzari, an Irish Catholic landlady in the unfashionable London suburb of Camberwell. Spark lived there, at 13 Baldwin Crescent, for a decade from 1955. Her much-acclaimed first novel, *The Comforters* (1957), was completed there and it remained her London base when she became an international celebrity with *The Prime of Miss Jean Brodie* and for three years (1962–5) spent half her life in New York. She loved Tiny Lazzari dearly as a kind of surrogate mother and as her first 'dragon' gatekeeper. An affectionate portrait of her appears in *Loitering with Intent* (1981) as Milly Sanders. It was only in 1965, when Spark was planning to move to Rome, that she relinquished her Camberwell flat.

Always experimental in her fiction, Spark might be considered the first British post-modernist. At the same time she was a theological (rather than a religious or proselytizing) writer. *The Comforters*, in the words of the *Times Literary Supplement*, is 'a novel about a character in a novel who has finished writing a study of the Novel and goes away to write a novel', and the heroine might either be a character in that novel or its author (*TLS*, 22 July 1957). The moral problem is how to love, as her religion demands, her repulsive and interfering co-religionist Mrs Hogg. The intellectual problem is how to represent the apparent disjunction between body and soul. Caroline's sense of being part of someone else's story reflects the sense throughout Spark's work of alienation and of the human race's being part of God's (incomprehensible) story. Time is elastic in her fiction, plunging backwards and forwards through analepsis and prolepsis, rendering the narrative present fragile and illusory. There is mankind's time and there is God's time. The two overlap and interweave.

Crucial to Spark's theology was the book of Job. She abandoned writing a book on the subject when her breakdown overwhelmed her. In 1955 she reviewed Jung's *Answer to Job*. Her *The Only Problem* (1974) concentrates on a character writing a treatise on Job. The 'only problem', and one to which Spark constantly returned, was how a benevolent and omniscient God could create a world of ubiquitous suffering. In this respect the holocaust represented a particular difficulty. The only answer was that the anthropomorphic notion of God must collapse.

Spark's early satires, written in London between 1957 and 1961, generate a powerful, yet comic, sense of loss in a fallen world. In *Memento Mori* (1959) the Catholic characters feel unthreatened by anonymous telephone messages reminding the elderly cast that they must die. *The Bachelors* (1960) reads like a pastiche of Eliot's *The Waste Land* (1922). A sense of evil, both terrifying and playful, haunts all her writing. Dougal Douglas in *The Ballad of Peckham Rye* (1960), a likeable mischief-maker with two bumps on his head, lies throughout to subvert the hypocrisy of those who surround him. 'What she has devised', Gerald Sykes noted, 'is an unponderous way of putting matters like Good and Evil and Death and Revelation back into a novel which also deals with contemporary British life' (*New York Times Book Review*, 28 Aug 1960). Her Catholicism was unconventional. She found the blind faith of her co-religionists tiresome, rarely attended church, and confessed only on her deathbed. Yet her faith was absolute.

Spark's life was characterized by continuous transformation: from humble Edinburgh childhood to the epitome of literary chic; from poet to novelist; from agnostic to Anglican to Roman Catholic; from the metropolitan to the rural. This she described in 1962 as a movement 'from exile into exile' ('Edinburgh-born', *New Statesman*, 10 Aug 1962). She abandoned each existence, closed the door on it, and began again, leaving in her wake a litter of disputes with friends, lovers, and publishers. Among these, in her early days as a novelist, in addition to Sergeant and Stanford, were Alan Barnsley (1916–1986, the novelist Gabriel Fielding), Rayner Heppenstall (1911–1981), who produced her first radio plays, Alan Maclean (1924–2006), and Christine Brooke-Rose (*b.* 1923) and her husband, Jerzy Peterkiewicz (1916–2007).

In New York Spark lived in a functional service apartment in the Beaux Arts Hotel. After the *New Yorker* devoted an entire issue to *The Prime of Miss Jean Brodie* the novel began to generate a small fortune. Jay Presson Allen's adaptation became a West End and Broadway hit, followed by a film directed by Ronald Neame (1969), for which Maggie Smith won an Oscar. The *New Yorker* provided an office overlooking Times Square and its flashing Time / Life sign. 'When it says "Time"', she told Shirley Hazzard, her confidante there until Hazzard married Francis Steegmuller, 'I write. When it says "Life" I want to go out' (Stannard, *Muriel Spark*). She often did go out, with Hazzard to concerts and films, with her much-prized agent, Ivan von Auw, to jazz clubs, and with younger friends to bars and discotheques. In New York she quickly transformed her public image with the help of Elizabeth Arden, diets, designer clothes, and jewellery. She bought a racehorse. Photographs of her over the next decade appear to reveal her steadily increasing youth. She became a star, not only in the literary firmament but also in her whole appearance. In New York she wrote what was perhaps her masterpiece, *The Girls of Slender Means* (1963), and what was intended to be her magnum opus, *The Mandelbaum Gate* (1965). But, despite the fact that the latter won the James Tait Black memorial prize, she was unhappy with the book. It concerns a gentile Jewess and was based on Spark's trip to Israel and attendance at Adolf Eichmann's trial in 1961, an experience she found acutely distressing.

Queen of letters: Italy, 1966–2006 In 1966, when New York's literary culture became too invasive for her, Spark moved to Rome. There she lived first in the elegant Hotel Raphael, just off Piazza Navona, and then in three rented flats. The second of these, in Palazzo Taverna, was distinctly grand with a vast Renaissance *salone* of which she furnished only one corner. Throughout, she kept herself to herself, her closest companions being homosexual males: Eugene Walter, Dario Ambrosiani, Brian de Breffny, and Count Lanfranco Rasponi. Having begun as her parents' princess, she transformed herself into a queen of letters. In Rome the settings of her novels—*The Public Image* (1968), *The Driver's Seat* (1970), *Not to Disturb* (1971), *The Hothouse by the East River* (1973), and *The Abbess of Crewe* (1974)—became more international and their style even more experimental, influenced by the work of Alain Robbe-Grillet and often written in the present tense. *The Driver's Seat* she considered her best, because best constructed, the story of a woman seeking her own murderer. Neurosis (epitomized by New York itself in *Hothouse*) seethes through them all: human cruelty, sexual perversity, and political corruption render human life bestial. *Abbess*, a black comedy loosely based on the Watergate scandal, is set in a nunnery.

In 1968 Penelope Jardine (*b.* 1932), daughter of the colonial governor Sir Douglas Jardine, became Spark's part-time secretary to support her own creative life as a painter and sculptor. They grew to be close friends but did not at first consider a shared household. Spark was buying a studio apartment overlooking Lake Nemi (the setting of *The Takeover*, 1976), and Jardine San Giovanni, a dilapidated priest's house and adjoining deconsecrated church in rural Tuscany near Arezzo. Spark, however, soon sold the studio, bought the small flat that Jardine rented in Vicolo del Gallo in Rome, and by the early 1970s had made San Giovanni her home, with Jardine as devoted companion, cook, housekeeper, driver, and secretary. They remained together until Spark's death, relentlessly travelling Europe. At San Giovanni Spark wrote her autobiography and nine more novels, mellowing as she adjusted to rustic life and as the house was steadily renovated. At first her work dealt with the very rich and their servants: *The Takeover* and *Territorial Rights* (1979). Two quasi-autobiographical works—*Loitering* and *A Far Cry from Kensington* (1988)—were followed by *Reality and Dreams* (1996), *Aiding and Abetting* (2000), and *The Finishing School* (2004), taking her back to where she had begun: to the contemplation of the creative process and its relation to spirituality, to transformations and transfigurations. All her later writings, particularly *Symposium* (1990), discuss love and how to distinguish this from possessiveness. The moral problems of her fiction often centre on resistance to attempted 'takeovers', the complicated truth of lived experience airbrushed because one person's identity requires the demolition of another's.

Spark saw this scenario in her relationship with Stanford and with her son. Stanford became an incubus to her, writing *Muriel Spark: a Biographical and Critical Study* (1963), and selling her letters to him. *A Far Cry from Kensington* lampoons him as the *pisseur de copie*, Hector Bartlett. Ultimately, however, it was Robin who presented the greater irritation. As an orthodox Jew, he insisted that Spark and her mother were Jewish through the female line and in 1998 revealed that he possessed his grandparents' ketubah, or Jewish marriage certificate, with the implication that Spark had suppressed this information in her autobiography. When a storm blew up about this in the British press, she was furious and responded with cutting remarks. Philip Camberg, who had married a Jewish woman and emigrated to America to become a research chemist and then a 'value engineer' (cost-cutter) for US Naval Systems Air Command, fully supported his sister's account and received poison-pen letters for his trouble. Spark cut Robin out of her will, leaving everything to Jardine.

Among those who expressed admiration for Spark's work were W. H. Auden, Graham Greene, Sir Frank Kermode, David Lodge, Evelyn Waugh, Tennessee Williams, and John Updike. She became a fellow of the Royal Society of Literature in 1963, and was appointed OBE in 1967 and DBE in 1993. She received numerous honorary doctorates, was appointed CLit in 1991 and a commander of the Ordre des Arts and des Lettres in 1996, and won the David Cohen British Literature prize for lifetime achievement in 1997. She sold her literary manuscripts to the University of Tulsa and her personal archive to the National Library of Scotland.

After fourteen years of terrible suffering from osteoporosis, malfunctioning hip replacements, fractured ribs and vertebrae, shingles, and post-herpetic neuralgia, Spark finally succumbed to cancer of the kidneys on 13 April 2006, at Villa Cherubini, a private hospital in Florence, and was buried in the village cemetery at Civitella, Val di Chiana, close to San Giovanni. Her funeral on 15 April was quiet, some forty people, mostly local, attending, including one male cousin from her father's side, who had come from London for his first visit to be a representative of her family. The news was broken on the day of the burial and immediately the international media were log-jammed with grief at her death and praise for her achievements.

'No other writer', Jenny Turner remarked, 'has ever come close to imitating [Spark's] special narrative voice. In its waspishness, its spirit, its curiously posh Scottish-camp, it is one of the great creations of postwar writing' (*The Guardian*, 17 April 2006). MARTIN STANNARD

Sources M. Spark, 'How I became a novelist', *John O'London's Weekly* (1 Dec 1960) · M. Spark, 'The poet's house', *The Critic* [Chicago], 19/4 (Feb–March 1961); repr. in *Encounter*, 30 (May 1965), 48–50 · M. Spark, 'Edinburgh-born', *New Statesman* (10 Aug 1962); repr. as 'What images return', *Memoirs of modern Scotland*, ed. K. Miller (1970), 151–3 · F. Kermode, 'The house of fiction: interviews with seven English novelists', *Partisan Review*, 30/1 (1963), 61–82; repr. in *The novel today: contemporary writers on modern fiction*, ed. M. Bradbury (1977), 111–35 · D. Stanford, *Muriel Spark: a biographical and critical study* (1963) · M. Spark, 'The desegregation of art', *Proceedings of the American Academy of Arts and Letters* (1971), 21–7; repr. in *Month*, 5 (1972), 152–3 · A. Hamilton, 'Alex Hamilton interviews Muriel Spark', *The Guardian* (8 Nov 1974) · D. Stanford, *Inside the forties: literary memoirs, 1937–57* (1977) · M. Spark, 'My Rome', *New York Times Magazine* (13 March 1983) · J. Mortimer, 'The culture of an anarchist', *Sunday Telegraph Magazine* (20 March 1988) · M. Spark, *Curriculum vitae* (1992) · S. Schiff, 'Muriel Spark between the lines', *New Yorker* (24 May 1993) · M. Stannard, 'The letter killeth', *The Spectator* (6 June 1998) · *Sunday Herald* (16 April 2006) · *Scotland on Sunday* (16 April 2006) · *The Times* (17 April 2006) · *Daily Telegraph* (17 April 2006) · *The Guardian* (17 April 2006) · *The Independent* (17 April 2006); (24 April 2006) · *The Herald* [Glasgow] (17 April 2006) · M. Stannard, *Muriel Spark* (2009) · *WW* (2006) · Burke, *Peerage* · personal knowledge (2010) · private information (2010) · b. cert.

Archives NL Scot., personal archive · University of Tulsa, McFarlin Library, literary manuscripts | BBC WAC · BFI, Joseph Losey MSS · Emory University, Atlanta, Robert Woodruff Library for Advanced Studies, Derek Stanford MSS · Georgetown University, Washington, DC, Lauinger Library, Alan G. Barnsley papers · Princeton University Libraries, Harold Ober archive · Ransom HRC · Saint Michael's College, Vermont · University of Delaware · University of Victoria Library, Canada, literary notebook · Washington University, St Louis Library, John Smith archive | FILM BFINA, *Booked*, N. Bigsby (director), Channel 4, 27 May 1998 · BFINA, documentary footage

Likenesses photographs, 1955–74, Getty Images, London, Hult. Arch. · M. Gerson, modern bromide print, 1961, NPG · M. Gerson, photographs, 1963, NPG · J. Bown, photograph, 1965, repro. in *The Observer* (19 July 1992) · C. Mydans, photographs, 1965, Getty Images, London, Time and Life Pictures · photographs, 1967–97, PA Photos, London · photographs, 1983–2005, Camera Press, London · S. Hyde, bromide print, 1984, NPG · J. Bauer, photograph, 1985, PA Photos, London · photographs, 1987–91, Rex Features, London, Sipa Press · T. Leighton, bromide fibre prints, 1988, NPG · U. Andersen, photographs, 1991–2002, Getty Images, London · B. Tulloch, pencil and wash, 1993, NPG · S. Pyke, photographs, 1997, Getty Images, London, Premium Archive · photograph, 1997, Rex Features, London · M. Hardie, photographs, 2004, Rex Features, London · A. Moffat, oils, Scot. NPG · F. Monaco, photograph, Rex Features, London [*see illus.*] · T. Pilston, photograph, repro. in *The Independent* (1 Aug 1992) · obituary photographs

Spencer, John (1935–2006), snooker player, was born on 18 September 1935 at Bealey Maternity Home, Radcliffe, near Bury, Lancashire, the youngest in the family of three sons and two daughters of William Spencer, night watchman and bookmaker's runner, of 44 Hollinhurst Road, Radcliffe, and his wife, Annie, formerly Hoadley, *née* Bleakley. (His father accidentally registered Spencer's birth date as 15 September, his own mother's birthday, and to avoid having to explain this Spencer used that date on all official documents throughout his life.) He was brought up in

John Spencer (1935–2006), by Central Press, 1974

Radcliffe, and attended Stand Grammar School in Whitefield, Manchester. He was introduced to snooker by his father, who had lost his right arm in action during the First World War and used a small clothes brush as a rest. He was soon a regular at The Grott in Radcliffe, and made his first century break when he was fifteen, but at this time snooker as a game was in the doldrums and his fame remained purely local. Also at the age of fifteen he left school, taking a variety of menial jobs.

Called up for national service in the RAF when he was eighteen, Spencer decided to enlist for three years rather than the standard two, since this enabled him to receive better pay and longer leave. On leaving the RAF he again took a series of mundane jobs until finding secure employment in a bookmaker's office. Meanwhile, having given up playing snooker on joining the RAF, he did not hit a ball for eleven years until an old friend recruited him for a £5-a-head challenge match between two Manchester billiard halls. After he had anchored Longsight to victory it struck him that if these were the best amateurs in Lancashire he had been underrating himself. He reached the final of the English amateur championship at his first attempt in 1964, losing to Ray Reardon, who later won six world titles. He became English amateur champion in 1966, and returned as runner-up from the world amateur championship in Karachi that year, on the point of retirement after a row over expenses. He initially had no thought of a professional career as there was then no tournament circuit. Players survived through exhibitions (including trick shots) in clubs for various charities. Out of the blue the National Spastics Society offered him £14 per engagement, plus a small commission on what he could raise through auctions and raffles. Pontins, in Blackpool, then offered him £20 a week for a summer season and his professional career was born. On 5 April 1969, now able to describe himself as a 'professional snooker player', he married Margaret Anni (Margot) Sawbridge, a twenty-year-old clothier's dresser from Radcliffe, and daughter of Frederick Sawbridge, shopkeeper. There were no children of the marriage.

In 1969 a new BBC2 television series, *Pot Black*, showed snooker in full colour for the first time and helped transform it from a subterranean working-class sport into a television entertainment. Spencer was one of its new generation of heroes and won the tournament three times, in 1970, 1971, and 1976. When John Player decided to sponsor a revived knock-out world championship, also in 1969 (originally held in 1927, it had for a number of years been conducted on a challenge basis), Spencer won the first prize of £1780. Beaten by Reardon in the April 1970 championship semi-final, he recaptured the title in Sydney in November that year, making three centuries in four frames in the final. A hot favourite to retain the title in 1972, he nevertheless lost that final to a fiery young Irishman, Alex Higgins, whose emergence was to be an important factor in the game's unexpected commercial success.

Spencer's cue, an unprepossessing 15 oz Excalibur, held together by a nail in its butt, that he had bought for 8 shillings from The Grott, was broken into four pieces when he fell asleep at the wheel of his car in 1974. He was lucky not to kill himself. Incredibly the cue was pinned together, and with it Spencer won the inaugural Benson and Hedges masters in 1975, but it never felt quite the same. Eventually, two months before the 1977 world championship, he changed to a new Canadian two-piece and regained the title not in his old assertive style but with a percentage game underpinned by concentration, tenacity, tactical acumen, and experience. In 1979, in the Holsten international tournament at Slough, he became the first player ever to make a 147 maximum in competition, albeit denied television exposure because Thames TV, anxious to avoid overtime payments, had awarded the crew a meal break.

Spencer's career and life were shattered on 9 May 1985 when he woke up with double vision, quickly diagnosed as myasthenia gravis, a disease that in his case had caused a deterioration of his eye muscles. Steroids fought the problem with intermittent success but the side effects were hellish. He managed to keep going as a BBC television summarizer and was from 1990 to 1996 chairman of the World Professional Billiards and Snooker Association. Nevertheless his condition and medication produced deep depressions, ungovernable spasms of aggression, and an obsession with suicide. It was all a dreadful contrast to his sunny, good natured younger self, a great lover of practical jokes, golf, and gambling on horses. In 2003 he was diagnosed with stomach cancer. In 2005 he declined further treatment, preferring to feel relatively normal for, as it proved, about a year, to suffering several years of misery from the side effects of drugs. He remained, as he had been for twenty years, a dedicated fund-raiser for the Myasthenia Gravis Association, and in his last months completed his autobiography, *Out of the Blue, into the Black* (2005). His marriage having ended in separation, though on good terms, he was supported by his partner of fifteen years, Jean Shepherd. He died at the Bury Hospice in Dumers Lane, Radcliffe (built in the grounds of the former Bealey Maternity Home), on 11 July 2006.

CLIVE EVERTON

Sources J. Spencer, *Out of the blue, into the black* (2005) • *The Times* (12 July 2006) • *Daily Telegraph* (13 July 2006) • *The Guardian* (13 July 2006) • *The Independent* (13 July 2006) • personal knowledge (2010) • private information (2010) • b. cert. • m. cert. • d. cert.

Archives FILM BFINA, documentary footage • BFINA, light entertainment footage • BFINA, performance footage

Likenesses photographs, 1965–90, PA Photos, London • photographs, 1969–74, Getty Images, London, Hult. Arch. • Central Press, photograph, 1974, Hult. Arch., London [*see illus.*] • photographs, 1975–84, Photoshot, London • D. Muscroft, photograph, 1981, Rex Features, London • obituary photographs • photographs, repro. in Spencer, *Out of the blue*

Spender, (John) Humphrey (1910–2005), photojournalist and artist, was born at 47 Campden House Court, Kensington, London, on 19 April 1910, the third son and youngest of the four children of (Edward) Harold Spender (1864–1926), journalist and author, and his wife, Violet Hilda, *née* Schuster (1878–1921). He was a brother of the poet Sir Stephen *Spender. In early life his myopia was, bizarrely, misdiagnosed as a symptom of congenital syphilis, and he was forbidden to read, initially for a year, and later in artificial light, contributing, he believed, to his much heightened visual sense. He was educated at Charlcote School, Worthing, at a school in London, and at Gresham's School, Norfolk, before spending a year in Freiburg im Breisgau studying art history and perfecting his German. He then spent four years at the Architectural Association School of Architecture, London, qualifying in 1933. He never practised as an architect, however, instead setting up a photographic studio in the Strand with his lover Bill Edmiston. Much of his income initially came from portraiture, but an assignment photographing housing conditions in the East End of London led to commissions from the *Left Review* to take pictures of the Jarrow marchers and the British Union of Fascists' rally at the Albert Hall.

In 1935 Spender joined the *Daily Mirror* for which, as Lensman, he covered numerous stories in the UK and abroad before resigning on a point of principle in 1937. He travelled frequently to Germany, where he was almost arrested at the Nazis' notorious Degenerate Art exhibition of 1937, after he had been overheard praising the art on display. He and his brother Stephen travelled often with Christopher Isherwood, and Humphrey Spender designed the dust jacket of Isherwood's *Goodbye to Berlin* (1939) and took the iconic photograph of Isherwood standing at a window, which was later reproduced on the jacket of *Christopher and his Kind* (1973). Meanwhile he had been persuaded by Tom Harrisson to join the team of Mass-Observation, and took more than 900 photographs in Bolton (Worktown). These he always took covertly, declaring that a photograph was 'spoiled' if its subjects had noticed his presence. He took a similar series of documentary photographs elsewhere for Stefan Lorant's *Picture Post*, whose staff he joined soon after its launch in 1938. At one point the mayor of Newcastle was driven to complain that Spender's photographs only ever showed the seamier side of Newcastle life. He was conscripted in 1941, and after a brief period in the Royal Army Service Corps spent the rest of the Second World War as an official photographer and interpreter of photo-reconnaissance pictures.

On demobilization Spender returned briefly to the *Picture Post*, but after he had won a textile design competition (judged by his friend Henry Moore) Robin Darwin, rector of the Royal College of Art, invited him to join the staff of the textile department, where he remained as a tutor from 1953 until 1975. He won four awards from the Council for Industrial Design for his textile and wallpaper designs, and his work was reproduced by companies including Sandersons and the Edinburgh Weavers. He also painted—his greatest passion—and designed murals for the television pavilion at the Festival of Britain, and for the P&O liners *Canberra* and *Oriana*. Solo exhibitions of his work were held at the Leicester and Redfern galleries, the New Art Centre, and various provincial galleries. In 1982 he published some of his Mass-Observation photographs in *Worktown People*, and others were included in David Jury's boxed set, *In Darkest England* (1998). Deborah Frizzell's book *Humphrey Spender's Humanist Landscapes: Photo-Documents, 1932–1942* had meanwhile been published the previous year, to coincide with an exhibition at the Yale Center for British Art. His final publication, *Morocco* (2004), was a record of a *Daily Mirror* assignment in 1935.

Spender was married three times. His first marriage, on 13 July 1937, was to Margaret (Lolly) Low, a 28-year-old architect whom he had met at the Architectural Association, and daughter of V. Warnen Low, surgeon. They adopted a son. Her death on Christmas day 1945 inspired Stephen Spender's 'Elegy for Margaret'. Spender married second, on 20 March 1948, Pauline Wynn, a 29-year-old actress and radio dramatist, and daughter of Group Captain Wynn Elias Wynn, RAF officer. They had one son. She died in 2003, and on 18 June that year he married his by then long-term companion, Rachel Anne Hewitt, a photographer and artist, and daughter of James Roy Hewitt, painter. She was fifty-five years his junior. Spender's wives were aware of his bisexuality, and the first two tolerated his many affairs with both men and women, who reputedly included Frederick Ashton and Paul Robeson's wife, Eslanda. From 1968 he lived at The Studio, Ulting, Maldon, Essex, a modernist building that was the first built work by the then unknown architect Richard Rogers. He died there on 11 March 2005, of heart failure, and was survived by his wife, Rachel, and his two sons. His Worktown photographs are now owned by Bolton Museum and Art Gallery.

ALEX MAY

Sources M. Hallett, *The real story of Picture Post* (1994) · *The Independent* (14 March 2005) · *The Times* (15 March 2005) · *Daily Telegraph* (15 March 2005) · *The Guardian* (15 March 2005); (31 March 2005) · www.spender.boltonmuseums.org.uk, 1 April 2008 · b. cert. · m. certs. · d. cert.

Archives Trinity Cam., Julian Otto Trevelyan papers · U. Sussex, Mass-Observation papers | FILM BFINA, documentary footage | SOUND BL NSA, photographers' gallery recordings, interview, 1980s, F4036 · BL NSA, oral history of photography, interviews with G. Robertson, 18–19 Dec 1992, F3742–F3751 · BL NSA, National Life Story Collection, interviews with C. Courtney, 1999, 2000, 2001, 2002, 2004, F7805–F7809, F8793–F8802

Likenesses group portrait, photograph, *c*.1916, priv. coll. · J. Siegieda, bromide print, 1978, NPG · S. Pyke, bromide fibre print, 1984, NPG · J. Bown, photographs, 2003, Camera Press, London · obituary photographs

Wealth at death £491,211: probate, 27 Jan 2006, *CGPLA Eng. & Wales*

Spriggs [*née* Williams], **Elizabeth Jean** (1929–2008), actress, was born at Ivy Cottage, Torr Street, Buxton, Derbyshire, on 18 September 1929, the second of four children of Arthur Lovell Williams (1907–1992), a journeyman joiner, later a master builder and farmer, and his wife, Laura May, *née* Potts (1907–1984). She was educated at Wheatley Street High School for Girls in Coventry, and studied opera at the Royal School of Music. She said that she 'grew up entirely without affection' (*Daily Mail*, 12 Dec 1994), although her parents were open minded about whether or not she should pursue a career in music (she had a strong mezzo-soprano voice), as an actress, or as a painter. Bronchial asthma prevented her from becoming a singer, so she went on to teach music and drama at Coventry Technical College. She married on 3 March 1951 at Green Lane Methodist Church, Coventry, Kenneth Spriggs (*b.* 1925), a local government officer, and son of Charles Spriggs, tool maker. They had one daughter, Wendy.

From an early age Elizabeth Spriggs had been passionate about acting. As a teacher she found no satisfaction—'I felt as if I was dying inside. The desire to act was like a weight within me, and I knew if I didn't do anything it would destroy me' (*Daily Mail*, 12 Dec 1994). She then made what she said was 'the most painful decision' of her life, and left her husband and two-year-old daughter to pursue her dream. At this time she was a member of a local amateur theatre group and she wrote to the theatre in Stockport, asking if they had any jobs. She was taken on, and when she first stood on a professional stage it was with a feeling of elation—'I am home, I am never going to leave' (ibid.). From Stockport she went to the Grand Theatre in Halifax, the Bristol Old Vic, and in 1954 the prestigious Birmingham Repertory Theatre, under the aegis of Sir Barry Jackson. She stayed at Birmingham for several seasons, graduating to challenging leading roles such as Cleopatra in *Antony and Cleopatra* and Madame Ranevsky in *The Cherry Orchard*.

In 1962 Spriggs joined the Royal Shakespeare Company in Stratford upon Avon, founded by Peter Hall two years earlier. Initially she experienced some frustration at the amount of understudying, but she was patient, and stayed with the company for ten years. Her early roles included Mrs Vixen in Peter Wood's convict-ship production of *The Beggar's Opera*, an asylum inmate in Peter Weiss's *Marat/Sade*, and a courtesan in *Comedy of Errors*. Eventually more significant roles came her way, starting with an acclaimed Gertrude to David Warner's student Hamlet (1965), in

Peter Hall's revelatory production. Her Gertrude was blowsy and morally weak, and she was, wrote J. C. Trewin, 'among the best in living memory, a shallow woman terrified by the pressure of events she could not comprehend' (Trewin, 134–5). As she moved between Stratford and the company's London base at the Aldwych Theatre her other parts included Mistress Quickly, the Nurse, and Mistress Ford, all of which revealed 'her gift for earthy comedy' (*The Independent*, 5 July 2008). Then, in 1969, she had a wonderful opportunity which she grabbed with relish. As Claire, the alcoholic sister of Agnes, played by Peggy Ashcroft, in Edward Albee's *A Delicate Balance*, she gave a blazing performance, full of pathos and understanding, and won the Clarence Derwent award as best supporting actress. Before then she had appeared at Stratford as a heartfelt Emilia in John Barton's colonialist *Othello*, and, at last given the chance in a leading role, a warm and witty Beatrice, opposite Derek Godfrey's Benedick. Her Beatrice was, according to the *New Statesman*'s critic, Benedict Nightingale, 'a sunny, complacent, busy lady, the sort anyone would approach if a concert party had to be arranged or an invalid visited' who 'rediscovered a capacity for love she had long since laid aside'.

In 1970, now a key player with the company, Spriggs was Paulina in *The Winter's Tale*, Maria in *Twelfth Night*, and Lady Britomart in *Major Barbara*, and scored a particular success as the splendidly named Lady Gay Spanker in Ronald Eyre's gleeful rediscovery of Dion Boucicault's Victorian comedy *London Assurance*. Her riding-whip-wielding Lady Gay, like a hunt in full cry, was a brilliant comic creation, and when the play transferred triumphantly to Broadway in 1974 she received Tony and Drama Desk award nominations as best supporting actress.

When Hall took over from Laurence Olivier as the artistic director of the National Theatre in 1973 Spriggs found a London base at last, and performed regularly with the company over the next few years. She was a delightfully brisk Madame Arcati in Noël Coward's *Blithe Spirit* (1976), directed by Harold Pinter; appeared in a brilliant double-act with John Gielgud, as Sir Politick and Lady Would-Be, in *Volpone* (1977); was 'gloriously lubricious' (*The Independent*, 5 July 2008) as Lady Fidget in *The Country Wife* (also 1977); and then gave one of her most moving performances, in a role she had previously played on television, as the stoical wife of Michael Gough's dying trade unionist in Arnold Wesker's *Love Letters on Blue Paper* (1978), for which she won the best supporting actress award from the Society of West End Theatres.

From the early 1970s Spriggs had been heavily in demand for television work, making notable appearances in such plays as Colin Welland's *Leeds United!* (1974) and Alan Bennett's *Our Winnie* (1982). She appeared in many costume dramas, including adaptations of *Middlemarch* and *Wives and Daughters*. She excelled as Inge Middleton in Angus Wilson's *Anglo-Saxon Attitudes*, as the gin-soaked midwife Sairey Gamp in *Martin Chuzzlewit*, and as the God-fearing gossip in *Oranges Are Not the Only Fruit*. Other television roles included countless appearances in such popular series as *Doctor Who*, *Poirot*, *Midsomer Murders*, *Lovejoy*, and *Sherlock Holmes*, and as P. G. Wodehouse's formidable Aunt Agatha in *Jeeves and Wooster*, a part Spriggs seemed born to play. Her greatest popular television successes were in two long-running series, as Connie Fox, the matriarch of a south London gang family, in *Fox* (1980), and as Harvey Moon's warm-hearted but tough old mum in *Shine on Harvey Moon* (1982–5 and 1995). Her feature film début came in *Work is a Four-Letter Word* (1968), directed by Peter Hall, but the opportunities she had on film were few. Her performance as the uproariously blunt Mrs Jennings in *Sense and Sensibility* (1995) showed what the cinema had neglected. In her later years her television work kept her away from the stage, although she had one more great success, in Ronald Eyre's revival of J. B. Priestley's *When We Are Married* (1986), more than holding her own in a brilliant cast that included Bill Fraser, Patricia Hayes, Prunella Scales, and Patricia Routledge.

'A large, jolly woman with an ample bosom and twinkling eyes' (*The Times*, 7 July 2008), Elizabeth Spriggs was superb in comic roles, but also had great reserves of emotion and warmth. Her performances had 'fresh air' (*The Guardian*, 7 July 2008). Her first marriage, to Kenneth Spriggs, ended in divorce. On 4 June 1965 she married Michael Waterman Jones (1928–2007), a fellow Royal Shakespeare Company actor and son of Charles Waterman Jones, process operator, but that marriage also ended in divorce. On 27 July 1977 she married (John) Murray Manson (*b.* 1944), a guitarist, and son of William Myles Manson, a ship's stockbroker. They had met in 1972, when he was working as a minicab driver and Spriggs was playing her unforgettable Lady Gay Spanker. She died in Oxford on 2 July 2008, and was survived by him and by her daughter, Wendy. ALEX JENNINGS

Sources B. Nightingale, 'The RSC ascendant', *Theatre 72*, ed. S. Morley (1972), 63–75 · J. C. Trewin, *Five and eighty Hamlets* (1987) · *Daily Mail* (12 Dec 1994) · *Daily Telegraph* (4 July 2008) · *The Independent* (5 July 2008) · *The Times* (7 July 2008) · *The Guardian* (7 July 2008) · *The Stage* (11 July 2008) · *WW* (2008) · personal knowledge (2012) · private information (2012) · b. cert. · m. certs.

Archives FILM BFINA, performance footage | SOUND BL NSA, performance recordings

Likenesses photographs, 1980–2007, Rex Features, London · photographs, 1994–2001, PA Photos, London · J. Watson, group portrait, photograph, Camera Press, London · obituary photographs · photographs, Photoshot, London

Wealth at death £311,053: probate, 3 Feb 2009, *CGPLA Eng. & Wales*

Stammers, Katharine Esther [Kay] (1914–2005), tennis player, was born on 3 April 1914 at 31 Glenferrie Road, St Albans, Hertfordshire, the only child of Hubert Charles Stammers, insurance clerk, and his wife, Alice Louise, *née* Curchod. She was educated at St Albans High School for Girls. Stammers learned to play tennis on a grass court at home after her parents moved to Wood Walk, in Sandpit Lane, St Albans. She developed into a talented and attacking left hander, and reached the final of the British junior championships in 1931. She made her Wimbledon début that year, from the qualifying competition, and took four games from Dorothy Round in their first round match. The following year she reached the fourth round at

Katharine Esther Stammers (1914–2005), by Bassano, 1935

Wimbledon, and won the Surrey hard court championship at Roehampton. By 1934 she had risen to third in the Lawn Tennis Association rankings, and in 1935 she scored a notable victory over Helen Wills Moody in the Kent championships at Beckenham. That year she won the women's doubles at Roland Garros in Paris with Margaret Scriven, and at Wimbledon with Freda James: they enjoyed 'a scintillating victory in the final against the formidable combination of [Simone] Mathieu and [Hilde] Sperling', 6–1 6–4 (Macaulay and Smyth, 107). The following year, 1936, Stammers and James successfully defended their Wimbledon title against Sarah Fabyan and Helen Jacobs, 6–2 6–1.

The Wimbledon doubles victories, coupled with appearances in the American championships and the Wightman cup, made Stammers known on both sides of the Atlantic. She was an exciting and popular player, with an indefinable physical grace, and attracted attention as much for her looks as for her tennis. The Wightman cup was a society event, and the British and American press enjoyed the spectacle offered by the annual exchange of athletic young women between the two countries. One British journalist wrote in 1939: 'Our six Wightman Cup girls, who start for America next Wednesday, are good lookers. For shorts, morning costume or evening dress, they will win admiration anywhere' (*St Louis Post-Dispatch*). A New York reporter greeted 'Kutey Kay Stammers and Co.' with less restraint: 'Gentlemen … We're not a glamour agent for these British beauties, but we think we ought to let you in on the fact that they're all knockouts' (ibid.). On one visit to America Stammers caught the eye of the young John F. Kennedy and she was his guest at Hyannis Port: she thought him 'divine' and a 'terrific catch', but recognized that he could, and would, play the field (*The Times*, 27 Dec 2005).

Although the Americans won the Wightman cup every year from 1931 to 1939 the British women offered real competition, and none more so than Stammers. In 1935 she won a hard-fought victory over Helen Jacobs, 5–7 6–1 9–7, and in 1938 she defeated the top-ranked American Alice Marble. The pair met again the following year in what is regarded as an era-defining Wimbledon final. Stammers, the British number one, was in top form, but Marble played brilliantly to win 6–2 6–0 in thirty minutes. Stammers 'actually hit more winning shots than she conceded errors', but she could not counter Marble's serve and volley game (Davidson and Jones, 53). The American did not drop a set in the singles that year and, fittingly, won the triple crown. Her victory foreshadowed the complete American dominance of the post-war era, with its greater emphasis on power and athleticism.

After the outbreak of the Second World War Stammers's tennis was largely confined to charity exhibition matches, in which she had appeared regularly before the war. On 24 January 1940 she married Michael Menzies, an officer in the Welsh Guards, at the parish church of St Peter, Pimlico; the bride 'wore a gown of oyster-pink satin, made on close fitting lines' (*The Times*, 25 Jan 1940). The couple had a daughter and two sons. The first child was born in 1943, but Stammers returned to tennis within a year, and in the first post-war Wimbledon, in 1946, she reached the quarter-final of the singles and the semi-final of the women's doubles, a feat that she repeated in 1947. She also played in the Wightman cup. The British were relatively confident of their 1946 selection, but were whitewashed that year and the next, and Stammers later reflected on dispiriting times:

> There we were, rather emaciated married women and mothers. The reason why we had to struggle away was because there was nobody in England coming on … It was hard work. I'm afraid by that time the American girls were very much better than we were. They played a stronger game. (Wade and Rafferty, 79)

Peter Ustinov, a tennis aficionado, once named Kay Stammers as his favourite woman player: 'So beautiful, so elegant, so delicate, such a fragile English rose. She never won anything, of course, but she always lost so gracefully' (*Daily Mail*, 3 June 1998). In fact Stammers was tougher and more successful than her looks allowed. She won two Wimbledon titles and one French; defeated both Helens—Wills Moody and Jacobs—and Dorothy Round; and reached the quarter- or the semi-final of the American championships every year between 1934 and 1939. It is a testimony to her fortitude that in August 1939, weeks after losing so heavily to Alice Marble at Wimbledon, she won a 'tremendous battle' against the American Dorothy Bundy in a quarter-final encounter in the eastern grass court championships, resurrecting her game at the end of the second set to win 10–8 0–6 8–6 (*The Times*, 11 Aug 1939).

Stammers was fun-loving and enjoyed society, but if she never quite fulfilled her undoubted potential she had to contend with the lack of resources and often inclement weather that afflicted the English game: 'we all had Dan Maskell at Wimbledon as our coach, for an hour or two twice a week. Half the time you'd go plodding down there and there'd be frost on the court or it'd be raining. It was quite hard work just getting the practice' (Wade and Rafferty, 72).

Stammers captained the British team in 1948 and 1949, but by then she was edging towards retirement. In 1951 her husband took up a post with Hill Samuel in Johannesburg, and the family lived there until, in March 1968, Menzies was transferred to New York. The couple divorced in 1974 and the following year Stammers married the American lawyer Thomas Walker Bullitt, whom she had met on the American tennis circuit. They lived at the Bullitt family home at Oxmoor Farm, near Louisville, Kentucky, where Stammers created an English garden, and involved herself in charity work. She continued to live at Oxmoor after her husband's death in 1991, and attended Wimbledon annually until she could no longer travel. She died on 23 December 2005. She was survived by her three children. MARK POTTLE

Sources *Wimbledon who's who* (1934) • *The Times* (11 April 1938); (11 Aug 1939); (14 Aug 1939); (25 Jan 1940); (29 April 1940); (9 June 1944); (6 April 1946); (4 Sept 1946); (8 Dec 1967); (16 May 1990); (27 Dec 2005) • *Time* (26 Aug 1935); (9 Sept 1935); (14 Sept 1936); (30 Aug 1937); (20 June 1938); (17 July 1939); (15 July 1946) • A. D. C. Macaulay and J. Smyth, *Behind the scenes at Wimbledon* (1965) • O. Davidson and C. M. Jones, *Great women tennis players* (1971) • A. Little and L. Tingay, *Wimbledon ladies: a centenary record, 1884–1984, the single champions* (1984) • V. Wade and J. Rafferty, *Ladies of the court: a century of women at Wimbledon* (1984) • *St Louis Post-Dispatch* [Missouri] (3 Feb 1939) • *Daily Mail* (3 June 1998) • *Daily Telegraph* (30 Dec 2005) • b. cert. • m. cert. [1940]

Archives FILM BFINA, news footage

Likenesses photographs, 1931–46, Getty Images, London • Bassano, vintage print, 1935, NPG [*see illus.*] • H. Tomlin, photograph, 1936, *Daily Herald*, NPG • Bassano, vintage print, 1938, NPG • obituary photographs

Stanier, Sir John Wilfred (1925–2007), army officer, was born at Little Eden, The Heath, Hatfield Broad Oak, Essex, on 6 October 1925, the son of Harold Allan Stanier (1897–1932) and his wife, Penelope Rose, *née* Price (1896–1974). His father, badly wounded in the First World War, managed the farming interests of John Spedan Lewis, the founder of the John Lewis Partnership, at Stockbridge in Hampshire. Stanier was educated at Marlborough College. As a boy he suffered problems with his feet, being told by a consultant that his arches had collapsed and that he would never be able to run. While at Marlborough he was introduced to a Swedish chiropractor who gave him a three-month treatment that, although extremely painful, had the desired effect. By the end of the treatment he could run without pain, going on to captain the second rugby fifteen.

On leaving school Stanier took up a short wartime place at Merton College, Oxford, before volunteering for the army in 1943. Following training at the Royal Military Academy, Sandhurst, and at the Royal Tank Corps school, Bovington, he was commissioned into the 7th Queen's Own hussars in 1946. On joining his regiment in Italy, he attended courts martial of former members of the SS, and witnessed several executions; a traumatic experience, he observed later. Following a home posting he returned to Trieste in Italy, where he served as a general staff officer grade 3 in the intelligence branch. He then rejoined his regiment serving in Germany, before a posting as an instructor at the Mons officer cadet training unit at Aldershot. On 19 November 1955, at the parish church in Danbury, Essex, he married Cicely Constance Lambert (*b.* 1930), daughter of Denis Malet Lambert, fruit farmer, of Manor Farm, Danbury. They had four daughters.

Stanier served with his regiment in Hong Kong before taking up a place at the Staff College, Camberley. Following graduation in 1957, he was appointed to the War Office as military assistant to the vice-chief of the imperial general staff. It was in this post that he first saw the cut and thrust of life in Whitehall, at a time when Britain's defence effort was evolving from post-imperial commitments to NATO deterrence on the central front in West Germany. The experience he gained was invaluable to his later career. During this tour he also demonstrated his formidable character. The vice-chief, Sir William Stratton, a Catholic, having written a critical report of a subordinate who had recently been divorced, was told directly by Stanier that he felt the comments to be unfair, being based on religious rather than military logic. 'When you are VCIGS ... I will ask your opinion' replied Stratton. Despite this rebuke it is clear that Stanier's first appointment at the ministry had been a success, since he was appointed MBE at its conclusion. In 1978, when he became vice-chief of the general staff, Stratton wrote to congratulate him. 'Now ... you may give me your opinion', he added (private information).

Stanier returned to his regiment in 1962 to command C squadron, 7th Queen's Own hussars, in Germany. Promoted lieutenant-colonel in 1963, he returned to Camberley as a member of the directing staff. Five years earlier his regiment had been amalgamated with the 3rd King's Royal hussars, and it was a considerable disappointment to him that he was not selected to command the regiment. He resolved to leave the army, and applied, albeit unsuccessfully, for the vacant post of defence correspondent of *The Times*. In the event he was selected to command the Royal Scots Greys in 1966. Through this association in due course he met Tam Dalyell, who had served as a national serviceman in the Scots Greys in the early 1950s. Dalyell recalled that Stainer's arrival as commanding officer 'created a seismic shock throughout the regiment'. He described him as 'ferocious', observing with gentle amusement 'the awe in which mature ex-officers regarded' him and the respect he was afforded by successive regimental sergeant-majors and in the sergeants' mess (*The Independent*, 14 Nov 2007). Stanier himself said that his period of command of the regiment was one of the most challenging and rewarding periods of his life.

In 1968 Stanier attended the Imperial Defence College,

and the following year he assumed command of 20th armoured brigade in Germany. This was followed by a return to the Ministry of Defence as director of public relations (army), where his plain talking and humour found its mark with journalists and reporters alike. Later, in 1997, he wrote a book with Miles Hudson as joint author, entitled *War and the Media*, covering the relationship between the media and the military, from the Crimea to the 1990s.

Meanwhile, in 1973 Stanier was promoted major-general and, as general officer commanding 1st armoured division, made an important contribution to the restructuring of the 1st British corps in Germany, a consequence of the 1975–6 defence review. His next appointment was as commandant of the Army Staff College, a role to which his forceful intellect, charisma, and energy were ideally suited. As commandant he led a delegation to the Frunze Military Academy in Moscow, the first visit of its kind. It was during this visit that he told the Russians that it was the British army's fate invariably to 'attack uphill … and along the join between two maps' (private information).

In 1978 Stanier was promoted lieutenant-general on appointment as vice-chief of the general staff, overseeing the army's equipment programme and readjustments to some of the less successful changes following the earlier defence review (for example the replacement of the brigade level of command by a 'field force'). In 1981, in the rank of general, he was appointed commander-in-chief, United Kingdom land forces, and in 1982 he oversaw the preparation and deployment of the land element of the South Atlantic task force during the Falklands War. His last active appointment was as chief of the general staff, a post he assumed in the autumn of 1982. His tenure coincided with a period of retrenchment following the Falklands War, but was also a time when he fiercely fought the army's corner in order to obtain the next generation of equipment, including the Challenger 2 main battle tank. He was promoted field marshal in 1985 on his last day in office as chief of the general staff.

In retirement Stanier frequently wrote letters to national newspapers on a range of subjects (for example dealing with terrorism, and the Iraq war of 2003, which he opposed), and was chairman of the Royal United Services Institution (1986–9), and constable of the Tower of London (1990–96). He listed his recreations in *Who's Who* as 'fishing, sailing, talking', and he was active in local affairs in Hampshire, where he lived. He served as aide-de-camp to the queen (1981–5) and was appointed KCB (1978), GCB (1982), and a deputy lieutenant of Hampshire (1987). He also served as colonel of the Royal Scots dragoon guards (1979–84) and colonel commandant of the Royal Armoured Corps (1982–5).

Stanier was a forceful and charismatic officer, with a sharp intellect and a sense of humour to match. He always spoke his mind, was never likely to suffer fools, and was capable of instilling fear among those around him when he deemed it necessary. He stirred strong emotions among those officers and soldiers who knew or served with him, but he was certainly respected by many. He died at his home, the Old Farmhouse, Hazeley Bottom, Hartley Wintney, Hampshire, on 10 November 2007, of cancer, and was survived by his wife and their four daughters. A memorial service was held at the Guards' Chapel, Wellington Barracks, London, on 10 April 2008.

SIMON DOUGHTY

Sources *The Times* (13 Nov 2007) · *Daily Telegraph* (13 Nov 2007) · *The Independent* (14 Nov 2007) · *Army List* · Burke, *Peerage* · *WW* (2007) · personal knowledge (2011) · private information (2011) · b. cert. · m. cert. · d. cert.

Likenesses obituary photographs · portrait, Cavalry and Guards Club, London

Wealth at death £374,363: probate, 11 Feb 2009, *CGPLA Eng. & Wales*

Stewart, Lorn Alastair [Johnnie] (1917–2005), television producer, was born at 3 Yardley Park Road, Tonbridge, Kent, on 7 November 1917, the only son of Haldane Campbell Stewart (1868–1942), director of music at Tonbridge School, and later choirmaster and organist at Magdalen College, Oxford, and his wife, Elinor Dorothy, *née* Hunt. His elder sister Jean Stewart (1914–2002) was a distinguished viola player. As a young boy he learned to play the piano, and in 1937, after leaving school, he joined the sound effects department of BBC radio drama. During the Second World War he served as a wireless operator in the Middle East and worked in intelligence. On demobilization he returned to the BBC, initially as a programme engineer. On 6 April 1946 he married Sheila Mary Williamson, the 24-year-old daughter of Frank Williamson, shipbroker. They had a daughter, Judith. The marriage later ended in divorce.

At the BBC Stewart progressed up the hierarchy and was able to indulge his interest in new music. He produced music programmes that included *Sing It Again* and *BBC Jazz Club*, and secured Frank Sinatra for Cyril Stapleton's *Show Band Show* for a mere £50. In 1958 he transferred to BBC television and produced *Juke Box Jury*, hosted by David Jacobs. The disc jockey Jimmy Savile hosted the popular *Teen and Twenty Disc Club* on Radio Luxembourg, and in 1963 the BBC producer Barney Colehan recorded a pilot for television. After discussion it became a chart show, produced by Johnnie Stewart, who named it *Top of the Pops*. The first programme was broadcast on new year's day 1964, with Savile as host. Because of the explosion of British beat groups, the charts were filled with home product and Stewart was confident of success.

At first *Top of the Pops* was broadcast from a converted church in Dickinson Road, Manchester. For three years Stewart used four presenters, alternating Savile, Alan Freeman, Pete Murray, and David Jacobs. Stewart devised simple rules: the programme would always end with the number one record, which was the only record that could be repeated from the previous week. He included the highest new entry and the highest climber and nothing going down was included. Quality was not the issue: the record-buyers determined the content, although Stewart did include a 'Tip for the Top'. Stewart's only mistake was not to archive all the programmes. Harry Goodwin's still photographs were used in the chart rundowns, and he shot the silhouette of Stewart that ended each programme, though many assumed that the still was of Billy Fury. The programme was screened at peak time and, although aimed at the young, it attracted a family audience spanning the generations. In a brilliant move Stewart created a popular female dance troupe, which became Pan's People. The audience was also an important ingredient of *Top of the Pops*. The hysterical screaming was genuine. As Stewart put it, '*Top of the Pops* was the simplest show in the world and also pure murder on the ears' (*Music Week*, 28 Jan 1995). Initially all records were mimed. The Musicians' Union felt that asking artists to mime was depriving their members of work, but Stewart argued that many acts could not create the same sound live. In the end Johnny Pearson formed a Top of the Pops orchestra with experienced session musicians.

Stewart sometimes felt antipathy towards the music he was promoting. In 1965, after the Small Faces had appeared on *Top of the Pops*, Stewart thanked them politely. Their leader, Steve Marriott, felt insulted by Stewart's patronizing comments, and as a consequence of Marriott's rude response Stewart broke his own rules so that the Small Faces could never play *Top of the Pops* again. Presenting the show from Manchester created problems as many of the bigger acts did not want to travel. In 1967 *Top of the Pops* moved to the Lime Grove Studios in west London. The new presenters included Stuart Henry, 'Emperor' Rosko, Simon Dee, and Kenny Everett, who were all connected with BBC Radio 1. John Peel made such a mess of presenting a programme in 1968 that Stewart told him he would never work on TV again. Later, after Stewart had moved on, Peel proved to be a witty and sardonic host. Stewart started the *Top of the Pops* review of the year, the first of which was broadcast before the queen's speech on Christmas day 1967. He also produced Alan Freeman's magazine show *All Systems Freeman*.

Stewart was given a year's sabbatical in 1971 and went to North America. His set designer, Stanley Dorfman, took over as producer of *Top of the Pops* and amended Stewart's rules, adding an LP spot, which one week included a ten-minute piece by Yes. Stewart returned and reinstated the original concept. His return coincided with another wave of home-grown British talent, with the 'glam rock' of Slade and T. Rex doing well. The presenters now included Noel Edmonds, Dave Lee Travis, and Tony Blackburn.

Stewart left *Top of the Pops* in 1974. In 1978 he produced the pop quiz *Cheggers Plays Pop* with Keith Chegwin. He then worked in South Africa on a local version of *Top of the Pops*. He retired to Ibiza but returned to the UK when his health deteriorated, living latterly at Dorrington House residential nursing home, Quebec Road, Dereham, Norfolk. He died there on 30 April 2005 of bronchopneumonia and severe peripheral vascular disease. He was survived by his daughter, Judith. *Top of the Pops* outlived him, finally being taken off the air in 2006.

SPENCER LEIGH

Sources *The Independent* (4 May 2005) · *The Times* (5 May 2005) · *Daily Post* [Liverpool] (5 May 2005) · *The Guardian* (6 May 2005) · personal knowledge (2009) · private information (2009) · b. cert. · m. cert. · d. cert.

Likenesses double portrait, photograph, 1960 (with Humphrey Lyttelton), Getty Images, London · H. Goodwin, photographs, priv. coll. · obituary photographs

Wealth at death under £229,000: probate, 17 June 2005, *CGPLA Eng. & Wales*

Stewart, (Atwell) Roy (1925–2008), actor and businessman, was born in Jamaica on 15 May 1925. He arrived in Liverpool on 2 October 1948 on the *Orbita*, just a few months after the *Empire Windrush* docked at Tilbury with the first wave of post-war settlers from the Caribbean. He entered his profession on the passenger list as 'electrician'. Planning to be a doctor, he was drawn into the world of theatre, working as a bit player in several stage productions. When he discovered that white stuntmen were 'blacking up' because of the lack of black stuntmen, he offered his services. Realizing he needed to build up his physique, in 1954 he opened a gymnasium bearing his name in Powis Square, Kensington, west London. A number of actors used Stewart's gym, including Sean Connery and Dave Prowse, who became a close friend and later found fame as Darth Vader in the film *Star Wars*. Stewart also gave advice to another client, Arnold Schwarzenegger, when he was preparing for the Mr Universe competition in London.

In addition to running his gym, Stewart opened The Globe, a popular Caribbean restaurant in Bayswater where his many famous patrons included Jimi Hendrix, Bob Marley, Van Morrison, and Bono. He also continued his acting career. During the 1960s and 1970s his television appearances included small roles in a number of popular drama series such as *Out of the Unknown* (1965), *Adam Adamant Lives!* (1967), *The Avengers* (1968), *Doomwatch* (1970), *The Troubleshooters* (1970), and *I, Claudius* (1976). However, the names of his characters reveal the limitations imposed on him: 'bodyguard', 'weightlifter', 'guard', 'muscle man', 'security man', and 'slave'.

Stewart's appearances in two *Doctor Who* stories earned him a place in the history of the cult favourite as one of the few black actors to appear in the first two decades of the series. In *The Tomb of the Cybermen* (1967) he appeared as the physically imposing but silent servant Toberman. His fight with a Cyberman ended with his death, and complaints from sensitive viewers who found the confrontation too graphic. This was followed four years later by his role as the circus strongman who fights the Doctor (Jon Pertwee) in *Terror of the Autons* (1971). Though Stewart's contribution to the success of the series was minor, the actor Fraser James later argued that it was groundbreaking, for three reasons: first that it was a breakthrough that black actors were working in the series at all, second that he was playing key roles and was not just in the background, and third that it was important at that time for black audiences in Britain to see representations of themselves in a popular television series seen by millions of viewers (*Race against Time*, BBC TV, 2010).

In films Stewart made an early appearance in Zoltan

Korda's *Storm over the Nile* (1955), but it was not until the 1960s that more regular film work came his way. He had small roles in exotic adventure dramas such as *She* (1965), and in comedies such as *Carry On up the Jungle* (1970). He also appeared in John Boorman's art house success *Leo the Last* (1970) and Charlton Heston's *Julius Caesar* (1970). More interesting were his roles in Jean-Luc Godard's film *Sympathy for the Devil* (1968), in which his scenes as a black power activist were intercut with footage of the rock group the Rolling Stones in rehearsal, and *Lady Caroline Lamb* (1972), in which his role as the Black Pug—who fights with Lord Byron (played by Richard Chamberlain)—acknowledged the existence of black boxers in Britain in the early part of the nineteenth century. A year later he appeared in Roger Moore's first James Bond film, *Live and Let Die* (1973). He played Quarrel jun., the son of Quarrel (John Kitzmiller), who was prominently featured in the first Bond movie, *Dr No* (1962).

Stewart retired from acting in the early 1980s, but continued to run The Globe until he died at his home, 86 Moreland Court, Church Walk, Golders Green, London, on 27 October 2008 from coronary heart disease. He was survived by two daughters. STEPHEN BOURNE

Sources *The Guardian* (4 Feb 2009) · www.itzcaribbean.com/roystewart.php, 10 Nov 2011 · www.imdb.com/name/nm0829796/, 10 Nov 2011 · UK incoming passenger lists, 1878–1960 · d. cert.
Archives FILM BFINA, performance footage
Likenesses photographs, repro. in www.itzcaribbean.com/roystewart.php

Donald Gresham Stokes, Baron Stokes (1914–2008), by unknown photographer

Stokes, Donald Gresham, Baron Stokes (1914–2008), industrialist, was born on 22 March 1914 at Lowood, Freta Road, Bexleyheath, Kent, the son of Harry Potts Stokes and his wife, Marie Elizabeth Gresham, *née* Yates. His father was an electrical engineer who ran the Bexley and Dartford tramway and electricity department and later the Plymouth Corporation tramways department.

Early career at Leyland Motors After education at Blundell's School in Devon, Stokes took up an engineering apprenticeship at Leyland Motors, a truck and bus manufacturer based in Lancashire; his training included a period at the Harris Institute of Technology in Preston. On 25 May 1939 he married Laura Elizabeth Courtenay Lamb (1915–1995), daughter of Frederick Courtenay Lamb, merchant; they had one son. He joined the Royal North Lancashire regiment in 1938 and spent the duration of the Second World War in the Royal Electrical and Mechanical Engineers. He ended it as a lieutenant-colonel and assistant director of mechanical engineering (technical), central Mediterranean forces.

Returning to Leyland after the war, Stokes was appointed export manager in 1946 and later general sales manager. In these posts he won a reputation as one of Britain's outstanding overseas salesmen. A notable coup was the sale of 620 buses to Cuba in 1964 at a time when the USA had imposed an embargo on trade with that country and was encouraging other countries to follow suit. The American government was irritated by the Leyland order, but Stokes was unrepentant. 'This is an English company doing a deal with Cuba,' he said; 'I have no knowledge of having to go to America for permission to sell buses' (*Time*, 17 Jan 1964). In 1965 he was asked by Denis Healey, minister of defence in the Labour government, to advise on how to improve the sale of British defence equipment overseas. He was knighted at the end of that year for services to export.

Stokes had joined the board of Leyland in 1954, and, together with Henry Spurrier, the chairman, and Stanley Markland, who was responsible for production and engineering, was part of the team that oversaw a rapid expansion of the company. The purchase of Albion, Scammell, and later AEC made Leyland the dominant British manufacturer of heavy trucks and buses, and in 1961 Spurrier took the fateful decision to enter the car business. Believing that Leyland was at a disadvantage in overseas markets because, unlike Mercedes in Germany, it did not offer cars as well as trucks, he acquired Standard-Triumph, the smallest of the 'big five' car manufacturers. (The others were the British Motor Corporation, Ford, Vauxhall, and Rootes.) Markland was made managing director of the new subsidiary, with Stokes as sales director. At the end of 1962 Spurrier fell seriously ill. He was succeeded as chairman by William Black, and the post of deputy chairman and managing director went to Stokes. Markland, who had been regarded as Spurrier's heir apparent, resigned from the company soon after this change. Stokes took on the additional title of chairman after Black's retirement in 1967.

Stokes now had personal responsibility for a federation of car and truck companies, each of which was run as a largely autonomous business. Yet Leyland was still substantially smaller than its principal overseas competitors even after these acquisitions, and Stokes looked for ways of enlarging the group. One possibility was to join forces with the British Motor Corporation (BMC). This company, the product of an earlier merger between Austin and Morris, was the biggest British-owned car manufacturer; it also made light trucks and vans that complemented Leyland's range. In 1964 Stokes had informal discussions with his BMC counterpart, Sir George Harriman, but at that time BMC's profits were much higher than Leyland's, and no agreement could be reached on the financial terms of a merger. The talks were resumed in 1966, but were discontinued when BMC made a separate agreement to buy Jaguar, a profitable manufacturer of luxury cars. Stokes had also had his eye on Jaguar, and his response to the BMC deal was to buy the Rover Company, which, like Jaguar, competed at the expensive end of the market; it also had a successful cross-country vehicle, the Land Rover.

These mergers came at a time when the Labour government was taking a close interest in the motor industry's affairs. The government, led by Harold Wilson, had been elected in 1964 on a manifesto that promised vigorous action to modernize British industry. As part of this programme, a new agency, the Industrial Reorganization Corporation (IRC), was set up to promote mergers in industries that were deemed to be too fragmented to compete effectively in world markets. Both Wilson and his minister of technology, Anthony Wedgwood Benn, believed that the motor industry urgently needed rationalization. Having reluctantly approved the takeover of Rootes by Chrysler of the USA, they were determined to create a strong British-owned national champion. In the government's view, the best way of achieving this was through a merger between Leyland and what was now called, following the Jaguar deal, British Motor Holdings (BMH).

With the IRC acting as matchmaker, Stokes and Harriman entered into a tortuous and often acrimonious negotiation which lasted for most of 1967. One of the main sticking points was the question of who would run the enlarged group. The IRC's view and that of the government was that Stokes, on the basis of his record at Leyland and at Standard-Triumph (which had been partially revived under Leyland's ownership), was the only credible candidate. This was fiercely resisted by Harriman and his colleagues, but their bargaining power was undermined by BMH's deteriorating financial position. The Austin and Morris operations had never been properly integrated, and, despite the success of the Mini and the 1100/1300, BMH was losing market share to Ford. Leyland was now the stronger partner, at least in financial terms, and the deal that was finally announced in April 1968 was effectively a takeover of BMH by Leyland. Harriman and several of his senior colleagues resigned soon after the new company, British Leyland Motor Corporation, was established.

Chairman of British Leyland British Leyland had 180,000 employees, forty-eight factories, and nine car marques; its annual output of vehicles was exceeded only by the three big American manufacturers (General Motors, Ford, and Chrysler) and by Volkswagen in Germany. The hope was that Stokes and his team would rectify the management weaknesses of BMH and achieve the economies of scale that would enable British Leyland to compete profitably in the world market. But the size of the task was grossly underestimated by the politicians—and by Stokes himself. The two merging companies had been created out of earlier acquisitions which had not been properly digested. The old BMC, as well as the smaller car makers, had been run by dominant leaders on the basis of intuition and practical experience, without the systems and disciplines in manufacturing, engineering, and product development that characterized professionally run companies such as Ford. To make matters worse, the factories, especially those located in the midlands, suffered from anarchic labour relations, with production constantly disrupted by strikes.

As chairman and managing director of the new company, Stokes had a huge weight of responsibility on his shoulders. He was widely admired as one of the country's most dynamic managers—he was given a life peerage in 1969—but he had no experience of running a company as large and complex as British Leyland. His involvement in cars had been confined to the relatively low-volume operations of Standard-Triumph and Rover. The problems faced by what was now called the Austin Morris division, competing against Ford and General Motors in the mass market, were of an entirely different order. If British Leyland was to fulfil the government's goals, Stokes needed to make rapid progress on three fronts: the development of a competitive range of cars for each of the market segments in which it was operating; a reform of the labour relations system; and, most important of all, the creation of a coherent organization in which the responsibilities of the head office and the operating subsidiaries were clearly defined.

The Mini and the 1100/1300, conceived by BMC's innovative designer Alec Issigonis, were based on front-wheel-drive technology. The next member of this family, the Maxi, was launched shortly after the merger, and plans for the 1100/1300 replacement, the Allegro, were well advanced. Stokes decided to continue with this programme, but at the same time to develop a range of rear-wheel-drive cars, sold under the Morris name, which would compete directly against Ford. The effect was to spread the Austin Morris division's meagre engineering resources over two separate families, neither of which came up to expectations. The Morris Marina never came near to catching up with the Ford Cortina, and the Austin Allegro was 'stylistically and mechanically inferior to the 1100/1300 series it had been created to replace, shortcomings that were compounded by a deterioration in corporate build quality' (Wood, 193). John Barber, a former Ford executive who was appointed director of product planning and finance shortly after the merger, thought it was a mistake to launch a frontal attack on Ford. He wanted to move Austin and Morris upmarket in quality and styling, drawing on the skills of the specialist car companies, even at the cost of some loss of volume. But that would have required extensive rationalization, including factory closures, a course that Stokes was determined to avoid. He was well aware that even the threat of closure might provoke official or unofficial strikes, which would disrupt production and cripple large parts of the business. Stokes, an optimist by nature, believed that he could keep the existing labour force fully employed by expanding sales. To a critic who questioned his strategy, he replied: 'we shall produce 1.5m vehicles a year and with the same number of people, and sucks to you and everyone else' (Turner, 210–11).

The main source of instability in labour relations at British Leyland lay in unregulated shop-floor bargaining over piece rates. Stokes decided to replace piecework with measured day work along 'Fordist' lines. On paper the new system had clear advantages. It would remove control over the pay–effort bargain from the shop stewards and permit the establishment of appropriate performance standards for each job. But implementing the reform was fraught with difficulties. The new system was installed before foremen and supervisors had been fully trained for their new responsibilities. Moreover, the principle of 'mutuality'—that changes in pay and working arrangements should not be introduced without union agreement—was left intact. Since pay was now fixed, shop stewards turned their attention to other issues, such as manning levels, worker effort, and security of earnings. The incentive to work hard was less than under piecework, and there was just as much scope as before for sectional bargaining, and just as many disputes.

At the root of many of British Leyland's problems was organizational uncertainty, reflecting unresolved tensions between former Leyland men from a small-company background and former Ford managers (many of them recruited by Barber) who brought a different conception of how a large car manufacturer should be run. Stokes himself was at heart a small-company man and preferred to retain much of the management style associated with his days at Leyland, including personal control over all capital spending requests over £2000. There were frequent disagreements between Barber, who favoured a Ford-type structure, and George Turnbull, the former Triumph engineer who ran Austin Morris and wanted a greater degree of divisional autonomy. That conflict was resolved in 1973 when Turnbull resigned and Barber was made deputy chairman of the company, but by that time the internal problems of the company had reached a point where recovery was probably impossible.

The demise of British Leyland Although British Leyland made a profit of just over £50 million in 1973, the highest in its short history, this was mainly due to the strength of domestic demand, and the company's underlying weaknesses were exposed when the market collapsed in 1974, following the increase in world oil prices and the subsequent economic recession. In December of that year Stokes was forced to ask the government for financial assistance to keep the company afloat. The government was then in the hands of the same group of men—principally Harold Wilson and Anthony Wedgwood Benn—who had presided over the creation of British Leyland in 1968. For them the collapse of the company was unthinkable, and they decided, first, to provide sufficient short-term finance to keep the company afloat, and, second, to set up a committee under Sir Don Ryder to review the long-term future of the company. The outcome, under the so-called Ryder plan, was that the government took control of the business (although there remained a significant minority of outside shareholders) and agreed to provide over £1 billion of public funds over an eight-year period in order to re-establish the company as a national champion, competing in all segments of the industry as it had been trying to do since 1968. Stokes was replaced as chairman after the government had accepted the Ryder report, and although he was given the honorific title of president, he played no further part in the company's affairs. Within the space of little more than two years it was clear that the assumptions on which the Ryder plan was based were far too optimistic. The company continued to make heavy losses and to lose market share, and there was no improvement in labour relations. The long overdue adjustment to reality did not begin until the appointment of Michael Edwardes as chairman and managing director in October 1977. What followed under Edwardes and his successors was a drastic downsizing of the business, leading ultimately to the break-up of British Leyland and the sale of its component parts to other, mostly non-British, companies.

The collapse of British Leyland was the greatest disaster in Britain's post-war industrial history. A large part of the blame belongs to the politicians who promoted the merger; they had a naïve belief in the virtues of size and had no conception of the managerial problems involved in making the BMH–Leyland merger work. There were serious weaknesses in BMH, but the merger with Leyland made them harder to solve. The merger also contributed to the decline of the Leyland truck and bus business. There, too, modernization was badly needed, but Stokes and his colleagues, preoccupied with the problems of the car business, failed to make the changes that might have enabled Leyland to keep pace with foreign competitors such as Volvo and Scania.

Stokes was at fault in allowing his personal ambition to blind him to the size of the task he was taking on. (That misjudgement, it must be said, was shared by his financial advisers and by Leyland's shareholders, who raised no objection to the merger with BMH.) He was a natural leader, a skilful persuader, and a consummate salesman, with a warmth and ebullience that elicited great loyalty from his subordinates. While he lacked big company experience, that gap would have been less serious if he had been able to build and work with a balanced and cohesive group of senior executives with appropriate backgrounds and skills. As an outward-looking chairman, dealing with customers and governments, he would have played to his strengths, while organizational issues could have been left to better qualified colleagues. But for that division of responsibilities to have worked Stokes would have needed a clearer vision of what sort of company he wanted British Leyland to be.

For some historians, Stokes's failure is part of a larger story that encompasses all the British-owned vehicle manufacturers. According to this view, these companies achieved their biggest success with labour-intensive production of semi-specialist models in low annual volumes. As long as the British market, and the Commonwealth markets that were the principal outlets for the industry's exports, were protected from international competition, this approach worked well, but it was wholly unsuitable for the more competitive markets that emerged in the 1960s and 1970s. What this new environment required was high-volume production of well-engineered products. The British-owned manufacturers, locked into a set of institutions and attitudes that had grown up under protected markets, could not adapt to it.

Final years After retiring from British Leyland, Stokes lived in Poole, Dorset. He took on several directorships, mostly linked to the motor industry, and was actively involved in setting up the local commercial radio station. A keen sailor, he was a member, and for three years commodore, of the Royal Motor Yacht Club in Poole Harbour. His first wife, Laura, died in 1995, and on 25 June 2000 he married Patricia June Pascall (*b.* 1929), a widow, daughter of Harry Arthur Silvester, engineer. He died at his home, Flat 2, Branksome Cliff, Westminster Road, Poole, on 21 July 2008. He was survived by his second wife, Patricia, and the son of his first marriage. GEOFFREY OWEN

Sources G. Turner, *The Leyland papers* (1971) • D. Hague and G. Wilkinson, *The IRC: an experiment in industrial intervention* (1983) • J. Wood, *Wheels of misfortune: the rise and fall of the British motor industry* (1988) • T. R. Whisler, *The British motor industry, 1945–1994: a case study in industrial decline* (1999) • G. Owen, *From empire to Europe: the decline and revival of British industry since the Second World War* (1999) • *The Times* (22 July 2008) • *Daily Telegraph* (22 July 2008) • *The Guardian* (22 July 2008) • *The Independent* (22 July 2008) • Burke, *Peerage* • *WW* (2008) • personal knowledge (2012) • private information (2012) • b. cert. • m. certs. • d. cert.

Archives SOUND BL NSA, current affairs recording

Likenesses photographs, 1967–9, Photoshot, London • C. Beaton, pencil, 1970–73, NPG • G. W. Hales, photograph, 1972 (with John Peyton), Getty Images, London • bromide print, NPG [*see illus.*] • obituary photographs

Wealth at death £3,900,788: probate, 21 Nov 2008, *CGPLA Eng. & Wales*

Stonefrost, Maurice Frank (1927–2008), local government officer, was born on 1 September 1927 at 100 Garnet Street, Bedminster, a poor district of Bristol, the only child of Arthur Stonefrost (1899–1984) and his wife, Annie, *née* Williams (1900–1998), who both worked at a chocolate factory. He attended Merrywood Grammar School in the city. He began to train as an accountant in 1942, then did national service in the Royal Air Force from 1948 to 1951. In the latter year he started to work in local government finance, originally in his home city before moving to Slough in 1954, Coventry in 1956, and west Sussex, where he subsequently lived, in 1961. From 1964 to 1973 he was secretary (chief officer) of the Institute of Municipal Treasurers and Accountants, forerunner of the Chartered Institute of Public Finance and Accountancy. Meanwhile, on 19 September 1953 he married Audrey Jean Fishlock (*b.* 1926), secretary, also from Bristol, daughter of Charlie John Fishlock, dairyman. They had a daughter, Hilary (*b.* 1955), and a son, Mark (*b.* 1959).

In 1973 Stonefrost moved to the Greater London council (GLC), where he remained until 1985, first as comptroller of financial services, then in his last year as director-general and clerk. From 1974 to 1976 he was a member of the Layfield committee, which considered possible reforms to local government finance, including the possibility of introducing a local income tax. During his years at the GLC he worked with Labour administrations led by Sir Reg Goodwin (1973–7) and Ken Livingstone (1981–5), and also with a Conservative one under Sir Horace Cutler (1977–81). The Goodwin years were ones of high inflation and cuts to local government grants: this was the time when the United Kingdom had to seek a loan from the International Monetary Fund. During this difficult period Stonefrost found himself negotiating with the government and the City to ensure London avoided New York's financially disastrous condition.

It was during the period when Livingstone was leader of the GLC that Stonefrost found himself in the most politically charged and difficult period of his working life. The Labour Party won the 1981 GLC election under a moderate leader, Andrew McIntosh, who was deposed by Livingstone within twenty-four hours of the poll. Stonefrost worked to provide the robust financial framework that allowed Livingstone's radical administration to pursue its policies, notably the reduction of public transport fares in the capital. Such was the expertise of the finance team under Stonefrost that he was able to operate in a non-political way to deliver significant resources for the GLC in what turned out to be its final years. In the mid-1980s Margaret Thatcher's government decided to abolish the GLC. Stonefrost believed this policy was a mistake and produced evidence suggesting savings would be very small while there would be higher borrowing costs for the London boroughs once the GLC had gone. His officials also generated charts suggesting what London government might look like after abolition. In particular there was a 'spider diagram' which showed hundreds of lines linking the capital's boroughs and other organizations that would pick up GLC responsibilities. Stonefrost was made a CBE in 1983. He resigned from the council a year before it was abolished in 1986, having, in his own words, 'continued to provide services at standards which the public pay for and have the right to expect' (*Daily Telegraph*, 9 Dec 2008).

After leaving the GLC Stonefrost joined the board of the National Home Loans Corporation, and became chief executive of the British Rail Pension Fund in 1986, where he oversaw the profitable management of its old masters collection. In 1990 he went on to chair Municipal Mutual Insurance, which provided councils with insurance, and after that the CLF Municipal Bank, from 1993 to 1998. He also chaired the commission on citizenship (1989–90) and served on the Marre committee on the future of the legal profession (1989–90) and a committee reviewing the

Church of England's finances (1993). Having been president of the Chartered Institute of Public Finance and Accountancy in 1984–5, the institute's centenary year, he remained active in the organization for the remainder of his life. Working to improve training and education within public sector accountancy was an important feature of his entire career. Other appointments in a busy public life included being chairman of the Dolphin Square Trust (1993–2001), vice-chairman of the Architectural Heritage Fund (1996–8), and a member of the London Pensions Fund Authority (1996–2001). He was made a deputy lieutenant of Greater London in 1986. He was awarded an honorary doctorate by City University in 1987, and subsequently served as deputy pro-chancellor and vice-chairman of the university's council (1992–9).

Stonefrost was a local government official during a complex and politically charged period of public life in Britain. Councils were affected by reductions in their autonomy, cuts in central grants, top-down interference, and regular structural reform. Yet at the end of his long years in public life the quality and integrity of public sector accountants remained unchallenged. Stonefrost's career and work contributed to this achievement. George Jones, who sat on the Layfield committee, observed of him:

> He had a powerful, subtle intellect. He was not a simplifier but a complexifier, seeing the odd angle and giving a fresh perspective on any problem. He was not dogmatic and assertive, but spoke tentatively, hesitantly, taking his listener with him on a journey of intellectual discovery. He did not get people's backs up. (*The Guardian*, 5 Nov 2008)

He spoke with a gentle west country burr which strengthened perceptions of his kindness and wisdom in public office. He lived latterly in Chichester, west Sussex, and died on 25 October 2008 at St Richard's Hospital there, of cancer of the prostate and colon. He was survived by his wife, Audrey, and their two children. TONY TRAVERS

Sources *The Guardian* (5 Nov 2008) · *The Times* (7 Nov 2008); (24 Nov 2008) · *The Independent* (26 Nov 2008) · *Daily Telegraph* (9 Dec 2008) · *WW* (2008) · personal knowledge (2012) · private information (2012) · b. cert. · m. cert. · d. cert.
Likenesses photographs, 1987, Photoshot, London · obituary photographs

Storey, Graham (1920–2005), literary scholar, was born on 8 November 1920 at North Ferriby in the East Riding of Yorkshire, the elder son of Stanley Runton Storey, dental surgeon, and his wife, Winifred Emily, *née* Graham. His parents had considerable means from both Winifred and the family firm of wine merchants, Asher-Storey. The family early moved to Manting House, Meldreth, Cambridgeshire, and the expectations of his parents focused on Storey 'in a way that he sometimes found oppressive' (*The Independent*). He was educated at St Edward's School, Oxford, and then entered Trinity Hall, Cambridge. His undergraduate career was foreshortened by the Second World War, but he took firsts in law and English. He served in the Royal Artillery from 1941 to 1945, was mentioned in dispatches, and formed a close friendship with Robert Runcie, the future archbishop of Canterbury; he was Runcie's best man and later his colleague, when Runcie was dean at Trinity Hall. Storey was demobilized with the rank of lieutenant.

Called to the bar by the Middle Temple in 1950, though he never practised, Storey was for some time undecided between law and English. Offered fellowships in Cambridge in law (at Gonville and Caius College) and English (at Trinity Hall), he determined on English. He was a fellow of Trinity Hall from 1949 to 1988, and very much a college man, serving as senior tutor (1958–68) and vice-master (1970–74). He was also a university lecturer (1965–81) and reader (1981–8) in English. His wider commitment to English and the university was demonstrated in his two years as chairman of the faculty board of English (1972–4), at that time, more even than usual, a poisoned chalice, with Cambridge English 'riven with personal animosities and fierce ideological disputes'; but Storey, 'whom no one considered a threat, thanks to his modest and polite demeanour', steered through reforms acceptable to all parties (*Daily Telegraph*).

Storey's first publication came about through a lifetime friendship with John Chancellor, writer and antiquarian book dealer: he was invited by Chancellor's father, Sir Christopher Chancellor, chairman of Reuters, to write the firm's history to mark its centenary (*Reuters' Century*, 1951). Subsequent publications were founded in taking up other men's work and pursuing them successfully to publication. He completed Humphry House's edition of the *Journals and Papers of Gerard Manley Hopkins* (1959), following House's premature death in 1955, and edited A. P. Rossiter's Shakespeare essays, *Angel with Horns* (1961). His lasting affection for Hopkins and Renaissance drama was demonstrated in his *Preface to Hopkins* (1981) and in his general editorship of the Cambridge Renaissance and Restoration Dramatists (1975–89). It was also through Humphry House that Storey came to his sterling academic achievement. He had had 'digs' with Humphry and Madeline House in Cambridge after war service and Madeline's confidence in him led to the Hopkins *Journals* and to an invitation to complete House's work on Dickens. In 1949 House had begun work on a complete and thoroughly annotated edition of Dickens's letters and drew many enthusiasts and academics into the enterprise: much had been done before his death to collect and annotate letters. After his death Madeline House felt that Storey 'was the man' and in 1957 invited him to join her as general editor. Kathleen Tillotson joined as a general editor a little later and others were brought in as co-editors for individual volumes. Yet overall, more especially in the later volumes, Storey produced the bulk of the annotation and, while he could be hasty, feeling towards the end no doubt the need to see the work through, the completed twelve volumes (1965–2002) stand as tribute to his accuracy, determination, and assiduity.

After his mother's death Storey acquired Crown House, Ermine Street, Caxton, Cambridgeshire, an old coaching inn, a rambling and dark building, far from warm in winter. Here was the archive room of the Dickens edition, its walls lined with works of reference (notably the *DNB*) and box upon box of photocopies, notes, and correspondence;

here also, being a good cook, Storey gave a celebratory dinner on the publication of each volume of the letters for the immediate collaborators. The garden was long, with a pond (into which were blown, on at least one occasion, notes of a co-editor), and the venue for Storey's annual summer party, with a string quartet, for students and colleagues.

Both colleagues and students appreciated Storey's care, tact, and generosity. If for him literature was something that disturbed, touching the 'primal' or 'archetypal terror', students found him ready to help and support them personally as well as academically, and he would delight in driving a group to Stratford to see a play, give them dinner, and return them that night. In committees he was well prepared and alert, so that business went without hitch. He was in many ways a shy man, who did not find it easy to relax in company, despite his delight in people and occasions, and was often self-effacing, even at events he had organized. His manner, particularly on the phone, could be abrupt, until callers learned how to fit their own rhythms to his. A homosexual, he kept his personal life largely separate and apparently believed that his sexuality was concealed from others, whereas in fact it was generally known and simply accepted. In his last years, he became increasingly physically and mentally frail and died of multiple causes on 6 November 2005 at the Hope Residential and Nursing Care Home, Brooklands Avenue, Cambridge. He was buried at Holy Trinity Church, Meldreth, Cambridgeshire, on 14 November. He had already munificently funded the conversion of the old college library into a public reception room, named in his honour and opened by the queen in 2000. (In his lifetime he gave more than £1 million to his college.) A legacy, supported by Trinity Hall, established a biannual lecture on 'The English novel' in the English faculty in his name, the first being given in 2008. ANGUS EASSON

Sources *The Independent* (15 Nov 2005) · *The Times* (16 Nov 2005); (18 Nov 2005); (19 Nov 2005); (13 Feb 2006) · *Daily Telegraph* (19 Nov 2005) · *The Guardian* (24 Dec 2005) · Magnus Linklater, memorial address, Trinity Hall, 11 Feb 2006 · P. Collins, *The Dickensian*, 102 (spring 2006), 93–4 · *WW* (2005) · personal knowledge (2009) · private information (2009) · b. cert. · d. cert.
Archives Dickens House Museum, Doughty Street, London, corresp. and papers relating to the Dickens letters edition · Royal Holloway College, Kathleen Tillotson archive | SOUND BL NSA, documentary recording
Likenesses obituary photographs · photograph, Trinity Hall, Cambridge
Wealth at death £2,231,624: probate, 4 May 2006, *CGPLA Eng. & Wales*

Stott, Richard Keith (1943–2007), journalist and newspaper editor, was born at 165 Banbury Road, Oxford, on 17 August 1943, the third child of Fred Brooks (Freddie) Stott (1894–1964), a hard-drinking but not very hard-working engineer, and his wife, Bertha, *née* Pickford, a publican's daughter who let out rooms to university students. His sister, Judith, became an actress; his brother, John, his eldest sibling, an unsuccessful hotelier. He grew up in the shadow of Oxford University, and attended Christ Church Cathedral School. After Clifton College, Bristol, he was rejected by two Oxford colleges—less, he believed, because he had only two A-levels than because he was aggressively outspoken at his interview. He had already adopted the attitude that he claimed characterized him: 'My natural instinct was to set my face against both respectability and a cosy inside track' (*Dogs and Lampposts*, 133). Journalism offered better prospects than the career he first preferred, the stage, although the theatre was to remain a significant interest and influence. Like his well-informed interest in architecture and art, particularly the Victorian painters, it provided a counterbalance to an otherwise rambunctious lifestyle.

Stott's apprenticeship on the *Bucks Herald*, begun at the age of nineteen, required long stints of proofreading and other sub-journalistic tasks he found discouraging. Only in 1963 when the biggest crime story of the era, the 'great train robbery', took place on the paper's doorstep was he able to do any notable reporting. Running with the Fleet Street pack reassured him about his choice of career. Before he could join that ruffianly élite, however, he needed more experience. This he acquired at a busy news agency in Kent and with it his first patron, the owner, Dan Ferrari. He also found, in a fellow reporter, an exemplar and lifelong rival: Kelvin McKenzie, who was to become editor of *The Sun* in 1981.

When, in 1968, Ferrari became night news editor of the *Daily Mirror*, the established tabloid that the relatively new *Sun* set out to overtake, Stott followed him. He was soon demonstrating a talent for turning up important stories and tenacity pursuing them. There was no great investigative tradition at the *Mirror*. Its editorial genius Hugh Cudlipp had driven the daily circulation up to a record 5 million in 1964 without such stories and considered them more trouble than they were worth. Stott became a fearless and highly vocal critic of Cudlippian values and the nationally recognized bylines that underpinned them. In fact he rarely endorsed a reputation he had not played a part in making. This was sometimes construed as raw jealousy; even, in the view of an otherwise admiring female colleague, 'Richard's catty feminine streak' (private information).

Nevertheless, Stott was a genuine motivating force in the *Mirror* newsroom. The younger executives who took over after Cudlipp's retirement welcomed his well-researched accounts of questionable dealings by politicians, particularly Reginald Maudling and Ernest Marples. He was named reporter of the year in the British press awards for an account in 1977 about the England football manager Don Revie taking bribes to lose matches. Not all his investigative feats were of equal worth, but his reputation expanded to the point where even feeble ones, such as demonstrating that more 'Beaujolais' was sold in Britain than the region could produce, made *Mirror* 'spreads'. He also developed the knack of intercepting credit that might have been better directed at colleagues. Thus he emerged as the star of the spectacular discovery of John Stonehouse, a former MP who had faked death and disappearance, eclipsing the contributions of other reporters.

When, tired of reporting, Stott demanded executive status he was made features editor (1979–81), then an assistant editor (1981–4) with oversight of virtually all content. All around him were greatly entertained by his abrasive confrontations with departments such as advertising, circulation, and publicity, that he thought were failing to support editorial efforts. As one colleague said: 'His method of tackling any problem was to paw the ground, lower his horns and CHARGE!' (private information). Even when Stott was mellowed by his favourite Jack Daniel's whiskey, colleagues failed to penetrate the barrage of wisecracks and raillery with which he defended his private persona. Nevertheless, when his autobiography, *Dogs and Lampposts* (2002), was published many people he had frequently mocked were surprised to find that he had actually regarded them highly. Some, who imagined they had won his respect, discovered the opposite.

On 18 April 1970 Stott married Penelope Anne Scragg (*b.* 1947), a nurse, who had first encountered him stretched out on her bed when she came home from a night shift. He had been invited for drinks by her room-mate and needed a nap. Penny's father was Air Vice-Marshal Sir Colin Scragg, and the wedding took place in the RAF church of St Clement Danes, a short walk from Fleet Street. They had three children, Emily (*b.* 1972), Hannah (*b.* 1975), and Christopher (*b.* 1979).

By the late 1970s Stott had attracted a circle of junior executives and privileged columnists. All were capable, but their outstanding quality in common was readiness to acknowledge his leadership. Succumbing to his persistent pressure for total command, Cudlipp's successor as editorial director, Tony Miles, made him editor of the group's junior title, the *Sunday People* (*Sunday* had recently been added to reinforce an identity that was in danger of being lost). He took the chair on 14 January 1984, twenty-one years to the day after he had joined the *Bucks Herald*, and set about restoring the reputation for exposés the paper had once enjoyed.

Mirror Group Newspapers editors were bedevilled by a swollen and inept management that was no match for the anarchic print unions. Disenchanted, the group's owners, Reed International, let Robert Maxwell acquire the company in July 1984 for far less than its true value. Maxwell proved a disastrous proprietor but at first his colourful style came as a welcome change. The principal difficulty the editors had was in fighting off his ham-fisted interventions. It was in part the defensive tactics employed by Mike Molloy, who had edited the *Daily Mirror* for ten years, that led Maxwell to promote him to editor-in-chief in 1985 and to replace him with Stott.

Stott was often to boast that he was the only person on the *Mirror* who ever really defied Maxwell. It is more likely that Maxwell was ready to tolerate a single outspoken dissenter as a kind of court jester and that Stott's 'cheeky chappie' attitude fitted the role. Nevertheless, Stott's autobiography included a searing memo he wrote to Maxwell in an attempt to define their relationship:

> Only one person can be in charge of the paper's editorial content, either publisher or editor, but not both. One of the main reasons for the attack on the Mirror's credibility and morale over the past few months has been the alarm created by what many people inside and outside Fleet Street interpret as confusion over the two roles. (*Dogs and Lampposts*, 226)

Even if Maxwell ever read this declaration it would have been entirely against his nature to heed it, and after eighteen tumultuous months Stott discovered he was to be replaced by Roy Greenslade. In compensation—supposedly—Maxwell agreed to help him organize a buyout of *The People* (*Sunday* by then dropped), which in the meantime he would return to edit. Predictably enough, Maxwell reneged on his offer. Unpredictably, a year later Stott let Maxwell persuade him to go back and edit the *Mirror*. The group was being prepared for flotation and falling circulation required attention.

It is likely that Stott would have emerged as a great editor at the *Mirror* had he not been compelled to spend so much time fending off a capricious and untrustworthy proprietor. He was editing the paper when news came of Maxwell's death, and he wrote the subsequently contentious headline: 'The man who saved the Mirror'. Even after Maxwell's depredations were revealed his defence was 'if you judged a newspaper proprietor by whether he leaves the paper in a better state than he found it, then Maxwell, for all his many faults, had been a successful owner' (*Dogs and Lampposts*, 297). The turmoil among Maxwell's creditors set the Fleet Street roundabout spinning. It deposited at the *Mirror*'s door a former sub-editor on the paper, David Montgomery, recently sacked as editor of *Today*, a newspaper Rupert Murdoch was trying to develop as a competitor to the *Daily Express* and *Daily Mail*. Montgomery convinced a new Mirror Group board of his management ability and was appointed chief executive. He assured Stott that he would remain as editor. Three weeks later he sacked him.

In 1993 Murdoch, who described Stott as one of the best three editors he had known, offered him the job from which he had ousted Montgomery. Helped by a team of loyal refugees from the *Mirror*, Stott made a manful attempt to turn *Today* into 'an iconoclastic, left-of-centre, top-end of the popular market paper' (*Dogs and Lampposts*, 341). His efforts won the *What the Papers Say* award for editor of the year but the financial odds were against him. The paper closed in 1995.

Stott was far from finished with journalism. He was snapped up as a columnist by the *News of the World* and later by the *Sunday Mirror*. He continued writing for the latter, in addition to editing the memoirs of his former protégé Alastair Campbell, even after pancreatic cancer had been diagnosed. In a career that had begun in 1963 he had achieved the unequalled feat of becoming editor of a national newspaper on five occasions: twice at the *Daily Mirror*, twice at *The People*, once at the short-lived but noteworthy *Today*. Stocky, sharp-tongued, and domineering, 'Stotty' was described by a fellow executive as 'the editor from Central Casting' (private information). He died on 30 July 2007, at home at 20 Albany Park Road, Kingston upon Thames, Surrey, and was survived by his wife, Penny, and their three children. His memorial service was held on 16 January 2008 at St Clement Danes Church, where he had been married. ANTHONY DELANO

Sources R. Stott, *Dogs and lampposts* (2002) · *The Times* (31 July 2007) · *The Independent* (31 July 2007) · *Daily Mirror* (31 July 2007); (17 Jan 2008) · *The Guardian* (1 Aug 2007) · *Daily Telegraph* (2 Aug 2007) · *WW* (2007) · personal knowledge (2011) · private information (2011) · b. cert. · m. cert. · d. cert.
Archives University of Cardiff, Bute Resource Centre | FILM BFINA, documentary footage
Likenesses photographs, 1991, PA Photos, London · photograph, 1992, repro. in news.bbc.co.uk/1/hi/uk/6922740.stm
Wealth at death £645,645: probate, 4 March 2008, *CGPLA Eng. & Wales*

Stoyle, Roger John Blin- (1924–2007), physicist, was born on 24 December 1924 at the City Maternity Home, Westcotes Drive, Leicester, the only son and elder child of Cuthbert Basil St John Blin-Stoyle (1894–1978), an engineer's fitter, later a driver then foreman for the Birmingham and Midland Omnibus Company, and his wife, Ada Mary, *née* Nash (1893–1983). His education began in South Wigston, and in September 1935 he won a scholarship to Alderman Newton's Boys' School in Leicester. Not until the sixth form did physics, thanks to some inspirational teaching, become exciting for him. He was brought up an Anglican, and was a member of the Church Lads' Brigade and the Anglican Young People's Association. In 1943 he was awarded a senior scholarship in natural science at Wadham College, Oxford. However, he was conscripted for military service in September 1943 and in April 1945 was commissioned into the Royal Corps of Signals. After a brief posting in Cologne he served as an officer instructor at Mhow, a cantonment near Indore, India. After demobilization in September 1946 he started at Wadham. At Oxford he met Audrey Elizabeth Balmford (*b.* 1927), a mathematics student at St Hugh's College, and daughter of Joseph Clifford Balmford, schoolmaster, of Liverpool; they were married on 30 August 1949, just after his graduation with first-class honours in physics. They had a son, Tony, and daughter, Helena.

Blin-Stoyle continued at Oxford as a graduate student in the department of theoretical physics under the supervision of John Spiers, working initially on polarized nuclear reactions, and then on the general formulation of β-decay theory, the decay of radioactive atomic nuclei through the emission of an electron (or positron). This work led to his first paper, published in 1951, and, in the same year, his DPhil degree. A Pressed Steel research fellowship enabled him to stay at Oxford and immediately he became the 'house theorist' for the local experimental research group working on deuteron–deuteron collisions. This was the first of several close and fruitful interactions with experimental groups, which were a feature of his later work. In 1953 he spent one year in Birmingham as a lecturer in mathematical physics and was encouraged by Rudi Peierls to work on the calculation of nuclear magnetic moments; this led to his first book, *Theories of Nuclear Moments* (1957). After returning to Oxford as a senior research officer in theoretical physics he began a collaboration with Michael Grace, leader of a group doing experiments on polarized nuclei. About this time he also collaborated on mesonic exchange effects in β-decay with John Bell, a theorist at the Atomic Energy Research Establishment in Harwell, and with Henry Primakoff, a visitor from Washington University, St Louis, USA. The protons and neutrons (nucleons) that make the nucleus are subject to quantum fluctuations caused by the exchange of fleeting 'virtual' particles, such as mesons. These fluctuations affect the nuclear properties and permit their use as a 'laboratory' in which to discover properties of the possibly exotic virtual particles. Blin-Stoyle used this to great effect later. Following the arrival in 1957 of Denys Wilkinson in Oxford he became interested in the parity-violating internucleon potential generated by meson exchange, and this led to the publication in 1960 of a much cited paper, 'Parity nonconserving internucleon potentials', in the *Physics Review*. It was written while he was a visiting professor at the Massachusetts Institute of Technology, a year that changed his view of how physics and science generally should be taught at universities.

Fortuitously Blin-Stoyle had an opportunity to implement his ideas about the teaching of science when, in 1962, he was appointed professor of theoretical physics at the then very new University of Sussex, and dean of its first science school, the school of physical sciences, which contained three subject groups: mathematics, physics, and chemistry. Some courses, in mathematics and in the structure and properties of matter, taught by Blin-Stoyle himself, were compulsory for all first-year students. His research continued to use the nucleus as a laboratory, and in 1970 he and Joan Freeman, an experimentalist at Harwell, inferred the existence of heavy intermediate vector mesons, later called W- and Z-bosons, from precision data on (superallowed) β-decays; the direct detection of these particles at CERN was not made until 1983. In 1976 they received the Institute of Physics Rutherford medal and prize for this work, and in the same year Blin-Stoyle was elected a fellow of the Royal Society for his overall contributions to nuclear physics. His account of this field appeared in his book *Fundamental Interactions of the Nucleus* (1973).

Blin-Stoyle's many administrative posts at Sussex included a period as deputy vice-chancellor (to Asa Briggs) in 1970–72, and as pro-vice-chancellor (science) in 1977–9. Service in 1978–83 on the joint committee of the Royal Society and the Institute of Physics afforded him opportunities to influence science education from the age of five upwards, and in 1983–8 he chaired the School Curriculum Development Committee. He retired from Sussex in 1987, but continued to serve on various professional bodies. In 1990–92 he was president of the Institute of Physics; he and the chief executive, Alun Jones, launched a Campaign for Physics resulting in a 30 per cent increase in the institute's membership. His continuing interest in school science education led to his appointment in 1993 as president of the Association for Science Education, a task that was informed by his concurrent experience of teaching ten-year-olds in a Lewes primary school near his home. An accomplished pianist and organist—who had considered trying for an organ scholarship at Oxford if he failed to win a natural science scholarship, and who became an associate of the Royal College of Music in 1949—he played in most churches in Lewes and many further afield. He died at Claydon House nursing home, 8 Wallands Crescent, Lewes, on 31 January 2007, of acute on chronic heart disease, and was survived by his wife, Audrey, and their two children. His humanist funeral was in Brighton on 12 February, with a commemoration at the University of Sussex on 15 June. DAVID BAILIN

Sources *The Independent* (15 Feb 2007) • *The Guardian* (20 Feb 2007) • *The Times* (12 March 2007); (3 April 2007) • *Memoirs FRS*, 54 (12 Dec 2008), 31–45; rsbm.royalsocietypublishing.org/content/54/31.full.pdf, 10 June 2010 • *WW* (2007) • personal knowledge (2011) • private information (2011) [Audrey Blin-Stoyle, widow; Tony Blin-Stoyle, son; H. Bown] • b. cert. • m. cert. • d. cert.

Likenesses G. Argent, photograph, *c*.1977, repro. in *Memoirs FRS* • obituary photographs

Wealth at death under £156,000: probate, 4 April 2007, *CGPLA Eng. & Wales*

Stratford. For this title name *see* Banks, Anthony Louis, Baron Stratford (1942–2006). For other subjects who held this title name *see Oxford DNB*, 53.23.

Strawson, Sir Peter Frederick (1919–2006), philosopher, was born on 23 November 1919 at 55 Castlebar Road, Ealing, London, the second son and second of four children (three sons and a daughter) of Cyril Walter Strawson (1888–1937) and his wife, Nellie Dora, *née* Jewell (1890–1975), both schoolteachers. His younger brother, John (*b*. 1921), became a major-general in the British army and a distinguished military historian. Between them he and Strawson produced more than twenty books.

Strawson was educated at Christ's College in Finchley, from where he won an open scholarship to read English at St John's College, Oxford. Arriving there in 1937 he decided instead to read philosophy, politics, and economics. This was primarily because he had discovered the attractions of philosophy and his own talent for it, but also because he wished to pursue a course that might enable him to understand better the impending war and its political consequences. In philosophy he was tutored by J. D. (John) Mabbott, who later became the president of St John's, and also by H. P. (Paul) Grice, an extremely brilliant philosopher, with whom Strawson subsequently both collaborated and on some issues fundamentally disagreed. In 1940 Strawson was, amusingly and shamefully, awarded a second in finals. His philosophy answers produced admiration in one youthful examiner, Isaiah Berlin, but disapproval in an older one, A. D. (Sandy) Lindsay, the master of Balliol. They compromised, to Berlin's shame, on a second. Rumour had it that Berlin's ability to support Strawson was hampered by his having lost the disputed scripts in a taxi, though this may be apocryphal.

After leaving Oxford in the summer of 1940 Strawson was called up into the army, serving first in the Royal Artillery, before reaching the rank of captain in the Royal Electrical and Mechanical Engineers. He was demobilized in 1946, having on 27 October the previous year married

Sir Peter Frederick Strawson (1919–2006), by Peter Wardle, 1989

Grace Hall Martin (*b*. 1919), on whom he had conferred the nickname Ann, by which she was subsequently known. Peter and Ann Strawson shared the same date of birth. They had four children, Julia (*b*. 1950), Galen (*b*. 1952), later a philosopher, Robert (*b*. 1954), and Virginia (*b*. 1961).

Strawson was committed to a career in philosophy, but was handicapped by his degree. He went first to the University College of North Wales at Bangor, as an assistant lecturer, but after winning the John Locke scholarship in 1946, and receiving the backing of Gilbert Ryle, he went to University College, Oxford, initially as a lecturer, and then, from 1948, a fellow. He spent his career, and life, in Oxford, although he travelled widely, principally in America, Europe, China, and India, where he was especially highly regarded. He remained a fellow of University College until 1968, when he became Gilbert Ryle's successor as Waynflete professor of metaphysical philosophy, which meant transferring to Magdalen College. He held this post until he retired in 1987. Thereafter he continued an active philosophical life, resuming his working relation with University College, which provided him with rooms until his death. He received many honours during his life, most notably election as a fellow of the British Academy in 1960 and an honorary member of the American Academy of Arts and Sciences in 1971. He was knighted in 1977, and a volume devoted to him in the famous and exclusive Library of Living Philosophers series was published in 1998.

Strawson re-entered Oxford philosophy at the beginning of what was to prove its golden period. Around him was an array of highly talented and intellectually energetic philosophers, including Grice, Richard Hare, G. A. Paul, Geoffrey Warnock, J. O. Urmson, and Anthony Quinton, constituting a terrific powerhouse for the subject, along with the more senior figures of Ryle and J. L. Austin, the latter being the main influence on the group, given his combination of a frightening critical presence with a conception of philosophy as properly done only by a close attention to language as it is used, which seemed, initially at least, to represent a novel and liberating approach to the subject. Strawson eventually emerged as the most formidable philosopher within that group, not only because of a quite remarkable and wide-ranging creativity and an unsurpassed speed of understanding and critical response, but also because he helped to overturn the Austinian paradigm, both by having in many people's eyes the better of Austin in a famous disagreement between them about truth, but also by simply doing plausible philosophy, especially in his book *Individuals* (1959), in a non-Austinian but not obviously unsuccessful way. Strawson led Oxford away from the Austinian straitjacket.

One of Strawson's main interests was the philosophy of language, and it was in that area that he achieved international fame when he published, in *Mind* in 1950, what was almost his first article, 'On referring'. In it he criticized a widely accepted theory of Bertrand Russell's about the role in English of the definite article 'the'. Russell thought that 'The F is G' should be analysed as equivalent to 'There is one and only one F and it is G'. Strawson, by contrast, held that there is no uniform way to capture the role of 'the' and that there are uses that Russell's analysis does not cover, namely where it forms part of an expression picking out an object, rather than saying there is such a thing. Strawson introduced the notion of presupposition to capture the relation between such uses of 'the F' and the idea that there is an F, a notion that linguists subsequently took up. Strawson wrote much after that about reference, expanding and modifying his views, but always maintaining that Russell's theory was inadequate. His first book, *Introduction to Logical Theory* (1952), which was a study of the nature of formal logic, explored among other things the issue, related to the dispute with Russell, of how far expressions in ordinary language have the same meaning as expressions in formal languages. Strawson's view was that ordinary language has no precise logic. This was another theme in Strawson's writings about language, which placed him in opposition to some popular systems of his time, including the approach to language championed by the American philosopher Donald Davidson. Strawson himself did not construct a theory as to how language functions, but some later developments in linguistics indicated how it might be done.

Strawson described his book *Individuals* (1959) as an exercise in descriptive metaphysics. The aim in part 1, which immediately attracted considerable attention, was to describe the types of thing that we fundamentally refer to, an issue continuing his focus on reference. Strawson argues that they are bodies and persons, and he provides an account of how bodies in space and time constitute a framework that enables our thought about things, as well as an account of how we think about ourselves. In part 2, which attracted far less attention, he offered a theory of the distinction between subjects and predicates. As well as describing our thought Strawson argues that scepticism about our thought can be dismissed, since employing our basic categories even to locate claims to be uncertain about requires that we have knowledge of such facts. *Individuals* was therefore a work of metaphysics, epistemology, and philosophy of language.

Strawson had a deep knowledge of the history of philosophy, and illuminated his own thoughts by relating them to the ideas of important figures from the past, for example, Gottfried Leibniz in the case of *Individuals*. In his next book, *The Bounds of Sense* (1966), Strawson engaged with the philosophy of Immanuel Kant. He attempted to explain Kant's thought and to sift the good from the bad in it, dropping transcendental idealism and the idea of the synthetic a priori, and extracting (from the *Transcendental Deduction* and the *Analogies*) a rich, extended argument designed to show that it is a condition for self-consciousness that one's experience is of objects that are not oneself. Again the ultimate target was scepticism. Strawson's book acted as a major stimulus to regenerate an interest in Kant among analytical philosophers.

Strawson wrote three other important books. In *Subject and Predicate in Logic and Grammar* (1974), a book of which he was especially fond, he developed his approach to the distinction between subject and predicate and embedded it in a highly abstract account of grammar. *Scepticism and Naturalism: Some Varieties* (1985), Strawson's Woodbridge lectures at Columbia University, presented a further response to scepticism, and a defence of a relaxed realism about secondary qualities, meaning, value, and the mind. Finally, in *Analysis and Metaphysics* (1992), Strawson, with the aim of introducing philosophy to the reader, explained and engaged in philosophy according to his own conception of it. Strawson also published a large number of important articles, ranging over language, metaphysics, epistemology, and the history of philosophy, including a highly influential one entitled 'Freedom and resentment' (published in the *Proceedings of the British Academy* in 1960), and the most important of these were republished in collections, notably *Logico-Linguistic Papers* (1971) and *Freedom and Resentment and Other Essays* (1974).

Strawson's main preoccupation was to oppose the distortions about our language, thought, and knowledge that philosophers characteristically generate when they approach our thought with metaphysical or epistemological prejudices. We cannot justify our scheme from outside, nor do we need to reduce parts of it to other parts to maintain their validity, nor can we dispense with it. Two distortions he combated repeatedly were the misdescriptions of experience attractive to empiricists like A. J. Ayer, and the scepticism about meaning attractive to the American philosopher W. V. Quine. He aimed to contribute to our understanding by removing these distortions and displaying links, dependences, and structure within our conceptual scheme. Strawson's aim to remove distortion made him similar to Ludwig Wittgenstein, a philosopher whom he admired, but Strawson's more constructive analyses represent a dissimilarity. Strawson contributed to the discussion of a very wide range of topics. It is a measure of his importance that his work was discussed by the leading philosophers of his time, including Russell, Wilfrid Sellars, Quine, Hilary Putnam, Michael Dummett, Davidson, and Saul Kripke. A large number of books and editions of journals had, even before his death, been devoted to his thought.

Strawson was primarily committed to doing philosophy well, part of that being a philosophy teacher, a role in which he was superb, both with undergraduates and graduates. He accepted, without relish or enthusiasm, the administrative roles that Oxford required of him, which he performed diligently. Unlike, for example, Freddie Ayer or Bernard Williams, he had no desire to contribute to public debates about morality, nor any desire to be a famous intellectual. His passions were more private. As he put it, 'philosophy, friends and family apart, my life has been enriched by the enjoyment of literature, landscape, architecture, and the company of clever and beautiful women' (Hahn, 21). He read and could quote vast quantities of English literature, especially poetry, which he himself also wrote, and he averred that a poet is what he would have most liked to be. This side to him, though, came out in his own writings, which avoided jargon and modish formalism, but were stylish, elegant, and distinctive. Indeed, he personified elegance, in manner, appearance, and speech. He was extremely mild mannered, which was somewhat ironic given that he focused on resentment and anger in his account of freedom. He was witty and could be unserious, playing long military games in his garden. Above all he exuded an apparently effortless intelligence. His students described encounters with him as like encounters with God. His speed of response to questions so impressed G. A. Paul, his first colleague at University College, that he compared Strawson to a chocolate dispensing machine: you put in a question and out came an answer.

Strawson continued publishing, lecturing, and taking part in philosophical discussion after his retirement, with no apparent loss in critical acuity. He grew, without complaint, frailer over time, despite retaining a capacity to out-walk most of those around him. He died of acute renal failure and colitis in the John Radcliffe Hospital, Oxford, on 13 February 2006, and was buried at Wolvercote cemetery, Oxford, on 27 February. On 8 July 2006 there was a gathering in Magdalen College, Oxford, to celebrate his life, and a group of distinguished people, including Mary Warnock, his brother John, Tom Nagel, and John Searle, spoke movingly of him as a person and a philosopher.

PAUL SNOWDON

Sources L. E. Hahn, ed., *The philosophy of P. F. Strawson* (1998) • *The Times* (15 Feb 2006) • *Daily Telegraph* (15 Feb 2006) • *The Guardian* (15 Feb 2006) • *The Independent* (18 Feb 2006) • *A tribute to Sir Peter Strawson*, Magdalen College occasional paper, 7 (2008) • Burke, *Peerage* • *WW* (2006) • personal knowledge (2010) • private information (2010) • b. cert. • m. cert. • d. cert.

Archives SOUND documentary recordings

Likenesses photograph, 1977, Photoshot, London • P. Wardle, black and white chalks on blue paper, 1989, University College, Oxford • P. Wardle, coloured chalk, 1989, NPG [*see illus.*] • I. Myerscough, pencil, 2005, NPG • obituary photographs

Stubbs, John Francis Alexander Heath- (1918–2006), poet, was born at Streatham Manor, Leigham Avenue, Streatham, London, on 9 July 1918, the elder son of Francis Heath-Stubbs, of independent means, and his wife, Edith Louise Sara, *née* Marr. At this time his parents lived at 5 Ranulf Road, Hampstead. His father had qualified as a solicitor but never practised. His mother was a concert pianist of distinction, as Edie Marr. She gave up her professional career after her son was born but became a music teacher when her husband developed multiple sclerosis and their private income was reduced by the depression of the 1930s. Music was to play a major part in her son's life and poetry.

Most of Heath-Stubbs's boyhood was spent near the New Forest. The wild birds there, identified for him by his father, became a frequent source of inspiration. At the age of twelve he went to the recently founded Bembridge School on the Isle of Wight. He spent much of his free time in the school library, where he became absorbed in works of reference, namely *Encyclopaedia Britannica*, *Brewer's Dictionary of Phrase and Fable*, and *Lemprière's Classical Dictionary*. They were the foundation of his education, he said later. Though he was miserable on the whole at Bembridge it was there that his literary talent began to emerge. He wrote poetry, published in the school magazine, but thought of studying biology at university.

When he was eighteen Heath-Stubbs was diagnosed with glaucoma, unusual in one so young, inherited from his father. After an operation he lost the sight of his right eye but retained some vision in the left, which he was able to use for reading until 1961. He bore this misfortune with great stoicism and overcame the disability to a remarkable degree, becoming phenomenally well read. After the operation he was sent to Worcester College for the Blind where he learned Braille, though he never used it. He became editor of the college magazine and, most important, he came into contact with boys of a working-class background and began with them his lifelong enjoyment of beer-drinking and of mixing freely with people of all social classes in pubs. Meanwhile his parents had heard of the Barker exhibition at Queen's College, Oxford, given to someone who was either blind or in danger of losing his sight, to read English. Heath-Stubbs was awarded the exhibition in 1939 and at the age of twenty-one went to Oxford.

At Oxford Heath-Stubbs soon became friends with two Queen's undergraduates, Sidney Keyes and Drummond Allison, who were poets, and with the handsome Philip Rawson, also writing poetry, later to become a professor of Indian art and a sculptor. Heath-Stubbs found the Oxford English school a satisfying complement to his private

John Francis Alexander Heath-Stubbs (1918–2006), by Derek Parker, 1965

reading of poetry. He enjoyed listening to J. R. R. Tolkien lecture on *Beowulf* and *Gawain and the Green Knight*. He stored the alliterative metre in his mind for future use. His tutors were Herbert Brett-Smith for literature and John Bryson for language, but it was attending lectures by Nevill Coghill and above all C. S. Lewis that he found most rewarding. He also went to lectures by Lewis's friend Charles Williams, who seemed a saint-like presence to many in Oxford at that time. Williams's account of the English poetic tradition made a powerful impression on Heath-Stubbs, who later wrote the pamphlet on him for the British Council's Writers and their Work series.

Herbert Read, the poetry adviser to Routledge, published *Eight Oxford Poets* in 1941, edited by Sidney Keyes and Michael Meyer, the future biographer of Ibsen, then at Christ Church. Heath-Stubbs was one of the eight, as was Keith Douglas. In a preface Keyes wrote: 'we are … *Romantic* writers, though by that I mean little more than that our greatest fault is a tendency to floridity, and that we have on the whole little sympathy with the Audenian school of poets' (*Eight Oxford Poets*, vii). This volume was followed a year later by Keyes's *The Iron Laurel* and Heath-Stubbs's *Wounded Thammuz*, a booklet of twenty-four pages containing an elegy celebrating the Babylonian deity mentioned by Milton in *Paradise Lost*, a poetic reworking of the dying god myth. Both books were published by Routledge.

Heath-Stubbs took first-class honours in his final schools in 1942 and stayed on for a BLitt on the background to James Thomson's *The Seasons*, but after a preliminary year's work both he and his supervisor, David Nichol Smith, came to the conclusion that in spite of his wide knowledge of literature, scholarship was not his forte. Part of his trouble was emotional: he had by now discovered his homosexuality and fallen desperately in love with Philip Rawson who, while admiring Heath-Stubbs's intellect and offering him firm friendship, was not of the same sexual orientation. *Beauty and the Beast*, the volume by Heath-Stubbs published by Routledge in 1943, contains 'The Heart's Forest', a moving poem of unrequited love. *The Divided Ways* (1945), dedicated to Rawson, has for its title-poem Heath-Stubbs's elegy for Keyes, killed in action in 1943 at the age of twenty. Allison was also killed in the war.

During this period William Bell, a poet from Merton College, introduced Heath-Stubbs to the college's literary society, the Bodley Club. He met there the atomic research scientist Ronald Bright, who later converted to Roman Catholicism to become Laurence Bright, a Dominican friar. Under his influence and that of Charles Williams, Heath-Stubbs reverted to the Anglican faith of his upbringing and became a regular churchgoer. Bell published a generous selection of poems by Heath-Stubbs in his anthology *Poetry from Oxford in Wartime* (1945) and several by Philip Larkin, an Oxford contemporary of Heath-Stubbs, excluded by Keyes and Meyer from *Eight Oxford Poets*. Heath-Stubbs and Larkin shared a dislike of each other's work. Larkin and his friend Kingsley Amis, both at St John's College, derided the use made by the Queen's poets of myth and legend. Three years later Bell, a keen mountaineer, died while climbing the Matterhorn. Heath-Stubbs edited and introduced a posthumous volume of Bell's poems, *Mountains Beneath the Horizon* (1950). These early deaths of his compeers left Heath-Stubbs the sole post-war survivor of Oxford's wartime poetic romantics.

After leaving Oxford Heath-Stubbs went to live in London, taking lodgings in a boarding-house in west Hampstead. Poetry was his vocation but he needed a job. He obtained one as a schoolmaster at The Hall preparatory school, where he read *The Ancient Mariner* to his pupils but found keeping them in order at other times to be beyond him. He resigned halfway through his second term. His next job was on a popular illustrated encyclopaedia in preparation at Hutchinson. He contributed articles not only on literature, music, and theology but also on plants, birds, insects, and cookery. He was also commissioned to write a book about Edgar Allan Poe but gave it up when it was half-written, having, as he put it, 'seen through Poe'. He gave up the Hutchinson job, too, after eighteen months, and apart from temporary university appointments became a freelance for the rest of his life.

Heath-Stubbs soon began to make his mark as a poet in London. His poems and articles appeared in Wrey Gardiner's *Poetry Quarterly*, Hugh Kingsmill's *New English Review*, and above all in John Lehmann's *Penguin New Writing*. He gave readings of his poetry with other poets, including Dylan Thomas, George Barker, and James Kirkup, at the Ethical Church in Bayswater. His work was noticed by Edith Sitwell who, when she was in London, invited him to luncheons at the Sesame Club. He encountered T. S. Eliot, who asked him to edit *The Faber Book of Twentieth-Century Verse*, which he compiled with his Oxford friend David Wright, a poet who was deaf. With Wright he also edited, for Lehmann's publishing imprint, *The Forsaken Garden*, an anthology of English poetry from 1824 to 1905. His critical study of some of the poets of this period was published in 1950 as *The Darkling Plain*.

Heath-Stubbs's social life centred on what came to be known (though not strictly accurately, as he was fond of pointing out) as Soho. He became almost as much a fixture in the Wheatsheaf, Rathbone Place, off Oxford Street, as the short-story writer Julian Maclaren-Ross. In between drinking pints of beer, he would discourse at length on literary matters ranging over vast areas of poetry and mythology to anyone prepared to listen to him. He was as unstoppable and mesmerizing an impromptu talker as was Coleridge in the eyes of his contemporaries.

Heath-Stubbs's next collection was rejected by Routledge, where Geoffrey Grigson had taken over as poetry adviser, but this did nothing to arrest the steady flow of poetry from his pen. He brought out fresh collections at regular intervals with various publishers: *The Swarming of the Bees* (1950) with Eyre and Spottiswode, *A Charm Against the Toothache* (1954) with Methuen, and *The Blue Fly in His Head* (1958) and *The Triumph of the Muse* (1962), both with Oxford University Press, which also published his translations from Leopardi, the beginning of his work of translation, usually with a collaborator, of exotic poets he considered too little known in England. He found a permanent home for his own work with Michael Schmidt's Carcanet Press in Manchester. Carcanet published *The Watchman's Flute* (1978), *Naming of the Beasts* (1982), *The Imitation of Aleph* (1985), and several other volumes, though his major work, *Artorius* (King Arthur), 'a heroic poem in four books and eight episodes', was first published in a limited edition of 315 copies by Alan Clodd's Enitharmon Press in 1973. This lengthy poem's sources were Malory, Geoffrey of Monmouth, the *Mabinogion*, and more immediately, as Heath-Stubbs explained in his memoirs, *Hindsights* (1993), Robert Graves's suggestion in *Count Belisarius* that

> if we had learnt about King Arthur … from an historian like Procopius … we might have had a very different picture of the British leader—as a general trying to preserve what was left of Roman civilisation in western Britain against the barbarian incursion of the Anglo-Saxons. (*Hindsights*, 284)

The poem may also be seen as an act of homage to Charles Williams, whose Arthurian poems *Taliessen Through Logres* and *The Region of the Summer Stars* Heath-Stubbs considered to be among the greatest poetry of the twentieth century.

Heath-Stubbs's early work had been notable for Browning-like monologues put into the mouths of literary or mythological figures. He now repudiated this kind of poetry and adopted a much more direct manner, speaking in his own voice rather than through masks, and experimenting in a wide variety of metrical forms. His technical versatility, comparable in its vast scope to that of Auden, became apparent with the publication by Carcanet of his *Collected Poems, 1943–1987* (1988), where he relegated the poetry of his youthful 'romantic' period to the back of the book. The poem 'Epitaph', written in 1956, began:

> Mr Heath-Stubbs as you must understand
> Came of a gentleman's family out Staffordshire
> Of as good blood as any in England
> But he was wall-eyed and his legs too spare.

His most anthologized poem, he grew to hate and wish he had never written it. Nevertheless, its gentle ironic humour pervades much of his later work. His admiration for the style of such masters as Dryden, Pope, and Crabbe emerged in his *Literary Essays* (1998).

Heath-Stubbs was rescued from the hardship of trying to live on literary earnings boosted by a small inherited income by his appointment as Gregory fellow of poetry at Leeds University in 1952. He was highly successful in this role, making a friend of Bonamy Dobrée, head of the English department, and the composer Peter Dickinson, for whom Heath-Stubbs wrote the libretto of an opera never staged, *The Unicorns*. As a contribution to the revival of poetic drama he wrote *Helen in Egypt* and other verse plays.

After three years at Leeds Heath-Stubbs was made visiting professor of English literature at the University of Alexandria in Egypt. His tenure there coincided with the Suez crisis and he gave an entertaining account in *Hindsights* of his continuing lecturing and teaching while under surveillance by the police as a potential British spy. His next appointments were at Ann Arbor, Michigan, in 1960–61, and then as a lecturer in London at the College of St Mark and St John, Chelsea. Another part-time teaching post followed at Merton College, Oxford, where John Jones, whom he had met as one of William Bell's friends, was the fellow in English. Jones needed someone to look after his pupils while he was engaged on research and working as the professor of poetry. Heath-Stubbs, though by now with only minimal sight, would travel from London to Oxford and back alone. On one occasion he suffered a serious fall while going down the steps at Oxford station and had to go to hospital with a broken hip.

In London he lived alone, too, in a small ground-floor flat in Bayswater but next door to his close friend Guthrie McKie. He had no difficulty in doing his shopping by himself. He was well known to the local shopkeepers, a tall man with a white stick, a glass eye, and a penetrating voice. He enjoyed the company of many friends who called, some of whom regularly read to him. He also enjoyed attending the spring and winter dinners of the Omar Khayyam Club, an all-male sodality aimed at celebrating the life of Edward Fitzgerald and the *Rubáiyát*. Heath-Stubbs had himself made an English version with Peter Avery, published in 1979. He contributed several poems to the club's illustrated menus and made a memorable speech when proposing the toast to the master. His sixtieth and eightieth birthdays were celebrated in special issues of the poetry magazine *Aquarius*, edited by his friend Eddie Linden. He was awarded the queen's gold medal for poetry in 1973 and made an OBE in 1989. Latterly he was cared for at the Athlone House nursing home in Woodfield Road, Westminster. He died in London on 26 December 2006. ANTHONY CURTIS

Sources J. Heath-Stubbs, *Hindsights* (1993) · *Daily Telegraph* (27 Dec 2006); (8 Jan 2007) · *The Independent* (27 Dec 2006) · *The Guardian* (29 Dec 2006); (6 Jan 2007) · *The Times* (30 Dec 2006); (9 Jan 2007); (20 Jan 2007) · *WW* (2006) · personal knowledge (2010) · private information (2010) [J. Jones; T. Braun] · b. cert.

Archives BL., Add. MSS 70795, 71240 · Emory University, Atlanta, papers · Indiana University, Lilly Library, papers · JRL · SUNY, Buffalo State College · U. Leeds, Brotherton L., papers · Washington University, St Louis, typescript of one poem | SOUND U. Leeds, Brotherton L.
Likenesses H. Coster, photographs, 1942, NPG · J. Whitlock Codner, oils, 1947; Bonhams, 21 Sept 2004 · D. Parker, 35mm black and white negative, 1965, NPG [*see illus.*] · N. Foxell, bromide print, 1978, NPG · P. Edwards, oils, 1988–9, NPG · S. Barker, bromide fibre print, 1998, NPG · A. Foxell, bromide fibre print, 1998, NPG · C. Barker, photograph, repro. in S. Barker, ed., *Portraits of poets* (1986) · obituary photographs
Wealth at death £681,944: probate, 7 June 2007, *CGPLA Eng. & Wales*

Swan, (Richard) Kenneth [Ken] **(1919–2005)**, tour operator, was born on 3 April 1919 at 175 High Street, Guildford, Surrey, the only child of William Frederic Swan, founder of Swan's Travel Bureau, and his wife, Gladys, *née* Lumley. He was educated at the City of London School, before leaving in 1935 to join his father's travel agency, where he worked until the outbreak of the Second World War. During the war he organized troop movements, mainly in the Middle East, ending the war with the rank of major. He was married twice: his first marriage, on 6 June 1942, to Lesley Muriel Parker, a twenty-year-old shorthand typist, and daughter of Basil Mason Parker, bank clerk, ended in divorce. After the war he rejoined his father's business, which was renamed W. F. and R. K. Swan Travel Ltd. On 21 November 1951 he married Marion Ethel Knight, a 28-year-old secretary, daughter of Reginald Herbert Balls, grocer's assistant, and former wife of Jack Coldham Knight; they had one son and one daughter.

Before the First World War Swan's father had been private secretary to Sir Henry Lunn, the travel agent and organizer of the first Hellenic Cruise to Troy and the Greek islands in 1908, and founder of the Hellenic Travellers' Club. When in 1951 Swan was asked by the Society for the Promotion of Hellenic Studies to arrange a tour to Greece for its members, he decided to organize it as a cruise. This led the Swans to revive the old Hellenic cruises, and the first cruise was advertised in 1955. From the start the Swans set high academic standards for the guest lecturers on the cruises, who included the archaeologist Sir Mortimer Wheeler, who was also television personality of the year in 1954 as a result of his appearances on *Animal, Vegetable or Mineral*. Wheeler was on the first cruise, and became a director of the company and subsequently chairman of the Hellenic Cruise division. He was in charge of choosing the lecturers, and wrote the detailed handbook to the sites. The lecturers gave talks on board ship, and helped to guide the passengers around the historical sites. Most of the passengers were retired members of the upper and professional classes, and many were as learned as the lecturers, including university dons, headmasters, bishops, judges, and diplomats, all intent on improving their knowledge of the ancient Mediterranean world: dinner-table conversation was at a high intellectual level. The cruises lasted two weeks, and there were usually eight a year, following a varied itinerary, concentrating on classical sites in the Aegean, but also visiting sites in the eastern Mediterranean and on the coast of north Africa. The ships chartered by the company were small—the first, the *Ankara*, took 300 passengers—and this helped to create an intimate atmosphere. Various traditions soon developed: one guest lecturer would be designated chaplain, and read the Acts of the Apostles in the theatre at Ephesus, and cast a wreath as the ship passed Gallipoli. Swan's wartime experience in the logistics of troop movements was the key to his success: everything was meticulously planned, and not only was he there to see the passengers off and welcome them back, but he would, if necessary, fly in during a cruise to deal with any crisis. Thus, for example, in August 1968, when the *Ankara* was in the Black Sea at the time of the Soviet invasion of Czechoslovakia, Swan flew in and directed the cruise to continue as planned to Odessa.

In 1961 Swan succeeded his father as managing director of W. K. and R. K. Swan Travel Ltd. He widened the scope of the cruises, including a 600 mile trip up the Nile, and introduced art treasures tours, including one to India and Ceylon. But in the 1960s other travel companies were developing the idea of cultural cruises, and competition became more intense. In 1968 Swan sold Swan Hellenic to Trust House Forte, remaining as managing director of Swan Hellenic, and also becoming managing director of THF Travel. When Forte decided to sell his travel companies Swan did not buy back Swan Hellenic, and in 1983 it was sold to P&O. His retirement party, Swan's last cruise, was organized by the archbishop of Canterbury, Robert Runcie, and the president of the British Academy, Owen Chadwick, both former Swan Hellenic lecturers: the party was held on the Thames, and the guests included over 100 past and present lecturers. Swan became president of Swan Hellenic, and concerned himself with chartering new ships, *Minerva* in 1996, and the much larger *Minerva II* in 2003. Although many regulars disliked the new large ship, Swan and his wife loved it, and went on several cruises in it.

Swan also helped to create the Association of British Travel Agents (ABTA) in 1950, and played an active part on its councils and committees. He was appointed OBE in 1996 for services to the travel industry. Having lived for many years at Rathmore, Horsell Vale, Woking, Surrey, he died on 21 August 2005 in St Peter's Hospital, Chertsey, Surrey, of heart failure. He was survived by his wife, Marion, and their two children. ANNE PIMLOTT BAKER

Sources *The Times* (14 Aug 1971); (30 Sept 2005); (18 Nov 2006) · J. Hawkes, *Mortimer Wheeler* (1982), ch. 11 · S. Platten, ed., *Runcie: on reflection* (2002), 116–24 · *Daily Telegraph* (4 Oct 2005) · *The Guardian* (10 Oct 2005) · b. cert. · m. certs. · d. cert. · private information (2009)
Likenesses obituary photographs
Wealth at death £596,388: probate, 5 Dec 2005, *CGPLA Eng. & Wales*

Tannahill, (Margery) Reay (1929–2007), food historian and historical novelist, was born on 9 December 1929 at 20 Queen Square, Glasgow, the daughter of James Cowan Tannahill, engineer's draughtsman and estimator, and his wife, Olive Margery, *née* Reay. She was educated at Shawlands Academy and would have liked to have gone to art school or drama school, but instead went to Glasgow University, where she took an MA degree in history and a postgraduate certificate in social sciences. She then worked as a probation officer, an advertising copywriter, a newspaper reporter, and a graphic designer before she secured a job in publishing. On 8 August 1958, at Marylebone register office, she married (Frank Harper) Michael Edwardes (1923–1990), a London publisher, the son of Frank Edwardes, master printer. There were no children of the marriage, which ended in divorce in 1983.

Reay Tannahill (she continued to use her maiden name) was almost an accidental pioneer of food history. Her *Food in History* (1973) was one of the earliest general books on the subject, and though she had no particular qualification for writing it, it remained one of the best. It originated in a commission in the 1960s for the Folio Society, for which she was a press officer, to put together two illustrated presentation books, *Regency England: the Great Age of the Colour Print* (1964) and *Paris in the Revolution* (1966). Asked to think of another subject suitable for an illustrated book, she chose *The Fine Art of Food* (1968). She said that when she embarked on the research she thought it would be easy, 'but I soon discovered just how feeble most of the other books were'. In the 1960s such books as there were on the history of food started with ancient Rome and 'jumped to the Renaissance'. It took her six or seven years to complete the research for *Food in History*. She said she had learned a major lesson when working on the volume on the French Revolution, an illustrated anthology of eyewitness accounts, namely, 'to look very carefully at my sources. Some of the perfectly orthodox sources were totally untrustworthy.' She cited a nineteenth-century French authority who 'did not believe that the French had ever eaten with their fingers', but always

> with knives and forks. When he quoted medieval texts, he twisted them so that the French … were not eating with their fingers. Now a lot of people when they do research just go to the last chap who has written a book, so you get myths like that carried on quite uncritically … I seriously avoided … any book on food history published in the last 150 years. (*The Guardian*, 2 June 1990)

As there was no faculty or school of food history to validate Tannahill's work, some academic historians were reserved about her work. As she later said, 'I had to contend with a certain amount of resistance … if I had crammed half a million years of food history into 400 pages, it must be superficial' (*The Guardian*, 2 June 1990). She was one of the first to recognize the importance of the prehistoric aspect of her subject and to turn to archaeology for an account of the early human diet, just as she was one of the first to realize that the history of agriculture was fundamental. Before her book historians of food had drawn on accounts of feasts and banquets and early cookery books, all of which recorded largely what was eaten by the literate upper classes. Few historians thought it important or interesting to discover what the masses were actually eating, the details of which were more likely to be contained in accounts of crop failures and successes than in glittering tales of court festivities. Though her ambitions were not scholarly in the narrow, academic sense,

> I had enough material so that every paragraph could have been a chapter, and every sentence … a paragraph … I was trying … to produce a panoramic view so that people who were only ever going to read one book about food could know as much as is reasonable for your average educated reader. (ibid.)

She was proud that in the second revision of this title (in 1988) she was one of the first to write at length about genetically modified organisms entering the food supply. A third revision was published in 2002.

Tannahill's next book was *Flesh and Blood: a History of the Cannibal Complex* (1975), using material she had had to omit from *Food in History*. At the urging of her publishers, she tackled the other basic human drive, in *Sex in History* (1980), which was translated into a dozen languages. Tiring of non-fiction, she turned her hand to historical novels, and wrote seven between 1983 and 2001. Latterly she lived a quiet private life in a flat in a smart terrace house near Tate Britain, and gave her recreation as 'work', though she belonged to the Arts Club and the Authors' Club, and was chairman of the latter from 1997 to 2000. Her last books were a pair set in a medieval castle belonging to a formidable widow, Dame Constance de Chair, *Having the Builders In* (2006) and *Having the Decorators In* (2007), the latter published the day before her death, at St Thomas's Hospital, Lambeth, London, on 2 November 2007, of heart disease and septicaemia. PAUL LEVY

Sources *The Guardian* (2 June 1990) • *The Herald* [Glasgow] (21 Nov 2007) • *The Independent* (27 Nov 2007) • *The Times* (27 Dec 2007) • interview with Claire Clifton, 1990 • personal knowledge (2011) • private information (2011) • b. cert. • m. cert. • d. cert.
Archives SOUND BL NSA, documentary recording
Likenesses obituary photographs
Wealth at death £599,150: probate, 14 May 2008, *CGPLA Eng. & Wales*

Tawney, Cyril Francis (1930–2005), folk-singer and songwriter, was born on 12 October 1930 at 6 Caroline Place, off Cobden Street, Forton, Gosport, Hampshire, the younger son of Archibald Stephen Edward Tawney (1896–1961), a telegraphist stationed at the Royal Navy barracks in Portsmouth, and his wife, Rose, *née* Moan (1897–1971). Like his brother, Archibald (Archie), ten years his senior, he went into the Royal Navy: 'I didn't come in from the heart of England to a seaport and join the Navy. I was in the Navy from the cradle' (Hunt, 'Navy man', 39). Four days short of his sixteenth birthday, on 8 October 1946, he joined up and was based at the artificer training establishment at Torpoint (commissioned that December as HMS *Fisgard*). John Gould, Tawney's contemporary, recalled that 'discipline was hard', with the new recruits at the bottom of the naval base's hierarchical pyramid; the base still operated a public school-like fagging system. Tawney became an electrical artificer, or 'tiffy' in naval slang, serving on surface craft and in submarines. His song 'The Lean and Unwashed Tiffy' was sparked by finding Hubert refer to 'Another lean and unwash'd artificer' in Shakespeare's

King John. During his four-year apprenticeship, under the influence of the American folk-singer Burl Ives, he began writing scripts and songs and playing the guitar, going on to appear in shipboard shows, some produced by Lieutenant David Attenborough.

Even then Tawney's songs ranked as more than short-life ditties or show throwaways. The finest were literate and intelligent. His songs were effectively English *chansons* and frequently used folk-song-like models. These traits can be heard in his 'Five-Foot Flirt' (1950), inspired by Red Ingle and the Natural Seven's 'Cigareets, Whuskey, and Wild Wild Women'. While naval allusions populated his songs of this period, more tellingly it was the vernacularity of songs like 'Sally Free and Easy' and 'The Ballad of Sammy's Bar' (both 1958) that enabled them to grow legs and travel.

In 1956, on a visit to London, Tawney performed at an English Folk Dance and Song Society concert, setting in train events that led to him making his wireless début on the BBC Home Service's *Sing Christmas and the Turn of the Year* on Christmas day 1957. This was a feat of live broadcasting linking England, Northern Ireland, Scotland, and Wales, with the American Alan Lomax as anchor-man (though the word only had a nautical meaning then). Tawney, waiting in the Plymouth studio with the local producer Peter Kennedy, was announced as 'Petty Officer Tawney of HMS *Murray*' before launching into the broadcast's longest live solo piece, a John Jacob Niles-styled 'I Wonder as I Wander' to his own guitar accompaniment.

Tawney bought himself out of the navy on 4 May 1959 and became a full-time professional folk-singer that month. At this point there was hardly any folk-club circuit, but, still a bachelor, he managed on income from radio and television. He obtained his first solo folk-club date in October 1961 and, based in the west country, he started a folk-club in January 1962 in Plympton, relocated to Plymouth that June. In 1960 he appeared in two anthologies, *Rocket Along* and *A Pinch of Salt*; his solo début, *Baby Lie Easy*, followed in 1962. On 28 October 1966 he married Rosemary June Radmore (1934–2012), dental nurse, and only child of Harold Albert Charles Radmore, a gardener for Plymouth corporation. They had no children.

Tawney had gone into the navy straight from grammar school without taking school certificate examinations. In 1972 he was accepted as a mature student by Lancaster University on the strength of his extensive private research and writings about folk-song; he graduated BA in English and history in 1975. His dissertation, 'Project Albatross, an investigation into the extent of folk song creativity in the Royal Navy of the 20th century' formed the basis of the introduction and 'sternpiece' to *Grey Funnel Lines: traditional song and verse of the Royal Navy, 1900–1970* (1987), a model of erudition about lower-deck song and versification.

From early in his career Tawney sought out and championed traditional west country folk-songs, notably those in the Baring-Gould collections, conveniently housed in Plymouth's main library. His research in these collections led to recordings that included *The Outlandish Knight* (1969), *Children's Songs From Devon and Cornwall* (1970), *A Mayflower Garland* (1970), and *The Unbuttoned Baring-Gould*, eventually retitled *Down Among the Barley Straw* (1976). It was his proud, and unchallenged, boast that he sang folk-songs for a living longer than anyone else in Britain.

Before he founded Neptune Tapes from his terraced house at 521 Meanwood Road, Leeds, in 1988, initially to present songs from his *Grey Funnel Lines* collection, Tawney's recorded output was scattered across the Argo, HMV, Polydor, Topic, Elektra, Leader, and Free Reed record labels. His songs achieved an extraordinary currency. They were performed and recorded by, among others, Peter Bellamy, Alex Campbell, Adge Cutler and the Wurzels, Lonnie Donegan, Bob Dylan, Marianne Faithfull, Davy Graham, Carolyn Hester, Emmylou Harris and Dolores Keane, Dorris Henderson, Louis Killen, the Silly Sisters (Maddy Prior and June Tabor), Martin Simpson, the Watersons, the Yetties (who sang 'Five-Foot Flirt' at his funeral service), and the Young Tradition. His work appeared in both *The Oxford Book of English Traditional Verse* (1983) and *The Oxford Book of Sea Songs* (1986). He died at the Royal Devon and Exeter Hospital, Wonford, Exeter, on 21 April 2005, after a protracted illness; his death certificate gave bilateral pneumonia and chronic osteomyelitis as the primary causes of death. He was survived by his wife, Rosemary. KEN HUNT

Sources J. Gilbert, 'British folk's father figure', *Sounds* (10 July 1971), 27 · C. Tawney, *Grey funnel lines: traditional song and verse of the Royal Navy, 1900–1970* (1987) · K. Hunt, *Sing Christmas and the turn of the year*, CD booklet notes, Rounder Records, 2000 · *Western Morning News* (23 April 2005) · *The Guardian* (27 April 2005) · *The Independent* (27 April 2005) · *The Times* (29 April 2005); (5 May 2005) · K. Hunt, 'The navy man', *fRoots* (Oct 2005), 39–41 · *Folk Music Journal*, 9/1 (2006), 141–2 · R. Tawney and C. Tawney, *Celebrating Cyril: a commemorative programme* (2007) · personal knowledge (2011) · private information (2011) [Rosemary Tawney, wife; Les Smith, cousin; J. Gould; P. Webb; A. Measom] · b. cert. · m. cert. · d. cert.

Archives Vaughan Williams Memorial Library, London, English Folk Dance and Song Society archive | FILM R. Smedley, *Folk like folk*, black and white film, BBC, 1964 · BFINA, documentary footage · BFINA, light entertainment footage | SOUND Vaughan Williams Memorial Library, London, English Folk Dance and Song Society archive, Cyril Tawney archive · BL NSA, performance recordings · BL NSA, documentary recordings · BL NSA, light entertainment recordings · Rounder Records, Cambridge, Massachusetts, *Sing Christmas and the turn of the year*, 11661-1850-2 · *Sing Chistmas*, BBC Radio 4, 'Archive hour', broadcast 25 Dec 2004 · Neptune Records, Meanwood, Leeds, Yorkshire, *Down the hatch: songs about drink & drinkers*, 1994, NGL 101 CD · ADA Recordings, Belper, Derbyshire, *The song goes on*, 2007, ADA108CD · ADA Recordings, Belper, Derbyshire, *Live at Holsteins*, 2007, ADA109CD

Likenesses B. Shuel, photographs, 1962–5, Getty Images, London

Wealth at death under £136,000: probate, 7 Nov 2005, *CGPLA Eng. & Wales*

Telford, Sir Robert [Bob] **(1915–2008)**, engineer and industrialist, was born on 1 October 1915 at 9 Auburn Road, West Derby, Liverpool, the eldest child in the family of three sons and one daughter of Robert Telford, a clerk in a timber exporting firm, and his wife, Sarah Annie, *née* Mercer, a farmer's daughter. He was not a direct descendant of the famous engineer Thomas Telford, but there was a family connection. As a child he was already interested in radios, taking apart and putting together crystal radio sets. Educated at Quarry Bank high school, Liverpool, until 1929, he moved to Queen Elizabeth's Grammar School, Tamworth, when his parents left Liverpool to take over a farm near Tamworth, Staffordshire. In 1934 he went to Christ's College, Cambridge, to read mechanical sciences, graduating with a third-class degree in 1937.

Telford joined the Marconi Wireless Telegraph Company in 1937 as a management trainee, concentrating on manufacture, and in 1939 he was appointed assistant works manager at the Chelmsford factory. From 1940 he was manager of the Hackbridge works, responsible for the wartime manufacture of airborne and portable radio equipment for the Royal Air Force. On 15 November 1941 he married Isabel Lucy Glover (*b*. 1919/1920), a tracer, daughter of George Cobert Whittenbury Glover, merchant; they had one son. The marriage ended in divorce in 1950.

Following the takeover of Marconi by English Electric in 1946, Telford spent four years in Brazil as managing director of the Companhia Marconi Brasileira, producing radio transmitters and receivers, before returning to Chelmsford in 1950 as assistant to the general manager of Marconi, F. N. Sutherland. Sutherland, who had recently moved to Marconi from English Electric, had been impressed by Telford when they met in Brazil. In 1953 Telford became general works manager, responsible for production in all the Marconi factories, which were mainly concentrated in Essex. He was one of the first to see an early model of the hovercraft in action, when the inventor, Christopher Cockerell, a former Marconi research engineer, and a great friend, demonstrated it to him in his bathroom. On 20 February 1958 he married his second wife, Elizabeth Mary (Betty) Cass, *née* Shelley (*b*. 1927), daughter of Frederick Charles William Shelley, a traffic superintendent. They had two daughters, in addition to one daughter from her previous marriage to Hilton G. Cass.

Telford succeeded Sutherland as general manager in 1958, and when Sutherland was appointed chairman in 1965, Telford became managing director of Marconi. Between 1950 and 1965 he was increasingly involved in developing new products and establishing new factories, moving out from Marconi's traditional area of radio communications to develop a range of new electronic products. By 1965 there were thirteen manufacturing divisions, including satellite communications and aeronautical engineering, compared with only four in 1948, and turnover had grown from £3 million to £33 million. In 1966 exports comprised 50 per cent of the order book.

When the General Electric Company (GEC) merged with English Electric in 1968, the Marconi Company was able to keep its own identity within the newly formed GEC-Marconi Electronics Ltd, which was created out of a group of GEC subsidiaries, including Elliott Automation. This became the defence division of GEC. Telford was appointed managing director of GEC-Marconi Electronics, a position he held for the next sixteen years, while remaining managing director of the Marconi Company Ltd until 1981, when he was elected chairman. He was also chairman of GEC Avionics, the largest part of GEC-Marconi Electronics, from 1982. GEC-Marconi Electronics products included military radar systems, communications equipment, torpedoes, and battlefield command and control systems, and by 1977 the group consisted of thirty-seven companies in the United Kingdom and overseas, with a turnover of £500 million, half of which was earned overseas. The group was awarded nineteen queen's awards, including eleven for export, and in 1978 Telford was knighted for services to export (having been appointed CBE in 1967). Under Telford, GEC-Marconi Electronics was in the forefront of international developments in defence electronics and technology, especially in the field of airborne communications systems.

Telford retired in 1984, after forty-seven years with the Marconi Company, and was appointed life president, a position previously held only by Guglielmo Marconi, the founder of the company. He had risen through the company because of his managerial skills more than because of his ability as an engineer. Of the eleven senior managers appointed by Arnold Weinstock, managing director of GEC, to run the new divisions formed after the 1968 merger, Telford was the only one who had not been a GEC manager. According to one of his former colleagues, 'Bob was a manager not a changer' (Aris, 120).

Always committed to improving the education of engineers, Telford served as a member of the Engineering Industry Training Board from 1968 to 1982. From 1985 to 1988 he was an adviser to the Comett programme, the first European Union education programme, designed to stimulate exchanges between universities and industry. In 1992 the European Society for Engineering Education awarded him the Leonardo da Vinci medal, given to a person who has made a contribution of international significance to engineering education. He held honorary degrees from Salford, Cranfield, Bath, Aston, Bradford, and Birmingham universities, and was a member of the council and court of the University of Essex. He held a number of public positions: he was deputy lieutenant of Essex from 1981, president of the Institution of Production Engineers from 1982 to 1983, a member of the council of the Industrial Society from 1982 to 1986, and chairman of the information technology advisory group set up by the Department of Trade and Industry in 1985. Telford enjoyed country life, 'messing about with a few acres of land' (*Essex Chronicle*, 5 Nov 1965), keeping poultry and ponies, and gardening at his home, Rettendon House, near Chelmsford; he was passionate about cricket, athletics, and Liverpool Football Club. He died of a heart attack on 10 March 2008 in Broomfield Hospital, Broomfield, Essex, and was survived by his second wife, Betty, and his children. A memorial service was held in Chelmsford Cathedral on 30 May 2008. ANNE PIMLOTT BAKER

Sources W. J. Baker, *A history of the Marconi Company* (1970); rev. edn (1996) • S. Aris, *Arnold Weinstock and the making of GEC* (1998) • *The Times* (10 April 2008) • *Essex Chronicle* (24 April 2008); (5 June 2008) • J. Cowdrey and D. Speake, memorial service addresses, Chelmsford Cathedral, 30 May 2008 • Marconi archives, Bodl.

Oxf. • Burke, *Peerage* • *WW* (2008) • private information (2012) • b. cert. • m. certs. • d. cert.
Archives Bodl. Oxf., Marconi archives, MS Marconi 687 | SOUND BL NSA, current affairs and documentary recordings
Likenesses photographs, 1983, Rex Features, London • photographs, Bodl. Oxf., Marconi archives, MS 687
Wealth at death £756,299: probate, 20 Oct 2008, *CGPLA Eng. & Wales*

Templeton, Sir John Marks (1912–2008), investment adviser and philanthropist, was born on 29 November 1912 in Winchester, Tennessee, USA, one of two sons of Harvey Maxwell Templeton, a lawyer who also dealt in property, and his wife, Vella, *née* Handly. Inheriting his parents' active presbyterianism, Templeton was a Sunday school supervisor at fifteen, and a mentor to his schoolfellows. When he found that his high school did not offer the mathematics course he needed for college entry, he taught himself and his fellow students so that they all passed. He went on to study at Yale, reputedly the first from his town to enter college, although his mother was, unusually, a graduate.

In Templeton's second year at Yale, his father lost money in the Wall Street crash and could no longer pay the fees, but Templeton succeeded in paying his own way, partly from the advertising revenue from a newspaper he started and also through winnings at poker. Graduating top of his class, he was awarded a Rhodes scholarship and studied jurisprudence at Balliol College, Oxford, the source of his later Anglophilia. He graduated with a second-class degree in 1936. He then eked out seven formative months on £90 travelling the world with a friend before moving to New York in 1937 as an investment adviser, where he was struck by the insularity of American investors. 'I couldn't find any investment counsellor who specialised in helping people invest outside America. So I saw a wide-open opportunity' (*Smart Money*, 1 April 2004). On 17 April 1937 he married Judith Dudley Folk (*d.* 1950), a Wellesley College student whom he had known in Tennessee. They had two sons and a daughter.

Templeton enjoyed only modest success until 1939 when, on Hitler's invasion of Poland, he borrowed $10,000 and invested $100 on each of the 104 stocks on the New York stock exchange valued at under $1 a share, taking the view that 'during war, everything that was in surplus and therefore unprofitable becomes scarce and profitable' (*The Times*, 9 July 2008). Three years later he had a profit on 100 out of the 104. Meanwhile he opened his own fund management company in 1940, with five wealthy clients. After the war he was one of the first to invest in Japan, following his aphorism that 'the time of maximum pessimism is the time to buy'.

In 1954 Templeton established the Templeton Growth Fund, the foundation of his fortune, a mutual fund headquartered in Canada (to save his clients capital gains tax) which specialized in international stocks. It grew at an astonishing 16 per cent a year between then and Templeton's retirement in 1992, the top performing growth fund in the second half of the twentieth century. It was estimated that $10,000 invested at the start would have been worth $7 million by the time of his death. In part this was due to Templeton's international focus. He called Warren Buffett, his only rival for the title of the USA's most successful investor, 'small-sighted': 'If he had spent more time in foreign nations, he would be better off' (Newsmax, *Financial Intelligence Report*, 16, 2005). He was also the arch-contrarian, declaring mischievously, 'When people are desperately trying to sell, help them and buy. When people are enthusiastically trying to buy, help them and sell' (*The Times*, 9 July 2008). *Money Magazine* dubbed him 'the greatest global stock-picker of the century' (*Money Magazine*, Jan 1999).

Templeton's attention to investment was paralleled by his active and positive Christianity. The fund's annual meetings, like all his business meetings, started with prayer. It was, he argued, not praying for success but a way of calming the mind: 'If you begin with prayer, you will think more clearly and make fewer mistakes.' In an attempt to reconcile any apparent conflicts between his capitalist and Christian beliefs, he argued that competitive business had similarities with religious aims—'it enriches the poor more than any other system humanity has had' (www.sirjohntempleton.org).

In 1951 Templeton's wife died in a cycling accident and he was left to bring up three small children on his own, but on 31 December 1958 he married a widowed neighbour, Irene Reynolds Butler (*d.* 1998). In 1968 they moved to Lyford Cay at Nassau in the Bahamas, where he renounced his American citizenship and became a British subject. There were obvious tax advantages but he argued that he made better decisions at a distance from Wall Street, where it was 'much more difficult to go opposite to the crowd' (*The Times*, 9 July 2008). He sold the Growth Fund in 1992 to Franklin Resources for $913 million, of which $440 million went to him. But he continued to invest and his contrarian views continued to deliver as he liquidated his own and his clients' technology stocks in the 1990s before the internet bubble burst.

Templeton, a lean, spare man, lived relatively frugally in Nassau, running an old car, sending his instructions by fax machine, keeping fit by walking against the ocean current, even travelling around Europe in a Volkswagen van with young relatives, and much of his fortune was spent on his religious interests. 'My neighbours go golfing and yachting,' he said, 'but my viewpoint is that it's far more important to be useful' (*The Times*, 9 July 2008). In 1972 he established the annual Templeton prize 'for progress towards research or discoveries about spiritual realities'. The prize was intended to balance the lack of a religious Nobel prize, and Templeton made sure that it was always worth more than the Nobel awards. (In the year of his death it was worth £820,000.) First awarded to Mother Teresa, its recipients were determined by panels that included Margaret Thatcher and the prince of Wales as well as the Dalai Lama. He was a regular visitor to the United Kingdom, where he was best known for his endowment in 1983 of Templeton College, Oxford, a graduate institution previously known as the Oxford Centre for Management Studies.

Templeton became increasingly fascinated by the idea

of using scientific methods to validate religion: 'No human has grasped one percent of what can be known about spiritual realities. So we are encouraging people to start using the same methods of science that have been so productive in other areas' (Newsmax, *Financial Intelligence Report*, 16, 2005). In 1987 he established the John Templeton Foundation 'as a philanthropic catalyst for discoveries relating to the Big Questions of human purpose and ultimate reality' and to support research on subjects 'ranging from complexity, evolution, and infinity to creativity, forgiveness, love, and free will'. Its motto was 'How little we know, how eager to learn'. In 2004 he put in a further $550 million, allowing the foundation to distribute $60 million a year. The foundation was a major influence in encouraging courses on spirituality and medicine, which became part of the curriculum in most medical schools in the USA. But it was criticized for using its riches to set the agenda for psychological research. Templeton rejected suggestions that he was also trying to finance creationism, insisting that he was encouraging debate. Of science and faith, he said, 'Don't argue—maybe you're both right' (*The Guardian*, 10 July 2008).

Templeton liked to stress the need for humility, pointing out that a third of his clients would have done even better had they not followed his advice. *The Humble Approach* (1981) was the title of the first of ten books, which also included *Is God the Only Reality?* (1993) and *Evidence of Purpose* (1994). Another, *Worldwide Laws of Life* (1998), selecting spiritual principles from a range of different faiths, reflected his belief in the 'diversity of gifts' within major religions which he did not see as conflicting with his personal presbyterian Christian beliefs. He served for forty-two years on the board of the Princeton Theological Seminary, with two terms as president. He was a trustee of Westminster Abbey Trust and a member of the council of Templeton College. He was knighted in 1987. He died in Nassau on 8 July 2008 and was survived by his two sons, Jack and Christopher, his daughter, Anne, having died in 2005. MARTIN ADENEY

Sources *Slate* (8 June 1997) · T. G. Harris, 'Sir John Templeton: mixing science, religion and humility', *Spirituality and Health* (9 Jan 2001) · *Smart Money* (1 April 2004) · *Business Week* (28 Nov 2005) · *Globe and Mail* [Toronto] (22 March 2008) · *The Times* (9 July 2008) · *Daily Telegraph* (9 July 2008) · *The Guardian* (10 July 2008) · *The Independent* (9 July 2008) · www.sirjohntempleton.org, 25 April 2011 · Burke, *Peerage* · *WW* (2008)
Archives SOUND BL NSA, documentary recording
Likenesses L. Pelham, photograph, 1980, Getty Images, London · photographs, 1987–2007, Photoshot, London · E. Bailey, photographs, 2003, PA Photos, London · obituary photographs
Wealth at death wealthy

Tennant, Sir Iain Mark (1919–2006), television executive and businessman, was born on 11 March 1919 at Hyndford House, North Berwick, Haddingtonshire, the only child of Lieutenant-Colonel John Edward Tennant (1890–1941), army and air force officer, and his first wife, Georgina Helen, daughter of General Sir George Macaulay Kirkpatrick. He was descended from Charles Tennant, a fabulously rich Glasgow chemical manufacturer. His father, who had served in the Scots Guards and then commanded the Royal Flying Corps in Mesopotamia at the end of the First World War, divorced his wife in 1925 and was remarried the following year to Victoria Duff, daughter of Sir Robert Duff, second baronet, with whom he had four further children (two son and two daughters). Despite these family upheavals Tennant had a happy childhood. During holidays he developed a love of Scotland at Innes House in Moray, the home of his grandfather Francis John Tennant, and at the Hambro home at Glendoe, near Fort Augustus—Jocelyn Hambro being a lifelong friend.

Tennant was educated at Eton College, where he rowed for the school, and then at Magdalene College, Cambridge, where his passion for the cinema and playing bridge led to his going down after his first year. With an ambition to enter the film industry, in which his family had interests, he worked briefly in studios at Welwyn Garden City before being called up on the outbreak of the Second World War. He was commissioned into the 2nd battalion of the Scots Guards as an intelligence officer in 1940. He was captured at Tobruk in 1942. In prisoner-of-war camps in Italy and Germany he was much involved in entertainment essential to maintaining morale, sometimes staging productions five times a week. His father (who had joined the Royal Air Force Volunteer Reserve as a group captain) was killed in action in 1941 and his grandfather died the following year, leaving him Innes House and part of his estate. The remainder, with Lochnabo House near Lhanbryde, was left to Tennant's only surviving uncle, (Francis) Michael Tennant. He left the army in 1946 with the rank of captain and settled at Innes House. On 11 July that year he married Lady Margaret Isla Helen Marion Ogilvy (*b.* 1920), second daughter of David Lyulph Gore Wolseley Ogilvy, seventh or twelfth earl of Airlie, with whom he had three children, Mark (*b.* 1947), Christopher (1950–2003), and Emma (*b.* 1954).

After the war Tennant worked briefly for the Inverness-based Caledonian Associated Cinemas, which had a string of some fifty cinemas across Scotland and was partly owned by the Tennants. Chaired by Sir Alexander Boyne King, Caledonian was a serious Scottish challenger to the dominant American ABC Films. Tennant became a non-executive director in 1950, a position he held until the business was sold thirty years later. When the film *The Dam Busters* was made in the early 1950s he acted as a gofer in the production. Such was his enthusiasm for the silver screen that he had a cinema fitted up in the old kitchen at Innes House where he could preview films. During the 1950s and early 1960s Caledonian continued to acquire new cinemas and through King formed a close relationship with Films of Scotland. In 1960 King, by way of a subsidiary, Caledonian Television, bid successfully for the franchise for commercial television in the north of Scotland. Renamed Grampian Television, with King as chairman and Tennant as vice-chairman, it went on air the following year, assisted by Howard Steele of Associated-British Picture Corporation. On King's retirement in 1968 Tennant succeeded him as chairman of both Grampian and Caledonian, positions he was to hold for a further twenty years. Under his chairmanship the brevity of

Grampian's board meetings was compensated for by extensive peregrinations around the transmission area as far north as Shetland and as far west as the Hebrides.

Tennant's skill as a non-executive director earned him directorships of the Times Publishing Company from 1962 to 1966 and from 1968 to 1989 of the Clydesdale Bank, a subsidiary of the Midland Bank until 1987. His greatest delight was his chairmanship of Glenlivet Distillers from 1964 until 1984. This was a period of expansion for both blended whisky and single malts. Tennant oversaw the merger with the blenders Hill Thomson & Co. of Edinburgh and with Longmorn-Glenlivet Distilleries in 1972. Although annoyed that the Imperial Group without telling him sold its stake in the company to the Canadian Seagram Corporation in 1977 to give it control, he continued to serve as chairman and joined the Seagram board. During his time as chairman of the company he visited over forty countries as an ambassador for its brands.

Tennant devoted time and energy to public service, particularly in Moray. He served as a county councillor, founded the Moray Sea School in 1949, and in 1963 was appointed lord lieutenant. He became a governor of Gordonstoun School in 1951 and served as chairman from 1957 to 1970; he brought his business acumen to bear in restoring its precarious financial position. During his time as chairman the prince of Wales was a pupil at the school, often spending weekends at Innes House. A member of the Royal Company of Archers from 1950, Tennant was an usher at the coronation in 1953 when he had to sit on the steps beside the pew he was guarding. On sitting down the seam of his trousers split with a loud retort, whereupon a peeress leaned forward to enquire if he needed a needle and thread, as she had one tucked in her coronet. The official appointment he cherished above every other position he held was as crown estate commissioner for Scotland from 1970 to 1990. Although the bulk of the crown lands in Scotland were on Speyside, there were holdings scattered across the country. In just the same way as he made the board of Grampian Television patrol its territory he insisted on visiting crown property in every part of the country to ensure it was well managed and the tenants satisfied. From 1981 to 1986 he served on the newspaper panel of the Monopolies and Mergers Committee. The queen appointed him a knight of the Thistle in 1986 and lord high commissioner to the general assembly of the Church of Scotland in 1988 and 1989.

Tennant's wife never cared for Innes House and when he was unexpectedly left Lochnabo House on the death of his uncle Michael in 1973 the family moved there and Innes House remained empty for some twenty years. Tennant died at Lochnabo on 25 September 2006 of bronchopneumonia and immobility, having suffered increasingly from Parkinson's disease. The funeral service was held at Gordonstoun School on 14 October. He was survived by his wife, Margaret, and two of their children.

Michael S. Moss

Sources *Press and Journal* [Aberdeen] (27 Sept 2006); (28 Sept 2006); (16 Oct 2006); (19 April 2007) • *Daily Telegraph* (30 Oct 2006) • *The Times* (31 Oct 2006) • *The Herald* [Glasgow] (19 April 2007) • Burke, *Peerage* • *WW* (2006) • private information (2010) • b. cert. • m. cert. • d. cert.

Wealth at death £3,565,184.65: confirmation, 19 March 2007, *CCI*

Tennant, Pauline Laetitia [*married names* Pitt-Rivers, Graham, Rumbold], **Lady Rumbold** (**1927–2008**), actress and poet, was born on 6 February 1927 at 13 Beaumont Street, in London's West End, the daughter of David Pax Tennant (1902–1968), son of Edward Priaulx Tennant, first Baron Glenconner, and his wife, Hermione Youlanda Ruby Clinton *Baddeley (1906–1986), actress. Her childhood was divided between the Gargoyle Club in Meard Street, run by her father, and her uncle Stephen Tennant's Gothic pile in Teffont Magna, Wiltshire. She was a close friend of Michael Wishart, the artist, and of her father's second wife, Virginia Parsons (later marchioness of Bath). Through her parents she also got to know well Dylan Thomas, Cyril Connolly, Tambimuttu, Francis Bacon, and Lucian Freud; the latter painted her in 1945. She made her stage début as a chorus girl before starring in Ben Travers's *She Follows Me About* (1943), with Robertson Hare, and in 1945 appeared on the front cover of *Theatre World*. She made her screen début in *Great Day* (1945), with Eric Portman and Sheila Sim. In *The Queen of Spades* (1949) she played the 'young countess' who sells her soul to the devil. She was married three times: first on 17 August 1946 to the social anthropologist Julian Alfred Lane Fox Pitt-*Rivers (1919–2001); second on 3 June 1954 to Euan Douglas Graham (1924–2007), grandson of the fifth duke of Montrose, and principal clerk of bills of the House of Lords, with whom she adopted a son, Andrew; and third on 14 December 1974 to Sir (Horace) Anthony Claude Rumbold, tenth baronet (1911–1983), a retired diplomat. They lived in Tisbury, Wiltshire, before moving to Dorchester, Dorset, where she was at the centre of an extensive social life. In 1989 she published a translation of the Dorset poet William Barnes's dialect verse, and in 1992 a book of her own poems, *Loaves and Fishes*. Towards the end of her life she moved back to Wiltshire, to a townhouse at Wilton, near Salisbury. She died on 6 December 2008 and was survived by her adopted son.

Sources *The Independent* (13 Dec 2008) • *Daily Telegraph* (18 Dec 2008) • *The Times* (24 Dec 2008) • b. cert. • m. certs.

Likenesses L. Freud, oils, 1945 • obituary photographs

Thoday, John Marion (**1916–2008**), radiobiologist and geneticist, was born on 30 August 1916 at 5 Lyme Park, Chinley, Derbyshire, the third of four sons of David *Thoday (1883–1964), botanist, and his wife, Mary Gladys, *née* Sykes (1884–1943), also a botanist. From the ages of two to six he was brought up in South Africa, where his father was professor of botany at the University of Cape Town; the family then settled in Bangor on his father's appointment as professor of botany at the University College of North Wales. He was educated at Bootham School, York, and then (much influenced by both his parents) read botany at Bangor, where his father was still head of department. In 1939 he graduated with an upper-second-class degree and began research into the effects of neutrons on chromosomes for a PhD at Trinity College, Cambridge, supervised by David Catcheside. His research was interrupted by the Second World War, and from 1941 to 1946 he worked as a photographic intelligence officer in the RAF, in Britain, north Africa, and Italy; he was promoted squadron leader in 1944. He eventually completed his Cambridge PhD in 1948.

On demobilization in 1946 Thoday found work as a cytologist and radiobiologist at the Mount Vernon Hospital and Radium Institute, at Northwood, Middlesex. His work there with John Read on the biological effects of radiation was highly significant, leading to ground-breaking papers showing, first, that the radiotherapeutic effect of X-rays on tissue growth was largely due to chromosome breakage, and, second, that X-rays are far more effective at causing chromosome breakage in the presence of oxygen.

In 1947 Thoday was appointed assistant lecturer in cytogenetics at the University of Sheffield. There he introduced the teaching of genetics to students of botany and zoology, and in 1954, appointed a senior lecturer, founded and led the university's new department of genetics. By this time his interests had switched from radiobiology to quantitative and evolutionary genetics, and in 1953 he published in the *Symposia of the Society for Experimental Biology* a highly influential theoretical paper, 'Components of Fitness', which underscored the importance of genetic flexibility for evolutionary potential. While at Sheffield he served the university in a number of ways, including as sub-warden of Crewe Hall, secretary of the non-professorial staff association, and secretary then president of the University Philosophical Society. He also, on 4 July 1950, married Doris Joan Rich (*b.* 1923), a sociologist, and daughter of Samuel Rich, draper; they had a daughter, Antonia (*b.* 1954), and a son, Jonathan (*b.* 1961).

In 1959 Thoday returned to Cambridge as the Arthur Balfour professor of genetics (succeeding the eminent geneticist R. A. Fisher), head of the department of genetics, and fellow of Emmanuel College. Within a few years he had succeeded where his predecessors had failed, in having genetics taught in part one of the natural sciences tripos. He also oversaw two moves of his department, first from its cramped quarters in Storeys Way to a much more spacious site on Milton Road, and then in 1976, following the move of the Cavendish Laboratory, to the central Downing site.

At Cambridge Thoday continued the work he had started at Sheffield on the mechanisms of genetic variance and evolutionary change, illustrating the ways in which individual species adapt and respond to their environments. Perhaps his most significant work, in collaboration with J. B. Gibson, was on the common fruit fly, *Drosophila melanogaster.* Thoday and Gibson selected two groups from a single culture of *Drosophila*, differentiated by high and low bristle numbers, finding that, despite the two groups being allowed to interbreed freely, they continued to show significant genetic divergence in subsequent generations when placed in distinctively different environments, albeit within a short distance of each other. This work confirmed the hypothesis of 'disruptive selection' first noticed by Charles Darwin among the finch populations of the Galapagos Islands (with the emergence of two different populations of finches, one with long beaks adapted to retrieving large seeds, and another with small beaks adapted to retrieving small seeds). The accepted wisdom at the time suggested that animal and plant populations could only exhibit sustained genetic differences when they were geographically separated, whereas Thoday and Gibson's work suggested that species could adapt selectively to different 'niches' within a single locality. Hence genetic separation was not a prerequisite for genetic divergence; indeed, genetic divergence could result from localized environmental factors and could lead in time to the development of separate species.

A gregarious, ebullient man who enjoyed controversy and the cut-and-thrust of debate, Thoday was also an excellent supervisor and much-loved head of department, who interested himself in his students' research and loved nothing better than to play darts and discuss research problems over a lunchtime pint. He was elected a fellow of the Royal Society in 1965, and served as president of the Genetical Society in 1975–8. He retired in 1983 (becoming an emeritus professor at Cambridge and a life fellow of Emmanuel College), but from 1982 to 1988 was active as the chairman of the UK National Committee for Biology. He was devoted to his college, presenting it with two chimeric trees, one a hawthorn core with a layer of medlar, and the other a laburnum core with a layer of creeping broom. A humanist—'since I was about sixteen I have found religion makes no sense', he said (John Thoday website, 'funeral service')—he described his political views as those of an 'old-fashioned liberal' (*The Guardian*, 3 Oct 2008). In line with his research, he had no truck with either extreme in the nature versus nurture debate, emphasizing the creative interplay of inheritance and environment. He remained in Cambridge in retirement, and died at his home, 7 Clarkson Road, on 25 August 2008, following a stroke. He was survived by his wife, Doris, an emeritus fellow of Lucy Cavendish College, and their two children. His funeral was held on 16 September and a memorial service was held in Emmanuel College chapel on 22 November 2008. ALEX MAY

Sources *Cambridge News* (4 Sept 2008) • *The Times* (12 Sept 2008); (24 Nov 2008) • *Daily Telegraph* (15 Sept 2008) • *The Guardian* (3 Oct 2008) • www.professorjohnthoday.com, 18 Aug 2011 • *WW* (2008) • b. cert. • m. cert. • d. cert.

Likenesses obituary photographs

Wealth at death £751,266: probate, 25 Nov 2008, *CGPLA Eng. & Wales*

Thomas, Marjorie Gwendolen (1923–2008), singer, was born on 5 June 1923 at 144 Hastings Street, Sunderland, the daughter of Alfred Evan Thomas, marine engine draughtsman, and his wife, Christina, *née* Neish. She moved to Oldham, Lancashire, with her parents at the age of two. Although born in the north-east of England, and brought up on the other side of the Pennines, she was of Welsh and Scottish descent. Her parents were amateur musicians and it was with her mother that she had her first piano lessons before transferring to William Walton's brother Noel. After attending Hulme and Manchester grammar schools for girls, she won a scholarship to study piano at the Royal Manchester College of Music in 1940. But at the beginning of her second term she transferred to singing and was taught by Elsie Thurston, later the teacher of Elisabeth Harewood. After graduating in 1944, she taught at Stockport High School for Girls, where one of her singing students was Joan Bakewell.

Thomas quickly made an impact in Manchester and soon came to the attention of John Barbirolli, the permanent conductor of the city's Hallé Orchestra. A passionate Elgarian, Barbirolli was always on the lookout for young singers who could do justice to Elgar's music. After auditioning for him in 1944, Thomas was engaged to sing Elgar's *Sea Pictures* at Manchester's Albert Hall under his baton that November. In December 1945 she was invited by Barbirolli's arch-nemesis Sir Thomas Beecham to sing the role of Konchakovna for a broadcast performance of Alexander Borodin's *Prince Igor* for the BBC. It was during those sessions at the corporation's Maida Vale studios that she met the sound engineer Edwin Robert James Gower (1902–1982), the son of Robert Gower, mechanical engineer, whom she married (following his divorce from Anne, *née* Gold) on 5 June 1947.

Impressed by her performance in Borodin's opera, Beecham asked Thomas to sing a group of songs at his London Delius festival at the Central Hall, Westminster, in 1946, and to sing the contralto part for the second of his three *Messiah* recordings, which he documented for Columbia in 1947. The next year, she gave birth to her only child, Eileen, before taking a year off singing. Her absence from the concert platform did not harm her career, and in 1950 (retaining her maiden name for professional purposes) she sang the role of Nancy in Benjamin Britten's *Albert Herring* at the Cheltenham festival and the part of Dryade in Richard Strauss's *Ariadne auf Naxos* at the Glyndebourne festival, which she revived for the company in 1953, the same year that she sang in Sidney Gilliat and Frank Launder's film *The Story of Gilbert and Sullivan*, starring Robert Morley and Maurice Evans.

In 1951 Thomas sang for Sir Malcolm Sargent for the first time. Captivated by her luminous vocal timbre, he engaged her immediately and went on to become her most decisive influence. He regularly used her for performances with the Royal and Huddersfield choral societies, and considered her his ideal interpreter for his orchestration of Brahms's *Four Serious Songs*. In 1954 he chose her for the part of the Angel for his critically acclaimed EMI recording of *The Dream of Gerontius* with the Huddersfield Choral Society and the Royal Liverpool Philharmonic Orchestra. She then went on to record with Sargent Handel's *Messiah* (twice), Mendelssohn's *Elijah*, Vaughan Williams's *Serenade to Music*, and *The Gondoliers*, *Iolanthe*, *The Mikado*, *The Yeoman of the Guard*, *HMS Pinafore*, *The Pirates of Penzance*, and *Patience* by Gilbert and Sullivan. Of Sargent, she said that 'his interpretations always had such elasticity. He was always prepared to give soloists a great deal of freedom in interpretation and one never felt rushed or dragged back' (Aldous, 54–5), qualities that she considered essential in any conductor.

In 1953 Thomas sang the roles of the Rhinemaiden Flosshilde and the Valkyrie Rossweisse for Rudolf Kempe's much-praised reading of Wagner's *Der Ring des Nibelungen* at the Royal Opera House, Covent Garden. There, she later sang the part of Magdalene in *Die Meistersinger von Nürnberg* under Rafael Kubelik, with whom she recorded Mahler's symphony no. 3 with the Bavarian Radio Symphony Orchestra for Deutsche Grammophon in 1967. In 1954 she took part in the English Opera Group's staging of *The Beggar's Opera* at Sadler's Wells, and the following year she sang at EMI's first stereo session for Bach's cantata no. 6 with the Bach Choir under Reginald Jacques. In 1960 Benjamin Britten invited her to sing Hermia in *A Midsummer Night's Dream* at Aldeburgh, the Holland Festival, and Covent Garden, and in 1963 she represented Britain in a performance of Bach's B minor mass at the Vatican with other international artists to mark the accession of Pope Paul VI. Six years later she sang for the investiture of the prince of Wales at Caernarfon.

In December 1973 Thomas left the concert hall and the opera house. Fittingly, the last work that she sang publicly was Handel's *Messiah* with the Huddersfield Choral Society, a performance later described as 'unlikely to be forgotten by those present' (*The Times*, 9 Oct 2008). After returning to her alma mater in Manchester as a singing teacher, she was invited by Sir Thomas Armstrong to succeeded Astra Desmond as professor of singing at the Royal Academy of Music, London, where she was later appointed its first head of vocal studies in 1984. She retired from teaching in 1990 but took up a number of hobbies, including gardening, knitting, tapestry, and lace-making. She lived latterly at 121 Coleraine Road, Greenwich, and died in London on 12 September 2008, survived by her daughter.

Marjorie Thomas was one of Britain's most distinguished twentieth-century singers. At the peak of her career, she worked with many of the world's leading conductors and was often their first choice when engaging contraltos and mezzo-sopranos. Her velvety tone meant that she was ideally suited to oratorio singing and was renowned for her interpretations of the Angel in Elgar's *Dream of Gerontius* and the alto part in Handel's *Messiah*. Like her predecessors, Dame Clara Butt and Kathleen Ferrier, she was a role model for many young singers and was celebrated by audiences on both sides of the Atlantic.

RAYMOND HOLDEN

Sources H. Rosenthal, *Two centuries of opera at Covent Garden* (1958) · S. Hughes, *Glyndebourne* (1965) · R. Aldous, *Tunes of glory: the life of Malcolm Sargent* (2001) · *The Guardian* (25 Sept 2008) · *Daily Telegraph* (27 Sept 2008) · *The Times* (3 Oct 2008); (9 Oct 2008) · *The Independent* (19 Nov 2008) · archive, Royal Academy of Music, London · personal knowledge (2012) · private information (2012) · b. cert. · m. cert.

Archives SOUND BL NSA, performance recordings

Likenesses obituary photographs · photograph, Lebrecht Music and Arts Photo Library, London

Wealth at death £495,083: probate, 15 Oct 2009, *CGPLA Eng. & Wales*

Thomas, Peter Kynaston (1926–2008), neurologist, was born on 28 June 1926 at St James Nursing Home, Swansea, the eldest of three sons of Heber Lesley Thomas (1901–1950), timber importer and author, of Caswell Bay, Gower, and his wife, Beatrice Ida Carmen, *née* Couch (1903–1978), daughter of Thomas Henry Couch, shipping and travel agent. Educated at the Parents' National Education Union school in Swansea and Emmanuel Grammar School (formerly the Bible College of Wales), Swansea, where he acquired a reputation for outstanding essays characterized by careful and exact use of language and correct punctuation, he matriculated at University College, London, as an open entrance scholar in 1944. Graduating BSc in 1947 and MB BS in 1950, he was a part-time demonstrator in anatomy at University College and part-time lecturer in physical anthropology at Birkbeck College, London, both from 1947 to 1950. He did his national service with the Royal Army Medical Corps as a physiologist and secretary to the military personnel research committee (1952–4); held junior hospital appointments at University College Hospital and the Middlesex Hospital, London (1950–57); trained in neurology at the National Hospital for Nervous Diseases, London (1957–61); and was briefly assistant professor of neurology at McGill University, Montreal (1961–2), before taking up appointments as neurologist to the Royal Free Hospital Group (1962–91), the National Hospital (1963–91), and the Royal National Orthopaedic Hospital, London (1965–74). He was contemporaneously senior lecturer at the Institute of Neurology, University of London (1963–74), then professor of neurology in the University of London (1974–91).

Thomas was a versatile and intuitive clinical neurologist who drew effortlessly on a vast font of knowledge and experience in shaping his clinical opinions and writings, and a talented investigator who played a key role in the evolution of clinical neuroscience in the United Kingdom during the second half of the twentieth century. While he was loyal to the National Hospital where he had trained and worked throughout his career, the school of clinical neuroscience that he developed and nurtured at the Royal Free Hospital School of Medicine started the necessary process of devolving modern neurology away from the epicentre of Queen Square. He was foundation president of the European Neurological Society, which he helped to form in 1988; served as president of the Association of British Neurologists in 1990–91, having acted as honorary secretary from 1977 to 1980; and was awarded the association's medal in 1997. He was made a CBE in 1997. As a young man he styled himself Peter Kynaston Thomas, but in the late 1950s became known universally as 'PK' and that sobriquet stuck thereafter.

Thomas married first, on 8 March 1952, Mary Truscott Cox (1928–1977), daughter of Frederick Truscott Cox, architect and building contractor; they had two sons, Adrian (*b.* 1954) and Nicholas (*b.* 1955). Following her death he married, on 17 September 1977, Anita Elizabeth Harding (1952–1995), a neurologist then working as a registrar at the National Hospital (later professor of clinical neurology at the Institute of Neurology), adopted daughter of George Alfred Harding, chiropodist. Widowed a second time, on 7 August 1999 he married Sawanthana (Sam) Ponsford, *née* Hemachudha, neurophysiologist, daughter of Chitt Hemachudha, medical practitioner, of Bangkok; by this marriage he became stepfather to her son, Mark (*b.* 1987), from her former marriage to another neurologist, Richard Ponsford.

The shape of Thomas's scientific career was set early: his lifelong interest in structure and function of the peripheral nervous system began through contact as an undergraduate with J. Z. (John Zachary) Young, who encouraged him to study the lateral line nerve of the trout. Thomas was quick to apply new techniques to the study of human peripheral nerve disease as experimental neurology flowered from the 1950s: his use of nerve biopsy, electrophysiology, electron microscopy, tissue culture, experimental models of common disorders such as the neuropathy that often complicates maturity onset diabetes, and eventually transgenic mouse models of human peripheral neuropathy, meant that his work over five decades remained innovative, creative, and influential. Early on he showed that, in health, nerve fibre diameter and internodal length determine the speed of electrical conduction; and, with Roger Gilliatt, he described neurophysiological features that distinguish degeneration of peripheral nerve fibres from those disorders primarily causing loss of the surrounding myelin sheath. This led to his work, especially with Anita Harding, on the classification and clinical phenotypes of a range of genetically determined peripheral neuropathies. Many important discoveries relating to the mechanisms of inherited neuropathies followed; and, despite Harding's untimely death in 1995, new disorders were systematically described throughout the rest of Thomas's professional career. These always involved careful clinical and laboratory examination, sometimes performed in remote places: loss of vision and painful sensory neuropathy attributed to nutritional deficiency in Cuba (where reputedly Fidel Castro took something of a shine to Thomas); hitherto unrecognized disorders of the Roma Gypsies in Bulgaria; and, in the last clinical study with which he was directly involved, climbing to 15,000 feet in remote regions of the Peruvian Andes to perform nerve biopsies and conduction studies for a study of altitudinal neuropathy.

Thomas was a prodigiously energetic and diligent editor of neurological journals. He served as co-chief editor of the *Journal of Neurology* (formerly *Zeitschrift für Neurologie*) with Marco Mumenthaler (1979–81) and subsequently as editor of *Brain* (1982–91) and the *Journal of Anatomy* (1990–2001). Colleagues remembered him weighed down by his shoulder bag in which papers currently under consideration were carried; anywhere and everywhere—airport lounge, conference auditorium, restaurant, before and after an out-patient clinic, and at any time when no other essential activity was taking place—he would be altering, polishing, and invariably improving the style and narrative of these manuscripts. Despite his place of education he was not above insisting on withdrawal of a reference to Deuteronomy, in which the author claimed the condition of interest was first described, on the grounds that the citation was 'of a religious nature', declaring his editorial judgement to be 'Solomonic' (private information). As editor of the *Journal of Anatomy* he revolutionized the appearance of the journal and modernized its content and distribution. Filling in for delinquent authors and committing to rigorous copy-editing of manuscripts were skills honed in the 1970s when he co-edited, with Peter Dyck and Edward Lambert, a monograph, *Peripheral Neuropathy* (1975; 4th edn, 2005); and, also with Peter Dyck, *Diabetic Neuropathy* (1987; 2nd edn, 1999), the definitive work on the subject.

Outwardly shy, terse in his spontaneous conversation, and capable of falling asleep in any company at any time—little surprise given the pace he and Anita Harding set for revelling and late nights—Thomas attracted and retained friends of many ages. He had an impish smile and sense of humour; could entertain a small child sitting on his knee with Welsh nursery rhymes; out-ski people half his age; and offer penetrating intellectual conclusions in speech or writing while apparently dozing or listening intently to the minimalist, electronic, and atonal modern compositions that seemed to resonate with the ancient rhythms of his Welsh roots. In 2001 he suffered a stroke which left him badly disabled and unable to maintain the professional activities on which he had thrived. He died of a chest infection at his home at 33 West Hill Park, Highgate, on 25 January 2008, and was survived by his wife, Sam, his two sons, and his stepson.

ALASTAIR COMPSTON

Sources *World Neurology*, 23/1 (March 2008), 16 · *BMJ*, 336 (22 March 2008), 674 · *The Guardian* (27 March 2008) · *The Times* (28 March 2008) · *Neurology Today*, 8/7 (3 April 2008), 32 · *Journal of the Neurological Sciences*, 273 (15 Oct 2008), 1–2 · *Journal of Neurology*, 255/3 (2008), 317 · *Archives of Neurology*, 65/7 (2008), 989 · A. K. Asbury and others, 'Professor P. K. Thomas: clinician, investigator, editor, and leader—a retrospective appreciation', *Brain*, 134 (2011), 618–26 · personal knowledge (2012) · private information (2012) · b. cert. · m. certs. · d. cert.
Likenesses obituary photographs
Wealth at death £1,053,068: probate, 16 Dec 2008, *CGPLA Eng. & Wales*

Thompson, Donald James [Don] (**1933–2006**), athlete, was born on 20 January 1933 at 6 Cleveland Road, Hillingdon, London, the son of Lauri James Thompson, aircraft draughtsman, and his wife, Doris Alice, *née* Denny. At the time of the registration of his birth his parents lived at 61 Keith Road, Hayes. He was educated locally. He took up running as a child, but an injury to his Achilles tendon when he was eighteen made him switch his attention to race walking as a member of the Metropolitan Walking Club. While working in insurance, he started to make an impact in the amateur racing world in 1954, when he finished second in his first London to Brighton walk, a distance of 52.5 miles.

In 1955 Thompson achieved national and international success as a race walker, winning the London to Brighton race and the 100 km Milan race. His diminutive frame—he was 5 feet 5 inches at his tallest—and his powerful performance earned him the nickname of *il topolino* (the little mouse) from the Italian spectators, a sobriquet that stuck. In 1956 he successfully defended his London to Brighton title, won the Race Walking Association (RWA) 50 km at Enfield, and represented Great Britain in the 50 km race at the Melbourne Olympic games. However, he suffered from dehydration in the Melbourne race, and withdrew after 45 km while in fifth place. Thompson dominated the sport in the late 1950s and early 1960s, regularly winning the RWA 50 km and the London to Brighton race, setting a course record of 7 hours 35 minutes 12 seconds in the latter in 1957. He also challenged for the European 50 km title in 1958, finishing in fifth place. In all, he won the RWA 50 km title eight times (from 1956 to 1962 and again in 1966), and the London to Brighton race nine times (from 1955 to 1962 and in 1967). His performances in the RWA's events won him that association's Edgar Horton cup in 1956, 1957, 1958, and 1961, while his performances on the London to Brighton race led him to be known as Mr Brighton in the race-walking world.

Thompson's fame spread beyond the relatively small world of British race walking in 1960 when he won the gold medal in the 50 km walk at the Rome Olympic games. He had learnt the lesson of his dehydration in Melbourne, and included some home-made climate training in his preparation for Rome. As well as concentrating on distance and stamina in his regular road training around his home in Cranford, Middlesex, he turned the bathroom of his mother's house into a heat chamber, blocking the doors and windows and using steam and an oil heater to get the temperature up to 43°C. He carried out close to twenty of these sessions, exercising in the heat and humidity for up to three quarters of an hour each time. The carbon monoxide fumes from the heater were a problem, but when he got to Rome, and had to race in 38°C heat, he found himself well prepared. With sunglasses and his trademark sunhat, made of a handkerchief sewn on to a cap, he started well, and when two of the early leaders were disqualified for losing contact with the ground, Thompson found himself battling for gold with John Ljunggren of Sweden. Thompson led for the last 5 km, and won by just 17 seconds in a new Olympic record of 4.25.30. Thompson later described himself as 'smugly happy' (*The Times*) with his victory, which was the only British athletics gold at Rome. He added to his international success later in 1960 by winning the Milan 100 km, and became the first—and at the time of his death only—race walker to be named sportsman of the year by the Sports Writers' Association.

As well as continuing to dominate domestic competition in the early 1960s and breaking British records at all distances from 20 to 30 miles and 25 to 50 km, Thompson also competed internationally, coming third in the European 50 km championship in 1962. He defended his Olympic title in Tokyo in 1964, but failed to retain the gold, ending in tenth place. However, his time of 4.22.39 was almost three minutes faster than his Rome time. He competed in the 1966 Commonwealth games in Kingston, Jamaica, switching down to the 20 km and finishing in fourth place. He also raced in the European championship and the Lugano cup in 1967, the last international performances of his race walking career.

On 26 May 1967, at Epsom register office, Thompson married Margaret (Maggie) Ball, a 28-year-old secretary at a teachers' training college, and daughter of John Arthur Ball, local government officer. They had one son and one daughter. They settled in Hythe, Kent, with Thompson joining the Folkestone Running Club. Although withdrawing from international competition, he remained active in both race walking and in long-distance running, managing over 150 marathons with a personal best time of 2.51. He maintained high mileage training for the rest of his life, combining his work as a self-employed gardener with training walks and runs of over 100 miles per week. In 1978 he achieved race walking's centurion status by completing the Leicester to Skegness 100 mile walk. He made an unlikely international return in 1991, when he was a member of the British team in a 200 km walk in France. He remained dedicated to the sport at club level, and was still active into his seventies as 'the elder statesman of English Walking' (Erickson). In March 2006, Thompson and his wife moved from Hythe to Fleet in Hampshire to be closer to their children's families. In October of that year, Thompson suffered an aneurysm. He died of a subarachnoid haemorrhage and pneumonia on 3 October 2006 at Frimley Park Hospital, Surrey. He was survived by his wife and their two children.

MARTIN POLLEY

Sources *The games of the XVII Olympiad, Rome 1960: the official report of the organizing committee* (1960) • D. Thompson, *The Don Thompson story* (1960) • I. Buchanan, *British Olympians: a hundred years of gold medallists* (1991) • *The Times* (10 Oct 2006) • *The Independent* (10 Oct 2006) • *The Guardian* (24 Oct 2006) • T. Erickson, *Centurion Footnotes*, 15 (2006), 6–10 • b. cert. • m. cert. • d. cert.

Likenesses photograph, 1960, Getty Images, London, Popperfoto • photographs, 1960–64, Getty Images, London, Hult. Arch. • obituary photographs • photograph, repro. in www.sportingheroes.net

Wealth at death under £189,000: probate, 22 Dec 2006, *CGPLA Eng. & Wales*

Thomson, (Robert Howard) Garry (1925–2007), museum conservator and author, was born on Carey Island, Malaya, on 13 September 1925, the son of Robert Thomson, a planter engaged in the production of plant oil, and his wife, Moira, *née* Spence. He was educated at Charterhouse School and served in India with the Royal Electrical and Mechanical Engineers during the final phase of the war in Asia. On demobilization he studied chemistry at Magdalene College, Cambridge, where he also established a Buddhist group, the start of a lifelong association as a writer on and teacher of its practices. In 1951 Thomson joined the editorial staff of the ICI-funded *History of Technology*, the first comprehensive survey of the subject (5 vols., 1954–8). On 28 September 1954, at Kensington register office, London, he married Mom Rajawongse Saisvasdi Svasti (known as Noy), the 23-year-old daughter of the Thai prince Mom Choa Subhai Svasti; they had four sons.

Thomson made his decisive move into conservation in 1955 when he became a research chemist in the scientific department of the National Gallery, London. Within five years he had risen to head the department as scientific adviser to the trustees, a position he held until his retirement in 1985. In the decades before his joining the National Gallery there had been relatively few scientifically trained conservators at British museums and galleries. Conservation, moreover, was principally understood as the repair and restoration of already damaged art works and objects, a procedure that inevitably compromised the appearance and authenticity of the original work. In the post-war period the National Gallery began to review this approach and to employ greater numbers of scientifically trained conservatorial staff, Thomson included. However, it was he—as the gallery's scientific adviser—who initiated a new discipline (subsequently known as preventative conservation) that sought to limit the need for intrusive restoration work through improvements to the conditions in which collections were kept. Thomson's particular interest was the effect of light on old master paintings and, from this, the maintenance of environments for storage and display—conditioned by light, heat, humidity, and air quality—that would minimize the risk of deterioration or damage. An appearance on the BBC's popular science programme *Tomorrow's World*, on which he advocated the need for paintings to be displayed under low-level lighting, is said to have earned him the nickname Twilight Thomson. Members of his small team at the National Gallery were also encouraged to study the composition and use of historical pigments, canvases, and other organic materials to understand better the optimal conditions for preservation, while links between art conservation and scientific research were strengthened with the involvement of university-based physicists in the gallery's work. These collaborations led to the development of new gallery practices, such as the analysis of cross-sections of paint layers, and the introduction of techniques used in forensic science, including electron microscopy and gas chromatography with mass spectrometry.

Thomson dedicated considerable time to the promotion of new standards and methods among his fellow curators and conservators. His edited collections *Recent Advances in Conservation* and *Museum Climatology* appeared in 1963 and 1967, and between 1959 and 1967 he was honorary editor of *Studies in Conservation*, the journal of the International Institute for the Conservation of Historic and Artistic Works, of which he was later president (1983–6). In September 1967 he organized the institute's first conference on museum climatology; six years later he devised and taught a course on the scientific principles of conservation for UNESCO's International Centre for the Study of the Preservation and Restoration of Cultural Property, for which he also advised on collections in north Africa, the Middle East, and Asia. In 1978 he published his most important work, *The Museum Environment* (1978), in which he set out the principles and practices of preventive conservation in a form accessible to those without a scientific background. The book, revised in 1986, proved highly influential in promoting a discipline later adopted in museums and galleries worldwide, and became a standard text in the teaching of conservation.

In 1983 Thomson was appointed CBE for services to conservation and in 1999 he became the first recipient of the Plowden gold medal, awarded by the Royal Warrant Holders' Association and named after Anna Plowden. Having retired from the National Gallery in 1985 he maintained his professional interests as a trustee of the National Museums and Galleries on Merseyside and continued to lecture for the International Centre for the Preservation and Restoration of Cultural Property. He was also able to dedicate greater time to the study and practice of Buddhism. For a decade from 1978 he was vice-president of the Buddhist Society, London, of which he had been a long-standing member, and for which he gave public talks and taught basic meditation. A regular contributor to the society's journal, he was also the author of two books, *Reflections on the Life of the Buddha* (1982) and *The Sceptical Buddhist* (1995), to which he brought a characteristic openness, generosity, and practicality. Thomson suffered from Parkinson's disease and died at his home, Squires Hill, Tilford, Surrey, of bronchopneumonia on 23 May 2007; he was survived by his wife and four sons.

PHILIP CARTER

Sources *The Independent* (25 June 2007) · *Daily Telegraph* (25 June 2007) · *The Times* (25 June 2007) · *WW* (2007) · m. cert. · d. cert.
Likenesses obituary photographs
Wealth at death £1,479,353: probate, 12 Oct 2007, *CGPLA Eng. & Wales*

George Morgan Thomson, Baron Thomson of Monifieth (1921–2008), by Bassano, 1966

Thomson, George Morgan, **Baron Thomson of Monifieth** (**1921–2008**), politician and public servant, was born on 16 January 1921 at 67b Port Street, Stirling, the son of James Thomson, commercial traveller, and his wife, Caroline Reid, *née* Morgan. His family, of the respectable lower middle class, moved shortly to Monifieth on the outskirts of Dundee, where he was educated at Grove Academy. After leaving school at sixteen he became a trainee journalist with the prominent Dundee publisher D. C. Thomson (no relation). In his later career he was happy to claim that he had briefly edited *The Dandy*, a popular 1930s children's comic.

After six years' wartime service in the RAF Thomson began to turn towards politics, becoming the assistant editor, then editor, of *Forward*, a Scottish Labour Party newspaper (which he helped relaunch nationwide in support of Hugh Gaitskell, the Labour Party leader in 1954). On 23 December 1948, at Hillhead register office, Glasgow, he married Grace Jenkins, a trainee teacher four years his junior, daughter of Cunningham Jenkins, museum attendant. Although Thomson had not hitherto played a significant part in local politics, he was chosen as the Labour candidate for the Hillhead constituency in the 1950 general election. He lost and the seat remained Conservative until Roy Jenkins (with Thomson's blessing) won a 1982 by-election for the Social Democratic Party.

Thomson did not contest the 1951 general election, but after the death of the incumbent Labour MP for Dundee East, Thomas Fotheringham Cook, he fought a by-election in July 1952, winning with 22,161 votes against 14,035 for his National Liberal (Conservative) opponent. Henceforth he was a member of parliament for over twenty years (sometimes known in Scotland as Morgan Thomson). Perhaps influenced by his constituency neighbour, John Strachey, he was initially inclined to lean towards Aneurin Bevan in the increasingly bitter arguments with Hugh Gaitskell for the soul of the Labour Party. But experience of parliament led him to move quickly to the middle-of-the-road 'keep calm' group and then to give support to Gaitskell, now Labour leader. Thomson was not of Gaitskell's inner circle but he was by instinct a Fabian and he was trusted and respected during Labour's troubled times of the 1950s. He was also friendly with James Callaghan, a rising and ambitious colleague, who served with him in the Council of Europe at Strasbourg.

Apart from obligatory references to Dundee, Thomson spoke in his maiden speech about the economic situation and the consequences of the recent American presidential election. A few weeks later he made a substantial speech hostile to the Central African Federation; and another on a bill to set up a Press Council. These two themes remained important throughout his career. Soon after his election Thomson and his family moved from Scotland, and at a time when MPs' salaries were modest, rented a house in Harlow New Town with reasonable access to London and Westminster, but he returned to his constituency conscientiously. When he left the House of Commons in 1972, his colleagues from both sides of the house praised him warmly for his service to Dundee and the whole of Tayside. But Thomson's vision was wide: he had no wish to become secretary of state for Scotland and he never wore a kilt.

After ten years of parliament Thomson had been well established, but in Labour's shadow cabinet annual popularity stakes he was bottom of the list. However, Gaitskell recognized his quality and asked him to become a Commonwealth and colonial spokesman. When Gaitskell died in 1963 Thomson was campaign manager for Callaghan's bid for the Labour leadership, in which Callaghan came third behind Harold Wilson and George Brown. Nevertheless, when the Labour government came into power in October 1964, Wilson appointed him a minister of state in the Foreign Office, then in 1966 chancellor of the duchy of Lancaster (though without a cabinet seat) as 'minister for Europe'. Except for a brief interval as minister without portfolio in 1968–9—when he was involved in local government reform—his ministerial life was absorbed by overseas affairs. He and his wife, Grace, enjoyed their relationship with the Foreign Office, the grandest government department, run by clever and sophisticated officials. In turn, they were respected by 'The Office' as loyal and committed, and Thomson was valued for his balanced judgement and his strength in making necessary decisions. A cabinet colleague, Richard Crossman, called the Thomsons 'the perfect, professional External Affairs Minister and wife … absolutely inoffensive', and Thomson one of the prime minister's 'henchmen' (Crossman, 204, 403). This was a mischievous and characteristic comment but even some of his younger parliament friends were disappointed when Thomson fell silent during a tense and restless political period following the devaluation of the pound.

In August 1967 Thomson was brought into the cabinet as secretary of state for Commonwealth affairs, with the responsibility for winding up the Commonwealth Office and merging it with the Foreign Office (an outcome achieved in October 1968). His principal policy role was to seek a solution when Ian Smith declared Rhodesia's unilateral independence. Thomson was seen to be a tough but fair negotiator, visiting Salisbury to seek a settlement, and accompanying the prime minister to HMS *Fearless* in another attempted agreement. By 1969 he was back at the Foreign Office where, again as chancellor of the duchy of Lancaster, but now with a seat in cabinet, he picked up his earlier European brief. Events had moved on, President de Gaulle had resigned, and Harold Wilson was now firmly committed to negotiating membership of the European Economic Community. It was up to Thomson to work out the details. By early 1970 it seemed likely that the Labour government would win another parliamentary term, during which Britain would join the existing European 'Six'. Enjoying his successful ministerial life, Thomson's future seemed secure but within two years this expectation fell apart.

In the June 1970 election Edward Heath and the Conservatives won a modest majority, and although Thomson won in Dundee, his vote was squeezed by the emerging Scottish National Party. Heath had been a consistent European and he pressed ahead to complete the negotiations for joining the community. Anthony Barber initially inherited Thomson's ministerial title and brief and, on the face of it, there would now be close to a consensus in the House of Commons. However, in opposition, Harold Wilson chose to turn turtle and to reject the terms of membership. Thomson, who had become the shadow defence secretary, was shocked by what he saw as unprincipled behaviour on a great historic issue. After painful months of internal debate he resigned, together with Roy Jenkins and Harold Lever, from Labour's shadow cabinet. In a House of Commons speech, heckled by the Labour left, he justified his resignation by referring to 'the sudden and complete change of policy by my party' (*Hansard 5C*, 835.262, 18 April 1972).

When the European Communities Act was finally put on the statute book, it was for the prime minister to appoint two commissioners—one Conservative, the other Labour—to serve in Brussels from January 1973 for four years. A ministerial colleague, Fred Mulley, was seen as the favoured choice but Heath preferred Thomson, who became commissioner for the regions. This was a new portfolio and it matched Labour's long-standing 'two nations' concern about a prosperous south and a deprived, declining industrial north. Within weeks of his arrival Thomson made a controversial innovation—'a historic meeting', he called it—in welcoming a House of Commons select committee to Brussels to take evidence from him and another member of the commission. Hitherto regional policy had not been a major interest for the Six but soon it was being said that Thomson's quiet and persuasive style could be good in raising its profile. From Brussels he travelled around the member regions and nations, not neglecting Scotland, speaking to political and business groups and conferences. Thus he became a successful commissioner—loyal to his country, on good terms with his other British commissioner, Sir Christopher Soames, and also collegiate within the commission. He had every reason to expect a further four-year term. But the president of France, Giscard d'Estaing, and the German chancellor, Helmut Schmidt, urged the case for Roy Jenkins to become the first British president of the commission. When Jenkins accepted, Thomson was out of a job.

Thomson might have chosen to re-enter the House of Commons but the Labour Party was in serious decline, and he did not welcome unpleasant ideological conflict. As an alternative to the Commons he accepted a peerage in the 1977 new year's honours. As Britain was unfamiliar with the European communities' political and business ways, he soon found that he was much in demand for his experience. From 1977 to 1980 he was the chairman of the Advertising Standards Authority, giving it a new lease of life, and where he was fondly remembered by its staff many years later. He also accepted directorships of the Royal Bank of Scotland, ICI, and the Woolwich Building Society, in all of which he played an active role. He was drawn into 'the great and the good' by the Pilgrims Trust, the Ditchley

Foundation, and the Leeds Castle Foundation; the queen appointed him a knight of the Thistle in 1981. But in this period his major and most influential role was as chairman of the Independent Broadcasting Authority, from 1981 to 1988. It was an exciting and expansionary time for television and the content of programmes was often bold and controversial. Thomson proved much more than a safe pair of hands, and was prepared to defend the broadcasters when politicians and campaigners demanded censorship. He dealt effectively both with Mary Whitehouse and her concern on moral—mainly sexual—issues and with those of Margaret Thatcher's ministers who were over-anxious on matters said to be crucial to the national interest.

At the end of his chairmanship of the Independent Broadcasting Authority and with his business commitments diminished, Thomson felt free to identify his political loyalties again, and in 1989 he joined the Liberal Democrats. He spoke mainly on broadcasting and European affairs (on which he was a party spokesman in the upper house from 1990 to 1998) but later he ranged widely. Although he had suffered a heart attack in his fifties and suffered skin cancer from much earlier, he remained fully active well into his eighties. He remained close to his wife during sixty years of marriage and they brought up two successful daughters, Caroline, (*b.* 1954) and Ailsa, (*b.* 1956), in a warm family environment. He was considerate towards his ministerial staff and in the European Commission, and in his closing years he found time to encourage and give confidence to new life peers. He had an easy sense of humour, rich with anecdotes, and was frequently asked to speak on celebrations and informal occasions. In his manner and appearance, he was open and he bore lightly a career of public success. He died in London on 3 October 2008 and was survived by his wife, Grace, and his two daughters. A memorial service was held at St Martin-in-the-Fields on 13 January 2009.

Thomson was a mainstream social democrat who made his way from modest beginnings to the establishment. He was not a thrusting competitor: his success emerged naturally from his quiet strength and steady integrity. When his political future seemed secure, he faced a political crisis; and when he was squeezed out of his European role, he was deeply disappointed. But he was resilient and on each occasion found important new roles.

WILLIAM RODGERS

Sources R. H. S. Crossman, *The diaries of a cabinet minister*, 3 (1977) · *The Times* (6 Oct 2008) · *Daily Telegraph* (6 Oct 2008) · *The Guardian* (6 Oct 2008) · *The Independent* (6 Oct 2008) · *The Herald* [Glasgow] (6 Oct 2008) · *The Scotsman* (7 Oct 2008) · www.royalsoced.org.uk/cms/files/fellows/obits_alpha/thomson_g_m.pdf, 1 June 2011 · *WW* (2008) · Burke, *Peerage* · personal knowledge (2012) · private information (2012) · b. cert. · m. cert.

Archives priv. coll. | FILM BFINA, current affairs footage

Likenesses Bassano, half-plate film negative, 1966, NPG [*see illus.*] · photographs, 1995–2001, Photoshot, London · obituary photographs

Wealth at death £791,049: probate, 3 Aug 2009, *CGPLA Eng. & Wales*

Thomson, Kenneth Roy [Ken], **second Baron Thomson of Fleet** (**1923–2006**), businessman and newspaper proprietor, was born on 1 September 1923, in Toronto, Ontario, Canada, the only son of Roy Herbert *Thomson, first Baron Thomson of Fleet (1894–1976), businessman and publisher, and his wife, Edna Alice (*d.* 1951), daughter of John Irvine. Both his parents were Canadian. His early years were spent in North Bay, Ontario. The family moved back to Toronto when he was fourteen. He attended Upper Canada College, then for a year the University of Toronto, before serving in the public relations department of the Royal Canadian Air Force from 1942 to 1945.

After the war Thomson took a degree in economics and law at Cambridge University. Back in Canada, he then began learning the newspaper business and joined *Timmins Daily Press* in 1947 as a cub reporter. A year later he became an advertising salesman for the *Galt Reporter*, based in Cambridge, Ontario, before serving as its general manager from 1950 to 1953. After his father purchased *The Scotsman* in 1953 and moved to Scotland in 1954 Ken Thomson became the president of Thomson Newspapers Limited, which then owned eighteen newspapers in Canada. On 13 June 1956 he married (Nora) Marilyn, daughter of Albert Vernard Lavis, of Toronto. They had two sons and one daughter.

Although his father had moved to Britain partly to give him a free run in developing the Canadian business, the rapid expansion of the British business in the late 1950s and in the 1960s inevitably led to Thomson becoming more involved in the British business. In 1957 his father had acquired the franchise for Scottish television and in 1959 he purchased the Kemsley Group, comprising UK national and regional newspapers including the *Sunday Times*. In 1964 his father received a hereditary British peerage; two years later he purchased *The Times*.

Ken Thomson, who was already a director of the UK business, became deputy chairman of Times Newspapers in 1966, chairman in 1968, and president in 1971. By the time of his father's death it was already apparent that the newspaper business in Britain faced critical decisions. The central problem was relations with the trade unions. Thomson backed attempts by the management of Times Newspapers (which was losing £1 million a month) to negotiate a deal with the unions that would end union disruptions and allow the introduction of modern printing technology. However, these negotiations made little progress, and in 1978 management decided to stop publication of both titles pending negotiation of a satisfactory settlement. After eleven months, with no prospect of achieving the original objectives, the stoppage was settled on terms that fell short of securing the economic future of the newspapers. In October 1980, after a strike by *Times* journalists, Thomson decided to sell Times Newspapers. The purchaser, the following year, was Rupert Murdoch, who paid £12 million. The union disputes continued after the sale and were only resolved by the move of printing to Wapping. Thomson had done his best for Times Newspapers and enjoyed the considerable goodwill of those who had worked for the company in his period of ownership.

Under Thomson's leadership Thomson Newspapers, which had become a public company in 1965 and had undergone major expansion in both Canada and the United States, would ultimately own the largest number of daily newspapers of any group in North America. Thomson's proudest newspaper acquisition, in 1980, was the *Globe and Mail* of Toronto, which shortly afterwards, with his full support, began printing at sites across Canada by satellite transmission, the first major newspaper to accomplish this feat. Thomson knew how pleased his father would have been with his purchase and the subsequent development of *The Globe* to become Canada's national newspaper. Roy Thomson had failed in his bid to acquire *The Globe* in the early 1950s, just before his move to Britain. For Ken Thomson, ownership of *The Globe* more than made up for the loss of Times Newspapers. Meanwhile, in 1979, the Woodbridge Company Ltd, the family's principal holding company, had acquired a 75 per cent interest in Hudson's Bay Company, Canada's oldest company and largest retailer. Thomson disposed of this interest in the 1990s on very satisfactory terms.

Until his father's death in 1976 Thomson was primarily focused on running the Canadian business. His father ran the UK business, which not only continued to acquire other publishing companies but moved into the travel business in 1965 and into North Sea oil in 1971. In 1978 activities in the UK were restructured and a new company, International Thomson Organisation Limited (ITOL), was formed. This then embarked on a major expansion into specialized information and publishing businesses, primarily in the USA, financed largely with cash flows from North Sea oil. In 1989 the new company disposed of its interests in North Sea oil and then merged with Thomson Newspapers to form the Thomson Corporation (TTC). In its final withdrawal from British newspapers, TTC sold its regional newspaper group in 1995. During this period it continued its acquisition of specialized information and publishing companies including West Publishing, an American legal publishing company, acquired in 1996 for $3.4 billion. The sale of the UK-based travel business followed in 1998 by way of the largest initial public offering ever made in the UK, and then in 2000 all of the North American community newspapers were disposed of. These steps led to the acceleration of the Thomson Corporation's transformation into one of the world's leading information companies, providing electronically delivered information to businesses and professionals around the world.

When Roy Thomson died in 1976 his family's fortune amounted to about $500 million. When Ken Thomson died thirty years later it had grown under his leadership to over $21 billion, the largest fortune of any family in Canada and among the world's top ten fortunes.

Renowned for his frugality (he neither smoked nor drank, lived in a relatively modest house, flew economy class, and reputedly had his hair cut by his wife), Thomson had a deep love of animals, especially dogs, and a lifelong interest in collecting works of art. Towards the end of his career he decided upon a major project involving the Art Gallery of Ontario. In 2002, in the most substantial act of philanthropy in Canadian history, he agreed to give $70 million in cash together with his priceless collection to the gallery, which was be renovated by the architect Frank Gehry.

Thomson died in Toronto on 12 June 2006 and was survived by his wife, Marilyn, and their two sons, David and Peter, and daughter, Taylor. David had become chairman of the Thomson Corporation in 2002 and, on their father's death, David (who succeeded his father as third Baron Thomson of Fleet) and Peter became co-chairmen of Woodbridge, which in addition to its ownership of over 70 per cent of the Thomson Corporation held a major interest in Canada's largest media company (including the *Globe and Mail*) as well as other interests. REES-MOGG

Sources *The Times* (13 June 2006) · *Daily Telegraph* (13 June 2006) · *The Guardian* (13 June 2006) · *The Independent* (13 June 2006) · Burke, *Peerage* · *WW* (2006) · personal knowledge (2010) · private information (2010)

Likenesses photographs, 1980–2004, PA Photos, London · N. Betts, photographs, 2006, Rex Features, London · obituary photographs

Wealth at death between £4000,000,000 and £9500,000,000

Thornes, John Barrie (1940–2008), geographer and geomorphologist, was born on 27 February 1940 in Horbury, near Wakefield, Yorkshire, the only child of Edwin Thornes, engineering foreman, and his wife, Gladys, *née* Carpenter. After primary schooling in Horbury he went to Ossett grammar school, where he acquired a lifetime commitment to the understanding of landscape, which was awakened by walking, scouting, and school fieldwork. He went on to study geography, with subsidiary geology, at Queen Mary College, University of London. He received a first-class degree in August 1962, and on 8 September the same year married Rosemary (Rose) Ransford (*b.* 1940), a fellow student at Queen Mary College, and daughter of Christopher Ransford, civil engineer. They had two children, Clare (*b.* 1967) and Christopher (*b.* 1968).

After graduating Thornes was awarded a two-year Commonwealth scholarship (1962–4) to McGill University in Montreal, where he studied advanced geomorphology, climatology, and glaciology, strongly influenced by F. K. (Kenneth) Hare. His MSc thesis was 'Late glacial stages in the development of the Coaticook valley, southern Quebec'. When Hare took the chair of geography at King's College, London, Thornes quickly followed to take up a studentship funded by the Department of Scientific and Industrial Research. In 1967 he completed his PhD thesis, 'Erosion and sedimentation in the Alto Duero, Spain'.

In London Thornes found himself in an academic geomorphological environment of great excitement. The British Geomorphological Research Group had been established. The subject was leaving behind the qualitative, Davisean, geological approach to landscape evolution established at King's by S. W. Wooldridge. The young turks of the group began to follow the ideas of the 'Columbia school' of A. N. Strahler, Stanley Schumm, and others.

Thornes was captivated by the work of Luna B. Leopold, M. Gordon ('Reds') Wolman, W. B. Langbein, and R. E. Horton, who were leading the way toward a new understanding of fluvial processes. He was deeply influenced by the quantitative, model based, general systems theory paradigm being taught by R. J. (Dick) Chorley at Cambridge. He was also inspired by the exciting changes in human geography between 1960 and 1980, especially the ideas of Peter Haggett, Ron Johnston, and David Harvey. His close colleagues and mentors at the London School of Economics were Michael Wise and Emrys Jones, human geographers who, he felt, understood the importance of physical geography in the man-and-environment equation.

Appointed assistant lecturer at the London School of Economics in 1966, Thornes became lecturer in 1968 and reader in 1978. He was then professor and head of department (1981–5), dean of science (1983–4), and deputy principal (1984–5) at Bedford College, London. In 1985 he moved to the University of Bristol as professor and head of department (1985–9) and dean of graduate studies (1989–92). He returned to his alma mater of King's College as professor and head of department in 1992, charged with rebuilding a major research school after the depredations of university reconstruction and retrenchment in London.

Thornes's early work in Spain blossomed into a lifelong research interest into the origins, evolution, and management of Spanish and other Mediterranean landscapes. Throughout his career and perhaps because he spoke Spanish, albeit only in the present tense, he also developed an interest in the rain forests of Amazonia from Manaus to the Xingu–Araguaia headwaters. This began with his membership of the spectacular Royal Geographical Society hovercraft expedition to the Casaquiare and Orinoco rivers. With Stephen Nortcliff he produced a series of innovative papers on the nutrient status of the soils, the hydraulic geometry of the streams, seasonal variations in hydrology, and cation exchange, which greatly increased the understanding of forest ecosystems.

Thornes's wide-ranging, almost furious, reading and enthusiasm for new ideas and concepts quickly led to other themes. An early interest was palaeohydrology. Generations of students experienced his enthusiasm for the autogeometry of river channels, channel changes with time, the processes of ephemeral streams, and the influence of catastrophic floods. Almost all of the photographs of him during his teaching career show him standing by or in streams, usually with a survey pole or current meter in his hands. Dominant in his thoughts, however, was an interest in the importance of vegetation and ecology to geomorphology, soil erosion, and, later, desertification. He led internationally acclaimed European Commission projects on Mediterranean desertification and land use, which in 1991–9 helped to establish the methodology, models, and data sets used to evaluate and mitigate the problems of land degradation in the region. An exciting consequence was that his academic colleagues first from Spain and then from many other European countries became involved in fruitful scientific exchanges and collaboration. Thornes also travelled widely to disseminate the knowledge gained through such collaboration. In addition to Europe he worked in Arctic Canada, Iceland, Brazil, Argentina, Brunei, the Mojave desert, Nepal, China, and South Africa.

Thornes was an innovative and strategic but pragmatic thinker who influenced research and teaching in all the departments, research groups, academic societies, and international institutions with which he was associated. At Bristol and King's he developed research schools or themes that focused on clearly defined objectives and enabled successful research funding applications. He received nearly £3 million in research funds over his career. Under Thornes these departments did not neglect teaching but placed it firmly within the chosen research interests. Students lived at the cutting edge of their subject. His own research was transmitted to generations of undergraduates in annual joint King's College, London, and London School of Economics fieldwork programmes between 1968 and 1989.

Above all Thornes was a team player. He undertook a full role in student societies, departmental administration, examination boards, and studentship grant committees. He served on the Natural Environment Research Council, the academic councils of Bedford and King's colleges, the editorial boards of several major journals, and the governing councils of the European Society for Soil Conservation, the British Association for the Advancement of Science, and the Institute of British Geographers, as president in 1992. In this latter role he encouraged the successful merger of the institute with the Royal Geographical Society. He was an assessor for Commonwealth universities, and an adviser to the Spanish Ministry of Education, the European Commission (DGXII), and the Hong Kong Universities Funding Council. Among many other honours he received the patron's medal of the Royal Geographical Society in 1996, and in 1998 the Linton award, the highest honour in the UK that his chosen subject could bestow.

Thornes was a prolific author of more than 130 academic papers and chapters in books. His early work was summarized in *Semi-arid Erosional Systems* (1977), which established a pattern that became a hallmark for his subsequent work. It drew together a clear exposition of an academic problem, relevant observation, description, and measurement of the system components underpinned by innovative conceptual models. Eleven major books and numerous research volumes followed. His conceptual interests were first expressed in *Geomorphology and Time* (1977), with Denys Brunsden, with whom he also wrote an important theoretical paper, 'Landscape sensitivity and change' (published in the *Transactions of the Institute of British Geographers*, 1979). His teaching style is clearly shown in *Process in Geomorphology* (1979), with Clifford Embleton, a compendium of lectures given in the mid-1970s. *Land Use and Prehistory in South-East Spain* (1985) and several classic papers with Antonio Gilman rewrote the way in which geographers conceptualized the influence of man on land use and soil erosion. His palaeohydrological work was summarized in *Palaeohydrology in Practice* (1987) and *Temperate Palaeohydrology* (1991), both co-edited with K. J. Gregory, John Lewin, and Leszek Starkel. *Vegetation and Erosion* (1990), *Mediterranean Desertification and Land Use* (1996) with Jane Brandt, *Atlas of Mediterranean Environments in Europe: the Desertification Context* (1997) with P. Mairota and N. A. Geeson, and *Environmental Issues in the Mediterranean* (2002) with John Wainwright, together with numerous research monographs, consolidated a remarkable lifetime's achievement.

Thornes was a kind, generous man, full of energy and life. Throughout his career his first consideration was his wife, Rosemary, and their family. Those who knew them both knew that her strength was essential to him. His urgent need to 'move on', to follow every new idea, to contribute to every field meeting and conference, meant that he needed organizing. In her he found the perfect partnership. After his stroke, in 1996, she became his lifeline. He suffered a heart attack on 17 July 2008 doing what he did best, on a field trip in south Shropshire, close to Shrewsbury where he was happily retired. He was declared dead at Shrewsbury Hospital. He was cremated at Shrewsbury crematorium on 31 July. His wife and children survived him. DENYS BRUNSDEN

Sources *The Times* (4 Aug 2008) • *Bristol Evening Post* (27 Aug 2008) • *Geophemera*, 104 (autumn 2008), 5–6 • *GJ*, 174/4 (Dec 2008), 387–8 • www.bristol.ac.uk/news/2008/5855.html, 13 Oct 2010 • CV, priv. coll. • personal knowledge (2012) • private information (2012) • m. cert. • d. cert.

Likenesses photograph, repro. in *GJ* (2008)

Wealth at death under £176,000: probate, 4 Nov 2008, *CGPLA Eng. & Wales*

Thorneycroft [*née* Cappi], **Contessa Carla Maria Concetta Francesca, Lady Thorneycroft** (1914–2007), fashion editor and conservationist, was born on 12 February 1914 in Paris, the daughter of Count Guido Malagola Cappi (1883–1941), archivist and interior designer, and his American wife, Alexandra, *née* Dunbar-Marshall (1893–1977). She had been born *en route* from Venice (where her father was keeper of the archives at the Frari) to London (where her mother's parents, distrusting Italian medical care, had insisted her mother go to give birth). She spent her early years in Venice, then Rome. Her parents divorced in 1924. She first met (George Edward) Peter *Thorneycroft, later Baron Thorneycroft (1909–1994), politician, when she was sixteen: she and her mother had met Thorneycroft's father while holidaying on Capri, and he had invited them to stay at Dunston Hall. They fell in love but failed to keep in touch, and both subsequently married: on 9 April 1934 Carla married Count Giorgio Roberti (*b.* 1905), chemist. They had a son and a daughter. During the Second World War she worked as a nurse at the Principessa Piemonte hospital in Rome. When the Italians capitulated and the Germans occupied the city and took over the hospital, she took in the Italian wounded at her apartment in via Panama. Operations were performed on her kitchen table; the cook complained when Carla used her saucepans for sterilizing instruments.

Carla Roberti's first marriage ended in divorce in 1946, and she decided to move with her two children to England (reputedly arriving with twenty-three suitcases). She was soon taken on as a fashion editor at *Vogue*. She met Peter Thorneycroft again at a party given by Henry (Chips) Channon. They married on 2 April 1949. After their marriage she continued working at *Vogue* until 1951, but also increasingly played her part in her husband's political career, both as a renowned hostess and as a talented public speaker. She and Thorneycroft had one daughter.

In 1966, when both Florence and Venice were flooded, Carla Thorneycroft, along with Sir Ashley Clarke and Natalie Brooke (the wife of Humphrey Brooke, secretary to the Royal Academy), was a founder of the Italian Art and Archives Rescue Fund, launched within a week of the floods in Florence. She served as vice-chairman of the organization, and received the Italian order of Merit in 1967. The fund also raised money for restoration work in Venice, and in 1971 was transformed into the Venice in Peril Fund. Carla Thorneycroft was a trustee and vice-chairman from 1971 to 1996, and president thereafter. By the time of her death the charity had funded the restoration of more than forty buildings or works of art in the city. She was also founding president of the League of Friends of the Italian Hospital (1956–89), vice-president of the British-Italian Society (1957–2007), founder member, trustee, and patron of the Rosehill Arts Theatre (1959–77), founder member and trustee of the Chichester Festival Theatre Trust (1962–88), a trustee of the Royal School of Needlework (1964–76; she was an expert at needlepoint), and a member of council of the Friends of Westminster Cathedral (1976–2007, vice-president from 1993). She was appointed DBE in 1995. She died at her flat in Eaton Square, Westminster, on 7 March 2007 of heart failure. She was survived by her two daughters and a stepson, her son having predeceased her.

Sources *Daily Telegraph* (15 March 2007) • *The Times* (24 March 2007) • d. cert.

Likenesses Lenare, nitrate negatives, 1949, NPG • D. Miller, photographs, 1957 (with Peter Thorneycroft), Getty Images, London, Hult. Arch. • photograph, repro. in www.veniceinperil.org

Wealth at death £184,000: probate, 20 July 2007, *CGPLA Eng. & Wales*

Thould, Anthony Keith [Tony] (1930–2005), physician and rheumatologist, was born on 4 October 1930 at Elmina, Church Path Road, St Thomas, Exeter, the only son and second child of Harry Bevis Thould (1898–1974), bank accountant and later bank manager, from the Severn valley, and his wife, Daisy, *née* Behenna (1894–1990), only child of William George Behenna, builder, and fiancée of a comrade killed at Harry Thould's side in the Mesopotamian trenches during the First World War. Thould's childhood was spent in south and west England, where his father's posts ensured a comfortable life but were insufficiently lucrative to pay public-school fees. Fortunately he won scholarships to three, choosing Stowe School (coinciding with the final five years of his hero, the influential founding headmaster, J. F. Roxburgh). Initially intending to be an architect, he switched to medicine and entered St Bartholomew's Hospital medical school, London, in 1948, graduating MB BS with distinction in 1954. After house appointments there and in Norwich, he volunteered to work in Hong Kong for national service in the Royal Army Medical Corps. There he met his future wife, Bernine Tivey (Bernie) Furner (*b.* 1932), a teacher, and daughter of Harold Hughes Furner, a New South Wales farmer, and his wife, both with roots going back to convicts transported to Australia in the first fleet. After Thould's demobilization they married at St Mary the Boltons, Kensington, on 24 August 1957 and had three sons. Returning to work at St Bartholomew's and University College Hospital, Thould was admitted MRCP in 1958 and proceeded MD in 1960.

Soberly dressed, copying Roxburgh's trademark red pocket handkerchief, outwardly Thould seemed a typical establishment figure (and later was twice lobbied to be Conservative candidate for Truro). The truth was quite otherwise, both professionally and personally. As well as official duties in Hong Kong, tackling epidemics of Asian flu and of polio (taking a fortnight's leave in bed to cure his own forme fruste), he volunteered to work in the local hospital and leprosy colony. In his final teaching hospital years he elected to work in rheumatology (then a despised and officially unrecognized speciality) and concentrated on applying for consultant posts in district hospitals (then a stigma of professional failure). He was asked to apply for a post at St Bartholomew's, but the hospital was at its intellectual nadir, and anyway he hated London, preferring the work in district hospitals. His appointment as consultant physician in general medicine at the Royal Cornwall Hospital, Truro, in 1965 therefore fulfilled a dream. Not only was the new hospital one of the first to be built in Britain after the war, taking medicine in Cornwall out of the dark ages, but the quality of life was ideal for his family, and his maternal roots were there, his mother's ancestors being Tregions, longstanding Cornish gentry.

In an early incident at Truro Thould had to resuscitate someone with cardiac arrest in full view of the other outpatients, fortunately successfully. Persuading the passing hospital photographer to record the scene, however, he then cajoled the management into building a dedicated coronary care unit, to which he arranged to be added an intensive care unit and facilities for dialysis (allocating half of his own beds for the units). His general physician's life was hectic; he responded to extensive demands for county-wide domiciliary visits and participated increasingly in important regional and national committees, becoming a familiar figure on the railway sleeping car. After ten years, however, he resolved to practise rheumatology full time, starting an appeal to construct the first custom-built unit in a British district hospital. With Sir John Betjeman as patron this raised £1 million, and the eighteen-bed unit was opened in May 1978 by Prince Charles, who insisted that it should be called the duke of Cornwall rheumatology department. An upper research floor was added the following year, and thereafter Thould concentrated on the specialism, travelling to rheumatological centres and meetings worldwide, undertaking research into osteoarthritis, publishing papers, and becoming an innovative editor of the *Annals of Rheumatic Diseases*. He had been elected FRCP in 1974.

Thould had an attractive, open personality, and patients loved his warm smile, while he revolutionized medical practice in one of the most deprived parts of Britain. Yet his career well illustrates the cliché 'it's wonderful what you can achieve if you don't want any credit'. Forced in 1989 to retire immediately after a transient stroke, and found to have severe hypertension, he received not even a letter of thanks from the authorities, either local or national. Though hurt, he was hardly surprised: even his colleagues had initially opposed his having any beds at the main hospital, challenged his move into rheumatology, and blocked his plans for a specialist rehabilitation unit. Now, however, he could indulge his latent wide outside interests. Though his illness forced him to stop sailing his self-built boat, he could still travel extensively, especially to the USA and Australia. As a trustee of the Cornish Heritage Trust he was responsible for its properties. Together with his wife he walked the entire 600-mile western coastal path in separate stretches. At Idless, near Truro, he purchased the neighbouring mill, connecting it with his own house with a new great room, while for the millennium he dug a lake and planted an arboretum. In that year he had a successful operation for colon cancer, but was later found to have myelomatosis. Undaunted, he continued to travel, read avidly, and write: among the unpublished manuscripts he left at his death were an autobiography, two volumes of children's stories, and a history of his village. He died at his home, Idless Mill, Idless, on 11 July 2005. He was survived by his wife and their three sons: one a schoolmaster, one a specialist in communicable diseases, and one an information technology consultant. A memorial service was held on 22 July at Kenwyn parish church, Truro. STEPHEN LOCK

Sources A. K. Thould, 'One man's journey', priv. coll. • A. K. Thould, 'A feast of lanterns', priv. coll. • A. K. Thould, 'Tales from my backyard', priv. coll. • Munk, *Roll* [vol. 12] • personal knowledge (2009) • private information (2009) • b. cert. • m. cert. • d. cert.
Archives Wellcome L., autobiography
Wealth at death £28,261: probate, 14 Nov 2005, *CGPLA Eng. & Wales*

Timpson, John Harry Robert (1928–2005), broadcaster and writer, was born on 2 July 1928 at Ridgeholme, The Ridgeway, Kenton, Middlesex, one of two children of John Hubert Victor Timpson, bank clerk, and his wife, Caroline, *née* Willson. In 1945, at the age of sixteen, he left Merchant Taylors' School in Northwood, Middlesex, abandoned youthful hopes for the theatrical life, and joined his local paper, the *Wembley News*, as a cub reporter. His early journalistic career was interrupted by two years of compulsory national service with the Royal Army Service Corps—a 'monumental bore', as he later recalled (*Today and Yesterday*, 16). Soon after returning to civilian life he became a district reporter for the Norfolk-based *Eastern*

Daily Press, where he remained for eight years, covering a succession of council meetings, court cases, and darts club dinners. On 2 June 1951 he married (Muriel) Patricia Whale, a 24-year-old nurse he had met at a church social event. She was the daughter of Albert Edward Whale, storeman and packer. They had two sons, Jeremy and Nicholas.

In 1959 Timpson joined the BBC as a general reporter, and was mentored by the former war reporter and court correspondent Godfrey Talbot. Between 1962 and 1967 he acted as Talbot's deputy, commentating on royal tours to Tunisia, Australia, and Ethiopia. Radio soon played to his strengths. He possessed a facility with words and reviewers noted, too, his 'rich, dark, deep-brown chocolate voice' (*Evening Standard*, 2 March 1979). This eased his path to a succession of presenting jobs. In 1970 he joined BBC Radio 4's *Today* programme, alongside—though very much the junior partner of—Jack de Manio. After de Manio's departure in 1971, Timpson co-presented with Robert Robinson and other up-and-coming broadcasters, such as Libby Purves and Sue MacGregor. *Today* had begun with a reputation for being nothing more than a pleasant 'morning miscellany', and Timpson's role had been to help 'harden' its news coverage. In the event he found himself drawn to the programme's more amusing stories, and developed a penchant for corny jokes, newspaper misprints, and ambiguous headlines. His trademark 'ho ho' quips spoke of a firm belief in the need to leaven often depressing news, especially for early morning listeners.

Timpson had two brief, largely unfulfilling flirtations with television. Before joining *Today* he had worked on Britain's first half-hour television news programme, BBC 2's *Newsroom* (1968–70), and in 1976 he joined *Tonight* as a presenter. After just eighteen months he returned to radio, somewhat dispirited. 'I didn't like TV', he told one magazine; it demanded too many 'false smiles' (*Woman*, 10 Dec 1983). By 1978 *Today* had been relaunched, and he provided a useful foil to the bumptiousness, northern pride, and cutting political commentary of his regular co-presenter, Brian Redhead. Timpson—southern, something of a John Bull figure, invariably polite and calm—sounded as if he was 'seeing things through with a rueful sense of humour' (*Daily Telegraph*, 10 Oct 1973). It was said that he made listeners feel they belonged 'to a rather good club' (*The Guardian*, 21 Nov 2005). For their next few years at the helm he and Redhead were a 'perfect and unbeatable duo' (Donovan, 79). *Today*, however, became more of a political heavyweight as the 1980s progressed, and seemed, increasingly, to favour an abrasive interviewing style that Timpson disliked. He left in 1986, but continued to appear regularly elsewhere on Radio 4, chairing *Any Questions?* (which he had joined in 1984) and presenting the occasional travelogue.

Though he spent much of his BBC career living in Chorleywood, apparently reconciled to the life of a suburban commuter, Timpson had always wanted to return to the country, and above all to his beloved Norfolk. In 1985 he bought a weekend cottage at Wellingham and moved there permanently in 1987, the same year he left *Any Questions?* and was appointed OBE for services to broadcasting. He subsequently moved to a larger house in Weasenham St Peter, overlooking the village green. Now retired from the BBC, he started spending more time than ever writing, mostly on the pleasures and oddities of country life. There was, for example, a regular column for the *Daily Mail*, in which he described the annual cycle of church fêtes and flower festivals taking place on his doorstep. He had already published his autobiography, *Today and Yesterday*, in 1976. There now followed a stream of other slight but highly readable books on country byways and characters, notably *Timpson's England* (1987) and *Timpson's English Eccentrics* (1991). In 1989 he published his first novel, *Paper Trail*, the semi-autobiographical story of a young newspaperman in Norfolk. This was followed by *Sound Track* in 1991. His last book was *Timpson on the Verge* (2002), about Norfolk village signs. Despite his prolific output, Timpson was never frenetic. More than anything he enjoyed simply 'idling' at home, in the garden, or on his four-berth cabin cruiser. He was, he happily admitted, 'a bit of a stick-in-the-mud' (*Sunday Express*, 12 Feb 1984). He died at the Queen Elizabeth Hospital, King's Lynn, Norfolk, on 19 November 2005, from multiple organ failure, sepsis, and a perforated ulcer. He was survived by his wife, Patricia, and son Jeremy, his son Nicholas having died suddenly a month earlier. DAVID HENDY

Sources J. Timpson, *Today and yesterday* (1976) · J. Timpson, *The lighter side of Today* (1983) · P. Donovan, *All our todays: forty years of Radio 4's 'Today' programme* (1997) · S. MacGregor, *Woman of today: an autobiography* (2002) · D. Hendy, *Life on air: a history of Radio Four* (2007) · *Daily Telegraph* (10 Oct 1973); (21 Nov 2005) · *Evening Standard* (2 March 1979) · *Woman* (10 Dec 1983) · *Sunday Express* (12 Feb 1984) · *The Times* (21 Nov 2005) · *The Guardian* (21 Nov 2005) · *The Independent* (21 Nov 2005) · radio programme review board, 10 June 1970, 15 May 1974, 18 Sept 1974, 9 July 1975, 10 Dec 1975, 12 July 1978, 7 Feb 1979, BBC WAC · letters from listeners, Aug 1972, BBC WAC, file R101/314/1 · annual report of the managing director of radio (Ian Trethowan), June 1973, BBC WAC, file R78/1389/1 · *WW* (2005) · b. cert. · m. cert. · d. cert.

Archives FILM BFINA, current affairs footage · BFINA, performance footage | SOUND BL NSA, current affairs recordings · BL NSA, documentary recordings · BL NSA, news recordings · BL NSA, performance recordings

Likenesses group portraits, photographs, 1971–9, PA Photos, London · Wesley, group portrait, photograph, 1978, Getty Images, London · obituary photographs · photographs, BBC

Wealth at death £507,669: probate, 4 April 2006, *CGPLA Eng. & Wales*

Tippet, Sir Anthony Sanders (1928–2006), naval officer and public servant, was born on 2 October 1928 at Loughrigg, South Molton, Devon, the son of William Kirby Roberts Tippet (1898–1985), bank clerk, and his wife, Henrietta Winifred Parker, *née* Sanders (1904–2004). At the time of his birth registration his parents lived at Hawthorn, Middle Road, Lymington, Hampshire. He was educated at West Buckland School, then joined the Royal Naval College, when it was still at its wartime home at Eaton Hall on the Grosvenor estate in Cheshire, as a paymaster cadet. He was top cadet in his term, and impressed from his initial appointment when his first and subsequent reports noted his sense of duty, boundless energy, intelligence, and leadership. He made a particular impact as judge advocate at an infamous court martial in Malta in 1950 when an officer (Lieutenant-Commander Christopher Swabey) was tried and found guilty of indecent assault and dismissed from the service. Although many years later the conviction was quashed, there was never any suggestion but that Tippet, though unqualified, had run the court martial impeccably. On 21 October the same year (Trafalgar day) he married Lola Audrey Bassett, aged twenty-three, daughter of Walter Bassett, commercial dealer, of Okehampton, Devon. They had three sons and a daughter.

After a number of shore and seagoing appointments Tippet qualified as a barrister, being called to the bar by Gray's Inn in 1959. On promotion to commander in 1963 he was secretary to the director of naval intelligence and then to the flag officer, Middle East, where he stayed to command HMS *Jufair* at Bahrain. Though not a warfare expert, he easily became an accomplished assistant director of naval plans from 1970 to 1972, when he ignored a formal warning, given for his health's sake, not to take on too much. Aged forty-nine he survived a heart attack. Meanwhile he was chief staff officer to the flag officer, Plymouth (1972–4), and captain of the barracks at Chatham (1976–9) before becoming, as a rear-admiral, assistant chief of fleet support (1979–81) and then flag officer and port admiral, Portsmouth (1981–3). Over the weekend of 2–3 April 1982 his leadership at Portsmouth was a key factor in preparing the fleet (which had just been given Easter leave) for the Falklands War.

From 1983 to 1986 Tippet was fourth sea lord, or chief of fleet support, responsible for the repair and maintenance of the fleet, the supply of armaments, stores, aircraft repairs, and the administration of all support services to the Royal Navy at bases throughout Britain and abroad. He controlled some 50,000 civilian staff and managed an annual budget of more than £2.5 billion, and an estate valued at £6 billion. He had reporting lines to every Conservative minister in the Ministry of Defence and at the behest of the secretary of state, Michael Heseltine, he took the royal dockyards into commercial management. The process, against opposition from vested interests on the left and right and from other senior officers, involved competitive bidding and the drafting of an act of parliament. Seemingly intransigent labour problems were thrashed out with trade union officials over late-night glasses of whisky in his office. The changes Tippet wrought in the dockyards were the model for many subsequent privatizations of military facilities. He also played a full part as a member of the Board of Admiralty in the overall direction and operations of the Royal Navy.

Tippet was knighted KCB in 1984 and retired from the navy two years later, at the relatively young age of fifty-eight. In 1987 he was appointed after open competition as general manager of the Hospitals for Sick Children Special Health Authority (which included Great Ormond Street Hospital) and he led this into NHS trust status, becoming chief executive of Great Ormond Street Hospital in 1994. His enthusiasm infected everyone from senior clinician to hospital porter and, with his naval style and charm but undoubted authority, he ensured the survival of Great Ormond Street. He was the driving force behind the Wishing Well campaign in 1987–9, with its trademark cartoon of a child's face with a teardrop. The appeal raised £54 million in two years and was at the time Britain's most successful fund-raising campaign. Once the core of the hospital had been rebuilt Tippet set himself the target of raising £10 million per annum to extend Great Ormond Street's research and clinical services. He retired in 1995, after eight strenuous years.

He might have chosen to walk the hills of his beloved Dartmoor or to sail or to holiday in his villa in south-west Turkey, but in September 1997 Tippet became chairman of the Funding Agency for Schools, responsible to the Labour secretary of state for education and employment for the funding and performance of 1200 grant-maintained schools in England. With a budget of £4 billion per annum he was set the task of handing the schools back to the superintendence of their local authorities within two years and to close the agency. Liaising with civil servants, education authorities, and local government, he achieved this task in October 1999, with little fuss and without controversy. Meanwhile, in 1998, following a critical Ofsted report on Calderdale local education authority, he had become chairman of the Halifax Learning Zone, with direct responsibility to the secretary of state for twenty-nine schools and their nine partnerships in industry, commerce, education, and the arts. The education action zone which he led closed in December 2003 when he had changed it into one of New Labour's 'excellence clusters'. His final public duty was to chair Bradford council's Interim Policy Partnership (2001–2) which, also following a critical Ofsted report, outsourced Bradford's education services.

Tippet's wide range of public duties extended to leading roles in more than a dozen naval, medical, and education charities, including the National Appeal for Music Therapy and the Peter Pan Children's Fund, a worldwide charity to encourage the young to support children's hospitals. He was also a governor and president of his old school, a trustee of the sea cadets, and a trustee and chairman of the Royal Naval Benevolent Society for Officers.

Tippet was hardworking, purposeful, and determined: problems of any nature were a challenge to him. He had a phenomenal memory for names and faces, could engage anyone in conversation, and was a forceful leader. As senior instructor at Dartmouth he once sailed the yacht *Wyvern* in the teeth of a south-westerly gale to Ushant for the weekend: his exhausted crew of midshipmen were expecting a slap-up meal in France but Tippet, having seen the lighthouse, turned and ran before the wind to Devon to write a lengthy dissertation in the boat's journal about the differences between his dead reckoning (the Dartmouth boats were in those days equipped with only basic navigation aids) and his observed positions. He collapsed on the London Underground on his way home on 13 October 2006, after giving a talk at dinner at the Institute of Child Health. He was survived by his wife, Lola, and three of their children, one son having predeceased him.

PETER HORE

Sources *Camden New Journal* (19 Oct 2006) · *The Times* (30 Oct 2006) · *North Devon Journal* (16 Nov 2006) · *Western Morning News* (12 Dec 2006) · *WW* (2006) · Burke, *Peerage* · personal knowledge (2012) · private information (2012) [B. Brown] · b. cert. · m. cert.
Archives TNA: PRO, ADM
Likenesses obituary photographs
Wealth at death £203,238: probate, 22 Feb 2007, *CGPLA Eng. & Wales*

Todd, Ronald [Ron] (**1927–2005**), trade unionist, was born on 11 March 1927 at 4 Apsley Road, Walthamstow, Essex, the fifth of six children of George Thomas Todd, builder's labourer, and later builder, and his wife, Emily, *née* Pauline. His parents were also market traders in Walthamstow market. The Todd family was a characteristic product of traditional east London cockney culture, and showed an almost tribal élan in sustaining its claim to be among the few born within the sound of Bow bells—which on a clear day in Walthamstow was just about validated.

The Todd family were practising Catholics and Ron Todd went to St Patrick's Roman Catholic School in Walthamstow, which he left at fourteen to get his first job sweeping the floor in a local barber's shop, after which he worked as a plumber's mate. His father, George, had been a regular in the Royal Marines and as soon as Todd was eighteen in 1945 he joined his father's regiment and for a brief spell they were actually together in the same camp. At the very end of the Second World War he was posted to Hong Kong as a marine commando and served for two years on the China border, during which time he had a spell in charge of Japanese prisoners of war. On 17 November 1945, at Our Lady's Church, Walthamstow, he married Josephine Mary Elsie (Jo) Tarrant (*d.* 1996), a nineteen-year-old factory worker, daughter of Samuel Joseph Tarrant, builder. They had a son and two daughters.

Todd's first job after demobilization was as a gas fitter in London's East End, but needing a better-paid job in 1954 he joined Ford Motors as an assembly line worker in the Dagenham plant, then one of the largest car plants in Europe. At the same time he also joined the Transport and General Workers' Union (TGWU)—and began his long climb to the leadership of that union. He worked for eight years on the Ford production lines and within five years was voted deputy convenor for the whole Dagenham plant—then with about 40,000 workers. In 1962 he became a full-time official of the TGWU—in the metal, engineering, and chemical group of the union—and seven years later was appointed senior regional officer which, in 1975, led to his appointment as regional secretary for the entire London and south-east area. Three years later he was promoted to the role of national organizer.

On 28 June 1984 Todd was elected general secretary of the TGWU to succeed Moss Evans. The union was then the largest in the country with nearly 1,500,000 members, and Todd won his election on a 41 per cent turnout of union members—unusually high for any union ballot—with a majority of 44,817 over his main challenger, George Wright, a Labour moderate. Wright immediately challenged Todd's victory by questioning the validity of the ballot. Moss Evans, having conducted the ballot through the independent Electoral Reform Society, repudiated the charges made by Wright and declared Todd the winner. Yet Todd refused to duck Wright's challenge and demanded a second ballot—despite all efforts to dissuade him—saying, 'I am determined that the members of this union should have the full democratic right to elect a leader whose credibility is beyond doubt' (*The Guardian*, 2 May 2005). He was, of course, also sensitive to a national mood distrustful of the unions and on the whole approving of Margaret Thatcher's recent trade-union reforms. The second ballot was a triumph for Todd. The turnout, in June 1985, was again above 40 per cent and his majority over Wright increased to 76,840. It established Todd as 'the trade unions' Mr Honest'—a reputation that helped carry him through the most challenging years any trade-union leader experienced in post-war Britain.

Todd made no pretences to be an intellectual figure; posturing was alien to his character. Nor was he an electrifying orator. He never commanded the same attention as his illustrious predecessors such as Ernest Bevin, Frank Cousins, or Jack Jones. Yet he won enormous respect as a down-to-earth 'man of the people' whose word was his bond—qualities that certainly put him on equal terms with those earlier more famous figures. He never betrayed his working-class background, always rejected honours and baubles, and insisted on remaining plain Mr Ron Todd.

None of this prevented a difficult life for him on both the industrial and political fronts. Much of Todd's period as leader of the TGWU coincided with the most turbulent years in Britain's post-war industrial affairs. Margaret Thatcher's campaign to 'tame the unions', aided by Norman Tebbitt, reached a peak during Todd's watch. In addition there was the government drive to privatize the old state industries, which led to increased unemployment and, together with new legislation curbing union powers, provoked widespread conflict, social unrest (including the year-long miners' strike), falling union membership, and a decline in the overall authority and influence of trade unionism. Todd also faced internal problems within the TGWU, notably from his thirty-nine-member executive committee, which sought a more militant political response to Thatcher's policies. One of his most emotive battles came with the government's abolition, in 1989, of the national dock labour scheme—the legacy of Ernest Bevin's wartime plan to end casual dock labour when he was minister of labour in Churchill's war cabinet. Todd was prepared to call a national dock strike to fight government plans but in the end backed down when he recognized that a strike would almost certainly end in failure because of the government's new legal restrictions and, perhaps more telling, a rank-and-file fear of challenging those new powers.

Nor was life any easier with Todd's political allies in the

Labour Party. Todd clashed fiercely with the Labour leader Neil Kinnock, especially after Labour's defeat in the general election of 1987—Thatcher's third victory in succession. It was after that defeat that Kinnock set about reforming Labour policies, notably discarding the party's policy on nuclear disarmament, and effectively laying the basis for what was to become Tony Blair's 'new' Labour Party. This provoked major conflict between Kinnock and Todd, starting at the Labour Party conference of 1988 and continuing until they both left the scene after the election of 1992. The primary cause was Kinnock's abandonment of unilateral nuclear disarmament. Todd denounced this as a betrayal, recalling how his predecessor Frank Cousins had started the party on the road to nuclear disarmament in 1960 by defeating the then Labour leader, Hugh Gaitksell. But in addition to this Todd objected to Kinnock's arguments in favour of 'modernizing' the Labour Party to increase its electoral appeal. What was particularly surprising at the time was that Todd's criticism of Kinnock was resented even by many of his friends on the left, not least because his strident and inflexible views seemed uncharacteristic—especially since Kinnock was a long-standing member of the TGWU. The truth is that there was an almost chemical lack of rapport between the two men: Kinnock had become impatient with what he, and others, were persuaded was a failure among the trade-union leadership to recognize changing social and political mores. On Todd's side there was a deepening fear that Labour's historic mission was being abandoned in favour of populism. It was a breach between Labour leadership and trade unions never to be resolved and that continued into and through the Blair era, long after Todd had departed the scene.

In many ways Todd was a most unusual trade-union 'baron'. He was a committed patriot—his friendship with the queen mother and his stance as an unapologetic royalist enabled him to recruit her as an honorary member of the TGWU. He was also a man who cherished his service in the Royal Marines, always attending their annual reunions. Yet none of this detracted from Todd's holding firmly to his socialist convictions—and possibly an even greater paradox, to his commitment to nuclear disarmament.

It was Todd's warmly effusive and generous cockney character quite as much as his ardent socialism and trade unionism that combined to establish him in the public eye as one of the most popular of all trade-union leaders during the most testing period for post-war trade unionism. Todd possessed a very British quality of presenting a face of humour amid considerable turbulence. It was, indeed, that character of patient courage that helped sustain him during a period of tremendous pressures and political tensions in his seven years as leader of the largest trade union in the country. Being elected general secretary of the TGWU in those days was akin to joining the royal household of Britain's labour movement. It was an inheritance Todd fought to sustain with humility, humanity, palpable integrity, and dedication—and always against the tide as Margaret Thatcher's policy to curb trade-union influence bit deeply into the nation's industrial life.

Todd served as a TUC member of the National Economic Development Committee (1985–92), a member of the Employment Appeal Tribunal (1986–9, and president for most of that time), honorary vice-president of the Campaign for Nuclear Disarmament, a patron of the Margaret Centre Macmillan Appeal, TUC representative on various anti-apartheid committees, and chairman of Trade Unions for Labour Victory, which successfully organized the retention of the Labour Party political levy among trade unionists following the Trade Union Act of 1984. He played a leading role in the trade-union campaign against apartheid in South Africa and in preparing for Nelson Mandela's release from prison, remaining a close friend of Mandela thereafter. He was also powerfully influential in paving the way for his successor, Bill Morris, to become the first black leader of any British trade union—indeed the first black man to head any major British institution. He retired as TGWU general secretary in the spring of 1992 and a few months later from the TUC general council, on which he had served since 1984, and of whose international committee he was chairman.

In retirement Todd spent much time on his long-standing hobby, palaeontology. He had a collection of 300 fossils, which evoked the nickname from his critics of Toddosaurus, to which he would respond with the quip, 'Don't knock the dinosaurs—they ruled the earth for 200 million years' (private information). He also collected Victorian songbooks and in retirement took a course in sign language to help the deaf and dumb. Even more unusually for a trade-union leader he wrote poetry and published five booklets of poems. He died of acute myeloblastic leukaemia on 30 April 2005 at Oldchurch Hospital, Romford, Essex. He was survived by his three children.

GEOFFREY GOODMAN

Sources *The Times* (2 May 2005) • *Daily Telegraph* (2 May 2005) • *The Guardian* (2 May 2005) • *The Independent* (2 May 2005) • Transport & General Workers' library and records • TUC annual reports and records • Labour Party annual reports and records • *WW* (2005) • personal knowledge (2009) • private information (2009) • b. cert. • m. cert. • d. cert.

Archives U. Warwick Mod. RC | FILM BFINA, current affairs footage [also BL NSA] | SOUND BL NSA, current affairs recordings; documentary recording

Likenesses photographs, 1980–90, Getty Images, London • photographs, 1984–91, PA Photos, London • photographs, 1990–2004, Photoshot, London • N. Sinclair, bromide print, 1991, NPG • banner, in or before 1992, National Museum of Labour History, Manchester • obituary photographs

Wealth at death under £189,000: probate, 21 Nov 2005, *CGPLA Eng. & Wales*

Tomkins, Sir Edward Emile (1915–2007), diplomatist, was born on 16 November 1915 in Jubbulpore, India, the eldest of the three children of Lieutenant-Colonel Ernest Leith Tomkins, army officer, and his wife, Marie-Louise, *née* de Marigny. Having an English father and French mother, Eddie, as he was commonly known, had a bilingual upbringing which was later to stand him in good stead. After going to Ampleforth College and Trinity College, Cambridge, he joined the foreign service in 1939.

Having enlisted in the army the following year he served as liaison officer with the Free French forces in north Africa. In 1942, while making his way across uncharted desert from the fort of Bir Hakeim, south of Tobruk, towards the British lines, he had the misfortune to run into a German unit and was taken prisoner. After being sent to a prisoner-of-war camp in northern Italy, the following year he and a colleague escaped and spent eighty-one days walking 500 miles across the Apennines and through the German lines to join up with the allied forces.

In 1944 Tomkins resumed his diplomatic career and served for two years in the Moscow embassy. That he was already marked out as a high-flyer is evident from his subsequent progress through a series of prestigious appointments: in 1948 assistant private secretary to the foreign secretary, Ernest Bevin; in 1951 first secretary in Washington; and in 1954 counsellor in Paris in charge of relations with the press. In Paris he met Gillian (Jill) Benson (1923–2003), the social secretary to Lady Jebb, wife of the ambassador, Sir Gladwyn Jebb. She was the daughter of Air Commodore Constantine Evelyn Benson of the banking family and his wife, Lady Morvyth, younger daughter of the second earl of Dudley. They married at the Catholic church in Park Road, Rickmansworth, on 15 November 1955 and had a son and two daughters.

In 1963 Tomkins became minister in Bonn; in 1967 minister in Washington; in 1970 ambassador in The Hague; and finally in 1972 ambassador in Paris. In every sense this was the crowning point of his career and he could not have had better credentials for it: a French mother, complete command of the language, and the legacy of his wartime liaison service with the Free French forces. He received a warm welcome from the French press. Agence France Presse, for example, greeted him as 'the first of Her Majesty's Ambassadors here to be of French origin on his mother's side, and the second Catholic Ambassador to represent the British Sovereign, Defender of the Anglican Faith' (quoted in *Daily Telegraph*, 25 Sept 2007). By nature he was calm, undemonstrative, and reflective; there was no question of his trying to emulate the flamboyant style of his predecessor, Christopher Soames. If his style was different he was no less firm, when necessary, in the defence of British interests. For their part the French government regarded him as a reliable interlocutor and he had a large circle of contacts in all walks of French life. He was promoted GCMG in 1975, having been made CVO in 1957 and CMG in 1960, and having been knighted KCMG in 1969. In addition to decorating him with the Croix de Guerre in 1944, the French government appointed him a *grand officier* of the Légion d'honneur in 1984.

On his retirement from the diplomatic service in 1975 Tomkins and his wife went to live in Winslow Hall, a beautiful seventeenth-century house in Buckinghamshire designed by Christopher Wren, which they had bought in 1959, when it was in such a run-down state that it was about to be demolished, and which they then painstakingly restored to its former glory over a number of years. They also had a property in France that gave them and their family and friends much pleasure. In 1958, just before they acquired Winslow Hall, they had bought some land on an old goat track at Meribel in Savoy and built a ski chalet on it, thereby becoming founder members of what became a popular winter sports resort.

Unlike many retiring diplomats who took up jobs in London, Tomkins chose instead to play an active part in local affairs. He served as a Conservative member of Buckinghamshire county council from 1977 to 1985, and was chairman of the governors of Stowe School and a patron of the University of Buckingham. From 1976 to 1998 he was president of the Federation of Alliances Françaises in Great Britain and in 1993 he became a founder member of an appeal committee chaired by Lady Soames to erect a statue of Charles de Gaulle in London.

Tomkins's outwardly impassive manner belied the fact that underneath the surface he was shrewd, clever, and, when necessary, calculating. He was also brave in standing up for what he believed. He made no secret, for example, of his strong conviction that Britain should play a forward role in Europe. He died of heart failure at Sibbertoft Manor Nursing Home, Church Street, Sibbertoft, Northamptonshire, on 20 September 2007. He was survived by his son and two daughters. JOHN LEAHY

Sources *Daily Telegraph* (25 Sept 2007) • *Buckingham and Winslow Advertiser* (25 Sept 2007); (1 Nov 2007) • *The Guardian* (27 Sept 2007) • *The Times* (28 Sept 2007); (13 Oct 2007); (18 Oct 2007) • Burke, *Peerage* • *WW* (2007) • personal knowledge (2011) • private information (2011) [Julian Tomkins, son; S. Wall] • m. cert. • d. cert.
Likenesses F. Barratt, photograph, 1970, Getty Images, London, Hult. Arch. • obituary photographs
Wealth at death £1,838,734: probate, 12 Feb 2010, *CGPLA Eng. & Wales*

Tomlinson [*née* Goward], **Jane Emily** (**1964–2007**), amateur athlete and charity fund-raiser, was born on 21 February 1964 at the Maternity Hospital, Wakefield, Yorkshire, the sixth of ten children of Paul Eric Goward (1932–1990), dentist, and his wife, Anne, *née* Morgan (*b.* 1933), a state registered nurse, midwife, and secondary schoolteacher. Her mother's ancestry was embedded in Merseyside Catholicism, while her father's family roots were in rural Leicestershire nonconformity, although he subsequently converted to Catholicism and their large family received a devoutly Catholic upbringing. Jane was baptized (a week after her birth) and later confirmed as a member of the Roman Catholic church, and was educated initially at St Peter and St Paul's Roman Catholic Primary School, Crosby, Liverpool, from 1968 to 1975. When her father was appointed to the South Australian dental service the family emigrated and she continued her education at the Dominican Cabra College, Adelaide, from 1975 to 1978 and then, after the family returned to Yorkshire, at Notre Dame High School, Leeds, from 1978 until 1982.

Following a turbulent period of uncharacteristic disorientation after leaving school, when she moved to Hull but never actually enrolled on her intended university course, stability returned to Jane Goward's life with her

Jane Emily Tomlinson (1964–2007), by Matt Cardy, 2004

marriage at the Church of Our Lady of Lourdes, Headingley, Leeds, on 20 June 1987 to Michael (Mike) Tomlinson (*b.* 1962), a law graduate of Manchester Polytechnic, employed at a bank in Wakefield, who hailed from a Catholic family from Settle in the Yorkshire dales. A wedding photograph (reproduced in *The Luxury of Time*, facing p. 184) reveals Jane as a petite, slim figure, with long, glossy, brown hair, sparkling eyes, and broad grin, linking arms with her father, whose heavy neck brace testified to his own debilitating struggle with bone marrow cancer, which he endured with great forbearance and good humour over a five-year period before his death in November 1990, leaving a deep impression on his devoted daughter. Notwithstanding her diminutive, five foot two inch stature Jane displayed qualities of determination and fortitude, inherited also from her mother and both of her grandmothers, which enabled her to demonstrate extraordinary courage in her own fight against cancer, which was diagnosed just months before her father's death, evoking his resigned, sardonic response: 'Welcome to the club, love' (*Luxury of Time*, 38). Indeed her husband, Mike, recalled after their first meeting in a Leeds nightclub that Jane had been so 'argumentative' and 'feisty' that he was 'staggered' when she gave him her contact number scribbled on an old beer mat in mascara, enabling their burgeoning relationship to develop (*How Good is That?*, 248). Moreover, even as her illness progressed and she lost her hair as a result of chemotherapy she retained a glint in her eyes and a hint of mischief in her smile, which endeared her both to her family and friends and to an increasingly wider public supporting her cancer fund-raising campaigns.

Tomlinson's ordeal began when in August 1990 at the age of twenty-six she discovered lumps in her breast, which proved malignant. Following a mastectomy and further treatment she experienced periods of remission between 1994 and August 2000, when she was informed by a consultant that her cancer, which had spread to her bones and her lungs, was incurable and that she probably had no more than six months to live. By this time she had three children, Suzanne, born in Leeds in June 1985, Rebecca, born in Peterborough in March 1988, and Steven, born in Leeds in May 1997. She was determined that they should retain positive memories of their mother during this most challenging phase of her life. Remarkably her decision to enrol as a trainee radiographer at the Leeds teaching hospitals occurred while she was herself undergoing radiotherapy as part of her cancer treatment. Her perseverance resulted in her being awarded a diploma of the College of Radiographers in 1993 and a postgraduate certificate in paediatric medical imaging by Sheffield Hallam University in 2002. Moreover she determinedly remained in employment as a radiographer up to the time of her death. Even more astonishingly the most strenuous physical challenges in her life were undertaken during a period when her cancer was spreading into her bones, lungs, and ultimately her liver. She had not previously exhibited the slightest interest in athletics or sport of any kind and only took up membership of a local gym and later of a local running club when she realized the potential of competitive running to raise funds for cancer research.

Tomlinson progressed from local runs over relatively short distances to more strenuous challenges, commencing with the first 5 kilometre Race for Life in Roundhay Park, Leeds, in May 2001; doubling the distance in the Leeds Abbey dash, in December 2001; then running her first half-marathon in York in January 2002, followed by the London marathon in April (which she completed in a respectable 4 hours 53 minutes) and the Great North Run in October. In March 2003 she cycled 1300 miles from John O'Groats to Lands End with her brother Luke; in April she became the first person to run the London marathon on chemotherapy and in August the first terminal cancer patient to complete the half ironman triathlon, comprising a 1.2 mile swim, a 56 mile bike ride and a half-marathon, finishing in the first half of the field. In 2004 she cycled 1900 miles from Rome to Leeds with her brother Luke, and in November completed the full ironman (a 2.4 mile swim, 112 mile cycle ride, and 26 mile marathon) in Florida, in 15 hours 47 minutes. In November 2005 she completed the New York marathon and in the summer of 2006 she embarked on her last expedition, a 4200 mile, 63 day cycle ride from San Francisco to New York, crossing the Nevada and Utah deserts and the Rocky Mountains. Her courage in facing her terminal illness and her athletic feats of endurance won her widespread admiration and affection and enabled her to raise, with the support of her husband, who managed the publicity and fund-raising, over £1.75 million during her lifetime for cancer charities.

Tomlinson's fund-raising activities brought her increasing public recognition. She was appointed MBE in 2003 and CBE in 2007, won more than fifteen media awards, and received five honorary university degrees. She was selected to present the jubilee baton to the queen in Leeds in 2002, awarded the freedom of the city of Leeds in 2005, and became an ambassador for Britain's bid to host the 2012 Olympics. Despite her growing celebrity status, however, as her husband commented in the final volume of a series of three best-selling, candid, and poignant published autobiographical diaries which she co-wrote with him, she remained 'essentially the same person, her sense of joy in life and family untainted' (*How Good is That?*, 344).

She died at St Gemma's Hospice, Harrogate Road, Leeds, from metastatic breast cancer on 3 September 2007. Her requiem mass on 14 September at St Anne's Roman Catholic Cathedral, Leeds, attended by civic dignitaries and watched by thousands, preceded a private cremation at Lawnswood crematorium, Leeds. The prime minister, Gordon Brown, paid tribute to her 'amazing spirit and strength', and her 'exceptional charity work' which would remain as an inspiration to others 'to fight on against the terrible scourge of cancer' (*The Independent*, 5 Sept 2007). Jane's Appeal continued to raise large sums of money for a variety of cancer charities after her death.

JOHN A. HARGREAVES

Sources J. Tomlinson and M. Tomlinson, *The luxury of time* (2005) • J. Tomlinson and M. Tomlinson, *You can't take it with you* (2006) • J. Tomlinson and M. Tomlinson, *How good is that?* (2008) • *The Times* (5 Sept 2007) • *The Guardian* (5 Sept 2007) • *The Independent* (5 Sept 2007) • *Daily Mail* (5 Sept 2007) • *Daily Telegraph* (6 Sept 2007) • www.janetomlinsonappeal.com, 20 July 2010 • private information (2011) • b. cert. • m. cert. • d. cert.

Likenesses photographs, 2002–6, Rex Features, London • photographs, 2002–6, Camera Press, London • photographs, 2002–7, PA Photos, London • M. Cardy, photograph, 2004, Getty Images, London [*see illus.*] • photographs, 2004–6, Photoshot, London • photographs, 2004–6, Getty Images, London • obituary photographs • photographs, repro. in www.janetomlinsonappeal.com • photographs, repro. in Tomlinson and Tomlinson, *Luxury of time* • photographs, repro. in Tomlinson and Tomlinson, *Can't take it with you* • photographs, repro. in Tomlinson and Tomlinson, *How good is that?*

Wealth at death under £19,000: probate, 27 Oct 2008, *CGPLA Eng. & Wales*

Tomlinson, John Race Godfrey (1932–2005), educationist, was born at the nursing home, Sandiway Road, Ashton upon Mersey, Cheshire, on 24 April 1932, the only son and eldest of five children of John Angell Tomlinson, a man of independent means, and his wife, Beatrice Elizabeth Race, *née* Godfrey. The family lived at 120 Urmston Lane, Stretford, a town then famous for growing rhubarb. He attended Moss Park primary school and Stretford Boys' Grammar School. From his childhood he loved history, which he studied at Manchester University. There he was influenced by Sir Lewis Namier, who was to become a close friend and who inspired Tomlinson to enrol on a graduate course at the Institute of Historical Research, London University, where he worked on the history of parliament. His collection of the Grenville papers was published in 1962. On 27 March 1954, while still a student, he married Audrey Maria Barrett (*b.* 1933), whom he had first met at a ballroom dancing class in 1947. They had two sons and two daughters.

Tomlinson was commissioned in the RAF in 1955 and took charge of education at a fighter squadron station. The experience of these three years undoubtedly influenced his decision to devote his career to education. After his national service he taught history for two years at Longton high school, simultaneously working as an evening lecturer for the Workers' Educational Association. But his ambition drew him towards a career in educational administration. In 1960 he became administrative assistant with responsibility for further education in Shropshire county council. During this time the family lived in Bayston Hill, near Shrewsbury. Having served three years in a rural county, he then successfully applied for the post of assistant education officer in Lancashire. There he gained valuable experience of urban education and was responsible for implementing comprehensive schooling—a move he welcomed, appreciating the enhanced opportunity it provided for all pupils. During this time the family lived in New Longton, just outside Preston. Four years later he was appointed deputy director of education for Cheshire. His new responsibilities included teacher supply and teacher training. The family took up residence at Bromborough, a small historic town which was then part of Cheshire.

In 1972, at a remarkably young age, Tomlinson was appointed director of education for Cheshire. Such was his standing with the county council that he was appointed following unanimous acclamation by the education committee. Over the next twelve years he established himself as one of the most outstanding of his generation of education administrators (he served as president of the Society of Education Officers in 1982). He was also involved with national activities such as the Committee on Child Health Services, chaired by Donald Court; he contributed to the Gulbenkian enquiries into drama, dance, and music, and chaired the Schools Council (1978–81), a body supported by the teachers' trades unions but increasingly distrusted by the Conservative government.

Even before the passing of the 1988 Education Reform Act Tomlinson perceived that local government was likely to lose its ability to plan and manage all aspects of schooling. He opted for a change of occupation and a return to the realm of scholarship. His application for a chair at Warwick, with no background in university teaching and no research record since his study of the history of parliament, was unusual. It is a tribute both to his reputation and to the perspicacity of the appointment panel that his potential value to the university was recognized. He was duly appointed professor of education and director of the Warwick Institute of Education. The family set up home in the village of Allesley, near Coventry, in 1985. In making this move Tomlinson hoped to free up his time for thinking and writing, but government changes in the training of teachers stymied this. The new developments ensured that his deft skills and extensive experience of reorganizing posts were put to good use.

Outside the university Tomlinson enjoyed many education-related activities. He was a governor of both the Chetham's and the Menuhin music schools. He chaired the inner London education authority's inquiry into freedom of information and produced an excellent report in 1987, but to no avail as the authority was closed down by the Thatcher government. He later chaired a three-year inquiry into disability and learning difficulties in further education that culminated in the report *Inclusive Learning* (1996). He also played a vital role in the Royal Society of Arts, being in turn a member of council, vice-president, and from 1989 to 1991 chairman of council. In all these different ways, he demonstrated his eagerness to serve the public good.

Leaving Warwick as an emeritus professor in 1996, Tomlinson accepted a part-time post as academic secretary of the University Council for the Education of Teachers, a body that co-ordinated university-based teacher education. From 1997 to 2000 he played a crucial role in delicate negotiations over teacher training. After his retirement he was appointed vice-chairman of the General Teaching Council, which he had persuaded David Blunkett to establish in 2000. He also chaired the National Forum for Learners with Learning Difficulties and Disabilities (2001–5). He received many honours: a clutch of honorary degrees and fellowships, a CBE in 1983, and in 1989 freedom of the City of London followed by appointment as a liveryman of the Goldsmiths' Company. These honours recognized not just his capacity for hard work but his integrity and regard for others, especially for those with any kind of disability.

Tomlinson was a complex man: a confirmed member of the Church of England yet a free thinker; a leader, whom people wanted to follow; a skilled teacher and a persevering learner; a member of the Athenaeum yet (perhaps influenced by his four sisters) a champion of women's rights; devoted to his wife and family yet utterly committed to public service. He died of prostate cancer in Walsgrave Hospital, Coventry, on 6 August 2005. He was cremated on 17 August. He was survived by his wife, Audrey, and their four children. PETER MORTIMORE

Sources preface, *Living education: essays in honour of John Tomlinson*, ed. P. Mortimore and V. Little (1997) • *The Independent* (17 Aug 2005) • *The Times* (27 Aug 2005) • *The Guardian* (30 Aug 2005) • V. Little, N. Parton, and G. Pugh, *Children and Society*, 19/5 (Nov 2005), 346–7 • *WW* (2005) • private information (2009) [Audrey Tomlinson, widow] • personal knowledge (2009) • b. cert. • m. cert. • d. cert.
Archives SOUND BL NSA, current affairs recordings
Likenesses obituary photographs
Wealth at death under £249,000: probate, 7 Nov 2005, *CGPLA Eng. & Wales*

Tomlinson, (Philip) Richard Henry (1943–2006), teacher and theatre director, was born on 10 August 1943 at 32 Mansion House Road, Glasgow, the only son (there were two daughters) of David Alan Tomlinson, chartered accountant and teacher, and his wife, Dorothy Maria, *née* Owston. At the time of his birth his parents lived at 66 Newlands Road, Glasgow. The family had moved to Glasgow from Cheltenham during the war, and returned afterwards. Tomlinson was educated at Cheltenham College, which instilled in him his lifelong love of cricket. After reading history at London University he travelled across South Africa, where he met (Yvonne) Mavoureen Bryceland, the daughter of the actress Yvonne Bryceland. They married in 1967 and later had two daughters, Jemimah and Maisie.

After their marriage Tomlinson and his wife hitchhiked back to Britain through Europe, and Tomlinson began teaching history at the National Star College, Cheltenham, which specialized in students with physical disabilities and associated learning difficulties. He moved in 1970 to the Sandford Centre, Cheltenham, then in 1971 to Hereward College for the Disabled in Coventry. It was there that in 1973 he met the aspiring actor Nabil Shaban, during an interview for a place on a business studies course. Having been rejected by every drama school in the country because of his disability, Shaban had reasoned that the only way he would get into the theatrical profession was to set up his own company. By coincidence Tomlinson's only question was whether or not Shaban was interested in drama. (Tomlinson had the previous year begun a series of drama workshops at the college.) Shaban sought Tomlinson out as soon as he arrived at Hereward, and became part of the stage management team on a show Tomlinson and his cast were devising called *Never Mind You'll Soon Get Better*. The show took its name from the platitudinous nature of attitudes towards the disabled, and, in particular, a remark a doctor had made to a young man who had broken his neck in a diving accident. It explored the stories of the cast and their experiences of being disabled. Their next show, *Ready Salted Crips* (1974), expanded on this theme and consisted of sketches focusing in a satirical way on 'disabled people's perspectives and experiences of education (which was usually second-class), the medical profession and model, family, parents, employment, lack of employment' (Shaban). A key part of the show was 'Blind, Crippled, and Black', a parody of 'Young, Gifted, and Black'. Shaban and Tomlinson shared a sense of humour influenced by Monty Python and the Goons and a determination to shock people out of their complacent and patronizing attitudes to people with disabilities. *Ready Salted Crips* toured Warwickshire, performing in schools, colleges, and amateur dramatic groups as well as in Coventry Cathedral and at Warwick University. The group followed this with Harold Pinter's *The Dumb Waiter*, which also toured and garnered excellent reviews from the local press. In 1975 Shaban and Tomlinson made a pact to set up a theatre company when Shaban had finished his degree. Tomlinson meanwhile went to the University of Illinois to study for an MA degree in education, specializing in child psychology, and while there he directed American students in a version of *Ready Salted Crips*, which he called *Sideshow*. He returned to London in 1976 to take up the post of senior adviser to disabled students at the

Open University and began to plan the establishment of the theatre company with Shaban.

When the United Nations announced that 1981 would be designated international year of disabled people Tomlinson and Shaban decided that their company would need to be ready with a show by 1980. An opportunity to perform at an international conference on disability and rehabilitation in Canada in 1980 spurred them on, and by the end of 1978 the company had a show, *Sideshow*, and a name, Graeae. The Graeae were three sisters in Greek legend with only an eye and a tooth between them, betrayed by Perseus and left blind, screaming, and defenceless. The company's work was dedicated to overturning this popular perception of the disabled and providing work and a showcase for disabled practitioners. *Sideshow*, coupled with a BBC documentary about the group broadcast in 1981, gained the company international recognition. In the same year Tomlinson became headmaster of the Thomas Delarue School for the disabled in Tonbridge, where once again he used drama to challenge the preconceptions of the staff and students. One of the latter, Jamie Beddard (who would go on to work for Graeae), later described him as 'a man with no preconceptions and an absolute faith in the individual'. Tomlinson's book *Disability, Theatre and Education* (1982) was a manifesto for theatre as a unique means of communication between the disabled and the able-bodied.

Tomlinson remained at the Thomas Delarue School until its closure in 1989. From 1993 to 2003 he was client services director for a national consultancy for people with learning disabilities, MacIntyre Care. He and his family had moved to Plaxtol in Kent where he resumed his cricketing career and joined the local amateur dramatic society, writing and appearing in pantomime. When Mavoureen died, in 1998, he moved to Manchester and set up a management training consultancy before becoming chief executive of the Royal School for the Deaf and Communication Disorders in Cheshire in 2004. He moved back to Tonbridge to live with his daughter Maisie when he became seriously ill with bone cancer. He died at her home, 37 Mortley Close, on 3 May 2006. Both daughters survived him. KATE DORNEY

Sources *Sevenoaks Chronicle* (11 May 2006) · *The Guardian* (7 Sept 2006) · J. Beddard, disabilityarts.info/etcetera/archive/etc331.html, 7 July 2009 · N. Shaban, *Early history of Graeae*, http://uk.geocities.com/jinghiz53, 8 May 2009 · b. cert. · d. cert.

Wealth at death under £177,000: probate, 9 June 2006, *CGPLA Eng. & Wales*

Torrance, Thomas Forsyth (1913–2007), theologian, was born in Chengdu (Chengtu), in the province of Szechwan (Sichuan), China, on 30 August 1913, the second of six children of Thomas Torrance (1871–1959) and his wife, Annie Elizabeth, *née* Sharpe, both missionaries. He carried his parents' evangelical devotion and sense of vocation into a long and distinguished career in Scotland as an academic theologian and churchman. His early education was at Chengdu Canadian School, but he and his siblings moved to Lanarkshire in 1927, where they were raised by their mother after their father's return to China. After schooling at Bellshill Academy he took an arts degree at the University of Edinburgh before proceeding to its faculty of divinity at New College. There his teachers included H. R. Mackintosh and John Baillie. A period of graduate study was undertaken with Karl Barth in Basel from 1937. He later completed his doctoral dissertation on the theology of the second-century church, begun under Barth, while a graduate student at Oriel College, Oxford. He was awarded his DTheol degree by Basel in 1946, by which time he had already acquired teaching experience during a brief sojourn at Auburn Seminary in New York (1938–9).

In 1940 Torrance was inducted as a Church of Scotland minister to his first pastoral charge at Alyth, Perthshire. His ministry there was interrupted by a period of wartime chaplaincy service, initially with the Huts and Canteens organization in the Middle East and later with the 10th Indian division in Italy, for which he was made MBE in 1945. After returning to parish ministry in Scotland he moved to Beechgrove Church, Aberdeen, in 1947, where he remained until his appointment three years later as professor of church history at his alma mater in Edinburgh. In 1952 he translated to the chair of Christian dogmatics, a position he held until his retirement in 1979. On 10 October 1946 he had married, at Holy Trinity Church, Combe Down, near Bath, Margaret Edith Spear (*b*. 1919), daughter of George Frederick Spear. They had two sons and one daughter.

Torrance was a theologian of international distinction; his academic career was marked by a prolific scholarly output and a range of projects that were of significance for Reformed and ecumenical church life. With his early enthusiasm for the work of Karl Barth, the leading theologian of the twentieth century, he soon became his foremost exponent in the English-speaking world. This involved, with Geoffrey Bromiley, the supervision of the English translation of the thirteen volumes of *Church Dogmatics* and a full-length study of the development of Barth's theology. Together with J. K. S. Reid he founded the *Scottish Journal of Theology*, a periodical that remained at the forefront of the field. He was also a co-founder of the Scottish Church Theology Society and the (UK) Society for the Study of Theology in 1952.

A series of essays produced in the 1950s on doctrinal disagreement and convergence were later gathered into two volumes that remained among Torrance's most useful contributions to international ecumenical dialogue. In 1957 he supported the 'bishops' report' at the general assembly of the Church of Scotland. Had it been approved it would have led to the union of the national churches north and south of the border. Yet, despite the backing of Torrance and other leading Scottish churchmen, the proposals suffered defeat after a campaign of resistance led by the *Scottish Daily Express*. Torrance, however, would often say that he was proud to have been born in China to an Anglican mother and later to have married an Anglican wife. Narrow nationalist or ecclesiastical sentiments were alike abhorrent to him. Within the Church of Scotland he led the highly influential baptismal commission that concluded its work in 1963. This affirmed a high doctrine of sacramental grace together with the catholic practice of infant baptism. His position on baptism dominated the doctrine of the Church of Scotland until its later gesture towards dual practice, a flexibility that he would surely have deplored just as he had earlier regretted Karl Barth's abandonment of infant baptism.

Torrance's ecumenical enthusiasm was particularly marked by his cordial relations with the Orthodox churches. Deeply committed to the theology of the early church, he stressed the catholic dimension of the Reformed tradition, never losing an opportunity to note the indebtedness of Calvin to the Greek fathers. For many years he led the Reformed–Orthodox doctrinal conversations and had the unusual distinction as a Reformed minister of being consecrated a protopresbyter of the Greek Orthodox church by Methodios Fouyas, metropolitan of Aksum, within the patriarchate of Alexandria.

Torrance's own theological publications exhibited his extraordinary energy, determination, and erudition. As a scholar of Christian dogma he published on almost every topic, but especially on the doctrines of the Trinity, the person and work of Christ, the Holy Spirit, and the sacraments. His position was broadly Barthian but was increasingly shaped by his reading of the Greek tradition, especially Athanasius, Cyril, and Gregory of Nazianzus. He championed the theology of the Nicene creed, his important study *The Trinitarian Faith* (1988) being structured by its teaching. Although he was viewed as resolutely orthodox by more liberal thinkers, he could be deeply critical of hyper-Calvinism, particularly its doctrines of predestination, substitutionary atonement, and biblical inerrancy. All these he regarded as displacing in different ways the person and work of Christ from the centre of a properly evangelical theology. He had almost nothing positive to say about the seventeenth-century Westminster confession of faith, the Church of Scotland's subordinate standard for more than 350 years.

As a teacher at New College, Edinburgh, Torrance was a dominant figure for almost thirty years. He attracted large numbers of students from across the world, particularly the USA, many being supervised for doctoral dissertations. To a large extent theology in Edinburgh was synonymous with his name during his time there. Other members of his family shared his vocation and theological commitments: his brother James (1923–2003) held the chair of systematic theology in the University of Aberdeen; his son Iain (*b*. 1949) became president of Princeton Theological Seminary. Torrance's forceful personality and combative style, however, could generate conflict as well as command allegiance. This became most intense with the public attack on aspects of his work by his distinguished colleague James Barr in *Semantics of Biblical Language* (1961), which argued that philosophical and theological conclusions about Hebraic thought could not be derived simply from an account of the semantic roots of key words. Barr later left Edinburgh for a chair in Manchester. Years afterwards Torrance remarked ruefully (if apocryphally) that Barr had been a brilliant tail-gunner in the RAF and had carried on shooting throughout his academic life. Choosing to remain in Edinburgh until his retirement—he appears to have rejected an opportunity to succeed Barth in Basel in 1961—Torrance exercised a significant influence over several generations of ministers. In 1976–7 he was appointed moderator of the general assembly of the Church of Scotland, and in this capacity he welcomed the queen to Edinburgh during her jubilee celebrations.

Torrance's most original work comprised a body of writings from the late 1960s onwards which sought to form a disciplinary alliance between the natural sciences and Christian theology. Although sometimes difficult to follow, this brought him into close contact with several leading scientists, particularly Michael Polanyi, whose literary executor he became. Torrance's commitment to a rapprochement with the natural sciences led him beyond the work of Karl Barth, who was always more inclined to stress the unique character of theology. Yet Torrance strove to identify common methodological approaches, a shared commitment to critical objectivity, and an implicit belief in the intelligibility of the physical universe, which, he argued, must point unmistakably to a transcendent ground of its rationality. This rehabilitation of natural theology was never allowed to compromise the distinctive commitments of his doctrinal work, yet it represented one of the most determined efforts in the twentieth century to establish a fruitful conversation between theology and science in search of a unified world view.

For much of his career Torrance was a distinctive and leading figure in English-speaking theology. Within the UK he stood apart from a theological culture that was often inhibited by logical positivism, secularization, and historical criticism from articulating a confident theological vision based on scripture and the fathers of the church. Together with Donald MacKinnon he maintained for a generation of British students the possibility of a strong theology that was intellectually robust and adequate to the needs of the churches. If his output did not sufficiently register the ethical and societal themes that later became standard in contemporary theology, it surely demonstrated that the task of the theologian could be accomplished only through extensive acquaintance with the historical traditions of the ecumenical church.

Many accolades were accorded to Torrance, including election as a fellow of the Royal Society of Edinburgh (1979) and of the British Academy (1983), the conferment of honorary degrees, and the award in 1978 of the Templeton prize for progress in religion in recognition of his work on theology and science. In retirement he maintained his prolific output, publishing a steady stream of monographs, while continuing to travel and lecture throughout the world. On three occasions he revisited Chengdu in China; the welfare of its revitalized churches there mattered deeply to him. Although his final years of confinement to a nursing home were inevitably frustrating, his interest in theology and his former pupils remained undiminished. Always he was sustained by his wife and family, the still point at the centre of an extraordinarily energetic lifestyle. He died at Braid Hills Nursing Centre, Edinburgh, on 2 December 2007; his wife and children survived him.

It is not unreasonable to claim Torrance as the leading British theologian of the twentieth century. Several full-length discussions of his work appeared in his lifetime, while a scholarly society and an electronic journal devoted to the study of his theology were established in the USA. Catalogued by the library of Princeton Theological Seminary, his papers form a vast archival collection that will command the close attention of future generations of scholars. DAVID FERGUSSON

Sources R. Spjuth, *Creation, contingency and divine presence in the theologies of Thomas F. Torrance and Eberhard Jüngel* (1995) · A. E. McGrath, *Thomas F. Torrance: an intellectual biography* (1999) · E. Colyer, *How to read T. F. Torrance* (2001) · T. Luoma, *Incarnation and physics: natural science in the theology of Thomas F. Torrance* (2002) · K. W. Lee, *Living in union with Christ: the practical theology of Thomas F. Torrance* (2002) · R. J. Stamps, *The sacrament of the word made flesh: the eucharistic theology of Thomas F. Torrance* (2007) · *The Herald* [Glasgow] (5 Dec 2007) · *The Independent* (7 Dec 2007) · *Daily Telegraph* (10 Dec 2007) · *The Times* (11 Dec 2007) · *The Guardian* (23 Jan 2008) · *International Journal of Systematic Theology*, 10/4 (2008), 369–71 · P. D. Molnar, *Thomas F. Torrance: theologian of the Trinity* (2009) · M. Habets, *Theosis in the theology of Thomas Torrance* (2009) · *WW* (2007) · personal knowledge (2011) · private information (2011) · m. cert. · d. cert.

Archives Princeton Theological Seminary, New Jersey

Likenesses photograph, group portrait, 1976, PA Photos, London · G. Squire, oils, 1991, U. Edin., New Coll. · R. Nigh, drawing, repro. in en.wikipedia.org/wiki/Thomas_Torrance · obituary photographs · photograph, repro. in www.tftorrance.org · photograph, repro. in www.templetonprize.org/previouswinner.html · photograph, repro. in *The Telegraph* (10 Dec 2007)

Townsend, Peter (1919–2006), Sinologist and art magazine editor, was born on 24 August 1919 at 21 Cyril Mansions, East Battersea, London, the third son and fourth of five children of Lewis William Townsend, dentist, poet, and biographer of Oliver Wendell Holmes, and his wife, Jessica Gertrude (Jessie), *née* Ramsey. His parents were Christian socialists; during the First World War his father had delivered anti-war speeches, and both parents had converted from Baptism to Quakerism. Lewis Townsend's cultural sensibilities combined with applied social responsibility were constant influences throughout his son's life. William Townsend, Peter's eldest brother (ten years older than him), later became painting professor at the Slade School of Art; Peter sat for him variously from the age of seven. The second son, Robert, an architect, was initially a communist but later converted to Catholicism. Peter's older sister, Margaret, was later headmistress of a girls' grammar school, and Janet, the youngest, was later children's book editor at Random House.

Townsend attended King's School, Canterbury, from 1932 to 1938. There he formed a discussion group to expose the British government's ineffectual role in addressing fascism in Italy, Germany, and Spain. He wrote to George Bernard Shaw, who invited him to London. Townsend later delighted in recounting how his apprehension melted away on reading the note Shaw's housekeeper gave him, saying, 'I too, am nervous about this meeting'. From 1938 to 1939 he studied history at Worcester College, Oxford.

In 1939 Townsend volunteered for the Friends' Ambulance Unit instead of returning to Oxford for his second year. He served in military hospitals in Bristol, and in London hospitals during the blitz. In 1941 the unit called for volunteers for a six-member unit in China, and after a course in Mandarin with E. R. Hughes, Townsend left in a convoy for China via South Africa and the Indian Ocean. He arrived in Singapore the day before the Japanese first bombed the city. The passage out was difficult, and the unit's arrival in Rangoon coincided with the first air raid there also; Townsend drove a lorry, without headlamps, out of the city through 'the flame lit horror', then on to Kunming (*China Phoenix*, 9).

After an accident Townsend left the Friends Ambulance Unit to become the English publicity secretary to the north-west headquarters in Baoji of the Chinese Industrial Co-operatives, which had been established with the support of foreign charities to sustain small-scale industrial development after the Japanese takeover of China's industrial belt. Townsend later described how he 'was numbed by the conditions that became part of [his] daily life', and by 'the injustices in Chinese society his history books had not prepared him for'. He empathized with the desire for change: 'revolution was preferable to no revolution' (*China Phoenix*, 13). While in China he learned many Chinese dialects, and he continued to speak Mandarin throughout his life. When, disgusted by the atrocities he had witnessed, he renounced his pacifism and travelled to the British embassy in Chunking (Chongqing) to enlist, the ambassador told him that his position in the Chinese Industrial Co-operatives was more significant for the war effort than becoming a soldier.

Among Townsend's friends in China was Zhou Enlai, who gave him a woodcut; this began his extensive collection of rare Chinese woodcuts, later sold to the National Gallery of Australia. It was also Zhou Enlai who arranged for Townsend to meet Mao Zedong in Ya'nan, travelling on an American military plane under the Chinese name T'ang Sun, which puzzled the lieutenant in command. He found Mao living with his wife in a simply furnished house, wearing his famous dusty blue uniform unbuttoned at the neck, smoking constantly; while his wife poured tea 'his wide ranging mind discussed international affairs as easily as the state of the border region' (*China Phoenix*, 76). Townsend felt inadequately equipped to answer questions on trade unions in Britain, but they agreed on the necessity of keeping the co-operatives going.

Townsend remained in China throughout the civil war. In 1947 he married Rose Yardumian, an Armenian-American journalist who wrote for the English language newspaper *People's China*. Townsend meanwhile contributed to the *New Statesman*, reported for the BBC, and was a stringer for Reuters. He witnessed the fall of Shanghai to the People's Liberation Army in 1949 and vividly described the terror of being hounded by wild dogs while attempting to reach a safe house. The Townsends eventually returned to London in 1951, living first in Canonbury and later in Kentish Town. Townsend wrote a sympathetic account of the Chinese revolution, *China Phoenix* (1955), and several other books and pamphlets on China, and was the editor of *China Monthly*, while his wife trained and practised as a primary school teacher. They had two daughters, Sally and Catherine.

In 1965 Tony Adams, director of Cory Adams McKay, invited Townsend to take up the position of editor of *Studio International* magazine. Founded as *The Studio* in 1893 and renamed *Studio International* in 1964, the magazine had lost its radical principles and become provincial; indeed, despite the name change it did not embrace an international outlook until Townsend's appointment. Townsend's editorial genius was twofold: on the production side he exerted high standards of professionalism, and for content he gave his assistants responsibility for decisions. They included Charles Harrison, Frank Whitford, Tim Hilton, and John McEwen. Indeed the roster of contributing editors and writers included such future luminaries as John Elderfield, Lucy Lippard, Seth Siegelaub, Jasia Reichardt, Clement Greenberg, Barbara Reise, Patrick Heron, Dore Ashton, David Sylvester, Robert Hughes, Jindrich Chalupecky, Eugene Brinkus, and Wieslaw Borowski. The decision to set up an international advisory committee created a British and European base for discussion of art practice from across the world that did not defer to American cultural hegemony. Townsend initiated artists' covers. The commissions were honorific, but artists regarded the opportunity as being more significant than a solo show. Seminal covers included those by Marcel Broodthaers, Patrick Caulfield, Jan Dibbets, Roger Hilton, Patrick Heron, Liliane Lijn, Richard Long, and Bridget Riley. Another innovation was artists' books, then a newly evolving form.

Townsend was regarded by many as the centre of the contemporary British art world from the end of the 1960s through to the early 1980s. Naturally shy, he instinctively nurtured artists and brought people together socially and in print. His meetings became legendary; lunch at Bertorelli's restaurant with Carl Andre became dinner. Local pubs were extensions of the office in Museum Street. He adopted unusual tactics to extract copy from writers, on one occasion arriving with a whisky bottle in the middle of the night to wait for completion. Meanwhile he served as chairman of the Greater London Arts Association and of Art Services Grants, which ran the Artists' Information Registry (AIR) and Space Provision, Artistic, Cultural and Educational (SPACE), which provided low-rent artists' studios. However, in 1975 the new owner of *Studio International*, the architect Michael Spens, asked him to make room for a younger editor. This and the rapid decline of the magazine enraged him.

In 1976 Townsend co-founded *Art Monthly* with Jack Wendler, an American who had previously run an innovative gallery in London and also funded artists' projects. It was conceived to be polemical and printed cheaply. In 1983 Townsend was invited to Australia for a lecture tour, which led to the founding of *Art Monthly Australia* in 1987. Thereafter he divided his time between London and Sydney. He edited both magazines until 1992 when his partnership with Wendler ended acrimoniously.

Townsend and his wife, Rose, separated in 1985, and she died in 1990. His partner for the last eleven years of his life was Pat Barnes, an American businesswoman, who nursed him through his final illness. He died from prostate cancer at his home, 12 Alwyne Road, Islington, London, on 21 July 2006. He was survived by Pat Barnes and his two daughters. JO MELVIN

Sources P. Townsend, *China phoenix* (1955) · *The Times* (24 July 2006) · *The Independent* (24 July 2006) · *The Guardian* (26 July 2006) · *Daily Telegraph* (7 Aug 2006) · BL NSA, National Life Story Collection, artists' lives, F18228–F18239 · priv. coll., personal papers · Tate collection, Peter Townsend papers, TGA 2009 · University of Sheffield, Peter Townsend China papers · Tate collection, *Studio International* papers, TGA 2002/8 · Tate collection, Charles Harrison papers, TGA 839 · Tate collection, Barbara Reise papers, TGA 786 · UCL, special collections, William Townsend's journals · personal knowledge (2010) · private information (2010) · b. cert. · d. cert.

Archives priv. coll. · Tate collection · University of Sheffield, papers relating to China | Tate collection, *Studio International* papers, TGA 2002/8 · Tate collection, Charles Harrison papers, TGA 839 · Tate collection, Barbara Reise papers, TGA 786 · UCL, William Townsend papers | FILM documentary footage, BFINA | SOUND BL, National Life Story Collection, artists' lives, F18228–F18239 · BL NSA, current affairs recordings · BL NSA, documentary recordings

Likenesses B. Flanagan, intaglio print on paper, 1972, Tate collection · W. Townsend, portraits, priv. coll. · obituary photographs

Wealth at death under £243,000: probate, 3 Oct 2006, *CGPLA Eng. & Wales*

Train, Christopher John (1932–2007), civil servant and historian, was born at 34 Wimbledon Road, Sherwood, Nottingham, on 12 March 1932, the son of Keith Sidney Sayer Train (1905–1985), schoolmaster and local historian, and his wife, Edna Ashby, *née* Ellis (1904–1991), a schoolteacher. He had one sister, Janet (*b.* 1939). He attended Haydn Road school, Nottingham high school, and Christ Church, Oxford, where he read Greats, taking a second in classical moderations in 1953 and another second in *literae humaniores* in 1955. At school and Oxford he acquired his lifelong love of cricket, together with rugby football and athletics, and developed a taste for paintings, theatre, and poetry. He captained the cricket first eleven at school and at Christ Church, and was a member of the Oxford Authentics. Towards the end of his national service in the Royal Navy (on HMS *Ark Royal*), he married, on 24 August 1957, at St Leodegarius Church, Basford, Nottingham, Sheila Mary Watson (*b.* 1933), daughter of Wilfred Watson; he had known her since their schooldays. They had one son and one daughter. From 1957 to 1967 he was a master at St Paul's School, London, teaching classical Greek to candidates for Oxford or Cambridge scholarships, as well as Latin, Greek, and ancient history through the school. He coached cricket and rugby.

In 1968 Train changed careers and joined the Home

Office, where he held a succession of pioneering appointments. From 1975 to 1978 he was the head of the crime policy planning unit, carrying forward a programme of work that linked different interests and services—for instance reducing the prison population and promoting crime prevention. In 1978 he was appointed secretary of the royal commission on criminal procedure, which was set up to tackle deficiencies in the investigation and prosecution of offences. He secured a sound rational base for its recommendations by arranging for research into how confessions were obtained. The recommendations of the commission, which were near-unanimous and owed much to Train's good humour and intellectual passion, were rapidly implemented in the Police and Criminal Evidence Act of 1984. Then for two years he was an innovative principal finance officer at the Home Office when cash limits and the test of 'value for money' were being introduced into government departments.

In 1983 Train was promoted to be director-general of the prison service. The prison service had been slow to pick up the modern style of management. Resources were seen as a constraint, and industrial relations problems were regarded as insoluble. Train, by strong and courageous leadership (without fuss) and the rigorous application of sound management principles, secured the adoption and implementation of many lasting changes: the abolition of prison officer overtime, with better basic pay and greater productivity; accelerated promotion to the governor grades; and a recognizable management structure, with the introduction of private-sector experience. A record number of new prisons was built, more swiftly and at a lower cost than before, and all cells were provided with integral sanitation. But prisoner unrest and staff discontent continued. There was a serious riot at Strangeways prison, Manchester, in April 1990, and the escape, with a smuggled gun, of two terrorist prisoners from Brixton prison in July 1991. Train retired later that year. He had already told a few colleagues that, in order to take up a house for retirement in Shropshire, he would retire in 1991, rather than when he was sixty in March 1992. It was publicly suggested that his early retirement was a consequence of the prison troubles. Train was hurt by this, but kept quiet.

The move to Clunbury in Shropshire started Train's third career. He immersed himself in local history, local literature, and even local language, learning Welsh to a good standard. His books of this period included a history of Clunbury, *Quietest under the Sun* (1996, the title echoing his deep knowledge of the poetry of A. E. Housman), and *Of Steam and Sheep* (2000), a history of Craven Arms. He devoted much energy to the local parish church and local history societies. Cricket also continued to entrance him. He would try to go to all the test matches in England, and using his MCC membership he invited a circle of old colleagues to join him at Lord's, where the merits of bygone cricketers were exhaustively appraised.

Train was always a schoolmaster and scholar. A subject had to be properly learned before he would talk about it. He would pause in silence in the middle of addressing a meeting to be sure of what he was about to say. As director-general of the prison service he visited every prison every two years and talked to the staff. He knew exactly what life in prison was like. A probing question to him about sanitation in prison cells at a meeting of a committee of the House of Commons was answered with a detailed description of 'slopping out', and the subject was dropped. In his talks about the Norman castles in the Welsh marches he would explain that the Normans by subjugating the country through castles used only a fraction of the number of soldiers the Romans needed for their occupation of Britain. The scholar and schoolmaster wanted to push back the frontiers of knowledge and understanding for colleagues and students alike. The reserve of the schoolmaster made it difficult for him to engage with some prison governors, who were used to a more emotional and outgoing form of leadership. Yet, privately, Train felt deeply about people and his jobs, and about buildings and music.

Train was a devoted, and much loved, husband and father. After a short illness he died at Bishops Castle Community Hospital on 7 May 2007 of cancer of the pancreas; his funeral was on 24 May at St Swithin's, Clunbury. He was survived by his wife and their two children.

Brian Cubbon

Sources *Nottingham Evening Post* (19 May 2007) • *The Times* (24 May 2007) • *The Pauline* (2007) • *Old Nottinghamians' Year Book* (2007) • *WW* (2007) • personal knowledge (2011) • private information (2011) • b. cert. • m. cert. • d. cert.

Likenesses obituary photographs

Wealth at death £338,500: probate, 30 Aug 2007, *CGPLA Eng. & Wales*

Trapp, Joseph Burney (1925–2005), librarian, historian, and literary scholar, was born at Carterton in the southern part of North Island, New Zealand, on 16 July 1925, the son of (Henry Mansfield) Burney Trapp and his wife, Frances Melanie, *née* Wolters. His maternal grandfather had founded the agency for distributing and registering land tenure, which his father had joined. As a boy he went to Dannevirke high school, a small state boarding-school further north of Carterton, where his elder sister was head of English. From there he went with a national scholarship to Victoria University College, Wellington, in 1943. Already fascinated by the classics and with a good grounding in Latin, he now added Greek, its rudiments firmly implanted by his elder sister, Phyllis, but afterwards largely self-taught.

Trapp graduated BA in English and Greek from Victoria in 1945, adding an MA in English and English literature with honours (there was then no doctoral system) in 1946. In the following year he started work at the Alexander Turnbull Library in Wellington, an independent institution with an outstandingly good collection, notably of Milton. The four years that he spent there taught him a lot about libraries and the way they work, but he was still thinking of an academic career, and was glad to return to Victoria as a junior lecturer in 1950. There he had to teach

Joseph Burney Trapp (1925–2005), by Mary Price, *c.*1976

a wide range of subjects, including a course on the classical background for English students. He might have remained at Victoria, but for an unexpected chance. Donald Gordon, professor of English at Reading University, decided to advertise in New Zealand a new short-term post as an assistant lecturer in his own department. Trapp saw the advertisement, applied for the post, and was appointed.

Trapp arrived at Reading for the new academic year in 1951. He was one of a number of notable immigrants from New Zealand who arrived in Britain, still in the grip of post-war austerity, at this time, including Robert Burchfield and Donald McKenzie. The colleagues he met at Reading, among them John Wain and Frank Kermode, remained friends. To Gordon he remained more than grateful, gratitude reciprocated in the dedication of Gordon's *The Renaissance Imagination* (1976). While at Reading he married, at the parish church in Mapledurham on 9 June 1953, Elayne Margaret Falla, the daughter of Sir Robert Alexander Falla, ornithologist and director of the Dominion Museum, Wellington. They had two sons.

Before Trapp's contract at Reading expired, another post, as assistant librarian at the Warburg Institute, came up. Gordon, who had greatly admired its director, Fritz Saxl, urged him to apply: 'it's just your sort of place', he said. So Trapp left Reading, not without regret. He arrived in London in 1953, becoming librarian in 1966, a post he held for ten more years. They were, perhaps, the happiest working years of his life. He took easily to the Warburg's eclectic system of arranging its books (he became an expert, perhaps the last surviving, on the 'Prussian instructions' of 1899 on which it was based), and through it to the institute itself.

Over these years Trapp became the guide, philosopher, and friend of all who used the library, not least the staff. His knowledge of its books was encyclopaedic, due not least to the fact that he handled most of them when the institute moved from South Kensington to Woburn Square in 1958. He opened the parcels of new acquisitions, as well as cataloguing them. He made a point of introducing himself to readers, in turn introducing them to books they had never heard of. He and his wife kept open house for the staff, taking in Leopold Ettlinger, head of the photographic collection, when he was bereft of his wife in 1956. Others, graduating from pupil to the staff, found that he continued to look after their interests, in and outside the institute. To all he offered the same courtesy and help, unawed by the great but especially tender to the tyro.

Trapp also took to the Warburg's equally eclectic scholarly objectives, linking the sources of imagery and literature. He was joint editor of the *Journal of the Warburg and Courtauld Institutes* from 1956 to 1976. His first major article (published in C. A. Patrides, ed., *Approaches to 'Paradise Lost'*, 1958) was 'The iconography of the fall of man'. He had an abiding interest in poetic garlands, the portraits and tombs of classical authors, and their counterparts in modern literature. 'Ovid's tomb: the growth of a legend from Eusebius to Laurence Sterne, Chateaubriand and George Richmond' (published in the *Journal of the Warburg and Courtauld Institutes* in 1973) artfully linked Renaissance and Enlightenment. He developed a special interest in the English followers of the Italian Renaissance, and was early associated with the Yale edition of the complete works of Thomas More. He undertook the volume devoted to *The Apology of Sir Thomas More*. It was not completed until 1979 but it remains a model of its kind, as sound on More's English as on the classical and biblical allusions, pursued with patient care. This led to a visiting professorship at the University of Toronto in 1969, and a hectic but enjoyable visit to Dartmouth College, where the American *Oxford Anthology of English Literature* (he was responsible for the medieval volume, published in 1973) was planned.

To succeed Ernst Gombrich as director of the institute in 1979 was a surprise to Trapp, as also to some others. The sequence of continental predecessors, Saxl, Henri Frankfort, Gertrud Bing, and Gombrich himself, seemed to predicate another in that mould. But Gombrich and others in the institute had had time to observe not only how efficiently the library ran, how seamlessly new acquisitions had added to its original strength and amplified its scope, but also the real scholarship in Trapp's work, his articles, short or long, carefully and imaginatively expressed. More important than all these, they recognized one on whom they could rely to maintain the old Warburg tradition, but lead it into closer connection with the University of London. This was not an easy task. It needed all Trapp's patience and diplomacy, suffering long meetings (which he could not bear) in a good cause, overcoming obstacles laid in the path by acquisitive or disapproving forces in the surrounding university, rallying the very varied troops on his own side, to bring this off. But he did it. The Warburg's staff and work were as richly diverse as they had been when he took over, but both were deployed in a way that fused gently with the rest of the university, by now hardly less various. The staff held positions within the university (Trapp was himself professor of the history of the classical tradition).

Trapp was never one to be overwhelmed by mere administration; if he knew that time could be better spent (and that prompted the odd outburst, more endearing than alarming), he always found time for what mattered, whether his own or other people's work. They benefited immediately; he read their manuscripts, invited them to lecture, and introduced them to audience or colleagues with equal sympathy. His own work was collected in *Essays on the Renaissance and the Classical Tradition* (1990) and *Studies of Petrarch and his Influence* (2003). The rise of 'the portrait of the author' became his Gray lectures at Cambridge in 1990, and as Lyell reader at Oxford (1994) he dealt as vividly with the illustration of Petrarch. This was followed by his Panizzi lectures at the British Library, published as *Erasmus, Colet and More* (1991). With Lotte Hellinga he edited the *Cambridge History of the Book in Britain, 1400–1557* (1999). 'Illustrations of Petrarch: an iconographic survey' (with Elizabeth McGrath) was in preparation at the time of his death.

Trapp also found time for other public duties. He was on the advisory boards of the Victoria and Albert Museum (1977–83) and the British Library (1980–87), and on the council of the British School at Rome (1984–95); he was chairman and trustee of Lambeth Palace Library (1987–98). Elected a fellow of the British Academy in 1980, he was its vice-president (1983–5) and foreign secretary (1988–95). He was a visiting professor at the University of Melbourne in 1980, and at Iowa State and Princeton universities in 1984. To all these institutions he gave the same degree of care and thought as he had to the Warburg. On his retirement in 1990 he was appointed CBE.

Retirement, however, was only the signal for more work, happily free of other entanglements. Although he was increasingly lame from arthritis, most days saw Trapp's little car parked outside the Warburg; he never intruded on his successor, but welcomed the many who called to ask for advice and help. He was always glad to see them, even if they interrupted his work. They always got more than they asked for: facts unknown, drawn from his vast reading, advice on organizing work, sympathy and encouragement. Humanity came naturally to one to whom the humanities were second nature.

He died at Ravenscourt Park Hospital, Hammersmith, on 13 July 2005; he was survived by his wife and two sons.

NICOLAS BARKER

Sources E. Chaney and P. Mack, eds., *England and the continental renaissance: essays in honour of J. B. Trapp* (1990) • *The Independent* (21 July 2005) • *The Guardian* (27 July 2005) • *The Times* (3 Aug 2005) • *Daily Telegraph* (19 Aug 2005) • *A commemoration: Professor Joseph Burney Trapp, 1925–2005* (2007) [a collection of tributes from friends and colleagues] • *WW* (2005) • personal knowledge (2009) • private information (2009) • b. cert. • m. cert. • d. cert.

Archives U. Lond., Warburg Institute

Likenesses M. Price, photograph, *c.*1976, NPG [*see illus.*] • obituary photographs • photographs, U. Lond., Warburg Institute

Wealth at death £90,773: probate, 27 Sept 2005, *CGPLA Eng. & Wales*

Treadgold, Mary (1910–2005), children's writer and radio producer, was born on 16 April 1910 at 51 Woodberry Crescent, Muswell Hill, Middlesex, the daughter of John Reginald Walter (Jack) Treadgold, stockbroker, and his wife, Hilda, *née* Edwards. She was educated at the Ginner-Mawer School of Dance and Drama (1916–22), Challoner's School (1921–3), and St Paul's Girls' School, London (1923–8), the latter at a time when Gustav Holst was music master and the writer Catherine Storr and the actress Celia Johnson pupils. She studied at Bedford College, University of London, from 1930 to 1936, and graduated MA in English literature.

After leaving university Mary Treadgold worked in publishing, first with Raphael Tuck and afterwards as William Heinemann's first children's editor, from 1938 to 1940. It was at this point that she was faced with 'a staggering number of manuscripts about Ponies and Pony Clubs—a few, a very few, outstanding, the majority quite frightful', and decided, 'I could do better myself!' (Carnegie medal archive). She resigned her post, and occupied her hours spent sheltering from air-raids during the blitz between September and December 1940 by writing her first, and most famous, children's book, *We Couldn't Leave Dinah*, published in England in 1941 and in the USA in the following year as *Left Till Called For*. Late in 1940 Treadgold moved to work for the BBC, where she became a literary editor and producer in various arms of the General Overseas Services, then temporarily based in buildings at Bedford College because of bomb damage at Bush House. While working at the Bedford College site she became close friends with Una Marson, the Jamaican writer and feminist, who had also joined the BBC Overseas Services. She later shared an office (possibly the famous Room 101) with Eric Blair (George Orwell), who was not only employed in propaganda broadcasting, but also edited the poetry programme *Voice*. When Marson became ill in 1945 and then returned to Jamaica, Treadgold was asked to take over her role in the African service for three months, and then became talks producer on the west African service. Of the twenty years she spent at the BBC, eleven were as literary editor of *Books to Read*, before eventually leaving to concentrate on her writing.

Treadgold described herself in 1978 as 'a good example of the "hobby writer"—writing … never taken over-seriously' (Kirkpatrick, 774). Nevertheless her first novel, which made use of her own childhood experience of the Channel Islands, won the highest possible accolade for a children's book, the Library Association's Carnegie medal for 1941. *We Couldn't Leave Dinah* describes the adventures of the pony-mad Templeton children who unwittingly miss the evacuation from a fictional island, and covertly assist the resistance during the German occupation. Seeking to transcend the typical pony book, Treadgold combined evocative landscape descriptions with a gripping adventure story, giving a powerful and moving account of the complexities of divided loyalties, collaboration, and threatened relationships in an occupied country, seen through the analytical eyes of teenagers. The sequel, *The Polly Harris* (1948), published in the USA in 1951 as *Mystery of the Polly Harris*, follows the Templeton children to the problems of post-war London, where they become involved in terrorist bombings and smuggling. Once again Treadgold debated issues beyond those of a standard children's story, portraying through her young characters the devastating effects of loneliness and the uncertainty of adolescence. In *No Ponies* (1946) she considered the delicate question of collaborators in France after the retreat of the Germans in 1944, emphasizing both the desperate aftermath of occupation and the continuing threat of a Nazi resurgence. Translations into several European languages were made.

In 1962 Treadgold published the first of her novels for younger readers, *The Winter Princess*, in which she sensitively drew on her knowledge of west African countries and their recent independence. *The Heron Ride* (1962) and *Return to the Heron* (1963) continued to demonstrate her concern with social and ethical issues, relating the adventures of impoverished orphan siblings whose desire for a horse is matched by that for a real home. In a prequel, *Journey from the Heron* (1982), set in London during the First World War, she again showed how experience is heightened and given meaning by the dramatic events of history.

Although Treadgold wrote in 1983 that 'writing for a child's *imaginative* future is of greater moment than I at first realised' (Kirkpatrick, 774), her writing had always stimulated her readers' imaginations. Her output was far more varied than was often assumed, including a novel for adults, *The Running Child* (1951), and at least one short ghost story, 'The Telephone' (1956), which reflected her ongoing interest in the supernatural. She lived in London for most of her life, and she died in St Teresa's Home, 42/46 Roland Gardens, Kensington, on 14 May 2005, of cancer. She never married. BRIDGET CARRINGTON

Sources M. Crouch, *Chosen for children* (1957) • D. L. Kirkpatrick, ed., *Twentieth century children's writers* (1983) • H. Carpenter and M. Prichard, *The Oxford companion to children's literature* (1984) [2nd edn 1987] • P. Hunt, ed., *Children's literature: an illustrated history* (1995) • D. Jarrett-Macauley, *The life of Una Marson, 1905–1965* (1998) • M. Myers, 'Storying war: a capsule overview', *The Lion and the Unicorn*, 24/3 (Sept 2000), 327–36 • V. Watson, ed., *The Cambridge guide to children's books in English* (2001) • K. Agnew and G. Fox, *Children at war* (2001) • G. Griffith, 'Deconstructing nationalisms: Henry Swanzy, Caribbean voices and the development of West Indian literature', *Small Axe*, 10 (2001) • B. Schwartz, *West Indian intellectuals in Britain* (2003) • O. D. Edwards, *British children's fiction in the Second World War* (2007) • *The Times* (23 June 2005) • Archive of the Carnegie Medal, www.carnegiegreenaway.org.uk/livingarchive/, 14 March 2008 • b. cert. • d. cert.

Likenesses photograph, repro. in M. Treadgold, *Return to the heron* (1963)

Wealth at death £721,000: probate, 28 July 2006, *CGPLA Eng. & Wales*

Tremlett, Christopher William (1936–2008), boat designer and manufacturer, was born on 17 May 1936 at Halwill Lodge, Halwill, near Beaworthy, Devon, the second son in the family of three sons and two daughters of Colonel Colin Percy Tremlett (1880–1972), army officer and paper manufacturer, and his wife, Dorothy (1900–1972), daughter of Percy Gray, of the Indian Civil Service. He spent his childhood in Exmouth, where his parents moved when the Second World War broke out. He was later educated at Durlston Court preparatory school in Dorset before moving on to Bradfield College in Berkshire. He did not distinguish himself academically but did prove to have outstanding qualities of leadership and organization, achievements that were to prove invaluable later in life. He found a passion for the sea and sailing, from an early age spending most of his school holidays sailing and wildfowling on the River Exe. It was there that he built his first boat, in his parents' garage, at the age of ten. He became a very competitive helmsman, eventually racing a 14 foot international dinghy.

Tremlett completed his national service as a subaltern in his father's old regiment, the Devonshires, serving in northern Germany. On demobilization in 1958 he joined his uncle's company, Three Castles Leather in Exeter, before going to Grenoble University to study French. It was there that he gained a lifelong passion for snow skiing, entering several leading competitions in which he proved an outstanding contender in the giant slalom. On his return from Grenoble he joined the Byam Shaw School of Art in London, where he concentrated on drawing and design. He then developed a passion for water skiing, in which he also excelled. This, combined with an earlier interest in sailing and the period at Byam Shaw School of Art studying drawing, led to his designing water-skiing tow boats. In 1960 Tremlett opened Tremletts (Skicraft) Ltd in Devon, producing water skis and his first cold-moulded ski towing hull. The business grew when he rented a boat-building facility at Odhams Wharf, on the banks of the River Clyst, a tributary of the Exe near Topsham, Devon. Tremlett remained based there for the rest of his life, and on 22 August 1964, at the parish church of Littleham-cum-Exmouth, he married a fellow Devonian six years his junior, Diana Christina Sturges, daughter of Group-Captain John Arthur Dicken Sturges, RAF officer. She was to work alongside him throughout his life. They had two children, Kate (*b.* 1965) and Mark (*b.* 1967).

Tremlett's approach to the industry proved unique. His hulls were produced by laying thin strips of veneer over a wooden mould, each layer being glued together. Tremlett developed a method of bringing each layer together by covering the entire structure with a rubber blanket before evacuating trapped air by means of a vacuum pump. The compressed veneers and glue were then cured by a long blast of hot air, resulting in a strong, affordable hull. The early Tremlett craft were aimed at the popular sport of water skiing but it soon became apparent that there was a growing market in offshore powerboat racing, whose early fleets were almost entirely composed of adapted ski-boats. Although some owners of early Tremletts tried their luck in the world-renowned class I Cowes–Torquay offshore race, it was in the lower-powered class III area that the company's name began to be noticed. Although other builders were producing highly competitive racers, often costing twice as much, Tremlett boats were usually in the winning frame, particularly when competing in long-distance offshore events like the 220 mile Putney–Calais–Putney race, with its testing sea conditions. It was his economically priced hull that gave Tremlett the well-deserved reputation of bringing the relatively expensive sport of powerboat racing within reach of the working man.

Tremlett boats went from success to success. Hulls were also offered in kit form, with many taken by the Kent boat builder Ray Stapley, who completed them with his own deck and cockpit layout. 'Stapley-Tremletts' dominated the British class III offshore category in the 1970s and early 1980s before the arrival of the offshore multihull. By then the Tremlett name was well established both at home and abroad, with much of the range also built under licence in Mauritius. In 1967 Tremlett produced his first glass-fibre hull, the Seashell, which became one of his standard production boats. This was followed three years later by the 21 foot Sportsman day boat, perhaps one of Tremlett's most successful designs. By this time Tremlett had found yet another interest, aviation. He flew solo after only five hours' tuition and was soon piloting his own Cessna 337 around the UK and to his many customers in Europe.

By the 1980s the Tremlett yard on the banks of the River Exe had grown into a successful factory employing approximately fifty workers. By now, with the arrival of the offshore catamaran, racing boats had become a small part of the business. Tremlett hulls had a reputation for being easily driven. They required less power than craft of similar size and this, coupled with their speed and good sea-keeping qualities, attracted interest from the commercial world. The range of hulls had also expanded up to 53 foot, with much of the output exported to Europe, Africa, and the Middle East, both for pleasure and for commercial use as fishing, military patrol, and harbour craft. Tremlett opened his own boatyard in Mauritius in 2001, in response to demand for his craft from the islands of the Indian Ocean and Far East. The Tremlett company both at home and abroad was moving still further ahead when its founder was diagnosed in 2005 with cancer of the oesophagus, from which he died at his home, Sherbrook House, 23 Northview Road, Budleigh Salterton, Devon, on 13 January 2008. At the time of his death he was working on a new range of ridged inflatable boats, keeping the company in line with current design trends. His life was celebrated at a well-attended memorial service in St Peter's Church, Budleigh Salterton, on 17 March 2008. He was survived by his wife and children. RAY BULMAN

Sources *Motor Boat and Yachting* (1961–2008); (22 Jan 2008) • *Yachts and Yachting* (13 May 1966) • *The Times* (26 Jan 2008) • personal knowledge (2012) • private information (2012) • b. cert. • m. cert. • d. cert.

Wealth at death £1,207,461: probate, 15 Aug 2008, *CGPLA Eng. & Wales*

Tripp, William John Charles Spencer [Jack] (**1922–2005**), comedian and pantomime artist, was born in Plymouth on 4 February 1922, the only son of William Tripp, baker, and his wife, Lilian. He had two sisters. His family had no theatrical connections, but they loved music hall and attended the Plymouth Palace Theatre every Monday night, where dancing acts were the young Jack's favourites. He initially had no particular comedic aspirations although at three years old he amused a party by mimicking Felix the cat. He attended tap dancing classes with his sisters and won the Espinosa award with the previously unheard of mark of 100 per cent, subsequently appearing in local clubs as 'Plymouth's Fred Astaire'. He attended school locally, at Plymouth public secondary school.

During the Second World War Tripp served with the Royal Electrical Engineers, but claimed never to have mastered the assembling of a Bren gun. He was soon co-opted into directing his first forces revue, *That's the Spirit*, and discovered his remarkable talent for mimetic comedy—as well as dancing—in skits including a one-man take-off of the popular music hall act Wilson, Keppel, and Betty. He joined the Stars in Battledress unit and performed in Europe and the Middle East (in Cairo and Khartoum).

It was while appearing in a Stars in Battledress production that Tripp was discovered by the agent of the great comedian Sid Field, whom he understudied in *Piccadilly Hayride* (1946). He watched Field at work over 100 times and learned from him the gift of audience rapport, taking in the whole house with naïve complicitous eyes. In 1947 he was booked for the celebrated *Half Past Eight Show* in Glasgow, Edinburgh, and Ayr, alongside Beryl Reid and the Scottish comedians Dave Willis and Harry Gordon. From these shows he was chosen as principal comic for the Fol-de-Rols, the acclaimed concert party. Greatrex Newman, the producer, wrote clever sketches and lyrics: Tripp modestly said that he didn't always understand the words he was singing but Newman praised him, saying 'Jack always brings something extra' (private information). He stayed with the Fols for fourteen years, becoming a particular summer favourite on the south coast. He performed sketches by Robert Dhery, the French comedian, Dhery and Jacques Tati being special favourites. In 1955 he appeared at the Adelphi in London in the revue *Such is Life*, with Al Read and Shirley Bassey. Later, in the 1960s and 1970s, his own revue, *Take a Tripp*, appeared regularly at various south coast resorts each summer.

Meanwhile a successful parallel career had developed, in pantomime. Tripp started as second comic to such 'Mothers' as Douglas Byng who taught him how to 'attack' a part. He was a hilarious Johnny in *Mother Goose* at the Oxford New Theatre in 1954, performing his ballerina and rebellious recruit sketches. He first played a dame—the part for which he became best known—in 1959, at the Alhambra in Glasgow, subsequently playing the part thirty-five times. So popular was he with panto managements that he only worked for four—Howard and Wyndham, Derek Salberg (for fourteen years), Duncan Weldon

William John Charles Spencer [Jack] **Tripp (1922–2005)**, by unknown photographer, 1994

(for twelve years), and Paul Elliot. They always wanted him back, knowing he could save the show even if their starring television celebrity proved inadequate. Salberg called Tripp 'my insurance policy' (private information). His pantomime career culminated in outstanding appearances as Nurse Ribena in *Babes in the Wood* (Sadler's Wells, 1994–5) and a spectacular Mother Goose (Plymouth, 1995–6). In 1996 he was made an MBE for services to pantomime. His last appearance was as Lord Brockhurst in Sandy Wilson's 1930s pastiche *Divorce Me Darling* (Chichester, 1997). In other hands this elderly roué part could have lent itself to vulgarity: Tripp brought to it the innocent charm that pervaded all his work.

Small and stylish, with twinkling eyes and feet, Tripp was a comic through and through. His face, with its inquiring nose and wide mouth—changing in a flash from broad grin to purse-lipped pathos—was an open invitation to laughter, as was his voice, a husky drawl with an inbuilt chortle. In visual comedy his timing was perfection. As dame he was dainty and demure—as immaculately clean as his starched gingham outfits; he never relied on funny costumes for a laugh. Without a trace of effeminacy he managed to suggest a sprightly female character as well as a gentle children's playmate. His favourite pantomime foil was Roy Hudd who wrote and directed all Tripp's later Christmas shows. Hudd understood Tripp's talents perfectly, regarding him as 'the best Dame there is' (*Evening Herald* [Plymouth], 2 Jan 2004), a view shared by Tripp's peers.

Off stage Tripp was full of *joie de vivre* and humour, rejoicing in life's absurdities. A loyal and generous friend, he was always ready to offer shrewd professional advice. Despite his sunny temperament he could be keenly critical, especially of bad manners and conceit in fellow artistes, while never losing his sense of the ridiculous. He and his longstanding on- and off-stage partner, Allen Christie, were outstanding hosts in their sumptuous flat in Wilbury Road, Hove. He died on 10 July 2005 in the Royal Sussex County Hospital, Brighton, of acute pneumonia. He was survived by a nephew, Paul Andrews, Allen Christie having predeceased him. A service of celebration and thanksgiving was held at St Paul's, Covent Garden, on 28 October 2005. JONATHAN CECIL

Sources J. Cecil, 'There is nothing like a dame', *Independent Magazine* (Dec 1989) • *The Times* (12 July 2005) • *Evening Herald* [Plymouth] (13 July 2005); (16 July 2005) • *Argus* [Brighton] (14 July 2005) • *Western Morning News* (19 July 2005) • *The Stage* (21 July 2005); (4 Aug 2005) • *The Herald* [Glasgow] (30 July 2005) • *Daily Telegraph* (6 Aug 2005) • J. Cecil, 'Jack Tripp: a tribute', *Call Boy*, 42/3 (autumn 2005) [Journal of the British Musical Society] • *Herald Express* [Torquay] (2 May 2006) • personal knowledge (2009) • private information (2009) [Paul Andrews, nephew; A. Sharkey] • d. cert.

Archives FILM British Theatre Museum Archive, 'Babes in the wood', video recording, Sadler's Wells, Dec–Jan 1994

Likenesses double portrait, photographs, 1956 (with Shirley Bassey), PA Photos, London • photograph, 1994, Photoshot, London [*see illus.*] • photographs, 1994, Photoshot, London • obituary photographs

Wealth at death under £231,000: probate, 24 Aug 2005, *CGPLA Eng. & Wales*

Trotman, Alexander James [Alex], **Baron Trotman (1933–2005)**, industrialist, was born at 30 Twickenham Road, Isleworth, Middlesex, on 22 July 1933, the son of Charles Arthur Trotman, stoker, and later upholsterer, and his wife, Agnes Smith, *née* Thomson. At the time of his birth registration his parents lived at 12 Beaconsfield Road, east Twickenham, but they later moved to Edinburgh, where Trotman attended Boroughmuir high school and acquired his lifelong Scottish accent. After completing his secondary school education he joined the Royal Air Force as a national serviceman and served as a navigator, with the rank of flying officer. While in the RAF he married, at the Wesley Methodist Chapel, Brompton, on 22 January 1955, Lorna Fletcher, a 21-year-old GPO telephonist from the village of Brompton, near Northallerton in the North Riding of Yorkshire, and daughter of John James Fletcher, a bricklayer's labourer. The marriage was later dissolved and in 1963 Trotman married his second wife, Valerie Anne. In all he had four children. No mention was made of either wives or children (or recreations) in his *Who's Who* and *Burke's Peerage* entries.

On leaving the RAF Trotman joined the Ford Motor Company at Dagenham. He built his early career in the purchasing department, where he was charged with the task of chasing deliveries of components for the Ford Consul. This was followed in 1961 by his appointment as chief product analyst on the Archbishop project, which resulted in the production of the Cortina model, of which more than three million were sold. Such success caught the attention of Henry Ford, and in 1967 came an elevation to chief product planning director for Ford Europe, with the objective of bringing about greater co-ordination between Ford's British and German operations.

Trotman harboured a desire to work in the company's American arena, but found that it was impossible to transfer across the Atlantic. In consequence he resigned his position in Europe and, after paying his own fare to America, applied for and got a post at Dearborn, Michigan, in 1969, though initially at less than his British salary. In 1972 he gained an MBA from Michigan State University. He become chief car planning manager in 1975 before returning to Europe as vice-president of Ford's truck operations in 1979. Four years later he took up the post of president of Ford's Asia Pacific region. Based in Melbourne, Australia, he faced strong Japanese competition, especially from Toyota and Honda, but succeeded in making Ford the Australian market leader within a year. His success did not go unnoticed and in 1984 he was recalled to Europe as chairman of Ford Europe, where his chief challenge lay in raising productivity levels in Britain to those in Germany. He returned to the United States in 1989 as vice-president of the company, in charge of all North American operations. Success with cars such as the Taurus and the Mercury Sable led to his being appointed chairman and chief executive of the Ford Motor Company in 1993.

Trotman's tenure in office lasted five years, during which he set about trying to transform a group of regional organizations into a global company through the Ford 2000 project, to bring about higher levels of integration. Hitherto the European and American plants had had little to do with each other, each producing models with their own suppliers and model-specific technical specifications. Crucial to Trotman's plan was the standardization of components across as many models as possible to reduce costs by economies of scale in purchasing and production on a global scale, while leaving branding and marketing targeted at specific consumers. Also central to his plan was making the European operation responsible for the design and production of small and medium-sized models like the Mondeo, with the American counterpart taking responsibility for large cars and sports utility vehicles. Though traditionally Ford had always sourced all its component parts from within, Ford 2000 was to break this mould too. Internal suppliers such as Visteon were spun off and told to compete in the wider market, with other remaining internal firms being forced to compete for the first time with outsiders for contracts. This strategy generated massive savings in costs of $5 billion in 1995 alone and went a considerable way towards restoring Ford's short-term profitability. Nevertheless, a degree of tension was created within Ford owing to the way in which the programme was implemented. There were two camps on Ford's board. The first favoured rapid implementation and the second a more incremental approach. Trotman backed the former and started by getting rid of 15 per cent of senior management as well as a considerable number of middle managers in order to reduce administration costs.

Trotman portrayed his Ford 2000 strategy as one that would release chaotic creativity. The eventual outcome was rather different. Not all models created were successful when sold across markets. The European-designed Mondeo sold well in Europe, but its American variants, the Contour and the Mercury Mystique, both failed to make a significant impact. Perhaps critics were correct in their assertion that the European and North American markets were quite distinct and should be treated as discrete entities. A further outcome of the Detroit-driven policy was that Ford Europe felt it had lost its autonomy and its executives appear to have suffered considerable demoralization. Eventually in 1998 the tensions caused by Ford 2000 were such that Trotman was invited to step aside as chairman in favour of William Clay Ford, Henry's grandson, and as chief executive by Jac Nasser.

In essence Trotman was a visionary, who foresaw correctly that globalization was inevitable in the automotive industry and tried to meet the challenges it presented. He was knighted in 1996, and made a life peer in 1999, the year in which he led an inquiry into small businesses on behalf of the British government. With homes in Florida and north Yorkshire, he was a member of the board of directors of the IBM Corporation (1995–2005) and of the New York stock exchange (1996–2002), while also a non-executive director of ICI (1997–2003) and its chairman from 2002 to 2003. He was president of the Hakluyt Foundation from 2002. He died of leukaemia on 25 April 2005, at the Friarage Hospital, Northallerton, Yorkshire. He was survived by his wife, Valerie, and his four children.

TOM DONNELLY

Sources *The Independent* (27 April 2005) · *The Times* (28 April 2005) · *The Economist* (28 April 2005) · *Daily Telegraph* (3 May 2005) · *WW* (2005) · Burke, *Peerage* · b. cert. · m. cert. [1955] · d. cert.
Archives FILM BFINA, documentary footage
Likenesses photographs, 1995–2000, Getty Images, London · obituary photographs

Trueman, Frederick Sewards [Fred] (**1931–2006**), cricketer and broadcaster, was born on 6 February 1931 at 5 Scotch Springs, Stainton, near Maltby, Yorkshire, the fourth of eight children (four sons and four daughters) of Alan Thomas Trueman (1891/2–1970), colliery hewer, point-to-point jockey, and former stud groom, and his wife, Ethel Bennett, *née* Stimpson. Sewards was the maiden name of his maternal grandmother who delivered him (he was a large baby, weighing 14 lb 1 oz). Shortly after Trueman's death it was reported that, in the 1990s, he had discovered that his biological grandmother was Jewish and that his mother, Ethel, had been put up for adoption as a child. Despite his father's employment as a miner at the time of his birth Trueman always regarded himself as from a country family and took great pride in this. In 1943 the Truemans moved to 10 Tennyson Road, Maltby, and Fred attended Maltby Hall secondary school. His father, a keen weekend player, taught all his sons to play cricket. Fred honed his skills as a fast bowler at school

Frederick Sewards [Fred] **Trueman (1931–2006)**, by Carl Sutton, 1953

until a serious injury when aged twelve—he was struck in the groin while batting—forced him to miss a year's schooling and two seasons of cricket.

Early playing career Trueman left school at fourteen and worked variously as an apprentice bricklayer and factory hand in Sheffield and Rotherham, before in 1948 obtaining a job in the tally office at Maltby colliery, where he remained until 1951. From the age of fifteen he played cricket for a local side, Roche Abbey, and impressive performances led to a successful trial with Sheffield United cricket club, which he joined at sixteen, progressing to the Sheffield first team in 1948. In the same year he took part in the Yorkshire Federation tour of southern England and that winter he was coached at Headingley by the former Yorkshire and England players Bill Bowes and Arthur Mitchell, who noted his strong physique, splendid natural action, and genuine pace. He made his first appearance for Yorkshire on 2 May 1949 against Cambridge University, when he was erroneously described in *Wisden* as a 'slow left-arm spin bowler'. Initially he tended to sacrifice consistency for pace. He was ineffective on his county championship début—the 1949 Roses match against Lancashire—though his performances improved over the season and on his first appearance at Lord's he took 8 for 70 in the second innings against the Minor Counties. In 1950, though unable to secure a regular place in the Yorkshire first team, he was selected for the Rest against England in the test trial at Park Avenue, Bradford. He took the wicket of his county team-mate Len Hutton and impressed the Yorkshire captain, Norman Yardley, who dubbed him Fiery Fred, the nickname by which he was best known throughout his career. Though still not certain of selection, he played more regularly and effectively for Yorkshire in the 1951 season, winning his county cap and taking 90 first-class wickets at an average of 20.57—including innings figures of 8 for 68 and 8 for 53 in two matches against Nottinghamshire.

Yorkshire County Cricket Club's new ruling that capped players would be paid during national service prompted Trueman to leave Maltby colliery in autumn 1951 and to enter the RAF as a sports storeman based at Hemswell, Lincolnshire. A sympathetic commanding officer allowed him time to play for Yorkshire, where he now established himself as a formidable fast bowler and was widely spoken of as a future England player. During his national service he also played football for the RAF and Lincoln City reserves. Having taken 32 wickets in four championship games, in June 1952 he was selected for his first test match, against India at Headingley. Trueman's impact was dramatic: after 14 balls of their second innings India were 0 for 4, with Trueman having taken three wickets and the Indian batsmen clearly apprehensive about facing his bowling. But despite finishing the four-match series with 29 wickets, Trueman's place in the England side was not secure. In part this was due to his growing reputation for plain speaking and a refusal to behave deferentially to the game's governing establishment, many of whom he considered snobbish and unduly disrespectful. In the following year he played for England only in the final Ashes test, though shortly before this he had been selected for the MCC's winter tour of the West Indies. It was there that Fiery Fred revealed a less appealing side, combining (on what was a politically sensitive tour) blunt language, unruly behaviour, and dangerous bowling that led to him being mocked by spectators as Mr Bumper Man. That his performance in all but the first test was also below standard made this an unhappy and controversial tour, after which the MCC committee withheld his good conduct bonus. In 1954, and despite an impressive county performance (134 wickets at 15.00), Trueman was again omitted from the test sides to face Pakistan and Australia, only resuming as an occasional England player in 1955. On 19 March of that year he married, at All Saints Church, Scarborough, Enid Elizabeth Chapman (*b.* 1931), daughter of Rodney Chapman, auctioneer and mayor of Scarborough; the couple had two daughters, Karen and Rebecca, and a son, Rodney.

England and Yorkshire By the spring of 1957 Trueman had played only seven tests since his first appearance against India. But an impressive opening to that year's county season (during which he took 135 wickets for Yorkshire) led to his international recall for the test series against the West Indies, with Trueman playing in all five matches and recording figures of 9 for 143 at Trent Bridge in July. This was a turning point in his England career. Over the next five years he played consistently for the national side and reached his peak as a fast bowler of remarkable pace, variety, and stamina. At 5 feet 10 inches and weighing 13 stone, with a broad bottom and powerful legs, he was the ideal build for a fast bowler. Sleeves rolled up and dark hair flailing, he dispatched the ball with a classic side-on action that made possible an out-swinger that moved away, late and at great speed, from right-handed batsmen. He combined this—his self-declared 'special delivery'—with an armoury of bouncers, yorkers, in-swingers, and later an effective off-break. Trueman's international performances in this period included a first overseas Ashes series (1958–9), five tests against India (1959) in which he claimed 24 wickets (average 16.00), and a far more satisfactory, and well-tempered, Caribbean tour (1959–60) when he took 21 test wickets, then a record for an English player in the West Indies. These years also saw the formation of a highly effective bowling partnership with Brian Statham, whose careful, searching approach complemented his partner's pace and aggression. Trueman's finest display from this period—and perhaps of his career—came in 1961 during the second innings of the third, Headingley, test against Australia. There, on a shortened run-up, he took five wickets without conceding a run, finishing the innings with 6 for 30 and match figures of 11 for 88. Even so, and much to his disgust, he was dropped for the final match of the series.

The late 1950s and early 1960s also saw Yorkshire emerge as the dominant force in championship cricket. Between 1959 and 1962 Trueman bowled more than 1000 overs a season for his county, and wicket hauls of 140, 175, 155, and 153 in these years were a major contribution to Yorkshire becoming county champions three times, followed by a further championship in 1963. County cricket was at the heart of Trueman's twenty-year playing career and playing for Yorkshire—for whom he took 1488 wickets in 381 matches—was, according to his memoir *As It Was* (2004), an honour he placed above his appearances for England. Yet Trueman's relations with his club were seldom straightforward. His biographer John Arlott identified Yorkshire's unhappy dressing room during the 1950s as a principal cause of Trueman's later difficulties with the game's authorities, there being notably uncomfortable relationships with his county captains Len Hutton and Vic Wilson. In 1962 Trueman was sent home by Wilson for arriving late for a championship match against Somerset after having captained the last ever Gentlemen v. Players contest at Lord's. By contrast Wilson's successor, Brian Close, sought to stimulate and focus Trueman's resentments—what Bill Bowes described as his 'powerful menace'—for the good of the team. Appreciating the need to 'sense his moods' and 'to get at him', Close would then see Trueman 'work himself up and play magnificently' (private information).

Problems of status and conduct between player and the game's hierarchy were also evident in the test arena. Trueman's 8 wickets in the second Ashes test at Melbourne (1962–3), for example, were overshadowed by disputes over training, mistaken press reports of brawls, and the deduction of one-third of his £150 tour bonus following a critical report by England's manager, the duke of Norfolk. It was not opposition to the establishment *per se* that soured relations with the duke—indeed politically Trueman was and remained a committed Conservative—but rather his refusal to be ill treated by those who considered themselves his social superiors. That Trueman began his 2004 memoir with a summary of a fractious exchange with the duke after the Melbourne test indicates the importance he attached to his battles with the game's élite. Equally characteristic was the friendship that subsequently developed between manager and player once social pretensions had been put aside. Reflecting on the series Trueman later noted Norfolk's invitation to 'Call me Dukie, Fred' as one of the highlights of the tour (*As It Was*, 286).

300 test wickets Trueman had initially responded to this latest dispute with the MCC—and to what he saw as his unfair treatment by the English press—by stating that he would not play again for England. Within months, however, any lingering resentment was being channelled more productively as he sought to become the dominant figure in a resurgent Yorkshire and, in test cricket, to beat a talented West Indian touring side that included the excellent fast bowlers Wes Hall and Charlie Griffiths. Trueman's success at that summer's Edgbaston test—with match figures of 12 for 119—derived from a mature, thoughtful performance of 'venom and variety' during which, under cloudy conditions, pace gave way to 'late and vicious swing; off the seam it cut, like a rattlesnake, this way and that' (*The Times*, 10 July 1963). Trueman finished the 1963 season with the best test, English first-class, and Yorkshire bowling figures, as well as two centuries with the bat (including one for an England eleven) and another county championship. And yet, even while receiving accolades for his performance at Edgbaston, it was evident to some that 'under a hot sun and a thankless wicket' Trueman 'is no longer the force he was' (ibid.). After a poor performance against Australia in the third test at Headingley (July 1964) he was dropped for the fourth match with his test tally on 297 wickets. Recalled for the final test at the Oval, on 15 August Trueman bowled 26 overs without a wicket before taking two in successive deliveries immediately before lunch. Having missed the opportunity of a dramatic hat-trick, he claimed a third victim later that afternoon and so became the world's first cricketer to reach 300 test wickets. For *The Times*, Trueman's figures did not 'of themselves prove that he is the finest of all fast bowlers', the player having had 'more opportunity … than most of those before him'. But there was also praise for the 'beauty and skill and the manliness and the terror of his calling' from a man who 'has never compromised his background or tried to be someone other than himself' (*The Times*, 17 Aug 1964).

Trueman played his sixty-seventh and final international, against New Zealand, in the following year, finishing his test career with 307 wickets. For England he also scored 981 runs, averaging 13.81 an innings. Not one to doubt his ability or his contribution to the national side, Trueman expected further opportunities to increase his total of international wickets, but he was never selected again. Of course, his achievement would also have been greater had he played in one or more of the six series between 1954 and 1964 (fifty-one matches) for which he was available but not selected. He himself repeatedly attributed these omissions to selectors' 'personal' hostility to his forthright attitudes and direct approach. Trueman's record was broken in 1975 by the West Indian Lance Gibbs, and has since been passed by more than twenty players. However, at the time of his death only two English bowlers (Ian Botham and Bob Willis) had bettered 307 test wickets. Moreover, his test average of 21.55 and his strike rate of a wicket every 49 balls remain impressive when compared with those of later players.

Trueman played for Yorkshire for a further three years and with 111, 75, and 66 wickets in the 1966, 1967, and 1968 seasons was again instrumental in securing three more county championships. Between 1962 and 1968 he captained Yorkshire on thirty-one occasions, of which the most memorable was the victory in July 1968 over Australia by an innings and 69 runs at his favourite county ground, Bramall Lane, Sheffield. In two decades as a county and international player he took 2304 first-class wickets (exceeding 100 wickets for Yorkshire in twelve seasons), achieved a batting average of 15.56, and made 438 catches—the majority at short leg.

Later career Following his retirement from Yorkshire, Trueman played six one-day games for Derbyshire in 1972 and remained a regular charity player for more than twenty years. He was also titular proprietor of Freddie Trueman Sports Ltd, a sporting goods shop in Skipton. However, from the early 1970s it was as a cricket commentator and writer (as well as a television 'personality') that he made his career and remained a popular public figure. Trueman had provided a ghosted column for the *Sunday People* since 1959, and during the 1960s he published several studies of the game, as well as *The Freddie Trueman Story* (1965), the first of three autobiographical volumes, which was followed by *Ball of Fire* (1976) and *As It Was* (2004). Later reminiscences and reflections on the game included *On Cricket* (1977, with John Arlott), *Fred Trueman's Cricket Masterpieces* (1990, with Peter Grosvenor), and *Talking Cricket* (1997), co-written with Don Mosey, with whom he also produced several volumes on Yorkshire life, including *Fred Trueman's Dales Journeys* (1998). For more than thirty years until his death Trueman's home in England (winters were spent in Spain) was Bay Tree Cottage, Flasby, north of Skipton, where he lived with his second wife, Veronica Wilson (*b.* 1933), daughter of Michael Lundy, a retired furniture salesman. After Trueman's divorce in 1971 from his first wife, Enid (from whom he had long been separated), he and Veronica had married on 28 February 1973 at Staincliffe register office, Skipton; they had no children, although Trueman became stepfather to Veronica's son and daughter from her previous marriage.

The early 1970s also saw Trueman move into television as the host of *Indoor League* (broadcast within Yorkshire in 1972 and nationally in 1973–7) in which—with his trademark cardigan, pipe, beer mug, and colloquial sign-off, 'I'll sithee'—he championed northern pub games like arm-wrestling, skittles, and shove ha'penny. Following an unsuccessful spell as a stand-up club entertainer, he also became an accomplished and often unstoppable public speaker. A natural raconteur, with a love of cricketing anecdotes and jokes, he combined a frequently professed love of simple pleasures with flashes of showmanship, among them a Rolls-Royce with the number plate FST 307. A series of myths and tall stories, including a reputation as a heavy drinker, also emerged and were repeatedly denied. Trueman's speaking engagements, in addition to providing a private income, became a regular source of fundraising for his chosen (principally children's) charities. Charitable work was a significant part of Trueman's later life and it was rumoured that his appointment as OBE in 1989 was as much in recognition of this as it was for his cricketing achievements. Once described by Harold Wilson as 'the greatest living Yorkshireman', Trueman may have been expecting greater official recognition, and certainly before this date. His television work on *Indoor League* was followed over the next decade with regular appearances on talk-shows and quiz and magazine programmes. In 1990 the marriage of his daughter Rebecca to the son of the American actress Raquel Welch gained widespread coverage—much of it concerned with the apparent incongruity of the couple's in-laws.

Trueman reached many more cricket fans as a member of the BBC's *Test Match Special* commentary team, which he joined in 1974. In this role he combined expert analysis and banter with bleak assessments of the modern game, his claim not to know 'what's going off out there' being a regular lament on the ill-discipline, poor fitness, and questionable tactics of many younger players. In doing so Trueman developed a reputation as a curmudgeon, though many of his pronouncements were delivered with a characteristic dry and quick wit that further served to cultivate his uncompromising image. However, he was genuinely dismayed and angered when, without warning, he and his regular co-commentator Trevor Bailey were dropped by the BBC in 1999. Even friends admitted that his contributions to the programme divided listeners with many (including members of the English Cricket Board) unsympathetic to his negativity, though supporters pointed to his eloquent reflections on cricket history and tactics during breaks for rain.

Away from the commentary box one dispute, that with the Yorkshire batsman Geoff Boycott and his supporters, dominated all others. During the 1970s Trueman criticized what he considered to be Boycott's selfish playing style and its damaging effect on Yorkshire cricket, and so contributed to Boycott losing the captaincy in 1978. Relations with the club had remained awkward since his retirement from playing, with Trueman resentful at what he saw as the administration's lack of respect for his achievements. In 1982 he was elected to the club's general committee but two years later a membership vote in favour of renewing Boycott's contract prompted his resignation and was followed by his defeat at the committee elections in March 1984. Thereafter he cut his ties with the club, though he remained an honorary life member and was later reconciled with Boycott after the latter's diagnosis with cancer in 2002. To players of his own generation Trueman was more generous, and he led efforts to raise funds for his former colleague Brian Statham after the collapse of a business career.

In the spring of 2006 Trueman, a pipe smoker from the age of seventeen, was diagnosed with lung cancer. He died on 1 July 2006 at Airedale General Hospital, Steeton, Keighley, Yorkshire, and was buried on 6 July at the Priory Church, Bolton Abbey, Yorkshire, where he was a regular member of the congregation. News of his death coincided with a one-day international between England and Sri Lanka at Headingley and prompted appreciative applause and a minute's silence. JOHN MORGAN

Sources F. Trueman, *The Freddie Trueman story* (1965) • J. Arlott, *Fred: portrait of a fast bowler* (1971) • F. Trueman, *Ball of fire* (1976) • D. Hodgson, *The official history of Yorkshire County Cricket Club* (1989) • F. Trueman, *As it was: the memoirs of Fred Trueman* (2004) • *The Times* (3 July 2006) • *Daily Telegraph* (3 July 2006) • *The Guardian* (3 July 2006) • *The Independent* (3 July 2006) • *Jewish Chronicle* (7 July 2006) • *Wisden* (2007) • J. Morgan and D. Joy, *Trueman's tales: Fiery Fred, Yorkshire's cricketing giant* (2007) • P. Baxter, *Inside the box: my life with Test Match Special* (2009) • *WW* (2006) • personal knowledge (2010) • private information (2010) • b. cert. • m. certs. • d. cert.

Archives FILM BFINA, *Mining Review*, M. Stewart (director), 1953 • BFINA, documentary footage • BFINA, current affairs footage • BFINA, light entertainment footage • BFINA, *Play it again*, B. Preston (director), Thames Television, 12 Aug 1981 • BFINA, *Close encounters: Freddie Trueman*, ITV, 2 April 1981 • BFINA, *This is your life*, R. Mayoh (director), Thames Television, 5 Dec 1979 • BFINA, *Past masters: fiery Fred Trueman*, G. Ward (director), ITV, 13 Aug 1981 | SOUND BL NSA, performance recordings • BL NSA, documentary recordings

Likenesses photographs, 1949–77, Hult. Arch., London • photographs, 1949–2003, PA Photos, London • photographs, 1951–94, Photoshot, London • photographs, 1952–2005, Rex Features, London • C. Sutton, photograph, 1953, Hult. Arch., London [*see illus.*] • photographs, 1955–96, Getty Images, London, Popperfoto • W. Suschitzky, bromide print, 1960, NPG • Jon, caricatures, 1961–3, Rex Features, London, *Daily Mail* • R. Spear, oil on canvas, 1963, MCC • A. Murrell, photographs, 1980–85, Getty Images, London • B. Thomas, photographs, 1982–94, Getty Images, London, Bob Thomas Sports • photographs, 1996–2003, Camera Press, London • C. Mason, photograph, 1997, Getty Images, London • H. Philpott, photographs, 2001, Getty Images, London, AFP • I. Walton, photograph, 2001, Getty Images, London • B. Fantoni, gouache, repro. in *The Listener* (16 Aug 1979); priv. coll. • A. Ferling, group portraits, oils, MCC collection • photographs, repro. in Trueman, *Ball of fire*

Tuohy, Thomas (1917–2008), chemical engineer and nuclear industry executive, was born at Simpson's Hotel, Wallsend, Newcastle upon Tyne, on 7 November 1917, the elder son of Michael Tuohy, a former private in the Irish Guards who was then the manager of the hotel (in reality a lodging house catering mainly for homeless men), and later a radio engineer, and his wife, Isabella Chessels, *née* Robertson (1893–1975). His father hailed from Cobh, Ireland; his mother was born in North Shields, of Scottish descent. His brother Peter was born in 1918.

Tuohy was educated at St Cuthbert's Grammar School, Newcastle, and was awarded a BSc in chemistry from Reading University. During the Second World War he worked as a chemist in various Royal Ordnance factories. He married first, on 1 June 1940, (Evelyn) Una Crosthwaite Goodacre (*b.* 1916/17), a bank clerk, and daughter of Ralph William Goodacre, a captain in the merchant navy. They had two sons, Michael (*b.* 1942) and Philip (*b.* 1946). The marriage was dissolved in or before 1949, and on 27 August that year Tuohy married, second, Lilian May Barnes (1924–1971), a laundry charge hand, and daughter of Thomas James Barnes, stone quarryman. They had a daughter, Kathleen (*b.* 1950), and a son, Thomas (*b.* 1951).

Tuohy began work in the immediate post-war atomic industry, initially (from 1946) as a health physics manager at Springfields nuclear fuel production plant, in Lancashire (to which he returned briefly as works manager in 1952–4) then, in 1949, joining Windscale as a health physics manager for the plutonium production plant. Subsequently he became manager at the plutonium 'piles' and metal production plant, 1950–52, and Windscale deputy works manager, 1954–7. In 1950 he demonstrated his hands-on approach to solving nuclear problems. During the commissioning of the plutonium production piles, it became apparent that the reactivity of pile 1 could be improved by reducing the amount of neutron-absorbing material in the core. The Windscale management decided that this could be best done by trimming metal from the fins of the fuel cartridges, but the pressing timetable did not allow them to be shipped back to the cartridge workshop at the fuel production site, at Springfields. The UK Atomic Energy Authority's official historian, Lorna Arnold, later recorded: 'They were dealt with on the spot. Tom Tuohy, deputy works general manager, at Windscale, worked at the charge hoist [a large mobile platform at the front of the pile] where, by hand, they cut a strip one-sixteenth of an inch wide from each fin. A million fins were clipped in three weeks during August and September 1950' (Arnold, 15). Two years later, on 28 March 1952, it was Tuohy who opened the reaction vessel in the chemical separation plant at Sellafield, and handled the first piece of plutonium made in Britain, which was destined for use in the first British nuclear warhead test, off Australia's north-west coast, in October that year.

Tuohy's claim to fame was his bravery in dousing an out-of-control nuclear conflagration at the plutonium production Windscale piles, in October 1957, thus avoiding a nuclear disaster. When the fire was discovered Tuohy was at home on leave, looking after his family who all had flu, and had to be specially summoned on site. Several methods were tried to contain the fire: the use of large bellows only served to fan the flames, the attempts at bludgeoning the eleven tons of burning fuel cartridges through the reactor and into the cooling pond behind it with scaffolding poles proved totally ineffective ('they jammed solid', Tuohy revealed to the subsequent board of inquiry), as did use of liquefied carbon dioxide from the neighbouring Calder Hall reactor, then also managed by Tuohy.

Tuohy donned full protective equipment and breathing apparatus and scaled the eighty feet to the top of the pile reactor building, where he reported no flames, only a dull red luminescence. It was decided, early on the morning of Friday 10 October, as a last resort to use water. This option was very risky, as molten metal oxidizes in contact with water, stripping oxygen from the water molecules and leaving free hydrogen, which could mix with incoming air and cause an explosion. Tuohy told the subsequent inquiry: 'We were quite honestly frightened of the water because we didn't know whether there would be an explosion or not' (Windscale Fire Board of Enquiry Transcript, 1.14–15). But there was no other choice left, so Tuohy took full charge of operations. He reported that both yellow and blue flames could now be seen, indicating what was burning inside the inferno. The makeshift hoses delivered water into the reactor for fully thirty hours before being turned off. Tuohy recalled, 'I went up to check several times until I was satisfied that the fire was out. I did stand to one side, sort of hopefully, but if you're staring straight at the core of a shut down reactor you're going to get quite a bit of radiation' (*Daily Telegraph*, 26 March 2008).

Sir William Penney's board of inquiry report into the 1957 near-disaster concluded that the steps taken to deal with the accident were 'prompt and efficient and displayed considerable devotion to duty on the part of all concerned', but it also admitted with regard to the deleterious health implications that 'It appears to us unsatisfactory that tolerance levels in respect of several of the possible hazards should have had to be worked out in haste after the accident had happened' (*Accident at Windscale No. 1 Pile on 10th October, 1957*, Cmnd 302). It was later calculated that at least 240 people contracted life-shortening cancers as a result of the atmospheric radioactive releases. For a month afterwards millions of gallons of milk from the nearby countryside were destroyed, being poured, after dilution, down the drains flowing into the Irish Sea. But for Tuohy's actions the radiological consequences could have been very much worse in economic, environmental, and human health costs. The British government under Macmillan, then in delicate diplomatic negotiations with Washington over Anglo-American military nuclear collaboration, covered up the causes of the fire, with UK atomic officials allowing the Americans to think that Tuohy's staff were to blame, to which Tuohy is reported to have responded: 'I thought they [the officials] were a shower of bastards' (*Daily Telegraph*, 26 March 2008). 'Mankind had never faced a situation like this; there's no-one to give you any advice', Tuohy later said ('Windscale: a nuclear disaster', BBC, 5 Oct 2007).

Tuohy was promoted following the fire to become Windscale general manager (1958–64), then managing director of the UK Atomic Energy Authority Production Group (1964–71). He became the first managing director (production) of British Nuclear Fuels Ltd in 1971, when it was spun out of the Atomic Energy Authority, and then managing director of the new uranium enrichment company, Urenco, a tripartite venture with the Netherlands and West Germany, from 1973 to 1974. He was appointed CBE in 1969. However, he never received any formal recognition of his Herculean efforts to control the Windscale fire. Reportedly disillusioned with the way the nuclear business was progressing, he resigned and took early retirement in October 1974. He thereafter lived in Beckermet, Cumbria, for many years. His second wife having died more than thirty years earlier, on 1 October 2004 he married, third, Shirley Anne de Bernardo, formerly Glinski, a 66-year-old retired computer systems specialist, originally from California, daughter of John de Bernardo, finance director. They moved to Australia for the last few years of his life, and Tuohy died in Newcastle, New South Wales, Australia, on 12 March 2008. DAVID LOWRY

Sources 'A revised transcript of the proceedings of the board of enquiry into the fire at Windscale pile no. 1, October 1957', 1989, news.bbc.co.uk/1/shared/bsp/hi/pdfs/05_10_07_ukaea.pdf, 25 July 2011 • L. Arnold, *Windscale 1957: anatomy of a nuclear accident*, 2nd edn (1995) • P. Dwyer, 'Windscale: a nuclear disaster', BBC news, 5 Oct 2007, news.bbc.co.uk/1/hi/sci/tech/7030281.stm, 25 July 2011 • *Daily Telegraph* (26 March 2008) • *The Independent* (26 March 2008) • *The Times* (15 April 2008) • *The Guardian* (7 May 2008) • *WW* (2008) • personal knowledge (2012) • private information (2012) • b. cert. • m. certs.

Archives SOUND BL NSA, documentary recordings

Likenesses obituary photographs

Wealth at death £946: probate, 18 Dec 2008, *CGPLA Eng. & Wales*

Twitchett, Denis Crispin (1925–2006), historian, was born on 23 September 1925 at 147 Mellison Road, Tooting, London, the elder son of Crispin William Twitchett (1897–1979), architectural draughtsman, and his wife, Gladys Claire, *née* Goff (1898–1969). At the time of his birth registration his parents lived at Fernside, Broadwater Road, Balham, London. He was educated at Isleworth county grammar school and was awarded a state scholarship to read geography at St Catharine's College, Cambridge. His life course was then altered by the Second World War. He became a naval cadet in 1942 and subsequently underwent Japanese language training at the School of Oriental and African Studies, University of London, before service at Bletchley Park and in the Royal Naval intelligence division as a Japanese language officer.

On demobilization Twitchett returned to SOAS to study modern Chinese in 1946–7. He went on to St Catharine's College, Cambridge, where he took a first in oriental studies in 1950. Staying on for his doctorate he was funded to spend time in Japan studying under Professor Niida Noboru, a distinguished scholar of Tang history at Tokyo University. He thus gained a familiarity, unusual among Western scholars, with the excellent Japanese scholarship on Chinese history. Another result of this sojourn was that he met Umeko Ichikawa (1925–1993), daughter of Shosuke Ichikawa, a Tokyo dyer, whom he married at Ealing register office on 18 February 1956. They had two sons.

Twitchett's first post was as a lecturer in Far Eastern history at SOAS from 1954. He was university lecturer in classical Chinese at Cambridge from 1956, returning to SOAS as professor of Chinese in 1960. He was appointed to the chair in Chinese at Cambridge in 1968. He became a fellow of the British Academy in 1967, and took up two visiting professorships at Princeton (in 1973–4 and 1978–9) before moving there as Gordon Wu professor of Chinese studies from 1980 to 1994.

Twitchett was a prolific scholar who produced much important work on the Tang dynasty (618–907). He had completed his doctorate, a study of government and finance under the Tang, in 1955, and that research formed the basis of his first major book, *Financial Administration under the Tang Dynasty* (1963, second edition 1970), a volume soon regarded as a classic on this formative period in Chinese history. Like his other work it was marked by the conscientious use of traditional Chinese sources, including material from the Dunhuang site. However, he was probably best known for his role in planning and editing the *Cambridge History of China* with Professor J. K. Fairbank of Harvard University. This monumental fifteen-volume work was intended to cover the history of China from earliest recorded history to the first years of the economic reforms in the People's Republic after the death of Mao Zedong. By the time of Twitchett's death twelve volumes had appeared. This series, for which the contributors were the most distinguished scholars in their fields from all over the world (ironically with the exception of the People's Republic of China), did much to ensure that the history of China, long neglected in the history departments of universities in the English-speaking world, made a belated appearance on the undergraduate syllabus, if only as an option.

Twitchett's other books included *Confucian Personalities* (1961) and *Perspectives on the Tang* (1973), both co-edited with Arthur Wright; *The Birth of Chinese Meritocracy: Bureaucrats and Examinations in Tang China* (1976); *Printing and Publishing in Medieval China* (1983); *The Writing of Official History under the Tang* (1992); and *The Historian, his Readers and the Passage of Time* (1997). Returning to his earlier training in geography in the 1970s, Twitchett also co-edited both the *Times Atlas of China* (1974) and the impressive China section of the *Times Atlas of World History*, which dealt with China from the prehistoric Peking Man to the turbulent cultural revolution. He was a general editor of the *Cambridge History of Japan* and retained both academic and personal links with the country, where he was always happy to return to the beer and sushi bar culture.

Twitchett was one of the first of a generation of scholars of China who had come to Asian studies through service in the armed forces. His thorough training in classical Chinese and the history of China was undertaken far from the country's twentieth-century realities. He recognized that China's contemporary weakness was, comparatively speaking, a recent phenomenon and he sought to set it against the background of the history of the rise and fall of Chinese empires. His lifelong scholarly interest was in economic and political institutions, tax collection, and technical innovations such as the development of coinage and of printing: all key factors in the power and longevity of the vast and culturally complex empires of medieval China. He never achieved fluency in the modern vernacular and his lack of sympathy for contemporary China and its revolutions created a distance between him and some of his colleagues. However, he worked hard to increase academic interest in China and exerted considerable influence behind the scenes on the development of Chinese studies in the West and on careers and posts. He retired to Cambridge and died at Addenbrooke's Hospital from heart failure on 24 February 2006. His two sons, Peter and Nicholas, survived him. DELIA DAVIN

Sources *The Times* (15 March 2006) · *News@Princeton* (7 April 2006) · *The Guardian* (19 April 2006) · *The Independent* (19 April 2006); (5 May 2006) · D. McMullen, *PBA* (2011) · *WW* (2006) · personal knowledge (2010) · private information (2010) · b. cert. · m. cert. · d. cert.

Likenesses obituary photographs

Wealth at death £468,429: probate, 17 Aug 2006, *CGPLA Eng. & Wales*

Tyndall, John Hutchyns (1934–2005), political activist, was born at Stork Nest, Topsham Road, Exeter, on 14 July 1934, the son of George Francis Tyndall, manager of an aerated water company, and his wife, Nellie, *née* Parker. His father was later employed at St George's House, a YMCA hostel at Southwark, in London. His grandfather, from co. Waterford, had served in the Royal Irish Constabulary. Educated at Beckenham and Penge grammar school, Tyndall spent his national service in the Royal Artillery in Germany. He then took a succession of jobs as bookkeeper or salesman. He was drawn to right-wing politics, and at the age of twenty-two joined A. K. Chesterton's League of Empire Loyalists. This was an alliance of right-wing Conservatives and British fascists. It generated publicity by stunts at Conservative Party conferences, but had no electoral ambitions of its own.

In 1957 Tyndall left the League of Empire Loyalists to form the National Labour Party. In 1960 this group merged with the White Defence League, to form his first but the second British National Party (the first such party had fallen into decline at the end of the Second World War). The British National Party had a paramilitary wing, Spearhead. Tyndall was its deputy commander. In 1962 he published *The Authoritarian State*, espousing empire, the repatriation of black people and Asians from Britain, and a society in which work would be compulsory and gender roles strictly enforced. In the same year he was convicted under the Public Order Act for his activities with Spearhead, and left the British National Party to form a new party, the British National Socialist Movement. He was photographed in Nazi-style paramilitary regalia, a picture that would be repeatedly reproduced to his discomfort later. In 1963 he formed yet another party, the Greater Britain Movement. In the same year he was engaged to Françoise Dior, the niece of the fashion designer Christian. She was reported as saying that she wanted 'to give birth to a little Nazi' (*The Times*, 20 July 2005). The engagement was broken off, and she later married Colin Jordan, Tyndall's political colleague and rival.

Tyndall was influenced by different elder statesmen of the British far right. He was brought into politics by A. K. Chesterton. Later, in the early 1960s, he made use of funds from the estate of the antisemitic camel doctor Arnold Leese. In his public speeches he laboured to imitate the accent and vocabulary of Oswald Mosley. He was not averse to violence, or to infringing the law. In 1966 he was convicted of illegal possession of a firearm. In 1986 he received a six-month sentence for conspiracy to incite racial hatred. In 1999 the *Daily Mirror* published pictures of him with the bomber David Copeland. At the time of his death he was again facing trial on charges of incitement.

In 1967 the National Front (NF) was formed, as a merger of the League of Empire Loyalists, the Greater Britain Movement, and the British National Party. Soon it was buoyed by the controversy surrounding the anti-immigration speeches of Enoch Powell. In 1972 Tyndall became party chairman. The NF enjoyed greater success than its predecessors, winning 16 per cent of the vote in a by-election at West Bromwich in 1973. It won over 100,000 votes in the London elections of 1977 and announced plans to field over 300 candidates at the general election of 1979. In 1977 the Anti-Nazi League was launched, a mass alliance of students, trade unionists, activists, and musicians, to oppose the NF. Its success had a powerful negative effect on the NF's fortunes. The league produced anti-NF literature and organized huge anti-racist carnivals. The NF's opportunities were restricted, and in the 1979 election every single NF candidate's deposit was lost.

Tyndall resigned from the NF's leadership in 1980, going on to launch a further party, the New National Front. This group in turn adopted the name British National Party (BNP) in 1982. It enjoyed limited electoral success, with the election of a single councillor, Derek Beackon, in Tower Hamlets in 1993. Following further opposition, however, the seat was lost, and the BNP entered several years of decline. In 1996, Tyndall took the decision that would effectively bring an end to his active political career: he invited Nick Griffin to join the BNP. Griffin had until that point been a leading figure in the rump of the National Front, in which role he had enjoyed only limited success. On joining the BNP, Griffin first deposed Tyndall as leader, and then took that party into its longest sustained period of growth. Seen within the BNP increasingly as a malcontent, Tyndall retained control of his own paper, *Spearhead*, but was isolated and excluded from the party in 2003. Shortly before Tyndall's death the BNP fielded 119 candidates in the general election of 2005. Their tally of 192,750 votes was then the highest achieved by the far right at any election in British history.

Having until then lived with his mother, on 19 November 1977 Tyndall married Valerie Dawn Olliff, a 35-year-old divorcee, a fellow right-wing activist and election candidate, and daughter of Joseph Charles Parker, engineer. They had one daughter, Marina. He died on 19 July 2005 at his home, 52 Westbourne Villas, Hove, Sussex, of heart failure. He was survived by his wife and daughter.

DAVID RENTON

Sources *The Times* (20 July 2005) · *Daily Telegraph* (20 July 2005) · *The Guardian* (20 July 2005) · *The Independent* (21 July 2005) · b. cert. · m. cert. · d. cert.

Archives SOUND BL NSA, recorded speeches

Likenesses photographs, 1962–79, Getty Images, London · photographs, 1978–97, Camera Press, London · photographs, 1979–2005, PA Photos, London · photographs, 1985–99, Rex Features, London · obituary photographs

Wealth at death under £67,000: probate, 26 Aug 2005, *CGPLA Eng. & Wales*

Tyrrell, David Arthur John (1925–2005), virologist, was born at Kaombe, Salcombe Road, Ashford, Middlesex, on 19 June 1925, the elder son of Sidney Charles Tyrrell, an accountant who had fought in the First World War, and his wife, Agnes Kate, *née* Blewett, a schoolteacher specializing in French and mathematics, who subsequently gave up her career to care for her family. Tyrrell had a gift for languages, later speaking French fluently as well as German. At primary school he was somewhat 'dreamy, forgetful and untidy' (Kerr and Taylor-Robinson, 352) but he excelled at his grammar school in Ashford, where he came top of his class. During the Second World War the family moved to Sheffield, where Tyrrell was a pupil at King Edward VII School, excelling not only at science subjects, but also at German and music. Although he had to drop music this remained a major interest throughout his life.

Tyrrell contemplated teaching but was dissuaded by some aspects of his own school, particularly the attitude of some of his teachers. Stimulated by a family friend who was a general practitioner and an increasing interest in science, he embarked on a career in medicine, starting in the medical school of Sheffield University, where he came under the influence of Charles Stuart-Harris, who subsequently had a major role in Tyrrell's career. After qualifying Tyrrell was encouraged to become involved in clinical research, particularly relating to infectious diseases. He met his wife, (Betty) Moyra Wylie, a general practitioner, while investigating an outbreak of poliomyelitis. She was the daughter of John Wylie, also a medical practitioner. They married at the parish church in Woodlands, Yorkshire, on 15 April 1950, and had two daughters and a son.

The defining experience in Tyrrell's career was being appointed as a research assistant at the Rockefeller Institute in New York. There he gained experience in research methodology and an insight into the interaction between viruses, cells, and mechanisms of viral interference. Research departments in the USA were generally less formal than in the UK and this enabled Tyrrell to rub shoulders with eminent basic scientists who were able to fertilize his innate curiosity and inquiring mind. He especially enjoyed the interaction between those trained in clinical medicine, like himself, and those with experience in basic sciences. Throughout his career Tyrrell had the knack of bridging the divide between clinical and basic research. Informality, combined with the highest scientific standards, was of benefit to numerous younger research workers who either trained with him directly or who sought his advice during their careers.

In 1954 Tyrrell returned to Sheffield to work in the Virus Research Laboratory, but three years later Sir Harold Himsworth, secretary of the Medical Research Council (MRC), invited him to join the MRC's Common Cold Unit (CCU) in Salisbury, Wiltshire, to work on the common cold virus that hitherto had not been isolated. The research was carried out in the Harvard Hospital, originally funded by the American Red Cross to deal with wartime epidemics of infectious diseases. Subsequently, the prefabricated buildings were found to be ideal for housing and isolating volunteers for experimental work on the common cold. Tyrrell used the volunteers for studying the transmission and some aspects of the pathogenesis of common cold viruses, growing viruses (later designated rhinoviruses) in cell cultures in test tubes. His success resulted from his unique and ingenious but essentially simple idea that if cultures were not only oxygenated but also incubated, not at the conventional temperature of 35–7°C, but at 33°C, rhinoviruses could be readily cultivated. Indeed, using himself as an experimental model, Tyrrell showed that nasal temperature was a few degrees lower than body temperature.

Tyrrell then extended his work with cell cultures by collaborating with a Swedish ear, nose, and throat specialist, Bertil Hoorn, who had developed an organ culture system which was more physiologically akin to the natural condition than the *in vitro* cell culture system. Thus when fetal ciliated trachea and nasal epithelium were inoculated, if infected the cilia would stop beating after a few days. This technique resulted in the identification not only of more hitherto uncultivatable rhinoviruses, but also of a new group of human viruses, the corona viruses, which were shown to induce respiratory infections (SARS being an example). To identify these viruses elegant electronmicroscopy was carried out in conjunction with June Almeida at St Thomas's Hospital medical school. The discovery of the rhinoviruses provided Tyrrell with a worldwide reputation. His volunteer studies became renowned and many of his researchers returned to the Harvard Hospital regularly, often during holidays. By the time of his death well over 100 rhinovirus types had been identified but since they all differ from one another antigenically, vaccination against the common cold was considered unrealistic.

In 1967 Tyrrell was appointed to head the division of communicable diseases at the MRC's Clinical Research Centre at Northwick Park Hospital in Harrow, London. Although by 1970 he was the centre's deputy director he continued to visit and direct research at the CCU, covering such areas as gastrointestinal and respiratory infections in children, as well as identifying as many as possible of the causes of febrile convulsions in infants and children. In 1985, however, the MRC decided to close the Clinical Research Centre and Tyrrell returned to work full-time at the CCU. Together with John Pattison and Mary Anderson, then at University College, London, Tyrrell directed studies on adult volunteers relating to the pathogenesis of parvovirus B19. This virus had been established to be the cause of sickle cell crises in patients with chronic haemolytic anaemia. The virus also caused miscarriages if acquired in pregnancy. These studies showed that some of the features of infection, including rash and joint symptoms, were due to an immunological mechanism.

While at the Clinical Research Centre at Northwick Park, and during his last few years, Tyrrell was involved in research at the Chronic Fatigue Syndrome Research Foundation, which he also served as chairman. The reality of chronic fatigue syndrome (otherwise known as ME) as a disease entity was doubted by many medical practitioners, but as a result of Tyrrell's dedication, integrity, and persuasion, together with some of the research conducted by the research foundation, most practitioners became convinced that the syndrome, although not fatal, was debilitating and worthy of investigation.

Tyrrell, with his insatiable curiosity and breadth of knowledge, chaired many committees. Members were not only impressed by Tyrrell's chairmanship and leadership, but also came away having themselves acquired enhanced perception of some of the problems being discussed. Among the committees he chaired were the Advisory Committee on Dangerous Pathogens (1981–91), the Consultative Committee on Research into Spongiform Encephalopathies (1989–90), the Spongiform Encephalopathy Advisory Committee (1990–95), the Biological Sub-Committee of the Committee on Safety of Medicines (1989–92), and the Task Force on Chronic Fatigue Syndrome / Myalgic Encephalomyelitis / Post Viral Fatigue Syndrome (1993–99). He was also a managing trustee of the Nuffield Foundation (1977–92). Many honours were bestowed on him. He was elected a fellow of the Royal Society in 1970 and appointed CBE in 1980. He was also given honorary doctorates by Sheffield and Southampton, the Stuart prize of the British Medical Association (1977), the Ambuj Nath Bose prize (1983), and the Conway Evans prize, awarded jointly by the Royal College of Physicians (London) and the Royal Society (1986).

Tyrrell was a committed Christian and his musical interests involved acting as organist and choirmaster at All Saints' Church in Whiteparish, Salisbury, where he lived. He was president of the Christian Medical Fellowship and president of the Friends of the Christian Medical College at Ludhiana (Punjab) for almost twenty years. He died at Salisbury District Hospital of prostate cancer on 2 May 2005. He was survived by his wife, Moyra, and two daughters, his son having predeceased him. A symposium on RNA viruses and disease was held in his memory at the Royal Society, London, in October 2006. This was well attended by scientific colleagues, including many he had mentored, and friends. J. E. BANATVALA

Sources *The Times* (18 May 2005); (24 May 2005); (1 June 2005) · *The Independent* (30 May 2005) · J. R. Kerr and D. Taylor-Robinson, *Memoirs FRS*, 53 (2007), 349–63 · *WW* (2005) · personal knowledge (2009) · private information (2009) · b. cert. · m. cert. · d. cert.

Archives Wellcome L. | Wellcome L., Sir Graham Selby Wilson MSS | SOUND BL NSA, millennium memory bank, interview with P. Hibberd, 18 Feb 1999, C900/19062

Likenesses G. Argent Studio, photograph, 1978, RS · obituary photographs

Wealth at death £524,818: probate, 11 July 2005, *CGPLA Eng. & Wales*

Ucko, Peter John (1938–2007), archaeologist and anthropologist, was born on 27 July 1938 at the London Clinic, 20 Devonshire Place, Westminster, the only child of Hans Ucko (1900–1967), physician, professor of endocrinology, and a leading amateur orchestral conductor (founder of the Impresario Society), and his wife, Lotte Edith, *née* Nadelmann (1904/5–1967), child psychologist. His parents were non-observant German Jews who, after Hans Ucko had been forced to leave his position at Berlin University in 1933, moved first to Paris, then to London in 1935. Ucko was brought up in London and Buckinghamshire and went to Bryanston School, Dorset. He developed an interest in ancient Egypt, reflected in a passion for collecting figurines and other artefacts. After a year at the North Western Polytechnic, London, he went to University College, London, to study anthropology, opting for courses with a strong archaeological bias. After graduating in 1959 he went on to study for a PhD degree at the London Institute of Archaeology, on anthropomorphic figurines of the ancient Near East.

After taking his PhD in 1962 Ucko joined the anthropology department at University College, London, as a lecturer and founded the distinctive and influential school of material culture studies for which the department became known. It was during this time that he established his academic reputation. His publications included a book on palaeolithic rock art (1967), written with his partner, Andrée Rosenfeld (*d.* 2008); a monograph based on his PhD dissertation (1968), which became well known for its attack on the idea that the female figurines were representations of a widely worshipped 'mother goddess'; a widely influential assault on traditional archaeological interpretations of the evidence from early cemeteries (1969); and a soon legendary comparative study of penis sheaths (1969). During this time he also organized two extremely influential conferences that established a model for international conferences in archaeology, resulting in *The Domestication of Plants and Animals* (1969, co-edited with G. W. Dimbleby) and *Man, Settlement and Urbanism* (1972, co-edited with G. W. Dimbleby and R. Tringham).

In 1972 Ucko took up an appointment as principal of the Australian Institute of Aboriginal Studies in Canberra. When he arrived it was an entirely white institution whose remit deliberately excluded examination of the conditions in which contemporary Aboriginal people lived. Ucko responded to increasing Aboriginal political activism by involving the institute in issues of current concern to them, such as land claims, and by bringing Aboriginal people into the institute's organization as members of its council and committees. This was an opportune time as the new Whitlam Labor government was favourable to Aboriginal interests and Ucko was able to oversee a rapid expansion of the institute. By 1980 he had decided that he had done all that he could in Australia and stepped down, after ensuring, against strong resistance, that his successor as principal would be an Aborigine. Andrée Rosenfeld had gone with Ucko to Australia but there he met the anthropologist Jane Elizabeth de Bargue Hubert, then the wife of Anthony Forge, and she became his partner and essential support for the rest of his life.

In 1981 Ucko returned to England and was appointed professor of archaeology at the University of Southampton. Shortly afterwards he was invited by its British representatives to organize the eleventh congress of the International Union of Pre- and Proto-historic Sciences, which was to be held in Britain in 1986. Ucko accepted the invitation on condition that its structure would be thematic, including such contemporary issues as the social role of archaeology, and that it really would be a world meeting, to include participants from the 'third world', and members of indigenous communities, for example Australian Aborigines, whose pasts were being interpreted by archaeologists. As preparations went ahead in 1984 it became increasingly clear that the congress was under threat from the academic boycott of South Africa: that if participation by South African academics was to be permitted then the congress itself would be disrupted and many of those Ucko most wanted to attend would refuse to come. The eventual decision of the British organizing committee to exclude South African participation led to international uproar, a split in the archaeological world, and the withdrawal of the congress's recognition by the International Union. At a meeting of the British executive committee in early 1986 most of its members resigned, allowing Ucko to appoint a new committee and proceed with the congress. It took place as planned in Southampton in September 1986, now billed as the World Archaeological Congress, and was an enormous success, with almost 1000 participants. Some of its most memorable sessions revolved around the contributions by members of indigenous communities. Subsequently the World Archaeological Congress was constituted as a permanent organization, meeting in different venues every four years, while Ucko created and edited the equally successful One World Archaeology series of books, as well as writing a fascinating account of the events that led up to the first congress itself, *Academic Freedom and Apartheid* (1987). However, it was not just the World Archaeological Congress that occupied Ucko over these and the following years. He was very active in developing the archaeology syllabus at Southampton as well as in supporting the creation of materials for teaching archaeology in schools. This sort of 'outreach' later became commonplace, but at the time Ucko was characteristically a lone pioneer.

In 1996 Ucko returned to London as director of the Institute of Archaeology, now part of University College, London. This was not a popular appointment in some quarters, given his radicalism, though Sir Derek Roberts, the college's provost, had recognized in him a dynamic kindred spirit. Ucko moved with characteristic forcefulness, making new appointments, overturning existing structures, and completely overhauling the syllabus at all levels. He now had the opportunity to put his ideas into practice on a larger scale and for him the most important aspect of this continued to be the involvement of archaeology in issues of importance to groups not normally involved in archaeology, including indigenous communities around the world. Existing degrees in conservation and museum studies were completely revised to have greater social relevance, new degrees were developed, notably in public archaeology, and outreach initiatives encouraged.

Ucko was for many an inspirational teacher and leader

and his contributions had a major influence on the development of archaeology, leading to a recognition of its loss of political innocence and its need to engage with the wider world. He retired in 2005 and was presented with a Festschrift, *A Future for Archaeology: the Past in the Present*, in 2006. In the last few years before he retired he had established close relations with the school of archaeology and museology in Beijing University and a joint International Centre for Chinese Heritage and Archaeology was founded. This became his main focus after his retirement and he was actively developing it until well into his final illness. He died at his home, 6 Regent Square, London, on 14 June 2007 after a long struggle against the worsening effects of diabetes, and, after a funeral at St Michael's Church, Highgate, on 26 June, was buried in Highgate cemetery. He was survived by Jane Hubert and her two children, Tom and Olivia. STEPHEN SHENNAN

Sources P. Ucko, *Academic freedom and apartheid* (1987) • R. Layton, S. Shennan, and P. Stone, eds., *A future for archaeology: the past in the present* (2006) • www.ucl.ac.uk/iams/PeterUcko.htm, 16 Aug 2010 • *The Independent* (21 June 2007) • *Daily Telegraph* (25 June 2007) • *SALON* [Society of Antiquaries of London online newsletter], 25 June 2007, www.sal.org.uk/salon/index_html?id=628#section8, 16 Aug 2010 • *The Times* (26 June 2007) • *The Guardian* (9 July 2007) • *African Archaeological Review*, 24/3–4 (Dec 2007), 95–7 • antiquity.ac.uk/tributes/ucko.html, 29 July 2010 • www.worldarchaeologicalcongress.org/site/peter_ucko_photos.php, 29 July 2010 • personal knowledge (2011) • private information (2011) • b. cert. • d. cert.

Likenesses obituary photographs • photographs, repro. in www.worldarchaeologicalcongress.org/site/peter_ucko_photos.php

Wealth at death £419,257: probate, 18 Sept 2007, *CGPLA Eng. & Wales*

Vallat, Sir Francis Aimé (1912–2008), international lawyer, professor, and civil servant, was born on 25 May 1912 at St Quentin, France, the younger son and youngest of the four children of Colonel Frederick William Vallat (1875–1922), army officer and engineer, and his wife, Marie Irma Adèle Adeline, *née* Maillard (*b*. 1877/8). His father was of part-English and part-Belgian descent, and his mother French (also born in St Quentin); they had married in England in 1902 and their three older children, Helen (*b*. 1903), Phyllis (*b*. 1904), and Howard (*b*. 1907), were all born in London. After the First World War, Frederick Vallat took his family to farm in Canada; but his early death left them in straitened circumstances. Happily, after an unpromising start Francis Vallat attended Parkdale College and won a prize and bursary which enabled him to go to University College, Toronto, from where he graduated with high honours in law. He then went to Gonville and Caius College, Cambridge, where he was tutored by Arnold McNair, the leading scholar of international law, and was secretary of the League of Nations Society. He graduated LLB with first-class honours, and was called to the bar by Gray's Inn in 1935 (where, thirty-six years later, he was elected a bencher). In 1935 he also became an assistant lecturer in law at Bristol University, but in the following year he returned to London to practise at the bar. On 15 April 1939 he married Mary Alison Cockell (1913–2004), schoolmistress, and daughter of Frederick Harold Cockell, schoolmaster. They had a daughter, Judith (*b*. 1941), and a son, John (*b*. 1945).

During the Second World War, Vallat served with the RAF Volunteer Reserve as an instructor in signals and radio, based for the most part at RAF Cranwell. He was demobilized with the rank of flight lieutenant in 1945, and in the same year joined the Foreign Office as an assistant legal adviser. From 1950 to 1954 he was posted to New York as legal adviser to the UK permanent delegation to the United Nations. He then returned to the Foreign Office as deputy legal adviser. He succeeded Sir Gerald Fitzmaurice as legal adviser in 1960. He took silk in 1961 and was knighted KCMG in 1962 (having been made a CMG in 1955). As legal adviser he participated in several important international conferences and represented the UK in a number of significant cases at the International Court of Justice, the European Court of Human Rights, and the Permanent Court of Arbitration.

Unusually, in 1965–6 Vallat took a year's sabbatical from the Foreign Office to serve as acting director of the Institute of Air and Space Law and visiting professor of law at McGill University, Canada; this resulted in a short but well-regarded book, *International Law and the Practitioner* (1966). In 1968 he took early retirement from the Foreign and Commonwealth Office (as it had become), in order to become director of international law studies at King's College, London, initially with the rank of senior lecturer. He was promoted reader in 1969 and professor in 1970, and remained at King's College until 1976. During this time he edited another frequently consulted book, *Introduction to the Study of Human Rights* (1972), and was the driving force behind the introduction of the pioneering, and very successful, LLM course in human rights in the University of London. He made many other practical contributions to international law. From 1969 to 1973 he was director of studies of the International Law Association; and from 1973 to 1981 he was a member of the United Nations International Law Commission (and its chairman in 1977–8). He also served as expert consultant to the UN Conference on the Succession of States in Respect of Treaties (1977–8); as a member of the UK national group on the Permanent Court of Arbitration (1980–92); as a member, and in due course vice-president, of the curatorium of the Hague Academy of International Law (1982–98); and as vice-president of the David Davies Memorial Institute of International Studies (1982–2001). Parallel with his academic career and public service he had in 1968 resumed his legal practice, at 3 Essex Court. He was engaged in a number of important international law cases, his last, in 2001, being *Qatar* v. *Bahrain*, helping to resolve successfully a boundary dispute with its roots in the eighteenth century. He received an honorary doctorate from the University of Lausanne and was knighted a second time as GBE in 1982.

Despite his chair at King's College, London, and visiting appointment at McGill, Vallat's contribution lay less in the realm of scholarship than in the practical development, application, and administration of international law. In those realms he was one of the leading figures of his day. His judgement, though cautious, was good; and the gravity of his public demeanour, combined with his imposing physical presence, meant that he was always regarded with respect. For his part he treated the potentates with whom he dealt with the regard due to their rank, but without obsequiousness.

Vallat had many interests outside the law. He was an enthusiastic sailor and skier, carrying on the latter activity until an advanced age. He loved gardening, the theatre, and, later in life, music. He was an expert upholsterer, branching out, in later years, into antique restoration. Above all he had a great gift for friendship, and, in private, a robust sense of humour. Curiously, for someone who spent most of his career involved in diplomacy, his humour could occasionally be tactless when dealing with friends and colleagues; but it was not intended maliciously, so he was usually forgiven.

Vallat's first marriage ended in divorce in 1973, and on 8 April 1988 he married Patricia Maria Morton Anderson (1919–1995), daughter of Hamish Morton Anderson, surgeon. Following her death, on 23 March 1996 he married Joan Olive Parham, Lady Parham (*b.* 1930), widow of Admiral Sir Frederick Parham, and daughter of Marcus Albert Charig, accountant. He lived latterly in West Lavington, near Midhurst, Sussex, and died in Guildford, Surrey, on 6 April 2008. He was survived by his wife, Joan, and the children of his first marriage.

MAURICE MENDELSON

Sources *The Times* (1 May 2008); (3 May 2008) · *The Independent* (27 May 2008) · *British Year Book of International Law*, 79/1 (2009), 3–6 · Burke, *Peerage* · *WW* (2008) · personal knowledge (2012) · private information (2012) · m. certs.

Archives SOUND BL NSA, documentary recording

Likenesses G. Argent, bromide print, 1968, NPG · obituary photographs

Varah, (Edward) Chad (1911–2007), Church of England clergyman and founder of the Samaritans, was born on 12 November 1911 at the vicarage, Barton upon Humber, Lincolnshire, the eldest son and eldest of nine children of Canon William Edward Varah (1862–1945), a strict Tractarian and vicar of Barton upon Humber from 1911 to 1945, and his wife, Mary, *née* Atkinson (1888/9–1965). He was named after St Chad, founder of the eighth-century St Peter's Church at Barton. In his autobiography he described his father as 'a very strong character, a man of principle with firm beliefs and convictions, and furthermore a man with the moral courage to speak what he believed, whether it would make him popular or unpopular' (*Before I Die Again*, 15), characteristics which he was to inherit, indeed to exhibit to an even greater degree than his father.

Varah was educated at Worksop College in Nottinghamshire. In 1930 he entered Keble College, Oxford, as an exhibitioner in natural sciences, but soon switched to philosophy, politics, and economics. A keen linguist, he was secretary of the university Russian and Slavonic clubs and founding president of the Scandinavian club (later joking that he had founded the club mainly in order to acquaint himself with the prettiest girls in Oxford). He graduated with a third-class degree in 1933, and then went

(Edward) Chad Varah (1911–2007), by Lucinda Douglas-Menzies, 1988

to Lincoln Theological College (where he was taught by Michael Ramsey, later archbishop of Canterbury), and was ordained deacon in 1935 and priest in 1936. He served his curacies at St Giles, Lincoln (1935–8), St Mary's, Putney (1938–40), and St John's, Barrow in Furness (1940–42). On 27 January 1940, at St Mary's, Putney, he married (Doris) Susan Whanslaw (1916–1993), daughter of Henry Robert Whanslaw, fitter; they had four sons (three of them triplets) and one daughter. Susan Varah enjoyed a distinguished career in her own right as a voluntary worker with the Mothers' Union, of which she was president from 1970 to 1976; she was appointed OBE in the latter year.

Varah served as vicar of Holy Trinity, Blackburn, from 1942 to 1949, and also as editor of the diocesan magazine, *The Crosier*, and then as vicar of St Paul's, Clapham Junction, from 1949 to 1953, also serving as chaplain of St John's Hospital, Battersea. Meanwhile he earned extra money by working as a staff scriptwriter–visualizer for *Eagle* and *Girl*, both founded by his fellow cleric Marcus Morris, from 1950 to 1961, using his scientific knowledge to advise on the 'Dan Dare' stories in the former. From 1953 to 2003 he was rector of St Stephen Walbrook (in the gift of the Grocers' Company), designed by Christopher Wren; he was also chaplain to the lord mayor of London, and a prebendary of St Paul's Cathedral, from 1975 to 2003.

Varah's interest both in sex education and in problems facing the suicidal was sparked by his first funeral, in 1935, of a young girl who had committed suicide, fearing she had a sexually transmitted disease, when in fact she had just began to menstruate. At each of his churches he began marriage guidance (including what would later be called sex education) classes for young couples preparing for marriage, or experiencing difficulties, and also youth clubs. In 1952 he caused controversy with an article in the *Picture Post* in which he heralded the advent of (and seemed to many to be insufficiently condemnatory of) the 'permissive' society.

In the early 1950s there were more than a thousand suicides a year in London alone—despite the fact that attempted suicide remained illegal until 1963. In November 1953 Varah founded the Samaritans, 'to befriend the suicidal and despairing'; the organization was formally constituted in February 1954. Despite being run initially by Varah alone, from his parish office, the organization was from the start constituted as a non-religious and certainly non-proselytizing service, offering confidential 'befriending' (or 'active listening therapy') rather than 'counselling' as such. Varah served as director of the London branch from 1954 to 1974. In the latter year he was ousted as director, because of his alleged inability to delegate, but he served as president from 1974 to 1986. The organization expanded rapidly: there were twenty-one branches by 1964, and more than 200 by the time of his death, operated by some 17,000 trained volunteers, answering an estimated 5 million 'contacts' (face-to-face meetings, phone calls, letters, or other communications) a year, twenty-four hours a day, 365 days a year. The model was also rapidly adopted elsewhere in the world, and Varah served as chairman of Befrienders International (later Befrienders Worldwide) from 1974 to 1983, then as president from 1983 to 1986; by the time of his death there were over 400 Befrienders centres in forty countries. After 1986 Varah distanced himself from the movement, believing it to have forsaken its original mission as an emergency service (and in 2003 he even wrote to the Charity Commission asking for its charitable status to be removed), but was reconciled in 2005 (in which year his son Michael was elected to the Samaritans' board of trustees).

Meanwhile, at St Stephen Walbrook, Varah employed a professional quartet to sing at the Sunday morning eucharist, and built up a substantial congregation from among workers in the City of London. Subsidence (caused by the building of nearby high-rises) necessitated the closure of the church for extensive repairs from 1978 to 1987, but it was re-opened in the latter year after the expenditure of substantial funds raised by Varah's friend Lord Palumbo. Controversy surrounded the installation of a large circular altar designed by Henry Moore, when the chancellor of the diocese of London refused permission for its use; the matter was finally settled by Varah's successful appeal to the little known and infrequently convened Court of Ecclesiastical Causes Reserved in 1987.

The central purpose of Varah's life was a love of God and his fellow man. A completely non-evangelical, non-judgemental organization, the Samaritans represented the perfect fulfilment of this purpose. While ecclesiastical authorities frowned on the concept of reincarnation Varah was steadfast in his belief that he would return to earth in another life, as he had done already in previous incarnations.

Varah was also of the view that vision with action can not only make a difference, but can change the world. He epitomized the polymath as a scientist, man of God, mathematician, musician, linguist, traveller, journalist, and author; and he was that rarity among human beings: good, clever, incorruptible, wise, and compassionate. As a preacher he was a mesmerizing figure. His sermons, which seldom lasted for more than ten minutes, and whose themes were decided as he made his way to the pulpit, were gems of enlightenment: spontaneous, incisive, and direct, presented from a photographic memory, culled from a deep knowledge of theology, and delivered with a total command of the English language and an impeccable sense of timing.

Varah was also fiercely patriotic. 'Britain top nation' he would shout, punching his fist in the air as Concorde passed over his house in Barnes on its flight path to New York. France was never mentioned as an equal partner in the project. On one occasion in Paris he interceded in a fight that seemed inevitable between two men by roundly insulting first one, then the other, in perfect French, before pointing to his clerical collar and announcing to both that he was a member of the Anglican clergy. The men, nonplussed, paused before shrugging and shaking hands and heads in bewilderment at the sight and sound of an Englishman who was clearly an eccentric. Varah went on his way, delighted with the morning's work.

While his virtues were manifold Varah could also be, on occasion, prickly, difficult, intemperate, and stubborn. He was always his own man. He had no time for bigots, philistines, or fools, to whom he gave short shrift, as he did to those mired in prejudice, or appalled by the shock of the new. Unshockable himself, he could never resist the opportunity of shocking others.

Though Varah was primarily associated with the Samaritans he was also involved in many other organizations. He was a patron of the Outsiders' Club (a self-help group for people with physical and social disabilities) from 1984 to 2002, and of the Terrence Higgins Trust from 1987 to 1999. In 1992 he founded Men Against Genital Mutilation of Girls. Earlier he had been secretary of the Orthodox Churches Aid Fund (1952–69) and president of the Committee for Publishing Russian Orthodox Church Music (1960–76). He received numerous honours, including the Albert Schweitzer gold medal in 1972; a Pride of Britain award for lifetime achievement in 2000; honorary doctorates from Leicester, St Andrews, Leeds, City, De Montfort, and Lincolnshire and Humberside universities; and in 1981 an honorary fellowship of his old college, Keble, of which he was inordinately proud. He was appointed OBE in 1969, CBE in 1995, and CH in 2000. He published his autobiography, *Before I Die Again* (the title reflecting his belief in reincarnation) in 1992. His other writings included a television play, *Nobody Understands Miranda* (1972) and *Telephone Masturbators and How to Befriend Them* (1976), as well as two volumes of Russian Orthodox church music and books about the Samaritans. When he retired in 2003 he was the oldest incumbent in the Church of England. He spent his final months in a nursing home in

Alton, Hampshire, near his daughter, and died on 8 November 2007 at the North Hampshire Hospital, Basingstoke, of pneumonia. He was survived by three sons and a daughter, his son Michael having died in April 2007.

PETER PALUMBO

Sources C. Varah, *Before I die again* (1992) · *The Independent* (2 Oct 2003); (10 Nov 2007) · *The Times* (10 Nov 2007) · *Daily Telegraph* (10 Nov 2007) · *The Guardian* (10 Nov 2007) · www.samaritans.org, 13 May 2010 · *WW* (2007) · personal knowledge (2011) · private information (2011) · b. cert. · m. cert. · d. cert.

Archives FILM BFINA, documentary footage | SOUND BL NSA, current affairs recordings · BL NSA, documentary recordings

Likenesses photographs, 1954–75, Getty Images, London · photographs, 1978–2004, PA Photos, London · L. Douglas-Menzies, bromide print, 1988, NPG [*see illus.*] · S. Raphael, oils, 1993, NPG · photographs, 1993–2000, Rex Features, London · photographs, 1993–2000, Photoshot, London · obituary photographs · photograph, repro. in *Sunday Telegraph* (26 April 1992) · photographs, Camera Press, London

Wealth at death under £148,000: probate, 25 June 2008, *CGPLA Eng. & Wales*

Varley, Eric Graham, **Baron Varley** (1932–2008), politician, was born on 11 August 1932 at 15 Poolsbrook Square, Poolsbrook, Staveley, near Chesterfield, Derbyshire, the son of Frank Varley, coal miner, and his wife Eva, *née* Goring. He attended the local secondary modern school but left at the age of fourteen. His mother was determined that he should not go down the pit, and he began his working life as an apprentice turner at Staveley iron works, before qualifying as an engineer's turner in 1952. An observant Methodist all his life, on 11 June 1955 he married Marjorie Turner, a 21-year-old shop assistant, at Middle Duckmanton Methodist Church. She was the daughter of Alfred Turner, coal miner. They had one son, Roger.

Varley's heart was in the coal-mining industry, and in 1955 he left the iron works to become an (above-ground) mining craftsman. He was thus eligible to join the then powerful National Union of Mineworkers. He became a branch secretary in 1955 and a member of the Derbyshire area executive committee in 1956, and was earmarked as a protégé by Bert Wynn, the highly influential, far-left general secretary of the Derbyshire miners. He meanwhile attended Chesterfield Technical College and day-release classes at Sheffield University, and then won a scholarship to Ruskin College, Oxford. When his home-town constituency of Chesterfield became vacant, he was regarded as the ideal candidate to hold this safe Labour seat. He was duly selected and in 1964 was elected MP by a large majority. He held Chesterfield through each subsequent general election before retiring voluntarily in 1984. If it had not been for his political predilections his career could have gone in an entirely different direction, since in his youth he was regarded as a first-rate soccer player, became a semi-professional, and was believed by experts to have the makings of a leading professional footballer. At first, under Wynn's influence and according to his own inclinations, Varley was decidedly on the left in the parliamentary Labour Party, supporting unilateral nuclear disarmament, calling for the swift renationalization of steel, and opposing UK membership of the European Economic Community. However, his talent was so obvious that he was to spend only three years of his parliamentary career on the back benches. During this period he became a sponsor of a back-bench bill to legalize homosexuality among consenting adults, not the most obvious stance for a mining MP to take.

Labour had come to power in the election of 1964, the year Varley was elected to parliament. He was spotted by John Silkin, the government chief whip, and recruited to the whips' office in 1967. His real breakthrough came when the prime minister, Harold Wilson, offered him an appointment as his parliamentary private secretary in 1968, and from then on, whether in government or opposition, he was always to be in Labour's inner circle of power. One of the factors that influenced Wilson to appoint him was his role within the then extremely powerful Trade Union Group of Labour MPs. Within a year he had been appointed minister of state at the Ministry of Technology, whose secretary of state was Tony Benn. He expressed, privately, his determination to use this position to kill off the Concorde supersonic aircraft project, but this aspiration remained unfulfilled, and Varley himself, in a later ministerial incarnation, was to travel on the inaugural commercial flight of Concorde to New York.

When Labour lost power in 1970 Varley became a front-bench spokesman in Benn's shadow industrial team. However, when Labour squeaked back into office in February 1974, Wilson promoted Varley to be secretary of state for energy, the cabinet's youngest member at the age of forty-one. He presided over the creation of the public-sector British National Oil Corporation and was one of the first prominent exponents of what later became the fashionable cause of energy conservation, with a widely publicized 'Save It' campaign. He had taken advantage of Wilson's agreement-to-differ dispensation for cabinet ministers over the 1975 national referendum on whether the UK should remain a member of the Common Market. However, this stance did him no harm with the prime minister who, in a post-referendum reshuffle, decided to switch Varley and Benn, with Varley transferred to the Department of Industry whose secretary of state, Benn, was to go to Energy. Benn did not like it, and Varley at first refused to go, not wishing to be categorized as an instrument of Benn's downgrading. Varley had for many years been a self-taught aficionado of classical music. While brooding over this predicament he was persuaded to take his mind off his dilemma by going to the opera at Covent Garden. During the interval he was sought out by the manager to take a call from the prime minister, who told him that Benn had agreed to go to Energy. So Varley entered the Royal Opera House as secretary of state for energy and left it as secretary of state for industry. The opera performed that evening was Verdi's *La forza del destino*.

Varley was a tough incumbent at industry, impatient with Benn's hobby-horse of unviable workers' co-operatives. Circumstances compelled him to take the crisis-ridden British Leyland into public ownership, while his major legislative achievement was the nationalization of the aircraft and shipbuilding industries. However, he drew the line at paying a massive subsidy to prevent the

American Chrysler company from closing down its British subsidiary, the former Rootes group, with a loss of 25,000 jobs. He was willing to call Chrysler's bluff but Wilson, under pressure from Willie Ross, secretary of state for Scotland, launched a rescue plan, behind Varley's back, devised by the malleable cabinet minister Harold Lever. This went through, and Varley contemplated resigning. An even more worrying situation arose when the *Daily Mail* published a front-page splash alleging that Varley had 'nodded through' corrupt bribes payments abroad. He sued for libel and won damages on the day that Labour lost office in 1979.

In opposition after 1979 Varley, who was repeatedly elected to the shadow cabinet, was campaign manager for the leadership bid of Denis Healey when Wilson's successor, James Callaghan, resigned after Labour's defeat. Perhaps because of this, when Michael Foot defeated Healey, he tried to shift Varley from his role as shadow employment secretary, wishing to appoint Neil Kinnock, who had been his own campaign manager. That move was stymied by the Trade Union Group of Labour MPs, whom Varley had chaired from 1971 to 1974, and who waited upon Foot to tell him that such a switch was unacceptable. Varley had meanwhile become treasurer of the Labour Party, with a seat on the national executive committee, defeating the far-left Norman Atkinson. However, when Kinnock became leader in 1983, he had had enough. He accepted a previously refused offer to become chairman and chief executive of the local company Coalite, and retired from the House of Commons in 1984. When Coalite was taken over in 1989 he left. Meanwhile he was a regional director for Lloyds Bank from 1987 to 1991. He was also a director of Ashgate Hospice Ltd from 1987 to 1996, of Cathelco Ltd from 1989 to 1999, and of Laxgate Ltd in 1991–2. In 1990 he was made a life peer. Ironically, considering his past stance, he was a member of the European Communities select committee (1991–6).

Varley never moved his home from Chesterfield, where one of his greatest prides was cultivating a captivatingly landscaped garden, almost a park, at his home in Somersall Lane. His last years were blighted by the onset of cancer. He bore his final illness with immense fortitude, fulfilling, on 29 July 2008, his wish to die in his own bed. He was survived by his wife, Marjorie, and son, Roger. GERALD KAUFMAN

Sources *The Times* (31 July 2008) • *Daily Telegraph* (31 July 2008) • *The Guardian* (31 July 2008) • *The Independent* (31 July 2008) • *WW* (2008) • Burke, *Peerage* • personal knowledge (2012) • private information (2012) • b. cert. • m. cert. • d. cert.

Archives FILM BFINA, *People and politics*, S. Hall (director), Thames Television, 19 June 1975 • BFINA, current affairs footage | SOUND BL NSA, current affairs and documentary recordings

Likenesses Bassano, half-plate film negatives, 1965, NPG • photographs, 1969–82, PA Photos, London • E. Duff, modern bromide print from an original negative, 1974, NPG • photographs, 1974–8, Getty Images, London • group portrait, photograph, 1981, Camera Press, London • G. Lee, photographs, 1990, Photoshot, London • obituary photographs

Wealth at death £881,040: probate, 4 Nov 2008, *CGPLA Eng. & Wales*

Veale, Sir Alan John Ralph (1920–2006), engineer and industrialist, was born on 2 February 1920 at 86 Monks Road, Exeter, the son of Leslie Henry Veale (*d.* 1971), wholesale fruit merchant, and his wife, Eleanor, *née* Davies. Educated at Exeter School, he took an early interest in what was then the new technology of electricity generation, and he secured an apprenticeship at Metropolitan Vickers in Manchester, the premier training ground for electrical engineers. He also took a degree in engineering at the Manchester College of Technology. During the Second World War his job was classified as a reserved occupation, and he worked on the manufacture of radar equipment. His first assignment in Metropolitan Vickers after the war was as assistant superintendent of electrical control equipment. On 18 July 1946 he married Muriel Edwards, the 22-year-old daughter of John William Edwards, rubber manufacturer. They had three sons.

Metropolitan Vickers had its main factory at Trafford Park, Manchester, which had been built in 1904 by one of the American pioneers of the electrical industry, George Westinghouse. Control of the company, which was then called British Westinghouse, subsequently passed into the hands of British business interests, and it was renamed Metropolitan Vickers, often shortened to Metrovick, in 1918. In 1928 Metrovick merged with another British electrical company, which also had American connections, British Thomson-Houston, to form a new group, Associated Electrical Industries (AEI). The two parts of the group, Metrovick at Manchester and British Thomson-Houston at Rugby, continued to be run largely independently, and indeed continued to fight each other, as Veale remarked later, 'like drunken sailors' (Aris, 63).

During the 1950s, while Veale was building his career at Trafford Park, Lord Chandos, chairman of AEI, embarked on an ambitious expansion programme that included a new factory at Larne in Northern Ireland to make turbines and another at Wythenshawe, near Manchester, for transformers. These investments produced meagre returns, and by the time Chandos retired in 1963 the company was in a weak state. Despite attempts by Chandos's successors to revive the business, AEI succumbed to a takeover bid from Arnold Weinstock's General Electric Company (GEC) in 1967.

Shortly before the GEC takeover Veale had moved from Trafford Park to take charge of the British Thomson-Houston works at Rugby. Weinstock had a low opinion of AEI's senior management, but he recognized that there were several experienced and talented engineers, including Veale, whose services he could not afford to lose. Veale, for his part, welcomed what he saw as Weinstock's 'crisp decisiveness' after the vacillation of the previous AEI management (Aris, 69), and over the next few years the two men established a relationship that, while hardly warm, was based on mutual respect. When GEC merged with English Electric in 1968—effectively an acquisition, since GEC was the dominant partner—Weinstock was faced with the task of rationalizing an array of factories throughout the UK, many of them competing with each other. There were also conflicts of personality between the former AEI and English Electric managers, especially in the heavy engineering operations with which Veale was mainly concerned. All these plants were put together into GEC Power Engineering in 1970, and Veale was made managing director, a post he held until his retirement in 1985. He joined the main board of GEC in 1973.

Operating from his base in Rugby, Veale supervised an extensive programme of rationalization, involving a reduction in the number of factories in the UK from fifty-five to twenty-seven and a 50 per cent cut in the number of people employed. At the same time Veale and his team set in train an aggressive search for export business, winning some notable orders including the big Castle Peak power station project in Hong Kong. Working closely with Bob Davidson, former English Electric engineer, he substantially enlarged GEC's share of the world market for heavy electrical equipment. Veale was also involved, with Weinstock, in the lengthy and often acrimonious debate about the choice of reactor for the British nuclear power programme, a debate that ended with GEC's withdrawal from its intended role as leader of the programme—although it continued to be a major supplier of power generating equipment for nuclear stations in the UK and overseas. Gentle in manner, Veale was also forceful and determined, and prepared to stand his ground whenever he felt that Weinstock's policies might damage the businesses for which he was responsible. His contribution to GEC lay not just in rationalization but also in nurturing the growth of new businesses, of which the Ruston industrial gas turbine business at Lincoln (acquired by English Electric shortly before the merger with GEC) was a notable example.

Veale was knighted in 1984. After his retirement from GEC in 1985 he played an active role in public life. He was president of the Institute of Production Engineers in 1985–6, sat on the councils of Salford and Exeter universities, and was a founding member of the Worshipful Company of Engineers. He was also chairman of Rossmore Warwick Ltd (1986–8), RFS Industries Ltd (1987–92), and Exeter Enterprise Ltd (from 1990).

He died on 29 March 2006, of cancer of the pancreas, at Eversleigh Nursing Home, 2 Clarendon Place, Leamington Spa. He was survived by his wife, Muriel, and two sons, one son having predeceased him. A memorial service was held on 30 June at the Queen's Chapel of the Savoy in London. He was commemorated in the Midlands Manufacturing Group's annual Sir Alan Veale lecture, begun in 2000.

GEOFFREY OWEN

Sources R. Jones and O. Marriott, *Anatomy of a merger: a history of GEC, AEI, and English Electric* (1970) • S. Aris, *Arnold Weinstock and the making of GEC* (1998) • A. Brummer and R. Cowe, *Weinstock: the life and times of Britain's premier industrialist* (1998) • *The Times* (15 May 2006) • Burke, *Peerage* • *WW* (2006) • private information (2010) • b. cert. • m. cert. • d. cert.

Wealth at death £824,946: probate, 20 Sept 2006, *CGPLA Eng. & Wales*

Vickers, James Oswald Noel [Jon] (**1916–2008**), educationist and trade unionist, was born on 6 April 1916 at 11 Queen Street, Mayfair, London, the son of Noel Mushcamp Vickers, a barrister then serving as a lieutenant in the 13th Yorkshire regiment, and his wife, Linda, *née* Lindemann. His father was killed in action when Vickers was three months old. According to an unpublished family history later written by Vickers his father was distantly related to the Vickers family of engineering fame. Vickers was also reputedly related to Winston Churchill and because of this was later interrogated by Heinrich Himmler, the head of the Gestapo, while a prisoner of war.

Vickers attended Stowe School, where he became known to family and friends as Mouse. He went up to Queens' College, Cambridge, to study history and English. He also gained a boxing blue, and joined the Communist Party. It is said that he did so as a consequence of the death of a schoolfriend, John Cornford, in the Spanish Civil War. He was commissioned in the army at the outbreak of the Second World War in 1939 and sent to France with the British expeditionary force as a second lieutenant in the Royal Army Service Corps. While on leave he married Winifred Mary (Freddie) Lambert (1918–2006) in Cambridge on 5 February 1940. The daughter of Charles Frederick Lambert, a customs and excise officer, she was an undergraduate at Newnham College, Cambridge, studying geography, and a fellow member of the Communist Party.

During the German blitzkrieg on Belgium and France, Vickers was wounded and captured on 27 May 1940 at Utterdoon, Belgium, when a car he was travelling in was immobilized. He subsequently had a bullet removed from his leg without anaesthetic in a German field hospital. He remained a prisoner of war until 13 January 1945. He made several escape attempts, and was sent to Stalag 21D near Poznan where he was classified as 'subversive'. He escaped again near Kassel and reached the American lines. He was reunited with his wife, Freddie, in London. She had lost both her legs in a bombing raid on Cambridge on 27 July 1942, but showed enormous courage in overcoming her disability. She was later a psychiatric social worker and a lecturer in social work at Chiswick Polytechnic. They had a daughter, Salley, and a son, James.

After demobilization Vickers was in 1946 appointed warden of the Wedgwood Memorial College at Barlaston Hall, Staffordshire. The college was an important provider of adult education for working people, especially from the Potteries, with close links to the Oxford Delegacy for Extra-Mural Studies, which had a long association with adult education in the district. His role as warden fitted closely with his political philosophy that an educated working-class élite was needed to lead the labour movement. He was forced to resign in 1949 after complaints of communist bias were made to the University of Oxford. He then joined the staff of the Electrical Trades Union (ETU) in its research department. He subsequently became the ETU education officer and head of Esher College, the ETU-run training college which he founded. Along with his wife and many others he left the Communist Party in 1956 in response to the Soviet repression of the Hungarian uprising. He subsequently joined the Labour Party. He left the ETU at about the same time but was reputedly a player in the events which led to a court case concerning Communist electoral rigging in the union in 1961.

Vickers was appointed deputy general secretary of the Civil Service Union (CSU) in 1960. The most working-class of the civil service unions, the CSU had a disparate membership, including cleaners, messengers, instructors, and telephonists. These were largely unrecruited by the other, larger, longer-established civil service unions. Vickers was held in high regard and was appointed general secretary in 1962 following the retirement of Victor Carvell.

Vickers's achievements as deputy general secretary and general secretary of the CSU were considerable. Its membership and influence increased significantly during this time, which was the high water mark of 'Whitleyism' in the civil service. Certainly the CSU and Jon Vickers became recognized players within the co-ordinating body of the civil service unions, the National Staff Side, and within the civil service National Whitley Council. He worked hard to establish the CSU's position and to resolve membership disputes with other unions, especially the Association of Government Supervisors and Radio Officers. However, perhaps his greatest achievement in the CSU was to hold together the many disparate sections of the union, who often had different and conflicting interests. The union was certainly stronger as a result of his period in office. He was an early and powerful advocate for the need to tackle low pay, which was endemic among the CSU membership. He was also a champion of the almost completely female membership who worked, often unnoticed, as cleaners of government premises. He retired in 1977, and was succeeded by his deputy, Les Moody. He was appointed OBE the same year.

Following his retirement Vickers served on the civil service appeal board and on the employment appeal tribunal (both from 1978 to 1986). He had also served as a member of the Fabian Society's trade union and industrial relations committee (1964–81) and a member of the council of the Tavistock Institute (1976–80). He enjoyed reading poetry and other literature, and bird-watching. He died on 1 June 2008 at his home, Heath Mount, Rake, near Liss, Hampshire, and was survived by his two children.

CHARLES COCHRANE

Sources *The National Staff Side Bulletin* [passim] · K. Edwards, *The story of the Civil Service Union* (1975) · *The Guardian* (23 June 2008) · *WW* (2008) · personal knowledge (2012) · private information (2012) [C. Cooper, W. McCall, J. Sheldon, P. Jones, B. Sutherland] · b. cert. · m. cert. · d. cert.

Likenesses photograph, repro. in *The Guardian* (23 June 2008) · photographs, repro. in Edwards, *Civil Service Union*

Wealth at death £120,445: probate, 12 March 2009, *CGPLA Eng. & Wales*

Walbank, Frank William (1909–2008), ancient historian, was born on 10 December 1909 at Cleveland Terrace, Bingley, Yorkshire, the only son of Albert Joseph David Walbank (1879–1967), an elementary schoolmaster, and his wife, Clarice, *née* Fletcher (1880–1965). His father, a cobbler's son, had left the family business and won a scholarship to the Yorkshire College (later Leeds University). A serious train accident put an end to his undergraduate career, and it was left to his son to fulfil his ambitions.

Frank Walbank proceeded, on scholarships, to Bradford Grammar School (1920–28) and to Peterhouse, Cambridge (1928–31). He read classics at Cambridge, having been led to believe that classics was the only means of entry into a career in one of the professions or the higher civil service. In later years he would look back with appreciation at the breadth and depth of his training in classics at Bradford (the intense pressure and relentless discipline of the scholarship programme notwithstanding). One of his teachers, E. H. (Ned) Goddard (formerly Gropius) assigned him some Polybius (an unlikely author to set a schoolboy to read, and in this case portentous), and later gave him his own Pauly-Wissowa, the multi-volume German-language encyclopaedia of classical antiquity, together with other classic works of German and Italian scholarship. Walbank's time as an undergraduate at Cambridge was something of a let-down by comparison. He encountered some fine scholars there, but did not feel that he learned much from them. He noted that, with few exceptions, they gave little attention to the problem of making their material palatable to the ordinary student. In his own teaching career Walbank was able to resolve this 'problem' and without resort to theatricality. At Peterhouse he came across for the first time the divide between the public schools and the grammar schools (which provided all the scholars and most of the exhibitioners). A tea-party arranged for him by James Mason (Marlborough, Peterhouse, and Hollywood) to introduce him to a friend of his from Trinity who, like Walbank, had won a Hellenic Travellers' Club prize, was a 'one-off', and something of an ordeal.

In scholarship, however, Walbank was totally at ease. A first in part one and a first with distinction in part two, specializing in ancient history, was followed by a year of research (as Hugo de Balsham research student at Peterhouse). The essay which won him the Hellenic Travellers' Club prize, on 'Federalism in the Greek world', had introduced him to Aratus of Sicyon, the politician and general who made a major contribution to the rise of the Achaean League in the third century BC. On Frank Adcock's advice, or instruction, he spent the summer of 1930 in Jena learning German, and set his sights on writing a thesis on Aratus in a year, to be submitted for the Thirlwall prize, with the expectation, or understanding, that success in the competition would lead to the publication of the thesis as a book with Cambridge University Press. All went according to plan—*Aratus of Sicyon* won the prize and was published in September 1933. There was one consequence not at first foreseen: his successes ensured that the initial aim of becoming a schoolmaster, which led to his taking up a teaching post as senior classics master at North Manchester High School in September 1932 (and at a time of high unemployment this was a cause of great celebration), was overtaken by the appeal of the academic profession. He was appointed assistant lecturer in Latin at Liverpool from January 1934.

On 27 July 1935 Walbank married Mary Woodward Fox

(1913–1987), a textile operative, of Nab Wood, Shipley, near Bingley, eldest daughter of a businessman, Oswald Charles Alfred Fox. They had two daughters, Dorothy (*b.* 1939) and Elizabeth (Mitzi; *b.* 1942), and a son, Christopher (*b.* 1944). Both parents were active in the Communist Party, the Labour Party, and various action groups. Walbank was always more anti-Nazi than pro-Communist, just as he was influenced more by humanitarian motives than by any doctrinal allegiance; he broke with the Communist Party definitively following the Stalin–Hitler pact of August 1939. In consequence of his leftist sympathies and activities, and his share in the harbouring of an illegal immigrant (a Sudeten German who had fought in the International Brigade in Spain), he was constrained to resign from the Home Guard, had his applications to work in the Ministry of Trade and Bletchley Park rejected, and spent the war in Liverpool with the National Fire Service; he was allowed to retain his post at the university. In later years his political allegiances were centre-left. He had no religion.

Walbank's academic career was spent at Liverpool. He was promoted to lecturer in 1936 then to professor of Latin in 1946 in succession to his mentor J. F. Mountford. In 1951 he was appointed Rathbone professor of ancient history and classical archaeology, a post he held until his retirement in 1977. An active and admired administrator, he served on numerous university committees, often as chairman, and was also public orator (1955–60). In 1974–7 he was a widely admired dean of the arts faculty.

Walbank was one of the great ancient historians in the English-speaking world of the twentieth century. His immense scholarly reputation was built around his contribution to the study of Polybius, the Greek historian of Rome of the second century BC. More broadly he was instrumental in raising the status of the Hellenistic period in Greek history from a mere appendage to the classical age. Polybian studies before Walbank are difficult to imagine. In the mid-twentieth century the only full commentary was still Johann Schweighäuser's remarkable eight-volume work of 1789–95. Polybius, and Hellenistic history as a whole, were largely the preserve of continental scholars. At the centre of Walbank's contribution to Polybian studies stands *A Historical Commentary on Polybius* in three magisterial volumes, published in 1957, 1967, and 1979. In 1972 his *Polybius* appeared, still the most important general study of the historian. In addition to these four foundational volumes he produced a flood of articles on all aspects of Polybius's life, historical method, and thought, some of them reproduced in two collections: *Selected Papers: Studies in Greek and Roman History and Historiography* (1985), and *Polybius, Rome and the Hellenistic World: Essays and Reflections* (2002). For the latter volume Walbank, by now in his nineties, prepared a useful and thorough review of recent scholarship.

Walbank brought to his *Commentary* the qualities that he attributed in his preface to Schweighäuser, thoroughness and sound common sense. These qualities may not sound glamorous, but in this case they combined with a voluminous knowledge, not just of Polybius but of all the other literary and documentary sources for Hellenistic history, to produce a truly great work of classical scholarship. He was not interested in everything in equal measure (religion received short shrift), and inevitably later discoveries or views added to the picture (but were to an extent taken account of in the addenda and corrigenda of vols. 2 and 3). Walbank, however, was usually right, and in any case he consistently provided a helpful starting point for discussion. The approach was 'historical', as the title indicated, and as the preface explained, as distinct from philological or literary. This is not to say that he did not have a profound understanding of Polybian language, as is borne out by his review of de Foucault, published in the *Classical Review* of 1975. But he remained firmly of the view that history, for all its literary construction, was and would remain a 'discourse of the real'.

The three volumes of the *Commentary*, adding up to just under 2300 pages, together with the papers on Polybius which make up the majority of his grand total of around 350 publications, dominated Walbank's oeuvre. However, his interests and expertise extended well beyond Polybius. He needed to be a master of the Hellenistic period in general in order to produce a work as authoritative as the *Commentary*. His early works included *Aratus of Sicyon* (1933) and *Philip of Macedon* (1940), both valuable points of reference; and his later works included the impressive *History of Macedon* (vol. 3 with N. G. L. Hammond, 1988), and the highly influential and much translated *The Hellenistic World* (1981), revised as *The Hellenistic Age: the Greek World 336–146 B.C.* (2002). In this latter work he followed a traditional path in basing his account on the three great Hellenistic kingdoms, Antigonid Macedon, Ptolemaic Egypt, and Seleucid Asia, but in addition extended his coverage to take in the minor Hellenistic kingdoms and the Greek Far East, in the process making use of recent archaeological and artistic discoveries. Runner-up to this work in terms of outreach and circulation was, paradoxically, his least persuasive book, *The Decline of the Roman Empire in the West* (1946), reissued in a revised version as *The Awful Revolution: the Decline of the Roman Empire in the West* (1969), which sold over 13,000 copies in the Japanese translation alone.

Walbank was active throughout his life in advancing the cause of classics and ancient history in the United Kingdom as a whole. He was president of the Roman Society (1961–5), the Classical Association (1970), and the Cambridge Philological Society (1982–4); review editor of the *Journal of Roman Studies* (1959–69); and joint editor of the second edition of the *Cambridge Ancient History*, vols. VII.1–2 and VIII (1984–9). He was elected a fellow of the British Academy in 1953 and made a CBE in 1993. His other honours included the silver jubilee medal (1977); the Kenyon medal of the British Academy (1989); honorary doctorates from the universities of Exeter (1988) and Kentucky (1996); honorary fellowship of Peterhouse (1984); membership of the Honorable Order of Kentucky Colonels (1995), an honour which he particularly enjoyed; and honorary or corresponding membership of learned societies in Germany, Israel, the Netherlands, and the USA. He gave the J. H. Gray lectures at the University of Cambridge in 1959, the J. L. Myres lecture at the University of Oxford in 1965, and the Sather lectures at the University of California, Berkeley, in 1971. A volume in his honour, *Hellenistic Constructs: Essays in Culture, History and Historiography*, appeared in 1997. In 2007 the fiftieth anniversary of the publication of the first volume of his monumental *Historical Commentary on Polybius* was celebrated at a conference in Liverpool. Ill health prevented him from attending, but his recorded message of welcome was played to the gathering.

Walbank bore his distinction lightly. He was aware of his lofty position in the world of classical scholarship, but appeared pleasantly surprised by it and did not glory in it. Joined with this rare modesty was an extraordinary generosity of spirit, an openness towards and tolerance of others, including his critics. He was immensely helpful to younger scholars. He had strong opinions on scholarship, as on politics and religion, but by and large kept them to himself and did not dwell on them. His retirement in Cambridge was long and tranquil, made happier for the fact that his wife, Mary, had at last recovered from a lengthy and disruptive illness. It was also an extraordinarily productive period. The flow of papers—and books—continued (until 2007). Walbank engaged actively in the life of the classics faculty and his college, and travelled frequently on academic engagements in the UK and abroad, particularly to the USA (where he was Andrew Mellon visiting professor in 1964), Germany, and Italy. He maintained his connection with Albania, which pre-dated the Second World War. At home he was splendid company; he had a great fund of stories, which he told with wit and panache. His optimistic and positive attitude to life carried him through the loss of his wife and the various trials of old age, and was infectious and uplifting for others, particularly his family (to whom he was very close) and friends. This was a man of achievement, humanity, and integrity, who was regarded by all who knew him with the greatest respect and affection. He died at his home, 64 Grantchester Meadows, on 23 October 2008 of a pulmonary embolus, and was survived by his three children. Two conferences were held in his memory in 2009: 'Ptolemaic Waterways and Power', the third International Ptolemaic Colloquium, held in Athens on 18–20 September, and 'Politics and History in the Hellenistic World', held in Kazan, Russia, on 9–11 December, thus coinciding with what would have been his hundredth birthday.

PETER GARNSEY

Sources F. W. Walbank, *Hypomnemata*, unpublished memoir, priv. coll. · list of publications up to 1984, F. W. Walbank, *Selected papers* (1985), 344–60 · F. W. Walbank, 'Haec olim meminisse iuvabit: recollections of Peterhouse, 1928–32', *Peterhouse Annual Record* (2001–2), 20–26 · *The Independent* (28 Oct 2008) · *The Times* (13 Nov 2008) · *The Guardian* (19 Nov 2008) · *PBA* [forthcoming] · B. J. Gibson and T. E. Harrison, *Polybius and his world: politics and history in the Hellenistic world* [forthcoming] · Walbank papers, U. Lpool L., Sydney Jones Library · *WW* (2008) · personal knowledge (2012) · private information (2012) [Dorothy Thompson, daughter; S. Hornblower; B. McGing] · b. cert. · m. cert. · d. cert.

Likenesses obituary photographs

Wealth at death £1,283,245: probate, 17 March 2009, *CGPLA Eng. & Wales*

Walker, Diana Barnato [*née* Diana Barnato] (**1918–2008**), aviator, was born on 15 January 1918 at 39 Elsworthy Road, Hampstead, London, the younger daughter of Woolf Joel Barnato (1895–1948), financier and racing driver, and his American first wife, Dorothy Maitland, *née* Falk. Her father, who was a captain in the Royal Field Artillery in the First World War, had inherited, at the age of two, the millions accumulated by his father Barney Barnato, the South African diamond magnate. After the war he became one of the celebrated 'Bentley boys' (he also bought a majority share in the Bentley company, of which he became chairman in 1925), and a highly successful racing driver, winning the Le Mans 24 hour race in 1928, 1929, and 1930. During the Second World War he served as a wing commander in the RAF, with responsibility for the defence of airfields in southern England.

Diana Barnato and her sister, Virginia, enjoyed the pleasures of high society, though Woolf separated from their mother when Diana was four. While their mother brought the girls up she maintained an amicable relationship with their father (who had two sons with his second wife, and married a third time shortly before his death). Diana was educated at Queen's College in Harley Street, London, until 1936, when she came out as a débutante and 'did the season'. Disenchanted by the social rounds, she invested her allowance in flying lessons at the Brooklands Flying Club in Surrey at £3 per hour, rather than learn with the Civil Air Guard for a mere 7*s*. 6*d*. per hour. She wrote, 'I was far too much of a snob to go to learn to fly with what I thought would be the *hoi polloi*' (*Spreading my Wings*, 34). Having gone solo after six hours on a de Havilland Tiger Moth she ran out of money and had to stop.

Following the outbreak of the Second World War Diana Barnato worked as a Voluntary Aid Detachment nurse and with the Red Cross, but was attracted by the chance of flying with the Air Transport Auxiliary, although she had only ten hours' flying experience. She was tested by the chief flying instructor, but a riding injury then laid her up for six months. Meanwhile the Air Transport Auxiliary had set up a training programme, and after another test in December 1941 she became one of fewer than 170 'Atagirls' (of whom sixteen were to lose their lives during the conflict).

The ATA's pilots ferried all types of military aircraft, from trainers to bombers, from factories to RAF stations or from maintenance units to squadrons. They had minimal pilot's notes and no radios, and often flew in marginal weather conditions. Barnato flew such aircraft as the single-engine Spitfire, Hurricane, Defiant, Mustang, Avenger, Wildcat, Vengeance, Firefly, Barracuda, and Tempest, and twin-engine types like the Oxford, Anson, Wellington, Warwick, Mosquito, Hudson, and Mitchell. She had her share of incidents. While flying a Supermarine Walrus air-sea-rescue amphibian, her least-liked aeroplane, from Cosford to Eastleigh on 19 September 1944, the windscreen was obscured by oil from the failing engine as she approached the Southampton balloon barrage at 1500 feet. Without power she could only push down the nose to prevent a stall and make a steep descent into the sea fog.

Diana Barnato Walker (**1918–2008**), by Bill Cross, 1943

Luckily she missed the balloon cables and emerged from the cloud a few feet above Eastleigh's grass airfield.

Three weeks after Barnato first met the battle of Britain fighter ace Squadron Leader Humphrey Trench Gilbert in 1942 they became engaged, but days later he died in a flying accident. Two years later, on 6 May 1944, she married another pilot, Wing Commander Derek Ronald Walker, and was docked three months' pay for making an unauthorized honeymoon flight to Brussels four months later in a Spitfire, accompanied by her husband in another. Derek Walker was killed in a flying accident shortly after the war's end, on 14 November 1945.

After the war Diana Barnato Walker, as she was now known, studied for the exams for a commercial pilot's licence, in company with the racing driver and industrialist Whitney Willard *Straight (1912–1979), a naturalized American and former RAF air commodore. This led to a thirty-year relationship, and a son, Barney, was born in 1947, though Straight never left his wife, nor did Diana ask him to: 'I was perfectly content. I had my own identity' (*The Times*, 19 Nov 2005). Having gained her commercial licence she became a pilot for the Women's Junior Air Corps, giving the cadets air experience and training flights at weekends and accumulating many hours in the corps's Fairchild Argus and Auster aircraft. She had just taken off in the newly acquired Argus on 11 July 1948 when it burst into flames. Rather than bale out and lose a valuable aeroplane, she switched off the fuel and glided back to the airfield, where the flames were put out. In 1963, for her work with the corps, she was awarded the Jean Lennox Bird trophy, presented annually to a British woman pilot. On 26 August that year she became the first British woman to exceed the speed of sound, and the fastest woman in the world when she attained Mach 1.65 (1262 mph) in an English Electric Lightning T.4 trainer version of the RAF's front-line fighter. Shortly after this she won a battle with cancer.

In later years Diana Barnato Walker took up sheep farming and was master of the Old Surrey and Burstow foxhounds for thirteen seasons, while continuing to fly for the Women's Junior Air Corps (renamed in 1964 the Girls' Venture Corps). She also became commodore of the Air Transport Auxiliary Association. She died of pneumonia on 28 April 2008 in a hospital near her sheep farm in Surrey, and was survived by her son, Barney.

PHILIP JARRETT

Sources A. King, *Golden wings: the story of some of the women ferry pilots of the Air Transport Auxiliary* (1956) • L. Curtis, *The forgotten pilots*, 3rd edn (1985) • D. Barnato Walker, *Spreading my wings* (1994) • *The Times* (19 Nov 2005); (8 May 2008) • G. Whittell, *Spitfire women of World War II* (2008) • *Daily Telegraph* (5 May 2008) • *The Guardian* (8 May 2008) • *The Independent* (9 May 2008) • *New York Times* (12 May 2008) • *Aerospace Professional* (July 2008) • b. cert. • m. cert.

Archives SOUND BL NSA, documentary recording

Likenesses B. Cross, photograph, 1943, Rex Features, London [*see illus.*] • photographs, 1943–93, Rex Features, London • obituary photographs • photographs, repro. in Barnato Walker, *Spreading my wings* • photographs, PA Photos, London

Wealth at death £6,278,641: probate, 8 Jan 2009, *CGPLA Eng. & Wales*

Walker, George Patrick Leonard (**1926–2005**), geologist and vulcanologist, was born on 2 March 1926 at 24 Cecil Road, Harlesden, Middlesex, the son of Leonard Thomas Richard Walker, dynamo tester, and later farmer, and his wife, Eveline Frances, *née* McConkey. Brought up in London and then Northern Ireland, he became fascinated as a teenager by geology and the minerals in the lavas of Antrim. He was educated at Wallace High School, Lisburn. Following BSc and MSc degrees in geology at Queen's University, Belfast, from 1948 he studied zeolite mineralogy in ancient basalt lava sequences for his PhD degree at Leeds University, eventually awarded in 1956. He was appointed an assistant lecturer at Imperial College, London, in 1951, becoming lecturer in 1954 and reader in 1964. On 22 March 1958 he married Hazel Rosemary Smith, a 28-year-old nursery nurse, and daughter of Walter Smith, farmer. They had a daughter, Alison, and a son, Leonard.

Walker used his knowledge of zeolites brilliantly in his seminal studies of the geology of eastern Iceland, where he displayed his flair as a field geologist, and his ability to make critical observations and make fundamental inferences about volcanic processes. He mapped the lavas and zeolite zones, and the geological structure of a large part of the east coast of Iceland, showing that the distribution of the zeolite minerals was systematically related to the depth of burial of the lavas. From these observations he inferred the processes that formed Iceland. This work was one of the first studies to gather geological evidence for sea-floor spreading at the inception of the theory of plate tectonics. His research revolutionized understanding of the geology of Iceland and in 1980 Walker was one of the few foreign citizens to be awarded the Icelandic order of the Falcon, conferred by the president of Iceland. He also received an honorary doctorate from the University of Iceland in 1988.

In the late 1960s and through the 1970s Walker increasingly focused on volcanic eruptions and geological studies of young active volcanoes. He combined supreme observational skills with a remarkable ability to integrate apparently unconnected observations into coherent conceptual models that gave powerful new insights into how volcanoes worked. He adopted a quantitative approach of gathering prodigious quantities of systematic data, and using his imaginative powers and intuition to extract major advances in understanding. His work was the foundation of much later understanding in vulcanology. He played a major role in turning vulcanology from a qualitative and descriptive enterprise to a robust and quantitative science. Among his many achievements in this period were finding the controls on lava flow emplacement, elucidating the relationships between the geology of pyroclastic deposits and the explosive eruptions that formed them, advancing understanding of what controls the morphology of volcanoes, and establishing new ways to assess volcanic hazards.

In 1978 Walker took up a Captain James Cook research fellowship of the Royal Society of New Zealand, based at the University of Auckland. There he devoted his energy to studying the young explosive vulcanism of the North Island, centred on Lake Taupo, which he recognized as a volcano of remarkable violence. In 1981 he was appointed as the first Gordon Macdonald chair in vulcanology at the University of Hawaii, where he continued his highly innovative research, focusing on the evolution of basaltic volcanoes and the dynamics of basalt lava flows. He retired in 1996 and returned to the UK to live in Gloucester, but continued his research as a visiting professor at Bristol University. His achievements were recognized by many awards, including election as a fellow of the Royal Society in 1975, an honorary fellowship of the Royal Society of New Zealand in 1987, the Thorarinsson medal (the highest award in vulcanology) in 1989, and the Wollaston medal of the Geological Society of London in 1995.

Walker was a brilliant teacher and devoted much of his time to encouraging and nurturing young scientists. His first love was for field geology and he was inspirational when showing students how to read the rocks on field classes, or training graduate students how to extract the secrets of nature by simple systematic observations and logical deduction. He was supremely fit and could see off most students in marches across Scottish mountains or to volcanoes in exotic and remote places. An extended line of exhausted but still enthusiastic students or colleagues as the sun set was a common feature of his field trips. In Hawaii he gave countless presentations to schools and community groups. He helped and encouraged many scientists from the developing world, where most active volcanoes are located. He inspired thousands of people, from primary school children to eminent professors.

Walker never sought the limelight. He was at his happiest in the field in remote parts of the world. He was devoted to geology and much of his work was done on a shoestring budget, sometimes also at his own expense. His contributions to science were seminal and far-reaching, and he was remembered with admiration and great affection by everyone who crossed his path. He was a devoted husband and father. He died on 17 January 2005 at Woodstock Nursing Home, 35 Upton Lane, Barnwood, Gloucester. He was survived by his wife, Hazel, and their two children. STEPHEN SPARKS

Sources *Daily Telegraph* (31 Jan 2005) · *The Independent* (31 Jan 2005) · *The Guardian* (22 Feb 2005) · L. Kristjánsson, 'George P. L. Walker and his geological research in Iceland', *Jökull*, 55 (2005), 147–54 · S. Self and R. S. J. Sparks, *Memoirs FRS*, 52 (2006), 425–36 · R. S. J. Sparks, 'The legacy of George Walker to volcanology', ed. S. Self and T. Thdarsson, *Geological Society of London Special Publication* (2008) · *WW* (2005) · personal knowledge (2008) · private information (2008) · b. cert. · m. cert. · d. cert.
Likenesses obituary photographs · photograph, University of Bristol
Wealth at death under £97,000: probate, 5 Aug 2005, *CGPLA Eng. & Wales*

Walsh, Kathleen [Kay] (**1911–2005**), actress, was born at 2 Granville House, Tetcott Road, Chelsea, London, on 15 November 1911, the daughter of James Walsh, taxi driver and later mechanical engineer, and his wife, Elizabeth, *née* Murphy, both of Irish descent. Kay, as she was known (or sometimes Katy to friends and colleagues), and her sister Peggy were raised in a small Pimlico flat by their grandmother, who had moved from Ireland. Her early years were spent in poverty and instilled in her both a determination to shake off such indigence and a lifelong sympathy for left-wing views. She had little formal education, but was highly intelligent, read widely, and became a sharply articulate woman—a classic auto-didact.

Walsh's initial ambition was to be a dancer. She said in 1991: 'I can't remember a time when I didn't dance. The first memory of a public performance was darting into Church Street, Chelsea, and dancing to a barrel organ, aged three' (McFarlane, *Autobiography*, 594). She danced in André Charlot's revues and scored some success as a solo dancer in New York in the early 1930s, as well as in straight plays. In one of these, in 1934, she was spotted by a film talent scout and the rest of her career was spent in film, with just a few television appearances. She was fair-haired, pretty, and purveyed what one writer called 'the common touch' (Quinlan, 482), which would stand her in good stead for the next several decades of notable screen work. Though she never really became a fully fledged star, she was always incisive and convincing, with a demotic appeal uncommon among English film actresses of the time.

Walsh's first film role was an uncredited part in the long-forgotten musical comedy *How's Chances?* (1934), but, after being noticed on stage by the director Basil Dean, joint managing director of Ealing Studios, she appeared in sixteen further films during the decade. Many of these starred such scarcely remembered popular comics of the day as Sandy Powell and Ernie Lotinga, but also and most famously George Formby, with whom she co-starred twice (in *Keep Fit*, 1937, and *I See Ice*, 1938), under the watchful eye of Mrs Formby. Many actresses who cut their teeth on these unsophisticated entertainments went on to more demanding fare and Walsh was no exception. Perhaps her most significant film of the 1930s was *Secret of Stamboul* (1936), for, while making it, she met David *Lean (1908–1991), then a film editor, fell in love with him, lived with him for four years, and became his second wife on 23 November 1940. In 1937 he edited the sea-going romance *The Last Adventurers*, in which she had a starring role.

Kathleen [Kay] Walsh (1911–2005), by unknown photographer, 1952

Marriage to Lean was a mixed blessing: on the one hand Walsh did some of her finest screen work in films he directed; on the other, his serial womanizing (he married six times and conducted numerous affairs) and perhaps his sense of intellectual inferiority, compared with the clever, perceptive Walsh, made him a difficult partner. 'Being in love with David was a killer, and how I survived I don't know', she said later (*The Times*, 28 April 2005). He gained considerably from his association with her. When he was editing Gabriel Pascal's film version of *Pygmalion* (1938) she provided some 'filler' dialogue which even Shaw did not recognize as other than his own. She had dragged Lean to see a Steiner Hall production of *Great Expectations* before the war and assisted on the screenplay when he so memorably filmed it in 1946; and the powerful, mutely gothic opening of his *Oliver Twist* (1948) was her idea. Not himself a reader, Lean was influenced by her taste. Further, when she was starring with Peter Ustinov in the mildly amusing 'Victorian' comedy *Vice-Versa* (1947), she noted the talented young Anthony Newley and recommended him to Lean to play the Artful Dodger in *Oliver Twist*.

While claiming to be interested only in 'working, just working' (McFarlane, *Autobiography*, 595), Walsh reached a new stature with her 1940s films, especially in the three directed by Lean. She brought a brisk humanity to Freda, who marries the sailor played by John Mills in *In Which We Serve* (1942, co-directed by Noël Coward); was very believable as the rebellious lower-middle-class daughter in *This Happy Breed* (1944), enacting a moving scene of reconciliation with Celia Johnson near the film's end; and, though she felt the character had been softened, she was extremely poignant as life-battered Nancy in *Oliver Twist* (1948). By this time her marriage to Lean had fallen apart and they divorced in 1949. Walsh's second marriage, on 14 March 1953, to the Canadian psychologist Elliott Jaques (1917–2003), with whom she adopted a daughter, Gemma, in 1956, was also dissolved, though she retained his name in several official functions for the rest of her life.

From 1950 Walsh settled rather early into character parts, but there was a string of memorable and substantial roles throughout the decade. She was wonderfully sly and insinuating as the housekeeper in Alfred Hitchcock's *Stage Fright* (1950); a warmly sympathetic hotel manager in *Last Holiday* (1950), the second of five films with her friend Alec Guinness; touchingly fallible as the vicar's wife in *Lease of Life* (1954); and worldly and forthright as the woman who unmasks the murderer Dirk Bogarde in *Cast a Dark Shadow* (1955). Best of all, though, were perhaps the 'winter cruise' segment of the Somerset Maugham compendium *Encore* (1951), in which she played an unstoppably loquacious traveller, and her role as the barmaid Coker, her own favourite, with Guinness in *The Horse's Mouth* (1958). She went on acting until 1981, and there were cherishable moments such as her mean-spirited Aunt Cissie in *The Virgin and the Gypsy* (1970), based on the novel by D. H. Lawrence. She enjoyed working with Bette Davis in a bad film, *Connecting Rooms* (1970), less so with Joan Fontaine in a better one, *The Witches* (1966). Her television work was comparatively negligible, but everything she did was worth watching. A consummate actress, a woman of rare wit and character, and a spirited hostess, Walsh was working on her memoirs in her last years. She died at the Chelsea and Westminster Hospital, London, on 16 April 2005, of multiple burns, following an accident.

Brian McFarlane

Sources D. Quinlan, *The illustrated directory of film stars* (1981) • A. Silver and J. Ursini, *David Lean and his films* (1974); pbk edn (1992) • K. Brownlow, *David Lean* (1996) • B. McFarlane, *An autobiography of British cinema* (1997) • B. McFarlane, ed., *The encyclopedia of British film*, 2nd edn (2005) • G. Phillips, *Beyond the epic: the life and films of David Lean* (2006) • *The Times* (28 April 2005) • *Daily Telegraph* (28 April 2005) • *The Guardian* (29 April 2005) • BFI film and TV database, www.bfi.org.uk, 21 Sept 2007 • www.imdb.com, 21 Sept 2007 • personal knowledge (2009) • private information (2009) • b. cert. • m. certs. • d. cert.

Archives FILM BFINFTVA, performance footage | SOUND BFINA, interview with B. McFarlane

Likenesses photographs, 1937–54, Getty Images, London • photographs, 1944–72, Rex Features, London • photograph, 1952, Rex Features, London, ITV [*see illus.*] • photographs, 1959, PA Photos, London • obituary photographs

Wealth at death £649,581: 17 July 2008, *CGPLA Eng. & Wales*

Ward, John Stanton (1917–2007), painter, was born on 10 October 1917 at 2 Gruneisen Street, Hereford, the youngest son and seventh child of Russell Stanton Ward (1868–1929), picture restorer and antique dealer, and his wife, Jessie Elizabeth, *née* Watson. For most of his childhood the family lived in cramped and at times straitened circumstances above his father's shop in Church Street, in the shadow of the cathedral. Meals were taken in his father's studio, and he grew up never lacking the materials and encouragement to draw and paint. His was a strict upbringing, with fierce aunts much in evidence—Ward was eleven when his father died—yet he remembered on the whole a happy time, with picnics and fishing trips along the Wye. 'Something was always going to "turn up", and my mother would talk confidently of our ship coming home', he would later write (*The Paintings of John Ward*, 11).

Ward was educated at the local infants' school, and then at St Owen's elementary school, the headmaster of which, P. H. Alder-Barratt, was an early influence. On his failing to gain entrance to either the cathedral school or the local grammar school Alder-Barratt arranged for him to attend the junior classes of the Hereford School of Art, where at fifteen he became a full-time student. Another important figure in his early life was F. C. Morgan, the city librarian, who introduced him to the history of art, and took him on his first visit to a public gallery, the Birmingham City Museum and Art Gallery.

Ward flourished at the art school under the mild but effective regime of its principal, Vaughan Milligan, founded firmly on drawing from life. In 1936, furnished with a grant of £80 from the local authorities, he progressed to the Royal College of Art. There he was taught by the professor of painting, Gilbert Spencer, and such artists as Charles Mahoney, Alan Sorrell, Percy Horton, and Barnett Freedman. Robert Buhler, Michael Rothenstein, and Jehan Daly were among his friends and contemporaries.

The outbreak of the Second World War interrupted Ward's studies, and in October 1939 he and Jehan Daly enlisted in the Royal Engineers. In 1942 he was attached as draughtsman to the headquarters of the 3rd division, with which he remained for the rest of the war, taking part in the D-day landings and seeing active service in France and the Netherlands. He continued to draw and paint whenever possible, and in Ghent, a private soldier still with time on his hands as the war drew to a close, he organized studio classes for his fellow soldiers. There he also met his future wife, Alison Christine Mary Williams (*b.* 1924/5), a spirited ambulance driver in the Auxiliary Territorial Service, and daughter of Richard Myrddin Williams, businessman. They eventually married at St Mary's Church, Cossington, Somerset, on 18 April 1950, and had four sons and twin daughters.

Demobilized early in 1946, Ward returned to the Royal College of Art to complete his studies, leaving that summer with a travelling scholarship, which in the event was to take him no farther than Oxford and the Cotswolds. The following year a contact with the publisher Paul Elek, suggested by his friend Michael Rothenstein, led to work illustrating two of Elek's county guides, to Herefordshire and the North Riding of Yorkshire. He also taught life drawing at the Wimbledon School of Art one day a week. A more significant move, however, came through a fellow student from Hereford, John Parsons, who was now the art editor of *Vogue*, and for the next few years, at a time when fashion photography had not entirely supplanted drawing, he was one of the magazine's regular freelance illustrators. He remembered his days on *Vogue* 'with pleasure and affection … I liked the excitement of the deadline and the unexpected subjects, debutantes, corsets, jewellery, actors and actresses' (*Paintings of John Ward*).

By 1952 Ward felt the time had come to make his way as an artist in his own right. He gave up his studio in Chelsea, resigned from *Vogue*, and moved to Folkestone, keeping himself going with part-time teaching, gallery shows, portraits, and illustration; Laurie Lee's *Cider with Rosie* (1959) was a notable commission. His career soon prospered. In 1954 he was elected to the Royal Society of Portrait Painters, and in 1956 became an associate of the Royal Academy. He also joined the Royal Watercolour Society and the New English Art Club. In 1957, with the aid of a mortgage and a generous loan from his father-in-law, he bought Bilting Court, near Ashford, Kent, for £4250. It remained his home for the rest of his life.

Ward's gallery career began in 1948, with a show at the Alexander Gallery in Kensington, shared with Dennis Lucas and John Minton. Another mixed show followed at Wildenstein's London gallery in 1953. After several one-man shows with the Trafford Gallery through the mid-1950s he moved on to the Arthur Jeffries Gallery, and, when that closed, was taken on by Jeremy Maas at his gallery in Clifford Street. Later he moved on again to Agnew's, which gave him a retrospective in 1990. In his last years he showed regularly with Hazlitt, Gooden and Fox in St James's.

The Royal Academy was, however, Ward's principal shop-window; it was an institution he adored, and which perfectly suited his temperament. He was promoted a full Royal Academician in 1966, and was a trustee from 1976 to 1987. In 1997 he resigned in controversial circumstances, having grown increasingly disaffected by what he saw as the ever-growing influence of management at the expense of the artist-members. His final exasperation was at the decision to show the Sensation exhibition of the work of the young British artists in the collection of Charles Saatchi. Though the invitation remained open to him he never rejoined, choosing rather to stay loyal to the other old-established exhibiting societies, the Royal Society of Portrait Painters, the Royal Watercolour Society, and the New English Art Club.

As a painter of the figure, whether of the model in the studio or the commissioned portrait, Ward was pre-eminent, very much in the manner of artists of the earlier twentieth century tradition in which he was brought up, such as Lavery and Orpen, Gunn, Rothenstein, and William Nicholson, among whom he would have stood as an equal. As a topographical and architectural draughtsman again he was remarkable, standing in an older tradition going back to the major figures of the nineteenth century, like Holland and Callow, Prout and Bonington, and the young Turner. The great cities of northern Italy and southern France were a particular subject, with Venice an enduring love, amounting to obsession. The interior of Florian's and the quieter corners of the piazza he made his own, which pitches, when he was in town, would be jealously guarded against intruding artists by the local proprietors. His last working visit was made a month before his death, in advance of what was planned to be his ninetieth birthday exhibition.

Ward was both fortunate and unfortunate in being somewhat out of his time. Closely identified with the Royal Academy from the mid-twentieth century, when it was held to represent everything that was old-fashioned in art, he supported it wholeheartedly through the subsequent decades as it returned to the mainstream, yet felt himself increasingly isolated among a more avant-garde and to him unsympathetic membership. Such a situation accounted for his eventual disaffection, yet it afforded him a continuing singularity and distinction, so that his wider reputation, and demand for his work, continued undiminished. He was appointed CBE in 1985, was a freeman of both Hereford and Canterbury, and was made an honorary DLitt of the University of Kent.

A naturally friendly and clubbable man, Ward was a long-standing member of the Athenaeum, and painted group portraits for several of the major London clubs and for such companies as Christies. He was always interested and enthusiastic, and constant in his encouragement of his fellow artists; he took the watercolour-painting prince of Wales under his wing. Yet for all his relish of the good things in life, and whatever the company, he remained entirely natural and unaffected, always himself, and never losing the gentle Herefordshire burr of his youth. He died at his home, Bilting Court, on 14 June 2007, and was survived by his wife and their six children.

William Packer

Sources J. Ward, *The paintings of John Ward* (1991) • *The Independent* (16 June 2007) • *Daily Telegraph* (18 June 2007) • *The Guardian* (21 June 2007) • *The Times* (22 June 2007) • *WW* (2007) • personal knowledge (2011) • private information (2011) • b. cert. • m. cert. • d. cert.
Archives Tate archives, Lord Clark MSS
Likenesses N. Parkinson, C-type colour print, 1975, NPG • C. Amey, C-type colour print, 1986 (with Hugh Leggatt), NPG • F. Curzon, resin prints, 1987–8 (with Princess Anne), NPG • D. Neame, bromide fibre print, 1988, NPG • J. Galloway, C-type colour print, 2000, NPG • obituary photographs
Wealth at death £1,492,927: probate, 14 July 2008, *CGPLA Eng. & Wales*

Warner, Sir Jean-Pierre Frank Eugene (1924–2005), barrister and judge, was born at 39 Holland Park, Kensington, London, on 24 September 1924, the elder of two sons of Frank Cloudesley ffolliot Warner, silk and textile manufacturer, and his wife, Louise Marie Blanche, *née* Gouet, a Frenchwoman. On his father's death in 1928 Warner's mother returned to France, taking her two sons with her; Warner received his early education in France. In 1938 he was sent to Harrow School but, after the outbreak of the Second World War and to avoid cross-channel travelling, he returned to school in France, where he remained until the fall of France in 1940 when, with his mother and brother, he escaped to England and resumed his education at Harrow.

From Harrow, Warner went to Trinity College, Cambridge. After four terms he left to join the rifle brigade, into which he was commissioned. Demobilized in 1947 with the rank of acting major and after service with Lord Mountbatten's staff in the Far East, he returned to Trinity and took a first in law in 1948. He was called to the bar by Lincoln's Inn in 1950 and on 2 September the same year, at Lincoln's Inn chapel, he married Sylvia Frances Goodale, the 23-year-old daughter of Ernest William Goodale, like Warner's father a textile manufacturer; they had two daughters. Warner had joined the highly respected chancery chambers of J. H. Stamp, and quickly established a successful practice in the fields of trust and fiscal law. In 1961 he was appointed junior counsel to the registrar of restrictive trading agreements, the official entrusted with the administration and enforcement of the Restrictive Trade Practices Act of 1956, a major legislative innovation in what was, for the United Kingdom, a relatively new and undeveloped field of competition law. In 1964 Warner progressed to the post of junior counsel to the Treasury ('Treasury devil') on the chancery side, which involved responsibility for advising the government on a wide range of chancery and fiscal legal issues. He was appointed queen's counsel in November 1972. Despite the pressure of work at the bar, Warner found time to sit as a Conservative councillor in the borough of Kensington from 1959 to 1968 (between 1963 and 1965 he chaired its general purposes committee). He was also a non-executive director of the family firm of silk fabric manufacturers between 1952 and 1970, being elected as a liveryman of the Worshipful Company of Weavers in 1952. He was a noted oenophile (chevalier du tastevin, 1952; commandeur, 1960; member, Confrerie St Etienne d'Alsace, 1981).

In 1972, when the United Kingdom signed the treaty of accession to the European Communities, Warner was nominated as the first British advocate-general of the Court of Justice of the European Communities (the ECJ), a post he held from 1973 until 1981. He was exceptionally well qualified for this post since he was bilingual in English and French, the latter being the ECJ's 'working language' (as advocate-general he would read through the French translations of his opinions and correct them where necessary). He also had, unusually for a British lawyer at that time, a specialist knowledge of competition law, which then formed part of the staple diet of the ECJ. Finally, his position as Treasury junior had enabled him to observe the work of government particularly closely, again a real advantage as a member of the ECJ.

As advocate-general, Warner's responsibility was to deliver in open court an independent opinion on the merits of the cases assigned to him. An advocate-general's opinions provided important assistance to the judges hearing the case. By the 1970s, when Warner joined the ECJ, its case law had already begun to accumulate and Warner's experience at the English bar stood him in good stead in analysing it and, where necessary, drawing inspiration from the principles enunciated in the national courts of the member states in an eclectic and synthetic process which, especially in that period, characterized the development of EC law. Warner's contribution was not confined to proceeding down already opened avenues, however. In one case he persuaded the ECJ to take what was then the revolutionary step of declining to answer a reference made by a national court for a preliminary ruling on the ground that there was no genuine dispute before the referring court. In another it was Warner's influence that led the ECJ to give careful consideration to the principles underlying the different rules in the member states regarding the confidentiality of lawyer–client communications, which led to the ultimate establishment in EC law of principles similar to the English concept of legal professional privilege.

Warner returned to London in March 1981, having been appointed a judge of the chancery division of the High Court of Justice. A condition of his appointment at the ECJ was that he satisfied national requirements for appointment to the highest judicial office (in the United Kingdom, the House of Lords) and, as he had served with distinction as a member of the supreme court of the European Communities, many colleagues regretted that he was appointed only as a judge of first instance. After eight years' absence from London, appointment to a first instance post was not, in any event, Warner's métier and, dogged as he was by worsening health, it is doubtful whether, conscientiously though he performed his judicial duties, he enjoyed them as greatly as he had his time at the ECJ.

With Warner's appointment to the High Court bench in 1981 came a knighthood and, in 1982, appointment as a judge of the UK restrictive practices court. In 1985 he was elected treasurer of Lincoln's Inn, of which he had been a bencher since the relatively early age of forty-two. In 1994 he retired from the High Court. In 1998 he was awarded the grand cross, order of Merit, of Luxembourg, the country where the ECJ had its seat. The United Kingdom failed to give him similar public recognition. However, three British universities, Exeter, Leicester, and Edinburgh, conferred on him honorary doctorates, which reflected also his work as vice-president and then president of the UK Association for European Law between 1975 and 1989.

Warner (known to his friends as J.-P.) lived latterly in Kensington, London. He died at the Royal Marsden Hospital, Chelsea, on 1 February 2005. The building of the ECJ in Luxembourg was constructed with a lining of asbestos material, and this may have been the origin of the 'industrial disease of mesothelioma' recorded, following an inquest, as the cause of his death. He was survived by his wife and two daughters. A memorial service was held at Lincoln's Inn chapel on 18 May 2005. JEREMY LEVER

Sources *The Times* (23 Feb 2005); (17 March 2005) • N. Burrows and R. Greaves, *The advocate general and EC law* (2007) • *WW* (2005) • Burke, *Peerage* • personal knowledge (2009) • private information (2009) [P. Lasok, QC.] • b. cert. • m. cert. • d. cert.

Archives SOUND BL NSA, current affairs recording

Likenesses T. Ward, pastels (after photograph repro. in *The Times*), Lincoln's Inn • photograph, repro. in *The Times* (23 Feb 2005)

Wealth at death £473,969: probate, 27 April 2005, *CGPLA Eng. & Wales*

Warren, Eleanor Catherine Rutherford (1919–2005), cellist, was born at 65 Addison Road, Kensington, London, on 5 June 1919, the daughter of William Rutherford Warren, a retired army captain, and his wife, Elsa Julia, *née* Seligman. Her German-born mother was a serious amateur cellist, and at the age of five Warren became the youngest ever student at the London Cello School in Nottingham Place, where her contemporaries included Zara Nelsova and Olga Hegedus. She soon began to win prizes at competitions and festivals and in 1933 played for Gregor Piatigorsky, who gave her regular help and encouragement on his London visits. She gained further experience through work in London chamber orchestras and freelance orchestral engagements. Piatigorsky introduced her to the agent Harold Holt, who arranged her Wigmore Hall début concert in 1935, just after her sixteenth birthday. She received excellent reviews and was soon appearing at Holt celebrity concerts with such artists as John McCormack, Richard Tauber, and Paul Robeson. Solo and concerto dates soon followed, in England, Holland, Belgium, and Canada.

During the Second World War, like many other artists, Warren played for the armed services, factory workers, and hospitals in extremely arduous and sometimes dangerous conditions. Concerts were also given in the underground, where crowds congregated at night to escape the blitz. In 1942 Warren attended a concert at the Czech embassy, where she was struck by the musicianship of the Czech émigré (Jan) Walter Susskind (1913–1980), then pianist of the Czech Trio and already a noted conductor. He was the son of Bruno Susskind, accountant. They married on 22 December 1943 and her life took a new direction. The birth of their son, Peter, in 1944 meant a challenging mix of motherhood, practice, and engagements.

Walter Susskind became chief conductor of the Scottish Orchestra, from 1946 to 1952, and life was divided between Glasgow and London. After the war it was at last possible to travel abroad, and Warren studied with Pierre Fournier in Paris and Switzerland and, in 1949, with Pablo Casals in Prades. Susskind left Britain in 1953 for the Victorian Symphony Orchestra in Melbourne. Their marriage ended at this time and Warren plunged headlong into the London scene, working with the English Chamber Orchestra, the London Mozart Players, the Zorian Quartet, and the English Baroque Ensemble, as well as undertaking regular film sessions with Malcolm Arnold, Richard Rodney Bennett, and Jacques Loussier.

A back injury forced Warren to abandon the cello, and in 1964 her second career began when she joined the BBC as a music assistant, soon broadcasting and devising programmes and series (including *This Week's Composer*), for which she proved to have immense flair. In the 1970s she devised a new series of live recitals from the concert hall in Broadcasting House, featuring artists of the younger generation. Graham Johnson discovered, long after the fact, that she had secured his first BBC broadcasts.

After wartime bomb damage the church of St John's, Smith Square, had been rebuilt in 1969 as a concert hall. Warren realized the potential of the building and created the highly successful BBC Monday lunchtime concerts, which mixed some of the great performers and ensembles with emerging artists, from whom she had an uncanny knack of picking winners. It was, for example, Warren's suggestion that led to the creation of the Pauk–Kirshbaum–Frankl Piano Trio. She was promoted to chief producer in 1971 and became closely involved with the Leeds piano competition. Four years later she was appointed head of music programmes, BBC Radio. Sir Nicholas Kenyon, one of her staff at that time, later fondly recalled her interest in the most junior members, nurturing and guiding their progress with care and affection. It was in some respects a fulfilling role for her, but she frequently felt frustrated by BBC bureaucracy.

In 1977 a tempting offer from John Manduell led Warren to accept the post of head of strings at the newly created Royal Northern College of Music in Manchester. Her innate interest in young performers made the role perfect for her, and she quickly placed chamber music at the heart of the department. She established a tradition of recitals and master classes from the greatest musicians, including Pierre Fournier, the Vermeer Quartet, Julian Bream, and John Williams. As ever, her principal concern was for the students, and she inevitably became involved in the BBC young musician of the year competition when it began in 1978 at the college.

In 1984 Warren decided to return to London and was asked by John Hosier, principal of the Guildhall School of Music and Drama, to establish a system for embedding chamber music in the school. The following year Michael Gough Matthews, director of the Royal College of Music, asked her to become chamber music director. She continued in both posts for the next ten years. In 1911 she was appointed MBE. After her retirement in 1996 she remained constantly in demand as adjudicator, adviser, and mentor, and was delighted when Ralph Kirshbaum, one of the many cellists whom she befriended, created the Manchester International Cello Festival at the Royal Northern College of Music.

As cellist, broadcaster, and teacher, Eleanor Warren successfully fulfilled three careers in her long life and touched the lives of countless musicians, who appreciated her passion for music, her razor-sharp mind, and her wicked sense of humour. She died at the BUPA Hospital, Gartree Road, Oadby, Leicestershire, on 25 August 2005, of cancer, and was survived by her son. TONY FELL

Sources E. Warren, unfinished autobiography, priv. coll. • *The Independent* (9 Sept 2005) • *The Times* (5 Oct 2005) • *Daily Telegraph* (10 Oct 2005) • *The Guardian* (27 Oct 2005) • personal knowledge (2009) • private information (2009) • b. cert. • m. cert. • d. cert.
Archives FILM BFINA, performance footage | SOUND BL NSA, documentary recordings; performance recordings
Likenesses obituary photographs
Wealth at death £172,709: probate, 1 Dec 2005, *CGPLA Eng. & Wales*

Watkin, (Francis) David (1925–2008), cinematographer, was born on 23 March 1925 at 2 St Mildred's Road, Margate, Kent, the son of John Wilfrid Watkin, solicitor, and his wife, Beatrice Lynda, *née* Dadswell. In 1948 he joined the Southern Railway film unit, which was merged with British Transport Film two years later. This proved to be a highly stimulating environment and in 1956 Watkin earned his first credit as a fully fledged cameraman on the documentary *The Long Night Haul*. By the early 1960s he had moved into the innovative world of television commercials and it was during this period that he developed a strong inclination for reflected or bounced light, which produced the soft, naturalistic look that was to become his trademark. It was on a commercial for Shredded Wheat that Watkin met the director Richard Lester, who subsequently invited him to shoot his next feature film, *The Knack* (1965), quickly followed by *Help!* (1965), featuring the Beatles. Both of these productions were distinguished by Lester's frenetic visual style, but tempered by Watkin's sense of precision and taste. This led to a connection with Tony Richardson, beginning with *Mademoiselle* (1966) and followed by the ambitious production of *The Charge of the Light Brigade* (1968), for which Watkin used old Ross Express lenses to capture the qualities of Roger Fenton's famous photographs of the Crimean War. He also experimented with filters to create the post-apocalyptic half-light of Lester's surreal comedy *The Bed Sitting Room* (1969).

Watkin's burgeoning reputation caught the attention of the American director Mike Nichols, who hired him to shoot his adaptation of Joseph Heller's celebrated anti-war novel *Catch-22* (1970), made on location in Mexico and Rome with studio interiors filmed in Hollywood. On returning to the UK, Watkin started work on *The Devils* (1971), the notorious tale of alleged demonic possession in a seventeenth-century French town, directed by Ken Russell. Watkin's soft, naturalistic light provided an effective counterpoint to Russell's trademark dramatic pyrotechnics and Derek Jarman's highly stylized sets, including the convent, an antiseptic cavern where exterior light struggles to pierce the oppressive gloom. The 1970s saw Watkin maintain a number of key creative partnerships, with Russell on *The Boy Friend* (1972); with Richardson on *A Delicate Balance* (1973) and *Joseph Andrews* (1977); and with Lester on *The Three Musketeers* (1973), *The Four Musketeers* (1974), *Robin and Marian* (1976), and *Cuba* (1979). In 1977 he worked for the first time with the Italian director Franco Zeffirelli, on *Jesus of Nazareth*.

Maintaining his reputation for inventiveness, Watkin continued to seek ways of illuminating sets that would fulfil his desire to light the scene, not the set-up, allowing full scope to the directors and actors without the need for constant lighting adjustments. On *The Devils*, for example, he had adapted an old military searchlight that had been used as a prop on the Richard Lester film *How I Won the War* (1967) to create strong shafts of light on the cathedral set. But more significant was the invention of the 'Wendy light', devised to light a night-time exterior on the production of *Hanover Street* (1979). This involved the rigging up of more than 200 bulbs into a single unit which was mounted on a cherry picker 150 feet in the air. The power of the light allowed Watkin to place it some distance from the action, creating a huge area in which actors could move without becoming under-exposed; it was also much more naturalistic than conventional lighting techniques for night exteriors.

In 1981 Watkin shot the Oscar-winning *Chariots of Fire* for the director Hugh Hudson, which momentarily brought some optimism back into the British film industry. But he also continued to be much sought after in the wider international arena, with films including Tony Richardson's *The Hotel New Hampshire* (1984), for which, against the prevailing trend, he created a sharp, deep-focus style, Barbara Streisand's directorial début, *Yentl* (1983), Taylor Hackford's *White Nights* (1985), and Sidney Pollack's *Out of Africa* (1986), which won him the Oscar for best cinematography. The stunning images of the Kenyan landscapes were captured on AGFA film stock, Watkin having rejected the latest product from the market leaders Kodak, giving the German manufacturer a major publicity boost. Having been garlanded, Watkin continued to find his talents in great demand on both sides of the Atlantic, shooting films for established directors like Norman Jewison (*Moonstruck*, 1987), Franco Zeffirelli (*Hamlet*, 1990; *Jane Eyre*, 1996; and *Tea with Mussolini*, 1999), and, towards the end of his career, for Sidney Lumet (*Night Falls on Manhattan*, 1996; *Critical Care*, 1997; and *Gloria*, 1999). But he also enhanced the work of such relative newcomers as Michael Caton-Jones on *Memphis Belle* (1990) and *This Boy's Life* (1993), Beban Kidron on *Used People* (1992), the theatre director Peter Sellers on *The Cabinet of Dr Ramirez* (1991), and the Hollywood actor Morgan Freeman on *Bopha!* (1993).

Throughout his career Watkin earned a reputation as a charming, cultivated, and self-deprecating man, and was notorious for taking naps between set-ups. He was openly gay, earning him the nickname Wendy, after which his innovative lighting device was named. His partner for many years was Nicholas John (Nick) Hand, embalmer, with whom he registered a civil partnership in 2006. He produced two volumes of autobiography, *Why is There Only One Word for Thesaurus?* (1998) and *Was Clara Schumann a Fag Hag?* (2008). He died on 19 February 2008 at his home, 6 Sussex Mews, Brighton, of cancer, and was survived by his partner, Nick Hand. DUNCAN PETRIE

Sources D. Chase, 'David Watkin', *American Cinematographer* (March 1984), 42–6 • S. Hachem, 'Lights, camera, emulsions for *Out of Africa*', *American Cinematographer* (Feb 1986), 66–72 • C. Hewitt, 'Honest guv!', *Eyepiece*, 15/3 (1994), 15–23 • D. Petrie, *The British cinematographer* (1996) • D. Watkin, *Why is there only one word for thesaurus?* (1998) • D. Watkin, *Was Clara Schumann a fag hag?* (2008) • *The Times* (22 Feb 2008) • *Daily Telegraph* (22 Feb 2008) • *The Guardian* (23 Feb 2008) • *The Independent* (25 Feb 2008) • davidwatkin.co.uk, 30 April 2010 • b. cert. • d. cert.

Archives FILM BFINA, documentary footage

Likenesses obituary photographs

Wealth at death £736,368: probate, 4 Sept 2008, *CGPLA Eng. & Wales*

Watkins, Sir Tasker (1918–2007), judge, was born on 18 November 1918 at 9 Station Terrace, Nelson, Glamorgan, the son of Bertram Watkins, engine fitter, and his wife, Jane, *née* Phillips. He was educated at Pontypridd grammar school until his parents, like many of that generation living in the valleys of south Wales, went to England to seek work. They moved to Dagenham, Essex, and he completed

Sir Tasker Watkins (1918–2007), by unknown photographer, 1971

his education in Romford. Before the outbreak of the Second World War he worked for export agents and, when war broke out, was being trained as a commercial attaché and was about to travel to Brazil.

Watkins joined the Duke of Cornwall's light infantry on 16 October 1939 and, after attending an officer cadet training unit, was commissioned into the Welch regiment as a second lieutenant in 1941. On 17 May that year, at the parish church in Dagenham, he married (Margaret) Eirwen Evans, daughter of John Rees Evans, driver. They had a son and a daughter. Meanwhile, while the force for the liberation of Europe was being trained, he attended the Advanced Handling and Fieldcraft School near Llanberis, Caernarvonshire, and remained there as an instructor. He landed in Normandy a week after D-day in June 1944 and served with the 1st/5th battalion of the Welch regiment. He took part in the harsh battles in Normandy and was awarded the Victoria Cross for his conduct during desperate fighting near Bafour on 16 August, in the course of the crucial battles around Falaise. The citation read:

> Lieutenant Watkins's company had to cross open cornfields in which booby traps had been set. It was not yet dusk and the company soon came under heavy machine-gun fire from posts in the corn and farther back, and also fire from an 88 mm gun; many casualties were caused and the advance was slowed up.
>
> Lieutenant Watkins, the only officer left, placed himself at the head of his men and under short range fire charged two posts in succession, personally killing or wounding the occupants with his Sten gun. On reaching his objective he found an anti-tank gun manned by a German soldier; his Sten gun jammed, so he threw it in the German's face and shot him with his pistol before he had time to recover.
>
> Lieutenant Watkins's company now had only some 30 men left and was counter-attacked by 50 enemy infantry.

> Lieutenant Watkins directed the fire of his men and then led a bayonet charge, which resulted in the almost complete destruction of the enemy.
>
> It was now dusk and orders were given for the battalion to withdraw. These orders were not received by Lieutenant Watkins's company as the wireless set had been destroyed. They now found themselves alone and surrounded in depleted numbers and in failing light. Lieutenant Watkins decided to rejoin his battalion by passing round the flank of the enemy position through which he had advanced but while passing through the cornfields once more, he was challenged by an enemy post at close range. He ordered his men to scatter and himself charged the post with a Bren gun and silenced it. He then led the remnants of his company back to battalion headquarters.
>
> His superb gallantry and total disregard for his own safety during an extremely difficult period were responsible for saving the lives of his men, and had a decisive influence on the course of the battle. (*London Gazette*, 31 Oct 1944)

Within ten days units of the British Second Army were on the banks of the River Seine and the American Third Army had entered Paris.

Only very rarely did Watkins speak of the events of 16 August 1944, either in public or in private. A contemporary newspaper report records him as saying only 'The boys were wonderful. They were Welsh' (*Western Mail*, 9 May 1945). In 1955 he was persuaded to speak on Radio Wales about the Welsh soldier in Normandy. Referring to his battalion's engagements, including Bafour, he said:

> A good memory is a fine thing but for those who were there it should not be too good. It should be good enough, however, to recall the great comradeship we enjoyed and which we shall never experience again. (P. Hannan, *Wales on the Wireless*, 1988, 112)

Interviewed in 2001 he was a little more forthcoming:

> You must believe me when I say it was just another day in the life of a soldier. I did what needed doing to help colleagues and friends, just as others looked out for me during the fighting that summer … I didn't wake up the next day a better or braver person, just different. I'd seen more killing and death in 24 hours—indeed been part of that terrible process—than is right for anybody. From that point onwards I have tried to take a more caring view of my fellow human beings, and that, of course, always includes your opponent, whether it be in war, sport or just life generally. (*Daily Telegraph*, 8 Nov 2001)

The outlook revealed by those statements, and the courage that underlay them, guided Watkins throughout his life. At a service in Westminster Abbey on 25 June 2006 to mark the 150th anniversary of the inauguration of the Victoria Cross, and attended by eight of the twelve surviving holders of the award, Watkins, accurately described in a press report as 'a diminutive figure and an eminent judge', read the lesson. 'We are just the ones fortunate enough to be recognised in this way and who are still here', he added when interviewed (*Daily Telegraph*, 27 June 2006).

In the summer of 1944 the battalion, with the 53rd (Welsh) division, continued with the advance into Belgium and the Netherlands. Watkins was promoted captain, and then acting major. His active service ended when he was badly wounded during the seven-day battle in late October 1944 to liberate the Dutch city of 's-Hertogenbosch. The task had been assigned to the division, an operation later described by the army commander as 'brilliant'. During treatment for his wounds amputation of a leg had been contemplated but the determination of Watkins, reflected in the conduct of those treating him, prevented it. After his evacuation the award of the Victoria Cross was announced and he was decorated by George VI on 8 March 1945.

After his demobilization in 1946 Watkins's main home for the rest of his life was in Llandaff, Cardiff. He joined the Middle Temple, and studied at home near the cathedral close with periods of reflection in the war-damaged cathedral, which was his parish church. He was called to the bar in June 1948. Not only did he develop a large and wide-ranging practice in Cardiff and on the Wales and Chester circuit, he was prominent in transforming the Cardiff bar into a body of practitioners capable of dealing with growing legal requirements in Wales, including public inquiries as well as substantial civil and criminal work.

On taking silk in 1965 Watkins joined chambers in London but his links with Wales remained strong. He appeared, as deputy to the attorney-general, as counsel to the tribunal at the Aberfan disaster inquiry in 1966. The disaster had occurred only a few miles from his birthplace. His practice included major criminal trials in Wales and important civil cases and inquiries including litigation involving the coal industry, a major employer in Wales during his time at the bar, and medical issues. He was a brilliant advocate, whether before judge, jury, or inquiry inspector. He never failed to secure and to retain the ear of the court, sensitive to the needs of the case as it developed. While he was forceful in his advocacy his innate courtesy and dignity never diminished.

Having been circuit treasurer for many years, Watkins was leader of the Wales and Chester circuit from 1970 until his appointment to the High Court bench (with the customary knighthood) in 1971, first in the newly created Family Division and then, from 1974, in the Queen's Bench Division. He had been recorder successively of Merthyr Tudful (1968–70) and Swansea (1970–71). As circuit leader he played an important role in saving the Wales and Chester circuit from the original conclusion of the Beeching Commission in 1970 that south Wales should be incorporated into the western circuit and north Wales into the northern circuit. The implications for Welsh life of its retention were far-reaching. He was a presiding judge on the circuit from 1975 until his promotion to the Court of Appeal, and appointment to the privy council, in 1980.

In 1983 the lord chief justice, Lord Lane, appointed Watkins the first senior presiding judge for England and Wales, with the object of relieving the chief justice of some of the heavy and growing administrative burden on him. In his role as senior presiding judge Watkins was constant in his encouragement of and support for all levels of the judiciary and maintained an optimism that was readily communicated to others. They were a formidable team: Watkins's range of qualities linked with the high intellect and clarity of mind of Geoffrey Lane, together with the fortitude and sense of public duty they shared.

Lane appointed Watkins deputy chief justice in 1988. In that role he was robust in maintaining the status and role of the judiciary in the face of growing pressures and tensions, inevitable at times, between the executive and the judiciary, and in supporting judicial independence in a complex modern society. He recognized the importance to constitutional arrangements of maintaining the status of the High Court judge. The fieldcraft that had taken him and his men through Normandy served the judiciary and the nation well. He was steadfast in his support of Lane, including the lord chief justice's last difficult period in office (when Lane was immoderately criticized after the release of the Birmingham six, whose convictions he had failed to overturn at an earlier appeal). He supported equally Lord Taylor of Gosforth, who succeeded Lane in 1992 and retained Watkins as deputy chief justice until his retirement in 1993. He was appointed GBE in 1990.

Watkins was the founder chairman of the Judicial Studies Board (1979–80) and organized the growing crown office jurisdiction, which later became the Administrative Court. As leader of a working party he introduced procedures designed to speed up and control the cost of criminal trials. He conducted his own cases courteously and perceptively, with a gift for producing an apt remark to deflate at a stroke the pompous or over-enthusiastic. With Lane he encouraged, in his judgments, a simplified approach to the conduct of criminal trials, summing-up, and sentencing. In both criminal and civil cases he achieved incremental developments of the law to meet modern needs. His judgments troubled the House of Lords only rarely.

Watkins held a range of public offices in Wales. From 1947 to 1968 he was president of the British Legion, Wales, and he was chairman of the mental health appeal tribunal, Welsh region, from 1960 to 1971. He was appointed deputy lieutenant of the county of Glamorgan in 1956. From 1987 to 1998 he was president of the University of Wales college of medicine, conducting council meetings with characteristic flair. He was awarded doctorates by the University of Wales and Glamorgan University and, in 1992, an honorary fellowship of the Royal College of Surgeons. In later years he was chairman of the Glamorgan committee of the Army Benevolent Fund, which achieved a remarkable fund-raising record.

Rugby union football was an important part of Watkins's life. He had a long association with the Glamorgan Wanderers club, first as a player and official and, from 1968 until his death, as president. On his retirement from the bench in 1993 he was elected president of the Welsh Rugby Union, an office he held for eleven years. He oversaw and guided, though he did not fully welcome, the transition from an amateur to a professional game. In Wales the strength of the game in local communities, and the loyalties associated with that, made the transition difficult. The period of his presidency was not a vintage one for a national team coming to terms with the professional game but he maintained the morale of players and officials throughout. As one captain, Colin Charvis, put it: 'During good times and bad, he was always there with some words of inspiration for myself and the team' (*South Wales Argus*, 9 Sept 2007). His speeches, at post-match dinners as on other occasions, were notable for their warmth and good humour. From its inception in 1975 until his death he was chairman of the trustees of the Welsh Rugby Union Charitable Trust, formed to assist injured players.

Watkins's range of activities and achievements gave him a unique position in the life of Wales in the latter part of the twentieth century. That was further marked towards the end of his life by his appointment as honorary life vice-patron of the Welsh Rugby Union (a position created especially for him), freeman of the city of Cardiff, and a knight of the order of St John. For all his companionability and ability to communicate with and lead people of every outlook, he was an intensely private person with a strong inner and family life, based on a simple Christian faith. He died on 9 September 2007 at the University Hospital of Wales, Cardiff, and was survived by his wife, Eirwen, and his daughter, Mair. His son, Rhodri, died in 1982. Memorial services were held on 1 December 2007 simultaneously in Llandaff Cathedral and St John's Cathedral, 's-Hertogenbosch. A statue commemorating his life and achievements was unveiled at the entrance to the Millennium Stadium in Cardiff, in the presence of the lord chief justice, Lord Judge, the first minister for Wales, Rhodri Morgan, and many other dignitaries, on 15 November 2009. MALCOLM PILL

Sources *LondG* (31 Oct 1944) · *South Wales Argus* (9 Sept 2007) · *The Times* (10 Sept 2007) · *Daily Telegraph* (10 Sept 2007) · *The Guardian* (10 Sept 2007); (24 Sept 2007) · *The Independent* (10 Sept 2007) · *Western Mail* (10 Sept 2007); (3 Dec 2007) · *Western Morning News* (10 Sept 2007) · *South Wales Echo* (10 Sept 2007); (11 Sept 2007); (3 Dec 2007); (16 Nov 2009) · W. A. Williams, *Heart of a dragon* (2008) · *WW* (2007) · Burke, *Peerage* · personal knowledge (2011) · private information (2011) · b. cert. · m. cert. · d. cert.

Likenesses photographs, 1945–92, Photoshot, London · photograph, 1971, PA Photos, London [*see illus.*] · photographs, 1971–2006, PA Photos, London · photograph, 2005 (with Johnson Beharry), Camera Press, London · D. Griffiths, oils, repro. in www.david-griffiths.co.uk/users/www.david-griffiths.co.uk/upload/tasker_watkins.jpg · obituary photographs · statue, Millennium Stadium, Cardiff

Wealth at death £580,203: probate, 10 March 2008, *CGPLA Eng. & Wales*

Watson, John Hugh [Adam] (**1914–2007**), diplomatist and scholar of international relations, was born at Lazonby, Battenberg Avenue (later Carisbrooke Road), Leicester, on 10 August 1914, the elder son of Joseph Charlton Watson, banker, and his wife, Alice, *née* Tate. He spent his early years in Buenos Aires, Argentina, where his father was stationed, and became fluent in Spanish. During these early years his mother (lacking any other books with which to teach him English) instilled in him a lifelong love of poetry. He returned to England at the age of eight and was educated at Rugby School. He then spent a year in Madrid, Freiburg im Breisgau, and Marburg-an-der-Lahn, before going to King's College, Cambridge, initially to read modern languages. While there he switched to history and was tutored by Herbert Butterfield.

Watson entered the diplomatic service in 1937. It was at this time that he began to be known as Adam (since, he later said, every head in the Foreign Office seemed to turn when someone asked for John). His first overseas posting was to Bucharest as a third secretary, in 1939. There he struck up lifelong friendships with Reggie Smith, the broadcaster and writer, and his wife, the novelist Olivia Manning, who based one of the characters in her Balkan trilogy on Watson. When Romania joined the axis powers late in 1940 he was the last to leave the British embassy there, and was transferred to Cairo. There his tasks included liaising with the Free French force in north Africa, but also preparing for the surrender of Egypt should the British be forced to retreat. In 1944 he was sent to the embassy in Moscow, as a second then first secretary. On his return to the Foreign Office in 1947 he was engaged in 'grey' propaganda, from 1948 under the auspices of the information research department, recruiting left-leaning intellectuals to provide propaganda against Soviet communism. In 1950 he was transferred to Washington as a psychological warfare liaison officer. There, also in 1950, he married an American economist, Katharine Anne (Andy) Campbell, with whom he had two sons, Douglas (*b.* 1952) and Alaric (*b.* 1958), and a daughter, Katharine (Polly; *b.* 1953).

From 1956 Watson (who had been promoted counsellor in 1953) specialized in African affairs, first as head of the Foreign Office's African department (where he had to deal with some of the fallout from the Suez escapade) and then, from 1959 (the Foreign Office again taking advantage of his fluency in languages), as minister at the embassy in Paris, with special responsibility for the affairs of French-speaking west Africa. He was concurrently British consul-general at Dakar (1959), then British ambassador to the Federation of Mali (1960–61) and to Senegal, Mauritania, and Togo (1960–62). He was appointed CMG in 1958. In 1960 he was induced by his old tutor Herbert Butterfield and by Martin Wight to join the British Committee on the Theory of International Politics (which later gave rise to the 'English school' of international relations, with an emphasis on *Realpolitik* and on the way the states system operated within a broader international society). He was one of the few practising diplomats on the committee.

In 1962–3 Watson spent a year at Nuffield College, Oxford, as Gwilym Gibbon research fellow. Then, shortly after the Cuban missile crisis, he was appointed British ambassador to Cuba. He was there when President John F. Kennedy was assassinated. His final posting was as under-secretary at the Foreign Office (1966–8), dealing primarily with NATO affairs and strategic issues. He published his first book, *The War of the Goldsmith's Daughter*, relating an episode in the fifteenth-century Muslim conquest of southern India, in 1964. This was followed by *Emergent Africa* (1965), published pseudonymously at the request of the Foreign Office as by Scipio. This, the fruit of his year's study in Oxford, analysed sympathetically the problems faced by the newly independent African nations both in dealing with their colonial legacies and in reconciling their desire for full independence with the realities of their economic and political needs. In 1968 he published *The Nature and Problems of the Third World* (1968).

In want of new pastures rather than because he could not expect further preferment Watson took early retirement from the Foreign Office in 1968. He spent five ultimately frustrating years as diplomatic adviser to the British Leyland Motor Corporation, then in 1974 moved to Paris as director-general of the International Association for Cultural Freedom, and chairman of the Fondation pour une Entraide Intellectuelle Européenne, both concerned to aid dissenting intellectuals, particularly in eastern Europe and the Soviet Union.

For the last thirty years of his life Watson embarked on a second career as an academic. He had already spent a year at the Australian National University in Canberra as a visiting fellow in 1973–4, at the invitation of Hedley Bull. In 1978 he was visiting professor at the University of Virginia. In 1980 he was invited back as professor of international relations at the Center for Advanced Studies there. He then embarked upon his most productive phase as a writer. In 1981, as editor, he saw to fruition Herbert Butterfield's last and most wide-ranging work, *The Origins of History* (1981). His *Diplomacy: the Dialogue between Sovereign States* (1982) was acclaimed as an authoritative exposition of the role of diplomacy through the ages. He co-edited (with Hedley Bull) *The Expansion of International Society* (1984), which encapsulated the English school's analysis of international relations. His most influential book was *The Evolution of International Society* (1992), which in particular highlighted the norms governing international relations, and the influence and consequences of hegemonical power relations. *The Limits of Independence* (1997) again emphasized the realities of hegemony and dependence in shaping the modern states system. His last book, published shortly before he died, was *Hegemony and History* (2007), which summarized his thinking on international relations, but included a new emphasis on the roles of individuals and non-state actors. He had retired formally from the University of Virginia in 1995, but continued to teach and to play an active role in seminars there until the last few months of his life. (Indeed, he was scheduled to teach in the autumn of 2007.)

Watson could at first appear formal, even stiff, but his essential warmth and humanity soon shone through. His quick wit, breadth of knowledge, and kindly interest were much appreciated by his students in Virginia, many of whom kept in touch with him years after they had left. He was well read in many languages (towards the end of his life he worried that his Romanian was getting rusty), and translated plays from German, French, and Spanish for broadcast on BBC Radio 4. He was described by Martin Wight as 'an avid reader of everything, and a shrewd intellectual magpie' (Vigezzi, 414). From 1980 to 1997 he and his wife, Andy, kept homes both in Charlottesville and in Mayfield, Sussex. He died of cancer of the prostate at the

Nuffield Hospital, Kingswood Road, Tunbridge Wells, on 21 August 2007, and was survived by Andy and their three children. ALEX MAY

Sources R. J. Aldrich, *The hidden hand: Britain, America and cold war secret intelligence* (2002) · B. Vigezzi, *The British Committee on the Theory of International Politics* (2005) · N. Guilhot, 'A network of intellectual friendships: the Fondation pour une Entraide Intellectuelle Européenne and East-West cultural dialogue, 1957–1991', *Minerva*, 44/4 (2006), 379–409 · *Daily Progress* [Charlottesville, Virginia, USA] (5 Sept 2007) · *Washington Post* (14 Sept 2007) · *Daily Telegraph* (28 Sept 2007) · *The Times* (17 Oct 2007) · *PS: Political Science and Politics*, 41/1 (Jan 2008), 230–31 · *FO List* [1938–68] · adamwatson memorial.webly.com, 11 Aug 2010 · *WW* (2007) · private information (2011) · b. cert. · d. cert.
Archives CUL, Herbert Butterfield MSS
Likenesses Bassano, half-plate film negatives, 1963, NPG · obituary photographs
Wealth at death nil—net: probate, 27 June 2008

Watt, William Montgomery (1909–2006), Scottish Episcopal clergyman and scholar of Islam, was born on 14 March 1909 at the manse, Ceres, Fife, the only child of Andrew Watt, a minister in the Church of Scotland, and his wife, Mary, *née* Burns, primary school teacher. His early years were far from stable. His father died shortly after his birth and this misfortune necessitated frequent relocations during his childhood. An uncle and an aunt shared parenting duties with his mother and he grew up primarily in Edinburgh, where he attended George Watson's College.

Watt initially dreamed of a career in science, but because of financial considerations and lack of career guidance he abandoned that ambition in order to study classics at the University of Edinburgh. He completed his MA a year ahead of schedule and entered Balliol College, Oxford, in 1930 with a Warner exhibition. He showed great promise, winning several scholarships (including the Ferguson scholarship in classics in 1931), and was disappointed to receive only a second-class degree in *literae humaniores* in 1932. Fortunately scholarships allowed him to spend another year studying at Balliol. He made the most of his extra time and redeemed the disappointing BA by writing a thesis for the degree of BLitt (awarded in 1935) entitled 'Kant's view of the relation between teleology and ethics', under the guidance of Clement C. J. Webb, whose 'personalist' approach to the philosophy of religion proved stimulating. In the summer of 1934 he continued his explorations in German philosophy at the University of Jena in Germany. When he returned to Scotland in the autumn, he took up an assistant lectureship in moral philosophy at the University of Edinburgh, where he served until 1938.

The year 1937 proved to be both difficult and pivotal for Watt. His mother died, he was jilted, and his doctoral thesis at the University of Edinburgh was rejected with no option for revision. He also published his first book, *Can Christians Be Pacifists?*, which provided a manifesto for 'Christian internationalism' (p. 125). The book signalled the beginning of Watt's lifetime interest in the development of a universal religion that would supersede all previous particular religions. Watt believed that humanity required a common religion to help it manage the transition from allegiance to the nation state to support of a common world federation. However, he had little first-hand experience of the challenges of religious dialogue and reconciliation until he caught a 'glimpse of the profundity of the problem' through conversations with a Muslim flatmate from Pakistan (Watt, *Islamic Revelation in the Modern World*, 1969, v). These conversations piqued Watt's interest and proved the beginning of a lifetime of reflection on the relationship between Christianity and Islam.

Following the exchanges with his Muslim friend, Watt entered into correspondence with the Anglican bishop in Jerusalem, George Francis Graham Brown. Shortly thereafter Graham Brown invited Watt to join him in Jerusalem as his specialist in Arab affairs. This new post required several years of preparation, but Watt made rapid progress, receiving ordination in 1939 after training at Cuddesdon College and completing his curacy in 1943 (in which year he married Jean Macdonald Donaldson, a social worker; they had a son and four daughters). During this busy period he studied Arabic at the School of Oriental and African Studies in London and began work on his doctoral thesis, 'Free will and predestination in early Islam', under the direction of the Scottish Arabist Richard Bell at the University of Edinburgh. He was awarded his PhD in 1944.

Watt arrived in Jerusalem in 1943 and remained on the bishop's staff until 1946, when a friend's death in the bombing of the King David Hotel in Jerusalem impelled him to look for a change of scenery. By the time he had returned home to the University of Edinburgh to take up a lectureship, first in ancient philosophy in 1946 and subsequently in Arabic in 1947, he had refined his own view of the proper Christian approach to Islam. In Watt's assessment the cultivation of a vigorous indigenous Arab Christianity in a fiercely nationalistic climate required appreciation of the enduring values of Islam. He believed that attacking Islam would only strengthen the already rapidly spreading cancer of materialism, so he argued that Christians should instead focus primarily on helping Muslims become better Muslims.

Watt's missionary experience gave impetus to his development of a Christian critique of Western views of Islam that anticipated elements of later post-structuralist and Marxist critiques of Orientalism. Watt believed that misconceptions and stereotypes about Islam in the West could be traced back to the 'medieval war-propaganda' of the crusades (Watt, *Muhammad at Medina*, 1956, 324). From his position in Edinburgh, where he served as professor of Arabic and Islamic studies from 1964 to 1979, he set about countering false perceptions. His monumental two-volume biography of the prophet Muhammad, *Muhammad at Mecca* (1953) and *Muhammad at Medina* (1956), broke new ground through the sympathetic treatment of its protagonist. In addition he launched the successful Islamic Surveys series at Edinburgh University Press. He edited the series from 1961 to 1979 and contributed many volumes of his own work including *Islamic Philosophy and*

Theology (1962), *A History of Islamic Spain* (1965), *Islamic Political Thought* (1968), and *The Influence of Islam on Medieval Europe* (1972).

Methodologically Watt attempted to blend philology with sociology. Though he eschewed the social and psychological reductionism of Marx and Freud, their work made him aware of the ways in which political and social biases unconsciously shaped both ideas in the past and conclusions of supposedly neutral scholarship in the present. Since political commitment was unavoidable, he believed it important that scholarship should support the right cause. For Watt this cause was religious and political internationalism. While class conflict, racial prejudice, and nationalist chauvinism threatened to tear the world apart, he believed that religion could play a crucial role in helping humanity form 'a single harmonious society' (Watt, 'Thoughts on Islamic unity', *Islamic Quarterly*, 3, 1956–7, 193). In *Islam and the Integration of Society* (1961) he sought to determine how Islam had fostered social cohesion in a localized context in the past and how it might do so on a worldwide scale in the future. Concepts derived from the work of Carl Jung, whose work Watt greatly admired, figured prominently in the analysis. In 1968, Watt forecasted presciently that by 'the year AD 2000 it seems probable that Islam will be one of a half-dozen significant political forces in the world' (Watt, *Islamic Political Thought*, ix). At the time, he believed Islam's political re-emergence would mean the spread of global unity and he did not anticipate the subsequent rise of Islamist terrorism. Many years later he provided an analysis of why things had not turned out as he expected in *Islamic Fundamentalism and Modernity* (1988).

Watt's Christian faith was of a decidedly liberal orientation. Though he was sympathetic to aspects of Anglo-Catholic spirituality, the liberal theology of F. D. Maurice exercised an early and lasting influence on his 'intellectual attitude as an Anglican' (Watt, 'Towards the religion of the future', priv. coll.). His numerous theological writings reflected his concern to communicate traditional Christian doctrines in modern scientific terms. He served as a priest for the Scottish Episcopal church throughout his life, and though sceptical of institutional initiatives towards Christian unity, he supported ecumenism by joining the Iona community in 1960. Though his work was not without its critics, he earned wide acclaim as one of Britain's foremost interpreters of Islam in the twentieth century and garnered numerous awards, honorary doctorates, and visiting lectureships throughout the world. He died on 24 October 2006 at Liberton Hospital, Edinburgh, of bronchopneumonia, and was survived by his wife, Jean, and their five children.

TODD M. THOMPSON

Sources E. Said, *Orientalism* (1979) • A. T. Welch and P. Cachia, eds., *Islam: past influence and present challenge* (1979) • A. F. d'Souza, *The origin of Islam as interpreted by W. Montgomery Watt and A. Kenneth Cragg: an analysis and evaluation* (1979) • R. G. Hovannisian and S. Vryonis, eds., *Islam's understanding of itself* (1983) • A. Z. Yamani, foreword, in W. M. Watt, *Islam and Christianity today: a contribution to dialogue* (1983) • A. S. Ahmed, *Postmodernism and Islam* (1992) • H. M. Said, ed., *Essays on Islam: felicitation volume in honour of Prof. W. Montgomery Watt* (1993) • *The Herald* [Glasgow] (19 Nov 1994) • J. M. Buaben, *Image of the prophet Muhammad in the West: a study of Muir, Margoliouth and Watt* (1996) • M. M. Ali, *Sirat al-Nabi and the orientalists: with special reference to the writings of William Muir, D. S. Margoliouth and W. Montgomery Watt* (1997) • B. Maan and A. McIntosh, '"The whole house of Islam, and we Christians with them": an interview with "the last orientalist" (Professor William Montgomery Watt)', *The Coracle*, 3/51 (2000), 8–11 • M. Aydin, *Modern western Christian theological understandings of Muslims since the Second Vatican Council* (2002) • J. O. Bengtsson, *The worldview of personalism: origins and early developments* (2006) • *The Independent* (8 Nov 2006) • *The Guardian* (14 Nov 2006) • *Church Times* (17 Nov 2006) • *The Scotsman* (30 Nov 2006) • *The Times* (2 Jan 2007) • F. Whaling, 'In memory of Professor William Montgomery Watt (1909–2006)', *British Association for the Study of Religions*, 110 (May 2007), 11–12 • D. M. Varisco, *Reading orientalism: Said and the unsaid* (2007) • E. Burke and D. Prochaska, eds., *Genealogies of orientalism: history, theory, politics* (2008) • *WW* (2006) • priv. coll., Watt papers • private information (2010) • b. cert. • d. cert.

Archives priv. coll.

Wealth at death £492,273.75: confirmation, 24 May 2007, *CCI*

Watts, Sir Arthur Desmond (1931–2007), international lawyer and diplomatist, was born on 14 November 1931 at 28 Lingfield Road, Wimbledon, Surrey, the only child of Captain (later Colonel) Arthur Edward Watts (1891–1958) of the army education corps and his wife, Eileen May, *née* Challons (1901–1980). The family home at the time was at 26 Thornton Hill, Wimbledon, but service life took them from place to place, including to India, and later to Shrewsbury, so giving Watts a footing to play minor counties cricket for Shropshire in 1955. His father was a strong influence, and Watts followed in his steps to Haileybury, with the ambition of an active army career—for which his superiors at Sandhurst thought he would have been ideally suited—rather than academic study. A rugby injury put paid to that, however, leaving him with a permanent limp that became more pronounced as the years went on, but left his mobility untouched. Invalided out of Sandhurst, he went to Downing College, Cambridge, to read economics, in which he had done particularly well at school. An operation for acute appendicitis necessitated an *aegrotat* in part one of the tripos, and he then shifted, under the influence of Clive Parry, to law. Like others of his generation he was hugely influenced by the brilliant galaxy of international lawyers in Cambridge at the time, including Sir Arnold McNair and the young Robbie Jennings, with both of whom he was later to collaborate on book projects. First-class honours followed in the law tripos in 1954 and a year later in the LLB, bringing him the Whewell scholarship.

The next logical step was to qualify professionally, in preparation for recruitment to the Foreign Office, to a temporary position in 1956, made permanent two years later after Watts had been called to the bar by Gray's Inn in 1957. On 17 August the same year he married Iris Ann Collier (*b.* 1934), daughter of Harry Collier, professional musician. They had met when both were undergraduates at Cambridge, and she gave up schoolteaching on marriage, later becoming, to Watts's pride, an author of popular novels. They had a son, Christopher, and a daughter, Catherine.

The Foreign Office Watts joined was preoccupied with

the disastrous Suez adventure and its consequences, including the sequestration by the Egyptian government of an enormous quantity of British property. When in due course a complex intergovernmental agreement was concluded in 1959, providing for the lifting of the sequestrations and the payment of a large sum in compensation, together with a wide range of related matters, Egypt was not yet ready to resume diplomatic relations but accepted the establishment of a British property commission (later transformed into an embassy). It speaks for Watts's adventurousness, not to mention his competence, that despite his being so junior he was chosen to be its legal adviser. Circumstances in Cairo must have been very trying, but Watts achieved his task with distinction, to the praise both of the agents for British property owners and of his superiors in the embassy, who forecast a glowing career for him if he decided to join the diplomatic branch.

Watts preferred, however, to return to the legal track in the Foreign Office. A posting to Bonn followed in 1967, but was cut short in 1969 when Watts was called back to the Foreign and Commonwealth Office (as it had now become) for early promotion to counsellor, and a secondment to a key position in the law officers' department (1969–70) with the creation there for the first time of a specialist post in international law.

On his return to the Foreign and Commonwealth Office in 1970 Watts was drawn into the intense and complex web of negotiation and internal planning for British entry into the European communities. This made him the natural choice to become, in 1974, the first substantive legal adviser to the United Kingdom representation in Brussels following British entry the previous year. The role was formative in many respects: in the creation of a diplomatic mission of a wholly different kind and shape, including secondments from numerous government departments; in the forging of productive relationships within the established hierarchies of the legal services of the council and commission; and in helping open European law, including the opportunities it offered, to the British legal profession. With his passion for hard work, mastery of detail, and patient, tactful, and open manner, Watts excelled at them all. By now, however, his and Iris's lives had begun to drift apart. She preferred not to accompany him for the whole of the posting to Brussels, and a relationship began to form with his secretary, Cecilia Gillette, which was later to blossom into a full partnership that lasted until his death.

Watts's reputation was now so well established that advancement followed steadily after his return, culminating in his appointment as legal adviser to the Foreign and Commonwealth Office in 1987. He was appointed QC in 1988, and was knighted KCMG in 1989 (having been appointed CMG in 1977). He was immensely popular as legal adviser, principally for the fact that, far from passively waiting to be asked, he was ready astutely to volunteer legal advice, always of a highly practical kind and often as a crisis was about to break, but to do so with a modest lack of dogmatism, so that his interventions, far from being resented, were positively welcomed by senior policy makers. This, coupled with the gift he had developed of clear and straightforward exposition and his good relations with the rest of Whitehall, gave international law a strong place in the Foreign Office.

During this period Watts became passionately involved in the affairs of Antarctica: for the exotic travel, the adventurous company, and the opportunity to put international law to the practical service of the public good. Having been the principal organizer of a polynational cricket match as close as was feasible to the south pole he deployed his negotiating skill in nudging the editors of *Wisden* eventually into recognizing it. Of greater moment for international law the period saw also the fruition of his decades-long collaboration with Jennings on the long-awaited ninth edition of *Oppenheim's International Law*, which appeared in 1992, covering the law of peace, and instantly re-established itself as the essential first port of call for practitioners seeking what the co-editors self-effacingly described as 'a helpful beginning for an inquiry into particular problems'. How much of the product was due to each author remained veiled, but there is every reason to suppose that a good deal more was Watts than Jennings, and there is no doubt that it was Watts's persistence and good organization that saw the book through to completion.

Mandatory retirement at the statutory age of sixty kept Watts's tenure as legal adviser to the Foreign and Commonwealth Office to four years, at the end of which he went into practice at the bar. His hopes of balancing it with academic work were immediately jolted by the explosive growth of his international practice, beginning with the signal distinction of being the first British advocate to be retained by the French government for proceedings at the International Court. Briefs followed at the court for Nigeria, Indonesia, Slovakia, Colombia, Ukraine, and Jordan, and appointment to four inter-state arbitration tribunals, as well as to several tribunals in disputes over foreign private investment. He was called on by the reigning prince of Liechtenstein to see through an initiative on self-determination that had run into difficulties in the UN general assembly. His advocacy was highly praised by connoisseurs as some of the most effective the International Court had seen, for its precision, accuracy, and directness (infused sometimes with an underlying passion, as in his speech in the advisory proceedings on the *Wall in the Occupied Palestinian Territory*).

In 1999 Carl Bildt, the Swedish statesman, then the UN secretary-general's special envoy for the Balkans, asked Watts to mediate a settlement of the furiously contested issue of succession to the rights and liabilities of the former Yugoslavia, an ungrateful task which, though it played to Watts's strengths, posed a stern test to even his patience and good humour. Not many would have stuck to it for five years but, bringing to bear the same fair-minded determination and innate balance that had distinguished him as an arbitrator, Watts cajoled out of the successor states one of the few agreements to have held over time.

Fortunately for international law and practice, though, these professional demands failed to stop the flow of Watts's published work, some of it highly original. In particular, his Lauterpacht lectures of 1992, 'International law and the Antarctic treaty system', offered an insider's knowledge of the legal problems and techniques of this unique exemplar of international co-operation; and his Hague Academy lectures of 1994, 'The legal position in international law of heads of state, heads of government and foreign ministers', were the first systematic treatment of a topic that leapt into prominence a few years later with the extradition proceedings over General Pinochet, in the course of which Watts's careful analysis, fuelled by a meticulous survey of international practice, was the focus of detailed attention by counsel for all parties and by the law lords themselves. He found time, too, having stumbled by chance on the remains of the ruined twelfth-century Augustinian priory at Tortington, near Arundel, to devote himself to their restoration and conversion into a private home, the restoration so sympathetically achieved that it won three design awards and brought him the chairmanship of the Sussex Heritage Trust.

Watts was part of a long line of eminent practitioner-scholars springing from the legal advisers to the Foreign Office. His particular contribution lay in the huge range of his reading and careful attention to detail, joined to clarity of expression and a view of law as a practical tool designed to be used. Although reserved in his private life he generated immediate affection and respect in those with whom he had contact professionally, and it was this, together with a lack of showmanship and a patent sense of balance and of fairness, that lent automatic authority to his advice and to his argument in court. In addition to his British honours he was made a grand officer of the order of Istiqlal (Jordan) and received posthumously the order of the Dual White Cross from Slovakia.

Although he had been troubled for some years by an ailment that drained his energy but resisted initial diagnosis, Watts's death, when it came, was sudden and unexpected. He collapsed on the way to see a client, suffering irreversible brain damage that led to his death at St Thomas's Hospital, Lambeth, a few days later, on 16 November 2007; his funeral was held at Boxgrove Priory, Sussex, on 28 November. When the news came through, the International Court, unusually, rose for a minute's silence.

F. D. Berman

Sources A. D. Watts, 'Jurisdictional immunities of special missions: the French property commission in Egypt', *International and Comparative Law Quarterly*, 12 (1963), 1383 • *Tortington and the black canons* (2002) • *The Lawyer* (26 Nov 2007) • funeral service addresses, Boxgrove Priory, 28 Nov 2007 • *Daily Telegraph* (4 Dec 2007) • *The Independent* (5 Feb 2007) • *The Times* (7 Dec 2007); (17 Dec 2007) • *The Guardian* (18 Jan 2008) • *British Year Book of International Law*, 77 (2007), 7–16 • *Downing Association Newsletter* (2008) • *FO List* • Burke, *Peerage* • *WW* (2007) • personal knowledge (2011) • private information (2011) • b. cert. • m. cert. • d. cert.

Likenesses photograph, 1988, Photoshot, London • obituary photographs • photograph, repro. in www.biicl.org/files/4374_newsletter_spring_2009.htm • photograph, Foreign and Commonwealth Office • photograph, repro. in *British Yearbook of International Law*, 6 • portrait, repro. in *Receuil des Cours* [Hague Academy], 247/3 (1994), facing p. 9

Wealth at death £1,665,815: probate, 3 June 2008, *CGPLA Eng. & Wales*

Weatherill, Bruce Bernard [Jack], **Baron Weatherill** (**1920–2007**), speaker of the House of Commons, was born on 25 November 1920 at Borderdale, London Road, Sunningdale, Berkshire, the only son (there were two daughters) of Bernard Bruce Weatherill (1883–1962), master tailor, and his wife, Annie Gertrude, *née* Creak (1886–1966). He was always known as Jack, as his twin sister was known as Jill. His father had been a Fabian socialist who once led a tailors' strike before going on to found the family tailoring business. Weatherill attended Malvern College, and had hoped to go on to university, but his father decided he ought to be apprenticed as a tailor.

Like many of his generation, Weatherill's main formative experience came in the Second World War. He was commissioned in the 4th/7th Royal dragoon guards, but felt more at home after a transfer to the Indian army, where he served with the 19th King George V's own lancers, rising to the rank of captain. These years reinforced a sense of public service and responsibility. He later quoted the inscription on the grave of an East India Company administrator—'He was trusted absolutely'—as the memorial he would like. He became proficient in Urdu and, after seeing the severe famine in Bengal in 1943, a lifelong vegetarian. As a cavalryman he developed a liking for riding, and, four decades later as speaker, in the early morning he often helped to exercise the horses of the Household Cavalry. His letters to his father and his sisters (preserved in the Templeman Library at the University of Kent) reflected his wry, but always generous, observations on his life in the army.

After the war Weatherill returned to the family business, Bernard Weatherill Ltd, becoming managing director from 1957 until 1970, when he entered the government whip's office. After leaving the Commons he became president of the firm. He was always proud of his background, carrying a silver thimble in his pocket, including his speaker's robes, to 'keep me humble' (*Sunday Times*, 26 Nov 1989). On 16 July 1949, at St George's, Hanover Square, he married (Daphne Iola) Lyn Eatwell (*b.* 1928), daughter of Henry Thomas Eatwell, engineer. They had two sons and one daughter.

Meanwhile Weatherill had become closely involved in local Conservative politics, following a traditional route for that generation: joining the then mass membership Young Conservatives (becoming the first chairman in Guildford from 1946 to 1949) and rising up the ladder of the voluntary side of the party from local to regional, and then to national level. He was chairman of the Guildford association in 1959–63, vice-chairman of the south-east area council in 1962–4, and a member of the national union executive in 1963–4.

Weatherill entered the House of Commons at the October 1964 general election as Conservative MP for Croydon

North East. After a close shave in 1966, when his majority fell to 588, he held the seat comfortably for the rest of his time in the Commons. He joined a parliamentary party where the old shire and landowning MPs had not disappeared. When elected speaker nineteen years later, he recalled overhearing the comment of one backbencher in one of the Commons lavatories: 'Don't know what the place is coming to—I see my tailor has been elected a member!' (*Sunday Times*, 26 Nov 1989). As an MP he vigorously championed the interests of small businesses.

Weatherill's political career was, as before his entry to the Commons, as an insider within the party machine. He joined the Conservative whips' office in 1967, steadily rising up its hierarchy to become deputy chief whip in December 1973, towards the end of the Heath government. He was widely respected for his emollient and understanding style, especially with difficult backbenchers. He was retained by Margaret Thatcher when she became leader but the two never got on. She saw him as too consensual and did not forget that he had voted in favour of proportional representation for elections to the European parliament (albeit in a free vote).

Weatherill was passed over as chief whip after Thatcher won power in 1979 and, instead, became chairman of ways and means, or deputy to the speaker. He was sworn of the privy council in 1980. After George Thomas retired at the 1983 general election, Weatherill was the obvious successor, despite worries about his handling of the odd rowdy debate. However, Thatcher initially pushed forward other candidates, including Humphrey Atkins and Francis Pym, whom she had just sacked from her cabinet. But in hurried behind-the-scenes manoeuvrings Thatcher's intervention backfired among most Conservative and Labour MPs, and Weatherill was chosen as the 154th speaker.

Unlike Thomas, who was widely seen as too close to the executive, Weatherill was determined to champion the rights of backbenchers. His style was unpretentious, charming, and drily humorous, with his occasional irritation mostly muttered under his breath. He took time to establish his authority over a frequently fractious house when Labour members became frustrated during the bitter year-long miners' strike. He was criticized by some more partisan Conservatives, and their press allies, who said he should have done more to clamp down on Labour rowdies and to protect Thatcher in the chamber. He maintained that she should not be 'cocooned'. He described this sniping as the 'black glove', and in a successful counter-attack to later criticisms in an interview on London Weekend Television's *Weekend World* programme, broadcast on 8 May 1988, he argued that: 'My absolute intention is to ensure that everything that goes on in our nation is exposed in the house.' He demonstrated this approach, and his independence, by agreeing to many more private notice questions, which required ministers to appear in the Commons to deal with pressing topical issues. His willingness to allow such questions on issues that ministers would have preferred to keep quiet often annoyed the government. The Weatherill speakership was also marked by the final arrival of television cameras in November 1989, a move he welcomed as giving a more rounded view of what was happening in the chamber than had been provided just by sound broadcasting over the previous decade.

After nine years as speaker Weatherill retired at the 1992 general election, immediately becoming a life peer, taking the title Baron Weatherill. But this did not mark the end of his public life, since he became convenor of the cross-bench peers from 1995 until 1999, the demanding role of ensuring that the views of non-aligned peers were taken into account. He played a role in the debates over the 1999 legislation removing most of the hereditary peers from the Lords, being closely involved in the amendment that kept ninety-two of them in the house for an interim period until longer-term changes were put forward. He also kept a close interest in the affairs of the Commons, eager for the latest news and deploring the downgrading of the chamber under Tony Blair's administration.

Weatherill accumulated a wide range of honours, being a freeman of the City of London and the borough of Croydon, an honorary bencher of Lincoln's Inn, a deputy lieutenant of Kent, and vice-chancellor of the order of St John of Jerusalem. He was high bailiff of Westminster Abbey from 1989 until 1998, when he resigned in protest at the handling of the removal of the organist. His interests included vintage cars (including a run in the 1977 London to Brighton rally) and tennis. In later life he relished his time with his seven grandchildren. After a two-year battle with prostate cancer he died on 6 May 2007 at North Downs Hospital, Tupwood Lane, Caterham, Surrey, near where most of his political and family life had been spent. His memorial service in Westminster Abbey on 23 October 2007 was packed with MPs of all parties. He was survived by his wife, Lyn, and their three children.

Peter Riddell

Sources *Sunday Times* (26 Nov 1989) · *BBC News Online* (7 May 2007) · *The Times* (8 May 2007) · *Daily Telegraph* (8 May 2007) · *The Guardian* (8 May 2007) · *The Independent* (8 May 2007) · Weatherill papers, University of Kent, Canterbury, Templeman Library · Burke, *Peerage* · *WW* (2007) · personal knowledge (2011) · private information (2011) · b. cert. · m. cert. · d. cert.

Archives University of Kent, Templeman Library | FILM BFINA, documentary footage | SOUND BL NSA, current affairs recordings · BL NSA, performance recordings

Likenesses Bassano, half-plate film negatives, 1965, NPG · Bassano, half-plate film negatives, 1978, NPG · photographs, 1981–2004, Photoshot, London · photographs, 1983–95, PA Photos, London · R.-L. Hall, oils, 1991, Parliamentary Art Collection, London · photographs, 1992–8, Rex Features, London · D. Moore, photograph, Camera Press, London · obituary photographs

Wealth at death £417,834: probate, 2 Jan 2008, *CGPLA Eng. & Wales*

Webster, Henry George [Harry] (**1917–2007**), automotive engineer, was born on 27 May 1917 at 53 Sir Thomas White's Road, Coventry, the only son of William George Webster, engineer (and later hotel proprietor), and his wife, Daisy Maud, *née* Thompson. He was educated at Welshpool county school, Montgomeryshire, after which he studied engineering at Coventry Technical College. On leaving college in 1932 he took up an apprenticeship at Coventry's Standard Motor Company. After six years he became an assistant technical engineer, a post held until 1940, when he was appointed deputy chief inspector in Standard's aircraft department. A year after the war ended he reverted to automotive engineering. Meanwhile, on 1 August 1943, at St Barbara's Church, Earlsdon, he married Margaret Alice (Peggy) Sharp (1916–2003), also from Coventry, daughter of Harry Sharp, engineer. They had one daughter.

In 1948, under the auspices of the firm's director of engineering, Ted Grinham, Webster was appointed Standard Motor's chief chassis engineer; in 1955 he was promoted chief engineer. He was made a director of Standard Triumph International, as the firm became in 1957, while remaining chief engineer. He held these positions until 1968 when, following the creation of British Leyland (BL) through a series of mergers in the car industry, he became technical director of BL's Austin Morris division at Longbridge, Birmingham, where he remained until 1974.

From 1948 until 1952 Webster's prime responsibility at Standard was for the design and refinement of the Triumph sports car, which was in great need of regeneration and modernization. The TR2, launched in 1953, proved a sporting, commercial, and export success. On his subsequent appointment as director of engineering in 1957 he assembled an enthusiastic team of engineers at Standard's Canley site and between them they established a pre-eminent reputation in developing sports cars and derivatives within a short time and with limited finance. Throughout its post-war history Standard was extremely short of investment capital until it was taken over by the truck-maker Leyland in 1960–61. Webster's personal relationship with the Italian car designer Giovanni Michelotti of Turin began in 1957 and lasted for many years.

When Standard was taken over by Leyland, Triumph sports cars were beginning to show their worth in the marketplace. Consequently Webster's superiors, including Alick Dick, Stanley Markland, and Donald Stokes, gave him their support. Crucial to Standard's success in this niche market was the advent of the Triumph Herald in 1959. The sleek lines of the Herald were Italian in origin and it was sold as a saloon, a coupé, and a convertible. Remarkably the car had a better turning circle than a London taxi. It also enjoyed an initial basic selling price of £702, representing excellent value in the early 1960s. The car was designed very quickly, and with precious little finance available Webster had to prove resourceful. Normally a car of this period would have had a monocoque body and chassis unit, but the sums of money required for this were far beyond Standard's resources. To compensate for this there was a reversion to pre-Second World War technology. This involved using a strong separate chassis and then adding modern all-independent suspension. This type of thinking was considered ingenious and helped define Webster's reputation in the field of automotive engineering. Additionally the Herald helped establish Triumph cars as 'sexy', which was unusual for such a small firm and led to the identification and exploitation of several niche markets. From the Triumph stable then flowed a range of cars like the sporty Triumph Vitesse, the Spitfire, and the GT6. Perhaps the most remarkable was the Triumph Dolomite 2000, an executive car that rivalled both BMW and Rover as well as bringing refinement to middle-class motoring in Britain, while the TR5 was the first UK-produced vehicle to have fuel injection as a standard feature. This period represented the high point of success for Triumph, especially when in 1961 its TRS racing sports car won the team prize at Le Mans and its Spitfires claimed victory in the capacity class there.

On the creation of BL in 1968 Webster was transferred to Longbridge, the firm's Austin Morris division. Although BL enjoyed 33 per cent of the UK market in 1968 it had little capital and suffered from the problem of ageing models with few new ones on the immediate horizon. Within six years of its foundation the firm was all but bankrupt and taken into public ownership under the National Enterprise Board. Webster found Longbridge quite different from his Coventry base at Canley. In addition to having little money, weak management, and a seeming lack of corporate vision, the company was racked by industrial disputes. Moreover, his job at BL included confronting Sir Alec Issigonis, whose Mini 1100 and 1300 designs were technically excellent and popular but singularly unprofitable, leaving Webster little choice but to shunt Issigonis aside and put him in command of the company's research arm. This left Webster free to work on such new models as the Austin Allegro and the Morris Marina, but under financial constraints so severe that neither product was developed properly and both were failures in the marketplace. In 1974 Webster left BL to become group technical director at the automotive component manufacturer Automotive Products, based in Leamington Spa. He retired in 1983. He was chairman of SKF Steel UK from 1982 to 1987. He was a fellow of the Society of Automotive Engineers, and was appointed CBE in 1974.

Throughout his career Webster appears to have been a modest man and was 'flabbergasted' when after his retirement from public life several of his vehicles were designated as 'classic cars' (*The Independent*, 17 Feb 2007). He himself was somewhat revered by a group of Triumph car owners who had formed the Triumph Sports Six club at Lubenham in Leicestershire, where a walkway on the premises was named Webster Way. He died of heart disease at his home, the Old School House, 2 Barrowfield Lane, Kenilworth, Warwickshire, on 6 February 2007. His daughter as well as his wife predeceased him, but he was survived by grandchildren. TOM DONNELLY

Sources *Daily Telegraph* (9 Feb 2007) • *The Times* (12 Feb 2007) • *The Independent* (17 Feb 2007) • *WW* (2007) • b. cert. • m. cert. • d. cert.
Likenesses obituary photographs
Wealth at death £1,265,786: probate, 16 July 2007, *CGPLA Eng. & Wales*

Webster, John Brighton (1934–2006), advertising executive, was born on 17 December 1934 at the Hertford British Hospital, Levallois-Perret, Paris, the only child of Brighton

Webster, a buyer for Unilever, and later personnel manager, and his wife, Beatrice Sarah, *née* Hill. After a few months in Bordeaux at the beginning of 1940 the family returned to England before the German occupation of Paris. His father continued to work for Unilever, moving several times, and Webster was educated at St Olave's School, York (1943–6), the Royal Grammar School, Newcastle (1946–7), and Hendon county grammar school (1947–51). He enrolled at Hornsey College of Art in 1952, and from 1954 to 1956 did his national service in the RAF, working as a photographer, and also painting aircraft hangars (he had declared an interest in painting), before returning to Hornsey for a final year. He had intended to become a painter, but after his art director showed him some American television commercials he was inspired to go into advertising: he was to be greatly influenced by the wit and style of American advertising of the 1960s. On 12 March 1960 he married Maureen Ann Griffiths, a 22-year-old secretary and later teacher, and daughter of Ernest John Griffiths, fireman; they had two daughters.

While still at Hornsey College of Art, Webster did work experience at the advertising agency Mather and Crowther, and after leaving Hornsey in 1957 he was offered a job there. He moved to Hobson Bates in 1965 and in 1967 to Pritchard Wood, where he devised the 'Have a new year' cinema campaign for National Provincial Bank life savings, warning of the dangers of drink driving. In 1968 three directors left Pritchard Wood to set up their own agency, Boase Massimi Pollitt (BMP), and Webster was one of those who left with them. He became creative director in 1971, and executive creative director in 1980. Based on 'account planning', the new system—developed at Pritchard Wood by Stanley Pollitt and at J. Walter Thompson by Stephen King—in which the account planner became an integral part of the team, directing the market research and the use of focus groups to test new advertisements before the launch of a campaign, BMP became one of the leading advertising agencies in the United Kingdom in the 1970s. Webster later compared the atmosphere at BMP in those early days to that of a university rather than an advertising agency. BMP was floated on the stock exchange in 1983, and bought by DDB (formerly Doyle Dane Bernbach) in 1989; it was integrated into the company, and became DDB London in 2004.

Webster's first and most famous television advertising campaign at BMP was for Cadbury's Smash instant mashed potatoes in 1973. He invented the Smash Martians, metallic puppets who visited earth to see how the inhabitants lived, and were highly amused, and scornful, to find them washing, peeling, boiling, and mashing potatoes by hand instead of just pouring hot water onto powder. This was a new approach to food advertising and the promotion of convenience foods, and was very successful: the campaign, with its slogan 'for mash get Smash', lasted ten years, and Cadbury's Smash became the brand leader. In 1999 *Campaign* magazine chose the Smash Martians as its 'campaign of the century', and in 2005 it was voted ITV's 'best ad ever'.

During the 1970s and 1980s Webster created many award-winning characters, including the Cresta bear (1972), an animated polar bear wearing sunglasses who promoted Cresta's soft drinks ('it's frothy, man'); the Honey Monster, launched in 1976 for Quaker Oats Sugar Puffs cereal ('tell them about the honey, Mummy'); George, the Hofmeister bear ('follow the bear'), played by a Hungarian circus performer (1989), which was later banned because it supposedly encouraged 'lager louts'; and the PG Tips chimps in 1990. He also used well-known personalities, including the actors and comedians Rowan Atkinson and Stephen Fry in his series for Barclaycard in the 1980s, and the footballer Gary Lineker to promote Walker's crisps. Lineker was known as 'Mr Nice Guy' because he had never been booked, and Webster used this in his 'No more Mr Nice Guy' campaign starting in 1995, in a series of scenes in which Lineker steals crisps from children and old ladies, and makes his fellow footballer Paul Gascoigne cry. He also ran many campaigns for *The Guardian* newspaper, including the points of view campaign in 1986: 'Skinhead' was voted the best British ad of the 1980s, and won a golden lion at Cannes. Other *Guardian* campaigns included one in 1989 based on the slogan 'a paper with a mind of its own for people with minds of their own', with a series of witty dialogues. Webster created Arkwright and his performing dog for John Smith's Yorkshire bitter in 1981—this campaign ran for nine years—and a popular campaign for Courage best bitter in 1979, set in an east London pub to the sound track of 'Gertcha' sung by Chas 'n' Dave. Webster never lost his enthusiasm or his creativity: his later campaigns included 'the flame with a brain' for British Gas (1990); the characters Betty Beep and Tom Beeb for BT (1994); the chocolate orange-utans for Terry's chocolate oranges (1995), starring Dawn French and Jennifer Saunders dressed as orang-utans; Parrots for Tropicana orange juice (2003); and Rabbit for *The Guardian* (2004)—in which a rabbit sits in the middle of the road weighing up the arguments for and against going to one side of the road or another. Shortly after he makes his choice, a juggernaut roars past on the other side, and the voiceover says, 'before you decide it's wise to be properly informed'.

Webster won more awards than any other 'creative' in Europe. His prizes included two grand prix and many gold lions at the Cannes International Advertising Film Festival, twenty-four British Television Advertising Awards gold awards, the Design and Art Direction president's award in 1982, and the British Television Advertising Awards chairman's award in 1990, the latter for his outstanding contribution to the commercials industry. Although he wanted to keep out of the limelight he valued his awards, claiming they gave him confidence: 'when someone walks into my office, they listen to what I say. When an account man wants to turn down my script, he thinks twice' (*Campaign*, 13 Jan 2006).

Unlike the stereotype of an advertising man, Webster was modest and unassuming. He loved the films and humour of Jacques Tati, and like Tati he drew his inspiration from his observations of everyday life. His campaigns were characterized by their wit and charm, and he wanted to entertain people, while at the same time selling the product. 'The people John wanted to impress were not in Cannes. They were in Stoke Newington, Liverpool, Sunderland, on the bus, in the supermarket, in the playground', according to his fellow advertising 'creative' Dave Trott (*Campaign*, 'Hall of fame', 2008). He took the comments of the focus groups seriously, often rewriting scripts up to the last minute. He was executive creative director for one episode of *Washes Whiter* (1990), a documentary examining the history of British television advertising. In 2002 he won a British Animation award for his script for *Hamilton Mattress* (2001), an animated film about an aardvark.

Webster was passionate about cricket and France. In 1974 he and his wife bought a house in the Var, moving in 1989 to a house in the same village with a small vineyard, which he tended, using the grapes to make his own wine. He loved what he perceived as the uncomplicated and calm life of a French peasant. Indeed he liked to say that 'there were two ways you could go in life: you could go into advertising and work excessively long hours in a highly competitive environment, eventually having enough money to buy a small house in France. Or you could just be a French peasant and not bother with the other bit' (*The Independent*, 13 Jan 2006). He suffered a heart attack on 6 January 2006 while out jogging near his home in Barnet, Hertfordshire, and was declared dead on arrival at Barnet General Hospital; he was survived by his wife and children. ANNE PIMLOTT BAKER

Sources J. Gable, *The tuppenny Punch and Judy show* (1980), 91–5 · P. Kleinman, *The Saatchi and Saatchi story* (1987), 129–32 · *Campaign* (23 Oct 1998) [suppl.]; (29 Dec 1999); (23 Sept 2005); (13 Jan 2006); (24 Oct 2008), 92–3 · M. Robinson, *100 greatest TV ads* (2000) · J. Myerson and G. Vickers, *Rewind: forty years of design and advertising* (2002), 125–8 · *The Independent* (13 Jan 2006); (16 Jan 2006); (1 May 2006) · *The Guardian* (17 Jan 2006) · M. Tungate, *Adland* (2007), 88–93 · W. Fletcher, *Powers of persuasion: the inside story of British advertising, 1951–2000* (2008), 106–8 · DBB London archive, History of Advertising Trust, Norwich · private information (2010) · m. cert. · d. cert.

Archives History of Advertising Trust, Norwich, DBB London archive

Likenesses P. Rudge, photograph, 1998, repro. in *Campaign* (24 Oct 2008) · obituary photographs · photograph, repro. in H. Vaske, *Standing on the shoulders of giants: Hermann Vaske's conversations with the masters of advertising* (2001)

Wealth at death £55,522: probate, 13 Dec 2006, *CGPLA Eng. & Wales*

Wedgwood, John (1919–2007), consultant geriatrician, was born on 28 September 1919 at Providence Cottage, Well Road, Hampstead, London, the eldest child of Josiah *Wedgwood (1899–1968), master potter, and his wife, Dorothy Mary Haskins, *née* Winser (1893–1974). He had a brother, Josiah, and a sister, Jennifer. He was the grandson of Josiah Clement *Wedgwood, first Baron Wedgwood, and his family tree was linked by marriage to the Darwin family and included Ralph Vaughan Williams, the Keyneses, the Huxleys, and the Trevelyans. His early life was spent in Hampstead Garden Suburb and Staffordshire until he was sent to Abbotsholme School, Derbyshire. During his holidays he and his brother made model soldiers, boated, climbed mountains, built a kayak, and

John Wedgwood (1919–2007), by Lucinda Douglas-Menzies

rebuilt an old Fiat. The only instructions from their parents were 'if in trouble send a telegram—use Latin: it takes fewer words' (private information). In 1938 he went to Trinity College, Cambridge, to read medicine; he completed his studies at Guy's Hospital, London, and qualified in 1943. On 17 July 1943 he married Margaret Webb Mason (*b.* 1920), an assistant almoner, and daughter of Alfred Mason, schoolmaster. They had three sons and two daughters.

In 1944 Wedgwood was commissioned surgeon-lieutenant in the Royal Naval Volunteer Reserve. He served in the Mediterranean and later in the Far East on the minesweeper HMS *Squirrel*, which was mined and sunk off Phuket Island on 24 July 1945. Wedgwood was wounded in his back and right leg and spent several hours in the sea before rescue. These injuries caused increasing discomfort with age and influenced his career direction.

After demobilization Wedgwood completed his Cambridge medical degrees and passed the MRCP examination in 1949. His father wanted him to work in the family's pottery business but he planned to be a surgeon. However, his wartime injuries caused such pain when standing that he decided to be a physician instead. Medical registrar appointments followed and later a senior registrar post at Addenbrooke's Hospital in Cambridge, where he completed his MD. His initial thoughts were to become a cardiologist, and senior registrar posts followed at St Bartholomew's and the National Heart hospitals. However, at Cambridge he had surveyed 200 neglected chronically sick patients in a local workhouse. What he saw influenced his final career decision: he had always wanted to specialize in an untapped field of medicine and geriatric medicine beckoned.

Wedgwood's first consultant post was in 1960 at Bury St Edmunds, where he had no medical, rehabilitation, or secretarial staffs. He was responsible for 243 patients in old, overcrowded infirmaries, one of which still had gas lighting. Bedpans were washed out in the patients' bath and the sister's office doubled as a day room. Eventually he persuaded the authorities to build a new forty-five bed geriatric unit, a day hospital, and a postgraduate medical centre, upgrade his remaining old wards, and close a 180 bed workhouse. Meanwhile he joined the British Geriatrics Society, serving as treasurer (1966–72), chairman of the executive committee (1968–73), and chairman of the editorial board of the society's journal, *Age and Ageing* (1969–86). While treasurer he placed the society on a firm business footing and established it as a registered charity.

In 1968 Wedgwood was appointed consultant geriatrician at the Middlesex Hospital, where he actively promoted the multidisciplinary teaching of geriatric medicine. He was elected FRCP in 1968, was an examiner for the MB and MRCP, and published extensively. His first marriage was dissolved in 1971 and on 20 May 1972 he married Joan Alice (Jo) Tamlyn (*b.* 1927), daughter of Harold Swann Ripsher, shopkeeper, and former wife of Robert J. Tamlyn. He thereby acquired one stepson.

In 1980 Wedgwood moved to the Royal Hospital for Incurables in Putney, as medical director and chairman of the board of management until he retired in 1986. He raised £3.5 million for new facilities, helping to create a centre of excellence with a new brain injury unit, a rehabilitation unit, a day centre, an engineering workshop, improved accommodation for patients, and research offices. He was a member of the council of the Royal Society of Arts (1981–5), a liveryman of the Worshipful Society of Apothecaries of London, and served on several national committees on the disabled. Between 1986 and 2003 he was chairman of the Royal Surgical Aid Society (AgeCare), whose meetings he opened with a prayer. He organized multidisciplinary conferences and teaching, and opened new residential homes. In 1987 he was appointed CBE, and in 1994 he was awarded the British Geriatrics Society's presidential medal.

Wedgwood was proud of his family history and was a non-executive director of the Wedgwood firm from 1967 to 1987. He was kind, gracious, supportive, always willing to give credit to others, and a skilled negotiator. He engendered great loyalty in staff and was affectionately known to many as Dr John. His Christian philosophy strengthened his determination to improve the care of the disadvantaged and older people. For many years he lived at 156 Ashley Gardens, Thirleby Road, Westminster. He died of bronchopneumonia in the Bradbury Centre, Manygate Lane, Shepperton, Surrey, on 30 August 2007. A celebration of his life was held on 29 November 2007 at the church of St Sepulchre-without-Newgate in London. He was survived by his wife, Jo, his stepson, and the five children of his first marriage. MICHAEL JOHN DENHAM

Sources *Daily Telegraph* (1 Sept 2007) · *The Times* (19 Sept 2007); (29 Sept 2007); (2 Oct 2007) · *BMJ*, 335 (2007), 999 · memorial order of service, 29 Nov 2007, priv. coll. · 'Geriatrics as a medical speciality', BL NSA, F3278–9 · British Geriatrics Society archives · Burke, *Peerage* · personal knowledge (2011) · private information (2011) · b. cert. · m. certs. · d. cert.

Archives British Geriatrics Society | SOUND BL NSA, 'Geriatrics as a medical speciality', F3278-9

Likenesses L. Douglas-Menzies, photograph, British Geriatrics Society, London [*see illus.*] · portrait, repro. in memorial order of service, 29 Nov 2007 · portrait, repro. in *Daily Telegraph* · portrait, British Geriatrics Society, London

Wealth at death £22,425: probate, 14 Dec 2007, *CGPLA Eng. & Wales*

Weir, Sir Michael Scott (1925–2006), diplomatist, was born on 28 January 1925 at 16 Howard Crescent, Dunfermline, Fife, the only son and elder child of Archibald Weir (*d.* 1943), a primary school headmaster, and his wife, Agnes Blanche Stewart, *née* Gass (*d.* 1975). He was educated at Dunfermline high school. He left early, despite being dux of the school, to take up a state scholarship at the School of Oriental and African Studies, London University, in 1943, to study Persian. Later in 1943 he joined the Royal Air Force and after further training in Persian and at the officer cadet training unit, he was commissioned in 1944. He served as intelligence officer to squadrons in Wales, Burma, and India, and in 1946 was posted as flight lieutenant to the Combined Intelligence Centre, Iraq, first in Baghdad and later at Habbaniyyah.

After demobilization in 1947 Weir went to Balliol College, Oxford, where he gained a first in classical moderations in 1948 and a second in *literae humaniores* in 1950. In September that year he joined the Foreign Service, and in January 1951 was sent to the Middle East Centre for Arabic Studies, at Shemlan, Lebanon. Early in 1952 he was posted to the Persian Gulf, where Britain exercised by treaty the role of protecting power over a number of Gulf states. After serving as acting political officer in Qatar, where he had a hand in bringing the ruler to abolish slavery, he was moved in the summer of 1952 to Sharjah as acting political agent in the Trucial States. There he was much involved in the frontier disputes with Saudi Arabia, whose occupation in 1952 of the Buraimi oasis, sovereignty over which was divided between Oman and Abu Dhabi, caused a crisis in Saudi relations with Britain. On 30 September 1953 at Culter parish church, Culter, Lanarkshire, he married (Agnes May) Alison Walker, a 27-year-old schoolteacher and daughter of Hugh Stewart Walker, headmaster; they had two sons and two daughters.

In 1954 Weir returned to the Foreign Office in London to serve in the south-east Asia department, and attended the final stages of the Geneva conference on Indochina that year. After appointment in 1956 as consul in San Francisco, he was transferred in 1958 as a first secretary to the British embassy in Washington, DC. In 1961 he was posted to Cairo. He returned to the Foreign Office in 1963 and after promotion to counsellor in 1966 became head of the Arabian department in 1967. The following year he moved to Bahrain as deputy political resident. There he was involved in the arrangements for Britain's withdrawal from the treaty relationships with the Persian Gulf states, the negotiation of the abandonment of Iran's claim to Bahrain, and the creation of the federation of the Trucial States as the United Arab Emirates. He was able to continue a role in this work when in 1971 he was appointed head of chancery in the UK mission to the United Nations in New York, where the issues of the Rhodesian unilateral declaration of independence and the Arab–Israeli problem were also priorities.

Weir returned to London in 1974 as assistant under-secretary in the Foreign and Commonwealth Office in charge of Middle Eastern affairs, with the rank of minister. In 1977 he was again involved briefly in Rhodesian issues as political adviser to the resident commissioner designate, Field Marshal Lord Carver. In 1979 he took up his final diplomatic post, as ambassador to Egypt. He narrowly escaped injury on 6 October 1981 when seated behind President Sadat at the parade at which the president was assassinated. It was a period of greatly improved relations between Britain and Egypt and, making many Egyptian friends, Weir was able to play a significant part in that process. He retired from the diplomatic service in January 1985 on reaching the statutory retirement age of sixty. Meanwhile, his first marriage having ended in divorce in 1973, on 23 October 1976 he married, second, Hilary Beatrice Reid (1945–2008), a colleague in the Foreign Office, and daughter of Allan Robert Reid, shipbroker. They had two sons.

Weir (who was made a CMG in 1974 and knighted KCMG in 1980) was one of the foreign, later diplomatic, service's most experienced Arabists, on whose advice successive ministers came to rely. Of his thirty-five years' service, all but six were passed either in the Middle East or in work directly related to the problems of the area, especially the Arab–Israeli problem, which weighed heavily on him. He was an able diplomat and a sound operator who brought to his work a deep knowledge of history and a gift for establishing relations of friendship and trust with people both in and out of office. This earned him many friends, especially in Egypt and the United States, friendships he maintained into his retirement.

It was perhaps in retirement that Weir's most significant and lasting work was done. In 1990 he became director of the 21st Century Trust, a body devoted to bringing together young people of ability from many countries in seminars on topical issues, founded and largely funded by Sir David Wills. Weir succeeded over a period of sixteen years, ten of them as director, in building up the trust into a thriving institution with a significant reputation. After his death the trustees established in his memory the Michael Weir fellowships, for the support of outstanding younger leaders from the Middle East. He was also president from 1988 until his death of the Egyptian Exploration Society and founding chairman from 1990 to 2006 of the British–Egyptian Society. The latter established an annual lecture in his name. In 2002 he was awarded by the German Federal Republic the order of merit, officer's class, in recognition of his work through the 21st Century Trust in building up co-operation with Germany.

Weir was excellent company, a ready listener and a witty talker, with a relaxed manner and a large fund of anecdotes. He enjoyed travelling, both within the Middle East and elsewhere, and for relaxation enjoyed golf and music. He made light of the ill health that increasingly afflicted him in his final years. He died at his home, 37 Lansdowne Gardens, Lambeth, London, on 22 June 2006, of bronchopneumonia and prostate cancer. He was survived by his wife, Hilary, and his six children. He was buried in the cemetery at Durisdeer, Dumfriesshire, on 7 July 2006. JOHN GRAHAM

Sources M. S. Weir, autobiography to 1982, priv. coll. • *The Independent* (28 June 2006); (7 July 2006) • *The Guardian* (3 July 2006) • *The Times* (17 July 2006) • *Daily Telegraph* (14 Aug 2006) • *WW* (2006) • Burke, *Peerage* • *FO List* • personal knowledge (2010) • private information (2010) • b. cert. • m. certs. • d. cert.

Wealth at death £1,223,213: probate, 10 Oct 2006, *CGPLA Eng. & Wales*

Weir, Thomas [Tom] (**1914–2006**), mountaineer, naturalist, and broadcaster, was born on 29 December 1914 at 310 Springburn Road, Glasgow, the youngest of the four children of Thomas Weir (1887–1916), engine fitter, and his wife, Jeanie (1887–1960), daughter of Alexander Davidson. Tom Weir—he used the diminutive form of his name almost exclusively—was born into a family of railway workers employed in the Springburn locomotive industry. His father, a lance-corporal in the Black Watch, was killed in action in Basrah, Mesopotamia, on 13 March 1916. He and his two surviving siblings, Mary (Molly) *Weir and William, were largely brought up by their widowed maternal grandmother, Jessie Davidson (*née* McCulloch), since Jeanie Weir was obliged to work as a wagon-painter in the locomotive works to support her family.

Weir did not prosper at school, and left in 1929 to work as a grocer's assistant in the Cowlairs Co-operative Society. He soon began to explore the highlands at every opportunity, and fell in with Matt Forrester and Peter Currie, who respectively stimulated his interest in the natural world—especially ornithology—and in writing about his experiences. A pivotal experience was his encounter with Pelmanism. He took a short course in this approach to work and life, and formed a firm resolve to make his living by writing about mountains and the associated natural world, taking as models the naturalist Seton Gordon and the explorer and writer Frank Smythe. He set about putting right the deficiencies of his education, and adding the skills he would need for his intended career. He left his hated grocery job, and took odd jobs instead, leaving him more time to wander in the highlands, and to develop his writing and photography.

The outbreak of the Second World War in 1939 came just at the wrong time for Weir, putting a stop to his plans as he was on the point of executing them. He served in various heavy artillery units, mostly in the defence of the channel coast, and when he was demobilized the surveying skills acquired led to a job with the Ordnance Survey, which suited him well. In the next few years he climbed extensively in Scotland and in the Alps, and completed his first book, *Highland Days* (1948), an account of exploration in the highlands similar to Alastair Borthwick's *Always a Little Further* (1939) and Bill Murray's *Mountaineering in Scotland* (1947). Together these three books brought the hitherto recondite activity of Scottish mountaineering to a wider public. In the same period Weir befriended Douglas Scott. Scott was a keen and able mountaineer and photographer who had spent part of his war service in northern India, allowing some tentative Himalayan exploration. Scott invited Weir to join him in an expedition to the Garhwal Himalaya. Bill Murray and Tom MacKinnon were soon added, and formed the Scottish Himalayan expedition of 1950. The party completed a difficult route on Uja Tirche, and attempted other peaks, but its real success was to traverse a huge area of unknown ground. Both Murray (*The Scottish Himalayan Expedition*, 1951) and Weir (*The Ultimate Mountains*, 1953) published books describing this expedition.

Weir's course as an explorer and mountaineer was now firmly set, and continued through a decade of concentrated activity with expeditions to northern Norway with Scott and Adam Watson in 1951 (*Camps and Climbs in Arctic Norway*, 1953); to the Gauri Sankar group in Nepal with MacKinnon and George Roger in 1952 (*East of Katmandu*, 1955); to the High Atlas with Scott and James Green in 1955; to the Cilo Dag Mountains of Turkish Kurdestan with Scott in 1956; to the Atlas and Anti-Atlas ranges again with Alfred Gregory in 1958; and to Scoresby Land with Iain Smart as part of Sir John Hunt's Greenland expedition in 1960.

During this period Weir and Scott maintained themselves by photography and journalism, sharing a darkroom in Glasgow, at one point with the noted portrait photographer J. Stephens Orr. In 1956 Weir began a series of illustrated pieces, 'My month', in the *Scots Magazine*, which he carried on without gaps well into the 1990s. These were broadened to cover aspects of rural life and work, as well as mountains and the natural world. This formula proved very successful, and led to other magazine work, notably a long series about the work of Scottish conservation organizations published in *Scotland's Magazine* under the pen-name of Ward Clarke. On 22 July 1959 he married Rhona Murray Dickson (*b*. 1920), primary school headteacher and daughter of Donald McIntyre Dickson, master mariner. After a honeymoon spent camping on the island of Foula observing seabirds the Weirs established themselves in the Dunbartonshire village of Gartocharn, where they remained.

In the late 1950s Weir began to work with 16 mm cine film, and to make radio programmes, and this prepared him well for the opportunity that came in the 1970s to make short television programmes, following the formula of his 'My month' pieces, for Scottish Television. These mostly appeared as the long-running series *Weir's Way*, launched in 1976, which turned Weir into a minor celebrity, not only renowned throughout Scotland, but also loved: his easy good manners, unintimidating person, and gentle approach brought out the best in those he interviewed, and he seldom allowed his own opinions to interfere with those of his guests, or to shape them. For this work he received some media awards, and was appointed MBE in 1978. During the same period his sister Molly also achieved success in acting and broadcasting, and published a series of six autobiographical books.

In 1984 Weir became president of the Scottish Mountaineering Club, an honour he valued highly. Throughout the 1980s he continued to write for magazines and also published a number of books dealing with the Scottish countryside. His final major effort as an author was to write *Weir's World: an Autobiography of Sorts* (1994), for which he was honoured by the annual festival of mountain literature at Bretton Hall in Leeds. The subtitle 'of Sorts' acknowledged his adherence to a principle he kept to so far as possible, and better than most non-fiction writers, namely not to repeat material already published. He became president of the Scottish Rights of Way Society in 1996, and served until 2001. He was also honoured with the John Muir Trust's first lifetime achievement award in 2000 for his work in bringing environmental issues to public notice. This award recognized Weir's part in several campaigns to prevent damage to the countryside by unsuitable development, notably the hydro-electric schemes proposed for Glen Nevis in 1960, and for Craigroyston above Loch Lomond in the 1970s. Following the latter campaign the Friends of Loch Lomond were formed in 1978, with Weir as a founding member. He was honorary president of the Friends from 1995 until his death. In the early 2000s his health began to fail, and he spent his last few years in Sunningdale Retirement Home in Balloch. He died there on 6 July 2006 and was buried in Kilmaronock churchyard on 14 July. He was survived by his wife, Rhona.

Tom Weir was not in the first rank as mountaineer, writer, or photographer, but he developed what talents he possessed in these spheres to the fullest possible extent—almost entirely though self-help and self-education—and harnessed them effectively and with the determination enjoined by his early course of Pelmanism. His work combined integrity and accuracy with enthusiasm and passion. Although he was best known for his television work, his greatest achievement was perhaps the extended and comprehensive picture drawn of life and work in the small communities of the Scottish countryside recorded through forty years in his *Scots Magazine* contributions.

ROBIN N. CAMPBELL

Sources *Tom Weir at 70*, interview by Magnus Magnusson for Scottish Television, 1984 · T. Weir, *Weir's world: an autobiography of sorts* (1994) · R. Aitken, laudation for John Muir Trust's lifetime achievement award, 2000, priv. coll. · *Evening Times* [Glasgow] (7 July 2006) · *The Scotsman* (8 July 2006) · *The Herald* [Glasgow] (8 July 2006) · *Daily Record* (8 July 2006) · *Daily Telegraph* (8 July 2006) · *The Times* (10 July 2006) · *The Observer* (16 July 2006) · *Scottish Mountaineering Club Journal*, 39 (2007), 643–6 · NL Scot., Tom Weir papers · personal knowledge (2010) · private information (2010) · b. cert. · m. cert. · d. cert.

Archives NL Scot. | FILM Scottish Screen Archive, Glasgow, *Weir's Way*, Scottish Television · Scottish Screen Archive, Glasgow, interview with Magnus Magnusson, Scottish Television, 1984

Likenesses J. Stephens Orr, photograph, 1956, priv. coll. • K. McFall, oils, 2004, priv. coll. • obituary photographs • photographs, NL Scot., Tom Weir collection • photographs, Scottish Mountaineering Club
Wealth at death £586,273: confirmation, 29 March 2007, *CCI*

Weschke, Karl Martin (1925–2005), artist, was born on 7 June 1925 in Taubenpreskeln, near Gera, Thuringia, Germany, the second of three children, by different fathers, of Else Emma Weschke. He met his father, Heinrich Hermann Hanke (*b.* 1905), only once, in 1936. On his marriage certificates he listed Hanke's occupation as politician or political activist, but in his Buchenwald concentration camp record Hanke was listed as a merchant. Hanke may have died at Buchenwald during the Second World War. He was certainly dead by 1947.

Else, whom Weschke described as a woman of loose morals, abandoned her son to an orphanage in 1927, but reclaimed him in 1932. She enrolled him in the local *Volkschule*, but two years later they moved to Gera, where Else found a job as an ice cream vendor, with Weschke pulling the carts. He spent his spare time drawing the fine buildings. He left school in 1940 and found an apprenticeship with an ornamental blacksmith. However, his mother insisted that he take up a post with a state insurance office, first in Gera, then in Gotha. Bored by this work, and imbued with the spirit of the Third Reich, in 1942 he volunteered for *Arbeitsdienst* (labour service) followed by service, behind the lines, in the Luftwaffe. Then, in 1945, tired of inaction, he volunteered to be a paratrooper and was thrown into the defence of 's-Hertogenbosch, where he was captured by the Canadians and dispatched to Britain as a prisoner of war.

Shunted around the country from camp to camp, by the summer of 1947 Weschke found himself at camp 180 in Radwinter, near Saffron Walden. There he came under the kindly care of Charles Stambrook (formerly Karl Sternberg), a Jewish refugee. Camp 180 was relatively open and prisoners were allowed out two nights a week to study. Weschke enrolled with the Cambridge University extramural board to study 'Wesen der Sprache der Kunst' ('the nature and language of art'), a course presented by Rudolph Wallfried at St John's College. Weschke's mind was opened to a world of European culture and, in particular, his German heritage, of which he had little prior knowledge. Another important contact at Radwinter was the Quaker Bessie Midgley, a member of the Fry family, who held open house to German prisoners and introduced him to Tom Driberg. Weschke was then transferred to Wilton Park where he was re-educated in political matters. In his spare time he was taken by Driberg to see exhibitions in London.

On 12 July 1948, soon after his release, Weschke married Alison Frances de Vere (1927–2001), a student at the Royal Academy, whom he had met through Driberg. He registered for the sculpture course at St Martin's School of Art but abandoned it after one term and took up painting, picking up the craft as he went along. While at St Martin's he met the painter Dorothy Mead, who introduced him to

Karl Martin Weschke (1925–2005), by Derrick Santini, *c.*1995

members of the Borough Group, followers of David Bomberg, with whom he felt a certain affinity. To hone his drawing skills he observed the dance classes of Vera Volkova in Covent Garden and sketched rapidly from life. He also spent many hours looking at the collections of the Tate and National galleries. A trip to Spain in 1953 left a lasting impression.

Although they were to remain lifelong friends, in 1950 Weschke and de Vere parted company. In 1954 he travelled to Sweden with a new partner, Lore Grage, a German national, with whom he fathered his first child, Rachel (*b.* 1955). In Sweden he painted and drew the landscape as a dark brooding presence, influenced not only by the German expressionist heritage with which he had come to identify but by the paintings of Goya and Velázquez. Still classed as an alien, he was helped to return to Britain by de Vere and Driberg. After a brief sojourn in Scotland, in 1955 he moved to Zennor in Cornwall, where he was joined temporarily by Lore. However, without a permit she had to return to Germany, taking Rachel with her. Lore and Weschke agreed that Weschke would have no further contact with his daughter. In 1956 he fathered a second child, Benjamin (Ben), this time with de Vere. They subsequently divorced, in 1958.

Weschke had come to Cornwall with the help of the painter Bryan Wynter. Wynter found him a place to rent, Tregerthen Cottages, where D. H. Lawrence had once resided. Weschke soon became part of the community of artists identified with St Ives, although he always remained on its fringes. He developed close friendships with Roger Hilton and the Scottish poet W. S. Graham, both of whom regarded themselves, like Weschke, as outsiders in Cornwall. At this time his paintings bore some stylistic community with those of the St Ives artists. He painted abstracted landscapes and figure subjects with a thick impasto influenced by the then fashionable Nicolas de Staël, but his palette of colours was significantly different, being sombre and limited in tonal variation. Unlike most of his colleagues he did not confine himself to landscape but tackled major themes relating to religion and history. On the recommendation of Bryan Robertson his *Deposition Triptych* (1958–9) was purchased by the Art Gallery of New South Wales from his exhibition at the Woodstock Gallery.

A second son, Lucas, was born in 1958, to Jan Green. In 1960 Weschke moved to a house on Cape Cornwall, where, with the exception of a few years in Gloucestershire, he spent the rest of his life. It was a one-storey, former tin mine engine house with views over the moors and cliffs and down to the Atlantic Ocean. Remote and subject to the full force of Atlantic storms, it was an appropriate dwelling for a painter of expressive landscapes and figure paintings. Two years later he and Jan split up and, on 24 December 1963, he had a brief marriage to Marie-Liese Norma Cynthia (Liese) Dennis (1939–2005), a fashion model. In spite of his turbulent private life his painting career was beginning to go well, with exhibitions at Matthiessens Gallery and the Grosvenor Gallery and inclusion in a number of important group exhibitions, such as 'British Painting in the Sixties' (1963) at the Tate and Whitechapel art galleries. After separation from Liese (they were divorced in 1968) his relationship with Jan was rekindled and a fourth child, Lore, was born in 1966. Within two years the relationship encountered difficulties and, with his career put on hold, he moved to Gloucestershire, where he began a relationship with Madeleine Frye.

The female nude had by then become a central motif in Weschke's paintings, frequently depicted in distressing situations with mythological overtones. Sometimes the nude was shown molested by a dog modelled on a borzoi, named Dankoff, that Weschke owned. Nearly always the theme was suggested by a common-day event Weschke had witnessed. Vulnerability, violation, and isolation were the themes of his work, painted in his characteristic ochre and earth colours, sometimes punctuated by a claret red or sombre blue. In *Study for the Women of Berlin* (1969–70), painted at the height of the Vietnam war, Weschke brought all these themes together. In 1971 he held a solo exhibition at the Bear Lane Gallery, Oxford, and a further show in Plymouth, Bristol, Leeds, and Glasgow. That same year, with Madeleine, he moved back to Cape Cornwall. Lucas and Lore came to live with them. In 1972 Madeleine bore him a fifth child, Rachel, named after his lost first-born. Within months, however, the relationship foundered and they separated.

Weschke's career seemed to have reached a high point when he was offered a one-man show at the Whitechapel Art Gallery in 1974, but the exhibition was greeted by critical silence, largely, he maintained, on account of hostility towards its new director, Jasia Reichardt, whose appointment had aroused controversy. Apart from inclusion in occasional group exhibitions, for five years his career entered the doldrums. In 1980, however, he was invited to hold a solo exhibition at Kettle's Yard Gallery, Cambridge. Earlier that year the Arts Council had purchased *The Meeting* (1974) and following the Kettle's Yard show the Tate Gallery acquired *Body on the Beach* (1977). Weschke's art, with its sombre palette and undertones of violence, represented his existentialist outlook on life. The landscape was that of the moors viewed from his studio window; the women depicted were, more often than not, his partners. There was also an erotic side to his imagination that emerged in various studies of the female nude, often cloaked in mythology, such as in *Leda and the Swan* (1985–6).

Around this time Weschke began a relationship with Petronilla Spencer-Silver, then working at the Contemporary Art Society, which was to endure for the rest of his life. In 1988 Television South West made a documentary about him, *Memory of Sweetness*. The following year he made drawings for an animated film, *Psyche and Eros* (1994), directed by de Vere. Success now followed success as the Tate Gallery acquired three further paintings and he was shortlisted for the Jerwood painting prize (1995). Sales generated the ability to travel and Weschke went to Egypt in 1990, 1992, and 1997. The trips had a direct impact on his art, not only in his choice of subjects, which now included Egyptian temples, the pyramids, and the Nile landscape, but also in the brightening of his palette, in particular by the introduction of cobalt blue, a colour that earlier in his career he had not been able to afford. Even when painting the familiar nude theme back in a Cornish setting his treatment was marked by the experience of Egypt. There was a new boldness to his vision and a sense of liberation, of having left the oppressiveness of his early life behind. The publication in 1998 of *Karl Weschke: Portrait of a Painter* by Jeremy Lewison, shortly after Weschke underwent a heart bypass operation, provided a further stimulus to his reputation. He became the subject of a German documentary film, *Karl Weschke: Ein deutscher Maler in Cornwall*, and was invited to hold a retrospective exhibition at the Kunstsammlung Gera, his first show in Germany. The broadcast of this documentary on German television led to contact from his first-born child, Rachel, with whom he was ultimately reunited.

Weschke remained a German citizen throughout his life and was finally recognized in his native Germany by the award of the order of merit by the Federal Republic of Germany in 2003. On 12 October the same year he married Petronilla. The enjoyment of such recognition was short-lived, however. In 2004, the year of his retrospective exhibition at Tate St Ives, he was diagnosed with cancer of the brain. He died at St Julia's Hospice, Hayle, on 20 February 2005 and was cremated at Penmount crematorium, Truro, on 28 February. His long-standing friend, David Cornwell (known as John le Carré), paid tribute to him at a celebratory memorial meeting held on 15 March 2005.

JEREMY LEWISON

Sources J. Lewison, *Karl Weschke: portrait of a painter* (1998) • F. Whitford and B. Tufnell, *Karl Weschke, beneath a black sky: paintings and drawings, 1953–2004* (2004) • *Daily Telegraph* (23 Feb 2005) • *The Independent* (23 Feb 2005) • *The Times* (24 Feb 2005) • *The Guardian* (25 Feb 2005) • J. le Carré, 'Karl', *Karl Weschke, 1925–2005* (2005) •

J. Lewison, 'A tribute to Karl Weschke', *Karl Weschke, 1925–2005* (2005) · personal knowledge (2009) · private information (2009) · m. certs. · d. cert.

Archives Tate Britain, Hyman Kreitman Research Centre | FILM Central Office of Information, *UK Today* · 'Karl Weschke', Illuminations, 2004 | SOUND BL NSA, National Life Story Collection, artists' lives, interviews with A. Lambirth, 12 Nov 2000, 25 June 2003, F11432–F11438, F14796–F14797 · BL NSA, documentary recordings · Tate Britain, Hyman Kreitman Research Centre

Likenesses D. Santini, C-type colour print, *c*.1995, NPG [*see illus.*] · obituary photographs · photographs, repro. in Lewison, *Karl Weschke*

Wealth at death £2,506,447: probate, 6 June 2006, *CGPLA Eng. & Wales*

Whale, John Hilary (1931–2008), journalist and newspaper editor, was born on 19 December 1931 at 6 Bevington Road, Oxford, the third child and eldest son of the Revd John Seldon *Whale (1896–1997), Congregational and later United Reformed minister and theologian, and his wife, Mary, *née* Carter (1904–2001). There were two older sisters and two younger brothers. He won a scholarship to Winchester College (where he was confirmed into the Church of England) and, after national service in the intelligence corps, went on an open scholarship to Corpus Christi College, Oxford, to read classics. There he met Judith Laurie (Judy) Hackett (*b*. 1932), an undergraduate at St Hugh's College, when both had roles in a Shakespeare play. He graduated with a second-class degree in *literae humaniores* in 1954.

Whale's first choice of career was the stage, which had attracted him since his schooldays. He appeared in provincial theatres and wrote radio plays with varying success. In 1957 he and Judy married in Minneapolis, Minnesota, USA, where he had taken a teaching post. They soon moved to Paris, where they taught English and worked as translators. In 1959 Whale joined the English-language section of French radio and a year later secured a position as a television reporter and scriptwriter with ITN. In a field where extroverts flourished, his quiet modesty made him a rarity but his stage experience served him well and he was promoted in 1963 to political correspondent on the eve of Labour's revival under Harold Wilson. In 1967 he became ITN's first resident correspondent in Washington.

Growing frustration with television's limitations in handling ideas or events which could not be pictured was explored in Whale's book, *The Half-Shut Eye* (1969), and he was more than ready to try print journalism when in 1969 he was invited by Harold Evans, editor of the *Sunday Times*, to join its political staff. There he worked happily with the lively team assembled by Evans, whom he liked and admired. He reported on British politics, on home affairs in general, and on the Northern Ireland conflict, uncovering the first evidence of the torture of IRA prisoners. While his findings occupied the news columns, the campaigning Evans allowed him to pass judgement in the leader columns on these and other British failings, a dual role with which only the most scrupulous could have been entrusted.

In 1979 Evans accepted Whale's suggestion that a new post of religious affairs correspondent should be created and that he should fill it. A stickler for literacy, Whale also volunteered to spend his Saturdays in weeding grammatical errors from the next day's edition, a huge task. He was appointed assistant editor (concurrently with his post as religious affairs correspondent) in 1981. His devotion to good English yielded a weekly column which later became a book, *Put it in Writing* (1984), which for years remained unmatched as a guide to sound usage. In 1984, unhappy with a new editor, he moved to become head of religious programmes at the BBC. Though he stayed there five years, he was never comfortable managing an often unbiddable staff of fifty.

In 1989 Whale was appointed editor of the weekly Anglican newspaper, the *Church Times*. A devout Anglican—he had been rector's warden in his parish church at Barnes, west London, and written its history, *One Church, One Lord* (1979), to help raise funds for its restoration after a fire—he had long wanted this post. His management skills and his nerve were tested as he presided over a change of premises, a revolution in print technology, and a complete change of design, which his readers did not readily accept. Building on his predecessor's work to broaden the paper's appeal, he strove to expunge the last traces of its partisan Anglo-Catholic origins. He wanted readers, whether of high or low churchmanship, to feel as easy in his columns as they would in the pews of his ideal church. His leading articles were framed both to stimulate and to moderate debate rather than take sides, notably where there was serious division as over the priesting of women. He brought in new writers and, for contributors and staff alike, new and higher standards of literacy. In his six years in the chair, the paper's reputation steadily grew. Its circulation, to his sorrow, did not. He resigned in 1995 when told he had prostate cancer and perhaps three years to live. In the event he had thirteen years of active, happy retirement.

Whale's intelligence—a distinguished Winchester contemporary said he was 'the cleverest man of our year' (private information)—and capacity for work might have brought success in any career. His final post, as editor of the *Church Times*, gave scope to his gifts and reflected his character. His standards were strict but with kindness for those who fell short. Truth was for him the *summum bonum* and he gloried in the English tongue as a vehicle for it. His use of language, written or spoken, marked him in his colleagues' judgement as one of the finest stylists of his day. His work and life were governed by his faith. He once wrote of the model Anglican parson as one in whom 'the chief expression of his love of God will be a love of truth' (*One Church, One Lord*, 167). The pattern of his own life is there displayed. He died at his home, 45 Shakespeare Road, Acton, London, on 17 June 2008, of a brain tumour, and was survived by his wife, Judy, and their only child, Toby.

JULIAN HAVILAND

Sources *The Times* (18 June 2008) · *The Guardian* (18 June 2008) · *Church Times* (20 June 2008) · *The Independent* (20 June 2008) · *WW* (2008) · personal knowledge (2012) · private information (2012) · b. cert. · d. cert.

Archives FILM BFINA, current affairs footage | SOUND BL NSA, documentary recording
Likenesses obituary photographs
Wealth at death £54,088: probate, 29 Aug 2008, *CGPLA Eng. & Wales*

Wharton, Michael Bernard (1913–2006), satirical journalist, was born Michael Bernhard Nathan on 19 April 1913 at 7 Glenhurst Road, Shipley, Yorkshire, the youngest child in the family of two sons and a daughter of Paul Sigismund Nathan, a woollen stuff merchant from a family of German-Jewish origin, and his wife, Bertha, *née* Wharton. As his father's wealth dwindled, his mother's conviction grew that her son should have been heir to Wharton Hall, Westmorland, with its deer park and long gallery, as he recounted in his memoir, *The Missing Will* (1984). This title referred both to a lost testament that might restore his inheritance and to a lack of drive. As a boy he would stare for hours from the window at Nab Wood, where he first experienced the numinous.

From Bradford grammar school Michael Nathan went in 1932 to Lincoln College, Oxford, on a county scholarship. He learnt to drink and, in 'an unremitting war on reality', joined a fellow Bradfordian in a game of their invention, West Riding Knife Throwing. This also entailed catching, and their hands were often bandaged (*The Missing Will*, 45). Another friend said: 'He seemed to look at people as though they were animals at a fair' (ibid., 62). He took a third in classical moderations in 1934 but in the summer of 1936 was sent down for throwing a Scotch egg at high table in hall. He returned to Oxford one morning by permission to take his viva, very drunk. He did not gain a degree. On 17 July 1936, at Bournemouth register office, he married Joan Atkey, the 21-year-old daughter of William Atkey, estate agent. He described himself on the marriage certificate rather grandly as 'author'. At that time he was finishing a novel, 'Sheldrake', featuring Tibetan thought-forms in a Yorkshire mill-town, an adumbration of his journalism. It found a publisher only in 1958.

His marriage was hidden from his parents until a son was born in February 1938, when he changed his surname to Wharton. He and his wife lived in a cottage in the Eden valley, Westmorland, a place he ever after loved, and campaigned to preserve. The rent was 10 shillings a month, and he regularly contributed to *Punch* under the name Simon Crabtree, at £12 for 1000 words. He kept up contributions even while serving in the army during the Second World War. He rose to acting lieutenant-colonel as a staff officer in India. He was demobilized in 1946. Having left his wife and child he lived raffishly after the war, finding work with the BBC (where a report he saw said he was 'not really BBC material'; *Missing Will*, 214). For more than a decade he spent a day a week selecting morning stories for the radio.

On 1 January 1957, having 'passed the night in a drunken phantasmagoria' (*Dubious Codicil*, 3), Wharton began his first permanent job, writing a column in the *Daily Telegraph* that he continued for forty-nine years. At first he assisted Colin Welch, who had begun the column fifteen months earlier, but from 1960 he wrote its 1000 words four days a week single-handed, resisting assistants. Headed 'Way of the world', it was signed Peter Simple. Readers were ignorant of its author, and the vignettes drawn by Michael ffolkes included one of Peter Simple as a tall, moustachio'd figure in a deerstalker. Sir Colin Coote, the editor of the *Daily Telegraph*, was not encouraging. 'Not too many skits please, Wharton', he would say (ibid., 12). His successor Maurice Green occasionally laughed at what he called Wharton's 'notes' (ibid., 167).

Peter Simple's humour was black pessimism tempered by fantasy, influenced not by Beachcomber of the *Daily Express* but by Myles na Gopaleen (Brian O'Nolan) of the *Irish Times*. The columnar characters attracted Homeric epithets, such as Dr Spacely-Trellis, the go-ahead bishop of Bevindon, or Alderman Foodbotham, the 25 stone, crag-visaged, iron-watch-chained perpetual chairman of the Bradford city tramways and fine arts committee. A tutelary hero was Colonel Sibthorp (1783–1855), the reactionary MP who repelled the mainline railway from Lincoln. Wharton sided with such hated groups as Afrikaaners in South Africa and Serbs in the former Yugoslavia.

Wharton was dogged by self-doubt, 'like an evil spirit, blighting life and hope', and haunted by a school report judging him 'passive and lacking in initiative'. Fascinated by his part-Jewish identity, he was aware of a 'persistent dream of literary fame and corresponding inability to live' (*Dubious Codicil*, 72). In the 1960s attacks of unease and dread increased. In 1963, after being declared columnist of the year by Granada Television's *What the Papers Say*, his depression deepened. He spent ten days voluntarily in an asylum, and underwent electro-convulsive treatment, returning to work after five weeks.

Wharton labelled his private life 'a horror comic' (*Dubious Codicil*, 137). His second wife, Catherine Mary (Kate) Derrington (1931–1992; daughter of John George Frederick Derrington, electrical engineer), whom he had married on 19 December 1952, shared his taste for fantasy, and nocturnal drunken charades enacting the French Revolution or the battle of the Somme brought pyjama'd neighbours onto the pavement to dance with rage outside their windows. Despite ties of 'affection and intermittent lust', Wharton disliked Kate's growing dominance (ibid., 254). She had become the lover of Colin Welch, who spent part of his time with his own wife. In 1964 Wharton met Susan Daughne Moller, a schoolteacher thirteen years his junior, and daughter of Nils Henry Moller, barrister. They were to marry on 4 January 1974, but not until 1971, when his daughter with Kate was at university, did Wharton leave the house in Putney where Kate was bringing up two children of Colin Welch. Between marriages, alone in Prince of Wales Drive, Battersea, he invariably ate five fish-fingers for dinner, read into the small hours, and each day caught a combination of buses to Fleet Street, creating the column on the way. He often used the word 'masochism' to characterize his chosen 'life of routine boredom' (ibid., 221).

In his early seventies Wharton seemed an inward man, peering through the upper lenses of his spectacles and making quiet remarks. He ended his column when the

Telegraph moved to the Isle of Dogs in 1987, but was persuaded to resume it for the *Sunday Telegraph* by its editor, Charles Moore, then weekly for the *Daily Telegraph* when Moore took up its editorship in 1995. Meanwhile *The Missing Will* (1984) took his life to 1957; its sequel, *A Dubious Codicil* (1991), painted astonishing comic scenes of drunken Fleet Street life, with a nightly theatre of the absurd in a pub called the Kings and Keys. Critics were struck by the vividness and honesty of these volumes. His last column appeared three days before his death, on 23 January 2006, of pneumonia in Wycombe Hospital. He was survived by his wife, Susan, and his two children.

CHRISTOPHER HOWSE

Sources R. West, 'The funniest writer in England', *The Spectator* (8 Nov 1980) • M. Wharton, *The missing will* (1984) • A. N. Wilson, 'Peter Simple's triumph', *The Spectator* (17 Nov 1984) • M. Wharton, *A dubious codicil* (1991) • *Daily Telegraph* (24 Jan 2006) • *The Times* (25 Jan 2006); (9 Feb 2006) • *The Guardian* (25 Jan 2006) • *The Independent* (26 Jan 2006); (30 Jan 2006) • *WW* (2006) • personal knowledge (2010) • private information (2010) • b. cert. • m. certs. • d. cert.

Archives SOUND BL NSA, documentary recording

Likenesses obituary photographs

Wealth at death under £244,000: probate, 18 May 2006, *CGPLA Eng. & Wales*

Wheeler, Sir Selwyn Charles Cornelius- [*known as* Sir Charles Wheeler] (**1923–2008**), journalist and broadcaster, was born on 26 March 1923 in Rheinbeck, Bremen, Germany, the younger son of Charles Cornelius-Wheeler (1892–1971), shipping company representative, and his wife, Winifred Agnes, *née* Rees (1889–1972). Sent home from Germany, where his father, a former wing commander in the RAF, worked as a shipping agent for a company based in Hamburg, he attended Cranbrook School in Kent, which he left in 1939 with the avowed intention of joining the forces. At sixteen too young to be accepted even as a volunteer, he took a job as a copy-boy with Lord Kemsley's tabloid *Daily Sketch*, where his duties included reviving flagging sub-editors with quarter bottles of whisky brought in from a nearby pub. A wiry, spare figure with a shock of dark hair (later to change to an equally distinctive silver) he, not surprisingly, soon became a welcome presence in the *Daily Sketch* newsroom, where he spent the next eighteen months.

When his elder brother, serving with RAF Coastal Command, was killed in 1940 Wheeler (as he preferred to be known) immediately redoubled his efforts to join up and in 1942 was commissioned into the Royal Marines, where he rose to the rank of captain and was mentioned in dispatches in 1944. He took part in the D-day landings in June of that year and, having fought his way through north-west Europe, was eventually assigned—after the allied victory of May 1945—to Berlin, where his fluent German (a language he had spoken since childhood) made him exceptionally useful for intelligence and interrogation purposes.

Demobilized in 1946 and unable to find a job in newspapers, Wheeler finally settled for a sub-editor's post in the BBC's external services, situated in Bush House in the Aldwych 'where', as he wryly remarked, 'they ignored my facility in German and put me straight into the Spanish-speaking Latin American service' (private information). For eighteen months he wrote news bulletins in English, subsequently to be translated into Spanish, before he was transferred to the general newsroom to help with the coverage of the 1948 Olympic games, held in London. Two years later came his first real break when, at very short notice, he was appointed to replace the German service's resident correspondent in Berlin, who had been invalided home with a bad case of alcoholism. Originally expecting to stay for only three months, Wheeler succeeded in remaining in post for three years—years that witnessed the Berlin uprising of 1953, enabling him not only to make his name as a foreign correspondent but also to win the gratitude and affection of his listeners (a substantial proportion of them based in communist east Berlin).

Sir Selwyn Charles Cornelius-Wheeler (1923–2008), by Jane Bown

Brought back to another desk job in London, Wheeler proceeded to kick his heels in Bush House until in 1956 his friendship with a BBC television executive led him to apply successfully for a producer's post with *Panorama*, then under the guiding hand of Richard Dimbleby. So impressive was his work for *Panorama* behind the camera that within two years he found himself being offered the programme's editorship, which he astonished his colleagues by declining. The truth was that he could not wait to get back into the field. That was never likely to happen through *Panorama*, which at the time had its own full cast of reporters in the shape of such distinguished figures as Malcolm Muggeridge, Woodrow Wyatt, and John Freeman. Wheeler therefore decided on a bold strategy. Abandoning the position he had established for himself in current affairs he took the revolutionary step of applying for a reporter's post with the traditional great rival to current affairs within the BBC, the news division. Once the initial shock had been got over he was swiftly rewarded with the offer of a posting to south Asia, working out of New Delhi. Although he had only just contracted his first marriage—to a 26-year-old fellow *Panorama* producer, Catherine Dove (daughter of Harold Dove, planter) at the Roman Catholic church of Our Lady of the Assumption and St Gregory, Soho, on 31 May 1958—Wheeler did not hesitate: he leapt at the opportunity, even though it meant he had to go to India initially on his own.

Wheeler stayed in New Delhi for four years, though only two or three months of those were to be spent with his first wife, who had meanwhile formed an attachment to John Freeman (whom she married in 1962). The BBC south Asia correspondent's parish extended well beyond India: it was, indeed, in Ceylon that Wheeler provoked an outraged reaction by referring in a broadcast to the country's prime minister as 'an inexperienced eccentric at the head of a cabinet of mediocrities' (it required all of the Macmillan government's finesse to calm down the subsequent Commonwealth row). At the end of his tour, however, no one could doubt the success that he had made of the New Delhi job. Wheeler's style—and his distinctive voice and diction—proved sufficiently memorable for the viewer or listener to have no difficulty in recognizing his handiwork. Justifiably he soon acquired the reputation of being one of the most articulate and literate of BBC broadcasters (shining particularly in the essay format of such a programme as Radio 4's *From Our Own Correspondent*). In New Delhi itself he had become an increasingly well-known figure, marrying in 1962 Dip Singh, the youngest daughter of Haibans Singh, a distinguished Sikh physician and landowner who had fled from west Punjab at the time of partition in 1947.

In its wisdom, however, the BBC decided in 1962 to change its India correspondent and Wheeler found himself sent back to his old stamping-ground of Berlin, though this time for the domestic, rather than the overseas, service. Return stays seldom match the excitement of the original venture and, while his second tour enabled him to cover the cost to the divided city of the Berlin Wall (erected in August 1961) and the response to it delivered by President Kennedy in his visit of June 1963, it was probably with some relief that Wheeler learned in 1965 that his next posting was to be to Washington as joint correspondent with Gerald Priestland, who had been his immediate predecessor in India. Wheeler was to spend eight years in all in Washington, the first four in not always easy double harness with Priestland and the remaining four as very much the solo star of the BBC's North American news output. It helped, of course, that the latter period included Watergate, when Wheeler's tenacious reporting easily outstripped that available anywhere else in the British media. He did not, in fact, see the story through to its dénouement, with President Nixon's resignation in August 1974; but it was at his own request that he left Washington in 1973 to take up a new post as chief European correspondent. This did not prove an entirely fortunate move, the arcane intricacies of the European Community and Brussels, where Wheeler and his wife and family were based, proving too much even for his exceptional explanatory gifts.

Having spurned the chance of climbing up the executive ladder—he had turned down the BBC controller's job in Northern Ireland on his return from Washington—Wheeler was content, once his time in Brussels came to an end in 1976, to leave the BBC's staff and (well short of retirement age) become a freelance. With his wife and two daughters he lived in Sussex, where he soon turned into a passionate gardener. But he was by no means professionally idle. After a hesitant start as a not particularly relaxed presenter for *Panorama* (1977–9), from 1980 to 1995 he presented *Newsnight*, his new freelance status turning into an inspired choice, enabling him to enjoy an Indian summer doing the thing he did best, which was the crafting and writing of programmes. For a sexagenarian, a septuagenarian, and ultimately even an octogenarian, his output was prodigious: he continued making programmes even after leaving *Newsnight*, and his last documentary series was broadcast in 2006. His achievement was recognized not only by his own profession in awarding him virtually every available prize for broadcasters but also by the government in (highly unusually for a journalist) appointing him CMG in 2001 and then in 2006 conferring a knighthood on him. A lifelong cigarette smoker, he died at his home, the Garden Cottage, Broomhall, Warnham, Sussex, of lung cancer on 4 July 2008 after a brief illness. His funeral was held at Worthing crematorium on 14 July 2008 and a service of thanksgiving took place in Westminster Abbey on 20 January 2009. The inaugural lecture accompanying an annual award set up in his honour was given on 20 May 2009 by Mark Thompson, director-general of the BBC, who declared Charles Wheeler to have been 'the finest reporter the BBC ever had' (*British Journalism Review*, Sept 2009, 80). His wife and two daughters survived him.

ANTHONY HOWARD

Sources *The Times* (5 July 2008) · *Daily Telegraph* (5 July 2008) · *The Guardian* (5 July 2008) · *The Independent* (5 July 2008) · *British Journalism Review* (Sept 2009) · *WW* (2008) · personal knowledge (2012) · private information (2012) · m. cert. [1958] · d. cert.

Archives FILM BFINA, 'Charles Wheeler: edge of frame', *Time Shift*, BBC4, 4 March 2004 · BFINA, 'Charles Wheeler: a tribute', BBC2, 22 July 2008 · BFINA, current affairs and documentary footage | SOUND BL NSA, current affairs and documentary recordings

Likenesses I. Kar, vintage bromide prints, 1958 (with Stephen S. Churakov and V. M. Zimenko), NPG · photographs, 1958–89, BBC · R. Barber, archival digital print, 1989, NPG · photographs, 1989–95, PA Photos, London · photographs, 1994–2000, Photoshot, London · S. Pyke, photographs, 2000, Getty Images, London · W. Conran, photograph, 2004, Getty Images, London · photograph, 2007, Rex Features, London · J. Bown, photograph,

Camera Press, London [*see illus.*] · C. Djanogly, photographs, Camera Press, London · obituary photographs

Wealth at death £611,573: probate, 6 Feb 2009, *CGPLA Eng. & Wales*

Whitehead, Phillip (1937–2005), television producer and politician, was born David Stuart Locke on 30 May 1937 at Masson House, Matlock Bath, Derbyshire, the son of (Marguerite) Elaine Clarke Locke, a dentist's daughter, and an unnamed British army officer. He was adopted by a childless couple, distantly related to his mother, on 22 October 1937, becoming thereafter Philip, later Phillip, Whitehead, the son of Harold Whitehead, a carpenter, and his wife, Frances May Whitehead, of Rowsley, Derbyshire.

Whitehead went to Lady Manners Grammar School in Bakewell and won a scholarship to Exeter College, Oxford, where he graduated with second-class honours in philosophy, politics, and economics in 1961; he was president of the Oxford Union in the same year. Surprisingly, considering his later career in Labour politics, he was also an officeholder in the Oxford University Conservative Association. His move towards the Labour Party was related to his friendship with Julia Gaitskell. He was influenced by the moderate, determined socialism of her father, the Labour leader Hugh Gaitskell, whom he got to know at the Gaitskells' home in Frognal Gardens, Hampstead, where he was a frequent visitor. He had an interest in the emergent nations of Africa. Indeed, as secretary of the Conservative Association he had moved an adjournment at the Oxford Union during Harold Macmillan's visit, in protest at the detention of Hastings Banda, and in 1961 he visited Nyasaland at Banda's invitation. After being commissioned into the Sherwood Foresters for his national service, he chose secondment to the Royal West African Frontier Force and spent eighteen months in Gambia training African soldiers.

Whitehead joined the BBC in 1961 as a graduate trainee, quickly becoming a producer. He met his future wife, Christine Hilary Usborne (*b.* 1943), there, where she was working as a production assistant. She was the daughter of Thomas George Usborne, an assistant secretary at the Ministry of Transport. They were married at Paddington register office on 1 April 1967; they had two sons and one daughter. At the BBC Whitehead became a producer on the current affairs flagship *Panorama*. When Jeremy Isaacs was sacked as editor of the series and departed for independent television, he poached the best of his former colleagues from the BBC, including Whitehead, who became editor of Thames Television's current affairs series *This Week* from 1967 to 1970. Under Isaacs Whitehead contributed two films to *The World at War*, which has often been described as the best British television documentary series ever made.

By various clues Whitehead had come to understand his adopted status, but refrained from overt contact with his family of birth for fear of upsetting his adoptive parents. In the 1966 general election while standing (unsuccessfully) for Labour in West Derbyshire he deliberately canvassed the house where he had been born and thus met his grandparents. After his adoptive parents' deaths he felt free to make contact with his natural mother. With typical self-deprecating humour he described the meeting between himself at thirty, bearded and balding, with his plump, blonde mother in her forties: 'We must have looked the same age, an uneasy assignation between troubled lovers' (*Daily Mail*, 19 Oct 1996).

In 1970 Whitehead successfully contested Derby North for Labour, a seat he held until 1983. Always a committed European, he was one of the rebel Labour MPs who voted for entry into the Common Market against his party's instructions in October 1971. He was later described as a 'back-room' man with a 'huge reputation among his colleagues as a heavyweight figure of principle and a highly effective issue politician' (*The Independent*, 3 Jan 2006). He was one of the sponsors of the Children's Bill of 1975, which gave adopted children the right to trace their natural parents. He described it as 'one of the best day's work I ever did as an MP' (*Daily Mail*, 19 Oct 1996). His friend Melvyn Bragg described him on the stump at this time: 'He dresses carelessly but badly, looks like a nineteenth-century Methodist minister … drinks little and takes on everyone' (Bragg, 'Diary of a canvasser', 65). He was not given office when Labour was in power from 1974 to 1979 but in his last three years he served as parliamentary spokesman on higher education and on the arts. It was said that he would have risen higher, but he was one of the 'lost generation' of Labour politicians who were in opposition or out of parliament during the Thatcher years.

After losing the 1983 election Whitehead returned to television, where he continued to work even after he re-entered politics. At the company he co-founded, Brook Associates (later Brook Lapping), he excelled in the production of history series with an emphasis on families, as in *The Windsors* (1994), *The Kennedys* (1993), and *The Dynasty: the Nehru–Gandhi Story* (1997). As a member of the Annan committee on the future of broadcasting from 1974 to 1977 he had had much to do with the creation of Channel 4 as a medium for minority interests. Channel 4 was to become immensely successful, but in the late 1990s it disappointed him. 'What have they done to our channel?' he lamented, regretting the move of Channel 4 to broadcast sensational, popular entertainment in a search for ratings success. He talked with contempt of pitching ideas for serious documentaries to commissioning editors who replied with such comments as, 'we don't want history about dead people' (personal knowledge). He collaborated on several books related to television programmes. The only book he wrote entirely himself, *The Writing on the Wall: Britain in the Seventies* (1985), based on his television history of the same title, gives a good indication of his elegant and witty conversational style. He was invited to give the prestigious MacTaggart lecture at the Edinburgh international television festival in 1987. His subject was 'Power and pluralism in broadcasting'.

Whitehead was chairman of the Fabian Society (1978–9), New Society Ltd (1986), Statesman and Nation Publications Ltd, publishers of the *New Statesman* (1985–90), and the Consumers' Association (1990–94). He was elected to the European Parliament as MEP for Staffordshire East and Derbyshire in 1994, and from 1999 until his death for East Midlands. He made a particular contribution on consumer affairs, and worked for the enlargement of the European Union, having long supported eastern European countries in their desire for self-determination. In recognition of this he was presented with the Polish solidarity medal by Lech Wałęsa in 2005.

Phillip Whitehead lived voraciously and enjoyed a busy life. He always wanted to cram more into a day; this often meant that projects were started, left, and then rushed or abandoned. His lack of punctuality was a television industry legend; colleagues waited until past the point of exasperation and were finally just glad to see him when he turned up. His contributions were often considered worth the delay. Nevertheless the wide range of his interests did not always serve him well: political colleagues seeing him with piles of papers related to television programmes questioned how serious he was about politics, while television colleagues waiting for him to return from interminable political meetings asked the reverse question. He excelled at both politics and television production but, paradoxically, would have achieved more if he had done less. He died suddenly of a heart attack on 31 December 2005 after falling ill in the house in Rowsley, Derbyshire, that had been his home since childhood, and was pronounced dead at the Royal Hospital, Chesterfield. His funeral was held on 13 January 2006 at St Katherine's Church in Rowsley, Derbyshire. He was survived by his wife and their three children. JAD ADAMS

Sources *The Times* (4 Dec 1959); (14 April 1961); (4 Jan 2006); (6 Jan 2006) · M. Bragg, 'Diary of a canvasser', *New Review*, 1/2 (May 1974), 65–74 · *Daily Mail* (19 Oct 1996) · *The Guardian* (2 Jan 2006); (16 Jan 2006) · *Daily Telegraph* (3 Jan 2006) · *The Independent* (3 Jan 2006) · M. Bragg, 'Remembering Phillip', *Fabian Review* (spring 2006) · *WW* (2005) · personal knowledge (2009) · private information (2009) · adoption certificate · b. cert. · m. cert. · d. cert.

Archives U. Warwick, corresp. with Richard Crossman | FILM BFINA, current affairs footage · BFINA, performance footage | SOUND BL NSA, current affairs recordings

Likenesses obituary photographs · photograph, PA Photos, London

Wealth at death £479,193: 10 April 2006, *CGPLA Eng. & Wales*

Whitelaw, James Hunter (1936–2006), engineer, was born on 28 January 1936 at 87 Stewart Crescent, Newmains, near Wishaw, Lanarkshire, the only child of James Whitelaw, a clerk in an ironworks, later an accountant and manager with the National Coal Board, and his wife, Jean Ross, *née* Scott. He was educated at Glasgow high school and Glasgow University, where he followed a sandwich course in mechanical engineering with industrial placements in the UK and Bahrain. Shortly after his return from Bahrain he met Elizabeth (Elspeth) Shields (*b.* 1935), a schoolteacher, and daughter of David Dewar Williamson Shields. They married on 10 July 1959 at Cardonald church, Glasgow, and had three sons, Alan (*b.* 1962), Stuart (*b.* 1964), and Jamie (*b.* 1968).

Following the completion of his undergraduate studies in 1957 and a brief period with Rolls-Royce as a graduate trainee, Whitelaw returned to Glasgow University to pursue doctoral studies on the thermo-physical properties of gases, for which he was awarded his PhD in 1961. He subsequently continued his research as a Fulbright scholar under the supervision of Joseph Kestin at Brown University, Rhode Island, in 1961–3. The guidance provided by Kestin was a lasting influence. Whitelaw returned to the UK in 1963 as a lecturer in the mechanical engineering department of Imperial College, led by Owen Saunders, to work in the thermodynamics and fluid mechanics division headed by Brian Spalding. The focus of the group's activities was on the development and application of 'universal' calculation methods for turbulent flows. The advent of such computational methods required experimental confirmation, and Whitelaw's groundbreaking research resulted in the development and application of non-intrusive laser-based instrumentation for flow characterization.

The early helium-neon lasers were highly unstable in operation, and difficulties in aligning the different optical components made progress slow. A key development, pursued jointly by Whitelaw and his research assistant, Franz Durst, resulted in a compact integrated system that formed the basis for subsequent commercial instruments. Further contributions were made in the area of counter-type processors and in the treatment of data through time-averaging. Together with Adrian Melling, Whitelaw and Durst wrote the first, highly influential book on the subject of laser Doppler anemometry (a technique for measuring the direction and speed of fluids). The experimental techniques developed under Whitelaw's charismatic leadership found wide application, for example in the study of the dynamics of combustion processes in furnaces and engines. Whitelaw's main research goal was to reveal the nature of aerodynamic and thermo-physical processes rather than simply to develop instrumentation. His research covered fundamental topics, like the anisotropy of turbulent stresses and the extinction/re-ignition of turbulent flames, as well as practical devices, including complex industrial burners, automotive engines, and gas turbines. Further developments followed, such as the phase-Doppler anemometer (PDA) for spray research and the shadow-Doppler anemometer for irregular particles, the latter in collaboration with colleagues at Keio University in Japan. During thirty-six years at Imperial Whitelaw published over 300 research papers and successfully supervised eighty-six PhD students. In addition, with colleagues from around the world, he organized a series of symposia on the application of laser-based methods to fluid mechanics at the Gulbenkian Institute in Lisbon. With Wolfgang Merzkirch he launched the archival journal *Experiments in Fluids* in 1981, and served as editor from 1983 to 1999.

Whitelaw advanced rapidly at Imperial College, becoming reader in 1969 and professor of convective heat transfer in 1974. He held the position of deputy head of department and was head of the thermofluids section for twenty-five years. He also developed close links with colleagues at overseas institutions and held visiting professorships at the universities of Arizona, California at Berkeley, and Minnesota, and at Hong Kong Polytechnic

University. He received honorary degrees from the Technical University of Lisbon (1980), the Polytechnic University of Valencia (1996), Trinity College, Dublin (1999), and the National Technical University of Athens (2001). He was elected a fellow of the Royal Academy of Engineering (1991), a fellow of the Royal Society (1996), a fellow of the City and Guilds Institute (1998), and a foreign associate of the US National Academy of Engineering (2000).

Whitelaw's enthusiasm for life and research was evident to the very end of his typically determined and dignified battle against the advance of motor neurone disease, during which he was fully supported by his wife, Elspeth, and their three sons. He died on 16 August 2006 at his home in Kingston upon Thames, Surrey.

PETER LINDSTEDT

Sources *The Times* (28 Sept 2006) · *International Journal of Heat and Fluid Flow*, 27 (2006), 978–9 · *Memoirs FRS*, 53 (2007), 385–99 · personal knowledge (2010) · private information (2010) · b. cert. · m. cert. · d. cert.

Likenesses photograph, repro. in *Memoirs FRS* · photograph, repro. in *International Journal of Heat and Fluid Flow*

Wealth at death £155,963: probate, 8 Nov 2006, *CGPLA Eng. & Wales*

Whiteside, Derek Thomas [Tom] (**1932–2008**), historian of mathematics, was born on 23 July 1932 at the Corporation Maternity Home, Devonshire Road, Blackpool, the second son of Ernest Whiteside, photographer, and his wife, Edith, *née* Watts (1899/1900–1937). The family lived in Blacow Street, Blackpool, a slum street that was later demolished. Whiteside's mother died at the age of thirty-seven when he was five years old. He and his brother were brought up by their father, who had been disabled by poison gas injuries suffered during the First World War. A childhood accident with a bus left Whiteside himself prone to increasingly severe epilepsy in later life.

From 1943 to 1950 Whiteside was educated at Blackpool grammar school. In the sixth form he studied languages but also displayed a precocious interest in mathematics. He went on to read French and Latin at Bristol University, and graduated with first-class honours in 1954. After two years of national service with the 5th Royal Tank Regiment in Libya he entered Cambridge University in 1956 as a graduate student. His PhD thesis, 'Patterns of mathematical thought in the later seventeenth century', was published in 1961 as the first issue of the newly established *Archive for History of the Exact Sciences*.

In the course of his research Whiteside worked his way through practically the entire corpus of seventeenth-century mathematical literature. In 1958 he began to examine the Portsmouth collection of Newton's manuscripts in Cambridge University Library; from 1959 to 1961 a Leverhulme fellowship enabled him to continue working on them. The story he himself liked to tell was that in 1960 he dropped in to Cambridge University Press to offer them an edition of Newton's mathematical papers. The offer was verbally accepted and thus began the many years of intensive work that eventually resulted in the eight volumes of *The Mathematical Papers of Isaac Newton* (1967–81).

For two years (1961–3) Whiteside was supported by a research fellowship from the Department of Scientific and Industrial Research. During this period, on 28 December 1962, he married Ruth Isabel Robinson (1940–1997), from Blackpool, daughter of Harold Robinson, market gardener. Their children, Simon and Philippa, were born in 1967 and 1970 respectively. From 1963 until his retirement in 1999 Whiteside was employed by the University of Cambridge. He was a research assistant (1963–72) and then director of research (1972–6) at the Whipple Science Museum. He was made a university reader in the history of mathematics in 1976, and university professor of the history of mathematics and the exact sciences in 1987.

In the early years of editing Newton's papers Whiteside (who published as D. T. Whiteside, but was known as Tom) had some assistance from Michael Hoskin, one of his PhD supervisors, and later from his great friend Adolf Prag, but otherwise he accomplished the prodigious task single-handed. He was proud that the completed volumes were so often referred to as 'Whiteside's papers'. Besides transcripts and translations of Newton's mathematical manuscripts the volumes contained lengthy introductory essays offering detailed insight into Newton's intellectual development. Before Whiteside began his work scholars understood very little of Newton's private mathematical world. Whiteside's extensive knowledge of seventeenth-century mathematical literature enabled him to set Newton's work into historical context, while his profound understanding of Newton's approach enabled him to interpret many difficult and often obscure calculations. The portrait that emerged of Newton as a mathematician underpinned all subsequent research in the field.

Various honours came in the wake of the Newton volumes: the médaille Alexandre Koyré of the Académie Internationale d'Histoire des Sciences in 1968; fellowship of the British Academy in 1975; the Sarton medal of the American History of Science Society in 1977; the Euler medal of the Soviet Union's Academy of Sciences in 1985; and an honorary degree of DLitt from the University of Lancaster in 1987.

For much of his career Whiteside was a solitary scholar. He never held a teaching position and had no research student. Nevertheless, he was enormously generous to those he regarded as serious researchers. To his friends he sent long handwritten letters, full of invaluable information and Whitesidean idiosyncrasies, greatly treasured by many of the recipients.

Whiteside completed his work on Newton while he was still in his intellectual prime. He afterwards turned his attention to the papers of Kepler and of the English mathematician Thomas Harriot, but failed to find in them the inspiration he had found in Newton and published very little on these or other historical topics. For the last few years of his life he was housebound by ill health and lived alone, his wife, Ruth, having died in 1997. He occupied himself for some of this time with a history of Blackpool grammar school, to which he felt himself so greatly indebted. He died at West Oak care home, Murray Road,

Wokingham, near his daughter's home, on 22 April 2008, from complications of epilepsy. Proud of his humble beginnings he asked for his ashes to be scattered in Blackpool. He was survived by his two children.

JACQUELINE STEDALL

Sources *Blackpool Gazette* (1 May 2008) · *The Independent* (3 May 2008) · *The Guardian* (5 May 2008) · *The Times* (7 May 2008) · *Regeneration and Renewal* (16 May 2008) · *BSHM Bulletin*, 23 (2008), 189–92 · *Historia Mathematica*, 36 (2009), 4–9 · *WW* (2008) · personal knowledge (2012) · private information (2012) [Philippa Whiteside Tomkins, daughter; N. Guicciardini] · b. cert. · m. cert. · d. cert.
Archives priv. coll.
Likenesses obituary photographs
Wealth at death £143,825: probate, 7 Nov 2008, *CGPLA Eng. & Wales*

Whyte, James Aitken (1920–2005), Church of Scotland minister, was born at 15 Pitt Street, Leith, on 28 January 1920, the second son of Andrew Whyte, produce broker, and his wife, Barbara Janet Pittillo, *née* Aitken. He was educated at Daniel Stewart's College, Edinburgh, and Edinburgh University, gaining first-class honours in philosophy in 1942. On 4 July the same year, at Greyfriars Church, Edinburgh, he married Elisabeth Wilson Mill (*d.* 1988), a 21-year-old schoolteacher, and daughter of George Scott Mill, Church of Scotland minister and missionary in India. They had two sons and one daughter. Whyte remained at Edinburgh to train for ministry in the Church of Scotland, and was ordained in 1945. He served as a chaplain to the forces until in 1948 he was called to be minister of Dunollie Road Church in Oban, where he served until 1954. From 1954 to 1958 he was minister of Mayfield North Church in Edinburgh. He was then, until his retirement in 1987, professor of practical theology and Christian ethics at the University of St Andrews, where he also served terms as dean of the faculty of divinity (1968–72) and principal of St Mary's College (1978–82). He served on many church committees, and in 1988–9 he was moderator of the general assembly of the Church of Scotland.

As an academic Whyte built up a reputation as a dynamic teacher who was passionately committed to the Scottish tradition that the university is the proper place to educate and form ministers. He published little, even in the area of his most serious theological inquiry—the design and ordering of church buildings according to the Reformed tradition. He published two books of sermons, *Laughter and Tears: Thoughts on Faith in Face of Suffering* (1993) and *The Dream and the Grace: Sermons on Healthy and Unhealthy Religion* (2001). In the former was printed the remarkable sermon he delivered in 1989 at the memorial service for the victims of the Lockerbie air disaster the previous year. Whyte was himself grieving the recent death of his first wife, Elisabeth, and was able to grapple honestly and effectively with the grief and pain and anger that those involved, and many others as well, suffered. Addressing those who sought vengeance, Whyte declared, 'Justice yes, retaliation no. For if we move in the way of retaliation we move right outside of the fellowship of Christ's sufferings, outside of the divine consolation. There is nothing that way but bitterness and the destruction of our own humanity' (p. 94). These words reverberated around the world, and may have helped to inhibit hasty armed reactions. Among the memorable sermons in Whyte's second volume was that preached at the memorial service for the sixteen pupils and their teacher who were killed by Thomas Hamilton in their primary school in Dunblane in 1996.

As moderator Whyte presided over the general assembly when the prime minister, Margaret Thatcher, addressed the assembly, claiming rather stridently that the policies of her government were based on Christian truths. She was received politely but suspiciously by the assembly, and at the end of her address the moderator distanced himself, and by implication, the church, from her message by giving her two books produced in the Scottish church—a study of housing especially for poor people, and a study of the Christian principles that should inform the distribution of wealth, income, and benefits in a decent society.

In an earlier general assembly, in 1984, Whyte had also played a major role. Two men who had been in prison for serious offences, embezzlement and murder, had felt a call to the ministry in the Church of Scotland, and now asked the church to test their call. This, understandably, aroused a great deal of controversy in the church, and the matter was taken to the assembly, where a vigorous debate ensued. The opponents of allowing the two men to be ordained claimed that if this were done the moral standing and the respectability of the whole church would be undermined. The debate seemed to be going strongly in the direction of denying the possibility of ordination to the two petitioners when Whyte rose and in a remarkable and moving speech declared that the real issue was whether the church really believed in the forgiveness of sins. This speech swung the assembly, and the two men were allowed to proceed to ordination. An Edinburgh prison chaplain reported that a few days after this assembly decision a prisoner who was an elder of the kirk came to him in tears and said that his wife had visited him and told him that last Sunday she had gone to church for the first time since his conviction because, she said, 'I now realise that the Church believes in the forgiveness of sins' (private information).

James Whyte was the very epitome of the practical theologian, deeply involved simultaneously in the work of the church and the academy, and covering in his lectures a wide field of pastoral care and counselling, and a range of ethical topics, as well as liturgy and homiletics. In his theology and his practice he was strongly Presbyterian, and although he devoted much energy to inter-church issues, he became increasingly suspicious of the ecumenical movement, and in particular of any proposals for reconciliation or unity with Episcopalians. He was made an honorary LLD of Dundee University in 1981, an honorary DD of St Andrews in 1989, and an honorary DUniv of Stirling in 1994. On 26 June 1993, at St Leonard's Chapel, St Andrews, he married his second wife, Ishbel Christina Rathie, *née*

Macaulay (*b.* 1925), a former schoolteacher, widow of William Rathie, and daughter of Alexander Macaulay, schoolteacher. He died at his home, 13 Hope Street, St Andrews, on 17 June 2005, of cancer, and was survived by his wife and the three children of his first marriage.

DUNCAN B. FORRESTER

Sources *The Times* (21 June 2005); (12 July 2005) · *The Herald* [Glasgow] (22 June 2005); (24 June 2005) · *The Guardian* (28 July 2005) · *WW* (2005) · James A. Whyte papers, New College, University of Edinburgh · personal knowledge (2009) · private information (2009) [Ishbel Whyte, widow] · b. cert. · m. certs. · d. cert.
Archives University of Edinburgh, New College
Likenesses photograph, 1988, The Scotsman · obituary photographs
Wealth at death £549,673.37: confirmation, 14 Dec 2005, *CCI*

Wiles, Maurice Frank (1923–2005), theologian, was born at 24 Dingwall Gardens, Golders Green, Middlesex, on 17 October 1923, the third and youngest son of Sir Harold Herbert Wiles (1892–1965), civil servant, and his wife, Stella, daughter of the Revd J. H. Wilkinson of West Grinstead, Wiltshire. His father served as deputy secretary at the Ministry of Labour and National Service from 1946 to 1955, and was knighted KBE in 1947. Wiles was educated at Tonbridge School, then gained an open scholarship to Christ's College, Cambridge, to read classics. At school he had participated in the evangelical children's special service camps and the varsities and public schools camps at Iwerne Minster in Dorset. In 1942 he was called up, learning Japanese, and working on military codes at Bletchley Park. He went to Christ's in 1945, changing to read philosophy, despite a conversation with the evangelical leader John Stott, who tried to get him to change his mind. He gained a second-class degree in moral sciences and a first in theology. At Christ's he came under the influence of the chaplain, Ian Ramsey, later bishop of Durham, who had sought to combine theology and linguistic philosophy, and he slowly moved away from his initial enthusiastic conservative evangelicalism. A long-standing friendship with C. F. D. (Charlie) Moule showed him that evangelicalism could be combined with a critical approach to the tradition. Nevertheless he remained thoroughly orthodox, moving to the evangelical theological college, Ridley Hall, in Cambridge to prepare for ordination in the Church of England. He was ordained deacon in 1950, and served a curacy at St George's, Stockport, under Wilfrid Garlick, a well-known broadcaster. On 1 April the same year he married, at All Saints' Church, Lindfield, Sussex, Patricia Margaret (Paddy) Mowll, the 22-year-old daughter of Robert James Mowll, schoolmaster. They had two sons and one daughter.

After his curacy Wiles commenced his academic career as chaplain at Ridley Hall from 1952 to 1955. In preparation for a Cambridge prize essay he began his detailed studies of Origen and other patristic thinkers, which led to two important monographs on early Christian hermeneutics, *The Spiritual Gospel: the Interpretation of the Fourth Gospel in the Early Church* (1960) and *The Divine Apostle: the Interpretation of St Paul's Epistles in the Early Church* (1967). After a period as lecturer in New Testament studies at the University College of Ibadan in Nigeria (1955–9), he was appointed dean of Clare College and university lecturer in divinity at Cambridge, succeeding Henry Chadwick, another long-standing friend. Still regarded as wholly orthodox, he was appointed by Geoffrey Fisher, archbishop of Canterbury, as an examining chaplain, a role he continued under Michael Ramsey. At Cambridge he published his first general work and highly regarded textbook, *The Christian Fathers* (1966).

Wiles was an ardent enthusiast for cricket, regularly playing for the Oxford diocese as well as the village of Stonor. It was perhaps a sense of fair play, combined with a liberal protestant approach to study, that meant that he was able to approach early Christianity in a way which refused to use the labels of orthodoxy and heresy. By the mid-1960s he was beginning to recognize that serious study of the early church 'had turned out to pose much more serious questions to the traditional understanding of the faith than I had previously realised' (*Scholarship and Faith*, 145). As early as 1962 he had published an article entitled 'In defence of Arius', and the following year a highly critical discussion of Cyprian (a saint with many Anglican adherents). He developed a keen interest in the relevance of early Christian doctrine to the post-Enlightenment world, publishing what was probably his most widely read book, *The Making of Christian Doctrine*, in 1967. In this he sought to explain patristic theology in its own terms rather than in the light of later tradition: 'We ought not … to begin with any preconceived theory concerning the pattern of doctrinal development. We can only proceed by a patient study of the historical evidence' (p. 15). In the same year he became professor of Christian doctrine at King's College, London. His inaugural lecture, 'Looking into the sun', and other writings including 'Does Christology rest on a mistake?', both of which were republished in *Working Papers in Doctrine* (1976), typified his approach to doctrine, which sought to test commonly held traditions.

In 1970 Wiles was appointed by the crown as regius professor of divinity and canon of Christ Church, Oxford, where again he was able to combine ecclesiastical, pastoral, and preaching duties with the life of an academic. He did not appear hampered by his church position and continued to explore the boundaries of theology, publishing his Hulsean lectures, *The Remaking of Christian Doctrine*, in 1974, which noted the 'continually changing' (p. 2) character of doctrine and its restatement in terms acceptable to the modern world. He was appointed as chairman of the Church of England doctrine commission, which produced its controversial report, *Christian Believing*, in 1976; this was, he noted, 'not an easy report to write' (p. xi) since its contributors could not reach complete consensus. Afterwards Donald Coggan, archbishop of Canterbury, reorganized the commission, removing Wiles as chairman. The following year he was embroiled in the controversy over *The Myth of God Incarnate* (edited by John Hick), to which he had contributed an essay calling for the metaphorical reinterpretation of ancient sources. He remained a loyal churchman, who understood the Christian life as 'commitment to the struggle to interpret and to live by the confused images that we are enabled to glimpse with the help of what our predecessors have seen' ('Worship and theology', in D. W. Hardy and P. H. Sedgewick, eds., *The Weight of Glory*, 1991, 77). His introductory lectures became the basis for his widely read textbook, *What is Theology?* (1976).

Wiles was elected a fellow of the British Academy in 1981, and shortly afterwards produced a small and personal book, *Faith and the Mystery of God* (1982), which won the Collins religious book award, and which saw mystery as a warning 'against the speciously attractive answers that could dissolve it' and as a way of encouraging 'us to continue with the looking, for we can never tell whether we have reached the limits of human understanding' (p. 129). More philosophical themes were approached in his Bampton lectures at Oxford in 1986, which were published the same year as *God's Action in the World*, and which again questioned the established orthodoxy. He was widely in demand as a lecturer, and among others gave the Kellogg lectures at the Episcopal Divinity School in Cambridge, Massachusetts, in 1977, which provided the basis for much of his collection *Explorations in Theology 4* (1979). The breadth of his interests was shown in his judicious Ferguson lectures delivered at Manchester University and published as *Christian Theology and Inter-Religious Dialogue* (1992). For much of his time in Oxford he also held the chair of the Oxford patristic conference, and helped to edit a number of its collections.

After retirement in 1991 Wiles continued to edit the *Journal of Theological Studies*, which he had taken over in 1985, until its centenary in 1999, and was keen to promote the work of younger and less-established scholars. For his seventieth birthday in 1993 he was presented with an affectionately critical Festschrift (*The Making and Remaking of Christian Doctrine*, edited by Sarah Coakley and David Pailin). In an active retirement he continued his research into the history of doctrine, publishing a scholarly account of the development of Arianism into modern times in *Archetypal Heresy: Arianism through the Centuries* (1996), which was inspired by William Whiston, a predecessor at Clare who was dismissed for maintaining the 'Arian heresy' in the eighteenth century. This book adopted Wiles's customary approach to the study of history which sought to 'free us from the restrictive shackles that that history is liable to impose upon us' (p. 186). Three years later, at the suggestion of his wife, he published a popular work of apologetics, *Reason to Believe*. His final book, *Scholarship and Faith: a Tale of Two Grandfathers* (2003), was a fascinating account of his two clergyman grandfathers, one a Strict and Particular Baptist, and the other an Anglican, which traced the conflicts between academic study and the Christian faith. It also contained a brief autobiographical chapter.

Although he was a naturally shy and private man most at home among his talented family, Wiles was also a gifted teacher and lecturer, as well as a respected and careful supervisor. He was immensely courteous, open-minded, and generous to people of all opinions, and had an unusual diffidence and humility. His theology was often developed in dialogue with friends, which was exemplified by a collection of articles mainly from Festschriften: *A Shared Search: Doing Theology in Conversation with One's Friends* (1994). His life work was perhaps best summarized at the end of *Reason to Believe*: the 'faith by which a Christian lives is fully compatible with a continuing search to understand better what the content of that faith should be' (p. 119). In his final years he suffered from prostate cancer, from which he died at his home, 11 Bay Tree Close, Iffley, Oxford, on 3 June 2005. He was survived by his wife, Paddy, and their three children. His son Sir Andrew John Wiles (*b.* 1953), mathematician, was best known for proving Fermat's last theorem. MARK D. CHAPMAN

Sources S. Coakley and D. Pailin, eds., *The making and remaking of Christian doctrine* (1993) · M. Wiles, *Scholarship and faith: a tale of two grandfathers* (2003), 137–54 · *The Times* (7 June 2005) · *Daily Telegraph* (7 June 2005) · *The Guardian* (10 June 2005) · *The Independent* (11 June 2005) · *WW* (2005) · personal knowledge (2009) · private information (2009) · b. cert. · m. cert. · d. cert.

Likenesses A. Newman, group portrait, bromide print, 1978 (*Regius professors*), NPG · obituary photographs

Wealth at death under £100,000: probate, 15 Sept 2005, *CGPLA Eng. & Wales*

Wilford, Sir (Kenneth) Michael (1922–2006), diplomatist, was born on 31 January 1922 in Wellington, New Zealand, the son of George McLean Wilford (*d.* 1965), an engineer who worked for BP, and his wife, Dorothy Veronica, *née* Wilson (*d.* 1945). His grandfather was Sir Thomas Mason Wilford, a barrister who served as New Zealand high commissioner in London from 1929 to 1933. Wilford went as a child in 1925 to Shanghai with his parents. After they separated he was sent to stay with his maternal grandmother in Dublin, where he attended Castle Park preparatory school; he later went to Wrekin College in Shropshire. He did well both in class and in sport. He became a keen cricketer and developed a passion for golf that he retained almost until his death. He went to Pembroke College, Cambridge, where he read mechanical sciences and played golf and cricket for the university.

When he was called up in 1940 Wilford joined the Royal Engineers. As a captain in 82nd assault squadron, part of the Guards' 79th armoured division, he took part in the landing in Normandy. He was wounded by a mortar bomb and evacuated for hospital treatment. He recovered from his wounds and returned to active service in August 1944. He took part in November 1944 in the landings on the Dutch island of Walcheren, where he was again wounded, this time more seriously, and was mentioned in dispatches. On 12 April 1944 he had married Joan Mary Law, the 25-year-old daughter of Captain Edward France Bold Law, naval officer. They had three daughters.

From March 1945 to October 1946 Wilford was an instructor at the School of Military Engineering while completing his degree in mechanical sciences at Cambridge. In 1947 he was accepted for the Foreign Service. His first posting, in 1947, was to the allied control commission in Berlin. From 1949 to 1952 he served in the private offices of the successive foreign secretaries Ernest Bevin, Herbert Morrison, and Anthony Eden. This gave him valuable experience in dealing with his political masters. In

1952 he was transferred to the embassy in Paris, where he worked under the ambassadors Sir Oliver Harvey and Sir Gladwyn Jebb. In 1955 he was posted to the commissioner general's office in Singapore, where he developed his interest in Far Eastern affairs. He returned to London in 1959 as assistant private secretary to Selwyn Lloyd, then foreign secretary, later becoming private secretary to Edward Heath, the lord privy seal, who was responsible for negotiating British entry to the European Common Market. He accompanied Lord Lansdowne to the Congo in 1961, where the United Nations secretary-general Dag Hammarskjöld was attempting to broker peace. Lansdowne and he escaped death in the crash that killed the secretary-general, as they had had to withdraw from the flight to send an urgent telegram to London.

In 1962 Wilford was posted to Rabat in Morocco. Two years later he was appointed counsellor in Peking (Beijing) at the outset of the cultural revolution. This posting was followed by a break in 1966–7 as a visiting fellow at All Souls College, Oxford. In 1967, after a short spell as political adviser to the governor of Hong Kong, he was transferred as counsellor in the British embassy in Washington, with particular responsibility for liaison with the Americans on Asian affairs at the height of the Vietnam War. This was followed by a stint in London first as assistant under-secretary and then as deputy under-secretary supervising relations with half the world including the Far East and south-east Asia. This led to his appointment as British ambassador to Japan where he served from 1975 until his retirement in 1980.

Wilford was almost unique in the diplomatic service in having a degree in mechanical sciences. This helped him to understand the needs of industry, for whose interests he worked hard as ambassador to Japan. He was an outstanding golfer, if sometimes irascible towards less able players. He believed that golf gave him a special advantage in Japan, where it is so widely played by politicians and businessmen. He was rightly proud of being asked to play an occasional game with Japanese ministers including Prime Minister Ohira, and with the presidents of leading Japanese companies. As ambassador in Tokyo, without previous experience of the country and with no knowledge of Japanese, his task was not an easy one, but he had in Sydney Giffard, as his minister and deputy, a Japanese expert, and he knew when to take advice. He was appointed KCMG in 1976 and GCMG in 1980. He had hoped to succeed Sir Murray Maclehose as governor of Hong Kong, but this was not to be.

After his retirement Wilford worked for various companies, including Lloyds Bank and Barings. He also played an active role in the Japan Association in London, of which he was honorary president, and in the UK–Japan 2000 Group, for which he acted as honorary treasurer. He was chairman of the council of the Royal Society of Asian Affairs and patron of the Japan Animal Welfare Society.

Michael Wilford was a man of integrity with a clear head and sharp mind. He worked and played hard. He did not suffer fools easily but his staff knew where they stood with him. His military training may at times have made him seem imperious and his short fuse could be intimidating, but he liked people and could be charming. He continued to play golf until his final years. He was a devoted husband to his wife, Joan, whom he nursed through illness towards the end of their lives. They celebrated their diamond wedding anniversary in 2004. After his retirement from the diplomatic service they lived at Brook Cottage, Cattle Lane, Abbotts Ann, Andover, Hampshire. He died there of prostate cancer on 28 June 2006; his wife died shortly after. They were survived by their three daughters. HUGH CORTAZZI

Sources *The Guardian* (18 July 2006) · *The Times* (25 July 2006); (1 Aug 2006) · Burke, *Peerage* · *WW* (2006) · personal knowledge (2010) · private information (2010) · m. cert. · d. cert.

Likenesses photographs, 1975, Photoshot, London · obituary photographs

Wealth at death £399,590: probate, 5 Sept 2006, *CGPLA Eng. & Wales*

Willett, Frank (1925–2006), museum director, archaeologist, and art historian, was born on 18 August 1925 at 60 Clarendon Street, Bolton, Lancashire, the only child of Thomas Willett (*d.* 1965), car salesman and later printer, and his wife, Frances, *née* Latham. He was educated at Bolton municipal secondary school, but his university education was delayed by the Second World War. He was called up in 1943 for military service in the Royal Air Force and trained as a translator in Japanese. Following his discharge on medical grounds in 1944, he took up his place at University College, Oxford, where he read English and became an active member of the archaeology society. He gained further archaeological experience at the Musée de l'Homme, Paris, in 1948, while studying for a diploma in anthropology at Oxford. He met his wife, Mary Constance (Connie) Hewitt (*b.* 1925), daughter of Charles Hewitt, leather worker, when they were both at school in Bolton, and they married in Bolton on 24 July 1950, by which time she was working as a schoolteacher. She introduced him to the Roman Catholic church, and his faith was a significant factor in his life, as was his commitment to her and to their children, a son, Steven, and three daughters, Margaret Mary, Pauline, and Jean.

Initially employed by Portsmouth City Museum in 1950, Willett moved in the same year to the Manchester Museum as keeper of the department of ethnology and general archaeology. The collections he curated there were wide-ranging and covered subjects as diverse as Maori woodcarving and Romano-British remains. In 1956, encouraged by William Fagg, curator of the African collections at the British Museum, and his brother Bernard Fagg, Nigerian government archaeologist, Willett made his first visit to Nigeria to take up a six-month excavation contract, returning a year later to conduct a rescue dig at the city of Ife. The remarkable finds of lifelike brass and ceramic sculptures inspired in Willett a fascination with Ife art, and in 1958 he moved his family to Nigeria and took up the position of archaeologist with the department of antiquities, with responsibility also for Ife Museum.

The educational needs of their children led the Willetts

to return to Britain in 1963, and in the following year Willett was offered a research fellowship at Nuffield College, Oxford. Three years later he took up the new chair in African art and archaeology at Northwestern University, Evanston, Illinois, and over the next decade inspired a generation of students in the study of African art. His own research saw fruition in the publication of *Ife in the History of West African Sculpture* (1967), which covered all known Ife sculptures and the evidence for their historical context. His ability to convey his knowledge in a clear and engaging manner was demonstrated with an enduringly popular book for the general reader, *African Art: an Introduction* (1971), which went through three editions by 2002.

In 1976 Willett returned to Britain as director of the Hunterian Museum and Art Gallery and titular professor in the University of Glasgow, and saw the new Hunterian Art Gallery, including its reconstructed Charles Rennie Mackintosh House, completed and opened to public acclaim in 1981. He also organized exhibitions of Nigerian art in the Hunterian Museum, and in 1980 collaborated on the major international touring exhibition 'Treasures of ancient Nigeria' and its associated publication. He was vice-chairman of the Scottish Museums Council from 1986 to 1989, and took the lead in an ambitious project to record all the ethnographic collections in Scottish museums, which was completed in 1994.

On his retirement from the Hunterian Museum and Art Gallery in 1990, Willett assumed the role of emeritus professor. He was frequently consulted in connection with international exhibitions on African art, and his encyclopaedic knowledge was sought by curators and collectors in establishing issues of authenticity, and in suspected cases of illegal art trafficking, a practice he did much to expose. His research continued unabated, often with collaborators, for example the Smithsonian Institution, and in 2004 he produced the culmination of a lifetime's work, *The Art of Ife: a Descriptive Catalogue*, a compilation of the entire corpus of Ife art, as a CD-ROM. This massive achievement was recognized by the Amaury Talbot prize of the Royal Anthropological Institute.

One of the most highly respected scholars of his day in the field of African art studies, Willett was appointed CBE in 1985. The Arts Council of the African Studies Association, the pre-eminent body in African art scholarship, presented him with their leadership award in 1995, and in 1997 he was awarded the bicentenary medal of the Royal Society of Edinburgh, of which he had been a fellow since 1979, and honorary curator from 1992 to 1997. Unfailingly generous and supportive to others, he wore his scholarship lightly. Yet he was a rigorous and thorough researcher, who pioneered the application of new scientific techniques, such as thermoluminescence and lead isotope analysis, to the cast brass and ceramic sculptures of early Nigerian civilization, greatly enhancing contemporary knowledge of these traditions. He died at St Margaret's Hospice, Clydebank, Glasgow, on 15 June 2006, and was survived by his wife, Connie, and their four children.

DALE IDIENS

Sources *The Herald* [Glasgow] (27 June 2006) · *Daily Telegraph* (26 July 2006) · *The Times* (27 July 2006) · *The Independent* (1 Aug 2006) · J. Picton, *African Arts*, 40/2 (2007), 13–15 · L. Pole, *Journal of Museum Ethnography*, 19 (March 2007), 1–6 · *WW* (2006) · personal knowledge (2010) · private information (2010) [Connie Willett, widow] · b. cert. · m. cert. · d. cert.

Archives U. Glas. | Royal Anthropological Institute, papers relating to brasses from Ife and Benin

Likenesses photograph, 1979, Royal Society of Edinburgh · obituary photographs · photographs, repro. in Picton, *African Arts*

Wealth at death £183,995.63: confirmation, 24 May 2007, *CCI*

Williams, Charles Adolphus [Charlie] (**1927–2006**), footballer and comedian, was born on 23 December 1927 at Anchor House, Church Hill, Royston, Barnsley, Yorkshire, the son of Charles Augustus Williams and Fanny Cook (formerly Harrison). Whether his white mother ever married his black father is unclear. His father was not named on the birth certificate and Charlie himself was first known as Cook until his mother left him to be brought up by his father. The latter was a Barbadian who served in the Royal Engineers in the First World War before settling in Yorkshire, where he sold groceries from a horse and cart, though the long-term effects of trench foot later rendered him disabled.

Williams attended South Hiendley primary school and Ryhill secondary school before leaving at the age of fourteen to work underground at Monkton colliery. After the death of his father in 1942 he transferred to Upton colliery and went to live with West Indian relatives. After the war, while playing in the colliery football team, he was spotted by scouts from league clubs. He first joined Leeds United as an amateur before signing semi-professional forms with Doncaster Rovers in 1948. He turned full-time professional in 1950 but did not secure a regular first-team place until the 1955/6 season. As one of only a few black players in professional football he helped Doncaster gain promotion to the second division of the Football League. By his own admission he was never a fancy player but, as a journeyman centre-half, he could 'stop them buggers that were' (*Daily Telegraph*, 4 Sept 2006). During his time as a footballer he met a machinist, Audrey Crump, daughter of Arthur Crump, a coalminer, and they married at Ryhill parish church on 1 April 1957, when she was aged nineteen. One of the witnesses was Dorris Cooke, otherwise Cook, his half-sister, of whose existence he was unaware until 1953. He and Audrey had two children, Melford and Beverley. The marriage was later dissolved.

In 1962 Williams received a lucrative offer to become a player–coach in Sydney but was refused a visa to Australia because of his colour. Aware that his football career would start to wane, he had already begun singing in the northern clubs as a member of a trio headed by Alick Jeffrey, a team-mate at Doncaster. His singing, like his football, was solid rather than spectacular, but audiences appreciated his patter between songs. The jokes took over and he began a new life as a comedian, though he was not an overnight success and his other jobs, when he was not on the dole, included window-cleaning and driving a scrap lorry.

Being a black man, born and brought up in Yorkshire,

Charles Adolphus [Charlie] **Williams (1927–2006)**, by unknown photographer, 1972

and with a strong local accent, was a novelty that Williams played upon in his act. As a footballer he had sought to improve his game by analysing every performance; likewise he did post-mortems after each stage routine. With his catch phrase 'Eh up me old flower' he eventually became Britain's first well-known black comedian, thanks to a long residence, beginning in 1971, on ITV's *The Comedians*, a prime-time show that highlighted talent from the club circuit. In 1972 he featured in the royal variety show, had a six-month engagement at the London Palladium, and was a subject of *This Is Your Life* when inveigled to the Batley Variety Club, one of the first instances of the show being held outside a studio. The next year he hosted *The Golden Shot*, a television game show, and published a joke-book-cum-autobiography, *Ee, I've Had Some Laughs*. At this time he was earning some £20,000 a year, a far cry from his £20 a week as a footballer. He was a non-smoker and a moderate drinker, but his extravagance was cars, though these were necessary to his employment on the working men's club circuit.

Much of Williams's act was self-parody and played up to his audience's prejudices, though he claimed that he was mocking racism. ('If you don't shut up, I'll come and move in next door to you', he would tell hecklers.) Unlike later black radical comedians his style was essentially nonconfrontational. Critics felt that he reinforced white stereotypes of blacks by his jokes about cannibals and 'darkies'. This was, of course, an era when the BBC still offered *The Black and White Minstrel Show* (in which white singers 'blacked up') and the National Front attacked black immigration. In later years he also upset the liberal-minded by defending the 'golliwog' mascot of Robertson's jams and having little truck with multi-culturalism, insisting that immigrants should abandon their traditional customs when settling in Britain. He argued that he was a black man rooted in British working-class culture, and certainly his northern audiences identified with his stories of terraced houses with outside lavatories, of working down the mines, and of living under the constraints of rationing. By the 1980s the political and entertainment environment had changed and he was no longer in demand as top billing. He settled down to a life of clubs, pantomime, and opening stores. He finally retired in 1995, though he made a surprise appearance in the BBC's *Windrush Gala Concert* in 1998 to mark the fiftieth anniversary of the start of mass West Indian migration to Britain. In 1999 he was made an MBE for his charity work and in 2000, criticisms put aside, he received a lifetime achievement award at the Black Comedy Awards. However, as a proud Yorkshireman he might have appreciated more his selection in 2004 by Doncaster Rovers' supporters as their 'all-time cult hero'. This for a man who scored but a single goal, against Barnsley, in 171 appearances for the club.

On 28 March 1992, at Birdwell Methodist Church, Williams married 47-year-old Janice Brenda Williams, at the time a canteen cook and later an auxiliary nurse. She had previously changed her name to Williams by deed poll. She cared for him as his health declined as a result of Parkinson's disease and dementia. He died on 2 September 2006 at Barnsley General Hospital from pulmonary thrombo-embolism and deep vein thrombosis. He was survived by Janice and the two children of his first marriage. WRAY VAMPLEW

Sources C. Williams, *Ee, I've had some laughs* (1973) · *The Times* (4 Sept 2006) · *Daily Telegraph* (4 Sept 2006) · *The Guardian* (4 Sept 2006) · *The Independent* (4 Sept 2006) · private information (2010) [D. Vamplew] · b. cert. · m. certs. · d. cert.

Archives FILM BFINA, documentary footage · BFINA, light entertainment footage · BFINA, performance footage [also BL NSA] · BFINA, *Look who's talking*, H. King (director), ITV, 21 Dec 1983 | SOUND [only videotape found]

Likenesses photograph, 1972, Rex Features, London [*see illus.*] · I. Tyas, photograph, 1973, Getty Images, London, Hult. Arch. · obituary photographs · photographs, repro. in Williams, *Laughs* · photographs, Photoshot, London · photographs, PA Photos, London · photographs, Rex Features, London

Wealth at death £179,000: probate, 28 Nov 2006, *CGPLA Eng. & Wales*

Williams, Sir Glanmor (1920–2005), historian, was born on 5 May 1920 at 3 Cross Francis Street, Dowlais, Glamorgan, the only son of Daniel Williams (*d.* 1957), a haulier in a coalmine, later a clerk, and his wife, Ceinwen, *née* Evans (*d.* 1970). In spite of the family's straitened economic circumstances during the depression his parents plied him with books and planted within him a pugnacious desire to make something of himself. Among his fondest memories of his upbringing were the warmth, altruism, and bravery of working-class people in Dowlais, and these values deeply affected his own moral and intellectual development. A devout Baptist chapel-goer throughout his life (his father was a deacon in a Baptist chapel), he became so immersed in nonconformist culture that at one stage he aspired to becoming a Baptist minister. At the age of eight he enthralled an audience at Calfaria Chapel on Dowlais Top by reciting Welsh prose and poetry for an hour and a half.

Educated at Cyfarthfa Castle Grammar School, formerly the home of the tyrannical Crawshay family, Williams swiftly developed a profound understanding of the privations suffered by the Welsh working class and of the democratic socialism that underpinned its community life. At the age of seventeen he won a scholarship to study history and Welsh at the University College of Wales, Aberystwyth, where, inspired by the proverbial 'Aber spirit' and by the tuition of E. A. Lewis, a well-regarded economic historian, he graduated with first-class honours in history and Welsh. Lewis's untimely death, however, robbed him of a suitable supervisor for his graduate research and he was also mortified by his failure, on medical grounds, to join the armed forces. In 1942 he was appointed to teach history and Welsh at Merthyr Intermediate School, where he spent his leisure hours researching for an MA thesis on the Welsh renaissance scholar Bishop Richard Davies.

Williams was still impelled by a strong desire to succeed in academe, and his fortunes took a turn for the better when he was appointed to a temporary lectureship in history at the University College of Wales, Swansea, in 1945. He was to spend the rest of his life living in this 'ugly-lovely' town. During his student days he had met (Margaret) Fay Davies, two years his junior, a native of Cardiff and a fellow historian. Then working as a secondary school teacher, she married Williams on 6 April 1946. They had a son and a daughter. Williams swiftly earned tenure and was raised to a senior lectureship in 1952. Five years later, amid some hurtful controversy, triggered by supporters of a rival candidate, he was appointed to the chair of history at Swansea, a post he held until his retirement in 1982.

Over the course of Williams's career no Welsh historian—not even Sir John Edward Lloyd—exercised a greater influence on the study of the history of Wales and in transforming it into a respectable and fruitful discipline than he did. Always busy and energetic as a writer, an entrepreneur, and a talent-spotter, Williams enticed high-quality teachers and researchers to his department, where Welsh history was taught within a broad academic and intellectual framework. He radiated an infectious sense of enjoyment in the classroom and was famously generous with his time and advice. His scholarly reputation was enormously enhanced when he published his ground-breaking book *The Welsh Church from Conquest to Reformation* (1962), a magisterial volume that at the time of his death remained unsurpassed in breadth and scope. His achievement was all the more remarkable given that, by training and choice, he was an early modern historian. But he had realized that he could not possibly write a convincing account of the protestant Reformation in Wales without having first assessed the condition of the Welsh church in the middle ages. His *Welsh Reformation Essays* (1967) further bolstered his reputation, but administrative chores and public duties prevented him from bringing his long-promised work on the Reformation to a successful conclusion. When *Wales and the Reformation* was eventually published in 1997 there was less originality in it than would have been the case had he completed it much earlier, but it was nevertheless respectfully received as an elegant analysis of how the Welsh embarked on a path that made them a protestant, and eventually nonconformist, people. He cared passionately about the cultural heritage of Wales, and in works such as *Religion, Language and Nationality in Wales* (1979) and *The Welsh and their Religion* (1991) he showed how the native tongue, a strong sense of spirituality, and a keen sense of nationhood had served as an active leaven in the lump.

In other ways too Williams was a strikingly successful mover and shaker. He persuaded the University of Wales Board of Celtic Studies to sponsor a series of monographs entitled Studies in Welsh History, which, under his joint editorship from 1977 onwards, produced a rich crop of works by young scholars. Just as important was the multi-volume History of Wales, an authoritative, standard work, published from 1981 onwards under his general editorship. His own *Recovery, Reorientation and Reformation: Wales, c.1415–1642* (1987) was one of the highlights of this series. Williams also transformed the prospects of the long-standing but incomplete *Glamorgan County History*. First conceived in 1931, this project had only one volume to its name when he agreed to become general editor in 1960. His colleagues feared that he had taken leave of his senses, but he was absolutely certain that writing and editing works associated with regional and local history was a perfectly legitimate activity. Once more he pursued the undertaking with conspicuous success. By the time of the centenary of the founding of Glamorgan county council in 1989 six bulky volumes had been guided through the press. Each of these initiatives was a striking example of how a persuasive, single-minded individual was able to bring a sense of purpose and unity to the mission of Welsh historians.

A productive and wide-ranging scholar, Williams also wrote in Welsh. Indeed, scarcely a year went by without a Welsh-language publication or review appearing under his name. His Welsh-language biography of Richard Davies, published in 1953, was awarded the Ellis Griffith prize by the University of Wales. A highly readable, abbreviated, Welsh-language version of *The Welsh Church from Conquest to Reformation* was published in 1968, and *Grym tafodau tân* (1984), a compendium of sparkling essays devoted to preachers, poets, and prose writers who had exercised the 'power of tongues of fire', was rewarded with a Welsh Arts Council prize for literature. At the age of eighty he produced another collection of beautifully written essays on religion and politics in *Cymru a'r gorffennol: côr o leisiau* (2000). Even though he claimed that speaking or writing in Welsh never came easily to him, and even though he made no secret of his Britishness—he once said that he was 'too British for many a Welsh-speaking Welshman and too Welsh for an English-speaking one'-

(*The Independent*, 28 Feb 2005)—he was an ardent devolutionist and supporter of Welsh culture.

The prolific Williams would surely have published even more had he not played such an active part in the public life of Wales. As president, vice-president, or chairman, he served on virtually every institution of cultural importance in Wales. Aware of his reputation for wisdom and equanimity, public bodies jostled for his services and by serving them Williams deepened his own knowledge of the architectural, archaeological, historical, and cultural heritage of Wales. Among other posts he was chairman of the Royal Commission on Ancient and Historical Monuments in Wales from 1986 to 1990 (and a member since 1962), chairman of the Ancient Monuments Board (Wales) from 1983 to 1995, and a member of the Welsh Arts Council from 1978 to 1981. He was one of three appointees to a commission (1963–5) that produced the celebrated Hughes Parry report on the legal status of the Welsh language, and when he became chairman of the Broadcasting Council for Wales and a governor of the BBC (1965–71) he valiantly defended Welsh interests within this highly London-centric institution. Never did any historian in Wales exert more influence on public affairs. His distinction as a scholar and public servant was widely recognized. Honorary fellowships were conferred upon him by Swansea, Aberystwyth, and Carmarthen; the University of Wales made him a DLitt in 1963 and an honorary LLD in 1998; and in 1991 he was presented with the coveted medal of the Honourable Society of Cymmrodorion. Elected a fellow of the Royal Historical Society in 1954, he served as its vice-president from 1979 to 1983. In 1970 the Society of Antiquaries elected him a fellow, as did the British Academy in 1986. He was appointed CBE in 1981 and in 1995 he was raised to a knighthood 'for services to the history, culture and heritage of Wales'. It gave him great joy, too, to be made a freeman of the borough of Merthyr Tudful in 2002.

Physically Glanmor Williams was a tiny man. Barely five feet tall, he was adept at turning his smallness to advantage. Never one to indulge in airs and graces, he preferred to be known as Glan and as the quintessential 'little boy from Dowlais'. A deeply humanitarian figure, his warmth and generosity were proverbial, and those who met him were instantly struck by his cheery greeting, high-pitched chuckle, and words of encouragement. Blessed with a lively sense of fun, he was a splendid raconteur and mimic. The Christian religion and classical music played a large part in his life and he was an active walker on hills and coastline. But few realized that this distinguished remembrancer, even when he was at the height of his career, was often assailed by bouts of depression and insecurity. Nevertheless his commitment to the cause of Welsh history remained undimmed to the end. Following a short illness he died of heart failure at Morriston Hospital, Swansea, on 24 February 2005, and was cremated at Swansea crematorium, where hundreds of his friends, colleagues, and admirers assembled to pay their tribute. He was survived by his wife and their two children.

Geraint H. Jenkins

Sources G. H. Jenkins, 'Dau fachan bech o Ddowlish', *Merthyr a Thaf*, ed. H. T. Edwards (2001), 192–226 · G. Williams, *A life* (2002) · *The Independent* (28 Feb 2005) · *The Guardian* (25 March 2005) · *The Times* (11 April 2005) · *Journal of Welsh Religious History*, 5 (2005), 1–3 · *Archaeologia Cambrensis*, 152 (2005), 192–4 · *Studia Celtica*, 39/1 (2005), 201–3 · *Y Traethodydd*, 160/675 (2005), 197–212 · *Trafodion Cymdeithas Hanes Bedyddwyr Cymru* (2005), 48–50 · *Welsh History Review*, 22/4 (2005), 762–6 · G. H. Jenkins, 'Glanmor Williams, 1920–2005', *PBA*, 138 (2006), 401–23 · *Morgannwg*, 49 (2006), 5–8 · *Llafur*, 9/3 (2006), 7–11 · *Renaissance Studies*, 20/3 (2006), 379–82 · G. H. Jenkins and G. E. Jones, eds., *Degrees of influence: a memorial volume for Glanmor Williams* (2008) · *WW* (2005) · Burke, *Peerage* · personal knowledge (2009) · private information (2009) · b. cert. · m. cert. · d. cert.

Archives NL Wales, diaries

Likenesses J. Roberts, portrait, NL Wales · obituary photographs

Wealth at death £40,785: probate, 11 Nov 2005, *CGPLA Eng. & Wales*

Williams, Sir (John) Kyffin (1918–2006), painter, was born on 9 May 1918 at Tanygraig, a house on the outskirts of Llangefni, Anglesey, the younger son of Henry Inglis Wynne Williams (1870–1942), bank manager, and his wife, Essyllt Mary, *née* Williams (1883–1964), daughter of Richard Hughes Williams, rector of Llansadwrn. He was descended on both sides from Anglican clergymen and landowners, long established in Anglesey, whom he traced back to the seventeenth century. The name Kyffin (which rhymes with puffin) came from his paternal grandmother, who was of Montgomeryshire stock; in his own family he was known as John.

Williams first went to school at Chirk in Denbighshire, where his father had been appointed manager of a branch of the Midland Bank, but in 1928 the family, reduced to near-penury by a lawsuit brought against them by a malevolent cousin, moved to Plas Gwyn, 'an ugly castellated house' (*Across the Straits*, 44) near the village of Pentrefelin between Cricieth and Porthmadog on the Llŷn peninsula. There, 'surrounded by some of the most glorious landscape in Britain, I began to assemble unknowingly a vast library of feelings, sensations and knowledge that were to form the foundations of my future life as a landscape painter' (ibid.). He received his early education at Tre-Arddur House School on Holy Island, Anglesey, where he was very happy despite frail health, and at Shrewsbury School, 'a hard philistine place' (ibid., 68), which he entered in 1931 and where he suffered on account of his small physique and bullying by older boys; he left at Christmas 1935. Back home at Plas Gwyn, he played tennis and cricket and began following the local hunt.

At the age of seventeen Williams was articled to Messrs Yale and Hardcastle, a firm of land agents with offices in Pwllheli, the work affording him opportunities of visiting most of the estates on the Llŷn peninsula. Shortly before receiving a commission in the 6th battalion of the Royal Welch Fusiliers (Territorial Army) in April 1937, he was diagnosed as having a form of epilepsy brought on by the polioencephalitis he had contracted at Shrewsbury. On being discharged from the army in 1940 he was told by a doctor that, as he was 'abnormal', he should take up art,

Sir (John) Kyffin Williams (1918–2006), by David Carpanini, 1987

which he did almost immediately. In October 1941, without any work to show and believing himself to be talentless, he enrolled at the Slade School of Fine Art, which had been evacuated to Oxford for the duration of the war, and he stayed there for three years. One day in the Ashmolean Library's print room, where the school was temporarily housed, he opened a book about Piero della Francesca and was overcome by the compassion in Christ's eyes in the painting *Resurrection*, and after this epiphany he returned to his art studies 'with a new sense of purpose and direction' (*Across the Straits*, 114). Unable to draw at first, he was advised to take up oils and this he did with instant pleasure and some success: he left the Slade with a prize for portraiture and a Robert Ross leaving scholarship.

In 1944 Williams was appointed senior art master at Highgate secondary school in London, and when the post became part-time he was able to make regular visits to north Wales and, from his lodgings in Bisham Gardens and later in West Hampstead and Holland Park, to begin painting the massive bulk of the mountains of Snowdonia in which he found an inexhaustible source of inspiration. As his epilepsy took a turn for the worse he felt more and more compelled to paint and it was not long before he had his first exhibition—at Colnaghi's in 1948. He was eventually obliged to give up teaching and in 1973 returned to his native island, living alone at Pwllfanogl, a small cottage on the shore of the Menai Strait which he rented from the marquess and marchioness of Anglesey, and from which there are splendid views of the Snowdonia range.

The typical Kyffin Williams painting shows a peak under dark cloud, a lowering sky, and perhaps a shepherd, with hazel stick and dog, making his way down a rocky or snowy slope, or a small farmhouse, its whitewashed walls a refuge from the sombre majesty of its setting. The predominant colours are olive green, slate grey, ochre, and umber, the paint applied lusciously with a palette knife in the thick, bold swathes of pigment in which the artist delighted. He worked prodigiously, turning out about 100 oil paintings a year, as well as countless gouaches and watercolours.

Almost immediately after his first exhibitions in London galleries Williams began to enjoy a reputation as the Welsh landscape painter *par excellence*. His inclusion in the Arts Council of Great Britain's 'Twenty-five paintings by contemporary Welsh artists' in 1949 confirmed his standing as a major presence in Wales, and one-man exhibitions followed at regular intervals. Many of the great and good sat for him and there was hardly a public body in Wales that did not have at least one of his pictures in its boardroom. His landscapes, in particular, seemed to satisfy the Welsh middle class's nostalgia for the countryside they had left and, as a consequence, the prices asked by galleries soared well beyond the pockets of most art buyers in Wales. A selection of his studies of old country people, especially women and children, was published in his book *Portraits* (1996). He was aware of his weaknesses as a painter. Almost as if to escape the confines of what he knew he could do, in 1968, with the help of a Winston Churchill fellowship, he spent several months in the Welsh-descended communities of Patagonia. The pictures he brought back were very different from his earlier work in their brighter colours and their depiction of this arid region and its gaucho people. Most of the watercolours and gouaches he made during the trip were donated, together with much else, to the National Library of Wales.

Williams was an accomplished raconteur who wrote with panache about the people and places he had known in two volumes of autobiography, *Across the Straits* (1973) and *A Wider Sky* (1991), the most important of his prose works. Curiously, given his conservative temperament and his dependence on official and corporate patronage, he was not averse to expressing acerbic views on the policies of such bodies as the Welsh Arts Council, which had neglected him for many years, and the art colleges where, to his dismay, draughtsmanship was no longer taught. He was passionately in favour of a national art gallery for Wales (as long as it stopped at 1950) and did much to create Oriel Ynys Môn, the major gallery in Anglesey, in 1996, donating 350 of his drawings and a number of canvases.

By the end of his life Williams enjoyed a reputation as the pre-eminent Welsh painter and many honours came his way. He served as president of the Royal Cambrian Academy, vice-president of the Honourable Society of Cymmrodorion, and deputy lieutenant of Gwynedd. He was elected to the Royal Academy in 1974, appointed OBE in 1982, made an honorary DLitt of the University of Wales in 1993, and knighted in 1999. He never married, though he was reputed to have been engaged three times. He died of cancer of the lung and prostate on 1 September 2006 at the St Tysilio Home, Llanfair Pwyllgwyngyll, Anglesey, and was buried at Llanfair-yng-Nghornwy, Anglesey.

MEIC STEPHENS

Sources K. Williams, *Across the straits* (1973) • K. Williams, *A wider sky* (1991) • I. Jeffrey, introduction, in N. Sinclair, *Kyffin Williams* (2004) • *Cambria*, 6/5 (Sept–Oct 2004), 70 • *The Times* (2 Sept 2006) • *Daily Telegraph* (2 Sept 2006) • *The Independent* (2 Sept 2006) • *The Guardian* (4 Sept 2006) • D. Meredith, ed., *Kyffin Williams, bro o bywyd / his life, his land* (2007) • I. Skidmore, *Kyffin: a figure in a Welsh landscape* (2008) • *WW* (2006) • Burke, *Peerage* • personal knowledge (2010) • private information (2010) • b. cert. • d. cert.

Archives NL Wales, corresp., diaries, and papers • Oriel Ynys Môn, Anglesey | SOUND BL NSA, performance recording

Likenesses H. M. Bateman, pencil sketch, 1943, NL Wales • M. Thomas, oils, *c*.1950, NL Wales • K. Williams, self-portrait, ink and watercolour on paper, 1956, repro. in D. Fraser-Jenkins and S. Fox-Pitt, *Portrait of the artist: artists' portraits published by Art News Review 1949–1960* (1989), 111 • I. Roberts-Jones, plaster bust, 1959, repro. in P. Cannon-Brookes, *Ivor Roberts-Jones: the journey to Harlech* (1983), 39, no. 22 • M. Cosman, pen and wash, *c*.1960, repro. in *Exhibition Catalogue: Belgrave Gallery* (1996) • D. Williams, photographs, *c*.1980, NL Wales • A. Keith, pencil and charcoal, 1986, NL Wales • D. Carpanini, etching, 1987, NL Wales [*see illus.*] • N. Sinclair, selenium-toned silver print, 1987, NPG • N. Sinclair, photographs, 1987–2003, NL Wales; repro. in A. Sumner, *Faces of Wales* (2006) • N. Sinclair, bromide print, 1992, NPG • D. Griffiths, oils, 1993, NL Wales • N. Sinclair, gelatin silver print, 1993, NPG • B. Mitchell, photographs, 1998, NL Wales • B. Batchelor, photograph, 1999, PA Photos, London • G. L. Hughes, photographs, 1999, NL Wales • W. Jones, acrylic on canvas, 2000, priv. coll. • D. Backhouse, bust; exh. Society of Portrait Sculptors, 24–29 April 2000 • E. Jackson, photograph, NL Wales • I. Roberts-Jones, pastel and pencil; Christies, 24 November 2005 • obituary photographs • photograph, repro. in *RA Magazine*, 11 (1986), 23 • portraits, repro. in Meredith, *Williams*

Wealth at death £6,187,017: probate, 11 July 2007, *CGPLA Eng. & Wales*

Williams, Nigel Prichard (1955–2006), charity worker and children's commissioner, was born on 21 January 1955 at Highfield Maternity Home, Barnstaple, Devon, the son of Idwal Prichard Williams, a valuer for the Inland Revenue, and his wife, Phyllis Irene, *née* Ley. When he was very young the family moved to Limavady, Northern Ireland, where he grew up. When he was twelve the family moved to Portadown, where he attended Portadown College. He later went to Cambridge University, where he graduated in geography. In 1976 he was recruited by the Northern Ireland civil service as a graduate trainee to work in the Department of Economic Development. On 21 December 1978 he married, at the registrar's office in Belfast, Heather (*b*. 1949), teacher, and daughter of George Ross, farmer. They had four children.

In 1984 Williams left the civil service to set up his own computer training company. He then became head of public policy for the charity Christian Action Research and Education (CARE), moving to London. He lived in Peckham for the next fifteen years and was active in the area in All Saints' Church and with the Liberal Democrats. He served from 1994 to 1998 as a Southwark borough councillor.

In 1995 Williams founded Childnet International, a charity set up to protect children both from abuse by adults and from bullying by other children through the internet. It began in a small way—'from my bedroom' as he put it (*Irish News*, 2 Oct 2003)—but came to have an international reputation, not least because of its prescience about the subject with which it was concerned. It was founded at a time when the internet was beginning to develop but the full implications about the uses to which it could be put and the need for international co-ordination, among regulators, industry, education, and law enforcement agencies, was lacking. Williams was especially concerned about pornography and had written a book, *False Images* (1991), on the subject. He was alerted partly by the use of the internet by his own children, as well as by what he had learned at CARE. He began Childnet International with a Christian ethos of service and support for others. He wanted it to serve as a catalyst to promote interaction between the different sectors, both serving and challenging people to ensure that the internet became a safe and helpful place for children. The agency was also intended to offer advice to children, schools, and families, and show the positive part that the internet could play in helping them. Williams was a board member of the Internet Watch Foundation and the Internet Rating Association and in 2001 was appointed by the home secretary to the government task force on child protection on the internet.

In October 2003 Williams took up the new post of children's commissioner in Northern Ireland (the second to take such a position in the UK, Wales being the first to create the position in April 2001). He moved from London with his wife, who worked with children with special needs, and their children to Glenarm, co. Antrim. As early as 1995 Williams had met the children's commissioners in Australia and New Zealand (the UK was far behind in recognizing the need for such posts) during a trip that he had made for Childnet International. He learned from them that while dealing with complaints was an important part of the role, there was as great a need to take a positive, proactive stance. When, thirteen years later, he found himself in their position, this is what he did. During his three years in the post he commissioned Queen's University, Belfast, to undertake a review of the state of children's social and human rights, including the situation of refugee and asylum-seeking children (a subject that in time became of increasing concern to his three fellow commissioners in the UK). This revealed weaknesses in the vetting of people working in schools and of children's treatment by the legal system.

Williams advanced the cause of children and young people in many areas in his three years in post, where he enjoyed some of the widest powers and the greatest independence of government granted to any civil servant. Short though his tenure was, it offered the secure base and political and public regard from which the new organization could proceed. Among the areas on which he focused were speech and language therapy services (for which he commissioned a review), and direct work with children and young people in several areas. He built a team that worked on matters as diverse as mental health and antisocial behaviour orders. These issues were important but, given his background, it was perhaps not unexpected that he should have placed especial emphasis on the internet. This was his greatest contribution: not only the stress on the subject by the commission, but also the fact that he was one of the few who so early understood the way the internet would affect the lives of the young and what action needed to be taken to ensure that it was a force for the good. He did all of this—and more—despite the fact that cancer had been diagnosed only a year after he took up office.

In January 2006 Williams became the first non-academic to receive the International Federation for Information Processing's biennial Namur award for work on understanding the social impact of information technology; he entitled his award lecture 'A parallel universe: children and young people's love affair with the internet'. While living in Northern Ireland he also wrote extensively, including an award-winning series of articles on places to visit in Northern Ireland, 'Off the beaten track', for the *Belfast Telegraph*. He died of cancer at his home, 75 Dickeystown Road, Glenarm, on 28 March 2006, and was survived by his wife, Heather, and their four children.

TERRY PHILPOT

Sources *Belfast Telegraph* (27 June 2003); (28 March 2006) · *Belfast News Letter* (27 June 2003); (2 Oct 2003) · *Irish News* (27 June 2003); (2 Oct 2003); (29 March 2006) · *The Guardian* (31 March 2006) · L. Neilands, *Children's champion: the story of Nigel Williams* (2009) · private information (2010) · b. cert. · m. cert. · d. cert.
Likenesses photographs, 2005, PA Photos, London · obituary photographs · photograph, repro. in Neilands, *Champion*, jacket
Wealth at death under £138,000: probate, 31 Aug 2006, *CGPLA NIre.*

Williams, Ursula Moray (1911–2006), children's writer and illustrator, was born on 19 April 1911 at Cherrycroft, Bell Hill, Petersfield, Hampshire, the younger of identical twins of Arthur Moray Williams (1878–1959), a classics tutor at Bedales School and amateur archaeologist, and his wife, Mabel Lizzie, *née* Unwin (1874–*c*.1954), a Froebel-trained teacher and sister of the publisher Stanley Unwin. Her paternal grandfather was John Alfred Williams, vicar of Alderminster, Warwickshire, and grandson of another John Alfred Williams, who had built up a fortune in Birmingham pin manufacturing. Her father liked to be known as Mr Moray Williams and gave each of his children the middle name Moray, but this was never formally part of their surname. After the First World War the family moved to Southampton, where her father took up a full-time post with the Red Cross. Living in part of a large, crumbling, eccentric mansion, Williams and her identical twin sister Barbara (*d*. 1975) spent a happy childhood full of reading, storytelling, imaginative games, ponies, and writing their own books for family consumption. They were educated mainly at home, first by their devoutly religious mother and later with governesses, before spending a year at a girls' school near Lake Annecy, France, at the age of seventeen, and then moving on together to Winchester College of Art. While Barbara went on to the Royal College of Art, later achieving distinction as the wood engraver and sculptor Barbara Árnason, Ursula stayed only a year at Winchester before deciding that writing was, for her, more than a childhood interest and could develop into her chosen career. Her parents supported her to stay at home and write, and her uncle Stanley Unwin encouraged her early ambitions and later steered her towards a good agent.

Williams's books often drew on her girlhood experiences; her first book, *Jean-Pierre* (1931), about a little boy and his pet goat, was published when she was just twenty. She provided her own pen and ink illustrations for almost half her books; some were illustrated by her sister, but with Barbara's marriage and move to Iceland, long-distance collaboration became more difficult, and over time Williams worked with many other well-known illustrators, including Edward Ardizzone, Shirley Hughes, Faith Jaques, and Eileen Soper.

On 28 September 1935 Williams married Conrad Southey (known as Peter) John, a thirty-year-old aircraft manufacturer, later contracts manager, and great-grandson of the poet Robert Southey. While pregnant with the first of their four sons she wrote *Adventures of the Little Wooden Horse* (1938). A long episodic story about a wooden horse in search of his master through many ups and downs, its 'read-aloud' style owed something to her enjoyment of being read to as a child, and perhaps the storytelling she herself had done as a Brownie Guide leader. Charmingly illustrated by Joyce Lankester Brisley (better known as the author and illustrator of the Milly-Molly-Mandy stories), the book was an immediate publishing success. Arrangements with nannies left afternoons free for work, so that Williams was able to combine writing and motherhood, and she was one of relatively few children's writers to be published throughout the Second World War, despite the paper shortage. She wrote mostly under her maiden name, although as Ursula John she had written *The Adventures of Boss and Dingbat* (1937), with photographs by Peter John, and also under that name was a contributor to *The Robin* magazine and annual in the 1950s and early 1960s.

A recurring theme of Williams's writing is the 'sentient toy' that identifies with human needs and emotions. Thus the Little Wooden Horse has an indomitable spirit through many adventures, as well as kindness and persistence, and the clockwork doll-child Marta (in *The Toymaker's Daughter*, 1968) longs to experience what it is to be human. Williams's writing unselfconsciously recalled the fairytales and imaginative games she enjoyed in childhood. In an interview with Elaine Moss in 1971 she mentioned the toy hobby horses she and her sister owned when young; and how much she had adored the story of Pinocchio. Moss then went on to speculate: 'had it ever occurred to her that her childhood passion for Pinocchio might have been partly responsible for the creation of the little wooden horse? Clearly it hadn't' (Moss, 55). Many children's writers of the 1950s and 1960s owed something to this earlier, much-loved episodic toy fantasy; those who developed new 'read-aloud' expressions of the 'sentient toy' theme included Joan G. Robinson (the Teddy Robinson series, 1953 onwards), Modwena Sedgwick (the Galldora stories, about a rag doll, from 1960), and Rumer Godden (in various doll stories).

Williams was modest about her work, and never achieved a literary award. However, some of her best-loved books, including *Adventures of the Little Wooden Horse* and *Gobbolino the Witch's Cat* (1942), about a reluctant witch's accomplice seeking a more domestic life, were enjoyed by several generations and remained in print more than half a century later, testimonies to the pleasure her work, full of adventure, loyalty, fun, and kindness, gave to many. Her productive writing career covered some seventy years, and after her husband died in 1974 she continued with writing, gardening, giving talks to schools, and involvement in local life in the village of Beckford, in Worcestershire, where she had lived since 1945, serving as a magistrate on the Evesham juvenile bench for many years. She died at Tewkesbury Nursing Home, Bushley, Tewkesbury, Gloucestershire, on 17 October 2006, and was survived by three of her four sons.

BELINDA COPSON

Sources interview with E. Moss, *Signal* (1971); repr. in E. Moss, *Part of the pattern* (1986) • D. L. Kirkpatrick, ed., *Twentieth-century children's writers*, 3rd edn (1989) • *Daily Telegraph* (1 Nov 2006) • *The Independent* (7 Nov 2006) • *The Guardian* (15 Nov 2006) • C. Davison, *Through the magic door: Ursula Moray Williams, Gobbolino and the little wooden horse* (2011) • DLitB, online edition • private information (2010) [C. Davison; Andrew John, son] • b. cert. • m. cert. • d. cert.
Archives Seven Stories (Centre for Children's Books), Newcastle upon Tyne, MSS, artwork, corresp., papers
Likenesses obituary photographs
Wealth at death under £20,000: probate, 22 Dec 2006, *CGPLA Eng. & Wales*

Williamson, Duncan James (1928–2007), storyteller and singer, was born on 11 April 1928, the son of John Williamson (1892–1963), basket maker, and his wife, Betsy, *née* Townsley. His registered place of birth was Sandhole in the parish of Glassary, Cumlodden, Argyll. In an essay of 1987 the folklorist Hamish Henderson put this more poetically, possibly with an echo of Ewan MacColl's 'Moving On Song' in mind, as 'born in a tent on the shores of Loch Fyne, near the village of Furnace' (Henderson, 226). Informally he was called Duncan MacCallum Williamson, having been born two hours after his mother's friend named MacCallum had died. He was one of sixteen children, three of whom died young.

Williamson was of Scots Traveller descent. Historically they were a nomadic people, distinct from Romany people. His parents encouraged him and his siblings to attend school—in part to acquire the requisite number of school attendances to allow them to go travelling, in part to avoid the official child-catchers who could remove a child from its family permanently. Alongside getting his letters, he grew up steeped in the oral transmission of knowledge, craft, lore, and storytelling. He learned Traveller trades like basket weaving, hawking, agricultural work of all kinds including berry picking at Blairgowrie's famed raspberry fields, drystone dyking, and general labouring. In 1933, on a trip with his father, the realization came that he was 'moich on horses' ('mad about horses'), hence the title of his autobiographical *The Horsieman: Memories of a Traveller, 1928–1958* (1994), based on conversations transcribed by his second wife. Like Gypsies, from whom they were rarely differentiated, Travellers suffered prejudice and marginalization. In his own 'Hawker's Lament' he sang:

> But maybe someday when we're gone from this world
> And buried deep down in the ground
> Will God make us welcome, will he give us a home
> Or will he tell us to keep moving on?
> (MacIntyre)

Helen Fullerton, an activist for Traveller rights, was the first collector to record Williamson. Although she had met members of his family, she met Williamson only in 1967 when she collected original poetry, songs, and ballads from him. Fullerton told Geordie MacIntyre and the two collectors made further recordings that November, including a five-verse fragment of 'Lady Margaret'; 'In time', wrote MacIntyre, 'Duncan rebuilt a complete "Tam Lin" [its other title], drawing from other members of his extended family. This is one of many examples of his resourcefulness as well as an instinctive act' (MacIntyre). Word of their find soon spread. In April 1968 Williamson appeared at Folksong and Ballad, a Glasgow folk club run by Carl McDougal, Ian Philip, Ron Clark, and MacIntyre—on a bill with the folk-singer and folklorist A. L. (Bert) Lloyd—and later that year at the Blairgowrie folk festival, organized by the Traditional Music and Song Association of Scotland.

Williamson described storytelling as 'the second oldest form of human entertainment' (private information) and achieved international recognition in his lifetime for his creativity as a storyteller, singer, and occasional composer of songs. His repertory of songs included 'Sir Patrick Spens', 'Thomas the Rhymer', 'Fortune Turns the Wheel', and 'Queen Amang the Heather'. With his second wife championing him, a succession of story books appeared, examples being *Fireside Tales of the Traveller Children* (1983), *The Broonie, Silkies and Fairies: Travellers' Tales* (1985), and *The Genie and the Fisherman, and Other Tales from the Travelling People* (1991). In time he was acknowledged as one of the foremost voices of Scots Traveller culture. Henderson marked him out as destined to be 'possibly the most extraordinary tradition-bearer of the whole traveller tribe' (Henderson, 220). His was a name to speak of in the same respectful tones as other leading exponents of Traveller culture, such as Lizzie Higgins, Jeannie Robertson, Stanley Robertson, Belle Stewart, and Sheila Stewart.

In his radio history of storytelling, 'Something understood: a chain of voices', Hugh Lupton recalled:

> It was Duncan who told me that when you tell a story or sing a song the person you heard it from is standing behind you. When that person spoke he, in turn, had a teller behind him, and so on, back and back and back. I love this idea, the story has to speak to its own time, but the teller has also to be true to the chain of voices that inform him or her.

Williamson had seven children—Edith (*b.* 1949), Jimmy (*b.* 1951), Willie (*b.* 1953), Betty (*b.* 1955), John (*b.* 1957), Isabelle (*b.* 1963), and Sandra (*b.* 1970)—with his first wife, Jeanie, *née* Townsley (1932–1971), whom he married in 1949, and two—Betsy Jane (*b.* 1977) and Thomas Jeffrey (*b.* 1979)—with his American second wife, Linda Jane, formerly Headlee, *née* Rast (*b.* 1949), whom he married on 22 February 1977. He had another child, Nancy, with Martha Stewart. He died of aspiration pneumonia and a stroke at Victoria Hospital, Hayfield Road, Kirkcaldy, Fife, on 8 November 2007, and was buried in the parish church cemetery in Strathmiglo, Fife. After his death the Scottish Storytelling Centre inscribed a carved chair with his name and life years. KEN HUNT

Sources D. Williamson, *Fireside tales of the Traveller children*, ed. L. Williamson (1983); 2nd edn (2009) • H. Henderson, introduction, in D. Williamson and L. Williamson, *A thorn in the king's foot: folktales of the Scottish travelling people* (1987); repr. in H. Henderson, *Alias MacAlias* (1992) • D. Williamson, *The horsieman: memoirs of a Traveller, 1928–58* (1994) • T. Neat and J. MacInnes, eds., *The voice of the bard: living poets and ancient tradition in the highlands and islands of Scotland* (2001) • *The Scotsman* (14 Dec 2003); (13 Nov 2007) • D. Williamson, 'Born under canvas', BBC Radio Scotland, broadcast 22 Dec 2003 • H. Lupton, 'Something understood: a chain of voices', transcript of Radio 4 broadcast, 13 Feb 2005, www.angelfire.com/folk/hughlupton/interview.htm, 20 July 2010 • *The Herald* [Glasgow] (9 Nov 2007) • *The Independent* (13 Nov 2007) • *The Times* (16 Nov 2007) • *Fife Free Press* (16 Nov 2007) • *The Guardian* (22 Nov 2007) • G. MacIntyre, www.scottishstorytellingcentre.co.uk/network/2007%20News%20Archive.pdf, 20 July 2010 • *Living Tradition* (Jan–Feb 2008), 13 • *Folk Music Journal*, 9/4 (2009), 685–7 • private information (2011) [Linda Williamson, wife; Jimmy Williamson, son; Nancy Williamson, daughter-in-law] • b. cert. • m. cert. [1977] • d. cert.

Archives NL Scot. | Appalachian Regional Studies Center, Radford University, Radford, Virginia, USA • Scottish Storytelling Centre, Edinburgh • U. Edin., school of Scottish studies | FILM London Centre for International Storytelling • U. Cal., Berkeley, department of English | SOUND BL NSA, documentary recordings • BL NSA, performance recordings • London Centre for International Storytelling • *Mary and the seal and other folktales: traditional storytelling by Duncan Williamson* (Springthyme Records, 1987) • *Put another log on the fire: songs and tunes from a Scots Traveller* (Veteran, 1994) • *Travellers' tales*, vols. 1 and 2 (Kyloe Records, 2002)

Likenesses A. Wynne, photographs, U. Edin., school of Scottish studies • photograph, repro. in www.celtarctic.com/moira_specialfeature.htm

Wilson, Anthony Howard [Tony] (1950–2007), television broadcaster and music entrepreneur, was born at Hope Hospital, Salford, Lancashire, on 20 February 1950, the only child of Sydney Wilson (1917–1997), tobacconist, and his wife, Doris Emily, *née* Knupfer (1904–1975). Thirteen years older than her husband and a widow when they married in 1948, Doris—whose father had emigrated from Freiburg, Germany—had earlier established their shop and residence at 448 Regent Road, Salford, with her first husband, Tom McNulty. She was known in the family for being steely and shrewd, while Sydney—with his plummy accent and penchant for bow ties—was regarded as kind and theatrical, the latter a reference to his earlier acting ambitions (his hazy past included a spell in ENSA in India), as well as being a euphemism for his sexuality.

Granada Television If Tony Wilson combined his parents' calculating and flamboyant personalities, he was also the product between 1961 and 1968 of Salford's leading school, De La Salle, a Catholic boys' grammar school. Although home from the age of five was a detached house

Anthony Howard [Tony] **Wilson (1950–2007)**, by Harry Goodwin, 1970s

on Ladythorn Avenue in leafy Marple, Cheshire (his family's business interests had by now extended to several stores), his connection with Salford was always proudly emphasized during his professional career. A place reading English at Jesus College, Cambridge, followed, where he was involved with student journalism and left-wing politics. He gained a lower second-class degree in 1971 and joined Independent Television News as a trainee journalist in London.

After a couple of years Wilson realized that his personality was too brash for a senior onscreen position at ITN, but rather than temper his individuality he returned north to Granada Television in Manchester and became a reporter for its early evening magazine programme, *Granada Reports*. His daredevil antics (which included hang-gliding, abseiling, and parachuting), posh accent, and general exuberance soon gained him some of the prominence he desired, albeit at a local rather than national level. Privately, though, the death of his mother clearly affected him, and his outwardly lapsed Catholicism was routinely revived for attendance at mass. His similarly distraught father later moved in with a male photographer in Manchester. The family quietly accepted this development.

Wilson's professional connection with music began with a ten-minute arts and entertainment slot, 'What's On', at the end of the Friday *Granada Reports* show. This soon led to a half-hour programme, *So It Goes*. First broadcast in July 1976 and optioned out to two other ITV regions, the first series boasted the début television appearance of the Sex Pistols (performing 'Anarchy in the UK', broadcast on 28 August). The second series in late 1977 included the Clash, the Jam, and Siouxsie and the Banshees. On 14 May 1977 Wilson married Lindsay Carole Reade (*b.* 1952), schoolteacher, later music promoter, and daughter of Arnold Reade, remedial therapist. Their often tempestuous relationship ended in divorce in 1983.

With a third series of *So It Goes* cancelled midway through the second series because of an expletive-riddled performance by Iggy Pop, Wilson's links to the music industry needed bolstering if he was to capitalize on the punk-inspired creative explosion that was in full swing. He therefore welcomed the suggestion made by his actor friend Alan Erasmus to co-manage a new band led by the guitarist Vini Reilly, later christened Durutti Column. Eager to find other groups, in April 1978 Wilson and Erasmus attended a 'battle of the bands' contest at Rafters, a small cellar venue on Manchester's Oxford Road, and were impressed by the intensity of the last of seventeen acts to appear. The group was Joy Division and with Wilson's help they went on to become the defining band of the post-punk era.

Factory The first outlet for Wilson's moonlighting in the music business (his job with Granada was maintained throughout) was to hire the Russell Club in Manchester's rundown Hulme district, and rename it The Factory for four gigs in May–June 1978. It was about this time that the graphic design student Peter Saville approached Wilson and agreed to produce posters for the enterprise. Anxious to distance the name from its connotations with Andy Warhol's Factory studio in New York, Saville appropriated the design of an industrial safety sign he had come across at college, which warned workers in striking yellow, black, and white graphics to use hearing protection. The industrial aesthetic for much of what followed was thereby established, and Saville became a long-standing business partner, despite being notoriously tardy about delivering his work. If some critics later accused Wilson of putting style over substance (the punk ethos was meant to be about a 'do-it-yourself' raggedness) the legacy of the Factory brand—with its clean codified language based on minimal information and an emphasis on index numbers—was arguably as significant for design as the music was for broader popular culture.

The next entrepreneurial step by Wilson was to establish a record label, also called Factory. The first release, in January 1979, showcased artists who had played at the Hulme venue: Cabaret Voltaire, the comedian John Dowie, Durutti Column, and Joy Division each claimed a side in a double 7 inch EP, *A Factory Sample*. It cost £3600 for 5000 copies, and it was Wilson who provided the funding, drawing on a £5000 inheritance from his mother. As Saville later observed, 'Tony's income and profession were fundamental elements in the formula of Factory happening' (Nice, 48). With Wilson also contributing the strategic ideas, Erasmus carrying out day-to-day management at his flat on 86 Palatine Road (the original business address of Factory Records), and Saville articulating a distinctive modernist aesthetic, the foundations for future releases were laid, but there was still relatively little to suggest that the label was likely to stand out commercially.

It took a personal tragedy to catapult the label to international renown and thereby provide the bedrock for what Wilson—whose self-confessed weakness was 'an excess of civic pride' (*The Guardian*, 20 May 2002)—saw as the creative regeneration of post-industrial Manchester. The tragedy was the suicide of Ian Curtis in May 1980, just as Joy Division were achieving considerable critical acclaim for their début album, *Unknown Pleasures* (1979), and were on the cusp of wider success with their imminent follow-up, *Closer* (1980). Like other friends of Curtis, Wilson chided himself for not being of more help to the distressed singer, having been preoccupied with making a documentary for Granada's flagship current affairs programme *World in Action*, a new role he had secured at the end of 1979. Wilson's high-profile persona and fondness for marijuana made him unsuitable for *World in Action*, however, and he was soon sacked from that particular role.

The Haçienda In 1981, with Factory Records benefiting financially from Joy Division's success after Curtis's death, Wilson turned his attention to putting something back into his beloved Manchester. Working with Rob Gretton, the manager of New Order, the band that had (with Wilson's encouragement) emerged out of Joy Division's ashes, he planned to give Mancunians the sort of trend-setting club for which New York was then renowned. However, converting a former yacht showroom on Whitworth Street in central Manchester into a modernistic dance and performing space did not come cheaply. The costs were estimated at £70,000, but came in at over £340,000. Given that the club continued to haemorrhage money long after it opened on 21 May 1982 it was just as well that New Order went on to exceed the commercial success of Joy Division. Meanwhile Wilson's imprint on the project was ubiquitous, from the club's name, the Haçienda (after the situationist tract *The Haçienda Must be Built*), to the location of the stage: New Order had wanted it to be prominent so as to create a focus for audiences, but Wilson insisted that it be located in the middle of the bar area so as not to impinge on the main floor space.

The increased stresses associated with the Haçienda project almost certainly contributed to the collapse of Wilson's marriage to Reade in 1981–2, a period that also saw him move to 36 Old Broadway in Withington, south Manchester. In early 1984 he began a relationship with Hilary J. Sherlock (*b.* 1955), and they quickly married, opting for a New York courtroom rather than a British register office. They had two children, Oliver (*b.* 1984) and Isabel (*b.* 1990), but once again the marriage failed.

Meanwhile, thanks to New Order's continuing commercial achievements (which included setting a sales record for a 12 inch single with 'Blue Monday' in 1983) and artistic acumen (they helped shape a new electronic dance-orientated music culture), Wilson's stature as a creative entrepreneur grew steadily throughout the 1980s and with it his wider ambitions for the reinvention of Manchester as a cultural capital. After a rocky start the Haçienda found its niche as a groundbreaking dance club, in no small part due to the arrival of the illegal recreational drug ecstasy in 1987. The venue went on to assume a legendary status. However, any suggestion that Wilson had a Midas touch when it came to talent-spotting and artist development would be misplaced. Factory's reluctance to promote its artists meant that most failed to get the attention they deserved. The Factory ethos also seemed a little smug for some. Morrissey, for instance, preferred to take his archly Mancunian band the Smiths to the London-based label Rough Trade. Yet there was one other major success for Wilson's Factory label by the turn of the decade, the Happy Mondays.

Wilson's job as a television presenter also received a fillip in 1987 when he hosted a new Channel 4 discussion programme, *After Dark*. Its unstructured, conversational format was perfect for Wilson's style of presenting and met with widespread critical acclaim. Though hardly prime-time television, it was national and prestigious: Tony Wilson accordingly became Anthony H. Wilson. Another music programme followed in 1988—*The Other Side of Midnight*—that was notable for an early performance by the Stone Roses, a band Wilson had deliberately ignored because his ex-wife Lindsay had been their manager.

In 1989 Factory opened a bar called Dry, again co-owned with New Order. Rather than locate it on the Oxford Road so as to be convenient for Manchester's huge student population Wilson successfully pressed for Oldham Street, in what was a rundown part of the city centre. The effect was to cost Factory and New Order dear, but Dry—as Wilson had hoped—provided the spark for the regeneration of Manchester's northern quarter.

Later years After the high of the late 1980s came the low of the early 1990s. Wilson's indulgence of the unruly excesses of the Happy Mondays resulted in the band going massively over budget for the troubled follow-up to their acclaimed album *Pills 'n' Thrills and Bellyaches* (1990). Around the same time the New Order cash cow dried up as squabbles in the band delayed the recording of a successor to the acid house-influenced *Technique* album of 1989. The Haçienda, in addition, was beset by gang-related violence, prompting intermittent closures. Amid all this Wilson hubristically focused on a new flagship headquarters for Factory on Charles Street, costing three-quarters of a million pounds. Wilson's personal life became newspaper gossip in 1991 when he left Hilary for Yvette Livesey (*b.* 1968), a model who had been Miss UK in 1987. Finally, in November 1992, two months after the release of the Happy Mondays' justly ignored *Yes Please!* album (it sold as few as 10,000 copies in its initial chart run), Factory was declared bankrupt with debts of £2.5 million. With a crash in Britain's property market and exceptionally high interest rates to contend with, Factory had been beset by cash-flow problems and crippling negative equity. Potential investors had fled after seeing the label's shambolic organization and learning about Wilson's radical policy of letting artists own the copyright to their own recordings. Formal contracts had only been introduced in late 1988—too late to affect much of the blue chip back catalogue. While Wilson would later claim that Factory's demise was part of a situationist master plan his anguish at the time indicated otherwise. The Haçienda staggered on for another five years before closing for good in June 1997, and was subsequently knocked down to make way for an apartment building, an ironic twist to Wilson's ambitions for the creative regeneration of Manchester.

Although Wilson's involvement in the music industry was maintained by a link with Polygram's subsidiary London Records (which had also scooped the New Order and Joy Division catalogue in the dying days of Factory), the reality was that his new label, Factory Too, was a pale shadow of its predecessor. Band-spotting proved especially difficult for the forty-something Wilson, as his lacklustre signings demonstrated. His Granada profile was also on the wane. An annual retainer of £15,000 for punditry and occasional presenting felt more like a pension than a job. While *Content*, another arts and music programme, helped pay the bills for a while in 1999–2000, money was becoming increasingly tight. In 2001 a lifetime achievement award from the Royal Television Society was received by Wilson with bitterness: 'This piece of shit … implies closure, old age and maturity', he told the award ceremony audience (Nolan, 170). Interest in the Factory story increased in 2002 with the release of Michael Winterbottom's mythologizing feature film *24 Hour Party People*, with the comic actor Steve Coogan playing Wilson. A hastily written book by Wilson with the same title was published that same year.

The extra attention Wilson received failed to revive his television career and by 2003 he was still doing piecework for Granada. Reading short news bulletins throughout the daily schedule was one such responsibility until his habit of swearing like a trooper caught up with him. Not realizing that a microphone was on during a live broadcast (just prior to the start of *Thomas the Tank Engine*) Wilson alerted his production crew in colourful terms that a red light on a camera had broken. A suspension and reprieve followed before Wilson decided his own fate by resigning from Granada, ostensibly to concentrate on campaigning for a devolved parliament for the north-west. Occasional reporting and presenting work for the BBC kept his connection with television going. When a 'biopic' version of Ian Curtis's life was mooted in 2004 Wilson was brought in as a co-producer. *Control*, directed by Anton Corbijn, was eventually released in October 2007.

In December 2006 Wilson was diagnosed with kidney cancer. Despite his friends contributing to a fund so that he could receive an expensive new drug treatment not available in his region of the NHS, he succumbed to the illness at the Christie Hospital, Withington, Manchester, on 10 August 2007. Manchester Town Hall lowered its flag to half mast. He was buried at the Southern cemetery, Charlton-Cum-Hardy, on 20 August, his coffin bearing the

Factory catalogue number FAC 501. He was survived by his partner, Yvette, and by his two children.

MICHAEL T. THORNHILL

Sources D. Nolan, *You're entitled to an opinion* (2009) • J. Nice, *Shadowplayers* (2010) • D. Curtis, *Touching from a distance* (1995) • D. Haslam, *Manchester, England* (1999) • T. Wilson, *24 hour party people* (2002) • *The Guardian* (20 May 2002); (13 Aug 2007); (21 Aug 2007) • S. Reynolds, *Rip it up and start again* (2005) • M. Robertson, *Factory records* (2006) • *The Times* (11 Aug 2007); (13 Aug 2007) • *Daily Telegraph* (13 Aug 2007) • *The Independent* (13 Aug 2007) • P. Hook, *The Haçienda* (2009) • K. Cummins, *Manchester: looking for the light through the pouring rain* (2009) • L. Reade, *Mr Manchester and the Factory girl: the story of Tony and Lindsay Wilson* (2010) • b. cert. • m. cert. [1977] • d. cert.

Archives FILM BFINA, performance footage • BFINA, documentary footage | SOUND BL NSA, documentary recordings

Likenesses H. Goodwin, photograph, 1970–79, Rex Features, London [*see illus.*] • H. Goodwin, photographs, 1970–79, Rex Features, London • photographs, 1970–2006, Rex Features, London • photographs, 1970–2006, Getty Images, London • photographs, 1975–2007, PA Photos, London • K. Cummins, bromide fibre print, 1985, NPG • photographs, 2002–6, PA Photos, London • P. Diggle, oils, 2007, priv. coll. • obituary photographs • photographs, Camera Press, London • photographs, repro. in Wilson, *24 hour party people* • photographs, repro. in Nolan, *You're entitled*

Wealth at death £484,747: probate, 13 March 2008, *CGPLA Eng. & Wales*

Sir Colin Alexander St John Wilson (1922–2007), by Anne-Katrin Purkiss, 1994

Wilson, Sir Colin Alexander St John [Sandy] (**1922–2007**), architect, was born on 14 March 1922 at St Mary's rectory, Cheltenham, Gloucestershire, the youngest of five children of Henry Albert Wilson (1876–1961), rector and rural dean of Cheltenham, bishop of Chelmsford from 1929 to 1950, and his wife, Dorothy Mary Marston, *née* Daniels (1883–1972), daughter of G. Walter Daniels, cloth merchant. His father was known as the Bolshie Bishop or the Red Rev because of his republican sympathies during the Spanish Civil War.

Wilson was born after an older brother, Roger (1913–1918), had died of tuberculosis, and considered himself a substitute. He was educated at Eversley House School, Southwold, and Felsted School, near Dunmow, Essex. In 1940 he entered Corpus Christi College, Cambridge, switching from history to architecture 'because there was an element of drawing in it' (Menin and Kite, 19). After service with the Royal Naval Volunteer Reserve in 1941–6 (latterly as a lieutenant) he used his demobilization pay to buy his first painting. He completed his training at the Bartlett School of Architecture, University College, London, in 1950, and worked for the classicist Verner Rees before joining the London county council (LCC)'s architect's department later that year.

Wilson's training had been rooted in the arts and crafts movement and in classicism. But at the LCC he found himself in the vanguard of modernism, working in a group of young graduates under the supervision of Robert Matthew and Leslie Martin. He joined a dynamic team that designed a prototype narrow-fronted maisonette, realized as ten-storey slab blocks inspired by Le Corbusier's *unité d'habitation*; Wilson's version appeared at the Bentham Road estate, completed in 1955. Wilson and a colleague, Peter Carter, meanwhile (unsuccessfully) entered the competition for Coventry Cathedral in 1950 with a square, centralized design under an early space frame roof.

Of greater significance was Wilson's involvement in the exhibition 'This is Tomorrow' at the Whitechapel Gallery in 1956, a collaboration between groups of architects and artists triggered by a meeting with Paule Vézelay, introduced to him by Martin. Already Wilson had joined the Independent Group, after finding himself the neighbour of Reyner and Mary Banham, through whom he met James Stirling, Eduardo Paolozzi, and the Smithsons. The Banhams also introduced Wilson to his first wife, Muriel Lavender (*b.* 1933), an art student and later gallery manager, daughter of Alfred Joel Lavender, schoolmaster. They married at the parish church of St Peter with St Thomas, Marylebone, London, on 20 August 1955. That year Wilson left the LCC to work for a developer, John de Vere Hunt, producing one scheme, in Hereford Square, Kensington. This block of flats was strikingly similar to Stirling and Gowan's contemporary flats at Ham Common in its honest expression of brick and concrete, and was a refinement of an idiom used by Le Corbusier at his Maisons Jaoul. Wilson's first independent work thus established him as one of the 'new brutalists', and he worked on a series of housing proposals, 'Habitat', with the Smithsons, Bill Howell, Stirling, and others.

In June 1956 Martin invited Wilson to work in Cambridge, where he had become professor of architecture and set up a private practice. Wilson's addition to the school of architecture, made with Alex Hardy and their students, repeated the Jaoul idiom on a rigorous proportional grid. With impeccable credentials in both the academic and local authority sectors, Martin was flooded with work, and as an adviser to potential clients he influenced 1960s university architecture out of all measure to the buildings he and Wilson designed. The nature of the collaboration, with Martin realizing his ideas through others, means that it is hard to unravel the precise authorship of many works. Wilson married the traditional Cambridge court with the raised, stepped internal courtyard of Alvar Aalto's Säynätsalo town hall in an unrealized scheme for King's; something of this plan appears at Harvey Court (1957–61) in a scheme developed by another assistant, Patrick Hodgkinson. Wilson planned a looser series of courtyards for Leicester University with Martin, and realized the physics laboratory and science lecture theatre, a three-sided block completed in 1961.

A seminal moment in Wilson's career was meeting Aalto in 1957, followed by his first visit to Finland and an introduction to Louis Kahn. Aalto's influence can be seen in the staggered plan of the William Stone Building (1963–4), an eight-storey brick accommodation tower for Peterhouse, Cambridge. Kahn's influence may have inspired the pair of houses that Wilson built in 1962–4 in Grantchester Road, one of them for himself and Muriel, a complex geometry realized in concrete block to a tartan grid that extends into the yard behind. The Wilsons' house is set behind a rigorous colonnade that supports an architect's office; the double-height drawing room behind housed a growing art collection. These influences matured at the St Cross Library in Oxford (opened in 1964), three libraries set off a broad, straight external stair (a Martin trait) and a cranked internal one. Though the final scheme was largely Martin's, in the largest library, for the law faculty, the complex layering of galleries and clerestories that defines Wilson's later work is apparent. St Cross led in 1962 to Martin and Wilson being jointly commissioned to extend the British Museum Library in Bloomsbury, and their first design, a series of libraries set off an L-shaped catalogue room that were expressed externally by colonnades, contained elements of the Grantchester Road and Oxford designs on a massive scale.

Wilson spent much of 1964 teaching at Yale. His students included Mary Jane (M. J.) Long (*b.* 1939), who came to work for him when he set up independent practice in 1965. They married in 1972, following the dissolution of his first marriage in 1971; a daughter, born in 1974, was followed by a son in 1976. Their first architectural collaboration was the Cambridge house they designed for the artist Christopher Cornford in 1965–7, featuring an atrium and gallery, and where Aalto's influence was strong. A commission for an ambitious new civic centre at Liverpool, also won in 1965, was aborted due to rising costs in 1973. Subsequently Wilson's career was dominated by the British Library, for which he took sole charge in 1968 and prepared a revised scheme in 1972–3 that included accommodation for the science and patents departments as well as for humanities, the two sections set either side of Hawksmoor's St George's Church in a scheme that also included terraces of public housing. Eventually, all that was realized in Bloomsbury was a gallery, restaurants, and offices, tucked to the west of the British Museum's portico and completed in 1979.

A new site for the British Library at St Pancras was confirmed in 1975. An initial study by Long kept the division between humanities and sciences, the former requiring large numbers of seats and closed stacks, the latter requiring more open shelving. Thus the development evolved around a central circulation space and catalogue hall as in the Bloomsbury schemes. The approved design of 1977 was, however, truncated by the government in 1987–8, and only about half was realized. A major revision was the setting of the King's Library in a giant glass case into the intended catalogue hall. Beset by uncertain funding, criticism from the prince of Wales—who in 1988 called it 'an academy for secret police' (*The Times*, 29 Oct 1988)—and delays, many caused by shelving problems, the British Library finally opened in 1997. Yet, with its integrated works of art by Wilson's friends, including Paolozzi and R. B. Kitaj, the building caught the mood of the late 1990s for a gentle neo-modernism, and while unsubtly referencing Aalto in such details as handrails its interior is almost heroic in scale. Lord Palumbo called it 'the greatest British public building of the twentieth century' (Barber). Wilson advocated this alternative modernism in two books written in the darkest hours of the British Library saga. *Architectural Reflections* (1992) arose out of his lectures to undergraduates, and *The Other Tradition of Modern Architecture* (1995) recorded his belief in the continuing relevance of architecture's humane mission, traced through the work of Aalto and other Scandinavian architects. He also wrote *The Artist at Work* (1999), on the working methods of the painters William Coldstream and Michael Andrews.

Wilson and Long came to specialize in libraries, with a circular library at Springfield, Chelmsford, commemorating Wilson's father, completed in 1984, and a library at Queen Mary College, London, built in 1989 and again following an L-plan. Indeed, Wilson argued, like Aalto, that one job should evolve out of another, each building on the experience of the last, and the homogeneity of his designs supports this tenet. Long set up her own practice, and a partnership with Rolfe Kentish in 1994. They worked with Wilson, notably on a large but quietly constructionist addition to the Pallant House Gallery in Chichester, opened in 2006, which houses Wilson's collection of modern British art and is a powerful memorial to his life and work.

In 1975, Wilson (known professionally as Colin St John Wilson, but by friends and family as Sandy) was appointed to the chair of architecture at Cambridge, which he held until 1989. A popular and inspiring teacher, he sought to expand the architectural debate, building on Martin's scientific research while introducing a critical and philosophical dimension. He was appointed a trustee of the Tate Gallery (1973–80) and of the National Gallery (1977–80). He was knighted in 1998. He died at St John's Hospice, Westminster, on 14 May 2007, of multiple myeloma, and was survived by his wife, Mary Jane, and their two children. ELAIN HARWOOD

Sources F. MacCarthy, 'Written in stone', *Guardian Weekend* (26 Aug 1995) · L. Barber, 'A job for life', *Telegraph Magazine* (27 April 1996) · C. St J. Wilson, *The design and construction of the British Library* (1998) · R. Stonehouse and G. Stromberg, *The architecture of the*

British Library (2004) · S. Menin and S. Kite, *An architecture of invitation: Colin St John Wilson* (2005) · R. Stonehouse, *Colin St John Wilson: buildings and projects* (2007) · *Daily Telegraph* (16 May 2007) · *The Guardian* (16 May 2007) · *The Times* (17 May 2007) · *The Independent* (19 May 2007) · Burke, *Peerage* · *WW* (2007) · personal knowledge (2011) · private information (2011) · b. cert. · m. cert. [1955] · d. cert.

Archives SOUND BL NSA, documentary recordings

Likenesses B. Seed, photographs, 1965, Camera Press, London · R. B. Kitaj, oil on canvas, 1981 (with M. J. Long), Pallant House Gallery, Chichester · W. Coldstream, portrait, 1982–3, Pallant House Gallery, Chichester · self-portrait, 1986, Pallant House Gallery, Chichester · B. Bernard, colour print, 1994, NPG · A.-K. Purkiss, bromide fibre print, 1994, NPG [*see illus.*] · S. Back, photographs, 1998, Rex Features, London · T. Kyriacou, photographs, 1998, Rex Features, London · obituary photographs

Wealth at death £9,884,208: probate, 27 March 2008, *CGPLA Eng. & Wales*

Wilson, Eric Charles Twelves (1912–2008), army officer and colonial administrator, was born on 2 October 1912 at Sheredale, Station Avenue, Sandown, Isle of Wight, the only son of Cyril Charles Clissold Wilson (1884–1971), curate at Sandown, later wartime chaplain, and rector of Hunsdon, Hertfordshire, and his wife, Evelyn, *née* Twelves. His paternal grandfather was Charles Thomas Wilson, the first Christian Missionary Society missionary to go to Buganda, in 1877.

Wilson was educated at Marlborough College (1926–31), which offered reduced fees for the sons of Anglican clergy (and has produced thirteen recipients of the Victoria Cross, and at least one Soviet spy). Tall and athletic, he became house captain, but never rose above private in the officer training corps. Inspired by the college memorial to Richard Conyngham Corfield, killed in Somaliland in 1913, he decided on a military career. He passed the entrance examination for the Royal Military College, Sandhurst, while still at school and, despite wearing spectacles, was accepted. He attended Sandhurst from August 1931 to December 1932. He was a prize cadet (receiving a scholarship or bursary) but in August 1932 forfeited his prize cadetship. He passed in 19th but passed out 115th (of 206). In February 1933 he was commissioned second lieutenant in the East Surrey regiment, and was promoted lieutenant three years later.

In July 1937 Wilson was seconded to the King's African rifles and served in Tanganyika with the 2nd (Nyasaland) battalion, becoming a Nyanja speaker. In 1939 he was seconded to the Somaliland camel corps. In August 1940 a large Italian force under General Guglielmo Nasi invaded British Somaliland. The British imperial force there was outnumbered, outgunned, and short of barbed wire. A principal British defensive position was at the Tug Argan gap, where the British occupied the overlooking hills. Wilson (by now an acting captain) commanded part of the camel corps machine-gun company, with Vickers machine-guns, on Observation Hill. From 11 August his posts engaged the invaders, inflicting many casualties. Under artillery fire Wilson, his spectacles shattered (fragments were visible under his skin for the rest of his life), with untreated wounds to his right shoulder and left eye, and suffering from malaria, fought on, repairing damaged

Eric Charles Twelves Wilson (1912–2008), by unknown photographer

weapons. His terrier Vicky was killed. On 13 August an order to withdraw was sent to Wilson but never received. About 5 p.m. on 15 August the enemy overran Wilson's post and he was captured. The British believed him killed and the Italians failed to inform the Red Cross that he was a prisoner of war.

In October 1940 Wilson was awarded a 'posthumous' Victoria Cross, 'for most conspicuous gallantry … Captain Wilson, fighting to the last, was killed' (*London Gazette*, 14 Oct 1940): the *Daily Sketch* headline was 'Another Rorke's Drift'. Despite official contradiction (reported in *The Times* on 16 Oct 1940), the error that he had been killed persisted. After medical treatment he was held in a prison camp at Adi Ugri, Eritrea, where a newly captured RAF officer, surprised to meet 'the late' Captain Wilson, told him of his Victoria Cross. Following the British liberation of the camp in early 1941 Wilson returned to England. He received his cross from the king at Buckingham Palace in July 1942.

Promoted captain in February 1941 and temporary major in November, Wilson served in north Africa as adjutant of the Long Range Desert Group. He then served in Burma as second in command of the 11th (Kenyan) King's African rifles on the advance down the Kabaw valley to the Chindwin. He contracted scrub typhus, spent two months in hospital, and was medically downgraded. Promoted acting lieutenant-colonel in June 1945, he spent the last months of the war commanding the infantry training centre at Jinja, Uganda. In 1946 he was seconded to the Northern Rhodesia regiment, and in 1949 he retired from the army. On 1 May 1943, at St Peter's Church, Pimlico, he had married Ann Pleydell-Bouverie (*b.* 1923), daughter of Major Humphrey Pleydell-Bouverie, and descended from the earls of Radnor and Harewood; they had two sons but divorced in 1953. In the same year he married Angela Joy Gordon, daughter of Lieutenant-Colonel J. McK. Gordon; they had one son.

From 1949 to 1961 Wilson served in the overseas civil service in Tanganyika, learning four local languages. Sympathetic towards Africans, he was district commissioner in North Mara, where he ended cattle raiding between the Masai and Kuria, and later in Mbeya. He left at Tanganyikan independence. He was then deputy warden (1962–6) and warden (1966–77) of London House, Mecklenburgh Square, London, a residence for graduate students from overseas. He remained attached to the Somali people, and was honorary secretary of the Anglo-Somali Society (1972–7 and 1988–90), organizing relief for the 1975 Somalia famine. He retired to Stowell in Dorset, where he enjoyed country life and wrote *Stowell in the Blackmore Vale* (1986). Towards the end of his life the oldest holder of the Victoria Cross and much in demand as a speaker and guest, he was active in the Victoria Cross and George Cross Association.

Latterly Wilson suffered from cancer of the prostate. He died on 23 December 2008 at Bydand, Watery Lane, Stowell, Dorset, after a stroke, and was buried on 29 December in the churchyard of St Peter and St Paul, Stowell. He was survived by his wife, Angela, and two sons, one of the sons of his first marriage having predeceased him.

ROGER T. STEARN

Sources *The Times* (12 Oct 1940); (16 Oct 1940); (30 Dec 2008); (5 Jan 2009) · *LondG* (14 Oct 1940) · H. Moyse-Bartlett, *The King's African rifles: a study in the military history of east and central Africa, 1890–1945* (1956) · J. Smyth, *Sandhurst: the history of the Royal Military Academy, Woolwich, the Royal Military College, Sandhurst, and the Royal Military Academy, Sandhurst, 1741–1961* (1961) · M. Langley, *The East Surrey regiment* (1972) · *The register of the Victoria Cross* (1981) · *Services of British army officers &c., 1939–1945* (1999) · M. C. Smith, *Awarded for valour: a history of the Victoria Cross and the evolution of British heroism* (2008) · *Daily Telegraph* (30 Dec 2008) · *The Independent* (2 Jan 2009) · *The Guardian* (20 Jan 2009) · *Medal News* (Feb 2009) · *WW* (2008) · army lists, 1933–49 · L. W. James, ed., *Marlborough College register: 1843–1952*, 9th edn (1952) · private information (2012) [A. R. Morton, T. E. Rogers] · b. cert. · m. cert. [1943] · d. cert.

Likenesses photograph, 1942, Rex Features, London · photograph, 1999 (with Queen Elizabeth II), Camera Press, London · photographs, 1999–2005, PA Photos, London · photograph, repro. in *Daily Telegraph* [*see illus.*]

Wilson, John (1927–2006), police officer, was born on 24 February 1927 at 25 Amos Avenue, Newton Heath, Manchester, the son of Joseph Wilson, linen salesman, and his wife, Hannah, *née* Pinch. The family moved to Lincoln where he was educated at the City School. Called up as the Second World War was ending he served in the intelligence corps in Palestine, a fitting background for his later career, and an experience that also gave him his first brush with terrorists when Irgun gunmen, fighting for an independent Jewish state, infiltrated his base. The terrorists, disguised as British soldiers, arrived on a jeep and planned to raid the officers' mess for hostages. Nineteen-year-old Wilson found himself lined up against a wall with a sten gun stuck in his back and later dryly recalled that the only thing he could think of was his mother.

Demobilized in 1948, Wilson drifted through a number of jobs, including working as an advertising salesman for the *Lincolnshire Echo* and trading in fruit and vegetables in the London docks. He started an economics course at Manchester University, which proved to be a poor choice; Wilson, uninspired, played squash by day and bridge by night. On 23 September 1950, while still a student, he married (Marjorie) Joan Suthrell (1928–2003), a chiropodist. Unsure of his career, Wilson consulted his former headmaster, who advised him to join the police.

Wilson began his career in the Metropolitan Police at the age of twenty-seven. After two unhappy years on the beat he decided to apply for special branch. The branch was then regarded as an élite in which officers often stayed for the rest of their careers. Formed in the 1870s as the special Irish branch to combat Fenian terrorism, the department by the 1950s covered counter-terrorism, extremism, subversion and counter-espionage, and the protection of politicians and VIPs, and also ran a national ports unit monitoring passenger arrivals and departures. Wilson had been turned down when he first applied but succeeded the second time. His introduction was inauspicious: a senior officer greeted Wilson's intake by telling the young officers that they should abandon hopes of reaching high rank because none would rise above sergeant. By the late 1960s Wilson was indeed still a detective sergeant after working in the branch's C squad, watching suspected political extremists, and A squad, which provided protection for VIPs. On one embarrassing occasion he was guarding General Ne Win, the Burmese dictator, and was chased round the garden of the general's London home by a curious guest who demanded to see his gun. Wilson, who loathed firearms, had left his weapon at home.

The re-emergence of the IRA was the spark that ignited Wilson's career after he was drafted into the branch's largely dormant B squad, devoted to Irish terrorism. In 1971 Wilson received intelligence that the Provisional IRA was planning its first major attack on London under cover of a rail strike. Extra police were poured into central London. They could not prevent car bombs from being planted outside the Old Bailey, where one man was killed, at Scotland Yard itself, and at two other establishment targets; but the bombers, the 'Belfast ten', were caught within hours and the chaos could have been far worse if the police had not been alerted. Wilson received commendations from the commissioner of the Metropolitan Police, Sir Robert Mark, and from the trial judge for his work.

Throughout the 1970s Wilson, awarded a second commissioner's commendation in 1974, was a key figure in the fight against the IRA and loyalist extremists, repairing and building strong relationships with the Royal Ulster Constabulary, the Garda Siochana, the cabinet office, and politicians. He became an acknowledged expert on Irish terrorism and in 1976 was promoted to chief superintendent and head of the Irish section. Often blunt and forthright, he was also extremely loyal and supportive of his officers. In 1977 he was appointed MBE and in 1978 became commander heading all special branch operations. He was awarded the queen's police medal shortly before he retired in 1983.

Wilson spent eight years as security chief for Britoil, based in Glasgow, before settling in North Walsham, Norfolk. Always loyal to his service, in retirement he lobbied against the expansion of MI5 in the 1990s into Irish counter-terrorism. He argued that other threats like Islamic extremism might be ignored. He died at his home, South Cottage, Crostwight Hall, North Walsham, Norfolk, on 6 February 2006, of alcohol poisoning, and was cremated at St Faith crematorium, Horsham St Faith, Norfolk. He was predeceased by his wife and was survived by two daughters and a son. STEWART TENDLER

Sources B. Huntley, *Bomb squad: my war against the terrorists* (1977) • M. Fido and K. Skinner, *The official encyclopedia of Scotland Yard* (1999) • *Daily Telegraph* (27 Feb 2006) • *The Times* (10 March 2006) • personal knowledge (2010) • private information (2010) • b. cert. • m. cert. • d. cert.
Likenesses obituary photographs
Wealth at death £315,402: probate, 7 June 2006, *CGPLA Eng. & Wales*

Wimbush, Mary (1924–2005), actress, was born on 19 March 1924, at 60 Carlton Avenue, Kenton, Middlesex, the daughter of (Nelson) Norman Wimbush, schoolmaster and lecturer in economics for London county council, and his wife, Ida Margaret, *née* Hughes. The family moved to Berkhamsted, Hertfordshire, when she was four. Her mother had attended the Royal Academy of Dramatic Art, and her father (who was facially disfigured in the First World War) was keen on amateur dramatics. She was educated at the Masonic School, Bushey, Berkhamsted School for Girls, and the convent school of St Agnes and St Michael, East Grinstead, Sussex, before training at the Central School of Speech and Drama, London. Leaving a few months before the Second World War ended, she joined ENSA to give entertainment to servicemen along the south coast, at a time when flying bombs were frequently overhead—an experience she found unnerving as she never knew when they were going to 'cut out and fall on you', as she put it years later (*The Independent*, 2 Nov 2005).

Wimbush began her peacetime acting career at Amersham repertory theatre and on 29 June 1946 married, as his second wife, the already well-known actor Howard Francis Marion-Crawford (1914–1969), who was then frequently employed by BBC producers in the Home Service and the new Third Programme. He was the son of Howard Francis Marion-Crawford, a lieutenant in the Irish Guards. They had one son, Charles. After her marriage Mary Wimbush (who continued acting under her maiden name) was soon also appearing on BBC radio, including in one of the first radio soap operas, *Mrs Dale's Diary*; the connection with the BBC Drama Repertory Company lasted into the 1970s and she did other radio work for the rest of her life. Her marriage to Howard Marion-Crawford ended in divorce in 1954. Four years later, from 1958 until his death, she was the lover of the poet (Frederick) Louis *MacNeice (1907–1963), who dedicated his last book of poems to her. She declined to participate in a BBC programme in which their relationship was discussed years later, a diffidence that was lived out in a modest cottage near Sherborne, Dorset, which for a long time was her home: she said that she was lucky in that she needed little in life except her work.

As a radio performer Wimbush's range was wide. She was cast as the heroine in H. L. V. Fletcher's drama *The Storm* in 1961, and the drama producer Audrey Cameron cast her in two Margery Allingham adaptations, *Look to the Lady* (1961) and *Black Plumes* (1964). But she could also be easily cast in the lighter roles of Alan Melville, such as *At Your Service* (1976). Auburn-haired and blue-eyed, hers was virtually an unknown face (as distinct from voice) until, in 1969, she appeared as the 'universal mother' character Mary Smith in Richard Attenborough's film of *Oh! What a Lovely War*. She got the part because Attenborough remembered that, years before, they had both been in a radio play in which she had played a mother who had to be told by her doctor that her son was dead. 'Every time she went through the scene, even at rehearsal, just standing by a microphone with a script in her hand, she made me cry', remembered Attenborough. 'I promised myself that if ever I were able to offer her a job, I would.' Her own reaction to the job was less flamboyant: 'Now at last they can see what I look like!' (*The Guardian*, 2 Nov 2005).

Wimbush's next films, *Fragment of Fear* (1970) and *Vampire Circus* (1972), and her television work in the 1970s and 1980s, including *Lady Killer* (1973), *Fall of Eagles*, and *Country Matters* (both 1974), were less notable, but her regular television appearances as Prudie Paynter in the Winston Graham series *Poldark* (1975–6) for the first time made her a prominent figure in British television. Meanwhile she was establishing herself on the stage across a wide range of parts and venues, including working for the National Theatre as the Duchess of York in *Richard III* and Mrs Sorby in *The Wild Duck*; creating Edna Shaft in Simon Gray's *Butley* in the West End; and at Birmingham Repertory Theatre playing the loyal wife of Sir Thomas More in *A Man for All Seasons*, Queen Gertrude in *Hamlet*, Clara in J. B. Priestley's *When we are Married*, and the Countess of Henslowe in *Elizabeth Rex*. In a production of *The Prime of Miss Jean Brodie*, at the Royal Exchange Theatre, Manchester, she played Miss Mackay.

Nevertheless it was radio, and in particular the highly popular and long-running soap opera *The Archers*, that was to utilize to the full Wimbush's flair for strong-voiced roles with flashes of humour, and crown her career. She began in *The Archers* in 1965 by playing the village schoolteacher Elsie Catcher, but that character retired in 1967 and it was not until two years later that she was recalled to the programme as the snobbish Lady Isabel Lander—until she too was written out. In 1992 she became Nigel Pargetter's over-assertive, manipulative mother Julia Pargetter, who for a time takes to drink before reforming. This was a character Wimbush expected to die off or otherwise disappear, but the outcome was rather different, and the character was killed off only after Wimbush's own death. Wimbush was able to use her distinctive voice to create a memorably pretentious character from a very ordinary background whose son was the heir to Lower

Loxley Hall and whose vulnerability made her just tolerable. The actress herself maintained that she had found the character most stimulating to play when she was on the bottle, but Julia Pargetter was a survivor like the actress who played her.

In 1991 Wimbush won the Sony Radio award for best actress for her performances in *The Horse's Mouth* and *The Mystery of Edwin Drood*, and two years later played Lady Edith in *The Governor's Consort*, a role written specifically for her by Peter Tinniswood. She was determined never to retire, and in 2004 was in a two-month tour of Arthur Miller's *The Crucible*. 'I intend to go on enjoying myself to the last', she said (*Birmingham Post*, 4 Oct 2004). She was taken ill with a retroperitoneal haemorrhage at the BBC Birmingham studios on 31 October 2005 after playing Julia Pargetter in a recording of an episode of *The Archers*, and was declared dead at the City Hospital, Winson Green. She was a modest but firm and distinctive favourite of radio, television, and theatre audiences, whose acting career had lasted more than sixty years. She was survived by her son Charles. DENNIS BARKER

Sources *The Times* (2 Nov 2005) · *Daily Telegraph* (2 Nov 2005) · *The Guardian* (2 Nov 2005) · *The Independent* (2 Nov 2005) · personal knowledge (2009) · private information (2009) · b. cert. · m. cert. · d. cert.
Archives FILM BFINA, performance footage | SOUND BL NSA, documentary recordings · BL NSA, performance recordings
Likenesses obituary photographs · photograph, BBC
Wealth at death £282,016: probate, 20 April 2006, *CGPLA Eng. & Wales*

Winskill, Sir Archibald Little (1917–2005), air force officer, was born on 24 January 1917 at 3 Middlegate, Penrith, Cumberland, the son of James Winskill, a motor mechanic then serving in the navy, later a car dealer, and his wife, Caroline, *née* Little. He was educated at Queen Elizabeth Grammar School, Penrith, and Carlisle grammar school; then, having shown a decided mechanical bent, from 1934 to 1939 was a trainee for a traffic apprenticeship at the London and North Eastern Railway works in Edinburgh. In 1937, in a move which was to determine the whole course of his future career, he joined the Royal Air Force Volunteer Reserve as a trainee pilot and was given basic flying training.

Like hundreds of other reservists Winskill was mobilized on the outbreak of the Second World War. On 24 August 1940 he was commissioned as a pilot officer in the RAF, and his first posting was to no. 8 bombing and gunnery school; then he was sent to an operational training unit—no. 7 at Harwarden—and from there to 54 squadron, a Spitfire squadron at Hornchurch. He then served briefly with 72 and 603 squadrons before being posted to 41 squadron, where he was appointed a flight commander.

On 14 August 1941 Winskill was reported missing. As part of the Tangmere wing he had been escorting Blenheims in an attack on a target near Lille when they were intercepted by Messerschmitt Bf 109s, one of which he shot down. His Spitfire was then hit and set on fire, forcing him to bale out. A French farmer took him to a cornfield, where he hid until nightfall; then the farmer's son took him into the farmhouse, where he was fed, and subsequently provided him with food daily until he could be sent to a 'safe house'. After two weeks his escape odyssey began—by bicycle, dressed as a farm worker, to a series of other houses until he was put on a train for Paris. There he was taken over by the Pat O'Leary escape line, which had a very successful record of escorting allied airmen and soldiers through occupied France into Spain. He went by train to Marseilles, then to Aix-les-Thermes in the Pyrenean foothills. With two other evaders he was guided over the mountains by an Andorran with local knowledge; they reached Barcelona, where the British consul-general arranged for them to be sent to Gibraltar via Madrid. Three months after being shot down Winskill was safely back in the UK, though forbidden to fly over Europe again because of his knowledge of escape routes. He was subsequently awarded the DFC.

From December 1941 Winskill served in three fighter squadrons—145, 611, and 165—before being given his first commands as squadron leader, briefly of 72 and 222 squadrons and finally of 232 squadron, eastern air command, Africa. This squadron provided close air support for the British First Army in Algeria and Tunisia. On 18 January 1943 he was shot down off the Tunisian coast and forced to bale out for the second time, coming down in the sea. He swam ashore, behind enemy lines, evaded capture, and rejoined his squadron. From April 1943 he was back on operations, shooting down a Stuka dive-bomber, sharing in the destruction of another, and ground strafing retreating axis forces. His north African tour ended in June 1943, when he was awarded a bar to his DFC. He served for the rest of the war at the Central Gunnery School, Sutton Bridge; he was promoted wing commander in March 1944. On 3 May 1947, at Hampstead register office, he married Christiane Amelie Pauline van het Kaar, formerly Kerbiriou, the former wife of Cornelius van het Kaar, and daughter of Emillieu Bailleux, of Calais. They had one son and one daughter.

In August 1947 Winskill was posted to Japan, with 17 squadron, part of the British component, Air Japan, serving there until April 1948 when sent to air headquarters, Malta. He then held a special appointment as air adviser to the Belgian government from December 1949, before returning to a series of UK postings at the Flying College, Manby, Stradishall, and Turnhouse. From June 1957 he was at the headquarters of the 2nd Tactical Air Force and in 1958 went to visit Felix Carron, the French farmboy who had helped him to evade capture—a meeting he described as a 'very emotional moment' (*Daily Telegraph*). By now a group captain, he was appointed to the staff of the air secretary and then, promoted air commodore, served as air attaché in Paris. From August 1967 he was director of RAF public relations, a post held then by an officer with a distinctive and inspiring war record.

In February 1968 Winskill was appointed captain of the queen's flight, following the death of group captain J. H. L. Blount in a Whirlwind helicopter accident. He had the task of restoring confidence, helped by the acquisition of

Wessex helicopters and Andovers, and was well liked by the royal family—especially the queen mother—for his charm and courtesy. Having been appointed CBE in 1960, he was appointed an extra equerry to the queen in 1968, CVO in 1973, and KCVO in 1980. He retired in 1982, and pursued his recreations of golf and bridge. Having lived latterly in Henley-on-Thames, he died in the Royal Berkshire Hospital, Reading, on 9 August 2005, of pneumonia and pulmonary fibrosis. He was survived by his wife, Christiane, and their daughter, his son having predeceased him. HUMPHREY WYNN

Sources *Daily Telegraph* (15 Aug 2005) · *Cumberland News* (19 Aug 2005) · *The Times* (26 Aug 2005) · RAF record of service, RAF Cranwell (Sleaford, Lincs.) · Burke, *Peerage* · *WW* (2005) · private information (2009) · b. cert. · m. cert. · d. cert.
Likenesses Hay Wrightson, three cream-toned bromide prints, NPG · obituary photographs
Wealth at death under £12,000: probate, 20 Feb 2006, *CGPLA Eng. & Wales*

(Cecile) Pearl Witherington (**1914–2008**), by unknown photographer, *c.*1943–*c.*1944

Witherington [*married name* Cornioley], **(Cecile) Pearl** (**1914–2008**), special operations officer, was born in Paris on 24 June 1914, the eldest of the four daughters of Wallace Seckham Witherington (1879–1932), the last surviving male member of an old Northumbrian fighting family, and his wife, Gertrude, née Hearn. She also had four brothers, all of whom died in infancy. Her family were gentry in reduced circumstances—her father drank heavily—and lived in Paris to save money. She was brought up there, becoming bilingual in French and English. Once she remembered coming home from school and finding the family's furniture in the street, because the apartment's rent was so long overdue. She later described her father (on her marriage certificate) as an architect, but it is doubtful that he ever practised. (His father, Walter Seckham Witherington, was an architect who designed, among other buildings, Carlyle Mansions in Chelsea.) When her parents separated, she and her sisters stayed with their mother. She went to elementary school in Paris, and learned to type.

When the Second World War broke out in September 1939 Pearl Witherington went to the British embassy, where the family was known, and volunteered for war work; she became an extra cipher clerk for the air attaché. Early in June 1940 she found the embassy closed—no one had remembered to tell her that the other staff had fled to Tours. She then realized the Germans were approaching Paris and took her mother and sisters down to Marseilles, crossing the demarcation line into unoccupied France illegally—her first clandestine operation.

The family was repatriated to England, and the air ministry found Pearl a post as personal assistant to a senior staff officer. She decided that this was no way for a Witherington to make war. She heard of the Special Operations Executive and volunteered for its independent French section. She learned guerrilla and sabotage skills, proved herself the best shot of her intake, was commissioned into the Women's Auxiliary Air Force, and was parachuted into France on the night of 22–3 September 1943. She was initially courier to Maurice Southgate's enormous Stationer circuit, which covered much of central France, and for over seven months travelled incessantly, by train, bicycle, or on foot, carrying arms and messages, disguised as Genevieve Touzalin, a cosmetics saleswoman. Though frequently passing through police and security controls, she was never arrested, despite many close shaves. The circuit was preparing groups of saboteurs who would make the Germans' rear areas unavailable to them after the impending invasion, and executed some useful coups, including blowing up a big Michelin tyre factory at Montluçon.

On 1 May 1944 Southgate fell into a Gestapo trap, which Witherington avoided. She then settled down to run a smaller circuit of her own, codenamed Wrestler, in the Sologne. Though a woman, at a time when women had no votes in France, and a foreigner, she accumulated a private army nearly 3000 strong, armed with hand weapons parachuted to her from England. The Germans heard of her, and offered a million francs for her capture; no one who knew her betrayed her. Henri Charles Willy Cornioley (1910–1999), a French pharmaceutical chemist to whom she had become engaged before the outbreak of war, joined her *en maquis* and fought beside her. (Neither family had approved the engagement: his because she was a protestant, hers because they did not think him a gentleman.) Her circuit brought rail traffic across the Sologne almost to a standstill after the Normandy landings, and ambushed road convoys heading for the front. It also helped to corral and force the surrender of a body of 18,000 German troops trying to retreat from south-western France back into the Reich. The region was overrun by the United States army late in August. She took Henri back to England with her, and they were married in Kensington register office on 26 October 1944. They had one daughter, Claire.

After the liberation of France, Pearl Cornioley was sent to the USA on a propaganda mission. This was not a great success because this small, correct, uniformed woman had none of the glamour an American audience expected of a secret agent. Her superiors sent her a civil MBE; she sent it back, saying she had done nothing civil. The air ministry secured her a military MBE, and she was advanced to CBE in 2004. The French also appointed her to the Légion d'honneur. In 1946 she returned to Paris, to a small flat she and Henri bought in the rue Pergolèse. She ran the secretarial side of the World Bank for many years. When she retired, and Henri's health began to fail, she sold the flat and moved with him to a *maison de retraite* at Châteauvieux, on the edge of Wrestler's former fighting area. She masterminded the erection of a memorial to F section's dead at Valençay (Indre), inaugurated by the queen mother in 1991 on the fiftieth anniversary of F section's first parachute drop, not far away. In 1996, in collaboration with a French journalist, Hervé Larroque, she published her autobiography, *Pauline*. She was a woman of unusual strength of character, courage, and directness of speech. Henri died at Châteauvieux in 1999; she died there on 24 February 2008. She was survived by her daughter.

M. R. D. Foot

Sources P. Cornioley and H. Larroque, *Pauline: la vie d'un agent du SOE* (Paris, 1996) • M. Binney, *The women who lived for danger* (2002) • M. R. D. Foot, *SOE in France*, 3rd edn (2003) • S. Helm, *A life in secrets: the story of Vera Atkins and the lost agents of SOE* (2005) • *The Times* (26 Feb 2008); (28 Feb 2008); (1 April 2008) • *Daily Telegraph* (26 Feb 2008) • *The Independent* (28 Feb 2008); (1 April 2008) • *The Guardian* (6 March 2008) • personal knowledge (2012) • private information (2012) • m. cert.

Archives TNA: PRO, H55/355/2, H59/356

Likenesses photograph, *c*.1943–*c*.1944, Heritage Image Partnership, London [*see illus.*] • photograph, 2004 (with Queen Elizabeth II), PA Photos, London • A. Jocard, photographs, 2006, Getty Images, London • obituary photographs • photographs, repro. in Cornioley and Larroque, *Pauline* • photographs, Rex Features, London

Wolf, Peter Otto (1918–2007), civil engineer and hydrologist, was born on 9 May 1918 in Vienna, the only son and elder child of Richard Wolf (1885–1967), civil engineer, and his wife, Dora (1889–1966), daughter of Julius Bondy. The latter, known in Vienna legal circles as 'the polite Dr Bondy' (a characteristic inherited by his grandson), was an adviser to the governments of Austria-Hungary, Turkey, and Persia, and was knighted by each.

Wolf went to school in St Pölten, Austria. His father, anxious that his son should not blindly follow him into an engineering career, enrolled him in the classical stream. But the boy did so well that he convinced his father that his desire to become an engineer did not stem from inability to do anything else. In 1936 he volunteered for service in the Austrian army as an officer cadet and in 1937 he started civil engineering studies at the Technische Hochschule, Vienna. When Germany annexed Austria in 1938 his father was the local chairman of the government party, the Patriotic Front, and was imprisoned by the Nazis; he was released through the efforts of the New York Ethical Union, arriving in England the day before war was declared on Germany. Meanwhile Wolf himself had escaped to England, obtaining a place as a student at King's College, London.

Peter Otto Wolf (1918–2007), by Janet Wolf

In 1939 Wolf was allowed to join the officer training corps and volunteered for service, but the recruiting board decided that he should continue with his studies. He gained a first-class degree in engineering from the University of London in 1941 but he also had a lively interest in theology, philosophy, and ethics, so he attended the additional course that led to his being awarded the Barry prize and becoming an associate of King's College. After graduating he was sent to work on land drainage and coast-defence in Yorkshire and Lincolnshire. Although initially classified as an enemy alien, he was in 1944 transferred by the intelligence unit of the War Office to work in the planning for naval combined operations in the run-up to the D-day landings, especially in relation to the canal and inland harbour systems in Europe. On 12 August that year he married Jennie Robinson (*b*. 1920), physiotherapist, and daughter of Arthur Robinson, bank manager. They had a daughter, Ann, and two sons, John and Michael. In 1945 Wolf chose to stay in Britain; his father returned to Austria, where he became engineering director of the Austrian Railways, but one month later he came back to live in England.

On leaving the War Office Wolf returned to flood protection works in Norfolk, but later in 1945, as part of the immediate post-war drive to build hydro-electric schemes, he joined James Williamson, consultant to the North of Scotland Hydro-electric Board, becoming chief designer for the Loch Sloy project and working on proposals for a system of hydro-electric schemes in the western highlands. In 1947 he moved to John Cochrane & Sons, contractors, and was senior engineer for the Mullardoch dam, which he would describe as the 'largest lump of concrete in the UK' (private information). In 1949 he changed direction and was appointed lecturer in fluid mechanics and hydraulic engineering at Imperial College, London; in 1955 he became reader in hydrology. In response to a request from hydrologists in Africa he founded the MSc course in the subject at Imperial College. It became the standard of comparison for subsequent graduate training in engineering hydrology and was still running fifty years later. At the same time he ran a private consulting office in London, specializing in floods, storm water, and water resources.

Wolf was to acquire the sobriquet 'the father of British Hydrology' (*Circulation*, 95, November 2007, 1). He said that his fascination with water started when he was three years old, playing with his ducks in the bath, and that he was lucky that for the rest of his life his work was his hobby. With his special expertise in flood protection, he was called upon to investigate and produce the hydrological analysis of the Lynmouth flood disaster of 1952, for which he was awarded (jointly with Charles Dobbie) the Telford premium of the Institution of Civil Engineers in 1953. In the latter year he became heavily involved with analysing the North Sea 'surge', which had resulted in the death of more than 2000 people in the UK and the Netherlands. In 1966 he was promoted to professor and head of the new civil engineering department at City University, positions he held until his retirement in 1982. He realized the importance of linking the degree course to the needs of the profession and by doing so built up the department to become the largest in the country. At the same time he thoroughly enjoyed his role as visiting professor at Stanford and Cornell universities, and at academic institutions in Mexico, Thailand, and Germany. Meanwhile, his first marriage having ended in divorce, on 17 September 1977 he married Janet Elizabeth Robertson (*b.* 1938), physicist and visual scientist at City University, and daughter of Thomas Reid Robertson, colonial civil servant in Mauritius. She was the rock, he frequently said, that made his last thirty years so happy.

In 1984–5 Wolf chaired the British government's research consultative committee on flood protection, producing the Wolf report. If its proposals had been implemented, the British floods of 2006 would have been much reduced. He regretted not having fought harder for them at the time. He then joined Pell Frischmann Consulting Engineers and became a director in 1993, working on many hydrological projects. He was particularly interested in the contamination of the water supply in the Upper Elbe Valley, caused by the bombing of the munition dumps by the Russians in the post-war period, and he headed the European Union investigation. Later he worked on the plan to provide power and desalinated water to the troubled region of the Dead Sea and Aqaba, using natural gas from adjacent wells in Saudi Arabia. At the time of his death he was advising Iraq's minister of water resources on how best to strengthen the huge earth dam at Mosul, in order to avoid a catastrophic collapse, which would result in flooding along the Tigris all the way to Baghdad.

Wolf served for almost thirty years on the Royal Society's hydrology sub-committee, in addition to Department of Scientific and Industrial Research and Natural Environment Research Council hydrology committees. He was a founder member of the Hazards Forum, becoming chairman of the standing committee on natural hazards from 1991 to 1993. He was a member of British delegations to many international meetings and a member of editorial boards of several international journals concerned especially with flood hydrology and hydraulics. He was elected a fellow of the Royal Academy of Engineering in 1982 and was a fellow of the Institution of Civil Engineers and many other institutions. He was also a founder member of the Company of Engineers. In 1988 he was delighted to be the first recipient of the Ray Linsley award (from the American Institute of Hydrology) set up to 'recognise individuals who have made outstanding contributions in surface water hydrology'. He helped set up the British Hydrological Society, of which he was president in 1987–9. He was awarded an honorary doctorate by Dresden University of Technology in 1987 for his achievements in hydrology and hydraulic engineering.

Raised in the turmoil of pre-war central Europe, international in his scholarship, his outlook, and his friendships, Peter Wolf became that increasingly rare phenomenon, an English gentleman. He was formal in an almost old-fashioned way. A loyal member of the Athenaeum, he represented the acme of what that club stood for in British society. He was noted for his gentle courtesy, gift for listening and taking interest, and the equal kindness he extended to all. His friendship and devotion to his students and their careers was legendary.

Wolf lived in Highgate for his last twenty-five years. He enjoyed classical music, reading, walking, sailing, and Viennese chocolate cake, but his lifelong passion was skiing. In Davos even in his eighties he would be first on the mountains in the morning and last off in the evening, and was amused to be given the reduced rate ski pass for the elderly. He had two ski holidays booked at the time of his death, of a heart attack on 6 October 2007 at the Royal Free Hospital, Hampstead, London. A memorial celebration of his life was held at the Athenaeum on 2 March 2008, and his ashes were buried in Highgate cemetery (west) on 1 February 2009, appropriately a day of great snow. He was survived by his wife, Janet, and the three children of his first marriage. WILEM FRISCHMANN

Sources *Circulation* [newsletter of the British Hydrological Society], 95 (Nov 2007), 1–2 · *The Times* (29 Nov 2007) · *Hazards Forum Newsletter*, 58 (autumn 2007) · *Hydrolink* [newsletter of the International Association for Hydro-Environment Engineering], 1/8

(2008), 15 · papers, Royal Academy of Engineering · papers, Institution of Civil Engineering · papers, Pell Frischmann Consulting Engineers · memorial celebration booklet, Athenaeum Club, 2 March 2007 · *WW* (2007) · personal knowledge (2011) · private information (2011) [Janet Wolf, widow] · m. certs. · d. cert.

Archives priv. coll. | Institution of Civil Engineering, London · Pell Frischmann Consulting Engineers, London · Royal Academy of Engineering, London | SOUND British Hydrological Society, interview by James Porter, CD

Likenesses J. Wolf, photograph, priv. coll. [*see illus.*] · photograph, repro. in *Hydrolink* · photograph, repro. in www3.imperial.ac.uk/ewre/aboutus/history · photographs, priv. coll.

Wolfson, Sir Brian Gordon (1935–2007), businessman, was born on 2 August 1935 at Braemar, Sandown Park, Liverpool, the son of Gabriel Wolfson (1906–1951), master builder and businessman, and his wife, Eve, *née* Carr. Educated at Liverpool College, he left at the age of sixteen to read law at Liverpool University, but dropped out after one year in order to help rescue Carrs Motors, the family motor car distribution and engineering company. The company had been in difficulties after the death of his father the previous year. On 9 March 1958, at Princes Road Synagogue, Liverpool, he married Helen Grodner (*b.* 1939), daughter of Lewis Grodner, company director; they had one son and one daughter.

After selling Carrs Motors Wolfson was recruited by Sidney Bernstein to develop the Granada television rental business, and joined Granada Group in 1961. Having established a chain of rental shops in Britain, he expanded the business to Europe and the United States. He was appointed a joint managing director of the Granada Group in 1967, but left in 1970 to pursue his own business activities in south-east Asia, Europe, and the United States. He started a group of businesses manufacturing cement machinery, and developed his own chain of companies leasing television sets. In 1976 he became chairman of Anglo-Nordic Holdings, and was so successful in the United States that in 1979 he was appointed the first non-American head of the Young Presidents' Organization.

Wolfson returned to Britain in 1985 to put together a consortium that was able to take over control of Wembley Stadium, which had been in severe financial straits since the early 1980s. He became chairman of Wembley Stadium Ltd in 1986, and floated the company on the stock market in 1987. He had many ideas for expanding the activities at Wembley, including boxing, which was reintroduced in 1986 after a twenty-year gap, and American football. Wembley became a major venue for rock and pop music concerts following the success of Live Aid in July 1985, and events there included two concerts in 1988 and 1990 dedicated to Nelson Mandela, and seven sold-out shows by Michael Jackson during his Bad World Tour in 1988. Wolfson also expanded the surrounding facilities, making more use of the conference centre, the exhibition halls, and Wembley arena. Football was not attracting capacity crowds, even for international matches, but as a lifelong supporter of Liverpool football club Wolfson was able to celebrate the victory of Liverpool over its rival Everton in the 1989 cup final. Even before the Hillsborough disaster of 1989 he had considered getting rid of the standing terraces, and in 1990 Wembley Stadium hosted its first all-seated events, with the creation of 4000 new seats. But to finance all this the company bought other leisure businesses, including bingo halls, night clubs, and film distribution companies, borrowing heavily to do so, and during the recession of the early 1990s Wolfson had to sell some of these at a loss. The modernization of the stadium was piecemeal, and it was becoming clear that it needed to be completely rebuilt, but by 1994 Wembley plc faced a £140 million debt, and the value of the shares collapsed in 1995. Wolfson was forced to resign as chairman. In 1996 Wembley's application for lottery funding to build a millennium stadium was successful.

Wolfson made a more lasting contribution to British business as chairman of the National Training Task Force, formed in 1988, which became Investors in People in 1993, and was chaired by Wolfson until 1999. Lacking any formal training himself, he nevertheless saw the importance of training, and retraining, the workforce, especially in light of reports that showed that Britain's workers held fewer qualifications than those of its major competitors. The National Training Task Force was set up by the government after the publication of the white paper *Employment for the 1990s*, and its main job was to set up a network of training and enterprise councils throughout the country, and to persuade employers of the necessity of investing in the skills of the working population. An Investors in People standard was launched in 1990, to be awarded to companies which met its criteria. As Wolfson was often quoted as saying, 'investment in equipment depreciates, whilst investment in people appreciates'. He was knighted in 1990.

Wolfson was a strong believer in the idea of 'action learning', developed by his friend Reginald Revans, and applied this to management training. He taught on a number of management courses at universities in Britain and the United States, and he was on the advisory board of the Joseph H. Lauder Institute of Management and International Studies at the Wharton Center of the University of Pennsylvania. He was also a governor of Ashridge Management College in Hertfordshire from 1991, and the first chairman of the Ashridge MBA programme, from 1988 to 1993. At the end of his life he was collaborating with a colleague at Ashridge, Andrew McGeorge, on a book about management theory. He was awarded honorary doctorates by Liverpool Polytechnic and Liverpool University.

After he left Wembley plc Wolfson developed new business interests, mainly in the United States. He liked to buy ailing companies, turn them round, and then sell them on, and so in 2000 he agreed to become chairman of Fruit of the Loom, a T-shirt manufacturer with branches all over the world, which was in danger of collapse. He restructured its finances, and sold it in 2002. In Britain, however, he was unable to save Colorvision, a television rental chain. He was chairman of the American management consultancy Kepner-Tregoe from 2000, and a member of the board of Playboy and the Scientific Games Corporation.

Addicted to work—'you've got to go out and work bloody hard and then work bloody hard again', he would say (*The Times*, 17 May 2007)—Wolfson had time for few outside interests, apart from Chinese archaeology and filming wildlife. He died on 10 May 2007 at his London home, Flat 17, 35–7 Grosvenor Square, Mayfair, of a heart attack. He was survived by his wife, Helen, from whom he was separated, and their two children.

ANNE PIMLOTT BAKER

Sources B. Evans, *The politics of the training market* (1992), 139–40 · *The Independent* (12 April 1995); (14 May 2007) · T. Watt and K. Palmer, *Wembley: the greatest stage* (1998) · P. Taylor and B. Thackwray, *Investors in people explained*, 3rd edn (1999) · *The Times* (17 May 2007) · *Daily Telegraph* (18 May 2007) · Burke, *Peerage* · *WW* (2007) · b. cert. · m. cert. · d. cert.

Likenesses A. Butler, group portrait, photograph, 1988, PA Photos, London · photographs, 1994, Photoshot, London · photograph, repro. in *The Times* (17 May 2007) · photograph, repro. in www.liv.ac.uk/www/alumni/recorder/Oct2002/11.html

Wealth at death £291,756: probate, 7 Jan 2008, *CGPLA Eng. & Wales*

Wollaston, Nicholas William [Nick] (**1926–2007**), novelist and travel writer, was born on 23 June 1926 at Bencombe House, Uley, Gloucestershire, the son of Alexander Frederick Richmond (Sandy) *Wollaston (1875–1943), naturalist and explorer, and his wife, Mary, *née* Meinertzhagen (1889–1930). His father was a medical doctor, collector of plants and insects, a celebrated explorer, and a fellow of King's College, Cambridge; he was shot dead in his college rooms when Wollaston was three. Wollaston was educated at Winchester College and (after service in the Royal Navy in the Mediterranean and the Pacific) at King's College, Cambridge. 'When I arrived', he later recalled,

> the head porter doffed his bowler and said he was proud to meet my father's son. How could I compete? I've always felt this inadequacy, not living up to my father's name and fame. I did no work. I played the flute, drank a lot of beer in the Eagle, and got a third. (*The Times*, 7 April 2003)

After a short period working at a leather tannery in Kenya owned by an uncle, then as a jackaroo on an Australian sheep station, he embarked on a career as a travel writer, starting with *Handles of Chance: a Journey from the Solomon Islands to Istanbul* (1956). On 11 August 1961 he married Deirdre Johnston (*b*. 1939/40), daughter of Patrick Murdoch Johnston, British ambassador to Cameroon then Nicaragua; they had three children, Sophy, Sam, and Josh. Wollaston's first book after his marriage, *Red Rumba: a Journey through the Caribbean and Central America* (1962), was particularly acclaimed, Graham Greene ranking it with Patrick Leigh Fermor's *The Traveller's Tree*. Besides other travel books he published a biography of August Courtauld, *The Man on the Ice Cap* (1980), seven novels, from *Jupiter Laughs* (1967) to *Café de Paris* (1988), each critically well received but none a bestseller, a semi-autobiographical account of a journey to La Mancha, *Tilting at Don Quixote* (1990), and *My Father, Sandy* (2003), in which he finally explored his relationship with the father he hardly knew. Much of his later writing remained unpublished, and in 2000 he was incensed by a publisher's report that suggested it was too 'late in the author's career': 'At a pinch, I'd change my name and borrow a photo of the barmaid in my local pub … if it would do the trick' (*The Observer*, 6 Aug 2000). For the last thirty years of his life he and Deirdre were tenants of a National Trust house, Thorington Hall, Stoke by Nayland, Suffolk, where she ran a bed and breakfast business. He died on 23 April 2007 at Colchester General Hospital, of bronchopneumonia and chronic obstructive pulmonary disease, and was survived by Deirdre and their three children.

Sources N. Wollaston, *My father, Sandy* (2003) · *The Times* (7 April 2003) · *The Guardian* (9 May 2007) · b. cert. · m. cert. · d. cert.

Wealth at death under £97,000: probate, 12 July 2007, *CGPLA Eng. & Wales*

Wooderson, Sydney Charles (**1914–2006**), athlete, was born at 11 Baldwin Crescent, Camberwell, London, on 30 August 1914, the second son of George Thomas Wooderson, fruit merchant, and his wife, Jeannette Emma, *née* Tindall. He and his two brothers, Alfred and Stanley, were all educated at Sutton Valence School in Kent. Taking inspiration from the athletic success of his elder brother, Alfred, Wooderson took up running as a schoolboy, and joined a local athletic club, the Blackheath Harriers. In 1933 he won the London Athletic Club's public schools championship, and became the first schoolboy to run faster than 4 minutes and 30 seconds for the mile. In that year he left school and became articled as a solicitor's clerk in the City of London; he later became a solicitor.

Wooderson's talent was noticed, and he soon became coached by Albert Hill, the double Olympic champion of 1920. Under Hill's guidance he flourished: he finished second to Jack Lovelock of New Zealand in the mile at the second empire games in London in 1934 (Jerry Cornes, who had finished second in the 1500 metres at the 1932 Olympic games, was third), and in 1935 took the first of five successive Amateur Athletic Association (AAA) one mile championships (a record that was never matched in his lifetime), beating Lovelock in the process. After a second defeat by Wooderson in Glasgow in that year (where Wooderson set his first British record of 4 minutes 12.7 seconds for the mile) Lovelock recorded in his journal that '[I] made up my mind to defeat Wooderson next year or die', and it was the threat from Wooderson that shaped Lovelock's preparation for the 1936 Olympic games (Colquhoun, 18).

In 1936 Wooderson set a new British record of 4 minutes 10.8 seconds for the mile, and defeated Lovelock in the AAA championships. However, he injured his left ankle while out walking and failed to qualify for the final of the 1500 metres at the Olympic games in Berlin in that year. Outwardly he showed no sign of his disappointment that the much anticipated contest between himself and Lovelock (who took gold with a new world record) in the Olympic final failed to take place. On 28 August 1937, however, in a handicap race at a Blackheath Harriers' meeting at London University's Motspur Park track, Wooderson set a new world record for the mile of 4 minutes 6.4 seconds.

Sydney Charles Wooderson (1914–2006), by A. Hudson, 1938

Watching in the crowd were not only Wooderson's parents and his coach, Hill, but Walter George, who as a professional had set a record of 4 minutes 12¾ seconds in 1886. Afterwards George was photographed congratulating Wooderson; fifty years later Wooderson himself was present at a meeting at Crystal Palace organized as a tribute to mark the anniversary of his world record which featured the generation of British middle distance athletes of the 1980s, including Sebastian Coe, his successor as world record holder for the mile.

Wooderson's record stood for five years until it was broken by the Swede, Gunder Haegg, in 1942, and it stood as a British record until broken by Roger Bannister in May 1953. Although Wooderson's comparatively light training and approach to the sport (he was scrupulous in returning overpaid expenses) epitomized the British amateur ethos of the day, there was nothing accidental about the world record attempt: four AAA timekeepers were present, and the track had been remeasured in advance and found to be slightly short, so that the start line had been adjusted by 10 inches. Wooderson later recalled 'I was quite amazed and could not sleep undisturbed for some days after' (Thurlow, 17).

The following year, at the same meeting, on 20 August 1937, Wooderson set world records for the 800 metres (1 minute 48.4 seconds) and the 880 yards (1 minute 49.2 seconds), the latter standing as a world record for seventeen years. He was unable to compete in the 1938 empire games (held in Sydney, Australia) because he was taking his legal exams; however, he won the European 1500 metres championship in Paris that year, in a time of 3 minutes 48.4 seconds. Earlier in that year he had declared his ambition to try to run a mile in 4 minutes. In 1939, running on a grass track at Fallowfield in Manchester, he became the first man ever to break 3 minutes for three-quarters of a mile (setting a world record of 2:59.5), and was seen as a strong contender for the 1500 metres at the 1940 Olympic games, originally due to be held in Tokyo, then in Helsinki. His one notable appearance outside Europe, which took place at the 'mile of the century' in Princeton that year, was a disappointment, and he finished fifth.

Wooderson's unlikely appearance for a leading world athlete was much commented upon; he was short (5 feet 6 inches tall) and slight (weighing less than 9 stone). He was also short-sighted and wore rimmed spectacles when racing. His appearance captured the public imagination, particularly in the immediate post-war period, and one observer has commented that this 'frail, bespectacled figure' symbolized the 'courage and endurance of the indomitable Englishman' (Holt, 275). Harold Abrahams wrote of a 'tiny figure … buffeted and almost apologising for occupying any space at all … the last person you would pick out as a king among milers' (Bryant, 102). One account characterized his defeats of Lovelock as 'like a goods train passing an express' (Lovesey, 86). His contests with the stylish Lovelock were one of the high points of athletics in the 1930s. Wooderson's frailty was deceptive, however: on the running track he cultivated an unmatchable finishing pace, and Lovelock commented in his private journal that Wooderson was 'so cool, clever and fast' (Colquhoun, 141).

The outbreak of the Second World War interrupted Wooderson's athletic career, and undoubtedly prevented him from fulfilling his potential as an athlete. Although his poor eyesight precluded him from active service, he joined the National Fire Service and was stationed in Croydon during the blitz, and then the Pioneer Corps and the Royal Electrical and Mechanical Engineers. He also participated in a number of wartime exhibition races, but in 1944 suffered a bout of rheumatic flu, which led to four months in hospital, and he received medical advice that he would never run competitively again.

Remarkably, Wooderson made a full recovery, and it was his appearances in front of large crowds in the athletic meetings of the immediate post-war period that undoubtedly confirmed his iconic status for spectators of sport of that generation. Among the estimated 60,000 people who saw his narrow defeat by Arne Andersson at the White City stadium on 6 August 1945 was the sixteen-year-old Roger Bannister, who later recalled that from this day Wooderson became his hero and gave him a schoolboy dream of becoming a runner (Bannister, 30). In a rematch in Göteborg, Sweden, a few weeks later on 9 September, Wooderson was again defeated, but ran his fastest ever mile of 4 minutes 4.2 seconds. In 1946 he set a British record for the 3 miles, winning the AAA championship at that distance, and then won the European 5000 metre championship in Oslo in a time of 14 minutes 8.6 seconds, beating the young Emil Zatopek in the process. An injury in a 2 mile race at Motspur Park track later that year ended his track career, but he competed for Blackheath Harriers in the English national cross-country championships between 1947 and 1949, winning the title in 1948. He was president of Blackheath Harriers in 1946 and 1969 (the latter their centennial year) and continued to support the club for many years. In 1947, on his retirement from track competition, the AAA arranged for a dinner in his honour, a 'unique tribute to a phenomenal runner and a man as popular with other athletes as with the public' (Lovesey, 95). In 1952 he was part of a small group of Britain's most famous athletes presented to the new Queen Elizabeth at the AAA championships in that year.

Wooderson married Pamela Lucy Willcocks, a 25-year-old secretary, and daughter of William Willcocks, gardener, on 15 April 1950, at St Paul's Church, Kingston Hill, Surrey. They had a son and a daughter. Always a modest man, after retirement from athletics Wooderson avoided public attention and retired to Devon and then Dorset. There was some discussion as to whether he was snubbed by the organizers of the 1948 London Olympic games, who failed to ask him to participate in bringing the Olympic torch into the stadium at Wembley, preferring instead a lesser known but more classically stylish athlete; one account states that Queen Elizabeth commented, 'of course we couldn't have had poor little Sydney', and late in life Wooderson claimed he had arrived on the opening day of the games as requested to bring the Olympic torch into the stadium, only to be told he was not required (*The Times*, 23 December 2006). A campaign led by Chris Brasher resulted in Wooderson being made an MBE in 2000, by which time he was virtually blind. He died at Anglebury Court residential care home in Wareham, Dorset, on 21 December 2006, suffering from Parkinson's disease and Crohn's disease. He was survived by his wife, Pamela, and their two children. A memorial service took place on 8 September 2007, and the Blackheath Harriers' clubhouse was renamed in his honour.

M. A. BRYANT

Sources P. Lovesey, *The official centenary history of the Amateur Athletic Association* (1979) • D. Thurlow, *Sydney Wooderson: forgotten champion* (1989) • T. Mason, ed., *Sport in Britain* (1989) • R. Holt, *Sport and the British: a modern history* (1989) • M. Sheridan, *A gentle cyclone: the running career of Sydney Wooderson* (1999) • R. Bannister, *The first four minutes* (2004) • J. Bryant, *3:59.4: the quest to break the four-minute mile* (2004) • I. Wooldridge, *Daily Mail* (13 Dec 2000) • *Athletics Weekly* (22 Dec 2006) • *The Times* (23 Dec 2006) • *Daily Telegraph* (23 Dec 2006) • *The Independent* (29 Dec 2006) • *The Guardian* (3 Jan 2007) • *IAAF News* (8 Jan 2007), www.iaaf.org • 'A tribute to Sydney Charles Wooderson MBE', Blackheath Harriers, 2007 • *As if running on air: the journals of Jack Lovelock*, ed. D. Colquhoun (2008) • Blackheath and Bromley Harriers website, www.bandbhar.org.uk, 5 July 2009 • b. cert. • m. cert. • d. cert.

Likenesses photographs, 1935–46, Getty Images, London, Hult. Arch. • photographs, 1937–8, Getty Images, London, Popperfoto • A. Hudson, photograph, 1938, Getty Images, London [*see illus.*] • photographs, 1938–46, PA Photos, London • photograph, 1954, Photoshot, London • obituary photographs • photographs, repro. in Thurlow, *Wooderson* • photographs, repro. in Sheridan, *Wooderson*

Woodrow, Joash (1927–2006), painter, was born at Leeds Maternity Hospital on 6 April 1927, the fifth of seven children of Harry Woodrow (formerly Herzl Wiadrow) and his wife, Rebecca (formerly Rifka), *née* Brostoff, who were both of Jewish descent, born in Russian Poland; his birth certificate recorded his name as Jehoash. Woodrow's parents had each come to Leeds with their own parents in the early 1900s. They married on a long visit to Boston, Massachusetts, in 1911, and returned to live in Leeds the following year.

Until 1932 the Woodrow family lived at 53 Chapeltown Road in Leeds. On the ground floor, the studious Harry opened a bookshop, which, however, did not prosper. He was therefore forced to return to work as a tailor's machinist, at the Leeds factory of Montague Burton, though the family was able to move to a large house, also in the Chapeltown area.

As a small boy Woodrow showed an artistic streak, making immaculate cardboard copies of board games that his family was unable to afford. In a small gouache painting of about 1945 showing a homburg-hatted male figure (a memory of his father) peering into a shop window of a sooty Victorian building, *Mr Woodrow's Bookshop*, Woodrow recalled his early childhood milieu. From 1942 to 1945 he was a student at Leeds College of Art. During this period—like members of an earlier generation of English Jewish artists, notably Isaac Rosenberg and Mark Gertler in London's East End, and the Ukrainian-born painter Jacob Kramer in Leeds—Woodrow made compassionate studies of his careworn immigrant parents, usually showing his father reading, and his mother resting or sleeping. His father died in 1951, his mother ten years later.

From 1945 to 1948 Woodrow did two years' national service, working mostly as a cartographer in a Cairo office. He then returned to Leeds College of Art to complete his studies. A fellow student there, Jack Coulthard, recalled him as 'an exotic and quite cosmopolitan figure' who 'read Sartre and Kafka, and was very interested in Matisse and Picasso'; he was 'warm, charismatic' yet 'somehow vulnerable, delicate' (Vann and Wullschlager, 26). From 1950 to 1953 he attended the Royal College of Art in London on a scholarship. The artist Cyril Satorsky, who attended art college in Leeds and London with Woodrow, recalled him as a young man as 'under average height, thickly built, square-faced with a very Russian-looking face. He had a Yorkshire accent but not a broad one. He was extremely shy and ultra-sensitive' (ibid., 23). This shyness and ultra-sensitivity meant that throughout his adult life Woodrow hardly ever revealed anything about his personal emotions to friends and family. It is not known if he had any romantic associations or attractions.

On graduating, Woodrow received glowing testimonials from his teachers. Ruskin Spear wrote, 'He shows great enthusiasm, intensity and ability' (Vann and Wullschlager, 28); Rodrigo Moynihan noted his paintings' 'mature richness of colour and expression' (ibid.), and Carel Weight, while noting his 'distinct sense of humour', saw him as 'a young artist of marked originality' (ibid.). His paintings of city parks and streets dating from the 1950s are remarkable for their painterly intensity and disciplined spontaneity of mark-making. Satorsky later described Woodrow's radical approach: 'it was as though he was defying the brush—there'd be paint on bristles sticking out in all directions … what looks like a careless brushstroke reveals the deepest consideration' (ibid., 27).

Woodrow stayed on in London for a while after leaving the Royal College of Art, but suffered a nervous crisis and returned to Leeds. In 1955 the Woodrow family moved to a small new semi-detached house in Allerton Grange Gardens, Leeds. The household now consisted of Rebecca, her son Israel, her nephew Paul (who was born in 1940), and Joash. Paul and Joash enjoyed one escape from post-war Leodensian austerity in a mid-1950s trip by train to Paris, where they visited art galleries and sat in fashionable left bank cafés. This was Woodrow's only post-war trip abroad. There was also a 1960 visit to London with Paul, where the Picasso exhibition at the Tate greatly impressed him.

Following Woodrow's mother's death, the family home began to fill up with artworks. Furniture was moved to make space for paintings; walls were so densely multi-layered with canvases that it became difficult to pass. Over the next four decades, living in relative seclusion and supported by modest stipends from two elder brothers and, latterly, his state pension, Woodrow painted and drew prolifically. He also made bizarrely inventive assemblages and, in the early 1960s, decorated a series of Victorian art books with his own hilariously surreal interventions. His late 1950s and 1960s portraits of handsome young men, rabbis, Leeds businessmen, and both stylish and sometimes somewhat grotesque-looking women, show a gracefully expressive use of line. Dozens of notebooks detail acute observations of Leeds city streets, its impressive Victorian architecture, its pedestrians and buskers, as well as succinct, dynamic studies of the Yorkshire countryside and coast.

Woodrow's most considerable achievement was the large body of paintings he made of Leeds from the early 1960s until about 1995. City centre panoramas, and semi-industrial sites around town, are the subjects of tautly structured, richly impastoed, shimmering oils. Inspiration was almost literally on his doorstep in the form of the local Gledhow Valley allotments, whose derelict huts, white picket fences, trees, and flowers were portrayed with a jousting use of line and a diaphanous palette. There is a poignant affinity between the appearance of Woodrow's allotments, with their huts, fences, and muddy tracks, and the tragically extinguished world of the shtetls and towns of Jewish Poland, where his parents had come from.

For over forty years Woodrow painted in Leeds with astonishing perseverance and dedication, free from public scrutiny. Not having to exhibit his works or having to compromise to the demands of critics or dealers, he enjoyed extraordinary inner freedom. In 2000 he left Leeds to live in sheltered accommodation in Manchester, and never painted again. The first solo exhibition of his work, at 108 Fine Art Gallery, Harrogate, drew a remarkable degree of press attention and critical acclaim. In August 2005 his brother Saul took him to see the first retrospective exhibition of his paintings, held at Manchester Art Gallery, the first time he had seen his work on public display. Further exhibitions at the Ben Uri Gallery and the Royal College of Art the same year drew critical acclaim. He died at North Manchester General Hospital on 15 February 2006, of a bowel obstruction.

PHILIP VANN

Sources N. Usherwood and C. P. Wood, *Joash Woodrow* (2004) · *Yorkshire Evening Post* (4 March 2006) · *Daily Telegraph* (11 April 2006) · *The Guardian* (27 April 2006) · P. Vann and J. Wullschlager, *Joash Woodrow: landscapes* (2007) · A. Stewart, introduction, *Joash Woodrow: portraits* (2008), 9–10 · D. Padmore, 'A personal recollection', *Joash Woodrow: portraits* (2008), 11–14 · personal knowledge (2010) · private information (2010) · b. cert. · d. cert.

Archives 108 Fine Art Gallery, Harrogate, paintings, drawings, notebooks

Likenesses J. Woodrow, self-portraits, *c.*1950–*c.*1980, 108 Fine Art Gallery, Harrogate

Wealth at death £503,345: probate, 5 July 2006, *CGPLA Eng. & Wales*

Woof, Robert Samuel (1931–2005), literary scholar and museum director, was born on 20 April 1931 at Royal Albert Farm, Lancaster, the third child of William Woof, a progressive farm manager, and his wife, Annie, *née* Mason. He became head boy at Lancaster Royal Grammar School and in 1950 won an open scholarship to read history at Pembroke College, Oxford; he soon changed to English literature, graduating with a second-class degree in 1953. A Goldsmith's fellowship in the same year took him to the University of Toronto, where his graduate studies were supervised by the distinguished Romantic scholars Kathleen Coburn and J. R. MacGillivray; he began at this time to study manuscripts at the Wordsworth Library, Grasmere. In 1959 he made the first of many contributions to Romantic scholarship when he completed his PhD thesis at Toronto on 'The literary relations of Wordsworth and Coleridge'. The previous year he had been appointed a lecturer in English at Toronto and had married Pamela Shirley Moore, who had also read English at Oxford. They had two sons and two daughters. Pamela Woof went on to her own career as a literary scholar, and biographer and editor of Dorothy Wordsworth.

In 1961 Woof resigned his lectureship at Toronto to become Lord Adams of Ennerdale research fellow at King's College, University of Durham (later the University of Newcastle upon Tyne). The following year he was appointed lecturer in English, and from 1971 to 1992 he was reader in English literature. At Newcastle he did not confine himself to teaching: with characteristic energy he played a leading role in many aspects of the city's cultural life. At the university he took charge of creative writing, then not an academic discipline. He acted as a judge in literary competitions, and was assessor for the work of the Morden Tower, a significant poetry venue. He was also instrumental in setting up a two-year poetry fellowship at the universities of Newcastle and Durham; among the poets he helped appoint were Tony Harrison, Basil Bunting, and Fleur Adcock. The theatre was another lifelong passion: he represented the university on the board of the Tyne and Wear Theatre Company, helped student amateur groups, and every spring brought the Royal Shakespeare Company to Newcastle for a six-week season of performances, workshops, and seminars. A confirmed bibliophile, he was chairman of the Friends of the University Library.

Beyond Newcastle, Woof was vice-chairman of Northern Arts from 1974 to 1981, and in the 1980s held a number of positions on the Arts Council of Great Britain, including vice-chairman of drama and chairman of literature. In 1991 he was invited to take over the chairmanship of the Century Theatre in Keswick, which he successfully split into two companies: first, Theatre by the Lake, which remained in Keswick; and second, English Touring Theatre, which became under his leadership one of Britain's leading classical touring companies.

Woof's greatest achievement, however, was his work at the Wordsworth Trust in Grasmere; it was there that his combination of erudition, creativity, and practical ingenuity found its fullest expression. Since its foundation in 1891, the trust had preserved Dove Cottage, William Wordsworth's home from 1799 to 1808, for 'lovers of English poetry from all over the world'. The trust was also the guardian of some 90 per cent of the poet's manuscripts. When Woof was appointed a trustee in 1970 it had remained essentially the same since the 1930s; he at once saw its hidden potential, and over the next thirty-five years, with rare dedication, he set about transforming it into a centre of international standing. As honorary keeper of collections he sought funding, and oversaw the conservation, first of Dove Cottage itself, and then, personally transporting manuscripts to the Cockerell workshop in Cambridge, of some 15,000 books and manuscripts. Further, thanks to his enlightened approach to acquisition, the collections in Grasmere widened in scope to include rare editions and manuscripts of most of the literary and political figures of the Romantic age; the work of the many artists who visited the lakes, such as Turner, Constable, and Wright of Derby, was included.

The trustees supported Woof's transformation of an old coach house into a museum, which was opened in 1981 with a permanent Wordsworth exhibition and space for changing displays. It also, crucially, had the security and environmental controls needed to persuade both institutions and private collectors to lend priceless treasures to the series of special exhibitions on Romantic themes that Woof created, supported by brilliant catalogues. On top of this there were winter and summer international residential and scholarly conferences held in Grasmere; an award-winning educational programme for schools; and, under Woof's direction, an advanced training in museum studies that helped hundreds of recent graduates to gain an awareness of career possibilities. In return the trainees helped with the trust's activities and responsibilities to the public.

In 1992 Woof resigned from the University of Newcastle to become the first director of the Wordsworth Trust. He encouraged a contemporary as well as a historical creativity, initiating the linking of the art and poetry of the past with that of the present through poet and artist residencies, weekly readings by contemporary writers, and contemporary art exhibitions. He kept the place as well as the trust's activities in mind, and by purchasing a number of nearby properties extended a quiet, unobtrusive protection around Dove Cottage and its garden. The culmination of his work in Grasmere was the planning and construction of a superb new building to house the collections. The Jerwood Centre at the Wordsworth Trust, modern yet sympathetic, was an architectural triumph, a great library, and a repository of Romantic works; it was formally opened in June 2005 by the poet Seamus Heaney.

This development of the Wordsworth Trust was achieved against the odds, and the constant need to raise money was mentally and emotionally demanding. Nevertheless Woof still found time for the scholarship that provided the foundation for all this activity. His memorable lectures (lasting anywhere between an hour and half a morning) embraced literature, art, history, and the Lake District; some exhibitions went on to the New York Public Library, the British Library, and the National Library of Scotland. The interdisciplinary nature of the work enabled Woof to make the surprising intellectual connections in which he delighted and excelled. The many catalogues published by the Wordsworth Trust were indeed books. His edition of T. W. Thompson's *Wordsworth's Hawkshead* (1970) was a treasure house of original research. Many articles testified to his scholarship. His magisterial account, from unpublished manuscripts as well as printed works, of Wordsworth criticism, *Wordsworth: the Critical Heritage*, was published in 2001. In his last years he brought out an edition of Hazlitt's *Spirit of the Age* (2004), with his own essays matching Hazlitt's; in 2005 his *Treasures of the Wordsworth Trust* appeared, a historical and scholarly account. Posthumously, in 2007, came his edition of Wordsworth's masterpiece completed in 1805, the thirteen-book *Prelude*.

In person Woof was animated, intense, humorous, generous, and immensely and immediately likeable. Blessed with a formidable memory, he drew lightly upon an astonishing range of reference, and in conversation was always persuasive, often inspirational. He was a fine reader of Wordsworth's poetry. His contribution to the artistic life of Britain was recognized in a number of awards and honours: honorary degrees from the universities of Lancaster, Newcastle, and Central Lancashire; the Northern Electric award in 1995; and the Creative Briton award in 1999. He was appointed CBE in 1998.

A non-smoker, Woof died of lung cancer on 7 November 2005 at the Freeman Hospital, Newcastle upon Tyne. The funeral was at St Oswald's Church, Grasmere, on 24 November 2005, and a memorial gathering, overwhelmingly attended, was held at the National Portrait Gallery, London, on 28 March 2006. He was survived by his wife, Pamela, and their four children. STEPHEN HEBRON

Sources *Daily Telegraph* (10 Nov 2005) · *The Guardian* (11 Nov 2005) · *The Times* (14 Nov 2005) · *The Independent* (17 Nov 2005) · *WW* (2005) · private information (2009) · personal knowledge (2009) · b. cert. · d. cert.

Archives The Wordsworth Trust, Grasmere, Cumbria

Likenesses C. Atkinson, digitally altered print on canvas with oil pastel and collage, 2006 (*Robert with ivy and laurel*), priv. coll. · obituary photographs

Wealth at death under £42,000: probate, 21 April 2006, *CGPLA Eng. & Wales*

Wooldridge, Ian Edmund (1932–2007), sporting journalist and broadcaster, was born on 14 January 1932 at Boscombe Hospital, near Bournemouth, Hampshire, the son of Edmund James Wooldridge (1895–1971), sub-postmaster at Wootton, New Milton, Hampshire, later an antiques dealer, and his wife, Bertha, *née* Stickland (1897–1982). After leaving Brockenhurst grammar school at the age of sixteen he joined the *New Milton Advertiser*, where with bicycle and pencil he spent his weekdays in the local magistrates' court, at council meetings, inquests, flower shows, weddings, and funerals. Under an editor whom he was later to describe as a benevolent bully, convinced that the National Union of Journalists had been personally founded by Lenin, his weekends were spent writing up local cricket, darts, and football events. After three years at the *Advertiser* and eighteen months' national service in the Royal Navy he found a job on the *Bournemouth Times*. It was from there, in 1956, that he made the move to London, first during the final year of the *News Chronicle*, then briefly at the *Sunday Dispatch* before joining the *Daily Mail* in 1961. He remained there for the next forty-six years. Meanwhile, on 5 October 1957, at the parish church of New Milton, he married Veronica Ann Phyllis Churcher (*b.* 1935), secretary, daughter of Arthur Henry Churcher, grocer. They had three sons.

Sport, especially cricket, had been a serious interest from early in Wooldridge's life. Selection for Hampshire schoolboys was his highest achievement on the playing side but in 1962 he was made cricket correspondent of the *Daily Mail*. His first major assignment was to cover the 1962–3 England tour of Australia, his first visit to a country that he came to appreciate above all others. Keith Miller and Richie Benand were surpassed in the list of Wooldridge sporting heroes only by Denis Compton. In 1964–5 he was in South Africa for his second England tour overseas. In many respects the cricket on both occasions was grim but Wooldridge's enjoyment was undisturbed. As he became more assured and moved up the *Mail* hierarchy he found reasons to be sent to Australia every winter, whether English cricketers were there or not. His love of cricket was severely tested later as at international level in particular it developed an unappetizing brutality. In 1986 at Port of Spain, Trinidad, he characterized the play between the West Indies and England as not being played under the Queensberry rules. Watching was almost as nerve-racking as playing, with test bowlers sending down four bouncers an over. He blamed the needs of television for the violence that he thought could destroy the game. He had a growing dislike of the trappings of sporting modernity.

Wooldridge had always been ambivalent about boxing, although he admired the courage of those who took part in it. His last column (on 26 February 2007) took the form of an appeal for support for a benefit night for a young boxer confined to a wheelchair. He wished that 'as a profession, [boxing] would pay more attention to its fallen'. He had earlier, in 1989, written a shrewd piece about Frank Bruno in which he told the boxer's two young daughters that their father had secured a good life for them by entering the ring with Mike Tyson.

Tennis was another sport that Wooldridge looked on with some distaste, particularly Wimbledon. In the early 1970s the Wimbledon club, looking to improve the grounds, was involved in a dispute with Merton council during which it threatened to move elsewhere. Wooldridge wrote a piece labelling the Wimbledon fortnight as the last of the great middle-class festivals, which could almost function without the tennis, and suggested an appropriate relocation would be to Basingstoke.

But it was the changes in football that provoked Wooldridge most sorely, especially as symbolized by the avaricious and near monopolistic premier league. As the twenty-first century opened he saw football not as the beautiful game but something out of control, run by elderly men often filmed embracing each other with diplomatic hugs while waiting to stab one another in the back and living high on the hog the while. He remarked that only in Bhutan, a country without television, could someone have avoided the world cup in 2002.

Wooldridge enjoyed the big occasions of horse racing, especially over the jumps, and was a great admirer of the skill and bravery of the jockeys. He liked a bet and once wrote that the Cheltenham festival without a bet was like being invited to a vegetarian, teetotal restaurant. He admired another famous equestrian, Princess Anne, and wrote several pieces underlining her prowess as an international sportswoman. There was also a touch of Ernest Hemingway, notably when he went through a period in which he tested his own mind and body by experiencing the action rather than just writing about it. In January 1985 he took twelve young readers of the *Mail* to experience the Cresta run to prove that 'guts was not exclusive to any one generation', and he also went down himself. He thought it his second greatest thrill but was very frightened and swore a lot. The following year he spent five months in Australia covering that country's challenge for the America's cup, which included one 20 minute period at the helm. He also covered the 1100 mile dog sled race in Alaska from the second seat of a single-engined plane. He flew with the Red Arrows and took part in the notorious bull-running in Pamplona on several occasions.

Wooldridge's writing won him four sports writer of the year awards and two each of sports feature writer of the year and sports columnist of the year. It has been calculated that he wrote some 7 million words during his working life. In his early days at the *Daily Mail* he ghosted columns for others, including Matt Busby and Max Faulkner. Critics sometimes accused him of writing with an irritating lightness of touch, and he could be tempted by the attractions of hyperbole. Of a cover drive by Ted Dexter during the Lord's test match against the West Indies in 1963 he wrote that Dexter's 'bat flashed through like a scimitar and the crash was like a British rifle sending death down into some deep, echoing gorge along the North West Frontier' (*Searching for Heroes*, 36). But he had a turn of phrase not often found among writers on sport, displayed during a piece on the Japanese grand prix of 1976 when he noted that Japan had yet to produce a driver who could keep his foot to the floor when all around him were easing theirs. He saw himself, increasingly, as a sports columnist rather than a sports reporter, in part at least due to a growing admiration for American sports writers like Thomas Boswell, Paul Gallico, Ring Lardner, and Red Smith. Gallico's *Farewell to Sport* was a particular favourite. Several of his colleagues speculated about how he might have developed if he had written for one of the more thoughtful if less popular papers, and been given more time and space. However, when the *Press Gazette* set up the newspaper hall of fame in November 2006 and included the forty most influential journalists of the previous forty years, the only two sports writers included were Hugh McIlvanny and Wooldridge. He was appointed OBE in 1991.

Wooldridge was and remained a *Mail* man, but not through and through. He had supported John Arlott when he spoke out against playing sport with teams representing the apartheid regime in South Africa as early as 1969. Although an admirer of Margaret Thatcher, he was a vigorous opponent of her attempt to prevent British athletes from competing in the Moscow Olympics and reminded her of her support for British rugby players who had wanted to play in South Africa. He thought that the Munich Olympics should have been abandoned after the shooting of the Israeli athletes in 1972. He refused to support the policy of the *Mail* when it subsidized the bringing of the South African runner Zola Budd to run for England. But he supported fox-hunting and preferred Sebastian Coe to Steve Ovett, characterizing the former as 'an increasingly rare phenomenon in British life, a person who would prefer to be pleasant rather than bloody minded' (*Searching for Heroes*, 122). He liked good food and drink as well as expensive hotels and preferred places like Seoul and Dubai, with no graffiti, no litter, and virtually no crime, to eastern Europe. He once wrote that cricket tours of India were like four months in prison without remission. He embraced a late twentieth-century version of the Corinthian spirit and preferred his winners to manifest the effortless superiority that was inseparable from the supposed British amateur tradition.

In the 1970s and 1980s Wooldridge was involved in the making of several eccentrically unsuccessful television programmes, two linked to fishing competitions and one, entitled *Calum Kennedy's Commando Course*, following a troupe of Scottish entertainers taking culture and fun to the highlands and islands. (Although shot in 1979, for legal reasons it was not shown until 1985.) He also found the time to write five books, including a short memoir, *Travelling Reserve* (1982). His first marriage was dissolved in 1979, and on 1 December 1980 he married Sarah Margaret Lourenço (*b.* 1946), secretary, daughter of Leonard Waller Andrews Chappell, insurance underwriter, and former wife of Antonio Lourenço. He had had a serious heart operation in 1997. He died at the Chelsea and Westminster Hospital on 4 March 2007, of sepsis following a *Clostridium difficile* infection. He was survived by his second wife, Sarah, and the three sons of his first marriage.

TONY MASON

Sources I. Wooldridge, *Travelling reserve* (1982) · *The Times* (6 March 2007) · *Daily Telegraph* (6 March 2007) · *The Guardian* (6 March 2007) · *The Independent* (6 March 2007) · I. Wooldridge, *Searching for heroes* (2007) · *WW* (2007) · b. cert. · m. certs. · d. cert.

Archives SOUND BL NSA, current affairs recordings · BL NSA, documentary recordings

Likenesses photographs, 1966–99, Rex Features, London · photographs, 1984–2005, Photoshot, London · obituary photographs · photograph, repro. in www.sportsjournalists.co.uk/blog/?p=483#more-483 · photograph, repro. in news.bbc.co.uk/1/hi/uk/6418435.stm

Wealth at death £571,099: probate, 8 June 2007, *CGPLA Eng. & Wales*

Woolmer, Robert Andrew [Bob] (**1948–2007**), cricketer and cricket coach, was born in Kanpur, India, on 14 May 1948, the son of Clarence Shirley Woolmer, an English insurance executive who had once played in India's domestic cricket championship, and his wife, Stella Kathleen, *née* Birks. He was ten when his father took him to Karachi to see Hanif Mohammed break the first-class record by scoring 499. (In 1994, after Brian Lara beat Hanif by scoring 501 for Warwickshire, whom Woolmer then coached, it was widely reported that he was unique in witnessing both innings.) The family moved back to England in the mid-1950s, settling in Kent, where Woolmer impressed at Skinners' School in Tunbridge Wells as a seam-bowling all-rounder, joining the county cricket club at the age of twenty. He made his one-day international début for England in 1972. In 1974 he married (Shirley) Gillian Hall, who had been brought up in South Africa. They had two sons.

The influence of Colin Cowdrey, a sedate, graceful stroke-player, Woolmer's team-mate at Kent and his driving companion, and another Indian-born Englishman, became increasingly plain—in girth as well as approach—and in 1975 Woolmer was picked for the Lord's test against Australia's intimidating pace duo of Dennis Lillee and Jeff Thomson. By the summer's end he had embarked on a sequence of three centuries in consecutive Ashes encounters. If the first was a painstaking, match-saving innings—in expending fully 396 minutes in reaching three figures he set an Ashes record for sluggishness—the other two, in 1977, were far more fluent and commanding.

The year 1977 also saw Woolmer join world series cricket, Kerry Packer's revolutionary breakaway venture in Australia. Banned from county cricket, along with the other Packer players, Woolmer was reprieved in the High Court and resumed his England career in 1980. Despite taking his aggregate beyond 1000 runs, he struggled in his four remaining tests, plunging his final average, in nineteen appearances, to a modest thirty-three. In 1982, beset by the back problems that would impel an early retirement, and spurred in part by the belief that maintaining links with South Africa was the best way of defeating prejudice, he undermined the international policy of sporting isolation by accepting a reported £50,000 to join

Robert Andrew [Bob] **Woolmer (1948–2007)**, by Philip Brown, 2006

the first 'rebel' tour of apartheid South Africa, where he was playing for Western Province, and was accordingly banned from national duty.

An affable, sensitive man, Woolmer now found his true calling as a coach, blazing a trail at a time when coaches were only just starting to challenge the captain's autocracy. Motivated by 'curiosity and challenge' (*The Times*, 15 Oct 2007), he became coach at Avendale Cricket Club, a club for 'non-white' cricketers in Athlone, Cape Town, and then had one season at Kent before he made his name at Warwickshire, admired for his use of computer technology and thirst for innovation, notably in his enthusiasm for the 'reverse sweep'. He also presided over a remarkable season in 1994 that saw Warwickshire, unprecedentedly, win three trophies and only narrowly fail to secure all four. In 1994 he became coach of the South African national cricket team, remaining until 1999. He had ceased to be the South African coach when in 2000 the scandal broke following revelations that the South African captain, Hansie Cronje, had accepted bribes in return for 'fixing' matches. Nevertheless Woolmer's defence of Cronje did his own reputation, and that of the game, no good.

Woolmer returned to Warwickshire for three troubled years from 2000 to 2002, and then became the International Cricket Council's performance manager before taking on the immense task, daunting enough even if he had spoken Urdu, of coaching Pakistan. His tenure of this post was a difficult one. During the 2006 Oval test against England, Pakistan's captain, Inzamam-ul-Haq, furious at allegations of ball-tampering, refused to resume play, and Pakistan became the first team to forfeit a test. The following year Pakistan was knocked out of the world cup, shockingly, by Ireland.

To Allan Donald, who broke South Africa's test wicket-taking record under Woolmer's aegis, Woolmer was the game's foremost technical coach. He 'looked at every aspect of the game', affirmed the long-time national wicket-keeper Dave Richardson. 'He didn't force anything down anyone's throat. You could always talk back to him if he got over-technical or over-enthusiastic' (interview, 2 Oct 2009, www.cricinfo.com). 'He was too generous with his time', wrote the journalist Ivo Tennant, who ghosted Woolmer's autobiography (*Pirate and Rebel?* 1984) and was more aware than most of the physical and mental toll. 'Any player could go to his room at any hour for advice' (*The Times*, 15 Oct 2007). The culmination of this accumulated wisdom was *Bob Woolmer's Art and Science of Cricket*, written in collaboration with a sports scientist, Tim Noakes. Technical instructions abounded alongside psychological advice: 'Remember, [the reverse sweep] is a shot that takes flair and confidence and, if you get it wrong, don't expect many sympathetic voices in the dressing room'. Woolmer also wrote *Skilful Cricket* (1993) and *Woolmer on Cricket* (2000).

On 18 March 2007, the day after Pakistan had been knocked out of the world cup, Woolmer, by now overweight and diabetes-stricken, was found dead in his room in the Jamaica Pegasus Hotel, Kingston, inciting all manner of speculation, even in nations immune to cricket. The Kingston police cited strangulation, fanning the flames. *The Observer*'s crime correspondent encapsulated the giddying confusion:

> The murderer was an enraged Pakistan fan. It was the cricket mafia. The Pakistan team captain. A terrorist plot by Islamic extremists. An underworld bookmaker who had lost millions. Who killed Bob Woolmer? Frankly, back then, it felt as if anyone might have murdered him, and that there were many who wanted him dead. (*Observer Sports Monthly*, 1 July 2007)

Two months later overseas pathologists disproved the police's claim, but uncertainty persisted. In November 2007 an open verdict was returned. His body was cremated in Cape Town on 4 May 2007. He was survived by his wife, Gill, and sons Russell and Dale. ROB STEEN

Sources B. Woolmer, *Pirate and rebel?* (1984) · *The Times* (19 March 2007); (8 June 2007); (15 Oct 2007) · *Daily Telegraph* (19 March 2007) · *The Guardian* (20 March 2007) · *The Independent* (20 March 2007) · *Observer Sports Monthly* (1 July 2007) · *WW* (2007)

Likenesses photographs, 1969–2006, Rex Features, London · photographs, 1970–2007, Getty Images, London · photographs, 1973–2000, Photoshot, London · photographs, 1999–2007, Camera Press, London · P. Brown, photograph, 2006, Rex Features, London [*see illus.*] · obituary photographs

Wragg, Edward Conrad [Ted] **(1938–2005)**, educationist, was born on 26 June 1938 at 158 Clarence Street, Sheffield, the only child of George William Wragg, fruit and flower hawker, and his wife, Maria, *née* Brandstetter, a cook. His father's first wife had died and he had a half-brother from that marriage. His mother had been born in Urfahr, Austria, and Wragg's uncle had been at school with Adolf Hitler. Wragg's mother had come to the UK on a passage assisted by the Austrian government, worked in service, and met her husband when he came to the house with flowers to sell. She was ambitious for her son and rather than send him to the inner-city school local to the family's terraced home she took him on the tram to Hunters Bar primary school, then considered the best in the city. When early signs of Wragg's promise emerged his father, a strong, opinionated, and determined working-class man, was proud of him, but his mother remained the driving force.

Wragg inherited a fine singing voice from his mother, who had sung on Austrian radio, and every Friday he was expected to sing in his primary school assembly. He would become physically sick with apprehension but his mother insisted he do it, sending him in with a biscuit to settle his stomach. In his last year at Hunters Bar an inspirational class teacher had a lasting impact. The teacher used projects to help his pupils learn at a time when projects were not generally done in schools. He took the class on trips, including one to Sheffield reference library to show them how to use reference materials. Wragg continued to use the library when he was a university student and met former classmates there. He passed the entrance examination for the city's King Edward VII Grammar School, where he excelled and pursued his loves of music, acting, and sport—he was a lifelong Sheffield Wednesday fan even though he was discouraged from playing football at King Edward's because it was 'working class' (*The Independent*). Later he coached university sides and was a qualified referee.

Wragg could have studied music at university but instead chose to study German at Durham University and contented his musical side by playing guitar in a skiffle band. His mother's native tongue had not been spoken at home. She and her sister, who also lived in England, had been reported for speaking in German when to do so during the Second World War risked internment, and abandoned their first language. Wragg grew up during the Second World War experiencing anti-German feeling and was the only child in his street not invited to VE-day celebrations, because he was known as the 'little German' (*Times Educational Supplement*, 3 Feb 2006).

At Durham Wragg was joined by his girlfriend, Judith King, whom he had met at a Congregational church conference at Easter 1956. The daughter of Beaumont King, steelworker, she annoyed her teachers by giving up a local authority exhibition to read geography and history at Durham to take a shorter teacher training course so that they would finish their studies at the same time. Wragg graduated with a first-class degree and a distinction in the oral, and followed this with a first in his postgraduate certificate of education. He then spent four years as an assistant master at Queen Elizabeth Grammar School, Wakefield, from 1960. He and Judith, who had qualified as a primary school teacher, married at Netherfield Independent Chapel, Thurlstone, Yorkshire, on 29 December that year—the start of a highly successful marriage that produced three much loved children, Josie, Caroline, and Christopher. Meanwhile Wragg's ability was spotted early, and he was appointed head of German at Wyggeston Boys' School, Leicester, at the age of twenty-six. He stayed only two years but left a clear impression on his pupils. One of them, Paul Fletcher, later said: 'He was an inspiring teacher ... His teaching style was effortless, his classroom control flawless, his humour still memorable' (http://newsvote.bbc.co.uk/mpapps, 10 Nov 2005).

In 1966 Wragg became a lecturer in education at Exeter University, where he also studied for his PhD, awarded in 1972 (he had taken the degree of MEd at Leicester University in 1967). In 1973 he was appointed to the chair of education at Nottingham University, at thirty-five the youngest professor of education in the country. At Nottingham he led an intensive two-year project looking at mixed ability teaching that found that bright children were not sufficiently stretched as effort focused on bringing the less able up to standard. He wrote: 'It is probably true that only exceptional teachers can manage unstreamed classes. I have tried it myself, and it is the hardest thing I have ever done' (*The Times*, 11 Nov 2005). But he thought it should be left to the schools to decide whether to stream classes or not, rather than to 'some moronic teenager in the Number 10 Policy Unit', as he later put it (*The Guardian*, 1 Feb 2005). He vehemently opposed the 'marketization' of education. His overriding aim was to see all children get a better education, not just children lucky enough to get into good schools. He railed against the testing regime and the league tables that followed the introduction of the national curriculum by the Conservative government of Margaret Thatcher, but his branding as an educational establishment 'leftie' by the political right later in his career failed to take on board the traditionalist side of this progressive educator.

In 1978 Wragg became director of the Institute of Education at Exeter University after he dazzled the interview board, and under his leadership it became pre-eminent in education research. During his time there he became the acerbic and witty spokesman for a generation of teachers who felt he uniquely understood what they did. For twenty-five years his columns in the *Times Educational Supplement*, and later *The Independent* and *The Guardian*, poured jargon-free comic vitriol on policies that diminished and demeaned the professionalism of teachers. He was on the teachers' side. As he said in one of his columns, 'There is no higher calling; without [teachers] society would slide back into primitive squalor' (*Times Educational Supplement*, 19 April 2002). Successive education ministers from Shirley Williams to Estelle Morris consulted him, and if they didn't he would ring and give the benefit of his advice. He was an ideal point of contact for journalists, since he seemed to know exactly what was going on in the corridors of power. He kept on teaching in schools whenever he could and was in touch with the realities of the job. Shortly before his death he took part in a television series that he masterminded, in which a group of disaffected teenagers was taught in a specially tailored school. At one point Wragg confessed to camera: 'I like all the kids and love them, but I could cheerfully take them behind a tree and ruin my career by smacking the hell out of them' (*Times Educational Supplement*, 9 Sept 2005). Teachers took comfort from someone who knew how frustrating teaching could be.

During the course of his career Wragg wrote more than

fifty books and 800 academic articles but it was his newspaper columns and his frequent appearances on television and radio that made him the most famous man in education of his day. He lampooned government ministers and educationists who had come up with what he described as wheezes, and created such unforgettable characters as Tony Zoffis (as in 'Tony's office')—a man who supposedly always did what the prime minister of the day, Tony Blair, wanted. His arch enemy Chris Woodhead, a controversial right-wing chief inspector of schools, was described as Woodentop. But Wragg was no dogmatist. In his book *The Cubic Curriculum* (1997), which looked at theories of how children best absorb information and nurture their imagination, he said: 'Learners need the excitement of finding out, just as they need the confirmation of being told. It should not be a matter of one versus the other' (p. 89). As an example of his pragmatism, if asked whether he favoured 'phonics' or 'look and say' when teaching children to read, he would ask his interlocutor whether they favoured a fork or a knife when eating.

Wragg stood down as director of the Institute of Education at Exeter in 1994 but continued as professor of education until 2003, when he retired, and was made professor emeritus. He had received numerous honorary degrees and had been a specialist adviser to parliamentary select committees on education and worked on numerous educational bodies, often from the chairman's seat. He was particularly influential as chairman of the School Broadcasting Council and its successor, the Educational Broadcasting Council (1981–7). He worked with Lord Puttnam to found the national teaching awards and from 2000 chaired the judging panel. His work in leading a commission investigating the struggling education system in Birmingham was seminal and helped the city's schools turn a corner. He suggested performance targets set by teachers, not governments, and entitlements to school trips and cultural visits, harking back to things that had excited his intellect and imagination as a boy. In 2008 cultural entitlements for all schoolchildren were introduced nationally. At the time of his death it was rumoured that he was about to join the House of Lords as a Liberal Democrat peer.

Wragg had huge energy, rising at 4 or 5 a.m. to write articles before the working day began. He lived life in the fast lane both metaphorically and literally: his much loved BMW had a driver who liked to get a move on. He was an editor's dream, delivering sparkling copy on time and to length and, if necessary, at very short notice. He was a reporter's dream, too, whose formidable memory calling up complex background made further research redundant. He was also a man of great kindness and warmth.

Wragg had taken up jogging in his mid-thirties and tried to jog every day. Once, in Belfast during the height of the troubles, he had jogged in his suit, his wife, Judith, having hidden his running kit because she didn't think it was safe out on the streets; he had a deliciously stubborn streak. It was while jogging one Sunday that he collapsed near his home and was taken to the Royal Devon and Exeter Hospital, where he died on 10 November 2005 of myocardial infarction. He was survived by his wife and their three children. When the news was released website message boards at the BBC, Exeter University, and the *Times Educational Supplement* among others were inundated with messages of condolence. In February 2006 Exeter Cathedral was packed with 700 people for a memorial service. A tribute evening later that month at London's Institute of Education attracted more than 900 participants and speakers included John Prescott, the deputy prime minister; Neil Kinnock, the former leader of the Labour Party; and Rory Bremner, the impressionist and comedian (for whom Wragg had written sketches). A memorial fund was launched during the evening to provide educational opportunities for disadvantaged young people in Wragg's home town of Sheffield. WENDY BERLINER

Sources *Daily Telegraph* (11 Nov 2005) · *The Independent* (11 Nov 2005) · *The Guardian* (11 Nov 2005); (12 Nov 2005); (15 Nov 2005) · *The Times* (11 Nov 2005); (16 Nov 2005) · cv, www.education.ex.ac.uk/tedwragg/cv.php, 1 April 2008 · *Times Educational Supplement* (18 Nov 2005); (3 Feb 2006) · www.tes.co.uk/blogs, 1 April 2008 · www.news.bbc.co.uk/1/hi/education, 1 April 2008 · *WW* (2005) · personal knowledge (2009) · private information (2009) [Judith Wragg, widow; T. Brighouse; R. Pring; P. Fletcher] · b. cert. · m. cert. · d. cert.

Archives FILM BFINA, current affairs footage | SOUND BL NSA, current affairs recordings

Likenesses obituary photographs · photograph, U. Lond., Institute of Education

Wealth at death £491,401: probate, 17 Feb 2006, *CGPLA Eng. & Wales*

Wright, Sir Denis Arthur Hepworth (1911–2005), diplomatist, was born in his paternal grandparents' house, 80 Durlston Road, Kingston upon Thames, Surrey, on 23 March 1911, the elder son and eldest of four children of Arthur Edgar Wright (1880–1949), assistant director of public works, Hong Kong, and his wife, Margery Hepworth, *née* Chapman (1888–1973). He spent nine years in Hong Kong, where he attended the Peak School, before returning to England with his parents in 1921. From Brentwood School, Essex (1921–9), where, in his words, his sole distinction was a prize for 'Virtue, Learning and Manners' (Wright, 1.13), he went to St Edmund Hall, Oxford, to read modern history, with financial support from his parents, his schoolmaster, an educational trust, and Essex county council. To learn to ride, he joined the cavalry squadron of the Oxford University officer training corps. He was a founder member of the Cosmopolitans, a small society for the discussion of international issues. He left Oxford in 1932 with a second-class degree in modern history.

Failing to win an eastern cadetship for the colonial service, Wright first took two ill-paid jobs in advertising and in 1936 joined Gallahers, the tobacco firm, at £350 a year. He became engaged in 1938 to Iona Carmen, an artist, daughter of Granville Craig, and niece of Lord Craigavon, the first prime minister of Northern Ireland. They had met through the Labour Club at Oxford (though he described himself as a 'non-political animal'; Wright, 1.26). Wright travelled alone on holiday to Romania in August 1939. Reaching Constanta on the outbreak of war, he was immediately recruited by the British consulate. Iona joined him and they were married in the consulate at

Galatz on the Danube on 10 November 1939. There were no children of the marriage.

In 1939–40 Constanta was a hive of covert activity, including the smuggling out of £20 million of Polish government gold, an abortive plan to block the Iron Gate gorge on the Danube, and spirited attempts to frustrate German activity. In 1940 Wright moved to the legation in Bucharest. When relations with Romania were broken in 1941, Wright was appointed vice-consul in Trebizond in north-east Turkey, a solitary post, with supplies short, communications slow, and little congenial company. The German advance into Russia raised the importance of the region and Wright made three difficult journeys into the hinterland to report on communications, earning a commendation from the embassy in Ankara. In May 1943 he became acting consul in Mersin, in south-eastern Turkey, an important port for supplies.

Returning to London in 1945, Wright took a job with the Ottoman Bank but soon resigned and joined the foreign service. His first posting was as first secretary (commercial) in Belgrade (1946–8). His subsequent career followed a more conventional path, although he spent ten of his twenty-six years' service in one country, eight of them as ambassador, a rarity in the twentieth-century diplomatic service. In 1949 he was appointed superintending trade consul in Chicago, and in 1951 head of the economic relations department at the Foreign Office. In 1953 he was chosen to reopen the embassy in Tehran after the fall of Mossadeq, first as chargé d'affaires and later as counsellor. This marked a turning point in his life. He was appointed CMG in 1954. After serving from 1955 as an assistant under-secretary in the Foreign Office, he was appointed in 1959 ambassador to Ethiopia and in 1963, after a brief spell in the Foreign Office, to Iran, where he remained until his retirement from the diplomatic service in 1971. He was appointed KCMG in 1961 and GCMG on retirement.

Wright proved to be a model representative of his country. Completely straightforward, he displayed a gift for friendship without condescension and an ability to engender trust. A shrewd judge of character, a firm and fair disciplinarian, he won the respect and affection of his staff and of the expatriate British. He learned the local languages and spoke Farsi well. He and Iona toured widely in their various posts, by Land Rover, horse, mule, or on foot, making a point everywhere of meeting the local population. He combined loyalty to his own government, albeit severely tested in 1956 by the Suez débâcle, with empathy with the people of the countries in which he served. This did not blind him to their faults. In his farewell dispatch from Addis Ababa he described Ethiopians as 'elusive, evasive, secretive and obstinate' (Wright, 2.361). After demonstrations in Iran in 1963, inspired largely by the religious community and suppressed with some bloodshed, he noted in his diary that the shah's weakness of character and judgement remained, and added prophetically: 'So long as the army and security forces remain loyal (and without them the Shah is doomed) … the country will probably tag along for some time' (ibid., 2.380).

The trust he established often enabled Wright to play a key part in furthering British interests. In Belgrade, after the break with Moscow, one Yugoslav official confided in Wright that the economic situation was desperate: if Britain valued Tito's survival, aid was essential. His report led to the reversal of British policy on aid. In Ethiopia in 1961, when the imperial guard mounted a coup, Wright's loyalist contacts turned to him to alert the emperor, who was absent in Brazil. The embassy provided a haven for the British community during the fighting. Most notably, from 1953 on, he established an unprecedentedly close but wary relationship with the shah of Iran. This contributed significantly to the success of the oil negotiations following the fall of Mossadeq in 1953. In 1959, while on holiday in Tehran, Wright was urged by an Iranian minister to see the shah to dissuade him from concluding a pact with the Soviet Union; and in 1969–70 he was instrumental in persuading the shah to drop Iran's claim to Bahrain, subject to a test of opinion there by the UN secretary-general. He failed, however, to move the shah over claims to other smaller islands.

After his retirement from the diplomatic service Wright was approached by the British government in May 1979 to break to the shah, in exile at Nassau, that they 'could not for the moment … offer [him] asylum' (Wright, 3.40). Wright agreed on condition that his mission should be secret. Disguised and travelling on a false passport as Edward Wilson, born on 1 April, he saw the shah and brought him to 'understand and accept' the decision (ibid., 3.41). In 1980, in his last direct service to the government, Wright joined a group of observers of the Rhodesian elections that followed the Lancaster House agreement of the previous December.

In retirement in Haddenham, Buckinghamshire, the Wrights kept open house for their many friends at their home, Duck Bottom. He became a director of several companies, including Shell, the Chartered (later Standard Chartered) Bank, and Mitchell Cotts (all 1971–81). He was elected an honorary fellow of both St Edmund Hall (1972) and St Antony's College (1975), Oxford. He was chairman of the Iran Society (1976–9; and president, 1989–95), a member of the executive committee of the British Institute for Persian Studies (1973–87; president, 1978–87), a member of the executive committee of the Anglo-Ethiopian Society (1972–7), and a governor of the Overseas Service College, Farnham Castle (1972–86). In 1990 he was awarded the Sir Percy Sykes memorial medal by the Royal Society for Asian Affairs. He was additionally chairman or committee member of some smaller societies or charities, including in 1975 a campaigning group, Haddenham into Europe. He made several lecture tours of North America and India. During this time he made serious contributions to scholarship, notably with two important and admired books, *The English amongst the Persians* (1977) and *The Persians amongst the English* (1985). He contributed, jointly with James Morris and Roger Wood, to *Persia* (1969) and published a collection of essays, *Britain and Iran, 1790–1980* (Iran Society, 2003). He died at his home in Haddenham, on 18 May 2005, of cancer of the prostate. His funeral took place on 2 June at St Mary's Church, Haddenham. He was survived by his wife, Iona. One of the most distinguished British diplomats of his generation, he remained endearingly modest about his abilities and achievements.

JOHN GRAHAM

Sources Bodl. Oxf., Wright papers [incl. 'Memoirs, 1911–1971', 3 vols., typescript] • FO papers, National Archives, Kew • BDOHP (interview by E. Cox), 26 July 2000, CAC Cam. • I. Wright, *Black Sea bride* (1997) • C. Kadivar, 'Our best bet: tea with former British ambassador to Iran', *The Iranian* (13 July 2000) • *Daily Telegraph* (21 May 2005) • *The Guardian* (23 May 2005) • *The Times* (3 June 2005); (20 June 2005) • *The Independent* (10 June 2005) • J. Gurney, 'Denis Arthur Hepworth Wright', *St Antony's Record* (2005), 150–52 • H. Carless, 'Obituary: Sir Denis Wright GCMG', *Asian Affairs*, 36/3 (Nov 2005), 440–41 • J. Gurney, 'Sir Denis Wright', *Iran: the Journal of Persian Studies*, 43 (2005) • *WW* (2005) • Burke, *Peerage* • diplomatic service list, 1970 • personal knowledge (2008) • private information (2008) • b. cert. • m. cert. • d. cert.

Archives Bodl. Oxf., papers • St Antony's College, Oxford, papers | TNA: PRO, FO | SOUND CAC Cam., diplomatic oral history programme, interview with E. Cox, 26 July 2000

Likenesses W. Bird, bromide print, 1961, NPG • obituary photographs • photographs (in 'Memoirs. 1911–1971'), Bodl. Oxf., Wright papers

Wealth at death £892,695: probate, 10 Jan 2006, *CGPLA Eng. & Wales*

Wright, Sir Edward Maitland (1906–2005), mathematician, was born on 13 February 1906 at Park Side House, Farnley, near Leeds, the son of Maitland Turner Wright (*d.* 1943), soap manufacturer, and his wife, Kate, *née* Owen (*d.* 1954), music teacher. When he was three his father's business (manufacturing Wright's Washall soap) failed; his parents separated, and he moved south with his mother. She worked at boarding schools, where he was able to study for free, with a reduction in his mother's salary. He worked as a teacher from the early age of fourteen, though he was sacked at the age of sixteen for being too young for his post. He was able to find another post, at Chard grammar school in Somerset, where he taught from 1923 to 1926. Until the age of fourteen he knew no mathematics beyond elementary arithmetic, but on being exposed to algebra fell in love with mathematics, which he taught himself to degree level. It was then possible to study for an external degree from the University of London without attending lectures, which, having a full-time teaching job, he was unable to do. He obtained his first degree in this way. On being told by a colleague that a London degree was only equivalent to scholarship standard at Oxford or Cambridge, he investigated the Oxford and Cambridge scholarships available. He was then twenty, and found that he was too old for all except one scholarship, at Jesus College, Oxford, which was unrestricted in subject or age. He successfully applied for this, and took up his scholarship in 1926 to study mathematics.

Wright's years at Oxford were happy and successful. He achieved firsts in mathematical moderations in 1927 and mathematics in 1929, and won the junior mathematical scholarship in 1928 and a senior studentship in 1929. He was then a research student of G. H. Hardy at Christ Church, Oxford, where he took his DPhil and was a junior research fellow from 1930 to 1933; during this time he spent a year in Göttingen and a year as a lecturer at King's College, London. He spent 1933–5 at Christ Church as a lecturer. At Oxford he met (Elizabeth) Phyllis Harris (*d.* 1987), a student of English at St Hilda's College, cox of the Oxford women's eight, and daughter of Harry Percy Harris, mining engineer. They married on 15 August 1934, when she was twenty-seven. They had one son, John.

In 1935, at the unusually early age of twenty-nine, Wright became professor of mathematics at Aberdeen University. While at Christ Church he had learned to fly with the university air squadron (though he never learned to drive). His year in Göttingen convinced him that war was coming. This was a belief he shared with his Christ Church colleague F. A. Lindemann, later Lord Cherwell and Churchill's scientific adviser, and Lindemann's pupil R. V. Jones, who became prominent in scientific and technical intelligence. As a result of his connection with Lindemann he was seconded to work as principal scientific officer with the Air Ministry, working in intelligence, from 1943 to 1945, having previously served as a flight lieutenant in the Royal Air Force Volunteer Reserve (1941–3). After the war he returned to Aberdeen, where he remained until his retirement in 1976. Having served as vice-principal in 1961–2, he became principal and vice-chancellor of the university, from 1962 until 1976. As principal he oversaw a significant expansion of student numbers and facilities and (despite a reputation for working on mathematical problems during meetings) an effective and respected committee chairman. When offered a post in Oxford he turned it down, preferring to remain in Aberdeen. The Edward Wright Building on Dunbar Street was later named in his honour.

Wright's mathematical papers were principally on number theory (including the theory of partitions, the representation of integers as sums of squares of integers, or generalizations of this such as Waring's problem, and the Erdös-Selberg elementary proof of the prime number theorem), combinatorial theory (including enumeration problems for labelled and unlabelled graphs), and complex analysis. But the greatest impact of his work was through his book with G. H. Hardy, *An Introduction to the Theory of Numbers* (1938), always referred to as 'Hardy and Wright'. This book was widely praised by number theory specialists for its excellent exposition, very broad range, and good judgement in the selection of material. Its continuing sales, through five editions (the last in 1979), was testimony to the great use made of it by mathematicians generally, as a textbook and as a work of reference.

Wright was elected a fellow of the Royal Society of Edinburgh in 1937, and received various honorary degrees and academic prizes and distinctions. He was knighted in 1977. He lived in retirement in Aberdeen until after his wife's death in 1987, and then in Reading. He died at the Royal Berkshire Hospital, Reading, on 2 February 2005, of septicaemia caused by a urinary tract infection. He was survived by his son, John, also a distinguished mathematician.

N. H. BINGHAM

Sources *Daily Telegraph* (10 Feb 2005) • *The Times* (11 Feb 2005); (24 Feb 2005) • N. H. Bingham, 'Sir Edward Maitland Wright', LMS newsletter 335, www.lms.ac.uk/newsletter/335, 18 June 2008 • J. J. O'Connor and E. F. Robertson, 'Edward Maitland Wright', www.groups.dcs.st-and.ac.uk/~history/Biographies, 18 June 2008 • A. R. Pears, *Bulletin of the London Mathematical Society*, 39 (2007), 857–65 • Burke, *Peerage* • *WW* (2005) • personal knowledge (2009) • private information (2009) • b. cert. • m. cert. • d. cert.

Archives Nuffield College, Oxford, Cherwell MSS

Likenesses obituary photographs • photograph, U. Aberdeen; repro. in *The Times* (11 Feb 2005)

Wealth at death £80,739: probate, 20 June 2005, *CGPLA Eng. & Wales*

Wright, Richard William [Rick] (**1943–2008**), keyboard player, was born on 28 July 1943 at Brookdale Nursing Home, Hatch End, Middlesex, the son of Robert Charles Wright, a research chemist at Unigate Dairies, and his wife, Daisy, *née* Hughes. The family lived in Pinner, Middlesex, where Wright grew up with his two sisters. He was educated at Haberdashers' Aske's Boys' School, then a direct grant school in Cricklewood, north-west London. He showed an early aptitude for music, especially jazz, and played a number of instruments including the piano, trumpet, trombone, and guitar. On leaving school he went to the Regent Street Polytechnic to study architecture and met there Roger Waters and Nick Mason. They initially formed a rhythm and blues band, Sigma 6, with Waters on bass, Mason on drums, and Wright on keyboards, and were sometimes joined by a female vocalist, Juliette Sylvia Veronica Cecilia Gale (*b.* 1945), daughter of Harold Gale, motor mechanic. Wright later married her on 7 August 1969.

Sigma 6 renamed themselves the Architectural Abdabs (also known as the Screaming Abdabs) and went through various changes of personnel, though the trio of Wright, Mason, and Waters remained constant. In 1964 Wright left the Regent Street Polytechnic and enrolled at the London College of Music. In the following year the band was joined by one of Waters's neighbours, Syd *Barrett, then a student at the Camberwell School of Art. The resulting quartet first took the name the Tea Set and then the Pink Floyd Sound after the two bluesmen, Pink Anderson and Floyd Council, but Pink Floyd it soon became. They signed for the record company EMI in February 1967.

Under Barrett's influence Pink Floyd became known around London's new 'underground' scene for their experimental music, innovative use of film, and dramatic light shows. They produced quirky and eccentric songs such as 'Arnold Layne' and 'See Emily Play', their first two singles written by Barrett. Barrett largely wrote their first album, *The Piper at the Gates of Dawn*, released in 1967, as well. But he was increasingly dependent on drugs and went into a mental decline. He was replaced in the following year by a new lead guitarist, David Gilmour. Wright played on Barrett's two single albums released in 1970, *The Madcap Laughs* and *Barrett*.

Pink Floyd's second album, *A Saucerful of Secrets*, released in July 1968, was less whimsical. The extended title track to the album was in the distinctively dreamy and ethereal style that defined the group's music at this stage, arguably their most creative period. Wright's instrumental versatility, training in different styles—from blues and jazz to classical and avant-garde—and virtuosity on keyboards and newly emerging synthesizers was a great advantage to a band experimenting with new styles of music, sometimes dubbed 'psychedelic' or 'progressive', and new musical and recording technologies. He was also able to sing lead vocals. Pink Floyd scored three films in this period, itself an innovation in the world of pop music: *More* (1969), a film by the French director Barbet Schroeder, about heroin addiction; Michelangelo Antonioni's trance-like *Zabriskie Point* (1970), about the American counter-culture in the 1960s; and Schroeder's *La Vallée* (1972), about an encounter with the Mapuga tribe in New Guinea, the music for which became the album *Obscured by Clouds*.

Before this in 1969 Pink Floyd had released perhaps the most demanding of all their albums, *Ummagumma*. A double album, one record was of live performances and the other gave half a side to each of the members of the band for studio compositions. Wright's piece entitled 'Sysyphus—Parts 1–4' was influenced by the music of Karlheinz Stockhausen. In the following year Pink Floyd released their most successful album to date, *Atom Heart Mother*, which was premièred at the Bath Festival and required a full orchestra and choir. Arguably it was on their next album, *Meddle* (1971), that Wright and the other members of the group made their most notable contribution in co-writing the celebrated piece 'Echoes', which took up the whole of the second side. This was the apotheosis of the Pink Floyd sound. If earlier pieces such as 'Interstellar Overdrive' and 'Set the Controls for the Heart of the Sun' had tried to capture the sense of flight and space in deliberately futuristic compositions, 'Echoes' was oceanic and subterranean. Developing from the sound of a sonar, it induced in the listener a sense of floating and drifting before building through a slow crescendo to a sudden, multi-layered electronic climax. The band played 'Echoes' in their 1974 film *Pink Floyd at Pompeii*.

A year earlier Pink Floyd had released their most commercially successful album, *The Dark Side of the Moon*, which sold 20 million copies around the world, and was a fixture in the British album chart for six years and in the American chart for more than fourteen. In its focus on money, the rat race, madness—the dark sides of modern life, in short—it marked a new phase as the band moved towards the composition of so-called 'concept albums'. Wright wrote or co-wrote a number of the most notable tracks including 'The Great Gig in the Sky', 'Breathe', and 'Us and Them'. His piano-playing was important to the album's most immediately accessible song, 'Money', but as an instrumentalist it was his use of synthesizers on the instrumental 'Any Colour You Like' which was most memorable. Here the many strands and textures of the melody envelop the listener, laying a basis for a powerful guitar solo from Gilmour.

Dark Side of the Moon looked back to the electronic experimentation of the early Pink Floyd sound and forward to a more popular and accessible style favoured by Roger Waters that would ultimately divide the band. Three more albums followed in the later 1970s: *Wish You Were Here*

(1975), which was a tribute to Barrett that included the memorable song 'Shine On You Crazy Diamond'; *Animals* (1977); and *The Wall* (1979), a double album which explored modern alienation. By the time of its release, however, Waters and Wright had argued and Wright had left the band. Ostensibly over Wright's cocaine addiction and his late return from a holiday, the division also had personal and artistic roots. Wright played on as a salaried musician, however, which was not to his disadvantage: the vast spectacles that the band provided at each venue when they went on tour with *The Wall* were so expensive to mount that the three remaining members of Pink Floyd were saddled with a considerable financial loss.

Eventually the tensions between Wright and Waters were so uncontainable that Wright decided to leave altogether. The last appearance of the classic Pink Floyd line-up was at Earl's Court, London, in July 1981. In 1985 Waters himself split with Mason and Gilmour, allowing Wright to rejoin them in a reconstituted Pink Floyd in 1987. He contributed to the album *A Momentary Lapse of Reason* in that year and became a full member of the band again in the following year. Two final albums followed: one, in 1992, was the improbable soundtrack to *La Carrera Panamerica*, the Mexican classic car race; the other, in which Wright was very prominent, was the highly successful *The Division Bell* (1995), for which he co-wrote five songs and provided the lead vocals on 'Wearing the Inside Out'. The four band members came together for a 'Live 8' concert in Hyde Park in July 2005 but this was an unrepeatable event: Wright, for one, did not favour any further collaboration as a group, though he continued to work with Gilmour, contributing to his album *On an Island* in 2006 and touring with Gilmour in that year.

Wright released an unsuccessful solo album himself in 1978 under the unpromising title of *Wet Dream*. From 1983 to 1985 he worked with Dave Harris, who had been a member of the post-punk, new-romantic group Fashion, in a duo called Zee. But their album *Identity* failed to establish one, or to find an audience. In 1996 he released *Broken China*, a collaboration with Sinead O'Connor and the lyricist Anthony Moore on songs about depression.

Wright's marriage to Juliette Gale, with whom he had a son and a daughter, James and Gala, was dissolved in 1982. He married his second wife, Franka, a Greek fashion designer, in 1984; they divorced in 1994. On 16 June 1995 he married Mildred Irene (Millie) Hobbs, a writer, and daughter of Carlton David Hobbs, insurance broker. They had a son, Ben, but were later divorced. Wright, who had homes in France and the British Virgin Islands, died of cancer on 15 September 2008. LAWRENCE GOLDMAN

Sources N. Schaffner, *Saucerful of secrets: the Pink Floyd odyssey* (2005) · N. Mason and P. Dodd, *Inside out: a personal history of Pink Floyd* (2004) · J. Harris, *The dark side of the moon: the making of the Pink Floyd masterpiece* (2006) · T. Manning, *The rough guide to Pink Floyd* (2006) · P. Anderson and M. Watkinson, *Crazy diamond: Syd Barrett and the dawn of Pink Floyd* (1991); new edn (2006) · G. Povey, *Echoes: the complete history of Pink Floyd* (2007) · M. Blake, *Pigs might fly: the inside story of Pink Floyd* (2008) · *The Times* (16 Sept 2008) · *Daily Telegraph* (17 Sept 2008) · *The Guardian* (16 Sept 2008) · *The Independent* (17 Sept 2008) · b. cert. · m. certs. [1969, 1995]

Archives FILM BFINA, documentary and performance footage | SOUND BL NSA, performance recordings

Likenesses photographs, 1960–2006, Getty Images, London · photographs, 1960–2006, Rex Features, London · photographs, c.1965–1994, Lebrecht Music and Arts Photo Library, London · V. Singh, group portrait, C-type colour print, 1967 (*Pink Floyd*), NPG · L. Lewis, group portrait, C-type colour print, 1970–79 (*Pink Floyd*), NPG · K. Grant, photograph, 1994, Camera Press, London · obituary photographs

Wealth at death £23,695,914: probate, 28 Sept 2009, *CGPLA Eng. & Wales*

Wyre, Raymond Keith [Ray] (**1951–2008**), probation officer and sexual crime consultant, was born at the Royal Victoria Hospital, Bournemouth, on 2 November 1951, the younger son of Derrick Claude Wyre (*b.* 1925), a chief petty officer in the Royal Navy (later a stores manager for a textiles firm, and later still a jeweller), and his wife, Ada Mary, *née* Bourner (*b.* 1928). At the time of his birth the family lived at 187 Seafield Road, Bournemouth. He left school at fifteen to join the Royal Navy, training as an electrician and submariner. On 16 September 1972, at Elim Pentecostal Church, Plymouth, he married Shirley Harris (*b.* 1953), originally from Newcastle, a shorthand typist for an estate agent, and daughter of Charles Frederick Varley Harris, a salesman for a tyre company. They had three children: Timothy (*b.* 1973), Matthew (*b.* 1975), and Rebecca (*b.* 1979).

When he was discharged from the Royal Navy owing to problems with his feet Wyre took a change of direction and attended a theological college. His experiences as a volunteer warden at a working men's hospital led him to decide against ordination, and in the late 1970s he obtained employment as a trainee probation officer at Winson Green Prison in Birmingham, where his first client was a sex offender. Following this he was employed as a probation officer at Albany Prison, Isle of Wight, between 1981 and 1985. It was during this period that he pioneered and developed group therapy for sex offenders (initially simply by scheduling several one-to-one appointments to coincide, since the prison authorities frowned on the idea of group therapy) and began to establish himself as an authority working with this client group. Through skilful questioning he would challenge the belief systems of offenders; many were reported to believe that he could read their minds.

In 1988 Wyre founded the Gracewell Clinic in Birmingham, with the support of a local entrepreneur, Trevor Price. This was the first residential clinic for sex offenders in the UK, initially taking referrals from the probation service of individuals convicted of sex offences, but later accepting men who had thus far managed to avoid the criminal justice system. The clinic was highly successful (none of its residents was caught re-offending), but a combination of financial pressures and local opposition to the housing of so many sex offenders in one building led to the closure of the clinic in 1993. He later said that he was

> always fighting the system because no one wanted me to do this kind of work. They thought sex offenders were one-offs and wouldn't do it again; they didn't understand that it's a lifelong pattern of behaviour and that unless people go

> through therapy … they'll go straight out and resume where they left off. (*The Independent*, 12 July 1994)

He also said that 'we are not working for the offender but for the children' (*The Times*, 3 Aug 1995).

Following the closure of the Gracewell Clinic, Wyre worked as an independent sexual crime consultant until 1999, when he founded Ray Wyre Associates with Derek Green and Paul Roffey. Ray Wyre Associates continued to promote and develop the work of Wyre and his colleagues, gaining increasing recognition within the courts and statutory agencies around the country and running training courses for police and other professionals in Europe, the United States, and the former Soviet Union.

Wyre was one of the pioneers of working with sex offenders and during his career his name was associated with a number of investigations involving the abduction and sexual abuse of children. He worked with some of the UK's most dangerous offenders, including the child-murderer Robert Black. At the time that Wyre interviewed Black the latter was appealing against a life sentence for child abduction and assault, but when he read Wyre's report he cancelled his appeal; he was later convicted of four child murders. Wyre also worked with Anne Marie West as the police prepared the case against her parents, Fred and Rosemary, for their trial in 1994. Among his many legacies was legislative change provoked by work he did with the television journalist Roger Cook (presenter of *The Cook Report*): after one of their programmes child pornography was made illegal in the UK in 1987. He also worked closely with Action for Children in helping to bring about legislation to enable British citizens who had sexually abused children abroad to be prosecuted in the UK; this eventually reached the statute book in the form of the Sexual Offences (Conspiracy and Incitement) Act 1996. He wrote numerous articles in professional journals. He also co-wrote three books: *Women, Men and Rape* (1986) with Anthony Swift; *Murder Squad* (1992) with Tim Tate, a researcher for *The Cook Report*; and, following his work with Robert Black, *The Murder of Childhood: Inside the Mind of One of Britain's Most Notorious Child Murderers* (1995), again with Tim Tate.

Wyre's knowledge and understanding of this hidden world of child sexual abuse was often utilized to inform all forms of print and broadcast media. He was the first point of contact for many journalists and he was always keen to assist them, welcoming the opportunity to promote greater understanding of his work. He was often on television providing insight into the world of child sexual abuse or participating in a live debate.

Small, round-faced, and somewhat dishevelled in appearance, but very astute—a colleague later described him as 'the sharpest man I have ever met', able to pick up on 'what was said, what was not said and what someone was feeling in a way that was at times quite disarming' (*The Times*, 1 July 2008)—Wyre was, despite the grim nature of his work, a natural optimist. He was a keen poker player. His first marriage ended in divorce, and on 26 March 1999, at Milton Keynes register office, he married Charmaine Therese Richardson, otherwise Charmaine Therese Manito (*b.* 1954), counsellor, former wife of Peter Manito, and daughter of Joe Ekanayake, television engineer. There were no children of this second marriage.

Wyre was a diabetic who struggled with the restrictions this placed on his lifestyle, and following a period of serious illness in 2004–5 he took the decision to retire from his post as director of Ray Wyre Associates. However, he continued to play an active role in the field of child protection and carried on his work as a conference speaker, trainer, practitioner, and authority in the field of child sexual abuse, until his death on 20 June 2008; he died in his sleep, of a massive stroke. He was survived by his wife, Charmaine, and the three children of his first marriage.

DEREK GREEN

Sources *The Independent* (12 July 1994) · *The Times* (3 Aug 1995); (1 July 2008); (4 July 2008) · *The Scotsman* (29 June 2008) · *The Herald* [Glasgow] (3 July 2008) · *The Guardian* (8 Aug 2008) · personal knowledge (2012) · private information (2012) · b. cert. · m. certs.
Archives FILM BFINA, current affairs and documentary footage
Likenesses obituary photographs
Wealth at death under £5000: probate, 29 Aug 2008, *CGPLA Eng. & Wales*

Yahya Ali Omar (1924–2008), Swahili scholar, was born in June 1924 in Mombasa, Kenya protectorate, the only son, a twin, and the youngest of three children of Ali bin Omar, fisherman, and his wife, Sudi binti Athman, both Swahili from northern Swahililand. When Yahya was four his father died, and the family moved to a house near the Anisa mosque. By day he learnt the Koran at the local *chuo*; by night he attended classes in Arabic and Islamic studies taught by Sheikh Abdallah al-Husni. As a boy, he wore a *kizibau* (waistcoat) over his *k'anzu* (an ankle-length garment); out of doors he was never bareheaded. From 1935 he continued his education at the Ghazali Muslim School, the first madrasa in Mombasa to enrol pupils of both sexes. He read voraciously in Arabic, including translations of Spinoza and Nietzsche, while, prone to depression, he found solace in the life and work of Heinrich Heine. He never mastered spoken or written English. When Sheikh Ghazali's school closed in the late 1930s he returned to Sheikh Abdallah al-Husni, while at night he attended other classes, including those at the Mazrui mosque, paying especial attention to Sheikh al-Amin bin Ali Mazrui, whose publications he admired.

In 1953 Yahya was employed as a teacher (*muʿallim*) at the government Arab Boys' School, Serani, teaching Arabic and Koranic studies and Swahili, remaining there for sixteen years. When Wilfrid Whiteley came from Makerere to study the Swahili speech of Mombasa he turned to Muʿallim Yahya—the first foreigner to employ Yahya as an informant. Over the next forty years there would be many more from many lands. During those teaching years Yahya translated three children's stories from Arabic into Swahili. These stories, displaying Yahya's humour, learning, and command of Swahili, transformed a mere translation into a literary gem. They were first broadcast in Mombasa in the late 1950s. Later they were published as *Three Prose Texts in the Swahili of Mombasa* (1998). In 1961 Yahya submitted evidence to the Robertson commission concerning the future of the Kenya coastal strip. Harmless though his submission was, it merited a special branch file, or so Yahya claimed.

When J. W. T. Allen visited Mombasa in the 1960s he considered Sheikh Yahya to be the leading Swahili scholar of the town. In 1969 Whiteley, who by now was professor of Bantu languages and head of the department of Africa, invited Yahya to work at the School of Oriental and African Studies (SOAS) in London. Yahya came not only with Whiteley's support but also to support him. This he did until Whiteley's death in 1972, when he was shipped back to east Africa. He then spent five years in Nairobi, the first three with the Islamic Foundation, proof-reading Sheikh Abdallah al-Farsi's Swahili interpretation of the Koran. He then worked for the Arab League. Finally he was employed by UNESCO, attached to Nairobi University, collecting Swahili poetry, both oral and written, in a dozen or so dialects. At this time Yahya was renowned as a *khattat* (calligrapher), and examples of his handwriting in Swahili-Arabic script are to be found in Dar es Salaam University, the British Library, and at SOAS.

In 1977 Yahya was invited to return to SOAS as Swahili assistant—the least significant academic title available. From then until 1982 he had a series of one-year contracts, without pension rights, and without a housing allowance—housing was always a problem. From 1982 the school employed him on an hourly basis. In 1985 Yahya was enabled to perform *umrah* (the lesser pilgrimage to Mecca). In 1995 he acquired British citizenship, never to return to Mombasa. Almost at the very end of his SOAS service he was awarded the diploma in Swahili (established in 1924 by Alice Werner). It was too little too late.

In Goa the archives contain a number of seventeenth- and eighteenth-century Swahili letters, one of which Yahya selected for study (1994; repr. 2001). At SOAS the archives contain verses of the nineteenth-century Mombasa poet Bwana Muyaka bin Haji, some of which are now obscure. Yahya was an authority on this poet, and listening to him declaim stanzas from Bwana Muyaka was a joy. Also in the archives is a collection of nineteenth-century Swahili letters formerly in the possession of W. E. Taylor. Yahya studied these letters, easily reading the script and comprehending the language. He even seemed to be on nodding terms with the personalities in the letters. The two articles that resulted were, in effect, a window opening onto nineteenth-century Mombasa. No one else could have worked on this material so competently. W. E. Taylor was one of only a handful of foreigners who attained eminence in Swahili studies. Both Taylor and Yahya devoted their lives to Swahili, and it was interesting to note how often Yahya's scholarship agreed with that of Taylor.

The library of SOAS holds the largest collection of Swahili manuscripts in the British Isles, dating from the end of the eighteenth century. A project to create an online catalogue, funded by the Leverhulme Trust, began in 2001. Yahya was the essential component, the only person in Britain who could read and comment intelligently on the material. Yet Yahya, hopeless with machinery of every sort, needed help. As Mrs Einstein said of the genius to whom she was married, 'The Herr Professor does not drive. It is too complicated.' Needless to say, Yahya did not use computers, let alone the internet. He was provided with technically competent assistants, but they knew little about Swahili manuscripts. In due course an online catalogue, replete with errors and omissions, appeared.

Yahya devoted his life to strengthening the three pillars of the Swahili world: Islam, the speech of the Swahili people (he argued that 'Swahili' Swahili had already become an endangered language, leaving the standardizers of the language, not mother-tongue speakers, in control), and Swahili culture (including Swahili in Swahili-Arabic script, and the observance of the Swahili new year). In 1891 W. E. Taylor had noted that his Swahili teacher Muʿallim Sikujua was 'in his time acknowledged the best Swahili antiquary in Mombasa' (Taylor, *African Aphorisms*, 1891, 82). A century later a similar observation was true of Yahya. Like Sikujua, Taylor himself, Charles Sacleux, H. E. Lambert, and J. W. T. Allen, Yahya was a talented scholar with an assured place among the giants. He died, unmarried, on 11 October 2008 at his home in Coram Street, Bloomsbury, London, after a stroke. He was buried three days later in the Garden of Peace Muslim cemetery in Hainault, London. P. J. L. Frankl

Sources *Coastweek* (31 Oct 2008) · M. Bakari, 'The legacy of Sheikh Yahya Ali Omar in Swahili studies', *Afrika und Übersee*, 90 (2008–9), 85–92 · P. J. L. Frankl, 'Yahya Ali Omar (1924–2008), Swahili scholar: an appreciation together with a bibliography of his writings', *Afrika und Übersee*, 90 (2008–9), 93–108 · personal knowledge (2012) · b. cert. · d. cert.
Archives Research Institute of Swahili Studies in East Africa, Mombasa, Kenya · SOAS | FILM SOAS, www.swahilimanuscripts.soas.ac.uk/swahili | SOUND SOAS, www.swahilimanuscripts.soas.ac.uk/swahili
Likenesses photograph, repro. in *Coastweek*

Yates, John (1925–2008), bishop of Gloucester, was born on 17 April 1925 at 75 Hotham Road, Putney, London, the son of Frank Yates, a civil service clerk in the General Register Office, and his wife, Edith Ethel, *née* Pasco (*b.* 1885), the widow of William John Stow. He was educated at Battersea grammar school and, during wartime evacuation, at Blackpool grammar school. He was called up into the Royal Air Force Volunteer Reserve in 1943, and subsequently served as an air crew member. On demobilization in 1947 he entered Jesus College, Cambridge, as a scholar and took a first-class degree in history in 1949. Training at Lincoln Theological College, and ordination in 1951, were followed by a curacy at Christ Church, Southgate, north London. While there he met Jean Kathleen Dover (1931–1995), a speech therapist, and daughter of Henry William Dover, valuer. They married at Christ Church, Southgate, on 2 January 1954 and had a son and two daughters.

Also in 1954, Yates returned to Lincoln Theological College as tutor and chaplain, where he remained until 1959. Although the quasi-monastic environment was unsuitable for the married men training with young families, Yates was happy and students found him a captivating teacher, academically sure-footed. There followed six tough years as vicar of Bottesford with Ashby, a large new housing estate on the outskirts of Scunthorpe. He was appointed principal of Lichfield Theological College in 1966 with a brief to develop a less narrowly academic style of training, rooted more in practical experience in parishes. He added pastoralia to the Anglican credentials of word and sacrament. But the subsequent radical reorganization of the church's theological colleges led to several closures, among them Lichfield in 1972. The archbishop of York, Donald Coggan, asked Yates to join him as suffragan bishop of Whitby, where for three years he made a significant impact on the church in industrial Teesside, in collaboration with the diocese of Durham.

In 1975 Yates became the thirty-ninth bishop of Gloucester. At first he found the diocese a bit stuffy and one professedly in favour of change just so long as it did not make any difference. His liberal values, concern for social justice, ecumenical outreach, advocacy of women priests, and struggle to fetch mission from the periphery to the centre of diocesan consciousness, were received with a mixture of caution and alarm. Clergy were not bombarded with innovations, though carefully thought-out initiatives were successful. He gained trust and respect for his belief that the strength of the Church of England was in its parishes. He admitted to a lack of confidence as a forceful leader. Gradually a new kind of leadership was revealed, one of collegiality, which combated the Gloucester tendency to isolationism. His own style was characterized by discursive decision-making rather than autocracy. He realized how irritating and time-consuming this often was for his colleagues.

Yates regarded Church House in Westminster as the Anglican Kremlin and did not become a recognizable national churchman until 1979, with the publication of *Homosexual Relationships: a Contribution to Discussion*, the findings of a working party set up by the board for social responsibility in 1974 under Yates's chairmanship. Among the report's findings was the contentious declaration that, 'there are circumstances in which individuals may justifiably choose to enter into a homosexual relationship with the hope of enjoying a companionship and physical expression of sexual love similar to that which is to be found in marriage' (para 168). The unanimous report was 'received' by the board in 1978, effectively damning it without faint praise. After ten months the board insisted that their critical observations be included in the published report. It was a shabby business. The general synod debated the report in February 1981 before it was shelved. Yates was taken aback by the venom directed at him.

In 1987 Yates was appointed chairman of the general synod board for social responsibility, in succession to Hugh Montefiore. Yates brought a more relaxed style and humour, and it was easier for members to say what they thought. But as a result the board seemed to fall apart with centrifugal pressures. Writing in his official capacity as chairman, he rattled the prime minister, Margaret Thatcher, by challenging her emphasis on individual, as opposed to collective, duties, and saying that he found it difficult to justify the creation of wealth regardless of the welfare of the rest of the community. Though determined, he was never a campaigner.

Yates left Gloucester in 1991. There was a glow of gratitude for his genial temper, shrewd mind, plain speaking, generosity in counsel, sanctified ordinariness, and pastoral availability. The new archbishop of Canterbury, George Carey, recruited him as head of staff, with the title of bishop at Lambeth; his experience and wisdom were a much needed counterbalance to Carey's own episcopal inexperience and evangelicalism. He finally retired in 1994. After the death of his first wife in 1995, he married Beryl Kathleen Wensley (1929–2006), a retired clergywoman, at St Barnabas's Church, Winchester, on 25 March 1998. She was the daughter of Edward Albert Perrott, accountant, and widow of John E. Wensley. Yates died at Brendan Nursing Trust, Park Road, Winchester, on 26 February 2008. He was survived by the three children of his first marriage. JOHN S. PEART-BINNS

Sources *The Independent* (1 March 2008) • *Daily Telegraph* (3 March 2008) • *Scunthorpe Evening Telegraph* (4 March 2008) • *The Guardian* (14 March 2008) • *Church Times* (14 March 2008) • *The Times* (8 April 2008); (7 May 2008) • *WW* (2008) • personal knowledge (2012) • private information (2012) • b. cert. • m. certs. • d. cert.
Archives University of Bradford, J. B. Priestley Library, Peart-Binns episcopal biography archive | SOUND BL NSA, documentary recording
Likenesses J. Redvers, portrait, Church House, College Green, Gloucester • obituary photographs
Wealth at death £369,879: probate, 2 June 2008, *CGPLA Eng. & Wales*

Yellowlees, Sir Henry (1919–2006), medical officer, was born on 16 April 1919 at 3 Cumin Place, Edinburgh, the elder son and eldest of three children of Henry Yellowlees (1888–1971), psychiatrist, and his wife, Dorothy, *née* Davis, a professional cellist. He spent his early childhood with his siblings David and Dorothy at The Retreat, a Quaker psychiatric centre in York, where his father was medical superintendent from 1922 to 1929 before moving to St Thomas's Hospital, London. He was educated at Bramcote preparatory school in Scarborough and then at Stowe School before reading medicine at University College, Oxford. In 1941 he joined the Royal Air Force, serving as a pilot and instructor until 1945. This delayed his entry into medical school at the Middlesex Hospital, and he graduated BM BCh in 1950. Meanwhile, on 21 August 1948, he had married Gwyneth Bramwell (Sally) Comber, (*d.* 2001), a nurse two years his senior, the divorced wife of Andrew Stephen Charles Comber, and the daughter of Francis Joseph William Maddox, naval engineer. They had two daughters and one son.

Yellowlees's first post was at the Middlesex as resident medical officer, and his effective management of an outbreak of meningitis among the staff was noted by the chief medical officer, Sir George Godber. Yellowlees gained extensive experience in the medical management of the National Health Service through appointments at the south-west regional hospital board (1954–9) and the north-west metropolitan regional hospital board (1959–63). In 1963 he accepted an invitation from Godber for a secondment to a civil service post at the Ministry of Health as a principal medical officer, and two years later he was appointed as a permanent senior principal medical officer. He worked closely with Godber, and was promoted to the position of deputy chief medical officer in 1967, shortly before the Ministry of Health was amalgamated into the Department of Health and Social Security.

Yellowlees succeeded Godber as chief medical officer in 1973 and served in that post for the next ten years, until his retirement in 1983, working for five secretaries of state for health: Sir Keith Joseph, Barbara Castle, David Ennals, Patrick Jenkin, and Norman Fowler. The post of chief medical officer was widely recognized as one of the most arduous within government. The occupant acted as a 'gatekeeper', ensuring that appropriate medical advice was provided for the secretary of state to react to health crises and also to develop new health policies and medical services; had responsibility for medical advice given to other government departments, including the Ministry of Agriculture, Fisheries and Food, the Department of Education and Science, and the Home Office; and acted as a conduit between the government and the medical profession, helping with negotiations on such sensitive issues as doctors' pay, working conditions, medical education, and fitness to practise. It is testimony to Yellowlees's considerable managerial skills that he steered the governments he served through a number of crises, in addition to furthering the development of the medical profession and health service in Britain.

Some of the most difficult situations that Yellowlees handled were related to the economic crises of the 1970s, which forced rationalizations in NHS budgets. The matter became politically complicated in 1974 when Barbara Castle determined to push through Labour's long-held manifesto pledge to remove 'pay beds'—one of the final vestiges of private medicine—from NHS hospitals. Yellowlees worked hard to restore the relations between the government and the medical profession, and was knighted KCB in 1975 (having been made a CB in 1971). During his tenure he also initiated some key health policies. He enabled the development of community medicine and accident and emergency medicine, drafted legislation that reduced the amount of lead in petrol, and made the wearing of car seat belts compulsory. He chaired the Committee on Medical Aspects of Food which developed daily nutritional guidelines, a topic he further promoted through his membership of the Council of the British Nutrition Foundation from 1973 to 1995. He was instrumental in reducing the number of hours worked by junior doctors, and helping women doctors to continue with their careers while raising families.

Like previous chief medical officers Yellowlees served as a member of the General Medical Council (1979–89) and the Medical Research Council (1974–83). He was well-connected within the medical establishment both in Britain and overseas. He participated in annual meetings with American and Canadian health officials, and those of the World Health Organization. His time in office also coincided with the global elimination of smallpox, the discovery of Lassa fever, and the first cases of legionnaires' disease in Britain. When he retired as chief medical officer in 1983 he was appointed an adviser to the Ministry of Defence on the restructuring of the medical services of the armed forces. He then became a consultant for the European office of the World Health Organization, and played a significant role in the 1980s Balkans dispute by successfully negotiating with the Turks and Bulgarians for the provision of healthcare for refugees. He remained engaged with British medicine through his position on the council of the British Medical Association from 1986 to 1990, and chaired its group on euthanasia policy.

Yellowlees's colleagues found him 'a joy to work with, always considerate of staff and aware of pressures on them, approachable, modest about his own considerable achievements, with a strong sense of humour and a charming manner' (*The Guardian*, 12 April 2006). He was divorced in 1984, and in the same year he met (Patricia) Mary Porter (*b.* 1947/8), healthcare consultant, and daughter of William John McGowan, account supervisor; they married on 7 February 2001. Heart bypass surgery in 1997 gave Yellowlees a new lease of life, and he continued to enjoy gardening, walking by the sea, and listening to Gilbert and Sullivan operas. In his last years he found in humanism an expression of his core beliefs and requested a humanist funeral. He died at his home, 33 Lea Road, Harpenden, Hertfordshire, on 22 March 2006 of heart failure, and was cremated at Watford. He was survived by his second wife, Mary, and by the three children of his first marriage, Ian, Rosemary, and Linda, all of whom had followed their parents into medical or nursing careers.

SALLY SHEARD

Sources S. Sheard and L. Donaldson, *The nation's doctor: the role of the chief medical officer, 1855–1998* (2005) · *The Times* (12 April 2006) · *The Guardian* (12 April 2006) · *BMJ*, 332 (29 April 2006), 1037 · Plarr's lives of the fellows, http://livesonline.rcseng.ac.uk/, 10 Oct 2008 · *WW* (2006) · Burke, *Peerage* · b. cert. · m. certs. · d. cert.

Likenesses photograph, 1973, PA Photos, London · obituary photographs

Wealth at death £313,892: probate, 9 June 2006, *CGPLA Eng. & Wales*

Young [*née* Cohen], **Aida** (**1920–2007**), film producer, was born on 11 August 1920 at 234 Mile End Road, Stepney Green, London, one of four daughters of Abraham Cohen, a watch repairer and jeweller, and his wife, Deby, *née* Cramer. She came from a Jewish Orthodox family, which regarded secretarial work or teaching as the most suitable jobs for a grammar school scholarship girl. Her early ambition to become an actress was discouraged, but she demonstrated the wilful independence that would later help her overcome the obstacles she encountered throughout her career by rejecting a teacher training place at Bedford College and secretly joining the leftist Unity Theatre. Unity's contacts within the thriving wartime documentary movement, particularly Albert Pearl of

Realist Films, encouraged her to try to enter the film business. As there were no formal training routes, opportunities depended largely on knowing the right people. Shortly after the war she was given a job as an assistant director by the Data Film Unit, a co-operative that, with missionary zeal, made government-sponsored documentaries. Having blithely lied about her capabilities to get the job, she was initially reliant on Pearl to teach her the basics of editing and production, but the enthusiasm of her colleagues for film was infectious and, over three years, she gained experience in a variety of roles.

On 21 July 1948, at Golders Green Synagogue, London, she married Gideon Young (*b.* 1919/20), a master printer one year her senior, and son of Isaac Young. They had two daughters, Ruth and Jane. Meanwhile, as state sponsorship contracted, Aida Young left documentary making to try her luck in the world of commercial feature films, taking an inferior job as a 'runner' at Rank's B film studios at Highbury in 1948. However, the studios were one of the first casualties of the recession that gripped British film production until the early 1950s, and she was obliged to try to make a living as a freelance. Freelancing was a precarious existence at the best of times, and particularly so for a woman as studios closed around her. 'You might as well have cut your throat', she commented later (BECTU interview), but she continued to fight the prevailing prejudices against the employment of a woman in occupations reserved almost exclusively for men. She recalled one American producer telling her 'we don't use girls in those roles—we don't use blacks either' (Koetting). Often mocked by other members of the crew, she worked as second or third assistant director—sometimes uncredited—on a number of low-budget productions, eventually achieving more regular employment with Douglas Fairbanks junior's unit at the National Studios in 1953. About the same time she began her association with Hammer Films, a company with which she eventually established herself as a fully fledged producer. Her work as second assistant director there included the company's breakthrough film, *The Quatermass Xperiment* (1955). She remembered Hammer fondly as a company with the atmosphere of a family, in which people willingly tried their hardest.

In the late 1950s, however, independent television offered more opportunities to women working in production, and Aida Young developed her career as production manager on television shows like *William Tell* (1958–9) and *The Invisible Man* (1959) and finally achieved a credit as producer on *Danger Man* in 1964. When she returned to Hammer at the invitation of her mentor, Michael Carreras, son of the company's founder, as an associate producer, she immediately enjoyed major box-office success with two fantasy adventures starring contemporary 'glamour queens': *She* (1965), featuring Ursula Andress, and *One Million Years BC* (1966), starring Raquel Welch. On the latter, a production beset with bad weather, location problems, and union disputes, Young was further tasked with preventing the press from revealing that the star, 'Miss Welch', was married with children. She succeeded, but was so disillusioned by the obstructive attitude of shop stewards that she left the technicians' union, the Association of Cinematograph, Television and Allied Technicians, soon afterwards.

After the success of *She*, Young was given the opportunity to work as a full producer on a sequel, *The Vengeance of She* (1968). Considering Hammer's stock-in-trade, it was perhaps inevitable that she would become a producer of horror films, although it was a genre for which she had no particular liking. Her first was *Dracula Has Risen from the Grave* (1968), but she preferred *Taste the Blood of Dracula* (1970) for its critique of repression and hypocrisy. Then, as Hammer foundered in the recession of the 1970s, Young switched to EMI, producing feature film versions of such television comedies as *Steptoe and Son* (1972), *Steptoe and Son Ride Again* (1973), and *The Likely Lads* (1976), before ending her career in the 1980s making, mainly for the American networks, teleplays and mini series, including the Emmy award-winning *The Bunker* (1981), made in Paris for NBC, *The Secret Life of Ian Fleming* (1990), and adaptations of books by Edna O'Brien (*The Country Girls*, 1984) and Barbara Taylor Bradford (*To Be the Best*, 1992).

In retirement at Osprey Court on London's Finchley Road, Aida Young developed Parkinson's disease and eventually suffered a stroke, finally dying from pneumonia at the Royal Free Hospital, Hampstead, on 12 August 2007. Her husband predeceased her, and she was survived by her daughters, whom she had discouraged from following her into a film industry that she believed still retained the capacity to frustrate ambition. In fact she had helped to open up employment opportunities for women and remained a role model for young female film-makers.

STEVE CHIBNALL

Sources *Screen International*, 14 (6 Dec 1975), 10–11; 520 (26 Oct 1985), 23–4 · C. Koetting, 'The young and the restless dead', *Fangoria*, 144 (July 1995), 14–19, 81 · interview, *The House that Hammer Built*, 10 (Oct 1998), 80–88 · *The Guardian* (19 Sept 2007) · *The Times* (24 Sept 2007) · *Hammer: the studio that dripped blood*, BBC television, 1987 · A. Young, audio recording, 29 Sept 1995, BFI, BECTU oral history project, interview 368 · www.imdb.com/name/nm0949239, 22 June 2010 · private information (2011) · b. cert. · m. cert. · d. cert.

Archives SOUND BFI, BECTU oral history project, interview 368, 29 Sept 1995

Likenesses photograph, repro. in www.britishtheatreguide.info/news/aidayoung.htm

Wealth at death £413,489: probate, 4 Feb 2008, *CGPLA Eng. & Wales*

Young, Priscilla Helen Ferguson (1925–2006), social worker, was born on 25 November 1925 at her grandparents' home, Walcot Rectory, 22 The Circus, Bath, Somerset, the elder child of Fergus Ferguson Young, a teacher and social worker, and his wife, Helen Frances Graham, *née* Murphy, who had worked at the Foreign Office until her marriage. At the time of her birth her father was secretary of the Bradford Council of Social Service, and lived at 14 Cleveland Road, Heaton, Bradford. There were relatives of Scottish, Irish, and English descent.

When Young was four she went to Kenya with her parents, where her father taught in a rural area. Her brother, Angus, was born there in 1933. As a young white child she was relatively isolated. She did not go to school but was taught by her mother and examined by her father. She spent a good deal of time on her own, watching the dung beetles scurry around, and practising the skills to avoid charging rhinos, seeing every day the tall Maasai passing by. She developed a sturdy self-reliance and a capacity to enjoy her own company.

Young returned to England with her parents and infant brother in 1936. She went to Kingsley School in Leamington and thence to Edinburgh University where, after an honours degree, she took a course in social studies. She then worked in London for four years with the Family Welfare Association. From 1948 there were opportunities to work in the newly created children's departments in local government to provide services for children who had to live away from home. Young worked in Somerset from 1951 to 1953 and then from 1953 to 1958 in Oxford, where she became deputy children's officer. In the late 1950s she decided to widen her experience by working with the Child and Family Services in Portland, Maine, USA, where she remained for three years.

On returning to the UK in 1961 Young took a post as lecturer in social work at the University of Leicester, where she remained, becoming a senior lecturer, until 1971. This was a time of very rapid expansion both within social work and in education for an emerging profession. In 1971 the government decided to set up a statutory body to promote and validate social work training, the Central Council for Education and Training in Social Work (CCETSW). Young was appointed to head it and she began fifteen years of unremittingly demanding work, based in London. These years coincided with a period of heavy caring responsibilities, as her parents aged and grew ill.

For more than ten years the council of CCETSW was unwieldy and too big. Young herself said that 'it was like trying to work with a parliament without a government' (*Social Services Insight*). CCETSW was pulled hither and thither by the conflicting interests of employers, trade unions, and academics, as well as service users. Young and her colleagues had to modify, reconcile, resist, or accept the diverse influences. In the years of her leadership there was a sharply increased awareness of the role of social workers in the area of children's services, especially in relation to child protection. The government had set a target—that the numbers in training should increase by 60 per cent in the first five years. This was achieved, but against a background of difficulties in resourcing and disagreement about ways forward. CCETSW had been set up without earmarked finance and was thus exposed to the chill winds of the oil crisis in the 1970s. The newly formed British Association of Social Workers, fleeing from 'élitism', removed professional qualification as a criterion for membership. Trade unions resisted post-qualifying training as the knowledge base grew. Educational establishments clashed with employers about the shape and content of courses. Issues concerning race began to emerge and caused much pain to many. Politicians were ambivalent and unclear about direction. Behind it all lay big questions about the range of tasks which should be described as social work and the extent to which a common basic training was appropriate.

Throughout the difficult years at CCETSW Young kept the ship steady. She remained true to her professional values, underpinned by a deep but unostentatious religious faith. She had a particular gift for making good working relationships with people at all levels in the organization from the chair to the cleaning ladies. She was least comfortable in adversarial situations, such as arose with trade unions or in relation to racial issues. She commented that 'one of the greatest stresses of the job was the diversity and levels of things that had to be dealt with' ('Recollections'). These years took their toll because CCETSW became an easy target for those with vested interests. She said—ruefully—that 'there have been times when I have thought of trying to establish a self-help group for Aunt Sallies' (*Social Services Insight*). Nevertheless she led CCETSW with a powerful commitment, integrity, humanity, a sense of proportion, and a keen sense of humour, and played an important role in establishing social work as a valuable and recognized profession.

Young was appointed CBE in 1982 for her services to social-work education. Her retirement in 1986 was marked by the award of an honorary DLitt by the University of Ulster. She lived in the west country for most of the time after she retired and engaged in a range of charitable and voluntary activities, enjoying her talent for home-making. She spent her last few years at The Rectory, Church Road, Leonard Stanley, Gloucestershire, with a friend, the Revd Sue Phillipson-Masters, who cared for her at home in her last illness. She died there, of cerebrovascular disease, on 8 January 2006, and her funeral was at the local church. She was survived by her brother, Angus.

OLIVE STEVENSON

Sources *Social Work Today* (28 July 1986) · *CCETSW Reporting*, 5 (Dec 1986) · *Social Services Insight* (6 Feb 1987) · F. Gibson, oration at award of an honorary DLitt, University of Ulster, 1987 · 'Recollections of Miss Young', 1990, BL NSA · *The Guardian* (4 Feb 2006) · *The Times* (24 March 2006) · *WW* (2006) · personal knowledge (2010) · private information (2010) · b. cert. · d. cert.

Archives University of Warwick, CCETSW papers | SOUND BL NSA, documentary recording [talking about her time at CCETSW, 1971–6] · BL NSA, 'Recollections of Miss Young', 1990

Likenesses obituary photographs · photographs, repro. in *Social Services Insight* (6 Feb 1987)

Wealth at death £178,763: probate, 31 May 2006, *CGPLA Eng. & Wales*

Zarnecki, Jerzy [George] (**1915–2008**), art historian, was born on 12 September 1915 at Stara Osota, near Kiev, Ukraine, the third of five children of Zygmunt Zarnecki, civil engineer, and his wife, Julia, *née* Wolszczan. His father was a convert from Judaism, his mother Catholic. His parents moved to Poland at the Russian revolution and Zarnecki grew up in Rataje, a small village beside the Vistula, where he attended the mathematical Gymnasium. He then went on to Cracow University where he obtained his MA degree in 1938 and became junior assistant in the Art History Institute. His career was cut short at the beginning of the Second World War, during which he served in the Polish army in France, where he was taken prisoner in

1940. His escape with the help of forged documents in 1942, his adventures in occupied southern France, internment in Spain, and escape to England make a dramatic narrative. His war service was recognized by the award of the Polish cross of valour and the Croix de Guerre. While still in the Polish army in the UK, taking shelter during an air raid at Regent's Park tube station in 1944, he met Anne Leslie Frith (1923–2009), daughter of John Leslie Frith, actor, whom he married on 22 March the following year and who remained his lifelong support. They had one son and one daughter.

After the war Zarnecki undertook a PhD degree at the Courtauld Institute under the inspiring supervision of Fritz Saxl, director of the Warburg Institute. Completed in 1950, his dissertation was on the regional schools in English sculpture in the twelfth century, and it set the course of his academic career. In 1945 he had obtained his first employment at the Courtauld as assistant in the Conway Library, the unrivalled photographic archive of medieval art and architecture, and scholars in this field owed much to his photographic campaigns abroad. After ten years as Conway librarian, he joined the teaching staff with the rank of reader in 1959, became deputy director in 1961, and professor in 1963. It was a period of expansion for the institute under Anthony Blunt's directorship and it was Zarnecki who carried the main administrative burden. His diplomatic and managerial skills were much admired and it was widely thought that he would become director when Blunt retired in 1974. But he felt that he wanted to return to more teaching and research and declined to apply. His achievements as scholar and deputy director received recognition from the 1960s: most notably, he was elected a fellow of the British Academy in 1968, made a CBE in 1970, and received several honorary doctorates. He was Slade professor of fine art at Oxford in 1960–61 and received the gold medal of the Society of Antiquaries in 1986. His generous help to Polish students and scholars was recognized by the award of several Polish distinctions.

Zarnecki published a considerable body of work, which was both authoritative and accessible. His two volumes *English Romanesque Sculpture, 1066–1140* (1951) and *Later English Romanesque Sculpture, 1140–1210* (1953) are deceptively modest in length and format. They were the first to propose a widely accepted structure of dates and sequence of the main monuments. These general books were followed by detailed studies of *English Romanesque Lead Sculpture* (1957), *Early Sculpture at Ely Cathedral* (1958), and *Romanesque Sculpture at Lincoln Cathedral* (1963; expanded edn, 1988) as well as numerous innovative articles collected in his two-volume *Studies in Romanesque Sculpture* (1979–92). Of his major publications only *Gislebertus, Sculptor of Autun* (1961) concentrated on a continental monument. The eleventh century saw the revival of monumental architectural sculpture and most of the surviving sculpture of the period forms an integral part of ecclesiastical buildings. Accordingly, a study of the history of the architectural setting was Zarnecki's first concern, followed by a close analysis of the sculpture itself. Comparisons, particularly with English illuminated manuscripts and continental sculpture, were adduced to fix sources of inspiration, dates, and sequences of development. If stylistic analysis was the main concern, his expertise also covered questions of material, patronage, and iconography. One of his most valued early studies demonstrated that the coronation of the Virgin, an image best known from thirteenth-century French sculpture and mosaics in Roman churches, in fact had its earliest development in England, as seen in a capital of about 1130 from Reading Abbey.

Shortly after his retirement in 1982 Zarnecki achieved a particular triumph with the Arts Council's magnificent exhibition 'English Romanesque Art' at the Hayward Gallery in 1984. His was the inspiration behind the exhibition, which for the first time brought the subject to a really wide audience. Indeed, although his reputation was that of a specialist, his ability to cover large fields for a more general public was demonstrated as early as 1945 by his brief introduction, *Polish Art*, and more fully with his *Art and the Medieval World* (1975). His achievements were matched by the warmth of his personality. Immediately striking was the old-world continental charm that remained with him to the end. But the charm was matched by a deep-seated kindness, concern for others, and gift for friendship. He died of bronchopneumonia at Barnet General Hospital, London, on 8 September 2008, and was buried on 22 September at Golders Green crematorium. His wife died nine months later. They were survived by their two children. C. M. Kauffmann

Sources N. Stratford, ed., *Romanesque and gothic: essays for George Zarnecki* (1987) · *The Guardian* (11 Sept 2008); (1 Nov 2008) · *The Times* (13 Sept 2008); (27 Sept 2008) · *The Independent* (16 Sept 2008) · *Daily Telegraph* (18 Sept 2008) · *Burlington Magazine* (Dec 2008) · *WW* (2008) · personal knowledge (2012) · private information (2012) · m. cert. · d. cert.

Likenesses L. A. Dickens, C-type colour print, 2001, NPG · obituary photographs

Ziman, John Michael (1925–2005), physicist and philosopher of science, was born into a cultured Jewish family at 21 Rustat Road, Cambridge, on 16 May 1925, the elder son and eldest of three children of Solomon Netheim Ziman and his wife, Nellie Frances, *née* Gaster. His father, who was born of Ashkenazi parents who had emigrated to New Zealand, was a Rhodes scholar, joined the Indian Civil Service, and rose to be secretary of the government of Bombay; his mother came from an English Sephardi tradition, well-to-do and crossed with a brilliant and strongly intellectual Romanian line. He was taken to New Zealand as a baby and was educated at Hamilton high school and Victoria University College, Wellington, where he graduated with first-class honours in physics. In 1947 he moved to Balliol College, Oxford, obtaining a first-class degree in mathematics in 1949 and a DPhil in theoretical physics in 1952. His first paper, on antiferromagnetism, published in 1951, began 'Some recent experiments', heralding what would become a theme of his research in physics, namely the close connection of theory to observations on real materials. On 14 September 1951, at Exmoor register office, he married Rosemary Milnes Dixon (*d.*

2001), a thirty-year-old schoolteacher, of Brushford, Somerset, daughter of Robert Stanley Dixon, architect. They adopted two sons and two daughters.

After switching to the theory of the conduction of heat and electricity in solids, Ziman moved to Cambridge in 1954 as a lecturer and (from 1957) fellow of King's College. His research was summarized in his treatise *Electrons and Phonons* (1960), which became a classic text. His interests shifted to more subtle aspects of solid metals, in which the quantum behaviour of electrons plays a central part. This phase of his scientific life led to his textbook *Principles of the Theory of Solids* (1965). Overlapping with the work on solid metals was the research for which he was perhaps best known: the application of quantum mechanics to conduction in liquid metals. The first of two innovations was to treat the atomic nuclei together with their inner electrons as structural units, weakly scattering the outer electrons that move nearly freely through the material. The second was to incorporate the fact that the random positions of the atoms were not independent but possessed statistical correlations. In this way he explained a wide variety of experimental data. His research was recognized by his election as a fellow of the Royal Society in 1967.

In 1964 Ziman moved to Bristol University, initially as professor of theoretical physics, becoming Melville Wills professor of physics in 1969, then Henry Overton Wills professor of physics and director of the H. H. Wills Physics Laboratory from 1976. Immediately after his move to Bristol he began to build up the theoretical physics group there. His gentle inclusiveness and abundant personal hospitality created a near-perfect working environment within the friendly and successful larger physics department, leading to developments not only in metal physics but also theories of liquid state structure and surfaces, geometry of waves and quantum chaos, and high-energy physics. His research in Bristol took a more formal turn, prompted by the realization that there were liquid metals, and, later, disordered alloys, for which the scattering was not weak. His work involved the study of waves interacting with disordered arrangements of spherical scattering objects, for which a wider literature already existed in acoustics and optics. The move towards formalism led in 1969 to another textbook, *Elements of Advanced Quantum Theory*. His gift for lucidly conveying complex phenomena was shown in his observation that the image of quantum theory as a pyramid

> is misleading if it calls to mind a uniformly sloping edifice up which one may laboriously clamber … quantum theory is much more like a *ziggurat*, with sudden high cliffs to be surmounted before one can move freely on the next plane of abstraction. (p. v)

Ziman's final contribution to theoretical physics was his book *Models of Disorder: the Theoretical Physics of Homogenously Disordered Systems* (1979). Its philosophy, diametrically opposed to that of idealized perfect crystals explained in *Principles of the Theory of Solids*, was based on the observation that 'Condensed-matter physics has expanded in recent years and shifted its centre of interest to encompass a whole new range of materials and phenomena … steel and glass, earth and water' (p. ix). The book ended with a valediction for his career as a physicist: 'I … take the opportunity of a natural break to announce that this is, as far as I am concerned, THE END' (p. 491).

In Cambridge Ziman had already been drawn into what would become his second career, based on the realization that the key to understanding how science works lay as much in sociology as in philosophy. With the first of his half-dozen books exploring this theme, *Public Knowledge: an Essay concerning the Social Dimension of Science* (1968), he became established as a leading figure in the emerging field of 'science studies', exceptional for being able to speak with first-hand authority as a practising scientist. This sustained effort was later summarized by Peter Lipton under four themes:

> The first theme is *naturalism* … According to Ziman, science should itself be studied empirically, with priority given to causal rather than logical analysis. The second theme may be called … *socialism*. As Ziman shows, any account of science that relies on the model of the lone heroic scientist is doomed to failure, because science is by its nature a social process. The third theme is *evolutionary epistemology*: Scientific models are imperfect maps … Ziman exploits a biological analogy with natural selection to illuminate the way in which these maps evolve. The last of Ziman's themes … is the emergence of *post-academic science* … roughly the difference between blue-sky research and work strongly constrained by interests of funding bodies, public and private. (Lipton, 108–10)

In 1982 Ziman left Bristol to pursue these interests as a visiting professor in the department of social and economic studies at Imperial College, London. He also had a private reason for moving: to begin life with his second cousin, fellow scientist, and intellectual soulmate Joan Henriette Solomon, the daughter of Abraham Sigismund Diamond, lawyer. They eventually married on 27 October 2002, at the West London Synagogue, after Rosemary Ziman's death.

Ziman's interest in science as a social phenomenon was practical as well as theoretical: he was an active member of the Council for Science and Society (of which he was chairman, 1976–90), the Science Policy Support Group, the working party on science and the media set up by the British Association for the Advancement of Science, and the Bodmer committee of the Royal Society, which reported in 1985. Several books on how to teach the social aspects of science followed, including *Teaching and Learning about Science and Society* (1980) and *An Introduction to Science Studies* (1984). His passionate advocacy of scientific freedom, which included visiting Moscow to support the Jewish refuseniks, resulted in his book with Paul Sieghart and John Humphrey, *The World of Science and the Rule of Law* (1986), which connected the norms of academic science with the legal principles of human rights. He was also involved in the Achievement Project of the Renaissance Trust, which focused on Western economic growth and technological innovation since 1500 and was based in Oxford in the 1990s. His final book was *Real Science* (2000).

He lived latterly at Oakley, near Aylesbury, Buckinghamshire. He died of heart failure, following complications after an infection of the heart valves, at the John Radcliffe Hospital, Oxford, on 2 January 2005. He was survived by his wife, Joan, and by three of his four adopted children, one son having predeceased him. MICHAEL BERRY

Sources P. Lipton, 'The science of science', *Notes and Records of the Royal Society*, 57 (2003), 108–111 [review of J. M. Ziman, *Real science: what it is and what it means*] • *The Times* (1 Feb 2005) • *The Guardian* (2 Feb 2005) • *Daily Telegraph* (17 Feb 2005) • M. V. Berry and J. F. Nye, 'John Michael Ziman', *Memoirs FRS*, 52 (2006), 479–91 • *WW* (2005) • personal knowledge (2009) • private information (2009) • b. cert. • m. certs. • d. cert.

Likenesses G. Argent Studio, photograph, 1985, RS; repro. in Berry and Nye, 'John Michael Ziman', 480 • W. Bird, photograph, RS • obituary photographs

Wealth at death £520,092: probate, 23 Nov 2005, *CGPLA Eng. & Wales*

PICTURE CREDITS

Abse, Leopold [Leo] (1917–2008)—© National Portrait Gallery, London

Allen, Dave (1936–2005)—Camera Press, London

Allen, Philip, Baron Allen of Abbeydale (1912–2007)—© National Portrait Gallery, London

Anson, Thomas Patrick John, fifth earl of Lichfield [*known as* Patrick Lichfield] (1939–2005)—courtesy of the Cecil Beaton Studio Archive at Sotheby's

Appiah, Enid Margaret [Peggy] (1921–2006)—Getty Images

Appleby, (Florence) Lucy (1920–2008)—by kind permission of the Appleby family

Aprahamian, (Abraham) Felix Barter (1914–2005)—© Pete Wicker; collection National Portrait Gallery, London

Arden, Don (1926–2007)—Evening News / Rex Features

Argent, (Bernard) Godfrey (1937–2006)—© National Portrait Gallery, London

Arnold, Sir Malcolm Henry (1921–2006)—Getty Images

Aspinall, Neil Stanley (1941–2008)—Getty Images

Badawi, (Mohammed Aboulkhair) Zaki (1922–2006)—Getty Images

Bailey, Derek (1930–2005)—© Mephisto / Rex Features

Baker, Harold Brooks Brooks- (1933–2005)—© Photoshot

Ball, Alan James (1945–2007)—Bob Thomas / Getty Images

Banks, Anthony Louis [Tony], Baron Stratford (1942–2006)—Camera Press, London

Barker, Ronald William George (1929–2005)—Getty Images

Barrett, Roger Keith [Syd] (1946–2006)—Getty Images

Baxter, Raymond Frederic (1922–2006)—© BBC

Bedford, Sybille (1911–2006)—© Lucinda Douglas-Menzies / National Portrait Gallery, London

Beeson, Paul Bruce (1908–2006)—© reserved; by kind permission of the Yale school of medicine

Bell, (Ernest) Arthur (1926–2006)—© Royal Botanic Gardens, Kew

Benenson, Peter James Henry (1921–2005)—© Carolyn Djanogly; collection National Portrait Gallery, London

Beresford, Maurice Warwick (1920–2005)—© Zigmund Baumann

Best, George (1946–2005)—© Sefton Samuels / National Portrait Gallery, London

Bevan, Natalie Alice (1909–2007)—© National Portrait Gallery, London

Biffen, (William) John, Baron Biffen (1930–2007)—Getty Images

Blatch, Emily May, Baroness Blatch (1937–2005)—© Photoshot

Bloom, Alan Herbert Vauser (1906–2005)—© Tessa Traeger / National Portrait Gallery, London

Blow, Isabella (1958–2007)—Mario Testino / Art Partner; hat by Philip Treacy

Blow, Sandra Betty (1925–2006)—© Roger Mayne / National Portrait Gallery, London

Brainin, Norbert (1923–2005)—© Milein Cosman / National Portrait Gallery, London

Brett, Sir Charles Edward Bainbridge (1928–2005)—Country Life Picture Library

Brooks, Anthony Morris [Tony] (1922–2007)—© reserved

Browne, George Edric (1920–2007)—© Val Wilmer

Browse, Lillian Gertrude (1906–2005)—© National Portrait Gallery, London

Cabrera Infante, Guillermo (1929–2005)—Camera Press, London

Cahn, Robert Wolfgang (1924–2007)—© Godfrey Argent Studio

Callaghan, Leonard James [Jim], Baron Callaghan of Cardiff (1912–2005)—© National Portrait Gallery, London

Carpenter, Humphrey William Bouverie (1946–2005)—© Mark Gerson / National Portrait Gallery, London

Carrier, Robert (1923–2006)—© National Portrait Gallery, London

Carter, Denis Victor, Baron Carter (1932–2006)—© Photoshot

Chadwick, Henry (1920–2008)—© David Poole; Master and Fellows of Peterhouse, Cambridge

Chan, Michael Chew Koon, Baron Chan (1940–2006)—© Photoshot

Channon, (Henry) Paul Guinness, Baron Kelvedon (1935–2007)—Getty Images

Charles, Dame (Mary) Eugenia (1919–2005)—National Geographic / Getty Images

Chrysostomides, Iouliane (1928–2008)—Hellenic Institute, Royal Holloway College

Clarke, Sir Arthur Charles (1917–2008)—Everett Collection / Rex Features

Clarke, Nicholas Campbell (1948–2006)—© BBC

Cleland, William Paton (1912–2005)—© Dr A Hollman

Cockfield, (Francis) Arthur, Baron Cockfield (1916–2007)—Popperfoto / Getty Images

Cole, Grace Elizabeth Agnes Annie [Gracie] (1924–2006)—© Val Wilmer

Colledge, (Magdalena) Cecilia (1920–2008)—Lake Placid Olympic Museum

Colvin, Sir Howard Montagu (1919–2007)—© Lucy Dickens / National Portrait Gallery, London

Cook, Beryl Frances (1926–2008)—© Beryl Cook 1977. Reproduced by permission of the Cook Estate c/o Rogers, Coleridge & White Ltd, 20 Powis Mews, London W11 1JN

Cook, Robert Finlayson [Robin] (1946–2005)—Getty Images

Coren, Alan (1938–2007)—Getty Images

Cotton, Sir William Frederick [Bill] (1928–2008)—© BBC

Cresswell, (Elizabeth) Helen (1934–2005)—Empics Sport / PA Photos

Crick, Sir Bernard Rowland (1929–2008)—© Colin McPherson / Corbis

Cuckney, John Graham, Baron Cuckney (1925–2008)—© PLA collection / Museum of London

Cutler, Ivor (1923–2006)—Getty Images

Dacie, Sir John Vivian (1912–2005)—© National Portrait Gallery, London

Dacres, Desmond Adolphus [Desmond Dekker] (1941–2006)—Getty Images

Daiches, David (1912–2005)—Scottish National Portrait Gallery

Deakin, Sir (Frederick) William Dampier (1913–2005)—© National Portrait Gallery, London

Deedes, William Francis [Bill], Baron Deedes (1913–2007)—© Andrew Festing

DeLorean, John Zachary (1925–2005)—Getty Images

Dempster, Nigel Richard Patton (1941–2007)—© Trevor Leighton / National Portrait Gallery, London

Deniz, Francisco Antonio (1912–2005)—© Val Wilmer

Doll, Sir (William) Richard Shaboe (1912–2005)—© Troika Photos

Donaldson, John Francis, Baron Donaldson of Lymington (1920–2005)—© Photoshot

Donaldson, (Charles) William [*pseud.* Henry Root] (1935–2005)—Getty Images

Douglas, Dame (Margaret) Mary (1921–2007)—© Mayotte Magnus; collection National Portrait Gallery, London

Drake, Charles Edward [Charlie] (1925–2006)—Getty Images

Drummond, Sir John Richard Gray (1934–2006)—© BBC

Duke, Neville Frederick (1922–2007)—Royal Air Force Museum, PC 98/173/6537/5

Dunwoody, Gwyneth Patricia (1930–2008)—Camera Press / Jane Bown

Ervine, David Walter (1953–2007)—Ross Wilson / photograph © Alice Burns

Evans, Gwynfor Richard (1912–2005)—PA Archive / PA Photos

Ewing [Bain], Margaret Anne (1945–2006)—© Victoria Carew Hunt / National Portrait Gallery, London

Faulkner, (Herbert Gustavus) Max (1916–2005)—Bob Thomas / Getty Images

Fewtrell, (Ernest) Malcolm (1909–2005)—Time and Life Pictures / Getty Images

Fitt, Gerard Martin, Baron Fitt (1926–2005)—Getty Images

Fort, Dame Maeve Geraldine (1940–2008)—© PA Photos

Forte, Charles, Baron Forte (1908–2007)—Getty Images

Fowles, John Robert (1926–2005)—© National Portrait Gallery, London

Franca, Celia (1921–2007)—courtesy of the National Ballet of Canada archives

Fraser, George Macdonald (1925–2008)—© Neil Drabble; collection National Portrait Gallery, London

Fraser, Ian Edward (1920–2008)—private collection

Freeman, Alan Leslie (1927–2006)—PA Photos

Gardiner, Margaret Emilia (1904–2005)—Pier Arts Centre; licensor SCRAN

Garson, Mary Sunniva (1921–2007)—by kind permission of the Grace and Compassion Benedictines

Ghoussoub, Mai (1952–2007)—Saqi Books

Gilmour, Ian Hedworth John Little, Baron Gilmour of Craigmillar (1926–2007)—© Photoshot

Glyn, Andrew John (1943–2007)—private collection

Goobey, Alastair Ross (1945–2008)—Rex Features

Graham, David Michael Gordon [Davey], (1940–2008)—© Brian Shuel/ National Portrait Gallery, London

Gravell, Raymond William Robert [Ray] (1951–2007)—www.sporting-heroes.net

Gray, Patience Jean (1917–2005)—© Guardian News and Media Ltd 1987

Gray, Sally (1915–2006)—from the Mander & Mitchenson Theatre Collection

Gray, Simon James Holliday (1936–2008)—Camera Press / Martin Pope

Green, Vivian Hubert Howard (1915–2005)—reproduced by kind permission of the Rector and Fellows of Lincoln College, Oxford

Hall, Terence (1926–2007)—© reserved; private collection

Handley, Vernon George [Tod] (1930–2008)—G.MacDomnic / Lebrecht Music & Arts

Harris, Ralph, Baron Harris of High Cross (1924–2006)—© Institute of Economic Affairs

Hastings, Sir Stephen Lewis Edmonstone (1921–2005)—© National Portrait Gallery, London

Hatto, Joyce Hilda (1928–2006)—© reserved

Hawkes, John Gregory (1915–2007)—© reserved

Haynes, John Norman (1934–2005)—© Ken Coton; collection National Portrait Gallery, London

Hayter, Althea Catharine (1911–2006)—by kind permission of Lady Hamilton of Epsom

Hazlehurst, Ronald (1928–2007)—Chris George / SWNS

Heath, Sir Edward Richard George (1916–2005)—© Guardian News and Media Ltd 2005

Heilbron, Dame Rose (1914–2005)—© National Portrait Gallery, London
Henshaw, Alexander Adolphus Dumphries (1912–2007)—collection of Philip Jarrett
Herbert, Sir Walter William [Wally] (1934–2007)—© Herbert collection, Polarworld
Hermon, Sir John Charles (1928–2008)—Bobbie Hanvey Photographic Archives, John J. Burns Library, Boston College
Hetherington, Sir Thomas Chalmers [Tony] (1926–2007)—© Howard Lloyd
Hickox, Richard Sidney (1948–2008)—Nigel Luckhurst / Lebrecht Music & Arts
Hockley, Sir Anthony Heritage Farrar-(1924–2006)—© National Portrait Gallery, London
Hudson, John Pilkington (1910–2007)—by kind permission of Richard Hudson
Hunt, John Joseph Benedict, Baron Hunt of Tanworth (1919–2008)—© National Portrait Gallery, London
Hussey, Joan Mervyn (1907–2006)—© Porphyrogenitus Ltd
Hussey, Marmaduke James [Duke], Baron Hussey of North Bradley (1923–2006)—Getty Images
Jacobs, Louis (1920–2006)—© John R. Rifkin
Jeger, Lena May, Baroness Jeger (1915–2007)—© Photoshot
Jellicoe, George Patrick John Rushworth, second Earl Jellicoe and Baron Jellicoe of Southampton (1918–2007)—© National Portrait Gallery, London
Jenkins, (John) Robin (1912–2005)—Scottish National Portrait Gallery
Johnson, William Henry [Peerie Willie] (1920–2007)—© Billy Fox Photography
Jones, Grenfell [Gren] (1934–2007)—Media Wales Ltd
Jones, Sir John Henry Harvey- (1924–2008)—Camera Press / Gemma Levine
Juda, Anneliese Emily [Annely] (1914–2006)—courtesy of Annely Juda Fine Art, London
Kavanagh, Patricia Olive [Pat] (1940–2008)—© Derek Thompson
Keenan, Brian Paschal (1941–2008)—Martin McCullough / Rex Features
Kelly, Barbara (1924–2007)—Getty Images
Kerr, Deborah (1921–2007)—Getty Images
King, John Leonard, Baron King of Wartnaby (1917–2005)—© Chris Hay; collection National Portrait Gallery, London
King, Dame Thea (1925–2007)—© Suzie Maeder
Kington, Miles Beresford (1941–2008)—Rex Features
Kirkwood, Patricia [Pat] (1921–2007)—Camera Press, London
Kitaj, Ronald Brooks (1932–2007)—© estate of R. B. Kitaj / National Portrait Gallery, London
Kossoff, David (1919–2005)—Rex Features
Laker, Sir Frederick Alfred [Freddie] (1922–2006)—Camera Press, London
Lambert, Verity Ann (1935–2007)—© BBC
Lane, Geoffrey Dawson, Baron Lane (1918–2005)—© Photoshot
Large, Sir Peter (1931–2005)—© Lady Sheenagh Large
La Rose, John Anthony (1927–2006)—© Julian Stapleton
Lloyd, Christopher (1921–2006)—© Jonathan Buckley
Lloyd, June Kathleen, Baroness Lloyd of Highbury (1928–2006)—courtesy of the Royal College of Paediatrics and Child Health
Lympany, Dame Moura (1916–2005)—Getty Images
Lyons, (Isidore) Jack (1916–2008)—© Stephen Lock / Telegraph Media Group Limited 1996
Lyttelton, Humphrey Richard Adeane (1921–2008)—© reserved; collection National Portrait Gallery, London
McLaren, Dame Anne Laura Dorinthea (1927–2007)—© PA Photos
Macquarrie, John [Ian] (1919–2007)—senior common room, Christ Church, Oxford
McRae, Colin Steele (1968–2007)—AFP / Getty Images
Macsween, John Angus (1939–2006)—© reserved
Maddox, Conroy Ronald (1912–2005)—by kind permission of Silvano Levy
Magnusson, Magnus (1929–2007)—© BBC
Mander, Noel Percy (1912–2005)—© private collection
Manning, Bernard John (1930–2007)—Harry Goodwin / Rex Features
Markham, Edward Archibald (1939–2008)—Kathy de Witt / Lebrecht Music & Arts
Marshall, Sir Arthur Gregory George (1903–2007)—Marshall of Cambridge
Masefield, Sir Peter Gordon (1914–2006)—Royal Aeronautical Society (National Aerospace Library)
May, Pamela (1917–2005)—© reserved
Mayne, Michael Clement Otway (1929–2006)—Great St Mary's Collection
Melly, (Alan) George Heywood (1926–2007)—© National Portrait Gallery, London
Michie, (Janet) Ray, Baroness Michie of Gallanach (1934–2008)—© BBC
Millar, George Reid (1910–2005)—Getty Images
Mills, Sir John Lewis Ernest Watts (1908–2005)—© Cornel Lucas; collection National Portrait Gallery, London
Minghella, Anthony (1954–2008)—© PA Photos
Mishcon, Victor, Baron Mishcon (1915–2006)—Camera Press, London
Mitchell, Adrian Christopher (1932–2008)—© Brian Shuel / National Portrait Gallery, London
Mitchell, John [Mitch] (1947–2008)—Redferns
Moore, Sir (John) Jeremy (1928–2007)—© PA Photos
Moss, Patricia Ann (1934–2008)—Frank Hudson / Sendtoppo / Rex Features
Mowlam, Marjorie (1949–2005)—© National Portrait Gallery, London
Mumford, Enid Mary (1924–2006)—Manchester Business School
Nerina, Nadia (1927–2008)—Washington Post / Getty Images
Newby, (George) Eric (1919–2006)—© Fergus Greer; collection National Portrait Gallery, London
Nolan, Michael Patrick, Baron Nolan (1928–2007)—© National Portrait Gallery, London
Norwood, Melita Stedman (1912–2005)—© Chris Harris / Rex Features
Obote, (Apolo) Milton (1925–2005)—AP / PA Photos
O'Brien, Conor Cruise (1917–2008)—Getty Images
Odell, John William [Jack] (1920–2007)—Getty Images
Osgood, Peter Leslie (1947–2006)—Getty Images
Pallo, Jackie (1926–2006)—Evening News / Associated Newspapers / Rex Features
Paolozzi, Sir Eduardo Luigi (1924–2005)—© National Portrait Gallery, London
Perkins, Geoffrey Howard (1953–2008)—© BBC
Pimlott, Steven Charles (1953–2007)—© Clare Park
Pinter, Harold (1930–2008)—© National Portrait Gallery, London
Pippard, Sir (Alfred) Brian (1920–2008)—© Godfrey Argent Studio
Podro, Michael Isaac (1931–2008)—© The Estate of R. B. Kitaj, courtesy Marlborough Gallery, New York
Porter, Sir Leslie (1920–2005)—© Robin Laurance / National Portrait Gallery, London
Postgate, (Richard) Oliver (1925–2008)—Smallfilms
Powell, Sir Richard Royle (1909–2006)—© National Portrait Gallery, London
Profumo, John Dennis (1915–2006)—Getty Images
Pym, Francis Leslie, Baron Pym (1922–2008)—© National Portrait Gallery, London
Rae, John Malcolm (1931–2006)—© National Portrait Gallery, London
Randle, Sir Philip John (1926–2006)—© Godfrey Argent Studio
Ratcliffe, Derek Almey (1929–2005)—© Des Thompson
Raymond, Paul (1925–2008)—PA Wire
Rees, Merlyn Merlyn-, Baron Merlyn-Rees (1920–2006)—© National Portrait Gallery, London
Reger, (Esther) Janet (1935–2005)—PA Archive / PA Photos
Rheinberg, Netta (1911–2006)—PA Photos
Roberts, Sir Gareth Gwyn (1940–2007)—CVCP (now Universities UK)
Roddick, Dame Anita Lucia (1942–2007)—Getty Images
Roll, Eric, Baron Roll of Ipsden (1907–2005)—© National Portrait Gallery, London
Rotblat, Sir Joseph (1908–2005)—© Dominick Tyler
Roth, Sir Martin (1917–2006)—© National Portrait Gallery, London
Rothschild, Dame Miriam Louisa (1908–2005)—© Tessa Traeger / National Portrait Gallery, London
Routh, John Reginald Surdeval [Jonathan] (1927–2008)—Rex Features
Roza, Lilian Patricia (1926–2008)—© BBC
Sandbrook, (John) Richard (1946–2005)—PA Archive / PA Photos
Saunders, Dame Cicely Mary Strode (1918–2005)—© Carolyn Djanogly; collection National Portrait Gallery, London
Schwarzkopf, Dame (Olga Maria) Elisabeth Friederike (1915–2006)—Getty Images
Scofield, (David) Paul (1922–2008)—© Cornel Lucas; collection National Portrait Gallery, London
Shearer [Kennedy], Moira (1926–2006)—Getty Images
Sheppard, David Stuart, Baron Sheppard of Liverpool (1929–2005)—© Sefton Samuels / National Portrait Gallery, London
Shepperd, Sir Alfred Joseph (1925–2007)—Wellcome Library, London
Sherrin, Edward George [Ned] (1931–2007)—© Patrick Jackson; collection National Portrait Gallery, London
Simon, Jocelyn Edward Salis, Baron Simon of Glaisdale (1911–2006)—© National Portrait Gallery, London
Smith, Ian Douglas (1919–2007)—Getty Images
Smith, Linda Helen (1958–2006)—Camera Press, London
Spark, Dame Muriel Sarah (1918–2006)—Frank Monaco / Rex Features
Spencer, John (1935–2006)—Getty Images
Stammers, Katharine Esther (1914–2005)—© National Portrait Gallery, London
Stokes, Donald Gresham, Baron Stokes (1914–2008)—© reserved; collection National Portrait Gallery, London
Strawson, Sir Peter Frederick (1919–2006)—© National Portrait Gallery, London
Stubbs, John Francis Alexander Heath-(1918–2006)—© National Portrait Gallery, London
Thomson, George Morgan, Baron Thomson of Monifieth (1921–2008)—© National Portrait Gallery
Tomlinson, Jane Emily (1964–2007)—Getty Images
Trapp, Joseph Burney (1925–2005)—© Warburg Institute
Tripp, William John Charles Spencer [Jack] (1922–2005)—© Photoshot
Trueman, Frederick Sewards [Fred] (1931–2006)—Getty Images
Varah, (Edward) Chad (1911–2007)—© Lucinda Douglas-Menzies / National Portrait Gallery, London
Walker, Diana Barnato (1918–2008)—Bill Cross / Rex Features
Walsh, Kathleen (1911–2005)—© ITV / Rex Features
Watkins, Sir Tasker (1918–2007)—© PA Photos
Wedgwood, John (1919–2007)—© Lucinda Douglas-Menzies
Weschke, Karl Martin (1925–2005)—© National Portrait Gallery, London
Wheeler, Sir Selwyn Charles Cornelius-(1923–2008)—Camera Press / Jane Bown
Williams, Charles Adolphus [Charlie] (1927–2006)—ITV / Rex Features
Williams, Sir (John) Kyffin (1918–2006)—© David Carpanini; by permission of Llyfrgell Genedlaethol Cymru / National Library of Wales
Wilson, Anthony Howard [Tony] (1950–2007)—Harry Goodwin / Rex Features
Wilson, Sir Colin Alexander St John (1922–2007)—© National Portrait Gallery, London
Wilson, Eric Charles Twelves (1912–2008)—Christopher Cox / Telegraph Media Group 2001
Witherington, (Cecile) Pearl (1914–2008)—© The National Archives / Heritage Images
Wolf, Peter Otto (1918–2007)—by kind permission of Janet Wolf
Wooderson, Sydney Charles (1914–2006)—© Getty Images
Woolmer, Robert Andrew [Bob] (1948–2007)—Philip Brown / Rex Features

INDEX OF CONTRIBUTORS

Acland, Antony
Campbell, Sir Alan Hugh (1919–2007)

Adams, Bernard
O'Malley, Mary Margaret (1918–2006)

Adams, Jad
Banks, Anthony Louis [Tony], Baron Stratford (1942–2006)
Whitehead, Phillip (1937–2005)

Adams, John
Brandt, George William (1920–2007)

Addison, Paul
Calder, Angus Lindsay Ritchie (1942–2008)

Adeney, Martin
Bide, Sir Austin Ernest (1915–2008)
Cadbury, Peter Egbert (1918–2006)
Cuckney, John Graham, Baron Cuckney (1925–2008)
Fraser, Sir (James) Campbell (1923–2007)
King, John Leonard, Baron King of Wartnaby (1917–2005)
Murphy, Sir Leslie Frederick (1915–2007)
Smith, Sir Leslie Edward George (1919–2006)
Templeton, Sir John Marks (1912–2008)

Aitken, Ian
Clements, Richard Harry (1928–2006)

Aldrich, Richard
Elvin, (Herbert) Lionel (1905–2005)
Marland, (Peter) Michael (1934–2008)

Alexander, Geraldine
Godwin, Fay Suzette (1931–2005)

Allen, Brian
Hayes, John Trevor (1929–2005)

Allen, Geraldine
Dobrée, Georgina (1930–2008)

Allen, J. R. L.
Allen, Percival (1917–2008)

Allum, Roger
Roberts, Sir Gareth Gwyn (1940–2007)

Anderton, Stephen
Lloyd, Christopher (1921–2006)

Ansari, Khizar Humayun
Badawi, (Mohammed Aboulkhair) Zaki (1922–2006)

Ashcroft, Stephen J. H.
Randle, Sir Philip John (1926–2006)

Ashton, S. R.
Johnston, Sir John Baines (1918–2005)

Aslet, Clive
Smith, Sir John Lindsay Eric (1923–2007)

Backhouse, Roger
Hutchison, Terence Wilmot (1912–2007)

Bagchi, Amiya Kumar
Posner, Michael Vivian (1931–2006)

Bailin, David
Stoyle, Roger John Blin- (1924–2007)

Bairner, Alan
Dougan, (Alexander) Derek (1938–2007)

Baker, Alan R. H.
Donkin, Robert Arthur (1928–2006)
Pounds, Norman John Greville (1912–2006)

Baker, Anne Pimlott
Bywater, (Richard) Arthur Samuel (1913–2005)
Cole, Michael (1928–2008)
Ellis, Susan Caroline Williams- (1918–2007)
Fry, Jeremy Joseph (1924–2005)
Henshaw, Michael Noel (1930–2007)
Hornby, Richard Phipps (1922–2007)
Hunt, Edgar Hubert (1909–2006)
Marre, (Romola) Mary, Lady Marre (1920–2005)
Matthews, Sir Peter Alec (1922–2006)
Parkes, Margaret, Lady Parkes (1925–2007)
Porter, Sir Leslie (1920–2005)
Roberts, Eirlys Rhiwen Cadwaladr (1911–2008)
Rooke, Sir Denis Eric (1924–2008)
Russell, William Morris (1920–2006)
Schofield, Sylvia Anne Terry (1916–2006)
Swan, (Richard) Kenneth (1919–2005)
Telford, Sir Robert (1915–2008)
Webster, John Brighton (1934–2006)
Wolfson, Sir Brian Gordon (1935–2007)

Baker, Mark
Ritchie, (Joseph) Murdoch (1925–2008)

Baker, William
Daiches, David (1912–2005)
Hamburger, Michael Peter Leopold (1924–2007)
Hobsbaum, Philip Dennis (1932–2005)

Baldwin, Peter
Cox, Lawrence Jack [John] (1920–2007)

Banatvala, J. E.
Almeida, June Dalziel (1930–2007)
Tyrrell, David Arthur John (1925–2005)

Barfield, Norman
Duke, Neville Frederick (1922–2007)
Henshaw, Alexander Adolphus Dumphries (1912–2007)
Laker, Sir Frederick Alfred [Freddie] (1922–2006)
Masefield, Sir Peter Gordon (1914–2006)
Page, Sir Frederick William (1917–2005)

Barker, Dennis
Allen, Dave (1936–2005)
Beadle, Jeremy James Anthony Gibson (1948–2008)
Griffith, Kenneth Reginald (1921–2006)
Kossoff, David (1919–2005)
Raymond, Paul (1925–2008)
Routh, John Reginald Surdeval [Jonathan] (1927–2008)
Wimbush, Mary (1924–2005)

Barker, Nicolas
Trapp, Joseph Burney (1925–2005)

Barker, Steve
Aitken, Laurel (1925–2005)
Dacres, Desmond Adolphus [Desmond Dekker] (1941–2006)

Baron, Wendy
Browse, Lillian Gertrude (1906–2005)

Barr, William
Koerner, Roy Martindale (1932–2008)

Bartley, Keith
Adams, Carol (1948–2007)

Barton, Anthony
Puxon, (Christine) Margaret (1915–2008)

Bartrip, P. W. J.
Blackmore, Frank Cuendet (1916–2008)

Bátiz-Lazo, Bernardo
Nixon, Sir Edwin Ronald (1925–2008)

Baxter, Christopher
Franks, Sir Arthur Temple [Dick] (1920–2008)

Beesley, Ian
Hunt, John Joseph Benedict, Baron Hunt of Tanworth (1919–2008)

Bellenger, Dominic Aidan
Garson, Mary Sunniva (1921–2007)

Beloff, Michael
Ackner, Desmond James Conrad, Baron Ackner (1920–2006)
Alexander, Robert Scott, Baron Alexander of Weedon (1936–2005)
Grayson, Edward (1925–2008)

Beral, Valerie
Doll, Sir (William) Richard Shaboe (1912–2005)

Bergfelder, Tim
Hiller, Erwin [Erwin Hillier] (1911–2005)

Berliner, Wendy
Wragg, Edward Conrad (1938–2005)

Berman, F. D.
Evans, Sir (William) Vincent John (1915–2007)
Watts, Sir Arthur Desmond (1931–2007)

Berry, Jacqueline
Mawer, (Elizabeth) Barbara (1936–2006)

Berry, Michael
Ziman, John Michael (1925–2005)

Bhadeshia, H. K. D. H.
Honeycombe, Sir Robert William Kerr (1921–2007)

Bhatia, Gautam
Baker, Laurence Wilfred (1917–2007)

Billington, Michael
Fry, Christopher (1907–2005)
Pinter, Harold (1930–2008)

Bingham, N. H.
Pitt, Sir Harry Raymond (1914–2005)
Wright, Sir Edward Maitland (1906–2005)

Bingham, Neil
Buzás, Stefan (1915–2008)

Birch, Sebastian
Cockfield, (Francis) Arthur, Baron Cockfield (1916–2007)

Bird, Margaret M.
Keatinge, William Richard (1931–2008)

Blacker, Terence
Donaldson, (Charles) William [Henry Root] (1935–2005)

Blundell, Tom L.
Orgel, Leslie Eleazer (1927–2007)

Blythe, Max
Baskett, Peter John Firth (1934–2008)
Goodwin, Leonard George (1915–2008)
Gray, (Thomas) Cecil (1913–2008)

Bourne, Stephen
Cole, Henry Alfred (1930–2008)
Mogotsi, Pearl Cynthia Connor- (1924–2005)
Stewart, (Atwell) Roy (1925–2008)

Bradley, Joseph M.
Burns, Thomas [Tommy] (1956–2008)
Johnstone, James Connelly [Jimmy, Jinky] (1944–2006)

Bragg, Melvyn
Jones, David Hugh (1934–2008)

Breckenridge, Alasdair
Goldberg, Sir Abraham (1923–2007)
Inman, William Howard Wallace (1929–2005)

Brewerton, David
Higgs, Sir Derek Alan (1944–2008)
Lyons, (Isidore) Jack (1916–2008)
Mobbs, Sir (Gerald) Nigel (1937–2005)
Morrow, Sir Ian Thomas (1912–2006)

Broadie, Alexander
Davie, George Elder (1912–2007)

Brock, W. H.
Fowden, Sir Leslie (1925–2008)

Brocken, Michael
Hall, Clifford Samuel (1925–2008)

Brooks, Stephen J.
Corbet, Philip Steven (1929–2008)

Brown, Kenneth D.
Odell, John William [Jack] (1920–2007)
Smith, Leslie Charles (1918–2005)

Brownjohn, Alan
Scannell, Vernon (1922–2007)

Brownlee, Colin
Denton, Sir Eric James (1923–2007)

Bruce, Gordon
Marshall, Sir Arthur Gregory George (1903–2007)

Brunsden, Denys
Thornes, John Barrie (1940–2008)

Bryant, M. A.
Peyton, John Wynne William, Baron Peyton of Yeovil (1919–2006)
Wooderson, Sydney Charles (1914–2006)

Bryant, Mark
Jones, Grenfell [Gren] (1934–2007)

Bryer, Anthony
Hussey, Joan Mervyn (1907–2006)

Buchan, Ursula
Finnis, Valerie Margaret Steriker (1924–2006)

Buchanan, J. Grant
Baddiley, Sir James (1918–2008)

Buchanan, Tom
Benenson, Peter James Henry (1921–2005)

Buczacki, Stefan
Burnett, Sir John Harrison (1922–2007)
Lambert, Joyce Mildred (1916–2005)

Bulman, Ray
Tremlett, Christopher William (1936–2008)

Burgen, Arnold
Hart, Philip Montagu D'Arcy (1900–2006)

Burke, David
Norwood, Melita Stedman (1912–2005)

Burke, Philip G.
Seaton, Michael John (1923–2007)

Burn, Gordon
Caulfield, Patrick Joseph (1936–2005)

Burton, Alan
Bond, Derek William Douglas (1920–2006)
Francis, Frederick William [Freddie] (1917–2007)
Green, Guy Mervin Charles (1913–2005)

Burton, Graham
Fort, Dame Maeve Geraldine (1940–2008)

Burton, Humphrey
Drummond, Sir John Richard Gray (1934–2006)

Burton-Page, Piers
Arnold, Sir Malcolm Henry (1921–2006)

Butland, Godfrey
Sheppard, David Stuart, Baron Sheppard of Liverpool (1929–2005)

Butts, Dennis
Selwyn, Victor (1917–2005)

Cairncross, Frances
Roll, Eric, Baron Roll of Ipsden (1907–2005)

Callaghan, John
Grant, Ted (1913–2006)

Campbell, Robin N.
Weir, Thomas [Tom] (1914–2006)

Campbell-Kelly, Martin
Michie, Donald (1923–2007)

Cantor, Harvey
Boyse, Edward Arthur (1923–2007)

Carrington, Bridget
Treadgold, Mary (1910–2005)

Carswell, Robert
Brett, Sir Charles Edward Bainbridge (1928–2005)
Kelly, Sir (John William) Basil (1920–2008)

Carter, David
Shields, Sir Robert (1930–2008)

Carter, Philip
Argent, (Bernard) Godfrey (1937–2006)
Badham, Molly Winifred (1914–2007)
Grima, Andrew Peter (1921–2007)
Juda, Anneliese Emily [Annely] (1914–2006)
Thomson, (Robert Howard) Garry (1925–2007)

Castell, William
Shepperd, Sir Alfred Joseph (1925–2007)

Cathcart, Brian
Hill, Sir John McGregor (1921–2008)
Rotblat, Sir Joseph (1908–2005)

Catling, H. W.
Megaw, Arthur Hubert Stanley [Peter] (1910–2006)

Cecil, Jonathan
Tripp, William John Charles Spencer [Jack] (1922–2005)

Chalke, Stephen
Cartwright, Thomas William [Tom] (1935–2007)

Chaloner, William G.
Fogg, Gordon Elliot [Tony] (1919–2005)

Chance, Michael
Hetherington, Sir Thomas Chalmers [Tony] (1926–2007)

Chapman, Don
Hauser, Frank Ivor (1922–2007)

Chapman, Mark D.
Macquarrie, John [Ian] (1919–2007)
Wiles, Maurice Frank (1923–2005)

Chaundy, Bob
Perkins, Geoffrey Howard (1953–2008)

Chibnall, Steve
Guest, Val (1911–2006)
Young, Aida (1920–2007)

Chinner, Graham
Deer, William Alexander [Alex] (1910–2008)

Clements, Ronald E.
Ackroyd, Peter Runham (1917–2005)

Close, Frank
Dalitz, Richard Henry (1925–2006)

Clout, Hugh
Chandler, Tony John (1928–2008)

Cochrane, Charles
Vickers, James Oswald Noel [Jon] (1916–2008)

Cockerill, Geoffrey
Smieton, Dame Mary Guillan (1902–2005)

Coleman, Edward
Jones, Philip James (1921–2006)

Coleridge, Gill
Kington, Miles Beresford (1941–2008)

Collins, Tony
Ashton, Eric (1935–2008)

Colston, Colin
Lane, Geoffrey Dawson, Baron Lane (1918–2005)

Colvin, Clare
Haycraft, Anna Margaret [Alice Thomas Ellis] (1932–2005)

Compston, Alastair
Davis, John Michael Newsom- (1932–2007)
McDonald, (William) Ian (1933–2006)
Thomas, Peter Kynaston (1926–2008)

Conway, Martin
Morgan, Philip (1930–2005)

Cooper, Emmanuel
Fournier, Robert Charles Privett (1915–2008)
Pearson, Colin James (1923–2007)

Copson, Belinda
Williams, Ursula Moray (1911–2006)

Corbett, Anne
Kogan, Maurice (1930–2007)

Cornish, W. R.
Lipstein, Kurt (1909–2006)

Cortazzi, Hugh
Wilford, Sir (Kenneth) Michael (1922–2006)

Coveney, Michael
Sherrin, Edward George [Ned] (1931–2007)

Cowley, R. A.
Bleaney, Brebis (1915–2006)

Craft, Alan W.
Chan, Michael Chew Koon, Baron Chan (1940–2006)
Lloyd, June Kathleen, Baroness Lloyd of Highbury (1928–2006)

Craig, Cairns
Finlay, Ian Hamilton (1925–2006)

Cranston, Ross
Mishcon, Victor, Baron Mishcon (1915–2006)

Crawford, Catherine
Dally, Ann Gwendolen (1926–2007)

Crawford, Michael H.
Brunt, Peter Astbury (1917–2005)

Cretney, S. M.
Simon, Jocelyn Edward Salis, Baron Simon of Glaisdale (1911–2006)

Crick, Michael
Best, George (1946–2005)

Crofts, Roger
Magnusson, Magnus (1929–2007)

Crystal, Michael
Hunter, Muir Vane Skerrett (1913–2008)

Cubbon, Brian
Allen, Philip, Baron Allen of Abbeydale (1912–2007)
Train, Christopher John (1932–2007)

Curtis, Anthony
Stubbs, John Francis Alexander Heath- (1918–2006)

Dalyell, Tam
Orme, Stanley, Baron Orme (1923–2005)

Darling, Elizabeth
MacEwen, Ann Maitland (1918–2008)

Dartington, Tim
Lyth, Isabel Edgar Punton (1917–2008)

Davenport-Hines, Richard
Baker, Harold Brooks Brooks- (1933–2005)
Birley, Marcus Oswald Hornby Lecky [Mark] (1930–2007)
Bonham, Derek Charles (1943–2007)
DeLorean, John Zachary (1925–2005)
Forte, Charles, Baron Forte (1908–2007)
Hastings, Sir Stephen Lewis Edmonstone (1921–2005)
Roddick, Dame Anita Lucia (1942–2007)
Smithers, Sir Peter Henry Berry Otway (1913–2006)

Davies, D. E. N.
Morris, Sir (James) Richard Samuel (1925–2008)

Davies, Peter
Bowen, Denis Arthur (1921–2006)

Davies, Philip
Feilden, Sir Bernard Melchior (1919–2008)

Davies, Sam
Bolton, Sir Frederic Bernard [Tim] (1921–2005)

Davin, Delia
Twitchett, Denis Crispin (1925–2006)

Delano, Anthony
Stott, Richard Keith (1943–2007)

Dendrinos, Charalambos
Chrysostomides, Iouliane (1928–2008)

Denham, Michael John
Wedgwood, John (1919–2007)

Denton, Richard M.
Randle, Sir Philip John (1926–2006)

Desmond, Ray
Craig, Stella Ross- (1906–2006)

Dewhurst, Keith
Shivas, Mark (1938–2008)

Dickinson, Peter
Mellers, Wilfrid Howard (1914–2008)

Dilks, David
Deakin, Sir (Frederick) William Dampier (1913–2005)
Parker, Sir (Arthur) Douglas Dodds- (1909–2006)

Donnelly, Tom
Corley, Sir Kenneth Sholl Ferrand (1908–2005)
Duckworth, (David) Keith (1933–2005)
Hart, Frederick Leslie (1914–2008)
Trotman, Alexander James, Baron Trotman (1933–2005)
Webster, Henry George (1917–2007)

Doran, David
Sandberg, Alexander Christer Edward (1923–2008)

Dorney, Kate
Banbury, (Frederick Harold) Frith (1912–2008)
Black, Dorothy [Kitty] (1914–2006)
Tomlinson, (Philip) Richard Henry (1943–2006)

Double, Oliver
Hardee, Malcolm Gerrard (1950–2005)
Manning, Bernard John (1930–2007)
Smith, Linda Helen (1958–2006)

Doughty, Simon
Stanier, Sir John Wilfred (1925–2007)

Doyle, William
McManners, John (1916–2006)

Drazin, Charles
Fowles, John Robert (1926–2005)

Driver, Felix
Cosgrove, Denis Edmund (1948–2008)

Dunkley, Christopher
Gill, (George) Michael (1923–2005)

Dyer, Christopher
Beresford, Maurice Warwick (1920–2005)

Easson, Angus
Storey, Graham (1920–2005)

Eccleshare, Julia
Baynes, Pauline Diana (1922–2008)

Hodgson, Miriam Ann (1938–2005)

Edmunds, Mike
Pagel, Bernard Ephraim Julius (1930–2007)

Ehrman, Edwina
Blow, Isabella (1958–2007)
Hayward, Douglas Frederick Cornelius (1934–2008)

Elliott, Ann
Lynton, Norbert Casper (1927–2007)

Emery, Fred
Hussey, Marmaduke James [Duke], Baron Hussey of North Bradley (1923–2006)

Emsley, Clive
Marwick, Arthur John Brereton (1936–2006)

Erskine-Hill, Howard
Jack, Ian Robert James (1923–2008)

Espiner, Mark
Cutler, Ivor (1923–2006)

Evans, Harriet
Croll, Elisabeth Joan (1944–2007)

Evans, Magdalen
Adams, Norman Edward Albert (1927–2005)

Evans, R. J. W.
Davies, Sir (Robert) Rees (1938–2005)

Evans, Rhys
Evans, Gwynfor Richard (1912–2005)

Everton, Clive
Spencer, John (1935–2006)

Eyre, Richard
Gray, Simon James Holliday (1936–2008)

Fall, Brian
Bullard, Sir Julian Leonard (1928–2006)

Fardon, Richard
Douglas, Dame (Margaret) Mary (1921–2007)

Fell, Tony
Warren, Eleanor Catherine Rutherford (1919–2005)

Fellowes, Robert
Ford, Sir Edward William Spencer (1910–2006)

Fenby, Jonathan
Boston, Richard (1938–2006)
Lyttelton, Humphrey Richard Adeane (1921–2008)

Ferguson-Smith, Malcolm A.
Edwards, John Hilton (1928–2007)

Fergusson, David
Torrance, Thomas Forsyth (1913–2007)

Fergusson, James
Hughes, David John (1930–2005)
Jolliffe, Peter Benedict (1947–2007)

Ferry, Georgina
Caminer, David Tresman (1915–2008)

Fielding, Michael
Rudduck, Jean (1937–2007)

Fisher, Richard
Faulkner, (Herbert Gustavus) Max (1916–2005)

Fitter, Alastair
Bradshaw, Anthony David (1926–2008)

Foot, M. R. D.
Cammaerts, Francis Charles Albert (1916–2006)
Millar, George Reid (1910–2005)
Witherington, (Cecile) Pearl (1914–2008)

Forbes, Elizabeth
Davies, (Albert) Meredith (1922–2005)
Glossop, (Cyril) Peter (1928–2008)
Ingpen, Joan Mary Eileen (1916–2007)

Forrester, Duncan B.
Whyte, James Aitken (1920–2005)

Forty, A. J.
Menter, Sir James Woodham (1921–2006)

Foster, Paul
Mander, Noel Percy (1912–2005)

Fox, Paul
Douglas, Margaret Elizabeth (1934–2008)
Miall, (Rowland) Leonard (1914–2005)

Frankl, P. J. L.
Yahya Ali Omar (1924–2008)

Franklin, Stuart
Griffiths, Philip Jones (1936–2008)

Fraser, Peter D.
Carter, Sir John Gregorio (1919–2005)
Fryer, Peter James (1927–2006)

Frayling, Christopher
Guyatt, Richard Gerald Talbot (1914–2007)

Freedland, Michael
Cass, Frank (1930–2007)

Frischmann, Wilem
Wolf, Peter Otto (1918–2007)

Galeotti, Mark
Litvinenko, Aleksandr Valterovich (1962–2006)

Gamble, Andrew
Crick, Sir Bernard Rowland (1929–2008)

Garnett, Mark
Channon, (Henry) Paul Guinness, Baron Kelvedon (1935–2007)
Lambton, Antony Claud Frederick, styled Lord Lambton (1922–2006)
Lockhart, Alexander John [Sandy] Bruce-, Baron Bruce-Lockhart (1942–2008)

Garnsey, Peter
Walbank, Frank William (1909–2008)

Gee, Maggie
Ghoussoub, Mai (1952–2007)

Gelder, M. G.
Roth, Sir Martin (1917–2006)

Gibson, Peter
Fox, Sir Michael John (1921–2007)
Megarry, Sir Robert Edgar (1910–2006)

Gildea, Robert
Johnson, Douglas William John (1925–2005)

Gillespie, Gordon
Ervine, David Walter (1953–2007)

Glanville, Philippa
Benney, (Adrian) Gerald Sallis (1930–2008)

Goldman, Lawrence
Barron, John Penrose (1934–2008)
Brightman, John Anson, Baron Brightman (1911–2006)
Brooks, Anthony Morris [Tony] (1922–2007)
Hardman, Leslie Henry (1913–2008)
Hodges, Sir Lewis Macdonald [Bob] (1918–2007)
Hogg, Richard Milne (1944–2007)
Jackson, Michael (1942–2007)
Jeger, Lena May, Baroness Jeger (1915–2007)
Milton, (Clement) Arthur (1928–2007)
Mitchell, Adrian Christopher (1932–2008)
Nuttall, Anthony David (1937–2007)
Osgood, Peter Leslie (1947–2006)
Riddelsdell, Dame Mildred (1913–2006)
Wright, Richard William [Rick] (1943–2008)

Gooding, Mel
Blow, Sandra Betty (1925–2006)

Goodman, Geoffrey
Bruce, Donald William Trevor, Baron Bruce of Donington (1912–2005)
Neal, Sir Leonard Francis (1913–2008)
Todd, Ronald (1927–2005)

Goodwin, Noël
May, Pamela (1917–2005)

Gough, Janet
Munro, Dame Alison (1914–2008)

Gourvish, Terry
Brech, Edward Francis Leopold (1909–2006)
Serpell, Sir David Radford (1911–2008)

Grade, Michael
Cotton, Sir William Frederick [Bill] (1928–2008)

Graham, John
Weir, Sir Michael Scott (1925–2006)
Wright, Sir Denis Arthur Hepworth (1911–2005)

Granger, Derek
Plowright, David Ernest (1930–2006)

Green, Derek
Wyre, Raymond Keith (1951–2008)

Greene, Graham C.
Ingrams, Leonard Victor (1941–2005)

Greenoak, Francesca
Bloom, Alan Herbert Vauser (1906–2005)

Greenwood, Jeremy J. D.
Fitter, Richard Sidney Richmond (1913–2005)

Greer, A. Lindsay
Cahn, Robert Wolfgang (1924–2007)

Grove, Eric J.
Scott, Sir (William) David Stewart (1921–2006)

Gubbins, Paul
Auld, William (1924–2006)

Gudjonsson, Gisli
MacKeith, James Alexander Culpin (1938–2007)

Hagan, Paul
McGregor, Sir Ian Alexander (1922–2007)

Haines, Catharine M. C.
Datta, Naomi (1922–2008)
Rothschild, Dame Miriam Louisa (1908–2005)

Hale, Brenda
Bracewell, Dame Joyanne Winifred (1934–2007)
Heilbron, Dame Rose (1914–2005)

Hall, Edward
Fraser, Jill (1946–2006)

Hamilton, A. C.
Macfadyen, Donald James Dobbie, Lord Macfadyen (1945–2008)

Hands, Terry
Farrah, Abd'Elkader (1926–2005)

Hanson, Brian J. T.
Pattinson, Sir (William) Derek (1930–2006)

Hardingham, Tim
Muir, (Isabella) Helen Mary (1920–2005)

Hargreaves, John A.
Hughes, Selwyn (1928–2006)
Tomlinson, Jane Emily (1964–2007)

Harper, Peter S.
Polani, Paul Emanuel (1914–2006)

Harrod, Tanya
Beyer, Ralph Alexander (1921–2008)

Hartcup, Guy
Beckett, Allan Harry (1914–2005)

Harvey, A. E.
Mayne, Michael Clement Otway (1929–2006)
Moule, Charles Francis Digby (1908–2007)

Harvie, Christopher
Cook, Robert Finlayson [Robin] (1946–2005)
Ewing [McAdam; Bain], Margaret Anne (1945–2006)

Harwood, Elain
Boyne, (Donald Arthur) Colin Aydon (1921–2006)
Erskine, Ralph (1914–2005)
Wilson, Sir Colin Alexander St John (1922–2007)

Hastings, Selina
Bedford, Sybille (1911–2006)

Hattersley, Roy
Callaghan, Leonard James [Jim], Baron Callaghan of Cardiff (1912–2005)

Hattersley-Smith, G.
Heap, John Arnfield (1932–2006)
Herbert, Sir Walter William [Wally] (1934–2007)

Haviland, Julian
Whale, John Hilary (1931–2008)

Hawes, Donald
Battiscombe, (Esther) Georgina (1905–2006)

Hawkesworth, Celia
Partridge, Monica Agnes (1915–2008)

Hawkins, Stephen J.
Southward, Alan James (1928–2007)

Haynes, Richard
Cowgill, (George) Bryan (1927–2008)

Hayward, Anthony
Barkworth, Peter Wynn (1929–2006)
Bell, Thomas George [Tom] (1933–2006)
Exton, Clive (1930–2007)
Orton, Peter Charles (1943–2007)
Postgate, (Richard) Oliver (1925–2008)
Prior, Allan (1922–2006)

Hazlett, W. Ian P.
Frend, William Hugh Clifford (1916–2005)

Hebron, Stephen
Woof, Robert Samuel (1931–2005)

Hedley, Gill
Gardiner, Margaret Emilia (1904–2005)

Heffer, Simon
Biffen, (William) John, Baron Biffen (1930–2007)
Gilmour, Ian Hedworth John Little, Baron Gilmour of Craigmillar (1926–2007)
Handley, Vernon George [Tod] (1930–2008)
Profumo, John Dennis (1915–2006)

Heilbron, J. L.
North, John David (1934–2008)

Hendy, David
Clarke, Nicholas Campbell (1948–2006)
Timpson, John Harry Robert (1928–2005)

Herbert, Amanda
Macgregor, (Janet) Elizabeth (1920–2005)

Herbert, David T.
Balchin, William George Victor (1916–2007)

Hill, Richard
Law, Sir Horace Rochfort (1911–2005)
McGeoch, Sir Ian Lachlan Mackay (1914–2007)
Pollock, Sir Michael Patrick (1916–2006)

Hines, James R.
Colledge, (Magdalena) Cecilia (1920–2008)

Hinnells, John R.
Boyce, (Nora Elisabeth) Mary (1920–2006)

Hoare, Philip
Melly, (Alan) George Heywood (1926–2007)

Holbrook, David
Marshall, Sybil Mary (1913–2005)

Holden, Raymond
Brainin, Norbert (1923–2005)
Bronhill, June (1929–2005)
Fretwell, Elizabeth Drina [Betty] (1920–2006)
Graham, Colin (1931–2007)
Rothwell, Rosalind Alice, Lady Barbirolli (1911–2008)
Schwarzkopf, Dame (Olga Maria) Elisabeth Friederike (1915–2006)
Thomas, Marjorie Gwendolen (1923–2008)

Holden, Anthony
Allan, Elkan Philip (1922–2006)

Hollman, Arthur
Cleland, William Paton (1912–2005)
Melrose, Denis Graham (1921–2007)

Holt, Richard
Court, Audrey Kathleen (1913–2005)

Honychurch, Lennox
Charles, Dame (Mary) Eugenia (1919–2005)

Hope, David
Jauncey, Charles Eliot, Baron Jauncey of Tullichettle (1925–2007)

Hopkinson, Amanda
Pomeras, Arnold Julius [Arno] (1920–2005)

Hore, Peter
Dunlop, Samuel Clarke (1922–2008)
Tippet, Sir Anthony Sanders (1928–2006)

Horwood, Joseph
Cushing, David Henry (1920–2008)

Howard, Anthony
Abse, Leopold [Leo] (1917–2008)
Kyle, (John) Keith (1925–2007)
Wheeler, Sir Selwyn Charles Cornelius- (1923–2008)

Howe, Geoffrey
Rawlinson, Peter Anthony Grayson, Baron Rawlinson of Ewell (1919–2006)

Howell, David
Dunwoody, Gwyneth Patricia (1930–2008)

Howse, Christopher
Wharton, Michael Bernard (1913–2006)

Humphries, Patrick
Smith, Michael George (1943–2008)

Hunt, Ken
Graham, David Michael Gordon [Davey], (1940–2008)
Johnson, William Henry [Peerie Willie] (1920–2007)
McEwen, Alexander Dundas (1935–2008)
Tawney, Cyril Francis (1930–2005)
Williamson, Duncan James (1928–2007)

Hurd, Douglas
Heath, Sir Edward Richard George (1916–2005)

Pym, Francis Leslie, Baron Pym (1922–2008)

Idiens, Dale
Willett, Frank (1925–2006)

Ingram, Derek
Keatley, Patrick Crawford (1920–2005)

Iversen, Margaret
Podro, Michael Isaac (1931–2008)

Jackson, Caroline
Blatch, Emily May, Baroness Blatch (1937–2005)

Jackson, Michael T.
Hawkes, John Gregory (1915–2007)

James, Louis
Heath, Roy Aubrey Kelvin (1926–2008)

Jarrett, Philip
Walker, Diana Barnato (1918–2008)

Jarvis, Adrian
Page, Sir John Joseph Joffre (1915–2006)

Jarvis, Anthea
Reger, (Esther) Janet (1935–2005)

Jenkins, Geraint H.
Williams, Sir Glanmor (1920–2005)

Jennings, Alex
Cummings, Constance (1910–2005)
Gish, Sheila (1942–2005)
Richardson, Ian William (1934–2007)
Scofield, (David) Paul (1922–2008)
Spriggs, Elizabeth Jean (1929–2008)

John, Gus
La Rose, John Anthony (1927–2006)

Johnston, Ron
Jones, Emrys (1920–2006)

Johnston, Alan
Coldstream, (John) Nicolas (1927–2008)

Jolly, Richard
Singer, Sir Hans Wolfgang (1910–2006)

Jones, Geoffrey
Durham, Sir Kenneth (1924–2005)

Jones, Peter
Kemp, Sir (Edward) Peter (1934–2008)

Judge, Igor
Lane, Geoffrey Dawson, Baron Lane (1918–2005)

Kauffmann, C. M.
Farr, Dennis Larry Ashwell (1929–2006)
Zarnecki, Jerzy (1915–2008)

Kaufman, Gerald
Varley, Eric Graham, Baron Varley (1932–2008)

Kavanagh, Dennis
Barber, Anthony Perrinott Lysberg, Baron Barber (1920–2005)
Holme, Richard Gordon, Baron Holme of Cheltenham (1936–2008)
Rees, Peter Wynford Innes, Baron Rees (1926–2008)

Seldon, Arthur (1916–2005)
Sherman, Sir Alfred (1919–2006)

Kay, Jackie
Darling, Julia Rose (1956–2005)

Kay, Joyce
Hill, Albert Edwin (1927–2005)
Moss, Patricia Ann (1934–2008)

Kenney, E. J.
Bailey, David Roy Shackleton (1917–2005)

Kerslake, Celia
Lewis, Geoffrey Lewis (1920–2008)

King, Emily
Fletcher, Alan Gerard (1931–2006)

King, Ursula
Parrinder, (Edward) Geoffrey Simons (1910–2005)

Kingman, J. F. C.
Kendall, David George (1918–2007)

Lachmann, Peter J.
Coombs, Robert Royston Amos [Robin] (1921–2006)

Laing, Margaret
McIntosh, Angus (1914–2005)

Lamb, Andrew
Slade, Julian Penkivil (1930–2006)

Lamont, William
Cohn, Norman Rufus Colin (1915–2007)

Land, Frank
Mumford, Enid Mary (1924–2006)

Langdale, Allan
Baxandall, Michael David Kighley (1933–2008)

Langford, Paul
Green, Vivian Hubert Howard (1915–2005)

Latham, Alison
Sadie, Stanley John (1930–2005)

Laws, John
Bridge, Nigel Cyprian, Baron Bridge of Harwich (1917–2007)

Leahy, John
Tomkins, Sir Edward Emile (1915–2007)

Leapman, Michael
Chipp, David Allan (1927–2008)
Cudlipp, Reginald William (1910–2005)
Rogers, Sir Frank Jarvis (1920–2005)
Singer, Aubrey Edward (1927–2007)

Ledingham, John G. G.
Beeson, Paul Bruce (1908–2006)
Hoffenberg, Sir Raymond [Bill] (1923–2007)

Lee, Hermione
Kavanagh, Patricia Olive [Pat] (1940–2008)

Leeson, Edward
Barker, Ronald William George (1929–2005)

Leigh, Spencer
Baldry, John William [Long John Baldry] (1941–2005)

Garrity, Frederick [Freddie] (1936–2006)
Hazlehurst, Ronald (1928–2007)
Ridley, Walter John (1913–2007)
Roza, Lilian Patricia (1926–2008)
Stewart, Lorn Alastair [Johnnie] (1917–2005)

Lennard-Jones, John
Bingley, Juliet Martin, Lady Bingley (1925–2005)

Lepschy, Giulio
Meneghello, Luigi (1922–2007)

Lever, Jeremy
Warner, Sir Jean-Pierre Frank Eugene (1924–2005)

Levy, Paul
Anson, Thomas Patrick John, fifth earl of Lichfield [Patrick Lichfield] (1939–2005)
Appleby, (Florence) Lucy (1920–2008)
Carrier, Robert (1923–2006)
Gray, Patience Jean (1917–2005)
Tannahill, (Margery) Reay (1929–2007)

Levy, Silvano
Maddox, Conroy Ronald (1912–2005)

Lewis, Jeremy
Michie, James Crain (1927–2007)

Lewis, John E.
McCrum, Michael William (1924–2005)

Lewis, S. Mitchell
Dacie, Sir John Vivian (1912–2005)

Lewison, Jeremy
Weschke, Karl Martin (1925–2005)

Liardet, Guy
Fraser, Ian Edward (1920–2008)
Hezlet, Sir Arthur Richard (1914–2007)

Limb, Roger
Cary, Tristram Ogilvie (1925–2008)

Lindstedt, Peter
Whitelaw, James Hunter (1936–2006)

Linklater, Magnus
Mackay, Eric Beattie (1922–2006)

Llewellyn-Smith, Elizabeth
Powell, Sir Richard Royle (1909–2006)

Lloyd, Christopher
Millar, Sir Oliver Nicholas (1923–2007)

Lock, Stephen
Smith, Antony John (1934–2008)
Thould, Anthony Keith (1930–2005)

Locke, Patrick
Ridley, Dame (Mildred) Betty (1909–2005)

Longair, Malcolm S.
Pippard, Sir (Alfred) Brian (1920–2008)

Lowry, David
Tuohy, Thomas (1917–2008)

MacCarthy, Fiona
Harling, (Henry) Robert (1910–2008)

McCave, I. Nicholas
Shackleton, Sir Nicholas John (1937–2006)

MacClancy, Jeremy
Needham, Rodney (1923–2006)

McFarlane, Brian
Court, Hazel Marjorie (1926–2008)
Gray, Sally (1915–2006)
Handford, Peter Thomas (1919–2007)
Herlie, Eileen (1918–2008)
Kerr, Deborah (1921–2007)
Lister, Moira (1923–2007)
Lloyd, (Hugh) Russell (1916–2008)
Mills, Sir John Lewis Ernest Watts (1908–2005)
Scott, Margaretta Mary Winifred (1912–2005)
Walsh, Kathleen (1911–2005)

MacGregor, Sue
Mawer, June Knox- (1930–2006)

McGuinness, Patrick
Raitt, Alan William (1930–2006)

MacIver, Matthew
Macintosh, Farquhar (1923–2007)

Mackenzie, Ann L.
McClelland, Ivy Lilian (1908–2006)

MacKenzie, John M.
Anderson, Alfred (1896–2005)

McLeod, John
Orr, Robert Kemsley [Robin] (1909–2006)

Macmillan, Duncan
Campbell, Steven Macmillan (1953–2007)

Maloney, Nicholas
Harris, Ralph, Baron Harris of High Cross (1924–2006)

Marquand, David
Cattermole, James (1910–2007)

Mason, Tony
Ball, Alan James (1945–2007)
Greenwood, Ronald [Ron] (1921–2006)
Haynes, John Norman (1934–2005)
Hughes, Margaret Patricia (1919–2005)
Wooldridge, Ian Edmund (1932–2007)

Massie, Alastair W.
Akehurst, Sir John Bryan (1930–2007)

Massie, Bert
Large, Sir Peter (1931–2005)

Matthew, Christopher
Morley, Sheridan Robert (1941–2007)

May, Alex
Allbeury, Theodore Edward Le Bouthillier [Ted] (1917–2005)
Aprahamian, (Abraham) Felix Barter (1914–2005)
Barraclough, Sir John (1918–2008)
Eltringham, (Stewart) Keith (1929–2006)
Fewtrell, (Ernest) Malcolm (1909–2005)
Franca, Celia (1921–2007)
Hobbs, John Raymond (1929–2008)
Keeble, Sir (Herbert Ben) Curtis (1922–2008)
King, Alexander (1909–2007)
McLaren, Dame Anne Laura Dorinthea (1927–2007)
Richardson, Joanna Leah (1925–2008)
Smalls, Derek Crighton [Bertie] (1937–2008)
Spender, (John) Humphrey (1910–2005)
Thoday, John Marion (1916–2008)
Watson, John Hugh [Adam] (1914–2007)

May, Robert M.
Southwood, Sir (Thomas) Richard Edmund (1931–2005)

Maynard, Robert
Lawther, Patrick Joseph (1921–2008)

Mayr-Harting, Henry
Chadwick, Henry (1920–2008)

Medway, Peter
Rosen, Harold (1919–2008)

Meek, Jo
Chisnall, (James) Arthur White (1925–2006)

Meisner, Nadine
Nerina, Nadia (1927–2008)

Mellor, Roger Philip
Kirkwood, Patricia [Pat] (1921–2007)

Melvin, Jo
Townsend, Peter (1919–2006)

Mendelson, Maurice
Vallat, Sir Francis Aimé (1912–2008)

Metcalf, D. M.
Grierson, Philip (1910–2006)

Michael, Ian
Russell, Sir Peter Edward Lionel (1913–2006)

Millington, Mark
Cabrera Infante, Guillermo (1929–2005)

Mills, David
Hill, Mary Eglantyne [Polly] (1914–2005)

Moffatt, H. K.
Saffman, Philip Geoffrey (1931–2008)

Monroe, Barbara
Saunders, Dame Cicely Mary Strode (1918–2005)

Moore, Charles
Johnson, Frank Robert (1943–2006)

Moore, Patrick
Robinson, John Ebdon [John Ebdon] (1923–2005)

Moorhouse, Paul
Latham, John Aubrey Clarendon (1921–2006)

Morgan, John
Trueman, Frederick Sewards [Fred] (1931–2006)

Morris, Peter J. T.
Mason, Stephen Finney (1923–2007)

Morris, Terence
Challenor, Harold Gordon (1922–2008)

Morrison, Bryce
Lympany, Dame Moura (1916–2005)

Mortimore, Peter
Tomlinson, John Race Godfrey (1932–2005)

Morton, James
Pallo, Jackie (1926–2006)
Sheridan, Bernard (1927–2007)

Moss, Ann
Lawton, Harold Walter (1899–2005)

Moss, Michael S.
Bell, (Alexander) Scott (1941–2007)
Macsween, John Angus (1939–2006)
Tennant, Sir Iain Mark (1919–2006)

Moss, Nicholas
Baxter, Raymond Frederic (1922–2006)

Murphy, Paul
Mowlam, Marjorie (1949–2005)

Murphy, Robert
Rigby, Terence Christopher Gerald (1937–2008)

Murrell, Colin
Dalton, Sir Howard (1944–2008)

Murrell, Kevin
Gearing, Harold William George (1912–2005)

Neill, Patrick
Fisher, Sir Henry Arthur Pears (1918–2005)
Nolan, Michael Patrick, Baron Nolan (1928–2007)

Neuberger, Julia
Rayner, John Desmond (1924–2005)

Neumann, Peter M.
Higman, Graham (1917–2008)

Newley, Patrick
Halliwell, David Wiliam (1936–2006)

Nicholls of Birkenhead
Oliver, Peter Raymond, Baron Oliver of Aylmerton (1921–2007)

Nicoll, William
Denman, Sir (George) Roy (1924–2006)

Niven, Alastair
Markham, Edward Archibald (1939–2008)
Rao, Raja (1908–2006)

Noltie, H. J.
Burtt, Brian Laurence (1913–2008)

Norquay, Glenda
Jenkins, (John) Robin (1912–2005)

Norris, Christopher
Hoddinott, Alun (1929–2008)

Norton, Michael
FitzHerbert, Luke Jos (1937–2007)

Owen, Geoffrey
Bond, Sir Kenneth Raymond Boyden (1920–2006)
Jones, Sir John Henry Harvey- (1924–2008)
Stokes, Donald Gresham, Baron Stokes (1914–2008)
Veale, Sir Alan John Ralph (1920–2006)

Ozanne, William I.
Hall, Mary (1928–2008)

Packer, William
Ward, John Stanton (1917–2007)

Palmer, Nigel F.
Ganz, Peter Felix (1920–2006)

Palumbo, Peter
Varah, (Edward) Chad (1911–2007)

Parker, R. C. T.
Inwood, Christiane Sourvinou- (1945–2007)

Parker, Roger
Budden, Julian Medforth (1924–2007)

Parry, Jonathan
Cowling, Maurice John (1926–2005)

Paterson, Lindsay
Cox, (Charles) Brian (1928–2008)

Paul, Geoffrey D.
Frankel, William (1917–2008)

Peart-Binns, John S.
Montefiore, Hugh William (1920–2005)
Noakes, George (1924–2008)
Yates, John (1925–2008)

Peden, G. C.
Goldman, Sir Samuel (1912–2007)

Penley, W. H.
Macfarlane, Sir George Gray (1916–2007)

Percival, John
Barnes, Clive Alexander (1927–2008)
Morrice, Norman Alexander (1931–2008)
Shearer, Moira [Moira Shearer King; Moira Shearer Kennedy, Lady Kennedy] (1926–2006)

Peto, Richard
Doll, Sir (William) Richard Shaboe (1912–2005)

Petrie, Duncan
Watkin, (Francis) David (1925–2008)

Phillips, Chloe
Elgar, Sybil Lillian (1914–2007)

Philpot, Terry
Clarke, Peter William Hanwell (1948–2007)
Gomm, Richard Culling Carr- (1922–2008)
Williams, Nigel Prichard (1955–2006)

Phimister, Ian
Smith, Ian Douglas (1919–2007)

Pill, Malcolm
Watkins, Sir Tasker (1918–2007)

Pirouet, M. Louise
Obote, (Apolo) Milton (1925–2005)

Plowden, William
Bishop, Sir Frederick Arthur (1915–2005)

Plumb of Coleshill
Carter, Denis Victor, Baron Carter (1932–2006)

Pointon, Michael
Fletcher, Cyril Trevellian (1913–2005)

Polkinghorne, John
Peacocke, Arthur Robert (1924–2006)

Polley, Martin
Norman, Andrew John (1943–2007)
Thompson, Donald James (1933–2006)

Porritt, Jonathon
Sandbrook, (John) Richard (1946–2005)

Porter, Vincent
Knatchbull, John Ulick, seventh Baron Brabourne of Brabourne [John Brabourne] (1924–2005)
Plaschkes, Otto (1929–2005)

Pottle, Mark
Rheinberg, Netta (1911–2006)
Stammers, Katharine Esther (1914–2005)

Powell, Kenneth
Papadakis, Andreas Constantine (1938–2008)

Prance, Ghillean T.
Bell, (Ernest) Arthur (1926–2006)

Prichard, Mari
Cresswell, (Elizabeth) Helen (1934–2005)

Pring, Richard
Morris, Max (1913–2008)

Pringle, Roger
Fox, Levi (1914–2006)

Prosser, William D.
Elliott, Walter Archibald, Lord Elliott (1922–2008)

Purser, Philip
Cox, Sir Geoffrey Sandford (1910–2008)
Kneale, (Thomas) Nigel (1922–2006)
Scott, Peter Graham (1923–2007)

Purves, Libby
Carpenter, Humphrey William Bouverie (1946–2005)
Coren, Alan (1938–2007)

Purvis, June
Banks, Olive Lucy (1923–2006)

Quinnell, Henrietta
Fox, Aileen Mary, Lady Fox (1907–2005)

Raikes, Sophie
Meadows, Bernard William (1915–2005)

Raines, Ronald T.
Knowles, Jeremy Randall (1935–2008)

Read, Donald
Renfrew, Glen McGarvie (1928–2006)

Reed, Jane
Kerr, Antonella Reuss, marchioness of Lothian (1922–2007)

Reed, T. J.
Luke, Frederic Davey [David] (1921–2005)

Rees-Mogg [Baron Rees-Mogg]
Thomson, Kenneth Roy, second Baron Thomson of Fleet (1923–2006)

Reid, Brian Holden
Gutteridge, William Frank [Bill] (1919–2008)
Hockley, Sir Anthony Heritage Farrar- (1924–2006)

Rellie, Alastair
Figures, Sir Colin Frederick (1925–2006)

Renton, David
Tyndall, John Hutchyns (1934–2005)

Richard, Ivor
Rees, Merlyn Merlyn-, Baron Merlyn-Rees (1920–2006)

Richards, Huw
Foster, Trevor John French (1914–2005)
Gravell, Raymond William Robert [Ray] (1951–2007)
Jones, Kenneth Jeffrey (1921–2006)

Riddell, Peter
Weatherill, Bruce Bernard [Jack], Baron Weatherill (1920–2007)

Riley, Barry
Leslie, Sir Peter Evelyn (1931–2007)

Roberts, Richard
Castleman, Christopher Norman Anthony (1941–2006)
Goobey, Alastair Ross (1945–2008)
Reeves, Christopher Reginald (1936–2007)

Rodgers, William
Thomson, George Morgan, Baron Thomson of Monifieth (1921–2008)

Roffey, Paul
Wyre, Raymond Keith (1951–2008)

Rogan, Johnny
Arden, Don (1926–2007)

Rogerson, J. W.
Barr, James (1924–2006)

Rooksby, Rikky
Barrett, Roger Keith [Syd] (1946–2006)
Mitchell, John [Mitch] (1947–2008)

Rosen, Aaron
Kitaj, Ronald Brooks (1932–2007)

Roxburgh, Ian
Bondi, Sir Hermann (1919–2005)

Roy, Donald
Minghella, Anthony (1954–2008)

Russell, Colin A.
Rees, Charles Wayne (1927–2006)

Rutter, Carol Chillington
Hunter, George Kirkpatrick (1920–2008)

Ryder, Chris
Fitt, Gerard Martin, Baron Fitt (1926–2005)
Hermon, Sir John Charles (1928–2008)

Salmon, Bridget
Sainsbury, Simon David Davan (1930–2006)

Sawyer, Andy
Clarke, Sir Arthur Charles (1917–2008)

Scott, Derek B.
Farnon, Robert Joseph (1917–2005)

Seabright, Paul
Hurley, Susan Lynn (1954–2007)

Seifert, Michael
Sapper, Alan Louis Geoffrey (1931–2006)

Self, Brian
Hudson, John Pilkington (1910–2007)

Sells, Robert
Medawar, Jean Shinglewood, Lady Medawar (1913–2005)

Sergeant, Jean-Claude
Charlot, Monica (1933–2005)

Serota, Nicholas
Manton, Sir Edwin Alfred Grenville (1909–2005)

Sheard, Sally
Yellowlees, Sir Henry (1919–2006)

Shennan, Stephen
Ucko, Peter John (1938–2007)

Sheppard, F. H. W.
Hibbert, Arthur Raymond [Christopher] (1924–2008)

Sheringham, Michael
Bowie, Malcolm McNaughtan (1943–2007)

Sherry, Patrick
Phillips, Dewi Zephaniah (1934–2006)

Sibley, Brian
Ellenshaw, Peter (1913–2007)

Slater, Michael
Collins, Philip Arthur William (1923–2007)

Slinn, Judy
Orr, Sir David Alexander (1922–2008)

Snowdon, Paul
Strawson, Sir Peter Frederick (1919–2006)

Sorley Walker, Kathrine
Meyer, Laverne Ignatius Henry (1935–2008)

Spalding, Julian
Cook, Beryl Frances (1926–2008)

Sparks, Stephen
Walker, George Patrick Leonard (1926–2005)

Spencer, John
Donaldson, John Francis, Baron Donaldson of Lymington (1920–2005)

Spencer, Maureen
Donaldson, John Francis, Baron Donaldson of Lymington (1920–2005)

Spencer, Robin
Paolozzi, Sir Eduardo Luigi (1924–2005)

Spicer, Andrew H.
Berman, Nestor Montague [Monty] (1913–2006)
Daly, John (1937–2008)
Drake, Charles Edward [Charlie] (1925–2006)

Stanley, E. G.
Brewer, Derek Stanley (1923–2008)

Stannard, Martin
Spark, Dame Muriel Sarah (1918–2006)

Stead, Peter
Emmanuel, Ivor Lewis (1927–2007)

Stearn, Roger T.
Wilson, Eric Charles Twelves (1912–2008)

Stedall, Jacqueline
Whiteside, Derek Thomas (1932–2008)

Steen, Rob
Woolmer, Robert Andrew [Bob] (1948–2007)

Steiner, Lisa A.
Ingram, Vernon Martin (1924–2006)

Stephens, Meic
Eames, (Gwladys) Marion (1921–2007)
Mathias, Roland Glyn (1915–2007)
Norris, (George) Leslie (1921–2006)
Williams, Sir (John) Kyffin (1918–2006)

Stephenson, Chris
Mark, Janet Marjorie [Jan] (1943–2006)

Stevens, David
Corner, Beryl Dorothy (1910–2007)

Stevenson, Olive
Young, Priscilla Helen Ferguson (1925–2006)

Stone, Humphrey
McLean, (John David) Ruari McDowall Hardie (1917–2006)

Strang, Alice
Bevan, Natalie Alice (1909–2007)

Street, Sean
Kelly, Barbara (1924–2007)

Stuart, Mark
Bethell, Nicholas William, fourth Baron Bethell (1938–2007)
Forth, Eric (1944–2006)
Johnston, (David) Russell Russell-, Baron Russell-Johnston (1932–2008)
Monro, Hector Seymour Peter, Baron Monro of Langholm (1922–2006)
Scott, Sir Nicholas Paul (1933–2005)

Stubley, Peter
Bailey, Derek (1930–2005)

Surowiec, Catherine A.
Box, John Allan Hyatt (1920–2005)

Sutcliffe, Bob
Glyn, Andrew John (1943–2007)

Swan, Sean
Keenan, Brian Paschal (1941–2008)

Szreter, S. R. S.
Banks, Joseph Ambrose (1920–2005)

Taylor, C. C. W.
Ackrill, John Lloyd (1921–2007)

Taylor, D. J.
Fraser, George Macdonald (1925–2008)

Teasdale, Graham
Jennett, (William) Bryan (1926–2008)

Tendler, Stewart
Nevill, James Francis (1927–2007)
Wilson, John (1927–2006)

Thomas, Christine G.
Simmons, John Simon Gabriel (1915–2005)

Thompson, Colin
Mill, Robert Duguid Forrest Pring- (1924–2005)

Thompson, David M.
Macarthur, Arthur Leitch (1913–2008)

Thompson, Des
Ratcliffe, Derek Almey (1929–2005)

Thompson, Dorothy J.
Fraser, Peter Marshall (1918–2007)

Thompson, Julian
Moore, Sir (John) Jeremy (1928–2007)

Thompson, Richard
Bayliss, Sir Richard Ian Samuel (1917–2006)

Thompson, Todd M.
Kerr, David Allan (1945–2008)
Lings, Martin (1909–2005)
Watt, William Montgomery (1909–2006)

Thoms, David
Burns, Richard Alexander (1971–2005)
McRae, Colin Steele (1968–2007)
Rolt, Anthony Peter Roylance (1918–2008)

Thorne, Robert
Ahm, Povl Borge (1926–2005)

Thornhill, Michael T.
Wilson, Anthony Howard [Tony] (1950–2007)

Thorpe, D. R.
Rae, John Malcolm (1931–2006)

Tinker, Anthea
Askham, Janet Mary (1941–2008)

Tomlinson, Jim
Robertson, Sir Lewis Findlay (1922–2008)

Toms, Edward
Foggon, George (1913–2006)

Torrance, David
Campbell, Gordon Thomas Calthrop, Baron Campbell of Croy (1921–2005)
Michie, (Janet) Ray, Baroness Michie of Gallanach (1934–2008)

Toye, John
Maizels, Alfred (1917–2006)

Tracy, Sheila
Cole, Grace Elizabeth Agnes Annie [Gracie] (1924–2006)
Lusher, Gordon Douglas [Don] (1923–2006)

Travers, Tony
Stonefrost, Maurice Frank (1927–2008)

Trelford, Donald
Davie, Michael (1924–2005)
Harris, (David) Kenneth (1919–2005)

Tucker, Nicholas
Appiah, Enid Margaret [Peggy] (1921–2006)
Keen, Douglas Henry George (1913–2008)
Pearce, (Ann) Philippa (1920–2006)

Tuckett, Alan
Sargant, Naomi Ellen, Lady McIntosh of Haringey (1933–2006)

Uglow, Jenny
Hayter, Alethea Catharine (1911–2006)

Ure, John
Jellicoe, George Patrick John Rushworth, second Earl Jellicoe and Baron Jellicoe of Southampton (1918–2007)
Newby, (George) Eric (1919–2006)

Vaizey, Marina
Holland, Joan Mary Crossley- (1912–2005)
Russell, John (1919–2008)

Vamplew, Wray
Crampsey, Robert Anthony (1930–2008)
Nicholson, David (1939–2006)
Williams, Charles Adolphus [Charlie] (1927–2006)

Vann, Philip
Kalman, Andras (1919–2007)
Woodrow, Joash (1927–2006)

Vaughan, Paul
Brien, Alan (1925–2008)

Vaver, David
Laddie, Sir Hugh Ian Lang (1946–2008)

Vickers, Hugo
Massingberd, Hugh John Montgomery- (1946–2007)

Waghmar, Burzine K.
Lambton, Ann Katharine Swynford (1912–2008)

Wainwright, Martin
Hartley, Marie (1905–2006)

Walker, Tim
Dempster, Nigel Richard Patton (1941–2007)

Wall, David S.
Osmond, Sir Douglas (1914–2006)

Warrack, John
Chissell, Joan Olive (1919–2007)
King, Dame Thea (1925–2007)

Waterhouse, Keith
Hall, Willis Edward (1929–2005)

Watt, Adam A.
Painter, George Duncan (1914–2005)

Webber, Christopher
Hatto, Joyce Hilda (1928–2006)
Hickox, Richard Sidney (1948–2008)
Pimlott, Steven Charles (1953–2007)

Wellings, Martin
Frost, Robert William (1950–2007)

West, Nigel
Bagot, Milicent Jessie Eleanor (1907–2006)

West, R. G.
Pennington, Winifred Anne (1915–2007)

Wetherell, David
Hand, (Geoffrey) David (1918–2006)

Wheatcroft, Geoffrey
O'Brien, Conor Cruise (1917–2008)

Wheatley, Helen
Lambert, Verity Ann (1935–2007)

White, Chris
Aspinall, Neil Stanley (1941–2008)
Freeman, Alan Leslie (1927–2006)

White, Christopher
Levey, Sir Michael Vincent (1927–2008)

Whyte, William
Colvin, Sir Howard Montagu (1919–2007)

Wilks, Yorick
Jones, Karen Ida Boalth Spärck (1935–2007)

Wilmer, Val
Browne, George Edric (1920–2007)
Campbell, Ambrose (1919–2006)
Deniz, Francisco Antonio (1912–2005)

Wilson, David M.
Eames, Elizabeth Sara (1918–2008)

Wilson, John F.
Jones, Sir (John) Derek Alun- (1933–2008)

Wilson, Simon Casimir
Reid, Sir Norman Robert (1915–2007)

Wittenberg, Jonathan
Jacobs, Louis (1920–2006)

Wood, Alan Muir
Brown, William Christopher (1928–2005)

Worrall, Anne
Curran, Agnes (1920–2005)

Worrall, James
Johnson, Henry James [Jim] (1924–2008)

Worsthorne, Peregrine
Deedes, William Francis [Bill], Baron Deedes (1913–2007)

Wroe, David
Hibbert, Sir Jack (1932–2005)

Wyatt, Will
Hatch, Sir David Edwin (1939–2007)

Wykes, David L.
Nuttall, Geoffrey Fillingham (1911–2007)

Wynn, Humphrey
Rowlands, Sir John Samuel (1915–2006)
Winskill, Sir Archibald Little (1917–2005)

Yapp, M. E.
Philips, Sir Cyril Henry (1912–2005)

Young, Cy
Hall, Terence (1926–2007)

Younger, Sam
Kenrick, Bruce Henderson (1920–2007)

Zhen, Willa
Kwok, Sui King [Lily] (1918–2007)